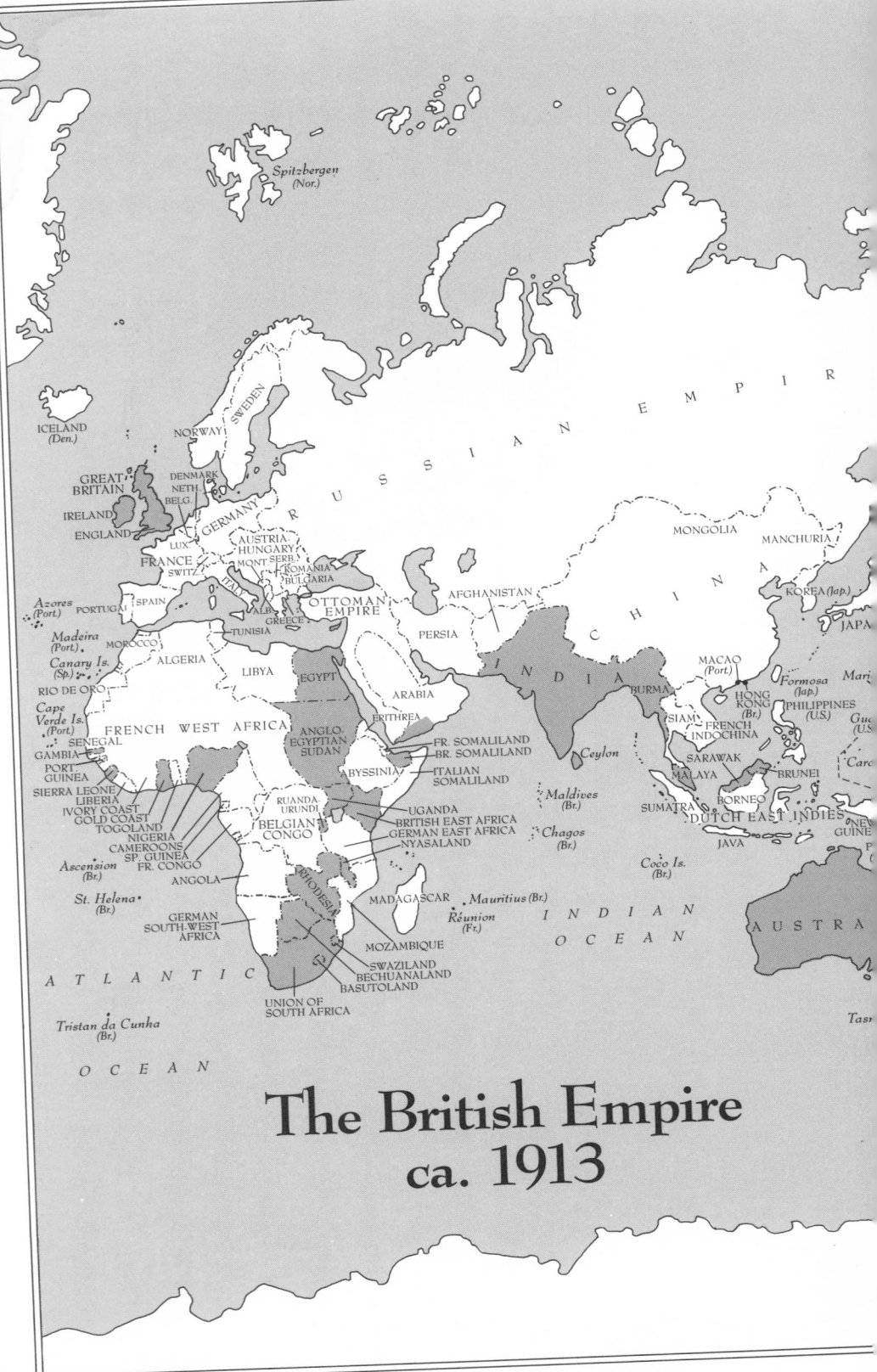

Spitzbergen
(Nor.)

R U S S I A N   E M P I R E

ICELAND
(Den.)

SWEDEN

NORWAY

GREAT
BRITAIN

DENMARK
NETH.
BELG.

IRELAND

ENGLAND

GERMANY

MONGOLIA   MANCHURIA

FRANCE

LUX.

AUSTRIA-
HUNGARY

SWITZ.

MONT.
SERB.

ROMANIA

BULGARIA

C H I N A

KOREA (Jap.)

Azores
(Port.)

PORTUGAL

SPAIN

ITALY

ALB.

GREECE

OTTOMAN
EMPIRE

AFGHANISTAN

JAPAN

Madeira
(Port.)

MOROCCO

TUNISIA

PERSIA

I N D I A

MACAO
(Port.)

Formosa
(Jap.)

Canary Is.
(Sp.)

ALGERIA

LIBYA

EGYPT

ARABIA

BURMA

HONG
KONG
(Br.)

PHILIPPINES
(U.S.)

RIO DE ORO

ERITREA

SIAM

FRENCH
INDOCHINA

Mari

*Cape
Verde Is.*
(Port.)

FRENCH   WEST   AFRICA

ANGLO-
EGYPTIAN
SUDAN

FR. SOMALILAND

BR. SOMALILAND

Ceylon

MALAYA

SARAWAK

BRUNEI

Caro

SENEGAL

ABYSSINIA

ITALIAN
SOMALILAND

Maldives
(Br.)

SUMATRA

BORNEO

DUTCH EAST INDIES

GAMBIA

PORT.
GUINEA

RUANDA-
URUNDI

UGANDA

BRITISH EAST AFRICA

GERMAN EAST AFRICA

NYASALAND

Chagos
(Br.)

JAVA

NEW
GUINE

SIERRA LEONE

LIBERIA

IVORY COAST

GOLD COAST

TOGOLAND

NIGERIA

CAMEROONS

SP. GUINEA

FR. CONGO

BELGIAN
CONGO

Coco Is.
(Br.)

Ascension
(Br.)

ANGOLA

St. Helena
(Br.)

RHODESIA

MADAGASCAR

Mauritius (Br.)

Réunion
(Fr.)

I N D I A N

O C E A N

A U S T R A

GERMAN
SOUTH-WEST
AFRICA

MOZAMBIQUE

A T L A N T I C

SWAZILAND

BECHUANALAND

BASUTOLAND

UNION OF
SOUTH AFRICA

Tristan da Cunha
(Br.)

Tasr

O C E A N

The British Empire
ca. 1913

GREENLAND
(Den.)

ALASKA
(U.S.)

C A N A D A

U N I T E D
S T A T E S

ATLANTIC

OCEAN

Bermuda
(Br.)

Bahamas (Br.)

HAITI

MEXICO

Hawaiian Islands
(U.S.)

BR.
HONDURAS

CUBA

DOMINICAN REPUBLIC
Puerto Rico (U.S.)

Guadeloupe (Fr.)
Martinique (Fr.)

JAMAICA

Grenada
(Br.)

Barbados (Br.)
Trinidad (Br.)

Marshall Is.

man
cific
nds

GUATEMALA
EL SALVADOR
HONDURAS
NICARAGUA
COSTA RICA

PANAMA

VENEZUELA

BR. GUIANA
DUTCH GUIANA
FR. GUIANA

arck
pelago

Solomon Is. (Br.)

COLOMBIA

New Hebrides
(Br. & Fr.)

Galapagos Is.

ECUADOR

B R A Z I L

Caledonia
(Fr.)

Marquesas Is.

French Polynesia

PERU

Tahiti

BOLIVIA

P A C I F I C

C I F I C

O C E A N

O C E A N

PARAGUAY

NEW
ZEALAND

CHILE

ARGENTINA

URUGUAY

Falkland Is.
(Br.)

Chazaud

Visit *Norton Topics Online*

at www.wwnorton.com/nael

Prepared by the Norton Anthology editors, *Norton Topics Online*, a freely accessible Web resource for *The Norton Anthology of English Literature*, Seventh Edition, offers:

- Annotated **Texts and Contexts** grouped by topic
- Over **1000 Illustrations**
- **250 Explorations** to stimulate critical thinking and generate paper topics
- **Annotated Links** to related sites
- **Cross-References** to the *Norton Anthology*
- A student-friendly **"How to Use This Site"** section

"Thanks for *The Norton Anthology of English Literature* companion Web site; it is what my students like and what I need in the way of an 'electronic T.A.'!"
— Jesse Airaudi, Baylor University

"As an English major in college, I find the resources, guides, and links within your Web site to be a useful supplement to assigned readings and class lectures."
— Kevin Coats, student

Coming in January 2000: *The Norton Online Archive*, an electronic library of over 180 literary texts, annotated by the editors, to supplement *The Norton Anthology of English Literature*, Seventh Edition.

THE NORTON ANTHOLOGY
ENGLISH LITERATURE

THE NORTON ANTHOLOGY
ENGLISH LITERATURE

W. W. Norton & Company ✂ Electronic Media
www.wwnorton.com/college/english

VOLUME 1

THE MIDDLE AGES
David / Donaldson

THE SIXTEENTH CENTURY
Logan / Greenblatt

THE EARLY SEVENTEENTH CENTURY
Lewalski / Adams

THE RESTORATION AND THE EIGHTEENTH CENTURY
Lipking / Monk

VOLUME 2

THE ROMANTIC PERIOD
Abrams / Stillinger

THE VICTORIAN AGE
Christ / Ford

THE TWENTIETH CENTURY
Stallworthy / Daiches

The Norton Anthology of English Literature

SEVENTH EDITION
VOLUME 2

Alfred David
PROFESSOR OF ENGLISH EMERITUS, INDIANA UNIVERSITY

E. Talbot Donaldson
LATE OF INDIANA UNIVERSITY

George M. Logan
JAMES CAPPON PROFESSOR OF ENGLISH, QUEEN'S UNIVERSITY

Hallett Smith
LATE OF THE HUNTINGTON LIBRARY

Barbara K. Lewalski
WILLIAM R. KENAN PROFESSOR OF ENGLISH AND OF HISTORY AND LITERATURE, HARVARD UNIVERSITY

Robert M. Adams
LATE OF THE UNIVERSITY OF CALIFORNIA AT LOS ANGELES

Lawrence Lipking
PROFESSOR OF ENGLISH AND CHESTER D. TRIPP PROFESSOR OF HUMANITIES, NORTHWESTERN UNIVERSITY

Samuel Holt Monk
LATE OF THE UNIVERSITY OF MINNESOTA

Jack Stillinger
CENTER FOR ADVANCED STUDY PROFESSOR OF ENGLISH, UNIVERSITY OF ILLINOIS

Carol T. Christ
PROFESSOR OF ENGLISH AND EXECUTIVE VICE CHANCELLOR AND PROVOST, UNIVERSITY OF CALIFORNIA AT BERKELEY

George H. Ford
LATE OF THE UNIVERSITY OF ROCHESTER

Jon Stallworthy
PROFESSOR OF ENGLISH LITERATURE, OXFORD UNIVERSITY

David Daiches
FORMERLY DIRECTOR OF THE INSTITUTE OF ADVANCED STUDIES, UNIVERSITY OF EDINBURGH

Tam o' Shanter: A Tale   109
Robert Bruce's March to Bannockburn   114
A Red, Red Rose   115
Song: For a' that and a' that   116

THE FRENCH REVOLUTION
AND THE "SPIRIT OF THE AGE"   117

ENGLISH CONTROVERSY ABOUT THE REVOLUTION   117
Richard Price: *From* A Discourse on the Love of Our Country   118
Edmund Burke: *From* Reflections on the Revolution in France   121
Mary Wollstonecraft: *From* A Vindication of the Rights of Men   128
Thomas Paine: *From* Rights of Man   133

APOCALYPTIC EXPECTATIONS BY PREACHERS AND POETS   137
Elhanan Winchester: *From* The Three Woe-Trumpets   139
Joseph Priestley: *From* The Present State of Europe Compared with
    Antient Prophecies   143
William Blake: *From* The French Revolution   144
    From America: A Prophecy   146
Robert Southey: *From* Joan of Arc: An Epic Poem   147
William Wordsworth: *From* Descriptive Sketches   149
    From The Excursion   150
Samuel Taylor Coleridge: *From* Religious Musings   153
Percy Bysshe Shelley: *From* Queen Mab: A Philosophical Poem   156

APOCALYPSE BY IMAGINATION   161

MARY WOLLSTONECRAFT (1759–1797)   163
A Vindication of the Rights of Woman   166
    Introduction   166
    Chap. 2. The Prevailing Opinion of a Sexual Character
        Discussed   170
    From Chap. 4. Observations on the State of Degradation . . .   185
Letters Written during a Short Residence in Sweden, Norway, and
        Denmark   192
    Advertisement   192
    Letter 1   193
    Letter 4   199
    Letter 8   201
    Letter 19   205

JOANNA BAILLIE (1762–1851)   209
A Winter's Day   210
Up! quit thy bower   217
Song: Woo'd and married and a'   217

WILLIAM WORDSWORTH (1770–1850)   219
LYRICAL BALLADS   222
Simon Lee   222
We Are Seven   224
Lines Written in Early Spring   226

Expostulation and Reply   227
The Tables Turned   228
The Thorn   229
Lines Composed a Few Miles above Tintern Abbey   235
Preface to Lyrical Ballads (1802)   238
  [The Subject and Language of Poetry]   239
  ["What Is a Poet?"]   246
  ["Emotion Recollected in Tranquillity"]   250

Strange fits of passion have I known   251
She dwelt among the untrodden ways   252
Three years she grew   252
A slumber did my spirit seal   254
I travelled among unknown men   254
Lucy Gray   254
The Two April Mornings   256
Nutting   258
The Ruined Cottage   259
Michael   270
Resolution and Independence   280
I wandered lonely as a cloud   284
My heart leaps up   285
Ode: Intimations of Immortality   286
Ode to Duty   292
The Solitary Reaper   293
Elegiac Stanzas   294

SONNETS   296
Composed upon Westminster Bridge, September 3, 1802   296
It is a beauteous evening   297
London, 1802   297
The world is too much with us   297
Surprised by joy   298
Mutability   298
Steamboats, Viaducts, and Railways   299

Extempore Effusion upon the Death of James Hogg   299
Prospectus to The Recluse   301

The Prelude, or Growth of a Poet's Mind   303
  Book First. Introduction, Childhood, and School-time   305
  Book Second. School-time continued   319
  Book Third. Residence at Cambridge   330
    [Experiences at St. John's College. The "Heroic Argument"]   330
  Book Fourth. Summer Vacation   334
    [The Walks with His Terrier. The Circuit of the Lake]   334
    ["The Surface of Past Time." The Walk Home from the Dance. The
      Discharged Soldier]   336
  Book Fifth. Books   341
    [The Dream of the Arab]   341
    [The Boy of Winander]   343
    ["The Mystery of Words"]   344

Contents

PREFACE TO THE SEVENTH EDITION   xxxiii
ACKNOWLEDGMENTS   xliii

"The Persistence of English" by Geoffrey Nunberg   xlvii

The Romantic Period (1785–1830)   1

Introduction   1
Timeline   22

ANNA LETITIA BARBAULD (1743–1825)   24
  A Summer Evening's Meditation   24
  The Rights of Woman   27
  To a Little Invisible Being Who Is Expected Soon to Become
     Visible   28
  Washing-Day   29
  Life   31

CHARLOTTE SMITH (1749–1806)   32
  ELEGIAC SONNETS   33
  Written at the Close of Spring   33
  To Sleep   33
  To Night   33
  Written in the Church-Yard at Middleton in Sussex   34
  On Being Cautioned against Walking on an Headland Overlooking the
     Sea, Because It Was Frequented by a Lunatic   34
  The Sea View   35

WILLIAM BLAKE (1757–1827)   35
  POETICAL SKETCHES   39
  To Spring   39
  To Autumn   40
  To the Evening Star   40
  All Religions Are One   41
  There Is No Natural Religion [a]   41
  There Is No Natural Religion [b]   42
  SONGS OF INNOCENCE AND OF EXPERIENCE   43
  Songs of Innocence   43
    Introduction   43
    The Ecchoing Green   43
    The Lamb   45

The Little Black Boy   45
The Chimney Sweeper   46
The Divine Image   47
Holy Thursday   47
Nurse's Song   48
Infant Joy   48
Songs of Experience   49
Introduction   49
Earth's Answer   50
The Clod & the Pebble   51
Holy Thursday   51
The Chimney Sweeper   52
Nurse's Song   52
The Sick Rose   52
The Fly   53
The Tyger   54
My Pretty Rose Tree   55
Ah Sun-flower   55
The Garden of Love   56
London   56
The Human Abstract   57
Infant Sorrow   57
A Poison Tree   58
To Tirzah   58
A Divine Image   59

The Book of Thel   59
Visions of the Daughters of Albion   64
The Marriage of Heaven and Hell   72
A Song of Liberty   82

BLAKE'S NOTEBOOK   84
Mock on, Mock on, Voltaire, Rousseau   84
Never pain to tell thy love   84
I askèd a thief   85

And did those feet   85
From A Vision of the Last Judgment   86
Two Letters on Sight and Vision   88

MARY ROBINSON (1758–1800)   91
London's Summer Morning   92
January, 1795   93
The Poor Singing Dame   94
The Haunted Beach   96
To the Poet Coleridge   98

ROBERT BURNS (1759–1796)   99
Green grow the rashes   101
Holy Willie's Prayer   102
To a Mouse   105
To a Louse   106
Auld Lang Syne   108

The Norton Anthology
of English Literature

SEVENTH EDITION

VOLUME 2

M. H. Abrams, *General Editor*

CLASS OF 1916 PROFESSOR OF ENGLISH EMERITUS,
CORNELL UNIVERSITY

Stephen Greenblatt, *Associate General Editor*

HARRY LEVIN PROFESSOR OF LITERATURE,
HARVARD UNIVERSITY

WWNORTON
W · W · NORTON & COMPANY · *New York ·* *London*

The text of this book is composed in Fairfield Medium
with the display set in Bernhard Modern.
Composition by Binghamton Valley Composition.
Manufacturing by R. R. Donnelley, Inc.
Cover illustration: Stanley Spencer, *Swan Upping at Cookham* (detail) (1914–19).
Tate Gallery, London. Photo: Tate Gallery, London/Art Resource, NY.

Editor: Julia Reidhead
Developmental Editor/Associate Managing Editor: Marian Johnson
Production Manager: Diane O'Connor
Manuscript and Project Editors: Candace Levy, Barry Katzen, David Hawkins,
Ann Tappert, Will Rigby
Editorial Assistant: Christa Grenawalt
Permissions Manager: Kristin Sheerin
Cover and Text Design: Antonina Krass
Art Research: Neil Ryder Hoos

Library of Congress Cataloging-in-Publication Data

The Norton anthology of English literature / M. H. Abrams, general
editor : Stephen Greenblatt, associate general editor. — 7th ed.
p.   cm.
Includes bibliographical references and index.

ISBN 0-393-97486-3 (v. 1). — ISBN 0-393-97487-1 (pbk.: v. 1).
ISBN 0-393-97490-1 (v. 2). — ISBN 0-393-97491-X (pbk.: v. 2).

1. English literature.   2. Great Britain—Literary collections.
I. Abrams, M. H. (Meyer Howard), 1912–   .   II. Greenblatt, Stephen, 1943–   .
III.   Title: Anthology of English literature.
PR1109.A2   1999
820.8—dc21   99-43298
CIP

W. W. Norton & Company, Inc., 500 Fifth Avenue, New York, N.Y. 10110
www.wwnorton.com

W. W. Norton & Company Ltd., 10 Coptic Street, London WC1A 1PU

1 2 3 4 5 6 7 8 9 0

Song [I hid my love]   810
Song [I peeled bits of straw]   811

FELICIA DOROTHEA HEMANS (1793–1835)   812
England's Dead   813
The Landing of the Pilgrim Fathers in New England   814
Casabianca   815
The Homes of England   817
A Spirit's Return   818

JOHN KEATS (1795–1821)   823
On First Looking into Chapman's Homer   826
Sleep and Poetry   827
[O for Ten Years]   827
On Seeing the Elgin Marbles   828
Endymion: A Poetic Romance   829
Preface   829
Book 1   830
[A Thing of Beauty]   830
[The "Pleasure Thermometer"]   831
On Sitting Down to Read King Lear Once Again   833
When I have fears that I may cease to be   833
To Homer   834
The Eve of St. Agnes   834
Why did I laugh tonight? No voice will tell   844
Bright star, would I were stedfast as thou art   845
La Belle Dame sans Merci: A Ballad   845
Sonnet to Sleep   847
Ode to Psyche   847
Ode to a Nightingale   849
Ode on a Grecian Urn   851
Ode on Melancholy   853
Ode on Indolence   854
Lamia   856
To Autumn   872
The Fall of Hyperion: A Dream   873
LETTERS   886
To Benjamin Bailey (Nov. 22, 1817)   887
To George and Thomas Keats (Dec. 21, 27 [?], 1817)   889
To John Hamilton Reynolds (Feb. 3, 1818)   890
To John Taylor (Feb. 27, 1818)   891
To John Hamilton Reynolds (May 3, 1818)   892
To Richard Woodhouse (Oct. 27, 1818)   894
To George and Georgiana Keats (Feb. 14–May 3, 1819)   896
To Fanny Brawne (July 25, 1819)   900
To Percy Bysshe Shelley (Aug. 16, 1820)   901
To Charles Brown (Nov. 30, 1820)   902

MARY WOLLSTONECRAFT SHELLEY (1797–1851)   903
Frankenstein; or, The Modern Prometheus   905

LETITIA ELIZABETH LANDON (1802–1838)   1034
The Proud Ladye   1035

Love's Last Lesson   1037
Revenge   1040
The Little Shroud   1041

The Victorian Age (1830–1901)   1043

Introduction   1043
Timeline   1064

THOMAS CARLYLE (1795–1881)   1066
    [Carlyle's Portraits of His Contemporaries]   1070
        [Queen Victoria at Eighteen]   1070
        [Samuel Taylor Coleridge at Fifty-three]   1070
        [William Wordsworth in His Seventies]   1074
        [Alfred Tennyson at Thirty-four]   1076
    Sartor Resartus   1077
        The Everlasting No   1077
        Centre of Indifference   1082
        The Everlasting Yea   1089
        Natural Supernaturalism   1096
    The French Revolution   1103
        September in Paris   1103
        Place de la Révolution   1106
        From Cause and Effect   1109
    Past and Present   1110
        Democracy   1110
        Captains of Industry   1115

JOHN HENRY CARDINAL NEWMAN (1801–1890)   1119
    The Idea of a University   1121
        From Discourse 5. Knowledge Its Own End   1121
        From Discourse 7. Knowledge Viewed in Relation to Professional
            Skill   1123
    Apologia Pro Vita Sua   1128
        From Chapter 1. History of My Religious Opinions to the Year
            1833   1128
        From Liberalism   1135

JOHN STUART MILL (1806–1873)   1137
    What Is Poetry?   1139
    On Liberty   1146
        From Chapter 3. Of Individuality as One of the Elements of Well-
            Being   1146
    The Subjection of Women   1155
        From Chapter 1   1156
    Autobiography   1166
        From Chapter 5. A Crisis in My Mental History. One Stage
            Onward   1166

Preliminary Confessions   530
     [The Prostitute Ann]   530
Introduction to the Pains of Opium   533
     [The Malay]   533
The Pains of Opium   535
     [Opium Reveries and Dreams]   535
On the Knocking at the Gate in *Macbeth*   543
Alexander Pope   547
     [The Literature of Knowledge and the Literature of Power]   547

GEORGE GORDON, LORD BYRON (1788–1824)   551
Written after Swimming from Sestos to Abydos   555
She walks in beauty   556
They say that Hope is happiness   557
When we two parted   557
Stanzas for Music   558
Darkness   559
So, we'll go no more a roving   560
When a man hath no freedom to fight for at home   561
Stanzas Written on the Road between Florence and Pisa   561
January 22nd. Missolonghi   562

CHILDE HAROLD'S PILGRIMAGE   563
Canto 1   564
     ["Sin's Long Labyrinth"]   564
Canto 3   565
     ["Once More Upon the Waters"]   565
     [Waterloo]   569
     [Napoleon]   572
     [Switzerland]   575
Canto 4   582
     [Venice]   582
     ["Farewell!"]   585

Manfred   588

DON JUAN   621
Fragment   622
Canto 1   623
     [Juan and Donna Julia]   623
Canto 2   651
     [The Shipwreck]   651
     [Juan and Haidee]   658
Canto 3   672
     [Juan and Haidee]   672
Canto 4   680
     [Juan and Haidee]   680

LETTERS   689
To Leigh Hunt (Sept.–Oct. 30, 1815)   689
To Thomas Moore (Jan. 28, 1817)   691
To John Cam Hobhouse and Douglas Kinnaird (Jan. 19, 1819)   693

To Douglas Kinnaird (Oct. 26, 1819)   695
To Percy Bysshe Shelley (Apr. 26, 1821)   697

PERCY BYSSHE SHELLEY (1792–1822)   698
   Mutability   701
   To Wordsworth   701
   Alastor; or, The Spirit of Solitude   702
   Mont Blanc   720
   Hymn to Intellectual Beauty   723
   Ozymandias   725
   Stanzas Written in Dejection—December 1818, near Naples   726
   A Song: "Men of England"   727
   England in 1819   728
   To Sidmouth and Castlereagh   728
   The Indian Girl's Song [The Indian Serenade]   729
   Ode to the West Wind   730
   Prometheus Unbound   732
      Preface   733
      From Act 1   736
      Act 2   742
         Scene 4   742
         Scene 5   746
      Act 3   749
         Scene 1   749
         From Scene 4   751
      From Act 4   754
   The Cloud   763
   To a Sky-Lark   765
   To Night   767
   To ―――― [Music, when soft voices die]   768
   The flower that smiles today   768
   O World, O Life, O Time   769
   Choruses from Hellas   769
      Worlds on worlds   769
      The world's great age   771
   Adonais   772
   A Dirge   786
   When the lamp is shattered   786
   To Jane (The keen stars were twinkling)   787
   Lines Written in the Bay of Lerici   788
   From A Defence of Poetry   789

JOHN CLARE (1793–1864)   802
   The Nightingale's Nest   803
   Pastoral Poesy   805
   Mouse's Nest   807
   A Vision   807
   I Am   808
   An Invite to Eternity   808
   Clock a Clay   809
   The Peasant Poet   810

Book Sixth. Cambridge, and the Alps 345
["Human Nature Seeming Born Again"] 345
[Crossing Simplon Pass] 346
Book Seventh. Residence in London 348
[The Blind Beggar. Bartholomew Fair] 348
Book Eighth. Retrospect, Love of Nature leading to Love of
Man 351
[The Shepherd in the Mist. Man Still Subordinate to Nature] 351
Book Ninth. Residence in France 354
[Paris and Orléans. Becomes a "Patriot"] 354
Book Tenth. France continued 357
[The Revolution: Paris and England] 357
[The Reign of Terror. Nightmares] 359
Book Eleventh. France, concluded 360
[Retrospect: "Bliss Was It in That Dawn." Recourse to "Reason's
Naked Self"] 360
[Crisis, Breakdown, and Recovery] 363
Book Twelfth. Imagination and Taste, how impaired and
restored 364
Book Thirteenth. Subject concluded 372
[Return to "Life's Familiar Face"] 372
[Discovery of His Poetic Subject. Salisbury Plain. Sight of "a New
World"] 373
Book Fourteenth. Conclusion 377
[The Vision on Mount Snowdon. Fear vs. Love Resolved.
Imagination] 377
[Conclusion: "The Mind of Man"] 382

DOROTHY WORDSWORTH (1771–1855) 383
From The Alfoxden Journal 385
From The Grasmere Journals 387
Grasmere—A Fragment 397
Thoughts on My Sick-Bed 399

SIR WALTER SCOTT (1771–1832) 401
The Heart of Midlothian 402
Chapter I. Being Introductory 402
Lochinvar 413
Jock of Hazeldean 415
Proud Maisie 415

SAMUEL TAYLOR COLERIDGE (1772–1834) 416
The Eolian Harp 419
This Lime-Tree Bower My Prison 420
The Rime of the Ancient Mariner 422
Kubla Khan 439
Christabel 441
Frost at Midnight 457
Dejection: An Ode 459
The Pains of Sleep 462
To William Wordsworth 464
On Donne's Poetry 466

Work without Hope   467
Epitaph   467
Biographia Literaria   467
  Chapter 1   468
    [The discipline of his taste at school]   468
    [Bowles's sonnets]   470
    [Comparison between the poets before and since Mr. Pope]   471
  Chapter 4   474
    [Mr. Wordsworth's earlier poems]   474
    [On fancy and imagination—the investigation of the distinction
      important to the fine arts]   476
  Chapter 13   477
    [On the imagination, or esemplastic power]   477
  Chapter 14. Occasion of the *Lyrical Ballads,* and the objects originally
    proposed—preface to the second edition—the ensuing controversy,
    its causes and acrimony—philosophic definitions of a poem and
    poetry with scholia   478
  Chapter 17   483
    [Examination of the tenets peculiar to Mr. Wordsworth]   483
    [Rustic life (above all, *low* and rustic life) especially unfavorable to the
      formation of a human diction—the best parts of language the
      products of philosophers, not clowns or shepherds]   484
    [The language of Milton as much the language of *real* life, yea,
      incomparably more so than that of the cottager]   484
Lectures on Shakespeare   486
  [Fancy and Imagination in Shakespeare's Poetry]   486
  [Mechanic vs. Organic Form]   488
The Statesman's Manual   489
  [On Symbol and Allegory]   489
  [The Satanic Hero]   491

WALTER SAVAGE LANDOR (1775–1864)   492
  Mother, I cannot mind my wheel   492
  Rose Aylmer   493
  Past ruined Ilion   493
  Twenty years hence   493

CHARLES LAMB (1775–1834)   494
  Christ's Hospital Five-and-Thirty Years Ago   495
  Old China   505

WILLIAM HAZLITT (1778–1830)   509
  On Gusto   510
  My First Acquaintance with Poets   513

THOMAS MOORE (1779–1852)   527
  Believe me, if all those endearing young charms   527
  The harp that once through Tara's halls   527
  The time I've lost in wooing   528

THOMAS DE QUINCEY (1785–1859)   529
  Confessions of an English Opium-Eater   530

We Must Look at the Harebell   2436
In the Children's Hospital   2437
Another Epitaph on an Army of Mercenaries   2437

JEAN RHYS (1894?–1979)   2437
Mannequin   2438
On Not Shooting Sitting Birds   2442

ROBERT GRAVES (1895–1985)   2444
Down, Wanton, Down!   2445
Love Without Hope   2446
The Cool Web   2446
The Reader Over My Shoulder   2446
To Juan at the Winter Solstice   2447
The White Goddess   2448
The Blue-Fly   2449
A Slice of Wedding Cake   2450

STEVIE SMITH (1902–1971)   2450
Is It Wise?   2451
Our Bog Is Dood   2451
Not Waving but Drowning   2452
The New Age   2453
Thoughts About the Person from Porlock   2453
Pretty   2455

GEORGE ORWELL (1903–1950)   2456
Shooting an Elephant   2457
Politics and the English Language   2462

SAMUEL BECKETT (1906–1989)   2471
Endgame   2472

W. H. AUDEN (1907–1973)   2500
Petition   2501
On This Island   2502
Spain 1937   2502
Musée des Beaux Arts   2505
Lullaby   2505
In Memory of W. B. Yeats   2506
Their Lonely Betters   2508
In Praise of Limestone   2509
The Shield of Achilles   2511

LOUIS MacNEICE (1907–1963)   2513
Sunday Morning   2513
The Sunlight on the Garden   2514
Bagpipe Music   2514
Soap Suds   2515
Star-Gazer   2516

Modern Fiction   2148
A Room of One's Own   2153
Professions for Women   2214
A Sketch of the Past   2218
  [Moments of Being and Non-Being]   2218
The Legacy   2226

JAMES JOYCE (1882–1941)   2231
Araby   2236
The Dead   2240
Ulysses   2269
  [Proteus]   2269
  [Lestrygonians]   2283
Finnegans Wake   2309
  From Anna Livia Plurabelle   2310

D. H. LAWRENCE (1885–1930)   2313
Odour of Chrysanthemums   2316
The Horse Dealer's Daughter   2330
Why the Novel Matters   2341
Love on the Farm   2346
Piano   2347
Tortoise Shell   2348
Tortoise Shout   2349
Bavarian Gentians   2351
Snake   2352
Cypresses   2354
How Beastly the Bourgeois Is   2356
The Ship of Death   2357

T. S. ELIOT (1888–1965)   2360
The Love Song of J. Alfred Prufrock   2364
Sweeney Among the Nightingales   2367
The Waste Land   2368
The Hollow Men   2383
Journey of the Magi   2386
Marina   2388

FOUR QUARTETS   2389
Little Gidding   2389

Tradition and the Individual Talent   2395
The Metaphysical Poets   2401

KATHERINE MANSFIELD (1888–1923)   2408
The Daughters of the Late Colonel   2409
The Garden Party   2423

HUGH MacDIARMID (1892–1978)   2433
A Drunk Man Looks at the Thistle   2435
  1. Farewell to Dostoevski   2435
  2. Yet Ha'e I Silence Left   2435
In Memoriam James Joyce   2436

The House of Life   1580
  The Sonnet   1580
  Nuptial Sleep   1580
   19. Silent Noon   1581
   77. Soul's Beauty   1581
   78. Body's Beauty   1581
   97. A Superscription   1582
   101. The One Hope   1582

CHRISTINA ROSSETTI (1830–1894)   1583
  Song ("She sat and sang alway")   1584
  Song ("When I am dead, my dearest")   1584
  After Death   1585
  Dead before Death   1585
  Cobwebs   1585
  A Triad   1586
  In an Artist's Studio   1586
  A Birthday   1587
  An Apple-Gathering   1587
  Winter: My Secret   1588
  Up-Hill   1589
  Goblin Market   1589
  "No, Thank You, John"   1601
  Promises Like Pie-Crust   1602
  In Progress   1603
  A Life's Parallels   1603
  Later Life   1603
   17 ("Something this foggy day, a something which")   1603
  Cardinal Newman   1604
  Sleeping at Last   1604

WILLIAM MORRIS (1834–1896)   1605
  The Defense of Guenevere   1606
  The Haystack in the Floods   1614
  How I Became a Socialist   1618

ALGERNON CHARLES SWINBURNE (1837–1909)   1621
  Choruses from Atalanta in Calydon   1623
   When the Hounds of Spring   1623
   Before the Beginning of Years   1624
  Hymn to Proserpine   1625
  The Garden of Proserpine   1628
  Ave Atque Vale   1631

WALTER PATER (1839–1894)   1636
  The Renaissance   1638
   Preface   1638
   ["La Gioconda"]   1641
   Conclusion   1642
  Appreciations   1645
   From Style   1645

ARTHUR HUGH CLOUGH (1819–1861)   1451
   Epi-strauss-ium   1452
   The Latest Decalogue   1452
   Say Not the Struggle Nought Availeth   1453

GEORGE ELIOT (1819–1880)   1454
   Margaret Fuller and Mary Wollstonecraft   1456
   Silly Novels by Lady Novelists   1461
   The Mill on the Floss   1469
     Book First. Boy and Girl   1469
      Chapter 1. Outside Dorlcote Mill   1469

MATTHEW ARNOLD (1822–1888)   1471
   The Forsaken Merman   1475
   Isolation. To Marguerite   1478
   To Marguerite—Continued   1479
   The Buried Life   1480
   Memorial Verses   1482
   Lines Written in Kensington Gardens   1484
   The Scholar Gypsy   1485
   Dover Beach   1492
   Stanzas from the Grande Chartreuse   1493
   Thyrsis   1498
   Preface to *Poems* (1853)   1504
   From The Function of Criticism at the Present Time   1514
   Culture and Anarchy   1528
     From Chapter 1. Sweetness and Light   1528
     From Chapter 2. Doing As One Likes   1530
     From Chapter 5. *Porro Unum Est Necessarium*   1532
   From The Study of Poetry   1534
   Literature and Science   1545

THOMAS HENRY HUXLEY (1825–1895)   1558
   Science and Culture   1559
     [The Values of Education in the Sciences]   1559
   Agnosticism and Christianity   1566
     [Agnosticism Defined]   1566

GEORGE MEREDITH (1828–1909)   1570
   Modern Love   1570
     1 ("By this he knew she wept with waking eyes")   1570
     2 ("It ended, and the morrow brought the task")   1571
     17 ("At dinner, she is hostess, I am host")   1571
     49 ("He found her by the ocean's moaning verge")   1572
     50 ("Thus piteously Love closed what he begat")   1572
   Lucifer in Starlight   1572

DANTE GABRIEL ROSSETTI (1828–1882)   1573
   The Blessed Damozel   1574
   My Sister's Sleep   1578
   The Woodspurge   1579

ELIZABETH GASKELL (1810–1865)   1318
   The Old Nurse's Story   1319

CHARLES DICKENS (1812–1870)   1333
   A Visit to Newgate   1335

ROBERT BROWNING (1812–1889)   1345
   Porphyria's Lover   1349
   Soliloquy of the Spanish Cloister   1350
   My Last Duchess   1352
   The Laboratory   1353
   The Lost Leader   1355
   How They Brought the Good News from Ghent to Aix   1356
   Home-Thoughts, from Abroad   1358
   Home-Thoughts, from the Sea   1358
   The Bishop Orders His Tomb at Saint Praxed's Church   1359
   Meeting at Night   1362
   Parting at Morning   1362
   A Toccata of Galuppi's   1363
   Memorabilia   1365
   Love among the Ruins   1365
   "Childe Roland to the Dark Tower Came"   1367
   Fra Lippo Lippi   1373
   The Last Ride Together   1382
   Andrea del Sarto   1385
   Two in the Campagna   1390
   A Grammarian's Funeral   1392
   An Epistle Containing the Strange Medical Experience of Karshish, the
         Arab Physician   1396
   Caliban upon Setebos   1402
   Prospiace   1409
   Abt Vogler   1410
   Rabbi Ben Ezra   1413

EMILY BRONTË (1818–1848)   1418
   I'm Happiest When Most Away   1419
   The Night-Wind   1420
   Remembrance   1421
   Stars   1421
   The Prisoner. A Fragment   1423
   No Coward Soul Is Mine   1424

JOHN RUSKIN (1819–1900)   1425
   Modern Painters   1428
      [A Definition of Greatness in Art]   1428
      ["The Slave Ship"]   1429
      From Of the Pathetic Fallacy   1430
   The Stones of Venice   1432
      [The Savageness of Gothic Architecture]   1432
   The Storm-Cloud of the Nineteenth Century   1443
      Lecture 1   1443

ELIZABETH BARRETT BROWNING (1806–1861)   1173
    The Cry of the Children   1174
    To George Sand: A Desire   1178
    To George Sand: A Recognition   1178
    Sonnets from the Portuguese   1179
        21 ("Say over again, and yet once over again")   1179
        22 ("When our two souls stand up erect and strong")   1179
        32 ("The first time that the sun rose on thine oath")   1180
        43 ("How do I love thee? Let me count the ways")   1180
    Aurora Leigh   1180
      Book 1   1180
        [The Feminine Education of Aurora Leigh]   1180
      Book 2   1186
        [Aurora's Aspirations]   1186
        [Aurora's Rejection of Romney]   1189
      Book 5   1192
        [Poets and the Present Age]   1192
    Mother and Poet   1195

ALFRED, LORD TENNYSON (1809–1892)   1198
    The Kraken   1201
    Mariana   1202
    The Lady of Shalott   1204
    The Lotos-Eaters   1208
    Ulysses   1213
    Tithonus   1215
    Break, Break, Break   1216
    The Epic [Morte d'Arthur]   1217
    The Eagle: A Fragment   1219
    Locksley Hall   1219

    THE PRINCESS   1225
    Sweet and Low   1225
    The Splendor Falls   1226
    Tears, Idle Tears   1226
    Ask Me No More   1227
    Now Sleeps the Crimson Petal   1227
    Come Down, O Maid   1228
    ["The Woman's Cause Is Man's"]   1229

    From In Memoriam A. H. H.   1230
    The Charge of the Light Brigade   1280

    IDYLLS OF THE KING   1282
    The Coming of Arthur   1282
    The Passing of Arthur   1293

    Flower in the Crannied Wall   1304
    Crossing the Bar   1304

EDWARD FITZGERALD (1809–1883)   1304
    The Rubáiyát of Omar Khayyám   1305

INDUSTRIALISM: PROGRESS OR DECLINE?   1696
  Thomas Babington Macaulay: A Review of Southey's *Colloquies*   1697
    [Evidence of Progress]   1697
  Friedrich Engels: *From* The Great Towns   1702
  Charles Kingsley: Alton Locke   1710
    [A London Slum]   1710
  Charles Dickens: Hard Times   1711
    [Coketown]   1711
  Anonymous: Poverty Knock   1712
  Henry Mayhew: London Labour and the London Poor   1714
    [Boy Inmate of the Casual Wards]   1714
  Annie Besant: The "White Slavery" of London Match Workers   1715
  Ada Nield Chew: A Living Wage for Factory Girls at Crewe   1717

THE "WOMAN QUESTION": THE VICTORIAN DEBATE ABOUT
       GENDER   1719
  Sarah Stickney Ellis: The Women of England: Their Social Duties and
    Domestic Habits   1721
    [Disinterested Kindness]   1721
  Coventry Patmore: The Angel in the House   1723
    The Paragon   1723
  Harriet Martineau: *From* Autobiography   1725
  Anonymous: The Great Social Evil   1728
  Dinah Maria Mulock: A Woman's Thoughts about Women   1732
    [Something to Do]   1732
  Florence Nightingale: Cassandra   1734
    [Nothing to Do]   1734
  Walter Besant: The Queen's Reign   1738
    [The Transformation of Women's Status between 1837 and
      1897]   1738

THE NINETIES   1740

MICHAEL FIELD (Katherine Bradley: 1846–1914; and Edith Cooper:
     1862–1913)   1742
    [Maids, not to you my mind doth change]   1742
    [A girl]   1743
    Unbosoming   1743
    [It was deep April, and the morn]   1744
    To Christina Rossetti   1744
    Nests in Elms   1745
    Eros   1745

WILLIAM ERNEST HENLEY (1849–1903)   1746
    In Hospital   1746
    Invictus   1747

OSCAR WILDE (1854–1900)   1747
    Impression du Matin   1749
    Hélas   1749
    E Tenebris   1750

GERARD MANLEY HOPKINS (1844–1889)   1648
  God's Grandeur   1651
  The Starlight Night   1651
  As Kingfishers Catch Fire   1652
  Spring   1652
  The Windhover   1652
  Pied Beauty   1653
  Hurrahing in Harvest   1653
  Binsey Poplars   1654
  Duns Scotus's Oxford   1654
  Felix Randal   1655
  Spring and Fall: to a young child   1655
  [Carrion Comfort]   1656
  No Worst, There Is None   1657
  I Wake and Feel the Fell of Dark, Not Day   1657
  That Nature Is a Heraclitean Fire   1658
  Thou Art Indeed Just, Lord   1658
  From Journal   1659

LIGHT VERSE   1662
EDWARD LEAR (1812–1888)   1662
  Limerick ("There was an Old Man who supposed")   1663
  How Pleasant to Know Mr. Lear   1663
  The Jumblies   1664
  Cold Are the Crabs   1665

LEWIS CARROLL (1832–1898)   1666
  Jabberwocky   1666
  [Humpty Dumpty's Explication of *Jabberwocky*]   1667
  The White Knight's Song   1668
  The Walrus and the Carpenter   1670
  The Hunting of the Snark   1672
    The Baker's Tale   1672

W. S. GILBERT (1836–1911)   1674
  When I, Good Friends, Was Called to the Bar   1675
  If You're Anxious for to Shine in the High Aesthetic Line   1676
  When Britain Really Ruled the Waves   1678

VICTORIAN ISSUES   1679
EVOLUTION   1679
  Charles Darwin: The Origin of Species   1679
    Struggle for Existence   1679
    Recapitulation and Conclusion   1682
  Charles Darwin: The Descent of Man   1686
    [Natural Selection and Sexual Selection]   1686
  Leonard Huxley: The Life and Letters of Thomas Henry Huxley   1690
    [The Huxley-Wilberforce Debate at Oxford]   1690
  Sir Edmund Gosse: Father and Son   1693
    [The Dilemma of the Fundamentalist and Scientist]   1694

The Harlot's House   1750
The Critic as Artist   1752
  [Criticism Itself an Art]   1752
Preface to *The Picture of Dorian Gray*   1760
The Importance of Being Earnest   1761
From De Profundis   1805

BERNARD SHAW (1856–1950)   1808
  Mrs. Warren's Profession   1810

FRANCIS THOMPSON (1859–1907)   1856
  The Hound of Heaven   1857

MARY ELIZABETH COLERIDGE (1861–1907)   1861
  The Other Side of a Mirror   1861
  The Witch   1862

RUDYARD KIPLING (1865–1936)   1863
  The Man Who Would Be King   1865
  Danny Deever   1888
  The Widow at Windsor   1889
  The Ladies   1890
  Recessional   1892
  The Hyenas   1893

ERNEST DOWSON (1867–1900)   1894
  Cynara   1894
  They Are Not Long   1895
  Carthusians   1895

The Twentieth Century   1897

Introduction   1897
Timeline   1914

THOMAS HARDY (1840–1928)   1916
  On the Western Circuit   1918
  Hap   1934
  The Impercipient   1935
  Neutral Tones   1935
  I Look into My Glass   1936
  A Broken Appointment   1936
  Drummer Hodge   1937
  The Darkling Thrush   1937
  The Ruined Maid   1938
  A Trampwoman's Tragedy   1939
  One We Knew   1942
  She Hears the Storm   1943

Channel Firing   1944
The Convergence of the Twain   1945
Ah, Are You Digging on My Grave?   1946
Under the Waterfall   1947
The Walk   1948
The Voice   1949
The Workbox   1949
During Wind and Rain   1950
In Time of "The Breaking of Nations"   1951
He Never Expected Much   1951

JOSEPH CONRAD (1857–1924)   1952
  Preface to The Nigger of the "Narcissus"   1954
    [The Task of the Artist]   1954
  Heart of Darkness   1957

                    THE RISE AND FALL OF EMPIRE   2017

JOHN RUSKIN: From Lectures on Art   2018
  [Imperial Duty]   2019

JOHN ATKINSON HOBSON: The Political Significance of
      Imperialism   2020

ANONYMOUS: Easter 1916 Proclamation of an Irish Republic   2023

RICHARD MULCAHY: [On the Treaty between Great Britain and
      Ireland]   2025

JAMES MORRIS: [The Partition of India]   2027

JAWAHARLAL NEHRU: Tryst with Destiny   2034

CHINUA ACHEBE: From An Image of Africa: Racism in
      Conrad's Heart of Darkness   2035

A. E. HOUSMAN (1859–1936)   2041
  Loveliest of Trees   2042
  When I Was One-and-Twenty   2042
  To an Athlete Dying Young   2042
  On Wenlock Edge   2043
  With Rue My Heart Is Laden   2044
  Terence, This Is Stupid Stuff   2044
  The Chestnut Casts His Flambeaux   2046
  Epitaph on an Army of Mercenaries   2047

DYLAN THOMAS (1914–1953)   2516
    The Force That Through the Green Fuse Drives the Flower   2517
    After the Funeral   2518
    There Was a Saviour   2519
    The Hunchback in the Park   2520
    Poem in October   2521
    Fern Hill   2522
    Do Not Go Gentle into That Good Night   2524

                  VOICES FROM WORLD WAR II   2525

EDITH SITWELL (1887–1964)   2527
    Still Falls the Rain   2527

HENRY REED (1914–1986)   2528
    Lessons of the War   2529
        1. Naming of Parts   2529
        2. Judging Distances   2530

RICHARD HILLARY (1919–1943)   2531
    From The Last Enemy   2532

KEITH DOUGLAS (1920–1944)   2535
    Gallantry   2536
    Vergissmeinnicht   2537
    Aristocrats   2537
    From Alamein to Zem Zem   2538

CHARLES CAUSLEY (b. 1917)   2539
    At the British War Cemetery, Bayeux   2540
    Armistice Day   2540

DORIS LESSING (b. 1919)   2541
    To Room Nineteen   2542

PHILIP LARKIN (1922–1985)   2564
    Church Going   2565
    MCMXIV   2566
    Talking in Bed   2567
    Ambulances   2568
    High Windows   2568
    Sad Steps   2569
    The Explosion   2570
    Aubade   2570

NADINE GORDIMER (b. 1923)   2572
    The Moment before the Gun Went Off   2573

THOM GUNN (b. 1929)   2576
    Considering the Snail   2576

A Map of the City   2577
Black Jackets   2577
My Sad Captains   2578
From the Wave   2579

DEREK WALCOTT (b. 1930)   2580
A Far Cry from Africa   2580
Nights in the Gardens of Port of Spain   2581
The Glory Trumpeter   2582
The Schooner *Flight*   2583
  1 Adios, Carenage   2583
Midsummer   2584
Omeros   2585
  Chapter XXX   2585

TED HUGHES (1930–1998)   2587
Wind   2587
Relic   2588
Pike   2589
Examination at the Womb-Door   2590
Theology   2590
The Seven Sorrows   2591
Daffodils   2592

HAROLD PINTER (b. 1930)   2594
The Dumb Waiter   2594

CHINUA ACHEBE (b. 1930)   2616
Things Fall Apart   2617

ALICE MUNRO (b. 1931)   2706
Walker Brothers Cowboy   2707

GEOFFREY HILL (b. 1932)   2717
In Memory of Jane Fraser   2717
Requiem for the Plantagenet Kings   2718
September Song   2718
Mercian Hymns   2719
  6 ("The princes of Mercia were badger and raven. Thrall")   2719
  7 ("Gasholders, russet among fields. Milldams, marlpools")   2719
  28 ("Processes of generation; deeds of settlement. The")   2720
  30 ("And it seemed, while we waited, he began to walk")   2720
An Apology for the Revival of Christian Architecture in England   2721
  9. The Laurel Axe   2721

V. S. NAIPAUL (b. 1932)   2722
One Out of Many   2722

EDNA O'BRIEN (b. 1932)   2745
Sister Imelda   2746

FLEUR ADCOCK (b. 1934)   2759
The Ex-Queen Among the Astronomers   2759

Poem Ended by a Death   2760
The Soho Hospital for Women   2761

TONY HARRISON (b. 1937)   2763
  Heredity   2764
  National Trust   2764
  Book Ends   2765
  Long Distance   2766
  Turns   2767
  Marked with D.   2767

ANITA DESAI (b. 1937)   2768
  Scholar and Gypsy   2768

TOM STOPPARD (b. 1937)   2785
  The Real Inspector Hound   2786

LES MURRAY (b. 1938)   2815
  Noonday Axeman   2816
  Morse   2818

SEAMUS HEANEY (b. 1939)   2818
  Digging   2819
  The Forge   2820
  Punishment   2821
  Casualty   2822
  The Skunk   2825
  Station Island   2825
    12 ("Like a convalescent, I took the hand")   2825
  The Sharping Stone   2827

J. M. COETZEE (b. 1940)   2829
  From Waiting for the Barbarians   2829

EAVAN BOLAND (b. 1944)   2834
  That the Science of Cartography Is Limited   2835
  The Dolls Museum in Dublin   2836
  The Lost Land   2837

CRAIG RAINE (b. 1944)   2838
  The Onion, Memory   2839
  A Martian Sends a Postcard Home   2840

SALMAN RUSHDIE (b. 1947)   2842
  The Prophet's Hair   2843

JAMES FENTON (b. 1949)   2853
  A German Requiem   2853
  Wind   2855

PAUL MULDOON (b. 1951)   2856
  Gathering Mushrooms   2856
  Milkwood and Monarch   2858

POEMS IN PROCESS   2859
  William Blake   2860
    The Tyger   2860
  William Wordsworth   2862
    She dwelt among the untrodden ways   2862
  Lord Byron   2863
    Don Juan   2863
      Canto 3, Stanza 9   2863
      Canto 14, Stanza 95   2864
  Percy Bysshe Shelley   2864
    O World, O Life, O Time   2865
  John Keats   2867
    The Eve of St. Agnes   2867
    To Autumn   2868
  Alfred, Lord Tennyson   2869
    The Lady of Shalott   2869
    Tithonus   2872
  Gerard Manley Hopkins   2873
    Thou art indeed just, Lord   2873
  William Butler Yeats   2873
    The Sorrow of Love   2874
    Leda and the Swan   2875
    After Long Silence   2877
  D. H. Lawrence   2879
    The Piano   2879

SELECTED BIBLIOGRAPHIES   2881
  Suggested General Readings   2881
  The Romantic Period   2883
  The Victorian Age   2891
  The Twentieth Century   2899

GEOGRAPHIC NOMENCLATURE   2916
MAP: London in the 19th and 20th Centuries   2917
BRITISH MONEY   2918
THE BRITISH BARONAGE   2921
  The Royal Lines of England and Great Britain   2923
RELIGIONS IN ENGLAND   2926
POETIC FORMS AND LITERARY TERMINOLOGY   2928

PERMISSIONS ACKNOWLEDGMENTS   2945

INDEX   2950

Preface to the Seventh Edition

The outpouring of English literature overflows all boundaries, including the capacious boundaries of *The Norton Anthology of English Literature.* But these pages manage to contain many of the most remarkable works written in English during centuries of restless creative effort. We have included epic poems and short lyrics; love songs and satires; tragedies and comedies written for performance on the commercial stage and private meditations meant to be perused in silence; prayers, popular ballads, prophecies, ecstatic visions, erotic fantasies, sermons, short stories, letters in verse and prose, critical essays, polemical tracts, several entire novels, and a great deal more. Such works generally form the core of courses that are designed to introduce students to the history of English literature, a history not only of gradual development, continuity, and dense internal echoes, but also of radical contingency, sudden change, and startling innovation.

One of the joys of literature in English is its spectacular abundance. Even from within the geographical confines of Great Britain and Ireland, where the majority of texts brought together in this collection originated, there are more than enough distinguished and exciting works to fill the pages of this anthology many times over. The abundance is all the greater if one takes, as the editors of these volumes do, a broad understanding of the term *literature.* The meaning of the term has in the course of several centuries shifted from the whole body of writing produced in a particular language to a subset of that writing consisting of works that claim special attention because of their formal beauty or expressive power. But any individual text's claim to attention is subject to constant debate and revision; established texts are jostled both by new arrivals and by previously neglected claimants; and the boundaries between the literary and whatever is thought to be "non-literary" are constantly challenged and redrawn. The heart of this collection consists of poems, plays, and prose fiction, but these categories are themselves products of ongoing historical transformations, and we have included many texts that call into question any conception of literature as denoting only a limited set of particular kinds of writing.

The designation "English" provides some obvious limits to the unwieldy, unstable, constantly shifting field of literature, but these limits are themselves in constant flux, due in part to the complexity of the territory evoked by the term (as explained in our appendix on "Geographical Nomenclature") and in part to the multinational, multicultural, and hugely expansive character of the language. As Geoffrey Nunberg's informative essay "The Persistence of English" (p. xlvii), commissioned for this Seventh Edition, makes clear, the variations in the forms of the spoken language that all go by the name of English are so great as to call into question the very notion of a single tongue, and the complex history and diffusion of the language have helped ensure that its literature is enormous. In the momentous process that transformed England into Great Britain and eventually into the center of a huge empire, more and more writers from outside England, beginning with the strong Irish and Scottish presence in the eighteenth century and gradually fanning out into the colonies, were absorbed into "English literature." Moreover, English has constantly interacted with other languages and has been transformed by this interaction. The scope of the cross-currents may be gauged by our medieval section, which includes selections in Old Irish and Middle Welsh, along with works by Bede, Geoffrey of Monmouth, Wace, and Marie de France—all of them authors living in the British Isles writing in languages other than English. Their works are important in themselves and also provide cultural contexts for understanding aspects of what we have come to think of as "English literature." Certain literary texts—many of them included in these volumes—have achieved sufficient prominence to serve as widespread models for other writers and as objects of enduring admiration, and thus to constitute a loose-boundaried canon. But just as there have never been academies in English-speaking countries established to regulate the use of language, so too there have never been firm and settled guidelines for canonizing particular texts. English literature as a field arouses not a sense of order but what the poet Yeats calls "the emotion of multitude."

The term "English Literature" in our title designates two different things. First, it refers to all the literary productions of a particular part of the world: the great preponderance of the works we include were written by authors living in England, Scotland, Wales, and Ireland. Second, it refers to literary works in the English language, a language that has extended far beyond the boundaries of its point of origin. Following the lead of most college courses, we have separated off, for purposes of this anthology, English literature from American literature, but in the selections for the latter half of the twentieth century we have incorporated a substantial number of texts by authors from other countries.

The linguistic mobility and cultural intertwining reflected in these twentieth-century texts are not new. It is fitting that among the first works in this anthology is *Beowulf,* a powerful epic written in the Germanic language known as Old English about a singularly restless Scandinavian hero, an epic newly translated for this edition by the Irish poet Seamus Heaney. Heaney, who was awarded the Nobel Prize for Literature in 1995, is one of the contemporary masters of English literature, but it would be potentially misleading to call him an "English poet," for he was born in Northern Ireland and is not in fact English. It would be still more misleading to call him a "British poet," as if his having been born in a country that was part of the British Empire were the most salient fact about the language he speaks and writes or the culture by which he was shaped. What does matter is that the language in which Heaney writes is English, and this fact links him powerfully with the authors assembled in these volumes, a linguistic community that stubbornly refuses to fit comfortably within any firm geographical or ethnic or national boundaries. So too, to glance at authors and writings included in the anthology, in the sixteenth century William Tyndale, in exile in the Low Countries and inspired by German religious reformers, translated the New

Testament from Greek and thereby changed the course of the English language; in the seventeenth century Aphra Behn touched her readers with a story that moves from Africa, where its hero is born, to South America, where she may have witnessed some of the tragic events she describes; and early in the twentieth century Joseph Conrad, born in Ukraine of Polish parents, wrote in eloquent English a celebrated novella whose vision of European empire was trenchantly challenged at the century's end by the Nigerian-born writer in English, Chinua Achebe.

A vital literary culture is always on the move. The Seventh Edition of *The Norton Anthology of English Literature* has retained the body of works that have traditionally been taught as the principal glories of English literature, but many of our new selections reflect the fact that the *national* conception of literary history, the conception by which English Literature meant the literature of England or at most of Great Britain, has begun to give way to something else. Writers like William Butler Yeats (born in Dublin), Hugh MacDiarmid (born in Dumfriesshire, Scotland), Virginia Woolf (born in London), and Dylan Thomas (born in Swansea, Wales) are now being taught, and are here anthologized, alongside such writers as Nadine Gordimer (born in the Transvaal, South Africa), Alice Munro (born in Wingham, Ontario), Derek Walcott (born on Saint Lucia in the West Indies), Chinua Achebe (born in Ogidi, Nigeria), and Salman Rushdie (born in Bombay, India). English literature, like so many other collective enterprises in our century, has ceased to be principally the product of the identity of a single nation; it is a global phenomenon.

A central feature of *The Norton Anthology of English Literature,* established by its original editors, was a commitment to provide periodic revisions in order to take advantage of newly recovered or better-edited texts, reflect scholarly discoveries and the shifting interests of readers, and keep the anthology in touch with contemporary critical and intellectual concerns. To help us honor this commitment we have, as in past years, profited from a remarkable flow of voluntary corrections and suggestions proposed by students, as well as teachers, who view the anthology with a loyal but critical eye. Moreover, we have again solicited and received detailed information on the works actually assigned, proposals for deletions and additions, and suggestions for improving the editorial matter, from over two hundred reviewers from around the world, almost all of them teachers who use the books in a course. In its evolution, then, this anthology has been the product of an ongoing collaboration among its editors, teachers, and students.

The active participation of an engaged community of readers has been crucial as the editors grapple with the challenging task of retaining (and indeed strengthening) the selection of more traditional texts even while adding many texts that reflect the transformation and expansion of the field of English studies. The challenge is heightened by the wish to keep each volume manageable, in size and weight, so that students will actually carry the book to class. The final decisions on what to include were made by the editors, but we were immeasurably assisted, especially in borderline cases, by the practical experience and the detailed opinions of teachers and scholars.

In addition to the new translation of *Beowulf* and to the greatly augmented global approach to twentieth-century literature in English, several other features of this Seventh Edition merit special mention. We have greatly expanded the selection of writing by women in all of the historical periods. The extraordinary work of scholars in recent years has recovered dozens of significant authors who had been marginalized or neglected by a male-dominated literary tradition and has deepened our understanding of those women writers who had managed, against considerable odds, to claim a place in that tradition. The First Edition of the *Norton Anthology* was ahead of its time in including six women writers; this Seventh Edition includes sixty, of whom twenty-one are newly added and twenty are reselected or expanded. Poets and prose writers whose names were scarcely mentioned even in the specialized literary histories of earlier generations—Isabella Whitney, Aemilia Lanyer, Lady Mary Wroth, Elizabeth Cary, Margaret Cavendish, Mary Leapor, Anna Letitia Barbauld, Charlotte Smith, Letitia Elizabeth Landon, and many others—now appear in the company of their male contemporaries. There are in addition three complete long prose works by women: Aphra Behn's *Oroonoko,* Mary Shelley's *Frankenstein,* and Virginia Woolf's *A Room of One's Own.*

The novel is, of course, a stumbling block for an anthology. The length of many great novels defies their incorporation in any volume that hopes to include a broad spectrum of literature. At the same time it is difficult to excerpt representative passages from narratives whose power often depends upon amplitude or upon the slow development of character or upon the on-rushing urgency of the story. Therefore, better to represent the remarkable achievements of novelists, the publisher is making available, in inexpensive and well-edited Norton Anthology Editions, a range of novels, including Jane Austen's *Pride and Prejudice,* Charles Dickens's *Hard Times,* Charlotte Brontë's *Jane Eyre,* and Emily Brontë's *Wuthering Heights.*

A further innovation in the Seventh Edition is our inclusion of new and expanded clusters of texts that resonate with one another culturally and thematically. Using the "Victorian Issues" section long featured in *The Norton Anthology of English Literature* as our model, we devised for each period groupings that serve to suggest some ways in which the pervasive concepts, images, and key terms that haunt major literary works can often be found in other written traces of a culture. Hence, for example, the adventures of Edmund Spenser's wandering knights resonate with the excerpts from Elizabethan travel accounts brought together in "The Wider World": Frobisher's violent encounters with the Eskimos of Baffin Island, Drake's attempt to lay claim to California, Amadas and Barlowe's idealizing vision of the Indians as the inhabitants of the Golden Age, and Hariot's subtle attempt to analyze and manipulate native beliefs. Similarly, the millenarian expectations voiced in the texts grouped in "The French Revolution and the 'Spirit of the Age' " helped shape the major writings of poets from William Blake to Percy Bysshe Shelley, while the historical struggles reflected in texts by Jawaharlal Nehru and others in "The Rise and Fall of Empire" echo in the fiction of Chinua Achebe, V. S. Naipaul, and J. M. Coetzee. We supplement the clusters for each period with several more topical groupings of texts and copious illustrations on the *Norton Anthology* Web site.

Period-by-Period Revisions

The scope of the revisions we have undertaken, the most extensive in the long publishing history of *The Norton Anthology of English Literature,* can be conveyed more fully by a list of some of the principal additions.

The Middle Ages. Better to represent the complex multilingual situation of the period, the section has been reorganized and divided into three parts: Anglo-Saxon England, Anglo-Norman England, and Middle English Literature of the Fourteenth and Fifteenth Centuries. Nearly fifteen years in the making, Seamus Heaney's translation of *Beowulf* comes closer to conveying the full power of the Anglo-Saxon epic than any existing rendering and will be of major interest as well to students of modern poetry. The selection of Anglo-Saxon poems has also been augmented by *The Wife's Lament.* We have added a new section, Anglo-Norman England, which provides a key bridge between the Anglo-Saxon period and the time of Chaucer, highlighting a cluster of texts that trace the origins of Arthurian romance. This section includes selections from the chronicle account of the Norman conquest; legendary histories by Geoffrey of Monmouth, Wace, and Layamon; Marie de France's *Lanval* (a Breton lay about King Arthur's court, here in a new verse translation by Alfred David), along with two of her fables; a selection from the *Ancrene Riwle* (Rule for Anchoresses); and two Celtic narratives: the Irish *Exile of the Sons of Uisliu* and the Welsh *Lludd and Lleuelys.* To Chaucer's works we have added *The Man of Law's Epilogue* and *Troilus's Song*; we have added to the grouping of Late Middle English lyrics and strengthened the already considerable selection from the revelations of the visionary anchoress Julian of Norwich; and we have included for the first time a work by Robert Henryson, *The Cock and the Fox.*

The Sixteenth Century. Shakespeare's magnificent comedy of cross-dressing and cross-purposes, *Twelfth Night,* is for the first time included in the *Norton Anthology,* providing a powerful contrast with his bleakest tragedy, *King Lear.* The raucous *Tunning of Elinour Rumming* has been added to Skelton's poems and the somber *Stand whoso list* to Wyatt's, while Gascoigne is now represented by his poem *Woodmanship.* Additions in poetry and prose works have similarly been made to Roger Ascham, Henry Howard, Earl of Surrey, Sir Walter Ralegh, Fulke Greville, Samuel Daniel, Thomas Campion, and Thomas Nashe. Along with the grouping of travel texts described above, another new cluster, "Literature of the Sacred," brings together contrasting Bible translations; writings by William Tyndale and Richard Hooker; Anne Askew's account, smuggled from the Tower, of her interrogation and torture, along with the martyrologist John Foxe's account of her execution; selections from the Book of Common Prayer and the Book of Homilies; and an Elizabethan translation of John Calvin's influential account of predestination. In addition to Anne Askew, another Elizabethan woman writer, Isabella Whitney, makes her appearance in the *Norton Anthology,* along with a new selection of texts by Mary Herbert and a newly added speech and letters by Queen Elizabeth.

The Early Seventeenth Century. In response to widespread demand and to our own sense of the work's commanding importance, both in its own time and in the history of English literature, we have for the first time included the whole of Milton's *Paradise Lost.* Other substantial works that newly appear in this section include Ben Jonson's *Masque of Blackness* and Andrew Marvell's *Upon Appleton House*, extensive selections from Elizabeth Cary's *Tragedy of Mariam*, and poetry and prose by Aemilia Lanyer and Margaret Cavendish. Additions have been made to the works of John Donne, Jonson, Lady Mary Wroth, George Herbert, Henry Vaughan, Richard Crashaw, Robert Herrick, and John Suckling. The "Voices of the War" cluster, introduced in the last edition, now includes Anna Trapnel's narrative of her eventful voyage from London to Cornwall; and a new cluster, "The Science of Self and World," brings together meditative texts, poems, and essays by Francis Bacon, Martha Moulsworth, Robert Burton, Rachel Speght, Sir Thomas Browne, Izaak Walton, and Thomas Hobbes.

The Restoration and the Eighteenth Century. John Gay's *The Beggar's Opera*—familiar to modern audiences as the source of Bertolt Brecht's *Threepenny Opera*—makes its appearance in the *Norton Anthology*, along with William Hogarth's illustration of a scene from the play. Hogarth's "literary" graphic art is represented by his satiric *Marriage A-la-Mode*. Two new clusters of texts enable readers to engage more fully with key controversies in the period. "Debating Women: Arguments in Verse" presents the war between the sexes in spirited poems by Jonathan Swift, Lady Mary Wortley Montagu, Alexander Pope, Anne Finch, Anne Ingram, and Mary Leapor. The period's sexual politics is illuminated as well in added texts by Samuel Pepys, John Wilmot, Second Earl of Rochester, and Aphra Behn. "Slavery and Freedom" brings together the disquieting exchange on the enslavement of African peoples between Ignatius Sancho and Laurence Sterne, along with Olaudah Equiano's ground-breaking history of his own enslavement. The narrative gifts of Frances Burney, whose long career spans this period and the next, are newly presented by six texts, including her famous, harrowing account of her mastectomy.

The Romantic Period. The principal changes here center on the greatly increased representation of women writers in the period: Mary Robinson and Letitia Elizabeth Landon are included for the first time, and there are substantially increased selections by Anna Letitia Barbauld, Charlotte Smith, Joanna Baillie, Dorothy Wordsworth, and Felicia Hemans; to Mary Wollstonecraft's epochal *Vindication of the Rights of Women*, we have now added a selection from her *Letters Written in Sweden*. Conjoined with Mary Shelley's *Frankenstein*, presented here in its entirety, these texts restore women writers, once marginalized in literary histories of the period, to the significant place they in fact occupied. A new thematic cluster focusing on the period's cataclysmic event, the French Revolution, brings together texts in prose and verse by Richard Price, Edmund Burke, Mary Wollstonecraft, Thomas Paine, Elhanan Winchester, Joseph Priestley, William Black, Robert Southey, William Wordsworth, Samuel Taylor Coleridge, and Percy Bysshe Shelley. The selection of poems by the peasant poet John Clare has been expanded and is printed in a new text prepared for this edition. We have also added to Sir Walter Scott the introductory chapter of his *Heart of Midlothian*, and to William Wordsworth his long and moving lyrical ballad *The Thorn*.

The Victorian Age. The important novelist, short story writer, and biographer Elizabeth Gaskell makes her appearance in the *Norton Anthology*, along with two late-nineteenth-century poets, Michael Field and Mary Elizabeth Coleridge. Rudyard Kipling's powerful story *The Man Who Would Be King* is a significant new addition, as is the selection from Oscar Wilde's prison writings, *De Profundis*. Dickens's somber reflection *A Visit to Newgate* has been added. There are new texts in the selections of many authors as well, including John Henry Cardinal Newman, Elizabeth Barrett Browning, Alfred, Lord Tennyson, Elizabeth Gaskell, George Eliot, Dante Gabriel Rossetti, William Morris, and Gerard Manley Hopkins. Bernard Shaw's play *Mrs. Warren's Profession* has been moved to its chronological place in this section. New texts have also been added to the "Victorian Issues" clusters on evolution, industrialism, and the debate about gender.

The Twentieth Century. The principal addition here, in length and in symbolic significance, is Chinua Achebe's celebrated novel *Things Fall Apart*, presented in its entirety, and, with Joseph Conrad's *Heart of Darkness* and Virginia Woolf's *A Room of One's Own,* the third complete prose work in this section. But there are many other changes as well, in keeping with a thoroughgoing rethinking of this century's literary history. We begin with Thomas Hardy (now shown as fiction writer as well as poet) and Joseph Conrad, both liminal figures poised between two distinct cultural worlds. These are followed by groupings of texts that articulate some of the forces that helped pull these worlds asunder. A cluster on "The Rise and Fall of Empire" brings together John Ruskin, John Hobson, the Easter Proclamation of the Irish Republic, Richard Mulcahy, James Morris, Jawaharlal Nehru, and Chinua Achebe, and these texts of geo-political crisis in turn resonate with "Voices from World War I" and "Voices from World War II," both sections newly strengthened by prose texts. We have added selections to E. M. Forster, James Joyce, and T. S. Eliot, among others, and for the first time present the work of the West Indian writer Jean Rhys and the Irish poet Paul Muldoon. Samuel Beckett is now represented by the complete text of his masterful tragicomedy, *Endgame.* Above all, the explosion of writing in English in "postcolonial" countries around the world shapes our revision of this section, not only in our inclusion of Achebe but also in new texts by Derek Walcott, V. S. Naipaul, Anita Desai, Les Murray, J. M. Coetzee, Eavan Boland, Alice Munro, and Salman Rushdie. Seamus Heaney's works, to which another poem has been added, provide the occasion to look back again to the beginning of these volumes with Heaney's new translation of *Beowulf.* This translation is a reminder that the history of literature is not a straightforward sequence, that the most recent works can double back upon the distant past, and that the words set down by men and women who have crumbled into dust can speak to us with astonishing directness.

Editorial Procedures

The scope of revisions to the editorial apparatus in the Seventh Edition is the most extensive ever undertaken in *The Norton Anthology of English Literature*. As in past editions, period introductions, headnotes, and annotation are designed to give students the information needed, without imposing an interpretation. The aim of these editorial materials is to make the anthology self-sufficient, so that it can be read anywhere—in a coffeehouse, on a bus, or under a tree. In this edition, this apparatus has been thoroughly revised in response to new scholarship. The period introductions and many headnotes have been either entirely or substantially rewritten to be more helpful to students, and all the Selected Bibliographies have been thoroughly updated.

Several new features reflect the broadened scope of the selections in the anthology. The new introductory essay, "The Persistence of English" by Geoffrey Nunberg, Stanford University and Xerox Palo Alto Research Center, explores the emergence and spread of English and its apparent present-day "triumph" as a world language. It provides a lively point of departure for the study of literature in English. The endpaper maps have been reconceived and redrawn. New timelines following each period introduction help students place their reading in historical and cultural context. So that students can explore literature as a visual medium, the anthology introduces visual materials from several periods—Hogarth's *Marriage A-la-Mode*, engravings by Blake, and Dante Gabriel Rossetti's illustrations for poems by Tennyson, Christina Rossetti, and Rossetti himself. These illustrations can be supplemented by the more than 350 images available on Norton Topics Online, the Web companion to the *Norton Anthology*.

Each volume of the anthology includes an appendix, "Poems in Process," which reproduces from manuscripts and printed texts the genesis and evolution of a number of poems whose final form is printed in that volume. Both volumes contain a useful section on "Poetic Forms and Literary Terminology," much revised in the Seventh Edition, as well as brief appendices on the intricacies of English money, the baronage, and religions. A new appendix, "Geographic Nomenclature," has been added to clarify the shifting place-names applied to regions of the British Isles.

Students, no less than scholars, deserve the most accurate texts available; in keeping with this policy, we continue to introduce improved versions of the selections where available. In this edition, for example, in addition to Seamus Heaney's new verse translation of *Beowulf*, we introduce Alfred David's new verse translation of Marie de France's *Lanval*, the Norton/Oxford text of *Twelfth Night*, and Jack Stillinger's newly edited texts of the poems of John Clare. To ease a student's access, we have normalized spelling and capitalization in texts up to and including the Victorian period to follow the conventions of modern English; we leave unaltered, however, texts in which modernizing would change semantic or metrical qualities and those texts for which we use specially edited versions (identified in a headnote or footnote); these include Wollstonecraft's *Vindication*, William Wordsworth's *Ruined Cottage* and *Prelude*, Dorothy Wordsworth's *Journals*, the verse and prose of P. B. Shelley and Keats, and Mary Shelley's *Frankenstein*. In The Twentieth Century, we have restored original spelling and punctuation to selections retained from the previous edition in the belief that the authors' choices, when they pose no difficulties for student readers, should be respected.

We continue other editorial procedures that have proved useful in the past. After each work, we cite (when known) the date of composition on the left and the date of first publication on the right; in some instances, the latter is followed by the date of a revised edition for which the author was responsible. We have used square brackets to indicate titles supplied by the editors for the convenience of readers. Whenever a portion of a text has been omitted, we have indicated that omission with three asterisks. If the omitted portion is important for following the plot or argument, we have provided a brief summary within the text or in a footnote. We have extended our longstanding practice of providing marginal glossing of single words and short phrases from medieval and dialect poets (such as Robert Burns) to all the poets in the anthology. Finally, we have adopted a bolder typeface and redesigned the page, so as to make the text more readable.

The Course Guide to Accompany "The Norton Anthology of English Literature," by Katherine Eggert and Kelly Hurley, University of Colorado at Boulder, based on an earlier version by Alfred David, Indiana University, has been thoroughly revised and expanded; it contains detailed syllabi for a variety of approaches to the course, teaching notes on individual authors, periods, and works, study and essay questions, and suggested ways to integrate the printed texts with material on the Norton Web site. A copy of the *Guide* may be obtained on request from the publisher.

The Norton Topics Online Web site (*www.wwnorton.com/nael*) augments the anthology's already broad representation of the sweep of English literature. For students who wish to extend their exploration of literary and cultural contexts, the Web site offers a huge range of related texts, prepared by the anthology editors, and by Myron Tuman, University of Alabama, and Philip Schwyzer, University of California, Berkeley. An ongoing venture, the Web site currently offers twenty-one thematic clusters—three per period—of texts and visual images, cross-referenced to the anthology, together with overviews, study explorations, and annotated links to related sites. In addition, the Audio Companion to *The Norton Anthology of English Literature* is available without charge upon request by teachers who adopt the anthology. It consists of two compact discs of readings by the authors of the works represented in the anthology, readings of poems in Old and Middle English and in English dialects, and performances of poems that were written to be set to music.

The editors are deeply grateful to the hundreds of teachers worldwide who have helped us to improve *The Norton Anthology of English Literature.* A list of the advisors who prepared in-depth reviews and of the instructors who replied to a detailed questionnaire follows on a separate page, under Acknowledgments. The editors would like to express appreciation for their assistance to Tiffany Beechy (Harvard University), Mitch Cohen (Wissenschaftskolleg zu Berlin), Sandie Byrne (Oxford University), Sarah Cole (Columbia University), Dianne Ferriss (Cornell University), Robert Folkenflik (University of California, Irvine), Robert D. Fulk (Indiana University), Andrew Gurr (The University of Reading), Wendy Hyman (Harvard University), Elissa Linke (Wissenschaftskolleg zu Berlin), Joanna Lipking (Northwestern University), Linda O'Riordan (Wissenschaftskolleg zu Berlin), Ruth Perry (M.I.T.), Leah Price (Harvard University), Ramie Targoff (Yale University), and Douglas Trevor (Harvard University). The editors give special thanks to Paul Leopold, who drafted the appendix on Geographic Nomenclature and revised the appendix on Religions in England, and to Philip Schwyzer (University of California, Berkeley), whose wide-ranging contributions include preparing texts and study materials for the Web site, assisting with the revision of numerous headnotes, and updating appendices on the British baronage and British money. We also thank the many people at Norton who contributed to the Seventh Edition: Julia Reidhead, who served not only as the inhouse supervisor but also as an unfailingly wise and effective collaborator in every aspect of planning and accomplishing this Seventh Edition; Marian Johnson, developmental editor, who kept the project moving forward with a remarkable blend of focused energy, intelligence, and common sense; Candace Levy, Ann Tappert, Barry Katzen, David Hawkins, and Will Rigby, project and manuscript editors; Anna Karvellas and Kirsten Miller, Web site editors; Diane O'Connor, production manager; Kristin Sheerin, permissions manager; Toni Krass, designer; Neil Ryder Hoos, art researcher; and Christa Grenawalt, editorial assistant and map coordinator. All these friends provided the editors with indispensable help in meeting the challenge of representing, justly and in only two volumes, the unparalleled range and variety of English literature.

M. H. ABRAMS
STEPHEN GREENBLATT

Acknowledgments

Among our many critics, advisors, and friends, the following were of especial help toward the preparation of the Seventh Edition, either with advice or by providing critiques of particular periods of the anthology: Judith H. Anderson (Indiana University), Paula Backsheider (Auburn University), Elleke Boehmer (Leeds University), Rebecca Brackmann (University of Illinois), James Chandler (University of Chicago), Valentine Cunningham (Oxford University), Lennard Davis (SUNY Binghamton), Katherine Eggert (University of Colorado), P. J. C. Field (University of Wales), Vincent Gillespie (Oxford University), Roland Greene (University of Oregon), A. C. Hamilton (Queen's University), Emrys Jones (Oxford University), Laura King (Yale University), Noel Kinnamon (Mars Hill College), John Leonard (University of Western Ontario), William T. Liston (Ball State University), F. P. Lock (Queen's University), Lee Patterson (Yale University), Jahan Ramazani (University of Virginia), John Regan (Oxford University), John Rogers (Yale University), Herbert Tucker (University of Virginia), Mel Wiebe (Queen's University).

The editors would like to express appreciation and thanks to the hundreds of teachers who provided reviews: Porter Abbott (University of California, Santa Barbara), Robert Aguirre (University of California, Los Angeles), Alan Ainsworth (Houston Community College Central), Jesse T. Airaudi (Baylor University), Edward Alexander (University of Washington), Michael Alexander (University of St. Andrews), Gilbert Allen (Furman University), Jill Angelino (George Washington University), Linda M. Austin (Oklahoma State University), Sonja S. Baghy (State University of West Georgia), Vern D. Bailey (Carleton College), William Barker (Fitchburg State University), Carol Barret (Northridge Campus, Austin Community College), Mary Barron (University of North Florida), Jackson Barry (University of Maryland), Dean Bevan (Baker University), Carol Beran (St. Mary's College), James Biester (Loyola University, Chicago), Nancy B. Black (Brooklyn College), Alan Blackstock (Wharton Community Junior College), Alfred F. Boe (San Diego State University), Cheryl D. Bohde (McLennan Community College), Karin Boklund-Lagopoul,oou (Aristotle University of Thessaloniki), Scott Boltwood (Emory and Henry College), Troy Boone (University of California, Santa Cruz), James L. Boren (University of Oregon), Ellen Brinks (Princeton University), Douglas Bruster (University of Texas, San Antonio), John Bugge (Emory University), Maria Bullon-Fernandez (Seattle University), John J. Burke (University of Alabama), Deborah G. Burks (Ohio State University), James Byer (Western Carlonia University), Gregory Castle (Arizona State University), Paul William Child (Sam Houston State University), Joe R. Christopher (Tarleton State University), A. E. B. Coldiron (Towson State University), John Constable (University of Leeds), C. Abbott Conway (McGill University), Patrick Creevy (Mississippi State University), Thomas M. Curley (Bridgewater State College), Clifford Davidson (Western Michigan University), Craig R. Davis (Smith College), Frank Day (Clemson University), Marliss Desens (Texas Tech University), Jerome Donnelly (University of Central Florida), Terrance Doody (Rice University), Max Dorsinville (McGill University), David Duff (University of Aberdeen), Alexander Dunlop (Auburn University), Richard J. DuRocher (St. Olaf College), Dwight Eddins (University of Alabama), Caroline L. Eisner (George Washington University), Andrew Elfenbein (University of Minnesota), Doris Williams Elliott (University of Kansas), Nancy S. Ellis (Mississippi State University), Kevin Eubanks (University of Tennessee), Gareth Euridge (Denison University), Deanna Evans (Bemidji State University), Julia A. Fesmire (Middle Tennessee State University), Michael Field (Bemidji State University), Judith L. Fisher (Trinity University), Graham Forst (Capilano College), Marilyn Francus (West Virginia University), Susan S. Frisbie (Santa Clara University), Shearle Furnish (West Texas A&M University), Arthur Ganz (City College of CUNY; The New School), Stephanie Gauper (Western Michigan University), Donna A. Gessell (North Georgia College and State University), Reid Gilbert (Capilano College), Jonathan C. Glance (Mercer University), I. Gopnik (McGill University), William Gorski (Northwestern State University of Louisiana), Roy Gottfried (Vanderbilt University), Timothy Gray (University of California, Santa Barbara), Patsy Griffin (Georgia Southern University), M. J. Gross (Southwest Texas State University), Gillian Hanson (University of Houston), Linda Hatchel (McLennan Community College), James Heldman (Western Kentucky University), Stephen Hemenway (Hope College), Michael Hennessy (Southwest Texas State University), Peter C. Herman (San Diego State University), James Hirsh (Georgia State University), Diane Long Hoeveler (Marquette University), Jerrold E. Hogle (University of Arizona), Brian Holloway (College of West Virginia), David Honick (Bentley College), Catherine E. Howard (University of Houston), David Hudson (Augsburg College), Steve Hudson (Portland Community College), Clark Hulse (University of Illinois, Chicago), Jefferson Hunter (Smith College), Vernon Ingraham (University of Massachusetts, Dartmouth), Thomas Jemielity (University of Notre Dame), R. Jothiprakash (Wiley College), John M. Kandl (Walsh University), David Kay (University of Illinois, Urbana-Champaign), Richard Kelly (University of Tennessee), Elizabeth Keyser (Hollins College), Gail Kienitz (Wheaton College), Richard Knowles (University of Wisconsin, Madison), Deborah Knuth (Colgate University), Albert Koinm (Sam Houston State University), Jack Kolb (University of California, Los Angeles), Valerie Krishna (City College, CUNY), Richard Kroll (University of California, Irvine), Jameela Lares (University of Southern Mississippi), Beth Lau (California State University, Long Beach), James Livingston (Northern Michigan University), Christine Loflin (Grinnell College), W. J. Lohman Jr. (University of Tampa), Suzanne H. MacRae (University of Arkansas, Fayettesville), Julia Maia (West Valley College), Sarah R. Marino (Ohio Northern University), Louis Martin (Elizabethtown College), Irene Martyniuk (Fitchburg State College), Frank T. Mason (University of South Florida), Mary Massirer (Baylor University), J. C. C. Mays (University College, Dublin), James McCord (Union College), Brian McCrea (University of Florida), Claie McEachern (University of California, Los Angeles), Joseph McGowan (University of San Diego), Alexander Menocal (University of North Florida), John Mercer (Northeastern State University),

Teresa Michals (George Mason University), Michael Allen Mikolajezak (University of St. Thomas), Jonathan Middlebrook (San Francisco State University), Sal Miroglotta (John Carroll University), James H. Morey (Emory University), Maryclaire Moroney (John Carroll University), William E. Morris (University of South Florida), Charlotte C. Morse (Virginia Commonwealth University), Alan H. Nelson (University of California, Berkeley), Jeff Nelson (University of Alabama, Huntsville), Richard Newhauser (Trinity University), Ashton Nichols (Dickinson College), Noreen O'Connor (George Washington University), Peter Okun (Davis and Elkins College), Nora M. Olivares (San Antonio College), Harold Orel (University of Kansas), Sue Owen (University of Sheffield), Diane Parkin-Speer (Southwest Texas State University), C. Patton (Texas Tech University), Paulus Pimoma (Central Washington University), John F. Plummer (Vanderbilt University), Alan Powers (Bristol Community College), William Powers (Michigan Technological University), Nicholas Radel (Furman University), Martha Rainbolt (DePauw University), Robert L. Reid (Emory and Henry College), Luke Reinsina (Seattle Pacific University), Cedric D. Reverand II (University of Wyoming), Mary E. Robbins (Georgia State University), Mark Rollins (Ohio State University, Athens), Charles Ross (Purdue University), Donelle R. Ruwe (Fitchburg State College), John Schell (University of Central Florida), Walter Scheps (SUNY Stony Brook), Michael Schoenfeldt (University of Michigan), Robert Scotto (Baruch College), Asha Sen (University of Wisconsin, Eau Claire), Lavina Shankar (Bates College), Michael Shea (Southern Connecticut State University), R. Allen Shoaf (University of Florida), Michael N. Stanton (University of Vermont), Massie C. Stinson Jr. (Longwood College), Andrea St. John (University of Miami), Donald R. Stoddard (Anne Arundel Community College), Joyce Ann Sutphen (Gustavas Adolphus College), Max K. Sutton (University of Kansas), Margaret Thomas (Wilberforce University), John M. Thompson (U.S. Naval Academy), Dinny Thorold (University of Westminster), James B. Twitchell (University of Florida), J. K. Van Dover (Lincoln University), Karen Van Eman (Wayne State University), Paul V. Voss (Georgia State University), Leon Waldoff (University of Illinois, Urbana-Champaign), Donald J. Weinstock (California State University, Long Beach), Susan Wells (Temple University), Winthrop Wetherbee (Cornell University), Thomas Willard (University of Arizona), J. D. Williams (Hunter College), Charles Workman (Stanford University), Margaret Enright Wye (Rockhurst College), R. O. Wyly (University of Southern Florida), James J. Yoch (University of Oklahoma), Marvin R. Zirker (Indiana University, Bloomington).

The Persistence of English

If you measure the success of a language in purely quantitative terms, English is entering the twenty-first century at the moment of its greatest triumph. It has between 400 and 450 million native speakers, perhaps 300 million more who speak it as a second language—well enough, that is, to use it in their daily lives—and somewhere between 500 and 750 million who speak it as a foreign language with various degrees of fluency. The resulting total of between 1.2 billion and 1.5 billion speakers, or roughly a quarter of the world's population, gives English more speakers than any other language (though Chinese has more native speakers). Then, too, English is spoken over a much wider geographical area than any other language and is the predominant lingua franca of most fields of international activity, such as diplomacy, business, travel, science, and technology.

But figures like these can obscure a basic question: what exactly do we mean when we talk about the "English language" in the first place? There is, after all, an enormous range of variation in the forms of speech that go by the name of English in the various parts of the world—or often, even within the speech of a single nation—and it is not obvious why we should think of all of these as belonging to a single language. Indeed, there are some linguists who prefer to talk about "world Englishes," in the plural, with the implication that these varieties may not have much more to unite them than a single name and a common historical origin.

To the general public, these reservations may be hard to understand; people usually assume that languages are natural kinds like botanical species, whose boundaries are matters of scientific fact. But as linguists observe, there is nothing in the forms of English themselves that tells us that it is a single language. It may be that the varieties called "English" have a great deal of vocabulary and structure in common and that English-speakers can usually manage to make themselves understood to one another, more or less (though films produced in one part of the English-speaking world often have to be dubbed or subtitled to make them intelligible to audiences in another). But there are many cases where we find linguistic varieties that are mutually intelligible and grammatically similar, but where speakers nonetheless identify separate languages—for example, Danish and Norwegian, Czech and Slovak, or Dutch and Afrikaans. And on the other hand, there are cases where speakers identify varieties as belonging to a single language even though they are linguistically quite distant from one another: the various "dialects" of Chinese are more different from one another than the Latin offshoots that we identify now as French, Italian, Spanish, and so forth.

Philosophers sometimes compare languages to games, and the analogy is apt here, as well. Trying to determine whether American English and British English or Dutch and Afrikaans are "the same language" is like trying to determine whether baseball and softball are "the same game"—it is not something you can find out just by looking at their rules. It is not surprising, then, that linguists should throw up their hands when someone asks them to determine on linguistic grounds alone whether two varieties belong to a single language. That, they answer, is a political or social determination, not a linguistic one, and they usually go on to cite a well-known quip: "a language is just a dialect with an army and a navy."

There is something to this remark. Since the eighteenth century, it has been widely believed that every nation deserved to have its own language, and declarations of political independence have often been followed by declarations of linguistic independence. Until recently, for example, the collection of similar language varieties that were spoken in most of central Yugoslavia was regarded as a single language, Serbo-Croatian, but once the various regions became independent, their inhabitants began to speak of Croatian, Serbian, and Bosnian as separate languages, even though they are mutually comprehensible and grammatically almost identical.

The English language has avoided this fate (though on occasion it has come closer to breaking up than most people realize). But the unity of a language is never a foregone conclusion. In any speech-community, there are forces always at work to create new differences and varieties: the geographic and social separation of speech-communities, their distinct cultural and practical interests, their contact with other cultures and other languages, and, no less important, a universal fondness for novelty for its own sake, and a desire to speak differently from one's parents or the people in the next town. Left to function on their own, these centrifugal pressures can rapidly lead to the linguistic fragmentation of the speech-community. That is what happened, for example, to the vulgar (that is, "popular") Latin of the late Roman Empire, which devolved into hundreds or thousands of separate dialects (the emergence of the eight or ten standard varieties that we now think of as the Romance languages was a much later development).

Maintaining the unity of a language over an extended time and space, then, requires a more or less conscious determination by its speakers that they have certain communicative interests in common that make it worthwhile to try to curb or modulate the natural tendency to fragmentation and isolation. This determination can be realized in a number of ways. The speakers of a language may decide to use a common spelling system even when dialects become phonetically distinct, to defer to the same set of literary models, to adopt a common format for their dictionaries and grammars, or to make instruction in the standard language a part of the general school curriculum, all of which the English-speaking world has done to some degree. Or in some other places, the nations of the linguistic community may establish academies or other state institutions charged with regulating the use of the language, and even go so far as to publish lists of words that are unacceptable for use in the press or in official publications, as the French government has done in recent years. Most important, the continuity of the language rests on speakers' willingness to absorb the linguistic and cultural influences of other parts of the linguistic community.

THE EMERGENCE OF THE ENGLISH LANGUAGE

To recount the history of a language, then, is not simply to trace the development of its various sounds, words, and constructions. Seen from that exclusively linguistic point of view, there would be nothing to distinguish the evolution of Anglo-Saxon into the varieties of modern English from the evolution of Latin into modern French, Italian, and so forth—we would not be able to tell, that is, why English continued to be considered a single language while the Romance languages did not. We also have to follow the play of centrifugal and centripetal forces that kept the language always more or less a unity—the continual process of creation of new dialects and varieties, the countervailing rise of new standards and of mechanisms aimed at maintaining the linguistic center of gravity.

Histories of the English language usually put its origin in the middle of the fifth century, when several Germanic peoples first landed in the place we now call England and began to displace the local inhabitants, the Celts. There is no inherent linguistic reason why we should locate the beginning of the language at this time, rather than with the Norman Conquest of 1066 or in the fourteenth century, say, and in fact the determination that English began with the Anglo-Saxon period was not generally accepted until the nineteenth century. But this point of view has been to a certain extent self-justifying, if only because it has led to the addition of Anglo-Saxon works to the canon of English literature, where they remain. Languages are constructions over time as well as over space.

Wherever we place the beginnings of English, though, there was never a time when the language was not diverse. The Germanic peoples who began to arrive in England in the fifth century belonged to a number of distinct tribes, each with its own dialect, and tended to settle in different parts of the country—the Saxons in the southwest, the Angles in the east and north, the Jutes (and perhaps some Franks) in Kent. These differences were the first source of the distinct dialects of the language we now refer to as Anglo-Saxon or Old English. As time went by, the linguistic divisions were reinforced by geography and by the political fragmentation of the country, and later, through contact with the Vikings who had settled the eastern and northern parts of England in the eighth through eleventh centuries.

Throughout this period, though, there were also forces operating to consolidate the language of England. Over the centuries, cultural and political dominance passed from Northumbria in the north to Mercia in the center and then to Wessex in the southwest, where a literary standard emerged in the ninth century, owing in part to the unification of the kingdom and in part to the singular efforts of Alfred the Great (849–899), who encouraged literary production in English and himself translated Latin works into the language. The influence of these standards and the frequent communication between the regions worked to level many of the dialect differences. There is a striking example of the process in the hundreds of everyday words derived from the language of the Scandinavian settlers, which include *dirt, lift, sky, skin, die, birth, weak, seat,* and *want.* All of these spread to general usage from the northern and eastern dialects in which they were first introduced, an indication of how frequent and ordinary were the contacts among the

Anglo-Saxons of various parts of the country—and initially, between the Anglo-Saxons and the Scandinavians themselves. (By contrast, the Celtic peoples that the Anglo-Saxons had displaced made relatively few contributions to the language, apart from place-names like *Thames, Avon,* and *Dover.*)

The Anglo-Saxon period came to an abrupt end with the Norman Conquest of 1066. With the introduction of a French-speaking ruling class, the written use of English was greatly reduced for 150 years. English did not reappear extensively in written records until the beginning of the thirteenth century, and even then it was only one of the languages of a multilingual community: French was widely used for another two hundred years or so (Parliament was conducted in French until 1362), and Latin was the predominant language of scholarship until the Renaissance. The English language that re-emerged in this period was considerably changed from the language of Alfred's period. Its grammar was simplified, continuing a process already under way before the Conquest, and its vocabulary was enriched by thousands of French loan words. Not surprisingly, given the preeminent role of French among the elite, these included the language of government (*majesty, state, rebel*); of religion (*pastor, ordain, temptation*); of fashion and social life (*button, adorn, dinner*); and of art, literature, and medicine (*painting, chapter, paper, physician*). But the breadth of French influence was not limited to those domains; it also provided simple words like *move, aim, join, solid, chief, clear, air,* and *very.* All of this left the language sufficiently different from Old English to warrant describing it with the name of Middle English, though we should bear in mind that language change is always gradual and that the division of English into neat periods is chiefly a matter of scholarly convenience.

Middle English was as varied a language as Old English was: Chaucer wrote in *Troilus and Criseyde* that "ther is so gret diversite in Englissh" that he was fearful that the text would be misread in other parts of the country. It was only in the fifteenth century or so that anything like a standard language began to emerge, based in the speech of the East Midlands and in particular of London, which reflected the increased centralization of political and economic power in that region. Even then, though, dialect differences remained strong; the scholar John Palsgrave complained in 1540 that the speech of university students was tainted by "the rude language used in their native countries [i.e., counties]," which left them unable to express themselves in their "vulgar tongue."

The language itself continued to change as it moved into what scholars describe as the Early Modern English period, which for convenience's sake we can date from the year 1500. Around this time, it began to undergo the Great Vowel Shift, as the long vowels engaged in an intricate dance that left them with new phonetic values. (In Chaucer's time, the word *bite* had been pronounced roughly as "beet," *beet* as "bate," *name* as "nahm," and so forth.) The grammar was changing as well; for example, the pronoun *thee* began to disappear, as did the verbal suffix-*eth*, and the modern form of questions began to emerge: in place of "See you that house?" people began to say "Do you see that house?" Most significantly, at least so far as contemporary observers were concerned, the Elizabethans and their successors coined thousands of new words based on Latin and Greek in an effort to make English an adequate replacement for Latin in the writing of philosophy, science, and literature. Many of these words now seem quite ordinary to us—for example, *accommodation*, *frugal*, *obscene*, *premeditated*, and *submerge*, all of which are recorded for the first time in Shakespeare's works. A large proportion of these linguistic experiments, though, never gained a foothold in the language—for example, *illecebrous* for "delicate," *deruncinate* for "to weed," *obtestate* for "call on," or Shakespeare's *disquantity* to mean "diminish." Indeed, some contemporaries ridiculed the pretension and obscurity of these "inkhorn words" in terms that sound very like modern criticisms of bureaucratic and corporate jargon—the rhetorician Thomas Wilson wrote in 1540 of the writers who affected "outlandish English" such that "if some of their mothers were alive, they were not able to tell what they say." But this effect was inevitable: The additions to the standard language that made it a suitable vehicle for art and scholarship could only increase the linguistic distance between the written language used by the educated classes and the spoken language used by other groups.

DICTIONARIES AND RULES

These were essentially growing pains for the standard language, which continued to gain ground in the sixteenth and seventeenth centuries, abetted by a number of developments: the ever-increasing dominance of London and the Southeast, the growth in social and geographic mobility, and in particular the introduction and spread of print, which led both to higher levels of literacy and schooling and to the gradual standardization of English spelling. But even as this process was going on, other developments were both creating new distinctions and investing existing ones with a new importance. For one thing, people were starting to pay more attention to accents based on social class, rather than region, an understandable preoccupation as social mobility increased and speech became a more important indicator of social background. Not surprisingly, the often imperfect efforts of the emerging middle class to speak and dress like their social superiors occasioned some ridicule; Thomas Gainsford wrote in 1616 of the "foppish mockery" of commoners who tried to imitate gentlemen by altering "habit, manner of life, conversation, and even their phrase of speech." Yet even the upper classes were paying more attention to speech as a social indicator than they had in previous ages; as one writer put it, "it is a pitty when a Noble man is better distinguished from a Clowne by his golden laces, than by his good language." (Shakespeare plays on this theme in *1 Henry IV* [3.1.250, 257–58] when he has Hotspur tease his wife for swearing too daintily, which makes her sound like "a comfit-maker's wife," rather than "like a lady as thou art," who swears with "a good mouth-filling oath.")

Over the course of the seventeenth and eighteenth centuries, print began to exercise a paradoxical effect on the perception of the language: even as it was serving to codify the standard, it was also making people more aware of variation and more anxious about its consequences. This was largely the result of the growing importance of print, as periodicals, novels, and other new forms became increasingly influential in shaping public opinion, together with the perception that the contributors to the print discourse were drawn from a wider range of backgrounds than in previous periods. As Samuel Johnson wrote: "The present age . . . may be styled, with great propriety, the Age of Authors; for, perhaps, there was never a time when men of all degrees of ability, of every kind of education, of every profession and employment were posting with ardor so general to the press. . . . "

This anxiety about the language was behind the frequent eighteenth-century lamentations that English was "unruled," "barbarous," or, as Johnson put it, "copious without order, and energetick without rule." Some writers looked for a remedy in public institutions modeled on the French Academy. This idea was advocated by John Dryden, Daniel Defoe, Joseph Addison, and most notably by Jonathan Swift, in a 1712 pamphlet called A Proposal for Correcting, Improving, and Ascertaining [i.e., "fixing"] the English Tongue, which did receive some official attention from the Tory government. But the idea was dropped as a Tory scheme when the Whigs came to power two years later, and by the middle of the eighteenth century, there was wide agreement among all parties that an academy would be an unwarranted intervention in the free conduct of public discourse. Samuel Johnson wrote in the Preface to his Dictionary of 1775 that he hoped that "the spirit of English liberty will hinder or destroy" any attempt to set up an academy; and the scientist and radical Joseph Priestly called such an institution "unsuitable to the genius of a free nation."

The rejection of the idea of an academy was to be important in the subsequent development of the language. From that time forward, it was clear that the state was not to play a major role in regulating and reforming the language, whether in England or in the other nations of the language community—a characteristic that makes English different from many other languages. (In languages like French and German, for example, spelling reforms can be introduced by official commissions charged with drawing up rules which are then adopted in all textbooks and official publications, a procedure that would be unthinkable in any of the nations of the English-speaking world.) Instead, the task of determining standards was left to private citizens, whose authority rested on their ability to gain general public acceptance.

The eighteenth century saw an enormous growth in the number of grammars and handbooks, which formulated most of the principles of correct English that, for better or worse, are still with us today—the rules for using who and whom, for example, the injunction against constructions like "very unique," and the curious prejudice against the split infinitive. Even more important was the development of the modern English dictionary. Before 1700, English speakers had to make do with alphabetical lists of "hard-words," a bit like the vocabulary improvement books that are still frequent today; it was only in the early 1700s that scholars began to produce anything like a comprehensive dictionary in the modern sense, a process that culminated in the publication of Samuel Johnson's magisterial Dictionary of 1755. It would be hard to argue that these dictionaries did much in fact to reduce variation or to arrest the process of linguistic change (among the words that Johnson objected to, for example, were belabor, budge, cajole, coax, doff, gambler, and job, all of which have since become part of the standard language). But they did serve to ease the sense of linguistic crisis, by providing a structure for describing the language and points of reference for resolving disputes about grammar and meaning. And while both the understanding of language and the craft of lexicography have made a great deal of progress since Johnson's time, the form of the English-language dictionary is still pretty much as he laid it down. (In this regard, Johnson's *Dictionary* is likely to present a much more familiar appearance to a modern reader than his poetry or periodical essays.)

THE DIFFUSION OF ENGLISH

The Modern English period saw the rise of another sort of variation, as well, as English began to spread over an increasingly larger area. By Shakespeare's time, English was displacing the Celtic languages in Wales, Cornwall, and Scotland, and then in Ireland, where the use of Irish was brutally repressed on the assumption—in retrospect a remarkably obtuse one—that people who were forced to become English in tongue would soon become English in loyalty as well. People in these new parts of the English-speaking world—a term we can begin to use in this period, for English was no longer the language of a single country—naturally used the language in accordance with their own idiom and habits of thought and mixed it with words drawn from the Celtic languages, a number of which eventually entered the speech of the larger linguistic community, for example, *baffle, bun, clan, crag, drab, galore, hubbub, pet, slob, slogan,* and *trousers.*

The development of the language in the New World followed the same process of differentiation. English settlers in North America rapidly developed their own characteristic forms of speech. They retained a number of words that had fallen into disuse in England (*din, clod, trash,* and *fall* for *autumn*) and gave old words new senses (like *corn,* which in England meant simply "grain," or *creek,* originally "an arm of the sea"). They borrowed freely from the other languages they came in contact with. By the time of the American Revolution, the colonists had already taken *chowder, cache, prairie,* and *bureau* from French; *noodle* and *pretzel* from German; *cookie, boss,* and *scow* and *yankee* from the Dutch; and *moose, skunk, chipmunk, succotash, toboggan,* and *tomahawk* from various Indian languages. And they coined new words with abandon. Some of these answered to their specific needs and interests—for example, *squatter, clearing, foothill, watershed, congressional, sidewalk*—but there were thousands of others that had no close connection to the American experience as such, many of which were ultimately adopted by the other varieties of English. *Belittle, influential, reliable, comeback, lengthy, turn down, make good*—all of these were originally American creations; they and other words like them indicate how independently the language was developing in the New World.

This process was repeated wherever English took root—in India, Africa, the Far East, the Caribbean, and Australia and New Zealand; by the late nineteenth century, English bore thousands of souvenirs of its extensive travels. From Africa (sometimes via Dutch) came words like *banana, boorish, palaver, gorilla,* and *guinea;* from the aboriginal languages of Australia came *wombat* and *kangaroo;* from the Caribbean languages came *cannibal, hammock, potato,* and *canoe;* and from the languages of India came *bangle, bungalow, chintz, cot, dinghy, jungle, loot, pariah, pundit,* and *thug.* And even lists like these are misleading, since they include only words that worked their way into the general English vocabulary and don't give a sense of the thousands of borrowings and coinages that were used only locally. Nor do they touch on the variation in grammar from one variety to the next. This kind of variation occurs everywhere, but it is particularly marked in regions like the Caribbean and Africa, where the local varieties of English are heavily influenced by English-based creoles—that is, language varieties that use English-based vocabulary with grammars largely derived from spoken—in this case, African—languages. This is the source, for example, of a number of the distinctive syntactic features of the variety used by many inner-city African Americans, like the "invariant *be*" of sentences like *We be living in Chicago*, which signals a state of affairs that holds for an extended period. (Some linguists have suggested that Middle English, in fact, could be thought of as a kind of creolized French.)

The growing importance of these new forms of English, particularly in America, presented a new challenge to the unity of the language. Until the eighteenth century, English was still thought of as essentially a national language. It might be spoken in various other nations and colonies under English control, but it was nonetheless rooted in the speech of England and subject to a single standard. Not surprisingly, Americans came to find this picture uncongenial, and when the United States first declared its independence from Britain, there was a strong sentiment for declaring that "American," too, should be recognized as a separate language. This was the view held by John Adams, Thomas Jefferson, and above all by America's first and greatest lexicographer, Noah Webster, who argued that American culture would naturally come to take a distinct form in the soil of the New World, free from what he described as "the old feudal and hierarchical establishments of England." And if a language was naturally the product and reflection of a national culture, then Americans could scarcely continue to speak "English." As Webster wrote in 1789: "Culture, habits, and language, as well as government should be national. America should have her own distinct from the rest of the world. . . ." It was in the interest of symbolically distinguishing American from English that Webster introduced a variety of spelling changes, such as *honor* and *favor* for *honour* and *favour*, *theater* for *theatre*, *traveled* for *travelled*, and so forth—a procedure that new nations often adopt when they want to make their variety of a language look different from its parent tongue.

In fact Webster's was by no means an outlandish suggestion. Even at the time of American independence, the linguistic differences between America and Britain were as great as those that separate many languages today, and the differences would have become much more salient if Americans had systematically adopted all of the spelling reforms that Webster at one time proposed, such as *wurd, reezon, tung, iz*, and so forth, which would ultimately have left English and American looking superficially no more similar than German and Dutch. Left to develop on their own, English and American might soon have gone their separate ways, perhaps paving the way for the separation of the varieties of English used in other parts of the world.

In the end, of course, the Americans and British decided that neither their linguistic nor their cultural and political differences warranted recognizing distinct languages. Webster himself conceded the point in 1828, when he entitled his magnum opus *An American Dictionary of the English Language*. And by 1862 the English novelist Anthony Trollope could write:

An American will perhaps consider himself to be as little like an English man as he is like a Frenchman. But he reads Shakespeare through the medium of his own vernacular, and has to undergo the penance of a foreign tongue before he can understand Molière. He separates himself from England in politics and perhaps in affection; but he cannot separate himself from England in mental culture.

ENGLISH AND ENGLISHNESS

This was a crucial point of transition, which set the English language on a very different course from most of the European languages, where the association of language and national culture was being made more strongly than ever before. But the detachment of English from Englishness did not take place overnight. For Trollope and his Victorian contemporaries, the "mental culture" of the English-speaking world was still a creation of England, the embodiment of English social and political values. "The English language," said G. C. Swayne in 1862, "is like the English constitution . . . and perhaps also the English Church, full of inconsistencies and anomalies, yet flourishing in defiance of theory." The monumental *Oxford English Dictionary* that the Victorians undertook was conceived in this patriotic spirit. In the words of Archbishop Richard Chevenix Trench, one of the guiding spirits of the OED project:

> We could scarcely have a lesson on the growth of our English tongue, we could scarcely follow upon one of its significant words, without having unawares a lesson in English history as well, without not merely falling upon some curious fact illustrative of our national life, but learning also how the great heart which is beating at the centre of that life, was being gradually shaped and moulded.

It was this conception of the significance of the language that led, too, to the insistence that the origin of the English language should properly be located in Anglo-Saxon, rather than in the thirteenth or fourteenth century, as scholars argued that contemporary English laws and institutions could be traced to a primordial "Anglo-Saxon spirit" in an almost racial line of descent, and that the Anglo-Saxon language was "immediately connected with the original introduction and establishment of their present language and their laws, their liberty, and their religion."

This view of English as the repository of "Anglo-Saxon" political ideals had its appeal in America, as well, particularly in the first decades of the twentieth century, when the crusade to "Americanize" recent immigrants led a number of states to impose severe restrictions on the use of other languages in schools, newspapers, and public meetings, a course that was often justified on the grounds that only speakers of English were in a position to fully appreciate the nuances of democratic thought. As a delegate to a New York State constitutional convention in 1916 put the point: "You have got to learn our language because that is the vehicle of the thought that has been handed down from the men in whose breasts first burned the fire of freedom at the signing of the Magna Carta."

But this view of the language is untenable on both linguistic and historical grounds. It is true that the nations of the English-speaking world have a common political heritage that makes itself known in similar legal systems and an (occasionally shaky) predilection for democratic forms of government. But while there is no doubt that the possession of a common language has helped to reinforce some of these connections, it is not responsible for them. Languages do work to create a common worldview, but not at such a specific level. Words like *democracy* move easily from one language to the next, along with the concepts they name—a good thing for the English-speaking world, since a great many of those ideals of "English democracy," as the writer calls it, owe no small debt to thinkers in Greece, Italy, France, Germany, and a number of other places, and those ideals have been established in many nations that speak languages other than English. (Thirteenth-century England was one of them. We should bear in mind that the Magna Carta that people sometimes like to mention in this context was a Latin document issued by a French-speaking king to French-speaking barons.) For that matter, there are English-speaking nations where democratic institutions have not taken root—nor should we take their continuing health for granted even in the core nations of the English-speaking world.

In the end, the view of English as the repository of Englishness has the effect of marginalizing or disenfranchising large parts of the English-speaking world, particularly those who do not count the political and cultural imposition of Englishness as an unmixed blessing. In most of the places where English has been planted, after all, it has had the British flag flying above it. And for many nations, it has been hard to slough off the sense of English as a colonial language. There is a famous passage in James Joyce's *Portrait of the Artist as a Young Man*, for example, where Stephen Daedelus says of the speech of an English-born dean, "The language in which we are speaking is his not mine," and there are still many people in Ireland and other parts of the English-speaking world who have mixed feelings about the English language: they may use and even love English, but they resent it, too.

Today the view of English as an essentially English creation is impossible to sustain even on purely linguistic grounds; the influences of the rest of the English-speaking world have simply been too great. Already in Trollope's time there were vociferous complaints in England about the growing use of Americanisms, a sign that the linguistic balance of payments between the two communities was tipping westward, and a present-day English writer would have a hard time producing a single paragraph that contained no words that originated in other parts of the linguistic community. Nor, what is more important, could you find a modern British or North American writer whose work was not heavily influenced, directly or indirectly, by the literature of the rest of the linguistic community, particularly after the extraordinary twentieth-century efflorescence of the English-language literatures of other parts of the world. Trying to imagine modern English literature without the contributions of writers like Yeats, Shaw, Joyce, Beckett, Heaney, Walcott, Lessing, Gordimer, Rushdie, Achebe, and Naipaul (to take only some of the writers who are included in this collection) is like trying to imagine an "English" cuisine that made no use of potatoes, tomatoes, corn, noodles, eggplant, olive oil, almonds, bay leaf, curry, or pepper.

THE FEATURES OF "STANDARD ENGLISH"

Where should we look, then, for the common "mental culture" that English-speakers share? This is always a difficult question to answer, partly because the understanding of the language changes from one place and time to the next, and partly because it is hard to say just what sorts of things languages are in the abstract. For all that we may want to think of the English-speaking world as a single community united by a common worldview, it is not a social group comparable to a tribe or people or nation—the sorts of groups that can easily evoke the first-person plural pronoun *we*. (Americans and Australians do not travel around saying "We gave the world Shakespeare," even though one might think that as paid-up members of the English-speaking community they would be entirely within their rights to do so.)

But we can get some sense of the ties that connect the members of the English-speaking community by starting with the language itself—not just in its forms and rules, but in the centripetal forces spoken of earlier. Forces like these are operating in every language community, it's true, but what gives each language its unique character is the way they are realized, the particular institutions and cultural commonalties which work to smooth differences and create a basis for continued communication—which ensure, in short, that English will continue as a single language, rather than break up into a collection of dialects that are free to wander wherever they will.

People often refer to this basis for communication as "Standard English," but that term is misleading. There are many linguistic communities that do have a genuine standard variety, a fixed and invariant form of the language that is used for certain kinds of communication. But that notion of the standard would be unsuitable to a language like English, which recognizes no single cultural center and has to allow for a great deal of variation even in the language of published texts. (It is rare to find a single page of an English-language novel or newspaper that does not reveal what nation it was written in.) What English does have, rather, is a collection of standard features—of spelling, of grammar, and of word use—which taken together ensure that certain kinds of communication will be more or less comprehensible in any part of the language community.

The standard features of English are as notable for what they don't contain as for what they do. One characteristic of English, for example, is that it has no standard pronunciation. People pronounce the language according to whatever their regional practice happens to be, and while certain pronunciations may be counted as "good" or "bad" according to local standards, there are no general rules about this, the way there are in French or Italian. (Some New Yorkers may be stigmatized for pronouncing words like *car* and *bard* as 'kah' and 'bahd', but roughly the same *r*-less pronunciation is standard in parts of the American South and in England, South Africa, Australia, and New Zealand.) In this sense, "standard English" exists only as a written language. Of course there is some variation in the rules of written English, as well, such as the American spellings that Webster introduced, but these are relatively minor and tend to date from earlier periods. A particular speech-community can pronounce the words *half* or *car* however it likes, but it can't unilaterally change the way the words are spelled. Indeed, this is one of the unappreciated advantages of the notoriously irregular English spelling system—it is so plainly *un*phonetic that there's no temptation to take it as codifying any particular spoken variety. When you want to define a written standard in a linguistic community that embraces no one standard accent, it's useful to have a spelling system that doesn't tip its hand.

The primacy of the written language is evident in the standard English vocabulary, too, if only indirectly. The fact is that English as such does not give us a complete vocabulary for talking about the world, but only for certain kinds of topics. If you want to talk about vegetables in English, for example, you have to choose among the usages common in one or another region: Depending on where you do your shopping, you will talk about *rutabagas, scallions,* and *string beans* or *Swedes, spring onions,* and *French beans.* That is, you can only talk about vegetables in your capacity as an American, an Englishman, or whatever, not in your capacity as an English-speaker in general. And similarly for fashion (*sweater* vs. *jumper, bobby pin* vs. *hair grip, vest* vs. *waistcoat*), for car parts (*hood* vs. *bonnet, trunk* vs. *boot*), and for food, sport, transport, and furniture, among many other things.

The English-language vocabulary is much more standardized, though, in other areas of the lexicon. We have a large common vocabulary for talking about aspects of our social and moral life—*blatant, vanity, smug, indifferent,* and the like. We have a common repertory of grammatical constructions and "signpost" expressions—for example, adverbs like *arguably, literally,* and *of course*—which we use to organize our discourse and tell readers how to interpret it. And there is a large number of common words for talking about the language itself—for example, *slang, usage, jargon, succinct,* and *literate.* (It is striking how many of these words are particular to English. No other language has an exact synonym for *slang,* for example, or a single word that covers the territory that *literate* covers in English, from "able to read and write" to "knowledgeable or educated.")

The common "core vocabulary" of English is not limited to these notions, of course—for example, it includes as well the thousands of technical and scientific terms that are in use throughout the English-speaking world, like *global warming* and *penicillin,* which for obvious reasons are not particularly susceptible to cultural variation. Nor would it be accurate to say that the core vocabulary includes all the words we use to refer to our language or to our social and moral life, many of which have a purely local character. But the existence of a core vocabulary of common English words, as fuzzy as it may prove to be, is an indication of the source of our cultural commonalities. What is notable about words like *blatant, arguably,* and *succinct* is that their meanings are defined by reference to our common literature, and in particular to the usage of what the eighteenth-century philosopher George Campbell described as "authors of reputation"—writers whose authority is determined by "the esteem of the public." We would not take the usage of Ezra Pound or Bernard Shaw as authoritative in deciding what words like *sweater* or *rutabaga* mean—they could easily have been wrong about either— but their precedents carry a lot of weight when we come to talking about the meaning of *blatant* and *succinct.* In fact the body of English-language "authors of reputation" *couldn't* be wrong about the meanings of words like these, since it is their usage by these authors that collectively determines what these words mean. And for purposes of defining these words it does not matter where a writer is from. The *American Heritage Dictionary*, for example, uses citations from the Irish writer Samuel Beckett to illustrate the meanings of *exasperate* and *impulsion*, from the Persian-born Doris Lessing, raised in southern Africa, to illustrate the meaning of *efface*, and from the Englishman E. M. Forster to illustrate the meaning of *solitude*; and dictionaries from other communities feel equally free to draw on the whole of English literature to illustrate the meanings of the words of the common vocabulary.

It is this strong connection between our common language and our common literature that gives both the language and the linguistic community their essential unity. Late in the eighteenth century, Samuel Johnson said that Britain had become "a nation of readers," by which he meant not just that people were reading more than ever before, but that participation in the written discourse of English had become in some sense constitutive of the national identity. And while the English-speaking world and its ongoing conversation can no longer be identified with a single nation, that world is still very much a community of readers in this sense. Historically, at least, we use the language in the same way because we read and talk about the same books—not *all* the same books, of course, but a loose and shifting group of works that figure as points of reference for our use of language.

This sense of the core vocabulary based on a common literature is intimately connected to the linguistic culture that English-speakers share—the standards, beliefs, and institutions that keep the various written dialects of the language from flying apart. The English dictionary is a good example. It is true that each part of the linguistic community requires its own dictionaries, given the variation in vocabulary and occasionally in spelling and the rest, but they are all formed on more or less the same model, which is very different from that of the French or the Germans. They all organize their entries in the same way, use the same form of definitions, include the same kind of information, and so on, to the point where we often speak of "*the* dictionary," as if the book were a single, invariant text like "the periodic table." By the same token, the schools in every English-speaking nation generally teach the same principles of good usage, a large number of which date from the grammarians of the eighteenth century. There are a few notable exceptions to this generality (Americans and most other communities outside England abandoned some time ago the effort to keep *shall* and *will* straight and seem to be none the worse off for it), but even in these cases grammarians justify their prescriptions using the same terminology and forms of argument.

THE CONTINUITY OF ENGLISH

To be sure, our collective agreement on standards of language and literature is never more than approximate and is always undergoing redefinition and change. Things could hardly be otherwise, given the varied constitution of the English-speaking community, the changing social background, and the insistence of English-speakers that they must be left to decide these matters on their own, without the intervention of official commissions or academies. It is not surprising that the reference points that we depend on to maintain the continuity of the language should often be controversial, even within a single community, and even less so that different national communities should have different ideas as to who counts as authority or what kinds of texts should be relevant to defining the common core of English words. The most we can ask of our common linguistic heritage is that it give us a general format for adapting the language to new needs and for reinterpreting its significance from one time and place to another.

This is the challenge posed by the triumph of English. Granted, there is no threat to the hegemony of English as a worldwide medium for practical communication. It is a certainty that the nations of the English-speaking community will continue to use the various forms of English to communicate with each other, as well as with the hundreds of millions of people who speak English as a second language (and who in fact outnumber the native speakers of the language by a factor of two or three to one). And with the growth of travel and trade and of media like the Internet, the number of English-speakers is sure to continue to increase.

But none of this guarantees the continuing unity of English as a means of cultural expression. What is striking about the accelerating spread of English over the past two centuries is not so much the number of speakers that the language has acquired, but the remarkable variety of the cultures and communities who use it. The heterogeneity of the linguistic community is evident not just in the emergence of the rich new literatures of Africa, Asia, and the Caribbean, but also in the literatures of what linguists sometimes call the "inner circle" of the English-speaking world—nations like Britain, the United States, Australia, and Canada—where the language is being asked to describe a much wider range of experience than ever before, particularly on behalf of groups who until recently have been largely excluded or marginalized from the collective conversation of the English-speaking world.

Not surprisingly, the speakers of the "new Englishes" use the language with different voices and different rhythms and bring to it different linguistic and cultural backgrounds. The language of a writer like Chinua Achebe reflects the influence not just of Shakespeare and Wordsworth but of proverbs and other forms of discourse drawn from West African oral traditions. Indian writers like R. K. Narayan and Salman Rushdie ground their works not just in the traditional English-language canon but in Sanskrit classics like the epic *Rāmāyana*. The continuing sense that all English-speakers are engaged in a common discourse depends on the linguistic community's being able to accommodate and absorb these new linguistic and literary influences, as it has been able to do in the past.

In all parts of the linguistic community, moreover, there are questions posed by the new media of discourse. Over the past hundred years, the primacy of print has been challenged first by the growth of film, recordings, and the broadcast media, and more recently by the remarkable growth of the Internet, each of which has had its effects on the language. With film and the rest, we have begun to see the emergence of spoken standards that coexist with the written standard of print, not in the form of a standardized English pronunciation—if anything, pronunciation differences among the communities of the English-speaking world have become more marked over the course of the century—but rather in the use of words, expressions, and rhythms that are particular to speech (there is no better example of this than the universal adoption of the particle *okay*). And the Internet has had the effect of projecting what were previously private forms of written communication, like the personal letter, into something more like models of public discourse, but with a language that is much more informal than the traditional discourse of the novel or newspaper.

It is a mistake to think that any of these new forms of discourse will wholly replace the discourse of print (the Internet, in particular, has shown itself to be an important vehicle for marketing and diffusing print works with much greater efficiency than has ever been possible before). It seems reasonable to assume that a hundred years from now the English-speaking world will still be at heart a community of readers—and of readers of books, among other things. And it is likely, too, that the English language will still be at heart a means of written expression, not just for setting down air schedules and trade statistics, but for doing the kind of cultural work that we have looked for literature to do for us in the past; a medium, that is, for poetry, criticism, history, and fiction. But only time will tell if English will remain a single language—if in the midst of all the diversity, cultural and communicative, people will still be able to discern a single "English literature" and a characteristic English-language frame of mind.

GEOFFREY NUNBERG
Stanford University and Xerox Palo Alto Research Center

The Norton Anthology
of English Literature

SEVENTH EDITION

VOLUME 2

The Romantic Period
1785–1830

1789–1815:   Revolutionary and Napoleonic period in France.—1789: The Revolution begins with the assembly of the States-General in May and the storming of the Bastille on July 14.—1793: King Louis XVI executed; England joins the alliance against France.—1793–94: The Reign of Terror under Robespierre. 1804: Napoleon crowned emperor.—1815: Napoleon defeated at Waterloo

1807:   British slave trade outlawed (slavery abolished throughout the empire, including the West Indies, twenty-six years later)

1811–20:   The Regency—George, Prince of Wales, acts as regent for George III, who has been declared incurably insane

1820:   Accession of George IV

The British Romantic period is at least as complex and diverse as any other period in literary history. For many decades of the twentieth century, scholars singled out five poets—Wordsworth, Coleridge, Byron, Percy Shelley, and Keats, adding Blake belatedly to make a sixth—and constructed notions of a unified Romanticism on the basis of their works. But there were problems all along: even the two closest collaborators of the 1790s, Wordsworth and Coleridge, interacting on a daily basis, would fit no single definition; Byron despised both Coleridge's metaphysics and Wordsworth's theory and practice of poetry; Shelley and Keats were at opposite poles from each other stylistically and philosophically; Blake was not at all like any of the other five.

Nowadays, although the six poets are still the principal canonical figures by any measure of canonicity, we recognize a much greater range of activities and accomplishments, literary and otherwise. In 1798, the year of Wordsworth and Coleridge's first *Lyrical Ballads,* neither of the authors had much of a reputation; Wordsworth was not even included among the 1112 entries in David Rivers's *Literary Memoirs of Living Authors of Great Britain* of that year, and *Lyrical Ballads* was published anonymously because, as Coleridge told the publisher, "Wordsworth's name is nothing—to a large number of persons mine *stinks.*" Some of the best-regarded poets of the time were women—Anna Barbauld, Charlotte Smith, Mary Robinson—and Wordsworth and Coleridge (both of whom were junior colleagues of Robinson when she was poetry editor of the *Morning Post* in the late 1790s) looked up to them and learned some of their craft from them. The rest of the then-established figures were the later eighteenth-century poets who are printed at the end of volume 1 of this anthology—Gray, Collins, Crabbe, and Cowper

1

in particular. Only Byron, among the principal poets, was instantly famous; and Felicia Hemans and Letitia Landon ran him a close race as best-sellers. The Romantic period had a great many more participants than the six canonical poets and was interinvolved with a multitude of political, social, and economic changes.

REVOLUTION AND REACTION

Following a widespread practice of historians of English literature, we denote by the "Romantic period" the span between the year 1785, the midpoint of the decade in which Samuel Johnson died and Blake and Burns published their first poems, and 1830, by which time the major writers of the preceding century were either dead or no longer productive. This was a turbulent period, during which England experienced the ordeal of change from a primarily agricultural society, where wealth and power had been concentrated in the landholding aristocracy, to a modern industrial nation, in which the balance of economic power shifted to large-scale employers, who found themselves ranged against an immensely enlarging and increasingly restive working class. And this change occurred in a context of revolution—first the American and then the much more radical French— and of wars, of economic cycles of inflation and depression, and of the constant threat to the social structure from imported revolutionary ideologies to which the ruling classes responded by the repression of traditional liberties.

The early period of the French Revolution, marked by the Declaration of the Rights of Man and the storming of the Bastille to release imprisoned political offenders, evoked enthusiastic support from English liberals and radicals alike. Three important books epitomize the radical social thinking stimulated by the Revolution. Mary Wollstonecraft's *A Vindication of the Rights of Men* (1790) justified the French Revolution against Edmund Burke's attack in his *Reflections on the Revolution in France* (1790). Tom Paine's *Rights of Man* (1791–92) also advocated for England a democratic republic that was to be achieved, if lesser pressures failed, by popular revolution. More important as an influence on Wordsworth, Percy Shelley, and other poets was William Godwin's *Inquiry Concerning Political Justice* (1793), which foretold an inevitable but peaceful evolution of society to a final stage in which all property would be equally distributed and all government would wither away. But English sympathizers dropped off as the Revolution followed its increasingly grim and violent course: the accession to power by Jacobin extremists; the "September Massacres" of the imprisoned and helpless nobility in 1792, followed by the execution of the king and queen; the invasion by the French Republic of the Rhineland and Netherlands, and its offer of armed assistance to all countries desiring to overthrow their governments, which brought England into the war against France; the guillotining of thousands in the Reign of Terror under Robespierre; and, after the execution in their turn of the men who had directed the Terror, the emergence of Napoleon first as dictator and then as emperor of France. As Wordsworth wrote in *The Prelude* (11.206–09),

> become Oppressors in their turn,
> Frenchmen had changed a war of self-defence
> For one of Conquest, losing sight of all
> Which they had struggled for. . . .

For Wordsworth and other English observers of liberal inclinations, these events posed a dilemma that became familiar again after the 1920s, in a parallel era of wars, revolutions, and the struggle by competing social ideologies—liberals had no side they could wholeheartedly espouse. Napoleon, the child and champion of the French Revolution, had become an arch-aggressor, a despot, and the founder of a new dynasty; yet almost all those who opposed him did so for the wrong reasons, with the result that his final defeat at Waterloo in 1815 proved to be the triumph, not of progress and reform, but of reactionary despotisms throughout continental Europe.

In England this was a period of harsh, repressive measures. Public meetings were prohibited, habeas corpus was suspended for the first time in over a hundred years, and advocates of even moderate political change were charged with high treason in time of war. The outlook of the Napoleonic wars put an end to reform for nearly three decades.

Yet this was the very time when profound economic and social changes were creating a desperate need for corresponding changes in political arrangements, and new classes—manufacturing, rather than agricultural—were beginning to demand a voice in government proportionate to their wealth. The "Industrial Revolution"—the shift in manufacturing that resulted from the invention of power-driven machinery to replace hand labor—had begun in the mid-eighteenth century with improvements in machines for processing textiles, and was given immense impetus when James Watt perfected the steam engine in 1765. In the succeeding decades steam replaced wind and water as the primary source of power in one after another type of manufacturing, and after centuries of almost imperceptibly slow change, there began that ever-accelerating alteration in economic and social conditions which shows no signs of slowing down in the foreseeable future. A new laboring population massed in the sprawling mill towns that burgeoned in central and northern England. In rural communities the destruction of home industry was accompanied by a rapid growth of the process—lamented by Oliver Goldsmith in *The Deserted Village* as early as 1770—of enclosing open fields and communally worked farms into privately owned agricultural holdings. Enclosure was by and large necessary for the more efficient methods of agriculture and animal breeding required to supply a growing population (although some of the land thus acquired was turned into vast private estates); in any case, it created a new landless class that either migrated to the industrial towns or remained as farm laborers, subsisting on starvation wages eked out by an inadequate dole. The landscape of England began to take on its modern appearance—the hitherto open rural areas subdivided into a checkerboard of fields enclosed by hedges and stone walls, with the factories of the industrial and trading cities casting a pall of smoke over vast areas of jerry-built houses and slum tenements. Meanwhile, the population was becoming increasingly polarized into what Disraeli later called the "Two Nations"—the two classes of capital and labor, the large owner or trader and the possessionless wageworker, the rich and the poor.

No attempt was made to regulate this shift from the old economic world to the new, not only because of inertia and the power of vested interests but because even liberal reformers were dominated by the social philosophy of laissez-faire. This theory of "let alone" holds that the general welfare can be ensured only by the free operation of economic laws; the government should maintain a policy of strict noninterference and leave people to pursue their private interests. For the great majority of the laboring class the results of this policy were inadequate wages, long hours of work under harsh discipline in sordid conditions, and the large-scale employment of women and children for tasks that destroyed both the body and the spirit. Reports by investigating committees on the coal mines, where male and female children of ten or even five years of age were harnessed to heavy coal-sledges that they dragged by crawling on their hands and knees, read like scenes from Dante's *Inferno*. In 1815 the conclusion of the French war, when the enlargement of the working force by demobilized troops coincided with the fall in the wartime demand for goods, brought on the first modern industrial depression. Since the workers had no vote and were prevented by law from unionizing, their only recourses were petitions, protest meetings, agitation, and hunger riots, which only frightened the ruling class into more repressive measures. In addition the introduction of new machines resulted in further loss of jobs, and this provoked sporadic attempts by dispossessed workers to destroy the machines. After one such outbreak, the House of Lords—despite Lord Byron's eloquent protest—passed a bill (1812) making death the penalty for destroying the frames used for weaving in the stocking industry. In 1819 meetings of workers were organized to demand parliamentary reform. In August of that year, a huge but orderly assembly at St. Peter's Fields, Manchester, was charged by troops, who killed nine and severely injured hundreds more; this was the notorious "Peterloo Massacre," so named with ironic reference to the Battle of Waterloo. The event incited Percy Shelley to write his poems for the working class, *England in 1819, A Song: "Men of England,"* and *To Sidmouth and Castlereagh.*

Suffering was largely confined to the poor, however, for all this while the landed classes, the industrialists, and many of the merchants prospered. The British Empire expanded aggressively both westward and eastward, becoming the most powerful colonial presence in the world. The British East India Company ruled the entire Indian subcontinent at this time, and black slave labor in the West Indies generated great wealth for British plantation owners and their overseers. In London the Regency period (1811–20) was for the leisure class a time of lavish display and moral laxity. In the provinces the gentry in their country houses carried on their family and social concerns—reflected in the novels of Jane Austen—almost untouched by great national and international events.

As in earlier English history, women constituted a deprived class that cut across social classes, for they were widely regarded as inferior to men in intellect and in all but domestic talents. They were therefore provided limited schooling and no facilities for higher education, had only lowly vocations open to them, were subjected to a rigid code of sexual behavior, and possessed (especially after marriage) almost no legal rights. In spite of these disabilities, this was the first era in British literature in which women writers began to rival men in their numbers, their success in sales, their literary reputations—and as poets and social commentators as well as novelists; just in the category of poetry, some nine hundred women are listed in J. R. de J. Jackson's recent bibliography, *Romantic Poetry by Women*. Unlike the men, they had, as a class, much in the way of deprivation and prejudice to contend with. In the revolutionary period, women finally acquired a strong and eloquent champion. Mary Wollstonecraft, who had written an early defense of the French Revolution, *A Vindication of the Rights of Men* (1790), followed this two years later with *A Vindication of the Rights of Woman*, a founding classic of the women's movement. Wollstonecraft asserted that women possess equal intellectual capacity and talents as men and demanded for them a greater share of social, educational, and vocational privileges. The cause of women's rights, however, was not taken up by effective proponents until the Victorian era, and even partial achievement of its aims was delayed until well along in the twentieth century.

But the pressures for reform in the privileges of men, as distinct from women, could not be eliminated in the early nineteenth century, especially since political disabilities were not limited to laborers. Gradually the working-class reformers acquired the support of the middle classes and the liberal Whigs. Finally, at a time of acute economic distress, and after unprecedented agitation and disorders that threatened to break out into revolution, the first Reform Bill was passed in 1832, amid widespread rejoicing. It eliminated the rotten boroughs (depopulated areas whose seats in Commons were at the disposal of a nobleman), redistributed parliamentary representation to include the new industrial cities, and extended the vote. Although about half the middle class, almost all the working class, and all women remained still without a franchise, the principle of the peaceful adjustment of conflicting interests by parliamentary majority had been firmly established, and reform was to go on, by stages, until England acquired universal adult suffrage in 1928.

THE "SPIRIT OF THE AGE"

Writers in Wordsworth's lifetime did not think of themselves as "Romantic"; the word was not applied until half a century later, by English historians. Contemporary critics and reviewers treated them as independent individuals, or else grouped them (often invidiously, but with some basis in fact) into a number of separate schools: "the Lake School" of Wordsworth, Coleridge, and Robert Southey; "the Cockney School," a derogatory term for the Londoners Leigh Hunt, William Hazlitt, and associated writers, including Keats; and "the Satanic School" of Byron, Percy Shelley, and their followers.

Many of the writers, however, did feel that there was something distinctive about their time—not a shared doctrine or literary quality, but a pervasive intellectual and imaginative climate, which some of them called "the spirit of the age." They had the sense that (as Keats said in one of his sonnets) "Great spirits now on earth are sojourning," and that there was evidence of a release of energy, experimental boldness, and creative power that marks a literary renaissance. In his *Defence of Poetry* Shelley claimed that the literature of the age "has arisen as it were from a new birth," and that "an electric life burns" within the words of its best writers which is "less their spirit than the spirit of the age." Shelley explained this literary spirit as an accompaniment of political and social revolution, and other writers agreed. Francis Jeffrey, the foremost conservative reviewer of the day, connected "the revolution in our literature" with "the agitations of the French Revolution, and the discussions as well as the hopes and terrors to which it gave occasion." Hazlitt, who published a book of essays called *The Spirit of the Age*, described how in his early youth the French Revolution had seemed "the dawn of a new era, a new impulse had been given to men's minds." The new poetry of the school of Wordsworth, he maintained, "had its origin in the French Revolution. . . . It was a time of promise, a renewal of the world—and of letters."

The imagination of many Romantic writers was, indeed, preoccupied with the fact and idea of revolution. In the early period of the French Revolution all the leading English writers except Edmund Burke were in sympathy with it, and Robert Burns, William Blake, Wordsworth, Coleridge, Southey, and Mary Wollstonecraft were among its fervent adherents. Later, even after the first boundless expectations had been disappointed by the events in France, the younger writers, including Hazlitt, Hunt, Shelley, and Byron, felt that its example, when purged of its errors, still constituted humanity's best hope. The Revolution generated a pervasive feeling that this was an age of new beginnings when, by discarding traditional procedures and outworn customs, everything was possible, and not only in the political and social realm but in intellectual and literary enterprises as well. In his *Prelude* Wordsworth wrote the classic description of the spirit of the early 1790s, with "France standing on the top of golden hours, / And human nature seeming born again," so that "the whole Earth, / The beauty wore of promise." Something of this sense of limitless possibilities survived the shock of first disappointment at events in France and carried over to the year 1797, when Wordsworth and Coleridge, in excited daily communion, revolutionized, on grounds analogous to the politics of democracy, the theory and practice of poetry. The product of these discussions was the *Lyrical Ballads* of 1798.

POETIC THEORY AND POETIC PRACTICE

Wordsworth undertook to justify the new poetry by a critical manifesto, or statement of poetic principles, first as a short Advertisement in the original *Lyrical Ballads*, then in the form of an extended Preface to the second edition in 1800, which he enlarged still further in the third edition of 1802. In it he set himself in opposition to the literary *ancien régime*, those writers of the eighteenth century who, in his view, had imposed on poetry artificial conventions that distorted its free and natural expression. Many of Wordsworth's later critical writings were attempts to clarify, buttress, or qualify points made in his first declaration. Coleridge said that the Preface was "half a child of my own brain"; and although he soon developed doubts about some of Wordsworth's unguarded statements, and undertook to correct them in *Biographia Literaria* (1817), he did not question the rightness of Wordsworth's attempt to overturn the reigning tradition. In the course of the eighteenth century there had been increasing opposition to the tradition of Dryden, Pope, and Johnson; and especially in the 1740s and later there had emerged many of the critical concepts, as well as a number of the poetic subjects and forms, that were later exploited by Wordsworth and his contemporaries. Wordsworth's Preface nevertheless deserves its reputation as a turning point in English literature, for Wordsworth gathered up isolated ideas, organized them into a coherent theory based on explicit critical principles, and made them the rationale for his own achievements as a poet. We can conveniently use the concepts in this influential essay as points of departure for a survey of distinctive elements that are widespread in the theory and poetry of the Romantic period.

1. The Concept of Poetry and the Poet

Representative eighteenth-century theorists had regarded poetry as primarily an imitation of human life—in a frequent figure, "a mirror held up to nature"—that the poet artfully renders and puts into an order designed to instruct and give artistic pleasure to the reader. Wordsworth, on the other hand, repeatedly described all good poetry as, at the moment of composition, "the spontaneous overflow of powerful feelings." Reversing earlier theory, he thus located the source of a poem not in the outer world, but in the individual poet, and specified that the essential materials of a poem were not external people and events, but the inner feelings of the author, or external objects only after these have been transformed or irradiated by the author's feelings. Other Romantic theories, however diverse in other aspects, concurred by referring primarily to the mind, emotions, and imagination of the poet, instead of to the outer world as perceived by the senses, for the origin, content, and defining attributes of a poem. Many writers, such as Charlotte Smith, identified poetry (in metaphors parallel to Wordsworth's "overflow") as the "expression" or "utterance" or "exhibition" of emotion. Blake and Shelley described a poem as an embodiment of the poet's imaginative vision, which they opposed to the ordinary world of common experience. Coleridge, following German precedents, introduced into English criticism an organic theory, based on the model of the growth of a plant. That is, he conceived a great work of literature to be a self-originating and self-organizing process that begins with a seedlike idea in the poet's imagination, grows by assimilating both the poet's feelings and the diverse materials of sense-experience, and evolves into an organic whole in which the parts are integrally related to each other and to the whole.

In accord with the view that poetry expresses the poet's own feelings and temperament, the lyric poem written in the first person, earlier regarded as a minor kind, became a major Romantic form, and was often described as the most essentially poetic of all the genres. And in the Romantic lyric the "I" often is not a conventionally typical lyric speaker, such as the Petrarchan lover or Cavalier gallant of Elizabethan and seventeenth-century love poems, but has recognizable traits of the poet's own person and circumstances. In the poems of Wordsworth, Coleridge, Shelley, Keats, Smith, Letitia Landon, and others, the experiences and states of mind expressed by the lyric speaker often accord closely with the known facts of the poet's life and with the personal confessions in the poet's letters and journals. Even in his ostensibly fictional writings (narrative and dramatic), Byron usually invites his readers to identify the hero with the author, whether the hero is presented romantically (as in *Childe Harold, Manfred*, and the Oriental tales) or in an ironic perspective (as in *Don Juan*). An extreme instance of this tendency to self-reference is Wordsworth's *Prelude*, which is a poem of epic length and epic seriousness about the growth of the poet's own mind.

The Prelude exemplifies two other important tendencies in the period. Like Blake, Coleridge in his early poems, and later on Shelley, Wordsworth presents himself as what he calls "a chosen son," or "Bard." That is, he assumes the persona and voice of a poet-prophet, modeled on Milton and the prophets in the Bible, and puts himself forward as a spokesman for traditional Western civilization at a time of profound crisis—a time, as Wordsworth said in book 2 of *The Prelude*, "of dereliction and dismay" and the "melancholy waste of hopes o'erthrown." (*Son* and *spokesman* are appropriate here; almost always, the bardic poet-prophet was a distinctively male persona.) As bards, Wordsworth and the other visionary poets set out to revise the biblical promise of divine redemption by reconstituting the grounds of hope and pronouncing the coming of a time in which a renewed humanity will inhabit a renovated earth on which men and women will feel thoroughly at home. *The Prelude* also is an instance of a central literary form of English, as of European, Romanticism—a long work about the formation of the self, often centering on a crisis, and presented in the radical metaphor of an interior journey in quest of one's true identity and destined spiritual home. Other English examples of this form are Blake's *Milton*, the crucial episode of Asia's underground journey in Shelley's *Prometheus Unbound*, Keats's *Endymion* and *The Fall of Hyperion*, and, in Victorian poetry, Elizabeth Barrett Browning's *Aurora Leigh*. There are equivalent developments in contemporary prose: the self-revelation in the personal essays of Lamb, Hazlitt, and Leigh Hunt and the currency of spiritual autobiography, whether fictionalized (Thomas Carlyle's *Sartor Resartus*) or presented as fact (Coleridge's *Biographia Literaria*, Thomas De Quincey's *Confessions of an English Opium Eater* and *Autobiographic Sketches*).

2. Poetic Spontaneity and Freedom

Wordsworth defined good poetry not merely as the overflow but as "the *spontaneous* overflow" of feelings. In traditional aesthetic theory, poetry had been regarded as supremely an art—an art that in modern times is practiced by poets who have assimilated classical precedents, are aware of the "rules" governing the kind of poem they are writing, and (except for the felicities that, as Pope said, are "beyond the reach of art") deliberately employ tested means to achieve foreknown effects upon an audience. But to Wordsworth, although the composition of a poem originates from "emotion recollected in tranquillity" and may be preceded and followed by reflection, the immediate act of composition must be spontaneous—that is, arising from impulse, and free from all rules and the artful manipulation of means to foreseen ends. Other important Romantic critics also voiced declarations of artistic independence from inherited precepts. Keats listed as an "axiom" that "if poetry comes not as naturally as the leaves to a tree it had better not come at all." Blake insisted that he wrote from "Inspiration and Vision" and that his long "prophetic" poem *Milton* was given to him by an agency not himself and "produced without Labor or Study." Shelley also thought it "an error to assert that the finest passages of poetry are produced by labor and study," and suggested instead that they are the products of an unconscious creativity: "A great statue or picture grows under the power of the artist as a child in the mother's womb." "The definition of genius," Hazlitt remarked, "is that it acts unconsciously." The surviving manuscripts of the Romantic poets, however, as well as the testimony of observers, show that they worked and reworked their texts no less arduously—if perhaps more immediately under the impetus of first conception—than the poets of earlier ages. Coleridge, who believed that truth lies in a union of opposites, came closer to the facts of Romantic practice when he claimed that the act of composing poetry involves the psychological contraries "of passion and of will, of *spontaneous* impulse and of *voluntary* purpose."

The emphasis in this period on the free activity of the imagination is related to an insistence on the essential role of instinct, intuition, and the feelings of "the heart" to supplement the judgments of the purely logical faculty, "the head," whether in the province of artistic beauty, philosophical and religious truth, or moral goodness. "Deep thinking," Coleridge wrote, "is attainable only by a man of deep feeling, and all truth is a species of revelation"; hence, "a metaphysical solution that does not tell you something in the heart is grievously to be suspected as apocryphal."

3. *Romantic "Nature Poetry"*

In his Preface, Wordsworth wrote that "I have at all times endeavored to look steadily at my subject," and in a supplementary Essay he complained that from Dryden through Pope there is scarcely an image from external nature "from which it can be inferred that the eye of the poet had been steadily fixed on his object." A glance at the table of contents of any collection of Romantic poems will show the degree to which the natural scene has become a primary poetic subject, while Wordsworth, Shelley, and even more Coleridge and Keats, described natural phenomena with an accuracy of observation that had no earlier match in its ability to capture the sensuous nuance.

Because of the prominence of landscape in this period, "Romantic poetry" has to the popular mind become almost synonymous with "nature poetry." Neither Romantic theory nor practice, however, justifies the opinion that the aim of this poetry was description for its own sake. Wordsworth in fact insisted that the ability to observe and describe objects accurately, although a necessary, is not at all a sufficient condition for poetry, "as its exercise supposes all the higher qualities of the mind to be passive, and in a state of subjection to external objects." And while many of the great Romantic lyrics—Wordsworth's *Tintern Abbey* and *Ode: Intimations of Immortality*, Coleridge's *Frost at Midnight* and *Dejection*, Shelley's *Ode to the West Wind*, Keats's *Nightingale*—begin with an aspect or change of aspect in the natural scene, this serves only as stimulus to the most characteristic human activity, that of thinking. The longer Romantic "nature poems" are in fact usually meditative poems, in which the presented scene serves to raise an emotional problem or personal crisis whose development and resolution constitute the organizing principle of the poem. As Wordsworth said in his Prospectus to *The Recluse*, not nature but "the Mind of Man" is "my haunt, and the main region of my song."

In addition, Romantic poems habitually endow the landscape with human life, passion, and expressiveness. In part such descriptions represent the poetic equivalent of the metaphysical concept of nature, which had developed in deliberate revolt against the worldviews of the scientific philosophers of the seventeenth and eighteenth centuries, who represented the ultimate reality as a mechanical world consisting of physical particles in motion. What is needed in philosophy, Coleridge wrote, is "the substitution of life and intelligence . . . for the philosophy of mechanism, which, in everything that is most worthy of the human intellect, strikes *Death*." But for many Romantic poets it was a matter of immediate experience to respond to the outer universe as a living entity that participates in the feelings of the observer. James Thomson and other descriptive poets of the preceding century had depicted the created universe as giving direct access to God, and even as itself possessing the attributes of divinity. In *Tintern Abbey* and other poems Wordsworth exhibits toward the landscape attitudes and sentiments that human beings had earlier felt not only for God, but also for a father, a mother, or a beloved. Elsewhere, as in the great passage on crossing Simplon Pass (*The Prelude* 6.625ff.), Wordsworth also revives the ancient theological concept that God's creation constitutes a symbol system, a physical revelation parallel to the written Apocalypse, the Book of Revelation in the Bible—

> Characters of the great Apocalypse,
> The types and symbols of Eternity,
> Of first, and last, and midst, and without end.

This view that natural objects correspond to an inner or a spiritual world underlay a tendency, especially in Blake and Percy Shelley, to write a symbolist poetry in which a rose, a sunflower, a mountain, a cave, or a cloud is presented as an object imbued with a significance beyond itself. "I always seek in what I see," Shelley said, "the likeness of something beyond the present and tangible object." And by Blake mere nature, as perceived by the physical eye and unhumanized by the imagination, was spurned "as the dirt upon my feet, no part of me."

4. The Glorification of the Ordinary and the Outcast

In two lectures on Wordsworth, Hazlitt declared that the school of poetry founded by Wordsworth was the literary equivalent of the French Revolution, translating political changes into poetical experiments. "Kings and queens were dethroned from their rank and station in legitimate tragedy or epic poetry, as they were decapitated elsewhere. . . . The paradox [these poets] set out with was that all things are by nature equally fit subjects for poetry; or that if there is any preference to be given, those that are the meanest and most unpromising are the best."

Hazlitt had in mind Wordsworth's statement that the aim of *Lyrical Ballads* was "to choose incidents and situations from common life" and to use a "selection of language really spoken by men," for which the source and model is "humble and rustic life." As Hazlitt shrewdly saw, this was a social rather than a distinctively literary definition of the proper materials and language for poetry. Versifiers of the later decades of the eighteenth century had experimented with the simple treatment of simple subjects, and Robert Burns—like Wordsworth, a sympathizer with the French Revolution—had achieved great poetic success in the serious representation of humble life in a language really spoken by rustics; the women poets especially—Barbauld, Robinson, Baillie—assimilated to their poems the subject matter of everyday life. But

Wordsworth underwrote his poetic practice with a theory that inverted the traditional hierarchy of poetic genres, subjects, and style by elevating humble and rustic life and the plain style, which in earlier theory were appropriate only to the lowly pastoral, into the principal subject and medium for poetry in general. And in his own practice, as Hazlitt also noted, Wordsworth went even further and turned for the subjects of his serious poems not only to humble people but to the ignominious, the outcast, the delinquent—to "convicts, female vagrants, gypsies . . . idiot boys and mad mothers," as well as to "peasants, peddlers, and village barbers." Hence the outrage of Lord Byron, who alone among his major contemporaries insisted that Dryden and Pope had laid out the proper road for poetry, and who—in spite of his liberalism in politics—maintained his literary allegiance both to aristocratic proprieties and to traditional poetic decorum:

> "Peddlers," and "Boats," and "Wagons"! Oh! ye shades
> Of Pope and Dryden, are we come to this?

Hazlitt also insisted that, in his democratization of poetry, Wordsworth was "the most original poet now living." Certainly Wordsworth in *Lyrical Ballads* was, in this respect, more radical than any of his contemporaries. He enlarged greatly his readers' imaginative sympathies and brought into the province of serious literature a range of materials and interests which are still being explored by writers of the present day.

It should be noted, however, that Wordsworth's aim in *Lyrical Ballads* was not simply to represent the world as it is but, as he announced in his Preface, to throw over "situations from common life . . . a certain coloring of imagination, whereby ordinary things should be presented to the mind in an unusual aspect." As this passage indicates, Wordsworth's concern in his poetry was not only with "common life" but with "ordinary *things*"; no one can read his poems without noticing the extraordinary reverence with which he invests words that in earlier writers had been derogatory—words like "common," "ordinary," "everyday," "humble," whether applied to people or to objects in the visible scene. His aim throughout is to shatter the lethargy of custom so as to refresh our sense of wonder—indeed, of divinity—in the everyday, the commonplace, the trivial, and the lowly.

Samuel Johnson had said that "wonder is a pause of reason" and that "all wonder is the effect of novelty upon ignorance." But for many Romantic writers, to arouse in the sophisticated mind that sense of wonder presumed to be felt by the ignorant and the innocent was a primary power of imagination and a major function of poetry. Commenting on the special imaginative quality of Wordsworth's early poetry (*Biographia Literaria*, chapter 6), Coleridge remarked: "To combine the child's sense of wonder and novelty with the appearances, which every day for perhaps forty years had rendered familiar . . . this is the character and privilege of genius," and its prime service is to awaken in the reader "freshness of sensation" in the representation of "familiar objects." Poetry, said Shelley in his *Defense of Poetry*, "reproduces the common universe" but "purges from our inward sight the film of familiarity which obscures from us the wonder of our being," and "creates anew the universe, after it has been blunted by reiteration." And in Carlyle's *Sartor Resartus* (1833–34), the chief—indeed the only—effect of the conversion of the protagonist from despairing unbelief is that he is able to sustain a sense of the "Natural Supernaturalism" in ordinary experience and so overcome the "custom" which "blinds us to the miraculousness of daily-recurring miracles." The great power of the imagination, according to all these writers, is that it makes the old world new again.

5. The Supernatural and "Strangeness in Beauty"

In most of his poems Coleridge, like Wordsworth, dealt with the everyday things of this world, and in *Frost at Midnight* he showed how well he too could achieve the effect of wonder in the familiar. But Coleridge tells us (*Biographia Literaria*, chapter 14) that according to the division of labor in *Lyrical Ballads*, his special function was to achieve wonder by a frank violation of natural laws and the ordinary course of events in poems of which "the incidents and agents were to be, in part at least, supernatural." And in *The Rime of the Ancient Mariner, Christabel*, and *Kubla Khan*, Coleridge opened up to poets in the modern world the realm of mystery and magic, in which materials from ancient folklore, superstition, and demonology are used to impress upon the reader the sense of occult powers and unknown modes of being. Such poems are usually set in the distant past or in faraway places, or both; the milieu of *Kubla Khan*, for example, exploits the exoticism both of the Middle Ages and of the Orient. Next to Coleridge, the greatest master of this Romantic mode—in which supernatural events have a deep psychological import—was John Keats. In *La Belle Dame sans Merci* and *The Eve of St. Agnes* he adapted the old forms of ballad and romance to modern sophisticated use and, like Coleridge, established a medieval setting for events that violate our sense of realism and the natural order. Hence the term *medieval revival*, frequently attached to the Romantic period, which comprehends also the ballad imitations and some of the verse tales and historical novels of Sir Walter Scott.

Another side of the tendency that Walter Pater later called "the addition of strangeness to beauty" was the Romantic interest in unusual modes of experience, of a kind that earlier writers had largely ignored as either too trivial or too aberrant for serious literary concern. Blake, Wordsworth, and Coleridge in their poetry explored visionary states of consciousness that are common among children but violate the standard categories of adult judgment. Coleridge was interested in mesmerism (what we now call hypnotism) and, like Blake and Shelley, studied the literature of the occult and the esoteric. Coleridge also shared with De Quincey a concern with dreams and nightmares; both authors exploited in their writings the altered consciousness and distorted perceptions they experienced under their addiction to opium. Byron made repeated use of the fascination with the forbidden and the appeal of the terrifying Satanic hero. And Keats was extraordinarily sensitive to the ambivalences of human experience—to the mingling, at their highest intensity, of pleasure and pain, to destructive aspects of sexuality, and to the erotic quality of the longing for death. These phenomena had already been explored by eighteenth-century writers of terror tales and Gothic fiction, and later in the nineteenth century all of them, sometimes exaggerated to perversity, became the special literary province of Charles Baudelaire, Algernon Charles Swinburne, and writers of the European "Decadence."

INDIVIDUALISM, INFINITE STRIVING,
AND NONCONFORMITY

Through the greater part of the eighteenth century, humans had for the most part been viewed as limited beings in a strictly ordered and essentially unchanging world. A variety of philosophical and religious systems in that century coincided in a distrust of radical innovation, a respect for the precedents established through the ages by the common sense of humanity, and the recommendation to set accessible goals and to avoid extremes, whether in politics, intellect, morality, or art. Many of the great literary works of the period joined in attacking what was called "pride," or aspirations beyond the limits natural to our species. "The bliss of man," Pope wrote in *An Essay on Man*, "(could pride that blessing find) / Is not to act or think beyond mankind":

> This kind, this due degree
> Of blindness, weakness, Heaven bestows on thee.
> Submit.

The Romantic period, the age of unfettered free enterprise, industrial expansion, and boundless revolutionary hope, was also an age of radical individualism in which both the philosophers and poets put an extraordinarily high estimate on human potentialities and powers. In German post-Kantian philosophy, which generated many of the characteristic ideas of European Romanticism, the human mind—what was called the "Subject" or "Ego"— took over various functions that had hitherto been the sole prerogative of Divinity. Most prominent was the rejection by philosophers of a central eighteenth-century concept of the mind as a mirrorlike recipient of a universe already created, and its replacement by a new concept of the mind as itself creating the universe it perceives. In a parallel fashion, the poets of the new period also described the mind as creating its own experience. According to Blake, the mind creates its proper milieu only if it totally rejects the material world; in Coleridge and Wordsworth, however, the mind creates in collaboration with something given to it from without. Mind, wrote Coleridge in 1801, is "not passive" but "made in God's Image, and that too in the sublimest sense—the Image of the *Creator*." And Wordsworth declared in *The Prelude* (2.258–61) that the individual mind

> Doth, like an Agent of the one great Mind,
> Create, creator and receiver both,
> Working but in alliance with the works
> Which it beholds.

Many Romantic writers also agreed that the mind has access beyond sense to the transcendant and the infinite, through a special faculty they called either Reason or Imagination. In *The Prelude* (6.600ff.) Wordsworth describes a flash of imagination "that has revealed / The invisible world," and affirms:

> Our destiny, our being's heart and home,
> Is with infinitude, and only there;
> With hope it is, hope that can never die,

Effort, and expectation, and desire,
And something evermore about to be.

The desire beyond human limits that, to the moralists of the preceding age, had been an essential sin, or tragic error, now becomes a glory and a triumph: the human being refuses to submit to limitations and, though finite, persists in setting infinite, hence inaccessible, goals. Wordsworth characteristically goes on to declare that "under such banners militant, the soul / Seeks for no trophies, struggles for no spoils"; for him, the infinite striving ends in physical quietism and moral fortitude. But for other writers, especially in Germany, the proper human aim is ceaseless activity—a "*Streben nach dem Unendlichen,*" a striving for the infinite. This view is epitomized by Goethe's Faust, who in his quest for the unattainable violates ordinary moral limits, yet wins salvation by his very insatiability, which never stoops to contentment with the possibilities offered by this finite world. Infinite longing—in Shelley's phrase, "the desire of the moth for a star"—was a recurrent theme also in the English literature of the day. "Less than everything," Blake announced, "cannot satisfy man." Shelley's *Alastor* and Keats's *Endymion* both represent the quest for an indefinable and inaccessible goal, and Byron's *Manfred* has for its hero a man whose "powers and will" reach beyond the limits of that human clay "which clogs the ethereal essence," so that "his aspirations / Have been beyond the dwellers of the earth."

In a parallel fashion, Romantic theorists of art rejected the neoclassic ideal of a limited intention, perfectly accomplished, in favor of "the glory of the imperfect," in which the very failures of artists attest the unlimited reach of their aims. And in their own work, Romantic writers deliberately put themselves in competition with the greatest of their predecessors and experimented boldly in poetic language, versification, and design. Especially in their longer poems they struck out in new directions, and in the space of a few decades produced an astonishing variety of forms constructed on novel principles of organization and style. Blake's symbolic lyrics and visionary "prophetic" poems; Coleridge's haunting ballad-narrative of sin and retribution, *The Rime of the Ancient Mariner;* Wordsworth's epiclike spiritual autobiography, *The Prelude;* Shelley's cosmic symbolic drama, *Prometheus Unbound;* Keats's sequence of odes on the irreconcilable conflict in basic human desires; Byron's satiric survey of all European civilization, *Don Juan*—one can say of each of them, as Shelley said of Byron's poem, that it was "something wholly new and relative to the age."

The great eighteenth-century writers had typically dealt with men and women as members of an organized, and usually an urban, society. Literary authors regarded themselves as integral parts of this society, addressed their works to it, and undertook to express its highest ideals and its collective traditional wisdom. Some Romantic writers, on the other hand, deliberately isolated themselves from society to give scope to their individual vision. Wordsworth titled his masterwork *The Recluse*, and he described himself as "musing in solitude" on its subject, "the individual Mind that keeps her own / Inviolate retirement." And in almost all Wordsworth's poems, long or short, the words *single, solitary, by oneself, alone* constitute a leitmotif; typically, his imagination is released by the sudden apparition of a single figure or object, stark against a natural background. Coleridge also, and still more

strikingly Byron and Shelley, represented a solitary protagonist who is separated from society because he has rejected it, or because it has rejected him.
These last three poets introduced what became a persistent theme in many
Victorian and modern writers—the theme of exile, of the disinherited mind
that cannot find a spiritual home in its native land and society or anywhere
in the modern world. The solitary Romantic nonconformist was sometimes
represented as also a great sinner. Male writers of that time were fascinated
by the outlaws of myth, legend, or history—Cain, Satan, Faust, the Wandering Jew, or the great, flawed figure of Napoleon—on whom they modeled
a number of their villains or their heroes. In Coleridge's *Ancient Mariner* (as
in Wordsworth's *Guilt and Sorrow* and *Peter Bell*) the guilty outcast—"alone,
alone, all, all alone"—is made to realize and expiate his sin against the community of living things so that he may reassume his place in the social order.
But in Byron the violator of conventional laws and limits remains proudly
unrepentant. His hero Manfred, a compound of guilt and superhuman greatness, cannot be defeated by death, successfully defying the demons who, in
the tradition of Marlowe's *Dr. Faustus*, have come to drag his soul to hell: "I
. . . was my own destroyer, and will be / My own hereafter.—Back, ye baffled
fiends!" A more reputable Romantic hero, who turns up frequently in Byron
and other writers and is made the protagonist of Shelley's great lyrical drama,
is the Prometheus of Greek mythology. He shares with Satan the status of
superlative nonconformity, since he sets himself in opposition to deity itself;
unlike Satan, however, he is the champion rather than the enemy of the
human race. Mary Shelley makes ironic use of this figure in her subtitle of
1818: *Frankenstein; or, The Modern Prometheus*—Victor Frankenstein is
decidedly not the champion of humankind.

MILLENNIAL EXPECTATIONS

Nowhere is the Romantic combination of boundless aspiration and the reliance on the power of the individual mind and imagination more evident than
in the literary treatment of the ultimate hope of humanity. The French Revolution had aroused in many sympathizers the millennial expectations that
are profoundly rooted in Hebrew and Christian tradition. "Few persons but
those who have lived in it," Robert Southey reminisced in 1824, "can conceive or comprehend what the memory of the French Revolution was, nor
what a visionary world seemed to open upon those who were just entering
it. Old things seemed passing away, and nothing was dreamt of but the regeneration of the human race." Southey's language—like that of Wordsworth,
Coleridge, Hazlitt, and other writers when they described their early Revolutionary fervor—is biblical; and it reflects the extent to which, in England,
the Revolution was championed by members of radical Protestant sects, who
envisioned it on the model of biblical prophecy.

The Bible ends with the book of Apocalypse (literally, "Revelation"),
prophesying a return of human beings to their lost Edenic felicity, first in
the millennium ("a thousand years") of an earthly kingdom, then in the eternity of "a new heaven and a new earth"; this consummation of history is
symbolized by a marriage between the New Jerusalem and Christ the Lamb.
At the outbreak of the French Revolution, Joseph Priestley and other Uni-

tarian leaders hailed that event as the stage preceding the millennium prophesied in Revelation. Coleridge and Wordsworth, in their early poems, also interpreted the Revolution as the violent preliminary to the new earth and heaven of apocalyptic prophecy. And Blake's *The French Revolution* (1791) and *America, a Prophecy* (1793) represented both these revolutions as apocalyptic portents of the last days of the fallen world.

When the later events in France dashed their faith in political revolution as a means to the millennium, a number of Romantic writers salvaged their apocalyptic hope by giving it a new interpretation. They transferred the agency of apocalypse from mass action to the individual mind—from a political to a spiritual revolution—and proposed that "the new earth and new heaven" of Revelation is available here, now, to all of us, if only we can make our visionary imagination triumph over our senses and sensebound understanding. Hence the extraordinary Romantic emphasis on a new way of *seeing* (which is regarded as the restoration of a lost earlier way of seeing) as the chief aim in life. Blake's "Prophetic Books," for example, all deal with some aspects of the Fall and Redemption, and represent apocalypse as the recovery of the imaginative vision of things as they really are, seen "through and not with the eye." "The Nature of my Work," Blake wrote, "is Visionary or Imaginative; it is an Endeavor to Restore what the Ancients called the Golden Age." This concept of the imaginative re-creation of the old earth continues to be expressed by Romantic poets in the original biblical metaphor of a marriage—although now it is not a marriage of the New Jerusalem with the Lamb but a conjunction of the inner faculties into spiritual unity, or else a marriage between the mind and the external world. Coleridge put this latter version succinctly in *Dejection: An Ode*; it is the inner condition of "Joy," at life's highest moments, "Which, wedding nature to us, gives in dower / A new earth and new heaven." Wordsworth announced as his "high argument" in the Prospectus to *The Recluse* (the same theme serves as underpattern for *The Prelude*) that "Paradise, and groves Elysian" are not "a history only of departed things"—

> For the discerning intellect of Man
> When wedded to this goodly universe
> In love and holy passion, shall find these
> A simple produce of the common day.

In Shelley's *Prometheus Unbound*, Prometheus represents archetypal humanity whose total change in moral being frees the imaginative capacity to envision, and to achieve, a regenerate world; the fourth act symbolizes this event in the mode of a marriage festival in which the whole cosmos participates.

Carlyle's *Sartor Resartus,* to mention one other example, is the history of an individual's violent spiritual crisis and conversion, which turns out to be the achievement of an individual apocalypse: "And I awoke to a new Heaven and a new Earth." But, as Carlyle goes on to indicate, this new earth is the old earth, seen by his protagonist as though miraculously re-created, because he has learned to substitute the "Imaginative" faculty for what Carlyle represents as the chief faculty of the eighteenth-century Enlightenment, the "Logical, Mensurative faculty," or "Understanding." Writing in 1830–31, at the close of the period historians have labeled "Romantic," Carlyle thus summed up the tendency of a generation of writers to retain the ancient faith in apocalypse, but to interpret it not as a change of the world, but as a change in our worldview.

OTHER FORMS: THE FAMILIAR ESSAY

This was also, along with its apocalyptic expectations, the period when literature for the first time became big business. Enlightenment-inspired educational reform and a rapid growth in population produced an explosion of potential readership. A new aesthetics of valuing art and literature "as such" emphasized reading for pleasure (as opposed to strictly moral and utilitarian ends); and people in general had more leisure in which to read, as well as more disposable income with which to purchase reading materials. Technological improvements in printing facilitated production and distribution, and commercial and public lending libraries were established. Hence the provision of more literature of all kinds to satisfy the needs of a greatly enlarged literate public.

At the close of the eighteenth century, reviews and magazines were written largely by hacks who acceded to the political bias and financial interests of the publisher and advertisers. The essays they included were weak imitations of the type established nearly a century earlier by single-essay periodicals such as the *Tatler* and the *Spectator*. In 1802, however, the *Edinburgh Review* inaugurated the modern type of periodical publication. It allowed considerable latitude to its writers, set its literary standards high, and was able to meet these standards by paying its contributors rates good enough to command the best talents of the day.

The success of this new enterprise stimulated the founding of rival reviews and magazines. (A "review," usually issued four times yearly, consisted primarily of essays on important books and discussions of contemporary issues; a "magazine" was a monthly publication that printed more miscellaneous materials, including a high proportion of original essays, poems, and stories.) In 1820 appeared the *London Magazine*, liberal in politics and contemporary in literary interests; in its short but notable career until 1829 it printed the work of a group of brilliant writers, including the three men who soon established themselves as the greatest essayists of the age—Lamb, Hazlitt, and De Quincey. These new periodicals not only elevated the essay in literary dignity and quality but revolutionized its form and substance. They competed strenuously for talent, paying well enough so that an author (at least one as prolific as Hazlitt) could earn a living as a freelance essayist. And writers were treated as serious practitioners who were competent, within broad limits, to write as they pleased.

Under these new conditions the "familiar essay"—a commentary on a nontechnical subject written in a relaxed and intimate manner—flourished, and in a fashion that to some degree paralleled the course of Romantic poetry. Each of the three major essayists was in fact closely associated with important poets and supported at least some of the new poetic developments in critical commentaries whose perceptiveness and discrimination render them durably valuable. Like the poets, these essayists were personal and subjective; their essays are often candidly autobiographical, reminiscent, self-analytic; and when the writers treated other matters than themselves, they tended to do so impressionistically, so that the material is seen reflected in the temperament of the essayist. The subject matter of the essays, like that of the poetry, exhibits an extension of range and sympathy far beyond the earlier limits of the leisure class and its fashionable concerns; the essays now dealt with clerks, chimney sweeps, poor relations, handball players, prize-fighters, and murderers. Most strikingly, the essayists resemble the poets in rebelling against eighteenth-century conventions by reviving prose forms long disused and developing new prose styles and structural principles. The result was a notable variety of achievements, ranging from Hazlitt's hard-hitting plain style and seemingly casual order of topics, through Lamb's delicately contrived rhetoric and meticulously controlled organization, to De Quincey's elaborate experiments in applying to prose the rhythms, harmonies, and thematic structure of musical compositions.

THE DRAMA

Although favorable to the essay, literary conditions in the early nineteenth century were unfavorable in the extreme to writing for the stage. By a licensing act that was not repealed until 1843, only the Drury Lane and Covent Garden theaters had the right to produce "legitimate"—that is to say, spoken—drama; the other theaters were restricted by law to entertainments in which there could be no dialogue except to music, and so put on mainly dancing, pantomime, and various types of musical plays. The two monopoly theaters were vast and ill-lighted, and their audiences were noisy and unruly; as a result, actors played in a grandiose and orotund style. To succeed under such conditions, plays had to be blatant and magniloquent, so that the drama of that period (fettered also by rigid moral and political censorship) tended to the extremes of either farce or melodrama. None of the plays written by the professional playwrights of the time is read nowadays; they survive mainly in the limbo of scholarly monographs on the history of the theater.

Nonetheless, attracted irresistibly by the example of their idolized Shakespeare, all the major Romantic poets, and many minor ones, tried their hand at poetic plays. Some of these were written as closet drama—Byron's *Manfred* and Shelley's *Prometheus Unbound,* for example, and most of Joanna Baillie's widely read *Plays on the Passions*—but others were expressly written for the stage. The poets, however, lacked experience with the hard necessities of the practical theater, and they were for the most part unable to throw off the artifice of an archaic style dominated by Elizabethan and Jacobean models.

Above all, the genius of an age that excelled in subjective or visionary literary forms was ill adapted to the theater, which is a peculiarly social genre representing a variety of credible characters. Even Byron, the only important poet of his generation to produce major work in a literary kind that requires a highly developed social sensibility—satire—did not succeed as a practical dramatist. His stage plays, while readable, mainly exhibit various aspects of the Byronic hero; they lack theatrical vigor and variety, and their thin-skinned author wisely refused to let them be put on before the merciless and demonstrative audiences of his day. Coleridge achieved a minor hit with his tragedy *Remorse*, which ran for twenty nights at the Drury Lane in 1813. The most capable Romantic dramatist was, surprisingly, Shelley. In *The Cenci* (1820) Shelley, with great tact and genuine theatrical acumen, converts a true story of the Italian Renaissance—of a monstrous father who violates his daughter and is in turn murdered by her—into a powerful version of his own central fable of the instinctive desire of evil to destroy, by degrading, the defiant individual, and of the moral triumph of the unconquerable single spirit, even in death. The play was not staged, however, until long after Shelley's death.

THE NOVEL

Two new types of fiction were prominent in the late eighteenth century. One was the "Gothic novel," which had been inaugurated in 1764 by Horace Walpole's *The Castle of Otranto: A Gothic Story*, and continued by Clara Reeve in *The Champion of Virtue: A Gothic Story* (1777). The term derives from the frequent setting of these tales in a gloomy castle of the Middle Ages, but it has been extended to a larger group of novels, set somewhere in the past, that exploit the possibilities of mystery and terror in sullen, craggy landscapes; decaying mansions with dank dungeons, secret passages, and stealthy ghosts; chilling supernatural phenomena; and often, sexual persecution of a beautiful maiden by an obsessed and haggard villain. These novels opened up to later fiction the dark, irrational side of human nature—the savage egoism, the perverse impulses, and the nightmarish terrors that lie beneath the controlled and ordered surface of the conscious mind. Some of the most powerful and influential writings in the mode were by women— they doubtless afforded a fictional release for the submerged desires and compensatory fantasies of that rigidly restricted and disadvantaged class. In *The Mysteries of Udolpho* (1794), and better still in *The Italian* (1797), Ann Radcliffe developed the figure of the mysterious and solitary *homme fatal*, torturing others because he is himself tortured by unspeakable guilt, who, though a villain, usurps the place of the hero in the reader's interest. Matthew Gregory Lewis in *The Monk* (1797), which he wrote at the age of twenty, has a similar protagonist and brings to the fore the elements of diabolism, sensuality, and sadistic perversion that were pungent but submerged components in Radcliffe's Gothic formula. Gothicism is apparent also in Romantic poetry: in Coleridge's medieval terror poem *Christabel*, in Byron's recurrent hero-villain, in the setting and descriptive passages of Keats's *Eve of St. Agnes,* and in Shelley's inclinations (fostered by his early love for Gothic tales and his own youthful trials in that form) toward the fantastic, the macabre, and the exploration of the unconscious mind and of such aberrations as incest.

The second fictional mode popular at the turn of the century was the novel of purpose, often written to propagate the new social and political theories current in the period of the French Revolution. The best examples combine didactic intention with elements of Gothic terror. William Godwin, the political philosopher, wrote *Caleb Williams* (1794) to illustrate the thesis that the lower classes are helplessly subject to the power and privilege of the ruling class, but he did so in the form of a chilling story about the relentless pursuit and persecution by a wealthy squire of his young secretary, who has come upon evidence that the squire has committed murder. Mary Shelley—Percy Shelley's wife and the daughter of Mary Wollstonecraft, author of *A Vindication of the Rights of Woman*—wrote a thematic novel of terror that not only is a literary classic but has become a popular myth. Her *Frankenstein* (1818) transforms a story about a fabricated monster into a powerful representation of the moral distortion imposed on an individual who, because he diverges from the norm, is rejected by society. Maria Edgeworth's *Castle Rackrent* (1800), admired by Walter Scott, initiated what he later developed—the British regional novel and the British historical novel—and Hannah More's *Coelebs in Search of a Wife* (1808), a hugely successful novel about marriage and religion, was influential in both Britain and the United States.

The Romantic period produced, in addition to Mary Shelley, two novelists whose renown is worldwide, Jane Austen and Sir Walter Scott. Jane Austen (1775–1817) is the only major author who seems to be untouched by the political, intellectual, and artistic revolutions of her age. Charlotte Brontë, speaking for the Romantic sensibility, complained that Jane Austen's novels lack warmth, enthusiasm, energy; "she ruffles her reader by nothing vehement, disturbs him by nothing profound. The passions are perfectly unknown to her." But Austen deliberately elected to work within the circumference of her own experience—the life of provincial English gentlefolk—and to maintain the decorum of the novel of manners, based on such literary antecedents as the comedy of manners of William Congreve and Richard Brinsley Sheridan and the novels of the earlier women authors Fanny Burney and Maria Edgeworth. Within these elected limits both of subject and form, Austen achieved a fully particularized setting within which to examine and criticize the values men and women live by in their everyday social lives.

Sense and Sensibility and *Northanger Abbey* gently ridicule two later eighteenth-century deviations from the humanistic norm: the cult of sensibility and the taste for Gothic terrors. Austen's other novels, published between 1813 and 1818—*Mansfield Park, Persuasion*, and best of all, *Pride and Prejudice* and *Emma*—all deal with the subject of getting married. This was in fact a central preoccupation and problem for the young leisure-class lady of that age, who had no career open to her outside of domesticity; Austen, however, chose the subject because it provided her with the best realistic opportunities for testing her heroines' practical sense and moral integrity, their degree of knowledge of the world and of themselves, and their capacity to demonstrate grace under social and financial pressure.

Sir Walter Scott (1771–1832) was contemporary with Jane Austen, and admired her greatly, but his work in fiction was at an extreme from hers. In 1814, with the anonymous *Waverley*, he turned from narrative verse (in which Byron had displaced him in popularity) to narrative prose and managed to write almost thirty long works of fiction in the eighteen years before he died. They are in the mode that he himself defined as romance, "the interest of which turns upon marvelous and uncommon incidents," in contrast to the novel such as Jane Austen wrote, in which "the events are accommodated to the ordinary train of human events, and the modern state of society." Scott's originality lay in opening up to fiction the rich and lively realm of history; he sometimes alters the order of events for novelistic purposes, yet he maintains fidelity to the spirit of the past and a meticulous accuracy in antiquarian detail. His series of Scottish novels, including *Guy Mannering, The Antiquary, Old Mortality, Rob Roy,* and (most enduringly) *The Heart of Midlothian,* are rooted in historical events from the seventeenth century up to his own time; *Ivanhoe* is set in thirteenth-century England; *Kenilworth* takes place in the age of Elizabeth; and *Quentin Durward,* the best of his Continental romances, has for its background the French court of the fifteenth century.

Like Byron, Scott wrote with dash and grandiosity in a kind of sustained improvisation; his plotting is often loose, his romantic lovers pallid, and his kings and chieftains large-scale puppets. But in his great scenes of action there are a scope and sweep not to be exceeded in fiction for several decades. And although, unlike his liberal Romantic contemporaries, Scott's political sympathies were aristocratic and feudal, his most vivid and convincing characters are members of the middle and lower classes. His tradesmen, servants, peasantry, social outcasts, and demented old women, speaking a rich Scottish vernacular (Scott's language, like Robert Burns's in verse, tended to become stilted and conventional when he wrote in standard English), make up a populous world in which each person is an individual, rooted in the circumstances of time, place, class, and occupation.

Scott had an immense international vogue, equaling that of Byron and Goethe, and became the acknowledged master of some of the greatest nineteenth-century novelists, including Balzac and Tolstoy. Jane Austen, on the other hand, during her lifetime was admired only by a limited group of English readers. Her novels have, however, demonstrated greater staying power. Scott's combination of casualness in design and prodigality in detail puts off many readers who have formed their sensibilities on the fiction of the present century. But even after the achievements of such masters in the form as Henry James, Jane Austen remains the sovereign of the intricate, spare, and ironic art of the novel of manners.

THE ROMANTIC PERIOD

TEXTS	CONTEXTS
1774 J. W. von Goethe, *The Sorrows of Young Werther*	
	1775 American War of Independence (1775–83)
1776 Adam Smith, *The Wealth of Nations*	
1778 Frances Burney, *Evelina*	
1779 Samuel Johnson, *Lives of the English Poets* (1779–81)	
	1780 Gordon Riots in London
1781 Immanuel Kant, *Critique of Pure Reason*. Jean-Jacques Rousseau, *Confessions*. J. C. Friedrich Schiller, *The Robbers*	
	1783 William Pitt becomes prime minister (serving until 1801 and again in 1804–06)
1784 Charlotte Smith, *Elegiac Sonnets*	1784 Death of Samuel Johnson
1785 William Cowper, *The Task*	
1786 William Beckford, *Vathek*. Robert Burns, *Poems, Chiefly in the Scottish Dialect*	
	1787 W. A. Mozart, *Don Giovanni*
1789 Jeremy Bentham, *Principles of Morals and Legislation*. William Blake, *Songs of Innocence*	1789 Fall of the Bastille (beginning of the French Revolution)
1790 Joanna Baillie, *Poems*. Blake, *The Marriage of Heaven and Hell*. Edmund Burke, *Reflections on the Revolution in France*	1790 Henry James Pye succeeds Thomas Warton as poet laureate. J. M. W. Turner first exhibits at the Royal Academy
1791 William Gilpin, *Observations on the River Wye*. Thomas Paine, *Rights of Man*. Ann Radcliffe, *The Romance of the Forest*	
1792 Mary Wollstonecraft, *A Vindication of the Rights of Woman*	1792 September Massacres in Paris. First gas lights in Britain
1793 William Godwin, *Political Justice*	1793 Execution of Louis XVI and Marie Antoinette. France declares war against Britain (and then Britain against France). The Reign of Terror
1794 Blake, *Songs of Experience*. Godwin, *Caleb Williams*. Radcliffe, *The Mysteries of Udolpho*	1794 The fall of Robespierre
1796 Matthew Gregory Lewis, *The Monk*	
1798 Joanna Baillie, *Plays on the Passions*, volume 1. Bentham, *Political Economy*. Thomas Malthus, *An Essay on the Principle of Population*. William Wordsworth and Samuel Taylor Coleridge, *Lyrical Ballads*	
1800 Maria Edgeworth, *Castle Rackrent*. Mary Robinson, *Lyrical Tales*	

TEXTS	CONTEXTS
	1802 Treaty of Amiens. *Edinburgh Review* founded. John Constable first exhibits at the Royal Academy
	1804 Napoleon crowned emperor
	1805 The French fleet defeated by the British at Trafalgar
1807 Wordsworth, *Poems in Two Volumes*	**1807** Abolition of the slave trade in Britain
1808 Goethe, *Faust,* part 1	**1808** Ludwig van Beethoven, *Symphonies* 5 and 6
	1811 The Prince of Wales becomes regent for George III, who is declared incurably insane
1812 Lord Byron, *Childe Harold's Pilgrimage,* cantos 1 and 2. Felicia Hemans, *The Domestic Affections*	**1812** War between Britain and the United States (1812–15)
1813 Jane Austen, *Price and Prejudice*	**1813** Robert Southey succeeds Pye as poet laureate
1814 Walter Scott, *Waverley.* Wordsworth, *The Excursion*	
	1815 Napoleon defeated at Waterloo
1816 Byron, *Childe Harold,* cantos 3 and 4. Coleridge, *Christabel, Kubla Khan.* Percy Shelley, *Alastor*	
1817 Byron, *Manfred.* Coleridge, *Biographia Literaria* and *Sibylline Leaves.* John Keats, *Poems*	**1817** *Blackwood's Edinburgh Magazine* founded. Death of Princess Charlotte
1818 Austen, *Northanger Abbey.* Keats, *Endymion.* Thomas Love Peacock, *Nightmare Abbey.* Mary Shelley, *Frankenstein*	
1819 Byron, *Don Juan,* cantos 1 and 2	**1819** "Peterloo Massacre" in Manchester
1820 John Clare, *Poems Descriptive of Rural Life.* Keats, *Lamia, Isabella, The Eve of St. Agnes, and Other Poems.* Percy Shelley, *Prometheus Unbound*	**1820** Death of George III; accession of George IV. *London Magazine* founded
1821 Thomas De Quincey, *Confessions of an English Opium-Eater.* Percy Shelley, *Adonais*	**1821** Deaths of Keats in Rome and Napoleon at St. Helena
	1822 Franz Schubert, *Unfinished Symphony.* Death of Percy Shelley in the Bay of Spezia, near Lerici, Italy
1824 Letitia Landon, *The Improvisatrice*	**1824** Death of Byron in Missolonghi
1827 Clare, *The Shepherd's Calendar*	
1828 Hemans, *Records of Woman*	
1830 Charles Lyell, *Principles of Geology* (1830–33). Alfred Tennyson, *Poems, Chiefly Lyrical*	**1830** Death of George IV; accession of William IV
	1832 First Reform Bill

ANNA LETITIA BARBAULD
1743–1825

Anna Barbauld, born Anna Letitia Aiken, received an unusual education from her father, a nonconformist minister and schoolmaster, that enabled her to read English before she was three and to master French and Italian, and then both Latin and Greek, while still a child. She made her literary debut with *Poems,* a work that went through five editions between 1773 and 1777 and immediately established her as a leading poet. In 1774 she married Rochemont Barbauld, a dissenting minister, and with him co-managed a school at Palgrave, in Suffolk. Thereafter, becoming increasingly famous and respected in literary circles as (according to the custom of the day) "Mrs. Barbauld," she divided her time between the teaching of younger pupils at Palgrave and a series of writings focused on education, politics, and literature. She published *Devotional Pieces* (1775), three volumes of *Lessons for Children* (1778–79), and *Hymns in Prose for Children* (1781), all of which were reprinted many times. William Hazlitt records a common experience in recalling that he read her works "before those of any other author, male or female, when I was learning to spell words of one syllable in her story-books for children."

She wrote political pamphlets in the 1790s, defending dissenters, democratic government, and popular education and opposing Britain's declaration of war against France; she attacked the slave trade in a verse *Epistle to William Wilberforce* (1791). In the next decade she turned to editing, producing the *Correspondence of Samuel Richardson* (six volumes, 1804), *The British Novelists* (fifty volumes, beginning in 1810), and a popular anthology of poetry and prose for young women called *The Female Speaker* (1811). Her work *The British Novelists* was the first attempt to establish a national canon in fiction paralleling the multivolume collections of British poets (such as the one associated with Samuel Johnson's prefaces) that had been appearing since the 1770s. Her introductory essay, *On the Origin and Progress of Novel-Writing,* is a pioneering statement concerning the educational value of novels.

Barbauld's last major work in poetry was *Eighteen Hundred and Eleven* (1812), a 334-line tirade against contemporary Britain lamenting the war with France (then in its seventeenth year), the poverty of leadership, the fallen economy, colonialism, and the failure of genius (at the conclusion, the Spirit of Genius emigrates to South America). The critical response was anguished and unanimously negative, even from the more liberal critics; and Barbauld seems not to have attempted another long work after this (she was, by this time, in her late sixties). She continued to write shorter pieces, such as the sprightly *Life,* on into the 1820s.

A Summer Evening's Meditation[1]

> 'Tis past! The sultry tyrant of the south
> Has spent his short-lived rage; more grateful hours
> Move silent on; the skies no more repel
> The dazzled sight, but with mild maiden beams
> 5   Of tempered lustre court the cherished eye
> To wander o'er their sphere; where, hung aloft,
> Dian's bright crescent, like a silver bow

1. The excursion-and-return structure of this poem anticipates the high flights (and returns) of later lyrics by Coleridge, Percy Shelley, and Keats, among others. But Barbauld's journey, beginning with "mild maiden beams" in line 4 and continuing with Diana's crescent (line 7), Venus's sweetest beam (lines 10 and 11), and "meekened Eve" (line 14), is specifically gendered throughout: it is clearly a woman who is launching "into the trackless deeps of space" (line 82).

New strung in heaven, lifts high its beamy horns
Impatient for the night, and seems to push
10 Her brother down the sky. Fair Venus shines
Even in the eye of day; with sweetest beam
Propitious shines, and shakes a trembling flood
Of softened radiance from her dewy locks.
The shadows spread apace; while meekened[2] Eve,
15 Her cheek yet warm with blushes, slow retires
Through the Hesperian gardens of the west,
And shuts the gates of day. 'Tis now the hour
When Contemplation from her sunless haunts,
The cool damp grotto, or the lonely depth
20 Of unpierced woods, where wrapt in solid shade
She mused away the gaudy hours of noon,
And fed on thoughts unripened by the sun,
Moves forward; and with radiant finger points
To yon blue concave swelled by breath divine,
25 Where, one by one, the living eyes of heaven
Awake, quick kindling o'er the face of ether
One boundless blaze; ten thousand trembling fires,
And dancing lustres, where the unsteady eye,
Restless and dazzled, wanders unconfined
30 O'er all this field of glories; spacious field,
And worthy of the Master: he, whose hand
With hieroglyphics elder than the Nile
Inscribed the mystic tablet, hung on high
To public gaze, and said, "Adore, O man!
35 The finger of thy God." From what pure wells
Of milky light, what soft o'erflowing urn,
Are all these lamps so fill'd? these friendly lamps,
For ever streaming o'er the azure deep
To point our path, and light us to our home.
40 How soft they slide along their lucid spheres!
And silent as the foot of Time, fulfill
Their destined courses: Nature's self is hushed,
And, but a scattered leaf, which rustles through
The thick-wove foliage, not a sound is heard
45 To break the midnight air; though the raised ear,
Intensely listening, drinks in every breath.
How deep the silence, yet how loud the praise!
But are they silent all? or is there not
A tongue in every star, that talks with man,
50 And woos him to be wise? nor woos in vain:
This dead of midnight is the noon of thought,
And Wisdom mounts her zenith with the stars.
At this still hour the self-collected soul
Turns inward, and beholds a stranger there
55 Of high descent, and more than mortal rank;
An embryo God; a spark of fire divine,
Which must burn on for ages, when the sun,—
Fair transitory creature of a day!—

2. Softened, made meek.

Has closed his golden eye, and wrapt in shades
60 Forgets his wonted journey through the east.

Ye citadels of light, and seats of Gods!
Perhaps my future home, from whence the soul,
Revolving periods past, may oft look back
With recollected tenderness on all
65 The various busy scenes she left below,
Its deep-laid projects and its strange events,
As on some fond and doting tale that soothed
Her infant hours—O be it lawful now
To tread the hallowed circle of your courts,
70 And with mute wonder and delighted awe
Approach your burning confines. Seized in thought,
On Fancy's wild and roving wing I sail,
From the green borders of the peopled Earth,
And the pale Moon, her duteous fair attendant;
75 From solitary Mars; from the vast orb
Of Jupiter, whose huge gigantic bulk
Dances in ether like the lightest leaf;
To the dim verge, the suburbs of the system,
Where cheerless Saturn 'midst his watery moons
80 Girt with a lucid zone, in gloomy pomp,
Sits like an exiled monarch: fearless thence
I launch into the trackless deeps of space,
Where, burning round, ten thousand suns appear,
Of elder beam, which ask no leave to shine
85 Of our terrestrial star, nor borrow light
From the proud regent of our scanty day;
Sons of the morning, first-born of creation,
And only less than Him who marks their track,
And guides their fiery wheels. Here must I stop,
90 Or is there aught beyond? What hand unseen
Impels me onward through the glowing orbs
Of habitable nature, far remote,
To the dread confines of eternal night,
To solitudes of vast unpeopled space,
95 The deserts of creation, wide and wild;
Where embryo systems and unkindled suns
Sleep in the womb of chaos? fancy droops,
And thought astonished stops her bold career.
But O thou mighty mind! whose powerful word
100 Said, thus let all things be, and thus they were,
Where shall I seek thy presence? how unblamed
Invoke thy dread perfection?
Have the broad eyelids of the morn beheld thee?
Or does the beamy shoulder of Orion
105 Support thy throne? O look with pity down
On erring, guilty man! not in thy names
Of terror clad; not with those thunders armed
That conscious Sinai felt, when fear appalled

The scattered tribes;[3]—thou hast a gentler voice,
110 That whispers comfort to the swelling heart,
Abashed, yet longing to behold her Maker.

But now my soul, unused to stretch her powers
In flight so daring, drops her weary wing,
And seeks again the known accustomed spot,
115 Drest up with sun, and shade, and lawns, and streams,
A mansion fair, and spacious for its guest,
And full replete with wonders. Let me here,
Content and grateful, wait the appointed time,
And ripen for the skies: the hour will come
120 When all these splendours bursting on my sight
Shall stand unveiled, and to my ravished sense
Unlock the glories of the world unknown.

1773

The Rights of Woman[1]

Yes, injured Woman! rise, assert thy right!
Woman! too long degraded, scorned, opprest;
O born to rule in partial Law's despite,
Resume thy native empire o'er the breast!

5 Go forth arrayed in panoply divine;
That angel pureness which admits no stain;
Go, bid proud Man his boasted rule resign,
And kiss the golden sceptre of thy reign.

Go, gird thyself with grace; collect thy store
10 Of bright artillery glancing from afar;
Soft melting tones thy thundering cannon's roar,
Blushes and fears thy magazine of war.

Thy rights are empire: urge no meaner claim,—
Felt, not defined, and if debated, lost;
15 Like sacred mysteries, which withheld from fame,
Shunning discussion, are revered the most.

Try all that wit and art suggest to bend
Of thy imperial foe the stubborn knee;
Make treacherous Man thy subject, not thy friend;
20 Thou mayst command, but never canst be free.

Awe the licentious, and restrain the rude;
Soften the sullen, clear the cloudy brow:

3. When God came down to deliver the Ten Commandments "there were thunders and lightnings . . . so that all the people . . . trembled" (Exodus 19.16).

1. A response—seemingly favorable until the last two stanzas—to Mary Wollstonecraft's *A Vindication of the Rights of Woman* (1792).

Be, more than princes' gifts, thy favours sued;—
She hazards all, who will the least allow.

25 But hope not, courted idol of mankind,
   On this proud eminence secure to stay;
   Subduing and subdued, thou soon shalt find
   Thy coldness soften, and thy pride give way.

   Then, then, abandon each ambitious thought,
30 Conquest or rule thy heart shall feebly move,
   In Nature's school, by her soft maxims taught,
   That separate rights are lost in mutual love.

ca. 1792–95   1825

To a Little Invisible Being
Who Is Expected Soon to Become Visible

Germ of new life, whose powers expanding slow
For many a moon their full perfection wait,—
Haste, precious pledge of happy love, to go
Auspicious borne through life's mysterious gate.

5 What powers lie folded in thy curious frame,—
  Senses from objects locked, and mind from thought!
  How little canst thou guess thy lofty claim
  To grasp at all the worlds the Almighty wrought!

   And see, the genial season's warmth to share,
10 Fresh younglings shoot, and opening roses glow!
   Swarms of new life exulting fill the air,—
   Haste, infant bud of being, haste to blow!°   bloom

   For thee the nurse prepares her lulling songs,
   The eager matrons count the lingering day;
15 But far the most thy anxious parent longs
   On thy soft cheek a mother's kiss to lay.

   She only asks to lay her burden down,
   That her glad arms that burden may resume;
   And nature's sharpest pangs her wishes crown,
20 That free thee living from thy living tomb.

   She longs to fold to her maternal breast
   Part of herself, yet to herself unknown;
   To see and to salute the stranger guest,
   Fed with her life through many a tedious moon.

25 Come, reap thy rich inheritance of love!
   Bask in the fondness of a Mother's eye!

Nor wit nor eloquence her heart shall move
Like the first accents of thy feeble cry.

Haste, little captive, burst thy prison doors!
30   Launch on the living world, and spring to light!
Nature for thee displays her various stores,
Opens her thousand inlets of delight.

If charmed verse or muttered prayers had power,
With favouring spells to speed thee on thy way,
35   Anxious I'd bid my beads° each passing hour,   ° offer a prayer
Till thy wished smile thy mother's pangs o'erpay.°   ° more than compensate

ca. 1795?   1825

Washing-Day

> . . . and their voice,
> Turning again towards childish treble, pipes
> And whistles in its sound.[1]

The Muses are turned gossips; they have lost
The buskined° step, and clear high-sounding phrase,   ° tragic, elevated
Language of gods, Come then, domestic Muse,
In slipshod measure loosely prattling on
5   Of farm or orchard, pleasant curds and cream,
Or drowning flies, or shoe lost in the mire
By little whimpering boy, with rueful face;
Come, Muse; and sing the dreaded Washing-Day.
Ye who beneath the yoke of wedlock bend,
10   With bowed soul, full well ye ken the day
Which week, smooth sliding after week, brings on
Too soon;—for to that day nor peace belongs
Nor comfort;—ere the first gray streak of dawn,
The red-armed washers come and chase repose.
15   Nor pleasant smile, nor quaint device of mirth,
E'er visited that day: the very cat,
From the wet kitchen scared and reeking hearth,
Visits the parlour,—an unwonted guest.
The silent breakfast-meal is soon dispatched;
20   Uninterrupted, save by anxious looks
Cast at the lowering sky, if sky should lower.
From that last evil, O preserve us, heavens!
For should the skies pour down, adieu to all
Remains of quiet: then expect to hear
25   Of sad disasters,—dirt and gravel stains
Hard to efface, and loaded lines at once
Snapped short,—and linen-horse° by dog thrown down,   ° drying rack
And all the petty miseries of life.

1. Loosely quoted from Shakespeare's *As You Like It* 2.7.160–62.

Saints have been calm while stretched upon the rack,
30 And Guatimozin² smiled on burning coals;
But never yet did housewife notable
Greet with a smile a rainy washing-day.
—But grant the welkin° fair, require not thou   *sky*
Who call'st thyself perchance the master there,
35 Or study swept or nicely dusted coat,
Or usual 'tendance;—ask not, indiscreet,
Thy stockings mended, though the yawning rents
Gape wide as Erebus;° nor hope to find   *the underworld*
Some snug recess impervious: shouldst thou try
40 The 'customed garden walks, shine eye shall rue
The budding fragrance of thy tender shrubs,
Myrtle or rose, all crushed beneath the weight
Of coarse checked apron,—with impatient hand
Twitched off when showers impend: or crossing lines
45 Shall mar thy musings, as the wet cold sheet
Flaps in thy face abrupt. Woe to the friend
Whose evil stars have urged him forth to claim
On such a day the hospitable rites!
Looks, blank at best, and stinted courtesy,
50 Shall he receive. Vainly he feeds his hopes
With dinner of roast chicken, savoury pie,
Or tart or pudding:—pudding he nor tart
That day shall eat; nor, though the husband try,
Mending what can't be helped, to kindle mirth
55 From cheer deficient, shall his consort's brow
Clear up propitious:—the unlucky guest
In silence dines, and early slinks away.
I well remember, when a child, the awe
This day struck into me; for then the maids,
60 I scarce knew why, looked cross, and drove me from them:
Nor soft caress could I obtain, nor hope
Usual indulgencies; jelly or creams,
Relic of costly suppers, and set by
For me, their petted one; or buttered toast,
65 When butter was forbid; or thrilling tale
Of ghost or witch, or murder—so I went
And sheltered me beside the parlour fire:
There my dear grandmother, eldest of forms,
Tended the little ones, and watched from harm,
70 Anxiously fond, though oft her spectacles
With elfin cunning hid, and oft the pins
Drawn from her ravelled stocking, might have soured
One less indulgent.—
At intervals my mother's voice was heard,
75 Urging dispatch: briskly the work went on,
All hands employed to wash, to rinse, to wring,

2. The last of the Aztec emperors (Cuanhtémoc, d. 1525), who was tortured and executed by the Spanish conquistadors.

To fold, and starch, and clap,° and iron, and plait.   *flatten*
Then would I sit me down, and ponder much
Why washings were. Sometimes through hollow bowl
80 Of pipe amused we blew, and sent aloft
The floating bubbles; little dreaming then
To see, Mongolfier,[3] thy silken ball
Ride buoyant through the clouds—so near approach
The sports of children and the toils of men.
85 Earth, air, and sky, and ocean, hath its bubbles,[4]
And verse is one of them—this most of all.

                                                    1797

Life

Animula, vagula, blandula.[1]

Life! I know not what thou art,
But know that thou and I must part;
And when, or how, or where we met,
I own to me's a secret yet.
5 But this I know, when thou art fled,
Where'er they lay these limbs, this head,
No clod so valueless shall be,
As all that then remains of me.
O whither, whither dost thou fly,
10 Where bend unseen thy trackless course,
    And in this strange divorce,
Ah tell where I must seek this compound I?

To the vast ocean of empyreal flame,
    From whence thy essence came,
15 Dost thou thy flight pursue, when freed
From matter's base encumbering weed?
    Or dost thou, hid from sight,
    Wait, like some spell-bound knight,
Through blank oblivious years th' appointed hour,
20 To break thy trance and reassume thy power?
Yet canst thou without thought or feeling be?
O say what art thou, when no more thou 'rt thee?

    Life! we've been long together,
    Through pleasant and through cloudy weather;
25   'Tis hard to part when friends are dear;
    Perhaps 't will cost a sigh, a tear;
    Then steal away, give little warning,

3. Brothers Joseph-Michel and Jacques-Étienne Mongolfier successfully launched the first hot-air balloon, at Annonay, France, in 1783.
4. Cf. *Macbeth* 1.3.77: "The earth hath bubbles, as the water has."

1. From Aelius Spartianus's *Life of Hadrian* 25— the first line of a poem supposedly composed by the emperor Hadrian on his deathbed: "Charming little soul, hastening away."

Choose thine own time;
Say not Good night, but in some brighter clime
30   Bid me Good morning.

1825

CHARLOTTE SMITH
1749–1806

The melancholy of Charlotte Smith's *Elegiac Sonnets* was no mere literary posture. Smith married at fourteen and bore a dozen children (three of whom died in infancy or childhood) before permanently separating from her husband because of his abusive temper, infidelities, and financial irresponsibility. She began writing to make money when her husband was imprisoned for debt in 1783. Her first book, which came out in 1784 with the bold title *Elegiac Sonnets, and Other Essays by Charlotte Smith of Bignor Park, in Sussex*, went through nine expanding editions in the following sixteen years.

Beginning in the later 1780s, Smith had considerable success as a novelist, rapidly producing *Emmeline* (four volumes, 1788), *Ethelinde* (five volumes, 1789), *Celestina* (four volumes, 1791), *Desmond* (three volumes, 1792), *The Old Manor House* (four volumes, 1793), and several others. She also wrote children's stories, sketches, and several long poems. *The Emigrants* (1793), an eight-hundred-line descriptive-reflective work on the plight of French exiles in England during the early years of the French Revolution, has been called by Smith's modern editor, Stuart Curran, "the finest piece of extended blank verse in English between Cowper's *The Task* (1785) and Wordsworth's unpublished initial version of *The Prelude* (1799)."

The sonnet as a form, after its great flourishing in the Renaissance in the hands of Sidney, Spenser, Shakespeare, Donne, and Milton, dropped out of fashion in the eighteenth century. It was, Samuel Johnson declared in his *Dictionary* (1755), "not very suitable to the English language, and has not been used by any man of eminence since Milton." Its revival toward the end of that century—by Coleridge in the 1790s; Wordsworth (who wrote some five hundred sonnets beginning in 1802); and in the next generation, Shelley and Keats—was largely the result of Smith's influence. Coleridge noted in the introduction to his privately printed "sheet of sonnets" in 1796 that "Charlotte Smith and [William Lisle] Bowles are they who first made the Sonnet popular among the present English"; but Bowles's *Fourteen Sonnets* of 1789, imitating those that Smith first published five years earlier (which by 1789 had reached a fifth edition), rode on a wave of popularity of the form that she had already established.

Wordsworth, who read her sonnets when he was a student at Cambridge, observed in 1833 that Smith "wrote . . . with true feeling for rural nature, at a time when nature was not much regarded by English Poets." Coleridge in his 1796 introductory essay on the sonnet, using Smith as a principal example, remarked that "those Sonnets appear to me the most exquisite, in which moral Sentiments, Affections, or Feelings, are deduced from, and associated with, the scenery of Nature." Subsequently, of course, the connecting of feelings and nature became a central theme and strategy in Romantic poetry. Under the influence of Smith, Coleridge himself quickly progressed from the sonnet to the conversation poem, beginning with *The Eolian Harp*, and in turn influenced Wordsworth and subsequent writers of odes and kindred types of descriptive-meditative verse. Thus Smith helped to originate one of the most distinctive genres of English literature, what has been called "the greater Romantic lyric."

FROM ELEGIAC SONNETS

Written at the Close of Spring

The garlands fade that Spring so lately wove,
    Each simple flower, which she had nursed in dew,
Anemonies, that spangled every grove,
    The primrose wan, and hare-bell mildly blue.
5 No more shall violets linger in the dell,
    Or purple orchis variegate the plain,
Till Spring again shall call forth every bell,
    And dress with humid hands her wreaths again.—
Ah! poor humanity! so frail, so fair,
10   Are the fond visions of thy early day,
Till tyrant passion, and corrosive care,
    Bid all thy fairy colors fade away!
Another May new buds and flowers shall bring;
Ah! why has happiness—no second Spring?

1784

To Sleep

Come, balmy Sleep! tired nature's soft resort!
    On these sad temples all thy poppies shed;
And bid gay dreams, from Morpheus' airy court,
    Float in light vision round my aching head!
5 Secure of all thy blessings, partial Power!
    On his hard bed the peasant throws him down;
And the poor sea boy, in the rudest hour,
    Enjoys thee more than he who wears a crown.[1]
Clasp'd in her faithful shepherd's guardian arms,
10   Well may the village girl sweet slumbers prove
And they, O gentle Sleep! still taste thy charms,
    Who wake to labor, liberty, and love.
But still thy opiate aid dost thou deny
To calm the anxious breast; to close the streaming eye.

1784

To Night

I love thee, mournful, sober-suited Night!
    When the faint moon, yet lingering in her wane,

---

1. As Smith herself noted, lines 7 and 8 allude to King Henry's apostrophe to sleep in 2 *Henry IV* 3.1.5–31 (cf. Keats's *Sonnet to Sleep*, p. 847).

And veil'd in clouds, with pale uncertain light
    Hangs o'er the waters of the restless main.
5 In deep depression sunk, the enfeebled mind
    Will to the deaf cold elements complain,
    And tell the embosom'd grief, however vain,
To sullen surges and the viewless wind.
Though no repose on thy dark breast I find,
10   I still enjoy thee—cheerless as thou art;
    For in thy quiet gloom the exhausted heart
Is calm, though wretched; hopeless, yet resign'd.
While to the winds and waves its sorrows given,
May reach—though lost on earth—the ear of Heaven!

                                        1788

Written in the Church-Yard at Middleton in Sussex[1]

Press'd by the Moon, mute arbitress of tides,
    While the loud equinox its power combines,
    The sea no more its swelling surge confines,
But o'er the shrinking land sublimely rides.
5 The wild blast, rising from the Western cave,
    Drives the huge billows from their heaving bed;
    Tears from their grassy tombs the village dead,
And breaks the silent sabbath of the grave!
With shells and sea-weed mingled, on the shore
10   Lo! their bones whiten in the frequent wave;
    But vain to them the winds and waters rave;
They hear the warring elements no more:
While I am doom'd—by life's long storm opprest,
To gaze with envy on their gloomy rest.

                                        1789

On Being Cautioned against Walking on an Headland Overlooking the Sea, Because It Was Frequented by a Lunatic

Is there a solitary wretch who hies
    To the tall cliff, with starting pace or slow,
And, measuring, views with wild and hollow eyes
    Its distance from the waves that chide below;
5 Who, as the sea-born gale with frequent sighs
    Chills his cold bed upon the mountain turf,
With hoarse, half-utter'd lamentation, lies

1. Middleton is a village on the margin of the sea, in Sussex, containing only two or three houses. There were formerly several acres of ground between its small church and the sea, which now, by its continual encroachments, approaches within a few feet of this half ruined and humble edifice. The wall, which once surrounded the churchyard, is entirely swept away, many of the graves broken up, and the remains of bodies interred washed into the sea: whence human bones are found among the sand and shingles on the shore [Smith's note].

Murmuring responses to the dashing surf?
In moody sadness, on the giddy brink,
10   I see him more with envy than with fear;
He has no *nice felicities* that shrink
From giant horrors; wildly wandering here,
He seems (uncursed with reason) not to know
The depth or the duration of his woe.

1797

The Sea View[1]

The upland shepherd, as reclined he lies
    On the soft turf that clothes the mountain brow,
Marks the bright sea-line mingling with the skies;
    Or from his course celestial, sinking slow,
5   The summer-sun in purple radiance low,
Blaze on the western waters; the wide scene
    Magnificent, and tranquil, seems to spread
Even o'er the rustic's breast a joy serene,
    When, like dark plague-spots by the Demons shed,
10 Charged deep with death, upon the waves, far seen,
    Move the war-freighted ships; and fierce and red,
Flash their destructive fire.—The mangled dead
And dying victims then pollute the flood.
Ah! thus man spoils Heaven's glorious works with blood!

1797

1. Suggested by the recollection of having seen, some years since, on a beautiful evening of Summer, an engagement between two armed ships, from the high down called the Beacon Hill, near Brighthelmstone [Smith's note, referring to a location near Brighton].

WILLIAM BLAKE
1757–1827

What William Blake called his "Spiritual Life" was as varied, free, and dramatic as his "Corporeal Life" was simple, limited, and unadventurous. His father was a London haberdasher. His only formal education was in art: at the age of ten he entered a drawing school and later studied for a time at the school of the Royal Academy of Arts. At fourteen he entered an apprenticeship for seven years to a well-known engraver, James Basire, and began reading widely in his free time and trying his hand at poetry. At twenty-four he married Catherine Boucher, daughter of a market gardener. She was then illiterate, but Blake taught her to read and to help him in his engraving and printing. In the early and somewhat sentimentalized biographies, Catherine is represented as an ideal wife for an unorthodox and impecunious genius. Blake, however, must have been a trying domestic partner, and his vehement attacks on the torment caused by a possessive, jealous female will, which reached their height in 1793 and remained prominent in his writings for another decade, probably reflect a troubled period at home. The couple was childless.

The Blakes for a time enjoyed a moderate prosperity while Blake gave drawing lessons, illustrated books, and engraved designs made by other artists. When the demand for his work slackened, Blake in 1800 moved to a cottage at Felpham, on the Sussex seacoast, to take advantage of the patronage of the wealthy poetaster, biographer, and amateur of the arts William Hayley, who with the best of narrow intentions tried to transform Blake into a conventional artist and breadwinner. But the caged eagle soon rebelled. Hayley, Blake wrote, "is the Enemy of my Spiritual Life while he pretends to be the Friend of my Corporeal."

At Felpham in 1803 occurred an event that left a permanent mark on Blake's mind and art—an altercation with one John Schofield, a private in the Royal Dragoons. Blake ordered the soldier out of his garden and, when Schofield replied with threats and curses against Blake and his wife, pushed him the fifty yards to the inn where he was quartered. Schofield brought charges that Blake had uttered seditious statements about king and country. Since England was at war with France, sedition was a hanging offense. Blake was acquitted—an event, according to a newspaper account, "which so gratified the auditory that the court was . . . thrown into an uproar by their noisy exultations." Nevertheless Schofield, his fellow soldier Cock, and other participants in the trial haunted Blake's imagination and were enlarged to demonic characters who play a sinister role in *Jerusalem*. The event exacerbated Blake's sense that ominous forces were at work in the contemporary world and led him to complicate the symbolic and allusive style by which he veiled the radical religious, moral, and political opinions that he expressed in his poems.

After three years at Felpham, Blake moved back to London, determined to follow his "Divine Vision," though it meant a life of isolation, misunderstanding, and poverty. When his single bid for public recognition, a one-man show put on in 1809, proved a total failure, Blake passed into almost complete obscurity. Only when he was in his sixties did he finally attract a small but devoted group of young painters who served as an audience for his work and his talk. Blake's old age was serene and self-confident, largely free from the bursts of irascibility with which he had earlier responded to what he viewed as the shallowness and blindness of the English public. He died in his seventieth year.

Blake's first book of poems, *Poetical Sketches*, which he had printed when he was twenty-six years old, showed his dissatisfaction with the reigning poetic tradition and his restless quest for new forms and techniques. For lyric models he turned back to the Elizabethan and early seventeenth-century poets, to the Ossianic poems, and to Collins, Thomas Chatterton, and other eighteenth-century writers outside the tradition of Pope; he also experimented with partial rhymes and novel rhythms and employed bold figures of speech that at times approximate symbols. In 1788 he began to experiment with relief etching, a method that he called "illuminated printing" and used to produce most of his books of poems. Working directly on a copper plate with pens, brushes, and an acid-resistant medium, he wrote the text in reverse (so that it would print in the normal order) and also drew the illustration; he then etched the plate in acid to eat away the untreated copper and leave the design standing in relief. The pages printed from such plates were colored by hand in water colors and stitched together to make up a volume. This process was laborious and time-consuming, and Blake printed very few copies of his books; for example, of *Songs of Innocence and of Experience* only twenty-eight copies (some of them incomplete) are known to exist; of *The Book of Thel*, sixteen; of *The Marriage of Heaven and Hell*, nine; and of *Jerusalem*, five.

It must be remembered that to read a Blake poem in a printed text without the illustrations is to see only an abstraction from an integral and mutually enlightening combination of words and design. In this mode of relief etching, he published *Songs of Innocence* (1789), then added supplementary poems and printed *Songs of Inno-*

cence and of Experience in 1794. The two groups of poems represent the world as it is envisioned by what he calls "two contrary states of the human soul." In the best of the songs of experience, such as *The Tyger* and *London*, Blake achieved his mature lyric technique of compressed metaphor and symbol that explode into a multiplicity of references.

Gradually Blake's thinking about human history and his experience of life and suffering articulated themselves in the "Giant Forms" and their actions, which came to constitute a complete mythology. As Blake's mythical character Los said, speaking for all imaginative artists, "I must Create a System or be enslaved by another Man's." This coherent but constantly altering and enlarging system composed the subject matter first of Blake's "minor prophecies," completed by 1795, and then of the major prophetic books on which he continued working until about 1820: *The Four Zoas, Milton,* and *Jerusalem.*

In his sixties Blake gave up poetry to devote himself to pictorial art. In the course of his life he produced hundreds of paintings and engravings, many of them illustrations for the work of other poets, including a representation of Chaucer's Canterbury pilgrims, a superb set of designs for the Book of Job, and a series of illustrations of Dante, on which he was still hard at work when he died. At the time of his death Blake was little known as an artist and almost entirely unknown as a poet. In the mid-nineteenth century he acquired a group of admirers among the Pre-Raphaelites, who regarded him as a precursor. Since the mid-1920s, Blake has finally come into his own, both in poetry and in painting, as one of the most dedicated, intellectually challenging, and astonishingly original of artists. His marked influence ranges from William Butler Yeats, who edited Blake's writings and modeled his own system of mythology on Blake's, to Allen Ginsberg and other Beat and counterculture writers, beginning in the 1950s, who admired Blake's stress on a visionary poetry and his rebellious stance against the conventional life and pieties of his day.

The explication of Blake's cryptic prophetic books has been the preoccupation of many scholars. Blake wrote them in the persona, or "voice," of "the Bard! / Who Present, Past, & Future sees"—that is, as a British poet who follows Spenser, and especially Milton, in a lineage going back to the prophets of the Bible. "The Nature of my Work," he said, "is Visionary or Imaginative." What Blake meant by the key terms *vision* and *imagination*, however, is often misinterpreted by taking literally what he, speaking the traditional language of his great predecessors, intended in a figurative sense. "That which can be made Explicit to the Idiot," Blake declared, "is not worth my care." Blake was a born ironist who enjoyed mystifying his well-meaning but literal-minded friends and who took a defiant pleasure in shocking the dull and complacent "angels" of his day by being deliberately outrageous in representing his work and opinions.

Blake declared that "all he knew was in the Bible" and that "The Old & New Testaments are the Great Code of Art." This is an exaggeration of the truth that all his prophetic writings deal, in various formulations, with some aspects of the overall biblical plot of the creation and the Fall, the history of the generations of humanity in the fallen world, redemption, and the promise of a recovery of Eden and of a New Jerusalem. These events, however, Blake interprets in what he calls "the spiritual sense." For such a procedure he had considerable precedent, not in the neoplatonic and occult thinkers with whom some modern commentators align him, but in the "spiritual" interpreters of the Bible among the radical Protestant sects in seventeenth- and eighteenth-century England. In *The French Revolution, America: A Prophecy, Europe: A Prophecy,* and the trenchant prophetic satire *The Marriage of Heaven and Hell*—all of which Blake wrote in the early 1790s while he was an ardent supporter of the French Revolution—he, like Wordsworth, Coleridge, Southey, and a number of radical English theologians, represented the contemporary Revolution as the purifying violence that, according to biblical prophecy, portended the imminent redemption of humanity and the world. In Blake's later poems, Orc, the fiery spirit of violent revolution, gives way as a central personage to Los, the type of the visionary imagination in the fallen world. Even in his early writings, however, Blake had represented political and social revolution as correlative with a radical change within the mind and imagination of the individual, so that the replacement of Orc by Los does not indicate Blake's recantation of former beliefs, but a shift of emphasis from an apocalypse by revolution to an apocalypse by imagination.

BLAKE'S MATURE MYTH

Blake's first attempt to articulate his full myth of humanity's present, past, and future was *The Four Zoas*, begun in 1796 or 1797. A passage from the opening statement of its theme exemplifies the long verse line (what Blake called "the march of long resounding strong heroic verse") in which he wrote his Prophetic Books and will serve also to outline the visualizable imaginative form in which Blake's thought embodied itself:

> Four Mighty Ones are in every Man; a Perfect Unity
> Cannot Exist, but from the Universal Brotherhood of Eden,
> The Universal Man. To Whom be Glory Evermore, Amen. . . .
> Los was the fourth immortal starry one, & in the Earth
> Of a bright Universe Empery attended day & night
> Days & nights of revolving joy, Urthona was his name
> In Eden; in the Auricular Nerves of Human life
> Which is the Earth of Eden, he his Emanations propagated. . . .
>   Daughter of Beulah, Sing
> His fall into Division & his Resurrection to Unity.

Blake's mythical premise, or starting point, is not a transcendent God but the "Universal Man" who is himself God and who incorporates the cosmos as well. (Blake elsewhere describes this founding image as "the Human Form Divine" and names him "Albion.") The fall, in this myth, is not the fall of humanity away from God but a falling apart of primal people, a "fall into Division." In this event the original sin is what Blake calls "Selfhood," the attempt of an isolated part to be self-sufficient. The breakup of the all-inclusive Universal Man in Eden into exiled parts, it is evident, serves to identify the Fall with the creation—the creation not only of man and of nature as we ordinarily know them but also of a separate sky god who is alien from humanity. Universal Man divides first into the "Four Mighty Ones" who are the Zoas, or chief powers and component aspects of humanity, and these in turn divide sexually into male Spectres and female Emanations. (Thus in the quoted passage the Zoa known in the unfallen state of Eden as Urthona, the imaginative power, separates into the form of Los in the fallen world.) In addition to Eden there are three successively lower "states" of being in the fallen world, which Blake calls Beulah (a pastoral condition of easy and relaxed innocence, without clash of "contraries"), Generation (the realm of common human experience, suffering, and conflicting contraries), and Ulro (Blake's hell, the lowest state, or limit, of bleak rationality, tyranny, static negation, and isolated Selfhood). The fallen world moves through the cycles of its history, successively approaching and falling away from redemption, until, by the agency of the Redeemer (who is equated with the human imagination and is most potently operative in the prophetic poet), it will culminate in an apocalypse. In terms of his controlling image of the Universal Man, Blake describes this apocalypse as a return to the original, undivided condition, "his Resurrection to Unity."

What is confusing to many readers is that Blake alternates this representation of the Fall (as a fragmentation of the one Primal Man into separate parts) with a different kind of representation, in terms of two sharply opposed ways of seeing the universe. In this latter mode, the Fall is a catastrophic change from imaginative insight (which sees the cosmos as unified and humanized) to sight by the physical eye (which sees the cosmos as a multitude of isolated individuals in an inhuman and alien nature).

In terms of this distinction, the apocalypse toward which Blake as imaginative artist strives unceasingly will enable men and women once again to envision all beings as participant in the individual life that he calls "the Universal Brotherhood of Eden"— that is, a humanized world in which all individuals, in familial union, can feel at home.

Although Blake did not know it, he shared with a number of contemporary German philosophers the point of view—it has in our own time become the prevailing point of view—that our fall (that is, the malaise of modern culture) is essentially a mode of psychic disintegration and of resultant alienation from oneself, one's world, and one's fellow human beings, and that our hope of recovery lies in a process of reintegration. As a poet, however, Blake does not present this view in abstract conceptual terms, but embodies it in picturable agents acting out an epic plot.

The text for Blake's writings is that of *The Complete Poetry and Prose of William Blake*, edited by David V. Erdman and Harold Bloom (revised edition, Berkeley, 1982). Blake's erratic spelling and punctuation have been altered when the original form might mislead the reader. The editors are grateful for the expert advice of Joseph Viscomi and Robert Essick in editing the selections from Blake.

FROM POETICAL SKETCHES[1]

To Spring[2]

> O thou, with dewy locks, who lookest down
> Thro' the clear windows of the morning; turn
> Thine angel eyes upon our western isle,
> Which in full choir hails thy approach, O Spring!
>
> 5 The hills tell each other, and the list'ning
> Vallies hear; all our longing eyes are turned
> Up to thy bright pavillions: issue forth,
> And let thy holy feet visit our clime.
>
> Come o'er the eastern hills, and let our winds
> 10 Kiss thy perfumed garments; let us taste
> Thy morn and evening breath; scatter thy pearls
> Upon our love-sick land that mourns for thee.
>
> O deck her forth with thy fair fingers; pour
> Thy soft kisses on her bosom; and put
> 15 Thy golden crown upon her languish'd head,
> Whose modest tresses were bound up for thee!

1783

---

1. *Poetical Sketches,* Blake's only volume of poems to be set in type, went to press in 1783 but was never put on sale. A preface written by an anonymous friend apologized for the poems on the grounds that they had been composed between the ages of twelve and twenty. Although, like the work of other youthful poets, they echo earlier writers (including Spenser, Shakespeare, and Milton),

many of them are radical experiments in metaphor, meter, and rhyme.
2. *Poetical Sketches* includes four poems, each in the form of an invocation to one of the four seasons. *To Spring* is thronged with echoes from the poetry of the Old Testament as well as from Milton.

To Autumn

O Autumn, laden with fruit, and stained
With the blood of the grape, pass not, but sit
Beneath my shady roof; there thou may'st rest,
And tune thy jolly voice to my fresh pipe;
5 And all the daughters of the year shall dance!
Sing now the lusty song of fruits and flowers.

"The narrow bud opens her beauties to
The sun, and love runs in her thrilling veins;
Blossoms hang round the brows of morning, and
10 Flourish down the bright cheek of modest eve,
Till clust'ring Summer breaks forth into singing,
And feather'd clouds strew flowers round her head.

"The spirits of the air live on the smells
Of fruit; and joy, with pinions light, roves round
15 The gardens, or sits singing in the trees."
Thus sang the jolly Autumn as he sat;
Then rose, girded himself, and o'er the bleak
Hills fled from our sight; but left his golden load.

1783

To the Evening Star

Thou fair-hair'd angel of the evening,
Now, while the sun rests on the mountains, light
Thy bright torch of love;[1] thy radiant crown
Put on, and smile upon our evening bed!
5 Smile on our loves; and, while thou drawest the
Blue curtains of the sky, scatter thy silver dew
On every flower that shuts its sweet eyes
In timely sleep. Let thy west wind sleep on
The lake; speak silence with thy glimmering eyes,
10 And wash the dusk with silver. Soon, full soon,
Dost thou withdraw; then the wolf rages wide,
And the lion glares thro' the dun forest:
The fleeces of our flocks are cover'd with
Thy sacred dew: protect them with thine influence.[2]

1783

---

1. The evening star is Venus, goddess of love.
2. In astrology, the technical term for the occult power of stars over humans.

All Religions Are One[1]

The Voice of one crying in the Wilderness[2]

The Argument. As the true method of knowledge is experiment the true faculty of knowing must be the faculty which experiences. This faculty I treat of.

PRINCIPLE 1st. That the Poetic Genius is the true Man, and that the body or outward form of Man is derived from the Poetic Genius. Likewise that the forms of all things are derived from their Genius, which by the Ancients was call'd an Angel & Spirit & Demon.

PRINCIPLE 2d. As all men are alike in outward form, So (and with the same infinite variety) all are alike in the Poetic Genius.

PRINCIPLE 3d. No man can think write or speak from his heart, but he must intend truth. Thus all sects of Philosophy are from the Poetic Genius, adapted to the weaknesses of every individual.

PRINCIPLE 4. As none by travelling over known lands can find out the unknown, So from already acquired knowledge Man could not acquire more. Therefore an universal Poetic Genius exists.

PRINCIPLE 5. The Religions of all Nations are derived from each Nation's different reception of the Poetic Genius, which is every where call'd the Spirit of Prophecy.

PRINCIPLE 6. The Jewish & Christian Testaments are An original derivation from the Poetic Genius. This is necessary from the confined nature of bodily sensation.

PRINCIPLE 7th. As all men are alike (tho' infinitely various), So all Religions & as all similars have one source.

The true Man is the source, he being the Poetic Genius.

1788

There Is No Natural Religion[1]

[a]

The Argument. Man has no notion of moral fitness but from Education. Naturally he is only a natural organ subject to Sense.

I. Man cannot naturally Percieve but through his natural or bodily organs.

II. Man by his reasoning power can only compare & judge of what he has already perciev'd.

---

1. This and the following two selections are early illuminated works, probably etched in 1788. They are directed both against 18th-century Deism or "natural religion" (which bases its religious tenets not on scriptural revelation, but on evidences of God in the natural or "organic" world) and against Christian orthodoxy, whose creed is based on a particular Scripture. In this selection Blake ironically accepts the Deistic view that all particular religions are variants of the one true religion but rejects the Deists' "Argument" that this religion is grounded on reasoning from sense-experience. He attributes the one religion instead to the innate possession by all people of "Poetic Genius"—that is, of a capacity for imaginative vision.

2. Applied in the Gospels (e.g., Matthew 3.3) to John the Baptist, regarded as fulfilling the prophecy in Isaiah 39.3. Blake applies the phrase to himself, as a later prophetic voice in an alien time.

1. In this selection Blake presents his version of English empiricism, which derives all mental content (including the evidences from which, in "natural religion," reason is held to prove the existence of God) from perceptions by the physical senses.

III. From a perception of only 3 senses or 3 elements none could deduce a fourth or fifth.

IV. None could have other than natural or organic thoughts if he had none but organic perceptions.

V. Man's desires are limited by his perceptions; none can desire what he has not perciev'd.

VI. The desires & perceptions of man, untaught by any thing but organs of sense, must be limited to objects of sense.

Conclusion. If it were not for the Poetic or Prophetic character the Philosophic & Experimental would soon be at the ratio of all things, & stand still unable to do other than repeat the same dull round over again.

1788

There Is No Natural Religion[1]

[b]

I. Man's perceptions are not bounded by organs of perception; he percieves more than sense (tho' ever so acute) can discover.

II. Reason, or the ratio[2] of all we have already known, is not the same that it shall be when we know more.

[III lacking]

IV. The bounded is loathed by its possessor. The same dull round even of a universe would soon become a mill with complicated wheels.

V. If the many become the same as the few when possess'd, More! More! is the cry of a mistaken soul. Less than All cannot satisfy Man.

VI. If any could desire what he is incapable of possessing, despair must be his eternal lot.

VII. The desire of Man being Infinite, the possession is Infinite & himself Infinite.

Application. He who sees the Infinite in all things sees God. He who sees the Ratio only sees himself only.

Therefore God becomes as we are, that we may be as he is.

1788

---

1. In this third document Blake presents his assertions (in opposition to those in the preceding tract) that knowledge is not limited to the physical senses, but is as unbounded as the infinite desires of humankind and its godlike capacity for infinite vision.

2. In Latin *ratio* signifies both "reason" and "calculation." Blake applies the term derogatorily to the 18th-century concept of reason as a calculating faculty whose operations are limited to sense-perceptions.

FROM SONGS OF INNOCENCE AND OF EXPERIENCE[1]

SHEWING THE TWO CONTRARY STATES OF THE HUMAN SOUL

FROM SONGS OF INNOCENCE

Introduction

Piping down the valleys wild
Piping songs of pleasant glee
On a cloud I saw a child,
And he laughing said to me,

5 "Pipe a song about a Lamb";
So I piped with merry chear;
"Piper pipe that song again"—
So I piped, he wept to hear.

"Drop thy pipe thy happy pipe
10 Sing thy songs of happy chear";
So I sung the same again
While he wept with joy to hear.

"Piper sit thee down and write
In a book that all may read"—
15 So he vanish'd from my sight.
And I pluck'd a hollow reed,

And I made a rural pen,
And I stain'd the water clear,
And I wrote my happy songs
20 Every child may joy to hear.

1789

The Ecchoing Green

The Sun does arise,
And make happy the skies.
The merry bells ring
To welcome the Spring.

1. *Songs of Innocence* was etched in 1789, and in 1794 was combined with additional poems under the title *Songs of Innocence and of Experience;* this collection was reprinted at various later times with varying arrangements of the poems. In his songs of innocence Blake assumes the stance that he is writing "happy songs / Every child may joy to hear," but they do not all depict an innocent and happy world; many of them incorporate injustice, evil, and suffering. These aspects of the fallen world, however, are represented as they appear to a "state" of the human soul that Blake calls "innocence" and that he expresses in a simple pastoral language, in the tradition of Isaac Watts's widely read *Divine Songs for Children* (1715). The vision of the same world, as it appears to the "contrary" state of the soul that Blake calls "experience," is an ugly and terrifying one of poverty, disease, prostitution, war, and social, institutional, and sexual repression, epitomized in the ghastly representation of modern London. Though each stands as an independent poem, a number of the songs of innocence have a matched counterpart, or "contrary," in the songs of experience. Thus *Infant Joy* is paired with *Infant Sorrow*, and the meek *Lamb* reveals its other aspect of divinity in the flaming, wrathful *Tyger*.

Title page for *Songs of Innocence*
(1789)

5   The sky-lark and thrush,
     The birds of the bush,
     Sing louder around,
     To the bells' chearful sound.
     While our sports shall be seen
10   On the Ecchoing Green.

     Old John with white hair
     Does laugh away care,
     Sitting under the oak,
     Among the old folk.
15   They laugh at our play,
     And soon they all say:
     "Such, such were the joys.
     When we all, girls & boys,
     In our youth-time were seen,
20   On the Ecchoing Green."

     Till the little ones weary
     No more can be merry
     The sun does descend,
     And our sports have an end:
25   Round the laps of their mothers,

Many sisters and brothers,
Like birds in their nest,
Are ready for rest;
And sport no more seen,
30   On the darkening Green.

1789

The Lamb

Little Lamb, who made thee?
Dost thou know who made thee?
Gave thee life & bid thee feed,
By the stream & o'er the mead;
5   Gave thee clothing of delight,
Softest clothing wooly bright;
Gave thee such a tender voice,
Making all the vales rejoice!
Little Lamb who made thee?
10   Dost thou know who made thee?

Little Lamb I'll tell thee,
Little Lamb I'll tell thee!
He is callèd by thy name,
For he calls himself a Lamb;
15   He is meek & he is mild,
He became a little child;
I a child & thou a lamb,
We are callèd by his name.
Little Lamb God bless thee.
20   Little Lamb God bless thee.

1789

The Little Black Boy

My mother bore me in the southern wild,
And I am black, but O! my soul is white;
White as an angel is the English child,
But I am black as if bereav'd of light.

5   My mother taught me underneath a tree,
And sitting down before the heat of day,
She took me on her lap and kissèd me,
And pointing to the east, began to say:

"Look on the rising sun: there God does live
10   And gives his light, and gives his heat away;
And flowers and trees and beasts and men receive
Comfort in morning, joy in the noon day.

"And we are put on earth a little space,
That we may learn to bear the beams of love,
15   And these black bodies and this sun-burnt face
Is but a cloud, and like a shady grove.

"For when our souls have learn'd the heat to bear,
The cloud will vanish; we shall hear his voice,
Saying: 'Come out from the grove, my love & care,
20   And round my golden tent like lambs rejoice.' "

Thus did my mother say, and kissèd me;
And thus I say to little English boy:
When I from black and he from white cloud free,
And round the tent of God like lambs we joy,

25   I'll shade him from the heat till he can bear
To lean in joy upon our father's knee.
And then I'll stand and stroke his silver hair,
And be like him, and he will then love me.

1789

The Chimney Sweeper

When my mother died I was very young,
And my father sold me while yet my tongue
Could scarcely cry " 'weep! 'weep! 'weep! 'weep!"[1]
So your chimneys I sweep & in soot I sleep.

5   There's little Tom Dacre, who cried when his head
That curl'd like a lamb's back, was shav'd, so I said,
"Hush, Tom! never mind it, for when your head's bare,
You know that the soot cannot spoil your white hair."

And so he was quiet, & that very night,
10   As Tom was a-sleeping he had such a sight!
That thousands of sweepers, Dick, Joe, Ned, & Jack,
Were all of them lock'd up in coffins of black;

And by came an Angel who had a bright key,
And he open'd the coffins & set them all free;
15   Then down a green plain, leaping, laughing they run,
And wash in a river and shine in the Sun.

Then naked & white, all their bags left behind,
They rise upon clouds, and sport in the wind.
And the Angel told Tom, if he'd be a good boy,
20   He'd have God for his father & never want joy.

---

1. The child's lisping attempt at the chimney sweeper's street cry, "Sweep! Sweep!"

And so Tom awoke; and we rose in the dark
And got with our bags & our brushes to work.
Tho' the morning was cold, Tom was happy & warm;
So if all do their duty, they need not fear harm.

1789

The Divine Image

To Mercy, Pity, Peace, and Love,
All pray in their distress,
And to these virtues of delight
Return their thankfulness.

5 For Mercy, Pity, Peace, and Love,
Is God, our father dear:
And Mercy, Pity, Peace, and Love,
Is Man, his child and care.

For Mercy has a human heart,
10 Pity, a human face,
And Love, the human form divine,
And Peace, the human dress.

Then every man of every clime,
That prays in his distress,
15 Prays to the human form divine,
Love, Mercy, Pity, Peace.

And all must love the human form,
In heathen, Turk, or Jew.
Where Mercy, Love, & Pity dwell,
20 There God is dwelling too.

1789

Holy Thursday[1]

'Twas on a Holy Thursday, their innocent faces clean,
The children walking two & two, in red & blue & green;
Grey headed beadles[2] walkd before with wands as white as snow,
Till into the high dome of Paul's they like Thames' waters flow.

5 O what a multitude they seemd, these flowers of London town!
Seated in companies they sit with radiance all their own.
The hum of multitudes was there, but multitudes of lambs,
Thousands of little boys & girls raising their innocent hands.

1. In the Anglican Church, the Thursday celebrating the ascension of Jesus (thirty-nine days
after Easter). It was the custom on this day to
march the poor (frequently orphaned) children
from the charity schools of London to a service at
St. Paul's Cathedral.
2. Lower church officers, one of whose duties is
to keep order.

Now like a mighty wind they raise to heaven the voice of song,
10   Or like harmonious thunderings the seats of heaven among.
Beneath them sit the agèd men, wise guardians of the poor;
Then cherish pity, lest you drive an angel from your door.[3]

ca. 1784   1789

Nurse's Song

When the voices of children are heard on the green
And laughing is heard on the hill,
My heart is at rest within my breast
And everything else is still.

5   "Then come home my children, the sun is gone down
And the dews of night arise;
Come, come, leave off play, and let us away
Till the morning appears in the skies."

"No, no, let us play, for it is yet day
10   And we cannot go to sleep;
Besides, in the sky, the little birds fly
And the hills are all coverd with sheep."

"Well, well, go & play till the light fades away
And then go home to bed."
15   The little ones leaped & shouted & laugh'd
And all the hills ecchoèd.

ca. 1784   1789

Infant Joy

"I have no name,
I am but two days old."
What shall I call thee?
"I happy am,
5   Joy is my name."
Sweet joy befall thee!

Pretty joy!
Sweet joy but two days old,
Sweet joy I call thee;
10   Thou dost smile,
I sing the while—
Sweet joy befall thee.

1789

3. Cf. Hebrews 13.2: "Be not forgetful to entertain strangers: for thereby some have entertained angels unawares."

From Songs of Experience

Introduction

Hear the voice of the Bard!
Who Present, Past, & Future sees;
Whose ears have heard
The Holy Word
5   That walk'd among the ancient trees;[1]

Calling the lapsèd Soul[2]
And weeping in the evening dew,
That might controll[3]
The starry pole,
10   And fallen, fallen light renew!

Separate title page for *Songs of Experience* (1794)

1. Genesis 3.8: "And [Adam and Eve] heard the voice of the Lord God walking in the garden in the cool of the day." The Bard, or poet-prophet, whose imagination is not bound by time, has heard the voice of the Lord in Eden.
2. The syntax leaves it ambiguous whether it is "the Bard" or "the Holy Word" who calls to the fallen ("lapsèd") soul and to the fallen earth to stop the natural cycle of light and darkness.
3. The likely syntax is that "Soul" is the subject of "might controll."

"O Earth, O Earth, return!
Arise from out the dewy grass;
Night is worn,
And the morn
15 Rises from the slumberous mass.

"Turn away no more;
Why wilt thou turn away?
The starry floor
The watry shore[4]
20 Is giv'n thee till the break of day."

1794

Earth's Answer[1]

Earth rais'd up her head,
From the darkness dread & drear.
Her light fled:
Stony dread!
5 And her locks cover'd with grey despair.

"Prison'd on watry shore
Starry Jealousy does keep my den,
Cold and hoar
Weeping o'er
10 I hear the Father of the ancient men.[2]

"Selfish father of men,
Cruel, jealous, selfish fear!
Can delight
Chain'd in night
15 The virgins of youth and morning bear?

"Does spring hide its joy
When buds and blossoms grow?
Does the sower
Sow by night,
20 Or the plowman in darkness plow?

"Break this heavy chain
That does freeze my bones around;
Selfish! vain!
Eternal bane!
25 That free Love with bondage bound."

1794

4. In Blake's recurrent symbolism the starry sky
("floor") signifies rigid rational order, and the sea
signifies chaos.
1. The Earth's answer explains why she, the natural world, cannot by her unaided endeavors renew
the fallen light.

2. This is the character that Blake later named
"Urizen" in his prophetic works. He is the tyrant
who binds the mind to the natural world and also
imposes a moral bondage on sexual desire and
other modes of human energy.

The Clod & the Pebble

"Love seeketh not Itself to please,
Nor for itself hath any care;
But for another gives its ease,
And builds a Heaven in Hell's despair."

5 So sang a little Clod of Clay,
Trodden with the cattle's feet;
But a Pebble of the brook,
Warbled out these metres meet:

"Love seeketh only Self to please,
10 To bind another to its delight;
Joys in another's loss of ease,
And builds a Hell in Heaven's despite."

1794

Holy Thursday

Is this a holy thing to see,
In a rich and fruitful land,
Babes reduced to misery,
Fed with cold and usurous hand?

5 Is that trembling cry a song?
Can it be a song of joy?
And so many children poor?
It is a land of poverty!

And their sun does never shine,
10 And their fields are bleak & bare,
And their ways are fill'd with thorns;
It is eternal winter there.

For where-e'er the sun does shine,
And where-e'er the rain does fall,
15 Babe can never hunger there,
Nor poverty the mind appall.

1794

The Chimney Sweeper

A little black thing among the snow
Crying " 'weep, 'weep," in notes of woe!
"Where are thy father & mother? say?"
"They are both gone up to the church to pray.

5   "Because I was happy upon the heath,
And smil'd among the winter's snow;
They clothed me in the clothes of death,
And taught me to sing the notes of woe.

"And because I am happy, & dance & sing,
10 They think they have done me no injury,
And are gone to praise God & his Priest & King,
Who make up a heaven of our misery."

1790–92   1794

Nurse's Song

When the voices of children are heard on the green
And whisperings are in the dale,
The days of my youth rise fresh in my mind,
My face turns green and pale.

5   Then come home my children, the sun is gone down
And the dews of night arise;
Your spring & your day are wasted in play,
And your winter and night in disguise.

1794

The Sick Rose

O Rose, thou art sick.
The invisible worm
That flies in the night
In the howling storm

5   Has found out thy bed
Of crimson joy,
And his dark secret love
Does thy life destroy.

1794

The Fly

Little Fly
Thy summer's play
My thoughtless hand
Has brush'd away

5   Am not I
A fly like thee?
Or art not thou
A man like me?

For I dance
10   And drink & sing,
Till some blind hand
Shall brush my wing.

If thought is life
And strength & breath,

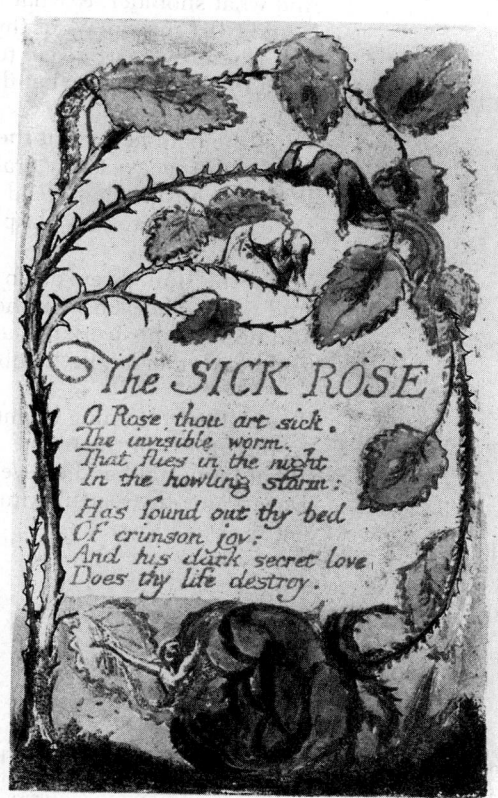

· *The Sick Rose*

15 And the want
Of thought is death;

Then am I
A happy fly,
If I live,
20 Or if I die.

1794

The Tyger[1]

Tyger! Tyger! burning bright
In the forests of the night,
What immortal hand or eye
Could frame thy fearful symmetry?

5 In what distant deeps or skies
Burnt the fire of thine eyes?
On what wings dare he aspire?
What the hand dare seize the fire?

And what shoulder, & what art,
10 Could twist the sinews of thy heart?
And when thy heart began to beat,
What dread hand? & what dread feet?

What the hammer? what the chain?
In what furnace was thy brain?
15 What the anvil? what dread grasp
Dare its deadly terrors clasp?

When the stars threw down their spears[2]
And water'd heaven with their tears,
Did he smile his work to see?
20 Did he who made the Lamb make thee?

Tyger! Tyger! burning bright
In the forests of the night,
What immortal hand or eye
Dare frame thy fearful symmetry?

1790–92

1794

---

1. For the author's revisions while composing *The Tyger*, see "Poems in Process," in the appendices to this volume.

2. "Threw down" is ambiguous and may signify that the stars either "surrendered" or "hurled down" their spears.

The Tyger

My Pretty Rose Tree

A flower was offerd to me;
Such a flower as May never bore,
But I said, "I've a Pretty Rose-tree,"
And I passed the sweet flower o'er.

5 Then I went to my Pretty Rose-tree,
To tend her by day and by night.
But my Rose turnd away with jealousy,
And her thorns were my only delight.

1794

Ah Sun-flower

Ah Sun-flower! weary of time,
Who countest the steps of the Sun,
Seeking after that sweet golden clime
Where the traveller's journey is done;

5 Where the Youth pined away with desire,
And the pale Virgin shrouded in snow,
Arise from their graves and aspire,
Where my Sun-flower wishes to go.

1794

The Garden of Love

I went to the Garden of Love,
And saw what I never had seen:
A Chapel was built in the midst,
Where I used to play on the green.

5 And the gates of this Chapel were shut,
And "Thou shalt not" writ over the door;
So I turn'd to the Garden of Love,
That so many sweet flowers bore,

And I saw it was filled with graves,
10 And tomb-stones where flowers should be;
And Priests in black gowns were walking their rounds,
And binding with briars my joys & desires.

1794

London

I wander thro' each charter'd[1] street,
Near where the charter'd Thames does flow,
And mark in every face I meet
Marks of weakness, marks of woe.

5 In every cry of every Man,
In every Infant's cry of fear,
In every voice, in every ban,[2]
The mind-forg'd manacles I hear:

How the Chimney-sweeper's cry
10 Every blackning Church appalls,
And the hapless Soldier's sigh
Runs in blood down Palace walls.

But most thro' midnight streets I hear
How the youthful Harlot's curse

---

1. "Given liberty," but also, ironically, "preempted as private property, and rented out."
2. The various meanings of *ban* are relevant (political and legal prohibition, curse, public condemnation) as well as "banns" (marriage proclamation).

15   Blasts the new-born Infant's tear,[3]
      And blights with plagues the Marriage hearse.[4]

                                                    1794

The Human Abstract[1]

        Pity would be no more,
        If we did not make somebody Poor;
        And Mercy no more could be,
        If all were as happy as we;

5   And mutual fear brings peace,
        Till the selfish loves increase;
        Then Cruelty knits a snare,
        And spreads his baits with care.

        He sits down with holy fears,
10   And waters the ground with tears;
        Then Humility takes its root
        Underneath his foot.

        Soon spreads the dismal shade
        Of Mystery over his head;
15   And the Catterpiller and Fly
        Feed on the Mystery.

        And it bears the fruit of Deceit,
        Ruddy and sweet to eat;
        And the Raven his nest has made
20   In its thickest shade.

        The Gods of the earth and sea,
        Sought thro' Nature to find this Tree,
        But their search was all in vain:
        There grows one in the Human Brain.

1790–92   1794

Infant Sorrow

        My mother groand! my father wept.
        Into the dangerous world I leapt,
        Helpless, naked, piping loud;
        Like a fiend hid in a cloud.

3. Most critics read this line as implying prenatal blindness, resulting from a parent's venereal disease (the "plagues" of line 16) by earlier infection from the harlot.
4. In the older sense: "converts the marriage bed into a bier." Or possibly, because the current sense of the word had also come into use in Blake's day, "converts the marriage coach into a funeral hearse."
1. The matched contrary to *The Divine Image* in *Songs of Innocence*. The virtues of the earlier poem, "Mercy, Pity, Peace, and Love," are now represented as possible marks for exploitation, cruelty, conflict, and hypocritical humility.

5 Struggling in my father's hands,
Striving against my swadling bands;
Bound and weary I thought best
To sulk upon my mother's breast.

1794

A Poison Tree

I was angry with my friend:
I told my wrath, my wrath did end.
I was angry with my foe:
I told it not, my wrath did grow.

5 And I waterd it in fears,
Night & morning with my tears;
And I sunnèd it with smiles,
And with soft deceitful wiles.

And it grew both day and night,
10 Till it bore an apple bright.
And my foe beheld it shine,
And he knew that it was mine,

And into my garden stole,
When the night had veild the pole;
15 In the morning glad I see
My foe outstretchd beneath the tree.

1794

To Tirzah[1]

Whate'er is Born of Mortal Birth
Must be consumèd with the Earth
To rise from Generation free;
Then what have I to do with thee?[2]

5 The Sexes sprung from Shame & Pride,
Blow'd° in the morn, in evening died;   blossomed
But Mercy changd Death into Sleep;
The Sexes rose to work & weep.

Thou, Mother of my Mortal part,
10 With cruelty didst mould my Heart,

1. Tirzah was the capital of the northern kingdom of Israel and is conceived by Blake in opposition to Jerusalem, capital of the southern kingdom of Judah, whose tribes had been redeemed from captivity. In this poem, which was added to late versions of *Songs of Experience,* Tirzah is represented as the mother—in the realm of material nature and "Generation"—of the mortal body, with its restrictive senses.
2. Echoing the words of Christ to his mother at the marriage in Cana, John 2.4: "Woman, what have I to do with thee? mine hour is not yet come."

And with false self-deceiving tears
Didst bind my Nostrils, Eyes, & Ears.

Didst close my Tongue in senseless clay
And me to Mortal Life betray.
15 The Death of Jesus set me free;
Then what have I to do with thee?

ca. 1805

A Divine Image[1]

Cruelty has a Human Heart
And Jealousy a Human Face,
Terror, the Human Form Divine,
And Secrecy, the Human Dress.

5 The Human Dress is forgèd Iron,
The Human Form, a fiery Forge,
The Human Face, a Furnace seal'd,
The Human Heart, its hungry Gorge.°   maw, stomach

1790–91

The Book of Thel   Although Blake dated the etched poem 1789, its composition probably extended to 1791, so that he was working on it at the time he was writing the *Songs of Innocence* and some of the *Songs of Experience*. *The Book of Thel* treats the same two "states"; now, however, Blake employs the narrative instead of the lyrical mode and embodies aspects of the developing myth that was fully enacted in his later prophetic books. And like the major prophecies, this poem is written in the fourteener, a long line of seven stresses.

The name *Thel* possibly derives from the Greek word for "wish" or "will" and may be intended to suggest the failure of desire, because of timidity, to fulfill itself. Thel is represented as a virgin dwelling in the Vales of Har, which seems equivalent to the sheltered state of pastoral peace and innocence in Blake's *Songs of Innocence*. Here, however, Thel feels useless and unfulfilled, and appeals for comfort, unavailingly, to various beings who are contented with their roles in Har. Finally, the Clay invites Thel to try the experiment of assuming embodied life. Part 4 (plate 6) expresses the brutal shock of the revelation to Thel of the world of sexual Generation and Experience—a revelation from which she flees in terror back to her sheltered, if unsatisfying, existence in Har.

Some commentators propose that Thel is an unborn soul who rejects the ordeal of an embodied life in the material world. Others propose that Thel is a human virgin who shrinks from experiencing a life of adult sexuality. It is possible, however, to read Blake's little myth as comprehending both these areas of significance. The reader does not need to be an adept in Blake's mythology to recognize the broad symbolic

1. Blake omitted this poem from all but one copy of *Songs of Experience,* probably because *The Human Abstract* served as a more comprehensive and subtle contrary to *The Divine Image* in *Songs of Innocence.*

reach of this poem in ordinary human experience—the elemental failure of nerve to meet the challenge of life as it is, the timid incapacity to risk the conflict, physicality, pain, and loss without which there is no possibility either of growth or of creativity.

The Book of Thel

PLATE i[1]

Thel's Motto

Does the Eagle know what is in the pit?
Or wilt thou go ask the Mole?
Can Wisdom be put in a silver rod?
Or Love in a golden bowl?[2]

PLATE 1

1

The daughters of Mne[3] Seraphim led round their sunny flocks,
All but the youngest; she in paleness sought the secret air,

Title page for *The Book of Thel* (1789),
plate ii. Copy N, ca. 1815

1. The plate numbers identify the page, each with its own pictorial design, as originally printed by Blake. These numbers are reproduced here because they are frequently used in references to Blake's writings.
2. Ecclesiastes 12.5–6 describes a time when "fears shall be in the way . . . and desire shall fail: because man goeth to his long home, and the mourners go about the streets: Or ever the silver cord be loosed, or the golden bowl be broken." Blake presumably changed the silver cord to a rod to make it, with the golden bowl, a sexual symbol.
3. There has been much speculation about this curious term. It may be an abbreviation for the name "Mnetha," the goddess of the Vales of Har in Blake's earlier poem *Tiriel*.

To fade away like morning beauty from her mortal day;
Down by the river of Adona[4] her soft voice is heard,
5 And thus her gentle lamentation falls like morning dew:

"O life of this our spring! why fades the lotus of the water?
Why fade these children of the spring? born but to smile & fall.
Ah! Thel is like a watry bow, and like a parting cloud,
Like a reflection in a glass, like shadows in the water,
10 Like dreams of infants, like a smile upon an infant's face,
Like the dove's voice, like transient day, like music in the air.
Ah! gentle may I lay me down, and gentle rest my head,
And gentle sleep the sleep of death, and gentle hear the voice
Of him that walketh in the garden in the evening time."[5]

15 The Lilly of the valley breathing in the humble grass
Answer'd the lovely maid and said: "I am a watry weed,
And I am very small, and love to dwell in lowly vales;
So weak, the gilded butterfly scarce perches on my head;
Yet I am visited from heaven, and he that smiles on all
20 Walks in the valley and each morn over me spreads his hand,
Saying: 'Rejoice, thou humble grass, thou new-born lilly flower,
Thou gentle maid of silent valleys and of modest brooks;
For thou shalt be clothed in light, and fed with morning manna,
Till summer's heat melts thee beside the fountains and the springs
25 To flourish in eternal vales.' Then why should Thel complain?

PLATE 2

Why should the mistress of the vales of Har utter a sigh?"

She ceasd & smild in tears, then sat down in her silver shrine.

Thel answerd: "O thou little virgin of the peaceful valley,
Giving to those that cannot crave, the voiceless, the o'ertired;
5 Thy breath doth nourish the innocent lamb, he smells thy milky
      garments,
He crops thy flowers, while thou sittest smiling in his face,
Wiping his mild and meekin° mouth from all contagious taints.   *humble*
Thy wine doth purify the golden honey; thy perfume,
Which thou dost scatter on every little blade of grass that springs,
10 Revives the milkèd cow, & tames the fire-breathing steed.
But Thel is like a faint cloud kindled at the rising sun:
I vanish from my pearly throne, and who shall find my place?"

"Queen of the vales," the Lilly answered, "ask the tender cloud,
And it shall tell thee why it glitters in the morning sky,
15 And why it scatters its bright beauty thro' the humid air.
Descend, O little cloud, & hover before the eyes of Thel."

4. Possibly suggesting an equation of the Vales of
Har to Spenser's Garden of Adonis in *The Faerie
Queene* 3.6, as well as to the paradisal garden in
Genesis (in line 14).

5. Genesis 3.8: "And they heard the voice of the
Lord God walking in the garden in the cool of the
day."

The Cloud descended, and the Lilly bowd her modest head,
And went to mind her numerous charge among the verdant grass.

PLATE 3

2

"O little Cloud," the virgin said, "I charge thee tell to me,
Why thou complainest not when in one hour thou fade away:
Then we shall seek thee but not find; ah, Thel is like to Thee.
I pass away, yet I complain, and no one hears my voice."

5   The Cloud then shew'd his golden head & his bright form emerg'd,
Hovering and glittering on the air before the face of Thel.

"O virgin, know'st thou not our steeds drink of the golden springs
Where Luvah[6] doth renew his horses? Look'st thou on my youth,
And fearest thou because I vanish and am seen no more,
10 Nothing remains? O maid, I tell thee, when I pass away,
It is to tenfold life, to love, to peace, and raptures holy:
Unseen descending, weigh my light wings upon balmy flowers,
And court the fair eyed dew, to take me to her shining tent;
The weeping virgin trembling kneels before the risen sun,
15 Till we arise link'd in a golden band, and never part,
But walk united, bearing food to all our tender flowers."

"Dost thou O little Cloud? I fear that I am not like thee;
For I walk through the vales of Har and smell the sweetest flowers,
But I feed not the little flowers; I hear the warbling birds,
20 But I feed not the warbling birds; they fly and seek their food;
But Thel delights in these no more, because I fade away,
And all shall say, 'Without a use this shining woman liv'd,
Or did she only live to be at death the food of worms?' "

The Cloud reclind upon his airy throne and answer'd thus:

25 "Then if thou art the food of worms, O virgin of the skies,
How great thy use, how great thy blessing! Every thing that lives
Lives not alone, nor for itself; fear not, and I will call
The weak worm from its lowly bed, and thou shalt hear its voice.
Come forth, worm of the silent valley, to thy pensive queen."

30 The helpless worm arose, and sat upon the Lilly's leaf,
And the bright Cloud saild on, to find his partner in the vale.

PLATE 4

3

Then Thel astonish'd view'd the Worm upon its dewy bed.

6. The earliest mention in Blake's work of one of his "Giant Forms," the Zoas. Luvah is the mythical embodiment of the passional and sexual aspect of humankind. He is represented here, like the Greek Phoebus Apollo, as the driver of the chariot of the sun; he repairs to the Vales of Har simply to rest and water his horses. The cloud in this passage describes the cycle of water, from cloud to rain and (by the vaporizing action of the sun on water) back to the cloud.

"Art thou a Worm? Image of weakness, art thou but a Worm?
I see thee like an infant wrapped in the Lilly's leaf;
Ah, weep not, little voice, thou can'st not speak, but thou can'st weep.
5 Is this a Worm? I see thee lay helpless & naked, weeping,
And none to answer, none to cherish thee with mother's smiles."

The Clod of Clay heard the Worm's voice, & raisd her pitying head;
She bow'd over the weeping infant, and her life exhal'd
In milky fondness; then on Thel she fix'd her humble eyes.

10 "O beauty of the vales of Har! we live not for ourselves;
Thou seest me the meanest thing, and so I am indeed;
My bosom of itself is cold, and of itself is dark,

PLATE 5

But he that loves the lowly, pours his oil upon my head,
And kisses me, and binds his nuptial bands around my breast,
And says: 'Thou mother of my children, I have lovèd thee,
And I have given thee a crown that none can take away.'
5 But how this is, sweet maid, I know not, and I cannot know;
I ponder, and I cannot ponder; yet I live and love."

The daughter of beauty wip'd her pitying tears with her white veil,
And said: "Alas! I knew not this, and therefore did I weep.
That God would love a Worm, I knew, and punish the evil foot
10 That, wilful, bruis'd its helpless form; but that he cherish'd it
With milk and oil I never knew; and therefore did I weep,
And I complaind in the mild air, because I fade away,
And lay me down in thy cold bed, and leave my shining lot."

"Queen of the vales," the matron Clay answered, "I heard thy sighs,
15 And all thy moans flew o'er my roof, but I have call'd them down.
Wilt thou, O Queen, enter my house? 'tis given thee to enter
And to return; fear nothing, enter with thy virgin feet."

PLATE 6

4

The eternal gates' terrific porter lifted the northern bar:[7]
Thel enter'd in & saw the secrets of the land unknown.
She saw the couches of the dead, & where the fibrous roots
Of every heart on earth infixes deep its restless twists:
5 A land of sorrows & of tears where never smile was seen.

She wanderd in the land of clouds thro' valleys dark, listning
Dolours & lamentations; waiting oft beside a dewy grave,
She stood in silence, listning to the voices of the ground,
Till to her own grave plot she came, & there she sat down,
10 And heard this voice of sorrow breathed from the hollow pit:

7. Homer, in *Odyssey* 13, described the Cave of the Naiades, of which the northern gate is for mortals and the southern gate for gods. The neoplatonist Porphyro had allegorized it as an account of the descent of the soul into matter and then its return.

"Why cannot the Ear be closed to its own destruction?
Or the glistning Eye to the poison of a smile?
Why are Eyelids stord with arrows ready drawn,
Where a thousand fighting men in ambush lie?
15 Or an Eye of gifts & graces, show'ring fruits & coinèd gold?
Why a Tongue impress'd with honey from every wind?
Why an Ear, a whirlpool fierce to draw creations in?
Why a Nostril wide inhaling terror, trembling, & affright?
Why a tender curb upon the youthful burning boy?
20 Why a little curtain of flesh on the bed of our desire?"[8]

The Virgin started from her seat, & with a shriek
Fled back unhinderd till she came into the vales of Har.

1789–91

Visions of the Daughters of Albion

This work, dated 1793 on the title page, is one of Blake's early illuminated books, and like his later and longer works is written in what Blake called "the long resounding strong heroic verse" of seven-foot lines. Unlike the timid heroine of *The Book of Thel*, the virgin Oothoon dares to break through into adult sexuality (symbolized by her plucking a marigold and placing it between her breasts) and sets out joyously to join her lover Theotormon, whose realm is the Atlantic Ocean. In her flight overseas she is waylaid and raped by Bromion in the figurative mode of a thunderstorm (1.16–17). The jealous Theotormon, condemning the victim as well as the rapist, binds the two "back to back" in a cave and sits weeping on the threshold. The rest of the work consists of monologues by the three characters, who remain fixed in these postures. Throughout this stage tableau the Daughters of Albion serve as the chorus who, in a recurrent refrain, echo the "woes" and "sighs" of Oothoon, but not her call to rebellion.

This simple drama is densely significant, for as Blake's compressed allusions indicate, the characters, events, and monologues have diverse areas of application. Blake's abrupt opening word, which he etched in very large letters, is *Enslav'd,* and the work as a whole embodies his view that contemporary men, and even more women, in a spiritual parallel to shackled black slaves, are in bondage to oppressive concepts and codes in all aspects of perception, thought, social institutions, and actions. As indicated by the refrain of the Daughters of Albion (that is, contemporary Englishwomen), Oothoon in one aspect represents the sexual disabilities and slavelike status of all women in a male-dominated society. But as "the soft soul of America" (1.3) she is also the revolutionary nation that had recently won political emancipation, yet continued to tolerate an agricultural system that involved black slavery and to acquiesce in the crass economic exploitation of her "soft American plains." At the same time, Oothoon is herself represented in the situation of a black female slave who has been branded, whipped, raped, and impregnated by her master.

Correlatively, the speeches of the boastful Bromion show him to be not only a sexual exploiter of women and a cruel and acquisitive slave owner but also a general proponent of the use of force to achieve mastery in wars, in an oppressive legal system, and in a religious morality based on the fear of hell (4.19–24). Theotormon is represented as even more contemptible. Broken and paralyzed by the prohibitions of a puritanical religion, he denies any possibility of achieving "joys" in this life, despairs of the power of intellect and imagination to improve the human condition and, ration-

---

8. This catalog of the life of Generation and Experience runs through the various senses to end with touch, the primary sexual sense.

alizing his own incapacity, bewails Oothoon's daring to think and act other than he does.

Oothoon's long and passionate oration that concludes the poem (plates 5–8) celebrates a free sexual life for both women and men. Blake, however, uses this open and unpossessive sexuality to typify the realization of all human potentialities and to represent an outgoing altruism, as opposed to an enclosed self-centeredness, "the self-love that envies all." To such a suspicious egotism, as her allusions indicate, Oothoon attributes the tyranny of uniform moral laws imposed on variable individuals, a rigidly institutional religion, the acquisitiveness that drives the system of commerce, and the property rights in another person that are established by the marriage contract.

Blake's poem reflects some prominent circumstances of the years of its composition, 1791–93. This was not only the time when the revolutionary spirit had moved from America to France and effected reverberations in England, but also the time of sporadic rebellions by black slaves in the Western Hemisphere and of widespread debate in England about the abolition of the slave trade. Blake himself, while composing the *Visions*, had illustrated the sadistic punishments inflicted on rebellious slaves in his engravings for J. G. Stedman's *A Narrative, of a Five Years' Expedition, against the Revolted Negroes of Surinam* (see David Erdman, *Blake: Prophet against Empire*, chapter 10). Blake's championing of women's liberation parallels some of the views expressed in the *Vindication of the Rights of Woman* published in 1792 by Mary Wollstonecraft, whom Blake knew and admired, and for whom he had illustrated a book the year before.

Visions of the Daughters of Albion
The Eye sees more than the Heart knows.

PLATE iii

The Argument

I loved Theotormon
And I was not ashamed
I trembled in my virgin fears
And I hid in Leutha's[1] vale!

5   I plucked Leutha's flower,
And I rose up from the vale;
But the terrible thunders tore
My virgin mantle in twain.

PLATE 1

Visions

ENSLAV'D, the Daughters of Albion weep: a trembling lamentation
Upon their mountains; in their valleys, sighs toward America.

For the soft soul of America, Oothoon[2] wandered in woe,
Along the vales of Leutha seeking flowers to comfort her;
5   And thus she spoke to the bright Marygold of Leutha's vale:

---

1. In some poems by Blake, Leutha is represented as a female figure who is beautiful and seductive, but treacherous.

2. The name is adapted by Blake from a character in James Macpherson's pretended translations, in the 1760s, from the ancient British bard Ossian.

Frontispiece, *Visions of the Daughters of Albion* (1793), plate i. Copy P, ca. 1815

"Art thou a flower! art thou a nymph! I see thee now a flower,
Now a nymph! I dare not pluck thee from thy dewy bed!"

The Golden nymph replied: "Pluck thou my flower Oothoon the mild.
Another flower shall spring, because the soul of sweet delight
10   Can never pass away." She ceas'd & closd her golden shrine.

Then Oothoon pluck'd the flower saying, "I pluck thee from thy bed,
Sweet flower, and put thee here to glow between my breasts,
And thus I turn my face to where my whole soul seeks."

Over the waves she went in wing'd exulting swift delight;
15   And over Theotormon's reign took her impetuous course.

Bromion rent her with his thunders. On his stormy bed
Lay the faint maid, and soon her woes appalld his thunders hoarse.

Bromion spoke: "Behold this harlot here on Bromion's bed,
And let the jealous dolphins sport around the lovely maid;
20   Thy soft American plains are mine, and mine thy north & south:
Stampt with my signet[3] are the swarthy children of the sun:
They are obedient, they resist not, they obey the scourge:
Their daughters worship terrors and obey the violent.

3. A small seal or stamp. The allusion is to the branding of black slaves by their owners.

PLATE 2

Now thou maist marry Bromion's harlot, and protect the child
Of Bromion's rage, that Oothoon shall put forth in nine moons' time."[4]

Then storms rent Theotormon's limbs; he rolld his waves around,
And folded his black jealous waters round the adulterate pair;
5   Bound back to back in Bromion's caves terror & meekness dwell.

At entrance Theotormon sits wearing the threshold hard
With secret tears; beneath him sound like waves on a desart shore
The voice of slaves beneath the sun, and children bought with money,
That shiver in religious caves beneath the burning fires
10   Of lust, that belch incessant from the summits of the earth.

Oothoon weeps not: she cannot weep! her tears are locked up;
But she can howl incessant, writhing her soft snowy limbs,
And calling Theotormon's Eagles to prey upon her flesh.[5]

"I call with holy voice! kings of the sounding air,
15   Rend away this defiled bosom that I may reflect
The image of Theotormon on my pure transparent breast."

The Eagles at her call descend & rend their bleeding prey;
Theotormon severely smiles; her soul reflects the smile,
As the clear spring mudded with feet of beasts grows pure & smiles.

20   The Daughters of Albion hear her woes, & eccho back her sighs.

"Why does my Theotormon sit weeping upon the threshold,
And Oothoon hovers by his side, perswading him in vain?
I cry, 'Arise O Theotormon, for the village dog
Barks at the breaking day, the nightingale has done lamenting,
25   The lark does rustle in the ripe corn, and the Eagle returns
From nightly prey, and lifts his golden beak to the pure east,
Shaking the dust from his immortal pinions to awake
The sun that sleeps too long. Arise my Theotormon, I am pure;
Because the night is gone that clos'd me in its deadly black.'
30   They told me that the night & day were all that I could see;
They told me that I had five senses to inclose me up,
And they inclos'd my infinite brain into a narrow circle,
And sunk my heart into the Abyss, a red round globe hot burning,
Till all from life I was obliterated and erased.
35   Instead of morn arises a bright shadow, like an eye
In the eastern cloud,[6] instead of night a sickly charnel house,
That Theotormon hears me not! to him the night and morn
Are both alike: a night of sighs, a morning of fresh tears;

4. Pregnancy enhanced the market value of a female slave in America.
5. The implied parallel is to Zeus's punishment of Prometheus for befriending the human race, by setting an eagle to devour his liver.

6. The contrast is between the physical sun perceived by the constricted ("inclos'd," line 32) sensible eye and "the breaking day" (line 24) of a new era perceived by Oothoon's liberated vision.

PLATE 3

And none but Bromion can hear my lamentations.

"With what sense is it that the chicken shuns the ravenous hawk?
With what sense does the tame pigeon measure out the expanse?
With what sense does the bee form cells? have not the mouse & frog
5   Eyes and ears and sense of touch? yet are their habitations
And their pursuits as different as their forms and as their joys.
Ask the wild ass why he refuses burdens, and the meek camel
Why he loves man; is it because of eye, ear, mouth, or skin,
Or breathing nostrils? No, for these the wolf and tyger have.
10 Ask the blind worm the secrets of the grave, and why her spires
Love to curl round the bones of death; and ask the rav'nous snake
Where she gets poison, & the wing'd eagle why he loves the sun,
And then tell me the thoughts of man, that have been hid of old.[7]

"Silent I hover all the night, and all day could be silent,
15 If Theotormon once would turn his loved eyes upon me.
How can I be defild when I reflect thy image pure?
Sweetest the fruit that the worm feeds on, & the soul prey'd on by woe,
The new wash'd lamb ting'd with the village smoke, & the bright swan
By the red earth of our immortal river:[8] I bathe my wings,
20 And I am white and pure to hover round Theotormon's breast."

Then Theotormon broke his silence, and he answered:

"Tell me what is the night or day to one o'erflowd with woe?
Tell me what is a thought? & of what substance is it made?
Tell me what is a joy? & in what gardens do joys grow?
25 And in what rivers swim the sorrows? and upon what mountains

PLATE 4

Wave shadows of discontent? and in what houses dwell the wretched
Drunken with woe, forgotten, and shut up from cold despair?

"Tell me where dwell the thoughts, forgotten till thou call them forth?
Tell me where dwell the joys of old! & where the ancient loves?
5   And when will they renew again & the night of oblivion past?
That I might traverse times & spaces far remote and bring
Comforts into a present sorrow and a night of pain.
Where goest thou, O thought? to what remote land is thy flight?
If thou returnest to the present moment of affliction
10 Wilt thou bring comforts on thy wings and dews and honey and balm,
Or poison from the desart wilds, from the eyes of the envier?"

Then Bromion said, and shook the cavern with his lamentation:

7. Oothoon implies that "thoughts" (powers of conceiving a liberated life in a better world) are as innate to human beings as instinctual patterns of behavior are to other species of living things.
8. "Red earth" is the etymological meaning of the Hebrew name "Adam" (cf. *The Marriage of Heaven and Hell* 2.13, p. 73). The "immortal river," accordingly, may refer to the "river" that "went out of Eden" (Genesis 2.10).

"Thou knowest that the ancient trees seen by thine eyes have fruit;
But knowest thou that trees and fruits flourish upon the earth
15 To gratify senses unknown? trees beasts and birds unknown:
Unknown, not unpercievd, spread in the infinite microscope,
In places yet unvisited by the voyager, and in worlds
Over another kind of seas, and in atmospheres unknown?
Ah! are there other wars, beside the wars of sword and fire?
20 And are there other sorrows, beside the sorrows of poverty?
And are there other joys, beside the joys of riches and ease?
And is there not one law for both the lion and the ox?[9]
And is there not eternal fire, and eternal chains?
To bind the phantoms of existence from eternal life?"

25 Then Oothoon waited silent all the day and all the night,

PLATE 5

But when the morn arose, her lamentation renewd.
The Daughters of Albion hear her woes, & eccho back her sighs.

"O Urizen![1] Creator of men! mistaken Demon of heaven:
Thy joys are tears! thy labour vain, to form men to thine image.
5 How can one joy absorb another? are not different joys
Holy, eternal, infinite! and each joy is a Love.

"Does not the great mouth laugh at a gift? & the narrow eyelids mock
At the labour that is above payment? and wilt thou take the ape
For thy councellor? or the dog for a schoolmaster to thy children?
10 Does he who contemns poverty, and he who turns with
         abhorrence
From usury, feel the same passion, or are they moved alike?
How can the giver of gifts experience the delights of the merchant?
How the industrious citizen the pains of the husbandman?
How different far the fat fed hireling with hollow drum,
15 Who buys whole corn fields into wastes,[2] and sings upon the
         heath:
How different their eye and ear! how different the world to them!
With what sense does the parson claim the labour of the farmer?
What are his nets & gins° & traps? & how does he surround him   *snares*
With cold floods of abstraction, and with forests of solitude,
20 To build him castles and high spires, where kings & priests may dwell?
Till she who burns with youth, and knows no fixed lot, is bound
In spells of law to one she loaths; and must she drag the chain
Of life, in weary lust? must chilling murderous thoughts obscure
The clear heaven of her eternal spring? to bear the wintry rage
25 Of a harsh terror, driv'n to madness, bound to hold a rod
Over her shrinking shoulders all the day, & all the night
To turn the wheel of false desire, and longings that wake her womb

9. The last line of *The Marriage of Heaven and Hell* proclaims: "One Law for the Lion & Ox is Oppression."
1. This is the first occurrence of the name "Urizen" in Blake. Oothoon's liberated vision recognizes the error in the way God is conceived in conventional religion.
2. Probably a compressed allusion both to the wealthy landowner who converts fertile fields into a game preserve and to the recruiting officer ("with hollow drum") who strips the land of its agricultural laborers.

To the abhorred birth of cherubs in the human form
That live a pestilence & die a meteor & are no more;
30 Till the child dwell with one he hates, and do the deed he loaths,
And the impure scourge force his seed into its unripe birth
E'er yet his eyelids can behold the arrows of the day?[3]

"Does the whale worship at thy footsteps as the hungry dog?
Or does he scent the mountain prey, because his nostrils wide
35 Draw in the ocean? does his eye discern the flying cloud
As the raven's eye? or does he measure the expanse like the vulture?
Does the still spider view the cliffs where eagles hide their young?
Or does the fly rejoice because the harvest is brought in?
Does not the eagle scorn the earth & despise the treasures beneath?
40 But the mole knoweth what is there, & the worm shall tell it thee.
Does not the worm erect a pillar in the mouldering church yard,

PLATE 6

And a palace of eternity in the jaws of the hungry grave?
Over his porch these words are written: 'Take thy bliss O Man!
And sweet shall be thy taste & sweet thy infant joys renew!'

"Infancy, fearless, lustful, happy! nestling for delight
5 In laps of pleasure; Innocence! honest, open, seeking
The vigorous joys of morning light, open to virgin bliss,
Who taught thee modesty, subtil modesty? Child of night & sleep,
When thou awakest wilt thou dissemble all thy secret joys,
Or wert thou not awake when all this mystery was disclos'd?
10 Then com'st thou forth a modest virgin, knowing to dissemble,
With nets found under thy night pillow to catch virgin joy,
And brand it with the name of whore, & sell it in the night,
In silence, ev'n without a whisper, and in seeming sleep.[4]
Religious dreams and holy vespers light thy smoky fires;
15 Once were thy fires lighted by the eyes of honest morn.
And does my Theotormon seek this hypocrite modesty,
This knowing, artful, secret, fearful, cautious, trembling hypocrite?
Then is Oothoon a whore indeed! and all the virgin joys
Of life are harlots, and Theotormon is a sick man's dream,
20 And Oothoon is the crafty slave of selfish holiness.

"But Oothoon is not so; a virgin fill'd with virgin fancies
Open to joy and to delight where ever beauty appears.
If in the morning sun I find it, there my eyes are fix'd

PLATE 7

In happy copulation; if in evening mild, wearied with work,
Sit on a bank and draw the pleasures of this free born joy.

"The moment of desire! the moment of desire! The virgin
That pines for man shall awaken her womb to enormous joys

3. The reference is to the begetting of children, both in actual slavery and in the metaphoric slavery of a loveless marriage, from generation to generation.

4. Oothoon contrasts the natural, innocent sensuality of an infant to the socially acquired, hypocritical modesty of the adult virgin; the latter is Theotormon's concept of female virtue.

5 In the secret shadows of her chamber; the youth shut up from
 The lustful joy shall forget to generate & create an amorous image
 In the shadows of his curtains and in the folds of his silent pillow.
 Are not these the places of religion? the rewards of continence?
 The self enjoyings of self denial? Why dost seek religion?
10 Is it because acts are not lovely, that thou seekest solitude,
 Where the horrible darkness is impressed with reflections of desire?

 "Father of Jealousy,[5] be thou accursed from the earth!
 Why hast thou taught my Theotormon this accursed thing?
 Till beauty fades from off my shoulders, darken'd and cast out,
15 A solitary shadow wailing on the margin of non-entity.

 "I cry, Love! Love! Love! happy happy Love! free as the mountain wind!
 Can that be Love, that drinks another as a sponge drinks water?
 That clouds with jealousy his nights, with weepings all the day,
 To spin a web of age around him, grey and hoary! dark!
20 Till his eyes sicken at the fruit that hangs before his sight.
 Such is self-love that envies all! a creeping skeleton
 With lamplike eyes watching around the frozen marriage bed.

 "But silken nets and traps of adamant[6] will Oothoon spread,
 And catch for thee girls of mild silver, or of furious gold;
25 I'll lie beside thee on a bank & view their wanton play
 In lovely copulation bliss on bliss with Theotormon:
 Red as the rosy morning, lustful as the first born beam,
 Oothoon shall view his dear delight, nor e'er with jealous cloud
 Come in the heaven of generous love; nor selfish blightings bring.

30 "Does the sun walk in glorious raiment on the secret floor

PLATE 8

 Where the cold miser spreads his gold? or does the bright cloud drop
 On his stone threshold? does his eye behold the beam that brings
 Expansion to the eye of pity? or will he bind himself
 Beside the ox to thy hard furrow? does not that mild beam blot
5 The bat, the owl, the glowing tyger, and the king of night?
 The sea fowl takes the wintry blast for a cov'ring to her limbs,
 And the wild snake the pestilence to adorn him with gems & gold.
 And trees & birds & beasts & men behold their eternal joy.
 Arise you little glancing wings, and sing your infant joy!
10 Arise and drink your bliss, for every thing that lives is holy!"[7]

 Thus every morning wails Oothoon, but Theotormon sits
 Upon the margind ocean conversing with shadows dire.

 The Daughters of Albion hear her woes, & eccho back her sighs.

1791–93   1793

5. I.e., Urizen (5.3), the false conceived God who
prohibits the satisfaction of human desires.
6. A legendary stone believed to be unbreakable.
(The name is derived from the Greek word for diamond.)
7. This last phrase is also the concluding line of
"A Song of Liberty," appended to *The Marriage of
Heaven and Hell.*

The Marriage of Heaven and Hell

This, the most immediately accessible of Blake's longer works, is a vigorous, deliberately outrageous, and at times comic onslaught against timidly conventional and self-righteous members of society as well as against stock opinions of orthodox Christian piety and morality. The seeming simplicity of Blake's satiric attitude, however, is deceptive.

Initially, Blake accepts the terminology of standard Christian morality ("what the religious call Good & Evil") but reverses its values. In this conventional use Evil, which is manifested by the class of beings called Devils and which consigns wrongdoers to the orthodox Hell, is everything associated with the body and its desires and consists essentially of energy, abundance, actions, and freedom. Conventional Good, which is manifested by Angels and guarantees its adherents a place in the orthodox Heaven, is associated with the Soul (regarded as entirely separate from the body) and consists of the contrary qualities of reason, restraint, passivity, and prohibition. Blandly adopting these conventional oppositions, Blake elects to assume the diabolic persona—what he calls "the voice of the Devil"—and to utter "Proverbs of Hell."

But this stance is only a first stage in Blake's complex irony, designed to startle the reader into recognizing the inadequacy of conventional moral categories. As he also says in the opening summary, "Without Contraries is no progression," and "Reason and Energy" are both "necessary to Human existence." It turns out that Blake subordinates his reversal of conventional values under a more inclusive point of view, according to which the real Good, as distinguished from the merely ironic Good, is not abandonment of all restraints but a "marriage," or union of the contraries, of desire and restraint, energy and reason, the promptings of Hell and the denials of Heaven—or as Blake calls these contraries in plate 16, "the Prolific" and "the Devouring." These two classes, he adds, "should be enemies," and "whoever tries to reconcile them seeks to destroy existence." Implicit in Blake's satire is the view that the good and abundant life consists in the sustained tension, without victory or suppression, of co-present oppositions.

Blake was stimulated to write this unique work in response to the writings of the visionary Swedish theologian Emanuel Swedenborg, whom he had at first admired but then had come to recognize as a conventional Angel in the disguise of a radical Devil. In plate 3 the writings of Swedenborg are described as the winding clothes Blake discards as he is resurrected from the tomb of his past self, as a poet-prophet who heralds the apocalyptic promise of his age. Blake wrote *The Marriage of Heaven and Hell* in the early 1790s, during the early years of the French Revolution, when he shared the expectations of a number of radical English writers, including the young poets Wordsworth, Coleridge, and Southey, that the revolution was the violent stage that, as the biblical prophets foresaw, immediately preceded the millennium. The double role of *The Marriage* as both satire and revolutionary prophecy is made explicit in *A Song of Liberty*, which Blake etched in 1792 and added as a coda.

The Marriage of Heaven and Hell

PLATE 2

The Argument

Rintrah[1] roars & shakes his fires in the burdend air;
Hungry clouds swag on the deep.

---

1. Rintrah plays the role of the angry Old Testament prophet Elijah as well as of John the Baptist, the voice "crying in the wilderness" (Matthew 3), preparing the way for Christ the Messiah. It has been plausibly suggested that stanzas 2–5 summarize the course of biblical history to the present

Once meek, and in a perilous path,
The just man kept his course along
5 The vale of death.
Roses are planted where thorns grow,
And on the barren heath
Sing the honey bees.

Then the perilous path was planted,
10 And a river, and a spring,
On every cliff and tomb;
And on the bleached bones
Red clay[2] brought forth;

Till the villain left the paths of ease,
15 To walk in perilous paths, and drive
The just man into barren climes.

Now the sneaking serpent walks
In mild humility,
And the just man rages in the wilds
20 Where lions roam.

Rintrah roars & shakes his fires in the burdend air;
Hungry clouds swag on the deep.

————————

PLATE 3

As a new heaven is begun, and it is now thirty-three years since its advent,
the Eternal Hell revives. And lo! Swedenborg[3] is the Angel sitting at the tomb;
his writings are the linen clothes folded up. Now is the dominion of Edom,
& the return of Adam into Paradise; see Isaiah xxxiv & XXXV Chap.[4]

Without Contraries is no progression. Attraction and Repulsion, Reason
and Energy, Love and Hate, are necessary to Human existence.

---

time. "Once" (line 3) refers to Old Testament history after the Fall; "Then" (line 9) is the time of the birth of Christ. "Till" (line 14) identifies the era when Christianity was perverted into an institutional religion. "Now" (line 17) is the time of the wrathful portent of the French Revolution. In this final era, the hypocritical serpent represents the priest of the "angels" in the poem, while "the just man" is embodied in Blake himself, a raging poet and prophet in the guise of a devil. "Swag" (line 2): sag, hang down.
2. In Hebrew, the literal meaning of "Adam," or created man. The probable reference is to the birth of the Redeemer, the new Adam.
3. Emanuel Swedenborg (1688–1772), Swedish scientist and religious philosopher, had predicted, on the basis of his visions, that the Last Judgment and the coming of the Kingdom of Heaven would occur in 1757. This was precisely the year of Blake's birth. Now, in 1790, Blake is thirty-three, the age at which Christ had been resurrected from the tomb; correspondingly, Blake rises from the tomb of his past life in his new role as imaginative artist who will redeem his age. But, Blake ironically comments, the works he will engrave in his resur-

rection will constitute the Eternal Hell, the contrary brought into simultaneous being by Swedenborg's limited New Heaven.
4. Isaiah 34 prophesies "the day of the Lord's vengeance," a time of violent destruction and bloodshed; Isaiah 35 prophesies the redemption to follow, in which "the desert shall . . . blossom as the rose," "in the wilderness shall waters break out, and streams in the desert," and "no lion shall be there," but "an highway shall be there . . . and it shall be called The way of holiness" (cf. "The Argument," lines 3–11, 20). Blake combines with these chapters Isaiah 63, in which "Edom" is the place from which comes the man whose garments are red with the blood he has spilled; for as he says, "the day of vengeance is in mine heart, and the year of my redeemed is come." Blake interprets this last phrase as predicting the time when Adam would regain his lost Paradise.
With reference to affairs in 1790, Edom can be taken to represent France, and the red man coming from Edom (to England) to be the spirit of the French Revolution, which Blake interprets as a portent of apocalyptic redemption and the recovery of Paradise.

From these contraries spring what the religious call Good & Evil. Good is the passive that obeys Reason. Evil is the active springing from Energy.

Good is Heaven. Evil is Hell.

PLATE 4

The Voice of the Devil

All Bibles or sacred codes have been the causes of the following Errors:

1. That Man has two real existing principles; Viz: a Body & a Soul.
2. That Energy, calld Evil, is alone from the Body, & that Reason, calld Good, is alone from the Soul.
3. That God will torment Man in Eternity for following his Energies.

But the following Contraries to these are True:

1. Man has no Body distinct from his Soul; for that calld Body is a portion of Soul discernd by the five Senses, the chief inlets of Soul in this age.
2. Energy is the only life, and is from the Body; and Reason is the bound or outward circumference of Energy.
3. Energy is Eternal Delight.

———————————

PLATE 5

Those who restrain desire, do so because theirs is weak enough to be restrained; and the restrainer or reason usurps its place & governs the unwilling.

And being restraind, it by degrees becomes passive, till it is only the shadow of desire.

The history of this is written in *Paradise Lost*,[5] & the Governor or Reason is call'd Messiah.

And the original Archangel, or possessor of the command of the heavenly host, is calld the Devil or Satan, and his children are call'd Sin & Death.[6]

But in the Book of Job, Milton's Messiah is call'd Satan.[7]

For this history has been adopted by both parties.

It indeed appear'd to Reason as if Desire was cast out; but the Devil's account is, that the Messi[PLATE 6]ah fell, & formed a heaven of what he stole from the Abyss.

This is shewn in the Gospel, where he prays to the Father to send the comforter or Desire that Reason may have Ideas to build on;[8] the Jehovah of the Bible being no other than he who dwells in flaming fire. Know that after Christ's death, he became Jehovah.

But in Milton, the Father is Destiny, the Son, a Ratio[9] of the five senses, & the Holy-ghost, Vacuum!

Note. The reason Milton wrote in fetters when he wrote of Angels & God,

5. What follows, to the end of this section, is Blake's "diabolical" reading of *Paradise Lost*.
6. Satan's giving birth to Sin and then incestuously begetting Death upon her is described in *Paradise Lost* 2.745ff.; the war in heaven, referred to three lines below, in which the Messiah defeated Satan and drove him out of heaven, is described in 6.824ff.
7. In the Book of Job, Satan plays the role of Job's moral accuser and physical tormentor.

8. Possibly John 14.16–17, where Christ says he "will pray the Father, and he shall give you another Comforter . . . Even the Spirit of truth."
9. The Latin *ratio* means both "reason" and "sum." Blake applies the term to the 18th-century view, following the empirical philosophy of John Locke, that the content of the mind, on which the faculty of reason operates, is limited to the sum of the experience acquired by the five senses.

and at liberty when of Devils & Hell, is because he was a true Poet and of the Devil's party without knowing it.

A Memorable Fancy[1]

As I was walking among the fires of hell, delighted with the enjoyments of Genius, which to Angels look like torment and insanity, I collected some of their Proverbs; thinking that as the sayings used in a nation mark its character, so the Proverbs of Hell shew the nature of Infernal wisdom better than any description of buildings or garments.

When I came home, on the abyss of the five senses, where a flat sided steep frowns over the present world, I saw a mighty Devil folded in black clouds, hovering on the sides of the rock; with cor[PLATE 7]roding fires he wrote the following sentence[2] now perceived by the minds of men, & read by them on earth:

> How do you know but ev'ry Bird that cuts the airy way,
> Is an immense world of delight, clos'd by your senses five?

Proverbs of Hell[3]

In seed time learn, in harvest teach, in winter enjoy.
Drive your cart and your plow over the bones of the dead.
The road of excess leads to the palace of wisdom.
Prudence is a rich ugly old maid courted by Incapacity.
5   He who desires but acts not, breeds pestilence.
The cut worm forgives the plow.
Dip him in the river who loves water.
A fool sees not the same tree that a wise man sees.
He whose face gives no light, shall never become a star.
10   Eternity is in love with the productions of time.
The busy bee has no time for sorrow.
The hours of folly are measur'd by the clock; but of wisdom, no clock can
       measure.
All wholsom food is caught without a net or a trap.
Bring out number, weight, & measure in a year of dearth.
15   No bird soars too high, if he soars with his own wings.
A dead body revenges not injuries.
The most sublime act is to set another before you.
If the fool would persist in his folly he would become wise.
Folly is the cloke of knavery.
20   Shame is Pride's cloke.

PLATE 8

Prisons are built with stones of Law, Brothels with bricks of Religion.
The pride of the peacock is the glory of God.

1. A parody of what Swedenborg called "memorable relations" of his literal-minded visions of the eternal world.
2. The "mighty Devil" is Blake, as he sees himself reflected in the shiny plate on which he is etching

this very passage with "corroding fires," i.e., acid. See also the third from last sentence in plate 14.
3. A "diabolic" version of the Book of Proverbs in the Old Testament.

The lust of the goat is the bounty of God.
The wrath of the lion is the wisdom of God.
5 The nakedness of woman is the work of God.
Excess of sorrow laughs. Excess of joy weeps.
The roaring of lions, the howling of wolves, the raging of the stormy sea,
and the destructive sword, are portions of eternity too great for the
eye of man.
The fox condemns the trap, not himself.
Joys impregnate. Sorrows bring forth.
10 Let man wear the fell of the lion, woman the fleece of the sheep.
The bird a nest, the spider a web, man friendship.
The selfish smiling fool & the sullen frowning fool shall be both thought
wise, that they may be a rod.
What is now proved was once only imagin'd.
The rat, the mouse, the fox, the rabbit watch the roots; the lion, the tyger,
the horse, the elephant, watch the fruits.
15 The cistern contains; the fountain overflows.
One thought fills immensity.
Always be ready to speak your mind, and a base man will avoid you.
Every thing possible to be believ'd is an image of truth.
The eagle never lost so much time as when he submitted to learn of the
crow.

PLATE 9

The fox provides for himself, but God provides for the lion.
Think in the morning, Act in the noon, Eat in the evening, Sleep in the
night.
He who has sufferd you to impose on him knows you.
As the plow follows words, so God rewards prayers.
5 The tygers of wrath are wiser than the horses of instruction.
Expect poison from the standing water.
You never know what is enough unless you know what is more than
enough.
Listen to the fool's reproach! it is a kingly title!
The eyes of fire, the nostrils of air, the mouth of water, the beard of earth.
10 The weak in courage is strong in cunning.
The apple tree never asks the beech how he shall grow, nor the lion the
horse, how he shall take his prey.
The thankful reciever bears a plentiful harvest.
If others had not been foolish, we should be so.
The soul of sweet delight can never be defil'd.
15 When thou seest an Eagle, thou seest a portion of Genius; lift up thy head!
As the catterpiller chooses the fairest leaves to lay her eggs on, so the
priest lays his curse on the fairest joys.
To create a little flower is the labour of ages.
Damn braces; Bless relaxes.
The best wine is the oldest, the best water the newest.
20 Prayers plow not! Praises reap not!
Joys laugh not! Sorrows weep not!

PLATE 10

The head Sublime, the heart Pathos, the genitals Beauty, the hands & feet
Proportion.

As the air to a bird or the sea to a fish, so is contempt to the contemptible.
The crow wish'd every thing was black, the owl that every thing was white.
Exuberance is Beauty.
5 If the lion was advised by the fox, he would be cunning.
Improvement makes strait roads, but the crooked roads without
     Improvement are roads of Genius.
Sooner murder an infant in its cradle than nurse unacted desires.
Where man is not, nature is barren.
Truth can never be told so as to be understood, and not be believ'd.
10   Enough! or Too much.

PLATE 11

    The ancient Poets animated all sensible objects with Gods or Geniuses, calling them by the names and adorning them with the properties of woods, rivers, mountains, lakes, cities, nations, and whatever their enlarged & numerous senses could perceive.

    And particularly they studied the genius of each city & country, placing it under its mental deity.

    Till a system was formed, which some took advantage of & enslav'd the vulgar by attempting to realize or abstract the mental deities from their objects; thus began Priesthood,

    Choosing forms of worship from poetic tales.

    And at length they pronounced that the Gods had ordered such things.

    Thus men forgot that All deities reside in the human breast.

PLATE 12

A Memorable Fancy[4]

    The Prophets Isaiah and Ezekiel dined with me, and I asked them how they dared so roundly to assert that God spake to them; and whether they did not think at the time that they would be misunderstood, & so be the cause of imposition.

    Isaiah answer'd: "I saw no God, nor heard any, in a finite organical perception; but my senses discover'd the infinite in every thing, and as I was then perswaded, & remain confirm'd, that the voice of honest indignation is the voice of God, I cared not for consequences, but wrote."

    Then I asked: "Does a firm perswasion that a thing is so, make it so?"

    He replied: "All poets believe that it does, & in ages of imagination this firm perswasion removed mountains; but many are not capable of a firm perswasion of any thing."

    Then Ezekiel said: "The philosophy of the East taught the first principles of human perception. Some nations held one principle for the origin & some another; we of Israel taught that the Poetic Genius (as you now call it) was the first principle and all the others merely derivative, which was the cause of our despising the Priests & Philosophers of other countries, and prophecying that all Gods [PL 13] would at last be proved to originate in ours & to be the tributaries of the Poetic Genius; it was this that our great poet, King David, desired so fervently & invokes so pathetically, saying by this he con-

---

4. Blake parodies Swedenborg's accounts, in his *Memorable Relations*, of his conversations with the inhabitants during his spiritual trips to heaven.

quers enemies & governs kingdoms; and we so loved our God, that we cursed in his name all the deities of surrounding nations, and asserted that they had rebelled; from these opinions the vulgar came to think that all nations would at last be subject to the Jews."

"This," said he, "like all firm perswasions, is come to pass, for all nations believe the Jews' code and worship the Jews' god, and what greater subjection can be?"

I heard this with some wonder, & must confess my own conviction. After dinner I ask'd Isaiah to favour the world with his lost works; he said none of equal value was lost. Ezekiel said the same of his.

I also asked Isaiah what made him go naked and barefoot three years? He answered, "the same that made our friend Diogenes,[5] the Grecian."

I then asked Ezekiel why he eat dung, & lay so long on his right & left side?[6] He answered, "the desire of raising other men into a perception of the infinite; this the North American tribes practise, & is he honest who resists his genius or conscience only for the sake of present ease or gratification?"

———————————

PLATE 14

The ancient tradition that the world will be consumed in fire at the end of six thousand years is true, as I have heard from Hell.

For the cherub with his flaming sword is hereby commanded to leave his guard at the tree of life;[7] and when he does, the whole creation will be consumed, and appear infinite and holy, whereas it now appears finite & corrupt.

This will come to pass by an improvement of sensual enjoyment.

But first the notion that man has a body distinct from his soul is to be expunged; this I shall do, by printing in the infernal method, by corrosives, which in Hell are salutary and medicinal, melting apparent surfaces away, and displaying the infinite which was hid.[8]

If the doors of perception were cleansed every thing would appear to man as it is, infinite.

For man has closed himself up, till he sees all things thro' narrow chinks of his cavern.

PLATE 15

A Memorable Fancy

I was in a Printing house in Hell & saw the method in which knowledge is transmitted from generation to generation.

In the first chamber was a Dragon-Man, clearing away the rubbish from a cave's mouth; within, a number of Dragons were hollowing the cave.

In the second chamber was a Viper folding round the rock & the cave, and others adorning it with gold, silver, and precious stones.

In the third chamber was an Eagle with wings and feathers of air; he

5. Greek Cynic (4th century), whose extreme repudiation of civilized customs gave rise to anecdotes that he had renounced clothing. In Isaiah 20.2–3, the prophet, at the command of the Lord, walked "naked and barefoot" for three years.
6. The Lord gave these instructions to the prophet

Ezekiel (4.4–6).
7. In Genesis 3.24, when the Lord drove Adam and Eve from the Garden of Eden, he had placed Cherubim and a flaming sword at the eastern end "to keep the way of the tree of life."
8. See n. 2, p. 75.

caused the inside of the cave to be infinite; around were numbers of Eagle-like men, who built palaces in the immense cliffs.

In the fourth chamber were Lions of flaming fire, raging around & melting the metals into living fluids.

In the fifth chamber were Unnam'd forms, which cast the metals into the expanse.

There they were receiv'd by Men who occupied the sixth chamber, and took the forms of books & were arranged in libraries.[9]

PLATE 16

The Giants[1] who formed this world into its sensual existence, and now seem to live in it in chains, are in truth the causes of its life & the sources of all activity; but the chains are the cunning of weak and tame minds which have power to resist energy; according to the proverb, the weak in courage is strong in cunning.

Thus one portion of being is the Prolific, the other, the Devouring; to the Devourer it seems as if the producer was in his chains, but it is not so; he only takes portions of existence and fancies that the whole.

But the Prolific would cease to be Prolific unless the Devourer as a sea received the excess of his delights.

Some will say, "Is not God alone the Prolific?" I answer, "God only Acts & Is, in existing beings or Men."

These two classes of men are always upon earth, & they should be enemies; whoever tries [PLATE 17] to reconcile them seeks to destroy existence.

Religion is an endeavour to reconcile the two.

Note. Jesus Christ did not wish to unite but to separate them, as in the Parable of sheep and goats! & he says, "I came not to send Peace but a Sword."[2]

Messiah or Satan or Tempter was formerly thought to be one of the Ante-diluvians[3] who are our Energies.

A Memorable Fancy

An Angel came to me and said: "O pitiable foolish young man! O horrible! O dreadful state! consider the hot burning dungeon thou art preparing for thyself to all eternity, to which thou art going in such career."

I said: "Perhaps you will be willing to shew me my eternal lot, & we will contemplate together upon it and see whether your lot or mine is most desirable."

So he took me thro' a stable & thro' a church & down into the church vault at the end of which was a mill; thro' the mill we went, and came to a cave; down the winding cavern we groped our tedious way till a void bound-less as a nether sky appeared beneath us, & we held by the roots of trees and hung over this immensity, but I said: "If you please, we will commit ourselves

---

9. In this "Memorable Fancy," Blake allegorizes his procedure in designing, etching, printing, and binding his works of imaginative genius.
1. In this section, human creative energies, called "the Prolific," in their relation to their indispen-sable contrary, "the Devourer."
2. Matthew 10.34. The parable of the sheep and the goats is in Matthew 25.32–33.
3. Those who lived before Noah's Flood.

to this void, and see whether Providence is here also, if you will not I will." But he answered: "Do not presume, O young man, but as we here remain, behold thy lot which will soon appear when the darkness passes away."[4]

So I remaind with him sitting in the twisted [PLATE 18] root of an oak; he was suspended in a fungus which hung with the head downward into the deep.

By degrees we beheld the infinite Abyss, fiery as the smoke of a burning city; beneath us at an immense distance was the sun, black but shining; round it were fiery tracks on which revolv'd vast spiders, crawling after their prey, which flew, or rather swum in the infinite deep, in the most terrific shapes of animals sprung from corruption; & the air was full of them, & seemed composed of them; these are Devils, and are called Powers of the air. I now asked my companion which was my eternal lot? He said, "Between the black & white spiders."

But now, from between the black & white spiders a cloud and fire burst and rolled thro the deep, blackning all beneath, so that the nether deep grew black as a sea & rolled with a terrible noise. Beneath us was nothing now to be seen but a black tempest, till looking east between the clouds & the waves, we saw a cataract of blood mixed with fire, and not many stones' throw from us appeared and sunk again the scaly fold of a monstrous serpent. At last to the east, distant about three degrees, appeared a fiery crest above the waves. Slowly it reared like a ridge of golden rocks till we discovered two globes of crimson fire, from which the sea fled away in clouds of smoke. And now we saw it was the head of Leviathan; his forehead was divided into streaks of green & purple like those on a tyger's forehead; soon we saw his mouth & red gills hang just above the raging foam, tinging the black deep with beams of blood, advancing toward [PLATE 19] us with all the fury of a spiritual existence.

My friend the Angel climb'd up from his station into the mill. I remain'd alone, & then this appearance was no more, but I found myself sitting on a pleasant bank beside a river by moon light, hearing a harper who sung to the harp, & his theme was: "The man who never alters his opinion is like standing water, & breeds reptiles of the mind."

But I arose, and sought for the mill, & there I found my Angel, who surprised asked me how I escaped?

I answerd: "All that we saw was owing to your metaphysics: for when you ran away, I found myself on a bank by moonlight hearing a harper. But now we have seen my eternal lot, shall I shew you yours? He laughd at my proposal; but I by force suddenly caught him in my arms, & flew westerly thro' the night, til we were elevated above the earth's shadow; then I flung myself with him directly into the body of the sun. Here I clothed myself in white, & taking in my hand Swedenborg's volumes, sunk from the glorious clime, and passed all the planets till we came to Saturn. Here I staid to rest & then leap'd into the void between Saturn & the fixed stars.[5]

4. The "stable" is that where Jesus was born, which, allegorically, leads to the "church" founded in his name and to the "vault" where this institution effectually buried him. The "mill" in Blake is a symbol of mechanical and analytic philosophy; through this the pilgrims pass into the twisting cave of rationalistic theology and descend to an underworld that is an empty abyss. The point of this Blakean equivalent of a carnival funhouse is that only after you have thoroughly confused yourself by this tortuous approach, and only if you then (as in the next two paragraphs) stare at this topsyturvy emptiness long enough, will the void gradually assume the semblance of the comic horrors of the fantasied Hell of angelic orthodoxy.

5. In the Ptolemaic world picture Saturn was in the outermost planetary sphere; beyond it was the sphere of the fixed stars.

"Here," said I, "is your lot, in this space, if space it may be calld." Soon we saw the stable and the church, & I took him to the altar and open'd the Bible, and lo! it was a deep pit, into which I descended, driving the Angel before me. Soon we saw seven houses of brick;[6] one we enterd; in it were a [PLATE 20] number of monkeys, baboons, & all of that species, chaind by the middle, grinning and snatching at one another, but withheld by the short-ness of their chains. However, I saw that they sometimes grew numerous, and then the weak were caught by the strong, and with a grinning aspect, first coupled with & then devourd, by plucking off first one limb and then another till the body was left a helpless trunk. This, after grinning & kissing it with seeming fondness, they devourd too; and here & there I saw one savourily picking the flesh off of his own tail. As the stench terribly annoyd us both, we went into the mill, & I in my hand brought the skeleton of a body, which in the mill was Aristotle's Analytics.[7]

So the Angel said: "Thy phantasy has imposed upon me, & thou oughtest to be ashamed."

I answered: "We impose on one another, & it is but lost time to converse with you whose works are only Analytics."

Opposition is true Friendship.

PLATE 21

I have always found that Angels have the vanity to speak of themselves as the only wise; this they do with a confident insolence sprouting from system-atic reasoning.

Thus Swedenborg boasts that what he writes is new; tho' it is only the Contents or Index of already publish'd books.

A man carried a monkey about for a shew, & because he was a little wiser than the monkey, grew vain, and conceiv'd himself as much wiser than seven men. It is so with Swedenborg; he shews the folly of churches & exposes hypocrites, till he imagines that all are religious, & himself the single [PLATE 22] one on earth that ever broke a net.

Now hear a plain fact: Swedenborg has not written one new truth. Now hear another: he has written all the old falshoods.

And now hear the reason: He conversed with Angels who are all religious, & conversed not with Devils, who all hate religion, for he was incapable thro' his conceited notions.

Thus Swedenborg's writings are a recapitulation of all superficial opinions, and an analysis of the more sublime, but no further.

Have now another plain fact: Any man of mechanical talents may from the writings of Paracelsus or Jacob Behmen[8] produce ten thousand volumes of equal value with Swedenborg's, and from those of Dante or Shakespear, an infinite number.

But when he has done this, let him not say that he knows better than his master, for he only holds a candle in sunshine.

---

6. The "seven churches which are in Asia," to which John addresses the Book of Revelation 1.4. Blake now forces on the angel his own diabolic view of angelic biblical exegesis, theological spec-ulation and disputation, and Hell.
7. Aristotle's treatises on logic.
8. Jakob Boehme (1575–1624), a German shoe-maker who developed a theosophical system that has had persisting influence both on theological and on metaphysical speculation. Paracelsus (1493–1541), a Swiss physician and a pioneer in empirical medicine, was also a prominent theorist of the occult.

A Memorable Fancy

Once I saw a Devil in a flame of fire, who arose before an Angel that sat on a cloud, and the Devil utterd these words:

"The worship of God is, Honouring his gifts in other men, each according to his genius, and loving the [PLATE 23] greatest men best. Those who envy or calumniate great men hate God, for there is no other God."

The Angel hearing this became almost blue; but mastering himself, he grew yellow, & at last white, pink, & smiling, and then replied:

"Thou Idolater, is not God One? & is not he visible in Jesus Christ? and has not Jesus Christ given his sanction to the law of ten commandments, and are not all other men fools, sinners, & nothings?"

The Devil answer'd; "Bray a fool in a mortar with wheat, yet shall not his folly be beaten out of him.[9] If Jesus Christ is the greatest man, you ought to love him in the greatest degree. Now hear how he has given his sanction to the law of ten commandments: did he not mock at the sabbath, and so mock the sabbath's God?[1] murder those who were murderd because of him? turn away the law from the woman taken in adultery?[2] steal the labor of others to support him? bear false witness when he omitted making a defence before Pilate?[3] covet when he pray'd for his disciples, and when he bid them shake off the dust of their feet against such as refused to lodge them?[4] I tell you, no virtue can exist without breaking these ten commandments. Jesus was all virtue, and acted from im[PLATE 24]pulse, not from rules."

When he had so spoken, I beheld the Angel, who stretched out his arms embracing the flame of fire, & he was consumed and arose as Elijah.[5]

Note. This Angel, who is now become a Devil, is my particular friend; we often read the Bible together in its infernal or diabolical sense, which the world shall have if they behave well.

I have also The Bible of Hell,[6] which the world shall have whether they will or no.

One Law for the Lion & Ox is Oppression.

1790–93   1790–93

PLATE 25

A Song of Liberty[1]

1. The Eternal Female groand! it was heard over all the Earth.
2. Albion's coast is sick, silent; the American meadows faint!

---

9. Proverbs 27.22: "Though thou shouldst bray a fool in a mortar among wheat with a pestle, yet will not his foolishness depart from him." "Bray": pound into small pieces.
1. Mark 2.27: "The sabbath was made for man."
2. Cf. John 8.2–11.
3. Cf. Matthew 27.13–14.
4. Matthew 10.14: "Whosoever shall not receive you . . . when ye depart . . . shake off the dust of your feet."
5. In 2 Kings 2.11 the prophet Elijah "went up by a whirlwind into heaven," borne by "a chariot of fire."
6. I.e., the poems and designs that Blake is work-

ing on.
1. Blake etched this poem in 1792 and sometimes bound it as an appendix to The Marriage of Heaven and Hell. It recounts the birth, manifested in the contemporary events in France, of the flaming Spirit of Revolution (whom Blake later called Orc), and describes his conflict with the tyrannical sky god (whom Blake later called Urizen). The poem ends with the portent of the Spirit of Revolution shattering the ten commandments, or prohibitions against political, religious, and moral liberty, and bringing in a free and joyous new world. "Albion's" (line 2): England's.

3. Shadows of Prophecy shiver along by the lakes and the rivers and mutter across the ocean. France, rend down thy dungeon![2]

4. Golden Spain, burst the barriers of old Rome!

5. Cast thy keys, O Rome,[3] into the deep down falling, even to eternity down falling,

6. And weep.[4]

7. In her trembling hands she took the new born terror, howling.

8. On those infinite mountains of light now barr'd out by the Atlantic sea,[5] the new born fire stood before the starry king![6]

9. Flag'd with grey brow'd snows and thunderous visages, the jealous wings wav'd over the deep.

10. The speary hand burned aloft, unbuckled was the shield, forth went the hand of jealousy among the flaming hair, and [PLATE 26] hurl'd the new born wonder thro' the starry night.

11. The fire, the fire, is falling!

12. Look up! look up! O citizen of London, enlarge thy countenance! O Jew, leave counting gold! return to thy oil and wine. O African! black African! (Go, wingèd thought, widen his forehead.)

13. The fiery limbs, the flaming hair, shot like the sinking sun into the western sea.

14. Wak'd from his eternal sleep, the hoary element[7] roaring fled away:

15. Down rushd, beating his wings in vain, the jealous king; his grey brow'd councellors, thunderous warriors, curl'd veterans, among helms, and shields, and chariots, horses, elephants; banners, castles, slings and rocks,

16. Falling, rushing, ruining! buried in the ruins, on Urthona's[8] dens;

17. All night beneath the ruins; then, their sullen flames faded, emerge round the gloomy king,

18. With thunder and fire, leading his starry hosts thro' the waste wilderness [PLATE 27] he promulgates his ten commands, glancing his beamy eyelids over the deep in dark dismay,

19. Where the son of fire in his eastern cloud, while the morning plumes her golden breast,

20. Spurning the clouds written with curses, stamps the stony law[9] to dust, loosing the eternal horses from the dens of night, crying:

"Empire is no more! and now the lion & wolf shall cease."[1]

Chorus

Let the Priests of the Raven of dawn, no longer in deadly black, with hoarse note curse the sons of joy. Nor his accepted brethren, whom, tyrant, he calls

2. The political prison, the Bastille, was destroyed by the French revolutionaries in 1789.
3. The keys of Rome, a symbol of Papal power.
4. John 11.35: "Jesus wept."
5. The legendary continent of Atlantis, sunk beneath the sea, which Blake uses to represent the condition before the Fall.
6. Blake often uses the stars, in their fixed courses, as a symbol of the law-governed Newtonian universe.
7. The sea, which to Blake represents a devouring chaos, such as had swallowed Atlantis.

8. In the later Prophetic Books, Urthona is the unfallen form of Los, who in the fallen world represents the poetic imagination, the agent working for the regeneration of humanity.
9. I.e., the Ten Commandments (verse 18), which the "finger of God" had written on "tables [tablets] of stone" (Exodus 31.18).
1. Cf. Isaiah's prophecy, 65.17–25, of "new heavens and a new earth," when "The wolf and the lamb shall feed together, and the lion shall eat straw like the bullock."

free, lay the bound or build the roof. Nor pale religious letchery call that
virginity, that wishes but acts not!

For every thing that lives is Holy.

1792   1792

FROM BLAKE'S NOTEBOOK[1]

Mock on, Mock on, Voltaire, Rousseau

Mock on, Mock on, Voltaire, Rousseau;[2]
Mock on, Mock on, 'tis all in vain.
You throw the sand against the wind,
And the wind blows it back again;

5   And every sand becomes a Gem
Reflected in the beams divine;
Blown back, they blind the mocking Eye,
But still in Israel's paths they shine.

The Atoms of Democritus
10 And Newton's Particles of light[3]
Are sands upon the Red sea shore,
Where Israel's tents do shine so bright.

Never pain to tell thy love

Never pain to tell thy love
Love that never told can be,
For the gentle wind does move
Silently, invisibly.

5   I told my love, I told my love,
I told her all my heart,
Trembling, cold, in ghastly fears—
Ah, she doth depart.

Soon as she was gone from me
10 A traveller came by
Silently, invisibly—
O, was no deny.

1. A commonplace book in which Blake drew
sketches and jotted down verses and memoranda
between the late 1780s and 1810. It is known as
the Rossetti manuscript because it later came into
the possession of the poet and painter Dante
Gabriel Rossetti. These poems were first published
in imperfect form in 1863, then transcribed from
the manuscript by Geoffrey Keynes in 1935.

2. Blake regards both Voltaire and Rousseau as
representing rationalism and Deism.
3. Newton in his Opticks hypothesized that light
consisted of minute material particles. Democritus
(460–362 B.C.E.) proposed that atoms were the
ultimate components of the universe.

I askèd a thief

I askèd a thief to steal me a peach,
He turned up his eyes;
I ask'd a lithe lady to lie her down,
Holy & meek she cries.

5 As soon as I went
An angel came.
He wink'd at the thief
And smild at the dame—

And without one word said
10 Had a peach from the tree
And still as a maid
Enjoy'd the lady.

1796

And did those feet[1]

And did those feet in ancient time
Walk upon England's mountains green?
And was the holy Lamb of God
On England's pleasant pastures seen?

5 And did the Countenance Divine
Shine forth upon our clouded hills?
And was Jerusalem builded here,
Among those dark Satanic Mills?[2]

Bring me my Bow of burning gold,
10 Bring me my Arrows of desire,
Bring me my Spear; O clouds unfold!
Bring me my Chariot of fire!

I will not cease from Mental Fight,
Nor shall my Sword sleep in my hand,

1. These quatrains occur in the preface to Blake's prophetic poem *Milton*. There is an ancient belief, still current in parts of England, that Jesus came to England with Joseph of Arimathea. Blake adapts the legend to his own conception of a spiritual Israel, in which the significance of biblical events is as relevant to England as to Palestine. By a particularly Blakean irony, this poem of mental war in the service of apocalyptic desire is widely used as a hymn by those of us whom Blake called "angels."
2. There may be an allusion here to industrial England, but the mill is primarily Blake's symbol for a mechanistic and utilitarian worldview, according to which, as he said elsewhere, "the same dull round, even of a universe" becomes "a mill with complicated wheels."

15   Till we have built Jerusalem
     In England's green & pleasant Land.
ca. 1804–10   ca. 1804–10

From A Vision of the Last Judgment[1]

For the Year 1810
Additions to Blake's Catalogue of Pictures &c

The Last Judgment [will be] when all those are Cast away who trouble
Religion with Questions concerning Good & Evil or Eating of the Tree of
those Knowledges or Reasonings which hinder the Vision of God turning all
into a Consuming fire. When Imaginative Art & Science & all Intellectual
Gifts, all the Gifts of the Holy Ghost, are lookd upon as of no use & only
Contention remains to Man, then the Last Judgment begins, & its Vision is
seen by the Imaginative Eye of Every one according to the situation he holds.

[PAGE 68] The Last Judgment is not Fable or Allegory but Vision. Fable
or Allegory are a totally distinct & inferior kind of Poetry. Vision, or Imagination, is a Representation of what Eternally Exists, Really & Unchangeably.
Fable or Allegory is Formd by the daughters of Memory. Imagination is Surrounded by the daughters of Inspiration, who in the aggregate are calld Jerusalem. [PAGE 69] Fable is Allegory, but what Critics call The Fable is Vision
itself. [PAGE 68] The Hebrew Bible & the Gospel of Jesus are not Allegory,
but Eternal Vision, or Imagination of All that Exists. Note here that Fable
or Allegory is Seldom without some Vision. Pilgrim's Progress is full of it, the
Greek Poets the same; but Allegory & Vision ought to be known as Two
Distinct Things, & so calld for the Sake of Eternal Life. Plato has made
Socrates say that Poets & Prophets do not know or Understand what they
write or Utter; this is a most Pernicious Falshood. If they do not, pray is an
inferior Kind to be calld Knowing? Plato confutes himself.[2]

The Last Judgment is one of these Stupendous Visions. I have represented
it as I saw it. To different People it appears differently, as [PAGE 69] every
thing else does; for tho on Earth things seem Permanent, they are less permanent than a Shadow, as we all know too well.

The Nature of Visionary Fancy, or Imagination, is very little Known, & the
Eternal nature & permanence of its ever Existent Images is considered as
less permanent than the things of Vegetative & Generative Nature; yet the
Oak dies as well as the Lettuce, but Its Eternal Image & Individuality never
dies, but renews by its seed. Just so the Imaginative Image returns by the
seed of Contemplative Thought. The Writings of the Prophets illustrate these
conceptions of the Visionary Fancy by their various sublime & Divine Images
as seen in the Worlds of Vision. * * *

1. In this essay Blake describes and comments on
his painting of the Last Judgment, now lost, which
is said to have measured seven by five feet and to
have included a thousand figures. The text has
been transcribed and rearranged, as the sequence
of the pages indicates, from the scattered fragments in Blake's Notebook. The opening and closing parts are reprinted here as Blake's fullest,
although cryptic, statements of what he means by
"vision." These sections deal with the relations of
imaginative vision to allegory, Greek fable, and the
biblical story; to uncurbed human passion and

intellectual power; to conventional and coercive
virtue; to what is seen by the "corporeal" eye; to
the arts; and to the Last Judgment and the apocalyptic redemption of humanity and of the created
world—an apocalypse that is to be achieved
through the triumph over the bodily eye by human
imagination, as manifested in the creative artist.
2. In Plato's dialogue Ion, in which Socrates traps
Ion into admitting that, because poets compose by
inspiration, they do so without knowing what they
are doing.

Let it here be Noted that the Greek Fables originated in Spiritual Mystery [PAGE 72] & Real Visions, Which are lost & clouded in Fable & Allegory, while the Hebrew Bible & the Greek Gospel are Genuine, Preservd by the Saviour's Mercy. The Nature of my Work is Visionary or Imaginative; it is an Endeavour to Restore what the Ancients calld the Golden Age.

[PAGE 69] This world of Imagination is the World of Eternity; it is the Divine bosom into which we shall all go after the death of the Vegetated body. This World of Imagination is Infinite & Eternal, whereas the world of Generation, or Vegetation, is Finite & Temporal. There Exist in that Eternal World the Permanent Realities of Every Thing which we see reflected in this Vegetable Glass of Nature.

All Things are comprehended in their Eternal Forms in the Divine [PAGE 70] body of the Saviour, the True Vine of Eternity, The Human Imagination, who appeard to Me as Coming to Judgment among his Saints & throwing off the Temporal that the Eternal might be Establishd. Around him were seen the Images of Existences according to a certain order suited to my Imaginative Eye. * * *

[PAGE 87] Men are admitted into Heaven not because they have curbed & governd their Passions, or have No Passions, but because they have Cultivated their Understandings. The Treasures of Heaven are not Negations of Passion, but Realities of Intellect from which All the Passions Emanate Uncurbed in their Eternal Glory. The Fool shall not enter into Heaven, let him be ever so Holy. Holiness is not The price of Enterance into Heaven. Those who are cast out Are All Those who, having no Passions of their own because No Intellect, Have spent their lives in Curbing & Governing other People's by the Various arts of Poverty & Cruelty of all kinds. Wo Wo Wo to you Hypocrites! Even Murder the Courts of Justice, more merciful than the Church, are compelld to allow, is not done in Passion but in Cool Blooded Design & Intention.

The Modern Church Crucifies Christ with the Head Downwards.

[PAGE 92] Many persons such as Paine & Voltaire,[3] with some of the Ancient Greeks, say: "We will not converse concerning Good & Evil; we will live in Paradise & Liberty." You may do so in Spirit, but not in the Mortal Body as you pretend, till after the last Judgment; for in Paradise they have no Corporeal & Mortal Body—that originated with the Fall & was calld Death & cannot be removed but by a Last Judgment; while we are in the world of Mortality we Must Suffer. The Whole Creation Groans to be deliverd; there will always be as many Hypocrites born as Honest Men & they will always have superior Power in Mortal Things. You cannot have Liberty in this World without what you call Moral Virtue, & you cannot have Moral Virtue without the Slavery of that half of the Human Race who hate what you call Moral Virtue.

*　　*　　*

Thinking as I do that the Creator of this World is a very Cruel Being, & being a Worshipper of Christ, I cannot help saying: "The Son, O how unlike

---

3. Blake represents Thomas Paine, author of *The Rights of Man* (1791), and Voltaire, the great author of the French Enlightenment, as proponents of the possibility of restoring an earthly paradise by political revolution. Such had been Blake's own view in the early 1790s (see, e.g., *The Marriage of Heaven and Hell*, p. 72).

the Father!" First God Almighty comes with a Thump on the Head. Then Jesus Christ comes with a balm to heal it.

The Last Judgment is an Overwhelming of Bad Art & Science. Mental Things are alone Real; what is Calld Corporeal Nobody Knows of its dwelling Place; it is in Fallacy & its Existence an Imposture. Where is the Existence Out of Mind or Thought? Where is it but in the Mind of a Fool? Some People flatter themselves that there will be No Last Judgment, & [PAGE 95] that Bad Art will be adopted & mixed with Good Art, That Error or Experiment will make a Part of Truth, & they Boast that it is its Foundation. These People flatter themselves; I will not Flatter them. Error is Created; Truth is Eternal. Error or Creation will be Burned Up, & then & not till then Truth or Eternity will appear. It is Burnt up the Moment Men cease to behold it. I assert for My self that I do not behold the Outward Creation & that to me it is hindrance & not Action; it is as the Dirt upon my feet, No part of Me. "What," it will be Questioned, "When the Sun rises, do you not see a round Disk of fire somewhat like a Guinea?" O no no, I see an Innumerable company of the Heavenly host crying "Holy Holy Holy is the Lord God Almighty." I question not my Corporeal or Vegetative Eye any more than I would Question a Window concerning a Sight: I look thro it & not with it.

1810   1810

Two Letters on Sight and Vision[1]

To Dr. John Trusler (Aug. 23, 1799)

Revd Sir

I really am sorry that you are falln out with the Spiritual World, Especially if I should have to answer for it. I feel very sorry that your Ideas & Mine on Moral Painting differ so much as to have made you angry with my method of Study. If I am wrong, I am wrong in good company. I had hoped your plan comprehended All Species of this Art, & Especially that you would not regret that Species which gives Existence to Every other, namely Visions of Eternity. You say that I want somebody to Elucidate my Ideas. But you ought to know that What is Grand is necessarily obscure to Weak men. That which can be made Explicit to the Idiot is not worth my care. The wisest of the Ancients considerd what is not too Explicit as the fittest for Instruction, because it rouzes the faculties to act. I name Moses, Solomon, Esop, Homer, Plato.

But as you have favored me with your remarks on my Design, permit me in return to defend it against a mistaken one, which is, That I have supposed Malevolence without a Cause.[2]—Is not Merit in one a Cause of Envy in

1. Blake wrote these pronouncements about the difference between "corporeal" sight and imaginative vision at times when a friend, a patron, or the need for money was putting pressure on him to turn from his visionary art to more fashionable modes of representation. The first letter is a passionate response to John Trusler (1735–1820), clergyman and author, who had objected to some of Blake's visionary art.

2. Blake had made a watercolor drawing (which has survived) illustrating Malevolence. He described this design in an earlier letter: "A Father, taking leave of his Wife & Child, Is watch'd by two Fiends incarnate, with intention that when his back is turned they will murder the mother & her infant."

another, & Serenity & Happiness & Beauty a Cause of Malevolence? But Want of Money & the Distress of A Thief can never be alleged as the Cause of his Thievery, for many honest people endure greater hardships with Fortitude. We must therefore seek the Cause elsewhere than in want of Money, for that is the Miser's passion, not the Thief's.

I have therefore proved your Reasonings Ill proportioned, which you can never prove my figures to be. They are those of Michael Angelo, Rafael, & the Antique, & of the best living Models. I perceive that your Eye is perverted by Caricature Prints, which ought not to abound so much as they do. Fun I love, but too much Fun is of all things the most loathsom. Mirth is better than Fun, & Happiness is better than Mirth—I feel that a Man may be happy in This World. And I know that This World Is a World of Imagination & Vision. I see Every thing I paint In This World, but Every body does not see alike. To the Eyes of a Miser a Guinea is more beautiful than the Sun, & a bag worn with the use of Money has more beautiful proportions than a Vine filled with Grapes. The tree which moves some to tears of joy is in the Eyes of others only a Green thing that stands in the way. Some See Nature all Ridicule & Deformity, & by these I shall not regulate my proportions; & Some Scarce see Nature at all. But to the Eyes of the Man of Imagination Nature is Imagination itself. As a man is, So he Sees. As the Eye is formed, such are its Powers. You certainly Mistake when you say that the Visions of Fancy are not to be found in This World. To Me This World is all One continued Vision of Fancy or Imagination, & I feel Flatterd when I am told So. What is it sets Homer, Virgil, & Milton in so high a rank of Art? Why is the Bible more Entertaining & Instructive than any other book? Is it not because they are addressed to the Imagination, which is Spiritual Sensation, & but mediately to the Understanding or Reason? Such is True Painting, and such was alone valued by the Greeks & the best modern Artists. Consider what Lord Bacon says, "Sense sends over to Imagination before Reason have judged, & Reason sends over to Imagination before the Decree can be acted." See Advancem^t of Learning, Part 2, P. 47 of first Edition.

But I am happy to find a Great Majority of Fellow Mortals who can Elucidate My Visions, & Particularly they have been Elucidated by Children, who have taken a greater delight in contemplating my Pictures than I even hoped. Neither Youth nor Childhood is Folly or Incapacity. Some Children are Fools, & so are some Old Men. But There is a vast Majority on the side of Imagination or Spiritual Sensation.

To Engrave after another Painter is infinitely more laborious than to Engrave one's own Inventions. And of the Size you require my price has been Thirty Guineas, & I cannot afford to do it for less. I had Twelve for the Head I sent you as a Specimen; but after my own designs, I could do at least Six times the quantity of labour in the same time, which will account for the difference of price, as also that Chalk Engraving is at least six times as laborious as Aqua tinta. I have no objection to Engraving after another Artist. Engraving is the profession I was apprenticed to, & should never have attempted to live by any thing else, If orders had not come in for my Designs & Paintings, which I have the pleasure to tell you are Increasing Every Day. Thus If I am a Painter, it is not to be attributed to Seeking after. But I am contented whether I live by Painting or Engraving.

I am Revd Sir Your very obedient servant,

William Blake

To George Cumberland[3] (Apr. 12, 1827)

Dear Cumberland

I have been very near the Gates of Death & have returned very weak & an Old Man feeble & tottering, but not in Spirit & Life not in The Real Man The Imagination which Liveth for Ever. In that I am stronger & stronger as this Foolish Body decays. I thank you for the Pains you have taken with Poor Job.[4] I know too well that a great majority of Englishmen are fond of The Indefinite, which they Measure by Newton's Doctrine of the Fluxions of an Atom,[5] a Thing that does not Exist. These are Politicians & think that Republican Art[6] is Inimical to their Atom. For a Line or Lineament is not formed by Chance; a Line is a Line in its Minutest Subdivision[s]; Strait or Crooked, It is Itself, & Not Intermeasurable with or by any Thing Else. Such is Job, but since the French Revolution Englishmen are all Intermeasurable One by Another; Certainly a happy state of Agreement, to which I for One do not Agree. God keep me from the Divinity of Yes & No too, The Yea Nay Creeping Jesus, from supposing Up & Down to be the same Thing, as all Experimentalists must suppose.

You are desirous, I know, to dispose of some of my Works & to make [them] Pleasing. I am obliged to you & to all who do so. But having none remaining of all that I had Printed, I cannot Print more Except at a great loss, for at the time I printed those things I had a whole House to range in; now I am shut up in a Corner, therefore am forced to ask a Price for them that I scarce expect to get from a Stranger. I am now Printing a Set of the Songs of Innocence & Experience for a Friend at Ten Guineas, which I cannot do under Six Months consistent with my other Work, so that I have little hope of doing any more of such things. The Last Work I produced is a Poem Entitled "Jerusalem the Emanation of the Giant Albion," but find that to Print it will Cost my Time the amount of Twenty Guineas. One I have Finishd; it contains 100 Plates but it is not likely that I shall get a Customer for it.[7]

As you wish me to send you a list with the Prices of these things they are as follows:

	£	s	d
America	6.	6.	0
Europe	6.	6.	0
Visions &^c	5.	5.	0
Thel	3.	3.	0
Songs of Inn. & Exp.	10.	10.	0
Urizen	6.	6.	0

3. A businessman who was an old and loyal friend of Blake and a buyer of his illuminated books. Blake wrote this letter only four months before he died on Aug. 4, 1827.
4. Cumberland was trying to interest his friends in buying a set of Blake's engravings, *Illustrations of the Book of Job.*
5. Isaac Newton's *Method of Fluxions* (1704)

announced his discovery of the infinitesimal calculus. To Blake, Newton was the archrepresentative of materialist philosophy.
6. I.e., a free art, not subject to authoritarian control.
7. This single colored copy of Blake's *Jerusalem* survives in the Mellon Collection.

The Little Card[8] I will do as soon as Possible, but when you Consider that I have been reduced to a Skeleton, from which I am slowly recovering, you will I hope have Patience with me.

Flaxman[9] is Gone & we must All soon follow, every one to his Own Eternal House, Leaving the Delusive Goddess Nature & her Laws to get into Freedom from all Law of the Members into The Mind, in which every one is King & Priest in his own House. God Send it so on Earth as it is in Heaven.

I am, Dear Sir, Yours Affectionately

WILLIAM BLAKE

8. A small illustrated name card that Blake executed for Cumberland; it was his last engraving.

9. John Flaxman, a well-known sculptor of the time, had died the preceding December.

MARY ROBINSON
1758–1800

Among poets of the Romantic period, Mary Robinson, whom the *Dictionary of National Biography,* at the beginning of a long entry, describes as "actress, author, and mistress of George, Prince of Wales (afterwards George IV)," lived a more sensational life than either Byron or Shelley. Her father was a Bristol whaler, her mother a woman of "genteel background" who, after her husband deserted the family, ran a school for girls. At fifteen Mary was married to Thomas Robinson, an articled law clerk who seemed a good match but quickly proved a gambler and libertine; he was arrested for debt, and Mary and her infant daughter spent a year with him in debtors' prison, where, to pass the time, she began writing poetry. Her first pieces appeared in a two-volume *Poems* published under the patronage of the duchess of Devonshire in 1775.

In December 1776, accepting a long-standing invitation of David Garrick, the actor-manager of the Drury Lane theater, Robinson made her stage debut as Juliet, and for the next four years she was constantly before the public—in thirty or more leading roles, nine of them in plays by Shakespeare (she once acted Lady Macbeth on a night when she was advertised for Cordelia in *King Lear*). A remarkable beauty, she attracted many suitors and was painted by the leading portraitists of the day, including George Romney; Thomas Gainsborough; and Sir Joshua Reynolds, president of the Royal Academy. At a command performance of *The Winter's Tale* in December 1779, playing the role of Perdita, Robinson captivated the prince of Wales and, after negotiating financial compensation in the form of a £20,000 bond (because she would have to give up her acting career), became his mistress. When he abandoned her a year later, she was unsuccessful in suing for the £20,000 but subsequently was granted a pension of £500 per year through the efforts of the Whig parliamentarian and foreign minister Charles James Fox, another of her lovers. At twenty-five she formed an attachment with an army officer, Colonel Banastre Tarleton, that lasted for ten years but ended, again, in abandonment, with the additional complication that she was in increasingly poor health and, from a miscarriage (in some accounts) or rheumatic fever (in others), was paralyzed from the waist down. Even then she made a striking public figure, as four liveried servants, covering their arms with long white sleeves, bore her from the opera house to her waiting carriage.

She took up writing as a principal activity at the beginning of the 1790s, her final decade, when she was in her early thirties.

Scholars are just now sorting out her various productions in poetry, fiction, drama, and other forms. She published long poems and further collections of verse in 1777, 1791, 1793, 1796 (*Sappho and Phaon,* a series of Petrarchan sonnets), and 1800 (*Lyrical Tales,* a collection on the principles of Wordsworth and Coleridge's 1798 *Lyrical Ballads*), and numerous separate pieces under a dozen different pseudonyms in the magazines and newspapers, including the *Morning Post,* where she succeeded Robert Southey as poetry editor. She authored seven multivolume novels in the 1790s, beginning with *Vancenza; or, The Dangers of Credulity* (1792), whose first edition sold out in a single day. In drama, she wrote a farce that was never published and a five-act tragedy that was published but never performed. Other writings include pamphlets titled *Impartial Reflections on the Present Situation of the Queen of France* (1793) and *Thoughts on the Condition of Women, and on the Injustice of Mental Subordination* (1799). Her posthumous *Memoirs* (1801), an extremely lively autobiography in a period seemingly dominated by male self-construction, went through many editions in several languages.

Robinson is one of the accomplished writers of blank verse in the 1790s (as in *London's Summer Morning*) as well as one of the most irrepressibly musical in many different forms of rhyme. Outspokenly liberal in her politics and social views, good-humored, satirical, and sentimental by turns, she is one of the voices of what Stuart Curran calls "the new realism that will impel English poetry into the nineteenth century." Her *Lyrical Tales* appeared a month before the second edition of Wordsworth and Coleridge's *Lyrical Ballads*—from the same publisher and printer and in exactly the same format and typography (Wordsworth, in reaction, tried to change his own title to *Poems by W. Wordsworth*). Robinson's *The Poor Singing Dame* is modeled on the most popular of Wordsworth's 1798 ballads, *Goody Blake and Harry Gill.* Wordsworth in turn based one of his pieces (*The Seven Sisters; or, The Solitude of Binnorie*) on the elaborate metrical scheme of Robinson's *The Haunted Beach,* a poem that prompted Coleridge to exclaim to Southey, when he first saw it in the *Morning Post,* "the Metre—ay! that Woman has an Ear." Coleridge admired her "undoubted Genius," and Robinson returned the compliment in one of her last poems, *To the Poet Coleridge,* a shrewd reading of *Kubla Khan* sixteen years before it first got into print.

London's Summer Morning

Who has not wak'd to list the busy sounds
Of summer's morning, in the sultry smoke
Of noisy London? On the pavement hot
The sooty chimney-boy, with dingy face
5   And tatter'd covering, shrilly bawls his trade,
Rousing the sleepy housemaid. At the door
The milk-pail rattles, and the tinkling bell
Proclaims the dustman's office; while the street
Is lost in clouds impervious. Now begins
10   The din of hackney-coaches, waggons, carts;
While tinmen's shops, and noisy trunk-makers,
Knife-grinders, coopers, squeaking cork-cutters,
Fruit-barrows, and the hunger-giving cries
Of vegetable venders, fill the air.
15   Now ev'ry shop displays its varied trade,
And the fresh-sprinkled pavement cools the feet

Of early walkers. At the private door
The ruddy housemaid twirls the busy mop,
Annoying the smart 'prentice, or neat girl,
20   Tripping with band-box[1] lightly. Now the sun
Darts burning splendor on the glitt'ring pane,
Save where the canvas awning throws a shade
On the gay merchandise. Now, spruce and trim,
In shops (where beauty smiles with industry)
25   Sits the smart damsel; while the passenger
Peeps through the window, watching ev'ry charm.
Now pastry dainties catch the eye minute
Of humming insects, while the limy snare
Waits to enthral them. Now the lamp-lighter
30   Mounts the tall ladder, nimbly venturous,
To trim the half-fill'd lamp; while at his feet
The pot-boy[2] yells discordant! All along
The sultry pavement, the old-clothes-man cries
In tone monotonous, and side-long views
35   The area for his traffic: now the bag
Is slily open'd, and the half-worn suit
(Sometimes the pilfer'd treasure of the base
Domestic spoiler), for one half its worth,
Sinks in the green abyss. The porter now
40   Bears his huge load along the burning way;
And the poor poet wakes from busy dreams,
To paint the summer morning.

ca. 1795   1804

January, 1795

Pavement slipp'ry, people sneezing,
Lords in ermine, beggars freezing;
Titled gluttons dainties carving,
Genius in a garret starving.

5   Lofty mansions, warm and spacious;
Courtiers cringing and voracious;
Misers scarce the wretched heeding;
Gallant soldiers fighting, bleeding.

Wives who laugh at passive spouses;
10   Theatres, and meeting-houses;
Balls, where simp'ring misses languish;
Hospitals, and groans of anguish.

Arts and sciences bewailing;
Commerce drooping, credit failing;
15   Placemen° mocking subjects loyal;   *political appointees*
Separations, weddings royal.

---

1. Box for hats, gloves, etc.   2. Servant from a nearby pub.

Authors who can't earn a dinner;
Many a subtle rogue a winner;
Fugitives for shelter seeking;
20   Misers hoarding, tradesmen breaking.

Taste and talents quite deserted;
All the laws of truth perverted;
Arrogance o'er merit soaring;
Merit silently deploring.

25   Ladies gambling night and morning;
Fools the works of genius scorning;
Ancient dames for girls mistaken,
Youthful damsels quite forsaken.

Some in luxury delighting;
30   More in talking than in fighting;
Lovers old, and beaux decrepid;
Lordlings empty and insipid.

Poets, painters, and musicians;
Lawyers, doctors, politicians:
35   Pamphlets, newspapers, and odes,
Seeking fame by diff'rent roads.

Gallant souls with empty purses;
Gen'rals only fit for nurses;
School-boys, smit with martial spirit,
40   Taking place of vet'ran merit.

Honest men who can't get places,
Knaves who shew unblushing faces;
Ruin hasten'd, peace retarded;
Candor spurn'd, and art rewarded.

1795   1806

The Poor Singing Dame

Beneath an old wall, that went round an old castle,
   For many a year, with brown ivy o'erspread,
A neat little hovel, its lowly roof raising,
   Defied the wild winds that howl'd over its shed:
5 The turrets, that frown'd on the poor simple dwelling,
   Were rock'd to and fro, when the tempest would roar,
And the river, that down the rich valley was swelling,
   Flow'd swiftly beside the green step of its door.

The summer sun gilded the rushy roof slanting,
10   The bright dews bespangled its ivy-bound hedge,
And above, on the ramparts, the sweet birds were chanting,
   And wild buds thick dappled the clear river's edge.

When the castle's rich chambers were haunted and dreary,
   The poor little hovel was still and secure;
15 And no robber e'er enter'd, nor goblin nor fairy,
   For the splendors of pride had no charms to allure.

The Lord of the castle, a proud surly ruler,
   Oft heard the low dwelling with sweet music ring,
For the old Dame that liv'd in the little hut cheerly,
20   Would sit at her wheel, and would merrily sing:
When with revels the castle's great hall was resounding,
   The old Dame was sleeping, not dreaming of fear;
And when over the mountains the huntsmen were bounding
   She would open her lattice, their clamors to hear.

25 To the merry-ton'd horn she would dance on the threshold,
   And louder, and louder, repeat her old song:
And when winter its mantle of frost was displaying,
   She caroll'd, undaunted, the bare woods among:
She would gather dry fern, ever happy and singing,
30   With her cake of brown bread, and her jug of brown beer,
And would smile when she heard the great castle-bell ringing,
   Inviting the proud—to their prodigal cheer.

Thus she liv'd, ever patient and ever contented,
   Till envy the Lord of the castle possess'd,
35 For he hated that poverty should be so cheerful,
   While care could the fav'rites of fortune molest;
He sent his bold yeomen with threats to prevent her,
   And still would she carol her sweet roundelay;
At last, an old steward relentless he sent her—
40   Who bore her, all trembling, to prison away!

Three weeks did she languish, then died broken-hearted,
   Poor Dame! how the death-bell did mournfully sound!
And along the green path six young bachelors bore her,
   And laid her for ever beneath the cold ground!
45 And the primroses pale 'mid the long grass were growing,
   The bright dews of twilight bespangled her grave,
And morn heard the breezes of summer soft blowing
   To bid the fresh flow'rets in sympathy wave.

The Lord of the castle, from that fatal moment
50   When poor singing Mary was laid in her grave,
Each night was surrounded by screech-owls appalling,
   Which o'er the black turrets their pinions would wave!
On the ramparts that frown'd on the river, swift flowing,
   They hover'd, still hooting a terrible song,
55 When his windows would rattle, the winter blast blowing,
   They would shriek like a ghost, the dark alleys among!

Wherever he wander'd they follow'd him crying,
   At dawnlight, at eve, still they haunted his way!
When the moon shone across the wide common they hooted,

60   Nor quitted his path till the blazing of day.
        His bones began wasting, his flesh was decaying,
            And he hung his proud head, and he perish'd with shame;
        And the tomb of rich marble, no soft tear displaying,
            O'ershadows the grave of the Poor Singing Dame!

1799–1800   1800

The Haunted Beach

        Upon a lonely desert Beach,
            Where the white foam was scatter'd,
        A little shed uprear'd its head,
            Though lofty barks° were shatter'd.   *ships*
    5   The sea-weeds gath'ring near the door
            A somber path display'd;
        And, all around, the deaf'ning roar
        Re-echo'd on the chalky shore,
            By the green billows made.

    10 Above a jutting cliff was seen
            Where Sea Birds hover'd, craving;
        And all around the craggs were bound
            With weeds—for ever waving.
        And here and there, a cavern wide
    15   Its shad'wy jaws display'd;
        And near the sands, at ebb of tide,
        A shiver'd mast was seen to ride
            Where the green billows stray'd.

        And often, while the moaning wind
    20   Stole o'er the Summer Ocean,
        The moonlight scene was all serene,
            The waters scarce in motion;
        Then, while the smoothly slanting sand
            The tall cliff wrapp'd in shade,
    25 The Fisherman beheld a band
        Of Spectres gliding hand in hand—
            Where the green billows play'd.

        And pale their faces were as snow,
            And sullenly they wander'd;
    30 And to the skies with hollow eyes
            They look'd as though they ponder'd.
        And sometimes, from their hammock shroud,
            They dismal howlings made,
        And while the blast blew strong and loud
    35 The clear moon mark'd the ghastly crowd,
            Where the green billows play'd!

        And then above the haunted hut
            The Curlews screaming hover'd;

And the low door, with furious roar,
40   The frothy breakers cover'd.
For in the Fisherman's lone shed
    A murder'd man was laid,
With ten wide gashes in his head,
And deep was made his sandy bed
45   Where the green billows play'd.

A shipwreck'd Mariner was he,
    Doom'd from his home to sever;
Who swore to be through wind and sea
    Firm and undaunted ever!
50   And when the wave resistless roll'd,
    About his arm he made
A packet rich of Spanish gold,
And, like a British sailor bold,
    Plung'd where the billows play'd!

55   The Spectre band, his messmates brave,
    Sunk in the yawning ocean,
While to the mast he lash'd him fast,
    And brav'd the storm's commotion.
The winter moon upon the sand
60   A silv'ry carpet made,
And mark'd the Sailor reach the land,
And mark'd his murd'rer wash his hand
    Where the green billows play'd.

And since that hour the Fisherman
65   Has toil'd and toil'd in vain;
For all the night the moony light
    Gleams on the specter'd main!
And when the skies are veil'd in gloom,
    The Murd'rer's liquid way
70   Bounds o'er the deeply yawning tomb,
And flashing fires the sands illume,
    Where the green billows play!

Full thirty years his task has been
    Day after day more weary;
75   For Heav'n design'd his guilty mind
    Should dwell on prospects dreary.
Bound by a strong and mystic chain,
    He has not pow'r to stray;
But destin'd mis'ry to sustain,
80   He wastes, in Solitude and Pain,
    A loathsome life away.

1800

To the Poet Coleridge[1]

Rapt in the visionary theme!
  Spirit divine! with thee I'll wander,
Where the blue, wavy, lucid stream,
  'Mid forest glooms, shall slow meander!
5 With thee I'll trace the circling bounds
  Of thy new Paradise extended;
And listen to the varying sounds
  Of winds, and foamy torrents blended.

Now by the source which lab'ring heaves
10 The mystic fountain, bubbling, panting,
While gossamer° its net-work weaves,   *filmy cobweb*
  Adown the blue lawn slanting!
I'll mark thy *sunny dome*, and view
  Thy *caves of ice*, thy fields of dew!
15 Thy ever-blooming mead, whose flow'r
Waves to the cold breath of the moonlight hour!
Or when the day-star, peering bright
On the grey wing of parting night;
While more than vegetating pow'r
20 Throbs grateful to the burning hour,
As summer's whisper'd sighs unfold
Her million, million buds of gold;
Then will I climb the breezy bounds,
  Of thy new Paradise extended,
25 And listen to the distant sounds
  Of winds, and foamy torrents blended!

Spirit divine! with thee I'll trace
Imagination's boundless space!
With thee, beneath thy *sunny dome*,
30 I'll listen to the minstrel's lay,
  Hymning the gradual close of day;
In *caves of ice* enchanted roam,
Where on the glitt'ring entrance plays
The moon's-beam with its silv'ry rays;
35 Or, when the glassy stream,
    That through the deep dell flows,
Flashes the noon's hot beam;
  The noon's hot beam, that midway shows
Thy flaming temple, studded o'er
40 With all Peruvia's° lustrous store!   *Peru's*
There will I trace the circling bounds
  Of thy new Paradise extended!
And listen to the awful sounds,
  Of winds, and foamy torrents blended!

45 And now I'll pause to catch the moan
  Of distant breezes, cavern-pent;

---

1. This poem is a tribute to, and running commentary on, Coleridge's *Kubla Khan*, which Robinson read in manuscript (Coleridge had drafted it in 1797 but did not publish it until 1816).

Now, ere the twilight tints are flown,
Purpling the landscape, far and wide,
On the dark promontory's side
50   I'll gather wild flow'rs, dew besprent,
And weave a crown for thee,
Genius of Heav'n-taught poesy!
While, op'ning to my wond'ring eyes,
Thou bidst a new creation rise,
55   I'll raptur'd trace the circling bounds
    Of thy rich Paradise extended,
And listen to the varying sounds
    Of winds, and foaming torrents blended.

And now, with lofty tones inviting,
60   Thy nymph, her dulcimer swift smiting,
Shall wake me in ecstatic measures!
Far, far remov'd from mortal pleasures!
    In cadence rich, in cadence strong,
Proving the wondrous witcheries of song!
65   I hear her voice! thy *sunny dome*,
Thy *caves of ice*, aloud repeat,
Vibrations, madd'ning sweet,
Calling the visionary wand'rer home.
She sings of thee, O favor'd child
70   Of *minstrelsy*, sublimely wild!
Of thee, whose soul can feel the tone
Which gives to airy dreams *a magic* all thy own!

Oct. 1800   1801

ROBERT BURNS
1759–1796

A favorite myth of later eighteenth-century primitivists was that there exist natural poets who warble their native woodnotes wild, independent of art or literary tradition. These artless poets were sought among peasants and proletarians, whose caste or rural habitation, it was thought, protected them from the artificialities of civilized life and culture. When Robert Burns published his first volume of *Poems* in 1786, he was at once hailed by the literati of Edinburgh as an instance of the natural genius, a "Heaven-taught plowman" whose poems were the spontaneous overflow of his native feelings. Burns rather enjoyed playing the role of the poet by instinct. But in fact he was a well-read (although largely self-educated) man whose quick intelligence and sensibility enabled him to make the most of limited opportunities. And although he broke clear of the contemporary conventions of decayed English neoclassicism, he did so not by instinct but as a deliberate craftsman who turned to two earlier traditions for his models. One of these was the oral tradition of Scottish folklore and folk song; the other was the highly developed literary tradition of poems written in the Scots dialect of English.

His father—William Burnes, as he spelled his name—was a God-fearing and hard-working farmer of Ayrshire, a county in southwestern Scotland, who, unable to make a go of it in a period of hard times and high rents, died in 1784 broken in body and spirit. Robert, with his brother Gilbert, was forced to do the toil of a man while still a boy and began to show signs of the heart trouble of which he was to die when only thirty-seven. Although his father had the Scottish esteem for education and saw to it that his sons attended school whenever they could, Burns's education in literature, theology, politics, and philosophy came mainly from his own reading. At the age of fifteen he fell in love, and was inspired by that event to write his first song. "Thus," he said, "with me began Love and Poesy." After he reached maturity, he cultivated assiduously both these propensities. He began a series of amorous affairs, fathering in 1785 the first of a number of illegitimate children; he also extended greatly the range and quantity of his attempts at poetry. So rapid was his development that by the time he published the Kilmarnock edition, at the age of twenty-seven, he had written all but a few of his greatest long poems.

The Kilmarnock volume (so named from the town in which it was published) is one of the most remarkable first volumes by any British poet, and it had a great and immediate success. Burns was acclaimed "Caledonia's Bard" and lionized by the intellectuals and gentlefolk when he visited Edinburgh soon after his book came out. The peasant-poet demonstrated that he could more than hold his own as a brilliant conversationalist and debater. But he was also wise enough to realize that once the novelty wore off, his eminence in this society would not endure. He had a fierce pride that was quick to resent any hint of contempt or condescension toward himself as a man of low degree. His sympathies were democratic, and he was an outspoken admirer of the republican revolutions in America and France. In religion, too, he was a radical, professing "the Religion of Sentiment and Reason" in opposition to the strict Calvinism in which he had been raised, and he offended many pious Presbyterians by his devastating satires against the rigid tenets and the moral authoritarianism of the Scottish kirk. Furthermore, his sexual irregularities were notorious, less because they were out of the common order at that time than because he flaunted them before the "unco guid"—as his biographer DeLancey Ferguson has said, "it was not so much that he was conspicuously sinful as that he sinned conspicuously." Most of Burns's friends in high station quickly fell away, and his later visits to Edinburgh did not repeat the social success of the first.

In 1788 Burns was given a commission as excise officer, or tax inspector, and he settled down with Jean Armour, a former lover, now his wife, at Ellisland, near Dumfries, combining his official duties with farming. This was the fourth farm on which Burns had worked; and when it, like the others, failed, he moved his family to the lively country town of Dumfries. Here he was fairly happy, despite recurrent illness and a chronic shortage of money. He performed his official duties efficiently and was respected by his fellow townspeople and esteemed by his superiors; he was a devoted family man and father; and he accumulated a circle of intimates to whom he could repair for conversation and conviviality. In 1787 James Johnson, an engraver, had enlisted Burns's aid in collecting Scottish folk songs for an anthology called *The Scots Musical Museum*. Burns soon became the real editor for several volumes of this work, devoting all of his free time to collecting, editing, restoring, and imitating traditional songs, and to writing verses of his own to traditional dance tunes. Almost all of his creative work during the last twelve years of his life went into the writing of songs for the *Musical Museum* and for George Thomson's *Select Collection of Original Scottish Airs*. This was for Burns a devoted labor of love and patriotism, done anonymously, for which he refused to accept any pay, although badly in need of money; and he continued the work when he was literally on his deathbed.

Burns's best poetry was written in Scots, a northern dialect of English spoken by rural people and (on other than formal occasions) by most eighteenth-century Scottish gentlefolk as well. When Burns attempted to write in standard English, the result—except in an occasional lyric such as the lucid and graceful *Afton Water*—

tended to be stilted and conventional, with the stock phrasing, sententiousness, and sentimentality of the genteel poetic tradition of his day. He is often considered a "pre-Romantic" who, anticipating Wordsworth, revived the lyric, exploited the literary forms and legends of folk culture, and wrote in the language really spoken by the common people. This reputation is based primarily on his songs. By far the major portion of the poems that Burns published under his own name are concerned with men and manners and are written in the literary forms that had been favored by earlier eighteenth-century poets; they include brilliant satire in a variety of modes, a number of fine verse epistles to friends and fellow poets, and one masterpiece of mock-heroic (or at any rate seriocomic) narrative, *Tam o' Shanter*. The claim could be supported that, next to Pope, Burns is the greatest eighteenth-century master of these literary types. Yet his writings in satire, epistle, and mock-heroic are very remote from Pope's in their heartiness and verve, no less than in their dialect and intricate stanza forms. The reason for the difference is that Burns turned for his models not to Horace and the English neoclassic tradition but to the native tradition that had been established in the golden age of Scottish poetry by Robert Henryson, William Dunbar, Gavin Douglas, and other Scottish Chaucerians of the fifteenth and sixteenth centuries. He knew this literature through his eighteenth-century Scottish predecessors, especially Allan Ramsay and Robert Fergusson, who had collected some of the old poems and written new ones based on the old models. Burns improved greatly on these predecessors, but he derived from them much that is characteristic in his literary forms, subjects, diction, and stanzas.

Burns's songs, however, are more widely known than his longer works and have in themselves been adequate to sustain his poetic reputation. He wrote over three hundred of them, in unequaled abundance and variety. In his songs he gives himself over wholeheartedly to the emotion of the moment, evoked by all the standard lyric subjects: love, drink, work, friendship, patriotism, and bawdry. His poetic character is hearty, generous, rollicking, tender, with a sympathy that encompasses humans of all types, from national heroes to tavern roarers. Burns is not only the national poet of Scotland but a song writer for all English-speaking people. Wherever in the world they may be on New Year's Eve, when, helped by drink and the reminder of their bondage to time, men and women indulge their instinct of a common humanity, they join hands and sing a song of Burns.

The texts printed here are based on *The Poems and Songs of Robert Burns*, ed. James Kinsley, 3 vols. (Oxford, 1968).

Green grow the rashes[1]

Chorus

Green grow the rashes,° O;   *rushes*
Green grow the rashes, O;
The sweetest hours that e'er I spend,
Are spent among the lasses, O.

I

There's nought but care on ev'ry han',
In ev'ry hour that passes, O:
What signifies the life o' man,
An' 'twere na for the lasses, O.
               Green grow, &c.

---

1. Burns's revision of a song long current in a number of versions, most of them bawdy.

2

5   The warly° race may riches chase,   *worldly*
      An' riches still may fly them, O;
      An' tho' at last they catch them fast,
      Their hearts can ne'er enjoy them, O.
          Green grow, &c.

3

      But gie me a canny° hour at e'en,   *quiet*
10   My arms about my Dearie, O;
      An' warly cares, an' warly men,
      May a' gae tapsalteerie,° O!   *topsy-turvy*
          Green grow, &c.

4

      For you sae douse,° ye sneer at this,   *sober*
      Ye're nought but senseless asses, O:
15   The wisest Man[2] the warl' saw,
      He dearly lov'd the lasses, O.
          Green grow, &c.

5

      Auld Nature swears, the lovely Dears
      Her noblest work she classes, O:
      Her prentice han' she try'd on man,
20   An' then she made the lasses, O.
          Green grow, &c.

1784   1787

Holy Willie's Prayer[1]

And send the Godly in a pet to pray—
                      POPE

Argument

Holy Willie was a rather oldish batchelor Elder in the parish of Mauchline, and much and justly famed for that polemical chattering which ends in tippling Orthodoxy, and for that Spiritualized Bawdry which refines to Liquorish Devotion.—In a Sessional process with a gentleman in Mauchline, a Mr. Gavin Hamilton, Holy Willie, and his priest, Father Auld, after full hearing in the Presbytry of Ayr, came off but second best; owing partly to the oratorical powers of Mr. Robt. Aiken, Mr. Hamilton's Counsel; but chiefly to Mr. Hamilton's being one of the most irreproachable and truly respectable

2. King Solomon.
1. This satire, in the form of a dramatic monologue, was inspired by one William Fisher, a self-righteous elder in the parish of Mauchline, and is directed against a basic Calvinist tenet of

the old Scottish kirk. Holy Willie assumes that he is one of a small minority, God's "elect"—in other words that he has been predestined for grace, no matter what works he does in this vale of tears. The epigraph is from *The Rape of the Lock*.

characters in the country.—On losing his Process, the Muse overheard him
at his devotions as follows—

O thou that in the heavens does dwell!
Wha, as it pleases best thysel,
Sends ane to heaven and ten to h-ll,
      A' for thy glory!
5 And no for ony gude or ill
        They've done before thee.

I bless and praise thy matchless might,
When thousands thou has left in night,
That I am here before thy sight,
10   For gifts and grace,
A burning and a shining light
        To a' this place.

What was I, or my generation,
That I should get such exaltation?
15 I, wha deserv'd most just damnation,
      For broken laws
Sax° thousand years ere my creation,   *six*
        Thro' Adam's cause!

When from my mother's womb I fell,
20 Thou might hae plunged me deep in hell,
To gnash my gooms, and weep, and wail,
      In burning lakes,
Where damned devils roar and yell
        Chain'd to their stakes.

25 Yet I am here, a chosen sample,
To shew thy grace is great and ample:
I'm here, a pillar o' thy temple
        Strong as a rock,
A guide, a ruler and example
30   To a' thy flock.

O Lord thou kens what zeal I bear,
When drinkers drink, and swearers swear,
And singin' there, and dancin' here,
      Wi' great an' sma';
35 For I am keepet by thy fear,
        Free frae them a'.

But yet—O Lord—confess I must—
At times I'm fash'd° wi' fleshly lust;   *troubled*
And sometimes too, in warldly trust
40   Vile Self gets in;
But thou remembers we are dust,
        Defil'd wi' sin.

O Lord—yestreen—thou kens—wi' Meg—
Thy pardon I sincerely beg!
45 O may't ne'er be a living plague,
   To my dishonor!
And I'll ne'er lift a lawless leg
   Again upon her.

Besides, I farther maun° avow,   *must*
50 Wi' Leezie's lass, three times—I trow°—   *believe*
But Lord, that Friday I was fou°   *drunk*
   When I cam near her;
Or else, thou kens, thy servant true
   Wad never steer° her.   *molest*

55 Maybe thou lets this fleshly thorn
Buffet thy servant e'en and morn,
Lest he o'er proud and high should turn,
   That he's sae gifted;
If sae, thy hand maun e'en be borne
60   Untill thou lift it.

Lord bless thy Chosen in this place,
For here thou has a chosen race:
But God, confound their stubborn face,
   And blast their name,
65 Wha bring thy rulers to disgrace
   And open shame.

Lord mind Gaun Hamilton's[2] deserts!
He drinks, and swears, and plays at cartes,°   *cards*
Yet has sae mony taking arts
70   Wi' Great and Sma',
Frae God's ain priest the people's hearts
   He steals awa.

And when we chasten'd him therefore,
Thou kens how he bred sic a splore,°   *disturbance*
75 And set the warld in a roar
   O' laughin at us:
Curse thou his basket and his store,
   Kail° and potatoes.   *broth*

Lord hear my earnest cry and prayer
80 Against that Presbytry of Ayr!
Thy strong right hand, Lord, make it bare
   Upon their heads!
Lord visit them, and dinna spare,
   For their misdeeds!

2. Burns's friend Gavin Hamilton, whom Holy Willie had brought up on moral charges before the Kirk Session of the Presbytery of Ayr. As Burns explains in the Argument, Hamilton was successfully defended by his counsel, Robert Aiken (referred to in line 85).

85 O Lord my God, that glib-tongu'd Aiken!
My very heart and flesh are quaking
To think how I sat, sweating, shaking,
            And piss'd wi' dread,
While Auld wi' hingin° lip gaed sneaking   *hanging*
90   And hid his head!

Lord, in thy day o'vengeance try him!
Lord visit him that did employ him!
And pass not in thy mercy by them,
            Nor hear their prayer;
95 But for thy people's sake destroy them,
            And dinna spare!

But Lord, remember me and mine
Wi' mercies temporal and divine!
That I for grace and gear° may shine,   *wealth*
100   Excell'd by nane!
And a' the glory shall be thine!
            Amen! Amen!

1789   1789

To a Mouse

On Turning Her up in Her Nest with the Plough, November, 1785[1]

Wee, sleeket,° cowran, tim'rous beastie,   *sleek*
O, what a panic's in thy breastie!
Thou need na start awa sae hasty,
            Wi' bickering brattle![2]
5 I wad be laith° to rin an' chase thee   *loath*
            Wi' murd'ring pattle!°   *plowstaff*

I'm truly sorry Man's dominion
Has broken Nature's social union,
An' justifies that ill opinion,
10   Which makes thee startle,
At me, thy poor, earth-born companion,
            An' fellow mortal!

I doubt na, whyles,° but thou may thieve;   *sometimes*
What then? poor beastie, thou maun° live!   *must*
15 A daimen-icker in a thrave[3]
            'S a sma' request:
I'll get a blessin wi' the lave,°   *remainder*
            An' never miss 't!

1. Burns's brother claimed that this poem was composed while the poet was actually holding the plow.
2. With headlong scamper.
3. An occasional ear in twenty-four sheaves.

Thy wee-bit housie, too, in ruin!
20 It's silly° wa's the win's are strewin!   *feeble*
An' naething, now, to big° a new ane,   *build*
        O' foggage° green!   *coarse grass*
An' bleak December's winds ensuin,
        Baith snell° an' keen!   *bitter*

25 Thou saw the fields laid bare an' waste,
An' weary Winter comin fast,
An' cozie here, beneath the blast,
        Thou thought to dwell,
Till crash! the cruel coulter° past   *cutter blade*
30   Out thro' thy cell.

That wee-bit heap o' leaves an' stibble°   *stubble*
Has cost thee monie a weary nibble!
Now thou 's turn'd out, for a' thy trouble,
        But° house or hald,[4]   *without*
35 To thole° the Winter's sleety dribble,   *endure*
        An' cranreuch° cauld!   *hoarfrost*

But Mousie, thou art no thy-lane,°   *not alone*
In proving foresight may be vain:
The best laid schemes o' Mice an' Men
40   Gang aft agley,[5]
An' lea'e us nought but grief an' pain,
        For promis'd joy!

Still, thou art blest, compar'd wi' me!
The present only toucheth thee:
45 But Och! I backward cast my e'e,
        On prospects drear!
An' forward tho' I canna see,
        I guess an' fear!

1785   1786

To a Louse

On Seeing One on a Lady's Bonnet at Church

Ha! whare ye gaun, ye crowlan° ferlie!°   *crawling / wonder*
Your impudence protects you sairly:°   *sorely*
I canna say but ye strunt° rarely,   *strut*
        Owre gawze and lace;
5 Tho' faith, I fear ye dine but sparely,
        On sic a place.

Ye ugly, creepan, blastet wonner,°   *wonder*
Detested, shunn'd, by saunt an' sinner,

---

4. Hold, holding (i.e., land).   5. Go oft awry.

How daur ye set your fit° upon her,   *foot*
10   Sae fine a Lady!
Gae somewhere else and seek your dinner,
      On some poor body.

Swith,° in some beggar's haffet° squattle;°   *swift / locks / sprawl*
There ye may creep, and sprawl, and sprattle,°   *struggle*
15 Wi' ither kindred, jumping cattle,
      In shoals and nations;
Whare horn nor bane[1] ne'er daur unsettle,
      Your thick plantations.

Now haud you there, ye're out o' sight,
20 Below the fatt'rels,° snug and tight,   *ribbon ends*
Na faith ye yet![2] ye'll no be right,
      Till ye've got on it,
The vera tapmost, towrin height
      O' Miss's bonnet.

25 My sooth! right bauld ye set your nose out,
As plump an' gray as onie grozet:°   *gooseberry*
O for some rank, mercurial rozet,°   *rosin*
      Or fell,° red smeddum,°   *sharp / powder*
I'd gie you sic a hearty dose o't,
30   Wad dress your droddum!°   *buttocks*

I wad na been surpriz'd to spy
You on an auld wife's flainen toy,°   *flannel cap*
Or aiblins° some bit duddie° boy,   *perhaps / ragged*
      On 's wylecoat;°   *undershirt*
35 But Miss's fine Lunardi,[3] fye!
      How daur ye do 't?

O Jenny dinna toss your head,
An' set your beauties a' abroad!°   *abroad*
Ye little ken what cursed speed
40   The blastie's° makin!   *creature's*
Thae° winks and finger-ends, I dread,   *those*
      Are notice takin!

O wad some Pow'r the giftie gie us
To see oursels as others see us!
45 It wad frae monie a blunder free us
      An' foolish notion:
What airs in dress an' gait wad lea'e us,
      And ev'n Devotion![4]

1785   1786

1. I.e., fine-tooth comb made of horn or bone ("bane").
2. Confound you!
3. A balloon-shaped bonnet, named after Vin-
cenzo Lunardi, who made a number of balloon flights in the mid-1780s.
4. I.e., even pretended piety.

Auld Lang Syne[1]

Should auld acquaintance be forgot
And never brought to mind?
Should auld acquaintance be forgot,
And auld lang syne!

Chorus

5 For auld lang syne, my jo,
For auld lang syne,
We'll tak a cup o' kindness yet
For auld lang syne.

And surely ye'll be° your pint stowp!°   *pay for / pint cup*
10 And surely I'll be mine!
And we'll tak a cup o' kindness yet,
For auld lang syne.
For auld, &c.

We twa hae run about the braes°   *slopes*
And pou'd the gowans° fine;   *daisies*
15 But we've wander'd many a weary fitt,
Sin auld lang syne.
For auld, &c.

We twa hae paidl'd in the burn°   *stream*
Frae morning sun till dine;°   *dinner, noon*
But seas between us braid° hae roar'd,   *broad*
20 Sin auld lang syne.
For auld, &c.

And there's a hand, my trusty fiere!°   *friend*
And gie's a hand o' thine!
And we'll tak a right gude-willie-waught,
For auld lang syne.
For auld, &c.

1788   1796

Afton Water[1]

Flow gently, sweet Afton, among thy green braes,°   *slopes*
Flow gently, I'll sing thee a song in thy praise;
My Mary's asleep by thy murmuring stream,
Flow gently, sweet Afton, disturb not her dream.

---

1. Long ago.   1. The Afton is a small river in Ayrshire.

5 Thou stock dove whose echo resounds thro' the glen,
Ye wild whistling blackbirds in yon thorny den,
Thou green crested lapwing thy screaming forbear,
I charge you disturb not my slumbering Fair.

How lofty, sweet Afton, thy neighbouring hills,
10 Far mark'd with the courses of clear winding rills;
There daily I wander as noon rises high,
My flocks and my Mary's sweet Cot° in my eye.   *cottage*

How pleasant thy banks and green vallies below,
Where wild in the woodlands the primroses blow;
15 There oft as mild ev'ning weeps over the lea,
The sweet scented birk° shades my Mary and me.   *birch*

Thy chrystal stream, Afton, how lovely it glides,
And winds by the cot where my Mary resides;
How wanton thy waters her snowy feet lave,
20 As gathering sweet flowerets she stems thy clear wave.

Flow gently, sweet Afton, among thy green braes,
Flow gently, sweet River, the theme of my lays;
My Mary's asleep by thy murmuring stream,
Flow gently, sweet Afton, disturb not her dream.

1789   1792

Tam o' Shanter: A Tale[1]

Of Brownyis and of Bogillis full is this buke.
GAWIN DOUGLAS.

When chapman billies[2] leave the street,
And drouthy° neebors neebors meet,   *thirsty*
As market-days are wearing late,
An' folk begin to tak the gate;°   *road*
5 While we sit bousing at the nappy,°   *strong ale*
And getting fou° and unco° happy,   *drunk / very*
We think na on the lang Scots miles,
The mosses, waters, slaps,° and styles,   *gaps (in walls)*
That lie between us and our hame,

1. This poem, written to order for a book on Scottish antiquities, is based on a witch story told about Alloway Kirk, an old ruin near Burns's house in Ayr. As a mock-heroic rendering of folk material, *Tam o' Shanter* is comparable to *The Nun's Priest's Tale* of Chaucer. Burns recognized that the poem was his most sustained and finished artistic performance; it discovers "a spice of roguish waggery" but also shows "a force of genius and a finishing polish that I despair of ever excelling." The verve and seriocomic sympathy with which Burns manages this misadventure of a confirmed tippler won Wordsworth, a water drinker, to passionate advocacy against the moralists who objected to Burns's ribaldry: "Who, but some impenetrable dunce or narrow-minded puritan in works of art, ever read without delight the picture which he has drawn of the convivial exaltation of the rustic adventurer, Tam o' Shanter? . . . I pity him who cannot perceive that, in all this, though there was no moral purpose, there is a moral effect" (*Letter to a Friend of Burns*, 1816).
2. Peddler fellows.

10   Whare sits our sulky sullen dame,
     Gathering her brows like gathering storm,
     Nursing her wrath to keep it warm.

       This truth fand° honest Tam o' Shanter,   *found*
     As he frae Ayr ae night did canter,
15   (Auld Ayr, wham ne'er a town surpasses,
     For honest men and bonny lasses).

       O Tam! hadst thou but been sae wise,
     As ta'en thy ain wife Kate's advice!
     She tauld thee weel thou was a skellum,°   *good-for-nothing*
20   A blethering,° blustering, drunken blellum;°   *chattering / babbler*
     That frae November till October,
     Ae market-day thou was nae sober;
     That ilka° melder,³ wi' the miller,   *every*
     Thou sat as lang as thou had siller;°   *silver, money*
25   That every naig° was ca'd° a shoe on,   *nag / driven*
     The smith and thee gat roaring fou on;
     That at the Lord's house, even on Sunday,
     Thou drank wi' Kirkton Jean till Monday.
     She prophesied that late or soon,
30   Thou would be found deep drown'd in Doon;
     Or catch'd wi' warlocks° in the mirk,°   *wizards / night*
     By Alloway's auld haunted kirk.

       Ah, gentle dames! it gars° me greet°   *makes / weep*
     To think how mony counsels sweet,
35   How mony lengthen'd sage advices,
     The husband frae the wife despises!

       But to our tale: Ae market-night,
     Tam had got planted unco right;
     Fast by an ingle,° bleezing° finely,   *fireplace / blazing*
40   Wi' reaming swats,° that drank divinely;   *foaming new ale*
     And at his elbow, Souter° Johnny,   *Cobbler*
     His ancient, trusty, drouthy crony;
     Tam lo'ed him like a vera brither;
     They had been fou for weeks thegither.
45   The night drave on wi' sangs and clatter;
     And ay the ale was growing better:
     The landlady and Tam grew gracious,
     Wi' favours secret, sweet, and precious:
     The Souter tauld his queerest stories;
50   The landlord's laugh was ready chorus:
     The storm without might rair° and rustle,   *roar*
     Tam did na mind the storm a whistle.

       Care, mad to see a man sae happy,
     E'en drown'd himsel amang the nappy:

3. The amount of corn processed at a single grinding.

55 As bees flee hame wi' lades o' treasure,
The minutes wing'd their way wi' pleasure:
Kings may be blest, but Tam was glorious,
O'er a' the ills o' life victorious!

But pleasures are like poppies spread,
60 You seize the flower, its bloom is shed;
Or like the snow falls in the river,
A moment white—then melts for ever;
Or like the borealis race,
That flit ere you can point their place;
65 Or like the rainbow's lovely form
Evanishing amid the storm.—
Nae man can tether time or tide;
The hour approaches Tam maun° ride;   *must*
That hour, o' night's black arch the key-stane,
70 That dreary hour, he mounts his beast in;
And sic a night he taks the road in,
As ne'er poor sinner was abroad in.

The wind blew as 'twad blawn its last;
The rattling showers rose on the blast;
75 The speedy gleams the darkness swallow'd;
Loud, deep, and lang, the thunder bellow'd:
That night, a child might understand,
The Deil had business on his hand.

Weel mounted on his gray mare, Meg,
80 A better never lifted leg,
Tam skelpit° on thro' dub° and mire,   *slapped / puddle*
Despising wind, and rain, and fire;
Whiles holding fast his gude blue bonnet;
Whiles crooning o'er some auld Scots sonnet;
85 Whiles glowring° round wi' prudent cares,   *staring*
Lest bogles° catch him unawares.   *hobgoblins*
Kirk-Alloway was drawing nigh,
Whare ghaists° and houlets° nightly cry.— *ghosts / owls*

By this time he was cross the ford,
90 Whare in the snaw, the chapman smoor'd;[4]
And past the birks° and meikle stane,° *birches / big stone*
Whare drunken Charlie brak's neck-bane;
And thro' the whins, and by the cairn,[5]
Whare hunters fand the murder'd bairn;
95 And near the thorn, aboon the well,
Where Mungo's mither hang'd hersel.—
Before him Doon pours all his floods;
The doubling storm roars thro' the woods;
The lightnings flash from pole to pole;

4. The peddler smothered.
5. Stones heaped up as a memorial. "Whins": furze (an evergreen shrub).

100 Near and more near the thunders roll:
When, glimmering thro' the groaning trees,
Kirk-Alloway seemed in a bleeze;°   *blaze*
Thro' ilka bore° the beams were glancing;   *hole*
And loud resounded mirth and dancing.—

105   Inspiring bold John Barleycorn!
What dangers thou canst make us scorn!
Wi' tippeny,[6] we fear nae evil;
Wi' usquabae,° we'll face the devil!—   *whisky*
The swats sae ream'd in Tammie's noddle,
110 Fair play, he car'd na deils a boddle.[7]
But Maggie stood right sair astonish'd,
Till, by the heel and hand admonish'd,
She ventured forward on the light;
And, vow! Tam saw an unco° sight!   *strange*
115 Warlocks and witches in a dance;
Nae cotillion brent° new frae France,   *brand*
But hornpipes, jigs, strathspeys,[8] and reels,
Put life and mettle in their heels.
A winnock-bunker° in the east,   *window seat*
120 There sat auld Nick, in shape o' beast;
A touzie tyke,° black, grim, and large,   *shaggy dog*
To gie them music was his charge:
He screw'd the pipes and gart° them skirl,°   *made / screech*
Till roof and rafters a' did dirl.°—   *rattle*
125 Coffins stood round, like open presses,
That shaw'd the dead in their last dresses;
And by some devilish cantraip° slight   *charm, trick*
Each in its cauld hand held a light.—
By which heroic Tam was able
130 To note upon the haly° table,   *holy*
A murderer's banes in gibbet airns;°   *irons*
Twa span-lang,[9] wee, unchristened bairns;
A thief, new-cutted frae a rape,°   *rope*
Wi' his last gasp his gab° did gape;   *mouth*
135 Five tomahawks, wi' blude red-rusted;
Five scymitars, wi' murder crusted;
A garter, which a babe had strangled;
A knife, a father's throat had mangled,
Whom his ain son o' life bereft;
140 The grey hairs yet stack to the heft;
Wi' mair o' horrible and awefu',
Which even to name wad be unlawfu'.

    As Tammie glowr'd, amaz'd, and curious,
The mirth and fun grew fast and furious:
145 The piper loud and louder blew;
The dancers quick and quicker flew;

---

6. Twopenny (of drink).
7. I.e., he didn't care a farthing about devils (a "boddle" is a very small copper coin).
8. Slow Highland dance.
9. Two spans long (a span is the distance from outstretched thumb to little finger).

They reel'd, they set, they cross'd, they cleekit,°   *joined hands*
Till ilka carlin° swat and reekit,   *old woman*
And coost her duddies to the wark,[1]
150 And linket° at it in her sark!°   *tripped lightly / shirt*

Now, Tam, O Tam! had thae been queans,°   *girls*
A' plump and strapping in their teens,
Their sarks, instead o' creeshie flannen,°   *greasy flannel*
Been snaw-white seventeen hunder linnen![2]
155 Thir° breeks o' mine, my only pair,   *these*
That ance were plush, o' gude blue hair,
I wad hae gi'en them off my hurdies,°   *buttocks*
For ae blink o' the bonie burdies!°   *maidens*

But wither'd beldams, auld and droll,
160 Rigwoodie° hags wad spean° a foal,   *bony / wean*
Lowping° and flinging on a crummock,°   *leaping / staff*
I wonder didna turn thy stomach.

But Tam kend what was what fu' brawlie,°   *finely*
There was ae winsome wench and wawlie°   *strapping*
165 That night enlisted in the core,°   *corps*
(Lang after kend on Carrick shore;
For mony a beast to dead she shot,
And perish'd mony a bony boat,
And shook baith meikle corn and bear,°   *barley*
170 And kept the country-side in fear:)
Her cutty° sark, o' Paisley harn,°   *short / yarn*
That while a lassie she had worn,
In longitude tho' sorely scanty,
It was her best, and she was vauntie.°—   *proud*
175 Ah! little kend thy reverend grannie,
That sark she coft° for her wee Nannie,   *bought*
Wi' twa pund Scots ('twas a' her riches),
Wad ever grac'd a dance of witches!

But here my Muse her wing maun cour;°   *lower*
180 Sic flights are far beyond her pow'r;
To sing how Nannie lap and flang,
(A souple jade she was, and strang),
And how Tam stood, like ane bewitch'd,
And thought his very een° enrich'd;   *eyes*
185 Even Satan glowr'd, and fidg'd fu' fain,[3]
And hotch'd° and blew wi' might and main: *jerked*
Till first ae caper, syne° anither,   *then*
Tam tint° his reason a' thegither,   *lost*
And roars out, 'Weel done, Cutty-sark!'
190 And in an instant all was dark:
And scarcely had he Maggie rallied,
When out the hellish legion sallied.

1. Cast off her clothes for the work.
2. Very fine linen, woven on a loom with seven-   teen hundred strips.
3. Fidgeted with pleasure.

As bees bizz out wi' angry fyke,°   *fuss*
When plundering herds° assail their byke;°   *herdsmen / hive*
195   As open° pussie's mortal foes,   *begin to bark*
When, pop! she starts before their nose;
As eager runs the market-crowd,
When 'Catch the thief!' resounds aloud;
So Maggie runs the witches follow,
200   Wi' mony an eldritch° skreech and hollow.   *unearthly*

Ah, Tam! Ah, Tam! thou'll get thy fairin'!°   *deserts*
In hell they'll roast thee like a herrin!
In vain thy Kate awaits thy comin!
Kate soon will be a woefu' woman!
205   Now, do thy speedy utmost, Meg,
And win the key-stane of the brig;°   *bridge*
There at them thou thy tail may toss,
A running stream they dare na cross.
But ere the key-stane she could make,
210   The fient a tail she had to shake!⁴
For Nannie, far before the rest,
Hard upon noble Maggie prest,
And flew at Tam wi' furious ettle;°   *intent*
But little wist she Maggie's mettle—
215   Ae spring brought off her master hale,°   *whole*
But left behind her ain gray tail:
The carlin claught° her by the rump,   *clutched*
And left poor Maggie scarce a stump.

Now, wha this tale o' truth shall read,
220   Ilk man and mother's son, take heed:
Whene'er to drink you are inclin'd,
Or cutty-sarks run in your mind,
Think, ye may buy the joys o'er dear,
Remember Tam o' Shanter's mare.

1790   1791

Robert Bruce's March to Bannockburn[1]

[SCOTS, WHA HAE]

Scots, wha hae wi' Wallace[2] bled,
Scots, wham Bruce has aften led,
Welcome to your gory bed,—
    Or to victorie.—

5   Now's the day, and now's the hour;
See the front o' battle lour;

---

4. I.e., she had no tail left at all.
1. In this best-known of Burns's patriotic songs
Robert Bruce is addressing his army before the
great victory at Bannockburn (1314), at which the

English were driven from Scotland.
2. Sir William Wallace (ca. 1272–1305), the great
Scottish warrior in the wars against the English.

See approach proud Edward's power,
    Chains and Slaverie.—

Wha will be a traitor-knave?
10 Wha can fill a coward's grave?
Wha sae base as be a Slave?
    —Let him turn and flie:—

Wha for Scotland's king and law,
Freedom's sword will strongly draw,
15 Free-man stand, or Free-man fa',
    Let him follow me.—

By Oppression's woes and pains!
By your Sons in servile chains!
We will drain our dearest veins,
20   But they *shall* be free!

Lay the proud Usurpers low!
Tyrants fall in every foe!
Liberty's in every blow!
    Let us Do—or Die!!!

1793   1794, 1815

A Red, Red Rose[1]

O my Luve's like a red, red rose,
    That's newly sprung in June;
O my Luve's like the melodie
    That's sweetly played in tune.

5 As fair art thou, my bonie lass,
    So deep in luve am I;
And I will love thee still, my Dear,
    Till a' the seas gang dry.

Till a' the seas gang dry, my Dear,
10   And the rocks melt wi' the sun:
O I will love thee still, my Dear,
    While the sands o' life shall run.

And fare thee weel, my only Luve!
    And fare thee weel, a while!
15 And I will come again, my Luve,
    Tho' it were ten thousand mile!

1794   1796

---

1. Like many of Burns's lyrics, this one incorporates elements from several current folk songs.

Song: For a' that and a' that

Is there, for honest Poverty
    That hangs his head, and a' that;
The coward-slave, we pass him by,
    We dare be poor for a' that!
5   For a' that, and a' that,
    Our toils obscure, and a' that,
The rank is but the guinea's stamp,
    The Man's the gowd° for a' that.   *gold*

What though on hamely fare we dine,
10   Wear hodden grey,[1] and a' that.
Gie fools their silks, and knaves their wine,
    A Man's a Man for a' that.
For a' that, and a' that,
    Their tinsel show, and a' that;
15   The honest man, though e'er sae poor,
    Is king o' men for a' that.

Ye see yon birkie° ca'd a lord,   *brisk young fellow*
    Wha struts, and stares, and a' that,
Though hundreds worship at his word,
20   He's but a coof° for a' that.   *dolt*
For a' that, and a' that,
    His ribband, star and a' that,
The man of independant mind,
    He looks and laughs at a' that.

25   A prince can mak a belted knight,
    A marquis, duke, and a' that;
But an honest man's aboon° his might,   *above*
    Guid faith he mauna fa' that![2]
For a' that, and a' that,
30   Their dignities, and a' that,
The pith o' Sense, and pride o' Worth,
    Are higher rank than a' that.

Then let us pray that come it may,
    As come it will for a' that,
35   That Sense and Worth, o'er a' the earth
    Shall bear the gree,[3] and a' that.
For a' that, and a' that,
    It's coming yet for a' that,
That Man to Man the warld o'er,
40   Shall brothers be for a' that.

1795   1795

---

1. A coarse cloth of undyed wool.   3. Win the prize.
2. Must not claim that.

The French Revolution and the "Spirit of the Age"

In a letter to Byron in 1816, Percy Shelley called the French Revolution "the master theme of the epoch in which we live"; and in various letters and essays, he declared that, as the result of the repercussions of the Revolution, the literature of England "has arisen as it were from a new birth," and that "the electric life that burns" within the great poets of the time expresses "less their spirit than the spirit of the age." (See, for example, the concluding paragraph of Shelley's *Defence of Poetry,* page 802.) With these judgments, many of Shelley's contemporaries concurred. Writers during Shelley's lifetime were obsessed with the possibility of a drastic and inclusive change in the human condition; and the works of a number of major Romantic poets cannot be understood, historically, without awareness of the extent to which their distinctive themes, plot forms, imagery, and modes of imagining and feeling were shaped first by the boundless promise, then by the tragedy, of the great events in neighboring France. And for a number of young poets in the early years (1789–93) the enthusiasm for the Revolution had the impetus and intensity of a religious awakening, because they interpreted the events in France in accordance with the apocalyptic prophecies in the Hebrew and Christian Scriptures; that is, they viewed these events as fulfilling the promise, guaranteed by an infallible text, that a short period of retributive and cleansing violence would usher in an era of universal peace and felicity equivalent to a restored Paradise. Even after what they considered the failure of the revolutionary promise—signaled by the execution of the king and queen, the massacres during the Reign of Terror under Robespierre, and later the wars of imperial conquest under Napoleon—these poets did not surrender their hope for a radical transformation of the political and social world. Instead, they transferred the basis of that hope from violent political revolution to an inner revolution in the moral and imaginative nature of the human race.

ENGLISH CONTROVERSY ABOUT THE REVOLUTION

The French Revolution began with the storming of the Bastille and freeing of a handful of political prisoners by an angry mob of Parisians on July 14, 1789. A month later, the new French National Assembly passed the Declaration of the Rights of Man. Six weeks after that (in early October), citizens marched to the royal palace at Versailles, just south of the city, and arrested King Louis XVI and his queen, Marie Antoinette, confining them to the Tuileries palace in Paris. These happenings were quickly reported in the London newspapers. The British liberals applauded; the radicals were ecstatic; many ordinary people were confused by the events, which seemed to promise improvement of the common lot but at the cost of toppling long-standing traditions of royalty and aristocracy.

One reaction on the English side of the Channel was the so-called war of pamphlets, initiated by Richard Price's sermon *A Discourse on the Love of Our Country*, which he delivered on November 4, 1789, a month after the imprisonment of the king and queen. The controversy accelerated in the wake of Edmund Burke's response to Price a year later, *Reflections on the Revolution in France*, which itself drew more than fifty further responses, among which the two most famous are Mary Wollstonecraft's *A Vindication of the Rights of Men* and Thomas Paine's *Rights of Man*. The works of Burke and Wollstonecraft and part 1 of Paine's *Rights* appeared in a very short span, from November 1790 to March 1791.

All four of the writers in this section are concerned with the same questions: justification of hereditary rule, ownership of property, interpretation of the English constitution, and the "rights of men"—and women—in such things as (in Price's words) "liberty of conscience in religious matters," the "right to resist power when abused," the "right to chuse our own governors; to cashier them for misconduct; and to frame a government for ourselves." But the extracts have been chosen mainly to illustrate the *tones* of the debate: celebratory in Price, congratulating himself and his audience on having lived to see "Thirty Millions of people, indignant and resolute, spurning at slavery, and demanding liberty with an irresistible voice"; blatantly sensationalist in Burke, depicting the rude treatment of the king and especially the queen, in her nightgown ("almost naked"), "forced to abandon the sanctuary of the most splendid palace in the world, which they left swimming in blood, polluted by massacre, and strewed with scattered limbs and mutilated carcases"; forthrightly contemptuous in Wollstonecraft, who describes Burke's work as "many ingenious arguments in a very specious garb"; basically pointed and plain in Paine: "I am contending for the rights of the *living*, and against their being willed away, and controuled and contracted for, by the . . . assumed authority of the dead."

RICHARD PRICE

Richard Price (1723–1791) was a Unitarian minister in London and a writer on moral philosophy, population, and the national debt, among other topics. The full title of his sermon, which prompted Burke's *Reflections* and in turn the scores of responses to Burke, is *A Discourse on the Love of Our Country, Delivered on Nov. 4, 1789, at the Meeting-House in the Old Jewry, to the Society for Commemorating the Revolution in Great Britain*. The London Revolution Society had been founded a year earlier to mark the hundredth anniversary of the "bloodless" Glorious Revolution of 1688, which ended the short reign of King James II and produced the Declaration of Right, establishing a limited monarchy and guaranteeing the civil rights of privileged classes. The first two-thirds of the extracts given here commemorate that Revolution; in the final third, beginning "What an eventful period is this!" Price greets with religious fervor "two other Revolutions, both glorious," the American and the French. The *Discourse* went through six editions in its first year of publication.

From A Discourse on the Love of Our Country

We are met to thank God for that event in this country to which the name of THE REVOLUTION has been given; and which, for more than a century, it has been usual for the friends of freedom, and more especially Protestant Dissenters, under the title of the REVOLUTION SOCIETY, to celebrate with expressions of joy and exultation. * * * By a bloodless victory, the fetters which despotism had been long preparing for us were broken; the rights of the people were asserted, a tyrant expelled, and a Sovereign of our own choice appointed in his room. Security was given to our property, and our consciences were emancipated. The bounds of free enquiry were enlarged; the volume in which are the words of eternal life, was laid more open to our examination; and that *aera* of light and liberty was introduced among us, by which we have been made an example to other kingdoms, and became the instructors of the world. Had it not been for this deliverance, the probability is, that, instead of being thus distinguished, we should now have been a base people, groaning under the infamy and misery of popery and slavery. Let us, therefore, offer thanksgivings to God, the author of all our blessings. * * *

It is well known that King James was not far from gaining his purpose; and that probably he would have succeeded, had he been less in a hurry. But he was a fool as well as a bigot. He wanted courage as well as prudence; and, therefore, fled, and left us to settle quietly for ourselves that constitution of government which is now our boast. We have particular reason, as Protestant Dissenters, to rejoice on this occasion. It was at this time we were rescued from persecution, and obtained the liberty of worshipping God in the manner we think most acceptable to him. It was then our meeting houses were opened, our worship was taken under the protection of the law, and the principles of toleration gained a triumph. We have, therefore, on this occasion, peculiar reasons for thanksgiving.—But let us remember that we ought not to satisfy ourselves with thanksgivings. Our gratitude, if genuine, will be accompanied with endeavours to give stability to the deliverance our country has obtained, and to extend and improve the happiness with which the Revolution has blest us.—Let us, in particular, take care not to forget the principles of the Revolution. This Society has, very properly, in its Reports, held out these principles, as an instruction to the public. I will only take notice of the three following:

First: The right to liberty of conscience in religious matters.

Secondly: The right to resist power when abused. And,

Thirdly: The right to chuse our own governors; to cashier them for misconduct; and to frame a government for ourselves.

* * *

I would farther direct you to remember, that though the Revolution was a great work, it was by no means a perfect work; and that all was not then gained which was necessary to put the kingdom in the secure and complete possession of the blessings of liberty.—In particular, you should recollect, that the toleration then obtained was imperfect. It included only those who could declare their faith in the doctrinal articles of the church of England. It has, indeed, been since extended, but not sufficiently; for there still exist penal laws on account of religious opinions, which (were they carried into execution) would shut up many of our places of worship, and silence and imprison some of our ablest and best men.—The TEST LAWS are also still in force; and deprive of eligibility to civil and military offices, all who cannot conform to the established worship. It is with great pleasure I find that the body of Protestant Dissenters, though defeated in two late attempts to deliver their country from this disgrace to it, have determined to persevere. Should they at last succeed, they will have the satisfaction, not only of removing from themselves a proscription they do not deserve, but of contributing to lessen the number of public iniquities. For I cannot call by a gentler name, laws which convert an ordinance appointed by our Saviour to commemorate his death, into an instrument of oppressive policy, and a qualification of rakes and atheists for civil posts.—I have said, *should* they succeed—but perhaps I ought not to suggest a doubt about their success. And, indeed, when I consider that in Scotland the established church is defended by no such test—that in Ireland it has been abolished—that in a great neighbouring country it has been declared to be an indefeasible right of all citizens to be equally eligible to public offices—that in the same kingdom a professed Dissenter from the established church holds the first office in the state—that in the Emperor's dominions *Jews* have been lately admitted to the enjoyment of equal privileges with other citizens—and that in this very country, a Dissenter, though excluded from the power of *executing* the laws, yet is allowed to be employed in *making* them.—When, I say, I consider such facts as these, I am disposed to think it impossible that the enemies of the repeal of the Test Laws should not soon become ashamed, and give up their opposition.

But the most important instance of the imperfect state in which the Revolution left our constitution, is the *inequality of our representation*. I think, indeed, this defect in our constitution so gross and so palpable, as to make it excellent chiefly in form and theory. You should remember that a representation in the legislature of a kingdom is the *basis* of constitutional liberty in it, and of all legitimate government; and that without it a government is nothing but an usurpation. When the representation is fair and equal, and at the same time vested with such powers as our House of Commons possesses, a kingdom may be said to govern itself, and consequently to possess true liberty. When the representation is partial, a kingdom possesses liberty only partially; and if extremely partial, it only gives a *semblance* of liberty; but if not only extremely partial, but corruptly chosen, and under corrupt influence after being chosen, it becomes a *nuisance*, and produces the worst of all forms of government—a government by corruption, a government carried on and supported by spreading venality and profligacy through a kingdom. May heaven preserve this kingdom from a calamity so dreadful! It is the point of depravity to which abuses under such a government as ours naturally tend, and the last stage of national unhappiness. We are, at present, I hope, at a great distance from it. But it cannot be pretended that there are no advances towards it, or that there is no reason for apprehension and alarm.

* * *

What an eventful period is this! I am thankful that I have lived to it; and I could almost say, *Lord, now lettest thou thy servant depart in peace, for mine eyes have seen thy salvation* [Luke 2.29–30]. I have lived to see a diffusion of knowledge, which has undermined superstition and error—I have lived to see the rights of men better understood than ever; and nations panting for liberty, which seemed to have lost the idea of it.—I have lived to see THIRTY MILLIONS of people, indignant and resolute, spurning at slavery, and demanding liberty with an irresistible voice; their king led in triumph, and an arbitrary monarch surrendering himself to his subjects.—After sharing in the benefits of one Revolution, I have been spared to be a witness to two other Revolutions, both glorious.——And now, methinks, I see the ardour for liberty catching and spreading; a general amendment beginning in human affairs; the dominion of kings changed for the dominion of laws, and the dominion of priests giving way to the dominion of reason and conscience.

Be encouraged, all ye friends of freedom, and writers in its defence! The times are auspicious. Your labours have not been in vain. Behold kingdoms, admonished by you, starting from sleep, breaking their fetters, and claiming justice from their oppressors! Behold, the light you have struck out, after setting *America* free, reflected to *France,* and there kindled into a blaze that lays despotism in ashes, and warms and illuminates *Europe!*

Tremble all ye oppressors of the world! Take warning all ye supporters of slavish governments, and slavish hierarchies! Call no more (absurdly and wickedly) REFORMATION, innovation. You cannot now hold the world in darkness. Struggle no longer against increasing light and liberality. Restore to mankind their rights; and consent to the correction of abuses, before they and you are destroyed together.

1789

EDMUND BURKE

The great statesman and political theorist Edmund Burke (1729–1797) read Price's *Discourse* in January 1790 and immediately began drafting his *Reflections on the Revolution in France* as a reply in the form of a letter (as the lengthy subtitle describes it) "Intended to Have Been Sent to a Gentleman in Paris." The work was published at the beginning of November and was an instant best-seller: thirteen thousand copies were purchased in the first five weeks, and by the following September it had gone through eleven editions. Clearly, part of its appeal to contemporary readers lay in the highly wrought accounts of the mob's violent treatment of the French king and queen (who at the time Burke was writing were imprisoned in Paris and would be executed three years later, in January and October 1793). *Reflections* has become the classic, most eloquent statement of British conservatism favoring monarchy, aristocracy, property, hereditary succession, and the wisdom of the ages. Earlier in his career Burke had championed many liberal causes and sided with the Americans in their war for independence; opponents and allies alike were surprised at the strength of his conviction that the French Revolution was a disaster and the revolutionists "a swinish multitude."

From Reflections on the Revolution in France

* * * All circumstances taken together, the French revolution is the most astonishing that has hitherto happened in the world. The most wonderful things are brought about in many instances by means the most absurd and ridiculous; in the most ridiculous modes; and apparently, by the most contemptible instruments. Every thing seems out of nature in this strange chaos of levity and ferocity, and of all sorts of crimes jumbled together with all sorts of follies. In viewing this monstrous tragi-comic scene, the most opposite passions necessarily succeed, and sometimes mix with each other in the mind; alternate contempt and indignation; alternate laughter and tears; alternate scorn and horror.

* * *

You will observe, that from Magna Charta to the Declaration of Right,[1] it has been the uniform policy of our constitution to claim and assert our liberties, as an *entailed inheritance* derived to us from our forefathers, and to be transmitted to our posterity; as an estate specially belonging to the people of this kingdom without any reference whatever to any other more general or prior right. By this means our constitution preserves an unity in so great a diversity of its parts. We have an inheritable crown; an inheritable peerage; and an house of commons and a people inheriting privileges, franchises, and liberties, from a long line of ancestors.

This policy appears to me to be the result of profound reflection; or rather the happy effect of following nature, which is wisdom without reflection, and above it. A spirit of innovation is generally the result of a selfish temper and confined views. People will not look forward to posterity, who never look backward to their ancestors. Besides, the people of England well know, that the idea of inheritance furnishes a sure principle of conservation, and a sure principle of transmission; without at all excluding a principle of improvement. It leaves acquisition free; but it secures what it acquires. Whatever advantages are obtained by a state proceeding on these maxims, are locked fast as in a sort of family settlement; grasped as in a kind of mortmain[2] for ever. By a constitutional policy, working after the pattern of nature, we receive, we hold, we transmit our government and our privileges, in the same manner in which we enjoy and transmit our property and our lives. The institutions of policy, the goods of fortune, the gifts of Providence, are handed down, to us and from us, in the same course and order. Our political system is placed in a just correspondence and symmetry with the order of the world, and with the mode of existence decreed to a permanent body composed of transitory parts; wherein, by the disposition of a stupendous wisdom, moulding together the great mysterious incorporation of the human race, the whole, at one time, is never old,

1. The Magna Carta, the "great charter" of English personal and political liberty, dates from 1215. The Declaration of Right, another cornerstone of the English constitution, was a product of the Glorious Revolution of 1688.
2. A legal term (literally, "dead hand") for the perpetual holding of lands by an ecclesiastical or other corporation.

or middle-aged, or young, but in a condition of unchangeable constancy, moves on through the varied tenour of perpetual decay, fall, renovation, and progression. Thus, by preserving the method of nature in the conduct of the state, in what we improve we are never wholly new; in what we retain we are never wholly obsolete. By adhering in this manner and on those principles to our forefathers, we are guided not by the superstition of antiquarians, but by the spirit of philosophic analogy. In this choice of inheritance we have given to our frame of polity the image of a relation in blood; binding up the constitution of our country with our dearest domestic ties; adopting our fundamental laws into the bosom of our family affections; keeping inseparable, and cherishing with the warmth of all their combined and mutually reflected charities, our state, our hearths, our sepulchres, and our altars.

Through the same plan of a conformity to nature in our artificial institutions, and by calling in the aid of her unerring and powerful instincts, to fortify the fallible and feeble contrivances of our reason, we have derived several other, and those no small benefits, from considering our liberties in the light of an inheritance. Always acting as if in the presence of canonized forefathers, the spirit of freedom, leading in itself to misrule and excess, is tempered with an awful gravity. This idea of a liberal descent inspires us with a sense of habitual native dignity, which prevents that upstart insolence almost inevitably adhering to and disgracing those who are the first acquirers of any distinction. By this means our liberty becomes a noble freedom. It carries an imposing and majestic aspect. It has a pedigree and illustrating ancestors. It has its bearings and its ensigns armorial. It has its gallery of portraits; its monumental inscriptions; its records, evidences, and titles. We procure reverence to our civil institutions on the principle upon which nature teaches us to revere individual men; on account of their age; and on account of those from whom they are descended. All your sophisters cannot produce any thing better adapted to preserve a rational and manly freedom than the course that we have pursued, who have chosen our nature rather than our speculations, our breasts rather than our inventions, for the great conservatories and magazines of our rights and privileges.

* * *

Far am I from denying in theory; full as far is my heart from withholding in practice (if I were of power to give or to withhold) the *real* rights of men. In denying their false claims of right, I do not mean to injure those which are real, and are such as their pretended rights would totally destroy. If civil society be made for the advantage of man, all the advantages for which it is made become his right. It is an institution of beneficence; and law itself is only beneficence acting by a rule. Men have a right to live by that rule; they have a right to justice; as between their fellows, whether their fellows are in politic function or in ordinary occupation. They have a right to the fruits of their industry; and to the means of making their industry fruitful. They have a right to the acquisitions of their parents; to the nourishment and improvement of their offspring; to instruction in life, and to consolation in death. Whatever each man can separately do, without trespassing upon others, he has a right to do for himself; and he has a right to a fair portion of all which society, with all its combinations of skill and force, can do in his favor. In this partnership all men have equal rights; but not to equal things. He that has but five shillings in the partnership, has as good a right to it, as he that has five hundred pound has to his larger proportion. But he has not a right to an equal dividend in the product of the joint stock; and as to the share of power, authority, and direction which each individual ought to have in the management of the state, that I must deny to be amongst the direct original rights of man in civil society; for I have in my contemplation the civil social man, and no other. It is a thing to be settled by convention.

* * *

* * * History, who keeps a durable record of all our acts, and exercises her awful censure over the proceedings of all sorts of sovereigns, will not forget, either those events, or the aera of this liberal refinement in the intercourse of mankind. History will record, that on the morning of the 6th of October 1789, the king and queen of France, after a day of confusion, alarm, dismay, and slaughter, lay down, under the pledged security of public faith, to indulge nature in a few hours of respite, and troubled melancholy repose. From this sleep the queen was first startled by the voice of the centinel at her door, who cried out to her, to save herself by flight— that this was the last proof of fidelity he could give—that they were upon him, and he was dead. Instantly he was cut down. A band of cruel ruffians and assassins, reeking with his blood, rushed into the chamber of the queen, and pierced with an hundred strokes of bayonets and poniards the bed, from whence this persecuted woman had but just time to fly almost naked, and through ways unknown to the murderers had escaped to seek refuge at the feet of a king and husband, not secure of his own life for a moment.

This king, to say no more of him, and this queen, and their infant children (who once would have been the pride and hope of a great and generous people) were then forced to abandon the sanctuary of the most splendid palace in the world, which they left swimming in blood, polluted by massacre, and strewed with scattered limbs and mutilated carcases. Thence they were conducted into the capital of their kingdom. Two had been selected from the unprovoked, unresisted, promiscuous slaughter, which was made of the gentlemen of birth and family who composed the king's body guard. These two gentlemen, with all the parade of an execution of justice, were cruelly and publickly dragged to the block, and beheaded in the great court of the palace. Their heads were stuck upon spears, and led the procession; whilst the royal captives who followed in the train were slowly moved along, amidst the horrid yells, and shrilling screams, and frantic dances, and infamous contumelies, and all the unutterable abominations of the furies of hell, in the abused shape of the vilest of women. After they had been made to taste, drop by drop, more than the bitterness of death, in the slow torture of a journey of twelve miles, protracted to six hours, they were, under a guard, composed of those very soldiers who had thus conducted them through this famous triumph, lodged in one of the old palaces of Paris, now converted into a Bastile for kings.

* * *

I hear that the august person, who was the principal object of our preacher's triumph,[3] though he supported himself, felt much on that shameful occasion. As a man, it became him to feel for his wife and his children, and the faithful guards of his person, that were massacred in cold blood about him; as a prince, it became him to feel for the strange and frightful transformation of his civilized subjects, and to be more grieved for them, than solicitous for himself. It derogates little from his fortitude, while it adds infinitely to the honor of his humanity. I am very sorry to say it, very sorry indeed, that such personages are in a situation in which it is not unbecoming in us to praise the virtues of the great.

I hear, and I rejoice to hear, that the great lady, the other object of the triumph, has borne that day (one is interested that beings made for suffering should suffer well) and that she bears all the succeeding days, that she bears the imprisonment of her husband, and her own captivity, and the exile of her friends, and the insulting adulation of addresses, and the whole weight of her accumulated wrongs, with a serene patience, in a manner suited to her rank and race, and becoming the offspring of a sovereign distinguished for her piety and her courage;[4] that like her she has lofty sentiments; that she feels with the dignity of a Roman matron; that in the last extremity she will save herself from the last disgrace, and that if she must fall, she will fall by no ignoble hand.

It is now sixteen or seventeen years since I saw the queen of France, then the dauphiness,[5] at Versailles; and surely never lighted on this orb, which she hardly seemed to touch, a more delightful vision. I saw her just above the horizon, decorating and cheering the elevated sphere she just began to move in,—glittering like the morning-star, full of life, and splendor, and joy. Oh! what a revolution! and what an heart must I have, to contemplate without emotion that elevation and that fall! Little did I dream when she added titles of veneration to those of enthusiastic, distant, respectful love, that she should ever be obliged to carry the sharp antidote against disgrace concealed in that bosom; little did I dream that I should have lived to see such disasters fallen upon her in a nation of gallant men, in a nation of men of honor and of cavaliers. I thought ten thousand swords must have leaped from their scabbards to avenge even a look that threatened her with insult.—But the age of chivalry is gone.—That of sophisters, oeconomists, and calculators, has succeeded; and the glory of Europe is extinguished for ever. Never, never more, shall we behold that generous loyalty to rank and sex, that proud submission, that dignified obedience, that subordination of the heart, which kept alive, even in servitude itself, the spirit of an exalted freedom. The unbought grace of life, the cheap defence of nations, the nurse of manly sentiment and heroic enterprize is gone! It is gone, that sensibility of principle, that chastity of honor, which felt a stain like a wound, which inspired

3. A reference to Price's exclamation, in the final selection printed above from A Discourse on the Love of Our Country, that he has lived to see the French "king led in triumph . . . an arbitrary monarch surrendering himself to his subjects." "August person": King Louis XVI.

4. Marie Antoinette was the daughter of Maria Theresa, empress of Austria.

5. I.e., wife of the dauphin, who was heir to the throne of France.

courage whilst it mitigated ferocity, which ennobled whatever it touched, and under which vice itself lost half its evil, by losing all its grossness.

This mixed system of opinion and sentiment had its origin in the antient chivalry; and the principle, though varied in its appearance by the varying state of human affairs, subsisted and influenced through a long succession of generations, even to the time we live in. If it should ever be totally extinguished, the loss I fear will be great. It is this which has given its character to modern Europe. It is this which has distinguished it under all its forms of government, and distinguished it to its advantage, from the states of Asia, and possibly from those states which flourished in the most brilliant periods of the antique world. It was this, which, without confounding ranks, had produced a noble equality, and handed it down through all the gradations of social life. It was this opinion which mitigated kings into companions, and raised private men to be fellows with kings. Without force, or opposition, it subdued the fierceness of pride and power; it obliged sovereigns to submit to the soft collar of social esteem, compelled stern authority to submit to elegance, and gave a domination vanquisher of laws, to be subdued by manners.

But now all is to be changed. All the pleasing illusions, which made power gentle, and obedience liberal, which harmonized the different shades of life, and which, by a bland assimilation, incorporated into politics the sentiments which beautify and soften private society, are to be dissolved by this new conquering empire of light and reason. All the decent drapery of life is to be rudely torn off. All the superadded ideas, furnished from the wardrobe of a moral imagination, which the heart owns, and the understanding ratifies, as necessary to cover the defects of our naked shivering nature, and to raise it to dignity in our own estimation, are to be exploded as a ridiculous, absurd, and antiquated fashion.

On this scheme of things, a king is but a man; a queen is but a woman; a woman is but an animal; and an animal not of the highest order. All homage paid to the sex in general as such, and without distinct views, is to be regarded as romance and folly. Regicide, and parricide, and sacrilege, are but fictions of superstition, corrupting jurisprudence by destroying its simplicity. The murder of a king, or a queen, or a bishop, or a father, are only common homicide; and if the people are by any chance, or in any way gainers by it, a sort of homicide much the most pardonable, and into which we ought not to make too severe a scrutiny.

On the scheme of this barbarous philosophy, which is the offspring of cold hearts and muddy understandings, and which is as void of solid wisdom, as it is destitute of all taste and elegance, laws are to be supported only by their own terrors, and by the concern, which each individual may find in them, from his own private speculations, or can spare to them from his own private interests. In the groves of *their* academy, at the end of every visto, you see nothing but the gallows. Nothing is left which engages the affections on the part of the commonwealth. On the principles of this mechanic philosophy, our institutions can never be embodied, if I may use the expression, in persons; so as to create in us love, veneration, admiration, or attachment. But that sort of reason which banishes the affections is incapable of filling their place. These public affections, combined with manners, are required sometimes as supplements, sometimes as correctives, always as aids to law. The precept given by a wise man, as well as a great critic, for the construction of poems, is equally true as to states. *Non satis est pulchra esse poemata, dulcia sunto.*[6] There ought to be a system of manners in every nation which a well-formed mind would be disposed to relish. To make us love our country, our country ought to be lovely.

But power, of some kind or other, will survive the shock in which manners and opinions perish; and it will find other and worse means for its support. The usurpation which, in order to subvert antient institutions, has destroyed antient principles, will hold power by arts similar to those by which it has acquired it. When the old feudal and chivalrous spirit of *Fealty,*[7] which, by freeing kings from fear, freed both kings and subjects from the precautions of tyranny, shall be extinct in the minds of men, plots and assassinations will be anticipated by preventive murder and preventive confiscation, and that long roll of grim and bloody maxims, which form the political code of all power, not standing on its own honor, and the honor of those who are to obey it. Kings will be tyrants from policy when subjects are rebels from principle.

When antient opinions and rules of life are taken away, the loss cannot possibly be estimated. From that moment we have no compass to govern us; nor can we know distinctly to what port we steer. Europe undoubtedly, taken in a mass, was in a flourishing condition the day on which your Revolution was compleated. How much of that prosperous state was owing to the spirit of our old manners and opinions is not easy to say; but as such causes cannot be indifferent in their operation, we must presume, that, on the whole, their operation was beneficial.

We are but too apt to consider things in the state in which we find them, without sufficiently adverting to the causes by which they have been produced, and possibly may be upheld. Nothing is more certain, than that our manners, our civilization, and all the good things which are connected with manners, and with civilization, have, in this European world of ours, depended for ages upon two principles; and were indeed the result of both combined; I mean the spirit of a gentleman, and the spirit of religion. The nobility and the clergy, the one by profession, the other by patronage, kept learning in existence, even in the midst of arms and confusions, and whilst governments were rather in their causes than formed. Learning paid back what it received to nobility and to priesthood; and paid it with usury, by enlarging their ideas, and by furnishing their minds. Happy if they had all continued to know their indissoluble union, and their proper place! Happy if learning, not debauched by ambition, had been satisfied to continue the instructor, and not aspired to be the master! Along with its natural protectors and guardians, learning will be cast into the mire, and trodden down under the hoofs of a swinish multitude.

If, as I suspect, modern letters owe more than they are always willing to own to antient manners, so do other interests which we value full as much as they are worth. Even commerce, and trade, and manufacture, the gods of our oeconomical politicians, are themselves perhaps but creatures; are themselves but effects, which, as first causes, we choose to worship. They certainly

---

6. It is not enough for poems to have beauty; they must be sweet, tender, affecting (Latin; Horace's *Ars Poetica* 99).

7. Fidelity of a vassal or feudal tenant to his lord.

grew under the same shade in which learning flourished. They too may decay with their natural protecting principles. With you, for the present at least, they all threaten to disappear together. Where trade and manufactures are wanting to a people, and the spirit of nobility and religion remains, sentiment supplies, and not always ill supplies their place; but if commerce and the arts should be lost in an experiment to try how well a state may stand without these old fundamental principles, what sort of a thing must be a nation of gross, stupid, ferocious, and at the same time, poor and sordid barbarians, destitute of religion, honor, or manly pride, possessing nothing at present, and hoping for nothing hereafter?

I wish you may not be going fast, and by the shortest cut, to that horrible and disgustful situation. Already there appears a poverty of conception, a coarseness and vulgarity in all the proceedings of the assembly and of all their instructors. Their liberty is not liberal. Their science is presumptuous ignorance. Their humanity is savage and brutal.

* * *

1790

MARY WOLLSTONECRAFT

The first of the many published replies to Burke's *Reflections* was by Mary Wollstone-craft (1759–1797), who appears elsewhere in this anthology as author of *A Vindication of the Rights of Woman* (1792), the earliest substantial work in the history of the women's movement in Great Britain, and *Letters Written during a Short Residence in Sweden, Norway, and Denmark* (1796). Toward the end of 1790, when Burke's *Reflections* came out, she was working in London as a writer and translator for the radical publisher Joseph Johnson. Reading Burke, she was outraged at the weakness of his arguments and the exaggerated rhetoric with which he depicted the revolutionists as violators of royalty and womanhood. Always a rapid writer, she composed her reply, *A Vindication of the Rights of Men*, in a matter of days, and Johnson's printer set it in type as fast as the sheets of manuscript were turned in. It was published anonymously in November, less than a month after Burke's *Reflections* first appeared, and a second edition (this time with her name on the title page) was called for almost immediately.

From A Vindication of the Rights of Men

Advertisement

Mr. Burke's Reflections on the French Revolution first engaged my attention as the transient topic of the day; and reading it more for amusement than information, my indignation was roused by the sophistical arguments, that every moment crossed me, in the questionable shape of natural feelings and common sense.

Many pages of the following letter were the effusions of the moment; but, swelling imperceptibly to a considerable size, the idea was suggested of publishing a short vindication of *the Rights of Men*.

Not having leisure or patience to follow this desultory writer through all the devious tracks in which his fancy has started fresh game, I have confined my strictures, in a great measure, to the grand principles at which he has levelled many ingenious arguments in a very specious garb.

A Letter to the Right Honorable Edmund Burke

Sir,

It is not necessary, with courtly insincerity, to apologize to you for thus intruding on your precious time, nor to profess that I think it an honor to discuss an important subject with a man whose literary abilities have raised him to notice in the state. I have not yet learned to twist my periods, nor, in the equivocal idiom of politeness, to disguise my sentiments, and imply what I should be afraid to utter: if, therefore, in the course of this epistle, I chance to express contempt, and even indignation, with some emphasis, I beseech you to believe that it is not a flight of fancy; for truth, in morals, has ever appeared to me the essence of the sublime; and, in taste, simplicity the only criterion of the beautiful. But I war not with an individual when I contend for the *rights of men* and the liberty of reason. You see I do not condescend to cull my words to avoid the invidious phrase, nor shall I be prevented from giving a manly definition of it, by the flimsy ridicule which a lively fancy has interwoven with the present acceptation of the term. Reverencing the rights of humanity, I shall dare to assert them; not intimidated by the horse laugh that you have raised, or waiting till time has wiped away the compassionate tears which you have elaborately labored to excite.

From the many just sentiments interspersed through the letter before me, and from the whole tendency of it, I should believe you to be a good, though a vain man, if some circumstances in your conduct did not render the inflexibility of your integrity doubtful; and for this vanity a knowledge of human nature enables me to discover such extenuating circumstances, in the very texture of your mind, that I am ready to call it amiable, and separate the public from the private character.

* * *

Quitting now the flowers of rhetoric, let us, Sir, reason together; and, believe me, I should not have meddled with these troubled waters, in order to point out your inconsistencies, if your wit had not burnished up some rusty, baneful opinions, and swelled the shallow current of ridicule till it resembled the flow of reason, and presumed to be the test of truth.

I shall not attempt to follow you through "horse-way and foot-path;"[1] but, attacking the foundation of your opinions, I shall leave the superstructure to find a center of gravity on which it may lean till some strong blast puffs it into the air; or your teeming fancy, which the ripening judgment of sixty years has not tamed, produces another Chinese erection,[2] to stare, at every

1. *King Lear* 4.1.55.
2. Chinese pagodas were popular ornaments in late-eighteenth-century British landscaping.

turn, the plain country people in the face, who bluntly call such an airy edifice—a folly.

The birthright of man, to give you, Sir, a short definition of this disputed right, is such a degree of liberty, civil and religious, as is compatible with the liberty of every other individual with whom he is united in a social compact, and the continued existence of that compact.

Liberty, in this simple, unsophisticated sense, I acknowledge, is a fair idea that has never yet received a form in the various governments that have been established on our beauteous globe; the demon of property has ever been at hand to encroach on the sacred rights of men, and to fence round with awful pomp laws that war with justice. But that it results from the eternal foundation of right—from immutable truth—who will presume to deny, that pretends to rationality—if reason has led them to build their morality[3] and religion on an everlasting foundation—the attributes of God?

I glow with indignation when I attempt, methodically, to unravel your slavish paradoxes, in which I can find no fixed first principle to refute; I shall not, therefore, condescend to shew where you affirm in one page what you deny in another; and how frequently you draw conclusions without any previous premises:—it would be something like cowardice to fight with a man who had never exercised the weapons with which his opponent chose to combat, and irksome to refute sentence after sentence in which the latent spirit of tyranny appeared.

I perceive, from the whole tenor of your Reflections, that you have a mortal antipathy to reason; but, if there is any thing like argument, or first principles, in your wild declamation, behold the result:—that we are to reverence the rust of antiquity, and term the unnatural customs, which ignorance and mistaken self-interest have consolidated, the sage fruit of experience: nay, that, if we do discover some errors, our *feelings* should lead us to excuse, with blind love, or unprincipled filial affection, the venerable vestiges of ancient days. These are gothic[4] notions of beauty—the ivy is beautiful, but, when it insidiously destroys the trunk from which it receives support, who would not grub it up?

Further, that we ought cautiously to remain for ever in frozen inactivity, because a thaw, whilst it nourishes the soil, spreads a temporary inundation; and the fear of risking any personal present convenience should prevent a struggle for the most estimable advantages. This is sound reasoning, I grant, in the mouth of the rich and short-sighted.

Yes, Sir, the strong gained riches, the few have sacrificed the many to their vices; and, to be able to pamper their appetites, and supinely exist without exercising mind or body, they have ceased to be men.—Lost to the relish of true pleasure, such beings would, indeed, deserve compassion, if injustice was not softened by the tyrant's plea—necessity; if prescription was not raised as an immortal boundary against innovation. Their minds, in fact, instead of being cultivated, have been so warped by education, that it may require some ages to bring them back to nature, and enable them to see their true interest, with that degree of conviction which is necessary to influence their conduct.

3. As religion is included in my idea of morality, I should not have mentioned the term without specifying all the simple ideas which that comprehensive word generalizes; but as the charge of atheism has been very freely banded about in the letter I am considering, I wish to guard against misrepresentation [Wollstonecraft's note].

4. Barbarous.

The civilization which has taken place in Europe has been very partial, and, like every custom that an arbitrary point of honour has established, refines the manners at the expence of morals, by making sentiments and opinions current in conversation that have no root in the heart, or weight in the cooler resolves of the mind.—And what has stopped its progress?—hereditary property—hereditary honors. The man has been changed into an artificial monster by the station in which he was born, and the consequent homage that benumbed his faculties like the torpedo's[5] touch;—or a being, with a capacity of reasoning, would not have failed to discover, as his faculties unfolded, that true happiness arose from the friendship and intimacy which can only be enjoyed by equals; and that charity is not a condescending distribution of alms, but an intercourse of good offices and mutual benefits, founded on respect for justice and humanity.

* * *

It is necessary emphatically to repeat, that there are rights which men inherit at their birth, as rational creatures, who were raised above the brute creation by their improvable faculties; and that, in receiving these, not from their forefathers but, from God, prescription can never undermine natural rights.

A father may dissipate his property without his child having any right to complain;—but should he attempt to sell him for a slave, or fetter him with laws contrary to reason; nature, in enabling him to discern good from evil, teaches him to break the ignoble chain, and not to believe that bread becomes flesh, and wine blood, because his parents swallowed the Eucharist with this blind persuasion.

There is no end to this implicit submission to authority—some where it must stop, or we return to barbarism; and the capacity of improvement, which gives us a natural sceptre on earth, is a cheat, an ignis-fatuus, that leads us from inviting meadows into bogs and dung-hills. And if it be allowed that many of the precautions, with which any alteration was made, in our government, were prudent, it rather proves its weakness than substantiates an opinion of the soundness of the stamina, or the excellence of the constitution.

But on what principle Mr. Burke could defend American independence, I cannot conceive; for the whole tenor of his plausible arguments settles slavery on an everlasting foundation. Allowing his servile reverence for antiquity, and prudent attention to self-interest, to have the force which he insists on, the slave trade ought never to be abolished; and, because our ignorant forefathers, not understanding the native dignity of man, sanctioned a traffic that outrages every suggestion of reason and religion, we are to submit to the inhuman custom, and term an atrocious insult to humanity the love of our country, and a proper submission to the laws by which our property is secured.—Security of property! Behold, in a few words, the definition of English liberty. And to this selfish principle every nobler one is sacrificed.—The Briton takes place of the man, and the image of God is lost in the citizen! But it is not that enthusiastic flame which in Greece and Rome consumed every sordid passion: no, self is the focus; and the disparting rays rise not above our foggy atmosphere. But softly—it is only the property of the rich

5. Stingray, a fish with a whiplike, poisonous tail.

that is secure; the man who lives by the sweat of his brow has no asylum from oppression; the strong man may enter—when was the castle of the poor sacred? and the base informer steal him from the family that depend on his industry for subsistence.

*   *   *

But, among all your plausible arguments, and witty illustrations, your contempt for the poor always appears conspicuous, and rouses my indignation. The following paragraph in particular struck me, as breathing the most tyrannic spirit, and displaying the most factitious feelings. "Good order is the foundation of all good things. To be enabled to acquire, the people, without being servile, must be tractable and obedient. The magistrate must have his reverence, the laws their authority. The body of the people must not find the principles of natural subordination by art rooted out of their minds. They must respect that property of which they *cannot* partake. *They must labor to obtain what by labor can be obtained; and when they find, as they commonly do, the success disproportioned to the endeavor, they must be taught their consolation in the final proportions of eternal justice.* Of this consolation, whoever deprives them, deadens their industry, and strikes at the root of all acquisition as of all conservation. He that does this, is the cruel oppressor, the merciless enemy, of the poor and wretched; at the same time that, by his wicked speculations, he exposes the fruits of successful industry, and the accumulations of fortune, (ah! there's the rub)[6] to the plunder of the negligent, the disappointed, and the unprosperous."

This is contemptible hard-hearted sophistry, in the specious form of humility, and submission to the will of Heaven.—It is, Sir, *possible* to render the poor happier in this world, without depriving them of the consolation which you gratuitously grant them in the next. They have a right to more comfort than they at present enjoy; and more comfort might be afforded them, without encroaching on the pleasures of the rich: not now waiting to enquire whether the rich have any right to exclusive pleasures. What do I say?—encroaching! No; if an intercourse were established between them, it would impart the only true pleasure that can be snatched in this land of shadows, this hard school of moral discipline.

I know, indeed, that there is often something disgusting in the distresses of poverty, at which the imagination revolts, and starts back to exercise itself in the more attractive Arcadia of fiction. The rich man builds a house, art and taste give it the highest finish. His gardens are planted, and the trees grow to recreate the fancy of the planter, though the temperature of the climate may rather force him to avoid the dangerous damps they exhale, than seek the umbrageous retreat. Every thing on the estate is cherished but man; —yet, to contribute to the happiness of man, is the most sublime of all enjoyments. But if, instead of sweeping pleasure-grounds, obelisks, temples, and elegant cottages, as *objects* for the eye, the heart was allowed to beat true to nature, decent farms would be scattered over the estate, and plenty smile around. Instead of the poor being subject to the griping hand of an avaricious steward, they would be watched over with fatherly solicitude, by the man whose duty and pleasure it was to guard their happiness, and shield

6. *Hamlet* 3.1.67.

from rapacity the beings who, by the sweat of their brow, exalted him above his fellows.

I could almost imagine I see a man thus gathering blessings as he mounted the hill of life; or consolation, in those days when the spirits lag, and the tired heart finds no pleasure in them. It is not by squandering alms that the poor can be relieved, or improved—it is the fostering sun of kindness, the wisdom that finds them employments calculated to give them habits of virtue, that meliorates their condition. Love is only the fruit of love; condescension and authority may produce the obedience you applaud; but he has lost his heart of flesh who can see a fellow-creature humbled before him, and trembling at the frown of a being, whose heart is supplied by the same vital current, and whose pride ought to be checked by a consciousness of having the same infirmities.

* * *

1790

THOMAS PAINE

Although he was born and lived his first thirty-seven years in England, Thomas Paine (1737–1809) enters the debate as a visitor from America, where by writing *Common Sense* (1776) and the sixteen *Crisis* pamphlets, beginning "These are the times that try men's souls" (1776–83), he had served as the most effective propagandist for American independence. His *Rights of Man: Being an Answer to Mr. Burke's Attack on the French Revolution*, published in March 1791 with a dedication "To George Washington, President of the United States of America," has the full weight of the American revolutionary experience behind it and is the strongest statement against hereditary monarchy of any of the works replying to Burke in this "war of pamphlets." Paine published a second part of *Rights of Man* the following year and, when charged with treason by the British, fled to France, where he was made a citizen and a member of the Convention. With the fall of the more moderate Girondists, he was imprisoned by the Jacobins for a year in 1793–94, during which he wrote his last famous work, *The Age of Reason* (1794).

From Rights of Man

Among the incivilities by which nations or individuals provoke and irritate each other, Mr. Burke's pamphlet on the French Revolution is an extraordinary instance. Neither the people of France, nor the National Assembly, were troubling themselves about the affairs of England, or the English Parliament; and why Mr. Burke should commence an unprovoked attack upon them, both in parliament and in public, is a conduct that cannot be pardoned on the score of manners, nor justified on that of policy.

There is scarcely an epithet of abuse to be found in the English language with which Mr. Burke has not loaded the French nation and the National

Assembly. Every thing which rancor, prejudice, ignorance or knowledge could suggest, are poured forth in the copious fury of near four hundred pages. In the strain and on the plan Mr. Burke was writing, he might have written on to as many thousands. When the tongue or the pen is let loose in a frenzy of passion, it is the man, and not the subject, that becomes exhausted.

Hitherto Mr. Burke has been mistaken and disappointed in the opinions he had formed of the affairs of France; but such is the ingenuity of his hope, or the malignancy of his despair, that it furnishes him with new pretences to go on. There was a time when it was impossible to make Mr. Burke believe there would be any revolution in France. His opinion then was, that the French had neither spirit to undertake it, nor fortitude to support it; and now that there is one, he seeks an escape by condemning it.

* * *

There never did, there never will, and there never can exist a parliament, or any description of men, or any generation of men, in any country, possessed of the right or the power of binding and controuling posterity to the *"end of time,"* or of commanding for ever how the world shall be governed, or who shall govern it; and therefore, all such clauses, acts or declarations, by which the makers of them attempt to do what they have neither the right nor the power to do, nor the power to execute, are in themselves null and void.—Every age and generation must be as free to act for itself, *in all cases*, as the ages and generations which preceded it. The vanity and presumption of governing beyond the grave, is the most ridiculous and insolent of all tyrannies. Man has no property in man; neither has any generation a property in the generations which are to follow. The parliament or the people of 1688, or of any other period, had no more right to dispose of the people of the present day, or to bind or to controul them *in any shape whatever*, than the parliament or the people of the present day have to dispose of, bind or controul those who are to live a hundred or a thousand years hence. Every generation is, and must be, competent to all the purposes which its occasions require. It is the living, and not the dead, that are to be accommodated. When man ceases to be, his power and his wants cease with him; and having no longer any participation in the concerns of this world, he has no longer any authority in directing who shall be its governors, or how its government shall be organized, or how administered.

I am not contending for nor against any form of government, nor for nor against any party here or elsewhere. That which a whole nation chooses to do, it has a right to do. Mr. Burke says, No. Where then *does* the right exist? I am contending for the rights of the *living*, and against their being willed away, and controuled and contracted for, by the manuscript assumed authority of the dead; and Mr. Burke is contending for the authority of the dead over the rights and freedom of the living.* * *

* * *

"We have seen," says Mr. Burke, "the French rebel against a mild and lawful Monarch, with more fury, outrage, and insult, than any people

has been known to rise against the most illegal usurper, or the most san-
guinary tyrant."—This is one among a thousand other instances, in which
Mr. Burke shews that he is ignorant of the springs and principles of the
French revolution.

It was not against Louis the XVIth, but against the despotic principles of
the government, that the nation revolted. These principles had not their
origin in him, but in the original establishment, many centuries back; and
they were become too deeply rooted to be removed, and the augean stable[1]
of parasites and plunderers too abominably filthy to be cleansed, by any thing
short of a complete and universal revolution. When it becomes necessary to
do a thing, the whole heart and soul should go into the measure, or not
attempt it. That crisis was then arrived, and there remained no choice but
to act with determined vigor, or not to act at all. The King was known to be
the friend of the nation, and this circumstance was favorable to the enterprise. Perhaps no man bred up in the style of an absolute King, ever possessed
a heart so little disposed to the exercise of that species of power as the present
King of France. But the principles of the government itself still remained
the same. The Monarch and the monarchy were distinct and separate things;
and it was against the established despotism of the latter, and not against
the person or principles of the former, that the revolt commenced, and the
revolution has been carried.

Mr. Burke does not attend to the distinction between *men* and *principles*;
and therefore, he does not see that a revolt may take place against the despotism of the latter, while there lies no charge of despotism against the
former.

The natural moderation of Louis the XVIth contributed nothing to alter
the hereditary despotism of the monarchy. All the tyrannies of former reigns,
acted under that hereditary despotism, were still liable to be revived in the
hands of a successor. It was not the respite of a reign that would satisfy
France, enlightened as she was then become. A casual discontinuance of the
practice of despotism, is not a discontinuance of its *principles*; the former
depends on the virtue of the individual who is in immediate possession of
power; the latter, on the virtue and fortitude of the nation. In the case of
Charles I and James II of England, the revolt was against the personal despotism of the men;[2] whereas in France, it was against the hereditary despotism of the established government. But men who can consign over the
rights of posterity for ever on the authority of a moldy parchment, like Mr.
Burke, are not qualified to judge of this revolution. It takes in a field too vast
for their views to explore, and proceeds with a mightiness of reason they
cannot keep pace with.

But there are many points of view in which this revolution may be considered. When despotism has established itself for ages in a country, as in
France, it is not in the person of the King only that it resides. It has the
appearance of being so in show, and in nominal authority; but it is not so in
practice, and in fact. It has its standard every where. Every office and depart-

---

1. King Augeas's stable, housing three thousand
oxen and neglected for decades, was a classical
symbol of filth and corruption. Hercules cleaned it
by changing the course of a river.

2. Charles I was overthrown by the Civil War and
executed in 1649. His son, James II, was
dethroned in the Glorious Revolution of 1688.

ment has its despotism founded upon custom and usage. Every place has its Bastille,[3] and every Bastille its despot. The original hereditary despotism resident in the person of the King, divides and subdivides itself into a thousand shapes and forms, till at last the whole of it is acted by deputation. This was the case in France; and against this species of despotism, proceeding on through an endless labyrinth of office till the source of it is scarcely perceptible, there is no mode of redress. It strengthens itself by assuming the appearance of duty, and tyrannises under the pretence of obeying.

When a man reflects on the condition which France was in from the nature of her government, he will see other causes for revolt than those which immediately connect themselves with the person or character of Louis XVI. There were, if I may so express it, a thousand despotisms to be reformed in France, which had grown up under the hereditary despotism of the monarchy, and became so rooted as to be in a great measure independent of it. Between the monarchy, the parliament, and the church, there was a *rivalship* of despotism; besides the feudal despotism operating locally, and the ministerial despotism operating every where. But Mr. Burke, by considering the King as the only possible object of a revolt, speaks as if France was a village, in which every thing that passed must be known to its commanding officer, and no oppression could be acted but what he could immediately control. Mr. Burke might have been in the Bastille his whole life, as well under Louis XVI as Louis XIV and neither the one nor the other have known that such a man as Mr. Burke existed. The despotic principles of the government were the same in both reigns, though the dispositions of the men were as remote as tyranny and benevolence.

What Mr. Burke considers as a reproach to the French Revolution (that of bringing it forward under a reign more mild than the preceding ones), is one of its highest honors. The revolutions that have taken place in other European countries, have been excited by personal hatred. The rage was against the man, and he became the victim. But, in the instance of France, we see a revolution generated in the rational contemplation of the rights of man, and distinguishing from the beginning between persons and principles.

But Mr. Burke appears to have no idea of principles, when he is contemplating governments. "Ten years ago," says he, "I could have felicitated France on her having a government, without enquiring what the nature of that government was, or how it was administered." Is this the language of a rational man? Is it the language of a heart feeling as it ought to feel for the rights and happiness of the human race? On this ground, Mr. Burke must compliment every government in the world, while the victims who suffer under them, whether sold into slavery, or tortured out of existence, are wholly forgotten. It is power, and not principles, that Mr. Burke venerates; and under this abominable depravity, he is disqualified to judge between them.— Thus much for his opinion as to the occasions of the French Revolution. * * *

* * *

As to the tragic paintings by which Mr. Burke has outraged his own imagination, and seeks to work upon that of his readers, they are very well calculated for theatrical representation, where facts are manufactured for the

---

3. France's political prison (where the French Revolution began on July 14, 1789).

sake of show, and accommodated to produce, through the weakness of sympathy, a weeping effect. But Mr. Burke should recollect that he is writing History, and not *Plays;* and that his readers will expect truth, and not the spouting rant of high-toned exclamation.

When we see a man dramatically lamenting in a publication intended to be believed, that, *"The age of chivalry is gone!* that *The glory of Europe is extinguished for ever!* that *The unbought grace of life* (if any one knows what it is), *the cheap defence of nations, the nurse of manly sentiment and heroic enterprize, is gone!"* and all this because the Quixote age of chivalric nonsense is gone, What opinion can we form of his judgment, or what regard can we pay to his facts? In the rhapsody of his imagination, he has discovered a world of wind-mills, and his sorrows are, that there are no Quixotes to attack them. But if the age of aristocracy, like that of chivalry, should fall, and they had originally some connection, Mr. Burke, the trumpeter of the Order, may continue his parody to the end, and finish with exclaiming, *"Othello's occupation's gone!"*[4]

Notwithstanding Mr. Burke's horrid paintings, when the French Revolution is compared with that of other countries, the astonishment will be, that it is marked with so few sacrifices; but this astonishment will cease when we reflect that *principles,* and not *persons,* were the meditated objects of destruction. The mind of the nation was acted upon by a higher stimulus than what the consideration of persons could inspire, and sought a higher conquest than could be produced by the downfall of an enemy.* * *

1791

APOCALYPTIC EXPECTATIONS BY PREACHERS AND POETS

Looking back to his early radical years from his conservative middle age, Robert Southey declared:

> Few persons but those who have lived in it can conceive or comprehend what the memory of the French Revolution was, nor what a visionary world seemed to open upon those who were just entering it. Old things seemed passing away, and nothing was dreamt of but the regeneration of the human race. (*The Correspondence of Robert Southey with Caroline Bowles,* ed. Edward Dowden, 1881)

In the prologue to his highly successful play *The Road to Ruin* (1792), Thomas Holcroft used the occasion to predict that the French Revolution would "fertilize a world, and renovate old earth!" And in *The Prelude* (p. 346), Wordsworth remembered the early years of the Revolution as a time when all Europe

was thrilled with joy,
France standing on the top of golden hours,
And human nature seeming born again.
(6.340–42)

Human nature regenerated in a world made new: this was the theme of many enthusiasts in England during the first four or five years after the outbreak of the French

---

4. *Othello* 3.3.362 (Othello's feeling, when he thinks Desdemona has been unfaithful, that his life is over). "Quixote" as an adjective, referring to the hero of Cervantes's romance, means "impractically idealistic."

Revolution in 1789. The concepts are patently theological. They originate in the apocalyptic and millennial passages of the Hebrew and Christian Scriptures, and their use indicates that for a number of British idealists, the early enthusiasm for the Revolution had the fervor and conviction of a religious movement.

The term *apocalypse,* derived from the Greek word meaning "revelation," designates the disclosure, in the Bible, of God's providential design for the end of human history. In its developed form, an apocalypse is a prophetic vision, in elaborately symbolic form, of the imminent events that will abruptly end the existing order and replace it with a new and perfected condition both of humanity and of the world. The root elements of apocalypse are the concern of the Hebrew prophets with the catastrophic punishments to be visited upon an errant Israel and its enemies in "the latter end of the days," as well as with the expectation of a messiah, a deliverer from suffering in this disaster-ridden world. These elements were collected in the writings attributed to the prophet Isaiah, which foretell, after God has vented His wrath, the advent of a renovated world of ease, joy, and peace. "For, behold, I create new heavens and a new earth," in which "the wolf and the lamb shall feed together, and the lion shall eat straw like the bullock" (Isaiah 65.17–25). The Old Testament of the Bible also contains a full-fledged apocalypse, the Book of Daniel, which includes a symbolic vision of four beasts, signifying four successive monarchies; following the Fourth Monarchy, after a violent preliminary, "one like the Son of man came with the clouds of heaven" and was given by the "Ancient of days" "an everlasting dominion, which shall not pass away" (Isaiah 7.13–14).

Passages predicting an imminent apocalypse occur in the New Testament both in the Synoptic Gospels and in the Epistles of Paul. The New Testament concludes with the most spectacular, awesome, and intricately ordered of all apocalyptic prophecies, the Book of Revelation. A series of symbolic events—seven angels blow seven trumpet blasts and pour out seven vials of wrath—represent the conflict between the forces of Christ and of the Antichrist, culminating in a prodigious violence in which the stars fall like ripe figs (Revelation 6.13) and the harvest of the earth is cast "into the great winepress of the wrath of God . . . and blood came out of the winepress, even unto the horse bridles" (14.19–20). This fierce destruction, however, is a cleansing one, preparatory to the Second Coming of Christ to inaugurate the Kingdom of God on earth, which will last one thousand years—in Latin, a "millennium," from which are derived the terms *millennial* and *millenarian* to signify the belief in a blissful earthly condition at the end of history. After the millennium, the forces of evil will be loosed again and finally defeated, after which the original creation, its function in the divine plot accomplished, will pass away, to be replaced by a new creation and by a new Jerusalem that will reconstitute, for the deserving elect, the paradise that had been lost at the Fall: "And there shall be no more death . . . neither shall there be any more pain: for the former things are passed away" (Revelation 21.4).

Two distinctive images recur persistently in later writings that derive from biblical apocalypses. One is the image of a sacred marriage that signifies the consummation of history. In Isaiah (62.2–5), the final redemption is figured as a marriage between the people of Israel and their land; in Revelation (21.2, 9–10), it is figured as a marriage between Christ and the new, or purified, Jerusalem, "coming down from God out of heaven, prepared as a bride adorned for her husband." The second recurrent image represents the final condition of blessedness as a renovated heaven and earth: "For, behold," the Lord said to Isaiah, "I create new heavens and a new earth" (Isaiah 65.17 and 66.22). Thus also Revelation (21.1, 5): "And I saw a new heaven and a new earth: for the first heaven and the first earth were passed away."

The apocalyptic and millennial prophecies in the Bible are readily convertible into a program for violent political revolution, because they consist of an infallible text that ordains a necessary and total destruction of the forces of the evil and guarantees the outcome of this violence in an enduring condition of peace, plenty, and consummate happiness. In the civil wars in seventeenth-century England, for example, there were fervent apocalyptic expectations among radical parliamentary sects that were shared by Oliver Cromwell, as well as by John Milton, who voiced his conviction of an imminent millennium in the traditional figures of an apocalyptic marriage and a universal renovation: "Thy Kingdome is now at hand. . . . come forth out of thy Royall Chambers, O Prince of all the Kings of the earth . . . for now the voice of thy Bride calls thee, and all creatures sigh to be renewed" (1.707, *Animadversions*, in *Complete Prose Works*; see also 1.616).

The late eighteenth century was another age of apocalyptic expectation, when the promise of the American Revolution, followed by the greater and more radical hopes raised by the early years of the French Revolution, revived within some English Nonconforming sects the millenarian excitement of Milton and other seventeenth-century predecessors. The Unitarian Richard Price had in 1785 hailed the American Revolution as a crucial step in fulfilling the "old prophecies" of a reign of reason, virtue, and peace, when the wolf will "dwell with the lamb and the leopard with the kid." *Discourse on the Love of Our Country*—excerpted above as a major provocation of Burke's *Reflections on the Revolution in France*—although delivered less than three months after the fall of the Bastille—already envisioned the uprising in terms of biblical prophecy. Other preachers such as Joseph Fawcett (a model for the millenarian preachings by the Solitary in Wordsworth's *Excursion*), Elhanan Winchester (who delivered his apocalyptic discourses to the British Parliament), and Joseph Priestley (who was not only a great chemist but a founder of the Unitarian Society) all interpreted the convulsions in France as fulfilling the prophecies of the last days. They thus invested the promise of France with the explosive power of the great Western myth of apocalypse, expanding a local historical event into the perfervid expectation that all humanity, everywhere, was at the violent threshold of an earthly paradise.

This phenomenon is of special importance for literature because, during the formative period in the early 1790s, the first generation of Romantic poets shared this millenarian excitement and incorporated in their poems apocalyptic expectations— or at least apocalyptic imaginings—of the French Revolution as prelude to the abrupt culmination of history, in the emergence of a new humanity on a new paradisal earth. The poetic selections printed here are from some of the works, written in 1793 and 1794, in which Southey, Blake, Wordsworth, and Coleridge present their versions of the expected historical sequence that Coleridge, in the prose "Argument" prefixed to *Religious Musings* (1794), tersely summarized: "The French Revolution. Millennium. Universal Redemption. Conclusion." The selections end with a passage from *Queen Mab* (1813), in which the youthful Shelley recapitulates the millenarian hopes that had been expressed by his older contemporaries in the early stage of the revolution, two decades before.

ELHANAN WINCHESTER

Elhanan Winchester (1751–1797) was an American evangelist whose sermons at the Baptist Church of Philadelphia attracted large and enthusiastic audiences. In 1787, Winchester felt divinely called to go to London in order to preach his "universalist" doctrine that, at the end of time, all humans would be saved, including even the worst of sinners.

On February 3 and 24, 1793, Winchester delivered to the British Parliament two discourses, the substance of which were published that same year with the resounding title *The Three Woe-Trumpets, of which the first and second are already past and the third is now begun: under which the seven vials of the wrath of God are to be poured out upon the world.* The title page added that the discourses were a commentary on Revelation 11.14–18:

> 14. The second woe is past; and, behold, the third woe cometh quickly.
>
> 15. And the seventh angel sounded; and there were great voices in heaven, saying, The kingdoms of his world are become the kingdoms of our Lord, and of his Christ; and he shall reign for ever and ever.
>
> 16. And the four and twenty elders, which sat before God on their seats, fell upon their faces, and worshipped God,
>
> 17. Saying, We give thee thanks, O Lord God Almighty, which art, and wast, and art to come; because thou hast taken to thee thy great power, and hast reigned.
>
> 18. And the nations were angry, and thy wrath is come, and the time of the dead, that they should be judged, and that thou shouldest give reward unto thy servants the prophets, and to the saints, and them that fear thy name, small and great: and shouldest destroy them which destroy the earth.

Winchester elaborates his depiction of the divine wrath and of the coming kingdom by reference to other passages in Revelation and to other books in the Bible, considering them to be prophecies of the contemporary revolution in France and of events that are to follow. That Winchester's discourses were delivered to Parliament indicates the currency of the belief that the convulsions in France precede a millennial restoration, everywhere and to all peoples, of the felicity that had been lost at the fall of Adam and Eve. Winchester, who was a poet as well as a preacher, published that same year, 1793, *The Process and Empire of Christ: An Heroic Poem*, written in blank verse. Books 8–12 deal with the Second Coming, the millennium, and the "New Creation; or The Renovation of the Heavens and Earth after the Conflagration."

From The Three Woe-Trumpets

* * *

By the great earthquake, we are to understand a great political shaking of some nation, whereby the government shall be overthrown and broken in pieces, as really as any part of the earth was ever broken and destroyed by a natural earthquake. * * * And in this earthquake, which will be a sudden and surprizing Revolution, different from all others, there will be slain of names of men seven thousand; or, the whole number of the titles, or names of distinction will be destroyed; and all this will take place in a most sudden and unexpected manner.

Now look at the Revolution, and overturning of the government in France, and see if this prophecy is not exactly fulfilled, and therein a full proof given that *the second woe is past*, beyond all dispute; and this epoch is therefore interesting to all Christians in the highest degree.

* * *

I regard the late events in France, therefore, as Signs of the Times, and they mark the close of the preceding period with great exactness; and in this light their consequence is very great: they shew us whereabouts we are, and tend to confirm the authority of the Scriptures, and especially the book of the Revelation of St. John.

A new and very important period is now beginning to take place, under the sound of the Seventh Trumpet, which will continue to sound from this time, 'till after the personal appearance of JESUS, 'till all the seven vials of the wrath of God are poured out, and until *the kingdoms of this world are become the kingdoms of our Lord, and of his Christ.*

But great will be the woes and desolations that will come upon the world before this happy event will take place. And for this reason, the seventh trumpet is properly denominated *a woe trumpet*, for the woes that will take place while it is sounding, will be great beyond example, and terrible beyond description.

* * *

Under the seventh trumpet our glorious Savior will personally appear: I have already observed, that he will come between the time of the sixth and seventh vial; all these awful dispensations that are taking place are solemn preparations for that event; and therefore our Lord charges us when we hear of wars and rumors of wars, to see that we *be not troubled; for all these things must come to pass.** * * The coming of our Savior in glory, is such a joyful event in itself, and will be followed by so many glorious consequences, that it is almost impossible for a true christian to think of it without exultation. And this will actually take place under the sound of the seventh trumpet.

* * *

It is very easy to see that in a very short time all nations shall be brought to yield obedience to him; *and the kingdoms of this world* shall *become the kingdoms of our Lord and of his Christ, and he shall reign, eis tous aionas tan aionon*; which our translators have translated *forever and ever*, but which appears (in Chap. xx.2, 3, 4, 5, 6, 7) to be only *a thousand years*, and is six times limited to that period. So that here the words which are used imply *hidden duration*, or *ages of ages*, without specifying the exact length of the periods: But in Chap. xx the time is made known with great exactness. * * * There is nothing in this view of the kingdom of Christ, that has any tendency to give umbrage or dissatisfaction to the present monarchs, kings, rulers, or governors of the earth, for though all the kingdoms of the world shall become the Lord's, and his Christ's, yet this is no encouragement for any usurpers to rise and seize upon them, under a pretence of their being the Lord's people, and that they are going to take possession of the kingdoms for him; for Christ himself will come in person, to take the kingdoms of this world under his government, so that this part of my text will not be accomplished till after his appearing in glory, and the first resurrection has taken place.

* * *

I will now as a close of this discourse, just mention the blessings of the Millennium, or the personal kingdom of our Lord upon the earth. * * *

The kingdom or government of Christ shall be absolutely universal, and shall extend over the whole earth: All nations shall know his name, and shall serve and obey him. * * *

His government shall be *just, equitable, righteous*, friendly to mankind, especially to the poor and needy. * * *

Another blessing that shall take place under the Messiah's government, shall be universal and constant peace during the whole period of his reign. * * *

The earth shall be filled with plenty as well as peace, and neither war, famine, pestilence, nor the terrible fierceness of wild beasts shall annoy, hurt, destroy, or even terrify the inhabitants of the earth in those blessed days. * * *

In those blessed times there shall be no differences of sentiment: All shall be harmony and love: No contradiction in the public instructions: All ministers shall agree, in principle and practice, in faith and worship. * * *

* * * When this perfect unity takes place among believers, the conversion of the whole world shall commence, and all shall bow at the scepter of Jesus and become the willing subjects of his kingdom. * * *

1793

JOSEPH PRIESTLEY

Joseph Priestley (1733–1804) was a Unitarian minister, political theorist, and philosopher, as well as an eminent scientist who helped establish modern chemistry by discovering oxygen. In 1791 he wrote and published *Letters to the Right Honorable Edmund Burke*, a reply to Burke's *Reflections on the French Revolution*, in which he hailed the American and French Revolutions as inaugurating the state of universal peace and happiness that was "distinctly and repeatedly foretold in many prophecies, delivered more than two thousand years ago" (Birmingham, 1791, p. 150). Priestley's enthusiastic endorsement of the French Revolution led to the destruction of his house, library, and laboratory in Birmingham by rioters on the second anniversary of the fall of the Bastille, July 14, 1791.

Three years later, on February 28, 1794, Priestley published the sermon *The Present State of Europe Compared with Antient Prophecies*, in which he interpreted the events in France by detailed reference to apocalyptic and millennial passages in the Bible, especially the Book of Revelation. Soon after publishing this sermon, he emigrated to Pennsylvania, where he lived the last ten years of his life. In a sermon that he did not live to deliver, Priestley reaffirmed his millennial faith: "Let us then be ever *looking for*, as we are *hastening into*, the coming of this great day of God. . . ."

From The Present State of Europe Compared with Antient Prophecies:

A Sermon, Preached at the Gravel Pit Meeting in Hackney,
February 28, 1794,
Being the Day Appointed for a General Fast[1]

* * *

If we can learn any thing concerning what is before us, from the language of prophecy, great calamities, such as the world has never yet experienced, will precede that happy state of things, in which "the kingdoms of this world will become the kingdom of our Lord Jesus Christ;" and these calamities will chiefly affect those nations which have been the seat of the great antichristian power; or, as all Protestants, and I believe justly, suppose, have been subject to the see of Rome. And it appears to me highly probable, as I hinted in my last discourse on this occasion, that the present disturbances in Europe are the beginning of those very calamitous times.* * *

* * * It is enough for us to know the certainty of these great events, that our faith may not fail on the approach of the predicted calamity, confident that it will have the happiest issue in God's own time. For the same Being who foretold the evil which we shall see come to pass, has likewise foretold the good that is to follow it.

That the second coming of Christ will be coincident with the commencement of the millennium, or the future peaceable and happy state of the world (which, according to all the prophecies, will take place after the restoration of the Jews) is evident from what Peter said, in his address to the Jews, on the occasion of his healing the lame man at the gate of the temple, Acts iii.19. * * *

This great event of the late revolution in France appears to me, and many others, to be not improbably the accomplishment of the following part of the Revelation, chap. xi.3: "And the same hour there was a great earthquake, and the tenth part of the city fell, and in the earthquake were slain of men (or literally, *names of men*) seven thousand, and the remnant were affrighted, and gave glory to God."

An earthquake, as I have observed, may signify a great convulsion, and revolution, in states; and as the Papal dominions were divided into ten parts, one of which, and one of the principal of them, was France, it is properly called *a tenth part of the city*, or of the mystical *Babylon*. And if by *names of men*, we understand their *titles*, such as those of the nobility, and other hereditary distinctions, all of which are now abolished, the accomplishment of the prediction will appear to be wonderfully exact. * * *

* * * What could have been more unexpected than the events of any one of the last four years, at the beginning of it? What a total revolution in the ideas, and conduct of a whole nation! What a total subversion of principles, what reverses of fortune, and what a waste of life! In how bloody and eventful a war are we engaged, how inconsiderable in its beginning, how rapid and wide in its progress, and how dark with respect to its termina-

---

1. Fasts were proclaimed by the British government to obtain divine sanction for the war against France, which had begun in February 1793. Priest- ley's sermon, however, was not what the government had in mind.

tion! At first it resembled Elijah's cloud, appearing no bigger than a *man's hand* [1 Kings 18.44]; but now it covers, and darkens, the whole European hemisphere!

Now, whatever we may think, as politicians (and with us every man will have his own opinion, on a subject so interesting to us all) I would, in this place, admonish you not to overlook the hand of God in the great scene that is now opening upon us. Nothing can ever come to pass without his appointment, or permission; and then, whatever be the views of men, we cannot doubt, but that his are always wise, righteous, and good. Let us, therefore, exercise faith in him, believing that though "clouds and darkness are round about him, righteousness and judgment are for ever the habitation of his throne" [Psalm 97.2]. All those who appear in the theatre of public affairs, in the field, or the cabinet, both those whom we praise, and those whom we blame, are equally instruments in his hands, and execute all his pleasure. Let this reflection, then, in our cooler moments (and I hope we shall endeavour, in all the tumult of affairs, to make these as many as possible), lead us to look more to God, and less to man; and consequently, in all the troubles in which we may be involved, repose the most unshaken confidence in him, and thence "in patience possess our own souls" [Luke 21.19], especially when it is evident that it is wholly out of our power to alter the course of events. If we be careful so to live as to be at all times prepared to die, what have we to fear, even though, as the Psalmist says, the "earth be removed, and the mountains be carried into the midst of the sea?" [Psalm 46.2]. Whatever turn the course of things may take, it cannot then be to our disadvantage. What, then, should hinder our contemplating the great scene, that seems now to be opening upon us, awful as it is, with tranquillity, and even with satisfaction, from our firm persuasion, that its termination will be glorious and happy?

1794

WILLIAM BLAKE

The narrative poems that William Blake (1757–1827) wrote in the early 1790s show that he, like the radical preachers of the time, envisioned the French Revolution as the portent of apocalypse. He planned *The French Revolution* as an epic poem in seven books. Of these, only the first book survives, in a single set of page proofs set in type in 1791. It traces, largely without symbolism, the events of the revolution shortly before and just after the fall of the Bastille on July 14, 1789, and incorporates the prophecy of a millennial condition in which "men walk with their fathers in bliss." The next year, 1792, Blake wrote *A Song of Liberty* (p. 82), which represents Energy as a revolutionary "son of fire," moving from America to France and crying the advent of an Isaian peaceable kingdom: "Empire is no more! And now the lion & wolf shall cease."

In what are known as the "minor prophecies," whose composition ended in 1795, Blake reshaped the large-scaled but still historical agents of his *French Revolution* into what he called the "Giant Forms" of his mythical system. These works are represented here by *America: A Prophecy*, which Blake dated 1793. In this poem the tyrant King George becomes "Albion's Angel" and is presented as an advocate of Urizen, the misconceived sky god of rationality, prohibition, and oppression. The opponent of Urizen is "red Orc," who represents the spirit of energy, bursting out not only in political revolution but in rebellion against all forms of physical, religious, and sexual repression. The triumph of Orc will result in a universal human state of peace and exuberant joy.

From The French Revolution: A Poem in Seven Books[1]

* * * Then the Abbe de S[i]eyes rais'd his feet
On the steps of the Louvre; like a voice of God following a storm, the
    Abbe follow'd
The pale fires of Aumont into the chamber, as a father that bows to his
    son;
Whose rich fields inheriting spread their old glory, so the voice of the
    people bowed
205   Before the ancient seat of the kingdom and mountains to be renewed.
"Hear, O Heavens of France, the voice of the people, arising from valley
    and hill,
O'erclouded with power. Hear the voice of vallies, the voice of meek cities,
Mourning oppressed on village and field, till the village and field is a
    waste.
For the husbandman weeps at blights of the fife, and blasting of trumpets
    consume
210   The souls of mild France; the pale mother nourishes her child to the
    deadly slaughter.
When the heavens were seal'd with a stone, and the terrible sun clos'd in
    an orb, and the moon
Rent from the nations, and each star appointed for watchers of night,
The millions of spirits immortal were bound in the ruins of sulphur
    heaven
To wander inslav'd; black, deprest in dark ignorance, kept in awe with the
    whip,
215   To worship terrors, bred from the blood of revenge and breath of desire,
In beastial forms; or more terrible men, till the dawn of our peaceful
    morning,
Till dawn, till morning, till the breaking of clouds, and swelling of winds,
    and the universal voice,
Till man raise his darken'd limbs out of the caves of night, his eyes and his
    heart
Expand: where is space? where O Sun is thy dwelling? where thy tent, O
    faint slumb'rous Moon?
220   Then the valleys of France shall cry to the soldier, 'Throw down thy sword
    and musket,

1. The speaker in this extract is the revolutionist and statesman Abbé Sieyès (1748–1836), who on July 6, 1789, addressed the French National Assembly to urge that the troops be withdrawn from Paris. The abbé's speech refers to the abolition of black slavery (lines 214–19) and to religious as well as political oppression (lines 223–26).

And run and embrace the meek peasant.' Her Nobles shall hear and shall
    weep, and put off
The red robe of terror, the crown of oppression, the shoes of contempt,
    and unbuckle
The girdle of war from the desolate earth; then the Priest in his thund'rous
    cloud
Shall weep, bending to earth embracing the valleys, and putting his hand
    to the plow
225   Shall say, 'No more I curse thee; but now I will bless thee: No more in
    deadly black
Devour thy labour; nor lift up a cloud in thy heavens, O laborious plow,
That the wild raging millions, that wander in forests, and howl in law
    blasted wastes,
Strength madden'd with slavery, honesty, bound in the dens of
    superstition,
May sing in the village, and shout in the harvest, and woo in pleasant
    gardens
230   Their once savage loves, now beaming with knowledge, with gentle awe
    adorned;
And the saw, and the hammer, the chisel, the pencil, the pen, and the
    instruments
Of heavenly song sound in the wilds once forbidden, to teach the laborious
    plowman
And shepherd deliver'd from clouds of war, from pestilence, from night-
    fear, from murder,
From falling, from stifling, from hunger, from cold, from slander, discon-
    tent and sloth;
235   That walk in beasts and birds of night, driven back by the sandy desert
Like pestilent fogs round cities of men: and the happy earth sing in its
    course,
The mild peaceable nations be opened to heav'n, and men walk with their
    fathers in bliss.'
Then hear the first voice of the morning: 'Depart, O clouds of night, and
    no more
Return; be withdrawn cloudy war, troops of warriors depart, nor around
    our peaceable city
240   Breathe fires, but ten miles from Paris, let all be peace, nor a soldier be
    seen!' ''

1791

From America: A Prophecy[1]

PLATE 6

"The morning comes, the night decays, the watchmen leave their stations;
The grave is burst, the spices shed, the linen wrapped up;
The bones of death, the cov'ring clay, the sinews shrunk & dry'd,

1. This "minor prophecy" (i.e., a short poem of
epiclike narrative) is dated 1793 but was drafted
and revised over several years. It relates the American Revolution to current events in France. Blake
identifies the speaker in plate 6 as "a voice" that
"came forth"—presumably, the voice of prophetic
vision. "Albion's Angel," who speaks in plate 7, is
George III of England. The speaker in plate 8 is
Orc, who appears to the terrified king in the serpent form of Satan, whom Blake regards as the
original revolutionary against oppression by a
tyrant God.

Reviving shake, inspiring move, breathing! awakening!
5   Spring like redeemed captives when their bonds & bars are burst.
Let the slave grinding at the mill run out into the field:
Let him look up into the heavens & laugh in the bright air;
Let the inchained soul shut up in darkness and in sighing,
Whose face has never seen a smile in thirty weary years,
10 Rise and look out; his chains are loose, his dungeon doors are open.
And let his wife and children return from the opressor's scourge.
They look behind at every step & believe it is a dream,
Singing, 'The Sun has left his blackness, & has found a fresher morning
And the fair Moon rejoices in the clear & cloudless night;
15 For Empire is no more, and now the Lion & Wolf shall cease.' "

PLATE 7
In thunders ends the voice. Then Albion's Angel wrathful burnt
Beside the Stone of Night; and like the Eternal Lion's howl
In famine & war, reply'd, "Art thou not Orc; who serpent-form'd
Stands at the gate of Enitharmon to devour her children?
5   Blasphemous Demon, Antichrist, hater of Dignities;
Lover of wild rebellion, and transgresser of God's Law,
Why dost thou come to Angels' eyes in this terrific form?"

PLATE 8
The terror answer'd: "I am Orc, wreath'd round the accursed tree:
The times are ended; shadows pass, the morning 'gins to break;
The fiery joy, that Urizen perverted to ten commands,
What night he led the starry hosts thro' the wide wilderness:
5   That stony law I stamp to dust: and scatter religion abroad
To the four winds as a torn book, & none shall gather the leaves;
But they shall rot on desart sands, & consume in bottomless deeps,
To make the desarts blossom, & the deeps shrink to their fountains,
And to renew the fiery joy, and burst the stony roof,
10 That pale religious letchery, seeking Virginity,
May find it in a harlot, and in coarse-clad honesty
The undefil'd, tho' ravish'd in her cradle night and morn:
For every thing that lives is holy, life delights in life;
Because the soul of sweet delight can never be defil'd.
15 Fires inwrap the earthly globe, yet man is not consumed;
Amidst the lustful fires he walks: his feet become like brass,
His knees and thighs like silver, & his breast and head like gold."

1793

ROBERT SOUTHEY

Robert Southey (1774–1843), although in his time a prolific and distinguished author, is now remembered mainly for his close association with Coleridge and Wordsworth, for Byron's savage lampoons of him in *Don Juan* and *The Vision of*

Judgment, and for his story *The Three Bears*, a piece so often retold that it has acquired the status of an anonymous folktale. He attended Oxford; was for a short time a fervent supporter of the French Revolution; and developed with Coleridge (who became his brother-in-law) the abortive scheme to found Pantisocracy, a utopian community on the banks of the Susquehanna River in Pennsylvania. In 1803 he moved to Keswick in the Lake Country, within long walking distance of his friend Wordsworth. With advancing age, he settled into a Tory viewpoint more conservative than those of Wordsworth and Coleridge. All his life a learned and hardworking professional author, he wrote thousands of pages of epics and short poems, histories, essays, biographies, and reviews. He was awarded the poet laureateship in 1813.

In 1830 Southey confided to Caroline Bowles (whom he married nine years later, after the death of his first wife) that "forty years ago I could partake in the hopes of those who expected that political revolutions were to bring about a political millennium." During that radical period he wrote *Wat Tyler* (1794), a play about the English Peasants' Revolt in 1381, with obvious implications for his own time. He also wrote in 1793, but did not publish until 1796, *Joan of Arc: An Epic Poem*, which represents Joan as a martyr in the cause of liberation from tyranny. In the printed excerpt here from book 9 of the epic, the angel Theodore appears to Joan in a vision and reveals to her the paradisal state of the early world, the fall of humanity through its lust for power and wealth, and then (by a violent event that in manuscript Southey identified as the French Revolution) the future recovery of the blissful condition of the initial Paradise.

From Joan of Arc: An Epic Poem

     "These are the Daemons that pervert the power
825 Of Love," said Theodore. "The time was once
     When LOVE and HAPPINESS went hand in hand,
     In that blest era of the infant world
     Ere man had learnt to bow the knee to man.
     Was there a youth whom warm affection fill'd,
830 He spake his honest heart; the earliest fruits
     His toil produced, the sweetest flowers that deck'd
     The sunny bank, he gather'd for the maid,
     Nor she disdain'd the gift—for VICE not yet
     Had burst the dungeons of her hell, and rear'd
835 Those artificial boundaries that divide
     Man from his species. State of blessedness!
     Till that ill-omen'd hour when Cain's stern son
     Delved in the bowels of the earth for gold,
     Accursed bane of virtue! of such force
840 As poets feign dwelt in the Gorgon's locks,
     Which whoso saw, felt instant the life-blood
     Cold curdle in his veins, the creeping flesh
     Grew stiff with horror, and the heart forgot
     To beat. Accursed hour! for man no more
845 To JUSTICE paid his homage, but forsook
     Her altars, and bow'd down before the shrine
     Of WEALTH and POWER, the Idols he had made.
     Then HELL enlarg'd herself, her gates flew wide,
     Her legion fiends rush'd forth. OPPRESSION came
850 Whose frown is desolation, and whose breath

Blasts like the Pestilence; and POVERTY,
A meager monster, who with withering touch
Makes barren all the better part of man,
MOTHER OF MISERIES; then the goodly earth
855 Which God had framed for happiness, became
One theatre of woe, and all that God
Had given to bless free men, these tyrant fiends
His bitterest curses made. Yet for the best
Hath he ordained all things, the ALL-WISE!
860 For by experience rous'd shall man at length
Dash down his Moloch-gods, Samson-like
And burst his fetters—only strong whilst strong
Believed; then in the bottomless abyss
OPPRESSION shall be chain'd, and POVERTY
865 Die, and with her, her Brood of Miseries;
And VIRTUE and EQUALITY preserve
The reign of LOVE, and Earth shall once again
Be Paradise, whilst WISDOM shall secure
The state of bliss which IGNORANCE betrayed."

870 "Oh age of happiness!" the Maid exclaim'd,
"Roll fast thy current, Time, till that blest age
Arrive! and happy thou my Theodore,
Permitted thus to see the sacred depths
Of wisdom!"

1796

WILLIAM WORDSWORTH

Descriptive Sketches is one of William Wordsworth's (1770–1850) first two books. It was published simultaneously with *An Evening Walk* by the radical publisher Joseph Johnson in January 1793. The poem describes Wordsworth's observations during a walking tour through the Alps with his Welsh friend Robert Jones in the summer of 1790, when the French were celebrating the first anniversary of the fall of the Bastille. (Wordsworth later represented the same tour in *The Prelude*, book 6; see p. 345.) The concluding section of *Descriptive Sketches*, written at the height of Wordsworth's republican enthusiasm, describes the promise of the French Revolution in terms that conjoin biblical millennialism with the Roman poet Virgil's fourth eclogue, which envisions the return of the primeval golden age. In the final text of *Descriptive Sketches* published in Wordsworth's lifetime, that of 1849–50, Wordsworth retracts his confidence in the millennial outcome of the French Revolution but does not renounce his millennial hope:

Lo, from the flames a great and glorious birth;
As if a new-made heaven were hailing a new earth!
—All cannot be: the promise is too fair
For creatures doomed to breathe terrestrial air:
Yet not for this will sober reason frown

Upon that promise, nor the hope disown;
She knows that only from high aims ensue
Rich guerdons, and to them alone are due.

From Descriptive Sketches

—Tho' Liberty shall soon, indignant, raise
775 Red on his hills his beacon's comet blaze;
Bid from on high his lonely cannon sound,
And on ten thousand hearths his shout rebound;
His larum-bell from village-tow'r to tow'r
Swing on th' astounded ear its dull undying roar:
780 Yet, yet rejoice, tho' Pride's perverted ire
Rouze Hell's own aid, and wrap thy hills in fire.
Lo! from th' innocuous flames, a lovely birth!
With its own Virtues springs another earth;
Nature, as in her prime, her virgin reign
785 Begins, and Love and Truth compose her train;
With pulseless hand, and fix'd unwearied gaze,
Unbreathing Justice her still beam surveys:
No more, along thy vales and viny groves,
Whole hamlets disappearing as he moves,
790 With cheeks o'erspread by smiles of baleful glow,
On his pale horse shall fell Consumption go.
    Oh give, great God, to Freedom's waves to ride
Sublime o'er Conquest, Avarice, and Pride,
To break, the vales where Death with Famine scow'rs,
795 And dark Oppression builds her thick-ribb'd tow'rs;
Where Machination her fell soul resigns,
Fled panting to the center of her mines;
Where Persecution decks with ghastly smiles
Her bed, his mountains mad Ambition piles;
800 Where Discord stalks dilating, every hour,
And crouching fearful at the feet of Pow'r,
Like Lightnings eager for th' almighty word,
Look up for sign of havoc, Fire, and Sword;
—Give them, beneath their breast while Gladness springs,
805 To brood the nations o'er with Nile-like wings;
And grant that every sceptred child of clay,
Who cries, presumptuous, "here their tides shall stay,"
Swept in their anger from th' affrighted shore,
With all his creatures sink—to rise no more.

1793

The Excursion

The Excursion, published in 1814, was Wordsworth's longest poem and was the subject of some noted negative reviews (Francis Jeffrey's in the *Edinburgh Review* began "This will never do"). It was, nonetheless, highly valued by John Keats and others and became one of the most influential works of its time. The passage printed here—from the late text of 1849–50 but virtually identical with that of the first edition—is spoken by the character called "the Solitary," who in the "Argument" to book 3 is described at first as "Roused by the French Revolution" but later oppressed by "Disappointment and Disgust." Wordsworth's account of the Solitary's early enthusiasm for the revolution reflects in part his own experience but is modeled also on Joseph Fawcett, a preacher and poet who had succeeded Richard Price, after Price's death in 1791, at the Dissenting Chapel in Old Jewry. During his residence in London in 1791, Wordsworth had attended Fawcett's sermons, which attracted a large and fashionable audience. The Solitary, in poems as well as sermons, projects the dazzling promise of the French Revolution in terms that like Wordsworth's autobiographical passage in *Descriptive Sketches*, fuse biblical prophecy with Virgil's prediction of a recurrence in the present of the golden age of humanity during the reign of the god Saturn.

From The Excursion
From *Book 3, Despondency*

* * *

    "From that abstraction I was roused,—and how?
Even as a thoughtful shepherd by a flash
Of lightning startled in a gloomy cave
Of these wild hills. For, lo! the dread Bastille,
710   With all the chambers in its horrid towers,
Fell to the ground:—by violence overthrown
Of indignation; and with shouts that drowned
The crash it made in falling! From the wreck
A golden palace rose, or seemed to rise,
715   The appointed seat of equitable law
And mild paternal sway. The potent shock
I felt: the transformation I perceived,
As marvellously seized as in that moment
When, from the blind mist issuing, I beheld
720   Glory—beyond all glory ever seen,
Confusion infinite of heaven and earth,
Dazzling the soul. Meanwhile, prophetic harps
In every grove were ringing, 'War shall cease;
Did ye not hear that conquest is abjured?
725   Bring garlands, bring forth choicest flowers, to deck
The tree of Liberty.'—My heart rebounded;
My melancholy voice the chorus joined;
—'Be joyful all ye nations; in all lands,
Ye that are capable of joy be glad!
730   Henceforth, whate'er is wanting to yourselves
In others ye shall promptly find;—and all,
Enriched by mutual and reflected wealth,
Shall with one heart honour their common kind.'

    "Thus was I reconverted to the world;
735   Society became my glittering bride,
And airy hopes my children.—From the depths

Of natural passion, seemingly escaped,
My soul diffused herself in wide embrace
Of institutions, and the forms of things;
740 As they exist, in mutable array,
Upon life's surface. What, though in my veins
There flowed no Gallic blood, nor had I breathed
The air of France, not less than Gallic zeal
Kindled and burned among the sapless twigs
745 Of my exhausted heart. If busy men
In sober conclave met, to weave a web
Of amity, whose living threads should stretch
Beyond the seas, and to the farthest pole,
There did I sit, assisting. If, with noise
750 And acclamation, crowds in open air
Expressed the tumult of their minds, my voice
There mingled, heard or not. The powers of song
I left not uninvoked; and, in still groves,
Where mild enthusiasts tuned a pensive lay
755 Of thanks and expectation, in accord
With their belief, I sang Saturnian rule
Returned,—a progeny of golden years
Permitted to descend, and bless mankind.
—With promises the Hebrew Scriptures teem:
760 I felt their invitation; and resumed
A long-suspended office in the House
Of public worship, where, the glowing phrase
Of ancient inspiration serving me,
I promised also,—with undaunted trust
765 Foretold, and added prayer to prophecy;
The admiration winning of the crowd;
The help desiring of the pure devout.

  "Scorn and contempt forbid me to proceed!
But History, time's slavish scribe, will tell
770 How rapidly the zealots of the cause
Disbanded—or in hostile ranks appeared;
Some, tired of honest service; these, outdone,
Disgusted therefore, or appalled, by aims
Of fiercer zealots—so confusion reigned,
775 And the more faithful were compelled to exclaim,
As Brutus did to Virtue, 'Liberty,
I worshipped thee, and find thee but a Shade!'

  "Such recantation had for me no charm,
Nor would I bend to it; who should have grieved
780 At aught, however fair, that bore the mien
Of a conclusion, or catastrophe.
Why then conceal, that, when the simply good
In timid selfishness withdrew, I sought
Other support, not scrupulous whence it came;
785 And, by what compromise it stood, not nice?
Enough if notions seemed to be high-pitched,

And qualities determined.—Among men
So charactered did I maintain a strife
Hopeless, and still more hopeless every hour;
790   But, in the process, I began to feel
That, if the emancipation of the world
Were missed, I should at least secure my own,
And be in part compensated. For rights,
Widely—inveterately usurped upon,
795   I spake with vehemence; and promptly seized
All that Abstraction furnished for my needs
Or purposes; nor scrupled to proclaim,
And propagate, by liberty of life,
Those new persuasions."

* * *

1814

SAMUEL TAYLOR COLERIDGE

Samuel Taylor Coleridge (1772–1834) was twenty-two when he drafted *Religious Musings: A Desultory Poem, Written on Christmas' Eve, in the Year of Our Lord, 1784.* It was first published in his *Poems* of 1796 and was his most ambitious poem up to that time. On it, Coleridge then said, "I build all my poetic pretensions." In the turbulence and excitement of the early period of the French Revolution, Coleridge felt the need to give public voice to his political, religious, and philosophical beliefs, and poetized such materials by assuming a visionary and oracular persona and adopting the elaborate rhetoric, allegorical tactics and contorted syntax of the late eighteenth-century "sublime ode." Soon, however, he rejected this mode (in which, he wrote in December 1794, "my Poetry . . . sweats beneath a heavy burthen of Ideas and Imagery! It has seldom Ease") for the relaxed style of heightened conversation represented at its best by *Frost at Midnight* (1798; see p. 457).

The passage of *Religious Musings* printed here, in the text and line numbering of 1796, covers the first three of the last four items listed in Coleridge's Argument for the poem: "The French Revolution. Millennium. Universal Redemption. Conclusion." Coleridge's notes stress his conviction that the contemporary events in France fulfil the prophecies in the Book of Revelation that a period of violence is the necessary prelude to an earthly millennium. Wordsworth judged the concluding section on "earth reparadis'd" to be the best in Coleridge's *Poems* of 1796—in considerable part, doubtless, because it matched his own prophetic vision in *Descriptive Sketches*, published the year before.

From Religious Musings

Argument

Introduction. Person of Christ. His Prayer on the Cross. The process of his Doctrines on the mind of the Individual. Character of the Elect. Superstition. Digression to the present War. Origin and Uses of Government and Property. The present State of Society. The French Revolution. Millennium. Universal Redemption. Conclusion.

* * *

O ye numberless,
Whom foul Oppression's ruffian gluttony
Drives from life's plenteous feast! O thou poor Wretch,
Who nurs'd in darkness and made wild by want

300   Dost roam for prey, yea thy unnatural hand
Liftest to deeds of blood! O pale-eyed Form,
The victim of seduction, doom'd to know
Polluted nights and days of blasphemy;
Who in loath'd orgies with lewd wassailers
305   Must gaily laugh, while thy remember'd Home
Gnaws like a viper at thy secret heart!
O aged Women! ye who weekly catch
The morsel tost by law-forc'd Charity,
And die so slowly, that none call it murder!
310   O loathly-visag'd Suppliants! ye that oft
Rack'd with disease, from the unopen'd gate
Of the full Lazar-house, heart-broken crawl!
O ye to scepter'd Glory's gore-drench'd field
Forc'd or ensnar'd, who swept by Slaughter's scythe,
315   (Stern nurse of Vultures!) steam in putrid heaps!
O thou poor Widow, who in dreams dost view
Thy Husband's mangled corse, and from short doze
Start'st with a shriek: or in thy half-thatch'd cot
Wak'd by the wintry night-storm, wet and cold,
320   Cow'rest o'er thy screaming baby! Rest awhile,
Children of Wretchedness! More groans must rise,
More blood must steam, or ere your wrongs be full.
Yet is the day of Retribution nigh:
The Lamb of God hath open'd the fifth seal:[1]
325   And upward rush on swiftest wing of fire
Th' innumerable multitude of Wrongs
By man on man inflicted! Rest awhile,
Children of Wretchedness! The hour is nigh:
And lo! the Great, the Rich, the Mighty Men,
330   The Kings and the Chief Captains of the World,
With all that fix'd on high like stars of Heaven
Shot baleful influence, shall be cast to earth,
Vile and down-trodden, as the untimely fruit

---

1. See the sixth chapter of the Revelation of St. John the Divine.—And I looked and beheld a pale horse; and his name that sat on him was Death, and Hell followed with him. And power was given unto them over the FOURTH part of the Earth to kill with sword, and with hunger, and with pestilence, and with the beasts of the Earth.—And when he had opened the fifth seal, I saw under the altar the souls of them that were slain for the word of God, and for the testimony which they held: and white robes were given unto every one of them; and it was said unto them, that they should rest yet for a little season, until their fellow servants also, and their brethren, that should be killed as they were should be fulfilled. And I beheld when he had opened the sixth seal, the stars of Heaven fell unto the Earth, even as a fig tree casteth her untimely figs when she is shaken of a mighty wind: And the Kings of the earth, and the great men, and the rich men, and the chief captains, &c. [Coleridge's note].

Shook from the fig-tree by a sudden storm.
335 Ev'n now the storm begins:[2] each gentle name,
Faith and meek Piety, with fearful joy
Tremble far-off—for lo! the Giant FRENZY
Uprooting empires with his whirlwind arm
Mocketh high Heaven; burst hideous from the cell
340 Where the old Hag, unconquerable, huge,
Creation's eyeless drudge, black RUIN, sits
Nursing th' impatient earthquake.

O return!
Pure FAITH! meek PIETY! The abhorred Form[3]
Whose scarlet robe was stiff with earthly pomp,
345 Who drank iniquity in cups of gold,
Whose names were many and all blasphemous,
Hath met the horrible judgment! Whence that cry?
The mighty army of foul Spirits shriek'd
Disherited of earth! For She hath fallen
350 On whose black front was written MYSTERY;
She that reel'd heavily, whose wine was blood;
She that work'd whoredom with the DAEMON POWER
And from the dark embrace all evils things
Brought forth and nurtur'd: mitred ATHEISM!
355 And patient FOLLY who on bended knee
Gives back the steel that stabb'd him; and pale FEAR
Hunted by ghastlier terrors than surround
Moon-blasted Madness when he yells at midnight!
Return pure FAITH! return meek PIETY!
360 The kingdoms of the world are yours: each heart
Self-govern'd, the vast family of Love
Rais'd from the common earth by common toil
Enjoy the equal produce. Such delights
As float to earth, permitted visitants!
365 When on some solemn jubilee of Saints
The sapphire-blazing gates of Paradise
Are thrown wide open, and thence voyage forth
Detachments wild of seraph-warbled airs,
And odors snatch'd from beds of amaranth,
370 And they, that from the crystal river of life
Spring up on freshen'd wing, ambrosial gales!
The favor'd good man in his lonely walk
Perceives them, and his silent spirit drinks
Strange bliss which he shall recognize in heaven.
375 And such delights, such strange beatitude
Seize on my young anticipating heart
When that blest future rushes on my view!
For in his own and in his Father's might

2. The French Revolution [Coleridge's note].
3. And there came one of the seven Angels which
had the seven vials and talked with me, saying unto
me, come hither! I will shew unto thee the judgment of the great Whore, that sitteth upon many
waters: with whom the Kings of the earth have
committed fornication, &c. Revelation of St. John
the Divine, chapter the seventeenth [Coleridge's
note].

The SAVIOR comes! While as to solemn strains
380 The THOUSAND YEARS[4] lead up their mystic dance,
Old OCEAN claps his hands! The DESERT shouts!
And soft gales wafted from the haunts of Spring
Melt the primaeval North! The mighty Dead
Rise to new life, whoe'er from earliest time
385 With conscious zeal had urg'd Love's wond'rous plan,
Coadjutors of God. To MILTON'S trump
The odorous groves of earth reparadis'd
Unbosom their glad echoes: inly hush'd
Adoring NEWTON his serener eye
390 Raises to heaven: and he of mortal kind
Wisest, he[5] first who mark'd the ideal tribes
Down the fine fibers from the sentient brain
Roll subtly-surging. Pressing on his steps
Lo! Priestley[6] there, Patriot, and Saint, and Sage,
395 Whom that my fleshly eye hath never seen
A childish pang of impotent regret
Hath thrill'd my heart. Him from his native land
Statesmen blood-stain'd and Priests idolatrous
By dark lies mad'ning the blind multitude
400 Drove with vain hate: calm, pitying he retir'd,
And mus'd expectant on these promis'd years.

O Years! the blest preeminence of Saints!
Sweeping before the rapt prophetic Gaze
Bright as what glories of the jasper throne
405 Stream from the gorgeous and face-veiling plumes
Of Spirits adoring! Ye, blest Years! must end,
And all beyond is darkness!

＊　＊　＊

1794

4. The Millennium:—in which I suppose, that Man will continue to enjoy the highest glory, of which his human nature is capable.—That all who in past ages have endeavored to ameliorate the state of man, will rise and enjoy the fruits and flowers, the imperceptible seeds of which they had sown in their former Life: and that the wicked will during the same period, be suffering the remedies adapted to their several bad habits. I suppose that this period will be followed by the passing away of this Earth, and by our entering the state of pure intellect; when all Creation shall rest from its labors [Coleridge's note, added in the 1797 edition].
5. David Hartley [Coleridge's note].
6. Sir Isaac Newton (line 390), Hartley (line 392), and Joseph Priestley were believers in apocalyptic prophecies, and all three had written interpretive commentaries on the Book of Revelation.

PERCY BYSSHE SHELLEY

Queen Mab, Percy Shelley's (1792–1822) first long work in verse, was written mainly in 1812, when the poet was twenty years old; it was printed and distributed privately (but never published by the author) in February 1813. It is an allegorical dream-vision in which the fairy queen Mab takes the mortal maiden Ianthe on an extra-terrestrial excursion to show her the past, present, and future states of the human world. The past is irrational, the woeful product of one human error after another. The ghastly present is corrupted by the institutions of king, priests, and statesmen. But the future, set forth in cantos 8 and 9, is one of human blessedness, when "A garden shall arise, in loveliness / Surpassing fabled Eden" (4.88–89). Shelley's is not a religious but a secular apocalypse, with the Spirit of Necessity replacing God's providence as the agent of redemption. Nonetheless, Shelley's anticipation of a "taint-less" humanity in a renovated world is for the most part imported from biblical millennialism, especially in Isaiah and Revelation. In the selections printed here from cantos 8 and 9, Queen Mab is speaking to Ianthe.

From Queen Mab: A Philosophical Poem

From Canto 8

* * *

Then in her triumph spoke the Fairy Queen:
"I will not call the ghost of ages gone
To unfold the frightful secrets of its lore;
    The present now is past,
45 And those events that desolate the earth
Have faded from the memory of Time,
Who dares not give reality to that
Whose being I annul. To me is given
The wonders of the human world to keep,
50 Space, matter, time, and mind. Futurity
Exposes now its treasure; let the sight
Renew and strengthen all thy failing hope.
O human Spirit! spur thee to the goal
Where virtue fixes universal peace,
55 And midst the ebb and flow of human things,
Show somewhat stable, somewhat certain still,
A lighthouse o'er the wild of dreary waves.

"The habitable earth is full of bliss;
Those wastes of frozen billows that were hurled
60 By everlasting snow-storms round the poles,
Where matter dared not vegetate or live,
But ceaseless frost round the vast solitude
Bound its broad zone of stillness, are unloosed;
And fragrant zephyrs there from spicy isles
65 Ruffle the placid ocean-deep, that rolls
Its broad, bright surges to the sloping sand,
Whose roar is wakened into echoings sweet
To murmur through the heaven-breathing groves
And melodize with man's blest nature there.

70 "Those desarts of immeasurable sand,
Whose age-collected fervors scarce allowed

A bird to live, a blade of grass to spring,
Where the shrill chirp of the green lizard's love
Broke on the sultry silentness alone,
75   Now teem with countless rills and shady woods,
Corn-fields and pastures and white cottages;
And where the startled wilderness beheld
A savage conqueror stained in kindred blood,
A tygress sating with the flesh of lambs
80   The unnatural famine of her toothless cubs,
Whilst shouts and howlings through the desart rang,
Sloping and smooth the daisy-spangled lawn,
Offering sweet incense to the sun-rise, smiles
To see a babe before his mother's door,
85   Sharing his morning's meal
    With the green and golden basilisk[1]
        That comes to lick his feet.

"Those trackless deeps, where many a weary sail
Has seen above the illimitable plain,
90   Morning on night, and night on morning rise,
Whilst still no land to greet the wanderer spread
Its shadowy mountains on the sun-bright sea,
Where the loud roarings of the tempest-waves
So long have mingled with the gusty wind
95   In melancholy loneliness, and swept
The desart of those ocean solitudes,
But vocal to the sea-bird's harrowing shriek,
The bellowing monster, and the rushing storm,
Now to the sweet and many mingling sounds
100   Of kindliest human impulses respond.
Those lonely realms bright garden-isles begem,
With lightsome clouds and shining seas between,
And fertile vallies, resonant with bliss,
Whilst green woods overcanopy the wave,
105   Which like a toil-worn labourer leaps to shore,
To meet the kisses of the flowrets there.

"All things are recreated, and the flame
Of consentaneous love inspires all life:
The fertile bosom of the earth gives suck
110   To myriads, who still grow beneath her care,
Rewarding her with their pure perfectness:
The balmy breathings of the winds inhale
Her virtues, and diffuse them all abroad:
Health floats amid the gentle atmosphere,
115   Glows in the fruits, and mantles on the stream:
No storms deform the beaming brow of heaven,
Nor scatter in the freshness of its pride
The foliage of the ever verdant trees;
But fruits are ever ripe, flowers ever fair,

1. A legendary serpent whose breath and glance are death-dealing.

120 And autumn proudly bears her matron grace,
    Kindling a flush on the fair cheek of spring,
    Whose virgin bloom beneath the ruddy fruit
    Reflects its tint, and blushes into love.

    "The lion now forgets to thirst for blood:
125 There might you see him sporting in the sun
    Beside the dreadless kid; his claws are sheathed,
    His teeth are harmless, custom's force has made
    His nature as the nature of a lamb.
    Like passion's fruit, the nightshade's tempting bane
130 Poisons no more the pleasure it bestows:
    All bitterness is past; the cup of joy
    Unmingled mantles to the goblet's brim,
    And courts the thirsty lips it fled before.

    "But chief, ambiguous man, he that can know
135 More misery, and dream more joy than all;
    Whose keen sensations thrill within his breast
    To mingle with a loftier instinct there,
    Lending their power to pleasure and to pain,
    Yet raising, sharpening, and refining each;
140 Who stands amid the ever-varying world,
    The burthen or the glory of the earth;
    He chief perceives the change, his being notes
    The gradual renovation, and defines
    Each movement of its progress on his mind.

145 "Man, where the gloom of the long polar night
    Lowers o'er the snow-clad rocks and frozen soil,
    Where scarce the hardiest herb that braves the frost
    Basks in the moonlight's ineffectual glow,
    Shrank with the plants, and darkened with the night;
150 His chilled and narrow energies, his heart,
    Insensible to courage, truth, or love,
    His stunted stature and imbecile frame,
    Marked him for some abortion of the earth,
    Fit compeer of the bears that roamed around,
155 Whose habits and enjoyments were his own:
    His life a feverish dream of stagnant woe,
    Whose meagre wants, but scantily fulfilled,
    Apprised him ever of the joyless length
    Which his short being's wretchedness had reached;
160 His death a pang which famine, cold and toil,
    Long on the mind, whilst yet the vital spark
    Clung to the body stubbornly, had brought:
    All was inflicted here that earth's revenge
    Could wreak on the infringers of her law;
165 One curse alone was spared—the name of God.

    "Nor where the tropics bound the realms of day
    With a broad belt of mingling cloud and flame,

Where blue mists through the unmoving atmosphere
Scattered the seeds of pestilence, and fed
170 Unnatural vegetation, where the land
Teemed with all earthquake, tempest and disease,
Was man a nobler being; slavery
Had crushed him to his country's bloodstained dust;
Or he was bartered for the fame of power,
175 Which all internal impulses destroying,
Makes human will an article of trade;
Or he was changed with Christians for their gold,
And dragged to distant isles, where to the sound
Of the flesh-mangling scourge, he does the work
180 Of all-polluting luxury and wealth,
Which doubly visits on the tyrants' heads
The long-protracted fulness of their woe;
Or he was led to legal butchery,
To turn to worms beneath that burning sun,
185 Where kings first leagued against the rights of men,
And priests first traded with the name of God.

"Even where the milder zone afforded man
A seeming shelter, yet contagion there,
Blighting his being with unnumbered ills,
190 Spread like a quenchless fire; nor truth till late
Availed to arrest its progress, or create
That peace which first in bloodless victory waved
Her snowy standard o'er this favored clime:
There man was long the train-bearer of slaves,
195 The mimic of surrounding misery,
The jackal of ambition's lion-rage,
The bloodhound of religion's hungry zeal.

"Here now the human being stands adorning
This loveliest earth with taintless body and mind;
200 Blest from his birth with all bland impulses,
Which gently in his noble bosom wake
All kindly passions and all pure desires.
Him, still from hope to hope the bliss pursuing
Which from the exhaustless lore of human weal
205 Dawns on the virtuous mind, the thoughts that rise
In time-destroying infiniteness, gift
With self-enshrined eternity, that mocks
The unprevailing hoariness of age,
And man, once fleeting o'er the transient scene
210 Swift as an unremembered vision, stands
Immortal upon earth: no longer now
He slays the lamb that looks him in the face,
And horribly devours his mangled flesh,
Which still avenging nature's broken law,
215 Kindled all putrid humors in his frame,
All evil passions, and all vain belief,

Hatred, despair, and loathing in his mind,
The germs of misery, death, disease, and crime.
No longer now the winged habitants,
220 That in the woods their sweet lives sing away,
Flee from the form of man; but gather round,
And prune their sunny feathers on the hands
Which little children stretch in friendly sport
Towards these dreadless partners of their play.
225 All things are void of terror: man has lost
His terrible prerogative, and stands
An equal amidst equals: happiness
And science dawn though late upon the earth;
Peace cheers the mind, health renovates the frame;
230 Disease and pleasure cease to mingle here,
Reason and passion cease to combat there;
Whilst each unfettered o'er the earth extend
Their all-subduing energies, and wield
The sceptre of a vast dominion there;
235 Whilst every shape and mode of matter lends
Its force to the omnipotence of mind,
Which from its dark mine drags the gem of truth
To decorate its paradise of peace."

From *Canto 9*

"O happy Earth! reality of Heaven!
To which those restless souls that ceaselessly
Throng through the human universe, aspire;
Thou consummation of all mortal hope!
5 Thou glorious prize of blindly-working will!
Whose rays, diffused throughout all space and time,
Verge to one point and blend for ever there:
Of purest spirits thou pure dwelling-place!
Where care and sorrow, impotence and crime,
10 Languor, disease, and ignorance dare not come:
O happy Earth, reality of Heaven!"

* * *

1813

APOCALYPSE BY IMAGINATION

Reminiscing in 1815, Thomas Noon Talfourd—an eminent jurist who was also a poet and a playwright—attributed to the French Revolution a primary part in shaping the literature of what we now call the Romantic period. The revolution, which "shook society to its deepest foundations," also "completed the regeneration of our poetry":

At one moment, all was hope and joy and rapture; the corruption and iniquity of ages seemed to vanish like a dream; the unclouded heavens seemed once more to ring with the exulting chorus of peace on earth and good-will to men; and the

spirit of a mighty and puissant nation, long confined in the dungeons of superstition, seemed rising in native majesty to draw new inspiration from the rejoicing
heavens.

But "on a sudden," Talfourd says, "all was changed," in the release of barbaric passions that resulted in actions that far exceeded "the darkest imaginings of the past."
The effect of "this moral hurricane, this breaking up of the surface of society, this
rending of the general heart," was "to raise and darken the imagination" and so contributed "to form that great age of poetry which is now flourishing around us" ("An
Attempt to Estimate the Poetical Talent of the Present Age," 1815).

Talfourd clearly recognized the religious and millenarian nature of the high enthusiasm and unbounded hopes incited during the early revolutionary years. He saw also,
however, that an essential feature of the revolution as a cultural and literary influence
was, in the general estimate, the fact that it had failed. The greatest and most enduring
poetry of the age was written not in the mood of revolutionary exaltation but in the
mood of revolutionary disenchantment and despair, after the succession of disasters
that began with the massacres, the executions, and the Reign of Terror in 1793–94.
A number of major Romantic poets, however, did not break from the formative past
but set out to salvage the grounds for hope in the coming of a renewed and perfected
world. Romantic thinking and imagination, that is, remained apocalyptic in form, but
with a radical shift from violent political revolution to a revolution of consciousness
as the agency that will transform the world.

The continuity between the earlier and later Romantic hopes for transformation is
indicated by the persistence of the two central apocalyptic images: the sacred marriage
and the advent of a new heaven and new earth. Coleridge combined the two figures
in the fifth stanza *Dejection: An Ode* (1802), where an inner harmony that he calls
"Joy" is

> the spirit and the power,
> Which wedding Nature to us gives in dower
> A new Earth and new Heaven. . . .
> (lines 67–69; see p. 460)

In the "Prospectus" to his major poetic enterprises, Wordsworth announced that his
"high argument" is a marriage hymn—a "spousal verse"—that will effect a "creation"
equivalent to a restored Paradise; but as in Coleridge, the ground for the apocalyptic
hope has been shifted from political revolution to an inner spiritual revolution, and
the marriage between the Lamb and the New Jerusalem has been converted into a
marriage between the human mind and the nature from which it has been alienated:

> Paradise, and groves
> Elysian, Fortunate Fields . . .
> . . . the discerning intellect of Man,
> When wedded to this goodly universe
> In love and holy passion, shall find these
> A simple produce of the common day.
> (lines 47–71; see p. 302)

William Blake's confidence in a millennial result of political revolution was short-
lived, but his imagination remained stubbornly apocalyptic. In his major prophetic
poem *Jerusalem* (ca. 1809–20), the concluding chapter is prefaced with the voice of
the Bard arousing Albion (universal mankind) from his "sleep of death," so that he
may reunite with his separated female emanation Jerusalem. The poem closes with
"the Eternal Day" of universal resurrection in a restored Paradise, and this event is
illustrated by Blake's rendering of the apocalyptic marriage—an etching of Albion and
Jerusalem in an embrace of love. Some two decades later, Percy Shelley manifested

a parallel evolution in his thinking. He lost his faith in the millennial possibility of political revolution, but his long poems continued to embody his vision of a total renovation of humanity and its world. In his *Prometheus Unbound*, this world is one that reveals itself to the purged human imagination, and only after humanity has achieved a total revolution of its moral nature. Shelley continues to represent this imaginative achievement of a new heaven on earth in the form of an apocalyptic marriage, the reunion between Prometheus and Asia—an erotic as well as a spiritual reunion, with which, in the fourth act, the entire cosmos exuberantly participates (act 3.4 and act 4; see pp. 751 and 754).

The myth of apocalypse has remained deeply ingrained in Western culture and has continued into the twentieth century to provide a scenario, or interpretive frame, for a violent political revolution of which the expected result on human well-being will be sudden, absolute, and universal. In *New Year Letter* (1940), for example, the poet W. H. Auden drew a parallel between Wordsworth's early view of the French Revolution as an apocalyptic Second Coming ("Parousia")—he "Saw in the fall of the Bastille / The Parousia of liberty"—and the response of political idealists in his own generation to the Communist revolution in Russia that began in 1917. As in the Romantic period, so in the twentieth century, he comments ruefully,

> We hoped; we waited for the day
> The State would wither clean away,
> Expecting the Millennium
> That theory promised us would come,
> It didn't.

MARY WOLLSTONECRAFT
1759–1797

Mary Wollstonecraft's father inherited a substantial fortune and set himself up as a gentleman farmer. He was, however, both extravagant and incompetent, and as one farm after another failed, he became moody and violent and sought solace in heavy bouts of drinking and in tyrannizing over his submissive wife. Mary was the second of five children and the oldest daughter. She later told her husband, William Godwin, that she used to throw herself in front of her mother to protect her from her husband's blows, and that she sometimes slept outside the door of her parents' bedroom to intervene if her father should break out in a drunken rage. The solace of Mary's early life was her fervent attachment to Fanny Blood, an accomplished girl two years her senior; their friendship, which began when Mary was sixteen, endured and deepened until Fanny's death.

At the age of nineteen Mary Wollstonecraft left home to take a position as companion to a well-to-do widow living in Bath, where she for the first time had the opportunity to observe—and scorn—the social life of the upper classes at the most fashionable of English resort cities. Having left her job in 1780 to nurse her dying mother through a long and harrowing illness, Wollstonecraft next went to live with the Bloods, where her work helped to sustain the struggling family. Her sister Eliza meanwhile had married and, in 1784, after the birth of a daughter, suffered a nervous breakdown. Convinced that her sister's collapse was the result of her husband's cruelty and abuse, Wollstonecraft persuaded her to abandon husband and child and flee to London; because a divorce at that time was not commonly available, and a fugitive wife could be forced to return to her husband, the two women hid in secret quarters while awaiting the grant of a legal separation. The infant, automatically given into the father's custody, died before she was a year old.

The penniless women, together with Fanny Blood and Wollstonecraft's other sister, Everina, established a girls' school at Newington Green, near London. The project flourished at first, and at Newington, Wollstonecraft was befriended by the Reverend Richard Price, a leading radical author and reformer whose kindly guidance helped shape her social and political opinions. Blood, although already ill with tuberculosis, went to Lisbon to marry her longtime suitor, Hugh Skeys, and quickly became pregnant. Wollstonecraft rushed to Lisbon to attend her friend's childbirth, only to have Fanny die in her arms; the infant died soon afterward. The loss threw Wollstonecraft (already subject to bouts of depression) into black despair, which was heightened when she found that the school at Newington was in bad financial straits and had to be closed. Tormented by creditors, she rallied her energies to write her first book, *Thoughts on the Education of Daughters* (1786), a conventional and pious series of essays, and took up a position as governess for several daughters in the Anglo-Irish family of Viscount Kingsborough, a man of great wealth whose seat was in County Cork, Ireland.

The Kingsboroughs were well intentioned and did their best to introduce Wollstonecraft into the busy trivialities of their social life. But the ambiguity of her position as governess, halfway between a servant and member of the family, was galling. An antagonism developed between Wollstonecraft and Lady Kingsborough, in part because the children feared their mother and adored their governess. Wollstonecraft was dismissed. She returned to London, where Joseph Johnson in 1788 published her first novel, *Mary, a Fiction,* a partly autobiographical but conventionally sentimental novel written while she was in Ireland, as well as a book for children, *Original Stories from Real Life.* The latter, a considerable success, was translated into German and quickly achieved a second English edition illustrated with engravings by William Blake. Wollstonecraft was befriended and subsidized by Johnson, the major publisher in England of radical and reformist books, and she took a prominent place among the notable writers whom he regularly entertained at his rooms in St. Paul's Churchyard. She published translations from French and German (she had taught herself both languages) and began reviewing books for Johnson's newly founded journal, the *Analytical Review.* Though still in straitened circumstances, she helped support her two sisters and her improvident and importunate father, and was also generous with funds—and with advice—to one of her brothers and to the indigent family of Fanny Blood.

In 1790 Edmund Burke's *Reflections on the Revolution in France*—an eloquent and powerful attack on the French Revolution and its English sympathizers—quickly evoked Wollstonecraft's response, *A Vindication of the Rights of Men.* This was a formidable piece of argumentation; its most potent passages are those that represent the disabilities and sufferings of the English lower classes and impugn the motives and sentiments of Burke. This work, the first book-length reply to Burke, scored an immediate success, although it was soon submerged in the flood of other replies, most notably Tom Paine's classic *Rights of Man* (1791–92). In 1792 Wollstonecraft focused her defense of the underprivileged on her own sex and wrote, in six weeks of intense effort, *A Vindication of the Rights of Woman.*

Earlier writers both in France and England had proposed that, given an equivalence in education, women would equal men in achievement. Wollstonecraft was particularly indebted to Catharine Macaulay's *Letters on Education* (1790), of which she had written an enthusiastic review. But Wollstonecraft's *Vindication* was unprecedented in its firsthand observations of the disabilities and indignities suffered by women and in the articulateness and passion with which it exposed and decried this injustice. Wollstonecraft's views were conspicuously radical at a time when women had no political rights; were limited to a few lowly vocations as servants, nurses, governesses, and petty shopkeepers; and were legally nonpersons who lost their property to their husbands at marriage and were incapable of instituting an action in the courts of law. An impressive feature of her book, for all its vehemence, is the clear-sightedness and balance of her analysis of the social conditions of the time, as they affect men as well as women. She perceives that women constitute an oppressed class that cuts across the standard hierarchy of social classes; she shows that women, because they are denied political and domestic privileges, have been forced to seek their ends by means of coquetry and cunning; and she also recognizes that men, no less than women, inherit their roles, and that the wielding of irresponsible power corrupts the oppressor no less than it distorts the oppressed. Hence her surprising and telling comparisons between women on the one hand and men of the nobility and military on the other as classes whose values and behavior have been distorted because their social roles prevent them from becoming fully human. In writing this pioneering work, Wollstonecraft found the cause that she was to pursue the rest of her life.

In December 1792, Wollstonecraft went to Paris to observe the French Revolution at firsthand. The years that she lived in France, 1793–94, were those in which the early period of moderation was succeeded by extremism and violence. In Paris she joined a group of English, American, and European expatriates sympathetic to the Revolution and fell in love with Gilbert Imlay, a personable American who had briefly been an officer in the American Revolutionary Army and was the author of a widely read book on the Kentucky backwoods, where he had been an explorer. He played the role in Paris of an American frontiersman and child of nature, but was in fact an adventurer who had left America to avoid prosecution for debt and for freewheeling speculations in Kentucky land; he was also unscrupulous in his relations with women. The two became lovers, and Wollstonecraft bore a daughter, Fanny Imlay, in May 1794. Imlay, who was often absent on mysterious business deals, left mother and daughter for a visit to London that he kept protracting. After the publication of her book *An Historical and Moral View of the Origin and Progress of the French Revolution* (1795), Wollstonecraft followed Imlay to London, where, persuaded that he no longer loved her, she tried to commit suicide; the attempt, however, was discovered and prevented by Imlay. To get her out of the way, he persuaded her to take a trip as his business envoy to the Scandinavian countries. Although this was then a region of poor or impassible roads and primitive accommodations, the intrepid Wollstonecraft traveled there for four months, sometimes in the wilds, accompanied by the year-old Fanny and a French nurse.

Back in London, Wollstonecraft discovered that Imlay was living with a new mistress, a strolling actress. Finally convinced he was lost to her, she hurled herself from a bridge into the Thames but was rescued by a passerby. Imlay departed with his actress to Paris. Wollstonecraft, resourceful as always, used the letters she had written to Imlay to compose a book, *Letters Written during a Short Residence in Sweden, Norway, and Denmark* (1796), full of sharp observations of human character, the conditions of Scandinavian women, and the austere northern landscape.

In the same year Wollstonecraft renewed an earlier acquaintance with the philosopher William Godwin. His *Inquiry Concerning Political Justice* (1793), the most drastic proposal for restructuring the political and social order yet published in England, together with his novel of terror, *Caleb Williams* (1794), which embodies his social views, had made him the most famed radical writer of his time. The austerely rationalistic philosopher, then forty years of age, had an unexpected capacity for deep feeling, and what began as a flirtation soon ripened into affection and (as their letters show) passionate physical love. She wrote Godwin, with what was for the time remarkable outspokenness on the part of a woman: "Now by these presents [i.e., this document] let me assure you that you are not only in my heart, but my veins, this morning. I turn from you half abashed—yet you haunt me, and some look, word or touch thrills through my whole frame. . . . When the heart and reason accord there is no flying from voluptuous sensations, do what a woman can." Wollstonecraft was soon again with child, and Godwin (who had in his *Inquiry* attacked the institution of marriage as a base form of property rights in human beings) braved the ridicule of his radical friends and conservative enemies by marrying her.

They set up a household together, but Godwin also kept separate quarters in which to do his writing, and they further salvaged their principles by agreeing to live separate social lives. Wollstonecraft was happy for a brief six months. On August 30 she gave birth to a daughter, Mary Wollstonecraft Godwin, later the author of *Frankenstein* and wife of Percy Shelley. The delivery was not difficult, but resulted in massive blood poisoning. After ten days of agony, she lapsed into a coma and died. Her last whispered words were about her husband: "He is the kindest, best man in the world." Godwin wrote to a friend, announcing her death: "I firmly believe that there does not exist her equal in the world. I know from experience we were formed to make each other happy."

To distract himself in his grief Godwin published in 1798 *Memoirs of the Author of "A Vindication of the Rights of Woman"* in which he told, with the total candor on which he prided himself, of her affairs with Imlay and himself, her attempts at suicide, and her free thinking in matters of religion and sexual relationships; in four companion volumes of her *Posthumous Works* he included her outspoken love letters to Imlay. The unintended result was to saddle Wollstonecraft with a scandalous reputation so enduring that through the Victorian era advocates of the equality of women circumspectly avoided references to her *Vindication;* even John Stuart Mill, in his *Subjection of Women* (1869), neglected to mention the work. It was only in the twentieth century, and especially in the later decades, that Wollstonecraft's *Vindication* gained recognition as a classic in the literature not only of women's rights but of social analysis as well.

From A Vindication of the Rights of Woman[1]

Introduction

After considering the historic page, and viewing the living world with anxious solicitude, the most melancholy emotions of sorrowful indignation have depressed my spirits, and I have sighed when obliged to confess, that either nature has made a great difference between man and man, or that the civilization which has hitherto taken place in the world has been very partial. I have turned over various books written on the subject of education, and patiently observed the conduct of parents and the management of schools; but what has been the result?—a profound conviction that the neglected education of my fellow-creatures is the grand source of the misery I deplore; and that women, in particular, are rendered weak and wretched by a variety of concurring causes, originating from one hasty conclusion. The conduct and manners of women, in fact, evidently prove

1. The text is from the second revised edition of 1792, as edited by Carol H. Poston for the Norton Critical Edition of *A Vindication* (1975). The editors gratefully acknowledge Poston's permission to use the information in her annotations.

that their minds are not in a healthy state; for, like the flowers which are planted in too rich a soil, strength and usefulness are sacrificed to beauty; and the flaunting leaves, after having pleased a fastidious eye, fade, disregarded on the stalk, long before the season when they ought to have arrived at maturity.—One cause of this barren blooming I attribute to a false system of education, gathered from the books written on this subject by men who, considering females rather as women than human creatures, have been more anxious to make them alluring mistresses than affectionate wives and rational mothers; and the understanding of the sex has been so bubbled[2] by this specious homage, that the civilized women of the present century, with a few exceptions, are only anxious to inspire love, when they ought to cherish a nobler ambition, and by their abilities and virtues exact respect.

In a treatise, therefore, on female rights and manners, the works which have been particularly written for their improvement must not be overlooked; especially when it is asserted, in direct terms, that the minds of women are enfeebled by false refinement; that the books of instruction, written by men of genius, have had the same tendency as more frivolous productions; and that, in the true style of Mahometanism, they are treated as a kind of subordinate beings, and not as a part of the human species,[3] when improvable reason is allowed to be the dignified distinction which raises men above the brute creation, and puts a natural sceptre in a feeble hand.

Yet, because I am a woman, I would not lead my readers to suppose that I mean violently to agitate the contested question respecting the equality or inferiority of the sex; but as the subject lies in my way, and I cannot pass it over without subjecting the main tendency of my reasoning to misconstruction, I shall stop a moment to deliver, in a few words, my opinion.—In the government of the physical world it is observable that the female in point of strength is, in general, inferior to the male. This is the law of nature; and it does not appear to be suspended or abrogated in favor of woman. A degree of physical superiority cannot, therefore, be denied—and it is a noble prerogative! But not content with this natural pre-eminence, men endeavor to sink us still lower, merely to render us alluring objects for a moment; and women, intoxicated by the adoration which men, under the influence of their senses, pay them, do not seek to obtain a durable interest in their hearts, or to become the friends of the fellow creatures who find amusement in their society.

I am aware of an obvious inference:—from every quarter have I heard exclamations against masculine women; but where are they to be found? If by this appellation men mean to inveigh against their ardor in hunting, shooting, and gaming, I shall most cordially join in the cry; but if it be against the imitation of manly virtues, or, more properly speaking, the attainment of those talents and virtues, the exercise of which ennobles the human character, and which raise females in the scale of animal being, when they are comprehensively termed mankind;—all those who view them with a philosophic eye must, I should think, wish with me, that they may every day grow more and more masculine.

2. In an archaic sense, deluded, cheated.
3. It was a common but mistaken opinion among
Europeans that the Koran, the sacred text of Islam, teaches that women have no souls.

This discussion naturally divides the subject. I shall first consider women in the grand light of human creatures, who, in common with men, are placed on this earth to unfold their faculties; and afterwards I shall more particularly point out their peculiar designation.

I wish also to steer clear of an error which many respectable writers have fallen into; for the instruction which has hitherto been addressed to women, has rather been applicable to *ladies*, if the little indirect advice, that is scattered through Sandford and Merton,[4] be excepted; but, addressing my sex in a firmer tone, I pay particular attention to those in the middle class, because they appear to be in the most natural state.[5] Perhaps the seeds of false refinement, immorality, and vanity, have ever been shed by the great. Weak, artificial beings, raised above the common wants and affections of their race, in a premature unnatural manner, undermine the very foundation of virtue, and spread corruption through the whole mass of society! As a class of mankind they have the strongest claim to pity; the education of the rich tends to render them vain and helpless, and the unfolding mind is not strengthened by the practice of those duties which dignify the human character.—They only live to amuse themselves, and by the same law which in nature invariably produces certain effects, they soon only afford barren amusement.

But as I purpose taking a separate view of the different ranks of society, and of the moral character of women, in each, this hint is, for the present, sufficient, and I have only alluded to the subject, because it appears to me to be the very essence of an introduction to give a cursory account of the contents of the work it introduces.

My own sex, I hope, will excuse me, if I treat them like rational creatures, instead of flattering their *fascinating* graces, and viewing them as if they were in a state of perpetual childhood, unable to stand alone. I earnestly wish to point out in what true dignity and human happiness consists—I wish to persuade women to endeavor to acquire strength, both of mind and body, and to convince them that the soft phrases, susceptibility of heart, delicacy of sentiment, and refinement of taste, are almost synonymous with epithets of weakness, and that those beings who are only the objects of pity and that kind of love, which has been termed its sister, will soon become objects of contempt.

Dismissing then those pretty feminine phrases, which the men condescendingly use to soften our slavish dependence, and despising that weak elegancy of mind, exquisite sensibility, and sweet docility of manners, supposed to be the sexual characteristics of the weaker vessel, I wish to shew that elegance is inferior to virtue, that the first object of laudable ambition is to obtain a character as a human being, regardless of the distinction of sex; and that secondary views should be brought to this simple touchstone.

This is a rough sketch of my plan; and should I express my conviction with the energetic emotions that I feel whenever I think of the subject, the dictates of experience and reflection will be felt by some of my readers. Animated by this important object, I shall disdain to cull[6] my phrases or

4. *The History of Sandford and Merton*, by Thomas Day, was a very popular story for children, published in three volumes (1786–89). In it a tutor, the Reverend Mr. Barlow, frequently cites the superiority in moral principles of Harry Sandford, the son of a poor farmer, over Tommy Merton, the

spoiled son of a rich family.
5. The middle class is viewed as more "natural" than the upper classes because it is uncorrupted by the artificialities of leisure-class life.
6. Be selective in.

polish my style;—I aim at being useful, and sincerity will render me unaffected; for, wishing rather to persuade by the force of my arguments, than dazzle by the elegance of my language, I shall not waste my time in rounding periods,[7] or in fabricating the turgid bombast of artificial feelings, which, coming from the head, never reach the heart. I shall be employed about things, not words!—and, anxious to render my sex more respectable members of society, I shall try to avoid that flowery diction which has slided from essays into novels, and from novels into familiar letters and conversation.

These pretty superlatives, dropping glibly from the tongue, vitiate the taste, and create a kind of sickly delicacy that turns away from simple unadorned truth; and a deluge of false sentiments and over-stretched feelings, stifling the natural emotions of the heart, render the domestic pleasures insipid, that ought to sweeten the exercise of those severe duties, which educate a rational and immortal being for a nobler field of action.

The education of women has, of late, been more attended to than formerly; yet they are still reckoned a frivolous sex, and ridiculed or pitied by the writers who endeavour by satire or instruction to improve them. It is acknowledged that they spend many of the first years of their lives in acquiring a smattering of accomplishments; meanwhile strength of body and mind are sacrificed to libertine notions of beauty, to the desire of establishing themselves,—the only way women can rise in the world,—by marriage. And this desire making mere animals of them, when they marry they act as such children may be expected to act:—they dress; they paint, and nickname God's creatures.[8]—Surely these weak beings are only fit for a seraglio![9]—Can they be expected to govern a family with judgment, or take care of the poor babes whom they bring into the world?

If then it can be fairly deduced from the present conduct of the sex, from the prevalent fondness for pleasure which takes place of ambition and those nobler passions that open and enlarge the soul; that the instruction which women have hitherto received has only tended, with the constitution of civil society, to render them insignificant objects of desire— mere propagators of fools!—if it can be proved that in aiming to accomplish them, without cultivating their understandings, they are taken out of their sphere of duties, and made ridiculous and useless when the short-lived bloom of beauty is over,[1] I presume that *rational* men will excuse me for endeavoring to persuade them to become more masculine and respectable.

Indeed the word masculine is only a bugbear: there is little reason to fear that women will acquire too much courage or fortitude; for their apparent inferiority with respect to bodily strength, must render them, in some degree, dependent on men in the various relations of life; but why should it be

7. I.e., in rounding out elaborate sentences. "Period": a formal sentence composed of balanced clauses.
8. Hamlet, charging Ophelia with the faults characteristic of women, says: "You jig, you amble, and you lisp, and / nickname God's creatures, and make your wantonness your ignorance" (*Hamlet* 3.1.143–45).
9. Harem, the women's quarters in a Muslim household.

1. A lively writer, I cannot recollect his name, asks what business women turned of forty have to do in the world? [Wollstonecraft's note]. Poston, in her edition of the *Vindication*, suggests that Wollstonecraft is recalling a passage in Fanny Burney's novel *Evelina* (1778), where the licentious Lord Merton exclaims: "I don't know what the devil a woman lives for after thirty; she is only in other folks' way."

increased by prejudices that give a sex to virtue, and confound simple truths with sensual reveries?

Women are, in fact, so much degraded by mistaken notions of female excellence, that I do not mean to add a paradox when I assert, that this artificial weakness produces a propensity to tyrannize, and gives birth to cunning, the natural opponent of strength, which leads them to play off those contemptible infantine airs that undermine esteem even whilst they excite desire. Let men become more chaste and modest, and if women do not grow wiser in the same ratio it will be clear that they have weaker understandings. It seems scarcely necessary to say, that I now speak of the sex in general. Many individuals have more sense than their male relatives; and, as nothing preponderates where there is a constant struggle for an equilibrium, without[2] it has naturally more gravity, some women govern their husbands without degrading themselves, because intellect will always govern.

Chap. 2. The Prevailing Opinion of a Sexual Character Discussed

To account for, and excuse the tyranny of man, many ingenious arguments have been brought forward to prove, that the two sexes, in the acquirement of virtue, ought to aim at attaining a very different character: or, to speak explicitly, women are not allowed to have sufficient strength of mind to acquire what really deserves the name of virtue. Yet it should seem, allowing them to have souls, that there is but one way appointed by Providence to lead *mankind* to either virtue or happiness.

If then women are not a swarm of ephemeron[3] triflers, why should they be kept in ignorance under the specious name of innocence? Men complain, and with reason, of the follies and caprices of our sex, when they do not keenly satirize our headstrong passions and groveling vices.—Behold, I should answer, the natural effect of ignorance! The mind will ever be unstable that has only prejudices to rest on, and the current will run with destructive fury when there are no barriers to break its force. Women are told from their infancy, and taught by the example of their mothers, that a little knowledge of human weakness, justly termed cunning, softness of temper, *outward* obedience, and a scrupulous attention to a puerile kind of propriety, will obtain for them the protection of man; and should they be beautiful, every thing else is needless, for, at least, twenty years of their lives.

Thus Milton describes our first frail mother; though when he tells us that women are formed for softness and sweet attractive grace,[4] I cannot comprehend his meaning, unless, in the true Mahometan strain, he meant to deprive us of souls, and insinuate that we were beings only designed by sweet attractive grace, and docile blind obedience, to gratify the senses of man when he can no longer soar on the wing of contemplation.

How grossly do they insult us who thus advise us only to render ourselves gentle, domestic brutes! For instance, the winning softness so warmly, and frequently, recommended, that governs by obeying. What childish expressions, and how insignificant is the being—can it be an immortal one? who

2. Unless.
3. A flying insect that lives only one day.
4. Milton asserts the authority of man over woman, on the grounds that "for contemplation he and valor formed, / For softness she and sweet attractive grace; / He for God only, she for God in him" (*Paradise Lost* 4.298ff.).

will condescend to govern by such sinister methods! "Certainly," says Lord Bacon, "man is of kin to the beasts by his body; and if he be not of kin to God by his spirit, he is a base and ignoble creature!"[5] Men, indeed, appear to me to act in a very unphilosophical manner when they try to secure the good conduct of women by attempting to keep them always in a state of childhood. Rousseau[6] was more consistent when he wished to stop the progress of reason in both sexes, for if men eat of the tree of knowledge, women will come in for a taste; but, from the imperfect cultivation which their understandings now receive, they only attain a knowledge of evil.

Children, I grant, should be innocent; but when the epithet is applied to men, or women, it is but a civil term for weakness. For if it be allowed that women were destined by Providence to acquire human virtues, and by the exercise of their understandings, that stability of character which is the firmest ground to rest our future hopes upon, they must be permitted to turn to the fountain of light, and not forced to shape their course by the twinkling of a mere satellite. Milton, I grant, was of a very different opinion; for he only bends to the indefeasible right of beauty, though it would be difficult to render two passages which I now mean to contrast, consistent. But into similar inconsistencies are great men often led by their senses.

> To whom thus Eve with *perfect beauty* adorn'd.
> My Author and Disposer, what thou bidst
> *Unargued* I obey; So God ordains;
> God is *thy law, thou mine*: to know no more
> Is Woman's *happiest* knowledge and her *praise.*[7]

These are exactly the arguments that I have used to children; but I have added, your reason is now gaining strength, and, till it arrives at some degree of maturity, you must look up to me for advice—then you ought to *think*, and only rely on God.

Yet in the following lines Milton seems to coincide with me; when he makes Adam thus expostulate with his Maker.

> Hast thou not made me here thy substitute,
> And these inferior far beneath me set?
> Among *unequals* what society
> Can sort, what harmony or true delight?
> Which must be mutual, in proportion due
> Giv'n and receiv'd; but in *disparity*
> The one intense, the other still remiss
> Cannot well suit with either, but soon prove
> Tedious alike: of *fellowship* I speak
> Such as I seek, fit to participate
> All rational delight[8]—

In treating, therefore, of the manners of women, let us, disregarding sensual arguments, trace what we should endeavor to make them in order to cooperate, if the expression be not too bold, with the supreme Being.

5. Francis Bacon's *Of Atheism* (1597).
6. Jean-Jacques Rousseau (1712–1778), who proposed limiting the role of rationality, as opposed to reliance on intuition and instinct. Rousseau's opinions about women and their appropriate education, as alluded to in this chapter, are expressed in

his treatise *Émile* (1762), especially book 5, "Sophy, or Woman."
7. *Paradise Lost* 4.634–38 (Wollstonecraft's italics).
8. *Paradise Lost* 8.381–91 (Wollstonecraft's italics).

By individual education, I mean, for the sense of the word is not precisely defined, such an attention to a child as will slowly sharpen the senses, form the temper,[9] regulate the passions as they begin to ferment, and set the understanding to work before the body arrives at maturity; so that the man may only have to proceed, not to begin, the important task of learning to think and reason.

To prevent any misconstruction, I must add, that I do not believe that a private education can work the wonders which some sanguine writers have attributed to it. Men and women must be educated, in a great degree, by the opinions and manners of the society they live in. In every age there has been a stream of popular opinion that has carried all before it, and given a family character, as it were, to the century. It may then fairly be inferred, that, till society be differently constituted, much cannot be expected from education. It is, however, sufficient for my present purpose to assert, that, whatever effect circumstances have on the abilities, every being may become virtuous by the exercise of its own reason; for if but one being was created with vicious inclinations, that is positively bad, what can save us from atheism? or if we worship a God, is not that God a devil?

Consequently, the most perfect education, in my opinion, is such an exercise of the understanding as is best calculated to strengthen the body and form the heart. Or, in other words, to enable the individual to attain such habits of virtue as will render it independent. In fact, it is a farce to call any being virtuous whose virtues do not result from the exercise of its own reason. This was Rousseau's opinion respecting men: I extend it to women, and confidently assert that they have been drawn out of their sphere by false refinement, and not by an endeavour to acquire masculine qualities. Still the regal homage which they receive is so intoxicating, that till the manners of the times are changed, and formed on more reasonable principles, it may be impossible to convince them that the illegitimate power, which they obtain, by degrading themselves, is a curse, and that they must return to nature and equality, if they wish to secure the placid satisfaction that unsophisticated affections impart. But for this epoch we must wait—wait, perhaps, till kings and nobles, enlightened by reason, and, preferring the real dignity of man to childish state,[1] throw off their gaudy hereditary trappings: and if then women do not resign the arbitrary power of beauty—they will prove that they have *less* mind than man.

I may be accused of arrogance; still I must declare what I firmly believe, that all the writers who have written on the subject of female education and manners from Rousseau to Dr. Gregory,[2] have contributed to render women more artificial, weak characters, than they would otherwise have been; and, consequently, more useless members of society. I might have expressed this conviction in a lower key; but I am afraid it would have been the whine of affectation, and not the faithful expression of my feelings, of the clear result, which experience and reflection have led me to draw. When I come to that division of the subject, I shall advert to the passages that I more particularly disapprove of, in the works of the authors I have just alluded to; but it is first necessary to observe, that my objection extends to the whole purport of those

9. Temperament, character.
1. Pomp, costly display.
2. John Gregory, Scottish author of a widely read

book on the education of women, *A Father's Legacy to His Daughters* (1774).

books, which tend, in my opinion, to degrade one half of the human species, and render women pleasing at the expense of every solid virtue.

Though, to reason on Rousseau's ground, if man did attain a degree of perfection of mind when his body arrived at maturity, it might be proper, in order to make a man and his wife *one*, that she should rely entirely on his understanding; and the graceful ivy, clasping the oak that supported it, would form a whole in which strength and beauty would be equally conspicuous. But, alas! husbands, as well as their helpmates, are often only overgrown children; nay, thanks to early debauchery, scarcely men in their outward form—and if the blind lead the blind, one need not come from heaven to tell us the consequence.

Many are the causes that, in the present corrupt state of society, contribute to enslave women by cramping their understandings and sharpening their senses. One, perhaps, that silently does more mischief than all the rest, is their disregard of order.

To do every thing in an orderly manner, is a most important precept, which women, who, generally speaking, receive only a disorderly kind of education, seldom attend to with that degree of exactness that men, who from their infancy are broken into method, observe. This negligent kind of guess-work, for what other epithet can be used to point out the random exertions of a sort of instinctive common sense, never brought to the test of reason? prevents their generalizing matters of fact—so they do to-day, what they did yesterday, merely because they did it yesterday.

This contempt of the understanding in early life has more baneful consequences than is commonly supposed; for the little knowledge which women of strong minds attain, is, from various circumstances, of a more desultory kind than the knowledge of men, and it is acquired more by sheer observations on real life, than from comparing what has been individually observed with the results of experience generalized by speculation. Led by their dependent situation and domestic employments more into society, what they learn is rather by snatches; and as learning is with them, in general, only a secondary thing, they do not pursue any one branch with that persevering ardour necessary to give vigor to the faculties, and clearness to the judgment. In the present state of society, a little learning is required to support the character of a gentleman; and boys are obliged to submit to a few years of discipline. But in the education of women, the cultivation of the understanding is always subordinate to the acquirement of some corporeal accomplishment; even while enervated by confinement and false notions of modesty, the body is prevented from attaining that grace and beauty which relaxed half-formed limbs never exhibit. Besides, in youth their faculties are not brought forward by emulation; and having no serious scientific study, if they have natural sagacity it is turned too soon on life and manners. They dwell on effects, and modifications, without tracing them back to causes; and complicated rules to adjust behaviour are a weak substitute for simple principles.

As a proof that education gives this appearance of weakness to females, we may instance the example of military men, who are, like them, sent into the world before their minds have been stored with knowledge or fortified by principles. The consequences are similar; soldiers acquire a little superficial knowledge, snatched from the muddy current of conversation, and, from continually mixing with society, they gain, what is termed a knowledge of the world; and this acquaintance with manners and customs has frequently been confounded with a knowledge of the human heart. But can the crude fruit of casual observation, never brought to the test of judgment, formed by comparing speculation and experience, deserve such a distinction? Soldiers, as well as women, practice the minor virtues with punctilious politeness. Where is then the sexual difference, when the education has been the same? All the difference that I can discern, arises from the superior advantage of liberty, which enables the former to see more of life.

It is wandering from my present subject, perhaps, to make a political remark; but, as it was produced naturally by the train of my reflections, I shall not pass it silently over.

Standing armies can never consist of resolute, robust men; they may be well disciplined machines, but they will seldom contain men under the influence of strong passions, or with very vigorous faculties. And as for any depth of understanding, I will venture to affirm, that it is as rarely to be found in the army as amongst women; and the cause, I maintain, is the same. It may be further observed, that officers are also particularly attentive to their persons, fond of dancing, crowded rooms, adventures, and ridicule.[3] Like the *fair* sex, the business of their lives is gallantry.—They were taught to please, and they only live to please. Yet they do not lose their rank in the distinction of sexes, for they are still reckoned superior to women, though in what their superiority consists, beyond what I have just mentioned, it is difficult to discover.

The great misfortune is this, that they both acquire manners before morals, and a knowledge of life before they have, from reflection, any acquaintance with the grand ideal outline of human nature. The consequence is natural; satisfied with common nature, they become a prey to prejudices, and taking all their opinions on credit, they blindly submit to authority. So that, if they have any sense, it is a kind of instinctive glance, that catches proportions, and decides with respect to manners; but fails when arguments are to be pursued below the surface, or opinions analyzed.

May not the same remark be applied to women? Nay, the argument may be carried still further, for they are both thrown out of a useful station by the unnatural distinctions established in civilized life. Riches and hereditary honours have made cyphers of women to give consequence to the numerical figure; and idleness has produced a mixture of gallantry and despotism into society, which leads the very men who are the slaves of their mistresses to tyrannize over their sisters, wives, and daughters. This is only keeping them in rank and file, it is true. Strengthen the female mind by enlarging it, and there will be an end to blind obedience; but, as blind obedience is ever sought for by power, tyrants and sensualists are in the right when they endeavour to keep women in the dark, because the former only want slaves, and the latter a play-thing. The sensualist, indeed, has been the most dangerous of tyrants, and women have been duped by their lovers, as princes by their ministers, whilst dreaming that they reigned over them.

I now principally allude to Rousseau, for his character of Sophia[4] is, undoubtedly, a captivating one, though it appears to me grossly unnatural;

---

3. Why should women be censured with petulant acrimony, because they seem to have a passion for a scarlet coat? Has not education placed them more on a level with soldiers than any other class of men? [Wollstonecraft's note].

4. The title of book 5 of Rousseau's *Émile*.

however it is not the superstructure, but the foundation of her character, the principles on which her education was built, that I mean to attack; nay, warmly as I admire the genius of that able writer, whose opinions I shall often have occasion to cite, indignation always takes place of admiration, and the rigid frown of insulted virtue effaces the smile of complacency, which his eloquent periods are wont to raise, when I read his voluptuous reveries. Is this the man, who, in his ardor for virtue, would banish all the soft arts of peace, and almost carry us back to Spartan discipline? Is this the man who delights to paint the useful struggles of passion, the triumphs of good dispositions, and the heroic flights which carry the glowing soul out of itself?—How are these mighty sentiments lowered when he describes the pretty foot and enticing airs of his little favorite! But, for the present, I waive the subject, and, instead of severely reprehending the transient effusions of overweening sensibility, I shall only observe, that whoever has cast a benevolent eye on society, must often have been gratified by the sight of a humble mutual love, not dignified by sentiment, or strengthened by a union in intellectual pursuits. The domestic trifles of the day have afforded matters for cheerful converse, and innocent caresses have softened toils which did not require great exercise of mind or stretch of thought: yet, has not the sight of this moderate felicity excited more tenderness than respect? An emotion similar to what we feel when children are playing, or animals sporting,[5] whilst the contemplation of the noble struggles of suffering merit has raised admiration, and carried our thoughts to that world where sensation will give place to reason.

Women are, therefore, to be considered either as moral beings, or so weak that they must be entirely subjected to the superior faculties of men.

Let us examine this question. Rousseau declares that a woman should never, for a moment, feel herself independent, that she should be governed by fear to exercise her natural cunning, and made a coquetish slave in order to render her a more alluring object of desire, a *sweeter* companion to man, whenever he chooses to relax himself. He carries the arguments, which he pretends to draw from the indications of nature, still further, and insinuates that truth and fortitude, the corner stones of all human virtue, should be cultivated with certain restrictions, because, with respect to the female character, obedience is the grand lesson which ought to be impressed with unrelenting rigor.[6]

What nonsense! when will a great man arise with sufficient strength of mind to puff away the fumes which pride and sensuality have thus spread over the subject! If women are by nature inferior to men, their virtues must be the same in quality, if not in degree, or virtue is a relative idea; consequently, their conduct should be founded on the same principles, and have the same aim.

Connected with man as daughters, wives, and mothers, their moral char-

5. Similar feelings has Milton's pleasing picture of paradisiacal happiness ever raised in my mind; yet, instead of envying the lovely pair, I have, with conscious dignity, or Satanic pride, turned to hell for sublimer objects. In the same style, when viewing some noble monument of human art, I have traced the emanation of the Deity in the order I admired, till, descending from that giddy height, I have caught myself contemplating the grandest of all human sights;—for fancy quickly placed, in some solitary recess, an outcast of fortune, rising superior to passion and discontent [Wollstonecraft's note].

6. Rousseau had written in *Émile*: "What is most wanted in a woman is gentleness; formed to obey a creature so imperfect as man, a creature often vicious and always faulty, she should early learn to submit to injustice and to suffer the wrongs inflicted on her by her husband without complaint."

acter may be estimated by their manner of fulfilling those simple duties; but the end, the grand end of their exertions should be to unfold their own faculties and acquire the dignity of conscious virtue. They may try to render their road pleasant; but ought never to forget, in common with man, that life yields not the felicity which can satisfy an immortal soul. I do not mean to insinuate, that either sex should be so lost in abstract reflections or distant views, as to forget the affections and duties that lie before them, and are, in truth, the means appointed to produce the fruit of life; on the contrary, I would warmly recommend them, even while I assert, that they afford most satisfaction when they are considered in their true, sober light.

Probably the prevailing opinion, that woman was created for man, may have taken its rise from Moses's poetical story;[7] yet, as very few, it is presumed, who have bestowed any serious thought on the subject, ever supposed that Eve was, literally speaking, one of Adam's ribs, the deduction must be allowed to fall to the ground; or, only be so far admitted as it proves that man, from the remotest antiquity, found it convenient to exert his strength to subjugate his companion, and his invention to shew that she ought to have her neck bent under the yoke, because the whole creation was only created for his convenience or pleasure.

Let it not be concluded that I wish to invert the order of things; I have already granted, that, from the constitution of their bodies, men seem to be designed by Providence to attain a greater degree of virtue.[8] I speak collectively of the whole sex; but I see not the shadow of a reason to conclude that their virtues should differ in respect to their nature. In fact, how can they, if virtue has only one eternal standard? I must therefore, if I reason consequentially, as strenuously maintain that they have the same simple direction, as that there is a God.

It follows then that cunning should not be opposed to wisdom, little cares to great exertions, or insipid softness, varnished over with the name of gentleness, to that fortitude which grand views alone can inspire.

I shall be told that woman would then lose many of her peculiar graces, and the opinion of a well known poet might be quoted to refute my unqualified assertion. For Pope has said, in the name of the whole male sex,

> Yet ne'er so sure our passion to create,
> As when she touch'd the brink of all we hate.[9]

In what light this sally places men and women, I shall leave to the judicious to determine; meanwhile I shall content myself with observing, that I cannot discover why, unless they are mortal, females should always be degraded by being made subservient to love or lust.

To speak disrespectfully of love is, I know, high treason against sentiment and fine feelings; but I wish to speak the simple language of truth, and rather to address the head than the heart. To endeavor to reason love out of the world, would be to out-Quixote Cervantes,[1] and equally offend against common sense; but an endeavor to restrain this tumultuous passion, and prove

---

7. The story of the creation of Eve from the rib of Adam (Genesis 2.21–22). Traditionally, the first five books of the Old Testament were attributed to the authorship of Moses.
8. In the third paragraph of her Introduction, Wollstonecraft had said that men are, in general,

physically stronger than women.
9. Alexander Pope's *Moral Essays 2, Of the Characters of Women*, lines 51–52.
1. I.e., to outdo the hero of Cervantes's *Don Quixote* (1605) in trying to accomplish the impossible.

that it should not be allowed to dethrone superior powers, or to usurp the sceptre which the understanding should ever coolly wield, appears less wild.

Youth is the season for love in both sexes; but in those days of thoughtless enjoyment provision should be made for the more important years of life, when reflection takes place of sensation. But Rousseau, and most of the male writers who have followed his steps, have warmly inculcated that the whole tendency of female education ought to be directed to one point:—to render them pleasing.

Let me reason with the supporters of this opinion who have any knowledge of human nature, do they imagine that marriage can eradicate the habitude of life? The woman who has only been taught to please will soon find that her charms are oblique sunbeams, and that they cannot have much effect on her husband's heart when they are seen every day, when the summer is passed and gone. Will she then have sufficient native energy to look into herself for comfort, and cultivate her dormant faculties? or, is it not more rational to expect that she will try to please other men; and, in the emotions raised by the expectation of new conquests, endeavor to forget the mortification her love or pride has received? When the husband ceases to be a lover—and the time will inevitably come, her desire of pleasing will then grow languid, or become a spring of bitterness; and love, perhaps, the most evanescent of all passions, gives place to jealousy or vanity.

I now speak of women who are restrained by principle or prejudice; such women, though they would shrink from an intrigue with real abhorrence, yet, nevertheless, wish to be convinced by the homage of gallantry that they are cruelly neglected by their husbands; or, days and weeks are spent in dreaming of the happiness enjoyed by congenial souls till their health is undermined and their spirits broken by discontent. How then can the great art of pleasing be such a necessary study? it is only useful to a mistress; the chaste wife, and serious mother, should only consider her power to please as the polish of her virtues, and the affection of her husband as one of the comforts that render her task less difficult and her life happier.—But, whether she be loved or neglected, her first wish should be to make herself respectable,[2] and not to rely for all her happiness on a being subject to like infirmities with herself.

The worthy Dr. Gregory fell into a similar error. I respect his heart; but entirely disapprove of his celebrated Legacy to his Daughters.

He advises them to cultivate a fondness for dress, because a fondness for dress, he asserts, is natural to them. I am unable to comprehend what either he or Rousseau mean, when they frequently use this indefinite term.[3] If they told us that in a pre-existent state the soul was fond of dress, and brought this inclination with it into a new body, I should listen to them with a half smile, as I often do when I hear a rant about innate elegance.—But if he only meant to say that the exercise of the faculties will produce this fondness—I deny it.—It is not natural; but arises, like false ambition in men, from a love of power.

Dr. Gregory goes much further; he actually recommends dissimulation, and advises an innocent girl to give the lie to her feelings, and not dance with spirit, when gaiety of heart would make her feel eloquent without mak-

2. I.e., morally worthy of respect.   3. I.e., "natural."

ing her gestures immodest. In the name of truth and common sense, why should not one woman acknowledge that she can take more exercise than another? or, in other words, that she has a sound constitution; and why, to damp innocent vivacity, is she darkly to be told that men will draw conclusions which she little thinks of?[4]—Let the libertine draw what inference he pleases; but, I hope, that no sensible mother will restrain the natural frankness of youth by instilling such indecent cautions. Out of the abundance of the heart the mouth speaketh;[5] and a wiser than Solomon hath said, that the heart should be made clean,[6] and not trivial ceremonies observed, which is not very difficult to fulfill with scrupulous exactness when vice reigns in the heart.

Women ought to endeavor to purify their heart; but can they do so when their uncultivated understandings make them entirely dependent on their senses for employment and amusement, when no noble pursuit sets them above the little vanities of the day, or enables them to curb the wild emotions that agitate a reed over which every passing breeze has power? To gain the affections of a virtuous man is affectation necessary? Nature has given woman a weaker frame than man; but, to ensure her husband's affections, must a wife, who by the exercise of her mind and body whilst she was discharging the duties of a daughter, wife, and mother, has allowed her constitution to retain its natural strength, and her nerves a healthy tone, is she, I say, to condescend to use art and feign a sickly delicacy in order to secure her husband's affection? Weakness may excite tenderness, and gratify the arrogant pride of man; but the lordly caresses of a protector will not gratify a noble mind that pants for, and deserves to be respected. Fondness is a poor substitute for friendship!

In a seraglio, I grant, that all these arts are necessary; the epicure must have his palate tickled, or he will sink into apathy; but have women so little ambition as to be satisfied with such a condition? Can they supinely dream life away in the lap of pleasure, or the languor of weariness, rather than assert their claim to pursue reasonable pleasures and render themselves conspicuous by practising the virtues which dignify mankind? Surely she has not an immortal soul who can loiter life away merely employed to adorn her person, that she may amuse the languid hours, and soften the cares of a fellow-creature who is willing to be enlivened by her smiles and tricks, when the serious business of life is over.

Besides, the woman who strengthens her body and exercises her mind will, by managing her family and practising various virtues, become the friend, and not the humble dependent of her husband; and if she, by possessing such substantial qualities, merit his regard, she will not find it necessary to conceal her affection, nor to pretend to an unnatural coldness of constitution to excite her husband's passions. In fact, if we revert to history, we shall find that the women who have distinguished themselves have neither been the most beautiful nor the most gentle of their sex.

Nature, or, to speak with strict propriety, God, has made all things right;

---

4. In *A Father's Legacy to His Daughters*, Gregory had advised a girl, when she dances, not "to forget the delicacy of [her] sex," lest she be "thought to discover a spirit she little dreams of."
5. Matthew 12.34.

6. Psalm 24 (attributed to David, the "wiser than Solomon"), 3–4: "Who shall ascend into the hill of the Lord? or who shall stand in his holy place? He that hath clean hands, and a pure heart."

but man has sought him out many inventions to mar the work. I now allude to that part of Dr. Gregory's treatise, where he advises a wife never to let her husband know the extent of her sensibility or affection. Voluptuous precaution, and as ineffectual as absurd.—Love, from its very nature, must be transitory. To seek for a secret that would render it constant, would be as wild a search as for the philosopher's stone, or the grand panacea:[7] and the discovery would be equally useless, or rather pernicious to mankind. The most holy band of society is friendship. It has been well said, by a shrewd satirist, "that rare as true love is, true friendship is still rarer."[8]

This is an obvious truth, and the cause not lying deep, will not elude a slight glance of inquiry.

Love, the common passion, in which chance and sensation take place of choice and reason, is, in some degree, felt by the mass of mankind; for it is not necessary to speak, at present, of the emotions that rise above or sink below love. This passion, naturally increased by suspense and difficulties, draws the mind out of its accustomed state, and exalts the affections; but the security of marriage, allowing the fever of love to subside, a healthy temperature is thought insipid, only by those who have not sufficient intellect to substitute the calm tenderness of friendship, the confidence of respect, instead of blind admiration, and the sensual emotions of fondness.

This is, must be, the course of nature.—Friendship or indifference inevitably succeeds love.—And this constitution seems perfectly to harmonize with the system of government which prevails in the moral world. Passions are spurs to action, and open the mind; but they sink into mere appetites, become a personal and momentary gratification, when the object is gained, and the satisfied mind rests in enjoyment. The man who had some virtue whilst he was struggling for a crown, often becomes a voluptuous tyrant when it graces his brow; and, when the lover is not lost in the husband, the dotard, a prey to childish caprices, and fond jealousies, neglects the serious duties of life, and the caresses which should excite confidence in his children are lavished on the overgrown child, his wife.

In order to fulfil the duties of life, and to be able to pursue with vigour the various employments which form the moral character, a master and mistress of a family ought not to continue to love each other with passion. I mean to say, that they ought not to indulge those emotions which disturb the order of society, and engross the thoughts that should be otherwise employed. The mind that has never been engrossed by one object wants vigor—if it can long be so, it is weak.

A mistaken education, a narrow, uncultivated mind, and many sexual prejudices, tend to make women more constant than men; but, for the present, I shall not touch on this branch of the subject. I will go still further, and advance, without dreaming of a paradox, that an unhappy marriage is often very advantageous to a family, and that the neglected wife is, in general, the best mother.[9] And this would almost always be the consequence if the female mind were more enlarged: for, it seems to be the common dispensation of

7. A medicine reputed to cure all diseases. "The philosopher's stone," in alchemy, had the power of transmuting base metals into gold.
8. Maxim 473 of La Rochefoucauld (1613–1680), the great French writer of epigrams.

9. Wollstonecraft's point is that a woman who is not preoccupied with her husband (and his attentions to her) has more time and attention for her children.

Providence, that what we gain in present enjoyment should be deducted from the treasure of life, experience; and that when we are gathering the flowers of the day and revelling in pleasure, the solid fruit of toil and wisdom should not be caught at the same time. The way lies before us, we must turn to the right or left; and he who will pass life away in bounding from one pleasure to another, must not complain if he acquire neither wisdom nor respectability of character.

Supposing, for a moment, that the soul is not immortal, and that man was only created for the present scene,—I think we should have reason to complain that love, infantine fondness, ever grew insipid and palled upon the sense. Let us eat, drink, and love for to-morrow we die, would be, in fact, the language of reason, the morality of life; and who but a fool would part with a reality for a fleeting shadow? But, if awed by observing the improbable[1] powers of the mind, we disdain to confine our wishes or thoughts to such a comparatively mean field of action; that only appears grand and important, as it is connected with a boundless prospect and sublime hopes, what necessity is there for falsehood in conduct, and why must the sacred majesty of truth be violated to detain a deceitful good that saps the very foundation of virtue? Why must the female mind be tainted by coquetish arts to gratify the sensualist, and prevent love from subsiding into friendship, or compassionate tenderness, when there are not qualities on which friendship can be built? Let the honest heart shew itself, and *reason* teach passion to submit to necessity; or, let the dignified pursuit of virtue and knowledge raise the mind above those emotions which rather imbitter than sweeten the cup of life, when they are not restrained within due bounds.

I do not mean to allude to the romantic passion, which is the concomitant of genius.—Who can clip its wing? But that grand passion not proportioned to the puny enjoyments of life, is only true to the sentiment, and feeds on itself. The passions which have been celebrated for their durability have always been unfortunate. They have acquired strength by absence and constitutional melancholy.—The fancy has hovered around a form of beauty dimly seen—but familiarity might have turned admiration into disgust; or, at least, into indifference, and allowed the imagination leisure to start fresh game. With perfect propriety, according to his view of things, does Rousseau make the mistress of his soul, Eloisa, love St. Preux, when life was fading before her;[2] but this is no proof of the immortality of the passion.

Of the same complexion is Dr. Gregory's advice respecting delicacy of sentiment,[3] which he advises a woman not to acquire, if she have determined to marry. This determination, however, perfectly consistent with his former advice, he calls *indelicate*, and earnestly persuades his daughters to conceal it, though it may govern their conduct;—as if it were indelicate to have the common appetites of human nature.

Noble morality! and consistent with the cautious prudence of a little soul that cannot extend its views beyond the present minute division of existence.

---

1. Poston points out that this may be a misprint in the second edition for "improvable," which occurs in the first edition.
2. In Rousseau's *Julie, ou la Nouvelle Héloise* (1761), Julie, after a life of fidelity to her husband, reveals on her deathbed that she has never lost her passion for St. Preux, her lover when she was young. Wollstonecraft accepts the common opinion that Julie represents Madame d'Houdetot, with whom Rousseau was in love when he wrote the novel.
3. I.e., too elevated and refined a notion of what to expect in a man.

If all the faculties of woman's mind are only to be cultivated as they respect her dependence on man; if, when a husband be obtained, she have arrived at her goal, and meanly proud rests satisfied with such a paltry crown, let her grovel contentedly, scarcely raised by her employments above the animal kingdom; but, if, struggling for the prize of her high calling, she look beyond the present scene, let her cultivate her understanding without stopping to consider what character the husband may have whom she is destined to marry. Let her only determine, without being too anxious about present happiness, to acquire the qualities that ennoble a rational being, and a rough inelegant husband may shock her taste without destroying her peace of mind. She will not model her soul to suit the frailties of her companion, but to bear with them: his character may be a trial, but not an impediment to virtue.

If Dr. Gregory confined his remark to romantic expectations of constant love and congenial feelings, he should have recollected that experience will banish what advice can never make us cease to wish for, when the imagination is kept alive at the expence of reason.

I own it frequently happens that women who have fostered a romantic unnatural delicacy of feeling, waste their[4] lives in *imagining* how happy they should have been with a husband who could love them with a fervid increasing affection every day, and all day. But they might as well pine married as single—and would not be a jot more unhappy with a bad husband than longing for a good one. That a proper education; or, to speak with more precision, a well stored mind, would enable a woman to support a single life with dignity, I grant; but that she should avoid cultivating her taste, lest her husband should occasionally shock it, is quitting a substance for a shadow. To say the truth, I do not know of what use is an improved taste, if the individual be not rendered more independent of the casualties of life; if new sources of enjoyment, only dependent on the solitary operations of the mind, are not opened. People of taste, married or single, without distinction, will ever be disgusted by various things that touch not less observing minds. On this conclusion the argument must not be allowed to hinge; but in the whole sum of enjoyment is taste to be denominated a blessing?

The question is, whether it procures most pain or pleasure? The answer will decide the propriety of Dr. Gregory's advice, and shew how absurd and tyrannic it is thus to lay down a system of slavery; or to attempt to educate moral beings by any other rules than those deduced from pure reason, which apply to the whole species.

Gentleness of manners, forbearance, and long-suffering, are such amiable Godlike qualities, that in sublime poetic strains the Deity has been invested with them; and, perhaps, no representation of his goodness so strongly fastens on the human affections as those that represent him abundant in mercy and willing to pardon. Gentleness, considered in this point of view, bears on its front all the characteristics of grandeur, combined with the winning graces of condescension; but what a different aspect it assumes when it is the submissive demeanour of dependence, the support of weakness that loves, because it wants protection; and is forbearing, because it must silently endure injuries; smiling under the lash at which it dare not snarl. Abject as

---

4. For example, the herd of Novelists [Wollstonecraft's note]. The author's reference is to women who have formed their expectations of love as it is misrepresented in the sentimental novels of their time.

this picture appears, it is the portrait of an accomplished woman, according to the received opinion of female excellence, separated by specious reasoners from human excellence. Or, they[5] kindly restore the rib, and make one moral being of a man and woman; not forgetting to give her all the "submissive charms."[6] How women are to exist in that state where there is to be neither marrying nor giving in marriage,[7] we are not told. For though moralists have agreed that the tenor of life seems to prove that *man* is prepared by various circumstances for a future state, they constantly concur in advising *woman* only to provide for the present. Gentleness, docility, and a spaniel-like affection are, on this ground, consistently recommended as the cardinal virtues of the sex; and, disregarding the arbitrary economy of nature, one writer has declared that it is masculine for a woman to be melancholy. She was created to be the toy of man, his rattle, and it must jingle in his ears whenever, dismissing reason, he chooses to be amused.

To recommend gentleness, indeed, on a broad basis is strictly philosophical. A frail being should labor to be gentle. But when forbearance confounds right and wrong, it ceases to be a virtue; and, however convenient it may be found in a companion—that companion will ever be considered as an inferior, and only inspire a vapid tenderness, which easily degenerates into contempt. Still, if advice could really make a being gentle, whose natural disposition admitted not of such a fine polish, something towards the advancement of order would be attained; but if, as might quickly be demonstrated, only affectation be produced by this indiscriminate counsel, which throws a stumbling-block in the way of gradual improvement, and true melioration of temper, the sex is not much benefited by sacrificing solid virtues to the attainment of superficial graces, though for a few years they may procure the individuals regal sway.

As a philosopher, I read with indignation the plausible epithets which men use to soften their insults; and, as a moralist, I ask what is meant by such heterogeneous associations, as fair defects, amiable weaknesses, &c.?[8] If there be but one criterion of morals, but one archetype of man, women appear to be suspended by destiny, according to the vulgar tale of Mahomet's coffin;[9] they have neither the unerring instinct of brutes, nor are allowed to fix the eye of reason on a perfect model. They were made to be loved, and must not aim at respect, lest they should be hunted out of society as masculine.

But to view the subject in another point of view. Do passive indolent women make the best wives? Confining our discussion to the present moment of existence, let us see how such weak creatures perform their part. Do the women who, by the attainment of a few superficial accomplishments, have strengthened the prevailing prejudice, merely contribute to the happiness of their husbands? Do they display their charms merely to amuse them?

---

5. *Vide* [see] Rousseau and Swedenborg [Wollstonecraft's note]. Rousseau's view was that a wife constituted an integral moral being only in concert with her husband. Emanuel Swedenborg (1688–1772), the Swedish theosophist, held that in the married state in heaven male and female are embodied in a single angelic form.
6. Milton says of Adam and Eve in *Paradise Lost* 4.497–99 that "he in delight / Both of her beauty and submissive charms / Smiled with superior love."
7. "For in the resurrection they neither marry, nor are given in marriage, but are as the angels of God in heaven" (Matthew 22.30).
8. In *Paradise Lost* 10.891–92 the fallen Adam refers to Eve as "this fair defect / Of Nature"; and in *Moral Essays* 2.43 Pope describes women as "Fine by defect, and delicately weak."
9. A legend has it that Mohammed's coffin hovers suspended in his tomb.

And have women, who have early imbibed notions of passive obedience, sufficient character to manage a family or educate children? So far from it, that, after surveying the history of woman, I cannot help, agreeing with the severest satirist, considering the sex as the weakest as well as the most oppressed half of the species. What does history disclose but marks of inferiority, and how few women have emancipated themselves from the galling yoke of sovereign man?—So few, that the exceptions remind me of an ingenious conjecture respecting Newton: that he was probably a being of a superior order, accidentally caged in a human body.[1] Following the same train of thinking, I have been led to imagine that the few extraordinary women who have rushed in eccentrical directions out of the orbit prescribed to their sex, were *male* spirits, confined by mistake in female frames. But if it be not philosophical to think of sex when the soul is mentioned, the inferiority must depend on the organs; or the heavenly fire, which is to ferment the clay, is not given in equal portions.

But avoiding, as I have hitherto done, any direct comparison of the two sexes collectively, or frankly acknowledging the inferiority of woman, according to the present appearance of things, I shall only insist that men have increased that inferiority till women are almost sunk below the standard of rational creatures. Let their faculties have room to unfold, and their virtues to gain strength, and then determine where the whole sex must stand in the intellectual scale. Yet let it be remembered, that for a small number of distinguished women I do not ask a place.

It is difficult for us purblind mortals to say to what height human discoveries and improvements may arrive when the gloom of despotism subsides, which makes us stumble at every step; but, when morality shall be settled on a more solid basis, then, without being gifted with a prophetic spirit, I will venture to predict that woman will be either the friend or slave of man. We shall not, as at present, doubt whether she is a moral agent, or the link which unites man with brutes.[2] But, should it then appear, that like the brutes they were principally created for the use of man, he will let them patiently bite the bridle, and not mock them with empty praise; or, should their rationality be proved, he will not impede their improvement merely to gratify his sensual appetites. He will not, with all the graces of rhetoric, advise them to submit implicitly their understanding to the guidance of man. He will not, when he treats of the education of women, assert that they ought never to have the free use of reason, nor would he recommend cunning and dissimulation to beings who are acquiring, in like manner as himself, the virtues of humanity.

Surely there can be but one rule of right, if morality has an eternal foundation, and whoever sacrifices virtue, strictly so called, to present convenience, or whose *duty* it is to act in such a manner, lives only for the passing day, and cannot be an accountable creature.

1. A possible reminiscence of Pope's *An Essay on Man* 2.31–34: "Superior beings [i.e., angels] . . . / Admired such wisdom in an earthly shape, / And showed a Newton as we show an ape."
2. Rousseau doubted that a woman, of herself, was a moral agent. There had been a long dispute about the question of woman being part of humankind. In the *Summa Theologica* (Question XVII, Art. 1) St. Thomas Aquinas concedes, with Aris-

totle, that the "production of woman comes from a defect in the active power, or from some material indisposition, or even from some external influence, such as that of a south wind, which is moist" (English Dominican translation of St. Thomas, edited by Anton C. Pegis, *The Basic Writings of Saint Thomas Aquinas* [New York, 1945], I, 880) [Poston's note].

The poet then should have dropped his sneer when he says,

> If weak women go astray,
> The stars are more in fault than they.[3]

For that they are bound by the adamantine chain of destiny is most certain, if it be proved that they are never to exercise their own reason, never to be independent, never to rise above opinion, or to feel the dignity of a rational will that only bows to God, and often forgets that the universe contains any being but itself and the model of perfection to which its ardent gaze is turned, to adore attributes that, softened into virtues, may be imitated in kind, though the degree overwhelms the enraptured mind.

If, I say, for I would not impress by declamation when Reason offers her sober light, if they be really capable of acting like rational creatures, let them not be treated like slaves; or, like the brutes who are dependent on the reason of man, when they associate with him; but cultivate their minds, give them the salutary, sublime curb of principle, and let them attain conscious dignity by feeling themselves only dependent on God. Teach them, in common with man, to submit to necessity, instead of giving, to render them more pleasing, a sex to morals.

Further, should experience prove that they cannot attain the same degree of strength of mind, perseverance, and fortitude, let their virtues be the same in kind, though they may vainly struggle for the same degree; and the superiority of man will be equally clear, if not clearer; and truth, as it is a simple principle, which admits of no modification, would be common to both. Nay, the order of society as it is at present regulated would not be inverted, for woman would then only have the rank that reason assigned her, and arts could not be practised to bring the balance even, much less to turn it.

These may be termed Utopian dreams.—Thanks to that Being who impressed them on my soul, and gave me sufficient strength of mind to dare to exert my own reason, till, becoming dependent only on him for the support of my virtue, I view, with indignation, the mistaken notions that enslave my sex.

I love man as my fellow; but his scepter, real or usurped, extends not to me, unless the reason of an individual demands my homage; and even then the submission is to reason, and not to man. In fact, the conduct of an accountable being must be regulated by the operations of its own reason; or on what foundation rests the throne of God?

It appears to me necessary to dwell on these obvious truths, because females have been insulated, as it were; and, while they have been stripped of the virtues that should clothe humanity, they have been decked with artificial graces that enable them to exercise a short-lived tyranny. Love, in their bosoms, taking place of every nobler passion, their sole ambition is to be fair, to raise emotion instead of inspiring respect; and this ignoble desire, like the servility in absolute monarchies, destroys all strength of character. Liberty is the mother of virtue, and if women be, by their very constitution, slaves, and not allowed to breathe the sharp invigorating air of freedom, they must ever languish like exotics, and be reckoned beautiful flaws in nature.

---

3. Matthew Prior, *Hans Carvel*, lines 11–12, alluding to *Julius Caesar* 1.2.141–42: "The fault, dear Brutus, is not in our stars, / But in ourselves."

As to the argument respecting the subjection in which the sex has ever been held, it retorts on man. The many have always been enthralled by the few; and monsters, who scarcely have shewn any discernment of human excellence, have tyrannized over thousands of their fellow-creatures. Why have men of superiour endowments submitted to such degradation? For, is it not universally acknowledged that kings, viewed collectively, have ever been inferior, in abilities and virtue, to the same number of men taken from the common mass of mankind—yet, have they not, and are they not still treated with a degree of reverence that is an insult to reason? China is not the only country where a living man has been made a God.[4] *Men* have submitted to superior strength to enjoy with impunity the pleasure of the moment—*women* have only done the same, and therefore till it is proved that the courtier, who servilely resigns the birthright of a man, is not a moral agent, it cannot be demonstrated that woman is essentially inferior to man because she has always been subjugated.

Brutal force has hitherto governed the world, and that the science of politics is in its infancy, is evident from philosophers scrupling to give the knowledge most useful to man that determinate distinction.

I shall not pursue this argument any further than to establish an obvious inference, that as sound politics diffuse liberty, mankind, including woman, will become more wise and virtuous.

From *Chap. 4. Observations on the State of Degradation to Which Woman Is Reduced by Various Causes*

* * *

In the middle rank of life, to continue the comparison,[5] men, in their youth, are prepared for professions, and marriage is not considered as the grand feature in their lives; whilst women, on the contrary, have no other scheme to sharpen their faculties. It is not business, extensive plans, or any of the excursive flights of ambition, that engross their attention; no, their thoughts are not employed in rearing such noble structures. To rise in the world, and have the liberty of running from pleasure to pleasure, they must marry advantageously, and to this object their time is sacrificed, and their persons often legally prostituted. A man when he enters any profession has his eye steadily fixed on some future advantage (and the mind gains great strength by having all its efforts directed to one point), and, full of his business, pleasure is considered as mere relaxation; whilst women seek for pleasure as the main purpose of existence. In fact, from the education, which they receive from society, the love of pleasure may be said to govern them all; but does this prove that there is a sex in souls? It would be just as rational to declare that the courtiers in France, when a destructive system of despotism had formed their character, were not men, because liberty, virtue, and humanity, were sacrificed to pleasure and vanity.—Fatal passions, which have ever domineered over the *whole* race!

The same love of pleasure, fostered by the whole tendency of their edu-

4. The emperors of China were regarded as deities.
5. I.e., her comparison between the social condi-tions of men and of women, which conduce to the degradation of women.

cation, gives a trifling turn to the conduct of women in most circumstances: for instance, they are ever anxious about secondary things; and on the watch for adventures, instead of being occupied by duties.

A man, when he undertakes a journey, has, in general, the end in view; a woman thinks more of the incidental occurrences, the strange things that may possibly occur on the road; the impression that she may make on her fellow-travellers; and, above all, she is anxiously intent on the care of the finery that she carries with her, which is more than ever a part of herself, when going to figure on a new scene; when, to use an apt French turn of expression, she is going to produce a sensation.—Can dignity of mind exist with such trivial cares?

In short, women, in general, as well as the rich of both sexes, have acquired all the follies and vices of civilization, and missed the useful fruit. It is not necessary for me always to premise, that I speak of the condition of the whole sex, leaving exceptions out of the question. Their senses are inflamed, and their understandings neglected, consequently they become the prey of their senses, delicately termed sensibility, and are blown about by every momentary gust of feeling. Civilized women are, therefore, so weakened by false refinement, that, respecting morals, their condition is much below what it would be were they left in a state nearer to nature. Ever restless and anxious, their over exercised sensibility not only renders them uncomfortable themselves, but troublesome, to use a soft phrase, to others. All their thoughts turn on things calculated to excite emotion; and feeling, when they should reason, their conduct is unstable, and their opinions are wavering—not the wavering produced by deliberation or progressive views, but by contradictory emotions. By fits and starts they are warm in many pursuits; yet this warmth, never concentrated into perseverance, soon exhausts itself; exhaled by its own heat, or meeting with some other fleeting passion, to which reason has never given any specific gravity, neutrality ensues. Miserable, indeed, must be that being whose cultivation of mind has only tended to inflame its passions! A distinction should be made between inflaming and strengthening them. The passions thus pampered, whilst the judgment is left unformed, what can be expected to ensue?—Undoubtedly, a mixture of madness and folly!

This observation should not be confined to the *fair* sex; however, at present, I only mean to apply it to them.

Novels, music, poetry, and gallantry, all tend to make women the creatures of sensation, and their character is thus formed in the mold of folly during the time they are acquiring accomplishments, the only improvement they are excited, by their station in society, to acquire. This overstretched sensibility naturally relaxes the other powers of the mind, and prevents intellect from attaining that sovereignty which it ought to attain to render a rational creature useful to others, and content with its own station: for the exercise of the understanding, as life advances, is the only method pointed out by nature to calm the passions.

Satiety has a very different effect, and I have often been forcibly struck by an emphatical description of damnation:—when the spirit is represented as continually hovering with abortive eagerness round the defiled body, unable to enjoy any thing without the organs of sense. Yet, to their senses, are women made slaves, because it is by their sensibility that they obtain present power.

And will moralists pretend to assert, that this is the condition in which one half of the human race should be encouraged to remain with listless inactivity and stupid acquiescence? Kind instructors! what were we created for? To remain, it may be said, innocent; they mean in a state of childhood.— We might as well never have been born, unless it were necessary that we should be created to enable man to acquire the noble privilege of reason, the power of discerning good from evil, whilst we lie down in the dust from whence we were taken, never to rise again.—

It would be an endless task to trace the variety of meannesses, cares, and sorrows, into which women are plunged by the prevailing opinion, that they were created rather to feel than reason, and that all the power they obtain, must be obtained by their charms and weakness:

Fine by defect, and amiably weak![6]

And, made by this amiable weakness entirely dependent, excepting what they gain by illicit sway, on man, not only for protection, but advice, is it surprising that, neglecting the duties that reason alone points out, and shrinking from trials calculated to strengthen their minds, they only exert themselves to give their defects a graceful covering, which may serve to heighten their charms in the eye of the voluptuary, though it sink them below the scale of moral excellence?

Fragile in every sense of the word, they are obliged to look up to man for every comfort. In the most trifling dangers they cling to their support, with parasitical tenacity, piteously demanding succour; and their *natural* protector extends his arm, or lifts up his voice, to guard the lovely trembler—from what? Perhaps the frown of an old cow, or the jump of a mouse; a rat, would be a serious danger. In the name of reason, and even common sense, what can save such beings from contempt; even though they be soft and fair?

These fears, when not affected, may produce some pretty attitudes; but they shew a degree of imbecility which degrades a rational creature in a way women are not aware of—for love and esteem are very distinct things.

I am fully persuaded that we should hear of none of these infantine airs, if girls were allowed to take sufficient exercise, and not confined in close rooms till their muscles are relaxed, and their powers of digestion destroyed. To carry the remark still further, if fear in girls, instead of being cherished, perhaps, created, were treated in the same manner as cowardice in boys, we should quickly see women with more dignified aspects. It is true, they could not then with equal propriety be termed the sweet flowers that smile in the walk of man; but they would be more respectable members of society, and discharge the important duties of life by the light of their own reason. "Educate women like men," says Rousseau, "and the more they resemble our sex the less power will they have over us."[7] This is the very point I aim at. I do not wish them to have power over men; but over themselves.

In the same strain have I heard men argue against instructing the poor;

6. Pope's actual words were "Fine by defect, and delicately weak" (*Moral Essays* 2.43).
7. In *Émile* Rousseau means this as a warning to women that if they are brought up to be like men, they will lose their sexual power over men.

for many are the forms that aristocracy assumes. "Teach them to read, and write," say they, "and you take them out of the station assigned them by nature." An eloquent Frenchman has answered them, I will borrow his sentiments. But they know not, when they make man a brute, that they may expect every instant to see him transformed into a ferocious beast.[8] Without knowledge there can be no morality!

Ignorance is a frail base for virtue! Yet, that it is the condition for which woman was organized, has been insisted upon by the writers who have most vehemently argued in favor of the superiority of man; a superiority not in degree, but essence; though, to soften the argument, they have labored to prove, with chivalrous generosity, that the sexes ought not to be compared; man was made to reason, woman to feel: and that together, flesh and spirit, they make the most perfect whole, by blending happily reason and sensibility into one character.

And what is sensibility? "Quickness of sensation; quickness of perception; delicacy." Thus is it defined by Dr. Johnson;[9] and the definition gives me no other idea than of the most exquisitely polished instinct. I discern not a trace of the image of God in either sensation or matter. Refined seventy times seven,[1] they are still material; intellect dwells not there; nor will fire ever make lead gold!

I come round to my old argument; if woman be allowed to have an immortal soul, she must have, as the employment of life, an understanding to improve. And when, to render the present state more complete, though every thing proves it to be but a fraction of a mighty sum, she is incited by present gratification to forget her grand destination, nature is counteracted, or she was born only to procreate and rot. Or, granting brutes, of every description, a soul, though not a reasonable one, the exercise of instinct and sensibility may be the step, which they are to take, in this life, towards the attainment of reason in the next; so that through all eternity they will lag behind man, who, why we cannot tell, had the power given him of attaining reason in his first mode of existence.

When I treat of the peculiar duties of women, as I should treat of the peculiar duties of a citizen or father, it will be found that I do not mean to insinuate that they should be taken out of their families, speaking of the majority. "He that hath wife and children," says Lord Bacon, "hath given hostages to fortune; for they are impediments to great enterprises, either of virtue or mischief. Certainly the best works, and of greatest merit for the public, have proceeded from the unmarried or childless men."[2] I say the same of women. But, the welfare of society is not built on extraordinary exertions; and were it more reasonably organized, there would be still less need of great abilities, or heroic virtues.

In the regulation of a family, in the education of children, understanding, in an unsophisticated sense, is particularly required: strength both of body and mind; yet the men who, by their writings, have most earnestly labored

---

8. Poston suggests that Wollstonecraft has in mind the comment by Mirabeau, the Revolutionary statesman, to the Abbé Siéyès, who had been rudely treated in the French Constituent Assembly in 1790: "My dear abbé, you have loosed the bull: do you expect he is not to make use of his horns?"
9. In his *Dictionary of the English Language*

(1747).
1. Jesus replies, when asked whether a brother's repeated sin should be forgiven "till seven times": "I say not unto thee, Until seven times: but, Until seventy times seven" (Matthew 18.22).
2. From Francis Bacon's essay *Of Marriage and the Single Life*.

to domesticate women, have endeavored, by arguments dictated by a gross appetite, which satiety had rendered fastidious, to weaken their bodies and cramp their minds. But, if even by these sinister methods they really *persuaded* women, by working on their feelings, to stay at home, and fulfil the duties of a mother and mistress of a family, I should cautiously oppose opinions that led women to right conduct, by prevailing on them to make the discharge of such important duties the main business of life, though reason were insulted. Yet, and I appeal to experience, if by neglecting the understanding they be as much, nay, more detached from these domestic employments, than they could be by the most serious intellectual pursuit, though it may be observed, that the mass of mankind will never vigorously pursue an intellectual object,[3] I may be allowed to infer that reason is absolutely necessary to enable a woman to perform any duty properly, and I must again repeat, that sensibility is not reason.

The comparison with the rich still occurs to me; for, when men neglect the duties of humanity, women will follow their example; a common stream hurries them both along with thoughtless celerity. Riches and honors prevent a man from enlarging his understanding, and enervate all his powers by reversing the order of nature, which has ever made true pleasure the reward of labor. Pleasure—enervating pleasure is, likewise, within women's reach without earning it. But, till hereditary possessions are spread abroad, how can we expect men to be proud of virtue? And, till they are, women will govern them by the most direct means, neglecting their dull domestic duties to catch the pleasure that sits lightly on the wing of time.

"The power of the woman," says some author, "is her sensibility";[4] and men, not aware of the consequence, do all they can to make this power swallow up every other. Those who constantly employ their sensibility will have most: for example; poets, painters, and composers.[5] Yet, when the sensibility is thus increased at the expence of reason, and even the imagination, why do philosophical men complain of their fickleness? The sexual attention of man particularly acts on female sensibility, and this sympathy has been exercised from their youth up. A husband cannot long pay those attentions with the passion necessary to excite lively emotions, and the heart, accustomed to lively emotions, turns to a new lover, or pines in secret, the prey of virtue or prudence. I mean when the heart has really been rendered susceptible, and the taste formed; for I am apt to conclude, from what I have seen in fashionable life, that vanity is oftener fostered than sensibility by the mode of education, and the intercourse between the sexes, which I have reprobated; and that coquetry more frequently proceeds from vanity than from that inconstancy, which overstrained sensibility naturally produces.

Another argument that has had great weight with me, must, I think, have some force with every considerate benevolent heart. Girls who have been thus weakly educated, are often cruelly left by their parents without any

---

3. The mass of mankind are rather the slaves of their appetites than of their passions [Wollstonecraft's note].
4. The sentiment is a commonplace, but Wollstonecraft may be referring to Edmund Burke's phrase: "The beauty of women is considerably owing to their weakness, or delicacy . . ." (Edmund Burke, *A Philosophical Enquiry into the Origin of Our Ideas of the Sublime and Beautiful* [London,

1759 (repr. The Scolar Press, 1970)], p. 219) [Poston's note].
5. Men of these descriptions pour it into their compositions, to amalgamate the gross materials; and, molding them with passion, give to the inert body a soul; but, in woman's imagination, love alone concentrates these ethereal beams [Wollstonecraft's note].

provision; and, of course, are dependent on, not only the reason, but the bounty of their brothers. These brothers are, to view the fairest side of the question, good sort of men, and give as a favor, what children of the same parents had an equal right to. In this equivocal humiliating situation, a docile female may remain some time, with a tolerable degree of comfort. But, when the brother marries, a probable circumstance, from being considered as the mistress of the family, she is viewed with averted looks as an intruder, an unnecessary burden on the benevolence of the master of the house, and his new partner.

Who can recount the misery, which many unfortunate beings, whose minds and bodies are equally weak, suffer in such situations—unable to work, and ashamed to beg? The wife, a cold-hearted, narrow-minded, woman, and this is not an unfair supposition; for the present mode of education does not tend to enlarge the heart any more than the understanding, is jealous of the little kindness which her husband shews to his relations; and her sensibility not rising to humanity, she is displeased at seeing the property of *her* children lavished on an helpless sister.

These are matters of fact, which have come under my eye again and again. The consequence is obvious, the wife has recourse to cunning to undermine the habitual affection, which she is afraid openly to oppose; and neither tears nor caresses are spared till the spy is worked out of her home, and thrown on the world, unprepared for its difficulties; or sent, as a great effort of generosity, or from some regard to propriety, with a small stipend, and an uncultivated mind, into joyless solitude.

These two women may be much upon a par, with respect to reason and humanity; and changing situations, might have acted just the same selfish part; but had they been differently educated, the case would also have been very different. The wife would not have had that sensibility, of which self is the centre, and reason might have taught her not to expect, and not even to be flattered by, the affection of her husband, if it led him to violate prior duties. She would wish not to love him merely because he loved her, but on account of his virtues; and the sister might have been able to struggle for herself instead of eating the bitter bread of dependence.

I am, indeed, persuaded that the heart, as well as the understanding, is opened by cultivation; and by, which may not appear so clear, strengthening the organs; I am not now talking of momentary flashes of sensibility, but of affections. And, perhaps, in the education of both sexes, the most difficult task is so to adjust instruction as not to narrow the understanding, whilst the heart is warmed by the generous juices of spring, just raised by the electric fermentation of the season; nor to dry up the feelings by employing the mind in investigations remote from life.

With respect to women, when they receive a careful education, they are either made fine ladies, brimful of sensibility, and teeming with capricious fancies; or mere notable women.[6] The latter are often friendly, honest creatures, and have a shrewd kind of good sense joined with worldly prudence, that often render them more useful members of society than the fine sentimental lady, though they possess neither greatness of mind nor taste. The intellectual world is shut against them; take them out of their family or

6. I.e., energetic in running a household.

neighborhood, and they stand still; the mind finding no employment, for literature affords a fund of amusement which they have never sought to relish, but frequently to despise. The sentiments and taste of more cultivated minds appear ridiculous, even in those whom chance and family connections have led them to love; but in mere acquaintance they think it all affectation.

A man of sense can only love such a woman on account of her sex, and respect her, because she is a trusty servant. He lets her, to preserve his own peace, scold the servants, and go to church in clothes made of the very best materials. A man of her own size of understanding would, probably, not agree so well with her; for he might wish to encroach on her prerogative, and manage some domestic concerns himself. Yet women, whose minds are not enlarged by cultivation, or the natural selfishness of sensibility expanded by reflection, are very unfit to manage a family; for, by an undue stretch of power, they are always tyrannizing to support a superiority that only rests on the arbitrary distinction of fortune. The evil is sometimes more serious, and domestics are deprived of innocent indulgences, and made to work beyond their strength, in order to enable the notable woman to keep a better table, and outshine her neighbours in finery and parade. If she attend to her children, it is, in general, to dress them in a costly manner—and, whether this attention arise from vanity or fondness, it is equally pernicious.

Besides, how many women of this description pass their days; or, at least, their evenings, discontentedly. Their husbands acknowledge that they are good managers, and chaste wives; but leave home to seek for more agreeable, may I be allowed to use a significant French word, *piquant*[7] society; and the patient drudge, who fulfils her task, like a blind horse in a mill, is defrauded of her just reward; for the wages due to her are the caresses of her husband; and women who have so few resources in themselves, do not very patiently bear this privation of a natural right.

A fine lady, on the contrary, has been taught to look down with contempt on the vulgar employments of life; though she has only been incited to acquire accomplishments that rise a degree above sense; for even corporeal accomplishments cannot be acquired with any degree of precision unless the understanding has been strengthened by exercise. Without a foundation of principles taste is superficial, grace must arise from something deeper than imitation. The imagination, however, is heated, and the feelings rendered fastidious, if not sophisticated; or, a counterpoise of judgment is not acquired, when the heart still remains artless, though it becomes too tender.

These women are often amiable; and their hearts are really more sensible to general benevolence, more alive to the sentiments that civilize life, than the square-elbowed family drudge; but, wanting a due proportion of reflection and self-government, they only inspire love; and are the mistresses of their husbands, whilst they have any hold on their affections; and the platonic friends of his male acquaintance. These are the fair defects in nature; the women who appear to be created not to enjoy the fellowship of man, but to save him from sinking into absolute brutality, by rubbing off the rough angles of his character; and by playful dalliance to give some dignity to the appetite that draws him to them.—Gracious Creator of the whole human race! hast thou created such a being as woman, who can trace thy wisdom

7. Stimulating.

in thy works, and feel that thou alone art by thy nature exalted above her,—
for no better purpose?—Can she believe that she was only made to submit
to man, her equal, a being, who, like her, was sent into the world to acquire
virtue?—Can she consent to be occupied merely to please him; merely to
adorn the earth, when her soul is capable of rising to thee?—And can she
rest supinely dependent on man for reason, when she ought to mount with
him the arduous steeps of knowledge?—

Yet, if love be the supreme good, let women be only educated to inspire
it, and let every charm be polished to intoxicate the senses; but, if they be
moral beings, let them have a chance to become intelligent; and let love to
man be only a part of that glowing flame of universal love, which, after
encircling humanity, mounts in grateful incense to God.

* * *

1792

Letters Written in Sweden, Norway, and Denmark In June 1795

Mary Wollstonecraft undertook an arduous and sometimes dangerous five-month trip
through the Scandinavian countries, taking with her Fanny, her year-old infant, and
Marguerite, a French maid she had brought from Paris to London. Wollstonecraft's
American lover Gilbert Imlay—author, inaugurator of sometimes shady commercial
deals, and inveterate philanderer—had conceived the scheme of sending her as his
business emissary to the northern countries, thus leaving himself free to pursue an
affair with another woman. Upon returning to London in September, Wollstonecraft
prepared for publication the letters she had written to Imlay during her trip; they
were issued the next year (1796) by her friend, the radical publisher Joseph Johnson.
Contemporary readers were left to guess at the identity of the *you* to whom the letters
were addressed and to speculate about the author's hints at a love relationship with
the addressee and about the causes of her present unhappiness.

In the letters Wollstonecraft comments insightfully and incisively about the class
divisions, manners, commerce, and conduct of the people she observed and especially
about the care of children and the situation and disabilities of women. She is also a
sensitive connoisseur, in the mode of that time, on natural scenery and moves easily
from aesthetic contemplation to solitary meditations on life, death, and the possibility
of an afterlife—meditations interspersed with sharply realistic observations of the
world about her. And always, she manifests her own doughty, passionate, and impetuous temperament.

Carol Poston, who has edited both Wollstonecraft's *Vindication of the Rights of
Woman* and her *Letters* from Scandinavia, justly describes the latter as "her most
delightful work" and remarks that, in the unsystematic freedom that it permits, "it is
possible that the epistolary journal is the perfect literary mode for Wollstonecraft's
strengths as a writer and thinker."

From Letters Written during a Short Residence in Sweden, Norway, and Denmark

Advertisement

The writing travels, or memoirs, has ever been a pleasant employment; for
vanity or sensibility always renders it interesting. In writing these desultory

letters, I found I could not avoid being continually the first person—"the little hero of each tale." I tried to correct this fault, if it be one, for they were designed for publication; but in proportion as I arranged my thoughts, my letter, I found, became stiff and affected: I, therefore, determined to let my remarks and reflections flow unrestrained, as I perceived that I could not give a just description of what I saw, but by relating the effect different objects had produced on my mind and feelings, whilst the impression was still fresh.

A person has a right, I have sometimes thought, when amused by a witty or interesting egotist, to talk of himself when he can win on our attention by acquiring our affection. Whether I deserve to rank amongst this privileged number, my readers alone can judge—and I give them leave to shut the book, if they do not wish to become better acquainted with me.

My plan was simply to endeavor to give a just view of the present state of the countries I have passed through, as far as I could obtain information during so short a residence; avoiding those details which, without being very useful to travelers who follow the same route, appear very insipid to those who only accompany you in their chair.

Letter 1

Eleven days of weariness on board a vessel not intended for the accommodation of passengers have so exhausted my spirits, to say nothing of the other causes, with which you are already sufficiently acquainted, that it is with some difficulty I adhere to my determination of giving you my observations, as I travel through new scenes, whilst warmed with the impression they have made on me.

The captain, as I mentioned to you, promised to put me on shore at Arendall, or Gothenburg, in his way to Elsineur;[1] but contrary winds obliged us to pass both places during the night. In the morning, however, after we had lost sight of the entrance of the latter bay, the vessel was becalmed; and the captain, to oblige me, hanging out a signal for a pilot, bore down towards the shore.

My attention was particularly directed to the lighthouse; and you can scarcely imagine with what anxiety I watched two long hours for a boat to emancipate me—still no one appeared. Every cloud that flitted on the horizon was hailed as a liberator, till approaching nearer, like most of the prospects sketched by hope, it dissolved under the eye into disappointment.

Weary of expectation, I then began to converse with the captain on the subject; and, from the tenor of the information my questions drew forth, I soon concluded, that, if I waited for a boat, I had little chance of getting on shore at this place. Despotism, as is usually the case, I found had here cramped the industry of man. The pilots being paid by the king, and scantily, they will not run into any danger, or even quit their hovels, if they can possibly avoid it, only to fulfil what is termed their duty. How different is it on the English coast, where, in the most stormy weather, boats immediately hail you, brought out by the expectation of extraordinary profit.

Disliking to sail for Elsineur, and still more to lie at anchor, or cruise about

---

1. Helsingør, Denmark. "Arendall": in Norway [Wollstonecraft's note]. "Gothenburg": Göteborg, Sweden.

the coast for several days, I exerted all my rhetoric to prevail on the captain to let me have the ship's boat; and though I added the most forcible of arguments, I for a long time addressed him in vain.

It is a kind of rule at sea, not to send out a boat. The captain was a good-natured man; but men with common minds seldom break through general rules. Prudence is ever the resort of weakness; and they rarely go as far as they may in any undertaking, who are determined not to go beyond it on any account. If, however, I had some trouble with the captain, I did not lose much time with the sailors; for they, all alacrity, hoisted out the boat, the moment I obtained permission, and promised to row me to the lighthouse.

I did not once allow myself to doubt of obtaining a conveyance from thence round the rocks—and then away for Gothenburg—confinement is so unpleasant.

The day was fine; and I enjoyed the water till, approaching the little island, poor Marguerite, whose timidity always acts as a feeler before her adventuring spirit, began to wonder at our not seeing any inhabitants. I did not listen to her. But when, on landing, the same silence prevailed, I caught the alarm, which was not lessened by the sight of two old men, whom we forced out of their wretched hut. Scarcely human in their appearance, we with difficulty obtained an intelligible reply to our questions—the result of which was, that they had no boat, and were not allowed to quit their post, on any pretense. But, they informed us, that there was at the other side, eight or ten miles over, a pilot's dwelling; two guineas[2] tempted the sailors to risk the captain's displeasure, and once more embark to row me over.

The weather was pleasant, and the appearance of the shore so grand, that I should have enjoyed the two hours it took to reach it, but for the fatigue which was too visible in the countenances of the sailors who, instead of uttering a complaint, were, with the thoughtless hilarity peculiar to them, joking about the possibility of the captain's taking advantage of a slight westerly breeze, which was springing up, to sail without them. Yet, in spite of their good humor, I could not help growing uneasy when the shore, receding, as it were, as we advanced, seemed to promise no end to their toil. This anxiety increased when, turning into the most picturesque bay I ever saw, my eyes sought in vain for the vestige of a human habitation. Before I could determine what step to take in such a dilemma, for I could not bear to think of returning to the ship, the sight of a barge relieved me, and we hastened towards it for information. We were immediately directed to pass some jutting rocks when we should see a pilot's hut.

There was a solemn silence in this scene, which made itself be felt. The sunbeams that played on the ocean, scarcely ruffled by the lightest breeze, contrasted with the huge, dark rocks, that looked like the rude materials of creation forming the barrier of unwrought space, forcibly struck me; but I should not have been sorry if the cottage had not appeared equally tranquil. Approaching a retreat where strangers, especially women, so seldom appeared, I wondered that curiosity did not bring the beings who inhabited it to the windows or door. I did not immediately recollect that men who remain so near the brute creation, as only to exert themselves to find the food necessary to sustain life, have little or no imagination to call forth the

---

2. A British gold coin worth one pound and a shilling.

curiosity necessary to fructify the faint glimmerings of mind which entitles them to rank as lords of the creation.—Had they either, they could not contentedly remain rooted in the clods they so indolently cultivate.

Whilst the sailors went to seek for the sluggish inhabitants, these conclusions occurred to me; and, recollecting the extreme fondness which the Parisians ever testify for novelty, their very curiosity appeared to me a proof of the progress they had made in refinement. Yes; in the art of living—in the art of escaping from the cares which embarrass the first steps towards the attainment of the pleasures of social life.

The pilots informed the sailors that they were under the direction of a lieutenant retired from the service, who spoke English; adding, that they could do nothing without his orders; and even the offer of money could hardly conquer their laziness, and prevail on them to accompany us to his dwelling. They would not go with me alone which I wanted them to have done, because I wished to dismiss the sailors as soon as possible. Once more we rowed off, they following tardily, till, turning round another bold protuberance of the rocks, we saw a boat making towards us, and soon learnt that it was the lieutenant himself, coming with some earnestness to see who we were.

To save the sailors any further toil, I had my baggage instantly removed into his boat; for, as he could speak English, a previous parley was not necessary; though Marguerite's respect for me could hardly keep her from expressing the fear, strongly marked on her countenance, which my putting ourselves into the power of a strange man excited. He pointed out his cottage; and, drawing near to it, I was not sorry to see a female figure, though I had not, like Marguerite, been thinking of robberies, murders, or the other evil which instantly, as the sailors would have said, runs foul of a woman's imagination.

On entering, I was still better pleased to find a clean house, with some degree of rural elegance. The beds were of muslin, coarse it is true, but dazzlingly white; and the floor was strewed over with little sprigs of juniper (the custom, as I afterwards found, of the country), which formed a contrast with the curtains and produced an agreeable sensation of freshness, to soften the ardor of noon. Still nothing was so pleasing as the alacrity of hospitality— all that the house afforded was quickly spread on the whitest linen.— Remember I had just left the vessel, where, without being fastidious, I had continually been disgusted. Fish, milk, butter, and cheese, and I am sorry to add, brandy, the bane of this country, were spread on the board. After we had dined, hospitality made them, with some degree of mystery, bring us some excellent coffee. I did not then know that it was prohibited.[3]

The good man of the house apologized for coming in continually, but declared that he was so glad to speak English, he could not stay out. He need not have apologized; I was equally glad of his company. With the wife I could only exchange smiles; and she was employed observing the make of our clothes. My hands, I found, had first led her to discover that I was the lady. I had, of course, my quantum of reverences; for the politeness of the north seems to partake of the coldness of the climate, and the rigidity of its iron sinewed rocks. Amongst the peasantry, there is, however, so much of

---

3. The law then prohibited the import or consumption of coffee.

the simplicity of the golden age in this land of flint—so much overflowing of heart, and fellow-feeling, that only benevolence, and the honest sympathy of nature, diffused smiles over my countenance when they kept me standing, regardless of my fatigue, whilst they dropt courtesy after courtesy.

The situation of this house was beautiful, though chosen for convenience. The master being the officer who commanded all the pilots on the coast, and the person appointed to guard wrecks, it was necessary for him to fix on a spot that would overlook the whole bay. As he had seen some service, he wore, not without a pride I thought becoming, a badge to prove that he had merited well of his country. It was happy, I thought, that he had been paid in honor; for the stipend he received was little more than twelve pounds a year.—I do not trouble myself or you with the calculation of Swedish ducats. Thus, my friend, you perceive the necessity of *perquisites*.[4] This same narrow policy runs through every thing. I shall have occasion further to animadvert on it.

Though my host amused me with an account of himself, which gave me an idea of the manners of the people I was about to visit, I was eager to climb the rocks to view the country, and see whether the honest tars had regained their ship. With the help of the lieutenant's telescope I saw the vessel underway with a fair though gentle gale. The sea was calm, playful even as the most shallow stream, and on the vast bason[5] I did not see a dark speck to indicate the boat. My conductors were consequently arrived.

Straying further my eye was attracted by the sight of some heart's-ease[6] that peeped through the rocks. I caught at it as a good omen, and going to preserve it in a letter that had not conveyed balm to my heart, a cruel remembrance suffused my eyes; but it passed away like an April shower. If you are deep read in Shakspeare, you will recollect that this was the little western flower tinged by love's dart, which "maidens call love in idleness."[7] The gaiety of my babe was unmixed; regardless of omens or sentiments, she found a few wild strawberries more grateful than flowers or fancies.

The lieutenant informed me that this was a commodious bay. Of that I could not judge, though I felt its picturesque beauty. Rocks were piled on rocks, forming a suitable bulwark to the ocean. Come no further, they emphatically said, turning their dark sides to the waves to augment the idle roar. The view was sterile: still little patches of earth, of the most exquisite verdure, enameled with the sweetest wild flowers, seemed to promise the goats and a few straggling cows luxurious herbage. How silent and peaceful was the scene. I gazed around with rapture, and felt more of that spontaneous pleasure which gives credibility to our expectation of happiness, than I had for a long, long time before. I forgot the horrors I had witnessed in France,[8] which had cast a gloom over all nature, and suffering the enthusiasm of my character, too often, gracious God! damped by the tears of disappointed affection, to be lighted up afresh, care took wing while simple fellow feeling expanded my heart.

---

4. Payments in addition to salary. The suggestion is of income derived from bribes or smuggling.
5. I.e., basin.
6. A small wildflower, variously colored. Wollstonecraft goes on to make the first of many veiled allusions to her faithless lover Gilbert Imlay, to whom these letters are addressed.

7. Popular name for the pansy, whose juice Oberon put on the sleeping Titania's eyes to make her dote on the next person she saw (*A Midsummer Night's Dream* 2.1.165–72).
8. Wollstonecraft had lived in France at the time of the Reign of Terror under Robespierre (1793–94).

To prolong this enjoyment, I readily assented to the proposal of our host to pay a visit to a family, the master of which spoke English, who was the drollest dog in the country, he added, repeating some of his stories, with a hearty laugh.

I walked on, still delighted with the rude beauties of the scene; for the sublime often gave place imperceptibly to the beautiful, dilating the emotions which were painfully concentrated.

When we entered this abode, the largest I had yet seen, I was introduced to a numerous family; but the father, from whom I was led to expect so much entertainment, was absent. The lieutenant consequently was obliged to be the interpreter of our reciprocal compliments. The phrases were awkwardly transmitted, it is true; but looks and gestures were sufficient to make them intelligible and interesting. The girls were all vivacity, and respect for me could scarcely keep them from romping with my host, who, asking for a pinch of snuff, was presented with a box, out of which an artificial mouse, fastened to the bottom, sprung. Though this trick had doubtless been played time out of mind, yet the laughter it excited was not less genuine.

They were overflowing with civility; but to prevent their almost killing my babe with kindness, I was obliged to shorten my visit; and two or three of the girls accompanied us, bringing with them a part of whatever the house afforded to contribute towards rendering my supper more plentiful; and plentiful in fact it was, though I with difficulty did honor to some of the dishes, not relishing the quantity of sugar and spices put into every thing. At supper my host told me bluntly that I was a woman of observation, for I asked him *men's questions.*

The arrangements for my journey were quickly made; I could only have a car with post-horses, as I did not choose to wait till a carriage could be sent for to Gothenburg. The expense of my journey, about one or two and twenty English miles, I found would not amount to more than eleven or twelve shillings, paying, he assured me, generously. I gave him a guinea and a half. But it was with the greatest difficulty that I could make him take so much, indeed any thing for my lodging and fare. He declared that it was next to robbing me, explaining how much I ought to pay on the road. However, as I was positive, he took the guinea for himself; but, as a condition, insisted on accompanying me, to prevent my meeting with any trouble or imposition on the way.

I then retired to my apartment with regret. The night was so fine, that I would gladly have rambled about much longer; yet recollecting that I must rise very early, I reluctantly went to bed: but my senses had been so awake, and my imagination still continued so busy, that I sought for rest in vain. Rising before six, I scented the sweet morning air; I had long before heard the birds twittering to hail the dawning day, though it could scarcely have been allowed to have departed.

Nothing, in fact, can equal the beauty of the northern summer's evening and night; if night it may be called that only wants the glare of day, the full light, which frequently seems so impertinent; for I could write at midnight very well without a candle. I contemplated all nature at rest; the rocks, even grown darker in their appearance, looked as if they partook of the general repose, and reclined more heavily on their foundation.—What, I exclaimed, is this active principle which keeps me still awake?—Why fly my thoughts abroad when every thing around me appears at home? My child was sleeping with equal calmness—innocent and sweet as the closing flowers.—Some recollections, attached to the idea of home, mingled with reflections respecting the state of society I had been contemplating that evening, made a tear drop on the rosy cheek I had just kissed; and emotions that trembled on the brink of ectasy and agony gave a poignancy to my sensations, which made me feel more alive than usual.

What are these imperious sympathies? How frequently has melancholy and even misanthropy taken possession of me, when the world has disgusted me, and friends have proved unkind. I have then considered myself as a particle broken off from the grand mass of mankind;—I was alone, till some involuntary sympathetic emotion, like the attraction of adhesion,[9] made me feel that I was still a part of a mighty whole, from which I could not sever myself—not, perhaps, for the reflection has been carried very far, by snapping the thread of an existence which loses its charms in proportion as the cruel experience of life stops or poisons the current of the heart. Futurity, what hast thou not to give to those who know that there is such a thing as happiness! I speak not of philosophical contentment, though pain has afforded them the strongest conviction of it.

After our coffee and milk, for the mistress of the house had been roused long before us by her hospitality, my baggage was taken forward in a boat by my host, because the car could not safely have been brought to the house.

The road at first was very rocky and troublesome; but our driver was careful, and the horses accustomed to the frequent and sudden acclivities and descents; so that not apprehending any danger, I played with my girl, whom I would not leave to Marguerite's care, on account of her timidity.

Stopping at a little inn to bait[1] the horses, I saw the first countenance in Sweden that displeased me, though the man was better dressed than any one who had as yet fallen in my way. An altercation took place between him and my host, the purport of which I could not guess, excepting that I was the occasion of it, be it what it would. The sequel was his leaving the house angrily; and I was immediately informed that he was the custom-house officer. The professional had indeed effaced the national character, for living as he did with these frank hospitable people, still only the exciseman appeared,—the counterpart of some I had met with in England and France. I was unprovided with a passport, not having entered any great town. At Gothenburg I knew I could immediately obtain one, and only the trouble made me object to the searching my trunks. He blustered for money; but the lieutenant was determined to guard me, according to promise, from imposition.

To avoid being interrogated at the town-gate, and obliged to go in the rain to give an account of myself, merely a form, before we could get the refreshment we stood in need of, he requested us to descend, I might have said step, from our car, and walk into town.

I expected to have found a tolerable inn, but was ushered into a most comfortless one; and, because it was about five o'clock, three or four hours

9. The physical attraction between two different   1. Feed.
substances.

after their dining hour, I could not prevail on them to give me any thing warm to eat.

The appearance of the accommodations obliged me to deliver one of my recommendatory letters, and the gentleman, to whom it was addressed, sent to look out for a lodging for me whilst I partook of his supper. As nothing passed at this supper to characterize the country, I shall here close my letter.

Your's truly.

Letter 4

The severity of the long Swedish winter tends to render the people sluggish; for, though this season has its peculiar pleasures, too much time is employed to guard against its inclemency. Still, as warm cloathing is absolutely necessary, the women spin, and the men weave, and by these exertions get a fence to keep out the cold. I have rarely passed a knot of cottages without seeing cloth laid out to bleach; and when I entered, always found the women spinning or knitting.

A mistaken tenderness, however, for their children, makes them, even in summer, load them with flannels; and, having a sort of natural antipathy to cold water, the squalid appearance of the poor babes, not to speak of the noxious smell which flannel and rugs retain, seems a reply to a question I had often asked—Why I did not see more children in the villages I passed through? Indeed the children appear to be nipt in the bud, having neither the graces nor charms of their age. And this, I am persuaded, is much more owing to the ignorance of the mothers than to the rudeness of the climate. Rendered feeble by the continual perspiration they are kept in, whilst every pore is absorbing unwholesome moisture, they give them, even at the breast, brandy, salt fish, and every other crude substance, which air and exercise enables the parent to digest.

The women of fortune here, as well as every where else, have nurses to suckle their children; and the total want of chastity in the lower class of women frequently renders them very unfit for the trust.[2]

You have sometimes remarked to me the difference of the manners of the country girls in England and in America; attributing the reserve of the former to the climate—to the absence of genial suns. But it must be their stars, not the zephyrs gently stealing on their senses, which here lead frail women astray.—Who can look at these rocks, and allow the voluptuousness[3] of nature to be an excuse for gratifying the desires it inspires? We must, therefore, find some other cause beside voluptuousness, I believe, to account for the conduct of the Swedish and American country girls; for I am led to conclude, from all the observations I have made, that there is always a mixture of sentiment and imagination in voluptuousness, to which neither of them have much pretension.

The country girls of Ireland and Wales equally feel the first impulse of nature, which, restrained in England by fear or delicacy, proves that society is there in a more advanced state. Besides, as the mind is cultivated, and

2. Because of the possibility of syphilis or other sexual disease.

3. Erotic sensuality.

taste gains ground, the passions become stronger, and rest on something more stable than the casual sympathies of the moment. Health and idleness will always account for promiscuous amors; and in some degree I term every person idle, the exercise of whose mind does not bear some proportion to that of the body.

The Swedish ladies exercise neither sufficiently; of course, grow very fat at an early age; and when they have not this downy[4] appearance, a comfortable idea, you will say, in a cold climate, they are not remarkable for fine forms. They have, however, mostly fine complexions; but indolence makes the lily soon displace the rose. The quantity of coffee, spices, and other things of that kind, with want of care, almost universally spoil their teeth, which contrast but ill with their ruby lips.

The manners of Stockholm are refined, I hear, by the introduction of gallantry; but in the country, romping and coarse freedoms, with coarser allusions, keep the spirits awake. In the article of cleanliness, the women, of all descriptions, seem very deficient; and their dress shews that vanity is more inherent in women than taste.

The men appear to have paid still less court to the graces. They are a robust, healthy race, distinguished for their common sense and turn for humor, rather than for wit or sentiment. I include not, as you may suppose, in this general character, some of the nobility and officers, who having traveled, are polite and well informed.

I must own to you, that the lower class of people here amuse and interest me much more than the middling, with their apish good breeding and prejudices. The sympathy and frankness of heart conspicuous in the peasantry produces even a simple gracefulness of deportment, which has frequently struck me as very picturesque; I have often also been touched by their extreme desire to oblige me, when I could not explain my wants, and by their earnest manner of expressing that desire. There is such a charm in tenderness!—It is so delightful to love our fellow-creatures, and meet the honest affections as they break forth. Still, my good friend, I begin to think that I should not like to live continually in the country, with people whose minds have such a narrow range. My heart would frequently be interested; but my mind would languish for more companionable society.

The beauties of nature appear to me now even more alluring than in my youth, because my intercourse with the world has formed, without vitiating my taste. But, with respect to the inhabitants of the country, my fancy has probably, when disgusted with artificial manners, solaced itself by joining the advantages of cultivation with the interesting sincerity of innocence, forgetting the lassitude that ignorance will naturally produce. I like to see animals sporting, and sympathize in their pains and pleasures. Still I love sometimes to view the human face divine, and trace the soul, as well as the heart, in its varying lineaments.

A journey to the country, which I must shortly make, will enable me to extend my remarks.—Adieu!

4. Softly plump.

Letter 8

Tonsberg[5] was formerly the residence of one of the little sovereigns of Norway; and on an adjacent mountain the vestiges of a fort remain, which was battered down by the Swedes; the entrance of the bay lying close to it.

Here I have frequently strayed, sovereign of the waste, I seldom met any human creature; and sometimes, reclining on the mossy down, under the shelter of a rock, the prattling of the sea amongst the pebbles has lulled me to sleep—no fear of any rude satyr's approaching to interrupt my repose. Balmy were the slumbers, and soft the gales, that refreshed me, when I awoke to follow, with an eye vaguely curious, the white sails, as they turned the cliffs, or seemed to take shelter under the pines which covered the little islands that so gracefully rose to render the terrific ocean beautiful. The fishermen were calmly casting their nets; whilst the seagulls hovered over the unruffled deep. Every thing seemed to harmonize into tranquillity—even the mournful call of the bittern was in cadence with the tinkling bells on the necks of the cows, that, pacing slowly one after the other, along an inviting path in the vale below, were repairing to the cottages to be milked. With what ineffable pleasure have I not gazed—and gazed again, losing my breath through my eyes—my very soul diffused itself in the scene—and, seeming to become all senses, glided in the scarcely-agitated waves, melted in the freshening breeze, or, taking its flight with fairy wing, to the misty mountains which bounded the prospect, fancy tript over new lawns, more beautiful even than the lovely slopes on the winding shore before me.—I pause, again breathless, to trace, with renewed delight, sentiments which entranced me, when, turning my humid eyes from the expanse below to the vault above, my sight pierced the fleecy clouds that softened the azure brightness; and, imperceptibly recalling the reveries of childhood, I bowed before the awful throne of my Creator, whilst I rested on its footstool.

You have sometimes wondered, my dear friend, at the extreme affection of my nature—But such is the temperature of my soul—It is not the vivacity of youth, the hey-day of existence. For years have I endeavored to calm an impetuous tide—laboring to make my feelings take an orderly course.—It was striving against the stream.—I must love and admire with warmth, or I sink into sadness. Tokens of love which I have received have rapt me in elysium—purifying the heart they enchanted.—My bosom still glows.—Do not saucily ask, repeating Sterne's question, "Maria, is it still so warm?"[6] Sufficiently, O my God! has it been chilled by sorrow and unkindness—still nature will prevail—and if I blush at recollecting past enjoyment, it is the rosy hue of pleasure heightened by modesty; for the blush of modesty and shame are as distinct as the emotions by which they are produced.

I need scarcely inform you, after telling you of my walks, that my constitution has been renovated here; and that I have recovered my activity, even whilst attaining a little *embonpoint*.[7] My imprudence last winter, and some untoward accidents just at the time I was weaning my child, had reduced

---

5. Tönsberg, Norway.
6. In Laurence Sterne's novel *A Sentimental Journey* (1768), Parson Yorick, a man of acute sensibility, drenches his handkerchief with tears at hearing of young Maria's misfortunes. When

Maria offers to wash the handkerchief in the stream, then dry it in her bosom, Yorick asks, "And is your heart still so warm, Maria?"
7. Plumpness (French).

me to a state of weakness which I never before experienced.[8] A slow fever preyed on me every night, during my residence in Sweden, and after I arrived at Tonsberg. By chance I found a fine rivulet filtered through the rocks, and confined in a bason for the cattle. It tasted to me like a chaly-beat;[9] at any rate it was pure; and the good effect of the various waters which invalids are sent to drink, depends, I believe, more on the air, exercise and change of scene, than on their medicinal qualities. I therefore determined to turn my morning walks towards it, and seek for health from the nymph of the fountain; partaking of the beverage offered to the tenants of the shade.

Chance likewise led me to discover a new pleasure, equally beneficial to my health. I wished to avail myself of my vicinity to the sea, and bathe; but it was not possible near the town; there was no convenience. The young woman whom I mentioned to you, proposed rowing me across the water, amongst the rocks; but as she was pregnant, I insisted on taking one of the oars, and learning to row. It was not difficult; and I do not know a pleasanter exercise. I soon became expert, and my train of thinking kept time, as it were, with the oars, or I suffered the boat to be carried along by the current, indulging a pleasing forgetfulness, or fallacious hopes.—How fallacious! yet, without hope, what is to sustain life, but the fear of annihilation—the only thing of which I have ever felt a dread—I cannot bear to think of being no more—of losing myself—though existence is often but a painful consciousness of misery; nay, it appears to me impossible that I should cease to exist, or that this active, restless spirit, equally alive to joy and sorrow, should only be organized dust—ready to fly abroad the moment the spring snaps, or the spark goes out, which kept it together. Surely something resides in this heart that is not perishable—and life is more than a dream.

Sometimes, to take up my oar, once more, when the sea was calm, I was amused by disturbing the innumerable young star fish which floated just below the surface: I had never observed them before; for they have not a hard shell, like those which I have seen on the seashore. They look like thickened water, with a white edge; and four purple circles, of different forms, were in the middle, over an incredible number of fibers, or white lines. Touching them, the cloudy substance would turn or close, first on one side, then on the other, very gracefully; but when I took one of them up in the ladle with which I heaved the water out of the boat, it appeared only a colorless jelly.

I did not see any of the seals, numbers of which followed our boat when we landed in Sweden; for though I like to sport in the water, I should have had no desire to join in their gambols.

Enough, you will say, of inanimate nature, and of brutes, to use the lordly phrase of man; let me hear something of the inhabitants.

The gentleman with whom I had business, is the mayor of Tonsberg; he speaks English intelligibly; and, having a sound understanding, I was sorry that his numerous occupations prevented my gaining as much information from him as I could have drawn forth, had we frequently conversed. The people of the town, as far as I had an opportunity of knowing their sentiments, are extremely well satisfied with his manner of discharging his office.

8. Wollstonecraft tells of these events in letters to Gilbert Imlay, January 1795, printed in *The Love Letters of Mary Wollstonecraft to Gilbert Imlay*, ed.

Roger Ingpen (1908).
9. Mineral water containing salts of iron, taken as a tonic.

He has a degree of information and good sense which excites respect, whilst a cheerfulness, almost amounting to gaiety, enables him to reconcile differences, and keep his neighbors in good humor.—"I lost my horse," said a woman to me; "but ever since, when I want to send to the mill, or go out, the mayor lends me one.—He scolds if I do not come for it."

A criminal was branded, during my stay here, for the third offense; but the relief he received made him declare that the judge was one of the best men in the world.

I sent this wretch a trifle, at different times, to take with him into slavery. As it was more than he expected, he wished very much to see me; and this wish brought to my remembrance an anecdote I heard when I was in Lisbon.[1]

A wretch who had been imprisoned several years, during which period lamps had been put up, was at last condemned to a cruel death; yet, in his way to execution, he only wished for one night's respite, to see the city lighted.

Having dined in company at the mayor's, I was invited with his family to spend the day at one of the richest merchant's houses.—Though I could not speak Danish, I knew that I could see a great deal: yes; I am persuaded that I have formed a very just opinion of the character of the Norwegians, without being able to hold converse with them.

I had expected to meet some company; yet was a little disconcerted at being ushered into an apartment full of well-dressed people; and, glancing my eyes round, they rested on several very pretty faces. Rosy cheeks, sparkling eyes, and light brown or golden locks; for I never saw so much hair with a yellow cast; and, with their fine complexions, it looked very becoming.

These women seem a mixture of indolence and vivacity; they scarcely ever walk out, and were astonished that I should, for pleasure; yet they are immoderately fond of dancing. Unaffected in their manners, if they have no pretensions to elegance, simplicity often produces a gracefulness of deportment, when they are animated by a particular desire to please—which was the case at present. The solitariness of my situation, which they thought terrible, interested them very much in my favor. They gathered round me—sung to me—and one of the prettiest, to whom I gave my hand, with some degree of cordiality, to meet the glance of her eyes, kissed me very affectionately.

At dinner, which was conducted with great hospitality, though we remained at table too long, they sung several songs, and, amongst the rest, translations of some patriotic French ones.[2] As the evening advanced, they became playful, and we kept up a sort of conversation of gestures. As their minds were totally uncultivated, I did not lose much, perhaps gained, by not being able to understand them; for fancy probably filled up, more to their advantage, the void in the picture. Be that as it may, they excited my sympathy; and I was very much flattered when I was told, the next day, that they said it was a pleasure to look at me, I appeared so good-natured.

The men were generally captains of ships. Several spoke English very tolerably; but they were merely matter of fact men, confined to a very narrow circle of observation. I found it difficult to obtain from them any information

1. Wollstonecraft had gone to Lisbon in 1785, to nurse her dying friend Fanny Blood.

2. To indicate sympathy with the French Revolution.

respecting their own country, when the fumes of tobacco did not keep me at a distance.

I was invited to partake of some other feasts, and always had to complain of the quantity of provision, and the length of time taken to consume it; for it would not have been proper to have said devour, all went on so fair and softly. The servants wait as slowly as their mistresses carve.

The young women here, as well as in Sweden, have commonly bad teeth, which I attribute to the same causes. They are fond of finery, but do not pay the necessary attention to their persons, to render beauty less transient than a flower; and that interesting expression which sentiment and accomplishments give, seldom supplies its place.

The servants have likewise an inferior sort of food here; but their masters are not allowed to strike them with impunity. I might have added mistresses; for it was a complaint of this kind, brought before the mayor, which led me to a knowledge of the fact.

The wages are low, which is particularly unjust, because the price of clothes is much higher than provisions. A young woman, who is wet nurse to the mistress of the inn where I lodge, receives only twelve dollars[3] a year, and pays ten for the nursing of her own child; the father had run away to get clear of the expense. There was something in this most painful state of widowhood which excited my compassion, and led me to reflections on the instability of the most flattering plans of happiness, that were painful in the extreme, till I was ready to ask whether this world was not created to exhibit every possible combination of wretchedness. I asked these questions of a heart writhing with anguish, whilst I listened to a melancholy ditty sung by this poor girl. It was too early for thee to be abandoned, thought I, and I hastened out of the house, to take my solitary evening's walk—And here I am again, to talk of any thing, but the pangs arising from the discovery of estranged affection, and the lonely sadness of a deserted heart.

The father and mother, if the father can be ascertained, are obliged to maintain an illegitimate child at their joint expense; but, should the father disappear, go up the country or to sea, the mother must maintain it herself. However, accidents of this kind do not prevent their marrying; and then it is not unusual to take the child or children home; and they are brought up very amicably with the marriage progeny.

I took some pains to learn what books were written originally in their language; but for any certain information respecting the state of Danish literature, I must wait till I arrive at Copenhagen.

The sound of the language is soft, a great proportion of the words ending in vowels; and there is a simplicity in the turn of some of the phrases which have been translated to me, that pleased and interested me. In the country, the farmers use the *thou* and *thee*; and they do not acquire the polite plurals of the towns by meeting at market. The not having markets established in the large towns appears to me a great inconvenience. When the farmers have any thing to sell, they bring it to the neighboring town, and take it from house to house. I am surprised that the inhabitants do not feel how very incommodious this usage is to both parties, and redress it. They indeed perceive it; for when I have introduced the subject, they acknowledged that they were often in want of necessaries, there being no butchers, and they were

---

3. The local currency was the rixdollar, worth about one-fifth of a British pound sterling.

often obliged to buy what they did not want; yet it was the *custom*; and the changing of customs of a long standing requires more energy than they yet possess. I received a similar reply, when I attempted to persuade the women that they injured their children by keeping them too warm. The only way of parrying off my reasoning was, that they must do as other people did. In short, reason on any subject of change, and they stop you by saying that "the town would talk." A person of sense, with a large fortune, to insure respect, might be very useful here, by inducing them to treat their children, and manage their sick properly, and eat food dressed in a simpler manner: the example, for instance, of a count's lady.

Reflecting on these prejudices made me revert to the wisdom of those legislators who established institutions for the good of the body, under the pretext of serving heaven for the salvation of the soul. These might with strict propriety be termed pious frauds; and I admire the Peruvian pair[4] for asserting that they came from the sun, when their conduct proved that they meant to enlighten a benighted country, whose obedience, or even attention, could only be secured by awe.

Thus much for conquering the *inertia* of reason; but, when it is once in motion, fables, once held sacred, may be ridiculed; and sacred they were, when useful to mankind.—Prometheus alone stole fire to animate the first man; his posterity need not supernatural aid to preserve the species, though love is generally termed a flame; and it may not be necessary much longer to suppose men inspired by heaven to inculcate the duties which demand special grace, when reason convinces them that they are the happiest who are the most nobly employed.

In a few days I am to set out for the western part of Norway, and then shall return by land to Gothenburg. I cannot think of leaving this place without regret. I speak of the place before the inhabitants, though there is a tenderness in their artless kindness which attaches me to them; but it is an attachment that inspires a regret very different from that I felt at leaving Hull, in my way to Sweden. The domestic happiness, and good-humored gaiety, of the amiable family where I and my Frances were so hospitably received, would have been sufficient to insure the tenderest remembrance, without the recollection of the social evenings to stimulate it, when good-breeding gave dignity to sympathy, and wit, zest to reason.

Adieu!—I am just informed that my horse has been waiting this quarter of an hour. I now venture to ride out alone. The steeple serves as a landmark. I once or twice lost my way, walking alone, without being able to inquire after a path. I was therefore obliged to make to the steeple, or windmill, over hedge and ditch.

Your's truly.

Letter 19

Business having obliged me to go a few miles out of town this morning, I was surprised at meeting a crowd of people of every description; and inquiring the cause, of a servant who spoke French, I was informed that a man

---

4. Probably a reference to the Inca of Peru and his daughter Orazia in John Dryden and Robert Howard's drama *The Indian Queen* (1663). When the Aztec emperor Montezuma, as a reward for his military service, requests Orazia in marriage, the Inca, addressing him as "Thou glorious sun," says that Montezuma deserves to die for wanting to mix "such base blood" with his divine blood.

had been executed two hours before, and the body afterwards burnt. I could not help looking with horror around—the fields lost their verdure—and I turned with disgust from the well-dressed women, who were returning with their children from this sight. What a spectacle for humanity! The seeing such a flock of idle gazers, plunged me into a train of reflections, on the pernicious effects produced by false notions of justice. And I am persuaded that till capital punishments be entirely abolished, executions ought to have every appearance of horror given to them; instead of being, as they are now, a scene of amusement for the gaping crowd, where sympathy is quickly effaced by curiosity.

I have always been of opinion that the allowing actors to die, in the presence of the audience, has an immoral tendency; but trifling when compared with the ferocity acquired by viewing the reality as a show; for it seems to me, that in all countries the common people go to executions to see how the poor wretch plays his part, rather than to commiserate his fate, much less to think of the breach of morality which has brought him to such a deplorable end. Consequently executions, far from being useful examples to the survivors, have, I am persuaded, a quite contrary effect, by hardening the heart they ought to terrify. Besides, the fear of an ignominious death, I believe, never deterred any one from the commission of a crime; because, in committing it, the mind is roused to activity about present circumstances. It is a game at hazard,[5] at which all expect the turn of the die in their own favor; never reflecting on the chance of ruin, till it comes. In fact, from what I saw, in the fortresses of Norway, I am more and more convinced that the same energy of character, which renders a man a daring villain, would have rendered him useful to society, had that society been well organized. When a strong mind is not disciplined by cultivation, it is a sense of injustice that renders it unjust.

Executions, however, occur very rarely at Copenhagen; for timidity, rather than clemency, palsies all the operations of the present government. The malefactor, who died this morning, would not, probably, have been punished with death at any other period; but an incendiary excites universal execration; and as the greater part of the inhabitants are still distressed by the late conflagration,[6] an example was thought absolutely necessary; though, from what I can gather, the fire was accidental.

Not, but that I have very seriously been informed, that combustible materials were placed at proper distances, by the emissaries of Mr. Pitt;[7] and, to corroborate the fact, many people insist, that the flames burst out at once in different parts of the city; not allowing the wind to have any hand in it. So much for the plot. But the fabricators of plots in all countries build their conjectures on the "baseless fabric of a vision";[8] and, it seems even a sort of poetical justice, that whilst this minister is crushing at home, plots of his own conjuring up,[9] that on the continent, and in the north, he should, with as little foundation, be accused of wishing to set the world on fire.

I forgot to mention, to you, that I was informed, by a man of veracity, that two persons came to the stake to drink a glass of the criminal's blood, as an

5. A game played with dice, similar to craps.
6. Earlier in that year (1795) a great fire in Copenhagen had destroyed nearly a thousand houses and public buildings. "Incendiary": arsonist.
7. William Pitt, then prime minister of England.
8. Prospero in Shakespeare's *The Tempest*

4.1.151–54: "And like the baseless fabric of this vision, . . . shall dissolve."
9. Pitt was prosecuting what he claimed to be Jacobin plots against Great Britain, at a time of war with revolutionary France.

infallible remedy for the apoplexy. And when I animadverted in the company, where it was mentioned, on such a horrible violation of nature, a Danish lady reproved me very severely, asking how I knew that it was not a cure for the disease? adding, that every attempt was justifiable in search of health. I did not, you may imagine, enter into an argument with a person the slave of such a gross prejudice. And I allude to it not only as a trait of the ignorance of the people, but to censure the government, for not preventing scenes that throw an odium on the human race.

Empiricism[1] is not peculiar to Denmark; and I know no way of rooting it out, though it be a remnant of exploded witchcraft, till the acquiring a general knowledge of the component parts of the human frame, become a part of public education.

Since the fire, the inhabitants have been very assiduously employed in searching for property secreted during the confusion; and it is astonishing how many people, formerly termed reputable, had availed themselves of the common calamity to purloin what the flames spared. Others, expert at making a distinction without a difference, concealed what they found, not troubling themselves to enquire for the owners, though they scrupled to search for plunder any where, but amongst the ruins.

To be honester than the laws require, is by most people thought a work of supererogation;[2] and to slip through the grate of the law, has ever exercised the abilities of adventurers, who wish to get rich the shortest way. Knavery, without personal danger, is an art, brought to great perfection by the statesman and swindler; and meaner knaves are not tardy in following their footsteps.

It moves my gall to discover some of the commercial frauds practiced during the present war. In short, under whatever point of view I consider society, it appears, to me, that an adoration of property is the root of all evil. Here it does not render the people enterprising, as in America, but thrifty and cautious. I never, therefore, was in a capital where there was so little appearance of active industry; and as for gaiety, I looked in vain for the sprightly gait of the Norwegians, who in every respect appear to me to have got the start of them. This difference I attribute to their having more liberty: a liberty which they think their right by inheritance, whilst the Danes, when they boast of their negative happiness, always mention it as the boon of the prince royal, under the superintending wisdom of count Bernstorff. Vassallage[3] is nevertheless ceasing throughout the kingdom, and with it will pass away that sordid avarice which every modification of slavery is calculated to produce.

If the chief use of property be power, in the shape of the respect it procures, is it not among the inconsistencies of human nature most incomprehensible, that men should find a pleasure in hoarding up property which they steal from their necessities, even when they are convinced that it would be dangerous to display such an enviable superiority? Is not this the situation of serfs[4] in every country; yet a rapacity to accumulate money seems to become stronger in proportion as it is allowed to be useless.

Wealth does not appear to be sought for, amongst the Danes, to obtain

1. In the old sense: medical practices without a scientific basis.
2. More than is required.
3. Social system that holds servitors in legal bond-age to their masters. Andreas Peter Bernstorff was an able administrator in the Danish foreign service.
4. Servitors who are owned by their masters.

the elegant luxuries of life; for a want of taste is very conspicuous at Copenhagen; so much so, that I am not surprised to hear that poor Matilda[5]
offended the rigid Lutherans, by aiming to refine their pleasures. The elegance which she wished to introduce, was termed lasciviousness: yet I do
not find that the absence of gallantry renders the wives more chaste, or the
husbands more constant. Love here seems to corrupt the morals, without
polishing the manners, by banishing confidence and truth, the charm as well
as cement of domestic life. A gentleman, who has resided in this city some
time, assures me that he could not find language to give me an idea of the
gross debaucheries into which the lower order of people fall; and the promiscuous amors of the men of the middling class with their female servants,
debases both beyond measure, weakening every species of family affection.

I have every where been struck by one characteristic difference in the
conduct of the two sexes; women, in general, are seduced by their superiors,
and men jilted by their inferiors; rank and manners awe the one, and cunning
and wantonness subjugate the other; ambition creeping into the woman's
passion, and tyranny giving force to the man's; for most men treat their
mistresses as kings do their favorites: *ergo* is not man then the tyrant of the
creation?

Still harping on the same subject, you will exclaim—How can I avoid it,
when most of the struggles of an eventful life have been occasioned by the
oppressed state of my sex:[6] we reason deeply, when we forcibly feel.

But to return to the straight road of observation. The sensuality so prevalent appears to me to arise rather from indolence of mind, and dull senses,
than from an exuberance of life, which often fructifies the whole character
when the vivacity of youthful spirits begins to subside into strength of mind.

I have before mentioned that the men are domestic tyrants, considering
them as fathers, brothers, or husband; but there is a kind of interregnum
between the reign of the father and husband, which is the only period of
freedom and pleasure that the women enjoy. Young people, who are attached
to each other, with the consent of their friends, exchange rings, and are
permitted to enjoy a degree of liberty together, which I have never noticed
in any other country. The days of courtship are therefore prolonged, till it
be perfectly convenient to marry: the intimacy often becomes very tender:
and if the lover obtain the privilege of a husband, it can only be termed half
by stealth, because the family is wilfully blind. It happens very rarely that
these honorary engagements are dissolved or disregarded, a stigma being
attached to a breach of faith, which is thought more disgraceful, if not so
criminal, as the violation of the marriage vow.

Do not forget that, in my general observations, I do not pretend to sketch
a national character; but merely to note the present state of morals and
manners, as I trace the progress of the world's improvement. Because, during
my residence in different countries, my principal object has been to take
such a dispassionate view of men as will lead me to form a just idea of the
nature of man. And, to deal ingenuously with you, I believe I should have

5. Caroline Matilda, sister of the Hanoverian
George III of Great Britain, was the young wife of
Christian VII of Denmark. By the plotting of
Crown Prince Frederick, who had become regent
in 1784 when his father was judged mentally unfit
to rule, she had been ordered imprisoned, but was
rescued by an English ship and taken to Hanover,
Germany, where she died in 1775 at the age of
twenty-four.
6. Wollstonecraft had published *A Vindication of
the Rights of Woman* three years earlier, in 1792.

been less severe in the remarks I have made on the vanity and depravity of the French,[7] had I travelled towards the north before I visited France.

The interesting picture frequently drawn of the virtues of a rising people has, I fear, been fallacious, excepting the accounts of the enthusiasm which various public struggles have produced. We talk of the depravity of the French, and lay a stress on the old age of the nation; yet where has more virtuous enthusiasm been displayed than during the two last years, by the common people of France and in their armies? I am obliged sometimes to recollect the numberless instances which I have either witnessed, or heard well authenticated, to balance the account of horrors, alas! but too true. I am, therefore, inclined to believe that the gross vices which I have always seen allied with simplicity of manners, are the concomitants of ignorance.

What, for example, has piety, under the heathen or christian system, been, but a blind faith in things contrary to the principles of reason? And could poor reason make considerable advances, when it was reckoned the highest degree of virtue to do violence to its dictates? Lutherans preaching reformation, have built a reputation for sanctity on the same foundation as the catholics; yet I do not perceive that a regular attendance on public worship, and their other observances, make them a whit more true in their affections, or honest in their private transactions. It seems, indeed, quite as easy to prevaricate[8] with religious injunctions as human laws, when the exercise of their reason does not lead people to acquire principles for themselves to be the criterion of all those they receive from others.

If travelling, as the completion of a liberal education, were to be adopted on rational grounds, the northern states ought to be visited before the more polished parts of Europe, to serve as the elements even of the knowledge of manners, only to be acquired by tracing the various shades in different countries. But, when visiting distant climes, a momentary social sympathy should not be allowed to influence the conclusions of the understanding; for hospitality too frequently leads travellers, especially those who travel in search of pleasure, to make a false estimate of the virtues of a nation; which, I am now convinced, bear an exact proportion to their scientific improvements.

Adieu.

1795   1796

7. See *Historical and Moral View of the French Revolution* [Wollstonecraft's note; she had published the book in 1794].
8. Evade or distort.

JOANNA BAILLIE
1762–1851

Joanna Baillie, who was born in Lanarkshire, Scotland, but lived in London and Hampstead from her early twenties until her death at the age of eighty-eight, is known primarily as a dramatist. Her first volume of *A Series of Plays: in Which It Is Attempted to Delineate the Stronger Passions of the Mind: Each Passion Being the Subject of a Tragedy and a Comedy*—now generally referred to as *Plays on the Passions*—appeared anonymously in 1798. It was an instant literary sensation, attracting as much speculation about its authorship as there was sixteen years later concerning Walter Scott's anonymous publication of *Waverley*. Two other volumes in the series followed in 1802 and 1812, winning acclaim for her as Britain's most distinguished woman playwright of the time—in some evaluations, the most distinguished regardless of gender. For Scott, she was "the best dramatic writer whom Britain has produced since the days of Shakespeare and Massinger"; Byron called her "our only dramatist since Otway and Southerne." She wrote and published, all told, twenty-eight plays—mostly as closet dramas (plays to be read rather than performed) but a number also for the stage—and exerted considerable sway on the serious drama of the first half of the nineteenth century.

Her preface to the original *Series of Plays*, a seventy-page "introductory discourse" advocating naturalness of language and subject matter, influenced both the Advertisement to Wordsworth and Coleridge's *Lyrical Ballads*, which appeared six months later, and Wordsworth's longer and more famous Preface two years later. "Those works," she wrote, "which most strongly characterize human nature in the middling and lower classes of society, where it is to be discovered by stronger and more unequivocal marks, will ever be the most popular"; the writer should forsake the "enchanted regions of simile, metaphor, allegory, and description" in favor of "the plain order of things in this every-day world." Baillie's prolonged focus on both the writer's and the reader's "sympathetick curiosity" in the essay probably also influenced William Hazlitt's concept of the sympathetic imagination and, through Hazlitt, Keats's notion of the self-effacing empathic "poetical Character."

Baillie's theories were better than her practice as a dramatist, and the modern reader is more likely to agree not with Scott and Byron but with Hazlitt's estimate of her plays: "With her the passions are, like the French republic, one and indivisible: they are not so in nature, or in Shakspeare." But Baillie's ideas about language and subject originated first of all in her poetry, with a volume of 1790 titled *Poems: Wherein It Is Attempted to Describe Certain Views of Nature and of Rustic Manners,* and she continues to be of interest as a poet today. The modern reader, admiring the homely but graceful blank verse of her *A Winter's Day*, can make connections with *The Prelude* (as in the descriptions of bird snaring, ice-skating, and the old discharged soldier), *The Excursion* (the character of the Wanderer), and *Michael* (Michael's thrift, Isabel's industrious spinning wheel)—works that were written a decade or more after Baillie's poem. Baillie also excelled as a songwriter both in standard English (as in *Up! quit thy bower*) and, like her contemporary Robert Burns, in the Scottish dialect (as in *Woo'd and married*).

A Winter's Day

The cock, warm roosting 'mid his feather'd mates,
Now lifts his beak and snuffs the morning air,
Stretches his neck and claps his heavy wings,
Gives three hoarse crows and, glad his task is done,
5   Low chuckling turns himself upon the roost,
Then nestles down again into his place.
The laboring hind,[1] who on his bed of straw
Beneath his home-made coverings, coarse but warm,

---

1. Hind does not perfectly express the condition of the person here intended, who is somewhat above a common laborer,—the tenant of a very small farm, which he cultivates with his own hands; a few cows, perhaps a horse, and some six or seven sheep being all the wealth he possessed. A class of men very common in the west of Scotland, ere political economy was thought of [Baillie's note].

Lock'd in the kindly arms of her who spun them,
10   Dreams of the gain that next year's crop should bring;
Or at some fair, disposing of his wool,
Or by some lucky and unlook'd-for bargain,
Fills his skin purse with store of tempting gold;
Now wakes from sleep at the unwelcome call,
15   And finds himself but just the same poor man
As when he went to rest.
He hears the blast against his window beat,
And wishes to himself he were a laird,°   *landowner, lord*
That he might lie a-bed. It may not be:
20   He rubs his eyes and stretches out his arms;
Heigh oh! heigh oh! he drawls with gaping mouth,
Then most unwillingly creeps from his lair,
And without looking-glass puts on his clothes.

    With rueful face he blows the smother'd fire,
25   And lights his candle at the reddening coal;
First sees that all be right among his cattle,
Then hies him to the barn with heavy tread,
Printing his footsteps on the new-fall'n snow.
From out the heap'd-up mow he draws his sheaves,
30   Dislodging the poor red-breast from his shelter
Where all the live-long night he slept secure;
But now, affrighted, with uncertain flight,
Flutters round walls and roof to find some hole
Through which he may escape.
35   Then whirling o'er his head, the heavy flail
Descends with force upon the jumping sheaves,
While every rugged wall and neighboring cot°   *cottage*
The noise re-echoes of his sturdy strokes.

    The family cares call next upon the wife
40   To quit her mean but comfortable bed.
And first she stirs the fire and fans the flame,
Then from her heap of sticks for winter stored
An armful brings; loud crackling as they burn,
Thick fly the red sparks upward to the roof,
45   While slowly mounts the smoke in wreathy clouds.
On goes the seething pot with morning cheer,
For which some little wistful folk await,
Who, peeping from the bed-clothes, spy well pleased
The cheery light that blazes on the wall,
50   And bawl for leave to rise.
Their busy mother knows not where to turn,
Her morning's work comes now so thick upon her.
One she must help to tie his little coat,
Unpin another's cap, or seek his shoe
55   Or hosen° lost, confusion soon o'er-master'd!   *breeches*
When all is o'er, out to the door they run
With new-comb'd sleeky hair and glistening faces,
Each with some little project in his head.

His new-soled shoes one on the ice must try;
60 To view his well-set trap another hies,
In hopes to find some poor unwary bird
(No worthless prize) entangled in his snare;
While one, less active, with round rosy cheeks,
Spreads out his purple fingers to the fire,
65 And peeps most wistfully into the pot.

But let us leave the warm and cheerful house
To view the bleak and dreary scene without,
And mark the dawning of a Winter day.
The morning vapor rests upon the heights,
70 Lurid and red, while growing gradual shades
Of pale and sickly light spread o'er the sky.
Then slowly from behind the southern hills
Enlarged and ruddy comes the rising sun,
Shooting athwart the hoary waste his beams
75 That gild the brow of every ridgy bank,
And deepen every valley with a shade.
The crusted window of each scatter'd cot,
The icicles that fringe the thatched roof,
The new-swept slide upon the frozen pool,
80 All keenly glance, new kindled with his rays;
And e'en the rugged face of scowling Winter
Looks somewhat gay. But only for a time
He shows his glory to the brightening earth,
Then hides his face behind a sullen cloud.

85 The birds now quit their holes and lurking sheds,
Most mute and melancholy, where through night,
All nestling close to keep each other warm,
In downy sleep they had forgot their hardships;
But not to chant and carol in the air,
90 Or lightly swing upon some waving bough,
And merrily return each other's notes;
No, silently they hop from bush to bush,
Can find no seeds to stop their craving want,
Then bend their flight to the low smoking cot,
95 Chirp on the roof, or at the window peck,
To tell their wants to those who lodge within.
The poor lank hare flies homeward to his den,
But little burthen'd with his nightly meal
Of wither'd coleworts[2] from the farmer's garden,
100 A wretched scanty portion, snatch'd in fear;
And fearful creatures, forced abroad by hunger,
Are now to every enemy a prey.

The husbandman lays by his heavy flail,
And to the house returns, where for him wait
105 His smoking breakfast and impatient children,

---

2. Kale or another cabbagelike vegetable.

Who, spoon in hand, and ready to begin,
Toward the door cast many an eager look
To see their dad come in.
Then round they sit, a cheerful company;
110   All quickly set to work, and with heap'd spoons
From ear to ear besmear their rosy cheeks.
The faithful dog stands by his master's side
Wagging his tail and looking in his face;
While humble puss pays court to all around,
115   And purrs and rubs them with her furry sides;
Nor goes this little flattery unrewarded.
But the laborious sit not long at table;
The grateful father lifts his eyes to heaven
To bless his God, whose ever bounteous hand
120   Him and his little ones doth daily feed,
Then rises satisfied to work again.

    The varied rousing sounds of industry
Are heard through all the village.
The humming wheel, the thrifty housewife's tongue,
125   Who scolds to keep her maidens to their work,
The wool-card's grating, most unmusical!
Issue from every house.
But hark! the sportsman from the neighboring hedge
His thunder sends! loud bark the village curs;
130   Up from her cards or wheel the maiden starts
And hastens to the door; the housewife chides,
Yet runs herself to look, in spite of thrift,
And all the little town is in a stir.

    Strutting before, the cock leads forth his train,
135   And, chuckling near the barn-door 'mid the straw,
Reminds the farmer of his morning's service.
His grateful master throws a liberal handful;
They flock about it, while the hungry sparrows,
Perch'd on the roof, look down with envious eye,
140   Then, aiming well, amidst the feeders light,
And seize upon the feast with greedy bill,
Till angry partlets° peck them off the field.   *hens*
But at a distance, on the leafless tree,
All woe-begone, the lonely blackbird sits;
145   The cold north wind ruffles his glossy feathers;
Full oft he looks, but dares not make approach,
Then turns his yellow beak to peck his side
And claps his wings close to his sharpen'd breast.
The wandering fowler from behind the hedge,
150   Fastens his eye upon him, points his gun,
And firing wantonly, as at a mark,
Of life bereaves him in the cheerful spot
That oft hath echo'd to his summer's song.

    The mid-day hour is near; the pent-up kine cows
155   Are driven from their stalls to take the air.

How stupidly they stare! and feel how strange!
They open wide their smoking mouths to low,
But scarcely can their feeble sound be heard,
Then turn and lick themselves and, step by step,
160   Move, dull and heavy, to their stalls again.

    In scatter'd groups the little idle boys,
With purple fingers molding in the snow
Their icy ammunition, pant for war;
And drawing up in opposite array,
165   Send forth a mighty shower of well-aim'd balls.
Each tiny hero tries his growing strength,
And burns to beat the foe-men off the field.
Or on the well-worn ice in eager throngs,
After short race, shoot rapidly along,
170   Trip up each other's heels, and on the surface
With studded shoes draw many a chalky line.
Untired and glowing with the healthful sport
They cease not till the sun hath run his course,
And threatening clouds, slow rising from the north,
175   Spread leaden darkness o'er the face of heaven;
Then by degrees they scatter to their homes,
Some with a broken head or bloody nose,
To claim their mother's pity, who, most skillful!
Cures all their troubles with a bit of bread.

180   The night comes on apace—
Chill blows the blast and drives the snow in wreaths;
Now every creature looks around for shelter,
And whether man or beast, all move alike
Towards their homes, and happy they who have
185   A house to screen them from the piercing cold!
Lo, o'er the frost a reverend form advances!
His hair white as the snow on which he treads,
His forehead mark'd with many a care-worn furrow,
Whose feeble body bending o'er a staff,
190   Shows still that once it was the seat of strength,
Though now it shakes like some old ruin'd tower.
Clothed indeed, but not disgraced with rags,
He still maintains that decent dignity
Which well becomes those who have served their country.
195   With tottering steps he gains the cottage door;
The wife within, who hears his hollow cough,
And pattering of his stick upon the threshold,
Sends out her little boy to see who's there.
The child looks up to mark the stranger's face,
200   And, seeing it enlighten'd with a smile,
Holds out his tiny hand to lead him in.
Round from her work the mother turns her head,
And views them, not ill pleased.
The stranger whines not with a piteous tale,

205 But only asks a little to relieve
A poor old soldier's wants.
The gentle matron brings the ready chair
And bids him sit to rest his weary limbs,
And warm himself before her blazing fire.
210 The children, full of curiosity,
Flock round, and with their fingers in their mouths
Stand staring at him, while the stranger, pleased,
Takes up the youngest urchin on his knee.
Proud of its seat, it wags its little feet,
215 And prates and laughs and plays with his white locks.
But soon a change comes o'er the soldier's face;
His thoughtful mind is turn'd on other days,
When his own boys were wont to play around him,
Who now lie distant from their native land
220 In honorable but untimely graves:
He feels how helpless and forlorn he is,
And big round tears course down his wither'd cheeks.
His toilsome daily labor at an end,
In comes the wearied master of the house,
225 And marks with satisfaction his old guest,
In the chief seat, with all the children round him.
His honest heart is fill'd with manly kindness,
He bids him stay and share their homely meal,
And take with them his quarters for the night.
230 The aged wanderer thankfully accepts,
And by the simple hospitable board,
Forgets the by-past hardships of the day.

When all are satisfied, about the fire
They draw their seats and form a cheerful ring.
235 The thrifty housewife turns her spinning-wheel;
The husband, useful even in his hour
Of ease and rest, a stocking knits, belike,
Or plaits stored rushes, which with after skill
Into a basket form'd may do good service,
240 With eggs or butter fill'd at fair or market.

Some idle neighbors now come dropping in,
Draw round their chairs and widen out the circle;
And every one in his own native way
Does what he can to cheer the social group.
245 Each tells some little story of himself,
That constant subject upon which mankind,
Whether in court or country, love to dwell.
How at a fair he saved a simple clown°   *peasant, rustic*
From being trick'd in buying of a cow;
250 Or laid a bet on his own horse's head
Against his neighbor's bought at twice his cost,
Which fail'd not to repay his better skill;
Or on a harvest day bound in an hour

More sheaves of corn than any of his fellows,
255   Though e'er so stark,° could do in twice the time;   *strong, powerful*
Or won the bridal race with savory broose[3]
And first kiss of the bonny bride, though all
The fleetest youngsters of the parish strove
In rivalry against him.
260   But chiefly the good man, by his own fire,
Hath privilege of being listen'd to,
Nor dares a little prattling tongue presume,
Though but in play, to break upon his story.
The children sit and listen with the rest;
265   And should the youngest raise its lisping voice,
The careful mother, ever on the watch,
And ever pleased with what her husband says,
Gives it a gentle tap upon the fingers,
Or stops its ill-timed prattle with a kiss.
270   The soldier next, but not unask'd, begins
His tale of war and blood. They gaze upon him,
And almost weep to see the man so poor,
So bent and feeble, helpless and forlorn,
Who has undaunted stood the battle's brunt
275   While roaring cannons shook the quaking earth,
And bullets hiss'd round his defenseless head.
Thus passes quickly on the evening hour,
Till sober folks must needs retire to rest;
Then all break up, and, by their several paths,
280   Hie homeward, with the evening pastime cheer'd
Far more, belike, than those who issue forth
From city theatre's gay scenic show,
Or crowded ball-room's splendid moving maze.
But where the song and story, joke and gibe,
285   So lately circled, what a solemn change
In little time takes place!
The sound of psalms, by mingled voices raised
Of young and old, upon the night air borne,
Haply to some benighted traveler,
290   Or the late parted neighbors on their way,
A pleasing notice gives, that those whose sires
In former days on the bare mountain's side,
In deserts, heaths, and caverns, praise and prayer,
At peril of their lives, in their own form
295   Of covenanted worship offered up,
In peace and safety in their own quiet home
Are—(as in quaint and modest phrase is termed)
Engaged now in *evening exercise*.[4]

---

3. A race, from the bride's former home to the bridegroom's house, run by the young men attending a country wedding.
4. In the first edition of the *Winter Day*, nothing regarding family worship was mentioned: a great omission, for which I justly take shame to myself.

"The Evening exercise," as it was called, prevailed in every house over the simple country parts of the West of Scotland, and I have often heard the sound of it passing through the twilight air, in returning from a late walk [Baillie's note]. Lines 281–98 are a later addition to the poem.

But long accustom'd to observe the weather,
300 The farmer cannot lay him down in peace
Till he has look'd to mark what bodes the night.
He lifts the latch, and moves the heavy door,
Sees wreaths of snow heap'd up on every side,
And black and dismal all above his head.
305 Anon the northern blast begins to rise;
He hears its hollow growling from afar,
Which, gathering strength, rolls on with doubled might,
And raves and bellows o'er his head. The trees
Like pithless saplings bend. He shuts his door,
310 And, thankful for the roof that covers him,
Hies him to bed.

1790

Up! quit thy bower[1]

Up! quit thy bower, late wears the hour;
Long have the rooks caw'd round thy tower;
On flower and tree, loud hums the bee;
The wilding kid[2] sports merrily:
5 A day so bright, so fresh, so clear,
Shineth when good fortune's near.

Up! lady fair, and braid thy hair,
And rouse thee in the breezy air;
The lulling stream, that sooth'd thy dream,
10 Is dancing in the sunny beam:
And hours so sweet, so bright, so gay,
Will waft good fortune on its way.

Up! time will tell; the friar's bell
Its service sound hath chimed well;
15 The aged crone keeps house alone,
And reapers to the fields are gone:
The active day, so boon and bright,
May bring good fortune ere the night.

1812

Song: Woo'd and married and a'

The bride she is winsome and bonny,
Her hair it is snooded[1] sae sleek,
And faithfu' and kind is her Johnny,
Yet fast fa' the tears on her cheek.
5 New pearlins° are cause of her sorrow,   lace trimmings

---

1. This song opens act 1 of Baillie's *The Beacon:*   2. Wild young goat.
A Serious Musical Drama in Two Acts (1812).   1. Bound up with a ribbon.

New pearlins and plenishing° too,   *furnishings*
The bride that has a' to borrow,
  Has e'en right mickle ado,
    Woo'd and married and a'!
10   Woo'd and married and a'!
  Is na' she very weel aff
    To be woo'd and married at a'?

Her mither then hastily spak,
  "The lassie is glaikit° wi' pride;   *foolish*
15 In my pouch I had never a plack°   *farthing*
  On the day when I was a bride.
E'en tak' to your wheel, and be clever,
  And draw out your thread in the sun;
The gear° that is gifted,° it never   *goods, wealth / given*
20   Will last like the gear that is won.°   *earned*
    Woo'd and married and a'!
     Wi' havins° and toucher° sae sma',   *possessions / dowry*
  I think ye are very weel aff,
    To be woo'd and married at a'!"

25 "Toot, toot!" quo' her gray-headed faither,
  "She's less o' a bride than a bairn;°   *child*
She's ta'en like a cout° frae the heather,   *colt*
  Wi' sense and discretion to learn.
Half husband, I trow, and half daddy,
30   As humor inconstantly leans,
The chiel° maun° be patient and steady,   *man / must*
  That yokes wi' a mate in her teens.
    A kerchief sae douce° and sae neat,   *sedate, respectable*
    O'er her locks that the winds used to blaw!
35   I'm baith like to laugh and to greet,°   *weep*
    When I think o' her married at a'!"

Then out spak' the wily bridegroom;
  Weel waled° were his wordies, I ween—   *chosen*
"I'm rich, though my coffer be toom,°   *empty*
40   Wi' the blinks o' your bonny blue een.°   *eyes*
I'm prouder o' thee by my side,
  Though thy ruffles or ribbons be few,
Than if Kate o' the Croft were my bride,
  Wi' purfles² and pearlins enow.
45   Dear and dearest of ony!
    Ye're woo'd and buikit³ and a'!"
And do ye think scorn o' your Johnny,
  And grieve to be married at a'?"

She turn'd, and she blush'd, and she smiled,
50   And she looket sae bashfully down;

2. Embroidered trimmings.
3. Booked, i.e., entered as betrothed in the official registry of the session clerk.

The pride o' her heart was beguiled,
   And she played wi' the sleeves o' her gown;
She twirled the tag o' her lace,
   And she nippet her boddice sae blue,
55 Syne° blinket sae sweet in his face,   *then*
   And aff like a maukin° she flew.   *hare*
     Woo'd and married and a'!
     Wi' Johnny to roose° her and a'!   *praise*
   She thinks hersel very weel aff,
60   To be woo'd and married at a'!

1822

WILLIAM WORDSWORTH
1770–1850

William Wordsworth was born in Cockermouth in West Cumberland, just on the northern fringe of the English Lake District. When his mother died, the eight-year-old boy was sent to school at Hawkshead, near Esthwaite Lake, in the heart of that thinly settled region that he and Coleridge were to transform into one of the poetic centers of England. William and his three brothers boarded in the cottage of Ann Tyson, who gave the boys simple comfort, ample affection, and freedom to roam the countryside at will. A vigorous, unruly, and sometimes moody boy, William spent his free days and occasionally "half the night" in the sports and rambles described in the first two books of *The Prelude*, "drinking in" (to use one of his favorite metaphors) the natural sights and sounds, and getting to know the cottagers, shepherds, and solitary wanderers who moved through his imagination into his later poetry. He also found time to read voraciously in the books owned by his young headmaster, William Taylor, who encouraged him in his inclination to poetry.

John Wordsworth, the poet's father, died suddenly when William was thirteen, leaving to his five children mainly the substantial sum owed him by Lord Lonsdale, whom he had served as attorney and as steward of the huge Lonsdale estate. That harsh and litigious nobleman managed to keep from paying the debt until he died in 1802. Wordsworth was nevertheless able to enter St. John's College, Cambridge, in 1787, where he found little in the limited curriculum of that time to appeal to him. He took his degree in 1791 without distinction.

During the summer vacation of his third year at Cambridge (1790), Wordsworth and his closest college friend, the Welshman Robert Jones, journeyed on foot through France and the Alps (described in *The Prelude* 6) at the time when the French were joyously celebrating the first anniversary of the fall of the Bastille. Upon completing his course at Cambridge, Wordsworth spent four months in London, set off on another walking tour with Robert Jones through Wales (the time of the memorable ascent of Mount Snowdon in *The Prelude* 14), and then went back alone to France to master the language and qualify as a traveling tutor.

During his year in France (November 1791 to December 1792) Wordsworth became a fervent "democrat" and proselyte of the French Revolution—which seemed to him, as to many other generous spirits, to promise a "glorious renovation"—and he fell in love with Annette Vallon, the impetuous and warm-hearted daughter of a French surgeon at Blois. It is clear that the two planned to marry, despite their differences in religion and political inclinations (Annette belonged to an old Catholic family whose sympathies were Royalist). But almost immediately after a daughter, Caroline, was born, lack of funds forced Wordsworth to return to England. The outbreak of war between England and France made it impossible for him to rejoin Annette until they had drifted so far apart in sympathies that a permanent union no longer seemed desirable. Wordsworth's agonies of guilt, his divided loyalties between England and France, his gradual disillusion with the course of the Revolution in France—according to his account in *The Prelude* 10 and 11—brought him to the verge of an emotional breakdown, when "sick, wearied out with contrarieties," he "yielded up moral questions in despair." His suffering, his near-collapse, and the successful effort, after his break with his past, to reestablish "a saving intercourse with my true self," are the experiences that underlie many of his greatest poems.

At this critical point a young friend, Raisley Calvert, died and left Wordsworth a sum of money just sufficient to enable him to live by his poetry. He settled in a rent-free house at Racedown, Dorsetshire, with his beloved sister, Dorothy, who now began her long career as confidante, inspirer, and secretary. At that same time Wordsworth met Samuel Taylor Coleridge; two years later he moved to Alfoxden House, Somersetshire, to be near Coleridge, who lived four miles away at Nether Stowey. Here he entered at the age of twenty-seven on the delayed springtime of his poetic career.

Even while he had been an undergraduate at Cambridge, Coleridge claimed that he had detected signs of genius in Wordsworth's rather conventional poem about his tour in the Alps, *Descriptive Sketches*, published in 1793. Now he hailed Wordsworth unreservedly as "the best poet of the age." The two men met almost daily, talked for hours about poetry, and composed prolifically. So close was their association that we find the same phrases occurring in poems by Wordsworth and Coleridge, as well as in the remarkable journals that Dorothy kept at the time; the two poets collaborated in some writings and freely traded thoughts and passages for others; and Coleridge even undertook to complete a few poems that Wordsworth had left unfinished.

The result of their joint efforts was a small volume, published anonymously in 1798, *Lyrical Ballads, with a Few Other Poems*. It opened with Coleridge's *Ancient Mariner;* included three other poems by Coleridge, a number of Wordsworth's verse anecdotes and psychological studies of humble people, and some lyrics in which Wordsworth celebrated impulses from a vernal wood; and closed with Wordsworth's great descriptive and meditative poem in blank verse (not a "lyrical ballad," but one of the "other poems" of the title), *Tintern Abbey*. In this last poem, Wordsworth inaugurated what some critics call his "myth of nature"; that is, his presentation of the "growth" of his mind to maturity, and the development of his emotional and moral life, as an interaction between his mind and the outer world. The volume of *Lyrical Ballads* clearly announces a new literary departure. William Hazlitt said that when he heard Coleridge read some of these newly written poems aloud, "the sense of a new style and a new spirit in poetry came over me," with something of the effect "that arises from the turning up of the fresh soil, or of the first welcome breath of spring." The professional reviewers were less enthusiastic. Nevertheless *Lyrical Ballads* sold out in two years, and Wordsworth published under his own name a new edition, dated 1800, to which he added a second volume of poems, many of them written in homesickness during a long, cold, and friendless winter that he and Dorothy had spent in Goslar, Germany, 1798–99. In his famous Preface to this edition, planned, like so many of the poems, in close consultation with Coleridge, Wordsworth enunciated the principles of the new criticism that served as rationale for the new poetry. Notable among the other works written in this prolific period is his austere and powerful tragic poem *The Ruined Cottage*.

Late in 1799 Wordsworth and Dorothy moved back permanently to their native lakes, settling at Grasmere in the little house later named Dove Cottage. Coleridge, following them, rented Greta Hall at Keswick, thirteen miles away. In 1802 Wordsworth finally came into his father's inheritance and, after an amicable settlement with Annette Vallon, married Mary Hutchinson, a Lake Country woman whom he had known since childhood. The course of his existence after that time was broken by various disasters: the drowning in 1805 of his favorite brother, John, a sea captain whose ship was wrecked in a storm; the death of two of his five children in 1812; a growing estrangement from Coleridge, culminating in a bitter quarrel (1810) from which they were not completely reconciled for almost two decades; and from the 1830s on, the physical and mental decline of his sister, Dorothy. The life of his middle age, however, was one of steadily increasing prosperity and reputation, as well as of political and religious conservatism. In 1813 an appointment as Stamp Distributor (that is, revenue collector) for Westmorland was concrete evidence of his recognition as a national poet. Gradually his residences, as he moved into more and more commodious quarters, became standard stops for tourists; he was awarded honorary degrees and, in 1843, was appointed poet laureate. He died in 1850 at the age of eighty; only then did his executors publish his masterpiece, *The Prelude*, the autobiographical poem that he had written in two parts in 1799, expanded to its full length in 1805, and then continued to revise almost to the last decade of his long life.

Most of Wordsworth's greatest poetry had been written by 1807, when he published *Poems in Two Volumes*; and after *The Excursion* (1814) and the first collected edition of his poems (1815), although he continued to write voluminously, there is an overall decline in his powers. The causes of the decline have been much debated; an important one seems to be inherent in the very nature of his most characteristic writing. Wordsworth is above all the poet of the remembrance of things past, or as he himself put it, of "emotion recollected in tranquillity." Some object or event in the present triggers a sudden renewal of feelings he had experienced in youth; the result is a poem exhibiting the sharp discrepancy between what Wordsworth called "two consciousnesses": himself as he is now and himself as he once was. But the memory of one's early emotional experience is not an inexhaustible resource for poetry, as Wordsworth himself recognized. He said in *The Prelude* 12, while describing the recurrence of "spots of time" from his memories of childhood:

> The days gone by
> Return upon me almost from the dawn
> Of life: the hiding places of Man's power
> Open; I would approach them, but they close.
> I see by glimpses now; when age comes on,
> May scarcely see at all.

The past that Wordsworth recollected was one of moments of intense experience, and of emotional turmoil which is ordered, in the calmer present, into a hard-won equilibrium. As time went on, however, he gained what, in the *Ode to Duty* (composed in 1804), he longed for, "a repose which ever is the same"—but at the expense of the agony and excitation which, under the calm surface, empowers his best and most characteristic poems.

Occasionally, in his middle and later life a jolting experience would revive the intensity of Wordsworth's remembered emotion, and also his earlier poetic strength. The moving sonnet *Surprised by Joy*, for example, was written in his forties at the abrupt realization that time was beginning to diminish his grief at the death some years earlier of his little daughter Catherine. And when Wordsworth was sixty-five years old, the sudden report of the death of James Hogg called up the memory of other and greater poets whom Wordsworth had loved and outlived; the result was his *Extempore Effusion*, written in a return to the simple quatrains of the early *Lyrical Ballads* and with a recovery of the elegiac voice that had uttered the dirges to Lucy, thirty-five years before.

FROM LYRICAL BALLADS

Simon Lee[1]

The Old Huntsman

WITH AN INCIDENT IN WHICH HE WAS CONCERNED

In the sweet shire of Cardigan,[2]
Not far from pleasant Ivor-hall,
An old man dwells, a little man,—
'Tis said he once was tall.
5   Full five-and-thirty years he lived
A running huntsman[3] merry;
And still the centre of his cheek
Is red as a ripe cherry.

No man like him the horn could sound,
10   And hill and valley rang with glee
When Echo bandied, round and round,
The halloo of Simon Lee.
In those proud days, he little cared
For husbandry or tillage;
15   To blither tasks did Simon rouse
The sleepers of the village.

He all the country could outrun,
Could leave both man and horse behind;
And often, ere the chase was done,
20   He reeled, and was stone-blind.°   totally blind
And still there's something in the world
At which his heart rejoices;
For when the chiming hounds are out,
He dearly loves their voices!

25   But, oh the heavy change![4]—bereft
Of health, strength, friends, and kindred, see!
Old Simon to the world is left
In liveried poverty.
His Master's dead,—and no one now
30   Dwells in the Hall of Ivor;
Men, dogs, and horses, all are dead;
He is the sole survivor.

1. This old man had been huntsman to the Squires of Alfoxden. . . . I have, after an interval of 45 years, the image of the old man as fresh before my eyes as if I had seen him yesterday. The expression when the hounds were out, "I dearly love their voices," was word for word from his own lips [Wordsworth's note, 1843]. Wordsworth and Dorothy had lived at Alfoxden House, Somer-

setshire, in 1797–98.
2. Wordsworth relocates the incident from Somersetshire to Cardiganshire in Wales.
3. Manager of the hunt and the person in charge of the hounds.
4. Milton's *Lycidas*, line 37: "But O the heavy change, now thou art gone."

And he is lean and he is sick;
His body, dwindled and awry,
35 Rests upon ankles swoln and thick;
His legs are thin and dry.
One prop he has, and only one,
His wife, an aged woman,
Lives with him, near the waterfall,
40 Upon the village Common.

Beside their moss-grown hut of clay,
Not twenty paces from the door,
A scrap of land they have, but they
Are poorest of the poor.
45 This scrap of land he from the heath
Enclosed when he was stronger;
But what to them avails the land
Which he can till no longer?

Oft, working by her Husband's side,
50 Ruth does what Simon cannot do;
For she, with scanty cause for pride,
Is stouter of the two.
And, though you with your utmost skill
From labour could not wean them,
55 'Tis very, very little—all
That they can do between them.

Few months of life has he in store
As he to you will tell,
For still, the more he works, the more
60 Do his weak ankles swell.
My gentle Reader, I perceive
How patiently you've waited,
And now I fear that you expect
Some tale will be related.

65 O Reader! had you in your mind
Such stores as silent thought can bring,
O gentle Reader! you would find
A tale in every thing.
What more I have to say is short,
70 And you must kindly take it:
It is no tale; but, should you think,
Perhaps a tale you'll make it.

One summer-day I chanced to see
This old Man doing all he could
75 To unearth the root of an old tree,
A stump of rotten wood.
The mattock tottered in his hand;
So vain was his endeavour,

That at the root of the old tree
80 He might have worked for ever.

"You're overtasked, good Simon Lee,
Give me your tool," to him I said;
And at the word right gladly he
Received my proffered aid.
85 I struck, and with a single blow
The tangled root I severed,
At which the poor old Man so long
And vainly had endeavoured.

The tears into his eyes were brought,
90 And thanks and praises seemed to run
So fast out of his heart, I thought
They never would have done.
—I've heard of hearts unkind, kind deeds
With coldness still returning;
95 Alas! the gratitude of men
Hath oftener left me mourning.

1798   1798

We Are Seven[1]

————A simple Child,
That lightly draws its breath,
And feels its life in every limb,
What should it know of death?

5 I met a little cottage Girl:
She was eight years old, she said;
Her hair was thick with many a curl
That clustered round her head.

She had a rustic, woodland air,
10 And she was wildly clad:
Her eyes were fair, and very fair;
—Her beauty made me glad.

"Sisters and brothers, little Maid,
How many may you be?"
15 "How many? Seven in all," she said,
And wondering looked at me.

"And where are they? I pray you tell."
She answered, "Seven are we;
And two of us at Conway[2] dwell,
20 And two are gone to sea.

1. Written at Alfoxden in the spring of 1798. . . .
The little girl who is the heroine I met within the
area of Goodrich Castle [in the Wye Valley north
of Tintern Abbey] in the year 1793 [Wordsworth's

note]. Wordsworth also tells us that he composed
the last line of the last stanza first, and that Coleridge contributed the initial stanza.
2. A seaport town in north Wales.

"Two of us in the church-yard lie,
My sister and my brother;
And, in the church-yard cottage, I
Dwell near them with my mother."

25   "You say that two at Conway dwell,
And two are gone to sea,
Yet ye are seven! I pray you tell,
Sweet Maid, how this may be."

Then did the little Maid reply,
30   "Seven boys and girls are we;
Two of us in the church-yard lie,
Beneath the church-yard tree."

"You run about, my little Maid,
Your limbs they are alive;
35   If two are in the church-yard laid,
Then ye are only five."

"Their graves are green, they may be seen,"
The little Maid replied,
"Twelve steps or more from my mother's door,
40   And they are side by side.

"My stockings there I often knit,
My kerchief there I hem;
And there upon the ground I sit,
And sing a song to them.

45   "And often after sun-set, Sir,
When it is light and fair,
I take my little porringer,[3]
And eat my supper there.

"The first that died was sister Jane;
50   In bed she moaning lay,
Till God released her of her pain;
And then she went away.

"So in the church-yard she was laid;
And, when the grass was dry,
55   Together round her grave we played,
My brother John and I.

"And when the ground was white with snow,
And I could run and slide,
My brother John was forced to go,
60   And he lies by her side."

3. Bowl for porridge.

"How many are you, then," said I,
"If they two are in heaven?"
Quick was the little Maid's reply,
"O Master! we are seven."

65   "But they are dead; those two are dead!
Their spirits are in heaven!"
'Twas throwing words away; for still
The little Maid would have her will,
And said, "Nay, we are seven!"

1798   1798

Lines Written in Early Spring

I heard a thousand blended notes,
While in a grove I sate reclined,
In that sweet mood when pleasant thoughts
Bring sad thoughts to the mind.

5   To her fair works did Nature link
The human soul that through me ran;
And much it grieved my heart to think
What man has made of man.

Through primrose tufts, in that green bower,
10   The periwinkle[1] trailed its wreaths,
And 'tis my faith that every flower
Enjoys the air it breathes.

The birds around me hopped and played,
Their thoughts I cannot measure:—
15   But the least motion which they made,
It seemed a thrill of pleasure.

The budding twigs spread out their fan,
To catch the breezy air;
And I must think, do all I can,
20   That there was pleasure there.

If this belief from heaven be sent,
If such be Nature's holy plan,[2]
Have I not reason to lament
What man has made of man?

1798   1798

---

1. A trailing evergreen plant with small blue flowers (U.S. myrtle).
2. The version of these two lines in the *Lyrical*
Ballads of 1798 reads: "If I these thoughts may not prevent, / If such be of my creed the plan."

Expostulation and Reply[1]

"Why, William, on that old grey stone,
Thus for the length of half a day,
Why, William, sit you thus alone,
And dream your time away?

5 "Where are your books?—that light bequeathed
To Beings else forlorn and blind!
Up! up! and drink the spirit breathed
From dead men to their kind.

"You look round on your Mother Earth,
10 As if she for no purpose bore you;
As if you were her first-born birth,
And none had lived before you!"

One morning thus, by Esthwaite lake,
When life was sweet, I knew not why,
15 To me my good friend Matthew spake,
And thus I made reply.

"The eye—it cannot choose but see;
We cannot bid the ear be still;
Our bodies feel, where'er they be,
20 Against or with our will.

"Nor less I deem that there are Powers
Which of themselves our minds impress;
That we can feed this mind of ours
In a wise passiveness.

25 "Think you, 'mid all this mighty sum
Of things for ever speaking,
That nothing of itself will come,
But we must still be seeking?

"—Then ask not wherefore, here, alone,
30 Conversing[2] as I may,
I sit upon this old grey stone,
And dream my time away."

Spring 1798   1798

---

1. This and the following companion poem have often been attacked—and defended—as Wordsworth's solemn deliverance on the comparative merits of nature and of books. But they are a dialogue between two friends who rally one another by the usual device of overstating parts of a whole truth. Wordsworth said that the pieces originated in a conversation "with a friend who was somewhat unreasonably attached to modern books of moral philosophy," and also that the lore of "a wise passiveness" made the poem a favorite among Quakers.
2. In the old sense of "communing" (with the "things for ever speaking").

The Tables Turned

An Evening Scene on the Same Subject

Up! up! my Friend, and quit your books;
Or surely you'll grow double:
Up! up! my Friend, and clear your looks;
Why all this toil and trouble?

5   The sun, above the mountain's head,
A freshening lustre mellow
Through all the long green fields has spread,
His first sweet evening yellow.

Books! 'tis a dull and endless strife:
10   Come, hear the woodland linnet,°   *small finch*
How sweet his music! on my life,
There's more of wisdom in it.

And hark! how blithe the throstle° sings!   *song thrush*
He, too, is no mean preacher:
15   Come forth into the light of things,
Let Nature be your Teacher.

She has a world of ready wealth,
Our minds and hearts to bless—
Spontaneous wisdom breathed by health,
20   Truth breathed by cheerfulness.

One impulse from a vernal wood
May teach you more of man,
Of moral evil and of good,
Than all the sages can.

25   Sweet is the lore which Nature brings;
Our meddling intellect
Mis-shapes the beauteous forms of things:—
We murder to dissect.

Enough of Science and of Art;
30   Close up those barren leaves;
Come forth, and bring with you a heart
That watches and receives.

1798   1798

The Thorn[1]

1

"There is a Thorn—it looks so old,
In truth, you'd find it hard to say
How it could ever have been young,
It looks so old and grey.
5   Not higher than a two years' child
It stands erect, this aged Thorn;
No leaves it has, no prickly points;
It is a mass of knotted joints,
A wretched thing forlorn.
10   It stands erect, and like a stone
With lichens is it overgrown.

2

"Like rock or stone, it is o'ergrown,
With lichens to the very top,
And hung with heavy tufts of moss,
15   A melancholy crop:
Up from the earth these mosses creep,
And this poor Thorn they clasp it round
So close, you'd say that they are bent
With plain and manifest intent
20   To drag it to the ground;
And all have joined in one endeavour
To bury this poor Thorn for ever.

3

"High on a mountain's highest ridge,
Where oft the stormy winter gale
25   Cuts like a scythe, while through the clouds
It sweeps from vale to vale;
Not five yards from the mountain path,
This Thorn you on your left espy;

1. Arose out of my observing, on the ridge of Quantock Hill [in Somersetshire], on a stormy day, a thorn which I had often past, in calm and bright weather, without noticing it. I said to myself, "Cannot I by some invention do as much to make this Thorn permanently an impressive object as the storm has made it to my eyes at this moment?" I began the poem accordingly, and composed it with great rapidity [Wordsworth's note, 1843]. In the prefatory Advertisement to the 1798 *Lyrical Ballads* Wordsworth wrote, "The poem of the Thorn . . . is not supposed to be spoken in the author's own person: the character of the loquacious narrator will sufficiently shew itself in the course of the story." In the editions of 1800–05 he elaborated in a separate note that reads, in part: "The character which I have here introduced speaking is sufficiently common. The Reader will perhaps have a general notion of it, if he has ever known a man, a Captain of a small trading vessel, for example, who, being past the middle age of life, had retired upon an annuity or small independent income to some village or country town of which he was not a native. . . . Such men, having little to do, become credulous and talkative from indolence; and from the same cause . . . they are prone to superstition. On which account it appeared to me proper to select a character like this to exhibit some of the general laws by which superstition acts upon the mind. Superstitious men are almost always men of slow faculties and deep feelings: their minds are not loose but adhesive; they have a reasonable share of imagination, by which word I mean the faculty which produces impressive effects out of simple elements. . . . It was my wish in this poem to show the manner in which such men cleave to the same ideas; and to follow the turns of passion . . . by which their conversation is swayed." "Thorn": hawthorn, a thorny shrub or small tree.

And to the left, three yards beyond,
30   You see a little muddy pond
Of water—never dry
Though but of compass small, and bare
To thirsty suns and parching air.

4

"And, close beside this aged Thorn,
35   There is a fresh and lovely sight,
A beauteous heap, a hill of moss,
Just half a foot in height.
All lovely colours there you see,
All colours that were ever seen;
40   And mossy network too is there,
As if by hand of lady fair
The work had woven been;
And cups, the darlings of the eye,
So deep is their vermilion dye.

5

45   "Ah me! what lovely tints are there
Of olive green and scarlet bright,
In spikes, in branches, and in stars,
Green, red, and pearly white!
This heap of earth o'ergrown with moss,
50   Which close beside the Thorn you see,
So fresh in all its beauteous dyes,
Is like an infant's grave in size,
As like as like can be:
But never, never any where,
55   An infant's grave was half so fair.

6

"Now would you see this aged Thorn,
This pond, and beauteous hill of moss,
You must take care and choose your time
The mountain when to cross.
60   For oft there sits between the heap
So like an infant's grave in size,
And that same pond of which I spoke,
A Woman in a scarlet cloak,
And to herself she cries,
65   'Oh misery! oh misery!
Oh woe is me! oh misery!'

7

"At all times of the day and night
This wretched Woman thither goes;
And she is known to every star,
70   And every wind that blows;
And there, beside the Thorn, she sits

When the blue daylight's in the skies,
And when the whirlwind's on the hill,
Or frosty air is keen and still,
75   And to herself she cries,
'Oh misery! oh misery!
Oh woe is me! oh misery!' "

8

"Now wherefore, thus, by day and night,
In rain, in tempest, and in snow,
80   Thus to the dreary mountain-top
Does this poor Woman go?
And why sits she beside the Thorn
When the blue daylight's in the sky
Or when the whirlwind's on the hill,
85   Or frosty air is keen and still,
And wherefore does she cry?—
O wherefore? wherefore? tell me why
Does she repeat that doleful cry?"

9

"I cannot tell; I wish I could;
90   For the true reason no one knows:
But would you gladly view the spot,
The spot to which she goes;
The hillock like an infant's grave,
The pond—and Thorn, so old and grey;
95   Pass by her door—'tis seldom shut—
And, if you see her in her hut—
Then to the spot away!
I never heard of such as dare
Approach the spot when she is there."

10

100   "But wherefore to the mountain-top
Can this unhappy Woman go,
Whatever star is in the skies,
Whatever wind may blow?"
"Full twenty years are past and gone
105   Since she (her name is Martha Ray)
Gave with a maiden's true good-will
Her company to Stephen Hill;
And she was blithe and gay,
While friends and kindred all approved
110   Of him whom tenderly she loved.

11

"And they had fixed the wedding day,
The morning that must wed them both;
But Stephen to another Maid
Had sworn another oath;

115 And, with this other Maid, to church
Unthinking Stephen went—
Poor Martha! on that woeful day
A pang of pitiless dismay
Into her soul was sent;
120 A fire was kindled in her breast,
Which might not burn itself to rest.

12

"They say, full six months after this,
While yet the summer leaves were green,
She to the mountain-top would go,
125 And there was often seen.
What could she seek?—or wish to hide?
Her state to any eye was plain;
She was with child, and she was mad;
Yet often was she sober sad
130 From her exceeding pain.
O guilty Father—would that death
Had saved him from that breach of faith!

13

"Sad case for such a brain to hold
Communion with a stirring child!
135 Sad case, as you may think, for one
Who had a brain so wild!
Last Christmas-eve we talked of this,
And grey-haired Wilfred of the glen
Held that the unborn infant wrought
140 About its mother's heart, and brought
Her senses back again:
And, when at last her time drew near,
Her looks were calm, her senses clear.

14

"More know I not, I wish I did,
145 And it should all be told to you;
For what became of this poor child
No mortal ever knew;
Nay—if a child to her was born
No earthly tongue could ever tell;
150 And if 'twas born alive or dead,
Far less could this with proof be said;
But some remember well,
That Martha Ray about this time
Would up the mountain often climb.

15

155 "And all that winter, when at night
The wind blew from the mountain-peak,
'Twas worth your while, though in the dark,

The churchyard path to seek:
For many a time and oft were heard
160 Cries coming from the mountain head:
Some plainly living voices were;
And others, I've heard many swear,
Were voices of the dead:
I cannot think, whate'er they say,
165 They had to do with Martha Ray.

16

"But that she goes to this old Thorn,
The Thorn which I described to you,
And there sits in a scarlet cloak,
I will be sworn is true.
170 For one day with my telescope,
To view the ocean wide and bright,
When to this country first I came,
Ere I had heard of Martha's name,
I climbed the mountain's height:—
175 A storm came on, and I could see
No object higher than my knee.

17

" 'Twas mist and rain, and storm and rain:
No screen, no fence could I discover;
And then the wind! in sooth, it was
180 A wind full ten times over.
I looked around, I thought I saw
A jutting crag,—and off I ran,
Head-foremost, through the driving rain,
The shelter of the crag to gain;
185 And, as I am a man,
Instead of jutting crag, I found
A Woman seated on the ground.

18

"I did not speak—I saw her face;
Her face!—it was enough for me;
190 I turned about and heard her cry,
'Oh misery! oh misery!'
And there she sits, until the moon
Through half the clear blue sky will go;
And, when the little breezes make
195 The waters of the pond to shake,
As all the country know,
She shudders, and you hear her cry,
'Oh misery! oh misery!' "

19

"But what's the Thorn? and what the pond?
200 And what the hill of moss to her?

And what the creeping breeze that comes
The little pond to stir?"
"I cannot tell; but some will say
She hanged her baby on the tree;
205 Some say she drowned it in the pond,
Which is a little step beyond:
But all and each agree,
The little Babe was buried there,
Beneath that hill of moss so fair.

20

210 "I've heard, the moss is spotted red
With drops of that poor infant's blood;
But kill a new-born infant thus,
I do not think she could!
Some say, if to the pond you go,
215 And fix on it a steady view,
The shadow of a babe you trace,
A baby and a baby's face,
And that it looks at you;
Whene'er you look on it, 'tis plain
220 The baby looks at you again.

21

"And some had sworn an oath that she
Should be to public justice brought;
And for the little infant's bones
With spades they would have sought.
225 But instantly the hill of moss
Before their eyes began to stir!
And, for full fifty yards around,
The grass—it shook upon the ground!
Yet all do still aver
230 The little Babe lies buried there,
Beneath that hill of moss so fair.

22

"I cannot tell how this may be,
But plain it is the Thorn is bound
With heavy tufts of moss that strive
235 To drag it to the ground;
And this I know, full many a time,
When she was on the mountain high,
By day, and in the silent night,
When all the stars shone clear and bright,
240 That I have heard her cry,
'Oh misery! oh misery!
Oh woe is me! oh misery!' "

Mar.–Apr. 1798   1798

Lines[1]

Composed a Few Miles above Tintern Abbey, on Revisiting the Banks of the Wye during a Tour, July 13, 1798

Five years have past; five summers, with the length
Of five long winters! and again I hear
These waters, rolling from their mountain-springs
With a soft inland murmur.—Once again
5 Do I behold these steep and lofty cliffs,
That on a wild secluded scene impress
Thoughts of more deep seclusion; and connect
The landscape with the quiet of the sky.
The day is come when I again repose
10 Here, under this dark sycamore, and view
These plots of cottage-ground, these orchard-tufts,
Which at this season, with their unripe fruits,
Are clad in one green hue, and lose themselves
'Mid groves and copses. Once again I see
15 These hedge-rows, hardly hedge-rows, little lines
Of sportive wood run wild: these pastoral farms,
Green to the very door; and wreaths of smoke
Sent up, in silence, from among the trees!
With some uncertain notice, as might seem
20 Of vagrant dwellers in the houseless woods,
Or of some Hermit's cave, where by his fire
The Hermit sits alone.

                      These beauteous forms,
Through a long absence, have not been to me
As is a landscape to a blind man's eye:
25 But oft, in lonely rooms, and 'mid the din
Of towns and cities, I have owed to them
In hours of weariness, sensations sweet,
Felt in the blood, and felt along the heart;
And passing even into my purer mind,
30 With tranquil restoration:—feelings too
Of unremembered pleasure: such, perhaps,
As have no slight or trivial influence
On that best portion of a good man's life,
His little, nameless, unremembered, acts
35 Of kindness and of love. Nor less, I trust,
To them I may have owed another gift,

1. No poem of mine was composed under circumstances more pleasant for me to remember than this. I began it upon leaving Tintern, after crossing the Wye, and concluded it just as I was entering Bristol in the evening, after a ramble of 4 or 5 days, with my sister. Not a line of it was altered, and not any part of it written down till I reached Bristol [Wordsworth's note]. The poem was printed as the last item in *Lyrical Ballads*.

Wordsworth had first visited the Wye valley and the ruins of Tintern Abbey, in Monmouthshire, while on a solitary walking tour in August 1793, when he was twenty-three years old. The puzzling difference between the present landscape and the remembered "picture of the mind" (line 61) gives rise to an intricately organized meditation, in which the poet reviews his past, evaluates the present, and (through his sister as intermediary) anticipates the future; he ends by rounding back quietly on the scene that had been his point of departure.

Of aspect more sublime; that blessed mood,
In which the burthen of the mystery,
In which the heavy and the weary weight
40   Of all this unintelligible world,
Is lightened:—that serene and blessed mood,
In which the affections gently lead us on,—
Until, the breath of this corporeal frame
And even the motion of our human blood
45   Almost suspended, we are laid asleep
In body, and become a living soul:
While with an eye made quiet by the power
Of harmony, and the deep power of joy,
We see into the life of things.

                     If this
50   Be but a vain belief, yet, oh! how oft—
In darkness and amid the many shapes
Of joyless daylight; when the fretful stir
Unprofitable, and the fever of the world,
Have hung upon the beatings of my heart—
55   How oft, in spirit, have I turned to thee,
O sylvan Wye! thou wanderer thro' the woods,
How often has my spirit turned to thee!

    And now, with gleams of half-extinguished thought,
With many recognitions dim and faint,
60   And somewhat of a sad perplexity,
The picture of the mind revives again:
While here I stand, not only with the sense
Of present pleasure, but with pleasing thoughts
That in this moment there is life and food
65   For future years. And so I dare to hope,
Though changed, no doubt, from what I was when first
I came among these hills; when like a roe
I bounded o'er the mountains, by the sides
Of the deep rivers, and the lonely streams,
70   Wherever nature led: more like a man
Flying from something that he dreads, than one
Who sought the thing he loved. For nature then
(The coarser pleasures of my boyish days,
And their glad animal movements all gone by)
75   To me was all in all.—I cannot paint
What then I was. The sounding cataract
Haunted me like a passion: the tall rock,
The mountain, and the deep and gloomy wood,
Their colours and their forms, were then to me
80   An appetite; a feeling and a love,
That had no need of a remoter charm,
By thought supplied, nor any interest
Unborrowed from the eye.—That time is past,
And all its aching joys are now no more,

85   And all its dizzy raptures.[2] Not for this
      Faint° I, nor mourn nor murmur; other gifts   *lose heart*
      Have followed; for such loss, I would believe,
      Abundant recompense. For I have learned
      To look on nature, not as in the hour
90   Of thoughtless youth; but hearing oftentimes
      The still, sad music of humanity,
      Nor harsh nor grating, though of ample power
      To chasten and subdue. And I have felt
      A presence that disturbs me with the joy
95   Of elevated thoughts; a sense sublime
      Of something far more deeply interfused,
      Whose dwelling is the light of setting suns,———
      And the round ocean and the living air,
      And the blue sky, and in the mind of man:
100 A motion and a spirit, that impels
      All thinking things, all objects of all thought,
      And rolls through all things. Therefore am I still
      A lover of the meadows and the woods,
      And mountains; and of all that we behold
105 From this green earth; of all the mighty world
      Of eye, and ear,—both what they half create,[3]
      And what perceive; well pleased to recognise
      In nature and the language of the sense,
      The anchor of my purest thoughts, the nurse,
110 The guide, the guardian of my heart, and soul
      Of all my moral being.

                              Nor perchance,
      If I were not thus taught, should I the more
      Suffer my genial spirits[4] to decay:
      For thou art with me here upon the banks
115 Of this fair river; thou my dearest Friend,[5]
      My dear, dear Friend; and in thy voice I catch
      The language of my former heart, and read
      My former pleasures in the shooting lights
      Of thy wild eyes. Oh! yet a little while
120 May I behold in thee what I was once,
      My dear, dear Sister! and this prayer I make,
      Knowing that Nature never did betray
      The heart that loved her; 'tis her privilege,
      Through all the years of this our life, to lead
125 From joy to joy: for she can so inform
      The mind that is within us, so impress

2. Lines 66ff. contain Wordsworth's famed description of the three stages of his growing up, defined in terms of his evolving relations to the natural scene: the young boy's purely physical responsiveness (lines 73–74); the postadolescent's aching, dizzy, and equivocal passions—a love that is more like dread (lines 67–72, 75–85: this was his state of mind on the occasion of his first visit);

his present state (lines 85ff.), in which for the first time he adds thought to sense.
3. This view that the "creative sensibility" contributes to its own perceptions is often reiterated in *The Prelude*.
4. Creative powers. ("Genial" is here the adjectival form of the noun "genius.")
5. His sister, Dorothy.

With quietness and beauty, and so feed
With lofty thoughts, that neither evil tongues,
Rash judgments, nor the sneers of selfish men,
130 Nor greetings where no kindness is, nor all
The dreary intercourse of daily life,
Shall e'er prevail against us, or disturb
Our cheerful faith, that all which we behold
Is full of blessings. Therefore let the moon
135 Shine on thee in thy solitary walk;
And let the misty mountain-winds be free
To blow against thee: and, in after years,
When these wild ecstasies shall be matured
Into a sober pleasure; when thy mind
140 Shall be a mansion for all lovely forms,
Thy memory be as a dwelling-place
For all sweet sounds and harmonies; oh! then,
If solitude, or fear, or pain, or grief,
Should be thy portion, with what healing thoughts
145 Of tender joy wilt thou remember me,
And these my exhortations! Nor, perchance—
If I should be where I no more can hear
Thy voice, nor catch from thy wild eyes these gleams
Of past existence⁶—wilt thou then forget
150 That on the banks of this delightful stream
We stood together; and that I, so long
A worshipper of Nature, hither came
Unwearied in that service; rather say
With warmer love—oh! with far deeper zeal
155 Of holier love. Nor wilt thou then forget,
That after many wanderings, many years
Of absence, these steep woods and lofty cliffs,
And this green pastoral landscape, were to me
More dear, both for themselves and for thy sake!

July 1798   1798

Preface to *Lyrical Ballads* (1802)

To the first edition of *Lyrical Ballads*, published jointly with Coleridge in 1798, Wordsworth prefixed an "advertisement" asserting that the majority of the poems were "to be considered as experiments" to determine "how far the language of conversation in the middle and lower classes of society is adapted to the purposes of poetic pleasure." In the second, two-volume edition of 1800 Wordsworth, aided by frequent conversations with Coleridge, expanded the Advertisement into a preface that justified the new poetry not as experiments, but as exemplifying the principles of all good poetry. The Preface was enlarged for the third edition of *Lyrical Ballads*, published two years later; this last version of 1802 is the one that is reprinted here.

Although some of its individual ideas had antecedents in the later eighteenth century, the Preface as a whole deserves its reputation as a revolutionary manifesto about

6. I.e., reminders of his own "past existence" five years earlier (see lines 116–19).

the nature of poetry. Like many radical statements, however, it claims to go back to the implicit principles that governed the great poetry of the past but have been perverted in recent practice. Most discussions of the Preface, following the lead of Coleridge in his *Biographia Literaria*, have focused on Wordsworth's assertions about the valid language of poetry, on which he bases his attack on the "poetic diction" of eighteenth-century poets. As Coleridge pointed out, Wordsworth's argument about this issue is far from clear. It is apparent, however, that Wordsworth undertook to overthrow the basic theory, as well as the reigning practice, of neoclassic poetry. That is, his Preface implicitly denies the traditional assumption that the poetic genres constitute a hierarchy, from epic and tragedy at the top down through comedy, satire, pastoral, to the short lyric at the lowest reaches of the poetic scale; he also rejects the traditional principle of "decorum," according to which the subject matter (especially the social class of the protagonists) and the level of diction are contrived by the poet to conform to the status of the literary kind on the poetic scale.

When Wordsworth asserted in the Preface that he deliberately chose to represent "incidents and situations from common life," he translated his democratic sympathies into critical terms, justifying his use of peasants, children, outcasts, criminals, and idiot boys as serious subjects of poetic and even tragic concern. He also undertook to write in "a selection of language really used by men," on the grounds that there can be no "essential difference between the language of prose and metrical composition." In making this claim, Wordsworth subverted the neoclassic principle that, in many kinds of poem, the language must be elevated over standard speech by a special diction and by artful figures of speech, to match the language to the height and dignity of a particular genre. Wordsworth's own views about the valid language of poetry are based on the new premise that "all good poetry is the spontaneous overflow of powerful feelings"—spontaneous, that is, at the moment of composition, even though the process is influenced by prior thought and acquired poetic skill.

Wordsworth's assertions about the materials and diction of poetry have been greatly influential in expanding the range of serious literature to include the common people and ordinary things and events, as well as in justifying a poetry of sincerity rather than of artifice, expressed in the ordinary language of its time. But in the long view, other aspects of his Preface have been no less significant in establishing its importance, not only as a turning point in English criticism but also as a central document in modern culture. Wordsworth attributed to imaginative literature the primary role in keeping human beings emotionally alive and morally sensitive—that is, keeping them essentially human—in the modern era of a technological and increasingly urban society, with its mass media and mass culture that threaten, in his view, to blunt the mind's "discriminatory powers" and to "reduce it to a state of almost savage torpor."

From Preface to *Lyrical Ballads, with Pastoral and Other Poems* (1802)

[THE SUBJECT AND LANGUAGE OF POETRY]

The first volume of these poems has already been submitted to general perusal. It was published, as an experiment, which, I hoped, might be of some use to ascertain, how far, by fitting to metrical arrangement a selection of the real language of men in a state of vivid sensation, that sort of pleasure and that quantity of pleasure may be imparted, which a poet may rationally endeavour to impart.

I had formed no very inaccurate estimate of the probable effect of those poems: I flattered myself that they who should be pleased with them would read them with more than common pleasure: and, on the other hand, I was well aware, that by those who should dislike them they would be read with more than common dislike. The result has differed from my expectation in this only, that I have pleased a greater number than I ventured to hope I should please.

For the sake of variety, and from a consciousness of my own weakness, I was induced to request the assistance of a friend, who furnished me with the poems of the *Ancient Mariner*, the *Foster-Mother's Tale*, the *Nightingale*, and the poem entitled *Love*. I should not, however, have requested this assistance, had I not believed that the poems of my friend[1] would in a great measure have the same tendency as my own, and that, though there would be found a difference, there would be found no discordance in the colours of our style; as our opinions on the subject of poetry do almost entirely coincide.

Several of my friends are anxious for the success of these poems from a belief, that, if the views with which they were composed were indeed realized, a class of poetry would be produced, well adapted to interest mankind permanently, and not unimportant in the multiplicity, and in the quality of its moral relations: and on this account they have advised me to prefix a systematic defence of the theory upon which the poems were written. But I was unwilling to undertake the task, because I knew that on this occasion the reader would look coldly upon my arguments, since I might be suspected of having been principally influenced by the selfish and foolish hope of *reasoning* him into an approbation of these particular poems: and I was still more unwilling to undertake the task, because, adequately to display my opinions, and fully to enforce my arguments, would require a space wholly disproportionate to the nature of a preface. For to treat the subject with the clearness and coherence of which I believe it susceptible, it would be necessary to give a full account of the present state of the public taste in this country, and to determine how far this taste is healthy or depraved; which, again, could not be determined, without pointing out, in what manner language and the human mind act and re-act on each other, and without retracing the revolutions, not of literature alone, but likewise of society itself. I have therefore altogether declined to enter regularly upon this defence; yet I am sensible, that there would be some impropriety in abruptly obtruding upon the public, without a few words of introduction, poems so materially different from those upon which general approbation is at present bestowed.

It is supposed, that by the act of writing in verse an author makes a formal engagement that he will gratify certain known habits of association; that he not only thus apprizes the reader that certain classes of ideas and expressions will be found in his book, but that others will be carefully excluded. This exponent or symbol held forth by metrical language must in different eras of literature have excited very different expectations: for example, in the age of Catullus, Terence, and Lucretius and that of Statius or Claudian,[2] and in

---

1. The "friend" of course is Coleridge. When he read this *Preface* and the new poems included in the 1802 edition of *Lyrical Ballads*, Coleridge wrote to Robert Southey that although Wordsworth's Preface of 1800 had been "half a child of my own brain," he now suspects that "there is a radical difference in our theoretical opinions respecting poetry—this I shall endeavour to go to the bottom of." The results of this endeavor are

Coleridge's discussions, fifteen years later, of Wordsworth's Preface in *Biographia Literaria*, chaps. 14 and 17.
2. Wordsworth's implied contrast is between the naturalness and simplicity of the first three Roman poets (who wrote in the last two centuries B.C.E.) and the elaborate artifice of the last two Roman poets (Statius wrote in the 1st and Claudian in the 4th century C.E.).

our own country, in the age of Shakespeare and Beaumont and Fletcher, and that of Donne and Cowley, or Dryden, or Pope. I will not take upon me to determine the exact import of the promise which by the act of writing in verse an author, in the present day, makes to his reader; but I am certain, it will appear to many persons that I have not fulfilled the terms of an engagement thus voluntarily contracted. They who have been accustomed to the gaudiness and inane phraseology of many modern writers, if they persist in reading this book to its conclusion, will, no doubt, frequently have to struggle with feelings of strangeness and awkwardness: they will look round for poetry, and will be induced to inquire by what species of courtesy these attempts can be permitted to assume that title. I hope therefore the reader will not censure me, if I attempt to state what I have proposed to myself to perform; and also (as far as the limits of a preface will permit) to explain some of the chief reasons which have determined me in the choice of my purpose: that at least he may be spared any unpleasant feeling of disappointment, and that I myself may be protected from the most dishonorable accusation which can be brought against an author, namely, that of an indolence which prevents him from endeavouring to ascertain what is his duty, or, when this duty is ascertained, prevents him from performing it.

The principal object, then, which I proposed to myself in these poems was to choose incidents and situations from common life, and to relate or describe them, throughout, as far as was possible, in a selection of language really used by men; and, at the same time, to throw over them a certain colouring of imagination, whereby ordinary things should be presented to the mind in an unusual way; and, further, and above all, to make these incidents and situations interesting by tracing in them, truly though not ostentatiously, the primary laws of our nature: chiefly, as far as regards the manner in which we associate ideas in a state of excitement.[3] Low and rustic life was generally chosen, because in that condition, the essential passions of the heart find a better soil in which they can attain their maturity, are less under restraint, and speak a plainer and more emphatic language; because in that condition of life our elementary feelings co-exist in a state of greater simplicity, and, consequently, may be more accurately contemplated, and more forcibly communicated; because the manners of rural life germinate from those elementary feelings; and, from the necessary character of rural occupations, are more easily comprehended; and are more durable; and lastly, because in that condition the passions of men are incorporated with the beautiful and permanent forms of nature. The language, too, of these men is adopted (purified indeed from what appear to be its real defects, from all lasting and rational causes of dislike or disgust) because such men hourly communicate with the best objects from which the best part of language is originally derived; and because, from their rank in society and the sameness and narrow circle of their intercourse, being less under the influence of social vanity they convey their feelings and notions in simple and unelaborated expressions. Accordingly, such a language, arising out of repeated experience and regular feelings, is a more permanent, and a far more philosophical language, than that which is frequently substituted for it by poets, who think that they are conferring honour upon themselves and their art, in proportion

---

3. Cf. Coleridge's account of their plan in *Biographia Literaria*, the beginning of chap. 14.

as they separate themselves from the sympathies of men, and indulge in arbitrary and capricious habits of expression, in order to furnish food for fickle tastes, and fickle appetites, of their own creation.[4]

I cannot, however, be insensible of the present outcry against the triviality and meanness both of thought and language, which some of my contemporaries have occasionally introduced into their metrical compositions; and I acknowledge, that this defect, where it exists, is more dishonorable to the writer's own character than false refinement or arbitrary innovation, though I should contend at the same time that it is far less pernicious in the sum of its consequences. From such verses the poems in these volumes will be found distinguished at least by one mark of difference, that each of them has a worthy *purpose*. Not that I mean to say, that I always began to write with a distinct purpose formally conceived; but I believe that my habits of meditation have so formed my feelings, as that my descriptions of such objects as strongly excite those feelings, will be found to carry along with them a *purpose*. If in this opinion I am mistaken, I can have little right to the name of a poet. For all good poetry is the spontaneous overflow of powerful feelings: but though this be true, poems to which any value can be attached, were never produced on any variety of subjects but by a man who, being possessed of more than usual organic sensibility, had also thought long and deeply. For our continued influxes of feeling are modified and directed by our thoughts, which are indeed the representatives of all our past feelings; and, as by contemplating the relation of these general representatives to each other we discover what is really important to men, so, by the repetition and continuance of this act, our feelings will be connected with important subjects, till at length, if we be originally possessed of much sensibility, such habits of mind will be produced, that, by obeying blindly and mechanically the impulses of those habits, we shall describe objects, and utter sentiments, of such a nature and in such connection with each other, that the understanding of the being to whom we address ourselves, if he be in a healthful state of association, must necessarily be in some degree enlightened, and his affections ameliorated.

I have said that each of these poems has a purpose. I have also informed my reader what this purpose will be found principally to be: namely, to illustrate the manner in which our feelings and ideas are associated in a state of excitement. But, speaking in language somewhat more appropriate, it is to follow the fluxes and refluxes of the mind when agitated by the great and simple affections of our nature. This object I have endeavored in these short essays to attain by various means; by tracing the maternal passion through many of its more subtile windings, as in the poems of the *Idiot Boy* and the *Mad Mother*; by accompanying the last struggles of a human being, at the approach of death, cleaving in solitude to life and society, as in the poem of the *Forsaken Indian*; by shewing, as in the stanzas entitled *We Are Seven*, the perplexity and obscurity which in childhood attend our notion of death, or rather our utter inability to admit that notion; or by displaying the strength of fraternal, or to speak more philosophically, of moral attachment when early associated with the great and beautiful objects of nature, as in *The Brothers*; or, as in the Incident of *Simon Lee*, by placing my reader in the

---

4. It is worth while here to observe that the affecting parts of Chaucer are almost always expressed in language pure and universally intelligible even to this day [Wordsworth's note].

way of receiving from ordinary moral sensations another and more salutary impression than we are accustomed to receive from them. It has also been part of my general purpose to attempt to sketch characters under the influence of less impassioned feelings, as in the *Two April Mornings, The Fountain, The Old Man Travelling, The Two Thieves,* &c., characters of which the elements are simple, belonging rather to nature than to manners, such as exist now, and will probably always exist, and which from their constitution may be distinctly and profitably contemplated. I will not abuse the indulgence of my reader by dwelling longer upon this subject; but it is proper that I should mention one other circumstance which distinguishes these poems from the popular poetry of the day; it is this, that the feeling therein developed gives importance to the action and situation, and not the action and situation to the feeling. My meaning will be rendered perfectly intelligible by referring my reader to the poems entitled *Poor Susan* and the *Childless Father,* particularly to the last stanza of the latter poem.

I will not suffer a sense of false modesty to prevent me from asserting, that I point my reader's attention to this mark of distinction, far less for the sake of these particular poems than from the general importance of the subject. The subject is indeed important! For the human mind is capable of being excited without the application of gross and violent stimulants; and he must have a very faint perception of its beauty and dignity who does not know this, and who does not further know, that one being is elevated above another, in proportion as he possesses this capability. It has therefore appeared to me, that to endeavour to produce or enlarge this capability is one of the best services in which, at any period, a writer can be engaged; but this service, excellent at all times, is especially so at the present day. For a multitude of causes, unknown to former times, are now acting with a combined force to blunt the discriminating powers of the mind, and, unfitting it for all voluntary exertion, to reduce it to a state of almost savage torpor. The most effective of these causes are the great national events which are daily taking place, and the increasing accumulation of men in cities, where the uniformity of their occupations produces a craving for extraordinary incident, which the rapid communication of intelligence hourly gratifies.[5] To this tendency of life and manners the literature and theatrical exhibitions of the country have conformed themselves. The invaluable works of our elder writers, I had almost said the works of Shakespeare and Milton, are driven into neglect by frantic novels, sickly and stupid German tragedies,[6] and deluges of idle and extravagant stories in verse.—When I think upon this degrading thirst after outrageous stimulation, I am almost ashamed to have spoken of the feeble effort with which I have endeavoured to counteract it; and, reflecting upon the magnitude of the general evil, I should be oppressed with no dishonorable melancholy, had I not a deep impression of certain inherent and indestructible qualities of the human mind, and likewise of certain powers in the great and permanent objects that act upon it which are equally inherent and indestructible; and did I not further add to this impression a belief, that the time is approaching when the evil will be sys-

5. This was the period of the wars against France, of industrial urbanization, and of the rapid proliferation in England of daily newspapers.
6. Wordsworth had in mind the "Gothic" terror novels by writers such as Ann Radcliffe and Matthew Gregory Lewis and the sentimental melodrama, then immensely popular in England, of August von Kotzebue and his German contemporaries.

tematically opposed, by men of greater powers, and with far more distinguished success.

Having dwelt thus long on the subjects and aim of these poems, I shall request the reader's permission to apprize him of a few circumstances relating to their *style*, in order, among other reasons, that I may not be censured for not having performed what I never attempted. The reader will find that personifications of abstract ideas rarely occur in these volumes; and, I hope, are utterly rejected as an ordinary device to elevate the style, and raise it above prose. I have proposed to myself to imitate, and, as far as is possible, to adopt the very language of men; and assuredly such personifications do not make any natural or regular part of that language. They are, indeed, a figure of speech occasionally prompted by passion, and I have made use of them as such; but I have endeavoured utterly to reject them as a mechanical device of style, or as a family language which writers in metre seem to lay claim to by prescription. I have wished to keep my reader in the company of flesh and blood, persuaded that by so doing I shall interest him. I am, however, well aware that others who pursue a different track may interest him likewise; I do not interfere with their claim, I only wish to prefer a different claim of my own. There will also be found in these volumes little of what is usually called poetic diction;[7] I have taken as much pains to avoid it as others ordinarily take to produce it; this I have done for the reason already alleged, to bring my language near to the language of men, and further, because the pleasure which I have proposed to myself to impart is of a kind very different from that which is supposed by many persons to be the proper object of poetry. I do not know how, without being culpably particular, I can give my reader a more exact notion of the style in which I wished these poems to be written than by informing him that I have at all times endeavoured to look steadily at my subject, consequently, I hope that there is in these poems little falsehood of description, and that my ideas are expressed in language fitted to their respective importance. Something I must have gained by this practice, as it is friendly to one property of all good poetry, namely, good sense; but it has necessarily cut me off from a large portion of phrases and figures of speech which from father to son have long been regarded as the common inheritance of poets. I have also thought it expedient to restrict myself still further, having abstained from the use of many expressions, in themselves proper and beautiful, but which have been foolishly repeated by bad poets, till such feelings of disgust are connected with them as it is scarcely possible by any art of association to overpower.

If in a poem there should be found a series of lines, or even a single line, in which the language, though naturally arranged and according to the strict laws of metre, does not differ from that of prose, there is a numerous class of critics, who, when they stumble upon these prosaisms as they call them, imagine that they have made a notable discovery, and exult over the poet as over a man ignorant of his own profession. Now these men would establish a canon of criticism which the reader will conclude he must utterly reject, if he wishes to be pleased with these volumes. And it would be a most easy task to prove to him, that not only the language of a large portion of every

---

7. In the sense of words, phrases, and figures of speech not commonly used in conversation or prose that are regarded as especially appropriate to poetry.

good poem, even of the most elevated character, must necessarily, except with reference to the metre, in no respect differ from that of good prose, but likewise that some of the most interesting parts of the best poems will be found to be strictly the language of prose, when prose is well written. The truth of this assertion might be demonstrated by innumerable passages from almost all the poetical writings, even of Milton himself. I have not space for much quotation; but, to illustrate the subject in a general manner, I will here adduce a short composition of Gray, who was at the head of those who by their reasonings have attempted to widen the space of separation betwixt prose and metrical composition, and was more than any other man curiously elaborate in the structure of his own poetic diction.[8]

> In vain to me the smiling mornings shine,
> And reddening Phoebus lifts his golden fire:
> The birds in vain their amorous descant join,
> Or cheerful fields resume their green attire:
> These ears, alas! for other notes repine;
> *A different object do these eyes require;*
> *My lonely anguish melts no heart but mine;*
> *And in my breast the imperfect joys expire;*
> Yet Morning smiles the busy race to cheer,
> And new-born pleasure brings to happier men;
> The fields to all their wonted tribute bear;
> To warm their little loves the birds complain.
> *I fruitless mourn to him that cannot hear*
> *And weep the more because I weep in vain.*

It will easily be perceived that the only part of this sonnet which is of any value is the lines printed in italics: it is equally obvious, that, except in the rhyme, and in the use of the single word "fruitless" for fruitlessly, which is so far a defect, the language of these lines does in no respect differ from that of prose.

By the foregoing quotation I have shewn that the language of prose may yet be well adapted to poetry; and I have previously asserted that a large portion of the language of every good poem can in no respect differ from that of good prose. I will go further. I do not doubt that it may be safely affirmed, that there neither is, nor can be, any essential difference between the language of prose and metrical composition. We are fond of tracing the resemblance between poetry and painting, and, accordingly, we call them sisters: but where shall we find bonds of connection sufficiently strict to typify the affinity betwixt metrical and prose composition? They both speak by and to the same organs; the bodies in which both of them are clothed may be said to be of the same substance, their affections are kindred and almost identical, not necessarily differing even in degree; poetry[9] sheds no

---

8. Thomas Gray had written, in a letter to Richard West, that "the language of the age is never the language of poetry." The poem that follows is Gray's *Sonnet on the Death of Richard West*.
9. I here use the word "poetry" (though against my own judgment) as opposed to the word "prose," and synonymous with metrical composition. But much confusion has been introduced into criticism by this contradistinction of poetry and prose, instead of the more philosophical one of poetry and matter of fact, or science. The only strict antithesis to prose is metre; nor is this, in truth, a *strict* antithesis; because lines and passages of metre so naturally occur in writing prose, that it would be scarcely possible to avoid them, even were it desirable [Wordsworth's note].

tears "such as Angels weep,"[1] but natural and human tears; she can boast of no celestial ichor[2] that distinguishes her vital juices from those of prose; the same human blood circulates through the veins of them both.

* * *

["WHAT IS A POET?"]

Taking up the subject, then, upon general grounds, I ask what is meant by the word "poet"? What is a poet? To whom does he address himself? And what language is to be expected from him? He is a man speaking to men: a man, it is true, endued with more lively sensibility, more enthusiasm and tenderness, who has a greater knowledge of human nature, and a more comprehensive soul, than are supposed to be common among mankind; a man pleased with his own passions and volitions, and who rejoices more than other men in the spirit of life that is in him; delighting to contemplate similar volitions and passions as manifested in the goings-on of the universe, and habitually impelled to create them where he does not find them. To these qualities he has added a disposition to be affected more than other men by absent things as if they were present; an ability of conjuring up in himself passions, which are indeed far from being the same as those produced by real events, yet (especially in those parts of the general sympathy which are pleasing and delightful) do more nearly resemble the passions produced by real events, than any thing which, from the motions of their own minds merely, other men are accustomed to feel in themselves; whence, and from practice, he has acquired a greater readiness and power in expressing what he thinks and feels, and especially those thoughts and feelings which, by his own choice, or from the structure of his own mind, arise in him without immediate external excitement.

But, whatever portion of this faculty we may suppose even the greatest poet to possess, there cannot be a doubt but that the language which it will suggest to him, must, in liveliness and truth, fall far short of that which is uttered by men in real life, under the actual pressure of those passions, certain shadows of which the poet thus produces, or feels to be produced, in himself. However exalted a notion we would wish to cherish of the character of a poet, it is obvious, that, while he describes and imitates passions, his situation is altogether slavish and mechanical, compared with the freedom and power of real and substantial action and suffering. So that it will be the wish of the poet to bring his feelings near to those of the persons whose feelings he describes, nay, for short spaces of time perhaps, to let himself slip into an entire delusion, and even confound and identify his own feelings with theirs; modifying only the language which is thus suggested to him, by a consideration that he describes for a particular purpose, that of giving pleasure. Here, then, he will apply the principle on which I have so much insisted, namely, that of selection; on this he will depend for removing what would otherwise be painful or disgusting in the passion; he will feel that there is no necessity to trick out or to elevate nature: and, the more industriously he applies this principle, the deeper will be his faith that no

1. *Paradise Lost* 1.620.
2. In Greek mythology, the fluid in the veins of the gods.

words, which his fancy or imagination can suggest, will be to be compared with those which are the emanations of reality and truth.

But it may be said by those who do not object to the general spirit of these remarks, that, as it is impossible for the poet to produce upon all occasions language as exquisitely fitted for the passion as that which the real passion itself suggests, it is proper that he should consider himself as in the situation of a translator, who deems himself justified when he substitutes excellences of another kind for those which are unattainable by him; and endeavours occasionally to surpass his original, in order to make some amends for the general inferiority to which he feels that he must submit. But this would be to encourage idleness and unmanly despair. Further, it is the language of men who speak of what they do not understand; who talk of poetry as a matter of amusement and idle pleasure; who will converse with us as gravely about a *taste* for poetry, as they express it, as if it were a thing as indifferent as a taste for rope-dancing, or Frontiniac[3] or sherry. Aristotle, I have been told, hath said, that poetry is the most philosophic of all writing;[4] it is so: its object is truth, not individual and local, but general, and operative; not standing upon external testimony, but carried alive into the heart by passion; truth which is its own testimony, which gives strength and divinity to the tribunal to which it appeals, and receives them from the same tribunal. Poetry is the image of man and nature. The obstacles which stand in the way of the fidelity of the biographer and historian, and of their consequent utility, are incalculably greater than those which are to be encountered by the poet who has an adequate notion of the dignity of his art. The poet writes under one restriction only, namely, that of the necessity of giving immediate pleasure to a human being possessed of that information which may be expected from him, not as a lawyer, a physician, a mariner, an astronomer or a natural philosopher, but as a man. Except this one restriction, there is no object standing between the poet and the image of things; between this, and the biographer and historian there are a thousand.

Nor let this necessity of producing immediate pleasure be considered as a degradation of the poet's art. It is far otherwise. It is an acknowledgment of the beauty of the universe, an acknowledgment the more sincere because it is not formal, but indirect; it is a task light and easy to him who looks at the world in the spirit of love: further, it is a homage paid to the native and naked dignity of man, to the grand elementary principle of pleasure, by which he knows, and feels, and lives, and moves.[5] We have no sympathy but what is propagated by pleasure: I would not be misunderstood; but wherever we sympathize with pain it will be found that the sympathy is produced and carried on by subtle combinations with pleasure. We have no knowledge, that is, no general principles drawn from the contemplation of particular facts, but what has been built up by pleasure, and exists in us by pleasure alone. The man of science, the chemist and mathematician, whatever difficulties and disgusts they may have had to struggle with, know and feel this. However painful may be the objects with which the anatomist's knowledge is connected, he feels that his knowledge is pleasure; and where he has no

3. A sweet wine made from muscat grapes.
4. Aristotle in fact said that "poetry is more philosophic than history, since its statements are of the nature of universals, whereas those of history are singulars" (*Poetics* 1451b).
5. A bold echo of the words of St. Paul, that in God "we live, and move, and have our being" (Acts 17.28).

pleasure he has no knowledge. What then does the poet? He considers man and the objects that surround him as acting and re-acting upon each other, so as to produce an infinite complexity of pain and pleasure; he considers man in his own nature and in his ordinary life as contemplating this with a certain quantity of immediate knowledge, with certain convictions, intuitions, and deductions which by habit become of the nature of intuitions; he considers him as looking upon this complex scene of ideas and sensations, and finding every where objects that immediately excite in him sympathies which, from the necessities of his nature, are accompanied by an overbalance of enjoyment.

To this knowledge which all men carry about with them, and to these sympathies in which without any other discipline than that of our daily life we are fitted to take delight, the poet principally directs his attention. He considers man and nature as essentially adapted to each other,[6] and the mind of man as naturally the mirror of the fairest and most interesting qualities of nature. And thus the poet, prompted by this feeling of pleasure which accompanies him through the whole course of his studies, converses with general nature with affections akin to those, which, through labour and length of time, the man of science has raised up in himself, by conversing with those particular parts of nature which are the objects of his studies. The knowledge both of the poet and the man of science is pleasure; but the knowledge of the one cleaves to us as a necessary part of our existence, our natural and unalienable inheritance; the other is a personal and individual acquisition, slow to come to us, and by no habitual and direct sympathy connecting us with our fellow-beings. The man of science seeks truth as a remote and unknown benefactor; he cherishes and loves it in his solitude: the poet, singing a song in which all human beings join with him, rejoices in the presence of truth as our visible friend and hourly companion. Poetry is the breath and finer spirit of all knowledge; it is the impassioned expression which is in the countenance of all science. Emphatically may it be said of the poet, as Shakespeare hath said of man, "that he looks before and after."[7] He is the rock of defence of human nature; an upholder and preserver, carrying everywhere with him relationship and love. In spite of difference of soil and climate, of language and manners, of laws and customs, in spite of things silently gone out of mind and things violently destroyed, the poet binds together by passion and knowledge the vast empire of human society, as it is spread over the whole earth, and over all time. The objects of the poet's thoughts are every where; though the eyes and senses of man are, it is true, his favorite guides, yet he will follow wheresoever he can find an atmosphere of sensation in which to move his wings. Poetry is the first and last of all knowledge—it is as immortal as the heart of man. If the labours of men of science should ever create any material revolution, direct or indirect, in our condition, and in the impressions which we habitually receive, the poet will sleep then no more than at present, but he will be ready to follow the steps of the man of science, not only in those general indirect effects, but he will be at his side, carrying sensation into the midst of the objects of the science itself. The remotest discoveries of the chemist, the botanist, or mineralogist,

6. On the mutual adaptation of man's mind and nature, see Wordsworth's Prospectus to The *Recluse*, p. 302, lines 63–71.
7. *Hamlet* 4.4.37.

will be as proper objects of the poet's art as any upon which it can be employed, if the time should ever come when these things shall be familiar to us, and the relations under which they are contemplated by the followers of these respective sciences shall be manifestly and palpably material to us as enjoying and suffering beings.[8] If the time should ever come when what is now called science, thus familiarized to men, shall be ready to put on, as it were, a form of flesh and blood, the poet will lend his divine spirit to aid the transfiguration, and will welcome the being thus produced, as a dear and genuine inmate of the household of man.—It is not, then, to be supposed that any one, who holds that sublime notion of poetry which I have attempted to convey, will break in upon the sanctity and truth of his pictures by transitory and accidental ornaments, and endeavour to excite admiration of himself by arts, the necessity of which must manifestly depend upon the assumed meanness of his subject.

What I have thus far said applies to poetry in general; but especially to those parts of composition where the poet speaks through the mouth of his characters; and upon this point it appears to have such weight that I will conclude, there are few persons, of good sense, who would not allow that the dramatic parts of composition are defective, in proportion as they deviate from the real language of nature, and are coloured by a diction of the poet's own, either peculiar to him as an individual poet, or belonging simply to poets in general, to a body of men who, from the circumstance of their compositions being in metre, it is expected will employ a particular language.

It is not, then, in the dramatic parts of composition that we look for this distinction of language; but still it may be proper and necessary where the poet speaks to us in his own person and character. To this I answer by referring my reader to the description which I have before given of a poet. Among the qualities which I have enumerated as principally conducing to form a poet, is implied nothing differing in kind from other men, but only in degree. The sum of what I have there said is, that the poet is chiefly distinguished from other men by a greater promptness to think and feel without immediate external excitement, and a greater power in expressing such thoughts and feelings as are produced in him in that manner. But these passions and thoughts and feelings are the general passions and thoughts and feelings of men. And with what are they connected? Undoubtedly with our moral sentiments and animal sensations, and with the causes which excite these; with the operations of the elements and the appearances of the visible universe; with storm and sun-shine, with the revolutions of the seasons, with cold and heat, with loss of friends and kindred, with injuries and resentments, gratitude and hope, with fear and sorrow. These, and the like, are the sensations and objects which the poet describes, as they are the sensations of other men, and the objects which interest them. The poet thinks and feels in the spirit of the passions of men. How, then, can his language differ in any material degree from that of all other men who feel vividly and see clearly? It might be *proved* that it is impossible. But supposing that this were not the case, the poet might then be allowed to use a peculiar language, when expressing his feelings for his own gratification, or that of

---

8. Wordsworth is at least right in anticipating the poetry of the machine; he himself wrote an early instance, the sonnet *Steamboats, Viaducts, and Railways*.

men like himself. But poets do not write for poets alone, but for men. Unless therefore we are advocates for that admiration which depends upon ignorance, and that pleasure which arises from hearing what we do not understand, the poet must descend from this supposed height, and, in order to excite rational sympathy, he must express himself as other men express themselves. * * *

["EMOTION RECOLLECTED IN TRANQUILLITY"]

I have said that poetry is the spontaneous overflow of powerful feelings: it takes its origin from emotion recollected in tranquillity: the emotion is contemplated till by a species of reaction the tranquillity gradually disappears, and an emotion, kindred to that which was before the subject of contemplation, is gradually produced, and does itself actually exist in the mind. In this mood successful composition generally begins, and in a mood similar to this it is carried on; but the emotion, of whatever kind and in whatever degree, from various causes is qualified by various pleasures, so that in describing any passions whatsoever, which are voluntarily described, the mind will upon the whole be in a state of enjoyment. Now, if nature be thus cautious in preserving in a state of enjoyment a being thus employed, the poet ought to profit by the lesson thus held forth to him, and ought especially to take care, that whatever passions he communicates to his reader, those passions, if his reader's mind be sound and vigorous, should always be accompanied with an overbalance of pleasure. Now the music of harmonious metrical language, the sense of difficulty overcome, and the blind association of pleasure which has been previously received from works of rhyme or metre of the same or similar construction, an indistinct perception perpetually renewed of language closely resembling that of real life, and yet, in the circumstance of metre, differing from it so widely, all these imperceptibly make up a complex feeling of delight, which is of the most important use in tempering the painful feeling which will always be found intermingled with powerful descriptions of the deeper passions. This effect is always produced in pathetic and impassioned poetry; while, in lighter compositions, the ease and gracefulness with which the poet manages his numbers are themselves confessedly a principal source of the gratification of the reader. I might perhaps include all which it is *necessary* to say upon this subject by affirming, what few persons will deny, that, of two descriptions, either of passions, manners, or characters, each of them equally well executed, the one in prose and the other in verse, the verse will be read a hundred times where the prose is read once. * * *

I know that nothing would have so effectually contributed to further the end which I have in view, as to have shewn of what kind the pleasure is, and how the pleasure is produced, which is confessedly produced by metrical composition essentially different from that which I have here endeavoured to recommend: for the reader will say that he has been pleased by such composition; and what can I do more for him? The power of any art is limited; and he will suspect, that, if I propose to furnish him with new friends, it is only upon condition of his abandoning his old friends. Besides, as I have said, the reader is himself conscious of the pleasure which he has received from such composition, composition to which he has peculiarly attached the endearing name of poetry; and all men feel an habitual gratitude, and something of an honorable bigotry for the objects which have long continued to please them: we not only wish to be pleased, but to be pleased in that particular way in which we have been accustomed to be pleased. There is a host of arguments in these feelings; and I should be the less able to combat them successfully, as I am willing to allow, that, in order entirely to enjoy the poetry which I am recommending, it would be necessary to give up much of what is ordinarily enjoyed. But, would my limits have permitted me to point out how this pleasure is produced, I might have removed many obstacles, and assisted my reader in perceiving that the powers of language are not so limited as he may suppose; and that it is possible that poetry may give other enjoyments, of a purer, more lasting, and more exquisite nature. This part of my subject I have not altogether neglected; but it has been less my present aim to prove, that the interest excited by some other kinds of poetry is less vivid, and less worthy of the nobler powers of the mind, than to offer reasons for presuming, that, if the object which I have proposed to myself were adequately attained, a species of poetry would be produced, which is genuine poetry; in its nature well adapted to interest mankind permanently, and likewise important in the multiplicity and quality of its moral relations.

From what has been said, and from a perusal of the poems, the reader will be able clearly to perceive the object which I have proposed to myself: he will determine how far I have attained this object; and, what is a much more important question, whether it be worth attaining; and upon the decision of these two questions will rest my claim to the approbation of the public.

1800, 1802

Strange fits of passion have I known[1]

Strange fits of passion have I known:
And I will dare to tell,
But in the Lover's ear alone,
What once to me befel.

5   When she I loved looked every day
Fresh as a rose in June,
I to her cottage bent my way,
Beneath an evening moon.

Upon the moon I fixed my eye,
10   All over the wide lea;
With quickening pace my horse drew nigh
Those paths so dear to me.

1. This and the four following pieces are often grouped by editors as the "Lucy poems," even though *A slumber did my spirit seal* does not identify the "she" who is the subject of that poem. All but the last were written in 1799, while Wordsworth and his sister were in Germany, and homesick. There has been diligent speculation about the identity of Lucy, but it remains speculation. The one certainty is that she is not the girl of Wordsworth's *Lucy Gray*.

And now we reached the orchard-plot;
And, as we climbed the hill,
15 The sinking moon to Lucy's cot
Came near, and nearer still.

In one of those sweet dreams I slept,
Kind Nature's gentlest boon!
And all the while my eyes I kept
20 On the descending moon.

My horse moved on; hoof after hoof
He raised, and never stopped:
When down behind the cottage roof,
At once, the bright moon dropped.

25 What fond and wayward thoughts will slide
Into a Lover's head!
"O mercy!" to myself I cried,
"If Lucy should be dead!"[2]

1799   1800

She dwelt among the untrodden ways[1]

She dwelt among the untrodden ways
 Beside the springs of Dove,[2]
A Maid whom there were none to praise
 And very few to love:

5 A violet by a mossy stone
 Half hidden from the eye!
—Fair as a star, when only one
 Is shining in the sky.

She lived unknown, and few could know
10 When Lucy ceased to be;
But she is in her grave, and, oh,
 The difference to me!

1799   1800

Three years she grew

Three years she grew in sun and shower,
Then Nature said, "A lovelier flower
On earth was never sown;

---

2. An additional stanza in an earlier manuscript version demonstrates how a poem can be improved by omission of a passage that is, in itself, excellent poetry: "I told her this: her laughter light / Is ringing in my ears; / And when I think upon that night / My eyes are dim with tears."

1. For the author's revisions while composing this poem, see "Poems in Process," in the appendices to this volume.
2. There are several rivers by this name in England, including one in the Lake District.

This Child I to myself will take;
5 She shall be mine, and I will make
A Lady of my own.[1]

"Myself will to my darling be
Both law and impulse: and with me
The Girl, in rock and plain,
10 In earth and heaven, in glade and bower,
Shall feel an overseeing power
To kindle or restrain.

"She shall be sportive as the fawn
That wild with glee across the lawn
15 Or up the mountain springs;
And hers shall be the breathing balm,
And hers the silence and the calm
Of mute insensate things.

"The floating clouds their state shall lend
20 To her; for her the willow bend;
Nor shall she fail to see
Even in the motions of the Storm
Grace that shall mould the Maiden's form
By silent sympathy.

25 "The stars of midnight shall be dear
To her; and she shall lean her ear
In many a secret place
Where rivulets dance their wayward round,
And beauty born of murmuring sound
30 Shall pass into her face.

"And vital feelings of delight
Shall rear her form to stately height,
Her virgin bosom swell;
Such thoughts to Lucy I will give
35 While she and I together live
Here in this happy dell."

Thus Nature spake—the work was done—
How soon my Lucy's race was run!
She died, and left to me
40 This heath, this calm, and quiet scene;
The memory of what has been,
And never more will be.

1799   1800

1. I.e., Lucy was three years old at the time when Nature made this promise; line 37 makes clear that Lucy had reached the maturity foretold in the sixth stanza when she died.

A slumber did my spirit seal

A slumber did my spirit seal;
   I had no human fears:
She seemed a thing that could not feel
   The touch of earthly years.

5 No motion has she now, no force;
   She neither hears nor sees;
Rolled round in earth's diurnal° course,   *daily*
   With rocks, and stones, and trees.

1799   1800

I travelled among unknown men

I travelled among unknown men,
   In lands beyond the sea;
Nor, England! did I know till then
   What love I bore to thee.

5 'Tis past, that melancholy dream!
   Nor will I quit thy shore
A second time; for still I seem
   To love thee more and more.

Among thy mountains did I feel
10   The joy of my desire;
And she I cherished turned her wheel
   Beside an English fire.

Thy mornings showed, thy nights concealed
   The bowers where Lucy played;
15 And thine too is the last green field
   That Lucy's eyes surveyed.

ca. 1801   1807

Lucy Gray[1]

Or, Solitude

Oft I had heard of Lucy Gray:
   And, when I crossed the wild,

---

1. Written in 1799 while Wordsworth was in Germany, and founded on a true account of a young girl who drowned when she lost her way in a snowstorm. "The body however was found in the canal. The way in which the incident was treated and the spiritualizing of the character might furnish hints for contrasting the imaginative influences which I have endeavored to throw over common life with Crabbe's matter-of-fact style of treating subjects of the same kind" [Wordsworth's note]. Cf. Wordsworth's statement, in the Preface to *Lyrical Ballads*, of his undertaking to throw over ordinary things "a certain colouring of imagination" (p. 241).

I chanced to see at break of day
The solitary child.

5 No mate, no comrade Lucy knew;
She dwelt on a wide moor,
—The sweetest thing that ever grew
Beside a human door!

You yet may spy the fawn at play,
10 The hare upon the green;
But the sweet face of Lucy Gray
Will never more be seen.

"To-night will be a stormy night—
You to the town must go;
15 And take a lantern, Child, to light
Your mother through the snow."

"That, Father! will I gladly do:
'Tis scarcely afternoon—
The minster°-clock has just struck two,   *church*
20 And yonder is the moon!"

At this the Father raised his hook,
And snapped a faggot-band;[2]
He plied his work;—and Lucy took
The lantern in her hand.

25 Not blither is the mountain roe:
With many a wanton stroke
Her feet disperse the powdery snow,
That rises up like smoke.

The storm came on before its time:
30 She wandered up and down;
And many a hill did Lucy climb:
But never reached the town.

The wretched parents all that night
Went shouting far and wide;
35 But there was neither sound nor sight
To serve them for a guide.

At day-break on a hill they stood
That overlooked the moor;
And thence they saw the bridge of wood,
40 A furlong[3] from their door.

---

2. Cord binding a bundle of sticks to be used for   3. One eighth of a mile.
fuel.

They wept—and, turning homeward, cried,
"In heaven we all shall meet;"
—When in the snow the mother spied
The print of Lucy's feet.

45 Then downwards from the steep hill's edge
They tracked the footmarks small;
And through the broken hawthorn hedge,
And by the long stone-wall;

And then an open field they crossed:
50 The marks were still the same;
They tracked them on, nor ever lost;
And to the bridge they came.

They followed from the snowy bank
Those footmarks, one by one,
55 Into the middle of the plank;
And further there were none!

—Yet some maintain that to this day
She is a living child;
That you may see sweet Lucy Gray
60 Upon the lonesome wild.

O'er rough and smooth she trips along,
And never looks behind;
And sings a solitary song
That whistles in the wind.

1799   1800

The Two April Mornings[1]

We walked along, while bright and red
Uprose the morning sun;
And Matthew stopped, he looked, and said,
"The will of God be done!"

5 A village schoolmaster was he,
With hair of glittering grey;
As blithe a man as you could see
On a spring holiday.

And on that morning, through the grass,
10 And by the steaming rills,°   small streams
We travelled merrily, to pass
A day among the hills.

1. In this poem and another called *Matthew*, both written in 1799, the central figure is named after a onetime schoolmaster at Hawkshead School, which Wordsworth attended.

"Our work," said I, "was well begun,
Then, from thy breast what thought,
15 Beneath so beautiful a sun,
So sad a sigh has brought?"

A second time did Matthew stop;
And fixing still his eye
Upon the eastern mountain-top,
20 To me he made reply:

"Yon cloud with that long purple cleft
Brings fresh into my mind
A day like this which I have left
Full thirty years behind.

25 "And just above yon slope of corn
Such colours, and no other,
Were in the sky, that April morn,
Of this the very brother.

"With rod and line I sued the sport
30 Which that sweet season gave,
And, to the church-yard come, stopped short
Beside my daughter's grave.

"Nine summers had she scarcely seen,
The pride of all the vale;
35 And then she sang;—she would have been
A very nightingale.

"Six feet in earth my Emma lay;
And yet I loved her more,
For so it seemed, than till that day
40 I e'er had loved before.

"And, turning from her grave, I met,
Beside the churchyard yew,
A blooming Girl, whose hair was wet
With points of morning dew.

45 "A basket on her head she bare;
Her brow was smooth and white:
To see a child so very fair,
It was a pure delight!

"No fountain from its rocky cave
50 E'er tripped with foot so free;
She seemed as happy as a wave
That dances on the sea.

"There came from me a sigh of pain
Which I could ill confine;

55 I looked at her, and looked again:
  And did not wish her mine!"

 Matthew is in his grave, yet now,
  Methinks, I see him stand,
 As at that moment, with a bough
60 Of wilding[2] in his hand.

1799   1800

Nutting[1]

————————It seems a day
(I speak of one from many singled out)
One of those heavenly days that cannot die;
When, in the eagerness of boyish hope,
5 I left our cottage-threshold, sallying forth
With a huge wallet o'er my shoulder slung,
A nutting-crook in hand; and turned my steps
Tow'rd some far-distant wood, a Figure quaint,
Tricked out in proud disguise of cast-off weeds°   _clothes_
10 Which for that service had been husbanded,
By exhortation of my frugal Dame[2]—
Motley accoutrement, of power to smile
At thorns, and brakes, and brambles,—and, in truth,
More ragged than need was! O'er pathless rocks,
15 Through beds of matted fern, and tangled thickets,
Forcing my way, I came to one dear nook
Unvisited, where not a broken bough
Drooped with its withered leaves, ungracious sign
Of devastation; but the hazels rose
20 Tall and erect, with tempting clusters hung,
A virgin scene!—A little while I stood,
Breathing with such suppression of the heart
As joy delights in; and, with wise restraint
Voluptuous, fearless of a rival, eyed
25 The banquet;—or beneath the trees I sate
Among the flowers, and with the flowers I played;
A temper known to those, who, after long
And weary expectation, have been blest
With sudden happiness beyond all hope.
30 Perhaps it was a bower beneath whose leaves
The violets of five seasons re-appear
And fade, unseen by any human eye;
Where fairy water-breaks[3] do murmur on
For ever; and I saw the sparkling foam,

2. An uncultivated tree or plant, especially the wild apple tree.
1. Wordsworth said that these lines, written in Germany in 1798, were "intended as part of a poem on my own mind [_The Prelude_], but struck out as not being wanted there." He published them in the second edition of _Lyrical Ballads_, 1800.
2. Ann Tyson, with whom Wordsworth lodged while at Hawkshead grammar school.
3. Places where the flow of a stream is broken by rocks.

35   And—with my cheek on one of those green stones
     That, fleeced with moss, under the shady trees,
     Lay round me, scattered like a flock of sheep—
     I heard the murmur and the murmuring sound,
     In that sweet mood when pleasure loves to pay
40   Tribute to ease; and, of its joy secure,
     The heart luxuriates with indifferent things,
     Wasting its kindliness on stocks[4] and stones,
     And on the vacant air. Then up I rose,
     And dragged to earth both branch and bough, with crash
45   And merciless ravage: and the shady nook
     Of hazels, and the green and mossy bower,
     Deformed and sullied, patiently gave up
     Their quiet being: and, unless I now
     Confound my present feelings with the past,
50   Ere from the mutilated bower I turned
     Exulting, rich beyond the wealth of kings,
     I felt a sense of pain when I beheld
     The silent trees, and saw the intruding sky.—
     Then, dearest Maiden,[5] move along these shades
55   In gentleness of heart; with gentle hand
     Touch—for there is a spirit in the woods.

1798   1800

The Ruined Cottage[1]

First Part

'Twas summer and the sun was mounted high.
     Along the south the uplands feebly glared
     Through a pale steam, and all the northern downs
     In clearer air ascending shewed far off
5   Their surfaces with shadows dappled o'er
     Of deep embattled clouds: far as the sight
     Could reach those many shadows lay in spots
     Determined and unmoved, with steady beams
     Of clear and pleasant sunshine interposed;
10 Pleasant to him who on the soft cool moss
     Extends his careless limbs beside the root
     Of some huge oak whose aged branches make

---

4. Tree stumps. ("Stocks and stones" is a conventional expression for "inanimate things.")
5. In a manuscript passage originally intended to lead up to *Nutting,* the maiden is called Lucy.
1. Wordsworth wrote *The Ruined Cottage* in 1797–98, then revised it several times before he finally published an expanded version of the story as book 1 of *The Excursion,* in 1814. *The Ruined Cottage* was not published as an independent poem until 1949, when it appeared in the fifth volume of *The Poetical Works of William Wordsworth,* edited by Ernest de Selincourt and Helen Darbishire, who printed a version known as "MS. B." The text reprinted here is from "MS. D," dated

1799, as transcribed by James Butler in the Cornell Wordsworth volume, *"The Ruined Cottage" and "The Pedlar"* (1979).
    This version is one of Wordsworth's earliest successes in verse narrative. The story presents the bleak facts of "a tale of silent suffering"—suffering that is undeserved, unrationalized, and irremissive. The event is "a common tale," and it poses the implicit question, What are we to make of human life, in which such things happen? The narrator confronts the fact of human suffering without reference to the creed of a beneficent power, whether in or out of nature.

A twilight of their own, a dewy shade
Where the wren warbles while the dreaming man,
15 Half-conscious of that soothing melody,
With side-long eye looks out upon the scene,
By those impending branches made more soft,
More soft and distant. Other lot was mine.
Across a bare wide Common I had toiled
20 With languid feet which by the slipp'ry ground
Were baffled still, and when I stretched myself
On the brown earth my limbs from very heat
Could find no rest nor my weak arm disperse
The insect host which gathered round my face
25 And joined their murmurs to the tedious noise
Of seeds of bursting gorse that crackled round.
I rose and turned towards a group of trees
Which midway in that level stood alone,
And thither come at length, beneath a shade
30 Of clustering elms that sprang from the same root
I found a ruined house, four naked walls
That stared upon each other. I looked round
And near the door I saw an aged Man,
Alone, and stretched upon the cottage bench;
35 An iron-pointed staff lay at his side.
With instantaneous joy I recognized
That pride of nature and of lowly life,
The venerable Armytage, a friend
As dear to me as is the setting sun.
40   Two days before
We had been fellow-travellers. I knew
That he was in this neighbourhood and now
Delighted found him here in the cool shade.
He lay, his pack of rustic merchandize
45 Pillowing his head—I guess he had no thought
Of his way-wandering life. His eyes were shut;
The shadows of the breezy elms above
Dappled his face. With thirsty heat oppress'd
At length I hailed him, glad to see his hat
50 Bedewed with water-drops, as if the brim
Had newly scoop'd a running stream. He rose
And pointing to a sun-flower bade me climb
The [   ]² wall where that same gaudy flower
Looked out upon the road. It was a plot
55 Of garden-ground, now wild, its matted weeds
Marked with the steps of those whom as they pass'd,
The goose-berry trees that shot in long lank slips,
Or currants hanging from their leafless stems
In scanty strings, had tempted to o'erleap
60 The broken wall. Within that cheerless spot,
Where two tall hedgerows of thick willow boughs

---

2. The brackets here and in later lines mark blank spaces left unfilled in the manuscript.

Joined in a damp cold nook, I found a well
Half-choked [with willow flowers and weeds.]³
I slaked my thirst and to the shady bench
65 Returned, and while I stood unbonneted
To catch the motion of the cooler air
The old Man said, "I see around me here
Things which you cannot see: we die, my Friend,
Nor we alone, but that which each man loved
70 And prized in his peculiar nook of earth
Dies with him or is changed, and very soon
Even of the good is no memorial left.
The Poets in their elegies and songs
Lamenting the departed call the groves,
75 They call upon the hills and streams to mourn,
And senseless rocks, nor idly; for they speak
In these their invocations with a voice
Obedient to the strong creative power
Of human passion. Sympathies there are
80 More tranquil, yet perhaps of kindred birth,
That steal upon the meditative mind
And grow with thought. Beside yon spring I stood
And eyed its waters till we seemed to feel
One sadness, they and I. For them a bond
85 Of brotherhood is broken: time has been
When every day the touch of human hand
Disturbed their stillness, and they ministered
To human comfort. When I stooped to drink,
A spider's web hung to the water's edge,
90 And on the wet and slimy foot-stone lay
The useless fragment of a wooden bowl;
It moved my very heart. The day has been
When I could never pass this road but she
Who lived within these walls, when I appeared,
95 A daughter's welcome gave me, and I loved her
As my own child. O Sir! the good die first,
And they whose hearts are dry as summer dust
Burn to the socket. Many a passenger
Has blessed poor Margaret for her gentle looks
100 When she upheld the cool refreshment drawn
From that forsaken spring, and no one came
But he was welcome, no one went away
But that it seemed she loved him. She is dead,
The worm is on her cheek, and this poor hut,
105 Stripp'd of its outward garb of household flowers,
Of rose and sweet-briar, offers to the wind
A cold bare wall whose earthy top is tricked
With weeds and the rank spear-grass. She is dead,
And nettles rot and adders sun themselves
110 Where we have sate together while she nurs'd

---

3. Wordsworth penciled the bracketed phrase into a gap left in the manuscript.

Her infant at her breast. The unshod Colt,
The wandring heifer and the Potter's ass,
Find shelter now within the chimney-wall
Where I have seen her evening hearth-stone blaze
115 And through the window spread upon the road
Its chearful light.—You will forgive me, Sir,
But often on this cottage do I muse
As on a picture, till my wiser mind
Sinks, yielding to the foolishness of grief.
120   She had a husband, an industrious man,
Sober and steady; I have heard her say
That he was up and busy at his loom
In summer ere the mower's scythe had swept
The dewy grass, and in the early spring
125 Ere the last star had vanished. They who pass'd
At evening, from behind the garden-fence
Might hear his busy spade, which he would ply
After his daily work till the day-light
Was gone and every leaf and flower were lost
130 In the dark hedges. So they pass'd their days
In peace and comfort, and two pretty babes
Were their best hope next to the God in Heaven.
—You may remember, now some ten years gone,
Two blighting seasons when the fields were left
135 With half a harvest.[4] It pleased heaven to add
A worse affliction in the plague of war:
A happy land was stricken to the heart;
'Twas a sad time of sorrow and distress:
A wanderer among the cottages,
140 I with my pack of winter raiment saw
The hardships of that season: many rich
Sunk down as in a dream among the poor,
And of the poor did many cease to be,
And their place knew them not. Meanwhile, abridg'd
145 Of daily comforts, gladly reconciled
To numerous self-denials, Margaret
Went struggling on through those calamitous years
With chearful hope: but ere the second autumn
A fever seized her husband. In disease
150 He lingered long, and when his strength returned
He found the little he had stored to meet
The hour of accident or crippling age
Was all consumed. As I have said, 'twas now
A time of trouble; shoals of artisans
155 Were from their daily labour turned away
To hang for bread on parish charity,
They and their wives and children—happier far
Could they have lived as do the little birds

---

4. As James Butler points out in his introduction, Wordsworth is purposely distancing his story in time. The "two blighting seasons" in fact occurred in 1794–95, only a few years before Wordsworth wrote *The Ruined Cottage*, when a bad harvest was followed by one of the worst winters on record. Much of the seed grain was destroyed in the ground, and the price of wheat nearly doubled.

That peck along the hedges or the kite
160   That makes her dwelling in the mountain rocks.
Ill fared it now with Robert, he who dwelt
In this poor cottage; at his door he stood
And whistled many a snatch of merry tunes
That had no mirth in them, or with his knife
165   Carved uncouth figures on the heads of sticks,
Then idly sought about through every nook
Of house or garden any casual task
Of use or ornament, and with a strange,
Amusing but uneasy novelty
170   He blended where he might the various tasks
Of summer, autumn, winter, and of spring.
But this endured not; his good-humour soon
Became a weight in which no pleasure was,
And poverty brought on a petted° mood   *ill-tempered*
175   And a sore temper: day by day he drooped,
And he would leave his home, and to the town
Without an errand would he turn his steps
Or wander here and there among the fields.
One while he would speak lightly of his babes
180   And with a cruel tongue: at other times
He played with them wild freaks of merriment:
And 'twas a piteous thing to see the looks
Of the poor innocent children. 'Every smile,'
Said Margaret to me here beneath these trees,
185   'Made my heart bleed,' " At this the old Man paus'd
And looking up to those enormous elms
He said, " 'Tis now the hour of deepest noon,
At this still season of repose and peace,
This hour when all things which are not at rest
190   Are chearful, while this multitude of flies
Fills all the air with happy melody,
Why should a tear be in an old man's eye?
Why should we thus with an untoward mind
And in the weakness of humanity
195   From natural wisdom turn our hearts away,
To natural comfort shut our eyes and ears,
And feeding on disquiet thus disturb
The calm of Nature with our restless thoughts?"

 END OF THE FIRST PART

Second Part

He spake with somewhat of a solemn tone:
200   But when he ended there was in his face
Such easy chearfulness, a look so mild
That for a little time it stole away
All recollection, and that simple tale
Passed from my mind like a forgotten sound.
205   A while on trivial things we held discourse,
To me soon tasteless. In my own despite

I thought of that poor woman as of one
Whom I had known and loved. He had rehearsed
Her homely tale with such familiar power,
210   With such a[n active]⁵ countenance, an eye
So busy, that the things of which he spake
Seemed present, and, attention now relaxed,
There was a heartfelt chillness in my veins.
I rose, and turning from that breezy shade
215   Went out into the open air and stood
To drink the comfort of the warmer sun.
Long time I had not stayed ere, looking round
Upon that tranquil ruin, I returned
And begged of the old man that for my sake
220   He would resume his story. He replied,
"It were a wantonness and would demand
Severe reproof, if we were men whose hearts
Could hold vain dalliance with the misery
Even of the dead, contented thence to draw
225   A momentary pleasure never marked
By reason, barren of all future good.
But we have known that there is often found
In mournful thoughts, and always might be found,
A power to virtue friendly; were't not so,
230   I am a dreamer among men, indeed
An idle dreamer. 'Tis a common tale,
By moving accidents⁶ uncharactered,
A tale of silent suffering, hardly clothed
In bodily form, and to the grosser sense
235   But ill adapted, scarcely palpable
To him who does not think. But at your bidding
I will proceed.
                    While thus it fared with them
To whom this cottage till that hapless year
Had been a blessed home, it was my chance
240   To travel in a country far remote,
And glad I was when, halting by yon gate
That leads from the green lane, again I saw
These lofty elm-trees. Long I did not rest:
With many pleasant thoughts I cheer'd my way
245   O'er the flat common. At the door arrived,
I knocked, and when I entered with the hope
Of usual greeting, Margaret looked at me
A little while, then turned her head away
Speechless, and sitting down upon a chair
250   Wept bitterly. I wist not what to do
Or how to speak to her. Poor wretch! at last
She rose from off her seat—and then, oh Sir!
I cannot tell how she pronounced my name:
With fervent love, and with a face of grief

---

5. Wordsworth penciled the bracketed phrase into a gap left in the manuscript.
6. Othello speaks "of most disastrous chances, /

Of moving accidents by flood and field, / Of hair-breadth 'scapes" (*Othello* 1.3.133–35).

255 Unutterably helpless, and a look
That seem'd to cling upon me, she enquir'd
If I had seen her husband. As she spake
A strange surprize and fear came to my heart,
Nor had I power to answer ere she told
260 That he had disappeared—just two months gone.
He left his house; two wretched days had passed,
And on the third by the first break of light,
Within her casement full in view she saw
A purse of gold.[7] 'I trembled at the sight,'
265 Said Margaret, 'for I knew it was his hand
That placed it there, and on that very day
By one, a stranger, from my husband sent,
The tidings came that he had joined a troop
Of soldiers going to a distant land.
270 He left me thus—Poor Man! he had not heart
To take a farewell of me, and he feared
That I should follow with my babes, and sink
Beneath the misery of a soldier's life.'
This tale did Margaret tell with many tears:
275 And when she ended I had little power
To give her comfort, and was glad to take
Such words of hope from her own mouth as serv'd
To cheer us both: but long we had not talked
Ere we built up a pile of better thoughts,
280 And with a brighter eye she looked around
As if she had been shedding tears of joy.
We parted. It was then the early spring;
I left her busy with her garden tools;
And well remember, o'er that fence she looked,
285 And while I paced along the foot-way path
Called out, and sent a blessing after me
With tender chearfulness and with a voice
That seemed the very sound of happy thoughts.
    I roved o'er many a hill and many a dale
290 With this my weary load, in heat and cold,
Through many a wood, and many an open ground,
In sunshine or in shade, in wet or fair,
Now blithe, now drooping, as it might befal,
My best companions now the driving winds
295 And now the 'trotting brooks'[8] and whispering trees
And now the music of my own sad steps,
With many a short-lived thought that pass'd between
And disappeared. I came this way again
Towards the wane of summer, when the wheat
300 Was yellow, and the soft and bladed grass
Sprang up afresh and o'er the hay-field spread

7. The "bounty" that her husband had been paid
for enlisting in the militia. The shortage of volunteers and England's sharply rising military needs
had in some counties forced the bounty up from
about £1 in 1757 to more than £16 in 1796 (J. R.
Western, *English Militia in the Eighteenth Century*, 1965, p. 276).
8. From Robert Burns (*To William Simpson*, line
87).

Its tender green. When I had reached the door
I found that she was absent. In the shade
Where now we sit I waited her return.
305 Her cottage in its outward look appeared
As chearful as before; in any shew
Of neatness little changed, but that I thought
The honeysuckle crowded round the door
And from the wall hung down in heavier wreathes,
310 And knots of worthless stone-crop⁹ started out
Along the window's edge, and grew like weeds
Against the lower panes. I turned aside
And stroll'd into her garden.—It was chang'd:
The unprofitable bindweed spread his bells
315 From side to side and with unwieldy wreaths
Had dragg'd the rose from its sustaining wall
And bent it down to earth; the border-tufts—
Daisy and thrift and lowly camomile
And thyme—had straggled out into the paths
320 Which they were used to deck. Ere this an hour
Was wasted. Back I turned my restless steps,
And as I walked before the door it chanced
A stranger passed, and guessing whom I sought
He said that she was used to ramble far.
325 The sun was sinking in the west, and now
I sate with sad impatience. From within
Her solitary infant cried aloud.
The spot though fair seemed very desolate,
The longer I remained more desolate.
330 And, looking round, I saw the corner-stones,
Till then unmark'd, on either side the door
With dull red stains discoloured and stuck o'er
With tufts and hairs of wool, as if the sheep
That feed upon the commons thither came
335 Familiarly and found a couching-place
Even at her threshold.—The house-clock struck eight;
I turned and saw her distant a few steps.
Her face was pale and thin, her figure too
Was chang'd. As she unlocked the door she said,
340 'It grieves me you have waited here so long,
But in good truth I've wandered much of late
And sometimes, to my shame I speak, have need
Of my best prayers to bring me back again.'
While on the board she spread our evening meal
345 She told me she had lost her elder child,
That he for months had been a serving-boy
Apprenticed by the parish. 'I perceive
You look at me, and you have cause. Today
I have been travelling far, and many days
350 About the fields I wander, knowing this
Only, that what I seek I cannot find.
And so I waste my time: for I am changed;

---

9. A plant with yellow flowers that grows on walls and rocks.

And to myself,' said she, 'have done much wrong,
And to this helpless infant. I have slept
355 Weeping, and weeping I have waked; my tears
Have flow'd as if my body were not such
As others are, and I could never die.
But I am now in mind and in my heart
More easy, and I hope,' said she, 'that heaven
360 Will give me patience to endure the things
Which I behold at home.' It would have grieved
Your very heart to see her. Sir, I feel
The story linger in my heart. I fear
'Tis long and tedious, but my spirit clings
365 To that poor woman: so familiarly
Do I perceive her manner, and her look
And presence, and so deeply do I feel
Her goodness, that not seldom in my walks
A momentary trance comes over me;
370 And to myself I seem to muse on one
By sorrow laid asleep or borne away,
A human being destined to awake
To human life, or something very near
To human life, when he shall come again
375 For whom she suffered. Sir, it would have griev'd
Your very soul to see her: evermore
Her eye-lids droop'd, her eyes were downward cast;
And when she at her table gave me food
She did not look at me. Her voice was low,
380 Her body was subdued. In every act
Pertaining to her house-affairs appeared
The careless stillness which a thinking mind
Gives to an idle matter—still she sighed,
But yet no motion of the breast was seen,
385 No heaving of the heart. While by the fire
We sate together, sighs came on my ear;
I knew not how, and hardly whence they came.
I took my staff, and when I kissed her babe
The tears stood in her eyes. I left her then
390 With the best hope and comfort I could give;
She thanked me for my will, but for my hope
It seemed she did not thank me.
      I returned
And took my rounds along this road again
Ere on its sunny bank the primrose flower
395 Had chronicled the earliest day of spring.
I found her sad and drooping; she had learn'd
No tidings of her husband: if he lived
She knew not that he lived; if he were dead
She knew not he was dead. She seemed the same
400 In person [or][1] appearance, but her house
Bespoke a sleepy hand of negligence;
The floor was neither dry nor neat, the hearth

---

1. The word *or* was erased here; later manuscripts read "and."

Was comfortless [   ],
The windows too were dim, and her few books,
405 Which, one upon the other, heretofore
Had been piled up against the corner-panes
In seemly order, now with straggling leaves
Lay scattered here and there, open or shut
As they had chanced to fall. Her infant babe
410 Had from its mother caught the trick of grief
And sighed among its playthings. Once again
I turned towards the garden-gate and saw
More plainly still that poverty and grief
Were now come nearer to her: the earth was hard,
415 With weeds defaced and knots of withered grass;
No ridges there appeared of clear black mould,
No winter greenness; of her herbs and flowers
It seemed the better part were gnawed away
Or trampled on the earth; a chain of straw
420 Which had been twisted round the tender stem
Of a young apple-tree lay at its root;
The bark was nibbled round by truant sheep.
Margaret stood near, her infant in her arms,
And seeing that my eye was on the tree
425 She said, 'I fear it will be dead and gone
Ere Robert come again.' Towards the house
Together we returned, and she inquired
If I had any hope. But for her Babe
And for her little friendless Boy, she said,
430 She had no wish to live, that she must die
Of sorrow. Yet I saw the idle loom
Still in its place. His Sunday garments hung
Upon the self-same nail, his very staff
Stood undisturbed behind the door. And when
435 I passed this way beaten by Autumn winds
She told me that her little babe was dead
And she was left alone. That very time,
I yet remember, through the miry lane
She walked with me a mile, when the bare trees
440 Trickled with foggy damps, and in such sort
That any heart had ached to hear her begg'd
That wheresoe'er I went I still would ask
For him whom she had lost. We parted then,
Our final parting, for from that time forth
445 Did many seasons pass ere I returned
Into this tract again.
                              Five tedious years
She lingered in unquiet widowhood,
A wife and widow. Needs must it have been
A sore heart-wasting. I have heard, my friend,
450 That in that broken arbour she would sit
The idle length of half a sabbath day—
There, where you see the toadstool's lazy head—
And when a dog passed by she still would quit

The shade and look abroad. On this old Bench
455 For hours she sate, and evermore her eye
Was busy in the distance, shaping things
Which made her heart beat quick. Seest thou that path?
(The green-sward now has broken its grey line)
There to and fro she paced through many a day
460 Of the warm summer, from a belt of flax
That girt her waist spinning the long-drawn thread
With backward steps.—Yet ever as there passed
A man whose garments shewed the Soldier's red,
Or crippled Mendicant in Sailor's garb,
465 The little child who sate to turn the wheel
Ceased from his toil, and she with faltering voice,
Expecting still to learn her husband's fate,
Made many a fond inquiry; and when they
Whose presence gave no comfort were gone by,
470 Her heart was still more sad. And by yon gate
Which bars the traveller's road she often stood
And when a stranger horseman came, the latch
Would lift, and in his face look wistfully,
Most happy if from aught discovered there
475 Of tender feeling she might dare repeat
The same sad question. Meanwhile her poor hut
Sunk to decay, for he was gone whose hand
At the first nippings of October frost
Closed up each chink and with fresh bands of straw
480 Chequered the green-grown thatch. And so she lived
Through the long winter, reckless and alone,
Till this reft house by frost, and thaw, and rain
Was sapped; and when she slept the nightly damps
Did chill her breast, and in the stormy day
485 Her tattered clothes were ruffled by the wind
Even at the side of her own fire. Yet still
She loved this wretched spot, nor would for worlds
Have parted hence; and still that length of road
And this rude bench one torturing hope endeared,
490 Fast rooted at her heart, and here, my friend,
In sickness she remained, and here she died,
Last human tenant of these ruined walls."
    The old Man ceased: he saw that I was mov'd;
From that low Bench, rising instinctively,
495 I turned aside in weakness, nor had power
To thank him for the tale which he had told.
I stood, and leaning o'er the garden-gate
Reviewed that Woman's suff'rings, and it seemed
To comfort me while with a brother's love
500 I blessed her in the impotence of grief.
At length [towards] the [Cottage I returned]²
Fondly, and traced with milder interest
That secret spirit of humanity

2. The words inside the brackets were added in MS. E.

Which, 'mid the calm oblivious tendencies
505 Of nature, 'mid her plants, her weeds, and flowers,
And silent overgrowings, still survived.
The old man, seeing this, resumed and said,
"My Friend, enough to sorrow have you given,
The purposes of wisdom ask no more;
510 Be wise and chearful, and no longer read
The forms of things with an unworthy eye.
She sleeps in the calm earth, and peace is here.
I well remember that those very plumes,
Those weeds, and the high spear-grass on that wall,
515 By mist and silent rain-drops silver'd o'er,
As once I passed did to my heart convey
So still an image of tranquillity,
So calm and still, and looked so beautiful
Amid the uneasy thoughts which filled my mind,
520 That what we feel of sorrow and despair
From ruin and from change, and all the grief
The passing shews of being leave behind,
Appeared an idle dream that could not live
Where meditation was. I turned away
525 And walked along my road in happiness."
      He ceased. By this the sun declining shot
A slant and mellow radiance which began
To fall upon us where beneath the trees
We sate on that low bench, and now we felt,
530 Admonished thus, the sweet hour coming on.
A linnet warbled from those lofty elms,
A thrush sang loud, and other melodies,
At distance heard, peopled the milder air.
The old man rose and hoisted up his load.
535 Together casting then a farewell look
Upon those silent walls, we left the shade
And ere the stars were visible attained
A rustic inn, our evening resting-place.

THE END

1797–ca.1799   1949

Michael[1]

A Pastoral Poem

If from the public way you turn your steps
Up the tumultuous brook of Green-head Ghyll,[2]

1. This poem is founded on the actual misfortunes of a family at Grasmere. For the account of the sheepfold, see Dorothy Wordsworth's *Grasmere Journals,* October 11, 1800 (p. 388). Wordsworth wrote to Thomas Poole, on April 9, 1801, that he had attempted to picture a mail "agitated by two of the most powerful affections of the human heart; the parental affection, and the love of property, *landed* property, including the feelings of inheritance, home, and personal and family independence." The subtitle shows Wordsworth's shift of the term "pastoral" from aristocratic make-believe to the tragic suffering of people in what he called "humble and rustic life."
2. A ravine forming the bed of a stream. Green-head Ghyll is not far from Wordsworth's cottage at Grasmere. The other places named in the poem are also in that vicinity.

You will suppose that with an upright path
Your feet must struggle; in such bold ascent
5   The pastoral mountains front you, face to face.
But, courage! for around that boisterous brook
The mountains have all opened out themselves,
And made a hidden valley of their own.
No habitation can be seen; but they
10   Who journey thither find themselves alone
With a few sheep, with rocks and stones, and kites°   *hawks*
That overhead are sailing in the sky.
It is in truth an utter solitude;
Nor should I have made mention of this Dell
15   But for one object which you might pass by,
Might see and notice not. Beside the brook
Appears a straggling heap of unhewn stones!
And to that simple object appertains
A story—unenriched with strange events,
20   Yet not unfit, I deem, for the fireside,
Or for the summer shade. It was the first
Of those domestic tales that spake to me
Of Shepherds, dwellers in the valleys, men
Whom I already loved;—not verily
25   For their own sakes, but for the fields and hills
Where was their occupation and abode.
And hence this Tale, while I was yet a Boy
Careless of books, yet having felt the power
Of Nature, by the gentle agency
30   Of natural objects, led me on to feel
For passions that were not my own, and think
(At random and imperfectly indeed)
On man, the heart of man, and human life.
Therefore, although it be a history
35   Homely and rude, I will relate the same
For the delight of a few natural hearts;
And, with yet fonder feeling, for the sake
Of youthful Poets, who among these hills
Will be my second self when I am gone.

40   Upon the forest-side in Grasmere Vale
There dwelt a Shepherd, Michael was his name;
An old man, stout of heart, and strong of limb.
His bodily frame had been from youth to age
Of an unusual strength: his mind was keen,
45   Intense, and frugal, apt for all affairs,
And in his shepherd's calling he was prompt
And watchful more than ordinary men.
Hence had he learned the meaning of all winds,
Of blasts of every tone; and, oftentimes,
50   When others heeded not, he heard the South
Make subterraneous music, like the noise
Of bagpipers on distant Highland hills.
The Shepherd, at such warning, of his flock

Bethought him, and he to himself would say,
55 "The winds are now devising work for me!"
And, truly, at all times, the storm, that drives
The traveller to a shelter, summoned him
Up to the mountains: he had been alone
Amid the heart of many thousand mists,
60 That came to him, and left him, on the heights.
So lived he till his eightieth year was past.
And grossly that man errs, who should suppose
That the green valleys, and the streams and rocks,
Were things indifferent to the Shepherd's thoughts.
65 Fields, where with cheerful spirits he had breathed
The common air; hills, which with vigorous step
He had so often climbed; which had impressed
So many incidents upon his mind
Of hardship, skill or courage, joy or fear;
70 Which, like a book, preserved the memory
Of the dumb animals, whom he had saved,
Had fed or sheltered, linking to such acts
The certainty of honourable gain;
Those fields, those hills—what could they less? had laid
75 Strong hold on his affections, were to him
A pleasurable feeling of blind love,
The pleasure which there is in life itself.

His days had not been passed in singleness.
His Helpmate was a comely matron, old—
80 Though younger than himself full twenty years.
She was a woman of a stirring life,
Whose heart was in her house: two wheels she had
Of antique form; this large, for spinning wool;
That small, for flax; and if one wheel had rest,
85 It was because the other was at work.
The Pair had but one inmate in their house,
An only Child, who had been born to them
When Michael, telling o'er his years, began
To deem that he was old,—in shepherd's phrase,
90 With one foot in the grave. This only Son,
With two brave sheep-dogs tried in many a storm,
The one of an inestimable worth,
Made all their household. I may truly say,
That they were as a proverb in the vale
95 For endless industry. When day was gone,
And from their occupations out of doors
The Son and Father were come home, even then,
Their labour did not cease; unless when all
Turned to the cleanly supper-board, and there,
100 Each with a mess of pottage and skimmed milk,
Sat round the basket piled with oaten cakes,
And their plain home-made cheese. Yet when the meal
Was ended, Luke (for so the Son was named)

And his old Father both betook themselves
105 To such convenient work as might employ
Their hands by the fire-side; perhaps to card
Wool for the Housewife's spindle, or repair
Some injury done to sickle, flail, or scythe,
Or other implement of house or field.

110   Down from the ceiling, by the chimney's edge,
That in our ancient uncouth country style
With huge and black projection overbrowed
Large space beneath, as duly as the light
Of day grew dim the Housewife hung a lamp;
115 An aged utensil, which had performed
Service beyond all others of its kind.
Early at evening did it burn—and late,
Surviving comrade of uncounted hours,
Which, going by from year to year, had found,
120 And left the couple neither gay perhaps
Nor cheerful, yet with objects and with hopes,
Living a life of eager industry.
And now, when Luke had reached his eighteenth year,
There by the light of his old lamp they sate,
125 Father and Son, while far into the night
The Housewife plied her own peculiar work,
Making the cottage through the silent hours
Murmur as with the sound of summer flies.
This light was famous in its neighbourhood,
130 And was a public symbol of the life
That thrifty Pair had lived. For, as it chanced,
Their cottage on a plot of rising ground
Stood single, with large prospect, north and south,
High into Easedale, up to Dunmail-Raise,
135 And westward to the village near the lake;
And from this constant light, so regular
And so far seen, the House itself, by all
Who dwelt within the limits of the vale,
Both old and young, was named THE EVENING STAR.

140   Thus living on through such a length of years,
The Shepherd, if he loved himself, must needs
Have loved his Helpmate; but to Michael's heart
This son of his old age was yet more dear—
Less from instinctive tenderness, the same
145 Fond spirit that blindly works in the blood of all—
Than that a child, more than all other gifts
That earth can offer to declining man,
Brings hope with it, and forward-looking thoughts,
And stirrings of inquietude, when they
150 By tendency of nature needs must fail.
Exceeding was the love he bare to him,
His heart and his heart's joy! For oftentimes

Old Michael, while he was a babe in arms,
Had done him female service, not alone
155 For pastime and delight, as is the use
Of fathers, but with patient mind enforced
To acts of tenderness; and he had rocked
His cradle, as with a woman's gentle hand.

And, in a later time, ere yet the Boy
160 Had put on boy's attire, did Michael love,
Albeit of a stern unbending mind,
To have the Young-one in his sight, when he
Wrought in the field, or on his shepherd's stool
Sate with a fettered sheep before him stretched
165 Under the large old oak, that near his door
Stood single, and, from matchless depth of shade,
Chosen for the Shearer's covert from the sun,
Thence in our rustic dialect was called
The CLIPPING TREE, a name which yet it bears.
170 There, while they two were sitting in the shade,
With others round them, earnest all and blithe,
Would Michael exercise his heart with looks
Of fond correction and reproof bestowed
Upon the Child, if he disturbed the sheep
175 By catching at their legs, or with his shouts
Scared them, while they lay still beneath the shears.

And when by Heaven's good grace the boy grew up
A healthy Lad, and carried in his cheek
Two steady roses that were five years old;
180 Then Michael from a winter coppice³ cut
With his own hand a sapling, which he hooped
With iron, making it throughout in all
Due requisites a perfect shepherd's staff,
And gave it to the Boy; wherewith equipt
185 He as a watchman oftentimes was placed
At gate or gap, to stem or turn the flock;
And, to his office prematurely called,
There stood the urchin, as you will divine,
Something between a hindrance and a help;
190 And for this cause not always, I believe,
Receiving from his Father hire of praise;
Though nought was left undone which staff, or voice,
Or looks, or threatening gestures, could perform.

But soon as Luke, full ten years old, could stand
195 Against the mountain blasts; and to the heights,
Not fearing toil, nor length of weary ways,
He with his Father daily went, and they
Were as companions, why should I relate
That objects which the Shepherd loved before

3. Grove of small trees.

200   Were dearer now? that from the Boy there came
        Feelings and emanations—things which were
        Light to the sun and music to the wind;
        And that the old Man's heart seemed born again?

        Thus in his Father's sight the Boy grew up:
205   And now, when he had reached his eighteenth year,
        He was his comfort and his daily hope.

        While in this sort the simple household lived
        From day to day, to Michael's ear there came
        Distressful tidings. Long before the time
210   Of which I speak, the Shepherd had been bound
        In surety for his brother's son, a man
        Of an industrious life, and ample means;
        But unforeseen misfortunes suddenly
        Had prest upon him; and old Michael now
215   Was summoned to discharge the forfeiture,
        A grievous penalty, but little less
        Than half his substance. This unlooked-for claim,
        At the first hearing, for a moment took
        More hope out of his life than he supposed
220   That any old man ever could have lost.
        As soon as he had armed himself with strength
        To look his trouble in the face, it seemed
        The Shepherd's sole resource to sell at once
        A portion of his patrimonial fields.
225   Such was his first resolve; he thought again,
        And his heart failed him. "Isabel," said he,
        Two evenings after he had heard the news,
        "I have been toiling more than seventy years,
        And in the open sunshine of God's love
230   Have we all lived; yet if these fields of ours
        Should pass into a stranger's hand, I think
        That I could not lie quiet in my grave.
        Our lot is a hard lot; the sun himself
        Has scarcely been more diligent than I;
235   And I have lived to be a fool at last
        To my own family. An evil man
        That was, and made an evil choice, if he
        Were false to us; and if he were not false,
        There are ten thousand to whom loss like this
240   Had been no sorrow. I forgive him;—but
        'Twere better to be dumb than to talk thus.

        "When I began, my purpose was to speak
        Of remedies and of a cheerful hope.
        Our Luke shall leave us, Isabel; the land
245   Shall not go from us, and it shall be free;
        He shall possess it, free as is the wind
        That passes over it. We have, thou know'st,
        Another kinsman—he will be our friend

In this distress. He is a prosperous man,
250 Thriving in trade—and Luke to him shall go,
And with his kinsman's help and his own thrift
He quickly will repair this loss, and then
He may return to us. If here he stay,
What can be done? Where every one is poor,
What can be gained?"
255   At this the old Man paused,
And Isabel sat silent, for her mind
Was busy, looking back into past times.
There's Richard Bateman,[4] thought she to herself,
He was a parish-boy—at the church-door
260 They made a gathering for him, shillings, pence
And halfpennies, wherewith the neighbours bought
A basket, which they filled with pedlar's wares;
And, with this basket on his arm, the lad
Went up to London, found a master there,
265 Who, out of many, chose the trusty boy
To go and overlook his merchandise
Beyond the seas; where he grew wondrous rich,
And left estates and monies to the poor,
And, at his birth-place, built a chapel floored
270 With marble, which he sent from foreign lands.
These thoughts, and many others of like sort,
Passed quickly through the mind of Isabel,
And her face brightened. The old Man was glad,
And thus resumed:—"Well, Isabel! this scheme
275 These two days, has been meat and drink to me.
Far more than we have lost is left us yet.
—We have enough—I wish indeed that I
Were younger;—but this hope is a good hope.
Make ready Luke's best garments, of the best
280 Buy for him more, and let us send him forth
To-morrow, or the next day, or to-night:
—If he *could* go, the Boy should go to-night."

    Here Michael ceased, and to the fields went forth
With a light heart. The Housewife for five days
285 Was restless morn and night, and all day long
Wrought on with her best fingers to prepare
Things needful for the journey of her son.
But Isabel was glad when Sunday came
To stop her in her work: for, when she lay
290 By Michael's side, she through the last two nights
Heard him, how he was troubled in his sleep:
And when they rose at morning she could see
That all his hopes were gone. That day at noon
She said to Luke, while they two by themselves
295 Were sitting at the door, "Thou must not go:
We have no other Child but thee to lose,
None to remember—do not go away,

---

4. The story alluded to here is well known in the country. The chapel is called Ings Chapel and is on the road leading from Kendal to Ambleside [Wordsworth's note].

For if thou leave thy Father he will die."
The Youth made answer with a jocund voice;
300 And Isabel, when she had told her fears,
Recovered heart. That evening her best fare
Did she bring forth, and all together sat
Like happy people round a Christmas fire.

With daylight Isabel resumed her work;
305 And all the ensuing week the house appeared
As cheerful as a grove in Spring: at length
The expected letter from their kinsman came,
With kind assurances that he would do
His utmost for the welfare of the Boy;
310 To which, requests were added, that forthwith
He might be sent to him. Ten times or more
The letter was read over; Isabel
Went forth to show it to the neighbours round;
Nor was there at that time on English land
315 A prouder heart than Luke's. When Isabel
Had to her house returned, the old Man said,
"He shall depart to-morrow." To this word
The Housewife answered, talking much of things
Which, if at such short notice he should go,
320 Would surely be forgotten. But at length
She gave consent, and Michael was at ease.

Near the tumultuous brook of Green-head Ghyll,
In that deep valley, Michael had designed
To build a Sheep-fold;⁵ and, before he heard
325 The tidings of his melancholy loss,
For this same purpose he had gathered up
A heap of stones, which by the streamlet's edge
Lay thrown together, ready for the work.
With Luke that evening thitherward he walked:
330 And soon as they had reached the place he stopped,
And thus the old Man spake to him:—"My Son,
To-morrow thou wilt leave me: with full heart
I look upon thee, for thou art the same
That wert a promise to me ere thy birth,
335 And all thy life hast been my daily joy.
I will relate to thee some little part
Of our two histories; 'twill do thee good
When thou art from me, even if I should touch
On things thou canst not know of.——After thou
340 First cam'st into the world—as oft befals
To new-born infants—thou didst sleep away
Two days, and blessings from thy Father's tongue
Then fell upon thee. Day by day passed on,
And still I loved thee with increasing love.
345 Never to living ear came sweeter sounds

5. A sheepfold [pen for sheep] in these mountains is an unroofed building of stone walls, with different divisions [Wordsworth's note].

Than when I heard thee by our own fire-side
First uttering, without words, a natural tune;
While thou, a feeding babe, didst in thy joy
Sing at thy Mother's breast. Month followed month,
350 And in the open fields my life was passed
And on the mountains; else I think that thou
Hadst been brought up upon thy Father's knees.
But we were playmates, Luke: among these hills,
As well thou knowest, in us the old and young
355 Have played together, nor with me didst thou
Lack any pleasure which a boy can know."
Luke had a manly heart; but at these words
He sobbed aloud. The old Man grasped his hand,
And said, "Nay, do not take it so—I see
360 That these are things of which I need not speak.
—Even to the utmost I have been to thee
A kind and a good Father: and herein
I but repay a gift which I myself
Received at others' hands; for, though now old
365 Beyond the common life of man, I still
Remember them who loved me in my youth.
Both of them sleep together: here they lived,
As all their Forefathers had done; and when
At length their time was come, they were not loth
370 To give their bodies to the family mould.
I wished that thou should'st live the life they lived:
But, 'tis a long time to look back, my Son,
And see so little gain from threescore years.
These fields were burthened° when they came to me;   mortgaged
375 Till I was forty years of age, not more
Than half of my inheritance was mine.
I toiled and toiled; God blessed me in my work,
And till these three weeks past the land was free.
—It looks as if it never could endure
380 Another Master. Heaven forgive me, Luke,
If I judge ill for thee, but it seems good
That thou should'st go."
                                    At this the old Man paused;
Then, pointing to the stones near which they stood,
Thus, after a short silence, he resumed:
385 "This was a work for us; and now, my Son,
It is a work for me. But, lay one stone—
Here, lay it for me, Luke, with thine own hands.
Nay, Boy, be of good hope;—we both may live
To see a better day. At eighty-four
390 I still am strong and hale;—do thou thy part;
I will do mine.—I will begin again
With many tasks that were resigned to thee:
Up to the heights, and in among the storms,
Will I without thee go again, and do
395 All works which I was wont to do alone,
Before I knew thy face.—Heaven bless thee, Boy!

Thy heart these two weeks has been beating fast
With many hopes; it should be so—yes—yes—
I knew that thou could'st never have a wish
400   To leave me, Luke: thou hast been bound to me
Only by links of love: when thou art gone,
What will be left to us!—But, I forget
My purposes. Lay now the corner-stone,
As I requested; and hereafter, Luke,
405   When thou art gone away, should evil men
Be thy companions, think of me, my Son,
And of this moment; hither turn thy thoughts,
And God will strengthen thee: amid all fear
And all temptation, Luke, I pray that thou
410   May'st bear in mind the life thy Fathers lived,
Who, being innocent, did for that cause
Bestir them in good deeds. Now, fare thee well—
When thou return'st, thou in this place wilt see
A work which is not here: a covenant
415   'Twill be between us; but, whatever fate
Befal thee, I shall love thee to the last,
And bear thy memory with me to the grave."

          The Shepherd ended here; and Luke stooped down,
And, as his Father had requested, laid
420   The first stone of the Sheep-fold. At the sight
The old Man's grief broke from him; to his heart
He pressed his Son, he kissèd him and wept;
And to the house together they returned.
—Hushed was that House in peace, or seeming peace,
425   Ere the night fell:—with morrow's dawn the Boy
Began his journey, and when he had reached
The public way, he put on a bold face;
And all the neighbours, as he passed their doors,
Came forth with wishes and with farewell prayers,
430   That followed him till he was out of sight.

          A good report did from their Kinsman come,
Of Luke and his well-doing: and the Boy
Wrote loving letters, full of wondrous news,
Which, as the Housewife phrased it, were throughout
435   "The prettiest letters that were ever seen."
Both parents read them with rejoicing hearts.
So, many months passed on: and once again
The Shepherd went about his daily work
With confident and cheerful thoughts; and now
440   Sometimes when he could find a leisure hour
He to that valley took his way, and there
Wrought at the Sheep-fold. Meantime Luke began
To slacken in his duty; and, at length,
He in the dissolute city gave himself
445   To evil courses: ignominy and shame

Fell on him, so that he was driven at last
To seek a hiding-place beyond the seas.

There is a comfort in the strength of love;
'Twill make a thing endurable, which else
450 Would overset the brain, or break the heart:
I have conversed with more than one who well
Remember the old Man, and what he was
Years after he had heard this heavy news.
His bodily frame had been from youth to age
455 Of an unusual strength. Among the rocks
He went, and still looked up to sun and cloud,
And listened to the wind; and, as before
Performed all kinds of labour for his sheep,
And for the land, his small inheritance.
460 And to that hollow dell from time to time
Did he repair, to build the Fold of which
His flock had need. 'Tis not forgotten yet
The pity which was then in every heart
For the old Man—and 'tis believed by all
465 That many and many a day he thither went,
And never lifted up a single stone.

There, by the Sheep-fold, sometimes was he seen
Sitting alone, or with his faithful Dog,
Then old, beside him, lying at his feet.
470 The length of full seven years, from time to time,
He at the building of this Sheep-fold wrought,
And left the work unfinished when he died.
Three years, or little more, did Isabel
Survive her Husband: at her death the estate
475 Was sold, and went into a stranger's hand.
The Cottage which was named the EVENING STAR
Is gone—the ploughshare has been through the ground
On which it stood; great changes have been wrought
In all the neighbourhood:—yet the oak is left
480 That grew beside their door; and the remains
Of the unfinished Sheep-fold may be seen
Beside the boisterous brook of Green-head Ghyll.

Oct. 11–Dec. 9, 1800   1800

Resolution and Independence[1]

I

There was a roaring in the wind all night;
The rain came heavily and fell in floods;

---

1. For the meeting with the old leech gatherer, see Dorothy Wordsworth's *Grasmere Journals*, October 3, 1800 (p. 387). Wordsworth himself tells us that "I was in the state of feeling described in the beginning of the poem, while crossing over Barton Fell from Mr. Clarkson's, at the foot of Ullswater, towards Askam. The image of the hare I then observed on the ridge of the Fell." He wrote the poem eighteen months after this event (see *Grasmere Journals*, May 4 and 7, 1802; pp. 393 and 394).

But now the sun is rising calm and bright;
The birds are singing in the distant woods;
Over his own sweet voice the Stock-dove broods;
The Jay makes answer as the Magpie chatters;
And all the air is filled with pleasant noise of waters.

2

All things that love the sun are out of doors;
The sky rejoices in the morning's birth;
The grass is bright with rain-drops;—on the moors
The hare is running races in her mirth;
And with her feet she from the plashy earth
Raises a mist; that, glittering in the sun,
Runs with her all the way, wherever she doth run.

3

I was a Traveller then upon the moor;
I saw the hare that raced about with joy;
I heard the woods and distant waters roar;
Or heard them not, as happy as a boy:
The pleasant season did my heart employ:
My old remembrances went from me wholly;
And all the ways of men, so vain and melancholy.

4

But, as it sometimes chanceth, from the might
Of joy in minds that can no further go,
As high as we have mounted in delight
In our dejection do we sink as low;
To me that morning did it happen so;
And fears and fancies thick upon me came;
Dim sadness—and blind thoughts, I knew not, nor could name.

5

I heard the sky-lark warbling in the sky;
And I bethought me of the playful hare:
Even such a happy Child of earth am I;
Even as these blissful creatures do I fare;
Far from the world I walk, and from all care;
But there may come another day to me—
Solitude, pain of heart, distress, and poverty.

6

My whole life I have lived in pleasant thought,
As if life's business were a summer mood;
As if all needful things would come unsought
To genial faith, still rich in genial good;
But how can He expect that others should
Build for him, sow for him, and at his call
Love him, who for himself will take no heed at all?

7

I thought of Chatterton,[2] the marvellous Boy,
The sleepless Soul that perished in his pride;
45 Of Him[3] who walked in glory and in joy
Following his plough, along the mountain-side:
By our own spirits are we deified:
We Poets in our youth begin in gladness;
But thereof come in the end despondency and madness.

8

50 Now, whether it were by peculiar grace,
A leading from above, a something given,
Yet it befel, that, in this lonely place,
When I with these untoward thoughts had striven,
Beside a pool bare to the eye of heaven
55 I saw a Man before me unawares:
The oldest man he seemed that ever wore grey hairs.

9

As a huge stone is sometimes seen to lie
Couched on the bald top of an eminence;
Wonder to all who do the same espy,
60 By what means it could thither come, and whence;
So that it seems a thing endued with sense:
Like a sea-beast crawled forth, that on a shelf
Of rock or sand reposeth, there to sun itself;

10

Such seemed this Man,[4] not all alive nor dead,
65 Nor all asleep—in his extreme old age:
His body was bent double, feet and head
Coming together in life's pilgrimage;
As if some dire constraint of pain, or rage
Of sickness felt by him in times long past,
70 A more than human weight upon his frame had cast.

11

Himself he propped, limbs, body, and pale face,
Upon a long grey staff of shaven wood:
And, still as I drew near with gentle pace,
Upon the margin of that moorish flood

2. Thomas Chatterton (1752–1770), a poet of great talent who, in his loneliness and dire poverty, poisoned himself at the age of seventeen and so became the prime Romantic symbol of neglected young genius.
3. Robert Burns, also considered at that time as a natural poet who died young and poor, without adequate recognition.
4. In Wordsworth's own analysis of this passage he says that the stone is endowed with something of life, the sea beast is stripped of some of its life

to assimilate it to the stone, and the old man divested of enough life and motion to make "the two objects unite and coalesce in just comparison." He used the passage to demonstrate his theory of how the "conferring, the abstracting, and the modifying powers of the Imagination . . . are all brought into conjunction" (Preface to the *Poems* of 1815). Cf. Coleridge's brief definitions of the imagination in *Biographia Literaria*, chap. 13 (p. 477).

75 Motionless as a cloud the old Man stood,
That heareth not the loud winds when they call;
And moveth all together, if it move at all.

12

At length, himself unsettling, he the pond
Stirred with his staff, and fixedly did look
80 Upon the muddy water, which he conned,
As if he had been reading in a book:
And now a stranger's privilege I took;
And, drawing to his side, to him did say,
"This morning gives us promise of a glorious day."

13

85 A gentle answer did the old Man make,
In courteous speech which forth he slowly drew:
And him with further words I thus bespake,
"What occupation do you there pursue?
This is a lonesome place for one like you."
90 Ere he replied, a flash of mild surprise
Broke from the sable orbs of his yet-vivid eyes.

14

His words came feebly, from a feeble chest,
But each in solemn order followed each,
With something of a lofty utterance drest—
95 Choice word and measured phrase, above the reach
Of ordinary men; a stately speech;
Such as grave Livers[5] do in Scotland use,
Religious men, who give to God and man their dues.

15

He told, that to these waters he had come
100 To gather leeches,[6] being old and poor:
Employment hazardous and wearisome!
And he had many hardships to endure:
From pond to pond he roamed, from moor to moor;
Housing, with God's good help, by choice or chance;
105 And in this way he gained an honest maintenance.

16

The old Man still stood talking by my side;
But now his voice to me was like a stream
Scarce heard; nor word from word could I divide;
And the whole body of the Man did seem
110 Like one whom I had met with in a dream;

5. Those who live gravely.
6. Used to draw blood for curative purposes. A leech gatherer, bare legged in shallow water, stirred the water to attract them and, when they fastened themselves to his legs, picked them off.

Or like a man from some far region sent,
To give me human strength, by apt admonishment.

17

My former thoughts returned: the fear that kills;
And hope that is unwilling to be fed;
115 Cold, pain, and labour, and all fleshly ills;
And mighty Poets in their misery dead.
—Perplexed, and longing to be comforted,
My question eagerly did I renew,
"How is it that you live, and what is it you do?"

18

120 He with a smile did then his words repeat;
And said, that, gathering leeches, far and wide
He travelled; stirring thus about his feet
The waters of the pools where they abide.
"Once I could meet with them on every side;
125 But they have dwindled long by slow decay;
Yet still I persevere, and find them where I may."

19

While he was talking thus, the lonely place,
The old Man's shape, and speech—all troubled me:
In my mind's eye I seemed to see him pace
130 About the weary moors continually,
Wandering about alone and silently.
While I these thoughts within myself pursued,
He, having made a pause, the same discourse renewed.

20

And soon with this he other matter blended,
135 Cheerfully uttered, with demeanour kind,
But stately in the main; and when he ended,
I could have laughed myself to scorn to find
In that decrepit Man so firm a mind.
"God," said I, "be my help and stay[7] secure;
140 I'll think of the Leech-gatherer on the lonely moor!"

May 3–July 4, 1802   1807

I wandered lonely as a cloud[1]

I wandered lonely as a cloud
That floats on high o'er vales and hills,
When all at once I saw a crowd,
A host, of golden daffodils;

---

7. Support (a noun).
1. For the original experience, two years earlier,

see Dorothy Wordsworth's *Grasmere Journals*,
April 15, 1802 (p. 391).

5   Beside the lake, beneath the trees,
Fluttering and dancing in the breeze.

Continuous as the stars that shine
And twinkle on the milky way,
They stretched in never-ending line
10   Along the margin of a bay:
Ten thousand saw I at a glance,
Tossing their heads in sprightly dance.

The waves beside them danced; but they
Out-did the sparkling waves in glee:
15   A poet could not but be gay,
In such a jocund company:
I gazed—and gazed—but little thought
What wealth the show to me had brought:

For oft, when on my couch I lie
20   In vacant or in pensive mood,
They flash upon that inward eye
Which is the bliss of solitude;
And then my heart with pleasure fills,
And dances with the daffodils.

1804   1807

My heart leaps up

My heart leaps up when I behold
   A rainbow in the sky:
So was it when my life began;
So is it now I am a man;
5   So be it when I shall grow old,
   Or let me die!
The Child is father of the Man;
And I could wish my days to be
Bound each to each by natural piety.[1]

Mar. 26, 1802   1807

1. As distinguished from piety based on the Scriptures, in which God makes the rainbow the token of his covenant with Noah and all his descendants (Genesis 9.12–17). The religious sentiment that binds Wordsworth's mature self to that of his childhood is a continuing responsiveness to the miracle of ordinary things.

Ode: Intimations of Immortality

In 1843, Wordsworth said about this *Ode* to Isabella Fenwick:

This was composed during my residence at Town End, Grasmere; two years at least passed between the writing of the four first stanzas and the remaining part. To the attentive and competent reader the whole sufficiently explains itself; but there may be no harm in adverting here to particular feelings or *experiences* of my own mind on which the structure of the poem partly rests. Nothing was more difficult for me in childhood than to admit the notion of death as a state applicable to my own being. I have said elsewhere [in the opening stanza of *We Are Seven*]:

> —A simple child,
> That lightly draws its breath,
> And feels its life in every limb,
> What should it know of death!—

But it was not so much from [feelings] of animal vivacity that *my* difficulty came as from a sense of the indomitableness of the spirit within me. I used to brood over the stories of Enoch and Elijah [Genesis 5.22–24; 2 Kings 2.11], and almost to persuade myself that, whatever might become of others, I should be translated, in something of the same way, to heaven. With a feeling congenial to this, I was often unable to think of external things as having external existence, and I communed with all that I saw as something not apart from, but inherent in, my own immaterial nature. Many times while going to school have I grasped at a wall or tree to recall myself from this abyss of idealism to the reality. At that time I was afraid of such processes. In later periods of life I have deplored, as we have all reason to do, a subjugation of an opposite character, and have rejoiced over the remembrances, as is expressed in the lines—

> Obstinate questionings
> Of sense and outward things,
> Fallings from us, vanishings; etc.

To that dreamlike vividness and splendor which invest objects of sight in childhood, everyone, I believe, if he would look back, could bear testimony, and I need not dwell upon it here: but having in the Poem regarded it as presumptive evidence of a prior state of existence, I think it right to protest against a conclusion, which has given pain to some good and pious persons, that I meant to inculcate such a belief. It is far too shadowy a notion to be recommended to faith, as more than an element in our instincts of immortality. But let us bear in mind that, though the idea is not advanced in revelation, there is nothing there to contradict it, and the fall of Man presents an analogy in its favor. Accordingly, a pre-existent state has entered into the popular creeds of many nations; and, among all persons acquainted with classic literature, is known as an ingredient in Platonic philosophy. Archimedes said that he could move the world if he had a point whereon to rest his machine. Who has not felt the same aspirations as regards the world of his own mind? Having to wield some of its elements when I was impelled to write this Poem on the 'Immortality of the Soul,' I took hold of the notion of pre-existence as having sufficient foundation in humanity for authorizing me to make for my purpose the best use of it I could as a Poet.

Plato, to whom Wordsworth refers, held the doctrine that the soul is immortal and exists separately from the body both before birth and after death. But while the *Ode* proposes that the soul only gradually loses "the vision splendid" after birth, Plato maintained the contrary: that the knowledge of the eternal Ideas, which the soul had acquired by direct acquaintance, is totally lost at the instant of birth and must be gradually "recollected" by philosophical discipline in the course of this life (*Phaedo* 73–77). Wordsworth's metaphorical use of the concept of preexistence in his poem resembles more closely the view of some neoplatonists that the glory of the unborn soul is gradually quenched by its descent into the darkness of matter.

When he dictated this long note to Isabella Fenwick, at the age of seventy-two or seventy-three, Wordsworth was troubled by objections that his apparent claim for the preexistence of the soul violated the Christian belief that the soul, although it survives after death, does not exist before the birth of an individual. His claim in the note is that he used preexistence not as a doctrine but only as a postulate enabling him to deal "as a poet" with a general human experience: that the passing of youth involves the loss of a freshness and radiance investing everything one sees. Coleridge's *Dejection: An Ode,* which he wrote (in its earliest version) after he had heard the first four stanzas of Wordsworth's poem, employs a similar figurative technique for a comparable, though more devastating, experience of loss.

The original published text of this poem (in 1807) had as its title only "Ode," and then as epigraph *"Paulo maiora canamus"* ("Let us sing of somewhat higher things") from Virgil's *Eclogue 4.*

Ode

Intimations of Immortality from Recollections of Early Childhood

> The Child is Father of the Man;
> And I could wish my days to be
> Bound each to each by natural piety.[1]

I

There was a time when meadow, grove, and stream,
The earth, and every common sight,
    To me did seem
    Apparelled in celestial light,
5 The glory and the freshness of a dream.
It is not now as it hath been of yore;—
    Turn wheresoe'er I may,
    By night or day,
The things which I have seen I now can see no more.

2

10   The Rainbow comes and goes,
    And lovely is the Rose,
    The Moon doth with delight
Look round her when the heavens are bare,
    Waters on a starry night
15   Are beautiful and fair;
    The sunshine is a glorious birth;
    But yet I know, where'er I go,
That there hath past away a glory from the earth.

3

Now, while the birds thus sing a joyous song,
20   And while the young lambs bound
    As to the tabor's[2] sound,

---

1. The concluding lines of Wordsworth's *My heart leaps up.*

2. A small drum often used to beat time for dancing.

To me alone there came a thought of grief:
A timely utterance[3] gave that thought relief,
    And I again am strong:
25 The cataracts blow their trumpets from the steep;
No more shall grief of mine the season wrong;
I hear the Echoes through the mountains throng,
The Winds come to me from the fields of sleep,[4]
    And all the earth is gay;
30   Land and sea
    Give themselves up to jollity,
        And with the heart of May
    Doth every Beast keep holiday;—
        Thou Child of Joy,
35 Shout round me, let me hear thy shouts, thou happy
    Shepherd-boy!

4

˅ Ye blessed Creatures, I have heard the call
    Ye to each other make; I see
The heavens laugh with you in your jubilee;
    My heart is at your festival,
40   My head hath its coronal,[5]
˅ The fulness of your bliss, I feel—I feel it all.
    Oh evil day! if I were sullen
    While Earth herself is adorning,
        This sweet May-morning,
45   And the Children are culling
        On every side,
    In a thousand valleys far and wide,
    Fresh flowers; while the sun shines warm,
And the Babe leaps up on his Mother's arm:—
50   I hear, I hear, with joy I hear!
    —But there's a Tree, of many, one,
A single Field which I have looked upon,
Both of them speak of something that is gone:
        The Pansy at my feet
55   Doth the same tale repeat:
Whither is fled the visionary gleam?
Where is it now, the glory and the dream?

5

Our birth is but a sleep and a forgetting:
The Soul that rises with us, our life's Star,[6]
60   Hath had elsewhere its setting,
        And cometh from afar:
    Not in entire forgetfulness,
    And not in utter nakedness,

3. Perhaps *My heart leaps up*, perhaps *Resolution and Independence,* perhaps not a poem at all.
4. Of the many suggested interpretations, the simplest is "from the fields where they were sleeping." Wordsworth often associated a rising wind with the revival of spirit and of poetic inspiration (see, e.g., the opening passage of *The Prelude*, p. 305).
5. Circlet of wildflowers, with which the shepherd boys trimmed their hats in May.
6. The sun, as metaphor for the soul.

|But trailing clouds of glory do we come
65   From God, who is our home:
Heaven lies about us in our infancy!
Shades of the prison-house begin to close
      Upon the growing Boy,
But He beholds the light, and whence it flows,
70   He sees it in his joy;
The Youth, who daily farther from the east
      Must travel, still is Nature's Priest,
      And by the vision splendid
      Is on his way attended;
75 At length the Man perceives it die away,
And fade into the light of common day.

6

Earth fills her lap with pleasures of her own;
Yearnings she hath in her own natural kind,
And, even with something of a Mother's mind,
80   And no unworthy aim,
      The homely[7] Nurse doth all she can
To make her Foster-child, her Inmate Man,
      Forget the glories he hath known,
And that imperial palace whence he came.

7

85 Behold the Child among his new-born blisses,
A six years' Darling of a pigmy size!
See, where 'mid work of his own hand he lies,
Fretted[8] by sallies of his mother's kisses,
With light upon him from his father's eyes!
90 See, at his feet, some little plan or chart,
Some fragment from his dream of human life,
Shaped by himself with newly-learnèd art;
      A wedding or a festival,
      A mourning or a funeral;
95   And this hath now his heart,
      And unto this he frames his song:
      Then will he fit his tongue
To dialogues of business, love, or strife;
      But it will not be long
100   Ere this be thrown aside,
      And with new joy and pride
The little Actor cons another part;
Filling from time to time his "humorous stage"[9]
With all the Persons, down to palsied Age,
105 That Life brings with her in her equipage;
      As if his whole vocation
      Were endless imitation.

7. In the old sense: simple and friendly.
8. Irritated; or possibly in the old sense: checkered over.
9. From a sonnet by the Elizabethan poet Samuel Daniel. In Daniel's age *humorous* meant "capricious" and also referred to the various characters and temperaments ("humors") represented in drama.

8

Thou, whose exterior semblance doth belie
    Thy Soul's immensity;
110 Thou best Philosopher, who yet dost keep
Thy heritage, thou Eye among the blind,
That, deaf and silent, read'st the eternal deep,
Haunted for ever by the eternal mind,—
    Mighty Prophet! Seer blest!
115   On whom those truths do rest,
Which we are toiling all our lives to find,
In darkness lost, the darkness of the grave;
Thou, over whom thy Immortality
Broods like the Day, a Master o'er a Slave,
120 A Presence which is not to be put by;
Thou little Child, yet glorious in the might
Of heaven-born freedom on thy being's height,
Why with such earnest pains dost thou provoke
The years to bring the inevitable yoke,
125 Thus blindly with thy blessedness at strife?
Full soon thy Soul shall have her earthly freight,
And custom lie upon thee with a weight,
Heavy as frost, and deep almost as life!

9

    O joy! that in our embers
130   Is something that doth live,
    That nature yet remembers
    What was so fugitive!
The thought of our past years in me doth breed
Perpetual benediction: not indeed
135 For that which is most worthy to be blest;
Delight and liberty, the simple creed
Of Childhood, whether busy or at rest,
With new-fledged hope still fluttering in his breast:—
    Not for these I raise
140   The song of thanks and praise;
    But for those obstinate questionings
    Of sense and outward things,
    Fallings from us, vanishings;
    Blank misgivings of a Creature
145 Moving about in worlds not realised,[1]
High instincts before which our mortal Nature
Did tremble like a guilty Thing surprised:
    But for those first affections,
    Those shadowy recollections,
150   Which, be they what they may,
Are yet the fountain light of all our day,
Are yet a master light of all our seeing;
    Uphold us, cherish, and have power to make
Our noisy years seem moments in the being

---

1. Not seeming real (see Wordsworth's comment in the headnote on p. 286).

155 Of the eternal Silence: truths that wake,
   To perish never;
 Which neither listlessness, nor mad endeavour,
   Nor Man nor Boy,
 Nor all that is at enmity with joy,
160 Can utterly abolish or destroy!
  Hence in a season of calm weather
   Though inland far we be,
 Our Souls have sight of that immortal sea
  Which brought us hither,
165 Can in a moment travel thither,
 And see the Children sport upon the shore,
 And hear the mighty waters rolling evermore.

      10
 Then sing, ye Birds, sing, sing a joyous song!
  And let the young Lambs bound
170 As to the tabor's sound!
 We in thought will join your throng,
  Ye that pipe and ye that play,
  Ye that through your hearts to-day
  Feel the gladness of the May!
175 What though the radiance which was once so bright
 Be now for ever taken from my sight,
  Though nothing can bring back the hour
 Of splendour in the grass, of glory in the flower;
  We will grieve not, rather find
180 Strength in what remains behind;
  In the primal sympathy
  Which having been must ever be;
  In the soothing thoughts that spring
  Out of human suffering;
185 In the faith that looks through death,
 In years that bring the philosophic mind.

      11
 And O, ye Fountains, Meadows, Hills, and Groves,
 Forebode not any severing of our loves!
 Yet in my heart of hearts I feel your might;
190 I only have relinquished one delight
 To live beneath your more habitual sway.
 I love the Brooks which down their channels fret,
 Even more than when I tripped lightly as they;
 The innocent brightness of a new-born Day
195   Is lovely yet;
 The Clouds that gather round the setting sun
 Do take a sober colouring from an eye
 That hath kept watch o'er man's mortality;
 Another race hath been, and other palms are won.[2]

2. In Greece foot races were often run for the prize of a branch or wreath of palm. Wordsworth's line echoes Paul, 1 Corinthians 9.24, who uses such races as a metaphor for life: "Know ye not that they which run in a race run all, but one receiveth the prize?"

200 Thanks to the human heart by which we live,
Thanks to its tenderness, its joys, and fears,
To me the meanest flower that blows can give
Thoughts that do often lie too deep for tears.

1802–04   1807

Ode to Duty[1]

Jam non consilio bonus, sed more eò perductus, ut non tantum rectè
facere possim, sed nisi rectè facere non possim.[2]

Stern Daughter of the Voice of God![3]
O Duty! if that name thou love
Who art a light to guide, a rod
To check the erring, and reprove;
5   Thou, who art victory and law
When empty terrors overawe;
From vain temptations dost set free;
And calm'st the weary strife of frail humanity!

There are who ask not if thine eye
10 Be on them; who, in love and truth,
Where no misgiving is, rely
Upon the genial sense[4] of youth:
Glad Hearts! without reproach or blot;
Who do thy work, and know it not:
15 Oh! if through confidence misplaced
They fail, thy saving arms, dread Power! around them cast.

Serene will be our days and bright,
And happy will our nature be,
When love is an unerring light,
20 And joy its own security.
And they a blissful course may hold
Even now, who, not unwisely bold,
Live in the spirit of this creed;
Yet seek thy firm support, according to their need.

1. "This Ode . . . is on the model of Gray's *Ode to Adversity* which is copied from Horace's *Ode to Fortune*. Many and many a time have I been twitted by my wife and sister for having forgotten this dedication of myself to the stern lawgiver" [Wordsworth's note].

In this poem, a striking departure from his earlier forms and ideas, Wordsworth abandons the descriptive-meditative pattern of his *Tintern Abbey* and *Ode: Intimations of Immortality* and reverts to the standard 18th-century form of an ode addressed to a personified abstraction. The poem also represents Wordsworth's reversion from his youthful reliance on natural impulse to a more orthodox ethical and religious tradition. It makes no reference to that "Nature" which earlier had

constituted for Wordsworth "both law and impulse" and, in *Tintern Abbey*, had been called "The guide, the guardian of my heart, and soul / Of all my moral being" (lines 110–11).
2. Now I am not good by conscious intent, but have been so trained by habit that I not only can act rightly but am unable to act other than rightly (Latin). Added in 1837, this epigraph is an adaptation from *Moral Epistles* 120.10 by Seneca (4 B.C.E.–65 C.E.), Stoic philosopher and writer of tragedies.
3. Cf. *Paradise Lost* 9.652–54: "God so commanded, and left that Command / Sole Daughter of his voice; the rest, we live / Law to ourselves, our Reason is our Law."
4. Innate vitality.

25   I, loving freedom, and untried;
      No sport of every random gust,
      Yet being to myself a guide,
      Too blindly have reposed my trust:
      And oft, when in my heart was heard
30   Thy timely mandate, I deferred
      The task, in smoother walks to stray;
      But thee I now would serve more strictly, if I may.

      Through no disturbance of my soul,
      Or strong compunction[5] in me wrought,
35   I supplicate for thy control;
      But in the quietness of thought:
      Me this unchartered freedom tires;
      I feel the weight of chance-desires:
      My hopes no more must change their name,
40   I long for a repose that ever is the same.

      Stern Lawgiver! yet thou dost wear
      The Godhead's most benignant grace;
      Nor know we any thing so fair
      As is the smile upon thy face:
45   Flowers laugh before thee on their beds
      And fragrance in thy footing treads;
      Thou dost preserve the stars from wrong;
      And the most ancient heavens, through Thee, are fresh and strong.

      To humbler functions, awful Power!
50   I call thee: I myself commend
      Unto thy guidance from this hour;
      Oh, let my weakness have an end!
      Give unto me, made lowly wise,[6]
      The spirit of self-sacrifice;
55   The confidence of reason give;
      And in the light of truth thy Bondman let me live!

1804   1807

The Solitary Reaper[1]

      Behold her, single in the field,
      Yon solitary Highland Lass!
      Reaping and singing by herself;
      Stop here, or gently pass!

5. In the older sense: sting of conscience, or remorse.
6. Another echo from Milton, whose Christian-humanist ethic pervades this ode. The angel Raphael had advised Adam (*Paradise Lost* 8.173–74), "Be lowly wise: / Think only what concerns thee and thy being."
1. One of the rare poems not based on Wordsworth's own experience. The poet tells us that it

was suggested by a passage in Thomas Wilkinson's *Tours to the British Mountains* (1824), which he had seen in manuscript: "Passed a female who was reaping alone: she sung in Erse [the Gaelic language of Scotland] as she bended over her sickle; the sweetest human voice I ever heard: her strains were tenderly melancholy, and felt delicious, long after they were heard no more."

5   Alone she cuts and binds the grain,
And sings a melancholy strain;
O listen! for the Vale profound
Is overflowing with the sound.

No Nightingale did ever chaunt
10   More welcome notes to weary bands
Of travellers in some shady haunt,
Among Arabian sands:
A voice so thrilling ne'er was heard
In spring-time from the Cuckoo-bird,
15   Breaking the silence of the seas
Among the farthest Hebrides.

Will no one tell me what she sings?[2]—
Perhaps the plaintive numbers flow
For old, unhappy, far-off things,
20   And battles long ago:
Or is it some more humble lay,
Familiar matter of to-day?
Some natural sorrow, loss, or pain,
That has been, and may be again?

25   Whate'er the theme, the Maiden sang
As if her song could have no ending;
I saw her singing at her work,
And o'er the sickle bending;—
I listened, motionless and still;
30   And, as I mounted up the hill,
The music in my heart I bore,
Long after it was heard no more.

Nov. 5, 1805   1807

Elegiac Stanzas

*Suggested by a Picture of Peele Castle, in a Storm,
Painted by Sir George Beaumont*[1]

I was thy neighbour once, thou rugged Pile!
Four summer weeks I dwelt in sight of thee:
I saw thee every day; and all the while
Thy Form was sleeping on a glassy sea.

5   So pure the sky, so quiet was the air!
So like, so very like, was day to day!

2. The poet does not understand Erse, the language in which she sings.
1. A wealthy landscape painter who was Wordsworth's patron and close friend. Peele Castle is on an island opposite Rampside, Lancashire, where Wordsworth had spent a month in 1794, twelve years before he saw Beaumont's painting. The poem has been interpreted as an expression of Wordsworth's loss of faith in nature. It should be noted, however, that the focus of the poem is not on an altered view of nature but on an altered knowledge of human life and on the moral values necessary to manage the inevitability of loss and suffering.

Whene'er I looked, thy Image still was there;
It trembled, but it never passed away.

How perfect was the calm! it seemed no sleep;
10 No mood, which season takes away, or brings:
I could have fancied that the mighty Deep
Was even the gentlest of all gentle Things.

Ah! THEN, if mine had been the Painter's hand,
To express what then I saw; and add the gleam,
15 The light that never was, on sea or land,
The consecration, and the Poet's dream;

I would have planted thee, thou hoary Pile
Amid a world how different from this!
Beside a sea that could not cease to smile;
20 On tranquil land, beneath a sky of bliss.

Thou shouldst have seemed a treasure-house divine
Of peaceful years; a chronicle of heaven;—
Of all the sunbeams that did ever shine
The very sweetest had to thee been given.

25 A Picture had it been of lasting ease,
Elysian² quiet, without toil or strife;
No motion but the moving tide, a breeze,
Or merely silent Nature's breathing life.

Such, in the fond illusion of my heart,
30 Such Picture would I at that time have made:
And seen the soul of truth in every part,
A stedfast peace that might not be betrayed.

So once it would have been,—'tis so no more;
I have submitted to a new control:
35 A power is gone, which nothing can restore;
A deep distress hath humanised my Soul.³

Not for a moment could I now behold
A smiling sea, and be what I have been:
The feeling of my loss will ne'er be old;
40 This, which I know, I speak with mind serene.

Then, Beaumont, Friend! who would have been the Friend,
If he had lived, of Him whom I deplore,°   mourn
This work of thine I blame not, but commend;
This sea in anger, and that dismal shore.

2. Referring to Elysium, in classical mythology the peaceful place where those favored by the gods dwelled after death.

3. Captain John Wordsworth, William's brother, had been drowned in a shipwreck on February 5, 1805. He is referred to in lines 41–42.

45   O 'tis a passionate Work!—yet wise and well,
     Well chosen is the spirit that is here;
     That Hulk which labours in the deadly swell,
     This rueful sky, this pageantry of fear!

     And this huge Castle, standing here sublime,
50   I love to see the look with which it braves,
     Cased in the unfeeling armour of old time,
     The lightning, the fierce wind, and trampling waves.

     Farewell, farewell the heart that lives alone,
     Housed in a dream, at distance from the Kind!°   *humankind*
55   Such happiness, wherever it be known,
     Is to be pitied; for 'tis surely blind.

     But welcome fortitude, and patient cheer,
     And frequent sights of what is to be borne!
     Such sights, or worse, as are before me here.—
60   Not without hope we suffer and we mourn.

Summer 1806   1807

SONNETS

Composed upon Westminster Bridge, September 3, 1802[1]

     Earth has not any thing to show more fair:
     Dull would he be of soul who could pass by
     A sight so touching in its majesty:
     This City now doth, like a garment, wear
5   The beauty of the morning; silent, bare,
     Ships, towers, domes, theatres, and temples lie
     Open unto the fields, and to the sky;
     All bright and glittering in the smokeless air.
     Never did sun more beautifully steep
10   In his first splendour, valley, rock, or hill;
     Ne'er saw I, never felt, a calm so deep!
     The river glideth at his own sweet will:
     Dear God! the very houses seem asleep;
     And all that mighty heart is lying still!

1802   1807

---

1. The date of this experience was not September 3, but July 31, 1802. Its occasion was a trip to France (see Dorothy Wordsworth's *Grasmere Journals,* July 1802, p. 395). The conflict of feelings attending Wordsworth's brief return to France, where he had once been a revolutionist and the lover of Annette Vallon, evoked a number of personal and political sonnets, among them the two that follow.

It is a beauteous evening

It is a beauteous evening, calm and free,
The holy time is quiet as a Nun
Breathless with adoration; the broad sun
Is sinking down in its tranquillity;
5   The gentleness of heaven broods o'er the Sea:
Listen! the mighty Being is awake,
And doth with his eternal motion make
A sound like thunder—everlastingly.
Dear Child! dear Girl! that walkest with me here,[2]
10   If thou appear untouched by solemn thought,
Thy nature is not therefore less divine:
Thou liest in Abraham's bosom[3] all the year;
And worshipp'st at the Temple's inner shrine,
God being with thee when we know it not.

Aug. 1802   1807

London, 1802[4]

Milton! thou should'st be living at this hour:
England hath need of thee: she is a fen
Of stagnant waters: altar, sword, and pen,
Fireside, the heroic wealth of hall and bower,
5   Have forfeited their ancient English dower
Of inward happiness. We are selfish men;
Oh! raise us up, return to us again;
And give us manners, virtue, freedom, power.
Thy soul was like a Star, and dwelt apart:
10   Thou hadst a voice whose sound was like the sea:
Pure as the naked heavens, majestic, free,
So didst thou travel on life's common way,
In cheerful godliness; and yet thy heart
The lowliest duties on herself did lay.

Sept. 1802   1807

The world is too much with us

The world is too much with us; late and soon,
Getting and spending, we lay waste our powers:
Little we see in Nature that is ours;

---

2. The girl walking with Wordsworth is Caroline, his daughter by Annette Vallon. For the event described, see Dorothy Wordsworth's *Grasmere Journals*, July 1802 (p. 395).
3. Where the souls destined for heaven rest after death. Luke 16.22: "And it came to pass, that the beggar died, and was carried by the angels into Abraham's bosom."

4. One of a series "written immediately after my return from France to London, when I could not but be struck, as here described, with the vanity and parade of our own country . . . as contrasted with the quiet, and I may say the desolation, that the revolution had produced in France" [Wordsworth's note].

We have given our hearts away, a sordid boon![5]
5   This Sea that bares her bosom to the moon;
The winds that will be howling at all hours,
And are up-gathered now like sleeping flowers;
For this, for every thing, we are out of tune;
It moves us not.—Great God! I'd rather be
10 A Pagan suckled in a creed outworn;
So might I, standing on this pleasant lea,
Have glimpses that would make me less forlorn;
Have sight of Proteus rising from the sea;
Or hear old Triton[6] blow his wreathèd horn.

1802–04   1807

Surprised by joy[7]

Surprised by joy—impatient as the Wind
I turned to share the transport—Oh! with whom
But Thee, deep buried in the silent tomb,
That spot which no vicissitude can find?
5   Love, faithful love, recalled thee to my mind—
But how could I forget thee? Through what power,
Even for the least division of an hour,
Have I been so beguiled as to be blind
To my most grievous loss!—That thought's return
10 Was the worst pang that sorrow ever bore,
Save one, one only, when I stood forlorn,
Knowing my heart's best treasure was no more;
That neither present time, nor years unborn
Could to my sight that heavenly face restore.

1813–14   1815

Mutability[8]

From low to high doth dissolution climb,
And sink from high to low, along a scale
Of awful notes, whose concord shall not fail;
A musical but melancholy chime,
5   Which they can hear who meddle not with crime,
Nor avarice, nor over-anxious care.
Truth fails not; but her outward forms that bear
The longest date do melt like frosty rime,

5. Gift. It is the act of giving the heart away that is sordid.
6. A sea deity, usually represented as blowing on a conch shell. Proteus was an old man of the sea who (in the *Odyssey*) could assume a variety of shapes. The description of Proteus echoes *Paradise Lost* 3.603–04, and that of Triton echoes Spenser's *Colin Clouts Come Home Againe*, lines 244–45. Milton and Spenser are the two English poets with

whom Wordsworth most closely allied himself.
7. This was in fact suggested by my daughter Catherine, long after her death [Wordsworth's note]. Catherine Wordsworth died June 4, 1812, at the age of four.
8. This sonnet was included in an otherwise rather pedestrian sequence, *Ecclesiastical Sonnets*, dealing with the history and ceremonies of the Church of England.

That in the morning whitened hill and plain
10 And is no more; drop like the tower sublime
Of yesterday, which royally did wear
His crown of weeds, but could not even sustain
Some casual shout that broke the silent air,
Or the unimaginable touch of Time.

1821   1822

Steamboats, Viaducts, and Railways[9]

Motions and Means, on land and sea at war
With old poetic feeling, not for this,
Shall ye, by Poets even, be judged amiss!
Nor shall your presence, howsoe'er it mar
5 The loveliness of Nature, prove a bar
To the Mind's gaining that prophetic sense
Of future change, that point of vision, whence
May be discovered what in soul ye are.
In spite of all that beauty may disown
10 In your harsh features, Nature doth embrace
Her lawful offspring in Man's art; and Time,
Pleased with your triumphs o'er his brother Space,
Accepts from your bold hands the proffered crown
Of hope, and smiles on you with cheer sublime.

1833   1835

Extempore Effusion upon the Death of James Hogg[1]

When first, descending from the moorlands,
I saw the Stream of Yarrow[2] glide
Along a bare and open valley,
The Ettrick Shepherd[3] was my guide.

5 When last along its banks I wandered,
Through groves that had begun to shed
Their golden leaves upon the pathways,
My steps the Border-minstrel[4] led.

9. In late middle age Wordsworth demonstrates, as he had predicted in the Preface to *Lyrical Ballads*, that the poet will assimilate to his subject matter the "material revolution" produced by science. Unlike most poets, furthermore, he boldly accepts as evidences of human progress even the unlovely encroachments of technology on his beloved natural scene.
1. Wordsworth's niece relates how he was deeply moved by finding unexpectedly in a newspaper an account of the death of the poet James Hogg. "Half an hour afterwards he came into the room where the ladies were sitting and asked Miss Hutchinson [his sister-in-law] to write down some lines which he had just composed." All the poets named here, several of Wordsworth's closest friends among them, had died between 1832 and 1835.
2. A river in the southeast of Scotland.
3. I.e., Hogg, who was born in Ettrick Forest and worked as a shepherd. He was discovered as a writer by Sir Walter Scott and became well known as a poet, essayist, and editor.
4. Sir Walter Scott.

The mighty Minstrel breathes no longer,
10 'Mid mouldering ruins low he lies;
And death upon the braes[5] of Yarrow,
Has closed the Shepherd-poet's eyes:

Nor has the rolling year twice measured,
From sign to sign, its stedfast course,
15 Since every mortal power of Coleridge
Was frozen at its marvellous source;

The rapt One, of the godlike forehead,
The heaven-eyed creature sleeps in earth:
And Lamb, the frolic and the gentle,
20 Has vanished from his lonely hearth.

Like clouds that rake the mountain-summits,
Or waves that own no curbing hand,
How fast has brother followed brother,
From sunshine to the sunless land!

25 Yet I, whose lids from infant slumber
Were earlier raised, remain to hear
A timid voice, that asks in whispers,
"Who next will drop and disappear?"

Our haughty life is crowned with darkness,
30 Like London with its own black wreath,
On which with thee, O Crabbe![6] forth-looking,
I gazed from Hampstead's breezy heath.

As if but yesterday departed,
Thou too art gone before; but why,
35 O'er ripe fruit, seasonably gathered,
Should frail survivors heave a sigh?

Mourn rather for that holy Spirit,
Sweet as the spring, as ocean deep;
For Her[7] who, ere her summer faded,
40 Has sunk into a breathless sleep.

No more of old romantic sorrows,
For slaughtered Youth or love-lorn Maid!
With sharper grief is Yarrow smitten,
And Ettrick mourns with her their Poet dead.

Nov. 21, 1835   1835

---

5. The sloping banks of a stream.
6. George Crabbe, the poet of rural and village life.

7. The poet Felicia Hemans, who died at forty-two.

Prospectus to *The Recluse*[1]

On Man, on Nature, and on Human Life,
Musing in solitude, I oft perceive
Fair trains of imagery before me rise,
Accompanied by feelings of delight
5   Pure, or with no unpleasing sadness mixed;
And I am conscious of affecting thoughts
And dear remembrances, whose presence soothes
Or elevates the Mind, intent to weigh
The good and evil of our mortal state.
10   —To these emotions, whencesoe'er they come,
Whether from breath of outward circumstance,
Or from the Soul—an impulse to herself—
I would give utterance in numerous verse.[2]
Of Truth, of Grandeur, Beauty, Love, and Hope,
15   And melancholy Fear subdued by Faith;
Of blessed consolations in distress;
Of moral strength, and intellectual Power;
Of joy in widest commonalty spread;
Of the individual Mind that keeps her own
20   Inviolate retirement, subject there
To Conscience only, and the law supreme
Of that Intelligence which governs all—
I sing:—"fit audience let me find though few!"[3]

So prayed, more gaining than he asked, the Bard—
25   In holiest mood. Urania,[4] I shall need
Thy guidance, or a greater Muse, if such
Descend to earth or dwell in highest heaven!
For I must tread on shadowy ground, must sink
Deep—and, aloft ascending, breathe in worlds
30   To which the heaven of heavens[5] is but a veil.
All strength—all terror, single or in bands,

1. Through most of his poetic life Wordsworth labored intermittently at a long philosophic poem called *The Recluse*, which he intended to be his masterwork. As he described this project in the Preface to *The Excursion* (1814), it was to consist of an autobiographical introduction (the poem now called *The Prelude*) and three long parts; of these three he completed only book 1 of part 1 (*Home at Grasmere*) and part 2, called *The Excursion*. In the Preface to *The Excursion*, Wordsworth printed this long extract (the concluding section of *Home at Grasmere*) to serve "as a kind of *Prospectus* of the design and scope of the whole Poem"—i.e., of the entire *Recluse*.

The first version of this Prospectus may have been drafted as early as 1798 or 1800. In language resonant with echoes of *Paradise Lost*, Wordsworth announces an undertaking that he conceives to be no less inspired and sublime than Milton's. In it he will move higher than Milton's heaven and deeper than Milton's hell, past scenes evoking greater fear than hell and greater awe than Jehovah; but without ever leaving "the Mind of Man— / My haunt,

and the main region of my song" (lines 40–41). And his "high argument" is that Paradise can be regained; not, however, as in Revelation 21 and in Milton, by the marriage between the New Jerusalem and Christ the Lamb, but by a marriage between the "intellect of Man" and "this goodly universe," and the resulting new "creation . . . which they with blended might / Accomplish" (lines 52–71). In no other passage does Wordsworth reveal so clearly the extent to which he assimilates in his poetry the biblical scheme of Milton's epic—assigning, however, the active role, from creation to redemption, to the human faculties, in their interaction with the external universe.

2. Harmonious verse; an echo of *Paradise Lost* 5.150. The inspiring "breath of outward circumstance" (line 11) parallels the "correspondent breeze" in the opening lines of *The Prelude*.

3. *Paradise Lost* 7.31.

4. The Muse whom Milton had invoked in *Paradise Lost* 7.1–39.

5. In *Paradise Lost* the dwelling place, beyond the visible heaven, of God and His angels.

That ever was put forth in personal form—
Jehovah—with his thunder, and the choir
Of shouting Angels, and the empyreal thrones[6]—
35 I pass them unalarmed. Not Chaos, not
The darkest pit of lowest Erebus,[7]
Nor aught of blinder vacancy, scooped out
By help of dreams—can breed such fear and awe
As fall upon us often when we look
40 Into our Minds, into the Mind of Man—
My haunt, and the main region of my song.
—Beauty—a living Presence of the earth,
Surpassing the most fair ideal Forms
Which craft of delicate Spirits hath composed
45 From earth's materials—waits upon my steps;
Pitches her tents before me as I move,
An hourly neighbour. Paradise, and groves
Elysian,[8] Fortunate Fields—like those of old
Sought in the Atlantic Main—why should they be
50 A history only of departed things,
Or a mere fiction of what never was?
For the discerning intellect of Man,
When wedded to this goodly universe
In love and holy passion, shall find these
55 A simple produce of the common day.
—I, long before the blissful hour arrives,
Would chant, in lonely peace, the spousal[9] verse
Of this great consummation:—and, by words
Which speak of nothing more than what we are,
60 Would I arouse the sensual from their sleep
Of Death, and win the vacant and the vain
To noble raptures; while my voice proclaims
How exquisitely the individual Mind
(And the progressive powers perhaps no less
65 Of the whole species) to the external World
Is fitted:—and how exquisitely, too—
Theme this but little heard of among men—
The external World is fitted to the Mind;
And the creation (by no lower name
70 Can it be called) which they with blended might
Accomplish:—this is our high argument.[1]
—Such grateful haunts foregoing, if I oft
Must turn elsewhere—to travel near the tribes
And fellowships of men, and see ill sights
75 Of madding passions mutually inflamed;
Must hear Humanity in fields and groves

---

6. Cf. *Paradise Lost* 2.430: "O progeny of Heaven, empyreal thrones!"
7. In classical myth, a dark region of the underworld; often used as a name for hell by Christian writers.
8. Elysium, in Greek myth, was the place where mortals favored by the gods live a happy life after death. It was sometimes identified with the

"Islands of the Blessed," reputed to be located far out in the western sea—hence "sought in the Atlantic Main" (line 49). See Horace, *Epodes* 16.
9. Marital. Hence a "spousal verse" is an epithalamion—a poem written to celebrate a marriage.
1. Theme, as in *Paradise Lost* 1.24: "the height of this great argument."

Pipe solitary anguish; or must hang
Brooding above the fierce confederate storm
Of sorrow, barricadoed[2] evermore
80 Within the walls of cities—may these sounds
Have their authentic comment; that even these
Hearing, I be not downcast or forlorn!—
Descend, prophetic Spirit! that inspir'st
The human Soul of universal earth,
85 Dreaming on things to come;[3] and dost possess
A metropolitan temple[4] in the hearts
Of mighty Poets; upon me bestow
A gift of genuine insight; that my Song
With star-like virtue in its place may shine,
90 Shedding benignant influence, and secure,
Itself, from all malevolent effect
Of those mutations that extend their sway
Throughout the nether sphere![5]—And if with this
I mix more lowly matter; with the thing
95 Contemplated, describe the Mind and Man
Contemplating; and who, and what he was—
The transitory Being that beheld
This Vision; when and where, and how he lived;[6]—
Be not this labour useless. If such theme
100 May sort with highest objects, then—dread Power!
Whose gracious favour is the primal source
Of all illumination—may my Life
Express the image of a better time,
More wise desires, and simpler manners;—nurse
105 My Heart in genuine freedom:—all pure thoughts
Be with me;—so shall thy unfailing love
Guide, and support, and cheer me to the end!

ca. 1798–1814   1814

The Prelude

The Prelude, now regarded as Wordsworth's crowning achievement, was unknown to the public at the time of his death in April 1850. When, three months later, it was published from manuscript by Wordsworth's literary executors, its title was given to it by the poet's wife. Wordsworth himself had referred to it variously as "the poem to Coleridge," "the poem on the growth of my own mind," and "the poem on my own poetical education."

For some seventy-five years this posthumous publication of 1850 was the only known text. Then in 1926 Ernest de Selincourt, working from manuscripts, printed an earlier version of the poem that Wordsworth had completed in 1805. Since that time other scholars have established the existence of a still earlier and much shorter

---

2. Barricaded, as in *Paradise Lost* 8.241: "Fast we found, fast shut / The dismal gates, and barricadoed strong."
3. Cf. Shakespeare's *Sonnet 107*: "the prophetic soul / Of the wide world dreaming on things to come."
4. The primary church of a religion.

5. In the Ptolemaic world picture, the spheres of the heavenly bodies were immutable, and only the earth (the "nether sphere," or region below the sphere of the moon) was subject to change. Cf. *Paradise Lost* 7.375 and 10.656–64.
6. Wordsworth thus justifies *The Prelude* and the autobiographical sections of *The Recluse*.

version of *The Prelude,* in two parts, that Wordsworth had composed in 1798–99. The following seems to have been the process of composition that produced the three principal versions of the poem:

1. The *Two-Part Prelude* of 1799. Wordsworth originally planned, early in 1798, to include an account of his own development as a poet in his projected but never-completed philosophical poem *The Recluse* (see the Prospectus to *The Recluse,* n. 1, p. 301). While living in Germany during the autumn and winter of 1798–99, he composed a number of passages about his early experiences with nature. What had been intended to be part of *The Recluse,* however, quickly evolved into an independent autobiographical poem, and by late 1799, when Wordsworth settled with his sister, Dorothy, at Grasmere, he had written a poem in two parts, 978 lines in length, which takes his life from infancy, through his years at Hawkshead School, to the age of seventeen. This poem corresponds, by and large, to the contents of books 1 and 2 of the later versions of *The Prelude.*

2. The 1805 *Prelude.* Late in 1801 Wordsworth began to expand the poem on his poetic life, and in 1804 he set to work intensively on the project. His initial plan was to write it in five books, but he soon decided to enlarge it to incorporate an account of his experiences in France and of his mental crisis after the failure of his hopes in the French Revolution, and to end the poem with his settlement at Grasmere and his taking up the great task of *The Recluse.* He completed the poem, in thirteen books, in May 1805. This is the version that Wordsworth read to Coleridge after the latter's return from Malta (see Coleridge's *To William Wordsworth,* p. 464).

3. The 1850 *Prelude.* For the next thirty-five years Wordsworth tinkered with the text, polishing the style and qualifying some of its radical statements about the divine sufficiency of the human mind in its communion with nature; he did not, however, in any essential way alter its subject matter or overall design. *The Prelude* that was published in July 1850 is in fourteen books and was printed from a fair copy; it incorporated Wordsworth's latest revisions, which had been made in 1839, as well as some alterations introduced by his literary executors. The selections printed here— from W. J. B. Owen's Cornell Wordsworth volume, *The Fourteen-Book Prelude* (1985)—are from the manuscript of this final version. Our reasons for choosing this version are set forth in Jack Stillinger's "Textual Primitivism and the Editing of Words-worth," *Studies in Romanticism* 28 (1989): 3–28.

When Wordsworth enlarged the two-part *Prelude* of 1799, he not only made it a poem of epic length but also heightened the style and introduced various thematic parallels with earlier epics, especially *Paradise Lost.* (For a central example, see Wordsworth's version of Milton's enterprise to "justify the ways of God to men," in 14.162–70, p. 380, and 14.384–89, p. 382.) The expanded poem, however, is a personal history that turns on a mental crisis and recovery, and for such a narrative design the chief prototype is not the classical or Christian epic but the spiritual autobiography of crisis. St. Augustine's *Confessions* established this central Christian form late in the fourth century, and it has had an uninterrupted history in European literature ever since.

As in Augustine's *Confessions* and many later versions of spiritual autobiography, Wordsworth's persistent metaphor is that of life as a circular journey whose end (as T. S. Eliot put it in *Four Quartets,* his adaptation of the traditional form) is "to arrive where we started / And know the place for the first time" (*Little Gidding,* lines 241–42). Wordsworth's *Prelude* opens with a literal journey whose chosen goal (1.72, 106–07) is "a known Vale whither my feet should turn"—that is, the Vale of Grasmere. *The Prelude* narrates a number of later journeys, most notably the crossing of the Alps in book 6 and, at the beginning of the final book, the climactic ascent of Mount Snowdon. In the course of the poem, such literal journeys become the metaphoric vehicle for an interior, spiritual journey in the quest, within the poet's memory, and in the very process of composing his poem, for his lost early self and his proper spiritual home. At its end the poem, adverting to its beginning, leaves the poet at home in the Vale of Grasmere, ready finally to begin his great project *The Recluse* (14.302–11, 374–85).

Throughout *The Prelude*, Wordsworth formulates the course of his life in accordance with an intricate artistic pattern and narrates it in a deliberately traditional voice. Although its episodes are recognizable events in his experience, they are interpreted in retrospect, reordered in sequence, retold as primarily a transaction between mind and nature, and shaped into the inherited design of crisis and recovery, from which the protagonist emerges as a new self in a transformed world, confirmed in his vocation as a poet. And although the narrator is recognizably William Wordsworth, addressing the entire poem as a communication to his friend Coleridge, he adopts the prophetic persona, modeled on the poet-prophets of the Bible, which John Milton had adopted in narrating *Paradise Lost* (13.300–11). In this way Wordsworth, like his great English predecessor, assumes the authority to speak as a national poet whose function is to reconstitute the grounds of hope in a dark time of postrevolutionary reaction and despair. As Wordsworth describes it (2.433–42), he speaks out

> in these times of fear,
> This melancholy waste of hopes overthrown,
> . . . 'mid indifference and apathy
> And wicked exultation, when good men,
> On every side, fall off, we know not how,
> To selfishness, disguised in gentle names
> Of peace and quiet and domestic love
> . . . this time
> Of dereliction and dismay. . . .

FROM THE PRELUDE

OR

GROWTH OF A POET'S MIND

AN AUTOBIOGRAPHICAL POEM

Book First
Introduction, Childhood, and School-time

O there is blessing in this gentle breeze,
A visitant that, while he fans my cheek,
Doth seem half-conscious of the joy he brings
From the green fields, and from yon azure sky.
5   Whate'er his mission, the soft breeze can come
To none more grateful than to me; escaped
From the vast City,[1] where I long have pined
A discontented Sojourner—Now free,
Free as a bird to settle where I will.
10   What dwelling shall receive me? in what vale
Shall be my harbour? underneath what grove
Shall I take up my home? and what clear stream
Shall with its murmur lull me into rest?
The earth is all before me:[2] with a heart

1. London. Wordsworth uses this city as a type representing a place of spiritual bondage from which he has finally escaped.
2. One of many echoes from *Paradise Lost*, where the line is applied to Adam and Eve as, at the conclusion of the poem, they begin their new life after being expelled from Eden: "The world was all before them" (12.646).

15 Joyous, nor scared at its own liberty,
    I look about; and should the chosen guide
    Be nothing better than a wandering cloud,
    I cannot miss my way. I breathe again;
    Trances of thought and mountings of the heart
20 Come fast upon me: it is shaken off,
    That burthen of my own unnatural self,
    The heavy weight of many a weary day
    Not mine, and such as were not made for me.
    Long months of peace (if such bold word accord
25 With any promises of human life),
    Long months of ease and undisturbed delight
    Are mine in prospect; whither shall I turn,
    By road or pathway, or through trackless field,
    Up hill or down, or shall some floating thing
30 Upon the River point me out my course?
    Dear Liberty! Yet what would it avail,
    But for a gift that consecrates the joy?
    For I, methought, while the sweet breath of heaven
    Was blowing on my body, felt, within,
35 A correspondent breeze, that gently moved
    With quickening virtue,[3] but is now become
    A tempest, a redundant° energy,   abundant
    Vexing its own creation. Thanks to both,
    And their congenial° powers that, while they join   kindred
40 In breaking up a long continued frost,
    Bring with them vernal promises, the hope
    Of active days urged on by flying hours;
    Days of sweet leisure taxed with patient thought
    Abstruse, nor wanting punctual service high,
45 Matins and vespers, of harmonious verse![4]
        Thus far, O Friend![5] did I, not used to make
    A present joy the matter of a Song,[6]
    Pour forth, that day, my soul in measured strains,
    That would not be forgotten, and are here
50 Recorded:—to the open fields I told
    A prophecy:—poetic numbers came
    Spontaneously, to clothe in priestly robe
    A renovated Spirit singled out,

3. Revivifying power. ("To quicken" is to give or restore life.)
4. I.e., verses equivalent to morning prayers (matins) and evening prayers (vespers). The opening passage (lines 1–45), which Wordsworth calls in book 7, line 4, a "glad preamble," replaces the traditional epic device, such as Milton had adopted in *Paradise Lost*, of an opening prayer to the Muse for inspiration. To be "inspired," in the literal sense, is to be breathed or blown into by a divinity (in Latin *spirare* means both "to breathe" and "to blow"). Wordsworth begins his poem with a "blessing" from an outer "breeze," which (lines 34–45) is called the "breath of heaven" and evokes in him a correspondent inner breeze that signalizes a springlike revival of his spirit after a wintry season, and also a burst of poetic power that he goes on to

equate (lines 50–54) with the utterances of biblical prophets when inspired by the Holy Spirit. The revivifying breeze and breath, at once material and spiritual, recurs later in *The Prelude* as a kind of leitmotif. It also serves as the radical metaphor of other Romantic poems such as Coleridge's *The Eolian Harp* and *Dejection: An Ode*, and Shelley's *Ode to the West Wind*.
5. Samuel Taylor Coleridge, to whom Wordsworth addresses the whole of the *Prelude*. For Coleridge's response, after the poem was read to him, see *To William Wordsworth* (p. 464).
6. In the Preface to *Lyrical Ballads* Wordsworth says that his poetry usually originates in "emotion recollected in tranquillity"; hence not, as in the preceding preamble, during the experience that it records.

Such hope was mine, for holy services:
55 My own voice cheered me, and, far more, the mind's
Internal echo of the imperfect sound;
To both I listened, drawing from them both
A chearful confidence in things to come.
    Content, and not unwilling now to give
60 A respite to this passion, I paced on
With brisk and eager steps; and came at length
To a green shady place where down I sate
Beneath a tree, slackening my thoughts by choice,
And settling into gentler happiness.
65 'Twas Autumn, and a clear and placid day,
With warmth, as much as needed, from a sun
Two hours declined towards the west, a day
With silver clouds, and sunshine on the grass,
And, in the sheltered and the sheltering grove,
70 A perfect stillness. Many were the thoughts
Encouraged and dismissed, till choice was made
Of a known Vale[7] whither my feet should turn,
Nor rest till they had reached the very door
Of the one Cottage which methought I saw.
75 No picture of mere memory ever looked
So fair; and while upon the fancied scene
I gazed with growing love, a higher power
Than Fancy gave assurance of some work
Of glory, there forthwith to be begun,
80 Perhaps too there performed.[8] Thus long I mused,
Nor e'er lost sight of what I mused upon,
Save where, amid the stately grove of Oaks,
Now here—now there—an acorn, from its cup
Dislodged, through sere leaves rustled, or at once
85 To the bare earth dropped with a startling sound.
    From that soft couch I rose not, till the sun
Had almost touched the horizon; casting then
A backward glance upon the curling cloud
Of city smoke, by distance ruralized,
90 Keen as a Truant or a Fugitive,
But as a Pilgrim resolute, I took,
Even with the chance equipment of that hour,
The road that pointed tow'rd the chosen Vale.
    It was a splendid evening: and my Soul
95 Once more made trial of her strength, nor lacked
Eolian visitations;[9] but the harp
Was soon defrauded, and the banded host
Of harmony dispersed in straggling sounds;
And lastly utter silence! "Be it so;

---

7. Grasmere, where Wordsworth settled with his sister, Dorothy, in December 1799. Wordsworth uses his walk to that "Vale" to symbolize a new stage in the journey of his life—a stage in which he returns to what he calls (in the title of the opening book of *The Recluse,* designed to follow *The Prelude*) "Home at Grasmere."

8. I.e., *The Recluse,* which Wordsworth planned to be his major poetic work.
9. Influences to which his soul responded as an Eolian harp responds to gusts of a breeze. For a description of this instrument, see Coleridge's *The Eolian Harp,* n. 1, p. 419.

100 Why think of any thing but present good?"
So, like a Home-bound Labourer, I pursued
My way, beneath the mellowing sun, that shed
Mild influence;[1] nor left in me one wish
Again to bend the sabbath of that time[2]
105 To a servile yoke. What need of many words?
A pleasant loitering journey, through three days
Continued, brought me to my hermitage.
I spare to tell of what ensued, the life
In common things,—the endless store of things
110 Rare, or at least so seeming, every day
Found all about me in one neighbourhood;
The self-congratulation,° and from morn   self-rejoicing
To night unbroken cheerfulness serene.
But speedily an earnest longing rose
115 To brace myself to some determined aim,
Reading or thinking; either to lay up
New stores, or rescue from decay the old
By timely interference: and therewith
Came hopes still higher, that with outward life
120 I might endue some airy phantasies
That had been floating loose about for years;
And to such Beings temperately deal forth
The many feelings that oppressed my heart.
That hope hath been discouraged; welcome light
125 Dawns from the East, but dawns—to disappear
And mock me with a sky that ripens not
Into a steady morning: if my mind,
Remembering the bold promise of the past,
Would gladly grapple with some noble theme,
130 Vain is her wish: where'er she turns, she finds
Impediments from day to day renewed.
      And now it would content me to yield up
Those lofty hopes awhile for present gifts
Of humbler industry. But, O dear Friend!
135 The Poet, gentle Creature as he is,
Hath, like the Lover, his unruly times,
His fits when he is neither sick nor well,
Though no distress be near him but his own
Unmanageable thoughts: his mind, best pleas'd
140 While she, as duteous as the Mother Dove,
Sits brooding,[3] lives not always to that end,
But, like the innocent Bird, hath goadings on
That drive her, as in trouble, through the groves:
With me is now such passion, to be blamed
145 No otherwise than as it lasts too long.
      When as becomes a Man who would prepare

---

1. An astrological term for the effect of stars on human life. *Paradise Lost* 7.374–75: "The Pleiades [a cluster of stars] before him danced / Shedding sweet influence."
2. That time of rest.

3. An echo of Milton's reference in *Paradise Lost* to the original act of creation in his invocation to the Holy Spirit: Thou "Dovelike satst brooding on the vast Abyss / And mad'st it pregnant" (1.21–22).

For such an arduous Work, I through myself
Make rigorous inquisition, the report
Is often chearing; for I neither seem
150 To lack that first great gift, the vital Soul,
Nor general Truths, which are themselves a sort
Of Elements and Agents, Under-powers,
Subordinate helpers of the living Mind:
Nor am I naked of external things,
155 Forms, images, nor numerous other aids
Of less regard, though won perhaps with toil,
And needful to build up a Poet's praise.
Time, place, and manners do I seek, and these
Are found in plenteous store, but no where such
160 As may be singled out with steady choice:
No little band of yet remembered names
Whom I in perfect confidence might hope
To summon back from lonesome banishment,
And make them dwellers in the hearts of men
165 Now living, or to live in future years.
Sometimes the ambitious Power of choice, mistaking
Proud spring-tide swellings for a regular sea,
Will settle on some British theme, some old
Romantic Tale by Milton left unsung:[4]
170 More often turning to some gentle place
Within the groves of Chivalry, I pipe
To Shepherd Swains, or seated, harp in hand,
Amid reposing knights by a River side
Or fountain, listen to the grave reports
175 Of dire enchantments faced, and overcome
By the strong mind, and Tales of warlike feats
Where spear encountered spear, and sword with sword
Fought, as if conscious of the blazonry
That the shield bore, so glorious was the strife;
180 Whence inspiration for a song that winds
Through ever changing scenes of votive quest,[5]
Wrongs to redress, harmonious tribute paid
To patient courage and unblemished truth,
To firm devotion, zeal unquenchable,
185 And Christian meekness hallowing faithful loves.[6]
Sometimes, more sternly moved, I would relate
How vanquished Mithridates northward passed,
And, hidden in the cloud of years, became
Odin, the Father of a Race by whom
190 Perished the Roman Empire;[7] how the friends
And followers of Sertorius, out of Spain

---

4. In *Paradise Lost* 9.24–41 Milton relates that, in seeking a subject for his epic poem, he rejected "fabled Knights" and medieval romance.
5. A quest undertaken to fulfill a vow.
6. An echo of the prefatory statement to Spenser's *Faerie Queene*, line 9: "Fierce warres and faithfull loves shall moralize my song."
7. Mithridates VI, king of Pontus, was defeated by the Roman Pompey in 66 B.C.E. In chap. 10 of his *Decline and Fall of the Roman Empire*, Edward Gibbon associates him with Odin, a chieftain of the Goths, who hoped to produce descendants who would wreak revenge on the conquering Romans. All the protagonists that Wordsworth considered for his poem were heroes in fights against tyranny.

Flying, found shelter in the Fortunate Isles;
And left their usages, their arts, and laws
To disappear by a slow gradual death;
195 To dwindle and to perish, one by one,
Starved in those narrow bounds: but not the soul
Of Liberty, which fifteen hundred years
Survived, and, when the European came
With skill and power that might not be withstood,
200 Did, like a pestilence, maintain its hold,
And wasted down by glorious death that Race
Of natural Heroes;[8]—or I would record
How, in tyrannic times, some high-souled Man,
Unnamed among the chronicles of Kings,
205 Suffered in silence for truth's sake: or tell
How that one Frenchman, through continued force
Of meditation on the inhuman deeds
Of those who conquered first the Indian isles,
Went, single in his ministry, across
210 The Ocean;—not to comfort the Oppressed,
But, like a thirsty wind, to roam about,
Withering the Oppressor:[9]—how Gustavus sought
Help at his need in Dalecarlia's mines:[1]
How Wallace[2] fought for Scotland, left the name
215 Of Wallace to be found, like a wild flower,
All over his dear Country, left the deeds
Of Wallace, like a family of Ghosts,
To people the steep rocks and river banks,
Her natural sanctuaries, with a local soul
220 Of independence and stern liberty.
Sometimes it suits me better to invent
A Tale from my own heart, more near akin
To my own passions, and habitual thoughts,
Some variegated Story, in the main
225 Lofty, but the unsubstantial Structure melts
Before the very sun that brightens it,
Mist into air dissolving! Then, a wish,
My last and favourite aspiration, mounts,
With yearning, tow'rds some philosophic Song
230 Of Truth[3] that cherishes our daily life;
With meditations passionate, from deep
Recesses in man's heart, immortal verse
Thoughtfully fitted to the Orphean lyre;[4]

8. Sertorius, a Roman general allied with Mithridates, fought off the armies of Pompey and others until he was assassinated in 72 B.C.E. There is a legend that after his death his followers, to escape Roman tyranny, fled from Spain to the Canary Islands (known in ancient times as "the Fortunate Isles," line 192), where their descendants flourished until subjugated and decimated by invading Spaniards late in the 15th century.
9. Dominique de Gourges, a French gentleman who went in 1568 to Florida to avenge the massacre of the French by the Spaniards there [foot-

note in *The Prelude* of 1850].
1. In the 16th century Gustavus I of Sweden mustered supporters in Dalecarlia, a mining district, to help free Sweden from the tyranny of Denmark.
2. William Wallace, Scottish national hero, fought against the English until captured and executed in 1305.
3. I.e., *The Recluse*.
4. The lyre of Orpheus. In Greek myth Orpheus was able to enchant not only human listeners but the natural world by his singing and playing.

But from this awful burthen I full soon
235 Take refuge, and beguile myself with trust
That mellower years will bring a riper mind
And clearer insight. Thus my days are passed
In contradiction; with no skill to part
Vague longing, haply bred by want of power,
240 From paramount impulse—not to be withstood;
A timorous capacity from prudence;
From circumspection, infinite delay.[5]
Humility and modest awe themselves
Betray me, serving often for a cloke
245 To a more subtile selfishness; that now
Locks every function up in blank° reserve,°   absolute / inaction
Now dupes me, trusting to an anxious eye
That with intrusive restlessness beats off
Simplicity, and self-presented truth.
250   Ah! better far than this, to stray about
Voluptuously,° through fields and rural walks,   luxuriously
And ask no record of the hours, resigned
To vacant musing, unreproved neglect
Of all things, and deliberate holiday:
255 Far better never to have heard the name
Of zeal and just ambition, than to live
Baffled and plagued by a mind that every hour
Turns recreant to her task, takes heart again,
Then feels immediately some hollow thought
260 Hang like an interdict° upon her hopes.   prohibition
This is my lot; for either still I find
Some imperfection in the chosen theme;
Or see of absolute accomplishment
Much wanting, so much wanting, in myself
265 That I recoil and droop, and seek repose
In listlessness from vain perplexity;
Unprofitably travelling toward the grave,
Like a false Steward who hath much received,
And renders nothing back.[6]
                         Was it for this[7]
270 That one, the fairest of all rivers, loved
To blend his murmurs with my Nurse's song;
And, from his alder shades and rocky falls,
And from his fords and shallows, sent a voice
That flowed along my dreams? For this didst Thou,
275 O Derwent! winding among grassy holms[8]
Where I was looking on, a Babe in arms,
Make ceaseless music, that composed my thoughts
To more than infant softness, giving me,
Amid the fretful dwellings of mankind,

5. The syntax is complex and inverted; in outline, the sense of lines 238–42 seems to be, to put it shortly: "With no ability ('skill') to distinguish between vague desire (perhaps resulting from lack of power) and ruling impulse; between timidity and prudence; between endless delay and carefulness ('circumspection')."
6. The reference is to the parable of the false steward in Matthew 25.14–30.
7. The two-part *Prelude* that Wordsworth wrote in 1798–99 begins at this point.
8. Flat ground next to a river.

280 A foretaste, a dim earnest, of the calm
That Nature breathes among the hills and groves?
    When he had left the mountains, and received
On his smooth breast the shadow of those Towers
That yet survive, a shattered Monument
285 Of feudal sway, the bright blue River passed
Along the margin of our Terrace Walk;[9]
A tempting Playmate whom we dearly loved.
O many a time have I, a five years' Child,
In a small mill-race severed from his stream,
290 Made one long bathing of a summer's day;
Basked in the sun, and plunged, and basked again,
Alternate all a summer's day, or scoured[1]
The sandy fields, leaping through flow'ry groves
Of yellow ragwort; or when rock and hill,
295 The woods and distant Skiddaw's[2] lofty height,
Were bronzed with deepest radiance, stood alone
Beneath the sky, as if I had been born
On Indian plains, and from my Mother's hut
Had run abroad in wantonness, to sport,
300 A naked Savage, in the thunder shower.
    Fair seed-time had my soul, and I grew up
Fostered alike by beauty and by fear;[3]
Much favoured in my birth-place, and no less
In that beloved Vale[4] to which erelong
305 We were transplanted—there were we let loose
For sports of wider range. Ere I had told
Ten birth-days, when among the mountain slopes
Frost, and the breath of frosty wind, had snapped
The last autumnal Crocus, 'twas my joy,
310 With store of Springes° o'er my Shoulder slung,   *bird snares*
To range the open heights where woodcocks ran
Along the smooth green turf. Through half the night,
Scudding away from snare to snare, I plied
That anxious visitation;—moon and stars
315 Were shining o'er my head; I was alone,
And seemed to be a trouble to the peace
That dwelt among them. Sometimes it befel,
In these night-wanderings, that a strong desire
O'erpowered my better reason, and the Bird
320 Which was the Captive of another's toil[5]
Became my prey; and when the deed was done
I heard, among the solitary hills,

9. The Derwent River flows by Cockermouth
Castle and then past the garden terrace behind
Wordsworth's father's house in Cockermouth,
Cumberland.
1. Run swiftly over.
2. A mountain nine miles east of Cockermouth.
3. Wordsworth introduces here a dialectic that
plays a central role in the evolution of *The Prelude*.
He represents his mind, confronting nature, as fostered in its growth by two antithetic principles, one
associated with love and the other with fear. These

principles correspond to the two main categories,
"the beautiful" and "the sublime," into which theorists of the landscape during the preceding century had classified the antithetic aspects of the
natural scene (see, e.g., 1.351–56, 466–75, 546).
In the concluding book (in 14.162–70), this
antithesis is finally resolved (see n. 3, p. 000).
4. The valley of Esthwaite, the location of Hawkshead, where Wordsworth attended school.
5. Snare or labor.

Low breathings coming after me, and sounds
Of undistinguishable motion, steps
325　Almost as silent as the turf they trod.
　　　Nor less, when Spring had warmed the cultured° Vale,　　*cultivated*
Roved we as plunderers where the Mother-bird
Had in high places built her lodge; though mean
Our object, and inglorious, yet the end°　　　　　　　　　*outcome*
330　Was not ignoble. Oh! when I have hung
Above the Raven's nest, by knots of grass
And half-inch fissures in the slippery rock
But ill-sustained; and almost (so it seemed)
Suspended by the blast that blew amain,
335　Shouldering the naked crag; Oh, at that time,
While on the perilous ridge I hung alone,
With what strange utterance did the loud dry wind
Blow through my ears! the sky seemed not a sky
Of earth, and with what motion moved the clouds!
340　　　Dust as we are, the immortal Spirit grows
Like harmony in music; there is a dark
Inscrutable workmanship that reconciles
Discordant elements, makes them cling together
In one society. How strange that all
345　The terrors, pains, and early miseries,
Regrets, vexations, lassitudes, interfused
Within my mind, should e'er have borne a part,
And that a needful part, in making up
The calm existence that is mine when I
350　Am worthy of myself! Praise to the end!
Thanks to the means which Nature deigned to employ!
Whether her fearless visitings or those
That came with soft alarm like hurtless lightning
Opening the peaceful clouds, or she would use
355　Severer interventions, ministry
More palpable, as best might suit her aim.[6]
　　　One summer evening (led by her) I found
A little Boat tied to a Willow-tree
Within a rocky cave, its usual home.
360　Straight I unloosed her chain, and, stepping in,
Pushed from the shore. It was an act of stealth
And troubled pleasure, nor without the voice
Of mountain-echoes did my Boat move on,
Leaving behind her still, on either side,
365　Small circles glittering idly in the moon,
Until they melted all into one track!
Of sparkling light. But now, like one who rows
(Proud of his skill) to reach a chosen point
With an unswerving line, I fixed my view
370　Upon the summit of a craggy ridge,
The horizon's utmost boundary; for above

---

6. A restatement of the double ministry of nature described in line 302. What follows is a second example of discipline by fear.

Was nothing but the stars and the grey sky.
She was an elfin Pinnace;° lustily   *small boat*
I dipped my oars into the silent lake;
375   And, as I rose upon the stroke, my boat
Went heaving through the Water like a swan:
When, from behind that craggy Steep, till then
The horizon's bound, a huge peak, black and huge,
As if with voluntary power instinct,°   *endowed*
380   Upreared its head.[7]—I struck, and struck again,
And, growing still in stature, the grim Shape
Towered up between me and the stars, and still,
For so it seemed, with purpose of its own
And measured motion, like a living Thing
385   Strode after me. With trembling oars I turned,
And through the silent water stole my way
Back to the Covert of the Willow-tree;
There, in her mooring-place, I left my Bark,—
And through the meadows homeward went, in grave
390   And serious mood; but after I had seen
That spectacle, for many days, my brain
Worked with a dim and undetermined sense
Of unknown modes of being; o'er my thoughts
There hung a darkness, call it solitude
395   Or blank desertion. No familiar Shapes
Remained, no pleasant images of trees,
Of sea or Sky, no colours of green fields,
But huge and mighty Forms, that do not live
Like living men, moved slowly through the mind
400   By day, and were a trouble to my dreams.
       Wisdom and Spirit of the Universe!
Thou Soul that art the eternity of thought,
That giv'st to forms and images a breath
And everlasting Motion! not in vain,
405   By day or star-light, thus from my first dawn
Of Childhood didst thou intertwine for me
The passions that build up our human Soul,
Not with the mean and vulgar° works of man,   *commonplace*
But with high objects, with enduring things,
410   With life and nature, purifying thus
The elements of feeling and of thought,
And sanctifying, by such discipline,
Both pain and fear; until we recognize
A grandeur in the beatings of the heart.
415   Nor was this fellowship vouchsafed to me
With stinted kindness. In November days
When vapours, rolling down the valley, made
A lonely scene more lonesome; among woods
At noon, and 'mid the calm of summer nights,

7. To direct his boat in a straight line, the rower (sitting facing the stern of the boat) has fixed his eye on a point on the ridge above the nearby shore, which blocks out the landscape behind. As he moves farther out, the black peak rises into his altering angle of vision and seems to stride closer with each stroke of the oars.

420　When, by the margin of the trembling Lake,
　　　Beneath the gloomy hills homeward I went
　　　In solitude, such intercourse was mine:
　　　Mine was it, in the fields both day and night,
　　　And by the waters, all the summer long.
425　—And in the frosty season, when the sun
　　　Was set, and visible for many a mile,
　　　The cottage windows blazed through twilight gloom,
　　　I heeded not their summons,—happy time
　　　It was indeed for all of us; for me
430　It was a time of rapture!—Clear and loud
　　　The village Clock toll'd six—I wheeled about,
　　　Proud and exulting like an untired horse
　　　That cares not for his home.—All shod with steel,
　　　We hissed along the polished ice, in games
435　Confederate, imitative of the chase
　　　And woodland pleasures,—the resounding horn,
　　　The Pack loud-chiming and the hunted hare.
　　　So through the darkness and the cold we flew,
　　　And not a voice was idle: with the din
440　Smitten, the precipices rang aloud;
　　　The leafless trees and every icy crag
　　　Tinkled like iron; while far distant hills
　　　Into the tumult sent an alien sound
　　　Of melancholy, not unnoticed while the stars,
445　Eastward, were sparkling clear, and in the west
　　　The orange sky of evening died away.
　　　Not seldom from the uproar I retired
　　　Into a silent bay,—or sportively
　　　Glanced sideway,[8] leaving the tumultous throng
450　To cut across the reflex° of a star　　　　　　　　　*reflection*
　　　That fled, and, flying still before me, gleamed
　　　Upon the glassy plain: and oftentimes,
　　　When we had given our bodies to the wind,
　　　And all the shadowy banks on either side
455　Came sweeping through the darkness, spinning still
　　　The rapid line of motion, then at once
　　　Have I, reclining back upon my heels,
　　　Stopped short; yet still the solitary cliffs
　　　Wheeled by me—even as if the earth had rolled
460　With visible motion her diurnal° round!　　　　　　*daily*
　　　Behind me did they stretch in solemn train,°　　*succession*
　　　Feebler and feebler, and I stood and watched
　　　Till all was tranquil as a dreamless sleep.
　　　　　Ye presences of Nature, in the sky,
465　And on the earth! Ye visions of the hills!
　　　And Souls[9] of lonely places! can I think
　　　A vulgar hope was yours when ye employed
　　　Such ministry, when ye, through many a year,

8. Moved off obliquely.
9. Wordsworth refers both to a single "Spirit" or "Soul" of the universe as a whole (e.g., lines 401–02) and to plural "Presences" and "Souls" inanimating the various parts of the universe.

Haunting me thus among my boyish sports,
470   On caves and trees, upon the woods and hills,
Impressed upon all forms the characters°   *signs*
Of danger or desire; and thus did make
The surface of the universal earth
With triumph and delight, with hope and fear,
Work° like a sea?   *seethe*
475   Not uselessly employed,
Might I pursue this theme through every change
Of exercise and play, to which the year
Did summon us in his delightful round.
     —We were a noisy crew; the sun in heaven
480   Beheld not vales more beautiful than ours,
Nor saw a Band in happiness and joy
Richer, or worthier of the ground they trod.
I could record with no reluctant voice
The woods of Autumn, and their hazel bowers
485   With milk-white clusters hung; the rod and line,
True symbol of hope's foolishness, whose strong
And unreproved enchantment led us on,
By rocks and pools shut out from every star
All the green summer, to forlorn cascades
490   Among the windings hid of mountain brooks.
     —Unfading recollections! at this hour
The heart is almost mine with which I felt,
From some hill-top on sunny afternoons,
The paper-Kite, high among fleecy clouds,
495   Pull at her rein, like an impatient Courser;
Or, from the meadows sent on gusty days,
Beheld her breast the wind, then suddenly
Dashed headlong, and rejected by the storm.
     Ye lowly Cottages in which we dwelt,
500   A ministration of your own was yours!
Can I forget you, being as ye were
So beautiful among the pleasant fields
In which ye stood? or can I here forget
The plain and seemly countenance with which
505   Ye dealt out your plain Comforts? Yet had ye
Delights and exultations of your own.
Eager and never weary, we pursued
Our home-amusements by the warm peat-fire
At evening, when with pencil, and smooth slate
510   In square divisions parcelled out, and all
With crosses and with cyphers scribbled o'er,
We schemed and puzzled, head opposed to head,
In strife too humble to be named in verse;[1]
Or round the naked table, snow-white deal,°   *pine or fir*
515   Cherry, or maple, sate in close array,
And to the Combat, Lu or Whist, led on

---

1. I.e., ticktacktoe. By his phrasing in this passage, Wordsworth pokes fun at 18th-century poetic diction, which avoided homely terms by using circumlocutions.

A thick-ribbed Army, not as in the world
Neglected and ungratefully thrown by
Even for the very service they had wrought,
520 But husbanded through many a long campaign.
Uncouth assemblage was it, where no few
Had changed their functions; some, plebeian cards
Which Fate, beyond the promise of their birth,
Had dignified, and called to represent
525 The Persons of departed Potentates.
Oh, with what echoes on the board they fell!
Ironic diamonds; Clubs, Hearts, Diamonds, Spades,
A congregation piteously akin!
Cheap matter offered they to boyish wit,
530 Those sooty Knaves, precipitated down
With scoffs and taunts like Vulcan[2] out of heaven;
The paramount Ace, a moon in her eclipse,
Queens gleaming through their Splendor's last decay,
And Monarchs surly at the wrongs sustained
535 By royal visages.[3] Meanwhile abroad
Incessant rain was falling, or the frost
Raged bitterly, with keen and silent tooth;
And, interrupting oft that eager game,
From under Esthwaite's splitting fields of ice
540 The pent-up air, struggling to free itself,
Gave out to meadow-grounds and hills, a loud
Protracted yelling, like the noise of wolves
Howling in Troops along the Bothnic Main.[4]
      Nor, sedulous° as I have been to trace   *diligent*
545 How Nature by extrinsic passion first
Peopled the mind with forms sublime or fair[5]
And made me love them, may I here omit
How other pleasures have been mine, and joys
Of subtler origin; how I have felt,
550 Not seldom even in that tempestuous time,
Those hallowed and pure motions of the sense
Which seem, in their simplicity, to own
An intellectual[6] charm;—that calm delight
Which, if I err not, surely must belong
555 To those first-born° affinities that fit   *innate*
Our new existence to existing things,
And, in our dawn of being, constitute
The bond of union between life and joy.
      Yes, I remember when the changeful earth
560 And twice five summers on my mind had stamped
The faces of the moving year, even then

2. Roman god of fire and forge. His mother, Juno,
when he was born lame, threw him down from
Olympus, the abode of the gods.
3. Wordsworth implicitly parallels the boys' card
games to the mock-epic description of the aristocratic game of ombre in Pope's *The Rape of the
Lock* 3.37–98.
4. A northern gulf of the Baltic Sea.

5. The passion at first was "extrinsic" because it
was felt not for nature itself but for nature as associated with the outdoor activities he loved. Wordsworth now goes on to distinguish other "subtler"
pleasures, felt in the very process of sensing the
natural objects.
6. Spiritual, as opposed to sense perceptions.

I held unconscious intercourse with beauty
Old as creation, drinking in a pure
Organic pleasure from the silver wreaths
565 Of curling mist, or from the level plain
Of waters, colored by impending° clouds.   *overhanging*
    The sands of Westmorland, the creeks and bays
Of Cumbria's° rocky limits, they can tell   *Cumberland's*
How, when the Sea threw off his evening shade,
570 And to the Shepherd's hut on distant hills
Sent welcome notice of the rising moon,
How I have stood, to fancies such as these
A Stranger, linking with the Spectacle
No conscious memory of a kindred sight,
575 And bringing with me no peculiar sense
Of quietness or peace, yet have I stood,
Even while mine eye hath moved o'er many a league[7]
Of shining water, gathering, as it seemed,
Through every hair-breadth in that field of light,
580 New pleasure, like a bee among the flowers.
    Thus oft amid those fits of vulgar[8] joy
Which, through all seasons, on a Child's pursuits
Are prompt Attendants; 'mid that giddy bliss
Which like a tempest works along the blood
585 And is forgotten: even then I felt
Gleams like the flashing of a shield,—the earth
And common face of Nature spake to me
Rememberable things; sometimes, 'tis true,
By chance collisions and quaint accidents
590 (Like those ill-sorted unions, work supposed
Of evil-minded fairies), yet not vain
Nor profitless, if haply they impressed
Collateral[9] objects and appearances,
Albeit lifeless then, and doomed to sleep
595 Until maturer seasons called them forth
To impregnate and to elevate the mind.
—And, if the vulgar joy by its own weight
Wearied itself out of the memory,
The scenes which were a witness of that joy
600 Remained, in their substantial lineaments
Depicted on the brain, and to the eye
Were visible, a daily sight: and thus
By the impressive discipline of fear,
By pleasure and repeated happiness,
605 So frequently repeated, and by force
Of obscure feelings representative
Of things forgotten; these same scenes so bright,
So beautiful, so majestic in themselves,
Though yet the day was distant, did become
610 Habitually dear; and all their forms

7. A measure equal to approximately three miles.   9. Accompanying but subordinate.
8. Ordinary, commonplace.

And changeful colours by invisible links
Were fastened to the affections.°   *feelings*
               I began
My Story early, not misled, I trust,
By an infirmity of love for days
615 Disowned by memory,[1] fancying flowers where none,
Not even the sweetest, do or can survive
For him at least whose dawning day they cheered;
Nor will it seem to Thee, O Friend! so prompt
In sympathy, that I have lengthened out,
620 With fond and feeble tongue, a tedious tale.
Meanwhile, my hope has been, that I might fetch
Invigorating thoughts from former years;
Might fix the wavering balance of my mind,
And haply meet reproaches too, whose power
625 May spur me on, in manhood now mature,
To honorable toil. Yet should these hopes
Prove vain, and thus should neither I be taught
To understand myself, nor thou to know
With better knowledge how the heart was framed
630 Of him thou lovest, need I dread from thee
Harsh judgments, if the Song be loth to quit
Those recollected hours that have the charm
Of visionary things, those lovely forms
And sweet sensations that throw back our life,
635 And almost make remotest infancy
A visible scene, on which the sun is shining?
    One end at least hath been attained—my mind
Hath been revived; and, if this genial[2] mood
Desert me not, forthwith shall be brought down
640 Through later years the story of my life:
The road lies plain before me,—'tis a theme
Single, and of determined bounds; and hence
I chuse it rather, at this time, than work
Of ampler or more varied argument,
645 Where I might be discomfited and lost;
And certain hopes are with me that to thee
This labour will be welcome, honoured Friend!

Book Second
School-time continued

Thus far, O Friend! have we, though leaving much
Unvisited, endeavoured to retrace
The simple ways in which my childhood walked,
Those chiefly, that first led me to the love
5 Of rivers, woods, and fields. The passion yet
Was in its birth, sustained, as might befal,

---

1. I.e., he hopes that he has not mistakenly attributed his later thoughts and feelings to a time of life
he can no longer remember.
2. Productive, creative.

By nourishment that came unsought; for still,
From week to week, from month to month, we lived
A round of tumult. Duly° were our games   *appropriately*
10   Prolonged in summer till the day-light failed;
No chair remained before the doors, the bench
And threshold steps were empty; fast asleep
The Labourer, and the old Man who had sate,
A later Lingerer, yet the revelry
15   Continued, and the loud uproar; at last,
When all the ground was dark, and twinkling stars
Edged the black clouds, home and to bed we went,
Feverish, with weary joints and beating minds.
Ah! is there One who ever has been young
20   Nor needs a warning voice to tame the pride
Of intellect, and virtue's self-esteem?
One is there,[1] though the wisest and the best
Of all mankind, who covets not at times
Union that cannot be; who would not give,
25   If so he might, to duty and to truth
The eagerness of infantine desire?
A tranquillizing spirit presses now
On my corporeal frame, so wide appears
The vacancy between me and those days,
30   Which yet have such self-presence° in my mind,   *actuality*
That, musing on them, often do I seem
Two consciousnesses, conscious of myself
And of some other Being. A rude mass
Of native rock, left midway in the Square
35   Of our small market Village, was the goal
Or centre of these sports; and, when, returned
After long absence, thither I repaired,
Gone was the old grey stone, and in its place
A smart Assembly-room usurped the ground
40   That had been ours.[2] There let the fiddle scream,
And be ye happy! Yet, my Friends,[3] I know
That more than one of you will think with me
Of those soft starry nights, and that old Dame
From whom the Stone was named, who there had sate
45   And watched her table with its huckster's wares
Assiduous, through the length of sixty years.
—We ran a boisterous course, the year span round
With giddy motion. But the time approached
That brought with it a regular desire
50   For calmer pleasures, when the winning forms
Of Nature were collaterally attached[4]
To every scheme of holiday delight,
And every boyish sport, less grateful° else   *pleasing*
And languidly pursued.
                          When summer came,

1. I.e., "Is there anyone . . . ?"
2. The Hawkshead Town Hall, built in 1790.
3. Coleridge and John Wordsworth (William's
brother), who had visited Hawkshead together
with William in November 1799.
4. Associated as an accompaniment.

55 Our pastime was, on bright half-holidays,
    To sweep along the plain of Windermere
    With rival oars; and the selected bourne°   *destination*
    Was now an Island musical with birds
    That sang and ceased not; now a sister isle,
60 Beneath the oaks' umbrageous° covert, sown   *shaded*
    With lilies of the valley like a field;
    And now a third small island,[5] where survived,
    In solitude, the ruins of a shrine
    Once to our Lady dedicate, and served
65 Daily with chaunted rites. In such a race,
    So ended, disappointment could be none,
    Uneasiness, or pain, or jealousy;
    We rested in the Shade, all pleased alike,
    Conquered and Conqueror. Thus the pride of strength,
70 And the vain-glory of superior skill,
    Were tempered, thus was gradually produced
    A quiet independence of the heart:
    And, to my Friend who knows me, I may add,
    Fearless of blame, that hence, for future days,
75 Ensued a diffidence and modesty;
    And I was taught to feel, perhaps too much,
    The self-sufficing power of solitude.
        Our daily meals were frugal, Sabine fare![6]
    More than we wished we knew the blessing then
80 Of vigorous hunger—hence corporeal strength
    Unsapped by delicate viands; for, exclude
    A little weekly stipend,[7] and we lived
    Through three divisions of the quartered year
    In pennyless poverty. But now, to school
85 From the half-yearly holidays returned,
    We came with weightier purses, that sufficed
    To furnish treats more costly than the Dame
    Of the old grey stone, from her scanty board, supplied.
    Hence rustic dinners on the cool green ground,
90 Or in the woods, or by a river side,
    Or shady fountains,° while among the leaves   *springs, streams*
    Soft airs were stirring, and the mid-day sun
    Unfelt shone brightly round us in our joy.
        Nor is my aim neglected if I tell
95 How sometimes, in the length of those half years,
    We from our funds drew largely—proud to curb,
    And eager to spur on, the galloping Steed:
    And with the cautious Inn-keeper, whose Stud
    Supplied our want, we haply might employ
100 Sly subterfuges, if the Adventure's bound
    Were distant, some famed Temple[8] where of yore

5. The island of Lady Holm, former site of a chapel dedicated to the Virgin Mary.
6. Like the meals of the Roman poet Horace on his Sabine farm.
7. In his last year at school Wordsworth had an allowance of sixpence a week, and his younger

brother Christopher, threepence. After the Midsummer and Christmas holidays (line 85), the boys received a larger sum, ranging up to a guinea.
8. The stone circle at Swinside, on the lower Duddon River, mistakenly believed at the time to have been a Druid temple.

The Druids worshipped, or the antique Walls
Of that large Abbey which within the Vale
Of Nightshade, to St Mary's honour built,
105 Stands yet, a mouldering Pile, with fractured arch,
Belfry, and Images, and living Trees;
A holy Scene![9]—Along the smooth green Turf
Our Horses grazed:—to more than inland peace
Left by the west wind sweeping overhead
110 From a tumultuous ocean, trees and towers
In that sequestered Valley may be seen
Both silent and both motionless alike;
Such the deep shelter that is there, and such
The safeguard for repose and quietness.
115 Our Steeds remounted, and the summons given,
With whip and spur we through the Chauntry[1] flew
In uncouth race, and left the cross-legged Knight
And the Stone-abbot, and that single Wren
Which one day sang so sweetly in the Nave
120 Of the old Church, that, though from recent Showers
The earth was comfortless, and, touched by faint
Internal breezes, sobbings of the place
And respirations, from the roofless walls
The shuddering ivy dripped large drops, yet still
125 So sweetly 'mid the gloom the invisible Bird
Sang to herself, that there I could have made
My dwelling-place, and lived for ever there
To hear such music. Through the Walls we flew,
And down the Valley, and, a circuit made
130 In wantonness of heart, through rough and smooth
We scampered homewards. Oh, ye rocks and streams,
And that still Spirit shed from evening air!
Even in this joyous time I sometimes felt
Your presence, when with slackened step we breathed[2]
135 Along the sides of the steep hills, or when,
Lighted by gleams of moonlight from the sea,
We beat with thundering hoofs the level sand.
Midway on long Winander's Eastern shore,
Within the crescent of a pleasant Bay,
140 A Tavern[3] stood, no homely-featured House,
Primeval like its neighbouring Cottages;
But 'twas a splendid place, the door beset
With Chaises, Grooms, and Liveries,—and within
Decanters, Glasses, and the blood-red Wine.
145 In ancient times, or ere the Hall was built
On the large Island,[4] had this Dwelling been
More worthy of a Poet's love, a Hut
Proud of its one bright fire and sycamore shade.
But, though the rhymes were gone that once inscribed

---

9. Furness Abbey, some twenty miles south of Hawkshead.
1. A chapel endowed for masses to be sung to the donor.
2. Stopped to let the horses catch their breath.
3. The White Lion at Bowness.
4. The Hall on Belle Isle in Lake Windermere had been built in the early 1780s.

150 The threshold, and large golden characters
Spread o'er the spangled sign-board had dislodged
The old Lion, and usurped his place in slight
And mockery of the rustic Painter's hand,
Yet to this hour the spot to me is dear
155 With all its foolish pomp. The garden lay
Upon a slope surmounted by the plain
Of a small Bowling-green: beneath us stood
A grove, with gleams of water through the trees
And over the tree-tops; nor did we want
160 Refreshment, strawberries, and mellow cream.
There, while through half an afternoon we played
On the smooth platform, whether skill prevailed
Or happy blunder triumphed, bursts of glee
Made all the mountains ring. But ere night-fall,
165 When in our pinnace we returned, at leisure
Over the shadowy Lake, and to the beach
Of some small Island steered our course with one,
The Minstrel of our Troop,[5] and left him there,
And rowed off gently, while he blew his flute
170 Alone upon the rock,—Oh then the calm
And dead still water lay upon my mind
Even with a weight of pleasure, and the sky,
Never before so beautiful, sank down
Into my heart, and held me like a dream!
175   Thus were my sympathies enlarged, and thus
Daily the common range of visible things
Grew dear to me: already I began
To love the sun; a boy I loved the sun,
Not as I since have loved him, as a pledge
180 And surety of our earthly life, a light
Which we behold, and feel we are alive;
Nor for his bounty to so many worlds,
But for this cause, that I had seen him lay
His beauty on the morning hills, had seen
185 The western mountain touch his setting orb,
In many a thoughtless hour, when, from excess
Of happiness, my blood appear'd to flow
For its own pleasure, and I breathed with joy;
And from like feelings, humble though intense,
190 To patriotic and domestic love
Analogous, the moon to me was dear;
For I would dream away my purposes,
Standing to gaze upon her while she hung
Midway between the hills, as if she knew
195 No other region; but belonged to thee,
Yea, appertained by a peculiar right
To thee, and thy grey huts,[6] thou one dear Vale!
    Those incidental charms which first attached

---

5. Identified by Christopher Wordsworth, *Memoirs* (1857), as Robert Greenwood, who became senior fellow of Trinity College, Cambridge.
6. Cottages built of gray stones.

My heart to rural objects, day by day
200 Grew weaker, and I hasten on to tell
How Nature, intervenient[7] till this time
And secondary, now at length was sought
For her own sake. But who shall[8] parcel out
His intellect, by geometric rules,
205 Split like a province into round and square?
Who knows the individual hour in which
His habits were first sown, even as a seed?
Who that shall point, as with a wand, and say,
"This portion of the river of my mind
210 Came from yon fountain"? Thou, my friend! art one
More deeply read in thy own thoughts; to thee
Science[9] appears but what in truth she is,
Not as our glory and our absolute boast,
But as a succedaneum,[1] and a prop
215 To our infirmity. No officious slave
Art thou of that false secondary power[2]
By which we multiply distinctions, then
Deem that our puny boundaries are things
That we perceive, and not that we have made.
220 To thee, unblinded by these formal arts,
The unity of all hath been revealed;
And thou wilt doubt with me, less aptly skilled
Than many are to range the faculties
In scale and order, class the cabinet[3]
225 Of their sensations, and in voluble phrase[4]
Run through the history and birth of each
As of a single independent thing.
Hard task, vain hope, to analyse the mind,
If each most obvious and particular thought,
230 Not in a mystical and idle sense,
But in the words of reason deeply weighed,
Hath no beginning.   Blest the infant Babe,
(For with my best conjecture I would trace
Our Being's earthly progress) blest the Babe,
235 Nursed in his Mother's arms, who sinks to sleep
Rocked on his Mother's breast; who, when his soul
Claims manifest kindred with a human soul,
Drinks in the feelings of his Mother's eye![5]
For him, in one dear Presence, there exists
240 A virtue which irradiates and exalts
Objects through widest intercourse of sense.
No outcast he, bewildered and depressed;

---

7. I.e., entering incidentally into his other concerns.
8. Is able to.
9. In the old sense: learning.
1. In medicine, a drug substituted for a different drug. Wordsworth, however, uses the term to signify a remedy, or palliative.
2. The analytic faculty, as opposed to the power

to apprehend "the unity of all" (line 221).
3. To classify, as if arranged in a display case.
4. In fluent phraseology.
5. Like the modern psychologist, Wordsworth recognized the importance of earliest infancy in the development of the individual mind, although he had then to invent the terms with which to analyze the process.

Along his infant veins are interfused
The gravitation and the filial bond
245   Of nature that connect him with the world.
Is there a flower to which he points with hand
Too weak to gather it, already love
Drawn from love's purest earthly fount for him
Hath beautified that flower; already shades
250   Of pity cast from inward tenderness
Do fall around him upon aught that bears
Unsightly marks of violence or harm.
Emphatically such a Being lives,
Frail Creature as he is, helpless as frail,
255   An inmate of this active universe.
For feeling has to him imparted power
That through the growing faculties of sense
Doth, like an Agent of the one great Mind,
Create, creator and receiver both,
260   Working but in alliance with the works
Which it beholds.[6]—Such, verily, is the first
Poetic spirit of our human life,
By uniform control of after years
In most abated or suppressed, in some,
265   Through every change of growth and of decay,
Preeminent till death.
                    From early days,
Beginning not long after that first time
In which, a Babe, by intercourse of touch,
I held mute dialogues with my Mother's heart,[7]
270   I have endeavoured to display the means
Whereby this infant sensibility,
Great birth-right of our being, was in me
Augmented and sustained. Yet is a path
More difficult before me, and I fear
275   That, in its broken windings, we shall need
The chamois'[8] sinews, and the eagle's wing:
For now a trouble came into my mind
From unknown causes. I was left alone,
Seeking the visible world, nor knowing why.
280   The props of my affections were removed,[9]
And yet the building stood, as if sustained
By its own spirit! All that I beheld
Was dear, and hence to finer influxes°   *influences*
The mind lay open, to a more exact
285   And close communion. Many are our joys

6. The infant, in the sense of security and love shed by his mother's presence on outer things, perceives what would otherwise be an alien world as a place to which he has a relationship like that of a son to a mother (lines 239–45). On such grounds Wordsworth asserts that the mind partially creates, by altering, the world it seems simply to perceive.
7. I.e., both infant and mother feel the pulse of the other's heart.
8. An agile species of antelope inhabiting mountainous regions of Europe.
9. Wordsworth's mother had died the month before his eighth birthday. It is unclear from the context whether the "trouble" that came into his mind (line 277) refers to the loss of his mother, in whose arms he had established his initial relationship to the natural world, or to the mysterious processes of the continued development and diversification of this relationship.

In youth, but Oh! what happiness to live
When every hour brings palpable access
Of knowledge, when all knowledge is delight,
And sorrow is not there! The seasons came,
290 And every season, wheresoe'er I moved,
Unfolded transitory qualities
Which, but for this most watchful power of love,
Had been neglected, left a register
Of permanent relations, else unknown.[1]
295 Hence life, and change, and beauty; solitude
More active even than "best society,"[2]
Society made sweet as solitude
By inward concords, silent, inobtrusive;
And gentle agitations of the mind
300 From manifold distinctions, difference
Perceived in things where, to the unwatchful eye,
No difference is, and hence, from the same source,
Sublimer joy: for I would walk alone
Under the quiet stars, and at that time
305 Have felt whate'er there is of power in sound
To breathe an elevated mood, by form
Or Image unprofaned: and I would stand,
If the night blackened with a coming storm,
Beneath some rock, listening to notes that are
310 The ghostly° language of the ancient earth,   *disembodied*
Or make their dim abode in distant winds.
Thence did I drink the visionary power;
And deem not profitless those fleeting moods
Of shadowy exultation: not for this,
315 That they are kindred to our purer mind
And intellectual life;[3] but that the soul,
Remembering how she felt, but what she felt
Remembering not, retains an obscure sense
Of possible sublimity, whereto
320 With growing faculties she doth aspire,
With faculties still growing, feeling still
That, whatsoever point they gain, they yet
Have something to pursue.[4]
                              And not alone
'Mid gloom and tumult, but no less 'mid fair
325 And tranquil scenes, that universal power
And fitness in the latent qualities
And essences of things, by which the mind
Is moved with feelings of delight, to me
Came strengthened with a superadded soul,

1. I.e., had it not been for the watchful power of love (line 292), the "transitory qualities" (291) would have been neglected, and the "permanent relations" now recorded in his memory would have been unknown.
2. A partial quotation of a line spoken by Adam to Eve in *Paradise Lost* 9.249: "For solitude some-

times is best society."
3. I.e., not because they are related to the non-sensuous ("intellectual") aspect of our life.
4. Cf. the revelation, while crossing Simplon Pass, that our destiny is with "something evermore about to be" (6.604–08, pp. 347–48).

330 A virtue not its own.—My morning walks
   Were early;—oft before the hours of School
   I travelled round our little Lake, five miles
   Of pleasant wandering; happy time! more dear
   For this, that One was by my side, a Friend[5]
335 Then passionately loved; with heart how full
   Would he peruse these lines! for many years
   Have since flowed in between us, and, our minds
   Both silent to each other, at this time
   We live as if those hours had never been.
340 Nor seldom did I lift our Cottage latch
   Far earlier, and ere one smoke-wreath had risen
   From human dwelling, or the thrush, high perched,
   Piped to the woods his shrill *reveillé*,[6] sate
   Alone upon some jutting eminence
345 At the first gleam of dawn-light, when the Vale,
   Yet slumbering, lay in utter solitude.
   How shall I seek the origin, where find
   Faith in the marvellous things which then I felt?
   Oft in those moments such a holy calm
350 Would overspread my soul, that bodily eyes
   Were utterly forgotten, and what I saw
   Appeared like something in myself, a dream,
   A prospect° in the mind.   scene
                        'Twere long to tell
   What spring and autumn, what the winter snows,
355 And what the summer shade, what day and night,
   Evening and morning, sleep and waking thought,
   From sources inexhaustible, poured forth
   To feed the spirit of religious love,
   In which I walked with Nature. But let this
360 Be not forgotten, that I still retained
   My first creative sensibility,[7]
   That by the regular action of the world
   My soul was unsubdued. A plastic° power   shaping
   Abode with me, a forming hand, at times
365 Rebellious, acting in a devious mood,
   A local Spirit of his own, at war
   With general tendency, but, for the most,
   Subservient strictly to external things
   With which it communed. An auxiliar light
370 Came from my mind which on the setting sun
   Bestowed new splendor; the melodious birds,
   The fluttering breezes, fountains that ran on
   Murmuring so sweetly in themselves, obeyed
   A like dominion; and the midnight storm
375 Grew darker in the presence of my eye;
   Hence my obeisance, my devotion hence,

5. Identified as John Fleming in a note to the edition of 1850.
6. Military parlance for a signal call.

7. I.e., the creative perception manifested by the
babe in his mother's arms (lines 235ff.).

And hence my transport.°   *exaltation*
          Nor should this, perchance,
Pass unrecorded, that I still° had loved   *always*
The exercise and produce of a toil
380   Than analytic industry to me
More pleasing, and whose character I deem
Is more poetic, as resembling more
Creative agency. The Song would speak
Of that interminable building reared
385   By observation of affinities
In objects where no brotherhood exists
To passive minds. My seventeenth year was come;
And, whether from this habit rooted now
So deeply in my mind, or from excess
390   Of the great social principle of life
Coercing all things into sympathy,
To unorganic Natures were transferred
My own enjoyments; or the Power of truth,
Coming in revelation, did converse
395   With things that really are;[8] I, at this time,
Saw blessings spread around me like a sea.
Thus while the days flew by and years passed on,
From Nature overflowing on my soul
I had received so much, that every thought
400   Was steeped in feeling; I was only then
Contented when with bliss ineffable
I felt the sentiment of Being spread
O'er all that moves, and all that seemeth still;
O'er all that, lost beyond the reach of thought
405   And human knowledge, to the human eye
Invisible, yet liveth to the heart;
O'er all that leaps, and runs, and shouts, and sings,
Or beats the gladsome air; o'er all that glides
Beneath the wave, yea, in the wave itself,
410   And mighty depth of waters. Wonder not
If high the transport, great the joy I felt,
Communing in this sort through earth and Heaven
With every form of Creature, as it looked
Towards the Uncreated with a countenance
415   Of adoration, with an eye of love.[9]
One song they sang, and it was audible,
Most audible, then, when the fleshly ear,
O'ercome by humblest prelude of that strain,
Forgot her functions and slept undisturbed.
420   If this be error, and another faith
Find easier access to the pious mind,[1]

---

8. Wordsworth is careful to indicate that there are alternative explanations for his sense that life pervades the inorganic as well as the organic world: it may be the result either of a way of perceiving that has been habitual since infancy or of a projection of his own inner life or else it may be the perception of an objective truth.
9. Wordsworth did not add lines 412–14, giving a Christian frame to his experience of the "one life," until the last revision of *The Prelude*, in 1839.
1. With lines 416–21 cf. *Tintern Abbey*, lines 43–50 (p. 236).

Yet were I grossly destitute of all
Those human sentiments that make this earth
So dear, if I should fail with grateful voice
425   To speak of you, Ye Mountains, and Ye Lakes,
And sounding Cataracts, Ye Mists and Winds
That dwell among the Hills where I was born.
If in my Youth I have been pure in heart,
If, mingling with the world, I am content
430   With my own modest pleasures, and have lived,
With God and Nature communing, removed
From little enmities and low desires,
The gift is yours: if in these times of fear,
This melancholy waste° of hopes o'erthrown,   *wasteland*
435   If, 'mid indifference and apathy
And wicked exultation, when good men,
On every side, fall off, we know not how,
To selfishness, disguised in gentle names
Of peace and quiet and domestic love,
440   Yet mingled, not unwillingly, with sneers
On visionary minds; if, in this time
Of dereliction and dismay,[2] I yet
Despair not of our Nature, but retain
A more than Roman confidence, a faith
445   That fails not, in all sorrow my support,
The blessing of my life, the gift is yours,
Ye Winds and sounding Cataracts, 'tis yours,
Ye Mountains! thine, O Nature! Thou hast fed
My lofty speculations; and in thee,
450   For this uneasy heart of ours, I find
A never-failing principle of joy
And purest passion.
                    Thou, my Friend! wert reared
In the great City, 'mid far other scenes;[3]
But we, by different roads, at length have gained
455   The self-same bourne. And for this cause to Thee
I speak, unapprehensive of contempt,
The insinuated scoff of coward tongues,
And all that silent language which so oft,
In conversation between Man and Man,
460   Blots from the human countenance all trace
Of beauty and of love. For Thou hast sought
The truth in solitude, and, since the days
That gave thee liberty, full long desired,
To serve in Nature's Temple, thou hast been
465   The most assiduous of her Ministers,[4]

2. The era, some ten years after the outbreak of the French Revolution, was one of violent reaction, in which many earlier sympathizers were recanting their radical beliefs.
3. A reminiscence of Coleridge's *Frost at Midnight*, lines 51–52: "For I was reared / In the great city, pent 'mid cloisters dim."

4. Wordsworth may be recalling the conclusion of Coleridge's *France: An Ode* (1798), where, disillusioned about the promise of liberty by the French Revolution, he writes that, while standing on a "sea-cliff's verge," "O Liberty! my spirit felt thee there." Wordsworth added lines 461–64 some years after Coleridge's death in 1834.

In many things my Brother, chiefly here
In this our deep devotion.
                Fare Thee well!
Health, and the quiet of a healthful mind,
Attend Thee! seeking oft the haunts of Men,
470   And yet more often living with thyself
And for thyself, so haply shall thy days
Be many, and a blessing to mankind.

From Book Third
Residence at Cambridge

[EXPERIENCES AT ST. JOHN'S COLLEGE. THE "HEROIC ARGUMENT"]

It was a dreary Morning when the Wheels
Rolled over a wide plain o'erhung with clouds,
And nothing cheered our way till first we saw
The long-roof'd Chapel of King's College lift
5   Turrets, and pinnacles in answering files
Extended high above a dusky grove.
    Advancing, we espied upon the road
A Student, clothed in Gown and tasselled Cap,
Striding along, as if o'ertasked by Time
10   Or covetous of exercise and air.
He passed—nor was I Master of my eyes
Till he was left an arrow's flight behind.
As near and nearer to the Spot we drew,
It seemed to suck us in with an eddy's force;
15   Onward we drove beneath the Castle, caught,
While crossing Magdalene Bridge, a glimpse of Cam,[1]
And at the *Hoop* alighted, famous Inn![2]
    My Spirit was up, my thoughts were full of hope;
Some friends I had, acquaintances who there
20   Seemed friends, poor simple School-boys! now hung round
With honor and importance: in a world
Of welcome faces up and down I roved;
Questions, directions, warnings, and advice
Flowed in upon me, from all sides; fresh day
25   Of pride and pleasure! to myself I seemed
A man of business and expence, and went
From shop to shop, about my own affairs,
To Tutor or to Tailor, as befel,
From street to street, with loose and careless mind.
30   I was the Dreamer, they the dream: I roamed
Delighted through the motley spectacle;
Gowns grave or gaudy, Doctors, Students, Streets,
Courts, Cloisters, flocks of Churches, gateways, towers.
Migration strange for a Stripling of the Hills,

---

1. The river that flows through Cambridge.
2. Wordsworth renders some of his early college experiences, when he was a callow country boy

(lines 34–35), in a deliberately inflated, or mock-epic, manner.

35   A Northern Villager! As if the change
      Had waited on some Fairy's wand, at once
      Behold me rich in monies; and attired
      In splendid garb, with hose of silk, and hair
      Powdered like rimy[3] trees, when frost is keen.
40   My lordly dressing-gown, I pass it by,
      With other signs of manhood that supplied
      The lack of beard.—The weeks went roundly on
      With invitations, suppers, wine and fruit,
      Smooth housekeeping within, and all without
45   Liberal, and suiting Gentleman's array!
          The Evangelist St. John my Patron was;[4]
      Three gothic Courts are his, and in the first
      Was my abiding-place, a nook obscure!
      Right underneath, the College Kitchens made
50   A humming sound, less tuneable than bees,
      But hardly less industrious; with shrill notes
      Of sharp command and scolding intermixed.
      Near me hung Trinity's loquacious Clock,
      Who never let the quarters, night or day,
55   Slip by him unproclaimed, and told the hours
      Twice over, with a male and female voice.
      Her pealing Organ was my neighbour too;
      And from my pillow, looking forth by light
      Of moon or favoring stars, I could behold
60   The Antechapel, where the Statue stood
      Of Newton, with his prism,[5] and silent face:
      The marble index of a Mind for ever
      Voyaging through strange seas of Thought, alone.
          Of College labors, of the Lecturer's room
65   All studded round, as thick as chairs could stand,
      With loyal Students faithful to their books,
      Half-and-half Idlers, hardy Recusants,[6]
      And honest Dunces—of important days,
      Examinations when the man was weighed
70   As in a balance! of excessive hopes,
      Tremblings withal, and commendable fears;
      Small jealousies, and triumphs good or bad,
      Let others, that know more, speak as they know.
      Such glory was but little sought by me
75   And little won. Yet, from the first crude days
      Of settling time in this untried abode,
      I was disturbed at times by prudent thoughts,
      Wishing to hope, without a hope; some fears
      About my future worldly maintenance;[7]
80   And, more than all, a strangeness in the mind,
      A feeling that I was not for that hour,

---

3. Covered with rime, frosted over.
4. Wordsworth was a student at St. John's College, Cambridge University, in 1787–91. Book 3 deals with his first year there.
5. In the west end of Trinity Chapel, adjoining St. John's College, stands Roubiliac's statue of New-

ton holding the prism with which he had conducted the experiments described in his *Optics*.
6. Those who refused to work at their studies.
7. Wordsworth was troubled by the expectation of his family that he would be appointed a fellow of St. John's College.

Nor for that place. But wherefore be cast down?
For (not to speak of Reason and her pure
Reflective acts to fix the moral law

85   Deep in the conscience; nor of Christian Hope
Bowing her head before her Sister Faith
As one far mightier),[8] hither I had come,
Bear witness, Truth, endowed with holy powers
And faculties, whether to work or feel.

90   Oft when the dazzling shew no longer new
Had ceased to dazzle, ofttimes did I quit
My Comrades, leave the Crowd, buildings and groves,
And as I paced alone the level fields
Far from those lovely sights and sounds sublime

95   With which I had been conversant, the mind
Drooped not, but there into herself returning
With prompt rebound, seemed fresh as heretofore.
At least I more distinctly recognized
Her native instincts; let me dare to speak

100   A higher language, say that now I felt
What independent solaces were mine
To mitigate the injurious sway of place
Or circumstance, how far soever changed
In youth, or to be changed in manhood's prime;

105   Or, for the few who shall be called to look
On the long shadows, in our evening years,
Ordained Precursors to the night of death.
As if awakened, summoned, roused, constrained,
I looked for universal things, perused

110   The common countenance of earth and sky;
Earth no where unembellished by some trace
Of that first paradise whence man was driven;
And sky whose beauty and bounty are expressed
By the proud name she bears, the name of heaven.

115   I called on both to teach me what they might;
Or, turning the mind in upon herself,
Pored, watched, expected, listened, spread my thoughts
And spread them with a wider creeping; felt
Incumbencies more awful,[9] visitings

120   Of the Upholder, of the tranquil Soul
That tolerates the indignities of Time;
And, from his centre of eternity
All finite motions overruling, lives
In glory immutable. But peace!—enough

125   Here to record I had ascended now
To such community with highest truth.
—A track pursuing, not untrod before,
From strict analogies by thought supplied,
Or consciousnesses not to be subdued,

130   To every natural form, rock, fruit or flower,

8. This pious qualification, lines 83–87, was added by Wordsworth in late revisions of The Prelude. In the version of 1805, he wrote: "I was a chosen son. / For hither I had come with holy powers / And faculties, whether to work or feel."
9. I.e., the weight of more awe-inspiring moods.

Even the loose stones that cover the high-way,
I gave a moral life; I saw them feel,
Or linked them to some feeling: the great mass
Lay bedded in a quickening° soul, and all   *life-giving*
135 That I beheld respired with inward meaning.
Add, that whate'er of Terror or of Love
Or Beauty, Nature's daily face put on
From transitory passion, unto this
I was as sensitive as waters are
140 To the sky's influence: in a kindred mood
Of passion, was obedient as a lute
That waits upon the touches of the wind.[1]
Unknown, unthought of, yet I was most rich;
I had a world about me; 'twas my own,
145 I made it; for it only lived to me,
And to the God who sees into the heart.
Such sympathies, though rarely, were betrayed
By outward gestures and by visible looks:
Some called it madness—so, indeed, it was,
150 If child-like fruitfulness in passing joy,
If steady moods of thoughtfulness, matured
To inspiration, sort with such a name;
If prophecy be madness; if things viewed
By Poets in old time, and higher up
155 By the first men, earth's first inhabitants,
May in these tutored days no more be seen
With undisordered sight. But, leaving this,
It was no madness: for the bodily eye
Amid my strongest workings evermore
160 Was searching out the lines of difference
As they lie hid in all external forms,
Near or remote, minute or vast, an eye
Which from a tree, a stone, a withered leaf,
To the broad ocean, and the azure heavens
165 Spangled with kindred multitudes of Stars,
Could find no surface where its power might sleep;
Which spake perpetual logic to my Soul,
And by an unrelenting agency
Did bind my feelings, even as in a chain.
170   And here, O friend! have I retraced my life
Up to an eminence, and told a tale
Of matters which not falsely may be called
The glory of my Youth. Of genius, power,
Creation, and Divinity itself,
175 I have been speaking, for my theme has been
What passed within me. Not of outward things
Done visibly for other minds; words, signs,
Symbols, or actions, but of my own heart
Have I been speaking, and my youthful mind.
180 O Heavens! how awful is the might of Souls

---

1. I.e., as a wind harp.

And what they do within themselves, while yet
The yoke of earth is new to them, the world
Nothing but a wild field where they were sown.
This is, in truth, heroic argument,
185 This genuine prowess, which I wished to touch
With hand however weak,[2] but in the main
It lies far hidden from the reach of words.
Points have we, all of us, within our Souls,
Where all stand single: this I feel, and make
190 Breathings for incommunicable powers.[3]
But is not each a memory to himself?
And, therefore, now that we must quit this theme,
I am not heartless;° for there's not a man   *disheartened*
That lives who hath not known his god-like hours,
195 And feels not what an empire we inherit,
As natural Beings, in the strength of Nature.
     No more:—for now into a populous plain
We must descend.—A Traveller I am
Whose tale is only of himself; even so,
200 So be it, if the pure of heart be prompt
To follow, and if Thou, O honored Friend!
Who in these thoughts art ever at my side,
Support, as heretofore, my fainting steps.[4]

*   *   *

Thus in submissive idleness, my Friend,
The laboring time of Autumn, Winter, Spring,
Eight months! rolled pleasingly away—the ninth
635 Came and returned me to my native hills.

From Book Fourth
Summer Vacation[1]

[THE WALKS WITH HIS TERRIER. THE CIRCUIT OF THE LAKE]

Among the favorites whom it pleased me well
To see again, was one, by ancient right
95 Our Inmate, a rough terrier of the hills,
By birth and call of nature pre-ordained
To hunt the badger, and unearth the fox,
Among the impervious crags; but having been
From youth our own adopted, he had passed
100 Into a gentler service. And when first
The boyish spirit flagged, and day by day
Along my veins I kindled with the stir,
The fermentation and the vernal heat

---

2. Wordsworth describes the innovative epic
theme ("heroic argument") for his projected long
poem. Cf. his Prospectus to *The Recluse*, lines 25–
41 (pp. 301–02).
3. This obscure assertion may mean that he tries,
inadequately, to express the inexpressible.

4. The terms of this behest to Coleridge suggest
the relation to Dante of Virgil, his guide in the
Inferno.
1. Wordsworth returned to Hawkshead for his
first summer vacation in 1788.

Of poesy, affecting private shades
105 Like a sick lover, then this Dog was used
To watch me, an attendant and a friend
Obsequious to my steps, early and late,
Though often of such dilatory walk
Tired, and uneasy at the halts I made.
110 A hundred times when, roving high and low,
I have been harrassed with the toil of verse,
Much pains and little progress, and at once
Some lovely Image in the Song rose up
Full-formed, like Venus rising from the Sea;[2]
115 Then have I darted forwards and let loose
My hand upon his back, with stormy joy;
Caressing him again, and yet again.
And when at evening on the public Way
I sauntered, like a river murmuring
120 And talking to itself, when all things else
Are still, the Creature trotted on before—
Such was his custom; but whene'er he met
A passenger° approaching, he would turn   *foot traveler*
To give me timely notice; and, straitway,
125 Grateful for that admonishment, I hushed
My voice, composed my gait, and with the air
And mien of one whose thoughts are free, advanced
To give and take a greeting, that might save
My name from piteous rumours, such as wait
130 On men suspected to be crazed in brain.
    Those walks, well worthy to be prized and loved,
Regretted! that word too was on my tongue,
But they were richly laden with all good,
And cannot be remembered but with thanks
135 And gratitude, and perfect joy of heart;
Those walks, in all their freshness, now came back,
Like a returning Spring. When first I made
Once more the circuit of our little Lake,
If ever happiness hath lodged with man,
140 That day consummate° happiness was mine,   *perfect*
Wide-spreading, steady, calm, contemplative.
The sun was set, or setting, when I left
Our cottage door, and evening soon brought on
A sober hour,—not winning or serene,
145 For cold and raw the air was, and untuned:
But as a face we love is sweetest then
When sorrow damps it; or, whatever look
It chance to wear, is sweetest if the heart
Have fulness in herself, even so with me
150 It fared that evening. Gently did my Soul
Put off her veil, and, self-transmuted, stood
Naked, as in the presence of her God.[3]

2. Aphrodite (the Roman Venus), goddess of love, was born from the foam of the sea.
3. In Exodus 34.30–34, when Moses descended from Mount Sinai, he wore a veil to hide from the Israelites the shining of his face, but removed the veil when, in privacy, he talked to God.

While on I walked, a comfort seemed to touch
A heart that had not been disconsolate;
155　Strength came where weakness was not known to be,
At least not felt; and restoration came,
Like an intruder, knocking at the door
Of unacknowledged weariness. I took
The balance, and with firm hand weighed myself.
160　—Of that external scene which round me lay
Little, in this abstraction, did I see,
Remembered less; but I had inward hopes
And swellings of the Spirit: was rapt and soothed,
Conversed with promises; had glimmering views
165　How life pervades the undecaying mind,
How the immortal Soul with God-like power
Informs, creates, and thaws the deepest sleep[4]
That time can lay upon her; how on earth,
Man, if he do but live within the light
170　Of high endeavours, daily spreads abroad
His being armed with strength that cannot fail.
Nor was there want of milder thoughts, of love,
Of innocence, and holiday repose;
And more than pastoral quiet 'mid the stir
175　Of boldest projects; and a peaceful end
At last, or glorious, by endurance won.
Thus musing, in a wood I sate me down,
Alone, continuing there to muse; the slopes
And heights, meanwhile, were slowly overspread
180　With darkness; and before a rippling breeze
The long lake lengthened out its hoary line:
And in the sheltered coppice[5] where I sate,
Around me from among the hazel leaves,
Now here, now there, moved by the straggling wind,
185　Came ever and anon a breath-like sound,
Quick as the pantings of the faithful Dog,
The off and on Companion of my walk;
And such, at times, believing them to be,
I turned my head, to look if he were there;
190　Then into solemn thought I passed once more.

["THE SURFACE OF PAST TIME." THE WALK HOME FROM THE DANCE. THE
DISCHARGED SOLDIER]

As one who hangs down-bending from the side
Of a slow-moving boat, upon the breast
Of a still water, solacing himself
With such discoveries as his eye can make,
260　Beneath him, in the bottom of the deep,
Sees many beauteous sights, weeds, fishes, flowers,
Grots, pebbles, roots of trees, and fancies more;

---

4. "Informs" and "creates" are probably to be read
as intransitive verbs, whereas "thaws" has "sleep"
for its direct object. "Sleep" Wordsworth uses, here
and elsewhere in *The Prelude*, for the deadening
effect of routine experience.
5. A clump of small trees and underbrush.

Yet often is perplexed, and cannot part
The shadow from the substance, rocks and sky,
265　Mountains and clouds reflected in the depth
Of the clear flood, from things which there abide
In their true Dwelling: now is crossed by gleam
Of his own image, by a sun-beam now,
And wavering motions, sent he knows not whence,
270　Impediments that make his task more sweet—
Such pleasant office have we long pursued,
Incumbent o'er the surface of past time,
With like success, nor often have appeared
Shapes fairer, or less doubtfully discerned
275　Than these to which the Tale, indulgent Friend!
Would now direct thy notice.[6] Yet in spite
Of pleasure won and knowledge not withheld,
There was an inner falling-off. I loved,
Loved deeply, all that had been loved before,
280　More deeply even than ever: but a swarm
Of heady schemes, jostling each other, gawds,°　　　　　*pastimes*
And feast, and dance, and public revelry;
And sports, and games (too grateful in themselves,
Yet in themselves less grateful, I believe,
285　Than as they were a badge, glossy and fresh,
Of manliness and freedom) all conspired
To lure my mind from firm habitual quest
Of feeding pleasures;[7] to depress the zeal
And damp those daily yearnings which had once been mine—
290　A wild unworldly-minded youth, given up
To his own eager thoughts. It would demand
Some skill, and longer time than may be spared,
To paint these vanities, and how they wrought
In haunts where they, till now, had been unknown.
295　It seemed the very garments that I wore
Preyed on my strength, and stopped the quiet stream
Of self-forgetfulness.
　　　　　　　　　　Yes, that heartless[8] chase
Of trivial pleasures was a poor exchange
For books and nature at that early age.
300　'Tis true some casual knowledge might be gained
Of character or life; but at that time,
Of manners put to School[9] I took small note;
And all my deeper passions lay elsewhere.
Far better had it been to exalt the mind
305　By solitary Study; to uphold
Intense desire through meditative peace.
And yet, for chastisement of these regrets,
The memory of one particular hour
Doth here rise up against me.—'Mid a throng

---

6. In this sustained simile Wordsworth describes his endeavors to distinguish facts from fancies, and his present self from his former self, in his remembrance of things past.

7. Pleasures that would nourish the mind.
8. Dispirited, without deep feeling.
9. Made a subject of systematic study.

310   Of Maids and Youths, old Men and Matrons staid,
       A medley of all tempers,[1] I had passed
       The night in dancing, gaiety, and mirth;
       With din of instruments, and shuffling feet,
       And glancing forms, and tapers glittering,
315   And unaimed prattle flying up and down—
       Spirits upon the stretch, and here and there
       Slight shocks of young love-liking interspersed,
       Whose transient pleasure mounted to the head,
       And tingled through the veins. Ere we retired
320   The cock had crowed; and now the eastern sky
       Was kindling, not unseen from humble copse
       And open field through which the pathway wound
       That homeward led my steps. Magnificent
       The Morning rose, in memorable pomp,
325   Glorious as e'er I had beheld; in front
       The Sea lay laughing at a distance;—near,
       The solid mountains shone bright as the clouds,
       Grain-tinctured,° drenched in empyrean[2] light;   *crimson-colored*
       And, in the meadows and the lower grounds,
330   Was all the sweetness of a common dawn;
       Dews, vapours, and the melody of birds;
       And Labourers going forth to till the fields.
          Ah! need I say, dear Friend, that to the brim
       My heart was full: I made no vows, but vows
335   Were then made for me; bond unknown to me
       Was given, that I should be, else sinning greatly,
       A dedicated Spirit.[3] On I walked
       In thankful blessedness which yet survives.
          Strange rendezvous my mind was at that time,
340   A party-colored shew of grave and gay,
       Solid and light, short-sighted and profound;
       Of inconsiderate habits and sedate,
       Consorting in one mansion, unreproved.
       The worth I knew of powers that I possessed,
345   Though slighted and too oft misused. Besides,
       That summer, swarming as it did with thoughts
       Transient and idle, lacked not intervals
       When Folly from the frown of fleeting Time
       Shrunk, and the Mind experienced in herself
350   Conformity as just as that of old[4]
       To the end and written spirit of God's works,
       Whether held forth in Nature or in Man,
       Through pregnant vision, separate or conjoined.
          When from our better selves we have too long
355   Been parted by the hurrying world, and droop,
       Sick of its business, of its pleasures tired,

---

1. Temperaments, types of character.
2. Celestial, referring to the outer sphere of the universe, composed of pure fire.
3. Wordsworth describes later in *The Prelude* his discovery that the specific vocation to which he felt

dedicated was to be the agent of a new kind of poetry (13.232ff.).
4. I.e., an immediacy of response similar to his mental experience before he indulged in these present distractions.

How gracious, how benign is Solitude!
How potent a mere image of her sway!
Most potent when impressed upon the mind
360 With an appropriate human centre—Hermit
Deep in the bosom of the Wilderness;
Votary[5] (in vast Cathedral, where no foot
Is treading and no other face is seen)
Kneeling at prayer; or Watchman on the top
365 Of Lighthouse beaten by Atlantic Waves;
Or as the soul of that great Power is met
Sometimes embodied on a public road,
When, for the night deserted, it assumes
A character of quiet more profound
Than pathless Wastes.

370   Once, when those summer Months
Were flown, and Autumn brought its annual shew
Of oars with oars contending, sails with sails,
Upon Winander's[6] spacious breast, it chanced
That—after I had left a flower-decked room
375 (Whose in-door pastime, lighted-up, survived
To a late hour) and spirits overwrought[7]
Were making night do penance for a day
Spent in a round of strenuous idleness—
My homeward course led up a long ascent
380 Where the road's watery surface, to the top
Of that sharp rising, glittered to the moon
And bore the semblance of another stream
Stealing with silent lapse[8] to join the brook
That murmured in the Vale. All else was still;
385 No living thing appeared in earth or air,
And, save the flowing Water's peaceful voice,
Sound was there none: but lo! an uncouth shape
Shewn by a sudden turning of the road,
So near, that, slipping back into the shade
390 Of a thick hawthorn, I could mark him well,
Myself unseen. He was of stature tall,
A span[9] above man's *common* measure tall.
Stiff, lank, and upright;—a more meagre° man   *emaciated*
Was never seen before by night or day.
395 Long were his arms, pallid his hands;—his mouth
Looked ghastly° in the moonlight. From behind,   *ghostly*
A mile-stone propped him; I could also ken
That he was clothed in military garb,
Though faded, yet entire. Companionless,
400 No dog attending, by no staff sustained

5. A person devoted to God's service.
6. Lake Windermere's.
7. Worked up to a high pitch. Wordsworth is describing a party at which the "pastime" had been dancing. The description of the meeting with the discharged soldier that follows was written in 1798 as an independent poem, which Wordsworth later incorporated in *The Prelude*.

8. Flowing. Wordsworth is remembering a description that his sister, Dorothy, had entered into her journal in January 1798, a few days before he composed this passage: "The road to the village of Holford glittered like another stream."
9. About nine inches (the distance between extended thumb and little finger).

He stood; and in his very dress appeared
A desolation, a simplicity
To which the trappings of a gaudy world
Make a strange background. From his lips erelong
405 Issued low muttered sounds, as if of pain
Or some uneasy thought; yet still his form
Kept the same awful steadiness;—at his feet
His shadow lay and moved not. From self-blame
Not wholly free, I watched him thus; at length
410 Subduing my heart's specious cowardice,[1]
I left the shady nook where I had stood,
And hailed him. Slowly, from his resting-place
He rose; and, with a lean and wasted arm
In measured gesture lifted to his head,
415 Returned my salutation: then resumed
His station as before; and when I asked
His history, the Veteran, in reply,
Was neither slow nor eager; but, unmoved,
And with a quiet uncomplaining voice,
420 A stately air of mild indifference,
He told, in few plain words, a Soldier's tale—
That in the Tropic Islands he had served,
Whence he had landed, scarcely three weeks past,
That on his landing he had been dismissed,[2]
425 And now was travelling towards his native home.
This heard, I said in pity, "Come with me."
He stooped, and straightway from the ground took up
An oaken staff, by me yet unobserved—
A staff which must have dropped from his slack hand
430 And lay till now neglected in the grass.
       Though weak his step and cautious, he appeared
To travel without pain, and I beheld,
With an astonishment but ill suppressed,
His ghastly figure moving at my side;
435 Nor could I, while we journeyed thus, forbear
To turn from present hardships to the past,
And speak of war, battle, and pestilence,
Sprinkling this talk with questions, better spared,
On what he might himself have seen or felt.
440 He all the while was in demeanour calm,
Concise in answer; solemn and sublime
He might have seemed, but that in all he said
There was a strange half-absence, as of one
Knowing too well the importance of his theme,
445 But feeling it no longer. Our discourse
Soon ended, and together on we passed,
In silence, through a wood, gloomy and still.
Up-turning then along an open field,
We reached a Cottage. At the door I knocked,

---

1. I.e., he had been deceiving himself in thinking that the motive for his delay was not cowardice.
2. The Tropic Islands are the West Indies. Tens of thousands of British soldiers serving there contracted tropical fevers and died, or else were rendered unfit for further service and discharged.

450 And earnestly to charitable care
Commended him, as a poor friendless Man
Belated, and by sickness overcome.
Assured that now the Traveller would repose
In comfort, I entreated, that henceforth
455 He would not linger in the public ways,
But ask for timely furtherance and help,
Such as his state required.—At this reproof,
With the same ghastly mildness in his look,
He said, "My trust is in the God of Heaven,
460 And in the eye of him who passes me."
    The Cottage door was speedily unbarred,
And now the Soldier touched his hat once more
With his lean hand; and, in a faltering voice
Whose tone bespake reviving interests
465 Till then unfelt, he thanked me; I returned
The farewell blessing of the patient Man,
And so we parted. Back I cast a look,
And lingered near the door a little space;
Then sought with quiet heart my distant home.
470   This passed, and He who deigns to mark with care
By what rules governed, with what end in view
This Work proceeds, *he* will not wish for more.

From Book Fifth
Books

[THE DREAM OF THE ARAB]

45   * * * Oh! why hath not the Mind
Some element to stamp her image on
In nature somewhat nearer to her own?
Why gifted with such powers to send abroad
Her spirit, must it lodge in shrines so frail?[1]
50   One day, when from my lips a like complaint
Had fallen in presence of a studious friend,
He with a smile made answer that in truth
'Twas going far to seek disquietude,
But, on the front of his reproof, confessed
55 That he himself had oftentimes given way
To kindred hauntings. Whereupon I told
That once in the stillness of a summer's noon,
While I was seated in a rocky cave
By the sea-side, perusing, so it chanced,
60 The famous history of the errant Knight
Recovered by Cervantes,[2] these same thoughts
Beset me, and to height unusual rose,
While listlessly I sate, and, having closed

1. Wordsworth is describing his recurrent fear that some holocaust might wipe out all books, the frail and perishable repositories of all human wisdom and poetry.

2. I.e., *Don Quixote.* Wordsworth's dream involves all the elements of the poet's last waking experience.

The Book, had turned my eyes tow'rd the wide Sea.
65 On Poetry, and geometric truth,
And their high privilege of lasting life,
From all internal injury exempt,
I mused; upon these chiefly: and, at length,
My senses yielding to the sultry air,
70 Sleep seized me, and I passed into a dream.
I saw before me stretched a boundless plain,
Of sandy wilderness, all blank and void;
And as I looked around, distress and fear
Came creeping over me, when at my side,
75 Close at my side, an uncouth Shape appeared
Upon a Dromedary, mounted high.
He seemed an Arab of the Bedouin Tribes:[3]
A Lance he bore, and underneath one arm
A Stone; and, in the opposite hand, a Shell
80 Of a surpassing brightness. At the sight
Much I rejoiced, not doubting but a Guide
Was present, one who with unerring skill
Would through the desert lead me; and while yet
I looked, and looked, self-questioned what this freight
85 Which the New-comer carried through the Waste
Could mean, the Arab told me that the Stone
(To give it in the language of the Dream)
Was Euclid's Elements;[4] "and this," said he,
"This other," pointing to the Shell, "this book
90 Is something of more worth": and, at the word,
Stretched forth the Shell, so beautiful in shape,
In color so resplendent, with command
That I should hold it to my ear. I did so,—
And heard, that instant, in an unknown tongue,
95 Which yet I understood, articulate sounds,
A loud prophetic blast of harmony—
An Ode, in passion uttered, which foretold
Destruction to the Children of the Earth,
By Deluge now at hand. No sooner ceased
100 The Song than the Arab with calm look declared
That all would come to pass, of which the voice
Had given forewarning, and that he himself
Was going then to bury those two Books:
The One that held acquaintance with the stars,
105 And wedded Soul to Soul in purest bond
Of Reason, undisturbed by space or time:
Th'other, that was a God, yea many Gods,
Had voices more than all the winds, with power
To exhilarate the Spirit, and to soothe,
110 Through every clime, the heart of human kind.
While this was uttering, strange as it may seem,
I wondered not, although I plainly saw

3. Mathematics had flourished among the Arabs—
hence the Arabian rider.
4. Celebrated book on plane geometry and the
theory of numbers by the Greek mathematician
Euclid; it continued to be used as a textbook into
the 19th century.

The One to be a Stone, the Other a Shell,
Nor doubted once but that they both were Books;
115 Having a perfect faith in all that passed.
Far stronger now grew the desire I felt
To cleave unto this Man; but when I prayed
To share his enterprize, he hurried on,
Reckless° of me: I followed, not unseen,   *heedless*
120 For oftentimes he cast a backward look,
Grasping his twofold treasure. Lance in rest,
He rode, I keeping pace with him; and now
He to my fancy had become the Knight
Whose tale Cervantes tells; yet not the Knight,
125 But was an Arab of the desert, too,
Of these was neither, and was both at once.
His countenance, meanwhile, grew more disturbed,
And looking backwards when he looked, mine eyes
Saw, over half the wilderness diffused,
130 A bed of glittering light: I asked the cause.
"It is," said he, "the waters of the Deep
Gathering upon us"; quickening then the pace
Of the unwieldy Creature he bestrode,
He left me; I called after him aloud,—
135 He heeded not; but with his twofold charge
Still in his grasp, before me, full in view,
Went hurrying o'er the illimitable Waste
With the fleet waters of a drowning World
In chase of him; whereat I waked in terror;
140 And saw the Sea before me, and the Book,
In which I had been reading, at my side.

[THE BOY OF WINANDER]

There was a Boy;[5]—ye knew him well, Ye Cliffs
And Islands of Winander!—many a time
At evening, when the earliest stars began
To move along the edges of the hills,
370 Rising or setting, would he stand alone,
Beneath the trees, or by the glimmering lake;
And there, with fingers interwoven, both hands
Pressed closely palm to palm and to his mouth
Uplifted, he, as through an instrument,
375 Blew mimic hootings to the silent owls
That they might answer him.—And they would shout
Across the watery Vale, and shout again,
Responsive to his call,—with quivering peals,
And long halloos, and screams, and echoes loud
380 Redoubled and redoubled; concourse wild
Of jocund din! and when a lengthened pause
Of silence came, and baffled his best skill,

---

5. In an early manuscript version of this passage Wordsworth uses the first-person pronoun. The experience he describes was thus apparently his own.

Then, sometimes, in that silence, while he hung
Listening, a gentle shock of mild surprize
385 Has carried far into his heart the voice
Of mountain torrents; or the visible scene
Would enter unawares into his mind
With all its solemn imagery, its rocks,
Its woods, and that uncertain heaven, received
390 Into the bosom of the steady lake.[6]
　　This Boy was taken from his Mates, and died
In childhood, ere he was full twelve years old.
Fair is the Spot, most beautiful the Vale
Where he was born: the grassy Church-yard hangs
395 Upon a slope above the Village School;
And through that Church-yard when my way has led
On summer evenings, I believe that there
A long half-hour together I have stood
Mute—looking at the grave in which he lies!
400 　　Even now appears before the mind's clear eye
That self-same Village Church; I see her sit
(The thronèd Lady whom erewhile we hailed)
On her green hill, forgetful of this Boy
Who slumbers at her feet, forgetful, too,
405 Of all her silent neighbourhood of graves,
And listening only to the gladsome sounds
That, from the rural School ascending, play
Beneath her, and about her. May she long
Behold a race of Young Ones like to those
410 With whom I herded! (easily, indeed,
We might have fed upon a fatter soil
Of Arts and Letters, but be that forgiven)
A race of *real* children; not too wise,
Too learnèd, or too good: but wanton, fresh,
415 And bandied up and down by love and hate;
Not unresentful where self-justified;
Fierce, moody, patient, venturous, modest, shy;
Mad at their sports like withered leaves in winds:
Though doing wrong and suffering, and full oft
420 Bending beneath our life's mysterious weight
Of pain, and doubt, and fear; yet yielding not
In happiness to the happiest upon earth.
Simplicity in habit, truth in speech,
Be these the daily strengtheners of their minds!
425 May books and nature be their early joy!
And knowledge, rightly honored with that name,
Knowledge not purchased by the loss of power!

["THE MYSTERY OF WORDS"]

Here must we pause; this only let me add,
From heart-experience, and in humblest sense

---

6. Coleridge wrote of the last line and a half ("that uncertain heaven . . . lake"): "Had I met these lines running wild in the deserts of Arabia, I should instantly have screamed out, 'Wordsworth.' "

Of modesty, that he, who, in his youth,
A daily Wanderer among woods and fields,
590 With living Nature hath been intimate,
Not only in that raw unpractised time
Is stirred to extasy, as others are,
By glittering verse; but, further, doth receive,
In measure only dealt out to himself,
595 Knowledge and increase of enduring joy
From the great Nature that exists in works
Of mighty Poets.[7] Visionary Power
Attends the motions of the viewless° winds   *invisible*
Embodied in the mystery of words:
600 There darkness makes abode, and all the host
Of shadowy things work endless changes there,
As in a mansion like their proper home.
Even forms and substances are circumfused
By that transparent veil with light divine;
605 And, through the turnings intricate of verse,
Present themselves as objects recognized,
In flashes, and with glory not their own.
      Thus far a scanty record is deduced
Of what I owed to Books in early life;
610 Their later influence yet remains untold;
But as this work was taking in my mind
Proportions that seemed larger than had first
Been meditated, I was indisposed
To any further progress, at a time
615 When these acknowledgments were left unpaid.

From Book Sixth
Cambridge, and the Alps

["HUMAN NATURE SEEMING BORN AGAIN"]

When the third summer freed us from restraint,[1]
A youthful Friend, he too a Mountaineer,
325 Not slow to share my wishes, took his staff,
And, sallying forth, we journeyed, side by side,
Bound to the distant Alps. A hardy slight
Did this unprecedented course imply
Of College studies and their set rewards;[2]
330 Nor had, in truth, the scheme been formed by me
Without uneasy forethought of the pain,
The censures, and ill-omening of those
To whom my worldly interests were dear.

7. Having found a set of symbols in nature, Wordsworth now finds nature in the symbol systems of "mighty poets."
1. After reviewing briefly his second and third years at Cambridge, Wordsworth here describes his trip through France and Switzerland with a college friend, Robert Jones, during the succeeding summer vacation, in 1790. France was then in the

"golden hours" of the early period of the Revolution; the fall of the Bastille had occurred on July 14 of the preceding year.
2. English universities allow much longer vacations than those in the United States, on the optimistic assumption that they will be used primarily for intensive study. Wordsworth is facing his final examinations in the next college year.

But Nature then was Sovereign in my mind,
335 And mighty Forms, seizing a youthful fancy,
Had given a charter[3] to irregular hopes.
In any age of uneventful calm
Among the Nations, surely would my heart
Have been possessed by similar desire;
340 But Europe at that time was thrilled with joy,
France standing on the top of golden hours,
And human nature seeming born again.

[CROSSING SIMPLON PASS]

* * * That very day,
525 From a bare ridge we also first beheld
Unveiled the summit of Mont Blanc, and grieved
To have a soulless image on the eye
Which had usurped upon a living thought
That never more could be.[4] The wondrous Vale
530 Of Chamouny[5] stretched far below, and soon
With its dumb cataracts, and streams of ice,
A motionless array of mighty waves,
Five rivers broad and vast, made rich amends,
And reconciled us to realities.
535 There small birds warble from the leafy trees,
The eagle soars high in the element;
There doth the Reaper bind the yellow sheaf,
The Maiden spread the hay-cock in the sun,
While Winter like a well-tamed lion walks,
540 Descending from the Mountain to make sport
Among the Cottages by beds of flowers.
Whate'er in this wide circuit we beheld,
Or heard, was fitted to our unripe state
Of intellect and heart. With such a book
545 Before our eyes we could not chuse but read
Lessons of genuine brotherhood, the plain
And universal reason of mankind,
The truths of Young and Old. Nor, side by side
Pacing, two social Pilgrims, or alone
550 Each with his humour,[6] could we fail to abound
In dreams and fictions pensively composed,
Dejection taken up for pleasure's sake,
And gilded sympathies; the willow wreath,[7]
And sober posies[8] of funereal flowers
555 Gathered, among those solitudes sublime,
From formal gardens of the Lady Sorrow,
Did sweeten many a meditative hour.
Yet still in me with those soft luxuries

3. Privileged freedom.
4. The "image" is the actual sight of Mont Blanc, as against what the poet has imagined the famous Swiss mountain to be.
5. Chamonix, a valley in eastern France, north of Mont Blanc.
6. Temperament, or state of mind.
7. Symbolizing sorrow. "Gilded": laid on like gilt; i.e., superficial.
8. Small bunches of flowers.

Mixed something of stern mood, an under thirst
560 Of vigor seldom utterly allayed.
And from that source how different a sadness
Would issue, let one incident make known.
When from the Vallais we had turned, and clomb°   climbed
Along the Simplon's steep and rugged road,[9]
565 Following a band of Muleteers, we reached
A halting-place where all together took
Their noon-tide meal. Hastily rose our Guide,
Leaving *us* at the Board; awhile we lingered,
Then paced the beaten downward way that led
570 Right to a rough stream's edge and there broke off.
The only track now visible was one
That from the torrent's further brink held forth
Conspicuous invitation to ascend
A lofty mountain. After brief delay
575 Crossing the unbridged stream, that road we took
And clomb with eagerness, till anxious fears
Intruded, for we failed to overtake
Our Comrades gone before. By fortunate chance,
While every moment added doubt to doubt,
580 A Peasant met us, from whose mouth we learned
That to the Spot which had perplexed us first
We must descend, and there should find the road,
Which in the stony channel of the Stream
Lay a few steps, and then along its banks,
585 And that our future course, all plain to sight,
Was downwards, with the current of that Stream.
Loth to believe what we so grieved to hear,
For still we had hopes that pointed to the clouds,
We questioned him again, and yet again;
590 But every word that from the Peasant's lips
Came in reply, translated by our feelings,
Ended in this, *that we had crossed the Alps.*[1]
        Imagination—here the Power so called
Through sad incompetence of human speech—
595 That awful Power rose from the Mind's abyss
Like an unfathered vapour[2] that enwraps
At once some lonely Traveller. I was lost,
Halted without an effort to break through;
But to my conscious soul I now can say,
600 "I recognize thy glory"; in such strength
Of usurpation, when the light of sense
Goes out, but with a flash that has revealed
The invisible world, doth Greatness make abode,
There harbours, whether we be young or old;
605 Our destiny, our being's heart and home,

9. The Simplon Pass through the Alps.
1. As Dorothy Wordsworth baldly put it later on,
"The ambition of youth was disappointed at these
tidings." The visionary experience that follows
(lines 593–617) occurred not in the Alps but at the
time of writing the passage, as the 1805 text explicitly says: "Imagination! lifting up itself / Before
the eye and progress of my Song."
2. Sudden vapor from no apparent source.

Is with infinitude, and only there;
With hope it is, hope that can never die,
Effort, and expectation, and desire,
And something evermore about to be.[3]
610 Under such banners militant the Soul
Seeks for no trophies, struggles for no spoils,
That may attest her prowess, blest in thoughts
That are their own perfection and reward,
Strong in herself, and in beatitude[4]
615 That hides her like the mighty flood of Nile
Poured from his fount of Abyssinian clouds
To fertilize the whole Egyptian plain.
   The melancholy slackening that ensued
Upon those tidings by the Peasant given
620 Was soon dislodged; downwards we hurried fast
And, with the half-shaped road, which we had missed,
Entered a narrow chasm. The brook and road
Were fellow-Travellers in this gloomy Strait,
And with them did we journey several hours
625 At a slow pace. The immeasurable height
Of woods decaying, never to be decayed,
The stationary blasts of waterfalls,
And in the narrow rent at every turn
Winds thwarting winds, bewildered and forlorn,
630 The torrents shooting from the clear blue sky,
The rocks that muttered close upon our ears,
Black drizzling crags that spake by the way-side
As if a voice were in them, the sick sight
And giddy prospect of the raving stream,
635 The unfettered clouds, and region of the Heavens,
Tumult and peace, the darkness and the light—
Were all like workings of one mind, the features
Of the same face, blossoms upon one tree,
Characters of the great Apocalypse,[5]
640 The types and symbols of Eternity,
Of first and last, and midst, and without end.[6]

From Book Seventh
Residence in London[1]

[THE BLIND BEGGAR. BARTHOLOMEW FAIR]

As the black storm upon the mountain top
620 Sets off the sunbeam in the Valley, so

---

3. At the time, Wordsworth had not been able to understand why he had felt such grievous disappointment at finding that he had already crossed the Alps, while still expecting to climb upward (lines 587–92). Now, a flash of vision reveals the symbolic significance of that experience: that the glory of humankind is to aim infinitely high, even though our capabilities are finite.
4. The ultimate blessedness or happiness.
5. The objects in this natural scene, exhibiting a coincidence of all opposites, are like the written words of the Apocalypse—i.e., of the Book of Revelation, the last book of the New Testament.
6. Cf. Revelation 1.8: "I am Alpha and Omega, the beginning and the ending, saith the Lord." The phrase is repeated in Revelation 21.6, after the fulfillment of the last things. In *Paradise Lost* 5.153–65 Milton says that the things created declare their Creator, and calls on all to extol "him first, him last, him midst, and without end."
1. Wordsworth spent three and a half months in London in 1791.

That huge fermenting Mass of human-kind
Serves as a solemn background or relief
To single forms and objects, whence they draw,
For feeling and contemplative regard,
625　More than inherent liveliness and power.
How oft amid those overflowing streets
Have I gone forward with the Crowd, and said
Unto myself, "The face of every one
That passes by me is a mystery!"
630　Thus have I looked, nor ceased to look, oppressed
By thoughts of what and whither, when and how,
Until the Shapes before my eyes became
A second-sight procession, such as glides
Over still mountains, or appears in dreams.
635　And once, far-travelled in such mood, beyond
The reach of common indication, lost
Amid the moving pageant, I was smitten
Abruptly with the view (a sight not rare)
Of a blind Beggar who, with upright face,
640　Stood propped against a Wall; upon his chest
Wearing a written paper to explain
His Story, whence he came, and who he was.
Caught by the spectacle, my mind turned round
As with the might of waters; an apt type
645　This Label seemed, of the utmost we can know
Both of ourselves and of the universe;
And on the Shape of that unmoving Man,
His steadfast face, and sightless eyes, I gazed
As if admonished from another world.
650　　Though reared upon the base of outward things,
Structures like these the excited Spirit mainly
Builds for herself. Scenes different there are,
Full-formed, that take, with small internal help,
Possession of the faculties—the peace
655　That comes with night; the deep solemnity
Of Nature's intermediate hours of rest,
When the great tide of human life stands still,
The business of the day to come—unborn,
Of that gone by—locked up as in the grave;[2]
660　The blended calmness of the heavens and earth,
Moonlight, and stars, and empty streets, and sounds
Unfrequent as in deserts: at late hours
Of winter evenings when unwholesome rains
Are falling hard, with people yet astir,
665　The feeble salutation from the voice
Of some unhappy woman, now and then
Heard as we pass; when no one looks about,
Nothing is listened to. But these, I fear,
Are falsely catalogued;[3] things that are, are not,
670　As the mind answers to them, or the heart

2. The sonnet *Composed upon Westminster Bridge* describes a similar response to London when its "mighty heart is lying still."

3. I.e., mistakenly classified as scenes (lines 652–54) whose effects on the perceiver depend but little on contributions by the perceiving mind.

Is prompt or slow to feel. What say you, then,
To times when half the City shall break out
Full of one passion, vengeance, rage, or fear?
To executions,[4] to a Street on fire,
675   Mobs, riots, or rejoicings? From these sights
Take one, that annual Festival, the Fair
Holden where Martyrs suffered in past time,
And named of St. Bartholomew;[5] there see
A work completed to our hands, that lays,
680   If any spectacle on earth can do,
The whole creative powers of Man asleep!
For once the Muse's help will we implore,
And she shall lodge us, wafted on her wings,
Above the press and danger of the Crowd,
685   Upon some Shewman's platform. What a shock
For eyes and ears! what anarchy and din
Barbarian and infernal—a phantasma[6]
Monstrous in color, motion, shape, sight, sound!
Below, the open space, through every nook
690   Of the wide area, twinkles, is alive
With heads; the midway region and above
Is thronged with staring pictures, and huge scrolls,
Dumb proclamations of the Prodigies!
With chattering monkeys dangling from their poles,
695   And children whirling in their roundabouts;°   *merry-go-rounds*
With those that stretch the neck, and strain the eyes;
And crack the voice in rivalship, the crowd
Inviting; with buffoons against buffoons
Grimacing, writhing, screaming, him who grinds
700   The hurdy-gurdy,[7] at the fiddle weaves,
Rattles the salt-box,[8] thumps the Kettle-drum;
And him who at the trumpet puffs his cheeks;
The silver-collared Negro with his timbrel;°   *tambourine*
Equestrians, tumblers, women, girls, and boys,
705   Blue-breeched, pink-vested, with high-towering plumes.
—All moveables of wonder from all parts
And here, Albinos, painted-Indians, Dwarfs,
The Horse of Knowledge,[9] and the learned Pig,
The Stone-eater, the Man that swallows fire—
710   Giants, Ventriloquists, the Invisible-girl,
The Bust that speaks, and moves its goggling eyes,
The Wax-work, Clock-work, all the marvellous craft
Of modern Merlins,[1] Wild-beasts, Puppet-shews,
All out-o'th'-way, far-fetched, perverted things,
715   All freaks of Nature, all Promethean[2] thoughts

---

4. Executions were public events in England until 1868.
5. This huge fair was long held in Smithfield, the place where, on St. Bartholomew's Day, August 24, Protestants had been executed in Queen Mary's reign (1553–58).
6. Fantasy of a disordered mind.
7. A stringed instrument, sounded by a turning wheel covered by rosin.

8. A wooden box, rattled and beaten with a stick.
9. A horse trained to tap out answers to numerical questions, etc.
1. Magicians. Merlin was the magician in Arthurian romance.
2. Creative, or highly inventive. In Greek mythology Prometheus made man out of clay and taught him the arts.

Of man; his dullness, madness, and their feats,
All jumbled up together, to compose
A Parliament of Monsters. Tents and Booths,
Meanwhile, as if the whole were one vast mill,
720   Are vomiting, receiving, on all sides,
Men, Women, three-years' Children, Babes in arms.
   Oh blank confusion! true epitome
Of what the mighty City is herself
To thousands upon thousands of her Sons,
725   Living amid the same perpetual whirl
Of trivial objects, melted and reduced
To one identity, by differences
That have no law, no meaning, and no end;
Oppression under which even highest minds
730   Must labour, whence the strongest are not free!
But though the picture weary out the eye,
By nature an unmanageable sight,
It is not wholly so to him who looks
In steadiness, who hath among least things
735   An undersense of greatest; sees the parts
As parts, but with a feeling of the whole.

*   *   *

This did I feel in London's vast Domain;
The Spirit of Nature was upon me there;
The Soul of Beauty and enduring life
Vouchsafed her inspirations; and diffused,
770   Through meagre lines and colours, and the press
Of self-destroying transitory things,
Composure, and ennobling harmony.

From Book Eighth
Retrospect, Love of Nature leading
to Love of Man[1]

[THE SHEPHERD IN THE MIST. MAN STILL SUBORDINATE TO NATURE]

* * * A rambling School-boy, thus
I felt his presence in his own domain
As of a Lord and Master; or a Power
Or Genius,[2] under Nature, under God
260   Presiding; and severest solitude
Had more commanding looks when he was there.
When up the lonely brooks on rainy days
Angling I went, or trod the trackless hills

---

1. In this book Wordsworth reviews the first twenty-one years of his life to trace the transfer of his earlier feelings for nature to shepherds and other humble people who carry on their lonely duties almost as though they were animate parts of the landscape (cf. *Michael*, lines 1–39, pp. 270–71). Wordsworth's central concern is to describe the early development in his relatively inexperi-

enced mind of an image, or conceptual model, of the largeness, worth, and almost sacred dignity of generic Man (lines 256–81), an image that proved invulnerable to the acid bath of his later experience of the vulgarity, meanness, and evil of which individuals are capable (lines 317–22).
2. Presiding spirit.

By mists bewildered, suddenly mine eyes
265 Have glanced upon him distant a few steps,
In size a Giant, stalking through thick fog,
His sheep like Greenland bears;° or, as he stepped   *polar bears*
Beyond the boundary line of some hill-shadow,
His form hath flashed upon me, glorified
270 By the deep radiance of the setting sun:[3]
Or him have I descried in distant sky,
A solitary object and sublime,
Above all height! like an aerial cross
Stationed alone upon a spiry rock
275 Of the Chartreuse,[4] for worship. Thus was Man
Ennobled outwardly before my sight,
And thus my heart was early introduced
To an unconscious love and reverence
Of human nature; hence the human Form
280 To me became an index of delight,
Of grace, and honor, power, and worthiness.
Meanwhile this Creature, spiritual almost
As those of Books, but more exalted far;
Far more of an imaginative Form
285 Than the gay Corin of the groves, who lives
For his own fancies, or to dance by the hour
In coronal, with Phillis[5] in the midst—
Was, for the purposes of Kind,[6] a Man
With the most common; husband, father; learned,
290 Could teach, admonish, suffered with the rest
From vice and folly, wretchedness and fear;
Of this I little saw, cared less for it;
But something must have felt.
                      Call ye these appearances
Which I beheld of Shepherds in my youth,
295 This sanctity of Nature given to man—
A shadow, a delusion, ye who pore
On the dead letter, miss the spirit of things;
Whose truth is not a motion or a shape
Instinct with vital functions, but a Block
300 Or waxen image which yourselves have made,
And ye adore. But blessed be the God
Of Nature and of Man, that this was so,
That men before my inexperienced eyes
Did first present themselves thus purified,
305 Removed, and to a distance that was fit.
And so we all of us in some degree
Are led to knowledge, whencesoever led
And howsoever; were it otherwise,

---

3. A "glory" is a mountain phenomenon in which the enlarged figure of a person is seen projected by the sun on the mist, with a radiance about its head. Cf. Coleridge's *Dejection: An Ode*, line 54 (p. 460).
4. In his tour of the Alps, Wordsworth had been deeply impressed by the Chartreuse, a Carthusian monastery in France, with its soaring cross visible against the sky. There is an overtone here of the Christ-like divinity investing the "common" man (line 289).
5. Corin and Phillis, dancing in their coronals, or wreaths of flowers, were stock characters in earlier pastoral literature.
6. I.e., in carrying out the tasks of humankind.

And we found evil fast as we find good
310 In our first years, or think that it is found,
How could the innocent heart bear up and live?
But doubly fortunate my lot; not here
Alone, that something of a better life
Perhaps was round me than it is the privilege
315 Of most to move in, but that first I looked
At Man through objects that were great or fair,
First communed with him by their help. And thus
Was founded a sure safeguard and defence
Against the weight of meanness, selfish cares,
320 Coarse manners, vulgar passions, that beat in
On all sides from the ordinary world
In which we traffic. Starting from this point,
I had my face turned tow'rd the truth, began
With an advantage furnished by that kind
325 Of prepossession without which the soul
Receives no knowledge that can bring forth good,
No genuine insight ever comes to her.
From the restraint of over-watchful eyes
Preserved, I moved about, year after year
330 Happy, and now most thankful, that my walk
Was guarded from too early intercourse
With the deformities of crowded life,
And those ensuing laughters and contempts
Self-pleasing, which, if we would wish to think
335 With a due reverence on earth's rightful Lord,
Here placed to be the Inheritor of heaven,[7]
Will not permit us; but pursue the mind
That to devotion willingly would rise,
Into the Temple, and the Temple's heart.[8]
340   Yet deem not, Friend, that human-kind with me
Thus early took a place preeminent;
Nature herself was at this unripe time
But secondary to my own pursuits
And animal activities, and all
345 Their trivial pleasures:[9] and when these had drooped
And gradually expired, and Nature, prized
For her own sake, became my joy, even then—
And upwards through late youth, until not less
Than two and twenty summers had been told—
350 Was Man in my affections and regards
Subordinate to her; her visible Forms
And viewless agencies: a passion she,
A rapture often, and immediate love
Ever at hand; *he* only a delight
355 Occasional, an accidental grace,
His hour being not yet come. * * *

7. This pious line was a later addition to the version of 1805.
8. I.e., into the devotional recesses of the inner-most mind.
9. Cf. his account of the stages of his development in lines 65–92 of *Tintern Abbey* (n. 2, p. 237).

From Book Ninth
Residence in France[1]

[PARIS AND ORLÉANS. BECOMES A "PATRIOT"]

Even as a River—partly (it might seem)
Yielding to old remembrances, and swayed
In part by fear to shape a way direct
That would engulph him soon in the ravenous Sea—
5 Turns, and will measure back his course, far back,
Seeking the very regions which he crossed
In his first outset; so have we, my Friend!
Turned and returned with intricate delay.
Or as a Traveller, who has gained the brow
10 Of some aerial Down,[2] while there he halts
For breathing-time, is tempted to review
The region left behind him; and if aught
Deserving notice have escaped regard,
Or been regarded with too careless eye,
15 Strives, from that height, with one, and yet one more
Last look, to make the best amends he may,
So have we lingered. Now we start afresh
With courage, and new hope risen on our toil.
Fair greetings to this shapeless eagerness,
20 Whene'er it comes! needful in work so long,
Thrice needful to the argument° which now   *theme*
Awaits us! Oh, how much unlike the past![3]

    Free as a Colt, at pasture on the hill,
I ranged at large through London's wide Domain
25 Month after Month. Obscurely did I live,
Not seeking frequent intercourse with men
By literature, or elegance, or rank
Distinguished. Scarcely was a year thus spent[4]
Ere I forsook the crowded Solitude;
30 With less regret for its luxurious pomp
And all the nicely-guarded shews of Art,
Than for the humble Bookstalls in the Streets,
Exposed to eye and hand where'er I turned.
—France lured me forth, the realm that I had crossed
35 So lately, journeying toward the snow-clad Alps.
But now relinquishing the scrip° and staff[5]   *knapsack*
And all enjoyment which the summer sun
Sheds round the steps of those who meet the day
With motion constant as his own, I went

1. Wordsworth's second visit to France, while he was twenty-one and twenty-two years of age (1791–92), came during a crucial period of the French Revolution. This book deals with his stay at Paris, Orléans, and Blois, when he developed his passionate partisanship for the French people and the revolutionary cause.
2. Treeless high land.
3. This preface parallels in function Milton's pref- ace to the equivalent ninth book of *Paradise Lost*, in which he announces that, having narrated the blameless life of Adam and Eve in Eden, he "now must change / Those notes to tragic," and tell of their fall.
4. His stay in London in fact lasted only four or five months, January–May 1791.
5. Traditional emblems of the foot pilgrim.

40 Prepared to sojourn in a pleasant Town[6]
Washed by the current of the stately Loire.
   Through Paris lay my readiest course, and there
Sojourning a few days, I visited
In haste each spot, of old or recent fame,
45 The latter chiefly; from the field of Mars[7]
Down to the suburbs of St. Anthony;[8]
And from Mont Martyr[9] southward to the Dome
Of Genevieve.[1] In both her clamorous Halls,
The National Synod and the Jacobins,[2]
50 I saw the Revolutionary Power
Toss like a Ship at anchor, rocked by storms;
The Arcades I traversed, in the Palace huge
Of Orleans,[3] coasted round and round the line
Of Tavern, Brothel, Gaming-house, and Shop,
55 Great rendezvous of worst and best, the walk
Of all who had a purpose, or had not;
I stared, and listened with a Stranger's ears
To Hawkers and Haranguers, hubbub wild!
And hissing Factionists, with ardent eyes,
60 In knots, or pairs, or single. Not a look
Hope takes, or Doubt or Fear are forced to wear,
But seemed there present, and I scanned them all,
Watched every gesture uncontrollable
Of anger, and vexation, and despite,
65 All side by side, and struggling face to face
With Gaiety and dissolute Idleness.
—Where silent zephyrs sported with the dust
Of the Bastille,[4] I sate in the open sun,
And from the rubbish gathered up a stone
70 And pocketed the Relic in the guise
Of an Enthusiast; yet, in honest truth,
I looked for Something that I could not find,
Affecting more emotion than I felt;
For 'tis most certain that these various sights,
75 However potent their first shock, with me
Appeared to recompence the Traveller's pains
Less than the painted Magdalene of Le Brun,[5]
A Beauty exquisitely wrought, with hair
Dishevelled, gleaming eyes, and rueful cheek
80 Pale, and bedropp'd with everflowing tears.
   But hence to my more permanent Abode[6]

6. Orléans, on the Loire River, where Wordsworth stayed from December 1791 until he moved to Blois early the next year.
7. The Champ de Mars, where Louis XVI swore fidelity to the new constitution.
8. Faubourg St. Antoine, near the Bastille, a working-class quarter and center of revolutionary violence.
9. Montmartre, a hill on which revolutionary meetings were held.
1. Became the Panthéon, a burial place for notable Frenchmen.
2. The club of radical democratic revolutionists,

named for the ancient convent of St. Jacques, their meeting place. "National Synod": the newly formed National Assembly.
3. The arcades in the courtyard of the Palais d'Orléans, a fashionable shopping center and Parisian rendezvous.
4. The political prison, which had been demolished after being stormed and sacked on July 14, 1789.
5. Charles Le Brun (1619–1690) painted the weeping Mary Magdalene, then regarded as a religious masterpiece.
6. In Orléans.

I hasten; there by novelties in speech,
Domestic manners, customs, gestures, looks,
And all the attire of ordinary life,
85 Attention was engrossed; and, thus amused,
I stood 'mid those concussions unconcerned,
Tranquil almost, and careless as a flower
Glassed in a green-house, or a Parlour shrub
That spreads its leaves in unmolested peace
90 While every bush and tree, the country through,
Is shaking to the roots; indifference this
Which may seem strange; but I was unprepared
With needful knowledge, had abruptly passed
Into a theatre whose stage was filled,
95 And busy with an action far advanced.
Like Others I had skimmed, and sometimes read
With care, the master pamphlets of the day;[7]
Nor wanted such half-insight as grew wild
Upon that meagre soil, helped out by talk
100 And public news; but having never seen
A Chronicle that might suffice to shew
Whence the main Organs[8] of the public Power
Had sprung, their transmigrations when and how
Accomplished, giving thus unto events
105 A form and body; all things were to me
Loose and disjointed, and the affections left
Without a vital interest. At that time,
Moreover, the first storm was overblown,
And the strong hand of outward violence
110 Locked up in quiet.[9] For myself, I fear
Now, in connection with so great a Theme,
To speak (as I must be compelled to do)
Of one so unimportant; night by night
Did I frequent the formal haunts of men
115 Whom, in the City, privilege of birth
Sequestered from the rest: societies
Polished in Arts, and in punctilio[1] versed;
Whence, and from deeper causes, all discourse
Of good and evil of the time was shunned
120 With scrupulous care: but these restrictions soon
Proved tedious, and I gradually withdrew
Into a noisier world, and thus erelong
Became a Patriot;[2] and my heart was all
Given to the People, and my love was theirs.

---

7. Wordsworth probably refers to the numerous English pamphlets (including Paine's *Rights of Man*, part 1, and Wollstonecraft's *A Vindication of the Rights of Men*) published in response to Edmund Burke's attack on the revolution, *Reflections on the Revolution in France* (1790).
8. Institutions, instruments.

9. After the storming of the Bastille in 1789 there was a period of calm until the massacre of three thousand Royalists in September 1792, after the deposition and imprisonment of Louis XVI.
1. The niceties of social manners.
2. I.e., became committed to the people's side in the Revolution.

From Book Tenth
France continued[1]
[THE REVOLUTION: PARIS AND ENGLAND]

Cheared with this hope,[2] to Paris I returned;
And ranged, with ardor heretofore unfelt,
50   The spacious City, and in progress passed
The Prison[3] where the unhappy Monarch lay,
Associate with his Children and his Wife,
In Bondage; and the Palace[4] lately stormed,
With roar of Cannon, by a furious Host.
55   I crossed the Square (an empty Area then!)
Of the Carousel, where so late had lain
The Dead, upon the Dying heaped; and gazed
On this and other Spots, as doth a Man
Upon a Volume whose contents he knows
60   Are memorable, but from him locked up,
Being written in a tongue he cannot read;
So that he questions the mute leaves with pain,
And half-upbraids their silence. But, that night,
I felt most deeply in what world I was,
65   What ground I trod on, and what air I breathed.
High was my Room and lonely, near the roof
Of a large Mansion or Hotel,° a Lodge   *town house*
That would have pleased me in more quiet times,
Nor was it wholly without pleasure, then.
70   With unextinguished taper I kept watch,
Reading at intervals; the fear gone by
Pressed on me almost like a fear to come.
I thought of those September massacres,
Divided from me by one little month,
75   Saw them and touched;[5] the rest was conjured up
From tragic fictions, or true history,
Remembrances and dim admonishments.
The Horse is taught his manage,[6] and no Star
Of wildest course but treads back his own steps;
80   For the spent hurricane the air provides
As fierce a Successor; the tide retreats
But to return out of its hiding place
In the great Deep; all things have second birth;
The earthquake is not satisfied at once;
85   And in this way I wrought upon myself
Until I seemed to hear a voice that cried

1. At this period, October 1792–August 1794, Wordsworth's revolutionary enthusiasm was at its height.
2. I.e., that the moderates were now taking over and would eliminate further violence.
3. I.e., the "Temple" (it had once housed the religious Order of Templars), where Louis XVI was held prisoner.

4. The Tuileries. In front of this is the great square of "the Carousel" (line 56), where a number of the mob storming the palace had been killed.
5. I.e., his imagination of the September massacres was so vivid as to be palpable.
6. The French *manège*, the prescribed action and paces of a trained horse.

To the whole City, "Sleep no more."[7] The Trance
Fled with the Voice to which it had given birth,
But vainly comments of a calmer mind
90   Promised soft peace and sweet forgetfulness.
The place, all hushed and silent as it was,
Appeared unfit for the repose of Night,
Defenceless as a wood where Tygers roam.

* * * In this frame of mind,
Dragged by a chain of harsh necessity,
So seemed it,—now I thankfully acknowledge,
Forced by the gracious providence of Heaven—
225   To England I returned,[8] else (though assured
That I both was, and must be, of small weight,
No better than a Landsman on the deck
Of a ship struggling with a hideous storm)
Doubtless I should have then made common cause
230   With some who perished, haply perished too,[9]
A poor mistaken and bewildered offering,
Should to the breast of Nature have gone back
With all my resolutions, all my hopes,
A Poet only to myself, to Men
235   Useless, and even, belovèd Friend, a Soul
To thee unknown![1]

* * *

What then were my emotions, when in Arms
Britain put forth her free-born strength in league,
265   O pity and shame! with those confederate Powers?[2]
Not in my single self alone I found,
But in the minds of all ingenuous Youth,
Change and subversion from that hour. No shock
Given to my moral nature had I known
270   Down to that very moment; neither lapse
Nor turn of sentiment that might be named
A revolution, save at this one time;
All else was progress on the self-same path
On which, with a diversity of pace,
275   I had been travelling: this a stride at once
Into another region.—As a light
And pliant hare-bell swinging in the breeze
On some gray rock, its birth-place, so had I
Wantoned, fast rooted on the ancient tower

---

7. *Macbeth* 2.2.33–34: "Methought I heard a voice cry, 'Sleep no more, / Macbeth does murder sleep.' "
8. Forced by the "harsh necessity" of a lack of money, Wordsworth returned to England late in 1792.
9. Wordsworth had allied his sympathies with the party of the Girondins, almost all of whom were guillotined or committed suicide.
1. Wordsworth did not meet Coleridge, the "beloved Friend," until 1795.

2. England joined the war against France in February 1793. The great moral crisis that almost wrecked Wordsworth's life began with this sudden split between his profound attachments to the English land (the development of which he had described in the early books of *The Prelude*) and his later but heartfelt identification with the cause of the French Revolution. What had seemed a single and coherent development suddenly became split into conflicting parts.

280 Of my beloved Country, wishing not
     A happier fortune than to wither there.
     Now was I from that pleasant station torn
     And tossed about in whirlwind. I rejoiced,
     Yea, afterwards, truth most painful to record!
285 Exulted, in the triumph of my Soul,
     When Englishmen by thousands were o'erthrown,
     Left without glory on the field, or driven,
     Brave hearts, to shameful flight.[3] It was a grief,—
     Grief call it not, 'twas any thing but that,—
290 A conflict of sensations without name,
     Of which *he* only who may love the sight
     Of a Village Steeple as I do can judge,
     When, in the Congregation bending all
     To their great Father, prayers were offered up,
295 Or praises, for our Country's victories,
     And, 'mid the simple Worshippers, perchance
     I only, like an uninvited Guest,
     Whom no one owned, sate silent, shall I add,
     Fed on the day of vengeance yet to come?

                    *   *   *

[THE REIGN OF TERROR. NIGHTMARES]

     —Domestic carnage now filled the whole year
     With Feast-days;[4] old Men from the Chimney-nook,
     The Maiden from the bosom of her Love,
     The Mother from the Cradle of her Babe,
360 The Warrior from the Field, all perished, all,
     Friends, enemies, of all parties, ages, ranks,
     Head after head, and never heads enough
     For those that bade them fall. They found their joy,
     They made it, proudly eager as a Child
365 (If like desires of innocent little ones
     May with such heinous appetites be compared),
     Pleased in some open field to exercise
     A toy that mimics with revolving wings
     The motion of a windmill, though the air
370 Do of itself blow fresh and make the Vanes
     Spin in his eyesight, *that* contents him not,
     But, with the play-thing at arm's length, he sets
     His front against the blast, and runs amain
     That it may whirl the faster.

                    *   *   *

     Most melancholy at that time, O Friend!
     Were my day-thoughts, my nights were miserable;

3. The French defeated the English in the battle of Hondschoote, September 6, 1793.
4. I.e., festivals celebrated by human slaughter ("carnage"). Lines 356–63 give a description of the height of the Reign of Terror under Robespierre. In 1794, a total of 1,376 people were guillotined in Paris in forty-nine days.

Through months, through years, long after the last beat
400 Of those atrocities, the hour of sleep
To me came rarely charged with natural gifts,
Such ghastly Visions had I of despair
And tyranny, and implements of death,
And innocent victims sinking under fear,
405 And momentary hope, and worn-out prayer,
Each in his separate cell, or penned in crowds
For sacrifice, and struggling with forced mirth
And levity in dungeons where the dust
Was laid with tears. Then suddenly the scene
410 Changed, and the unbroken dream entangled me
In long orations which I strove to plead
Before unjust tribunals—with a voice
Labouring, a brain confounded, and a sense
Death-like of treacherous desertion, felt
415 In the last place of refuge, my own soul.

From Book Eleventh
France, concluded[1]

[RETROSPECT: "BLISS WAS IT IN THAT DAWN." RECOURSE TO
"REASON'S NAKED SELF"]

105   O pleasant exercise of hope and joy![2]
For mighty were the Auxiliars which then stood
Upon our side, we who were strong in Love!
Bliss was it in that dawn to be alive,
But to be young was very Heaven! O times,
110 In which the meagre, stale, forbidding ways
Of custom, law, and statute, took at once
The attraction of a Country in Romance!
When Reason seemed the most to assert her rights,
When most intent on making of herself
115 A prime Enchantress—to assist the work
Which then was going forward in her name!
Not favored spots alone, but the whole earth
The beauty wore of promise—that which sets
(As at some moments might not be unfelt
120 Among the bowers of Paradise itself)
The budding rose above the rose full blown.[3]
What Temper° at the prospect did not wake   temperament
To happiness unthought of? The inert
Were roused, and lively natures rapt away![4]

---

1. Book 11 deals with the year from August 1794 through September 1795: Wordsworth's growing disillusionment with the French Revolution, his recourse to abstract theories of man and politics, his despair and nervous breakdown, and the beginning of his recovery when he moved from London to Racedown.

2. Wordsworth in this passage turns back to the summer of 1792, when his enthusiasm for the Revolution was at its height.
3. A statement of the Romantic theme of the glory of the imperfect, which sets a higher value on promise than on achievement.
4. Enraptured; carried away by enthusiasm.

125   They who had fed their Childhood upon dreams,
The play-fellows of Fancy, who had made
All powers of swiftness, subtilty, and strength
Their ministers,—who in lordly wise had stirred
Among the grandest objects of the Sense,
130   And dealt with whatsoever they found there
As if they had within some lurking right
To wield it;—they, too, who of gentle mood
Had watched all gentle motions, and to these
Had fitted their own thoughts, schemers more mild,
135   And in the region of their peaceful selves;—
Now was it that *both* found, the Meek and Lofty
Did both find helpers to their hearts' desire,
And stuff at hand, plastic° as they could wish,—   *malleable*
Were called upon to exercise their skill,
140   Not in Utopia,—subterranean Fields,—
Or some secreted Island, Heaven knows where!
But in the very world, which is the world
Of all of us,—the place where in the end
We find our happiness, or not at all!
145   Why should I not confess that Earth was then
To me what an Inheritance new-fallen
Seems, when the first time visited, to one
Who thither comes to find in it his home?
He walks about and looks upon the spot
150   With cordial transport, moulds it and remoulds,
And is half-pleased with things that are amiss,
'Twill be such joy to see them disappear.
      An active partisan, I thus convoked°   *called up*
From every object pleasant circumstance
155   To suit my ends; I moved among mankind
With genial feelings still° predominant;   *always*
When erring, erring on the better part,
And in the kinder spirit; placable,
Indulgent, as not uninformed that men
160   See as they have been taught, and that Antiquity[5]
Gives rights to error; and aware no less
That throwing off oppression must be work
As well of licence as of liberty;
And above all, for this was more than all,
165   Not caring if the wind did now and then
Blow keen upon an eminence that gave
Prospect so large into futurity;
In brief, a Child of Nature, as at first,
Diffusing only those affections wider
170   That from the cradle had grown up with me,
And losing, in no other way than light
Is lost in light, the weak in the more strong.
      In the main outline, such, it might be said,

---

5. Classical antiquity.

Was my condition, till with open war
175 Britain opposed the Liberties of France;[6]
This threw me first out of the pale° of love,   *enclosure*
Soured, and corrupted, upwards to the source,
My sentiments; was not,[7] as hitherto,
A swallowing up of lesser things in great;
180 But change of them into their contraries;
And thus a way was opened for mistakes
And false conclusions, in degree as gross,
In kind more dangerous. What had been a pride
Was now a shame; my likings and my loves
185 Ran in new channels, leaving old ones dry,
And hence a blow that in maturer age
Would but have touched the judgement, struck more deep
Into sensations near the heart; meantime,
As from the first, wild theories were afloat
190 To whose pretensions sedulously urged[8]
I had but lent a careless ear, assured
That time was ready to set all things right,
And that the multitude so long oppressed
Would be oppressed no more.
                                        But when events
195 Brought less encouragement, and unto these
The immediate proof of principles no more
Could be entrusted, while the events themselves,
Worn out in greatness, stripped of novelty,
Less occupied the mind; and sentiments
200 Could through my understanding's natural growth
No longer keep their ground, by faith maintained
Of inward consciousness, and hope that laid
Her hand upon her object; evidence
Safer, of universal application, such
205 As could not be impeached, was sought elsewhere.
        But now, become Oppressors in their turn,
Frenchmen had changed a war of self-defence
For one of Conquest, losing sight of all
Which they had struggled for:[9] and mounted up,
210 Openly in the eye of Earth and Heaven,
The scale of Liberty.[1] I read her doom
With anger vexed, with disappointment sore,
But not dismayed, nor taking to the shame
Of a false Prophet. While resentment rose,
215 Striving to hide, what nought could heal, the wounds
Of mortified presumption, I adhered
More firmly to old tenets, and, to prove[2]
Their temper, strained them more; and thus, in heat
Of contest, did opinions every day

6. On February 11, 1793, England declared war
against France.
7. I.e., there was not (in my sentiments).
8. Diligently argued for.
9. In late 1794 and early 1795 French troops had
successes in Spain, Italy, Holland, and Germany—

even though, in the constitution written in 1790,
they had renounced all foreign conquest.
1. I.e., the desire for power now outweighed the
love of liberty.
2. Test. The figure is that of testing a tempered
steel sword.

220 Grow into consequence, till round my mind
They clung, as if they were its life, nay more,
The very being of the immortal Soul.
      This was the time when, all things tending fast
To depravation, speculative schemes
225 That promised to abstract the hopes of Man
Out of his feelings, to be fixed thenceforth
For ever in a purer element,
Found ready welcome.[3] Tempting region *that*
For Zeal to enter and refresh herself,
230 Where passions had the privilege to work,
And never hear the sound of their own names:
But, speaking more in charity, the dream
Flattered the young, pleased with extremes, nor least
With that which makes our Reason's naked self
235 The object of its fervour. * * *

[CRISIS, BREAKDOWN, AND RECOVERY]

I summoned my best skill, and toiled, intent
280 To anatomize° the frame of social life,   *analyze*
Yea, the whole body of society
Searched to its heart. Share with me, Friend! the wish
That some dramatic tale indued with shapes
Livelier, and flinging out less guarded words
285 Than suit the Work we fashion, might set forth
What then I learned, or think I learned, of truth,
And the errors into which I fell, betrayed
By present objects, and by reasonings false
From their beginnings, inasmuch as drawn
290 Out of a heart that had been turned aside
From Nature's way by outward accidents,
And which was thus confounded more and more,
Misguided and misguiding. So I fared,
Dragging all precepts, judgments, maxims, creeds,
295 Like culprits to the bar; calling the mind,
Suspiciously, to establish in plain day
Her titles[4] and her honors, now believing,
Now disbelieving, endlessly perplexed
With impulse, motive, right and wrong, the ground
300 Of obligation, what the rule and whence
The sanction, till, demanding formal *proof*
And seeking it in every thing, I lost
All feeling of conviction, and, in fine,°   *the end*
Sick, wearied out with contrarieties,
305 Yielded up moral questions in despair.
      This was the crisis of that strong disease,

3. I.e., schemes that undertook to separate ("abstract") people's hopes for future happiness from reliance on the emotional part of human nature, and instead to ground those hopes on their rational natures ("a purer element"). The allusion is primarily to William Godwin's *Inquiry Concern-* *ing Political Justice* (1793), which attempted to ground ethical and political principles, and the expectation of human progress, exclusively on rational principles.
4. Legal entitlements.

This the soul's last and lowest ebb; I drooped,
Deeming our blessed Reason of least use
Where wanted most. * * *

         * * * Then it was,
Thanks to the bounteous Giver of all good!
335   That the beloved Woman[5] in whose sight
Those days were passed, now speaking in a voice
Of sudden admonition—like a brook
That does but *cross* a lonely road, and now
Seen, heard, and felt, and caught at every turn,
340   Companion never lost through many a league—
Maintained for me a saving intercourse
With my true self:[6] for, though bedimmed and changed
Both as a clouded and a waning moon,
She whispered still that brightness would return,
345   She in the midst of all preserved me still
A Poet, made me seek beneath that name,
And that alone, my office upon earth.
And lastly, as hereafter will be shewn,
If willing audience fail not, Nature's self,
350   By all varieties of human love
Assisted, led me back through opening day
To those sweet counsels between head and heart
Whence grew that genuine knowledge fraught with peace
Which, through the later sinkings of this cause,
355   Hath still upheld me, and upholds me now
In the catastrophe (for so they dream,
And nothing less), when, finally to close
And rivet down the gains of France, a Pope
Is summoned in, to crown an Emperor:[7]
360   This last opprobrium, when we see a people
That once looked up in faith, as if to Heaven
For manna, take a lesson from the Dog
Returning to his vomit. * * *

Book Twelfth
Imagination and Taste, how impaired and restored[1]

Long time have human ignorance and guilt
Detained us, on what spectacles of woe
Compelled to look, and inwardly oppressed
With sorrow, disappointment, vexing thoughts,
5   Confusion of the judgment, zeal decayed,

---

5. After a long separation, Dorothy Wordsworth came to live with her brother at Racedown in 1795 and remained a permanent member of his household.
6. Dorothy and the renewed influence of nature (line 349) healed the inner fracture between his earlier and later selves, which Wordsworth had described in 10.268ff.

7. The ultimate blow to liberal hopes for France occurred when on December 2, 1804, Napoleon summoned Pope Pius VII to officiate at the ceremony elevating him to emperor. At the last moment, Napoleon took the crown and donned it himself.
1. Book 12 reviews the "impairment" and gradual recovery of Wordsworth's creative sensibility in response to the natural world.

And, lastly, utter loss of hope itself
And things to hope for! Not with these began
Our Song, and not with these our Song must end.[2]
Ye motions of delight, that haunt the sides
10 Of the green hills; ye breezes and soft airs,
Whose subtile intercourse with breathing flowers,
Feelingly watched, might teach Man's haughty race
How without injury to take, to give
Without offence; ye who, as if to shew
15 The wondrous influence of power gently used,
Bend the complying heads of lordly pines,
And with a touch shift the stupendous clouds
Through the whole compass of the sky; ye brooks
Muttering along the stones, a busy noise
20 By day, a quiet sound in silent night;
Ye waves that out of the great deep steal forth
In a calm hour to kiss the pebbly shore,
Not mute, and then retire, fearing no storm;
And you, ye Groves, whose ministry it is
25 To interpose the covert of your shades,
Even as a sleep, between the heart of man
And outward troubles, between man himself,
Not seldom, and his own uneasy heart!
Oh that I had a music and a voice
30 Harmonious as your own, that I might tell
What Ye have done for me! The morning shines,
Nor heedeth Man's perverseness; Spring returns,
I saw the Spring return and could rejoice,
In common with the Children of her love
35 Piping on boughs, or sporting on fresh fields,
Or boldly seeking pleasure nearer heaven
On wings that navigate cerulean skies.
So neither were complacency° nor peace   satisfaction
Nor tender yearnings wanting for my good
40 Through those distracted times;[3] in Nature still
Glorying, I found a counterpoise in her,
Which, when the Spirit of evil reached its height,
Maintained for me a secret happiness.
    This Narrative, my Friend, hath chiefly told
45 Of intellectual power,[4] fostering love,
Dispensing truth, and over men and things,
Where reason yet might hesitate, diffusing
Prophetic sympathies of genial faith.
So was I favored, such my happy lot,
50 Until that natural graciousness of mind
Gave way to overpressure from the times
And their disastrous issues. What availed,

---

2. The reference is back to the joyous preamble
with which *The Prelude* began. Wordsworth goes
on (line 10) to invoke the breeze described in the
opening line of the poem.
3. I.e., the period of spiritual crisis that he had

described in 11.293–309.
4. The power of the integral mind (as distinguished from the limited capacity of "reason"
alone, line 47).

When spells forbade the Voyager to land,
That fragrant notice of a pleasant shore
55 Wafted at intervals from many a bower
Of blissful gratitude and fearless peace?
Dare I avow that wish was mine to see,
And hope that future times *would* surely see,
The man to come parted as by a gulph
60 From him who had been, that I could no more
Trust the elevation which had made me one
With the great Family that still survives
To illuminate the abyss of ages past,
Sage, Warrior, Patriot, Hero?—for it seemed
65 That their best virtues were not free from taint
Of something false and weak, that could not stand
The open eye of Reason.[5] Then I said,
"Go to the Poets; they will speak to thee
More perfectly of purer Creatures; yet
70 If Reason be nobility in Man,
Can aught be more ignoble than the Man
Whom they delight in, blinded as he is
By prejudice, the miserable slave
Of low ambition, or distempered love?"
75   In such strange passion (if I may once more
Review the past) I warred against myself,
A Bigot to a New Idolatry;
Like a cowled Monk who hath forsworn the world,
Zealously labour'd to cut off my heart
80 From all the sources of her former strength;
And as by simple waving of a Wand
The wizard instantaneously dissolves
Palace or grove, even so could I unsoul
As readily by syllogistic words[6]
85 Those mysteries of being which have made,
And shall continue evermore to make,
Of the whole human race one brotherhood.
     What wonder, then, if to a mind so far
Perverted, even the visible Universe
90 Fell under the dominion of a taste
Less Spiritual, with microscopic view
Was scanned, as I had scanned the moral world?[7]

---

5. This passage is both elliptical and contorted in its syntax. The fragrance wafted to the sailor from the shore—i.e., his remembered experiences of human feelings of gratitude and love (lines 54–56)—serves also as evidence of the shared emotions that had earlier united him to the family of past humanity (lines 61–63). The "spells" that prevented the sailor from landing on that shore (line 53) consist of his fascination with a limited mode of analytic reasoning, which engendered the hope that in the future people would be purely rational beings, hence utterly different from the feelingful, passionate creatures of the past (lines 58–60). This mode of reasoning, in addition, not only made Wordsworth distrust the earlier emotional evidences of his unity with humanity but also led him

to believe that the actions of even the greatest men recorded in human history were tainted, because they were motivated by feelings rather than by reason alone (lines 64–67).

   In his allusions to the rational "spells" and his hope for a new type of humanity, Wordsworth is describing the period in his life when he had succumbed to the views of William Godwin's Inquiry Concerning Political Justice (1793), which derogated the role of the feelings and passions as motives and confidently anticipated a future in which the actions of humanity will be determined solely by dispassionate reason.
6. Logical reasoning.
7. I.e., the habit of logical analysis perverted his way of perceiving the natural world.

     Oh Soul of Nature, excellent and fair!
     That didst rejoice with me, with whom I too
95   Rejoiced, through early Youth, before the winds
     And roaring waters, and in lights and shades
     That marched and countermarched about the hills
     In glorious apparition, powers on whom
     I daily waited, now all eye and now
100 All ear; but never long without the heart
     Employed, and Man's unfolding intellect!
     Oh Soul of Nature! that, by laws divine
     Sustained and governed, still dost overflow
     With an impassioned life, what feeble ones
105 Walk on this earth! how feeble have I been
     When thou wert in thy strength! Nor this through stroke
     Of human suffering, such as justifies
     Remissness and inaptitude of mind,
     But through presumption;[8] even in pleasure pleased
110 Unworthily, disliking here, and there
     Liking; by rules of mimic Art transferred
     To things above all Art; but more,—for this,
     Although a strong infection of the age,
     Was never much my habit—giving way
115 To a comparison of scene with scene,
     Bent overmuch on superficial things,
     Pampering myself with meagre novelties
     Of colour and proportion, to the moods
     Of time and season, to the moral power,
120 The affections and the spirit of the Place,
     Insensible.[9] Nor only did the love
     Of sitting thus in judgment interrupt
     My deeper feelings, but another cause,
     More subtile and less easily explained,
125 That almost seems inherent in the Creature,
     A twofold frame of body and of mind.
     I speak in recollection of a time
     When the bodily eye, in every stage of life
     The most despotic of our senses, gained
130 Such strength in *me* as often held my mind
     In absolute dominion. Gladly here,
     Entering upon abstruser Argument,
     Could I endeavour to unfold the means
     Which Nature studiously employs to thwart
135 This tyranny, summons all the senses each
     To counteract the other, and themselves,
     And makes them all, and the Objects with which all
     Are conversant, subservient in their turn

---

8. Presumptuousness, arrogance.
9. Unresponsive. Wordsworth has described his temporary participation in the cult of the picturesque—i.e., judging a natural scene by criteria derived from the "Art" of landscape painting (lines 111–12)—and then his acquired tendency to judge the comparative value of natural scenes by superficial, purely aesthetic criteria (lines 115–18).

To the great ends of Liberty and Power.[1]
140   But leave we this: enough that my delights
(Such as they were) were sought insatiably.
Vivid the transport, vivid, though not profound;
I roamed from hill to hill, from rock to rock,
Still craving combinations of new forms,
145   New pleasure, wider empire for the sight,
Proud of her own endowments, and rejoiced
To lay the inner faculties asleep.
Amid the turns and counterturns, the strife
And various trials of our complex being,
150   As we grow up, such thraldom of that sense[2]
Seems hard to shun. And yet I knew a Maid,
A young Enthusiast, who escaped these bonds;[3]
Her eye was not the Mistress of her heart;
Far less did rules prescribed by passive taste
155   Or barren intermeddling subtleties
Perplex her mind; but, wise as women are
When genial circumstance[4] hath favoured them,
She welcomed what was given and craved no more;
Whate'er the scene presented to her view,
160   That was the best, to that she was attuned
By her benign simplicity of life
And through a perfect happiness of Soul
Whose variegated feelings were in this
Sisters, that they were each some new delight.
165   Birds in the bower, and lambs in the green field,
Could they have known her, would have loved; methought
Her very presence such a sweetness breathed
That flowers, and trees, and even the silent hills,
And every thing she looked on should have had
170   An intimation how she bore herself
Towards them and to all creatures. God delights
In such a being; for her common thoughts
Are piety, her life is gratitude.
      Even like this Maid, before I was called forth
175   From the retirement of my native hills,
I loved whate'er I saw: nor lightly loved,
But most intensely; never dreamt of aught
More grand, more fair, more exquisitely framed
Than those few nooks to which my happy feet
180   Were limited. I had not at that time
Lived long enough, nor in the least survived
The first diviner influence of this world
As it appears to unaccustomed eyes.
Worshipping then among the depth of things
185   As piety ordained,[5] could I submit

1. I.e., the ways in which Nature uses an individual's other senses to counteract the tyranny of the eye—as well as the tyranny of any other single sense—so as to make all the senses (and the external objects they enable us to perceive) subordinate to the free, creative power of the human mind. Later in this book Wordsworth attributes this power of free creativity to the imagination.
2. I.e., subservience to the sense of sight.
3. Mary Hutchinson, whom Wordsworth had known since childhood and whom he married in 1802.
4. Beneficent conditions (of a woman's life).
5. In the 1805 text: "As my soul bade me."

To measured admiration, or to aught
That should preclude humility and love?
I felt, observed, and pondered; did not judge,
Yea, never thought of judging; with the gift
190 Of all this glory filled and satisfied.
And afterwards, when through the gorgeous Alps
Roaming, I carried with me the same heart:[6]
In truth, the degradation,[7] howsoe'er
Induced, effect in whatsoe'er degree
195 Of custom that prepares a partial scale
In which the little oft outweighs the great,
Or any other cause that hath been named;
Or lastly, aggravated by the times,
And their empassioned sounds,[8] which well might make
200 The milder minstrelsies of rural scenes
Inaudible, was transient; I had known
Too forcibly, too early in my life,
Visitings of imaginative power
For this to last: I shook the habit off
205 Entirely and for ever, and again
In Nature's presence stood, as now I stand,
A sensitive Being, a *creative* Soul.
    There are in our existence spots of time,[9]
That with distinct pre-eminence retain
210 A renovating virtue, whence, depressed
By false opinion and contentious thought,
Or aught of heavier or more deadly weight,
In trivial occupations, and the round
Of ordinary intercourse, our minds
215 Are nourished and invisibly repaired;
A virtue by which pleasure is inhanced,
That penetrates, enables us to mount,
When high, more high, and lifts us up when fallen.
This efficacious Spirit chiefly lurks
220 Among those passages of life that give
Profoundest knowledge how and to what point
The mind is lord and master—outward sense
The obedient Servant of her will. Such moments
Are scattered every where, taking their date
225 From our first Childhood. I remember well
That once, while yet my inexperienced hand
Could scarcely hold a bridle, with proud hopes
I mounted, and we journied towards the hills:
An ancient Servant of my Father's house
230 Was with me, my encourager and Guide.
We had not travelled long ere some mischance

6. In his walk across the Alps in 1790, described in book 6.
7. I.e., the deterioration (of a full, unreflective response to nature) that he has described in lines 109–51.
8. I.e., by the high passions aroused by the French Revolution. Wordsworth speculates that these may have been a contributing factor in diminishing his attention and responsiveness to the natural world.

9. Moments of experience in which something ordinary (line 254) suddenly becomes profoundly significant. Because this significance is bestowed by the perceiver, it demonstrates the freedom and creative power of the imaginative mind (lines 220–23, 275–77). The remembrance of such moments nourishes and repairs the mind in periods of depression or distraction when the imagination flags (lines 210–15).

Disjoined me from my Comrade, and, through fear
Dismounting, down the rough and stony Moor
I led my horse, and, stumbling on, at length
235 Came to a bottom,° where in former times   valley
A Murderer had been hung in iron chains.
The Gibbet mast[1] had mouldered down, the bones
And iron case were gone, but on the turf
Hard by, soon after that fell deed was wrought,
240 Some unknown hand had carved the Murderer's name.
The monumental Letters were inscribed
In times long past, but still from year to year,
By superstition of the neighbourhood,
The grass is cleared away, and to that hour
245 The characters were fresh and visible.
A casual glance had shewn them, and I fled,
Faultering and faint and ignorant of the road:
Then, reascending the bare common, saw
A naked Pool that lay beneath the hills,
250 The Beacon on its summit, and, more near,
A Girl who bore a Pitcher on her head,
And seemed with difficult steps to force her way
Against the blowing wind. It was in truth
An ordinary sight; but I should need
255 Colors and words that are unknown to man
To paint the visionary dreariness
Which, while I looked all round for my lost Guide,
Invested Moorland waste and naked Pool,
The Beacon crowning the lone eminence,
260 The Female and her garments vexed and tossed
By the strong wind.—When, in the blessed hours
Of early love, the loved One[2] at my side,
I roamed, in daily presence of this scene,
Upon the naked Pool and dreary Crags,
265 And on the melancholy Beacon, fell
A spirit of pleasure, and Youth's golden gleam;
And think ye not with radiance more sublime
For these remembrances, and for the power
They had left behind? So feeling comes in aid
270 Of feeling, and diversity of strength
Attends us, if but once we have been strong.
Oh! mystery of Man, from what a depth
Proceed thy honors! I am lost, but see
In simple child-hood something of the base
275 On which thy greatness stands; but this I feel,
That from thyself it comes, that thou must give,
Else never canst receive. The days gone by
Return upon me almost from the dawn
Of life: the hiding-places of Man's power
280 Open; I would approach them, but they close.
I see by glimpses now; when age comes on

1. The post with a projecting arm used for hanging   2. Mary Hutchinson.
criminals.

May scarcely see at all, and I would give,
While yet we may, as far as words can give,
Substance and life to what I feel, enshrining,
285   Such is my hope, the spirit of the past
For future restoration.—Yet another
Of these memorials.
                  One Christmas-time,[3]
On the glad Eve of its dear holidays,
Feverish, and tired, and restless, I went forth
290   Into the fields, impatient for the sight
Of those led Palfreys[4] that should bear us home,
My Brothers and myself. There rose a Crag
That, from the meeting point of two highways
Ascending, overlooked them both, far stretched;
295   Thither, uncertain on which road to fix
My expectation, thither I repaired,
Scout-like, and gained the summit; 'twas a day
Tempestuous, dark, and wild, and on the grass
I sate, half-sheltered by a naked wall;
300   Upon my right hand couched a single sheep,
Upon my left a blasted hawthorn stood:
With those Companions at my side, I sate,
Straining my eyes intensely, as the mist
Gave intermitting prospect of the copse
305   And plain beneath. Ere we to School returned
That dreary time, ere we had been ten days
Sojourners in my Father's House, he died,[5]
And I and my three Brothers, Orphans then,
Followed his Body to the Grave. The Event,
310   With all the sorrow that it brought, appeared
A chastisement; and when I called to mind
That day so lately passed, when from the Crag
I looked in such anxiety of hope,
With trite reflections of morality,
315   Yet in the deepest passion, I bowed low
To God, who thus corrected my desires;
And afterwards, the wind and sleety rain
And all the business[6] of the Elements,
The single Sheep, and the one blasted tree,
320   And the bleak music of that old stone wall,
The noise of wood and water, and the mist
That on the line of each of those two Roads
Advanced in such indisputable shapes;[7]
All these were kindred spectacles and sounds
325   To which I oft repaired, and thence would drink
As at a fountain; and on winter nights,
Down to this *very* time, when storm and rain
Beat on my roof, or haply at noon-day,
While in a grove I walk whose lofty trees,

---

3. In 1783. Wordsworth, aged thirteen, was at
Hawkshead School with two of his brothers.
4. Small saddle horses.
5. John Wordsworth died on December 30, 1783.

William's mother had died five years earlier.
6. Busy-ness; motions.
7. I.e., shapes one did not dare question.

330 Laden with summer's thickest foliage, rock
In a strong wind, some working of the spirit,
Some inward agitations, thence are brought,[8]
Whate'er their office, whether to beguile
Thoughts over-busy in the course they took,
335 Or animate an hour of vacant ease.

From Book Thirteenth
Subject concluded

[RETURN TO "LIFE'S FAMILIAR FACE"]

From Nature doth emotion come, and moods
Of calmness equally are Nature's gift:
This is her glory; these two attributes
Are sister horns that constitute her strength.[1]
5 Hence Genius,[2] born to thrive by interchange
Of peace and excitation, finds in her
His best and purest friend, from her receives
That energy by which he seeks the truth,
From her that happy stillness of the mind
10 Which fits him to receive it, when unsought.
    Such benefit the humblest intellects
Partake of, each in their degree: 'tis mine
To speak of what myself have known and felt.
Smooth task! for words find easy way, inspired
15 By gratitude and confidence in truth.
Long time in search of knowledge did I range
The field of human life, in heart and mind
Benighted, but the dawn beginning now
To reappear,[3] 'twas proved that not in vain
20 I had been taught to reverence a Power
That is the visible quality and shape
And image of right reason,[4] that matures
Her processes by steadfast laws, gives birth
To no impatient or fallacious hopes,
25 No heat of passion or excessive zeal,
No vain conceits,—provokes to no quick turns
Of self-applauding intellect,—but trains
To meekness, and exalts by humble faith;[5]
Holds up before the mind, intoxicate
30 With present objects, and the busy dance
Of things that pass away, a temperate shew
Of objects that endure; and by this course
Disposes her, when over-fondly set
On throwing off incumbrances, to seek

8. Another instance of Wordsworth's inner response to an outer breeze (cf. 1.33–38, p. 306).
1. In the Old Testament, the horn of an animal signifies power.
2. A person capable of creativity.
3. I.e., he is beginning to recover from the spiri-

tual crisis recorded in 11.293–309.
4. Wordsworth follows Milton's use of the term "right reason" to denote a human faculty that is inherently attuned to truth.
5. In the text of 1805: "but lifts / The being into magnanimity."

35 In Man, and in the frame of social life,
    Whate'er there is desireable and good
    Of kindred permanence, unchanged in form
    And function, or through strict vicissitude
    Of life and death revolving. Above all
40 Were re-established now those watchful thoughts
    Which (seeing little worthy or sublime
    In what the Historian's pen so much delights
    To blazon, Power and Energy detached
    From moral purpose) early tutored me
45 To look with feelings of fraternal love
    Upon the unassuming things that hold
    A silent station in this beauteous world.[6]
      Thus moderated, thus composed, I found
    Once more in Man an object of delight,
50 Of pure imagination, and of love;
    And, as the horizon of my mind enlarged,
    Again I took the intellectual eye[7]
    For my Instructor, studious more to see
    Great Truths, than touch and handle little ones.
55 Knowledge was given accordingly; my trust
    Became more firm in feelings that had stood
    The test of such a trial; clearer far
    My sense of excellence—of right and wrong:
    The promise of the present time retired
60 Into its true proportions; sanguine[8] schemes,
    Ambitious projects, pleased me less; I sought
    For present good in life's familiar face,
    And built thereon my hopes of good to come.

[DISCOVERY OF HIS POETIC SUBJECT. SALISBURY PLAIN.
SIGHT OF "A NEW WORLD"]

220   Here, calling up to mind what then I saw,[9]
      A youthful Traveller, and see daily now
      In the familiar circuit of my home,
      Here might I pause and bend in reverence
      To Nature, and the power of human minds,
225   To Men as they are Men within themselves.
      How oft high service is performed within,
      When all the external Man is rude in shew!
      Not like a Temple rich with pomp and gold,

6. Here Wordsworth begins his account of how he came to feel bonds to, and to love, the silent, lowly, common things whose celebration he considers to be his special vocation as an innovative poet-prophet (see lines 301–08).
7. Perception by the integral mind.
8. Optimistic. Wordsworth apparently refers back to his earlier "ambitious projects" for a long poem, described in 1.166–220, as well as to the optimistic schemes for humankind that had been engendered by his commitment to the French Revolution.
9. Wordsworth has described, as part of his imaginative recovery, his learning to look again with

sympathy upon "the unassuming things that hold / A silent station in this beauteous world" (lines 46–47) and his finding again "in Man an object of delight" (line 49). Now he shows how, in reaction against his concern with great actions detached from moral purpose that constituted the French Revolution, he came to embrace the poetic doctrines of the Preface to Lyrical Ballads. That is, he will write of simple, lowly people, whose patient endurance of suffering redounds to the glory of humankind and who speak a language that is the spontaneous overflow of powerful feelings (lines 263–64).

But a mere mountain Chapel that protects
230 Its simple Worshippers from sun and shower.
Of these, said I, shall be my song, of these,
If future years mature me for the task,
Will I record the praises, making Verse
Deal boldly with substantial things; in truth
235 And sanctity of passion speak of these,
That justice may be done, obeisance paid
Where it is due: thus haply shall I teach,
Inspire, through unadulterated° ears   uncorrupted
Pour rapture, tenderness, and hope, my theme
240 No other than the very heart of Man
As found among the best of those who live
Not unexalted by religious faith,
Nor uninformed by Books, good books, though few,
In Nature's presence: thence may I select
245 Sorrow, that is not sorrow, but delight,
And miserable love that is not pain
To hear of, for the glory that redounds
Therefrom to human kind and what we are.
Be mine to follow with no timid step
250 Where knowledge leads me; it shall be my pride
That I have dared to tread this holy ground,
Speaking no dream, but things oracular,
Matter not lightly to be heard by those
Who to the letter of the outward promise
255 Do read the invisible Soul,[1] by Men adroit
In speech, and for communion with the world
Accomplished, minds whose faculties are then
Most active when they are most eloquent,
And elevated most, when most admired.
260 Men may be found of other mold than these,
Who are their own Upholders, to themselves
Encouragement, and energy, and will,
Expressing liveliest thoughts in lively words
As native passion dictates.[2] Others, too,
265 There are, among the walks of homely life,
Still higher, men for contemplation framed,
Shy, and unpractised in the strife of phrase,[3]
Meek men, whose very souls perhaps would sink
Beneath them, summoned to such intercourse:
270 Theirs is the language of the heavens, the power,
The thought, the image, and the silent joy;
Words are but under-agents in their Souls;
When they are grasping with their greatest strength
They do not breathe among them;[4] this I speak
275 In gratitude to God, who feeds our hearts

1. I.e., this doctrine will not be lightly accepted by those who judge inner worth by exterior seeming.
2. In his Preface to *Lyrical Ballads* of 1800, Wordsworth said that he chose characters from low and rustic life because in them "the essential passions of the heart . . . are less under restraint, and speak a plainer and more emphatic language."
3. The rhetoric of controversy.
4. I.e., even in the greatest strength of their intuitive grasp, they do not utter words, which (line 272) are for them merely subsidiary to the fullness of their response to an experience.

For his own service; knoweth, loveth us
When we are unregarded by the world.
   Also, about this time did I receive
Convictions still more strong than heretofore
280 Not only that the inner frame is good,
And graciously composed, but that, no less,
Nature for all conditions wants not power
To consecrate, if we have eyes to see,
The outside of her Creatures, and to breathe
285 Grandeur upon the very humblest face
Of human life. I felt that the array
Of act and circumstance, and visible form,
Is mainly, to the pleasure of the mind,
What passion makes them, that meanwhile the forms
290 Of Nature have a passion in themselves
That intermingles with those works of man
To which she summons him; although the works
Be mean, have nothing lofty of their own;
And that the Genius of the Poet hence
295 May boldly take his way among mankind
Wherever Nature leads, that he hath stood
By Nature's side among the Men of old,
And so shall stand for ever. Dearest Friend,
If thou partake the animating faith
300 That Poets, even as Prophets, each with each
Connected in a mighty scheme of truth,
Have each his own peculiar faculty,
Heaven's gift, a sense that fits him to perceive
Objects unseen before, thou wilt not blame
305 The humblest of this band[5] who dares to hope
That unto him hath also been vouchsafed
An insight, that in some sort he possesses
A Privilege, whereby a Work of his,
Proceeding from a source of untaught things,
310 Creative and enduring, may become
A Power like one of Nature's. To a hope
Not less ambitious once among the Wilds
Of Sarum's Plain[6] my youthful Spirit was raised;
There, as I ranged at will the pastoral downs[7]
315 Trackless and smooth, or paced the bare white roads
Lengthening in solitude their dreary line,
Time with his retinue of ages fled
Backwards, nor checked his flight until I saw
Our dim Ancestral Past in Vision clear;[8]
320 Saw multitudes of men, and here and there
A single Briton clothed in Wolf-skin vest,
With shield and stone-axe, stride across the wold;[9]

---

5. Wordsworth himself.
6. Salisbury Plain, which Wordsworth crossed alone on foot in the summer of 1793.
7. Open hills used to pasture sheep.
8. Wordsworth shared the common, but mistaken, belief of his time that Stonehenge, the giant meg-

alithic structure on Salisbury Plain, had been a temple of the Celtic priests, the Druids, and that the Druids had there performed the rite of human sacrifice; hence the imaginings and vision that he goes on to relate.
9. High open country.

The voice of Spears was heard, the rattling spear
Shaken by arms of mighty bone, in strength,
325 Long mouldered, of barbaric majesty.
I called on Darkness—but before the word
Was uttered, midnight darkness seemed to take
All objects from my sight; and lo! again
The Desart visible by dismal flames;
330 It is the Sacrificial Altar, fed
With living Men—how deep the groans! the voice
Of those that crowd the giant wicker thrills
The monumental hillocks,[1] and the pomp
Is for both worlds, the living and the dead.
335 At other moments (for through that wide waste
Three summer days I roamed) where'er the Plain
Was figured o'er with circles, lines, or mounds,
That yet survive, a work, as some divine,[2]
Shaped by the Druids, so to represent
340 Their knowledge of the heavens, and image forth
The constellations; gently was I charmed
Into a waking dream, a reverie
That with believing eyes, where'er I turned,
Beheld long-bearded Teachers with white wands
345 Uplifted, pointing to the starry sky
Alternately, and Plain below, while breath
Of music swayed their motions, and the Waste
Rejoiced with them and me in those sweet Sounds.
    This for the past, and things that may be viewed
350 Or fancied, in the obscurity of years
From monumental hints:[3] and thou, O Friend!
Pleased with some unpremeditated strains
That served those wanderings to beguile, hast said
That then and there my mind had exercised
355 Upon the vulgar forms of present things,
The actual world of our familiar days,
Yet higher power, had caught from them a tone,
An image, and a character, by books
Not hitherto reflected.[4] Call we this
360 A partial judgement—and yet why? for *then*
We were as Strangers;[5] and I may not speak
Thus wrongfully of verse, however rude,
Which on thy young imagination, trained
In the great City, broke like light from far.

---

1. The many bronze age burial mounds on Salisbury Plain. "Giant wicker": Aylett Sammes, in *Britannia Antiqua Illustrata* (1676), had described, as a rite of the ancient Britons, that they wove a huge wicker structure in the shape of a man, filled it with living humans, and set it afire.
2. Conjecture (a verb).
3. I.e., from what the monumental remains on Salisbury Plain suggested to him.
4. Wordsworth refers to an event that Coleridge narrates in *Biographia Literaria*, chap. 4. In November 1795 Wordsworth had read to Coleridge a manuscript version of his poem *Adventures on Salisbury*

Plain. What impressed Coleridge, as he tells us, was Wordsworth's "fine balance of truth in observing with the imaginative faculty in modifying the objects observed, and above all, the original gift of spreading . . . the depth and height of the ideal world, around forms, incidents, and situations of which, for the common view, custom had bedimmed all the luster." "This," Coleridge concludes, "is the character and privilege of genius."
5. Though Coleridge and Wordsworth had met in September 1795, they did not become close friends until 1797. "Partial": biased (in Wordsworth's favor).

365 Moreover, each man's mind is to herself
Witness and judge; and I remember well
That in Life's every-day appearances
I seemed about this time to gain clear sight
Of a new world, a world, too, that was fit
370 To be transmitted and to other eyes
Made visible, as ruled by those fixed laws
Whence spiritual dignity originates,
Which do both give it being and maintain
A balance, an ennobling interchange
375 Of action from without, and from within;
The excellence, pure function, and best power
Both of the object seen, and eye that sees.

From Book Fourteenth
Conclusion

[THE VISION ON MOUNT SNOWDON. FEAR VS. LOVE RESOLVED.
IMAGINATION]

In one of those Excursions (may they ne'er
Fade from remembrance!), through the Northern tracts
Of Cambria ranging with a youthful Friend,
I left Bethgellert's huts at couching-time,
5 And westward took my way, to see the sun
Rise from the top of Snowdon.[1] To the door
Of a rude Cottage at the Mountain's base
We came, and rouzed the Shepherd who attends
The adventurous Stranger's steps, a trusty Guide;
10 Then, cheered by short refreshment, sallied forth.
—It was a close, warm, breezeless summer night,
Wan, dull, and glaring,[2] with a dripping fog
Low-hung and thick, that covered all the sky.
But, undiscouraged, we began to climb
15 The mountain-side. The mist soon girt us round,
And, after ordinary Travellers' talk
With our Conductor, pensively we sank
Each into commerce with his private thoughts:
Thus did we breast the ascent, and by myself
20 Was nothing either seen or heard that checked
Those musings or diverted, save that once
The Shepherd's Lurcher,[3] who, among the crags,
Had to his joy unearthed a Hedgehog, teased
His coiled-up Prey with barkings turbulent.
25 This small adventure, for even such it seemed

1. Wordsworth climbed Mount Snowdon—the highest peak in Wales ("Cambria"), and some ten miles from the sea—with Robert Jones, the friend with whom he had also tramped through the Alps (book 6). The climb started from the village of Bethgelert at "couching-time" (line 4), the time of night when the sheep lie down to sleep. This event had taken place in 1791 (or possibly 1793); Wordsworth presents it out of its chronological order to introduce at this point a great natural "type" or "emblem" (lines 66, 70) for the mind, and especially for the activity of the imagination, whose "restoration" he has described in the two preceding books.
2. In north of England dialect, *glairie,* applied to the weather, means dull, rainy.
3. A crossbred dog used to hunt hares.

In that wild place, and at the dead of night,
Being over and forgotten, on we wound
In silence as before. With forehead bent
Earthward, as if in opposition set
30 Against an enemy, I panted up
With eager pace, and no less eager thoughts.
Thus might we wear a midnight hour away,
Ascending at loose distance each from each,
And I, as chanced, the foremost of the Band:
35 When at my feet the ground appeared to brighten,
And with a step or two seemed brighter still;
Nor was time given to ask, or learn, the cause;
For instantly a light upon the turf
Fell like a flash; and lo! as I looked up,
40 The Moon hung naked in a firmament
Of azure without cloud, and at my feet
Rested a silent sea of hoary mist.
A hundred hills their dusky backs upheaved
All over this still Ocean;[4] and beyond,
45 Far, far beyond, the solid vapours stretched,
In Headlands, tongues, and promontory shapes,
Into the main Atlantic, that appeared
To dwindle, and give up his majesty,
Usurped upon far as the sight could reach.
50 Not so the ethereal Vault; encroachment none
Was there, nor loss;[5] only the inferior stars
Had disappeared, or shed a fainter light
In the clear presence of the full-orbed Moon;
Who, from her sovereign elevation, gazed
55 Upon the billowy ocean, as it lay
All meek and silent, save that through a rift
Not distant from the shore whereon we stood,
A fixed, abysmal, gloomy breathing-place,
Mounted the roar of waters—torrents—streams
60 Innumerable, roaring with one voice!
Heard over earth and sea, and in that hour,
For so it seemed, felt by the starry heavens.
    When into air had partially dissolved
That Vision, given to Spirits of the night,
65 And three chance human Wanderers, in calm thought
Reflected, it appeared to me the type
Of a majestic Intellect, its acts
And its possessions, what it has and craves,
What in itself it is, and would become.
70 There I beheld the emblem of a Mind
That feeds upon infinity, that broods
Over the dark abyss, intent to hear
Its voices issuing forth to silent light
In one continuous stream; a mind sustained

---

4. In Milton's description of the creation of the world, "the mountains huge appear / Emergent, and their broad bare backs upheave / Into the clouds" (*Paradise Lost* 7.285–87).

5. The mist projected in various shapes over the Atlantic Ocean, but did not "encroach" on the heavens overhead.

75   By recognitions of transcendent power
      In sense, conducting to ideal form;
      In soul, of more than mortal privilege.[6]
      One function, above all, of such a mind
      Had Nature shadowed there, by putting forth,
80   'Mid circumstances awful and sublime,
      That mutual domination which she loves
      To exert upon the face of outward things,
      So moulded, joined, abstracted; so endowed
      With interchangeable supremacy,
85   That Men least sensitive see, hear, perceive,
      And cannot chuse but feel. The power which all
      Acknowledge when thus moved, which Nature thus
      To bodily sense exhibits, is the express
      Resemblance of that glorious faculty
90   That higher minds bear with them as their own.[7]
      This is the very spirit in which they deal
      With the whole compass of the universe:
      They, from their native selves, can send abroad
      Kindred mutations; for themselves create
95   A like existence; and whene'er it dawns
      Created for them, catch it;—or are caught
      By its inevitable mastery,
      Like angels stopped upon the wing by sound
      Of harmony from heaven's remotest spheres.
100   Them the enduring and the transient both
      Serve to exalt; they build up greatest things
      From least suggestions; ever on the watch,
      Willing to work and to be wrought upon,
      They need not extraordinary calls
105   To rouse them, in a world of life they live;
      By sensible impressions not enthralled,
      But, by their quickening impulse, made more prompt
      To hold fit converse with the spiritual world,
      And with the generations of mankind
110   Spread over time, past, present, and to come,
      Age after age, till Time shall be no more.
      Such minds are truly from the Deity,
      For they are powers; and hence the highest bliss
      That flesh can know is theirs,—the consciousness
115   Of whom they are, habitually infused
      Through every image, and through every thought,
      And all affections° by communion raised   *emotions*
      From earth to heaven, from human to divine.
      Hence endless occupation for the Soul,
120   Whether discursive or intuitive;[8]

6. The sense of lines 74–77 seems to be that the mind of someone who is gifted beyond the ordinary lot of mortals recognizes its power to transcend the senses by converting sensory objects into ideal forms.
7. The "glorious faculty" is the imagination, which in its exhibition of mastery over sense—through its power to alter and re-create what is given to it in perception (lines 93–105)—is analogous to that aspect of the outer scene in which the ordinary landscape is transfigured by the moonlit mist. Cf. the mind as "lord and master" of outward sense in 12.219–23 (p. 369).
8. An echo of *Paradise Lost* 5.488. The "discursive" reason undertakes to reach truths through a logical sequence of premises, observations, and conclusions; the "intuitive" reason comprehends truths immediately.

Hence chearfulness for acts of daily life,
Emotions which best foresight need not fear,
Most worthy then of trust when most intense:
Hence, amid ills that vex, and wrongs that crush
125 Our hearts, if here the words of holy Writ
May with fit reverence be applied, that peace
Which passeth understanding,⁹—that repose
In moral judgements which from this pure source
Must come, or will by Man be sought in vain.
130   Oh! who is he that hath his whole life long
Preserved, enlarged, this freedom in himself?
For this alone is genuine Liberty.
Where is the favoured Being who hath held
That course, unchecked, unerring, and untired,
135 In one perpetual progress smooth and bright?
—A humbler destiny have we retraced,
And told of lapse and hesitating choice,
And backward wanderings along thorny ways:
Yet, compassed round by Mountain Solitudes
140 Within whose solemn temple I received
My earliest visitations, careless then
Of what was given me; and which now I range
A meditative, oft a suffering Man,
Do I declare, in accents which, from truth
145 Deriving chearful confidence, shall blend
Their modulation with these vocal streams,
That, whatsoever falls my better mind
Revolving¹ with the accidents of life
May have sustained, that, howsoe'er misled,
150 Never did I, in quest of right and wrong,
Tamper with conscience from a private aim;
Nor was in any public hope the dupe
Of selfish passions; nor did ever yield,
Wilfully, to mean cares or low pursuits;
155 But shrunk with apprehensive jealousy
From every combination which might aid
The tendency, too potent in itself,
Of use and custom to bow down the Soul
Under a growing weight of vulgar sense,
160 And substitute a universe of death²
For that which moves with light and life informed,
Actual, divine, and true. To fear and love,
To love as prime and chief, for there fear ends,
Be this ascribed; to early intercourse
165 In presence of sublime or beautiful forms
With the adverse principles of pain and joy—
Evil, as one is rashly named by men
Who know not what they speak. By love subsists

---

9. Philippians 4.7: "The peace of God, which passeth all understanding." This passage of Christian
piety was added by Wordsworth in a late revision.
1. Allusion to the ancient concept of fortune's

revolving wheel.
2. Milton's description of hell in *Paradise Lost*
2.622–23: "A universe of death, which God by
curse / Created evil."

All lasting grandeur, by pervading love;
170 That gone, we are as dust.³—Behold the fields
In balmy spring-time full of rising flowers
And joyous Creatures; see that Pair, the lamb
And the lamb's Mother, and their tender ways
Shall touch thee to the heart; thou callest this love,
175 And not inaptly so, for love it is,
Far as it carries thee. In some green Bower
Rest, and be not alone, but have thou there
The One who is thy choice of all the world:
There linger, listening, gazing with delight
180 Impassioned, but delight how pitiable!
Unless this love by a still higher love
Be hallowed, love that breathes not without awe;
Love that adores, but on the knees of prayer,
By heaven inspired; that frees from chains the soul,
185 Bearing in union with the purest, best
Of earth-born passions, on the wings of praise,
A mutual tribute to the Almighty's Throne.⁴
　　This spiritual love acts not, nor can exist
Without Imagination, which in truth
190 Is but another name for absolute power
And clearest insight, amplitude of mind,
And reason, in her most exalted mood.
This faculty hath been the feeding source
Of our long labor: we have traced the stream
195 From the blind cavern whence is faintly heard
Its natal murmur; followed it to light
And open day; accompanied its course
Among the ways of Nature; for a time
Lost sight of it, bewildered and engulphed;
200 Then given it greeting as it rose once more
In strength, reflecting from its placid breast
The works of man, and face of human life;
And lastly, from its progress have we drawn
Faith in life endless, the sustaining thought
205 Of human being, Eternity, and God.⁵
—Imagination having been our theme,
So also hath that intellectual love,
For they are each in each, and cannot stand
Dividually.°—Here must thou be, O Man!　　　　　　*separately*
210 Power to thyself; no Helper hast thou here;

---

3. Wordsworth's mind, he had said early in *The Prelude*, had been "fostered alike by beauty and by fear" (1.302 and n. 3, p. 312); that is, by the opposing but equally necessary principles of the beautiful and the terrifying, or "sublime," aspects of nature. Now, in his conclusion, the principles of fear and pain are said to be mistakenly equated with "evil," and to be ultimately transcended by their "adverse principles" of love and joy. This passage is equivalent to the theodicy of *Paradise Lost*, in which Milton justifies evil and pain ("the ways of God to men," 1.26) by reference to the fall and redemption; Wordsworth, however, translates this into a natural theodicy of the interaction of man's mind with the external world (cf. the Prospectus to *The Recluse*, lines 8–9 and n. 1, p. 301).

4. In place of lines 182–87, the text of 1805 has: "a love that comes into the heart / With awe and a diffusive sentiment. / Thy love is human merely: this proceeds / More from the brooding soul, and is divine."

5. The 1805 version reads: "The feeling of life endless, the great thought / By which we live, Infinity and God."

Here keepest thou in singleness thy state;
No other can divide with thee this work;
No secondary hand can intervene
To fashion this ability; 'tis thine,
215 The prime and vital principle is thine
In the recesses of thy nature, far
From any reach of outward fellowship,
Else is not thine at all. * * *

[CONCLUSION: "THE MIND OF MAN"]

And now, O Friend![6] this History is brought
To its appointed close: the discipline
And consummation of a Poet's mind
305 In every thing that stood most prominent
Have faithfully been pictured; we have reached
The time (our guiding object from the first)
When we may, not presumptuously, I hope,
Suppose my powers so far confirmed, and such
310 My knowledge, as to make me capable
Of building up a Work that shall endure.

* * * Having now
Told what best merits mention, further pains
Our present purpose seems not to require,
And I have other tasks. Recall to mind
375 The mood in which this labour was begun.
O Friend! the termination of my course
Is nearer now, much nearer; yet even then,
In that distraction, and intense desire,
I said unto the life which I had lived,
380 Where art thou? Hear I not a voice from thee
Which 'tis reproach to hear?[7] Anon I rose
As if on wings, and saw beneath me stretched
Vast prospect of the world which I had been
And was; and hence this Song, which like a Lark
385 I have protracted, in the unwearied heavens
Singing, and often with more plaintive voice
To earth attempered and her deep-drawn sighs,
Yet centering all in love, and in the end
All gratulant,° if rightly understood.[8]   *congratulatory*

*   *   *

Oh! yet a few short years of useful life,
And all will be complete, thy[9] race be run,

---

6. Coleridge.

7. As he approaches the end, Wordsworth recalls
the beginning of *The Prelude*. The reproachful
voice is that which asked the question, "Was it for
this?" in 1.269ff. This query called forth a vision
of his remembered life, which he proceeded to
explore in search of both the sources of his poetic
powers and the impediments to their fulfillment.
The "Song" (line 384) describing this quest, which

he then began, is the poem he is now completing.

8. The poet finds that suffering and frustration are
justified, when seen as part of the overall design of
the life he has just reviewed. The passage echoes
the conclusion of Pope's theodicy (the justification
of evil) in *An Essay on Man* 1.291–92: "All discord,
harmony not understood; / All partial evil, universal good."

9. Coleridge's.

Thy monument of glory will be raised;
435 Then, though, too weak to tread the ways of truth,
This Age fall back to old idolatry,
Though Men return to servitude as fast
As the tide ebbs, to ignominy and shame
By Nations sink together,[1] we shall still
440 Find solace—knowing what we have learnt to know,
Rich in true happiness if allowed to be
Faithful alike in forwarding a day
Of firmer trust, joint laborers in the Work
(Should Providence such grace to us vouchsafe)
445 Of their deliverance,[2] surely yet to come.
Prophets of Nature, we to them will speak
A lasting inspiration, sanctified
By reason, blest by faith: what we have loved
Others will love, and we will teach them how,
450 Instruct them how the mind of Man becomes
A thousand times more beautiful than the earth
On which he dwells, above this Frame of things
(Which 'mid all revolutions in the hopes
And fears of Men doth still remain unchanged)
455 In beauty exalted, as it is itself
Of quality and fabric more divine.[3]

1798–1839   1850

1. I.e., though men—whole nations of them together—sink to ignominy and shame.
2. In the 1805 text: "redemption." Wordsworth reaffirms his belief in a millennial outcome of human history, though he now bases that belief not on political "revolutions" (cf. line 453) but on a revolution in the mind of man.
3. Cf. Wordsworth's assertion that "the Mind of Man" is "My haunt, and the main region of my song" in the Prospectus to *The Recluse*, lines 40–41 (p. 302).

DOROTHY WORDSWORTH
1771–1855

Dorothy Wordsworth has an enduring place in English literature even though she wrote almost no word for publication. Not until long after her death did scholars gradually retrieve and print her letters, a few poems, and a series of journals that she kept sporadically between 1798 and 1828 because, she wrote, "I shall give William Pleasure by it." It has always been known, from tributes to her by her brother and Coleridge, that she exerted an important influence on the lives and writings of both these men. It is now apparent that she also possessed a power surpassing that of the two poets for precise observation of people and the natural world, together with a genius for terse, luminous, and delicately nuanced description in prose. Her hastily scribbled journals are an incomparable record of what Coleridge, in *Frost at Midnight*, called "all the numberless goings-on of life" in "sea, hill, and wood" as well as in the "populous village," noted by one who lived her life among rural folk.

Dorothy was born on Christmas Day 1771, twenty-one months after William; she was the only girl of five Wordsworth children. From her seventh year, when her mother died, she lived with various relatives—some of them tolerant and affectionate, others rigid and tyrannical—and saw William and her other brothers only occasionally, during the boys' summer vacations from school. In 1795, when she was twenty-four, the bequest to William by Raisley Calvert enabled her to carry out a long-held plan to join her brother in a house at Racedown, and the two spent the rest of their long lives together, first in Dorsetshire and Somersetshire, in the southwest of England, then in their beloved Lake District. She uncomplainingly subordinated her own talents to looking after her brother and his household.

All her adult life she was overworked and troubled by a variety of ailments. Suddenly, after a severe illness in 1835, she suffered a physical and mental collapse. She spent the rest of her existence as an invalid. Hardest for her family to endure was the drastic change in her temperament: from a high-spirited and compassionate woman she became (save for brief intervals of lucidity) querulous, demanding, and at times violent. In this half-life she lingered for twenty years, attended devotedly by William until his death five years before her own in 1855.

Our principal selections are from the journal Dorothy kept in 1798 at Alfoxden, Somersetshire, where the Wordsworths had moved from Racedown to be near Coleridge at Nether Stowey, as well as from her journals while at Grasmere (1800–03), with Coleridge residing some thirteen miles away at Greta Hall, Keswick. Her records cover the period when both men emerged as major poets, and in their achievements Dorothy played an indispensable role. In book 11 of *The Prelude* William says that, in the time of his spiritual crisis, Dorothy "maintained for me a saving intercourse / With my true self" and "preserved me still / A Poet"; and in a letter of 1797 Coleridge stressed the delicacy and tact in the responses of William's "exquisite sister" to the world of sense: "Her manners are simple, ardent, impressive. . . . Her information various—her eye watchful in minutest observation of nature—and her taste a perfect electrometer—it bends, protrudes, and draws in, at subtlest beauties & most recondite faults."

The passages from her journals reprinted below include many verbal sketches of natural appearances that recur in Wordsworth's and Coleridge's poems. Of at least equal importance for Wordsworth was her chronicling of the busy wayfaring life of rural England. These were exceedingly hard times for country people, when the suffering caused by the displacement of small farms and of household crafts by large-scale farms and industries was aggravated by the economic distress caused by protracted Continental wars (see Wordsworth's comment in *The Ruined Cottage*, lines 133ff., p. 262). Peddlers, maimed war veterans, leech gatherers, adult and infant beggars, ousted farm families, fugitives, and women abandoned by husbands or lovers streamed along the rural roads and into William's brooding poetic imagination—often by way of Dorothy's prose records.

The journals also show the intensity of Dorothy's love for her brother. Inevitably in our era, the mutual devotion of the orphaned brother and sister has evoked psychoanalytic speculation. It is important to note that Mary Hutchinson, a gentle and open-hearted young woman, had been Dorothy's closest friend ever since childhood, and that Dorothy encouraged William's courtship and marriage, even though she realized that it entailed her own displacement as a focus of her brother's life. All the evidence indicates that their lives in a single household never strained the affectionate relationship between the two women; indeed Dorothy, until she became an invalid, added to her former functions as William's chief support, housekeeper, and scribe a loving ministration to her brother's children.

Because the manuscript of the Alfoxden journal has disappeared, the text printed here is from the transcript published by William Knight in 1897. The selections from the Grasmere journals reproduce Pamela Woof's exact transcription of the manuscripts in the Wordsworth Library at Dove Cottage (Oxford University Press, 1991). Dorothy Wordsworth's poems, written mainly for children in her brother's household and surviving as manuscripts in one or another family commonplace book, were not collected until 1987, when Susan M. Levin edited thirty of them in an appendix ("The Collected Poems of Dorothy Wordsworth") to her *Dorothy Wordsworth and Romanticism.* The two poems included here are reprinted from this source.

From The Alfoxden Journal

Jan. 31, 1798. Set forward to Stowey[1] at half-past five. A violent storm in the wood; sheltered under the hollies. When we left home the moon immensely large, the sky scattered over with clouds. These soon closed in, contracting the dimensions of the moon without concealing her.[2] The sound of the pattering shower, and the gusts of wind, very grand. Left the wood when nothing remained of the storm but the driving wind, and a few scattering drops of rain. Presently all clear, Venus first showing herself between the struggling clouds; afterwards Jupiter appeared. The hawthorn hedges, black and pointed, glittering with millions of diamond drops; the hollies shining with broader patches of light. The road to the village of Holford glittered like another stream. On our return, the wind high—a violent storm of hail and rain at the Castle of Comfort.[3] All the Heavens seemed in one perpetual motion when the rain ceased; the moon appearing, now half veiled, and now retired behind heavy clouds, the stars still moving, the roads very dirty.

*   *   *

Feb. 3. A mild morning, the windows open at breakfast, the redbreasts singing in the garden. Walked with Coleridge over the hills. The sea at first obscured by vapour; that vapour afterwards slid in one mighty mass along the sea-shore; the islands and one point of land clear beyond it. The distant country (which was purple in the clear dull air), overhung by straggling clouds that sailed over it, appeared like the darker clouds, which are often seen at a great distance apparently motionless, while the nearer ones pass quickly over them, driven by the lower winds. I never saw such a union of earth, sky, and sea. The clouds beneath our feet spread themselves to the water, and the clouds of the sky almost joined them. Gathered sticks in the wood; a perfect stillness. The redbreasts sang upon the leafless boughs. Of a great number of sheep in the field, only one standing. Returned to dinner at five o'clock. The moonlight still and warm as a summer's night at nine o'clock.

Feb. 4. Walked a great part of the way to Stowey with Coleridge. The morning warm and sunny. The young lasses seen on the hill-tops, in the villages and roads, in their summer holiday clothes—pink petticoats and blue. Mothers with their children in arms, and the little ones that could just walk, tottering by their side. Midges or small flies spinning in the sunshine; the songs of the lark and redbreast; daisies upon the turf; the hazels in blossom; honeysuckles budding. I saw one solitary strawberry flower under a

1. Coleridge's cottage at Nether Stowey, three miles from Alfoxden.
2. Cf. Coleridge's *Christabel,* lines 16–19

(p. 442).
3. A tavern halfway between Holford and Nether Stowey.

hedge. The furze gay with blossom. The moss rubbed from the pailings by the sheep, that leave locks of wool, and the red marks with which they are spotted, upon the wood.[4]

* * *

Feb. 8. Went up the Park, and over the tops of the hills, till we came to a new and very delicious pathway, which conducted us to the Coombe.[5] Sat a considerable time upon the heath. Its surface restless and glittering with the motion of the scattered piles of withered grass, and the waving of the spiders' threads.[6] On our return the mist still hanging over the sea, but the opposite coast clear, and the rocky cliffs distinguishable. In the deep Coombe, as we stood upon the sunless hill, we saw miles of grass, light and glittering, and the insects passing.

Feb. 9. William gathered sticks.

Feb. 10. Walked to Woodlands, and to the waterfall. The adder's-tongue and the ferns green in the low damp dell. These plants now in perpetual motion from the current of the air; in summer only moved by the drippings of the rocks.[7] A cloudy day.

* * *

Mar. 7. William and I drank tea at Coleridge's. A cloudy sky. Observed nothing particularly interesting—the distant prospect obscured. One only leaf upon the top of a tree—the sole remaining leaf—danced round and round like a rag blown by the wind.[8]

Mar. 8. Walked in the Park in the morning. I sate under the fir trees. Coleridge came after dinner, so we did not walk again. A foggy morning, but a clear sunny day.

Mar. 9. A clear sunny morning, went to meet Mr and Mrs Coleridge. The day very warm.

Mar. 10. Coleridge, Wm, and I walked in the evening to the top of the hill. We all passed the morning in sauntering about the park and gardens, the children playing about, the old man at the top of the hill gathering furze; interesting groups of human creatures, the young frisking and dancing in the sun, the elder quietly drinking in the life and soul of the sun and air.

Mar. 11. A cold day. The children went down towards the sea. William and I walked to the top of the hills above Holford. Met the blacksmith. Pleasant to see the labourer on Sunday jump with the friskiness of a cow upon a sunny day.

* * *

1798   1897

4. Cf. Wordsworth's *The Ruined Cottage*, lines 330–36 (p. 266).
5. Hodder's Coombe in the Quantock Hills, near Alfoxden. A combe is a deep valley on the flank of a hill.
6. Cf. Coleridge's *The Rime of the Ancient Mari-*

ner, line 184 (p. 427).
7. Cf. the description of the dell in Coleridge's *This Lime-Tree Bower My Prison*, lines 13–20 (p. 421).
8. Cf. *Christabel*, lines 49ff. (p. 443).

From The Grasmere Journals

1800

May 14 1800 [*Wednesday*]. Wm & John set off into Yorkshire[1] after dinner at ½ past 2 o'clock—cold pork in their pockets. I left them at the turning of the Low-wood bay under the trees. My heart was so full that I could hardly speak to W when I gave him a farewell kiss. I sate a long time upon a stone at the margin of the lake, & after a flood of tears my heart was easier. The lake looked to me I knew not why dull and melancholy, and the weltering on the shores seemed a heavy sound. I walked as long as I could amongst the stones of the shore. The wood rich in flowers. A beautiful yellow, palish yellow flower, that looked thick round & double, & smelt very sweet—I supposed it was a ranunculus—Crowfoot, the grassy-leaved Rabbit-toothed white flower, strawberries, geranium—scentless violet, anemones two kinds, orchises, primroses. The heckberry very beautiful, the crab coming out as a low shrub. Met a blind man, driving a very large beautiful Bull & a cow—he walked with two sticks. Came home by Clappersgate. The valley very green, many sweet views up to Rydale head when I could juggle away the fine houses, but they disturbed me even more than when I have been happier— one beautiful view of the Bridge, without Sir Michael's.[2] Sate down very often, tho' it was cold. I resolved to write a journal of the time till W & J return, & I set about keeping my resolve because I will not quarrel with myself, & because I shall give Wm Pleasure by it when he comes home again. At Rydale a woman of the village, stout & well-dressed, begged a halfpenny— she had never she said done it before—but these hard times!—Arrived at home with a bad head-ache, set some slips of privett. The evening cold, had a fire—my face now flame-coloured. It is nine o'clock. I shall soon go to bed. A young woman begged at the door—she had come from Manchester on Sunday morn with two shillings & a slip of paper which she supposed a Bank note—it was a cheat. She had buried her husband & three children within a year & a half—all in one grave—burying very dear—paupers all put in one place—20 shillings paid for as much ground as will bury a man—a stone to be put over it or the right will be lost—11 / 6 each time the ground is opened. Oh! that I had a letter from William!

* * *

Friday 3rd October. Very rainy all the morning—little Sally learning to mark. Wm walked to Ambleside after dinner. I went with him part of the way—he talked much about the object of his Essay for the 2nd volume of LB.[3] I returned expecting the Simpsons—they did not come. I should have met Wm but my teeth ached & it was showery & late—he returned after 10. Amos Cottle's[4] death in the Morning Post. Wrote to S. Lowthian.[5]

    N.B. When Wm & I returned from accompanying Jones we met an old

---

1. William and his younger brother John, on the way to visit Mary Hutchinson, whom William was to marry two and a half years later.
2. Sir Michael le Fleming's estate, Rydal Hall. "Without": outside or beyond.
3. The Preface to the second edition of *Lyrical*

Ballads, 1800.
4. The brother of Joseph Cottle, Bristol publisher of the first edition of *Lyrical Ballads*.
5. Sally Lowthian, who had been a servant in the house of the Wordsworths' father.

man almost double,[6] he had on a coat thrown over his shoulders above his waistcoat & coat. Under this he carried a bundle & had an apron on & a night cap. His face was interesting. He had dark eyes & a long nose—John who afterwards met him at Wythburn took him for a Jew. He was of Scotch parents but had been born in the army. He had had a wife "& a good woman & it pleased God to bless us with ten children"—all these were dead but one of whom he had not heard for many years, a sailor—his trade was to gather leeches, but now leeches are scarce & he had not strength for it—he lived by begging & was making his way to Carlisle where he should buy a few godly books to sell. He said leeches were very scarce partly owing to this dry season, but many years they have been scarce—he supposed it owing to their being much sought after, that they did not breed fast, & were of slow growth. Leeches were formerly 2 / 6 [per] 100; they are now 30 /. He had been hurt in driving a cart his leg broke his body driven over his skull fractured—he felt no pain till he recovered from his first insensibility. It was then late in the evening—when the light was just going away.

* * *

Saturday [Oct.] *11th.* A fine October morning—sat in the house working all the morning. Wm composing—Sally Ashburner learning to mark. After Dinner we walked up Greenhead Gill in search of a sheepfold.[7] We went by Mr Oliff's & through his woods. It was a delightful day & the views looked excessively chearful & beautiful chiefly that from Mr Oliff's field where our house is to be built. The colours of the mountains soft & rich, with orange fern—The Cattle pasturing upon the hill-tops Kites sailing as in the sky above our heads—Sheep bleating & in lines & chains & patterns scattered over the mountains. They come down & feed on the little green islands in the beds of the torrents & so may be swept away. The Sheepfold is falling away it is built nearly in the form of a heart unequally divided. Look down the brook & see the drops rise upwards & sparkle in the air, at the little falls, the higher sparkles the tallest. We walked along the turf of the mountain till we came to a Cattle track—made by the cattle which come upon the hills. We drank tea at Mr Simpson's returned at about nine—a fine mild night.

Sunday 12th October. Beautiful day. Sate in the house writing in the morning while Wm went into the Wood to compose. Wrote to John in the morning—copied poems for the LB, in the evening wrote to Mrs Rawson. Mary Jameson & Sally Ashburner dined. We pulled apples after dinner, a large basket full. We walked before tea by Bainriggs to observe the many coloured foliage the oaks dark green with yellow leaves—The birches generally still green, some near the water yellowish. The Sycamore crimson & crimson-tufted—the mountain ash a deep orange—the common ash Lemon colour but many ashes still fresh in their summer green. Those that were discoloured chiefly near the water. William composing in the Evening. Went to bed at 12 o'clock.

* * *

6. William's *Resolution and Independence*, composed one and a half years later, incorporated various details of Dorothy's description of the leech gatherer. See May 4 and 7, 1802 (pp. 393 and 394), for William working on the poem he originally called *The Leech Gatherer*.

7. The sheepfold in William's *Michael*; lines 1–17 of the poem describe the walk up Greenhead Ghyll.

1801

Tuesday [Nov.] 24th. A rainy morning. We all were well except that my head ached a little & I took my Breakfast in bed. I read a little of Chaucer, prepared the goose for dinner, & then we all walked out—I was obliged to return for my fur tippet & Spenser[8] it was so cold. We had intended going to Easedale but we shaped our course to Mr Gell's cottage. It was very windy & we heard the wind everywhere about us as we went along the Lane but the walls sheltered us—John Green's house looked pretty under Silver How—as we were going along we were stopped at once, at the distance perhaps of 50 yards from our favorite Birch tree it was yielding to the gusty wind with all its tender twigs, the sun shone upon it & it glanced in the wind like a flying sunshiny shower—it was a tree in shape with stem & branches but it was like a Spirit of water—The sun went in & it resumed its purplish appearance the twigs still yielding to the wind but not so visibly to us. The other Birch trees that were near it looked bright & chearful—but it was a Creature by its own self among them. We could not get into Mr Gell's grounds—the old tree fallen from its undue exaltation above the Gate. A shower came on when we were at Benson's. We went through the wood—it became fair, there was a rainbow which spanned the lake from the Island house to the foot of Bainriggs. The village looked populous & beautiful. Catkins are coming out palm trees budding—the alder with its plumb coloured buds. We came home over the stepping stones the Lake was foamy with white waves. I saw a solitary butter flower in the wood. *I* found it not easy to get over the stepping stones—reached home at dinner time. Sent Peggy Ashburner some goose. She sent me some honey—with a thousand thanks—"alas the gratitude of men has & c"[9] I went in to set her right about this & sate a while with her. She talked about Thomas's having sold his land—"Ay" says she I said many a time "He's not come fra London to buy our Land however" then she told me with what pains & industry they had made up their taxes interest &c &c—how they all got up at 5 o'clock in the morning to spin & Thomas carded, & that they had paid off a hundred pound of the interest. She said she used to take such pleasure in the cattle & sheep—"O how pleased I used to be when they fetched them down, & when I had been a bit poorly I would gang out upon a hill & look over t' fields & see them & it used to do me so much good you cannot think"—Molly said to me when I came in "poor Body! she's very ill but one does not know how long she may last. Many a fair face may gang before her." We sate by the fire without work for some time then Mary read a poem of Daniell upon Learning.[1] After tea Wm read Spenser now & then a little aloud to us. We were making his waistcoat. We had a note from Mrs C., with bad news from poor C very ill. William walked to John's grove—I went to meet him—moonlight but it rained. I met him before I had got as far as John Baty's he had been surprized & terrified by a sudden rushing of winds which seemed to bring earth sky & lake together, as if the whole were going to enclose him in—he was glad he was in a high Road.

---

8. A close-fitting jacket worn by women and children.
9. A quotation from William's *Simon Lee*: "Alas! the gratitude of men / Has oft'ner left me mourn-ing."
1. Samuel Daniel's long poem *Musophilus: Containing a General Defense of Learning* (1599).

In speaking of our walk on Sunday Evening the 22nd November I forgot to notice one most impressive sight—it was the moon & the moonlight seen through hurrying driving clouds immediately behind the Stone man upon the top of the hill on the Forest side. Every tooth & every edge of Rock was visible, & the Man stood like a Giant watching from the Roof of a lofty castle. The hill seemed perpendicular from the darkness below it. It was a sight that I could call to mind at any time it was so distinct.

* * *

1802

Thursday [*Mar. 4*]. Before we had quite finished Breakfast Calvert's man brought the horses for Wm.[2] We had a deal to do to shave—pens to make—poems to put in order for writing, to settle the dress pack up &c &. The man came before the pens were made & he was obliged to leave me with only two—Since he has left me (at ½ past 11) it is now 2 I have been putting the Drawers into order, laid by his clothes which we had thrown here & there & everywhere, filed two months' newspapers & got my dinner 2 boiled eggs & 2 apple tarts. I have set Molly on to clear the garden a little, & I myself have helped. I transplanted some snowdrops—The Bees are busy—Wm has a nice bright day. It was hard frost in the night—The Robins are singing sweetly—Now for my walk. I *will* be busy, I *will* look well & be well when he comes back to me. O the Darling! Here is one of his bitten apples! I can hardly find in my heart to throw it into the fire. I must wash myself, then off—I walked round the two Lakes crossed the stepping stones at Rydale Foot. Sate down where we always sit. I was full of thoughts about my darling. Blessings on him. I came home at the foot of our own hill under Loughrigg. They are making sad ravages in the woods—Benson's Wood is going & the wood above the River. The wind has blown down a small fir tree on the Rock that terminates John's path—I suppose the wind of Wednesday night. I read German after my return till tea time. After tea I worked & read the LB, enchanted with the Idiot Boy. Wrote to Wm then went to Bed. It snowed when I went to Bed.

* * *

Monday [*Mar. 22*]. A rainy day—William very poorly. Mr Luff came in after dinner & brought us 2 letters from Sara H. & one from poor Annette. I read Sara's letters while he was here. I finished my letters to M. & S. & wrote to my Br Richard. We talked a good deal about C. & other interesting things. We resolved to see Annette, & that Wm should go to Mary.[3] We wrote to Coleridge not to expect us till Thursday or Friday.

Tuesday [*Mar. 23*]. A mild morning William worked at the Cuckow poem.[4] I sewed beside him. After dinner he slept I read German, & at the closing in of day went to sit in the Orchard—he came to me, & walked backwards & forwards. We talked about C—Wm repeated the poem to me—I left him there & in 20 minutes he came in, rather tired with attempting to write—

---

2. For a journey to Keswick, to visit Coleridge.
3. It had been arranged several months earlier that William was to marry Mary Hutchinson ("Sara H" is Mary's sister, with whom Coleridge had fallen in love). Now the Wordsworths resolve to go to France to settle affairs with Annette Vallon, mother of William's daughter, Caroline. William did not conceal the facts of his early love affair from his family, or from Mary Hutchinson.
4. *To the Cuckoo.*

he is now reading Ben Jonson I am going to read German it is about 10 o'clock, a quiet night. The fire flutters & the watch ticks I hear nothing else save the Breathing of my Beloved & he now & then pushes his book forward & turns over a leaf. Fletcher is not come home. No letter from C.

* * *

Thursday [Apr.] 15th. It was a threatening misty morning—but mild. We set off after dinner from Eusemere—Mrs Clarkson went a short way with us but turned back. The wind was furious & we thought we must have returned. We first rested in the large Boat-house, then under a furze Bush opposite Mr Clarksons, saw the plough going in the field. The wind seized our breath the Lake was rough. There was a Boat by itself floating in the middle of the Bay below Water Millock—We rested again in the Water Millock Lane. The hawthorns are black & green, the birches here & there greenish but there is yet more of purple to be seen on the Twigs. We got over into a field to avoid some cows—people working, a few primroses by the roadside, wood-sorrel flower, the anemone, scentless violets, strawberries, & that starry yellow flower which Mrs C calls pile wort. When we were in the woods beyond Gowbarrow park we saw a few daffodils close to the water side.[5] We fancied that the lake had floated the seeds ashore & that the little colony had so sprung up—But as we went along there were more & yet more & at last under the boughs of the trees, we saw that there was a long belt of them along the shore, about the breadth of a country turnpike road. I never saw daffodils so beautiful they grew among the mossy stones about & about them, some rested their heads upon these stones as on a pillow for weariness & the rest tossed & reeled & danced & seemed as if they verily laughed with the wind that blew upon them over the lake, they looked so gay ever glancing ever changing. This wind blew directly over the lake to them. There was here & there a little knot & a few stragglers a few yards higher up but they were so few as not to disturb the simplicity & unity & life of that one busy high-way—We rested again & again. The Bays were stormy & we heard the waves at different distances & in the middle of the water like the sea—Rain came on, we were wet when we reached Luffs but we called in. Luckily all was chearless & gloomy so we faced the storm—we *must* have been wet if we had waited—put on dry clothes at Dobson's. I was very kindly treated by a young woman, the Landlady looked sour but it is her way. She gave us a goodish supper. Excellent ham & potatoes. We paid 7 / when we came away. William was sitting by a bright fire when I came downstairs. He soon made his way to the Library piled up in a corner of the window. He brought out a volume of Enfield's Speaker,[6] another miscellany, & an odd volume of Congreve's plays. We had a glass of warm rum & water—We enjoyed ourselves & wished for Mary. It rained & blew when we went to bed. NB Deer in Gowbarrow park like skeletons.

Friday 16th April (Good Friday). When I undrew my curtains in the morning, I was much affected by the beauty of the prospect & the change. The sun shone, the wind has passed away, the hills looked chearful, the river was

5. William did not compose his poem on the daffodils, *I wandered lonely as a cloud,* until two years later. Comparison with the poem will show how extensive was his use of Dorothy's prose descrip- tion (see p. 284).

6. William Enfield's *The Speaker* (1774), a volume of selections suitable for elocution.

very bright as it flowed into the lake. The Church rises up behind a little knot of Rocks, the steeple not so high as an ordinary 3 story house. Bees, in a row in the garden under the wall. After Wm had shaved we set forward. The valley is at first broken by little rocky woody knolls that make retiring places, fairy valleys in the vale, the river winds along under these hills travelling not in a bustle but not slowly to the lake. We saw a fisherman in the flat meadow on the other side of the water. He came towards us & threw his line over the two arched Bridge. It is a Bridge of a heavy construction, almost bending inwards in the middle, but it is grey & there is a look of ancientry in the architecture of it that pleased me. As we go on the vale opens out more into one vale with somewhat of a cradle Bed. Cottages with groups of trees on the side of the hills. We passed a pair of twin Children 2 years old— & Sate on the next bridge which we crossed a single arch. We rested again upon the Turf & looked at the same Bridge. We observed arches in the water occasioned by the large stones sending it down in two streams—a Sheep came plunging through the river, stumbled up the Bank & passed close to us, it had been frightened by an insignificant little Dog on the other side, its fleece dropped a glittering shower under its belly—Primroses by the roadside, pile wort that shone like stars of gold in the Sun, violets, strawberries, retired & half buried among the grass. When we came to the foot of Brothers water I left William sitting on the Bridge & went along the path on the right side of the Lake through the wood—I was delighted with what I saw. The water under the boughs of the bare old trees, the simplicity of the mountains & the exquisite beauty of the path. There was one grey cottage. I repeated the Glowworm[7] as I walked along—I hung over the gate, & thought I could have stayed for ever. When I returned I found William writing a poem descriptive of the sights & sounds we saw & heard. There was the gentle flowing of the stream, the glittering lively lake, green fields without a living creature to be seen on them, behind us, a flat pasture with 42 cattle feeding to our left the road leading to the hamlet, no smoke there, the sun shone on the bare roofs. The people were at work ploughing, harrowing & sowing— Lasses spreading dung, a dog's barking now & then, cocks crowing, birds twittering, the snow in patches at the top of the highest hills, yellow palms, purple & green twigs on the Birches, ashes with their glittering spikes quite bare. The hawthorn a bright green with black stems under the oak. The moss of the oak glossy. We then went on, passed two sisters at work, *they first passed us,* one with two pitch forks in her hand. The other had a spade. We had some talk with them. They laughed aloud after we were gone perhaps half in wantonness, half boldness. William finished his poem before we got to the foot of Kirkstone.[8] * * *

* * *

Thursday [Apr.] 29. A beautiful morning. The sun shone & all was pleasant. We sent off our parcel to Coleridge by the waggon. Mr Simpson heard the Cuckow today. Before we went out after I had written down the Tinker (which William finished this morning)[9] Luff called. He was very lame, limped into the kitchen—he came on a little Pony. We then went to John's Grove,

---

7. William's poem beginning "Among all lovely things my Love had been," composed four days earlier; "my Love" in this line is Dorothy.

8. The short lyric *Written in March.*
9. William never published his comic poem *The Tinker.* It was first printed in 1897.

sate a while at first. Afterwards William lay, & I lay in the trench under the fence—he with his eyes shut & listening to the waterfalls & the Birds. There was no one waterfall above another[1]—it was a sound of waters in the air— the voice of the air. William heard me breathing & rustling now & then but we both lay still, & unseen by one another—he thought that it would be as sweet thus to lie so in the grave, to hear the *peaceful* sounds of the earth & just to know that our dear friends were near. The Lake was still. There was a Boat out. Silver How reflected with delicate purple & yellowish hues as I have seen Spar—Lambs on the island & running races together by the half dozen in the round field near us. The copses green*ish,* hawthorn green.— Came home to dinner then went to Mr Simpson. We rested a long time under a wall. Sheep & lambs were in the field—cottages smoking. As I lay down on the grass, I observed the glittering silver line on the ridges of the Backs of the sheep, owing to their situation respecting the Sun—which made them look beautiful but with something of strangeness, like animals of another kind—as if belonging to a more splendid world. Met old Mr S at the door—Mrs S poorly—I got mullens & pansies—I was sick & ill & obliged to come home soon. We went to bed immediately—I slept up stairs. The air coldish where it was felt somewhat frosty.

* * *

Tuesday May 4th. William had slept pretty well & though he went to bed nervous & jaded in the extreme he rose refreshed. I wrote the Leech Gatherer[2] for him which he had begun the night before & of which he wrote several stanzas in bed this Monday morning. It was very hot, we called at Mr Simpson's door as we passed but did not go in. We rested several times by the way, read & repeated the Leech Gatherer. We were almost melted before we were at the top of the hill. We saw Coleridge on the Wytheburn side of the water. He crossed the Beck to us. Mr Simpson was fishing there. William & I ate a Luncheon, then went on towards the waterfall. It is a glorious wild solitude under that lofty purple crag. It stood upright by itself. Its own self & its shadow below, one mass—all else was sunshine. We went on further. A Bird at the top of the crags was flying round & round & looked in thinness & transparency, shape & motion like a moth. We climbed the hill but looked in vain for a shade except at the foot of the great waterfall, & there we did not like to stay on account of the loose stones above our heads. We came down & rested upon a moss covered Rock, rising out of the bed of the River. There we lay ate our dinner & stayed there till about 4 o'clock or later—Wm & C repeated & read verses. I drank a little Brandy & water & was in Heaven. The Stags horn is very beautiful & fresh springing upon the fells. Mountain ashes, green. We drank tea at a farm house. The woman had not a pleasant countenance, but was civil enough. She had a pretty Boy a year old whom she suckled. We parted from Coleridge at Sara's Crag after having looked at the Letters which C carved in the morning. I kissed them all. Wm deepened the T with C's penknife.[3] We sate afterwards on the wall, seeing the sun go

---

1. I.e., no waterfall could be heard individually.
2. The poem that was published as *Resolution and Independence.* For its origin, see the entry for October 3, 1800 (p. 387).
3. The rock, which has since been blasted away to make room for a new road, contained the carved letters: W. W., M. H., D. W., S. T. C., J. W., S. H. (M. H. and S. H. are Mary and Sara Hutchinson; J. W. is John Wordsworth.)

down & the reflections in the still water. C looked well & parted from us chearfully, hopping up upon the side stones. On the Rays we met a woman with 2 little girls one in her arms the other about 4 years old walking by her side, a pretty little thing, but half starved. She had on a pair of slippers that had belonged to some gentleman's child, down at the heels—it was not easy to keep them on—but, poor thing! young as she was, she walked carefully with them. Alas too young for such cares & such travels—The Mother when we accosted her told us that her husband had left her & gone off with another woman & how she *"pursued"* them. Then her fury kindled & her eyes rolled about. She changed again to tears. She was a Cockermouth woman—30 years of age a child at Cockermouth when I was—I was moved & gave her a shilling, I believe 6^d more than I ought to have given. We had the crescent moon with the "auld moon in her arms."[4]—We rested often:—always upon the Bridges. Reached home at about 10 o'clock. The Lloyds had been here in our absence. We went soon to bed. I repeated verses to William while he was in bed—he was soothed & I left him. "This is the Spot"[5] over & over again.

* * *

6th May Thursday 1802. A sweet morning we have put the finishing stroke to our Bower & here we are sitting in the orchard. It is one o'clock. We are sitting upon a seat under the wall which I found my Brother building up when I came to him with his apple—he had intended that it should have been done before I came. It is a nice cool shady spot. The small Birds are singing—Lambs bleating, Cuckow calling—The Thrush sings by Fits. Thomas Ashburner's axe is going quietly (without passion) in the orchard—Hens are cackling, Flies humming, the women talking together at their doors—Plumb & pear trees are in Blossom—apple trees greenish—the opposite woods green, the crows are cawing. We have heard Ravens. The ash trees are in blossom, Birds flying all about us. The stitchwort is coming out, there is one budding Lychnis, the primroses are passing their prime. Celandine violets & wood sorrel for ever more little—geraniums & pansies on the wall. We walked in the evening to Tail End to enquire about hurdles for the orchard shed & about Mr Luff's flower—The flower dead—no hurdles. I went to look at the falling wood—Wm also when he had been at Benson's went with me. They have left a good many small oak trees but we dare not hope that they are all to remain. The Ladies are come to Mr Gell's cottage. We saw them as we went & their light when we returned. When we came in we found a Magazine & Review & a letter from Coleridge with verses to Hartley & Sara H. We read the Review,[6] &c. The moon was a perfect Boat a silver Boat when we were out in the evening. The Birch Tree is all over green in *small* leaf more light & elegant than when it is full out. It bent to the breezes as if for the love of its own delightful motions. Sloe thorns & Hawthorns in the hedges.

Friday 7th May. William had slept uncommonly well so, feeling himself strong, he fell to work at the Leech gatherer—He wrote hard at it till dinner time, then he gave over tired to death—he had finished the poem.[7] * * *

---

4. From the *Ballad of Sir Patrick Spens*. Coleridge quoted the stanza, of which this phrase is part, as epigraph to *Dejection: An Ode*.
5. William never completed this poem.

6. The *Monthly Review* for March 1802.
7. Later entries show, however, that William kept working on the manuscript until July 4.

＊　＊　＊

[*July.*] On Thursday morning, 29th, we arrived in London.[8] Wm left me at the Inn—I went to bed &c &c &c—After various troubles and disasters we left London on Saturday morning at ½ past 5 or 6, the 31st of July (I have forgot which). We mounted the Dover Coach at Charing Cross. It was a beautiful morning. The City, St. Paul's, with the River & a multitude of little Boats, made a most beautiful sight as we crossed Westminster Bridge. The houses were not overhung by their cloud of smoke & they were spread out endlessly, yet the sun shone so brightly with such a pure light that there was even something like the purity of one of nature's own grand spectacles.[9] We rode on chearfully now with the Paris Diligence before us, now behind— we walked up the steep hills, beautiful prospects everywhere, till we even reached Dover. ＊ ＊ ＊ We arrived at Calais at 4 o'clock on Sunday morning the 31st of July.[1] We stayed in the vessel till ½ past 7, then Wm went for Letters, at about ½ past 8 or 9. We found out Annette & C chez Madame Avril dans la Rue de la Tête d'or. We lodged opposite two Ladies in tolerably decent-sized rooms but badly furnished, & with large store of bad smells & dirt in the yard, & all about. The weather was very hot. We walked by the sea-shore almost every evening with Annette & Caroline or Wm & I alone. I had a bad cold & could not bathe at first but William did. It was a pretty sight to see as we walked upon the Sands when the tide was low perhaps a hundred people bathing about ¼ of a mile distant from us, and we had delightful walks after the heat of the day was passed away—seeing far off in the west the Coast of England like a cloud crested with Dover Castle, which was but like the summit of the cloud—the Evening star & the glory of the sky. The Reflections in the water were more beautiful than the sky itself, purple waves brighter than precious stones for ever melting away upon the sands. ＊ ＊ ＊

＊　＊　＊

[*Sept. 24 and following.*] Mary first met us in the avenue. She looked so fat and well that we were made very happy by the sight of her—then came Sara, & last of all Joanna.[2] Tom was forking corn standing upon the corn cart. We dressed ourselves immediately & got tea—the garden looked gay with asters & sweet peas—I looked at everything with tranquillity & happiness but I was ill both on Saturday & Sunday & continued to be poorly most of the time of our stay. Jack & George came on Friday Evening 1st October. On Saturday 2nd we rode to Hackness, William Jack George & Sara single, I behind Tom. On Sunday 3rd Mary & Sara were busy packing. On Monday 4th October 1802, my Brother William was married to Mary Hutchinson. I slept a good deal of the night & rose fresh & well in the morning—at a little after 8 o'clock I saw them go down the avenue towards the Church. William had parted from me up stairs. I gave him the wedding ring—with how deep

8. On the way to France to visit Annette Vallon and Caroline (see the entry for March 22, 1802; p. 390).
9. Cf. William's sonnet *Composed upon Westminster Bridge* (p. 296).
1. The actual date was August 1. One of the walks by the sea that Dorothy goes on to describe was the occasion for William's sonnet *It is a beauteous evening.*

2. The Wordsworths have come to Gallow Hill, Yorkshire, for the marriage of William and Mary. The people mentioned are Mary's sisters and brothers (Sara, Joanna, Tom, Jack, and George Hutchinson). Out of consideration for Dorothy's overwrought feelings, only Joanna, Jack, and Tom attended the ceremony at Brampton Church.

a blessing! I took it from my forefinger where I had worn it the whole of the night before—he slipped it again onto my finger and blessed me fervently. When they were absent my dear little Sara prepared the breakfast. I kept myself as quiet as I could, but when I saw the two men running up the walk, coming to tell us it was over, I could stand it no longer & threw myself on the bed where I lay in stillness, neither hearing or seeing any thing, till Sara came upstairs to me & said "They are coming." This forced me from the bed where I lay & I moved I knew not how straight forward, faster than my strength could carry me till I met my beloved William & fell upon his bosom. He & John Hutchinson led me to the house & there I stayed to welcome my dear Mary. As soon as we had breakfasted we departed.[3] It rained when we set off. Poor Mary was much agitated when she parted from her Brothers & Sisters & her home. Nothing particular occurred till we reached Kirby. We had sunshine & showers, pleasant talk, love & chearfulness. * * * It rained very hard when we reached Windermere. We sate in the rain at Wilcock's to change horses, & arrived at Grasmere at about 6 o'clock on Wednesday Evening, the 6th of October 1802. Molly was overjoyed to see us,—for my part I cannot describe what I felt, & our dear Mary's feelings would I dare say not be easy to speak of. We went by candle light into the garden & were astonished at the growth of the Brooms, Portugal Laurels, &c &c &—The next day, Thursday, we unpacked the Boxes. On Friday 8th we baked Bread, & Mary & I walked, first upon the Hill side, & then in John's Grove, then in view of Rydale, the first walk that I had taken with my Sister.

* * *

24th December 1802, Christmas Eve. William is now sitting by me at ½ past 10 o'clock. I have been beside him ever since tea running the heel of a stocking, repeating some of his sonnets to him, listening to his own repeating, reading some of Milton's & the Allegro & Penseroso. It is a quiet keen frost. Mary is in the parlour below attending to the baking of cakes & Jenny Fletcher's pies. Sara is in bed in the tooth ache, & so we are—beloved William is turning over the leaves of Charlotte Smith's sonnets, but he keeps his hand to his poor chest pushing aside his breastplate.[4] Mary is well & I am well, & Molly is as blithe as last year at this time. Coleridge came this morning with Wedgwood.[5] We all turned out of Wm's bedroom one by one to meet him—he looked well. We had to tell him of the Birth of his little Girl, born yesterday morning at 6 o'clock.[6] W went with them to Wytheburn in the Chaise, & M & I met Wm on the Rays. It was not an unpleasant morning to the feelings—far from it—the sun shone now & then, & there was no wind, but all things looked chearless & distinct, no meltings of sky into mountains—the mountains like stone-work wrought up with huge hammers.—Last Sunday was as mild a day as I ever remember—We all set off together to walk. I went to Rydale & Wm returned with me. M & S[7] went round the Lakes. There were flowers of various kinds the topmost bell of a fox-glove, geraniums, daisies—a buttercup in the water (but this I saw two

---

3. Dorothy accompanied William and Mary on the three-day journey back to their cottage at Grasmere.
4. Probably an undergarment covering the chest.
5. Tom Wedgwood, whose father had founded the

famous pottery works, was a friend and generous patron of Coleridge.
6. Coleridge's daughter, Sara (1802–1852).
7. Mary and her sister Sara Hutchinson.

or three days before) small yellow flowers (I do not know their name) in the turf a large bunch of strawberry blossoms. Wm sate a while with me, then went to meet M. & S.—Last Saturday I dined at Mr Simpson's also a beautiful mild day. Monday was a frosty day, & it has been frost ever since. On Saturday I dined with Mrs Simpson. It is today Christmas-day Saturday 25th December 1802. I am 31 years of age.—It is a dull frosty day.

* * *

1800–02   1897

Grasmere—A Fragment

Peaceful our valley, fair and green,
And beautiful her cottages,
Each in its nook, its sheltered hold,
Or underneath its tuft of trees.

5   Many and beautiful they are;
But there is *one* that I love best,
A lowly shed, in truth, it is,
A brother of the rest.

Yet when I sit on rock or hill,
10   Down looking on the valley fair,
That Cottage with its clustering trees
Summons my heart; it settles there.

Others there are whose small domain
Of fertile fields and hedgerows green
15   Might more seduce a wanderer's mind
To wish that *there* his home had been.

Such wish be his! I blame him not,
My fancies they perchance are wild
—I love that house because it is
20   The very Mountains' child.

Fields hath it of its own, green fields,
But they are rocky steep and bare;
Their fence is of the mountain stone,
And moss and lichen flourish there.

25   And when the storm comes from the North
It lingers near that pastoral spot,
And, piping through the mossy walls,
It seems delighted with its lot.

And let it take its own delight;
30   And let it range the pastures bare;

Until it reach that group of trees,
—It may not enter there!

A green unfading grove it is,
Skirted with many a lesser tree,
35   Hazel and holly, beech and oak,
A bright and flourishing company.

Precious the shelter of those trees;
They screen the cottage that I love;
The sunshine pierces to the roof,
40   And the tall pine-trees tower above.

When first I saw that dear abode,
It was a lovely winter's day:
After a night of perilous storm
The west wind ruled with gentle sway;

45   A day so mild, it might have been
The first day of the gladsome spring;
The robins warbled, and I heard
One solitary throstle sing.

A Stranger, Grasmere, in thy Vale,
50   All faces then to me unknown,
I left my sole companion-friend
To wander out alone.

Lured by a little winding path,
I quitted soon the public road,
55   A smooth and tempting path it was,
By sheep and shepherds trod.

Eastward, toward the lofty hills,
This pathway led me on
Until I reached a stately Rock,
60   With velvet moss o'ergrown.

With russet oak and tufts of fern
Its top was richly garlanded;
Its sides adorned with eglantine
Bedropp'd with hips of glossy red.

65   There, too, in many a sheltered chink
The foxglove's broad leaves flourished fair,
And silver birch whose purple twigs
Bend to the softest breathing air.

Beneath that Rock my course I stayed,
70   And, looking to its summit high,
"Thou wear'st," said I, "a splendid garb,
Here winter keeps his revelry."

"Full long a dweller on the Plains,
I griev'd when summer days were gone;
75 No more I'll grieve; for Winter here
Hath pleasure gardens of his own.

"What need of flowers? The splendid moss
Is gayer than an April mead;
More rich its hues of various green,
80 Orange, and gold, & glittering red."

—Beside that gay and lovely Rock
There came with merry voice
A foaming streamlet glancing by;
It seemed to say "Rejoice!"

85 My youthful wishes all fulfill'd,
Wishes matured by thoughtful choice,
I stood an Inmate of this vale
How *could* I but rejoice?

ca. 1802–05   1892

Thoughts on My Sick-Bed[1]

And has the remnant of my life
Been pilfered of this sunny Spring?
And have its own prelusive sounds
Touched in my heart no echoing string?

5 Ah! say not so—the hidden life
Couchant° within this feeble frame   *lying*
Hath been enriched by kindred gifts,
That, undesired, unsought-for, came

With joyful heart in youthful days
10 When fresh each season in its Round
I welcomed the earliest Celandine
Glittering upon the mossy ground;

With busy eyes I pierced the lane
In quest of known and *un*known things,
15 —The primrose a lamp on its fortress rock,
The silent butterfly spreading its wings,

The violet betrayed by its noiseless breath,
The daffodil dancing in the breeze,

1. In a letter of May 25, 1832, William Wordsworth's daughter Dora mentions this as "an affecting poem which she [her aunt Dorothy] has written
on the pleasure she received from the first spring
flowers that were carried up to her when confined
to her sick room." The lines refer to half a dozen
or more poems by William, including *I wandered
lonely as a cloud* (in line 18) and *Tintern Abbey*
(lines 45–52).

The carolling thrush, on his naked perch,
20   Towering above the budding trees.

Our cottage-hearth no longer our home,
Companions of Nature were we,
The Stirring, the Still, the Loquacious, the Mute—
To all we gave our sympathy.

25   Yet never in those careless days
When spring-time in rock, field, or bower
Was but a fountain of earthly hope
A promise of fruits & the *splendid* flower.

No! then I never felt a bliss
30   That might with *that* compare
Which, piercing to my couch of rest,
Came on the vernal air.

When loving Friends an offering brought,
The first flowers of the year,
35   Culled from the precincts of our home,
From nooks to Memory dear.

With some sad thoughts the work was done,
Unprompted and unbidden,
But joy it brought to my *hidden* life,
40   To consciousness no longer hidden.

I felt a Power unfelt before,
Controlling weakness, languor, pain;
It bore me to the Terrace walk
I trod the Hills again;—

45   No prisoner in this lonely room,
I *saw* the green Banks of the Wye,
Recalling thy prophetic words,
Bard, Brother, Friend from infancy!

No need of motion, or of strength,
50   Or even the breathing air:
—I thought of Nature's loveliest scenes;
And with Memory I was there.

May 1832   1978

SIR WALTER SCOTT
1771–1832

Walter Scott was born in Edinburgh, but as a small boy, to improve his health, he lived for some years with his grandparents on their farm in the Scottish Border country (the part of southern Scotland lying immediately north of the border with England). This region was rich in ballad and folklore, much of it associated with the Border warfare between northern English and southern Scottish raiders. As a child, Scott listened eagerly to stories about old events and battles as well as to accounts of their experiences by survivors of the Jacobite rebellion of 1745. He early acquired what he exploited in his prose fiction—a sense of history as associated with a specific place and a sense of the past that is kept alive in the oral traditions of the present.

Scott's father was a lawyer and he himself was trained in the law, becoming in 1799 sheriff (local judge) of Selkirkshire, a Border county, and in 1806 clerk of session— i.e., secretary to the highest civil court in Scotland—in Edinburgh. Scott viewed the law, in its development over the centuries, as embodying the changing social customs of the country and an important element in social history, and he often used it (as in *The Heart of Midlothian*) to give a special dimension to his fiction.

From early childhood, Scott was an avid reader of ballads and poetic romances, which with his phenomenal memory he effortlessly memorized. He began his literary career as a poet, first as a translator of German ballad imitations, then as a writer of such imitations, then as a collector and editor of Border ballads (*Minstrelsy of the Scottish Border*, 1802–03), some of which he revised to smooth out roughness and to add striking touches. He then moved on to compose long narrative poems, which were widely read; the best known are *Marmion* (1808) and *The Lady of the Lake* (1810). He gave up narrative poetry for prose fiction because, as he said, "Byron beat me" in the writing of verse romances. In 1811 he began building his great country house at Abbotsford, in his beloved Border country; he furnished the house with historical relics and at the same time incorporated the latest technological developments, such as lighting by gas.

Scott continued to write lyric poems, which he inserted in his novels. Some of the lyrics, including *Jock of Hazeldean* and *Proud Maisie*, are based on the folk ballad and capture remarkably the terse suggestiveness of the oral form. His first novel, *Waverley* (1814), which deals with the Jacobite rebellion, introduced a motif that recurs in much of his best fiction, such as *Old Mortality* (1816) and *The Heart of Midlothian* (1818): the protagonist mediates between a heroic but violent old world that can no longer survive and an emerging new world that has something to learn from the past it rejects. It is this recognition of continuity-in-change between the past and the present that made Scott the founder of the true historical novel, as distinguished from the "Gothic" novel, which had represented the past primarily for its exotic appeal.

Scott published all his novels anonymously, but their author was soon identified and became the most internationally famous as well as the most prolific writer of his day. He was made baronet in 1820. His ambition was to become, as laird of Abbotsford, a great and benevolent landowner of the old school. To achieve this status, he kept adding to his house and buying more land; and to support such expenditures, he associated himself with a number of commercial ventures in printing and publishing. In the crash of 1826, as a result of the failure of the publishing firm of Constable, Scott was financially ruined. He insisted on working off his huge debts by his pen and exhausted himself in the effort to do so. Not until after his death were his creditors finally paid off in full with the proceeds of the continuing sale of his novels.

From The Heart of Midlothian[1]

Chapter I. Being Introductory

So down thy hill, romantic Ashbourn, glides
The Derby dilly, carrying six insides.

Frere.[2]

The times have changed in nothing more (we follow as we were wont the manuscript of Peter Pattieson) than in the rapid conveyance of intelligence and communication betwixt one part of Scotland and another. It is not above twenty or thirty years, according to the evidence of many credible witnesses now alive, since a little miserable horse-cart, performing with difficulty a journey of thirty miles *per diem,* carried our mails from the capital of Scotland to its extremity. Nor was Scotland much more deficient in these accommodations, than our richer sister had been about eighty years before. Fielding, in his *Tom Jones,* and Farquhar, in a little farce called the *Stage-Coach,*[3] have ridiculed the slowness of these vehicles of public accommodation. According to the latter authority, the highest bribe could only induce the coachman to promise to anticipate by half an hour the usual time of his arrival at the Bull and Mouth.

But in both countries these ancient, slow, and sure modes of conveyance, are now alike unknown; mail-coach races against mail-coach, and high-flyer[4] against high-flyer, through the most remote districts of Britain. And in our village alone, three post-coaches, and four coaches with men armed, and in scarlet cassocks, thunder through the streets each day, and rival in brilliancy and noise the invention of the celebrated tyrant:—

Demens, qui nimbos et non imitabile fulmen,
Aere et cornipedum pulsu, simularat, equorum.[5]

Now and then, to complete the resemblance, and to correct the presumption of the venturous charioteers, it does happen that the career of these dashing rivals of Salmoneus[6] meets with as undesirable and violent a termination as that of their prototype. It is on such occasions that the Insides and Outsides, to use the appropriate vehicular phrases, have reason to rue the exchange of the slow and safe motion of the ancient Fly-coaches, which, compared with the chariots of Mr. Palmer,[7] so ill deserve the name. The

---

1. Scott's novel, written and published in 1818, takes its title and central focus from the old Edinburgh Tolbooth, a prison familiarly called, after the name of Edinburgh's county, "the heart of Midlothian." The work brings together historical events connected with the Porteous Riot of 1736 and the stories of Effie Deans, who like Porteous is imprisoned in the Tolbooth under sentence of death, and her sister Jeanie, who wins her pardon. The chapter printed here, exemplifying Scott's complex framing of his historical fiction, provides a narrator (Peter Pattieson), an assemblage of minor characters, a great many jokes and satirical comments on the law, and discussion of the conflict between historical truth and the novelist's invention.
2. John Hookham Frere's *The Loves of the Triangles: A Mathematical and Philosophical Poem* (1798), 1.181–82. "Dilly": short form of *diligence,*

a public stagecoach. "Insides": the passengers riding inside a coach, in contrast to the "outsides," the passengers riding outside on the roof of the coach.
3. George Farquhar's popular farce *The Stage Coach* was first produced in 1704. Henry Fielding comments on the slowness of coaches in *Tom Jones,* book 11, chap. 9.
4. A fast stagecoach.
5. Madman! to mimic the storm-clouds and inimitable thunder with brass and the tramp of horn-footed horses! (Latin; Virgil's *Aeneid* 6.590–91).
6. Virgil's "celebrated tyrant" (above), a king who, wishing to be thought a god, imitated lightning by throwing torches from his chariot. To punish his impiety, Jupiter destroyed him with a thunderbolt.
7. John Palmer (1742–1818), inventor of the British mail-coach system in the mid-1780s.

ancient vehicle used to settle quietly down, like a ship scuttled and left to sink by the gradual influx of the waters, while the modern is smashed to pieces with the velocity of the same vessel hurled against breakers, or rather with the fury of a bomb bursting at the conclusion of its career through the air. The late ingenious Mr. Pennant,[8] whose humor it was to set his face in stern opposition to these speedy conveyances, had collected, I have heard, a formidable list of such casualties, which, joined to the imposition of innkeepers, whose charges the passengers had no time to dispute, the sauciness of the coachman, and the uncontrolled and despotic authority of the tyrant called the Guard, held forth a picture of horror, to which murder, theft, fraud, and peculation, lent all their dark coloring. But that which gratifies the impatience of the human disposition will be practiced in the teeth of danger, and in defiance of admonition; and, in despite of the Cambrian antiquary,[9] mail-coaches not only roll their thunders round the base of Penman-Maur and Cader-Edris, but

> Frighted Skiddaw hears afar
> The rattling of the unscythed car.

And perhaps the echoes of Ben-Nevis[1] may soon be awakened by the bugle, not of a warlike chieftain, but of the guard of a mail-coach.

It was a fine summer day, and our little school had obtained a half holyday, by the intercession of a good-humored visitor.[2] I expected by the coach a new number of an interesting periodical publication, and walked forward on the highway to meet it, with the impatience which Cowper has described as actuating the resident in the country when longing for intelligence from the mart of news:

> "The grand debate,
> The popular harangue,—the tart reply,—
> The logic, and the wisdom, and the wit,
> And the loud laugh,—I long to know them all;—
> I burn to set the imprison'd wranglers free,
> And give them voice and utterance once again."[3]

It was with such feelings that I eyed the approach of the new coach, lately established on our road, and known by the name of the Somerset, which, to say truth, possesses some interest for me, even when it conveys no such important information. The distant tremulous sound of its wheels was heard just as I gained the summit of the gentle ascent, called the Goslin-brae, from which you command an extensive view down the valley of the river Gander. The public road, which comes up the side of that stream, and crosses it at a bridge about a quarter of a mile from the place where I was standing, runs partly through enclosures and plantations, and partly through open pasture land. It is a childish amusement perhaps,—but my life has been spent with children, and why should not my pleasures be like theirs?—childish as it is

---

8. Thomas Pennant (1726–1798), naturalist and travel writer, who published, among other works, *A Tour in Scotland* (1771).
9. I.e., Pennant. "Cambrian": Welsh.
1. The highest mountain in Great Britain, near Fort William, Scotland. Penmaenmawr and Cader Idris are peaks in northwest Wales. Skiddaw is in the English Lake District.
2. His Honor Gilbert Goslinn of Gandercleugh; for I love to be precise in matters of importance.— J. C. [Scott's note, in his character as Jedediah Cleishbotham, the presenter of this novel in a series designated *Tales of My Landlord*].
3. William Cowper's *The Task* 4.30–35.

then, I must own I have had great pleasure in watching the approach of the carriage, where the openings of the road permit it to be seen. The gay glancing of the equipage, its diminished and toy-like appearance at a distance, contrasted with the rapidity of its motion, its appearance and disappearance at intervals, and the progressively increasing sounds that announce its nearer approach, have all to the idle and listless spectator, who has nothing more important to attend to, something of awakening interest. The ridicule may attach to me, which is flung upon many an honest citizen, who watches from the window of his villa the passage of the stage-coach; but it is a very natural source of amusement notwithstanding, and many of those who join in the laugh are perhaps not unused to resort to it in secret.

On the present occasion, however, fate had decreed that I should not enjoy the consummation of the amusement by seeing the coach rattle past me as I sat on the turf, and hearing the hoarse grating voice of the guard as he skimmed forth for my grasp the expected packet, without the carriage checking its course for an instant. I had seen the vehicle thunder down the hill that leads to the bridge with more than its usual impetuosity, glittering all the while by flashes from a cloudy tabernacle of the dust which it had raised, and leaving a train behind it on the road resembling a wreath of summer mist. But it did not appear on the top of the nearer bank within the usual space of three minutes, which frequent observation had enabled me to ascertain was the medium time for crossing the bridge and mounting the ascent. When double that space had elapsed, I became alarmed, and walked hastily forward. As I came in sight of the bridge, the cause of delay was too manifest, for the Somerset had made a summerset[4] in good earnest, and overturned so completely, that it was literally resting upon the ground, with the roof undermost, and the four wheels in the air. The "exertions of the guard and coachman," both of whom were gratefully commemorated in the newspapers, having succeeded in disentangling the horses by cutting the harness, were now proceeding to extricate the *insides* by a sort of summary and Caesarean process of delivery, forcing the hinges from one of the doors which they could not open otherwise. In this manner were two disconsolate damsels set at liberty from the womb of the leathern conveniency. As they immediately began to settle their clothes, which were a little deranged, as may be presumed, I concluded they had received no injury, and did not venture to obtrude my services at their toilette, for which, I understand, I have since been reflected upon by the fair sufferers. The *outsides*, who must have been discharged from their elevated situation by a shock resembling the springing of a mine, escaped, nevertheless, with the usual allowance of scratches and bruises, excepting three, who, having been pitched into the river Gander, were dimly seen contending with the tide, like the relics of Aeneas's shipwreck,—

Rari apparent nantes in gurgite vasto.[5]

I applied my poor exertions where they seemed to be most needed, and with the assistance of one or two of the company who had escaped unhurt, easily succeeded in fishing out two of the unfortunate passengers, who were stout active young fellows; and but for the preposterous length of their great-

---

4. Or somerset, a play on the name of the coach ("Somerset") and a form of modern *somersault*.

5. *Aeneid* 1.118: "Here and there are seen swimmers in the vast abyss."

coats, and the equally fashionable latitude and longitude of their Wellington trousers, would have required little assistance from any one. The third was sickly and elderly, and might have perished but for the efforts used to preserve him.

When the two great-coated gentlemen had extricated themselves from the river, and shaken their ears like huge water-dogs, a violent altercation ensued betwixt them and the coachman and guard, concerning the cause of their overthrow. In the course of the squabble, I observed that both my new acquaintances belonged to the law, and that their professional sharpness was likely to prove an over-match for the surly and official tone of the guardians of the vehicle. The dispute ended in the guard assuring the passengers that they should have seats in a heavy coach which would pass that spot in less than half an hour, providing it were not full. Chance seemed to favor this arrangement, for when the expected vehicle arrived, there were only two places occupied in a carriage which professed to carry six. The two ladies who had been disinterred out of the fallen vehicle were readily admitted, but positive objections were stated by those previously in possession to the admittance of the two lawyers, whose wetted garments being much of the nature of well-soaked sponges, there was every reason to believe they would refund a considerable part of the water they had collected, to the inconvenience of their fellow-passengers. On the other hand, the lawyers rejected a seat on the roof, alleging that they had only taken that station for pleasure for one stage, but were entitled in all respects to free egress and regress from the interior, to which their contract positively referred. After some altercation, in which something was said upon the edict *Nautae, caupones, stabularii*,[6] the coach went off, leaving the learned gentlemen to abide by their action of damages.

They immediately applied to me to guide them to the next village and the best inn; and from the account I gave them of the Wallace-Head, declared they were much better pleased to stop there than to go forward upon the terms of that impudent scoundrel the guard of the Somerset. All that they now wanted was a lad to carry their travelling bags, who was easily procured from an adjoining cottage; and they prepared to walk forward, when they found there was another passenger in the same deserted situation with themselves. This was the elderly and sickly-looking person, who had been precipitated into the river along with the two young lawyers. He, it seems, had been too modest to push his own plea against the coachman when he saw that of his betters rejected, and now remained behind with a look of timid anxiety, plainly intimating that he was deficient in those means of recommendation which are necessary passports to the hospitality of an inn.

I ventured to call the attention of the two dashing young blades, for such they seemed, to the desolate condition of their fellow-traveller. They took the hint with ready good-nature.

"O, true, Mr. Dunover," said one of the youngsters, "you must not remain on the pavé[7] here; you must go and have some dinner with us—Halkit and I must have a post-chaise to go on, at all events, and we will set you down wherever suits you best."

The poor man, for such his dress, as well as his diffidence, bespoke him,

---

6. A Roman law that imposed strict liability on shipmasters, innkeepers, and stablekeepers for the safety of property entrusted to them.
7. Pavement.

made the sort of acknowledging bow by which says a Scotchman, "It's too much honor for the like of me"; and followed humbly behind his gay patrons, all three besprinkling the dusty road as they walked along with the moisture of their drenched garments, and exhibiting the singular and somewhat ridiculous appearance of three persons suffering from the opposite extreme of humidity, while the summer sun was at its height, and everything else around them had the expression of heat and drought. The ridicule did not escape the young gentlemen themselves, and they had made what might be received as one or two tolerable jests on the subject before they had advanced far on their peregrination.

"We cannot complain, like Cowley," said one of them, "that Gideon's fleece remains dry, while all around is moist; this is the reverse of the miracle."[8]

"We ought to be received with gratitude in this good town; we bring a supply of what they seem to need most," said Halkit.

"And distribute it with unparalleled generosity," replied his companion; "performing the part of three water-carts for the benefit of their dusty roads."

"We come before them, too," said Halkit, "in full professional force—counsel and agent—"

"And client," said the young advocate, looking behind him. And then added, lowering his voice, "that looks as if he had kept such dangerous company too long."

It was, indeed, too true, that the humble follower of the gay young men had the threadbare appearance of a worn-out litigant, and I could not but smile at the conceit, though anxious to conceal my mirth from the object of it.

When we arrived at the Wallace Inn, the elder of the Edinburgh gentlemen, and whom I understood to be a barrister,[9] insisted that I should remain and take part of their dinner; and their enquiries and demands speedily put my landlord and his whole family in motion to produce the best cheer which the larder and cellar afforded, and proceed to cook it to the best advantage, a science in which our entertainers seemed to be admirably skilled. In other respects they were lively young men, in the hey-day of youth and good spirits, playing the part which is common to the higher classes of the law at Edinburgh, and which nearly resembles that of the young templars in the days of Steele and Addison.[1] An air of giddy gaiety mingled with the good sense, taste, and information which their conversation exhibited; and it seemed to be their object to unite the character of men of fashion and lovers of the polite arts. A fine gentleman, bred up in the thorough idleness and inanity of pursuit, which I understand is absolutely necessary to the character in perfection, might in all probability have traced a tinge of professional pedantry which marked the barrister in spite of his efforts, and something of active bustle in his companion, and would certainly have detected more than a fashionable mixture of information and animated interest in the language of both. But to me, who had no pretensions to be so critical, my companions seemed to form a very happy mixture of good-breeding and liberal informa-

---

8. Abraham Cowley's *The Complaint* (1663), lines 68–74, referring to Judges 6.36–40.
9. One who can plead cases in the superior courts of law. Halkit is a solicitor, admitted only to the lower courts.

1. Richard Steele and Joseph Addison, principal authors of the *Spectator* papers (1711–12, 1714). "Templars": lawyers.

tion, with a disposition to lively rattle, pun, and jest, amusing to a grave man, because it is what he himself can least easily command.

The thin pale-faced man, whom their good-nature had brought into their society, looked out of place, as well as out of spirits; sate on the edge of his seat, and kept the chair at two feet distance from the table; thus incommoding himself considerably in conveying the victuals to his mouth, as if by way of penance for partaking of them in the company of his superiors. A short time after dinner, declining all entreaty to partake of the wine, which circulated freely round, he informed himself of the hour when the chaise had been ordered to attend; and saying he would be in readiness, modestly withdrew from the apartment.

"Jack," said the barrister to his companion, "I remember that poor fellow's face; you spoke more truly than you were aware of; he really is one of my clients, poor man."

"Poor man!" echoed Halkit—"I suppose you mean he is your one and only client?"

"That's not my fault, Jack," replied the other, whose name I discovered was Hardie. "You are to give me all your business, you know; and if you have none, the learned gentleman here knows nothing can come of nothing."[2]

"You seem to have brought something to nothing though, in the case of that honest man. He looks as if he were just about to honor with his residence the HEART OF MIDLOTHIAN."

"You are mistaken—he is just delivered from it.—Our friend here looks for an explanation. Pray, Mr. Pattieson, have you been in Edinburgh?"

I answered in the affirmative.

"Then you must have passed, occasionally at least, though probably not so faithfully as I am doomed to do, through a narrow intricate passage, leading out of the north-west corner of the Parliament Square, and passing by a high and antique building, with turrets and iron grates,

> Making good the saying odd,
> Near the church and far from God"—[3]

Mr. Halkit broke in upon his learned counsel, to contribute his moiety to the riddle—"Having at the door the sign of the Red Man———"

"And being on the whole," resumed the counsellor, interrupting his friend in his turn, "a sort of place where misfortune is happily confounded with guilt, where all who are in wish to get out———"

"And where none who have the good luck to be out, wish to get in," added his companion.

"I conceive you, gentlemen," replied I; "you mean the prison."

"The prison," added the young lawyer—"You have hit it—the very reverend Tolbooth itself; and let me tell you, you are obliged to us for describing it with so much modesty and brevity; for with whatever amplifications we might have chosen to decorate the subject, you lay entirely at our mercy, since the Fathers Conscript of our city have decreed, that the venerable edifice itself shall not remain in existence to confirm or to confute us."

---

2. The Aristotelian maxim "*Ex nihilo nihil fit*" (the basis of Lear's famous response to his daughter Cordelia, "Nothing will come of nothing," *King* *Lear* 1.1.88).
3. A proverb dating back to medieval times.

"Then the Tolbooth of Edinburgh is called the Heart of Midlothian?" said I.

"So termed and reputed, I assure you."

"I think," said I, with the bashful diffidence with which a man lets slip a pun in presence of his superiors, "the metropolitan county may, in that case, be said to have a sad heart."

"Right as my glove, Mr. Pattieson," added Mr. Hardie; "and a close heart, and a hard heart—Keep it up, Jack."

"And a wicked heart, and a poor heart," answered Halkit, doing his best.

"And yet it may be called in some sort a strong heart, and a high heart," rejoined the advocate. "You see I can put you both out of heart."

"I have played all my hearts," said the younger gentleman.

"Then we'll have another lead," answered his companion.—"And as to the old and condemned Tolbooth, what pity the same honor cannot be done to it as has been done to many of its inmates. Why should not the Tolbooth have its 'Last Speech, Confession, and Dying Words'? The old stones would be just as conscious of the honor as many a poor devil who has dangled like a tassel[4] at the west end of it, while the hawkers[5] were shouting a confession the culprit had never heard of."

"I am afraid," said I, "if I might presume to give my opinion, it would be a tale of unvaried sorrow and guilt."

"Not entirely, my friend," said Hardie; "a prison is a world within itself, and has its own business, griefs, and joys, peculiar to its circle. Its inmates are sometimes short-lived, but so are soldiers on service; they are poor relatively to the world without, but there are degrees of wealth and poverty among them, and so some are relatively rich also. They cannot stir abroad, but neither can the garrison of a besieged fort, or the crew of a ship at sea; and they are not under a dispensation quite so desperate as either, for they may have as much food as they have money to buy, and are not obliged to work whether they have food or not."

"But what variety of incident," said I (not without a secret view to my present task), "could possibly be derived from such a work as you are pleased to talk of?"

"Infinite," replied the young advocate. "Whatever of guilt, crime, imposture, folly, unheard-of misfortunes, and unlooked-for change of fortune, can be found to chequer life, my Last Speech of the Tolbooth should illustrate with examples sufficient to gorge even the public's all-devouring appetite for the wonderful and horrible. The inventor of fictitious narratives has to rack his brains for means to diversify his tale, and after all can hardly hit upon characters or incidents which have not been used again and again, until they are familiar to the eye of the reader, so that the developement, *enlèvement*,[6] the desperate wound of which the hero never dies, the burning fever from which the heroine is sure to recover, become a mere matter of course. I join with my honest friend Crabbe, and have an unlucky propensity to hope when hope is lost, and to rely upon the cork-jacket, which carries the heroes of romance safe through all the billows of affliction." He then declaimed the following passage, rather with too much than too little emphasis:

4. I.e., has been hanged.
5. Sellers of broadsides supposedly reporting the

condemned criminal's confession.
6. Kidnapping.

"Much have I fear'd, but am no more afraid,
When some chaste beauty, by some wretch betray'd,
Is drawn away with such distracted speed,
That she anticipates a dreadful deed.
Not so do I—Let solid walls impound
The captive fair, and dig a moat around;
Let there be brazen locks and bars of steel,
And keepers cruel, such as never feel;
With not a single note the purse supply,
And when she begs, let men and maids deny;
Be windows there from which she dares not fall,
And help so distant, 'tis in vain to call;
Still means of freedom will some Power devise,
And from the baffled ruffian snatch his prize."[7]

"The end of uncertainty," he concluded, "is the death of interest; and hence it happens that no one now reads novels."

"Hear him, ye gods!" returned his companion. "I assure you, Mr. Pattieson, you will hardly visit this learned gentleman, but you are likely to find the new novel most in repute lying on his table,—snugly intrenched, however, beneath Stair's *Institutes*, or an open volume of Morrison's *Decisions*."[8]

"Do I deny it?" said the hopeful jurisconsult, "or wherefore should I, since it is well known these Dalilahs seduce my wisers and my betters? May they not be found lurking amidst the multiplied memorials of our most distinguished counsel, and even peeping from under the cushion of a judge's armchair? Our seniors at the bar, within the bar, and even on the bench, read novels; and, if not belied,[9] some of them have written novels into the bargain. I only say, that I read from habit and from indolence, not from real interest; that, like Ancient Pistol devouring his leek,[1] I read and swear till I get to the end of the narrative. But not so in the real records of human vagaries—not so in the State Trials, or in the Books of Adjournal, where every now and then you read new pages of the human heart, and turns of fortune far beyond what the boldest novelist ever attempted to produce from the coinage of his brain."

"And for such narratives," I asked, "you suppose the History of the Prison of Edinburgh might afford appropriate materials?"

"In a degree unusually ample, my dear sir," said Hardie—"Fill your glass, however, in the meanwhile. Was it not for many years the place in which the Scottish parliament met? Was it not James's[2] place of refuge, when the mob, inflamed by a seditious preacher, broke forth on him with the cries of 'The sword of the Lord and of Gideon—bring forth the wicked Haman'?[3] Since that time how many hearts have throbbed within these walls, as the tolling of the neighbouring bell announced to them how fast the sands of their life were ebbing; how many must have sunk at the sound—how many were supported by stubborn pride and dogged resolution—how many by the consolations of religion? Have there not been some, who, looking back on

---

7. George Crabbe's *The Borough* (1810), letter 20, lines 78–91.
8. Standard treatises on Scottish law.
9. Misrepresented, described falsely.
1. The Welshman Fluellen makes the bombastic Pistol eat a leek, the national emblem of Wales, in

Shakespeare's *Henry V* 5.1.
2. The unpopular, autocratic James II (1633–1701).
3. The mob was conflating Judges 7.20 ("The sword of the Lord, and of Gideon") and Esther 3–9 (the wicked Haman).

the motives of their crimes, were scarce able to understand how they should have had such temptation as to seduce them from virtue? and have there not, perhaps, been others, who, sensible of their innocence, were divided between indignation at the undeserved doom which they were to undergo, consciousness that they had not deserved it, and racking anxiety to discover some way in which they might yet vindicate themselves? Do you suppose any of these deep, powerful, and agitating feelings, can be recorded and perused without exciting a corresponding depth of deep, powerful, and agitating interest?—O! do but wait till I publish the *Causes Célèbres* of Caledonia,[4] and you will find no want of a novel or a tragedy for some time to come. The true thing will triumph over the brightest inventions of the most ardent imagination. *Magna est veritas, et praevalebit.*"[5]

"I have understood," said I, encouraged by the affability of my rattling entertainer, "that less of this interest must attach to Scottish jurisprudence than to that of any other country. The general morality of our people, their sober and prudent habits——"

"Secure them," said the barrister, "against any great increase of professional thieves and depredators, but not against wild and wayward starts of fancy and passion, producing crimes of an extraordinary description, which are precisely those to the detail of which we listen with thrilling interest. England has been much longer a highly civilized country; her subjects have been very strictly amendable to laws administered without fear or favor, a complete division of labor has taken place among her subjects, and the very thieves and robbers form a distinct class in society, subdivided among themselves according to the subject of their depredations, and the mode in which they carry them on, acting upon regular habits and principles, which can be calculated and anticipated at Bow Street, Hatton Garden, or the Old Bailey.[6] Our sister kingdom is like a cultivated field,—the farmer expects that, in spite of all his care, a certain number of weeds will rise with the corn, and can tell you beforehand their names and appearance. But Scotland is like one of her own Highland glens, and the moralist who reads the records of her criminal jurisprudence, will find as many curious anomalous facts in the history of mind, as the botanist will detect rare specimens among her dingles[7] and cliffs."

"And that's all the good you have obtained from three perusals of the Commentaries on Scottish Criminal Jurisprudence?" said his companion. "I suppose the learned author very little thinks that the facts which his erudition and acuteness have accumulated for the illustration of legal doctrines, might be so arranged as to form a sort of appendix to the half-bound and slip-shod volumes of the circulating library."

"I'll bet you a pint of claret," said the elder lawyer, "that he will not feel sore at the comparison. But as we say at the bar, 'I beg I may not be interrupted'; I have much more to say upon my Scottish collection of *Causes Célèbres.* You will please recollect the scope and motive given for the contrivance and execution of many extraordinary and daring crimes, by the long civil dissensions of Scotland—by the hereditary jurisdictions, which, until 1748, rested the investigation of crimes in judges, ignorant, partial, or inter-

---

4. Famous cases of Scotland.
5. From the Apocrypha in the Vulgate (the Latin Bible), 1 Esdras 4.41: "The truth is powerful, and

will prevail."
6. London locations associated with the law.
7. Wooded valleys.

ested—by the habits of the gentry, shut up in their distant and solitary man-
sion-houses, nursing their revengeful passions just to keep their blood from
stagnating—not to mention that amiable national qualification, called the
perfervidum ingenium Scotorum,[8] which our lawyers join in alleging as a
reason for the severity of some of our enactments. When I come to treat of
matters so mysterious, deep, and dangerous, as these circumstances have
given rise to, the blood of each reader shall be curdled, and his epidermis
crisped into goose skin.—But, hist!—here comes the landlord, with tidings,
I suppose, that the chaise is ready."

It was no such thing—the tidings bore, that no chaise could be had that
evening, for Sir Peter Plyem had carried forward my landlord's two pairs of
horses that morning to the ancient royal borough of Bubbleburgh, to look
after his interest there. But as Bubbleburgh is only one of a set of five boroughs which club their shares[9] for a member of parliament, Sir Peter's adversary had judiciously watched his departure, in order to commence a canvass
in the no less royal borough of Bitem, which, as all the world knows, lies at
the very termination of Sir Peter's avenue, and has been held in leading-
strings[1] by him and his ancestors for time immemorial. Now Sir Peter was
thus placed in the situation of an ambitious monarch, who, after having
commenced a daring inroad into his enemies' territories, is suddenly recalled
by an invasion of his own hereditary dominions. He was obliged in consequence to return from the half-won borough of Bubbleburgh, to look after
the half-lost borough of Bitem, and the two pairs of horses which had carried
him that morning to Bubbleburgh, were now forcibly detained to transport
him, his agent, his valet, his jester, and his hard-drinker, across the country
to Bitem. The cause of this detention, which to me was of as little consequence as it may be to the reader, was important enough to my companions
to reconcile them to the delay. Like eagles, they smelled the battle afar off,
ordered a magnum of claret and beds at the Wallace, and entered at full
career into the Bubbleburgh and Bitem politics, with all the probable "petitions and complaints" to which they were likely to give rise.

In the midst of an anxious, animated, and, to me, most unintelligible discussion, concerning provosts, bailies, deacons, sets of boroughs, leets, town-
clerks, burgesses resident and non-resident,[2] all of a sudden the lawyer
recollected himself. "Poor Dunover, we must not forget him"; and the landlord was dispatched in quest of the *pauvre hontēux*,[3] with an earnestly civil
invitation to him for the rest of the evening. I could not help asking the
young gentlemen if they knew the history of this poor man; and the counsellor applied himself to his pocket to recover the memorial or brief from
which he had stated his cause.

"He has been a candidate for our *remedium miserabile*," said Mr. Hardie,
"commonly called a *cessio bonorum*.[4] As there are divines who have doubted
the eternity of future punishments, so the Scotch lawyers seem to have
thought that the crime of poverty might be atoned for by something short of
perpetual imprisonment. After a month's confinement, you must know, a

---

8. The treacherous disposition of the Scots
(Latin).
9. I.e., combine their votes (to elect a candidate).
1. In a state of dependence.
2. Political terms. "Bailies": chief magistrates.
"Leets": lists of candidates eligible for some office.

3. Pauper who is ashamed to beg.
4. In Roman and old Scots law, the surrender of
all one's property to creditors (to avoid imprisonment for debt). "*Remedium miserable*": sad remedy
(Latin).

prisoner for debt is entitled, on a sufficient statement to our Supreme Court, setting forth the amount of his funds, and the nature of his misfortunes, and surrendering all his effects to his creditors, to claim to be discharged from prison."

"I had heard," I replied, "of such a humane regulation."

"Yes," said Halkit, "and the beauty of it is, as the foreign fellow said, you may get the *cessio* when the *bonorums* are all spent—But what, are you puzzling in your pockets to seek your only memorial among old play-bills, letters requesting a meeting of the Faculty, rules of the Speculative Society, syllabus' of lectures—all the miscellaneous contents of a young advocate's pocket, which contains every thing but briefs and bank notes? Can you not state a case of *cessio* without your memorial? Why, it is done every Saturday. The events follow each other as regularly as clock-work, and one form of condescendence might suit every one of them."

"This is very unlike the variety of distress which this gentleman stated to fall under the consideration of your judges," said I.

"True," replied Halkit; "but Hardie spoke of criminal jurisprudence, and this business is purely civil. I could plead a *cessio* myself without the inspiring honours of a gown and three-tailed periwig[5]—Listen.—My client was bred a journeyman weaver—made some little money—took a farm—(for conducting a farm, like driving a gig, comes by nature)—late severe times— induced to sign bills with a friend, for which he received no value—landlord sequestrates—creditors accept a composition—pursuer sets up a public-house—fails a second time—is incarcerated for a debt of ten pounds, seven shillings and sixpence—his debts amount to blank—his losses to blank—his funds to blank—leaving a balance of blank in his favor. There is no opposition; your lordships will please grant commission to take his oath."

Hardie now renounced this ineffectual search, in which there was perhaps a little affectation, and told us the tale of poor Dunover's distresses, with a tone in which a degree of feeling, which he seemed ashamed of as unprofessional, mingled with his attempts at wit, and did him more honor. It was one of those tales which seem to argue a sort of ill-luck or fatality attached to the hero. A well-informed, industrious, and blameless, but poor and bashful man, had in vain essayed all the usual means by which others acquire independence, yet had never succeeded beyond the attainment of bare subsistence. During a brief gleam of hope, rather than of actual prosperity, he had added a wife and family to his cares, but the dawn was speedily overcast. Everything retrograded with him towards the verge of the miry Slough of Despond,[6] which yawns for insolvent debtors; and after catching at each twig, and experiencing the protracted agony of feeling them one by one elude his grasp, he actually sunk into the miry pit whence he had been extricated by the professional exertions of Hardie.

"And, I suppose, now you have dragged this poor devil ashore, you will leave him half naked on the beach to provide for himself?" said Halkit. "Hark ye,"—and he whispered something in his ear, of which the penetrating and insinuating words, "Interest with my Lord," alone reached mine.

"It is *pessimi exempli*,"[7] said Hardie, laughing, "to provide for a ruined

5. The gown and wig that Halkit wears in court.
6. From John Bunyan's *Pilgrim's Progress*.

7. The worst of examples (Latin).

client; but I was thinking of what you mention, provided it can be managed—But hush! here he comes."

The recent relation of the poor man's misfortunes had given him, I was pleased to observe, a claim to the attention and respect of the young men, who treated him with great civility, and gradually engaged him in a conversation, which, much to my satisfaction, again turned upon the *Causes Célèbres* of Scotland. Emboldened by the kindness with which he was treated, Mr. Dunover began to contribute his share to the amusement of the evening. Jails, like other places, have their ancient traditions, known only to the inhabitants, and handed down from one set of the melancholy lodgers to the next who occupy their cells. Some of these, which Dunover mentioned, were interesting, and served to illustrate the narratives of remarkable trials, which Hardie had at his finger ends, and which his companion was also well skilled in. This sort of conversation passed away the evening till the early hour when Mr. Dunover chose to retire to rest, and I also retreated to take down memorandums of what I had learned, in order to add another narrative to those which it had been my chief amusement to collect, and to write out in detail. The two young men ordered a broiled bone, Madeira negus, and a pack of cards, and commenced a game at picquet.[8]

Next morning the travelers left Gandercleugh. I afterwards learned from the papers that both have been since engaged in the great political cause of Bubbleburgh and Bitem, a summary case, and entitled to particular dispatch; but which, it is thought, nevertheless, may outlast the duration of the parliament to which the contest refers. Mr. Halkit, as the newspapers informed me, acts as agent or solicitor; and Mr. Hardie opened for Sir Peter Plyem with singular ability, and to such good purpose, that I understand he has since had fewer play-bills and more briefs in his pocket. And both the young gentlemen deserve their good fortune; for I learned from Dunover, who called on me some weeks afterwards, and communicated the intelligence with tears in his eyes, that their interest had availed to obtain him a small office for the decent maintenance of his family; and that, after a train of constant and uninterrupted misfortune, he could trace a dawn of prosperity to his having the good fortune to be flung from the top of a mail-coach into the river Gander, in company with an advocate and a writer to the signet.[9] The reader will not perhaps deem himself equally obliged to the accident, since it brings upon him the following narrative, founded upon the conversation of the evening.

1818   1818

Lochinvar[1]

O young Lochinvar is come out of the west,
Through all the wide Border his steed was the best;
And save his good broadsword he weapons had none,
He rode all unarm'd, and he rode all alone.

8. A card game for two players. "Madeira negus": a mixture of wine (here, Madeira), hot water, sugar, nutmeg, and lemons.
9. I.e., with a barrister (Hardie) and the highest grade of legal solicitor (Halkit).
1. An inset poem in the long narrative poem *Marmion*.

5 So faithful in love, and so dauntless in war,
 There never was knight like the young Lochinvar.

 He staid not for brake, and he stopp'd not for stone,
 He swam the Eske river where ford there was none;
 But ere he alighted at Netherby gate,
10 The bride had consented, the gallant came late:
 For a laggard in love, and a dastard in war,
 Was to wed the fair Ellen of brave Lochinvar.

 So boldly he enter'd the Netherby Hall,
 Among bride's-men, and kinsmen, and brothers and all:
15 Then spoke the bride's father, his hand on his sword,
 (For the poor craven bridegroom said never a word,)
 "O come ye in peace here, or come ye in war,
 Or to dance at our bridal, young Lord Lochinvar?"

 "I long woo'd your daughter, my suit you denied;—
20 Love swells like the Solway, but ebbs like its tide—
 And now I am come, with this lost love of mine,
 To lead but one measure, drink one cup of wine.
 There are maidens in Scotland more lovely by far,
 That would gladly be bride to the young Lochinvar."

25 The bride kiss'd the goblet: the knight took it up,
 He quaff'd off the wine, and he threw down the cup.
 She look'd down to blush, and she look'd up to sigh,
 With a smile on her lips and a tear in her eye.
 He took her soft hand, ere her mother could bar,—
30 "Now tread we a measure!" said young Lochinvar.

 So stately his form, and so lovely her face,
 That never a hall such a galliard[2] did grace;
 While her mother did fret, and her father did fume,
 And the bridegroom stood dangling his bonnet and plume;
35 And the bride-maidens whisper'd, " 'twere better by far
 To have match'd our fair cousin with young Lochinvar."

 One touch to her hand, and one word in her ear,
 When they reach'd the hall-door, and the charger stood near;
 So light to the croupe[3] the fair lady he swung,
40 So light to the saddle before her he sprung!
 "She is won! we are gone, over bank, bush, and scaur;°   *rocky crag*
 They'll have fleet steeds that follow," quoth young Lochinvar.

 There was mounting 'mong Graemes of the Netherby clan;
 Forsters, Fenwicks, and Musgraves, they rode and they ran:
45 There was racing and chasing on Cannobie Lee,
 But the lost bride of Netherby ne'er did they see.

---

2. A man of courage and spirit.   3. The rump of the horse.

So daring in love, and so dauntless in war,
Have ye e'er heard of gallant like young Lochinvar?

1808

Jock of Hazeldean[1]

"Why weep ye by the tide, ladie?
  Why weep ye by the tide?
I'll wed ye to my youngest son,
  And ye sall be his bride:
5 And ye sall be his bride, ladie,
    Sae comely to be seen"—
But ay she loot the tears down fa'
  For Jock of Hazeldean.

"Now let this willfu' grief be done,
10   And dry that cheek so pale;
Young Frank is chief of Errington
  And lord of Langley Dale;
His step is first in peaceful ha',
  His sword in battle keen"—
15 But ay she loot the tears down fa'
  For Jock of Hazeldean.

"A chain of gold ye sall not lack,
  Nor braid to bind your hair;
Nor mettled hound, nor managed° hawk,   *trained*
20   Nor palfrey fresh and fair;
And you, the foremost o' them a',
  Shall ride our forest queen"—
But ay she loot the tears down fa'
  For Jock of Hazeldean.

25 The kirk was decked at morningtide,
   The tapers glimmered fair;
The priest and bridegroom wait the bride,
  And dame and knight are there.
They sought her baith by bower and ha';
30   The ladie was not seen!
She's o'er the Border and awa'
  Wi' Jock of Hazeldean.

1816

Proud Maisie[1]

Proud Maisie is in the wood
  Walking so early;

---

1. The first stanza is from a traditional Scottish ballad.

1. Sung by crazy Madge Wildfire on her deathbed in *The Heart of Midlothian* (chap. 40).

Sweet Robin sits on the bush,
    Singing so rarely.

5   "Tell me, thou bonny bird,
      When shall I marry me?"—
    "When six braw° gentlemen   *fine*
      Kirward shall carry ye."

    "Who makes the bridal bed,
10   Birdie, say truly?"—
    "The gray-headed sexton
    That delves the grave duly.

    "The glowworm o'er grave and stone
    Shall light thee steady,
15   The owl from the steeple sing,
    'Welcome, proud lady.' "

                                              1818

SAMUEL TAYLOR COLERIDGE
1772–1834

In *The Prelude* Wordsworth, recording his gratitude to the mountains, lakes, and winds "that dwell among the hills where I was born," commiserates with Coleridge because "thou, my Friend! wert reared / In the great City, 'mid far other scenes." Samuel Taylor Coleridge had in fact been born in the small town of Ottery St. Mary, in rural Devonshire, but on the death of his father he had been sent to school at Christ's Hospital, in London. He was a dreamy, enthusiastic, and extraordinarily precocious schoolboy; Charles Lamb, his schoolmate and lifelong friend, in his essay on Christ's Hospital has given us a vivid sketch of Coleridge's loneliness, his learning, and his eloquence. When in 1791 Coleridge entered Jesus College, Cambridge, he was an accomplished scholar; but he found little intellectual stimulation at the university, fell into idleness, dissoluteness, and debt, then in despair fled to London and enlisted in the Light Dragoons under the alias of Silas Tomkyn Comberbache—one of the most inept cavalrymen in the long history of the British army. Although rescued by his brothers and sent back to Cambridge, he left in 1794 without a degree.

    In June 1794 Coleridge met Robert Southey, then a student at Oxford who, like himself, had poetic aspirations, was a radical in religion and politics, and sympathized with the republican experiment in France. Together the two young men planned to establish an ideal democratic community in America for which Coleridge coined the name "Pantisocracy," signifying an equal rule by all. A plausible American real-estate agent persuaded them that the ideal location would be on the banks of the Susquehanna, in Pennsylvania. Twelve men undertook to go; and because perpetuation of the scheme required offspring, hence wives, Coleridge dutifully became engaged to Sara Fricker, conveniently at hand as the sister of Southey's fiancée. The Pantisocracy scheme collapsed, but at Southey's insistence Coleridge went through with the marriage, "resolved," as he said, "but wretched." Later Coleridge's radicalism waned, and he became a conservative in politics—a highly philosophical one—and a staunch Anglican in religion.

In 1795 Coleridge met Wordsworth and at once judged him to be "the best poet of the age." When in 1797 Wordsworth brought his sister, Dorothy, to settle at Alfoxden, only three miles from the Coleridges at Nether Stowey, the period of intimate communication and poetic collaboration began that was the golden time of Coleridge's life. An annuity of £150, granted to Coleridge by Thomas and Josiah Wedgwood, sons of the founder of the famous pottery firm, came just in time to deflect him from assuming a post as a Unitarian minister. After their joint publication of *Lyrical Ballads* in 1798, Coleridge and the Wordsworths spent a winter in Germany, where Coleridge attended the University of Göttingen and began the lifelong study of Kant and the post-Kantian German philosophers and critics that helped alter profoundly his thinking about philosophy, religion, and aesthetics.

Back in England, Coleridge in 1800 followed the Wordsworths to the Lake District, settling at Greta Hall, Keswick. He had become gradually disaffected from his wife, and now he fell helplessly and hopelessly in love with Sara Hutchinson, whose sister, Mary, Wordsworth married in 1802. In accord with the medical prescription of that time, Coleridge had been taking laudanum (opium dissolved in alcohol) to ease the painful physical ailments from which he had suffered from an early age. In 1800–01 heavy dosages during attacks of rheumatism made opium a necessity to him, and Coleridge soon recognized that the drug was a greater evil than the diseases it did not cure. *Dejection: An Ode*, published in 1802, was Coleridge's despairing farewell to health, happiness, and poetic creativity. A two-year sojourn on the Mediterranean island of Malta, intended to restore his health, instead completed his decline. When he returned to England in the late summer of 1806 he was a broken man, an inveterate drug addict, estranged from his wife, suffering from agonies of remorse, and subject to terrifying nightmares of guilt and despair from which his own shrieks awakened him. A bitter quarrel with Wordsworth in 1810 marked the nadir of his life and expectations.

Under these conditions Coleridge's literary efforts, however sporadic and fragmentary, were little short of heroic. In 1808 he gave a course of public lectures in London and, in the next eleven years, followed these with other series on both literary and philosophical topics. He wrote for newspapers and single-handedly undertook to write, publish, and distribute a periodical, *The Friend*, which lasted for some ten months beginning in June 1809. A tragedy, *Remorse*, had in 1813 a successful run of twenty performances at the Drury Lane theater. In 1816 he took up residence at Highgate, a northern suburb of London, under the supervision of the excellent and endlessly forbearing physician James Gillman, who managed to control, although not to eliminate, Coleridge's consumption of opium. The next three years were Coleridge's most sustained period of literary activity: while continuing to lecture and to write for the newspapers on a variety of subjects, he published *Biographia Literaria, Zapolya* (a drama), a book consisting of the essays in *The Friend* (revised and greatly enlarged), two collections of poems, and several important treatises on philosophical and religious subjects. In these last he undertook to establish a philosophical basis for the Trinitarian theology to which he had turned after his youthful period of Unitarianism.

The remaining years of his life, which he spent with Dr. and Mrs. Gillman, were quieter and happier than any he had known since the turn of the century. He came to a peaceful understanding with his wife and was reconciled with Wordsworth, with whom he toured the Rhineland in 1828. His rooms at Highgate became a center for friends, for the London literati, and for a steady stream of pilgrims from England and America. They came to hear one of the wonders of the age, the Sage of Highgate's conversation—or monologue—for even in his decline, Coleridge's talk never lost the almost incantatory power that Hazlitt has immortalized in *My First Acquaintance with Poets*. When he died, Coleridge left his friends with the sense that an incomparable intellect had vanished from the world. "The most *wonderful* man that I have ever known," Wordsworth declared, his voice breaking; and Charles Lamb wrote, "His great and dear spirit haunts me. . . . Never saw I his likeness, nor probably the world can see again."

Coleridge's friends, however, abetted by his own merciless self-judgments, set current the opinion, still common, that he was great in promise but not in performance. Even in his buoyant youth he described his own character as "indolence capable of energies"; and it is true that while his mind was incessantly active and fertile, he lacked application and staying power. He also manifested early in life a profound sense of guilt and a need for public expiation. After drug addiction sapped his strength and will, he often adapted (or simply adopted) passages from other writers, with little or no acknowledgment, and sometimes in a context that seems designed to reveal that he is reliant on sources that he does not credit. Whatever the tangled motives for his procedure, Coleridge has repeatedly been charged with gross plagiarism, from his day to our own. After *The Rime of the Ancient Mariner*, most of the poems he completed were written, like the first version of *Dejection: An Ode*, in a spasm of intense effort. Writings that required sustained planning and application were either left unfinished or, like *Biographia Literaria*, made up of brilliant sections eked out with filler, sometimes lifted from other writers, in a desperate effort to meet a deadline. Many of his speculations Coleridge merely confided to his notebooks and the ears of his friends, incorporated in letters, and poured out in the margins of his own and other people's books.

Even so, it is only when measured against his own potentialities that Coleridge's achievements appear limited. In opposition to the prevailing British philosophy of empiricism and associationism, Coleridge for most of his mature life expounded his views of the mind as creative in perception, intuitive in its discovery of the first premises of metaphysics and religion, and capable of a poetic re-creation of the world of sense by the fusing and formative power of the imagination. Within the decade after Coleridge died, John Stuart Mill, an acute student of contemporary thought, announced that Coleridge was one of "the two great seminal minds of England," the most important instigator and representative of the conservative intellectual movement of the day. Time has proved Mill's estimate of Coleridge to be just, for his influence is strongly evident in nineteenth-century English and American traditions of philosophical idealism, enlightened political conservatism, and liberal interpretations of Trinitarian theology. By present consensus, Coleridge is also one of the most important and influential of literary theorists; a number of his central ideas were adopted even by some New Critics of the mid-twentieth century who derogated the Romantic poetry for which his criticism provided a rationale. Above all, Coleridge's writings in verse, although small in quantity, are the achievements of a remarkably innovative poet.

In the course of a few years, he wrote his poems of mystery and demonism, *The Rime of the Ancient Mariner, Christabel*, and *Kubla Khan*. No less impressive in their own way are the blank-verse poems of the lonely and meditative mind that, by an extension of Coleridge's term for one of them, are called "Conversation Poems"; in the best of these, *Frost at Midnight*, Coleridge perfected the characteristic pattern of integrally related description and meditation, which Wordsworth immediately used in *Tintern Abbey*. Coleridge himself adapted this pattern to *Dejection: An Ode*, a high achievement in a genre in which few poets have been successful, the irregular English ode. And even when he had mainly given up poetry, after 1805, Coleridge continued to write occasional short lyrics (printed here) that are notable both for their quality and for the extent to which they have been neglected by anthologists.

The Eolian Harp[1]

Composed at Clevedon, Somersetshire

My pensive Sara! thy soft cheek reclined
Thus on mine arm, most soothing sweet it is
To sit beside our cot, our cot o'ergrown
With white-flowered jasmin, and the broad-leaved myrtle,
5   (Meet emblems they of Innocence and Love!)
And watch the clouds, that late were rich with light,
Slow saddening round, and mark the star of eve
Serenely brilliant (such should wisdom be)
Shine opposite! How exquisite the scents
10 Snatched from yon bean-field! and the world so hushed!
The stilly murmur of the distant sea
Tells us of silence.

            And that simplest lute,
Placed length-ways in the clasping casement, hark!
How by the desultory breeze caressed,
15 Like some coy maid half yielding to her lover,
It pours such sweet upbraiding, as must needs
Tempt to repeat the wrong! And now, its strings
Boldlier swept, the long sequacious° notes   *successive*
Over delicious surges sink and rise,
20 Such a soft floating witchery of sound
As twilight Elfins make, when they at eve
Voyage on gentle gales from Fairy-Land,
Where Melodies round honey-dropping flowers,
Footless and wild, like birds of Paradise,[2]
25 Nor pause, nor perch, hovering on untamed wing!
O the one life within us and abroad,
Which meets all motion and becomes its soul,
A light in sound, a sound-like power in light,
Rhythm in all thought, and joyance every where—
30 Methinks, it should have been impossible
Not to love all things in a world so filled;

1. Named for Aeolus, god of the winds, the harp has strings stretched over a rectangular sounding box. The strings are tuned in unison. When placed in an opened window, the harp (also called "Eolian lute," "Eolian lyre," "wind harp") responds to the altering wind by sequences of musical chords. This instrument, which seems to voice nature's own music, was a favorite household furnishing in the period and was repeatedly alluded to in Romantic poetry. It served also as one of the recurrent Romantic images for the mind—either the mind in poetic inspiration, as in the last stanza of Shelley's *Ode to the West Wind* (p. 732), or else the mind in perception, responding to an intellectual breeze by trembling into consciousness, as in this poem, lines 44–48. Coleridge, however, no sooner puts forward this concept than he retracts it, for it comes too close to the heresy of pantheism, which identifies God with the nature that, in the orthodox view, is His creation.

Coleridge wrote this poem to Sara Fricker, whom he married on October 4, 1795, and took to a cottage (the "cot" of lines 3 and 64) at Clevedon, overlooking the Bristol Channel. He later several times expanded and altered the original version; the famous lines 26–29, for example, were not added until 1817. The poem was Coleridge's first achievement in the important Romantic form of the sustained blank-verse lyric of description and meditation, in the mode of conversation addressed to a silent auditor—a form that he perfected in *Frost at Midnight*, and that Wordsworth adopted in *Tintern Abbey*.

2. Brilliantly colored birds found in New Guinea and adjacent islands. The native practice of removing the legs when preparing the skin led Europeans to believe that the birds were footless and spent their lives hovering in the air and feeding on nectar.

Where the breeze warbles, and the mute still air
Is Music slumbering on her instrument.

And thus, my love! as on the midway slope
35 Of yonder hill I stretch my limbs at noon,
Whilst through my half-closed eye-lids I behold
The sunbeams dance, like diamonds, on the main,
And tranquil muse upon tranquillity;
Full many a thought uncalled and undetained,
40 And many idle flitting phantasies,
Traverse my indolent and passive brain,
As wild and various as the random gales
That swell and flutter on this subject lute!

And what if all of animated nature
45 Be but organic harps diversely framed,
That tremble into thought, as o'er them sweeps
Plastic and vast, one intellectual breeze,
At once the Soul of each, and God of All?

But thy more serious eye a mild reproof
50 Darts, O beloved woman! nor such thoughts
Dim and unhallowed dost thou not reject,
And biddest me walk humbly with my God.
Meek daughter in the family of Christ!
Well hast thou said and holily dispraised
55 These shapings of the unregenerate mind;
Bubbles that glitter as they rise and break
On vain Philosophy's aye-babbling spring.
For never guiltless may I speak of him,
The Incomprehensible! save when with awe
60 I praise him, and with Faith that inly feels;
Who with his saving mercies healed me,
A sinful and most miserable man,
Wildered and dark, and gave me to possess
Peace, and this cot, and thee, heart-honored Maid!

1795   1796

This Lime-Tree Bower My Prison

In the June of 1797, some long-expected Friends paid a visit to the
author's cottage; and on the morning of their arrival, he met with
an accident, which disabled him from walking during the whole
time of their stay. One evening, when they had left him for a few
hours, he composed the following lines in the garden-bower.[1]

1. The time was in fact July 1797; the visiting
friends were William and Dorothy Wordsworth
and Charles Lamb; the accident was the fault of
Mrs. Coleridge—"dear Sara," Coleridge wrote,
"accidentally emptied a skillet of boiling milk on
my foot"; and the bower consisted of lime (i.e., lin-
den) trees in the garden of Thomas Poole, next

door to Coleridge's cottage at Nether Stowey.
Coleridge related these facts in a letter to Robert
Southey, July 17, 1797, in which he transcribed
the first version of this fine "conversation poem."
In the earliest printed text, the title is followed by
"Addressed to Charles Lamb, of the India-House,
London."

Well, they are gone, and here must I remain,
This lime-tree bower my prison! I have lost
Beauties and feelings, such as would have been
Most sweet to my remembrance even when age
5   Had dimmed mine eyes to blindness! They, meanwhile,
Friends, whom I never more may meet again,
On springy[2] heath, along the hill-top edge,
Wander in gladness, and wind down, perchance,
To that still roaring dell, of which I told;
10   The roaring dell, o'erwooded, narrow, deep,
And only speckled by the mid-day sun;
Where its slim trunk the ash from rock to rock
Flings arching like a bridge;—that branchless ash,
Unsunned and damp, whose few poor yellow leaves
15   Ne'er tremble in the gale, yet tremble still,
Fanned by the water-fall! and there my friends
Behold the dark green file of long lank weeds,
That all at once (a most fantastic sight!)
Still nod and drip beneath the dripping edge
Of the blue clay-stone.[3]

20   Now, my friends emerge
Beneath the wide wide Heaven—and view again
The many-steepled tract magnificent
Of hilly fields and meadows, and the sea,
With some fair bark, perhaps, whose sails light up
25   The slip of smooth clear blue betwixt two Isles
Of purple shadow! Yes! they wander on
In gladness all; but thou, methinks, most glad,
My gentle-hearted Charles! for thou hast pined
And hungered after Nature, many a year,
30   In the great City pent,[4] winning thy way
With sad yet patient soul, through evil and pain
And strange calamity![5] Ah! slowly sink
Behind the western ridge, thou glorious sun!
Shine in the slant beams of the sinking orb,
35   Ye purple heath-flowers! richlier burn, ye clouds!
Live in the yellow light, ye distant groves!
And kindle, thou blue ocean! So my Friend
Struck with deep joy may stand, as I have stood,
Silent with swimming sense; yea, gazing round
40   On the wide landscape, gaze till all doth seem
Less gross than bodily; and of such hues
As veil the Almighty Spirit, when yet he makes
Spirits perceive his presence.

                    A delight
Comes sudden on my heart, and I am glad

2. *Elastic*, I mean [Coleridge's note].
3. Cf. Dorothy Wordsworth's description of the "low damp dell" in her *Alfoxden Journal*, February 10, 1798 (p. 386).
4. Despite Coleridge's claim, Charles Lamb emi-

nently preferred London over what he called "dead Nature."
5. Some ten months earlier Charles Lamb's sister, Mary, had stabbed their mother to death in a fit of insanity.

45   As I myself were there! Nor in this bower,
This little lime-tree bower, have I not marked
Much that has soothed me. Pale beneath the blaze
Hung the transparent foliage; and I watched
Some broad and sunny leaf, and loved to see
50   The shadow of the leaf and stem above
Dappling its sunshine! And that walnut-tree
Was richly tinged, and a deep radiance lay
Full on the ancient ivy, which usurps
Those fronting elms, and now, with blackest mass
55   Makes their dark branches gleam a lighter hue
Through the late twilight: and though now the bat
Wheels silent by, and not a swallow twitters,
Yet still the solitary humble bee
Sings in the bean-flower! Henceforth I shall know
60   That Nature ne'er deserts the wise and pure;
No plot so narrow, be but Nature there,
No waste so vacant, but may well employ
Each faculty of sense, and keep the heart
Awake to Love and Beauty! and sometimes
65   'Tis well to be bereft of promised good,
That we may lift the Soul, and contemplate
With lively joy the joys we cannot share.
My gentle-hearted Charles! when the last rook
Beat its straight path along the dusky air
70   Homewards, I blessed it! deeming its black wing
(Now a dim speck, now vanishing in light)
Had crossed the mighty orb's dilated glory,
While thou stood'st gazing; or when all was still,
Flew creeking o'er thy head, and had a charm
75   For thee, my gentle-hearted Charles, to whom
No sound is dissonant which tells of Life.

1797   1800

 The Rime of the Ancient Mariner[1]

IN SEVEN PARTS

*Facile credo, plures esse Naturas invisibiles quam visibiles in rerum
universitate. Sed horum [sic] omnium familiam quis nobis enarrabit,
et gradus et cognationes et discrimina et singulorum munera? Quid
agunt? quae loca habitant? Harum rerum notitiam semper ambivit
ingenium humanum, nunquam attigit. Juvat, interea, non diffiteor,
quandoque in animo, tanquam in tabulâ, majoris et melioris mundi*

1. Coleridge describes the origin of this poem in the opening section of chap. 14 of *Biographia Literaria*. In a comment made to the Reverend Alexander Dyce in 1835 and in a note on *We Are Seven* dictated in 1843, Wordsworth added some details. The poem, based on a dream of Coleridge's friend Cruikshank, was originally planned as a collaboration between Coleridge and Wordsworth, to pay the expense of a walking tour they took with Dorothy Wordsworth in November 1797. Before he dropped out of the enterprise, Wordsworth suggested the shooting of the albatross and the navigation of the ship by the dead men; he also contributed lines 13–16 and 226–27.

The version of *The Rime of the Ancient Mariner* printed in *Lyrical Ballads* (1798) contained many archaic words and spellings. In later editions Coleridge greatly improved the poem by pruning the archaisms and by other revisions; he also added the Latin epigraph and the marginal glosses.

*imaginem contemplari: ne mens assuefacta hodiernae vitae minutiis
se contrahat nimis, et tota subsidat in pusillas cogitationes. Sed ver-
itati interea invigilandum est, modusque servandus, ut certa ab incer-
tis, diem a nocte, distinguamus.*

T. BURNET, *Archaeol. Phil.* p. 68.[2]

Part 1

An ancient Mariner
meeteth three gal-
lants bidden to a
wedding-feast, and
detaineth one.

It is an ancient Mariner
And he stoppeth one of three.
"By thy long grey beard and glittering eye,
Now wherefore stopp'st thou me?

The Bridegroom's doors are opened wide,   5
And I am next of kin;
The guests are met, the feast is set:
May'st hear the merry din."

He holds him with his skinny hand,
"There was a ship," quoth he.   10
"Hold off! unhand me, grey-beard loon!"
Eftsoons[3] his hand dropt he.

The wedding guest is
spellbound by the eye
of the old sea-faring
man, and con-
strained to hear his
tale.

He holds him with his glittering eye—
The wedding-guest stood still,
And listens like a three years' child: 15
The Mariner hath his will.[4]

The wedding-guest sat on a stone:
He cannot choose but hear;
And thus spake on that ancient man,
The bright-eyed Mariner.   20

"The ship was cheered, the harbor cleared,
Merrily did we drop
Below the kirk,[5] below the hill,
Below the light house top.

The Mariner tells
how the ship sailed
southward with a
good wind and fair
weather, till it
reached the line.

The sun came up upon the left,   25
Out of the sea came he!
And he shone bright, and on the right
Went down into the sea.

Higher and higher every day,
Till over the mast at noon[6]—"   30

2. "I readily believe that there are more invisible than visible Natures in the universe. But who will explain for us the family of all these beings, and the ranks and relations and distinguishing features and functions of each? What do they do? What places do they inhabit? The human mind has always sought the knowledge of these things, but never attained it. Meanwhile I do not deny that it is helpful sometimes to contemplate in the mind, as on a tablet, the image of a greater and better world, lest the intellect, habituated to the petty things of daily life, narrow itself and sink wholly into trivial thoughts. But at the same time we must be watchful for the truth and keep a sense of proportion, so that we may distinguish the certain from the uncertain, day from night." Adapted by Coleridge from Thomas Burnet, *Archaeologiae Philosophicae* (1692).

3. At once.

4. I.e., the Mariner has gained control of the will of the wedding guest by hypnosis—or, as it was called in Coleridge's time, by "mesmerism."

5. Church.

6. The ship had reached the equator.

The wedding-guest here beat his breast,
For he heard the loud bassoon.

The Wedding Guest heareth the bridal music; but the mariner continueth his tale.

The bride hath paced into the hall,
Red as a rose is she;
Nodding their heads before her goes   35
The merry minstrelsy.

The wedding-guest he beat his breast,
Yet he cannot choose but hear;
And thus spake on that ancient man,
The bright-eyed Mariner.   40

The ship driven by a storm toward the south pole.

"And now the storm-blast came, and he
Was tyrannous and strong:
He struck with his o'ertaking wings,
And chased us south along.

With sloping masts and dipping prow,   45
As who pursued with yell and blow
Still treads the shadow of his foe,
And forward bends his head,
The ship drove fast, loud roared the blast,
And southward aye we fled.   50

And now there came both mist and snow,
And it grew wondrous cold:
And ice, mast-high, came floating by,
As green as emerald.

The land of ice, and of fearful sounds where no living thing was to be seen.

And through the drifts the snowy clifts   55
Did send a dismal sheen:
Nor shapes of men nor beasts we ken—
The ice was all between.

The ice was here, the ice was there,
The ice was all around: 60
It cracked and growled, and roared and howled,
Like noises in a swound![7]

Till a great sea-bird, called the Albatross, came through the snow-fog, and was received with great joy and hospitality.

At length did cross an Albatross,
Thorough the fog it came;
As if it had been a Christian soul,   65
We hailed it in God's name.

It ate the food it ne'er had eat,
And round and round it flew.
The ice did split with a thunder-fit;
The helmsman steered us through!   70

7. Swoon.

And lo! the Albatross proveth a bird of good omen, and followeth the ship as it returned northward through fog and floating ice.

And a good south wind sprung up behind;
The Albatross did follow,
And every day, for food or play,
Came to the mariners' hollo!

In mist or cloud, on mast or shroud,[8]   75
It perched for vespers nine;
Whiles all the night, through fog-smoke white,
Glimmered the white moon-shine."

The ancient Mariner inhospitably killeth the pious bird of good omen.

"God save thee, ancient Mariner!
From the fiends, that plague thee thus!—   80
Why look'st thou so?"—With my cross-bow
I shot the Albatross.

Part 2

The Sun now rose upon the right:[9]
Out of the sea came he,
Still hid in mist, and on the left   85
Went down into the sea.

And the good south wind still blew behind,
But no sweet bird did follow,
Nor any day for food or play
Came to the mariners' hollo!   90

His shipmates cry out against the ancient Mariner, for killing the bird of good luck.

And I had done a hellish thing,
And it would work 'em woe:
For all averred, I had killed the bird
That made the breeze to blow.
Ah wretch! said they, the bird to slay,   95
That made the breeze to blow!

But when the fog cleared off, they justify the same, and thus make themselves accomplices in the crime.

Nor dim nor red, like God's own head,
The glorious Sun uprist:
Then all averred, I had killed the bird
That brought the fog and mist.   100
'Twas right, said they, such birds to slay,
That bring the fog and mist.

The fair breeze continues; the ship enters the Pacific Ocean, and sails northward, even till it reaches the Line.[1]

The fair breeze blew, the white foam flew,
The furrow followed free;
We were the first that ever burst   105
Into that silent sea.

The ship hath been suddenly becalmed.

Down dropt the breeze, the sails dropt down,
'Twas sad as sad could be;

8. Rope supporting the mast.
9. Having rounded Cape Horn, the ship heads north into the Pacific.
1. I.e., the equator. Unless it is simply an error (Coleridge misreading his own poem), this gloss anticipates the ship's later arrival at the equator, on its trip north from the region of the South Pole, as described in lines 381–84.

And we did speak only to break
The silence of the sea!   110

All in a hot and copper sky,
The bloody Sun, at noon,
Right up above the mast did stand,
No bigger than the Moon.

Day after day, day after day,   115
We stuck, nor breath nor motion;
As idle as a painted ship
Upon a painted ocean.

And the Albatross
begins to be avenged.

Water, water, every where,
And all the boards did shrink;   120
Water, water, every where,
Nor any drop to drink.

The very deep did rot: O Christ!
That ever this should be!
Yea, slimy things did crawl with legs   125
Upon the slimy sea.

About, about, in reel and rout
The death-fires[2] danced at night;
The water, like a witch's oils,
Burnt green, and blue and white.   130

A spirit had followed
them; one of the
invisible inhabitants
of this planet, neither
departed souls nor
angels; concerning
whom the learned

And some in dreams assured were
Of the spirit that plagued us so;
Nine fathom deep he had followed us
From the land of mist and snow.

Jew, Josephus, and the Platonic Constantinopolitan, Michael Psellus, may be consulted. They are very
numerous, and there is no climate or element without one or more.

And every tongue, through utter drought,   135
Was withered at the root;
We could not speak, no more than if
We had been choked with soot.

The shipmates, in
their sore distress,
would fain throw
the whole guilt on
the ancient Mariner:
in sign whereof they
hang the dead sea
bird round his
neck.

Ah! well-a-day! what evil looks
Had I from old and young!   140
Instead of the cross, the Albatross
About my neck was hung.

Part 3

There passed a weary time. Each throat
Was parched, and glazed each eye.

2. Usually glossed as the corposant, or St. Elmo's fire—an atmospheric electricity on a ship's mast or rigging—believed by superstitious sailors to portend disaster. Possibly the image is instead a type of oceanic *ignis fatuus* ("foolish fire") resulting from the decomposition of putrescent matter in the sea (see line 123).

The ancient Mariner beholdeth a sign in the element afar off.

A weary time! a weary time!   145
How glazed each weary eye,
When looking westward, I beheld
A something in the sky.

At first it seemed a little speck,
And then it seemed a mist;   150
It moved and moved, and took at last
A certain shape, I wist.[3]

A speck, a mist, a shape, I wist!
And still it neared and neared:
As if it dodged a water-sprite,[4]   155
It plunged and tacked and veered.

At its nearer approach, it seemeth him to be a ship; and at a dear ransom he freeth his speech from the bonds of thirst.

With throats unslaked, with black lips baked,
We could nor laugh nor wail;
Through utter drought all dumb we stood!
I bit my arm, I sucked the blood,   160
And cried, A sail! a sail!

A flash of joy;

With throats unslaked, with black lips baked,
Agape they heard me call:
Gramercy![5] they for joy did grin,
And all at once their breath drew in,   165
As they were drinking all.

And horror follows. For can it be a ship that comes onward without wind or tide?

See! see! (I cried) she tacks no more!
Hither to work us weal;[6]
Without a breeze, without a tide,
She steadies with upright keel!   170

The western wave was all a-flame.
The day was well nigh done!
Almost upon the western wave
Rested the broad bright Sun;
When that strange shape drove suddenly   175
Betwixt us and the Sun.

It seemeth him but the skeleton of a ship.

And straight the Sun was flecked with bars,
(Heaven's Mother send us grace!)
As if through a dungeon-grate he peered
With broad and burning face.   180

Alas! (thought I, and my heart beat loud)
How fast she nears and nears!
Are those her sails that glance in the Sun,
Like restless gossameres?[7]

3. Knew.
4. A supernatural being that supervises the natural elements (but Coleridge may in fact have been using the term to mean water-*spout*).
5. Great thanks; from the French *grand-merci*.
6. Benefit.
7. Filmy cobwebs floating in the air.

And its ribs are seen as bars on the face of the setting Sun. The specter-woman and her death-mate, and no other on board the skeleton-ship.

Are those her ribs through which the Sun 185
Did peer, as through a grate?
And is that Woman all her crew?
Is that a Death? and are there two?
Is Death that woman's mate?

Like vessel, like crew!

Her lips were red, her looks were free, 190
Her locks were yellow as gold:
Her skin was as white as leprosy,
The Night-mare Life-in-Death was she,
Who thicks man's blood with cold.

Death and Life-in-death have diced for the ship's crew, and she (the latter) winneth the ancient Mariner.

The naked hulk alongside came, 195
And the twain were casting dice;
"The game is done! I've won! I've won!"
Quoth she, and whistles thrice.

No twilight within the courts of the sun.

The Sun's rim dips; the stars rush out:
At one stride comes the dark; 200
With far-heard whisper, o'er the sea,
Off shot the spectre-bark.

At the rising of the Moon,

We listened and looked sideways up!
Fear at my heart, as at a cup,
My life-blood seemed to sip! 205
The stars were dim, and thick the night,
The steersman's face by his lamp gleamed white;
From the sails the dew did drip—
Till clomb above the eastern bar
The horned Moon, with one bright star 210
Within the nether tip.[8]

One after another,

One after one, by the star-dogged Moon,
Too quick for groan or sigh,
Each turned his face with a ghastly pang,
And cursed me with his eye. 215

His shipmates drop down dead.

Four times fifty living men,
(And I heard nor sigh nor groan)
With heavy thump, a lifeless lump,
They dropped down one by one.

But Life-in-Death begins her work on the ancient Mariner.

The souls did from their bodies fly,— 220
They fled to bliss or woe!
And every soul, it passed me by,
Like the whizz of my cross-bow!

Part 4

The wedding guest feareth that a spirit is talking to him.

"I fear thee, ancient Mariner!
I fear thy skinny hand! 225
And thou art long, and lank, and brown,
As is the ribbed sea-sand.

8. An omen of impending evil.

I fear thee and thy glittering eye,
And thy skinny hand, so brown."—
Fear not, fear not, thou wedding-guest!   230
This body drop not down.

But the ancient Mar-
iner assureth him of
his bodily life, and
proceedeth to relate
his horrible penance.

Alone, alone, all, all alone,
Alone on a wide wide sea!
And never a saint took pity on
My soul in agony.   235

He despiseth the
creatures of the
calm,

The many men, so beautiful!
And they all dead did lie:
And a thousand thousand slimy things
Lived on; and so did I.

And envieth that
they should live, and
so many lie dead.

I looked upon the rotting sea,   240
And drew my eyes away;
I looked upon the rotting deck,
And there the dead men lay.

I looked to heaven, and tried to pray;
But or ever a prayer had gusht,   245
A wicked whisper came, and made
My heart as dry as dust.

I closed my lids, and kept them close,
And the balls like pulses beat;
For the sky and the sea, and the sea and the sky   250
Lay like a load on my weary eye,
And the dead were at my feet.

But the curse liveth
for him in the eye of
the dead men.

The cold sweat melted from their limbs,
Nor rot nor reek did they:
The look with which they looked on me   255
Had never passed away.

An orphan's curse would drag to hell
A spirit from on high;
But oh! more horrible than that
Is the curse in a dead man's eye!   260
Seven days, seven nights, I saw that curse,
And yet I could not die.

In his loneliness and
fixedness he yearneth
towards the journey-
ing Moon, and the
stars that still
sojourn, yet still
move onward; and

The moving Moon went up the sky,
And no where did abide:
Softly she was going up,   265
And a star or two beside—

everywhere the blue sky belongs to them, and is their appointed rest, and their native country and their
own natural homes, which they enter unannounced, as lords that are certainly expected and yet there
is a silent joy at their arrival.

Her beams bemocked the sultry main,
Like April hoar-frost spread;
But where the ship's huge shadow lay,
The charmed water burnt alway   270
A still and awful red.

By the light of the Moon he beholdeth God's creatures of the great calm.

Beyond the shadow of the ship,
I watched the water-snakes:
They moved in tracks of shining white,
And when they reared, the elfish light
Fell off in hoary flakes.   275

Within the shadow of the ship
I watched their rich attire:
Blue, glossy green, and velvet black,
They coiled and swam; and every track   280
Was a flash of golden fire.

Their beauty and their happiness.

O happy living things! no tongue
Their beauty might declare:
A spring of love gushed from my heart,

He blesseth them in his heart.

And I blessed them unaware: 285
Sure my kind saint took pity on me,
And I blessed them unaware.

The spell begins to break.

The selfsame moment I could pray;
And from my neck so free
The Albatross fell off, and sank   290
Like lead into the sea.

Part 5

Oh sleep! it is a gentle thing,
Beloved from pole to pole!
To Mary Queen the praise be given!
She sent the gentle sleep from Heaven,   295
That slid into my soul.

By grace of the holy Mother, the ancient Mariner is refreshed with rain.

The silly⁹ buckets on the deck,
That had so long remained,
I dreamt that they were filled with dew;
And when I awoke, it rained.   300

My lips were wet, my throat was cold,
My garments all were dank;
Sure I had drunken in my dreams,
And still my body drank.

I moved, and could not feel my limbs: 305
I was so light—almost
I thought that I had died in sleep,
And was a blessed ghost.

He heareth sounds and seeth strange sights and commotions in the sky and the element.

And soon I heard a roaring wind:
It did not come anear;   310
But with its sound it shook the sails,
That were so thin and sere.

9. Simple, homely.

The upper air burst into life!
And a hundred fire-flags sheen,[1]
To and fro they were hurried about!   315
And to and fro, and in and out,
The wan stars danced between.

And the coming wind did roar more loud,
And the sails did sigh like sedge;[2]
And the rain poured down from one black cloud;   320
The Moon was at its edge.

The thick black cloud was cleft, and still
The Moon was at its side:
Like waters shot from some high crag,
The lightning fell with never a jag,   325
A river steep and wide.

The bodies of the
ship's crew are
inspired, and the
ship moves on;

The loud wind never reached the ship,
Yet now the ship moved on!
Beneath the lightning and the moon
The dead men gave a groan.   330

They groaned, they stirred, they all uprose,
Nor spake, nor moved their eyes;
It had been strange, even in a dream,
To have seen those dead men rise.

The helmsman steered, the ship moved on;   335
Yet never a breeze up blew;
The mariners all 'gan work the ropes,
Where they were wont to do;
They raised their limbs like lifeless tools—
We were a ghastly crew.   340

The body of my brother's son
Stood by me, knee to knee:
The body and I pulled at one rope,
But he said nought to me.

But not by the souls
of the men, nor by
dæmons[3] of earth or
middle air, but by a
blessed troop of
angelic spirits, sent
down by the invoca-
tion of the guardian
saint.

"I fear thee, ancient Mariner!"   345
Be calm, thou Wedding-Guest!
'Twas not those souls that fled in pain,
Which to their corses[4] came again,
But a troop of spirits blest:

For when it dawned—they dropped their arms,   350
And clustered round the mast;

1. Shone. These fire-flags are probably St. Elmo's
fire (see n. 2, p. 426), but Coleridge may be
describing the Aurora Australis, or Southern
Lights, and possibly also lightning.
2. A rushlike plant growing in wet soil.

3. Supernatural beings halfway between mortals
and gods (the type of spirit that Coleridge describes
in the gloss beside lines 131–34).
4. Corpses.

Sweet sounds rose slowly through their mouths,
And from their bodies passed.

Around, around, flew each sweet sound,
Then darted to the Sun;   355
Slowly the sounds came back again,
Now mixed, now one by one.

Sometimes a-dropping from the sky
I heard the sky-lark sing;
Sometimes all little birds that are,   360
How they seemed to fill the sea and air
With their sweet jargoning![5]

And now 'twas like all instruments,
Now like a lonely flute;
And now it is an angel's song,   365
That makes the heavens be mute.

It ceased; yet still the sails made on
A pleasant noise till noon,
A noise like of a hidden brook
In the leafy month of June,   370
That to the sleeping woods all night
Singeth a quiet tune.

Till noon we quietly sailed on,
Yet never a breeze did breathe:
Slowly and smoothly went the ship,   375
Moved onward from beneath.

The lonesome spirit   Under the keel nine fathom deep,
from the south-pole
carries on the ship as From the land of mist and snow,
far as the line, in   The spirit slid: and it was he
obedience to the
angelic troop, but   That made the ship to go.   380
still requireth ven- The sails at noon left off their tune,
geance.
                 And the ship stood still also.

The Sun, right up above the mast,
Had fixed her to the ocean:
But in a minute she 'gan stir,   385
With a short uneasy motion—
Backwards and forwards half her length
With a short uneasy motion.

Then like a pawing horse let go,
She made a sudden bound: 390
It flung the blood into my head,
And I fell down in a swound.

5. Warbling (Middle English).

The Polar Spirit's fellow dæmons, the invisible inhabitants of the element, take part in his wrong; and two of them relate, one to the other, that penance long and heavy for the ancient Mariner hath been accorded to the Polar Spirit, who returneth southward.

How long in that same fit I lay,
I have not[6] to declare;
But ere my living life returned,   395
I heard and in my soul discerned
Two voices in the air.

"Is it he?" quoth one, "Is this the man?
By him who died on cross,
With his cruel bow he laid full low   400
The harmless Albatross.

The spirit who bideth by himself
In the land of mist and snow,
He loved the bird that loved the man
Who shot him with his bow."   405

The other was a softer voice,
As soft as honey-dew:
Quoth he, "The man hath penance done,
And penance more will do."

Part 6

FIRST VOICE
"But tell me, tell me! speak again,   410
Thy soft response renewing—
What makes that ship drive on so fast?
What is the ocean doing?"

SECOND VOICE
"Still as a slave before his lord,
The ocean hath no blast;   415
His great bright eye most silently
Up to the Moon is cast—

If he may know which way to go;
For she guides him smooth or grim.
See, brother, see! how graciously   420
She looketh down on him."

FIRST VOICE
The Mariner hath been cast into a trance; for the angelic power causeth the vessel to drive northward faster than human life could endure.
"But why drives on that ship so fast,
Without or wave or wind?"

SECOND VOICE
"The air is cut away before,
And closes from behind.   425

Fly, brother, fly! more high, more high!
Or we shall be belated:

6. I.e., have not the knowledge.

For slow and slow that ship will go,
When the Mariner's trance is abated."

I woke, and we were sailing on   430
As in a gentle weather:
'Twas night, calm night, the moon was high;
The dead men stood together.

All stood together on the deck,
For a charnel-dungeon fitter: 435
All fixed on me their stony eyes,
That in the Moon did glitter.

The pang, the curse, with which they died,
Had never passed away:
I could not draw my eyes from theirs,   440
Nor turn them up to pray.

And now this spell was snapt: once more
I viewed the ocean green,
And looked far forth, yet little saw
Of what had else been seen—   445

Like one, that on a lonesome road
Doth walk in fear and dread,
And having once turned round walks on,
And turns no more his head;
Because he knows, a frightful fiend   450
Doth close behind him tread.

But soon there breathed a wind on me,
Nor sound nor motion made:
Its path was not upon the sea,
In ripple or in shade.   455

It raised my hair, it fanned my cheek
Like a meadow-gale of spring—
It mingled strangely with my fears,
Yet it felt like a welcoming.

Swiftly, swiftly flew the ship,   460
Yet she sailed softly too:
Sweetly, sweetly blew the breeze—
On me alone it blew.

Oh! dream of joy! is this indeed
The light-house top I see?   465
Is this the hill? is this the kirk?
Is this mine own countree?

We drifted o'er the harbour-bar,
And I with sobs did pray—

O let me be awake, my God!   470
Or let me sleep alway.

The harbour-bay was clear as glass,
So smoothly it was strewn!
And on the bay the moonlight lay,
And the shadow of the moon.   475

The rock shone bright, the kirk no less,
That stands above the rock:
The moonlight steeped in silentness
The steady weathercock.

And the bay was white with silent light,   480
Till rising from the same,

The angelic spirits
leave the dead bod-   Full many shapes, that shadows were,
ies,   In crimson colours came.

And appear in their   A little distance from the prow
own forms of light.   Those crimson shadows were: 485
I turned my eyes upon the deck—
Oh, Christ! what saw I there!

Each corse lay flat, lifeless and flat,
And, by the holy rood!
A man all light, a seraph-man,[7]   490
On every corse there stood.

This seraph-band, each waved his hand:
It was a heavenly sight!
They stood as signals to the land,
Each one a lovely light;   495

This seraph-band, each waved his hand,
No voice did they impart—
No voice; but oh! the silence sank
Like music on my heart.

But soon I heard the dash of oars,   500
I heard the Pilot's cheer;
My head was turned perforce away,
And I saw a boat appear.

The Pilot and the Pilot's boy,
I heard them coming fast: 505
Dear Lord in Heaven! it was a joy
The dead men could not blast.

I saw a third—I heard his voice:
It is the Hermit good!
He singeth loud his godly hymns   510

7. A shining celestial being, highest in the ranks of the angels. "Rood": cross.

That he makes in the wood.
He'll shrieve my soul, he'll wash away
The Albatross's blood.

Part 7

The Hermit of the wood,

This Hermit good lives in that wood
Which slopes down to the sea.   515
How loudly his sweet voice he rears!
He loves to talk with marineres
That come from a far countree.

He kneels at morn, and noon, and eve—
He hath a cushion plump: 520
It is the moss that wholly hides
The rotted old oak-stump.

The skiff-boat neared: I heard them talk,
"Why, this is strange, I trow!
Where are those lights so many and fair,   525
That signal made but now?"

Approacheth the ship with wonder.

"Strange, by my faith!" the Hermit said—
"And they answered not our cheer!
The planks looked warped! and see those sails,
How thin they are and sere!   530
I never saw aught like to them,
Unless perchance it were

Brown skeletons of leaves that lag
My forest-brook along;
When the ivy-tod[8] is heavy with snow,   535
And the owlet whoops to the wolf below,
That eats the she-wolf's young."

"Dear Lord! it hath a fiendish look"—
(The Pilot made reply)
"I am a-feared"—"Push on, push on!"   540
Said the Hermit cheerily.

The boat came closer to the ship,
But I nor spake nor stirred;
The boat came close beneath the ship,
And straight a sound was heard.   545

The ship suddenly sinketh.

Under the water it rumbled on,
Still louder and more dread:
It reached the ship, it split the bay;
The ship went down like lead.

8. Clump of ivy.

The ancient Mariner is saved in the Pilot's boat.

Stunned by that loud and dreadful sound,   550
Which sky and ocean smote,
Like one that hath been seven days drowned
My body lay afloat;
But swift as dreams, myself I found
Within the Pilot's boat.   555

Upon the whirl, where sank the ship,
The boat spun round and round;
And all was still, save that the hill
Was telling of the sound.

I moved my lips—the Pilot shrieked   560
And fell down in a fit;
The holy Hermit raised his eyes,
And prayed where he did sit.

I took the oars: the Pilot's boy,
Who now doth crazy go,   565
Laughed loud and long, and all the while
His eyes went to and fro.
"Ha! ha!" quoth he, "full plain I see,
The Devil knows how to row."

And now, all in my own countree,   570
I stood on the firm land!
The Hermit stepped forth from the boat,
And scarcely he could stand.

The ancient Mariner earnestly entreateth the Hermit to shrieve him; and the penance of life falls on him.

"O shrieve me, shrieve me, holy man!"
The Hermit crossed his brow.[9]   575
"Say quick," quoth he, "I bid thee say—
What manner of man art thou?"

Forthwith this frame of mine was wrenched
With a woful agony,
Which forced me to begin my tale;   580
And then it left me free.

And ever and anon throughout his future life an agony constraineth him to travel from land to land.

Since then, at an uncertain hour,
That agony returns:
And till my ghastly tale is told,
This heart within me burns.   585

I pass, like night, from land to land;
I have strange power of speech;
That moment that his face I see,
I know the man that must hear me:
To him my tale I teach.   590

What loud uproar bursts from that door!
The wedding-guests are there:

9. Made the sign of the cross on his forehead. "Shrieve me": hear my confession and grant me absolution.

But in the garden-bower the bride
And bride-maids singing are:
And hark the little vesper bell,   595
Which biddeth me to prayer!

O Wedding-Guest! this soul hath been
Alone on a wide wide sea:
So lonely 'twas, that God himself
Scarce seemed there to be.   600

O sweeter than the marriage-feast,
'Tis sweeter far to me,
To walk together to the kirk
With a goodly company!—

To walk together to the kirk,   605
And all together pray,
While each to his great Father bends,
Old men, and babes, and loving friends,
And youths and maidens gay!

And to teach, by his own example, love and reverence to all things that God made and loveth.

Farewell, farewell! but this I tell   610
To thee, thou Wedding-Guest!
He prayeth well, who loveth well
Both man and bird and beast.

He prayeth best, who loveth best
All things both great and small;   615
For the dear God who loveth us,
He made and loveth all.[1]

The Mariner, whose eye is bright,
Whose beard with age is hoar,
Is gone: and now the Wedding-Guest   620
Turned from the bridegroom's door.

He went like one that hath been stunned,
And is of sense forlorn:[2]
A sadder and a wiser man,
He rose the morrow morn.   625

1797   1798

---

1. Coleridge said in 1830, answering the objection of the poet Anna Barbauld that the poem "lacked a moral": "I told her that in my own judgment the poem had too much; and that the only, or chief fault, if I might say so, was the obtrusion of the moral sentiment so openly on the reader as a principle or cause of action in a work of pure imagination. It ought to have had no more moral than the *Arabian Nights'* tale of the merchant's sitting down to eat dates by the side of a well and throwing the shells aside, and lo! a genie starts up and says he *must* kill the aforesaid merchant *because* one of the date shells had, it seems, put out the eye of the genie's son."
2. Forsaken.

Kubla Khan

Or, A Vision in a Dream. A Fragment

In[1] the summer of the year 1797, the Author, then in ill health, had retired to a lonely farm house between Porlock and Linton, on the Exmoor confines of Somerset and Devonshire. In consequence of a slight indisposition, an anodyne had been prescribed, from the effect of which he fell asleep in his chair at the moment that he was reading the following sentence, or words of the same substance, in *Purchas's Pilgrimage:* "Here the Khan Kubla commanded a palace to be built, and a stately garden thereunto: and thus ten miles of fertile ground were inclosed with a wall."[2] The author continued for about three hours in a profound sleep, at least of the external senses,[3] during which time he has the most vivid confidence, that he could not have composed less than from two to three hundred lines; if that indeed can be called composition in which all the images rose up before him as things, with a parallel production of the correspondent expressions, without any sensation or consciousness of effort. On awaking he appeared to himself to have a distinct recollection of the whole, and taking his pen, ink, and paper, instantly and eagerly wrote down the lines that are here preserved. At this moment he was unfortunately called out by a person on business from Porlock, and detained by him above an hour, and on his return to his room, found, to his no small surprise and mortification, that though he still retained some vague and dim recollection of the general purport of the vision, yet, with the exception of some eight or ten scattered lines and images, all the rest had passed away like the images on the surface of a stream into which a stone had been cast, but, alas! without the after restoration of the latter:

> Then all the charm
> Is broken—all that phantom-world so fair
> Vanishes, and a thousand circlets spread,
> And each mis-shape[s] the other. Stay awhile,
> Poor youth! who scarcely dar'st lift up thine eyes—
> The stream will soon renew its smoothness, soon
> The visions will return! And lo! he stays,
> And soon the fragments dim of lovely forms
> Come trembling back, unite, and now once more
> The pool becomes a mirror.
>   [From Coleridge's *The Picture; or, the Lover's Resolution,*
>   lines 91–100]

1. In the texts of 1816–29, this note began with an additional short paragraph: "The following fragment is here published at the request of a poet of great and deserved celebrity, and, as far as the Author's own opinions are concerned, rather as a psychological curiosity, than on the ground of any supposed *poetic* merits." The "poet of . . . celebrity" was Lord Byron.
2. "In Xamdu did Cublai Can build a stately Palace, encompassing sixteene miles of plaine ground with a wall, wherein are fertile Meddowes, pleasant Springs, delightfull Streames, and all sorts of beasts of chase and game, and in the middest

thereof a sumptuous house of pleasure, which may be removed from place to place." From Samuel Purchas, *Purchas his Pilgrimage* (1613). The historical Kublai Khan founded the Mongol dynasty in China in the 13th century.
3. In a note on a manuscript copy of *Kubla Khan,* Coleridge gave a more precise account of the nature of this "sleep": "This fragment with a good deal more, not recoverable, composed, in a sort of reverie brought on by two grains of opium, taken to check a dysentery, at a farmhouse between Porlock and Linton, a quarter of a mile from Culbone Church, in the fall of the year, 1797."

Yet from the still surviving recollections in his mind, the Author has frequently purposed to finish for himself what had been originally, as it were, given to him. Αὔριον ἄδιον ἄσω:[4] but the to-morrow is yet to come.

As a contrast to this vision, I have annexed a fragment of a very different character, describing with equal fidelity the dream of pain and disease.[5]—1816.

In Xanadu did Kubla Khan
A stately pleasure-dome decree:
Where Alph,[6] the sacred river, ran
Through caverns measureless to man
5   Down to a sunless sea.
So twice five miles of fertile ground
With walls and towers were girdled round:
And there were gardens bright with sinuous rills
Where blossomed many an incense-bearing tree;
10 And here were forests ancient as the hills,
Enfolding sunny spots of greenery.

But oh! that deep romantic chasm which slanted
Down the green hill athwart a cedarn cover!
A savage place! as holy and enchanted
15 As e'er beneath a waning moon was haunted
By woman wailing for her demon-lover!
And from this chasm, with ceaseless turmoil seething,
As if this earth in fast thick pants were breathing,
A mighty fountain momently was forced:
20 Amid whose swift half-intermitted burst
Huge fragments vaulted like rebounding hail,
Or chaffy grain beneath the thresher's flail:
And 'mid these dancing rocks at once and ever
It flung up momently the sacred river.
25 Five miles meandering with a mazy motion
Through wood and dale the sacred river ran,
Then reached the caverns measureless to man,
And sank in tumult to a lifeless ocean:
And 'mid this tumult Kubla heard from far
30 Ancestral voices prophesying war!

The shadow of the dome of pleasure
Floated midway on the waves;
Where was heard the mingled measure
From the fountain and the caves.
35 It was a miracle of rare device,
A sunny pleasure-dome with caves of ice!

4. I shall sing a sweeter song tomorrow (Greek; recalled from Theocritus's *Idyls* 1.145).

A number of Coleridge's assertions in this preface have been debated by critics: whether the poem was written in 1797 or later, whether it was actually composed in a "dream" or opium reverie, even whether it is a fragment or in fact complete. All critics agree, however, that this visionary poem

of demonic inspiration is much more than a mere "psychological curiosity."

5. Coleridge refers to *The Pains of Sleep*.

6. Derived probably from the Greek river Alpheus, which flows into the Ionian Sea. Its waters were fabled to rise again in Sicily as the fountain of Arethusa.

A damsel with a dulcimer
In a vision once I saw:
It was an Abyssinian maid,
40   And on her dulcimer she played,
Singing of Mount Abora.[7]
Could I revive within me
Her symphony and song,
To such a deep delight 'twould win me,
45   That with music loud and long,
I would build that dome in air,
That sunny dome! those caves of ice!
And all who heard should see them there,
And all should cry, Beware! Beware!
50   His flashing eyes, his floating hair!
Weave a circle round him thrice,[8]
And close your eyes with holy dread,
For he on honey-dew hath fed,
And drunk the milk of Paradise.[9]

ca. 1797–98   1816

Christabel[1]

Preface

The first part of the following poem was written in the year 1797, at Stowey, in the county of Somerset. The second part, after my return from Germany, in the year 1800, at Keswick, Cumberland. It is probable, that if the poem had been finished at either of the former periods, or if even the first and second part had been published in the year 1800, the impression of its originality would have been much greater than I dare at present expect. But for this, I have only my own indolence to blame. The dates are mentioned for the exclusive purpose of precluding charges of plagiarism or servile imitation from myself. For there is amongst us a set of critics, who seem to hold, that every possible thought and image is traditional; who have no notion that there are such things as fountains in the world, small as well as great; and who would therefore charitably derive every rill they behold flowing, from a perforation made in some other man's tank. I am confident, however, that as far as the present poem is concerned, the celebrated poets[2] whose writings I might be suspected of having imitated, either in particular passages, or in

---

7. Apparently a reminiscence of *Paradise Lost* 4.280–82: "where Abassin Kings their issue guard / Mount Amara (though this by some supposed / True Paradise) under the Ethiop line."
8. A magic ritual, to protect the inspired poet from intrusion.
9. Lines 50ff. echo in part the description, in Plato's *Ion* 533–34, of inspired poets, who are "like Bacchic maidens who draw milk and honey from the rivers when they are under the influence of Dionysus but not when they are in their right mind."
1. Coleridge had planned to publish *Christabel* in the 2nd edition of *Lyrical Ballads* (1800) but had not been able to complete the poem. When *Chris-*

tabel was finally published in 1816 in its present fragmentary state, he still had hopes of finishing it, for the Preface contained this sentence (deleted in the edition of 1834): "But as, in my very first conception of the tale, I had the whole present to my mind, with the wholeness, no less than with the liveliness of a vision; I trust that I shall be able to embody in verse the three parts yet to come, in the course of the present year."
2. Sir Walter Scott and Lord Byron, who had read and admired *Christabel* while it circulated in manuscript. Coleridge has in mind Scott's *Lay of the Last Minstrel* (1805) and Byron's *Siege of Corinth* (1816), which showed the influence of *Christabel*, especially in their meter.

the tone and the spirit of the whole, would be among the first to vindicate me from the charge, and who, on any striking coincidence, would permit me to address them in this doggerel version of two monkish Latin hexameters.

> Tis mine and it is likewise yours;
> But an if this will not do;
> Let it be mine, good friend! for I
> Am the poorer of the two.

I have only to add, that the metre of the Christabel is not, properly speaking, irregular, though it may seem so from its being founded on a new principle: namely, that of counting in each line the accents, not the syllables.[3] Though the latter may vary from seven to twelve, yet in each line the accents will be found to be only four. Nevertheless this occasional variation in number of syllables is not introduced wantonly, or for the mere ends of convenience, but in correspondence with some transition, in the nature of the imagery or passion.

Part 1

'Tis the middle of night by the castle clock,
And the owls have awakened the crowing cock;
Tu—whit!———Tu—whoo!
And hark, again! the crowing cock,
5   How drowsily it crew.

Sir Leoline, the Baron rich,
Hath a toothless mastiff bitch;
From her kennel beneath the rock
She maketh answer to the clock,
10   Four for the quarters, and twelve for the hour;
Ever and aye, by shine and shower,
Sixteen short howls, not over loud;
Some say, she sees my lady's shroud.

Is the night chilly and dark?
15   The night is chilly, but not dark.
The thin gray cloud is spread on high,
It covers but not hides the sky.
The moon is behind, and at the full;
And yet she looks both small and dull.
20   The night is chill, the cloud is gray:
'Tis a month before the month of May,
And the Spring comes slowly up this way.

The lovely lady, Christabel,
Whom her father loves so well,
25   What makes her in the wood so late,
A furlong from the castle gate?

---

3. Much of the older English versification, following the example of Anglo-Saxon poetry, had been based on stress, or "accent," and some of it shows as much freedom in varying the number of syllables as does Christabel. The poem, however, is a radical departure from the theory and practice of versification in the 18th century, which had been based on a recurrent number of syllables in each line.

She had dreams all yesternight
Of her own betrothed knight;
And she in the midnight wood will pray
30 For the weal° of her lover that's far away.   *well-being*

She stole along, she nothing spoke,
The sighs she heaved were soft and low,
And naught was green upon the oak,
But moss and rarest mistletoe:[4]
35 She kneels beneath the huge oak tree,
And in silence prayeth she.

The lady sprang up suddenly,
The lovely lady, Christabel!
It moaned as near, as near can be,
40 But what it is, she cannot tell.—
On the other side it seems to be,
Of the huge, broad-breasted, old oak tree.

The night is chill; the forest bare;
Is it the wind that moaneth bleak?
45 There is not wind enough in the air
To move away the ringlet curl
From the lovely lady's cheek—
There is not wind enough to twirl
The one red leaf, the last of its clan,
50 That dances as often as dance it can,
Hanging so light, and hanging so high,
On the topmost twig that looks up at the sky.

Hush, beating heart of Christabel!
Jesu, Maria, shield her well!
55 She folded her arms beneath her cloak,
And stole to the other side of the oak.
   What sees she there?

There she sees a damsel bright,
Drest in a silken robe of white,
60 That shadowy in the moonlight shone:
The neck that made that white robe wan,
Her stately neck, and arms were bare;
Her blue-veined feet unsandal'd were,
And wildly glittered here and there
65 The gems entangled in her hair.
I guess, 'twas frightful there to see
A lady so richly clad as she—
Beautiful exceedingly!

"Mary mother, save me now!"
70 (Said Christabel,) "And who art thou?"

---

4. In Celtic Britain the mistletoe (a parasitic plant) had been held in veneration when it was found growing—as it rarely does—on an oak tree. (Its usual host is the apple tree.)

The lady strange made answer meet,
And her voice was faint and sweet:—
"Have pity on my sore distress,
I scarce can speak for weariness:
75   Stretch forth thy hand, and have no fear!"
Said Christabel, "How camest thou here?"
And the lady, whose voice was faint and sweet,
Did thus pursue her answer meet:—

"My sire is of a noble line,
80   And my name is Geraldine:
Five warriors seized me yestermorn,
Me, even me, a maid forlorn:
They choked my cries with force and fright,
And tied me on a palfrey white.
85   The palfrey was as fleet as wind,
And they rode furiously behind.
They spurred amain,[5] their steeds were white:
And once we crossed the shade of night.
As sure as Heaven shall rescue me,
90   I have no thought what men they be;
Nor do I know how long it is
(For I have lain entranced I wis[6])
Since one, the tallest of the five,
Took me from the palfrey's back,
95   A weary woman, scarce alive.
Some muttered words his comrades spoke:
He placed me underneath this oak;
He swore they would return with haste;
Whither they went I cannot tell—
100   I thought I heard, some minutes past,
Sounds as of a castle bell.
Stretch forth thy hand" (thus ended she),
"And help a wretched maid to flee."

Then Christabel stretched forth her hand
105   And comforted fair Geraldine:
"O well, bright dame! may you command
The service of Sir Leoline;
And gladly our stout chivalry
Will he send forth and friends withal
110   To guide and guard you safe and free
Home to your noble father's hall."

She rose: and forth with steps they passed
That strove to be, and were not, fast.
Her gracious stars the lady blest,
115   And thus spake on sweet Christabel:
"All our household are at rest,

5. At top speed.
6. I believe (Coleridge's misinterpretation of the Middle English adverb *ywis*, meaning "certainly").

The hall as silent as the cell;
Sir Leoline is weak in health,
And may not well awakened be,
120 But we will move as if in stealth,
And I beseech your courtesy,
This night, to share your couch with me."

They crossed the moat, and Christabel
Took the key that fitted well;
125 A little door she opened straight,
All in the middle of the gate;
The gate that was ironed within and without,
Where an army in battle array had marched out.
The lady sank, belike through pain,
130 And Christabel with might and main
Lifted her up, a weary weight,
Over the threshold of the gate:[7]
Then the lady rose again,
And moved, as she were not in pain.

135 So free from danger, free from fear,
They crossed the court: right glad they were.
And Christabel devoutly cried
To the Lady by her side;
"Praise we the Virgin all divine
140 Who hath rescued thee from thy distress!"
"Alas, alas!" said Geraldine,
"I cannot speak for weariness."
So free from danger, free from fear,
They crossed the court: right glad they were.

145 Outside her kennel the mastiff old
Lay fast asleep, in moonshine cold.
The mastiff old did not awake,
Yet she an angry moan did make!
And what can ail the mastiff bitch?
150 Never till now she uttered yell
Beneath the eye of Christabel.
Perhaps it is the owlet's scritch:
For what can ail the mastiff bitch?

They passed the hall, that echoes still,
155 Pass as lightly as you will!
The brands were flat, the brands were dying,
Amid their own white ashes lying;
But when the lady passed, there came
A tongue of light, a fit of flame;
160 And Christabel saw the lady's eye,
And nothing else saw she thereby,

---

7. According to legend, a witch cannot cross the threshold by her own power because it has been blessed against evil spirits.

Save the boss of the shield of Sir Leoline tall,
Which hung in a murky old niche in the wall.
"O softly tread," said Christabel,
165 "My father seldom sleepeth well."

Sweet Christabel her feet doth bare,
And, jealous of the listening air,
They steal their way from stair to stair,
Now in glimmer, and now in gloom,
170 And now they pass the Baron's room,
As still as death with stifled breath!
And now have reached her chamber door;
And now doth Geraldine press down
The rushes[8] of the chamber floor.

175 The moon shines dim in the open air,
And not a moonbeam enters here.
But they without its light can see
The chamber carved so curiously,
Carved with figures strange and sweet,
180 All made out of the carver's brain,
For a lady's chamber meet:
The lamp with twofold silver chain
Is fastened to an angel's feet.
The silver lamp burns dead and dim;
185 But Christabel the lamp will trim.
She trimmed the lamp, and made it bright,
And left it swinging to and fro,
While Geraldine, in wretched plight,
Sank down upon the floor below.

190 "O weary lady, Geraldine,
I pray you, drink this cordial wine!
It is a wine of virtuous powers;
My mother made it of wild flowers."

"And will your mother pity me,
195 Who am a maiden most forlorn?"
Christabel answered—"Woe is me!
She died the hour that I was born.
I have heard the grey-haired friar tell,
How on her death-bed she did say,
200 That she should hear the castle-bell
Strike twelve upon my wedding day.
O mother dear! that thou wert here!"
"I would," said Geraldine, "she were!"

But soon with altered voice, said she—
205 "Off, wandering mother! Peak and pine!
I have power to bid thee flee."

8. Often used as a floor covering in the Middle Ages.

Alas! what ails poor Geraldine?
Why stares she with unsettled eye?
Can she the bodiless dead espy?
210 And why with hollow voice cries she,
"Off, woman, off! this hour is mine—
Though thou her guardian spirit be,
Off, woman, off! 'tis given to me."

Then Christabel knelt by the lady's side,
215 And raised to heaven her eyes so blue—
"Alas!" said she, "this ghastly ride—
Dear lady! it hath wildered you!"
The lady wiped her moist cold brow,
And faintly said, " 'tis over now!"

220 Again the wild-flower wine she drank:
Her fair large eyes 'gan glitter bright,
And from the floor whereon she sank,
The lofty lady stood upright;
She was most beautiful to see,
225 Like a lady of a far countrée.

And thus the lofty lady spake—
"All they who live in the upper sky,
Do love you, holy Christabel!
And you love them, and for their sake
230 And for the good which me befell,
Even I in my degree will try,
Fair maiden, to requite you well.
But now unrobe yourself; for I
Must pray, ere yet in bed I lie."

235 Quoth Christabel, "So let it be!"
And as the lady bade, did she.
Her gentle limbs did she undress,
And lay down in her loveliness.

But through her brain of weal and woe
240 So many thoughts moved to and fro,
That vain it were her lids to close;
So half-way from the bed she rose,
And on her elbow did recline
To look at the lady Geraldine.

245 Beneath the lamp the lady bowed,
And slowly rolled her eyes around;
Then drawing in her breath aloud,
Like one that shuddered, she unbound
The cincture° from beneath her breast: *belt*
250 Her silken robe, and inner vest,
Dropt to her feet, and full in view,
Behold! her bosom and half her side——

A sight to dream of, not to tell!
O shield her! shield sweet Christabel!

255 Yet Geraldine nor speaks nor stirs;
Ah! what a stricken look was hers!
Deep from within she seems half-way
To lift some weight with sick assay,°   *attempt*
And eyes the maid and seeks delay;
260 Then suddenly as one defied
Collects herself in scorn and pride,
And lay down by the maiden's side!—
And in her arms the maid she took,
      Ah well-a-day!
265 And with low voice and doleful look
These words did say:
"In the touch of this bosom there worketh a spell,
Which is lord of thy utterance, Christabel!
Thou knowest to-night, and wilt know to-morrow
270 This mark of my shame, this seal of my sorrow;
      But vainly thou warrest,
        For this is alone in
        Thy power to declare,
        That in the dim forest
275   Thou heard'st a low moaning,
And found'st a bright lady, surpassingly fair:
And didst bring her home with thee in love and in charity,
To shield her and shelter her from the damp air."

The Conclusion to Part 1

It was a lovely sight to see
280 The lady Christabel, when she
Was praying at the old oak tree.
      Amid the jagged shadows
      Of mossy leafless boughs,
      Kneeling in the moonlight,
285   To make her gentle vows;
Her slender palms together prest,
Heaving sometimes on her breast;
Her face resigned to bliss or bale°—   *evil, sorrow*
Her face, oh call it fair not pale,
290 And both blue eyes more bright than clear,
Each about to have a tear.

With open eyes (ah woe is me!)
Asleep, and dreaming fearfully,
Fearfully dreaming, yet I wis,
295 Dreaming that alone, which is—
O sorrow and shame! Can this be she,
The lady, who knelt at the old oak tree?
And lo! the worker of these harms,
That holds the maiden in her arms,

300   Seems to slumber still and mild,
      As a mother with her child.

      A star hath set, a star hath risen,
      O Geraldine! since arms of thine
      Have been the lovely lady's prison.
305   O Geraldine! one hour was thine—
      Thou'st had thy will! By tairn[9] and rill,
      The night-birds all that hour were still.
      But now they are jubilant anew,
      From cliff and tower, tu—whoo! tu—whoo!
310   Tu—whoo! tu—whoo! from wood and fell![1]

      And see! the lady Christabel
      Gathers herself from out her trance;
      Her limbs relax, her countenance
      Grows sad and soft; the smooth thin lids
315   Close o'er her eyes; and tears she sheds—
      Large tears that leave the lashes bright!
      And oft the while she seems to smile
      As infants at a sudden light!
      Yea, she doth smile, and she doth weep,
320   Like a youthful hermitess,
      Beauteous in a wilderness,
      Who, praying always, prays in sleep.
      And, if she move unquietly,
      Perchance, 'tis but the blood so free,
325   Comes back and tingles in her feet.
      No doubt, she hath a vision sweet.
      What if her guardian spirit 'twere?
      What if she knew her mother near?
      But this she knows, in joys and woes,
330   That saints will aid if men will call:
      For the blue sky bends over all!

Part 2

      "Each matin bell," the Baron saith,
      "Knells us back to a world of death."
      These words Sir Leoline first said,
335   When he rose and found his lady dead:
      These words Sir Leoline will say,
      Many a morn to his dying day!

      And hence the custom and law began,
      That still at dawn the sacristan,°   *sexton*
340   Who duly pulls the heavy bell,
      Five and forty beads must tell[2]
      Between each stroke—a warning knell,

---

9. Tarn, a mountain pool.
1. Elevated moor, or hill.

2. Pray while "telling" (keeping count on) the beads of a rosary.

Which not a soul can choose but hear
From Bratha Head to Wyndermere.[3]

345 Saith Bracy the bard, "So let it knell!
And let the drowsy sacristan
Still count as slowly as he can!
There is no lack of such, I ween,
As well fill up the space between.
350 In Langdale Pike° and Witch's Lair,   *Peak*
And Dungeon-ghyll[4] so foully rent,
With ropes of rock and bells of air
Three sinful sextons' ghosts are pent,
Who all give back, one after t'other,
355 The death-note to their living brother;
And oft too, by the knell offended,
Just as their one! two! three! is ended,
The devil mocks the doleful tale
With a merry peal from Borodale."

360 The air is still! through mist and cloud
That merry peal comes ringing loud;
And Geraldine shakes off her dread,
And rises lightly from the bed;
Puts on her silken vestments white,
365 And tricks her hair in lovely plight,°   *plait*
And nothing doubting of her spell
Awakens the lady Christabel.
"Sleep you, sweet lady Christabel?
I trust that you have rested well."

370 And Christabel awoke and spied
The same who lay down by her side—
O rather say, the same whom she
Raised up beneath the old oak tree!
Nay, fairer yet! and yet more fair!
375 For she belike hath drunken deep
Of all the blessedness of sleep!
And while she spake, her looks, her air
Such gentle thankfulness declare,
That (so it seemed) her girded vests
380 Grew tight beneath her heaving breasts.
"Sure I have sinned!" said Christabel,
"Now heaven be praised if all be well!"
And in low faltering tones, yet sweet,
Did she the lofty lady greet
385 With such perplexity of mind
As dreams too lively leave behind.

So quickly she rose, and quickly arrayed
Her maiden limbs, and having prayed

---

3. These and the following names are of localities
in the English Lake District.   4. Ravine forming the bed of a stream.

That He, who on the cross did groan,
390 Might wash away her sins unknown,
She forthwith led fair Geraldine
To meet her sire, Sir Leoline.

The lovely maid and the lady tall
Are pacing both into the hall,
395 And pacing on through page and groom,
Enter the Baron's presence room.

The Baron rose, and while he prest
His gentle daughter to his breast,
With cheerful wonder in his eyes
400 The lady Geraldine espies,
And gave such welcome to the same,
As might beseem so bright a dame!

But when he heard the lady's tale,
And when she told her father's name,
405 Why waxed Sir Leoline so pale,
Murmuring o'er the name again,
Lord Roland de Vaux of Tryermaine?

Alas! they had been friends in youth;
But whispering tongues can poison truth;
410 And constancy lives in realms above;
And life is thorny; and youth is vain;
And to be wroth with one we love,
Doth work like madness in the brain.
And thus it chanced, as I divine,
415 With Roland and Sir Leoline.
Each spake words of high disdain
And insult to his heart's best brother:
They parted—ne'er to meet again!
But never either found another
420 To free the hollow heart from paining—
They stood aloof, the scars remaining,
Like cliffs which had been rent asunder;
A dreary sea now flows between;—
But neither heat, nor frost, nor thunder,
425 Shall wholly do away, I ween,
The marks of that which once hath been.

Sir Leoline, a moment's space,
Stood gazing on the damsel's face:
And the youthful Lord of Tryermaine
430 Came back upon his heart again.

O then the Baron forgot his age,
His noble heart swelled high with rage;
He swore by the wounds in Jesu's side,
He would proclaim it far and wide

435 With trump and solemn heraldry,
That they who thus had wronged the dame,
Were base as spotted infamy!
"And if they dare deny the same,
My herald shall appoint a week,
440 And let the recreant traitors seek
My tourney court—that there and then
I may dislodge their reptile souls
From the bodies and forms of men!"
He spake: his eye in lightning rolls!
445 For the lady was ruthlessly seized; and he kenned
In the beautiful lady the child of his friend!

And now the tears were on his face,
And fondly in his arms he took
Fair Geraldine, who met the embrace,
450 Prolonging it with joyous look.
Which when she viewed, a vision fell
Upon the soul of Christabel,
The vision of fear, the touch and pain!
She shrunk and shuddered, and saw again—
455 (Ah, woe is me! Was it for thee,
Thou gentle maid! such sights to see?)
Again she saw that bosom old,
Again she felt that bosom cold,
And drew in her breath with a hissing sound:
460 Whereat the Knight turned wildly round,
And nothing saw, but his own sweet maid
With eyes upraised, as one that prayed.

The touch, the sight, had passed away,
And in its stead that vision blest,
465 Which comforted her after-rest,
While in the lady's arms she lay,
Had put a rapture in her breast,
And on her lips and o'er her eyes
Spread smiles like light!
      With new surprise,
470 "What ails then my beloved child?"
The Baron said—His daughter mild
Made answer, "All will yet be well!"
I ween, she had no power to tell
Aught else: so mighty was the spell.

475 Yet he, who saw this Geraldine,
Had deemed her sure a thing divine.
Such sorrow with such grace she blended,
As if she feared, she had offended
Sweet Christabel, that gentle maid!
480 And with such lowly tones she prayed,
She might be sent without delay
Home to her father's mansion.
         "Nay!

Nay, by my soul!" said Leoline.
"Ho! Bracy, the bard, the charge be thine!
485   Go thou, with music sweet and loud,
And take two steeds with trappings proud,
And take the youth whom thou lov'st best
To bear thy harp, and learn thy song,
And clothe you both in solemn vest,
490   And over the mountains haste along,
Lest wandering folk, that are abroad,
Detain you on the valley road.
And when he has crossed the Irthing flood,
My merry bard! he hastes, he hastes
495   Up Knorren Moor, through Halegarth Wood,
And reaches soon that castle good
Which stands and threatens Scotland's wastes.

"Bard Bracy! bard Bracy! your horses are fleet,
Ye must ride up the hall, your music so sweet,
500   More loud than your horses' echoing feet!
And loud and loud to Lord Roland call,
Thy daughter is safe in Langdale hall!
Thy beautiful daughter is safe and free—
Sir Leoline greets thee thus through me.
505   He bids thee come without delay
With all thy numerous array;
And take thy lovely daughter home:
And he will meet thee on the way
With all his numerous array
510   White with their panting palfreys' foam:
And by mine honour! I will say,
That I repent me of the day
When I spake words of fierce disdain
To Roland de Vaux of Tryermaine!—
515   —For since that evil hour hath flown,
Many a summer's sun hath shone;
Yet ne'er found I a friend again
Like Roland de Vaux of Tryermaine."

The lady fell, and clasped his knees,
520   Her face upraised, her eyes o'erflowing;
And Bracy replied, with faltering voice,
His gracious hail on all bestowing!—
"Thy words, thou sire of Christabel,
Are sweeter than my harp can tell;
525   Yet might I gain a boon of thee,
This day my journey should not be,
So strange a dream hath come to me;
That I had vowed with music loud
To clear yon wood from thing unblest,
530   Warned by a vision in my rest!
For in my sleep I saw that dove,
That gentle bird, whom thou dost love,
And call'st by thy own daughter's name—

Sir Leoline! I saw the same
535 Fluttering, and uttering fearful moan,
Among the green herbs in the forest alone.
Which when I saw and when I heard,
I wonder'd what might ail the bird;
For nothing near it could I see,
540 Save the grass and green herbs underneath the old tree.

"And in my dream methought I went
To search out what might there be found;
And what the sweet bird's trouble meant,
That thus lay fluttering on the ground.
545 I went and peered, and could descry
No cause for her distressful cry;
But yet for her dear lady's sake
I stooped, methought, the dove to take,
When lo! I saw a bright green snake
550 Coiled around its wings and neck,
Green as the herbs on which it couched,
Close by the dove's its head it crouched;
And with the dove it heaves and stirs,
Swelling its neck as she swelled hers!
555 I woke; it was the midnight hour,
The clock was echoing in the tower;
But though my slumber was gone by,
This dream it would not pass away—
It seems to live upon my eye!
560 And thence I vowed this self-same day,
With music strong and saintly song
To wander through the forest bare,
Lest aught unholy loiter there."

Thus Bracy said: the Baron, the while,
565 Half-listening heard him with a smile;
Then turned to Lady Geraldine,
His eyes made up of wonder and love;
And said in courtly accents fine,
"Sweet maid, Lord Roland's beauteous dove,
570 With arms more strong than harp or song,
Thy sire and I will crush the snake!"
He kissed her forehead as he spake,
And Geraldine, in maiden wise,
Casting down her large bright eyes,
575 With blushing cheek and courtesy fine
She turned her from Sir Leoline;
Softly gathering up her train,
That o'er her right arm fell again;
And folded her arms across her chest,
580 And couched her head upon her breast,
And looked askance at Christabel——
Jesu Maria, shield her well!

A snake's small eye blinks dull and shy,
And the lady's eyes they shrunk in her head,

585 Each shrunk up to a serpent's eye,
And with somewhat of malice, and more of dread,
At Christabel she looked askance!—
One moment—and the sight was fled!
But Christabel in dizzy trance
590 Stumbling on the unsteady ground
Shuddered aloud, with a hissing sound;
And Geraldine again turned round,
And like a thing, that sought relief,
Full of wonder and full of grief,
595 She rolled her large bright eyes divine
Wildly on Sir Leoline.

The maid, alas! her thoughts are gone,
She nothing sees—no sight but one!
The maid, devoid of guile and sin,
600 I know not how, in fearful wise
So deeply had she drunken in
That look, those shrunken serpent eyes,
That all her features were resigned
To this sole image in her mind;
605 And passively did imitate
That look of dull and treacherous hate!
And thus she stood, in dizzy trance,
Still picturing that look askance
With forced unconscious sympathy
610 Full before her father's view——
As far as such a look could be,
In eyes so innocent and blue!
And when the trance was o'er, the maid
Paused awhile, and inly prayed:
615 Then falling at the Baron's feet,
"By my mother's soul do I entreat
That thou this woman send away!"
She said: and more she could not say:
For what she knew she could not tell,
620 O'er-mastered by the mighty spell.

Why is thy cheek so wan and wild,
Sir Leoline? Thy only child
Lies at thy feet, thy joy, thy pride,
So fair, so innocent, so mild;
625 The same, for whom thy lady died!
O by the pangs of her dear mother
Think thou no evil of thy child!
For her, and thee, and for no other,
She prayed the moment ere she died:
630 Prayed that the babe for whom she died,
Might prove her dear lord's joy and pride!
That prayer her deadly pangs beguiled,
Sir Leoline!
And wouldst thou wrong thy only child,
635 Her child and thine?

Within the Baron's heart and brain
If thoughts, like these, had any share,
They only swelled his rage and pain,
And did but work confusion there.
640 His heart was cleft with pain and rage,
His cheeks they quivered, his eyes were wild,
Dishonoured thus in his old age;
Dishonoured by his only child,
And all his hospitality
645 To the wrong'd daughter of his friend
By more than woman's jealousy
Brought thus to a disgraceful end—
He rolled his eye with stern regard
Upon the gentle minstrel bard,
650 And said in tones abrupt, austere—
"Why, Bracy! dost thou loiter here?
I bade thee hence!" The bard obeyed;
And turning from his own sweet maid,
The aged knight, Sir Leoline,
655 Led forth the lady Geraldine!

The Conclusion to Part 2

A little child, a limber elf,
Singing, dancing to itself,
A fairy thing with red round cheeks,
That always finds, and never seeks,
660 Makes such a vision to the sight
As fills a father's eyes with light;
And pleasures flow in so thick and fast
Upon his heart, that he at last
Must needs express his love's excess
665 With words of unmeant bitterness.
Perhaps 'tis pretty to force together
Thoughts so all unlike each other;
To mutter and mock a broken charm,
To dally with wrong that does no harm.
670 Perhaps 'tis tender too and pretty
At each wild word to feel within
A sweet recoil of love and pity.
And what, if in a world of sin
(O sorrow and shame should this be true!)
675 Such giddiness of heart and brain
Comes seldom save from rage and pain,
So talks as it's most used to do.

1798–1800   1816

Frost at Midnight[1]

The frost performs its secret ministry,
Unhelped by any wind. The owlet's cry
Came loud—and hark, again! loud as before.
The inmates of my cottage, all at rest,
5   Have left me to that solitude, which suits
Abstruser musings: save that at my side
My cradled infant slumbers peacefully.
'Tis calm indeed! so calm, that it disturbs
And vexes meditation with its strange
10   And extreme silentness. Sea, hill, and wood,
This populous village! Sea, and hill, and wood,
With all the numberless goings on of life,
Inaudible as dreams! the thin blue flame
Lies on my low burnt fire, and quivers not;
15   Only that film,[2] which fluttered on the grate,
Still flutters there, the sole unquiet thing.
Methinks, its motion in this hush of nature
Gives it dim sympathies with me who live,
Making it a companionable form,
20   Whose puny flaps and freaks the idling Spirit
By its own moods interprets, every where
Echo or mirror seeking of itself,
And makes a toy of Thought.

                    But O! how oft,
How oft, at school, with most believing mind,
25   Presageful, have I gazed upon the bars,
To watch that fluttering stranger! and as oft
With unclosed lids, already had I dreamt
Of my sweet birth-place,[3] and the old church-tower,
Whose bells, the poor man's only music, rang
30   From morn to evening, all the hot Fair-day,
So sweetly, that they stirred and haunted me
With a wild pleasure, falling on mine ear
Most like articulate sounds of things to come!
So gazed I, till the soothing things I dreamt
35   Lulled me to sleep, and sleep prolonged my dreams!
And so I brooded all the following morn,
Awed by the stern preceptor's[4] face, mine eye
Fixed with mock study on my swimming book:
Save if the door half opened, and I snatched
40   A hasty glance, and still my heart leaped up,
For still I hoped to see the stranger's face,

---

1. The scene is Coleridge's cottage at Nether
Stowey; the infant in line 7 is his son Hartley, then
aged seventeen months.
2. In all parts of the kingdom these films are called
strangers and supposed to portend the arrival of
some absent friend [Coleridge's note]. The "film"
is a piece of soot fluttering on the bar of the grate.

3. Coleridge was born at Ottery St. Mary, Devonshire, but went to school in London, beginning at
the age of nine.
4. The Reverend James Boyer at Coleridge's
school, Christ's Hospital; Coleridge describes him
in *Biographia Literaria*, chap. 1.

Townsman, or aunt, or sister more beloved,
My play-mate when we both were clothed alike!⁵

Dear Babe, that sleepest cradled by my side,
45　Whose gentle breathings, heard in this deep calm,
Fill up the interspersed vacancies
And momentary pauses of the thought!
My babe so beautiful! it thrills my heart
With tender gladness, thus to look at thee,
50　And think that thou shalt learn far other lore
And in far other scenes! For I was reared
In the great city, pent 'mid cloisters dim,
And saw nought lovely but the sky and stars.
But thou, my babe! shalt wander like a breeze
55　By lakes and sandy shores, beneath the crags
Of ancient mountain, and beneath the clouds,
Which image in their bulk both lakes and shores
And mountain crags: so shalt thou see and hear
The lovely shapes and sounds intelligible
60　Of that eternal language, which thy God
Utters, who from eternity doth teach
Himself in all, and all things in himself.
Great universal Teacher! he shall mould
Thy spirit, and by giving make it ask.

65　Therefore all seasons shall be sweet to thee,
Whether the summer clothe the general earth
With greenness, or the redbreast sit and sing
Betwixt the tufts of snow on the bare branch
Of mossy apple-tree, while the nigh thatch
70　Smokes in the sun-thaw; whether the eave-drops fall
Heard only in the trances of the blast,
Or if the secret ministry of frost
Shall hang them up in silent icicles,
Quietly shining to the quiet Moon.

Feb. 1798   1798

---

5. I.e., when both Coleridge and his sister Ann still wore infant clothes.

Dejection: An Ode[1]

Late, late yestreen I saw the new Moon,
With the old Moon in her arms;
And I fear, I fear, my Master dear!
We shall have a deadly storm.
Ballad of Sir Patrick Spence

I

Well! If the Bard was weather-wise, who made
The grand old ballad of Sir Patrick Spence,
This night, so tranquil now, will not go hence
Unroused by winds, that ply a busier trade
5 Than those which mould yon cloud in lazy flakes,
Or the dull sobbing draft, that moans and rakes
    Upon the strings of this Eolian lute,[2]
    Which better far were mute.
For lo! the New-moon winter-bright!
10 And overspread with phantom light,
    (With swimming phantom light o'erspread
    But rimmed and circled by a silver thread)
I see the old Moon in her lap, foretelling
    The coming on of rain and squally blast.
15 And oh! that even now the gust were swelling,
    And the slant night-shower driving loud and fast!
Those sounds which oft have raised me, whilst they awed,
    And sent my soul abroad,
Might now perhaps their wonted° impulse give,   customary
20 Might startle this dull pain, and make it move and live!

2

A grief without a pang, void, dark, and drear,
A stifled, drowsy, unimpassioned grief,
Which finds no natural outlet, no relief,
    In word, or sigh, or tear—
25 O Lady![3] in this wan and heartless mood,
To other thoughts by yonder throstle woo'd,
    All this long eve, so balmy and serene,
Have I been gazing on the western sky,
    And its peculiar tint of yellow green:

1. This poem originated in a verse letter of 340 lines, called *A Letter to ———*, that Coleridge wrote on the night of April 4, 1802, after hearing the opening stanzas of *Ode: Intimations of Immortality*, which Wordsworth had just composed. The *Letter* was addressed to Sara Hutchinson (whom Coleridge sometimes called "Asra"), the sister of Wordsworth's fiancée, Mary. It picked up the theme of a loss in the quality of perceptual experience that Wordsworth had presented at the beginning of his *Ode*. In his original poem Coleridge lamented at length his unhappy marriage and the hopelessness of his love for Sara Hutchinson. In the next six months Coleridge deleted more than half the original lines, revised and reordered the remaining passages, and so transformed a long verse confession into the compact and dignified *Dejection: An Ode*. He published the *Ode*, in substantially its present form, on October 4, 1802, Wordsworth's wedding day—and also the seventh anniversary of Coleridge's own disastrous marriage to Sara Fricker. Note Coleridge's use of marriage as a metaphor in lines 49 and 67–70.
2. A stringed instrument played upon by the wind (see *The Eolian Harp*, n. 1, p. 419).
3. In the original version "Sara"—i.e., Sara Hutchinson. After intervening versions, in which the poem was addressed first to "William" (Wordsworth) and then to "Edmund," Coleridge introduced the noncommittal "Lady" in 1817.

30 And still I gaze—and with how blank an eye!
And those thin clouds above, in flakes and bars,
That give away their motion to the stars;
Those stars, that glide behind them or between,
Now sparkling, now bedimmed, but always seen:
35 Yon crescent Moon as fixed as if it grew
In its own cloudless, starless lake of blue;
I see them all so excellently fair,
I see, not feel, how beautiful they are!

3

My genial[4] spirits fail;
40 And what can these avail
To lift the smothering weight from off my breast?
It were a vain endeavour,
Though I should gaze for ever
On that green light that lingers in the west:
45 I may not hope from outward forms to win
The passion and the life, whose fountains are within.

4

O Lady! we receive but what we give,
And in our life alone does nature live:
Ours is her wedding-garment, ours her shroud![5]
50 And would we aught behold, of higher worth,
Than that inanimate cold world allowed
To the poor loveless ever-anxious crowd,
Ah! from the soul itself must issue forth,
A light, a glory,[6] a fair luminous cloud
55 Enveloping the Earth—
And from the soul itself must there be sent
A sweet and potent voice, of its own birth,
Of all sweet sounds the life and element!

5

O pure of heart! thou need'st not ask of me
60 What this strong music in the soul may be!
What, and wherein it doth exist,
This light, this glory, this fair luminous mist,
This beautiful and beauty-making power.
Joy,[7] virtuous Lady! Joy that ne'er was given,
65 Save to the pure, and in their purest hour,
Life, and Life's effluence, cloud at once and shower,
Joy, Lady! is the spirit and the power,

4. In its old use as the adjectival form of *genius:*
"My innate powers fail."
5. I.e., whether nature is experienced as "inanimate" (line 51) or in living interchange with the observer depends on the apathy or joyous vitality of the observer's own spirit.
6. Coleridge commonly used "glory" not in the sense of a halo, merely, but as a term for a moun-

tain phenomenon in which a walker sees his own figure projected by the sun in the mist, enlarged, and with a circle of light around its head.
7. Coleridge often uses "Joy" for a sense of abounding vitality and of harmony between one's inner life and the life of nature. He sometimes calls the contrary "exsiccation," or spiritual dryness.

Which wedding Nature to us gives in dower,
  A new Earth and new Heaven,[8]
70 Undreamt of by the sensual and the proud—
Joy is the sweet voice, Joy the luminous cloud—
    We in ourselves rejoice!
And thence flows all that charms or ear or sight,
  All melodies the echoes of that voice,
75 All colours a suffusion from that light.

6

There was a time when, though my path was rough,
  This joy within me dallied with distress,
And all misfortunes were but as the stuff
  Whence Fancy made me dreams of happiness:
80 For hope grew round me, like the twining vine,
And fruits, and foliage, not my own, seemed mine.
But now afflictions bow me down to earth:
Nor care I that they rob me of my mirth,
    But oh! each visitation
85 Suspends what nature gave me at my birth,
  My shaping spirit of Imagination.
For not to think of what I needs must feel,
  But to be still and patient, all I can;
And haply by abstruse research to steal
90   From my own nature all the natural man—
This was my sole resource, my only plan:
Till that which suits a part infects the whole,
And now is almost grown the habit of my soul.

7

Hence, viper thoughts, that coil around my mind,
95   Reality's dark dream!
I turn from you, and listen to the wind,
  Which long has raved unnoticed. What a scream
Of agony by torture lengthened out
That lute sent forth! Thou Wind, that ravest without,
100   Bare crag, or mountain-tairn,[9] or blasted tree,
Or pine-grove whither woodman never clomb,
Or lonely house, long held the witches' home,
    Methinks were fitter instruments for thee,
Mad Lutanist! who in this month of showers,
105 Of dark brown gardens, and of peeping flowers,
Mak'st Devils' yule,[1] with worse than wintry song,
The blossoms, buds, and timorous leaves among.
    Thou Actor, perfect in all tragic sounds!

---

8. The sense becomes clearer if line 68 is punctuated in the way that Coleridge himself punctuated it when quoting the passage in one of his essays: "Which, wedding Nature to us, gives in dower." The idea is that "Joy" is the condition that (overcoming the alienation between mind and its milieu) marries us to "Nature" and gives by way of wedding portion ("dower") the experience of a renovated world.
9. Tarn, or mountain pool.
1. Christmas as, in a perverted form, it is celebrated by devils.

Thou mighty Poet, e'en to frenzy bold!
110   What tell'st thou now about?
      'Tis of the rushing of a host in rout,
With groans of trampled men, with smarting wounds—
At once they groan with pain, and shudder with the cold!
But hush! there is a pause of deepest silence!
115   And all that noise, as of a rushing crowd,
With groans, and tremulous shudderings—all is over—
      It tells another tale, with sounds less deep and loud!
        A tale of less affright,
        And tempered with delight,
120 As Otway's[2] self had framed the tender lay,
        'Tis of a little child
        Upon a lonesome wild,
Not far from home, but she hath lost her way:
And now moans low in bitter grief and fear,
125 And now screams loud, and hopes to make her mother hear.

8

'Tis midnight, but small thoughts have I of sleep:
Full seldom may my friend such vigils keep!
Visit her, gentle Sleep! with wings of healing,
      And may this storm be but a mountain-birth,[3]
130 May all the stars hang bright above her dwelling,
      Silent as though they watched the sleeping Earth!
        With light heart may she rise,
        Gay fancy, cheerful eyes,
      Joy lift her spirit, joy attune her voice;
135 To her may all things live, from pole to pole,
      Their life the eddying of her living soul!
        O simple spirit, guided from above,
Dear Lady! friend devoutest of my choice,
Thus mayest thou ever, evermore rejoice.

Apr. 4, 1802   1802

The Pains of Sleep[1]

Ere on my bed my limbs I lay,
It hath not been my use to pray
With moving lips or bended knees;
But silently, by slow degrees,

2. Thomas Otway (1652–1685), a dramatist noted for the pathos of his tragic passages. The poet originally named was "William," and the allusion was probably to Wordsworth's *Lucy Gray*.
3. Probably, "May this be a typical mountain storm, short though violent," although it is possible that Coleridge intended an allusion to Horace's phrase, "the mountain labored and brought forth a mouse."
1. Coleridge included a draft of this poem in a letter to Robert Southey, September 11, 1803, in which he wrote that "my spirits are dreadful, owing entirely to the Horrors of every night—I truly dread to sleep. It is no shadow with me, but substantial Misery foot-thick, that makes me sit by my bedside of a morning, & cry—. I have abandoned all opiates except Ether be one; & that only in *fits.* . . . " The last sentence indicates what Coleridge did not know—that his guilty nightmares were probably withdrawal symptoms from opium. The dreams he describes are very similar to those that De Quincey represents as "The Pains of Opium" in his *Confessions of an English Opium-Eater*.

5   My spirit I to Love compose,
In humble trust mine eye-lids close,
With reverential resignation,
No wish conceived, no thought exprest,
Only a sense of supplication;
10 A sense o'er all my soul imprest
That I am weak, yet not unblest,
Since in me, round me, every where
Eternal strength and wisdom are.

But yester-night I prayed aloud
15 In anguish and in agony,
Up-starting from the fiendish crowd
Of shapes and thoughts that tortured me:
A lurid light, a trampling throng,
Sense of intolerable wrong,
20 And whom I scorned, those only strong!
Thirst of revenge, the powerless will
Still baffled, and yet burning still!
Desire with loathing strangely mixed
On wild or hateful objects fixed.
25 Fantastic passions! maddening brawl!
And shame and terror over all!
Deeds to be hid which were not hid,
Which all confused I could not know,
Whether I suffered, or I did:
30 For all seemed guilt, remorse or woe,
My own or others still the same
Life-stifling fear, soul-stifling shame.

So two nights passed: the night's dismay
Saddened and stunned the coming day.
35 Sleep, the wide blessing, seemed to me
Distemper's worst calamity.
The third night, when my own loud scream
Had waked me from the fiendish dream,
O'ercome with sufferings strange and wild,
40 I wept as I had been a child;
And having thus by tears subdued
My anguish to a milder mood,
Such punishments, I said, were due
To natures deepliest stained with sin,—
45 For aye entempesting anew
The unfathomable hell within,
The horror of their deeds to view,
To know and loathe, yet wish and do!
Such griefs with such men well agree,
50 But wherefore, wherefore fall on me?
To be beloved is all I need,
And whom I love, I love indeed.

1803   1816

To William Wordsworth

Composed on the Night after His Recitation of a Poem on the Growth of an Individual Mind[1]

Friend of the wise! and teacher of the good!
Into my heart have I received that lay
More than historic, that prophetic lay
Wherein (high theme by thee first sung aright)
5   Of the foundations and the building up
Of a Human Spirit thou hast dared to tell
What may be told, to the understanding mind
Revealable; and what within the mind
By vital breathings secret as the soul
10 Of vernal growth, oft quickens in the heart
Thoughts all too deep for words![2]—

                                Theme hard as high!
Of smiles spontaneous, and mysterious fears
(The first-born they of Reason and twin birth),
Of tides obedient to external force,
15 And currents self-determined, as might seem,
Or by some inner power; of moments awful,
Now in thy inner life, and now abroad,
When power streamed from thee, and thy soul received
The light reflected, as a light bestowed—
20 Of fancies fair, and milder hours of youth,
Hyblean[3] murmurs of poetic thought
Industrious in its joy, in vales and glens
Native or outland, lakes and famous hills!
Or on the lonely high-road, when the stars
25 Were rising; or by secret mountain-streams,
The guides and the companions of thy way!

    Of more than Fancy, of the Social Sense
Distending wide, and man beloved as man,
Where France in all her towns lay vibrating
30 Like some becalmed bark beneath the burst
Of Heaven's immediate thunder, when no cloud
Is visible, or shadow on the main.
For thou wert there, thine own brows garlanded,
Amid the tremor of a realm aglow,
35 Amid a mighty nation jubilant,
When from the general heart of human kind
Hope sprang forth like a full-born Deity!

1. This was the poem (later called *The Prelude*), addressed to Coleridge, that Wordsworth had completed in 1805. After Coleridge returned from Malta, very low in health and spirits, Wordsworth read the poem aloud to him during the evenings of almost two weeks. Coleridge wrote most of the present response immediately after the reading was completed, on January 7, 1807.

2. Wordsworth had described the effect on his mind of the animating breeze ("vital breathings") in *The Prelude* 1.1–44. "Thoughts . . . words" echoes the last line of Wordsworth's *Intimations* ode. Coleridge goes on to summarize the major themes and events of *The Prelude*.

3. Sweet. Hybla, in ancient Sicily, was famous for its honey.

———Of that dear Hope afflicted and struckd
So summoned homeward, thenceforth calm a
40 From the dread watch-tower of man's absolute
With light unwaning on her eyes, to look
Far on—herself a glory to behold,
The Angel of the vision! Then (last strain)
Of Duty, chosen laws controlling choice,
45 Action and joy!—An Orphic song[4] indeed,
A song divine of high and passionate thoughts
To their own music chanted!

               O great Bard!
Ere yet that last strain dying awed the air,
With steadfast eye I viewed thee in the choir
50 Of ever-enduring men. The truly great
Have all one age, and from one visible space
Shed influence! They, both in power and act,
Are permanent, and Time is not with them,
Save as it worketh for them, they in it.
55 Nor less a sacred roll, than those of old,
And to be placed, as they, with gradual fame
Among the archives of mankind, thy work
Makes audible a linked lay of Truth,
Of Truth profound a sweet continuous lay,
60 Not learnt, but native, her own natural notes!
Ah! as I listened with a heart forlorn,
The pulses of my being beat anew:
And even as life returns upon the drowned,[5]
Life's joy rekindling roused a throng of pains—
65 Keen pangs of Love, awakening as a babe
Turbulent, with an outcry in the heart;
And fears self-willed, that shunned the eye of hope;
And hope that scarce would know itself from fear;
Sense of past youth, and manhood come in vain,
70 And genius given, and knowledge won in vain;
And all which I had culled in wood-walks wild,
And all which patient toil had reared, and all,
Commune with thee had opened out—but flowers
Strewed on my corse, and borne upon my bier,
75 In the same coffin, for the self-same grave!

    That way no more! and ill beseems it me,
Who came a welcomer in herald's guise,
Singing of glory, and futurity,
To wander back on such unhealthful road,
80 Plucking the poisons of self-harm! And ill
Such intertwine beseems triumphal wreaths
Strewed before thy advancing!

4. As enchanting and oracular as the song of the legendary Orpheus. There may also be an allusion to the Orphic mysteries, involving spiritual death and rebirth (see lines 61–66). "The Angel of the vision" (line 43) probably alludes to "the great vision of the guarded mount" in Milton's *Lycidas*, line 161.

5. A death-in-life is also described in, e.g., *Dejection: An Ode* and *Epitaph*.

Nor do thou,
rd! inpair the memory of that hour
communion with my nobler mind[6]
ꓹy or grief, already felt too long!
ꓲet my words import more blame than needs.
ꓱ tumult rose and ceased: for peace is nigh
ꓱhere wisdom's voice has found a listening heart.
ꓲmid the howl of more than wintry storms,
The halcyon[7] hears the voice of vernal hours
Already on the wing.

Eve following eve,[8]
Dear tranquil time, when the sweet sense of Home
Is sweetest! moments for their own sake hailed
And more desired, more precious for thy song,
95   In silence listening, like a devout child,
My soul lay passive, by thy various strain
Driven as in surges now beneath the stars,
With momentary stars of my own birth,
Fair constellated foam, still darting off
100   Into the darkness; now a tranquil sea,
Outspread and bright, yet swelling to the moon.

And when—O Friend! my comforter and guide!
Strong in thyself, and powerful to give strength!—
Thy long sustained Song finally closed,
105   And thy deep voice had ceased—yet thou thyself
Wert still before my eyes, and round us both
That happy vision of beloved faces—
Scarce conscious, and yet conscious of its close
I sate, my being blended in one thought
110   (Thought was it? or aspiration? or resolve?)
Absorbed, yet hanging still upon the sound—
And when I rose, I found myself in prayer.

1807   1817

On Donne's Poetry[1]

With Donne, whose muse on dromedary[2] trots,
Wreathe iron pokers into true-love knots;
Rhyme's sturdy cripple, fancy's maze and clue,
Wit's forge and fire-blast, meaning's press and screw.

ca. 1818   1836

6. I.e., during the early association between the
two poets (1797–98).
7. A fabled bird, able to calm the sea where it
nested in winter.
8. The evenings during which Wordsworth read
his poem aloud.
1. John Donne as a poet had been in eclipse for

most of the 18th century. This terse and penetrating comment shows the Romantic poet's great,
though ironically qualified, respect for the master
of the metaphysical style.
2. The one-humped Arabian camel, trained to be
ridden.

Work without Hope
Lines Composed 21st February 1825

All Nature seems at work. Slugs leave their lair—
The bees are stirring—birds are on the wing—
And Winter slumbering in the open air,
Wears on his smiling face a dream of Spring!
5   And I the while, the sole unbusy thing,
Nor honey make, nor pair, nor build, nor sing.

Yet well I ken the banks where amaranths[1] blow,
Have traced the fount whence streams of nectar flow.
Bloom, O ye amaranths! bloom for whom ye may,
10   For me ye bloom not! Glide, rich streams, away!
With lips unbrightened, wreathless brow, I stroll:
And would you learn the spells that drowse my soul?
Work without hope draws nectar in a sieve,
And hope without an object cannot live.

1825   1828

Epitaph[1]

Stop, Christian Passer-by!—Stop, child of God,
And read with gentle breast. Beneath this sod
A poet lies, or that which once seem'd he.—
O, lift one thought in prayer for S. T. C.;
5   That he who many a year with toil of breath
Found death in life, may here find life in death!
Mercy for praise—to be forgiven for[2] fame
He ask'd, and hoped, through Christ. Do thou the same!

1833   1834

Biographia Literaria   In March 1815 Coleridge was preparing a collected
edition of his poems and planned to include "a general preface . . . on the principles
of philosophic and genial criticism." Characteristically, the materials developed as
Coleridge worked on them until, on July 29, he declared that the preface had been
extended into a complete work, "an Autobiographia Literaria"; it was to consist of two
main parts, "my literary life and opinions, as far as poetry and *poetical* criticism [are]
concerned" and a critique of Wordsworth's theory of poetic diction. This work was
ready by September 17, 1815, but the *Biographia Literaria*, in two volumes, was not
published until July 1817. The delay was caused by a series of miscalculations by his

---

1. Mythical flowers that bloom perpetually.
1. Written by Coleridge the year before he died.
One version that he sent in a letter had as a title:
"Epitaph on a Poet little known, yet better known

by the Initials of his name than by the Name
Itself."
2. "For" in the sense of "instead of" [Coleridge's
note].

printer, which forced Coleridge to add 150 pages of miscellaneous materials to pad out the length of the second volume.

Coleridge had been planning a detailed critique of Wordsworth's theory of poetic diction ever since 1802, when he had detected "a radical difference in our theoretical opinions respecting poetry." In the selection from chapter 17, Coleridge agrees with Wordsworth's general aim of reforming the artifices of current poetic diction, but he sharply denies Wordsworth's claim that there is no essential difference between the language of poetry and the language spoken by people in real life. The other selections printed here are devoted mainly to the central principle of Coleridge's own critical theory, the distinction between the mechanical "fancy" and the organic "imagination." The biographical section of the *Biographia* (chapters 1 and 4), dealing with the development of his poetic taste and theory, describes his gradual realization, climaxed by his first exposure to Wordsworth's poetry, "that fancy and imagination were two distinct and widely different faculties." The conclusion to chapter 13 tersely summarizes this distinction; and the definition of poetry, at the end of chapter 14, develops at greater length the nature of the process and products of the "synthetic and magical power . . . of imagination." These paragraphs, whose meaning is much disputed, have become a central reference in English literary criticism.

From Biographia Literaria

From *Chapter 1*

[THE DISCIPLINE OF HIS TASTE AT SCHOOL][1]

At school I enjoyed the inestimable advantage of a very sensible, though at the same time a very severe master. He[2] early molded my taste to the preference of Demosthenes to Cicero, of Homer and Theocritus to Virgil, and again of Virgil to Ovid. He habituated me to compare Lucretius (in such extracts as I then read), Terence, and, above all, the chaster poems of Catullus not only with the Roman poets of the so-called silver and brazen ages but with even those of the Augustan era; and, on grounds of plain sense and universal logic, to see and assert the superiority of the former in the truth and nativeness both of their thoughts and diction. At the same time that we were studying the Greek tragic poets, he made us read Shakespeare and Milton as lessons; and they were the lessons, too, which required most time and trouble to *bring up*, so as to escape his censure. I learnt from him that poetry, even that of the loftiest and, seemingly, that of the wildest odes, had a logic of its own as severe as that of science; and more difficult, because more subtle, more complex, and dependent on more, and more fugitive, causes. In the truly great poets, he would say, there is a reason assignable, not only for every word, but for the position of every word; and I well remember that, availing himself of the synonyms to the Homer of Didymus,[3] he made us attempt to show, with regard to each, *why* it would not have answered the same purpose, and *wherein* consisted the peculiar fitness of the word in the original text.

---

1. Coleridge heads each chapter with a list of topics. In instances where we excerpt from chapters, we introduce these headings in brackets before the relevant selection.
2. The Rev. James Bowyer, many years Head Master of the Grammar School, Christ's Hospital

[Coleridge's note]. See also Charles Lamb's essay *Christ's Hospital Five-and-Thirty Years Ago* (p. 495).
3. Didymus of Alexandria (ca. 65 B.C.E.–10 C.E.) was the author of a commentary on the text of Homer.

In our own English compositions (at least for the last three years of our school education) he showed no mercy to phrase, metaphor, or image unsupported by a sound sense, or where the same sense might have been conveyed with equal force and dignity in plainer words. Lute, harp, and lyre, muse, muses, and inspirations, Pegasus, Parnassus, and Hippocrene were all an abomination to him. In fancy I can almost hear him now, exclaiming, "Harp? Harp? Lyre? Pen and ink, boy, you mean! Muse, boy, muse? Your nurse's daughter, you mean! Pierian spring? Oh, aye! the cloister pump, I suppose!" Nay, certain introductions, similes, and examples were placed by name on a list of interdiction. Among the similes there was, I remember, that of the manchineel fruit,[4] as suiting equally well with too many subjects, in which, however, it yielded the palm at once to the example of Alexander and Clytus,[5] which was equally good and apt whatever might be the theme. Was it ambition? Alexander and Clytus! Flattery? Alexander and Clytus! Anger? Drunkenness? Pride? Friendship? Ingratitude? Late repentance? Still, still Alexander and Clytus! At length, the praises of agriculture having been exemplified in the sagacious observation that, had Alexander been holding the plow, he would not have run his friend Clytus through with a spear, this tried and serviceable old friend was banished by public edict *in secula seculorum*.[6] I have sometimes ventured to think that a list of this kind or an *index expurgatorius*[7] of certain well-known and ever returning phrases, both introductory and transitional, including the large assortment of modest egoisms and flattering illeisms,[8] etc., etc., might be hung up in our law courts and both Houses of Parliament with great advantage to the public as an important saving of national time, an incalculable relief to his Majesty's ministers; but, above all, as insuring the thanks of country attorneys and their clients, who have private bills to carry through the House.

Be this as it may, there was one custom of our master's which I cannot pass over in silence, because I think it imitable and worthy of imitation. He would often permit our theme exercises, under some pretext of want of time, to accumulate till each lad had four or five to be looked over. Then placing the whole number *abreast* on his desk, he would ask the writer why this or that sentence might not have found as appropriate a place under this or that other thesis; and if no satisfying answer could be returned and two faults of the same kind were found in one exercise, the irrevocable verdict followed, the exercise was torn up, and another on the same subject to be produced, in addition to the tasks of the day. The reader will, I trust, excuse this tribute of recollection to a man whose severities, even now, not seldom furnish the dreams by which the blind fancy would fain interpret to the mind the painful sensations of distempered sleep; but neither lessen nor dim the deep sense of my moral and intellectual obligations. He sent us to the university excellent Latin and Greek scholars and tolerable Hebraists. Yet our classical knowledge was the least of the good gifts which we derived from his zealous and conscientious tutorage. He is now gone to his final reward, full of years and full of honors, even of those honors which were dearest to his heart as gratefully bestowed by that school, and still binding him to the interests of

---

4. Poisonous, though attractive in appearance.
5. Plutarch's *Life* of Alexander the Great relates that the king killed his friend Clytus in a drunken quarrel.
6. Literally, for centuries of centuries (Latin); forever.
7. Index of things to be deleted (Latin).
8. Excessive use of the pronoun *he* (in Latin, *ille*).

that school, in which he had been himself educated and to which during his whole life he was a dedicated thing. * * *

[BOWLES'S SONNETS]

I had just entered on my seventeenth year, when the sonnets of Mr. Bowles,[9] twenty in number, and just then published in a quarto pamphlet, were first made known and presented to me by a schoolfellow who had quitted us for the university and who, during the whole time that he was in our first form (or in our school language, a Grecian),[1] had been my patron and protector. I refer to Dr. Middleton, the truly learned and every way excellent Bishop of Calcutta. * * *

It was a double pleasure to me, and still remains a tender recollection, that I should have received from a friend so revered the first knowledge of a poet by whose works, year after year, I was so enthusiastically delighted and inspired. My earliest acquaintances will not have forgotten the undisciplined eagerness and impetuous zeal with which I laboured to make proselytes, not only of my companions, but of all with whom I conversed, of whatever rank and in whatever place. As my school finances did not permit me to purchase copies, I made, within less than a year and a half, more than forty transcriptions, as the best presents I could offer to those who had in any way won my regard. And with almost equal delight did I receive the three or four following publications of the same author.

Though I have seen and known enough of mankind to be well aware that I shall perhaps stand alone in my creed, and that it will be well if I subject myself to no worse charge than that of singularity, I am not therefore deterred from avowing that I regard and ever have regarded the obligations of intellect among the most sacred of the claims of gratitude. A valuable thought, or a particular train of thoughts, gives me additional pleasure when I can safely refer and attribute it to the conversation or correspondence of another. My obligations to Mr. Bowles were indeed important and for radical good. At a very premature age, even before my fifteenth year, I had bewildered myself in metaphysics and in theological controversy. Nothing else pleased me. History and particular facts lost all interest in my mind. Poetry (though for a schoolboy of that age I was above par in English versification and had already produced two or three compositions which, I may venture to say without reference to my age, were somewhat above mediocrity, and which had gained me more credit than the sound good sense of my old master was at all pleased with), poetry itself, yea novels and romances, became insipid to me. In my friendless wanderings on our leave-days (for I was an orphan, and had scarce any connections in London), highly was I delighted if any passenger, especially if he were dressed in black,[2] would enter into conversation with me. For I soon found the means of directing it to my favorite subjects

---

9. William Lisle Bowles (1762–1850) published in 1789 two editions of a collection of sonnets setting forth the meditations evoked from a traveler by the changing scene.

1. Gifted students in the final class at Christ's Hospital who were being prepared for a university.
2. I.e., if he were a clergyman.

> Of providence, fore-knowledge, will, and fate,
> Fixed fate, free will, fore-knowledge absolute,
> And found no end, in wandering mazes lost.[3]

This preposterous pursuit was, beyond doubt, injurious both to my natural powers and to the progress of my education. It would perhaps have been destructive had it been continued; but from this I was auspiciously withdrawn, partly indeed by an accidental introduction to an amiable family,[4] chiefly however by the genial influence of a style of poetry so tender and yet so manly, so natural and real, and yet so dignified and harmonious, as the sonnets, etc., of Mr. Bowles! Well were it for me, perhaps, had I never relapsed into the same mental disease; if I had continued to pluck the flower and reap the harvest from the cultivated surface, instead of delving in the unwholesome quicksilver mines of metaphysic depths. But if in after time I have sought a refuge from bodily pain and mismanaged sensibility in abstruse researches, which exercised the strength and subtlety of the understanding without awakening the feelings of the heart; still there was a long and blessed interval, during which my natural faculties were allowed to expand and my original tendencies to develop themselves: my fancy, and the love of nature, and the sense of beauty in forms and sounds.

[COMPARISON BETWEEN THE POETS BEFORE AND SINCE MR. POPE]

The second advantage which I owe to my early perusal and admiration of these poems (to which let me add, though known to me at a somewhat later period, the *Lewesdon Hill* of Mr. Crow)[5] bears more immediately on my present subject. Among those with whom I conversed there were, of course, very many who had formed their taste and their notions of poetry from the writings of Mr. Pope and his followers: or to speak more generally, in that school of French poetry condensed and invigorated by English understanding which had predominated from the last century. I was not blind to the merits of this school, yet as from inexperience of the world and consequent want of sympathy with the general subjects of these poems they gave me little pleasure, I doubtless undervalued the *kind*, and with the presumption of youth withheld from its masters the legitimate name of poets. I saw that the excellence of this kind consisted in just and acute observations on men and manners in an artificial state of society as its matter and substance, and in the logic of wit conveyed in smooth and strong epigrammatic couplets as its *form*. Even when the subject was addressed to the fancy or the intellect, as in the *Rape of the Lock* or the *Essay on Man;* nay, when it was a consecutive narration, as in that astonishing product of matchless talent and ingenuity, Pope's translation of the *Iliad*; still a *point* was looked for at the end of each second line, and the whole was as it were a sorites or, if I may exchange a logical for a grammatical metaphor, a *conjunction disjunctive*,[6] of epigrams.

3. *Paradise Lost* 2.559–61.
4. The family of Mary Evans, with whom Coleridge fell in love in 1788.
5. William Crow(e) (1745–1829) published in 1788 *Lewesdon Hill*, a long poem in blank verse that, like Bowles's sonnets, combined descriptions of the natural scene with associated moral and personal reflections.
6. A word that connects the parts of a sentence but expresses an alternative or opposition: "or," "but," "lest," etc. "Sorites": a sequence of interconnected syllogisms.

Meantime the matter and diction seemed to me characterized not so much by poetic thoughts as by thoughts *translated* into the language of poetry. On this last point I had occasion to render my own thoughts gradually more and more plain to myself by frequent amicable disputes concerning Darwin's *Botanic Garden*,[7] which for some years was greatly extolled, not only by the *reading* public in general, but even by those whose genius and natural robustness of understanding enabled them afterwards to act foremost in dissipating these "painted mists" that occasionally rise from the marshes at the foot of Parnassus. During my first Cambridge vacation I assisted a friend in a contribution for a literary society in Devonshire, and in this I remember to have compared Darwin's work to the Russian palace of ice, glittering, cold, and transitory. In the same essay too I assigned sundry reasons, chiefly drawn from a comparison of passages in the Latin poets with the original Greek from which they were borrowed, for the preference of Collins's odes to those of Gray, and of the simile in Shakespeare:

> How like a younker or a prodigal
> The scarfed bark puts from her native bay,
> Hugged and embraced by the strumpet wind!
> How like the prodigal doth she return,
> With over-weathered ribs and ragged sails,
> Lean, rent and beggared by the strumpet wind![8]

to the imitation in the *Bard*:

> Fair laughs the morn, and soft the zephyr blows
> While proudly riding o'er the azure realm
> In gallant trim the gilded vessel goes;
> YOUTH on the prow, and PLEASURE at the helm;
> Regardless of the sweeping whirlwind's sway,
> That, hushed in grim repose, expects its evening prey.[9]

(In which, by the bye, the words "realm" and "sway" are rhymes dearly purchased.) I preferred the original, on the ground that in the imitation it depended wholly in the compositor's putting, or not putting, a small capital both in this and in many other passages of the same poet whether the words should be personifications or mere abstracts. I mention this because, in referring various lines in Gray to their original in Shakespeare and Milton, and in the clear perception how completely all the propriety was lost in the transfer, I was at that early period led to a conjecture which, many years afterwards, was recalled to me from the same thought having been started in conversation, but far more ably, and developed more fully, by Mr. Wordsworth; namely, that this style of poetry which I have characterized above as translations of prose thoughts into poetic language had been kept up by, if it did not wholly arise from, the custom of writing Latin verses and the great importance attached to these exercises in our public schools. Whatever might have been the case in the fifteenth century, when the use of the Latin tongue was so general among learned men that Erasmus is said to have forgotten his native language; yet in the present day it is not to be supposed

---

7. Published in 1789–91 by Erasmus Darwin (1731–1802); a long poem in closed couplets, presenting the science of botany in elaborate allegories.
8. *Merchant of Venice* 2.6.14–19.
9. Thomas Gray's *The Bard* (1757).

that a youth can think in Latin, or that he can have any other reliance on the force or fitness of his phrases but the authority of the author from whence he had adopted them. Consequently he must first prepare his thoughts and then pick out from Virgil, Horace, Ovid, or perhaps more compendiously, from his *Gradus*,[1] halves and quarters of lines in which to embody them.

I never object to a certain degree of disputatiousness in a young man from the age of seventeen to that of four or five and twenty, provided I find him always arguing on one side of the question. The controversies occasioned by my unfeigned zeal for the honor of a favorite contemporary, then known to me only by his works, were of great advantage in the formation and establishment of my taste and critical opinions. In my defense of the lines running into each other instead of closing at each couplet, and of natural language, neither bookish nor vulgar, neither redolent of the lamp nor of the kennel, such as *I will remember thee;* instead of the same thought tricked up in the rag-fair finery of

> ———Thy image on her wing
> Before my FANCY'S eye shall MEMORY bring,

I had continually to adduce the meter and diction of the Greek poets from Homer to Theocritus inclusive; and still more of our elder English poets from Chaucer to Milton. Nor was this all. But as it was my constant reply to authorities brought against me from later poets of great name that no authority could avail in opposition to Truth, Nature, Logic, and the Laws of Universal Grammar; actuated too by my former passion for metaphysical investigations, I labored at a solid foundation on which permanently to ground my opinions in the component faculties of the human mind itself and their comparative dignity and importance. According to the faculty or source from which the pleasure given by any poem or passage was derived I estimated the merit of such poem or passage. As the result of all my reading and meditation, I abstracted two critical aphorisms, deeming them to comprise the conditions and criteria of poetic style: first, that not the poem which we have *read*, but that to which we *return* with the greatest pleasure, possesses the genuine power and claims the name of *essential* poetry. Second, that whatever lines can be translated into other words of the same language without diminution of their significance, either in sense of association or in any worthy feeling, are so far vicious in their diction. Be it however observed that I excluded from the list of worthy feelings the pleasure derived from mere novelty in the reader, and the desire of exciting wonderment at his powers in the author. Oftentimes since then, in perusing French tragedies, I have fancied two marks of admiration at the end of each line, as hieroglyphics of the author's own admiration at his own cleverness. Our genuine admiration of a great poet is a continuous undercurrent of feeling; it is everywhere present, but seldom anywhere as a separate excitement. I was wont boldly to affirm that it would be scarcely more difficult to push a stone out from the pyramids with the bare hand than to alter a word, or the position of a word, in Milton or Shakespeare (in their most important works at least), without making the author say something else, or something worse, than he

---

1. *Gradus ad Parnassum* ("Stairway to Parnassus"), a dictionary of Latin words, synonyms, and descriptive epithets, illustrated from the Latin poets. It was long used as a school text in Latin composition.

does say. One great distinction I appeared to myself to see plainly, between even the characteristic faults of our elder poets and the false beauties of the moderns. In the former, from Donne to Cowley, we find the most fantastic out-of-the-way thoughts, but in the most pure and genuine mother English; in the latter, the most obvious thoughts, in language the most fantastic and arbitrary. Our faulty elder poets sacrificed the passion and passionate flow of poetry to the subtleties of intellect and to the starts of wit; the moderns to the glare and glitter of a perpetual yet broken and heterogeneous imagery, or rather to an amphibious something, made up half of image and half of abstract[2] meaning. The one sacrificed the heart to the head, the other both heart and head to point and drapery. * * *

From *Chapter 4*

[MR. WORDSWORTH'S EARLIER POEMS]

* * * During the last year of my residence at Cambridge, I became acquainted with Mr. Wordsworth's first publication, entitled *Descriptive Sketches*;[3] and seldom, if ever, was the emergence of an original poetic genius above the literary horizon more evidently announced. In the form, style, and manner of the whole poem, and in the structure of the particular lines and periods, there is a harshness and acerbity connected and combined with words and images all a-glow which might recall those products of the vegetable world, where gorgeous blossoms rise out of the hard and thorny rind and shell within which the rich fruit was elaborating. The language was not only peculiar and strong, but at times knotty and contorted, as by its own impatient strength; while the novelty and struggling crowd of images, acting in conjunction with the difficulties of the style, demanded always a greater closeness of attention than poetry (at all events than descriptive poetry) has a right to claim. It not seldom therefore justified the complaint of obscurity. In the following extract I have sometimes fancied that I saw an emblem of the poem itself and of the author's genius as it was then displayed:

> 'Tis storm; and hid in mist from hour to hour,
> All day the floods a deepening murmur pour;
> The sky is veiled, and every cheerful sight:
> Dark is the region as with coming night;
> And yet what frequent bursts of overpowering light!
> Triumphant on the bosom of the storm,
> Glances the fire-clad eagle's wheeling form;
> Eastward, in long perspective glittering, shine
> The wood-crowned cliffs that o'er the lake recline;
> Wide o'er the Alps a hundred streams unfold,
> At once to pillars turned that flame with gold;
> Behind his sail the peasant strives to shun
> The West, that burns like one dilated sun,

2. I remember a ludicrous instance in the poem of a young tradesman: "No more will I endure Love's pleasing pain, / Or round my *heart's leg* tie his galling chain" [Coleridge's note].
3. Published 1793, the year before Coleridge left

Cambridge; a long descriptive-meditative poem in closed couplets, recounting Wordsworth's walking tour in the Alps in 1790. Wordsworth describes the same tour in *The Prelude*, book 6.

> Where in a mighty crucible expire
> The mountains, glowing hot, like coals of fire.[4]

The poetic Psyche, in its process to full development, undergoes as many changes as its Greek namesake, the butterfly.[5] And it is remarkable how soon genius clears and purifies itself from the faults and errors of its earliest products; faults which, in its earliest compositions, are the more obtrusive and confluent because, as heterogeneous elements which had only a temporary use, they constitute the very *ferment* by which themselves are carried off. Or we may compare them to some diseases, which must work on the humors and be thrown out on the surface in order to secure the patient from their future recurrence. I was in my twenty-fourth year when I had the happiness of knowing Mr. Wordsworth personally;[6] and, while memory lasts, I shall hardly forget the sudden effect produced on my mind by his recitation of a manuscript poem which still remains unpublished, but of which the stanza and tone of style were the same as those of *The Female Vagrant* as originally printed in the first volume of the *Lyrical Ballads*.[7] There was here no mark of strained thought or forced diction, no crowd or turbulence of imagery, and, as the poet hath himself well described in his lines on revisiting the Wye,[8] manly reflection and human associations had given both variety and an additional interest to natural objects which in the passion and appetite of the first love they had seemed to him neither to need or permit. The occasional obscurities, which had risen from an imperfect control over the resources of his native language, had almost wholly disappeared, together with that worse defect of arbitrary and illogical phrases, at once hackneyed and fantastic, which hold so distinguished a place in the *technique* of ordinary poetry and will, more or less, alloy the earlier poems of the truest genius, unless the attention has been specifically directed to their worthlessness and incongruity. I did not perceive anything particular in the mere style of the poem alluded to during its recitation, except indeed such difference as was not separable from the thought and manner; and the Spenserian stanza which always, more or less, recalls to the reader's mind Spenser's own style, would doubtless have authorized in my then opinion a more frequent descent to the phrases of ordinary life than could, without an ill effect, have been hazarded in the heroic couplet. It was not however the freedom from false taste, whether as to common defects or to those more properly his own, which made so unusual an impression on my feelings immediately, and subsequently on my judgment. It was the union of deep feeling with profound thought; the fine balance of truth in observing with the imaginative faculty in modifying the objects observed; and above all the original gift of spreading the tone, the *atmosphere*, and with it the depth and height of the ideal world, around forms, incidents, and situations of which, for the common view, custom had bedimmed all the luster, had dried up the sparkle and the dewdrops. "To find no contradiction in the union of old and new, to contemplate the

---

4. *Descriptive Sketches* (1815 version), lines 332ff.
5. In Greek, Psyche is the common name for the soul and the butterfly [Coleridge's note].
6. The meeting occurred in September 1795.
7. *Salisbury Plain* (1793–94), which was left in manuscript until Wordsworth published a revised version in 1842 under the title *Guilt and Sorrow*. An excerpt from *Salisbury Plain* was printed as *The Female Vagrant*, in *Lyrical Ballads* (1798).
8. Wordsworth's *Tintern Abbey*, lines 76ff.

Ancient of Days and all his works with feelings as fresh as if all had then sprang forth at the first creative fiat, characterizes the mind that feels the riddle of the world and may help to unravel it. To carry on the feelings of childhood into the powers of manhood; to combine the child's sense of wonder and novelty with the appearances which every day for perhaps forty years had rendered familiar;

> With sun and moon and stars throughout the year,
> And man and woman;[9]

this is the character and privilege of genius, and one of the marks which distinguish genius from talents. And therefore it is the prime merit of genius, and its most unequivocal mode of manifestation, so to represent familiar objects as to awaken in the minds of others a kindred feeling concerning them, and that freshness of sensation which is the constant accompaniment of mental no less than of bodily convalescence. Who has not a thousand times seen snow fall on water? Who has not watched it with a new feeling from the time that he has read Burns' comparison of sensual pleasure

> To snow that falls upon a river
> A moment white—then gone forever![1]

In poems, equally as in philosophic disquisitions, genius produces the strongest impressions of novelty while it rescues the most admitted truths from the impotence caused by the very circumstance of their universal admission. Truths of all others the most awful and mysterious, yet being at the same time of universal interest, are too often considered as *so* true, that they lose all the life and efficiency of truth and lie bedridden in the dormitory of the soul side by side with the most despised and exploded errors." *The Friend*, p. 76, no. 5.[2]

[ON FANCY AND IMAGINATION—THE INVESTIGATION OF THE DISTINCTION IMPORTANT TO THE FINE ARTS]

This excellence, which in all Mr. Wordsworth's writings is more or less predominant and which constitutes the character of his mind, I no sooner felt than I sought to understand. Repeated meditations led me first to suspect (and a more intimate analysis of the human faculties, their appropriate marks, functions, and effects, matured my conjecture into full conviction) that fancy and imagination were two distinct and widely different faculties, instead of being, according to the general belief, either two names with one meaning, or at furthest the lower and higher degree of one and the same power. It is not, I own, easy to conceive a more apposite translation of the Greek *phantasia* than the Latin *imaginatio*; but it is equally true that in all societies there exists an instinct of growth, a certain collective unconscious good sense working progressively to desynonymize those words originally of the same meaning which the conflux of dialects had supplied to the more homogeneous languages, as the Greek and German: and which the same

---

9. Altered from Milton's sonnet *To Mr. Cyriack Skinner upon His Blindness.*
1. Altered from Burns's *Tam o' Shanter*, lines 61–62.
2. A periodical published by Coleridge (1809–10).

cause, joined with accidents of translation from original works of different countries, occasion in mixed languages like our own. The first and most important point to be proved is, that two conceptions perfectly distinct are confused under one and the same word, and (this done) to appropriate that word exclusively to one meaning, and the synonym (should there be one) to the other. But if (as will be often the case in the arts and sciences) no synonym exists, we must either invent or borrow a word. In the present instance the appropriation had already begun and been legitimated in the derivative adjective: Milton had a highly *imaginative,* Cowley a very *fanciful,* mind. If therefore I should succeed in establishing the actual existence of two faculties generally different, the nomenclature would be at once determined. To the faculty by which I had characterized Milton we should confine the term *imagination;* while the other would be contra-distinguished as *fancy.* Now were it once fully ascertained that this division is no less grounded in nature than that of delirium from mania, or Otway's

Lutes, lobsters, seas of milk, and ships of amber,[3]

from Shakespeare's

What! have his daughters brought him to this pass?[4]

or from the preceding apostrophe to the elements, the theory of the fine arts and of poetry in particular could not, I thought, but derive some additional and important light. It would in its immediate effects furnish a torch of guidance to the philosophical critic, and ultimately to the poet himself. In energetic minds truth soon changes by domestication into power; and from directing in the discrimination and appraisal of the product becomes influencive in the production. To admire on principle is the only way to imitate without loss of originality. * * *

From *Chapter 13*

[ON THE IMAGINATION, OR ESEMPLASTIC[5] POWER]

* * * The IMAGINATION, then, I consider either as primary, or secondary. The primary IMAGINATION I hold to be the living power and prime agent of all human perception, and as a repetition in the finite mind of the eternal act of creation in the infinite I AM. The secondary I consider as an echo of the former, coexisting with the conscious will, yet still as identical with the primary in the *kind* of its agency, and differing only in *degree,* and in the *mode* of its operation. It dissolves, diffuses, dissipates, in order to recreate; or where this process is rendered impossible, yet still, at all events, it struggles to idealize and to unify. It is essentially *vital,* even as all objects (*as* objects) are essentially fixed and dead.

FANCY, on the contrary, has no other counters to play with but fixities and definites. The fancy is indeed no other than a mode of memory emancipated from the order of time and space; and blended with, and modified by that

3. Thomas Otway, in *Venice Preserved* (1682), wrote "laurels" in place of "lobsters" (5.2.151).
4. *King Lear* 3.4.59.

5. Coleridge coined this word and used it to mean "molding into unity."

empirical phenomenon of the will which we express by the word CHOICE. But equally with the ordinary memory it must receive all its materials ready made from the law of association.[6] * * *

Chapter 14

OCCASION OF THE *LYRICAL BALLADS*, AND THE OBJECTS ORIGINALLY PROPOSED—PREFACE TO THE SECOND EDITION—THE ENSUING CONTROVERSY, ITS CAUSES AND ACRIMONY—PHILOSOPHIC DEFINITIONS OF A POEM AND POETRY WITH SCHOLIA.[7]

During the first year that Mr. Wordsworth and I were neighbours,[8] our conversations turned frequently on the two cardinal points of poetry, the power of exciting the sympathy of the reader by a faithful adherence to the truth of nature, and the power of giving the interest of novelty by the modifying colors of imagination.[9] The sudden charm which accidents of light and shade, which moonlight or sunset diffused over a known and familiar landscape, appeared to represent the practicability of combining both. These are the poetry of nature. The thought suggested itself (to which of us I do not recollect) that a series of poems might be composed of two sorts. In the one, the incidents and agents were to be, in part at least, supernatural; and the excellence aimed at was to consist in the interesting of the affections by the dramatic truth of such emotions as would naturally accompany such situations, supposing them real. And real in *this* sense they have been to every human being who, from whatever source of delusion, has at any time believed himself under supernatural agency. For the second class, subjects were to be chosen from ordinary life; the characters and incidents were to be such as will be found in every village and its vicinity where there is a meditative and feeling mind to seek after them, or to notice them when they present themselves.

In this idea originated the plan of the *Lyrical Ballads*; in which it was agreed that my endeavours should be directed to persons and characters supernatural, or at least romantic; yet so as to transfer from our inward nature a human interest and a semblance of truth sufficient to procure for these shadows of imagination that willing suspension of disbelief for the moment, which constitutes poetic faith. Mr. Wordsworth, on the other hand, was to propose to himself as his object to give the charm of novelty to things of every day, and to excite a feeling analogous to the supernatural, by awakening the mind's attention from the lethargy of custom and directing it to the loveliness and the wonders of the world before us; an inexhaustible treasure, but for which, in consequence of the film of familiarity and selfish

6. Coleridge conceives God's creation to be a continuing process, which has an analogy in the creative perception ("primary imagination") of all human minds. The creative process is repeated, or "echoed," on still a third level, by the "secondary imagination" of the poet, which dissolves the products of primary perception in order to shape them into a new and unified creation—the imaginative passage or poem. The "fancy," on the other hand, can only manipulate "fixities and definites" that, linked by association, come to it ready-made from perception. Its products, therefore, are not re-creations (echoes of God's original creative process) but mosaic-like reassemblies of existing bits and pieces.
7. Additional remarks, after a philosophic demonstration.
8. At Nether Stowey and Alfoxden, Somerset, in 1797.
9. Cf. Wordsworth's account in his Preface to *Lyrical Ballads* (p. 239).

solicitude, we have eyes yet see not, ears that hear not, and hearts that neither feel nor understand.[1]

With this view I wrote *The Ancient Mariner,* and was preparing, among other poems, *The Dark Ladie,* and the *Christabel,* in which I should have more nearly realized my ideal than I had done in my first attempt. But Mr. Wordsworth's industry had proved so much more successful and the number of his poems so much greater, that my compositions, instead of forming a balance, appeared rather an interpolation of heterogeneous matter.[2] Mr. Wordsworth added two or three poems written in his own character, in the impassioned, lofty, and sustained diction which is characteristic of his genius. In this form the *Lyrical Ballads* were published; and were presented by him, as an *experiment,*[3] whether subjects which from their nature rejected the usual ornaments and extra-colloquial style of poems in general might not be so managed in the language of ordinary life as to produce the pleasurable interest which it is the peculiar business of poetry to impart. To the second edition[4] he added a preface of considerable length; in which, notwithstanding some passages of apparently a contrary import, he was understood to contend for the extension of this style to poetry of all kinds, and to reject as vicious and indefensible all phrases and forms of style that were not included in what he (unfortunately, I think, adopting an equivocal expression) called the language of *real* life. From this preface, prefixed to poems in which it was impossible to deny the presence of original genius, however mistaken its direction might be deemed, arose the whole long-continued controversy.[5] For from the conjunction of perceived power with supposed heresy I explain the inveteracy and in some instances, I grieve to say, the acrimonious passions with which the controversy has been conducted by the assailants.

Had Mr. Wordsworth's poems been the silly, the childish things which they were for a long time described as being; had they been really distinguished from the compositions of other poets merely by meanness of language and inanity of thought; had they indeed contained nothing more than what is found in the parodies and pretended imitations of them; they must have sunk at once, a dead weight, into the slough of oblivion, and have dragged the preface along with them. But year after year increased the number of Mr. Wordsworth's admirers. They were found too not in the lower classes of the reading public, but chiefly among young men of strong sensibility and meditative minds; and their admiration (inflamed perhaps in some degree by opposition) was distinguished by its intensity, I might almost say, by its *religious* fervor. These facts, and the intellectual energy of the author, which was more or less consciously felt where it was outwardly and even boisterously denied, meeting with sentiments of aversion to his opinions and of alarm at their consequences, produced an eddy of criticism which would of itself have borne up the poems by the violence with which it whirled them round and round. With many parts of this preface, in the sense attributed to them and which the words undoubtedly seem to authorize, I never

---

1. Cf. Isaiah 6.9–10.
2. The first edition of *Lyrical Ballads,* published anonymously in 1798, contained nineteen poems by Wordsworth, four by Coleridge.
3. *Experiments* was the word used by Wordsworth

in his *Advertisement* to the first edition.
4. Published in 1800.
5. The controversy over Wordsworth's theory and poetical practice in the literary journals of the day.

concurred; but, on the contrary objected to them as erroneous in principle, and as contradictory (in appearance at least) both to other parts of the same preface and to the author's own practice in the greater number of the poems themselves. Mr. Wordsworth in his recent collection[6] has, I find, degraded this prefatory disquisition to the end of his second volume, to be read or not at the reader's choice. But he has not, as far as I can discover, announced any change in his poetic creed. At all events, considering it as the source of a controversy in which I have been honored more than I deserve by the frequent conjunction of my name with his, I think it expedient to declare once for all in what points I coincide with his opinions, and in what points I altogether differ. But in order to render myself intelligible I must previously, in as few words as possible, explain my ideas, first, of a POEM; and secondly, of POETRY itself, in *kind* and in *essence*.

The office of philosophical *disquisition* consists in just *distinction*; while it is the privilege of the philosopher to preserve himself constantly aware that distinction is not division. In order to obtain adequate notions of any truth, we must intellectually separate its distinguishable parts; and this is the technical *process* of philosophy. But having so done, we must then restore them in our conceptions to the unity in which they actually coexist; and this is the *result* of philosophy. A poem contains the same elements as a prose composition; the difference therefore must consist in a different combination of them, in consequence of a different object proposed. According to the difference of the object will be the difference of the combination. It is possible that the object may be merely to facilitate the recollection of any given facts or observations by artificial arrangement; and the composition will be a poem, merely because it is distinguished from prose by meter, or by rhyme, or by both conjointly. In this, the lowest sense, a man might attribute the name of a poem to the well-known enumeration of the days in the several months:

> Thirty days hath September,
> April, June, and November, etc.

and others of the same class and purpose. And as a particular pleasure is found in anticipating the recurrence of sounds and quantities, all compositions that have this charm superadded, whatever be their contents, *may* be entitled poems.

So much for the superficial *form*. A difference of object and contents supplies an additional ground of distinction. The immediate purpose may be the communication of truths; either of truth absolute and demonstrable, as in works of science; or of facts experienced and recorded, as in history. Pleasure, and that of the highest and most permanent kind, may *result* from the *attainment* of the end; but it is not itself the immediate end. In other works the communication of pleasure may be the immediate purpose; and though truth, either moral or intellectual, ought to be the *ultimate* end, yet this will distinguish the character of the author, not the class to which the work belongs. Blessed indeed is that state of society in which the immediate purpose would be baffled by the perversion of the proper ultimate end; in which

6. *Poems*, 2 vols., 1815.

no charm of diction or imagery could exempt the Bathyllus even of an Anacreon, or the Alexis of Virgil,[7] from disgust and aversion!

But the communication of pleasure may be the immediate object of a work not metrically composed; and that object may have been in a high degree attained, as in novels and romances. Would then the mere superaddition of meter, with or without rhyme, entitle *these* to the name of poems? The answer is that nothing can permanently please which does not contain in itself the reason why it is so, and not otherwise. If meter be superadded, all other parts must be made consonant with it. They must be such as to justify the perpetual and distinct attention to each part which an exact correspondent recurrence of accent and sound are calculated to excite. The final definition then, so deduced, may be thus worded. A poem is that species of composition which is opposed to works of science by proposing for its *immediate* object pleasure, not truth; and from all other species (having *this* object in common with it) it is discriminated by proposing to itself such delight from the *whole* as is compatible with a distinct gratification from each component *part*.

Controversy is not seldom excited in consequence of the disputants attaching each a different meaning to the same word; and in few instances has this been more striking than in disputes concerning the present subject. If a man chooses to call every composition a poem which is rhyme, or measure, or both, I must leave his opinion uncontroverted. The distinction is at least competent to characterize the writer's intention. If it were subjoined that the whole is likewise entertaining or affecting as a tale or as a series of interesting reflections, I of course admit this as another fit ingredient of a poem and an additional merit. But if the definition sought for be that of a *legitimate* poem, I answer it must be one the parts of which mutually support and explain each other; all in their proportion harmonizing with, and supporting the purpose and known influences of metrical arrangement. The philosophic critics of all ages coincide with the ultimate judgment of all countries in equally denying the praises of a just poem on the one hand to a series of striking lines or distichs,[8] each of which absorbing the whole attention of the reader to itself disjoins it from its context and makes it a separate whole, instead of a harmonizing part; and on the other hand, to an unsustained composition, from which the reader collects rapidly the general result unattracted by the component parts. The reader should be carried forward, not merely or chiefly by the mechanical impulse of curiosity, or by a restless desire to arrive at the final solution; but by the pleasurable activity of mind excited by the attractions of the journey itself. Like the motion of a serpent, which the Egyptians made the emblem of intellectual power; or like the path of sound through the air; at every step he pauses and half recedes, and from the retrogressive movement collects the force which again carries him onward. "*Praecipitandus est* liber *spiritus*,"[9] says Petronius Arbiter most happily. The epithet *liber* here balances the preceding verb; and it is not easy to conceive more meaning condensed in fewer words.

7. The reference is to poems of homosexual love. Bathyllus was a beautiful boy praised by Anacreon, a Greek lyric poet (ca. 560–475 B.C.E.); Alexis was a young man loved by the shepherd Corydon in Virgil's *Eclogue* 2.

8. Pairs of lines.
9. "The *free* spirit [of the poet] must be hurled onward." From the *Satyricon*, by the lively Roman satirist Petronius Arbiter (1st century C.E.).

But if this should be admitted as a satisfactory character of a poem, we have still to seek for a definition of poetry. The writings of Plato, and Bishop Taylor, and the *Theoria Sacra* of Burnet,[1] furnish undeniable proofs that poetry of the highest kind may exist without meter, and even without the contradistinguishing objects of a poem. The first chapter of Isaiah (indeed a very large proportion of the whole book) is poetry in the most emphatic sense; yet it would be not less irrational than strange to assert that pleasure, and not truth, was the immediate object of the prophet. In short, whatever *specific* import we attach to the word poetry, there will be found involved in it, as a necessary consequence, that a poem of any length neither can be, nor ought to be, all poetry.[2] Yet if a harmonious whole is to be produced, the remaining parts must be preserved in *keeping* with the poetry; and this can be no otherwise effected than by such a studied selection and artificial arrangement as will partake of *one*, though not a *peculiar*, property of poetry. And this again can be no other than the property of exciting a more continuous and equal attention than the language of prose aims at, whether colloquial or written.

My own conclusions on the nature of poetry, in the strictest use of the word, have been in part anticipated in the preceding disquisition on the fancy and imagination. What is poetry? is so nearly the same question with, what is a poet? that the answer to the one is involved in the solution of the other. For it is a distinction resulting from the poetic genius itself, which sustains and modifies the images, thoughts, and emotions of the poet's own mind.

The poet, described in *ideal* perfection, brings the whole soul of man into activity, with the subordination of its faculties to each other, according to their relative worth and dignity. He diffuses a tone and spirit of unity that blends and (as it were) *fuses*, each into each, by that synthetic and magical power to which we have exclusively appropriated the name of imagination. This power, first put in action by the will and understanding and retained under their irremissive, though gentle and unnoticed, control (*laxis effertur habenis*)[3] reveals itself in the balance or reconciliation of opposite or discordant qualities:[4] of sameness, with difference; of the general, with the concrete; the idea, with the image; the individual, with the representative; the sense of novelty and freshness, with old and familiar objects; a more than usual state of emotion, with more than usual order; judgment ever awake and steady self-possession, with enthusiasm and feeling profound or vehement; and while it blends and harmonizes the natural and the artificial, still subordinates art to nature; the manner to the matter; and our admiration of the poet to our sympathy with the poetry. "Doubtless," as Sir John Davies observes of the soul (and his words may with slight alteration be applied, and even more appropriately, to the poetic IMAGINATION):

1. Thomas Burnet (1635?–1715), author of *The Sacred Theory of the Earth*. Bishop Jeremy Taylor (1613–1667), author of *Holy Living* and *Holy Dying*. Coleridge greatly admired the elaborate and sonorous prose of both these writers. He took from a work by Burnet the Latin motto for *The Rime of the Ancient Mariner*.
2. Coleridge does not use the word *poetry* in the usual way, as a term for the class of all metrical compositions, or of all "poems," but to designate those passages, whether in verse or prose, produced by the mind of genius in its supreme moments of imaginative activity.
3. Driven with loosened reins (Latin).
4. Here Coleridge introduces the concept that the highest poetry incorporates and reconciles opposite or discordant elements. Under the names of "irony" and "paradox," this concept became a primary criterion of the American New Critics.

Doubtless this could not be, but that she turns
   Bodies to spirit by sublimation strange,
As fire converts to fire the things it burns,
   As we our food into our nature change.

From their gross matter she abstracts their forms,
   And draws a kind of quintessence from things;
Which to her proper nature she transforms,
   To bear them light on her celestial wings.

Thus does she, when from individual states
   She doth abstract the universal kinds;
Which then reclothed in divers names and fates
   Steal access through our senses to our minds.[5]

Finally, GOOD SENSE is the BODY of poetic genius, FANCY its DRAPERY, MOTION its LIFE, and IMAGINATION the SOUL that is everywhere, and in each; and forms all into one graceful and intelligent whole.

From *Chapter 17*

[EXAMINATION OF THE TENETS PECULIAR TO MR. WORDSWORTH]

As far then as Mr. Wordsworth in his preface contended, and most ably contended, for a reformation in our poetic diction, as far as he has envinced the truth of passion, and the *dramatic* propriety of those figures and metaphors in the original poets which, stripped of their justifying reasons and converted into mere artifices of connection or ornament, constitute the characteristic falsity in the poetic style of the moderns; and as far as he has, with equal acuteness and clearness, pointed out the process by which this change was effected and the resemblances between that state into which the reader's mind is thrown by the pleasurable confusion of thought from an unaccustomed train of words and images and that state which is induced by the natural language of impassioned feeling, he undertook a useful task and deserves all praise, both for the attempt and for the execution. The provocations to this remonstrance in behalf of truth and nature were still of perpetual recurrence before and after the publication of this preface. * * *

My own differences from certain supposed parts of Mr. Wordsworth's theory ground themselves on the assumption that his words had been rightly interpreted, as purporting that the proper diction for poetry in general consists altogether in a language taken, with due exceptions, from the mouths of men in real life, a language which actually constitutes the natural conversation of men under the influence of natural feelings.[6] My objection is, first, that in *any* sense this rule is applicable only to *certain* classes of poetry; secondly, that even to these classes it is not applicable, except in such a sense as hath never by anyone (as far as I know or have read) been denied or doubted; and, lastly, that as far as, and in that degree in which it is

---

5. Adapted from John Davies's *Nosce Teipsum* ("Know Thyself"), a philosophical poem (1599).
6. Wordsworth's Preface to *Lyrical Ballads* (1800): "A selection of the real language of men in a state of vivid sensation. . . . Low and rustic life was generally chosen. . . . The language, too, of these men is adopted."

practicable, yet as a *rule* it is useless, if not injurious, and therefore either need not or ought not to be practiced. * * *

[RUSTIC LIFE (ABOVE ALL, *LOW* AND RUSTIC LIFE) ESPECIALLY UNFAVORABLE TO THE FORMATION OF A HUMAN DICTION—THE BEST PARTS OF LANGUAGE THE PRODUCTS OF PHILOSOPHERS, NOT CLOWNS[7] OR SHEPHERDS]

As little can I agree with the assertion that from the objects with which the rustic hourly communicates the best part of language is formed. For first, if to communicate with an object implies such an acquaintance with it, as renders it capable of being discriminately reflected on; the distinct knowledge of an uneducated rustic would furnish a very scanty vocabulary. The few things, and modes of action, requisite for his bodily conveniences, would alone be individualized; while all the rest of nature would be expressed by a small number of confused general terms. Secondly, I deny that the words and combinations of words derived from the objects, with which the rustic is familiar, whether with distinct or confused knowledge, can be justly said to form the *best* part of language. It is more than probable that many classes of the brute creation possess discriminating sounds, by which they can convey to each other notices of such objects as concern their food, shelter, or safety. Yet we hesitate to call the aggregate of such sounds a language, otherwise than metaphorically. The best part of human language, properly so called, is derived from reflection on the acts of the mind itself. It is formed by a voluntary appropriation of fixed symbols to internal acts, to processes and results of imagination, the greater part of which have no place in the consciousness of uneducated man; though in civilized society, by imitation and passive remembrance of what they hear from their religious instructors and other superiors, the most uneducated share in the harvest which they neither sowed or reaped. * * *

[THE LANGUAGE OF MILTON AS MUCH THE LANGUAGE OF *REAL* LIFE, YEA, INCOMPARABLY MORE SO THAN THAT OF THE COTTAGER]

Here let me be permitted to remind the reader that the positions which I controvert are contained in the sentences—"a selection of the REAL language of men"; "the language of these men (i.e., men in low and rustic life) I propose to myself to imitate, and as far as possible to adopt the very language of men." "Between the language of prose and that of metrical composition there neither is, nor can be any essential difference." It is against these exclusively that my opposition is directed.

I object, in the very first instance, to an equivocation in the use of the word "real." Every man's language varies according to the extent of his knowledge, the activity of his faculties, and the depth or quickness of his feelings. Every man's language has, first, its *individualities;* secondly, the common properties of the *class* to which he belongs; and thirdly, words and phrases of *universal* use. The language of Hooker, Bacon, Bishop Taylor, and Burke

7. Rustic people.

differs from the common language of the learned class only by the superior number and novelty of the thoughts and relations which they had to convey. The language of Algernon Sidney[8] differs not at all from that which every well-educated gentleman would wish to write, and (with due allowances for the undeliberateness and less connected train of thinking natural and proper to conversation) such as he would wish to talk. Neither one nor the other differ half as much from the general language of cultivated society as the language of Mr. Wordsworth's homeliest composition differs from that of a common peasant. For "real" therefore we must substitute *ordinary*, or *lingua communis*.[9] And this, we have proved, is no more to be found in the phraseology of low and rustic life than in that of any other class. Omit the peculiarities of each, and the result of course must be common to all. And assuredly the omissions and changes to be made in the language of rustics before it could be transferred to any species of poem, except the drama or other professed imitation, are at least as numerous and weighty as would be required in adapting to the same purpose the ordinary language of tradesmen and manufacturers. Not to mention that the language so highly extolled by Mr. Wordsworth varies in every county, nay, in every village, according to the accidental character of the clergyman, the existence or nonexistence of schools; or even, perhaps, as the exciseman, publican, or barber happen to be, or not to be, zealous politicians and readers of the weekly newspaper *pro bono publico*.[1] Anterior to cultivation the *lingua communis* of every country, as Dante has well observed, exists every where in parts and no where as a whole.[2]

Neither is the case rendered at all more tenable by the addition of the words "in a state of excitement."[3] For the nature of a man's words, when he is strongly affected by joy, grief, or anger, must necessarily depend on the number and quality of the general truths, conceptions, and images, and of the words expressing them, with which his mind had been previously stored. For the property of passion is not to *create*, but to set in increased activity. At least, whatever new connections of thoughts or images, or (which is equally, if not more than equally, the appropriate effect of strong excitement) whatever generalizations of truth or experience the heat of passion may produce, yet the terms of their conveyance must have pre-existed in his former conversations, and are only collected and crowded together by the unusual stimulation. It is indeed very possible to adopt in a poem the unmeaning repetitions, habitual phrases, and other blank counters which an unfurnished or confused understanding interposes at short intervals in order to keep hold of his subject which is still slipping from him, and to give him time for recollection; or in mere aid of vacancy, as in the scanty companies of a country stage the same player pops backwards and forwards, in order to prevent the appearance of empty spaces, in the procession of *Macbeth* or *Henry VIIIth*. But what assistance to the poet or ornament to the poem these can supply, I am at a loss to conjecture. Nothing assuredly can differ either in origin or in mode more widely from the apparent tautologies of intense

8. Republican soldier and statesmen (1622–1683), author of *Discourses Concerning Government*.
9. The common language (Latin).
1. For the public welfare (Latin).

2. In *De vulgari eloquentia* (On the speech of the people) Dante discusses—and affirms—the fitness for poetry of the unlocalized Italian vernacular.
3. Wordsworth: "the manner in which we associate ideas in a state of excitement."

and turbulent feeling in which the passion is greater and of longer endurance than to be exhausted or satisfied by a single representation of the image or incident exciting it. Such repetitions I admit to be a beauty of the highest kind; as illustrated by Mr. Wordsworth himself from the song of Deborah. "At her feet he bowed, he fell, he lay down; at her feet he bowed, he fell; where he bowed, there he fell down dead."[4]

1815   1817

From Lectures on Shakespeare[1]

[FANCY AND IMAGINATION IN SHAKESPEARE'S POETRY]

In the preceding lecture we have examined with what armor clothed and with what titles authorized Shakespeare came forward as a poet to demand the throne of fame as the dramatic poet of England; we have now to observe and retrace the excellencies which compelled even his contemporaries to seat him on that throne, although there were giants in those days contending for the same honor. Hereafter we shall endeavor to make out the title of the English drama, as created by and existing in Shakespeare, and its right to the supremacy of dramatic excellence in general. I have endeavored to prove that he had shown himself a *poet*, previously to his appearance as a dramatic poet—and that had no *Lear*, no *Othello*, no *Henry the Fourth*, no *Twelfth Night* appeared, we must have admitted that Shakespeare possessed the chief if not all the requisites of a poet—namely, deep feeling and exquisite sense of beauty, both as exhibited to the eye in combinations of form, and to the ear in sweet and appropriate melody (with the exception of Spenser he is [the sweetest of English poets]); that these feelings were under the command of *his own will*—that in his very first productions he projected his mind out of his own particular being, and felt and made others feel, on subjects [in] no way connected with himself, except by force of contemplation, and that sublime faculty, by which a great mind becomes that which it meditates on. To this we are to add the affectionate love of nature and natural objects, without which no man could have observed so steadily, or painted so truly and passionately the very minutest beauties of the external world. Next, we have shown that he possessed fancy, considered as the faculty of bringing together images dissimilar in the main by some one point or more of likeness distinguished.[2]

> Full gently now she takes him by the hand,
> A lily prisoned in a jail of snow,

4. Judges 5.27. Cited by Wordsworth in a note to *The Thorn* as an example of the natural tautology of "impassioned feelings."
1. Although Coleridge's series of public lectures on Shakespeare and other poets contained much of his best criticism, he published none of this material, leaving only fragmentary remains of his lectures in notebooks, scraps of manuscript, and notes written in the margins of books. The following selections, which develop some of the principal ideas presented in *Biographia Literaria*, reproduce the text of T. M. Raysor's edition—based on Coleridge's manuscripts and on contemporary reports—

of *Coleridge's Shakespearean Criticism* (1930); four minor corrections in wording have been taken from R. A. Foakes's edition of Coleridge's *Lectures 1808–1819: On Literature* (1987).
2. Coleridge here applies the distinction between fancy and imagination presented in *Biographia Literaria*, chap. 13. This passage from the narrative poem *Venus and Adonis* (lines 361–64) is an instance of fancy because the elements brought together remain an assemblage of recognizable and independent "fixities and definites," despite the isolated points of likeness which form the grounds of the comparison.

> Or ivory in an alabaster band—
> So white a friend engirts so white a foe.

Still mounting, we find undoubted proof in his mind of imagination, or the power by which one image or feeling is made to modify many others and by a sort of *fusion to force many into one*—that which after showed itself in such might and energy in *Lear*, where the deep anguish of a father spreads the feeling of ingratitude and cruelty over the very elements of heaven. Various are the workings of this greatest faculty of the human mind—both passionate and tranquil. In its tranquil and purely pleasurable operation, it acts chiefly by producing out of many things, as they would have appeared in the description of an ordinary mind, described slowly and in unimpassioned succession, a oneness, even as nature, the greatest of poets, acts upon us when we open our eyes upon an extended prospect. Thus the flight of Adonis from the enamored goddess in the dusk of evening—

> Look how a bright star shooteth from the sky—
> So glides he in the night from Venus' eye.[3]

How many images and feelings are here brought together without effort and without discord—the beauty of Adonis—the rapidity of his flight—the yearning yet hopelessness of the enamored gazer—and a shadowy ideal character thrown over the whole.[4]—Or it acts by impressing the stamp of humanity, of human feeling, over inanimate objects * * *

> Lo, here the gentle lark, weary of rest,
> From his moist cabinet mounts up on high
> And wakes the morning, from whose silver breast
> The sun ariseth in his majesty;
> Who doth the world so gloriously behold
> That cedar tops and hills seem burnished gold.

And lastly, which belongs only to a great poet, the power of so carrying on the eye of the reader as to make him almost lose the consciousness of words—to make him *see* everything—and this without exciting any painful or laborious attention, without any *anatomy* of description (a fault not uncommon in descriptive poetry) but with the sweetness and easy movement of nature.

Lastly, he previously to his dramas, gave proof of a most profound, energetic, and philosophical mind, without which he might have been a very delightful poet, but not the great dramatic poet. * * * But chance and his powerful instinct combined to lead him to his proper province—in the conquest of which we are to consider both the difficulties that opposed him, and the advantages.

1808

---

3. *Venus and Adonis*, lines 815–16.
4. This passage is an instance of imagination, Coleridge claims, because the component parts— the shooting star and the flight of Adonis, together with the feelings with which both are perceived— dissolve into a new and seamless unity, different in character from the sum of its parts. In the following instance (lines 853–58), the imagination is claimed to fuse the neutral and inanimate objects with the human nature and feelings of the observer.

[MECHANIC VS. ORGANIC FORM][5]

The subject of the present lecture is no less than a question submitted to your understandings, emancipated from national prejudice: Are the plays of Shakespeare works of rude uncultivated genius, in which the splendor of the parts compensates, if aught can compensate, for the barbarous shapelessness and irregularity of the whole? To which not only the French critics, but even his own English admirers, say [yes]. Or is the form equally admirable with the matter, the judgment of the great poet not less deserving of our wonder than his genius? Or to repeat the question in other words, is Shakespeare a great dramatic poet on account only of those beauties and excellencies which he possesses in common with the ancients, but with diminished claims to our love and honor to the full extent of his difference from them? Or are these very differences additional proofs of poetic wisdom, at once results and symbols of living power as contrasted with lifeless mechanism, of free and rival originality as contradistinguished from servile imitation, or more accurately, [from] a blind copying of effects instead of a true imitation of the essential principles? Imagine not I am about to oppose genius to rules. No! the comparative value of these rules is the very cause to be tried. The spirit of poetry, like all other living powers, must of necessity circumscribe itself by rules, were it only to unite power with beauty. It must embody in order to reveal itself; but a living body is of necessity an organized one—and what is organization but the connection of parts to a whole, so that each part is at once end and means! This is no discovery of criticism; it is a necessity of the human mind—and all nations have felt and obeyed it, in the invention of meter and measured sounds as the vehicle and involucrum[6] of poetry, itself a fellow growth from the same life, even as the bark is to the tree.

No work of true genius dare want its appropriate form; neither indeed is there any danger of this. As it must not, so neither can it, be lawless! For it is even this that constitutes its genius—the power of acting creatively under laws of its own origination. How then comes it that not only single Zoili,[7] but whole nations have combined in unhesitating condemnation of our great dramatist, as a sort of African nature, fertile in beautiful monsters, as a wild heath where islands of fertility look greener from the surrounding waste, where the loveliest plants now shine out among unsightly weeds and now are choked by their parasitic growth, so intertwined that we cannot disentangle the weed without snapping the flower. In this statement I have had no reference to the vulgar abuse of Voltaire,[8] save as far as his charges are coincident with the decisions of his commentators and (so they tell you) his almost idolatrous admirers. The true ground of the mistake, as has been well

---

5. Coleridge is opposing the earlier view that, because he violates the critical "rules" based on classical drama, Shakespeare is a highly irregular dramatist whose occasional successes are the result of innate and untutored genius, operating without artistry or judgment. Coleridge's refutation is based on his distinction between the "mechanical form" conceived by neoclassical criticism and "organic form." Mechanical form results from imposing a pattern of preexisting rules on the literary material. Shakespeare's organic form, on the other hand, evolves like a plant by an inner principle, according not to rules but to the laws of its own growth, until it achieves an organic unity—a living interdependence of parts and whole in which, as Coleridge says, "each part is at once end and means." The concept of "organic form," in one or another interpretation, became a cardinal principle in much 20th-century criticism.
6. Outer covering of part of a plant.
7. Plural of "Zoilus," who in classical times was the standard example of a bad critic.
8. Voltaire (1694–1778) wrote critiques treating Shakespeare as a barbarous, irregular, and sometimes indecent natural genius.

remarked by a continental critic,[9] lies in the confounding mechanical regularity with organic form. The form is mechanic when on any given material we impress a predetermined form, not necessarily arising out of the properties of the material, as when to a mass of wet clay we give whatever shape we wish it to retain when hardened. The organic form, on the other hand, is innate; it shapes as it develops itself from within, and the fullness of its development is one and the same with the perfection of its outward form. Such is the life, such the form. Nature, the prime genial[1] artist, inexhaustible in diverse powers, is equally inexhaustible in forms. Each exterior is the physiognomy of the being within, its true image reflected and thrown out from the concave mirror. And even such is the appropriate excellence of her chosen poet, of our own Shakespeare, himself a nature humanized, a genial understanding directing self-consciously a power and an implicit wisdom deeper than consciousness.[2]

1812   1930

From The Statesman's Manual

[ON SYMBOL AND ALLEGORY][1]

The histories and political economy[2] of the present and preceding century partake in the general contagion of its mechanic philosophy, and are the *product* of an unenlivened generalizing Understanding. In the Scriptures they are the living *educts*[3] of the Imagination; of that reconciling and mediatory power, which incorporating the Reason in Images of the Sense, and organizing (as it were) the flux of the Senses by the permanence and self-circling energies of the Reason, gives birth to a system of symbols, harmonious in themselves, and consubstantial with the truths, of which they are the *conductors*. These are the Wheels which Ezekiel beheld, when the hand of the Lord was upon him, and he saw visions of God as he sat among the captives by the river of Chebar. *Whithersoever the Spirit was to go, the wheels went, and thither was their spirit to go: for the spirit of the living creature was in the wheels also.*[4] The truths and the symbols that represent them move in conjunction and form the living chariot that bears up (for *us*) the throne of the Divine Humanity. Hence, by a derivative, indeed, but not a divided, influence, and though in a secondary yet in more than a metaphorical sense,

9. August Wilhelm Schlegel, German critic and literary historian, whose *Lectures on Dramatic Art and Literature* (1808–09) proposed the distinction between mechanical and organic form that Coleridge develops in this lecture.
1. The adjectival form of *genius*.
2. I.e., the organic process of the imagination is in part unconscious.
1. Coleridge published *The Statesman's Manual, or The Bible the Best Guide to Political Skill and Foresight* in 1816; it was intended to show that the Scriptures, properly interpreted, provide the universal principles that should guide lawmakers in meeting the political and economic emergencies of that troubled era. His discussion there of symbol, in contradistinction both to allegory and to metaphor, has been often cited and elaborated in recent treatments of symbolism in poetry. Coleridge's

analysis, however, is specifically directed not to poetry but to his view that the persons and events in biblical history signify timeless and universal, as well as particular and local, truths and that in God's created nature, each element and power is in essential interrelation with the whole that is manifested within that part.
2. Economic theory.
3. Those things that are educed—i.e., brought forth, evolved.
4. Slightly altered from the prophet Ezekiel's vision of the Chariot of God, when he had been "among the captives by the river of Chebar" (Ezekiel 1.1–20). Ezekiel was among the Jews who had been taken into captivity in Babylonia by King Nebuchadnezzar in 597 B.C.E. He was put in a community of Jewish captives at Tel-Abib on the banks of the Chebar canal.

the Sacred Book is worthily intitled *the* WORD OF GOD. Hence too, its contents present to us the stream of time continuous as Life and a symbol of Eternity, inasmuch as the Past and the Future are virtually contained in the Present. According therefore to our relative position on its banks the Sacred History becomes prophetic, the Sacred Prophecies historical, while the power and substance of both inhere in its Laws, its Promises, and its Comminations.[5] In the Scriptures therefore both Facts and Persons must of necessity have a twofold significance, a past and a future, a temporary and a perpetual, a particular and a universal application. They must be at once Portraits and Ideals.

Eheu! paupertina philosophia in paupertinam religionem ducit:[6]—A hunger-bitten and idea-less philosophy naturally produces a starveling and comfortless religion. It is among the miseries of the present age that it recognizes no medium between *Literal* and *Metaphorical*. Faith is either to be buried in the dead letter,[7] or its name and honors usurped by a counterfeit product of the mechanical understanding, which in the blindness of self-complacency confounds SYMBOLS with ALLEGORIES. Now an Allegory is but a translation of abstract notions into a picture-language which is itself nothing but an abstraction from objects of the senses; the principal being more worthless even than its phantom proxy, both alike unsubstantial, and the former shapeless to boot. On the other hand a Symbol (ὁ ἔστιν ἄει ταυτηγόρικον)[8] is characterized by a translucence of the Special[9] in the Individual or of the General in the Especial or of the Universal in the General. Above all by the translucence of the Eternal through and in the Temporal. It always partakes of the Reality which it renders intelligible; and while it enunciates the whole, abides itself as a living part in that Unity, of which it is the representative. The other are but empty echoes which the fancy arbitrarily associates with apparitions of matter, less beautiful but not less shadowy than the sloping orchard or hillside pasture-field seen in the transparent lake below. Alas! for the flocks that are to be led forth to such pastures! *"It shall even be as when the hungry dreameth, and behold! he eateth; but he waketh and his soul is empty: or as when the thirsty dreameth, and behold he drinketh; but he awaketh and is faint!"*[1] * * *

* * * The fact therefore, that the mind of man in its own primary and constitutional forms represents the laws of nature, is a mystery which of itself should suffice to make us religious:[2] for it is a problem of which God is the only solution, God, the one before all, and of all, and through all!—True natural philosophy is comprised in the study of the science and language of *symbols*. The power delegated to nature is all in every part: and by a symbol I mean, not a metaphor or allegory or any other figure of speech or form of fancy, but an actual and essential part of that, the whole of which it represents. Thus our Lord speaks symbolically when he says that "the eye is the light of the body."[3] The genuine naturalist is a dramatic poet in his own line:

---

5. Divine threats of punishment for sins.
6. Alas! a poverty-stricken philosophy leads to a poverty-stricken religion (Latin).
7. I.e., the Scriptures read entirely literally.
8. Which is always tautegorical (Greek). Coleridge coined this word and elsewhere defined "*tautegorical*" as "expressing the *same* subject but with a

difference."
9. That which pertains to the species.
1. Slightly altered from Isaiah 29.8.
2. This paragraph is from appendix C of *The Statesman's Manual*.
3. Matthew 6.22: "The light of the body is the eye."

and such as our myriad-minded Shakespeare is, compared with the Racines and Metastasios,[4] such and by a similar process of self-transformation would the man be, compared with the Doctors of the mechanic school,[5] who should construct his physiology on the heaven-descended, Know Thyself.[6]

[THE SATANIC HERO][7]

* * * In its state of immanence (or indwelling) in reason and religion, the WILL appears indifferently, as wisdom or as love: two names of the same power, the former more intelligential,[8] the latter more spiritual, the former more frequent in the Old, the latter in the New Testament. But in its utmost abstraction and consequent state of reprobation,[9] the Will becomes satanic pride and rebellious self-idolatry in the relations of the spirit to itself, and remorseless despotism relatively to others; the more hopeless as the more obdurate by its subjugation of sensual impulses, by its superiority to toil and pain and pleasure; in short, by the fearful resolve to find in itself alone the one absolute motive of action, under which all other motives from within and from without must be either subordinated or crushed.

This is the character which Milton has so philosophically as well as sublimely embodied in the Satan of his Paradise Lost. Alas! too often has it been embodied in *real* life! Too often has it given a dark and savage grandeur to the historic page! And wherever it has appeared, under whatever circumstances of time and country, the same ingredients have gone to its composition; and it has been identified by the same attributes. Hope in which there is no Cheerfulness; Steadfastness within and immovable Resolve, with outward Restlessness and whirling Activity; Violence with Guile; Temerity with Cunning; and, as the result of all, Interminableness of Object with perfect Indifference of Means; these are the qualities that have constituted the COMMANDING GENIUS! these are the Marks that have characterized the Masters of Mischief, the Liberticides, and mighty Hunters of Mankind, from NIMROD[1] to NAPOLEON. And from inattention to the possibility of such a character as well as from ignorance of its elements, even men of honest intentions too frequently become fascinated. Nay, whole nations have been so far duped by this want of insight and reflection as to regard with palliative admiration, instead of wonder and abhorrence, the Molochs[2] of human nature, who are indebted, for the far larger portion of their meteoric success, to their total

---

4. Pietro Metastasio (1698–1782), a minor Italian poet and author of opera librettos. Jean Racine (1639–1699), the great French author of verse tragedies. Coleridge delighted in derogating French philosophy and culture, venting what he called his "Gall contra Gallois"—his gall against the Gauls. "Naturalist": one who studies natural science.
5. I.e., learned men who hold a mechanistic philosophy of nature.
6. The Roman Juvenal, in *Satires* 11.27 of Horace (Quintas Horatius Flaccus), had said that "From Heaven it descends, 'Know Thyself.' " The original saying, "Know Thyself," was attributed by classical authors to the Delphic oracle.
7. From *The Statesman's Manual*, appendix C. Coleridge analyzes the character of Milton's Satan

and goes on to recognize, and to warn his age against, the appeal of that type of Romantic hero (exemplified above all by the protagonists in Byron's romances and in his drama, *Manfred*), which was in large part modeled on the Satan of *Paradise Lost*.
8. Intellectual.
9. In its theological sense: rejection by God.
1. In Genesis 10.9 Nimrod is described as "a mighty hunter before the Lord." The passage was traditionally interpreted to signify that Nimrod hunted down men, hence that he was the prototype of all tyrants and bloody conquerors.
2. Molochs, monsters of evil. In the Old Testament Moloch is an idol to whom firstborn children are sacrificed. Milton adopted the name for the warlike fallen angel (see *Paradise Lost* 2.43–107).

want of principle, and who surpass the generality of their fellow creatures in one act of courage only, that of daring to say with their whole heart, "Evil, be thou my good!"[3]—All *system* so far is power; and a *systematic* criminal, self-consistent and entire in wickedness, who entrenches villainy within villainy, and barricades crime by crime, has removed a world of obstacles by the mere decision, that he will have no obstacles, but those of force and brute matter.

1816

3. Spoken by Satan, *Paradise Lost* 4.110.

WALTER SAVAGE LANDOR
1775–1864

Walter Savage Landor was born well-to-do and with a violently independent and combative temper. He quarreled with the authorities at Rugby and Oxford, with his wife and family, with servants and officials, with the governments of Europe (he was a revolutionary sympathizer, and unlike most of his literary contemporaries never wavered in his republicanism), and with his neighbors, first in Wales and then in Italy; he was constantly embroiled in expensive litigation. But in the course of his long life, the generous-hearted and outspoken poet also acquired many friends and admirers, ranging from Robert Southey and William Hazlitt in the Romantic period to Robert Browning, Charles Dickens, and Algernon Charles Swinburne among the Victorians. He lived in Italy from 1815 to 1835. When he returned to England he was lionized for a time as an active Romantic poet when all the others were dead or silent; but a violent outburst, which led to court action, forced him in 1857 to take up once more his exile in Italy, where he died in his ninetieth year.

Most of the writings of this greatly irascible man, whether in prose or verse, have characteristics to which critics apply the terms *serene* and *marmoreal* (marblelike). His best-known prose works are the numerous *Imaginary Conversations* (1824–53), mainly between historical figures and on literary, philosophic, and political topics. These have their admirers, but they are written in a style so elevated and remote that they sometimes suggest dialogues between heroic-size Greek statues. He wrote many long narrative and dramatic poems, of which the most durable is the epic *Gebir*, published in 1798, the same year as Wordsworth and Coleridge's *Lyrical Ballads*. But Landor's best achievement, in which he emulated Greek and Roman models, is in the short lyric, usually an elegy or a courtly compliment that is stripped down until it approximates an epigram. He is master of the spare, elegant, and severely formal utterance of lyric feelings.

Mother, I cannot mind my wheel

Mother, I cannot mind my wheel;
   My fingers ache, my lips are dry:
Oh! if you felt the pain I feel!
But oh, who ever felt as I!

5   No longer could I doubt him true,
    All other men may use deceit;
    He always said my eyes were blue,
    And often swore my lips were sweet.

1806

Rose Aylmer[1]

Ah, what avails the sceptered race,
    Ah, what the form divine!
What every virtue, every grace!
    Rose Aylmer, all were thine.

5   Rose Aylmer, whom these wakeful eyes
    May weep, but never see,
A night of memories and of sighs
    I consecrate to thee

1806

Past ruined Ilion

Past ruined Ilion Helen[1] lives,
    Alcestis rises from the shades;[2]
Verse calls them forth; 'tis verse that gives
    Immortal youth to mortal maids.

5   Soon shall oblivion's deepening veil
    Hide all the peopled hills you see,
The gay, the proud, while lovers hail
    These many summers you and me.

The tear for fading beauty check,
10   For passing glory cease to sigh;
One form shall rise above the wreck,
    One name, Ianthe, shall not die.

1831

Twenty years hence

Twenty years hence my eyes may grow
    If not quite dim, yet rather so,
Still yours from others they shall know
    Twenty years hence.

---

1. The daughter of the fourth Baron Aylmer
(hence "the sceptered race," line 1). She became
a friend of Landor's in 1794 at the age of seventeen
and died suddenly in Calcutta, six years later.

1. Helen of Troy ("Ilion").
2. Alcestis gave her own life in exchange for that
of her husband but was rescued from Hades ("the
shades") by Hercules.

⁵ Twenty years hence though it may hap
That I be called to take a nap
In a cool cell where thunderclap
    Was never heard,

There breathe but o'er my arch of grass
¹⁰ A not too sadly sighed *Alas*,
And I shall catch, ere you can pass,
    That wingèd word.

1846

CHARLES LAMB
1775–1834

Charles Lamb was a near contemporary of Wordsworth and Coleridge; he numbered these two poets among his close friends, published his own early poems in combination with those of Coleridge in 1796 and 1797, and supported the *Lyrical Ballads* and some of the other avant-garde poetry of his time. Yet Lamb lacks almost all the traits and convictions we think of as characteristically "Romantic." He happily lived all his life in the city and its environs, sharing Samuel Johnson's opinion that he who tires of London tires of life. He could not abide Shelley or his poetry, and he distrusted Coleridge's supernaturalism and Wordsworth's oracular sublimities and religion of nature, preferring those elements in their poems that were human and realistic. In an age when many of the important writers were fervent radicals and some became equally fervent reactionaries, Lamb remained uncommitted in both politics and religion, and although on intimate terms with such dedicated reformers as William Hazlitt, William Godwin, Thomas Holcroft, and Leigh Hunt, he chose them as friends, as he said, not for their opinions but "for some individuality of character which they manifested." In his own writings the one attribute he shared with his great contemporaries was that of *l'étalage du moi,* "the display of one's own personality": many of his best familiar essays, like Wordsworth's poems, are made up of his early experiences and feelings, recollected in tranquility. But, although the expression of private experiences in a personal poetry was a new and distinctive Romantic form, the personal essay was an established genre that had been developed by Montaigne as early as the sixteenth century.

    Lamb was born in London at the Inner Temple, where his father was clerk and assistant to a lawyer. At the age of seven he entered Christ's Hospital, the "Bluecoat School" of his essay *Christ's Hospital Five-and-Thirty Years Ago.* He left the school before he was fifteen and soon thereafter became a clerk in the accounting department of the East India Company, a huge commercial house, where he remained for thirty-three years. His adult life was quiet and unadventurous; but under its calm surface, as Walter Pater said, lay "something of the fateful domestic horror, of the beautiful heroism and devotedness too, of old Greek tragedy." When he was twenty-two his beloved sister, Mary, ten years his senior, broke down under the strain of caring for her invalid parents and stabbed her mother in the heart. Upon her recovery, Mary was released to the care of her brother, who devoted the rest of his life to her and to their common household. Mary's attacks recurred, briefly but periodically, and when the terribly familiar symptoms began to show themselves, Charles and Mary would walk arm in arm and weeping to the asylum, carrying a straitjacket with them.

Most of the time, however, Mary was her normally serene and gracious self, and shared her brother's love of company and genius for friendship. The Wednesday- (sometimes Thursday-) night gatherings at the Lambs' attracted a varied company that included many of the leading writers and artists of England. Charles drew furiously on a pipe of strong tobacco and drank copiously; as the alcohol eased his habitual stammer, his puns and practical jokes grew ever more outrageous. He had, in fact, a complex temperament, in which the playfulness overlay a somber melancholy and the freakishness sometimes manifested a touch of malice. To requests from Wordsworth and Coleridge for criticism of their poems he replied with a caustic candor not entirely appreciated by its beneficiaries, and he never encountered pretentiousness or complacency without puncturing it by a well-honed witticism. "What choice venom!" exclaimed his friend Hazlitt, an expert on the subject—but while Hazlitt managed to antagonize almost everyone by his outspokenness, few could take offense, and none could long sustain it, at Lamb's behavior.

To supplement his salary at the East India House, Lamb had early turned to writing in a variety of literary forms, including minor verse; a sentimental novel; a blank- verse tragedy; and a farce, *Mr. H——*, which was hissed by the audience (including the honest author) when it was produced at Drury Lane. He also collaborated with his sister, Mary, on an excellent children's book, *Tales from Shakespeare*, and wrote some brilliant critical commentaries in his anthology, important for the Elizabethan revival of that period, titled *Specimens of English Dramatic Poets Who Lived about the Time of Shakespeare*. Not until 1820, however, at the age of forty-five, did Lamb begin to contribute to the *London Magazine* the *Essays of Elia*, written in a uniquely distinctive style.

In the familiar essay, Lamb was able to exploit his major subject: himself and his connoisseurship of literature, people, and strong local attachments—"old chairs, old tables, streets, squares, where I have sunned myself, my old school." Under the pseudonym of an Italian clerk named Elia, whom he had known while briefly employed in the South Sea House, Lamb projects in his essays the character of a man who is whimsical but strong-willed, self-deprecating yet self-absorbed, a specialist in nostalgia and in that humor which balances delicately on the verge of pathos. His seemingly ingenuous self-revelation is, however, achieved by the cunning of a deliberate and dedicated artist in prose. He wrote, as he said, "for antiquity"; his prose style, like that of Edmund Spenser's in verse, is an invented style. Although its basis is plain modern English, it is colored throughout by archaic words, expressions, and turns of syntax. In the manner of earlier literary eccentrics such as Robert Burton and Laurence Sterne, Lamb delights in tricks of words and thought and in the elaborate exploration of a literary conceit. Close imitators of his style invariably fall into archness and sentimentality; Lamb's feat was to transform whimsy into a highly distinctive personal essay.

Christ's Hospital Five-and-Thirty Years Ago[1]

In Mr. Lamb's *Works*, published a year or two since, I find a magnificent eulogy on my old school, such as it was, or now appears to him to have been, between the years 1782 and 1789. It happens very oddly that my own standing at Christ's was nearly corresponding with his; and, with all gratitude to

1. Christ's Hospital, London (founded in 1552 by Edward VI), was run as a free boarding school for the sons of middle-class parents in straitened financial circumstances. Its students were known as "Bluecoat Boys," from their uniform of a long blue gown and yellow stockings. Lamb had in 1813 published a magazine article, *Recollections of*

Christ's Hospital, that the present essay undertakes to supplement by presenting the less formal side of school life. The "I" or narrator of the essay is Elia— a device that allows Lamb to combine his own circumstances and experiences with those of Coleridge, his older contemporary at the school.

him for his enthusiasm for the cloisters, I think he has contrived to bring together whatever can be said in praise of them, dropping all the other side of the argument most ingeniously.

I remember L. at school, and can well recollect that he had some peculiar advantages, which I and others of his schoolfellows had not. His friends lived in town, and were near at hand; and he had the privilege of going to see them almost as often as he wished, through some invidious distinction, which was denied to us. The present worthy subtreasurer to the Inner Temple[2] can explain how that happened. He had his tea and hot rolls in a morning, while we were battening upon our quarter of a penny loaf—our *crug*—moistened with attenuated small beer, in wooden piggins, smacking of the pitched leathern jack[3] it was poured from. Our Monday's milk porritch, blue and tasteless, and the pease soup of Saturday, coarse and choking, were enriched for him with a slice of "extraordinary bread and butter," from the hot loaf of the Temple. The Wednesday's mess of millet, somewhat less repugnant—(we had three banyan to four meat days[4] in the week)—was endeared to his palate with a lump of double-refined, and a smack of ginger (to make it go down the more glibly) or the fragrant cinnamon. In lieu of our *half-pickled* Sundays, or *quite fresh* boiled beef on Thursdays (strong as *caro equina*[5]), with detestable marigolds floating in the pail to poison the broth—our scanty mutton scrags on Friday—and rather more savory, but grudging, portions of the same flesh, rotten-roasted[6] or rare, on the Tuesdays (the only dish which excited our appetites, and disappointed our stomachs, in almost equal proportion)—he had his hot plate of roast veal, or the more tempting griskin[7] (exotics unknown to our palates), cooked in the paternal kitchen (a great thing), and brought him daily by his maid or aunt! I remember the good old relative (in whom love forbade pride) squatting down upon some odd stone in a by-nook of the cloisters, disclosing the viands (of higher regale than those cates which the ravens ministered to the Tishbite);[8] and the contending passions of L. at the unfolding. There was love for the bringer; shame for the thing brought, and the manner of its bringing; sympathy for those who were too many to share in it; and, at top of all, hunger (eldest, strongest of the passions!) predominant, breaking down the stony fences of shame, and awkwardness, and a troubling over-consciousness.

I was a poor friendless boy. My parents, and those who should care for me, were far away. Those few acquaintances of theirs, which they could reckon upon being kind to me in the great city, after a little forced notice, which they had the grace to take of me on my first arrival in town, soon grew tired of my holiday visits. They seemed to them to recur too often, though I thought them few enough; and, one after another, they all failed me, and I felt myself alone among six hundred playmates.

O the cruelty of separating a poor lad from his early homestead! The yearnings which I used to have towards it in those unfledged years! How, in my

---

2. Randal Norris, who had befriended young Charles Lamb. The Inner Temple is one of the four Inns of Court, the center of the English legal profession.
3. A leather vessel coated on the outside with pitch. "Crug": bread (slang). "Small beer": beer low in alcoholic content. "Piggins": small wooden pails.
4. "Banyan . . . days": nautical term for days when

no meat is served; it derives from *banian*, a member of a Hindu caste to whom meat is forbidden. "Millet": a cereal.
5. Horsemeat (Latin).
6. Overdone. "Scrags": necks.
7. The lean part of a loin of pork.
8. The prophet Elijah, who was fed by the ravens in 1 Kings 17. "Cates": delicacies.

dreams, would my native town (far in the west) come back, with its church, and trees, and faces! How I would wake weeping, and in the anguish of my heart exclaim upon sweet Calne in Wiltshire![9]

To this late hour of my life, I trace impressions left by the recollections of those friendless holidays. The long warm days of summer never return but they bring with them a gloom from the haunting memory of those *whole-day leaves*, when, by some strange arrangement, we were turned out for the live-long day, upon our own hands, whether we had friends to go to or none. I remember those bathing excursions to the New River which L. recalls with such relish, better, I think, than he can—for he was a home-seeking lad, and did not much care for such water pastimes: How merrily we would sally forth into the fields; and strip under the first warmth of the sun; and wanton like young dace[1] in the streams; getting us appetites for noon, which those of us that were penniless (our scanty morning crust long since exhausted) had not the means of allaying—while the cattle, and the birds, and the fishes were at feed about us and we had nothing to satisfy our cravings—the very beauty of the day, and the exercise of the pastime, and the sense of liberty, setting a keener edge upon them! How faint and languid, finally, we would return, towards nightfall, to our desired morsel, half-rejoicing, half-reluctant that the hours of our uneasy liberty had expired!

It was worse in the days of winter, to go prowling about the streets object-less—shivering at cold windows of print shops, to extract a little amusement; or haply, as a last resort in the hopes of a little novelty, to pay a fifty-times repeated visit (where our individual faces should be as well known to the warden as those of his own charges) to the Lions in the Tower—to whose levee, by courtesy immemorial, we had a prescriptive title to admission.[2]

L.'s governor (so we called the patron who presented us to the foundation)[3] lived in a manner under his paternal roof. Any complaint which he had to make was sure of being attended to. This was understood at Christ's, and was an effectual screen to him against the severity of masters, or worse tyranny of the monitors. The oppressions of these young brutes are heart-sickening to call to recollection. I have been called out of my bed, and *waked for the purpose*, in the coldest winter nights—and this not once, but night after night—in my shirt, to receive the discipline of a leathern thong and eleven other sufferers, because it pleased my callow overseer, when there has been any talking heard after we were gone to bed, to make the six last beds in the dormitory, where the youngest children of us slept, answerable for an offense they neither dared to commit nor had the power to hinder. The same execrable tyranny drove the younger part of us from the fires, when our feet were perishing with snow; and, under the cruelest penalties, forbade the indulgence of a drink of water when we lay in sleepless summer nights fevered with the season and the day's sports.

There was one H——, who, I learned, in after days was seen expiating some maturer offense in the hulks.[4] (Do I flatter myself in fancying that this

9. Coleridge had come to school from Ottery St. Mary, Devonshire, in the southwest of England.
1. A small quick-darting fish.
2. The Bluecoat Boys had the right of free admission to the royal menagerie, then housed in the Tower of London. "Levee": a formal morning reception.

3. I.e., who vouched for a candidate for entrance to Christ's Hospital. Lamb's patron was Samuel Salt, a lawyer and Member of Parliament for whom Lamb's father served as clerk.
4. Prison ship. (In Lamb's time the plural "hulks" had come to be used for the singular.)

might be the planter of that name, who suffered—at Nevis, I think, or St. Kitts[5]—some few years since? My friend Tobin was the benevolent instrument of bringing him to the gallows.) This petty Nero actually branded a boy who had offended him with a red-hot iron; and nearly starved forty of us with exacting contributions, to the one-half of our bread, to pamper a young ass, which, incredible as it may seem, with the connivance of the nurse's daughter (a young flame of his) he had contrived to smuggle in, and keep upon the leads[6] of the *ward*, as they called our dormitories. This game went on for better than a week, till the foolish beast, not able to fare well but he must cry roast meat—happier than Caligula's minion,[7] could he have kept his own counsel—but foolisher, alas! than any of his species in the fables—waxing fat, and kicking, in the fullness of bread, one unlucky minute would needs proclaim his good fortune to the world below; and, laying out his simple throat, blew such a ram's-horn blast, as (toppling down the walls of his own Jericho)[8] set concealment any longer at defiance. The client was dismissed, with certain attentions, to Smithfield; but I never understood that the patron underwent any censure on the occasion. This was in the stewardship of L.'s admired Perry.[9]

Under the same *facile* administration, can L. have forgotten the cool impunity with which the nurses used to carry away openly, in open platters, for their own tables, one out of two of every hot joint, which the careful matron had been seeing scrupulously weighed out for our dinners? These things were daily practiced in that magnificent apartment which L. (grown connoisseur since, we presume) praises so highly for the grand paintings "by Verrio,[1] and others," with which it is "hung round and adorned." But the sight of sleek, well-fed bluecoat boys in pictures was, at that time, I believe, little consolatory to him, or us, the living ones, who saw the better part of our provisions carried away before our faces by harpies; and ourselves reduced (with the Trojan in the hall of Dido)

> To feed our mind with idle portraiture.[2]

L. has recorded the repugnance of the school to *gags*, or the fat of fresh beef boiled; and sets it down to some superstition. But these unctuous morsels are never grateful to young palates (children are universally fat-haters), and in strong, coarse, boiled meats, *unsalted*, are detestable. A *gag-eater* in our time was equivalent to a *ghoul*, and held in equal detestation. ———— suffered under the imputation.

> . . . 'Twas said
> He ate strange flesh.[3]

He was observed, after dinner, carefully to gather up the remnants left at his table (not many nor very choice fragments, you may credit me)—and, in an especial manner, these disreputable morsels, which he would convey away

<hr>

5. Islands in the West Indies.
6. A flat roof.
7. The favorite horse of the Roman emperor Caligula, who was fed gilded oats and appointed to the post of chief consul.
8. Joshua toppled the walls of Jericho by trumpet blasts (Joshua 6.16–20).
9. John Perry, steward of the school, described in Lamb's earlier essay. "Smithfield": a market for horses and cattle.

1. Antonio Verrio, Italian painter of the 17th century. While living in England, he painted a large picture of the mathematics students of Christ's Hospital being received by James II.
2. Virgil's *Aeneid* 1.464; Aeneas is inspecting the paintings in Dido's temple to Juno.
3. Loosely quoted from *Antony and Cleopatra* 1.4.67.

and secretly stow in the settle that stood at his bedside. None saw when he ate them. It was rumored that he privately devoured them in the night. He was watched, but no traces of such midnight practices were discoverable. Some reported that on leave-days he had been seen to carry out of the bounds a large blue check handkerchief, full of something. This then must be the accursed thing. Conjecture next was at work to imagine how he could dispose of it. Some said he sold it to the beggars. This belief generally prevailed. He went about moping. None spake to him. No one would play with him. He was excommunicated; put out of the pale of the school. He was too powerful a boy to be beaten, but he underwent every mode of that negative punishment which is more grievous than many stripes. Still he persevered. At length he was observed by two of his schoolfellows, who were determined to get at the secret, and had traced him one leave-day for the purpose, to enter a large worn-out building, such as there exist specimens of in Chancery Lane, which are let out to various scales of pauperism, with open door and a common staircase. After him they silently slunk in, and followed by stealth up four flights, and saw him tap at a poor wicket, which was opened by an aged woman, meanly clad. Suspicion was now ripened into certainty. The informers had secured their victim. They had him in their toils. Accusation was formally preferred, and retribution most signal was looked for. Mr. Hathaway, the then steward (for this happened a little after my time), with that patient sagacity which tempered all his conduct, determined to investigate the matter before he proceeded to sentence. The result was that the supposed mendicants, the receivers or purchasers of the mysterious scraps, turned out to be the parents of ———, an honest couple come to decay—whom this seasonable supply had, in all probability, saved from mendicancy; and that this young stork, at the expense of his own good name, had all this while been only feeding the old birds!—The governors on this occasion, much to their honor, voted a present relief to the family of ———, and presented him with a silver medal. The lesson which the steward read upon RASH JUDGMENT, on the occasion of publicly delivering the medal to ———, I believe would not be lost upon his auditory.—I had left school then, but I well remember ———. He was a tall, shambling youth, with a cast in his eye, not at all calculated to conciliate hostile prejudices. I have since seen him carrying a baker's basket. I think I heard he did not do quite so well by himself as he had done by the old folks.

I was a hypochondriac lad;[4] and the sight of a boy in fetters, upon the day of my first putting on the blue clothes, was not exactly fitted to assuage the natural terrors of initiation. I was of tender years, barely turned of seven; and had only read of such things in books, or seen them but in dreams. I was told he had *run away*. This was the punishment for the first offense.— As a novice I was soon after taken to see the dungeons. These were little, square, Bedlam[5] cells, where a boy could just lie at his length upon straw and a blanket—a mattress, I think, was afterwards substituted—with a peep of light, let in askance, from a prison orifice at top, barely enough to read by. Here the poor boy was locked in by himself all day, without sight of any but the porter who brought him his bread and water—who *might not speak*

---

4. From this point on Elia speaks as Lamb, rather than as Coleridge.

5. St. Mary of Bethlehem, an insane asylum in London.

to him—or of the beadle, who came twice a week to call him out to receive his periodical chastisement, which was almost welcome, because it separated him for a brief interval from solitude—and here he was shut up by himself *of nights* out of the reach of any sound, to suffer whatever horrors the weak nerves, and superstition incident to his time of life, might subject him to. This was the penalty for the second offense. Wouldst thou like, reader, to see what became of him in the next degree?

The culprit, who had been a third time an offender, and whose expulsion was at this time deemed irreversible, was brought forth, as at some solemn auto da fé, arrayed in uncouth and most appalling attire—all trace of his late "watchet weeds"[6] carefully effaced, he was exposed in a jacket resembling those which London lamplighters formerly delighted in, with a cap of the same. The effect of this divestiture was such as the ingenious devisers of it could have anticipated. With his pale and frighted features, it was as if some of those disfigurements in Dante[7] had seized upon him. In this disguisement he was brought into the hall (*L.'s favorite state room*), where awaited him the whole number of his schoolfellows, whose joint lessons and sports he was thenceforth to share no more; the awful presence of the steward, to be seen for the last time; of the executioner beadle, clad in his state robe for the occasion; and of two faces more, of direr import, because never but in these extremities visible. These were governors; two of whom by choice, or charter, were always accustomed to officiate at these *Ultima Supplicia;*[8] not to mitigate (so at least we understood it), but to enforce the uttermost stripe. Old Bamber Gascoigne, and Peter Aubert, I remember, were colleagues on one occasion, when the beadle turning rather pale, a glass of brandy was ordered to prepare him for the mysteries. The scourging was, after the old Roman fashion, long and stately. The lictor[9] accompanied the criminal quite round the hall. We were generally too faint, with attending to the previous disgusting circumstances, to make accurate report with our eyes of the degree of corporal suffering inflicted. Report, of course, gave out the back knotty and livid. After scourging, he was made over, in his *San Benito,*[1] to his friends, if he had any (but commonly such poor runagates were friendless), or to his parish officer, who, to enhance the effect of the scene, had his station allotted to him on the outside of the hall gate.

These solemn pageantries were not played off so often as to spoil the general mirth of the community. We had plenty of exercise and recreation *after* school hours; and, for myself, I must confess that I was never happier than *in* them. The Upper and the Lower Grammar Schools were held in the same room; and an imaginary line only divided their bounds. Their character was as different as that of the inhabitants on the two sides of the Pyrenees. The Rev. James Boyer[2] was the Upper master; but the Rev. Matthew Field presided over that portion of the apartment of which I had the good fortune to be a member. We lived a life as careless as birds. We talked and did just what we pleased, and nobody molested us. We carried an accidence, or a grammar, for form; but, for any trouble it gave us, we might take two years

---

6. Blue clothes. "Auto da fé": act of faith (literal trans.), the ceremony before the execution of heretics under the Spanish Inquisition.
7. I.e., of the sinners in Dante's *Inferno;* see canto 20.
8. Extreme punishments (Latin).

9. A Roman officer who cleared the way for the chief magistrates.
1. The yellow robe worn by the condemned heretic at an auto da fé.
2. This teacher is also described by Coleridge in *Biographia Literaria,* chap. 1.

in getting through the verbs deponent,[3] and another two in forgetting all that we had learned about them. There was now and then the formality of saying a lesson, but if you had not learned it, a brush across the shoulders (just enough to disturb a fly) was the sole remonstrance. Field never used the rod; and in truth he wielded the cane with no great good will—holding it "like a dancer." It looked in his hands rather like an emblem than an instrument of authority; and an emblem, too, he was ashamed of. He was a good, easy man, that did not care to ruffle his own peace, nor perhaps set any great consideration upon the value of juvenile time. He came among us, now and then, but often stayed away whole days from us; and when he came it made no difference to us—he had his private room to retire to, the short time he stayed, to be out of the sound of our noise. Our mirth and uproar went on. We had classics of our own, without being beholden to "insolent Greece or haughty Rome,"[4] that passed current among us—*Peter Wilkins*—the *Adventures of the Hon. Captain Robert Boyle*—the *Fortunate Bluecoat Boy*[5]—and the like. Or we cultivated a turn for mechanic and scientific operations; making little sun-dials of paper; or weaving those ingenious parentheses called *cat cradles*; or making dry peas to dance upon the end of a tin pipe; or studying the art military over that laudable game "French and English,"[6] and a hundred other such devices to pass away the time—mixing the useful with the agreeable—as would have made the souls of Rousseau and John Locke[7] chuckle to have seen us.

Matthew Field belonged to that class of modest divines who affect to mix in equal proportion the *gentleman,* the *scholar,* and the *Christian;* but, I know not how, the first ingredient is generally found to be the predominating dose in the composition. He was engaged in gay parties, or with his courtly bow at some episcopal levee, when he should have been attending upon us. He had for many years the classical charge of a hundred children, during the four or five first years of their education, and his very highest form seldom proceeded further than two or three of the introductory fables of Phaedrus.[8] How things were suffered to go on thus, I cannot guess. Boyer, who was the proper person to have remedied these abuses, always affected, perhaps felt, a delicacy in interfering in a province not strictly his own. I have not been without my suspicions, that he was not altogether displeased at the contrast we presented to his end of the school. We were a sort of Helots to his young Spartans.[9] He would sometimes, with ironic deference, send to borrow a rod of the Under Master, and then, with sardonic grin, observe to one of his upper boys, "how neat and fresh the twigs looked." While his pale students were battering their brains over Xenophon and Plato, with a silence as deep as that enjoined by the Samite, we were enjoying ourselves at our ease in our little Goshen.[1] We saw a little into the secrets of his discipline, and the

3. Verbs with an active meaning but passive form. "Accidence": a table of the declension of nouns and conjugation of verbs in Greek and Latin.
4. Ben Jonson's *To the Memory of . . . William Shakespeare,* line 39.
5. All three were popular adventure stories or romances of the day.
6. A game in which contestants, with eyes closed, draw lines on a sheet of paper covered with dots. The winner is the contestant whose line touches the most dots.
7. Two philosophers who recommended systems of education that combined theory with practical experience.
8. A Roman of the 1st century C.E., author of a verse translation of Aesop's fables.
9. The Spartans exhibited drunken Helots (slaves) as a warning example to their children.
1. Where the Jews dwelled, protected from the swarms of flies with which the Lord plagued the Egyptians in Exodus 8.22. "Samite": Pythagoras of Samos, Greek mathematician and philosopher (6th century B.C.E.), who forbade his pupils to speak until they had studied with him five years.

prospect did but the more reconcile us to our lot. His thunders rolled innocuous for us: his storms came near, but never touched us; contrary to Gideon's miracle, while all around were drenched, our fleece was dry.[2] His boys turned out the better scholars; we, I suspect, have the advantage in temper. His pupils cannot speak of him without something of terror allaying their gratitude; the remembrance of Field comes back with all the soothing images of indolence, and summer slumbers, and work like play, and innocent idleness, and Elysian exemptions, and life itself a "playing holiday."

Though sufficiently removed from the jurisdiction of Boyer, we were near enough (as I have said) to understand a little of his system. We occasionally heard sounds of the *Ululantes,* and caught glances of Tartarus.[3] B. was a rabid pedant. His English style was cramped to barbarism. His Easter anthems (for his duty obliged him to those periodical flights) were grating as scrannel pipes.[4]—He would laugh, aye, and heartily, but then it must be at Flaccus's quibble about *Rex*[5]—or at the *tristis severitas in vultu,* or *inspicere in patinas,* of Terence[6]—thin jests, which at their first broaching could hardly have had *vis*[7] enough to move a Roman muscle.—He had two wigs, both pedantic, but of different omen. The one serene, smiling, fresh powdered, betokening a mild day. The other, an old, discolored, unkempt, angry caxon,[8] denoting frequent and bloody execution. Woe to the school, when he made his morning appearance in his *passy,* or *passionate wig.* No comet expounded surer.[9]—J. B. had a heavy hand. I have known him double his knotty fist at a poor trembling child (the maternal milk hardly dry upon its lips) with a "Sirrah, do you presume to set your wits at me?"—Nothing was more common than to see him make a headlong entry into the schoolroom, from his inner recess, or library, and, with turbulent eye, singling out a lad, roar out, "Od's my life, sirrah" (his favorite adjuration), "I have a great mind to whip you"—then, with as sudden a retracting impulse, fling back into his lair—and, after a cooling lapse of some minutes (during which all but the culprit had totally forgotten the context) drive headlong out again, piecing out his imperfect sense, as if it had been some Devil's Litany, with the expletory yell—"*and I* WILL, *too.*"—In his gentler moods, when the *rabidus furor* was assuaged, he had resort to an ingenious method, peculiar, for what I have heard, to himself, of whipping the boy, and reading the Debates,[1] at the same time; a paragraph, and a lash between; which in those times, when parliamentary oratory was most at a height and flourishing in these realms, was not calculated to impress the patient with a veneration for the diffuser graces of rhetoric.

Once, and but once, the uplifted rod was known to fall ineffectual from his hand—when droll squinting W—— having been caught putting the

2. Judges 6.37–38. As a sign to Gideon, the Lord soaked his sheepskin while leaving the earth around it dry.
3. In the *Aeneid* 6.557–58 Aeneas hears the groans and the sound of the lash from Tartarus, the infernal place of punishment for the wicked. "*Ululantes*": howling sufferers.
4. Harsh pipes, an echo of Milton's *Lycidas,* line 124.
5. In Horace's *Satires* 1.7 there is a pun on *Rex* as both a surname and the word for *king.*
6. In Terence's *Andrea* 5.2 one character says of

a notorious liar that he has "a sober severity in his countenance." In his *Adelphi* 3.3, after a father has advised his son to look into the lives of men as a mirror, the slave advises the kitchen scullions "to look into the stew pans" as a mirror.
7. Force (Latin); a term in rhetorical theory.
8. A type of wig.
9. Comets were superstitiously regarded as omens of disaster.
1. The record of debates in Parliament. "*Rabidus furor*": mad rage (Latin).

inside of the master's desk to a use for which the architect had clearly not designed it, to justify himself, with great simplicity averred, that *he did not know that the thing had been forewarned*. This exquisite irrecognition of any law antecedent to the *oral* or *declaratory* struck so irrestibly upon the fancy of all who heard it (the pedagogue himself not excepted)—that remission was unavoidable.

L. has given credit to B.'s great merits as an instructor. Coleridge, in his literary life, has pronounced a more intelligible and ample encomium on them. The author of the *Country Spectator*[2] doubts not to compare him with the ablest teachers of antiquity. Perhaps we cannot dismiss him better than with the pious ejaculation of C.—when he heard that his old master was on his deathbed: "Poor J. B.!—may all his faults be forgiven; and may he be wafted to bliss by little cherub boys all head and wings, with no *bottoms* to reproach his sublunary infirmities."

Under him were many good and sound scholars bred.—First Grecian[3] of my time was Lancelot Pepys Stevens, kindest of boys and men, since Co-grammar-master (and inseparable companion) with Dr. T———e. What an edifying spectacle did this brace of friends present to those who remembered the antisocialities of their predecessors!—You never met the one by chance in the street without a wonder, which was quickly dissipated by the almost immediate sub-appearance of the other. Generally arm-in-arm, these kindly coadjutors lightened for each other the toilsome duties of their profession, and when, in advanced age, one found it convenient to retire, the other was not long in discovering that it suited him to lay down the fasces[4] also. Oh, it is pleasant, as it is rare, to find the same arm linked in yours at forty, which at thirteen helped it to turn over the *Cicero De Amicitia*,[5] or some tale of Antique Friendship, which the young heart even then was burning to antic-ipate!—Co-Grecian with S. was Th———, who has since executed with ability various diplomatic functions at the Northern courts. Th——— was a tall, dark, saturnine youth, sparing of speech, with raven locks.—Thomas Fanshaw Middleton followed him (now Bishop of Calcutta), a scholar and a gentleman in his teens. He has the reputation of an excellent critic; and is author (besides the *Country Spectator*) of a *Treatise on the Greek Article*, against Sharpe. M. is said to bear his miter high in India, where the *regni novitas*[6] (I dare say) sufficiently justifies the bearing. A humility quite as primitive as that of Jewel or Hooker[7] might not be exactly fitted to impress the minds of those Anglo-Asiatic diocesans with a reverence for home institutions, and the church which those fathers watered. The manners of M. at school, though firm, were mild and unassuming.—Next to M. (if not senior to him) was Richards, author of the *Aboriginal Britons,* the most spirited of the Oxford Prize Poems; a pale, studious Grecian.—Then followed poor S———, ill-fated M———! of these the Muse is silent.[8]

2. Thomas Middleton, who was at school with Lamb and Coleridge, edited the magazine *Country Spectator* (1792–93) and later became bishop of Calcutta.

3. The Grecians were the small group of superior scholars selected to be sent to a university (usually Cambridge) on a Christ's Hospital scholarship.

4. The bundle of rods, serving as the handle of an ax, carried before the Roman magistrates as a sym-bol of office.

5. Cicero's essay *On Friendship*.

6. Newness of the reign (Latin).

7. Famous divines in the 16th century during the early period of the Anglican Church.

8. Lamb identified these students as Scott, who died insane, and Maunde, who was expelled from the school.

> Finding some of Edward's race
> Unhappy, pass their annals by.[9]

Come back into memory, like as thou wert in the dayspring of thy fancies, with hope like a fiery column before thee—the dark pillar not yet turned—Samuel Taylor Coleridge—Logician, Metaphysician, Bard!—How have I seen the casual passer through the cloisters stand still, entranced with admiration (while he weighed the disproportion between the *speech* and the *garb* of the young Mirandola[1]), to hear thee unfold, in thy deep and sweet intonations, the mysteries of Jamblichus, or Plotinus[2] (for even in those years thou waxedst not pale at such philosophic draughts), or reciting Homer in his Greek, or Pindar—while the walls of the old Grey Friars[3] re-echoed to the accents of the *inspired charity-boy!*—Many were the "wit combats" (to dally awhile with the words of old Fuller) between him and C. V. Le G——, "which two I behold like a Spanish great galleon, and an English man-of-war; Master Coleridge, like the former, was built far higher in learning, solid, but slow in his performances. C. V. L., with the English man-of-war, lesser in bulk, but lighter in sailing, could turn with all tides, tack about, and take advantage of all winds, by the quickness of his wit and invention."[4]

Nor shalt thou, their compeer, be quickly forgotten, Allen, with the cordial smile, and still more cordial laugh, with which thou wert wont to make the old cloisters shake, in thy cognition of some poignant jest of theirs; or the anticipation of some more material, and, peradventure, practical one, of thine own. Extinct are those smiles, with that beautiful countenance, with which (for thou wert the *Nireus formosus*[5] of the school), in the days of thy maturer waggery, thou didst disarm the wrath of infuriated town-damsel, who, incensed by provoking pinch, turning tigress-like round, suddenly converted by thy angel look, exchanged the half-formed terrible "*bl——,*" for a gentler greeting—"*bless thy handsome face!*"

Next follow two, who ought to be now alive, and the friends of Elia—the junior Le G—— and F——; who impelled, the former by a roving temper, the latter by too quick a sense of neglect—ill capable of enduring the slights poor Sizars[6] are sometimes subject to in our seats of learning—exchanged their Alma Mater for the camp; perishing, one by climate, and one on the plains of Salamanca: Le G——, sanguine, volatile, sweet-natured; F——, dogged, faithful, anticipative of insult, warmhearted, with something of the old Roman height about him.

Fine, frank-hearted Fr——, the present master of Hertford, with Marmaduke T——,[7] mildest of missionaries—and both my good friends still—close the catalogue of Grecians in my time.

1820   1823

---

9. Altered from Matthew Prior's *Carmen Seculare* (1700). "Edward's race": applied to the students of Christ's Hospital, founded by Edward VI.
1. Pico della Mirandola, the brilliant and charming humanist and philosopher of the Italian Renaissance, who died in 1494 at the age of thirty-one.
2. Neoplatonic philosophers.
3. Christ's Hospital was located in buildings that had once belonged to the Grey Friars (i.e., Franciscans).
4. Lamb adapts to Coleridge and Charles Valentine Le Grice the famous description of the wit combats between Shakespeare (the "man-of-war") and Ben Jonson (the "great galleon") in Thomas Fuller's *Worthies of England* (1662).
5. The handsome Nireus; a Greek warrior in Homer's *Iliad* 2.
6. An undergraduate at Cambridge University who receives an allowance toward his expenses. "Le G——": Samuel Le Grice, who became an army officer and died in the West Indies. "F——": Joseph Favell.
7. Marmaduke Thompson. "Fr——": Frederick William Franklin.

Old China

I have an almost feminine partiality for old china. When I go to see any great house, I inquire for the china closet, and next for the picture gallery. I cannot defend the order of preference, but by saying that we have all some taste or other, of too ancient a date to admit of our remembering distinctly that it was an acquired one. I can call to mind the first play, and the first exhibition, that I was taken to; but I am not conscious of a time when china jars and saucers were introduced into my imagination.

I had no repugnance then—why should I now have?—to those little, lawless, azure-tinctured grotesques, that under the notion of men and women float about, uncircumscribed by any element, in that world before perspective—a china teacup.

I like to see my old friends—whom distance cannot diminish—figuring up in the air (so they appear to our optics), yet on terra firma still—for so we must in courtesy interpret that speck of deeper blue, which the decorous artist, to prevent absurdity, had made to spring up beneath their sandals.

I love the men with women's faces, and the women, if possible, with still more womanish expressions.

Here is a young and courtly mandarin, handing tea to a lady from a salver—two miles off. See how distance seems to set off respect! And here the same lady, or another—for likeness is identity on teacups—is stepping into a little fairy boat, moored on the hither side of this calm garden river, with a dainty mincing foot, which in a right angle of incidence (as angles go in our world) must infallibly land her in the midst of a flowery mead—a furlong off on the other side of the same strange stream!

Farther on—if far or near can be predicated of their world—see horses, trees, pagodas, dancing the hays.[1]

Here—a cow and rabbit couchant,[2] and coextensive—so objects show, seen through the lucid atmosphere of fine Cathay.[3]

I was pointing out to my cousin last evening, over our Hyson[4] (which we are old-fashioned enough to drink unmixed still of an afternoon), some of these *speciosa miracula*[5] upon a set of extraordinary old blue china (a recent purchase) which we were now for the first time using; and could not help remarking how favorable circumstances had been to us of late years that we could afford to please the eye sometimes with trifles of this sort—when a passing sentiment seemed to overshade the brows of my companion. I am quick at detecting these summer clouds in Bridget.[6]

"I wish the good old times would come again," she said, "when we were not quite so rich. I do not mean that I want to be poor; but there was a middle state"—so she was pleased to ramble on—"in which I am sure we were a great deal happier. A purchase is but a purchase, now that you have money enough and to spare. Formerly it used to be a triumph. When we coveted a cheap luxury (and, O! how much ado I had to get you to consent in those times!)—we were used to have a debate two or three days before,

---

1. An English country dance with a serpentining movement.
2. Lying down with the head raised (heraldry).
3. The old European name for China.

4. A Chinese green tea.
5. Shining wonders (Latin).
6. In Lamb's essays, his name for his sister, Mary.

and to weigh the *for* and *against,* and think what we might spare it out of, and what saving we could hit upon, that should be an equivalent. A thing was worth buying then, when we felt the money that we paid for it.

"Do you remember the brown suit, which you made to hang upon you, till all your friends cried shame upon you, it grew so threadbare—and all because of that folio Beaumont and Fletcher,[7] which you dragged home late at night from Barker's in Covent Garden? Do you remember how we eyed it for weeks before we could make up our minds to the purchase, and had not come to a determination till it was near ten o'clock of the Saturday night, when you set off from Islington,[8] fearing you should be too late—and when the old bookseller with some grumbling opened his shop, and by the twinkling taper (for he was setting bedwards) lighted out the relic from his dusty treasures— and when you lugged it home, wishing it were twice as cumbersome—and when you presented it to me—and when we were exploring the perfectness of it (*collating,* you called it)—and while I was repairing some of these loose leaves with paste, which your impatience would not suffer to be left till daybreak—was there no pleasure in being a poor man? or can those neat black clothes which you wear now, and are so careful to keep brushed, since we have become rich and finical, give you half the honest vanity with which you flaunted it about in that overworn suit—your old corbeau[9]—for four or five weeks longer than you should have done, to pacify your conscience for the mighty sum of fifteen—or sixteen shillings was it?—a great affair we thought it then—which you had lavished on the old folio. Now you can afford to buy any book that pleases you, but I do not see that you ever bring me home any nice old purchases now.

"When you came home with twenty apologies for laying out a less number of shillings upon that print after Leonardo,[1] which we christened the 'Lady Blanch'; when you looked at the purchase, and thought of the money—and thought of the money, and looked again at the picture—was there no pleasure in being a poor man? Now, you have nothing to do but to walk into Colnaghi's, and buy a wilderness of Leonardos. Yet do you?

"Then, do you remember our pleasant walks to Enfield, and Potter's Bar, and Waltham,[2] when we had a holiday—holidays, and all other fun, are gone now we are rich—and the little hand-basket in which I used to deposit our day's fare of savory cold lamb and salad—and how you would pry about at noontide for some decent house, where we might go in and produce our store—only paying for the ale that you must call for—and speculate upon the looks of the landlady, and whether she was likely to allow us a tablecloth—and wish for such another honest hostess as Izaak Walton has described many a one on the pleasant banks of the Lea, when he went a-fishing—and sometimes they would prove obliging enough, and sometimes they would look grudgingly upon us—but we had cheerful looks still for one another, and would eat our plain food savorily, scarcely grudging Piscator[3] his Trout Hall? Now—when we go out a day's pleasuring, which is seldom,

---

7. The Elizabethan dramatic collaborators, whose plays were first collected in a large folio volume in 1647.
8. In the north of London, where the Lambs had been living.
9. A dark green cloth, almost black (hence its name, the French for "raven").

1. Leonardo da Vinci (1452–1519), the great Italian painter. The painting is the one known as *Modesty and Vanity.*
2. All three are suburbs to the north of London.
3. The fisherman in Izaak Walton's *Complete Angler* (1653).

moreover, we *ride* part of the way—and go into a fine inn, and order the best of dinners, never debating the expense—which, after all, never has half the relish of those chance country snaps,[4] when we were at the mercy of uncertain usage and a precarious welcome.

"You are too proud to see a play anywhere now but in the pit. Do you remember where it was we used to sit, when we saw the *Battle of Hexham*, and the *Surrender of Calais*,[5] and Bannister and Mrs. Bland in the *Children in the Wood*[6]—when we squeezed out our shillings apiece to sit three or four times in a season in the one-shilling gallery—where you felt all the time that you ought not to have brought me—and more strongly I felt obligation to you for having brought me—and the pleasure was the better for a little shame—and when the curtain drew up, what cared we for our place in the house, or what mattered it where we were sitting, when our thoughts were with Rosalind in Arden, or with Viola at the Court of Ilyria.[7] You used to say that the gallery was the best place of all for enjoying a play socially—that the relish of such exhibitions must be in proportion to the infrequency of going—that the company we met there, not being in general readers of plays, were obliged to attend the more, and did attend, to what was going on, on the stage—because a word lost would have been a chasm, which it was impossible for them to fill up. With such reflections we consoled our pride then—and I appeal to you whether, as a woman, I met generally with less attention and accommodation than I have done since in more expensive situations in the house? The getting in indeed, and the crowding up those inconvenient staircases, was bad enough—but there was still a law of civility to woman recognized to quite as great an extent as we ever found in the other passages—and how a little difficulty overcome heightened the snug seat and the play, afterwards! Now we can only pay our money and walk in. You cannot see, you say, in the galleries now. I am sure we saw, and heard too, well enough then—but sight, and all, I think, is gone with our poverty.

"There was pleasure in eating strawberries, before they became quite common—in the first dish of peas, while they were yet dear—to have them for a nice supper, a treat. What treat can we have now? If we were to treat ourselves now—that is, to have dainties a little above our means, it would be selfish and wicked. It is the very little more that we allow ourselves beyond what the actual poor can get at that makes what I call a treat—when two people living together, as we have done, now and then indulge themselves in a cheap luxury, which both like; while each apologizes, and is willing to take both halves of the blame to his single share. I see no harm in people making much of themselves, in that sense of the word. It may give them a hint how to make much of others. But now—what I mean by the word—we never do make much of ourselves. None but the poor can do it. I do not mean the veriest poor of all, but persons as we were, just above poverty.

"I know what you were going to say, that it is mighty pleasant at the end of the year to make all meet—and much ado we used to have every Thirty-first Night of December to account for our exceedings—many a long face did you make over your puzzled accounts, and in contriving to make it out how we had spent so much—or that we had not spent so much—or that it

4. Snacks.
5. Comedies by George Colman (1762–1836).
6. By Thomas Morton (1764–1838).

7. Rosalind in *As You Like It* and Viola in *Twelfth Night*.

was impossible we should spend so much next year—and still we found our slender capital decreasing—but then, betwixt ways, and projects, and compromises of one sort or another, and talk of curtailing this charge, and doing without that for the future—and the hope that youth brings, and laughing spirits (in which you were never poor till now), we pocketed up our loss, and in conclusion, with 'lusty brimmers' (as you used to quote it out of *hearty cheerful Mr. Cotton*,[8] as you called him), we used to welcome in 'the coming guest.' Now we have no reckoning at all at the end of the old year—no flattering promises about the new year doing better for us."

Bridget is so sparing of her speech on most occasions that when she gets into a rhetorical vein, I am careful how I interrupt it. I could not help, however, smiling at the phantom of wealth which her dear imagination had conjured up out of a clear income of poor—— hundred pounds a year. "It is true we were happier when we were poorer, but we were also younger, my cousin. I am afraid we must put up with the excess, for if we were to shake the superflux into the sea, we should not much mend ourselves. That we had much to struggle with, as we grew up together, we have reason to be most thankful. It strengthened and knit our compact closer. We could never have been what we have been to each other, if we had always had the sufficiency which you now complain of. The resisting power—those natural dilations of the youthful spirit, which circumstances cannot straiten—with us are long since passed away. Competence to age is supplementary youth, a sorry supplement indeed, but I fear the best that is to be had. We must ride where we formerly walked: live better and lie softer—and shall be wise to do so—than we had means to do in those good old days you speak of. Yet could those days return—could you and I once more walk our thirty miles a day—could Bannister and Mrs. Bland again be young, and you and I be young to see them—could the good old one-shilling gallery days return—they are dreams, my cousin, now—but could you and I at this moment, instead of this quiet argument, by our well-carpeted fireside, sitting on this luxurious sofa—be once more struggling up those inconvenient staircases, pushed about, and squeezed, and elbowed by the poorest rabble of poor gallery scramblers—could I once more hear those anxious shrieks of yours—and the delicious *Thank God, we are safe,* which always followed when the topmost stair, conquered, let in the first light of the whole cheerful theater down beneath us—I know not the fathom line that ever touched a descent so deep as I would be willing to bury more wealth in than Croesus had, or the great Jew R——[9] is supposed to have, to purchase it. And now do just look at that merry little Chinese waiter holding an umbrella, big enough for a bed-tester, over the head of that pretty insipid half Madonnaish chit of a lady in that very blue summerhouse."

1823   1823

---

8. Charles Cotton (1630–1687), a favorite poet of Lamb's. The quotations are from his poem *The New Year*.

9. Nathan Meyer Rothschild (1777–1836) founded the English branch of the great European banking house.

WILLIAM HAZLITT
1778–1830

"I started in life," William Hazlitt wrote, "with the French Revolution, and I have lived, alas! to see the end of it. . . . Since then, I confess, I have no longer felt myself young, for with that my hopes fell." He was born into a radical circle, for the elder William Hazlitt, his father, was a Unitarian minister who declared from the pulpit his advocacy both of American independence and of the French Revolution. When young William was five years old, his father took the family to America in search of liberty and founded the first Unitarian church in Boston, but four years later he returned to settle at Wem, in Shropshire. Despite the persistent attacks of reviewers and the backsliding of his once-radical friends, Hazlitt himself never wavered in his loyalty to liberty, equality, and the principles behind the overthrow of the monarchy in France. His first literary production, at the age of thirteen, was a letter to a newspaper in indignant protest against the mob that sacked Joseph Priestley's house, when the scientist and preacher had celebrated publicly the second anniversary of the fall of the Bastille. His last book, published in the year he died, was a four-volume life of Napoleon, in which he expressed a vehement, but qualified, admiration of Napoleon as a man of heroic will and power in the service of the emancipation of mankind.

Hazlitt was a long time finding his vocation. When he attended the Hackney College, London, between the ages of fifteen and eighteen, he plunged into philosophical studies. In 1799 he took up the study of painting and did not relinquish the ambition to become a portraitist until 1812. His first books dealt with philosophy, economics, and politics; and his first job as a journalist was as parliamentary reporter for the *Morning Chronicle.* It was not until 1813, when he was thirty-six, that he began contributing dramatic criticism and miscellaneous essays to various periodicals and so discovered what he had been born to do. Years of wide reading and hard thinking had made him thoroughly ready: within the next decade he demonstrated himself to be a highly popular lecturer on Shakespeare, Elizabethan drama, and English poetry from Chaucer to his own day; a superb connoisseur of the theater and of painting; a master of the familiar essay; and with Coleridge, one of the two most important literary critics of his time. Coleridge is a systematic critic for whom theory precedes application and whose theory of poetry is part of a general philosophy of humanity and nature. Hazlitt, on the other hand, decries what he calls the "modern or metaphysical school of criticism"; his distinctive power is as a practical critic who communicates what he calls his "impressions," that is, the immediacy of his firsthand responses to a literary work or passage.

Unlike his contemporaries Coleridge, Lamb, and De Quincey, whose writings look back to the elaborate prose stylists of the earlier seventeenth century, Hazlitt developed a fast-moving, hard-hitting prose in a style that he called "plain, point-blank speaking." He wrote, indeed, nearly as fast as he talked, almost without correction and (despite the density of literary quotations) without reference to books or notes. This rapidity was possible only because his essays are relatively planless. Hazlitt characteristically lays down a topic, then piles up relevant observations and instances; the essay accumulates instead of developing; often, it does not round to a conclusion, but simply stops. Hazlitt's prose is unfailingly energetic, but his most satisfying essays, considered as works of literary art, are those that, like *My First Acquaintance with Poets,* have a narrative subject matter to give him a principle of organization.

In demeanor Hazlitt was awkward and self-conscious; Coleridge described him in 1803 as "brow-hanging, shoe-contemplative, strange." He had grown up as a member of a highly unpopular minority, in both religion and politics; he found his friends deserting to the side of reaction; and his natural combativeness was exacerbated by the persistent abuse directed against him by writers in the conservative press and periodicals. In the course of his life he managed to quarrel, in private and in print, with almost everyone whom he had once admired and liked, including Coleridge, Wordsworth, Leigh Hunt, and even his most intimate and enduring friend, Charles Lamb. But what appealed to his admirers, as to modern readers of his essays, is his courage and uncompromising honesty, and above all his zest for life in its diversity—including even, as he announced in the title of an essay, *The Pleasure of Hating*. He relished, and was able to convey completely, the particular qualities of things—a passage of poetry, a painting, a natural prospect, or a well-directed blow in a prize fight. Despite the recurrent frustrations of his fifty-two years of existence, he was able to say, with his last breath, "Well, I've had a happy life."

On Gusto[1]

Gusto in art is power or passion defining any object. It is not so difficult to explain this term in what relates to expression (of which it may be said to be the highest degree) as in what relates to things without expression, to the natural appearances of objects, as mere color or form. In one sense, however, there is hardly any object entirely devoid of expression, without some character of power belonging to it, some precise association with pleasure or pain: and it is in giving this truth of character from the truth of feeling, whether in the highest or the lowest degree, but always in the highest degree of which the subject is capable, that gusto consists.

There is a gusto in the coloring of Titian.[2] Not only do his heads seem to think—his bodies seem to feel. This is what the Italians mean by the *morbidezza*[3] of his flesh color. It seems sensitive and alive all over; not merely to have the look and texture of flesh, but the feeling in itself. For example, the limbs of his female figures have a luxurious softness and delicacy, which appears conscious of the pleasure of the beholder. As the objects themselves in nature would produce an impression on the sense, distinct from every other object, and having something divine in it, which the heart owns and the imagination consecrates, the objects in the picture preserve the same impression, absolute, unimpaired, stamped with all the truth of passion, the pride of the eye, and the charm of beauty. Rubens makes his flesh color like flowers; Albano's[4] is like ivory; Titian's is like flesh, and like nothing else. It is as different from that of other painters, as the skin is from a piece of white or red drapery thrown over it. The blood circulates here and there, the blue

---

1. In this critical essay of 1816 Hazlitt introduces one of his distinctive critical terms. In the 17th century, English writers had imported the Italian term *gusto*, meaning taste, to denote a spectator's artistic sensibility, and sometimes in the sense (which remains primary in our own day) of keen relish or zest. From Hazlitt's diverse statements we can make out that he transferred the application of "gusto" from the responsiveness of a spectator to an essential feature of a natural or human object—a feature that has been passionately rendered by the artist so that it appeals through the eye to the other senses and communicates (in what for Hazlitt is the highest commendation) a sense of "power." Most of Hazlitt's examples are from the visual art of painting, but he finds this quality in literature as well.

Keats, who was greatly influenced by Hazlitt's criticism, illuminated Hazlitt's notion of the capacity of great works of art to evoke a wide range of sensuous and emotional responses when, soon after reading Hazlitt *On Gusto*, he remarked (in a letter of December 21, 1817) about a painting by Benjamin West that "there is nothing to be intense upon; no women one feels mad to kiss; no face swelling into reality."

2. Tiziano Vecelli (ca. 1490–1576), greatest of the 16th-century Venetian painters.

3. Softness, delicacy.

4. Francesco Albani (1578–1660), Italian painter. Peter Paul Rubens (1577–1640), Flemish painter, was the most important artist of his time in northern Europe.

veins just appear, the rest is distinguished throughout only by that sort of tingling sensation to the eye, which the body feels within itself. This is gusto. Vandyke's[5] flesh color, though it has great truth and purity, wants gusto. It has not the internal character, the living principle in it. It is a smooth surface, not a warm, moving mass. It is painted without passion, with indifference. The hand only has been concerned. The impression slides off from the eye, and does not, like the tones of Titian's pencil,[6] leave a sting behind it in the mind of the spectator. The eye does not acquire a taste or appetite for what it sees. In a word, gusto in painting is where the impression made on one sense excites by affinity those of another.

Michael Angelo's forms are full of gusto. They everywhere obtrude the sense of power upon the eye. His limbs convey an idea of muscular strength, of moral grandeur, and even of intellectual dignity: they are firm, commanding, broad, and massy, capable of executing with ease the determined purposes of the will. His faces have no other expression than his figures, conscious power and capacity. They appear only to think what they shall do, and to know that they can do it. This is what is meant by saying that his style is hard and masculine. It is the reverse of Correggio's,[7] which is effeminate. That is, the gusto of Michael Angelo consists in expressing energy of will without proportionable sensibility, Correggio's in expressing exquisite sensibility without energy of will. In Correggio's faces as well as figures we see neither bones nor muscles, but then what a soul is there, full of sweetness and of grace—pure, playful, soft, angelical! There is sentiment enough in a hand painted by Correggio to set up a school of history painters. Whenever we look at the hands of Correggio's women or of Raphael's,[8] we always wish to touch them.

Again, Titian's landscapes have a prodigious gusto, both in the coloring and forms. We shall never forget one that we saw many years ago in the Orleans Gallery of Acteon hunting.[9] It had a brown, mellow, autumnal look. The sky was of the color of stone. The winds seemed to sing through the rustling branches of the trees, and already you might hear the twanging of bows resound through the tangled mazes of the wood. Mr. West,[1] we understand, has this landscape. He will know if this description of it is just. The landscape background of the St. Peter Martyr[2] is another well known instance of the power of this great painter to give a romantic interest and an appropriate character to the objects of his pencil, where every circumstance adds to the effect of the scene—the bold trunks of the tall forest trees, the trailing ground plants, with that tall convent spire rising in the distance, amidst the blue sapphire mountains and the golden sky.

Rubens has a great deal of gusto in his Fauns and Satyrs, and in all that expresses motion, but in nothing else. Rembrandt has it in everything; every-

---

5. Sir Anthony Vandyke (1599–1641), Flemish portrait-painter, who did some of his best-known work at the English court of Charles I.
6. In the archaic sense: a painter's brush.
7. Antonio Correggio (1494–1534), Italian artist.
8. Rafaello Sanzio (1488–1520), one of the supreme painters of the high Italian Renaissance.
9. Titian's *Diana and Actaeon,* shown in a celebrated sale-exhibition of old Italian masters, most of them from the collection of the Duc d'Orléans, in London, 1798–99. In *On the Pleasures of Paint-*

ing Hazlitt writes that this exhibition first revealed to him the high possibilities of the art of painting.
1. Benjamin West (1738–1820) was an American-born painter of historical scenes who achieved a high reputation in England. In 1792 he succeeded Sir Joshua Reynolds as president of the Royal Academy.
2. A celebrated altarpiece by Titian depicting the martyrdom of Peter, a 13th-century Dominican. It was destroyed by fire in 1867.

thing in his pictures has a tangible character. If he puts a diamond in the ear of a burgomaster's wife, it is of the first water; and his furs and stuffs are proof against a Russian winter. Raphael's gusto was only in expression; he had no idea of the character of anything but the human form. The dryness and poverty of his style in other respects is a phenomenon in the art. His trees are like sprigs of grass stuck in a book of botanical specimens. Was it that Raphael never had time to go beyond the walls of Rome? That he was always in the streets, at church, or in the bath? He was not one of the Society of Arcadians.[3]

Claude's[4] landscapes, perfect as they are, want gusto. This is not easy to explain. They are perfect abstractions of the visible images of things; they speak the visible language of nature truly. They resemble a mirror or a microscope. To the eye only they are more perfect than any other landscapes that ever were or will be painted; they give more of nature, as cognizable by one sense alone; but they lay an equal stress on all visible impressions. They do not interpret one sense by another; they do not distinguish the character of different objects as we are taught, and can only be taught, to distinguish them by their effect on the different senses. That is, his eye wanted imagination: it did not strongly sympathize with his other faculties. He saw the atmosphere, but he did not feel it. He painted the trunk of a tree or a rock in the foreground as smooth—with as complete an abstraction of the gross, tangible impression, as any other part of the picture. His trees are perfectly beautiful, but quite immovable; they have a look of enchantment. In short, his landscapes are unequaled imitations of nature, released from its subjection to the elements, as if all objects were become a delightful fairy vision, and the eye had rarefied and refined away the other senses.

The gusto in the Greek statues is of a very singular kind. The sense of perfect form nearly occupies the whole mind, and hardly suffers it to dwell on any other feeling. It seems enough for them *to be*, without acting or suffering. Their forms are ideal, spiritual. Their beauty is power. By their beauty they are raised above the frailties of pain or passion; by their beauty they are deified.

The infinite quantity of dramatic invention in Shakespeare takes from his gusto. The power he delights to show is not intense, but discursive. He never insists on anything as much as he might, except a quibble. Milton has great gusto. He repeats his blows twice; grapples with and exhausts his subject. His imagination has a double relish of its objects, an inveterate attachment to the things he describes, and to the words describing them.

——Or where Chineses drive
With sails and wind their *cany* waggons *light*.

Wild above rule or art, *enormous* bliss.[5]

3. I.e., someone who delights in the beauties of the countryside. Hazlitt adds a footnote: "Raphael not only could not paint a landscape; he could not paint people in a landscape. He could not have painted the heads or the figures, or even the dresses, of the St. Peter Martyr. His figures have always an *in-door* look, that is, a set, determined, voluntary, dramatic character, arising from their own passions, or a watchfulness of those of others, and want [lack] that wild uncertainty of expression, which is connected with the accidents of nature and the changes of the elements. He has nothing *romantic* about him."
4. Claude Lorraine (1600–1682), French painter renowned for his landscapes and seascapes.
5. *Paradise Lost* 3.438–39 and 5.297.

There is a gusto in Pope's compliments, in Dryden's satires, and Prior's tales;[6] and among prose writers Boccaccio and Rabelais had the most of it. We will only mention one other work which appears to us to be full of gusto, and that is the *Beggar's Opera.*[7] If it is not, we are altogether mistaken in our notions on this delicate subject.

1816   1817

My First Acquaintance with Poets[1]

My father was a Dissenting Minister, at Wem, in Shropshire; and in the year 1798 (the figures that compose that date are to me like the "dreaded name of Demogorgon"[2]) Mr. Coleridge came to Shrewsbury, to succeed Mr. Rowe in the spiritual charge of a Unitarian congregation there. He did not come till late on the Saturday afternoon before he was to preach; and Mr. Rowe, who himself went down to the coach, in a state of anxiety and expectation, to look for the arrival of his successor, could find no one at all answering the description but a round-faced man, in a short black coat (like a shooting jacket) which hardly seemed to have been made for him, but who seemed to be talking at a great rate to his fellow passengers. Mr. Rowe had scarce returned to give an account of his disappointment, when the round-faced man in black entered, and dissipated all doubts on the subject, by beginning to talk. He did not cease while he stayed; nor has he since, that I know of. He held the good town of Shrewsbury in delightful suspense for three weeks that he remained there, "fluttering the *proud Salopians,* like an eagle in a dovecote";[3] and the Welsh mountains that skirt the horizon with their tempestuous confusion, agree to have heard no such mystic sounds since the days of

High-born Hoel's harp or soft Llewellyn's lay![4]

As we passed along between Wem and Shrewsbury, and I eyed their blue tops seen through the wintry branches, or the red rustling leaves of the sturdy oak trees by the roadside, a sound was in my ears as of a Siren's song; I was stunned, startled with it, as from deep sleep; but I had no notion then that I should ever be able to express my admiration to others in motley imagery or quaint allusion, till the light of his genius shone into my soul, like the sun's rays glittering in the puddles of the road. I was at that time dumb, inarticulate, helpless, like a worm by the wayside, crushed, bleeding, lifeless; but now, bursting from the deadly bands that bound them,

6. A group of somewhat bawdy narrative poems by the early-18th-century poet Matthew Prior.
7. The extremely popular comic opera by John Gay, produced in 1728. At the end of his essay, Hazlitt apparently returns to the common use of "gusto" in the sense of "spirited, zestful."
1. This essay was written in 1823, a quarter century after the events it describes. By then Coleridge and Wordsworth had long given up their early radicalism, and both men had quarreled with Hazlitt— hence the essay's elegiac note in dealing with the genius of the two poets. Nevertheless, Hazlitt communicates the excitement he had felt when Cole-

ridge awakened him to the sense of his own literary possibilities, and the essay remains an incomparable portrait of Wordsworth and Coleridge early in 1798, the period of their closest collaboration.
2. *Paradise Lost* 2.964–65. To mythographers of the Renaissance, Demogorgon was a mysterious and terrifying demon, sometimes described as ancestor of all the gods. He plays a central role in Shelley's *Prometheus Unbound*.
3. Adapted from Shakespeare's *Coriolanus* 5.6.115–16. "Salopians": inhabitants of Shropshire.
4. Thomas Gray's *The Bard,* line 28.

> With Styx nine times round them,[5]

my ideas float on winged words, and as they expand their plumes, catch the golden light of other years. My soul has indeed remained in its original bondage, dark, obscure, with longings infinite and unsatisfied; my heart, shut up in the prison house of this rude clay, has never found, nor will it ever find, a heart to speak to; but that my understanding also did not remain dumb and brutish, or at length found a language to express itself, I owe to Coleridge. But this is not to my purpose.

My father lived ten miles from Shrewsbury, and was in the habit of exchanging visits with Mr. Rowe, and with Mr. Jenkins of Whitechurch (nine miles farther on) according to the custom of Dissenting Ministers in each other's neighborhood. A line of communication is thus established, by which the flame of civil and religious liberty is kept alive, and nourishes its smoldering fire unquenchable, like the fires in the *Agamemnon* of Aeschylus, placed at different stations, that waited for ten long years to announce with their blazing pyramids the destruction of Troy. Coleridge had agreed to come over to see my father, according to the courtesy of the country, as Mr. Rowe's probable successor; but in the meantime, I had gone to hear him preach the Sunday after his arrival. A poet and a philosopher getting up into a Unitarian pulpit to preach the Gospel was a romance in these degenerate days, a sort of revival of the primitive spirit of Christianity, which was not to be resisted.

It was in January of 1798, that I rose one morning before daylight, to walk ten miles in the mud, and went to hear this celebrated person preach. Never, the longest day I have to live, shall I have such another walk as this cold, raw, comfortless one, in the winter of the year 1798. *Il y a des impressions que ni le temps ni les circonstances peuvent effacer. Dusse-je vivre des siècles entiers, le doux temps de ma jeunesse ne peut renaître pour moi, ni s'effacer jamais dans ma mémoire.*[6] When I got there, the organ was playing the 100th psalm, and when it was done, Mr. Coleridge rose and gave out his text, "And he went up into the mountain to pray, *himself, alone.*"[7] As he gave out this text, his voice "rose like a steam of rich distilled perfume,"[8] and when he came to the two last words, which he pronounced loud, deep, and distinct, it seemed to me, who was then young, as if the sounds had echoed from the bottom of the human heart, and as if that prayer might have floated in solemn silence through the universe. The idea of St. John came into my mind, "of one crying in the wilderness, who had his loins girt about, and whose food was locusts and wild honey."[9] The preacher then launched into his subject, like an eagle dallying with the wind. The sermon was upon peace and war; upon church and state—not their alliance but their separation—on the spirit of the world and the spirit of Christianity, not as the same, but as opposed to one another. He talked of those who had "inscribed the cross of Christ on banners dripping with human gore." He made a poetical and pastoral excursion—and to show the fatal effects of war, drew a striking contrast

---

5. Adapted from Pope's *Ode on St. Cecilia's Day*, lines 90–91.
6. There are some impressions which neither time nor circumstances can efface. Might I live whole centuries, the sweet time of my youth cannot be reborn for me, nor ever erased from my memory

(French). Based on Rousseau's epistolary novel *La Nouvelle Héloïse* (1761), part 6, letter 7.
7. Cf. Matthew 14.23 and John 6.15.
8. Milton's *Comus*, line 556.
9. See Matthew 3.3–4 and Mark 1.3–6.

between the simple shepherd boy, driving his team afield, or sitting under the hawthorn, piping to his flock, "as though he should never be old,"[1] and the same poor country lad, crimped,[2] kidnapped, brought into town, made drunk, at an alehouse, turned into a wretched drummer boy, with his hair sticking on end with powder and pomatum, a long cue at his back, and tricked out in the loathsome finery of the profession of blood.

Such were the notes our once-loved poet sung.[3]

And for myself, I could not have been more delighted if I had heard the music of the spheres. Poetry and Philosophy had met together. Truth and Genius had embraced, under the eye and with the sanction of Religion. This was even beyond my hopes. I returned home well satisfied. The sun that was still laboring pale and wan through the sky, obscured by thick mists, seemed an emblem of the *good cause*;[4] and the cold dank drops of dew, that hung half melted on the beard of the thistle, had something genial and refreshing in them; for there was a spirit of hope and youth in all nature, that turned everything into good. The face of nature had not then the brand of *Jus Divinum*[5] on it:

Like to that sanguine flower inscribed with woe.[6]

On the Tuesday following, the half-inspired speaker came. I was called down into the room where he was, and went half-hoping, half-afraid. He received me very graciously, and I listened for a long time without uttering a word. I did not suffer in his opinion by my silence. "For those two hours," he afterwards was pleased to say, "he was conversing with W. H.'s forehead!" His appearance was different from what I had anticipated from seeing him before. At a distance, and in the dim light of the chapel, there was to me a strange wildness in his aspect, a dusky obscurity, and I thought him pitted with the smallpox. His complexion was at that time clear, and even bright—

As are the children of yon azure sheen.[7]

His forehead was broad and high, light as if built of ivory, with large projecting eyebrows, and his eyes rolling beneath them, like a sea with darkened luster. "A certain tender bloom his face o'erspread,"[8] a purple tinge as we see it in the pale thoughtful complexions of the Spanish portrait painters, Murillo and Velasquez. His mouth was gross, voluptuous, open, eloquent; his chin good-humored and round; but his nose, the rudder of the face, the index of the will, was small, feeble, nothing—like what he has done. It might seem that the genius of his face as from a height surveyed and projected him (with sufficient capacity and huge aspiration) into the world unknown of thought and imagination, with nothing to support or guide his veering purpose, as if Columbus had launched his adventurous course for the New World in a scallop,[9] with-out oars or compass. So at least I comment on it

1. Sir Philip Sidney's *Arcadia* 1.2.
2. Trapped into enlisting in military service.
3. The first line of Pope's *Epistle to Robert, Earl of Oxford*.
4. The cause of liberty, i.e., the French Revolution.
5. The divine right (of kings).
6. I.e., the hyacinth, believed to be marked with the Greek lament "AI AI"; the line is from Milton's *Lycidas* (106).
7. Adapted from James Thomson's *The Castle of Indolence* 2.33.
8. See Thomson's *The Castle of Indolence* 1.57.
9. Probably for *shallop*, a small boat.

after the event. Coleridge in his person was rather above the common size, inclining to the corpulent, or like Lord Hamlet, "somewhat fat and pursy."[1] His hair (now, alas! gray) was then black and glossy as the raven's, and fell in smooth masses over his forehead. This long pendulous hair is peculiar to enthusiasts, to those whose minds tend heavenward; and is traditionally inseparable (though of a different color) from the pictures of Christ. It ought to belong, as a character, to all who preach *Christ crucified*, and Coleridge was at that time one of those!

It was curious to observe the contrast between him and my father, who was a veteran in the cause, and then declining into the vale of years. He had been a poor Irish lad, carefully brought up by his parents, and sent to the University of Glasgow (where he studied under Adam Smith[2]) to prepare him for his future destination. It was his mother's proudest wish to see her son a Dissenting Minister. So if we look back to past generations (as far as eye can reach) we see the same hopes, fears, wishes, followed by the same disappointments, throbbing in the human heart; and so we may see them (if we look forward) rising up forever, and disappearing, like vaporish bubbles, in the human breast! After being tossed about from congregation to congregation in the heats of the Unitarian controversy, and squabbles about the American war,[3] he had been relegated to an obscure village, where he was to spend the last thirty years of his life, far from the only converse that he loved, the talk about disputed texts of Scripture and the cause of civil and religious liberty. Here he passed his days, repining but resigned, in the study of the Bible, and the perusal of the Commentators—huge folios, not easily got through, one of which would outlast a winter! Why did he pore on these from morn to night (with the exception of a walk in the fields or a turn in the garden to gather broccoli plants or kidney beans of his own rearing, with no small degree of pride and pleasure)? Here were "no figures nor no fantasies"[4]—neither poetry nor philosophy—nothing to dazzle, nothing to excite modern curiosity; but to his lackluster eyes there appeared, within the pages of the ponderous, unwieldy, neglected tomes, the sacred name of JEHOVAH in Hebrew capitals: pressed down by the weight of the style, worn to the last fading thinness of the understanding, there were glimpses, glimmering notions of the patriarchal wanderings, with palm trees hovering in the horizon, and processions of camels at the distance of three thousand years; there was Moses with the Burning Bush, the number of the Twelve Tribes, types, shadows,[5] glosses on the law and the prophets; there were discussions (dull enough) on the age of Methuselah, a mighty speculation! there were outlines, rude guesses at the shape of Noah's Ark and of the riches of Solomon's Temple; questions as to the date of the creation, predictions of the end of all things; the great lapses of time, the strange mutations of the globe were unfolded with the voluminous leaf, as it turned over; and though the soul might slumber with an hieroglyphic veil of inscrutable mysteries drawn over it, yet it was in a slumber ill-exchanged for all the sharpened realities of sense, wit, fancy, or reason. My father's life was comparatively a dream; but

1. Cf. *Hamlet* 3.4.144, 5.2.230.
2. Scottish philosopher and author of the great economic treatise *The Wealth of Nations* (1776).
3. The American Revolution, with which a number of radical Unitarian preachers were in sympathy.

4. *Julius Caesar* 2.1.230.
5. Old Testament foreshadowings of later events, or symbols of moral and theological truths. "Types": characters and events in the Old Testament believed to prefigure analogous matters in the New Testament.

it was a dream of infinity and eternity, of death, the resurrection, and a judgment to come!

No two individuals were ever more unlike than were the host and his guest. A poet was to my father a sort of nondescript: yet whatever added grace to the Unitarian cause was to him welcome. He could hardly have been more surprised or pleased if our visitor had worn wings. Indeed, his thoughts had wings; and as the silken sounds rustled round our little wainscoted parlor, my father threw back his spectacles over his forehead, his white hairs mixing with its sanguine hue; and a smile of delight beamed across his rugged cordial face, to think that Truth had found a new ally in Fancy! Besides, Coleridge seemed to take considerable notice of me, and that of itself was enough. He talked very familiarly, but agreeably, and glanced over a variety of subjects. At dinner time he grew more animated, and dilated in a very edifying manner on Mary Wollstonecraft and Mackintosh.[6] The last, he said, he considered (on my father's speaking of his *Vindiciae Gallicae* as a capital performance) as a clever scholastic[7] man—a master of the topics—or as the ready warehouseman of letters, who knew exactly where to lay his hand on what he wanted, though the goods were not his own. He thought him no match for Burke, either in style or matter. Burke was a metaphysician, Mackintosh a mere logician. Burke was an orator (almost a poet) who reasoned in figures, because he had an eye for nature: Mackintosh, on the other hand, was a rhetorician, who had only an eye to commonplaces. On this I ventured to say that I had always entertained a great opinion of Burke, and that (as far as I could find) the speaking of him with contempt might be made the test of a vulgar democratical mind. This was the first observation I ever made to Coleridge, and he said it was a very just and striking one. I remember the leg of Welsh mutton and the turnips on the table that day had the finest flavor imaginable. Coleridge added that Mackintosh and Tom Wedgwood[8] (of whom, however, he spoke highly) had expressed a very indifferent opinion of his friend Mr. Wordsworth, on which he remarked to them—"He strides on so far before you that he dwindles in the distance!" Godwin[9] had once boasted to him of having carried on an argument with Mackintosh for three hours with dubious success; Coleridge told him—"If there had been a man of genius in the room, he would have settled the question in five minutes." He asked me if I had ever seen Mary Wollstonecraft, and I said I had once for a few moments, and that she seemed to me to turn off Godwin's objections to something she advanced with quite a playful, easy air. He replied, that "this was only one instance of the ascendancy which people of imagination exercised over those of mere intellect." He did not rate Godwin very high (this was caprice or prejudice, real or affected) but he had a great idea of Mrs. Wollstonecraft's powers of conversation, none at all of her talent for book-making. We talked a little about Holcroft.[1] He had been asked if he was not much struck *with* him, and he said, he thought himself in more

6. Mary Wollstonecraft's *A Vindication of the Rights of Men* (1790) and the Scottish philosopher James Mackintosh's *Vindiciae Gallicae* ("Defense of France," 1791) were both written in opposition to Edmund Burke's *Reflections on the French Revolution* (1790).
7. The Scholastics, medieval philosophers and theologians, organized their thought systematically, often under various "topics"—standard headings, or "commonplaces" (see the third sentence following).
8. Son of Josiah Wedgwood (1730–1795), who founded the great pottery firm that still exists.
9. William Godwin (1756–1836), radical philosopher and didactic novelist, author of the influential *Inquiry Concerning Political Justice* (1793).
1. Thomas Holcroft (1749–1809), another radical contemporary, author of plays and novels.

danger of being struck *by* him. I complained that he would not let me get on at all, for he required a definition of even the commonest word, exclaiming, "What do you mean by a *sensation*, sir? What do you mean by an *idea?*" This, Coleridge said, was barricadoing the road to truth: it was setting up a turnpike gate at every step we took. I forget a great number of things, many more than I remember; but the day passed off pleasantly, and the next morning Mr. Coleridge was to return to Shrewsbury. When I came down to breakfast, I found that he had just received a letter from his friend, T. Wedgwood, making him an offer of £150 a year if he chose to waive his present pursuit, and devote himself entirely to the study of poetry and philosophy. Coleridge seemed to make up his mind to close with this proposal in the act of tying on one of his shoes. It threw an additional damp on his departure. It took the wayward enthusiast quite from us to cast him into Deva's winding vales,[2] or by the shores of old romance. Instead of living at ten miles' distance, of being the pastor of a Dissenting congregation at Shrewsbury, he was henceforth to inhabit the Hill of Parnassus, to be a Shepherd on the Delectable Mountains.[3] Alas! I knew not the way thither, and felt very little gratitude for Mr. Wedgwood's bounty. I was presently relieved from this dilemma; for Mr. Coleridge, asking for a pen and ink, and going to a table to write something on a bit of card, advanced towards me with undulating step, and giving me the precious document, said that that was his address, *Mr. Coleridge, Nether Stowey, Somersetshire;* and that he should be glad to see me there in a few weeks' time, and, if I chose, would come half-way to meet me. I was not less surprised than the shepherd boy (this simile is to be found in *Cassandra*[4]) when he sees a thunderbolt fall close at his feet. I stammered out my acknowledgments and acceptance of this offer (I thought Mr. Wedgwood's annuity a trifle to it) as well as I could; and this mighty business being settled, the poet-preacher took leave, and I accompanied him six miles on the road. It was a fine morning in the middle of winter, and he talked the whole way. The scholar in Chaucer is described as going

——sounding on his way.[5]

So Coleridge went on his. In digressing, in dilating, in passing from subject to subject, he appeared to me to float in air, to slide on ice. He told me in confidence (going along) that he should have preached two sermons before he accepted the situation at Shrewsbury, one on Infant Baptism, the other on the Lord's Supper, showing that he could not administer either, which would have effectually disqualified him for the object in view. I observed that he continually crossed me on the way by shifting from one side of the footpath to the other. This struck me as an odd movement; but I did not at that time connect it with any instability of purpose or involuntary change of principle, as I have done since. He seemed unable to keep on in a straight line. He spoke slightingly of Hume[6] (whose *Essay on Miracles* he said was stolen

---

2. Milton, *Lycidas*, line 55: "Nor yet where Deva spreads her wizard stream" ("Deva" is the river Dee, in Wales). Because Milton speaks in the passage of "Druid bards," Hazlitt means that Coleridge will devote himself to imaginative writing.
3. An allegorical locale in John Bunyan's *Pilgrim's Progress*, here used as another periphrasis for the occupation of poetry.
4. A romance by the 17th-century French writer La Calprenède.
5. *The Canterbury Tales, General Prologue,* line 309: "Souning in moral vertu was his speeche" (in Chaucer, the meaning of "souning in" is either "resounding in" or "consonant with").
6. David Hume, 18th-century Scottish philosopher.

from an objection started in one of South's sermons—*Credat Judaeus Appella!*[7]). I was not very much pleased at this account of Hume, for I had just been reading, with infinite relish, that completest of all metaphysical *choke-pears*,[8] his *Treatise on Human Nature*, to which the *Essays*, in point of scholastic subtlety and close reasoning, are mere elegant trifling, light summer reading. Coleridge even denied the excellence of Hume's general style, which I think betrayed a want of taste or candor. He however made me amends by the manner in which he spoke of Berkeley.[9] He dwelt particularly on his *Essay on Vision* as a masterpiece of analytical reasoning. So it undoubtedly is. He was exceedingly angry with Dr. Johnson for striking the stone with his foot, in allusion to this author's theory of matter and spirit, and saying, "Thus I confute him, sir."[1] Coleridge drew a parallel (I don't know how he brought about the connection) between Bishop Berkeley and Tom Paine.[2] He said the one was an instance of a subtle, the other of an acute mind, than which no two things could be more distinct. The one was a shopboy's quality, the other the characteristic of a philosopher. He considered Bishop Butler[3] as a true philosopher, a profound and conscientious thinker, a genuine reader of nature and of his own mind. He did not speak of his *Analogy*, but of his *Sermons at the Rolls' Chapel*, of which I had never heard. Coleridge somehow always contrived to prefer the *unknown* to the *known*. In this instance he was right. The *Analogy* is a tissue of sophistry, of wiredrawn, theological special-pleading; the *Sermons* (with the Preface to them) are in a fine vein of deep, matured reflection, a candid appeal to our observation of human nature, without pedantry and without bias. I told Coleridge I had written a few remarks, and was sometimes foolish enough to believe that I had made a discovery on the same subject (the *Natural Disinterestedness of the Human Mind*)[4]—and I tried to explain my view of it to Coleridge, who listened with great willingness, but I did not succeed in making myself understood. I sat down to the task shortly afterwards for the twentieth time, got new pens and paper, determined to make clear work of it, wrote a few meager sentences in the skeleton-style of a mathematical demonstration, stopped halfway down the second page; and, after trying in vain to pump up any words, images, notions, apprehensions, facts, or observations, from that gulf of abstraction in which I had plunged myself for four or five years preceding, gave up the attempt as labor in vain, and shed tears of helpless despondency on the blank unfinished paper. I can write fast enough now. Am I better than I was then? Oh no! One truth discovered, one pang of regret at not being able to express it, is better than all the fluency and flippancy in the world. Would that I could go back to what I then was! Why can we not revive past times as we can revisit old places? If I had the quaint Muse of Sir Philip Sidney to assist me, I would write a *Sonnet to the Road between Wem and Shrewsbury*, and immortalize every step of it by some fond

7. From Horace's *Satires* 1.5.100: "Let Appella the Jew believe it" (Latin); implying that he himself does not. Robert South (1634–1716), Anglican divine.
8. A very sour variety of pear; hence, anything hard to take in.
9. Bishop George Berkeley, 18th-century Irish idealist philosopher and author of an *Essay toward a New Theory of Vision* (1709).
1. The anecdote is in James Boswell's *The Life of*

Samuel Johnson.
2. Philosophical supporter of the American and French Revolutions and author of *Common Sense* and *The Rights of Man*.
3. Joseph Butler, 18th-century theologian and moral philosopher, author of the *Analogy of Religion* (1736).
4. Published as *An Essay on the Principles of Human Action* (1805).

enigmatical conceit. I would swear that the very milestones had ears, and that Harmer Hill stooped with all its pines, to listen to a poet, as he passed! I remember but one other topic of discourse in this walk. He mentioned Paley,[5] praised the naturalness and clearness of his style, but condemned his sentiments, thought him a mere time-serving casuist, and said that "the fact of his work on Moral and Political Philosophy being made a textbook in our universities was a disgrace to the national character." We parted at the six-mile stone; and I returned homeward pensive but much pleased. I had met with unexpected notice from a person whom I believed to have been preju-diced against me. "Kind and affable to me had been his condescension, and should be honored ever with suitable regard."[6] He was the first poet I had known, and he certainly answered to that inspired name. I had heard a great deal of his powers of conversation, and was not disappointed. In fact, I never met with anything at all like them, either before or since. I could easily credit the accounts which were circulated of his holding forth to a large party of ladies and gentlemen, an evening or two before, on the Berkeleian Theory, when he made the whole material universe look like a transparency of fine words; and another story (which I believe he has somewhere told himself)[7] of his being asked to a party at Birmingham, of his smoking tobacco and going to sleep after dinner on a sofa, where the company found him, to their no small surprise, which was increased to wonder when he started up of a sudden, and rubbing his eyes, looked about him, and launched into a three hours' description of the third heaven, of which he had had a dream, very different from Mr. Southey's *Vision of Judgment*, and also from that other *Vision of Judgment*, which Mr. Murray, the secretary of the Bridge Street Junto,[8] has taken into his especial keeping!

On my way back, I had a sound in my ears, it was the voice of Fancy: I had a light before me, it was the face of Poetry. The one still lingers there, the other has not quitted my side! Coleridge in truth met me half-way on the ground of philosophy, or I should not have been won over to his imagi-native creed. I had an uneasy, pleasurable sensation all the time, till I was to visit him. During those months the chill breath of winter gave me a wel-coming; the vernal air was balm and inspiration to me. The golden sunsets, the silver star of evening, lighted me on my way to new hopes and prospects. *I was to visit Coleridge in the spring.* This circumstance was never absent from my thoughts, and mingled with all my feelings. I wrote to him at the time proposed, and received an answer postponing my intended visit for a week or two, but very cordially urging me to complete my promise then. This delay did not damp, but rather increased my ardor. In the meantime, I went to Llangollen Vale,[9] by way of initiating myself in the mysteries of natural scenery; and I must say I was enchanted with it. I had been reading Cole-ridge's description of England in his fine *Ode on the Departing Year*, and I

5. William Paley, author of *Evidences of Christi-anity* (1794) and supporter of a utilitarian theology and morality.
6. Paraphrasing Adam's words about the angel Raphael in *Paradise Lost* 8.648–50.
7. See Coleridge's *Biographia Literaria*, chap. 10.
8. Robert Southey's *A Vision of Judgment* is a syc-ophantic memorial poem describing the entrance into heaven of George III. Charles Murray was

solicitor to an association, located at New Bridge Street, for "Opposing Disloyal and Seditious Prin-ciples." He prosecuted John Hunt for publishing Byron's *The Vision of Judgment*, a brilliant parody of Southey's poem. Hazlitt derisively refers to the association as a "junto," i.e., a group formed for political intrigue.
9. In north Wales (about thirty-five miles from Wem).

applied it, *con amore*,[1] to the objects before me. That valley was to me (in a manner) the cradle of a new existence: in the river that winds through it, my spirit was baptized in the waters of Helicon![2]

I returned home, and soon after set out on my journey with unworn heart and untired feet. My way lay through Worcester and Gloucester, and by Upton, where I thought of Tom Jones and the adventure of the muff.[3] I remember getting completely wet through one day, and stopping at an inn (I think it was at Tewkesbury) where I sat up all night to read *Paul and Virginia*.[4] Sweet were the showers in early youth that drenched my body, and sweet the drops of pity that fell upon the books I read! I recollect a remark of Coleridge's upon this very book that nothing could show the gross indelicacy of French manners and the entire corruption of their imagination more strongly than the behavior of the heroine in the last fatal scene, who turns away from a person on board the sinking vessel, that offers to save her life, because he has thrown off his clothes to assist him in swimming. Was this a time to think of such a circumstance? I once hinted to Wordsworth, as we were sailing in his boat on Grasmere lake, that I thought he had borrowed the idea of his *Poems on the Naming of Places* from the local inscriptions of the same kind in *Paul and Virginia*. He did not own the obligation, and stated some distinction without a difference in defense to his claim to originality. Any the slightest variation would be sufficient for this purpose in his mind; for whatever he added or omitted would inevitably be worth all that any one else had done, and contain the marrow of the sentiment. I was still two days before the time fixed for my arrival, for I had taken care to set out early enough. I stopped these two days at Bridgewater, and when I was tired of sauntering on the banks of its muddy river, returned to the inn and read *Camilla*.[5] So have I loitered my life away, reading books, looking at pictures, going to plays, hearing, thinking, writing on what pleased me best. I have wanted only one thing to make me happy; but wanting that, have wanted everything![6]

I arrived, and was well received. The country about Nether Stowey is beautiful, green and hilly, and near the seashore. I saw it but the other day, after an interval of twenty years, from a hill near Taunton. How was the map of my life spread out before me, as the map of the country lay at my feet! In the afternoon, Coleridge took me over to Alfoxden, a romantic old family mansion of the St. Aubins, where Wordsworth lived. It was then in the possession of a friend of the poet's, who gave him the free use of it.[7] Somehow, that period (the time just after the French Revolution) was not a time when *nothing was given for nothing*. The mind opened and a softness might be perceived coming over the heart of individuals, beneath "the scales that fence" our self-interest. Wordsworth himself was from home, but his sister kept house, and set before us a frugal repast; and we had free access to her brother's poems, the *Lyrical Ballads,* which were still in manuscript, or in the form of *Sybilline Leaves*.[8] I dipped into a few of these with great satisfaction, and with the faith of a novice. I slept that night in an old room with

---

1. "With love," fervently (Italian).
2. A mountain sacred to Apollo and the Muses.
3. Henry Fielding's *Tom Jones* 10.5ff.
4. A sentimental love idyll (1788) by the French writer Bernardin de Saint-Pierre.
5. A novel by Fanny Burney, published in 1796.

6. The love of Sarah Walker, the daughter of Hazlitt's landlord. He describes his infatuation with her in *Liber Amoris* (1823).
7. A mistake; Wordsworth paid rent.
8. I.e., "prophetic writings"; used by Coleridge as the title for his published poems in 1817.

blue hangings, and covered with the round-faced family portraits of the age of George I and II and from the wooded declivity of the adjoining park that overlooked my window, at the dawn of day, could

———hear the loud stag speak.[9]

In the outset of life (and particularly at this time I felt it so) our imagination has a body to it. We are in a state between sleeping and waking, and have indistinct but glorious glimpses of strange shapes, and there is always something to come better than what we see. As in our dreams the fullness of the blood gives warmth and reality to the coinage of the brain, so in youth our ideas are clothed, and fed, and pampered with our good spirits; we breathe thick with thoughtless happiness, the weight of future years presses on the strong pulses of the heart, and we repose with undisturbed faith in truth and good. As we advance, we exhaust our fund of enjoyment and of hope. We are no longer wrapped in *lamb's wool*, lulled in Elysium. As we taste the pleasures of life, their spirit evaporates, the sense palls; and nothing is left but the phantoms, the lifeless shadows of what *has been*!

That morning, as soon as breakfast was over, we strolled out into the park, and seating ourselves on the trunk of an old ash tree that stretched along the ground, Coleridge read aloud with a sonorous and musical voice, the ballad of *Betty Foy*.[1] I was not critically or skeptically inclined. I saw touches of truth and nature, and took the rest for granted. But in the *Thorn*, the *Mad Mother*, and the *Complaint of a Poor Indian Woman*, I felt that deeper power and pathos which have been since acknowledged,

In spite of pride, in erring reason's spite,[2]

as the characteristics of this author; and the sense of a new style and a new spirit in poetry came over me. It had to me something of the effect that arises from the turning up of the fresh soil, or of the first welcome breath of spring,

While yet the trembling year is unconfirmed.[3]

Coleridge and myself walked back to Stowey that evening, and his voice sounded high

Of Providence, foreknowledge, will, and fate,
Fixed fate, free will, foreknowledge absolute,[4]

as we passed through echoing grove, by fairy stream or waterfall, gleaming in the summer moonlight! He lamented that Wordsworth was not prone enough to believe in the traditional superstitions of the place, and that there was a something corporeal, a *matter-of-fact-ness*, a clinging to the palpable, or often to the petty, in his poetry, in consequence. His genius was not a spirit that descended to·him through the air; it sprung out of the ground like a flower, or unfolded itself from a green spray, on which the goldfinch sang. He said, however (if I remember right), that this objection must be confined to his descriptive pieces, that his philosophic poetry had a grand and comprehensive spirit in it, so that his soul seemed to inhabit the universe like a

9. Ben Jonson's poem *To Sir Robert Wroth*, line 22.
1. Wordsworth's *Idiot Boy*. Like the other poems mentioned, it was included in *Lyrical Ballads*.

2. Pope's *Essay on Man* 1.293.
3. James Thomson's *The Seasons: Spring*, line 18.
4. *Paradise Lost* 2.559–60.

palace, and to discover truth by intuition, rather than by deduction. The next day Wordsworth arrived from Bristol at Coleridge's cottage. I think I see him now. He answered in some degree to his friend's description of him, but was more gaunt and Don Quixote-like. He was quaintly dressed (according to the *costume* of that unconstrained period) in a brown fustian[5] jacket and striped pantaloons. There was something of a roll, a lounge in his gait, not unlike his own Peter Bell.[6] There was a severe, worn pressure of thought about his temples, a fire in his eye (as if he saw something in objects more than the outward appearance), an intense high narrow forehead, a Roman nose, cheeks furrowed by strong purpose and feeling, and a convulsive inclination to laughter about the mouth, a good deal at variance with the solemn, stately expression of the rest of his face. Chantry's bust wants the marking traits; but he was teased into making it regular and heavy; Haydon's[7] head of him, introduced into the *Entrance of Christ into Jerusalem,* is the most like his drooping weight of thought and expression. He sat down and talked very naturally and freely, with a mixture of clear gushing accents in his voice, a deep guttural intonation, and a strong tincture of the northern *burr,* like the crust on wine. He instantly began to make havoc of the half of a Cheshire cheese on the table, and said triumphantly that "his marriage with experience had not been so unproductive as Mr. Southey's in teaching him a knowledge of the good things of this life." He had been to see the *Castle Spectre* by Monk Lewis,[8] while at Bristol, and described it very well. He said "it fitted the taste of the audience like a glove." This *ad captandum*[9] merit was, however, by no means a recommendation of it, according to the severe principles of the new school, which reject rather than court popular effect. Wordsworth, looking out of the low, latticed window, said, "How beautifully the sun sets on that yellow bank!" I thought within myself, "With what eyes these poets see nature!" and ever after, when I saw the sunset stream upon the objects facing it, conceived I had made a discovery, or thanked Mr. Wordsworth for having made one for me! We went over to Alfoxden again the day following, and Wordsworth read us the story of *Peter Bell* in the open air; and the comment made upon it by his face and voice was very different from that of some later critics! Whatever might be thought of the poem, "his face was as a book where men might read strange matters,"[1] and he announced the fate of his hero in prophetic tones. There is a *chaunt* in the recitation both of Coleridge and Wordsworth, which acts as a spell upon the hearer, and disarms the judgment. Perhaps they have deceived themselves by making habitual use of this ambiguous accompaniment. Coleridge's manner is more full, animated, and varied; Wordsworth's more equable, sustained, and internal. The one might be termed more *dramatic,* the other more *lyrical.* Coleridge has told me that he himself liked to compose in walking over uneven ground, or breaking through the straggling branches of a copse wood; whereas Wordsworth always wrote (if he could) walking up and down a straight gravel walk, or in some spot where the continuity of his verse met with no collateral interruption. Returning that same evening, I got

---

5. A coarse and heavy cotton cloth.
6. The protagonist in Wordsworth's poem *Peter Bell.*
7. Benjamin Robert Haydon, painter of grandiose historical and religious pictures. Sir Francis Chantrey, a sculptor.

8. Matthew Gregory Lewis, called "Monk" Lewis from his horror tale *The Monk* (1795). *The Castle Spectre* was a play, also in the Gothic terror-mode.
9. "For the sake of captivating" an audience.
1. See *Macbeth* 1.5.60–61.

into a metaphysical argument with Wordsworth, while Coleridge was explaining the different notes of the nightingale to his sister, in which we neither of us succeeded in making ourselves perfectly clear and intelligible. Thus I passed three weeks at Nether Stowey and in the neighborhood, generally devoting the afternoons to a delightful chat in an arbor made of bark by the poet's friend Tom Poole, sitting under two fine elm trees, and listening to the bees humming round us while we quaffed our flip.[2] It was agreed, among other things, that we should make a jaunt down the Bristol Channel, as far as Linton. We set off together on foot, Coleridge, John Chester, and I. This Chester was a native of Nether Stowey, one of those who were attracted to Coleridge's discourse as flies are to honey, or bees in swarming-time to the sound of a brass pan. He "followed in the chase like a dog who hunts, not like one that made up the cry."[3] He had on a brown cloth coat, boots, and corduroy breeches, was low in stature, bowlegged, had a drag in his walk like a drover, which he assisted by a hazel switch, and kept on a sort of trot by the side of Coleridge, like a running footman by a state coach, that he might not lose a syllable or sound that fell from Coleridge's lips. He told me his private opinion, that Coleridge was a wonderful man. He scarcely opened his lips, much less offered an opinion the whole way: yet of the three, had I to choose during that journey, I would be John Chester. He afterwards followed Coleridge into Germany, where the Kantean philosophers were puzzled how to bring him under any of their categories. When he sat down at table with his idol, John's felicity was complete; Sir Walter Scott's, or Mr. Blackwood's, when they sat down at the same table with the King,[4] was not more so. We passed Dunster on our right, a small town between the brow of a hill and the sea. I remember eying it wistfully as it lay below us: contrasted with the woody scene around, it looked as clear, as pure, as *embrowned* and ideal as any landscape I have seen since, of Gaspar Poussin's or Domenichino's. We had a long day's march—(our feet kept time to the echoes of Coleridge's tongue)—through Minehead and by the Blue Anchor, and on to Linton, which we did not reach till near midnight, and where we had some difficulty in making a lodgment. We however knocked the people of the house up at last, and we were repaid for our apprehensions and fatigue by some excellent rashers of fried bacon and eggs. The view in coming along had been splendid. We walked for miles and miles on dark brown heaths overlooking the channel, with the Welsh hills beyond, and at times descended into little sheltered valleys close by the seaside, with a smuggler's face scowling by us, and then had to ascend conical hills with a path winding up through a coppice to a barren top, like a monk's shaven crown, from one of which I pointed out to Coleridge's notice the bare masts of a vessel on the very edge of the horizon and within the red-orbed disk of the setting sun, like his own specter-ship in the *Ancient Mariner*. At Linton the character of the seacoast becomes more marked and rugged. There is a place called the Valley of Rocks (I suspect this was only the poetical name for it) bedded among precipices overhanging the sea, with rocky caverns beneath, into which the waves dash, and where the seagull forever wheels its screaming flight. On the tops of these are huge stones thrown transverse, as if an earth-

---

2. Spiced and sweetened ale.
3. See *Othello* 2.3.337–38.
4. At a banquet given to George IV at Edinburgh,

in 1822. William Blackwood, publisher of *Blackwood's Magazine,* was, like Scott, a Tory and hence a supporter of the king.

quake had tossed them there, and behind these is a fretwork of perpendicular rocks, something like the Giant's Causeway.[5] A thunderstorm came on while we were at the inn, and Coleridge was running out bareheaded to enjoy the commotion of the elements in the Valley of Rocks, but as if in spite, the clouds only muttered a few angry sounds, and let fall a few refreshing drops. Coleridge told me that he and Wordsworth were to have made this place the scene of a prose tale, which was to have been in the manner of, but far superior to, the *Death of Abel*,[6] but they had relinquished the design. In the morning of the second day, we breakfasted luxuriously in an old-fashioned parlor, on tea, toast, eggs, and honey, in the very sight of the beehives from which it had been taken, and a garden full of thyme and wild flowers that had produced it. On this occasion Coleridge spoke of Virgil's *Georgics*, but not well. I do not think he had much feeling for the classical or elegant. It was in this room that we found a little worn-out copy of the *Seasons*,[7] lying in a window seat, on which Coleridge exclaimed, "*That* is true fame!" He said Thomson was a great poet, rather than a good one; his style was as meretricious as his thoughts were natural. He spoke of Cowper as the best modern poet. He said the *Lyrical Ballads* were an experiment about to be tried by him and Wordsworth, to see how far the public taste would endure poetry written in a more natural and simple style than had hitherto been attempted; totally discarding the artifices of poetical diction, and making use only of such words as had probably been common in the most ordinary language since the days of Henry II. Some comparison was introduced between Shakespeare and Milton. He said "he hardly knew which to prefer. Shakespeare appeared to him a mere stripling in the art; he was as tall and as strong, with infinitely more activity than Milton, but he never appeared to have come to man's estate; or if he had, he would not have been a man, but a monster." He spoke with contempt of Gray, and with intolerance of Pope. He did not like the versification of the latter. He observed that "the ears of these couplet-writers might be charged with having short memories, that could not retain the harmony of whole passages." He thought little of Junius[8] as a writer; he had a dislike of Dr. Johnson; and a much higher opinion of Burke as an orator and politician, than of Fox or Pitt. He however thought him very inferior in richness of style and imagery to some of our elder prose writers, particularly Jeremy Taylor.[9] He liked Richardson, but not Fielding; nor could I get him to enter into the merits of *Caleb Williams*.[1] In short, he was profound and discriminating with respect to those authors whom he liked, and where he gave his judgment fair play; capricious, perverse, and prejudiced in his antipathies and distastes. We loitered on the "ribbed sea-sands,"[2] in such talk as this, a whole morning, and I recollect met with a curious seaweed, of which John Chester told us the country name! A fisherman gave Coleridge an account of a boy that had been drowned the day before, and that they had tried to save him at the risk of their own lives. He

---

5. A mass of rocks on the northern Irish coast.
6. The "prose tale" exists as a fragment, *The Wanderings of Cain. The Death of Abel* (1758) is by the once celebrated Swiss poet, Salomon Gessner.
7. By James Thomson, published in 1726–30.
8. The pseudonym of the author (whose identity is still uncertain) of a series of attacks on George III and various politicians, 1769–72.

9. The 17th-century divine, author of *Holy Living* (1650) and *Holy Dying* (1651).
1. A 1794 novel by William Godwin. Samuel Richardson and Henry Fielding, the great 18th-century novelists.
2. Echoing *The Rime of the Ancient Mariner*, line 227.

said "he did not know how it was that they ventured, but, sir, we have a *nature* towards one another." This expression, Coleridge remarked to me, was a fine illustration of that theory of disinterestedness which I (in common with Butler) had adopted. I broached to him an argument of mine to prove that *likeness* was not mere association of ideas. I said that the mark in the sand put one in mind of a man's foot, not because it was part of a former impression of a man's foot (for it was quite new) but because it was like the shape of a man's foot. He assented to the justness of this distinction (which I have explained at length elsewhere, for the benefit of the curious) and John Chester listened; not from any interest in the subject, but because he was astonished that I should be able to suggest anything to Coleridge that he did not already know. We returned on the third morning, and Coleridge remarked the silent cottage-smoke curling up the valleys where, a few evenings before, we had seen the lights gleaming through the dark.

In a day or two after we arrived at Stowey, we set out, I on my return home, and he for Germany. It was a Sunday morning, and he was to preach that day for Dr. Toulmin of Taunton. I asked him if he had prepared anything for the occasion? He said he had not even thought of the text, but should as soon as we parted. I did not go to hear him—this was a fault—but we met in the evening at Bridgewater. The next day we had a long day's walk to Bristol, and sat down, I recollect, by a well-side on the road, to cool ourselves and satisfy our thirst, when Coleridge repeated to me some descriptive lines from his tragedy of *Remorse;* which I must say became his mouth and that occasion better than they, some years after, did Mr. Elliston's[3] and the Drury Lane boards,

> Oh memory! shield me from the world's poor strife,
> And give those scenes thine everlasting life.

I saw no more of him for a year or two, during which period he had been wandering in the Hartz Forest in Germany; and his return was cometary, meteorous, unlike his setting out. It was not till some time after that I knew his friends Lamb and Southey. The last always appears to me (as I first saw him) with a commonplace-book under his arm, and the first with a bon mot in his mouth. It was at Godwin's that I met him with Holcroft and Coleridge, where they were disputing fiercely which was the best—*Man as he was, or man as he is to be.* "Give me," says Lamb, "man as he is *not* to be." This saying was the beginning of a friendship between us, which I believe still continues.—Enough of this for the present.

> But there is matter for another rhyme,
> And I to this may add a second tale.[4]

1823

---

3. Robert William Elliston, a well-known actor. Coleridge's *Remorse* was produced at Drury Lane in 1813.

4. Wordsworth, *Hart-Leap Well*, lines 95–96.

THOMAS MOORE
1779–1852

Although he was an Irish Catholic and the son of a Dublin grocer, Tom Moore became the fashionable versifier of Regency England. His *Irish Melodies*, published between 1807 and 1834 with accompanying music (some of the tunes by Moore himself), were an immense success, and for many years his wit, charm, liberalism, and singing voice made him a brilliant figure in literary and social circles, especially among the aristocratic Whig reformers. The same qualities made him one of Byron's closest friends. He wrote numerous satires, lampoons, and prose pieces. He is chiefly remembered, however, for the Oriental verse romance *Lalla Rookh* (1817), which achieved a great European success; his fine *Life of Byron* (1830); and for a handful of songs—most of them in the tradition of amatory gallantry that goes back to the seventeenth-century Cavaliers—that have won their way into the repertory that is sung around the piano on a social evening.

Believe me, if all those endearing young charms

Believe me, if all those endearing young charms,
    Which I gaze on so fondly today,
Were to change by tomorrow, and fleet in my arms,
    Like fairy-gifts fading away,
5 Thou wouldst still be adored, as this moment thou art,
    Let thy loveliness fade as it will,
And around the dear ruin each wish of my heart
    Would entwine itself verdantly still.

It is not while beauty and youth are thine own,
10   And thy cheeks unprofaned by a tear
That the fervor and faith of a soul can be known,
    To which time will but make thee more dear;
No, the heart that has truly loved never forgets,
    But as truly loves on to the close,
15 As the sunflower turns on her god, when he sets,
    The same look which she turned when he rose.

1808

The harp that once through Tara's halls[1]

The harp that once through Tara's halls
    The soul of music shed,
Now hangs as mute on Tara's walls
    As if that soul were fled.—
5 So sleeps the pride of former days,
    So glory's thrill is o'er,

---

1. Tara, northwest of Dublin, was the capital of Ireland during the early Middle Ages, when that country was a center of European civilization and learning.

And hearts that once beat high for praise
Now feel that pulse no more.

No more to chiefs and ladies bright
10　　The harp of Tara swells;
The chord alone that breaks at night
Its tale of ruin tells.
Thus Freedom now so seldom wakes,
The only throb she gives,
15　Is when some heart indignant breaks,
To show that still she lives.

1834

The time I've lost in wooing

The time I've lost in wooing,
In watching and pursuing
The light that lies
In woman's eyes,
5　Has been my heart's undoing.
Though Wisdom oft has sought me,
I scorned the lore she brought me,
My only books
Were woman's looks,
10　And folly's all they've taught me.

Her smile when Beauty granted,
I hung with gaze enchanted,
Like him, the sprite,[1]
Whom maids by night
15　Oft meet in glen that's haunted.
Like him, too, Beauty won me,
But while her eyes were on me;
If once their ray
Was turned away,
20　Oh! winds could not outrun me.

And are those follies going?
And is my proud heart growing
Too cold or wise
For brilliant eyes
25　Again to set it glowing?
No, vain, alas! th' endeavor
From bonds so sweet to sever;
Poor Wisdom's chance
Against a glance
30　Is now as weak as ever.

1834

1. The Irish fairy; he can be controlled by mortals only when their eyes are fixed on him.

THOMAS DE QUINCEY
1785–1859

De Quincey's father was a wealthy merchant who died when Thomas was seven years old. The boy was a precocious scholar, especially in Latin and Greek, and a gentle and bookish introvert; he found it difficult to adapt himself to discipline and routine and was thrown into panic by any emergency that called for decisive action. He ran away from Manchester Grammar School and, after a summer spent tramping through Wales, broke off completely from his family and guardians and went to London in the hope that he could obtain from moneylenders an advance on his prospective inheritance. There at the age of seventeen he spent a terrible winter of loneliness and destitution, befriended only by some kindly streetwalkers. These early experiences with the sinister aspect of city life later became persistent elements in his dreams of terror.

After a reconciliation with his guardians he entered Worcester College, Oxford, on an inadequate allowance. He spent the years 1803–08 in sporadic attendance, isolated as usual, then left abruptly in the middle of his examination for the A.B. with honors because he could not face the ordeal of an oral examination.

De Quincey had been an early admirer of Wordsworth and Coleridge. No sooner did he come of age and into his inheritance than, with his usual combination of generosity and improvidence, he made Coleridge an anonymous gift of £300. He became an intimate friend of the Wordsworths at Grasmere, and when they left Dove Cottage for Allan Bank, took up his own residence at Dove Cottage to be near them. For a time he lived the life of a rural scholar, but then fell in love with Margaret Simpson, the daughter of a small local landholder and farmer and, after she had borne him a son, married her in February 1817. This affair led to an estrangement from the Wordsworths and left him in severe financial difficulties. Worse still, De Quincey at this time became completely enslaved to opium. Following the medical practice of the time, he had been taking the drug for a variety of painful ailments; but now, driven by poverty and despair as well as pain, he indulged in huge quantities of laudanum (opium dissolved in alcohol) and was never thereafter able to free himself from addiction to what he called "the pleasures and pains of opium." It was during periods of maximum use, and especially in the recurrent agonies of cutting down his opium dosage, that he experienced the grotesque and terrifying reveries and nightmares that he wove into his literary fantasies.

Desperate for income, De Quincey at last turned to writing at the age of thirty-six. *Confessions of an English Opium-Eater,* which he contributed to the *London Magazine,* scored an immediate success and was at once reprinted as a book, but it earned him little money. In 1828 he moved with his three children to Edinburgh, to write for *Blackwood's Magazine.* For almost the rest of his life, he led a harried existence, beset by many physical ills, struggling with his irresolution and melancholia and the horrors of the opium habit, dodging his creditors and the constant threat of imprisonment for debt. All the while he ground out articles on any salable subject in a ceaseless struggle to keep his children, who ultimately numbered eight, from starving to death. Only after his mother died and left him a small income was he able, in his sixties, to live in comparative ease and freedom under the care of his devoted and practical-minded daughters. His last decade he spent mainly in gathering, revising, and expanding his essays for his "Collective Edition"; the final volume appeared in 1860, the year after his death.

Although De Quincey's life was disorderly and his best-known writings were sensational, he was a conventional and conservative person—a rigid moralist, a Tory, and a faithful champion of the Church of England. Everybody who knew him testified to his gentleness, his courteous and musical speech, and his exquisite manners. Less obvious, under the surface timidity and irresolution, were the toughness and courage that sustained him through a long life of seemingly hopeless struggle.

Although more than 150 of De Quincey's anonymous essays have been identified, the great bulk of them were pieces of hasty journalism that are now read only by scholars. He served for a time as an important source of knowledge for Englishmen of the literature of the late eighteenth-century German renaissance. As a literary critic De Quincey was capable of a fine essay in critical impressionism, *On the Knocking at the Gate in "Macbeth,"* but he was too whimsical and unsystematic to rank with his greater contemporaries, Coleridge and Hazlitt. He wrote a number of vivid biographical sketches of writers he knew personally, most notably Wordsworth, Coleridge, Southey, and Lamb. His most distinctive and impressive achievements, however, are the writings that start with fact and move into macabre fantasy (*On Murder Considered as One of the Fine Arts*) and especially those that begin as quiet autobiography and develop into an elaborate construction made up from the materials of his reveries and dreams (*Confessions of an English Opium-Eater, Autobiographic Sketches, Suspiria de Profundis,* and *The English Mail Coach*). In these achievements, De Quincey opened up to English literature the nightside of human consciousness, with its grotesque strangeness, its *Angst* (anxiety), and its pervasive sense of guilt and alienation. "In dreams," he wrote, long before Sigmund Freud, "perhaps under some secret conflict of the midnight sleeper, lighted up to the consciousness at the time, but darkened to the memory as soon as all is finished, each several child of our mysterious race completes for himself the treason of the aboriginal fall." And for these dream writings he developed a mode of organization that is based on thematic statement, variation, and development in the art of music, in which he had a deep and abiding interest. Although by temperament a conservative, De Quincey was in his writings a radical innovator, whose experiments look ahead to the materials and methods of such later masters in prose and verse as James Joyce, Franz Kafka, and T. S. Eliot.

From Confessions of an English Opium-Eater[1]

From *Preliminary Confessions*[2]

[THE PROSTITUTE ANN]

* * * Another person there was at that time, whom I have since sought to trace with far deeper earnestness, and with far deeper sorrow at my failure.

1. The *Confessions* were published anonymously in two issues of the *London Magazine,* September and October 1821, and were reprinted as a book in the following year. In 1856 De Quincey revised the book for the collected edition of his writings, expanding it to more than twice its original length. The author was over seventy years old at the time and privately expressed the judgment that the expanded edition lacks the immediacy and artistic economy of the original. The selections here are from the version of the *Confessions* printed in 1822.

The work is divided into three parts. The first part, "Preliminary Confessions," deals with De Quincey's early experiences—at school, in Wales, and in London—before taking opium. Part Two, "The Pleasures of Opium" (omitted here), describes the early effects on his perceptions and reveries of his moderate and occasional indulgence in the drug. Part Three, "The Pains of Opium," is an elaborate and artful representation of his fantastic nightmares; these, in modern medical opinion, are in part withdrawal symptoms, during periods when he tried to cut down his use of opium.

In De Quincey's own lifetime, and ever since, the charge has been brought that the reports of these dreams were largely fabricated by the author. But De Quincey himself always insisted that they were substantially accurate; and both the fact and the content of such anguished nightmares are corroborated by the testimony of another laudanum addict, Samuel Taylor Coleridge, in his poem *The Pains of Sleep* (1803).

2. The seventeen-year-old De Quincey, unhappy at Manchester Grammar School, had run away and taken refuge in London, his whereabouts unknown to his mother and his guardians. He had slept outdoors for two months but has now been permitted, by a disreputable and seedy lawyer, to sleep in an unoccupied, unfurnished, and rat-infested house. There he and a ten-year-old girl, nameless and of uncertain parentage, huddle together for warmth, eking out a famished existence on whatever scraps he can scavenge from his landlord's frugal breakfast. He goes on to describe his friendship with a young prostitute, Ann.

This person was a young woman, and one of that unhappy class who subsist upon the wages of prostitution. I feel no shame, nor have any reason to feel it, in avowing, that I was then on familiar and friendly terms with many women in that unfortunate condition. The reader needs neither smile at this avowal, nor frown. For, not to remind my classical readers of the old Latin proverb—"*Sine Cerere*," &c.,[3] it may well be supposed that in the existing state of my purse, my connection with such women could not have been an impure one. But the truth is, that at no time of my life have I been a person to hold myself polluted by the touch or approach of any creature that wore a human shape: on the contrary, from my very earliest youth it has been my pride to converse familiarly, *more Socratico*,[4] with all human beings, man, woman, and child, that chance might fling in my way: a practice which is friendly to the knowledge of human nature, to good feelings, and to that frankness of address which becomes a man who would be thought a philosopher. For a philosopher should not see with the eyes of the poor limitary[5] creature, calling himself a man of the world, and filled with narrow and self-regarding prejudices of birth and education, but should look upon himself as a Catholic[6] creature, and as standing in an equal relation to high and low—to educated and uneducated, to the guilty and the innocent. Being myself at that time of necessity a peripatetic, or a walker of the street, I naturally fell in more frequently with those female peripatetics who are technically called street-walkers. Many of these women had occasionally taken my part against watchmen who wished to drive me off the steps of houses where I was sitting. But one amongst them, the one on whose account I have at all introduced this subject—yet no! let me not class thee, oh noble-minded Ann——, with that order of women; let me find, if it be possible, some gentler name to designate the condition of her to whose bounty and compassion, ministering to my necessities when all the world had forsaken me, I owe it that I am at this time alive.—For many weeks I had walked at nights with this poor friendless girl up and down Oxford Street, or had rested with her on steps and under the shelter of porticos. She could not be so old as myself: she told me, indeed, that she had not completed her sixteenth year. By such questions as my interest about her prompted, I had gradually drawn forth her simple history. Hers was a case of ordinary occurrence (as I have since had reason to think), and one in which, if London beneficence had better adapted its arrangements to meet it, the power of the law might oftener be interposed to protect, and to avenge. But the stream of London charity flows in a channel which, though deep and mighty, is yet noiseless and underground; not obvious or readily accessible to poor houseless wanderers; and it cannot be denied that the outside air and framework of London society is harsh, cruel, and repulsive. In any case, however, I saw that part of her injuries might easily have been redressed; and I urged her often and earnestly to lay her complaint before a magistrate: friendless as she was, I assured her that she would meet with immediate attention; and that English justice, which was no respecter of persons, would speedily and amply avenge her on the brutal ruffian who had plundered her little property. She promised me often that she would; but she delayed taking the steps I pointed out from

---

3. *Sine Cerere et Baccho friget Venus*—"without Ceres and Bacchus [food and wine], love grows cold."
4. "In the manner of Socrates"; i.e., by a dialogue

of questions and answers.
5. Limited.
6. In the sense of "inclusive in tastes and understanding."

time to time: for she was timid and dejected to a degree which showed how deeply sorrow had taken hold of her young heart: and perhaps she thought justly that the most upright judge, and the most righteous tribunals, could do nothing to repair her heaviest wrongs. Something, however, would perhaps have been done: for it had been settled between us at length, but unhappily on the very last time but one that I was ever to see her, that in a day or two we should go together before a magistrate, and that I should speak on her behalf. This little service it was destined, however, that I should never realize. Meantime, that which she rendered to me, and which was greater than I could ever have repaid her, was this:—One night, when we were pacing slowly along Oxford Street, and after a day when I had felt more than usually ill and faint, I requested her to turn off with me into Soho Square: thither we went; and we sat down on the steps of a house, which, to this hour, I never pass without a pang of grief, and an inner act of homage to the spirit of that unhappy girl, in memory of the noble action which she there performed. Suddenly, as we sat, I grew much worse: I had been leaning my head against her bosom; and all at once I sank from her arms and fell backwards on the steps. From the sensations I then had, I felt an inner conviction of the liveliest kind that without some powerful and reviving stimulus, I should either have died on the spot—or should at least have sunk to a point of exhaustion from which all re-ascent under my friendless circumstances would soon have become hopeless. Then it was, at this crisis of my fate, that my poor orphan companion—who had herself met with little but injuries in this world—stretched out a saving hand to me. Uttering a cry of terror, but without a moment's delay, she ran off into Oxford Street, and in less time than could be imagined, returned to me with a glass of port wine and spices, that acted upon my empty stomach (which at that time would have rejected all solid food) with an instantaneous power of restoration: and for this glass the generous girl without a murmur paid out of her own humble purse at a time—be it remembered!—when she had scarcely wherewithal to purchase the bare necessaries of life, and when she could have no reason to expect that I should ever be able to reimburse her.——Oh! youthful benefactress! how often in succeeding years, standing in solitary places, and thinking of thee with grief of heart and perfect love, how often have I wished that, as in ancient times the curse of a father was believed to have a supernatural power, and to pursue its object with a fatal necessity of self-fulfillment—even so the benediction of a heart oppressed with gratitude, might have a like prerogative; might have power given to it from above to chase—to haunt—to waylay[7]—to overtake—to pursue thee into the central darkness of a London brothel, or (if it were possible) into the darkness of the grave—there to awaken thee with an authentic message of peace and forgiveness, and of final reconciliation!

I do not often weep: for not only do my thoughts on subjects connected with the chief interests of man daily, nay hourly, descend a thousand fathoms "too deep for tears";[8] not only does the sternness of my habits of thought present an antagonism to the feelings which prompt tears—wanting of necessity to those who, being protected usually by their levity from any ten-

---

7. From Wordsworth's *She was a phantom of delight,* line 10: "To haunt, to startle, and way-lay." De Quincey was an early and enthusiastic admirer of Wordsworth's poetry.

8. From the last line of Wordsworth's *Ode: Intimations of Immortality.*

dency to meditative sorrow, would by that same levity be made incapable of resisting it on any casual access of such feelings:—but also, I believe that all minds which have contemplated such objects as deeply as I have done, must, for their own protection from utter despondency, have early encouraged and cherished some tranquilizing belief as to the future balances and the hieroglyphic meanings of human sufferings. On these accounts, I am cheerful to this hour; and, as I have said, I do not often weep. Yet some feelings, though not deeper or more passionate, are more tender than others; and often, when I walk at this time in Oxford Street by dreamy lamplight, and hear those airs played on a barrel-organ which years ago solaced me and my dear companion (as I must always call her), I shed tears, and muse with myself at the mysterious dispensation which so suddenly and so critically separated us for ever.[9] * * *

From *Introduction to the Pains of Opium*[1]

[THE MALAY]

* * * I remember, about this time, a little incident, which I mention, because, trifling as it was, the reader will soon meet it again in my dreams, which it influenced more fearfully than could be imagined. One day a Malay knocked at my door. What business a Malay could have to transact amongst English mountains, I cannot conjecture: but possibly he was on his road to a seaport about forty miles distant.

The servant who opened the door to him was a young girl born and bred amongst the mountains,[2] who had never seen an Asiatic dress of any sort: his turban, therefore, confounded her not a little: and, as it turned out that his attainments in English were exactly of the same extent as hers in the Malay, there seemed to be an impassable gulf fixed between all communication of ideas, if either party had happened to possess any. In this dilemma, the girl, recollecting the reputed learning of her master (and, doubtless, giving me credit for a knowledge of all the languages of the earth, besides, perhaps, a few of the lunar ones), came and gave me to understand that there was a sort of demon below, whom she clearly imagined that my art could exorcise from the house. I did not immediately go down: but, when I did, the group which presented itself, arranged as it was by accident, though not very elaborate, took hold of my fancy and my eye in a way that none of the statuesque attitudes exhibited in the ballets at the Opera House, though so ostentatiously complex, had ever done. In a cottage kitchen, but paneled on the wall with dark wood that from age and rubbing resembled oak, and looking more like a rustic hall of entrance than a kitchen, stood the Malay— his turban and loose trousers of dingy white relieved upon the dark paneling: he had placed himself nearer to the girl than she seemed to relish; though

9. De Quincey goes on to narrate that, having been given some money by a family friend who recognized him in the street, he had traveled to Eton to ask a young nobleman whom he knew to stand security for a loan that De Quincey was soliciting from a money-lender. When he returned to London three days later, Ann had disappeared.
1. It is 1816. De Quincy is living at Dove Cottage, Grasmere, and for three years has been addicted

to laudanum, i.e., opium dissolved in alcohol. At this time, he has succeeded in reducing his daily dosage from eight thousand to one thousand drops, with a consequent improvement in health and energy.
2. The lovely Barbara Lewthwaite, whom Wordsworth had described as a "child of beauty rare" in his poem *The Pet Lamb*.

her native spirit of mountain intrepidity contended with the feeling of simple awe which her countenance expressed as she gazed upon the tiger-cat before her. And a more striking picture there could not be imagined, than the beautiful English face of the girl, and its exquisite fairness, together with her erect and independent attitude, contrasted with the sallow and bilious skin of the Malay, enameled or veneered with mahogany, by marine air, his small, fierce, restless eyes, thin lips, slavish gestures and adorations. Half-hidden by the ferocious-looking Malay, was a little child from a neighboring cottage who had crept in after him, and was now in the act of reverting its head, and gazing upwards at the turban and the fiery eyes beneath it, whilst with one hand he caught at the dress of the young woman for protection. My knowledge of the Oriental tongues is not remarkably extensive, being indeed confined to two words—the Arabic word for barley, and the Turkish for opium (madjoon), which I have learnt from Anastasius.[3] And, as I had neither a Malay dictionary, nor even Adelung's *Mithridates,*[4] which might have helped me to a few words, I addressed him in some lines from the Iliad; considering that, of such languages as I possessed, Greek, in point of longitude, came geographically nearest to an Oriental one. He worshiped[5] me in a most devout manner, and replied in what I suppose was Malay. In this way I saved my reputation with my neighbors: for the Malay had no means of betraying the secret. He lay down upon the floor for about an hour, and then pursued his journey. On his departure, I presented him with a piece of opium. To him, as an Orientalist, I concluded that opium must be familiar: and the expression of his face convinced me that it was. Nevertheless, I was struck with some little consternation when I saw him suddenly raise his hand to his mouth, and (in the schoolboy phrase) bolt the whole, divided into three pieces, at one mouthful. The quantity was enough to kill three dragoons and their horses: and I felt some alarm for the poor creature: but what could be done? I had given him the opium in compassion for his solitary life, on recollecting that if he had traveled on foot from London, it must be nearly three weeks since he could have exchanged a thought with any human being. I could not think of violating the laws of hospitality, by having him seized and drenched with an emetic, and thus frightening him into a notion that we were going to sacrifice him to some English idol. No: there was clearly no help for it:—he took his leave: and for some days I felt anxious: but as I never heard of any Malay being found dead, I became convinced that he was used[6] to opium: and that I must have done him the service I designed, by giving him one night of respite from the pains of wandering.

This incident I have digressed to mention, because this Malay (partly from the picturesque exhibition he assisted to frame, partly from the anxiety I connected with his image for some days) fastened afterwards upon my dreams, and brought other Malays with him worse than himself, that ran "amuck" at me, and led me into a world of troubles. * * *

---

3. *Anastasius, or Memoirs of a Greek,* was a novel published anonymously by Thomas Hope in 1819. It included a description of the physical effects of opium that De Quincey considered to be a "grievous misrepresentation."
4. A book on Oriental languages by the German philologist J. C. Adelung (1732–1806).
5. Bowed down to.
6. This, however, is not a necessary conclusion: the varieties of effect produced by opium on different constitutions are infinite [De Quincey's note].

From *The Pains of Opium*

[OPIUM REVERIES AND DREAMS]

I have thus described and illustrated my intellectual torpor, in terms that apply, more or less, to every part of the four years during which I was under the Circean[7] spells of opium. But for misery and suffering, I might, indeed, be said to have existed in a dormant state. I seldom could prevail on myself to write a letter; an answer of a few words, to any that I received, was the utmost that I could accomplish; and often *that* not until the letter had lain weeks, or even months, on my writing table. Without the aid of M.[8] all records of bills paid, or *to be* paid, must have perished: and my whole domestic economy, whatever became of Political Economy,[9] must have gone into irretrievable confusion.—I shall not afterwards allude to this part of the case: it is one, however, which the opium-eater will find, in the end, as oppressive and tormenting as any other, from the sense of incapacity and feebleness, from the direct embarrassments incident to the neglect or procrastination of each day's appropriate duties, and from the remorse which must often exasperate the stings of these evils to a reflective and conscientious mind. The opium-eater loses none of his moral sensibilities, or aspirations: he wishes and longs, as earnestly as ever, to realize what he believes possible, and feels to be exacted by duty; but his intellectual apprehension of what is possible infinitely outruns his power, not of execution only, but even of power to attempt. He lies under the weight of incubus and nightmare: he lies in sight of all that he would fain perform, just as a man forcibly confined to his bed by the mortal languor of a relaxing disease, who is compelled to witness injury or outrage offered to some object of his tenderest love:—he curses the spells which chain him down from motion:—he would lay down his life if he might get up and walk; but he is powerless as an infant, and cannot even attempt to rise.

I now pass to what is the main subject of these latter confessions, to the history and journal of what took place in my dreams; for these were the immediate and proximate cause of my acutest suffering.

The first notice I had of any important change going on in this part of my physical economy, was from the re-awakening of a state of eye generally incident to childhood, or exalted states of irritability. I know not whether my reader is aware that many children, perhaps most, have a power of painting, as it were, upon the darkness, all sorts of phantoms; in some, that power is simply a mechanic affection of the eye; others have a voluntary, or a semi-voluntary power to dismiss or to summon them; or, as a child once said to me when I questioned him on this matter, "I can tell them to go, and they go; but sometimes they come, when I don't tell them to come." Whereupon I told him that he had almost as unlimited a command over apparitions, as a Roman centurion[1] over his soldiers.—In the middle of 1817, I think it was, that this faculty became positively distressing to me: at night, when I lay

---

7. Like those of Circe (the enchantress in the *Odyssey* who turned Odysseus's men into swine).
8. Margaret Simpson, whom De Quincey had married in 1817.
9. Inspired by David Ricardo's *Principles of Political Economy* (1817), De Quincey had begun to

write, but never completed, a work he called *Prolegomena to All Future Systems of Political Economy.*
1. A Roman officer commanding a troop of a hundred soldiers (a "century").

awake in bed, vast processions passed along in mournful pomp; friezes of never-ending stories, that to my feelings were as sad and solemn as if they were stories drawn from times before Oedipus or Priam—before Tyre—before Memphis.[2] And, at the same time, a corresponding change took place in my dreams; a theater seemed suddenly opened and lighted up within my brain, which presented nightly spectacles of more than earthly splendor. And the four following facts may be mentioned, as noticeable at this time:

1. That, as the creative state of the eye increased, a sympathy seemed to arise between the waking and the dreaming states of the brain in one point—that whatsoever I happened to call up and to trace by a voluntary act upon the darkness was very apt to transfer itself to my dreams; so that I feared to exercise this faculty; for, as Midas turned all things to gold, that yet baffled his hopes and defrauded his human desires,[3] so whatsoever things capable of being visually represented I did but think of in the darkness, immediately shaped themselves into phantoms of the eye; and, by a process apparently no less inevitable, when thus once traced in faint and visionary colors, like writings in sympathetic ink,[4] they were drawn out by the fierce chemistry of my dreams, into insufferable splendor that fretted my heart.

2. For this, and all other changes in my dreams, were accompanied by deep-seated anxiety and gloomy melancholy, such as are wholly incommunicable by words. I seemed every night to descend, not metaphorically, but literally to descend, into chasms and sunless abysses, depths below depths, from which it seemed hopeless that I could ever reascend. Nor did I, by waking, feel that I *had* re-ascended. This I do not dwell upon; because the state of gloom which attended these gorgeous spectacles, amounting at least to utter darkness, as of some suicidal despondency, cannot be approached by words.

3. The sense of space, and in the end, the sense of time, were both powerfully affected. Buildings, landscapes, &c. were exhibited in proportions so vast as the bodily eye is not fitted to receive. Space swelled, and was amplified to an extent of unutterable infinity. This, however, did not disturb me so much as the vast expansion of time; I sometimes seemed to have lived for 70 or 100 years in one night; nay, sometimes had feelings representative of a millennium passed in that time, or, however, of a duration far beyond the limits of any human experience.

4. The minutest incidents of childhood, or forgotten scenes of later years, were often revived: I could not be said to recollect them; for if I had been told of them when waking, I should not have been able to acknowledge them as parts of my past experience. But placed as they were before me, in dreams like intuitions, and clothed in all their evanescent circumstances and accompanying feelings, I *recognized* them instantaneously. I was once told by a near relative[5] of mine, that having in her childhood fallen into a river, and being on the very verge of death but for the critical assistance which reached her, she saw in a moment her whole life, in its minutest incidents, arrayed before her simultaneously as in a mirror; and she had a faculty developed as

---

2. De Quincey is calling the roll of great civilizations in the past. Oedipus was the king of Thebes. Priam was the king of Troy. Tyre was the chief city of Phoenicia. Memphis was the capital of ancient Egypt.
3. When granted his rash wish that all he touched

should turn to gold, King Midas was horrified to discover that his food, drink, and beloved daughter all became gold at his touch.
4. Invisible ink.
5. According to family report, De Quincey's mother.

suddenly for comprehending the whole and every part. This, from some opium experiences of mine, I can believe; I have, indeed, seen the same thing asserted twice in modern books, and accompanied by a remark which I am convinced is true; viz. that the dread book of account, which the Scriptures speak of,[6] is, in fact, the mind itself of each individual. Of this, at least, I feel assured, that there is no such thing as *forgetting* possible to the mind; a thousand accidents may, and will, interpose a veil between our present consciousness and the secret inscriptions on the mind; accidents of the same sort will also rend away this veil; but alike, whether veiled or unveiled, the inscription remains forever; just as the stars seem to withdraw before the common light of day, whereas, in fact, we all know that it is the light which is drawn over them as a veil—and that they are waiting to be revealed, when the obscuring daylight shall have withdrawn.

Having noticed these four facts as memorably distinguishing my dreams from those of health, I shall now cite a case illustrative of the first fact; and shall then cite any others that I remember, either in their chronological order, or any other that may give them more effect as pictures to the reader.

I had been in youth, and even since, for occasional amusement, a great reader of Livy,[7] whom, I confess, that I prefer, both for style and matter, to any of the Roman historians; and I had often felt as most solemn and appalling sounds, and most emphatically representative of the majesty of the Roman people, the two words so often occurring in Livy—*Consul Romanus*;[8] especially when the consul is introduced in his military character. I mean to say, that the words king—sultan—regent, &c. or any other titles of those who embody in their own persons the collective majesty of a great people, had less power over my reverential feelings. I had also, though no great reader of history, made myself minutely and critically familiar with one period of English history, viz. the period of the Parliamentary War, having been attracted by the moral grandeur of some who figured in that day, and by the many interesting memoirs which survive those unquiet times. Both these parts of my lighter reading, having furnished me often with matter of reflection, now furnished me with matter for my dreams. Often I used to see, after painting upon the blank darkness a sort of rehearsal whilst waking, a crowd of ladies, and perhaps a festival, and dances. And I heard it said, or I said to myself, "These are English ladies from the unhappy times of Charles I. These are the wives and the daughters of those who met in peace, and sat at the same tables, and were allied by marriage or by blood; and yet, after a certain day in August, 1642,[9] never smiled upon each other again, nor met but in the field of battle; and at Marston Moor, at Newbury, or at Naseby,[1] cut asunder all ties of love by the cruel saber, and washed away in blood the memory of ancient friendship."—The ladies danced, and looked as lovely as the court of George IV.[2] Yet I knew, even in my dream, that they had been in the grave for nearly two centuries.—This pageant would suddenly dissolve: and at a clapping of hands, would be heard the heart-quaking sound of

6. The book listing everyone's name at the Last Judgment (Revelation 20.12).
7. Titus Livius (59 B.C.E.–17 C.E.), author of a huge history of Rome in 142 books.
8. Roman consul (Latin); one of two officials, elected annually, who wielded the chief military and judicial authority in Republican Rome.

9. The raising of the king's banner on Castle Hill, Nottingham, on August 22, 1642, signaled the beginning of the English Civil War.
1. Scenes of the defeat of King Charles's forces in the Civil War.
2. The reigning monarch at the time De Quincey was writing.

Consul Romanus; and immediately came "sweeping by," in gorgeous palu-daments, Paulus or Marius,[3] girt round by a company of centurions, with the crimson tunic hoisted on a spear,[4] and followed by the *alalagmos*[5] of the Roman legions.

Many years ago, when I was looking over Piranesi's Antiquities of Rome, Mr. Coleridge, who was standing by, described to me a set of plates by that artist, called his *Dreams*,[6] and which record the scenery of his own visions during the delirium of a fever. Some of them (I describe only from memory of Mr. Coleridge's account) represented vast Gothic halls: on the floor of which stood all sorts of engines and machinery, wheels, cables, pulleys, lev-ers, catapults, &c. &c. expressive of enormous power put forth, and resis-tance overcome. Creeping along the sides of the walls, you perceived a staircase; and upon it, groping his way upwards, was Piranesi himself: follow the stairs a little further, and you perceive it come to a sudden abrupt ter-mination, without any balustrade, and allowing no step onwards to him who had reached the extremity, except into the depths below. Whatever is to become of poor Piranesi, you suppose, at least, that his labors must in some way terminate here. But raise your eyes, and behold a second flight of stairs still higher: on which again Piranesi is perceived, but this time standing on the very brink of the abyss. Again elevate your eye, and a still more aerial flight of stairs is beheld: and again is poor Piranesi busy on his aspiring labors: and so on, until the unfinished stairs and Piranesi both are lost in the upper gloom of the hall.—With the same power of endless growth and self-reproduction did my architecture proceed in dreams. In the early stage of my malady, the splendors of my dreams were indeed chiefly architectural: and I beheld such pomp of cities and palaces as was never yet beheld by the waking eye, unless in the clouds. From a great modern poet[7] I cite part of a passage which describes, as an appearance actually beheld in the clouds, what in many of its circumstances I saw frequently in sleep:

> The appearance, instantaneously disclosed,
> Was of a mighty city—boldly say
> A wilderness of building, sinking far
> And self-withdrawn into a wondrous depth,
> Far sinking into splendor—without end!
> Fabric it seem'd of diamond, and of gold,
> With alabaster domes, and silver spires,
> And blazing terrace upon terrace, high
> Uplifted; here, serene pavilions bright
> In avenues disposed; there towers begirt
> With battlements that on their restless fronts
> Bore stars—illumination of all gems!
> By earthly nature had the effect been wrought

3. Lucius Paulus (d. 160 B.C.E.) and Caius Marius (d. 86 B.C.E.) were Roman generals who won famous victories. "Paludaments": the cloaks worn by Roman generals.
4. The signal which announced a day of battle [De Quincey's note in the revised edition].
5. A word expressing collectively the gathering of the Roman war-cries [De Quincey's note in the revised edition]. The word is Greek.
6. Giovanni Piranesi (1720–1778), a Venetian

especially famed for his many etchings of ancient and modern Rome. He did not publish prints called *Dreams*; De Quincey doubtless refers to his series called *Carceri d'Invenzione*, "Imaginary pris-ons." The description that De Quincey recalls from Coleridge's conversation is remarkably apt for these terrifying architectural fantasies.
7. The quotation is from Wordsworth's *The Excur-sion*, book 2, lines 834ff. It describes a cloud struc-ture after a storm.

Upon the dark materials of the storm
Now pacified: on them, and on the coves,
And mountain-steeps and summits, whereunto
The vapors had receded,—taking there
Their station under a cerulean sky, &c. &c.

The sublime circumstance—"battlements that on their *restless* fronts bore stars"—might have been copied from my architectural dreams, for it often occurred.—We hear it reported of Dryden, and of Fuseli[8] in modern times, that they thought proper to eat raw meat for the sake of obtaining splendid dreams: how much better for such a purpose to have eaten opium, which yet I do not remember that any poet is recorded to have done, except the dramatist Shadwell:[9] and in ancient days, Homer is, I think, rightly reputed to have known the virtues of opium.[1]

To my architecture succeeded dreams of lakes—and silvery expanses of water:—these haunted me so much, that I feared (though possibly it will appear ludicrous to a medical man) that some dropsical[2] state or tendency of the brain might thus be making itself (to use a metaphysical word) *objective;* and the sentient organ *project* itself as its own object.—For two months I suffered greatly in my head—a part of my bodily structure which had hitherto been so clear from all touch or taint of weakness (physically, I mean), that I used to say of it, as the last Lord Orford[3] said of his stomach, that it seemed likely to survive the rest of my person.—Till now I had never felt a headache even, or any the slightest pain, except rheumatic pains caused by my own folly. However, I got over this attack, though it must have been verging on something very dangerous.

The waters now changed their character—from translucent lakes, shining like mirrors, they now became seas and oceans. And now came a tremendous change, which, unfolding itself slowly like a scroll, through many months, promised an abiding torment; and, in fact, it never left me until the winding up of my case. Hitherto the human face had mixed often in my dreams, but not despotically, nor with any special power of tormenting. But now that which I have called the tyranny of the human face began to unfold itself. Perhaps some part of my London life might be answerable for this. Be that as it may, now it was that upon the rocking waters of the ocean the human face began to appear: the sea appeared paved with innumerable faces, upturned to the heavens: faces, imploring, wrathful, despairing, surged upwards by thousands, by myriads, by generations, by centuries:—my agitation was infinite,—my mind tossed—and surged with the ocean.

May 1818

The Malay has been a fearful enemy for months. I have been every night, through his means, transported into Asiatic scenes. I know not whether others share in my feelings on this point; but I have often thought that if I were

---

8. John Henry Fuseli (1741–1825) was born in Switzerland and painted in England. He was noted for his paintings of nightmarish fantasies.
9. Thomas Shadwell was a Restoration dramatist and poet. He is now better known as the target of Dryden's satire (in *Mac Flecknoe* and elsewhere) than as a writer in his own right.
1. In the *Odyssey,* book 4, Homer lauded nepenthe

(which is probably opium) as a "drug to heal all pain and anger, and bring forgetfulness of every sorrow."
2. Afflicted with dropsy—an accumulation of fluid in the bodily tissues and cavities.
3. Horace Walpole, 18th-century wit and letter writer, author of the Gothic novel *The Castle of Otranto* (1764).

compelled to forego England, and to live in China, and among Chinese manners and modes of life and scenery, I should go mad. The causes of my horror lie deep; and some of them must be common to others. Southern Asia, in general, is the seat of awful images and associations. As the cradle of the human race, it would alone have a dim and reverential feeling connected with it. But there are other reasons. No man can pretend that the wild, barbarous, and capricious superstitions of Africa, or of savage tribes elsewhere, affect him in the way that he is affected by the ancient, monumental, cruel, and elaborate religions of Indostan, &c. The mere antiquity of Asiatic things, of their institutions, histories, modes of faith, &c. is so impressive, that to me the vast age of the race and name overpowers the sense of youth in the individual. A young Chinese seems to me an antediluvian man renewed. Even Englishmen, though not bred in any knowledge of such institutions, cannot but shudder at the mystic sublimity of *castes*[4] that have flowed apart, and refused to mix, through such immemorial tracts of time; nor can any man fail to be awed by the names of the Ganges, or the Euphrates. It contributes much to these feelings, that southern Asia is, and has been for thousands of years, the part of the earth most swarming with human life; the great *officina gentium*.[5] Man is a weed in those regions. The vast empires also, into which the enormous population of Asia has always been cast, give a further sublimity to the feelings associated with all Oriental names or images. In China, over and above what it has in common with the rest of southern Asia, I am terrified by the modes of life, by the manners, and the barrier of utter abhorrence, and want of sympathy, placed between us by feelings deeper than I can analyze. I could sooner live with lunatics, or brute animals. All this, and much more than I can say, or have time to say, the reader must enter into before he can comprehend the unimaginable horror which these dreams of Oriental imagery, and mythological tortures, impressed upon me. Under the connecting feeling of tropical heat and vertical sunlights, I brought together all creatures, birds, beasts, reptiles, all trees and plants, usages and appearances, that are found in all tropical regions, and assembled them together in China or Indostan. From kindred feelings, I soon brought Egypt and all her gods under the same law. I was stared at, hooted at, grinned at, chattered at, by monkeys, by paroquets, by cockatoos. I ran into pagodas: and was fixed, for centuries, at the summit, or in secret rooms; I was the idol; I was the priest; I was worshiped; I was sacrificed. I fled from the wrath of Brama through all the forests of Asia: Vishnu hated me: Seeva[6] laid wait for me. I came suddenly upon Isis and Osiris: I had done a deed, they said, which the ibis and the crocodile[7] trembled at. I was buried, for a thousand years, in stone coffins, with mummies and sphinxes, in narrow chambers at the heart of eternal pyramids. I was kissed, with cancerous kisses, by crocodiles; and laid, confounded with all unutterable slimy things, amongst reeds and Nilotic mud.

I thus give the reader some slight abstraction of my Oriental dreams, which

4. The reference is to the Hindu caste system, with its sharp division between four hereditary social classes.
5. Manufactory of populations (Latin).
6. In the Hindu triad, Brahma is the creative aspect of divine reality, Vishnu is its maintainer, and Shiva its destroyer.

7. The ibis (a long-legged wading bird) and the crocodile were considered sacred in ancient Egypt. Isis was the ancient Egyptian goddess of fertility. She was the sister and wife of Osiris, whose annual death and rebirth represented the seasonal cycle of nature.

always filled me with such amazement at the monstrous scenery, that horror seemed absorbed, for a while, in sheer astonishment. Sooner or later, came a reflux of feeling that swallowed up the astonishment, and left me, not so much in terror, as in hatred and abomination of what I saw. Over every form, and threat, and punishment, and dim sightless incarceration, brooded a sense of eternity and infinity that drove me into an oppression as of madness. Into these dreams only, it was, with one or two slight exceptions, that any circumstances of physical horror entered. All before had been moral and spiritual terrors. But here the main agents were ugly birds, or snakes, or crocodiles; especially the last. The cursed crocodile became to me the object of more horror than almost all the rest. I was compelled to live with him; and (as was always the case almost in my dreams) for centuries. I escaped sometimes, and found myself in Chinese houses, with cane tables, &c. All the feet of the tables, sofas, &c. soon became instinct with life: the abominable head of the crocodile, and his leering eyes, looked out at me, multiplied into a thousand repetitions: and I stood loathing and fascinated. And so often did this hideous reptile haunt my dreams, that many times the very same dream was broken up in the very same way: I heard gentle voices speaking to me (I hear every thing when I am sleeping); and instantly I awoke: it was broad noon; and my children were standing, hand in hand, at my bedside; come to show me their colored shoes, or new frocks, or to let me see them dressed for going out. I protest that so awful was the transition from the damned crocodile, and the other unutterable monsters and abortions of my dreams, to the sight of innocent *human* natures and of infancy, that, in the mighty and sudden revulsion of mind, I wept, and could not forbear it, as I kissed their faces.

June 1819

I have had occasion to remark, at various periods of my life, that the deaths of those whom we love, and indeed the contemplation of death generally, is (*ceteris paribus*)[8] more affecting in summer than in any other season of the year. And the reasons are these three, I think: first, that the visible heavens in summer appear far higher, more distant, and (if such a solecism may be excused) more infinite; the clouds, by which chiefly the eye expounds the distance of the blue pavilion stretched over our heads, are in summer more voluminous, massed, and accumulated in far grander and more towering piles: secondly, the light and the appearances of the declining and the setting sun are much more fitted to be types and characters of the Infinite: and, thirdly (which is the main reason), the exuberant and riotous prodigality of life naturally forces the mind more powerfully upon the antagonist thought of death, and the wintry sterility of the grave. For it may be observed, generally, that wherever two thoughts stand related to each other by a law of antagonism, and exist, as it were, by mutual repulsion, they are apt to suggest each other. On these accounts it is that I find it impossible to banish the thought of death when I am walking alone in the endless days of summer; and any particular death, if not more affecting, at least haunts my mind more obstinately and besiegingly in that season. Perhaps this cause, and a slight

8. Other things being the same (Latin).

incident which I omit, might have been the immediate occasions of the following dream; to which, however, a predisposition must always have existed in my mind; but having been once roused, it never left me, and split into a thousand fantastic varieties, which often suddenly reunited, and composed again the original dream.

I thought that it was a Sunday morning in May, that it was Easter Sunday, and as yet very early in the morning. I was standing, as it seemed to me, at the door of my own cottage. Right before me lay the very scene which could really be commanded from that situation, but exalted, as was usual, and solemnized by the power of dreams. There were the same mountains, and the same lovely valley at their feet; but the mountains were raised to more than Alpine height, and there was interspace far larger between them of meadows and forest lawns; the hedges were rich with white roses; and no living creature was to be seen, excepting that in the green churchyard there were cattle tranquilly reposing upon the verdant graves, and particularly round about the grave of a child whom I had tenderly loved,[9] just as I had really beheld them, a little before sunrise in the same summer, when that child died. I gazed upon the well-known scene, and I said aloud (as I thought) to myself, "It yet wants much of sunrise; and it is Easter Sunday; and that is the day on which they celebrate the first-fruits of resurrection. I will walk abroad; old griefs shall be forgotten today; for the air is cool and still, and the hills are high, and stretch away to heaven; and the forest-glades are as quiet as the churchyard; and, with the dew, I can wash the fever from my forehead, and then I shall be unhappy no longer." And I turned, as if to open my garden gate; and immediately I saw upon the left a scene far different; but which yet the power of dreams had reconciled into harmony with the other. The scene was an Oriental one; and there also it was Easter Sunday, and very early in the morning. And at a vast distance were visible, as a stain upon the horizon, the domes and cupolas of a great city—an image or faint abstraction, caught perhaps in childhood from some picture of Jerusalem. And not a bow-shot from me, upon a stone, and shaded by Judean palms, there sat a woman; and I looked; and it was—Ann! She fixed her eyes upon me earnestly; and I said to her at length: "So then I have found you at last." I waited: but she answered me not a word. Her face was the same as when I saw it last, and yet again how different! Seventeen years ago, when the lamplight fell upon her face, as for the last time I kissed her lips (lips, Ann, that to me were not polluted), her eyes were streaming with tears: the tears were now wiped away; she seemed more beautiful than she was at that time, but in all other points the same, and not older. Her looks were tranquil, but with unusual solemnity of expression; and I now gazed upon her with some awe, but suddenly her countenance grew dim, and, turning to the mountains, I perceived vapors rolling between us; in a moment, all had vanished; thick darkness came on; and, in the twinkling of an eye, I was far away from mountains, and by lamplight in Oxford Street, walking again with Ann—just as we walked seventeen years before, when we were both children.

As a final specimen, I cite one of a different character, from 1820.
The dream commenced with a music which now I often heard in dreams—

9. The child is Wordsworth's daughter Catherine, who died at the age of four. She is the subject of Wordsworth's sonnet *Surprised by joy.*

a music of preparation and of awakening suspense; a music like the opening of the Coronation Anthem,[1] and which, like *that,* gave the feeling of a vast march—of infinite cavalcades filing off—and the tread of innumerable armies. The morning was come of a mighty day—a day of crisis and of final hope for human nature, then suffering some mysterious eclipse, and laboring in some dread extremity. Somewhere, I knew not where—somehow, I knew not how—by some beings, I knew not whom—a battle, a strife, an agony, was conducting—was evolving like a great drama, or piece of music; with which my sympathy was the more insupportable from my confusion as to its place, its cause, its nature, and its possible issue. I, as is usual in dreams (where, of necessity, we make ourselves central to every movement), had the power, and yet had not the power, to decide it. I had the power, if I could raise myself, to will it; and yet again had not the power, for the weight of twenty Atlantics was upon me, or the oppression of inexpiable guilt. "Deeper than ever plummet sounded,"[2] I lay inactive. Then, like a chorus, the passion deepened. Some greater interest was at stake; some mightier cause than ever yet the sword had pleaded, or trumpet had proclaimed. Then came sudden alarms: hurryings to and fro: trepidations of innumerable fugitives, I knew not whether from the good cause or the bad: darkness and lights: tempest and human faces: and at last, with the sense that all was lost, female forms, and the features that were worth all the world to me, and but a moment allowed—and clasped hands, and heart-breaking partings, and then—everlasting farewells! and with a sigh, such as the caves of hell sighed when the incestuous mother uttered the abhorred name of death,[3] the sound was reverberated—everlasting farewells! and again, and yet again reverberated—everlasting farewells!

And I awoke in struggles, and cried aloud—"I will sleep no more!"[4]

1821   1821

On the Knocking at the Gate in *Macbeth*[1]

From my boyish days I had always felt a great perplexity on one point in *Macbeth.* It was this: The knocking at the gate which succeeds to the murder of Duncan produced to my feelings an effect for which I never could account. The effect was that it reflected back upon the murderer a peculiar awfulness and a depth of solemnity; yet, however obstinately I endeavored with my

---

1. Composed by George Frideric Handel for the coronation of George II in 1727.
2. *The Tempest* 3.3.101.
3. The reference is to *Paradise Lost,* book 2, lines 777ff. The "incestuous mother" is Sin, who is doubly incestuous: she is the daughter of Satan, who begot Death upon her, and she was in turn raped by her son and gave birth to a pack of "yelling Monsters."
4. Macbeth says: "Methought I heard a voice cry 'Sleep no more, / Macbeth does murder sleep' " (2.2.33–34).
1. This essay, one of the best-known critiques of Shakespeare, deals with the scene in *Macbeth* (2.2–3) in which, just after they have murdered

Duncan, Macbeth and his wife are startled by a loud knocking at the gate. De Quincey exhibits the procedure in Romantic criticism of making, as he says, the "understanding" wait upon the "feelings." That is, instead of judging the success or failure of a passage by its conformity to prior critical theory, De Quincey brings in theory only to explain his impression or immediate emotional response to the passage. The final paragraph demonstrates a weakness of Romantic criticism when it is driven to an extreme, for it converts the reasonable view that Shakespeare must be presumed right until shown to be wrong into the untenable view that Shakespeare is an artistic deity who can do no wrong.

understanding to comprehend this, for many years I never could see *why* it should produce such an effect.

Here I pause for one moment, to exhort the reader never to pay any attention to his understanding when it stands in opposition to any other faculty of his mind. The mere understanding, however useful and indispensable, is the meanest faculty in the human mind, and the most to be distrusted; and yet the great majority of people trust to nothing else—which may do for ordinary life, but not for philosophical purposes. Of this out of ten thousand instances that I might produce I will cite one. Ask of any person whatsoever who is not previously prepared for the demand by a knowledge of the perspective to draw in the rudest way the commonest appearance which depends upon the laws of that science—as, for instance, to represent the effect of two walls standing at right angles to each other, or the appearance of the houses on each side of a street as seen by a person looking down the street from one extremity. Now, in all cases, unless the person has happened to observe in pictures how it is that artists produce these effects, he will be utterly unable to make the smallest approximation to it. Yet why? For he has actually seen the effect every day of his life. The reason is that he allows his understanding to overrule his eyes. His understanding, which includes no intuitive knowledge of the laws of vision, can furnish him with no reason why a line which is known and can be proved to be a horizontal line should not *appear* a horizontal line: a line that made any angle with the perpendicular less than a right angle would seem to him to indicate that his houses were all tumbling down together. Accordingly, he makes the line of his houses a horizontal line, and fails, of course, to produce the effect demanded. Here, then, is one instance out of many in which not only the understanding is allowed to overrule the eyes, but where the understanding is positively allowed to obliterate the eyes, as it were; for not only does the man believe the evidence of his understanding in opposition to that of his eyes, but (what is monstrous) the idiot is not aware that his eyes ever gave such evidence. He does not know that he has seen (and therefore *quoad* his consciousness[2] has *not* seen) that which he *has* seen every day of his life.

But to return from this digression. My understanding could furnish no reason why the knocking at the gate in *Macbeth* should produce any effect, direct or reflected. In fact, my understanding said positively that it could not produce any effect. But I knew better; I felt that it did; and I waited and clung to the problem until further knowledge should enable me to solve it. At length, in 1812, Mr. Williams[3] made his debut on the stage of Ratcliffe Highway, and executed those unparalleled murders which have procured for him such a brilliant and undying reputation. On which murders, by the way, I must observe that in one respect they have had an ill effect, by making the connoisseur in murder very fastidious in his taste, and dissatisfied by anything that has been since done in that line. All other murders look pale by the deep crimson of his; and, as an amateur[4] once said to me in a querulous tone, "There has been absolutely nothing *doing* since his time, or nothing

---

2. I.e., so far as his consciousness is concerned.
3. John Williams, a sailor, had thrown London into a panic (the date was actually December 1811) by murdering the Marr family and, twelve days later, the Williamson family. De Quincey described these murders at length in the postscript to his two essays *On Murder Considered as One of the Fine Arts.*
4. I.e., a fancier or follower of an art or sport.

that's worth speaking of." But this is wrong; for it is unreasonable to expect all men to be great artists, and born with the genius of Mr. Williams. Now, it will be remembered that in the first of these murders (that of the Marrs) the same incident (of a knocking at the door[5] soon after the work of extermination was complete) did actually occur which the genius of Shakespeare has invented; and all good judges, and the most eminent dilettanti,[6] acknowledged the felicity of Shakespeare's suggestion as soon as it was actually realized. Here, then, was a fresh proof that I was right in relying on my own feeling, in opposition to my understanding; and I again set myself to study the problem. At length I solved it to my own satisfaction; and my solution is this: Murder, in ordinary cases, where the sympathy is wholly directed to the case of the murdered person, is an incident of coarse and vulgar horror; and for this reason—that it flings the interest exclusively upon the natural but ignoble instinct by which we cleave to life: an instinct which, as being indispensable to the primal law of self-preservation, is the same in kind (though different in degree) amongst all living creatures. This instinct, therefore, because it annihilates all distinctions, and degrades the greatest of men to the level of "the poor beetle that we tread on,"[7] exhibits human nature in its most abject and humiliating attitude. Such an attitude would little suit the purposes of the poet. What then must he do? He must throw the interest on the murderer. Our sympathy must be with *him* (of course I mean a sympathy of comprehension, a sympathy by which we enter into his feelings, and are made to understand them—not a sympathy of pity or approbation).[8] In the murdered person, all strife of thought, all flux and reflux of passion and of purpose, are crushed by one overwhelming panic; the fear of instant death smites him "with its petrific[9] mace." But in the murderer, such a murderer as a poet will condescend to, there must be raging some great storm of passion—jealousy, ambition, vengeance, hatred—which will create a hell within him; and into this hell we are to look.

In *Macbeth*, for the sake of gratifying his own enormous and teeming faculty of creation, Shakespeare has introduced two murderers: and, as usual in his hands, they are remarkably discriminated; but—though in Macbeth the strife of mind is greater than in his wife, the tiger spirit not so awake, and his feelings caught chiefly by contagion from her—yet, as both were finally involved in the guilt of murder, the murderous mind of necessity is finally to be presumed in both. This was to be expressed; and, on its own account, as well as to make it a more proportionable antagonist to the unoffending nature of their victim, "the gracious Duncan," and adequately to expound "the deep damnation of his taking off,"[1] this was to be expressed with peculiar energy. We were to be made to feel that the human nature—i.e., the divine nature of love and mercy, spread through the hearts of all creatures, and seldom utterly withdrawn from man—was gone, vanished, extinct, and that the fiendish nature had taken its place. And, as this effect is marvelously accomplished in the *dialogues* and *soliloquies* themselves, so

---

5. By a maidservant of the Marrs, returning from the purchase of oysters for supper.
6. Lovers of the fine arts.
7. *Measure for Measure* 3.1.77.
8. In a note De Quincey decries "the unscholarlike use of the word sympathy, at present so general, by which, instead of taking it in its proper sense, as the act of reproducing in our minds the feelings of another, whether for hatred, indignation, love, pity, or approbation, it is made a mere synonym of the word *pity*."
9. Petrifying, turning to stone (from *Paradise Lost* 10.294).
1. *Macbeth* 3.1.67 and 1.7.20.

it is finally consummated by the expedient under consideration; and it is to this that I now solicit the reader's attention. If the reader has ever witnessed a wife, daughter, or sister in a fainting fit, he may chance to have observed that the most affecting moment in such a spectacle is *that* in which a sigh and a stirring announce the recommencement of suspended life. Or, if the reader has ever been present in a vast metropolis on the day when some great national idol was carried in funeral pomp to his grave, and, chancing to walk near the course through which it passed, has felt powerfully, in the silence and desertion of the streets, and in the stagnation of ordinary business, the deep interest which at that moment was possessing the heart of man—if all at once he should hear the deathlike stillness broken up by the sound of wheels rattling away from the scene, and making known that the transitory vision was dissolved, he will be aware that at no moment was his sense of the complete suspension and pause in ordinary human concerns so full and affecting as at that moment when the suspension ceases, and the goings-on of human life are suddenly resumed. All action in any direction is best expounded, measured, and made apprehensible, by reaction. Now, apply this to the case in *Macbeth*. Here, as I have said, the retiring of the human heart and the entrance of the fiendish heart was to be expressed and made sensible. Another world has stepped in; and the murderers are taken out of the region of human things, human purposes, human desires. They are transfigured: Lady Macbeth is "unsexed";[2] Macbeth has forgot that he was born of woman; both are conformed to the image of devils; and the world of devils is suddenly revealed. But how shall this be conveyed and made palpable? In order that a new world may step in, this world must for a time disappear. The murderers and the murder must be insulated—cut off by an immeasurable gulf from the ordinary tide and succession of human affairs—locked up and sequestered in some deep recess; we must be made sensible that the world of ordinary life is suddenly arrested, laid asleep, tranced, racked into a dread armistice; time must be annihilated, relation to things without abolished; and all must pass self-withdrawn into a deep syncope[3] and suspension of earthly passion. Hence it is that, when the deed is done, when the work of darkness is perfect, then the world of darkness passes away like a pageantry in the clouds: the knocking at the gate is heard, and it makes known audibly that the reaction has commenced; the human has made its reflux upon the fiendish; the pulses of life are beginning to beat again; and the reestablishment of the goings-on of the world in which we live first makes us profoundly sensible of the awful parenthesis that had suspended them.

O mighty poet! Thy works are not as those of other men, simply and merely great works of art, but are also like the phenomena of nature, like the sun and the sea, the stars and the flowers, like frost and snow, rain and dew, hailstorm and thunder, which are to be studied with entire submission of our own faculties, and in the perfect faith that in them there can be no too much or too little, nothing useless or inert, but that, the farther we press in our discoveries, the more we shall see proofs of design and self-supporting arrangement where the careless eye had seen nothing but accident!

1823

2. Steeling herself to the murder, Lady Macbeth calls on the spirits of hell to "unsex me here" (1.5.39).
3. Fainting spell.

From Alexander Pope

[THE LITERATURE OF KNOWLEDGE AND THE LITERATURE OF POWER][1]

What is it that we mean by *literature*? Popularly, and amongst the thoughtless, it is held to include everything that is printed in a book. Little logic is required to disturb *that* definition. The most thoughtless person is easily made aware that in the idea of *literature* one essential element is some relation to a general and common interest of man—so that what applies only to a local, or professional, or merely personal interest, even though presenting itself in the shape of a book, will not belong to Literature. So far the definition is easily narrowed; and it is as easily expanded. For not only is much that takes a station in books not literature; but inversely, much that really *is* literature never reaches a station in books. The weekly sermons of Christendom, that vast pulpit literature which acts so extensively upon the popular mind—to warn, to uphold, to renew, to comfort, to alarm—does not attain the sanctuary of libraries in the ten-thousandth part of its extent. The Drama again—as, for instance, the finest of Shakespeare's plays in England, and all leading Athenian plays in the noontide of the Attic stage—operated as a literature on the public mind, and were (according to the strictest letter of that term) *published* through the audiences that witnessed[2] their representation some time before they were published as things to be read; and they were published in this scenical mode of publication with much more effect than they could have had as books during ages of costly copying or of costly printing.

Books, therefore, do not suggest an idea coextensive and interchangeable with the idea of Literature; since much literature, scenic, forensic, or didactic[3] (as from lecturers and public orators), may never come into books, and much that *does* come into books may connect itself with no literary interest.[4] But a far more important correction, applicable to the common vague idea of literature, is to be sought not so much in a better definition of literature as in a sharper distinction of the two functions which it fulfills. In that great social organ which, collectively, we call literature, there may be distinguished two separate offices that may blend and often *do* so, but capable, severally, of a severe insulation, and naturally fitted for reciprocal repulsion. There is,

1. This section of an essay on Alexander Pope (written in 1848, revised in 1858) has achieved independent status as a contribution to literary theory. In an earlier treatment of this topic in *Letters to a Young Man* (1823), De Quincey wrote that "the true antithesis to knowledge," in defining the effects of literature, "is not *pleasure*, but *power*"; then added in a footnote that he owed this distinction "to many years' conversation with Mr. Wordsworth." In his *Essay Supplementary* to the Preface to his *Poems* (1815), Wordsworth had written that "every great poet . . . has to call forth and communicate *power*," and that for an original writer "to create taste is to call forth and bestow power, of which knowledge is the effect."
2. Charles I, for example, when Prince of Wales, and many others in his father's court, gained their known familiarity with Shakespeare not through the original quartos, so slenderly diffused, nor through the first folio of 1623, but through the court representations of his chief dramas at Whitehall [De Quincey's note]. Whitehall was a royal palace in London. It was destroyed by fire in 1698.
3. Expository, designed to instruct. "Scenic": dramatic. "Forensic": argumentative, designed to persuade, especially in legal proceedings.
4. What are called *The Blue Books*—by which title are understood the folio reports issued every session of Parliament by committees of the two Houses, and stitched into blue covers—though often sneered at by the ignorant as so much wastepaper, will be acknowledged gratefully by those who have used them diligently as the main wellheads of all accurate information as to the Great Britain of this day. As an immense depository of faithful (*and not superannuated*) statistics, they are indispensable to the honest student. But no man would therefore class the *Blue Books* as literature [De Quincey's note].

first, the literature of *knowledge;* and, secondly, the literature of *power.* The function of the first is—to *teach;* the function of the second is—to *move:*[5] the first is a rudder; the second, an oar or a sail. The first speaks to the *mere discursive*[6] understanding; the second speaks ultimately, it may happen, to the higher understanding or reason, but always *through* affections of pleasure and sympathy. Remotely, it may travel towards an object seated in what Lord Bacon calls *dry* light;[7] but, proximately, it does and must operate—else it ceases to be a literature of *power*—on and through that *humid* light which clothes itself in the mists and glittering *iris* of human passions, desires, and genial[8] emotions. Men have so little reflected on the higher functions of literature as to find it a paradox if one should describe it as a mean or subordinate purpose of books to give information. But this is a paradox only in the sense which makes it honorable to be paradoxical. Whenever we talk in ordinary language of seeking information or gaining knowledge, we understand the words as connected with something of absolute novelty. But it is the grandeur of all truth which *can* occupy a very high place in human interests that it is never absolutely novel to the meanest of minds: it exists eternally by way of germ or latent principle in the lowest as in the highest, needing to be developed, but never to be planted. To be capable of transplantation is the immediate criterion of a truth that ranges on a lower scale. Besides which, there is a rarer thing than truth—namely, *power,* or deep sympathy with truth. What is the effect, for instance, upon society, of children? By the pity, by the tenderness, and by the peculiar modes of admiration, which connect themselves with the helplessness, with the innocence, and with the simplicity of children, not only are the primal affections strengthened and continually renewed, but the qualities which are dearest in the sight of heaven—the frailty, for instance, which appeals to forbearance, the innocence which symbolizes the heavenly, and the simplicity which is most alien from the worldly—are kept up in perpetual remembrance, and their ideals are continually refreshed. A purpose of the same nature is answered by the higher literature, viz. the literature of power. What do you learn from *Paradise Lost?* Nothing at all. What do you learn from a cookery book? Something new, something that you did not know before, in every paragraph. But would you therefore put the wretched cookery book on a higher level of estimation than the divine poem? What you owe to Milton is not any knowledge, of which a million separate items are still but a million of advancing steps on the same earthly level; what you owe is *power*—that is, exercise and expansion to your own latent capacity of sympathy with the infinite, where every pulse and each separate influx is a step upwards, a step ascending as upon a Jacob's ladder from earth to mysterious altitudes above the earth.[9] *All* the steps of knowledge, from first to last, carry you further on the same plane, but could never raise you one foot above your ancient level of earth: whereas the very *first* step in power is a flight—is an ascending movement into another element where earth is forgotten.

---

5. Through the 18th century many critical theorists, following classical precedent, asserted that the aims of poetry are to teach, to please, and to move the reader.
6. Ordered in a rational or logical way.
7. In his essay *Of Friendship,* Francis Bacon quotes Heraclitus, the early Greek philosopher, as saying "Dry light is ever the best," then goes on to distinguish between dry light and the light of an understanding, which is "ever infused and drenched" in an individual's own "affections and customs."
8. Pertaining to genius; creative. "Iris": rainbow colors.
9. The ladder that the patriarch Jacob saw in a dream, reaching from earth to heaven, on which angels were ascending and descending (Genesis 28.11–12).

Were it not that human sensibilities are ventilated and continually called out into exercise by the great phenomena of infancy, or of real life as it moves through chance and change, or of literature as it recombines these elements in the mimicries of poetry, romance, etc., it is certain that, like any animal power or muscular energy falling into disuse, all such sensibilities would gradually droop and dwindle. It is in relation to these great *moral* capacities of man that the literature of power, as contradistinguished from that of knowledge, lives and has its field of action. It is concerned with what is highest in man; for the Scriptures themselves never condescended to deal by suggestion or cooperation with the mere discursive understanding: when speaking of man in his intellectual capacity, the Scriptures speak not of the understanding, but of *"the understanding heart"*[1]—making the heart, i.e. the great *intuitive* (or nondiscursive) organ, to be the interchangeable formula for man in his highest state of capacity for the infinite. Tragedy, romance, fairy tale, or epopée,[2] all alike restore to man's mind the ideals of justice, of hope, of truth, of mercy, of retribution, which else (left to the support of daily life in its realities) would languish for want of sufficient illustration. What is meant, for instance, by *poetic justice*?[3]—It does not mean a justice that differs by its object from the ordinary justice of human jurisprudence; for then it must be confessedly a very bad kind of justice; but it means a justice that differs from common forensic justice by the degree in which it *attains* its object, a justice that is more omnipotent over its own ends, as dealing—not with the refractory elements of earthly life, but with the elements of its own creation, and with materials flexible to its own purest preconceptions. It is certain that, were it not for the Literature of Power, these ideals would often remain amongst us as mere arid notional forms; whereas, by the creative forces of man put forth in literature, they gain a vernal life of restoration, and germinate into vital activities. The commonest novel, by moving in alliance with human fears and hopes, with human instincts of wrong and right, sustains and quickens those affections. Calling them into action, it rescues them from torpor. And hence the preeminency over all authors that merely *teach* of the meanest that *moves*, or that teaches, if at all, indirectly *by* moving. The very highest work that has ever existed in the Literature of Knowledge is but a *provisional* work: a book upon trial and sufferance, and *quamdiu bene se gesserit*.[4] Let its teaching be even partially revised, let it be but expanded—nay, even let its teaching be but placed in a better order—and instantly it is superseded. Whereas the feeblest works in the Literature of Power, surviving at all, survive as finished and unalterable amongst men. For instance, the *Principia* of Sir Isaac Newton was a book *militant*[5] on earth from the first. In all stages of its progress it would have to fight for its existence: 1st, as regards absolute truth; 2dly, when that combat was over, as regards its form or mode of presenting the truth. And as soon as a La Place,[6] or anybody else, builds higher upon the foundations laid by this book, effectually he throws it out of the sunshine into decay and

1. In 1 Kings 3.9 King Solomon asks the Lord for "an understanding heart to judge thy people."
2. Epic poem (French).
3. A term in literary criticism for the distribution of earthly rewards and punishments, at the end of a work of literature, in proportion to the virtues and vices of the various characters.
4. As long as it shall conduct itself well (Latin).
5. Combative. "*Principia*": Isaac Newton's great

Philosophiae Naturalis Principia Mathematica (Mathematical principles of natural philosophy), published in 1687, set forth the laws of motion and the principle of universal gravitation.
6. Pierre-Simon, marquis de Laplace, mathematician and astronomer, author of *A Treatise on Celestial Mechanics* (1799–1825), was known as "the Newton of France."

darkness; by weapons won from this book he superannuates and destroys this book, so that soon the name of Newton remains as a mere *nominis umbra*,[7] but his book, as a living power, has transmigrated into other forms. Now, on the contrary, the *Iliad*, the *Prometheus* of Aeschylus, the *Othello* or *King Lear*, the *Hamlet* or *Macbeth*, and the *Paradise Lost*, are not militant, but triumphant forever as long as the languages exist in which they speak or can be taught to speak. They never *can* transmigrate into new incarnations. To reproduce *these* in new forms, or variations, even if in some things they should be improved, would be to plagiarize. A good steam engine is properly superseded by a better. But one lovely pastoral valley is not superseded by another, nor a statute of Praxiteles by a statue of Michael Angelo.[8] These things are separated not by imparity, but by disparity. They are not thought of as unequal under the same standard, but as different in *kind*, and, if otherwise equal, as equal under a different standard. Human works of immortal beauty and works of nature in one respect stand on the same footing: they never absolutely repeat each other, never approach so near as not to differ; and they differ not as better and worse, or simply by more and less: they differ by undecipherable and incommunicable differences, that cannot be caught by mimicries, that cannot be reflected in the mirror of copies, that cannot become ponderable in the scales of vulgar comparison.

Applying these principles to Pope as a representative of fine literature in general, we would wish to remark the claim which he has, or which any equal writer has, to the attention and jealous winnowing of those critics in particular who watch over public morals. Clergymen, and all organs of public criticism put in motion by clergymen, are more especially concerned in the just appreciation of such writers, if the two canons are remembered which we have endeavored to illustrate, viz. that all works in this class, as opposed to those in the literature of knowledge, 1st, work by far deeper agencies, and, 2dly, are more permanent; in the strictest sense they are κτήματα ἐς ἀεί[9] and what evil they do, or what good they do, is commensurate with the national language, sometimes long after the nation has departed. At this hour, five hundred years since their creation, the tales of Chaucer,[1] never equaled on this earth for their tenderness, and for life of picturesqueness, are read familiarly by many in the charming language of their natal day, and by others in the modernizations of Dryden, of Pope, and Wordsworth.[2] At this hour, one thousand eight hundred years since their creation, the Pagan tales of Ovid,[3] never equaled on this earth for the gaiety of their movement and the capricious graces of their narrative, are read by all Christendom. This man's people and their monuments are dust; but *he* is alive: he has survived them, as he told us that he had it in his commission to do, by a thousand years; "and *shall* a thousand more."

All the literature of knowledge builds only ground-nests, that are swept away by floods, or confounded by the plow; but the literature of power builds

---

7. Shadow of a name (Latin).
8. Michelangelo Buonarroti (1475–1564), Renaissance sculptor, painter, architect, and poet. Praxiteles (4th century B.C.E.), Greek sculptor.
9. Everlasting possessions (Greek).
1. The *Canterbury Tales* were not made public until 1380 or thereabouts; but the composition must have cost thirty or more years; not to mention

that the work had probably been finished for some years before it was divulged [De Quincey's note].
2. Following the example of various earlier poets who wrote modernized versions of Chaucer, Wordsworth had translated *The Prioress's Tale* and a section of *Troilus and Criseyde*.
3. Latin poet (43 B.C.E.–18 C.E.), author of *Metamorphoses* and other books of verse narratives.

nests in aerial altitudes of temples sacred from violation, or of forests inaccessible to fraud. *This* is a great prerogative of the *power* literature; and it is a greater which lies in the mode of its influence. The *knowledge* literature, like the fashion of this world, passeth away. An Encyclopedia is its abstract; and, in this respect, it may be taken for its speaking symbol—that before one generation has passed an Encyclopedia is superannuated; for it speaks through the dead memory and unimpassioned understanding, which have not the repose of higher faculties, but are continually enlarging and varying their phylacteries.[4] But all literature properly so called—literature κατ᾽ ἐξοχήν[5]—for the very same reason that it is so much more durable than the literature of knowledge, is (and by the very same proportion it is) more intense and electrically searching in its impressions. The directions in which the tragedy of this planet has trained our human feelings to play, and the combinations into which the poetry of this planet has thrown our human passions of love and hatred, of admiration and contempt, exercise a power for bad or good over human life that cannot be contemplated, when stretching through many generations, without a sentiment allied to awe.[6] And of this let everyone be assured—that he owes to the impassioned books which he has read many a thousand more of emotions than he can consciously trace back to them. Dim by their origination, these emotions yet arise in him, and mould him through life, like forgotten incidents of his childhood.

1848, 1858

4. I.e., preestablished texts. "Phylacteries" are leather boxes, inscribed with quotations from the Hebrew Scriptures, worn by Orthodox Jews during morning prayer.
5. In the highest degree (Greek).
6. The reason why the broad distinctions between the two literatures of power and knowledge so little fix the attention lies in the fact that a vast proportion of books—history, biography, travels, miscellaneous essays, etc.—lying in a middle zone, confound these distinctions by interblending them. All that we call "amusement" or "entertainment" is a diluted form of the power belonging to passion, and also a mixed form; and, where threads of direct *instruction* intermingle in the texture with these threads of *power*, this absorption of the duality into one representative *nuance* neutralizes the separate perception of either. Fused into a *tertium quid* [a third thing], or neutral state, they disappear to the popular eye as the repelling forces which, in fact, they are [De Quincey's note].

GEORGE GORDON, LORD BYRON
1788–1824

In his *History of English Literature*, written in the late 1850s, the French critic Hippolyte Taine gave only a few condescending pages to Wordsworth, Coleridge, Percy Shelley, and Keats and then devoted a long chapter to Lord Byron, "the greatest and most English of these artists; he is so great and so English that from him alone we shall learn more truths of his country and of his age than from all the rest together." This comment reflects the fact that Byron had achieved an immense European reputation during his own lifetime, while his English contemporaries were admired only by coteries in England and America. Through much of the nineteenth century he continued to be rated as one of the greatest of English poets and the very prototype of literary Romanticism. His influence was manifested everywhere, not only among minor writers—most European poets struck Byronic attitudes—but among the major poets and novelists (Goethe in Germany, Balzac and Stendhal in France, Pushkin and Dostoevsky in Russia, and Melville in America), painters (especially Delacroix), and composers (including Beethoven and Berlioz).

These facts may surprise the reader who is aware of the recent estimate of Byron as the least consequential of the great Romantic poets, whose achievements have little in common with the distinctive innovations of Wordsworth, Coleridge, Shelley, or Keats. Only Shelley, among these writers, thought highly of either Byron or his work; while Byron spoke slightingly of all of them except Shelley and, in fact, insisted that, measured against the poetic practice of Alexander Pope, he and his contemporaries were "all in the wrong, one as much as another . . . we are upon a wrong revolutionary poetical system, or systems, not worth a damn in itself." Byron's masterpiece, *Don Juan*, is an instance of that favorite neoclassic type, a satire against modern civilization, and shares many of the aims and methods of Pope, Swift, Voltaire, and Sterne. Even Byron's lyrics are old-fashioned: many are in the eighteenth-century gentlemanly mode of witty extemporization and epigram (*Written after Swimming from Sestos to Abydos*) or continue the Cavalier tradition of the elaborate development of a compliment to a lady (*She walks in beauty* and *Stanzas for Music*).

Byron's chief claim to be considered an arch-Romantic is that he provided his age with what Taine called its "ruling personage; that is, the model that contemporaries invest with their admiration and sympathy." This personage is the "Byronic hero." He is first sketched in the opening canto of *Childe Harold,* then recurs in various guises in the verse romances and dramas that followed. In his developed form, as we find it in *Manfred,* he is an alien, mysterious, and gloomy spirit, superior in his passions and powers to the common run of humanity, whom he regards with disdain. He harbors the torturing memory of an enormous, nameless guilt that drives him toward an inevitable doom. He is in his isolation absolutely self-reliant, pursuing his own ends according to his self-generated moral code against any opposition, human or supernatural. And he exerts an attraction on other characters that is the more compelling because it involves their terror at his obliviousness to ordinary human concerns and values. This figure, infusing the archrebel in a nonpolitical form with a strong erotic interest, was imitated in life as well as in art and helped shape the intellectual and the cultural history of the later nineteenth century. The literary descendants of the Byronic hero include Heathcliff in *Wuthering Heights,* Captain Ahab in *Moby-Dick,* and the hero of Pushkin's great poem *Eugene Onegin.* Bertrand Russell, in his *History of Western Philosophy,* gives a chapter to Byron—not because he was a systematic thinker but because "Byronism," the attitude of "Titanic cosmic self-assertion," established a stance toward humanity and the world that entered nineteenth-century philosophy and eventually helped form Nietzsche's concept of the Superman, the hero who is not subject to the ordinary criteria of good and evil.

Byron's contemporaries insisted on identifying the author with his fictional characters. But Byron's letters and the testimony of his friends show that, except for recurrent moods of deep depression, his own temperament was in many respects antithetic to that of his heroes. He was passionate and willful; but when in good humor, he could be very much a man of the world in the eighteenth-century style—gregarious, tolerant, and a witty conversationalist capable of taking an ironic attitude toward his own activities as well as those of others. The aloof hauteur he exhibited in public was largely a mask to hide his diffidence when in strange company. But although Byronism was largely a fiction, produced by a collaboration between Byron's imagination and that of his public, the fiction was historically more important than the actual person.

Byron was descended from two aristocratic families, both of them colorful, violent, and dissolute. His grandfather was an admiral nicknamed "Foulweather Jack"; his great-uncle was the fifth Baron Byron, known to his rural neighbors as the "Wicked Lord," who was tried by his peers for killing his kinsman William Chaworth in a drunken duel; his father, Captain John Byron, was a rake and fortune hunter who rapidly dissipated the patrimony of two wealthy wives. Byron's mother was a Scotswoman, Catherine Gordon of Gight, the last descendant of a line of lawless Scottish lairds. After her husband died (Byron was then three), she brought up her son in near poverty in Aberdeen, where he was indoctrinated with the Calvinistic morality of Scottish Presbyterianism. Catherine Byron was an ill-educated and extremely irascible woman who nevertheless had an abiding love for her son; they fought violently when together, but corresponded affectionately enough when apart, until her death in 1811.

When Byron was ten, the death of his great-uncle, preceded by that of more immediate heirs to the title, made him the sixth Lord Byron. In a fashion suitable to his new status he was sent to Harrow School, then to Trinity College, Cambridge. He had a deformed foot, made worse by inept surgical treatment, about which he felt acute embarrassment. His lameness made him avid for athletic prowess; he played cricket and made himself an expert boxer, fencer, and horseman and a powerful swimmer. He was also sexually precocious; when only seven, he fell in love with a little cousin, Mary Duff, and so violently that ten years later news of her marriage threw him into convulsions. Both at Cambridge and at his ancestral estate of Newstead, he engaged with more than ordinary zeal in the expensive pursuits and fashionable dissipations of a young Regency lord. As a result, despite a sizable and increasing income, he got into financial difficulties from which he did not entirely extricate himself until late in his life. In the course of his schooling he formed many close and devoted friendships, the most important with John Cam Hobhouse, a sturdy political liberal and commonsense moralist who exerted a steadying influence throughout Byron's turbulent life.

Despite his distractions at the university, Byron found time to try his hand at lyric verse, some of which was published in 1807 in a slim and conventional volume titled *Hours of Idleness*. This was treated so harshly by the pontifical *Edinburgh Review* that Byron was provoked to write in reply his first important poem, *English Bards and Scotch Reviewers,* a vigorous satire in the couplet style of the late-eighteenth-century followers of Pope, in which he incorporated brilliant but tactless ridicule (which he later came to regret) of important poetic contemporaries, including Scott, Wordsworth, and Coleridge.

After attaining his M.A. degree and his majority, Byron set out with Hobhouse in 1809 on a tour through Portugal and Spain to Malta, and then to little-known Albania, Greece, and Asia Minor. In this adventurous two-year excursion, he accumulated materials that he incorporated into many of his important poems, including his last work, *Don Juan*. The first literary product was *Childe Harold;* he wrote the opening two cantos while on the tour that the poem describes; published them in 1812 soon after his return to England; and, in his own oft-quoted phrase, "awoke one morning and found myself famous." He became the celebrity of fashionable London, and increased his literary success by a series of highly readable Near Eastern verse tales; in these the Byronic hero, in various embodiments, flaunts his misanthropy and undergoes a variety of violent and romantic adventures that current gossip attributed to the author himself. In his chronic shortage of money, Byron could well have used the huge income from these publications, but instead maintained his status as an aristocratic amateur by giving the royalties away. Occupying his inherited seat in the House of Lords, he also became briefly active on the extreme liberal side of the Whig party and spoke courageously in defense of the Nottingham weavers who had resorted to smashing the newly invented textile machines that had thrown them out of work. He also supported other liberal measures, including that of Catholic Emancipation.

Byron was extraordinarily handsome—"so beautiful a countenance," Coleridge wrote, "I scarcely ever saw . . . his eyes the open portals of the sun—things of light, and for light." Because of a constitutional tendency to obesity, however, he was able to maintain his looks only by resorting again and again to a starvation diet of biscuits, soda water, and strong cathartics. Often as a result of female initiative rather than his own, Byron entered into a sequence of liaisons with ladies of fashion. One of these, the flamboyant and eccentric young Lady Caroline Lamb, caused him so much distress by her pursuit and public tantrums that Byron turned for relief to marriage with Annabella Milbanke, who was in every way Lady Caroline's opposite, for she was naive, unworldly, intellectual (with a special passion for mathematics), and not a little priggish. This ill-starred marriage produced a daughter (Augusta Ada) and many scenes in which Byron, goaded by financial difficulties, behaved so frantically that his wife suspected his sanity; after only one year, the union ended in a legal separation. The final blow came when Lady Byron discovered her husband's incestuous relations with his half-sister, Augusta Leigh. The two had been raised apart, so that they were almost strangers when they met as adults. Byron's affection for his sister, however guilty, was genuine and endured all through his life. This affair proved a delicious morsel even to the jaded palate of the dissolute Regency society. Byron was ostracized by all but a few friends and was finally forced to leave England forever on April 25, 1816.

Byron now resumed the travels incorporated in the third and fourth cantos of *Childe Harold*. At Geneva he lived for several months in close and intellectually fruitful relation to Percy and Mary Shelley, who were accompanied by Mary's stepsister, Claire Clairmont—a misguided seventeen-year-old who had forced herself on Byron while he was still in England and who in January 1817 bore him a daughter, Allegra. In the fall of 1817 Byron established himself in Venice, where he inaugurated a period of frenzied debauchery that, he estimated, involved more than two hundred women. This period, however, was also one of great literary creativity: often working through the later hours of the night, he finished his tragedy *Manfred;* wrote the fourth canto of *Childe Harold;* and after turning out *Beppo,* a short preview of the narrative style and stanza of *Don Juan,* began the composition of *Don Juan* itself. In the colloquial ottava rima, he finally learned to write poetry as well as he had written the prose of his vivid, informative, and witty letters.

Exhausted and bored by promiscuity, Byron in 1819 settled into a placid and relatively faithful relationship with Teresa Guiccioli, the young wife of the elderly Count Alessandro Guiccioli; according to the Italian upper-class mores of the times, having contracted a marriage of convenience, she could now with propriety attach Byron to herself as a *cavaliere servente.* Through the countess's nationalistic family, the Gambas, Byron became involved in the Carbonari plot against Austrian control over northern Italy. When the Gambas were forced by the authorities to move to Pisa, Byron followed them there and, for the second time, joined the Shelleys. There grew up about them the "Pisan Circle," which in addition to the Gambas included their friends Thomas Medwin and Edward and Jane Williams, as well as the Greek nationalist leader Prince Mavrocordatos, the picturesque Irish Count Taaffe, and the flamboyant and mendacious adventurer Edward Trelawny, who seems to have stepped out of one of Byron's romances. The circle was gradually broken up, first by Shelley's anger over Byron's treatment of his daughter Allegra (Byron had sent the child to be brought up as a Catholic in an Italian convent, where she died of a fever in 1822); then by the expulsion of the Gambas, whom Byron followed to Genoa; and finally by the drowning of Shelley and Williams in July 1822.

Byron meanwhile had been steadily at work on a series of closet tragedies (including *Cain, Sardanapalus,* and *Marino Faliero*) and on his devastating satire on the life and death of George III, *The Vision of Judgment.* But increasingly he devoted himself to the continuation of *Don Juan.* He had always been diffident in his self-judgments and easily swayed by literary advice. But now, confident that he had at last found his métier, he kept on, in spite of persistent objections against the supposed immorality of the poem by the English public, by his publisher John Murray, by his friends and well-wishers, and by his extremely decorous lover, the Countess Guiccioli—by almost everyone, in fact, except the idealist Shelley, who thought *Juan* incomparably better than anything he himself could write and insisted "that every word of it is pregnant with immortality."

Byron finally broke off literature for action when he organized an expedition to assist in the Greek war for independence from the Turks. He knew too well the conditions in Greece, and had too skeptical an estimate of human nature, to entertain hope of success; but, in part because his own writings had helped to kindle European enthusiasm for the Greek cause, he now felt honor-bound to try what could be done. In the dismal, marshy town of Missolonghi he lived a Spartan existence, training troops whom he had himself subsidized and exhibiting practical grasp and a power of leadership amid a chaos of factionalism, intrigue, and military ineptitude. Worn out, he succumbed to a series of feverish attacks and died just after he had reached his thirty-sixth birthday. To this day Byron is revered by the Greek people as a national hero.

Students of Byron still feel, as his friends had felt, the magnetism of his volatile temperament. As Mary Shelley wrote six years after his death, when she read Thomas Moore's edition of his *Letters and Journals:* "The Lord Byron I find there is our Lord Byron—the fascinating—faulty—childish—philosophical being—daring the world— docile to a private circle—impetuous and indolent—gloomy and yet more gay than any other." Of his inner discordances, Byron himself was well aware; he told his friend Lady Blessington: "I am so changeable, being everything by turns and nothing long—I am such a strange *mélange* of good and evil, that it would be difficult to describe me." Yet he remained faithful to his code: a determination to tell the truth as he saw it about the world and about himself (his refusal to suppress or conceal any of his moods is in part what made him seem so contradictory) and a dedication to the freedom of nations and individuals. As he went on to say to Lady Blessington: "There are but two sentiments to which I am constant—a strong love of liberty, and a detestation of cant."

The poetry texts printed here are taken from Jerome J. McGann's edition, *Lord Byron: The Complete Poetical Works* (Oxford, 1980–93).

Written after Swimming from Sestos to Abydos[1]

May 9, 1810

I

If in the month of dark December
Leander, who was nightly wont
(What maid will not the tale remember?)
To cross thy stream, broad Hellespont!

2

5   If when the wintry tempest roared
He sped to Hero, nothing loth,

---

1. The Hellespont (now called the Dardanelles) is the narrow strait between Europe and Asia. In the ancient story, retold in Christopher Marlowe's *Hero and Leander,* young Leander of Abydos, on the Asian side, swam nightly to visit Hero, a priestess of the goddess Venus at Sestos, until he was drowned when he made the attempt in a storm. Byron and a young Lieutenant Ekenhead swam the Hellespont in the reverse direction on May 3, 1810. Byron alternated between complacency and humor in his many references to the event. In a note to the poem, he mentions that the distance was "upwards of four English miles, though the actual breadth is barely one. The rapidity of the current is such that no boat can row directly across. . . . The water was extremely cold, from the melting of the mountain snows."

And thus of old thy current pour'd,
Fair Venus! how I pity both!

3

For *me*, degenerate modern wretch,
10   Though in the genial month of May,
My dripping limbs I faintly stretch,
    And think I've done a feat to-day.

4

But since he cross'd the rapid tide,
    According to the doubtful story,
15 To woo,—and—Lord knows what beside,
    And swam for Love, as I for Glory;

5

'Twere hard to say who fared the best:
    Sad mortals! thus the Gods still plague you!
He lost his labour, I my jest:
20   For he was drown'd, and I've the ague.

1810   1812

She walks in beauty[1]

1

She walks in beauty, like the night
    Of cloudless climes and starry skies;
And all that's best of dark and bright
    Meet in her aspect and her eyes:
5 Thus mellow'd to that tender light
    Which heaven to gaudy day denies.

2

One shade the more, one ray the less,
    Had half impair'd the nameless grace
Which waves in every raven tress,
10   Or softly lightens o'er her face;
Where thoughts serenely sweet express
    How pure, how dear their dwelling place.

3

And on that cheek, and o'er that brow,
    So soft, so calm, yet eloquent,
15 The smiles that win, the tints that glow,
    But tell of days in goodness spent,

---

1. One of the lyrics in *Hebrew Melodies* (1815),
written to be set to adaptations of traditional Jewish tunes by the young musician Isaac Nathan.
Byron wrote the lines the morning after he had met
his beautiful young cousin by marriage, Mrs. Robert John Wilmot, who wore a black mourning gown
brightened with spangles.

A mind at peace with all below,
A heart whose love is innocent!

June 1814   1815

They say that Hope is happiness

Felix qui potuit rerum cognoscere causas.[1]
                                        VIRGIL

1

They say that Hope is happiness—
   But genuine Love must prize the past;
And Mem'ry wakes the thoughts that bless:
   They rose the first—they set the last.

2

5   And all that mem'ry loves the most
       Was once our only hope to be:
   And all that hope adored and lost
       Hath melted into memory.

3

   Alas! it is delusion all—
10   The future cheats us from afar:
   Nor can we be what we recall,
       Nor dare we think on what we are.

1814   1829

When we two parted

1

When we two parted
   In silence and tears,
Half broken-hearted
   To sever for years,
5   Pale grew thy cheek and cold,
       Colder thy kiss;
   Truly that hour foretold
       Sorrow to this.

2

   The dew of the morning
10   Sunk chill on my brow—
   It felt like the warning
       Of what I feel now.

1. Happy is he who has been able to learn the causes of things (Latin; *Georgics* 2.490).

Thy vows are all broken,
    And light is thy fame;
15 I hear thy name spoken,
    And share in its shame.

                3
They name thee before me,
    A knell to mine ear;
A shudder comes o'er me—
20   Why wert thou so dear?
They know not I knew thee,
    Who knew thee too well:—
Long, long shall I rue thee,
    Too deeply to tell.

                4
25 In secret we met—
    In silence I grieve,
That thy heart could forget,
    Thy spirit deceive.
If I should meet thee
30   After long years,
How should I greet thee!—
    With silence and tears.

1815   1815

Stanzas for Music

There be none of Beauty's daughters
    With a magic like thee;
And like music on the waters
    Is thy sweet voice to me:
5   When, as if its sound were causing
The charmed ocean's pausing,
The waves lie still and gleaming,
And the lulled winds seem dreaming.

And the midnight moon is weaving
10   Her bright chain o'er the deep;
Whose breast is gently heaving,
    As an infant's asleep.
So the spirit bows before thee,
    To listen and adore thee;
15 With a full but soft emotion,
    Like the swell of Summer's ocean.

1816   1816

Darkness[1]

I had a dream, which was not all a dream.
The bright sun was extinguish'd, and the stars
Did wander darkling[2] in the eternal space,
Rayless, and pathless, and the icy earth
5 Swung blind and blackening in the moonless air;
Morn came, and went—and came, and brought no day,
And men forgot their passions in the dread
Of this their desolation; and all hearts
Were chill'd into a selfish prayer for light:
10 And they did live by watchfires—and the thrones,
The palaces of crowned kings—the huts,
The habitations of all things which dwell,
Were burnt for beacons; cities were consumed,
And men were gathered round their blazing homes
15 To look once more into each other's face;
Happy were those who dwelt within the eye
Of the volcanos, and their mountain-torch:
A fearful hope was all the world contain'd;
Forests were set on fire—but hour by hour
20 They fell and faded—and the crackling trunks
Extinguish'd with a crash—and all was black.
The brows of men by the despairing light
Wore an unearthly aspect, as by fits
The flashes fell upon them; some lay down
25 And hid their eyes and wept; and some did rest
Their chins upon their clenched hands, and smiled;
And others hurried to and fro, and fed
Their funeral piles with fuel, and looked up
With mad disquietude on the dull sky,
30 The pall of a past world; and then again
With curses cast them down upon the dust,
And gnash'd their teeth and howl'd: the wild birds shriek'd,
And, terrified, did flutter on the ground,
And flap their useless wings; the wildest brutes
35 Came tame and tremulous; and vipers crawl'd
And twined themselves among the multitude,
Hissing, but stingless—they were slain for food:
And War, which for a moment was no more,
Did glut himself again;—a meal was bought
40 With blood, and each sate sullenly apart
Gorging himself in gloom: no love was left;
All earth was but one thought—and that was death,
Immediate and inglorious; and the pang
Of famine fed upon all entrails—men
45 Died, and their bones were tombless as their flesh;

---

1. A powerfully imagined blank-verse description of the end of life on earth—a speculation hardly
less common in Byron's time than in ours.
2. In the dark.

The meagre by the meagre were devoured,
Even dogs assail'd their masters, all save one,
And he was faithful to a corse, and kept
The birds and beasts and famish'd men at bay,
50 Till hunger clung° them, or the dropping dead   *withered*
Lured their lank jaws; himself sought out no food,
But with a piteous and perpetual moan,
And a quick desolate cry, licking the hand
Which answered not with a caress—he died.
55 The crowd was famish'd by degrees; but two
Of an enormous city did survive,
And they were enemies; they met beside
The dying embers of an altar-place,
Where had been heap'd a mass of holy things
60 For an unholy usage; they raked up,
And shivering scraped with their cold skeleton hands
The feeble ashes, and their feeble breath
Blew for a little life, and made a flame
Which was a mockery; then they lifted up
65 Their eyes as it grew lighter, and beheld
Each other's aspects—saw, and shriek'd, and died—
Even of their mutual hideousness they died,
Unknowing who he was upon whose brow
Famine had written Fiend. The world was void,
70 The populous and the powerful—was a lump,
Seasonless, herbless, treeless, manless, lifeless—
A lump of death—a chaos of hard clay.
The rivers, lakes, and ocean all stood still,
And nothing stirred within their silent depths;
75 Ships sailorless lay rotting on the sea,
And their masts fell down piecemeal; as they dropp'd
They slept on the abyss without a surge—
The waves were dead; the tides were in their grave,
The moon their mistress had expired before;
80 The winds were withered in the stagnant air,
And the clouds perish'd; Darkness had no need
Of aid from them—She was the universe.

1816   1816

So, we'll go no more a roving[1]

I

So, we'll go no more a roving
So late into the night,

---

1. Composed in the Lenten aftermath of a spell of feverish dissipation in the Carnival season in Venice, and included in a letter to Thomas Moore, February 28, 1817. Byron wrote, "I find 'the sword wearing out the scabbard,' though I have but just turned the corner of twenty-nine." The poem is based on the refrain of a Scottish song, *The Jolly Beggar*: "And we'll gang nae mair a roving / Sae late into the nicht."

Though the heart be still as loving,
　　And the moon be still as bright.

2

5　For the sword outwears its sheath,
　　And the soul wears out the breast,
　And the heart must pause to breathe,
　　And love itself have rest.

3

　Though the night was made for loving,
10　　And the day returns too soon,
　Yet we'll go no more a roving
　　By the light of the moon.

1817　　　　　　　　　　　　　　　　　　　　　　　　1830

When a man hath no freedom to fight for at home[1]

When a man hath no freedom to fight for at home,
　Let him combat for that of his neighbors;
Let him think of the glories of Greece and of Rome,
　And get knock'd on the head for his labours.

5　To do good to mankind is the chivalrous plan,
　　And is always as nobly requited;
Then battle for freedom wherever you can,
　　And, if not shot or hang'd, you'll get knighted.

Nov. 5, 1820　　　　　　　　　　　　　　　　　　　　　1830

Stanzas Written on the Road between Florence and Pisa

Oh, talk not to me of a name great in story—
The days of our youth are the days of our glory;
And the myrtle and ivy[1] of sweet two-and-twenty
Are worth all your laurels,[2] though ever so plenty.

5　What are garlands and crowns to the brow that is wrinkled?
'Tis but as a dead-flower with May-dew besprinkled:
Then away with all such from the head that is hoary!
What care I for the wreaths that can *only* give glory?

Oh FAME!—if I e'er took delight in thy praises,
10　'Twas less for the sake of thy high-sounding phrases,

1. The ironist's attitude toward gratuitous enlistment in a foreign war for national freedom—a cause to which Byron gave his own life less than four years later.

1. Sacred to Bacchus, god of wine and revelry. "Myrtle": sacred to Venus, goddess of love.
2. A laurel crown was awarded by the Greeks as a mark of high honor.

Than to see the bright eyes of the dear one discover
She thought that I was not unworthy to love her.

There chiefly I sought thee, *there* only I found thee;
Her glance was the best of the rays that surround thee;
15   When it sparkled o'er aught that was bright in my story,
I knew it was love, and I felt it was glory.

Nov. 1821   1830

January 22nd. Missolonghi

On this day I complete my thirty sixth year

'Tis time this heart should be unmoved,
    Since others it hath ceased to move:
Place let me love!
        Still let me love!

5   My days are in the yellow leaf;
    The flowers and fruits of Love are gone;
The worm—the canker, and the grief
        Are mine alone!

The fire that on my bosom preys
10   Is lone as some Volcanic Isle;
No torch is kindled at its blaze
        A funeral pile!

The hope, the fear, the jealous care,
    The exalted portion of the pain
15   And power of Love I cannot share,
        But wear the chain.

But 'tis not *thus*—and 'tis not *here*
    Such thoughts should shake my Soul, nor *now*
Where Glory decks the hero's bier
20   Or binds his brow.

The Sword, the Banner, and the Field,
    Glory and Greece around us see!
The Spartan borne upon his shield
        Was not more free!

25   Awake (not Greece—she *is* awake!)
    Awake, my Spirit! think through *whom*
Thy life-blood tracks its parent lake
        And then strike home!

Tread those reviving passions down
30   Unworthy Manhood—unto thee

> Indifferent should the smile or frown
> Of Beauty be.

> If thou regret'st thy Youth, *why live?*
> The land of honourable Death
> 35 Is here:—up to the Field, and give
> Away thy Breath!

> Seek out—less often sought than found—
> A Soldier's Grave, for thee the best;
> Then look around, and choose thy Ground,
> 40 And take thy Rest!

Jan. 1824   1824

Childe Harold's Pilgrimage

Childe Harold is a travelogue narrated by a melancholy, passionate, well-read, and very eloquent tourist. Byron wrote most of the first two cantos while on the tour through Spain, Portugal, Albania, and Greece that these cantos describe; when he published them, in 1812, they made him at one stroke the best known and most talked about poet in England. Byron took up *Childe Harold* again in 1816, during the European tour he made after the breakup of his marriage. Canto 3, published in 1816, moves through Belgium, up the Rhine, then to Switzerland and the Alps. Canto 4, published in 1818, describes the great cities and monuments of Italy.

Byron chose for his poem the Spenserian stanza, and like James Thomson (in the *Castle of Indolence*) and other eighteenth-century predecessors, he attempted in the first canto to imitate, in a seriocomic fashion, the archaic language of his Elizabethan model. (The word *Childe* itself is the ancient term for a young noble awaiting knighthood.) But he soon dropped the archaisms, and in the last two cantos he adapts Spenser's mellifluous stanza to his own assured and brassy magniloquence.

In the preface to his first two cantos, Byron had insisted that the narrator, Childe Harold, was "a fictitious character," merely "the child of imagination." In the manuscript version of these cantos, however, he had called his hero "Childe Burun," the early form of his own family name. The world insisted on identifying the character as well as the travels of the protagonist with those of the author, and in the fourth canto Byron, abandoning the third-person *dramatis persona,* spoke out frankly in the first person.

Childe Harold achieved a great European reputation, not only because of the character of its protagonist but also because of its high-pitched style, with its abrupt changes in subject, mood, and pace. Goethe applied to the poem the terms *Keckheit, Kühnheit, und Grandiosität:* "darling, dash, and grandiosity." Byron converted an accurate tourist's record of scenes, memorials, and museums into a dramatic experience in which everything is presented as it affects the violent sensibility of a new cultural phenomenon, the Romantic Man of Feeling.

FROM CHILDE HAROLD'S PILGRIMAGE

A ROMAUNT[1]

From Canto 1

["SIN'S LONG LABYRINTH"]

1

Oh, thou! in Hellas deem'd of heav'nly birth,
Muse! form'd or fabled at the minstrel's will!
Since sham'd full oft by later lyres on earth,
Mine dares not call thee from thy sacred hill:
5   Yet there I've wander'd by thy vaunted rill;
Yes! sigh'd o'er Delphi's long-deserted shrine,
Where, save that feeble fountain, all is still;
Nor mote° my shell awake the weary Nine[2]   *may*
To grace so plain a tale—this lowly lay of mine.

2

10   Whilome[3] in Albion's° isle there dwelt a youth,   *England's*
Who ne in virtue's ways did take delight;
But spent his days in riot most uncouth,
And vex'd with mirth the drowsy ear of Night.
Ah, me! in sooth he was a shameless wight,
15   Sore given to revel and ungodly glee;
Few earthly things found favour in his sight
Save concubines and carnal companie,
And flaunting wassailers[4] of high and low degree.

3

Childe Harold was he hight:—but whence his name
20   And lineage long, it suits me not to say;
Suffice it, that perchance they were of fame,
And had been glorious in another day:
But one sad losel[5] soils a name for aye,
However mighty in the olden time;
25   Nor all that heralds rake from coffin'd clay,
Nor florid prose, nor honied lies of rhyme
Can blazon evil deeds, or consecrate a crime.

4

Childe Harold bask'd him in the noon-tide sun,
Disporting there like any other fly;
30   Nor deem'd before his little day was done
One blast might chill him into misery.

1. A romance or narrative of adventure.
2. The Muses, whose "vaunted rill" (line 5) was the Castalian spring. "Shell": lyre. Hermes is fabled to have invented the lyre by stretching strings over the hollow of a tortoise shell.
3. Once upon a time.

4. Noisy, insolent drinkers (Byron is thought to refer to his own youthful carousing with friends at Newstead Abbey).
5. Rascal. Byron's great-uncle, the fifth Lord Byron, had killed a kinsman in a drunken duel.

But long ere scarce a third of his pass'd by,
Worse than adversity the Childe befell;
He felt the fulness of satiety:
35   Then loath'd he in his native land to dwell,
Which seem'd to him more lone than Eremite's[6] sad cell.

5

For he through Sin's long labyrinth had run,
Nor made atonement when he did amiss,
Had sigh'd to many though he lov'd but one,
40   And that lov'd one, alas! could ne'er be his.
Ah, happy she! to 'scape from him whose kiss
Had been pollution unto aught so chaste;
Who soon had left her charms for vulgar bliss,
And spoil'd her goodly lands to gild his waste,
45   Nor calm domestic peace had ever deign'd to taste.

6

And now Childe Harold was sore sick at heart,
And from his fellow bacchanals would flee;
'Tis said, at times the sullen tear would start,
But Pride congeal'd the drop within his ee:°   *eye*
50   Apart he stalk'd in joyless reverie,
And from his native land resolv'd to go,
And visit scorching climes beyond the sea;
With pleasure drugg'd he almost long'd for woe,
And e'en for change of scene would seek the shades below.

From Canto 3

["ONCE MORE UPON THE WATERS"]

1

Is thy face like thy mother's, my fair child!
Ada![1] sole daughter of my house and heart?
When last I saw thy young blue eyes they smiled,
And then we parted,—not as now we part,
But with a hope.—
5   Awaking with a start,
The waters heave around me; and on high
The winds lift up their voices: I depart,
Whither I know not; but the hour's gone by,
When Albion's lessening shores could grieve or glad mine eye.

2

10   Once more upon the waters! yet once more!
And the waves bound beneath me as a steed

---

6. A religious hermit.
1. Byron's daughter Augusta Ada, born in December 1816, a month before her parents separated.

Byron's "hope" (line 5) had been for a reconciliation, but he was never to see Ada again.

That knows his rider. Welcome, to their roar!
Swift be their guidance, wheresoe'er it lead!
Though the strain'd mast should quiver as a reed,
15 And the rent canvas fluttering strew the gale,
Still must I on; for I am as a weed,
Flung from the rock, on Ocean's foam, to sail
Where'er the surge may sweep, the tempest's breath prevail.

3

In my youth's summer[2] I did sing of One,
20 The wandering outlaw of his own dark mind;
Again I seize the theme then but begun,
And bear it with me, as the rushing wind
Bears the cloud onwards: in that Tale I find
The furrows of long thought, and dried-up tears,
25 Which, ebbing, leave a sterile track behind,
O'er which all heavily the journeying years
Plod the last sands of life,—where not a flower appears.

4

Since my young days of passion—joy, or pain,
Perchance my heart and harp have lost a string,
30 And both may jar:[3] it may be, that in vain
I would essay as I have sung to sing.
Yet, though a dreary strain, to this I cling;
So that it wean me from the weary dream
Of selfish grief or gladness—so it fling
35 Forgetfulness around me—it shall seem
To me, though to none else, a not ungrateful theme.

5

He, who grown aged in this world of woe,
In deeds, not years, piercing the depths of life,
So that no wonder waits him; nor below
40 Can love, or sorrow, fame, ambition, strife,
Cut to his heart again with the keen knife
Of silent, sharp endurance: he can tell
Why thought seeks refuge in lone caves, yet rife
With airy images, and shapes which dwell
45 Still unimpair'd, though old, in the soul's haunted cell.

6

'Tis to create, and in creating live
A being more intense, that we endow
With form our fancy, gaining as we give
The life we image, even as I do now.
50 What am I? Nothing; but not so art thou,
Soul of my thought![4] with whom I traverse earth,
Invisible but gazing, as I glow

2. Byron wrote canto 1 at age twenty-one; he is now twenty-eight.

3. Sound discordant.

4. I.e., Childe Harold, his literary creation.

Mix'd with thy spirit, blended with thy birth,
And feeling still with thee in my crush'd feelings' dearth.

7

55 Yet must I think less wildly:—I *have* thought
Too long and darkly, till my brain became,
In its own eddy boiling and o'erwrought,
A whirling gulf of phantasy and flame:
And thus, untaught in youth my heart to tame,
60 My springs of life were poison'd. 'Tis too late!
Yet am I chang'd; though still enough the same
In strength to bear what time can not abate,
And feed on bitter fruits without accusing Fate.

8

Something too much of this:—but now 'tis past,
65 And the spell closes with its silent seal.[5]
Long absent HAROLD re-appears at last;
He of the breast which fain no more would feel,
Wrung with the wounds which kill not, but ne'er heal;
Yet Time, who changes all, had alter'd him
70 In soul and aspect as in age: years steal
Fire from the mind as vigour from the limb;
And life's enchanted cup but sparkles near the brim.

9

His had been quaff'd too quickly, and he found
The dregs were wormwood; but he fill'd again,
75 And from a purer fount, on holier ground,
And deem'd its spring perpetual; but in vain!
Still round him clung invisibly a chain
Which gall'd for ever, fettering though unseen,
And heavy though it clank'd not; worn with pain,
80 Which pined although it spoke not, and grew keen,
Entering with every step, he took, through many a scene.

10

Secure in guarded coldness, he had mix'd
Again in fancied safety with his kind,
And deem'd his spirit now so firmly fix'd
85 And sheath'd with an invulnerable mind,
That, if no joy, no sorrow lurk'd behind;
And he, as one, might midst the many stand
Unheeded, searching through the crowd to find
Fit speculation! such as in strange land
90 He found in wonder-works of God and Nature's hand.

11

But who can view the ripened rose, nor seek
To wear it? who can curiously behold

5. I.e., he sets the seal of silence on his personal tale ("spell").

The smoothness and the sheen of beauty's cheek,
Nor feel the heart can never all grow old?
95 Who can contemplate Fame through clouds unfold
The star which rises o'er her steep, nor climb?
Harold, once more within the vortex, roll'd
On with the giddy circle, chasing Time,
Yet with a nobler aim than in his youth's fond° prime.   *foolish*

12

100 But soon he knew himself the most unfit
Of men to herd with Man; with whom he held
Little in common; untaught to submit
His thoughts to others, though his soul was quell'd
In youth by his own thoughts; still uncompell'd,
105 He would not yield dominion of his mind
To spirits against whom his own rebell'd;
Proud though in desolation; which could find
A life within itself, to breathe without mankind.

13

Where rose the mountains, there to him were friends;
110 Where roll'd the ocean, thereon was his home;
Where a blue sky, and glowing clime, extends,
He had the passion and the power to roam;
The desert, forest, cavern, breaker's foam,
Were unto him companionship; they spake
115 A mutual language, clearer than the tome
Of his land's tongue, which he would oft forsake
For Nature's pages glass'd° by sunbeams on the lake.   *made glassy*

14

Like the Chaldean,[6] he could watch the stars,
Till he had peopled them with beings bright
120 As their own beams; and earth, and earth-born jars,
And human frailties, were forgotten quite:
Could he have kept his spirit to that flight
He had been happy; but this clay will sink
Its spark immortal, envying it the light
125 To which it mounts, as if to break the link
That keeps us from yon heaven which woos us to its brink.

15

But in Man's dwellings he became a thing
Restless and worn, and stern and wearisome,
Droop'd as a wild-born falcon with clipt wing,
130 To whom the boundless air alone were home:
Then came his fit again, which to o'ercome,
As eagerly the barr'd-up bird will beat
His breast and beak against his wiry dome

---

6. A people of ancient Babylonia, expert in astronomy.

Till the blood tinge his plumage, so the heat
135 Of his impeded soul would through his bosom eat.

16

Self-exiled Harold wanders forth again,
With nought of hope left, but with less of gloom;
The very knowledge that he lived in vain,
That all was over on this side the tomb,
140 Had made Despair a smilingness assume,
Which, though 'twere wild,—as on the plundered wreck
When mariners would madly meet their doom
With draughts intemperate on the sinking deck,—
Did yet inspire a cheer, which he forbore to check.

[WATERLOO]

17

145 Stop!—for thy tread is on an Empire's dust!
An Earthquake's spoil is sepulchered below!
Is the spot mark'd with no colossal bust?
Nor column trophied for triumphal show?
None; but the moral's truth tells simpler so,
150 As the ground was before, thus let it be;—
How that red rain hath made the harvest grow!
And is this all the world has gained by thee,
Thou first and last of fields! king-making Victory?

18

And Harold stands upon this place of skulls,
155 The grave of France, the deadly Waterloo![7]
How in an hour the power which gave annuls
Its gifts, transferring fame as fleeting too!
In "pride of place" here last the eagle flew,[8]
Then tore with bloody talon the rent plain,
160 Pierced by the shaft of banded nations through;
Ambition's life and labours all were vain;
He wears the shattered links of the world's broken chain.[9]

19

Fit retribution! Gaul[1] may champ the bit
And foam in fetters;—but is Earth more free?
165 Did nations combat to make One submit;
Or league to teach all kings true sovereignty?
What! shall reviving Thraldom again be
The patched-up idol of enlightened days?
Shall we, who struck the Lion down, shall we

7. Napoleon's defeat at Waterloo, near Brussels, had occurred only the year before, on June 18, 1815.
8. The eagle was the standard of Napoleon. "Pride of place": from falconry, meaning the highest point of flight (cf. *Macbeth* 2.4.12).

9. Napoleon was then a prisoner at St. Helena.
1. France. Byron, like Shelley and other liberals, saw the defeat of the Napoleonic tyranny as also a victory for tyrannous kings and the forces of extreme reaction throughout Europe.

170   Pay the Wolf homage? proffering lowly gaze
    And servile knees to thrones? No; *prove*[2] before ye praise!

20

    If not, o'er one fallen despot boast no more!
    In vain fair cheeks were furrowed with hot tears
    For Europe's flowers long rooted up before
175   The trampler of her vineyards; in vain years
    Of death, depopulation, bondage, fears,
    Have all been borne, and broken by the accord
    Of roused-up millions: all that most endears
    Glory, is when the myrtle wreathes a sword
180   Such as Harmodius drew on Athens' tyrant lord.[3]

21

    There was a sound of revelry by night,[4]
    And Belgium's capital had gathered then
    Her Beauty and her Chivalry, and bright
    The lamps shone o'er fair women and brave men;
185   A thousand hearts beat happily; and when
    Music arose with its voluptuous swell,
    Soft eyes look'd love to eyes which spake again,
    And all went merry as a marriage-bell;
    But hush! hark! a deep sound strikes like a rising knell!

22

190   Did ye not hear it?—No; 'twas but the wind,
    Or the car rattling o'er the stony street;
    On with the dance! let joy be unconfined;
    No sleep till morn, when Youth and Pleasure meet
    To chase the glowing Hours with flying feet—
195   But, hark!—that heavy sound breaks in once more,
    As if the clouds its echo would repeat;
    And nearer, clearer, deadlier than before!
    Arm! Arm! and out—it is—the cannon's opening roar!

23

    Within a windowed niche of that high hall
200   Sate Brunswick's fated chieftain;[5] he did hear
    That sound the first amidst the festival,
    And caught its tone with Death's prophetic ear;
    And when they smiled because he deem'd it near,
    His heart more truly knew that peal too well
205   Which stretch'd his father on a bloody bier,
    And roused the vengeance blood alone could quell:
    He rush'd into the field, and, foremost fighting, fell.

---

2. Await the test (proof) of experience.
3. In 514 B.C.E. Harmodius and Aristogeiton, hiding their daggers in myrtle (symbol of love), killed Hipparchus, tyrant of Athens.
4. A famous ball, given by the duchess of Richmond on the eve of the battle of Quatre Bras,
which opened the conflict at Waterloo.
5. The duke of Brunswick, nephew of George III of England, was killed in the battle of Quatre Bras. His father, commanding the Prussian army against Napoleon, had been killed at Auerstedt in 1806 (line 205).

24

Ah! then and there was hurrying to and fro,
And gathering tears, and tremblings of distress,
210 And cheeks all pale, which but an hour ago
Blush'd at the praise of their own loveliness;
And there were sudden partings, such as press
The life from out young hearts, and choking sighs
Which ne'er might be repeated; who could guess
215 If ever more should meet those mutual eyes,
Since upon nights so sweet such awful morn could rise?

25

And there was mounting in hot haste: the steed,
The mustering squadron, and the clattering car,
Went pouring forward in impetuous speed,
220 And swiftly forming in the ranks of war;
And the deep thunder peal on peal afar;
And near, the beat of the alarming drum
Roused up the soldier ere the morning star;
While throng'd the citizens with terror dumb,
225 Or whispering, with white lips—"The foe! They come! they come!"

26

And wild and high the "Cameron's gathering" rose!
The war-note of Lochiel,[6] which Albyn's° hills   *Scotland's*
Have heard, and heard, too, have her Saxon foes:—
How in the noon of night that pibroch[7] thrills,
230 Savage and shrill! But with the breath which fills
Their mountain-pipe, so fill the mountaineers
With the fierce native daring which instils
The stirring memory of a thousand years,
And Evan's, Donald's[8] fame rings in each clansman's ears!

27

235 And Ardennes[9] waves above them her green leaves,
Dewy with nature's tear-drops, as they pass,
Grieving, if aught inanimate e'er grieves,
Over the unreturning brave,—alas!
Ere evening to be trodden like the grass
240 Which now beneath them, but above shall grow
In its next verdure, when this fiery mass
Of living valour, rolling on the foe
And burning with high hope, shall moulder cold and low.

28

Last noon beheld them full of lusty life,
245 Last eve in Beauty's circle proudly gay,

6. "Cameron's gathering" is the clan song of the Camerons, whose chief was called "Lochiel," after his estate.
7. Bagpipe music, usually warlike in character.
8. Sir Evan and Donald Cameron, famous warri-ors in the Stuart cause in the 17th and 18th centuries.
9. A forested region covering parts of Belgium, France, and Luxembourg.

The midnight brought the signal-sound of strife,
The morn the marshalling in arms,—the day
Battle's magnificently-stern array!
The thunder-clouds close o'er it, which when rent
250   The earth is covered thick with other clay,
Which her own clay shall cover, heaped and pent,
Rider and horse,—friend, foe,—in one red burial blent!

*   *   *

[NAPOLEON]

36

There sunk the greatest, nor the worst of men,[1]
Whose spirit antithetically mixt
One moment of the mightiest, and again
On little objects with like firmness fixt,
320   Extreme in all things! hadst thou been betwixt,
Thy throne had still been thine, or never been;
For daring made thy rise as fall: thou seek'st
Even now to re-assume the imperial mien,
And shake again the world, the Thunderer of the scene!

37

325   Conqueror and captive of the earth art thou!
She trembles at thee still, and thy wild name
Was ne'er more bruited in men's minds than now
That thou art nothing, save the jest of Fame,
Who wooed thee once, thy vassal, and became
330   The flatterer of thy fierceness, till thou wert
A god unto thyself; nor less the same
To the astounded kingdoms all inert,
Who deem'd thee for a time whate'er thou didst assert.

38

Oh, more or less than man—in high or low,
335   Battling with nations, flying from the field;
Now making monarchs' necks thy footstool, now
More than thy meanest soldier taught to yield;
An empire thou couldst crush, command, rebuild,
But govern not thy pettiest passion, nor,
340   However deeply in men's spirits skill'd,
Look through thine own, nor curb the lust of war,
Nor learn that tempted Fate will leave the loftiest star.

39

Yet well thy soul hath brook'd the turning tide
With that untaught innate philosophy,
345   Which, be it wisdom, coldness, or deep pride,

---

1. Napoleon, here portrayed with many of the characteristics of the Byronic hero.

Is gall and wormwood to an enemy.
When the whole host of hatred stood hard by,
To watch and mock thee shrinking, thou hast smiled
With a sedate and all-enduring eye;—
350   When Fortune fled her spoil'd and favourite child,
He stood unbowed beneath the ills upon him piled.

40

Sager than in thy fortunes; for in them
Ambition steel'd thee on too far to show
That just habitual scorn which could contemn
355   Men and their thoughts; 'twas wise to feel, not so
To wear it ever on thy lip and brow,
And spurn the instruments thou wert to use
Till they were turn'd unto thine overthrow:
'Tis but a worthless world to win or lose;
360   So hath it proved to thee, and all such lot[2] who choose.

41

If, like a tower upon a headlong rock,
Thou hadst been made to stand or fall alone,
Such scorn of man had help'd to brave the shock;
But men's thoughts were the steps which paved thy throne,
365   *Their* admiration thy best weapon shone;
The part of Philip's son[3] was thine, not then
(Unless aside thy purple had been thrown)
Like stern Diogenes[4] to mock at men;
For sceptred cynics earth were far too wide a den.

42

370   But quiet to quick bosoms is a hell,
And *there* hath been thy bane; there is a fire
And motion of the soul which will not dwell
In its own narrow being, but aspire
Beyond the fitting medium of desire;
375   And, but once kindled, quenchless evermore,
Preys upon high adventure, nor can tire
Of aught but rest; a fever at the core,
Fatal to him who bears, to all who ever bore.

43

This makes the madmen who have made men mad
380   By their contagion; Conquerors and Kings,
Founders of sects and systems, to whom add
Sophists, Bards, Statesmen, all unquiet things
Which stir too strongly the soul's secret springs,

---

2. An inversion: "all who choose such lot" (i.e., who choose to play such a game of chance).
3. Alexander the Great, son of Philip of Macedon.
4. The Greek philosopher of Cynicism, contemporary of Alexander. It is related that Alexander was so struck by his independence of mind that he said, "If I were not Alexander, I should wish to be Diogenes," hence the allusion in lines 367 and 369.

And are themselves the fools to those they fool;
385   Envied, yet how unenviable! what stings
Are theirs! One breast laid open were a school
Which would unteach mankind the lust to shine or rule:

44

Their breath is agitation, and their life
A storm whereon they ride, to sink at last,
390   And yet so nurs'd and bigotted to strife,
That should their days, surviving perils past,
Melt to calm twilight, they feel overcast
With sorrow and supineness, and so die;
Even as a flame unfed, which runs to waste
395   With its own flickering, or a sword laid by
Which eats into itself, and rusts ingloriously.

45

He who ascends to mountain-tops, shall find
The loftiest peaks most wrapt in clouds and snow;
He who surpasses or subdues mankind,
400   Must look down on the hate of those below.
Though high *above* the sun of glory glow,
And far *beneath* the earth and ocean spread,
Round him are icy rocks, and loudly blow
Contending tempests on his naked head,
405   And thus reward the toils which to those summits led.[5]

*   *   *

52

460   Thus Harold inly said, and pass'd along,
Yet not insensibly to all which here
Awoke the jocund birds to early song
In glens which might have made even exile dear:
Though on his brow were graven lines austere,
465   And tranquil sternness which had ta'en the place
Of feelings fierier far but less severe,
Joy was not always absent from his face,
But o'er it in such scenes would steal with transient trace.

53

Nor was all love shut from him, though his days
470   Of passion had consumed themselves to dust.
It is in vain that we would coldly gaze
On such as smile upon us; the heart must
Leap kindly back to kindness, though disgust
Hath wean'd it from all worldlings: thus he felt,
475   For there was soft remembrance, and sweet trust
In one fond breast,[6] to which his own would melt,
And in its tenderer hour on that his bosom dwelt.

---

5. In the stanzas here omitted, Harold is abruptly
sent sailing up the Rhine, meditating on the "thousand battles" that "have assailed thy banks."

6. Commentators agree that the reference is to
Byron's half-sister, Augusta Leigh.

54

And he had learn'd to love,—I know not why,
For this in such as him seems strange of mood,—
480 The helpless looks of blooming infancy,
Even in its earliest nurture; what subdued,
To change like this, a mind so far imbued
With scorn of man, it little boots to know;
But thus it was; and though in solitude
485 Small power the nipp'd affections have to grow,
In him this glowed when all beside had ceased to glow.

55

And there was one soft breast, as hath been said,
Which unto his was bound by stronger ties
Than the church links withal; and, though unwed,
490 *That* love was pure, and, far above disguise,
Had stood the test of mortal enmities
Still undivided, and cemented more
By peril, dreaded most in female eyes;
But this was firm, and from a foreign shore
495 Well to that heart might his these absent greetings pour!

*   *   *

[SWITZERLAND]

68

Lake Leman° woos me with its crystal face,   *Geneva*
645 The mirror where the stars and mountains view
The stillness of their aspect in each trace
Its clear depth yields of their far height and hue:
There is too much of man here, to look through
With a fit mind the might which I behold;
650 But soon in me shall Loneliness renew
Thoughts hid, but not less cherish'd than of old,
Ere mingling with the herd had penn'd me in their fold.

69

To fly from, need not be to hate, mankind;
All are not fit with them to stir and toil,
655 Nor is it discontent to keep the mind
Deep in its fountain, lest it overboil
In the hot throng, where we become the spoil
Of our infection, till too late and long
We may deplore and struggle with the coil,°   *tumult*
660 In wretched interchange of wrong for wrong
'Midst a contentious world, striving where none are strong.

70

There, in a moment, we may plunge our years
In fatal penitence, and in the blight
Of our own soul, turn all our blood to tears,

665 And colour things to come with hues of Night;
The race of life becomes a hopeless flight
To those that walk in darkness: on the sea,
The boldest steer but where their ports invite,
But there are wanderers o'er Eternity
670 Whose bark drives on and on, and anchored ne'er shall be.

71

Is it not better, then, to be alone,
And love Earth only for its earthly sake?
By the blue rushing of the arrowy Rhone,
Or the pure bosom of its nursing lake,
675 Which feeds it as a mother who doth make
A fair but froward infant her own care,
Kissing its cries away as these awake;—
Is it not better thus our lives to wear,
Than join the crushing crowd, doom'd to inflict or bear?

72

680 I live not in myself, but I become
Portion of that around me; and to me,
High mountains are a feeling, but the hum
Of human cities torture: I can see
Nothing to loathe in nature, save to be
685 A link reluctant in a fleshly chain,
Class'd among creatures, when the soul can flee,
And with the sky, the peak, the heaving plain
Of ocean, or the stars, mingle, and not in vain.[7]

73

And thus I am absorb'd, and this is life:
690 I look upon the peopled desert past,
As on a place of agony and strife,
Where, for some sin, to Sorrow I was cast,
To act and suffer, but remount at last
With a fresh pinion; which I feel to spring,
695 Though young, yet waxing vigorous, as the blast
Which it would cope with, on delighted wing,
Spurning the clay-cold bonds which round our being cling.

74

And when, at length, the mind shall be all free
From what it hates in this degraded form,
700 Reft of its carnal life, save what shall be
Existent happier in the fly and worm,—
When elements to elements conform,

---

7. Byron had lived in close contact with Shelley at Geneva and had toured the lake with him. At that time, he was introduced to concepts of nature in the poetry of Wordsworth, whom Shelley had pressed on Byron's attention. These ideas are reflected in canto 3, but the voice is Byron's own. For his comment on being "half mad" while writing canto 3, see his letter to Thomas Moore, January 28, 1817 (p. 691).

And dust is as it should be, shall I not
Feel all I see, less dazzling, but more warm?
705   The bodiless thought? the Spirit of each spot?
Of which, even now, I share at times the immortal lot?

75

Are not the mountains, waves, and skies, a part
Of me and of my soul, as I of them?
Is not the love of these deep in my heart
710   With a pure passion? should I not contemn
All objects, if compared with these? and stem
A tide of suffering, rather than forego
Such feelings for the hard and worldly phlegm
Of those whose eyes are only turn'd below,
715 Gazing upon the ground, with thoughts which dare not glow?

76

But this is not my theme; and I return
To that which is immediate, and require
Those who find contemplation in the urn,[8]
To look on One,[9] whose dust was once all fire,
720   A native of the land where I respire
The clear air for a while—a passing guest,
Where he became a being,—whose desire
Was to be glorious; 'twas a foolish quest,
The which to gain and keep, he sacrificed all rest.

77

725   Here the self-torturing sophist, wild Rousseau,
The apostle of affliction, he who threw
Enchantment over passion, and from woe
Wrung overwhelming eloquence, first drew
The breath which made him wretched; yet he knew
730   How to make madness beautiful, and cast
O'er erring deeds and thoughts, a heavenly hue
Of words, like sunbeams, dazzling as they past
The eyes, which o'er them shed tears feelingly and fast.

78

His love was passion's essence—as a tree
735   On fire by lightning; with ethereal flame
Kindled he was, and blasted; for to be
Thus, and enamoured, were in him the same.
But his was not the love of living dame,
Nor of the dead who rise upon our dreams,
740   But of ideal beauty, which became
In him existence, and o'erflowing teems
Along his burning page, distempered though it seems.

8. I.e., those who find matter for meditation in an
urn containing the ashes of the dead.
9. Jean-Jacques Rousseau, who had been born in
Geneva in 1712. Byron's characterization is based
on Rousseau's novel *La Nouvelle Héloise,* as well
as on his *Confessions.*

* * *

85

Clear, placid Leman! thy contrasted lake,
With the wild world I dwelt in, is a thing
Which warns me, with its stillness, to forsake
800 Earth's troubled waters for a purer spring.
This quiet sail is as a noiseless wing
To waft me from distraction; once I loved
Torn ocean's roar, but thy soft murmuring
Sounds sweet as if a sister's voice reproved,
805 That I with stern delights should e'er have been so moved.

86

It is the hush of night, and all between
Thy margin and the mountains, dusk, yet clear,
Mellowed and mingling, yet distinctly seen,
Save darken'd Jura,[1] whose capt heights appear
810 Precipitously steep; and drawing near,
There breathes a living fragrance from the shore,
Of flowers yet fresh with childhood; on the ear
Drops the light drip of the suspended oar,
Or chirps the grasshopper one good-night carol more;

87

815 He is an evening reveller, who makes
His life an infancy, and sings his fill;
At intervals, some bird from out the brakes,°   thickets
Starts into voice a moment, then is still.
There seems a floating whisper on the hill,
820 But that is fancy, for the starlight dews
All silently their tears of love instil,
Weeping themselves away, till they infuse
Deep into Nature's breast the spirit of her hues.

88

Ye stars! which are the poetry of heaven!
825 If in your bright leaves we would read the fate
Of men and empires,—'tis to be forgiven,
That in our aspirations to be great,
Our destinies o'erleap their mortal state,
And claim a kindred with you; for ye are
830 A beauty and a mystery, and create
In us such love and reverence from afar,
That fortune, fame, power, life, have named themselves a star.

89

All heaven and earth are still—though not in sleep,
But breathless, as we grow when feeling most;

1. The mountain range between Switzerland and France, visible from Lake Geneva.

835   And silent, as we stand in thoughts too deep:—
All heaven and earth are still: From the high host
Of stars, to the lull'd lake and mountain-coast,
All is concentered in a life intense,
Where not a beam, nor air, nor leaf is lost,
840   But hath a part of being, and a sense
Of that which is of all Creator and defence.

90

Then stirs the feeling infinite, so felt
In solitude, where we are *least* alone;
A truth, which through our being then doth melt
845   And purifies from self: it is a tone,
The soul and source of music, which makes known
Eternal harmony, and sheds a charm,
Like to the fabled Cytherea's zone,[2]
Binding all things with beauty;—'twould disarm
850 The spectre Death, had he substantial power to harm.

91

Not vainly did the early Persian make
His altar the high places and the peak
Of earth-o'ergazing mountains, and thus take
A fit and unwall'd temple, there to seek
855   The Spirit, in whose honour shrines are weak,
Uprear'd of human hands. Come, and compare
Columns and idol-dwellings, Goth or Greek,
With Nature's realms of worship, earth and air,
Nor fix on fond abodes to circumscribe thy prayer!

92

860   The sky is changed!—and such a change! Oh night,
And storm, and darkness, ye are wondrous strong,
Yet lovely in your strength, as is the light
Of a dark eye in woman! Far along,
From peak to peak, the rattling crags among
865   Leaps the live thunder! Not from one lone cloud,
But every mountain now hath found a tongue,
And Jura answers, through her misty shroud,
Back to the joyous Alps, who call to her aloud!

93

And this is in the night:—Most glorious night!
870   Thou wert not sent for slumber! let me be
A sharer in thy fierce and far delight,—
A portion of the tempest and of thee!
How the lit lake shines, a phosphoric sea,
And the big rain comes dancing to the earth!
875   And now again 'tis black,—and now, the glee

---

2. The sash of Venus, which conferred the power to attract love.

Of the loud hills shakes with its mountain-mirth,
As if they did rejoice o'er a young earthquake's birth.

94

Now, where the swift Rhone cleaves his way between
Heights which appear as lovers who have parted
880   In hate, whose mining depths so intervene,
That they can meet no more, though broken-hearted;
Though in their souls, which thus each other thwarted,
Love was the very root of the fond rage
Which blighted their life's bloom, and then departed:—
885   Itself expired, but leaving them an age
Of years all winters,—war within themselves to wage.

95

Now, where the quick Rhone thus hath cleft his way,
The mightiest of the storms hath ta'en his stand:
For here, not one, but many, make their play,
890   And fling their thunder-bolts from hand to hand,
Flashing and cast around: of all the band,
The brightest through these parted hills hath fork'd
His lightnings,—as if he did understand,
That in such gaps as desolation work'd,
895 There the hot shaft should blast whatever therein lurk'd.

96

Sky, mountains, river, winds, lake, lightnings! ye!
With night, and clouds, and thunder, and a soul
To make these felt and feeling, well may be
Things that have made me watchful; the far roll
900   Of your departing voices, is the knoll[3]
Of what in me is sleepless,—if I rest.
But where of ye, oh tempests! is the goal?
Are ye like those within the human breast?
Or do ye find, at length, like eagles, some high nest?

97

905 Could I embody and unbosom now
That which is most within me,—could I wreak
My thoughts upon expression, and thus throw
Soul, heart, mind, passions, feelings, strong or weak,
All that I would have sought, and all I seek,
910   Bear, know, feel, and yet breathe—into *one* word,
And that one word were Lightning, I would speak;
But as it is, I live and die unheard,
With a most voiceless thought, sheathing it as a sword.

98

The morn is up again, the dewy morn,
915   With breath all incense, and with cheek all bloom,

---

3. Knell (old form).

Laughing the clouds away with playful scorn,
And living as if earth contain'd no tomb,—
And glowing into day: we may resume
The march of our existence: and thus I,
920   Still on thy shores, fair Leman! may find room
And food for meditation, nor pass by
Much, that may give us pause, if pondered fittingly.

* * *

113

I have not loved the world, nor the world me;[4]
1050   I have not flattered its rank breath, nor bow'd
To its idolatries a patient knee,—
Nor coin'd my cheek to smiles,—nor cried aloud
In worship of an echo; in the crowd
They could not deem me one of such; I stood
1055   Among them, but not of them; in a shroud
Of thoughts which were not their thoughts, and still could,
Had I not filed[5] my mind, which thus itself subdued.

114

I have not loved the world, nor the world me,—
But let us part fair foes; I do believe,
1060   Though I have found them not, that there may be
Words which are things,—hopes which will not deceive,
And virtues which are merciful, nor weave
Snares for the failing: I would also deem
O'er others' griefs that some sincerely grieve;
1065   That two, or one, are almost what they seem,—
That goodness is no name, and happiness no dream.

115

My daughter! with thy name this song begun—
My daughter! with thy name thus much shall end—
I see thee not,—I hear thee not,—but none
1070   Can be so wrapt in thee; thou art the friend
To whom the shadows of far years extend:
Albeit my brow thou never should'st behold,
My voice shall with thy future visions blend,
And reach into thy heart,—when mine is cold,—
1075   A token and a tone, even from thy father's mould.

116

To aid thy mind's development,—to watch
Thy dawn of little joys,—to sit and see
Almost thy very growth,—to view thee catch
Knowledge of objects,—wonders yet to thee!
1080   To hold thee lightly on a gentle knee,
And print on thy soft cheek a parent's kiss,—

---

4. Harold utters this soliloquy as he stands at the summit of an Alpine pass, looking southward on Italy.

5. Defiled. In a note Byron refers to *Macbeth* 3.1.66 ("For Banquo's issue have I filed my mind").

This, it should seem, was not reserv'd for me;
Yet this was in my nature:—as it is,
I know not what is there, yet something like to this.

117

1085 Yet, though dull Hate as duty should be taught,
I know that thou wilt love me; though my name
Should be shut from thee, as a spell still fraught
With desolation,—and a broken claim:
Though the grave closed between us,—'twere the same,
1090 I know that thou wilt love me; though to drain
My blood from out thy being, were an aim,
And an attainment,—all would be in vain,—
Still thou would'st love me, still that more than life retain.

118

The child of love,—though born in bitterness,
1095 And nurtured in convulsion,—of thy sire
These were the elements,—and thine no less.
As yet such are around thee,—but thy fire
Shall be more tempered, and thy hope far higher.
Sweet be thy cradled slumbers! O'er the sea,
1100 And from the mountains where I now respire,
Fain would I waft such blessing upon thee,
As, with a sigh, I deem thou might'st have been to me!

From Canto 4

[VENICE]

1

I stood in Venice, on the Bridge of Sighs;[1]
A palace and a prison on each hand:
I saw from out the wave her structures rise
As from the stroke of the enchanter's wand:
5   A thousand years their cloudy wings expand
Around me, and a dying Glory smiles
O'er the far times, when many a subject land
Look'd to the winged Lion's[2] marble piles,
Where Venice sate in state, thron'd on her hundred isles!

2

10   She looks a sea Cybele,[3] fresh from ocean,
Rising with her tiara of proud towers
At airy distance, with majestic motion,
A ruler of the waters and their powers:

---

1. A covered bridge between the Doge's Palace and the prison of San Marco.
2. The emblem of St. Mark, patron saint of Venice.
3. A nature goddess, sometimes represented wearing a crown ("tiara," line 11) of towers.

And such she was;—her daughters had their dowers
15 From spoils of nations, and the exhaustless East
Pour'd in her lap all gems in sparkling showers.
In purple was she robed, and of her feast
Monarchs partook, and deem'd their dignity increas'd.

3

In Venice Tasso's echoes are no more,
20 And silent rows the songless gondolier;[4]
Her palaces are crumbling to the shore,
And music meets not always now the ear:
Those days are gone—but Beauty still is here.
States fall, arts fade—but Nature doth not die,
25 Nor yet forget how Venice once was dear,
The pleasant place of all festivity,
The revel of the earth, the masque[5] of Italy!

4

But unto us she hath a spell beyond
Her name in story, and her long array
30 Of mighty shadows, whose dim forms despond
Above the dogeless city's[6] vanish'd sway;
Ours is a trophy which will not decay
With the Rialto;[7] Shylock and the Moor,
And Pierre, can not be swept or worn away—
35 The keystones of the arch! though all were o'er,
For us repeopled were° the solitary shore.   *would be*

*   *   *

132

1180 And thou, who never yet of human wrong
Left'st the unbalanced scale, great Nemesis![8]
Here, where the ancient paid thee homage long—
Thou, who didst call the Furies from the abyss,
And round Orestes[9] bade them howl and hiss
1185 For that unnatural retribution—just,
Had it but been from hands less near—in this
Thy former realm, I call thee from the dust!
Dost thou not hear my heart?—Awake! thou shalt, and must.

133

It is not that I may not have incurr'd
1190 For my ancestral faults or mine the wound

4. The gondoliers formerly had the custom of chanting stanzas of Tasso's *Jerusalem Delivered*.
5. Masques were lavish dramatic entertainments popular in the courts of the Renaissance, involving songs, dances, and elaborate costumes and staging.
6. The last duke ("doge") of Venice had been deposed by Napoleon in 1797.
7. The business district in Venice, a setting in *The Merchant of Venice* and *Othello* ("the Moor"), and also in Thomas Otway's tragedy *Venice Preserved* (1682), in which Pierre (line 34) is a leading character.
8. The speaker has journeyed from Venice through Ferrara and Florence to Rome. In this city he invokes the Greek and Roman goddess Nemesis, who represented divine retribution for human transgressions, especially for presumption against the gods.
9. The Furies pursued Orestes for killing his mother, Clytemnestra, to avenge her murder of his father, Agamemnon, when he had returned from the Trojan war.

I bleed withal, and, had it been conferr'd
With a just weapon, it had flowed unbound;
But now my blood shall not sink in the ground;
To thee I do devote it—*thou* shalt take
1195   The vengeance, which shall yet be sought and found,[1]
Which if *I* have not taken for the sake—
But let that pass—I sleep, but thou shalt yet awake.

134

And if my voice break forth, 'tis not that now
I shrink from what is suffered: let him speak
1200   Who hath beheld decline upon my brow,
Or seen my mind's convulsion leave it weak;
But in this page a record will I seek.
Not in the air shall these my words disperse,
Though I be ashes; a far hour shall wreak
1205   The deep prophetic fullness of this verse,
And pile on human heads the mountain of my curse!

135

That curse shall be Forgiveness.—Have I not—
Hear me, my mother Earth! behold it, Heaven!—
Have I not had to wrestle with my lot?
1210   Have I not suffered things to be forgiven?
Have I not had my brain seared, my heart riven,
Hopes sapp'd, name blighted, Life's life lied away?
And only not to desperation driven,
Because not altogether of such clay
1215   As rots into the souls of those whom I survey.

136

From mighty wrongs to petty perfidy
Have I not seen what human things could do?
From the loud roar of foaming calumny
To the small whisper of the as paltry few,
1220   And subtler venom of the reptile crew,
The Janus glance[2] of whose significant eye,
Learning to lie with silence, would *seem* true,
And without utterance, save the shrug or sigh,
Deal round to happy fools its speechless obloquy.

137

1225   But I have lived, and have not lived in vain:
My mind may lose its force, my blood its fire,
And my frame perish even in conquering pain;
But there is that within me which shall tire
Torture and Time, and breathe when I expire;
1230   Something unearthly, which they deem not of,

---

1. He calls on Nemesis to avenge the injustices
that have driven him into his exiled wandering.
2. I.e., facing both ways. In Roman mythology

Janus was represented with two faces, one looking
before, the other behind.

Like the remembered tone of a mute lyre,
Shall on their softened spirits sink, and move
In hearts all rocky now the late remorse of love.

* * *

["FAREWELL!"]

175

But I forget.—My pilgrim's shrine is won,[3]
And he and I must part,—so let it be,—
His task and mine alike are nearly done;
1570 Yet once more let us look upon the sea;
The midland ocean breaks on him and me,
And from the Alban Mount[4] we now behold
Our friend of youth, that ocean, which when we
Beheld it last by Calpe's rock[5] unfold
1575 Those waves, we followed on till the dark Euxine[6] roll'd

176

Upon the blue Symplegades:[7] long years—
Long, though not very many, since have done
Their work on both; some suffering and some tears
Have left us nearly where we had begun:
1580 Yet not in vain our mortal race hath run,
We have had our reward—and it is here;
That we can yet feel gladden'd by the sun,
And reap from earth, sea, joy almost as dear
As if there were no man to trouble what is clear.

177

1585 Oh! that the Desert were my dwelling place,
With one fair Spirit for my minister,
That I might all forget the human race,
And, hating no one, love but only her!
Ye Elements!—in whose ennobling stir
1590 I feel myself exalted—Can ye not
Accord me such a being? Do I err
In deeming such inhabit many a spot?
Though with them to converse can rarely be our lot.

178

There is a pleasure in the pathless woods,
1595 There is a rapture on the lonely shore,
There is society, where none intrudes,
By the deep Sea, and music in its roar:

---

3. I.e., he has reached the goal of his religious pilgrimage.
4. The point of vantage is an Alban hill, looking over the Roman Campagna to the Mediterranean. In its concluding passage (lines 1573ff.) the poem thus rounds back to Harold's initial voyage, when

he had first looked upon that sea.
5. The Rock of Gibraltar.
6. Greek name for the Black Sea.
7. Two islands situated at the place where the Black Sea flows into the Bosphorus Strait.

I love not Man the less, but Nature more,
From these our interviews, in which I steal
1600 From all I may be, or have been before,
To mingle with the Universe, and feel
What I can ne'er express, yet can not all conceal.

179

Roll on, thou deep and dark blue ocean—roll!
Ten thousand fleets sweep over thee in vain;
1605 Man marks the earth with ruin—his control
Stops with the shore;—upon the watery plain
The wrecks are all thy deed, nor doth remain
A shadow of man's ravage, save his own,
When, for a moment, like a drop of rain,
1610 He sinks into thy depths with bubbling groan,
Without a grave, unknell'd, uncoffin'd, and unknown.

180

His steps are not upon thy paths,—thy fields
Are not a spoil for him,—thou dost arise
And shake him from thee; the vile strength he wields
1615 For earth's destruction thou dost all despise,
Spurning him from thy bosom to the skies,
And send'st him, shivering in thy playful spray
And howling, to his Gods, where haply lies
His petty hope in some near port or bay,
1620 And dashest him again to earth:—there let him lay.[8]

181

The armaments which thunderstrike the walls
Of rock-built cities, bidding nations quake,
And monarchs tremble in their capitals,
The oak leviathans,° whose huge ribs make   *warships*
1625 Their clay creator the vain title take
Of lord of thee, and arbiter of war;
These are thy toys, and, as the snowy flake,
They melt into thy yeast of waves, which mar
Alike the Armada's pride, or spoils of Trafalgar.[9]

182

1630 Thy shores are empires, changed in all save thee—
Assyria, Greece, Rome, Carthage, what are they?
Thy waters washed them power while they were free,
And many a tyrant since; their shores obey
The stranger, slave, or savage; their decay
1635 Has dried up realms to desarts:—not so thou,

---

8. For "lie," a much-noted solecism. Byron, like other English aristocrats of the time, affected a cavalier indifference to commonplace grammar.
9. A storm was responsible for the loss of a num-
ber of French ships that Nelson had captured at Trafalgar (1805). The Spanish Armada, defeated by the English in 1588, also lost many ships in a storm.

Unchangeable save to thy wild waves' play—
Time writes no wrinkle on thine azure brow—
Such as creation's dawn beheld, thou rollest now.

183

Thou glorious mirror, where the Almighty's form
1640   Glasses° itself in tempests; in all time,   *mirrors*
Calm or convuls'd—in breeze, or gale, or storm,
Icing the pole, or in the torrid clime
Dark-heaving;—boundless, endless, and sublime—
The image of Eternity—the throne
1645   Of the Invisible; even from out thy slime
The monsters of the deep are made; each zone
Obeys thee; thou goest forth, dread, fathomless, alone.

184

And I have loved thee, Ocean! and my joy
Of youthful sports was on thy breast to be
1650   Borne, like thy bubbles, onward: from a boy
I wantoned with thy breakers—they to me
Were a delight; and if the freshening sea
Made them a terror—'twas a pleasing fear,
For I was as it were a child of thee,
1655   And trusted to thy billows far and near,
And laid my hand upon thy mane—as I do here.

185

My task is done—my song hath ceased—my theme
Has died into an echo; it is fit
The spell should break of this protracted dream.
1660   The torch shall be extinguish'd which hath lit
My midnight lamp—and what is writ, is writ,—
Would it were worthier! but I am not now
That which I have been—and my visions flit
Less palpably before me—and the glow
1665 Which in my spirit dwelt, is fluttering, faint, and low.

186

Farewell! a word that must be, and hath been—
A sound which makes us linger;—yet—farewell!
Ye! who have traced the Pilgrim to the scene
Which is his last, if in your memories dwell
1670   A thought which once was his, if on ye swell
A single recollection, not in vain
He wore his sandal-shoon, and scallop-shell;[1]
Farewell! with *him* alone may rest the pain,
If such there were—with *you*, the moral of his strain!

1812, 1816, 1818

---

1. Sandals and a scallop shell (worn on the hat) were traditional emblems of pilgrims to holy shrines.

Manfred *Manfred* is Byron's first dramatic work. As its subtitle, "A Dramatic Poem," indicates, it was not intended to be produced on the stage; Byron also referred to it as a "metaphysical" drama—that is, a drama of ideas. He began writing it in the autumn of 1816 while living in the Swiss Alps, whose grandeur stimulated his imagination; he finished the drama the following year in Italy.

Manfred's literary forebears include the villains of Gothic fiction and melodrama; the Greek Titan Prometheus, rebel against Zeus, ruler of the gods; Milton's fallen angel, Satan; Ahasuerus, the legendary Wandering Jew who, having ridiculed Christ as he bore the Cross to Calvary, is doomed to live until Christ's Second Coming; and the story of Faust, who yielded his soul to the devil in exchange for superhuman powers. Byron denied that he had ever heard of Marlowe's *Doctor Faustus,* and because he knew no German he had not read Goethe's *Faust,* of which part 1 had been published in 1808. But his friend M. G. Lewis (author of the Gothic novel *The Monk*) had read parts of *Faust* to him in extempore translation during the summer of 1816, just before the composition of *Manfred,* and Byron worked his memories of this oral translation into his own drama in a way that evoked Goethe's admiration.

Like Byron's earlier heroes, Childe Harold and the protagonists of some of his verse romances, Manfred is hounded by remorse—in this instance, for a transgression that (it is hinted but never quite specified) is incest with his sister Astarte; it is also hinted that Astarte has taken her own life. While this element in the drama is often regarded as Byron's veiled confession of his incestuous relations with his half-sister, Augusta Leigh, the theme of incest was a common one both in Gothic fiction and in the writings of Romantic authors such as Goethe, Chateaubriand, Scott, and both the Shelleys.

The character of Manfred is its author's most impressive representation of the Byronic Hero. Byron's invention is to have Manfred, unlike Faust, disdainfully reject the offer of a pact with the powers of darkness. He thereby sets himself up as the totally autonomous man, independent of any external authority or power, whose own mind, as he says in the concluding scene (3.4.127–40), generates the values by which he lives "in sufferance or in joy," and by reference to which he judges, requites, and finally destroys himself. In his book *Ecce Homo,* Nietzsche, recognizing Byron's anticipation of his own *Übermensch* (the "superman" who posits for himself a moral code beyond all traditional standards of good and evil), asserted that the character of Manfred was greater than that of Goethe's Faust.

Manfred

A DRAMATIC POEM

"There are more things in heaven and earth, Horatio,
Than are dreamt of in your philosophy."[1]

DRAMATIS PERSONAE

MANFRED	WITCH OF THE ALPS
CHAMOIS HUNTER	ARIMANES
ABBOT OF ST. MAURICE	NEMESIS
MANUEL	THE DESTINIES
HERMAN	SPIRITS, ETC.

---

1. *Hamlet* 1.5.168–69.

*The scene of the Drama is amongst the Higher Alps—partly in
the Castle of Manfred, and partly in the Mountains.*

Act 1

SCENE 1. MANFRED *alone.—Scene, a Gothic gallery.*[2]*—Time, Midnight.*

MANFRED   The lamp must be replenish'd, but even then
It will not burn so long as I must watch:
My slumbers—if I slumber—are not sleep,
But a continuance of enduring thought,
5   Which then I can resist not: in my heart
There is a vigil, and these eyes but close
To look within; and yet I live, and bear
The aspect and the form of breathing men.
But grief should be the instructor of the wise;
10   Sorrow is knowledge: they who know the most
Must mourn the deepest o'er the fatal truth,
The Tree of Knowledge is not that of Life.
Philosophy and science, and the springs
Of wonder, and the wisdom of the world,
15   I have essayed, and in my mind there is
A power to make these subject to itself—
But they avail not: I have done men good,
And I have met with good even among men—
But this avail'd not: I have had my foes,
20   And none have baffled, many fallen before me—
But this avail'd not:—Good, or evil, life,
Powers, passions, all I see in other beings,
Have been to me as rain unto the sands,
Since that all-nameless hour. I have no dread,
25   And feel the curse to have no natural fear,
Nor fluttering throb, that beats with hopes or wishes,
Or lurking love of something on the earth.—
Now to my task.—
                 Mysterious Agency!
Ye spirits of the unbounded Universe!
30   Whom I have sought in darkness and in light—
Ye, who do compass earth about, and dwell
In subtler essence—ye, to whom the tops
Of mountains inaccessible are haunts,
And earth's and ocean's caves familiar things—
35   I call upon ye by the written charm
Which gives me power upon you—Rise! appear!   [*A pause.*]
They come not yet.—Now by the voice of him
Who is the first among you[3]—by this sign,
Which makes you tremble—by the claims of him
40   Who is undying,[4]—Rise! appear!—Appear!   [*A pause.*]

2. A large chamber built in the medieval Gothic
style with high, pointed arches.
3. Arimanes, who appears in 2.4.

4. Probably God, to whom traditional magic con-
jurations often allude.

If it be so.—Spirits of earth and air,
Ye shall not thus elude me: by a power,
Deeper than all yet urged, a tyrant-spell,
Which had its birth-place in a star condemn'd,
45   The burning wreck of a demolish'd world,
A wandering hell in the eternal space;
By the strong curse which is upon my soul,
The thought which is within me and around me,
I do compel ye to my will.—Appear!

[*A star is seen at the darker end of the gallery; it is stationary; and a voice is heard singing.*]

FIRST SPIRIT[5]
50   Mortal! to thy bidding bow'd,
From my mansion in the cloud,
Which the breath of twilight builds,
And the summer's sun-set gilds
With the azure and vermilion,
55   Which is mix'd for my pavilion;
Though thy quest may be forbidden,
On a star-beam I have ridd'n;
To thine adjuration bow'd,
Mortal—be thy wish avow'd!

Voice of the SECOND SPIRIT
60   Mont Blanc is the monarch of mountains,
They crowned him long ago
On a throne of rocks, in a robe of clouds,
With a diadem of snow.
Around his waist are forests braced,
65   The Avalanche in his hand;
But ere it fall, that thundering ball
Must pause for my command.
The Glacier's cold and restless mass
Moves onward day by day;
70   But I am he who bids it pass,
Or with its ice delay.
I am the spirit of the place,
Could make the mountain bow
And quiver to his cavern'd base—
75   And what with me wouldst *Thou?*

Voice of the THIRD SPIRIT
In the blue depth of the waters,
Where the wave hath no strife,
Where the wind is a stranger,
And the sea-snake hath life,
80   Where the Mermaid is decking

5. The Spirits, successively, are those of the Air, Mountain, Ocean, Earth, Winds, Night, and Manfred's guiding Star.

Her green hair with shells;
Like the storm on the surface
Came the sound of thy spells;
O'er my calm Hall of Coral
85   The deep echo roll'd—
To the Spirit of Ocean
Thy wishes unfold!

FOURTH SPIRIT

Where the slumbering earthquake
Lies pillow'd on fire,
90   And the lakes of bitumen
Rise boilingly higher;
Where the roots of the Andes
Strike deep in the earth,
As their summits to heaven
95   Shoot soaringly forth;
I have quitted my birth-place,
Thy bidding to bide—
Thy spell hath subdued me,
Thy will be my guide!

FIFTH SPIRIT

100 I am the Rider of the wind,
The Stirrer of the storm;
The hurricane I left behind
Is yet with lightning warm;
To speed to thee, o'er shore and sea
105   I swept upon the blast:
The fleet I met sailed well, and yet
'Twill sink ere night be past.

SIXTH SPIRIT

My dwelling is the shadow of the night,
Why doth thy magic torture me with light?

SEVENTH SPIRIT

110 The star which rules thy destiny,
Was ruled, ere earth began, by me:
It was a world as fresh and fair
As e'er revolved round sun in air;
Its course was free and regular,
115 Space bosom'd not a lovelier star.
The hour arrived—and it became
A wandering mass of shapeless flame,
A pathless comet, and a curse,
The menace of the universe;
120 Still rolling on with innate force,
Without a sphere, without a course,
A bright deformity on high,
The monster of the upper sky!
And thou! beneath its influence born—

125   Thou worm! whom I obey and scorn—
      Forced by a power (which is not thine,
      And lent thee but to make thee mine)
      For this brief moment to descend,
      Where these weak spirits round thee bend
130   And parley with a thing like thee—
      What wouldst thou, Child of Clay! with me?

              The SEVEN SPIRITS
    Earth, ocean, air, night, mountains, winds, thy star,
    Are at thy beck and bidding, Child of Clay!
    Before thee at thy quest their spirits are—
135   What wouldst thou with us, son of mortals—say?

MANFRED Forgetfulness—
FIRST SPIRIT   Of what—of whom—and why?
MANFRED   Of that which is within me; read it there—
    Ye know it, and I cannot utter it.
SPIRIT   We can but give thee that which we possess:
140   Ask of us subjects, sovereignty, the power
    O'er earth, the whole, or portion, or a sign
    Which shall control the elements, whereof
    We are the dominators, each and all,
    These shall be thine.
MANFRED   Oblivion, self-oblivion—
145   Can ye not wring from out the hidden realms
    Ye offer so profusely what I ask?
SPIRIT   It is not in our essence, in our skill;
    But—thou mayst die.
MANFRED   Will death bestow it on me?
SPIRIT   We are immortal, and do not forget;
150   We are eternal; and to us the past
    Is, as the future, present. Art thou answered?
MANFRED   Ye mock me—but the power which brought ye here
    Hath made you mine. Slaves, scoff not at my will!
    The mind, the spirit, the Promethean spark,[6]
155   The lightning of my being, is as bright,
    Pervading, and far-darting as your own,
    And shall not yield to yours, though coop'd in clay!
    Answer, or I will teach you what I am.
SPIRIT   We answer as we answered; our reply
    Is even in thine own words.
160 MANFRED   Why say ye so?
SPIRIT   If, as thou say'st, thine essence be as ours,
    We have replied in telling thee, the thing
    Mortals call death hath nought to do with us.
MANFRED   I then have call'd ye from your realms in vain;
    Ye cannot, or ye will not, aid me.
165 SPIRIT   Say;

---

6. In Greek myth, Prometheus molded man from clay, and stole fire from heaven to give it to humans.

What we possess we offer; it is thine:
Bethink ere thou dismiss us, ask again—
Kingdom, and sway, and strength, and length of days—
MANFRED   Accursed! what have I to do with days?
170   They are too long already.—Hence—begone!
SPIRIT   Yet pause: being here, our will would do thee service;
Bethink thee, is there then no other gift
Which we can make not worthless in thine eyes?
MANFRED   No, none: yet stay—one moment, ere we part—
175   I would behold ye face to face. I hear
Your voices, sweet and melancholy sounds,
As music on the waters; and I see
The steady aspect of a clear large star;
But nothing more. Approach me as ye are,
180   Or one, or all, in your accustom'd forms.
SPIRIT   We have no forms beyond the elements
Of which we are the mind and principle:
But choose a form—in that we will appear.
MANFRED   I have no choice; there is no form on earth
185   Hideous or beautiful to me. Let him,
Who is most powerful of ye, take such aspect
As unto him may seem most fitting.—Come!
SEVENTH SPIRIT [*appearing in the shape of a beautiful female figure*].[7]
Behold!
MANFRED   Oh God! if it be thus, and *thou*
Art not a madness and a mockery,
190   I yet might be most happy.—I will clasp thee,
And we again will be—   [*The figure vanishes.*]
My heart is crushed!   [MANFRED *falls senseless.*]

[*A voice is heard in the Incantation[8] which follows.*]

When the moon is on the wave,
     And the glow-worm in the grass,
And the meteor on the grave,
195   And the wisp on the morass;
When the falling stars are shooting,
And the answer'd owls are hooting,
And the silent leaves are still
In the shadow of the hill,
200   Shall my soul be upon thine,
With a power and with a sign.

Though thy slumber may be deep,
Yet thy spirit shall not sleep,
There are shades which will not vanish,

7. This shape may be a simulacrum of Astarte, whose phantom appears in 2.3.97; it probably represents, however, the ideal of the beautiful and good that Manfred had pursued in his uncorrupted youth.
8. Byron had published this "incantation" as a separate poem six months before *Manfred*.

205   There are thoughts thou canst not banish;
    By a power to thee unknown,
    Thou canst never be alone;
    Thou art wrapt as with a shroud,
    Thou art gathered in a cloud;
210   And for ever shalt thou dwell
    In the spirit of this spell.

    Though thou seest me not pass by,
    Thou shalt feel me with thine eye
    As a thing that, though unseen,
215   Must be near thee, and hath been;
    And when in that secret dread
    Thou hast turn'd around thy head,
    Thou shalt marvel I am not
    As thy shadow on the spot,
220   And the power which thou dost feel
    Shall be what thou must conceal.

    And a magic voice and verse
    Hath baptized thee with a curse;
    And a spirit of the air
225   Hath begirt thee with a snare;
    In the wind there is a voice
    Shall forbid thee to rejoice;
    And to thee shall Night deny
    All the quiet of her sky;
230   And the day shall have a sun,
    Which shall make thee wish it done.

    From thy false tears I did distil
    An essence which hath strength to kill;
    From thy own heart I then did wring
235   The black blood in its blackest spring;
    From thy own smile I snatch'd the snake,
    For there it coil'd as in a brake;°   *thicket*
    From thy own lip I drew the charm
    Which gave all these their chiefest harm;
240   In proving every poison known,
    I found the strongest was thine own.

    By thy cold breast and serpent smile,
    By thy unfathom'd gulfs of guile,
    By that most seeming virtuous eye,
245   By thy shut soul's hypocrisy;
    By the perfection of thine art
    Which pass'd for human thine own heart;
    By thy delight in others' pain,
    And by thy brotherhood of Cain,[9]

9. I.e., by your kinship with Cain, who murdered his brother, Abel.

250   I call upon thee! and compel
              Thyself to be thy proper Hell!

              And on thy head I pour the vial
              Which doth devote thee to this trial;
              Nor to slumber, nor to die,
255   Shall be in thy destiny;
              Though thy death shall still seem near
              To thy wish, but as a fear;
              Lo! the spell now works around thee,
              And the clankless chain hath bound thee;
260   O'er thy heart and brain together
              Hath the word been pass'd—now wither!

SCENE 2. *The Mountain of the Jungfrau.*[1]—Time, Morning.—
MANFRED *alone upon the Cliffs.*

MANFRED   The spirits I have raised abandon me—
              The spells which I have studied baffle me—
              The remedy I reck'd of tortured me;
              I lean no more on super-human aid,
5   It hath no power upon the past, and for
              The future, till the past be gulf'd in darkness,
              It is not of my search.—My mother Earth!
              And thou fresh breaking Day, and you, ye Mountains,
              Why are ye beautiful? I cannot love ye.
10   And thou, the bright eye of the universe,
              That openest over all, and unto all
              Art a delight—thou shin'st not on my heart.
              And you, ye crags, upon whose extreme edge
              I stand, and on the torrent's brink beneath
15   Behold the tall pines dwindled as to shrubs
              In dizziness of distance; when a leap,
              A stir, a motion, even a breath, would bring
              My breast upon its rocky bosom's bed
              To rest for ever—wherefore do I pause?
20   I feel the impulse—yet I do not plunge;
              I see the peril—yet do not recede;
              And my brain reels—and yet my foot is firm:
              There is a power upon me which withholds
              And makes it my fatality to live;
25   If it be life to wear within myself
              This barrenness of spirit, and to be
              My own soul's sepulchre, for I have ceased
              To justify my deeds unto myself—
              The last infirmity of evil. Ay,
30   Thou winged and cloud-cleaving minister,   *[An eagle passes.]*
              Whose happy flight is highest into heaven,
              Well may'st thou swoop so near me—I should be

1. A high Alpine mountain in south-central Switzerland.

Thy prey, and gorge thine eaglets; thou art gone
Where the eye cannot follow thee; but thine
35 Yet pierces downward, onward, or above,
With a pervading vision.—Beautiful!
How beautiful is all this visible world!
How glorious in its action and itself;
But we, who name ourselves its sovereigns, we,
40 Half dust, half deity, alike unfit
To sink or soar, with our mix'd essence make
A conflict of its elements, and breathe
The breath of degradation and of pride,
Contending with low wants and lofty will
45 Till our mortality predominates,
And men are—what they name not to themselves,
And trust not to each other. Hark! the note,
                    [*The Shepherd's pipe in the distance is heard.*]
The natural music of the mountain reed—
For here the patriarchal days² are not
50 A pastoral fable—pipes in the liberal° air,   free-moving
Mix'd with the sweet bells of the sauntering herd;
My soul would drink those echoes.—Oh, that I were
The viewless° spirit of a lovely sound,   invisible
A living voice, a breathing harmony,
55 A bodiless enjoyment—born and dying
With the blest tone which made me!
               Enter from below a CHAMOIS³ HUNTER.
CHAMOIS HUNTER   Even so
This way the chamois leapt: her nimble feet
Have baffled me; my gains to-day will scarce
Repay my break-neck travail.—What is here?
60 Who seems not of my trade, and yet hath reach'd
A height which none even of our mountaineers,
Save our best hunters, may attain: his garb
Is goodly, his mien manly, and his air
Proud as a free-born peasant's, at this distance.—
I will approach him nearer.
65 MANFRED [*not perceiving the other*]   To be thus—
Gray-hair'd with anguish, like these blasted pines,
Wrecks of a single winter, barkless, branchless,
A blighted trunk upon a cursed root,
Which but supplies a feeling to decay—
70 And to be thus, eternally but thus,
Having been otherwise! Now furrow'd o'er
With wrinkles, plough'd by moments, not by years;
And hours—all tortured into ages—hours
Which I outlive!—Ye toppling crags of ice!
75 Ye avalanches, whom a breath draws down

2. The days of the Old Testament patriarchs, who were shepherds.

3. A goatlike antelope found in the high regions of European mountains.

In mountainous o'erwhelming, come and crush me—
I hear ye momently above, beneath,
Crash with a frequent conflict; but ye pass,
And only fall on things which still would live;
On the young flourishing forest, or the hut
And hamlet of the harmless villager.

CHAMOIS HUNTER   The mists begin to rise from up the valley;
I'll warn him to descend, or he may chance
To lose at once his way and life together.

MANFRED   The mists boil up around the glaciers; clouds
Rise curling fast beneath me, white and sulphury,
Like foam from the roused ocean of deep Hell,
Whose every wave breaks on a living shore,
Heaped with the damn'd like pebbles.—I am giddy.

CHAMOIS HUNTER   I must approach him cautiously; if near,
A sudden step will startle him, and he
Seems tottering already.

MANFRED   Mountains have fallen,
Leaving a gap in the clouds, and with the shock
Rocking their Alpine brethren; filling up
The ripe green valleys with destruction's splinters;
Damming the rivers with a sudden dash,
Which crush'd the waters into mist, and made
Their fountains find another channel—thus,
Thus, in its old age, did Mount Rosenberg[4]—
Why stood I not beneath it?

CHAMOIS HUNTER   Friend! have a care,
Your next step may be fatal!—for the love
Of him who made you, stand not on that brink!

MANFRED [not hearing him]   Such would have been for me a fitting tomb;
My bones had then been quiet in their depth;
They had not then been strewn upon the rocks
For the wind's pastime—as thus—thus they shall be—
In this one plunge.—Farewell, ye opening heavens!
Look not upon me thus reproachfully—
Ye were not meant for me—Earth! take these atoms!

[As MANFRED is in act to spring from the cliff, the CHAMOIS HUNTER
seizes and retains him with a sudden grasp.]

CHAMOIS HUNTER   Hold, madman!—though aweary of thy life,
Stain not our pure vales with thy guilty blood.—
Away with me—I will not quit my hold.

MANFRED   I am most sick at heart—nay, grasp me not—
I am all feebleness—the mountains whirl
Spinning around me—I grow blind—What art thou?

CHAMOIS HUNTER   I'll answer that anon.—Away with me—
The clouds grow thicker—there—now lean on me—
Place your foot here—here, take this staff, and cling

---

4. In 1806, ten years before the composition of *Manfred*, a huge landslide on Mount Rossberg ("Rosen-berg") had destroyed four villages and killed 457 people.

A moment to that shrub—now give me your hand,
120 And hold fast by my girdle—softly—well—
The Chalet will be gained within an hour—
Come on, we'll quickly find a surer footing,
And something like a pathway, which the torrent
Hath wash'd since winter.—Come, 'tis bravely done—
125 You should have been a hunter.—Follow me.
        [As they descend the rocks with difficulty, the scene closes.]

Act 2

SCENE 1. A Cottage amongst the Bernese Alps.[5] MANFRED and
                the CHAMOIS HUNTER.

CHAMOIS HUNTER   No, no—yet pause—thou must not yet go forth:
    Thy mind and body are alike unfit
    To trust each other, for some hours, at least;
    When thou art better, I will be thy guide—
    But whither?
5 MANFRED   It imports not; I do know
    My route full well, and need no further guidance.
CHAMOIS HUNTER   Thy garb and gait bespeak thee of high lineage—
    One of the many chiefs, whose castled crags
    Look o'er the lower valleys—which of these
10 May call thee Lord? I only know their portals;
    My way of life leads me but rarely down
    To bask by the huge hearths of those old halls,
    Carousing with the vassals; but the paths,
    Which step from out our mountains to their doors,
15 I know from childhood—which of these is thine?
MANFRED   No matter.
CHAMOIS HUNTER   Well, sir, pardon me the question,
    And be of better cheer. Come, taste my wine;
    'Tis of an ancient vintage; many a day
    'T has thawed my veins among our glaciers, now
20 Let it do thus for thine—Come, pledge me fairly.
MANFRED   Away, away! there's blood upon the brim!
    Will it then never—never sink in the earth?
CHAMOIS HUNTER   What dost thou mean? thy senses wander from thee.
MANFRED   I say 'tis blood—my blood! the pure warm stream
25 Which ran in the veins of my fathers, and in ours
    When we were in our youth, and had one heart,
    And loved each other as we should not love,
    And this was shed: but still it rises up,
    Colouring the clouds, that shut me out from heaven,
30 Where thou art not—and I shall never be.
CHAMOIS HUNTER   Man of strange words, and some half-maddening sin,
    Which makes thee people vacancy, whate'er
    Thy dread and sufferance be, there's comfort yet—
    The aid of holy men, and heavenly patience—

5. A mountain range in south-central Switzerland.

35   MANFRED   Patience and patience! Hence—that word was made
    For brutes of burthen, not for birds of prey;
    Preach it to mortals of a dust like thine,—
    I am not of thine order.
  CHAMOIS HUNTER   Thanks to heaven!
    I would not be of thine for the free fame
40   Of William Tell;[6] but whatsoe'er thine ill,
    It must be borne, and these wild starts are useless.
  MANFRED   Do I not bear it?—Look on me—I live.
  CHAMOIS HUNTER   This is convulsion, and no healthful life.
  MANFRED   I tell thee, man! I have lived many years,
45   Many long years, but they are nothing now
    To those which I must number: ages—ages—
    Space and eternity—and consciousness,
    With the fierce thirst of death—and still unslaked!
  CHAMOIS HUNTER   Why, on thy brow the seal of middle age
50   Hath scarce been set; I am thine elder far.
  MANFRED   Think'st thou existence doth depend on time?
    It doth; but actions are our epochs: mine
    Have made my days and nights imperishable,
    Endless, and all alike, as sands on the shore,
55   Innumerable atoms, and one desart,
    Barren and cold, on which the wild waves break,
    But nothing rests, save carcases and wrecks,
    Rocks, and the salt-surf weeds of bitterness.
  CHAMOIS HUNTER   Alas! he's mad—but yet I must not leave him.
60   MANFRED   I would I were—for then the things I see
    Would be but a distempered dream.
  CHAMOIS HUNTER   What is it
    That thou dost see, or think thou look'st upon?
  MANFRED   Myself, and thee—a peasant of the Alps—
    Thy humble virtues, hospitable home,
65   And spirit patient, pious, proud and free;
    Thy self-respect, grafted on innocent thoughts;
    Thy days of health, and nights of sleep; thy toils,
    By danger dignified, yet guiltless; hopes
    Of cheerful old age and a quiet grave,
70   With cross and garland over its green turf,
    And thy grandchildren's love for epitaph;
    This do I see—and then I look within—
    It matters not—my soul was scorch'd already!
  CHAMOIS HUNTER   And would'st thou then exchange thy lot for mine?
75   MANFRED   No, friend! I would not wrong thee, nor exchange
    My lot with living being: I can bear—
    However wretchedly, 'tis still to bear—
    In life what others could not brook to dream,
    But perish in their slumber.
  CHAMOIS HUNTER   And with this—
80   This cautious feeling for another's pain,

---

6. The hero who, according to legend, liberated Switzerland from Austrian oppression in the 14th century.

Canst thou be black with evil?—say not so.
Can one of gentle thoughts have wreak'd revenge
Upon his enemies?
MANFRED   Oh! no, no, no!
My injuries came down on those who loved me—
On those whom I best loved: I never quell'd°   killed
An enemy, save in my just defence—
My wrongs were all on those I should have cherished—
But my embrace was fatal.
CHAMOIS HUNTER   Heaven give thee rest!
And penitence restore thee to thyself;
My prayers shall be for thee.
MANFRED   I need them not,
But can endure thy pity. I depart—
'Tis time—farewell!—Here's gold, and thanks for thee—
No words—it is thy due.—Follow me not—
I know my path—the mountain peril's past:—
And once again, I charge thee, follow not!

[*Exit* MANFRED.]

SCENE 2. *A lower Valley in the Alps.—A Cataract.*

Enter MANFRED.

It is not noon—the sunbow's rays still arch
The torrent with the many hues of heaven,
And roll the sheeted silver's waving column
O'er the crag's headlong perpendicular,
And fling its lines of foaming light along,
And to and fro, like the pale courser's tail,
The Giant steed, to be bestrode by Death,
As told in the Apocalypse.[7] No eyes
But mine now drink this sight of loveliness;
I should be sole in this sweet solitude,
And with the Spirit of the place divide
The homage of these waters.—I will call her.
    [MANFRED *takes some of the water into the palm of his hand, and flings*
    it in the air, muttering the adjuration. After a pause, the WITCH OF THE
    ALPS *rises beneath the arch of the sunbow of the torrent.*]
Beautiful Spirit! with thy hair of light,
And dazzling eyes of glory, in whose form
The charms of Earth's least-mortal daughters grow
To an unearthly stature, in an essence
Of purer elements; while the hues of youth,—
Carnation'd like a sleeping infant's cheek,
Rock'd by the beating of her mother's heart,
Or the rose tints, which summer's twilight leaves
Upon the lofty glacier's virgin snow,
The blush of earth embracing with her heaven,—

---

7. Revelation 6.8: "And I looked, and behold a pale horse: and his name that sat on him was Death, and
Hell followed with him."

Tinge thy celestial aspect, and make tame
The beauties of the sunbow which bends o'er thee.
25 Beautiful Spirit! in thy calm clear brow,
Wherein is glass'd° serenity of soul,   *reflected*
Which of itself shows immortality,
I read that thou wilt pardon to a Son
Of Earth, whom the abstruser powers permit
30 At times to commune with them—if that he
Avail him of his spells—to call thee thus,
And gaze on thee a moment.
WITCH   Son of Earth!
I know thee, and the powers which give thee power;
I know thee for a man of many thoughts,
35 And deeds of good and ill, extreme in both,
Fatal and fated in thy sufferings.
I have expected this—what wouldst thou with me?
MANFRED   To look upon thy beauty—nothing further.
The face of the earth hath madden'd me, and I
40 Take refuge in her mysteries, and pierce
To the abodes of those who govern her—
But they can nothing aid me. I have sought
From them what they could not bestow, and now
I search no further.
WITCH   What could be the quest
45 Which is not in the power of the most powerful,
The rulers of the invisible?
MANFRED   A boon;
But why should I repeat it? 'twere in vain.
WITCH   I know not that; let thy lips utter it.
MANFRED   Well, though it torture me, 'tis but the same;
50 My pang shall find a voice. From my youth upwards
My spirit walk'd not with the souls of men,
Nor look'd upon the earth with human eyes;
The thirst of their ambition was not mine,
The aim of their existence was not mine;
55 My joys, my griefs, my passions, and my powers,
Made me a stranger; though I wore the form,
I had no sympathy with breathing flesh,
Nor midst the creatures of clay that girded me
Was there but one who—but of her anon.
60 I said, with men, and with the thoughts of men,
I held but slight communion; but instead,
My joy was in the Wilderness, to breathe
The difficult air of the iced mountain's top,
Where the birds dare not build, nor insect's wing
65 Flit o'er the herbless granite; or to plunge
Into the torrent, and to roll along
On the swift whirl of the new breaking wave
Of river-stream, or ocean, in their flow.
In these my early strength exulted; or

70   To follow through the night the moving moon,
    The stars and their development; or catch
    The dazzling lightnings till my eyes grew dim;
    Or to look, list'ning, on the scattered leaves,
    While Autumn winds were at their evening song.
75   These were my pastimes, and to be alone;
    For if the beings, of whom I was one,—
    Hating to be so,—cross'd me in my path,
    I felt myself degraded back to them,
    And was all clay again. And then I dived,
80   In my lone wanderings, to the caves of death,
    Searching its cause in its effect; and drew
    From wither'd bones, and skulls, and heap'd up dust,
    Conclusions most forbidden. Then I pass'd
    The nights of years in sciences untaught,
85   Save in the old-time; and with time and toil,
    And terrible ordeal, and such penance
    As in itself hath power upon the air,
    And spirits that do compass air and earth,
    Space, and the peopled infinite, I made
90   Mine eyes familiar with Eternity,
    Such as, before me, did the Magi,[8] and
    He who from out their fountain dwellings raised
    Eros and Anteros, at Gadara,[9]
    As I do thee;—and with my knowledge grew
95   The thirst of knowledge, and the power and joy
    Of this most bright intelligence, until—
WITCH   Proceed.
MANFRED   Oh! I but thus prolonged my words,
    Boasting these idle attributes, because
    As I approach the core of my heart's grief—
100   But to my task. I have not named to thee
    Father or mother, mistress, friend, or being,
    With whom I wore the chain of human ties;
    If I had such, they seem'd not such to me—
    Yet there was one—
WITCH   Spare not thyself—proceed.
105 MANFRED   She was like me in lineaments—her eyes,
    Her hair, her features, all, to the very tone
    Even of her voice, they said were like to mine;
    But soften'd all, and temper'd into beauty;
    She had the same lone thoughts and wanderings,
110   The quest of hidden knowledge, and a mind
    To comprehend the universe: nor these
    Alone, but with them gentler powers than mine,
    Pity, and smiles, and tears—which I had not;
    And tenderness—but that I had for her;

8. Masters of occult knowledge (plural of *magus*).
9. Iamblicus, the 4th-century Neoplatonic philosopher, called up Eros, god of love, and Anteros, god of unrequited love, from the hot springs named after them at Gadara, in Syria.

115   Humility—and that I never had.
    Her faults were mine—her virtues were her own—
    I loved her, and destroy'd her!
    WITCH   With thy hand?
    MANFRED   Not with my hand, but heart—which broke her heart—
    It gazed on mine, and withered. I have shed
120   Blood, but not hers—and yet her blood was shed—
    I saw—and could not staunch it.
    WITCH   And for this—
    A being of the race thou dost despise,
    The order which thine own would rise above,
    Mingling with us and ours, thou dost forego
125   The gifts of our great knowledge, and shrink'st back
    To recreant mortality—Away!
    MANFRED   Daughter of Air! I tell thee, since that hour—
    But words are breath—look on me in my sleep,
    Or watch my watchings—Come and sit by me!
130   My solitude is solitude no more,
    But peopled with the Furies;—I have gnash'd
    My teeth in darkness till returning morn,
    Then cursed myself till sunset;—I have pray'd
    For madness as a blessing—'tis denied me.
135   I have affronted death—but in the war
    Of elements the waters shrunk from me,
    And fatal things pass'd harmless—the cold hand
    Of an all-pitiless demon held me back,
    Back by a single hair, which would not break.
140   In phantasy, imagination, all
    The affluence of my soul—which one day was
    A Croesus in creation[1]—I plunged deep,
    But, like an ebbing wave, it dash'd me back
    Into the gulf of my unfathom'd thought.
145   I plunged amidst mankind—Forgetfulness
    I sought in all, save where 'tis to be found,
    And that I have to learn—my sciences,[2]
    My long pursued and super-human art,
    Is mortal here—I dwell in my despair—
    And live—and live for ever.
150   WITCH   It may be
    That I can aid thee.
    MANFRED   To do this thy power
    Must wake the dead, or lay me low with them.
    Do so—in any shape—in any hour—
    With any torture—so it be the last.
155   WITCH   That is not in my province; but if thou
    Wilt swear obedience to my will, and do

---

1. I.e., my imagination had at one time been as rich as King Croesus in its creative powers. Manfred's self-description in this passage, as longing for a death that is denied him, is modeled on the legend, often treated in Romantic literature, of the Wandering Jew.
2. Occult bodies of knowledge.

My bidding, it may help thee to thy wishes.

MANFRED   I will not swear—Obey! and whom? the spirits
Whose presence I command, and be the slave
Of those who served me—Never!

160 WITCH   Is this all?
Hast thou no gentler answer—Yet bethink thee,
And pause ere thou rejectest.

MANFRED   I have said it.

WITCH   Enough!—I may retire then—say!

MANFRED   Retire!

                                 [The WITCH *disappears.*]

MANFRED [*alone*]   We are the fools of time and terror: Days

165   Steal on us and steal from us; yet we live,
Loathing our life, and dreading still to die.
In all the days of this detested yoke—
This heaving burthen, this accursed breath—
This vital weight upon the struggling heart,

170   Which sinks with sorrow, or beats quick with pain,
Or joy that ends in agony or faintness—
In all the days of past and future, for
In life there is no present, we can number
How few—how less than few—wherein the soul

175   Forbears to pant for death, and yet draws back
As from a stream in winter, though the chill
Be but a moment's. I have one resource
Still in my science—I can call the dead,
And ask them what it is we dread to be:

180   The sternest answer can but be the Grave,
And that is nothing—if they answer not—
The buried Prophet answered to the Hag
Of Endor;[3] and the Spartan Monarch drew
From the Byzantine maid's unsleeping spirit

185   An answer and his destiny—he slew
That which he loved, unknowing what he slew,
And died unpardon'd—though he call'd in aid
The Phyxian Jove, and in Phigalia roused
The Arcadian Evocators to compel

190   The indignant shadow to depose her wrath,[4]
Or fix her term of vengeance—she replied
In words of dubious import, but fulfill'd.
If I had never lived, that which I love
Had still been living; had I never loved,

195   That which I love would still be beautiful—

3. The Woman of Endor, at the behest of King Saul, summoned up the spirit of the dead prophet Samuel, who foretold that in an impending battle the Philistines would conquer the Israelites and kill Saul and his sons (1 Samuel 28.7–19).
4. Plutarch relates that King Pausanias ("the Spartan Monarch") had accidentally killed Cleonice ("the Byzantine maid"), whom he desired as his mistress. Her ghost haunted him until he called up her spirit to beg her forgiveness. She told him, enigmatically, that he would quickly be freed from his troubles; soon after that, he was killed. Another Pausanias, author of the *Description of Greece*, adds the details that King Pausanias, in the vain attempt to purge his guilt, had called for aid from Jupiter Phyxius and consulted the Evocators at Phigalia, in Arcadia, who had the power to call up the souls of the dead.

Happy and giving happiness. What is she?
What is she now?—a sufferer for my sins—
A thing I dare not think upon—or nothing.
Within few hours I shall not call in vain—
200 Yet in this hour I dread the thing I dare:
Until this hour I never shrunk to gaze
On spirit, good or evil—now I tremble,
And feel a strange cold thaw upon my heart,
But I can act even what I most abhor,
205 And champion human fears.—The night approaches.   [*Exit.*]

SCENE 3. *The Summit of the Jungfrau Mountain.*

Enter FIRST DESTINY.

The moon is rising broad, and round, and bright;
And here on snows, where never human foot
Of common mortal trod, we nightly tread,
And leave no traces; o'er the savage sea,
5 The glassy ocean of the mountain ice,
We skim its rugged breakers, which put on
The aspect of a tumbling tempest's foam,
Frozen in a moment—a dead whirlpool's image;
And this most steep fantastic pinnacle,
10 The fretwork of some earthquake—where the clouds
Pause to repose themselves in passing by—
Is sacred to our revels, or our vigils;
Here do I wait my sisters, on our way
To the Hall of Arimanes, for to-night
15 Is our great festival—'tis strange they come not.

A Voice without, singing
                    The Captive Usurper,[5]
                        Hurl'd down from the throne,
                    Lay buried in torpor,
                        Forgotten and lone;
20   I broke through his slumbers,
                        I shivered his chain,
                    I leagued him with numbers—
                        He's Tyrant again!
        With the blood of a million he'll answer my care,
25   With a nation's destruction—his flight and despair.

Second Voice, without
            The ship sail'd on, the ship sail'd fast,
            But I left not a sail, and I left not a mast;
            There is not a plank of the hull or the deck,
            And there is not a wretch to lament o'er his wreck;

5. Napoleon. The song of the first Voice alludes to Napoleon's escape from his captivity on the island of Elba in March 1815. After his defeat at the Battle of Waterloo he was interned on another island, St. Helena, in October 1815.

30   Save one, whom I held, as he swam, by the hair,
And he was a subject well worthy my care;
A traitor on land, and a pirate at sea—
But I saved him to wreak further havoc for me!

FIRST DESTINY, *answering*
The city lies sleeping;

35   The morn, to deplore it,
May dawn on it weeping:
       Sullenly, slowly,
The black plague flew o'er it—
       Thousands lie lowly;
40   Tens of thousands shall perish—
       The living shall fly from
The sick they should cherish;
       But nothing can vanquish
The touch that they die from.
45   Sorrow and anguish,
And evil and dread,
       Envelope a nation—
The blest are the dead,
Who see not the sight
50   Of their own desolation.—
This work of a night—
This wreck of a realm—this deed of my doing—
For ages I've done, and shall still be renewing!

Enter the SECOND *and* THIRD DESTINIES.

THE THREE
Our hands contain the hearts of men,

55   Our footsteps are their graves;
We only give to take again
    The spirits of our slaves!

FIRST DESTINY   Welcome!—Where's Nemesis?[6]
SECOND DESTINY   At some great work;
  But what I know not, for my hands were full.
THIRD DESTINY   Behold she cometh.
             Enter NEMESIS.
60 FIRST DESTINY   Say, where hast thou been?—
  My sisters and thyself are slow to-night.
NEMESIS   I was detain'd repairing shattered thrones,
  Marrying fools, restoring dynasties,
  Avenging men upon their enemies,
65 And making them repent their own revenge;
  Goading the wise to madness; from the dull
  Shaping out oracles to rule the world
  Afresh, for they were waxing out of date,

---

6. The Greek and Roman goddess of retribution, particularly of the sin of *hubris*, overweening presumption against the gods.

And mortals dared to ponder for themselves,
70 To weigh kings in the balance, and to speak
Of freedom, the forbidden fruit.—Away!
We have outstaid the hour—mount we our clouds!   [*Exeunt.*]

SCENE 4. *The Hall of* ARIMANES.[7]—ARIMANES *on his Throne, a
Globe of Fire, surrounded by the* SPIRITS.

Hymn of the SPIRITS

Hail to our Master!—Prince of Earth and Air!—
Who walks the clouds and waters—in his hand
The sceptre of the elements, which tear
Themselves to chaos at his high command!
5 He breatheth—and a tempest shakes the sea;
He speaketh—and the clouds reply in thunder;
He gazeth—from his glance the sunbeams flee;
He moveth—earthquakes rend the world asunder.
Beneath his footsteps the volcanos rise;
10 His shadow is the Pestilence; his path
The comets herald through the crackling skies;
And planets turn to ashes at his wrath.
To him War offers daily sacrifice;
To him Death pays his tribute; Life is his,
15 With all its infinite of agonies—
And his the spirit of whatever is!

Enter the DESTINIES *and* NEMESIS

FIRST DESTINY Glory to Arimanes! on the earth
His power increaseth—both my sisters did
His bidding, nor did I neglect my duty!
20 SECOND DESTINY Glory to Arimanes! we who bow
The necks of men, bow down before his throne!
THIRD DESTINY Glory to Arimanes!—we await
His nod!
NEMESIS Sovereign of Sovereigns! we are thine,
And all that liveth, more or less, is ours,
25 And most things wholly so; still to increase
Our power increasing thine, demands our care,
And we are vigilant—Thy late commands
Have been fulfilled to the utmost.

Enter MANFRED.

A SPIRIT   What is here?
A mortal!—Thou most rash and fatal wretch,
Bow down and worship!
30 SECOND SPIRIT   I do know the man—
A Magian° of great power, and fearful skill!   *magus*
THIRD SPIRIT Bow down and worship, slave!—What, know'st thou not
Thine and our Sovereign?—Tremble, and obey!
ALL THE SPIRITS Prostrate thyself, and thy condemned clay,
Child of the Earth! or dread the worst.

7. The name is derived from Ahriman, who in the dualistic Zoroastrian religion was the principle of darkness
and evil.

35 MANFRED   I know it;
    And yet ye see I kneel not.
    FOURTH SPIRIT   'Twill be taught thee.
    MANFRED   'Tis taught already;—many a night on the earth,
    On the bare ground, have I bow'd down my face,
    And strew'd my head with ashes; I have known
40 The fulness of humiliation, for
    I sunk before my vain despair, and knelt
    To my own desolation.
    FIFTH SPIRIT   Dost thou dare
    Refuse to Arimanes on his throne
    What the whole earth accords, beholding not
45 The terror of his Glory—Crouch! I say.
    MANFRED   Bid *him* bow down to that which is above him,
    The overruling Infinite—the Maker
    Who made him not for worship—let him kneel,
    And we will kneel together.
    THE SPIRITS   Crush the worm!
    Tear him in pieces!—
50 FIRST DESTINY   Hence! Avaunt!—he's mine.
    Prince of the Powers invisible! This man
    Is of no common order, as his port
    And presence here denote; his sufferings
    Have been of an immortal nature, like
55 Our own; his knowledge and his powers and will,
    As far as is compatible with clay,
    Which clogs the ethereal essence, have been such
    As clay hath seldom borne; his aspirations
    Have been beyond the dwellers of the earth,
60 And they have only taught him what we know—
    That knowledge is not happiness, and science
    But an exchange of ignorance for that
    Which is another kind of ignorance.
    This is not all—the passions, attributes
65 Of earth and heaven, from which no power, nor being,
    Nor breath from the worm upwards is exempt,
    Have pierced his heart; and in their consequence
    Made him a thing, which I, who pity not,
    Yet pardon those who pity. He is mine,
70 And thine, it may be—be it so, or not,
    No other Spirit in this region hath
    A soul like his—or power upon his soul.
    NEMESIS   What doth he here then?
    FIRST DESTINY   Let *him* answer that.
    MANFRED   Ye know what I have known; and without power
75 I could not be amongst ye: but there are
    Powers deeper still beyond—I come in quest
    Of such, to answer unto what I seek.
    NEMESIS   What wouldst *thou*?
    MANFRED   Thou canst not reply to me.
    Call up the dead—my question is for them.

80 NEMESIS   Great Arimanes, doth thy will avouch
  The wishes of this mortal?
ARIMANES   Yea.
NEMESIS   Whom would'st thou
  Uncharnel?
MANFRED   One without a tomb—call up
  Astarte.[8]

                        NEMESIS
                 Shadow! or Spirit!
85   Whatever thou art,
               Which still doth inherit
                 The whole or a part
               Of the form of thy birth,
                 Of the mould of thy clay,
90   Which returned to the earth,
                 Re-appear to the day!
               Bear what thou borest,
                 The heart and the form,
               And the aspect thou worest
95   Redeem from the worm.
               Appear!—Appear!—Appear!
             Who sent thee there requires thee here!

   [*The Phantom of* ASTARTE *rises and stands in the midst.*]

MANFRED   Can this be death? there's bloom upon her cheek;
  But now I see it is no living hue,
100 But a strange hectic°—like the unnatural red   *feverish flush*
  Which Autumn plants upon the perish'd leaf.
  It is the same! Oh, God! that I should dread
  To look upon the same—Astarte!—No,
  I cannot speak to her—but bid her speak—
105 Forgive me or condemn me.

                        NEMESIS
               By the power which hath broken
                 The grave which enthrall'd thee,
               Speak to him who hath spoken,
                 Or those who have call'd thee!
110 MANFRED   She is silent,
  And in that silence I am more than answered.
NEMESIS   My power extends no further. Prince of air!
  It rests with thee alone—command her voice.
ARIMANES   Spirit—obey this sceptre!
NEMESIS   Silent still!
115 She is not of our order, but belongs
  To the other powers. Mortal! thy quest is vain,
  And we are baffled also.
MANFRED   Hear me, hear me—
  Astarte! my beloved! speak to me:

8. Byron applies to Manfred's beloved the name of Astarte (also known as Ashtoreth), goddess of love and
fertility, the Eastern equivalent of the Greek goddess Aphrodite.

I have so much endured—so much endure—
120 Look on me! the grave hath not changed thee more
Than I am changed for thee. Thou lovedst me
Too much, as I loved thee: we were not made
To torture thus each other, though it were
The deadliest sin to love as we have loved.
125 Say that thou loath'st me not—that I do bear
This punishment for both—that thou wilt be
One of the blessed—and that I shall die,
For hitherto all hateful things conspire
To bind me in existence—in a life
130 Which makes me shrink from immortality—
A future like the past. I cannot rest.
I know not what I ask, nor what I seek:
I feel but what thou art—and what I am;
And I would hear yet once before I perish
135 The voice which was my music—Speak to me!
For I have call'd on thee in the still night,
Startled the slumbering birds from the hush'd boughs,
And woke the mountain wolves, and made the caves
Acquainted with thy vainly echoed name,
140 Which answered me—many things answered me—
Spirits and men—but thou wert silent all.
Yet speak to me! I have outwatch'd the stars,
And gazed o'er heaven in vain in search of thee.
Speak to me! I have wandered o'er the earth,
145 And never found thy likeness—Speak to me!
Look on the fiends around—they feel for me:
I fear them not, and feel for thee alone—
Speak to me! though it be in wrath;—but say—
I reck not what—but let me hear thee once—
This once—once more!
PHANTOM OF ASTARTE   Manfred!
150 MANFRED   Say on, say on—
I live but in the sound—it is thy voice!
PHANTOM   Manfred! To-morrow ends thine earthly ills.
Farewell!
MANFRED   Yet one word more—am I forgiven?
PHANTOM   Farewell!
MANFRED   Say, shall we meet again?
PHANTOM   Farewell!
155 MANFRED   One word for mercy! Say, thou lovest me.
PHANTOM   Manfred!   [*The Spirit of* ASTARTE *disappears.*]
NEMESIS   She's gone, and will not be recall'd;
Her words will be fulfill'd. Return to the earth.
A SPIRIT   He is convulsed—This is to be a mortal
And seek the things beyond mortality.
160 ANOTHER SPIRIT   Yet, see, he mastereth himself, and makes
His torture tributary to his will.
Had he been one of us, he would have made

An awful spirit.

NEMESIS   Hast thou further question
Of our great sovereign, or his worshippers?

MANFRED   None.

NEMESIS   Then for a time farewell.

165   MANFRED   We meet then—
Where? On the earth?

NEMESIS   That will be seen hereafter.

MANFRED   Even as thou wilt: and for the grace accorded
I now depart a debtor. Fare ye well!   [*Exit* MANFRED.]
     [*Scene closes.*]

Act 3

SCENE 1. *A Hall in the Castle of* MANFRED. MANFRED *and* HERMAN.

MANFRED   What is the hour?

HERMAN   It wants but one till sunset,
And promises a lovely twilight.

MANFRED   Say,
Are all things so disposed of in the tower
As I directed?

HERMAN   All, my lord, are ready;
Here is the key and casket.

5   MANFRED   It is well:
Thou mayst retire.   [*Exit* HERMAN.]

MANFRED [*alone*]   There is a calm upon me—
Inexplicable stillness! which till now
Did not belong to what I knew of life.
If that I did not know philosophy

10   To be of all our vanities the motliest,[9]
The merest word that ever fool'd the ear
From out the schoolman's jargon, I should deem
The golden secret, the sought "Kalon,"[1] found,
And seated in my soul. It will not last,

15   But it is well to have known it, though but once:
It hath enlarged my thoughts with a new sense,
And I within my tablets would note down
That there is such a feeling. Who is there?
                    Re-enter HERMAN.

HERMAN   My lord, the abbot of St. Maurice[2] craves
To greet your presence.
            Enter the ABBOT OF ST. MAURICE.

20   ABBOT   Peace be with Count Manfred!

MANFRED   Thanks, holy father! welcome to these walls;
Thy presence honours them, and blesseth those
Who dwell within them.

ABBOT   Would it were so, Count!—

---

9. "The most diverse" or, possibly, "the most fool-ish" (*motley* was the multicolored suit worn by a court jester).

1. Greek for both "the Beautiful" and "the Good."
2. In the Rhone Valley in Switzerland.

But I would fain confer with thee alone.
25 MANFRED   Herman, retire. What would my reverend guest?

[*Exit* HERMAN.]

ABBOT   Thus, without prelude:—Age and zeal, my office,[3]
And good intent, must plead my privilege;
Our near, though not acquainted neighbourhood,
May also be my herald. Rumours strange,
30 And of unholy nature, are abroad,
And busy with thy name; a noble name
For centuries; may he who bears it now
Transmit it unimpair'd!
MANFRED   Proceed,—I listen.
ABBOT   'Tis said thou holdest converse with the things
35 Which are forbidden to the search of man;
That with the dwellers of the dark abodes,
The many evil and unheavenly spirits
Which walk the valley of the shade of death,
Thou communest. I know that with mankind,
40 Thy fellows in creation, thou dost rarely
Exchange thy thoughts, and that thy solitude
Is as an anchorite's,[4] were it but holy.
MANFRED   And what are they who do avouch these things?
ABBOT   My pious brethren—the scared peasantry—
45 Even thy own vassals—who do look on thee
With most unquiet eyes. Thy life's in peril.
MANFRED   Take it.
ABBOT   I come to save, and not destroy—
I would not pry into thy secret soul;
But if these things be sooth, there still is time
50 For penitence and pity: reconcile thee
With the true church, and through the church to heaven.
MANFRED   I hear thee. This is my reply; whate'er
I may have been, or am, doth rest between
Heaven and myself.—I shall not choose a mortal
55 To be my mediator. Have I sinn'd
Against your ordinances? prove and punish!
ABBOT   My son! I did not speak of punishment,
But penitence and pardon;—with thyself
The choice of such remains—and for the last,
60 Our institutions and our strong belief
Have given me power to smooth the path from sin
To higher hope and better thoughts; the first
I leave to heaven—"Vengeance is mine alone!"
So saith the Lord,[5] and with all humbleness
65 His servant echoes back the awful word.
MANFRED   Old man! there is no power in holy men,
Nor charm in prayer—nor purifying form

3. Religious vocation.
4. A person who, for religious reasons, lives in
seclusion.

5. Romans 12.19: "Vengeance is mine; I will
repay, saith the Lord."

Of penitence—nor outward look—nor fast—
Nor agony—nor, greater than all these,
70   The innate tortures of that deep despair,
Which is remorse without the fear of hell,
But all in all sufficient to itself
Would make a hell of heaven—can exorcise
From out the unbounded spirit, the quick sense
75   Of its own sins, wrongs, sufferance, and revenge
Upon itself; there is no future pang
Can deal that justice on the self-condemn'd
He deals on his own soul.

ABBOT   All this is well;
For this will pass away, and be succeeded
80   By an auspicious hope, which shall look up
With calm assurance to that blessed place,
Which all who seek may win, whatever be
Their earthly errors, so they be atoned:
And the commencement of atonement is
85   The sense of its necessity.—Say on—
And all our church can teach thee shall be taught;
And all we can absolve thee, shall be pardon'd.

MANFRED   When Rome's sixth Emperor[6] was near his last,
The victim of a self-inflicted wound,
90   To shun the torments of a public death
From senates once his slaves, a certain soldier,
With show of loyal pity, would have staunch'd
The gushing throat with his officious robe;
The dying Roman thrust him back and said—
95   Some empire still in his expiring glance,
"It is too late—is this fidelity?"

ABBOT   And what of this?

MANFRED   I answer with the Roman—
"It is too late!"

ABBOT   It never can be so,
To reconcile thyself with thy own soul,
100   And thy own soul with heaven. Hast thou no hope?
'Tis strange—even those who do despair above,
Yet shape themselves some phantasy on earth,
To which frail twig they cling, like drowning men.

MANFRED   Ay—father! I have had those earthly visions
105   And noble aspirations in my youth,
To make my own the mind of other men,
The enlightener of nations; and to rise
I knew not whither—it might be to fall;
But fall, even as the mountain-cataract,
110   Which having leapt from its more dazzling height,
Even in the foaming strength of its abyss,

6. Otho. Byron attaches to his suicide a story that Suetonius tells about the death of an earlier emperor, Nero.

(Which casts up misty columns that become
Clouds raining from the re-ascended skies)
Lies low but mighty still.—But this is past,
My thoughts mistook themselves.

115 ABBOT   And wherefore so?

MANFRED   I could not tame my nature down; for he
Must serve who fain would sway—and soothe—and sue—
And watch all time—and pry into all place—
And be a living lie—who would become
120 A mighty thing amongst the mean, and such
The mass are; I disdained to mingle with
A herd, though to be leader—and of wolves.
The lion is alone, and so am I.

ABBOT   And why not live and act with other men?

125 MANFRED   Because my nature was averse from life;
And yet not cruel; for I would not make,
But find a desolation:—like the wind,
The red-hot breath of the most lone Simoom,[7]
Which dwells but in the desert, and sweeps o'er
130 The barren sands which bear no shrubs to blast,
And revels o'er their wild and arid waves,
And seeketh not, so that it is not sought,
But being met is deadly; such hath been
The course of my existence; but there came
Things in my path which are no more.

135 ABBOT   Alas!
I 'gin to fear that thou art past all aid
From me and from my calling; yet so young,
I still would—

MANFRED   Look on me! there is an order
Of mortals on the earth, who do become
140 Old in their youth, and die ere middle age,
Without the violence of warlike death;
Some perishing of pleasure—some of study—
Some worn with toil—some of mere weariness—
Some of disease—and some insanity—
145 And some of withered, or of broken hearts;
For this last is a malady which slays
More than are numbered in the lists of Fate,
Taking all shapes, and bearing many names.
Look upon me! for even of all these things
150 Have I partaken; and of all these things,
One were enough; then wonder not that I
Am what I am, but that I ever was,
Or, having been, that I am still on earth.

ABBOT   Yet, hear me still—

MANFRED   Old man! I do respect
155 Thine order, and revere thine years; I deem

---

7. A hot, sand-laden wind in the Sahara and Arabian deserts.

Thy purpose pious, but it is in vain:
Think me not churlish; I would spare thyself,
Far more than me, in shunning at this time
All further colloquy—and so—farewell.   [*Exit* MANFRED.]
160   ABBOT   This should have been a noble creature: he
Hath all the energy which would have made
A goodly frame of glorious elements,
Had they been wisely mingled; as it is,
It is an awful chaos—light and darkness—
165   And mind and dust—and passions and pure thoughts,
Mix'd, and contending without end or order,
All dormant or destructive: he will perish,
And yet he must not; I will try once more,
For such are worth redemption; and my duty
170   Is to dare all things for a righteous end.
I'll follow him—but cautiously, though surely.   [*Exit* ABBOT.]

SCENE 2. *Another Chamber.* MANFRED *and* HERMAN.

HERMAN   My Lord, you bade me wait on you at sunset:
He sinks beyond the mountain.
MANFRED   Doth he so?
I will look on him.
          [MANFRED *advances to the Window of the Hall.*]
                    Glorious Orb! the idol
Of early nature, and the vigorous race
5   Of undiseased mankind, the giant sons
Of the embrace of angels, with a sex
More beautiful than they, which did draw down
The erring spirits[8] who can ne'er return.—
Most glorious orb! that wert a worship, ere
10   The mystery of thy making was reveal'd!
Thou earliest minister of the Almighty,
Which gladden'd, on their mountain tops, the hearts
Of the Chaldean shepherds, till they pour'd
Themselves in orisons!° Thou material God!   *prayers*
15   And representative of the Unknown—
Who chose thee for his shadow! Thou chief star!
Centre of many stars! which mak'st our earth
Endurable, and temperest the hues
And hearts of all who walk within thy rays!
20   Sire of the seasons! Monarch of the climes,
And those who dwell in them! for near or far,
Our inborn spirits have a tint of thee,
Even as our outward aspects;—thou dost rise,
And shine, and set in glory. Fare thee well!

8. Genesis 6.4: "There were giants in the earth in those days; and also after that, when the sons of God came in unto the daughters of men, and they bare children to them, the same became mighty men which were of old, men of renown." Byron interprets "the sons of God" as denoting errant angels.

25 I ne'er shall see thee more. As my first glance
Of love and wonder was for thee, then take
My latest look: thou wilt not beam on one
To whom the gifts of life and warmth have been
Of a more fatal nature. He is gone:
30 I follow.   [*Exit* MANFRED.]

SCENE 3. *The Mountains.—The Castle of* MANFRED *at some distance.—A Terrace before a Tower.—Time, Twilight.* HERMAN, MANUEL, *and other Dependants of* MANFRED.

HERMAN   'Tis strange enough; night after night, for years,
He hath pursued long vigils in this tower,
Without a witness. I have been within it,—
So have we all been oft-times; but from it,
5 Or its contents, it were impossible
To draw conclusions absolute, of aught
His studies tend to. To be sure, there is
One chamber where none enter; I would give
The fee° of what I have to come these three years,   *ownership*
To pore upon its mysteries.
10 MANUEL   'Twere dangerous;
Content thyself with what thou knowest already.
HERMAN   Ah! Manuel! thou art elderly and wise,
And could'st say much; thou hast dwelt within the castle—
How many years is't?
MANUEL   Ere Count Manfred's birth,
15 I served his father, whom he nought resembles.
HERMAN   There be more sons in like predicament.
But wherein do they differ?
MANUEL   I speak not
Of features or of form, but mind and habits:
Count Sigismund was proud,—but gay and free,—
20 A warrior and a reveller; he dwelt not
With books and solitude, nor made the night
A gloomy vigil, but a festal time,
Merrier than day; he did not walk the rocks
And forests like a wolf, nor turn aside
From men and their delights.
25 HERMAN   Beshrew[9] the hour,
But those were jocund times! I would that such
Would visit the old walls again; they look
As if they had forgotten them.
MANUEL   These walls
Must change their chieftain first. Oh! I have seen
Some strange things in them, Herman.
30 HERMAN   Come, be friendly;
Relate me some to while away our watch:

---

9. Curse (used jocularly).

I've heard thee darkly speak of an event
Which happened hereabouts, by this same tower.
MANUEL   That was a night indeed; I do remember
35   'Twas twilight, as it may be now, and such
Another evening—yon red cloud, which rests
On Eigher's[1] pinnacle, so rested then,—
So like that it might be the same; the wind
Was faint and gusty, and the mountain snows
40   Began to glitter with the climbing moon;
Count Manfred was, as now, within his tower,—
How occupied, we knew not, but with him
The sole companion of his wanderings
And watchings—her, whom of all earthly things
45   That lived, the only thing he seem'd to love,—
As he, indeed, by blood was bound to do,
The Lady Astarte, his—
                Hush! who comes here?
              Enter the ABBOT.
ABBOT   Where is your master?
HERMAN
                 Yonder in the tower.
ABBOT   I must speak with him.
MANUEL
                 'Tis impossible;
50   He is most private, and must not be thus
Intruded on.
ABBOT   Upon myself I take
The forfeit of my fault, if fault there be—
But I must see him.
HERMAN   Thou hast seen him once
This eve already.
ABBOT   Sirrah! I command thee,
55   Knock, and apprize the Count of my approach.
HERMAN   We dare not.
ABBOT   Then it seems I must be herald
Of my own purpose.
MANUEL   Reverend father, stop—
I pray you pause.
ABBOT   Why so?
MANUEL   But step this way,
And I will tell you further.
                          [*Exeunt.*]

SCENE 4. *Interior of the Tower.*

MANFRED *alone*

The stars are forth, the moon above the tops
Of the snow-shining mountains.—Beautiful!
I linger yet with Nature, for the night
Hath been to me a more familiar face
5   Than that of man; and in her starry shade

1. A peak a few miles north of the Jungfrau.

Of dim and solitary loveliness,
I learn'd the language of another world.
I do remember me, that in my youth,
When I was wandering,—upon such a night
10 I stood within the Coloseum's wall,
'Midst the chief relics of almighty Rome;
The trees which grew along the broken arches
Waved dark in the blue midnight, and the stars
Shone through the rents of ruin; from afar
15 The watchdog bayed beyond the Tiber;[2] and
More near from out the Caesars' palace[3] came
The owl's long cry, and, interruptedly,
Of distant sentinels the fitful song
Begun and died upon the gentle wind.
20 Some cypresses beyond the time-worn breach
Appeared to skirt the horizon, yet they stood
Within a bowshot—where the Caesars dwelt,
And dwell the tuneless birds of night; amidst
A grove which springs through levell'd battlements,
25 And twines its roots with the imperial hearths,
Ivy usurps the laurel's place of growth;—
But the gladiators' bloody Circus[4] stands,
A noble wreck in ruinous perfection!
While Caesar's chambers, and the Augustan halls,
30 Grovel on earth in indistinct decay.—
And thou didst shine, thou rolling moon, upon
All this, and cast a wide and tender light,
Which soften'd down the hoar austerity
Of rugged desolation, and fill'd up,
35 As 'twere anew, the gaps of centuries;
Leaving that beautiful which still was so,
And making that which was not, till the place
Became religion, and the heart ran o'er
With silent worship of the great of old!—
40 The dead, but sceptred sovereigns, who still rule
Our spirits from their urns.—
                     'Twas such a night!
'Tis strange that I recall it at this time;
But I have found our thoughts take wildest flight
Even at the moment when they should array
Themselves in pensive order.
                  Enter the ABBOT.
45 ABBOT   My good Lord!
   I crave a second grace for this approach;
But yet let not my humble zeal offend
By its abruptness—all it hath of ill

2. The river that flows through Rome.
3. The palace of the Roman emperors. It stands on the Palatine hill, immediately southwest of the Coliseum.

4. The circular arena within the Coliseum where professional gladiators fought to the death as public entertainment.

Recoils on me; its good in the effect
50   May light upon your head—could I say *heart*—
Could I touch *that*, with words or prayers, I should
Recall a noble spirit which hath wandered,
But is not yet all lost.
MANFRED   Thou know'st me not;
My days are numbered, and my deeds recorded:
55   Retire, or 'twill be dangerous—Away!
ABBOT   Thou dost not mean to menace me?
MANFRED   Not I;
I simply tell thee peril is at hand,
And would preserve thee.
ABBOT   What dost mean?
MANFRED   Look there!
What dost thou see?
ABBOT   Nothing.
MANFRED   Look there, I say,
60   And steadfastly;—now tell me what thou seest?
ABBOT   That which should shake me,—but I fear it not—
I see a dusk and awful figure rise
Like an infernal god from out the earth;
His face wrapt in a mantle, and his form
65   Robed as with angry clouds; he stands between
Thyself and me—but I do fear him not.
MANFRED   Thou hast no cause—he shall not harm thee—but
His sight may shock thine old limbs into palsy.
I say to thee—Retire!
ABBOT   And, I reply—
70   Never—till I have battled with this fiend—
What doth he here?
MANFRED   Why—ay—what doth he here?
I did not send for him,—he is unbidden.
ABBOT   Alas! lost mortal! what with guests like these
Hast thou to do? I tremble for thy sake;
75   Why doth he gaze on thee, and thou on him?
Ah! he unveils his aspect; on his brow
The thunder-scars are graven; from his eye
Glares forth the immortality of hell—
Avaunt!—
MANFRED   Pronounce—what is thy mission?
SPIRIT   Come!
80   ABBOT   What art thou, unknown being? answer!—speak!
SPIRIT   The genius[5] of this mortal.—Come! 'tis time.
MANFRED   I am prepared for all things, but deny
The power which summons me. Who sent thee here?
SPIRIT   Thou'lt know anon—Come! come!
MANFRED   I have commanded
85   Things of an essence greater far than thine,

---

5. The spirit or deity presiding over a human being from birth.

And striven with thy masters. Get thee hence!
SPIRIT   Mortal! thine hour is come—Away! I say.
MANFRED   I knew, and know my hour is come, but not
  To render up my soul to such as thee:
90 Away! I'll die as I have lived—alone.
SPIRIT   Then I must summon up my brethren.—Rise!
                                    [*Other Spirits rise up.*]
ABBOT   Avaunt! ye evil ones!—Avaunt! I say,—
  Ye have no power where piety hath power,
  And I do charge ye in the name—
SPIRIT   Old man!
95 We know ourselves, our mission, and thine order;
  Waste not thy holy words on idle uses,
  It were in vain; this man is forfeited.
  Once more I summon him—Away! away!
MANFRED   I do defy ye,—though I feel my soul
100 Is ebbing from me, yet I do defy ye;
  Nor will I hence, while I have earthly breath
  To breathe my scorn upon ye—earthly strength
  To wrestle, though with spirits; what ye take
  Shall be ta'en limb by limb.
SPIRIT   Reluctant mortal!
105 Is this the Magian who would so pervade
  The world invisible, and make himself
  Almost our equal?—Can it be that thou
  Art thus in love with life? the very life
  Which made thee wretched!
MANFRED   Thou false fiend, thou liest!
110 My life is in its last hour,—*that* I know,
  Nor would redeem a moment of that hour;
  I do not combat against death, but thee
  And thy surrounding angels; my past power
  Was purchased by no compact with thy crew,
115 But by superior science—penance—daring—
  And length of watching—strength of mind—and skill
  In knowledge of our fathers—when the earth
  Saw men and spirits walking side by side,
  And gave ye no supremacy: I stand
120 Upon my strength—I do defy—deny—
  Spurn back, and scorn ye!—
SPIRIT   But thy many crimes
  Have made thee—
MANFRED   What are they to such as thee?
  Must crimes be punish'd but by other crimes,
  And greater criminals?—Back to thy hell!
125 Thou hast no power upon me, *that* I feel;
  Thou never shalt possess me, *that* I know:
  What I have done is done; I bear within
  A torture which could nothing gain from thine:
  The mind which is immortal makes itself

130 Requital for its good or evil thoughts—
Is its own origin of ill and end—
And its own place and time[6]—its innate sense,
When stripp'd of this mortality, derives
No colour from the fleeting things without,
135 But is absorb'd in sufferance or in joy,
Born from the knowledge of its own desert.
Thou didst not tempt me, and thou couldst not tempt me;
I have not been thy dupe, nor am thy prey—
But was my own destroyer, and will be
140 My own hereafter.—Back, ye baffled fiends!
The hand of death is on me—but not yours!

[*The Demons disappear.*]

ABBOT Alas! how pale thou art—thy lips are white—
And thy breast heaves—and in thy gasping throat
The accents rattle—Give thy prayers to Heaven—
145 Pray—albeit but in thought,—but die not thus.
MANFRED 'Tis over—my dull eyes can fix thee not;
But all things swim around me, and the earth
Heaves as it were beneath me. Fare thee well—
Give me thy hand.
ABBOT Cold—cold—even to the heart—
150 But yet one prayer—alas! how fares it with thee?—
MANFRED Old man! 'tis not so difficult to die.[7]

[MANFRED *expires.*]

ABBOT He's gone—his soul hath ta'en its earthless flight—
Whither? I dread to think—but he is gone.

1816–17   1817

Don Juan

Byron began his masterpiece (pronounced in the English fashion, *Don Joó-un*) in July of 1818, published it in installments beginning with cantos 1 and 2 in 1819, and continued working on it almost until his death. He extemporized the poem from episode to episode. "I *have* no plan," he said, "I *had* no plan; but I had or have materials." The work was composed with remarkable speed (the 888 lines of canto 13, for example, were dashed off within a week), and it aims at the effect of improvisation rather than of artful compression; it asks to be read rapidly, at a conversational pace.

The poem breaks off with the sixteenth canto, but even in its unfinished state *Don Juan* is the longest satirical poem, and indeed one of the longest poems of any kind, in English. Its hero, the Spanish libertine, had in the original legend been superhuman in his sexual energy and wickedness. Throughout Byron's version the unspoken but persistent joke is that this archetypal *homme fatal* of European legend is in fact more acted upon than active. Unfailingly amiable and well intentioned, he is

6. The last of several echoes by Manfred of Satan's claim that "The mind is its own place, and in itself / Can make a Heaven of Hell, and a Hell of Heaven" (*Paradise Lost* 1.254–55). See also 1.1.252 and 3.1.73, above.

7. When this line was omitted in the printing of the first edition, Byron wrote angrily to his publisher: "You have destroyed the whole effect and moral of the poem."

guilty largely of youth, charm, and a courteous and compliant spirit. The women do all the rest.

The chief models for the poem were the Italian seriocomic versions of medieval chivalric romances; the genre had been introduced by Pulci in the fifteenth century and was adopted by Ariosto in his *Orlando Furioso* (1532). From these writers Byron caught the mixed moods and violent oscillations between the sublime and the ridiculous as well as the colloquial management of the complex ottava rima—an eight-line stanza in which the initial interlaced rhymes (*ababab*) build up to the comic turn in the final couplet (*cc*). Byron was influenced in the English use of this Italian form by a mildly amusing poem published in 1817, under the pseudonym of "Whistlecraft," by his friend John Hookham Frere. Other recognizable antecedents of *Don Juan* are Jonathan Swift's *Gulliver's Travels* and Samuel Johnson's *Rasselas,* which had employed the naive traveler as a satiric device, and Laurence Sterne's novel *Tristram Shandy*, with its comic exploitation of a narrative medium blatantly subject to the whimsy of the author. But even the most original literary works play variations on inherited conventions. Shelley at once recognized his friend's poem as "something wholly new and relative to the age."

Byron's literary advisers thought the poem unacceptably immoral, and John Murray took the precaution of printing the first two installments without identifying either Byron as the author or himself as the publisher. But Byron insisted that *Don Juan* is "a *satire* on *abuses* of the present state of society" and "the most moral of poems." And the poem is zestfully on the side of life, in its abundant variety. "As to 'Don Juan,' " Byron wrote elatedly to a friend, "confess—confess, you dog—and be candid. . . . it may be profligate—but is it not *life*, is it not *the thing?*" (see his letter to Douglas Kinnaird, Oct. 26, 1819, p. 695).

The controlling element of *Don Juan* is not the narrative but the narrator, and his temperament gives the work its unity. The poem is really a continuous monologue, in the course of which a story manages to be told. It opens with the first-person pronoun and immediately lets us into the storyteller's predicament: "I want a hero. . . ." The voice then goes on, for almost two thousand stanzas, with effortless volubility and shifts of mood, using the occasion of Juan's misadventures to confide to us the speaker's thoughts and devastating judgments on the major institutions, activities, and values of Western society. The poet who in his brilliant successful youth created the gloomy and misanthropic Byronic hero, in his later and sadder life created a character (not the hero, but the narrator of *Don Juan*) who is one of the great comic inventions in English literature.

FROM DON JUAN

Fragment[1]

> I would to Heaven that I were so much Clay—
>   As I am blood—bone—marrow, passion—feeling—
> Because at least the past were past away—
>   And for the future—(but I write this reeling
> 5 Having got drunk exceedingly to day
>   So that I seem to stand upon the ceiling)

---

1. This stanza was written on the back of a page of the manuscript of canto 1. For the author's revisions while composing two stanzas of *Don Juan*, see "Poems in Process," in the appendices to this volume.

I say—the future is a serious matter—
And so—for Godsake—Hock[2] and Soda water.

From Canto 1

[JUAN AND DONNA JULIA]

I

I want a hero: an uncommon want,
    When every year and month sends forth a new one,
Till, after cloying the gazettes with cant,
    The age discovers he is not the true one;
5 Of such as these I should not care to vaunt,
    I'll therefore take our ancient friend Don Juan,
We all have seen him in the pantomime[1]
Sent to the devil, somewhat ere his time.

*   *   *

5

Brave men were living before Agamemnon[2]
    And since, exceeding valorous and sage,
35 A good deal like him too, though quite the same none;
    But then they shone not on the poet's page,
And so have been forgotten—I condemn none,
    But can't find any in the present age
Fit for my poem (that is, for my new one);
40 So, as I said, I'll take my friend Don Juan.

6

Most epic poets plunge in *"medias res,"*[3]
    (Horace makes this the heroic turnpike road)
And then your hero tells, whene'er you please,
    What went before—by way of episode,
45 While seated after dinner at his ease,
    Beside his mistress in some soft abode,
Palace, or garden, paradise, or cavern,
Which serves the happy couple for a tavern.

7

That is the usual method, but not mine—
50   My way is to begin with the beginning;
The regularity of my design
    Forbids all wandering as the worst of sinning,
And therefore I shall open with a line
    (Although it cost me half an hour in spinning)

---

2. A white Rhine wine, from the German *Hochheimer*.
1. The Juan legend was a popular subject in English pantomime.
2. In Homer's *Iliad*, the king commanding the Greeks in the siege of Troy. This line is translated from a Latin ode by Horace.
3. Into the middle of things (Latin; Horace's *Art of Poetry* 148).

55 Narrating somewhat of Don Juan's father,
And also of his mother, if you'd rather.

8

In Seville was he born, a pleasant city,
    Famous for oranges and women—he
Who has not seen it will be much to pity,
60   So says the proverb—and I quite agree;
Of all the Spanish towns is none more pretty,
    Cadiz perhaps—but that you soon may see:—
Don Juan's parents lived beside the river,
A noble stream, and call'd the Guadalquivir.

9

65 His father's name was Jóse[4]—*Don,* of course,
    A true Hidalgo, free from every stain
Of Moor or Hebrew blood, he traced his source
    Through the most Gothic gentlemen of Spain;
A better cavalier ne'er mounted horse,
70   Or, being mounted, e'er got down again,
Than Jóse, who begot our hero, who
Begot—but that's to come——Well, to renew:

10

His mother was a learned lady, famed
    For every branch of every science known—
75 In every christian language ever named,
    With virtues equall'd by her wit alone,
She made the cleverest people quite ashamed,
    And even the good with inward envy groan,
Finding themselves so very much exceeded
80 In their own way by all the things that she did.

11

Her memory was a mine: she knew by heart
    All Calderon and greater part of Lopé,[5]
So that if any actor miss'd his part
    She could have served him for the prompter's copy;
85 For her Feinagle's[6] were an useless art,
    And he himself obliged to shut up shop—he
Could never make a memory so fine as
That which adorn'd the brain of Donna Inez.

12

Her favourite science was the mathematical,
90   Her noblest virtue was her magnanimity,
Her wit (she sometimes tried at wit) was Attic[7] all,

---

4. Normally "José"; Byron transferred the accent to keep his meter.
5. Calderón de la Barca and Lope de Vega, the great Spanish dramatists of the early 17th century.
6. Gregor von Feinagle, a German expert on the art of memory, who had lectured in England in 1811.
7. Athenian. *Attic salt* signifies the famed wit of the Athenians.

Her serious sayings darken'd to sublimity;
In short, in all things she was fairly what I call
A prodigy—her morning dress was dimity,
95   Her evening silk, or, in the summer, muslin,
And other stuffs, with which I won't stay puzzling.

13

She knew the Latin—that is, "the Lord's prayer,"
And Greek—the alphabet—I'm nearly sure;
She read some French romances here and there,
100   Although her mode of speaking was not pure;
For native Spanish she had no great care,
At least her conversation was obscure;
Her thoughts were theorems, her words a problem,
As if she deem'd that mystery would ennoble 'em.

*   *   *

22

'Tis pity learned virgins ever wed
170   With persons of no sort of education,
Or gentlemen, who, though well-born and bred,
Grow tired of scientific conversation:
I don't choose to say much upon this head,
I'm a plain man, and in a single station,
175   But—Oh! ye lords of ladies intellectual,
Inform us truly, have they not hen-peck'd you all?

23

Don Jóse and his lady quarrell'd—*why*,
Not any of the many could divine,
Though several thousand people chose to try,
180   'Twas surely no concern of theirs nor mine;
I loathe that low vice curiosity,
But if there's any thing in which I shine
'Tis in arranging all my friends' affairs.
Not having, of my own, domestic cares.

24

185 And so I interfered, and with the best
Intentions, but their treatment was not kind;
I think the foolish people were possess'd,
For neither of them could I ever find,
Although their porter afterwards confess'd—
190   But that's no matter, and the worst's behind,
For little Juan o'er me threw, down stairs,
A pail of housemaid's water unawares.

25

A little curly-headed, good-for-nothing,
And mischief-making monkey from his birth;
195 His parents ne'er agreed except in doting

Upon the most unquiet imp on earth;
Instead of quarrelling, had they been but both in
Their senses, they'd have sent young master forth
To school, or had him soundly whipp'd at home,
200 To teach him manners for the time to come.

26

Don Jóse and the Donna Inez led
For some time an unhappy sort of life,
Wishing each other, not divorced, but dead;
They lived respectably as man and wife,
205 Their conduct was exceedingly well-bred,
And gave no outward signs of inward strife,
Until at length the smother'd fire broke out,
And put the business past all kind of doubt.

27

For Inez call'd some druggists and physicians,
210 And tried to prove her loving lord was *mad*,[8]
But as he had some lucid intermissions,
She next decided he was only *bad*;
Yet when they ask'd her for her depositions,
No sort of explanation could be had,
215 Save that her duty both to man and God
Required this conduct—which seem'd very odd.

28

She kept a journal, where his faults were noted,
And open'd certain trunks of books and letters,
All which might, if occasion served, be quoted;
220 And then she had all Seville for abettors,
Besides her good old grandmother (who doted);
The hearers of her case became repeaters,
Then advocates, inquisitors, and judges,
Some for amusement, others for old grudges.

29

225 And then this best and meekest woman bore
With such serenity her husband's woes,
Just as the Spartan ladies did of yore,
Who saw their spouses kill'd, and nobly chose
Never to say a word about them more—
230 Calmly she heard each calumny that rose,
And saw *his* agonies with such sublimity,
That all the world exclaim'd "What magnanimity!"

* * *

8. Lady Byron had thought her husband might be insane and sought medical advice on the matter. This and other passages obviously allude to his wife, although Byron insisted that Donna Inez was not intended to be a caricature of Lady Byron.

32

Their friends had tried at reconciliation,
250   Then their relations, who made matters worse;
('Twere hard to say upon a like occasion
      To whom it may be best to have recourse—
I can't say much for friend or yet relation):
      The lawyers did their utmost for divorce,
255 But scarce a fee was paid on either side
Before, unluckily, Don Jóse died.

33

He died: and most unluckily, because,
      According to all hints I could collect
From counsel learned in those kinds of laws,
260   (Although their talk's obscure and circumspect)
His death contrived to spoil a charming cause;
      A thousand pities also with respect
To public feeling, which on this occasion
Was manifested in a great sensation.

*   *   *

37

Dying intestate, Juan was sole heir
290   To a chancery suit, and messuages,[9] and lands,
Which, with a long minority and care,
      Promised to turn out well in proper hands:
Inez became sole guardian, which was fair,
      And answer'd but to nature's just demands;
295 An only son left with an only mother
Is brought up much more wisely than another.

38

Sagest of women, even of widows, she
      Resolved that Juan should be quite a paragon,
And worthy of the noblest pedigree:
300   (His sire was of Castile, his dam from Arragon).
Then for accomplishments of chivalry,
      In case our lord the king should go to war again,
He learn'd the arts of riding, fencing, gunnery,
And how to scale a fortress—or a nunnery.

39

305 But that which Donna Inez most desired,
      And saw into herself each day before all
The learned tutors whom for him she hired,
      Was, that his breeding should be strictly moral;
Much into all his studies she inquired,
310   And so they were submitted first to her, all,
Arts, sciences, no branch was made a mystery
To Juan's eyes, excepting natural history.[1]

9. Houses and the adjoining lands. "Chancery
suit": a case in what was then the highest English

court, notorious for its delays.
1. Includes biology and physiology.

40

The languages, especially the dead,
The sciences, and most of all the abstruse,
315 The arts, at least all such as could be said
To be the most remote from common use,
In all these he was much and deeply read;
But not a page of anything that's loose,
Or hints continuation of the species,
320 Was ever suffer'd, lest he should grow vicious.

41

His classic studies made a little puzzle,
Because of filthy loves of gods and goddesses,
Who in the earlier ages made a bustle,
But never put on pantaloons or boddices;
325 His reverend tutors had at times a tussle,
And for their Aeneids, Iliads, and Odysseys,
Were forced to make an odd sort of apology,
For Donna Inez dreaded the mythology.

42

Ovid's a rake, as half his verses show him,
330 Anacreon's morals are a still worse sample,
Catullus scarcely has a decent poem,
I don't think Sappho's Ode a good example,
Although Longinus[2] tells us there is no hymn
Where the sublime soars forth on wings more ample;
335 But Virgil's songs are pure, except that horrid one
Beginning with "*Formosum Pastor Corydon*."[3]

43

Lucretius' irreligion[4] is too strong
For early stomachs, to prove wholesome food;
I can't help thinking Juvenal[5] was wrong,
340 Although no doubt his real intent was good,
For speaking out so plainly in his song,
So much indeed as to be downright rude;
And then what proper person can be partial
To all those nauseous epigrams of Martial?

44

345 Juan was taught from out the best edition,
Expurgated by learned men, who place,
Judiciously, from out the schoolboy's vision,
The grosser parts; but fearful to deface
Too much their modest bard by this omission,

---

2. The Greek rhetorician Longinus praises a passage from Sappho in *On the Sublime* 10.
3. Virgil's *Eclogue* 2 begins: "The shepherd, Corydon, burned with love for the handsome Alexis."
4. In *De rerum natura* (On the nature of things)

Lucretius sets out to show that the universe can be explained without reference to any god.
5. The Latin satires of Juvenal attacked the corruption of Roman society in the 1st century C.E.

350   And pitying sore his mutilated case,
They only add them all in an appendix,[6]
Which saves, in fact, the trouble of an index.

*   *   *

52

For my part I say nothing—nothing—but
410   *This* I will say—my reasons are my own—
That if I had an only son to put
    To school (as God be praised that I have none)
'Tis not with Donna Inez I would shut
    Him up to learn his catechism alone,
415   No—No—I'd send him out betimes to college,
For there it was I pick'd up my own knowledge.

53

For there one learns—'tis not for me to boast,
    Though I acquired—but I pass over *that,*
As well as all the Greek I since have lost:
420   I say that there's the place—but *"Verbum sat,"*[7]
I think I pick'd up too, as well as most,
    Knowledge of matters—but no matter *what*—
I never married—but, I think, I know
That sons should not be educated so.

54

425   Young Juan now was sixteen years of age,
    Tall, handsome, slender, but well knit; he seem'd
Active, though not so sprightly, as a page;
    And every body but his mother deem'd
Him almost man; but she flew in a rage,
430   And bit her lips (for else she might have scream'd),
If any said so, for to be precocious
Was in her eyes a thing the most atrocious.

55

Amongst her numerous acquaintance, all
    Selected for discretion and devotion,
435   There was the Donna Julia, whom to call
    Pretty were but to give a feeble notion
Of many charms in her as natural
    As sweetness to the flower, or salt to ocean,
Her zone° to Venus, or his bow to Cupid,   belt, sash
440   (But this last simile is trite and stupid).

56

The darkness of her Oriental eye
    Accorded with her Moorish origin;

6. Fact! There is, or was, such an edition, with all the obnoxious epigrams of Martial placed by themselves at the end [Byron's note].

7. A word [to the wise] is sufficient (Latin).

(Her blood was not all Spanish, by the by;
    In Spain, you know, this is a sort of sin).
445 When proud Grenada fell, and, forced to fly,
    Boabdil wept,[8] of Donna Julia's kin
Some went to Africa, some staid in Spain,
Her great great grandmamma chose to remain.

57

She married (I forget the pedigree)
450   With an Hidalgo,[9] who transmitted down
His blood less noble than such blood should be;
    At such alliances his sires would frown,
In that point so precise in each degree
    That they bred *in and in,* as might be shown,
455 Marrying their cousins—nay, their aunts and nieces,
Which always spoils the breed, if it increases.

58

This heathenish cross restored the breed again,
    Ruin'd its blood, but much improved its flesh;
For, from a root the ugliest in Old Spain
460   Sprung up a branch as beautiful as fresh;
The sons no more were short, the daughters plain:
    But there's a rumour which I fain would hush,
'Tis said that Donna Julia's grandmamma
Produced her Don more heirs at love than law.

59

465 However this might be, the race went on
    Improving still through every generation,
Until it center'd in an only son,
    Who left an only daughter; my narration
May have suggested that this single one
470   Could be but Julia (whom on this occasion
I shall have much to speak about), and she
Was married, charming, chaste,[1] and twenty-three.

60

Her eye (I'm very fond of handsome eyes)
    Was large and dark, suppressing half its fire
475 Until she spoke, then through its soft disguise
    Flash'd an expression more of pride than ire,
And love than either; and there would arise
    A something in them which was not desire,
But would have been, perhaps, but for the soul
480 Which struggled through and chasten'd down the whole.

61

Her glossy hair was cluster'd o'er a brow
    Bright with intelligence, and fair and smooth;

---

8. The last Moorish king of Granada (then a province in Spain) wept when his capital fell to the Spaniards (1492).

9. A Spanish nobleman of the lower class.
1. I.e., faithful to her husband.

Her eyebrow's shape was like the aerial bow,
   Her cheek all purple with the beam of youth,
485 Mounting, at times, to a transparent glow,
   As if her veins ran lightning; she, in sooth,
Possess'd an air and grace by no means common:
Her stature tall—I hate a dumpy woman.

62

Wedded she was some years, and to a man
490   Of fifty, and such husbands are in plenty;
And yet, I think, instead of such a ONE
   'Twere better to have TWO of five and twenty,
Especially in countries near the sun:
   And now I think on't, "mi vien in mente,"[2]
495 Ladies even of the most uneasy virtue
Prefer a spouse whose age is short of thirty.

63

'Tis a sad thing, I cannot choose but say,
   And all the fault of that indecent sun,
Who cannot leave alone our helpless clay,
500   But will keep baking, broiling, burning on,
That howsoever people fast and pray
   The flesh is frail, and so the soul undone:
What men call gallantry, and gods adultery,
Is much more common where the climate's sultry.

64

505 Happy the nations of the moral north!
   Where all is virtue, and the winter season
Sends sin, without a rag on, shivering forth;
   ('Twas snow that brought St. Francis back to reason);
Where juries cast up what a wife is worth
510   By laying whate'er sum, in mulct,[3] they please on
The lover, who must pay a handsome price,
Because it is a marketable vice.

65

Alfonso was the name of Julia's lord,
   A man well looking for his years, and who
515 Was neither much beloved, nor yet abhorr'd;
   They lived together as most people do,
Suffering each other's foibles by accord,
   And not exactly either *one* or *two*;
Yet he was jealous, though he did not show it,
520 For jealousy dislikes the world to know it.

*   *   *

69

545 Juan she saw, and, as a pretty child,
   Caress'd him often, such a thing might be

---

2. It comes to my mind (Italian).   3. By way of a fine or legal penalty.

Quite innocently done, and harmless styled,
    When she had twenty years, and thirteen he;
But I am not so sure I should have smiled
550   When he was sixteen, Julia twenty-three,
These few short years make wondrous alterations,
Particularly amongst sun-burnt nations.

70

Whate'er the cause might be, they had become
    Changed; for the dame grew distant, the youth shy,
555 Their looks cast down, their greetings almost dumb,
    And much embarrassment in either eye;
There surely will be little doubt with some
    That Donna Julia knew the reason why,
But as for Juan, he had no more notion
560 Than he who never saw the sea of ocean.

71

Yet Julia's very coldness still was kind,
    And tremulously gentle her small hand
Withdrew itself from his, but left behind
    A little pressure, thrilling, and so bland
565 And slight, so very slight, that to the mind
    'Twas but a doubt; but ne'er magician's wand
Wrought change with all Armida's[4] fairy art
Like what this light touch left on Juan's heart.

72

And if she met him, though she smiled no more,
570   She look'd a sadness sweeter than her smile,
As if her heart had deeper thoughts in store
    She must not own, but cherish'd more the while,
For that compression in its burning core;
    Even innocence itself has many a wile,
575 And will not dare to trust itself with truth,
And love is taught hypocrisy from youth.

*   *   *

75

Poor Julia's heart was in an awkward state;
    She felt it going, and resolved to make
595 The noblest efforts for herself and mate,
    For honour's, pride's, religion's, virtue's sake;
Her resolutions were most truly great,
    And almost might have made a Tarquin[5] quake;
She pray'd the Virgin Mary for her grace,
600 As being the best judge of a lady's case.

---

4. The sorceress who seduces Rinaldo in Torquato Tasso's *Jerusalem Delivered*.
5. A member of a legendary family of Roman kings noted for tyranny and cruelty; perhaps a reference specifically to Lucius Tarquinus, the villain of Shakespeare's *The Rape of Lucrece*.

76

She vow'd she never would see Juan more,
   And next day paid a visit to his mother,
And look'd extremely at the opening door,
   Which, by the Virgin's grace, let in another;
605 Grateful she was, and yet a little sore—
   Again it opens, it can be no other,
'Tis surely Juan now—No! I'm afraid
That night the Virgin was no further pray'd.

77

She now determined that a virtuous woman
610   Should rather face and overcome temptation,
That flight was base and dastardly, and no man
   Should ever give her heart the least sensation;
That is to say, a thought beyond the common
   Preference, that we must feel upon occasion,
615 For people who are pleasanter than others,
But then they only seem so many brothers.

78

And even if by chance—and who can tell?
   The devil's so very sly—she should discover
That all within was not so very well,
620   And, if still free, that such or such a lover
Might please perhaps, a virtuous wife can quell
   Such thoughts, and be the better when they're over;
And if the man should ask, 'tis but denial:
I recommend young ladies to make trial.

79

625 And then there are such things as love divine,
   Bright and immaculate, unmix'd and pure,
Such as the angels think so very fine,
   And matrons, who would be no less secure,
Platonic, perfect, "just such love as mine":
630   Thus Julia said—and thought so, to be sure,
And so I'd have her think, were I the man
On whom her reveries celestial ran.

            *   *   *

86

So much for Julia. Now we'll turn to Juan,
   Poor little fellow! he had no idea
Of his own case, and never hit the true one;
   In feelings quick as Ovid's Miss Medea,[6]
685 He puzzled over what he found a new one,
   But not as yet imagined it could be a

---

6. In *Metamorphoses* 7 Ovid tells the story of Medea's mad infatuation for Jason.

Thing quite in course, and not at all alarming,
Which, with a little patience, might grow charming.

* * *

90

Young Juan wander'd by the glassy brooks
   Thinking unutterable things; he threw
715 Himself at length within the leafy nooks
   Where the wild branch of the cork forest grew;
There poets find materials for their books,
   And every now and then we read them through,
So that their plan and prosody are eligible,
720 Unless, like Wordsworth, they prove unintelligible.

91

He, Juan (and not Wordsworth), so pursued
   His self-communion with his own high soul,
Until his mighty heart, in its great mood,
   Had mitigated part, though not the whole
725 Of its disease; he did the best he could
   With things not very subject to control,
And turn'd, without perceiving his condition,
Like Coleridge, into a metaphysician.

92

He thought about himself, and the whole earth,
730   Of man the wonderful, and of the stars,
And how the deuce they ever could have birth;
   And then he thought of earthquakes, and of wars,
How many miles the moon might have in girth,
   Of air-balloons, and of the many bars
735 To perfect knowledge of the boundless skies;
And then he thought of Donna Julia's eyes.

93

In thoughts like these true wisdom may discern
   Longings sublime, and aspirations high,
Which some are born with, but the most part learn
740   To plague themselves withal, they know not why:
'Twas strange that one so young should thus concern
   His brain about the action of the sky;
If *you* think 'twas philosophy that this did,
I can't help thinking puberty assisted.

94

745 He pored upon the leaves, and on the flowers,
   And heard a voice in all the winds; and then
He thought of wood nymphs and immortal bowers,
   And how the goddesses came down to men:
He miss'd the pathway, he forgot the hours,
750   And when he look'd upon his watch again,

He found how much old Time had been a winner—
He also found that he had lost his dinner.

*   *   *

103

'Twas on a summer's day—the sixth of June:—
   I like to be particular in dates,
Not only of the age, and year, but moon;
820   They are a sort of post-house, where the Fates
Change horses, making history change its tune,
   Then spur away o'er empires and o'er states,
Leaving at last not much besides chronology,
Excepting the post-obits[7] of theology.

104

825 'Twas on the sixth of June, about the hour
   Of half-past six—perhaps still nearer seven,
When Julia sate within as pretty a bower
   As e'er held houri in that heathenish heaven
Described by Mahomet, and Anacreon Moore,[8]
830   To whom the lyre and laurels have been given,
With all the trophies of triumphant song—
He won them well, and may he wear them long!

105

She sate, but not alone; I know not well
   How this same interview had taken place,
835 And even if I knew, I should not tell—
   People should hold their tongues in any case;
No matter how or why the thing befell,
   But there were she and Juan, face to face—
When two such faces are so, 'twould be wise,
840 But very difficult, to shut their eyes.

106

How beautiful she look'd! her conscious[9] heart
   Glow'd in her cheek, and yet she felt no wrong.
Oh Love! how perfect is thy mystic art,
   Strengthening the weak, and trampling on the strong,
845 How self-deceitful is the sagest part
   Of mortals whom thy lure hath led along—
The precipice she stood on was immense,
So was her creed° in her own innocence.   *belief*

107

She thought of her own strength, and Juan's youth,
850   And of the folly of all prudish fears,

---

7. I.e., postobit bonds (*post obitum,* "after death" [Latin]): loans to an heir that fall due after the death of the person whose estate he or she is to inherit. Byron's meaning is probably that only theology purports to tell us what rewards are due in heaven.

8. Byron's friend the poet Thomas Moore, who had translated the *Odes* of Anacreon. Byron is alluding to the tale of *Paradise and the Peri* in Moore's Oriental poem *Lalla Rookh.*
9. Inwardly aware (of her feelings).

Victorious virtue, and domestic truth,
  And then of Don Alfonso's fifty years:
I wish these last had not occurr'd, in sooth,
  Because that number rarely much endears,
855   And through all climes, the snowy and the sunny,
  Sounds ill in love, whate'er it may in money.

* * *

113

The sun set, and up rose the yellow moon:
  The devil's in the moon for mischief; they
Who call'd her CHASTE, methinks, began too soon
900   Their nomenclature; there is not a day,
The longest, not the twenty-first of June,
  Sees half the business in a wicked way
On which three single hours of moonshine smile—
And then she looks so modest all the while.

114

905 There is a dangerous silence in that hour,
  A stillness, which leaves room for the full soul
To open all itself, without the power
  Of calling wholly back its self-control;
The silver light which, hallowing tree and tower,
910   Sheds beauty and deep softness o'er the whole,
Breathes also to the heart, and o'er it throws
A loving languor, which is not repose.

115

And Julia sate with Juan, half embraced
  And half retiring from the glowing arm,
915 Which trembled like the bosom where 'twas placed;
  Yet still she must have thought there was no harm,
Or else 'twere easy to withdraw her waist;
  But then the situation had its charm,
And then—God knows what next—I can't go on;
920 I'm almost sorry that I e'er begun.

116

Oh Plato! Plato! you have paved the way,
  With your confounded fantasies, to more
Immoral conduct by the fancied sway
  Your system feigns o'er the controlless core
925 Of human hearts, than all the long array
  Of poets and romancers:—You're a bore,
A charlatan, a coxcomb—and have been,
At best, no better than a go-between.

117

And Julia's voice was lost, except in sighs,
930   Until too late for useful conversation;

The tears were gushing from her gentle eyes,
　　I wish, indeed, they had not had occasion,
But who, alas! can love, and then be wise?
　　Not that remorse did not oppose temptation,
935　A little still she strove, and much repented,
　　And whispering "I will ne'er consent"—consented.

* * *

126

'Tis sweet to win, no matter how, one's laurels
　　By blood or ink; 'tis sweet to put an end
To strife; 'tis sometimes sweet to have our quarrels,
　　Particularly with a tiresome friend;
1005　Sweet is old wine in bottles, ale in barrels;
　　Dear is the helpless creature we defend
Against the world; and dear the schoolboy spot
We ne'er forget, though there we are forgot.

127

But sweeter still than this, than these, than all,
1010　Is first and passionate love—it stands alone,
Like Adam's recollection of his fall;
　　The tree of knowledge has been pluck'd—all's known—
And life yields nothing further to recall
　　Worthy of this ambrosial sin, so shown,
1015　No doubt in fable, as the unforgiven
Fire which Prometheus[1] filch'd for us from heaven.

* * *

133

Man's a phenomenon, one knows not what,
　　And wonderful beyond all wondrous measure;
'Tis pity though, in this sublime world, that
1060　Pleasure's a sin, and sometimes sin's a pleasure;
Few mortals know what end they would be at,
　　But whether glory, power, or love, or treasure,
The path is through perplexing ways, and when
The goal is gain'd, we die, you know—and then—

134

1065　What then?—I do not know, no more do you—
　　And so good night.—Return we to our story:
'Twas in November, when fine days are few,
　　And the far mountains wax a little hoary,
And clap a white cape on their mantles blue;
1070　And the sea dashes round the promontory,
And the loud breaker boils against the rock,
And sober suns must set at five o'clock.

---

1. The Titan Prometheus incurred the wrath of Zeus by stealing fire from heaven for humans.

135

'Twas, as the watchmen say, a cloudy night;
    No moon, no stars, the wind was low or loud
1075 By gusts, and many a sparkling hearth was bright
    With the piled wood, round which the family crowd;
There's something cheerful in that sort of light,
    Even as a summer sky's without a cloud:
I'm fond of fire, and crickets, and all that,
1080 A lobster-salad, and champagne, and chat.

136

'Twas midnight—Donna Julia was in bed,
    Sleeping, most probably—when at her door
Arose a clatter might awake the dead,
    If they had never been awoke before,
1085 And that they have been so we all have read,
    And are to be so, at the least, once more—
The door was fasten'd, but with voice and fist
First knocks were heard, then "Madam—Madam—hist!

137

"For God's sake, Madam—Madam—here's my master,
1090   With more than half the city at his back—
Was ever heard of such a curst disaster!
    'Tis not my fault—I kept good watch—Alack!
Do, pray undo the bolt a little faster—
    They're on the stair just now, and in a crack
1095 Will all be here; perhaps he yet may fly—
Surely the window's not so *very* high!"

138

By this time Don Alfonso was arrived,
    With torches, friends, and servants in great number;
The major part of them had long been wived,
1100   And therefore paused not to disturb the slumber
Of any wicked woman, who contrived
    By stealth her husband's temples to encumber:[2]
Examples of this kind are so contagious,
Were one not punish'd, all would be outrageous.

139

1105 I can't tell how, or why, or what suspicion
    Could enter into Don Alfonso's head;
But for a cavalier of his condition°   rank
    It surely was exceedingly ill-bred
Without a word of previous admonition,
1110   To hold a levee[3] round his lady's bed,
And summon lackeys, arm'd with fire and sword,
To prove himself the thing he most abhorr'd.

---

2. Horns growing on the forehead were the tra-   3. Morning reception.
ditional emblem of the cuckolded husband.

140

Poor Donna Julia! starting as from sleep,
  (Mind—that I do not say—she had not slept)
1115 Began at once to scream, and yawn, and weep;
  Her maid Antonia, who was an adept,
Contrived to fling the bed-clothes in a heap,
  As if she had just now from out them crept:
I can't tell why she should take all this trouble
1120 To prove her mistress had been sleeping double.

141

But Julia mistress, and Antonia maid,
  Appear'd like two poor harmless women, who
Of goblins, but still more of men afraid,
  Had thought one man might be deterr'd by two,
1125 And therefore side by side were gently laid,
  Until the hours of absence should run through,
And truant husband should return, and say,
"My dear, I was the first who came away."

142

Now Julia found at length a voice, and cried,
1130 "In heaven's name, Don Alfonso, what d'ye mean?
Has madness seized you? would that I had died
  Ere such a monster's victim I had been!
What may this midnight violence betide,
  A sudden fit of drunkenness or spleen?
1135 Dare you suspect me, whom the thought would kill?
Search, then, the room!"—Alfonso said, "I will."

143

He search'd, *they* search'd, and rummaged every where,
  Closet and clothes'-press, chest and window-seat,
And found much linen, lace, and seven pair
1140 Of stockings, slippers, brushes, combs, complete,
With other articles of ladies fair,
  To keep them beautiful, or leave them neat:
Arras[4] they prick'd and curtains with their swords,
And wounded several shutters, and some boards.

144

1145 Under the bed they search'd, and there they found—
  No matter what—it was not that they sought;
They open'd windows, gazing if the ground
  Had signs or footmarks, but the earth said nought;
And then they stared each others' faces round:
1150 'Tis odd, not one of all these seekers thought,
And seems to me almost a sort of blunder,
Of looking *in* the bed as well as under.

4. A tapestry hanging on a wall.

145

During this inquisition Julia's tongue
   Was not asleep—"Yes, search and search," she cried,
1155 "Insult on insult heap, and wrong on wrong!
   It was for this that I became a bride!
For this in silence I have suffer'd long
   A husband like Alfonso at my side;
But now I'll bear no more, nor here remain,
1160 If there be law, or lawyers, in all Spain."

146

"Yes, Don Alfonso! husband now no more,
   If ever you indeed deserved the name,
Is't worthy of your years?—you have threescore,
   Fifty, or sixty—it is all the same—
1165 Is't wise or fitting causeless to explore
   For facts against a virtuous woman's fame?
Ungrateful, perjured, barbarous Don Alfonso,
How dare you think your lady would go on so?"

         *   *   *

159

1265 The Senhor Don Alfonso stood confused;
   Antonia bustled round the ransack'd room,
And, turning up her nose, with looks abused
   Her master, and his myrmidons, of whom
Not one, except the attorney, was amused;
1270 He, like Achates,[5] faithful to the tomb,
So there were quarrels, cared not for the cause,
Knowing they must be settled by the laws.

160

With prying snub-nose, and small eyes, he stood,
   Following Antonia's motions here and there,
1275 With much suspicion in his attitude;
   For reputations he had little care;
So that a suit or action were made good,
   Small pity had he for the young and fair,
And ne'er believed in negatives, till these
1280 Were proved by competent false witnesses.

161

But Don Alfonso stood with downcast looks,
   And, truth to say, he made a foolish figure;
When, after searching in five hundred nooks,
   And treating a young wife with so much rigour,
1285 He gain'd no point, except some self-rebukes,
   Added to those his lady with such vigour

---

5. The *fidus Achates* ("faithful Achates") of Virgil's *Aeneid,* whose loyalty to Aeneas has become proverbial.

Had pour'd upon him for the last half-hour,
Quick, thick, and heavy—as a thunder-shower.

162

At first he tried to hammer an excuse,
1290   To which the sole reply was tears, and sobs,
And indications of hysterics, whose
     Prologue is always certain throes, and throbs,
Gasps, and whatever else the owners choose:—
     Alfonso saw his wife, and thought of Job's;[6]
1295   He saw too, in perspective, her relations,
And then he tried to muster all his patience.

163

He stood in act to speak, or rather stammer,
     But sage Antonia cut him short before
The anvil of his speech received the hammer,
1300   With "Pray sir, leave the room, and say no more,
Or madam dies."—Alfonso mutter'd "D—n her,"
     But nothing else, the time of words was o'er;
He cast a rueful look or two, and did,
He knew not wherefore, that which he was bid.

164

1305   With him retired his *"posse comitatus,"*[7]
     The attorney last, who linger'd near the door,
Reluctantly, still tarrying there as late as
     Antonia let him—not a little sore
At this most strange and unexplain'd *"hiatus"*
1310   In Don Alfonso's facts, which just now wore
An awkward look; as he resolved the case
The door was fasten'd in his legal face.

165

No sooner was it bolted, than—Oh shame!
     Oh sin! Oh sorrow! and Oh womankind!
1315   How can you do such things and keep your fame,
     Unless this world, and t'other too, be blind?
Nothing so dear as an unfilch'd good name!
     But to proceed—for there is more behind:
With much heart-felt reluctance be it said,
1320   Young Juan slipp'd, half-smother'd, from the bed.

166

He had been hid—I don't pretend to say
     How, nor can I indeed describe the where—
Young, slender, and pack'd easily, he lay,

6. Job's wife had advised her afflicted husband to "curse God, and die" (Job 2.9).
7. The complete form of the modern word *posse* (*posse comitatus* means literally "power of the county" [Latin], i.e., the body of citizens summoned by a sheriff to preserve order in the county).

No doubt, in little compass, round or square;
1325 But pity him I neither must nor may
His suffocation by that pretty pair;
'Twere better, sure, to die so, than be shut
With maudlin Clarence in his Malmsey butt.[8]

* * *

169

1345 What's to be done? Alfonso will be back
The moment he has sent his fools away.
Antonia's skill was put upon the rack,
But no device could be brought into play—
And how to parry the renew'd attack?
1350 Besides, it wanted but few hours of day:
Antonia puzzled; Julia did not speak,
But press'd her bloodless lip to Juan's cheek.

170

He turn'd his lip to hers, and with his hand
Call'd back the tangles of her wandering hair;
1355 Even then their love they could not all command,
And half forgot their danger and despair:
Antonia's patience now was at a stand—
"Come, come, 'tis no time now for fooling there,"
She whisper'd, in great wrath—"I must deposit
1360 This pretty gentleman within the closet."

* * *

173

Now, Don Alfonso entering, but alone,
Closed the oration of the trusty maid:
She loiter'd, and he told her to be gone,
1380 An order somewhat sullenly obey'd;
However, present remedy was none,
And no great good seem'd answer'd if she staid:
Regarding both with slow and sidelong view,
She snuff'd the candle, curtsied, and withdrew.

174

1385 Alfonso paused a minute—then begun
Some strange excuses for his late proceeding;
He would not justify what he had done,
To say the best, it was extreme ill-breeding;
But there were ample reasons for it, none
1390 Of which he specified in this his pleading:
His speech was a fine sample, on the whole,
Of rhetoric, which the learn'd call "rigmarole."[9]

* * *

8. Clarence, brother of Edward IV and of the
future Richard III, was reputed to have been assassinated by being drowned in a cask ("butt") of
malmsey, a sweet and aromatic wine.
9. Illogical sequence of vague statements.

180

Alfonso closed his speech, and begg'd her pardon,
 Which Julia half withheld, and then half granted,
1435 And laid conditions, he thought, very hard on,
 Denying several little things he wanted:
He stood like Adam lingering near his garden,
 With useless penitence perplex'd and haunted,
Beseeching she no further would refuse,
1440 When lo! he stumbled o'er a pair of shoes.

181

A pair of shoes!—what then? not much, if they
 Are such as fit with lady's feet, but these
(No one can tell how much I grieve to say)
 Were masculine; to see them, and to seize,
1445 Was but a moment's act.—Ah! Well-a-day!
 My teeth begin to chatter, my veins freeze—
Alfonso first examined well their fashion,
And then flew out into another passion.

182

He left the room for his relinquish'd sword,
1450 And Julia instant to the closet flew,
"Fly, Juan, fly! for heaven's sake—not a word—
 The door is open—you may yet slip through
The passage you so often have explored—
 Here is the garden-key—Fly—fly—Adieu!
1455 Haste—haste!—I hear Alfonso's hurrying feet—
Day has not broke—there's no one in the street."

183

None can say that this was not good advice,
 The only mischief was, it came too late;
Of all experience 'tis the usual price,
1460 A sort of income-tax laid on by fate:
Juan had reach'd the room-door in a trice,
 And might have done so by the garden-gate,
But met Alfonso in his dressing-gown,
Who threaten'd death—so Juan knock'd him down.

184

1465 Dire was the scuffle, and out went the light,
 Antonia cried out "Rape!" and Julia "Fire!"
But not a servant stirr'd to aid the fight.
 Alfonso, pommell'd to his heart's desire,
Swore lustily he'd be revenged this night;
1470 And Juan, too, blasphemed an octave higher,
His blood was up; though young, he was a Tartar,[1]
And not at all disposed to prove a martyr.

---

1. A formidable opponent.

185

Alfonso's sword had dropp'd ere he could draw it,
  And they continued battling hand to hand,
1475 For Juan very luckily ne'er saw it;
  His temper not being under great command,
If at that moment he had chanced to claw it,
  Alfonso's days had not been in the land
Much longer.—Think of husbands', lovers' lives!
1480 And how ye may be doubly widows—wives!

186

Alfonso grappled to detain the foe,
  And Juan throttled him to get away,
And blood ('twas from the nose) began to flow;
  At last, as they more faintly wrestling lay,
1485 Juan contrived to give an awkward blow,
  And then his only garment quite gave way;
He fled, like Joseph,[2] leaving it; but there,
I doubt, all likeness ends between the pair.

187

Lights came at length, and men, and maids, who found
1490   An awkward spectacle their eyes before;
Antonia in hysterics, Julia swoon'd,
  Alfonso leaning, breathless, by the door;
Some half-torn drapery scatter'd on the ground,
  Some blood, and several footsteps, but no more:
1495 Juan the gate gain'd, turn'd the key about,
And liking not the inside, lock'd the out.

188

Here ends this canto.—Need I sing, or say,
  How Juan, naked, favour'd by the night,
Who favours what she should not, found his way,
1500   And reach'd his home in an unseemly plight?
The pleasant scandal which arose next day,
  The nine days' wonder which was brought to light,
And how Alfonso sued for a divorce,
Were in the English newspapers, of course.

189

1505 If you would like to see the whole proceedings,
  The depositions, and the cause at full,
The names of all the witnesses, the pleadings
  Of counsel to nonsuit,[3] or to annul,
There's more than one edition, and the readings
1510   Are various, but they none of them are dull,

---

2. In Genesis 39.7ff. the chaste Joseph flees from the advances of Potiphar's wife, leaving "his garment in her hand."

3. Judgment against the plaintiff for failure to establish his case.

The best is that in shorthand ta'en by Gurney,[4]
Who to Madrid on purpose made a journey.

190

But Donna Inez, to divert the train
   Of one of the most circulating scandals
1515 That had for centuries been known in Spain,
     Since Roderic's Goths, or older Genseric's Vandals,[5]
First vow'd (and never had she vow'd in vain)
   To Virgin Mary several pounds of candles;
And then, by the advice of some old ladies,
1520 She sent her son to be embark'd at Cadiz.

191

She had resolved that he should travel through
   All European climes, by land or sea,
To mend his former morals, or get new,
   Especially in France and Italy,
1525 (At least this is the thing most people do).
   Julia was sent into a nunnery,
And there, perhaps, her feelings may be better
Shown in the following copy of her letter:

192

"They tell me 'tis decided; you depart:
1530   'Tis wise—'tis well, but not the less a pain;
I have no further claim on your young heart,
   Mine was the victim, and would be again;
To love too much has been the only art
   I used;—I write in haste, and if a stain
1535 Be on this sheet, 'tis not what it appears,
My eyeballs burn and throb, but have no tears.

193

"I loved, I love you, for that love have lost
   State, station, heaven, mankind's, my own esteem,
And yet can not regret what it hath cost,
1540   So dear is still the memory of that dream;
Yet, if I name my guilt, 'tis not to boast,
   None can deem harshlier of me than I deem:
I trace this scrawl because I cannot rest—
I've nothing to reproach, nor to request.

194

1545 "Man's love is of his life a thing apart,
   'Tis woman's whole existence; man may range
The court, camp, church, the vessel, and the mart,

---

4. William B. Gurney (1777–1855), official short-hand writer for the houses of Parliament and a famous court reporter.

5. The Germanic tribes that overran Spain and other parts of southern Europe in the 5th through 8th centuries, notorious for rape and violence.

Sword, gown, gain, glory, offer in exchange
Pride, fame, ambition, to fill up his heart,
1550   And few there are whom these can not estrange;
Man has all these resources, we but one,
To love again, and be again undone.

195

"My breast has been all weakness, is so yet;
    I struggle, but cannot collect my mind;
1555 My blood still rushes where my spirit's set,
    As roll the waves before the settled wind;
My brain is feminine, nor can forget—
    To all, except your image, madly blind;
As turns the needle[6] trembling to the pole
1560 It ne'er can reach, so turns to you, my soul.

196

"You will proceed in beauty, and in pride,
    Beloved and loving many; all is o'er
For me on earth, except some years to hide
    My shame and sorrow deep in my heart's core;
1565 These I could bear, but cannot cast aside
    The passion which still rends it as before,
And so farewell—forgive me, love me—No,
That word is idle now—but let it go.

197

"I have no more to say, but linger still,
1570   And dare not set my seal upon this sheet,
And yet I may as well the task fulfil,
    My misery can scarce be more complete:
I had not lived till now, could sorrow kill;
    Death flies the wretch who fain the blow would meet,
1575 And I must even survive this last adieu,
And bear with life, to love and pray for you!"

198

This note was written upon gilt-edged paper
    With a neat crow-quill, rather hard, but new;
Her small white fingers scarce could reach the taper,[7]
1580   But trembled as magnetic needles do,
And yet she did not let one tear escape her;
    The seal a sunflower; *"Elle vous suit partout,"*[8]
The motto, cut upon a white cornelian;
The wax was superfine, its hue vermilion.

199

1585 This was Don Juan's earliest scrape; but whether
    I shall proceed with his adventures is

---

6. Of a compass.
7. The candle (to melt wax to seal the letter).

8. She follows you everywhere (French).

Dependent on the public altogether;
   We'll see, however, what they say to this,
Their favour in an author's cap's a feather,
1590   And no great mischief's done by their caprice;
And if their approbation we experience,
   Perhaps they'll have some more about a year hence.

200

My poem's epic, and is meant to be
   Divided in twelve books; each book containing,
1595 With love, and war, a heavy gale at sea,
   A list of ships, and captains, and kings reigning,
New characters; the episodes are three:
   A panorama view of hell's in training,
After the style of Virgil and of Homer,
1600 So that my name of Epic's no misnomer.

201

All these things will be specified in time,
   With strict regard to Aristotle's rules,
The *vade mecum*[9] of the true sublime,
   Which makes so many poets, and some fools;
1605 Prose poets like blank-verse, I'm fond of rhyme,
   Good workmen never quarrel with their tools;
I've got new mythological machinery,
And very handsome supernatural scenery.

202

There's only one slight difference between
1610   Me and my epic brethren gone before,
And here the advantage is my own, I ween;
   (Not that I have not several merits more,
But this will more peculiarly be seen)
   They so embellish, that 'tis quite a bore
1615 Their labyrinth of fables to thread through,
Whereas this story's actually true.

203

If any person doubt it, I appeal
   To history, tradition, and to facts,
To newspapers, whose truth all know and feel,
1620   To plays in five, and operas in three acts;
All these confirm my statement a good deal,
   But that which more completely faith exacts
Is, that myself, and several now in Seville,
Saw Juan's last elopement with the devil.[1]

9. Go with me (Latin, literal trans.); handbook. Byron is deriding the neoclassic view that Aristotle's *Poetics* proposes "rules" for writing epic and tragedy.

1. The usual plays on the Juan legend ended with Juan in hell; an early-20th-century version is Bernard Shaw's *Man and Superman*.

204

1625 If ever I should condescend to prose,
　　　　I'll write poetical commandments, which
　　　Shall supersede beyond all doubt all those
　　　　That went before; in these I shall enrich
　　　My text with many things that no one knows,
1630　　And carry precept to the highest pitch:
　　　I'll call the work "Longinus o'er a Bottle,
　　　Or, Every Poet his *own* Aristotle."

205

　　　Thou shalt believe in Milton, Dryden, Pope;[2]
　　　　Thou shalt not set up Wordsworth, Coleridge, Southey;
1635　Because the first is crazed beyond all hope,
　　　　The second drunk, the third so quaint and mouthey:
　　　With Crabbe it may be difficult to cope,
　　　　And Campbell's Hippocrene[3] is somewhat drouthy:
　　　Thou shalt not steal from Samuel Rogers, nor—
1640　Commit—flirtation with the muse of Moore.

206

　　　Thou shalt not covet Mr. Sotheby's Muse,
　　　　His Pegasus,[4] nor any thing that's his;
　　　Thou shalt not bear false witness like "the Blues,"[5]
　　　　(There's one, at least, is very fond of this);
1645　Thou shalt not write, in short, but what I choose:
　　　　This is true criticism, and you may kiss—
　　　Exactly as you please, or not, the rod,
　　　But if you don't, I'll lay it on, by G—d!

207

　　　If any person should presume to assert
1650　　This story is not moral, first I pray
　　　That they will not cry out before they're hurt,
　　　　Then that they'll read it o'er again, and say,
　　　(But, doubtless, nobody will be so pert)
　　　　That this is not a moral tale, though gay;
1655　Besides, in canto twelfth, I mean to show
　　　The very place where wicked people go.

　　　　　　　　＊　＊　＊

213

　　　But now at thirty years my hair is gray—
　　　　(I wonder what it will be like at forty?
　　　I thought of a peruke° the other day)　　　　　　　　　　*wig*
1700　　My heart is not much greener; and, in short, I

---

2. This is one of many passages, in prose and verse, in which Byron vigorously defended Dryden and Pope against his Romantic contemporaries.
3. Fountain on Mount Helicon whose waters supposedly gave inspiration. George Crabbe, whom Byron admired, was the author of *The Village* and other realistic poems of rural life. Thomas Campbell, Samuel Rogers, and Thomas Moore (below)

were lesser poets of the Romantic period; the last two were close friends of Byron's.
4. The winged horse symbolizing poetic inspiration. William Sotheby, contemporary poet and translator, was a wealthy man (see line 1642).
5. I.e., bluestockings, a contemporary term for pedantic female intellectuals, among whom Byron numbered his wife (line 1644).

Have squander'd my whole summer while 'twas May,
  And feel no more the spirit to retort; I
Have spent my life, both interest and principal,
And deem not, what I deem'd, my soul invincible.

214

1705 No more—no more—Oh! never more on me
  The freshness of the heart can fall like dew,
Which out of all the lovely things we see
  Extracts emotions beautiful and new,
Hived in our bosoms like the bag o' the bee:
1710 Think'st thou the honey with those objects grew?
Alas! 'twas not in them, but in thy power
To double even the sweetness of a flower.

215

No more—no more—Oh! never more, my heart,
  Canst thou be my sole world, my universe!
1715 Once all in all, but now a thing apart,
  Thou canst not be my blessing or my curse:
The illusion's gone for ever, and thou art
  Insensible, I trust, but none the worse,
And in thy stead I've got a deal of judgment,
1720 Though heaven knows how it ever found a lodgement.

216

My days of love are over, me no more
  The charms of maid, wife, and still less of widow,
Can make the fool of which they made before,
  In short, I must not lead the life I did do;
1725 The credulous hope of mutual minds is o'er,
  The copious use of claret is forbid too,
So for a good old gentlemanly vice,
I think I must take up with avarice.

217

Ambition was my idol, which was broken
1730 Before the shrines of Sorrow and of Pleasure;
And the two last have left me many a token
  O'er which reflection may be made at leisure:
Now, like Friar Bacon's brazen head, I've spoken,
  "Time is, Time was, Time's past,"⁶ a chymic treasure⁷
1735 Is glittering youth, which I have spent betimes—
My heart in passion, and my head on rhymes.

218

What is the end of fame? 'tis but to fill
  A certain portion of uncertain paper:
Some liken it to climbing up a hill,

---

6. Spoken by a bronze bust in Robert Greene's comedy *Friar Bacon and Friar Bungay* (1594).

7. "Chymic": alchemic; i.e., the "treasure" is counterfeit gold.

1740 Whose summit, like all hills', is lost in vapour;
For this men write, speak, preach, and heroes kill,
And bards burn what they call their "midnight taper,"
To have, when the original is dust,
A name, a wretched picture, and worse bust.[8]

219

1745 What are the hopes of man? old Egypt's King
Cheops erected the first pyramid
And largest, thinking it was just the thing
To keep his memory whole, and mummy hid;
But somebody or other rummaging,
1750 Burglariously broke his coffin's lid:
Let not a monument give you or me hopes,
Since not a pinch of dust remains of Cheops.

220

But I, being fond of true philosophy,
Say very often to myself, "Alas!
1755 All things that have been born were born to die,
And flesh (which Death mows down to hay) is grass;
You've pass'd your youth not so unpleasantly,
And if you had it o'er again—'twould pass—
So thank your stars that matters are no worse,
1760 And read your Bible, sir, and mind your purse."

221

But for the present, gentle reader! and
Still gentler purchaser! the bard—that's I—
Must, with permission, shake you by the hand,
And so your humble servant, and good bye!
1765 We meet again, if we should understand
Each other; and if not, I shall not try
Your patience further than by this short sample—
'Twere well if others follow'd my example.

222

"Go, little book, from this my solitude!
1770 I cast thee on the waters, go thy ways!
And if, as I believe, thy vein be good,
The world will find thee after many days."
When Southey's read, and Wordsworth understood,
I can't help putting in my claim to praise—
1775 The four first rhymes are Southey's every line:[9]
For God's sake, reader! take them not for mine.

---

8. Byron was unhappy with the portrait bust of him recently made by the Danish sculptor Thorwaldsen.

9. The lines occur in the last stanza of Southey's *Epilogue to the Lay of the Laureate.*

From Canto 2

[THE SHIPWRECK]

8

But to our tale: the Donna Inez sent
   Her son to Cadiz only to embark;
To stay there had not answer'd her intent,
60   But why?—we leave the reader in the dark—
'Twas for a voyage that the young man was meant,
   As if a Spanish ship were Noah's ark,
To wean him from the wickedness of earth,
And send him like a dove of promise forth.

9

65 Don Juan bade his valet pack his things
   According to direction, then received
A lecture and some money: for four springs
   He was to travel; and though Inez grieved,
(As every kind of parting has its stings)
70   She hoped he would improve—perhaps believed:
A letter, too, she gave (he never read it)
Of good advice—and two or three of credit.

10

In the mean time, to pass her hours away,
   Brave Inez now set up a Sunday school
75 For naughty children, who would rather play
   (Like truant rogues) the devil, or the fool;
Infants of three years old were taught that day,
   Dunces were whipt, or set upon a stool:
The great success of Juan's education,
80 Spurr'd her to teach another generation.

11

Juan embark'd—the ship got under way,
   The wind was fair, the water passing rough;
A devil of a sea rolls in that bay,
   As I, who've cross'd it oft, know well enough;
85 And, standing upon deck, the dashing spray
   Flies in one's face, and makes it weather-tough:
And there he stood to take, and take again,
His first—perhaps his last—farewell of Spain.

12

I can't but say it is an awkward sight
90   To see one's native land receding through
The growing waters; it unmans one quite,
   Especially when life is rather new:
I recollect Great Britain's coast looks white,
   But almost every other country's blue,

95 When gazing on them, mystified by distance,
  We enter on our nautical existence.

*   *   *

17

 And Juan wept, and much he sigh'd and thought,
130 While his salt tears dropp'd into the salt sea,
 "Sweets to the sweet"; (I like so much to quote;
  You must excuse this extract, 'tis where she,
 The Queen of Denmark, for Ophelia brought
  Flowers to the grave);[1] and sobbing often, he
135 Reflected on his present situation,
 And seriously resolved on reformation.

18

 "Farewell, my Spain! a long farewell!" he cried,
  "Perhaps I may revisit thee no more,
 But die, as many an exiled heart hath died,
140 Of its own thirst to see again thy shore:
 Farewell, where Guadalquivir's waters glide!
  Farewell, my mother! and, since all is o'er,
 Farewell, too dearest Julia!,"—(here he drew
 Her letter out again, and read it through).

19

145 "And oh! if e'er I should forget, I swear—
  But that's impossible, and cannot be—
 Sooner shall this blue ocean melt to air,
  Sooner shall earth resolve itself to sea,
 Than I resign thine image, Oh! my fair!
150 Or think of any thing excepting thee;
 A mind diseased no remedy can physic—"
 (Here the ship gave a lurch, and he grew sea-sick.)

20

 "Sooner shall heaven kiss earth"—(here he fell sicker)
  "Oh, Julia! what is every other woe?—
155 (For God's sake let me have a glass of liquor,
  Pedro, Battista, help me down below.)
 Julia, my love!—(you rascal, Pedro, quicker)—
  Oh Julia!—(this curst vessel pitches so)—
 Beloved Julia, hear me still beseeching!"
160 (Here he grew inarticulate with retching.)

21

 He felt that chilling heaviness of heart,
  Or rather stomach, which, alas! attends,
 Beyond the best apothecary's art,
  The loss of love, the treachery of friends,

---

1. *Hamlet* 5.1.227.

165 Or death of those we doat on, when a part
　　　Of us dies with them as each fond hope ends:
　　No doubt he would have been much more pathetic,
　　　But the sea acted as a strong emetic.[2]

＊　＊　＊

49

385 'Twas twilight, and the sunless day went down
　　　Over the waste of waters; like a veil,
　　Which, if withdrawn, would but disclose the frown
　　　Of one whose hate is masked but to assail;
　　Thus to their hopeless eyes the night was shown
390　　And grimly darkled o'er their faces pale,
　　And the dim desolate deep; twelve days had Fear
　　Been their familiar, and now Death was here.

50

　　Some trial had been making at a raft,
　　　With little hope in such a rolling sea,
395 A sort of thing at which one would have laugh'd,
　　　If any laughter at such times could be,
　　Unless with people who too much have quaff'd,
　　　And have a kind of wild and horrid glee,
　　Half epileptical, and half hysterical:—
400　Their preservation would have been a miracle.

51

　　At half-past eight o'clock, booms, hencoops, spars,
　　　And all things, for a chance, had been cast loose,
　　That still could keep afloat the struggling tars,
　　　For yet they strove, although of no great use:
405 There was no light in heaven but a few stars,
　　　The boats put off o'ercrowded with their crews;
　　She gave a heel, and then a lurch to port,
　　And, going down head foremost—sunk, in short.

52

　　Then rose from sea to sky the wild farewell,
410　Then shriek'd the timid, and stood still the brave,
　　Then some leap'd overboard with dreadful yell,
　　　As eager to anticipate their grave;
　　And the sea yawn'd around her like a hell,
　　　And down she suck'd with her the whirling wave,
415 Like one who grapples with his enemy,
　　And strives to strangle him before he die.

53

　　And first one universal shriek there rush'd,
　　　Louder than the loud ocean, like a crash

2. In stanzas 22–48 (here omitted) the ship, bound for Leghorn, runs into a violent storm and is battered into a helpless, sinking wreck.

Of echoing thunder; and then all was hush'd,
420   Save the wild wind and the remorseless dash
Of billows; but at intervals there gush'd,
    Accompanied with a convulsive splash,
A solitary shriek, the bubbling cry
Of some strong swimmer in his agony.

*   *   *

56

Juan got into the long-boat, and there
    Contrived to help Pedrillo[3] to a place;
It seem'd as if they had exchanged their care,
    For Juan wore the magisterial face
445 Which courage gives, while poor Pedrillo's pair
    Of eyes were crying for their owner's case:
Battista, though (a name call'd shortly Tita),
Was lost by getting at some aqua-vita.°   *brandy*

57

Pedro, his valet, too, he tried to save,
450   But the same cause, conducive to his loss,
Left him so drunk, he jump'd into the wave
    As o'er the cutter's edge he tried to cross,
And so he found a wine-and-watery grave;
    They could not rescue him although so close,
455 Because the sea ran higher every minute,
And for the boat—the crew kept crowding in it.

*   *   *

66

'Tis thus with people in an open boat,
    They live upon the love of life, and bear
More than can be believed, or even thought,
    And stand like rocks the tempest's wear and tear;
525 And hardship still has been the sailor's lot,
    Since Noah's ark went cruising here and there;
She had a curious crew as well as cargo,
Like the first old Greek privateer, the Argo.[4]

67

But man is a carnivorous production,
530   And must have meals, at least one meal a day;
He cannot live, like woodcocks, upon suction,[5]
    But, like the shark and tiger, must have prey:
Although his anatomical construction
    Bears vegetables in a grumbling way,
535 Your labouring people think beyond all question,
Beef, veal, and mutton, better for digestion.

---

3. Juan's tutor.
4. In the Greek myth the *Argo* is the ship on which Jason set out in quest of the Golden Fleece. Byron ironically calls it a "privateer" (a private ship licensed by a government in wartime to attack and pillage enemy vessels).
5. Woodcocks probe the turf with their long flexible bills, seeming to suck air as they feed.

68

And thus it was with this our hapless crew,
   For on the third day there came on a calm,
And though at first their strength it might renew,
540   And lying on their weariness like balm,
   Lull'd them like turtles sleeping on the blue
    Of ocean, when they woke they felt a qualm,
And fell all ravenously on their provision,
Instead of hoarding it with due precision.

*   *   *

72

The seventh day,[6] and no wind—the burning sun
570   Blister'd and scorch'd, and, stagnant on the sea,
They lay like carcases; and hope was none,
   Save in the breeze that came not; savagely
They glared upon each other—all was done,
   Water, and wine, and food,—and you might see
575 The longings of the cannibal arise
(Although they spoke not) in their wolfish eyes.

73

At length one whisper'd his companion, who
   Whisper'd another, and thus it went round,
And then into a hoarser murmur grew,
580   An ominous, and wild, and desperate sound,
And when his comrade's thought each sufferer knew,
   'Twas but his own, suppress'd till now, he found:
And out they spoke of lots for flesh and blood,
And who should die to be his fellow's food.

74

585 But ere they came to this, they that day shared
   Some leathern caps, and what remain'd of shoes;
And then they look'd around them, and despair'd,
   And none to be the sacrifice would choose;
At length the lots were torn up, and prepared,
590   But of materials that must shock the Muse—
Having no paper, for the want of better,
They took by force from Juan Julia's letter.

75

The lots were made, and mark'd, and mix'd, and handed,
   In silent horror, and their distribution
595 Lull'd even the savage hunger which demanded,
   Like the Promethean vulture,[7] this pollution;
None in particular had sought or plann'd it,

6. On the fourth day the crew had killed and eaten Juan's pet spaniel. Byron based the episode of cannibalism that follows on various historical accounts of disasters at sea.

7. Because Prometheus had stolen fire from heaven to give to humans, Zeus punished him by chaining him to a mountain peak, where an eagle fed on his ever-renewing liver.

'Twas nature gnaw'd them to this resolution,
By which none were permitted to be neuter—
600   And the lot fell on Juan's luckless tutor.

76

He but requested to be bled to death:
    The surgeon had his instruments, and bled
Pedrillo, and so gently ebb'd his breath,
    You hardly could perceive when he was dead.
605   He died as born, a Catholic in faith,
    Like most in the belief in which they're bred,
And first a little crucifix he kiss'd,
And then held out his jugular and wrist.

77

The surgeon, as there was no other fee,
610   Had his first choice of morsels for his pains;
But being thirstiest at the moment, he
    Preferr'd a draught from the fast-flowing veins:
Part was divided, part thrown in the sea,
    And such things as the entrails and the brains
615   Regaled two sharks, who follow'd o'er the billow—
The sailors ate the rest of poor Pedrillo.

78

The sailors ate him, all save three or four,
    Who were not quite so fond of animal food;
To these was added Juan, who, before
620   Refusing his own spaniel, hardly could
Feel now his appetite increased much more;
    'Twas not to be expected that he should,
Even in extremity of their disaster,
Dine with them on his pastor and his master.

79

625   'Twas better that he did not; for, in fact,
    The consequence was awful in the extreme;
For they, who were most ravenous in the act,
    Went raging mad—Lord! how they did blaspheme!
And foam and roll, with strange convulsions rack'd,
630   Drinking salt-water like a mountain-stream,
Tearing, and grinning, howling, screeching, swearing,
And, with hyaena laughter, died despairing.

* * *

103

As they drew nigh the land, which now was seen
    Unequal in its aspect here and there,
They felt the freshness of its growing green,
820   That waved in forest-tops, and smooth'd the air,
And fell upon their glazed eyes like a screen

From glistening waves, and skies so hot and bare—
Lovely seem'd any object that should sweep
Away the vast, salt, dread, eternal deep.

104

825 The shore look'd wild, without a trace of man,
    And girt by formidable waves; but they
Were mad for land, and thus their course they ran,
    Though right ahead the roaring breakers lay:
A reef between them also now began
830   To show its boiling surf and bounding spray,
But finding no place for their landing better,
They ran the boat for shore, and overset her.

105

But in his native stream, the Guadalquivir,
    Juan to lave his youthful limbs was wont;
835 And having learnt to swim in that sweet river,
    Had often turn'd the art to some account:
A better swimmer you could scarce see ever,
    He could, perhaps, have pass'd the Hellespont,
As once (a feat on which ourselves we prided)
840 Leander, Mr. Ekenhead, and I did.[8]

106

So here, though faint, emaciated, and stark,
    He buoy'd his boyish limbs, and strove to ply
With the quick wave, and gain, ere it was dark,
    The beach which lay before him, high and dry:
845 The greatest danger here was from a shark,
    That carried off his neighbour by the thigh;
As for the other two, they could not swim,
So nobody arrived on shore but him.

107

Nor yet had he arrived but for the oar,
850   Which, providentially for him, was wash'd
Just as his feeble arms could strike no more,
    And the hard wave o'erwhelm'd him as 'twas dash'd
Within his grasp; he clung to it, and sore
    The waters beat while he thereto was lash'd;
855 At last, with swimming, wading, scrambling, he
Roll'd on the beach, half senseless, from the sea:

108

There, breathless, with his digging nails he clung
    Fast to the sand, lest the returning wave,
From whose reluctant roar his life he wrung,

8. Like Leander in the myth, Byron and Lieutenant Ekenhead had swum the Hellespont, on May 3, 1810.
See *Written after Swimming from Sestos to Abydos* (p. 555).

860   Should suck him back to her insatiate grave:
    And there he lay, full length, where he was flung,
       Before the entrance of a cliff-worn cave,
    With just enough of life to feel its pain,
    And deem that it was saved, perhaps, in vain.

109

865   With slow and staggering effort he arose,
       But sunk again upon his bleeding knee
    And quivering hand; and then he look'd for those
       Who long had been his mates upon the sea,
    But none of them appear'd to share his woes,
870   Save one, a corpse from out the famish'd three,
    Who died two days before, and now had found
    An unknown barren beach for burial ground.

110

    And as he gazed, his dizzy brain spun fast,
       And down he sunk; and as he sunk, the sand
875   Swam round and round, and all his senses pass'd:
       He fell upon his side, and his stretch'd hand
    Droop'd dripping on the oar, (their jury-mast)
       And, like a wither'd lily, on the land
    His slender frame and pallid aspect lay,
880   As fair a thing as e'er was form'd of clay.

[JUAN AND HAIDEE]

111

    How long in his damp trance young Juan lay
       He knew not, for the earth was gone for him,
    And Time had nothing more of night nor day
       For his congealing blood, and senses dim;
885   And how this heavy faintness pass'd away
       He knew not, till each painful pulse and limb,
    And tingling vein seem'd throbbing back to life,
    For Death, though vanquish'd, still retired with strife.

112

    His eyes he open'd, shut, again unclosed,
890   For all was doubt and dizziness; methought
    He still was in the boat, and had but dozed,
       And felt again with his despair o'erwrought,
    And wish'd it death in which he had reposed,
       And then once more his feelings back were brought,
895   And slowly by his swimming eyes was seen
    A lovely female face of seventeen.

113

    'Twas bending close o'er his, and the small mouth
       Seem'd almost prying into his for breath;

And chafing him, the soft warm hand of youth
900　　Recall'd his answering spirits back from death;
And, bathing his chill temples, tried to soothe
　　Each pulse to animation, till beneath
Its gentle touch and trembling care, a sigh
To these kind efforts made a low reply.

114

905　Then was the cordial pour'd, and mantle flung
　　Around his scarce-clad limbs; and the fair arm
Raised higher the faint head which o'er it hung;
　　And her transparent cheek, all pure and warm,
Pillow'd his death-like forehead; then she wrung
910　　His dewy curls, long drench'd by every storm;
And watch'd with eagerness each throb that drew
A sigh from his heaved bosom—and hers, too.

115

And lifting him with care into the cave,
　　The gentle girl, and her attendant,—one
915　Young, yet her elder, and of brow less grave,
　　And more robust of figure,—then begun
To kindle fire, and as the new flames gave
　　Light to the rocks that roof'd them, which the sun
Had never seen, the maid, or whatsoe'er
920　She was, appear'd distinct, and tall, and fair.

116

Her brow was overhung with coins of gold,
　　That sparkled o'er the auburn of her hair,
Her clustering hair, whose longer locks were roll'd
　　In braids behind, and though her stature were
925　Even of the highest for a female mould,
　　They nearly reach'd her heel; and in her air
There was a something which bespoke command,
As one who was a lady in the land.

117

Her hair, I said, was auburn; but her eyes
930　　Were black as death, their lashes the same hue,
Of downcast length, in whose silk shadow lies
　　Deepest attraction, for when to the view
Forth from its raven fringe the full glance flies,
　　Ne'er with such force the swiftest arrow flew;
935　'Tis as the snake late coil'd, who pours his length,
And hurls at once his venom and his strength.

*　　*　　*

123

And these two tended him, and cheer'd him both
　　With food and raiment, and those soft attentions,

Which are (as I must own) of female growth,
980　　And have ten thousand delicate inventions:
They made a most superior mess of broth,
　　A thing which poesy but seldom mentions,
But the best dish that e'er was cook'd since Homer's
Achilles order'd dinner for new comers.[9]

124

985　I'll tell you who they were, this female pair,
　　Lest they should seem princesses in disguise;
Besides, I hate all mystery, and that air
　　Of clap-trap, which your recent poets prize;
And so, in short, the girls they really were
990　　They shall appear before your curious eyes,
Mistress and maid; the first was only daughter
Of an old man, who lived upon the water.

125

A fisherman he had been in his youth,
　　And still a sort of fisherman was he;
995　But other speculations were, in sooth,
　　Added to his connection with the sea,
Perhaps not so respectable, in truth:
　　A little smuggling, and some piracy,
Left him, at last, the sole of many masters
1000　Of an ill-gotten million of piastres.[1]

126

A fisher, therefore, was he—though of men,
　　Like Peter the Apostle,[2]—and he fish'd
For wandering merchant vessels, now and then,
　　And sometimes caught as many as he wish'd;
1005　The cargoes he confiscated, and gain
　　He sought in the slave-market too, and dish'd
Full many a morsel for that Turkish trade,
By which, no doubt, a good deal may be made.

127

He was a Greek, and on his isle had built
1010　（One of the wild and smaller Cyclades)[3]
A very handsome house from out his guilt,
　　And there he lived exceedingly at ease;
Heaven knows what cash he got, or blood he spilt,
　　A sad[4] old fellow was he, if you please,
1015　But this I know, it was a spacious building,
Full of barbaric carving, paint, and gilding.

9. A reference to the lavish feast with which Achilles entertained Ajax, Phoenix, and Ulysses (*Iliad* 9.193ff.).
1. Near-Eastern coins.
2. Christ's words to Peter and Andrew, both fisher-

men: "Follow me, and I will make you fishers of men" (Matthew 4.19).
3. A group of islands in the Aegean Sea.
4. In the playful sense: wicked.

128

He had an only daughter, call'd Haidee,
   The greatest heiress of the Eastern Isles;
Besides, so very beautiful was she,
1020   Her dowry was as nothing to her smiles:
Still in her teens, and like a lovely tree
   She grew to womanhood, and between whiles
Rejected several suitors, just to learn
How to accept a better in his turn.

129

1025 And walking out upon the beach, below
   The cliff, towards sunset, on that day she found,
Insensible,—not dead, but nearly so,—
   Don Juan, almost famish'd, and half drown'd;
But being naked, she was shock'd, you know,
1030   Yet deem'd herself in common pity bound,
As far as in her lay, "to take him in,
A stranger"[5] dying, with so white a skin.

130

But taking him into her father's house
   Was not exactly the best way to save,
1035 But like conveying to the cat the mouse,
   Or people in a trance into their grave;
Because the good old man had so much "νους,"[6]
   Unlike the honest Arab thieves so brave,
He would have hospitably cured the stranger,
1040 And sold him instantly when out of danger.

131

And therefore, with her maid, she thought it best
   (A virgin always on her maid relies)
To place him in the cave for present rest:
   And when, at last, he open'd his black eyes,
1045 Their charity increased about their guest;
   And their compassion grew to such a size,
It open'd half the turnpike-gates to heaven—
(St. Paul says 'tis the toll which must be given).[7]

*   *   *

141

And Haidee met the morning face to face;
   Her own was freshest, though a feverish flush
Had dyed it with the headlong blood, whose race
   From heart to cheek is curb'd into a blush,
1125 Like to a torrent which a mountain's base,
   That overpowers some Alpine river's rush,

---

5. Cf. Matthew 25.35: "I was a stranger, and ye took me in."
6. *Nous,* "intelligence" (Greek); in England, pro-nounced so as to rhyme with *mouse.*
7. 1 Corinthians 13.13.

Checks to a lake, whose waves in circles spread;
Or the Red Sea—but the sea is not red.

142

And down the cliff the island virgin came,
1130   And near the cave her quick light footsteps drew,
While the sun smiled on her with his first flame,
   And young Aurora° kiss'd her lips with dew,   *dawn*
Taking her for a sister; just the same
   Mistake you would have made on seeing the two,
1135 Although the mortal, quite as fresh and fair,
Had all the advantage too of not being air.

143

And when into the cavern Haidee stepp'd
   All timidly, yet rapidly, she saw
That like an infant Juan sweetly slept;
1140   And then she stopp'd, and stood as if in awe,
(For sleep is awful) and on tiptoe crept
   And wrapt him closer, lest the air, too raw,
Should reach his blood, then o'er him still as death
Bent, with hush'd lips, that drank his scarce-drawn breath.

*   *   *

148

And she bent o'er him, and he lay beneath,
   Hush'd as the babe upon its mother's breast,
Droop'd as the willow when no winds can breathe,
1180   Lull'd like the depth of ocean when at rest,
Fair as the crowning rose of the whole wreath,
   Soft as the callow° cygnet° in its nest;   *young/swan*
In short, he was a very pretty fellow,
Although his woes had turn'd him rather yellow.

149

1185 He woke and gazed, and would have slept again,
   But the fair face which met his eyes forbade
Those eyes to close, though weariness and pain
   Had further sleep a further pleasure made;
For woman's face was never form'd in vain
1190   For Juan, so that even when he pray'd
He turn'd from grisly saints, and martyrs hairy,
To the sweet portraits of the Virgin Mary.

150

And thus upon his elbow he arose,
   And look'd upon the lady, in whose cheek
1195 The pale contended with the purple rose,
   As with an effort she began to speak;
Her eyes were eloquent, her words would pose,
   Although she told him, in good modern Greek,

With an Ionian accent, low and sweet,
1200   That he was faint, and must not talk, but eat.

*   *   *

168

And every day by day-break—rather early
   For Juan, who was somewhat fond of rest—
She came into the cave, but it was merely
1340   To see her bird reposing in his nest;
And she would softly stir his locks so curly,
    Without disturbing her yet slumbering guest,
Breathing all gently o'er his cheek and mouth,
As o'er a bed of roses the sweet south.[8]

169

1345 And every morn his colour freshlier came,
   And every day help'd on his convalescence;
'Twas well, because health in the human frame
   Is pleasant, besides being true love's essence,
For health and idleness to passion's flame
1350   Are oil and gunpowder; and some good lessons
Are also learnt from Ceres[9] and from Bacchus,
Without whom Venus will not long attack us.

170

While Venus fills the heart (without heart really
   Love, though good always, is not quite so good)
1355 Ceres presents a plate of vermicelli,—
   For love must be sustain'd like flesh and blood,—
While Bacchus pours out wine, or hands a jelly:
   Eggs, oysters too, are amatory food;
But who is their purveyor from above
1360 Heaven knows,—it may be Neptune, Pan, or Jove.

171

When Juan woke he found some good things ready,
   A bath, a breakfast, and the finest eyes
That ever made a youthful heart less steady,
   Besides her maid's, as pretty for their size;
1365 But I have spoken of all this already—
   And repetition's tiresome and unwise,—
Well—Juan, after bathing in the sea,
Came always back to coffee and Haidee.

172

Both were so young, and one so innocent,
1370   That bathing pass'd for nothing; Juan seem'd
To her, as 'twere, the kind of being sent,
   Of whom these two years she had nightly dream'd,

---

8. The south wind.   9. Goddess of the grain.

A something to be loved, a creature meant
   To be her happiness, and whom she deem'd
1375 To render happy; all who joy would win
Must share it,—Happiness was born a twin.

173

It was such pleasure to behold him, such
   Enlargement of existence to partake
Nature with him, to thrill beneath his touch,
1380   To watch him slumbering, and to see him wake:
To live with him for ever were too much;
   But then the thought of parting made her quake:
He was her own, her ocean-treasure, cast
Like a rich wreck—her first love, and her last.

174

1385 And thus a moon roll'd on, and fair Haidee
   Paid daily visits to her boy, and took
Such plentiful precautions, that still he
   Remain'd unknown within his craggy nook;
At last her father's prows put out to sea,
1390   For certain merchantmen upon the look,
Not as of yore to carry off an Io,[1]
But three Ragusan vessels, bound for Scio.[2]

175

Then came her freedom, for she had no mother,
   So that, her father being at sea, she was
1395 Free as a married woman, or such other
   Female, as where she likes may freely pass,
Without even the encumbrance of a brother,
   The freest she that ever gazed on glass:
I speak of christian lands in this comparison,
1400 Where wives, at least, are seldom kept in garrison.

176

Now she prolong'd her visits and her talk
   (For they must talk), and he had learnt to say
So much as to propose to take a walk,—
   For little had he wander'd since the day
1405 On which, like a young flower snapp'd from the stalk,
   Drooping and dewy on the beach he lay,—
And thus they walk'd out in the afternoon,
And saw the sun set opposite the moon.

177

It was a wild and breaker-beaten coast,
1410   With cliffs above, and a broad sandy shore,
Guarded by shoals and rocks as by an host,

---

1. A mistress of Zeus who was persecuted by his jealous wife, Hera, and kidnapped by Phoenician merchants.

2. The Italian name for Chios, an island near Turkey. "Ragusan": Ragusa (or Dubrovnik) is an Adriatic port.

With here and there a creek, whose aspect wore
  A better welcome to the tempest-tost;
  And rarely ceas'd the haughty billow's roar,
1415 Save on the dead long summer days, which make
  The outstretch'd ocean glitter like a lake.

178

And the small ripple spilt upon the beach
  Scarcely o'erpass'd the cream of your champagne,
When o'er the brim the sparkling bumpers reach,
1420   That spring-dew of the spirit! the heart's rain!
Few things surpass old wine; and they may preach
  Who please,—the more because they preach in vain,—
Let us have wine and woman, mirth and laughter,
Sermons and soda water the day after.

179

1425 Man, being reasonable, must get drunk;
  The best of life is but intoxication:
Glory, the grape, love, gold, in these are sunk
  The hopes of all men, and of every nation;
Without their sap, how branchless were the trunk
1430   Of life's strange tree, so fruitful on occasion:
But to return,—Get very drunk; and when
You wake with head-ache, you shall see what then.

180

Ring for your valet—bid him quickly bring
  Some hock and soda-water, then you'll know
1435 A pleasure worthy Xerxes[3] the great king;
  For not the blest sherbet, sublimed with snow,
Nor the first sparkle of the desert-spring,
  Nor Burgundy in all its sunset glow,
After long travel, ennui, love, or slaughter,
1440 Vie with that draught of hock and soda-water.

181

The coast—I think it was the coast that I
  Was just describing—Yes, it *was* the coast—
Lay at this period quiet as the sky,
  The sands untumbled, the blue waves untost,
1445 And all was stillness, save the sea-bird's cry,
  And dolphin's leap, and little billow crost
By some low rock or shelve, that made it fret
Against the boundary it scarcely wet.

182

And forth they wandered, her sire being gone,
1450   As I have said, upon an expedition;

---

3. The 5th-century Persian king was said to have offered a reward to anyone who could discover a new kind of pleasure.

And mother, brother, guardian, she had none,
 Save Zoe, who, although with due precision
She waited on her lady with the sun,
 Thought daily service was her only mission,
1455 Bringing warm water, wreathing her long tresses,
And asking now and then for cast-off dresses.

183

It was the cooling hour, just when the rounded
 Red sun sinks down behind the azure hill,
Which then seems as if the whole earth it bounded,
1460 Circling all nature, hush'd, and dim, and still,
With the far mountain-crescent half surrounded
 On one side, and the deep sea calm and chill
Upon the other, and the rosy sky,
With one star sparkling through it like an eye.

184

1465 And thus they wander'd forth, and hand in hand,
 Over the shining pebbles and the shells,
Glided along the smooth and harden'd sand,
 And in the worn and wild receptacles
Work'd by the storms, yet work'd as it were plann'd,
1470 In hollow halls, with sparry roofs and cells,
They turn'd to rest; and, each clasp'd by an arm,
Yielded to the deep twilight's purple charm.

185

They look'd up to the sky, whose floating glow
 Spread like a rosy ocean, vast and bright;
1475 They gazed upon the glittering sea below,
 Whence the broad moon rose circling into sight;
They heard the wave's splash, and the wind so low,
 And saw each other's dark eyes darting light
Into each other—and, beholding this,
1480 Their lips drew near, and clung into a kiss;

186

A long, long kiss, a kiss of youth and love,
 And beauty, all concentrating like rays
Into one focus, kindled from above;
 Such kisses as belong to early days,
1485 Where heart, and soul, and sense, in concert move,
 And the blood's lava, and the pulse a blaze,
Each kiss a heart-quake,—for a kiss's strength,
I think, it must be reckon'd by its length.

187

By length I mean duration; theirs endured
1490 Heaven knows how long—no doubt they never reckon'd;
And if they had, they could not have secured
 The sum of their sensations to a second:

They had not spoken; but they felt allured,
    As if their souls and lips each other beckon'd,
1495 Which, being join'd, like swarming bees they clung—
    Their hearts the flowers from whence the honey sprung.

188

They were alone, but not alone as they
    Who shut in chambers think it loneliness;
The silent ocean, and the starlight bay,
1500   The twilight glow, which momently grew less,
The voiceless sands, and dropping caves, that lay
    Around them, made them to each other press,
As if there were no life beneath the sky
Save theirs, and that their life could never die.

189

1505 They fear'd no eyes nor ears on that lone beach,
    They felt no terrors from the night, they were
All in all to each other: though their speech
    Was broken words, they *thought* a language there,—
And all the burning tongues the passions teach
1510   Found in one sigh the best interpreter
Of nature's oracle—first love,—that all
Which Eve has left her daughters since her fall.

190

Haidee[4] spoke not of scruples, ask'd no vows,
    Nor offer'd any; she had never heard
1515 Of plight and promises to be a spouse,
    Or perils by a loving maid incurr'd;
She was all which pure ignorance allows,
    And flew to her young mate like a young bird;
And, never having dreamt of falsehood, she
1520 Had not one word to say of constancy.

191

She loved, and was beloved—she adored,
    And she was worshipp'd; after nature's fashion,
Their intense souls, into each other pour'd,
    If souls could die, had perish'd in that passion,—
1525 But by degrees their senses were restored,
    Again to be o'ercome, again to dash on;
And, beating 'gainst *his* bosom, Haidee's heart
Felt as if never more to beat apart.

192

Alas! they were so young, so beautiful,
1530   So lonely, loving, helpless, and the hour
Was that in which the heart is always full,

---

4. Byron said, with reference to Haidee: "I was, and am, penetrated with the conviction that women only know evil from men, whereas men have no criterion to judge of purity or goodness but woman."

And, having o'er itself no further power,
Prompts deeds eternity can not annul,
But pays off moments in an endless shower
1535   Of hell-fire—all prepared for people giving
Pleasure or pain to one another living.

193

Alas! for Juan and Haidee! they were
So loving and so lovely—till then never,
Excepting our first parents, such a pair
1540   Had run the risk of being damn'd for ever;
And Haidee, being devout as well as fair,
Had, doubtless, heard about the Stygian river,[5]
And hell and purgatory—but forgot
Just in the very crisis she should not.

194

1545   They look upon each other, and their eyes
Gleam in the moonlight; and her white arm clasps
Round Juan's head, and his around hers lies
Half buried in the tresses which it grasps;
She sits upon his knee, and drinks his sighs,
1550   He hers, until they end in broken gasps;
And thus they form a group that's quite antique,
Half naked, loving, natural, and Greek.

195

And when those deep and burning moments pass'd,
And Juan sunk to sleep within her arms,
1555   She slept not, but all tenderly, though fast,
Sustain'd his head upon her bosom's charms;
And now and then her eye to heaven is cast,
And then on the pale cheek her breast now warms,
Pillow'd on her o'erflowing heart, which pants
1560   With all it granted, and with all it grants.

196

An infant when it gazes on a light,
A child the moment when it drains the breast,
A devotee when soars the Host[6] in sight,
An Arab with a stranger for a guest,
1565   A sailor when the prize has struck[7] in fight,
A miser filling his most hoarded chest,
Feel rapture; but not such true joy are reaping
As they who watch o'er what they love while sleeping.

197

For there it lies so tranquil, so beloved,
1570   All that it hath of life with us is living;

---

5. The Styx, which flows through Hades.
6. The Eucharistic wafer.

7. Has lowered its flag in token of surrender.

So gentle, stirless, helpless, and unmoved,
   And all unconscious of the joy 'tis giving;
All it hath felt, inflicted, pass'd, and proved,
   Hush'd into depths beyond the watcher's diving;
1575   There lies the thing we love with all its errors
   And all its charms, like death without its terrors.

198

The lady watch'd her lover—and that hour
   Of Love's, and Night's, and Ocean's solitude,
O'erflow'd her soul with their united power;
1580   Amidst the barren sand and rocks so rude
She and her wave-worn love had made their bower,
   Where nought upon their passion could intrude,
And all the stars that crowded the blue space
Saw nothing happier than her glowing face.

199

1585   Alas! the love of women! it is known
   To be a lovely and a fearful thing;
For all of theirs upon that die is thrown,
   And if 'tis lost, life hath no more to bring
To them but mockeries of the past alone,
1590   And their revenge is as the tiger's spring,
Deadly, and quick, and crushing; yet, as real
Torture is theirs, what they inflict they feel.

200

They are right; for man, to man so oft unjust,
   Is always so to women; one sole bond
1595   Awaits them, treachery is all their trust;
   Taught to conceal, their bursting hearts despond
Over their idol, till some wealthier lust
   Buys them in marriage—and what rests beyond?
A thankless husband, next a faithless lover,
1600   Then dressing, nursing, praying, and all's over.

201

Some take a lover, some take drams or prayers,
   Some mind their household, others dissipation,
Some run away, and but exchange their cares,
   Losing the advantage of a virtuous station;
1605   Few changes e'er can better their affairs,
   Theirs being an unnatural situation,
From the dull palace to the dirty hovel:
Some play the devil, and then write a novel.[8]

---

8. The impetuous Lady Caroline Lamb, having thrown herself at Byron and been after a time rejected, incorporated incidents from the affair in her novel *Glenarvon* (1816).

202

Haidee was Nature's bride, and knew not this;
   Haidee was Passion's child, born where the sun
Showers triple light, and scorches even the kiss
   Of his gazelle-eyed daughters; she was one
Made but to love, to feel that she was his
   Who was her chosen: what was said or done
Elsewhere was nothing—She had nought to fear,
Hope, care, nor love beyond, her heart beat *here*.

203

And oh! that quickening of the heart, that beat!
   How much it costs us! yet each rising throb
Is in its cause as its effect so sweet,
   That Wisdom, ever on the watch to rob
Joy of its alchymy, and to repeat
   Fine truths, even Conscience, too, has a tough job
To make us understand each good old maxim,
So good—I wonder Castlereagh[9] don't tax 'em.

204

And now 'twas done—on the lone shore were plighted
   Their hearts; the stars, their nuptial torches, shed
Beauty upon the beautiful they lighted:
   Ocean their witness, and the cave their bed,
By their own feelings hallow'd and united,
   Their priest was Solitude, and they were wed:
And they were happy, for to their young eyes
Each was an angel, and earth paradise.

*   *   *

208

But Juan! had he quite forgotten Julia?
   And should he have forgotten her so soon?
I can't but say it seems to me most truly a
   Perplexing question; but, no doubt, the moon
Does these things for us, and whenever newly a
   Strong palpitation rises, 'tis her boon,
Else how the devil is it that fresh features
Have such a charm for us poor human creatures?

209

I hate inconstancy—I loathe, detest,
   Abhor, condemn, abjure the mortal made
Of such quicksilver clay that in his breast
   No permanent foundation can be laid;
Love, constant love, has been my constant guest,
   And yet last night, being at a masquerade,

9. Robert Stewart, Viscount Castlereagh, British foreign secretary (1812–22).

I saw the prettiest creature, fresh from Milan,
Which gave me some sensations like a villain.

210

But soon Philosophy came to my aid,
   And whisper'd "think of every sacred tie!"
1675 "I will, my dear Philosophy!" I said,
   "But then her teeth, and then, Oh heaven! her eye!
I'll just inquire if she be wife or maid,
   Or neither—out of curiosity."
"Stop!" cried Philosophy, with air so Grecian,
1680 (Though she was masqued then as a fair Venetian).

211

"Stop!" so I stopp'd.—But to return: that which
   Men call inconstancy is nothing more
Than admiration due where nature's rich
   Profusion with young beauty covers o'er
1685 Some favour'd object; and as in the niche
   A lovely statue we almost adore,
This sort of adoration of the real
Is but a heightening of the "beau ideal."[1]

212

'Tis the perception of the beautiful,
1690   A fine extension of the faculties,
Platonic, universal, wonderful,
   Drawn from the stars, and filter'd through the skies,
Without which life would be extremely dull;
   In short, it is the use of our own eyes,
1695 With one or two small senses added, just
To hint that flesh is form'd of fiery dust.

213

Yet 'tis a painful feeling, and unwilling,
   For surely if we always could perceive
In the same object graces quite as killing
1700   As when she rose upon us like an Eve,
'Twould save us many a heart-ache, many a shilling,
   (For we must get them anyhow, or grieve),
Whereas, if one sole lady pleased for ever,
How pleasant for the heart, as well as liver!

* * *

216

In the mean time, without proceeding more
   In this anatomy, I've finish'd now
Two hundred and odd stanzas as before,

---

1. Ideal beauty (French).

That being about the number I'll allow
1725 Each canto of the twelve, or twenty-four;
And, laying down my pen, I make my bow,
Leaving Don Juan and Haidee to plead
For them and theirs with all who deign to read.

From Canto 3

[JUAN AND HAIDEE]

1

Hail, Muse! *et cetera.*—We left Juan sleeping,
   Pillow'd upon a fair and happy breast,
And watch'd by eyes that never yet knew weeping,
   And loved by a young heart, too deeply blest
5 To feel the poison through her spirit creeping,
   Or know who rested there, a foe to rest
Had soil'd the current of her sinless years,
And turn'd her pure heart's purest blood to tears.

2

Oh, Love! what is it in this world of ours
10   Which makes it fatal to be loved? Ah why
With cypress branches[1] hast thou wreathed thy bowers,
   And made thy best interpreter a sigh?
As those who dote on odours pluck the flowers,
   And place them on their breast—but place to die!
15 Thus the frail beings we would fondly cherish
Are laid within our bosoms but to perish.

3

In her first passion woman loves her lover,
   In all the others all she loves is love,
Which grows a habit she can ne'er get over,
20   And fits her loosely—like an easy glove,
As you may find, whene'er you like to prove her:
   One man alone at first her heart can move;
She then prefers him in the plural number,
Not finding that the additions much encumber.

4

25 I know not if the fault be men's or theirs;
   But one thing's pretty sure; a woman planted[2]—
(Unless at once she plunge for life in prayers)—
   After a decent time must be gallanted;
Although, no doubt, her first of love affairs
30   Is that to which her heart is wholly granted;

---

1. Signifying sorrow.
2. Abandoned (from the French *planter là,* to leave in the lurch).

Yet there are some, they say, who have had *none*,
But those who have ne'er end with only *one*.

5

'Tis melancholy, and a fearful sign
   Of human frailty, folly, also crime,
35 That love and marriage rarely can combine,
    Although they both are born in the same clime;
Marriage from love, like vinegar from wine—
    A sad, sour, sober beverage—by time
Is sharpen'd from its high celestial flavour
40 Down to a very homely household savour.

6

There's something of antipathy, as 'twere,
   Between their present and their future state;
A kind of flattery that's hardly fair
    Is used until the truth arrives too late—
45 Yet what can people do, except despair?
    The same things change their names at such a rate;
For instance—passion in a lover's glorious,
But in a husband is pronounced uxorious.

7

Men grow ashamed of being so very fond;
50   They sometimes also get a little tired
(But that, of course, is rare), and then despond:
    The same things cannot always be admired,
Yet 'tis "so nominated in the bond,"[3]
    That both are tied till one shall have expired.
55 Sad thought! to lose the spouse that was adorning
Our days, and put one's servants into mourning.

8

There's doubtless something in domestic doings,
   Which forms, in fact, true love's antithesis;
Romances paint at full length people's wooings,
60   But only give a bust of marriages;
For no one cares for matrimonial cooings,
    There's nothing wrong in a connubial kiss:
Think you, if Laura had been Petrarch's wife,
He would have written sonnets all his life?

9

65 All tragedies are finish'd by a death,
   All comedies are ended by a marriage;
The future states of both are left to faith,
    For authors fear description might disparage
The worlds to come of both, or fall beneath,

---

3. Spoken by Shylock in *The Merchant of Venice* 4.1.254: "Is it so nominated in the bond?"

70 And then both worlds would punish their miscarriage;
  So leaving each their priest and prayer-book ready,
  They say no more of Death or of the Lady.[4]

10

  The only two that in my recollection
   Have sung of heaven and hell, or marriage, are
75 Dante and Milton, and of both the affection
   Was hapless in their nuptials, for some bar
  Of fault or temper ruin'd the connexion
   (Such things, in fact, it don't ask much to mar);
  But Dante's Beatrice and Milton's Eve
80 Were not drawn from their spouses, you conceive.

11

  Some persons say that Dante meant theology
   By Beatrice, and not a mistress—I,
  Although my opinion may require apology,
   Deem this a commentator's phantasy,
85 Unless indeed it was from his own knowledge he
   Decided thus, and show'd good reason why;
  I think that Dante's more abstruse ecstatics
  Meant to personify the mathematics.

12

  Haidee and Juan were not married, but
90   The fault was theirs, not mine: it is not fair,
  Chaste reader, then, in any way to put
   The blame on me, unless you wish they were;
  Then if you'd have them wedded, please to shut
   The book which treats of this erroneous pair,
95 Before the consequences grow too awful;
  'Tis angerous to read of loves unlawful.

13

  Yet they were happy,—happy in the illicit
   Indulgence of their innocent desires;
  But more imprudent grown with every visit,
100   Haidee forgot the island was her sire's;
  When we have what we like, 'tis hard to miss it,
   At least in the beginning, ere one tires;
  Thus she came often, not a moment losing,
  Whilst her piratical papa was cruising.

14

105 Let not his mode of raising cash seem strange,
   Although he fleeced the flags of every nation,
  For into a prime minister but change
   His title, and 'tis nothing but taxation;
  But he, more modest, took an humbler range

---

4. Alluding to a popular ballad, *Death and the Lady*.

110 Of life, and in an honester vocation
Pursued o'er the high seas his watery journey,
And merely practised as a sea-attorney.

15

The good old gentleman had been detain'd
By winds and waves, and some important captures;
115 And, in the hope of more, at sea remain'd,
Although a squall or two had damp'd his raptures,
By swamping one of the prizes; he had chain'd
His prisoners, dividing them like chapters
In number'd lots; they all had cuffs and collars,
120 And averaged each from ten to a hundred dollars.

* * *

19

145 Then having settled his marine affairs,
Despatching single cruisers here and there,
His vessel having need of some repairs,
He shaped his course to where his daughter fair
Continued still her hospitable cares;
150 But that part of the coast being shoal and bare,
And rough with reefs which ran out many a mile,
His port lay on the other side o' the isle.

20

And there he went ashore without delay,
Having no custom-house nor quarantine
155 To ask him awkward questions on the way
About the time and place where he had been:
He left his ship to be hove down next day,
With orders to the people to careen;[5]
So that all hands were busy beyond measure,
160 In getting out goods, ballast, guns, and treasure.

* * *

27

He saw his white walls shining in the sun,
210 His garden trees all shadowy and green;
He heard his rivulet's light bubbling run,
The distant dog-bark; and perceived between
The umbrage of the wood so cool and dun
The moving figures, and the sparkling sheen
215 Of arms (in the East all arm)—and various dyes
Of colour'd garbs, as bright as butterflies.

28

And as the spot where they appear he nears,
Surprised at these unwonted signs of idling,
He hears—alas! no music of the spheres,

5. To tip a vessel on its side to clean and repair its hull.

220   But an unhallow'd, earthly sound of fiddling!
    A melody which made him doubt his ears,
      The cause being past his guessing or unriddling;
    A pipe, too, and a drum, and shortly after,
    A most unoriental roar of laughter.

*   *   *

38

He did not know (Alas! how men will lie)
    That a report (especially the Greeks)
Avouch'd his death (such people never die),
300   And put his house in mourning several weeks,
But now their eyes and also lips were dry;
    The bloom too had return'd to Haidee's cheeks.
Her tears too being return'd into their fount,
She now kept house upon her own account.

39

305   Hence all this rice, meat, dancing, wine, and fiddling,
    Which turn'd the isle into a place of pleasure;
The servants all were getting drunk or idling,
    A life which made them happy beyond measure.
Her father's hospitality seem'd middling,
310   Compared with what Haidee did with his treasure;
'Twas wonderful how things went on improving,
While she had not one hour to spare from loving.

40

Perhaps you think in stumbling on this feast
    He flew into a passion, and in fact
315   There was no mighty reason to be pleased;
    Perhaps you prophesy some sudden act,
The whip, the rack, or dungeon at the least,
    To teach his people to be more exact,
And that, proceeding at a very high rate,
320   He showed the royal *penchants* of a pirate.

41

You're wrong.—He was the mildest manner'd man
    That ever scuttled ship or cut a throat;
With such true breeding of a gentleman,
    You never could divine his real thought;
325   No courtier could, and scarcely woman can
    Gird more deceit within a petticoat;
Pity he loved adventurous life's variety,
He was so great a loss to good society.

*   *   *

48

Not that he was not sometimes rash or so,
    But never in his real and serious mood;

Then calm, concentrated, and still, and slow,
380   He lay coil'd like the boa in the wood;
With him it never was a word and blow,
     His angry word once o'er, he shed no blood,
But in his silence there was much to rue,
And his *one* blow left little work for *two.*

49

385   He ask'd no further questions, and proceeded
     On to the house, but by a private way,
So that the few who met him hardly heeded,
     So little they expected him that day;
If love paternal in his bosom pleaded
390   For Haidee's sake, is more than I can say,
But certainly to one deem'd dead returning,
This revel seem'd a curious mode of mourning.

50

If all the dead could now return to life,
     (Which God forbid!) or some, or a great many,
395   For instance, if a husband or his wife
     (Nuptial examples are as good as any),
No doubt whate'er might be their former strife,
     The present weather would be much more rainy—
Tears shed into the grave of the connexion
400   Would share most probably its resurrection.

51

He enter'd in the house no more his home,
     A thing to human feelings the most trying,
And harder for the heart to overcome,
     Perhaps, than even the mental pangs of dying;
405   To find our hearthstone turn'd into a tomb,
     And round its once warm precincts palely lying
The ashes of our hopes, is a deep grief,
Beyond a single gentleman's belief.

52

He enter'd in the house—his home no more,
410   For without hearts there is no home;—and felt
The solitude of passing his own door
     Without a welcome; *there* he long had dwelt,
There his few peaceful days Time had swept o'er,
     There his worn bosom and keen eye would melt
415   Over the innocence of that sweet child,
His only shrine of feelings undefiled.

53

He was a man of a strange temperament,
     Of mild demeanour though of savage mood,
Moderate in all his habits, and content

420 With temperance in pleasure, as in food,
  Quick to perceive, and strong to bear, and meant
   For something better, if not wholly good;
  His country's wrongs and his despair to save her
  Had stung him from a slave to an enslaver.

      * * *

96

  But let me to my story: I must own,
   If I have any fault, it is digression;
  Leaving my people to proceed alone,
860   While I soliloquize beyond expression;
  But these are my addresses from the throne,
   Which put off business to the ensuing session:
  Forgetting each omission is a loss to
  The world, not quite so great as Ariosto.[6]

97

865 I know that what our neighbours call *"longueurs,"*[7]
   (We've not so good a *word*, but have the *thing*
  In that complete perfection which ensures
   An epic from Bob Southey[8] every spring—)
  Form not the true temptation which allures
870   The reader; but 'twould not be hard to bring
  Some fine examples of the *épopée,*[9]
  To prove its grand ingredient is *ennui.*

98

  We learn from Horace, Homer sometimes sleeps;[1]
   We feel without him: Wordsworth sometimes wakes,
875 To show with what complacency he creeps,
   With his dear *"Waggoners,"*[2] around his lakes;
  He wishes for "a boat" to sail the deeps—
   Of ocean?—No, of air; and then he makes
  Another outcry for "a little boat,"
880 And drivels seas to set it well afloat.[3]

99

  If he must fain sweep o'er the etherial plain,
   And Pegasus[4] runs restive in his "waggon,"
  Could he not beg the loan of Charles's Wain?[5]
   Or pray Medea for a single dragon?[6]

---

6. Byron warmly admired this poet, author of *Orlando Furioso* (1532), the greatest of the Italian chivalric romances.
7. Boringly wordy passages of verse or prose (French).
8. Robert Southey (1774–1843), poet laureate and author of a number of epic-length narrative poems.
9. Epic poem (French).
1. Horace's *Art of Poetry* 359: "Sometimes great Homer nods."
2. A reference to Wordsworth's long narrative poem *The Waggoner* (1819).

3. In the prologue to his poem *Peter Bell* (1819), Wordsworth wishes for "a little boat, / In shape a very crescent-moon: / Fast through the clouds my boat can sail."
4. In Greek myth, the winged horse. He was said to have produced the fountain Hippocrene, sacred to the Muses, by stamping his hoof.
5. The constellation known in the United States as the Big Dipper.
6. When the Argonaut Jason abandoned Medea to take a new wife, she murdered their sons to punish him, then escaped in a chariot drawn by winged dragons.

885　　Or if too classic for his vulgar brain,
　　　　He fear'd his neck to venture such a nag on,
　　　And he must needs mount nearer to the moon,
　　　Could not the blockhead ask for a balloon?

100

　　　"Pedlars,"[7] and "boats," and "waggons!" Oh! Ye shades
890　　Of Pope and Dryden, are we come to this?
　　　That trash of such sort not alone evades
　　　　Contempt, but from the bathos' vast abyss
　　　Floats scumlike uppermost, and these Jack Cades[8]
　　　　Of sense and song above your graves may hiss—
895　The "little boatman" and his "Peter Bell"
　　　Can sneer at him who drew "Achitophel!"[9]

101

　　　T' our tale.—The feast was over, the slaves gone,
　　　　The dwarfs and dancing girls had all retired;
　　　The Arab lore and poet's song were done,
900　　And every sound of revelry expired;
　　　The lady and her lover, left alone,
　　　　The rosy flood of twilight's sky admired;—
　　　Ave Maria![1] o'er the earth and sea,
　　　That heavenliest hour of Heaven is worthiest thee!

102

905　Ave Maria! blessed be the hour!
　　　　The time, the clime, the spot, where I so oft
　　　Have felt that moment in its fullest power
　　　　Sink o'er the earth so beautiful and soft,
　　　While swung the deep bell in the distant tower,
910　　Or the faint dying day-hymn stole aloft,
　　　And not a breath crept through the rosy air,
　　　And yet the forest leaves seem'd stirr'd with prayer.

103

　　　Ave Maria! 'tis the hour of prayer!
　　　Ave Maria! 'tis the hour of love!
915　Ave Maria! may our spirits dare
　　　　Look up to thine and to thy Son's above!
　　　Ave Maria! oh that face so fair!
　　　　Those downcast eyes beneath the Almighty dove—
　　　What though 'tis but a pictured image strike—
920　That painting is no idol, 'tis too like.

---

7. Wordsworth's Peddler narrates the story of Margaret, from the early manuscript *The Ruined Cottage* (p. 259). Byron knew this story in the later form that Wordsworth incorporated into book 1 of *The Excursion* (1814).
8. An adventurer who led an uprising against Henry VI in 1450.
9. I.e., John Dryden, author of *Absalom and Ach-*

itophel (1681), whom Byron greatly admired. Wordsworth had derogated Dryden's poetry in the *Essay, Supplementary to the Preface* to his *Poems* (1815).
1. Hail, Mary, (Latin), the opening words of a Roman Catholic prayer. *Ave Maria* is sometimes used to refer to evening (or morning), because the prayer is part of the service at these times.

104

Some kinder casuists are pleased to say,
    In nameless print—that I have no devotion;
But set those persons down with me to pray,
    And you shall see who has the properest notion
925   Of getting into Heaven the shortest way;
    My altars are the mountains and the ocean,
Earth, air, stars,—all that springs from the great Whole,
Who hath produced, and will receive the soul.

* * *

From Canto 4

[JUAN AND HAIDEE]

3

As boy, I thought myself a clever fellow,
    And wish'd that others held the same opinion;
They took it up when my days grew more mellow,
20   And other minds acknowledged my dominion:
Now my sere fancy "falls into the yellow
    Leaf,"[1] and imagination droops her pinion,
And the sad truth which hovers o'er my desk
Turns what was once romantic to burlesque.

4

25 And if I laugh at any mortal thing,
    'Tis that I may not weep; and if I weep,
'Tis that our nature cannot always bring
    Itself to apathy, for we must steep
Our hearts first in the depths of Lethe's[2] spring
30   Ere what we least wish to behold will sleep:
Thetis baptized her mortal son in Styx;[3]
A mortal mother would on Lethe fix.

5

Some have accused me of a strange design
    Against the creed and morals of the land,
35 And trace it in this poem every line:
    I don't pretend that I quite understand
My own meaning when I would be *very* fine,
    But the fact is that I have nothing plann'd,
Unless it were to be a moment merry,
40 A novel word in my vocabulary.

---

1. Cf. *Macbeth* 5.3.22–24: "My way of life / Is
fall'n into the sere, the yellow leaf."
2. A river in Hades that brings oblivion of life.

3. The river in Hades into which the nymph Thetis
dipped Achilles, to make him invulnerable.

6

To the kind reader of our sober clime
　　This way of writing will appear exotic;
Pulci[4] was sire of the half-serious rhyme,
　　Who sang when chivalry was more Quixotic,
45　And revell'd in the fancies of the time,
　　　True knights, chaste dames, huge giants, kings despotic;
But all these, save the last, being obsolete,
I chose a modern subject as more meet.

7

How I have treated it, I do not know;
50　　Perhaps no better than they have treated me
Who have imputed such designs as show
　　Not what they saw, but what they wish'd to see;
But if it gives them pleasure, be it so,
　　This is a liberal age, and thoughts are free:
55　Meantime Apollo plucks me by the ear,
And tells me to resume my story here.

* * *

26

Juan and Haidee gazed upon each other
　　With swimming looks of speechless tenderness,
Which mix'd all feelings, friend, child, lover, brother,
　　All that the best can mingle and express
205　When two pure hearts are pour'd in one another,
　　　And love too much, and yet can not love less;
But almost sanctify the sweet excess
By the immortal wish and power to bless.

27

Mix'd in each other's arms, and heart in heart,
210　　Why did they not then die?—they had lived too long
Should an hour come to bid them breathe apart;
　　Years could but bring them cruel things or wrong,
The world was not for them, nor the world's art
　　For beings passionate as Sappho's song;
215　Love was born *with* them, *in* them, so intense,
It was their very spirit—not a sense.

28

They should have lived together deep in woods,
　　Unseen as sings the nightingale; they were
Unfit to mix in these thick solitudes
220　　Call'd social, haunts of Hate, and Vice, and Care:
How lonely every freeborn creature broods!
　　The sweetest song-birds nestle in a pair;

4. Author of the *Morgante Maggiore,* prototype of the Italian seriocomic romance from which Byron derived the stanza and manner of *Don Juan* (see headnote, p. 621).

The eagle soars alone; the gull and crow
Flock o'er their carrion, just like men below.

29

225   Now pillow'd cheek to cheek, in loving sleep,
     Haidee and Juan their siesta took,
A gentle slumber, but it was not deep,
     For ever and anon a something shook
Juan, and shuddering o'er his frame would creep;
230   And Haidee's sweet lips murmur'd like a brook
A wordless music, and her face so fair
Stirr'd with her dream as rose-leaves with the air;

30

Or as the stirring of a deep clear stream
     Within an Alpine hollow, when the wind
235 Walks o'er it, was she shaken by the dream,
     The mystical usurper of the mind—
O'erpowering us to be whate'er may seem
     Good to the soul which we no more can bind;
Strange state of being! (for 'tis still to be)
240 Senseless to feel, and with seal'd eyes to see.

31

She dream'd of being alone on the sea-shore,
     Chain'd to a rock; she knew not how, but stir
She could not from the spot, and the loud roar
     Grew, and each wave rose roughly, threatening her;
245 And o'er her upper lip they seem'd to pour,
     Until she sobb'd for breath, and soon they were
Foaming o'er her lone head, so fierce and high—
Each broke to drown her, yet she could not die.

32

Anon—she was released, and then she stray'd
250   O'er the sharp shingles° with her bleeding feet,   *loose pebbles*
And stumbled almost every step she made;
     And something roll'd before her in a sheet,
Which she must still pursue howe'er afraid;
     'Twas white and indistinct, nor stopp'd to meet
255 Her glance nor grasp, for still she gazed and grasp'd,
And ran, but it escaped her as she clasp'd.

33

The dream changed; in a cave she stood, its walls
     Were hung with marble icicles; the work
Of ages on its water-fretted halls,
260   Where waves might wash, and seals might breed and lurk;
Her hair was dripping, and the very balls

Of her black eyes seemed turn'd to tears, and murk
The sharp rocks look'd below each drop they caught,
Which froze to marble as it fell, she thought.

34

265   And wet, and cold, and lifeless at her feet,
        Pale as the foam that froth'd on his dead brow,
    Which she essay'd in vain to clear, (how sweet
        Were once her cares, how idle seem'd they now!)
    Lay Juan, nor could aught renew the beat
270   Of his quench'd heart; and the sea dirges low
    Rang in her sad ears like a mermaid's song,
    And that brief dream appear'd a life too long.

35

    And gazing on the dead, she thought his face
        Faded, or alter'd into something new—
275   Like to her father's features, till each trace
        More like and like to Lambro's aspect grew—
    With all his keen worn look and Grecian grace;
        And starting, she awoke, and what to view?
    Oh! Powers of Heaven! what dark eye meets she there?
280   'Tis—'tis her father's—fix'd upon the pair!

36

    Then shrieking, she arose, and shrieking fell,
        With joy and sorrow, hope and fear, to see
    Him whom she deem'd a habitant where dwell
        The ocean-buried, risen from death, to be
285   Perchance the death of one she loved too well:
        Dear as her father had been to Haidee,
    It was a moment of that awful kind—
    I have seen such—but must not call to mind.

37

    Up Juan sprung to Haidee's bitter shriek,
290   And caught her falling, and from off the wall
    Snatch'd down his sabre, in hot haste to wreak
        Vengeance on him who was the cause of all:
    Then Lambro, who till now forbore to speak,
        Smiled scornfully, and said, "Within my call,
295   A thousand scimitars await the word;
    Put up, young man, put up your silly sword."

38

    And Haidee clung around him; "Juan, 'tis—
        'Tis Lambro—'tis my father! Kneel with me—
    He will forgive us—yes—it must be—yes.
300   Oh! dearest father, in this agony

Of pleasure and of pain—even while I kiss
   Thy garment's hem with transport, can it be
That doubt should mingle with my filial joy?
Deal with me as thou wilt, but spare this boy."

39

305 High and inscrutable the old man stood,
   Calm in his voice, and calm within his eye—
Not always signs with him of calmest mood:
   He look'd upon her, but gave no reply;
Then turn'd to Juan, in whose cheek the blood
310   Oft came and went, as there resolved to die;
In arms, at least, he stood, in act to spring
On the first foe whom Lambro's call might bring.

40

"Young man, your sword"; so Lambro once more said:
   Juan replied, "Not while this arm is free."
315 The old man's cheek grew pale, but not with dread,
   And drawing from his belt a pistol, he
Replied, "Your blood be then on your own head."
   Then look'd close at the flint, as if to see
'Twas fresh—for he had lately used the lock[5]—
320 And next proceeded quietly to cock.

41

It has a strange quick jar upon the ear,
   That cocking of a pistol, when you know
A moment more will bring the sight to bear
   Upon your person, twelve yards off, or so;
325 A gentlemanly distance,[6] not too near,
   If you have got a former friend for foe;
But after being fired at once or twice,
The ear becomes more Irish, and less nice.[7]

42

Lambro presented, and one instant more
330   Had stopp'd this Canto, and Don Juan's breath,
When Haidee threw herself her boy before;
   Stern as her sire: "On me," she cried, "let death
Descend—the fault is mine; this fatal shore
   He found—but sought not. I have pledged my faith;
335 I love him—I will die with him: I knew
Your nature's firmness—know your daughter's too."

43

A minute past, and she had been all tears,
   And tenderness, and infancy: but now

5. The part of the gun that explodes the charge.
6. I.e., dueling distance.

7. Finicky. Byron alludes to the propensity of hot-headed young Irishmen to fight duels.

She stood as one who champion'd human fears—
340   Pale, statue-like, and stern, she woo'd the blow;
And tall beyond her sex, and their compeers,[8]
    She drew up to her height, as if to show
A fairer mark; and with a fix'd eye scann'd
Her father's face—but never stopp'd his hand.

44

345 He gazed on her, and she on him; 'twas strange
    How like they look'd! the expression was the same;
Serenely savage, with a little change
    In the large dark eye's mutual-darted flame;
For she too was as one who could avenge,
350   If cause should be—a lioness, though tame:
Her father's blood before her father's face
Boil'd up, and prov'd her truly of his race.

45

I said they were alike, their features and
    Their stature differing but in sex and years;
355 Even to the delicacy of their hand
    There was resemblance, such as true blood wears;
And now to see them, thus divided, stand
    In fix'd ferocity, when joyous tears,
And sweet sensations, should have welcomed both,
360 Show what the passions are in their full growth.

46

The father paused a moment, then withdrew
    His weapon, and replaced it; but stood still,
And looking on her, as to look her through,
    "Not *I*," he said, "have sought this stranger's ill;
365 Not *I* have made this desolation: few
    Would bear such outrage, and forbear to kill;
But I must do my duty—how thou hast
Done thine, the present vouches for the past.

47

"Let him disarm; or, by my father's head,
370   His own shall roll before you like a ball!"
He raised his whistle, as the word he said,
    And blew; another answer'd to the call,
And rushing in disorderly, though led,
    And arm'd from boot to turban, one and all,
375 Some twenty of his train came, rank on rank;
He gave the word, "Arrest or slay the Frank."[9]

8. I.e., she was the match in height of Lambro and Juan.

9. Term used in the Near East to designate a Western European.

48

Then, with a sudden movement, he withdrew
   His daughter; while compress'd within his clasp,
'Twixt her and Juan interposed the crew;
380   In vain she struggled in her father's grasp—
His arms were like a serpent's coil: then flew
   Upon their prey, as darts an angry asp,
The file of pirates; save the foremost, who
Had fallen, with his right shoulder half cut through.

49

385 The second had his cheek laid open; but
   The third, a wary, cool old sworder, took
The blows upon his cutlass, and then put
   His own well in; so well, ere you could look,
His man was floor'd, and helpless at his foot,
390   With the blood running like a little brook
From two smart sabre gashes, deep and red—
One on the arm, the other on the head.

50

And then they bound him where he fell, and bore
   Juan from the apartment: with a sign
395 Old Lambro bade them take him to the shore,
   Where lay some ships which were to sail at nine.
They laid him in a boat, and plied the oar
   Until they reach'd some galliots,[1] placed in line;
On board of one of these, and under hatches,
400 They stow'd him, with strict orders to the watches.

51

The world is full of strange vicissitudes,
   And here was one exceedingly unpleasant:
A gentleman so rich in the world's goods,
   Handsome and young, enjoying all the present,
405 Just at the very time when he least broods
   On such a thing is suddenly to sea sent,
Wounded and chain'd, so that he cannot move,
And all because a lady fell in love.

          *   *   *

56

Afric is all the sun's, and as her earth
   Her human clay is kindled; full of power
For good or evil, burning from its birth,
   The Moorish blood partakes the planet's hour,
445 And like the soil beneath it will bring forth:
   Beauty and love were Haidée's mother's dower;

---

1. A small, fast galley, propelled by both oars and sails.

But her large dark eye show'd deep Passion's force,
    Though sleeping like a lion near a source.

57

    Her daughter, temper'd with a milder ray,
450   Like summer clouds all silvery, smooth, and fair,
    Till slowly charged with thunder they display
      Terror to earth, and tempest to the air,
    Had held till now her soft and milky way;
      But overwrought with passion and despair,
455   The fire burst forth from her Numidian° veins,   *North African*
    Even as the Simoom[2] sweeps the blasted plains.

58

    The last sight which she saw was Juan's gore,
      And he himself o'ermaster'd and cut down;
    His blood was running on the very floor
460   Where late he trod, her beautiful, her own;
    Thus much she view'd an instant and no more,—
      Her struggles ceased with one convulsive groan;
    On her sire's arm, which until now scarce held
    Her writhing, fell she like a cedar fell'd.

59

465   A vein had burst, and her sweet lips' pure dyes
      Were dabbled with the deep blood which ran o'er;
    And her head droop'd as when the lily lies
      O'ercharged with rain: her summon'd handmaids bore
    Their lady to her couch with gushing eyes;
470   Of herbs and cordials they produced their store,
    But she defied all means they could employ,
    Like one life could not hold, nor death destroy.

60

    Days lay she in that state unchanged, though chill
      With nothing livid,[3] still her lips were red;
475   She had no pulse, but death seem'd absent still;
      No hideous sign proclaim'd her surely dead;
    Corruption came not in each mind to kill
      All hope; to look upon her sweet face bred
    New thoughts of life, for it seem'd full of soul,
480   She had so much, earth could not claim the whole.

*   *   *

69

545   Twelve days and nights she wither'd thus; at last,
      Without a groan, or sigh, or glance, to show
    A parting pang, the spirit from her past:

---

2. A violent, hot, dust-laden desert wind.   3. I.e., though she was ashen pale.

And they who watch'd her nearest could not know
The very instant, till the change that cast
550   Her sweet face into shadow, dull and slow,
Glazed o'er her eyes—the beautiful, the black—
Oh! to possess such lustre—and then lack!

70

She died, but not alone; she held within
A second principle of life, which might
555 Have dawn'd a fair and sinless child of sin;
But closed its little being without light,
And went down to the grave unborn, wherein
Blossom and bough lie wither'd with one blight;
In vain the dews of Heaven descend above
560 The bleeding flower and blasted fruit of love.

71

Thus lived—thus died she; never more on her
Shall sorrow light, or shame. She was not made
Through years or moons the inner weight to bear,
Which colder hearts endure till they are laid
565 By age in earth; her days and pleasures were
Brief, but delightful—such as had not staid
Long with her destiny; but she sleeps well
By the sea shore, whereon she loved to dwell.

72

That isle is now all desolate and bare,
570 Its dwellings down, its tenants past away;
None but her own and father's grave is there,
And nothing outward tells of human clay;
Ye could not know where lies a thing so fair,
No stone is there to show, no tongue to say
575 What was; no dirge, except the hollow sea's,
Mourns o'er the beauty of the Cyclades.

73

But many a Greek maid in a loving song
Sighs o'er her name; and many an islander
With her sire's story makes the night less long;
580 Valour was his, and beauty dwelt with her;
If she loved rashly, her life paid for wrong—
A heavy price must all pay who thus err,
In some shape; let none think to fly the danger,
For soon or late Love is his own avenger.

74

585 But let me change this theme, which grows too sad,
And lay this sheet of sorrows on the shelf;
I don't much like describing people mad,
For fear of seeming rather touch'd myself—

Besides I've no more on this head to add;
590   And as my Muse is a capricious elf,
We'll put about, and try another tack
With Juan, left half-kill'd some stanzas back.[4]

1818–23   1819–24

LETTERS[1]

To Leigh Hunt[2]

[WORDSWORTH AND POPE]

13 Terrace Piccadilly Septr.–Octr. 30th. 1815

My dear Hunt—Many thanks for your books of which you already know my opinion.—Their external splendour should not disturb you as inappropriate—they have still more within than without.——I take leave to differ from you on Wordsworth[3] as freely as I once agreed with you—at that time I gave him credit for promise which is unfulfilled—I still think his capacity warrants all you say of *it* only—but that his performances since "Lyrical Ballads"—are miserably inadequate to the ability which lurks within him:—there is undoubtedly much natural talent spilt over "the Excursion" but it is rain upon rocks where it stands & stagnates—or rain upon sands where it falls without fertilizing—who can understand him?—let those who do make him intelligible.—Jacob Behman—Swedenborg—& Joanna Southcote[4] are mere types of this Arch-Apostle of mystery & mysticism—but I have done:—no I have not done—for I have two petty & perhaps unworthy objections in small matters to make to him—which with his pretension to accurate observation & fury against Pope's false translation of the "Moonlight scene in Homer"[5] I wonder he should have fallen into—these be they.—He says of Greece in the body of his book—that it is a land of

---

4. Juan's adventures continue. He is sold as a slave in Constantinople to an enamored sultana; she disguises him as a girl and adds him to her husband's harem for convenience of access. Juan escapes, joins the Russian army that is besieging Ismail, and so distinguishes himself in the capture of the town that he is sent with despatches to St. Petersburg. There he becomes "man-mistress" to the insatiable Catherine the Great. As the result of her assiduous attentions, he falls into a physical decline and, for a salutary change of scene and climate, is sent on a diplomatic mission to England. In canto 16, the last that Byron finished, he is in the middle of an amorous adventure while a guest at the medieval country mansion of an English nobleman, Lord Henry Amundeville, and his very beautiful wife.

1. Three thousand of Byron's letters have survived—a remarkable number for so short a life. In general, they are our best single biographical source for the poet, providing running commentary on his day-to-day concerns and activities and giving us the clearest possible picture of his complex personality, a picture relatively (but not entirely) free of the posturings that pervade both the romantic poems and the satires. In addition, they are

independently valuable for their charm, energy, and sheer brilliance. The selections printed here focus primarily on Byron's own poetry and his ideas about writers and literature, but they also represent his wide-ranging interests, as well as his powers of amusing anecdote and vivid description of the society of his time. The texts are from Leslie A. Marchand's twelve-volume edition, *Byron's Letters and Journals* (1973–82).

2. The poet, journalist, and political radical who, as editor of the *Examiner*, introduced Keats and Shelley to the public.

3. Hunt discussed Wordsworth, generally favorably, in a lengthy note in the second edition of his *The Feast of the Poets* (1815).

4. Jakob Boehme, Emanuel Swedenborg, and Joanna Southcott were religious visionaries (German, Swedish, and English, respectively). Southcott, who claimed that she would give birth to a new Messiah, had died in 1814.

5. Wordsworth's criticism of Pope's "false and contradictory" translation of the moonlight scene (*Iliad* 8.687–708) had recently appeared in his *Essay, Supplementary to the Preface* in the first collected edition of his *Poems* (March 1815).

"*rivers—fertile* plains—& *sounding* shores
Under a cope of *variegated* sky"[6]

The rivers are dry half the year—the plains are barren—and the shores *still* & *tideless* as the Mediterranean can make them—the Sky is anything but variegated—being for months & months—but "darkly—deeply—beautifully blue."[7]—The next is in his notes—where he talks of our "Monuments crowded together in the busy &c. of a large town"—as compared with the "still seclusion of a Turkish cemetery in some *remote* place"[8]—this is pure stuff—for *one* monument in our Churchyards—there are *ten* in the Turkish—& so crowded that you cannot walk between them—they are always close to the walks of the towns—that is—merely divided by a path or road—and as to "*remote* places"—men never take the trouble in a barbarous country to carry their dead very far—they must have lived near to where they are buried—there are no cemeteries in "remote places"—except such as have the cypress & the tombstone still left when the olive & the habitation of the living have perished.——These things I was struck with as coming peculiarly in my own way—and in both of these he is wrong—yet I should have noticed neither but for his attack on Pope for a like blunder—and a peevish affectation about him of despising a popularity which he will never obtain.—I write in great haste—& I doubt—*not* much to the purpose—but you have it hot & hot—just as it comes—& so let it go.——By the way—both he & you go too far against Pope's "so when the Moon &c." it is no translation I know—but it is not such *false* description as asserted—I have read it on the spot—there is a burst—and a lightness—and a glow—about the night in the Troad[9]—which makes the "planets vivid"—& the "pole glowing" the moon is—at least the sky is clearness itself—and I know no more appropriate expression for the expansion of such a heaven—over the scene—the plain—the sea—the sky—Ida—the Hellespont—Simois—Scamander—and the isles—than that of a "flood of Glory."[1]——I am getting horribly lengthy—& must stop—to the whole of your letter I say "ditto to Mr. Burke" as the Bristol Candidate cried by way of Electioneering harangue:[2]—you need not speak of morbid feelings—& vexations to me—I have plenty—for which I must blame partly the times—& chiefly myself: but let us forget them—*I* shall be very apt to do so—when I see you next—will you come to the theatre & see our new Management?[3]—you shall cut it up to your heart's content root & branch afterwards if you like—but come & see it?—if not I must come & see you.—

ever yrs very truly & affectly.

BYRON

6. *The Excursion* 4.719–20 (text of the 1st edition, 1814).
7. Southey's *Madoc* 1.5.102.
8. In his first *Essay upon Epitaphs*, originally published in Coleridge's *The Friend* (1810) and then reprinted among the notes to book 5 of *The Excursion* (1814), Wordsworth says: "let a man only compare in imagination the unsightly manner in which our monuments are crowded together in the busy, noisy, unclean, and almost grassless churchyard of a large town, with the still seclusion of a Turkish cemetery, in some remote place."

9. Troas, the region around ancient Troy, in the present northwest Turkey.
1. The three short quotations (beginning with "planets vivid") are from Pope's translation of the moonlight scene, *Iliad* 8.691, 692, 696.
2. This is reported (in biographies of Edmund Burke) to have been the whole of Henry Cruger's campaign speech when he and Burke ran together for seats in Parliament in 1774.
3. Byron had become a member of the subcommittee of management of the Drury Lane theater in May 1815.

P.S.—Not a word from Moore for these 2 months.—Pray let me have the rest of "Rimini["]⁴ you have 2 excellent points in that poem—originality—& Italianism—I will back you as a bard against half the fellows on whom you throw away much good criticism & eulogy—but don't let your bookseller publish in *Quarto* it is the worst size possible for circulation—I say this on Bibliopolical authority—

again—yours ever

[B]

To Thomas Moore¹

[*CHILDE HAROLD*. A VENETIAN ADVENTURE]

Venice, January 28th, 1817

Your letter of the 8th is before me. The remedy for your plethora is simple—abstinence. I was obliged to have recourse to the like some years ago, I mean in point of *diet*, and, with the exception of some convivial weeks and days, (it might be months, now and then), have kept to Pythagoras² ever since. For all this, let me hear that you are better. You must not *indulge* in "filthy beer," nor in porter, nor eat *suppers*—the last are the devil to those who swallow dinner. * ³

I am truly sorry to hear of your father's misfortune⁴—cruel at any time, but doubly cruel in advanced life. However, you will, at least, have the satisfaction of doing your part by him, and, depend upon it, it will not be in vain. Fortune, to be sure, is a female, but not such a b * * as the rest (always excepting your wife and my sister from such sweeping terms); for she generally has some justice in the long run. I have no spite against her, though between her and Nemesis I have had some sore gauntlets to run—but then I have done my best to deserve no better. But to *you*, she is a good deal in arrear, and she will come round—mind if she don't: you have the vigour of life, of independence, of talent, spirit, and character all with you. What you can do for yourself, you have done and will do; and surely there are some others in the world who would not be sorry to be of use, if you would allow them to be useful, or at least attempt it.

I think of being in England in the spring. If there is a row, by the sceptre of King Ludd,⁵ but I'll be one; and if there is none, and only a continuance of "this meek, piping time of peace,"⁶ I will take a cottage a hundred yards to the south of your abode, and become your neighbour; and we will compose such canticles, and hold such dialogues, as shall be the terror of the *Times*

4. Hunt's narrative poem *The Story of Rimini* (1816).
1. Irish poet and a good friend of Byron since they met in 1811. Moore's *Life* of Byron in 1830 is the sole source for many of Byron's letters, including this one.
2. I.e., have eaten no flesh (the disciples of the Greek philosopher-mathematician Pythagoras were strict vegetarians).
3. These asterisks (as well as those in the next paragraph and near the end of the letter) are Moore's, representing omissions in his printed text.
4. Moore's father had been dismissed from his post as barrack-master at Dublin.
5. A mythical king of Britain.
6. *Richard III* 1.1.24.

(including the newspaper of that name), and the wonder, and honour, and praise, of the Morning Chronicle and posterity.

I rejoice to hear of your forthcoming in February[7]—though I tremble for the "magnificence," which you attribute to the new Childe Harold.[8] I am glad you like it; it is a fine indistinct piece of poetical desolation, and my favourite. I was half mad during the time of its composition, between metaphysics, mountains, lakes, love unextinguishable, thoughts unutterable, and the nightmare of my own delinquencies. I should, many a good day, have blown my brains out, but for the recollection that it would have given pleasure to my mother-in-law; and, even *then*, if I could have been certain to haunt her—but I won't dwell upon these trifling family matters.

Venice is in the *estro* of her carnival, and I have been up these last two nights at the ridotto[9] and the opera, and all that kind of thing. Now for an adventure. A few days ago a gondolier brought me a billet without a subscription, intimating a wish on the part of the writer to meet me either in gondola or at the island of San Lazaro, or at a third rendezvous, indicated in the note. "I know the country's disposition well"—in Venice "they do let Heaven see those tricks they dare not show," &c. &c.;[1] so, for all response, I said that neither of the three places suited me; but that I would either be at home at ten at night *alone*, or at the ridotto at midnight, where the writer might meet me masked. At ten o'clock I was at home and alone (Marianna was gone with her husband to a conversazione[2]), when the door of my apartment opened, and in walked a well-looking and (for an Italian) *bionda*[3] girl of about nineteen, who informed me that she was married to the brother of my *amorosa*, and wished to have some conversation with me. I made a decent reply, and we had some talk in Italian and Romaic (her mother being a Greek of Corfu), when lo! in a very few minutes, in marches, to my very great astonishment, Marianna S[egati], *in propria persona*, and after making polite courtesy to her sister-in-law and to me, without a single word seizes her said sister-in-law by the hair, and bestows upon her some sixteen slaps, which would have made your ear ache only to hear their echo. I need not describe the screaming which ensued. The luckless visitor took flight. I seized Marianna, who, after several vain efforts to get away in pursuit of the enemy, fairly went into fits in my arms; and, in spite of reasoning, eau de Cologne, vinegar, half a pint of water, and God knows what other waters beside, continued so till past midnight.

After damning my servants for letting people in without apprizing me, I found that Marianna in the morning had seen her sister-in-law's gondolier on the stairs, and, suspecting that his apparition boded her no good, had either returned of her own accord, or been followed by her maids or some other spy of her people to the conversazione, from whence she returned to perpetrate this piece of pugilism. I had seen fits before, and also some small scenery of the same genus in and out of our island: but this was not all. After about an hour, in comes—who? why, Signor S[egati], her lord and husband, and finds me with his wife fainting upon the sofa, and all the apparatus of confusion, dishevelled hair, hats, handkerchiefs, salts, smelling-bottles—and

---

7. Moore's Oriental romance *Lalla Rookh*.
8. Canto 3 of *Childe Harold's Pilgrimage* (1816).
9. An Italian social gathering. "Estro": fire, fervor.
1. *Othello* 3.3.206–07. The passage continues:

"dare not show their husbands."
2. An evening party. Marianna Segati, wife of a Venetian draper, was Byron's current *amorosa*.
3. Blonde (Italian).

the lady as pale as ashes without sense or motion. His first question was, "What is all this?" The lady could not reply—so I did. I told him the explanation was the easiest thing in the world; but in the mean time it would be as well to recover his wife—at least, her senses. This came about in due time of suspiration and respiration.

You need not be alarmed—jealousy is not the order of the day in Venice, and daggers are out of fashion; while duels, on love matters, are unknown— at least, with the husbands. But, for all this, it was an awkward affair; and though he must have known that I made love to Marianna, yet I believe he was not, till that evening, aware of the extent to which it had gone. It is very well known that almost all the married women have a lover; but it is usual to keep up the forms, as in other nations. I did not, therefore, know what the devil to say. I could not out with the truth, out of regard to her, and I did not choose to lie for my sake;—besides, the thing told itself. I thought the best way would be to let her explain it as she chose (a woman being never at a loss—the devil always sticks by them)—only determining to protect and carry her off, in case of any ferocity on the part of the Signor. I saw that he was quite calm. She went to bed, and next day—how they settled it, I know not, but settle it they did. Well—then I had to explain to Marianna about this never to be sufficiently confounded sister-in-law; which I did by swearing innocence, eternal constancy, &c. &c. * * * But the sister-in-law, very much discomposed with being treated in such wise, has (not having her own shame before her eyes) told the affair to half Venice, and the servants (who were summoned by the fight and the fainting) to the other half. But, here, nobody minds such trifles, except to be amused by them. I don't know whether you will be so, but I have scrawled a long letter out of these follies.

Believe me ever. &c.

To John Cam Hobhouse and Douglas Kinnaird[1]

[DON JUAN AND INDECENCY]

Venice January 19th. 1819

Dear H. and dear K.—I approve and sanction all your legal proceedings with regard to my affairs, and can only repeat my thanks & approbation—if you put off the payments of debts "till *after* Lady Noel's[2] death"—it is well—if till *after* her damnation—better—for that will last forever—yet I hope not:— for her sake as well as the Creditors'—I am willing to believe in Purgatory.— —With regard to the Poeshie—I will have no "cutting & slashing" as Perry[3] calls it—you may omit the stanzas on Castlereagh—indeed it is better—& the two "*Bobs*" at the end of the 3d. stanza of the dedication—which will leave "high" & "adry" good rhymes without any "*double* (or Single) Entendre"[4]—but no more—I appeal—not "to Philip fasting" but to Alexander

1. Hobhouse was a close friend of Byron from Cambridge days and had accompanied the poet on the first year of his grand tour to the East in 1809. Kinnaird, who also had been at Cambridge, was Byron's banker and literary agent in London.
2. Byron's mother-in-law.
3. James Perry, editor of the *Morning Chronicle*.
4. The 136-line dedication to Southey was omit-

ted entirely when the first two cantos of *Don Juan* were published anonymously in 1819. Stanza 3 ends in an outrageous sexual pun on Southey's first name ("dry bob" was slang for intercourse without emission), and several later stanzas attack Viscount Castlereagh, the British foreign secretary, as an "intellectual eunuch," a "cold-blooded, smooth-faced, placid miscreant."

drunk[5]—I appeal to Murray at his ledger—to the people—in short, Don Juan shall be an entire horse or none.—If the objection be to the indecency, the Age which applauds the "Bath Guide" & Little's[6] poems—& reads Fielding & Smollett still—may bear with that;—if to the poetry—I will take my chance.—I will not give way to all the Cant of Christendom—I have been cloyed with applause & sickened with abuse;—at present—I care for little but the Copyright,—I have imbibed a great love for money—let me have it— if Murray loses this time—he won't the next—he will be cautious—and I shall learn the decline of his customers by his epistolary indications.———But in no case will I submit to have the poem mutilated.—There is another Canto written—but not copied—in two hundred & odd Stanzas,—if this succeeds— as to the prudery of the present day—what is it? are we more moral than when Prior[7] wrote—is there anything in Don Juan so strong as in Ariosto—or Voltaire—or Chaucer?—Tell Hobhouse—his letter to De Breme has made a great Sensation—and is to be published in the Tuscan & other Gazettes— Count R[izzo] came to consult with me about it last Sunday—we think of Tuscany—for Florence and Milan are in literary war—but the Lombard league is headed by Monti[8]—& would make a difficulty of insertion in the Lombard Gazettes—once published in the Pisan—it will find its way through Italy—by translation or reply.———So Lauderdale[9] has been telling a story!—I suppose this is my reward for presenting him at Countess Benzone's—& shewing him—what attention I could.———Which "piece" does he mean?— since last year I have run the Gauntlet;—is it the Tarruscelli—the Da Mosti—the Spineda—the Lotti—the Rizzato—the Eleanora—the Carlotta— the Giulietta—the Alvisi—the Zambieri—The Eleanora da Bezzi—(who was the King of Naples' Gioaschino's mistress—at least one of them) the Theresina of Mazzurati—the Glettenheimer—& her Sister—the Luigia & her mother—the Fornaretta—the Santa—the Caligari—the Portiera [Vedova?]—the Bolognese figurante—the Tentora and her sister—cum multis aliis?[1]—some of them are Countesses—& some of them Cobblers wives— some noble—some middling—some low—& all whores—which does the damned old "Ladro—& porco fottuto"[2] mean?—I have had them all & thrice as many to boot since 1817—Since *he* tells a story about me—I will tell one about him;—when he landed at the *Custom house* from *Corfu*—he called for *"Post horses—directly"*— he was told that there were no horses except mine nearer than the Lido—unless he wished for the four bronze Coursers of St. Mark[3]—which were at his Service.—

I am yrs. ever—

Let me have H's Election[4] immediately—I mention it *last* as being what I was least likely to forget.——

5. A play on a phrase in Valerius Maximus, *Facta et dicta* 7.2: "appeal from Philip drunk to Philip sober." Philip of Macedon was the father of Alexander the Great.
6. "Thomas Little" was a pseudonym of Thomas Moore. Christopher Anstey's *New Bath Guide* (1766) was a humorous work in anapests describing the Blunderhead family at Bath.
7. Matthew Prior, a contemporary of Pope.
8. Vincenzo Monti was a poet whom Byron and Hobhouse had met in Milan. Ludovico di Breme wrote a defense of Italian writers against the criticism that had appeared in Hobhouse's *Historical Illustrations to the Fourth Canto of Childe Harold* (1818). Hobhouse in turn sent Byron an answer to di Breme. Count Francesco Rizzo-Patarol was an acquaintance in Venice.
9. James Maitland, eighth earl of Lauderdale, who along with his "story" about Byron's love affairs had carried back to England the manuscripts of *Don Juan* (canto 1) and some other poems.
1. With many others (Latin).
2. Thief—and filthy pig (Italian).
3. The four gilded bronze statues above the portal of St. Mark's Basilica in Venice.
4. Hobhouse had begun campaigning for the Westminster seat in Parliament in November 1818 but was defeated the following March. He succeeded in a subsequent election in 1820.

P.S.—Whatever Brain-money—you get on my account from Murray—pray remit me—I will never consent to pay away what I *earn*—that is *mine*—& what I get by my brains—I will spend on my b——ks—as long as I have a tester or a testicle remaining.—I shall not live long—& for that Reason—I must live while I can—so—let him disburse—& me receive—"for the Night cometh."[5]——If I had but had twenty thousand a year I should not have been living now—but all men are not born with a silver or Gold Spoon in their mouths.——My balance—also—my balance—& a Copyright—I have another Canto—too—ready—& then there will be my half year in June—recollect—*I care for nothing but "monies".*—January 20th. 1819.—You say nothing of Mazeppa[6]—did it arrive—with one other—besides that you mention?——

To Douglas Kinnaird

[*DON JUAN:* "IS IT NOT LIFE?"]

Venice. Octr. 26th. [1819]

My dear Douglas—My late expenditure has arisen from living at a distance from Venice and being obliged to keep up two establishments, from frequent journeys—and buying some furniture and books as well as a horse or two—and not from any renewal of the EPICUREAN system[1] as you suspect. I have been faithful to my honest liaison with Countess Guiccioli[2]—and I can assure you that *She* has never cost me directly or indirectly a sixpence—indeed the circumstances of herself and family render this no merit.—I never offered her but one present—a broach of brilliants—and she sent it back to me with her *own hair* in it (I shall *not* say of *what part* but *that* is an Italian custom) and a note to say that she was not in the habit of receiving presents of that value—but hoped that I would not consider her sending it back as an affront—nor the value diminished by the enclosure.—I have not had a whore this half-year—confining myself to the strictest adultery.——Why should you prevent Hanson from making a *peer*[3] if he likes it—I think the *"Garretting"* would be by far the best parliamentary privilege—I know of.—— Damn your delicacy.—It is a low commercial quality—and very unworthy a man who prefixes "honourable" to his nomenclature. If you say that I must sign the bonds—I suppose that I must—but it is very iniquitous to make me pay my debts—you have no idea of the pain it gives one.—Pray do three things—get my property out of the *funds*—get Rochdale[4] sold—get me some information from Perry about *South America*[5]—and 4thly. ask Lady Noel not to live so very long.——As to Subscribing to Manchester—if I do that—I will write a letter to Burdett[6]—for publication—to accompany the

---

5. John 9.4: "I must work the works of him that sent me, while it is day: the night cometh, when no man can work."

6. Murray published *Mazeppa* in June 1819.

1. I.e., money spent on pleasures of the senses.

2. Byron mentions having fallen in love with Teresa Guiccioli ("a Romagnuola Countess from Ravenna—who is nineteen years old & has a Count of fifty") in a letter of April 6, 1819. Their relationship lasted until Byron set sail for Greece in the summer of 1823.

3. I.e., being made a peer (of the realm). John

Hanson, Byron's solicitor and agent before Kinnaird took over his principal business affairs, never realized this ambition.

4. An estate that Byron had inherited in Lancashire.

5. Byron was considering the possibility of emigrating to South America, specifically to Venezuela.

6. Sir Francis Burdett, member of Parliament for Westminster, a reformer and leader of opposition to the Tories.

Subscription—which shall be more radical than anything yet rooted—but I feel lazy.—I have thought of this for some time—but alas! the air of this cursed Italy enervates—and disfranchises the thoughts of a man after nearly four years of respiration—to say nothing of emission.—As to "Don Juan"—confess—confess—you dog—and be candid—that it is the sublime of *that there* sort of writing—it may be bawdy—but is it not good English?—it may be profligate—but is it not *life*, is it not *the thing*?—Could any man have written it—who has not lived in the world?—and tooled in a post-chaise? in a hackney coach? in a Gondola? against a wall? in a court carriage? in a vis a vis?[7]—on a table?—and under it?—I have written about a hundred stanzas of a third Canto—but it is damned modest—the outcry has frightened me.— I had such projects for the Don—but the *Cant* is so much stronger than *Cunt*—now a days,—that the benefit of experience in a man who had well weighed the worth of both monosyllables—must be lost to despairing posterity.—After all what stuff this outcry is—Lalla Rookh and Little—are more dangerous than my burlesque poem can be—Moore has been here—we got tipsy together—and were very amicable—he is gone on to Rome—I put my life (in M.S.) into his hands[8]—(*not* for publication) you—or any body else may see it—at his return.—It only comes up to 1816.——He is a noble fellow—and looks quite fresh and poetical—nine years (the age of a poem's education) my Senior—he looks younger—this comes of marriage and being settled in the Country. I want to go to South America—I have written to Hobhouse all about it.—I wrote to my wife—three months ago—under care to Murray—has she got the letter—or is the letter got into Blackwood's magazine?——You ask after my Christmas pye—Remit it any how—*Circulars*[9] is the best—you are right about *income*—I must have it all—how the devil do I know that I may live a year or a month?—I wish I knew that I might regulate my spending in more ways than one.—As it is one always thinks that there is but a span.—A man may as well break or be damned for a large sum as a small one—I should be loth to pay the devil or any other creditor more than sixpence in the pound.—

[scrawl for signature]

P.S.—I recollect nothing of "Davies's landlord"—but what ever Davies *says*—I will *swear* to—and *that's* more than *he* would.—So pray pay—has he a landlady too?—perhaps I may owe her something.——With regard to the bonds I will sign them but—it goes against the grain.——As to the rest— you *can't* err—so long as you *don't* pay.——Paying is executor's or executioner's work.——You may write somewhat oftener—Mr. Galignani's messenger[1] gives the outline of your public affairs—but I see no results—you have no man yet—(always excepting Burdett—& you & H[obhouse] and the Gentlemanly leaven of your two-penny loaf of rebellion) don't forget however my charge of horse—and commission for the Midland Counties and by the holies!—You shall have your account in decimals.—Love to Hobby—but why leave the Whigs?——

---

7. A light carriage for two persons sitting face to face.
8. Byron's famous memoirs, which were later sold to John Murray and burned in the publisher's office.
9. Letters of credit.
1. *Galignani's Messenger*, an English newspaper published in Paris.

To Percy Bysshe Shelley

[KEATS AND SHELLEY]

Ravenna, April 26th, 1821

The child continues doing well, and the accounts are regular and favourable. It is gratifying to me that you and Mrs. Shelley do not disapprove of the step which I have taken, which is merely temporary.[1]

I am very sorry to hear what you say of Keats[2]—is it *actually* true? I did not think criticism had been so killing. Though I differ from you essentially in your estimate of his performances, I so much abhor all unnecessary pain, that I would rather he had been seated on the highest peak of Parnassus than have perished in such a manner. Poor fellow! though with such inordinate self-love he would probably have not been very happy. I read the review of "Endymion" in the Quarterly. It was severe,—but surely not so severe as many reviews in that and other journals upon others.

I recollect the effect on me of the Edinburgh on my first poem;[3] it was rage, and resistance, and redress—but not despondency nor despair. I grant that those are not amiable feelings; but, in this world of bustle and broil, and especially in the career of writing, a man should calculate upon his powers of *resistance* before he goes into the arena.

"Expect not life from pain nor danger free,
Nor deem the doom of man reversed for thee."[4]

You know my opinion of *that second-hand* school of poetry. You also know my high opinion of your own poetry,—because it is of *no* school. I read Cenci—but, besides that I think the *subject* essentially *un* dramatic, I am not an admirer of our old dramatists *as models*. I deny that the English have hitherto had a drama at all. Your Cenci, however, was a work of power, and poetry. As to *my* drama,[5] pray revenge yourself upon it, by being as free as I have been with yours.

I have not yet got your Prometheus, which I long to see. I have heard nothing of mine, and do not know that it is yet published. I have published a pamphlet on the Pope controversy, which you will not like. Had I known that Keats was dead—or that he was alive and so sensitive—I should have omitted some remarks upon his poetry, to which I was provoked by his *attack* upon *Pope*,[6] and my disapprobation of *his own* style of writing.

1. Byron had recently placed his four-year-old daughter Allegra in a convent school near Ravenna, against the wishes of her mother, Mary Shelley's stepsister Claire Clairmont.
2. In a letter to Byron, April 17, 1821: "Young Keats, whose 'Hyperion' showed so great a promise, died lately at Rome from the consequences of breaking a blood-vessel, in paroxysms of despair at the contemptuous attack on his book in the *Quarterly Review*" (see Shelley's *Adonais*, p. 772).
3. The review of Byron's *Hours of Idleness* in the *Edinburgh Review* prompted him to write his first major satire, *English Bards and Scotch Reviewers* (1809).
4. Johnson, *The Vanity of Human Wishes*, lines 155–56 (Byron is quoting from memory).

5. *Marino Faliero*, published in London on April 21, 1821. Shelley's *The Cenci* and *Prometheus Unbound* (next paragraph) were written in 1819 and published in 1820.
6. Keats attacked Augustan poetry (but not necessarily Pope) in *Sleep and Poetry*, lines 181–206. Byron's pamphlet, *Letter to ********[John Murray], on the Rev. W. L. Bowles' Strictures on the Life and Writings of Pope*, had just appeared in London. His best-known comment on Keats, written a year and a half later, is canto 11, stanza 60 in *Don Juan*, beginning "John Keats, who was killed off by one critique" and ending " 'Tis strange the mind, that very fiery particle, / Should let itself be snuffed out by an Article."

You want me to undertake a great Poem—I have not the inclination nor the power. As I grow older, the indifference—*not* to life, for we love it by instinct—but to the stimuli of life, increases. Besides, this late failure of the Italians[7] has latterly disappointed me for many reasons,—some public, some personal. My respects to Mrs. S.

Yours ever,

B

P.S.—Could not you and I contrive to meet this summer? Could not you take a run *alone?*

---

7. A planned uprising by the Carbonari, a secret revolutionary society into which Byron had been initiated by the father and brother of his mistress Teresa Guiccioli, failed in Feb. 1821.

PERCY BYSSHE SHELLEY
1792–1822

Percy Bysshe Shelley, a radical nonconformist in every aspect of his life and thought, emerged from a solidly conservative background. His ancestors had been Sussex aristocrats since early in the seventeenth century; his grandfather, Sir Bysshe Shelley, made himself the richest man in Horsham, Sussex; his father, Timothy Shelley, was a hardheaded and conventional Member of Parliament. Percy Shelley himself was in line for a baronetcy and, as befitted his station, was sent to be educated at Eton and Oxford. As a youth he was slight of build, eccentric in manner, and unskilled in sports or fighting and, as a consequence, was mercilessly baited by older and stronger boys. He later said that he saw the petty tyranny of schoolmasters and schoolmates as representative of man's general inhumanity to man, and dedicated his life to a war against injustice and oppression. As he described the experience in the Dedication to *Laon and Cythna*:

> So without shame, I spake:—"I will be wise,
> And just, and free, and mild, if in me lies
> Such power, for I grow weary to behold
> The selfish and the strong still tyrannise
> Without reproach or check." I then controuled
> My tears, my heart grew calm, and I was meek and bold.

At Oxford in the autumn of 1810 Shelley's closest friend was Thomas Jefferson Hogg, a self-centered, self-confident young man who shared Shelley's love of philosophy and scorn of orthodoxy. The two collaborated on a pamphlet, *The Necessity of Atheism,* which claimed that God's existence cannot be proved on empirical grounds, and, provocatively, they mailed it to the bishops and heads of the colleges at Oxford. Shelley refused to repudiate the document and, to his shock and grief, was peremptorily expelled, terminating a university career that had lasted only six months. This event opened a breach between Shelley and his father that widened over the years.

Shelley went to London, where he took up the cause of Harriet Westbrook, the pretty and warmhearted daughter of a well-to-do tavern keeper, whose father, Shelley wrote to Hogg, "has persecuted her in a most horrible way by endeavoring to compel her to go to school." Harriet threw herself on Shelley's protection, and "gratitude and admiration," he wrote, "all demand that I shall love her *forever.*" He eloped with Harriet to Edinburgh and married her, against his conviction that marriage was a tyrannical and degrading social institution. He was then eighteen years of age, and his bride sixteen. The young couple moved restlessly from place to place, living on a small allowance granted reluctantly by their families. In February 1812, accompanied by Harriet's sister Eliza, they traveled to Dublin to distribute Shelley's *Address to the Irish People* and otherwise take part in the movement for Catholic emancipation and for the amelioration of that oppressed and poverty-stricken people.

Back in London, Shelley became a disciple of the radical social philosopher William Godwin, author of the *Inquiry Concerning Political Justice.* In 1813 he printed privately his first important work, *Queen Mab,* a long poem set in the fantastic frame of the journey of a disembodied soul through space, to whom the fairy Mab reveals in visions the woeful past, the dreadful present, and a utopian future. Announcing that "there is no God!" Mab decries institutional religion and codified morality as the roots of social evil, prophesying that all institutions will wither away and humanity will return to its natural condition of goodness and felicity.

In the following spring Shelley, who had drifted apart from Harriet, fell in love with the beautiful Mary Wollstonecraft Godwin, daughter of Mary Wollstonecraft and William Godwin. Convinced that cohabitation without love is immoral, he abandoned Harriet, fled to France with Mary (taking along her stepsister, Claire Clairmont), and—in accordance with his belief in nonexclusive love—invited Harriet to come live with them in the relationship of a sister. Shelley's elopement with Mary outraged her father, despite the facts that his own views of marriage had been no less radical than Shelley's and that Shelley, himself in financial difficulties, had earlier taken over Godwin's very substantial debts. When he returned to London, Shelley found that the general public, his family, and most of his friends regarded him as not only an atheist and revolutionary but also a gross immoralist. When two years later Harriet, pregnant by an unknown lover, drowned herself in a fit of despair, the courts denied Shelley the custody of their two children. Shelley married Mary Godwin and in 1818 moved to Italy. Thereafter he envisioned himself as an alien and outcast, rejected by the human race to whose welfare he had dedicated his powers and his life.

In Italy he resumed his restless way of life, evading creditors by moving from town to town and house to house. His health was usually bad. Although the death of his grandfather in 1815 had provided a substantial income, he dissipated so much of it by his warmhearted but improvident support of William Godwin, Leigh Hunt, and other needy pensioners that he was constantly short of money and harried by creditors. Within nine months, in 1818–19, Clara and William, children of Percy and Mary Shelley, both died. This tragedy threw Mary into a state of apathy and self-absorption that destroyed the earlier harmony of her relationship with her husband, from which even the birth of another son, Percy Florence, could not entirely rescue her.

In these circumstances, close to despair and knowing that he almost entirely lacked an audience, Shelley wrote his greatest works. In 1819 he completed *Prometheus Unbound* and a tragedy, *The Cenci.* He wrote also numerous lyric poems; a visionary call for a proletarian revolution, *The Mask of Anarchy*; a witty satire on Wordsworth, *Peter Bell the Third*; and a penetrating political essay, *A Philosophical View of Reform.* His works of the next two years include *A Defence of Poetry*; *Epipsychidion,* a rhapsodic vision of love as a spiritual union beyond earthly limits; *Adonais,* his elegy on the death of Keats; and *Hellas,* a lyrical drama evoked by the Greek war for liberation from the Turks. These writings, unlike the early *Queen Mab,* are the products of a mind chastened by tragic experience, deepened by philosophical speculation, and stored with the harvest of his reading—which Shelley carried on, as his friend Hogg said, "in season and out of season, at table, in bed, and especially during a walk," until he became one of the most erudite of poets. His delight in scientific discoveries and speculations continued, but his earlier zest for Gothic terrors and the social theories of the radical eighteenth-century optimists gave way to an absorption in Greek tragedy, Milton's *Paradise Lost,* and the Bible. Although he did not give up his hopes for a millennial future (he wore a ring with the motto *Il buon tempo verrà*— "the good time will come"), he now attributed the evils of society to humanity's own moral failures and grounded the possibility of radical social reform on a reform of the moral and imaginative faculties through the redeeming power of love. Though often represented as a simpleminded doctrinaire, Shelley in fact possessed a complex and energetically inquisitive intelligence that never halted at a fixed mental position; his writings reflect stages in a ceaseless exploration.

The poems of Shelley's maturity also show the influence of his study of Plato and the Neoplatonists. Shelley found congenial the Platonic division of the cosmos into two worlds—the ordinary world of change, mortality, evil, and suffering and an ideal world of perfect and eternal Forms, of which the world of sense-experience is only a distant and illusory reflection. The earlier interpretations of Shelley as a downright Platonic idealist, however, have been drastically modified by modern investigations of his reading and writings. He was a close student of British empirical philosophy, which limits knowledge to valid reasoning on what is given in sense-experience, and within this tradition he felt a special affinity to the radical skepticism of David Hume. A number of Shelley's works, such as *Mont Blanc,* express his view of the narrow limits of what human beings can know with certainty and exemplify his refusal to let his hopes harden into a philosophical or religious creed. To what has been called the "skeptical idealism" of the mature Shelley (see the notes he appended to his lyrics from *Hellas*), hope in a redemption from present social ills is not an intellectual certainty but a moral obligation. Despair is self-fulfilling; we must continue to hope because, by keeping open the possibility of a better future, hope releases the imaginative and creative powers that are the only means of achieving that end.

When in 1820 the Shelleys settled finally at Pisa, he came closer to finding contentment than at any other time in his adult life. A group of friends, Shelley's "Pisan Circle," gathered around them, including for a while Lord Byron and the swashbuckling young Cornishman Edward Trelawny. Chief in Shelley's affections were Edward Williams, a retired lieutenant of a cavalry regiment serving in India, and his charming common-law wife, Jane, with whom Shelley carried on a flirtation and to whom he addressed some of his best lyrics and verse letters. The end came suddenly, and in a way previsioned in the last stanza of *Adonais,* in which he had described his spirit as a ship driven by a violent storm out into the dark unknown. On July 8, 1822, Shelley and Edward Williams were sailing their open boat, the *Don Juan,* on the Gulf of Spezia. A violent squall swamped the boat. When several days later the bodies were washed ashore they were cremated, and Shelley's ashes were buried in the Protestant Cemetery at Rome, near the graves of John Keats and William Shelley, the poet's young son.

Both Shelley's character and his poetry have been the subject of violently contradictory, and often partisan, estimates. His actions according to his deep convictions often led to disastrous consequences for himself and those near to him; and even recent scholars, while repudiating the vicious attacks by Shelley's contemporaries, attribute some of those actions to a self-assured egotism that masked itself as idealism. Yet Byron, who knew Shelley intimately and did not pay moral compliments lightly, wrote to his publisher John Murray, in response to attacks on Shelley at the time of his death: "You are all brutally mistaken about Shelley, who was, without exception, the *best* and least selfish man I ever knew." Shelley's politics, vilified during his lifetime, have made him a literary hero to later political radicals, as well as to the British Labour Party. As a poet, Shelley was greatly admired by Robert Browning, Swinburne, and other Victorians; but in the mid-twentieth century he was repeatedly charged with intellectual and emotional immaturity, shoddy workmanship, and incoherent imagery by such influential writers as F. R. Leavis and his followers in Britain and the New Critics in America. More recently, however, many sympathetic studies have revealed the coherent intellectual understructure of his poems and have confirmed Wordsworth's early recognition that "Shelley is one of the best *artists* of us all: I mean in workmanship of style." Shelley, it has become clear, greatly expanded the metrical and stanzaic resources of English versification. His poems exhibit a broad range of voices, from the high but ordered passion of *Ode to the West Wind,* through the heroic dignity of the utterances of Prometheus, to the approximation of what is inexpressible in the description of Asia's transfiguration and in the visionary conclusion of *Adonais.* Most surprising, for a poet who almost entirely lacked an audience, is the urbanity, the assured command of the tone and language of a cultivated man of the world, exemplified in passages that Shelley wrote all through his mature career and especially in the lyrics and verse letters that he composed during the last year of his life.

The texts printed here are those prepared by Donald H. Reiman and Sharon B. Powers for *Shelley's Poetry and Prose,* a Norton Critical Edition (1977); Reiman has also edited for this anthology a few poems not included in that edition.

Mutability

We are as clouds that veil the midnight moon;
  How restlessly they speed, and gleam, and quiver,
Streaking the darkness radiantly!—yet soon
  Night closes round, and they are lost for ever:

5 Or like forgotten lyres,° whose dissonant strings   *wind harps*
  Give various response to each varying blast,
To whose frail frame no second motion brings
  One mood or modulation like the last.

We rest.—A dream has power to poison sleep;
10   We rise.—One wandering thought pollutes the day;
We feel, conceive or reason, laugh or weep;
  Embrace fond woe, or cast our cares away:

It is the same!—For, be it joy or sorrow,
  The path of its departure still is free:
15 Man's yesterday may ne'er be like his morrow;
  Nought may endure but Mutability.

ca. 1814–15   1816

To Wordsworth[1]

Poet of Nature, thou hast wept to know
That things depart which never may return:
Childhood and youth, friendship and love's first glow,
Have fled like sweet dreams, leaving thee to mourn.
5 These common woes I feel. One loss is mine
Which thou too feel'st, yet I alone deplore.
Thou wert as a lone star, whose light did shine
On some frail bark in winter's midnight roar:
Thou hast like to a rock-built refuge stood

1. Shelley's grieved comment on the poet of nature and of social radicalism after his views had become conservative.

10   Above the blind and battling multitude:
      In honoured poverty thy voice did weave
      Songs consecrate to truth and liberty,—
      Deserting these, thou leavest me to grieve,
      Thus having been, that thou shouldst cease to be.

ca. 1814–15   1816

Alastor; or, The Spirit of Solitude

Alastor; or, The Spirit of Solitude   Shelley wrote *Alastor* in the fall and early winter of 1815 and published it in March 1816. According to his friend Thomas Love Peacock, the poet was "at a loss for a title, and I proposed that which he adopted: Alastor, or the Spirit of Solitude. The Greek word *Alastor* is an evil genius. . . . I mention the true meaning of the word because many have supposed *Alastor* to be the name of the hero" (*Memoirs of Shelley*). Peacock's definition of an *alastor* as "an *evil* genius" has compounded the problems in interpreting this work: the term *evil* does not seem to fit the attitude expressed within the poem toward the protagonist's solitary quest, the poem seems to clash with statements in Shelley's preface, and the first and second paragraphs of the preface seem inconsistent with each other. These problems, however, may be largely resolved if we recognize that, in this early achievement (he was only twenty-three when he wrote *Alastor*), Shelley established his characteristic procedure of working with multiple perspectives. Both preface and poem explore alternative and conflicting possibilities in what Shelley calls "doubtful knowledge"— matters that are humanly essential but in which no certainty is humanly possible.

By the term *allegorical* in the opening sentence of his preface, Shelley may be taken to signify that his poem, like medieval and Renaissance allegories such as Dante's *Divine Comedy* and Spenser's *Faerie Queene,* represents a need and aspiration in the spiritual realm by the allegorical vehicle of a journey and quest in the material world. Shelley's protagonist, for whom the objects in the natural world "cease to suffice," commits himself to the search for a female Other who will fulfill his intellectual, imaginative, and sensuous needs. Because, however, his desires are unlimited and the world's possibilities are finite, his quest is doomed to end in his early death.

The second paragraph of the preface passes judgment on the visionary protagonist in terms of the values of "actual men"—that is, the requirements of human and social life in this world. From this point of view, the visionary has been "avenged" (punished) for turning away from both human and natural community in pursuit of his own psychic needs. The preface goes on, however, to elevate the moral status of such a visionary over a second class of "meaner spirits" who also "keep aloof from sympathies with their kind," but only because they are unable to project their feelings beyond their own narrow selves and so are "morally dead."

The diversity of attitudes expressed within the poem itself becomes more intelligible if, on the basis of the many echoes of Wordsworth in the opening invocation, we identify the narrator of the story as a Wordsworthian poet for whom the natural world is sufficient to satisfy both the demands of his imagination and his need for community. This narrative poet, it can be assumed, undertakes to tell compassionately, but from his own perspective, the history of a nameless visionary who has surrendered everything in the quest for a goal beyond possibility.

In this early poem Shelley establishes a form, a conceptual frame, and the imagery for the Romantic quest that he reiterated in his later poems and that also served as a paradigm for many other poems, from Byron's *Manfred* and Keats's *Endymion* to the quest-poems of Shelley's later admirer William Butler Yeats.

Alastor; or, The Spirit of Solitude

Preface

The poem entitled "ALASTOR," may be considered as allegorical of one of the most interesting situations of the human mind. It represents a youth of uncorrupted feelings and adventurous genius led forth by an imagination inflamed and purified through familiarity with all that is excellent and majestic, to the contemplation of the universe. He drinks deep of the fountains of knowledge, and is still insatiate. The magnificence and beauty of the external world sinks profoundly into the frame of his conceptions, and affords to their modifications a variety not to be exhausted. So long as it is possible for his desires to point towards objects thus infinite and unmeasured, he is joyous, and tranquil, and self-possessed. But the period arrives when these objects cease to suffice. His mind is at length suddenly awakened and thirsts for intercourse with an intelligence similar to itself. He images to himself the Being whom he loves. Conversant with speculations of the sublimest and most perfect natures, the vision in which he embodies his own imaginations unites all of wonderful, or wise, or beautiful, which the poet, the philosopher, or the lover could depicture. The intellectual faculties, the imagination, the functions of sense, have their respective requisitions on the sympathy of corresponding powers in other human beings. The Poet is represented as uniting these requisitions, and attaching them to a single image.[1] He seeks in vain for a prototype of his conception. Blasted by his disappointment, he descends to an untimely grave.

The picture is not barren of instruction to actual men. The Poet's self-centred seclusion was avenged by the furies of an irresistible passion pursuing him to speedy ruin. But that Power which strikes the luminaries of the world with sudden darkness and extinction, by awakening them to too exquisite a perception of its influences, dooms to a slow and poisonous decay those meaner spirits that dare to abjure its dominion. Their destiny is more abject and inglorious as their delinquency is more contemptible and pernicious. They who, deluded by no generous error, instigated by no sacred thirst of doubtful knowledge, duped by no illustrious superstition, loving nothing on this earth, and cherishing no hopes beyond, yet keep aloof from sympathies with their kind, rejoicing neither in human joy nor mourning with human grief; these, and such as they, have their apportioned curse. They languish, because none feel with them their common nature. They are morally dead. They are neither friends, nor lovers, nor fathers, nor citizens of the world, nor benefactors of their country. Among those who attempt to exist without human sympathy, the pure and tender-hearted perish through the intensity and passion of their search after its communities, when the vacancy of their spirit suddenly makes itself felt. All else, selfish, blind, and

---

1. Shelley's view that the object of love is an idealized antitype to all that is best within the self is clarified by a passage in his *Essay on Love,* which may have been written at about the time of *Alastor:* "We dimly see within our intellectual nature . . . the ideal prototype of every thing excellent or lovely that we are capable of conceiving as belonging to the nature of men. . . . [This is] a soul within our soul. . . . The discovery of its anti-type . . . in such proportion as the type within demands; this is the invisible and unattainable point to which Love tends; and . . . without the possession of which there is no rest nor respite to the heart over which it rules."

torpid, are those unforeseeing multitudes who constitute, together with their own, the lasting misery and loneliness of the world. Those who love not their fellow-beings live unfruitful lives, and prepare for their old age a miserable grave.

> "The good die first,
> And those whose hearts are dry as summer dust,
> Burn to the socket!"[2]

December 14, 1815

Alastor; or, The Spirit of Solitude

Nondum amabam, et amare amabam, qæurebam quid amarem, amans amare.—Confess. St. August.[3]

Earth, ocean, air, beloved brotherhood!
If our great Mother[4] has imbued my soul
With aught of natural piety[5] to feel
Your love, and recompense the boon with mine;[6]
5 If dewy morn, and odorous noon, and even,
With sunset and its gorgeous ministers,[7]
And solemn midnight's tingling silentness;
If autumn's hollow sighs in the sere wood,
And winter robing with pure snow and crowns
10 Of starry ice the grey grass and bare boughs;
If spring's voluptuous pantings when she breathes
Her first sweet kisses, have been dear to me;
If no bright bird, insect, or gentle beast
I consciously have injured, but still loved
15 And cherished these my kindred; then forgive
This boast, beloved brethren, and withdraw
No portion of your wonted favour now!

Mother of this unfathomable world!
Favour my solemn song, for I have loved
20 Thee ever, and thee only; I have watched
Thy shadow, and the darkness of thy steps,
And my heart ever gazes on the depth
Of thy deep mysteries. I have made my bed
In charnels and on coffins, where black death
25 Keeps record of the trophies won from thee,
Hoping to still these obstinate questionings[8]
Of thee and thine, by forcing some lone ghost,

---

2. Wordsworth's *The Excursion* 1.519–21; the passage occurs also in *The Ruined Cottage* 96–98, which Wordsworth reworked into the first book of *The Excursion* (1814).

3. St. Augustine's *Confessions* 3.1: "Not yet did I love, though I loved to love, seeking what I might love, loving to love." Augustine thus describes his state of mind when he was addicted to illicit sexual love; the true object of his desire, which compels the tortuous spiritual journey of his life, he later discovered to be the infinite and transcendent God.

4. Nature, invoked as the common mother of the elements and of the poet.

5. Wordsworth, *My heart leaps up*, lines 8–9: "And I could wish my days to be / Bound each to each by natural piety." Wordsworth also used these lines as the epigraph to his *Ode: Intimations of Immortality*.

6. I.e., with my love.

7. The sunset colors.

8. Wordsworth, *Ode: Intimations of Immortality*, lines 141–42: "those obstinate questionings / Of sense and outward things."

Thy messenger, to render up the tale
Of what we are. In lone and silent hours,
30 When night makes a weird sound of its own stillness,
Like an inspired and desperate alchymist
Staking his very life on some dark hope,
Have I mixed awful talk and asking looks
With my most innocent love, until strange tears
35 Uniting with those breathless kisses, made
Such magic as compels the charmed night
To render up thy charge: . . . and, though ne'er yet
Thou hast unveil'd thy inmost sanctuary,
Enough from incommunicable dream,
40 And twilight phantasms, and deep noonday thought,
Has shone within me, that serenely now
And moveless, as a long-forgotten lyre
Suspended in the solitary dome
Of some mysterious and deserted fane,⁹
45 I wait thy breath, Great Parent, that my strain
May modulate with murmurs of the air,
And motions of the forests and the sea,
And voice of living beings, and woven hymns
Of night and day, and the deep heart of man.¹

50 There was a Poet whose untimely tomb
No human hands with pious reverence reared,
But the charmed eddies of autumnal winds
Built o'er his mouldering bones a pyramid
Of mouldering leaves in the waste wilderness:—
55 A lovely youth,—no mourning maiden decked
With weeping flowers, or votive cypress wreath,²
The lone couch of his everlasting sleep:—
Gentle, and brave, and generous,—no lorn° bard   *abandoned*
Breathed o'er his dark fate one melodious sigh:
60 He lived, he died, he sung, in solitude.
Strangers have wept to hear his passionate notes,
And virgins, as unknown he past, have pined
And wasted for fond love of his wild eyes.
The fire of those soft orbs has ceased to burn,
65 And Silence, too enamoured of that voice,
Locks its mute music in her rugged cell.

By solemn vision, and bright silver dream,
His infancy was nurtured. Every sight
And sound from the vast earth and ambient air,
70 Sent to his heart its choicest impulses.
The fountains of divine philosophy
Fled not his thirsting lips, and all of great

---

9. Temple. The narrator calls on the Mother, his natural muse, to make him her wind harp. Cf. the opening passage of Wordsworth's *Prelude*, Coleridge's *Dejection: An Ode*, and the conclusions of Shelley's *Ode to the West Wind* and *Adonais*.
1. Cf. Wordsworth, *Tintern Abbey* 94ff.: "A pres-
ence . . . / Whose dwelling is . . . the round ocean and the living air, / And the blue sky, and in the mind of man: / A motion and a spirit."
2. The cypress represented mourning. "Votive": offered to fulfill a vow to the gods.

Or good, or lovely, which the sacred past
In truth or fable consecrates, he felt
75 And knew. When early youth had past, he left
His cold fireside and alienated home
To seek strange truths in undiscovered lands.
Many a wide waste and tangled wilderness
Has lured his fearless steps; and he has bought
80 With his sweet voice and eyes, from savage men,
His rest and food. Nature's most secret steps
He like her shadow has pursued, where'er
The red volcano overcanopies
Its fields of snow and pinnacles of ice
85 With burning smoke, or where bitumen lakes[3]
On black bare pointed islets ever beat
With sluggish surge, or where the secret caves
Rugged and dark, winding among the springs
Of fire and poison, inaccessible
90 To avarice or pride, their starry domes
Of diamond and of gold expand above
Numberless and immeasurable halls,
Frequent° with crystal column, and clear shrines   *crowded*
Of pearl, and thrones radiant with chrysolite.[4]
95 Nor had that scene of ampler majesty
Than gems or gold, the varying roof of heaven
And the green earth lost in his heart its claims
To love and wonder; he would linger long
In lonesome vales, making the wild his home,
100 Until the doves and squirrels would partake
From his innocuous hand his bloodless food,[5]
Lured by the gentle meaning of his looks,
And the wild antelope, that starts whene'er
The dry leaf rustles in the brake,° suspend   *thicket*
105 Her timid steps to gaze upon a form
More graceful than her own.

               His wandering step
Obedient to high thoughts, has visited
The awful ruins of the days of old:
Athens, and Tyre, and Balbec,[6] and the waste
110 Where stood Jerusalem, the fallen towers
Of Babylon, the eternal pyramids,
Memphis and Thebes,[7] and whatsoe'er of strange
Sculptured on alabaster obelisk,
Or jasper tomb, or mutilated sphynx,
115 Dark Æthiopia in her desert hills
Conceals. Among the ruined temples there,
Stupendous columns, and wild images
Of more than man, where marble dæmons watch

---

3. Lakes of pitch, flowing from a volcano.
4. An olive green stone.
5. Shelley was himself a vegetarian.
6. An ancient city in what is now Lebanon. Tyre

was once an important commercial city on the
Phoenician coast.
7. The ancient capital of Upper Egypt. Memphis
is the ruined capital of Lower Egypt.

The Zodiac's[8] brazen mystery, and dead men
120   Hang their mute thoughts on the mute walls around,[9]
He lingered, poring on memorials
Of the world's youth, through the long burning day
Gazed on those speechless shapes, nor, when the moon
Filled the mysterious halls with floating shades
125   Suspended he that task, but ever gazed
And gazed, till meaning on his vacant mind
Flashed like strong inspiration, and he saw
The thrilling secrets of the birth of time.

Meanwhile an Arab maiden brought his food,
130   Her daily portion, from her father's tent,
And spread her matting for his couch, and stole
From duties and repose to tend his steps:—
Enamoured, yet not daring for deep awe
To speak her love:—and watched his nightly sleep,
135   Sleepless herself, to gaze upon his lips
Parted in slumber, whence the regular breath
Of innocent dreams arose: then, when red morn
Made paler the pale moon, to her cold home
Wildered,° and wan, and panting, she returned.   *bewildered*

140   The Poet wandering on, through Arabie
And Persia, and the wild Carmanian waste,[1]
And o'er the aërial mountains which pour down
Indus and Oxus[2] from their icy caves,
In joy and exultation held his way;
145   Till in the vale of Cashmire, far within
Its loneliest dell, where odorous plants entwine
Beneath the hollow rocks a natural bower,
Beside a sparkling rivulet he stretched
His languid limbs. A vision on his sleep
150   There came, a dream of hopes that never yet
Had flushed his cheek. He dreamed a veiled maid
Sate near him, talking in low solemn tones.
Her voice was like the voice of his own soul
Heard in the calm of thought; its music long,
155   Like woven sounds of streams and breezes, held
His inmost sense suspended in its web
Of many-coloured woof and shifting hues.
Knowledge and truth and virtue were her theme,
And lofty hopes of divine liberty,
160   Thoughts the most dear to him, and poesy,
Herself a poet.[3] Soon the solemn mood
Of her pure mind kindled through all her frame
A permeating fire: wild numbers then

---

8. In the temple of Isis at Denderah, Egypt, the
Zodiac is represented on the ceiling. "Daemons":
in Greek mythology, not evil spirits but minor deities or attendant spirits.
9. I.e., by quotations inscribed in the stone.
1. A desert in southern Persia.

2. Rivers in Asia.
3. The envisioned maiden embodies all three qualities specified in the preface: intellect (line 158),
imagination (lines 160–61), and the sexual and
other "functions of sense" (lines 176ff.).

She raised, with voice stifled in tremulous sobs
165 Subdued by its own pathos: her fair hands
Were bare alone, sweeping from some strange harp
Strange symphony, and in their branching veins
The eloquent blood told an ineffable tale.
The beating of her heart was heard to fill
170 The pauses of her music, and her breath
Tumultuously accorded with those fits
Of intermitted song. Sudden she rose,
As if her heart impatiently endured
Its bursting burthen: at the sound he turned,
175 And saw by the warm light of their own life
Her glowing limbs beneath the sinuous veil
Of woven wind, her outspread arms now bare,
Her dark locks floating in the breath of night,
Her beamy bending eyes, her parted lips
180 Outstretched, and pale, and quivering eagerly.
His strong heart sunk and sickened with excess
Of love. He reared his shuddering limbs and quelled
His gasping breath, and spread his arms to meet
Her panting bosom: . . . she drew back a while,
185 Then, yielding to the irresistible joy,
With frantic gesture and short breathless cry
Folded his frame in her dissolving arms.
Now blackness veiled his dizzy eyes, and night
Involved and swallowed up the vision; sleep,
190 Like a dark flood suspended in its course,
Rolled back its impulse on his vacant brain.

Roused by the shock he started from his trance—
The cold white light of morning, the blue moon
Low in the west, the clear and garish hills,
195 The distinct valley and the vacant woods,
Spread round him where he stood. Whither have fled
The hues of heaven that canopied his bower
Of yesternight? The sounds that soothed his sleep,
The mystery and the majesty of Earth,
200 The joy, the exultation? His wan eyes
Gaze on the empty scene as vacantly
As ocean's moon looks on the moon in heaven.
The spirit of sweet human love has sent
A vision to the sleep of him who spurned
205 Her choicest gifts. He eagerly pursues
Beyond the realms of dream that fleeting shade;
He overleaps the bounds. Alas! alas!
Were limbs, and breath, and being intertwined
Thus treacherously? Lost, lost, for ever lost,
210 In the wide pathless desart of dim sleep,
That beautiful shape! Does the dark gate of death
Conduct to thy mysterious paradise,
O Sleep?[4] Does the bright arch of rainbow clouds,

4. I.e., is death the only access to this maiden of his dream?

And pendent mountains seen in the calm lake,
215 Lead only to a black and watery depth,
While death's blue vault, with loathliest vapours hung,
Where every shade which the foul grave exhales
Hides its dead eye from the detested day,
Conduct,[5] O Sleep, to thy delightful realms?
220 This doubt with sudden tide flowed on his heart,
The insatiate hope which it awakened, stung
His brain even like despair.
             While day-light held
The sky, the Poet kept mute conference
With his still soul. At night the passion came,
225 Like the fierce fiend of a distempered dream,
And shook him from his rest, and led him forth
Into the darkness.—As an eagle grasped
In folds of the green serpent, feels her breast
Burn with the poison, and precipitates°   hastens
230 Through night and day, tempest, and calm, and cloud,
Frantic with dizzying anguish, her blind flight
O'er the wide aëry wilderness:[6] thus driven
By the bright shadow of that lovely dream,
Beneath the cold glare of the desolate night,
235 Through tangled swamps and deep precipitous dells,
Startling with careless step the moon-light snake,
He fled. Red morning dawned upon his flight,
Shedding the mockery of its vital hues
Upon his cheek of death. He wandered on
240 Till vast Aornos seen from Petra's[7] steep
Hung o'er the low horizon like a cloud;
Through Balk,[8] and where the desolated tombs
Of Parthian kings[9] scatter to every wind
Their wasting dust, wildly he wandered on,
245 Day after day, a weary waste of hours,
Bearing within his life the brooding care
That ever fed on its decaying flame.
And now his limbs were lean; his scattered hair
Sered by the autumn of strange suffering
250 Sung dirges in the wind; his listless hand
Hung like dead bone within its withered skin;
Life, and the lustre that consumed it, shone
As in a furnace burning secretly
From his dark eyes alone. The cottagers,
255 Who ministered with human charity
His human wants, beheld with wondering awe
Their fleeting visitant. The mountaineer,
Encountering on some dizzy precipice
That spectral form, deemed that the Spirit of wind
260 With lightning eyes, and eager breath, and feet

5. "Conduct" is a singular subjunctive verb; its subject is "vault" (line 216).
6. The eagle and serpent locked in mortal combat is a recurrent image in Shelley's poems (see *Prometheus Unbound* 3.1.72–73, p. 751).
7. The rock (literal trans.); "Petra's steep" is a mountain stronghold in the northern part of ancient Arabia. Aornos is a high mountain.
8. Bactria, in ancient Persia, is now part of Afghanistan.
9. The Parthians inhabited northern Persia.

Disturbing not the drifted snow, had paused
In its career: the infant would conceal
His troubled visage in his mother's robe
In terror at the glare of those wild eyes,
265 To remember their strange light in many a dream
Of after-times; but youthful maidens, taught
By nature, would interpret half the woe
That wasted him, would call him with false names
Brother, and friend,[1] would press his pallid hand
270 At parting, and watch, dim through tears, the path
Of his departure from their father's door.

At length upon the lone Chorasmian shore[2]
He paused, a wide and melancholy waste
Of putrid marshes. A strong impulse urged
275 His steps to the sea-shore. A swan was there,
Beside a sluggish stream among the reeds.
It rose as he approached, and with strong wings
Scaling the upward sky, bent its bright course
High over the immeasurable main.
280 His eyes pursued its flight.—"Thou hast a home,
Beautiful bird; thou voyagest to thine home,
Where thy sweet mate will twine her downy neck
With thine, and welcome thy return with eyes
Bright in the lustre of their own fond joy.
285 And what am I that I should linger here,
With voice far sweeter than thy dying notes,
Spirit more vast than thine, frame more attuned
To beauty, wasting these surpassing powers
In the deaf air, to the blind earth, and heaven
290 That echoes not my thoughts?" A gloomy smile
Of desperate hope wrinkled his quivering lips.
For sleep, he knew, kept most relentlessly
Its precious charge,[3] and silent death exposed,
Faithless perhaps as sleep, a shadowy lure,
295 With doubtful smile mocking its own strange charms.

Startled by his own thoughts he looked around.
There was no fair fiend[4] near him, not a sight
Or sound of awe but in his own deep mind.
A little shallop[5] floating near the shore
300 Caught the impatient wandering of his gaze.
It had been long abandoned, for its sides
Gaped wide with many a rift, and its frail joints
Swayed with the undulations of the tide.
A restless impulse urged him to embark
305 And meet lone Death on the drear ocean's waste;

1. The maidens call him "false" (i.e., mistaken) names signifying an affectionate earthly relationship instead of his unearthly love.
2. The shore of Lake Aral, about 175 miles east of the Caspian Sea.
3. I.e., the maiden in the sleeper's dream. The passage goes on to express the skeptical fear that neither sleep nor death may yield the Poet his desire.
4. Apparently he suspects there may have been an external agent luring him to the death described in the preceding lines.
5. A small open boat.

For well he knew that mighty Shadow loves
The slimy caverns of the populous deep.

    The day was fair and sunny; sea and sky
Drank its inspiring radiance, and the wind
310   Swept strongly from the shore, blackening the waves.
Following his eager soul, the wanderer
Leaped in the boat, he spread his cloak aloft
On the bare mast, and took his lonely seat,
And felt the boat speed o'er the tranquil sea
315   Like a torn cloud before the hurricane.

    As one that in a silver vision floats
Obedient to the sweep of odorous winds
Upon resplendent clouds, so rapidly
Along the dark and ruffled waters fled
320   The straining boat.—A whirlwind swept it on,
With fierce gusts and precipitating force,
Through the white ridges of the chafed sea.
The waves arose. Higher and higher still
Their fierce necks writhed beneath the tempest's scourge
325   Like serpents struggling in a vulture's grasp.
Calm and rejoicing in the fearful war
Of wave running on wave, and blast on blast
Descending, and black flood on whirlpool driven
With dark obliterating course, he sate:
330   As if their genii were the ministers
Appointed to conduct him to the light
Of those beloved eyes, the Poet sate
Holding the steady helm. Evening came on,
The beams of sunset hung their rainbow hues
335   High 'mid the shifting domes of sheeted spray
That canopied his path o'er the waste deep;
Twilight, ascending slowly from the east,
Entwin'd in duskier wreaths her braided locks
O'er the fair front and radiant eyes of day;
340   Night followed, clad with stars. On every side
More horribly the multitudinous streams
Of ocean's mountainous waste to mutual war
Rushed in dark tumult thundering, as to mock
The calm and spangled sky. The little boat
345   Still fled before the storm; still fled, like foam
Down the steep cataract of a wintry river;
Now pausing on the edge of the riven wave;
Now leaving far behind the bursting mass
That fell, convulsing ocean. Safely fled—
350   As if that frail and wasted human form,
Had been an elemental god.[6]
                     At midnight
The moon arose: and lo! the etherial cliffs[7]

6. A god of one of the natural elements (see line 1).

7. I.e., cliffs high in the air.

Of Caucasus, whose icy summits shone
Among the stars like sunlight, and around
355 Whose cavern'd base the whirlpools and the waves
Bursting and eddying irresistibly
Rage and resound for ever.—Who shall save?—
The boat fled on,—the boiling torrent drove,—
The crags closed round with black and jagged arms,
360 The shattered mountain overhung the sea,
And faster still, beyond all human speed,
Suspended on the sweep of the smooth wave,
The little boat was driven. A cavern there
Yawned, and amid its slant and winding depths
365 Ingulphed the rushing sea. The boat fled on
With unrelaxing speed.—"Vision and Love!"
The Poet cried aloud, "I have beheld
The path of thy departure. Sleep and death
Shall not divide us long!"

                        The boat pursued
370 The winding of the cavern.[8] Day-light shone
At length upon that gloomy river's flow;
Now, where the fiercest war among the waves
Is calm, on the unfathomable stream
The boat moved slowly. Where the mountain, riven,
375 Exposed those black depths to the azure sky,
Ere yet the flood's enormous volume fell
Even to the base of Caucasus, with sound
That shook the everlasting rocks, the mass
Filled with one whirlpool all that ample chasm;
380 Stair above stair the eddying waters rose,
Circling immeasurably fast, and laved
With alternating dash the knarled roots
Of mighty trees, that stretched their giant arms
In darkness over it. I' the midst was left,
385 Reflecting, yet distorting every cloud,
A pool of treacherous and tremendous calm.
Seized by the sway of the ascending stream,
With dizzy swiftness, round, and round, and round,
Ridge after ridge the straining boat arose,
390 Till on the verge of the extremest curve,
Where, through an opening of the rocky bank,
The waters overflow, and a smooth spot
Of glassy quiet mid those battling tides
Is left, the boat paused shuddering.—Shall it sink
395 Down the abyss? Shall the reverting stress
Of that resistless gulph embosom it?
Now shall it fall?—A wandering stream of wind,
Breathed from the west, has caught the expanded sail,
And, lo! with gentle motion, between banks

---

8. A boat beating upstream within a cave, like the eagle and serpent, is a recurrent Shelleyan image.

400 Of mossy slope, and on a placid stream,
    Beneath a woven grove it sails, and, hark!
    The ghastly torrent mingles its far roar,
    With the breeze murmuring in the musical woods.
    Where the embowering trees recede, and leave
405 A little space of green expanse, the cove
    Is closed by meeting banks, whose yellow flowers
    For ever gaze on their own drooping eyes,
    Reflected in the crystal calm. The wave
    Of the boat's motion marred their pensive task,
410 Which nought but vagrant bird, or wanton wind,
    Or falling spear-grass, or their own decay
    Had e'er disturbed before. The Poet longed
    To deck with their bright hues his withered hair,
    But on his heart its solitude returned,
415 And he forbore.⁹ Not the strong impulse hid
    In those flushed cheeks, bent eyes, and shadowy frame,
    Had yet performed its ministry: it hung
    Upon his life, as lightning in a cloud
    Gleams, hovering ere it vanish, ere the floods
    Of night close over it.
420   The noonday sun
    Now shone upon the forest, one vast mass
    Of mingling shade, whose brown magnificence
    A narrow vale embosoms. There, huge caves,
    Scooped in the dark base of their aëry rocks
425 Mocking¹ its moans, respond and roar for ever.
    The meeting boughs and implicated° leaves   *intertwined*
    Wove twilight o'er the Poet's path, as led
    By love, or dream, or god, or mightier Death,
    He sought in Nature's dearest haunt, some bank,
430 Her cradle, and his sepulchre. More dark
    And dark the shades accumulate. The oak,
    Expanding its immense and knotty arms,
    Embraces the light beech. The pyramids
    Of the tall cedar overarching, frame
435 Most solemn domes within, and far below.
    Like clouds suspended in an emerald sky,
    The ash and the acacia floating hang
    Tremulous and pale. Like restless serpents, clothed
    In rainbow and in fire, the parasites,
440 Starred with ten thousand blossoms, flow around
    The grey trunks, and, as gamesome infants' eyes,
    With gentle meanings, and most innocent wiles,
    Fold their beams round the hearts of those that love,
    These twine their tendrils with the wedded boughs
445 Uniting their close union; the woven leaves

9. Another recurrent image: flowers overhanging their own reflection. The "yellow flowers" (line 406), probably narcissus, may signify, in this passage, the temptation of the Poet to be satisfied with the projection of his own earthly nature. But his need for a supermundane Other revives, and "the strong impulse" (line 415) drives him on.

1. As often in Shelley, "mocking" has a double sense: mimicking as well as ridiculing the sounds of the forest (line 421).

Make net-work of the dark blue light of day,
And the night's noontide clearness, mutable
As shapes in the weird clouds. Soft mossy lawns
Beneath these canopies extend their swells,
450 Fragrant with perfumed herbs, and eyed with blooms
Minute yet beautiful. One darkest glen
Sends from its woods of musk-rose, twined with jasmine,
A soul-dissolving odour, to invite
To some more lovely mystery. Through the dell,
455 Silence and Twilight here, twin-sisters, keep
Their noonday watch, and sail among the shades,
Like vaporous shapes half seen; beyond, a well,
Dark, gleaming, and of most translucent wave,
Images all the woven boughs above,
460 And each depending leaf, and every speck
Of azure sky, darting between their chasms;
Nor aught else in the liquid mirror laves
Its portraiture, but some inconstant star
Between one foliaged lattice twinkling fair,
465 Or, painted bird, sleeping beneath the moon,
Or gorgeous insect floating motionless,
Unconscious of the day, ere yet his wings
Have spread their glories to the gaze of noon.

Hither the Poet came. His eyes beheld
470 Their own wan light through the reflected lines
Of his thin hair, distinct in the dark depth
Of that still fountain; as the human heart,
Gazing in dreams over the gloomy grave,
Sees its own treacherous likeness there. He heard
475 The motion of the leaves, the grass that sprung
Startled and glanced and trembled even to feel
An unaccustomed presence, and the sound
Of the sweet brook that from the secret springs
Of that dark fountain rose. A Spirit seemed
480 To stand beside him—clothed in no bright robes
Of shadowy silver or enshrining light,
Borrowed from aught the visible world affords
Of grace, or majesty, or mystery;—
But, undulating woods, and silent well,
485 And leaping rivulet, and evening gloom
Now deepening the dark shades, for speech assuming
Held commune with him, as if he and it
Were all that was,—only . . . when his regard
Was raised by intense pensiveness, . . . two eyes,
490 Two starry eyes, hung in the gloom of thought,
And seemed with their serene and azure smiles
To beckon him.[2]

Obedient to the light
That shone within his soul, he went, pursuing

---

2. The Poet sees the eyes of the maiden of his vision and, obedient to his inner light, resumes his quest (lines 491–93).

The windings of the dell.—The rivulet
495 Wanton and wild, through many a green ravine
Beneath the forest flowed. Sometimes it fell
Among the moss with hollow harmony
Dark and profound. Now on the polished stones
It danced; like childhood laughing as it went:
500 Then, through the plain in tranquil wanderings crept,
Reflecting every herb and drooping bud
That overhung its quietness.—"O stream!
Whose source is inaccessibly profound,
Whither do thy mysterious waters tend?
505 Thou imagest my life. Thy darksome stillness,
Thy dazzling waves, thy loud and hollow gulphs,
Thy searchless° fountain, and invisible course   *undiscoverable*
Have each their type in me: and the wide sky,
And measureless ocean may declare as soon
510 What oozy cavern or what wandering cloud
Contains thy waters, as the universe
Tell where these living thoughts reside, when stretched
Upon thy flowers my bloodless limbs shall waste
I' the passing wind!"

                          Beside the grassy shore
515 Of the small stream he went; he did impress
On the green moss his tremulous step, that caught
Strong shuddering from his burning limbs. As one
Roused by some joyous madness from the couch
Of fever, he did move; yet, not like him,
520 Forgetful of the grave, where, when the flame
Of his frail exultation shall be spent,
He must descend. With rapid steps he went
Beneath the shade of trees, beside the flow
Of the wild babbling rivulet; and now
525 The forest's solemn canopies were changed
For the uniform and lightsome° evening sky.   *illuminated*
Grey rocks did peep from the spare moss, and stemmed
The struggling brook: tall spires of windlestrae³
Threw their thin shadows down the rugged slope,
530 And nought but knarled roots⁴ of antient pines
Branchless and blasted, clenched with grasping roots
The unwilling soil. A gradual change was here,
Yet ghastly. For, as fast years flow away,
The smooth brow gathers, and the hair grows thin
535 And white, and where irradiate° dewy eyes   *illumined*
Had shone, gleam stony orbs:—so from his steps
Bright flowers departed, and the beautiful shade
Of the green groves, with all their odorous winds
And musical motions. Calm, he still pursued
540 The stream, that with a larger volume now
Rolled through the labyrinthine dell; and there
Fretted a path through its descending curves

---

3. Windlestraw (Scottish dialect); tall, dried stalks   4. Apparently an error for "trunks."
of grass.

With its wintry speed. On every side now rose
Rocks, which, in unimaginable forms,
545   Lifted their black and barren pinnacles
In the light of evening, and its precipice[5]
Obscuring the ravine, disclosed above,
Mid toppling stones, black gulphs and yawning caves,
Whose windings gave ten thousand various tongues
550   To the loud stream. Lo! where the pass expands
Its stony jaws, the abrupt mountain breaks,
And seems, with its accumulated crags,
To overhang the world: for wide expand
Beneath the wan stars and descending moon
555   Islanded seas, blue mountains, mighty streams,
Dim tracts and vast, robed in the lustrous gloom
Of leaden-coloured even, and fiery hills
Mingling their flames with twilight, on the verge
Of the remote horizon. The near scene,
560   In naked and severe simplicity,
Made contrast with the universe. A pine,[6]
Rock-rooted, stretched athwart the vacancy
Its swinging boughs, to each inconstant blast
Yielding one only response, at each pause
565   In most familiar cadence, with the howl
The thunder and the hiss of homeless streams
Mingling its solemn song, whilst the broad river,
Foaming and hurrying o'er its rugged path,
Fell into that immeasurable void
570   Scattering its waters to the passing winds.

    Yet the grey precipice and solemn pine
And torrent, were not all;—one silent nook
Was there. Even on the edge of that vast mountain,
Upheld by knotty roots and fallen rocks,
575   It overlooked in its serenity
The dark earth, and the bending vault of stars.
It was a tranquil spot, that seemed to smile
Even in the lap of horror. Ivy clasped
The fissured stones with its entwining arms,
580   And did embower with leaves for ever green,
And berries dark, the smooth and even space
Of its inviolated floor, and here
The children of the autumnal whirlwind bore,
In wanton sport, those bright leaves, whose decay,
585   Red, yellow, or etherially pale,
Rivals the pride of summer. 'Tis the haunt
Of every gentle wind, whose breath can teach
The wilds to love tranquillity. One step,
One human step alone, has ever broken
590   The stillness of its solitude:—one voice
Alone inspired its echoes,—even that voice
Which hither came, floating among the winds,

---

5. Headlong fall (of the stream, line 540).
6. Pine trees in Shelley often signify persistence and steadfastness amid change and vicissitudes.

And led the loveliest among human forms
To make their wild haunts the depository
595 Of all the grace and beauty that endued
Its motions, render up its majesty,
Scatter its music on the unfeeling storm,
And to the damp leaves and blue cavern mould,
Nurses of rainbow flowers and branching moss,
600 Commit the colours of that varying cheek,
That snowy breast, those dark and drooping eyes.

The dim and horned[7] moon hung low, and poured
A sea of lustre on the horizon's verge
That overflowed its mountains. Yellow mist
605 Filled the unbounded atmosphere, and drank
Wan moonlight even to fulness: not a star
Shone, not a sound was heard; the very winds,
Danger's grim playmates, on that precipice
Slept, clasped in his embrace.—O, storm of death!
610 Whose sightless[8] speed divides this sullen night:
And thou, colossal Skeleton, that, still
Guiding its irresistible career
In thy devastating omnipotence,
Art king of this frail world, from the red field
615 Of slaughter, from the reeking hospital,
The patriot's sacred couch, the snowy bed
Of innocence, the scaffold and the throne,
A mighty voice invokes thee. Ruin calls
His brother Death. A rare and regal prey
620 He hath prepared, prowling around the world;
Glutted with which thou mayst repose, and men
Go to their graves like flowers or creeping worms,
Nor ever more offer at thy dark shrine
The unheeded tribute of a broken heart.

625 When on the threshold of the green recess
The wanderer's footsteps fell, he knew that death
Was on him. Yet a little, ere it fled,
Did he resign his high and holy soul
To images of the majestic past,
630 That paused within his passive being now,
Like winds that bear sweet music, when they breathe
Through some dim latticed chamber. He did place
His pale lean hand upon the rugged trunk
Of the old pine. Upon an ivied stone
635 Reclined his languid head, his limbs did rest,
Diffused and motionless, on the smooth brink
Of that obscurest chasm;—and thus he lay,
Surrendering to their final impulses
The hovering powers of life. Hope and despair,
640 The torturers, slept; no mortal pain or fear
Marred his repose, the influxes of sense,

7. Crescent-shaped, with the points curved in.   8. Invisible, or perhaps "unseeing."

And his own being unalloyed by pain,
Yet feebler and more feeble, calmly fed
The stream of thought, till he lay breathing there
645   At peace, and faintly smiling:—his last sight
Was the great moon, which o'er the western line
Of the wide world her mighty horn suspended,
With whose dun° beams inwoven darkness seemed   darkened
To mingle. Now upon the jagged hills
650   It rests, and still as the divided frame
Of the vast meteor[9] sunk, the Poet's blood,
That ever beat in mystic sympathy
With nature's ebb and flow, grew feebler still:
And when two lessening points of light alone
655   Gleamed through the darkness, the alternate gasp
Of his faint respiration scarce did stir
The stagnate night:[1]—till the minutest ray
Was quenched, the pulse yet lingered in his heart.
It paused—it fluttered. But when heaven remained
660   Utterly black, the murky shades involved
An image, silent, cold, and motionless,
As their own voiceless earth and vacant air.
Even as a vapour° fed with golden beams   cloud
That ministered on[2] sunlight, ere the west
665   Eclipses it, was now that wonderous frame—
No sense, no motion, no divinity—
A fragile lute, on whose harmonious strings
The breath of heaven did wander—a bright stream
Once fed with many-voiced waves—a dream
670   Of youth, which night and time have quenched for ever,
Still, dark, and dry, and unremembered now.

O, for Medea's wondrous alchemy,
Which wheresoe'er it fell made the earth gleam
With bright flowers, and the wintry boughs exhale
675   From vernal blooms fresh fragrance![3] O, that God,
Profuse of poisons, would concede the chalice
Which but one living man[4] has drained, who now,
Vessel of deathless wrath, a slave that feels
No proud exemption in the blighting curse
680   He bears, over the world wanders for ever,
Lone as incarnate death! O, that the dream
Of dark magician in his visioned cave,[5]
Raking the cinders of a crucible
For life and power, even when his feeble hand
685   Shakes in its last decay, were the true law

9. I.e., the moon; "meteor" was once used for any phenomenon within the earth's atmosphere.
1. The Poet's life ebbs in consonance with the descent of the "horned moon," to the moment when only the two "points of light"—its horns—show above the hills.
2. Attended, acted as a servant to.
3. Medea brewed a magic potion to rejuvenate the dying Aeson; where some of the potion spilled on

the ground, flowers sprang up (Ovid, *Metamorphoses* 7.275ff.).
4. The Wandering Jew. According to a medieval legend, he had taunted Christ on the way to His crucifixion and was condemned to wander the world, deathless, until Christ's second coming.
5. Cave in which he has visions. "Dark magician": an alchemist attempting to produce the elixir of enduring life.

Of this so lovely world! But thou art fled
Like some frail exhalation; which the dawn
Robes in its golden beams,—ah! thou hast fled!
The brave, the gentle, and the beautiful,
690 The child of grace and genius. Heartless things
Are done and said i' the world, and many worms
And beasts and men live on, and mighty Earth
From sea and mountain, city and wilderness,
In vesper[6] low or joyous orison,°   *prayer*
695 Lifts still its solemn voice:—but thou art fled—
Thou canst no longer know or love the shapes
Of this phantasmal scene, who have to thee
Been purest ministers, who are, alas!
Now thou art not. Upon those pallid lips
700 So sweet even in their silence, on those eyes
That image sleep in death, upon that form
Yet safe from the worm's outrage, let no tear
Be shed—not even in thought. Nor, when those hues
Are gone, and those divinest lineaments,
705 Worn by the senseless° wind, shall live alone   *unfeeling*
In the frail pauses of this simple strain,
Let not high verse, mourning the memory
Of that which is no more, or painting's woe
Or sculpture, speak in feeble imagery
710 Their own cold powers. Art and eloquence,
And all the shews o' the world are frail and vain
To weep a loss that turns their lights to shade.
It is a woe too "deep for tears,"[7] when all
Is reft at once, when some surpassing Spirit,
715 Whose light adorned the world around it, leaves
Those who remain behind, not sobs or groans,
The passionate tumult of a clinging hope;
But pale despair and cold tranquillity,
Nature's vast frame, the web of human things,
720 Birth and the grave, that are not as they were.

1815   1816

6. Evening prayer.
7. From the last line of Wordsworth's *Ode: Inti-*   *mations of Immortality*: "Thoughts that do often lie
   too deep for tears."

Mont Blanc[1]

Lines Written in the Vale of Chamouni

1

The everlasting universe of things
Flows through the mind, and rolls its rapid waves,
Now dark—now glittering—now reflecting gloom—
Now lending splendour, where from secret springs
5   The source of human thought its tribute brings
Of waters,—with a sound but half its own.
Such as a feeble brook will oft assume
In the wild woods, among the mountains lone,
Where waterfalls around it leap forever,
10 Where woods and winds contend, and a vast river
Over its rocks ceaselessly bursts and raves.

2

Thus thou, Ravine of Arve—dark, deep Ravine—
Thou many-coloured, many-voiced vale,
Over whose pines, and crags, and caverns sail
15 Fast cloud shadows and sunbeams: awful° scene,   awe-inspiring
Where Power in likeness of the Arve comes down
From the ice gulphs that gird his secret throne,
Bursting through these dark mountains like the flame
Of lightning through the tempest;—thou dost lie,
20 Thy giant brood of pines around thee clinging,
Children of elder time, in whose devotion
The chainless winds still come and ever came
To drink their odours, and their mighty swinging
To hear—an old and solemn harmony;
25 Thine earthly rainbows stretched across the sweep
Of the etherial waterfall, whose veil
Robes some unsculptured[2] image; the strange sleep
Which when the voices of the desart fail
Wraps all in its own deep eternity;—
30 Thy caverns echoing to the Arve's commotion,
A loud, lone sound no other sound can tame;
Thou art pervaded with that ceaseless motion,
Thou art the path of that unresting sound—

1. Mont Blanc, near the French border with Italy, is the highest mountain in the Alps. When he conceived the poem, Shelley was standing on a bridge over the Arve River in the valley of Chamonix, in what is now southeastern France.
    Shelley wrote of this poem: "It was composed under the immediate impression of the deep and powerful feelings excited by the objects which it attempts to describe; and, as an indisciplined overflowing of the soul, rests its claim to approbation on an attempt to imitate the untamable wildness and inaccessible solemnity from which those feelings sprang."
    Shelley's comment points to two important attributes of *Mont Blanc*. First, he attempts, as in other poems (especially in *Ode to the West Wind*), to make the poem iconic or directly imitative of the alternating "wildness" and "solemnity" of the scene and the consonant thought and feelings it evokes. Second, this work belongs to the genre of the "local" poem, a descriptive-meditative presentation of a precisely identified landscape. In this respect it resembles Wordsworth's *Tintern Abbey*, the major influence on *Mont Blanc*. Shelley's poem, like Wordsworth's, poses the question of the significance of the interchange between nature and the human mind; he proposes, however, a very different answer to that question.

2. I.e., not formed by humans.

Dizzy Ravine! and when I gaze on thee
35 I seem as in a trance sublime and strange
To muse on my own separate phantasy,
My own, my human mind, which passively
Now renders and receives fast influencings,
Holding an unremitting interchange
40 With the clear universe of things around;[3]
One legion of wild thoughts, whose wandering wings
Now float above thy darkness, and now rest
Where that or thou art no unbidden guest,
In the still cave of the witch Poesy,[4]
45 Seeking among the shadows that pass by
Ghosts of all things that are, some shade of thee,
Some phantom, some faint image; till the breast
From which they fled recalls them, thou art there![5]

3

Some say that gleams of a remoter world
50 Visit the soul in sleep,—that death is slumber,
And that its shapes the busy thoughts outnumber
Of those who wake and live.—I look on high;
Has some unknown omnipotence unfurled
The veil of life and death? or do I lie
55 In dream, and does the mightier world of sleep
Spread far around and inaccessibly
Its circles? For the very spirit fails,
Driven like a homeless cloud from steep to steep
That vanishes among the viewless° gales!   *invisible*
60 Far, far above, piercing the infinite sky,
Mont Blanc appears,—still, snowy, and serene—
Its subject mountains their unearthly forms
Pile around it, ice and rock; broad vales between
Of frozen floods, unfathomable deeps,
65 Blue as the overhanging heaven, that spread
And wind among the accumulated steeps;
A desart peopled by the storms alone,
Save when the eagle brings some hunter's bone,
And the wolf tracts° her there—how hideously   *tracks*
70 Its shapes are heaped around! rude, bare, and high,
Ghastly, and scarred, and riven.—Is this the scene
Where the old Earthquake-dæmon[6] taught her young
Ruin? Were these their toys? or did a sea
Of fire, envelope once this silent snow?
75 None can reply—all seems eternal now.
The wilderness has a mysterious tongue

---

3. This passage is remarkably parallel to a passage
Shelley could not have read in *The Prelude*, first
published in 1850, in which Wordsworth discovers, in the landscape viewed from Mount Snowdon, the "type" or "emblem" of the human mind in
its interchange with nature (see *The Prelude*
14.63ff., p. 378).
4. I.e., in the part of the mind that creates poetry.

5. I.e., the thoughts (line 41) seek, in the poet's
creative faculty, some shade, phantom, or image of
the Arve; and when the breast, which has forgotten
these images, recalls them again—there, suddenly,
does the Arve exist.
6. A supernatural being, halfway between mortals
and the gods. Here it represents the force that
makes earthquakes.

Which teaches awful doubt, or faith so mild,
So solemn, so serene, that man may be
But for such faith[7] with nature reconciled;
80 Thou hast a voice, great Mountain, to repeal
Large codes of fraud and woe; not understood
By all, but which[8] the wise, and great, and good
Interpret, or make felt, or deeply feel.

4

The fields, the lakes, the forests, and the streams,
85 Ocean, and all the living things that dwell
Within the dædal[9] earth; lightning, and rain,
Earthquake, and fiery flood, and hurricane,
The torpor of the year when feeble dreams
Visit the hidden buds, or dreamless sleep
90 Holds every future leaf and flower;—the bound
With which from that detested trance they leap;
The works and ways of man, their death and birth,
And that of him and all that his may be;
All things that move and breathe with toil and sound
95 Are born and die; revolve, subside and swell.
Power dwells apart in its tranquillity
Remote, serene, and inaccessible:
And *this*, the naked countenance of earth,
On which I gaze, even these primæval mountains
100 Teach the adverting mind. The glaciers creep
Like snakes that watch their prey, from their far fountains,
Slow rolling on; there, many a precipice,
Frost and the Sun in scorn of mortal power
Have piled: dome, pyramid, and pinnacle,
105 A city of death, distinct with many a tower
And wall impregnable of beaming ice.
Yet not a city, but a flood of ruin
Is there, that from the boundaries of the sky
Rolls its perpetual stream; vast pines are strewing
110 Its destined path, or in the mangled soil
Branchless and shattered stand: the rocks, drawn down
From yon remotest waste, have overthrown
The limits of the dead and living world,
Never to be reclaimed. The dwelling-place
115 Of insects, beasts, and birds, becomes its spoil;
Their food and their retreat for ever gone,
So much of life and joy is lost. The race
Of man, flies far in dread; his work and dwelling
Vanish, like smoke before the tempest's stream,
120 And their place is not known. Below, vast caves
Shine in the rushing torrents' restless gleam,

7. I.e., "simply by holding such faith." In Shelley's balance of possibilities, the landscape is equally capable of instilling such a Wordsworthian faith (in the possibility of reconciling humans and nature, lines 78–79) or the "awful" (i.e., "awe-some") doubt (that nature is totally alien to human ends and values).
8. The reference is to "voice," line 80.
9. Intricately formed; derived from Daedalus, builder of the labyrinth in Crete.

Which from those secret chasms in tumult welling[1]
Meet in the vale, and one majestic River,[2]
The breath and blood of distant lands, for ever
125 Rolls its loud waters to the ocean waves,
Breathes its swift vapours to the circling air.

5

Mont Blanc yet gleams on high:—the power is there,
The still and solemn power of many sights,
And many sounds, and much of life and death.
130 In the calm darkness of the moonless nights,
In the lone glare of day, the snows descend
Upon that Mountain; none beholds them there,
Nor when the flakes burn in the sinking sun,
Or the star-beams dart through them:—Winds contend
135 Silently there, and heap the snow with breath
Rapid and strong, but silently! Its home
The voiceless lightning in these solitudes
Keeps innocently, and like vapour broods
Over the snow. The secret strength of things
140 Which governs thought, and to the infinite dome
Of heaven is as a law, inhabits thee!
And what were thou,° and earth, and stars, and sea,   *Mont Blanc*
If to the human mind's imaginings
Silence and solitude were vacancy?

1816   1817

Hymn to Intellectual Beauty[1]

I

The awful shadow of some unseen Power
   Floats though unseen amongst us,—visiting
   This various world with as inconstant wing
As summer winds that creep from flower to flower.—
5 Like moonbeams that behind some piny mountain shower,[2]
      It visits with inconstant glance
      Each human heart and countenance;
Like hues and harmonies of evening,—
      Like clouds in starlight widely spread,—
10   Like memory of music fled,—
      Like aught that for its grace may be
Dear, and yet dearer for its mystery.

1. This description (as well as that in lines 9–11) seems to be an echo of Coleridge's description of the chasm and sacred river in the recently published *Kubla Khan*, lines 12–24.
2. The Arve, which flows into Lake Geneva.
1. "Intellectual" means "nonsensible." "Intellectual Beauty" is thus beyond access by sense experience. It is simply postulated to account for occasional states of awareness that lend splendor, grace, and truth both to experience of the natural world and to people's moral consciousness. To this mystery (stanzas 5–7) Shelley had, at its early visitation, dedicated his powers, and to it he now prays as he passes the noon of life (stanza 7).
2. Used as a verb.

2

Spirit of BEAUTY, that dost consecrate
   With thine own hues all thou dost shine upon
15   Of human thought or form,—where art thou gone?
Why dost thou pass away and leave our state,
This dim vast vale of tears, vacant and desolate?
     Ask why the sunlight not forever
     Weaves rainbows o'er yon mountain river,
20   Why aught should fail and fade that once is shewn,
     Why fear and dream and death and birth
     Cast on the daylight of this earth
     Such gloom,—why man has such a scope
For love and hate, despondency and hope?

3

25 No voice from some sublimer world hath ever
     To sage or poet these responses given—
     Therefore the name of God and ghosts and Heaven,
Remain the records of their vain endeavour,[3]
Frail spells—whose uttered charm might not avail to sever,
30   From all we hear and all we see,
     Doubt, chance, and mutability.
Thy light alone—like mist o'er mountains driven,
     Or music by the night wind sent
     Through strings of some still instrument,°   *wind harp*
35   Or moonlight on a midnight stream,
Gives grace and truth to life's unquiet dream.

4

Love, Hope, and Self-esteem, like clouds depart
     And come, for some uncertain moments lent.
     Man were immortal, and omnipotent,
40 Didst thou, unknown and awful as thou art,
Keep with thy glorious train firm state within his heart.[4]
     Thou messenger of sympathies,
     That wax and wane in lovers' eyes—
Thou—that to human thought art nourishment,
45   Like darkness to a dying flame!
     Depart not as thy shadow came,
     Depart not—lest the grave should be,
Like life and fear, a dark reality.

5

While yet a boy I sought for ghosts, and sped
50   Through many a listening chamber, cave and ruin,
     And starlight wood, with fearful steps pursuing
Hopes of high talk with the departed dead.

3. The names (line 27) are nothing better than guesses at identifying the mystery by religious philosophers and poets (line 26).

4. I.e., "man would be immortal . . . if thou didst keep."

I called on poisonous names with which our youth is fed;[5]
    I was not heard—I saw them not—
55   When musing deeply on the lot
Of life, at that sweet time when winds are wooing
    All vital things that wake to bring
    News of buds and blossoming,—
    Sudden, thy shadow fell on me;
60 I shrieked, and clasped my hands in extacy!

6

I vowed that I would dedicate my powers
    To thee and thine—have I not kept the vow?
    With beating heart and streaming eyes, even now
I call the phantoms of a thousand hours
65 Each from his voiceless grave: they have in visioned bowers
    Of studious zeal or love's delight
    Outwatched with me the envious night[6]—
They know that never joy illumed my brow
    Unlinked with hope that thou wouldst free
70   This world from its dark slavery,
    That thou—O awful LOVELINESS,
Wouldst give whate'er these words cannot express.

7

The day becomes more solemn and serene
    When noon is past—there is a harmony
75   In autumn, and a lustre in its sky,
Which through the summer is not heard or seen,
As if it could not be, as if it had not been!
    Thus let thy power, which like the truth
    Of nature on my passive youth
80 Descended, to my onward life supply
    Its calm—to one who worships thee,
    And every form containing thee,
Whom, SPIRIT fair, thy spells did bind
To fear[7] himself, and love all human kind.

1816   1817

Ozymandias[1]

I met a traveller from an antique land,
Who said—"Two vast and trunkless legs of stone
Stand in the desert. . . . Near them, on the sand,

---

5. Lines 49–52 refer to Shelley's youthful experiments with magic. The "poisonous names" are probably those in the prayers he had been taught as a child.
6. I.e., stayed up until the night, envious of their delight, had reluctantly departed.
7. Probably in the old sense: "to stand in awe of."

1. According to Diodorus Siculus, Greek historian of the 1st century B.C.E., the largest statue in Egypt had the inscription: "I am Ozymandias, king of kings; if anyone wishes to know what I am and where I lie, let him surpass me in some of my exploits." Ozymandias was the Greek name for Ramses II of Egypt, 13th century B.C.E.

Half sunk a shattered visage lies, whose frown,
5 And wrinkled lip, and sneer of cold command,
Tell that its sculptor well those passions read
Which yet survive, stamped on these lifeless things,
The hand that mocked them, and the heart that fed;[2]
And on the pedestal, these words appear:
10 My name is Ozymandias, King of Kings,
Look on my Works, ye Mighty, and despair!
Nothing beside remains. Round the decay
Of that colossal Wreck, boundless and bare
The lone and level sands stretch far away."

1817   1818

Stanzas Written in Dejection—
December 1818, near Naples[1]

The Sun is warm, the sky is clear,
The waves are dancing fast and bright,
Blue isles and snowy mountains wear
The purple noon's transparent might,
5 The breath of the moist earth is light
Around its unexpanded buds;
Like many a voice of one delight
The winds, the birds, the Ocean-floods;
The City's voice itself is soft, like Solitude's.

10 I see the Deep's untrampled floor
With green and purple seaweeds strown;
I see the waves upon the shore
Like light dissolved in star-showers, thrown;
I sit upon the sands alone;
15 The lightning of the noontide Ocean
Is flashing round me, and a tone
Arises from its measured motion,
How sweet! did any heart now share in my emotion.

Alas, I have nor hope nor health
20 Nor peace within nor calm around,
Nor that content surpassing wealth
The sage[2] in meditation found,
And walked with inward glory crowned;
Nor fame nor power nor love nor leisure—
25 Others I see whom these surround,
Smiling they live and call life pleasure:
To me that cup has been dealt in another measure.

---

2. "The hand" is the sculptor's, who had "mocked" (both imitated and derided) the sculptured passions; "the heart" is the king's, which has "fed" his passions.
1. Shelley's first wife, Harriet, had drowned herself; Clara, his baby daughter with Mary Shelley,

had just died; and Shelley himself was plagued by ill health, pain, financial worries, and the sense that he had failed as a poet.
2. Probably the Roman emperor Marcus Aurelius (2nd century C.E.), Stoic philosopher who wrote twelve books of *Meditations*.

Yet now despair itself is mild,
Even as the winds and waters are;
30   I could lie down like a tired child
And weep away the life of care
Which I have borne and yet must bear
Till Death like Sleep might steal on me,
And I might feel in the warm air
35   My cheek grow cold, and hear the Sea
Breathe o'er my dying brain its last monotony.

Some might lament that I were cold,
As I, when this sweet day is gone,[3]
Which my lost heart, too soon grown old,
40   Insults with this untimely moan—
They might lament,—for I am one
Whom men love not, and yet regret;
Unlike this day, which, when the Sun
Shall on its stainless glory set,
45   Will linger though enjoyed, like joy in Memory yet.

1818   1824

A Song: "Men of England"[1]

Men of England, wherefore plough
For the lords who lay ye low?
Wherefore weave with toil and care
The rich robes your tyrants wear?

5   Wherefore feed and clothe and save
From the cradle to the grave
Those ungrateful drones who would
Drain your sweat—nay, drink your blood?

Wherefore, Bees of England, forge
10   Many a weapon, chain, and scourge,
That these stingless drones may spoil
The forced produce of your toil?

Have ye leisure, comfort, calm,
Shelter, food, love's gentle balm?
15   Or what is it ye buy so dear
With your pain and with your fear?

The seed ye sow, another reaps;
The wealth ye find, another keeps;

---

3. I.e., as I will lament this sweet day when it has
gone.
1. This and the two following poems were written
at a time of turbulent unrest, after the return of
troops from the Napoleonic Wars had precipitated

a great economic depression. The *Song*, expressing
Shelley's hope for a proletarian revolution, was
originally planned as one of a series for workers. It
has become, as the poet wished, a hymn of the
British labor movement.

The robes ye weave, another wears;
20   The arms ye forge, another bears.

Sow seed—but let no tyrant reap:
Find wealth—let no impostor heap:
Weave robes—let not the idle wear:
Forge arms—in your defence to bear.

25   Shrink to your cellars, holes, and cells—
In halls ye deck another dwells.
Why shake the chains ye wrought? Ye see
The steel ye tempered glance on ye.

With plough and spade and hoe and loom
30   Trace your grave and build your tomb
And weave your winding-sheet—till fair
England be your Sepulchre.

1819   1839

England in 1819

An old, mad, blind, despised, and dying King;[1]
Princes, the dregs of their dull race, who flow
Through public scorn,—mud from a muddy spring;
Rulers who neither see nor feel nor know,
5   But leechlike to their fainting country cling
Till they drop, blind in blood, without a blow.
A people starved and stabbed in th' untilled field;[2]
An army, whom liberticide and prey
Makes as a two-edged sword to all who wield;
10   Golden and sanguine laws[3] which tempt and slay;
Religion Christless, Godless—a book sealed;
A senate, Time's worst statute, unrepealed[4]—
Are graves from which a glorious Phantom[5] may
Burst, to illumine our tempestuous day.

1819   1839

To Sidmouth and Castlereagh[1]

As from their ancestral oak
Two empty ravens wind their clarion,

1. George III, who had been declared insane in 1811. He died in 1820.
2. Alluding to the Peterloo Massacre on August 16, 1819. In St. Peter's field, near Manchester, a troop of cavalry had charged into a crowd attending a peaceful rally in support of parliamentary reform. "Peterloo" is an ironic combination of "St. Peter's" and "Waterloo."
3. Laws bought with gold, and leading to bloodshed.
4. The law imposing disabilities on Dissenters and Roman Catholics.

5. I.e., a revolution.
1. Shelley's powerful satire is directed against Viscount Castlereagh, foreign secretary (1812–22), who took a leading part in the European settlement after the Battle of Waterloo, and Viscount Sidmouth (1757–1844), the home secretary, whose cruelly coercive measures (supported by Castlereagh) against unrest in the laboring classes were in large part responsible for the Peterloo Massacre.
    When this poem was reprinted by Mary Shelley in 1839, it was given the title *Similes for Two Political Characters of 1819*.

Yell by yell, and croak by croak,
    When they scent the noonday smoke
5   Of fresh human carrion:—

As two gibbering night-birds flit
    From their bowers of deadly yew
Through the night to frighten it—
    When the moon is in a fit,
10   And the stars are none, or few:—

As a shark and dogfish wait
    Under an Atlantic isle
For the Negro-ship, whose freight
    Is the theme of their debate,
15   Wrinkling their red gills the while—

Are ye—two vultures sick for battle,
    Two scorpions under one wet stone,
Two bloodless wolves whose dry throats rattle,
    Two crows perched on the murrained[2] cattle,
20   Two vipers tangled into one.

1819   1832

The Indian Girl's Song[1] [The Indian Serenade]

I arise from dreams of thee
    In the first sleep of night—
The winds are breathing low
    And the stars are burning bright.
5   I arise from dreams of thee—
    And a spirit in my feet
Has borne me—Who knows how?
    To thy chamber window, sweet!—

The wandering airs they faint
10 On the dark silent stream—
The champak[2] odours fail
    Like sweet thoughts in a dream;
The nightingale's complaint—
    It dies upon her heart—
15 As I must die on thine
    O beloved as thou art!

O lift me from the grass!
    I die, I faint, I fail!
Let thy love in kisses rain

2. A *murrain* is a malignant disease of domestic animals.
1. Usually headed *The Indian Serenade*. Shelley's title makes it clear that the poem is not a personal utterance but a dramatic lyric, sung by an imagined

East Indian girl. It manifests the conventional extravagance of an Oriental love poem.
2. An Indian species of magnolia, bearing fragrant orange flowers.

20   On my lips and eyelids pale.
My cheek is cold and white, alas!
My heart beats loud and fast.
Oh press it close to thine again
Where it will break at last.

1819   1822

Ode to the West Wind[1]

I

O wild West Wind, thou breath of Autumn's being,
Thou, from whose unseen presence the leaves dead
Are driven, like ghosts from an enchanter fleeing,

Yellow, and black, and pale, and hectic[2] red,
5   Pestilence-stricken multitudes: O Thou,
Who chariotest to their dark wintry bed

The winged seeds, where they lie cold and low,
Each like a corpse within its grave, until
Thine azure sister of the Spring[3] shall blow

10   Her clarion[4] o'er the dreaming earth, and fill
(Driving sweet buds like flocks to feed in air)
With living hues and odours plain and hill:

Wild Spirit, which art moving everywhere;
Destroyer and Preserver; hear, O hear!

2

15   Thou on whose stream, 'mid the steep sky's commotion,
Loose clouds like Earth's decaying leaves are shed,
Shook from the tangled boughs of Heaven and Ocean,[5]

1. This poem was conceived and chiefly written in a wood that skirts the Arno, near Florence, and on a day when that tempestuous wind, whose temperature is at once mild and animating, was collecting the vapours which pour down the autumnal rains [Shelley's note]. As in other major Romantic poems—for example, the opening of Wordsworth's *Prelude*, Coleridge's *Dejection: An Ode*, and the conclusion to Shelley's *Adonais*—the rising wind, linked with the cycle of the seasons, is presented as the outer correspondent to an inner change from apathy to spiritual vitality and from imaginative sterility to a burst of creative power that is paralleled to the inspiration of the biblical prophets. In Hebrew, Latin, Greek, and many other languages, the words for *wind, breath, soul,* and *inspiration* are all identical or related. Thus Shelley's west wind is a "spirit" (the Latin *spiritus:* wind, breath, soul, and the root word in "inspiration"), the "breath of Autumn's being," which on earth,

sky, and sea destroys in the autumn to revivify in the spring. Around this central image the poem weaves various cycles of death and regeneration—vegetational, human, and divine.

Shelley's sonnet-length stanza, developed from the interlaced three-line units of the Italian *terza rima* (*aba bcb cdc,* etc.), consists of a set of four such tercets, closed by a couplet rhyming with the middle line of the preceding tercet: *aba bcb cdc ded ee.*

2. Referring to the kind of fever that occurs in tuberculosis.
3. The west wind that will blow in the spring.
4. A high, shrill trumpet.
5. The fragmentary clouds ("leaves") are torn by the wind from the larger and higher clouds ("boughs"), which are formed by a union of air with vapor drawn up by the sun from the ocean. "Angels" (line 18) suggests the old sense: "messengers," "harbingers."

Angels of rain and lightning: there are spread
On the blue surface of thine aery surge,
20　Like the bright hair uplifted from the head

Of some fierce Mænad,[6] even from the dim verge
Of the horizon to the zenith's height,
The locks of the approaching storm. Thou Dirge

Of the dying year, to which this closing night
25　Will be the dome of a vast sepulchre,
Vaulted with all thy congregated might

Of vapours,° from whose solid atmosphere　　　　　　　　*clouds*
Black rain and fire and hail will burst: O hear!

3
Thou who didst waken from his summer dreams
30　The blue Mediterranean, where he lay,
Lulled by the coil of his chrystalline streams,[7]

Beside a pumice isle in Baiæ's bay,[8]
And saw in sleep old palaces and towers
Quivering within the wave's intenser day,

35　All overgrown with azure moss and flowers
So sweet, the sense faints picturing them! Thou
For whose path the Atlantic's level powers

Cleave themselves into chasms, while far below
The sea-blooms and the oozy woods which wear
40　The sapless foliage of the ocean, know

Thy voice, and suddenly grow grey with fear,
And tremble and despoil themselves:[9] O hear!

4
If I were a dead leaf thou mightest bear;
If I were a swift cloud to fly with thee;
45　A wave to pant beneath thy power, and share

The impulse of thy strength, only less free
Than thou, O Uncontrollable! If even
I were as in my boyhood, and could be

6. A female votary who danced frenziedly in the worship of Dionysus (Bacchus), the Greek god of wine and vegetation. As vegetation god, he was fabled to die in the fall and to be resurrected in the spring.
7. The currents that flow in the Mediterranean Sea, sometimes with a visible difference in color.

8. West of Naples, the locale of imposing villas erected by Roman emperors. "Pumice": a porous volcanic stone.
9. The vegetation at the bottom of the sea . . . sympathizes with that of the land in the change of seasons [Shelley's note].

The comrade of thy wanderings over Heaven,
50 As then, when to outstrip thy skiey speed
Scarce seemed a vision; I would ne'er have striven

As thus with thee in prayer in my sore need.
Oh! lift me as a wave, a leaf, a cloud!
I fall upon the thorns of life! I bleed!

55 A heavy weight of hours has chained and bowed
One too like thee: tameless, and swift, and proud.

5

Make me thy lyre,[1] even as the forest is:
What if my leaves are falling like its own!
The tumult of thy mighty harmonies

60 Will take from both a deep, autumnal tone,
Sweet though in sadness. Be thou, Spirit fierce,
My spirit! Be thou me, impetuous one!

Drive my dead thoughts over the universe
Like withered leaves to quicken a new birth!
65 And, by the incantation of this verse,

Scatter, as from an unextinguished hearth
Ashes and sparks, my words among mankind!
Be through my lips to unawakened Earth

The trumpet of a prophecy! O Wind,
70 If Winter comes, can Spring be far behind?

1819   1820

Prometheus Unbound

Shelley composed this work in Italy between the autumn of 1818 and the close of 1819 and published it the following summer. Upon its completion he wrote in a letter, "It is a drama, with characters and mechanism of a kind yet unattempted; and I think the execution is better than any of my former attempts." It is based on the *Prometheus Bound* of Aeschylus, which dramatizes the sufferings of Prometheus, unrepentant champion of humanity, who, because he had stolen fire from heaven, was condemned by Zeus to be chained to Mount Caucasus and to be tortured by a vulture feeding on his liver; in a lost sequel, Aeschylus reconciled Prometheus with his oppressor. Shelley continued Aeschylus's story but transformed it into a symbolic drama about the origin of evil and the possibility of overcoming it. In such earlier writings as *Queen Mab* Shelley had expressed his belief that injustice and suffering can be eliminated by an external revolution that will wipe out or radically reform the causes of evil, attributed to existing social, political, and religious institutions. Implicit in *Prometheus Unbound,* on the other hand, is the view that both evil and the possibility of reform are the moral responsibility of men and

---

1. The Eolian lyre, which responds to the wind with rising and falling musical chords.

women themselves. Social chaos and wars are a gigantic projection of human moral disorder and inner division and conflict; tyrants are the outer representatives of the tyranny of our baser over our better elements; hatred for others is a product of self-contempt; and external political reform is impossible unless we have first reformed our own nature at its roots, by substituting selfless love for divisive hatred. Shelley thus incorporates into his secular myth—of universal regeneration by a triumph of humanity's moral imagination—the ethical teaching of Christ on the Mount, together with the classical morality represented in the *Prometheus* of Aeschylus. Shelley however, adds the warning (4.562ff.) that even should such a regeneration take place, its maintenance will depend on an unremitting vigilance, lest the serpent deep in human nature break loose and start the cycle of evil all over again.

Shelley writes in his preface that it is a mistake to suppose that the poem contains "a reasoned system on the theory of human life. Didactic poetry is my abhorrence." *Prometheus Unbound* is not a dramatized philosophical essay or a moral allegory but a large and intricate imaginative construction that involves premises about human nature and the springs of morality and creativity. The non-Christian poet Yeats called it one of "the sacred books of the world," and the Christian critic C. S. Lewis found in it poetic powers matched only by Dante.

FROM PROMETHEUS UNBOUND

A Lyrical Drama in Four Acts

Audisne hæc Amphiarae, sub terram abdite?[1]

Preface

The Greek tragic writers, in selecting as their subject any portion of their national history or mythology, employed in their treatment of it a certain arbitrary discretion. They by no means conceived themselves bound to adhere to the common interpretation or to imitate in story as in title their rivals and predecessors. Such a system would have amounted to a resignation of those claims to preference over their competitors which incited the composition. The Agamemnonian story was exhibited on the Athenian theatre with as many variations as dramas.

I have presumed to employ a similar licence.—The *Prometheus Unbound* of Æschylus, supposed the reconciliation of Jupiter with his victim as the price of the disclosure of the danger threatened to his empire by the consummation of his marriage with Thetis. Thetis, according to this view of the subject, was given in marriage to Peleus, and Prometheus by the permission of Jupiter delivered from his captivity by Hercules.[2]—Had I framed my story

---

1. Cicero, *Tusculan Disputations* 2.60: "Do you hear this, O Amphiaraus, concealed under the earth?" In Greek myth Amphiaraus was a seer. Fleeing from an unsuccessful assault on Thebes, he was saved from his pursuers by Zeus, who by a thunderbolt opened a cleft in the earth that swallowed him up.

In his *Disputations* Cicero is arguing for the Stoic doctrine of the need to master pain and suffering. He quotes this line (a Latin translation from Aeschylus's lost drama *Epigoni*) in the course of an

anecdote about Dionysius of Heraclea, who, tormented by kidney stones, abjures the doctrine of his Stoic teacher Zeno that pain is not an evil. By way of reproof his fellow-Stoic Cleanthes strikes his foot on the ground and utters this line. Cicero interprets it as an appeal to Zeno the Stoic master (under the name of Amphiaraus).

2. Shelley's description of the subject of Aeschylus's lost drama, *Prometheus Unbound*, is a speculation based on surviving fragments.

on this model I should have done no more than have attempted to restore the lost drama of Æschylus; an ambition, which, if my preference to this mode of treating the subject had incited me to cherish, the recollection of the high comparison such an attempt would challenge, might well abate. But in truth I was averse from a catastrophe so feeble as that of reconciling the Champion with the Oppressor of mankind. The moral interest of the fable which is so powerfully sustained by the sufferings and endurance of Prometheus, would be annihilated if we could conceive of him as unsaying his high language, and quailing before his successful and perfidious adversary. The only imaginary being resembling in any degree Prometheus, is Satan; and Prometheus is, in my judgement, a more poetical character than Satan because, in addition to courage and majesty and firm and patient opposition to omnipotent force, he is susceptible of being described as exempt from the taints of ambition, envy, revenge, and a desire for personal aggrandisement, which in the Hero of *Paradise Lost,* interfere with the interest. The character of Satan engenders in the mind a pernicious casuistry which leads us to weigh his faults with his wrongs and to excuse the former because the latter exceed all measure. In the minds of those who consider that magnificent fiction with a religious feeling, it engenders something worse. But Prometheus is, as it were, the type of the highest perfection of moral and intellectual nature, impelled by the purest and the truest motives to the best and noblest ends.

This Poem was chiefly written upon the mountainous ruins of the Baths of Caracalla, among the flowery glades, and thickets of odoriferous blossoming trees which are extended in ever winding labyrinths upon its immense platforms and dizzy arches suspended in the air. The bright blue sky of Rome, and the effect of the vigorous awakening of spring in that divinest climate, and the new life with which it drenches the spirits even to intoxication, were the inspiration of this drama.

The imagery which I have employed will be found in many instances to have been drawn from the operations of the human mind, or from those external actions by which they are expressed. This is unusual in modern Poetry; although Dante and Shakespeare are full of instances of the same kind: Dante indeed more than any other poet and with greater success. But the Greek poets, as writers to whom no resource of awakening the sympathy of their contemporaries was unknown, were in the habitual use of this power, and it is the study of their works (since a higher merit would probably be denied me) to which I am willing that my readers should impute this singularity.

One word is due in candour to the degree in which the study of contemporary writings may have tinged my composition, for such has been a topic of censure with regard to poems far more popular, and indeed more deservedly popular than mine. It is impossible that any one who inhabits the same age with such writers as those who stand in the foremost ranks of our own, can conscientiously assure himself, that his language and tone of thought may not have been modified by the study of the productions of those extraordinary intellects. It is true, that, not the spirit of their genius, but the forms in which it has manifested itself, are due, less to the peculiarities of their own minds, than to the peculiarity of the moral and intellectual condition of the minds among which they have been produced. Thus a number of writers possess the form, whilst they want the spirit of those whom, it is alleged, they imitate; because the former is the endowment of the age in which they live, and the latter must be the uncommunicated lightning of their own mind.

The peculiar style of intense and comprehensive imagery which distinguishes the modern literature of England, has not been, as a general power, the product of the imitation of any particular writer. The mass of capabilities remains at every period materially the same; the circumstances which awaken it to action perpetually change. If England were divided into forty republics, each equal in population and extent to Athens, there is no reason to suppose but that, under institutions not more perfect than those of Athens, each would produce philosophers and poets equal to those who (if we except Shakespeare) have never been surpassed. We owe the great writers of the golden age of our literature to that fervid awakening of the public mind which shook to dust the oldest and most oppressive form of the Christian Religion. We owe Milton to the progress and developement of the same spirit; the sacred Milton was, let it ever be remembered, a Republican, and a bold enquirer into morals and religion. The great writers of our own age are, we have reason to suppose, the companions and forerunners of some unimagined change in our social condition or the opinions which cement it. The cloud of mind is discharging its collected lightning, and the equilibrium between institutions and opinions is now restoring, or is about to be restored.[3]

As to imitation; Poetry is a mimetic art. It creates, but it creates by combination and representation. Poetical abstractions are beautiful and new, not because the portions of which they are composed had no previous existence in the mind of man or in nature, but because the whole produced by their combination has some intelligible and beautiful analogy with those sources of emotion and thought, and with the contemporary condition of them: one great poet is a masterpiece of nature, which another not only ought to study but must study. He might as wisely and as easily determine that his mind should no longer be the mirror of all that is lovely in the visible universe, as exclude from his contemplation the beautiful which exists in the writings of a great contemporary. The pretence of doing it would be a presumption in any but the greatest; the effect, even in him, would be strained, unnatural and ineffectual. A Poet, is the combined product of such internal powers as modify the nature of others, and of such external influences as excite and sustain these powers; he is not one, but both. Every man's mind is in this respect modified by all the objects of nature and art, by every word and every suggestion which he ever admitted to act upon his consciousness; it is the mirror upon which all forms are reflected, and in which they compose one form. Poets, not otherwise than philosophers, painters, sculptors and musicians, are in one sense the creators and in another the creations of their age. From this subjection the loftiest do not escape. There is a similarity between Homer and Hesiod, between Æschylus and Euripides, between Virgil and Horace, between Dante and Petrarch, between Shakespeare and Fletcher, between Dryden and Pope; each has a generic resemblance under which

---

3. See Shelley's similar tribute to his great contemporaries in the concluding paragraph of his *Defence of Poetry* (p. 802).

their specific distinctions are arranged. If this similarity be the result of imitation, I am willing to confess that I have imitated.

Let this opportunity be conceded to me of acknowledging that I have, what a Scotch philosopher characteristically terms, "a passion for reforming the world:"[4] what passion incited him to write and publish his book, he omits to explain. For my part I had rather be damned with Plato and Lord Bacon, than go to Heaven with Paley and Malthus.[5] But it is a mistake to suppose that I dedicate my poetical compositions solely to the direct enforcement of reform, or that I consider them in any degree as containing a reasoned system on the theory of human life. Didactic poetry is my abhorrence; nothing can be equally well expressed in prose that is not tedious and supererogatory in verse. My purpose has hitherto been simply to familiarise the highly refined imagination of the more select classes of poetical readers with beautiful idealisms of moral excellence; aware that until the mind can love, and admire, and trust, and hope, and endure, reasoned principles of moral conduct are seeds cast upon the highway of life which the unconscious passenger tramples into dust, although they would bear the harvest of his happiness. Should I live to accomplish what I purpose, that is, produce a systematical history of what appear to me to be the genuine elements of human society,[6] let not the advocates of injustice and superstition flatter themselves that I should take Æschylus rather than Plato as my model.

The having spoken of myself with unaffected freedom will need little apology with the candid; and let the uncandid consider that they injure me less than their own hearts and minds by misrepresentation. Whatever talents a person may possess to amuse and instruct others, be they ever so inconsiderable, he is yet bound to exert them: if his attempt be ineffectual, let the punishment of an unaccomplished purpose have been sufficient; let none trouble themselves to heap the dust of oblivion upon his efforts; the pile they raise will betray his grave which might otherwise have been unknown.

Prometheus Unbound

From *Act 1*

SCENE: *A Ravine of Icy Rocks in the Indian Caucasus.* PROMETHEUS *is discovered bound to the Precipice.* PANTHEA *and* IONE *are seated at his feet. Time, Night. During the Scene, Morning slowly breaks.*

PROMETHEUS Monarch of Gods and Dæmons,[1] and all Spirits
   But One, who throng those bright and rolling Worlds
   Which Thou and I alone of living things

---

4. This is the title of chap. 16 in *The Principles of Moral Science* (1805) by the Scottish writer Robert Forsyth.
5. Thomas Malthus's *An Essay on the Principle of Population* (1798) argued that the rate of increase in population will soon exceed the rate of increase in the food supply necessary to sustain it. William Paley wrote *Evidences of Christianity* (1794), which undertakes to prove that the design apparent in natural phenomena, and especially in the

human body, entails the existence of God as the great Designer. Shelley ironically expresses his contempt for the doctrines of both these thinkers, which he conceives as arguments for accepting uncomplainingly the present state of the world.
6. Shelley did not live to write this history.
1. Demogorgon (see 2.4). "Daemons": supernatural beings, intermediary between gods and mortals. Prometheus is addressing Jupiter.

Behold with sleepless eyes! regard this Earth
5   Made multitudinous with thy slaves, whom thou
Requitest for knee-worship, prayer and praise,
And toil, and hecatombs[2] of broken hearts,
With fear and self contempt and barren hope;
Whilst me, who am thy foe, eyeless° in hate,   *blinded*
10   Hast thou made reign and triumph, to thy scorn,
O'er mine own misery and thy vain revenge.—
Three thousand years of sleep-unsheltered hours
And moments—aye° divided by keen pangs   *always*
Till they seemed years, torture and solitude,
15   Scorn and despair,—these are mine empire:—
More glorious far than that which thou surveyest
From thine unenvied throne, O Mighty God!
Almighty, had I deigned[3] to share the shame
Of thine ill tyranny, and hung not here
20   Nailed to this wall of eagle-baffling mountain,
Black, wintry, dead, unmeasured; without herb,
Insect, or beast, or shape or sound of life.
Ah me, alas, pain, pain ever, forever!

No change, no pause, no hope!—Yet I endure.
25   I ask the Earth, have not the mountains felt?
I ask yon Heaven—the all-beholding Sun,
Has it not seen? The Sea, in storm or calm,
Heaven's ever-changing Shadow, spread below—
Have its deaf waves not heard my agony?
30   Ah me, alas, pain, pain ever, forever!

The crawling glaciers pierce me with the spears
Of their moon-freezing chrystals; the bright chains
Eat with their burning cold into my bones.
Heaven's winged hound, polluting from thy lips
35   His beak in poison not his own, tears up
My heart;[4] and shapeless sights come wandering by,
The ghastly people of the realm of dream,
Mocking me: and the Earthquake-fiends are charged
To wrench the rivets from my quivering wounds
40   When the rocks split and close again behind;
While from their loud abysses howling throng
The genii of the storm, urging the rage
Of whirlwind, and afflict me with keen hail.
And yet to me welcome is Day and Night,
45   Whether one breaks the hoar frost of the morn,
Or starry, dim, and slow, the other climbs
The leaden-coloured East; for then they lead

2. Large sacrificial offerings.
3. I.e., you would have been all-powerful, if I had
deigned.

4. The vulture, tearing daily at Prometheus's
heart, was kissed by Jupiter by way of reward.

Their wingless, crawling Hours,[5] one among whom
—As some dark Priest hales° the reluctant victim—   drags
50 Shall drag thee, cruel King, to kiss the blood
From these pale feet,[6] which then might trample thee
If they disdained not such a prostrate slave.
Disdain? Ah no! I pity thee.[7]—What Ruin
Will hunt thee undefended through wide Heaven!
55 How will thy soul, cloven to its depth with terror,
Gape like a Hell within! I speak in grief,
Not exultation, for I hate no more,
As then, ere misery made me wise.—The Curse
Once breathed on thee I would recall. Ye Mountains,
60 Whose many-voiced Echoes, through the mist
Of cataracts, flung the thunder of that spell!
Ye icy Springs, stagnant with wrinkling frost,
Which vibrated to hear me, and then crept
Shuddering through India! Thou serenest Air,
65 Through which the Sun walks burning without beams!
And ye swift Whirlwinds, who on poised wings
Hung mute and moveless o'er yon hushed abyss,
As thunder louder than your own made rock
The orbed world! If then my words had power
70 —Though I am changed so that aught evil wish
Is dead within, although no memory be
Of what is hate—let them not lose it now![8]
What was that curse? for ye all heard me speak.[9]

* * *

PHANTASM

Fiend, I defy thee! with a calm, fixed mind,
    All that thou canst inflict I bid thee do;
Foul Tyrant both of Gods and Humankind,
265   One only being shalt thou not subdue.
        Rain then thy plagues upon me here,
        Ghastly disease and frenzying fear;
        And let alternate frost and fire
        Eat into me, and be thine ire
270 Lightning and cutting hail and legioned forms
Of furies, driving by upon the wounding storms.

Aye, do thy worst. Thou art Omnipotent.
    O'er all things but thyself I gave thee power,

5. The Hours were represented in Greek myth and art by human figures with wings.
6. One of a number of implied parallels between the agony of Prometheus and the passion of Christ.
7. At this early point occurs the crisis of the action: the beginning of Prometheus's change of heart from hate to compassion, consummated in lines 303–05. The rest of the symbolic drama gradually unfolds the consequences of this moral tri-

umph—of which Prometheus himself is unaware.
8. Let my words not lose their power now.
9. In the passage here omitted, none dares, for fear of the god's vengeance, to repeat the curse Prometheus had proclaimed against Jupiter. Prometheus is finally forced to call up the Phantasm of Jupiter himself, who, in the next excerpt, repeats the words of Prometheus's curse.

And my own will. Be thy swift mischiefs sent
275 To blast mankind, from yon etherial tower.
    Let thy malignant spirit move
    Its darkness over those I love:
    On me and mine I imprecate°   *pray for*
    The utmost torture of thy hate
280 And thus devote to sleepless agony
This undeclining head while thou must reign on high.

But thou who art the God and Lord—O thou
    Who fillest with thy soul this world of woe,
To whom all things of Earth and Heaven do bow
285   In fear and worship—all-prevailing foe!
    I curse thee! let a sufferer's curse
    Clasp thee, his torturer, like remorse,
    Till thine Infinity shall be
    A robe of envenomed agony;[1]
290 And thine Omnipotence a crown of pain
To cling like burning gold round thy dissolving brain.

Heap on thy soul by virtue of this Curse
    Ill deeds, then be thou damned, beholding good,
Both infinite as is the Universe,
295   And thou, and thy self-torturing solitude.
    An awful Image of calm power
    Though now thou sittest, let the hour
    Come, when thou must appear to be
    That which thou art internally.
300 And after many a false and fruitless crime
Scorn track thy lagging fall through boundless space and time.
                                          [*The Phantasm vanishes.*]

PROMETHEUS   Were these my words, O Parent?
THE EARTH   They were thine.
PROMETHEUS   It doth repent me: words are quick and vain;
    Grief for awhile is blind, and so was mine.
305   I wish no living thing to suffer pain.

THE EARTH

    Misery, O misery to me,
    That Jove at length should vanquish thee.[2]
    Wail, howl aloud, Land and Sea,
    The Earth's rent heart shall answer ye.
310 Howl, Spirits of the living and the dead,
Your refuge, your defence lies fallen and vanquished.

FIRST ECHO

Lies fallen and vanquished?

1. Like the poisoned shirt of the centaur Nessus, which consumed Hercules' flesh when he put it on. The next two lines allude to the mock crowning of Christ with a crown of thorns.

2. Earth mistakes mercy for submission and, therefore, interprets Prometheus's moral victory as his defeat.

SECOND ECHO
Fallen and vanquished!

IONE[3]
Fear not—'tis but some passing spasm,
The Titan is unvanquished still.[4]

* * *

FURY Behold, an emblem—those who do endure
595 Deep wrongs for man, and scorn and chains, but heap
Thousand-fold torment on themselves and him.
PROMETHEUS Remit the anguish of that lighted stare—
Close those wan lips—let that thorn-wounded brow
Stream not with blood—it mingles with thy tears
600 Fix, fix those tortured orbs in peace and death
So thy sick throes shake not that crucifix,
So those pale fingers play not with thy gore.—
O horrible! Thy name I will not speak,
It hath become a curse.[5] I see, I see
605 The wise, the mild, the lofty and the just,
Whom thy slaves hate for being like to thee,
Some hunted by foul lies from their heart's home,
An early-chosen, late-lamented home,
As hooded ounces[6] cling to the driven hind,°   doe
610 Some linked to corpses in unwholesome cells:
Some—hear I not the multitude laugh loud?—
Impaled in lingering fire: and mighty realms
Float by my feet like sea-uprooted isles
Whose sons are kneaded down in common blood
615 By the red light of their own burning homes.
FURY Blood thou canst see, and fire; and canst hear groans;
Worse things, unheard, unseen, remain behind.
PROMETHEUS Worse?
FURY   In each human heart terror survives
The ravin it has gorged:[7] the loftiest fear
620 All that they would disdain to think were true:
Hypocrisy and custom make their minds
The fanes° of many a worship, now outworn.   temples
They dare not devise good for man's estate
And yet they know not that they do not dare.
625 The good want power, but to weep barren tears.
The powerful goodness want: worse need for them.

---

3. Ione, Panthea, and Asia (in the following scene) are sisters and Oceanids—i.e., daughters of Oceanus.
4. In the omitted passage the herald Mercury, at Jupiter's command, brings a group of Furies (in Greek myth, avengers of crimes against the gods) who tempt Prometheus to despair by revealing the loathsome potentialities for evil in humankind's conscious and unconscious mind. In the climactic temptation a Fury tears aside a veil to reveal a rep-

resentation ("emblem," line 594) of the suffering Christ on the cross.
5. I.e., the name "Christ" has become, literally, a curse word, and metaphorically, a curse to humankind, in that His religion of love is used to justify religious wars and bloody oppression.
6. Cheetahs, or leopards, used in hunting (hoods were sometimes placed over their eyes to make them easier to control).
7. The prey that it has greedily devoured.

The wise want love, and those who love want wisdom;
And all best things are thus confused to ill.
Many are strong and rich,—and would be just,—
630   But live among their suffering fellow men
As if none felt: they know not what they do.[8]
PROMETHEUS   Thy words are like a cloud of winged snakes
And yet, I pity those they torture not.
FURY   Thou pitiest them? I speak no more!   [Vanishes.]
PROMETHEUS.   Ah woe!
635   Ah woe! Alas! pain, pain ever, forever!
I close my tearless eyes, but see more clear
Thy works within my woe-illumed mind,
Thou subtle Tyrant![9] . . . Peace is in the grave—
The grave hides all things beautiful and good—
640   I am a God and cannot find it there,
Nor would I seek it: for, though dread revenge,
This is defeat, fierce King, not victory.
The sights with which thou torturest gird my soul
With new endurance, till the hour arrives
. 645   When they shall be no types of things which are.
PANTHEA   Alas! what sawest thou?
PROMETHEUS   There are two woes:
To speak and to behold; thou spare me one.[1]
Names are there, Nature's sacred watchwords—they
Were borne aloft in bright emblazonry.[2]
650   The nations thronged around, and cried aloud
As with one voice, "Truth, liberty and love!"
Suddenly fierce confusion fell from Heaven
Among them—there was strife, deceit and fear;
Tyrants rushed in, and did divide the spoil.
655   This was the shadow of the truth I saw.
THE EARTH   I felt thy torture, Son, with such mixed joy
As pain and Virtue give.—To cheer thy state
I bid ascend those subtle and fair spirits
Whose homes are the dim caves of human thought
660   And who inhabit, as birds wing the wind,
Its world-surrounding ether;[3] they behold
Beyond that twilight realm, as in a glass,°   mirror
The future—may they speak comfort to thee![4]

*   *   *

8. The Fury ironically echoes Christ's plea for forgiveness of his crucifiers: "Father, forgive them: for
they know not what they do" (Luke 23.34). Lines
625–28 are Shelley's comment on his own age of
political reaction and oppression. This passage
underlies Yeats's description of the troubled era
after World War I in The Second Coming, lines
3–8.
9. Jupiter (also addressed as "fierce King," line
642).

1. I.e., spare me the woe of speaking (about what
I have beheld).
2. As in a brilliant display of banners.
3. A medium, weightless and infinitely elastic,
once supposed to permeate the universe.
4. The speech of the Earth ushers in a troop of
spirits representing the noble and virtuous potentialities of the mind, on which rests the hope of a
future felicity for humanity.

From *Act 2*

SCENE 4—*The Cave of* DEMOGORGON. ASIA *and* PANTHEA.[5]

PANTHEA   What veiled form sits on that ebon throne?
ASIA   The veil has fallen! . . .
PANTHEA   I see a mighty Darkness
    Filling the seat of power; and rays of gloom
    Dart round, as light from the meridian Sun,
5   Ungazed upon and shapeless—neither limb
    Nor form—nor outline;[6] yet we feel it is
    A living Spirit.
DEMOGORGON   Ask what thou wouldst know.
ASIA   What canst thou tell?
DEMOGORGON   All things thou dar'st demand.
ASIA   Who made the living world?
DEMOGORGON   God.
ASIA   Who made all
10   That it contains—thought, passion, reason, will,
    Imagination?
DEMOGORGON   God, Almighty God.
ASIA   Who made that sense[7] which, when the winds of Spring
    In rarest visitation, or the voice
    Of one beloved heard in youth alone,
15   Fills the faint eyes with falling tears, which dim
    The radiant looks of unbewailing flowers,
    And leaves this peopled earth a solitude
    When it returns no more?
DEMOGORGON   Merciful God.
ASIA   And who made terror, madness, crime, remorse,
20   Which from the links of the great chain of things
    To every thought within the mind of man
    Sway and drag heavily—and each one reels
    Under the load towards the pit of death;
    Abandoned hope, and love that turns to hate;
25   And self-contempt, bitterer to drink than blood;
    Pain whose unheeded and familiar speech
    Is howling and keen shrieks, day after day;
    And Hell, or the sharp fear of Hell?[8]
DEMOGORGON   He reigns.

---

5. Act 2 has opened with Asia—the feminine principle and embodiment of love, who was separated from Prometheus at the moment of his fall into divisive hate—in a lovely Indian valley at the first hour of the dawn of the spring season of redemption. Asia and her sister Panthea have been led, by a sweet and irresistible compulsion, first to the portal and then down into the depths of the cave of Demogorgon—the central enigma of Shelley's poem.
  Commentators have usually equated Demogorgon with necessity, but the interpretation may be too confining. More flexibly, he can be thought of as process, the inexorable way in which things evolve. But the ultimate mover of that process—

the ultimate reason for the way things are—must remain, Shelley skeptically insists, a mystery beyond the limits of accessible knowledge. Demogorgon is ignorant of the principle that controls him and can give merely riddling answers to Asia's questions about the "why" of creation, good, and evil.
6. Echoing Milton's description of Death, *Paradise Lost* 2.666–73.
7. Presumably the sense by which one is aware of the "unseen Power" that Shelley calls "Intellectual Beauty" (see *Hymn to Intellectual Beauty*, stanza 2, p. 724).
8. The nouns "hope," "love," etc. (lines 24–28) are all objects of the verb "made" (line 19).

ASIA   Utter his name—a world pining in pain
30   Asks but his name; curses shall drag him down.
DEMOGORGON   He reigns.
ASIA   I feel, I know it—who?
DEMOGORGON   He reigns.
ASIA   Who reigns? There was the Heaven and Earth at first
      And Light and Love;—then Saturn,[9] from whose throne
      Time fell, an envious shadow; such the state
35   Of the earth's primal spirits beneath his sway
      As the calm joy of flowers and living leaves
      Before the wind or sun has withered them
      And semivital worms; but he refused
      The birthright of their being, knowledge, power,
40   The skill which wields the elements, the thought
      Which pierces this dim Universe like light,
      Self-empire and the majesty of love,
      For thirst of which they fainted. Then Prometheus
      Gave wisdom, which is strength, to Jupiter
45   And with this law alone: "Let man be free,"
      Clothed him with the dominion of wide Heaven.
      To know nor faith nor love nor law, to be
      Omnipotent but friendless, is to reign;
      And Jove now reigned; for on the race of man
50   First famine, and then toil, and then disease,
      Strife, wounds, and ghastly death unseen before,
      Fell; and the unseasonable seasons drove,
      With alternating shafts of frost and fire,
      Their shelterless, pale tribes to mountain caves;
55   And in their desart° hearts fierce wants he sent   *empty*
      And mad disquietudes, and shadows idle
      Of unreal good, which levied mutual war,
      So ruining the lair wherein they raged.
      Prometheus saw, and waked the legioned hopes
60   Which sleep within folded Elysian flowers,
      Nepenthe, Moly, Amaranth,[1] fadeless blooms;
      That they might hide with thin and rainbow wings
      The shape of Death; and Love he sent to bind
      The disunited tendrils of that vine
65   Which bears the wine of life, the human heart;
      And he tamed fire which, like some beast of prey,
      Most terrible, but lovely, played beneath
      The frown of man, and tortured to his will
      Iron and gold, the slaves and signs of power,
70   And gems and poisons, and all subtlest forms,
      Hidden beneath the mountains and the waves.

---

9. In Greek myth Saturn's reign was the golden age. In Shelley's version Saturn refused to grant mortals knowledge and science, so that it was an age of ignorant innocence in which the deepest human needs remained unfulfilled.

1. These are medicinal drugs and flowers in Greek myth. Asia is describing (lines 59–97) the various sciences and arts given to humans by Prometheus, the culture bringer.

He gave man speech, and speech created thought,
Which is the measure of the Universe;
And Science struck the thrones of Earth and Heaven
Which shook, but fell not; and the harmonious mind
Poured itself forth in all-prophetic song,
And music lifted up the listening spirit
Until it walked, exempt from mortal care,
Godlike, o'er the clear billows of sweet sound;
And human hands first mimicked and then mocked[2]
With moulded limbs more lovely than its own
The human form, till marble grew divine,
And mothers, gazing, drank the love men see
Reflected in their race, behold, and perish.[3]—
He told the hidden power of herbs and springs,
And Disease drank and slept—Death grew like sleep.—
He taught the implicated° orbits woven   intertwined
Of the wide-wandering stars, and how the Sun
Changes his lair, and by what secret spell
The pale moon is transformed, when her broad eye
Gazes not on the interlunar[4] sea;
He taught to rule, as life directs the limbs,
The tempest-winged chariots of the Ocean,
And the Celt knew the Indian.[5] Cities then
Were built, and through their snow-like columns flowed
The warm winds, and the azure æther shone,
And the blue sea and shadowy hills were seen . . .
Such the alleviations of his state
Prometheus gave to man—for which he hangs
Withering in destined pain—but who rains down
Evil, the immedicable plague, which while
Man looks on his creation like a God
And sees that it is glorious, drives him on,
The wreck of his own will, the scorn of Earth,
The outcast, the abandoned, the alone?—
Not Jove: while yet his frown shook Heaven, aye when
His adversary from adamantine chains
Cursed him, he trembled like a slave. Declare
Who is his master? Is he too a slave?

DEMOGORGON   All spirits are enslaved which serve things evil:
Thou knowest if Jupiter be such or no.
ASIA   Whom calledst thou God?
DEMOGORGON   I spoke but as ye speak—
For Jove is the supreme of living things.
ASIA   Who is the master of the slave?
DEMOGORGON   —If the Abysm

2. I.e., sculptors first merely reproduced but later
improved on ("mocked" in the sense of "heightened") the beauty of the human form.
3. Expectant mothers looked at the beautiful statues so that their children might, by prenatal influence, be born with the beauty that makes

beholders die of love.
4. The phase between old and new moons, when
the moon is invisible.
5. The reference is to the ships in which the Celtic
(here, non-Greco-Roman) races of Europe were
able to sail to India.

115   Could vomit forth its secrets:—but a voice
         Is wanting, the deep truth is imageless;[6]
         For what would it avail to bid thee gaze
         On the revolving world? what to bid speak
         Fate, Time, Occasion, Chance and Change? To these
120   All things are subject but eternal Love.
ASIA   So much I asked before, and my heart gave
         The response thou hast given; and of such truths
         Each to itself must be the oracle.—
         One more demand . . . and do thou answer me
125   As my own soul would answer, did it know
         That which I ask.—Prometheus shall arise
         Henceforth the Sun of this rejoicing world:
         When shall the destined hour arrive?
DEMOGORGON   Behold![7]
ASIA   The rocks are cloven, and through the purple night
130   I see Cars drawn by rainbow-winged steeds
         Which trample the dim winds—in each there stands
         A wild-eyed charioteer, urging their flight.
         Some look behind, as fiends pursued them there
         And yet I see no shapes but the keen stars:
135   Others with burning eyes lean forth, and drink
         With eager lips the wind of their own speed,
         As if the thing they loved fled on before,
         And now—even now they clasped it; their bright locks
         Stream like a comet's flashing hair: they all
         Sweep onward.—
140 DEMOGORGON   These are the immortal Hours
         Of whom thou didst demand.—One waits for thee.
ASIA   A Spirit with a dreadful countenance
         Checks its dark chariot by the craggy gulph.
         Unlike thy brethren, ghastly charioteer,
145   What art thou? whither wouldst thou bear me? Speak!
SPIRIT   I am the shadow of a destiny
         More dread than is my aspect—ere yon planet
         Has set, the Darkness[8] which ascends with me
         Shall wrap in lasting night Heaven's kingless throne.
ASIA   What meanest thou?
150 PANTHEA   That terrible shadow floats
         Up from its throne, as may the lurid° smoke   red-glaring
         Of earthquake-ruined cities o'er the sea.—
         Lo! it ascends the Car . . . the coursers fly
         Terrified; watch its path among the stars
         Blackening the night!
155 ASIA   Thus I am answered—strange!
PANTHEA See, near the verge° another chariot stays;   horizon
         An ivory shell inlaid with crimson fire

6. I.e., ultimate truths can be neither known nor   the approaching chariots ("Cars").
expressed.   8. Demogorgon, who is ascending (lines 150–55)
7. Demogorgon's answer is a gesture: he points to   to effect the dethronement of Jupiter.

Which comes and goes within its sculptured rim
Of delicate strange tracery—the young Spirit
160   That guides it, has the dovelike eyes of hope.
How its soft smiles attract the soul!—as light
Lures winged insects[9] through the lampless air.

SPIRIT

My coursers are fed with the lightning,
    They drink of the whirlwind's stream
165   And when the red morning is brightning
        They bathe in the fresh sunbeam;
    They have strength for their swiftness, I deem:
        Then ascend with me, daughter of Ocean.

I desire—and their speed makes night kindle;
170   I fear—they outstrip the Typhoon;
    Ere the cloud piled on Atlas[1] can dwindle
        We encircle the earth and the moon:
    We shall rest from long labours at noon:
        Then ascend with me, daughter of Ocean.

SCENE 5—*The Car pauses within a Cloud on the Top of a snowy Mountain.*
ASIA, PANTHEA, *and the* SPIRIT OF THE HOUR.

SPIRIT

On the brink of the night and the morning
    My coursers are wont to respire,[2]
But the Earth has just whispered a warning
    That their flight must be swifter than fire:
5   They shall drink the hot speed of desire!

ASIA   Thou breathest on their nostrils—but my breath
    Would give them swifter speed.
SPIRIT   Alas, it could not.
PANTHEA   O Spirit! pause and tell whence is the light
    Which fills the cloud? the sun is yet unrisen.
10 SPIRIT   The sun will rise not until noon.[3]—Apollo
    Is held in Heaven by wonder—and the light
    Which fills this vapour, as the aerial hue
    Of fountain-gazing roses fills the water,
    Flows from thy mighty sister.
PANTHEA   Yes, I feel . . .
15 ASIA   What is it with thee, sister? Thou art pale.
PANTHEA   How thou art changed! I dare not look on thee;
    I feel, but see thee not. I scarce endure

9. The ancient image of the soul, or *psyche,* was a
moth. The chariot described here will carry Asia to
a reunion with Prometheus.
1. A mountain in North Africa that the Greeks

regarded as so high that it supported the heavens.
2. Catch their breath.
3. The time of the reunion of Prometheus and
Asia.

The radiance of thy beauty.[4] Some good change
Is working in the elements which suffer
20 Thy presence thus unveiled.—The Nereids tell
That on the day when the clear hyaline°   glassy sea
Was cloven at thy uprise, and thou didst stand
Within a veined shell,[5] which floated on
Over the calm floor of the chrystal sea,
25 Among the Ægean isles, and by the shores
Which bear thy name, love, like the atmosphere
Of the sun's fire filling the living world,
Burst from thee, and illumined Earth and Heaven
And the deep ocean and the sunless caves,
30 And all that dwells within them; till grief cast
Eclipse upon the soul from which it came:
Such art thou now, nor is it I alone,
Thy sister, thy companion, thine own chosen one,
But the whole world which seeks thy sympathy.
35 Hearest thou not sounds i' the air which speak the love
Of all articulate beings? Feelest thou not
The inanimate winds enamoured of thee?—List!   [Music.]
ASIA   Thy words are sweeter than aught else but his
Whose echoes they are—yet all love is sweet,
40 Given or returned; common as light is love
And its familiar voice wearies not ever.
Like the wide Heaven, the all-sustaining air,
It makes the reptile equal to the God . . .
They who inspire it most are fortunate
45 As I am now; but those who feel it most
Are happier still, after long sufferings
As I shall soon become.
PANTHEA   List! Spirits speak.

VOICE (*in the air, singing*)[6]
Life of Life! thy lips enkindle
    With their love the breath between them
50 And thy smiles before they dwindle
    Make the cold air fire; then screen them
In those looks where whoso gazes
Faints, entangled in their mazes.

Child of Light! thy limbs are burning
55   Through the vest which seems to hide them
As the radiant lines of morning
    Through the clouds ere they divide them,

---

4. In an earlier scene Panthea had envisioned in a dream the radiant and eternal inner form of Prometheus emerging through his "wound-worn limbs." The corresponding transfiguration of Asia, prepared for by her descent to the underworld, now takes place.
5. The story told by the Nereids (sea nymphs)

serves to associate Asia with Aphrodite, goddess of love, emerging (as in Botticelli's painting) from the Mediterranean on a seashell.
6. The voice attempts to describe, in a dizzying whirl of optical paradoxes, what it feels like to look on the naked essence of love and beauty.

And this atmosphere divinest
Shrouds thee wheresoe'er thou shinest.

60 Fair are others;—none beholds thee
    But thy voice sounds low and tender
Like the fairest, for it folds thee
    From the sight, that liquid splendour,
And all feel, yet see thee never
65 As I feel now, lost forever!

Lamp of Earth! where'er thou movest
    Its dim shapes are clad with brightness
And the souls of whom thou lovest
    Walk upon the winds with lightness
70 Till they fail, as I am failing,
Dizzy, lost . . . yet unbewailing!

ASIA

My soul is an enchanted Boat
Which, like a sleeping swan, doth float
Upon the silver waves of thy sweet singing,
75   And thine doth like an Angel sit
    Beside the helm conducting it
Whilst all the winds with melody are ringing.
    It seems to float ever—forever—
    Upon that many winding River
80   Between mountains, woods, abysses,
    A Paradise of wildernesses,
Till like one in slumber bound
Borne to the Ocean, I float down, around,
Into a Sea profound, of ever-spreading sound.

85   Meanwhile thy spirit lifts its pinions°   *wings*
    In Music's most serene dominions,
Catching the winds that fan that happy Heaven.
    And we sail on, away, afar,
    Without a course—without a star—
90 But by the instinct of sweet Music driven
    Till, through Elysian garden islets
    By thee, most beautiful of pilots,
    Where never mortal pinnace° glided,   *small boat*
    The boat of my desire is guided—
95 Realms where the air we breathe is Love
Which in the winds and on the waves doth move,
Harmonizing this Earth with what we feel above.

    We have past Age's icy caves,
    And Manhood's dark and tossing waves
100 And Youth's smooth ocean, smiling to betray;
    Beyond the glassy gulphs we flee

Of shadow-peopled Infancy,
Through Death and Birth to a diviner day,[7]
A Paradise of vaulted bowers
105   Lit by downward-gazing flowers
And watery paths that wind between
Wildernesses calm and green,
Peopled by shapes too bright to see,
And rest, having beheld—somewhat like thee,
110   Which walk upon the sea, and chaunt melodiously!

From Act 3

SCENE 1—*Heaven.* JUPITER *on his Throne;* THETIS *and the other Deities assembled.*

JUPITER   Ye congregated Powers of Heaven who share
    The glory and the strength of him ye serve,
    Rejoice! henceforth I am omnipotent.
    All else had been subdued to me—alone
5   The soul of man, like unextinguished fire,
    Yet burns towards Heaven with fierce reproach and doubt
    And lamentation and reluctant prayer,
    Hurling up insurrection, which might make
    Our antique empire insecure, though built
10   On eldest faith, and Hell's coeval,[8] fear.
    And though my curses through the pendulous° air   *suspending*
    Like snow on herbless peaks, fall flake by flake
    And cling to it[9]—though under my wrath's night
    It climb the crags of life, step after step,
15   Which wound it, as ice wounds unsandalled feet,
    It yet remains supreme o'er misery,
    Aspiring . . . unrepressed; yet soon to fall:
    Even now have I begotten a strange wonder,
    That fatal Child,[1] the terror of the Earth,
20   Who waits but till the destined Hour arrive,
    Bearing from Demogorgon's vacant throne
    The dreadful might of ever living limbs
    Which clothed that awful spirit unbeheld—
    To redescend, and trample out the spark[2] . . .

25   Pour forth Heaven's wine, Idæan Ganymede,
    And let it fill the dædal[3] cups like fire
    And from the flower-inwoven soil divine
    Ye all triumphant harmonies arise

7. Asia is describing what it feels like to be trans-figured—in the image of moving backward in the stream of time, through youth and infancy and birth itself, in order to die to this life and be born again to a "diviner" existence.
8. Of the same age.
9. "It" (as also in lines 14 and 16) is "the soul of man" (line 5).
1. The son of Jupiter and Thetis. Jupiter believes that he has begotten a child who will assume the bodily form of the conquered Demogorgon and then return to announce his victory and the defeat of the resistance of Prometheus.
2. Of Prometheus's defiance.
3. Skillfully wrought (from the name of the Greek craftsman Daedalus). Ganymede (line 25) had been seized on Mount Ida by an eagle and carried to heaven to be Jupiter's cupbearer.

As dew from Earth under the twilight stars;
Drink! be the nectar circling through your veins
The soul of joy, ye everliving Gods,
Till exultation burst in one wide voice
Like music from Elysian winds.—

                              And thou
Ascend beside me, veiled in the light
Of the desire which makes thee one with me,
Thetis, bright Image of Eternity!—
When thou didst cry, "Insufferable might!"[4]
God! spare me! I sustain not the quick flames,
The penetrating presence; all my being,
Like him whom the Numidian seps[5] did thaw
Into a dew with poison, is dissolved,
Sinking through its foundations"—even then
Two mighty spirits, mingling, made a third
Mightier than either—which unbodied now
Between us, floats, felt although unbeheld,
Waiting the incarnation, which ascends—
Hear ye the thunder of the fiery wheels
Griding[6] the winds?—from Demogorgon's throne.—
Victory! victory! Feel'st thou not, O World,
The Earthquake of his chariot thundering up
Olympus?

[*The Car of the* HOUR *arrives.* DEMOGORGON *descends and moves towards the Throne of* JUPITER.]

            Awful Shape, what art thou? Speak!
DEMOGORGON   Eternity—demand no direr name.
Descend, and follow me down the abyss;
I am thy child,[7] as thou wert Saturn's child,
Mightier than thee; and we must dwell together
Henceforth in darkness.—Lift thy lightnings not.
The tyranny of Heaven none may retain,
Or reassume, or hold succeeding thee . . .
Yet if thou wilt—as 'tis the destiny
Of trodden worms to writhe till they are dead—
Put forth thy might.

JUPITER   Detested prodigy!
Even thus beneath the deep Titanian prisons[8]
I trample thee! . . . thou lingerest?

                        Mercy! mercy!
No pity—no release, no respite! . . . Oh,
That thou wouldst make mine enemy my judge.
Even where he hangs, seared by my long revenge
On Caucasus—he would not doom me thus.—

---

4. This description of the sexual union of Jupiter and Thetis is a grotesque parody of the reunion of Prometheus and Asia.
5. A serpent of Numidia (North Africa) whose bite was thought to cause putrefaction.
6. Cutting with a rasping sound.

7. Ironically, and in a figurative sense: Demogorgon's function follows from Jupiter's actions.
8. After they overthrew the Titans, Jupiter and the Olympian gods imprisoned them in Tartarus, deep beneath the earth.

Gentle and just and dreadless, is he not
The monarch of the world?[9] what then art thou? . . .
No refuge! no appeal— . . .

70   Sink with me then—
We two will sink in the wide waves of ruin
Even as a vulture and a snake outspent
Drop, twisted in inextricable fight,[1]
Into a shoreless sea.—Let Hell unlock

75   Its mounded Oceans of tempestuous fire,
And whelm on them into the bottomless void
The desolated world and thee and me,
The conqueror and the conquered, and the wreck
Of that for which they combated.
                                              Ai! Ai!

80   The elements obey me not . . . I sink . . .
Dizzily down—ever, forever, down—
And, like a cloud, mine enemy above
Darkens my fall with victory!—Ai! Ai!

From SCENE 4—*A Forest. In the Background a Cave.* PROMETHEUS, ASIA, PAN-
THEA, IONE, *and the* SPIRIT OF THE EARTH.[2]

*   *   *

[*The* SPIRIT OF THE HOUR *enters.*]

PROMETHEUS   We feel what thou hast heard and seen—yet speak.
SPIRIT OF THE HOUR   Soon as the sound had ceased whose thunder filled
The abysses of the sky, and the wide earth,

100   There was a change . . . the impalpable thin air
And the all-circling sunlight were transformed
As if the sense of love dissolved in them
Had folded itself round the sphered world.
My vision then grew clear and I could see

105   Into the mysteries of the Universe.[3]
Dizzy as with delight I floated down,
Winnowing the lightsome air with languid plumes,
My coursers sought their birthplace in the sun
Where they henceforth will live exempt from toil,

110   Pasturing flowers of vegetable fire—
And where my moonlike car will stand within
A temple, gazed upon by Phidian forms,[4]

9. The ultimate irony: Jupiter appeals to those very
qualities of Prometheus for which he has hitherto
persecuted him, begging for a mercy that Prometheus has already granted him, but Prometheus's
change from vengefulness to mercy is in fact the
cause of Jupiter's present downfall.
1. The eagle (or vulture) and the snake locked in
equal combat—a favorite Shelleyan image (cf.
Alastor, lines 227–32, p. 000).
2. After Jupiter's annihilation (described in scene
2), Hercules unbinds Prometheus, who is reunited
with Asia and retires to a cave "where we will sit
and talk of time and change / . . . ourselves

unchanged." In the speech that concludes the act
(reprinted here) the Spirit of the Hour describes
what happened in the human world when he
sounded the apocalyptic trumpet.
3. I.e., the earth's atmosphere clarifies, no longer
refracting the sunlight, and so allows the Spirit of
the Hour to see what is happening on earth.
4. The crescent-shaped ("moonlike") chariot, its
apocalyptic mission accomplished, will be frozen
to stone and will be surrounded by the sculptured
forms of other agents in the drama. Phidias (5th
century B.C.E.) was the noblest of Greek sculptors.

Of thee, and Asia and the Earth, and me
And you fair nymphs, looking the love we feel,
115 In memory of the tidings it has borne,
Beneath a dome fretted with graven flowers,
Poised on twelve columns of resplendent stone
And open to the bright and liquid sky.
Yoked to it by an amphisæbnic snake[5]
120 The likeness of those winged steeds will mock[6]
The flight from which they find repose.—Alas,
Whither has wandered now my partial[7] tongue
When all remains untold which ye would hear!—
As I have said, I floated to the Earth:
125 It was, as it is still, the pain of bliss
To move, to breathe, to be; I wandering went
Among the haunts and dwellings of mankind
And first was disappointed not to see
Such mighty change as I had felt within
130 Expressed in outward things; but soon I looked,
And behold! thrones were kingless, and men walked
One with the other even as spirits do,
None fawned, none trampled; hate, disdain or fear,
Self-love or self-contempt on human brows
135 No more inscribed, as o'er the gate of hell,
"All hope abandon, ye who enter here";[8]
None frowned, none trembled, none with eager fear
Gazed on another's eye of cold command
Until the subject of a tyrant's will
140 Became, worse fate, the abject of his own[9]
Which spurred him, like an outspent horse, to death.
None wrought his lips in truth-entangling lines
Which smiled the lie his tongue disdained to speak;
None with firm sneer trod out in his own heart
145 The sparks of love and hope, till there remained
Those bitter ashes, a soul self-consumed,
And the wretch crept, a vampire among men,
Infecting all with his own hideous ill.
None talked that common, false, cold, hollow talk
150 Which makes the heart deny the *yes* it breathes
Yet question that unmeant hypocrisy
With such a self-mistrust as has no name.
And women too, frank, beautiful and kind
As the free Heaven which rains fresh light and dew
155 On the wide earth, past: gentle, radiant forms,
From custom's evil taint exempt and pure;
Speaking the wisdom once they could not think,

---

5. A mythical snake with a head at each end; it serves here as a symbolic warning that a reversal of the process is always possible.
6. "Imitate" and also, in their immobility, "mock at" the flight they represent.

7. Biased or, possibly, telling only part of the story.
8. The inscription over the gate of hell in Dante's *Inferno* 3.9.
9. I.e., he was so abjectly enslaved that his own will accorded with the tyrant's will.

Looking emotions once they feared to feel
And changed to all which once they dared not be,
160 Yet being now, made Earth like Heaven—nor pride
Nor jealousy nor envy nor ill shame,
The bitterest of those drops of treasured gall,
Spoilt the sweet taste of the nepenthe,[1] love.

Thrones, altars, judgement-seats and prisons; wherein
165 And beside which, by wretched men were borne
Sceptres, tiaras, swords and chains, and tomes
Of reasoned wrong glozed on[2] by ignorance,
Were like those monstrous and barbaric shapes,
The ghosts of a no more remembered fame,
170 Which from their unworn obelisks[3] look forth
In triumph o'er the palaces and tombs
Of those who were their conquerors, mouldering round.
Those imaged to the pride of Kings and Priests
A dark yet mighty faith, a power as wide
175 As is the world it wasted, and are now
But an astonishment; even so the tools
And emblems of its last captivity
Amid the dwellings of the peopled Earth,
Stand, not o'erthrown, but unregarded now.
180 And those foul shapes, abhorred by God and man—
Which under many a name and many a form
Strange, savage, ghastly, dark and execrable
Were Jupiter,[4] the tyrant of the world;
And which the nations panic-stricken served
185 With blood, and hearts broken by long hope, and love
Dragged to his altars soiled and garlandless
And slain amid men's unreclaiming tears,
Flattering the thing they feared, which fear was hate—
Frown, mouldering fast, o'er their abandoned shrines.
190 The painted veil, by those who were, called life,[5]
Which mimicked, as with colours idly spread,
All men believed and hoped, is torn aside—
The loathsome mask has fallen, the man remains
Sceptreless, free, uncircumscribed—but man:
195 Equal, unclassed, tribeless, and nationless,
Exempt from awe, worship, degree,—the King
Over himself; just, gentle, wise—but man:
Passionless? no—yet free from guilt or pain
Which were, for his will made, or suffered them,
200 Nor yet exempt, though ruling them like slaves,

1. A drug (probably opium) that brings forgetfulness of pain and sorrow.
2. Annotated, explained.
3. The Egyptian obelisks (tapering shafts of stone), brought to Rome by its conquering armies, included hieroglyphs that—because they were still undeciphered in Shelley's time—seemed "monstrous and barbaric shapes" (line 168).
4. The "foul shapes" (line 180) were statues of the gods who, whatever their names, were all really manifestations of Jupiter.
5. I.e., which was thought to be life by humans as they were before their regeneration.

From chance and death and mutability,
The clogs of that which else might oversoar
The loftiest star of unascended Heaven
Pinnacled dim in the intense inane.[6]

From Act 4[7]

SCENE—A Part of the Forest near the Cave of PROMETHEUS.

* * *

IONE   Even whilst we speak
185   New notes arise . . . What is that awful sound?
PANTHEA   'Tis the deep music of the rolling world,
    Kindling within the strings of the waved air
    Æolian modulations.[8]
IONE   Listen too,
    How every pause is filled with under-notes,
190   Clear, silver, icy, keen, awakening tones
    Which pierce the sense and live within the soul
    As the sharp stars pierce Winter's chrystal air
    And gaze upon themselves within the sea.
PANTHEA   But see, where through two openings in the forest
195   Which hanging branches overcanopy,
    And where two runnels of a rivulet
    Between the close moss violet-inwoven
    Have made their path of melody, like sisters
    Who part with sighs that they may meet in smiles,
200   Turning their dear disunion to an isle
    Of lovely grief, a wood of sweet sad thoughts;
    Two visions of strange radiance float upon
    The Ocean-like inchantment of strong sound
    Which flows intenser, keener, deeper yet
205   Under the ground and through the windless air.
IONE   I see a chariot like that thinnest boat
    In which the Mother of the Months is borne
    By ebbing light into her western cave
    When she upsprings from interlunar dreams,[9]

---

6. I.e., a dim point in the extreme of empty space. The sense of lines 198–204 is if regenerate man were to be released from all earthly and biological impediments ("clogs"), he would become what even the stars are not—a pure ideal.

7. The original drama, completed in the spring of 1819, consisted of three acts. Later that year Shelley added a jubilant fourth act. In Revelation 21, the apocalyptic replacement of the old world by "a new heaven and new earth" had been symbolized by the marriage of the Lamb with the New Jerusalem. Shelley's fourth act, somewhat like the conclusion of Blake's Jerusalem, expands this figure into a cosmic epithalamion, representing a union of divided elements that enacts everywhere the reunion of Prometheus and Asia taking place off-stage.

Shelley's model is the Renaissance masque, which combines song and dance with spectacular displays. Panthea and Ione serve as commentators on the action, which is divided into three episodes. In the first episode, omitted here, the purified "Spirits of the human mind" unite in a ritual dance with the Hours of the glad new day. In the second episode (lines 194–318), there appear emblematic representations of the moon and the earth, each bearing an infant whose hour has come round at last. Shelley based this description in part on Ezekiel 1, the vision of the chariot of divine glory, which had traditionally been interpreted as a portent of apocalypse. The third episode (lines 319–502) is the bacchanalian dance of the love-intoxicated Moon around her brother and paramour, the rejuvenescent Earth. By way of coda (line 549 to the end), Demogorgon calls on all beings to hear his proclamation of the moral significance of this great drama of humanity's self-betrayal and self-redemption.

8. Evoking music like that of the Eolian harp.

9. I.e., the chariot is a thin crescent shape, like the new Moon, when it carries within it the outline of the old Moon ("Mother of the Months") to the cave where she is reborn during the "interlunar" period—i.e., when the Moon is entirely invisible.

210 O'er which is curved an orblike canopy
Of gentle darkness, and the hills and woods
Distinctly seen through that dusk aery veil
Regard° like shapes in an enchanter's glass;   *look*
Its wheels are solid clouds, azure and gold,
215 Such as the genii of the thunderstorm
Pile on the floor of the illumined sea
When the Sun rushes under it; they roll
And move and grow as with an inward wind.
Within it sits a winged Infant, white
220 Its countenance, like the whiteness of bright snow,
Its plumes are as feathers of sunny frost,
Its limbs gleam white, through the wind-flowing folds
Of its white robe, woof of ætherial pearl.
Its hair is white,—the brightness of white light
225 Scattered in strings,[1] yet its two eyes are Heavens
Of liquid darkness, which the Deity
Within, seems pouring, as a storm is poured
From jagged clouds, out of their arrowy lashes,
Tempering the cold and radiant air around
230 With fire that is not brightness;[2] in its hand
It sways a quivering moonbeam, from whose point
A guiding power directs the chariot's prow
Over its wheeled clouds, which as they roll
Over the grass and flowers and waves, wake sounds
235 Sweet as a singing rain of silver dew.
PANTHEA   And from the other opening in the wood
Rushes with loud and whirlwind harmony
A sphere, which is as many thousand spheres,
Solid as chrystal, yet through all its mass
240 Flow, as through empty space, music and light:
Ten thousand orbs involving and involved,[3]
Purple and azure, white and green and golden,
Sphere within sphere, and every space between
Peopled with unimaginable shapes
245 Such as ghosts dream dwell in the lampless deep
Yet each intertranspicuous,[4] and they whirl
Over each other with a thousand motions
Upon a thousand sightless° axles spinning   *invisible*
And with the force of self-destroying swiftness,
250 Intensely, slowly, solemnly roll on—

1. The infant resembles "one like unto the Son of man" in Revelation 1.14: "His head and his hairs were white like wool, as white as snow." The description that follows, of the light radiated from the infant's eyes, echoes the description in Ezekiel's vision, 1.27–28, of the "brightness round about" that "was the appearance of the likeness of the glory of the Lord."
2. Shelley knew, from the account by Sir Humphry Davy, Herschel's discovery (1800) that there are what Herschel called "dark rays"—i.e., infrared radiation; Davy suggested that the moon gave off such rays.

3. The transparent sphere is an emblem of earth. The description of its spinning and that of its interior orbs echoes both Ezekiel 1.16—"the appearance of the wheels and their work . . . was as it were a wheel in the middle of a wheel"—and *Paradise Lost* 5.620–24, which describes the "mystical dance" of the angels in heaven, whose movements resemble the revolving spheres of the planets: "mazes intricate, / Eccentric, intervolved, yet regular / Then most, when most irregular they seem."
4. Transparent, so that each can be seen through the others.

Kindling with mingled sounds, and many tones,
Intelligible words and music wild.—
With mighty whirl the multitudinous Orb
Grinds the bright brook into an azure mist

255 Of elemental subtlety, like light,
And the wild odour of the forest flowers,
The music of the living grass and air,
The emerald light of leaf-entangled beams
Round its intense, yet self-conflicting[5] speed,

260 Seem kneaded into one aerial mass
Which drowns the sense. Within the Orb itself,
Pillowed upon its alabaster arms
Like to a child o'erwearied with sweet toil,
On its own folded wings and wavy hair

265 The Spirit of the Earth is laid asleep,
And you can see its little lips are moving
Amid the changing light of their own smiles
Like one who talks of what he loves in dream—

IONE   'Tis only mocking° the Orb's harmony . . .   *imitating*

270 PANTHEA   And from a star upon its forehead, shoot,
Like swords of azure fire, or golden spears
With tyrant-quelling myrtle[6] overtwined,
Embleming Heaven and Earth united now,
Vast beams like spokes of some invisible wheel

275 Which whirl as the Orb whirls, swifter than thought,
Filling the abyss with sunlike lightenings,
And perpendicular now, and now transverse,
Pierce the dark soil, and as they pierce and pass
Make bare the secrets of the Earth's deep heart,[7]

280 Infinite mine of adamant[8] and gold,
Valueless° stones and unimagined gems,   *priceless*
And caverns on chrystalline columns poised
With vegetable silver overspread,
Wells of unfathomed fire, and watersprings

285 Whence the great Sea, even as a child, is fed
Whose vapours clothe Earth's monarch mountain-tops
With kingly, ermine snow; the beams flash on
And make appear the melancholy ruins
Of cancelled cycles;[9] anchors, beaks of ships,

290 Planks turned to marble, quivers, helms° and spears   *helmets*
And gorgon-headed targes,[1] and the wheels
Of scythed chariots,[2] and the emblazonry
Of trophies, standards and armorial beasts[3]
Round which Death laughed, sepulchred emblems

---

5. Because its component spheres are spinning in opposed directions.
6. The myrtle, sacred to Venus, symbolizes love.
7. I.e., the star on the infant's forehead radiates penetrating beams that (like modern X rays) reveal what lies beneath the surface of the earth.
8. Very hard rock.

9. I.e., of civilizations that flourished, then disappeared.
1. Shields embossed with a gorgon's head.
2. Ancient war chariots sometimes had steel blades fastened to the wheels.
3. Animals in heraldic insignia.

295 Of dead Destruction, ruin within ruin!
The wrecks beside of many a city vast,
Whose population which the Earth grew over
Was mortal but not human;[4] see, they lie,
Their monstrous works and uncouth skeletons,
300 Their statues, homes, and fanes;° prodigious shapes   *temples*
Huddled in grey annihilation, split,
Jammed in the hard black deep; and over these
The anatomies° of unknown winged things,   *skeletons*
And fishes which were isles of living scale,
305 And serpents, bony chains, twisted around
The iron crags, or within heaps of dust
To which the tortuous strength of their last pangs
Had crushed the iron crags;—and over these
The jagged alligator and the might
310 Of earth-convulsing behemoth,[5] which once
Were monarch beasts, and on the slimy shores
And weed-overgrown continents of Earth
Increased and multiplied like summer worms
On an abandoned corpse, till the blue globe
315 Wrapt Deluge round it like a cloak, and they
Yelled, gaspt and were abolished; or some God
Whose throne was in a Comet, past, and cried—
"Be not!"—and like my words they were no more.[6]

THE EARTH

The joy, the triumph, the delight, the madness,
320 The boundless, overflowing, bursting gladness,
The vaporous exultation, not to be confined![7]
     Ha! ha! the animation of delight
     Which wraps me, like an atmosphere of light,
And bears me as a cloud is borne by its own wind!

THE MOON

325   Brother mine, calm wanderer,
     Happy globe of land and air,
Some Spirit[8] is darted like a beam from thee,
     Which penetrates my frozen frame
     And passes with the warmth of flame—
330 With love and odour and deep melody
     Through me, through me!—

---

4. That is, a prehuman race of beings that once overspread the earth.
5. The huge land animal described in Job 40.15–24.
6. According to the theory of "Catastrophism" proposed by G. F. Cuvier, *Researches on Fossil Bones* (1812), successive geologic layers of fossils are evidence of a sequence of catastrophes—each of which wiped out the forms of life that then existed. Shelley proposes two hypotheses (lines 314–18): either such floods originated from some cataclysm on earth or they were prodigious tides caused by the gravitational pull of a passing comet.
In writing this passage, Shelley recalled Keats's *Endymion* 3.123–36, which described the remains on the ocean floor of extinct cultures and animal species.
7. Literally, the earth's gases are bursting out through its volcanoes.
8. Physically, the gravitational force exerted by the earth on the satellite moon.

THE EARTH

Ha! ha! the caverns of my hollow mountains,
My cloven fire-crags, sound-exulting fountains
Laugh with a vast and inextinguishable laughter.
335   The Oceans and the Desarts and the Abysses
    And the deep air's unmeasured wildernesses
Answer from all their clouds and billows, echoing after.

    They cry aloud as I do—"Sceptred Curse,°   *Jupiter*
    Who all our green and azure Universe
340 Threatenedst to muffle round with black destruction, sending
    A solid cloud to rain hot thunderstones,
    And splinter and knead down my children's bones,
All I bring forth, to one void mass battering and blending,

    "Until each craglike tower and storied column,
345   Palace and Obelisk and Temple solemn,
My imperial mountains crowned with cloud and snow and fire,
    My sea-like forests, every blade and blossom
    Which finds a grave or cradle in my bosom,
Were stamped by thy strong hate into a lifeless mire,

350   "How art thou sunk, withdrawn, cover'd—drunk up
    By thirsty nothing, as the brackish° cup   *slightly salty*
Drained by a Desart-troop—a little drop for all;
    And from beneath, around, within, above,
    Filling thy void annihilation, Love
355 Bursts in like light on caves cloven by the thunderball."

THE MOON

    The snow upon my lifeless mountains
    Is loosened into living fountains,
My solid Oceans flow and sing and shine
    A spirit from my heart bursts forth,
    It clothes with unexpected birth
360 My cold bare bosom: Oh! it must be thine
    On mine, on mine!

    Gazing on thee I feel, I know,
    Green stalks burst forth, and bright flowers grow
And living shapes upon my bosom move:
365   Music is in the sea and air,
    Winged clouds soar here and there,
Dark with the rain new buds are dreaming of:
    'Tis Love, all Love!

THE EARTH

370   It interpenetrates my granite mass,
    Through tangled roots and trodden clay doth pass
Into the utmost leaves and delicatest flowers;
    Upon the winds, among the clouds 'tis spread,
    It wakes a life in the forgotten dead,
375 They breathe a spirit up from their obscurest bowers

And like a storm, bursting its cloudy prison
    With thunder and with whirlwind, has arisen
Out of the lampless caves of unimagined being,
    With earthquake shock and swiftness making shiver
380   Thought's stagnant chaos, unremoved forever,
Till Hate and Fear and Pain, light-vanquished shadows, fleeing,

    Leave Man, who was a many-sided mirror
    Which could distort to many a shape of error
This true fair world of things—a Sea reflecting Love;
385   Which over all his kind, as the Sun's Heaven
    Gliding o'er Ocean, smooth, serene and even,
Darting from starry depths radiance and light, doth move,

    Leave Man, even as a leprous child is left
    Who follows a sick beast to some warm cleft
390   Of rocks, through which the might of healing springs is poured:
    Then when it wanders home with rosy smile
    Unconscious, and its mother fears awhile
It is a Spirit—then weeps on her child restored.[9]

    Man, oh, not men![1] a chain of linked thought,
395   Of love and might to be divided not,
Compelling the elements with adamantine stress—
    As the Sun rules,[2] even with a tyrant's gaze,
    The unquiet Republic of the maze
Of Planets, struggling fierce towards Heaven's free wilderness.

400   Man, one harmonious Soul of many a soul
    Whose nature is its own divine controul
Where all things flow to all, as rivers to the sea;
    Familiar acts are beautiful through love;
    Labour and Pain and Grief in life's green grove
405   Sport like tame beasts—none knew how gentle they could be!

    His Will, with all mean passions, bad delights,
    And selfish cares, its trembling satellites,
A spirit ill to guide, but mighty to obey,
    Is as a tempest-winged ship, whose helm
410   Love rules, through waves which dare not overwhelm,
Forcing Life's wildest shores to own its sovereign sway.

    All things confess his strength.—Through the cold mass
    Of marble and of colour his dreams pass;
Bright threads, whence mothers weave the robes their children wear;
415   Language is a perpetual Orphic song,[3]
    Which rules with Dædal harmony a throng
Of thoughts and forms, which else senseless and shapeless were.

9. A reminiscence of the legend of King Bladud of Britain, who, a banished leper, was following a lost swine and stumbled on a hot spring (now in the town of Bath), which cured him.
1. Human society, once splintered by hate, is now united by love into a single macrocosmic "Man."
2. By gravitational force.
3. Like the music of Orpheus, which attracted and controlled beasts, rocks, and trees.

The Lightning is his slave;[4] Heaven's utmost deep
Gives up her stars, and like a flock of sheep
420 They pass before his eye, are numbered, and roll on!
The Tempest is his steed,—he strides the air;
And the abyss shouts from her depth laid bare,
"Heaven, hast thou secrets? Man unveils me; I have none."

THE MOON
The shadow of white Death has past
425 From my path in Heaven at last,
A clinging shroud of solid frost and sleep—
And through my newly-woven bowers
Wander happy paramours
Less mighty, but as mild as those who keep
430 Thy vales more deep.

THE EARTH
As the dissolving warmth of Dawn may fold
A half-unfrozen dewglobe, green and gold
And chrystalline, till it becomes a winged mist
And wanders up the vault of the blue Day,
435 Outlives the noon, and on the Sun's last ray
Hangs o'er the Sea—a fleece of fire and amethyst—

THE MOON
Thou art folded, thou art lying
In the light which is undying
Of thine own joy and Heaven's smile divine;
440 All suns and constellations shower
On thee a light, a life, a power
Which doth array thy sphere—thou pourest thine
On mine, on mine!

THE EARTH
I spin beneath my pyramid of night[5]
445 Which points into the Heavens, dreaming delight,
Murmuring victorious joy in my enchanted sleep;
As a youth lulled in love-dreams, faintly sighing,
Under the shadow of his beauty lying
Which round his rest a watch of light and warmth doth keep.

THE MOON
450 As in the soft and sweet eclipse
When soul meets soul on lovers' lips,
High hearts are calm and brightest eyes are dull;
So when thy shadow falls on me[6]
Then am I mute and still,—by thee

4. The Earth describes regenerate man's scientific
and technological triumphs.
5. The conical shadow cast by the earth as it intercepts the sun's light.
6. In the eclipse of the moon, when it enters the
earth's shadow.

455   Covered; of thy love, Orb most beautiful,
             Full, oh, too full!—

        Thou art speeding round the Sun,
        Brightest World of many a one,
        Green and azure sphere, which shinest
460   With a light which is divinest
        Among all the lamps of Heaven
        To whom life and light is given;
        I, thy chrystal paramour,
        Borne beside thee by a power
465   Like the polar Paradise,
        Magnet-like, of lovers' eyes;[7]
        I, a most enamoured maiden
        Whose weak brain is overladen
        With the pleasure of her love—
470   Maniac-like around thee move,
        Gazing, an insatiate bride,
        On thy form from every side
        Like a Mænad round the cup
        Which Agave[8] lifted up
475   In the weird Cadmæan forest.—
        Brother, wheresoe'er thou soarest
        I must hurry, whirl and follow
        Through the Heavens wide and hollow,
        Sheltered by the warm embrace
480   Of thy soul, from hungry space,
        Drinking, from thy sense and sight,
        Beauty, majesty, and might,
        As a lover or chameleon
        Grows like what it looks upon,
485   As a violet's gentle eye
        Gazes on the azure sky
      Until its hue grows like what it beholds,
        As a grey and watery mist
        Glows like solid amethyst
490   Athwart the western mountains it enfolds,
        When the sunset sleeps
          Upon its snow—

               THE EARTH
        And the weak day weeps[9]
          That it should be so.
495   O gentle Moon, the voice of thy delight
        Falls on me like thy clear and tender light
        Soothing the seaman, borne the summer night
          Through isles forever calm;
        O gentle Moon, thy chrystal accents pierce

---

7. As it circles the earth, the moon spins at a rate that keeps the same side constantly toward it.
8. Daughter of King Cadmus; in a blind frenzy she tore her own son Pentheus to bits when he was caught spying on the Dionysiac rites. "Maenad": a female participant in the ecstatic worship of Dionysus (Bacchus).
9. I.e., with the dew at nightfall.

500   The caverns of my Pride's deep Universe,
       Charming the tyger Joy, whose tramplings fierce
       Made wounds, which need thy balm.

                        *   *   *

                      DEMOGORGON
       Man, who wert once a despot and a slave,—
550   A dupe and a deceiver,—a Decay,
       A Traveller from the cradle to the grave
       Through the dim night of this immortal Day:

                         ALL
       Speak—thy strong words may never pass away.

                      DEMOGORGON
       This is the Day which down the void Abysm
555   At the Earth-born's spell[1] yawns for Heaven's Despotism,
          And Conquest is dragged Captive through the Deep;[2]
       Love from its awful throne of patient power
       In the wise heart, from the last giddy hour
          Of dread endurance, from the slippery, steep,
560   And narrow verge of crag-like Agony, springs
       And folds over the world its healing wings.

       Gentleness, Virtue, Wisdom and Endurance,—
       These are the seals of that most firm assurance
          Which bars the pit over Destruction's strength;
565   And if, with infirm hand, Eternity,
       Mother of many acts and hours, should free
          The serpent that would clasp her with his length[3]—
       These are the spells by which to reassume
       An empire o'er the disentangled Doom.[4]

570   To suffer woes which Hope thinks infinite;
       To forgive wrongs darker than Death or Night;
          To defy Power which seems Omnipotent;
       To love, and bear; to hope, till Hope creates
       From its own wreck the thing it contemplates;
575   Neither to change nor falter nor repent:
       This, like thy glory, Titan! is to be
       Good, great and joyous, beautiful and free;
       This is alone Life, Joy, Empire and Victory.

1818–19   1820

---

1. Prometheus's spell—i.e., his magically effective words of pity, in place of vengefulness.
2. Ephesians 4.8: "When [Christ] ascended up on high, he led captivity captive."
3. A final reminder that the serpent incessantly struggles to break loose and start the cycle of humanity's fall all over again. Felicity must continue to be earned.
4. Shelley's four cardinal virtues (line 562), which seal the serpent in the pit, also constitute the magic formulas ("spells") by which to remaster him, should he again break loose. These virtues are expanded on in the concluding lines (570–75).

The Cloud

I bring fresh showers for the thirsting flowers,
    From the seas and streams;
I bear light shade for the leaves when laid
    In their noon-day dreams.
5 From my wings are shaken the dews that waken
    The sweet buds every one,
When rocked to rest on their mother's° breast,   *earth's*
    As she dances about the Sun.
I wield the flail of the lashing hail,
10   And whiten the green plains under,
And then again I dissolve it in rain,
    And laugh as I pass in thunder.

I sift the snow on the mountains below,
    And their great pines groan aghast;
15 And all the night 'tis my pillow white,
    While I sleep in the arms of the blast.
Sublime on the towers of my skiey bowers,
    Lightning my pilot sits;
In a cavern under is fettered the thunder,
20   It struggles and howls at fits;°   *fitfully*
Over Earth and Ocean, with gentle motion,
    This pilot is guiding me,
Lured by the love of the genii that move
    In the depths of the purple sea;[1]
25 Over the rills, and the crags, and the hills,
    Over the lakes and the plains,
Wherever he dream, under mountain or stream,
    The Spirit he loves remains;
And I all the while bask in Heaven's blue smile,[2]
30   Whilst he is dissolving in rains.

The sanguine Sunrise, with his meteor eyes,
    And his burning plumes outspread,[3]
Leaps on the back of my sailing rack,[4]
    When the morning star shines dead;
35 As on the jag of a mountain crag,
    Which an earthquake rocks and swings,
An eagle alit one moment may sit
    In the light of its golden wings.
And when Sunset may breathe, from the lit Sea beneath,
40   Its ardours of rest and of love,
And the crimson pall° of eve may fall   *rich coverlet*
    From the depth of Heaven above,
With wings folded I rest, on mine aëry nest,
    As still as a brooding dove.

1. I.e., atmospheric electricity, guiding the cloud (line 18), discharges as lightning when "lured" by the attraction of an opposite charge.
2. The upper part of the cloud remains exposed to the sun.
3. The sun's corona. "Meteor eyes": as bright as a burning meteor.
4. High, broken clouds, driven by the wind.

45 That orbed maiden with white fire laden
    Whom mortals call the Moon,
Glides glimmering o'er my fleece-like floor,
    By the midnight breezes strewn;
And wherever the beat of her unseen feet,
50   Which only the angels hear,
May have broken the woof,° of my tent's thin roof,   *texture*
    The stars peep behind her, and peer;
And I laugh to see them whirl and flee,
    Like a swarm of golden bees,
55 When I widen the rent in my wind-built tent,
    Till the calm rivers, lakes, and seas,
Like strips of the sky fallen through me on high,
    Are each paved with the moon and these.⁵

I bind the Sun's throne with a burning zone°   *belt, sash*
60   And the Moon's with a girdle of pearl;
The volcanos are dim and the stars reel and swim
    When the whirlwinds my banner unfurl.
From cape to cape, with a bridge-like shape,
    Over a torrent sea,
65 Sunbeam-proof, I hang like a roof—
    The mountains its columns be!
The triumphal arch, through which I march
    With hurricane, fire, and snow,
When the Powers of the Air, are chained to my chair,
70   Is the million-coloured Bow;
The sphere-fire° above its soft colours wove   *sunlight*
    While the moist Earth was laughing below.

I am the daughter of Earth and Water,
    And the nursling of the Sky;
75 I pass through the pores, of the ocean and shores;
    I change, but I cannot die—
For after the rain, when with never a stain
    The pavilion of Heaven is bare,
And the winds and sunbeams, with their convex gleams,
80   Build up the blue dome of Air⁶—
I silently laugh at my own cenotaph,⁷
    And out of the caverns of rain,
Like a child from the womb, like a ghost from the tomb,
    I arise, and unbuild it again.—

1820   1820

---

5. The stars reflected in the water.
6. The blue color of the sky. The phenomenon, as Shelley indicates, results from the way "sunbeams" are filtered by the earth's atmosphere.

7. The memorial monument of the dead cloud is the cloudless blue dome of the sky. (The point is that a cenotaph is a monument that does not contain a corpse.)

To a Sky-Lark[1]

Hail to thee, blithe Spirit!
   Bird thou never wert—
That from Heaven, or near it,
   Pourest thy full heart
5   In profuse strains of unpremeditated art.

Higher still and higher
   From the earth thou springest
Like a cloud of fire;
   The blue deep thou wingest,
10   And singing still dost soar, and soaring ever singest.

In the golden lightning
   Of the sunken Sun—
O'er which clouds are brightning,
   Thou dost float and run;
15   Like an unbodied joy whose race is just begun.

The pale purple even
   Melts around thy flight,
Like a star of Heaven
   In the broad day-light
20   Thou art unseen,—but yet I hear thy shrill delight,

Keen as are the arrows
   Of that silver sphere,[2]
Whose intense lamp narrows
   In the white dawn clear
25   Until we hardly see—we feel that it is there.

All the earth and air
   With thy voice is loud,
As when Night is bare
   From one lonely cloud
30   The moon rains out her beams—and Heaven is overflowed.

What thou art we know not;
   What is most like thee?
From rainbow clouds there flow not
   Drops so bright to see
35   As from thy presence showers a rain of melody.

Like a Poet hidden
   In the light of thought,
Singing hymns unbidden,

1. The European skylark is a small bird that sings only in flight, often when it is too high to be visible. This bird, freed from the bonds of earth and soaring beyond the reach of all the physical senses except hearing, is made the emblem of a nonmaterial spirit of pure joy, beyond the possibility of human experience (see lines 15, 31).
2. The morning star.

Till the world is wrought
40   To sympathy with hopes and fears it heeded not:

Like a high-born maiden
    In a palace-tower,
Soothing her love-laden
    Soul in secret hour,
45   With music sweet as love—which overflows her bower:

Like a glow-worm golden
    In a dell of dew,
Scattering unbeholden
    Its aerial hue
50   Among the flowers and grass which screen it from the view:

Like a rose embowered
    In its own green leaves—
By warm winds deflowered—
    Till the scent it gives
55   Makes faint with too much sweet those heavy-winged thieves:[3]

Sound of vernal showers
    On the twinkling grass,
Rain-awakened flowers,
    All that ever was
60   Joyous, and clear and fresh, thy music doth surpass.

Teach us, Sprite° or Bird,   spirit
    What sweet thoughts are thine;
I have never heard
    Praise of love or wine
65   That panted forth a flood of rapture so divine:

Chorus Hymeneal[4]
    Or triumphal chaunt
Matched with thine would be all
    But an empty vaunt,
70   A thing wherein we feel there is some hidden want.

What objects are the fountains
    Of thy happy strain?
What fields or waves or mountains?
    What shapes of sky or plain?
75   What love of thine own kind? what ignorance of pain?

With thy clear keen joyance
    Languor cannot be—
Shadow of annoyance
    Never came near thee;
80   Thou lovest—but ne'er knew love's sad satiety.

3. The "warm winds," line 53.   4. Marital (from Hymen, Greek god of marriage).

Waking or asleep,
　　Thou of death must deem
Things more true and deep
　　Than we mortals dream,
85　Or how could thy notes flow in such a chrystal stream?

We look before and after,
　　And pine for what is not—
Our sincerest laughter
　　With some pain is fraught—
90　Our sweetest songs are those that tell of saddest thought.

Yet if we could scorn
　　Hate and pride and fear;
If we were things born
　　Not to shed a tear,
95　I know not how thy joy we ever should come near.

Better than all measures
　　Of delightful sound—
Better than all treasures
　　That in books are found—
100　Thy skill to poet were, thou Scorner of the ground!

Teach me half the gladness
　　That thy brain must know,
Such harmonious madness
　　From my lips would flow
105　The world should listen then—as I am listening now.

1820   1820

To Night[1]

Swiftly walk o'er the western wave,
　　Spirit of Night!
Out of the misty eastern cave
Where, all the long and lone daylight
　5　Thou wovest dreams of joy and fear,
Which make thee terrible and dear,
　　Swift be thy flight!

Wrap thy form in a mantle grey,
　　Star-inwrought!
　10　Blind with thine hair the eyes of day,
Kiss her until she be wearied out—
Then wander o'er City and sea and land,
Touching all with thine opiate wand—
　　Come, long-sought!

---

1. Night and darkness, as opposed to daylight, are often for Shelley symbols of the primordial powers and revelations of the poetic imagination.

15   When I arose and saw the dawn
      I sighed for thee;
  When Light rode high, and the dew was gone,
  And noon lay heavy on flower and tree,
  And the weary Day[2] turned to his rest,
20   Lingering like an unloved guest,
      I sighed for thee.

  Thy brother Death came, and cried,
      Wouldst thou me?
  Thy sweet child Sleep, the filmy-eyed,
25   Murmured like a noontide bee,
  Shall I nestle near thy side?
  Wouldst thou me? and I replied,
      No, not thee!

  Death will come when thou art dead,
30   Soon, too soon—
  Sleep will come when thou art fled;
  Of neither would I ask the boon
  I ask of thee, beloved Night—
  Swift be thine approaching flight,
35   Come soon, soon!

1820   1824

To ——— [Music, when soft voices die]

  Music, when soft voices die,
  Vibrates in the memory.—
  Odours, when sweet violets sicken,
  Live within the sense they quicken.—

5   Rose leaves, when the rose is dead,
  Are heaped for the beloved's bed[1]—
  And so thy thoughts,[2] when thou art gone,
  Love itself shall slumber on.

1821   1824

The flower that smiles today[1]

  The flower that smiles today
      Tomorrow dies;
  All that we wish to stay
      Tempts and then flies;
5   What is this world's delight?
  Lightning, that mocks the night,
      Brief even as bright.—

---

2. Here the "Day" is the male sun, not the female "day" with whom the Spirit of Night dallies in the preceding stanza.
1. The bed of the dead rose.

2. I.e., my thoughts of thee.
1. First printed, with the title *Mutability*, in Mary Shelley's edition of *Posthumous Poems of Percy Bysshe Shelley* (1824).

Virtue, how frail it is!—
        Friendship, how rare!—
10   Love, how it sells poor bliss
        For proud despair!
    But these though soon they fall,
    Survive their joy, and all
        Which ours we call.—

15   Whilst skies are blue and bright,
        Whilst flowers are gay,
    Whilst eyes that change ere night
        Make glad the day;
    Whilst yet the calm hours creep,
20   Dream thou—and from thy sleep
        Then wake to weep.

1821

1824

O World, O Life, O Time[1]

    O World, O Life, O Time,
    On whose last steps I climb,
Trembling at that where I had stood before,
    When will return the glory of your prime?
5   No more, O never more!

    Out of the day and night
    A joy has taken flight—
Fresh spring and summer [   ] and winter hoar
Move my faint heart with grief, but with delight
10   No more, O never more!

1824

Choruses from *Hellas*[1]

Worlds on worlds[2]

Worlds on worlds are rolling ever
From creation to decay,

1. For the author's revisions while composing this poem, see "Poems in Process," in the appendices to this volume.

1. *Hellas,* a closet drama written in the autumn of 1821, was inspired by the Greek war for independence against the Turks. In his preface, Shelley declared that he viewed this revolution as auguring the final overthrow of all tyranny. The choruses below are sung by captive Greek women. The first chorus describes the entrance of Christ into the revolving cycle of history; the second chorus concludes the drama.

2. The popular notions of Christianity are represented in this chorus as true in their relation to the worship they superseded . . . without considering their merits in a relation more universal. . . . The concluding verses indicate a progressive state of more or less exalted existence. . . . Let it not be supposed that I mean to dogmatise upon a subject [i.e., the problem of evil, and the possibility of its future elimination] upon which all men are equally ignorant. . . . That there is a true solution to the riddle, and that in our present state that solution is unattainable by us, are propositions that may be regarded as equally certain: meanwhile, as it is the province of the poet to attach himself to those ideas which exalt and ennoble humanity, let him be permitted to have conjectured the condition of that futurity towards which we are all impelled by an inextinguishable thirst for immortality [Shelley's note].

Like the bubbles on a river
    Sparkling, bursting, borne away.
5   But *they*³ are still immortal
    Who through Birth's orient° portal   *eastern*
And Death's dark chasm hurrying to and fro,
    Clothe their unceasing flight
    In the brief dust and light
10 Gathered around their chariots as they go;
    New shapes they still may weave,
    New Gods, new Laws receive,
Bright or dim are they as the robes they last
    On Death's bare ribs had cast.

15   A Power from the unknown God,
    A Promethean Conqueror,⁴ came;
    Like a triumphal path he trod
        The thorns of death and shame.
    A mortal shape to him
20   Was like the vapour dim
Which the orient planet animates with light;
    Hell, Sin, and Slavery came
    Like bloodhounds mild and tame,
Nor preyed, until their Lord had taken flight;
25   The moon of Mahomet⁵
    Arose, and it shall set,
While blazoned as on Heaven's immortal noon
    The cross leads generations on.⁶

    Swift as the radiant shapes of sleep
30   From one whose dreams are Paradise
Fly, when the fond wretch wakes to weep,
    And Day peers forth with her blank eyes;
    So fleet, so faint, so fair,
    The Powers of earth and air
35 Fled from the folding star⁷ of Bethlehem:
    Apollo, Pan, and Love,
    And even Olympian Jove
Grew weak, for killing Truth had glared on them;
    Our hills and seas and streams,
40   Dispeopled of their dreams,
Their waters turned to blood, their dew to tears,
    Wailed for the golden years.

---

3. Beings which inhabit the planets and . . . clothe
themselves in matter [Shelley's note].
4. Christ, whom Shelley compares with Prometheus, who brought fire and the arts of civilization
to humankind.
5. The crescent, emblem of Islam, which was
founded six centuries after the birth of Christ.

6. The Roman emperor Constantine was converted to Christianity when he saw a bright cross
imposed on the sun at noon.
7. The star of evening, the time when sheep are
driven into the sheepfold. Shelley goes on to
describe the pagan gods of earth and Olympus fleeing before the star of Bethlehem.

The world's great age[8]

The world's great age begins anew,
 The golden years[9] return,
The earth doth like a snake renew
 Her winter weeds[1] outworn;
5 Heaven smiles, and faiths and empires gleam
Like wrecks of a dissolving dream.

A brighter Hellas rears its mountains
 From waves serener far,
A new Peneus[2] rolls his fountains
10 Against the morning-star,
Where fairer Tempe bloom, there sleep
Young Cyclads[3] on a sunnier deep.

A loftier Argo[4] cleaves the main,
 Fraught with a later prize;
15 Another Orpheus[5] sings again,
 And loves, and weeps, and dies;
A new Ulysses leaves once more
Calypso[6] for his native shore.

O, write no more the tale of Troy,
20 If earth Death's scroll must be!
Nor mix with Laian[7] rage the joy
 Which dawns upon the free;
Although a subtler Sphinx renew
Riddles of death Thebes never knew.

25 Another Athens shall arise,
 And to remoter time
Bequeath, like sunset to the skies,
 The splendour of its prime,
And leave, if nought so bright may live,
30 All earth can take or Heaven can give.

Saturn and Love their long repose
 Shall burst, more bright and good

---

8. Prophecies of wars, and rumours of wars, etc., may safely be made by poet or prophet in any age, but to anticipate however darkly a period of regeneration and happiness is a more hazardous exercise of the faculty which bards possess or fain. It will remind the reader . . . of Isaiah and Virgil, whose ardent spirits . . . saw the possible and perhaps approaching state of society in which the "lion shall lie down with the lamb," and "*omnis feret omnia tellus.*" Let these great names be my authority and excuse [Shelley's note]. The quotations are from Isaiah's millennial prophecy (e.g., chaps. 25, 45), and Virgil's prediction, in *Eclogue* 4, of a return of the golden age, when "all the earth will produce all things."
9. In Greek myth, the first period of history, when Saturn reigned.

1. Clothes (especially mourning garments) as well as dead vegetation.
2. The river that flows through the beautiful vale of Tempe (line 11).
3. The Cyclades, islands in the Aegean Sea.
4. On which Jason sailed in his quest for the Golden Fleece.
5. The legendary player on the lyre who was torn to pieces by the frenzied Thracian women while he was mourning the death of his wife, Eurydice.
6. The nymph deserted by Ulysses on his voyage back from the Trojan War to his native Ithaca.
7. King Laius of Thebes was killed in a quarrel by his son Oedipus, who did not recognize his father. Shortly thereafter, Oedipus delivered Thebes from the ravages of the Sphinx by answering its riddle (lines 23–24).

> Than all who fell, than One who rose,
>   Than many unsubdued;[8]
> 35 Not gold, not blood their altar dowers
> But votive tears and symbol flowers.
>
> O cease! must hate and death return?
>   Cease! must men kill and die?
> Cease! drain not to its dregs the urn
> 40   Of bitter prophecy.
> The world is weary of the past,
> O might it die or rest at last!

1821   1822

Adonais   John Keats died in Rome on February 23, 1821, and was buried there in the Protestant Cemetery. Shelley had met Keats, had invited him to be his guest at Pisa, and had gradually come to to realize that he was "among the writers of the highest genius who have adorned our age" (Preface to *Adonais*). The name "Adonais" is derived from Adonis, the handsome youth who had been loved by the goddess Venus and slain by a wild boar; the function of the beast in this poem is attributed to the anonymous author of a vituperative review of Keats's *Endymion* in the *Quarterly Review,* April 1818 (now known to be John Wilson Croker), whom Shelley mistakenly believed to be responsible for Keats's illness and death.

   Shelley in a letter described *Adonais*, which he wrote in April–June 1821 and had printed in Pisa in July, as a "highly wrought piece of art." Its artistry consists in part in the care with which it follows the conventions of the pastoral elegy, established more than two thousand years earlier by the Greek Sicilian poets Theocritus, Bion, and Moschus—Shelley had himself translated into English Bion's *Lament for Adonis* and Moschus's *Lament for Bion.* We recognize the centuries-old poetic ritual in many verbal echoes and in such devices as the mournful and accusing invocation to a muse (stanzas 2–4), the sympathetic participation of nature in the grieving (stanzas 14–17), the procession of appropriate mourners (stanzas 30–35), the denunciation of unworthy practitioners of the pastoral or literary art (stanzas 17, 27–29, 36–37), and above all, in the turn from despair at the finality of human death (lines 1, 64, 190: "*He* will awake no more, oh, never more!") to consolation in the sudden and contradictory discovery that the grave is a gate to a higher existence (line 343: "Peace, peace! he is not dead, he doth not sleep").

   The first English publication of *Adonais,* in 1829 in an edition sponsored by the so-called Cambridge Apostles (R. M. Milnes, Alfred Tennyson, and A. H. Hallam) marked the beginning of Keats's posthumous emergence from obscurity as a poet.

Adonais

An Elegy on the Death of John Keats, Author of Endymion, Hyperion, etc.

> [Thou wert the morning star among the living,
>   Ere thy fair light had fled—

---

8. Saturn and Love were among the deities of a real or imaginary state of innocence and happiness. "All" those "who fell" [are] the Gods of Greece, Asia, and Egypt; the "One who rose" [is] Jesus Christ . . . and the "many unsubdued" [are] the monstrous objects of the idolatry of China, India, the Antarctic islands, and the native tribes of America [Shelley's note].

Now, having died, thou art as Hesperus, giving
New splendour to the dead.][1]

1

I weep for Adonais—he is dead!
O, weep for Adonais! though our tears
Thaw not the frost which binds so dear a head!
And thou, sad Hour,[2] selected from all years
5   To mourn our loss, rouse thy obscure compeers,
And teach them thine own sorrow, say: with me
Died Adonais; till the Future dares
Forget the Past, his fate and fame shall be
An echo and a light unto eternity!

2

10   Where wert thou mighty Mother,[3] when he lay,
When thy Son lay, pierced by the shaft which flies
In darkness?[4] where was lorn° Urania   *abandoned*
When Adonais died? With veiled eyes,
'Mid listening Echoes, in her Paradise
15   She sate, while one,[5] with soft enamoured breath,
Rekindled all the fading melodies,
With which, like flowers that mock the corse° beneath,   *corpse*
He had adorned and hid the coming bulk of death.

3

O, weep for Adonais—he is dead!
20   Wake, melancholy Mother, wake and weep!
Yet wherefore? Quench within their burning bed
Thy fiery tears, and let thy loud heart keep
Like his, a mute and uncomplaining sleep;
For he is gone, where all things wise and fair
25   Descend;—oh, dream not that the amorous Deep°   *abyss*
Will yet restore him to the vital air;
Death feeds on his mute voice, and laughs at our despair.

4

Most musical of mourners, weep again!
Lament anew, Urania!—He[6] died,
30   Who was the Sire of an immortal strain,
Blind, old, and lonely, when his country's pride,
The priest, the slave, and the liberticide,
Trampled and mocked with many a loathed rite

---

1. Shelley prefixed to *Adonais* a Greek epigram, attributed to Plato; this is Shelley's own translation of the Greek. The planet Venus appears both as the morning star, Lucifer, and as the evening star, Hesperus or Vesper. Shelley makes of this phenomenon a key symbol for Adonais's triumph over death, in stanzas 44–46.
2. Shelley follows the classical mode of personifying the hours, which mark the passage of time and turn of the seasons.
3. Urania. She had originally been the Muse of astronomy, but the name was also an epithet for

Venus. Shelley converts Venus Urania, who in Greek myth had been the lover of Adonis, into the mother of Adonais.
4. Alludes to the anonymity of the review of *Endymion*.
5. I.e., the echo of Keats's voice in his poems.
6. Milton, regarded as precursor of the great poetic tradition in which Keats wrote. He had adopted Urania as the muse of *Paradise Lost*. Lines 31–35 describe Milton's life during the restoration of the Stuart monarchy.

Of lust and blood; he went, unterrified,
35 Into the gulph of death; but his clear Sprite°   *spirit*
Yet reigns o'er earth; the third among the sons of light.[7]

5

Most musical of mourners, weep anew!
Not all to that bright station dared to climb;
And happier they their happiness who knew,
40 Whose tapers yet burn through that night of time
In which suns perished; others more sublime,
Struck by the envious wrath of man or God,
Have sunk, extinct in their refulgent prime;
And some yet live, treading the thorny road,
45 Which leads, through toil and hate, to Fame's serene abode.

6

But now, thy youngest, dearest one, has perished—
The nursling of thy widowhood, who grew,
Like a pale flower by some sad maiden cherished,
And fed with true love tears, instead of dew;[8]
50 Most musical of mourners, weep anew!
Thy extreme[9] hope, the loveliest and the last,
The bloom, whose petals nipt before they blew°   *bloomed*
Died on the promise of the fruit, is waste;
The broken lily lies—the storm is overpast.

7

55 To that high Capital,° where kingly Death   *Rome*
Keeps his pale court in beauty and decay,
He came; and bought, with price of purest breath,
A grave among the eternal.—Come away!
Haste, while the vault of blue Italian day
60 Is yet his fitting charnel-roof! while still
He lies, as if in dewy sleep he lay;
Awake him not! surely he takes his fill
Of deep and liquid rest, forgetful of all ill.

8

He will awake no more, oh, never more!—
65 Within the twilight chamber spreads apace,
The shadow of white Death, and at the door
Invisible Corruption waits to trace
His extreme way to her dim dwelling-place;
The eternal Hunger sits, but pity and awe
70 Soothe her pale rage, nor dares she to deface
So fair a prey, till darkness, and the law
Of change, shall 'oer his sleep the mortal curtain draw.

7. The three are Milton and his great predecessors
in epic poetry, Homer and Dante. The stanza following describes the lot of other poets, up to Shelley's own time.
8. An allusion to an incident in Keats's *Isabella*.
9. Last, as well as highest.

9

O, weep for Adonais!—The quick° Dreams,   *living*
The passion-winged Ministers of thought,
75   Who were his flocks,[1] whom near the living streams
Of his young spirit he fed, and whom he taught
The love which was its music, wander not,—
Wander no more, from kindling brain to brain,
But droop there, whence they sprung; and mourn their lot
80   Round the cold heart, where, after their sweet pain,
They ne'er will gather strength, or find a home again.

10

And one[2] with trembling hands clasps his cold head,
And fans him with her moonlight wings, and cries;
"Our love, our hope, our sorrow, is not dead;
85   See, on the silken fringe of his faint eyes,
Like dew upon a sleeping flower, there lies
A tear some Dream has loosened from his brain."
Lost Angel of a ruined Paradise!
She knew not 'twas her own; as with no stain
90   She faded, like a cloud which had outwept its rain.

11

One from a lucid° urn of starry dew   *luminous*
Washed his light limbs as if embalming them;
Another clipt her profuse locks, and threw
The wreath upon him, like an anadem,°   *rich garland*
95   Which frozen tears instead of pearls begem;
Another in her wilful grief would break
Her bow and winged reeds, as if to stem
A greater loss with one which was more weak;
And dull the barbed fire against his frozen cheek.

12

100   Another Splendour on his mouth alit,
That mouth, whence it was wont to draw the breath
Which gave it strength to pierce the guarded wit,[3]
And pass into the panting heart beneath
With lightning and with music: the damp death
105   Quenched its caress upon his icy lips;
And, as a dying meteor stains a wreath
Of moonlight vapour, which the cold night clips,°   *embraces*
It flushed through his pale limbs, and past to its eclipse.

13

And others came . . . Desires and Adorations,
110   Winged Persuasions and veiled Destinies,
Splendours, and Glooms, and glimmering Incarnations

1. The products of Keats's imagination, figuratively represented (according to pastoral convention) as his sheep.

2. One of the Dreams (line 73).
3. The cautious intellect (of the listener).

Of hopes and fears, and twilight Phantasies;
And Sorrow, with her family of Sighs,
And Pleasure, blind with tears, led by the gleam
115 Of her own dying smile instead of eyes,
Came in slow pomp;—the moving pomp might seem
Like pageantry of mist on an autumnal stream.

14

All he had loved, and moulded into thought,
From shape, and hue, and odour, and sweet sound,
120 Lamented Adonais. Morning sought
Her eastern watchtower, and her hair unbound,
Wet with the tears which should adorn the ground,
Dimmed the aerial eyes that kindle day;
Afar the melancholy thunder moaned,
125 Pale Ocean in unquiet slumber lay,
And the wild winds flew round, sobbing in their dismay.

15

Lost Echo sits amid the voiceless mountains,
And feeds her grief with his remembered lay,
And will no more reply to winds or fountains,
130 Or amorous birds perched on the young green spray,
Or herdsman's horn, or bell at closing day;
Since she can mimic not his lips, more dear
Than those for whose disdain she pined away
Into a shadow of all sounds:⁴—a drear
135 Murmur, between their songs, is all the woodmen hear.

16

Grief made the young Spring wild, and she threw down
Her kindling buds, as if she Autumn were,
Or they dead leaves; since her delight is flown
For whom should she have waked the sullen year?
140 To Phoebus was not Hyacinth so dear⁵
Nor to himself Narcissus, as to both
Thou Adonais: wan they stand and sere⁶
Amid the faint companions of their youth,
With dew all turned to tears; odour, to sighing ruth.°   pity

17

145 Thy spirit's sister, the lorn nightingale⁷
Mourns not her mate with such melodious pain;
Not so the eagle, who like thee could scale
Heaven, and could nourish in the sun's domain
Her mighty youth with morning,⁸ doth complain,

---

4. Because of her unrequited love for Narcissus, who was enamored of his own reflection (line 141), the nymph Echo pined away until she was only a reflected sound.
5. Young Hyacinthus was loved by Phoebus Apollo, who accidentally killed him in a game of quoits. Apollo made the hyacinth flower spring

from his blood.
6. Dried, withered.
7. To whom Keats had written *Ode to a Nightingale.*
8. In the legend, the aged eagle, to renew his youth, flies toward the sun until his old plumage is burned off and the film cleared from his eyes.

150   Soaring and screaming round her empty nest,
    As Albion° wails for thee: the curse of Cain   *England*
    Light on his head⁹ who pierced thy innocent breast,
   And scared the angel soul that was its earthly guest!

18

    Ah woe is me! Winter is come and gone,
155   But grief returns with the revolving year;
    The airs and streams renew their joyous tone;
    The ants, the bees, the swallows reappear;
    Fresh leaves and flowers deck the dead Seasons' bier;
    The amorous birds now pair in every brake,°   *thicket*
160   And build their mossy homes in field and brere;°   *briar*
    And the green lizard, and the golden snake,
  Like unimprisoned flames, out of their trance awake.

19

    Through wood and stream and field and hill and Ocean
    A quickening life from the Earth's heart has burst
165   As it has ever done, with change and motion,
    From the great morning of the world when first
    God dawned on Chaos; in its stream immersed
    The lamps of Heaven flash with a softer light;
    All baser things pant with life's sacred thirst;
170   Diffuse themselves; and spend in love's delight,
  The beauty and the joy of their renewed might.

20

    The leprous corpse touched by this spirit tender
    Exhales itself in flowers of gentle breath;
    Like incarnations of the stars, when splendour
175   Is changed to fragrance, they illumine death
    And mock the merry worm that wakes beneath;
    Nought we know, dies. Shall that alone which knows
    Be as a sword consumed before the sheath¹
    By sightless° lightning?—th' intense atom glows *invisible*
180 A moment, then is quenched in a most cold repose.

21

    Alas! that all we loved of him should be,
    But for our grief, as if it had not been,
    And grief itself be mortal! Woe is me!
    Whence are we, and why are we? of what scene
185   The actors or spectators? Great and mean
    Meet massed in death, who lends what life must borrow.
    As long as skies are blue, and fields are green,
    Evening must usher night, night urge the morrow,
  Month follow month with woe, and year wake year to sorrow.

---

9. The reviewer of *Endymion*.
1. The "sword" is the mind that knows; the "sheath" is its vehicle, the material body.

22

190 *He* will awake no more, oh, never more!
"Wake thou," cried Misery, "childless Mother, rise
Out of thy sleep, and slake,° in thy heart's core,   *assuage*
A wound more fierce than his with tears and sighs."
And all the Dreams that watched Urania's eyes,
195 And all the Echoes whom their sister's song[2]
Had held in holy silence, cried: "Arise!"
Swift as a Thought by the snake Memory stung,
From her ambrosial rest the fading Splendour° sprung.   *Urania*

23

She rose like an autumnal Night, that springs
200 Out of the East, and follows wild and drear
The golden Day, which, on eternal wings,
Even as a ghost abandoning a bier,
Had left the Earth a corpse. Sorrow and fear
So struck, so roused, so rapt Urania;
205 So saddened round her like an atmosphere
Of stormy mist; so swept her on her way
Even to the mournful place where Adonais lay.

24

Out of her secret Paradise she sped,
Through camps and cities rough with stone, and steel,
210 And human hearts, which to her aery tread
Yielding not, wounded the invisible
Palms of her tender feet where'er they fell:
And barbed tongues, and thoughts more sharp than they
Rent the soft Form they never could repel,
215 Whose sacred blood, like the young tears of May,
Paved with eternal flowers that undeserving way.

25

In the death chamber for a moment Death
Shamed by the presence of that living Might
Blushed to annihilation, and the breath
220 Revisited those lips, and life's pale light
Flashed through those limbs, so late her dear delight.
"Leave me not wild and drear and comfortless,
As silent lightning leaves the starless night!
Leave me not!" cried Urania: her distress
225 Roused Death: Death rose and smiled, and met her vain caress.

26

"Stay yet awhile! speak to me once again;
Kiss me, so long but as a kiss may live;
And in my heartless[3] breast and burning brain
That word, that kiss shall all thoughts else survive
230 With food of saddest memory kept alive,

---

2. I.e., the Echo in line 127.   3. Because her heart had been given to Adonais.

Now thou art dead, as if it were a part
Of thee, my Adonais! I would give
All that I am to be as thou now art!
But I am chained to Time, and cannot thence depart!

27

235 "Oh gentle child, beautiful as thou wert,
Why didst thou leave the trodden paths of men
Too soon, and with weak hands though mighty heart
Dare the unpastured dragon in his den?[4]
Defenceless as thou wert, oh where was then
240 Wisdom the mirrored shield, or scorn the spear?[5]
Or hadst thou waited the full cycle, when
Thy spirit should have filled its crescent sphere,[6]
The monsters of life's waste had fled from thee like deer.

28

"The herded wolves, bold only to pursue;
245 The obscene ravens, clamorous o'er the dead;
The vultures to the conqueror's banner true
Who feed where Desolation first has fed,
And whose wings rain contagion;—how they fled,
When like Apollo, from his golden bow,
250 The Pythian of the age[7] one arrow sped
And smiled!—The spoilers tempt no second blow,
They fawn on the proud feet that spurn them lying low.

29

"The sun comes forth, and many reptiles spawn;
He sets, and each ephemeral insect then
255 Is gathered into death without a dawn,
And the immortal stars awake again;
So is it in the world of living men:
A godlike mind soars forth, in its delight
Making earth bare and veiling heaven,[8] and when
260 It sinks, the swarms that dimmed or shared its light
Leave to its kindred lamps[9] the spirit's awful night."

30

Thus ceased she: and the mountain shepherds came,
Their garlands sere, their magic mantles rent;
The Pilgrim of Eternity,[1] whose fame
265 Over his living head like Heaven is bent,
An early but enduring monument,

4. I.e., the hostile reviewers.
5. The allusion is to Perseus, who had cut off Medusa's head while avoiding the direct sight of her (which would have turned him to stone) by looking only at her reflection in his shield.
6. I.e., when thy spirit, like the full moon, should have reached its maturity.
7. Byron, who had directed against critics of the age his satiric poem *English Bards and Scotch*

Reviewers (1809). The allusion is to Apollo, called "the Pythian" because he had slain the dragon Python.
8. As the sun reveals the earth but veils the other stars.
9. The other stars (i.e., creative minds), of lesser brilliance than the sun.
1. Byron, who had referred to his Childe Harold as one of the "wanderers o'er Eternity" (3.669).

Came, veiling all the lightnings of his song
In sorrow; from her wilds Ierne sent
The sweetest lyrist[2] of her saddest wrong,
270 And love taught grief to fall like music from his tongue.

31

Midst others of less note, came one frail Form,[3]
A phantom among men; companionless
As the last cloud of an expiring storm
Whose thunder is its knell; he, as I guess,
275 Had gazed on Nature's naked loveliness,
Actæon-like, and now he fled astray
With feeble steps o'er the world's wilderness,
And his own thoughts, along that rugged way,
Pursued, like raging hounds, their father and their prey.[4]

32

280 A pardlike° Spirit beautiful and swift—   leopardlike
A Love in desolation masked;—a Power
Girt round with weakness;—it can scarce uplift
The weight of the superincumbent hour;[5]
It is a dying lamp, a falling shower,
285 A breaking billow;—even whilst we speak
Is it not broken? On the withering flower
The killing sun smiles brightly: on a cheek
The life can burn in blood, even while the heart may break.

33

His head was bound with pansies overblown,
290 And faded violets, white, and pied, and blue;
And a light spear topped with a cypress cone,
Round whose rude shaft dark ivy tresses grew[6]
Yet dripping with the forest's noonday dew,
Vibrated, as the ever-beating heart
295 Shook the weak hand that grasped it; of that crew
He came the last, neglected and apart;
A herd-abandoned deer struck by the hunter's dart.

34

All stood aloof, and at his partial° moan   sympathetic
Smiled through their tears; well knew that gentle band
300 Who in another's fate now wept his own;
As in the accents of an unknown land,
He sung new sorrow; sad Urania scanned
The Stranger's mien, and murmured: "who art thou?"

2. Thomas Moore (1779–1852), from Ireland ("Ierne"), who had written poems about the oppression of his native land.
3. Shelley himself, represented in one of his aspects—like the Poet in *Alastor*, rather than the author of *Prometheus Unbound*.
4. Actaeon, while hunting, came upon the naked

Diana bathing and, as a punishment, was turned into a stag and torn to pieces by his own hounds.
5. The heavy, overhanging hour of Keats's death.
6. Like the thyrsus, the leaf-entwined and cone-topped staff carried by Dionysus. The pansies are emblems of sorrowful thought. The cypress is an emblem of mourning.

He answered not, but with a sudden hand
305   Made bare his branded and ensanguined brow,
Which was like Cain's or Christ's[7]—Oh! that it should be so!

35

What softer voice is hushed over the dead?
Athwart what brow is that dark mantle thrown?
What form leans sadly o'er the white death-bed,
310   In mockery of monumental stone,[8]
The heavy heart heaving without a moan?
If it be He,[9] who, gentlest of the wise,
Taught, soothed, loved, honoured the departed one;
Let me not vex, with inharmonious sighs
315 The silence of that heart's accepted sacrifice.

36

Our Adonais has drunk poison—oh!
What deaf and viperous murderer could crown
Life's early cup with such a draught of woe?
The nameless worm[1] would now itself disown:
320   It felt, yet could escape the magic tone
Whose prelude held all envy, hate, and wrong,
But what was howling in one breast alone,
Silent with expectation of the song,[2]
Whose master's hand is cold, whose silver lyre unstrung.

37

325   Live thou, whose infamy is not thy fame!
Live! fear no heavier chastisement from me,
Thou noteless blot on a remembered name!
But be thyself, and know thyself to be!
And ever at thy season be thou free
330   To spill the venom when thy fangs o'erflow:
Remorse and Self-contempt shall cling to thee;
Hot Shame shall burn upon thy secret brow,
And like a beaten hound tremble thou shalt—as now.

38

Nor let us weep that our delight is fled
335   Far from these carrion kites[3] that scream below;
He wakes or sleeps with the enduring dead;
Thou canst not soar where he is sitting now.—
Dust to the dust! but the pure spirit shall flow
Back to the burning fountain whence it came,

---

7. His bloody ("ensanguined") brow bore a mark like that with which God had branded Cain for murdering Abel—or like that left by Christ's crown of thorns.
8. In imitation of a memorial statue.
9. Leigh Hunt, close friend of both Keats and

Shelley.
1. Snake—the anonymous reviewer.
2. The promise of later greatness in Keats's early poems "held . . . silent" the expression of all malignant feelings except the reviewer's.
3. Birds of prey; a species of hawk.

340   A portion of the Eternal,[4] which must glow
       Through time and change, unquenchably the same,
    Whilst thy cold embers choke the sordid hearth of shame.

39

     Peace, peace! he is not dead, he doth not sleep—
     He hath awakened from the dream of life—
345   'Tis we, who lost in stormy visions, keep
     With phantoms an unprofitable strife,
     And in mad trance, strike with our spirit's knife
     Invulnerable nothings.—*We* decay
     Like corpses in a charnel; fear and grief
350   Convulse us and consume us day by day,
   And cold hopes swarm like worms within our living clay.

40

     He has outsoared the shadow of our night;[5]
     Envy and calumny and hate and pain,
     And that unrest which men miscall delight,
355   Can touch him not and torture not again;
     From the contagion of the world's slow stain
     He is secure, and now can never mourn
     A heart grown cold, a head grown grey in vain;
     Nor, when the spirit's self has ceased to burn,
360   With sparkless ashes load an unlamented urn.

41

     He lives, he wakes—'tis Death is dead, not he;
     Mourn not for Adonais.—Thou young Dawn
     Turn all thy dew to splendour, for from thee
     The spirit thou lamentest is not gone;
365   Ye caverns and ye forests, cease to moan!
     Cease ye faint flowers and fountains, and thou Air
     Which like a mourning veil thy scarf hadst thrown
     O'er the abandoned Earth, now leave it bare
  Even to the joyous stars which smile on its despair![6]

42

370   He is made one with Nature: there is heard
     His voice in all her music, from the moan
     Of thunder, to the song of night's sweet bird;[7]
     He is a presence to be felt and known
     In darkness and in light, from herb and stone,
375   Spreading itself where'er that Power may move

---

4. Shelley adopts for this poem the Neoplatonic view that all life and all forms emanate from the Absolute, the eternal One. The Absolute is imaged as both a radiant light source and an overflowing fountain, which circulates continuously through the dross of matter (stanza 43) and back to its source.

5. He has soared beyond the shadow cast by the earth as it intercepts the sun's light.
6. Shelley's science is, as usual, accurate: it is the envelope of air around the earth that, by diffusing and reflecting sunlight, veils the stars.
7. The nightingale, in allusion to Keats's *Ode to a Nightingale*.

Which has withdrawn his being to its own;
Which wields the world with never wearied love,
Sustains it from beneath, and kindles it above.

43

He is a portion of the loveliness
380 Which once he made more lovely: he doth bear
His part, while the one Spirit's plastic[8] stress
Sweeps through the dull dense world, compelling there,
All new successions to the forms they wear;
Torturing th' unwilling dross that checks its flight
385 To its own likeness, as each mass may bear;[9]
And bursting in its beauty and its might
From trees and beasts and men into the Heaven's light.

44

The splendours of the firmament of time
May be eclipsed, but are extinguished not;
390 Like stars to their appointed height they climb
And death is a low mist which cannot blot
The brightness it may veil.[1] When lofty thought
Lifts a young heart above its mortal lair,
And love and life contend in it, for what
395 Shall be its earthly doom,° the dead live there[2]   *destiny*
And move like winds of light on dark and stormy air.

45

The inheritors of unfulfilled renown[3]
Rose from their thrones, built beyond mortal thought,
Far in the Unapparent. Chatterton
400 Rose pale, his solemn agony had not
Yet faded from him; Sidney, as he fought
And as he fell and as he lived and loved
Sublimely mild, a Spirit without spot,
Arose; and Lucan, by his death approved:°   *justified*
405 Oblivion as they rose shrank like a thing reproved.

46

And many more, whose names on Earth are dark
But whose transmitted effluence cannot die
So long as fire outlives the parent spark,
Rose, robed in dazzling immortality.
410 "Thou art become as one of us," they cry,
"It was for thee yon kingless sphere has long

---

8. Formative, shaping.
9. I.e., to the degree that a particular substance will permit.
1. The radiance of stars (i.e., of poets) persists, even when they are temporarily "eclipsed" by another heavenly body, or obscured by the veil of the earth's atmosphere.
2. I.e., in the thought of the "young heart."

3. Poets who (like Keats) died young, before achieving their full measure of fame: Thomas Chatterton (1752–1770) committed suicide at seventeen, Sir Philip Sidney (1554–1586) died in battle at thirty-two, and the Roman poet Lucan (39–65 C.E.) killed himself at twenty-six to escape a sentence of death for having plotted against the tyrant Nero.

Swung blind in unascended majesty,
Silent alone amid an Heaven of song.
Assume thy winged throne, thou Vesper of our throng!"[4]

47

415   Who mourns for Adonais? oh come forth
Fond wretch! and know thyself and him aright.
Clasp with thy panting soul the pendulous[5] Earth;
As from a centre, dart thy spirit's light
Beyond all worlds, until its spacious might
420   Satiate the void circumference: then shrink
Even to a point within our day and night;[6]
And keep thy heart light lest it make thee sink
When hope has kindled hope, and lured thee to the brink.

48

Or go to Rome, which is the sepulchre
425   O, not of him, but of our joy: 'tis nought
That ages, empires, and religions there
Lie buried in the ravage they have wrought;
For such as he can lend,—they[7] borrow not
Glory from those who made the world their prey;
430   And he is gathered to the kings of thought
Who waged contention with their time's decay,
And of the past are all that cannot pass away.

49

Go thou to Rome,—at once the Paradise,
The grave, the city, and the wilderness;
435   And where its wrecks like shattered mountains rise,
And flowering weeds, and fragrant copses[8] dress
The bones of Desolation's nakedness
Pass, till the Spirit of the spot shall lead
Thy footsteps to a slope of green access[9]
440   Where, like an infant's smile, over the dead,
A light of laughing flowers along the grass is spread.

50

And grey walls moulder round,[1] on which dull Time
Feeds, like slow fire upon a hoary brand;[2]
And one keen pyramid with wedge sublime,[3]

---

4. Adonais assumes his place in the sphere of Vesper, the evening star, hitherto unoccupied ("kingless"), hence also "silent" amid the music of the other spheres.
5. Suspended, floating in space.
6. The poet bids the wretch who is foolish ("fond") enough to mourn Adonais to stretch his imagination so as to reach the poet's own cosmic viewpoint and then allow it to contract ("shrink") back to its ordinary vantage point on earth—where, unlike Adonais in his heavenly place, we have an alternation of day and night.
7. Poets like Keats, who can bestow ("lend") glory,

as opposed to the Roman conquerors, who borrowed glory from those they conquered.
8. Undergrowth. In Shelley's time the ruins of ancient Rome were overgrown with weeds and shrubbery.
9. The Protestant Cemetery, Keats's burial place. The next line is a glancing allusion to Shelley's three-year-old son, William, also buried there.
1. The wall of ancient Rome formed one boundary of the cemetery.
2. A burning log.
3. The tomb of Caius Cestius, a Roman tribune, just outside the cemetery.

445   Pavilioning the dust of him who planned
    This refuge for his memory, doth stand
    Like flame transformed to marble; and beneath,
    A field is spread, on which a newer band
    Have pitched in Heaven's smile their camp of death
450 Welcoming him we lose with scarce extinguished breath.

51

    Here pause: these graves are all too young as yet
    To have outgrown the sorrow which consigned
    Its charge to each; and if the seal is set,
    Here, on one fountain of a mourning mind,[4]
455   Break it not thou! too surely shalt thou find
    Thine own well full, if thou returnest home,
    Of tears and gall. From the world's bitter wind
    Seek shelter in the shadow of the tomb.
What Adonais is, why fear we to become?

52

460   The One remains, the many change and pass;
    Heaven's light forever shines, Earth's shadows fly;
    Life, like a dome of many-coloured glass,
    Stains the white radiance of Eternity,
    Until Death tramples it to fragments.[5]—Die,
465   If thou wouldst be with that which thou dost seek!
    Follow where all is fled!—Rome's azure sky,
    Flowers, ruins, statues, music, words, are weak
The glory they transfuse with fitting truth to speak.

53

    Why linger, why turn back, why shrink, my Heart?
470   Thy hopes are gone before; from all things here
    They have departed; thou shouldst now depart!
    A light is past from the revolving year,
    And man, and woman; and what still is dear
    Attracts to crush, repels to make thee wither.
475   The soft sky smiles,—the low wind whispers near:
    'Tis Adonais calls! oh, hasten thither,
No more let Life divide what Death can join together.

54

    That Light whose smile kindles the Universe,
    That Beauty in which all things work and move,
480   That Benediction which the eclipsing Curse
    Of birth can quench not, that sustaining Love
    Which through the web of being blindly wove
    By man and beast and earth and air and sea,
    Burns bright or dim, as each are mirrors of[6]

---

4. Shelley's mourning for his son.
5. Earthly life colors ("stains") the pure white light of the One, which is the source of all light (see lines 339–40, n. 4). The azure sky, flowers, etc., of lines 466–68 exemplify earthly colors that, how-ever beautiful, fall far short of the "glory" of the pure Light that they transmit but also refract ("transfuse").
6. I.e., according to the degree that each reflects.

485   The fire for which all thirst;[7] now beams on me,
    Consuming the last clouds of cold mortality.

55

    The breath whose might I have invoked in song[8]
    Descends on me; my spirit's bark is driven,
    Far from the shore, far from the trembling throng
490   Whose sails were never to the tempest given;
    The massy earth and sphered skies are riven!
    I am borne darkly, fearfully, afar;
    Whilst burning through the inmost veil of Heaven,
    The soul of Adonais, like a star,
495 Beacons from the abode where the Eternal are.

1821   1821

A Dirge

    Rough wind, that moanest loud
      Grief too sad for song;
    Wild wind, when sullen cloud
      Knells all the night long;
5   Sad storm, whose tears are vain,
    Bare woods, whose branches strain,
    Deep caves and dreary main,—
      Wail, for the world's wrong!

1821   1824

When the lamp is shattered

    When the lamp is shattered
    The light in the dust lies dead—
    When the cloud is scattered
    The rainbow's glory is shed—
5   When the lute is broken
    Sweet tones are remembered not—
    When the lips have spoken
    Loved accents are soon forgot.

    As music and splendour
10   Survive not the lamp and the lute,
    The heart's echoes render
    No song when the spirit is mute—
    No song—but sad dirges
    Like the wind through a ruined cell

---

7. The "thirst" of the human spirit is to return to
the fountain and fire (the "burning fountain," line
339) which is its source.

8. Two years earlier Shelley had "invoked" (prayed
to, and also asked for) "the breath of Autumn's
being" in his *Ode to the West Wind*.

15   Or the mournful surges
That ring the dead seaman's knell.

When hearts have once mingled
Love first leaves the well-built nest[1]—
The weak one is singled
20   To endure what it once possest.
O Love! who bewailest
The frailty of all things here,
Why choose you the frailest[2]
For your cradle, your home and your bier?

25   Its passions will rock thee
As the storms rock the ravens on high—
Bright Reason will mock thee
Like the Sun from a wintry sky—
From thy nest every rafter
30   Will rot, and thine eagle home[3]
Leave thee naked to laughter
When leaves fall and cold winds come.

1822   1824

To Jane[1] (The keen stars were twinkling)

The keen stars were twinkling
And the fair moon was rising among them,
    Dear Jane.
The guitar was tinkling
5   But the notes were not sweet 'till you sung them
    Again.—
As the moon's soft splendour
O'er the faint cold starlight of Heaven
    Is thrown—
10   So your voice most tender
To the strings without soul had then given
    Its own.

The stars will awaken,
Though the moon sleep a full hour later,
15   Tonight;
No leaf will be shaken
While the dews of your melody scatter
    Delight.
Though the sound overpowers
20   Sing again, with your dear voice revealing
    A tone
Of some world far from ours,

---

1. Love abandons first the sturdier heart.
2. I.e., the human heart.
3. Like the lofty, and therefore exposed, nest of the eagle.

1. Jane Williams, the common-law wife of Shelley's close friend Edward Williams.

Where music and moonlight and feeling
Are one.

1822   1832

Lines Written in the Bay of Lerici[1]

Bright wanderer,° fair coquette of Heaven,   *moon*
To whom alone it has been given
To change and be adored for ever. . . .
Envy not this dim world, for never
5   But once within its shadow grew
One fair as [thou], but far more true.
She left me at the silent time
When the moon had ceased to climb
The azure dome of Heaven's steep,
10   And like an albatross asleep,
Balanced on her wings of light,
Hovered in the purple night,
Ere she sought her Ocean nest
In the chambers of the west.—
15   She left me, and I staid alone
Thinking over every tone,
Which though now silent to the ear
The enchanted heart could hear
Like notes which die when born, but still
20   Haunt the echoes of the hill:
And feeling ever—O too much—
The soft vibrations of her touch
As if her gentle hand even now
Lightly trembled on my brow;
25   And thus although she absent were
Memory gave me all of her
That even fancy dares to claim.—
Her presence had made weak and tame
All passions, and I lived alone,
30   In the time which is our own;
The past and future were forgot
As they had been, and would be, not.—
But soon, the guardian angel gone,
The demon[2] reassumed his throne
35   In my faint heart . . . I dare not speak
My thoughts; but thus disturbed and weak
I sate and watched the vessels glide
Along the ocean bright and wide,
Like spirit-winged chariots sent
40   O'er some serenest element
To ministrations strange and far;

---

1. Another of Shelley's lyrics inspired by Jane Williams. He shared with the Williamses a summer house near Lerici, on the northeastern coast of Italy.
2. I.e., the passions, with their compulsion to look before and after (lines 29–32).

        As if to some Elysian star
        They sailed for drink to medicine
        Such sweet and bitter pain as mine.
45   And the wind that winged their flight
        From the land came fresh and light,
        And the scent of sleeping flowers
        And the coolness of the hours
        Of dew, and the sweet warmth of day
50   Was scattered o'er the twinkling bay;
        And the fisher with his lamp
        And spear, about the low rocks damp
        Crept, and struck the fish who came
        To worship the delusive flame:
55   Too happy, they whose pleasure sought
        Extinguishes all sense and thought
        Of the regret that pleasure [leaves][3]
        Destroying life alone not peace.

1822   1862

A Defence of Poetry

A Defence of Poetry   In 1820 Shelley's good friend Thomas Love Peacock published an ironic essay, *The Four Ages of Poetry,* implicitly directed against the towering claims for poetry and the poetic imagination made by his Romantic contemporaries. Peacock adopted the premise of Wordsworth and some other Romantic critics—that poetry in its origin was a primitive use of language and mind—but from this premise he proceeded to draw the conclusion that poetry has become a useless anachronism in this age of science and technology. Peacock was himself a poet as well as an excellent prose satirist, and Shelley saw the joke; but he also recognized that the view that Peacock, as a satirist, had assumed was very close to that actually held in his day by Utilitarian philosophers and the material-minded public, who either attacked or contemptuously ignored the imaginative faculty and its achievements. He therefore undertook, as he good-humoredly wrote to Peacock, "to break a lance with you . . . in honor of my mistress Urania," even though he was only "the knight of the shield of shadow and the lance of gossamere." The result was *A Defence of Poetry,* planned to consist of three parts. The last two parts were never written, and even the existing section, written in 1821, remained unpublished until 1840, eighteen years after Shelley's death.

Shelley's emphasis in this essay, like that of Blake in his critical commentaries, is not on the particularity of individual poems but on the universal and permanent qualities and values that, he believes, all great poems, as products of imagination, have in common. Shelley in addition extends the term *poet* to include all creative minds that break out of the conditions of their time and place to envision what he regards as the eternal and general forms of value. This category includes not only writers in prose as well as verse but also artists, legislators, prophets, and the founders of new social and religious institutions.

The *Defence* is an eloquent and enduring claim for the indispensability of the visionary and creative imagination in all the great human concerns. Few later social critics have equaled the cogency of Shelley's attack on our acquisitive society and its narrowly material concepts of utility and progress. Such a bias has opened the way

3. This word has been suggested by earlier editors; Shelley left a blank space.

to enormous advances in the physical sciences and our material well-being, but without a proportionate development of our "poetic faculty," the moral imagination. The result, Shelley says, is that "man, having enslaved the elements, remains himself a slave."

From A Defence of Poetry

or Remarks Suggested by an Essay Entitled "The Four Ages of Poetry"

According to one mode of regarding those two classes of mental action, which are called reason and imagination, the former may be considered as mind contemplating the relations borne by one thought to another, however produced; and the latter, as mind acting upon those thoughts so as to colour them with its own light, and composing from them, as from elements, other thoughts, each containing within itself the principle of its own integrity. The one[1] is the *to poiein*,[2] or the principle of synthesis, and has for its objects those forms which are common to universal nature and existence itself; the other is the *to logizein*,[3] or principle of analysis, and its action regards the relations of things, simply as relations; considering thoughts, not in their integral unity, but as the algebraical representations which conduct to certain general results. Reason is the enumeration of quantities already known; imagination is the perception of the value of those quantities, both separately and as a whole. Reason respects the differences, and imagination the similitudes of things. Reason is to Imagination as the instrument to the agent, as the body to the spirit, as the shadow to the substance.

Poetry, in a general sense, may be defined to be "the expression of the Imagination": and poetry is connate with the origin of man. Man is an instrument over which a series of external and internal impressions are driven, like the alternations of an ever-changing wind over an Æolian lyre,[4] which move it by their motion to ever-changing melody. But there is a principle within the human being, and perhaps within all sentient beings, which acts otherwise than in the lyre, and produces not melody, alone, but harmony, by an internal adjustment of the sounds or motions thus excited to the impressions which excite them. It is as if the lyre could accommodate its chords to the motions of that which strikes them, in a determined proportion of sound; even as the musician can accommodate his voice to the sound of the lyre. A child at play by itself will express its delight by its voice and motions; and every inflexion of tone and every gesture will bear exact relation to a corresponding antitype in the pleasurable impressions which awakened it; it will be the reflected image of that impression; and as the lyre trembles and sounds after the wind has died away, so the child seeks, by prolonging in its voice and motions the duration of the effect, to prolong also a consciousness of the cause. In relation to the objects which delight a child, these expressions are, what poetry is to higher objects. The savage (for the savage is to

---

1. The imagination. "The other" (later in the sentence) is the reason.
2. Making. The Greek word from which the English term *poet* derives means "maker," and "maker" was often used as equivalent to "poet" by Renaissance critics such as Sir Philip Sidney in his

Defence of Poesy, which Shelley had carefully studied.
3. Calculating, reasoning.
4. A wind harp (see Coleridge, *The Eolian Harp*, p. 419).

ages what the child is to years) expresses the emotions produced in him by surrounding objects in a similar manner; and language and gesture, together with plastic or pictorial imitation, become the image of the combined effect of those objects, and of his apprehension of them. Man in society, with all his passions and his pleasures, next becomes the object of the passions and pleasures of man; an additional class of emotions produces an augmented treasure of expressions; and language, gesture, and the imitative arts, become at once the representation and the medium, the pencil and the picture, the chisel and the statue, the chord and the harmony. The social sympathies, or those laws from which as from its elements society results, begin to develope themselves from the moment that two human beings coexist; the future is contained within the present as the plant within the seed; and equality, diversity, unity, contrast, mutual dependence, become the principles alone capable of affording the motives according to which the will of a social being is determined to action, inasmuch as he is social; and constitute pleasure in sensation, virtue in sentiment, beauty in art, truth in reasoning, and love in the intercourse of kind. Hence men, even in the infancy of society, observe a certain order in their words and actions, distinct from that of the objects and the impressions represented by them, all expression being subject to the laws of that from which it proceeds. But let us dismiss those more general considerations which might involve an enquiry into the principles of society itself, and restrict our view to the manner in which the imagination is expressed upon its forms.

In the youth of the world, men dance and sing and imitate natural objects, observing[5] in these actions, as in all others, a certain rhythm or order. And, although all men observe a similar, they observe not the same order, in the motions of the dance, in the melody of the song, in the combinations of language, in the series of their imitations of natural objects. For there is a certain order or rhythm belonging to each of these classes of mimetic representation, from which the hearer and the spectator receive an intenser and purer pleasure than from any other: the sense of an approximation to this order has been called taste, by modern writers. Every man in the infancy of art, observes an order which approximates more or less closely to that from which this highest delight results: but the diversity is not sufficiently marked, as that its gradations should be sensible, except in those instances where the predominance of this faculty of approximation to the beautiful (for so we may be permitted to name the relation between this highest pleasure and its cause) is very great. Those in whom it exists in excess are poets, in the most universal sense of the word; and the pleasure resulting from the manner in which they express the influence of society or nature upon their own minds, communicates itself to others, and gathers a sort of reduplication from that community. Their language is vitally metaphorical; that is, it marks the before unapprehended relations of things, and perpetuates their apprehension, until the words which represent them, become through time signs for portions or classes of thoughts[6] instead of pictures of integral thoughts; and then if no new poets should arise to create afresh the associations which have been thus disorganized, language will be dead to all the nobler purposes of human intercourse. These similitudes or relations are finely said by Lord

5. Following, obeying.   6. I.e., abstract concepts.

Bacon to be "the same footsteps of nature impressed upon the various subjects of the world"[7]—and he considers the faculty which perceives them as the storehouse of axioms common to all knowledge. In the infancy of society every author is necessarily a poet, because language itself is poetry; and to be a poet is to apprehend the true and the beautiful, in a word the good which exists in the relation, subsisting, first between existence and perception, and secondly between perception and expression. Every original language near to its source is in itself the chaos of a cyclic poem:[8] the copiousness of lexicography and the distinctions of grammar are the works of a later age, and are merely the catalogue and the form of the creations of Poetry.

But Poets, or those who imagine and express this indestructible order, are not only the authors of language and of music, of the dance and architecture and statuary and painting: they are the institutors of laws, and the founders of civil society and the inventors of the arts of life and the teachers, who draw into a certain propinquity with the beautiful and the true that partial apprehension of the agencies of the invisible world which is called religion.[9] Hence all original religions are allegorical, or susceptible of allegory, and like Janus[1] have a double face of false and true. Poets, according to the circumstances of the age and nation in which they appeared, were called in the earlier epochs of the world legislators or prophets:[2] a poet essentially comprises and unites both these characters. For he not only beholds intensely the present as it is, and discovers those laws according to which present things ought to be ordered, but he beholds the future in the present, and his thoughts are the germs of the flower and the fruit of latest time. Not that I assert poets to be prophets in the gross sense of the word, or that they can foretell the form as surely as they foreknow the spirit of events: such is the pretence of superstition which would make poetry an attribute of prophecy, rather than prophecy an attribute of poetry. A Poet participates in the eternal, the infinite, and the one; as far as relates to his conceptions, time and place and number are not. The grammatical forms which express the moods of time, and the difference of persons and the distinction of place are convertible with respect to the highest poetry without injuring it as poetry, and the choruses of Æschylus, and the book of Job, and Dante's Paradise would afford, more than any other writings, examples of this fact, if the limits of this essay did not forbid citation. The creations of sculpture, painting, and music, are illustrations still more decisive.

Language, colour, form, and religious and civil habits of action are all the instruments and materials of poetry; they may be called poetry by that figure of speech which considers the effect as a synonime of the cause. But poetry in a more restricted sense[3] expresses those arrangements of language, and especially metrical language, which are created by that imperial faculty, whose throne is curtained within the invisible nature of man. And this springs from the nature itself of language, which is a more direct represen-

---

7. Francis Bacon's *De Augmentis Scientiarum* (On the enlargement of the sciences) 1.3.
8. A group of poems (e.g., "the Arthurian cycle") that deal with the same subject.
9. Here Shelley enlarges the scope of the term *poetry* to denote all the creative achievements, or imaginative breakthroughs, of humankind, including noninstitutional religious insights.
1. Roman god of beginnings and endings, often represented by two heads facing opposite directions.
2. Sir Philip Sidney had pointed out, in his *Defence of Poesy,* that *vates,* the Roman term for "poet," signifies "a diviner, fore-seer, or Prophet."
3. I.e., restricted to specifically verbal poetry, as against the inclusive sense in which Shelley has been applying the term.

tation of the actions and passions of our internal being, and is susceptible of more various and delicate combinations, than colour, form, or motion, and is more plastic and obedient to the controul of that faculty of which it is the creation. For language is arbitrarily produced by the Imagination and has relation to thoughts alone; but all other materials, instruments and conditions of art, have relations among each other, which limit and interpose between conception and expression. The former[4] is as a mirror which reflects, the latter as a cloud which enfeebles, the light of which both are mediums of communication. Hence the fame of sculptors, painters and musicians, although the intrinsic powers of the great masters of these arts, may yield in no degree to that of those who have employed language as the hieroglyphic of their thoughts, has never equalled that of poets in the restricted sense of the term; as two performers of equal skill will produce unequal effects from a guitar and a harp. The fame of legislators and founders of religions, so long as their institutions last, alone seems to exceed that of poets in the restricted sense; but it can scarcely be a question whether, if we deduct the celebrity which their flattery of the gross opinions of the vulgar usually conciliates, together with that which belonged to them in their higher character of poets, any excess will remain.

We have thus circumscribed the meaning of the word Poetry within the limits of that art which is the most familiar and the most perfect expression of the faculty itself. It is necessary however to make the circle still narrower, and to determine the distinction between measured and unmeasured language; for the popular division into prose and verse is inadmissible in accurate philosophy.

Sounds as well as thoughts have relation both between each other and towards that which they represent, and a perception of the order of those relations has always been found connected with a perception of the order of the relations of thoughts. Hence the language of poets has ever affected a certain uniform and harmonious recurrence of sound, without which it were not poetry, and which is scarcely less indispensable to the communication of its influence, than the words themselves, without reference to that peculiar order. Hence the vanity of translation; it were as wise to cast a violet into a crucible that you might discover the formal principle of its colour and odour, as seek to transfuse from one language into another the creations of a poet. The plant must spring again from its seed or it will bear no flower—and this is the burthen of the curse of Babel.[5]

An observation of the regular mode of the recurrence of this harmony in the language of poetical minds, together with its relation to music, produced metre, or a certain system of traditional forms of harmony of language. Yet it is by no means essential that a poet should accommodate his language to this traditional form, so that the harmony which is its spirit, be observed. The practise is indeed convenient and popular, and to be preferred, especially in such composition as includes much form and action: but every great poet must inevitably innovate upon the example of his predecessors in the exact structure of his peculiar versification. The distinction between poets and

4. I.e., language, as opposed to the media of sculpture, painting, and music.
5. When the descendants of Noah, who spoke a single language, undertook to build the Tower of Babel that would reach heaven, God cut short the attempt by multiplying languages so that the builders could no longer communicate (see Genesis 11.1–9).

prose writers is a vulgar error. The distinction between philosophers and poets has been anticipated.[6] Plato was essentially a poet—the truth and splendour of his imagery and the melody of his language is the most intense that it is possible to conceive. He rejected the measure of the epic, dramatic, and lyrical forms, because he sought to kindle a harmony in thoughts divested of shape and action, and he forbore to invent any regular plan of rhythm which would include, under determinate forms, the varied pauses of his style. Cicero[7] sought to imitate the cadence of his periods but with little success. Lord Bacon was a poet.[8] His language has a sweet and majestic rhythm, which satisfies the sense, no less than the almost superhuman wisdom of his philosophy satisfies the intellect; it is a strain which distends, and then bursts the circumference of the hearer's mind, and pours itself forth together with it into the universal element with which it has perpetual sympathy. All the authors of revolutions in opinion are not only necessarily poets as they are inventors, nor even as their words unveil the permanent analogy of things by images which participate in the life of truth; but as their periods are harmonious and rhythmical and contain in themselves the elements of verse; being the echo of the eternal music. Nor are those supreme poets, who have employed traditional forms of rhythm on account of the form and action of their subjects, less capable of perceiving and teaching the truth of things, than those who have omitted that form. Shakespeare, Dante and Milton (to confine ourselves to modern writers) are philosophers of the very loftiest power.

A poem is the very image of life expressed in its eternal truth. There is this difference between a story and a poem, that a story is a catalogue of detached facts, which have no other bond of connexion than time, place, circumstance, cause and effect; the other is the creation of actions according to the unchangeable forms of human nature, as existing in the mind of the creator, which is itself the image of all other minds. The one is partial, and applies only to a definite period of time, and a certain combination of events which can never again recur; the other is universal, and contains within itself the germ of a relation to whatever motives or actions have place in the possible varieties of human nature. Time, which destroys the beauty and the use of the story of particular facts, stript of the poetry which should invest them, augments that of Poetry, and for ever develops new and wonderful applications of the eternal truth which it contains. Hence epitomes[9] have been called the moths of just history;[1] they eat out the poetry of it. The story of particular facts is as a mirror which obscures and distorts that which should be beautiful: Poetry is a mirror which makes beautiful that which is distorted.

The parts of a composition may be poetical, without the composition as a whole being a poem. A single sentence may be considered as a whole though it be found in a series of unassimilated portions; a single word even may be a spark of inextinguishable thought. And thus all the great historians, Herodotus, Plutarch, Livy,[2] were poets; and although the plan of these writers, especially that of Livy, restrained them from developing this faculty in its

---

6. I.e., in what Shelley has already said.
7. Marcus Tullius Cicero, the great Roman orator of the 1st century B.C.E.
8. See the *Filium Labyrinthi* and the *Essay on Death* particularly [Shelley's note].
9. Abstracts, summaries.
1. By Bacon in *The Advancement of Learning*

2.2.4.
2. Titus Livius (59 B.C.E.–17 C.E.) wrote an immense history of Rome. Herodotus (ca. 480–ca. 425 B.C.E.) wrote the first systematic history of Greece. Plutarch (ca. 46–ca. 120 C.E.) wrote *Parallel Lives* (of eminent Greeks and Romans).

highest degree, they make copious and ample amends for their subjection, by filling all the interstices of their subjects with living images.

Having determined what is poetry, and who are poets, let us proceed to estimate its effects upon society.

Poetry is ever accompanied with pleasure: all spirits on which it falls, open themselves to receive the wisdom which is mingled with its delight. In the infancy of the world, neither poets themselves nor their auditors are fully aware of the excellence of poetry: for it acts in a divine and unapprehended manner, beyond and above consciousness; and it is reserved for future generations to contemplate and measure the mighty cause and effect in all the strength and splendour of their union. Even in modern times, no living poet ever arrived at the fulness of his fame; the jury which sits in judgement upon a poet, belonging as he does to all time, must be composed of his peers: it must be impanelled by Time from the selectest of the wise of many generations. A Poet is a nightingale, who sits in darkness and sings to cheer its own solitude with sweet sounds; his auditors are as men entranced by the melody of an unseen musician, who feel that they are moved and softened, yet know not whence or why. The poems of Homer and his contemporaries were the delight of infant Greece; they were the elements of that social system which is the column upon which all succeeding civilization has reposed. Homer embodied the ideal perfection of his age in human character; nor can we doubt that those who read his verses were awakened to an ambition of becoming like to Achilles, Hector and Ulysses: the truth and beauty of friendship, patriotism and persevering devotion to an object, were unveiled to the depths in these immortal creations: the sentiments of the auditors must have been refined and enlarged by a sympathy with such great and lovely impersonations, until from admiring they imitated, and from imitation they identified themselves with the objects of their admiration. Nor let it be objected, that these characters are remote from moral perfection, and that they can by no means be considered as edifying patterns for general imitation. Every epoch under names more or less specious has deified its peculiar errors; Revenge is the naked Idol of the worship of a semi-barbarous age; and Self-deceit is the veiled Image of unknown evil before which luxury and satiety lie prostrate. But a poet considers the vices of his contemporaries as the temporary dress in which his creations must be arrayed, and which cover without concealing the eternal proportions of their beauty. An epic or dramatic personage is understood to wear them around his soul, as he may the antient armour or the modern uniform around his body; whilst it is easy to conceive a dress more graceful than either. The beauty of the internal nature cannot be so far concealed by its accidental vesture, but that the spirit of its form shall communicate itself to the very disguise, and indicate the shape it hides from the manner in which it is worn. A majestic form and graceful motions will express themselves through the most barbarous and tasteless costume. Few poets of the highest class have chosen to exhibit the beauty of their conceptions in its naked truth and splendour; and it is doubtful whether the alloy of costume, habit, etc., be not necessary to temper this planetary music[3] for mortal ears.

The whole objection, however, of the immorality of poetry[4] rests upon a

---

3. The music made by the revolving crystalline spheres of the planets, inaudible to human ears.
4. In the preceding paragraph Shelley has been implicitly dealing with the charge, voiced by Plato in his *Republic,* that poetry is immoral because it represents evil characters acting evilly.

misconception of the manner in which poetry acts to produce the moral improvement of man. Ethical science[5] arranges the elements which poetry has created, and propounds schemes and proposes examples of civil and domestic life: nor is it for want of admirable doctrines that men hate, and despise, and censure, and deceive, and subjugate one another. But Poetry acts in another and diviner manner. It awakens and enlarges the mind itself by rendering it the receptacle of a thousand unapprehended combinations of thought. Poetry lifts the veil from the hidden beauty of the world, and makes familiar objects be as if they were not familiar; it reproduces[6] all that it represents, and the impersonations clothed in its Elysian light stand thenceforward in the minds of those who have once contemplated them, as memorials of that gentle and exalted content[7] which extends itself over all thoughts and actions with which it coexists. The great secret of morals is Love; or a going out of our own nature, and an identification of ourselves with the beautiful which exists in thought, action, or person, not our own. A man, to be greatly good, must imagine intensely and comprehensively; he must put himself in the place of another and of many others; the pains and pleasures of his species must become his own. The great instrument of moral good is the imagination;[8] and poetry administers to the effect by acting upon the cause. Poetry enlarges the circumference of the imagination by replenishing it with thoughts of ever new delight, which have the power of attracting and assimilating to their own nature all other thoughts, and which form new intervals and interstices whose void for ever craves fresh food. Poetry strengthens that faculty which is the organ of the moral nature of man, in the same manner as exercise strengthens a limb. A Poet therefore would do ill to embody his own conceptions of right and wrong, which are usually those of his place and time, in his poetical creations, which participate in neither. By this assumption of the inferior office of interpreting the effect, in which perhaps after all he might acquit himself but imperfectly, he would resign the glory in a participation in the cause.[9] There was little danger that Homer, or any of the eternal Poets, should have so far misunderstood themselves as to have abdicated this throne of their widest dominion. Those in whom the poetical faculty, though great, is less intense, as Euripides, Lucan, Tasso,[1] Spenser, have frequently affected[2] a moral aim, and the effect of their poetry is diminished in exact proportion to the degree in which they compel us to advert to this purpose.[3]

* * *

It is difficult to define pleasure in its highest sense; the definition involving a number of apparent paradoxes. For, from an inexplicable defect of harmony

5. Moral philosophy.
6. Produces anew, re-creates.
7. Contentment.
8. Central to Shelley's theory is the concept (developed by 18th-century philosophers) of the sympathetic imagination—the faculty by which an individual is enabled to identify with the thoughts and feelings of others. Shelley insists that the faculty in poetry that enables us to share the joys and sufferings of invented characters is also the basis of all morality, for it compels us to feel for others as we feel for ourselves.
9. The "effect," or the explicit moral standards into which imaginative insights are translated at a particular time or place, is contrasted to the

"cause" of all morality, the imagination itself.
1. Tasso Torquato (1544–1595), Italian poet, author of *Jerusalem Delivered*, an epic poem about a crusade. Euripides (ca. 484–406 B.C.E.), Greek writer of tragedies. Lucan (39–65 C.E.), Roman poet, author of the *Pharsalia*.
2. Assumed, adopted.
3. In the following omitted passage Shelley reviews the history of drama and poetry in relation to civilization and morality and proceeds to refute the charge that poets are less useful than "reasoners and merchants." He begins by defining *utility* in terms of pleasure and then distinguishes between the lower (physical and material) and the higher (imaginative) pleasures.

in the constitution of human nature, the pain of the inferior is frequently connected with the pleasures of the superior portions of our being. Sorrow, terror, anguish, despair itself are often the chosen expressions of an approximation to the highest good. Our sympathy in tragic fiction depends on this principle; tragedy delights by affording a shadow of the pleasure which exists in pain. This is the source also of the melancholy which is inseparable from the sweetest melody. The pleasure that is in sorrow is sweeter than the pleasure of pleasure itself. And hence the saying, "It is better to go to the house of mourning, than to the house of mirth."[4] Not that this highest species of pleasure is necessarily linked with pain. The delight of love and friendship, the ecstasy of the admiration of nature, the joy of the perception and still more of the creation of poetry is often wholly unalloyed.

The production and assurance of pleasure in this highest sense is true utility. Those who produce and preserve this pleasure are Poets or poetical philosophers.

The exertions of Locke, Hume, Gibbon, Voltaire, Rousseau,[5] and their disciples, in favour of oppressed and deluded humanity, are entitled to the gratitude of mankind. Yet it is easy to calculate the degree of moral and intellectual improvement which the world would have exhibited, had they never lived. A little more nonsense would have been talked for a century or two; and perhaps a few more men, women, and children, burnt as heretics. We might not at this moment have been congratulating each other on the abolition of the Inquisition in Spain.[6] But it exceeds all imagination to conceive what would have been the moral condition of the world if neither Dante, Petrarch, Boccaccio, Chaucer, Shakespeare, Calderon, Lord Bacon, nor Milton, had ever existed; if Raphael and Michael Angelo had never been born; if the Hebrew poetry had never been translated; if a revival of the study of Greek literature had never taken place; if no monuments of antient sculpture had been handed down to us; and if the poetry of the religion of the antient world had been extinguished together with its belief. The human mind could never, except by the intervention of these excitements, have been awakened to the invention of the grosser sciences, and that application of analytical reasoning to the aberrations of society, which it is now attempted to exalt over the direct expression of the inventive and creative faculty itself.

We have more moral, political and historical wisdom, than we know how to reduce into practice; we have more scientific and economical knowledge than can be accommodated to the just distribution of the produce which it multiplies. The poetry in these systems of thought, is concealed by the accumulation of facts and calculating processes. There is no want of knowledge respecting what is wisest and best in morals, government, and political economy, or at least, what is wiser and better than what men now practise and endure. But we let "I dare not wait upon I would, like the poor cat i' the adage."[7] We want the creative faculty to imagine that which we know; we want the generous impulse to act that which we imagine; we want the poetry of life: our calculations have outrun conception; we have eaten more than we can digest. The cultivation of those sciences which have enlarged the

4. Ecclesiastes 7.2.
5. In a note Shelley says that, although Peacock had classified Rousseau with these other thinkers of the 17th and 18th centuries, "he was essentially a poet. The others, even Voltaire, were mere rea-

soners."
6. The Inquisition had been suspended in 1820, the year before Shelley wrote this essay; it was not abolished permanently until 1834.
7. *Macbeth* 1.7.44–45.

limits of the empire of man over the external world, has, for want of the poetical faculty, proportionally circumscribed those of the internal world; and man, having enslaved the elements, remains himself a slave. To what but a cultivation of the mechanical arts in a degree disproportioned to the presence of the creative faculty, which is the basis of all knowledge, is to be attributed the abuse of all invention for abridging and combining labour, to the exasperation of the inequality of mankind? From what other cause has it arisen that these inventions which should have lightened, have added a weight to the curse imposed on Adam? Poetry, and the principle of Self, of which money is the visible incarnation, are the God and Mammon of the world.[8]

The functions of the poetical faculty are two-fold; by one it creates new materials of knowledge, and power and pleasure; by the other it engenders in the mind a desire to reproduce and arrange them according to a certain rhythm and order which may be called the beautiful and the good. The cultivation of poetry is never more to be desired than at periods when, from an excess of the selfish and calculating principle, the accumulation of the materials of external life exceed the quantity of the power of assimilating them to the internal laws of human nature. The body has then become too unwieldy for that which animates it.

Poetry is indeed something divine. It is at once the centre and circumference of knowledge; it is that which comprehends all science, and that to which all science must be referred. It is at the same time the root and blossom of all other systems of thought; it is that from which all spring, and that which adorns all; and that which, if blighted, denies the fruit and the seed, and withholds from the barren world the nourishment and the succession of the scions of the tree of life. It is the perfect and consummate surface and bloom of things; it is as the odour and the colour of the rose to the texture of the elements which compose it, as the form and the splendour of unfaded beauty to the secrets of anatomy and corruption. What were Virtue, Love, Patriotism, Friendship etc.—what were the scenery of this beautiful Universe which we inhabit—what were our consolations on this side of the grave—and what were our aspirations beyond it—if Poetry did not ascend to bring light and fire from those eternal regions where the owl-winged faculty of calculation dare not ever soar? Poetry is not like reasoning, a power to be exerted according to the determination of the will. A man cannot say, "I will compose poetry." The greatest poet even cannot say it: for the mind in creation is as a fading coal which some invisible influence, like an inconstant wind, awakens to transitory brightness: this power arises from within, like the colour of a flower which fades and changes as it is developed, and the conscious portions of our natures are unprophetic either of its approach or its departure.[9] Could this influence be durable in its original purity and force, it is impossible to predict the greatness of the results; but when composition begins, inspiration is already on the decline, and the most glorious poetry that has ever been communicated to the world is probably a feeble

---

8. Matthew 6.24: "Ye cannot serve God and Mammon."
9. This passage reiterates the ancient belief that the highest poetry is "inspired" and therefore occurs independently of the intention, effort, or consciousness of the poet. Unlike earlier critics, however, Shelley attributes such poetry not to a god or a muse but to the unconscious depths of the poet's own mind.

shadow of the original conception of the poet. I appeal to the greatest Poets of the present day, whether it be not an error to assert that the finest passages of poetry are produced by labour and study. The toil and the delay recommended by critics can be justly interpreted to mean no more than a careful observation of the inspired moments, and an artificial connexion of the spaces between their suggestions by the intertexture of conventional expressions; a necessity only imposed by the limitedness of the poetical faculty itself. For Milton conceived the Paradise Lost as a whole before he executed it in portions. We have his own authority also for the Muse having "dictated" to him the "unpremeditated song,"[1] and let this be an answer to those who would allege the fifty-six various readings of the first line of the Orlando Furioso.[2] Compositions so produced are to poetry what mosaic is to painting. This instinct and intuition of the poetical faculty is still more observable in the plastic and pictorial arts: a great statue or picture grows under the power of the artist as a child in the mother's womb; and the very mind which directs the hands in formation is incapable of accounting to itself for the origin, the gradations, or the media of the process.

Poetry is the record of the best and happiest[3] moments of the happiest and best minds. We are aware of evanescent visitations of thought and feeling sometimes associated with place or person, sometimes regarding our own mind alone, and always arising unforeseen and departing unbidden, but elevating and delightful beyond all expression: so that even in the desire and the regret they leave, there cannot but be pleasure, participating as it does in the nature of its object. It is as it were the interpenetration of a diviner nature through our own; but its footsteps are like those of a wind over a sea, where the coming calm erases, and whose traces remain only as on the wrinkled sand which paves it. These and corresponding conditions of being are experienced principally by those of the most delicate sensibility and the most enlarged imagination; and the state of mind produced by them is at war with every base desire. The enthusiasm of virtue, love, patriotism, and friendship is essentially linked with these emotions; and whilst they last, self appears as what it is, an atom to a Universe. Poets are not only subject to these experiences as spirits of the most refined organization, but they can colour all that they combine with the evanescent hues of this etherial world; a word, or a trait in the representation of a scene or a passion, will touch the enchanted chord, and reanimate, in those who have ever experienced these emotions, the sleeping, the cold, the buried image of the past. Poetry thus makes immortal all that is best and most beautiful in the world; it arrests the vanishing apparitions which haunt the interlunations[4] of life, and veiling them or in language or in form sends them forth among mankind, bearing sweet news of kindred joy to those with whom their sisters abide—abide, because there is no portal of expression from the caverns of the spirit which they inhabit into the universe of things. Poetry redeems from decay the visitations of the divinity in man.

Poetry turns all things to loveliness; it exalts the beauty of that which is most beautiful, and it adds beauty to that which is most deformed; it marries

1. *Paradise Lost* 9.21–24.
2. The epic poem by the 16th-century Italian poet Ariosto, noted for his care in composition.
3. In the double sense of "most joyous" and "most

apt or felicitous in invention."
4. The dark intervals between the old and new moons.

exultation and horror, grief and pleasure, eternity and change; it subdues to union under its light yoke all irreconcilable things. It transmutes all that it touches, and every form moving within the radiance of its presence is changed by wondrous sympathy to an incarnation of the spirit which it breathes; its secret alchemy turns to potable gold[5] the poisonous waters which flow from death through life; it strips the veil of familiarity from the world, and lays bare the naked and sleeping beauty which is the spirit of its forms.

All things exist as they are perceived: at least in relation to the percipient. "The mind is its own place, and of itself can make a heaven of hell, a hell of heaven."[6] But poetry defeats the curse which binds us to be subjected to the accident of surrounding impressions. And whether it spreads its own figured curtain or withdraws life's dark veil from before the scene of things, it equally creates for us a being within our being. It makes us the inhabitants of a world to which the familiar world is a chaos. It reproduces the common universe of which we are portions and percipients, and it purges from our inward sight the film of familiarity which obscures from us the wonder of our being. It compels us to feel that which we perceive, and to imagine that which we know. It creates anew the universe after it has been annihilated in our minds by the recurrence of impressions blunted by reiteration.[7] It justifies that bold and true word of Tasso: *Non merita nome di creatore, se non Iddio ed il Poeta.*[8]

A Poet, as he is the author to others of the highest wisdom, pleasure, virtue and glory, so he ought personally to be the happiest, the best, the wisest, and the most illustrious of men. As to his glory, let Time be challenged to declare whether the fame of any other institutor of human life be comparable to that of a poet. That he is the wisest, the happiest, and the best, inasmuch as he is a poet, is equally incontrovertible: the greatest poets have been men of the most spotless virtue, of the most consummate prudence, and, if we could look into the interior of their lives, the most fortunate of men: and the exceptions, as they regard those who possessed the poetic faculty in a high yet inferior degree, will be found on consideration to confirm rather than destroy the rule. Let us for a moment stoop to the arbitration of popular breath, and usurping and uniting in our own persons the incompatible characters of accuser, witness, judge and executioner, let us decide without trial, testimony, or form that certain motives of those who are "there sitting where we dare not soar"[9] are reprehensible. Let us assume that Homer was a drunkard, that Virgil was a flatterer, that Horace was a coward, that Tasso was a madman, that Lord Bacon was a peculator, that Raphael was a libertine, that Spenser was a poet laureate.[1] It is inconsistent with this division of our subject to cite living poets, but Posterity has done ample justice to the great names now referred to. Their errors have been weighed and found to have

---

5. Alchemists aimed to produce a drinkable ("potable") form of gold that would be an elixir of life, curing all diseases.
6. Satan's speech, *Paradise Lost* 1.254–55.
7. Shelley's version of a widespread Romantic doctrine that the poetic imagination transforms the familiar into the miraculous and recreates the old world into a new world. See, e.g., Coleridge's *Biographia Literaria* on "freshness of sensation," chap. 4 (p. 474), and Carlyle's *Sartor Resartus*, "Natural Supernaturalism," book 3, chap. 8

(p. 1096).
8. "No one merits the name of Creator except God and the Poet." Quoted by Pierantonio Serassi in his *Life of Torquato Tasso* (1785).
9. *Paradise Lost* 4.829.
1. Charges that had in fact been made against these men. The use of "poet laureate" as a derogatory term was a dig at Robert Southey, who held that honor at the time Shelley was writing. "Peculator": a misappropriator of public money. Raphael is the 16th-century Italian painter.

been dust in the balance; if their sins "were as scarlet, they are now white as snow";[2] they have been washed in the blood of the mediator and the redeemer Time. Observe in what a ludicrous chaos the imputations of real or fictitious crime have been confused in the contemporary calumnies against poetry and poets;[3] consider how little is, as it appears—or appears, as it is; look to your own motives, and judge not, lest ye be judged.

Poetry, as has been said, in this respect differs from logic, that it is not subject to the controul of the active powers of the mind, and that its birth and recurrence has no necessary connexion with consciousness or will. It is presumptuous to determine that these[4] are the necessary conditions of all mental causation, when mental effects are experienced insusceptible of being referred to them. The frequent recurrence of the poetical power, it is obvious to suppose, may produce in the mind an habit of order and harmony correlative with its own nature and with its effects upon other minds. But in the intervals of inspiration, and they may be frequent without being durable, a poet becomes a man, and is abandoned to the sudden reflux of the influences under which others habitually live. But as he is more delicately organized than other men, and sensible to pain and pleasure, both his own and that of others, in a degree unknown to them, he will avoid the one and pursue the other with an ardour proportioned to this difference. And he renders himself obnoxious to calumny,[5] when he neglects to observe the circumstances under which these objects of universal pursuit and flight have disguised themselves in one another's garments.

But there is nothing necessarily evil in this error, and thus cruelty, envy, revenge, avarice, and the passions purely evil, have never formed any portion of the popular imputations on the lives of poets.

I have thought it most favourable to the cause of truth to set down these remarks according to the order in which they were suggested to my mind, by a consideration of the subject itself, instead of following that of the treatise that excited me to make them public.[6] Thus although devoid of the formality of a polemical reply; if the view they contain be just, they will be found to involve a refutation of the doctrines of the Four Ages of Poetry, so far at least as regards the first division of the subject. I can readily conjecture what should have moved the gall of the learned and intelligent author of that paper; I confess myself, like him, unwilling to be stunned by the Theseids of the hoarse Codri of the day. Bavius and Mævius[7] undoubtedly are, as they ever were, insufferable persons. But it belongs to a philosophical critic to distinguish rather than confound.

The first part of these remarks has related to Poetry in its elements and principles; and it has been shewn, as well as the narrow limits assigned them would permit, that what is called poetry, in a restricted sense, has a common source with all other forms of order and of beauty according to which the materials of human life are susceptible of being arranged, and which is poetry in an universal sense.

---

2. Isaiah 1.18.

3. Shelley alludes especially to the charges of immorality by contemporary reviewers against Lord Byron and himself.

4. I.e., consciousness or will. Shelley again proposes that some mental processes are unconscious—outside our control or awareness.

5. Exposed to slander.

6. Peacock's Four Ages of Poetry.

7. Would-be poets satirized by Virgil and Horace. "Theseids": epic poems about Theseus. Codrus (plural "Codri") was the Roman author of a long, dull Theseid attacked by Juvenal and others.

The second part[8] will have for its object an application of these principles to the present state of the cultivation of Poetry, and a defence of the attempt to idealize the modern forms of manners and opinions, and compel them into a subordination to the imaginative and creative faculty. For the literature of England, an energetic developement of which has ever preceded or accompanied a great and free developement of the national will, has arisen as it were from a new birth. In spite of the low-thoughted envy which would undervalue contemporary merit, our own will be a memorable age in intellectual achievements, and we live among such philosophers and poets as surpass beyond comparison any who have appeared since the last national struggle for civil and religious liberty.[9] The most unfailing herald, companion, and follower of the awakening of a great people to work a beneficial change in opinion or institution, is Poetry. At such periods there is an accumulation of the power of communicating and receiving intense and impassioned conceptions respecting man and nature. The persons in whom this power resides, may often, as far as regards many portions of their nature, have little apparent correspondence with that spirit of good of which they are the ministers. But even whilst they deny and abjure, they are yet compelled to serve, the Power which is seated upon the throne of their own soul. It is impossible to read the compositions of the most celebrated writers of the present day without being startled with the electric life which burns within their words. They measure the circumference and sound the depths of human nature with a comprehensive and all-penetrating spirit, and they are themselves perhaps the most sincerely astonished at its manifestations, for it is less their spirit than the spirit of the age.[1] Poets are the hierophants[2] of an unapprehended inspiration, the mirrors of the gigantic shadows which futurity casts upon the present, the words which express what they understand not; the trumpets which sing to battle, and feel not what they inspire: the influence which is moved not, but moves.[3] Poets are the unacknowledged legislators of the World.

1821   1840

8. Shelley, however, completed only the first part.
9. In the age of Milton and the English Civil Wars.
1. By attributing to the great poets and philosophers of his time a shared "spirit of the age," Shelley anticipates what later historians were to identify as "the Romantic movement."
2. Priests who are expositors of sacred mysteries.
3. Aristotle had said that God is the "Unmoved Mover" of the universe.

JOHN CLARE
1793–1864

John Clare was the nearest thing to the "natural poet" for whom primitivists had been searching ever since the mid-eighteenth century. An earlier and greater peasant poet, Robert Burns, had managed to acquire a solid liberal education. Clare, however, was born at Helpston, a Northamptonshire village, of a field laborer who was barely literate and a mother who was entirely illiterate, and he obtained only enough schooling to enable him to read and write. Although he was a sickly and fearful child, he had to work hard in the field, where he found himself composing verse "for downright pleasure in giving vent to my feelings." In 1820, publication of his *Poems Descriptive of Rural Life and Scenery* attracted critical attention, and on a trip to London, he was made much of by leading writers of the day. But his celebrity soon dimmed, and his three later books of verse were failures. Under these and other disappointments his mind gave way in 1837, and he spent almost all the rest of his life in an asylum. The place was for him a refuge as well as a confinement, for he was treated kindly, allowed to wander about the countryside, and encouraged to go on writing his verses. Some of his best achievements are the poems composed during his madness.

Clare did not, of course, write independently of literary influences, for he had studied the poetry of James Thomson, William Cowper, Burns, Milton, Wordsworth, and Coleridge. But he managed to stay true to his own experience of everyday country sights and customs and to capture in his verse the genuine idiom of rural people. His nightingale poem, written in a long-established literary tradition, has many more particulars of nature than any of those by his predecessors, and his homely mouse, in the third poem printed below, is a bit of pure rustic impressionism in a way that even Burns's moralized mouse is not (see *To a Mouse*, p. 105). Some of Clare's introspective asylum poems achieve so haunting a poignancy and are spoken in so quietly distinctive a voice that they have made the great mass of manuscripts he left at his death an exciting place of discovery for recent scholars.

Those same manuscripts are a site of contention among current textual theorists. Words are everywhere misspelled in them, standard syntax is regularly ignored, and there is almost no punctuation in the lines. In his own day, Clare was respelled, punctuated, and otherwise made presentable by his publisher, John Taylor (who did the same for John Keats, another of his poets who took a casual view of such matters). Modern scholars, eager to recover exactly what Clare wrote—in effect, to free him from the impositions and constraints of well-intentioned nineteenth-century editors— are restoring the idiosyncrasies but, in the process, are constructing a poet who is so full of what we would normally call mistakes as to be, for all practical purposes, inaccessible to the general reader. (For example, the manuscripts have "were" for "where," "your" for "you're," "anker" for "hanker," "hugh" for "huge.") The texts printed below, which are presented as "reading" versions of Clare's own words, are the product of a principled modernization by the editors of this anthology. They are based, where the materials are available, on authoritative manuscript versions recovered and now made standard by Eric Robinson and his associates in a succession of editions published by Oxford University Press.

The Nightingale's Nest

Up this green woodland ride° let's softly rove,   *riding path*
And list° the nightingale—she dwelleth here.   *listen to*
Hush! let the wood gate softly clap, for fear
The noise may drive her from her home of love;
5 For here I've heard her many a merry year—
At morn and eve, nay, all the livelong day,
As though she lived on song. This very spot,
Just where that old man's beard° all wildly trails   *Spanish moss*
Rude arbours o'er the road and stops the way—
10 And where that child its blue-bell flowers hath got,
Laughing and creeping through the mossy rails°—   *fence rails*
There have I hunted like a very boy,
Creeping on hands and knees through matted thorns
To find her nest and see her feed her young.

15 And vainly did I many hours employ:
   All seemed as hidden as a thought unborn.
   And where these crimping° fern leaves ramp° among   *curling/shoot up*
   The hazel's under-boughs, I've nestled down
   And watched her while she sung; and her renown
20 Hath made me marvel that so famed a bird[1]
   Should have no better dress than russet brown.
   Her wings would tremble in her ecstasy,
   And feathers stand on end, as 'twere with joy,
   And mouth wide open to release her heart
25 Of its out-sobbing songs. The happiest part
   Of summer's fame she shared, for so to me
   Did happy fancies shapen her employ;[2]
   But if I touched a bush or scarcely stirred,
   All in a moment stopt. I watched in vain:
30 The timid bird had left the hazel bush,
   And at a distance hid to sing again.
   Lost in a wilderness of listening leaves,
   Rich ecstasy would pour its luscious strain,
   Till envy spurred the emulating thrush
35 To start less wild and scarce inferior songs;
   For cares with him for half the year remain,
   To damp the ardour of his speckled breast,
   While nightingales to summer's life belongs,
   And naked trees and winter's nipping wrongs
40 Are strangers to her music and her rest.
   Her joys are evergreen, her world is wide—
   Hark! there she is as usual—let's be hush—
   For in this black-thorn clump, if rightly guessed,
   Her curious house is hidden. Part aside
45 These hazel branches in a gentle way,
   And stoop right cautious 'neath the rustling boughs,
   For we will have another search to-day,
   And hunt this fern-strewn thorn clump round and round;
   And where this seeded wood grass idly bows,
50 We'll wade right through, it is a likely nook:
   In such like spots, and often on the ground,
   They'll build where rude boys never think to look—
   Aye, as I live! her secret nest is here,
   Upon this whitethorn stulp!° I've searched about   *stump*
55 For hours in vain. There! put that bramble by—
   Nay, trample on its branches and get near.
   How subtle is the bird! she started out
   And raised a plaintive note of danger nigh,
   Ere we were past the brambles; and now, near
60 Her nest, she sudden stops—as choking fear
   That might betray her home. So even now

---

1. The nightingale had been celebrated by, among
others, Chaucer, Spenser, Shakespeare, Milton,
and, closer to Clare's own time, William Cowper,
Charlotte Smith, Mary Robinson, Coleridge,
Wordsworth, and Keats. In lines 22, 24–25, and

33, Clare echoes lines 57–58 of Keats's *Ode to a
Nightingale*.
2. Give shape to her (the nightingale's) regular
activities.

We'll leave it as we found it: safety's guard
Of pathless solitude shall keep it still.
See, there she's sitting on the old oak bough,
65 Mute in her fears; our presence doth retard
Her joys, and doubt turns all her rapture chill.

Sing on, sweet bird! may no worse hap befall
Thy visions, than the fear that now deceives.
We will not plunder music of its dower,
70 Nor turn this spot of happiness to thrall;°   *misery*
For melody seems hid in every flower,
That blossoms near thy home. These harebells all
Seems bowing with the beautiful in song;
And gaping cuckoo° with its spotted leaves   *a spring flower*
75 Seems blushing of the singing it has heard.
How curious is the nest; no other bird
Uses such loose materials, or weaves
Their dwellings in such spots: dead oaken leaves
Are placed without, and velvet moss within,
80 And little scraps of grass, and, scant and spare,
Of what seems scarce materials, down and hair;
For from man's haunts she seemeth nought to win.
Yet nature is the builder and contrives
Homes for her children's comfort even here;
85 Where solitude's disciples spend their lives
Unseen save when a wanderer passes near
That loves such pleasant places. Deep adown,
The nest is made an hermit's mossy cell.
Snug lie her curious eggs, in number five,
90 Of deadened green, or rather olive brown;
And the old prickly thorn-bush guards them well.
And here we'll leave them, still unknown to wrong,
As the old woodland's legacy of song.

1825–30   1835

Pastoral Poesy

True poesy is not in words,
    But images that thoughts express,
By which the simplest hearts are stirred
    To elevated happiness.

5   Mere books would be but useless things
        Where none had taste or mind to read,
    Like unknown lands where beauty springs
        And none are there to heed.

    But poesy is a language meet,
10   And fields are every one's employ;°   *concern*
    The wild flower 'neath the shepherd's feet
        Looks up and gives him joy;

A language that is ever green,
 That feelings unto all impart,
15 As hawthorn blossoms, soon as seen,
 Give May to every heart.

An image to the mind is brought,
 Where happiness enjoys
An easy thoughtlessness of thought
20 And meets excess of joys.

And such is poesy; its power
 May varied lights employ,
Yet to all minds it gives the dower
 Of self-creating joy.

25 And whether it be hill or moor,
 I feel where'er I go
A silence that discourses more
 That any tongue can do.

Unruffled quietness hath made
30 A peace in every place,
And woods are resting in their shade
 Of social loneliness.

The storm, from which the shepherd turns
 To pull his beaver° down,   *beaver hat*
35 While he upon the heath sojourns,
 Which autumn pleaches° brown,   *bleaches*

Is music, ay, and more indeed
 To those of musing mind
Who through the yellow woods proceed
40 And listen to the wind.

The poet in his fitful glee
 And fancy's many moods
Meets it as some strange melody,
 A poem of the woods,

45 And now a harp that flings around
 The music of the wind;
The poet often hears the sound
 When beauty fills the mind.

So would I my own mind employ,
50 And my own heart impress,
That poesy's self's a dwelling joy
 Of humble quietness.

1824–32   1935

Mouse's Nest

I found a ball of grass among the hay
And progged° it as I passed and went away;   *prodded*
And when I looked I fancied something stirred,
And turned again and hoped to catch the bird—
5   When out an old mouse bolted in the wheats
With all her young ones hanging at her teats;
She looked so odd and so grotesque to me,
I ran and wondered what the thing could be,
And pushed the knapweed[1] bunches where I stood;

10   Then the mouse hurried from the craking° brood.   *squawking*
The young ones squeaked, and as I went away
She found her nest again among the hay.
The water o'er the pebbles scarce could run
And broad old cesspools[2] glittered in the sun.

1835–37   1935

A Vision

I

I lost the love of heaven above;
I spurn'd the lust of earth below;
I felt the sweets of fancied love,—
And hell itself my only foe.

2

5   I lost earth's joys but felt the glow
Of heaven's flame abound in me:
Till loveliness and I did grow
The bard of immortality.

3

I loved, but woman fell away;
10   I hid me from her faded fame:
I snatch'd the sun's eternal ray,—
And wrote till earth was but a name.

4

In every language upon earth,
On every shore, o'er every sea,

---

1. A plant with knobs of purple flowers.   2. Low spots where water has collected.

15   I gave my name immortal birth,
      And kept my spirit with the free.

Aug. 2, 1844   1924

I Am

1

I am—yet what I am, none cares or knows;
    My friends forsake me like a memory lost:—
I am the self-consumer of my woes;—
    They rise and vanish in oblivion's host,
5 Like shadows in love's frenzied stifled throes:—
And yet I am, and live—like vapours tossed

2

Into the nothingness of scorn and noise,—
    Into the living sea of waking dreams,
Where there is neither sense of life or joys,
10   But the vast shipwreck of my life's esteems;
Even the dearest that I love the best
Are strange—nay, rather, stranger than the rest.

3

I long for scenes where man hath never trod,
    A place where woman never smiled or wept,
15 There to abide with my Creator, God,
    And sleep as I in childhood sweetly slept,
Untroubling and untroubled where I lie,
The grass below—above, the vaulted sky.

1842–46   1848

An Invite to Eternity

1

Wilt thou go with me, sweet maid,
Say maiden, wilt thou go with me
Through the valley depths of shade,
Of night and dark obscurity,
5 Where the path hath lost its way,
Where the sun forgets the day,
Where there's nor life nor light to see,
Sweet maiden, wilt thou go with me?

2

Where stones will turn to flooding streams,
10 Where plains will rise like ocean waves,
Where life will fade like visioned dreams

And mountains darken into caves,
Say maiden, wilt thou go with me
Through this sad non-identity,
15   Where parents live and are forgot
And sisters live and know us not?

3

Say maiden, wilt thou go with me
In this strange death of life to be,
To live in death and be the same
20   Without this life, or home, or name,
At once to be and not to be,
That was and is not—yet to see
Things pass like shadows—and the sky
Above, below, around us lie?

4

25   The land of shadows wilt thou trace
And look—nor know each other's face,
The present mixed with reasons gone
And past and present all as one?
Say maiden, can thy life be led
30   To join the living with the dead?
Then trace thy footsteps on with me—
We're wed to one eternity.

1847   1848

Clock a Clay[1]

1

In the cowslip's peeps I lie,[2]
Hidden from the buzzing fly,
While green grass beneath me lies,
Pearled wi' dew like fishes' eyes;
5   Here I lie, a Clock a Clay,
Waiting for the time o' day.

2

While grassy forests quake surprise,
And the wild wind sobs and sighs,
My gold home rocks as like to fall
10   On its pillars green and tall;
When the pattering rain drives by
Clock a Clay keeps warm and dry.

---

1. The ladybird, or ladybug. The sixth and last lines allude to the children's game of telling the hour by the number of taps it takes to make the ladybird fly away home.
2. Cf. the opening lines of Ariel's song in act 5 of Shakespeare's *Tempest:* "Where the bee sucks, there suck I: / In a cowslip's bell I lie." "Peeps": i.e., pips—single blossoms of flowers growing in a cluster. "Cowslip": a yellow primrose.

3

Day by day and night by night,
All the week I hide from sight;
15   In the cowslip's peeps I lie,
In rain and dew still warm and dry;
Day and night and night and day,
Red black-spotted Clock a Clay.

4

My home it shakes in wind and showers,
20   Pale green pillar topped wi' flowers,
Bending at the wild wind's breath,
Till I touch the grass beneath;
Here still I live, lone Clock a Clay,
Watching for the time of day.

ca. 1848   1873

The Peasant Poet

He loved the brook's soft sound,
The swallow swimming by;
He loved the daisy-covered ground,
The cloud-bedappled sky.
5   To him the dismal storm appeared
The very voice of God,
And where the evening rack° was reared   mass of clouds
Stood Moses with his rod.
And everything his eyes surveyed,
10   The insects i' the brake,
Were creatures God Almighty made—
He loved them for His sake:
A silent man in life's affairs,
A thinker from a boy,
15   A peasant in his daily cares—
The poet in his joy.

1842–64   1920

Song

I hid my love when young while I
Couldn't bear the buzzing of a fly;
I hid my love to my despite
Till I could not bear to look at light.
5   I dare not gaze upon her face
But left her memory in each place;
Where'er I saw a wild flower lie
I kissed and bade my love goodbye.

I met her in the greenest dells,
10   Where dewdrops pearl the wood bluebells;

The lost breeze kissed her bright blue eye,
The bee kissed and went singing by.
A sunbeam found a passage there,
A gold chain round her neck so fair;
As secret as the wild bee's song
She lay there all the summer long.

I hid my love in field and town
Till e'en the breeze would knock me down.
The bees seemed singing ballads o'er
The fly's buzz turned a lion's roar;
And even silence found a tongue
To haunt me all the summer long:
The riddle nature could not prove
Was nothing else but secret love.

1842–64   1920

Song

I peeled bits o' straws and I got switches too
From the grey peeling willow as idlers do,
And I switched at the flies as I sat all alone
Till my flesh, blood, and marrow wasted to dry bone.
My illness was love, though I knew not the smart,
But the beauty o' love was the blood o' my heart.

Crowded places, I shunned them as noises too rude
And flew to the silence of sweet solitude,
Where the flower in green darkness buds, blossoms, and fades,
Unseen of a' shepherds and flower-loving maids.
The hermit bees find them but once and away;
There I'll bury alive and in silence decay.

I looked on the eyes o' fair woman too long,
Till silence and shame stole the use o' my tongue;
When I tried to speak to her I'd nothing to say,
So I turned myself round, and she wandered away.
When she got too far off—why, I'd something to tell,
So I sent sighs behind her and talked to mysel'.

Willow switches I broke, and I peeled bits o' straws,
Ever lonely in crowds, in nature's own laws—
My ballroom the pasture, my music the bees,
My drink was the fountain, my church the tall trees.
Who ever would love or be tied to a wife
When it makes a man mad a' the days o' his life?

1842–64   1920

FELICIA DOROTHEA HEMANS
1793–1835

Born in Liverpool and brought up in Wales, Felicia Hemans published her first two volumes—*Poems* and *England and Spain, or Valour and Patriotism*—when she was fifteen. She followed these four years later with *The Domestic Affections and Other Poems* (1812) and from 1816 on into the 1830s produced new books of poetry almost annually: short sentimental lyrics, tales and "historic scenes," translations, songs for music, sketches of women, hymns for children. She also published literary criticism in the magazines and wrote three plays. Her work was widely read, anthologized, memorized, and set to music throughout the nineteenth century and was especially popular and influential in the United States, where the first of many collected editions of her poems appeared in 1825. When she died, she was eulogized by many poets, including William Wordsworth, Letitia Landon, and Elizabeth Barrett—a sign of the high regard in which she was held by her contemporaries.

A tablet erected by her brothers in the cathedral of St. Asaph, in north Wales, reads in part, "In memory of Felicia Hemans, whose character is best pourtrayed in her writings." But there are several characters in her poems, and some of them seem not entirely compatible with some of the others. She is frequently thought of as the poet (in the nineteenth century as "the poetess") of domestic affections, at the center of a cult of domesticity in which women are subservient to men, who carry on the important business of life, and patriarchy is the acknowledged if not always accepted standard. Among her most popular pieces in this vein, *Evening Prayer, at a Girls' School* depicts the happy ignorance of schoolgirls whose enjoyment of life will end when they reach womanhood, and *Indian Woman's Death-Song* is the lament of a Native American woman whose husband has abandoned her, sung as she plunges in her canoe over a cataract to suicide with an infant in her arms.

Many of Hemans's longer narratives, by contrast, recount the exploits of women warriors who, to avenge personal, family, or national injustice or insult, destroy enemies in a manner not conventionally associated with female behavior. In *The Widow of Crescentius*, Stephania stalks and poisons the German emperor Otho, the murderer of her husband; in *The Wife of Asdrubal*, a mother publicly kills her own children and herself to show contempt for her husband, a betrayer of the Carthaginians whom he governed; the heroine of *The Bride of the Greek Isle*, boarding the ship of the pirates who have killed her husband, annihilates them (and herself) in a conflagration rivaling the monumental explosion described in *Casabianca*. Among the numerous themes of her work, patriotism and military action recur frequently; there may be a biographical basis for these motifs, given that her two oldest brothers distinguished themselves in the Peninsular War and her military husband (who deserted her and their five sons in 1818) had also served in Spain. But some of her most famous patriotic and military poems are now being viewed as critiques of the virtues and ideologies they had been thought by earlier readers to inculcate. *The Homes of England*, for example, has been read as both asserting and undermining the idea that all homes are equal, ancestral estates and cottages alike; and in *Casabianca*, the boy's automatic steadfastness has been interpreted as empty obedience rather than admirable loyalty.

Hemans was the highest paid writer in *Blackwood's* during her day. Her books sold more copies than those of any other contemporary poet except Byron and Walter Scott. She was a shrewd calculator of the literary marketplace and a genius in her negotiations with publishers (which she carried on entirely through the mails). Her self-abasing women of the domestic affections and her scimitar-wielding superwomen of the revenge narratives exist side by side throughout her works. These and other seeming dissonances clearly enhanced the strong appeal of her poems to a wide range of readers, men as well as women.

England's Dead

Son of the ocean isle!
Where sleep your mighty dead?
Show me what high and stately pile
Is rear'd o'er Glory's bed.

5   Go, stranger! track the deep,
Free, free the white sail spread!
Wave may not foam, nor wild wind sweep,
Where rest not England's dead.

On Egypt's burning plains,
10   By the pyramid o'ersway'd,
With fearful power the noonday reigns,
And the palm trees yield no shade.[1]

But let the angry sun
From heaven look fiercely red,
15   Unfelt by those whose task is done!—
There slumber England's dead.

The hurricane hath might
Along the Indian shore,
And far by Ganges' banks at night,
20   Is heard the tiger's roar.

But let the sound roll on!
It hath no tone of dread,
For those that from their toils are gone;—
There slumber England's dead.

25   Loud rush the torrent floods
The western wilds among,
And free, in green Columbia's woods,
The hunter's bow is strung.

But let the floods rush on!
30   Let the arrow's flight be sped!
Why should *they* reck whose task is done?—
There slumber England's dead!

The mountain storms rise high
In the snowy Pyrenees,
35   And toss the pine boughs through the sky,
Like rose leaves on the breeze.

1. English forces defeated the French at Alexandria in the spring of 1801. The rest of the references—to 18th- and early-19th-century battles in India (lines 17–24), America (lines 25–32), Spain (lines 33–40), and on the sea (lines 41–48)—are more general.

But let the storm rage on!
Let the fresh wreaths be shed!
For the Roncesvalles' field[2] is won,—
40 *There* slumber England's dead.

On the frozen deep's repose
'Tis a dark and dreadful hour,
When round the ship the ice-fields close,
And the northern night clouds lower.

45 But let the ice drift on!
Let the cold-blue desert spread!
Their course with mast and flag is done,—
Even there sleep England's dead.

The warlike of the isles,
50 The men of field and wave!
Are not the rocks their funeral piles,
The seas and shores their grave?

Go, stranger! track the deep,
Free, free the white sail spread!
55 Wave may not foam, nor wild wind sweep,
Where rest not England's dead.

          1822

The Landing of the Pilgrim Fathers in New England

> Look now abroad—another race has fill'd
> Those populous borders—wide the wood recedes,
> And towns shoot up, and fertile realms are till'd;
> The land is full of harvests and green meads.
>   —BRYANT[1]

The breaking waves dash'd high
 On a stern and rock-bound coast,
And the woods against a stormy sky
 Their giant branches toss'd;

5 And the heavy night hung dark,
 The hills and waters o'er,
When a band of exiles moor'd their bark
 On the wild New England shore.

Not as the conqueror comes,
10 They, the true-hearted, came;

---

2. Roncesvalles, the mountain pass in the Pyrenees between France and Spain, was a scene of action during the Peninsular War (1808–14).

1. William Cullen Bryant, *The Ages* (1821), lines 280–83.

Not with the roll of the stirring drums,
  And the trumpet that sings of fame;

Not as the flying come,
  In silence and in fear;—
15 They shook the depths of the desert gloom
  With their hymns of lofty cheer.

Amidst the storm they sang,
  And the stars heard and the sea;
And the sounding aisles of the dim woods rang
20   To the anthem of the free!

The ocean eagle soar'd
  From his nest by the white wave's foam;
And the rocking pines of the forest roar'd—
  This was their welcome home!

25 There were men with hoary hair
  Amidst that pilgrim band;—
Why had *they* come to wither there,
  Away from their childhood's land?

There was woman's fearless eye,
30   Lit by her deep love's truth;
There was manhood's brow serenely high,
  And the fiery heart of youth.

What sought they thus afar?
  Bright jewels of the mine?
35 The wealth of seas, the spoils of war?—
  They sought a faith's pure shrine!

Aye, call it holy ground,
  The soil where first they trod.
They have left unstain'd what there they found—
40   Freedom to worship God.

1826

Casabianca[1]

The boy stood on the burning deck
  Whence all but he had fled;
The flame that lit the battle's wreck
  Shone round him o'er the dead.

1. Young Casabianca, a boy about thirteen years old, son to the Admiral of the *Orient*, remained at his post (in the Battle of the Nile) after the ship had taken fire, and all the guns had been abandoned; and perished in the explosion of the vessel, when the flames had reached the powder [Hemans's note]. The Battle of the Nile, in which Nelson captured and destroyed the French fleet in Aboukir Bay, took place on August 1, 1798.

5 Yet beautiful and bright he stood,
    As born to rule the storm;
A creature of heroic blood,
    A proud, though childlike form.

The flames roll'd on—he would not go
10   Without his father's word;
That father, faint in death below,
    His voice no longer heard.

He call'd aloud:—"Say, Father, say
    If yet my task is done?"
15 He knew not that the chieftain lay
    Unconscious of his son.

"Speak, Father!" once again he cried,
    "If I may yet be gone!"
And but the booming shots replied,
20   And fast the flames roll'd on.

Upon his brow he felt their breath,
    And in his waving hair,
And look'd from that lone post of death
    In still, yet brave despair.

25 And shouted but once more aloud,
    "My Father! must I stay?"
While o'er him fast, through sail and shroud,
    The wreathing fires made way.

They wrapt the ship in splendour wild,
30   They caught the flag on high,
And stream'd above the gallant child,
    Like banners in the sky.

There came a burst of thunder sound—
    The boy—oh! where was he?
35 Ask of the winds that far around
    With fragments strew'd the sea!—

With mast, and helm, and pennon fair,
    That well had borne their part,
But the noblest thing which perish'd there
40   Was that young faithful heart!

1826

The Homes of England

Where's the coward that would not dare
To fight for such a land?
—*Marmion*[1]

The stately Homes of England,
How beautiful they stand!
Amidst their tall ancestral trees,
O'er all the pleasant land.
5　The deer across their greensward bound
Through shade and sunny gleam,
And the swan glides past them with the sound
Of some rejoicing stream.

The merry Homes of England!
10　Around their hearths by night,
What gladsome looks of household love
Meet in the ruddy light!
There woman's voice flows forth in song,
Or childhood's tale is told,
15　Or lips move tunefully along
Some glorious page of old.

The blessed Homes of England!
How softly on their bowers
Is laid the holy quietness
20　That breathes from Sabbath-hours!
Solemn, yet sweet, the church-bell's chime
Floats through their woods at morn;
All other sounds, in that still time,
Of breeze and leaf are born.

25　The Cottage Homes of England!
By thousands on her plains,
They are smiling o'er the silvery brooks,
And round the hamlet-fanes.°　　　　　　　*village churches*
Through glowing orchards forth they peep,
30　Each from its nook of leaves,
And fearless there the lowly sleep,
As the bird beneath their eaves.

The free, fair Homes of England!
Long, long, in hut and hall,
35　May hearts of native proof be rear'd
To guard each hallow'd wall!
And green for ever be the groves,

---

1. From Sir Walter Scott's long poem *Marmion*
(1808), 4.633–34, a tale of betrayal and bloody
conflict between the English and the Scots. When
she first published the poem, in *Blackwood's*, April
1827, Hemans used as epigraph a passage from the
work of another Scottish author, Joanna Baillie's
Ethwald: A Tragedy, part 2 (1802), 1.2.76–82.

And bright the flowery sod,
Where first the child's glad spirit loves
40   Its country and its God!

1827

A Spirit's Return

"This is to be a mortal,
And seek the things beyond mortality!"
—MANFRED[1]

Thy voice prevails—dear friend, my gentle friend!
This long-shut heart for thee shall be unsealed,
And though thy soft eye mournfully will bend
Over the troubled stream, yet once revealed
5   Shall its freed waters flow; then rocks must close
For evermore, above their dark repose.

Come while the gorgeous mysteries of the sky
Fused in the crimson sea of sunset lie;
Come to the woods, where all strange wandering sound
10   Is mingled into harmony profound;
Where the leaves thrill with spirit, while the wind
Fills with a viewless being, unconfined,
The trembling reeds and fountains—our own dell,
With its green dimness and Aeolian° breath,   *wind-blown*
15   Shall suit th' unveiling of dark records well—
Hear me in tenderness and silent faith!

Thou knew'st me not in life's fresh vernal morn—
I would thou hadst!—for then my heart on thine
Had poured a worthier love; now, all o'erworn
20   By its deep thirst for something too divine,
It hath but fitful music to bestow,
Echoes of harp-strings broken long ago.

Yet even in youth companionless I stood,
As a lone forest-bird 'midst ocean's foam;
25   For me the silver cords of brotherhood
Were early loosed; the voices from my home
Passed one by one, and melody and mirth
Left me a dreamer by a silent hearth.

But, with the fulness of a heart that burned
30   For the deep sympathies of mind, I turned
From that unanswering spot, and fondly sought

1. A remark concerning Manfred's convulsion at the moment the Phantom of his beloved Astarte disappears (*Manfred* 2.4.158–59; see p. 610). Hemans's poem can be read as commentary on Byron's play, Percy Shelley's *Alastor*, and Keats's *Endymion* (see the note to lines 216–17 below), all of which depict a protagonist's problems in communicating with an otherworldly lover.

In all wild scenes with thrilling murmurs fraught,
In every still small voice and sound of power,
And flute-note of the wind through cave and bower,
35 A perilous delight!—for then first woke
My life's lone passion, the mysterious quest
Of secret knowledge; and each tone that broke
From the wood-arches or the fountain's breast,
Making my quick soul vibrate as a lyre,
40 But ministered to that strange inborn fire.
'Midst the bright silence of the mountain dells,
In noon-tide hours or golden summer-eves,
My thoughts have burst forth as a gale that swells
Into a rushing blast, and from the leaves
45 Shakes out response. O thou rich world unseen!
Thou curtained realm of spirits!—thus my cry
Hath troubled air and silence—dost thou lie
Spread all around, yet by some filmy screen
Shut from us ever? The resounding woods,
50 Do their depths teem with marvels?—and the floods,
And the pure fountains, leading secret veins
Of quenchless melody through rock and hill,
Have they bright dwellers?—are their lone domains
Peopled with beauty, which may never still
55 *Our* weary thirst of soul?—Cold, weak and cold,
Is earth's vain language, piercing not one fold
Of our deep being! Oh, for gifts more high!
For a seer's glance to rend mortality!
For a charmed rod, to call from each dark shrine
60 The oracles divine!

I woke from those high fantasies, to know
My kindred with the earth—I woke to love:
O gentle friend! to love in doubt and woe,
Shutting the heart the worshipped name above,
65 Is to love deeply—and *my* spirit's dower
Was a sad gift, a melancholy power
Of so adoring—with a buried care,
And with the o'erflowing of a voiceless prayer,
And with a deepening dream, that day by day,
70 In the still shadow of its lonely sway,
Folded me closer, till the world held nought
Save the *one* being to my centred thought.

There was no music but his voice to hear,
No joy but such as with *his* step drew near;
75 Light was but where he looked—life where he moved;
Silently, fervently, thus, thus I loved.
Oh! but such love is fearful!—and I knew
Its gathering doom:—the soul's prophetic sight
Even then unfolded in my breast, and threw
80 O'er all things round a full, strong, vivid light,
Too sorrowfully clear!—an undertone

Was given to Nature's harp, for me alone
Whispering of grief.—Of grief?—be strong, awake,
Hath not thy love been victory, O, my soul?
85 Hath not its conflict won a voice to shake
Death's fastnesses?—a magic to control
Worlds far removed?—from o'er the grave to thee
Love hath made answer; and *thy* tale should be
Sung like a lay of triumph!—Now return,
90 And take thy treasure from its bosomed urn,
And lift it once to light!

                  In fear, in pain,
I said I loved—but yet a heavenly strain
Of sweetness floated down the tearful stream,
A joy flashed through the trouble of my dream!
95 I knew myself beloved!—we breathed no vow,
No mingling visions might our fate allow,
As unto happy hearts; but still and deep,
Like a rich jewel gleaming in a grave,
Like golden sand in some dark river's wave,
100 So did my soul that costly knowledge keep
So jealously!—a thing o'er which to shed,
When stars alone beheld the drooping head,
Lone tears! yet ofttimes burdened with the excess
Of our strange nature's quivering happiness.

105 But, oh! sweet friend! we dream not of love's might
Till death has robed with soft and solemn light
The image we enshrine!—Before *that* hour,
We have but glimpses of the o'ermastering power
Within us laid!—*then* doth the spirit-flame
110 With sword-like lightning rend its mortal frame;
The wings of that which pants to follow fast
Shake their clay-bars, as with a prisoned blast—
The sea is in our souls!

                  He died—*he* died
On whom my lone devotedness was cast!
115 I might not keep one vigil by his side,
I, whose wrung heart watched with him to the last!
I might not once his fainting head sustain,
Nor bathe his parched lips in the hour of pain,
Nor say to him, "Farewell!"—He passed away—
120 Oh! had *my* love been there, its conquering sway
Had won him back from death! but thus removed,
Borne o'er the abyss no sounding-line hath proved,
Joined with the unknown, the viewless—he became
Unto my thoughts another, yet the same—
125 Changed—hallowed—glorified!—and his low grave
Seemed a bright mournful altar—mine, all mine:—
Brother and friend soon left me *that* sole shrine,

The birthright of the faithful!—*their* world's wave
Soon swept them from its brink.—Oh! deem thou not
130 That on the sad and consecrated spot
My soul grew weak!—I tell thee that a power
There kindled heart and lip—a fiery shower
My words were made—a might was given to prayer,
And a strong grasp to passionate despair,
135 And a dead triumph!—Know'st thou what I sought?
For what high boon my struggling spirit wrought?—
Communion with the dead!—I sent a cry,
Through the veiled empires of eternity,
A voice to cleave them! By the mournful truth,
140 By the lost promise of my blighted youth,
By the strong chain a mighty love can bind
On the beloved, the spell of mind o'er mind;
By words, which in themselves are magic high,
Armed and inspired, and winged with agony;
145 By tears, which comfort not, but burn, and seem
To bear the heart's blood in their passion stream;
I summoned, I adjured!—with quickened sense,
With the keen vigil of a life intense,
I watched, an answer from the winds to wring,
150 I listened, if perchance the stream might bring
Token from worlds afar: I taught *one* sound
Unto a thousand echoes—one profound
Imploring accent to the tomb, the sky—
One prayer to night—"Awake, appear, reply!"
155 Hast thou been told that from the viewless bourne,
The dark way never hath allowed return?
That all, which tears can move, with life is fled—
That earthly love is powerless on the dead?
Believe it not!—there is a large lone star
160 Now burning o'er yon western hill afar,
And under its clear light there lies a spot
Which well might utter forth—Believe it not!

I sat beneath that planet—I had wept
My woe to stillness, every night-wind slept;
165 A hush was on the hills; the very streams
Went by like clouds, or noiseless founts in dreams,
And the dark tree o'ershadowing me that hour,
Stood motionless, even as the gray church-tower
Whereon I gazed unconsciously:—there came
170 A low sound, like the tremor of a flame,
Or like the light quick shiver of a wing,
Flitting through twilight woods, across the air;
And I looked up!—Oh! for strong words to bring
Conviction o'er thy thought!—Before me there,
175 He, the departed, stood!—Ay, face to face,
So near, and yet how far!—his form, his mien,
Gave to remembrance back each burning trace

Within:—Yet something awfully serene,
Pure, sculpture-like, on the pale brow, that wore
180 Of the once-beating heart no token more;
And stillness on the lip—and o'er the hair
A gleam, that trembled through the breathless air;
And an unfathomed calm, that seemed to lie
In the grave sweetness of the illumined eye;
185 Told of the gulfs between our beings set,
And, as that unsheathed spirit-glance I met,
Made my soul faint:—with *fear?* Oh! *not* with fear!
With the sick feeling that in *his* far sphere
My love could be as nothing! But he spoke—
190 How shall I tell thee of the startling thrill
In that low voice, whose breezy tones could fill
My bosom's infinite? O, friend! I woke
Then first to heavenly life!—Soft, solemn, clear
Breathed the mysterious accents on mine ear,
195 Yet strangely seemed as if the while they rose
From depths of distance, o'er the wide repose
Of slumbering waters wafted, or the dells
Of mountains, hollow with sweet-echo cells;
But, as they murmured on, the mortal chill
200 Passed from me, like a mist before the morn,
And, to that glorious intercourse upborne
By slow degrees, a calm, divinely still,
Possessed my frame: I sought that lighted eye—
From its intense and searching purity
205 I drank in *soul!*—I questioned of the dead—
Of the hushed, starry shores their footsteps tread,
And I was answered:—if remembrance there,
With dreamy whispers fill the immortal air;
If thought, here piled from many a jewel-heap,
210 Be treasure in that pensive land to keep;
If love, o'ersweeping change, and blight, and blast
Find *there* the music of his home at last;
I asked, and I was answered:—Full and high
Was that communion with eternity,
215 Too rich for aught so fleeting!—Like a knell
Swept o'er my sense its closing words, "Farewell,
On earth we meet no more!"[2]—and all was gone—
The pale bright settled brow—the thrilling tone,
The still and shining eye! and never more
220 May twilight gloom or midnight hush restore
That radiant guest! One full-fraught hour of heaven,
To earthly passion's wild implorings given,
Was made my own—the ethereal fire hath shivered
The fragile censer[3] in whose mould it quivered

---

2. This is the answer to Manfred's question to the Phantom of Astarte (2.4.154): "Say, shall we meet again?" Astarte vanishes, and Nemesis says, "She's gone, and will not be recall'd." Hemans's lines also echo Endymion's renunciation of his dream god-dess at a crucial moment in Keats's *Endymion* (4.657–59): "The hour may come / When we shall meet in pure elysium. / On earth I may not love thee."
3. Container in which incense is burned.

225 Brightly, consumingly! What now is left?
A faded world, of glory's hues bereft—
A void, a chain!—I dwell 'midst throngs, apart,
In the cold silence of the stranger's heart;
A fixed, immortal shadow stands between
230 My spirit and life's fast receding scene;
A gift hath severed me from human ties,
A power is gone from all earth's melodies,
Which never may return: their chords are broken,
The music of another land hath spoken—
235 No after-sound is sweet!—this weary thirst!
And I have heard celestial fountains burst!—
What *here* shall quench it?
                                    Dost thou not rejoice,
When the spring sends forth an awakening voice
Through the young woods?—Thou dost!—And in the birth
240 Of early leaves, and flowers, and songs of mirth,
Thousands, like thee, find gladness!—Couldst thou know
How every breeze then summons *me* to go!
How all the light of love and beauty shed
By those rich hours, but woos me to the dead!
245 The *only* beautiful that change no more—
The only loved!—the dwellers on the shore
Of spring fulfilled!—The dead!—*whom* call we so?
They that breathe purer air, that feel, that know
Things wrapt from us!—Away!—within me pent,
250 That which is barred from its own element
Still droops or struggles!—But the day *will* come—
Over the deep the free bird finds its home,
And the stream lingers 'midst the rocks, yet greets
The sea at last; and the winged flower-seed meets
255 A soil to rest in:—shall not *I*, too, be,
My spirit-love! upborne to dwell with thee?
Yes! by the power whose conquering anguish stirred
The tomb, whose cry beyond the stars was heard,
Whose agony of triumph won thee back
260 Through the dim pass no mortal step may track,
Yet shall we meet!—that glimpse of joy divine
Proved thee for ever and for ever mine!

1830

JOHN KEATS
1795–1821

John Keats's father was head stableman at a London livery stable; he married his
employer's daughter and inherited the business. The poet's mother, by all reports,

was a strongly sensuous woman and a rather casual but affectionate rearer of her five children—John (the first born), his three brothers (one of whom died in infancy), and a sister. Keats was sent to the Reverend John Clarke's private school at Enfield, where he was a noisy, high-spirited boy; despite his small stature (when full-grown, he was barely over five feet in height), he distinguished himself in sports and fistfights. Here he had the good fortune to have as a mentor Charles Cowden Clarke, son of the headmaster, who later became a writer and editor; he encouraged Keats's passion for reading and, both at school and in the course of their later friendship, introduced him to Spenser and other poets, to music, and to the theater.

When Keats was eight his father was killed by a fall from a horse, and when he was fourteen his mother died of tuberculosis. Although the livery stable had prospered, and £8,000 had been left in trust to the children by Keats's grandmother, the estate remained tied up in the law courts for all of Keats's lifetime. The children's guardian, Richard Abbey, an unimaginative and practical-minded businessman, took Keats out of school at the age of fifteen and bound him apprentice to Thomas Hammond, a surgeon and apothecary at Edmonton. In 1815 Keats carried on his medical studies at Guy's Hospital, London, and the next year qualified to practice as an apothecary-surgeon—but almost immediately, over his guardian's protests, he abandoned medicine for poetry.

This decision was influenced by Keats's friendship with Leigh Hunt, then editor of the *Examiner* and a leading political radical, poet, and prolific writer of criticism and periodical essays. Hunt, the first successful author of Keats's acquaintance, added his enthusiastic encouragement of Keats's poetic efforts to that of Clarke. More important, he introduced him to writers greater than Hunt himself—William Hazlitt, Charles Lamb, and Percy Shelley—as well as to Benjamin Robert Haydon, painter of grandiose historical and religious canvases. Through Hunt, Keats also met John Hamilton Reynolds and then Charles Wentworth Dilke and Charles Brown, who became his intimate friends and provided him with an essential circumstance for a fledgling poet: a sympathetic and appreciative audience.

The rapidity and sureness of Keats's development has no match. He did not even undertake poetry until his eighteenth year and, for the following few years, produced album verse that was at best merely competent and at times manifested an arch sentimentality. Suddenly, in 1816, he spoke out loud and bold in the sonnet *On First Looking into Chapman's Homer*. Later that same year he wrote *Sleep and Poetry*, in which he laid out for himself a program deliberately modeled on the careers of the greatest poets, asking only

> for ten years, that I may overwhelm
> Myself in poesy; so I may do the deed
> That my own soul has to itself decreed.

For even while his health was good, Keats felt a foreboding of early death and applied himself to his art with a desperate urgency. In 1817 he went on to compose *Endymion*, an ambitious undertaking of more than four thousand lines. It is a profuse allegory of a mortal's quest for an ideal feminine counterpart and a flawless happiness beyond earthly possibility; in a number of passages, it already exhibits the sure movement and phrasing of his mature poetic style. But Keats's critical judgment and aspiration exceeded his achievement: long before he completed it, he declared impatiently that he carried on with the "slipshod" *Endymion* only as a "trial of invention" and began to block out *Hyperion*, conceived on the model of Milton's *Paradise Lost* in that most demanding of forms, the epic poem. His success in achieving the Miltonic manner is one of the reasons why Keats abandoned *Hyperion* before it was finished, for he recognized that he was uncommonly susceptible to poetic influences and regarded this as a threat to his individuality. "I will write independently," he insisted. "The Genius of Poetry must work out its own salvation in a man." He had refused the chance of intimacy with Shelley "that I might have my own unfettered scope"; he had broken away from Leigh Hunt's influence lest he get "the reputation of Hunt's *élève* [pupil]"; now he shied away from domination by Milton's powerfully infectious style.

With the year 1818 began a series of troubles that culminated in Keats's mortal illness. Sentimental legend used to fix the blame on two anonymous articles: a scurrilous attack on Keats as a member of the "Cockney School" (that is, Hunt's radical literary circle in London), which appeared in the heavily Tory *Blackwood's Magazine,* and a savage mauling of *Endymion* in the *Quarterly Review.* Shelley gave impetus to this myth by his description of Keats in *Adonais* as "a pale flower," and Byron, who knew even less about him, asserted that he was "snuffed out by an article." But in fact, Keats had the good sense to recognize that the attacks were motivated by Tory bias and class snobbery, and he had already passed his own severe judgment on *Endymion:* "My own domestic criticism," he said, "has given me pain without comparison beyond what *Blackwood* or the *Quarterly* could possibly inflict." More important was the financial distress of his brother George and his young bride, who emigrated to Kentucky and lost their money in an ill-advised investment; Keats, himself short of funds, had now to turn to literary journeywork to eke out the family income. His brother Tom contracted tuberculosis, and the poet, in devoted attendance, helplessly watched him waste away until his death that December. In the summer of that year Keats had taken a strenuous walking tour in the English Lake District, Scotland, and Ireland. It was a glorious adventure but a totally exhausting one in wet, cold weather, and he returned in August with a chronically ulcerated throat made increasingly ominous by the shadow of the tuberculosis that had killed his mother and brother. And in the late fall of that same year Keats fell unwillingly, helplessly in love with Fanny Brawne. This attractive, vivacious, and mildly flirtatious woman of eighteen had little interest in poetry, but she possessed an alert and sensible mind and loved Keats sincerely. They became engaged, but Keats's dedication to poetry, his poverty, and his growing illness made marriage impossible and love a torment.

In this period of acute distress and emotional turmoil, within five years of his first trying his hand at poetry, Keats achieved the culmination of his brief poetic career. Between January and September of 1819, masterpiece followed masterpiece in astonishing succession: *The Eve of St. Agnes, La Belle Dame sans Merci,* all of the "great odes," *Lamia,* and a sufficient number of fine sonnets to make him, with Wordsworth, the major Romantic craftsman in that form. All of these poems possess the distinctive qualities of the work of Keats's maturity: a slow-paced, gracious movement; a concreteness of description in which all the senses—tactile, gustatory, kinetic, visceral, as well as visual and auditory—combine to give the total apprehension of an experience; a delight at the sheer existence of things outside himself, the poet seeming to lose his own identity in a total identification with the object he contemplates; and a concentrated felicity of phrasing that reminded his friends, as it has many critics since, of the language of Shakespeare. Under the richly sensuous surface, we find Keats's characteristic presentation of all experience as a tangle of inseparable but irreconcilable opposites. He finds melancholy in delight and pleasure in pain; he feels the highest intensity of love as an approximation to death; he inclines equally toward a life of indolence and "sensation" and toward a life of thought; he is aware both of the attraction of an imaginative dream world without "disagreeables" and the remorseless pressure of the actual; he aspires at the same time to aesthetic detachment and to social responsibility.

His letters, hardly less remarkable than his poetry, show that Keats felt on his pulses the conflicts he dramatized in his major poems. Above all, they reveal him wrestling with the problem of evil and suffering—what to make of our lives in the discovery that "the world is full of misery and heartbreak, pain, sickness and oppression." To the end of his life, he refused to seek solace for the complexity and contradictions of experience either in the abstractions of inherited philosophical doctrines or in the absolutes of a religious creed. At the close of his poetic career, in the latter part of 1819, Keats began to rework the epic *Hyperion* into the form of a dream vision that he called *The Fall of Hyperion*. In the introductory section of this fragment the poet is told by the prophetess Moneta that he has hitherto been merely a dreamer; he must know that

> The poet and the dreamer are distinct,
> Diverse, sheer opposite, antipodes,

and that the height of poetry can be reached only by

> those to whom the miseries of the world
> Are misery, and will not let them rest.

He was seemingly planning to undertake a new direction and subject matter, when illness and death intervened.

On the night of February 3, 1820, he coughed up blood. As a physician, he refused to evade the truth: "I cannot be deceived in that colour; that drop of blood is my death warrant. I must die." That spring and summer a series of hemorrhages rapidly weakened him. In the autumn he allowed himself to be persuaded to seek the milder climate of Italy in the company of Joseph Severn, a young painter, but these last months were only what he called "a posthumous existence." He died in Rome on February 23, 1821, and was buried in the Protestant Cemetery. At times the agony of his disease, the seeming frustration of his hopes for great poetic achievement, and the despair of his passion for Fanny Brawne compelled even Keats's brave spirit to bitterness and jealousy, but he always recovered his gallantry. His last letter, written to Charles Brown, concludes: "I can scarcely bid you good bye even in a letter. I always made an awkward bow. God bless you! John Keats."

No one can read Keats's poems and letters without an undersense of the tragic waste of an extraordinary intellect and genius cut off so early. What he might have done is beyond conjecture; what we do know is that his poetry, when he stopped writing at the age of twenty-four, exceeds the accomplishment at the same age of Chaucer, Shakespeare, and Milton.

The texts here are taken from Jack Stillinger's edition, *The Poems of John Keats* (Cambridge, Mass., 1978).

On First Looking into Chapman's Homer[1]

Much have I travell'd in the realms of gold,
    And many goodly states and kingdoms seen;
    Round many western islands have I been
Which bards in fealty to Apollo hold.
5   Oft of one wide expanse had I been told
    That deep-brow'd Homer ruled as his demesne;[2]
    Yet did I never breathe its pure serene[3]
Till I heard Chapman speak out loud and bold:
Then felt I like some watcher of the skies
10   When a new planet swims into his ken;
Or like stout Cortez when with eagle eyes
    He star'd at the Pacific—and all his men

1. Keats's mentor Charles Cowden Clarke intro-duced him to Homer in the robust translation of the Elizabethan poet George Chapman. They read through the night, and Keats walked home at dawn. This sonnet reached Clarke by the ten o'clock mail that same morning. It was Balboa, not Cortez, who caught his first sight of the Pacific from the heights of Darien, in Panama, but none of Keats's contemporaries noticed the error.
2. Realm, feudal possession.
3. Clear expanse of air.

Look'd at each other with a wild surmise—
Silent, upon a peak in Darien.

Oct. 1816   1816

From Sleep and Poetry[1]

[O FOR TEN YEARS]

O for ten years, that I may overwhelm
Myself in poesy; so I may do the deed
That my own soul has to itself decreed.
Then will I pass the countries that I see
100 In long perspective, and continually
Taste their pure fountains. First the realm I'll pass
Of Flora, and old Pan:[2] sleep in the grass,
Feed upon apples red, and strawberries,
And choose each pleasure that my fancy sees;
105 Catch the white-handed nymphs in shady places,
To woo sweet kisses from averted faces,—
Play with their fingers, touch their shoulders white
Into a pretty shrinking with a bite
As hard as lips can make it: till agreed,
110 A lovely tale of human life we'll read.
And one will teach a tame dove how it best
May fan the cool air gently o'er my rest;
Another, bending o'er her nimble tread,
Will set a green robe floating round her head,
115 And still will dance with ever varied ease,
Smiling upon the flowers and the trees:
Another will entice me on, and on
Through almond blossoms and rich cinnamon;
Till in the bosom of a leafy world
120 We rest in silence, like two gems upcurl'd
In the recesses of a pearly shell.

And can I ever bid these joys farewell?
Yes, I must pass them for a nobler life,
Where I may find the agonies, the strife
125 Of human hearts: for lo! I see afar,
O'er sailing the blue cragginess, a car[3]
And steeds with streamy manes—the charioteer

1. At the early age of twenty-one, Keats set himself
a regimen of poetic training modeled on the course
followed by the greatest poets. Virgil had established the pattern of beginning with pastoral writing and proceeding gradually to the point at which
he was ready to undertake the epic, and this pattern had been deliberately followed by Spenser and
Milton. Keats's version of this program, as he
describes it here, is to begin with the realm "of
Flora, and old Pan" (line 102) and, within ten
years, to climb up to the level of poetry dealing with
"the agonies, the strife / Of human hearts" (lines
124–25). The latter achievement Keats found best
represented among his contemporaries by Wordsworth and, less successfully, Shelley; Keats's vision
of the chariot of poesy (lines 125–54) parallels
Shelley's allegorical visions. The program Keats set
himself is illuminated by his analysis of Wordsworth's progress in his letter to J. H. Reynolds of
May 3, 1818 (p. 892).
2. I.e., the carefree pastoral world. Flora was the
Roman goddess of flowers. Pan was the Greek god
of pastures, woods, and animal life.
3. This chariot, with its "charioteer" (line 127),
represents the higher poetic imagination, which
bodies forth the matters "of delight, of mystery,
and fear" (line 138) that characterize the grander
poetic genres.

Looks out upon the winds with glorious fear:
And now the numerous tramplings quiver lightly
130 Along a huge cloud's ridge; and now with sprightly
Wheel downward come they into fresher skies,
Tipt round with silver from the sun's bright eyes.
Still downward with capacious whirl they glide;
And now I see them on a green-hill's side
135 In breezy rest among the nodding stalks.
The charioteer with wond'rous gesture talks
To the trees and mountains; and there soon appear
Shapes of delight, of mystery, and fear,
Passing along before a dusky space
140 Made by some mighty oaks: as they would chase
Some ever-fleeting music on they sweep.
Lo! how they murmur, laugh, and smile, and weep:
Some with upholden hand and mouth severe;
Some with their faces muffled to the ear
145 Between their arms; some, clear in youthful bloom,
Go glad and smilingly athwart the gloom;
Some looking back, and some with upward gaze;
Yes, thousands in a thousand different ways
Flit onward—now a lovely wreath of girls
150 Dancing their sleek hair into tangled curls;
And now broad wings. Most awfully intent,
The driver of those steeds is forward bent,
And seems to listen: O that I might know
All that he writes with such a hurrying glow.

155 The visions all are fled—the car is fled
Into the light of heaven, and in their stead
A sense of real things comes doubly strong,
And, like a muddy stream, would bear along
My soul to nothingness: but I will strive
160 Against all doubtings, and will keep alive
The thought of that same chariot, and the strange
Journey it went.

* * *

Oct.–Dec. 1816   1817

On Seeing the Elgin Marbles[1]

My spirit is too weak—mortality
     Weighs heavily on me like unwilling sleep,
     And each imagined pinnacle and steep
     Of godlike hardship tells me I must die
5   Like a sick eagle looking at the sky.
          Yet 'tis a gentle luxury to weep

---

1. Lord Elgin had brought to England in 1806 the marble statues and friezes that adorned the Parthenon at Athens; in 1816 they were purchased by the government for the British Museum.

That I have not the cloudy winds to keep
Fresh for the opening of the morning's eye.
Such dim-conceived glories of the brain
10   Bring round the heart an undescribable feud;
So do these wonders a most dizzy pain,
    That mingles Grecian grandeur with the rude
Wasting of old time—with a billowy main—
A sun—a shadow of a magnitude.

Mar. 1 or 2, 1817   1817

From Endymion: A Poetic Romance[1]

"The stretched metre of an antique song"

INSCRIBED TO THE MEMORY OF THOMAS CHATTERTON

Preface

Knowing within myself the manner in which this Poem has been produced, it is not without a feeling of regret that I make it public.

What manner I mean, will be quite clear to the reader, who must soon
perceive great inexperience, immaturity, and every error denoting a feverish
attempt, rather than a deed accomplished. The two first books, and indeed
the two last, I feel sensible are not of such completion as to warrant their
passing the press; nor should they if I thought a year's castigation would do
them any good;—it will not: the foundations are too sandy. It is just that this
youngster should die away: a sad thought for me, if I had not some hope that
while it is dwindling I may be plotting, and fitting myself for verses fit to live.

This may be speaking too presumptuously, and may deserve a punishment:
but no feeling man will be forward to inflict it: he will leave me alone, with
the conviction that there is not a fiercer hell than the failure in a great object.
This is not written with the least atom of purpose to forestall criticisms of
course, but from the desire I have to conciliate men who are competent to
look, and who do look with a zealous eye, to the honour of English literature.

The imagination of a boy is healthy, and the mature imagination of a man
is healthy; but there is a space of life between, in which the soul is in a
ferment, the character undecided, the way of life uncertain, the ambition
thick-sighted: thence proceeds mawkishness, and all the thousand bitters
which those men I speak of must necessarily taste in going over the following
pages.

---

1. This poem of more than four thousand lines
(based on the classical myth of a mortal beloved by
the goddess of the moon) tells of Endymion's long
and agonized search for an immortal goddess
whom he had seen in several visions. In the course
of his wanderings he comes upon an Indian maid
who had been abandoned by the followers of Bacchus and, to his utter despair, succumbs to a sensual passion for her, in apparent betrayal of his love
for his heavenly ideal. In the resolution the Indian
maid reveals that she is herself Cynthia (Diana),
goddess of the moon, the celestial subject of his
earlier visions.

The verse epigraph is adapted from Shakespeare's Sonnet 17, line 12: "And stretchèd metre
of an antique song." Thomas Chatterton (1752–
1770), to whom *Endymion* is inscribed, wrote a
number of brilliant pseudoarchaic poems that he
attributed to an imaginary 15th-century poet, Thomas Rowley. Keats described him as "the most
English of poets except Shakespeare."

I hope I have not in too late a day touched the beautiful mythology of Greece, and dulled its brightness: for I wish to try once more,[2] before I bid it farewell.

Teignmouth, April 10, 1818

From *Book 1*

[A THING OF BEAUTY]

A thing of beauty is a joy for ever:
Its loveliness increases; it will never
Pass into nothingness; but still will keep
A bower quiet for us, and a sleep
5   Full of sweet dreams, and health, and quiet breathing.
Therefore, on every morrow, are we wreathing
A flowery band to bind us to the earth,
Spite of despondence, of the inhuman dearth
Of noble natures, of the gloomy days,
10   Of all the unhealthy and o'er-darkened ways
Made for our searching: yes, in spite of all,
Some shape of beauty moves away the pall
From our dark spirits. Such the sun, the moon,
Trees old, and young sprouting a shady boon
15   For simple sheep; and such are daffodils
With the green world they live in; and clear rills
That for themselves a cooling covert make
'Gainst the hot season; the mid forest brake,°   *thicket*
Rich with a sprinkling of fair musk-rose blooms:
20   And such too is the grandeur of the dooms°   *judgments*
We have imagined for the mighty dead;
All lovely tales that we have heard or read:
An endless fountain of immortal drink,
Pouring unto us from the heaven's brink.[3]

25   Nor do we merely feel these essences
For one short hour; no, even as the trees
That whisper round a temple become soon
Dear as the temple's self, so does the moon,
The passion poesy, glories infinite,
30   Haunt us till they become a cheering light
Unto our souls, and bound to us so fast,
That, whether there be shine, or gloom o'ercast,
They alway must be with us, or we die.

       Therefore, 'tis with full happiness that I
35   Will trace the story of Endymion.
The very music of the name has gone

---

2. In *Hyperion*, which Keats was already planning.
3. The poet sets up, and seeks to resolve, the basic opposition between the inevitably "mortal" pleasures in this life and the conceived possibility of "immortal" delight. Thus "essences" (line 25) seem to be the things of beauty in this world, purged of the mutability that is inescapable in ordinary experience. The central passage dealing with this theme is in book 1, lines 777ff.

Into my being, and each pleasant scene
Is growing fresh before me as the green
Of our own vallies. * * *

[THE "PLEASURE THERMOMETER"]

"Peona!4 ever have I long'd to slake
770 My thirst for the world's praises: nothing base,
No merely slumberous phantasm, could unlace
The stubborn canvas for my voyage prepar'd—
Though now 'tis tatter'd; leaving my bark bar'd
And sullenly drifting: yet my higher hope
775 Is of too wide, too rainbow-large a scope,
To fret at myriads of earthly wrecks.
Wherein lies happiness? In that which becks
Our ready minds to fellowship divine,
A fellowship with essence; till we shine,
780 Full alchemiz'd,5 and free of space. Behold
The clear religion of heaven! Fold
A rose leaf round thy finger's taperness,
And soothe thy lips: hist, when the airy stress
Of music's kiss impregnates the free winds,
785 And with a sympathetic touch unbinds
Eolian6 magic from their lucid wombs:
Then old songs waken from enclouded tombs;
Old ditties sigh above their father's grave;
Ghosts of melodious prophecyings rave
790 Round every spot where trod Apollo's foot;
Bronze clarions awake, and faintly bruit,7
Where long ago a giant battle was;
And, from the turf, a lullaby doth pass
In every place where infant Orpheus slept.
795 Feel we these things?—that moment have we stept
Into a sort of oneness, and our state
Is like a floating spirit's. But there are
Richer entanglements, enthralments far
More self-destroying, leading, by degrees,
800 To the chief intensity: the crown of these
Is made of love and friendship, and sits high
Upon the forehead of humanity.

4. The sister to whom Endymion confides his troubles. Of lines 769–857, Keats wrote to his publisher, John Taylor: "When I wrote it, it was the regular stepping of the Imagination towards a Truth. My having written that Argument will perhaps be of the greatest Service to me of anything I ever did—It set before me at once the gradations of Happiness even like a kind of Pleasure Thermometer, and is my first step towards the chief attempt in the Drama—the playing of different Natures with Joy and Sorrow." The gradations on this "Pleasure Thermometer" mark the stages on the way to what Keats calls "happiness" (line 777)—his secular version of the religious concept of "felicity" that, in the orthodox view, is to be achieved by a surrender of oneself to God. For Keats, the way to happiness lies through a fusion of ourselves, first sensuously, with the lovely objects of nature and art (lines 781–97), then on a higher level, with other human beings through "love and friendship" (line 801) and, ultimately, sexual love. By this "self-destroying," or loss of personal identity through our imaginative identification with a beloved person outside ourselves, we escape from the material limits and the self-centered condition of ordinary experience, to achieve a "fellowship with essence," which is a kind of immortality within our mortal existence (line 844).
5. Transformed by alchemy from a base to a precious metal.
6. From Aeolus, god of winds.
7. Make a sound.

All its more ponderous and bulky worth
Is friendship, whence there ever issues forth
805   A steady splendour; but at the tip-top
There hangs by unseen film, an orbed drop
Of light, and that is love: its influence,
Thrown in our eyes, genders a novel sense,
At which we start and fret; till in the end,
810   Melting into its radiance, we blend,
Mingle, and so become a part of it,—
Nor with aught else can our souls interknit
So wingedly: when we combine therewith,
Life's self is nourish'd by its proper pith,[8]
815   And we are nurtured like a pelican brood.[9]
Aye, so delicious is the unsating food,
That men, who might have tower'd in the van
Of all the congregated world, to fan
And winnow from the coming step of time
820   All chaff of custom, wipe away all slime
Left by men-slugs and human serpentry,
Have been content to let occasion die,
Whilst they did sleep in love's elysium.
And, truly, I would rather be struck dumb,
825   Than speak against this ardent listlessness:
For I have ever thought that it might bless
The world with benefits unknowingly;
As does the nightingale, upperched high,
And cloister'd among cool and bunched leaves—
830   She sings but to her love, nor e'er conceives
How tiptoe Night holds back her dark-grey hood.[1]
Just so may love, although 'tis understood
The mere commingling of passionate breath,
Produce more than our searching witnesseth:
835   What I know not: but who, of men, can tell
That flowers would bloom, or that green fruit would swell
To melting pulp, that fish would have bright mail,
The earth its dower of river, wood, and vale,
The meadows runnels, runnels pebble-stones,
840   The seed its harvest, or the lute its tones,
Tones ravishment, or ravishment its sweet,
If human souls did never kiss and greet?

    "Now, if this earthly love has power to make
Men's being mortal, immortal; to shake
845   Ambition from their memories, and brim
Their measure of content; what merest whim,
Seems all this poor endeavour after fame,
To one, who keeps within his stedfast aim
A love immortal, an immortal too.
850   Look not so wilder'd; for these things are true,

---

8. Its own elemental substance.
9. Young pelicans were once thought to feed on their mother's flesh. In a parallel way, our life is nourished by another's life, with which it fuses in love.
1. I.e., in order to hear better.

And never can be born of atomies°   *mites*
That buzz about our slumbers, like brain-flies,
Leaving us fancy-sick. No, no, I'm sure,
My restless spirit never could endure
855   To brood so long upon one luxury,
Unless it did, though fearfully, espy
A hope beyond the shadow of a dream."

Apr.–Nov. 1817   1818

On Sitting Down to Read *King Lear* Once Again[1]

O golden-tongued Romance, with serene lute!
    Fair plumed syren, queen of far-away!
    Leave melodizing on this wintry day,
Shut up thine olden pages, and be mute.
5   Adieu! for, once again, the fierce dispute
    Betwixt damnation and impassion'd clay
    Must I burn through; once more humbly assay
The bitter-sweet of this Shakespearean fruit.
Chief Poet! and ye clouds of Albion,[2]
10   Begetters of our deep eternal theme!
When through the old oak forest[3] I am gone,
    Let me not wander in a barren dream:
But, when I am consumed in the fire,
Give me new phoenix[4] wings to fly at my desire.

Jan. 22, 1818   1838

When I have fears that I may cease to be[1]

When I have fears that I may cease to be
    Before my pen has glean'd my teeming brain,
Before high piled books, in charactry,[2]
    Hold like rich garners the full ripen'd grain;
5   When I behold, upon the night's starr'd face,
    Huge cloudy symbols of a high romance,
And think that I may never live to trace
    Their shadows, with the magic hand of chance;
And when I feel, fair creature of an hour,
10   That I shall never look upon thee more,
Never have relish in the fairy power
    Of unreflecting love;—then on the shore

1. Keats pauses, while revising *Endymion: A Poetic Romance*, to read again Shakespeare's great tragedy. The word "syren" (line 2) indicates Keats's feeling that "Romance" was enticing him from the poet's prime duty, to deal with "the agonies, the strife / Of human hearts" (*Sleep and Poetry*, lines 124–25).
2. Old name for England. *King Lear* is set in Celtic Britain.
3. A reference either to *King Lear* or to *Endymion*.
4. The fabulous bird that periodically burns itself to death to rise anew from the ashes.
1. The first, and one of the most successful, of Keats's attempts at the sonnet in the Shakespearean rhyme scheme.
2. Characters; printed letters of the alphabet.

Of the wide world I stand alone, and think
Till love and fame to nothingness do sink.

Jan. 1818   1848

To Homer

Standing aloof in giant ignorance,
   Of thee I hear and of the Cyclades,[1]
As one who sits ashore and longs perchance
   To visit dolphin-coral in deep seas.
5 So wast thou blind;—but then the veil was rent,
   For Jove uncurtain'd heaven to let thee live,
And Neptune made for thee a spumy tent,
   And Pan made sing for thee his forest-hive;
Aye on the shores of darkness there is light,
10 And precipices show untrodden green,
There is a budding morrow in midnight,
   There is a triple sight in blindness keen;
Such seeing hadst thou, as it once befel
To Dian, Queen of Earth, and Heaven, and Hell.[2]

1818   1848

The Eve of St. Agnes[1]

I

St. Agnes' Eve—Ah, bitter chill it was!
The owl, for all his feathers, was a-cold;
The hare limp'd trembling through the frozen grass,
And silent was the flock in woolly fold:
5 Numb were the Beadsman's[2] fingers, while he told
His rosary, and while his frosted breath,
Like pious incense from a censer old,
Seem'd taking flight for heaven, without a death,
Past the sweet Virgin's picture, while his prayer he saith.

---

1. A group of islands in the Aegean Sea, off
Greece. Keats's allusion is to his ignorance of the
Greek language.
2. In late pagan cults Diana was worshiped as a
three-figured goddess, the deity of nature and of
the moon as well as the queen of hell. The "triple
sight" that blind Homer paradoxically commands
is of these three regions and also of heaven, sea,
and earth (the realms of Jove, Neptune, and Pan,
lines 6–8).
1. St. Agnes, martyred ca. 303 at the age of thirteen, is the patron saint of virgins. Legend has it that
if a chaste young woman performs the proper ritual,
she will dream of her future husband on the evening
before St. Agnes's Day, January 21. Keats combines
this superstition with the Romeo and Juliet theme
of young love thwarted by feuding families and tells
the story in a sequence of evolving Spenserian

stanzas. The luxurious product has been called "a
colored dream," but it is a complexly meaningful
dream, in which the strong contrasts of heat and
cold, crimson and silver, youth and age, revelry and
austere penance, sensuality and chastity, life and
death, and hell and heaven assume symbolic values.
They figure forth the extremes of spirituality and
physicality that are involved in sexuality, the difference between the dream and the reality of passion,
and the ambivalences at the center of both human
love and the imagination. The poem is Keats's first
complete success in sustained narrative. For the
author's revisions while composing stanzas 26 and
30 of The Eve of St. Agnes, see "Poems in Process,"
in the appendices to the volume.
2. One who is paid to pray for his benefactor. He
"tells" (counts) the beads of his rosary, to keep
track of his prayers.

2

His prayer he saith, this patient, holy man;
Then takes his lamp, and riseth from his knees,
And back returneth, meagre, barefoot, wan,
Along the chapel aisle by slow degrees:
The sculptur'd dead, on each side, seem to freeze,
Emprison'd in black, purgatorial rails:
Knights, ladies, praying in dumb° orat'ries,°   silent / chapels
He passeth by; and his weak spirit fails
To think³ how they may ache in icy hoods and mails.

3

Northward he turneth through a little door,
And scarce three steps, ere Music's golden tongue
Flatter'd° to tears this aged man and poor;   beguiled
But no—already had his deathbell rung;
The joys of all his life were said and sung:
His was harsh penance on St. Agnes' Eve:
Another way he went, and soon among
Rough ashes sat he for his soul's reprieve,
And all night kept awake, for sinners' sake to grieve.

4

That ancient Beadsman heard the prelude soft;
And so it chanc'd, for many a door was wide,
From hurry to and fro. Soon, up aloft,
The silver, snarling trumpets 'gan to chide:
The level chambers, ready with their pride,°   ostentation
Were glowing to receive a thousand guests:
The carved angels, ever eager-eyed,
Star'd, where upon their heads the cornice rests,
With hair blown back, and wings put cross-wise on their breasts.

5

At length burst in the argent revelry,⁴
With plume, tiara, and all rich array,
Numerous as shadows haunting fairily
The brain, new stuff'd, in youth, with triumphs gay
Of old romance. These let us wish away,
And turn, sole-thoughted, to one Lady there,
Whose heart had brooded, all that wintry day,
On love, and wing'd St. Agnes' saintly care,
As she had heard old dames full many times declare.

6

They told her how, upon St. Agnes' Eve,
Young virgins might have visions of delight,
And soft adorings from their loves receive
Upon the honey'd middle of the night,

---

3. I.e., when he thinks.   4. Silver-adorned revelers.

50   If ceremonies due they did aright;
       As, supperless to bed they must retire,
       And couch supine their beauties, lily white;
       Nor look behind, nor sideways, but require
    Of heaven with upward eyes for all that they desire.

7

55   Full of this whim was thoughtful Madeline:
       The music, yearning like a god in pain,
       She scarcely heard: her maiden eyes divine,
       Fix'd on the floor, saw many a sweeping train
       Pass by—she heeded not at all: in vain
60   Came many a tiptoe, amorous cavalier,
       And back retir'd, not cool'd by high disdain;
       But she saw not: her heart was otherwhere:
    She sigh'd for Agnes' dreams, the sweetest of the year.

8

       She danc'd along with vague, regardless eyes,
65   Anxious her lips, her breathing quick and short:
       The hallow'd hour was near at hand: she sighs
       Amid the timbrels,° and the throng'd resort   *small drums*
       Of whisperers in anger, or in sport;
       'Mid looks of love, defiance, hate, and scorn,
70   Hoodwink'd with faery fancy; all amort,[5]
       Save to St. Agnes and her lambs unshorn,[6]
    And all the bliss to be before to-morrow morn.

9

       So, purposing each moment to retire,
       She linger'd still. Meantime, across the moors,
75   Had come young Porphyro, with heart on fire
       For Madeline. Beside the portal doors,
       Buttress'd from moonlight,[7] stands he, and implores
       All saints to give him sight of Madeline,
       But for one moment in the tedious hours,
80   That he might gaze and worship all unseen;
    Perchance speak, kneel, touch, kiss—in sooth such things have been.

10

       He ventures in: let no buzz'd whisper tell:
       All eyes be muffled, or a hundred swords
       Will storm his heart, Love's fev'rous citadel:
85   For him, those chambers held barbarian hordes,
       Hyena foemen, and hot-blooded lords,
       Whose very dogs would execrations howl

5. As though dead. "Hoodwinked": covered by a hood or blindfolded.
6. On St. Agnes's Day it was the custom to offer lambs' wool at the altar, to be made into cloth by nuns.
7. Sheltered from the moonlight by the buttresses (the supports projecting from the wall).

Against his lineage: not one breast affords
Him any mercy, in that mansion foul,
90   Save one old beldame,[8] weak in body and in soul.

11

Ah, happy chance! the aged creature came,
Shuffling along with ivory-headed wand,°   *staff*
To where he stood, hid from the torch's flame,
Behind a broad hall-pillar, far beyond
95   The sound of merriment and chorus bland:°   *soft*
He startled her; but soon she knew his face,
And grasp'd his fingers in her palsied hand,
Saying, "Mercy, Porphyro! hie thee from this place;
They are all here to-night, the whole blood-thirsty race!

12

100   "Get hence! get hence! there's dwarfish Hildebrand;
He had a fever late, and in the fit
He cursed thee and thine, both house and land:
Then there's that old Lord Maurice, not a whit
More tame for his gray hairs—Alas me! flit!
105   Flit like a ghost away."—"Ah, Gossip[9] dear,
We're safe enough; here in this arm-chair sit,
And tell me how"—"Good Saints! not here, not here;
Follow me, child, or else these stones will be thy bier."

13

He follow'd through a lowly arched way,
110   Brushing the cobwebs with his lofty plume,
And as she mutter'd "Well-a—well-a-day!"
He found him in a little moonlight room,
Pale, lattic'd, chill, and silent as a tomb.
"Now tell me where is Madeline," said he,
115   "O tell me, Angela, by the holy loom
Which none but secret sisterhood may see,
When they St. Agnes' wool are weaving piously."

14

"St. Agnes! Ah! it is St. Agnes' Eve—
Yet men will murder upon holy days:
120   Thou must hold water in a witch's sieve,[1]
And be liege-lord of all the Elves and Fays,
To venture so: it fills me with amaze
To see thee, Porphyro!—St. Agnes' Eve!
God's help! my lady fair the conjuror plays[2]

---

8. Old (and usually, homely) woman; an ironic
development in English from the French meaning,
"lovely lady."
9. In the old sense: godmother or old friend.

1. A sieve made to hold water by witchcraft.
2. I.e., in her attempt to evoke the vision of her
lover.

125 This very night: good angels her deceive!
But let me laugh awhile, I've mickle° time to grieve."   *much*

15

Feebly she laugheth in the languid moon,
While Porphyro upon her face doth look,
Like puzzled urchin on an aged crone
130 Who keepeth clos'd a wond'rous riddle-book,
As spectacled she sits in chimney nook.
But soon his eyes grew brilliant, when she told
His lady's purpose; and he scarce could brook°   *restrain*
Tears, at the thought of those enchantments cold,
135 And Madeline asleep in lap of legends old.

16

Sudden a thought came like a full-blown rose,
Flushing his brow, and in his pained heart
Made purple riot: then doth he propose
A stratagem, that makes the beldame start:
140 "A cruel man and impious thou art:
Sweet lady, let her pray, and sleep, and dream
Alone with her good angels, far apart
From wicked men like thee. Go, go!—I deem
Thou canst not surely be the same that thou didst seem."

17

145 "I will not harm her, by all saints I swear,"
Quoth Porphyro: "O may I ne'er find grace
When my weak voice shall whisper its last prayer,
If one of her soft ringlets I displace,
Or look with ruffian passion in her face:
150 Good Angela, believe me by these tears;
Or I will, even in a moment's space,
Awake, with horrid shout, my foemen's ears,
And beard them, though they be more fang'd than wolves and bears."

18

"Ah! why wilt thou affright a feeble soul?
155 A poor, weak, palsy-stricken, churchyard thing,
Whose passing-bell° may ere the midnight toll;   *death knell*
Whose prayers for thee, each morn and evening,
Were never miss'd."—Thus plaining,° doth she bring   *complaining*
A gentler speech from burning Porphyro;
160 So woful, and of such deep sorrowing,
That Angela gives promise she will do
Whatever he shall wish, betide her weal or woe.

19

Which was, to lead him, in close secrecy,
Even to Madeline's chamber, and there hide
165 Him in a closet, of such privacy

That he might see her beauty unespied,
And win perhaps that night a peerless bride,
While legion'd fairies pac'd the coverlet,
And pale enchantment held her sleepy-eyed.
170   Never on such a night have lovers met,
Since Merlin paid his Demon all the monstrous debt.[3]

20

"It shall be as thou wishest," said the Dame:
"All cates° and dainties shall be stored there   *delicacies*
Quickly on this feast-night: by the tambour frame[4]
175   Her own lute thou wilt see: no time to spare,
For I am slow and feeble, and scarce dare
On such a catering trust my dizzy head.
Wait here, my child, with patience; kneel in prayer
The while: Ah! thou must needs the lady wed,
180   Or may I never leave my grave among the dead."

21

So saying, she hobbled off with busy fear.
The lover's endless minutes slowly pass'd;
The dame return'd, and whisper'd in his ear
To follow her; with aged eyes aghast
185   From fright of dim espial. Safe at last,
Through many a dusky gallery, they gain
The maiden's chamber, silken, hush'd, and chaste;
Where Porphyro took covert, pleas'd amain.°   *mightily*
His poor guide hurried back with agues in her brain.

22

190   Her falt'ring hand upon the balustrade,
Old Angela was feeling for the stair,
When Madeline, St. Agnes' charmed maid,
Rose, like a mission'd spirit,[5] unaware:
With silver taper's light, and pious care,
195   She turn'd, and down the aged gossip led
To a safe level matting. Now prepare,
Young Porphyro, for gazing on that bed;
She comes, she comes again, like ring-dove fray'd° and fled.   *frightened*

23

Out went the taper as she hurried in;
200   Its little smoke, in pallid moonshine, died:
She clos'd the door, she panted, all akin
To spirits of the air, and visions wide:
No uttered syllable, or, woe betide!
But to her heart, her heart was voluble,
205   Paining with eloquence her balmy side;

3. Probably the episode in the Arthurian legends
in which Merlin, the magician, lost his life when
the wily Vivien turned one of his own spells against
him.
4. A drum-shaped embroidery frame.
5. I.e., like an angel sent on a mission.

As though a tongueless nightingale should swell
Her throat in vain, and die, heart-stifled, in her dell.

24

A casement high and triple-arch'd there was,
All garlanded with carven imag'ries
210 Of fruits, and flowers, and bunches of knot-grass,
And diamonded with panes of quaint device,
Innumerable of stains and splendid dyes,
As are the tiger-moth's deep-damask'd wings;
And in the midst, 'mong thousand heraldries,
215 And twilight saints, and dim emblazonings,
A shielded scutcheon blush'd with blood of queens and kings.[6]

25

Full on this casement shone the wintry moon,
And threw warm gules[7] on Madeline's fair breast,
As down she knelt for heaven's grace and boon;°   gift, blessing
220 Rose-bloom fell on her hands, together prest,
And on her silver cross soft amethyst,
And on her hair a glory, like a saint:
She seem'd a splendid angel, newly drest,
Save wings, for heaven:—Porphyro grew faint:
225 She knelt, so pure a thing, so free from mortal taint.

26

Anon his heart revives: her vespers done,
Of all its wreathed pearls her hair she frees;
Unclasps her warmed jewels one by one;
Loosens her fragrant boddice; by degrees
230 Her rich attire creeps rustling to her knees:
Half-hidden, like a mermaid in sea-weed,
Pensive awhile she dreams awake, and sees,
In fancy, fair St. Agnes in her bed,
But dares not look behind, or all the charm is fled.

27

235 Soon, trembling in her soft and chilly nest,
In sort of wakeful swoon, perplex'd[8] she lay,
Until the poppied warmth of sleep oppress'd
Her soothed limbs, and soul fatigued away;
Flown, like a thought, until the morrow-day;
240 Blissfully haven'd both from joy and pain;
Clasp'd like a missal where swart Paynims pray;[9]
Blinded alike from sunshine and from rain,
As though a rose should shut, and be a bud again.

6. I.e., among the genealogical emblems ("heraldries") and other devices ("emblazonings"), a heraldic shield signified by its colors that the family was of royal blood.
7. Red (heraldry).
8. In a confused state between waking and sleeping.
9. Variously interpreted; perhaps: held tightly, cherished (or else kept shut, fastened with a clasp), like a Christian prayer book ("missal") in a land where the religion is that of dark-skinned pagans ("swart Paynims").

28

Stol'n to this paradise, and so entranced,
245   Porphyro gazed upon her empty dress,
And listen'd to her breathing, if it chanced
To wake into a slumberous tenderness;
Which when he heard, that minute did he bless,
And breath'd himself: then from the closet crept,
250   Noiseless as fear in a wide wilderness,
And over the hush'd carpet, silent, stept,
And 'tween the curtains peep'd, where, lo!—how fast she slept.

29

Then by the bed-side, where the faded moon
Made a dim, silver twilight, soft he set
255   A table, and, half anguish'd, threw thereon
A cloth of woven crimson, gold, and jet:—
O for some drowsy Morphean amulet![1]
The boisterous, midnight, festive clarion,[2]
The kettle-drum, and far-heard clarionet,
260   Affray his ears, though but in dying tone:—
The hall door shuts again, and all the noise is gone.

30

And still she slept an azure-lidded sleep,
In blanched linen, smooth, and lavender'd,
While he from forth the closet brought a heap
265   Of candied apple, quince, and plum, and gourd;°   melon
With jellies soother than the creamy curd,
And lucent syrops, tinct with cinnamon;
Manna and dates, in argosy transferr'd
From Fez,[3] and spiced dainties, every one,
270   From silken Samarcand to cedar'd Lebanon.

31

These delicates he heap'd with glowing hand
On golden dishes and in baskets bright
Of wreathed silver: sumptuous they stand
In the retired quiet of the night,
275   Filling the chilly room with perfume light.—
"And now, my love, my seraph[4] fair, awake!
Thou art my heaven, and I thine eremite:[5]
Open thine eyes, for meek St. Agnes' sake,
Or I shall drowse beside thee, so my soul doth ache."

32

280   Thus whispering, his warm, unnerved arm
Sank in her pillow. Shaded was her dream

---

1. Sleep-producing charm.
2. High-pitched trumpet.
3. I.e., jellies softer ("soother") than the curds of cream, clear ("lucent") syrops tinged with cinnamon, and sweet gums ("manna") and dates transported in a great merchant ship ("argosy") from Fez.
4. One of the highest orders of angels.
5. Hermit, religious solitary.

By the dusk curtains:—'twas a midnight charm
Impossible to melt as iced stream:
The lustrous salvers in the moonlight gleam;
285   Broad golden fringe upon the carpet lies:
It seem'd he never, never could redeem
From such a stedfast spell his lady's eyes;
So mus'd awhile, entoil'd in woofed phantasies.[6]

33

Awakening up, he took her hollow lute,—
290   Tumultuous,—and, in chords that tenderest be,
He play'd an ancient ditty, long since mute,
In Provence call'd, "La belle dame sans mercy":[7]
Close to her ear touching the melody;—
Wherewith disturb'd, she utter'd a soft moan:
295   He ceased—she panted quick—and suddenly
Her blue affrayed eyes wide open shone:
Upon his knees he sank, pale as smooth-sculptured stone.

34

Her eyes were open, but she still beheld,
Now wide awake, the vision of her sleep:
300   There was a painful change, that nigh expell'd
The blisses of her dream so pure and deep:
At which fair Madeline began to weep,
And moan forth witless words with many a sigh;
While still her gaze on Porphyro would keep;
305   Who knelt, with joined hands and piteous eye,
Fearing to move or speak, she look'd so dreamingly.

35

"Ah, Porphyro!" said she, "but even now
Thy voice was at sweet tremble in mine ear,
Made tuneable with every sweetest vow;
310   And those sad eyes were spiritual and clear:
How chang'd thou art! how pallid, chill, and drear!
Give me that voice again, my Porphyro,
Those looks immortal, those complainings dear!
Oh leave me not in this eternal woe,
315   For if thou diest, my love, I know not where to go."

36

Beyond a mortal man impassion'd far
At these voluptuous accents, he arose,
Ethereal, flush'd, and like a throbbing star
Seen mid the sapphire heaven's deep repose;
320   Into her dream he melted, as the rose
Blendeth its odour with the violet,—

6. Entangled in a weave of fantasies.
7. "The Lovely Lady without Pity," title of a work

by the medieval poet Alain Chartier. Keats later
adopted the title for his own ballad.

Solution sweet: meantime the frost-wind blows
Like Love's alarum pattering the sharp sleet
Against the window-panes; St. Agnes' moon hath set.

37

325 'Tis dark: quick pattereth the flaw-blown° sleet: *gust-blown*
"This is no dream, my bride, my Madeline!"
'Tis dark: the iced gusts still rave and beat:
"No dream, alas! alas! and woe is mine!
Porphyro will leave me here to fade and pine.—
330 Cruel! what traitor could thee hither bring?
I curse not, for my heart is lost in thine,
Though thou forsakest a deceived thing;—
A dove forlorn and lost with sick unpruned wing."

38

"My Madeline! sweet dreamer! lovely bride!
335 Say, may I be for aye thy vassal blest?
Thy beauty's shield, heart-shap'd and vermeil° dyed?   *vermilion*
Ah, silver shrine, here will I take my rest
After so many hours of toil and quest,
A famish'd pilgrim,—saved by miracle.
340 Though I have found, I will not rob thy nest
Saving of thy sweet self; if thou think'st well
To trust, fair Madeline, to no rude infidel.

39

"Hark! 'tis an elfin-storm from faery land,
Of haggard[8] seeming, but a boon indeed:
345 Arise—arise! the morning is at hand;—
The bloated wassaillers[9] will never heed:—
Let us away, my love, with happy speed;
There are no ears to hear, or eyes to see,—
Drown'd all in Rhenish and the sleepy mead:[1]
350 Awake! arise! my love, and fearless be,
For o'er the southern moors I have a home for thee."

40

She hurried at his words, beset with fears,
For there were sleeping dragons all around,
At glaring watch, perhaps, with ready spears—
355 Down the wide stairs a darkling[2] way they found.—
In all the house was heard no human sound.
A chain-droop'd lamp was flickering by each door;
The arras, rich with horseman, hawk, and hound,
Flutter'd in the besieging wind's uproar;
360 And the long carpets rose along the gusty floor.

8. Wild, untamed (originally, a wild hawk).
9. Drunken carousers.
1. Rhine wine and the sleep-producing mead (a

heavy fermented drink made with honey).
2. In the dark.

41

They glide, like phantoms, into the wide hall;
Like phantoms, to the iron porch, they glide;
Where lay the Porter, in uneasy sprawl,
With a huge empty flaggon by his side:
365 The wakeful bloodhound rose, and shook his hide,
But his sagacious eye an inmate owns:[3]
By one, and one, the bolts full easy slide:—
The chains lie silent on the footworn stones;—
The key turns, and the door upon its hinges groans.

42

370 And they are gone: ay, ages long ago
These lovers fled away into the storm.
That night the Baron dreamt of many a woe,
And all his warrior-guests, with shade and form
Of witch, and demon, and large coffin-worm,
375 Were long be-nightmar'd. Angela the old
Died palsy-twitch'd, with meagre face deform;
The Beadsman, after thousand aves[4] told,
For aye° unsought for slept among his ashes cold.   *ever*

Jan.–Feb. 1819   1820

Why did I laugh tonight? No voice will tell[1]

Why did I laugh tonight? No voice will tell:
    No god, no demon of severe response,
Deigns to reply from heaven or from hell.
    Then to my human heart I turn at once—
5 Heart! thou and I are here sad and alone;
    Say, wherefore did I laugh? O mortal pain!
O darkness! darkness! ever must I moan,
    To question heaven and hell and heart in vain!
Why did I laugh? I know this being's lease—
10 My fancy to its utmost blisses spreads:
Yet could I on this very midnight cease,
    And the world's gaudy ensigns° see in shreds.   *banners*
Verse, fame, and beauty are intense indeed,
But death intenser—death is life's high meed.

Mar. 1819   1848

---

3. Acknowledges a member of the household.
4. The prayers beginning *Ave Maria* ("Hail Mary").
1. In the letter to his brother and sister-in-law, George and Georgiana Keats, into which he copied this sonnet, March 19, 1819, Keats wrote: "Though the first steps to it were through my human passions, they went away, and I wrote with my Mind— and perhaps I must confess a little bit of my heart. . . . I went to bed, and enjoyed an uninterrupted sleep. Sane I went to bed and sane I arose."

Bright star, would I were stedfast as thou art[1]

Bright star, would I were stedfast as thou art—
    Not in lone splendor hung aloft the night,
And watching, with eternal lids apart,
    Like nature's patient, sleepless eremite,[2]
5 The moving waters at their priestlike task
    Of pure ablution[3] round earth's human shores,
Or gazing on the new soft-fallen mask
    Of snow upon the mountains and the moors;
No—yet still stedfast, still unchangeable,
10   Pillow'd upon my fair love's ripening breast,
To feel for ever its soft swell and fall,
    Awake for ever in a sweet unrest,
Still, still to hear her tender-taken breath,
And so live ever—or else swoon to death.[4]

1819   1838

La Belle Dame sans Merci: A Ballad[1]

1

O what can ail thee, knight at arms,
    Alone and palely loitering?
The sedge has wither'd from the lake,
    And no birds sing.

2

5 O what can ail thee, knight at arms,
    So haggard and so woe-begone?
The squirrel's granary is full,
    And the harvest's done.

3

I see a lily on thy brow
10   With anguish moist and fever dew,
And on thy cheeks a fading rose
    Fast withereth too.

1. While on a tour of the Lake District in 1818, Keats had said that the austere scenes "refine one's sensual vision into a sort of north star which can never cease to be open lidded and steadfast over the wonders of the great Power." The thought developed into this sonnet, which Keats drafted in 1819, then copied into his volume of Shakespeare's poems at the end of September or the beginning of October 1820, while on his way to Italy, where he died.
2. Hermit, religious solitary.
3. Washing, as part of a religious rite.
4. In the earlier version: "Half passionless, and so swoon on to death."

1. The title, though not the subject, was taken from a medieval poem by Alain Chartier and means "The Lovely Lady without Pity." The story of a mortal destroyed by his love for a supernatural femme fatale has been told repeatedly in myth, fairy tale, and ballad. The text printed here is Keats's earlier version of the poem, as transcribed by Charles Brown. The version published in 1820 begins, "Ah, what can ail thee, wretched wight."

Keats imitates a frequent procedure of folk ballads by casting the poem into the dialogue form. The first three stanzas are addressed to the knight, and the rest of the poem is his reply.

4

I met a lady in the meads,
    Full beautiful, a fairy's child;
15 Her hair was long, her foot was light,
    And her eyes were wild.

5

I made a garland for her head,
    And bracelets too, and fragrant zone;[2]
She look'd at me as she did love,
20   And made sweet moan.

6

I set her on my pacing steed,
    And nothing else saw all day long,
For sidelong would she bend, and sing
    A fairy's song.

7

25 She found me roots of relish sweet,
    And honey wild, and manna dew,
And sure in language strange she said—
    I love thee true.

8

She took me to her elfin grot,
30   And there she wept, and sigh'd full sore,
And there I shut her wild wild eyes
    With kisses four.

9

And there she lulled me asleep,
    And there I dream'd—Ah! woe betide!
35 The latest° dream I ever dream'd   last
    On the cold hill's side.

10

I saw pale kings, and princes too,
    Pale warriors, death pale were they all;
They cried—"La belle dame sans merci
40   Hath thee in thrall!"

11

I saw their starv'd lips in the gloam
    With horrid warning gaped wide,
And I awoke and found me here
    On the cold hill's side.

2. Belt (of flowers).

12

45 And this is why I sojourn here,
   Alone and palely loitering,
Though the sedge is wither'd from the lake,
   And no birds sing.

Apr. 1819   1820

Sonnet to Sleep

O soft embalmer of the still midnight,
   Shutting with careful fingers and benign
Our gloom-pleas'd eyes, embower'd from the light,
   Enshaded in forgetfulness divine:
5 O soothest° Sleep! if so it please thee, close,   *softest*
   In midst of this thine hymn, my willing eyes,
Or wait the Amen ere thy poppy[1] throws
   Around my bed its lulling charities.
Then save me or the passed day will shine
10   Upon my pillow, breeding many woes:
Save me from curious° conscience, that still hoards   *scrupulous*
   Its strength for darkness, burrowing like the mole;
Turn the key deftly in the oiled wards,[2]
   And seal the hushed casket of my soul.

Apr. 1819   1838

Ode to Psyche[1]

O Goddess! hear these tuneless numbers, wrung
   By sweet enforcement and remembrance dear,
And pardon that thy secrets should be sung
   Even into thine own soft-conched[2] ear:
5 Surely I dreamt to-day, or did I see
   The winged Psyche with awaken'd eyes?[3]
I wander'd in a forest thoughtlessly,

1. Opium is made from the dried juice of the opium poppy.
2. The ridges in a lock that correspond to the notches of the key.
1. This poem initiated the sequence of great odes that Keats wrote in the spring of 1819. It is copied into the same journal-letter that included the *Sonnet to Sleep* and several other sonnets as well as a comment about "endeavoring to discover a better sonnet stanza than we have." It is therefore likely that Keats's experiments with sonnet schemes led to the development of the intricate and varied stanzas of his odes and also that he abandoned the sonnet on discovering the richer possibilities of the more spacious form. In his journal-letter, on April 30, he said that of all his recent poems, *Psyche* "is the first and the only one with which I have taken even moderate pains. I have for the most part dashed off my lines in a hurry. This I have done

leisurely—I think it reads the more richly for it and will I hope encourage me to write other things in even a more peaceable and healthy spirit."
   In the story told by the Roman author Apuleius in the 2nd century, Psyche was a lovely mortal beloved by Cupid, "the winged boy," son of Venus. After various tribulations imposed by Venus because she was jealous of Psyche's beauty, Psyche was wedded to Cupid and translated to heaven as an immortal. To this latter-day goddess, Keats in the last two stanzas promises to establish a place of worship within his own mind, with himself as poet-priest and prophet.
2. Soft and shaped like a seashell.
3. Another of Keats's inquiries into the relation of dreams to poetic vision; see, e.g., *Sleep and Poetry*, the concluding lines of *Ode to a Nightingale*, and the opening section of *The Fall of Hyperion: A Dream*.

And, on the sudden, fainting with surprise,
Saw two fair creatures, couched side by side
10 In deepest grass, beneath the whisp'ring roof
Of leaves and trembled blossoms, where there ran
A brooklet, scarce espied:
'Mid hush'd, cool-rooted flowers, fragrant-eyed,
Blue, silver-white, and budded Tyrian,[4]
15 They lay calm-breathing on the bedded grass;
Their arms embraced, and their pinions° too;   *wings*
Their lips touch'd not, but had not bade adieu,
As if disjoined by soft-handed slumber,
And ready still past kisses to outnumber
20 At tender eye-dawn of aurorean love:[5]
The winged boy I knew;
But who wast thou, O happy, happy dove?
His Psyche true!

O latest born and loveliest vision far
25 Of all Olympus' faded hierarchy![6]
Fairer than Phoebe's sapphire-region'd star,[7]
Or Vesper,° amorous glow-worm of the sky;   *evening star*
Fairer than these, though temple thou hast none,
Nor altar heap'd with flowers;
30 Nor virgin-choir to make delicious moan
Upon the midnight hours;
No voice, no lute, no pipe, no incense sweet
From chain-swung censer teeming;
No shrine, no grove, no oracle, no heat
35 Of pale-mouth'd prophet dreaming.

O brightest! though too late for antique vows,
Too, too late for the fond believing lyre,
When holy were the haunted forest boughs,
Holy the air, the water, and the fire;
40 Yet even in these days so far retir'd
From happy pieties, thy lucent fans,°   *shining wings*
Fluttering among the faint Olympians,
I see, and sing, by my own eyes inspired.
So let me be thy choir, and make a moan
45 Upon the midnight hours;
Thy voice, thy lute, thy pipe, thy incense sweet
From swinged censer teeming;
Thy shrine, thy grove, thy oracle, thy heat
Of pale-mouth'd prophet dreaming.

50 Yes, I will be thy priest, and build a fane°   *temple*
In some untrodden region of my mind,

---

4. The purple dye anciently made in Tyre.
5. Aurora was the goddess of the dawn.
6. The ranks of the classic gods of Mount Olympus. "You must recollect that Psyche was not embodied as a goddess before the time of Apuleius the Platonist who lived after the Augustan age, and consequently the goddess was never worshiped or sacrificed to with any of the ancient fervor—and perhaps never thought of in the old religion" (Keats, journal-letter, April 30, 1819).
7. The moon, supervised by the goddess Phoebe (Diana).

Where branched thoughts, new grown with pleasant pain,
    Instead of pines shall murmur in the wind:
Far, far around shall those dark-cluster'd trees
55   Fledge the wild-ridged mountains steep by steep;[8]
And there by zephyrs, streams, and birds, and bees,
    The moss-lain Dryads° shall be lull'd to sleep;   *wood nymphs*
And in the midst of this wide quietness
A rosy sanctuary will I dress
60 With the wreath'd trellis of a working brain,
    With buds, and bells, and stars without a name,
With all the gardener Fancy e'er could feign,
    Who breeding flowers, will never breed the same:
And there shall be for thee all soft delight
65   That shadowy thought can win,
A bright torch, and a casement ope at night,
    To let the warm Love[9] in!

Apr. 1819

1820

Ode to a Nightingale[1]

I

My heart aches, and a drowsy numbness pains
    My sense, as though of hemlock[2] I had drunk,
Or emptied some dull opiate to the drains
    One minute past, and Lethe[3]-wards had sunk:
5 'Tis not through envy of thy happy lot,
    But being too happy in thine happiness,—
      That thou, light-winged Dryad of the trees,
      In some melodious plot
Of beechen green, and shadows numberless,
10   Singest of summer in full-throated ease.

2

O, for a draught of vintage! that hath been
    Cool'd a long age in the deep-delved earth,
Tasting of Flora[4] and the country green,
    Dance, and Provençal song,[5] and sunburnt mirth!
15 O for a beaker full of the warm South,
    Full of the true, the blushful Hippocrene,[6]

8. I.e., the trees shall stand, rank against rank, like layers of feathers.
9. I.e., Cupid, god of love.
1. Charles Brown, with whom Keats was then living in Hampstead, wrote: "In the spring of 1819 a nightingale had built her nest near my house. Keats felt a tranquil and continual joy in her song; and one morning he took his chair from the breakfast table to the grass plot under a plum tree, where he sat for two or three hours. When he came into the house, I perceived he had some scraps of paper in his hand, and these he was quietly thrusting behind the books. On inquiry, I found those scraps, four or five in number, contained his poetic

feeling on the song of our nightingale."
2. A poisonous herb, not the North American evergreen tree.
3. River in Hades whose waters cause forgetfulness.
4. Roman goddess of flowers, or the flowers themselves.
5. Provence, in southern France, was in the late Middle Ages renowned for its troubadours—writers and singers of love songs.
6. Fountain of the Muses on Mount Helicon, hence the waters of inspiration, here applied metaphorically to a beaker of wine.

With beaded bubbles winking at the brim,
    And purple-stained mouth;
That I might drink, and leave the world unseen,
20   And with thee fade away into the forest dim:

3

Fade far away, dissolve, and quite forget
    What thou among the leaves hast never known,
The weariness, the fever, and the fret
    Here, where men sit and hear each other groan;
25 Where palsy shakes a few, sad, last gray hairs,
    Where youth grows pale, and spectre-thin, and dies;[7]
        Where but to think is to be full of sorrow
           And leaden-eyed despairs,
    Where Beauty cannot keep her lustrous eyes,
30   Or new Love pine at them beyond to-morrow.

4

Away! away! for I will fly to thee,
    Not charioted by Bacchus and his pards,
But on the viewless wings of Poesy,[8]
    Though the dull brain perplexes and retards:
35 Already with thee! tender is the night,
    And haply the Queen-Moon is on her throne,
        Cluster'd around by all her starry Fays;°   *fairies*
        But here there is no light,
    Save what from heaven is with the breezes blown
40   Through verdurous° glooms and winding mossy ways.   *green-foliaged*

5

I cannot see what flowers are at my feet,
    Nor what soft incense hangs upon the boughs,
But, in embalmed° darkness, guess each sweet   *perfumed*
    Wherewith the seasonable month endows
45 The grass, the thicket, and the fruit-tree wild;
    White hawthorn, and the pastoral eglantine;[9]
        Fast fading violets cover'd up in leaves;
           And mid-May's eldest child,
    The coming musk-rose, full of dewy wine,
50   The murmurous haunt of flies on summer eves.

6

Darkling° I listen; and, for many a time   *in darkness*
    I have been half in love with easeful Death,
Call'd him soft names in many a mused° rhyme,   *meditated*
    To take into the air my quiet breath;
55 Now more than ever seems it rich to die,

---

7. Keats's brother Tom, wasted by tuberculosis, had died the preceding winter.
8. I.e., by getting drunk not on wine (the "vintage" of stanza 2) but on the invisible ("viewless") wings of the poetic imagination. (Bacchus, god of wine, was sometimes represented in a chariot drawn by "pards"—leopards.)
9. Sweetbrier or honeysuckle.

To cease upon the midnight with no pain,
    While thou art pouring forth thy soul abroad
        In such an ecstasy!
    Still wouldst thou sing, and I have ears in vain—
60   To thy high requiem become a sod.

7

Thou wast not born for death, immortal Bird!
    No hungry generations tread thee down;
The voice I hear this passing night was heard
    In ancient days by emperor and clown:
65 Perhaps the self-same song that found a path
    Through the sad heart of Ruth,[1] when, sick for home,
        She stood in tears amid the alien corn;°   *wheat*
            The same that oft-times hath
    Charm'd magic casements, opening on the foam
70   Of perilous seas, in faery lands forlorn.

8

Forlorn! the very word is like a bell
    To toll me back from thee to my sole self!
Adieu! the fancy[2] cannot cheat so well
    As she is fam'd to do, deceiving elf.
75 Adieu! adieu! thy plaintive anthem° fades   *hymn*
    Past the near meadows, over the still stream,
        Up the hill-side; and now 'tis buried deep
            In the next valley-glades:
    Was it a vision, or a waking dream?
80   Fled is that music:—Do I wake or sleep?[3]

May 1819   1819

Ode on a Grecian Urn[1]

1

Thou still unravish'd bride of quietness,
    Thou foster-child of silence and slow time,
Sylvan[2] historian, who canst thus express
    A flowery tale more sweetly than our rhyme:
5   What leaf-fring'd legend haunts about thy shape

---

1. The young widow in the biblical Book of Ruth.
2. I.e., imagination, "the viewless wings of Poesy" of line 33.
3. See n. 3, p. 847.
1. This urn, with its sculptured reliefs of Dionysian ecstasies, panting young lovers in flight and pursuit, a pastoral piper under spring foliage, and the quiet procession of priest and townspeople, resembles parts of various vases, sculptures, and paintings, but it existed in all its particulars only in Keats's imagination. In the urn—which captures moments of intense experience in attitudes of grace and immobilizes them in marble—Keats found the perfect correlative for his concern with

the longing for permanence in a world of change. The interpretation of the details with which he develops this concept, however, is hotly disputed, all the way from the opening phrase—is "still" an adverb ("as yet") or an adjective ("motionless")?—to the two concluding lines, which have already accumulated as much critical discussion as the "two-handed engine" in Milton's *Lycidas* or the cruxes in Shakespeare's plays. These disputes testify to the enigmatic richness of meaning in the five stanzas, as well as to the fact that the ode has become a central point of reference in the criticism of the English lyric.
2. Rustic, representing a woodland scene.

Of deities or mortals, or of both,
  In Tempe or the dales of Arcady?[3]
What men or gods are these? What maidens loth?
What mad pursuit? What struggle to escape?
10   What pipes and timbrels? What wild ecstasy?

2

Heard melodies are sweet, but those unheard
  Are sweeter; therefore, ye soft pipes, play on;
Not to the sensual ear,[4] but, more endear'd,
  Pipe to the spirit ditties of no tone:
15 Fair youth, beneath the trees, thou canst not leave
    Thy song, nor ever can those trees be bare;
      Bold lover, never, never canst thou kiss,
  Though winning near the goal—yet, do not grieve;
    She cannot fade, though thou hast not thy bliss,
20   For ever wilt thou love, and she be fair!

3

Ah, happy, happy boughs! that cannot shed
  Your leaves, nor ever bid the spring adieu;
And, happy melodist, unwearied,
  For ever piping songs for ever new;
25 More happy love! more happy, happy love!
    For ever warm and still to be enjoy'd,
      For ever panting, and for ever young;
All breathing human passion far above,
    That leaves a heart high-sorrowful and cloy'd,
30   A burning forehead, and a parching tongue.

4

Who are these coming to the sacrifice?
  To what green altar, O mysterious priest,
Lead'st thou that heifer lowing at the skies,
  And all her silken flanks with garlands drest?
35 What little town by river or sea shore,
    Or mountain-built with peaceful citadel,
      Is emptied of this folk, this pious morn?
And, little town, thy streets for evermore
    Will silent be; and not a soul to tell
40   Why thou art desolate, can e'er return.

5

O Attic[5] shape! Fair attitude! with brede
  Of marble men and maidens overwrought,[6]

---

3. The valleys of Arcadia, a state in ancient Greece often used as a symbol of the pastoral ideal. "Tempe": a beautiful valley in Greece that has come to represent supreme rural beauty.
4. The ear of sense (as opposed to that of the "spirit," or imagination).
5. Greek. Attica was the region of Greece in which Athens was located.
6. Ornamented all over ("overwrought") with an interwoven pattern ("brede").

With forest branches and the trodden weed;
    Thou, silent form, dost tease us out of thought
45 As doth eternity: Cold Pastoral!
    When old age shall this generation waste,
    Thou shalt remain, in midst of other woe
    Than ours, a friend to man, to whom thou say'st,
    "Beauty is truth, truth beauty,"[7]—that is all
50   Ye know on earth, and all ye need to know.

1819   1820

Ode on Melancholy   This is Keats's best-known statement of his recurrent theme of the mingled contrarieties of life. The remarkable last stanza, in which Melancholy becomes a veiled goddess in a mystery religion, implies that it is the tragic human destiny that beauty, joy, and life itself owe not only their quality but their value to the fact that they are transitory and turn into their opposites.

    The poem once had the following initial stanza, which Keats canceled in manuscript:

    Though you should build a bark of dead men's bones,
        And rear a phantom gibbet for a mast,
    Stitch creeds together for a sail, with groans
        To fill it out, bloodstained and aghast;
    Although your rudder be a Dragon's tail,
        Long sever'd, yet still hard with agony,
        Your cordage large uprootings from the skull
    Of bald Medusa: certes you would fail
    To find the Melancholy, whether she
        Dreameth in any isle of Lethe dull.

Ode on Melancholy

I

No, no, go not to Lethe,[1] neither twist
    Wolf's-bane, tight-rooted, for its poisonous wine;
Nor suffer thy pale forehead to be kiss'd
    By nightshade, ruby grape of Proserpine;[2]
5 Make not your rosary of yew-berries,[3]
    Nor let the beetle, nor the death-moth be

7. The quotation marks around this phrase are found in the volume of poems Keats published in 1820, but there are no quotation marks in the version printed in *Annals of the Fine Arts* that same year or in the transcripts of the poem made by Keats's friends. This discrepancy has multiplied the diversity of critical interpretations of the last two lines. Critics disagree whether the whole of these lines is said by the urn, or "Beauty is truth, truth beauty" by the urn and the rest by the lyric speaker; whether the "ye" in the last line is addressed to the lyric speaker, to the readers, to the urn, or to the figures on the urn; whether "all ye know" is that beauty is truth, or this plus the statement in lines 46–48; and whether "beauty is truth" is a profound metaphysical proposition, an overstatement representing the limited point of view of the urn, or simply nonsensical.

1. The waters of forgetfulness in Hades.
2. The wife of Pluto and queen of the infernal regions. "Nightshade" and "wolf's-bane" (line 2) are poisonous plants.
3. A symbol of death.

Your mournful Psyche,[4] nor the downy owl
A partner in your sorrow's mysteries;[5]
For shade to shade will come too drowsily,
10   And drown the wakeful anguish of the soul.[6]

2

But when the melancholy fit shall fall
    Sudden from heaven like a weeping cloud,
That fosters the droop-headed flowers all,
    And hides the green hill in an April shroud;
15 Then glut thy sorrow on a morning rose,
    Or on the rainbow of the salt sand-wave,
    Or on the wealth of globed peonies;
Or if thy mistress some rich anger shows,
    Emprison her soft hand, and let her rave,
20   And feed deep, deep upon her peerless eyes.

3

She[7] dwells with Beauty—Beauty that must die;
    And Joy, whose hand is ever at his lips
Bidding adieu; and aching Pleasure nigh,
    Turning to poison while the bee-mouth sips:
25 Ay, in the very temple of Delight
    Veil'd Melancholy has her sovran shrine,
        Though seen of none save him whose strenuous tongue
Can burst Joy's grape against his palate fine;[8]
His soul shall taste the sadness of her might,
30   And be among her cloudy trophies hung.[9]

1819   1820

Ode on Indolence[1]

"They toil not, neither do they spin."[2]

I

One morn before me were three figures seen,
    With bowed necks, and joined hands, side-faced;

---

4. In ancient times, Psyche (the soul) was sometimes represented as a butterfly or moth, fluttering out of the mouth of a dying man. The allusion may also be to the death's-head moth, which has skull-like markings on its back. The "beetle" of line 6 refers to replicas of the large black beetle, the scarab, which were often placed by Egyptians in their tombs as a symbol of resurrection.
5. Secret religious rites.
6. I.e., sorrow needs contrast to sustain its intensity.
7. Usually taken to refer to Melancholy rather than to "thy mistress" in line 18.
8. Sensitive, subtly discriminative.
9. A reference to the Greek and Roman practice

of hanging trophies in the temples of the gods.
1. On March 19, 1819, Keats wrote to George and Georgiana Keats: "This morning I am in a sort of temper indolent and supremely careless. . . . Neither Poetry, nor Ambition, nor Love have any alertness of countenance as they pass by me: they seem rather like three figures on a greek vase—a Man and two women—whom no one but myself could distinguish in their disguisement. This is the only happiness; and is a rare instance of advantage in the body overpowering the Mind." The ode was probably written soon after this time, but was not published until 1848, long after the poet's death.
2. Matthew 6.28.

And one behind the other stepp'd serene,
In placid sandals, and in white robes graced:
5 They pass'd, like figures on a marble urn,
When shifted round to see the other side;
They came again: as when the urn once more
Is shifted round, the first seen shades return;
And they were strange to me, as may betide
10 With vases, to one deep in Phidian[3] lore.

2

How is it, shadows, that I knew ye not?
How came ye muffled in so hush a masque?
Was it a silent deep-disguised plot
To steal away, and leave without a task
15 My idle days? Ripe was the drowsy hour;
The blissful cloud of summer-indolence
Benumb'd my eyes; my pulse grew less and less;
Pain had no sting, and pleasure's wreath no flower.
O, why did ye not melt, and leave my sense
20 Unhaunted quite of all but—nothingness?

3

A third time pass'd they by, and, passing, turn'd
Each one the face a moment whiles to me;
Then faded, and to follow them I burn'd
And ached for wings, because I knew the three:
25 The first was a fair maid, and Love her name;
The second was Ambition, pale of cheek,
And ever watchful with fatigued eye;
The last, whom I love more, the more of blame
Is heap'd upon her, maiden most unmeek,—
30 I knew to be my demon Poesy.

4

They faded, and, forsooth! I wanted wings:
O folly! What is Love? and where is it?
And for that poor Ambition—it springs
From a man's little heart's short fever-fit;
35 For Poesy!—no,—she has not a joy,—
At least for me,—so sweet as drowsy noons,
And evenings steep'd in honied indolence;
O, for an age so shelter'd from annoy,
That I may never know how change the moons,
40 Or hear the voice of busy common-sense!

5

A third time came they by;—alas! wherefore?
My sleep had been embroider'd with dim dreams;
My soul had been a lawn besprinkled o'er

---

3. Phidias was the great Athenian sculptor of the 5th century B.C.E. who designed the marble sculptures for the Parthenon.

With flowers, and stirring shades, and baffled beams:
45 The morn was clouded, but no shower fell,
Though in her lids hung the sweet tears of May;
The open casement press'd a new-leaved vine,
Let in the budding warmth and throstle's lay;
O shadows! 'twas a time to bid farewell!
50 Upon your skirts had fallen no tears of mine.

6

So, ye three ghosts, adieu! Ye cannot raise
My head cool-bedded in the flowery grass;
For I would not be dieted with praise,
A pet-lamb in a sentimental farce![4]
55 Fade softly from my eyes, and be once more
In masque-like figures on the dreamy urn;
Farewell! I yet have visions for the night,
And for the day faint visions there is store;
Vanish, ye phantoms, from my idle spright,°   *spirit*
60 Into the clouds, and never more return!

Spring 1819   1848

Lamia   In a note printed at the end of the poem, Keats cited as his source the
following story in Robert Burton's *Anatomy of Melancholy* (1621):

> One Menippus Lycius, a young man twenty-five years of age, that going betwixt
> Cenchreas and Corinth, met such a phantasm in the habit of a fair gentlewoman,
> which, taking him by the hand, carried him home to her house, in the suburbs
> of Corinth. . . . The young man, a philosopher, otherwise staid and discreet, able
> to moderate his passions, though not this of love, tarried with her a while to his
> great content, and at last married her, to whose wedding, amongst other guests,
> came Apollonius; who, by some probable conjectures, found her out to be a
> serpent, a lamia; and that all her furniture was, like Tantalus's gold, described
> by Homer, no substance but mere illusions. When she saw herself descried, she
> wept, and desired Apollonius to be silent, but he would not be moved, and
> thereupon she, plate, house, and all that was in it, vanished in an instant: many
> thousands took notice of this fact, for it was done in the midst of Greece.

In ancient demonology, a "lamia" was a monster in woman's form who preyed on
human beings. There are various clues that Keats invested the ancient legend with
allegorical significance (see especially 2.229–38). Its interpretation, however, and
even the inclination of Keats's own sympathies in the contest between Lamia and
Apollonius, have been disputed. Perhaps Keats simply failed to make up his mind or
wavered in the course of composition. In any case, the poem presents an inevitably
fatal situation, in which no one is entirely blameless or blameworthy and no character
monopolizes either our sympathy or antipathy. Lamia is an enchantress, a liar, and a

---

4. In a letter of June 9, 1819, Keats wrote: "I have
been very idle lately, very averse to writing; both
from the overpowering idea of our dead poets and
from abatement of my love of fame. I hope I am a
little more of a Philosopher than I was, consequently a little less of a versifying Pet-lamb. . . .
You will judge of my 1819 temper when I tell you
that the thing I have most enjoyed this year has
been writing an ode to Indolence."

calculating expert in *amour;* but she apparently intends no harm, is genuinely in love, and is very beautiful. And both male protagonists exhibit culpable extremes. Lycius, though an attractive young lover, is gullible, a slave to his passions, and capable of gratuitous cruelty; while Apollonius, though realistically clear-sighted, is rigid, puritanical, and inhumane.

The poem, written between late June and early September 1819, is a return, after the Spenserian stanzas of *The Eve of St. Agnes,* to the pentameter couplets Keats had used in *Endymion* and other early poems. But Keats had in the meantime been studying John Dryden's closed and strong-paced couplets. The initial lines of Dryden's version of Boccaccio's story *Cymon and Iphigenia* demonstrate the kind of narrative model that helped Keats make the technical transition from the fluent but sprawling gracefulness of the opening of *Endymion* to the vigor and economy of the opening of *Lamia:*

> In that sweet isle where Venus keeps her court,
> And every grace, and all the loves, resort;
> Where either sex is formed of softer earth,
> And takes the bent of pleasure from their birth;
> There lived a Cyprian lord, above the rest
> Wise, wealthy, with a numerous issue blessed. . . .

Lamia

Part 1

Upon a time, before the faery broods
Drove Nymph and Satyr[1] from the prosperous woods,
Before King Oberon's bright diadem,
Sceptre, and mantle, clasp'd with dewy gem,
5   Frighted away the Dryads and the Fauns
From rushes green, and brakes,° and cowslip'd lawns,   thickets
The ever-smitten Hermes[2] empty left
His golden throne, bent warm on amorous theft:
From high Olympus had he stolen light,
10 On this side of Jove's clouds, to escape the sight
Of his great summoner, and made retreat
Into a forest on the shores of Crete.
For somewhere in that sacred island dwelt
A nymph, to whom all hoofed Satyrs knelt;
15 At whose white feet the languid Tritons[3] poured
Pearls, while on land they wither'd and adored.
Fast by the springs where she to bathe was wont,
And in those meads where sometime she might haunt,
Were strewn rich gifts, unknown to any Muse,
20 Though Fancy's casket were unlock'd to choose.
Ah, what a world of love was at her feet!
So Hermes thought, and a celestial heat

---

1. Nymphs and satyrs—like the dryads and fauns in line 5—were minor classical deities of the woods and fields, said here to have been driven off by Oberon, king of the fairies, who were supernatural beings of the postclassical era.

2. Or Mercury; wing-footed messenger at the summons of Jove (line 11), Hermes was notoriously amorous.
3. Minor sea gods.

Burnt from his winged heels to either ear,
That from a whiteness, as the lily clear,
25 Blush'd into roses 'mid his golden hair,
Fallen in jealous curls about his shoulders bare.[4]

From vale to vale, from wood to wood, he flew,
Breathing upon the flowers his passion new,
And wound with many a river to its head,
30 To find where this sweet nymph prepar'd her secret bed:
In vain; the sweet nymph might nowhere be found,
And so he rested, on the lonely ground,
Pensive, and full of painful jealousies
Of the Wood-Gods, and even the very trees.
35 There as he stood, he heard a mournful voice,
Such as once heard, in gentle heart, destroys
All pain but pity: thus the lone voice spake:
"When from this wreathed tomb shall I awake!
When move in a sweet body fit for life,
40 And love, and pleasure, and the ruddy strife
Of hearts and lips! Ah, miserable me!"
The God, dove-footed,[5] glided silently
Round bush and tree, soft-brushing, in his speed,
The taller grasses and full-flowering weed,
45 Until he found a palpitating snake,
Bright, and cirque-couchant[6] in a dusky brake.

She was a gordian[7] shape of dazzling hue,
Vermilion-spotted, golden, green, and blue;
Striped like a zebra, freckled like a pard,°   *leopard*
50 Eyed like a peacock,[8] and all crimson barr'd;
And full of silver moons, that, as she breathed,
Dissolv'd, or brighter shone, or interwreathed
Their lustres with the gloomier tapestries—
So rainbow-sided, touch'd with miseries,
55 She seem'd, at once, some penanced lady elf,
Some demon's mistress, or the demon's self.
Upon her crest she wore a wannish[9] fire
Sprinkled with stars, like Ariadne's tiar:[1]
Her head was serpent, but ah, bitter-sweet!
60 She had a woman's mouth with all its pearls[2] complete:
And for her eyes: what could such eyes do there
But weep, and weep, that they were born so fair?
As Proserpine still weeps for her Sicilian air.[3]
Her throat was serpent, but the words she spake

---

4. I.e., the curls clung jealously to his bare shoulders. This line is the first of a number of Alexan-
drines, a six-foot line, used to vary the metrical
movement—a device that Keats learned from
Dryden. Another such device is the triplet, occurring first in lines 61–63.
5. I.e., quietly as a dove.
6. Lying in a circular coil.
7. Intricately twisted, like the knot tied by King
Gordius, which no one could undo.

8. Having multicolored spots, like the "eyes" in a
peacock's tail.
9. Rather dark.
1. Ariadne, who was transformed into a constellation, had been represented in a painting by Titian
wearing a symbolic crown, or tiara ("tiar"), of stars.
2. "Pearls" had become almost a synonym for
teeth in Elizabethan love poems.
3. Proserpine had been carried off to Hades by
Pluto from the field of Enna, in Sicily.

65 Came, as through bubbling honey, for Love's sake,
And thus; while Hermes on his pinions lay,
Like a stoop'd falcon[4] ere he takes his prey.

"Fair Hermes, crown'd with feathers, fluttering light,
I had a splendid dream of thee last night:
70 I saw thee sitting, on a throne of gold,
Among the Gods, upon Olympus old,
The only sad one; for thou didst not hear
The soft, lute-finger'd Muses chaunting clear,
Nor even Apollo when he sang alone,
75 Deaf to his throbbing throat's long, long melodious moan.
I dreamt I saw thee, robed in purple flakes,
Break amorous through the clouds, as morning breaks,
And, swiftly as a bright Phœbean dart,[5]
Strike for the Cretan isle; and here thou art!
80 Too gentle Hermes, hast thou found the maid?"
Whereat the star of Lethe[6] not delay'd
His rosy eloquence, and thus inquired:
"Thou smooth-lipp'd serpent, surely high inspired!
Thou beauteous wreath, with melancholy eyes,
85 Possess whatever bliss thou canst devise,
Telling me only where my nymph is fled,—
Where she doth breathe!" "Bright planet, thou hast said,"
Return'd the snake, "but seal with oaths, fair God!"
"I swear," said Hermes, "by my serpent rod,
90 And by thine eyes, and by thy starry crown!"
Light flew his earnest words, among the blossoms blown.
Then thus again the brilliance feminine:
"Too frail of heart! for this lost nymph of thine,
Free as the air, invisibly, she strays
95 About these thornless wilds; her pleasant days
She tastes unseen; unseen her nimble feet
Leave traces in the grass and flowers sweet;
From weary tendrils, and bow'd branches green,
She plucks the fruit unseen, she bathes unseen:
100 And by my power is her beauty veil'd
To keep it unaffronted, unassail'd
By the love-glances of unlovely eyes,
Of Satyrs, Fauns, and blear'd Silenus'[7] sighs.
Pale grew her immortality, for woe
105 Of all these lovers, and she grieved so
I took compassion on her, bade her steep
Her hair in weïrd° syrops, that would keep   *magical*
Her loveliness invisible, yet free
To wander as she loves, in liberty.
110 Thou shalt behold her, Hermes, thou alone,

---

4. *Stoop* is the term for the plunge of a falcon on his prey.
5. A ray of Phoebus Apollo, god of the sun.
6. Hermes, when he appeared like a star on the banks of Lethe, in the darkness of Hades. (One of Hermes' offices was to guide the souls of the dead to the lower regions.)
7. Satyr, tutor of Bacchus, usually represented as drunk.

If thou wilt, as thou swearest, grant my boon!"
Then, once again, the charmed God began
An oath, and through the serpent's ears it ran
Warm, tremulous, devout, psalterian.[8]
115 Ravish'd, she lifted her Circean head,
Blush'd a live damask,[9] and swift-lisping said,
"I was a woman, let me have once more
A woman's shape, and charming as before.
I love a youth of Corinth—O the bliss!
120 Give me my woman's form, and place me where he is.
Stoop, Hermes, let me breathe upon thy brow,
And thou shalt see thy sweet nymph even now."
The God on half-shut feathers sank serene,
She breath'd upon his eyes, and swift was seen
125 Of both the guarded nymph near-smiling on the green.
It was no dream; or say a dream it was,
Real are the dreams of Gods, and smoothly pass
Their pleasures in a long immortal dream.
One warm, flush'd moment, hovering, it might seem
130 Dash'd by the wood-nymph's beauty, so he burn'd;
Then, lighting on the printless verdure, turn'd
To the swoon'd serpent, and with languid arm,
Delicate, put to proof the lythe Caducean charm.[1]
So done, upon the nymph his eyes he bent
135 Full of adoring tears and blandishment,
And towards her stept: she, like a moon in wane,
Faded before him, cower'd, nor could restrain
Her fearful sobs, self-folding like a flower
That faints into itself at evening hour:
140 But the God fostering her chilled hand,
She felt the warmth, her eyelids open'd bland,°   *softly*
And, like new flowers at morning song of bees,
Bloom'd, and gave up her honey to the lees.°   *dregs*
Into the green-recessed woods they flew;
145 Nor grew they pale, as mortal lovers do.

     Left to herself, the serpent now began
To change; her elfin blood in madness ran,
Her mouth foam'd, and the grass, therewith besprent,°   *sprinkled*
Wither'd at dew so sweet and virulent;
150 Her eyes in torture fix'd, and anguish drear,
Hot, glaz'd, and wide, with lid-lashes all sear,
Flash'd phosphor and sharp sparks, without one cooling tear.
The colours all inflam'd throughout her train,
She writh'd about, convuls'd with scarlet pain:
155 A deep volcanian yellow took the place
Of all her milder-mooned body's grace;[2]

---

8. Either "like a psalm" or "like the sound of the psaltery" (an ancient stringed instrument).
9. The color of a damask rose (large and fragrant pink rose). "Circean": like that of Circe, the enchantress in the *Odyssey*.

1. I.e., put to the test the magic of the flexible Caduceus (Hermes' official staff).
2. I.e., the yellow of sulfur (thrown up by a volcano) replaced her former silvery moon color.

And, as the lava ravishes the mead,
Spoilt all her silver mail, and golden brede;[3]
Made gloom of all her frecklings, streaks and bars,
160 Eclips'd her crescents, and lick'd up her stars:
So that, in moments few, she was undrest
Of all her sapphires, greens, and amethyst,
And rubious-argent:° of all these bereft,   *silvery red*
Nothing but pain and ugliness were left.
165 Still shone her crown; that vanish'd, also she
Melted and disappear'd as suddenly;
And in the air, her new voice luting soft,
Cried, "Lycius! gentle Lycius!"—Borne aloft
With the bright mists about the mountains hoar
170 These words dissolv'd: Crete's forests heard no more.

Whither fled Lamia, now a lady bright,
A full-born beauty new and exquisite?
She fled into that valley they pass o'er
Who go to Corinth from Cenchreas' shore;[4]
175 And rested at the foot of those wild hills,
The rugged founts of the Peæran rills,
And of that other ridge whose barren back
Stretches, with all its mist and cloudy rack,
South-westward to Cleone. There she stood
180 About a young bird's flutter from a wood,
Fair, on a sloping green of mossy tread,
By a clear pool, wherein she passioned[5]
To see herself escap'd from so sore ills,
While her robes flaunted with the daffodils.

185 Ah, happy Lycius!—for she was a maid
More beautiful than ever twisted braid,
Or sigh'd, or blush'd, or on spring-flowered lea°   *meadow*
Spread a green kirtle° to the minstrelsy: *gown*
A virgin purest lipp'd, yet in the lore
190 Of love deep learned to the red heart's core:
Not one hour old, yet of sciential brain
To unperplex bliss from its neighbour pain;
Define their pettish limits, and estrange
Their points of contact, and swift counterchange;[6]
195 Intrigue with the specious chaos,[7] and dispart
Its most ambiguous atoms with sure art;
As though in Cupid's college she had spent
Sweet days a lovely graduate, still unshent,°   *unspoiled*
And kept his rosy terms[8] in idle languishment.

3. Embroidery, interwoven pattern. "Mail": interlinked rings, as in a coat of armor.
4. Cenchrea (Keats's "Cenchreas") was a harbor of Corinth, in southern Greece.
5. Felt intense excitement.
6. I.e., of knowledgeable ("sciential") brain to disentangle ("unperplex") bliss from its closely related pain, to define their quarreled-over ("pettish") lim-

its, and to separate out ("estrange") their points of contact and the swift changes of each condition into its opposite. Cf. Keats's *Ode on Melancholy*, lines 21–26 (p. 853).
7. I.e., turn to her own artful purpose the seeming ("specious") chaos.
8. The terms spent studying in "Cupid's college."

200   Why this fair creature chose so fairily
    By the wayside to linger, we shall see;
    But first 'tis fit to tell how she could muse
    And dream, when in the serpent prison-house,
    Of all she list,° strange or magnificent: *wished*
205   How, ever, where she will'd, her spirit went;
    Whether to faint Elysium, or where
    Down through tress-lifting waves the Nereids[9] fair
    Wind into Thetis' bower by many a pearly stair;
    Or where God Bacchus drains his cups divine,
210   Stretch'd out, at ease, beneath a glutinous pine;
    Or where in Pluto's gardens palatine°   *palatial*
    Mulciber's columns gleam in far piazzian line.[1]
    And sometimes into cities she would send
    Her dream, with feast and rioting to blend;
215   And once, while among mortals dreaming thus,
    She saw the young Corinthian Lycius
    Charioting foremost in the envious race,
    Like a young Jove with calm uneager face,
    And fell into a swooning love of him.
220   Now on the moth-time of that evening dim
    He would return that way, as well she knew,
    To Corinth from the shore; for freshly blew
    The eastern soft wind, and his galley now
    Grated the quaystones with her brazen prow
225   In port Cenchreas, from Egina isle
    Fresh anchor'd; whither he had been awhile
    To sacrifice to Jove, whose temple there
    Waits with high marble doors for blood and incense rare.
    Jove heard his vows, and better'd his desire;
230   For by some freakful chance he made retire
    From his companions, and set forth to walk,
    Perhaps grown wearied of their Corinth talk:
    Over the solitary hills he fared,
    Thoughtless at first, but ere eve's star appeared
235   His phantasy was lost, where reason fades,
    In the calm'd twilight of Platonic shades.[2]
    Lamia beheld him coming, near, more near—
    Close to her passing, in indifference drear,
    His silent sandals swept the mossy green;
240   So neighbour'd to him, and yet so unseen
    She stood: he pass'd, shut up in mysteries,
    His mind wrapp'd like his mantle, while her eyes
    Follow'd his steps, and her neck regal white
    Turn'd—syllabling thus, "Ah, Lycius bright,
245   And will you leave me on the hills alone?
    Lycius, look back! and be some pity shown."
    He did; not with cold wonder fearingly,

---

9. Sea nymphs, of whom Thetis (line 208, the mother of Achilles) was one.
1. I.e., columns made by Mulciber (Vulcan, god of fire and metalworking) gleam in long lines around open courts (piazzas).
2. I.e., he was absorbed in musing about the obscurities of Plato's philosophy.

But Orpheus-like at an Eurydice;[3]
For so delicious were the words she sung,
250 It seem'd he had lov'd them a whole summer long:
And soon his eyes had drunk her beauty up,
Leaving no drop in the bewildering cup,
And still the cup was full,—while he, afraid
Lest she should vanish ere his lip had paid
255 Due adoration, thus began to adore;
Her soft look growing coy, she saw his chain so sure:
"Leave thee alone! Look back! Ah, Goddess, see
Whether my eyes can ever turn from thee!
For pity do not this sad heart belie[4]—
260 Even as thou vanishest so I shall die.
Stay! though a Naiad of the rivers, stay!
To thy far wishes will thy streams obey:
Stay! though the greenest woods be thy domain,
Alone they can drink up the morning rain:
265 Though a descended Pleiad,[5] will not one
Of thine harmonious sisters keep in tune
Thy spheres, and as thy silver proxy shine?
So sweetly to these ravish'd ears of mine
Came thy sweet greeting, that if thou shouldst fade
270 Thy memory will waste me to a shade:—
For pity do not melt!"—"If I should stay,"
Said Lamia, "here, upon this floor of clay,
And pain my steps upon these flowers too rough,
What canst thou say or do of charm enough
275 To dull the nice[6] remembrance of my home?
Thou canst not ask me with thee here to roam
Over these hills and vales, where no joy is,—
Empty of immortality and bliss!
Thou art a scholar, Lycius, and must know
280 That finer spirits cannot breathe below
In human climes, and live: Alas! poor youth,
What taste of purer air hast thou to soothe
My essence? What serener palaces,
Where I may all my many senses please,
285 And by mysterious sleights a hundred thirsts appease?
It cannot be—Adieu!" So said, she rose
Tiptoe with white arms spread. He, sick to lose
The amorous promise of her lone complain,
Swoon'd, murmuring of love, and pale with pain.
290 The cruel lady, without any show
Of sorrow for her tender favourite's woe,
But rather, if her eyes could brighter be,
With brighter eyes and slow amenity,
Put her new lips to his, and gave afresh

---

3. As Orpheus looked at Eurydice in Hades.
Orpheus was allowed by Pluto to lead Eurydice
back to earth on condition that he not look back
at her, but he could not resist doing so, hence lost
her once more.

4. Be false to.
5. One of the seven sisters composing the constellation Pleiades.
6. Detailed, minutely accurate.

295　The life she had so tangled in her mesh:
　　And as he from one trance was wakening
　　Into another, she began to sing,
　　Happy in beauty, life, and love, and every thing,
　　A song of love, too sweet for earthly lyres,
300　While, like held breath, the stars drew in their panting fires.
　　And then she whisper'd in such trembling tone,
　　As those who, safe together met alone
　　For the first time through many anguish'd days,
　　Use other speech than looks; bidding him raise
305　His drooping head, and clear his soul of doubt,
　　For that she was a woman, and without
　　Any more subtle fluid in her veins
　　Than throbbing blood, and that the self-same pains
　　Inhabited her frail-strung heart as his,
310　And next she wonder'd how his eyes could miss
　　Her face so long in Corinth, where, she said,
　　She dwelt but half retir'd, and there had led
　　Days happy as the gold coin could invent
　　Without the aid of love; yet in content
315　Till she saw him, as once she pass'd him by,
　　Where 'gainst a column he leant thoughtfully
　　At Venus' temple porch, 'mid baskets heap'd
　　Of amorous herbs and flowers, newly reap'd
　　Late on that eve, as 'twas the night before
320　The Adonian feast;[7] whereof she saw no more,
　　But wept alone those days, for why should she adore?
　　Lycius from death awoke into amaze,
　　To see her still, and singing so sweet lays;
　　Then from amaze into delight he fell
325　To hear her whisper woman's lore so well;
　　And every word she spake entic'd him on
　　To unperplex'd delight[8] and pleasure known.
　　Let the mad poets say whate'er they please
　　Of the sweets of Fairies, Peris,[9] Goddesses,
330　There is not such a treat among them all,
　　Haunters of cavern, lake, and waterfall,
　　As a real woman, lineal indeed
　　From Pyrrha's pebbles[1] or old Adam's seed.
　　Thus gentle Lamia judg'd, and judg'd aright,
335　That Lycius could not love in half a fright,
　　So threw the goddess off, and won his heart
　　More pleasantly by playing woman's part,
　　With no more awe than what her beauty gave,
　　That, while it smote, still guaranteed to save.
340　Lycius to all made eloquent reply,
　　Marrying to every word a twinborn sigh;
　　And last, pointing to Corinth, ask'd her sweet,

---

7. The feast of Adonis, beloved by Venus.
8. I.e., delight not mixed with its neighbor, pain (see line 192).
9. Fairylike creatures in Persian mythology.

1. Descended from the pebbles with which, in Greek myth, Pyrrha and Deucalion repeopled the earth after the flood.

If 'twas too far that night for her soft feet.
The way was short, for Lamia's eagerness
345 Made, by a spell, the triple league decrease
To a few paces; not at all surmised
By blinded Lycius, so in her comprized.[2]
They pass'd the city gates, he knew not how,
So noiseless, and he never thought to know.

350 As men talk in a dream, so Corinth all,
Throughout her palaces imperial,
And all her populous streets and temples lewd,[3]
Mutter'd, like tempest in the distance brew'd,
To the wide-spreaded night above her towers.
355 Men, women, rich and poor, in the cool hours,
Shuffled their sandals o'er the pavement white,
Companion'd or alone; while many a light
Flared, here and there, from wealthy festivals,
And threw their moving shadows on the walls,
360 Or found them cluster'd in the corniced shade
Of some arch'd temple door, or dusky colonnade.

Muffling his face, of greeting friends in fear,
Her fingers he press'd hard, as one came near
With curl'd gray beard, sharp eyes, and smooth bald crown,
365 Slow-stepp'd, and robed in philosophic gown:
Lycius shrank closer, as they met and past,
Into his mantle, adding wings to haste,
While hurried Lamia trembled: "Ah," said he,
"Why do you shudder, love, so ruefully?
370 Why does your tender palm dissolve in dew?"—
"I'm wearied," said fair Lamia: "tell me who
Is that old man? I cannot bring to mind
His features:—Lycius! wherefore did you blind
Yourself from his quick eyes?" Lycius replied,
375 " 'Tis Apollonius sage, my trusty guide
And good instructor; but to-night he seems
The ghost of folly haunting my sweet dreams."

While yet he spake they had arrived before
A pillar'd porch, with lofty portal door,
380 Where hung a silver lamp, whose phosphor glow
Reflected in the slabbed steps below,
Mild as a star in water; for so new,
And so unsullied was the marble hue,
So through the crystal polish, liquid fine,
385 Ran the dark veins, that none but feet divine
Could e'er have touch'd there. Sounds Æolian[4]
Breath'd from the hinges, as the ample span
Of the wide doors disclos'd a place unknown

2. Bound up, absorbed.
3. Temples of Venus, whose worship sometimes involved ritual prostitution.
4. Like sounds from the wind harp (Aeolus is god of winds), which responds musically to a current of air.

Some time to any, but those two alone,
390 And a few Persian mutes, who that same year
Were seen about the markets: none knew where
They could inhabit; the most curious
Were foil'd, who watch'd to trace them to their house:
And but the flitter-winged verse must tell,
395 For truth's sake, what woe afterwards befel,
'Twould humour many a heart to leave them thus,
Shut from the busy world of more incredulous.

Part 2

Love in a hut, with water and a crust,
Is—Love, forgive us!—cinders, ashes, dust;
Love in a palace is perhaps at last
More grievous torment than a hermit's fast:—
5 That is a doubtful tale from faery land,
Hard for the non-elect to understand.
Had Lycius liv'd to hand his story down,
He might have given the moral a fresh frown,
Or clench'd it quite: but too short was their bliss
10 To breed distrust and hate, that make the soft voice hiss.
Besides, there, nightly, with terrific glare,
Love, jealous grown of so complete a pair,
Hover'd and buzz'd his wings, with fearful roar,
Above the lintel of their chamber door,
15 And down the passage cast a glow upon the floor.

For all this came a ruin: side by side
They were enthroned, in the even tide,
Upon a couch, near to a curtaining
Whose airy texture, from a golden string,
20 Floated into the room, and let appear
Unveil'd the summer heaven, blue and clear,
Betwixt two marble shafts:—there they reposed,
Where use had made it sweet, with eyelids closed,
Saving a tythe which love still open kept,
25 That they might see each other while they almost slept;
When from the slope side of a suburb hill,
Deafening the swallow's twitter, came a thrill
Of trumpets—Lycius started—the sounds fled,
But left a thought, a buzzing in his head.
30 For the first time, since first he harbour'd in
That purple-lined palace of sweet sin,
His spirit pass'd beyond its golden bourn
Into the noisy world almost forsworn.
The lady, ever watchful, penetrant,
35 Saw this with pain, so arguing a want
Of something more, more than her empery°   empire
Of joys; and she began to moan and sigh
Because he mused beyond her, knowing well
That but a moment's thought is passion's passing bell.°   death knell

40 "Why do you sigh, fair creature?" whisper'd he:
    "Why do you think?" return'd she tenderly:
    "You have deserted me;—where am I now?
    Not in your heart while care weighs on your brow:
    No, no, you have dismiss'd me; and I go
45 From your breast houseless: ay, it must be so."
    He answer'd, bending to her open eyes,
    Where he was mirror'd small in paradise,
    "My silver planet, both of eve and morn![5]
    Why will you plead yourself so sad forlorn,
50 While I am striving how to fill my heart
    With deeper crimson, and a double smart?
    How to entangle, trammel up and snare
    Your soul in mine, and labyrinth you there
    Like the hid scent in an unbudded rose?
55 Ay, a sweet kiss—you see your mighty woes.[6]
    My thoughts! shall I unveil them? Listen then!
    What mortal hath a prize, that other men
    May be confounded and abash'd withal,
    But lets it sometimes pace abroad majestical,
60 And triumph, as in thee I should rejoice
    Amid the hoarse alarm of Corinth's voice.
    Let my foes choke, and my friends shout afar,
    While through the thronged streets your bridal car
    Wheels round its dazzling spokes."—The lady's cheek
65 Trembled; she nothing said, but, pale and meek,
    Arose and knelt before him, wept a rain
    Of sorrows at his words; at last with pain
    Beseeching him, the while his hand she wrung,
    To change his purpose. He thereat was stung,
70 Perverse, with stronger fancy to reclaim
    Her wild and timid nature to his aim:
    Besides, for all his love, in self despite,
    Against his better self, he took delight
    Luxurious in her sorrows, soft and new.
75 His passion, cruel grown, took on a hue
    Fierce and sanguineous as 'twas possible
    In one whose brow had no dark veins to swell.
    Fine was the mitigated fury, like
    Apollo's presence when in act to strike
80 The serpent—Ha, the serpent! certes, she
    Was none. She burnt, she lov'd the tyranny,
    And, all subdued, consented to the hour
    When to the bridal he should lead his paramour.
    Whispering in midnight silence, said the youth,
85 "Sure some sweet name thou hast, though, by my truth,
    I have not ask'd it, ever thinking thee
    Not mortal, but of heavenly progeny,
    As still I do. Hast any mortal name,

5. The planet Venus, which is both the morning and the evening star.

6. Playfully: "You see how great your troubles were!"

Fit appellation for this dazzling frame?
90 Or friends or kinsfolk on the citied earth,
To share our marriage feast and nuptial mirth?"
"I have no friends," said Lamia, "no, not one;
My presence in wide Corinth hardly known:
My parents' bones are in their dusty urns
95 Sepulchred, where no kindled incense burns,
Seeing all their luckless race are dead, save me,
And I neglect the holy rite for thee.
Even as you list invite your many guests;
But if, as now it seems, your vision rests
100 With any pleasure on me, do not bid
Old Apollonius—from him keep me hid."
Lycius, perplex'd at words so blind and blank,
Made close inquiry; from whose touch she shrank,
Feigning a sleep; and he to the dull shade
105 Of deep sleep in a moment was betray'd.

It was the custom then to bring away,
The bride from home at blushing shut of day,
Veil'd, in a chariot, heralded along
By strewn flowers, torches, and a marriage song,
110 With other pageants: but this fair unknown
Had not a friend. So being left alone,
(Lycius was gone to summon all his kin)
And knowing surely she could never win
His foolish heart from its mad pompousness,
115 She set herself, high-thoughted, how to dress
The misery in fit magnificence.
She did so, but 'tis doubtful how and whence
Came, and who were her subtle servitors.
About the halls, and to and from the doors,
120 There was a noise of wings, till in short space
The glowing banquet-room shone with wide-arched grace.
A haunting music, sole perhaps and lone
Supportress of the faery-roof, made moan
Throughout, as fearful the whole charm might fade.
125 Fresh carved cedar, mimicking a glade
Of palm and plantain, met from either side,
High in the midst, in honour of the bride:
Two palms and then two plantains, and so on,
From either side their stems branch'd one to one
130 All down the aisled place; and beneath all
There ran a stream of lamps straight on from wall to wall.
So canopied, lay an untasted feast
Teeming with odours. Lamia, regal drest,
Silently paced about, and as she went,
135 In pale contented sort of discontent,
Mission'd her viewless servants to enrich
The fretted[7] splendour of each nook and niche.

---

7. Adorned with fretwork (interlaced patterns).

Between the tree-stems, marbled plain at first,
Came jasper pannels; then, anon, there burst
140 Forth creeping imagery of slighter trees,
And with the larger wove in small intricacies.
Approving all, she faded at self-will,
And shut the chamber up, close, hush'd and still,
Complete and ready for the revels rude,
145 When dreadful° guests would come to spoil her solitude.   *terrifying*

    The day appear'd, and all the gossip rout.
O senseless Lycius! Madman! wherefore flout
The silent-blessing fate, warm cloister'd hours,
And show to common eyes these secret bowers?
150 The herd approach'd; each guest, with busy brain,
Arriving at the portal, gaz'd amain,°   *intently*
And enter'd marveling: for they knew the street,
Remember'd it from childhood all complete
Without a gap, yet ne'er before had seen
155 That royal porch, that high-built fair demesne;°   *estate*
So in they hurried all, maz'd, curious and keen:
Save one, who look'd thereon with eye severe,
And with calm-planted steps walk'd in austere;
'Twas Apollonius: something too he laugh'd,
160 As though some knotty problem, that had daft°   *baffled*
His patient thought, had now begun to thaw,
And solve and melt:—'twas just as he foresaw.

    He met within the murmurous vestibule
His young disciple. " 'Tis no common rule,
165 Lycius," said he, "for uninvited guest
To force himself upon you, and infest
With an unbidden presence the bright throng
Of younger friends; yet must I do this wrong,
And you forgive me." Lycius blush'd, and led
170 The old man through the inner doors broad-spread;
With reconciling words and courteous mien
Turning into sweet milk the sophist's spleen.

    Of wealthy lustre was the banquet-room,
Fill'd with pervading brilliance and perfume:
175 Before each lucid pannel fuming stood
A censer fed with myrrh and spiced wood,
Each by a sacred tripod held aloft,
Whose slender feet wide-swerv'd upon the soft
Wool-woofed° carpets: fifty wreaths of smoke   *woven*
180 From fifty censers their light voyage took
To the high roof, still mimick'd as they rose
Along the mirror'd walls by twin-clouds odorous.
Twelve sphered tables, by silk seats insphered,
High as the level of a man's breast rear'd
185 On libbard's° paws, upheld the heavy gold   *leopard's*
Of cups and goblets, and the store thrice told

Of Ceres' horn,[8] and, in huge vessels, wine
Come from the gloomy tun with merry shine.
Thus loaded with a feast the tables stood,
190   Each shrining in the midst the image of a God.

When in an antichamber every guest
Had felt the cold full sponge to pleasure press'd,
By minist'ring slaves, upon his hands and feet,
And fragrant oils with ceremony meet
195   Pour'd on his hair, they all mov'd to the feast
In white robes, and themselves in order placed
Around the silken couches, wondering
Whence all this mighty cost and blaze of wealth could spring.

Soft went the music the soft air along,
200   While fluent Greek a vowel'd undersong
Kept up among the guests, discoursing low
At first, for scarcely was the wine at flow;
But when the happy vintage touch'd their brains,
Louder they talk, and louder come the strains
205   Of powerful instruments:—the gorgeous dyes,
The space, the splendour of the draperies,
The roof of awful richness, nectarous cheer,
Beautiful slaves, and Lamia's self, appear,
Now, when the wine has done its rosy deed,
210   And every soul from human trammels freed,
No more so strange; for merry wine, sweet wine,
Will make Elysian shades not too fair, too divine.

Soon was God Bacchus at meridian height;
Flush'd were their cheeks, and bright eyes double bright:
215   Garlands of every green, and every scent
From vales deflower'd, or forest-trees branch-rent,
In baskets of bright osier'd[9] gold were brought
High as the handles heap'd, to suit the thought
Of every guest; that each, as he did please,
220   Might fancy-fit his brows, silk-pillow'd at his ease.

What wreath for Lamia? What for Lycius?
What for the sage, old Apollonius?
Upon her aching forehead be there hung
The leaves of willow and of adder's tongue;[1]
225   And for the youth, quick, let us strip for him
The thyrsus,[2] that his watching eyes may swim
Into forgetfulness; and, for the sage,
Let spear-grass and the spiteful thistle wage
War on his temples. Do not all charms fly

---

8. The horn of plenty, overflowing with the products of Ceres, goddess of grain.
9. Plaited. An "osier" is a strip of willow used in weaving baskets.

1. A fern whose spikes resemble a serpent's tongue.
2. The vine-covered staff of Bacchus, used to signify drunkenness.

230   At the mere touch of cold philosophy?[3]
There was an awful° rainbow once in heaven: *awe-inspiring*
We know her woof, her texture; she is given
In the dull catalogue of common things.
Philosophy will clip an Angel's wings,
235   Conquer all mysteries by rule and line,
Empty the haunted air, and gnomed mine[4]—
Unweave a rainbow, as it erewhile made
The tender-person'd Lamia melt into a shade.

     By her glad Lycius sitting, in chief place,
240   Scarce saw in all the room another face,
Till, checking his love trance, a cup he took
Full brimm'd, and opposite sent forth a look
'Cross the broad table, to beseech a glance
From his old teacher's wrinkled countenance,
245   And pledge[5] him. The bald-head philosopher
Had fix'd his eye, without a twinkle or stir
Full on the alarmed beauty of the bride,
Brow-beating her fair form, and troubling her sweet pride.
Lycius then press'd her hand, with devout touch,
250   As pale it lay upon the rosy couch:
'Twas icy, and the cold ran through his veins;
Then sudden it grew hot, and all the pains
Of an unnatural heat shot to his heart.
"Lamia, what means this? Wherefore dost thou start?
255   Know'st thou that man?" Poor Lamia answer'd not.
He gaz'd into her eyes, and not a jot
Own'd° they the lovelorn piteous appeal: *acknowledged*
More, more he gaz'd: his human senses reel:
Some hungry spell that loveliness absorbs;
260   There was no recognition in those orbs.
"Lamia!" he cried—and no soft-toned reply.
The many heard, and the loud revelry
Grew hush; the stately music no more breathes;
The myrtle[6] sicken'd in a thousand wreaths.
265   By faint degrees, voice, lute, and pleasure ceased;
A deadly silence step by step increased,
Until it seem'd a horrid presence there,
And not a man but felt the terror in his hair.
"Lamia!" he shriek'd; and nothing but the shriek
270   With its sad echo did the silence break.
"Begone, foul dream!" he cried, gazing again
In the bride's face, where now no azure vein
Wander'd on fair-spaced temples; no soft bloom
Misted the cheek; no passion to illume
275   The deep-recessed vision:—all was blight;

---

3. In the sense of "natural philosophy," or science. Benjamin Haydon tells in his *Autobiography* how, at a hard-drinking and high-spirited dinner party, Keats had agreed with Charles Lamb (to what extent jokingly, it is not clear) that Newton's *Optics* "had destroyed all the poetry of the rainbow by reducing it to the prismatic colors."
4. Gnomes were guardians of mines.
5. Drink a toast to.
6. Sacred to Venus, hence an emblem of love.

Lamia, no longer fair, there sat a deadly white.
"Shut, shut those juggling[7] eyes, thou ruthless man!
Turn them aside, wretch! or the righteous ban
Of all the Gods, whose dreadful images
280 Here represent their shadowy presences,
May pierce them on the sudden with the thorn
Of painful blindness; leaving thee forlorn,
In trembling dotage to the feeblest fright
Of conscience, for their long offended might,
285 For all thine impious proud-heart sophistries,
Unlawful magic, and enticing lies.
Corinthians! look upon that gray-beard wretch!
Mark how, possess'd, his lashless eyelids stretch
Around his demon eyes! Corinthians, see!
290 My sweet bride withers at their potency."
"Fool!" said the sophist, in an under-tone
Gruff with contempt; which a death-nighing moan
From Lycius answer'd, as heart-struck and lost,
He sank supine beside the aching ghost.
295 "Fool! Fool!" repeated he, while his eyes still
Relented not, nor mov'd; "from every ill
Of life have I preserv'd thee to this day,
And shall I see thee made a serpent's prey?"
Then Lamia breath'd death breath; the sophist's eye,
300 Like a sharp spear, went through her utterly,
Keen, cruel, perceant,° stinging: she, as well   piercing
As her weak hand could any meaning tell,
Motion'd him to be silent; vainly so,
He look'd and look'd again a level—No!
305 "A Serpent!" echoed he; no sooner said,
Than with a frightful scream she vanished:
And Lycius' arms were empty of delight,
As were his limbs of life, from that same night.
On the high couch he lay!—his friends came round—
310 Supported him—no pulse, or breath they found,
And, in its marriage robe, the heavy body wound.

July–Aug. 1819   1820

To Autumn[1]

I

Season of mists and mellow fruitfulness,
  Close bosom-friend of the maturing sun;
Conspiring with him how to load and bless
  With fruit the vines that round the thatch-eves run;
5   To bend with apples the moss'd cottage-trees,
  And fill all fruit with ripeness to the core;

---

7. Deceiving, full of trickery.
1. Two days after this ode was composed, Keats wrote to J. H. Reynolds: "I never liked stubble fields so much as now—Aye, better than the chilly green of the spring. Somehow a stubble plain looks warm—in the same way that some pictures look warm—this struck me so much in my Sunday's walk that I composed upon it." For the author's revisions while composing To Autumn, see "Poems in Process," in the appendices to this volume.

To swell the gourd, and plump the hazel shells
With a sweet kernel; to set budding more,
And still more, later flowers for the bees,
10   Until they think warm days will never cease,
For summer has o'er-brimm'd their clammy cells.

2

Who hath not seen thee oft amid thy store?
Sometimes whoever seeks abroad may find
Thee sitting careless on a granary floor,
15   Thy hair soft-lifted by the winnowing[2] wind;
Or on a half-reap'd furrow sound asleep,
Drows'd with the fume of poppies, while thy hook°   scythe
Spares the next swath and all its twined flowers:
And sometimes like a gleaner thou dost keep
20   Steady thy laden head across a brook;
Or by a cyder-press, with patient look,
Thou watchest the last oozings hours by hours.

3

Where are the songs of spring? Ay, where are they?
Think not of them, thou hast thy music too,—
25   While barred clouds bloom the soft-dying day,
And touch the stubble-plains with rosy hue;
Then in a wailful choir the small gnats mourn
Among the river sallows,° borne aloft   willows
Or sinking as the light wind lives or dies;
30   And full-grown lambs loud bleat from hilly bourn;°   region
Hedge-crickets sing; and now with treble soft
The red-breast whistles from a garden-croft;[3]
And gathering swallows twitter in the skies.

Sept. 19, 1819   1820

The Fall of Hyperion: A Dream

Late in 1818, at about the end of his twenty-third year and while he was serving as nurse to his dying brother Tom, Keats planned to undertake an epic poem, modeled on *Paradise Lost,* which he called *Hyperion.* Its subject, the displacement of Saturn and his fellow Titans by Zeus and the other Olympians, was taken from Greek mythology, but the primary epic question, like that in *Paradise Lost,* was *unde malum?*—whence and why evil? Keats set out in his story to represent an answer, not according to any religious creed but in humanistic terms, delimited to humankind and its natural milieu. The Titans had been equable and benign gods, ruling in the Saturnian, or golden, age of general felicity. Yet at the beginning of the poem all the Titans except Hyperion, god of the sun, have been dethroned; and the uncomprehending Saturn again and again raises the questions Who? Why? How? Can blank unreason and injustice determine the course of things?

In book 3 of the original *Hyperion* the scenes among the Titans are supplemented by the experience of the Olympian Apollo, still a youth but destined to displace

2. To "winnow" is to fan the chaff from the grain.   3. An enclosed plot of farmland.

Hyperion among the heavenly powers. He lives in "aching ignorance" of the universe and its processes, but he is aware of his ignorance and avid for knowledge. Suddenly Apollo reads in the face of Mnemosyne—goddess of memory, who will be mother of the muses and so of all the arts—the silent record of the defeat of the Titans and at once soars to the knowledge that he seeks: the understanding, both intoxicating and agonizing, that life involves process, that process entails change and suffering, and that there can be no creative progress except by the defeat and destruction of the preceding stage. Apollo cries out:

> Knowledge enormous makes a God of me.
> Names, deeds, gray legends, dire events, rebellions,
> Majesties, sovran voices, agonies,
> Creations and destroyings, all at once
> Pour into the wide hollows of my brain,
> And deify me. . . .

This opening out of Apollo's awareness to the tragic nature of life is what the Titans lacked. As the fragment breaks off, Apollo is transfigured—like one who should "with fierce convulse / Die into life"—not only into one who has earned the right to displace Hyperion as god of the sun, but also into the god of the highest poetry.

Keats abandoned this extraordinary fragment in April 1819. Late that summer, however, he took up the theme again, under the title *The Fall of Hyperion: A Dream*. This time his primary model is Dante, whom he had been studying in Henry Cary's verse translation. In *The Divine Comedy* all the narrated events are represented as a vision granted to Dante at the beginning of the poem. In similar fashion, Keats begins his new poem with a long induction in which the poet, in a dream, earns the right to a vision finally granted him by Moneta (her Latin name suggests "the Admonisher"), who replaces Mnemosyne; this vision will incorporate the events narrated in the first *Hyperion*. The induction, in effect, shifts the center of poetic concern from the epic action to the evolving consciousness of the narrative poet himself, as he seeks his identity and status; it serves also to displace (or perhaps to parallel) the earlier ordeal through which Apollo had become god of poetry by the ordeal of this particular poet.

As early as *Sleep and Poetry* (1816), Keats had begun to explore the baffling relation of dreams to insight, of wishful fantasies to imaginative truth, and of the life of humane action to the contemplative vision of the poet. He continued to widen these speculations in *Endymion* and some of his shorter poems; and his letters show his ceaseless effort to assimilate his enlarging experience, his sharpening sense of suffering humanity, and his search for some equivalent of the "salvation" offered by a religious creed he could not accept into his theory and program of poetry. (See especially the letters included here subtitled "Milton, Wordsworth, and the Chambers of Human Life" and "The Vale of Soul-Making.") In the introduction to the long "Dream" that constitutes *The Fall of Hyperion*, Keats works the results of his experience and speculations into the form of a ritual initiation, in which he moves from stage to stage in his evolution as a poet. This agonizing rite of passage ends at the stage in which, having passed through and beyond the ordinary experience of human suffering, he achieves aesthetic insight and distance—the power "To see as a God sees" (line 304)—and so demonstrates his right to undertake this epic poem of tragic suffering.

A number of things caused Keats to abandon *The Fall of Hyperion* at the sixty-first line of the second canto. He wrote to Reynolds on September 21, 1819:

> I have given up Hyperion. . . . Miltonic verse cannot be written but in an artful or rather artist's humour. I wish to give myself up to other sensations. English ought to be kept up. It may be interesting to you to pick out some lines from Hyperion and put a mark × to the false beauty proceeding from art, and one ‖ to the true voice of feeling.

The two Hyperion fragments are impressive achievements, but as Keats with his acumen in self-criticism recognized, they have the air of artistic *tours de force,* written in an age in which the high artifice of the epic matter and style had ceased to be the natural voice of the poet. In the same letter, Keats mentions having composed two days earlier the ode *To Autumn.* In this, his last major poem, the poet had envisaged the circumstance of the cycle of life and death, and had articulated his experience in his own poetic voice.

The Fall of Hyperion: A Dream

Canto 1

Fanatics have their dreams, wherewith they weave
A paradise for a sect; the savage too
From forth the loftiest fashion of his sleep
Guesses at heaven: pity these have not
5   Trac'd upon vellum or wild Indian leaf
The shadows of melodious utterance.
But bare of laurel they live, dream, and die;
For Poesy alone can tell her dreams,
With the fine spell of words alone can save
10   Imagination from the sable charm
And dumb enchantment. Who alive can say
"Thou art no poet; may'st not tell thy dreams"?
Since every man whose soul is not a clod
Hath visions, and would speak, if he had lov'd
15   And been well nurtured in his mother tongue.
Whether the dream now purposed to rehearse
Be poet's or fanatic's will be known
When this warm scribe my hand is in the grave.

Methought I stood where trees of every clime,
20   Palm, myrtle, oak, and sycamore, and beech,
With plantane, and spice blossoms, made a screen;
In neighbourhood of fountains, by the noise
Soft showering in mine ears, and, by the touch
Of scent, not far from roses. Turning round,
25   I saw an arbour with a drooping roof
Of trellis vines, and bells, and larger blooms,
Like floral-censers swinging light in air;
Before its wreathed doorway, on a mound
Of moss, was spread a feast of summer fruits,
30   Which, nearer seen, seem'd refuse of a meal
By angel tasted, or our mother Eve;[1]
For empty shells were scattered on the grass,
And grape stalks but half bare, and remnants more,
Sweet smelling, whose pure kinds I could not know.
35   Still was more plenty than the fabled horn[2]
Thrice emptied could pour forth, at banqueting

---

1. In *Paradise Lost* 5.321ff. Eve serves the visiting angel Raphael with a meal of fruits and fruit juices. Keats thus adapts Milton's Eden to represent the early stage of his own experience and poetry.
2. The cornucopia, or horn of plenty.

For Proserpine return'd to her own fields,[3]
Where the white heifers low. And appetite
More yearning than on earth I ever felt
40 Growing within, I ate deliciously;
And, after not long, thirsted, for thereby
Stood a cool vessel of transparent juice,
Sipp'd by the wander'd bee, the which I took,
And, pledging all the mortals of the world,
45 And all the dead whose names are in our lips,
Drank. That full draught is parent of my theme.[4]
No Asian poppy, nor elixir fine
Of the soon fading jealous caliphat;[5]
No poison gender'd in close monkish cell
50 To thin the scarlet conclave of old men,[6]
Could so have rapt unwilling life away.
Among the fragrant husks and berries crush'd,
Upon the grass I struggled hard against
The domineering potion; but in vain:
55 The cloudy swoon came on, and down I sunk
Like a Silenus[7] on an antique vase.
How long I slumber'd 'tis a chance to guess.
When sense of life return'd, I started up
As if with wings; but the fair trees were gone,
60 The mossy mound and arbour were no more;
I look'd around upon the carved sides
Of an old sanctuary with roof august,
Builded so high, it seem'd that filmed clouds
Might spread beneath, as o'er the stars of heaven;
65 So old the place was, I remembered none
The like upon the earth; what I had seen
Of grey cathedrals, buttress'd walls, rent towers,
The superannuations of sunk realms,
Or nature's rocks toil'd hard in waves and winds,
70 Seem'd but the faulture° of decrepit things   *defects*
To° that eternal domed monument.   *compared to*
Upon the marble at my feet there lay
Store of strange vessels, and large draperies,
Which needs had been of dyed asbestus wove,
75 Or in that place the moth could not corrupt,[8]
So white the linen; so, in some, distinct
Ran imageries from a sombre loom.
All in a mingled heap confus'd there lay
Robes, golden tongs, censer, and chafing dish,
80 Girdles, and chains, and holy jewelries.[9]

Turning from these with awe, once more I rais'd
My eyes to fathom the space every way;

---

3. When Proserpine each year is released by her husband, Pluto, god of the underworld, for a sojourn on earth, it is the beginning of spring.
4. The drink puts the poet to sleep and effects the dream within a dream that constitutes the remainder of the fragment.
5. A council of caliphs, Muslim rulers, who plot to kill each other with a poisonous drink ("elixir").

6. The College of Cardinals.
7. An elderly satyr, usually represented as drunk.
8. Matthew 6.20: "Lay up for yourselves treasures in heaven, where neither moth nor rust doth corrupt."
9. Offerings to the gods were spread on the floor of Greek temples.

The embossed roof, the silent massy range
Of columns north and south, ending in mist
85 Of nothing, then to eastward, where black gates
Were shut against the sunrise evermore.
Then to the west I look'd,[1] and saw far off
An image, huge of feature as a cloud,
At level of whose feet an altar slept,
90 To be approach'd on either side by steps,
And marble balustrade, and patient travail
To count with toil the innumerable degrees.
Towards the altar sober-pac'd I went,
Repressing haste, as too unholy there;
95 And, coming nearer, saw beside the shrine
One minist'ring;[2] and there arose a flame.
When in mid-May the sickening east wind
Shifts sudden to the south, the small warm rain
Melts out the frozen incense from all flowers,
100 And fills the air with so much pleasant health
That even the dying man forgets his shroud;
Even so that lofty sacrificial fire,
Sending forth Maian[3] incense, spread around
Forgetfulness of every thing but bliss,
105 And clouded all the altar with soft smoke,
From whose white fragrant curtains thus I heard
Language pronounc'd. "If thou canst not ascend
These steps,[4] die on that marble where thou art.
Thy flesh, near cousin to the common dust,
110 Will parch for lack of nutriment—thy bones
Will wither in few years, and vanish so
That not the quickest eye could find a grain
Of what thou now art on that pavement cold.
The sands of thy short life are spent this hour,
115 And no hand in the universe can turn
Thy hour glass, if these gummed leaves be burnt
Ere thou canst mount up these immortal steps."
I heard, I look'd: two senses both at once
So fine, so subtle, felt the tyranny
120 Of that fierce threat, and the hard task proposed.
Prodigious seem'd the toil; the leaves were yet
Burning,—when suddenly a palsied chill
Struck from the paved level up my limbs,
And was ascending quick to put cold grasp
125 Upon those streams that pulse beside the throat:
I shriek'd; and the sharp anguish of my shriek
Stung my own ears—I strove hard to escape
The numbness; strove to gain the lowest step.
Slow, heavy, deadly was my pace: the cold
130 Grew stifling, suffocating, at the heart;

1. The poet cannot turn back to his origin in the east, and the ways north and south lead nowhere; he must travel the way of mortal life toward the sunset.
2. Who identifies herself in line 226 as Moneta.
3. Maia was one of the Pleiades, a daughter of Atlas and (by Zeus) the mother of Hermes.
4. These steps that the poet must ascend to knowledge were probably suggested by the stairs going up the steep side of the purgatorial Mount in Dante's *Purgatorio*.

And when I clasp'd my hands I felt them not.
One minute before death, my iced foot touch'd
The lowest stair; and as it touch'd, life seem'd
To pour in at the toes: I mounted up,
135 As once fair angels on a ladder flew
From the green turf to heaven.⁵—"Holy Power,"
Cried I, approaching near the horned shrine,⁶
"What am I that should so be sav'd from death?
What am I that another death come not
140 To choak my utterance sacrilegious here?"
Then said the veiled shadow—"Thou hast felt
What 'tis to die and live again before
Thy fated hour. That thou hadst power to do so
Is thy own safety; thou hast dated on
145 Thy doom."⁷—"High Prophetess," said I, "purge off
Benign, if so it please thee, my mind's film."
"None can usurp this height," return'd that shade,
"But those to whom the miseries of the world
Are misery, and will not let them rest.
150 All else who find a haven in the world,
Where they may thoughtless sleep away their days,
If by a chance into this fane° they come,   *temple*
Rot on the pavement where thou rotted'st half."⁸—
"Are there not thousands in the world," said I,
155 Encourag'd by the sooth voice of the shade,
"Who love their fellows even to the death;
Who feel the giant agony of the world;
And more, like slaves to poor humanity,
Labour for mortal good? I sure should see
160 Other men here: but I am here alone."
"They whom thou spak'st of are no vision'ries,"
Rejoin'd that voice—"They are no dreamers weak,
They seek no wonder but the human face;
No music but a happy-noted voice—
165 They come not here, they have no thought to come—
And thou art here, for thou art less than they.
What benefit canst thou do, or all thy tribe,
To the great world? Thou art a dreaming thing;
A fever of thyself—think of the earth;
170 What bliss even in hope is there for thee?
What haven? Every creature hath its home;
Every sole man hath days of joy and pain,
Whether his labours be sublime or low—
The pain alone; the joy alone; distinct:
175 Only the dreamer venoms all his days,
Bearing more woe than all his sins deserve.

5. The ladder by which, in a dream, Jacob saw angels passing between heaven and earth (Genesis 28.12 and *Paradise Lost* 3.510–15).
6. As, e.g., in Exodus 27.2, "And thou shalt make the horns of [the altar] upon the four corners thereof." In his description of the temple and its accouterments Keats deliberately mingles Hebrew,

Christian, and pagan elements to represent the poet's passage through the stage represented by all religions, which are "dreams" made into the creed for "a sect" (lines 1–18).
7. I.e., you have postponed the time when you will be judged.
8. I.e., where you halfway rotted.

Therefore, that happiness be somewhat shar'd,
Such things as thou art are admitted oft
Into like gardens thou didst pass erewhile,
180 And suffer'd in these temples; for that cause
Thou standest safe beneath this statue's knees."
"That I am favored for unworthiness,
By such propitious parley medicin'd
In sickness not ignoble, I rejoice,
185 Aye, and could weep for love of such award."
So answer'd I, continuing, "If it please,
Majestic shadow, tell me: sure not all[9]
Those melodies sung into the world's ear
Are useless: sure a poet is a sage;
190 A humanist, physician to all men.
That I am none I feel, as vultures feel
They are no birds when eagles are abroad.
What am I then? Thou spakest of my tribe:
What tribe?"—The tall shade veil'd in drooping white
195 Then spake, so much more earnest, that the breath
Mov'd the thin linen folds that drooping hung
About a golden censer from the hand
Pendent.—"Art thou not of the dreamer tribe?
The poet and the dreamer are distinct,
200 Diverse, sheer opposite, antipodes.
The one pours out a balm upon the world,
The other vexes it." Then shouted I
Spite of myself, and with a Pythia's spleen,[1]
"Apollo! faded, far flown Apollo!
205 Where is thy misty pestilence[2] to creep
Into the dwellings, through the door crannies,
Of all mock lyrists, large self worshipers,
And careless hectorers in proud bad verse.[3]
Though I breathe death with them it will be life
210 To see them sprawl before me into graves.[4]

9. Keats's friend Richard Woodhouse, whose manuscript copy of the poem is our principal source of the text, crossed out lines 187–210 with the marginal comment next to lines 197–99: "K. seems to have intended to erase this & the next 21 lines." Probably the basis for his opinion is the partial repetition of lines 187 and 194–98 in lines 211 and 216–20.
1. With the anger ("spleen") of the Pythia, the priestess who served at Delphi as the oracle of Apollo, the god of poetry.
2. Apollo was a sender of plagues, as well as the inspirer of prophecy and poetry.
3. This has been conjectured as referring to Byron, or else to several contemporaries, including Shelley and Wordsworth. But the poetic types, not individuals, are what matter to Keats's argument.
4. In lines 147–210 we find a series of progressive distinctions: (1) between humanitarians who feel for "the miseries of the world" and people who are "thoughtless" sleepers (lines 147–53); (2) within the class of humanitarians, between those who actively "benefit . . . the great world" and the poets who are "vision'ries" and "dreamers" (lines 161–

69); (3) and within the class of poets, between those who are merely dreamers and those who are sages and healers (lines 187–202). As in the colloquy between Asia and Demogorgon (see Shelley's *Prometheus Unbound* 2.4.1–128, p. 742), the interchange here may be taken to represent, in dramatized form, a process of inner analysis and self-discovery on the part of the questing poet. Moneta's charges are not final judgments but tests to determine the "tribe" to which the narrating poet belongs—tests he passes by the nature of the responses he makes. At this point, the fact that the narrator himself proceeds to bring charges against self-indulgent and irresponsible poets distinguishes him from the class of poets he denounces and thus shows that he is ready for the final stage of his ordeal, his initiation into the realm of the highest poetry, through the revelation of the "high tragedy" (line 277) of what it means to be human. This ultimate enlightenment, which begins with line 291 and presumably would have constituted the remainder of the poem, is a vision in a dream within a dream (see n. 4, p. 876).

Majestic shadow, tell me where I am:
Whose altar this; for whom this incense curls:
What image this, whose face I cannot see,
For the broad marble knees; and who thou art,
215   Of accent feminine, so courteous."
Then the tall shade in drooping linens veil'd
Spake out, so much more earnest, that her breath
Stirr'd the thin folds of gauze that drooping hung
About a golden censer from her hand
220   Pendent; and by her voice I knew she shed
Long treasured tears. "This temple sad and lone
Is all spar'd from the thunder of a war
Foughten long since by giant hierarchy
Against rebellion: this old image here,
225   Whose carved features wrinkled as he fell,
Is Saturn's; I, Moneta, left supreme
Sole priestess of his desolation."—
I had no words to answer; for my tongue,
Useless, could find about its roofed home
230   No syllable of a fit majesty
To make rejoinder to Moneta's mourn.
There was a silence while the altar's blaze
Was fainting for sweet food: I look'd thereon
And on the paved floor, where nigh were pil'd
235   Faggots of cinnamon, and many heaps
Of other crisped spice-wood—then again
I look'd upon the altar and its horns
Whiten'd with ashes, and its lang'rous flame,
And then upon the offerings again;
240   And so by turns—till sad Moneta cried,
"The sacrifice is done, but not the less
Will I be kind to thee for thy good will.
My power, which to me is still a curse,
Shall be to thee a wonder; for the scenes
245   Still swooning vivid through my globed brain
With an electral changing misery
Thou shalt with those dull mortal eyes behold,
Free from all pain, if wonder pain thee not."
As near as an immortal's sphered words
250   Could to a mother's soften, were these last:
But yet I had a terror of her robes,
And chiefly of the veils, that from her brow
Hung pale, and curtain'd her in mysteries
That made my heart too small to hold its blood.
255   This saw that Goddess, and with sacred hand
Parted the veils. Then saw I a wan face,
Not pin'd by human sorrows, but bright blanch'd
By an immortal sickness which kills not;
It works a constant change, which happy death
260   Can put no end to; deathwards progressing
To no death was that visage; it had pass'd
The lily and the snow; and beyond these

I must not think now, though I saw that face—
But for her eyes I should have fled away.
265 They held me back, with a benignant light,
Soft mitigated by divinest lids
Half closed, and visionless entire they seem'd
Of all external things—they saw me not,
But in blank splendor beam'd like the mild moon,
270 Who comforts those she sees not, who knows not
What eyes are upward cast. As I had found
A grain of gold upon a mountain's side,
And twing'd with avarice strain'd out my eyes
To search its sullen entrails rich with ore,
275 So at the view of sad Moneta's brow,
I ached to see what things the hollow brain
Behind enwombed: what high tragedy
In the dark secret chambers of her skull
Was acting, that could give so dread a stress
280 To her cold lips, and fill with such a light
Her planetary eyes; and touch her voice
With such a sorrow. "Shade of Memory!"
Cried I, with act adorant at her feet,
"By all the gloom hung round thy fallen house,
285 By this last temple, by the golden age,
By great Apollo, thy dear foster child,
And by thy self, forlorn divinity,
The pale Omega⁵ of a wither'd race,
Let me behold, according as thou said'st,
290 What in thy brain so ferments to and fro."—
No sooner had this conjuration pass'd
My devout lips, than side by side we stood,
(Like a stunt bramble by a solemn pine)
Deep in the shady sadness of a vale,⁶
295 Far sunken from the healthy breath of morn,
Far from the fiery noon, and eve's one star.
Onward I look'd beneath the gloomy boughs,
And saw, what first I thought an image huge,
Like to the image pedestal'd so high
300 In Saturn's temple. Then Moneta's voice
Came brief upon mine ear,—"So Saturn sat
When he had lost his realms."—Whereon there grew
A power within me of enormous ken,
To see as a God sees, and take the depth
305 Of things as nimbly as the outward eye
Can size and shape pervade. The lofty theme
At those few words hung vast before my mind,
With half unravel'd web. I set myself
Upon an eagle's watch, that I might see,
310 And seeing ne'er forget. No stir of life

---

5. The final letter of the Greek alphabet.
6. This had been the opening line of the original *Hyperion*. The rest of the poem is a revised version of part of that first narrative, with the poet now represented as allowed to envision the course of events that Moneta recalls in her memory (lines 282, 289–90).

Was in this shrouded vale, not so much air
As in the zoning° of a summer's day   *course*
Robs not one light seed from the feather'd grass,
But where the deaf leaf fell there did it rest:
315   A stream went voiceless by, still deaden'd more
By reason of the fallen divinity
Spreading more shade: the Naiad° mid her reeds   *water nymph*
Press'd her cold finger closer to her lips.
Along the margin sand large footmarks went
320   No farther than to where old Saturn's feet
Had rested, and there slept, how long a sleep!
Degraded, cold, upon the sodden ground
His old right hand lay nerveless, listless, dead,
Unsceptred; and his realmless[7] eyes were clos'd,
325   While his bow'd head seem'd listening to the Earth,
His antient mother,[8] for some comfort yet.

It seem'd no force could wake him from his place;
But there came one who with a kindred hand
Touch'd his wide shoulders, after bending low
330   With reverence, though to one who knew it not.
Then came the griev'd voice of Mnemosyne,[9]
And griev'd I hearken'd. "That divinity
Whom thou saw'st step from yon forlornest wood,
And with slow pace approach our fallen King,
335   Is Thea,[1] softest-natur'd of our brood."
I mark'd the goddess in fair statuary
Surpassing wan Moneta by the head,[2]
And in her sorrow nearer woman's tears.
There was a listening fear in her regard,
340   As if calamity had but begun;
As if the vanward clouds[3] of evil days
Had spent their malice, and the sullen rear
Was with its stored thunder labouring up.
One hand she press'd upon that aching spot
345   Where beats the human heart; as if just there,
Though an immortal, she felt cruel pain;
The other upon Saturn's bended neck
She laid, and to the level of his hollow ear
Leaning, with parted lips, some words she spake
350   In solemn tenor and deep organ tune;
Some mourning words, which in our feeble tongue
Would come in this-like accenting; how frail
To that large utterance of the early Gods!—
"Saturn! look up—and for what, poor lost King?[4]
355   I have no comfort for thee, no—not one:

---

7. Saturn's eyes, when open, express the fact that he has lost his realm.
8. Saturn and the other Titans were the children of Heaven and Earth.
9. As in 2.50, Keats substitutes for "Moneta" the "Mnemosyne" of the first *Hyperion.* This may be a slip but more likely indicates an alternative name for Moneta, in her role as participant in, as well as commentator on, the tragic action.
1. Sister and wife of Hyperion.
2. I.e., Thea was a head taller than Moneta.
3. The front line of clouds.
4. Keats several times recalls King Lear in representing the condition of Saturn.

I cannot cry, *Wherefore thus sleepest thou?*
For heaven is parted from thee, and the earth
Knows thee not, so afflicted, for a God;
And ocean too, with all its solemn noise,
360 Has from thy sceptre pass'd, and all the air
Is emptied of thine hoary majesty.
Thy thunder, captious at the new command,
Rumbles reluctant o'er our fallen house;
And thy sharp lightning in unpracticed hands
365 Scorches and burns our once serene domain.
With such remorseless speed still come new woes
That unbelief has not a space to breathe.[5]
Saturn, sleep on:—Me thoughtless,[6] why should I
Thus violate thy slumbrous solitude?
370 Why should I ope thy melancholy eyes?
Saturn, sleep on, while at thy feet I weep."

     As when, upon a tranced summer night,
Forests, branch-charmed by the earnest stars,[7]
Dream, and so dream all night, without a noise,
375 Save from one gradual solitary gust,
Swelling upon the silence; dying off;
As if the ebbing air had but one wave;
So came these words, and went; the while in tears
She press'd her fair large forehead to the earth,
380 Just where her fallen hair might spread in curls,
A soft and silken mat for Saturn's feet.
Long, long, those two were postured motionless,
Like sculpture builded up upon the grave
Of their own power. A long awful time
385 I look'd upon them; still they were the same;
The frozen God still bending to the earth,
And the sad Goddess weeping at his feet;
Moneta silent. Without stay or prop
But my own weak mortality, I bore
390 The load of this eternal quietude,
The unchanging gloom, and the three fixed shapes
Ponderous upon my senses a whole moon.
For by my burning brain I measured sure
Her silver seasons shedded on the night,
395 And every day by day methought I grew
More gaunt and ghostly. Oftentimes I pray'd
Intense, that death would take me from the vale
And all its burthens. Gasping with despair
Of change, hour after hour I curs'd myself:
400 Until old Saturn rais'd his faded eyes,
And look'd around, and saw his kingdom gone,
And all the gloom and sorrow of the place,

---

5. That disbelief has not an instant to catch its
breath.
6. I.e., how thoughtless I am!
7. The grander version in the first *Hyperion*,

1.72ff., reads: "As when, upon a tranced summer-
night / Those green-rob'd senators of mighty
woods, / Tall oaks, branch-charmed by the earnest
stars, / Dream."

And that fair kneeling Goddess at his feet.
As the moist scent of flowers, and grass, and leaves
405 Fills forest dells with a pervading air
Known to the woodland nostril, so the words
Of Saturn fill'd the mossy glooms around,
Even to the hollows of time-eaten oaks,
And to the windings in the foxes' hole,
410 With sad low tones, while thus he spake, and sent
Strange musings to the solitary Pan.

"Moan, brethren, moan; for we are swallow'd up
And buried from all godlike exercise
Of influence benign on planets pale,
415 And peaceful sway above man's harvesting,
And all those acts which deity supreme
Doth ease its heart of love in. Moan and wail.
Moan, brethren, moan; for lo! the rebel spheres
Spin round, the stars their antient courses keep,
420 Clouds still with shadowy moisture haunt the earth,
Still suck their fill of light from sun and moon,
Still buds the tree, and still the sea-shores murmur.
There is no death in all the universe,
No smell of death—there shall be death⁸—Moan, moan,
425 Moan, Cybele,⁹ moan, for thy pernicious babes
Have chang'd a God into a shaking palsy.
Moan, brethren, moan; for I have no strength left,
Weak as the reed—weak—feeble as my voice—
O, O, the pain, the pain of feebleness.
430 Moan, moan; for still I thaw—or give me help:
Throw down those imps¹ and give me victory.
Let me hear other groans, and trumpets blown
Of triumph calm, and hymns of festival
From the gold peaks of heaven's high piled clouds;
435 Voices of soft proclaim,° and silver stir   proclamation
Of strings in hollow shells; and let there be
Beautiful things made new for the surprize
Of the sky children."—So he feebly ceas'd,
With such a poor and sickly sounding pause,
440 Methought I heard some old man of the earth
Bewailing earthly loss; nor could my eyes
And ears act with that pleasant unison of sense
Which marries sweet sound with the grace of form,
And dolorous accent from a tragic harp
445 With large limb'd visions.² More I scrutinized:
Still fix'd he sat beneath the sable trees,
Whose arms spread straggling in wild serpent forms,
With leaves all hush'd: his awful presence there

---

8. The passing of the Saturnian golden age (paralleled by Keats with the fable of the loss of Eden) has introduced suffering, and will also introduce death.
9. The wife of Saturn and mother of the Olympian gods, who have overthrown their parents.
1. I.e., his rebellious children.
2. I.e., the narrator could not attach this speech, like that of a feebly complaining old mortal, to the visible form of the large-limbed god who uttered it.

(Now all was silent) gave a deadly lie
450   To what I erewhile heard: only his lips
Trembled amid the white curls of his beard.
They told the truth, though, round, the snowy locks
Hung nobly, as upon the face of heaven
A midday fleece of clouds. Thea arose
455   And stretch'd her white arm through the hollow dark,
Pointing some whither: whereat he too rose
Like a vast giant seen by men at sea
To grow pale from the waves at dull midnight.[3]
They melted from my sight into the woods:
460   Ere I could turn, Moneta cried—"These twain
Are speeding to the families of grief,
Where roof'd in by black rocks they waste in pain
And darkness for no hope."—And she spake on,
As ye may read who can unwearied pass
465   Onward from the antichamber of this dream,
Where even at the open doors awhile
I must delay, and glean my memory
Of her high phrase: perhaps no further dare.

Canto 2

"Mortal, that thou may'st understand aright,
I humanize my sayings to thine ear,
Making comparisons of earthly things;
Or thou might'st better listen to the wind,
5   Whose language is to thee a barren noise,
Though it blows legend-laden through the trees.
In melancholy realms big tears are shed,
More sorrow like to this, and such-like woe,
Too huge for mortal tongue, or pen of scribe.
10   The Titans fierce, self-hid, or prison-bound,
Groan for the old allegiance once more,
Listening in their doom for Saturn's voice.
But one of our whole eagle-brood still keeps
His sov'reignty, and rule, and majesty;
15   Blazing Hyperion on his orbed fire
Still sits, still snuffs the incense teeming up
From man to the Sun's God: yet unsecure;
For as upon the earth dire prodigies[4]
Fright and perplex, so also shudders he:
20   Nor at dog's howl, or gloom-bird's even screech,
Or the familiar visitings of one
Upon the first toll of his passing bell:[5]
But horrors portion'd to a giant nerve

3. I.e., like a giant who is seen at sea to emerge, pale, from the waves.
4. Terrifying omens.
5. Lines 20–22 might be paraphrased: "Not, however, at such portents as a dog's howl or the evening screech of the owl or with the well-known feelings ['visitings'] of someone when he hears the first stroke of his own death knell." It had been the English custom to ring the church bell when a person was close to death, to invite hearers to pray for his departing soul (see, e.g., Shakespeare, *Venus and Adonis*, lines 701–02; and for "visitings," *Macbeth* 1.5.43).

Make great Hyperion ache. His palace bright,
25 Bastion'd with pyramids of glowing gold,
And touch'd with shade of bronzed obelisks,
Glares a blood red through all the thousand courts,
Arches, and domes, and fiery galeries:
And all its curtains of Aurorian clouds
30 Flush angerly: when he would taste the wreaths
Of incense breath'd aloft from sacred hills,
Instead of sweets, his ample palate takes
Savour of poisonous brass, and metals sick.
Wherefore when harbour'd in the sleepy west,
35 After the full completion of fair day,
For rest divine upon exalted couch
And slumber in the arms of melody,
He paces through the pleasant hours of ease,
With strides colossal, on from hall to hall;
40 While, far within each aisle and deep recess,
His winged minions in close clusters stand
Amaz'd, and full of fear; like anxious men
Who on a wide plain gather in sad troops,
When earthquakes jar their battlements and towers.
45 Even now, while Saturn, rous'd from icy trance,
Goes, step for step, with Thea from yon woods,
Hyperion, leaving twilight in the rear,
Is sloping to the threshold of the west.
Thither we tend."—Now in clear light I stood,
50 Reliev'd from the dusk vale. Mnemosyne
Was sitting on a square edg'd polish'd stone,
That in its lucid depth reflected pure
Her priestess-garments. My quick eyes ran on
From stately nave to nave, from vault to vault,
55 Through bowers of fragrant and enwreathed light,
And diamond paved lustrous long arcades.
Anon rush'd by the bright Hyperion;
His flaming robes stream'd out beyond his heels,
And gave a roar, as if of earthly fire,
60 That scar'd away the meek ethereal hours
And made their dove-wings tremble: on he flared[6]

July–Sept. 1819   1857

Letters   Keats's letters serve as a running commentary on his life, reading, thinking, and writing. His early reputation as a poet of pure luxury, sensation, and art for
art's sake has undergone a radical change since, in the twentieth century, critics began
to pay close attention to the letters. For Keats thought hard and persistently about
life and art, and any seed of an ethical or critical idea that he picked up from his
contemporaries (in particular, Hazlitt, Coleridge, Wordsworth) instantly germinated
and flourished in the rich soil of his imagination. What T. S. Eliot said about the

6. The manuscript breaks off at this point.

Metaphysical poets applies to Keats in his letters: his "mode of feeling was directly and freshly altered by [his] reading and thought." And like Donne, he looked not only into the heart but, literally, "into the cerebral cortex, the nervous system, and the digestive tract." A number of Keats's casual comments on the poet and on poetry included here—especially those dealing with "negative capability" and with what we now call empathy—have become standard points of reference in aesthetic theory. But Keats himself regarded nothing that he said as final; each statement constituted only a stage in his continuing exploration into what he called "the mystery."

The text printed here is that of the edition of the *Letters* by Hyder E. Rollins (1958), which reproduces the original manuscripts precisely.

LETTERS

To Benjamin Bailey[1]

[THE AUTHENTICITY OF THE IMAGINATION]

[November 22, 1817]

My dear Bailey,

* * * O I wish I was as certain of the end of all your troubles as that of your momentary start about the authenticity of the Imagination. I am certain of nothing but of the holiness of the Heart's affections and the truth of Imagination—What the imagination seizes as Beauty must be truth[2]— whether it existed before or not—for I have the same Idea of all our Passions as of Love they are all in their sublime, creative of essential Beauty—In a Word, you may know my favorite Speculation by my first Book and the little song[3] I sent in my last—which is a representation from the fancy of the probable mode of operating in these Matters—The Imagination may be compared to Adam's dream[4]—he awoke and found it truth. I am the more zealous in this affair, because I have never yet been able to perceive how any thing can be known for truth by consequitive reasoning[5]—and yet it must be— Can it be that even the greatest Philosopher ever ~~when~~ arrived at his goal without putting aside numerous objections—However it may be, O for a Life of Sensations[6] rather than of Thoughts! It is "a Vision in the form of Youth" a Shadow of reality to come—and this consideration has further conv[i]nced me for it has come as auxiliary to another favorite Speculation of mine, that we shall enjoy ourselves here after by having what we called happiness on Earth repeated in a finer tone and so repeated[7]—And yet such a fate can only befall those who delight in sensation rather than hunger as you do after Truth—Adam's dream will do here and seems to be a conviction that Imagination and its empyreal reflection is the same as human Life and its spiritual

1. One of Keats's closest friends. Keats had stayed with him the month before at Oxford, where Bailey was an undergraduate.
2. The phrase occurs in a poetic context at the close of *Ode on a Grecian Urn*. Try substituting "real," or "reality," where Keats uses the word *truth*.
3. The song was "O Sorrow," from book 4 of *Endymion*.
4. In *Paradise Lost* 8.452–90, Adam dreams that

Eve has been created, and awakes to find her real. Adam also describes an earlier prefigurative dream in the same work, 8.283–311.
5. Consecutive reasoning—reasoning that moves by logical steps.
6. Probably not only sense experiences but also the intuitive perceptions of truths, as opposed to truth achieved by consecutive reasoning.
7. Cf. the "Pleasure Thermometer" in *Endymion* 1.777ff. (p. 831).

repetition. But as I was saying—the simple imaginative Mind may have its rewards in the repeti[ti]on of its own silent Working coming continually on the spirit with a fine suddenness—to compare great things with small—have you never by being surprised with an old Melody—in a delicious place—by a delicious voice, fe[l]t over again your very speculations and surmises at the time it first operated on your soul—do you not remember forming to yourself the singer's face more beautiful [than] it was possible and yet with the elevation of the Moment you did not think so—even then you were mounted on the Wings of Imagination so high—that the Prototype must be here after—that delicious face you will see—What a time! I am continually running away from the subject—sure this cannot be exactly the case with a complex Mind—one that is imaginative and at the same time careful of its fruits—who would exist partly on sensation partly on thought—to whom it is necessary that years should bring the philosophic Mind[8]—such an one I consider your's and therefore it is necessary to your eternal Happiness that you not only ~~have~~ drink this old Wine of Heaven which I shall call the redigestion of our most ethereal Musings on Earth; but also increase in knowledge and know all things. I am glad to hear you are in a fair Way for Easter—you will soon get through your unpleasant reading and then!—but the world is full of troubles and I have not much reason to think myself pesterd with many—I think Jane or Marianne has a better opinion of me than I deserve—for really and truly I do not think my Brothers illness connected with mine—you know more of the real Cause than they do—nor have I any chance of being rack'd as you have been[9]—you perhaps at one time thought there was such a thing as Worldly Happiness to be arrived at, at certain periods of time marked out—you have of necessity from your disposition been thus led away—I scarcely remember counting upon any Happiness—I look not for it if it be not in the present hour—nothing startles me beyond the Moment. The setting sun will always set me to rights—or if a Sparrow come before my Window I take part in its existence and pick about the Gravel. The first thing that strikes me on hea[r]ing a Misfortune having befalled another is this. "Well it cannot be helped.—he will have the pleasure of trying the resourses of his spirit, and I beg now my dear Bailey that hereafter should you observe any thing cold in me not to [put] it to the account of heartlessness but abstraction—for I assure you I sometimes feel not the influence of a Passion or Affection during a whole week—and so long this sometimes continues I begin to suspect myself and the genuiness of my feelings at other times—thinking them a few barren Tragedy-tears.

* * *

Your affectionate friend
John Keats—

---

8. An echo of Wordsworth, Ode: Intimations of Immortality, line 187.
9. Keats's friends Jane and Mariane Reynolds feared that his ill health at this time threatened tuberculosis, from which his brother Tom was suffering. Bailey had recently experienced pain (been "racked") because of an unsuccessful love affair.

To George and Thomas Keats

[NEGATIVE CAPABILITY]

[December 21, 27 (?), 1817]

My dear Brothers

I must crave your pardon for not having written ere this. * * * I spent Friday evening with Wells[1] & went the next morning to see *Death on the Pale horse*. It is a wonderful picture, when West's[2] age is considered; But there is nothing to be intense upon; no women one feels mad to kiss; no face swelling into reality. the excellence of every Art is its intensity, capable of making all disagreeables evaporate, from their being in close relationship with Beauty & Truth[3]—Examine King Lear & you will find this examplified throughout; but in this picture we have unpleasantness without any momentous depth of speculation excited, in which to bury its repulsiveness—The picture is larger than Christ rejected—I dined with Haydon[4] the sunday after you left, & had a very pleasant day, I dined too (for I have been out too much lately) with Horace Smith & met his two Brothers with Hill & Kingston & one Du Bois,[5] they only served to convince me, how superior humour is to wit in respect to enjoyment—These men say things which make one start, without making one feel, they are all alike; their manners are all alike; they all know fashionables; they have a mannerism in their very eating & drinking, in their mere handling a Decanter—They talked of Kean[6] & his low company— Would I were with that company instead of yours said I to myself! I know such like acquaintance will never do for me & yet I am going to Reynolds, on wednesday—Brown & Dilke[7] walked with me & back from the Christmas pantomime.[8] I had not a dispute but a disquisition with Dilke, on various subjects; several things dovetailed in my mind, & at once it struck me, what quality went to form a Man of Achievement especially in Literature & which Shakespeare possessed so enormously—I mean *Negative Capability*,[9] that is when man is capable of being in uncertainties, Mysteries, doubts, without any irritable reaching after fact & reason—Coleridge, for instance, would let go by a fine isolated verisimilitude caught from the Penetralium[1] of mystery,

1. Charles Wells, a former schoolmate of Tom Keats.
2. Benjamin West (1738–1820), painter of historical pictures, was an American who moved to England and became president of the Royal Academy. The *Christ Rejected* mentioned a few sentences farther on is also by West.
3. Keats's solution to a problem at least as old as Aristotle's *Poetics:* why do we take pleasure in the aesthetic representation of a subject that in life would be ugly or painful?
4. Keats's close friend Benjamin Haydon, painter of large-scale historical and religious pictures.
5. Smith was one of the best-known literary wits of the day; the others mentioned were men of letters or of literary interests.
6. Edmund Kean, noted Shakespearean actor of the early 19th century.
7. Charles Armitage Brown, John Hamilton Reynolds, and Charles Wentworth Dilke were all writers and friends of Keats. Keats interrupted the writing of this letter after the dash; beginning with "Brown

& Dilke" he is writing several days after the preceding sentences.
8. Christmas pantomimes were performed each year at Drury Lane and Covent Garden theaters.
9. This famous and elusive phrase has accumulated a sizable body of commentary. Two points may be offered here: (1) Keats is concerned with a central aesthetic question of his day: to distinguish between what was called the "objective" poet, who simply and impersonally presents material, and the "subjective" or "sentimental" poet, who presents material as it appears when viewed through the writer's personal interests, beliefs, and feelings. The poet of "negative capability" is the objective poet (see the letter to Reynolds, February 3, 1818, p. 890). (2) Keats goes on to propose that, within a poem, the presentation of subject matter in an artistic form that appeals to our "sense of Beauty" is enough, independently of its truth or falsity when considered outside the poem.
1. The Latin *penetralia* signified the innermost and most secret parts of a temple.

from being incapable of remaining content with half knowledge. This pursued through Volumes would perhaps take us no further than this, that with a great poet the sense of Beauty overcomes every other consideration, or rather obliterates all consideration.

Shelley's poem[2] is out & there are words about its being objected too, as much as Queen Mab was. Poor Shelley I think he has his Quota of good qualities, in sooth la!! Write soon to your most sincere friend & affectionate Brother

John

To John Hamilton Reynolds[1]

[WORDSWORTH'S POETRY]

[February 3, 1818]

My dear Reynolds,

* * * It may be said that we ought to read our Contemporaries. that Wordsworth &c should have their due from us. but for the sake of a few fine imaginative or domestic passages, are we to be bullied into a certain Philosophy engendered in the whims of an Egotist[2]—Every man has his speculations, but every man does not brood and peacock over them till he makes a false coinage and deceives himself—Many a man can travel to the very bourne[3] of Heaven, and yet want confidence to put down his halfseeing. Sancho[4] will invent a Journey heavenward as well as any body. We hate poetry that has a palpable design upon us—and if we do not agree, seems to put its hand in its breeches pocket. Poetry should be great & unobtrusive, a thing which enters into one's soul, and does not startle it or amaze it with itself but with its subject.—How beautiful are the retired flowers! how would they lose their beauty were they to throng into the highway crying out, "admire me I am a violet! dote upon me I am a primrose! Modern poets differ from the Elizabethans in this. Each of the moderns like an Elector of Hanover governs his petty state, & knows how many straws are swept daily from the Causeways in all his dominions & has a continual itching that all the Housewives should have their coppers well scoured: the antients were ~~Emperors of large~~ Emperors of vast Provinces, they had only heard of the remote ones and scarcely cared to visit them.—I will cut all this—I will have no more of Wordsworth or Hunt[5] in particular—Why should we be of the tribe of Manasseh, when we can wander with Esau?[6] why should we kick

---

2. *Laon and Cythna* (1817), which dealt with incest and had to be recalled by the author; Shelley revised and republished it as *The Revolt of Islam* (1818). *Queen Mab* (1813) was a youthful poem in which Shelley presented his radical program for the achievement of a millennial earthly state by the elimination of "kings, priests, and statesmen" and the reform of human institutions.
1. A close friend who was at this time an insurance clerk and also an able poet and man of letters.
2. Keats immensely admired Wordsworth, as succeeding letters will show, and learned more from him than from any poetic contemporary. He had reservations, however, about the subjective and

didactic qualities of Wordsworth's poetry—reservations that, in some moods, he stated in unflattering terms.
3. Boundary.
4. Sancho Panza, the earthy squire in Cervantes's *Don Quixote.*
5. Leigh Hunt, a poet who earlier had strongly influenced Keats's style.
6. I.e., why should we carry on a conventional way of life (as did the tribe of Manasseh in Old Testament history) when we can become adventurers (like Esau, who sold his birthright in Genesis 25.29–34 and became an outlaw).

against the Pricks, when we can walk on Roses? Why should we be owls, when we can be Eagles? Why be teased with "nice Eyed wagtails," when we have in sight "the Cherub Contemplation"?[7]—Why with Wordsworths "Matthew with a bough of wilding in his hand" when we can have Jacques "under an oak &c"[8]—The secret of the Bough of Wilding will run through your head faster than I can write it—Old Matthew spoke to him some years ago on some nothing, & because he happens in an Evening Walk to imagine the figure of the old man—he must stamp it down in black & white, and it is henceforth sacred—I don't mean to deny Wordsworth's grandeur & Hunt's merit, but I mean to say we need not be teazed with grandeur & merit—when we can have them uncontaminated & unobtrusive. Let us have the old Poets, & robin Hood[9] Your letter and its sonnets gave me more pleasure than will the 4th Book of Childe Harold[1] & the whole of any body's life & opinions.
* * *

Y[r] sincere friend and Coscribbler
John Keats.

To John Taylor[1]

[KEATS'S AXIOMS IN POETRY]

[February 27, 1818]

My dear Taylor,

Your alteration strikes me as being a great improvement—the page looks much better. * * * It is a sorry thing for me that any one should have to overcome Prejudices in reading my Verses—that affects me more than any hypercriticism on any particular Passage. In *Endymion* I have most likely but moved into the Go-cart from the leading strings. In Poetry I have a few Axioms, and you will see how far I am from their Centre. 1st I think Poetry should surprise by a fine excess and not by Singularity—it should strike the Reader as a wording of his own highest thoughts, and appear almost a Remembrance—2nd Its touches of Beauty should never be half way therby making the reader breathless instead of content: the rise, the progress, the setting of imagery should like the Sun come natural natural too him—shine over him and set soberly although in magnificence leaving him in the Luxury of twilight—but it is easier to think what Poetry should be than to write it—and this leads me on to another axiom. That if Poetry comes not as naturally as the Leaves to a tree it had better not come at all. However it may be with me I cannot help looking into new countries with "O for a Muse of fire to ascend!"[2]—If Endymion serves me as a Pioneer perhaps I ought to be content. I have great reason to be content, for thank God I can read and perhaps understand Shakspeare to his depths, and I have I am sure many friends, who, if I fail, will attribute any change in my Life and Temper to Humbleness

7. Milton, *Il Penseroso*, line 54. "Nice Eyed wagtails": from Hunt's *Nymphs*.
8. *As You Like It* 2.1.31. The Wordsworth phrase is from his poem *The Two April Mornings*. A "wilding" is a wild apple tree.
9. A reference to two sonnets on Robin Hood, written by Reynolds, which he had sent to Keats.

1. Canto 4 of Byron's *Childe Harold's Pilgrimage* was being eagerly awaited by English readers.
1. Partner in the publishing firm of Taylor and Hessey, to whom Keats wrote this letter while *Endymion* was being put through the press.
2. Altered from *Henry V*, Prologue, line 1.

rather than to Pride—to a cowering under the Wings of great Poets rather than to a Bitterness that I am not appreciated. I am anxious to get Endymion printed that I may forget it and proceed. * * *

Your sincere and oblig^d friend
John Keats—

P.S. You shall have a sho[r]t *Preface* in good time—

To John Hamilton Reynolds

[MILTON, WORDSWORTH, AND THE CHAMBERS OF HUMAN LIFE]

[May 3, 1818]

My dear Reynolds.

* * * Were I to study physic or rather Medicine again,—I feel it would not make the least difference in my Poetry; when the Mind is in its infancy a Bias in is in reality a Bias, but when we have acquired more strength, a Bias becomes no Bias. Every department of knowledge we see excellent and calculated towards a great whole. I am so convinced of this, that I am glad at not having given away my medical Books, which I shall again look over to keep alive the little I know thitherwards; and moreover intend through you and Rice to become a sort of Pip-civilian.[1] An extensive knowledge is needful to thinking people—it takes away the heat and fever; and helps, by widening speculation, to ease the Burden of the Mystery:[2] a thing I begin to understand a little, and which weighed upon you in the most gloomy and true sentence in your Letter. The difference of high Sensations with and without knowledge appears to me this—in the latter case we are falling continually ten thousand fathoms deep and being blown up again without wings and with all [the] horror of a ~~Case~~ bare shoulderd Creature—in the former case, our shoulders are fledged,[3] and we go thro' the same ~~Fir~~ air and space without fear. * * *

You say "I fear there is little chance of any thing else in this life." You seem by that to have been going through with a more painful and acute ~~test~~ zest the same labyrinth that I have—I have come to the same conclusion thus far. My Branchings out therefrom have been numerous: one of them is the consideration of Wordsworth's genius and as a help, in the manner of gold being the meridian Line of worldly wealth,—how he differs from Milton.[4]—And here I have nothing but surmises, from an uncertainty whether Miltons apparently less anxiety for Humanity proceeds from his seeing further or no than Wordsworth: And whether Wordsworth has in truth epic passions, and martyrs himself to the human heart, the main region of his song[5]—In regard to his genius alone—we find what he says true as far as we

---

1. Apparently "a small-scale layman." James Rice, a lawyer, was one of Keats's favorite friends.
2. Wordsworth, *Tintern Abbey*, line 38. Here begins Keats's insightful expansion of the significance of this and other phrases and passages in Wordsworth.
3. Grow wings.

4. I.e., as gold is the standard of material wealth (in the way that the meridian line of Greenwich Observatory, England, is the reference for measuring degrees of longitude), so Milton is the standard of poetic value, by which we may measure Wordsworth.
5. Cf. Prospectus to *The Recluse*, line 41 (p. 302).

have experienced and we can judge no further but by larger experience—for axioms in philosophy are not axioms until they are proved upon our pulses: We read fine——things but never feel them to [the] full until we have gone the same steps as the Author.—I know this is not plain; you will know exactly my meaning when I say, that now I shall relish Hamlet more than I ever have done—Or, better—You are sensible no man can set down Venery[6] as a bestial or joyless thing until he is sick of it and therefore all philosophizing on it would be mere wording. Until we are sick, we understand not;—in fine, as Byron says, "Knowledge is Sorrow";[7] and I go on to say that "Sorrow is Wisdom"—and further for aught we can know for certainty! "Wisdom is folly."

* * *

I will return to Wordsworth—whether or no he has an extended vision or a circumscribed grandeur—whether he is an eagle in his nest, or on the wing—And to be more explicit and to show you how tall I stand by the giant, I will put down a simile of human life as far as I now perceive it; that is, to the point to which I say we both have arrived at—Well—I compare human life to a large Mansion of Many Apartments, two of which I can only describe, the doors of the rest being as yet shut upon me—The first we step into we call the infant or thoughtless Chamber, in which we remain as long as we do not think—We remain there a long while, and notwithstanding the doors of the second Chamber remain wide open, showing a bright appearance, we care not to hasten to it; but are at length imperceptibly impelled by the awakening of the thinking principle—within us—we no sooner get into the second Chamber, which I shall call the Chamber of Maiden-Thought,[8] than we become intoxicated with the light and the atmosphere, we see nothing but pleasant wonders, and think of delaying there for ever in delight: However among the effects this breathing is father of is that tremendous one of sharpening one's vision into the ~~head~~ heart and nature of Man—of convincing ones nerves that the World is full of Misery and Heartbreak, Pain, Sickness and oppression—whereby This Chamber of Maiden Thought becomes gradually darken'd and at the same time on all sides of it many doors are set open—but all dark—all leading to dark passages—We see not the ballance of good and evil. We are in a Mist—*We* are now in that state—We feel the "burden of the Mystery," To this point was Wordsworth come, as far as I can conceive when he wrote "Tintern Abbey" and it seems to me that his Genius is explorative of those dark Passages. Now if we live, and go on thinking, we too shall explore them. he is a Genius and superior [to] us, in so far as he can, more than we, make discoveries, and shed a light in them—Here I must think Wordsworth is deeper than Milton—though I think it has depended more upon the general and gregarious advance of intellect, than individual greatness of Mind—From the Paradise Lost and the other Works of Milton, I hope it is not too presuming, even between ourselves to say, his Philosophy, human and divine, may be tolerably understood by one not much advanced in years, In his time englishmen were just emancipated from a great superstition—and Men had got hold of certain points and resting places in reasoning which were too newly born to be doubted, and too much ~~oppressed~~ opposed by the Mass of Europe not to be thought etherial and authentically

---

6. Sexual indulgence.
7. *Manfred* 1.1.10: "Sorrow is knowledge."

8. I.e., innocent thought, with the implication (as in "maiden voyage") of a first undertaking.

divine—who could gainsay his ideas on virtue, vice, and Chastity in Comus, just at the time of the dismissal of Cod-pieces[9] and a hundred other disgraces? who would not rest satisfied with his hintings at good and evil in the Paradise Lost, when just free from the inquisition and burrning in Smithfield?[1] The Reformation produced such immediate and greats benefits, that Protestantism was considered under the immediate eye of heaven, and its own remaining Dogmas and superstitions, then, as it were, regenerated, constituted those resting places and seeming sure points of Reasoning—from that I have mentioned, Milton, whatever he may have thought in the sequel,[2] appears to have been content with these by his writings—He did not think into the human heart, as Wordsworth has done—Yet Milton as a Philosop[h]er, had sure as great powers as Wordsworth—What is then to be inferr'd? O many things—It proves there is really a grand march of intellect—, It proves that a mighty providence subdues the mightiest Minds to the service of the time being, whether it be in human Knowledge or Religion— * * * Tom[3] has spit a leetle blood this afternoon, and that is rather a damper—but I know—the truth is there is something real in the World Your third Chamber of Life shall be a lucky and a gentle one—stored with the wine of love—and the Bread of Friendship— * * *

Your affectionate friend
John Keats.

To Richard Woodhouse[1]

[A POET HAS NO IDENTITY]

[October 27, 1818]

My dear Woodhouse,

Your Letter gave me a great satisfaction; more on account of its friendliness, than any relish of that matter in it which is accounted so acceptable in the "genus irritabile"[2] The best answer I can give you is in a clerklike manner to make some observations on two principle points, which seem to point like indices into the midst of the whole pro and con, about genius, and views and atchievements and ambition and cœtera. 1st As to the poetical Character itself, (I mean that sort of which, if I am any thing, I am a Member; that sort distinguished from the wordsworthian or egotistical sublime; which is a thing per se and stands alone) it is not itself—it has no self—it is every thing and nothing—It has no character—it enjoys light and shade; it lives in gusto, be it foul or fair, high or low, rich or poor, mean or elevated—It has as much delight in conceiving an Iago as an Imogen.[3] What shocks the vir-

---

9. In the 15th and 16th centuries, the codpiece was a flap, often ornamental, that covered an opening in the front of men's breeches.
1. An open place northwest of the walls of the City of London where, in the 16th century, heretics were burned.
2. Later on.
3. Keats's younger brother, then eighteen, who was dying of tuberculosis.

1. A young lawyer with literary interests who early recognized Keats's talents and prepared, or preserved, manuscript copies of many of his poems and letters.
2. "The irritable race," a phrase Horace had applied to poets (*Epistles* 2.2.102).
3. Iago is the villain in Shakespeare's *Othello* and Imogen the virtuous heroine in his *Cymbeline*.

tuous philosop[h]er, delights the camelion[4] Poet. It does no harm from its relish of the dark side of things any more than from its taste for the bright one; because they both end in speculation.[5] A Poet is the most unpoetical of any thing in existence; because he has no Identity—he is continually in for[6]—and filling some other Body—The Sun, the Moon, the Sea and Men and Women who are creatures of impulse are poetical and have about them an unchangeable attribute—the poet has none; no identity—he is certainly the most unpoetical of all God's Creatures. If then he has no self, and if I am a Poet, where is the Wonder that I should say I would ~~right~~ write no more? Might I not at that very instant [have] been cogitating on the Characters of saturn and Ops?[7] It is a wretched thing to confess; but is a very fact that not one word I ever utter can be taken for granted as an opinion growing out of my identical nature—how can it, when I have no nature? When I am in a room with People if I ever am free from speculating on creations of my own brain, then not myself goes home to myself: but the identity of every one in the room begins to to press upon me[8] that, I am in a very little time an[ni]hilated—not only among Men; it would be the same in a Nursery of children: I know not whether I make myself wholly understood: I hope enough so to let you see that no dependence is to be placed on what I said that day.

In the second place I will speak of my views, and of the life I purpose to myself—I am ambitious of doing the world some good: if I should be spared that may be the work of maturer years—in the interval I will assay to reach to as high a summit in Poetry as the nerve[9] bestowed upon me will suffer. The faint conceptions I have of Poems to come brings the blood frequently into my forehead—All I hope is that I may not lose all interest in human affairs—that the solitary indifference I feel for applause even from the finest Spirits, will not blunt any acuteness of vision I may have. I do not think it will—I feel assured I should write from the mere yearning and fondness I have for the Beautiful even if my night's labours should be burnt every morning and no eye ever shine upon them. But even now I am perhaps not speaking from myself; but from some character in whose soul I now live. I am sure however that this next sentence is from myself. I feel your anxiety, good opinion and friendliness in the highest degree, and am

Your's most sincerely

John Keats

4. The chameleon is a lizard that camouflages itself by changing its color to match its surroundings.
5. Possibly "in contemplation"—i.e., without affecting our practical judgment or actions.
6. Instead of "in for," Keats may have intended to write "informing."

7. Characters in Keats's *Hyperion*. Woodhouse had recently written Keats to express concern at a remark by the poet that, because former writers had preempted the best poetic materials and styles, there was nothing new left for the modern poet.
8. Perhaps "*so* to press upon me."
9. Sinew.

To George and Georgiana Keats[1]

[THE VALE OF SOUL-MAKING]

[February 14–May 3, 1819]

My dear Brother & Sister—

* * * I have this moment received a note from Haslam[2] in which he expects the death of his Father who has been for some time in a state of insensibility—his mother bears up he says very well—I shall go to [town] tommorrow to see him. This is the world—thus we cannot expect to give way many hours to pleasure—Circumstances are like Clouds continually gathering and bursting—While we are laughing the seed of some trouble is put into he the wide arable land of events—while we are laughing it sprouts [it] grows and suddenly bears a poison fruit which we must pluck—Even so we have leisure to reason on the misfortunes of our friends; our own touch us too nearly for words. Very few men have ever arrived at a complete disinterestedness of Mind: very few have been influenced by a pure desire of the benefit of others—in the greater part of the Benefactors of & to Humanity some meretricious motive has sullied their greatness—some melodramatic scenery has facinated them—From the manner in which I feel Haslam's misfortune I perceive how far I am from any humble standard of disinterestedness—Yet this feeling ought to be carried to its highest pitch, as there is no fear of its ever injuring society—which it would do I fear pushed to an extremity—For in wild nature the Hawk would loose his Breakfast of Robins and the Robin his of Worms The Lion must starve as well as the swallow—The greater part of Men make their way with the same instinctiveness, the same unwandering eye from their purposes, the same animal eagerness as the Hawk—The Hawk wants a Mate, so does the Man—look at them both they set about it and procure on[e] in the same manner—They want both a nest and they both set about one in the same manner—they get their food in the same manner— The noble animal Man for his amusement smokes his pipe—the Hawk balances about the Clouds—that is the only difference of their leisures. This it is that makes the Amusement of Life—to a speculative Mind. I go among the Feilds and catch a glimpse of a stoat[3] or a fieldmouse peeping out of the withered grass—the creature hath a purpose and its eyes are bright with it—I go amongst the buildings of a city and I see a Man hurrying along—to what? The Creature has a purpose and his eyes are bright with it. But then as Wordsworth says, "we have all one human heart"[4]—there is an ellectric fire in human nature tending to purify—so that among these human creature[s] there is continually some birth of new heroism—The pity is that we must wonder at it: as we should at finding a pearl in rubbish—I have no doubt that thousands of people never heard of have had hearts comp[l]etely disinterested: I can remember but two—Socrates and Jesus—their Histories evince it—What I heard a little time ago, Taylor observe with respect to

---

1. Keats's brother and his wife, who had emigrated to Louisville, Kentucky, in 1818. This is part of a long letter that Keats wrote over a period of several months. The date of this first extract is March 19.

2. William Haslam, a young businessman and close friend.
3. A weasel.
4. *The Old Cumberland Beggar*, line 153.

Socrates, may be said of Jesus—That he was so great as man that though he transmitted no writing of his own to posterity, we have his Mind and his sayings and his greatness handed to us by others. It is to be lamented that the history of the latter was written and revised by Men interested in the pious frauds of Religion. Yet through all this I see his splendour. Even here though I myself am pursueing the same instinctive course as the veriest human animal you can think of—I am however young writing at random—straining at particles of light in the midst of a great darkness—without knowing the bearing of any one assertion of any one opinion. Yet may I not in this be free from sin?[5] May there not be superior beings amused with any graceful, though instinctive attitude my mind [may] fall into, as I am entertained with the alertness of a Stoat or the anxiety of a Deer? Though a quarrel in the streets is a thing to be hated, the energies displayed in it are fine; the commonest Man shows a grace in his quarrel—By a superior being our reasoning[s] may take the same tone—though erroneous they may be fine—This is the very thing in which consists poetry; and if so it is not so fine a thing as philosophy—For the same reason that an eagle is not so fine a thing as a truth—Give me this credit—Do you not think I strive—to know myself? Give me this credit—and you will not think that on my own accou[n]t I repeat Milton's lines

> "How charming is divine Philosophy
> Not harsh and crabbed as dull fools suppose
> But musical as is Apollo's lute"—[6]

No—no for myself—feeling grateful as I do to have got into a state of mind to relish them properly—Nothing ever becomes real till it is experienced—Even a Proverb is no proverb to you till your Life has illustrated it— * * *

* * * I have been reading lately two very different books Robertson's America and Voltaire's Siecle De Louis xiv[7] It is like walking arm and arm between Pizarro and the great-little Monarch.[8] In How lementabl[e] a case do we see the great body of the people in both instances: in the first, where Men might seem to inherit quiet of Mind from unsophisticated senses; from uncontamination of civilisation; and especially from their being as it were estranged from the mutual helps of Society and its mutual injuries—and thereby more immediately under the Protection of Providence—even there they had mortal pains to bear as bad; or even worse than Baliffs,[9] Debts and Poverties of civilised Life—The whole appears to resolve into this—that Man is originally "a poor forked creature"[1] subject to the same mischances as the beasts of the forest, destined to hardships and disquietude of some kind or other. If

5. Keats speculates that though his instinctive course is not, any more than an animal's, "disinterested" (free from selfish interests), it may still, like an animal's, be natural, hence innocent and possessed of an innate grace and beauty. He further supposes that this may be the nature of poetry, also, as distinguished from the deliberate and self-conscious process of philosophical reasoning (cf. the letter to George and Thomas Keats on "Negative Capability," begun on December 21, 1817, p. 889).
6. Comus, lines 475–77.
7. Voltaire, Le Siècle de Louis XIV, 5 vols. (1751);

William Robertson, The History of America (1777—Keats was reading the 10th ed., 4 vols., 1803). In this second extract from the journal-letter Keats is writing toward the end of April (on the 21st or 28th).
8. Francisco Pizarro, the Spanish explorer whose exploits are described in Robertson's America. The "Monarch" is Louis XIV.
9. Bailiffs: officers of the law whose duties included making arrests for bad debts.
1. King Lear 3.4.95–97. Lear says: "Unaccommodated man is no more but such a poor, bare, forked animal as thou art."

he improves by degrees his bodily accommodations and comforts—at each stage, at each accent there are waiting for him a fresh set of annoyances— he is mortal and there is still a heaven with its Stars abov[e] his head. The most interesting question that can come before us is, How far by the persevering endeavours of a seldom appearing Socrates Mankind may be made happy—I can imagine such happiness carried to an extreme—but what must it end in?—Death—and who could in such a case bear with death—the whole troubles of life which are now frittered away in a series of years, would the[n] be accumulated for the last days of a being who instead of hailing its approach, would leave this world as Eve left Paradise—But in truth I do not at all believe in this sort of perfectibility—the nature of the world will not admit of it—the inhabitants of the world will correspond to itself—Let the fish philosophise the ice away from the Rivers in winter time and they shall be at continual play in the tepid delight of summer. Look at the Poles and at the sands of Africa, Whirlpools and volcanoes—Let men exterminate them and I will say that they may arrive at earthly Happiness—The point at which Man may arrive is as far as the paralel state in inanimate nature and no further—For instance suppose a rose to have sensation, it blooms on a beautiful morning it enjoys itself—but there comes a cold wind, a hot sun—it can not escape it, it cannot destroy its annoyances—they are as native to the world as itself: no more can man be happy in spite, the world[l]y elements will prey upon his nature—The common cognomen of this world among the misguided and superstitious is "a vale of tears" from which we are to be redeemed by a certain arbitrary interposition of God and taken to Heaven— What a little circumscribe[d] straightened notion! Call the world if you Please "The vale of Soul-making" Then you will find out the use of the world (I am speaking now in the highest terms for human nature admitting it to be immortal which I will here take for granted for the purpose of showing a thought which has struck me concerning it) I say *"Soul making"* Soul as distinguished from an Intelligence—There may be intelligences or sparks of the divinity in millions—but they are not Souls ~~the~~ till they acquire identities, till each one is personally itself. I[n]telligences are atoms of perception— they know and they see and they are pure, in short they are God—how then are Souls to be made? How then are these sparks which are God to have identity given them—so as ever to possess a bliss peculiar to each ones individual existence? How, but by the medium of a world like this? This point I sincerely wish to consider because I think it a grander system of salvation than the chrystean religion—or rather it is a system of Spirit-creation[2]— This is effected by three grand materials acting the one upon the other for a series of years—These three Materials are the *Intelligence*—the *human heart* (as distinguished from intelligence or Mind) and the *World* or *Elemental space* suited for the proper action of *Mind and Heart* on each other

---

2. Keats is struggling for an analogy that will embody his solution to the ancient riddle of evil, as an alternative to what he understands to be the Christian view: that evil exists as a test of the individual's merit of salvation in heaven, and this world is only a proving ground for a later and better life. Keats proposes that the function of the human experience of sorrow and pain is to feed and discipline the formless and unstocked "intelligence" that we possess at birth and thus to shape it into a rich and coherent "identity," or "soul." This result provides a justification ("salvation") for our suffering in terms of our earthly life itself: that is, experience is its own reward. The passage is analogous to what Wordsworth says in the last two stanzas of his *Ode: Intimations of Immortality*.

for the purpose of forming the *Soul* or *Intelligence destined to possess the sense of Identity*. I can scarcely express what I but dimly perceive—and yet I think I perceive it—that you may judge the more clearly I will put it in the most homely form possible—I will call the *world* a School instituted for the purpose of teaching little children to read—I will call the *human heart* the *horn Book*[3] used in that School—and I will call the *Child able to read, the Soul* made from that *school* and its *hornbook*. Do you not see how necessary a World of Pains and troubles is to school an Intelligence and make it a soul? A Place where the heart must feel and suffer in a thousand diverse ways! Not merely is the Heart a Hornbook, It is the Minds Bible, it is the Minds experience, it is the teat from which the Mind or intelligence sucks its identity—As various as the Lives of Men are—so various become their souls, and thus does God make individual beings, Souls, Identical Souls of the sparks of his own essence—This appears to me a faint sketch of a system of Salvation which does not affront our reason and humanity—I am convinced that many difficulties which christians labour under would vanish before it—There is one wh[i]ch even now Strikes me— the Salvation of Children—In them the Spark or intelligence returns to God without any identity—it having had no time to learn of, and be altered by, the heart—or seat of the human Passions—It is pretty generally suspected that the chr[i]stian scheme has been coppied from the ancient persian and greek Philosophers. Why may they not have made this simple thing even more simple for common apprehension by introducing Mediators and Personages in the same manner as in the hethen mythology abstractions are personified—Seriously I think it probable that this System of Soul-making— may have been the Parent of all the more palpable and personal Schemes of Redemption, among the Zoroastrians the Christians and the Hindoos. For as one part of the human species must have their carved Jupiter; so another part must have the palpable and named Mediatior and saviour, their Christ their Oromanes and their Vishnu[4]—If what I have said should not be plain enough, as I fear it may not be, I will [put] you in the place where I began in this series of thoughts—I mean, I began by seeing how man was formed by circumstances—and what are circumstances?—but touchstones of his heart—? and what are touch stones?—but proovings of his heartt?—and what are proovings of his heart but fortifiers or alterers of his nature? and what is his altered nature but his soul?—and what was his soul before it came into the world and had These provings and alterations and perfectionings?—An intelligences—without Identity—and how is this Identity to be made? Through the medium of the Heart? And how is the heart to become this Medium but in a world of Circumstances?—There now I think what with Poetry and Theology you may thank your Stars that my pen is not very long winded— * * *

This is the 3d of May & every thing is in delightful forwardness; the violets are not withered, before the peeping of the first rose; You must let me know every thing, how parcels go & come, what papers you have, & what

---

3. A child's primer, which used to consist of a sheet of paper mounted on thin wood, protected by a sheet of transparent horn.
4. The deity who creates and preserves the world, in Hindu belief. Oromanes (Ahriman) was the principle of evil, locked in a persisting struggle with Ormazd, the principle of good, in the Zoroastrian religion.

Newspapers you want, & other things—God bless you my dear Brother & Sister

Your ever Affectionate Brother
John Keats—

To Fanny Brawne

[FANNY BRAWNE AS KEATS'S "FAIR STAR"]

[July 25, 1819]

My sweet Girl,

I hope you did not blame me much for not obeying your request of a Letter on Saturday: we have had four in our small room playing at cards night and morning leaving me no undisturb'd opportunity to write. Now Rice and Martin are gone I am at liberty. Brown to my sorrow confirms the account you give of your ill health. You cannot conceive how I ache to be with you: how I would die for one hour——for what is in the world? I say you cannot conceive; it is impossible you should look with such eyes upon me as I have upon you: it cannot be. Forgive me if I wander a little this evening, for I have been all day employ'd in a very abstr[a]ct Poem[1] and I am in deep love with you—two things which must excuse me. I have, believe me, not been an age in letting you take possession of me; the very first week I knew you I wrote myself your vassal; but burnt the Letter as the very next time I saw you I thought you manifested some dislike to me. If you should ever feel for Man at the first sight what I did for you, I am lost. Yet I should not quarrel with you, but hate myself if such a thing were to happen—only I should burst if the thing were not as fine as a Man as you are as a Woman. Perhaps I am too vehement, then fancy me on my knees, especially when I mention a part of you Letter which hurt me; you say speaking of Mr. Severn[2] "but you must be satisfied in knowing that I admired you much more than your friend." My dear love, I cannot believe there ever was or ever could be any thing to admire in me especially as far as sight goes—I cannot be admired, I am not a thing to be admired. You are, I love you; all I can bring you is a swooning admiration of your Beauty. I hold that place among Men which snub-nos'd brunettes with meeting eyebrows do among women—they are trash to me—unless I should find one among them with a fire in her heart like the one that burns in mine. You absorb me in spite of myself—you alone: for I look not forward with any pleasure to what is call'd being settled in the world; I tremble at domestic cares—yet for you I would meet them, though if it would leave you the happier I would rather die than do so. I have two luxuries to brood over in my walks, your Loveliness and the hour of my death. O that I could have possession of them both in the same minute. I hate the world: it batters too much the wings of my self-will, and would I could take a sweet poison from your lips to send me out of it. From no others would I take it. I am indeed astonish'd to find myself so careless of all cha[r]ms but yours—

---

1. Probably *The Fall of Hyperion.*
2. Joseph Severn, who later looked after Keats during his final illness in Rome.

remembring as I do the time when even a bit of ribband was a matter of interest with me. What softer words can I find for you after this—what it is I will not read. Nor will I say more here, but in a Postscript answer any thing else you may have mentioned in your Letter in so many words—for I am distracted with a thousand thoughts. I will imagine you Venus tonight and pray, pray, pray to your star like a Hethen.[3]

Your's ever, fair Star,

John Keats.

To Percy Bysshe Shelley[1]

[LOAD EVERY RIFT WITH ORE]

[August 16, 1820]

My dear Shelley,

I am very much gratified that you, in a foreign country, and with a mind almost over occupied, should write to me in the strain of the Letter beside me. If I do not take advantage of your invitation it will be prevented by a circumstance I have very much at heart to prophesy[2]—There is no doubt that an english winter would put an end to me, and do so in a lingering hateful manner, therefore I must either voyage or journey to Italy as a soldier marches up to a battery. My nerves at present are the worst part of me, yet they feel soothed when I think that come what extreme may, I shall not be destined to remain in one spot long enough to take a hatred of any four particular bed-posts. I am glad you take any pleasure in my poor Poem;[3]— which I would willingly take the trouble to unwrite, if possible, did I care so much as I have done about Reputation. I received a copy of the Cenci,[4] as from yourself from Hunt. There is only one part of it I am judge of; the Poetry, and dramatic effect, which by many spirits now a days is considered the mammon. A modern work it is said must have a purpose,[5] which may be the God—*an artist* must serve Mammon—he must have "self concentration" selfishness perhaps. You I am sure will forgive me for sincerely remarking that you might curb your magnanimity and be more of an artist, and "load every rift"[6] of your subject with ore. The thought of such discipline must fall like cold chains upon you, who perhaps never sat with your wings furl'd for six Months together. And is not this extraordina[r]y talk for the writer of Endymion? whose mind was like a pack of scattered cards—I am pick'd up and sorted to a pip.[7] My Imagination is a Monastry and I am its Monk—you must explain my metap[cs][8] to yourself. I am in expectation of Prometheus[9]

---

3. See Keats's sonnet *Bright star* (p. 845) for parallels to this and other remarks in the present letter.

1. Written in reply to a letter urging Keats (who was ill) to spend the winter with the Shelleys in Pisa.

2. His own death.

3. Keats's *Endymion*, Shelley had written, contains treasures, "though treasures poured forth with indistinct profusion." Keats here responds with advice in kind.

4. Shelley's blank-verse tragedy, *The Cenci*, had been published in the spring of 1820.

5. Wordsworth had said this in his Preface to *Lyrical Ballads*. For "Mammon" see Matthew 6.24 and Luke 16.13: "Ye cannot serve God and mammon."

6. Spenser, *The Faerie Queene* 2.7.28: "With rich metall loaded every rifte."

7. Perfectly ordered; all the suits in the deck matched up ("pips" are the conventional spots on playing cards).

8. Metaphysics.

9. *Prometheus Unbound,* of which Shelley had promised Keats a copy.

every day. Could I have my own wish for its interest effected you would have it still in manuscript—or be but now putting an end to the second act. I remember you advising me not to publish my first-blights, on Hampstead heath—I am returning advice upon your hands. Most of the Poems in the volume I send you[1] have been written above two years, and would never have been publish'd but from a hope of gain; so you see I am inclined enough to take your advice now. I must exp[r]ess once more my deep sense of your kindness, adding my sincere thanks and respects for M[rs] Shelley. In the hope of soon seeing you I remain

most sincerely yours,
John Keats—

To Charles Brown[1]

[KEATS'S LAST LETTER]

Rome. 30 November 1820.

My dear Brown,

'Tis the most difficult thing in the world to me to write a letter. My stomach continues so bad, that I feel it worse on opening any book,—yet I am much better than I was in Quarantine.[2] Then I am afraid to encounter the proing and conning of any thing interesting to me in England. I have an habitual feeling of my real life having past, and that I am leading a posthumous existence. God knows how it would have been—but it appears to me—however, I will not speak of that subject. I must have been at Bedhampton nearly at the time you were writing to me from Chichester—how unfortunate—and to pass on the river too! There was my star predominant![3] I cannot answer any thing in your letter, which followed me from Naples to Rome, because I am afraid to look it over again. I am so weak (in mind) that I cannot bear the sight of any hand writing of a friend I love so much as I do you. Yet I ride the little horse,—and, at my worst, even in Quarantine, summoned up more puns, in a sort of desperation, in one week than in any year of my life. There is one thought enough to kill me—I have been well, healthy, alert &c, walking with her[4]—and now—the knowledge of contrast, feeling for light and shade, all that information (primitive sense) necessary for a poem are great enemies to the recovery of the stomach. There, you rogue, I put you to the torture,—but you must bring your philosophy to bear—as I do mine, really—or how should I be able to live? D[r] Clarke is very attentive to me; he says, there is very little the matter with my lungs, but my stomach, he says, is very bad. I am well disappointed in hearing good news from George,—for it runs in my head we shall all die young. I have not written to X X X X X yet,[5]

---

1. Keats's volume of 1820, including *Lamia, The Eve of St. Agnes*, and the odes. When Shelley drowned, he had this small book open in his pocket.
1. Written to Keats's friend Charles Armitage Brown from the house on the Spanish Stairs, in the Piazza di Spagna, where Keats was being tended in his mortal illness by the devoted Joseph Severn.

2. When it landed at Naples, Keats's ship had been quarantined for ten miserably hot days.
3. *The Winter's Tale* 1.2.202–03: "It is a bawdy planet, that will strike / Where 'tis predominant."
4. Fanny Brawne.
5. Charles Brown, whose manuscript transcription is the only text for this letter, substituted crosses for the names of Keats's friends to conceal their identities.

which he must think very neglectful; being anxious to send him a good account of my health, I have delayed it from week to week. If I recover, I will do all in my power to correct the mistakes made during sickness; and if I should not, all my faults will be forgiven. I shall write to X X X to-morrow, or next day. I will write to X X X X X in the middle of next week. Severn is very well, though he leads so dull a life with me. Remember me to all friends, and tell X X X X I should not have left London without taking leave of him, but from being so low in body and mind. Write to George as soon as you receive this, and tell him how I am, as far as you can guess;—and also a note to my sister—who walks about my imagination like a ghost—she is so like Tom.[6] I can scarcely bid you good bye even in a letter. I always made an awkward bow.

God bless you!
John Keats.

6. Keats's youngest brother, whom Fanny, his only sister, closely resembled, had died of tuberculosis on December 1, 1818. George was John Keats's younger brother.

MARY WOLLSTONECRAFT SHELLEY
1797–1851

Percy Shelley wrote of his young wife, in the Dedication to *Laon and Cythna:*

> They say that thou wert lovely from thy birth,
> Of glorious parents, thou aspiring Child.

The "glorious parents" were William Godwin, the leading reformer and radical philosopher of the time, and Mary Wollstonecraft, famed as the author of *A Vindication of the Rights of Woman;* Wollstonecraft had died as the result of childbed fever incurred when she gave birth to Mary. Four years later Godwin married a widow, Mary Jane Clairmont, who soon had more than she could cope with trying to manage a family of five children of diverse parentage, amid increasing financial difficulties. Mary bitterly resented her stepmother but adored her father, who, she later said, "was my God—and I remember many childish instances of the excess of attachment I bore for him."

To ease the situation, Mary was sent at the age of fourteen to live in Dundee, Scotland, with the family of William Baxter, an admirer of Godwin. After two pleasant years roaming the countryside, daydreaming, and writing stories (which have been lost), she returned in 1814 to her father's house in London. There at the age of sixteen she encountered the twenty-one-year-old poet Percy Bysshe Shelley, a devotee of Godwin's and an almost daily visitor, who had become estranged from his wife, Harriet. The young people fell in love; within a few months Mary was pregnant. On July 28 they ran off to Europe, taking with them her stepsister Jane Clairmont, who later changed her name to Claire. Mary described their happy though feckless wanderings through France, Switzerland, and Germany in her first book, *History of a Six Weeks' Tour,* published anonymously in 1817.

Back in England, she gave premature birth to a daughter who lived only a few weeks; a year later, in 1816, she bore a son, William. Shelley was usually in financial difficulties and often had to hide from his creditors to avoid arrest. Nonetheless, he contributed substantial sums (borrowed against his expectations as heir to his father, Sir Timothy) to Godwin's support, even though Godwin, despite his earlier advocacy of free love, refused to countenance Shelley's liaison with his daughter. Claire Clairmont meanwhile sought out and had a brief affair with Byron, who left her pregnant. In the spring of 1816 the Shelleys went abroad again with Claire, and at the latter's behest settled in Geneva, where Byron, accompanied by his physician and friend John William Polidori, set up residence in the nearby Villa Diodati. Mary Shelley tells us, in the introduction to *Frankenstein*, how her imagination was fired by their animated conversations during many social evenings. Encouraged and assisted by Shelley, she wrote *Frankenstein; or, The Modern Prometheus*, and published it anonymously in 1818.

The last six years of Mary's life with her husband, spent first in England and then in Italy, were filled with disasters. In October 1816, her sensitive and moody half-sister, Fanny Imlay, feeling herself an unloved burden on the Godwin household, committed suicide by an overdose of laudanum. Two months later Shelley's abandoned wife, Harriet, pregnant by an unknown lover, drowned herself in the Serpentine lake at Hyde Park in London. Shelley at once married Mary, but the courts denied him custody of Harriet's two children on the grounds that he was morally unfit to rear them. In September 1818 came the death of Mary's third baby, Clara, followed less than nine months later by the death of her adored son, William; so that at twenty-two Mary had been three times a mother and three times bereaved. These tragedies and her own ill health threw her into a depression that was only partly relieved by the birth of a second son, Percy Florence, in November 1819, and was deepened again the next spring by a miscarriage, as well as by the death of Claire's daughter Allegra, whom Byron had placed in an Italian convent. Mary Shelley's habitual reserve, which masked the depth of her feelings, now became an apathy that caused her to withdraw, emotionally, from her husband. When Shelley was drowned in the Gulf of Spezia in July 1822, she was left with a persisting sense that she had failed her husband when he most needed her.

An impoverished widow of twenty-four, she returned to England with two ambitions. One was to disseminate the poetry and to rescue the character of Shelley, whom she idolized in memory; the other was to support by her writings her surviving son. Her only financial assistance was a small allowance given her by Sir Timothy Shelley, which he threatened to cut off if she wrote a biography of his radical and scandal-haunted son. In the remaining quarter century of her life Mary Shelley became a notable success as a professional woman of letters. She wrote five more novels, of which the first two are the best. *The Last Man* (1826), a narrative of the destruction of humankind by a plague until there is only a single survivor, almost equals *Frankenstein* in its analysis of human isolation; and *Valperga* (1823), set in the Italian Middle Ages, is a romance about a quasi-Napoleonic figure who sacrifices his love and his humanity to a lust for political power. She wrote also some twenty-five short tales and left in manuscript a novella, *Mathilda* (written in 1819 but not published until 1959), which deals with the disastrous results of a father's incestuous passion for a daughter who resembles his dead wife. In 1835–39 she contributed to the *Cabinet Cyclopedia* five volumes of admirable biographical and critical studies of Continental authors. She also published several separate editions of her husband's writings in verse and prose. In accordance with what was then standard editorial procedure, she altered and emended Shelley's texts; she also added prefaces and notes, relating Shelley's writings to the circumstances of his life and thought, which have been an important resource for scholars of Romantic literature.

Not until old Sir Timothy died in 1844, leaving his title and estate to her son, did she find herself in comfortable circumstances. Her last years were cheered by the devotion of her son—who was an amiable man but entirely lacked the genius of his parents—and by her close friendship with Jane St. John, an admirer of Shelley's poetry, whom Sir Percy Florence married in 1848. Mary Shelley died three years later, at the age of fifty-three.

During her widowhood, she craved social acceptance and status and, although she maintained liberal principles, tried hard, by adapting herself to conventional standards in her writings and her life, to work free from the onus of what her contemporaries regarded as the scandalous careers of her mother, father, and husband. In later life she wrote an apologia in her journal, dated October 21, 1838, that reveals the stresses of a life spent trying to measure up to the example, yet escape the bad reputations, of her parents and husband.

> In the first place, with regard to "the good cause"—the cause of the advancement of freedom and knowledge, of the rights of women, etc.—I am not a person of opinions. . . . Some have a passion for reforming the world; others do not cling to particular opinions. That my parents and Shelley were of the former class, makes me respect it. . . . For myself, I earnestly desire the good and enlightenment of my fellow creatures, and see all, in the present course, tending to the same, and rejoice; but I am not for violent extremes, which only brings on an injurious reaction. . . .
>
> To hang back, as I do, brings a penalty. I was nursed and fed with a love of glory. To be something great and good was the precept given me by my father; Shelley reiterated it. . . . But Shelley died, and I was alone. . . . My total friendlessness, my horror of pushing, and inability to put myself forward unless led, cherished and supported—all this has sunk me in a state of loneliness no other human being ever before, I believe, endured—except Robinson Crusoe. . . .
>
> But I have never crouched to society—never sought it unworthily. If I have never written to vindicate the rights of women, I have ever defended women when oppressed. At every risk I have befriended and supported victims to the social system; but I make no boast, for in truth it is simple justice I perform; and so am I still reviled for being worldly. . . .
>
> Such as I have written appears to me the exact truth.

Frankenstein

Mary Shelley was eighteen when she began drafting *Frankenstein* in June 1816, nineteen when she completed it eleven months later, and twenty when it was published anonymously—in three slender volumes—early in 1818. It was a success from the beginning and has been a best-seller and a major literary and cultural presence ever since.

First-time readers are sometimes shocked to discover that "Frankenstein" is the name of the obsessed scientist rather than his monstrous creation and that the unnamed Creature, far from the wooden, grunting figure of popular films and television, is the most eloquent and rational character in the novel. Clues to Mary Shelley's intentions begin with the 1818 title page, on which the ironic subtitle likens Victor Frankenstein to Prometheus, the Titan in Greek mythology who championed humankind against tyranny, and a three-line epigraph from *Paradise Lost* just beneath the subtitle subversively equates Frankenstein with God and his Creature with the fallen Adam.

The epistolary frame introduces the explorer Robert Walton, who acts as a broker between the story's events and the reader. He is the first of the novel's three narrators; his letters give a first-person credibility to the fantasy and establish several principal themes at the outset—in particular the opposition of science and poetry (Walton is a failed poet who is now seeking glory as a scientist) and the theme of human connection, which is one of the main concerns of the Creature's long account of himself in the central chapters of volume 2. The other two narrators—Frankenstein (whose story is contained within Walton's) and the Creature (whose monologue is relayed by Frankenstein)—add myriad further concerns that would have been clear to the novel's original readers but have become obscured by time. Frankenstein's experiments have a basis in important scientific questions of the day: evolution, the so-called vitalist debate over the origins and nature of life, and the conflict between science and religion that is inherent in such topics. Frankenstein is a Faustian overreacher, and at various times both he and the Creature are types of Milton's Satan and, in a similar vein, Byronic heroes.

In several interesting chapters (volume 2, chapters 3 to 8), the Creature describes his self-education, starting with his earliest perceptions of natural phenomena and quickly advancing to language, logic, literature, philosophy, and politics. To some extent the Creature, who has no innate ideas and must learn everything through experience, is a clear example of John Locke's *tabula rasa,* the blank slate on which everything is to be written. But he also seems to have a core of natural goodness that can be corrupted through exposure to human behavior; this makes him resemble the romantic conceptions of human innocence associated with Jean-Jacques Rousseau. Some of the complex political content of *Frankenstein* comes via the lessons that the Creature overhears based on Volney's *Ruins of Empire* ("I heard of the division of property, of immense wealth and squalid poverty; of rank, descent, and noble blood. . . . I learned that the possessions most esteemed . . . were, high and unsullied descent united with riches"). An implied critique of colonial imperialism, beginning with Walton's zeal to discover a polar route to the Pacific, thus further expanding the British Empire, is observable in many of the later incidents.

Because this remarkable book was written by a woman, and because Mary Shelley's mother was so important to the history of feminism, *Frankenstein* has become a central text in feminist studies. Even though the women characters (except for the enlightened, high-spirited Safie in volume 2, chapter 6) are totally passive, many feminists today interpret the Creature himself as a symbol of the fate of women who do not conform to social expectations and are treated like "creatures" instead of human beings. The relation of Victor Frankenstein to the Creature may also be seen as a paradigm of bad family relationships, where a "parent" fails to assume loving responsibility for the "child" he has brought to life. The Creature profoundly needs sympathy and relationship but is cut off from humanity by his origin and monstrosity. Because his overtures to human beings evoke only horror and disgust, his love, rejected, turns into murderous hate. *Frankenstein* is not only a major Romantic achievement; its account of the monstrous potentiality of human creative power when severed from moral and social concerns has made it a modern myth that recurs persistently in fiction, melodrama, and film and haunts the popular consciousness.

There are two main versions of *Frankenstein*—that of the original edition of 1818 and that of a revised text that Mary Shelley published as the third edition in 1831. The text printed here, taken from the Norton Critical Edition of the novel prepared by J. Paul Hunter (1996), is a reprint of the version of 1818, correcting only obvious typographical errors.

Frankenstein;
or, The Modern Prometheus[1]

> Did I request thee, Maker, from my clay
> To mould me man? Did I solicit thee
> From darkness to promote me?——
> > Paradise Lost[2]

To William Godwin,[3]
Author of Political Justice, Caleb Williams, &c.
these volumes are respectfully inscribed by the Author

Preface[4]

The event on which this fiction is founded has been supposed, by Dr. Darwin,[5] and some of the physiological writers of Germany, as not of impossible occurrence. I shall not be supposed as according the remotest degree of serious faith to such an imagination; yet, in assuming it as the basis of a work of fancy, I have not considered myself as merely weaving a series of supernatural terrors. The event on which the interest of the story depends is exempt from the disadvantages of a mere tale of spectres or enchantment. It was recommended by, the novelty of the situations which it develops; and, however impossible as a physical fact, affords a point of view to the imagination for the delineating of human passions more comprehensive and commanding than any which the ordinary relations of existing events can yield.

I have thus endeavoured to preserve the truth of the elementary principles of human nature, while I have not scrupled to innovate upon their combinations. The *Iliad*, the tragic poetry of Greece—Shakespeare, in the *Tempest* and *Midsummer Night's Dream*,—and most especially Milton, in *Paradise Lost*, conform to this rule; and the most humble novelist, who seeks to confer or receive amusement from his labours, may, without presumption, apply to prose fiction a licence, or rather a rule, from the adoption of which so many exquisite combinations of human feeling have resulted in the highest specimens of poetry.

The circumstance on which my store rests was suggested in casual conversation. It was commenced, partly as a source of amusement, and partly as an expedient for exercising any untried resources of mind. Other motives were mingled with these, as the work proceeded. I am by no means indifferent to the manner in which whatever moral tendencies exist in the sentiments or characters it contains shall affect the reader; yet my chief concern in this respect has been limited to the avoiding the enervating effects of the

---

1. In Greek mythology, a Titan who created humankind, for whom he stole fire from the gods. As punishment, Zeus chained him on a cliff and set an eagle to tear at his liver.
2. Spoken by Adam after the Fall, *Paradise Lost* 10.743–45.
3. Father of Mary Shelley, a radical political philosopher who wrote *Inquiry Concerning Political Justice* (1793) and several novels, including the highly popular *The Adventures of Caleb Williams*

(1794).
4. In her Author's Introduction (1831), Mary Shelley says that this *Preface* "was entirely written" by Percy Shelley.
5. Erasmus Darwin (1731–1802), grandfather of Charles Darwin, wrote immensely popular treatments of biological and botanic science in verse. In *The Temple of Nature* (1803), he speculated that life may generate spontaneously.

novels of the present day, and to the exhibition of the amiableness of domestic affection, and the excellence of universal virtue. The opinions which naturally spring from the character and situation of the hero are by no means to be conceived as existing always in my own conviction; nor is any inference justly to be drawn from the following pages as prejudicing any philosophical doctrine of whatever kind.

It is a subject also of additional interest to the author, that this story was begun in the majestic region where the scene is principally laid, and in society which cannot cease to be regretted. I passed the summer of 1816 in the environs of Geneva. The season was cold and rainy, and in the evenings we crowded around a blazing wood fire, and, occasionally amused ourselves with some German stories of ghosts,[6] which happened to fall into our hands. These tales excited in us a playful desire of imitation. Two other friends[7] (a tale from the pen of one of whom would be far more acceptable to the public than any thing I can ever hope to produce) and myself agreed to write each a story, founded on some supernatural occurrence.

The weather, however, suddenly became serene; and my two friends left me on a journey among the Alps, and lost, in the magnificent scenes which they present, all memory of their ghostly visions. The following tale is the only one which has been completed.

Author's Introduction [1831][1]

The Publishers of the Standard Novels, in selecting "Frankenstein" for one of their series, expressed a wish that I should furnish them with some account of the origin of the story. I am the more willing to comply, because I shall thus give a general answer to the question, so very frequently asked me—"How I, then a young girl, came to think of, and to dilate upon, so very hideous an idea?" It is true that I am very averse to bringing myself forward in print; but as my account will only appear as an appendage to a former production, and as it will be confined to such topics as have connection with my authorship alone, I can scarcely accuse myself of a personal intrusion.

It is not singular that, as the daughter of two persons of distinguished literary celebrity,[2] I should very early in life have thought of writing. As a child I scribbled; and my favourite pastime, during the hours given me for recreation, was to "write stories." Still I had a dearer pleasure than this, which was the formation of castles in the air—the indulging in waking dreams—the following up trains of thought, which had for their subject the formation of a succession of imaginary incidents. My dreams were at once more fantastic and agreeable than my writings. In the latter I was a close

---

6. In a translation in French of *Fantasmagoriana* (1812), a collection of stories of the supernatural. See n. 6, p. 909.
7. Percy Shelley and Lord Byron.
1. Mary Shelley wrote this introduction for the 3rd edition of *Frankenstein* published in a series, "Standard Novels" (1831); it is thus fifteen years later than the events of 1816 that it recalls. In it

she undertakes to explain—in terms of outer events that engage with her fantasy life to effect an obsessive visionary experience—how it is that an author in her late teens could write a work that, as we now recognize, not only is a classic in the genre of terror tales but has become an enduring myth.
2. Mary Wollstonecraft and William Godwin.

imitator—rather doing as others had done, than putting down the suggestions of my own mind. What I wrote was intended at least for one other eye—my childhood's companion and friend;[3] but my dreams were all my own; I accounted for them to nobody; they were my refuge when annoyed—my dearest pleasure when free.

I lived principally in the country as a girl, and passed a considerable time in Scotland. I made occasional visits to the more picturesque parts; but my habitual residence was on the blank and dreary northern shores of the Tay, near Dundee. Blank and dreary on retrospection I call them; they were not so to me then. They were the eyry[4] of freedom, and the pleasant region where unheeded I could commune with the creatures of my fancy. I wrote then—but in a most common-place style. It was beneath the trees of the grounds belonging to our house, or on the bleak sides of the woodless mountains near, that my true compositions, the airy flights of my imagination, were born and fostered. I did not make myself the heroine of my tales. Life appeared to me too common-place an affair as regarded myself. I could not figure to myself that romantic woes or wonderful events would ever be my lot; but I was not confined to my own identity; and I could people the hours with creations far more interesting to me at that age, than my own sensations.

After this my life became busier, and reality stood in place of fiction. My husband,[5] however, was, from the first, very anxious that I should prove myself worthy of my parentage, and enrol myself on the page of fame. He was for ever inciting me to obtain literary reputation, which even on my own part I cared for then, though since I have become infinitely indifferent to it. At this time he desired that I should write, not so much with the idea that I could produce any thing worthy of notice, but that he might himself judge how far I possessed the promise of better things hereafter. Still I did nothing. Travelling, and the cares of a family, occupied my time; and study, in the way of reading, or improving my ideas in communication with his far more cultivated mind, was all of literary employment that engaged my attention.

In the summer of 1816, we visited Switzerland, and became the neighbours of Lord Byron. At first we spent our pleasant hours on the lake, or wandering on its shores; and Lord Byron, who was writing the third canto of Childe Harold, was the only one among us who put his thoughts upon paper. These, as he brought them successively to us, clothed in all the light and harmony of poetry, seemed to stamp as divine the glories of heaven and earth, whose influences we partook with him.

But it proved a wet, ungenial summer, and incessant rain often confined us for days to the house. Some volumes of ghost stories, translated from the German into French, fell into our hands.[6] There was the History of the Inconstant Lover, who, when he thought to clasp the bride to whom he had pledged his vows, found himself in the arms of the pale ghost of her whom he had deserted. There was the tale of the sinful founder of his race, whose

3. Isabel Baxter, the daughter of William Baxter, with whom Mary had lived in Dundee, Scotland (1812–14).
4. An eagle's nest, built high on a cliff or tree.
5. Mary and Percy Shelley did not in fact marry until December, some six months after the events described in this introduction.

6. The French translation, published anonymously in 1812, was called *Fantasmagoriana, or Collected Stories of Apparitions of Specters, Ghosts, Phantoms, etc.* The stories she goes on to describe, somewhat inaccurately, are *The Dead Fiancée* and *Family Portraits.*

miserable doom it was to bestow the kiss of death on all the younger sons of his fated house, just when they reached the age of promise. His gigantic, shadowy form, clothed like the ghost in Hamlet, in complete armour, but with the beaver[7] up, was seen at midnight, by the moon's fitful beams, to advance slowly along the gloomy avenue. The shape was lost beneath the shadow of the castle walls; but soon a gate swung back, a step was heard, the door of the chamber opened, and he advanced to the couch of the blooming youths, cradled in healthy sleep. Eternal sorrow sat upon his face as he bent down and kissed the forehead of the boys, who from that hour withered like flowers snapt upon the stalk. I have not seen these stories since then; but their incidents are as fresh in my mind as if I had read them yesterday.

"We will each write a ghost story," said Lord Byron; and his proposition was acceded to. There were four of us.[8] The noble author began a tale, a fragment of which he printed at the end of his poem of Mazeppa. Shelley, more apt to embody ideas and sentiments in the radiance of brilliant imagery, and in the music of the most melodious verse that adorns our language, than to invent the machinery of a story, commenced one founded on the experiences of his early life. Poor Polidori had some terrible idea about a skull-headed lady, who was so punished for peeping through a key-hole—what to see I forget—something very shocking and wrong of course; but when she was reduced to a worse condition than the renowned Tom of Coventry,[9] he did not know what to do with her, and was obliged to despatch her to the tomb of the Capulets,[1] the only place for which she was fitted. The illustrious poets also, annoyed by the platitude of prose, speedily relinquished their uncongenial task.

I busied myself to *think of a story*,—a story to rival those which had excited us to this task. One which would speak to the mysterious fears of our nature, and awaken thrilling horror—one to make the reader dread to look round, to curdle the blood, and quicken the beatings of the heart. If I did not accomplish these things, my ghost story would be unworthy of its name. I thought and pondered—vainly. I felt that blank incapability of invention which is the greatest misery of authorship, when dull Nothing replies to our anxious invocations. *Have you thought of a story?* I was asked each morning, and each morning I was forced to reply with a mortifying negative.

Every thing must have a beginning, to speak in Sanchean[2] phrase, and that beginning must be linked to something that went before. The Hindoos give the world an elephant to support it, but they make the elephant stand upon a tortoise. Invention, it must be humbly admitted, does not consist in creating out of void, but out of chaos; the materials must, in the first place, be afforded: it can give form to dark, shapeless substances, but cannot bring into being the substance itself. In all matters of discovery and invention, even of those that appertain to the imagination, we are continually reminded of the story of Columbus and his egg.[3] Invention consists in the capacity of

---

7. The hinged piece of armor that covers the face (see *Hamlet* 1.2.226–28).
8. Byron, Percy and Mary Shelley, and John William Polidori, Byron's physician and friend. Mary omits Claire Clairmont, her stepsister and Byron's former mistress, who was staying with the Shelleys at Geneva.
9. "Peeping Tom," who, according to the legend, was struck blind when he looked at Lady Godiva

as she rode naked through Coventry.
1. Where Romeo and Juliet died.
2. I.e., of Sancho Panza, the literal-minded squire in Cervantes's *Don Quixote* (1605).
3. According to popular legend, Christopher Columbus boasted that he could accomplish the impossible feat of making a hard-boiled egg stand on end. When challenged to do so, he lightly cracked one end and stood the egg upright.

seizing on the capabilities of a subject, and in the power of moulding and fashioning ideas suggested to it.

Many and long were the conversations between Lord Byron and Shelley, to which I was a devout but nearly silent listener. During one of these, various philosophical doctrines were discussed, and among others the nature of the principle of life, and whether there was any probability of its ever being discovered and communicated.[4] They talked of the experiments of Dr. Darwin,[5] (I speak not of what the Doctor really did, or said that he did, but, as more to my purpose, of what was then spoken of as having been done by him,) who preserved a piece of vermicelli in a glass case, till by some extraordinary means it began to move with voluntary motion. Not thus, after all, would life be given. Perhaps a corpse would be re-animated; galvanism[6] had given token of such things: perhaps the component parts of a creature might be manufactured, brought together, and endued with vital warmth.

Night waned upon this talk, and even the witching hour had gone by, before we retired to rest. When I placed my head on my pillow, I did not sleep, nor could I be said to think. My imagination, unbidden, possessed and guided me, gifting the successive images that arose in my mind with a vividness far beyond the usual bounds of reverie. I saw—with shut eyes, but acute mental vision,—I saw the pale student of unhallowed arts kneeling beside the thing he had put together. I saw the hideous phantasm of a man stretched out, and then, on the working of some powerful engine, show signs of life and stir with an uneasy, half vital motion. Frightful must it be; for supremely frightful would be the effect of any human endeavour to mock the stupendous mechanism of the Creator of the world. His success would terrify the artist; he would rush away from his odious handywork, horror-stricken. He would hope that, left to itself, the slight spark of life which he had communicated would fade; that this thing, which had received such imperfect animation, would subside into dead matter; and he might sleep in the belief that the silence of the grave would quench for ever the transient existence of the hideous corpse which he had looked upon as the cradle of life. He sleeps; but he is awakened; he opens his eyes; behold the horrid thing stands at his bedside, opening his curtains, and looking on him with yellow, watery, but speculative eyes.

I opened mine in terror. The idea so possessed my mind, that a thrill of fear ran through me, and I wished to exchange the ghastly image of my fancy for the realities around. I see them still; the very room, the dark *parquet*,[7] the closed shutters, with the moonlight struggling through, and the sense I had that the glassy lake and white high Alps were beyond. I could not so easily get rid of my hideous phantom; still it haunted me. I must try to think of something else. I recurred to my ghost story,—my tiresome unlucky ghost

---

4. James Rieger conjectures that Mary Shelley may in fact be remembering a conversation between Polidori and Shelley, which apparently took place a day before Byron suggested writing ghost stories and which, as Polidori records in his diary for June 15, 1816, was "about principles—whether man was to be thought merely an instrument." Polidori had recently published a treatise on sleepwalking.

5. In *The Temple of Nature* (1803) Erasmus Dar-

win describes an experiment with the pasta called vermicelli—literally, "little worms."

6. The use of electric current to induce muscle twitches in dead tissue. Mary Shelley probably has in mind a widely discussed experiment of 1803 in which Giovanni Aldini had effected spasmodic contractions in the corpse of a criminal executed at Newgate prison.

7. A floor made of wooden pieces arranged in a decorative pattern.

story! O! if I could only contrive one which would frighten my reader as I myself had been frightened that night!

Swift as light and as cheering was the idea that broke in upon me. "I have found it! What terrified me will terrify others; and I need only describe the spectre which had haunted my midnight pillow." On the morrow I announced that I had *thought of a story*. I began that day with the words, *It was on a dreary night of November*, making only a transcript of the grim terrors of my waking dream.

At first I thought but of a few pages—of a short tale; but Shelley urged me to develope the idea at greater length. I certainly did not owe the suggestion of one incident, nor scarcely of one train of feeling, to my husband, and yet but for his incitement, it would never have taken the form in which it was presented to the world. From this declaration I must except the preface. As far as I can recollect, it was entirely written by him.[8]

And now, once again, I bid my hideous progeny go forth and prosper. I have an affection for it, for it was the offspring of happy days, when death and grief were but words, which found no true echo in my heart. Its several pages speak of many a walk, many a drive, and many a conversation, when I was not alone; and my companion was one who, in this world, I shall never see more. But this is for myself; my readers have nothing to do with these associations.

I will add but one word as to the alterations I have made. They are principally those of style. I have changed no portion of the story, nor introduced any new ideas or circumstances. I have mended the language where it was so bald as to interfere with the interest of the narrative; and these changes occur almost exclusively in the beginning of the first volume. Throughout they are entirely confined to such parts as are mere adjuncts to the story, leaving the core and substance of it untouched.

M. W. S.

London, October 15, 1831

VOLUME 1

Letter 1.

TO MRS. SAVILLE, ENGLAND.

St. Petersburgh.[1] Dec. 11th, 17—

You will rejoice to hear that no disaster has accompanied the commencement of an enterprise which you have regarded with such evil forebodings. I arrived here yesterday; and my first task is to assure my dear sister of my welfare, and increasing confidence in the success of my undertaking.

I am already far north of London; and as I walk in the streets of Petersburgh, I feel a cold northern breeze play upon my cheeks, which braces my nerves, and fills me with delight. Do you understand this feeling? This breeze, which has travelled from the regions towards which I am advancing, gives

---

8. Percy Shelley's contributions to the text are analyzed and evaluated in the Norton Critical Edition of *Frankenstein*, edited by J. Paul Hunter.

Percy Shelley's *Preface* is reprinted on p. 907.
1. In northwestern Russia, on the Gulf of Finland.

me a foretaste of those icy climes. Inspirited by this wind of promise, my day dreams become more fervent and vivid. I try in vain to be persuaded that the pole is the seat of frost and desolation; it ever presents itself to my imagination as the region of beauty and delight. There, Margaret, the sun is for ever visible; its broad disk just skirting the horizon, and diffusing a perpetual splendour. There—for with your leave, my sister, I will put some trust in preceding navigators—there snow and frost are banished; and, sailing over a calm sea, we may be wafted to a land surpassing in wonders and in beauty every region hitherto discovered on the habitable globe. Its productions and features may be without example, as the phænomena of the heavenly bodies undoubtedly are in those undiscovered solitudes. What may not be expected in a country of eternal light? I may there discover the wondrous power which attracts the needle;[2] and may regulate a thousand celestial observations, that require only this voyage to render their seeming eccentricities consistent for ever. I shall satiate my ardent curiosity with the sight of a part of the world never before visited, and may tread a land never before imprinted by the foot of man. These are my enticements, and they are sufficient to conquer all fear of danger or death, and to induce me to commence this laborious voyage with the joy a child feels when he embarks in a little boat with his holiday mates, on an expedition of discovery up his native river. But, supposing all these conjectures to be false, you cannot contest the inestimable benefit which I shall confer on all mankind to the last generation, by discovering a passage near the pole to those countries, to reach which at present so many months are requisite; or by ascertaining the secret of the magnet, which, if at all possible, can only be effected by an undertaking such as mine.

These reflections have dispelled the agitation with which I began my letter, and I feel my heart glow with an enthusiasm which elevates me to heaven; for nothing contributes so much to tranquillize the mind as a steady purpose,—a point on which the soul may fix its intellectual eye. This expedition has been the favourite dream of my early years. I have read with ardour the accounts of the various voyages which have been made in the prospect of arriving at the North Pacific Ocean through the seas which surround the pole. You may remember, that a history of all the voyages made for purposes of discovery composed the whole of our good uncle Thomas's library. My education was neglected, yet I was passionately fond of reading. These volumes were my study day and night, and my familiarity with them increased that regret which I had felt, as a child, on learning that my father's dying injunction had forbidden my uncle to allow me to embark in a sea-faring life.

These visions faded when I perused, for the first time, those poets whose effusions entranced my soul, and lifted it to heaven. I also became a poet, and for one year lived in a Paradise of my own creation; I imagined that I also might obtain a niche in the temple where the names of Homer and Shakespeare are consecrated. You are well acquainted with my failure, and how heavily I bore the disappointment. But just at that time I inherited the fortune of my cousin, and my thoughts were turned into the channel of their earlier bent.

Six years have passed since I resolved on my present undertaking. I can, even now, remember the hour from which I dedicated myself to this great

2. Compass needle.

enterprise. I commenced by inuring my body to hardship. I accompanied the whale-fishers on several expeditions to the North Sea; I voluntarily endured cold, famine, thirst, and want of sleep; I often worked harder than the common sailors during the day, and devoted my nights to the study of mathematics, the theory of medicine, and those branches of physical science from which a naval adventurer might derive the greatest practical advantage. Twice I actually hired myself as an undermate in a Greenland whaler, and acquitted myself to admiration. I must own I felt a little proud, when my captain offered me the second dignity in the vessel, and entreated me to remain with the greatest earnestness; so valuable did he consider my services.

And now, dear Margaret, do I not deserve to accomplish some great purpose. My life might have been passed in ease and luxury; but I preferred glory to every enticement that wealth placed in my path. Oh, that some encouraging voice would answer in the affirmative! My courage and my resolution is firm; but my hopes fluctuate, and my spirits are often depressed. I am about to proceed on a long and difficult voyage; the emergencies of which will demand all my fortitude: I am required not only to raise the spirits of others, but sometimes to sustain my own, when their's are failing.

This is the most favourable period for travelling in Russia. They fly quickly over the snow in their sledges; the motion is pleasant, and, in my opinion, far more agreeable than that of an English stage-coach. The cold is not excessive, if you are wrapt in furs, a dress which I have already adopted; for there is a great difference between walking the deck and remaining seated motionless for hours, when no exercise prevents the blood from actually freezing in your veins. I have no ambition to lose my life on the post-road between St. Petersburgh and Archangel.[3]

I shall depart for the latter town in a fortnight or three weeks; and my intention is to hire a ship there, which can easily be done by paying the insurance for the owner, and to engage as many sailors as I think necessary among those who are accustomed to the whale-fishing. I do not intend to sail until the month of June: and when shall I return? Ah, dear sister, how can I answer this question? If I succeed, many, many months, perhaps years, will pass before you and I may meet. If I fail, you will see me again soon, or never.

Farewell, my dear, excellent, Margaret. Heaven shower down blessings on you, and save me, that I may again and again testify my gratitude for all your love and kindness.

Your affectionate brother,
R. WALTON.

Letter 2.

TO MRS. SAVILLE, ENGLAND.

Archangel, 28th March, 17—.

How slowly the time passes here, encompassed as I am by frost and snow; yet a second step is taken towards by my enterprise. I have hired a vessel,

---

3. A port in northern Russia, on an inlet of the Arctic Ocean. "Post-road": a main road, on which the mails were transported.

and am occupied in collecting my sailors; those whom I have already engaged appear to be men on whom I can depend, and are certainly possessed of dauntless courage.

But I have one want which I have never yet been able to satisfy; and the absence of the object of which I now feel as a most severe evil. I have no friend, Margaret: when I am glowing with the enthusiasm of success, there will be none to participate my joy; if I am assailed by disappointment, no one will endeavour to sustain me in dejection. I shall commit my thoughts to paper, it is true; but that is a poor medium for the communication of feeling. I desire the company of a man who could sympathize with me; whose eyes would reply to mine. You may deem me romantic, my dear sister, but I bitterly feel the want of a friend. I have no one near me, gentle yet courageous, possessed of a cultivated as well as of a capacious mind, whose tastes are like my own, to approve or amend my plans. How would such a friend repair the faults of your poor brother! I am too ardent in execution, and too impatient of difficulties. But it is a still greater evil to me that I am self-educated: for the first fourteen years of my life I ran wild on a common, and read nothing but our uncle Thomas's books of voyages. At that age I became acquainted with the celebrated poets of our own country, but it was only when it had ceased to be in my power to derive its most important benefits from such a conviction, that I perceived the necessity of becoming acquainted with more languages than that of my native country. Now I am twenty-eight, and am in reality more illiterate than many school-boys of fifteen. It is true that I have thought more, and that my day dreams are more extended and magnificent; but they want (as the painters call it) *keeping*;[4] and I greatly need a friend who would have sense enough not to despise me as romantic, and affection enough for me to endeavour to regulate my mind.

Well, these are useless complaints; I shall certainly find no friend on the wide ocean, nor even here in Archangel, among merchants and seamen. Yet some feelings, unallied to the dross of human nature,[5] beat even in these rugged bosoms. My lieutenant, for instance, is a man of wonderful courage and enterprise; he is madly desirous of glory. He is an Englishman, and in the midst of national and professional prejudices, unsoftened by cultivation, retains some of the noblest endowments of humanity. I first became acquainted with him on board a whale vessel: finding that he was unemployed in this city, I easily engaged him to assist in my enterprise.

The master is a person of an excellent disposition, and is remarkable in the ship for his gentleness, and the mildness of his discipline. He is, indeed, of so amiable a nature, that he will not hunt (a favourite, and almost the only amusement here), because he cannot endure to spill blood. He is, moreover, heroically generous. Some years ago he loved a young Russian lady, of moderate fortune; and having amassed a considerable sum in prize-money,[6] the father of the girl consented to the match. He saw his mistress once before the destined ceremony; but she was bathed in tears, and, throwing herself at his feet, entreated him to spare her, confessing at the same time that she loved another, but that he was poor, and that her father would never consent to the union. My generous friend reassured the suppliant, and on being

---

4. The proper proportion, in a painting, between near and distant objects.
5. I.e., unrelated to the bad elements in human nature.
6. For enemy ships captured in wartime.

informed of the name of her lover instantly abandoned his pursuit. He had already bought a farm with his money, on which he had designed to pass the remainder of his life; but he bestowed the whole on his rival, together with the remains of his prize-money to purchase stock,[7] and then himself solicited the young woman's father to consent to her marriage with her lover. But the old man decidedly refused, thinking himself bound in honour to my friend; who, when he found the father inexorable, quitted his country, nor returned until he heard that his former mistress was married according to her inclinations. "What a noble fellow!" you will exclaim. He is so; but then he has passed all his life on board a vessel, and has scarcely an idea beyond the rope and the shroud.[8]

But do not suppose that, because I complain a little, or because I can conceive a consolation for my toils which I may never know, that I am wavering in my resolutions. Those are as fixed as fate; and my voyage is only now delayed until the weather shall permit my embarkation. The winter has been dreadfully severe; but the spring promises well, and it is considered as a remarkably early season; so that, perhaps, I may sail sooner than I expected. I shall do nothing rashly; you know me sufficiently to confide in my prudence and considerateness whenever the safety of others is committed to my care.

I cannot describe to you my sensations on the near prospect of my undertaking. It is impossible to communicate to you a conception of the trembling sensation, half pleasurable and half fearful, with which I am preparing to depart. I am going to unexplored regions, to "the land of mist and snow;"[9] but I shall kill no albatross, therefore do not be alarmed for my safety.

Shall I meet you again, after having traversed immense seas, and returned by the most southern cape of Africa or America? I dare not expect such success, yet I cannot bear to look on the reverse of the picture. Continue to write to me by every opportunity: I may receive your letters (though the chance is very doubtful) on some occasions when I need them most to support my spirits. I love you very tenderly. Remember me with affection, should you never hear from me again.

Your affectionate brother,
ROBERT WALTON.

Letter 3.

TO MRS. SAVILLE, ENGLAND.

July 7th, 17—.

MY DEAR SISTER,

I write a few lines in haste, to say that I am safe, and well advanced on my voyage. This letter will reach England by a merchant-man now on its homeward voyage from Archangel; more fortunate than I, who may not see my native land, perhaps, for many years. I am, however, in good spirits: my men are bold, and apparently firm of purpose; nor do the floating sheets of ice that continually pass us, indicating the dangers of the region towards which we are advancing, appear to dismay them. We have already reached a very high latitude; but it is the height of summer, and although not so

---

7. Livestock, farm animals.
8. A rope that supports a ship's mast.

9. Coleridge, *The Ancient Mariner*, line 403.

warm as in England, the southern gales, which blow us speedily towards those shores which I so ardently desire to attain, breathe a degree of renovating warmth which I had not expected.

No incidents have hitherto befallen us, that would make a figure[1] in a letter. One or two stiff gales, and the breaking of a mast, are accidents which experienced navigators scarcely remember to record; and I shall be well content, if nothing worse happen to us during our voyage.

Adieu, my dear Margaret. Be assured, that for my own sake, as well as your's, I will not rashly encounter danger. I will be cool, persevering, and prudent.

Remember me to all my English friends.

Most affectionately yours,

R. W.

Letter 4.

TO MRS. SAVILLE, ENGLAND.

August 5th, 17—.

So strange an accident has happened to us, that I cannot forbear recording it, although it is very probable that you will see me before these papers can come into your possession.

Last Monday (July 31st), we were nearly surrounded by ice, which closed in the ship on all sides, scarcely leaving her the sea room in which she floated. Our situation was somewhat dangerous, especially as we were compassed round by a very thick fog. We accordingly lay to,[2] hoping that some change would take place in the atmosphere and weather.

About two o'clock the mist cleared away, and we beheld, stretched out in every direction, vast and irregular plains of ice, which seemed to have no end. Some of my comrades groaned, and my own mind began to grow watchful with anxious thoughts, when a strange sight suddenly attracted our attention, and diverted our solicitude from our own situation. We perceived a low carriage, fixed on a sledge and drawn by dogs, pass on towards the north, at the distance of half a mile: a being which had the shape of a man, but apparently of gigantic stature, sat in the sledge, and guided the dogs. We watched the rapid progress of the traveller with our telescopes, until he was lost among the distant inequalities of the ice.

This appearance excited our unqualified wonder. We were, as we believed, many hundred miles from any land; but this apparition seemed to denote that it was not, in reality, so distant as we had supposed. Shut in, however, by ice, it was impossible to follow his track, which we had observed with the greatest attention.

About two hours after this occurrence, we heard the ground sea;[3] and before night the ice broke, and freed our ship. We, however, lay to until the morning, fearing to encounter in the dark those large loose masses which float about after the breaking up of the ice. I profited of this time to rest for a few hours.

In the morning, however, as soon as it was light, I went upon deck, and

1. Be important enough.
2. Stopped the ship.
3. Deep, rolling waves.

found all the sailors busy on one side of the vessel, apparently talking to some one in the sea. It was, in fact, a sledge, like that we had seen before, which had drifted towards us in the night, on a large fragment of ice. Only one dog remained alive; but there was a human being within it, whom the sailors were persuading to enter the vessel. He was not, as the other traveller seemed to be, a savage inhabitant of some undiscovered island, but an European. When I appeared on deck, the master said, "Here is our captain, and he will not allow you to perish on the open sea."

On perceiving me, the stranger addressed me in English, although with a foreign accent. "Before I come on board your vessel," said he, "will you have the kindness to inform me whither you are bound?"

You may conceive my astonishment on hearing such a question addressed to me from a man on the brink of destruction, and to whom I should have supposed that my vessel would have been a resource which he would not have exchanged for the most precious wealth the earth can afford. I replied, however, that we were on a voyage of discovery towards the northern pole.

Upon hearing this he appeared satisfied, and consented to come on board. Good God! Margaret, if you had seen the man who thus capitulated[4] for his safety, your surprise would have been boundless. His limbs were nearly frozen, and his body dreadfully emaciated by fatigue and suffering. I never saw a man in so wretched a condition. We attempted to carry him into the cabin; but as soon as he had quitted the fresh air, he fainted. We accordingly brought him back to the deck, and restored him to animation by rubbing him with brandy, and forcing him to swallow a small quantity. As soon as he shewed signs of life, we wrapped him up in blankets, and placed him near the chimney of the kitchen-stove. By slow degrees he recovered, and ate a little soup, which restored him wonderfully.

Two days passed in this manner before he was able to speak; and I often feared that his sufferings had deprived him of understanding. When he had in some measure recovered, I removed him to my own cabin, and attended on him as much as my duty would permit. I never saw a more interesting creature: his eyes have generally an expression of wildness, and even madness; but there are moments when, if any one performs an act of kindness towards him, or does him any the most trifling service, his whole countenance is lighted up, as it were, with a beam of benevolence and sweetness that I never saw equalled. But he is generally melancholy and despairing; and sometimes he gnashes his teeth, as if impatient of the weight of woes that oppresses him.

When my guest was a little recovered, I had great trouble to keep off the men, who wished to ask him a thousand questions; but I would not allow him to be tormented by their idle curiosity, in a state of body and mind whose restoration evidently depended upon entire repose. Once, however, the lieutenant asked, Why he had come so far upon the ice in so strange a vehicle?

His countenance instantly assumed an aspect of the deepest gloom; and he replied, "To seek one who fled from me."

"And did the man whom you pursued travel in the same fashion?"

"Yes."

"Then I fancy we have seen him; for, the day before we picked you up, we saw some dogs drawing a sledge, with a man in it, across the ice."

---

4. Set definite conditions for surrendering.

This aroused the stranger's attention; and he asked a multitude of questions concerning the route which the dæmon,[5] as he called him, had pursued. Soon after, when he was alone with me, he said, "I have, doubtless, excited your curiosity, as well as that of these good people; but you are too considerate to make inquiries."

"Certainly; it would indeed be very impertinent and inhuman in me to trouble you with any inquisitiveness of mine."

"And yet you rescued me from a strange and perilous situation; you have benevolently restored me to life."

Soon after this he inquired, if I thought that the breaking up of the ice had destroyed the other sledge? I replied, that I could not answer with any degree of certainty; for the ice had not broken until near midnight, and the traveller might have arrived at a place of safety before that time; but of this I could not judge.

From this time the stranger seemed very eager to be upon deck, to watch for the sledge which had before appeared; but I have persuaded him to remain in the cabin, for he is far too weak to sustain the rawness of the atmosphere. But I have promised that some one should watch for him, and give him instant notice if any new object should appear in sight.

Such is my journal of what relates to this strange occurrence up to the present day. The stranger has gradually improved in health, but is very silent, and appears uneasy when any one except myself enters his cabin. Yet his manners are so conciliating and gentle, that the sailors are all interested in him, although they have had very little communication with him. For my own part, I begin to love him as a brother; and his constant and deep grief fills me with sympathy and compassion. He must have been a noble creature in his better days, being even now in wreck so attractive and amiable.

I said in one of my letters, my dear Margaret, that I should find no friend on the wide ocean; yet I have found a man who, before his spirit had been broken by misery, I should have been happy to have possessed as the brother of my heart.

I shall continue my journal concerning the stranger at intervals, should I have any fresh incidents to record.

August 13th, 17—.

My affection for my guest increases every day. He excites at once my admiration[6] and my pity to an astonishing degree. How can I see so noble a creature destroyed by misery without feeling the most poignant grief? He is so gentle, yet so wise; his mind is so cultivated; and when he speaks, although his words are culled with the choicest art, yet they flow with rapidity and unparalleled eloquence.

He is now much recovered from his illness, and is continually on the deck, apparently watching for the sledge that preceded his own. Yet, although unhappy, he is not so utterly occupied by his own misery, but that he interests himself deeply in the employments of others. He has asked me many questions concerning my design; and I have related my little history frankly to him. He appeared pleased with the confidence, and suggested several alterations in my plan, which I shall find exceedingly useful. There is no pedantry

5. In Greek mythology, a lower-order divinity. Shelley, however, probably uses "daemon" as an alternative spelling for *demon,* an evil spirit.
6. In an old sense: wonder, astonishment.

in his manner; but all he does appears to spring solely from the interest he instinctively takes in the welfare of those who surround him. He is often overcome by gloom, and then he sits by himself, and tries to overcome all that is sullen or unsocial in his humour. These paroxysms pass from him like a cloud from before the sun, though his dejection never leaves him. I have endeavoured to win his confidence; and I trust that I have succeeded. One day I mentioned to him the desire I had always felt of finding a friend who might sympathize with me, and direct me by his counsel. I said, I did not belong to that class of men who are offended by advice. "I am self-educated, and perhaps I hardly rely sufficiently upon my own powers. I wish therefore that my companion should be wiser and more experienced than myself, to confirm and support me; nor have I believed it impossible to find a true friend."

"I agree with you," replied the stranger, "in believing that friendship is not only a desirable, but a possible acquisition. I once had a friend, the most noble of human creatures, and am entitled, therefore, to judge respecting friendship. You have hope, and the world before you, and have no cause for despair. But I—I have lost every thing, and cannot begin life anew."

As he said this, his countenance became expressive of a calm settled grief, that touched me to the heart. But he was silent, and presently retired to his cabin.

Even broken in spirit as he is, no one can feel more deeply than he does the beauties of nature. The starry sky, the sea and every sight afforded by these wonderful regions, seems still to have the power of elevating his soul from earth. Such a man has a double existence: he may suffer misery, and be overwhelmed by disappointments; yet when he has retired into himself, he will be like a celestial spirit, that has a halo around him, within whose circle no grief or folly ventures.

Will you laugh at the enthusiasm I express concerning this divine wanderer? If you do, you must have certainly lost that simplicity which was once your characteristic charm. Yet, if you will, smile at the warmth of my expressions, while I find every day new causes for repeating them.

August 19th, 17—.

Yesterday the stranger said to me, "You may easily perceive, Captain Walton, that I have suffered great and unparalleled misfortunes. I had determined, once, that the memory of these evils should die with me; but you have won me to alter my determination. You seek for knowledge and wisdom, as I once did; and I ardently hope that the gratification of your wishes may not be a serpent to sting you, as mine has been. I do not know that the relation of my misfortunes will be useful to you, yet, if you are inclined, listen to my tale. I believe that the strange incidents connected with it will afford a view of nature, which may enlarge your faculties and understanding. You will hear of powers and occurrences, such as you have been accustomed to believe impossible: but I do not doubt that my tale conveys in its series internal evidence of the truth of the events of which it is composed."

You may easily conceive that I was much gratified by the offered communication; yet I could not endure that he should renew his grief by a recital of his misfortunes. I felt the greatest eagerness to hear the promised narrative, partly from curiosity, and partly from a strong desire to ameliorate his fate, if it were in my power. I expressed these feelings in my answer.

"I thank you," he replied, "for your sympathy, but it is useless; my fate is nearly fulfilled. I wait but for one event, and then I shall repose in peace. I understand your feeling," continued he, perceiving that I wished to interrupt him; "but you are mistaken, my friend, if thus you will allow me to name you; nothing can alter my destiny: listen to my history, and you will perceive how irrevocably it is determined."

He then told me, that he would commence his narrative the next day when I should be at leisure. This promise drew from me the warmest thanks. I have resolved every night, when I am not engaged, to record, as nearly as possible in his own words, what he has related during the day. If I should be engaged, I will at least make notes. This manuscript will doubtless afford you the greatest pleasure: but to me, who know him, and who hear it from his own lips, with what interest and sympathy shall I read it in some future day!

Chapter 1.

I am by birth a Genevese;[7] and my family is one of the most distinguished of that republic. My ancestors had been for many years counsellors and syndics;[8] and my father had filled several public situations with honour and reputation. He was respected by all who knew him for his integrity and indefatigable attention to public business. He passed his younger days perpetually occupied by the affairs of his country; and it was not until the decline of life that he thought of marrying, and bestowing on the state sons who might carry his virtues and his name down to posterity.

As the circumstances of his marriage illustrate his character, I cannot refrain from relating them. One of his most intimate friends was a merchant, who, from a flourishing state, fell, through numerous mischances, into poverty. This man, whose name was Beaufort, was of a proud and unbending disposition, and could not bear to live in poverty and oblivion in the same country where he had formerly been distinguished for his rank and magnificence. Having paid his debts, therefore, in the most honourable manner, he retreated with his daughter to the town of Lucerne, where he lived unknown and in wretchedness. My father loved Beaufort with the truest friendship, and was deeply grieved by his retreat in these unfortunate circumstances. He grieved also for the loss of his society, and resolved to seek him out and endeavour to persuade him to begin the world again through his credit and assistance.

Beaufort had taken effectual measures to conceal himself; and it was ten months before my father discovered his abode. Overjoyed at this discovery, he hastened to the house, which was situated in a mean street, near the Reuss. But when he entered, misery and despair alone welcomed him. Beaufort had saved but a very small sum of money from the wreck of his fortunes; but it was sufficient to provide him with sustenance for some months, and in the mean time he hoped to procure some respectable employment in a

7. I.e., from the republic of Geneva, Switzerland.
8. Legislators chosen from the leading families in Geneva.

merchant's house. The interval was consequently spent in inaction; his grief only became more deep and rankling, when he had leisure for reflection; and at length it took so fast hold of his mind, that at the end of three months he lay on a bed of sickness, incapable of any exertion.

His daughter attended him with the greatest tenderness; but she saw with despair that their little fund was rapidly decreasing, and that there was no other prospect of support. But Caroline Beaufort possessed a mind of an uncommon mould; and her courage rose to support her in her adversity. She procured plain work;[9] she plaited straw; and by various means contrived to earn a pittance scarcely sufficient to support life.

Several months passed in this manner. Her father grew worse; her time was more entirely occupied in attending him; her means of subsistence decreased; and in the tenth month her father died in her arms, leaving her an orphan and a beggar. This last blow overcame her; and she knelt by Beaufort's coffin, weeping bitterly, when my father entered the chamber. He came like a protecting spirit to the poor girl, who committed herself to his care, and after the interment of his friend he conducted her to Geneva, and placed her under the protection of a relation. Two years after this event Caroline became his wife.

When my father became a husband and a parent, he found his time so occupied by the duties of his new situation, that he relinquished many of his public employments, and devoted himself to the education of his children. Of these I was the eldest, and the destined successor to all his labours and utility. No creature could have more tender parents than mine. My improvement and health were their constant care, especially as I remained for several years their only child. But before I continue my narrative, I must record an incident which took place when I was four years of age.

My father had a sister, whom he tenderly loved, and who had married early in life an Italian gentleman. Soon after her marriage, she had accompanied her husband into his native country, and for some years my father had very little communication with her. About the time I mentioned she died; and a few months afterwards he received a letter from her husband, acquainting him with his intention of marrying an Italian lady, and requesting my father to take charge of the infant Elizabeth, the only child of his deceased sister. "It is my wish," he said, "that you should consider her as your own daughter, and educate her thus. Her mother's fortune is secured[1] to her, the documents of which I will commit to your keeping. Reflect upon this proposition; and decide whether you would prefer educating your niece yourself to her being brought up by a stepmother."

My father did not hesitate, and immediately went to Italy that he might accompany the little Elizabeth to her future home. I have often heard my mother say, that she was at that time the most beautiful child she had ever seen, and shewed signs even then of a gentle and affectionate disposition. These indications, and a desire to bind as closely as possible the ties of domestic love, determined my mother to consider Elizabeth as my future wife; a design which she never found reason to repent.

From this time Elizabeth Lavenza became my playfellow, and, as we grew

---

9. Basic sewing, as distinguished from fancy sewing.

1. Legally guaranteed.

older, my friend. She was docile and good tempered, yet gay and playful as a summer insect. Although she was lively and animated, her feelings were strong and deep, and her disposition uncommonly affectionate. No one could better enjoy liberty, yet no one could submit with more grace than she did to constraint and caprice. Her imagination was luxuriant, yet her capability of application was great. Her person was the image of her mind; her hazel eyes, although as lively as a bird's, possessed an attractive softness. Her figure was light and airy; and, though capable of enduring great fatigue, she appeared the most fragile creature in the world. While I admired her understanding and fancy, I loved to tend on her, as I should on a favourite animal; and I never saw so much grace both of person and mind united to so little pretension.

Every one adored Elizabeth. If the servants had any request to make, it was always through her intercession. We were strangers to any species of disunion and dispute; for although there was a great dissimilitude in our characters, there was an harmony in that very dissimilitude. I was more calm and philosophical than my companion; yet my temper was not so yielding. My application was of longer endurance; but it was not so severe whilst it endured. I delighted in investigating the facts relative to the actual world; she busied herself in following the aërial[2] creations of the poets. The world was to me a secret, which I desired to discover; to her it was a vacancy; which she sought to people with imaginations of her own.

My brothers were considerably younger than myself; but I had a friend in one of my schoolfellows, who compensated for this deficiency. Henry Clerval was the son of a merchant of Geneva, an intimate friend of my father. He was a boy of singular talent and fancy. I remember, when he was nine years old, he wrote a fairy tale, which was the delight and amazement of all his companions. His favorite study consisted in books of chivalry and romance; and when very young, I can remember, that we used to act plays composed by him out of these favourite books, the principal characters of which were Orlando, Robin Hood, Amadis, and St. George.[3]

No youth could have passed more happily than mine. My parents were indulgent, and my companions amiable. Our studies were never forced; and by some means we always had an end placed in view, which excited us to ardour in the prosecution of them. It was by this method, and not by emulation, that we were urged to application. Elizabeth was not incited to apply herself to drawing, that her companions might not outstrip her; but through the desire of pleasing her aunt, by the representation of some favorite scene done by her own hand. We learned Latin and English, that we might read the writings in those languages; and so far from study being made odious to us through punishment, we loved application, and our amusements would have been the labours of other children. Perhaps we did not read so many books, or learn languages so quickly, as those who are disciplined according to the ordinary methods; but what we learned was impressed the more deeply on our memories.

In this description of our domestic circle I include Henry Clerval; for he

2. Lofty, imaginative.
3. Robin Hood and St. George are legendary English heroes. Orlando is the hero of Ludovico Ariosto's Italian romance, *Orlando Furioso* (1532).

Amadis is the hero of the Spanish or Portuguese romance *Amadis of Gaul* (second half of the 15th century).

was constantly with us. He went to school with me, and generally passed the afternoon at our house; for being an only child, and destitute of companions at home, his father was well pleased that he should find associates at our house; and we were never completely happy when Clerval was absent.

I feel pleasure in dwelling on the recollections of childhood, before misfortune had tainted my mind, and changed its bright visions of extensive usefulness into gloomy and narrow reflections upon self. But, in drawing the picture of my early days, I must not omit to record those events which led, by insensible steps to my after tale of misery: for when I would account to myself for the birth of that passion, which afterwards ruled my destiny, I find it arise, like a mountain river, from ignoble and almost forgotten sources; but, swelling as it proceeded, it became the torrent which, in its course, has swept away all my hopes and joys.

Natural philosophy is the genius[4] that has regulated my fate; I desire therefore, in this narration, to state those facts which led to my predilection for that science. When I was thirteen years of age, we all went on a party of pleasure to the baths near Thonon: the inclemency of the weather obliged us to remain a day confined to the inn. In this house I chanced to find a volume of the works of Cornelius Agrippa.[5] I opened it with apathy; the theory which he attempts to demonstrate, and the wonderful facts which he relates, soon changed this feeling into enthusiasm. A new light seemed to dawn upon my mind; and, bounding with joy, I communicated my discovery to my father. I cannot help remarking here the many opportunities instructors possess of directing the attention of their pupils to useful knowledge, which they utterly neglect. My father looked carelessly at the title-page of my book, and said, "Ah! Cornelius Agrippa! My dear Victor, do not waste your time upon this; it is sad trash."

If, instead of this remark, my father had taken the pains to explain to me, that the principles of Agrippa had been entirely exploded, and that a modern system of science had been introduced, which possessed much greater powers than the ancient, because the powers of the latter were chimerical, while those of the former were real and practical; under such circumstances, I should certainly have thrown Agrippa aside, and, with my imagination warmed as it was, should probably have applied myself to the more rational theory of chemistry which has resulted from modern discoveries. It is even possible, that the train of my ideas would never have received the fatal impulse that led to my ruin. But the cursory glance my father had taken of my volume by no means assured me that he was acquainted with its contents; and I continued to read with the greatest avidity.

When I returned home, my first care was to procure the whole works of this author, and afterwards of Paracelsus and Albertus Magnus.[6] I read and studied the wild fancies of these writers with delight; they appeared to me treasures known to few beside myself; and although I often wished to communicate these secret stores of knowledge to my father, yet his indefinite censure of my favourite Agrippa always withheld me. I disclosed my discov-

---

4. Attendant spirit. "Natural philosophy": the sciences dealing with the physical universe.
5. Henricus Cornelius Agrippa (1486–1535), a writer on magic and the occult sciences.
6. A German monk and scholastic philosopher

(1193 or 1206–1280) whose great learning earned him the title "Doctor Universalis." Paracelsus (1493–1541), a Swiss physician who wrote works on alchemy and magic, as well as empirical chemistry and medicine.

eries to Elizabeth, therefore, under a promise of strict secrecy; but she did not interest herself in the subject, and I was left by her to pursue my studies alone.

It may appear very strange, that a disciple of Albertus Magnus should arise in the eighteenth century; but our family was not scientifical, and I had not attended any of the lectures given at the schools of Geneva. My dreams were therefore undisturbed by reality; and I entered with the greatest diligence into the search of the philosopher's stone and the elixir of life.[7] But the latter obtained my most undivided attention: wealth was an inferior object; but what glory would attend the discovery, if I could banish disease from the human frame, and render man invulnerable to any but a violent death!

Nor were these my only visions. The raising of ghosts or devils was a promise liberally accorded by my favourite authors, the fulfilment of which I most eagerly sought; and if my incantations were always unsuccessful, I attributed the failure rather to my own inexperience and mistake, than to a want of skill or fidelity in my instructors.

The natural phænomena that take place every day before our eyes did not escape my examinations. Distillation, and the wonderful effects of steam, processes of which my favourite authors were utterly ignorant, excited my astonishment; but my utmost wonder was engaged by some experiments on an airpump,[8] which I saw employed by a gentleman whom we were in the habit of visiting.

The ignorance of the early philosophers on these and several other points served to decrease their credit with me: but I could not entirely throw them aside, before some other system should occupy their place in my mind.

When I was about fifteen years old, we had retired to our house near Belrive, when we witnessed a most violent and terrible thunder-storm. It advanced from behind the mountains of Jura; and the thunder burst at once with frightful loudness from various quarters of the heavens. I remained, while the storm lasted, watching its progress with curiosity and delight. As I stood at the door, on a sudden I beheld a stream of fire issue from an old and beautiful oak, which stood about twenty yards from our house; and so soon as the dazzling light vanished, the oak had disappeared, and nothing remained but a blasted stump. When we visited it the next morning, we found the tree shattered in a singular manner. It was not splintered by the shock, but entirely reduced to thin ribbands of wood. I never beheld any thing so utterly destroyed.

The catastrophe of this tree excited my extreme astonishment; and I eagerly inquired of my father the nature and origin of thunder and lightning. He replied, "Electricity;" describing at the same time the various effects of that power. He constructed a small electrical machine, and exhibited a few experiments; he made also a kite, with a wire and string, which drew down that fluid from the clouds.[9]

This last stroke completed the overthrow of Cornelius Agrippa, Albertus Magnus, and Paracelsus, who had so long reigned the lords of my imagination. But by some fatality I did not feel inclined to commence the study of

---

7. Medieval alchemists aimed to produce the philosopher's stone, which would transmute base metals to gold, and the elixir of life, which would prolong life indefinitely.

8. A pump to effect a vacuum, used in physical experiments.

9. In emulation of Benjamin Franklin's experiments with a kite during lightning storms.

any modern system; and this disinclination was influenced by the following circumstance.

My father expressed a wish that I should attend a course of lectures upon natural philosophy, to which I cheerfully consented. Some accident prevented my attending these lectures until the course was nearly finished. The lecture, being therefore one of the last, was entirely incomprehensible to me. The professor discoursed with the greatest fluency of potassium and boron, of sulphates and oxyds, terms to which I could affix no idea; and I became disgusted with the science of natural philosophy, although I still read Pliny and Buffon[1] with delight, authors, in my estimation, of nearly equal interest and utility.

My occupations at this age were principally the mathematics, and most of the branches of study appertaining to that science. I was busily employed in learning languages; Latin was already familiar to me, and I began to read some of the easiest Greek authors without the help of a lexicon. I also perfectly understood English and German. This is the list of my accomplishments at the age of seventeen and you may conceive that my hours were fully employed in acquiring and maintaining a knowledge of this various literature.

Another task also devolved upon me, when I became the instructor of my brothers. Ernest was six years younger than myself, and was my principal pupil. He had been afflicted with ill health from his infancy, through which Elizabeth and I had been his constant nurses: his disposition was gentle, but he was incapable of any severe application. William, the youngest of our family, was yet an infant, and the most beautiful little fellow in the world, his lively blue eyes, dimpled cheeks, and endearing manners, inspired the tenderest affection.

Such was our domestic circle, from which care and pain seemed for ever banished. My father directed our studies, and my mother partook of our enjoyments. Neither of us possessed the slightest pre-eminence over the other; the voice of command was never heard amongst us; but mutual affection engaged us all to comply with and obey the slightest desire of each other.

Chapter 2.

When I had attained the age of seventeen, my parents resolved that I should become a student at the university of Ingolstadt.[2] I had hitherto attended the schools of Geneva; but my father thought it necessary, for the completion of my education, that I should be made acquainted with other customs than those of my native country. My departure was therefore fixed at an early date; but, before the day resolved upon could arrive, the first misfortune of my life occurred—an omen, as it were, of my future misery.

Elizabeth had caught the scarlet fever; but her illness was not severe, and she quickly recovered. During her confinement, many arguments had been urged to persuade my mother to refrain from attending upon her. She had, at first, yielded to our entreaties; but when she heard that her favourite was

1. The comte de Buffon (1707–1788), French author of a monumental *Histoire naturelle* in 36 volumes. Pliny (23–79 C.E.), the Roman compiler of *Historiae Naturalis*, an encyclopedic collection of popular science, much of it erroneous.
2. This Bavarian university was notorious as a base for the Illuminati, a secret society that fostered religious free thinking and republican politics.

recovering, she could no longer debar herself from her society, and entered her chamber long before the danger of infection was past. The consequences of this imprudence were fatal. On the third day my mother sickened; her fever was very malignant, and the looks of her attendants prognosticated the worst event. On her death-bed the fortitude and benignity of this admirable woman did not desert her. She joined the hands of Elizabeth and myself: "My children," she said, "my firmest hopes of future happiness were placed on the prospect of your union. This expectation will now be the consolation of your father. Elizabeth, my love, you must supply my place to your younger cousins. Alas! I regret that I am taken from you; and, happy and beloved as I have been, is it not hard to quit you all? But these are not thoughts befitting me; I will endeavour to resign myself cheerfully to death, and will indulge a hope of meeting you in another world."

She died calmly; and her countenance expressed affection even in death. I need not describe the feelings of those whose dearest ties are rent by that most irreparable evil, the void that presents itself to the soul, and the despair that is exhibited on the countenance. It is so long before the mind can persuade itself that she, whom we saw every day, and whose very existence appeared a part of our own, can have departed for ever—that the brightness of a beloved eye can have been extinguished, and the sound of a voice so familiar, and dear to the ear, can be hushed, never more to be heard. These are the reflections of the first days; but when the lapse of time proves the reality of the evil, then the actual bitterness of grief commences. Yet from whom has not that rude hand rent away some dear connexion; and why should I describe a sorrow which all have felt, and must feel? The time at length arrives, when grief is rather an indulgence than a necessity; and the smile that plays upon the lips, although it may be deemed a sacrilege, is not banished. My mother was dead, but we had still duties which we ought to perform; we must continue our course with the rest, and learn to think ourselves fortunate, whilst one remains whom the spoiler has not seized.

My journey to Ingolstadt, which had been deferred by these events, was now again determined upon. I obtained from my father a respite of some weeks. This period was spent sadly; my mother's death, and my speedy departure, depressed our spirits; but Elizabeth endeavoured to renew the spirit of cheerfulness in our little society. Since the death of her aunt, her mind had acquired new firmness and vigour. She determined to fulfil her duties with the greatest exactness; and she felt that that most imperious duty, of rendering her uncle and cousins happy, had devolved upon her. She consoled me, amused her uncle, instructed my brothers, and I never beheld her so enchanting as at this time, when she was continually endeavouring to contribute to the happiness of others, entirely forgetful of herself.

The day of my departure at length arrived. I had taken leave of all my friends, excepting Clerval, who spent the last evening with us. He bitterly lamented that he was unable to accompany me: but his father could not be persuaded to part with him, intending that he should become a partner with him in business, in compliance with his favourite theory, that learning was superfluous in the commerce of ordinary life. Henry had a refined mind; he had no desire to be idle, and was well pleased to become his father's partner, but he believed that a man might be a very good trader, and yet possess a cultivated understanding.

We sat late, listening to his complaints, and making many little arrangements for the future. The next morning early I departed. Tears gushed from the eyes of Elizabeth; they proceeded partly from sorrow at my departure, and partly because she reflected that the same journey was to have taken place three months before, when a mother's blessing would have accompanied me.

I threw myself into the chaise that was to convey me away, and indulged in the most melancholy reflections. I, who had ever been surrounded by amiable companions, continually engaged in endeavouring to bestow mutual pleasure, I was now alone. In the university, whither I was going, I must form my own friends, and be my own protector. My life had hitherto been remarkably secluded and domestic; and this had given me invincible repugnance to new countenances. I loved my brothers, Elizabeth, and Clerval, these were "old familiar faces;"[3] but I believed myself totally unfitted for the company of strangers. Such were my reflections as I commenced my journey; but as I proceeded, my spirits and hopes rose. I ardently desired the acquisition of knowledge. I had often, when at home, thought it hard to remain during my youth cooped up in one place, and had longed to enter the world, and take my station among other human beings. Now my desires were complied with, and it would, indeed, have been folly to repent.

I had sufficient leisure for these and many other reflections during my journey to Ingolstadt, which was long and fatiguing. At length the high white steeple of the town met my eyes. I alighted, and was conducted to my solitary apartment, to spend the evening as I pleased.

The next morning I delivered my letters of introduction, and paid a visit to some of the principal professors, and among others to M. Krempe, professor of natural philosophy. He received me with politeness, and asked me several questions concerning my progress in the different branches of science appertaining to natural philosophy. I mentioned, it is true, with fear and trembling, the only authors I had ever read upon those subjects. The professor stared: "Have you," he said, "really spent your time in studying such nonsense?"

I replied in the affirmative. "Every minute," continued M. Krempe with warmth, "every instant that you have wasted on those books is utterly and entirely lost. You have burdened your memory with exploded systems, and useless names. Good God! in what desert land have you lived, where no one was kind enough to inform you that these fancies, which you have so greedily imbibed, are a thousand years old, and as musty as they are ancient? I little expected in this enlightened and scientific age to find a disciple of Albertus Magnus and Paracelsus. My dear Sir, you must begin your studies entirely anew."

So saying, he stept aside, and wrote down a list of several books treating of natural philosophy, which he desired me to procure, and dismissed me, after mentioning that in the beginning of the following week he intended to commence a course of lectures upon natural philosophy in its general relations, and that M. Waldman, a fellow-professor, would lecture upon chemistry the alternate days that he missed.

I returned home, not disappointed, for I had long considered those authors

3. Title of a poem (1798) by Charles Lamb.

useless whom the professor had so strongly reprobated; but I did not feel much inclined to study the books which I procured at his recommendation. M. Krempe was a little squat man, with a gruff voice and repulsive countenance; the teacher, therefore, did not prepossess me in favour of his doctrine. Besides, I had a contempt for the uses of modern natural philosophy. It was very different, when the masters of the science sought immortality and power; such views, although futile, were grand: but now the scene was changed. The ambition of the inquirer seemed to limit itself to the annihilation of those visions on which my interest in science was chiefly founded. I was required to exchange chimeras of boundless grandeur for realities of little worth.

Such were my reflections during the first two or three days spent almost in solitude. But as the ensuing week commenced, I thought of the information which M. Krempe had given me concerning the lectures. And although I could not consent to go and hear that little conceited fellow deliver sentences[4] out of a pulpit, I recollected what he had said of M. Waldman, whom I had never seen, as he had hitherto been out of town.

Partly from curiosity, and partly from idleness, I went into the lecturing room, which M. Waldman entered shortly after. This professor was very unlike his colleague. He appeared about fifty years of age, but with an aspect expressive of the greatest benevolence; a few gray hairs covered his temples, but those at the back of his head were nearly black. His person was short, but remarkably erect; and his voice the sweetest I had ever heard. He began his lecture by a recapitulation of the history of chemistry and the various improvements made by different men of learning, pronouncing with fervour the names of the most distinguished discoverers. He then took a cursory view of the present state of the science, and explained many of its elementary terms. After having made a few preparatory experiments, he concluded with a panegyric upon modern chemistry, the terms of which I shall never forget:—

"The ancient teachers of this science," said he, "promised impossibilities, and performed nothing. The modern masters promise very little; they know that metals cannot be transmuted, and that the elixir of life is a chimera. But these philosophers, whose hands seem only made to dabble in dirt, and their eyes to pore over the microscope or crucible, have indeed performed miracles. They penetrate into the recesses of nature, and shew how she works in her hiding places. They ascend into the heavens; they have discovered how the blood circulates, and the nature of the air we breathe.[5] They have acquired new and almost unlimited powers; they can command the thunders of heaven, mimic the earthquake, and even mock the invisible world with its own shadows."

I departed highly pleased with the professor and his lecture, and paid him a visit the same evening. His manners in private were even more mild and attractive than in public; for there was a certain dignity in his mien during his lecture, which in his own house was replaced by the greatest affability and kindness. He heard with attention my little narration concerning my studies, and smiled at the names of Cornelius Agrippa and Paracelsus, but

---

4. Pronouncements, formally stated opinions.
5. William Harvey discovered in 1628 the circulation of the blood. In the 1770s Joseph Priestley published his *Experiments and Observations on Different Kinds of Air*, in which he identified the gas later named oxygen.

without the contempt that M. Krempe had exhibited. He said, that "these were men to whose indefatigable zeal modern philosophers were indebted for most of the foundations of their knowledge. They had left to us, as an easier task, to give new names, and arrange in connected classifications, the facts which they in a great degree had been the instruments of bringing to light. The labours of men of genius, however erroneously directed, scarcely ever fail in ultimately turning to the solid advantage of mankind." I listened to his statement, which was delivered without any presumption or affectation; and then added, that his lecture had removed my prejudices against modern chemists; and I, at the same time, requested his advice concerning the books I ought to procure.

"I am happy," said M. Waldman, "to have gained a disciple; and if your application equals your ability, I have no doubt of your success. Chemistry is that branch of natural philosophy in which the greatest improvements have been and may be made; it is on that account that I have made it my peculiar[6] study; but at the same time I have not neglected the other branches of science. A man would make but a very sorry chemist, if he attended to that department of human knowledge alone. If your wish is to become really a man of science, and not merely a petty experimentalist, I should advise you to apply to every branch of natural philosophy, including mathematics."

He then took me into his laboratory, and explained to me the uses of his various machines; instructing me as to what I ought to procure, and promising me the use of his own, when I should have advanced far enough in the science not to derange their mechanism. He also gave me the list of books which I had requested; and I took my leave.

Thus ended a day memorable to me; it decided my future destiny.

Chapter 3.

From this day natural philosophy, and particularly chemistry, in the most comprehensive sense of the term, became nearly my sole occupation. I read with ardour those works, so full of genius and discrimination, which modern inquirers have written on these subjects. I attended the lectures, and cultivated the acquaintance, of the men of science of the university; and I found even in M. Krempe a great deal of sound sense and real information, combined, it is true, with a repulsive physiognomy and manners, but not on that account the less valuable. In M. Waldman I found a true friend. His gentleness was never tinged by dogmatism; and his instructions were given with an air of frankness and good nature, that banished every idea of pedantry. It was, perhaps, the amiable character of this man that inclined me more to that branch of natural philosophy which he professed, than an intrinsic love for the science itself. But this state of mind had place only in the first steps towards knowledge: the more fully I entered into the science, the more exclusively I pursued it for its own sake. That application, which at first had been a matter of duty and resolution, now became so ardent and eager, that the stars often disappeared in the light of morning whilst I was yet engaged in my laboratory.

As I applied so closely, it may be easily conceived that I improved rapidly.

6. Special, particular.

My ardour was indeed the astonishment of the students; and my proficiency, that of the masters. Professor Krempe often asked me, with a sly smile, how Cornelius Agrippa went on? whilst M. Waldman expressed the most heartfelt exultation in my progress. Two years passed in this manner, during which I paid no visit to Geneva, but was engaged, heart and soul, in the pursuit of some discoveries, which I hoped to make. None but those who have experienced them can conceive of the enticements of science. In other studies you go as far as others have gone before you, and there is nothing more to know; but in a scientific pursuit there is continual food for discovery and wonder. A mind of moderate capacity, which closely pursues one study, must infallibly arrive at great proficiency in that study; and I, who continually sought the attainment of one object of pursuit, and was solely wrapt up in this, improved so rapidly, that, at the end of two years, I made some discoveries in the improvement of some chemical instruments, which procured me great esteem and admiration at the university. When I had arrived at this point, and had become as well acquainted with the theory and practice of natural philosophy as depended on the lessons of any of the professors at Ingolstadt, my residence there being no longer conducive to my improvements, I thought of returning to my friends and my native town, when an incident happened that protracted my stay.

One of the phænonema which had peculiarly attracted my attention was the structure of the human frame, and, indeed, any animal endued with life. Whence, I often asked myself, did the principle of life proceed? It was a bold question, and one which has ever been considered as a mystery; yet with how many things are we upon the brink of becoming acquainted, if cowardice or carelessness did not restrain our inquiries. I revolved these circumstances in my mind, and determined thenceforth to apply myself more particularly to those branches of natural philosophy which relate to physiology. Unless I had been animated by an almost supernatural enthusiasm, my application to this study would have been irksome, and almost intolerable. To examine the causes of life, we must first have recourse to death. I became acquainted with the science of anatomy: but this was not sufficient; I must also observe the natural decay and corruption of the human body. In my education my father had taken the greatest precautions that my mind should be impressed with no supernatural horrors. I do not ever remember to have trembled at a tale of superstition, or to have feared the apparition of a spirit. Darkness had no effect upon my fancy; and a church-yard was to me merely the receptacle of bodies deprived of life, which, from being the seat of beauty and strength, had become food for the worm. Now I was led to examine the cause and progress of this decay, and forced to spend days and nights in vaults and charnel houses.[7] My attention was fixed upon every object the most insupportable to the delicacy of the human feelings. I saw how the fine form of man was degraded and wasted; I beheld the corruption of death succeed to the blooming cheek of life; I saw how the worm inherited the wonders of the eye and brain. I paused, examining and analysing all the minutiæ of causation, as exemplified in the change from life to death, and death to life, until from the midst of this darkness a sudden light broke in upon me—a light so brilliant and wondrous, yet so simple, that while I became dizzy with the

---

7. Where the bodies of the dead are placed.

immensity of the prospect which it illustrated, I was surprised that among so many men of genius, who had directed their inquiries towards the same science, that I alone should be reserved to discover so astonishing a secret.

Remember, I am not recording the vision of a madman. The sun does not more certainly shine in the heavens, than that which I now affirm is true. Some miracle might have produced it, yet the stages of the discovery were distinct and probable. After days and nights of incredible labour and fatigue, I succeeded in discovering the cause of generation and life; nay, more, I became myself capable of bestowing animation upon lifeless matter.

The astonishment which I had at first experienced on this discovery soon gave place to delight and rapture. After so much time spent in painful labour, to arrive at once at the summit of my desires, was the most gratifying consummation of my toils. But this discovery was so great and overwhelming, that all the steps by which I had been progressively led to it were obliterated, and I beheld only the result. What had been the study and desire of the wisest men since the creation of the world, was now within my grasp. Not that, like a magic scene, it all opened upon me at once: the information I had obtained was of a nature rather to direct my endeavours so soon as I should point them towards the object of my search, than to exhibit that object already accomplished. I was like the Arabian who had been buried with the dead, and found a passage to life aided only by one glimmering, and seemingly ineffectual, light.[8]

I see by your eagerness, and the wonder and hope which your eyes express, my friend, that you expect to be informed of the secret with which I am acquainted; that cannot be: listen patiently until the end of my story, and you will easily perceive why I am reserved upon that subject. I will not lead you on, unguarded and ardent as I then was, to your destruction and infallible misery. Learn from me, if not by my precepts, at least by my example, how dangerous is the acquirement of knowledge, and how much happier that man is who believes his native town to be the world, than he who aspires to become greater than his nature will allow.

When I found so astonishing a power placed within my hands, I hesitated a long time concerning the manner in which I should employ it. Although I possessed the capacity of bestowing animation, yet to prepare a frame for the reception of it, with all its intricacies of fibres, muscles, and veins, still remained a work of inconceivable difficulty and labour. I doubted at first whether I should attempt the creation of a being like myself or one of simpler organization; but my imagination was too much exalted by my first success to permit me to doubt of my ability to give life to an animal as complex and wonderful as man. The materials at present within my command hardly appeared adequate to so arduous an undertaking; but I doubted not that I should ultimately succeed. I prepared myself for a multitude of reverses; my operations might be incessantly baffled, and at last my work be imperfect: yet, when I considered the improvement which every day takes place in science and mechanics, I was encouraged to hope my present attempts would at least lay the foundations of future success. Nor could I consider the magnitude and complexity of my plan as any argument of its impracticability. It was with these feelings that I began the creation of a human being. As the minuteness of the parts formed a great hindrance to my speed, I resolved,

---

8. The story, *Sinbad's Fourth Voyage*, is told in *A Thousand and One Nights*.

contrary to my first intention, to make the being of a gigantic stature; that is to say, about eight feet in height, and proportionably large. After having formed this determination, and having spent some months in successfully collecting and arranging my materials, I began.

No one can conceive the variety of feelings which bore me onwards, like a hurricane, in the first enthusiasm of success. Life and death appeared to me ideal bounds,[9] which I should first break through, and pour a torrent of light into our dark world. A new species would bless me as its creator and source; many happy and excellent natures would owe their being to me. No father could claim the gratitude of his child so completely as I should deserve their's. Pursuing these reflections, I thought, that if I could bestow animation upon lifeless matter, I might in process of time (although I now found it impossible) renew life where death had apparently devoted the body to corruption.

These thoughts supported my spirits, while I pursued my undertaking with unremitting ardour. My cheek had grown pale with study, and my person had become emaciated with confinement. Sometimes, on the very brink of certainty, I failed; yet still I clung to the hope which the next day or the next hour might realize. One secret which I alone possessed was the hope to which I had dedicated myself, and the moon gazed on my midnight labours, while, with unrelaxed and breathless eagerness, I pursued nature to her hiding places. Who shall conceive the horrors of my secret toil, as I dabbled among the unhallowed damps of the grave, or tortured the living animal to animate the lifeless clay? My limbs now tremble, and my eyes swim with the remembrance; but then a resistless, and almost frantic impulse, urged me forward; I seemed to have lost all soul or sensation but for this one pursuit. It was indeed but a passing trance, that only made me feel with renewed acuteness so soon as, the unnatural stimulus ceasing to operate, I had returned to my old habits. I collected bones from charnel houses; and disturbed, with profane fingers, the tremendous secrets of the human frame. In a solitary chamber, or rather cell, at the top of the house, and separated from all the other apartments by a gallery and staircase, I kept my workshop of filthy creation; my eyeballs were starting from their sockets in attending to the details of my employment. The dissecting room and the slaughter-house furnished many of my materials; and often did my human nature turn with loathing from my occupation, whilst, still urged on by an eagerness which perpetually increased, I brought my work near to a conclusion.

The summer months passed while I was thus engaged, heart and soul, in one pursuit. It was a most beautiful season; never did the fields bestow a more plentiful harvest, or the vines yield a more luxuriant vintage: but my eyes were insensible to the charms of nature. And the same feelings which made me neglect the scenes around me caused me also to forget those friends who were so many miles absent, and whom I had not seen for so long a time. I knew my silence disquieted them; and I well remembered the words of my father: "I know that while you are pleased with yourself, you will think of us with affection, and we shall hear regularly from you. You must pardon me, if I regard any interruption in your correspondence as a proof that your other duties are equally neglected."

I knew well therefore what would be my father's feelings; but I could not

9. Imagined limits.

tear my thoughts from my employment, loathsome in itself, but which had taken an irresistible hold of my imagination. I wished, as it were, to procrastinate all that related to my feelings of affection until the great object, which swallowed up every habit of my nature, should be completed.

I then thought that my father would be unjust if he ascribed my neglect to vice, or faultiness on my part; but I am now convinced that he was justified in conceiving that I should not be altogether free from blame. A human being in perfection ought always to preserve a calm and peaceful mind, and never to allow passion or a transitory desire to disturb his tranquillity. I do not think that the pursuit of knowledge is an exception to this rule. If the study to which you apply yourself has a tendency to weaken your affections, and to destroy your taste for those simple pleasures in which no alloy can possibly mix, then that study is certainly unlawful, that is to say, not befitting the human mind. If this rule were always observed; if no man allowed any pursuit whatsoever to interfere with the tranquillity of his domestic affections, Greece had not been enslaved; Cæsar would have spared his country; America would have been discovered more gradually; and the empires of Mexico and Peru had not been destroyed.[1]

But I forget that I am moralizing in the most interesting part of my tale; and your looks remind me to proceed.

My father made no reproach in his letters; and only took notice of my silence by inquiring into my occupations more particularly than before. Winter, spring, and summer, passed away during my labours; but I did not watch the blossom or the expanding leaves—sights which before always yielded me supreme delight, so deeply was I engrossed in my occupation. The leaves of that year had withered before my work drew near to a close; and now every day shewed me more plainly how well I had succeeded. But my enthusiasm was checked by my anxiety, and I appeared rather like one doomed by slavery to toil in the mines, or any other unwholesome trade, than an artist occupied by his favourite employment. Every night I was oppressed by a slow fever, and I became nervous to a most painful degree; a disease that I regretted the more because I had hitherto enjoyed most excellent health, and had always boasted of the firmness of my nerves. But I believed that exercise and amusement would soon drive away such symptoms; and I promised myself both of these, when my creation should be complete.

Chapter 4.

It was on a dreary night of November, that I beheld the accomplishment of my toils. With an anxiety that almost amounted to agony, I collected the instruments of life around me, that I might infuse a spark of being into the lifeless thing that lay at my feet. It was already one in the morning; the rain pattered dismally against the panes, and my candle was nearly burnt out, when, by the glimmer of the half-extinguished light, I saw the dull yellow eye of the creature open; it breathed hard, and a convulsive motion agitated its limbs.

1. Greece was at that time dominated by the Turks. The other allusions are to the civil war that broke out after Julius Caesar was assassinated by republicans who feared that he aspired to become king, the displacement of native Americans by the rapid influx of European settlers, and the destructive violence by Spanish conquistadors in Mexico and Peru.

How can I describe my emotions at this catastrophe, or how delineate the wretch whom with such infinite pains and care I had endeavoured to form? His limbs were in proportion, and I had selected his features as beautiful. Beautiful!—Great God! His yellow skin scarcely covered the work of muscles and arteries beneath; his hair was of a lustrous black, and flowing; his teeth of a pearly whiteness; but these luxuriances only formed a more horrid contrast with his watery eyes, that seemed almost of the same colour as the dun white sockets in which they were set, his shrivelled complexion, and straight black lips.

The different accidents of life are not so changeable as the feelings of human nature. I had worked hard for nearly two years, for the sole purpose of infusing life into an inanimate body. For this I had deprived myself of rest and health. I had desired it with an ardour that far exceeded moderation; but now that I had finished, the beauty of the dream vanished, and breathless horror and disgust filled my heart. Unable to endure the aspect of the being I had created, I rushed out of the room, and continued a long time traversing my bed-chamber, unable to compose my mind to sleep. At length lassitude succeeded to the tumult I had before endured; and I threw myself on the bed in my clothes, endeavouring to seek a few moments of forgetfulness. But it was in vain: I slept indeed, but I was disturbed by the wildest dreams. I thought I saw Elizabeth, in the bloom of health, walking in the streets of Ingolstadt. Delighted and surprised, I embraced her; but as I imprinted the first kiss on her lips, they became livid with the hue of death; her features appeared to change, and I thought that I held the corpse of my dead mother in my arms; a shroud enveloped her form, and I saw the grave-worms crawling in the folds of the flannel. I started from my sleep with horror; a cold dew covered my forehead, my teeth chattered, and every limb became convulsed; when, by the dim and yellow light of the moon, as it forced its way through the window-shutters, I beheld the wretch—the miserable monster whom I had created. He held up the curtain of the bed; and his eyes, if eyes they may be called, were fixed on me. His jaws opened, and he muttered some inarticulate sounds, while a grin wrinkled his cheeks. He might have spoken, but I did not hear; one hand was stretched out, seemingly to detain me, but I escaped, and rushed down stairs. I took refuge in the court-yard belonging to the house which I inhabited; where I remained during the rest of the night, walking up and down in the greatest agitation, listening attentively, catching and fearing each sound as if it were to announce the approach of the demoniacal corpse to which I had so miserably given life.

Oh! no mortal could support the horror of that countenance. A mummy again endued with animation could not be so hideous as that wretch. I had gazed on him while unfinished; he was ugly then; but when those muscles and joints were rendered capable of motion, it became a thing such as even Dante[2] could not have conceived.

I passed the night wretchedly. Sometimes my pulse beat so quickly and hardly, that I felt the palpitation of every artery; at others, I nearly sank to the ground through languor and extreme weakness. Mingled with this horror, I felt the bitterness of disappointment: dreams that had been my food and

---

2. Dante Alighieri (1265–1321), who described the ghastly tortures of the damned in *The Inferno*, the opening book of his *Divine Comedy*.

pleasant rest for so long a space, were now become a hell to me; and the change was so rapid, the overthrow so complete!

Morning, dismal and wet, at length dawned, and discovered to my sleepless and aching eyes the church of Ingolstadt, its white steeple and clock, which indicated the sixth hour. The porter opened the gates of the court, which had that night been my asylum, and I issued into the streets, pacing them with quick steps, as if I sought to avoid the wretch whom I feared every turning of the street would present to my view. I did not dare return to the apartment which I inhabited, but felt impelled to hurry on, although wetted by the rain, which poured from a black and comfortless sky.

I continued walking in this manner for some time, endeavouring, by bodily exercise, to ease the load that weighed upon my mind. I traversed the streets, without any clear conception of where I was, or what I was doing. My heart palpitated in the sickness of fear; and I hurried on with irregular steps, not daring to look about me:

> Like one who, on a lonely road,
> Doth walk in fear and dread,
> And, having once turn'd round, walks on,
> And turns no more his head;
> Because he knows a frightful fiend
> Doth close behind him tread.[3]

Continuing thus, I came at length opposite to the inn at which the various diligences[4] and carriages usually stopped. Here I paused, I knew not why; but I remained some minutes with my eyes fixed on a coach that was coming towards me from the other end of the street. As it drew nearer, I observed that it was the Swiss diligence: it stopped just where I was standing; and, on the door being opened, I perceived Henry Clerval, who, on seeing me, instantly sprung out. "My dear Frankenstein," exclaimed he, "how glad I am to see you! how fortunate that you should be here at the very moment of my alighting!"

Nothing could equal my delight on seeing Clerval; his presence brought back to my thoughts my father, Elizabeth, and all those scenes of home so dear to my recollection. I grasped his hand, and in a moment forgot my horror and misfortune; I felt suddenly, and for the first time during many months calm and serene joy. I welcomed my friend, therefore, in the most cordial manner, and we walked towards my college. Clerval continued talking for some time about our mutual friends and his own good fortune in being permitted to come to Ingolstadt. "You may easily believe," said he, "how great was the difficulty to persuade my father that it was not absolutely necessary for a merchant not to understand any thing except book-keeping; and, indeed, I believe I left him incredulous to the last, for his constant answer to my unwearied entreaties was the same as that of the Dutch schoolmaster in the Vicar of Wakefield: 'I have ten thousand florins a year without Greek, I eat heartily without Greek.'[5] But his affection for me at length overcame his dislike of learning, and he has permitted me to undertake a voyage of discovery to the land of knowledge."

"It gives me the greatest delight to see you; but tell me how you left my father, brothers, and Elizabeth."

---

3. Coleridge's The Ancient Mariner, lines 446–51.
4. Stagecoaches.
5. From Oliver Goldsmith's novel The Vicar of Wakefield (1766), chap. 20.

"Very well, and very happy, only a little uneasy that they hear from you so seldom. By the bye, I mean to lecture you a little upon their account myself.—But, my dear Frankenstein," continued he, stopping short, and gazing full in my face, "I did not before remark how very ill you appear; so thin and pale; you look as if you had been watching for several nights."

"You have guessed right; I have lately been so deeply engaged in one occupation, that I have not allowed myself sufficient rest, as you see: but I hope, I sincerely hope, that all these employments are now at an end, and that I am at length free."

I trembled excessively; I could not endure to think of, and far less to allude to the occurrences of the preceding night. I walked with a quick pace, and we soon arrived at my college. I then reflected, and the thought made me shiver, that the creature whom I had left in my apartment might still be there, alive, and walking about. I dreaded to behold this monster; but I feared still more that Henry should see him. Entreating him therefore to remain a few minutes at the bottom of the stairs, I darted up towards my own room. My hand was already on the lock of the door before I recollected myself. I then paused; and a cold shivering came over me. I threw the door forcibly open, as children are accustomed to do when they expect a spectre to stand in waiting for them on the other side; but nothing appeared. I stepped fearfully in: the apartment was empty; and my bedroom was also freed from its hideous guest. I could hardly believe that so great a good-fortune could have befallen me; but when I became assured that my enemy had indeed fled, I clapped my hands for joy, and ran down to Clerval.

We ascended into my room, and the servant presently brought breakfast; but I was unable to contain myself. It was not joy only that possessed me; I felt my flesh tingle with excess of sensitiveness, and my pulse beat rapidly. I was unable to remain for a single instant in the same place; I jumped over the chairs, clapped my hands, and laughed aloud. Clerval at first attributed my unusual spirits to joy on his arrival; but when he observed me more attentively, he saw a wildness in my eyes for which he could not account; and my loud, unrestrained, heartless laughter, frightened and astonished him.

"My dear Victor," cried he, "what, for God's sake, is the matter? Do not laugh in that manner. How ill you are! What is the cause of all this?"

"Do not ask me," cried I, putting my hands before my eyes, for I thought I saw the dreaded spectre glide into the room; "*he* can tell.—Oh, save me! save me!" I imagined that the monster seized me; I struggled furiously, and fell down in a fit.

Poor Clerval! what must have been his feelings? A meeting, which he anticipated with such joy, so strangely turned to bitterness. But I was not the witness of his grief; for I was lifeless, and did not recover my senses for a long, long time.

This was the commencement of a nervous fever, which confined me for several months. During all that time Henry was my only nurse. I afterwards learned that, knowing my father's advanced age, and unfitness for so long a journey, and how wretched my sickness would make Elizabeth, he spared them this grief by concealing the extent of my disorder. He knew that I could not have a more kind and attentive nurse than himself; and, firm in the hope he felt of my recovery, he did not doubt that, instead of doing harm, he performed the kindest action that he could towards them.

But I was in reality very ill; and surely nothing but the unbounded and unremitting attentions of my friend could have restored me to life. The form of the monster on whom I had bestowed existence was for ever before my eyes, and I raved incessantly concerning him. Doubtless my words surprised Henry: he at first believed them to be the wanderings of my disturbed imagination; but the pertinacity with which I continually recurred to the same subject persuaded him that my disorder indeed owed its origin to some uncommon and terrible event.

By very slow degrees, and with frequent relapses, that alarmed and grieved my friend, I recovered. I remember the first time I became capable of observing outward objects with any kind of pleasure, I perceived that the fallen leaves had disappeared, and that the young buds were shooting forth from the trees that shaded my window. It was a divine spring; and the season contributed greatly to my convalescence. I felt also sentiments of joy and affection revive in my bosom; my gloom disappeared, and in a short time I became as cheerful as before I was attacked by the fatal passion.

"Dearest Clerval," exclaimed I, "how kind, how very good you are to me. This whole winter, instead of being spent in study, as you promised yourself, has been consumed in my sick room. How shall I ever repay you? I feel the greatest remorse for the disappointment of which I have been the occasion; but you will forgive me."

"You will repay me entirely, if you do not discompose yourself, but get well as fast as you can; and since you appear in such good spirits, I may speak to you on one subject, may I not?"

I trembled. One subject! what could it be? Could he allude to an object on whom I dared not even think?

"Compose yourself," said Clerval, who observed my change of colour, "I will not mention it, if it agitates you; but your father and cousin would be very happy if they received a letter from you in your own hand-writing. They hardly know how ill you have been, and are uneasy at your long silence."

"Is that all? my dear Henry. How could you suppose that my first thought would not fly towards those dear, dear friends whom I love, and who are so deserving of my love?"

"If this is your present temper, my friend, you will perhaps be glad to see a letter that has been lying here some days for you: it is from your cousin, I believe."

Chapter 5.

Clerval then put the following letter into my hands.

"*TO* V. FRANKENSTEIN.

"MY DEAR COUSIN,

"I cannot describe to you the uneasiness we have all felt concerning your health. We cannot help imagining that your friend Clerval conceals the extent of your disorder: for it is now several months since we have seen your hand-writing; and all this time you have been obliged to dictate your letters to Henry. Surely, Victor, you must have been exceedingly ill; and this makes us all very wretched, as much so nearly as after the death of your dear mother. My uncle was almost persuaded that you were indeed dangerously ill, and could hardly be restrained from undertaking a journey to Ingolstadt. Clerval always writes that you are getting better; I eagerly hope that you will confirm this intelligence soon in your own hand-writing; for indeed, indeed, Victor, we are all very miserable on this account. Relieve us from this fear, and we shall be the happiest creatures in the world. Your father's health is now so vigorous, that he appears ten years younger since last winter. Ernest also is so much improved, that you would hardly know him: he is now nearly sixteen, and has lost that sickly appearance which he had some years ago; he is grown quite robust and active.

"My uncle and I conversed a long time last night about what profession Ernest should follow. His constant illness when young has deprived him of the habits of application; and now that he enjoys good health, he is continually in the open air, climbing the hills, or rowing on the lake. I therefore proposed that he should be a farmer; which you know, Cousin, is a favourite scheme of mine. A farmer's is a very healthy happy life; and the least hurtful, or rather the most beneficial profession of any. My uncle had an idea of his being educated as an advocate, that through his interest he might become a judge. But, besides that he is not at all fitted for such an occupation, it is certainly more creditable to cultivate the earth for the sustenance of man, than to be the confidant, and sometimes the accomplice, of his vices; which is the profession of a lawyer. I said, that the employments of a prosperous farmer, if they were not a more honourable, they were at least a happier species of occupation than that of a judge, whose misfortune it was always to meddle with the dark side of human nature. My uncle smiled, and said, that I ought to be an advocate myself, which put an end to the conversation on that subject.

"And now I must tell you a little story that will please, and perhaps amuse you. Do you not remember Justine Moritz? Probably you do not; I will relate her history, therefore, in a few words. Madame Moritz, her mother, was a widow with four children, of whom Justine was the third. This girl had always been the favourite of her father; but, through a strange perversity, her mother could not endure her, and, after the death of M. Moritz, treated her very ill. My aunt observed this; and, when Justine was twelve years of age, prevailed on her mother to allow her to live at her house. The republican institutions of our country have produced simpler and happier manners than those which prevail in the great monarchies that surround it. Hence there is less distinction between the several classes of its inhabitants; and the lower orders being neither so poor nor so despised, their manners are more refined and moral. A servant in Geneva does not mean the same thing as a servant in France and England. Justine, thus received in our family, learned the duties of a servant; a condition which, in our fortunate country, does not include the idea of ignorance, and a sacrifice of the dignity of a human being.

"After what I have said, I dare say you well remember the heroine of my little tale: for Justine was a great favourite of your's; and I recollect you once remarked, that if you were in an ill humour, one glance from Justine could dissipate it, for the same reason that Ariosto gives concerning the beauty of Angelica[6]—she looked so frank-hearted and happy. My aunt conceived a great attachment for her, by which she was induced to give her an education superior to that which she had at first intended. This benefit was fully repaid; Justine was the most grateful little creature in the world: I do not mean that she made any professions,[7] I never heard one pass her lips; but you could see by her eyes that she almost adored her protectress. Although her disposition was gay, and in many respects inconsiderate, yet she paid the greatest attention to every gesture of my aunt. She thought her the model of all excellence, and endeavoured to imitate her phraseology and manners, so that even now she often reminds me of her.

"When my dearest aunt died, every one was too much occupied in their own grief to notice poor Justine, who had attended her during her illness with the most anxious affection. Poor Justine was very ill; but other trials were reserved for her.

"One by one, her brothers and sister died; and her mother, with the exception of her neglected daughter, was left childless. The conscience of the woman was troubled; she began to think that the deaths of her favourites was a judgment from heaven to chastise her partiality. She was a Roman Catholic; and I believe her confessor confirmed the idea which she had conceived. Accordingly, a few months after your departure for Ingoldstadt, Justine was called home by her repentant mother. Poor girl! she wept when she quitted our house: she was much altered since the death of my aunt; grief had given softness and a winning mildness to her manners, which had before been remarkable for vivacity. Nor was her residence at her mother's house of a nature to restore her gaiety. The poor woman was very vacillating in her repentance. She sometimes begged Justine to forgive her unkindness, but much oftener accused her of having caused the deaths of her brothers and sister. Perpetual fretting at length threw Madame Moritz into a decline, which at first increased her irritability, but she is now at peace for ever. She died on the first approach of cold weather, at the beginning of this last winter. Justine has returned to us; and I assure you I love her tenderly. She is very clever and gentle, and extremely pretty; as I mentioned before, her mien and her expressions continually remind me of my dear aunt.

"I must say also a few words to you, my dear cousin, of little darling William. I wish you could see him; he is very tall of his age, with sweet laughing blue eyes, dark eye-lashes, and curling hair. When he smiles, two little dimples appear on each cheek, which are rosy with health. He has already had one or two little *wives*, but Louisa Biron is his favourite, a pretty little girl of five years of age.

"Now, dear Victor, I dare say you wish to be indulged in a little gossip concerning the good people of Geneva. The pretty Miss Mansfield has already received the congratulatory visits on her approaching marriage with a young Englishman John Melbourne, Esq. Her ugly sister,

6. The heroine of Ariosto's *Orlando Furioso* (1532). 7. Explicit statements.

Manon, married M. Duvillard, the rich banker, last autumn. Your favourite schoolfellow, Louis Manoir, has suffered several misfortunes since the departure of Clerval from Geneva. But he has already recovered his spirits, and is reported to be on the point of marrying a very lively pretty French-woman, Madame Tavernier. She is a widow, and much older than Manoir; but she is very much admired, and a favorite with every body.

"I have written myself into good spirits, dear cousin; yet I cannot conclude without again anxiously inquiring concerning your health. Dear Victor, if you are not very ill, write yourself, and make your father and all of us happy; or—I cannot bear to think of the other side of the question; my tears already flow. Adieu, my dearest cousin.

"ELIZABETH LAVENZA.
"Geneva, March 18th, 17—."

"Dear, dear Elizabeth!" I exclaimed when I had read her letter, "I will write instantly, and relieve them from the anxiety they must feel." I wrote, and this exertion greatly fatigued me; but my convalescence had commenced, and proceeded regularly. In another fortnight I was able to leave my chamber.

One of my first duties on my recovery was to introduce Clerval to the several professors of the university. In doing this, I underwent a kind of rough usage, ill befitting the wounds that my mind had sustained. Ever since the fatal night, the end of my labours, and the beginning of my misfortunes, I had conceived a violent antipathy even to the name of natural philosophy. When I was otherwise quite restored to health, the sight of a chemical instrument would renew all the agony of my nervous symptoms. Henry saw this and had removed all my apparatus from my view. He had also changed my apartment; for he perceived that I had acquired a dislike for the room which had previously been my laboratory. But these cares of Clerval were made of no avail when I visited the professors. M. Waldman inflicted torture when he praised, with kindness and warmth, the astonishing progress I had made in the sciences. He soon perceived that I disliked the subject; but, not guessing the real cause, he attributed my feelings to modesty, and changed the subject from my improvement to the science itself, with a desire, as I evidently saw, of drawing me out. What could I do? He meant to please, and he tormented me. I felt as if he had placed carefully, one by one, in my view those instruments which were to be afterwards used in putting me to a slow and cruel death. I writhed under his words, yet dared not exhibit the pain I felt. Clerval, whose eyes and feelings were always quick in discerning the sensations of others, declined the subject, alleging, in excuse, his total ignorance; and the conversation took a more general turn. I thanked my friend from my heart, but I did not speak. I saw plainly that he was surprised, but he never attempted to draw my secret from me; and although I loved him with a mixture of affection and reverence that knew no bounds, yet I could never persuade myself to confide to him that event which was so often present to my recollection, but which I feared the detail to another would only impress more deeply.

M. Krempe was not equally docile; and in my condition at that time, of almost insupportable sensitiveness, his harsh blunt encomiums gave me even more pain than the benevolent approbation of M. Waldman. "D—n the fellow!" cried he; "why, M. Clerval, I assure you he has outstript us all. Aye, stare if you please; but it is nevertheless true. A youngster who, but a few years ago, believed Cornelius Agrippa as firmly as the gospel, has now set himself at the head of the university; and if he is not soon pulled down, we shall all be out of countenance.—Aye, aye," continued he, observing my face expressive of suffering, "M. Frankenstein is modest; an excellent quality in a young man. Young men should be diffident of themselves, you know, M. Clerval; I was myself when young: but that wears out in a very short time."

M. Krempe had now commenced an eulogy on himself, which happily turned the conversation from a subject that was so annoying to me.

Clerval was no natural philosopher. His imagination was too vivid for the minutiæ of science. Languages were his principal study; and he sought, by acquiring their elements, to open a field for self-instruction on his return to Geneva. Persian, Arabic, and Hebrew, gained his attention, after he had made himself perfectly master of Greek and Latin. For my own part, idleness had ever been irksome to me; and now that I wished to fly from reflection, and hated my former studies, I felt great relief in being the fellow-pupil with my friend, and found not only instruction but consolation in the works of the orientalists. Their melancholy is soothing, and their joy elevating to a degree I never experienced in studying the authors of any other country. When you read their writings, life appears to consist in a warm sun and garden of roses,—in the smiles and frowns of a fair enemy, and the fire that consumes your own heart. How different from the manly and heroical poetry of Greece and Rome.

Summer passed away in these occupations, and my return to Geneva was fixed for the latter end of autumn; but being delayed by several accidents, winter and snow arrived, the roads were deemed impassable, and my journey was retarded until the ensuing spring. I felt this delay very bitterly; for I longed to see my native town, and my beloved friends. My return had only been delayed so long from an unwillingness to leave Clerval in a strange place, before he had become acquainted with any of its inhabitants. The winter, however, was spent cheerfully; and although the spring was uncommonly late, when it came, its beauty compensated for its dilatoriness.

The month of May had already commenced, and I expected the letter daily which was to fix the date of my departure, when Henry proposed a pedestrian tour in the environs of Ingoldstadt that I might bid a personal farewell to the country I had so long inhabited. I acceded with pleasure to this proposition: I was fond of exercise, and Clerval had always been my favourite companion in the rambles of this nature that I had taken among the scenes of my native country.

We passed a fortnight in these perambulations: my health and spirits had long been restored, and they gained additional strength from the salubrious air I breathed, the natural incidents of our progress, and the conversation of my friend. Study had before secluded me from the intercourse of my fellow-creatures, and rendered me unsocial; but Clerval called forth the better feelings of my heart; he again taught me to love the aspect of nature, and the cheerful faces of children. Excellent friend! how sincerely did you love me, and endeavour to elevate my mind, until it was on a level with your own. A selfish pursuit had cramped and narrowed me, until your gentleness and affection warmed and opened my senses; I became the same happy creature who, a few years ago, loving and beloved by all, had no sorrow or care. When happy, inanimate nature had the power of bestowing on me the most delightful sensations. A serene sky and verdant fields filled me with ecstacy. The present season was indeed divine; the flowers of spring bloomed in the hedges, while those of summer were already in bud: I was undisturbed by thoughts which during the preceding year had pressed upon me, notwithstanding my endeavours to throw them off, with an invincible burden.

Henry rejoiced in my gaiety, and sincerely sympathized in my feelings: he exerted himself to amuse me, while he expressed the sensations that filled his soul. The resources of his mind on this occasion were truly astonishing: his conversation was full of imagination; and very often, in imitation of the Persian and Arabic writers, he invented tales of wonderful fancy and passion. At other times he repeated my favourite poems, or drew me out into arguments, which he supported with great ingenuity.

We returned to our college on a Sunday afternoon: the peasants were dancing, and every one we met appeared gay and happy. My own spirits were high, and I bounded along with feelings of unbridled joy and hilarity.

Chapter 6.

On my return, I found the following letter from my father:—

"*TO* V. FRANKENSTEIN.

"MY DEAR VICTOR,

"You have probably waited impatiently for a letter to fix the date of your return to us; and I was at first tempted to write only a few lines, merely mentioning the day on which I should expect you. But that would be a cruel kindness, and I dare not do it. What would be your surprise, my son, when you expected a happy and gay welcome, to behold on the contrary, tears and wretchedness? And how, Victor, can I relate our misfortune? Absence cannot have rendered you callous to our joys and griefs; and how shall I inflict pain on an absent child? I wish to prepare you for the woeful news, but I know it is impossible; even now your eye skims over the page, to seek the words which are to convey to you the horrible tidings.

"William is dead!—that sweet child, whose smiles delighted and warmed my heart, who was so gentle, yet so gay! Victor, he is murdered!

"I will not attempt to console you; but will simply relate the circumstances of the transaction.

"Last Thursday (May 7th) I, my niece, and your two brothers, went to walk in Plainpalais. The evening was warm and serene, and we prolonged our walk farther than usual. It was already dusk before we thought of returning; and then we discovered that William and Ernest, who had gone on before, were not to be found. We accordingly rested on a seat until they should return. Presently Ernest came, and inquired if we had seen his brother: he said, that they had been playing together, that William had run away to hide himself, and that he vainly sought for him, and afterwards waited for him a long time, but that he did not return.

"This account rather alarmed us, and we continued to search for him until night fell, when Elizabeth conjectured that he might have returned to the house. He was not there. We returned again, with torches; for I could not rest, when I thought that my sweet boy had lost himself, and was exposed to all the damps and dews of night: Elizabeth also suffered extreme anguish. About five in the morning I discovered my lovely boy, whom the night before I had seen blooming and active in health, stretched on the grass livid and motionless: the print of the murderer's finger was on his neck.

"He was conveyed home, and the anguish that was visible in my countenance betrayed the secret to Elizabeth. She was very earnest to see the corpse. At first I attempted to prevent her; but she persisted, and entering the room where it lay, hastily examined the neck of the victim, and clasping her hands exclaimed, 'O God! I have murdered my darling infant!'

"She fainted, and was restored with extreme difficulty. When she again lived, it was only to weep and sigh. She told me, that that same evening William had teazed her to let him wear a very valuable miniature that she possessed of your mother. This picture is gone, and was doubtless the temptation which urged the murderer to the deed. We have no trace of him at present, although our exertions to discover him are unremitted; but they will not restore my beloved William.

"Come, dearest Victor; you alone can console Elizabeth. She weeps continually, and accuses herself unjustly as the cause of his death; her words pierce my heart. We are all unhappy; but will not that be an additional motive for you, my son, to return and be our comforter? Your dear mother! Alas, Victor! I now say, Thank God she did not live to witness the cruel, miserable death of her youngest darling!

"Come, Victor; not brooding thoughts of vengeance against the assassin, but with feelings of peace and gentleness, that will heal, instead of festering the wounds of our minds. Enter the house of mourning, my friend, but with kindness and affection for those who love you, and not with hatred for your enemies.

"Your affectionate and afflicted father,

"ALPHONSE FRANKENSTEIN.
"Geneva, May 12th, 17—."

Clerval, who had watched my countenance as I read this letter, was surprised to observe the despair that succeeded to the joy I at first expressed on receiving news from my friends. I threw the letter on the table, and covered my face with my hands.

"My dear Frankenstein," exclaimed Henry, when he perceived me weep with bitterness, "are you always to be unhappy? My dear friend, what has happened?"

I motioned to him to take up the letter, while I walked up and down the room in the extremest agitation. Tears also gushed from the eyes of Clerval, as he read the account of my misfortune.

"I can offer you no consolation, my friend," said he; "your disaster is irreparable. What do you intend to do?"

"To go instantly to Geneva: come with me, Henry, to order the horses."

During our walk, Clerval endeavoured to raise my spirits. He did not do this by common topics of consolation, but by exhibiting the truest sympathy. "Poor William!" said he, "that dear child; he now sleeps with his angel mother. His friends mourn and weep, but he is at rest: he does not now feel the murderer's grasp; a sod covers his gentle form, and he knows no pain. He can no longer be a fit subject for pity; the survivors are the greatest sufferers, and for them time is the only consolation. Those maxims of the Stoics, that death was no evil, and that the mind of man ought to be superior to despair on the eternal absence of a beloved object, ought not to be urged. Even Cato[8] wept over the dead body of his brother."

Clerval spoke thus as we hurried through the streets; the words impressed themselves on my mind, and I remembered them afterwards in solitude. But now, as soon as the horses arrived, I hurried into a cabriole,[9] and bade farewell to my friend.

My journey was very melancholy. At first I wished to hurry on, for I longed to console and sympathize with my loved and sorrowing friends; but when I drew near my native town, I slackened my progress. I could hardly sustain the multitude of feelings that crowded into my mind. I passed through scenes familiar to my youth, but which I had not seen for nearly six years. How altered every thing might be during that time? One sudden and desolating change had taken place; but a thousand little circumstances might have by degrees worked other alterations, which, although they were done more tranquilly, might not be the less decisive. Fear overcame me; I dared not advance dreading a thousand nameless evils that made me tremble, although I was unable to define them.

I remained two days at Lausanne, in this painful state of mind. I contemplated the lake: the waters were placid; all around was calm, and the snowy mountains, "the palaces of nature,"[1] were not changed. By degrees the calm and heavenly scene restored me, and I continued my journey towards Geneva.

The road ran by the side of the lake, which became narrower as I approached my native town. I discovered more distinctly the black sides of Jura, and the bright summit of Mont Blanc I wept like a child: "Dear mountains! my own beautiful lake! how do you welcome your wanderer? Your summits are clear; the sky and lake are blue and placid. Is this to prognosticate peace, or to mock at my unhappiness?"

I fear, my friend, that I shall render myself tedious by dwelling on these preliminary circumstances; but they were days of comparative happiness, and I think of them with pleasure. My country, my beloved country! who but a native can tell the delight I took in again beholding thy streams, thy mountains, and, more than all, thy lovely lake.

Yet, as I drew nearer home, grief and fear again overcame me. Night also closed around; and when I could hardly see the dark mountains, I felt still more gloomily. The picture appeared a vast and dim scene of evil, and I foresaw obscurely that I was destined to become the most wretched of

---

8. Although the Stoics advocated the restraint of the emotions by reason, the Stoic philosopher Cato the Younger (1st century B.C.E.) could not restrain his passionate grief at the death of his brother. The story is told in Plutarch's *Lives* (early 2nd century C.E.).
9. A two-wheeled horse-drawn carriage.
1. Byron describes "the Alps / The palaces of Nature" in *Childe Harold's Pilgrimage* (1816), 3.62.

human beings. Alas! I prophesied truly, and failed only in one single circumstance, that in all the misery I imagined and dreaded, I did not conceive the hundredth part of the anguish I was destined to endure.

It was completely dark when I arrived in the environs of Geneva; the gates of the town were already shut; and I was obliged to pass the night at Secheron, a village half a league to the east of the city. The sky was serene; and, as I was unable to rest, I resolved to visit the spot where my poor William had been murdered. As I could not pass through the town, I was obliged to cross the lake in a boat to arrive at Plainpalais. During this short voyage I saw the lightnings playing on the summit of Mont Blanc in the most beautiful figures. The storm appeared to approach rapidly; and, on landing, I ascended a low hill, that I might observe its progress. It advanced; the heavens were clouded, and I soon felt the rain coming slowly in large drops, but its violence quickly increased.

I quitted my seat, and walked on, although the darkness and storm increased every minute, and the thunder burst with a terrific crash over my head. It was echoed from Salêve, the Juras, and the Alps of Savoy; vivid flashes of lightning dazzled my eyes, illuminating the lake, making it appear like a vast sheet of fire; then for an instant every thing seemed of a pitchy darkness, until the eye recovered itself from the preceding flash. The storm, as is often the case in Switzerland, appeared at once in various parts of the heavens. The most violent storm hung exactly north of the town, over that part of the lake which lies between the promontory of Belrive and the village of Copêt. Another storm enlightened Jura with faint flashes; and another darkened and sometimes disclosed the Môle, a peaked mountain to the east of the lake.

While I watched the storm, so beautiful yet terrific,[2] I wandered on with a hasty step. This noble war in the sky elevated my spirits; I clasped my hands and exclaimed aloud, "William, dear angel! this is thy funeral, this thy dirge!" As I said these words, I perceived in the gloom a figure which stole from behind a clump of trees near me; I stood fixed, gazing intently: I could not be mistaken. A flash of lightning illuminated the object, and discovered its shape plainly to me; its gigantic stature, and the deformity of its aspect, more hideous than belongs to humanity, instantly informed me that it was the wretch, the filthy dæmon to whom I had given life. What did he there? Could he be (I shuddered at the conception) the murderer of my brother? No sooner did that idea cross my imagination, than I became convinced of its truth; my teeth chattered, and I was forced to lean against a tree for support. The figure passed me quickly, and I lost it in the gloom. Nothing in human shape could have destroyed that fair child. *He* was the murderer! I could not doubt it. The mere presence of the idea was an irresistible proof of the fact. I thought of pursuing the devil; but it would have been in vain, for another flash discovered him to me hanging among the rocks of the nearly perpendicular ascent of Mont Salêve, a hill that bounds Plainpalais on the south. He soon reached the summit, and disappeared.

I remained motionless. The thunder ceased; but the rain still continued, and the scene was enveloped in an impenetrable darkness. I revolved in my mind the events which I had until now sought to forget: the whole train of

2. Terrifying.

my progress towards the creation; the appearance of the work of my own hands alive at my bed side, its departure. Two years had now nearly elapsed since the night on which he first received life; and was this his first crime? Alas! I had turned loose into the world a depraved wretch, whose delight was in carnage and misery; had he not murdered my brother?

No one can conceive the anguish I suffered during the remainder of the night, which I spent, cold and wet, in the open air. But I did not feel the inconvenience of the weather; my imagination was busy in scenes of evil and despair. I considered the being whom I had cast among mankind, and endowed with the will and power to effect purposes of horror, such as the deed which he had now done, nearly in the light of my own vampire,[3] my own spirit let loose from the grave, and forced to destroy all that was dear to me.

Day dawned; and I directed my steps towards the town. The gates were open; and I hastened to my father's house. My first thought was to discover what I knew of the murderer, and cause instant pursuit to be made. But I paused when I reflected on the story that I had to tell. A being whom I myself had formed, and endued with life, had met me at midnight among the precipices of an inaccessible mountain. I remembered also the nervous fever with which I had been seized just at the time that I dated my creation, and which would give an air of delirium to a tale otherwise so utterly improbable. I well knew that if any other had communicated such a relation to me, I should have looked upon it as the ravings of insanity. Besides, the strange nature of the animal would elude all pursuit, even if I were so far credited as to persuade my relatives to commence it. Besides, of what use would be pursuit? Who could arrest a creature capable of scaling the overhanging sides of Mont Salêve? These reflections determined me, and I resolved to remain silent.

It was about five in the morning when I entered my father's house. I told the servants not to disturb the family, and went into the library to attend their usual hour of rising.

Six years had elapsed, passed as a dream but for one indelible trace, and I stood in the same place where I had last embraced my father before my departure for Ingolstadt. Beloved and respectable parent! He still remained to me. I gazed on the picture of my mother, which stood over the mantlepiece. It was an historical subject, painted at my father's desire, and represented Caroline Beaufort in an agony of despair, kneeling by the coffin of her dead father. Her garb was rustic, and her cheek pale; but there was an air of dignity and beauty, that hardly permitted the sentiment of pity. Below this picture was a miniature of William; and my tears flowed when I looked upon it. While I was thus engaged, Ernest entered; he had heard me arrive, and hastened to welcome me. He expressed a sorrowful delight to see me: "Welcome, my dearest Victor," said he. "Ah! I wish you had come three months ago, and then you would have found us all joyous and delighted. But we are now unhappy; and, I am afraid, tears instead of smiles will be your welcome. Our father looks so sorrowful: this dreadful event seems to have revived in his mind his grief on the death of Mamma. Poor Elizabeth also is quite inconsolable." Ernest began to weep as he said these words.

3. In folklore, a corpse, reanimated, which sucks the blood of sleeping persons. Victor feels as though his Creature were his own dead self, come back to life.

"Do not," said I, "welcome me thus; try to be more calm, that I may not be absolutely miserable the moment I enter my father's house after so long an absence. But, tell me, how does my father support his misfortunes? and how is my poor Elizabeth?"

"She indeed requires consolation; she accused herself of having caused the death of my brother, and that made her very wretched. But since the murderer has been discovered—"

"The murderer discovered! Good God! how can that be? who could attempt to pursue him? It is impossible; one might as well try to overtake the winds, or confine a mountain-stream with a straw."

"I do not know what you mean; but we were all very unhappy when she was discovered. No one would believe it at first; and even now Elizabeth will not be convinced, notwithstanding all the evidence. Indeed, who would credit that Justine Moritz, who was so amiable, and fond of all the family, could all at once become so extremely wicked?"

"Justine Moritz! Poor, poor girl, is she the accused? But it is wrongfully; every one knows that; no one believes it, surely, Ernest?"

"No one did at first; but several circumstances came out, that have almost forced conviction upon us: and her own behaviour has been so confused, as to add to the evidence of facts a weight that, I fear, leaves no hope for doubt. But she will be tried to-day, and you will then hear all."

He related that, the morning on which the murder of poor William had been discovered, Justine had been taken ill, and confined to her bed; and, after several days, one of the servants, happening to examine the apparel she had worn on the night of the murder, had discovered in her pocket the picture of my mother, which had been judged to be the temptation of the murderer. The servant instantly shewed it to one of the others, who, without saying a word to any of the family, went to a magistrate; and, upon their deposition, Justine was apprehended. On being charged with the fact, the poor girl confirmed the suspicion in a great measure, by her extreme confusion of manner.

This was a strange tale, but it did not shake my faith; and I replied earnestly, "You are all mistaken; I know the murderer. Justine, poor, good Justine, is innocent."

At that instant my father entered. I saw unhappiness deeply impressed on his countenance, but he endeavoured to welcome me cheerfully; and, after we had exchanged our mournful greeting, would have introduced some other topic than that of our disaster, had not Ernest exclaimed, "Good God, Papa! Victor says that he knows who was the murderer of poor William."

"We do also, unfortunately," replied my father; "for indeed I had rather have been for ever ignorant than have discovered so much depravity and ingratitude in one I valued so highly."

"My dear father, you are mistaken; Justine is innocent."

"If she is, God forbid that she should suffer as guilty. She is to be tried to-day, and I hope, I sincerely hope, that she will be acquitted."

This speech calmed me. I was firmly convinced in my own mind that Justine, and indeed every human being, was guiltless of this murder. I had no fear, therefore, that any circumstantial evidence could be brought forward strong enough to convict her; and, in this assurance, I calmed myself, expecting the trial with eagerness, but without prognosticating an evil result.

We were soon joined by Elizabeth. Time had made great alterations in her form since I had last beheld her. Six years before she had been a pretty, good-humoured girl, whom every one loved and caressed. She was now a woman in stature and expression of countenance, which was uncommonly lovely. An open and capacious forehead gave indications of a good understanding, joined to great frankness of disposition. Her eyes were hazel, and expressive of mildness, now through recent affliction allied to sadness. Her hair was of a rich dark auburn, her complexion fair, and her figure slight and graceful. She welcomed me with the greatest affection. "Your arrival, my dear cousin," said she, "fills me with hope. You perhaps will find some means to justify my poor guiltless Justine. Alas! who is safe, if she be convicted of crime? I rely on her innocence as certainly as I do upon my own. Our misfortune is doubly hard to us; we have not only lost that lovely darling boy, but this poor girl, whom I sincerely love, is to be torn away by even a worse fate. If she is condemned, I never shall know joy more. But she will not, I am sure she will not; and then I shall be happy again, even after the sad death of my little William."

"She is innocent, my Elizabeth," said I, "and that shall be proved; fear nothing, but let your spirits be cheered by the assurance of her acquittal."

"How kind you are! every one else believes in her guilt, and that made me wretched; for I knew that it was impossible: and to see every one else prejudiced in so deadly a manner, rendered me hopeless and despairing." She wept.

"Sweet niece," said my father, "dry your tears. If she is, as you believe, innocent, rely on the justice of our judges, and the activity with which I shall prevent the slightest shadow of partiality."

Chapter 7.

We passed a few sad hours, until eleven o'clock, when the trial was to commence. My father and the rest of the family being obliged to attend as witnesses, I accompanied them to the court. During the whole of this wretched mockery of justice, I suffered living torture. It was to be decided, whether the result of my curiosity and lawless devices would cause the death of two of my fellow-beings: one a smiling babe, full of innocence and joy; the other far more dreadfully murdered, with every aggravation of infamy that could make the murder memorable in horror. Justine also was a girl of merit, and possessed qualities which promised to render her life happy: now all was to be obliterated in an ignominious grave; and I the cause! A thousand times rather would I have confessed myself guilty of the crime ascribed to Justine; but I was absent when it was committed, and such a declaration would have been considered as the ravings of a madman, and would not have exculpated her who suffered through me.

The appearance of Justine was calm. She was dressed in mourning; and her countenance, always engaging, was rendered, by the solemnity of her feelings, exquisitely beautiful. Yet she appeared confident in innocence, and did not tremble, although gazed on and execrated by thousands; for all the kindness which her beauty might otherwise have excited, was obliterated in the minds of the spectators by the imagination of the enormity she was supposed to have committed. She was tranquil, yet her tranquillity was evidently constrained; and as her confusion had before been adduced as a proof of her guilt, she worked up her mind to an appearance of courage. When she entered the court, she threw her eyes round it, and quickly discovered where we were seated. A tear seemed to dim her eye when she saw us; but she quickly recovered herself, and a look of sorrowful affection seemed to attest her utter guiltlessness.

The trial began; and after the advocate against her had stated the charge, several witnesses were called. Several strange facts combined against her, which might have staggered any one who had not such proof of her innocence as I had. She had been out the whole of the night on which the murder had been committed, and towards morning had been perceived by a market-woman not far from the spot where the body of the murdered child had been afterwards found. The woman asked her what she did there; but she looked very strangely, and only returned a confused and unintelligible answer. She returned to the house about eight o'clock; and when one inquired where she had passed the night, she replied, that she had been looking for the child, and demanded earnestly, if any thing had been heard concerning him. When shewn the body, she fell into violent hysterics, and kept her bed for several days. The picture was then produced, which the servant had found in her pocket; and when Elizabeth, in a faltering voice, proved that it was the same which, an hour before the child had been missed, she had placed round his neck, a murmur of horror and indignation filled the court.

Justine was called on for her defence. As the trial had proceeded, her countenance had altered. Surprise, horror, and misery, were strongly expressed. Sometimes she struggled with her tears; but when she was desired to plead, she collected her powers, and spoke in an audible although variable voice:—

"God knows," she said, "how entirely I am innocent. But I do not pretend that my protestations should acquit me: I rest my innocence on a plain and simple explanation of the facts which have been adduced against me; and I hope the character I have always borne will incline my judges to a favourable interpretation, where any circumstance appears doubtful or suspicious."

She then related that, by the permission of Elizabeth, she had passed the evening of the night on which the murder had been committed, at the house of an aunt at Chêne, a village situated at about a league from Geneva. On her return, at about nine o'clock, she met a man, who asked her if she had seen any thing of the child who was lost. She was alarmed by this account, and passed several hours in looking for him, when the gates of Geneva were shut, and she was forced to remain several hours of the night in a barn belonging to a cottage, being unwilling to call up the inhabitants, to whom she was well known. Unable to rest or sleep, she quitted her asylum early, that she might again endeavour to find my brother. If she had gone near the spot where his body lay, it was without her knowledge. That she had been bewildered when questioned by the market-woman, was not surprising, since she had passed a sleepless night, and the fate of poor William was yet uncertain. Concerning the picture she could give no account.

"I know," continued the unhappy victim, "how heavily and fatally this one circumstance weighs against me, but I have no power of explaining it; and when I have expressed my utter ignorance, I am only left to conjecture concerning the probabilities by which it might have been placed in my pocket.

But here also I am checked. I believe that I have no enemy on earth, and none surely would have been so wicked as to destroy me wantonly. Did the murderer place it there? I know of no opportunity afforded him for so doing; or if I had, why should he have stolen the jewel, to part with it again so soon?

"I commit my cause to the justice of my judges, yet I see no room for hope. I beg permission to have a few witnesses examined concerning my character; and if their testimony shall not overweigh my supposed guilt, I must be condemned, although I would pledge my salvation on my innocence."

Several witnesses were called, who had known her for many years, and they spoke well of her; but fear, and hatred of the crime of which they supposed her guilty, rendered them timorous, and unwilling to come forward. Elizabeth saw even this last resource, her excellent dispositions and irreproachable conduct, about to fail the accused, when, although violently agitated, she desired permission to address the court.

"I am," said she, "the cousin of the unhappy child who was murdered, or rather his sister, for I was educated by and have lived with his parents ever since and even long before his birth. It may therefore be judged indecent in me to come forward on this occasion; but when I see a fellow-creature about to perish through the cowardice of her pretended friends, I wish to be allowed to speak, that I may say what I know of her character. I am well acquainted with the accused. I have lived in the same house with her, at one time for five, and at another for nearly two years. During all that period she appeared to me the most amiable and benevolent of human creatures. She nursed Madame Frankenstein, my aunt, in her last illness with the greatest affection and care; and afterwards attended her own mother during a tedious[4] illness, in a manner that excited the admiration of all who knew her. After which she again lived in my uncle's house, where she was beloved by all the family. She was warmly attached to the child who is now dead, and acted towards him like a most affectionate mother. For my own part, I do not hesitate to say, that, notwithstanding all the evidence produced against her, I believe and rely on her perfect innocence. She had no temptation for such an action: as to the bauble on which the chief proof rests, if she had earnestly desired it, I should have willingly given it to her; so much do I esteem and value her."

Excellent Elizabeth! A murmur of approbation was heard; but it was excited by her generous interference, and not in favour of poor Justine, on whom the public indignation was turned with renewed violence, charging her with the blackest ingratitude. She herself wept as Elizabeth spoke, but she did not answer. My own agitation and anguish was extreme during the whole trial. I believed in her innocence; I knew it. Could the dæmon, who had (I did not for a minute doubt) murdered my brother, also in his hellish sport have betrayed the innocent to death and ignominy. I could not sustain the horror of my situation; and when I perceived that the popular voice, and the countenances of the judges, had already condemned my unhappy victim, I rushed out of the court in agony. The tortures of the accused did not equal mine; she was sustained by innocence, but the fangs of remorse tore my bosom, and would not forego their hold.

I passed a night of unmingled wretchedness. In the morning I went to the

---

4. Long-lasting.

court; my lips and throat were parched. I dared not ask the fatal question; but I was known, and the officer guessed the cause of my visit. The ballots[5] had been thrown; they were all black, and Justine was condemned.

I cannot pretend to describe what I then felt. I had before experienced sensations of horror; and I have endeavoured to bestow upon them adequate expressions, but words cannot convey an idea of the heart-sickening despair that I then endured. The person to whom I addressed myself added, that Justine had already confessed her guilt. "That evidence," he observed, "was hardly required in so glaring a case, but I am glad of it; and, indeed, none of our judges like to condemn a criminal upon circumstantial evidence, be it ever so decisive."

When I returned home, Elizabeth eagerly demanded the result.

"My cousin," replied I, "it is decided as you may have expected; all judges had rather that ten innocent should suffer, than that one guilty should escape. But she has confessed."

This was a dire blow to poor Elizabeth, who had relied with firmness upon Justine's innocence. "Alas!" said she, "how shall I ever again believe in human benevolence? Justine, whom I loved and esteemed as my sister, how could she put on those smiles of innocence only to betray; her mild eyes seemed incapable of any severity or ill-humour, and yet she has committed a murder."

Soon after we heard that the poor victim had expressed a wish to see my cousin. My father wished her not to go; but said, that he left it to her own judgment and feelings to decide. "Yes," said Elizabeth, "I will go, although she is guilty; and you, Victor, shall accompany me: I cannot go alone." The idea of this visit was torture to me, yet I could not refuse.

We entered the gloomy prison-chamber, and beheld Justine sitting on some straw at the further end; her hands were manacled, and her head rested on her knees. She rose on seeing us enter; and when we were left alone with her, she threw herself at the feet of Elizabeth, weeping bitterly. My cousin wept also.

"Oh, Justine!" said she, "why did you rob me of my last consolation. I relied on your innocence; and although I was then very wretched, I was not so miserable as I am now."

"And do you also believe that I am so very, very wicked? Do you also join with my enemies to crush me?" Her voice was suffocated with sobs.

"Rise, my poor girl," said Elizabeth, "why do you kneel, if you are innocent? I am not one of your enemies; I believed you guiltless, notwithstanding every evidence, until I heard that you had yourself declared your guilt. That report, you say, is false; and be assured, dear Justine, that nothing can shake my confidence in you for a moment, but your own confession."

"I did confess; but I confessed a lie. I confessed, that I might obtain absolution; but now that falsehood lies heavier at my heart than all my other sins. The God of heaven forgive me! Ever since I was condemned, my confessor has besieged me; he threatened and menaced, until I almost began to think that I was the monster that he said I was. He threatened excommunication and hell fire in my last moments, if I continued obdurate. Dear lady, I had none to support me; all looked on me as a wretch doomed to ignominy and

5. Small balls used in secret votes.

perdition. What could I do? In an evil hour I subscribed to a lie; and now only am I truly miserable."

She paused, weeping, and then continued—"I thought with horror, my sweet lady, that you should believe your Justine, whom your blessed aunt had so highly honoured, and whom you loved, was a creature capable of a crime which none but the devil himself could have perpetrated. Dear William! dearest blessed child! I soon shall see you again in heaven, where we shall all be happy; and that consoles me, going as I am to suffer ignominy and death."

"Oh, Justine! forgive me for having for one moment distrusted you. Why did you confess? But do not mourn, my dear girl; I will every where proclaim your innocence, and force belief. Yet you must die; you, my playfellow, my companion, my more than sister. I never can survive so horrible a misfortune."

"Dear, sweet Elizabeth, do not weep. You ought to raise me with thoughts of a better life, and elevate me from the petty cares of this world of injustice and strife. Do not you, excellent friend, drive me to despair."

"I will try to comfort you; but this, I fear, is an evil too deep and poignant to admit of consolation, for there is no hope. Yet heaven bless thee, my dearest Justine, with resignation, and a confidence elevated beyond this world. Oh! how I hate its shews and mockeries! when one creature is murdered, another is immediately deprived of life in a slow torturing manner; then the executioners, their hands yet reeking with the blood of innocence, believe that they have done a great deed. They call this *retribution*. Hateful name! When that word is pronounced, I know greater and more horrid punishments are going to be inflicted than the gloomiest tyrant has ever invented to satiate his utmost revenge. Yet this is not consolation for you, my Justine, unless indeed that you may glory in escaping from so miserable a den. Alas! I would I were in peace with my aunt and my lovely William, escaped from a world which is hateful to me, and the visages of men which I abhor."

Justine smiled languidly. "This, dear lady, is despair, and not resignation. I must not learn the lesson that you would teach me. Talk of something else, something that will bring peace, and not increase of misery."

During this conversation I had retired to a corner of the prison-room, where I could conceal the horrid anguish that possessed me. Despair! Who dared talk of that? The poor victim, who on the morrow was to pass the dreary boundary between life and death, felt not as I did, such deep and bitter agony. I gnashed my teeth, and ground them together, uttering a groan that came from my inmost soul. Justine started. When she saw who it was, she approached me, and said, "Dear Sir, you are very kind to visit me; you, I hope, do not believe that I am guilty."

I could not answer. "No, Justine," said Elizabeth; "he is more convinced of your innocence than I was; for even when he heard that you had confessed, he did not credit it."

"I truly thank him. In these last moments I feel the sincerest gratitude towards those who think of me with kindness. How sweet is the affection of others to such a wretch as I am! It removes more than half my misfortune; and I feel as if I could die in peace, now that my innocence is acknowledged by you, dear lady, and your cousin."

Thus the poor sufferer tried to comfort others and herself. She indeed gained the resignation she desired. But I, the true murderer, felt the never-dying worm alive in my bosom,[6] which allowed of no hope or consolation. Elizabeth also wept, and was unhappy; but her's also was the misery of innocence, which, like a cloud that passes over the fair moon, for a while hides, but cannot tarnish its brightness. Anguish and despair had penetrated into the core of my heart; I bore a hell within me, which nothing could extinguish. We staid several hours with Justine; and it was with great difficulty that Elizabeth could tear herself away. "I wish," cried she, "that I were to die with you; I cannot live in this world of misery."

Justine assumed an air of cheerfulness, while she with difficulty repressed her bitter tears. She embraced Elizabeth, and said, in a voice of half-suppressed emotion, "Farewell, sweet lady, dearest Elizabeth, my beloved and only friend; may heaven in its bounty bless and preserve you; may this be the last misfortune that you will ever suffer. Live, and be happy, and make others so."

As we returned, Elizabeth said, "You know not, my dear Victor, how much I am relieved, now that I trust in the innocence of this unfortunate girl. I never could again have known peace, if I had been deceived in my reliance on her. For the moment that I did believe her guilty, I felt an anguish that I could not have long sustained. Now my heart is lightened. The innocent suffers; but she whom I thought amiable and good has not betrayed the trust I reposed in her, and I am consoled."

Amiable cousin! such were your thoughts, mild and gentle as your own dear eyes and voice. But I—I was a wretch, and none ever conceived of the misery that I then endured.

VOLUME 2

Chapter 1.

Nothing is more painful to the human mind, than, after the feelings have been worked up by a quick succession of events, the dead calmness of inaction and certainty which follows, and deprives the soul both of hope and fear. Justine died; she rested; and I was alive. The blood flowed freely in my veins, but a weight of despair and remorse pressed on my heart, which nothing could remove. Sleep fled from my eyes; I wandered like an evil spirit, for I had committed deeds of mischief beyond description horrible, and more, much more, (I persuaded myself) was yet behind. Yet my heart overflowed with kindness, and the love of virtue. I had begun life with benevolent intentions, and thirsted for the moment when I should put them in practice, and make myself useful to my fellow-beings. Now all was blasted:[1] instead of that serenity of conscience, which allowed me to look back upon the past with self-satisfaction, and from thence to gather promise of new hopes, I was seized by remorse and the sense of guilt, which hurried me away to a hell of intense tortures, such as no language can describe.

This state of mind preyed upon my health, which had entirely recovered

---

6. Jesus describes the sufferings of people in hell: "where their worm dieth not, and the fire is not quenched" (Mark 9.44).
1. Blighted, ruined.

from the first shock it had sustained. I shunned the face of man; all sound of joy or complacency was torture to me; solitude was my only consolation—deep, dark, death-like solitude.

My father observed with pain the alteration perceptible in my disposition and habits, and endeavoured to reason with me on the folly of giving way to immoderate grief. "Do you think, Victor," said he, "that I do not suffer also? No one could love a child more than I loved your brother;" (tears came into his eyes as he spoke); "but is it not a duty to the survivors, that we should refrain from augmenting their unhappiness by an appearance of immoderate grief? It is also a duty owed to yourself; for excessive sorrow prevents improvement or enjoyment, or even the discharge of daily usefulness, without which no man is fit for society."

This advice, although good, was totally inapplicable to my case; I should have been the first to hide my grief, and console my friends, if remorse had not mingled its bitterness with my other sensations. Now I could only answer my father with a look of despair, and endeavour to hide myself from his view.

About this time we retired to our house at Belrive. This change was particularly agreeable to me. The shutting of the gates regularly at ten o'clock, and the impossibility of remaining on the lake after that hour, had rendered our residence within the walls of Geneva very irksome to me. I was now free. Often, after the rest of the family had retired for the night, I took the boat, and passed many hours upon the water. Sometimes, with my sails set, I was carried by the wind; and sometimes, after rowing into the middle of the lake, I left the boat to pursue its own course, and gave way to my own miserable reflections. I was often tempted, when all was at peace around me, and I the only unquiet thing that wandered restless in a scene so beautiful and heavenly, if I except some bat, or the frogs, whose harsh and interrupted croaking was heard only when I approached the shore—often, I say, I was tempted to plunge into the silent lake, that the waters might close over me and my calamities for ever. But I was restrained, when I thought of the heroic and suffering Elizabeth, whom I tenderly loved, and whose existence was bound up in mine. I thought also of my father, and surviving brother: should I by my base desertion leave them exposed and unprotected to the malice of the fiend whom I had let loose among them?

At these moments I wept bitterly, and wished that peace would revisit my mind only that I might afford them consolation and happiness. But that could not be. Remorse extinguished every hope. I had been the author of unalterable evils; and I lived in daily fear, lest the monster whom I had created should perpetrate some new wickedness. I had an obscure feeling that all was not over, and that he would still commit some signal[2] crime, which by its enormity should almost efface the recollection of the past. There was always scope for fear, so long as any thing I loved remained behind. My abhorrence of this fiend cannot be conceived. When I thought of him, I gnashed my teeth, my eyes became inflamed, and I ardently wished to extinguish that life which I had so thoughtlessly bestowed. When I reflected on his crimes and malice, my hatred and revenge burst all bounds of moderation. I would have made a pilgrimage to the highest peak of the Andes, could

2. Conspicuous.

I, when there, have precipitated him to their base. I wished to see him again, that I might wreak the utmost extent of anger on his head, and avenge the deaths of William and Justine.

Our house was the house of mourning. My father's health was deeply shaken by the horror of the recent events. Elizabeth was sad and desponding; she no longer took delight in her ordinary occupations; all pleasure seemed to her sacrilege toward the dead; eternal woe and tears she then thought was the just tribute she should pay to innocence so blasted and destroyed. She was no longer that happy creature, who in earlier youth wandered with me on the banks of the lake, and talked with ecstacy of our future prospects. She had become grave, and often conversed of the inconstancy of fortune, and the instability of human life.

"When I reflect, my dear cousin," said she, "on the miserable death of Justine Moritz, I no longer see the world and its works as they before appeared to me. Before, I looked upon the accounts of vice and injustice, that I read in books or heard from others, as tales of ancient days, or imaginary evils; at least they were remote, and more familiar to reason than to the imagination; but now misery has come home, and men appear to me as monsters thirsting for each other's blood. Yet I am certainly unjust. Every body believed that poor girl to be guilty; and if she could have committed the crime for which she suffered, assuredly she would have been the most depraved of human creatures. For the sake of a few jewels, to have murdered the son of her benefactor and friend, a child whom she had nursed from its birth, and appeared to love as if it had been her own! I could not consent to the death of any human being; but certainly I should have thought such a creature unfit to remain in the society of men. Yet she was innocent. I know, I feel she was innocent; you are of the same opinion, and that confirms me. Alas! Victor, when falsehood can look so like the truth, who can assure themselves of certain happiness? I feel as if I were walking on the edge of a precipice, towards which thousands are crowding, and endeavouring to plunge me into the abyss. William and Justine were assassinated, and the murderer escapes; he walks about the world free, and perhaps respected. But even if I were condemned to suffer on the scaffold for the same crimes, I would not change places with such a wretch."

I listened to this discourse with the extremest agony. I, not in deed, but in effect, was the true murderer. Elizabeth read my anguish in my countenance, and kindly taking my hand said, "My dearest cousin, you must calm yourself. These events have affected me, God knows how deeply; but I am not so wretched as you are. There is an expression of despair, and sometimes of revenge, in your countenance, that makes me tremble. Be calm, my dear Victor; I would sacrifice my life to your peace. We surely shall be happy: quiet in our native country, and not mingling in the world, what can disturb our tranquillity?"

She shed tears as she said this, distrusting the very solace that she gave; but at the same time she smiled, that she might chase away the fiend that lurked in my heart. My father, who saw in the unhappiness that was painted in my face only an exaggeration of that sorrow which I might naturally feel, thought that an amusement suited to my taste would be the best means of restoring to me my wonted serenity. It was from this cause that he had removed to the country; and, induced by the same motive, he now proposed that we should all make an excursion to the valley of Chamounix.[3] I had been there before, but Elizabeth and Ernest never had; and both had often expressed an earnest desire to see the scenery of this place, which had been described to them as so wonderful and sublime. Accordingly we departed from Geneva on this tour about the middle of the month of August, nearly two months after the death of Justine.

The weather was uncommonly fine; and if mine had been a sorrow to be chased away by any fleeting circumstance, this excursion would certainly have had the effect intended by my father. As it was, I was somewhat interested in the scene; it sometimes lulled, although it could not extinguish my grief. During the first day we travelled in a carriage. In the morning we had seen the mountains at a distance, towards which we gradually advanced. We perceived that the valley through which we wound, and which was formed by the river Arve, whose course we followed, closed in upon us by degrees; and when the sun had set, we beheld immense mountains and precipices overhanging us on every side, and heard the sound of the river raging among rocks, and the dashing of waterfalls around.

The next day we pursued our journey upon mules; and as we ascended still higher, the valley assumed a more magnificent and astonishing character. Ruined castles hanging on the precipices of piny mountains; the impetuous Arve, and cottages every here and there peeping forth from among the trees, formed a scene of singular beauty. But it was augmented and rendered sublime by the mighty Alps, whose white and shining pyramids and domes towered above all, as belonging to another earth, the habitations of another race of beings.

We passed the bridge of Pelissier, where the ravine, which the river forms, opened before us, and we began to ascend the mountain that overhangs it. Soon after we entered the valley of Chamounix. This valley is more wonderful and sublime, but not so beautiful and picturesque as that of Servox, through which we had just passed. The high and snowy mountains were its immediate boundaries; but we saw no more ruined castles and fertile fields. Immense glaciers approached the road; we heard the rumbling thunder of the falling avalanche, and marked the smoke of its passage. Mont Blanc, the supreme and magnificent Mont Blanc, raised itself from the surrounding *aiguilles*, and its tremendous *dome*[4] overlooked the valley.

During this journey, I sometimes joined Elizabeth, and exerted myself to point out to her the various beauties of the scene. I often suffered my mule to lag behind, and indulged in the misery of reflection. At other times I spurred on the animal before my companions, that I might forget them, the world, and, more than all, myself. When at a distance, I alighted, and threw myself on the grass, weighed down by horror and despair. At eight in the evening I arrived at Chamounix. My father and Elizabeth were very much fatigued; Ernest, who accompanied us, was delighted, and in high spirits: the only circumstance that detracted from his pleasure was the south wind, and the rain it seemed to promise for the next day.

We retired early to our apartments, but not to sleep; at least I did not. I remained many hours at the window, watching the pallid lightning that

---

3. At the foot of Mont Blanc, the highest mountain in the Alps. The Shelleys toured the valley and its glacier in 1816—the occasion of Percy's poem

Mont Blanc (p. 720).
4. The rounded, snow-covered summit of Mont Blanc. "*Aiguilles*": narrow, pointed peaks.

played above Mont Blanc, and listening to the rushing of the Arve, which ran below my window.

Chapter 2.

The next day, contrary to the prognostications of our guides, was fine, although clouded. We visited the source of the Arveiron, and rode about the valley until evening. These sublime and magnificent scenes afforded me the greatest consolation that I was capable of receiving. They elevated me from all littleness of feeling; and although they did not remove my grief, they subdued and tranquillized it. In some degree, also, they diverted my mind from the thoughts over which it had brooded for the last month. I returned in the evening, fatigued, but less unhappy, and conversed with my family with more cheerfulness than had been my custom for some time. My father was pleased, and Elizabeth overjoyed. "My dear cousin," said she, "you see what happiness you diffuse when you are happy; do not relapse again!"

The following morning the rain poured down in torrents, and thick mists hid the summits of the mountains. I rose early, but felt unusually melancholy. The rain depressed me; my old feelings recurred, and I was miserable. I knew how disappointed my father would be at this sudden change, and I wished to avoid him until I had recovered myself so far as to be enabled to conceal those feelings that overpowered me. I knew that they would remain that day at the inn; and as I had ever inured myself to rain, moisture, and cold, I resolved to go alone to the summit of Montanvert. I remembered the effect that the view of the tremendous and ever-moving glacier had produced upon my mind when I first saw it. It had then filled me with a sublime ecstacy that gave wings to the soul, and allowed it to soar from the obscure world to light and joy. The sight of the awful[5] and majestic in nature had indeed always the effect of solemnizing my mind, and causing me to forget the passing cares of life. I determined to go alone, for I was well acquainted with the path, and the presence of another would destroy the solitary grandeur of the scene.

The ascent is precipitous, but the path is cut into continual and short windings, which enable you to surmount the perpendicularity of the mountain. It is a scene terrifically desolate. In a thousand spots the traces of the winter avalanche may be perceived, where trees lie broken and strewed on the ground; some entirely destroyed, others bent, leaning upon the jutting rocks of the mountain, or transversely upon other trees. The path, as you ascend higher, is intersected by ravines of snow, down which stones continually roll from above; one of them is particularly dangerous, as the slightest sound, such as even speaking in a loud voice, produces a concussion of air sufficient to draw destruction upon the head of the speaker. The pines are not tall or luxuriant, but they are sombre, and add an air of severity to the scene. I looked on the valley beneath; vast mists were rising from the rivers which ran through it, and curling in thick wreaths around the opposite mountains, whose summits were hid in the uniform clouds, while rain poured from the dark sky, and added to the melancholy impression I received

5. Awe-inspiring.

from the objects around me. Alas! why does man boast of sensibilities superior to those apparent in the brute; it only renders them more necessary[6] beings. If our impulses were confined to hunger, thirst, and desire, we might be nearly free; but now we are moved by every wind that blows, and a chance word or scene that that word may convey to us.

> We rest; a dream has power to poison sleep.
>   We rise; one wand'ring thought pollutes the day.
> We feel, conceive, or reason; laugh, or weep,
>   Embrace fond woe, or cast our cares away;
> It is the same: for, be it joy or sorrow,
>   The path of its departure still is free.
> Man's yesterday may ne'er be like his morrow;
>   Naught may endure but mutability![7]

It was nearly noon when I arrived at the top of the ascent. For some time I sat upon the rock that overlooks the sea of ice.[8] A mist covered both that and the surrounding mountains. Presently a breeze dissipated the cloud, and I descended upon the glacier. The surface is very uneven, rising like the waves of a troubled sea, descending low, and interspersed by rifts that sink deep. The field of ice is almost a league[9] in width, but I spent nearly two hours in crossing it. The opposite mountain is a bare perpendicular rock. From the side where I now stood Montanvert was exactly opposite, at the distance of a league; and above it rose Mont Blanc, in awful majesty. I remained in a recess of the rock, gazing on this wonderful and stupendous scene. The sea, or rather the vast river of ice, wound among its dependent mountains, whose aërial summits hung over its recesses. Their icy and glittering peaks shone in the sunlight over the clouds. My heart, which was before sorrowful, now swelled with something like joy; I exclaimed—"Wandering spirits, if indeed ye wander, and do not rest in your narrow beds, allow me this faint happiness, or take me, as your companion, away from the joys of life."

As I said this, I suddenly beheld the figure of a man, at some distance, advancing towards me with superhuman speed. He bounded over the crevices in the ice, among which I had walked with caution; his stature also, as he approached, seemed to exceed that of man. I was troubled: a mist came over my eyes, and I felt a faintness seize me; but I was quickly restored by the cold gale of the mountains. I perceived, as the shape came nearer, (sight tremendous and abhorred!) that it was the wretch whom I had created. I trembled with rage and horror, resolving to wait his approach, and then close with him in mortal combat. He approached; his countenance bespoke bitter anguish, combined with disdain and malignity, while its unearthly ugliness rendered it almost too horrible for human eyes. But I scarcely observed this; anger and hatred had at first deprived me of utterance, and I recovered only to overwhelm him with words expressive of furious detestation and contempt.

"Devil!" I exclaimed, "do you dare approach me? and do not you fear the

6. I.e., acting more by necessity than by free choice.
7. Shelley's Poems.—"On Mutability" [Mary Shelley's note]. This is the second half of the sixteen-line poem, (p. 701).
8. The glacier descending from Mont Blanc is named Mer de Glace (sea of ice).
9. Three miles.

fierce vengeance of my arm wreaked on your miserable head? Begone, vile insect! or rather stay, that I may trample you to dust! and, oh, that I could, with the extinction of your miserable existence, restore those victims whom you have diabolically murdered!"

"I expected this reception," said the dæmon. "All men hate the wretched; how then must I be hated, who am miserable beyond all living things! Yet you, my creator, detest and spurn me, thy creature, to whom thou art bound by ties only dissoluble by the annihilation of one of us. You purpose to kill me. How dare you sport thus with life? Do your duty towards me, and I will do mine towards you and the rest of mankind. If you will comply with my conditions, I will leave them and you at peace; but if you refuse, I will glut the maw of death, until it be satiated with the blood of your remaining friends."

"Abhorred monster! fiend that thou art! the tortures of hell are too mild a vengeance for thy crimes. Wretched devil! you reproach me with your creation; come on then, that I may extinguish the spark which I so negligently bestowed."

My rage was without bounds; I sprang on him, impelled by all the feelings which can arm one being against the existence of another.

He easily eluded me, and said,

"Be calm! I entreat you to hear me, before you give vent to your hatred on my devoted head. Have I not suffered enough, that you seek to increase my misery? Life, although it may only be an accumulation of anguish, is dear to me, and I will defend it. Remember, thou hast made me more powerful than thyself; my height is superior to thine; my joints more supple. But I will not be tempted to set myself in opposition to thee. I am thy creature and I will be even mild and docile to my natural lord and King, if thou wilt also perform thy part, the which thou owest me. Oh, Frankenstein, be not equitable to every other, and trample upon me alone, to whom thy justice, and even thy clemency and affection, is most due. Remember, that I am thy creature: I ought to be thy Adam; but I am rather the fallen angel, whom thou drivest from joy for no misdeed. Every where I see bliss, from which I alone am irrevocably excluded. I was benevolent and good; misery made me a fiend. Make me happy, and I shall again be virtuous."

"Begone! I will not hear you. There can be no community between you and me; we are enemies. Begone, or let us try our strength in a fight, in which one must fall."

"How can I move thee? Will no entreaties cause thee to turn a favourable eye upon thy creature, who implores thy goodness and compassion. Believe me, Frankenstein: I was benevolent; my soul glowed with love and humanity: but am I not alone, miserably alone? You, my creator, abhor me; what hope can I gather from your fellow-creatures, who owe me nothing? they spurn and hate me. The desert mountains and dreary glaciers are my refuge. I have wandered here many days; the caves of ice, which I only do not fear, are a dwelling to me, and the only one which man does not grudge. These bleak skies I hail, for they are kinder to me than your fellow-beings. If the multitude of mankind knew of my existence, they would do as you do, and arm themselves for my destruction. Shall I not then hate them who abhor me? I will keep no terms with my enemies. I am miserable, and they shall share my wretchedness. Yet it is in your power to recompense me, and deliver them from an evil which it only remains for you to make so great, that not only you and your family, but thousands of others, shall be swallowed up in the whirlwinds of its rage. Let your compassion be moved, and do not disdain me. Listen to my tale: when you have heard that, abandon or commiserate me, as you shall judge that I deserve. But hear me. The guilty are allowed, by human laws, bloody as they may be, to speak in their own defence before they are condemned. Listen to me, Frankenstein. You accuse me of murder; and yet you would, with a satisfied conscience, destroy your own creature. Oh, praise the eternal justice of man! Yet I ask you not to spare me: listen to me; and then, if you can, and if you will, destroy the work of your hands."

"Why do you call to my remembrance circumstances of which I shudder to reflect, that I have been the miserable origin and author? Cursed be the day, abhorred devil, in which you first saw light! Cursed (although I curse myself) be the hands that formed you! You have made me wretched beyond expression. You have left me no power to consider whether I am just to you, or not. Begone! relieve me from the sight of your detested form."

"Thus I relieve thee, my creator," he said, and placed his hated hands before my eyes, which I flung from me with violence; "thus I take from thee a sight which you abhor. Still thou canst listen to me, and grant me thy compassion. By the virtues that I once possessed, I demand this from you. Hear my tale; it is long and strange, and the temperature of this place is not fitting to your fine[1] sensations; come to the hut upon the mountain. The sun is yet high in the heavens; before it descends to hide itself behind yon snowy precipices, and illuminate another world, you will have heard my story, and can decide. On you it rests, whether I quit for ever the neighbourhood of man, and lead a harmless life, or become the scourge of your fellow-creatures, and the author of your own speedy ruin."

As he said this, he led the way across the ice: I followed. My heart was full, and I did not answer him; but, as I proceeded, I weighed the various arguments that he had used, and determined at least to listen to his tale. I was partly urged by curiosity, and compassion confirmed my resolution. I had hitherto supposed him to be the murderer of my brother, and I eagerly sought a confirmation or denial of this opinion. For the first time, also, I felt what the duties of a creator towards his creature were, and that I ought to render him happy before I complained of his wickedness. These motives urged me to comply with his demand. We crossed the ice, therefore, and ascended the opposite rock. The air was cold, and the rain again began to descend: we entered the hut, the fiend with an air of exultation, I with a heavy heart, and depressed spirits. But I consented to listen; and, seating myself by the fire which my odious companion had lighted, he thus began his tale.

Chapter 3.

"It is with considerable difficulty that I remember the original æra of my being: all the events of that period appear confused and indistinct. A strange multiplicity of sensations seized me, and I saw, felt, heard, and smelt, at the same time; and it was, indeed, a long time before I learned to distinguish

1. Delicate.

between the operations of my various senses. By degrees, I remember, a stronger light pressed upon my nerves, so that I was obliged to shut my eyes. Darkness then came over me, and troubled me; but hardly had I felt this, when, by opening my eyes, as I now suppose, the light poured in upon me again. I walked, and, I believe, descended; but I presently found a great alteration in my sensations. Before, dark and opaque bodies had surrounded me, impervious to my touch or sight; but I now found that I could wander on at liberty, with no obstacles which I could not either surmount or avoid. The light became more and more oppressive to me; and, the heat wearying me as I walked, I sought a place where I could receive shade. This was the forest near Ingolstadt; and here I lay by the side of a brook resting from my fatigue, until I felt tormented by hunger and thirst. This roused me from my nearly dormant state, and I ate some berries which I found hanging on the trees, or lying on the ground. I slaked my thirst at the brook; and then lying down, was overcome by sleep.

"It was dark when I awoke; I felt cold also, and half-frightened as it were instinctively, finding myself so desolate. Before I had quitted your apartment, on a sensation of cold, I had covered myself with some clothes; but these were insufficient to secure me from the dews of night. I was a poor, helpless, miserable wretch; I knew, and could distinguish, nothing; but, feeling pain invade me on all sides, I sat down and wept.

"Soon a gentle light stole over the heavens, and gave me a sensation of pleasure. I started up, and beheld a radiant form rise from among the trees. I gazed with a kind of wonder. It moved slowly, but it enlightened my path; and I again went out in search of berries. I was still cold, when under one of the trees I found a huge cloak, with which I covered myself, and sat down upon the ground. No distinct ideas occupied my mind; all was confused. I felt light, and hunger, and thirst, and darkness; innumerable sounds rung in my ears, and on all sides various scents saluted[2] me: the only object that I could distinguish was the bright moon, and I fixed my eyes on that with pleasure.

"Several changes of day and night passed, and the orb of night had greatly lessened when I began to distinguish my sensations from each other. I gradually saw plainly the clear stream that supplied me with drink, and the trees that shaded me with their foliage. I was delighted when I first discovered that a pleasant sound, which often saluted my ears, proceeded from the throats of the little winged animals who had often intercepted the light from my eyes. I began also to observe, with greater accuracy, the forms that surrounded me, and to perceive the boundaries of the radiant roof of light which canopied me. Sometimes I tried to imitate the pleasant songs of the birds, but was unable. Sometimes I wished to express my sensations in my own mode, but the uncouth and inarticulate sounds which broke from me frightened me into silence again.

"The moon had disappeared from the night, and again, with a lessened form, shewed itself, while I still remained in the forest. My sensations had, by this time, become distinct, and my mind received every day additional ideas. My eyes became accustomed to the light, and to perceive objects in their right forms; I distinguished the insect from the herb, and, by degrees,

2. Greeted.

one herb from another. I found that the sparrow uttered none but harsh notes, whilst those of the blackbird and thrush were sweet and enticing.

"One day, when I was oppressed by cold, I found a fire which had been left by some wandering beggars, and was overcome with delight at the warmth I experienced from it. In my joy I thrust my hand into the live embers, but quickly drew it out again with a cry of pain. How strange, I thought, that the same cause should produce such opposite effects! I examined the materials of the fire, and to my joy found it to be composed of wood. I quickly collected some branches; but they were wet, and would not burn. I was pained at this, and sat still watching the operation of the fire. The wet wood which I had placed near the heat dried, and itself became inflamed. I reflected on this; and, by touching the various branches, I discovered the cause, and busied myself in collecting a great quantity of wood, that I might dry it, and have a plentiful supply of fire. When night came on, and brought sleep with it, I was in the greatest fear lest my fire should be extinguished. I covered it carefully with dry wood and leaves, and placed wet branches upon it; and then, spreading my cloak, I lay on the ground, and sunk into sleep.

"It was morning when I awoke, and my first care was to visit the fire. I uncovered it, and a gentle breeze quickly fanned it into a flame. I observed this also, and contrived a fan of branches, which roused the embers when they were nearly extinguished. When night came again, I found, with pleasure, that the fire gave light as well as heat; and that the discovery of this element was useful to me in my food; for I found some of the offals that the travellers had left had been roasted, and tasted much more savoury than the berries I gathered from the trees. I tried, therefore, to dress my food in the same manner, placing it on the live embers. I found that the berries were spoiled by this operation, and the nuts and roots much improved.

"Food, however, became scarce; and I often spent the whole day searching in vain for a few acorns to assuage the pangs of hunger. When I found this, I resolved to quit the place that I had hitherto inhabited, to seek for one where the few wants I experienced would be more easily satisfied. In this emigration, I exceedingly lamented the loss of the fire which I had obtained through accident, and knew not how to reproduce it. I gave several hours to the serious consideration of this difficulty; but I was obliged to relinquish all attempt to supply it; and, wrapping myself up in my cloak, I struck across the wood towards the setting sun. I passed three days in these rambles, and at length discovered the open country. A great fall of snow had taken place the night before, and the fields were of one uniform white; the appearance was disconsolate, and I found my feet chilled by the cold damp substance that covered the ground.

"It was about seven in the morning, and I longed to obtain food and shelter; at length I perceived a small hut, on a rising ground, which had doubtless been built for the convenience of some shepherd. This was a new sight to me; and I examined the structure with great curiosity. Finding the door open, I entered. An old man sat in it, near a fire, over which he was preparing his breakfast. He turned on hearing a noise; and, perceiving me, shrieked loudly, and, quitting the hut, ran across the fields with a speed of which his debilitated form hardly appeared capable. His appearance, different from any I had ever before seen, and his flight, somewhat surprised me. But I was enchanted by the appearance of the hut: here the snow and rain could not penetrate; the ground was dry; and it presented to me then as exquisite and divine a retreat as Pandæmonium appeared to the dæmons of hell after their sufferings in the lake of fire.[3] I greedily devoured the remnants of the shepherd's breakfast, which consisted of bread, cheese, milk, and wine; the latter, however, I did not like. [Then] overcome by fatigue, I lay down among some straw, and fell asleep.

"It was noon when I awoke; and, allured by the warmth of the sun, which shone brightly on the white ground, I determined to recommence my travels; and, depositing the remains of the peasant's breakfast in a wallet[4] I found, I proceeded across the fields for several hours, until at sunset I arrived at a village. How miraculous did this appear! the huts, the neater cottages, and stately houses, engaged my admiration by turns. The vegetables in the gardens, the milk and cheese that I saw placed at the windows of some of the cottages, allured my appetite. One of the best of these I entered; but I had hardly placed my foot within the door, before the children shrieked, and one of the women fainted. The whole village was roused; some fled, some attacked me, until, grievously bruised by stones and many other kinds of missile weapons, I escaped to the open country, and fearfully took refuge in a low hovel, quite bare, and making a wretched appearance after the palaces I had beheld in the village. This hovel, however, joined a cottage of a neat and pleasant appearance; but, after my late dearly-bought experience, I dared not enter it. My place of refuge was constructed of wood, but so low, that I could with difficulty sit upright in it. No wood, however, was placed on the earth, which formed the floor, but it was dry; and although the wind entered it by innumerable chinks, I found it an agreeable asylum from the snow and rain.

"Here then I retreated, and lay down, happy to have found a shelter, however miserable, from the inclemency of the season, and still more from the barbarity of man.

"As soon as morning dawned, I crept from my kennel, that I might view the adjacent cottage, and discover if I could remain in the habitation I had found. It was situated against the back of the cottage, and surrounded on the sides which were exposed by a pig-stye and a clear pool of water. One part was open, and by that I had crept in; but now I covered every crevice by which I might be perceived with stones and wood, yet in such a manner that I might move them on occasion to pass out: all the light I enjoyed came through the stye, and that was sufficient for me.

"Having thus arranged my dwelling, and carpeted it with clean straw, I retired; for I saw the figure of a man at a distance, and I remembered too well my treatment the night before, to trust myself in his power. I had first, however, provided for my sustenance for that day, by a loaf of coarse bread, which I purloined, and a cup with which I could drink, more conveniently than from my hand, of the pure water which flowed by my retreat. The floor was a little raised, so that it was kept perfectly dry, and by its vicinity to the chimney of the cottage it was tolerably warm.

"Being thus provided, I resolved to reside in this hovel, until something should occur which might alter my determination. It was indeed a paradise,

---

3. Satan and the other fallen angels build the city of Pandemonium (all-demons) in the fiery regions of Hell. See *Paradise Lost* 1.670ff.
4. Knapsack or satchel.

compared to the bleak forest, my former residence, the rain-dropping branches, and dank earth. I ate my breakfast with pleasure, and was about to remove a plank to procure myself a little water, when I heard a step, and, looking through a small chink, I beheld a young creature, with a pail on her head, passing before my hovel. The girl was young and of gentle demeanour,[5] unlike what I have since found cottagers and farm-house servants to be. Yet she was meanly[6] dressed, a coarse blue petticoat and a linen jacket being her only garb; her fair hair was plaited, but not adorned; she looked patient, yet sad. I lost sight of her; and in about a quarter of an hour she returned, bearing the pail, which was now partly filled with milk. As she walked along, seemingly incommoded by the burden, a young man met her, whose countenance expressed a deeper despondence. Uttering a few sounds with an air of melancholy, he took the pail from her head, and bore it to the cottage himself. She followed, and they disappeared. Presently I saw the young man again, with some tools in his hand, cross the field behind the cottage; and the girl was also busied, sometimes in the house, and sometimes in the yard.

"On examining my dwelling, I found that one of the windows of the cottage had formerly occupied a part of it, but the panes had been filled up with wood. In one of these was a small and almost imperceptible chink, through which the eye could just penetrate. Through this crevice, a small room was visible, white-washed and clean, but very bare of furniture. In one corner, near a small fire, sat an old man, leaning his head on his hands in a disconsolate attitude. The young girl was occupied in arranging the cottage; but presently she took something out of a drawer, which employed her hands, and she sat down beside the old man, who, taking up an instrument, began to play, and to produce sounds, sweeter than the voice of the thrush or the nightingale. It was a lovely sight, even to me, poor wretch! who had never beheld aught beautiful before. The silver hair and benevolent countenance of the aged cottager, won my reverence; while the gentle manners of the girl enticed my love. He played a sweet mournful air, which I perceived drew tears from the eyes of his amiable companion, of which the old man took no notice, until she sobbed audibly; he then pronounced a few sounds, and the fair creature, leaving her work, knelt at his feet. He raised her, and smiled with such kindness and affection, that I felt sensations of a peculiar and overpowering nature: they were a mixture of pain and pleasure, such as I had never before experienced, either from hunger or cold, warmth or food; and I withdrew from the window, unable to bear these emotions.

"Soon after this the young man returned, bearing on his shoulders a load of wood. The girl met him at the door, helped to relieve him of his burden, and, taking some of the fuel into the cottage, placed it on the fire; then she and the youth went apart into a nook of the cottage, and he shewed her a large loaf and a piece of cheese. She seemed pleased; and went into the garden for some roots and plants, which she placed in water, and then upon the fire. She afterwards continued her work, whilst the young man went into the garden, and appeared busily employed in digging and pulling up roots. After he had been employed thus about an hour, the young woman joined him, and they entered the cottage together.

5. I.e., conducting herself like someone of good family and breeding.   6. Coarsely.

"The old man had, in the mean time, been pensive; but, on the appearance of his companions, he assumed a more cheerful air, and they sat down to eat. The meal was quickly dispatched. The young woman was again occupied in arranging the cottage; the old man walked before the cottage in the sun for a few minutes, leaning on the arm of the youth. Nothing could exceed in beauty the contrast between these two excellent creatures. One was old, with silver hairs and a countenance beaming with benevolence and love: the younger was slight and graceful in his figure, and his features were moulded with the finest symmetry; yet his eyes and attitude expressed the utmost sadness and despondency. The old man returned to the cottage; and the youth, with tools different from those he had used in the morning, directed his steps across the fields.

"Night quickly shut in; but, to my extreme wonder, I found that the cottagers had a means of prolonging light, by the use of tapers, and was delighted to find, that the setting of the sun did not put an end to the pleasure I experienced in watching my human neighbours. In the evening, the young girl and her companion were employed in various occupations which I did not understand; and the old man again took up the instrument, which produced the divine sounds that had enchanted me in the morning. So soon as he had finished, the youth began, not to play, but to utter sounds that were monotonous, and neither resembling the harmony of the old man's instrument or the songs of the birds; I since found that he read aloud, but at that time I knew nothing of the science of words or letters.

"The family, after having been thus occupied for a short time, extinguished their lights, and retired, as I conjectured, to rest."

Chapter 4.

"I lay on my straw, but I could not sleep. I thought of the occurrences of the day. What chiefly struck me was the gentle manners of these people; and I longed to join them, but dared not. I remembered too well the treatment I had suffered the night before from the barbarous villagers, and resolved, whatever course of conduct I might hereafter think it right to pursue, that for the present I would remain quietly in my hovel, watching, and endeavouring to discover the motives which influenced their actions.

"The cottagers arose the next morning before the sun. The young woman arranged the cottage, and prepared the food; and the youth departed after the first meal.

"This day was passed in the same routine as that which preceded it. The young man was constantly employed out of doors, and the girl in various laborious occupations within. The old man, whom I soon perceived to be blind, employed his leisure hours on his instrument, or in contemplation. Nothing could exceed the love and respect which the younger cottagers exhibited towards their venerable companion. They performed towards him every little office of affection and duty with gentleness; and he rewarded them by his benevolent smiles.

"They were not entirely happy. The young man and his companion often went apart, and appeared to weep. I saw no cause for their unhappiness; but I was deeply affected by it. If such lovely creatures were miserable, it was less strange that I, an imperfect and solitary being, should be wretched. Yet why were these gentle beings unhappy? They possessed a delightful house (for such it was in my eyes), and every luxury; they had a fire to warm them when chill, and delicious viands when hungry; they were dressed in excellent clothes; and, still more, they enjoyed one another's company and speech, interchanging each day looks of affection and kindness. What did their tears imply? Did they really express pain? I was at first unable to solve these questions; but perpetual attention, and time, explained to me many appearances which were at first enigmatic.

"A considerable period elapsed before I discovered one of the causes of the uneasiness of this amiable family; it was poverty: and they suffered that evil in a very distressing degree. Their nourishment consisted entirely of the vegetables of their garden, and the milk of one cow, who gave very little during the winter, when its masters could scarcely procure food to support it. They often, I believe, suffered the pangs of hunger very poignantly, especially the two younger cottagers; for several times they placed food before the old man, when they reserved none for themselves.

"This trait of kindness moved me sensibly. I had been accustomed, during the night, to steal a part of their store for my own consumption; but when I found that in doing this I inflicted pain on the cottagers, I abstained, and satisfied myself with berries, nuts, and roots, which I gathered from a neighbouring wood.

"I discovered also another means through which I was enabled to assist their labours. I found that the youth spent a great part of each day in collecting wood for the family fire; and, during the night, I often took his tools, the use of which I quickly discovered, and brought home firing sufficient for the consumption of several days.

"I remember, the first time that I did this, the young woman, when she opened the door in the morning, appeared greatly astonished on seeing a great pile of wood on the outside. She uttered some words in a loud voice, and the youth joined her, who also expressed surprise. I observed, with pleasure, that he did not go to the forest that day, but spent it in repairing the cottage, and cultivating the garden.

"By degrees I made a discovery of still greater moment. I found that these people possessed a method of communicating their experience and feelings to one another by articulate sounds. I perceived that the words they spoke sometimes produced pleasure or pain, smiles or sadness, in the minds and countenances of the hearers. This was indeed a godlike science, and I ardently desired to become acquainted with it. But I was baffled in every attempt I made for this purpose. Their pronunciation was quick; and the words they uttered, not having any apparent connexion with visible objects, I was unable to discover any clue by which I could unravel the mystery of their reference. By great application, however, and after having remained during the space of several revolutions of the moon in my hovel, I discovered the names that were given to some of the most familiar objects of discourse: I learned and applied the words *fire, milk, bread,* and *wood.* I learned also the names of the cottagers themselves. The youth and his companion had each of them several names, but the old man had only one, which was *father.* The girl was called *sister,* or *Agatha;* and the youth *Felix, brother,* or *son.* I cannot describe the delight I felt when I learned the ideas appropriated to each of these sounds, and was able to pronounce them. I distinguished several other words, without being able as yet to understand or apply them; such as *good, dearest, unhappy*.

"I spent the winter in this manner. The gentle manners and beauty of the cottagers greatly endeared them to me: when they were unhappy, I felt depressed; when they rejoiced, I sympathized in their joys. I saw few human beings beside them; and if any other happened to enter the cottage, their harsh manners and rude gait only enhanced to me the superior accomplishments of my friends. The old man, I could perceive, often endeavoured to encourage his children, as sometimes I found that he called them, to cast off their melancholy. He would talk in a cheerful accent, with an expression of goodness that bestowed pleasure even upon me. Agatha listened with respect, her eyes sometimes filled with tears, which she endeavoured to wipe away unperceived; but I generally found that her countenance and tone were more cheerful after having listened to the exhortations of her father. It was not thus with Felix. He was always the saddest of the group; and, even to my unpractised senses, he appeared to have suffered more deeply than his friends. But if his countenance was more sorrowful, his voice was more cheerful than that of his sister, especially when he addressed the old man.

"I could mention innumerable instances, which, although slight, marked the dispositions of these amiable cottagers. In the midst of poverty and want, Felix carried with pleasure to his sister the first little white flower that peeped out from beneath the snowy ground. Early in the morning before she had risen, he cleared away the snow that obstructed her path to the milk-house, drew water from the well, and brought the wood from the outhouse, where, to his perpetual astonishment, he found his store always replenished by an invisible hand. In the day, I believe, he worked sometimes for a neighbouring farmer, because he often went forth, and did not return until dinner, yet brought no wood with him. At other times he worked in the garden; but, as there was little to do in the frosty season, he read to the old man and Agatha.

"This reading had puzzled me extremely at first; but, by degrees, I discovered that he uttered many of the same sounds when he read as when he talked. I conjectured, therefore, that he found on the paper signs for speech which he understood, and I ardently longed to comprehend these also; but how was that possible, when I did not even understand the sounds for which they stood as signs? I improved, however, sensibly in this science, but not sufficiently to follow up any kind of conversation, although I applied my whole mind to the endeavour: for I easily perceived that, although I eagerly longed to discover myself to the cottagers, I ought not to make the attempt until I had first become master of their language; which knowledge might enable me to make them overlook the deformity of my figure; for with this also the contrast perpetually presented to my eyes had made me acquainted.

"I had admired the perfect forms of my cottagers—their grace, beauty, and delicate complexions: but how was I terrified, when I viewed myself in a transparent pool! At first I started back, unable to believe that it was indeed I who was reflected in the mirror; and when I became fully convinced that I was in reality the monster that I am, I was filled with the bitterest sensations of despondence and mortification. Alas! I did not yet entirely know the fatal effects of this miserable deformity.

"As the sun became warmer, and the light of day longer, the snow vanished, and I beheld the bare trees and the black earth. From this time Felix was more employed; and the heart-moving indications of impending famine disappeared. Their food, as I afterwards found, was coarse, but it was wholesome; and they procured a sufficiency of it. Several new kinds of plants sprung up in the garden, which they dressed; and these signs of comfort increased daily as the season advanced.

"The old man, leaning on his son, walked each day at noon, when it did not rain, as I found it was called when the heavens poured forth its waters. This frequently took place; but a high wind quickly dried the earth, and the season became far more pleasant than it had been.

"My mode of life in my hovel was uniform. During the morning I attended the motions of the cottagers; and when they were dispersed in various occupations, I slept: the remainder of the day was spent in observing my friends. When they had retired to rest, if there was any moon, or the night was starlight, I went into the woods, and collected my own food and fuel for the cottage. When I returned, as often as it was necessary, I cleared their path from the snow, and performed those offices that I had seen done by Felix. I afterwards found that these labours, performed by an invisible hand, greatly astonished them; and once or twice I heard them, on these occasions, utter the words *good spirit, wonderful*; but I did not then understand the signification of these terms.

"My thoughts now became more active, and I longed to discover the motives and feelings of these lovely creatures; I was inquisitive to know why Felix appeared so miserable, and Agatha so sad. I thought (foolish wretch!) that it might be in my power to restore happiness to these deserving people. When I slept, or was absent, the forms of the venerable blind father, the gentle Agatha, and the excellent Felix, flitted before me. I looked upon them as superior beings, who would be the arbiters of my future destiny. I formed in my imagination a thousand pictures of presenting myself to them, and their reception of me. I imagined that they would be disgusted, until, by my gentle demeanour and conciliating words, I should first win their favour, and afterwards their love.

"These thoughts exhilarated me, and led me to apply with fresh ardour to the acquiring the art of language. My organs were indeed harsh, but supple; and although my voice was very unlike the soft music of their tones, yet I pronounced such words as I understood with tolerable ease. It was as the ass and the lap-dog; yet surely the gentle ass, whose intentions were affectionate, although his manners were rude, deserved better treatment than blows and execration.[7]

"The pleasant showers and genial warmth of spring greatly altered the aspect of the earth. Men, who before this change seemed to have been hid in caves, dispersed themselves, and were employed in various arts of cultivation. The birds sang in more cheerful notes, and the leaves began to bud forth on the trees. Happy, happy earth! fit habitation for gods, which, so short a time before, was bleak, damp, and unwholesome. My spirits were elevated by the enchanting appearance of nature; the past was blotted from my memory, the present was tranquil, and the future gilded by bright rays of hope, and anticipations of joy."

7. The story is told in one of the verse fables by the French writer Jean de La Fontaine (1621–1695). Noting that the Lapdog is petted when he rubs against its master, the Ass imitates the action, but is beaten and berated for doing so.

Chapter 5.

"I now hasten to the more moving part of my story. I shall relate events that impressed me with feelings which, from what I was, have made me what I am.

"Spring advanced rapidly; the weather became fine, and the skies cloudless. It surprised me, that what before was desert and gloomy should now bloom with the most beautiful flowers and verdure. My senses were gratified and refreshed by a thousand scents of delight, and a thousand sights of beauty.

"It was on one of these days, when my cottagers periodically rested from labour—the old man played on his guitar, and the children listened to him—I observed that the countenance of Felix was melancholy beyond expression: he sighed frequently; and once his father paused in his music, and I conjectured by his manner that he inquired the cause of his son's sorrow. Felix replied in a cheerful accent, and the old man was recommencing his music, when some one tapped at the door.

"It was a lady on horseback, accompanied by a countryman as a guide. The lady was dressed in a dark suit, and covered with a thick black veil. Agatha asked a question; to which the stranger only replied by pronouncing, in a sweet accent, the name of Felix. Her voice was musical, but unlike that of either of my friends. On hearing this word, Felix came up hastily to the lady; who, when she saw him, threw up her veil, and I beheld a countenance of angelic beauty and expression. Her hair of a shining raven black, and curiously braided; her eyes were dark, but gentle, although animated; her features of a regular proportion, and her complexion wondrously fair, each cheek tinged with a lovely pink.

"Felix seemed ravished with delight when he saw her, every trait of sorrow vanished from his face, and it instantly expressed a degree of ecstatic joy, of which I could hardly have believed it capable; his eyes sparkled, as his cheek flushed with pleasure; and at that moment I thought him as beautiful as the stranger. She appeared affected by different feelings; wiping a few tears from her lovely eyes, she held out her hand to Felix, who kissed it rapturously, and called her, as well as I could distinguish, his sweet Arabian. She did not appear to understand him, but smiled. He assisted her to dismount, and, dismissing her guide, conducted her into the cottage. Some conversation took place between him and his father; and the young stranger knelt at the old man's feet, and would have kissed his hand, but he raised her, and embraced her affectionately.

"I soon perceived, that although the stranger uttered articulate sounds, and appeared to have a language of her own, she was neither understood by, or herself understood, the cottagers. They made many signs which I did not comprehend; but I saw that her presence diffused gladness through the cottage, dispelling their sorrow as the sun dissipates the morning mists. Felix seemed peculiarly happy, and with smiles of delight welcomed his Arabian. Agatha, the ever-gentle Agatha, kissed the hands of the lovely stranger; and, pointing to her brother, made signs which appeared to me to mean that he had been sorrowful until she came. Some hours passed thus, while they, by their countenances, expressed joy, the cause of which I did not comprehend. Presently I found, by the frequent recurrence of one sound which the stranger repeated after them, that she was endeavouring to learn their language; and the idea instantly occurred to me, that I should make use of the same instructions to the same end. The stranger learned about twenty words at the first lesson, most of them indeed were those which I had before understood, but I profited by the others.

"As night came on, Agatha and the Arabian retired early. When they separated, Felix kissed the hand of the stranger, and said, 'Good night, sweet Safie.' He sat up much longer, conversing with his father; and, by the frequent repetition of her name, I conjectured that their lovely guest was the subject of their conversation. I ardently desired to understand them, and bent every faculty towards that purpose, but found it utterly impossible.

"The next morning Felix went out to his work; and, after the usual occupations of Agatha were finished, the Arabian sat at the feet of the old man, and, taking his guitar, played some airs so entrancingly beautiful, that they at once drew tears of sorrow and delight from my eyes. She sang, and her voice flowed in a rich cadence, swelling or dying away, like a nightingale of the woods.

"When she had finished, she gave the guitar to Agatha, who at first declined it. She played a simple air, and her voice accompanied it in sweet accents, but unlike the wondrous strain of the stranger. The old man appeared enraptured, and said some words, which Agatha endeavoured to explain to Safie, and by which he appeared to wish to express that she bestowed on him the greatest delight by her music."

"The days now passed as peaceably as before, with the sole alteration, that joy had taken place of sadness in the countenances of my friends. Safie was always gay and happy; she and I improved rapidly in the knowledge of language, so that in two months I began to comprehend most of the words uttered by my protectors."

"In the meanwhile also the black ground was covered with herbage, and the green banks interspersed with innumerable flowers, sweet to the scent and the eyes, stars of pale radiance among the moonlight woods; the sun became warmer, the nights clear and balmy; and my nocturnal rambles were an extreme pleasure to me, although they were considerably shortened by the late setting and early rising of the sun; for I never ventured abroad during daylight, fearful of meeting with the same treatment as I had formerly endured in the first village which I entered."

"My days were spent in close attention, that I might more speedily master the language; and I may boast that I improved more rapidly than the Arabian, who understood very little, and conversed in broken accents, whilst I comprehended and could imitate almost every word that was spoken.

"While I improved in speech, I also learned the science of letters, as it was taught to the stranger; and this opened before me a wide field for wonder and delight."

"The book from which Felix instructed Safie was Volney's *Ruins of Empires*.[8] I should not have understood the purport of this book, had not Felix, in reading it, given very minute explanations. He had chosen this work, he said, because the declamatory style was framed in imitation of the eastern

---

8. The comte de Volney published *Les ruines, ou Méditations sur les révolutions des empires* in 1791, the early period of the French Revolution. It sur-veys the rise and fall of civilizations and looks forward to a future era of rationality, freedom, and justice.

authors. Through this work I obtained a cursory knowledge of history, and a view of the several empires at present existing in the world; it gave me an insight into the manners, governments, and religions of the different nations of the earth. I heard of the slothful Asiatics; of the stupendous genius and mental activity of the Grecians; of the wars and wonderful virtue of the early Romans—of their subsequent degeneration—of the decline of that mighty empire; of chivalry, christianity, and kings. I heard of the discovery of the American hemisphere, and wept with Safie over the hapless fate of its original inhabitants.

"These wonderful narrations inspired me with strange feelings. Was man, indeed, at once so powerful, so virtuous, and magnificent, yet so vicious and base? He appeared at one time a mere scion of the evil principle, and at another as all that can be conceived of noble and godlike. To be a great and virtuous man appeared the highest honour that can befall a sensitive being; to be base and vicious, as many on record have been, appeared the lowest degradation, a condition more abject than that of the blind mole or harmless worm. For a long time I could not conceive how one man could go forth to murder his fellow, or even why there were laws and governments; but when I heard details of vice and bloodshed, my wonder ceased, and I turned away with disgust and loathing.

"Every conversation of the cottagers now opened new wonders to me. While I listened to the instructions which Felix bestowed upon the Arabian, the strange system of human society was explained to me. I heard of the division of property, of immense wealth and squalid poverty; of rank, descent, and noble blood.

"The words induced me to turn towards myself. I learned that the possessions most esteemed by your fellow-creatures were, high and unsullied descent[9] united with riches. A man might be respected with only one of these acquisitions; but without either he was considered, except in very rare instances, as a vagabond and a slave, doomed to waste his powers for the profit of the chosen few. And what was I? Of my creation and creator I was absolutely ignorant; but I knew that I possessed no money, no friends, no kind of property. I was, besides, endowed with a figure hideously deformed and loathsome; I was not even of the same nature as man. I was more agile than they, and could subsist upon coarser diet; I bore the extremes of heat and cold with less injury to my frame; my stature far exceeded their's. When I looked around, I saw and heard of none like me. Was I then a monster, a blot upon the earth, from which all men fled, and whom all men disowned?

"I cannot describe to you the agony that these reflections inflicted upon me; I tried to dispel them, but sorrow only increased with knowledge. Oh, that I had for ever remained in my native wood, nor known or felt beyond the sensations of hunger, thirst, and heat!

"Of what a strange nature is knowledge! It clings to the mind, when it has once seized on it, like a lichen on the rock. I wished sometimes to shake off all thought and feeling; but I learned that there was but one means to overcome the sensation of pain, and that was death—a state which I feared yet did not understand. I admired virtue and good feelings, and loved the gentle manners and amiable qualities of my cottagers; but I was shut out from

---

9. Ancestry.

intercourse with them, except through means which I obtained by stealth, when I was unseen and unknown, and which rather increased than satisfied the desire I had of becoming one among my fellows. The gentle words of Agatha, and the animated smiles of the charming Arabian, were not for me. The mild exhortations of the old man, and the lively conversation of the loved Felix, were not for me. Miserable, unhappy wretch!

"Other lessons were impressed upon me even more deeply. I heard of the difference of sexes; of the birth and growth of children; how the father doted on the smiles of the infant, and the lively sallies of the older child; how all the life and cares of the mother were wrapt up in the precious charge; how the mind of youth expanded and gained knowledge; of brother, sister, and all the various relationships which bind one human being to another in mutual bonds.

"But where were my friends and relations? No father had watched my infant days, no mother had blessed me with smiles and caresses; or if they had, all my past life was now a blot, a blind vacancy in which I distinguished nothing. From my earliest remembrance I had been as I then was in height and proportion. I had never yet seen a being resembling me, or who claimed any intercourse with me. What was I? The question again recurred, to be answered only with groans.

"I will soon explain to what these feelings tended; but allow me now to return to the cottagers, whose story excited in me such various feelings of indignation, delight, and wonder, but which all terminated in additional love and reverence for my protectors (for so I loved, in an innocent, half painful self-deceit, to call them)."

Chapter 6.

"Some time elapsed before I learned the history of my friends. It was one which could not fail to impress itself deeply on my mind, unfolding as it did a number of circumstances each interesting and wonderful to one so utterly inexperienced as I was.

"The name of the old man was De Lacey. He was descended from a good family in France, where he had lived for many years in affluence, respected by his superiors, and beloved by his equals. His son was bred in the service of his country; and Agatha had ranked with ladies of the highest distinction. A few months before my arrival, they had lived in a large and luxurious city, called Paris, surrounded by friends, and possessed of every enjoyment which virtue, refinement of intellect, or taste, accompanied by a moderate fortune, could afford.

"The father of Safie had been the cause of their ruin. He was a Turkish merchant, and had inhabited Paris for many years, when, for some reason which I could not learn, he became obnoxious to the government. He was seized and cast into prison the very day that Safie arrived from Constantinople to join him. He was tried, and condemned to death. The injustice of his sentence was very flagrant; all Paris was indignant; and it was judged that his religion and wealth, rather than the crime alleged against him, had been the cause of his condemnation.

"Felix had been present at the trial; his horror and indignation were uncontrollable, when he heard the decision of the court. He made, at that moment, a solemn vow to deliver him, and then looked around for the means. After many fruitless attempts to gain admittance to the prison, he found a strongly grated window in an unguarded part of the building, which lighted the dungeon of the unfortunate Mahometan; who, loaded with chains, waited in despair the execution of the barbarous sentence. Felix visited the grate at night, and made known to the prisoner his intentions in his favour. The Turk, amazed and delighted, endeavoured to kindle the zeal of his deliverer by promises of reward and wealth. Felix rejected his offers with contempt; yet when he saw the lovely Safie, who was allowed to visit her father, and who, by her gestures, expressed her lively gratitude, the youth could not help owning to his own mind, that the captive possessed a treasure which would fully reward his toil and hazard.

"The Turk quickly perceived the impression that his daughter had made on the heart of Felix, and endeavoured to secure him more entirely in his interests by the promise of her hand in marriage, so soon as he should be conveyed to a place of safety. Felix was too delicate[1] to accept this offer; yet he looked forward to the probability of that event as to the consummation of his happiness.

"During the ensuing days, while the preparations were going forward for the escape of the merchant, the zeal of Felix was warmed by several letters that he received from this lovely girl, who found means to express her thoughts in the language of her lover by the aid of an old man, a servant of her father's, who understood French. She thanked him in the most ardent terms for his intended services towards her father; and at the same time she gently deplored her own fate.

"I have copies of these letters; for I found means, during my residence in the hovel, to procure the implements of writing; and the letters were often in the hands of Felix or Agatha. Before I depart, I will give them to you, they will prove the truth of my tale; but at present, as the sun is already far declined, I shall only have time to repeat the substance of them to you.

"Safie related, that her mother was a Christian Arab, seized and made a slave by the Turks; recommended by her beauty, she had won the heart of the father of Safie, who married her. The young girl spoke in high and enthusiastic terms of her mother, who, born in freedom spurned the bondage to which she was now reduced. She instructed her daughter in the tenets of her religion, and taught her to aspire to higher powers of intellect, and an independence of spirit, forbidden to the female followers of Mahomet. This lady died; but her lessons were indelibly impressed on the mind of Safie, who sickened at the prospect of again returning to Asia, and the being immured within the walls of a haram, allowed only to occupy herself with puerile amusements, ill suited to the temper of her soul, now accustomed to grand ideas and a noble emulation for virtue. The prospect of marrying a Christian, and remaining in a country where women were allowed to take a rank in society, was enchanting to her.

"The day for the execution of the Turk was fixed; but, on the night previous to it, he had quitted prison, and before morning was distant many leagues from Paris. Felix had procured passports in the name of his father, sister,

1. Morally sensitive.

and himself. He had previously communicated his plan to the former, who aided the deceit by quitting his house, under the pretence of a journey, and concealed himself, with his daughter, in an obscure part of Paris.

"Felix conducted the fugitives through France to Lyons, and across Mont Cenis to Leghorn, where the merchant had decided to wait a favourable opportunity of passing into some part of the Turkish dominions.

"Safie resolved to remain with her father until the moment of his departure, before which time the Turk renewed his promise that she should be united to his deliverer; and Felix remained with them in expectation of that event; and in the mean time he enjoyed the society of the Arabian, who exhibited towards him the simplest and tenderest affection. They conversed with one another through the means of an interpreter, and sometimes with the interpretation of looks; and Safie sang to him the divine airs of her native country.

"The Turk allowed this intimacy to take place, and encouraged the hopes of the youthful lovers, while in his heart he had formed far other plans. He loathed the idea that his daughter should be united to a Christian; but he feared the resentment of Felix if he should appear lukewarm; for he knew that he was still in the power of his deliverer, if he should choose to betray him to the Italian state which they inhabited. He revolved a thousand plans by which he should be enabled to prolong the deceit until it might be no longer necessary, and secretly to take his daughter with him when he departed. His plans were greatly facilitated by the news which arrived from Paris.

"The government of France were greatly enraged at the escape of their victim, and spared no pains to detect and punish his deliverer. The plot of Felix was quickly discovered, and De Lacey and Agatha were thrown into prison. The news reached Felix, and roused him from his dream of pleasure. His blind and aged father, and his gentle sister, lay in a noisome dungeon, while he enjoyed the free air, and the society of her whom he loved. This idea was torture to him. He quickly arranged with the Turk, that if the latter should find a favourable opportunity for escape before Felix could return to Italy, Safie should remain as a boarder at a convent at Leghorn; and then, quitting the lovely Arabian, he hastened to Paris, and delivered himself up to the vengeance of the law, hoping to free De Lacey and Agatha by this proceeding.

"He did not succeed. They remained confined for five months before the trial took place; the result of which deprived them of their fortune, and condemned them to a perpetual exile from their native country.

"They found a miserable asylum in the cottage in Germany, where I discovered them. Felix soon learned that the treacherous Turk, for whom he and his family endured such unheard-of oppression, on discovering that his deliverer was thus reduced to poverty and impotence, became a traitor to good feeling and honour, and had quitted Italy with his daughter, insultingly sending Felix a pittance of money to aid him, as he said, in some plan of future maintenance.

"Such were the events that preyed on the heart of Felix, and rendered him, when I first saw him, the most miserable of his family. He could have endured poverty, and when this distress had been the meed of his virtue, he would have gloried in it: but the ingratitude of the Turk, and the loss of his beloved Safie, were misfortunes more bitter and irreparable. The arrival of the Arabian now infused new life into his soul.

"When the news reached Leghorn, that Felix was deprived of his wealth and rank, the merchant commanded his daughter to think no more of her lover, but to prepare to return with him to her native country. The generous nature of Safie was outraged by this command; she attempted to expostulate with her father, but he left her angrily, reiterating his tyrannical mandate.

"A few days after, the Turk entered his daughter's apartment, and told her hastily, that he had reason to believe that his residence at Leghorn had been divulged, and that he should speedily be delivered up to the French government; he had, consequently, hired a vessel to convey him to Constantinople, for which city he should sail in a few hours. He intended to leave his daughter under the care of a confidential servant, to follow at her leisure with the greater part of his property, which had not yet arrived at Leghorn.

"When alone, Safie resolved in her own mind the plan of conduct that it would become her to pursue in this emergency. A residence in Turkey was abhorrent to her; her religion and feelings were alike adverse to it. By some papers of her father's, which fell into her hands, she heard of the exile of her lover, and learnt the name of the spot where he then resided. She hesitated some time, but at length she formed her determination. Taking with her some jewels that belonged to her, and a small sum of money, she quitted Italy, with an attendant, a native of Leghorn, but who understood the common language of Turkey, and departed for Germany.

"She arrived in safety at a town about twenty leagues from the cottage of De Lacey, when her attendant fell dangerously ill. Safie nursed her with the most devoted affection; but the poor girl died, and the Arabian was left alone, unacquainted with the language of the country, and utterly ignorant of the customs of the world. She fell, however, into good hands. The Italian had mentioned the name of the spot for which they were bound; and, after her death, the woman of the house in which they had lived took care that Safie should arrive in safety at the cottage of her lover."

Chapter 7.

"Such was the history of my beloved cottagers. It impressed me deeply. I learned, from the views of social life which it developed, to admire their virtues, and to deprecate the vices of mankind.

"As yet I looked upon crime as a distant evil; benevolence and generosity were ever present before me, inciting within me a desire to become an actor in the busy scene where so many admirable qualities were called forth and displayed. But, in giving an account of the progress of my intellect, I must not omit a circumstance which occurred in the beginning of the month of August of the same year.

"One night, during my accustomed visit to the neighbouring wood, where I collected my own food, and brought home firing for my protectors, I found on the ground a leathern portmanteau, containing several articles of dress and some books. I eagerly seized the prize, and returned with it to my hovel. Fortunately the books were written in the language the elements of which I had acquired at the cottage; they consisted of *Paradise Lost*, a volume of

Plutarch's Lives, and the *Sorrows of Werter*.[2] The possession of these treasures gave me extreme delight; I now continually studied and exercised my mind upon these histories, whilst my friends were employed in their ordinary occupations.

"I can hardly describe to you the effect of these books. They produced in me an infinity of new images and feelings, that sometimes raised me to ecstacy, but more frequently sunk me into the lowest dejection. In the *Sorrows of Werter*, besides the interest of its simple and affecting story, so many opinions are canvassed, and so many lights thrown upon what had hitherto been to me obscure subjects, that I found in it a never-ending source of speculation and astonishment. The gentle and domestic manners it described, combined with lofty sentiments and feelings, which had for their object something out of self,[3] accorded well with my experience among my protectors, and with the wants which were for ever alive in my own bosom. But I thought Werter himself a more divine being than I had ever beheld or imagined; his character contained no pretension, but it sunk deep. The disquisitions upon death and suicide were calculated to fill me with wonder. I did not pretend to enter into the merits of the case, yet I inclined towards the opinions of the hero, whose extinction I wept, without precisely understanding it.

"As I read, however, I applied much personally to my own feelings and condition. I found myself similar, yet at the same time strangely unlike the beings concerning whom I read, and to whose conversation I was a listener. I sympathized with, and partly understood them, but I was unformed in mind; I was dependent on none, and related to none. 'The path of my departure was free;'[4] and there was none to lament my annihilation. My person was hideous, and my stature gigantic: what did this mean? Who was I? What was I? Whence did I come? What was my destination? These questions continually recurred, but I was unable to solve them.

"The volume of *Plutarch's Lives* which I possessed, contained the histories of the first founders of the ancient republics. This book had a far different effect upon me from the *Sorrows of Werter*. I learned from Werter's imaginations despondency and gloom: but Plutarch taught me high thoughts; he elevated me above the wretched sphere of my own reflections, to admire and love the heroes of past ages. Many things I read surpassed my understanding and experience. I had a very confused knowledge of kingdoms, wide extents of country, mighty rivers, and boundless seas. But I was perfectly unacquainted with towns, and large assemblages of men. The cottage of my protectors had been the only school in which I had studied human nature; but this book developed new and mightier scenes of action. I read of men concerned in public affairs governing or massacring their species. I felt the greatest ardour for virtue rise within me, and abhorrence for vice, as far as I understood the signification of those terms, relative as they were, as I applied them, to pleasure and pain alone. Induced by these feelings, I was

2. The books are in French translations. *Plutarch's Lives*, by the Greek biographer Plutarch (ca. 50–ca. 125 C.E.), recounts the lives of Greek and Roman notables in parallel pairs. *The Sorrows of Young Werther* was an enormously popular and influential novel (1774) by the German author Johann Wolfgang von Goethe about a sensitive and passionate artist who, hopelessly in love with a young woman betrothed to another, shoots himself in despair.
3. Selfless.
4. Alteration of Percy Shelley's *Mutability*, line 14 (p. 701).

of course led to admire peaceable law-givers, Numa, Solon, and Lycurgus, in preference to Romulus and Theseus.[5] The patriarchal lives[6] of my protectors caused these impressions to take a firm hold on my mind; perhaps, if my first introduction to humanity had been made by a young soldier, burning for glory and slaughter, I should have been imbued with different sensations.

"But *Paradise Lost* excited different and far deeper emotions. I read it, as I had read the other volumes which had fallen into my hands, as a true history. It moved every feeling of wonder and awe, that the picture of an omnipotent God warring with his creatures was capable of exciting. I often referred the several situations, as their similarity struck me, to my own. Like Adam, I was created apparently united by no link to any other being in existence; but his state was far different from mine in every other respect. He had come forth from the hands of God a perfect creature, happy and prosperous, guarded by the especial care of his Creator; he was allowed to converse with, and acquire knowledge from beings of a superior nature: but I was wretched, helpless, and alone. Many times I considered Satan as the fitter emblem of my condition; for often, like him, when I viewed the bliss of my protectors, the bitter gall of envy rose within me.

"Another circumstance strengthened and confirmed these feelings. Soon after my arrival in the hovel, I discovered some papers in the pocket of the dress[7] which I had taken from your laboratory. At first I had neglected them; but now that I was able to decypher the characters in which they were written, I began to study them with diligence. It was your journal of the four months that preceded my creation. You minutely described in these papers every step you took in the progress of your work; this history was mingled with accounts of domestic occurrences. You, doubtless, recollect these papers. Here they are. Every thing is related in them which bears reference to my accursed origin; the whole detail of that series of disgusting circumstances which produced it is set in view; the minutest description of my odious and loathsome person is given, in language which painted your own horrors, and rendered mine ineffaceable. I sickened as I read. 'Hateful day when I received life!' I exclaimed in agony. 'Cursed creator! Why did you form a monster so hideous that even you turned from me in disgust? God in pity made man beautiful and alluring, after his own image; but my form is a filthy type of your's, more horrid from its very resemblance. Satan had his companions, fellow-devils, to admire and encourage him; but I am solitary and detested.'

"These were the reflections of my hours of despondency and solitude; but when I contemplated the virtues of the cottagers, their amiable and benevolent dispositions, I persuaded myself that when they should become acquainted with my admiration of their virtues, they would compassionate me, and overlook my personal deformity. Could they turn from their door one, however monstrous, who solicited their compassion and friendship? I

5. Only Solon is a historical figure; the others are legendary. Numa Pompilius, the second king of Rome, had a long and peaceful reign that was regarded as a kind of golden age. Solon (ca. 640–ca. 558 B.C.E.) was both a statesman and a poet, famed for instituting an enlightened constitution for Athens. Lycurgus was a reformer of the laws of Sparta. Romulus, held to be a cofounder of Rome with his twin brother Remus, later murdered his brother and planned the rape of the Sabine women. Theseus abandoned Ariadne, after she had given him a thread by which, after killing the Minotaur, he was able to find his way out of the monster's Labyrinth.
6. Lives that are governed by a wise and venerable man.
7. Protective outer garment.

resolved, at least, not to despair, but in every way to fit myself for an interview with them which would decide my fate. I postponed this attempt for some months longer; for the importance attached to its success inspired me with a dread lest I should fail. Besides, I found that my understanding improved so much with every day's experience, that I was unwilling to commence this undertaking until a few more months should have added to my wisdom.

"Several changes, in the mean time, took place in the cottage. The presence of Safie diffused happiness among its inhabitants; and I also found that a greater degree of plenty reigned there. Felix and Agatha spent more time in amusement and conversation, and were assisted in their labours by servants. They did not appear rich, but they were contented and happy; their feelings were serene and peaceful, while mine became every day more tumultuous. Increase of knowledge only discovered to me more clearly what a wretched outcast I was. I cherished hope, it is true; but it vanished, when I beheld my person reflected in water, or my shadow in the moon-shine, even as that frail image and that inconstant shade.

"I endeavoured to crush these fears, and to fortify myself for the trial which in a few months I resolved to undergo; and sometimes I allowed my thoughts, unchecked by reason, to ramble in the fields of Paradise, and dared to fancy amiable and lovely creatures sympathizing with my feelings and cheering my gloom; their angelic countenances breathed smiles of consolation. But it was all a dream: no Eve soothed my sorrows, or shared my thoughts; I was alone. I remembered Adam's supplication to his Creator;[8] but where was mine? he had abandoned me, and, in the bitterness of my heart, I cursed him.

"Autumn passed thus. I saw, with surprise and grief, the leaves decay and fall, and nature again assume the barren and bleak appearance it had worn when I first beheld the woods and the lovely moon. Yet I did not heed the bleakness of the weather; I was better fitted by my conformation[9] for the endurance of cold than heat. But my chief delights were the sight of the flowers, the birds, and all the gay apparel of summer; when those deserted me, I turned with more attention towards the cottagers. Their happiness was not decreased by the absence of summer. They loved, and sympathized with one another; and their joys, depending on each other, were not interrupted by the casualties that took place around them. The more I saw of them, the greater became my desire to claim their protection and kindness; my heart yearned to be known and loved by these amiable creatures: to see their sweet looks turned towards me with affection, was the utmost limit of my ambition. I dared not think that they would turn them from me with disdain and horror. The poor that stopped at their door were never driven away. I asked, it is true, for greater treasures than a little food or rest; I required kindness and sympathy; but I did not believe myself utterly unworthy of it.

"The winter advanced, and an entire revolution of the seasons had taken place since I awoke into life. My attention, at this time, was solely directed towards my plan of introducing myself into the cottage of my protectors. I revolved many projects; but that on which I finally fixed was, to enter the dwelling when the blind old man should be alone. I had sagacity enough to discover, that the unnatural hideousness of my person was the chief object

---

8. The solitary Adam begs God for "a human consort" in *Paradise Lost* 8.364–451. 9. Constitution.

of horror with those who had formerly beheld me. My voice, although harsh, had nothing terrible in it; I thought, therefore, that if, in the absence of his children, I could gain the good-will and mediation of the old De Lacy, I might, by his means, be tolerated by my younger protectors.

"One day, when the sun shone on the red leaves that strewed the ground, and diffused cheerfulness, although it denied warmth, Safie, Agatha, and Felix, departed on a long country walk, and the old man, at his own desire, was left alone in the cottage. When his children had departed, he took up his guitar, and played several mournful, but sweet airs, more sweet and mournful than I had ever heard him play before. At first his countenance was illuminated with pleasure, but, as he continued, thoughtfulness and sadness succeeded; at length, laying aside the instrument, he sat absorbed in reflection.

"My heart beat quick; this was the hour and moment of trial, which would decide my hopes, or realize my fears. The servants were gone to a neighbouring fair. All was silent in and around the cottage: it was an excellent opportunity; yet, when I proceeded to execute my plan, my limbs failed me, and I sunk to the ground. Again I rose; and, exerting all the firmness of which I was master, removed the planks which I had placed before my hovel to conceal my retreat. The fresh air revived me, and, with renewed determination, I approached the door of their cottage.

"I knocked. 'Who is there?' said the old man—'Come in.'

"I entered; 'Pardon this intrusion,' said I, 'I am a traveller in want of a little rest; you would greatly oblige me, if you would allow me to remain a few minutes before the fire.'

" 'Enter,' said De Lacy; 'and I will try in what manner I can relieve your wants; but, unfortunately, my children are from home, and, as I am blind, I am afraid I shall find it difficult to procure food for you.'

" 'Do not trouble yourself, my kind host, I have food; it is warmth and rest only that I need.'

"I sat down, and a silence ensued. I knew that every minute was precious to me, yet I remained irresolute in what manner to commence the interview; when the old man addressed me—

" 'By your language, stranger, I suppose you are my countryman;—are you French?'

" 'No; but I was educated by a French family, and understand that language only. I am now going to claim the protection of some friends, whom I sincerely love, and of whose favour I have some hopes.'

" 'Are these Germans?'

" 'No, they are French. But let us change the subject. I am an unfortunate and deserted creature; I look around, and I have no relation or friend upon earth. These amiable people to whom I go have never seen me, and know little of me. I am full of fears; for if I fail there, I am an outcast in the world for ever.'

" 'Do not despair. To be friendless is indeed to be unfortunate; but the hearts of men, when unprejudiced by any obvious self-interest, are full of brotherly love and charity. Rely, therefore, on your hopes; and if these friends are good and amiable, do not despair.'

" 'They are kind—they are the most excellent creatures in the world; but, unfortunately, they are prejudiced against me. I have good dispositions; my life has been hitherto harmless, and, in some degree, beneficial; but a fatal prejudice clouds their eyes, and where they ought to see a feeling and kind friend, they behold only a detestable monster.'

" 'That is indeed unfortunate; but if you are really blameless, cannot you undeceive them?'

" 'I am about to undertake that task; and it is on that account that I feel so many overwhelming terrors. I tenderly love these friends; I have, unknown to them, been for many months in the habits of daily kindness towards them; but they believe that I wish to injure them, and it is that prejudice which I wish to overcome.'

" 'Where do these friends reside?'

" 'Near this spot.'

"The old man paused, and then continued, 'If you will unreservedly confide to me the particulars of your tale, I perhaps may be of use in undeceiving them. I am blind, and cannot judge of your countenance, but there is something in your words which persuades me that you are sincere. I am poor, and an exile; but it will afford me true pleasure to be in any way serviceable to a human creature.'

" 'Excellent man! I thank you, and accept your generous offer. You raise me from the dust by this kindness; and I trust that, by your aid, I shall not be driven from the society and sympathy of your fellow-creatures.'

" 'Heaven forbid! even if you were really criminal; for that can only drive you to desperation, and not instigate you to virtue. I also am unfortunate; I and my family have been condemned, although innocent: judge, therefore, if I do not feel for your misfortunes.'

" 'How can I thank you, my best and only benefactor? from your lips first have I heard the voice of kindness directed towards me; I shall be for ever grateful; and your present humanity assures me of success with those friends whom I am on the point of meeting.'

" 'May I know the names and residence of those friends?'

"I paused. This, I thought, was the moment of decision, which was to rob me of, or bestow happiness on me for ever. I struggled vainly for firmness sufficient to answer him, but the effort destroyed all my remaining strength; I sank on the chair, and sobbed aloud. At that moment I heard the steps of my younger protectors. I had not a moment to lose; but, seizing the hand of the old man, I cried, 'Now is the time!—save and protect me! You and your family are the friends whom I seek. Do not you desert me in the hour of trial!'

" 'Great God!' exclaimed the old man, 'who are you?'

"At that instant the cottage door was opened, and Felix, Safie, and Agatha entered. Who can describe their horror and consternation on beholding me? Agatha fainted; and Safie, unable to attend to her friend, rushed out of the cottage. Felix darted forward, and with supernatural force tore me from his father, to whose knees I clung: in a transport of fury, he dashed me to the ground, and struck me violently with a stick. I could have torn him limb from limb, as the lion rends the antelope. But my heart sunk within me as with bitter sickness, and I refrained. I saw him on the point of repeating his blow, when, overcome by pain and anguish, I quitted the cottage, and in the general tumult escaped unperceived to my hovel."

Chapter 8.

"Cursed, cursed creator! Why did I live? Why, in that instant, did I not extinguish the spark of existence which you had so wantonly bestowed? I know not; despair had not yet taken possession of me; my feelings were those of rage and revenge. I could with pleasure have destroyed the cottage and its inhabitants, and have glutted myself with their shrieks and misery.

"When night came, I quitted my retreat, and wandered in the wood; and now, no longer restrained by the fear of discovery, I gave vent to my anguish in fearful howlings. I was like a wild beast that had broken the toils; destroying the objects that obstructed me, and ranging through the wood with a stag-like swiftness. Oh! what a miserable night I passed! the cold stars shone in mockery, and the bare trees waved their branches above me: now and then the sweet voice of a bird burst forth amidst the universal stillness. All, save I, were at rest or in enjoyment: I, like the arch fiend, bore a hell within me;[1] and, finding myself unsympathized with, wished to tear up the trees, spread havoc and destruction around me, and then to have sat down and enjoyed the ruin.

"But this was a luxury of sensation that could not endure; I became fatigued with excess of bodily exertion, and sank on the damp grass in the sick impotence of despair. There was none among the myriads of men that existed who would pity or assist me; and should I feel kindness towards my enemies? No: from that moment I declared everlasting war against the species, and, more than all, against him who had formed me, and sent me forth to this insupportable misery.

"The sun rose; I heard the voices of men, and knew that it was impossible to return to my retreat during that day. Accordingly I hid myself in some thick underwood, determining to devote the ensuing hours to reflection on my situation.

"The pleasant sunshine, and the pure air of day, restored me to some degree of tranquillity; and when I considered what had passed at the cottage, I could not help believing that I had been too hasty in my conclusions. I had certainly acted imprudently. It was apparent that my conversation had interested the father in my behalf, and I was a fool in having exposed my person to the horror of his children. I ought to have familiarized the old De Lacy to me, and by degrees have discovered myself to the rest of his family, when they should have been prepared for my approach. But I did not believe my errors to be irretrievable; and, after much consideration, I resolved to return to the cottage, seek the old man, and by my representations win him to my party.

"These thoughts calmed me, and in the afternoon I sank into a profound sleep; but the fever of my blood did not allow me to be visited by peaceful dreams. The horrible scene of the preceding day was for ever acting before my eyes; the females were flying, and the enraged Felix tearing me from his father's feet. I awoke exhausted; and, finding that it was already night, I crept forth from my hiding-place, and went in search of food.

"When my hunger was appeased, I directed my steps towards the well-known path that conducted to the cottage. All there was at peace. I crept

---

1. Echoing Satan, *Paradise Lost* 4.75: "Which way I fly is Hell; myself am Hell."

into my hovel, and remained in silent expectation of the accustomed hour when the family arose. That hour past, the sun mounted high in the heavens, but the cottagers did not appear. I trembled violently, apprehending some dreadful misfortune. The inside of the cottage was dark, and I heard no motion; I cannot describe the agony of this suspence.

"Presently two countrymen passed by; but, pausing near the cottage, they entered into conversation, using violent gesticulations; but I did not understand what they said, as they spoke the language of the country,[2] which differed from that of my protectors. Soon after, however, Felix approached with another man: I was surprised, as I knew that he had not quitted the cottage that morning, and waited anxiously to discover, from his discourse, the meaning of these unusual appearances.

" 'Do you consider,' said his companion to him, 'that you will be obliged to pay three months' rent, and to lose the produce of your garden? I do not wish to take any unfair advantage, and I beg therefore that you will take some days to consider of your determination.'

" 'It is utterly useless,' replied Felix, 'we can never again inhabit your cottage. The life of my father is in the greatest danger, owing to the dreadful circumstance that I have related. My wife and my sister will never recover their horror. I entreat you not to reason with me any more. Take possession of your tenement, and let me fly from this place.'

"Felix trembled violently as he said this. He and his companion entered the cottage, in which they remained for a few minutes, and then departed. I never saw any of the family of De Lacy more.

"I continued for the remainder of the day in my hovel in a state of utter and stupid despair. My protectors had departed, and had broken the only link that held me to the world. For the first time the feelings of revenge and hatred filled my bosom, and I did not strive to controul them; but, allowing myself to be borne away by the stream, I bent my mind towards injury and death. When I thought of my friends, of the mild voice of De Lacy, the gentle eyes of Agatha, and the exquisite beauty of the Arabian, these thoughts vanished, and a gush of tears somewhat soothed me. But again, when I reflected that they had spurned and deserted me, anger returned, a rage of anger; and, unable to injure any thing human, I turned my fury towards inanimate objects. As night advanced, I placed a variety of combustibles around the cottage; and, after having destroyed every vestige of cultivation in the garden, I waited with forced impatience until the moon had sunk to commence my operations.

"As the night advanced, a fierce wind arose from the woods, and quickly dispersed the clouds that had loitered in the heavens: the blast tore along like a mighty avalanche, and produced a kind of insanity in my spirits, that burst all bounds of reason and reflection. I lighted the dry branch of a tree, and danced with fury around the devoted cottage, my eyes still fixed on the western horizon, the edge of which the moon nearly touched. A part of its orb was at length hid, and I waved my brand; it sunk, and, with a loud scream, I fired the straw, and heath, and bushes, which I had collected. The wind fanned the fire, and the cottage was quickly enveloped by the flames, which clung to it, and licked it with their forked and destroying tongues.

2. German.

"As soon as I was convinced that no assistance could save any part of the habitation, I quitted the scene, and sought for refuge in the woods.

"And now, with the world before me, whither should I bend my steps?[3] I resolved to fly far from the scene of my misfortunes; but to me, hated and despised, every country must be equally horrible. At length the thought of you crossed my mind. I learned from your papers that you were my father, my creator; and to whom could I apply with more fitness than to him who had given me life? Among the lessons that Felix had bestowed upon Safie geography had not been omitted: I had learned from these the relative situations of the different countries of the earth. You had mentioned Geneva as the name of your native town; and towards this place I resolved to proceed.

"But how was I to direct myself? I knew that I must travel in a south-westerly direction to reach my destination; but the sun was my only guide. I did not know the names of the towns that I was to pass through, nor could I ask information from a single human being; but I did not despair. From you only could I hope for succour, although towards you I felt no sentiment but that of hatred. Unfeeling, heartless creator! you had endowed me with perceptions and passions, and then cast me abroad an object for the scorn and horror of mankind. But on you only had I any claim for pity and redress, and from you I determined to seek that justice which I vainly attempted to gain from any other being that wore the human form.

"My travels were long, and the sufferings I endured intense. It was late in autumn when I quitted the district where I had so long resided. I travelled only at night, fearful of encountering the visage of a human being. Nature decayed around me, and the sun became heatless; rain and snow poured around me; mighty rivers were frozen; the surface of the earth was hard, and chill, and bare, and I found no shelter. Oh, earth! how often did I imprecate curses on the cause of my being! The mildness of my nature had fled, and all within me was turned to gall and bitterness. The nearer I approached to your habitation, the more deeply did I feel the spirit of revenge enkindled in my heart. Snow fell, and the waters were hardened, but I rested not. A few incidents now and then directed me, and I possessed a map of the country; but I often wandered wide from my path. The agony of my feelings allowed me no respite: no incident occurred from which my rage and misery could not extract its food; but a circumstance that happened when I arrived on the confines of Switzerland, when the sun had recovered its warmth, and the earth again began to look green, confirmed in an especial manner the bitterness and horror of my feelings.

"I generally rested during the day, and travelled only when I was secured by night from the view of man. One morning, however, finding that my path lay through a deep wood, I ventured to continue my journey after the sun had risen; the day, which was one of the first of spring, cheered even me by the loveliness of its sunshine and the balminess of the air. I felt emotions of gentleness and pleasure, that had long appeared dead, revive within me. Half surprised by the novelty of these sensations, I allowed myself to be borne away by them; and, forgetting my solitude and deformity, dared to be happy. Soft tears again bedewed my cheeks, and I even raised my humid eyes with thankfulness towards the blessed sun which bestowed such joy upon me.

---

3. An allusion to the close of *Paradise Lost* 12.646–49, beginning: "The world was all before them, where to choose / Their place of rest."

"I continued to wind among the paths of the wood, until I came to its boundary, which was skirted by a deep and rapid river, into which many of the trees bent their branches, now budding with the fresh spring. Here I paused, not exactly knowing what path to pursue, when I heard the sound of voices, that induced me to conceal myself under the shade of a cypress. I was scarcely hid, when a young girl came running towards the spot where I was concealed, laughing as if she ran from some one in sport. She continued her course along the precipitous sides of the river, when suddenly her foot slipt; and she fell into the rapid stream. I rushed from my hiding place, and, with extreme labour from the force of the current, saved her, and dragged her to shore. She was senseless; and I endeavoured, by every means in my power, to restore animation, when I was suddenly interrupted by the approach of a rustic, who was probably the person from whom she had playfully fled. On seeing me, he darted towards me, and, tearing the girl from my arms, hastened towards the deeper parts of the wood. I followed speedily, I hardly knew why; but when the man saw me draw near, he aimed a gun, which he carried, at my body, and fired. I sunk to the ground, and my injurer, with increased swiftness, escaped into the wood.

"This was then the reward of my benevolence! I had saved a human being from destruction, and, as a recompence, I now writhed under the miserable pain of a wound, which shattered the flesh and bone. The feelings of kindness and gentleness, which I had entertained but a few moments before, gave place to hellish rage and gnashing of teeth. Inflamed by pain, I vowed eternal hatred and vengeance to all mankind. But the agony of my wound overcame me; my pulses paused, and I fainted.

"For some weeks I led a miserable life in the woods, endeavouring to cure the wound which I had received. The ball had entered my shoulder, and I knew not whether it had remained there or passed through; at any rate I had no means of extracting it. My sufferings were augmented also by the oppressive sense of the injustice and ingratitude of their infliction. My daily vows rose for revenge—a deep and deadly revenge, such as would alone compensate for the outrages and anguish I had endured.

"After some weeks my wound healed, and I continued my journey. The labours I endured were no longer to be alleviated by the bright sun or gentle breezes of spring; all joy was but a mockery, which insulted my desolate state, and made me feel more painfully that I was not made for the enjoyment of pleasure.

"But my toils now drew near a close; and, two months from this time, I reached the environs of Geneva.

"It was evening when I arrived, and I retired to a hiding-place among the fields that surround it, to meditate in what manner I should apply to you. I was oppressed by fatigue and hunger, and far too unhappy to enjoy the gentle breezes of evening, or the prospect of the sun setting behind the stupendous mountains of Jura.

"At this time a slight sleep relieved me from the pain of reflection, which was disturbed by the approach of a beautiful child, who came running into the recess I had chosen with all the sportiveness of infancy. Suddenly, as I gazed on him, an idea seized me, that this little creature was unprejudiced, and had lived too short a time to have imbibed a horror of deformity. If, therefore, I could seize him, and educate him as my companion and friend, I should not be so desolate in this peopled earth.

"Urged by this impulse, I seized on the boy as he passed, and drew him towards me. As soon as he beheld my form, he placed his hands before his eyes, and uttered a shrill scream: I drew his hand forcibly from his face, and said, 'Child, what is the meaning of this? I do not intend to hurt you; listen to me.'

"He struggled violently; 'Let me go,' he cried; 'monster! ugly wretch! you wish to eat me, and tear me to pieces—You are an ogre—Let me go, or I will tell my papa.'

" 'Boy, you will never see your father again; you must come with me.'

" 'Hideous monster! let me go; My papa is a Syndic—he is M. Frankenstein—he would punish you. You dare not keep me.'

" 'Frankenstein! you belong then to my enemy—to him towards whom I have sworn eternal revenge; you shall be my first victim.'

"The child still struggled, and loaded me with epithets which carried despair to my heart: I grasped his throat to silence him, and in a moment he lay dead at my feet.

"I gazed on my victim, and my heart swelled with exultation and hellish triumph: clapping my hands, I exclaimed, 'I, too, can create desolation; my enemy is not impregnable; this death will carry despair to him, and a thousand other miseries shall torment and destroy him.'

"As I fixed my eyes on the child, I saw something glittering on his breast. I took it; it was a portrait of a most lovely woman. In spite of my malignity, it softened and attracted me. For a few moments I gazed with delight on her dark eyes, fringerd by deep lashes, and her lovely lips; but presently my rage returned: I remembered that I was for ever deprived of the delights that such beautiful creatures could bestow; and that she whose resemblance I contemplated would, in regarding me, have changed that air of divine benignity to one expressive of disgust and affright.

"Can you wonder that such thoughts transported me with rage? I only wonder that at that moment, instead of venting my sensations in exclamations and agony, I did not rush among mankind, and perish in the attempt to destroy them.

"While I was overcome by these feelings, I left the spot where I had committed the murder, and was seeking a more secluded hiding-place, when I perceived a woman passing near me. She was young, not indeed so beautiful as her whose portrait I held, but of an agreeable aspect, and blooming in the loveliness of youth and health. Here, I thought, is one of those whose smiles are bestowed on all but me; she shall not escape: thanks to the lessons of Felix, and the sanguinary[4] laws of man, I have learned how to work mischief. I approached her unperceived, and placed the portrait securely in one of the folds of her dress.

"For some days I haunted the spot where these scenes had taken place; sometimes wishing to see you, sometimes resolved to quit the world and its miseries for ever. At length I wandered towards these mountains, and have ranged through their immense recesses, consumed by a burning passion which you alone can gratify. We may not part until you have promised to comply with my requisition.[5] I am alone, and miserable; man will not associate with me; but one as deformed and horrible as myself would not deny

4. Bloodthirsty.

5. Demand.

herself to me. My companion must be of the same species, and have the same defects. This being you must create."

Chapter 9.

The being finished speaking, and fixed his looks upon me in expectation of a reply. But I was bewildered, perplexed, and unable to arrange my ideas sufficiently to understand the full extent of his proposition. He continued—

"You must create a female for me, with whom I can live in the interchange of those sympathies necessary for my being. This you alone can do; and I demand it of you as a right which you must not refuse."

The latter part of his tale had kindled anew in me the anger that had died away while he narrated his peaceful life among the cottagers, and, as he said this, I could no longer suppress the rage that burned within me.

"I do refuse it," I replied; "and no torture shall ever extort a consent from me. You may render me the most miserable of men, but you shall never make me base in my own eyes. Shall I create another like yourself, whose joint wickedness might desolate the world. Begone! I have answered you; you may torture me, but I will never consent."

"You are in the wrong," replied the fiend; "and, instead of threatening, I am content to reason with you. I am malicious because I am miserable; am I not shunned and hated by all mankind? You, my creator, would tear me to pieces, and triumph; remember that, and tell me why I should pity man more than he pities me? You would not call it murder, if you could precipitate me into one of those ice-rifts, and destroy my frame, the work of your own hands. Shall I respect man, when he contemns[6] me? Let him live with me in the interchange of kindness, and, instead of injury, I would bestow every benefit upon him with tears of gratitude at his acceptance. But that cannot be; the human senses are insurmountable barriers to our union. Yet mine shall not be the submission of abject slavery. I will revenge my injuries: if I cannot inspire love, I will cause fear; and chiefly towards you my arch-enemy, because my creator, do I swear inextinguishable hatred. Have a care: I will work at your destruction, nor finish until I desolate your heart, so that you curse the hour of your birth."

A fiendish rage animated him as he said this; his face was wrinkled into contortions too horrible for human eyes to behold; but presently he calmed himself, and proceeded—

"I intended to reason. This passion is detrimental to me; for you do not reflect that you are the cause of its excess. If any being felt emotions of benevolence towards me, I should return them an hundred and an hundred fold; for that one creature's sake, I would make peace with the whole kind! But I now indulge in dreams of bliss that cannot be realized. What I ask of you is reasonable and moderate; I demand a creature of another sex, but as hideous as myself: the gratification is small, but it is all that I can receive, and it shall content me. It is true, we shall be monsters, cut off from all the world; but on that account we shall be more attached to one another. Our lives will not be happy, but they will be harmless, and free from the misery I now feel. Oh! my creator, make me happy; let me feel gratitude towards

---

6. Views with contempt.

you for one benefit! Let me see that I excite the sympathy of some existing thing; do not deny me my request!"

I was moved. I shuddered when I thought of the possible consequences of my consent; but I felt that there was some justice in his argument. His tale, and the feelings he now expressed, proved him to be a creature of fine sensations; and did I not, as his maker, owe him all the portion of happiness that it was in my power to bestow? He saw my change of feeling, and continued—

"If you consent, neither you nor any other human being shall ever see us again: I will go to the vast wilds of South America. My food is not that of man; I do not destroy the lamb and the kid, to glut my appetite; acorns and berries afford me sufficient nourishment. My companion will be of the same nature as myself, and will be content with the same fare. We shall make our bed of dried leaves; the sun will shine on us as on man, and will ripen our food. The picture I present to you is peaceful and human, and you must feel that you could deny it only in the wantonness of power and cruelty. Pitiless as you have been towards me, I now see compassion in your eyes; let me seize the favourable moment, and persuade you to promise what I so ardently desire."

"You propose," replied I, "to fly from the habitations of man, to dwell in those wilds where the beasts of the field will be your only companions. How can you, who long for the love and sympathy of man, persevere in this exile? You will return, and again seek their kindness, and you will meet with their detestation; your evil passions will be renewed, and you will then have a companion to aid you in the task of destruction. This may not be; cease to argue the point, for I cannot consent."

"How inconstant are your feelings! but a moment ago you were moved by my representations, and why do you again harden yourself to my complaints? I swear to you, by the earth which I inhabit, and by you that made me, that, with the companion you bestow, I will quit the neighbourhood of man, and dwell, as it may chance, in the most savage of places. My evil passions will have fled, for I shall meet with sympathy; my life will flow quietly away, and, in my dying moments, I shall not curse my maker."

His words had a strange effect upon me. I compassionated him, and sometimes felt a wish to console him; but when I looked upon him, when I saw the filthy mass that moved and talked, my heart sickened, and my feelings were altered to those of horror and hatred. I tried to stifle these sensations; I thought, that as I could not sympathize with him, I had no right to withhold from him the small portion of happiness which was yet in my power to bestow.

"You swear," I said, "to be harmless; but have you not already stewn a degree of malice that should reasonably make me distrust you? May not even this be a feint that will increase your triumph by affording a wider scope for your revenge?"

"How is this? I thought I had moved your compassion, and yet you still refuse to bestow on me the only benefit that can soften my heart, and render me harmless. If I have no ties and no affections, hatred and vice must be my portion; the love of another will destroy the cause of my crimes, and I shall become a thing, of whose existence every one will be ignorant. My vices are the children of a forced solitude that I abhor; and my virtues will necessarily arise when I live in communion with an equal. I shall feel the affections of a sensitive being, and become linked to the chain of existence and events, from which I am now excluded."

I paused some time to reflect on all he had related, and the various arguments which he had employed. I thought of the promise of virtues which he had displayed on the opening of his existence, and the subsequent blight of all kindly feeling by the loathing and scorn which his protectors had manifested towards him. His power and threats were not omitted in my calculations: a creature who could exist in the ice caves of the glaciers, and hide himself from pursuit among the ridges of inaccessible precipices, was a being possessing faculties it would be vain to cope with. After a long pause of reflection, I concluded, that the justice due both to him and my fellow-creatures demanded of me that I should comply with his request. Turning to him, therefore, I said—

"I consent to your demand, on your solemn oath to quit Europe for ever, and every other place in the neighborhood of man, as soon as I shall deliver into your hands a female who will accompany you in your exile."

"I swear," he cried, "by the sun, and by the blue sky of heaven, that if you grant my prayer, while they exist you shall never behold me again. Depart to your home, and commence your labours: I shall watch their progress with unutterable anxiety; and fear not but that when you are ready I shall appear."

Saying this, he suddenly quitted me, fearful, perhaps, of any change in my sentiments. I saw him descend the mountain with greater speed than the flight of an eagle, and quickly lost him among the undulations of the sea of ice.

His tale had occupied the whole day; and the sun was upon the verge of the horizon when he departed. I knew that I ought to hasten my descent towards the valley, as I should soon be encompassed in darkness; but my heart was heavy, and my steps slow. The labour of winding among the little paths of the mountains, and fixing my feet firmly as I advanced, perplexed me, occupied as I was by the emotions which the occurrences of the day had produced. Night was far advanced, when I came to the half-way resting-place, and seated myself beside the fountain. The stars shone at intervals, as the clouds passed from over them; the dark pines rose before me, and every here and there a broken tree lay on the ground: it was a scene of wonderful solemnity, and stirred strange thoughts within me. I wept bitterly; and, clasping my hands in agony, I exclaimed, "Oh! stars, and clouds, and winds, ye are all about to mock me: if ye really pity me, crush sensation and memory; let me become as nought; but if not, depart, depart and leave me in darkness."

These were wild and miserable thoughts; but I cannot describe to you how the eternal twinkling of the stars weighed upon me, and how I listened to every blast of wind, as if it were a dull ugly siroc[7] on its way to consume me.

Morning dawned before I arrived at the village of Chamounix; but my presence, so haggard and strange, hardly calmed the fears of my family, who had waited the whole night in anxious expectation of my return.

The following day we returned to Geneva. The intention of my father in coming had been to divert my mind, and to restore me to my lost tranquillity;

7. The sirocco, a hot wind that blows across the Mediterranean from North Africa.

but the medicine had been fatal. And, unable to account for the excess of misery I appeared to suffer, he hastened to return home, hoping the quiet and monotony of a domestic life would by degrees alleviate my sufferings from whatsoever cause they might spring.

For myself, I was passive in all their arrangements; and the gentle affection of my beloved Elizabeth was inadequate to draw me from the depth of my despair. The promise I had made to the dæmon weighed upon my mind, like Dante's iron cowl on the heads of the hellish hypocrites.[8] All pleasures of earth and sky passed before me like a dream, and that thought only had to me the reality of life. Can you wonder, that sometimes a kind of insanity possessed me, or that I saw continually about me a multitude of filthy animals inflicting on me incessant torture, that often extorted screams and bitter groans?

By degrees, however, these feelings became calmed. I entered again into the every-day scene of life, if not with interest, at least with some degree of tranquillity.

VOLUME 3

Chapter 1.

Day after day, week after week, passed away on my return to Geneva; and I could not collect the courage to recommence my work. I feared the vengeance of the disappointed fiend, yet I was unable to overcome my repugnance to the task which was enjoined me. I found that I could not compose a female without again devoting several months to profound study and laborious disquisition.[1] I had heard of some discoveries having been made by an English philosopher, the knowledge of which was material to my success, and I sometimes thought of obtaining my father's consent to visit England for this purpose; but I clung to every pretence of delay, and could not resolve to interrupt my returning tranquillity. My health, which had hitherto declined, was now much restored; and my spirits, when unchecked by the memory of my unhappy promise, rose proportionably. My father saw this change with pleasure, and he turned his thoughts towards the best method of eradicating the remains of my melancholy, which every now and then would return by fits, and with a devouring blackness overcast the approaching sunshine. At these moments I took refuge in the most perfect solitude. I passed whole days on the lake alone in a little boat, watching the clouds, and listening to the rippling of the waves, silent and listless. But the fresh air and bright sun seldom failed to restore me to some degree of composure; and, on my return, I met the salutations of my friends with a readier smile and a more cheerful heart.

It was after my return from one of these rambles that my father, calling me aside, thus addressed me:—

"I am happy to remark, my dear son, that you have resumed your former pleasures, and seem to be returning to yourself. And yet you are still unhappy, and still avoid our society. For some time I was lost in conjecture as to the

---

8. In Dante's *Inferno* 23.58ff., the hypocrites are crushed by the burden of monks' hoods that, although gilded on the outside, are lined with lead.
1. Investigation.

cause of this; but yesterday an idea struck me, and if it is well founded, I conjure you to avow it. Reserve on such a point would be not only useless, but draw down treble misery on us all."

I trembled violently at this exordium,[2] and my father continued—

"I confess, my son, that I have always looked forward to your marriage with your cousin as the tie of our domestic comfort, and the stay of my declining years. You were attached to each other from your earliest infancy; you studied together, and appeared, in dispositions and tastes, entirely suited to one another. But so blind is the experience of man, that what I conceived to be the best assistants to my plan may have entirely destroyed it. You, perhaps, regard her as your sister, without any wish that she might become your wife. Nay, you may have met with another whom you may love; and, considering yourself as bound in honour to your cousin, this struggle may occasion the poignant misery which you appear to feel."

"My dear father, re-assure yourself. I love my cousin tenderly and sincerely. I never saw any woman who excited, as Elizabeth does, my warmest admiration and affection. My future hopes and prospects are entirely bound up in the expectation of our union."

"The expression of your sentiments on this subject, my dear Victor, gives me more pleasure than I have for some time experienced. If you feel thus, we shall assuredly be happy, however present events may cast a gloom over us. But it is this gloom, which appears to have taken so strong a hold of your mind, that I wish to dissipate. Tell me, therefore, whether you object to an immediate solemnization of the marriage. We have been unfortunate, and recent events have drawn us from that every-day tranquillity befitting my years and infirmities. You are younger; yet I do not suppose, possessed as you are of a competent fortune, that an early marriage would at all interfere with any future plans of honour and utility that you may have formed. Do not suppose, however, that I wish to dictate happiness to you, or that a delay on your part would cause me any serious uneasiness. Interpret my words with candour,[3] and answer me, I conjure you, with confidence and sincerity."

I listened to my father in silence, and remained for some time incapable of offering any reply. I revolved rapidly in my mind a multitude of thoughts, and endeavoured to arrive at some conclusion. Alas! to me the idea of an immediate union with my cousin was one of horror and dismay. I was bound by a solemn promise, which I had not yet fulfilled, and dared not break; or, if I did, what manifold miseries might not impend over me and my devoted family! Could I enter into a festival with this deadly weight yet hanging round my neck, and bowing me to the ground. I must perform my engagement,[4] and let the monster depart with his mate, before I allowed myself to enjoy the delight of an union from which I expected peace.

I remembered also the necessity imposed upon me of either journeying to England, or entering into a long correspondence with those philosophers of that country, whose knowledge and discoveries were of indispensable use to me in my present undertaking. The latter method of obtaining the desired intelligence was dilatory and unsatisfactory: besides, any variation was agreeable to me, and I was delighted with the idea of spending a year or two in

2. Introductory part of a speech.
3. Impartiality.

4. Obligation.

change of scene and variety of occupation, in absence from my family; during which period some event might happen which would restore me to them in peace and happiness: my promise might be fulfilled, and the monster have departed; or some accident might occur to destroy him, and put an end to my slavery for ever.

These feelings dictated my answer to my father. I expressed a wish to visit England; but, concealing the true reasons of this request, I clothed my desires under the guise of wishing to travel and see the world before I sat down for life within the walls of my native town.

I urged my entreaty with earnestness, and my father was easily induced to comply; for a more indulgent and less dictatorial parent did not exist upon earth. Our plan was soon arranged. I should travel to Strasburgh, where Clerval would join me. Some short time would be spent in the towns of Holland, and our principal stay would be in England. We should return by France; and it was agreed that the tour should occupy the space of two years.

My father pleased himself with the reflection, that my union with Elizabeth should take place immediately on my return to Geneva. "These two years," said he, "will pass swiftly, and it will be the last delay that will oppose itself to your happiness. And, indeed, I earnestly desire that period to arrive, when we shall all be united, and neither hopes or fears arise to disturb our domestic calm."

"I am content," I replied, "with your arrangement. By that time we shall both have become wiser, and I hope happier, than we at present are." I sighed; but my father kindly forbore to question me further concerning the cause of my dejection. He hoped that new scenes, and the amusement of travelling, would restore my tranquillity.

I now made arrangements for my journey; but one feeling haunted me, which filled me with fear and agitation. During my absence I should leave my friends unconscious of the existence of their enemy, and unprotected from his attacks, exasperated as he might be by my departure. But he had promised to follow me wherever I might go; and would he not accompany me to England? This imagination was dreadful in itself, but soothing, inasmuch as it supposed the safety of my friends. I was agonized with the idea of the possibility that the reverse of this might happen. But through the whole period during which I was the slave of my creature, I allowed myself to be governed by the impulses of the moment; and my present sensations strongly intimated that the fiend would follow me, and exempt my family from the danger of his machinations.

It was in the latter end of August that I departed, to pass two years of exile. Elizabeth approved of the reasons of my departure, and only regretted that she had not the same opportunities of enlarging her experience, and cultivating her understanding. She wept, however, as she bade me farewell, and entreated me to return happy and tranquil. "We all," said she, "depend upon you; and if you are miserable, what must be our feelings?"

I threw myself into the carriage that was to convey me away, hardly knowing whither I was going, and careless of what was passing around. I remembered only, and it was with a bitter anguish that I reflected on it, to order that my chemical instruments should be packed to go with me: for I resolved to fulfill my promise while abroad, and return, if possible, a free man. Filled with dreary imaginations, I passed through many beautiful and majestic scenes; but my eyes were fixed and unobserving. I could only think of the bourne[5] of my travels, and the work which was to occupy me whilst they endured.

After some days spent in listless indolence, during which I traversed many leagues, I arrived at Strasburgh, where I waited two days for Clerval. He came. Alas, how great was the contrast between us! He was alive to every new scene; joyful when he saw the beauties of the setting sun, and more happy when he beheld it rise, and recommence a new day. He pointed out to me the shifting colours of the landscape, and the appearances of the sky. "This is what it is to live;" he cried, "now I enjoy existence! But you, my dear Frankenstein, wherefore are you desponding and sorrowful?" In truth, I was occupied by gloomy thoughts, and neither saw the descent of the evening star, nor the golden sun-rise reflected in the Rhine.—And you, my friend, would be far more amused with the journal of Clerval, who observed the scenery with an eye of feeling and delight, than to listen to my reflections. I, a miserable wretch, haunted by a curse that shut up every avenue to enjoyment.

We had agreed to descend the Rhine in a boat from Strasburgh to Rotterdam, whence we might take shipping for London. During this voyage, we passed by many willowy islands, and saw several beautiful towns. We staid a day at Manheim, and, on the fifth from our departure from Strasburgh, arrived at Mayence. The course of the Rhine below Mayence becomes much more picturesque. The river descends rapidly, and winds between hills, not high, but steep, and of beautiful forms. We saw many ruined castles standing on the edges of precipices, surrounded by black woods, high and inaccessible. This part of the Rhine, indeed, presents a singularly variegated landscape. In one spot you view rugged hills, ruined castles overlooking tremendous precipices, with the dark Rhine rushing beneath; and, on the sudden turn of a promontory, flourishing vineyards, with green sloping banks, and a meandering river, and populous towns, occupy the scene.

We travelled at the time of the vintage, and heard the song of the labourers, as we glided down the stream. Even I, depressed in mind, and my spirits continually agitated by gloomy feelings, even I was pleased. I lay at the bottom of the boat, and, as I gazed on the cloudless blue sky, I seemed to drink in a tranquillity to which I had long been a stranger. And if these were my sensations, who can describe those of Henry? He felt as if he had been transported to Fairy-land, and enjoyed a happiness seldom tasted by man. "I have seen," he said, "the most beautiful scenes of my own country; I have visited the lakes of Lucerne and Uri, where the snowy mountains descend almost perpendicularly to the water, casting black and impenetrable shades, which would cause a gloomy and mournful appearance, were it not for the most verdant islands that relieve the eye by their gay appearance; I have seen this lake agitated by a tempest, when the wind tore up whirlwinds of water, and gave you an idea of what the water-spout must be on the great ocean, and the waves dash with fury the base of the mountain, where the priest and his mistress were overwhelmed by an avalanche, and where their dying voices are still said to be heard amid the pauses of the nightly wind,[6] I have seen

---

5. Destination.
6. In her *History of a Six Weeks' Tour* (1817), describing her first trip to Europe with Percy Shel-

ley, Mary tells this story of a priest and his mistress who, to avoid persecution, lived in "a cottage at the foot of the snows."

the mountains of La Valais, and the Pays de Vaud: but this country, Victor, pleases me more than all those wonders. The mountains of Switzerland are more majestic and strange; but there is a charm in the banks of this divine river, that I never before saw equalled. Look at that castle which overhangs yon precipice; and that also on the island, almost concealed amongst the foliage of those lovely trees; and now that group of labourers coming from among their vines; and that village half-hid in the recess of the mountain. Oh, surely, the spirit that inhabits and guards this place has a soul more in harmony with man, than those who pile[7] the glacier, or retire to the inaccessible peaks of the mountains of our own country."

Clerval! beloved friend! even now it delights me to record your words, and to dwell on the praise of which you are so eminently deserving. He was a being formed in the "very poetry of nature."[8] His wild and enthusiastic imagination was chastened by the sensibility of his heart. His soul overflowed with ardent affections, and his friendship was of that devoted and wondrous nature that the worldly-minded teach us to look for only in the imagination. But even human sympathies were not sufficient to satisfy his eager mind. The scenery of external nature, which others regard only with admiration, he loved with ardour:

> ———"The sounding cataract
> Haunted *him* like a passion: the tall rock,
> The mountain, and the deep and gloomy wood,
> Their colours and their forms, were then to *him*
> An appetite; a feeling, and a love,
> That had no need of a remoter charm,
> By thought supplied, or any interest
> Unborrowed from the eye."[9]

And where does he now exist? Is this gentle and lovely being lost for ever? Has this mind so replete with ideas, imaginations fanciful and magnificent, which formed a world, whose existence depended on the life of its creator; has this mind perished? Does it now only exist in my memory? No, it is not thus; your form so divinely wrought, and beaming with beauty, has decayed, but your spirit still visits and consoles your unhappy friend.

Pardon this gush of sorrow; these ineffectual words are but a slight tribute to the unexampled worth of Henry, but they soothe my heart, overflowing with the anguish which his remembrance creates. I will proceed with my tale.

Beyond Cologne we descended to the plains of Holland; and we resolved to post[1] the remainder of our way; for the wind was contrary, and the stream of the river was too gentle to aid us.

Our journey here lost the interest arising from beautiful scenery; but we arrived in a few days at Rotterdam, whence we proceeded by sea to England. It was on a clear morning, in the latter days of December, that I first saw the white cliffs of Britain. The banks of the Thames presented a new scene;

---

7. Apparently, "who drive pilings into," as foundations for a building.
8. Leigh Hunt's "Rimini" [Mary Shelley's note]. Hunt's *The Story of Rimini* (1816) is based on Dante's account of the adulterous lovers, Paolo and Francesca, in *The Inferno*, canto 5.

9. Wordsworth's "Tintern Abbey" [Mary Shelley's note]. In the second and fourth lines of this quotation from *Lines Composed a Few Miles above Tintern Abbey*, Shelley changed "me" to "him."
1. Travel by relays of horses.

they were flat, but fertile, and almost every town was marked by the remembrance of some story. We saw Tilbury Fort, and remembered the Spanish armada; Gravesend, Woolwich, and Greenwich, places which I had heard of even in my country.

At length we saw the numerous steeples of London, St. Paul's towering above all, and the Tower famed in English history.

Chapter 2.

London was our present point of rest; we determined to remain several months in this wonderful and celebrated city. Clerval desired the intercourse of[2] the men of genius and talent who flourished at this time; but this was with me a secondary object; I was principally occupied with the means of obtaining the information necessary for the completion of my promise, and quickly availed myself of the letters of introduction that I had brought with me, addressed to the most distinguished natural philosophers.

If this journey had taken place during my days of study and happiness, it would have afforded me inexpressible pleasure. But a blight had come over my existence, and I only visited these people for the sake of the information they might give me on the subject in which my interest was so terribly profound. Company was irksome to me; when alone, I could fill my mind with the sights of heaven and earth; the voice of Henry soothed me, and I could thus cheat myself into a transitory peace. But busy uninteresting joyous faces brought back despair to my heart. I saw an insurmountable barrier placed between me and my fellow-men; this barrier was sealed with the blood of William and Justine; and to reflect on the events connected with those names filled my soul with anguish.

But in Clerval I saw the image of my former self; he was inquisitive, and anxious to gain experience and instruction. The difference of manners which he observed was to him an inexhaustible source of instruction and amusement. He was for ever busy; and the only check to his enjoyments was my sorrowful and dejected mien. I tried to conceal this as much as possible, that I might not debar him from the pleasures natural to one who was entering on a new scene of life, undisturbed by any care or bitter recollection. I often refused to accompany him, alleging another engagement, that I might remain alone. I now also began to collect the materials necessary for my new creation, and this was to me like the torture of single drops of water continually falling on the head. Every thought that was devoted to it was an extreme anguish, and every word that I spoke in allusion to it caused my lips to quiver, and my heart to palpitate.

After passing some months in London, we received a letter from a person in Scotland, who had formerly been our visitor at Geneva. He mentioned the beauties of his native country, and asked us if those were not sufficient allurements to induce us to prolong our journey as far north as Perth, where he resided. Clerval eagerly desired to accept this invitation; and I, although I abhorred society, wished to view again mountains and streams, and all the wondrous works with which Nature adorns her chosen dwelling-places.

We had arrived in England at the beginning of October, and it was now

2. Conversational exchanges with.

February. We accordingly determined to commence our journey towards the north at the expiration of another month. In this expedition we did not intend to follow the great road to Edinburgh, but to visit Windsor, Oxford, Matlock, and the Cumberland lakes, resolving to arrive at the completion of this tour about the end of July. I packed my chemical instruments, and the materials I had collected, resolving to finish my labours in some obscure nook in the northern highlands of Scotland.

We quitted London on the 27th of March, and remained a few days at Windsor, rambling in its beautiful forest. This was a new scene to us mountaineers; the majestic oaks, the quantity of game, and the herds of stately deer, were all novelties to us.

From thence we proceeded to Oxford. As we entered this city, our minds were filled with the remembrance of the events that had been transacted here more than a century and a half before. It was here that Charles I. had collected his forces. This city had remained faithful to him, after the whole nation had forsaken his cause to join the standard of parliament and liberty. The memory of that unfortunate king, and his companions, the amiable Falkland, the insolent Goring, his queen and son, gave a peculiar interest to every part of the city, which they might be supposed to have inhabited.[3] The spirit of elder days found a dwelling here, and we delighted to trace its footsteps. If these feelings had not found an imaginary gratification, the appearance of the city had yet in itself sufficient beauty to obtain our admiration. The colleges are ancient and picturesque; the streets are almost magnificent; and the lovely Isis, which flows beside it through meadows of exquisite verdure, is spread forth into a placid expanse of waters, which reflects its majestic assemblage of towers, and spires, and domes, embosomed among aged trees.

I enjoyed this scene; and yet my enjoyment was embittered both by the memory of the past, and the anticipation of the future. I was formed for peaceful happiness. During my youthful days discontent never visited my mind; and if I was ever overcome by *ennui*, the sight of what is beautiful in nature, or the study of what is excellent and sublime in the productions of man, could always interest my heart, and communicate elasticity to my spirits. But I am a blasted tree; the bolt has entered my soul; and I felt then that I should survive to exhibit, what I shall soon cease to be—a miserable spectacle of wrecked humanity, pitiable to others, and abhorrent to myself.

We passed a considerable period at Oxford, rambling among its environs, and endeavouring to identify every spot which might relate to the most animating epoch of English history. Our little voyages of discovery were often prolonged by the successive objects that presented themselves. We visited the tomb of the illustrious Hampden,[4] and the field on which that patriot fell. For a moment my soul was elevated from its debasing and miserable fears to contemplate the divine ideas of liberty and self-sacrifice, of which these sights were the monuments and the remembrancers. For an instant I

---

3. The city of Oxford served as the headquarters for Charles I during the Civil War in the 1640s. Viscount Falkland, although his convictions were with the Parliamentary forces, fought for the king and was killed in battle. "The insolent Goring" was Baron Goring, an ambitious general in the Royalist army who injured the king's cause by his intrigues.

Charles (the "son") became Charles II at the Restoration in 1660.
4. John Hampden (1599–1643), a powerful debater and popular leader in the Parliamentary cause, was killed in a military skirmish at Chalgrove Field, near Oxford.

dared to shake off my chains, and look around me with a free and lofty spirit; but the iron had eaten into my flesh, and I sank again, trembling and hopeless, into my miserable self.

We left Oxford with regret, and proceeded to Matlock, which was our next place of rest. The country in the neighbourhood of this village resembled, to a greater degree, the scenery of Switzerland; but every thing is on a lower scale, and the green hills want the crown of distant white Alps, which always attend on the piny mountains of my native country. We visited the wondrous cave, and the little cabinets of natural history, where the curiosities[5] are disposed in the same manner as in the collections at Servox and Chamounix. The latter name made me tremble, when pronounced by Henry; and I hastened to quit Matlock, with which that terrible scene was thus associated.

From Derby still journeying northward, we passed two months in Cumberland and Westmoreland.[6] I could now almost fancy myself among the Swiss mountains. The little patches of snow which yet lingered on the northern sides of the mountains, the lakes, and the dashing of the rocky streams, were all familiar and dear sights to me. Here also we made some acquaintances, who almost contrived to cheat me into happiness. The delight of Clerval was proportionably greater than mine; his mind expanded in the company of men of talent, and he found in his own nature greater capacities and resources than he could have imagined himself to have possessed while he associated with his inferiors. "I could pass my life here," said he to me; "and among these mountains I should scarcely regret Switzerland and the Rhine."

But he found that a traveller's life is one that includes much pain amidst its enjoyments. His feelings are for ever on the stretch, and when he begins to sink into repose, he finds himself obliged to quit that on which he rests in pleasure for something new, which again engages his attention, and which also he forsakes for other novelties.

We had scarcely visited the various lakes of Cumberland and Westmoreland, and conceived an affection for some of the inhabitants, when the period of our appointment with our Scotch friend approached, and we left them to travel on. For my own part I was not sorry. I had now neglected my promise for some time, and I feared the effects of the dæmon's disappointment. He might remain in Switzerland, and wreak his vengeance on my relatives. This idea pursued me, and tormented me at every moment from which I might otherwise have snatched repose and peace. I waited for my letters with feverish impatience: if they were delayed, I was miserable, and overcome by a thousand fears; and when they arrived, and I saw the superscription of Elizabeth or my father, I hardly dared to read and ascertain my fate. Sometimes I thought that the fiend followed me, and might expedite my remissness by murdering my companion. When these thoughts possessed me. I would not quit Henry for a moment, but followed him as his shadow, to protect him from the fancied rage of his destroyer. I felt as if I had committed some great crime, the consciousness of which haunted me. I was guiltless, but I had indeed drawn down a horrible curse upon my head, as mortal as that of crime.

5. Rooms where rarities were shown (including both natural objects and works of art and artisanry) were called "cabinets of curiosities."

6. The Lake District, associated with the poets Wordsworth, Coleridge, and Robert Southey.

I visited Edinburgh with languid eyes and mind; and yet that city might have interested the most unfortunate being. Clerval did not like it so well as Oxford; for the antiquity of the latter city was more pleasing to him. But the beauty and regularity of the new town of Edinburgh, its romantic castle, and its environs, the most delightful in the world, Arthur's Seat, St. Bernard's Well, and the Pentland Hills, compensated him for the change, and filled him with cheerfulness and admiration. But I was impatient to arrive at the termination of my journey.

We left Edinburgh in a week, passing through Coupar, St. Andrews, and along the banks of the Tay, to Perth, where our friend expected us. But I was in no mood to laugh and talk with strangers, or enter into their feelings or plans with the good humour expected from a guest; and accordingly I told Clerval that I wished to make the tour of Scotland alone. "Do you," said I, "enjoy yourself, and let this be our rendezvous. I may be absent a month or two; but do not interfere with my motions, I entreat you: leave me to peace and solitude for a short time; and when I return, I hope it will be with a lighter heart, more congenial to your own temper."

Henry wished to dissuade me; but, seeing me bent on this plan, ceased to remonstrate. He entreated me to write often. "I had rather be with you," he said, "in your solitary rambles, than with these Scotch people, whom I do not know: hasten then, my dear friend, to return, that I may again feel myself somewhat at home, which I cannot do in your absence."

Having parted from my friend, I determined to visit some remote spot of Scotland, and finish my work in solitude. I did not doubt but that the monster followed me, and would discover himself to me when I should have finished, that he might receive his companion.

With this resolution I traversed the northern highlands, and fixed on one of the remotest of the Orkneys[7] as the scene of my labours. It was a place fitted for such a work, being hardly more than a rock, whose high sides were continually beaten upon by the waves. The soil was barren, scarcely affording pasture for a few miserable cows, and oatmeal for its inhabitants, which consisted of five persons, whose gaunt and scraggy limbs gave tokens of their miserable fare. Vegetables and bread, when they indulged in such luxuries, and even fresh water, was to be procured from the main land, which was about five miles distant.

On the whole island there were but three miserable huts, and one of these was vacant when I arrived. This I hired. It contained but two rooms, and these exhibited all the squalidness of the most miserable penury. The thatch had fallen in, the walls were unplastered, and the door was off its hinges. I ordered it to be repaired, bought some furniture, and took possession; an incident which would, doubtless, have occasioned some surprise, had not all the senses of the cottagers been benumbed by want and squalid poverty. As it was, I lived ungazed at and unmolested, hardly thanked for the pittance of food and clothes which I gave; so much does suffering blunt even the coarsest sensations of men.

In this retreat I devoted the morning to labour; but in the evening, when the weather permitted, I walked on the stony beach of the sea, to listen to the waves as they roared, and dashed at my feet. It was a monotonous, yet ever-changing scene. I thought of Switzerland; it was far different from this

7. Islands north of Scotland.

desolate and appalling landscape. Its hills are covered with vines, and its cottages are scattered thickly in the plains. Its fair lakes reflect a blue and gentle sky; and, when troubled by the winds, their tumult is but as the play of a lively infant, when compared to the roarings of the giant ocean.

In this manner I distributed my occupations when I first arrived; but, as I proceeded in my labour, it became every day more horrible and irksome to me. Sometimes I could not prevail on myself to enter my laboratory for several days; and at other times I toiled day and night in order to complete my work. It was indeed a filthy process in which I was engaged. During my first experiment, a kind of enthusiastic frenzy had blinded me to the horror of my employment; my mind was intently fixed on the sequel of my labour, and my eyes were shut to the horror of my proceedings. But now I went to it in cold blood, and my heart often sickened at the work of my hands.

Thus situated, employed in the most detestable occupation, immersed in a solitude where nothing could for an instant call my attention from the actual scene in which I was engaged, my spirits became unequal;[8] I grew restless and nervous. Every moment I feared to meet my persecutor. Sometimes I sat with my eyes fixed on the ground, fearing to raise them lest they should encounter the object which I so much dreaded to behold. I feared to wander from the sight of my fellow-creatures, lest when alone he should come to claim his companion.

In the mean time I worked on, and my labour was already considerably advanced. I looked towards its completion with a tremulous and eager hope, which I dared not trust myself to question, but which was intermixed with obscure forebodings of evil, that made my heart sicken in my bosom.

Chapter 3.

I sat one evening in my laboratory; the sun had set, and the moon was just rising from the sea; I had not sufficient light for my employment, and I remained idle, in a pause of consideration of whether I should leave my labour for the night, or hasten its conclusion by an unremitting attention to it. As I sat, a train of reflection occurred to me, which led me to consider the effects of what I was now doing. Three years before I was engaged in the same manner, and had created a fiend whose unparalleled barbarity had desolated my heart, and filled it for ever with the bitterest remorse. I was now about to form another being, of whose dispositions I was alike ignorant; she might become ten thousand times more malignant than her mate, and delight, for its own sake, in murder and wretchedness. He had sworn to quit the neighbourhood of man, and hide himself in deserts; but she had not; and she, who in all probability was to become a thinking and reasoning animal, might refuse to comply with a compact made before her creation. They might even hate each other; the creature who already lived loathed his own deformity, and might he not conceive a greater abhorrence for it when it came before his eyes in the female form? She also might turn with disgust from him to the superior beauty of man; she might quit him, and he be again alone, exasperated by the fresh provocation of being deserted by one of his own species.

Even if they were to leave Europe, and inhabit the deserts of the new

8. Uneven, unsettled.

world, yet one of the first results of those sympathies for which the dæmon thirsted would be children, and a race of devils would be propagated upon the earth, who might make the very existence of the species of man a condition precarious and full of terror. Had I a right, for my own benefit, to inflict this curse upon everlasting generations? I had before been moved by the *sophisms*[9] of the being I had created; I had been struck senseless by his fiendish threats: but now, for the first time, the wickedness of my promise burst upon me; I shuddered to think that future ages might curse me as their pest, whose selfishness had not hesitated to buy its own peace at the price perhaps of the existence of the whole human race.

I trembled, and my heart failed within me; when, on looking up, I saw, by the light of the moon, the dæmon at the casement. A ghastly grin wrinkled his lips as he gazed on me, where I sat fulfilling the task which he had allotted to me. Yes, he had followed me in my travels; he had loitered in forests, hid himself in caves, or taken refuge in wide and desert heaths; and he now came to mark my progress, and claim the fulfilment of my promise.

As I looked on him, his countenance expressed the utmost extent of malice and treachery. I thought with a sensation of madness on my promise of creating another like to him, and, trembling with passion, tore to pieces the thing on which I was engaged. The wretch saw me destroy the creature on whose future existence he depended for happiness, and, with a howl of devilish despair and revenge, withdrew.

I left the room, and, locking the door, made a solemn vow in my own heart never to resume my labours; and then, with trembling steps, I sought my own apartment. I was alone; none were near me to dissipate the gloom, and relieve me from the sickening oppression of the most terrible reveries.

Several hours past, and I remained near my window gazing on the sea; it was almost motionless, for the winds were hushed, and all nature reposed under the eye of the quiet moon. A few fishing vessels alone specked the water, and now and then the gentle breeze wafted the sound of voices, as the fishermen called to one another. I felt the silence, although I was hardly conscious of its extreme profundity, until my ear was suddenly arrested by the paddling of oars near the shore, and a person landed close to my house.

In a few minutes after, I heard the creaking of my door, as if some one endeavoured to open it softly. I trembled from head to foot; I felt a presentiment of who it was, and wished to rouse one of the peasants who dwelt in a cottage not far from mine; but I was overcome by the sensation of helplessness, so often felt in frightful dreams, when you in vain endeavour to fly from an impending danger, and was rooted to the spot.

Presently I heard the sound of footsteps along the passage; the door opened, and the wretch whom I dreaded appeared. Shutting the door, he approached me, and said, in a smothered voice—

"You have destroyed the work which you began; what is it that you intend? Do you dare to break your promise? I have endured toil and misery: I left Switzerland with you; I crept along the shores of the Rhine, among its willow islands, and over the summits of its hills. I have dwelt many months in the heaths of England, and among the deserts of Scotland. I have endured incalculable fatigue, and cold, and hunger; do you dare destroy my hopes?"

---

9. Sophistries; plausible but misleading arguments.

"Begone! I do break my promise; never will I create another like yourself, equal in deformity and wickedness."

"Slave, I before reasoned with you, but you have proved yourself unworthy of my condescension. Remember that I have power; you believe yourself miserable, but I can make you so wretched that the light of day will be hateful to you. You are my creator, but I am your master;—obey!"

"The hour of my weakness is past, and the period[1] of your power is arrived. Your threats cannot move me to do an act of wickedness; but they confirm me in a resolution of not creating you a companion in vice. Shall I, in cool blood, set loose upon the earth a dæmon whose delight is in death and wretchedness? Begone! I am firm, and your words will only exasperate my rage."

The monster saw my determination in my face, and gnashed his teeth in the impotence of anger. "Shall each man," cried he, "find a wife for his bosom, and each beast have his mate, and I be alone? I had feelings of affection, and they were requited by detestation and scorn. Man, you may hate; but beware! Your hours will pass in dread and misery, and soon the bolt will fall which must ravish from you your happiness for ever. Are you to be happy, while I grovel in the intensity of my wretchedness? You can blast my other passions; but revenge remains—revenge, henceforth dearer than light or food! I may die; but first you, my tyrant and tormentor, shall curse the sun that gazes on your misery. Beware; for I am fearless, and therefore powerful. I will watch with the wiliness of a snake, that I may sting with its venom. Man, you shall repent of the injuries you inflict."

"Devil, cease; and do not poison the air with these sounds of malice. I have declared my resolution to you, and I am no coward to bend beneath words. Leave me; I am inexorable."

"It is well. I go; but remember, I shall be with you on your wedding-night."

I started forward, and exclaimed, "Villain! before you sign my death-warrant, be sure that you are yourself safe."

I would have seized him; but he eluded me, and quitted the house with precipitation: in a few moments I saw him in his boat, which shot across the waters with an arrowy swiftness, and was soon lost amidst the waves.

All was again silent; but his words rung in my ears. I burned with rage to pursue the murderer of my peace, and precipitate him into the ocean. I walked up and down my room hastily and perturbed, while my imagination conjured up a thousand images to torment and sting me. Why had I not followed him, and closed with him in mortal strife? But I had suffered him to depart, and he had directed his course towards the main land. I shuddered to think who might be the next victim sacrificed to his insatiate revenge. And then I thought again of his words—*"I will be with you on your wedding-night."* That then was the period fixed for the fulfilment of my destiny. In that hour I should die, and at once satisfy and extinguish his malice. The prospect did not move me to fear; yet when I thought of my beloved Elizabeth,—of her tears and endless sorrow, when she should find her lover so barbarously snatched from her,—tears, the first I had shed for many months, streamed from my eyes, and I resolved not to fall before my enemy without a bitter struggle.

1. End.

The night passed away, and the sun rose from the ocean; my feelings became calmer, if it may be called calmness, when the violence of rage sinks into the depths of despair. I left the house, the horrid scene of the last night's contention, and walked on the beach of the sea, which I almost regarded as an insuperable barrier between me and my fellow-creatures; nay, a wish that such should prove the fact stole across me. I desired that I might pass my life on that barren rock, wearily it is true, but uninterrupted by any sudden shock of misery. If I returned, it was to be sacrificed, or to see those whom I most loved die under the grasp of a dæmon whom I had myself created.

I walked about the isle like a restless spectre, separated from all it loved, and miserable in the separation. When it became noon, and the sun rose higher, I lay down on the grass, and was overpowered by a deep sleep. I had been awake the whole of the preceding night, my nerves were agitated, and my eyes inflamed by watching and misery. The sleep into which I now sunk refreshed me; and when I awoke, I again felt as if I belonged to a race of human beings like myself, and I began to reflect upon what had passed with greater composure; yet still the words of the fiend rung in my ears like a death-knell, they appeared like a dream, yet distinct and oppressive as a reality.

The sun had far descended, and I still sat on the shore, satisfying my appetite, which had become ravenous, with an oaten cake, when I saw a fishing-boat land close to me, and one of the men brought me a packet; it contained letters from Geneva, and one from Clerval, entreating me to join him. He said that nearly a year had elapsed since we had quitted Switzerland, and France was yet unvisited. He entreated me, therefore, to leave my solitary isle, and meet him at Perth, in a week from that time, when we might arrange the plan of our future proceedings. This letter in a degree recalled me to life, and I determined to quit my island at the expiration of two days.

Yet, before I departed, there was a task to perform, on which I shuddered to reflect: I must pack my chemical instruments; and for that purpose I must enter the room which had been the scene of my odious work, and I must handle those utensils, the sight of which was sickening to me. The next morning, at day-break, I summoned sufficient courage, and unlocked the door of my laboratory. The remains of the half-finished creature, whom I had destroyed, lay scattered on the floor, and I almost felt as if I had mangled the living flesh of a human being. I paused to collect myself, and then entered the chamber. With trembling hand I conveyed the instruments out of the room; but I reflected that I ought not to leave the relics of my work to excite the horror and suspicion of the peasants, and I accordingly put them into a basket, with a great quantity of stones, and laying them up, determined to throw them into the sea that very night; and in the mean time I sat upon the beach, employed in cleaning and arranging my chemical apparatus.

Nothing could be more complete than the alteration that had taken place in my feelings since the night of the appearance of the dæmon. I had before regarded my promise with a gloomy despair, as a thing that, with whatever consequences, must be fulfilled; but I now felt as if a film had been taken from before my eyes, and that I, for the first time, saw clearly. The idea of renewing my labours did not for one instant occur to me; the threat I had heard weighed on my thoughts, but I did not reflect that a voluntary act of mine could avert it. I had resolved in my own mind, that to create another like the fiend I had first made would be an act of the basest and most atrocious selfishness; and I banished from my mind every thought that could lead to a different conclusion.

Between two and three in the morning the moon rose; and I then, putting my basket aboard a little skiff, sailed out about four miles from the shore. The scene was perfectly solitary: a few boats were returning towards land, but I sailed away from them. I felt as if I was about the commission of a dreadful crime, and avoided with shuddering anxiety any encounter with my fellow-creatures. At one time the moon, which had before been clear, was suddenly overspread by a thick cloud, and I took advantage of the moment of darkness, and cast my basket into the sea; I listened to the gurgling sound as it sunk, and then sailed away from the spot. The sky became clouded; but the air was pure, although chilled by the north-east breeze that was then rising. But it refreshed me, and filled me with such agreeable sensations, that I resolved to prolong my stay on the water, and fixing the rudder in a direct position, stretched myself at the bottom of the boat. Clouds hid the moon, every thing was obscure, and I heard only the sound of the boat, as its keel cut through the waves; the murmur lulled me, and in a short time I slept soundly.

I do not know how long I remained in this situation, but when I awoke I found that the sun had already mounted considerably. The wind was high, and the waves continually threatened the safety of my little skiff. I found that the wind was north-east, and must have driven me far from the coast from which I had embarked. I endeavoured to change my course, but quickly found that if I again made the attempt the boat would be instantly filled with water. Thus situated, my only resource was to drive before the wind. I confess that I felt a few sensations of terror. I had no compass with me, and was so little acquainted with the geography of this part of the world that the sun was of little benefit to me. I might be driven into the wide Atlantic, and feel all the tortures of starvation, or be swallowed up in the immeasurable waters that roared and buffeted around me. I had already been out many hours, and felt the torment of a burning thirst, a prelude to my other sufferings. I looked on the heavens, which were covered by clouds that flew before the wind only to be replaced by others: I looked upon the sea, it was to be my grave. "Fiend," I exclaimed, "your task is already fulfilled!" I thought of Elizabeth, of my father, and of Clerval; and sunk into a reverie, so despairing and frightful, that even now, when the scene is on the point of closing before me for ever, I shudder to reflect on it.

Some hours passed thus; but by degrees, as the sun declined towards the horizon, the wind died away into a gentle breeze, and the sea became free from breakers. But these gave place to a heavy swell; I felt sick, and hardly able to hold the rudder, when suddenly I saw a line of high land towards the south.

Almost spent, as I was, by fatigue, and the dreadful suspense I endured for several hours, this sudden certainty of life rushed like a flood of warm joy to my heart, and tears gushed from my eyes.

How mutable are our feelings, and how strange is that clinging love we have of life even in the excess of misery! I constructed another sail with a part of my dress, and eagerly steered my course towards the land. It had a wild and rocky appearance; but as I approached nearer, I easily perceived the traces of cultivation. I saw vessels near the shore, and found myself suddenly transported back to the neighbourhood of civilized man. I eagerly traced the windings of the land, and hailed a steeple which I at length saw issuing from behind a small promontory. As I was in a state of extreme debility, I resolved to sail directly towards the town as a place where I could most easily procure nourishment. Fortunately I had money with me. As I turned the promontory, I perceived a small neat town and a good harbour, which I entered, my heart bounding with joy at my unexpected escape.

As I was occupied in fixing the boat and arranging the sails, several people crowded towards the spot. They seemed very much surprised at my appearance; but, instead of offering me any assistance, whispered together with gestures that at any other time might have produced in me a slight sensation of alarm. As it was, I merely remarked that they spoke English; and I therefore addressed them in that language: "My good friends," said I, "will you be so kind as to tell me the name of this town, and inform me where I am?"

"You will know that soon enough," replied a man with a gruff voice. "May be you are come to a place that will not prove much to your taste; but you will not be consulted as to your quarters, I promise you."

I was exceedingly surprised on receiving so rude an answer from a stranger; and I was also disconcerted on perceiving the frowning and angry countenances of his companions. "Why do you answer me so roughly?" I replied: "surely it is not the custom of Englishmen to receive strangers so inhospitably."

"I do not know," said the man, "what the custom of the English may be; but it is the custom of the Irish to hate villains."

While this strange dialogue continued, I perceived the crowd rapidly increase. Their faces expressed a mixture of curiosity and anger, which annoyed, and in some degree alarmed me. I inquired the way to the inn; but no one replied. I then moved forward, and a murmuring sound arose from the crowd as they followed and surrounded me; when an ill-looking man approaching, tapped me on the shoulder, and said, "Come, Sir, you must follow me to Mr. Kirwin's, to give an account of yourself."

"Who is Mr. Kirwin? Why am I to give an account of myself? Is not this a free country?"

"Aye, Sir, free enough for honest folks. Mr. Kirwin is a magistrate; and you are to give an account of the death of a gentleman who was found murdered here last night."

This answer startled me; but I presently recovered myself. I was innocent; that could easily be proved: accordingly I followed my conductor in silence, and was led to one of the best houses in the town. I was ready to sink from fatigue and hunger; but, being surrounded by a crowd, I thought it politic to rouse all my strength, that no physical debility might be construed into apprehension or conscious guilt. Little did I then expect the calamity that was in a few moments to overwhelm me and extinguish in horror and despair all fear of ignominy or death.

I must pause here; for it requires all my fortitude to recall the memory of the frightful events which I am about to relate, in proper detail, to my recollection.

Chapter 4.

I was soon introduced into the presence of the magistrate, an old benevolent man, with calm and mild manners. He looked upon me, however, with some degree of severity; and then, turning towards my conductors, he asked who appeared as witnesses on this occasion.

About half a dozen men came forward; and one being selected by the magistrate, he deposed, that he had been out fishing the night before with his son and brother-in-law, Daniel Nugent, when, about ten o'clock, they observed a strong northerly blast rising, and they accordingly put in for port. It was a very dark night, as the moon had not yet risen; they did not land at the harbour, but, as they had been accustomed, at a creek about two miles below. He walked on first, carrying a part of the fishing tackle, and his companions followed him at some distance. As he was proceeding along the sands, he struck his foot against something, and fell all his length on the ground. His companions came up to assist him; and, by the light of their lantern, they found that he had fallen on the body of a man, who was to all appearance dead. Their first supposition was, that it was the corpse of some person who had been drowned, and was thrown on shore by the waves; but, upon examination, they found that the clothes were not wet, and even that the body was not then cold. They instantly carried it to the cottage of an old woman near the spot, and endeavoured, but in vain, to restore it to life. He appeared to be a handsome young man, about five and twenty years of age. He had apparently been strangled; for there was no sign of any violence, except the black mark of fingers on his neck.

The first part of this deposition did not in the least interest me; but when the mark of the fingers was mentioned, I remembered the murder of my brother, and felt myself extremely agitated; my limbs trembled, and a mist came over my eyes, which obliged me to lean on a chair for support. The magistrate observed me with a keen eye, and of course drew an unfavourable augury from my manner.

The son confirmed his father's account: but when Daniel Nugent was called, he swore positively that, just before the fall of his companion, he saw a boat, with a single man in it, at a short distance from the shore; and, as far as he could judge by the light of a few stars, it was the same boat in which I had just landed.

A woman deposed, that she lived near the beach, and was standing at the door of her cottage, waiting for the return of the fishermen, about an hour before she heard of the discovery of the body, when she saw a boat, with only only one man in it, push off from that part of the shore where the corpse was afterwards found.

Another woman confirmed the account of the fishermen having brought the body into her house; it was not cold. They put it into a bed, and rubbed it; and Daniel went to the town for an apothecary, but life was quite gone.

Several other men were examined concerning my landing; and they agreed, that, with the strong north wind that had arisen during the night, it was very probable that I had beaten about for many hours, and had been obliged to return nearly to the same spot from which I had departed. Besides, they observed that it appeared that I had brought the body from another place, and it was likely, that as I did not appear to know the shore, I might have put into the harbour ignorant of the distance of the town of —— from the place where I had deposited the corpse.

Mr. Kirwin, on hearing this evidence, desired that I should be taken into the room where the body lay for interment, that it might be observed what effect the sight of it would produce upon me. This idea was probably suggested by the extreme agitation I had exhibited when the mode of the murder had been described. I was accordingly conducted, by the magistrate and several other persons, to the inn. I could not help being struck by the strange coincidences that had taken place during this eventful night; but, knowing that I had been conversing with several persons in the island I had inhabited about the time that the body had been found, I was perfectly tranquil as to the consequences of the affair.

I entered the room where the corpse lay, and was led up to the coffin. How can I describe my sensations on beholding it? I feel yet parched with horror, nor can I reflect on that terrible moment without shuddering and agony, that faintly reminds me of the anguish of the recognition. The trial, the presence of the magistrate and witnesses, passed like a dream from my memory, when I saw the lifeless form of Henry Clerval stretched before me. I gasped for breath; and, throwing myself on the body, I exclaimed, "Have my murderous machinations deprived you also, my dearest Henry, of life? Two I have already destroyed; other victims await their destiny: but you, Clerval, my friend, my benefactor"—

The human frame could no longer support the agonizing suffering that I endured, and I was carried out of the room in strong convulsions.

A fever succeeded to this. I lay for two months on the point of death: my ravings, as I afterwards heard, were frightful; I called myself the murderer of William, of Justine, and of Clerval. Sometimes I entreated my attendants to assist me in the destruction of the fiend by whom I was tormented; and, at others, I felt the fingers of the monster already grasping my neck, and screamed aloud with agony and terror. Fortunately, as I spoke my native language, Mr. Kirwin alone understood me; but my gestures and bitter cries were sufficient to affright the other witnesses.

Why did I not die? More miserable than man ever was before, why did I not sink into forgetfulness and rest? Death snatches away many blooming children, the only hopes of their doating parents: how many brides and youthful lovers have been one day in the bloom of health and hope, and the next a prey for worms and the decay of the tomb! Of what materials was I made, that I could thus resist so many shocks, which, like the turning of the wheel, continually renewed the torture.

But I was doomed to live; and, in two months, found myself as awaking from a dream, in a prison, stretched on a wretched bed, surrounded by gaolers, turnkeys, bolts, and all the miserable apparatus of a dungeon. It was morning, I remember, when I thus awoke to understanding: I had forgotten the particulars of what had happened, and only felt as if some great misfortune had suddenly overwhelmed me; but when I looked around, and saw the barred windows, and the squalidness of the room in which I was, all flashed across my memory, and I groaned bitterly.

This sound disturbed an old woman who was sleeping in a chair beside me. She was a hired nurse, the wife of one of the turnkeys, and her countenance expressed all those bad qualities which often characterize that class. The lines of her face were hard and rude, like that of persons accustomed to see without sympathizing in sights of misery. Her tone expressed her entire indifference; she addressed me in English, and the voice struck me as one that I had heard during my sufferings:

"Are you better now, Sir?" said she.

I replied in the same language, with a feeble voice, "I believe I am; but if it be all true, if indeed I did not dream, I am sorry that I am still alive to feel this misery and horror."

"For that matter," replied the old woman, "if you mean about the gentleman you murdered, I believe that it were better for you if you were dead, for I fancy it will go hard with you; but you will be hung when the next sessions[2] come on. However, that's none of my business, I am sent to nurse you, and get you well; I do my duty with a safe conscience, it were well if every body did the same."

I turned with loathing from the woman who could utter so unfeeling a speech to a person just saved, on the very edge of death; but I felt languid, and unable to reflect on all that had passed. The whole series of my life appeared to me as a dream; I sometimes doubted if indeed it were all true, for it never presented itself to my mind with the force of reality.

As the images that floated before me became more distinct, I grew feverish; a darkness pressed around me; no one was near me who soothed me with the gentle voice of love; no dear hand supported me. The physician came and prescribed medicines, and the old woman prepared them for me; but utter carelessness was visible in the first, and the expression of brutality was strongly marked in the visage of the second. Who could be interested in the fate of a murderer, but the hangman who would gain his fee?

These were my first reflections; but I soon learned that Mr. Kirwin had shewn me extreme kindness. He had caused the best room in the prison to be prepared for me (wretched indeed was the best); and it was he who had provided a physician and a nurse. It is true, he seldom came to see me; for, although he ardently desired to relieve the sufferings of every human creature, he did not wish to be present at the agonies and miserable ravings of a murderer. He came, therefore, sometimes to see that I was not neglected; but his visits were short, and at long intervals.

One day, when I was gradually recovering, I was seated in a chair, my eyes half open, and my cheeks livid like those in death, I was overcome by gloom and misery, and often reflected I had better seek death than remain miserably pent up only to be let loose in a world replete with wretchedness. At one time I considered whether I should not declare myself guilty, and suffer the penalty of the law, less innocent than poor Justine had been. Such were my thoughts, when the door of my apartment was opened, and Mr. Kirwin entered. His countenance expressed sympathy and compassion; he drew a chair close to mine, and addressed me in French—

"I fear that this place is very shocking to you; can I do any thing to make you more comfortable?"

"I thank you; but all that you mention is nothing to me: on the whole earth there is no comfort which I am capable of receiving."

---

2. Regular sittings of a court to try certain criminal cases.

"I know that the sympathy of a stranger can be but of little relief to one borne down as you are by so strange a misfortune. But you will, I hope, soon quit this melancholy abode; for, doubtless, evidence can easily be brought to free you from the criminal charge."

"That is my least concern: I am, by a course of strange events, become the most miserable of mortals. Persecuted and tortured as I am and have been, can death be any evil to me?"

"Nothing indeed could be more unfortunate and agonizing than the strange chances that have lately occurred. You were thrown, by some surprising accident, on this shore, renowned for its hospitality; seized immediately, and charged with murder. The first sight that was presented to your eyes was the body of your friend, murdered in so unaccountable a manner, and placed, as it were, by some fiend across your path."

As Mr. Kirwin said this, notwithstanding the agitation I endured on this retrospect of my sufferings, I also felt considerable surprise at the knowledge he seemed to possess concerning me. I suppose some astonishment was exhibited in my countenance; for Mr. Kirwin hastened to say—

"It was not until a day or two after your illness that I thought of examining your dress, that I might discover some trace by which I could send to your relations an account of your misfortune and illness. I found several letters, and, among others, one which I discovered from its commencement to be from your father. I instantly wrote to Geneva: nearly two months have elapsed since the departure of my letter.—But you are ill; even now you tremble: you are unfit for agitation of any kind."

"This suspense is a thousand times worse than the most horrible event: tell me what new scene of death has been acted, and whose murder I am now to lament."

"Your family is perfectly well," said Mr. Kirwin, with gentleness; "and some one, a friend, is come to visit you."

I know not by what chain of thought the idea presented itself, but it instantly darted into my mind that the murderer had come to mock at my misery, and taunt me with the death of Clerval, as a new incitement for me to comply with his hellish desires. I put my hand before my eyes, and cried out in agony—

"Oh! take him away! I cannot see him; for God's sake, do not let him enter!"

Mr. Kirwin regarded me with a troubled countenance. He could not help regarding my exclamation as a presumption of my guilt, and said, in rather a severe tone—

"I should have thought, young man, that the presence of your father would have been welcome, instead of inspiring such violent repugnance."

"My father!" cried I, while every feature and every muscle was relaxed from anguish to pleasure. "Is my father, indeed, come? How kind, how very kind. But where is he, why does he not hasten to me?"

My change of manner surprised and pleased the magistrate; perhaps he thought that my former exclamation was a momentary return of delirium, and now he instantly resumed his former benevolence. He rose, and quitted the room with my nurse, and in a moment my father entered it.

Nothing, at this moment, could have given me greater pleasure than the arrival of my father. I stretched out my hand to him, and cried—

"Are you then safe—and Elizabeth—and Ernest?"

My father calmed me with assurances of their welfare, and endeavoured, by dwelling on these subjects so interesting to my heart, to raise my desponding spirits; but he soon felt that a prison cannot be the abode of cheerfulness. "What a place is this that you inhabit, my son!" said he, looking mournfully at the barred windows, and wretched appearance of the room. "You travelled to seek happiness, but a fatality seems to pursue you. And poor Clerval—"

The name of my unfortunate and murdered friend was an agitation too great to be endured in my weak state; I shed tears.

"Alas! yes, my father," replied I; "some destiny of the most horrible kind hangs over me, and I must live to fulfil it, or surely I should have died on the coffin of Henry."

We were not allowed to converse for any length of time, for the precarious state of my health rendered every precaution necessary that could insure tranquillity. Mr. Kirwin came in, and insisted that my strength should not be exhausted by too much exertion. But the appearance of my father was to me like that of my good angel, and I gradually recovered my health.

As my sickness quitted me, I was absorbed by a gloomy and black melancholy, that nothing could dissipate. The image of Clerval was for ever before me, ghastly and murdered. More than once the agitation into which these reflections threw me made my friends dread a dangerous relapse. Alas! why did they preserve so miserable and detested a life? It was surely that I might fulfil my destiny, which is now drawing to a close. Soon, oh, very soon, will death extinguish these throbbings, and relieve me from the mighty weight of anguish that bears me to the dust; and, in executing the award of justice, I shall also sink to rest. Then the appearance of death was distant, although the wish was ever present to my thoughts; and I often sat for hours motionless and speechless, wishing for some mighty revolution that might bury me and my destroyer in its ruins.

The season of the assizes[3] approached. I had already been three months in prison; and although I was still weak, and in continual danger of a relapse, I was obliged to travel nearly a hundred miles to the county-town, where the court was held. Mr. Kirwin charged himself with every care of collecting witnesses, and arranging my defence. I was spared the disgrace of appearing publicly as a criminal, as the case was not brought before the court that decides on life and death. The grand jury rejected the bill, on its being proved that I was on the Orkney Islands at the hour the body of my friend was found, and a fortnight after my removal I was liberated from prison.

My father was enraptured on finding me freed from the vexations of a criminal charge, that I was again allowed to breathe the fresh atmosphere, and allowed to return to my native country. I did not participate in these feelings; for to me the walls of a dungeon or a palace were alike hateful. The cup of life was poisoned for ever; and although the sun shone upon me, as upon the happy and gay of heart, I saw around me nothing but a dense and frightful darkness, penetrated by no light but the glimmer of two eyes that glared upon me. Sometimes they were the expressive eyes of Henry, languishing in death, the dark orbs nearly covered by the lids, and the long black lashes that fringed them; sometimes it was the watery clouded eyes of the monster, as I first saw them in my chamber at Ingolstadt.

---

3. Sessions for administering civil and criminal justice.

My father tried to awaken in me the feelings of affection. He talked of Geneva, which I should soon visit—of Elizabeth, and Ernest; but these words only drew deep groans from me. Sometimes, indeed, I felt a wish for happiness; and thought, with melancholy delight, of my beloved cousin; or longed, with a devouring *maladie du pays*,[4] to see once more the blue lake and rapid Rhone, that had been so dear to me in early childhood: but my general state of feeling was a torpor, in which a prison was as welcome a residence as the divinest scene in nature; and these fits were seldom interrupted, but by paroxysms of anguish and despair. At these moments I often endeavoured to put an end to the existence I loathed; and it required unceasing attendance and vigilance to restrain me from committing some dreadful act of violence.

I remember, as I quitted the prison, I heard one of the men say, "He may be innocent of the murder, but he has certainly a bad conscience." These words struck me. A bad conscience! yes, surely I had one. William, Justine, and Clerval, had died through my infernal machinations; "And whose death," cried I, "is to finish the tragedy? Ah! my father, do not remain in this wretched country; take me where I may forget myself, my existence, and all the world."

My father easily acceded to my desire; and, after having taken leave of Mr. Kirwin, we hastened to Dublin. I felt as if I was relieved from a heavy weight, when the packet sailed with a fair wind from Ireland, and I had quitted for ever the country which had been to me the scene of so much misery.

It was midnight. My father slept in the cabin; and I lay on the deck, looking at the stars, and listening to the dashing of the waves. I hailed the darkness that shut Ireland from my sight, and my pulse beat with a feverish joy, when I reflected that I should soon see Geneva. The past appeared to me in the light of a frightful dream; yet the vessel in which I was, the wind that blew me from the detested shore of Ireland, and the sea which surrounded me, told me too forcibly that I was deceived by no vision, and that Clerval, my friend and dearest companion, had fallen a victim to me and the monster of my creation. I repassed, in my memory, my whole life; my quiet happiness while residing with my family in Geneva, the death of my mother; and my departure for Ingolstadt. I remembered shuddering at the mad enthusiasm that hurried me on to the creation of my hideous enemy, and I called to mind the night during which he first lived. I was unable to pursue the train of thought; a thousand feelings pressed upon me, and I wept bitterly.

Ever since my recovery from the fever I had been in the custom of taking every night a small quantity of laudanum;[5] for it was by means of this drug only that I was enabled to gain the rest necessary for the preservation of life. Oppressed by the recollection of my various misfortunes, I now took a double dose, and soon slept profoundly. But sleep did not afford me respite from thought and misery; my dreams presented a thousand objects that scared me. Towards morning I was possessed by a kind of night-mare; I felt the fiend's grasp in my neck, and could not free myself from it; groans and cries rung in my ears. My father, who was watching over me, perceiving my restlessness, awoke me, and pointed to the port of Holyhead,[6] which we were now entering.

4. Homesickness (French).
5. Opium dissolved in alcohol, prescribed at the time as a sedative.
6. On the island of Holyhead, which is just off the island of Anglesey, Wales.

Chapter 5.

We had resolved not to go to London, but to cross the country to Portsmouth, and thence to embark for Havre.[7] I preferred this plan principally because I dreaded to see again those places in which I had enjoyed a few moments of tranquillity with my beloved Clerval. I thought with horror of seeing again those persons whom we had been accustomed to visit together, and who might make inquiries concerning an event, the very remembrance of which made me again feel the pang I endured when I gazed on his lifeless form in the inn at ———.

As for my father, his desires and exertions were bounded to the[8] again seeing me restored to health and peace of mind. His tenderness and attentions were unremitting; my grief and gloom was obstinate, but he would not despair. Sometimes he thought that I felt deeply the degradation of being obliged to answer a charge of murder, and he endeavoured to prove to me the futility of pride.

"Alas! my father," said I, "how little do you know me. Human beings, their feelings and passions, would indeed be degraded, if such a wretch as I felt pride. Justine, poor unhappy Justine, was as innocent as I, and she suffered the same charge; she died for it; and I am the cause of this—I murdered her. William, Justine, and Henry—they all died by my hands."

My father had often, during my imprisonment, heard me make the same assertion; when I thus accused myself, he sometimes seemed to desire an explanation, and at others he appeared to consider it as caused by delirium, and that, during my illness, some idea of this kind had presented itself to my imagination, the remembrance of which I preserved in my convalescence. I avoided explanation, and maintained a continual silence concerning the wretch I had created. I had a feeling that I should be supposed mad, and this for ever chained my tongue, when I would have given the whole world to have confided the fatal secret.

Upon this occasion my father said, with an expression of unbounded wonder, "What do you mean, Victor? are you mad? My dear son, I entreat you never to make such an assertion again."

"I am not mad," I cried energetically; "the sun and the heavens, who have viewed my operations, can bear witness of my truth. I am the assassin of those most innocent victims; they died by my machinations. A thousand times would I have shed my own blood drop by drop, to have saved their lives but I could not, my father, indeed, could not sacrifice the whole human race."

The conclusion of this speech convinced my father that my ideas were deranged, and he instantly changed the subject of our conversation, and endeavoured to alter the course of my thoughts. He wished as much as possible to obliterate the memory of the scenes that had taken place in Ireland, and never alluded to them, or suffered me to speak of my misfortunes.

As time passed away I became more calm: misery had her dwelling in my heart, but I no longer talked in the same incoherent manner of my own crimes; sufficient for me was the consciousness of them. By the utmost self-violence, I curbed the imperious voice of wretchedness, which sometimes

---

7. Le Havre, French channel port.　　　　8. Limited to.

desired to declare itself to the whole world; and my manners were calmer and more composed than they had ever been since my journey to the sea of ice.

We arrived at Havre on the 8th of May, and instantly proceeded to Paris, where my father had some business which detained us a few weeks. In this city, I received the following letter from Elizabeth:—

"*TO* VICTOR FRANKENSTEIN.

"MY DEAREST FRIEND,

"It gave me the greatest pleasure to receive a letter from my uncle dated at Paris; you are no longer at a formidable distance, and I may hope to see you in less than a fortnight. My poor cousin, how much you must have suffered! I expect to see you looking even more ill than when you quitted Geneva. This winter has been passed most miserably, tortured as I have been by anxious suspense; yet I hope to see peace in your countenance, and to find that your heart is not totally devoid of comfort and tranquillity.

"Yet I fear that the same feelings now exist that made you so miserable a year ago, even perhaps augmented by time. I would not disturb you at this period, when so many misfortunes weigh upon you; but a conversation that I had with my uncle previous to his departure renders some explanation necessary before we meet.

"Explanation! you may possibly say; what can Elizabeth have to explain? If you really say this, my questions are answered, and I have no more to do than to sign myself your affectionate cousin. But you are distant from me, and it is possible that you may dread, and yet be pleased with this explanation; and, in a probability of this being the case, I dare not any longer postpone writing what, during your absence, I have often wished to express to you, but have never had the courage to begin.

"You well know, Victor, that our union had been the favourite plan of your parents ever since our infancy. We were told this when young, and taught to look forward to it as an event that would certainly take place. We were affectionate playfellows during childhood, and, I believe, dear and valued friends to one another as we grew older. But as brother and sister often entertain a lively affection towards each other, without desiring a more intimate union, may not such also be our case? Tell me, dearest Victor. Answer me, I conjure[9] you, by our mutual happiness, with simple truth—Do you not love another?

"You have travelled; you have spent several years of your life at Ingolstadt; and I confess to you, my friend, that when I saw you last autumn so unhappy, flying to solitude, from the society of every creature, I could not help supposing that you might regret our connexion, and believe yourself bound in honour to fulfil the wishes of your parents, although they opposed themselves to your inclinations. But this is false reasoning. I confess to you, my cousin, that I love you, and that in my

9. Entreat.

airy dreams of futurity you have been my constant friend and companion. But it is your happiness I desire as well as my own, when I declare to you, that our marriage would render me eternally miserable, unless it were the dictate of your own free choice. Even now I weep to think, that, borne down as you are by the cruelest misfortunes, you may stifle, by the word *honour*, all hope of that love and happiness which would alone restore you to yourself. I, who have so interested an affection for you, may increase your miseries ten-fold, by being an obstacle to your wishes. Ah, Victor, be assured that your cousin and playmate has too sincere a love for you not to be made miserable by this supposition. Be happy, my friend; and if you obey me in this one request, remain satisfied that nothing on earth will have the power to interrupt my tranquillity.

"Do not let this letter disturb you; do not answer it to-morrow, or the next day, or even until you come, if it will give you pain. My uncle will send me news of your health; and if I see but one smile on your lips when we meet, occasioned by this or any other exertion of mine, I shall need no other happiness.

"ELIZABETH LAVENZA.
"Geneva, May 18th, 17——."

This letter revived in my memory what I had before forgotten, the threat of the fiend—"*I will be with you on your wedding-night!*" Such was my sentence, and on that night would the dæmon employ every art to destroy me, and tear me from the glimpse of happiness which promised partly to console my sufferings. On that night he had determined to consummate his crimes by my death. Well, be it so; a deadly struggle would then assuredly take place, in which if he was victorious, I should be at peace, and his power over me be at an end. If he were vanquished, I should be a free man. Alas! what freedom? such as the peasant enjoys when his family have been massacred before his eyes, his cottage burnt, his lands laid waste, and he is turned adrift, homeless, pennyless, and alone, but free. Such would be my liberty, except that in my Elizabeth I possessed a treasure; alas! balanced by those horrors of remorse and guilt, which would pursue me until death.

Sweet and beloved Elizabeth! I read and re-read her letter, and some softened feelings stole into my heart, and dared to whisper paradisaical dreams of love and joy; but the apple was already eaten, and the angel's arm bared to drive me from all hope.[1] Yet I would die to make her happy. If the monster executed his threat, death was inevitable; yet, again, I considered whether my marriage would hasten my fate. My destruction might indeed arrive a few months sooner; but if my torturer should suspect that I postponed it, influenced by his menaces, he would surely find other, and perhaps more dreadful means of revenge. He had vowed *to be with me on my wedding-night*, yet he did not consider that threat as binding him to peace in the mean time; for, as if to shew me that he was not yet satiated with blood, he had murdered Clerval immediately after the enunciation of his threats. I resolved, therefore, that if my immediate union with my cousin would conduce either

1. Adam and Eve are led from the Garden of Eden by the archangel Michael, and the way back is barred by a flaming sword (*Paradise Lost* 12.636–44).

to her's or my father's happiness, my adversary's designs against my life should not retard it a single hour.

In this state of mind I wrote to Elizabeth. My letter was calm and affectionate. "I fear, my beloved girl," I said, "little happiness remains for us on earth; yet all that I may one day enjoy is concentered in you. Chase away your idle fears; to you alone do I consecrate my life, and my endeavour for contentment. I have one secret, Elizabeth, a dreadful one; when revealed to you, it will chill your frame with horror, and then, far from being surprised at my misery, you will only wonder that I survive what I have endured. I will confide this tale of misery and terror to you the day after our marriage shall take place; for, my sweet cousin, there must be perfect confidence between us. But until then, I conjure you, do not mention or allude to it. This I most earnestly entreat, and I know you will comply."

In about a week after the arrival of Elizabeth's letter, we returned to Geneva. My cousin welcomed me with warm affection; yet tears were in her eyes, as she beheld my emaciated frame and feverish cheeks. I saw a change in her also. She was thinner, and had lost much of that heavenly vivacity that had before charmed me; but her gentleness, and soft looks of compassion, made her a more fit companion for one blasted and miserable as I was.

The tranquillity which I now enjoyed did not endure. Memory brought madness with it; and when I thought on what had passed, a real insanity possessed me; sometimes I was furious, and burnt with rage, sometimes low and despondent. I neither spoke or looked, but sat motionless, bewildered by the multitude of miseries that overcame me.

Elizabeth alone had the power to draw me from these fits; her gentle voice would soothe me when transported by passion, and inspire me with human feelings when sunk in torpor. She wept with me, and for me. When reason returned, she would remonstrate, and endeavour to inspire me with resignation. Ah! it is well for the unfortunate to be resigned, but for the guilty there is no peace. The agonies of remorse poison the luxury there is otherwise sometimes found in indulging the excess of grief.

Soon after my arrival my father spoke of my immediate marriage with my cousin. I remained silent.

"Have you, then, some other attachment?"

"None on earth. I love Elizabeth, and look forward to our union with delight. Let the day therefore be fixed; and on it I will consecrate myself, in life or death, to the happiness of my cousin."

"My dear Victor, do not speak thus. Heavy misfortunes have befallen us; but let us only cling closer to what remains, and transfer our love for those whom we have lost to those who yet live. Our circle will be small, but bound close by the ties of affection and mutual misfortune. And when time shall have softened your despair, new and dear objects of care will be born to replace those of whom we have been so cruelly deprived."

Such were the lessons of my father. But to me the remembrance of the threat returned: nor can you wonder, that, omnipotent as the fiend had yet been in his deeds of blood, I should almost regard him as invincible; and that when he had pronounced the words, "*I shall be with you on your wedding-night*," I should regard the threatened fate as unavoidable. But death was no evil to me, if the loss of Elizabeth were balanced with it; and I therefore, with a contented and even cheerful countenance, agreed with my father, that if my cousin would consent, the ceremony should take place in ten days, and thus put, as I imagined, the seal to my fate.

Great God! if for one instant I had thought what might be the hellish intention of my fiendish adversary, I would rather have banished myself for ever from my native country, and wandered a friendless outcast over the earth, than have consented to this miserable marriage. But, as if possessed of magic powers, the monster had blinded me to his real intentions; and when I thought that I prepared only my own death, I hastened that of a far dearer victim.

As the period fixed for our marriage drew nearer, whether from cowardice or a prophetic feeling, I felt my heart sink within me. But I concealed my feelings by an appearance of hilarity, that brought smiles and joy to the countenance of my father, but hardly deceived the ever-watchful and nicer[2] eye of Elizabeth. She looked forward to our union with placid contentment, not unmingled with a little fear, which past misfortunes had impressed, that what now appeared certain and tangible happiness, might soon dissipate into an airy dream, and leave no trace but deep and everlasting regret.

Preparations were made for the event; congratulatory visits were received; and all wore a smiling appearance. I shut up, as well as I could, in my own heart the anxiety that preyed there, and entered with seeming earnestness into the plans of my father, although they might only serve as the decorations of my tragedy. A house was purchased for us near Cologny, by which we should enjoy the pleasures of the country, and yet be so near Geneva as to see my father every day; who would still reside within the walls, for the benefit of Ernest, that he might follow his studies at the schools.

In the mean time I took every precaution to defend my person, in case the fiend should openly attack me. I carried pistols and a dagger constantly about me, and was ever on the watch to prevent artifice; and by these means gained a greater degree of tranquillity. Indeed, as the period approached, the threat appeared more as a delusion, not to be regarded as worthy to disturb my peace, while the happiness I hoped for in my marriage wore a greater appearance of certainty, as the day fixed for its solemnization drew nearer, and I heard it continually spoken of as an occurrence which no accident could possibly prevent.

Elizabeth seemed happy; my tranquil demeanour contributed greatly to calm her mind. But on the day that was to fulfil my wishes and my destiny, she was melancholy, and a presentiment of evil pervaded her; and perhaps also she thought of the dreadful secret, which I had promised to reveal to her the following day. My father was in the mean time overjoyed, and, in the bustle of preparation, only observed in the melancholy of his niece the diffidence of a bride.

After the ceremony was performed, a large party assembled at my father's; but it was agreed that Elizabeth and I should pass the afternoon and night at Evian, and return to Cologny the next morning. As the day was fair, and the wind favourable, we resolved to go by water.

Those were the last moments of my life during which I enjoyed the feeling of happiness. We passed rapidly along: the sun was hot, but we were sheltered from its rays by a kind of canopy, while we enjoyed the beauty of the

2. More sensitive and discerning.

scene, sometimes on one side of the lake, where we saw Mont Salêve, the pleasant banks of Montalêgre, and at a distance, surmounting all, the beautiful Mont Blanc, and the assemblage of snowy mountains that in vain endeavour to emulate her; sometimes coasting the opposite banks, we saw the mighty Jura opposing its dark side to the ambition that would quit its native country, and an almost insurmountable barrier to the invader who should wish to enslave it.

I took the hand of Elizabeth: "You are sorrowful, my love. Ah! if you knew what I have suffered, and what I may yet endure, you would endeavour to let me taste the quiet, and freedom from despair, that this one day at least permits me to enjoy."

"Be happy, my dear Victor," replied Elizabeth; "there is, I hope, nothing to distress you; and be assured that if a lively joy is not painted in my face, my heart is contented. Something whispers to me not to depend too much on the prospect that is opened before us; but I will not listen to such a sinister voice. Observe how fast we move along, and how the clouds which sometimes obscure, and sometimes rise above the dome of Mont Blanc, render this scene of beauty still more interesting. Look also at the innumerable fish that are swimming in the clear waters, where we can distinguish every pebble that lies at the bottom. What a divine day! how happy and serene all nature appears!"

Thus Elizabeth endeavoured to divert her thoughts and mine from all reflection upon melancholy subjects. But her temper was fluctuating; joy for a few instants shone in her eyes, but it continually gave place to distraction and reverie.

The sun sunk lower in the heavens; we passed the river Drance, and observed its path through the chasms of the higher, and the glens of the lower hills. The Alps here come closer to the lake, and we approached the amphitheatre of mountains which forms its eastern boundary. The spire of Evian shone under the woods that surrounded it, and the range of mountain above mountain by which it was overhung.

The wind, which had hitherto carried us along with amazing rapidity, sunk at sunset to a light breeze; the soft air just ruffled the water, and caused a pleasant motion among the trees as we approached the shore, from which it wafted the most delightful scent of flowers and hay. The sun sunk beneath the horizon as we landed; and as I touched the shore, I felt those cares and fears revive, which soon were to clasp me, and cling to me for ever.

Chapter 6.

It was eight o'clock when we landed; we walked for a short time on the shore, enjoying the transitory light, and then retired to the inn, and contemplated the lovely scene of waters, woods, and mountains, obscured in darkness, yet still displaying their black outlines.

The wind, which had fallen in the south, now rose with great violence in the west. The moon had reached her summit in the heavens, and was beginning to descend; the clouds swept across it swifter than the flight of the vulture, and dimmed her rays, while the lake reflected the scene of the busy heavens, rendered still busier by the restless waves that were beginning to rise. Suddenly a heavy storm of rain descended.

I had been calm during the day; but so soon as night obscured the shapes of objects, a thousand fears arose in my mind. I was anxious and watchful, while my right hand grasped a pistol which was hidden in my bosom; every sound terrified me; but I resolved that I would sell my life dearly, and not relax the impending conflict until my own life, or that of my adversary, were extinguished.

Elizabeth observed my agitation for some time in timid and fearful silence; at length she said, "What is it that agitates you, my dear Victor? What is it you fear?"

"Oh! peace, peace, my love," replied I, "this night, and all will be safe: but this night is dreadful, very dreadful."

I passed an hour in this state of mind, when suddenly I reflected how dreadful the combat which I momentarily expected would be to my wife, and I earnestly entreated her to retire, resolving not to join her until I had obtained some knowledge as to the situation of my enemy.

She left me, and I continued some time walking up and down the passages of the house, and inspecting every corner that might afford a retreat to my adversary. But I discovered no trace of him, and was beginning to conjecture that some fortunate chance had intervened to prevent the execution of his menaces; when suddenly I heard a shrill and dreadful scream. It came from the room into which Elizabeth had retired. As I heard it, the whole truth rushed into my mind, my arms dropped, the motion of every muscle and fibre was suspended; I could feel the blood trickling in my veins, and tingling in the extremities of my limbs. This state lasted but for an instant; the scream was repeated, and I rushed into the room.

Great God! why did I not then expire! Why am I here to relate the destruction of the best hope, and the purest creature of earth? She was there, lifeless and inanimate, thrown across the bed, her head hanging down, and her pale and distorted features half covered by her hair. Every where I turn I see the same figure—her bloodless arms and relaxed form flung by the murderer on its bridal bier. Could I behold this, and live? Alas! life is obstinate, and clings closest where it is most hated. For a moment only did I lose recollection; I fainted.

When I recovered, I found myself surrounded by the people of the inn; their countenances expressed a breathless terror: but the horror of others appeared only as a mockery, a shadow of the feelings that oppressed me. I escaped from them to the room where lay the body of Elizabeth, my love, my wife, so lately living, so dear, so worthy. She had been moved from the posture in which I had first beheld her; and now, as she lay, her head upon her arm, and a handkerchief thrown across her face and neck, I might have supposed her asleep. I rushed towards her, and embraced her with ardour; but the deathly languor and coldness of the limbs told me, that what I now held in my arms had ceased to be the Elizabeth whom I had loved and cherished. The murderous mark of the fiend's grasp was on her neck, and the breath had ceased to issue from her lips.

While I still hung over her in the agony of despair, I happened to look up. The windows of the room had before been darkened; and I felt a kind of panic on seeing the pale yellow light of the moon illuminate the chamber. The shutters had been thrown back; and, with a sensation of horror not to be described, I saw at the open window a figure the most hideous and abhorred. A grin was on the face of the monster; he seemed to jeer, as with his fiendish finger he pointed towards the corpse of my wife. I rushed towards the window, and drawing a pistol from my bosom, shot; but he eluded me, leaped from his station, and, running with the swiftness of lightning, plunged into the lake.

The report of the pistol brought a crowd into the room. I pointed to the spot where he had disappeared, and we followed the track with boats; nets were cast, but in vain. After passing several hours, we returned hopeless, most of my companions believing it to have been a form conjured by my fancy. After having landed, they proceeded to search the country, parties going in different directions among the woods and vines.

I did not accompany them; I was exhausted: a film covered my eyes, and my skin was parched with the heat of fever. In this state I lay on a bed, hardly conscious of what had happened; my eyes wandered round the room, as if to seek something that I had lost.

At length I remembered that my father would anxiously expect the return of Elizabeth and myself, and that I must return alone. This reflection brought tears into my eyes, and I wept for a long time; but my thoughts rambled to various subjects, reflecting on my misfortunes, and their cause. I was bewildered in a cloud of wonder and horror. The death of William, the execution of Justine, the murder of Clerval, and lastly of my wife; even at that moment I knew not that my only remaining friends were safe from the malignity of the fiend; my father even now might be writhing under his grasp, and Ernest might be dead at his feet. This idea made me shudder, and recalled me to action. I started up, and resolved to return to Geneva with all possible speed.

There were no horses to be procured, and I must return by the lake; but the wind was unfavourable, and the rain fell in torrents. However, it was hardly morning, and I might reasonably hope to arrive by night. I hired men to row, and took an oar myself, for I had always experienced relief from mental torment in bodily exercise. But the overflowing misery I now felt, and the excess of agitation that I endured, rendered me incapable of any exertion. I threw down the oar; and, leaning my head upon my hands, gave way to every gloomy idea that arose. If I looked up, I saw the scenes which were familiar to me in my happier time, and which I had contemplated but the day before in the company of her who was now but a shadow and a recollection. Tears streamed from my eyes. The rain had ceased for a moment, and I saw the fish play in the waters as they had done a few hours before; they had then been observed by Elizabeth. Nothing is so painful to the human mind as a great and sudden change. The sun might shine, or the clouds might lour, but nothing could appear to me as it had done the day before. A fiend had snatched from me every hope of future happiness: no creature had ever been so miserable as I was; so frightful an event is single in the history of man.

But why should I dwell upon the incidents that followed this last overwhelming event. Mine has been a tale of horrors; I have reached their *acme*, and what I must now relate can but be tedious to you. Know that, one by one, my friends were snatched away; I was left desolate. My own strength is exhausted; and I must tell, in a few words, what remains of my hideous narration.

I arrived at Geneva. My father and Ernest yet lived; but the former sunk under the tidings that I bore. I see him now, excellent and venerable old man! his eyes wandered in vacancy, for they had lost their charm and their delight—his niece, his more than daughter, whom he doated on with all that affection which a man feels, who, in the decline of life, having few affections, clings more earnestly to those that remain. Cursed, cursed be the fiend that brought misery on his grey hairs, and doomed him to waste in wretchedness! He could not live under the horrors that were accumulated around him; an apoplectic fit was brought on, and in a few days he died in my arms.

What then became of me? I know not; I lost sensation, and chains and darkness were the only objects that pressed upon me. Sometimes, indeed, I dreamt that I wandered in flowery meadows and pleasant vales with the friends of my youth; but awoke, and found myself in a dungeon. Melancholy followed, but by degrees I gained a clear conception of my miseries and situation, and was then released from my prison. For they had called me mad; and during many months, as I understood, a solitary cell had been my habitation.

But liberty had been a useless gift to me had I not, as I awakened to reason, at the same time awakened to revenge. As the memory of past misfortunes pressed upon me, I began to reflect on their cause—the monster whom I had created, the miserable dæmon whom I had sent abroad into the world for my destruction. I was possessed by a maddening rage when I thought of him, and desired and ardently prayed that I might have him within my grasp to wreak a great and signal revenge on his cursed head.

Nor did my hate long confine itself to useless wishes; I began to reflect on the best means of securing him; and for this purpose, about a month after my release, I repaired to a criminal judge in the town, and told him that I had an accusation to make; that I knew the destroyer of my family; and that I required him to exert his whole authority for the apprehension of the murderer.

The magistrate listened to me with attention and kindness: "Be assured, sir," said he, "no pains or exertions on my part shall be spared to discover the villain."

"I thank you," replied I; "listen, therefore, to the deposition that I have to make. It is indeed a tale so strange, that I should fear you would not credit it, were there not something in truth which, however wonderful, forces conviction. The story is too connected to be mistaken for a dream, and I have no motive for falsehood." My manner, as I thus addressed him, was impressive, but calm; I had formed in my own heart a resolution to pursue my destroyer to death; and this purpose quieted my agony, and provisionally reconciled me to life. I now related my history briefly, but with firmness and precision, marking the dates with accuracy, and never deviating into invective or exclamation.

The magistrate appeared at first perfectly incredulous, but as I continued he became more attentive and interested; I saw him sometimes shudder with horror, at others a lively surprise, unmingled with disbelief, was painted on his countenance.

When I had concluded my narration, I said, "This is the being whom I accuse, and for whose detection and punishment I call upon you to exert your whole power. It is your duty as a magistrate, and I believe and hope that your feelings as a man will not revolt from the execution of those functions on this occasion."

This address caused a considerable change in the physiognomy of my auditor. He had heard my story with that half kind of belief that is given to a tale of spirits and supernatural events; but when he was called upon to act officially in consequence, the whole tide of his incredulity returned. He, however, answered mildly, "I would willingly afford you every aid in your pursuit; but the creature of whom you speak appears to have powers which would put all my exertions to defiance. Who can follow an animal which can traverse the sea of ice, and inhabit caves and dens, where no man would venture to intrude? Besides, some months have elapsed since the commission of his crimes, and no one can conjecture to what place he has wandered, or what region he may now inhabit."

"I do not doubt that he hovers near the spot which I inhabit; and if he has indeed taken refuge in the Alps, he may be hunted like the chamois,[3] and destroyed as a beast of prey. But I perceive your thoughts: you do not credit my narrative, and do not intend to pursue my enemy with the punishment which is his desert."

As I spoke, rage sparkled in my eyes; the magistrate was intimidated; "You are mistaken," said he, "I will exert myself; and if it is in my power to seize the monster, be assured that he shall suffer punishment proportionate to his crimes. But I fear, from what you have yourself described to be his properties, that this will prove impracticable, and that, while every proper measure is pursued, you should endeavour to make up your mind to disappointment."

"That cannot be; but all that I can say will be of little avail. My revenge is of no moment to you; yet, while I allow it to be a vice, I confess that it is the devouring and only passion of my soul. My rage is unspeakable, when I reflect that the murderer, whom I have turned loose upon society, still exists. You refuse my just demand: I have but one resource; and I devote myself, either in my life or death, to his destruction."

I trembled with excess of agitation as I said this; there was a phrenzy in my manner, and something, I doubt not, of that haughty fierceness, which the martyrs of old are said to have possessed. But to a Genevan magistrate, whose mind was occupied by far other ideas than those of devotion and heroism, this elevation of mind had much the appearance of madness. He endeavoured to soothe me as a nurse does a child, and reverted to my tale as the effects of delirium.

"Man," I cried, "how ignorant art thou in thy pride of wisdom! Cease; you know not what it is you say."

I broke from the house angry and disturbed, and retired to meditate on some other mode of action.

Chapter 7.

My present situation was one in which all voluntary thought was swallowed up and lost. I was hurried away by fury; revenge alone endowed me with strength and composure; it modelled my feelings, and allowed me to be calculating and calm, at periods when otherwise delirium or death would have been my portion.

My first resolution was to quit Geneva for ever; my country, which, when I was happy and beloved, was dear to me, now, in my adversity, became

3. A swift, horned animal inhabiting the Alps, hunted for the soft leather made from its hide.

hateful. I provided myself with a sum of money, together with a few jewels which had belonged to my mother, and departed.

And now my wanderings began, which are to cease but with life. I have traversed a vast portion of the earth, and have endured all the hardships which travellers, in deserts and barbarous countries, are wont to meet. How I have lived I hardly know; many times have I stretched my failing limbs upon the sandy plain, and prayed for death. But revenge kept me alive; I dared not die, and leave my adversary in being.

When I quitted Geneva, my first labour was to gain some clue by which I might trace the steps of my fiendish enemy. But my plan was unsettled; and I wandered many hours around the confines of the town, uncertain what path I should pursue. As night approached, I found myself at the entrance of the cemetery where William, Elizabeth, and my father, reposed. I entered it, and approached the tomb which marked their graves. Every thing was silent, except the leaves of the trees, which were gently agitated by the wind; the night was nearly dark; and the scene would have been solemn and affecting even to an uninterested observer. The spirits of the departed seemed to flit around, and to cast a shadow, which was felt but seen not, around the head of the mourner.

The deep grief which this scene had at first excited quickly gave way to rage and despair. They were dead, and I lived; their murderer also lived, and to destroy him I must drag out my weary existence. I knelt on the grass, and kissed the earth, and with quivering lips exclaimed, "By the sacred earth on which I kneel, by the shades[4] that wander near me, by the deep and eternal grief that I feel, I swear; and by thee, O Night, and by the spirits that preside over thee, I swear to pursue the dæmon, who caused this misery, until he or I shall perish in mortal conflict. For this purpose I will preserve my life: to execute this dear revenge, will I again behold the sun, and tread the green herbage of earth, which otherwise should vanish from my eyes for ever. And I call on you, spirits of the dead; and on you, wandering ministers of vengeance, to aid and conduct me in my work. Let the cursed and hellish monster drink deep of agony; let him feel the despair that now torments me."

I had begun my adjuration with solemnity, and an awe which almost assured me that the shades of my murdered friends heard and approved my devotion; but the furies possessed me as I concluded, and rage choaked my utterance.

I was answered through the stillness of night by a loud and fiendish laugh. It rung on my ears long and heavily; the mountains re-echoed it, and I felt as if all hell surrounded me with mockery and laughter. Surely in that moment I should have been possessed by phrenzy, and have destroyed my miserable existence, but that my vow was heard, and that I was reserved for vengeance. The laughter died away, when a well-known and abhorred voice, apparently close to my ear, addressed me in an audible whisper—"I am satisfied: miserable wretch! you have determined to live, and I am satisfied."

I darted towards the spot from which the sound proceeded; but the devil eluded my grasp. Suddenly the broad disk of the moon arose, and shone full upon his ghastly and distorted shape, as he fled with more than mortal speed.

I pursued him; and for many months this has been my task. Guided by a

4. Disembodied spirits.

slight clue, I followed the windings of the Rhone, but vainly. The blue Mediterranean appeared; and, by a strange chance, I saw the fiend enter by night, and hide himself in a vessel bound for the Black Sea. I took my passage in the same ship; but he escaped, I know not how.

Amidst the wilds of Tartary and Russia, although he still evaded me, I have ever followed in his track. Sometimes the peasants, scared by this horrid apparition, informed me of his path; sometimes he himself, who feared that if I lost all trace I should despair and die, often left some mark to guide me. The snows descended on my head, and I saw the print of his huge step on the white plain. To you first entering on life, to whom care is new and agony unknown, how can you understand what I have felt, and still feel. Cold, want, and fatigue, were the least pains which I was destined to endure. I was cursed by some devil, and carried about with me my eternal hell; yet still a spirit of good followed and directed my steps, and, when I most murmured, would suddenly extricate me from seemingly insurmountable difficulties. Sometimes, when nature overcome by hunger, sunk under the exhaustion, a repast was prepared for me in the desert, that restored and inspirited me. The fare was indeed coarse, such as the peasants of the country ate; but I may not doubt that it was set there by the spirits that I had invoked to aid me. Often, when all was dry, the heavens cloudless, and I was parched by thirst, a slight cloud would bedim the sky, shed the few drops that revived me, and vanish.

I followed, when I could, the courses of the rivers; but the dæmon generally avoided these, as it was here that the population of the country chiefly collected. In other places human beings were seldom seen; and I generally subsisted on the wild animals that crossed my path. I had money with me, and gained the friendship of the villagers by distributing it, or bringing with me some food that I had killed, which, after taking a small part, I always presented to those who had provided me with fire and utensils for cooking.

My life, as it passed thus, was indeed hateful to me, and it was during sleep alone that I could taste joy. O blessed sleep! often, when most miserable. I sank to repose, and my dreams lulled me even to rapture. The spirits that guarded me had provided these moments, or rather hours, of happiness that I might retain strength to fulfil my pilgrimage. Deprived of this respite, I should have sunk under my hardships. During the day I was sustained and inspirited by the hope of night: for in sleep I saw my friends, my wife, and my beloved country; again I saw the benevolent countenance of my father, heard the silver tones of my Elizabeth's voice, and beheld Clerval enjoying health and youth. Often, when wearied by a toilsome march, I persuaded myself that I was dreaming until night should come, and that I should then enjoy reality in the arms of my dearest friends. What agonizing fondness did I feel for them! how did I cling to their dear forms, as sometimes they haunted even my waking hours, and persuade myself that they still lived! At such moments vengeance, that burned within me, died in my heart, and I pursued my path towards the destruction of the dæmon, more as a task enjoined by heaven, as the mechanical impulse of some power of which I was unconscious, than as the ardent desire of my soul.

What his feelings were whom I pursued, I cannot know. Sometimes, indeed, he left marks in writing on the barks of the trees, or cut in stone, that guided me, and instigated my fury. "My reign is not yet over," (these words were legible in one of these inscriptions); "you live, and my power is complete. Follow me; I seek the everlasting ices of the north, where you will feel the misery of cold and frost, to which I am impassive. You will find near this place, if you follow not too tardily, a dead hare; eat, and be refreshed. Come on, my enemy; we have yet to wrestle for our lives; but many hard and miserable hours must you endure, until that period shall arrive."

Scoffing devil! Again do I vow vengeance; again do I devote thee, miserable fiend, to torture and death. Never will I omit my search, until he or I perish; and then with what ecstacy shall I join my Elizabeth, and those who even now prepare for me the reward of my tedious toil and horrible pilgrimage.

As I still pursued my journey to the northward, the snows thickened, and the cold increased in a degree almost too severe to support. The peasants were shut up in their hovels, and only a few of the most hardy ventured forth to seize the animals whom starvation had forced from their hiding-places to seek for prey. The rivers were covered with ice, and no fish could be procured; and thus I was cut off from my chief article of maintenance.

The triumph of my enemy increased with the difficulty of my labours. One inscription that he left was in these words: "Prepare! your toils only begin: wrap yourself in furs, and provide food, for we shall soon enter upon a journey where your sufferings will satisfy my everlasting hatred."

My courage and perseverance were invigorated by these scoffing words; I resolved not to fail in my purpose; and, calling on heaven to support me, I continued with unabated fervour to traverse immense deserts, until the ocean appeared at a distance, and formed the utmost boundary of the horizon. Oh! how unlike it was to the blue seas of the south! Covered with ice, it was only to be distinguished from land by its superior wildness and ruggedness. The Greeks wept for joy when they beheld the Mediterranean from the hills of Asia, and hailed with rapture the boundary of their toils.[5] I did not weep; but I knelt down, and, with a full heart, thanked my guiding spirit for conducting me in safety to the place where I hoped, notwithstanding my adversary's gibe, to meet and grapple with him.

Some weeks before this period I had procured a sledge and dogs, and thus traversed the snows with inconceivable speed. I know not whether the fiend possessed the same advantages; but I found that, as before I had daily lost ground in the pursuit, I now gained on him; so much so, that when I first saw the ocean, he was but one day's journey in advance, and I hoped to intercept him before he should reach the beach. With new courage, therefore, I pressed on, and in two days arrived at a wretched hamlet on the seashore. I inquired of the inhabitants concerning the fiend, and gained accurate information. A gigantic monster, they said, had arrived the night before, armed with a gun and many pistols; putting to flight the inhabitants of a solitary cottage, through fear of his terrific appearance. He had carried off their store of winter food, and, placing it in a sledge, to draw which he had seized on a numerous drove of trained dogs, he had harnessed them, and the same night, to the joy of the horror-struck villagers, had pursued his journey across the sea in a direction that led to no land; and they conjectured that he must speedily be destroyed by the breaking of the ice, or frozen by the eternal frosts.

---

5. A famed event during the Greek army's retreat from a failed expedition against Persia (401–399 B.C.E.), told by Xenophon in his *Anabasis*, book 4.

On hearing this information, I suffered a temporary access of despair. He had escaped me; and I must commence a destructive and almost endless journey across the mountainous ices of the ocean,—amidst cold that few of the inhabitants could long endure, and which I, the native of a genial and sunny climate, could not hope to survive. Yet at the idea that the fiend should live and be triumphant, my rage and vengeance returned, and, like a mighty tide, overwhelmed every other feeling. After a slight repose, during which the spirits of the dead hovered round, and instigated me to toil and revenge, I prepared for my journey.

I exchanged my land sledge for one fashioned for the inequalities of the frozen ocean; and, purchasing a plentiful stock of provisions, I departed from land.

I cannot guess how many days have passed since then; but I have endured misery, which nothing but the eternal sentiment of a just retribution burning within my heart could have enabled me to support. Immense and rugged mountains of ice often barred up my passage, and I often heard the thunder of the ground sea, which threatened my destruction. But again the frost came, and made the paths of the sea secure.

By the quantity of provision which I had consumed I should guess that I had passed three weeks in this journey; and the continual protraction of hope, returning back upon the heart, often wrung bitter drops of despondency and grief from my eyes. Despair had indeed almost secured her prey, and I should soon have sunk beneath this misery; when once, after the poor animals that carried me had with incredible toil gained the summit of a sloping ice mountain, and one sinking under his fatigue died, I viewed the expanse before me with anguish, when suddenly my eye caught a dark speck upon the dusky plain. I strained my sight to discover what it could be, and uttered a wild cry of ecstacy when I distinguished a sledge, and the distorted proportions of a well-known form within. Oh! with what a burning gush did hope revisit my heart! warm tears filled my eyes, which I hastily wiped away, that they might not intercept the view I had of the dæmon; but still my sight was dimmed by the burning drops, until, giving way to the emotions that oppressed me, I wept aloud.

But this was not the time for delay; I disencumbered the dogs of their dead companion, gave them a plentiful portion of food; and, after an hour's rest, which was absolutely necessary, and yet which was bitterly irksome to me, I continued my route. The sledge was still visible; nor did I again lose sight of it, except at the moments when for a short time some ice rock concealed it with its intervening crags. I indeed perceptibly gained on it; and when, after nearly two days' journey, I beheld my enemy at no more than a mile distant, my heart bounded within me.

But now, when I appeared almost within grasp of my enemy, my hopes were suddenly extinguished, and I lost all trace of him more utterly than I had ever done before. A ground sea was heard; the thunder of its progress, as the waters rolled and swelled beneath me, became every moment more ominous and terrific. I pressed on, but in vain. The wind arose; the sea roared; and, as with the mighty shock of an earthquake, it split, and cracked with a tremendous and overwhelming sound. The work was soon finished: in a few minutes a tumultuous sea rolled between me and my enemy, and I was left drifting on a scattered piece of ice, that was continually lessening, and thus preparing for me a hideous death.

In this manner many appalling hours passed; several of my dogs died; and I myself was about to sink under the accumulation of distress, when I saw your vessel riding at anchor, and holding forth to me hopes of succour and life. I had no conception that vessels ever came so far north, and was astounded at the sight. I quickly destroyed part of my sledge to construct oars; and by these means was enabled, with infinite fatigue, to move my ice-raft in the direction of your ship. I had determined, if you were going southward, still to trust myself to the mercy of the seas, rather than abandon my purpose. I hoped to induce you to grant me a boat with which I could still pursue my enemy. But your direction was northward. You took me on board when my vigour was exhausted, and I should soon have sunk under my multiplied hardships into a death, which I still dread,—for my task is unfulfilled.

Oh! when will my guiding spirit, in conducting me to the dæmon, allow me the rest I so much desire; or must I die, and he yet live? If I do, swear to me, Walton, that he shall not escape; that you will seek him, and satisfy my vengeance in his death. Yet, do I dare ask you to undertake my pilgrimage, to endure the hardships that I have undergone? No; I am not so selfish. Yet, when I am dead, if he should appear; if the ministers of vengeance should conduct him to you, swear that he shall not live—swear that he shall not triumph over my accumulated woes, and live to make another such a wretch as I am. He is eloquent and persuasive; and once his words had even power over my heart: but trust him not. His soul is as hellish as his form, full of treachery and fiend-like malice. Hear him not; call on the manes[6] of William, Justine, Clerval, Elizabeth, my father, and of the wretched Victor, and thrust your sword into his heart. I will hover near, and direct the steel aright.

WALTON, *in continuation.*

August 26th, 17—.

You have read this strange and terrific story, Margaret; and do you not feel your blood congealed with horror, like that which even now curdles mine? Sometimes, seized with sudden agony, he could not continue his tale; at others, his voice broken, yet piercing, uttered with difficulty the words so replete with agony. His fine and lovely eyes were now lighted up with indignation, now subdued to downcast sorrow, and quenched in infinite wretchedness. Sometimes he commanded his countenance and tones, and related the most horrible incidents with a tranquil voice, suppressing every mark of agitation; then, like a volcano bursting forth, his face would suddenly change to an expression of the wildest rage, as he shrieked out imprecations on his persecutor.

His tale is connected,[7] and told with an appearance of the simplest truth; yet I own to you that the letters of Felix and Safie, which he shewed me, and the apparition of the monster, seen from our ship, brought to me a greater conviction of the truth of his narrative than his asseverations, however earnest and connected. Such a monster has then really existence; I cannot doubt it; yet I am lost in surprise and admiration. Sometimes I endeavoured to gain from Frankenstein the particulars of his creature's formation; but on this point he was impenetrable.

---

6. Roman term for the spirits of dead ancestors.   7. Coherent.

"Are you mad, my friend?" said he, "or whither does your senseless curiosity lead you? Would you also create for yourself and the world a demoniacal enemy? Or to what do your questions tend? Peace, peace! learn my miseries, and do not seek to increase your own."

Frankenstein discovered that I made notes concerning his history: he asked to see them, and then himself corrected and augmented them in many places; but principally in giving the life and spirit to the conversations he held with his enemy. "Since you have preserved my narration," said he, "I would not that a mutilated one should go down to posterity."

Thus has a week passed away, while I have listened to the strangest tale that ever imagination formed. My thoughts, and every feeling of my soul, have been drunk up by the interest for my guest, which this tale, and his own elevated and gentle manners have created. I wish to soothe him; yet can I counsel one so infinitely miserable, so destitute of every hope of consolation, to live? Oh, no! the only joy that he can now know will be when he composes his shattered feelings to peace and death. Yet he enjoys one comfort, the offspring of solitude and delirium: he believes, that, when in dreams he holds converse with his friends, and derives from that communion consolation for his miseries, or excitements to his vengeance, that they are not the creations of his fancy, but the real beings who visit him from the regions of a remote world. This faith gives a solemnity to his reveries that render them to me almost as imposing and interesting as truth.

Our conversations are not always confined to his own history and misfortunes. On every point of general literature he displays unbounded knowledge, and a quick and piercing apprehension. His eloquence is forcible and touching; nor can I hear him, when he relates a pathetic incident, or endeavours to move the passions of pity or love, without tears. What a glorious creature must he have been in the days of his prosperity, when he is thus noble and godlike in ruin. He seems to feel his own worth, and the greatness of his fall.

"When younger," said he, "I felt as if I were destined for some great enterprise. My feelings are profound; but I possessed a coolness of judgment that fitted me for illustrious achievements. This sentiment of the worth of my nature supported me, when others would have been oppressed; for I deemed it criminal to throw away in useless grief those talents that might be useful to my fellow-creatures. When I reflected on the work I had completed, no less a one than the creation of a sensitive and rational animal, I could not rank myself with the herd of common projectors.[8] But this feeling, which supported me in the commencement of my career, now serves only to plunge me lower in the dust. All my speculations and hopes are as nothing; and, like the archangel who aspired to omnipotence, I am chained in an eternal hell. My imagination was vivid, yet my powers of analysis and application were intense; by the union of these qualities I conceived the idea, and executed the creation of a man. Even now I cannot recollect, without passion, my reveries while the work was incomplete. I trod heaven in my thoughts, now exulting in my powers, now burning with the idea of their effects. From my infancy I was imbued with high hopes and a lofty ambition; but how am I sunk! Oh! my friend, if you had known me as I once was, you would not

8. Devisers of schemes and experiments.

recognize me in this state of degradation. Despondency rarely visited my heart; a high destiny seemed to bear me on, until I fell, never, never again to rise."

Must I then lose this admirable being? I have longed for a friend; I have sought one who would sympathize with and love me. Behold, on these desert seas I have found such a one; but, I fear, I have gained him only to know his value, and lose him. I would reconcile him to life, but he repulses the idea.

"I thank you, Walton," he said, "for your kind intentions towards so miserable a wretch; but when you speak of new ties, and fresh affections, think you that any can replace those who are gone? Can any man be to me as Clerval was; or any woman another Elizabeth? Even where the affections are not strongly moved by any superior excellence, the companions of our childhood always possess a certain power over our minds, which hardly any later friend can obtain. They know our infantine dispositions, which, however they may be afterwards modified, are never eradicated; and they can judge of our actions with more certain conclusions as to the integrity of our motives. A sister or a brother can never, unless indeed such symptoms have been shewn early, suspect the other of fraud or false dealing, when another friend, however strongly he may be attached, may, in spite of himself, be invaded with suspicion. But I enjoyed friends, dear not only through habit and association, but from their own merits; and, wherever I am, the soothing voice of my Elizabeth, and the conversation of Clerval, will be ever whispered in my ear. They are dead; and but one feeling in such a solitude can persuade me to preserve my life. If I were engaged in any high undertaking or design, fraught with extensive utility to my fellow-creatures, then could I live to fulfil it. But such is not my destiny; I must pursue and destroy the being to whom I gave existence; then my lot on earth will be fulfilled, and I may die."

September 2d.

MY BELOVED SISTER,

I write to you, encompassed by peril, and ignorant whether I am ever doomed to see again dear England, and the dearer friends that inhabit it. I am surrounded by mountains of ice, which admit of no escape, and threaten every moment to crush my vessel. The brave fellows, whom I have persuaded to be my companions, look towards me for aid; but I have none to bestow. There is something terribly appalling in our situation, yet my courage and hopes do not desert me. We may survive; and if we do not, I will repeat the lessons of my Seneca, and die with a good heart.[9]

Yet what, Margaret, will be the state of your mind? You will not hear of my destruction, and you will anxiously await my return. Years will pass, and you will have visitings of despair, and yet be tortured by hope. Oh! my beloved sister, the sickening failings of your heart-felt expectations are, in prospect, more terrible to me than my own death. But you have a husband, and lovely children; you may be happy: heaven bless you, and make you so!

My unfortunate guest regards me with the tenderest compassion. He endeavours to fill me with hope; and talks as if life were a possession which

---

9. Seneca was a Roman playwright and Stoic philosopher of the first century C.E. When the emperor Nero, accusing him of conspiracy, ordered him to commit suicide, he slashed his veins and died with quiet dignity.

he valued. He reminds me how often the same accidents have happened to other navigators, who have attempted this sea, and, in spite of myself, he fills me with cheerful auguries. Even the sailors feel the power of his eloquence: when he speaks, they no longer despair; he rouses their energies, and, while they hear his voice, they believe these vast mountains of ice are mole-hills, which will vanish before the resolutions of man. These feelings are transitory; each day's expectation delayed fills them with fear, and I almost dread a mutiny caused by this despair.

September 5th.

A scene has just passed of such uncommon interest, that although it is highly probable that these papers may never reach you, yet I cannot forbear recording it.

We are still surrounded by mountains of ice, still in imminent danger of being crushed in their conflict. The cold is excessive, and many of my unfortunate comrades have already found a grave amidst this scene of desolation. Frankenstein has daily declined in health: a feverish fire still glimmers in his eyes; but he is exhausted, and, when suddenly roused to any exertion, he speedily sinks again into apparent lifelessness.

I mentioned in my last letter the fears I entertained of a mutiny. This morning, as I sat watching the wan countenance of my friend—his eyes half closed, and his limbs hanging listlessly,—I was roused by half a dozen of the sailors, who desired admission into the cabin. They entered; and their leader addressed me. He told me that he and his companions had been chosen by the other sailors to come in deputation to me, to make me a demand, which, in justice, I could not refuse. We were immured in ice, and should probably never escape; but they feared that if, as was possible, the ice should dissipate, and a free passage be opened, I should be rash enough to continue my voyage, and lead them into fresh dangers, after they might happily have surmounted this. They desired, therefore, that I should engage with a solemn promise, that if the vessel should be freed, I would instantly direct my course southward.

This speech troubled me. I had not despaired; nor had I yet conceived the idea of returning, if set free. Yet could I, in justice, or even in possibility, refuse this demand? I hesitated before I answered; when Frankenstein, who had at first been silent, and, indeed, appeared hardly to have force enough to attend, now roused himself, his eyes sparkled, and his cheeks flushed with momentary vigour. Turning towards the men, he said—

"What do you mean? What do you demand of your captain? Are you then so easily turned from your design? Did you not call this a glorious expedition? and wherefore was it glorious? Not because the way was smooth and placid as a southern sea but because it was full of dangers and terror; because, at every new incident, your fortitude was to be called forth and your courage exhibited; because danger and death surrounded, and these dangers you were to brave and overcome. For this was it a glorious, for this was it an honourable undertaking. You were hereafter to be hailed as the benefactors of your species; your name adored, as belonging to brave men who encountered death for honour and the benefit of mankind. And now, behold, with the first imagination of danger, or, if you will, the first mighty and terrific trial of your courage, you shrink away, and are content to be handed down as men who had not strength enough to endure cold and peril; and so, poor souls, they were chilly, and returned to their warm fire-sides. Why, that requires not this preparation; ye need not have come thus far, and dragged your captain to the shame of a defeat, merely to prove yourselves cowards. Oh! be men, or be more than men. Be steady to your purposes, and firm as a rock. This ice is not made of such stuff as your hearts might be; it is mutable, cannot withstand you, if you say that it shall not. Do not return to your families with the stigma of disgrace marked on your brows.[1] Return as heroes who have fought and conquered, and who know not what it is to turn their backs on the foe."

He spoke this with a voice so modulated to the different feelings expressed in his speech, with an eye so full of lofty design and heroism, that can you wonder that these men were moved. They looked at one another, and were unable to reply. I spoke; I told them to retire, and consider of what had been said: that I would not lead them further north, if they strenuously desired the contrary; but that I hoped that, with reflection, their courage would return.

They retired, and I turned towards my friend; but he was sunk in languor, and almost deprived of life.

How all this will terminate, I know not; but I had rather die, than return shamefully,—my purpose unfulfilled. Yet I fear such will be my fate; the men, unsupported by ideas of glory and honour, can never willingly continue to endure their present hardships.

September 7th.

The die is cast;[2] I have consented to return, if we are not destroyed. Thus are my hopes blasted by cowardice and indecision; I come back ignorant and disappointed. It requires more philosophy than I possess, to bear this injustice with patience.

September 12th.

It is past; I am returning to England. I have lost my hopes of utility and glory;—I have lost my friend. But I will endeavour to detail these bitter circumstances to you, my dear sister; and, while I am wafted towards England, and towards you, I will not despond.

September 9th, the ice began to move, and roarings like thunder were heard at a distance, as the islands split and cracked in every direction. We were in the most imminent peril; but, as we could only remain passive, my chief attention was occupied by my unfortunate guest, whose illness increased in such a degree, that he was entirely confined to his bed. The ice cracked behind us, and was driven with force towards the north; a breeze sprung from the west, and on the 11th the passage towards the south became perfectly free. When the sailors saw this, and that their return to their native country was apparently assured, a shout of tumultuous joy broke from them, loud and long-continued. Frankenstein, who was dozing, awoke, and asked

1. An allusion to the mark that the Lord set upon Cain after he killed his brother, Abel (Genesis 4.8–15).

2. Echoing Julius Caesar's remark when, in 49 B.C.E., he crossed the Rubicon and so inaugurated a war against his former ally, Pompey.

the cause of the tumult. "They shout," I said, "because they will soon return to England."

"Do you then really return?"

"Alas! yes; I cannot withstand their demands. I cannot lead them unwillingly to danger, and I must return."

"Do so, if you will; but I will not. You may give up your purpose; but mine is assigned to me by heaven, and I dare not. I am weak; but surely the spirits who assist my vengeance will endow me with sufficient strength." Saying this, he endeavoured to spring from the bed, but the exertion was too great for him; he fell back, and fainted.

It was long before he was restored; and I often thought that life was entirely extinct. At length he opened his eyes, but he breathed with difficulty, and was unable to speak. The surgeon gave him a composing draught,[3] and ordered us to leave him undisturbed. In the mean time he told me, that my friend had certainly not many hours to live.

His sentence was pronounced; and I could only grieve, and be patient. I sat by his bed watching him; his eyes were closed, and I thought he slept; but presently he called to me in a feeble voice, and, bidding me come near, said—"Alas! the strength I relied on is gone; I feel that I shall soon die, and he, my enemy and persecutor, may still be in being. Think not, Walton, that in the last moments of my existence I feel that burning hatred, and ardent desire of revenge, I once expressed, but I feel myself justified in desiring the death of my adversary. During these last days I have been occupied in examining my past conduct; nor do I find it blameable. In a fit of enthusiastic madness I created a rational creature, and was bound towards him, to assure, as far as was in my power, his happiness and well-being. This was my duty; but there was another still paramount to that. My duties towards my fellow-creatures had greater claims to my attention, because they included a greater proportion of happiness or misery. Urged by this view, I refused, and I did right in refusing, to create a companion for the first creature. He shewed unparalleled malignity and selfishness, in evil: he destroyed my friends; he devoted to destruction beings who possessed exquisite sensations, happiness, and wisdom; nor do I know where this thirst for vengeance may end. Miserable himself, that he may render no other wretched, he ought to die. The task of his destruction was mine, but I have failed. When actuated by selfish and vicious motives, I asked you to undertake my unfinished work; and I renew this request now, when I am only induced by reason and virtue.

"Yet I cannot ask you to renounce your country and friends, to fulfil this task; and now, that you are returning to England, you will have little chance of meeting with him. But the consideration of these points, and the well-balancing of what you may esteem your duties, I leave to you; my judgment and ideas are already disturbed by the near approach of death. I dare not ask you to do what I think right, for I may still be misled by passion.

"That he should live to be an instrument of mischief disturbs me; in other respects this hour, when I momentarily expect my release, is the only happy one which I have enjoyed for several years. The forms of the beloved dead flit before me, and I hasten to their arms. Farewell, Walton! Seek happiness in tranquillity, and avoid ambition, even if it be only the apparently innocent

---

3. Liquid medicine.

one of distinguishing yourself in science and discoveries. Yet why do I say this? I have myself been blasted in these hopes, yet another may succeed."

His voice became fainter as he spoke; and at length, exhausted by his effort, he sunk into silence. About half an hour afterwards he attempted again to speak, but was unable; he pressed my hand feebly, and his eyes closed for ever, while the irradiation of a gentle smile passed away from his lips.

Margaret, what comment can I make on the untimely extinction of this glorious spirit? What can I say, that will enable you to understand the depth of my sorrow? All that I should express would be inadequate and feeble. My tears flow; my mind is overshadowed by a cloud of disappointment. But I journey towards England, and I may there find consolation.

I am interrupted. What do these sounds portend? It is midnight; the breeze blows fairly, and the watch on deck scarcely stir. Again; there is a sound as of a human voice, but hoarser; it comes from the cabin where the remains of Frankenstein still lie. I must arise, and examine. Good night, my sister.

Great God! what a scene has just taken place! I am yet dizzy with the remembrance of it. I hardly know whether I shall have the power to detail it; yet the tale which I have recorded would be incomplete without this final and wonderful catastrophe.

I entered the cabin, where lay the remains of my ill-fated and admirable friend. Over him hung a form which I cannot find words to describe; gigantic in stature, yet uncouth and distorted in its proportions. As he hung over the coffin, his face was concealed by long locks of ragged hair; but one vast hand was extended, in colour and apparent texture like that of a mummy. When he heard the sound of my approach, he ceased to utter exclamations of grief and horror, and sprung towards the window. Never did I behold a vision so horrible as his face, of such loathsome, yet appalling hideousness. I shut my eyes involuntarily, and endeavoured to recollect what were my duties with regard to this destroyer. I called on him to stay.

He paused, looking on me with wonder; and, again turning towards the lifeless form of his creator, he seemed to forget my presence, and every feature and gesture seemed instigated by the wildest rage of some uncontrollable passion.

"That is also my victim!" he exclaimed; "in his murder my crimes are consummated; the miserable series of my being is wound to its close! Oh, Frankenstein! generous and self-devoted being! what does it avail that I now ask thee to pardon me? I, who irretrievably destroyed thee by destroying all thou lovedst. Alas! he is cold; he may not answer me."

His voice seemed suffocated; and my first impulses, which had suggested to me the duty of obeying the dying request of my friend, in destroying his enemy, were now suspended by a mixture of curiosity and compassion. I approached this tremendous being; I dared not again raise my looks upon his face, there was something so scaring and unearthly in his ugliness. I attempted to speak, but the words died away on my lips. The monster continued to utter wild and incoherent self-reproaches. At length I gathered resolution to address him, in a pause of the tempest of his passion: "Your repentance," I said, "is now superfluous. If you had listened to the voice of conscience, and heeded the stings of remorse, before you had urged your diabolical vengeance to this extremity, Frankenstein would yet have lived."

"And do you dream?" said the dæmon; "do you think that I was then dead to agony and remorse?—He," he continued, pointing to the corpse, "he suffered not more in the consummation of the deed;—oh! not the ten-thousandth portion of the anguish that was mine during the lingering detail of its execution. A frightful selfishness hurried me on, while my heart was poisoned with remorse. Think ye that the groans of Clerval were music to my ears? My heart was fashioned to be susceptible of love and sympathy; and, when wrenched by misery to vice and hatred, it did not endure the violence of the change without torture, such as you cannot even imagine.

"After the murder of Clerval, I returned to Switzerland, heart-broken and overcome. I pitied Frankenstein; my pity amounted to horror: I abhorred myself. But when I discovered that he, the author at once of my existence and of its unspeakable torments, dared to hope for happiness; that while he accumulated wretchedness and despair upon me, he sought his own enjoyment in feelings and passions from the indulgence of which I was for ever barred, then impotent envy and bitter indignation filled me with an insatiable thirst for vengeance. I recollected my threat, and resolved that it should be accomplished. I knew that I was preparing for myself a deadly torture; but I was the slave, not the master of an impulse, which I detested, yet could not disobey. Yet when she died!—nay, then I was not miserable. I had cast off all feeling, subdued all anguish to riot in the excess of my despair. Evil thenceforth became my good.[4] Urged thus far, I had no choice but to adapt my nature to an element which I had willingly chosen. The completion of my demoniacal design became an insatiable passion. And now it is ended; there is my last victim!"

I was at first touched by the expressions of his misery; yet when I called to mind what Frankenstein had said of his powers of eloquence and persuasion, and when I again cast my eyes on the lifeless form of my friend, indignation was re-kindled within me. "Wretch!" I said, "it is well that you come here to whine over the desolation that you have made. You throw a torch into a pile of buildings, and when they are consumed you sit among the ruins, and lament the fall. Hypocritical fiend! if he whom you mourn still lived, still would he be the object, again would he become the prey of your accursed vengeance. It is not pity that you feel; you lament only because the victim of your malignity is withdrawn from your power."

"Oh, it is not thus—not thus," interrupted the being; "yet such must be the impression conveyed to you by what appears to be the purport of my actions. Yet I seek not a fellow-feeling in my misery. No sympathy may I ever find. When I first sought it, it was the love of virtue, the feelings of happiness and affection with which my whole being overflowed, that I wished to be participated.[5] But now, that virtue has become to me a shadow, and that happiness and affection are turned into bitter and loathing despair, in what should I seek for sympathy? I am content to suffer alone, while my sufferings shall endure: when I die, I am well satisfied that abhorrence and opprobrium should load my memory. Once my fancy was soothed with dreams of virtue, of fame, and of enjoyment. Once I falsely hoped to meet with beings, who, pardoning my outward form, would love me for the excellent qualities which

---

4. Echoing Satan, *Paradise Lost* 4.109–10: "All good to me is lost; / Evil, be thou my good."   5. Shared with others.

I was capable of bringing forth. I was nourished with high thoughts of honour and devotion. But now vice has degraded me beneath the meanest animal. No crime, no mischief, no malignity, no misery, can be found comparable to mine. When I call over the frightful catalogue of my deeds, I cannot believe that I am he whose thoughts were once filled with sublime and transcendant visions of the beauty and the majesty of goodness. But it is even so; the fallen angel becomes a malignant devil.[6] Yet even that enemy of God and man had friends and associates in his desolation; I am quite alone.

"You, who call Frankenstein your friend, seem to have a knowledge of my crimes and his misfortunes. But, in the detail which he gave you of them, he could not sum up the hours and months of misery which I endured, wasting in impotent passions. For whilst I destroyed his hopes, I did not satisfy my own desires. They were for ever ardent and craving; still I desired love and fellowship, and I was still spurned. Was there no injustice in this? Am I to be thought the only criminal, when all human kind sinned against me? Why do you not hate Felix, who drove his friend from his door with contumely?[7] Why do you not execrate the rustic who sought to destroy the saviour of his child? Nay, these are virtuous and immaculate beings! I, the miserable and the abandoned, am an abortion, to be spurned at, and kicked, and trampled on. Even now my blood boils at the recollection of this injustice.

"But it is true that I am a wretch. I have murdered the lovely and the helpless; I have strangled the innocent as they slept, and grasped to death his throat who never injured me or any other living thing. I have devoted my creator, the select specimen of all that is worthy of love and admiration among men, to misery; I have pursued him even to that irremediable ruin. There he lies, white and cold in death. You hate me; but your abhorrence cannot equal that with which I regard myself. I look on the hands which executed the deed; I think on the heart in which the imagination of it was conceived, and long for the moment when they will meet my eyes, when it will haunt my thoughts, no more.

"Fear not that I shall be the instrument of future mischief. My work is nearly complete. Neither your's nor any man's death is needed to consummate the series of my being, and accomplish that which must be done; but it requires my own. Do not think that I shall be slow to perform this sacrifice. I shall quit your vessel on the ice-raft which brought me hither, and shall seek the most northern extremity of the globe; I shall collect my funeral pile, and consume to ashes this miserable frame, that its remains may afford no light to any curious and unhallowed wretch, who would create such another as I have been. I shall die. I shall no longer feel the agonies which now consume me, or be the prey of feelings unsatisfied, yet unquenched. He is dead who called me into being; and when I shall be no more, the very remembrance of us both will speedily vanish. I shall no longer see the sun or stars, or feel the winds play on my cheeks. Light, feeling, and sense, will pass away; and in this condition must I find my happiness. Some years ago, when the images which this world affords first opened upon me, when I felt the cheering warmth of summer, and heard the rustling of the leaves and the chirping

6. Like Satan, who before his rebellion against God had been the archangel Lucifer.

7. Contemptuous speech.

of the birds, and these were all to me, I should have wept to die; now it is my only consolation. Polluted by crimes, and torn by the bitterest remorse, where can I find rest but in death?

"Farewell! I leave you, and in you the last of human kind whom these eyes will ever behold. Farewell, Frankenstein! If thou wert yet alive, and yet cherished a desire of revenge against me, it would be better satiated in my life than in my destruction. But it was not so; thou didst seek my extinction, that I might not cause greater wretchedness; and if yet, in some mode unknown to me, thou hast not yet ceased to think and feel, thou desirest not my life for my own misery. Blasted as thou wert, my agony was still superior to thine; for the bitter sting of remorse may not cease to rankle in my wounds until death shall close them for ever.

"But soon," he cried, with sad and solemn enthusiasm, "I shall die, and what I now feel be no longer felt. Soon these burning miseries will be extinct. I shall ascend my funeral pile triumphantly, and exult in the agony of the torturing flames. The light of that conflagration will fade away; my ashes will be swept into the sea by the winds. My spirit will sleep in peace; or if it thinks, it will not surely think thus. Farewell."

He sprung from the cabin-window, as he said this, upon the ice-raft which lay close to the vessel. He was soon borne away by the waves, and lost in darkness and distance.

THE END.

1816–17   1818

LETITIA ELIZABETH LANDON
1802–1838

Letitia Elizabeth Landon, whose initials became one of the most famous literary pseudonyms of nineteenth-century Britain, was born and educated in Chelsea, London. She published her first poem in the weekly *Literary Gazette* in March 1820, when she was seventeen, and soon thereafter became a principal writer and reviewer for the magazine. Her first important collections of poems were *The Improvisatrice* (1824), which went through six editions in its first year, and *The Troubadour, Catalogue of Pictures, and Historical Sketches* (1825), which went through four. She quickly followed these with *The Golden Violet* (1827), the first of many editions of her *Poetical Works* (1827), and *The Venetian Bracelet* (1829). She also wrote essays, short fiction, children's stories, several novels, and a play; and she edited—and contributed hundreds of poems to—the albums, gift books, and annual anthologies that became a staple of British literary production of the 1820s and 1830s. All this highly remunerative work appeared from the pen of "L.E.L.," the pseudonym that she first used in the *Literary Gazette* and that attracted increasing numbers of readers and also poetic responses, as it was disclosed by stages that the author behind the initials was female, young, and a great beauty. To this day, many of Landon's books continue to be catalogued under the pseudonym, and a recently published "feminist companion" to literature in English has an entry for "L.E.L." but none for "Landon."

Landon and Felicia Hemans, as "L.E.L." and "Mrs. Hemans," were the two best-selling poets of their time—the decade and a half following the deaths of Keats, Percy Shelley, and Byron in the early 1820s—and were major inspirations to subsequent writers such as Elizabeth Barrett and Christina Rossetti. Unlike Hemans, Landon attracted scandal, partly because of her casual social relations with men and partly because of her principal subject matter, the joys and especially the sorrows of female passion. There were rumors of affairs with, among others, William Jerdan, who was editor of the *Literary Gazette*, the journalist William Maginn, and the artist Daniel Maclise. She was engaged to the editor John Forster, future biographer of Dickens, but had to break the engagement because of these rumors. In 1838 she finally married, someone she had known for only a short time, George Maclean, governor of the British settlement at Cape Coast Castle, west Africa (in what is now Ghana). She arrived with Maclean at Cape Coast in August 1838 and two months later was dead, reportedly from an overdose of prussic acid—though whether the cause was accident, suicide, or murder has never been determined.

Landon perfected, and the reviewers helped maintain, several personas in her work: the pseudonymous, therefore anonymous, writer of passionate love lyrics; the Romantic "improvisatrice" jotting down verses in the interstices of an intense social life; the renowned beauty who constantly fails in love and, in lamenting her crushed feelings, becomes the female equivalent of the Byronic hero; and an early version of the Victorian "poetess" inditing songs to appeal to a burgeoning cult of domesticity. As in Hemans's poetry, some of these personas are not wholly compatible with some of the others. But their variety and vitality captivated the readers and, during Landon's short life, provided her a fortune in sales and royalties.

The Proud Ladye[1]

Oh, what could the ladye's beauty match,
    An° it were not the ladye's pride?   *if*
An hundred knights from far and near
    Woo'd at that ladye's side.

5   The rose of the summer slept on her cheek,
    Its lily upon her breast,
And her eye shone forth like the glorious star
    That rises the first in the west.

There were some that woo'd for her land and gold,
10   And some for her noble name,

---

1. This ballad is . . . taken, with some slight change, from a legend in Russell's Germany [Landon's note]. The story, in John Russell's *A Tour in Germany* (1824), chap. 11, relates how "the fair Cunigunda, equally celebrated for her charms and her cruelty . . . would listen to no tale of love, and dreaded marriage as she did a prison. At length, to free herself from all importunities, she made a solemn vow never to give her hand but to the knight who should ride round the castle on the outer wall . . . [which] runs along the very brink of hideous precipices. . . . History has not recorded the precise number of those who actually made the attempt; it is only certain that every one of them broke his neck. . . . At length, a young and handsome knight appeared at the castle gate . . . [to] try his fortune. . . . In a short time, a shout from the menials announced that the adventure had been achieved; and Cunigunda, exulting that she was conquered, hastened into the court. . . . But the knight stood aloof, gloomy and severe. 'I can claim you,' said he; 'but I am come, and I have risked my life, not to win your hand, but to humble your pride and punish your barbarity'—and thereupon he read her a harsh lecture on the cruelty and arrogance of her conduct towards her suitors. The spirit of chivalry weeps at recording, that he finished his oration by giving the astonished beauty a box on the ear." Landon's ballad (in the same stanza as Keats's story of another *belle dame sans merci*) was included as a separate piece within a long poem, *The Troubadour*, that she published in 1825.

And more that woo'd for her loveliness;
    But her answer was still the same.

"There is a steep and lofty wall,
    Where my warders° trembling stand;   *guards*
15 He who at speed shall ride round its height,
    For him shall be my hand."

Many turn'd away from the deed,
    The hope of their wooing o'er;
But many a young knight mounted the steed
20   He never mounted more.

At last there came a youthful knight,
    From a strange and far countrie,
The steed that he rode was white as the foam
    Upon a stormy sea.

25 And she who had scorn'd the name of love,
    Now bow'd before its might,
And the ladye grew meek as if disdain
    Were not made for that stranger knight.

She sought at first to steal his soul
30   By dance, song, and festival;
At length on bended knee she pray'd
    He would not ride the wall.

But gaily the young knight laugh'd at her fears,
    And flung him on his steed,—
35 There was not a saint in the calendar
    That she pray'd not to in her need.

She dar'd not raise her eyes to see
    If heaven had granted her prayer,
Till she heard a light step bound to her side,—
40   The gallant knight stood there!

And took the ladye Adeline
    From her hair a jewell'd band,
But the knight repell'd the offer'd gift,
    And turn'd from the offer'd hand.

45 "And deemest thou that I dared this deed,
    Ladye, for love of thee?
The honour that guides the soldier's lance
    Is mistress enough for me.

"Enough for me to ride the ring,
50   The victor's crown to wear;
But not in honour of the eyes
    Of any ladye there.

"I had a brother whom I lost
    Through thy proud crueltie,
55 And far more was to me his love,
    Than woman's love can be.

"I came to triumph o'er the pride
    Through which that brother fell,
I laugh to scorn thy love and thee,
60   And now, proud dame, farewell!"

And from that hour the ladye pined,
    For love was in her heart,
And on her slumber there came dreams
    She could not bid depart.

65 Her eye lost all its starry light,
    Her cheek grew wan and pale,
Till she hid her faded loveliness
    Beneath the sacred veil.

And she cut off her long dark hair,
70   And bade the world farewell,
And she now dwells a veiled nun
    In Saint Marie's cell.

1825

Love's Last Lesson

"Teach it me, if you can,—forgetfulness![1]
I surely shall forget, if you can bid me;
I who have worshipp'd thee, my god on earth,
I who have bow'd me at thy lightest word.
5 Your last command, 'Forget me,' will it not
Sink deeply down within my inmost soul?
Forget thee!—ay, forgetfulness will be
A mercy to me. By the many nights
When I have wept for that I dared not sleep,—
10 A dream had made me live my woes again,
Acting my wretchedness, without the hope
My foolish heart still clings to, though that hope
Is like the opiate which may lull a while,
Then wake to double torture; by the days
15 Pass'd in lone watching and in anxious fears,
When a breath sent the crimson to my cheek,
Like the red gushing of a sudden wound;
By all the careless looks and careless words
Which have to me been like the scorpion's stinging;

1. An allusion to Byron's *Manfred* 1.1.135–36: "What wouldst thou with us, son of mortals— say?"—to which Manfred replies, "Forgetfulness." Other Byronic echoes in lines 14–15, 18–23, 85– 86, and 95–98 further link Landon's speaker to the protagonists of *Childe Harold* and *Manfred*.

20 By happiness blighted, and by thee, for ever;
    By thy eternal work of wretchedness;
    By all my wither'd feelings, ruin'd health,
    Crush'd hopes, and rifled heart, I will forget thee!
    Alas! my words are vanity. Forget thee!
25 Thy work of wasting is too surely done.
    The April shower may pass and be forgotten,
    The rose fall and one fresh spring in its place,
    And thus it may be with light summer love.
    It was not thus with mine: it did not spring,
30 Like the bright colour on an evening cloud,
    Into a moment's life, brief, beautiful;
    Not amid lighted halls, when flatteries
    Steal on the ear like dew upon the rose,
    As soft, as soon dispersed, as quickly pass'd;
35 But you first call'd my woman's feelings forth,
    And taught me love ere I had dream'd love's name.
    I loved unconsciously: your name was all
    That seem'd in language, and to me the world
    Was only made for you; in solitude,
40 When passions hold their interchange together,
    Your image was the shadow of my thought;
    Never did slave, before his Eastern lord,
    Tremble as I did when I met your eye,
    And yet each look was counted as a prize;
45 I laid your words up in my heart like pearls
    Hid in the ocean's treasure-cave. At last
    I learn'd my heart's deep secret: for I hoped,
    I dream'd you loved me; wonder, fear, delight,
    Swept my heart like a storm; my soul, my life,
50 Seem'd all too little for your happiness;
    Had I been mistress of the starry worlds
    That light the midnight, they had all been yours,
    And I had deem'd such boon but poverty.
    As it was, I gave all I could—my love,
55 My deep, my true, my fervent, faithful love;
    And now you bid me learn forgetfulness:
    It is a lesson that I soon shall learn.
    There is a home of quiet for the wretched,
    A somewhat dark, and cold, and silent rest,
60 But still it is rest,—for it is the grave."

    She flung aside the scroll, as it had part
    In her great misery. Why should she write?
    What could she write? Her woman's pride forbade
    To let him look upon her heart, and see
65 It was an utter ruin;—and cold words,
    And scorn and slight, that may repay his own,
    Were as a foreign language, to whose sound
    She might not frame her utterance. Down she bent
    Her head upon an arm so white that tears

70   Seem'd but the natural melting of its snow,
     Touch'd by the flush'd cheek's crimson; yet life-blood
     Less wrings in shedding than such tears as those.

         And this then is love's ending! It is like
     The history of some fair southern clime.
75   Hot fires are in the bosom of the earth,
     And the warm'd soil puts forth its thousand flowers,
     Its fruits of gold, summer's regality,
     And sleep and odours float upon the air:
     At length the subterranean element
80   Breaks from its secret dwelling-place, and lays
     All waste before it; the red lava stream
     Sweeps like the pestilence; and that which was
     A garden in its colours and its breath,
     Fit for the princess of a fairy tale,
85   Is as a desert, in whose burning sands,
     And ashy waters, who is there can trace
     A sign, a memory of its former beauty?
     It is thus with the heart; love lights it up
     With hopes like young companions, and with joys
90   Dreaming deliciously of their sweet selves.

         This is at first; but what is the result?
     Hopes that lie mute in their own sullenness,
     For they have quarrell'd even with themselves;
     And joys indeed like birds of Paradise:[2]
95   And in their stead despair coils scorpion-like
     Stinging itself; and the heart, burnt and crush'd
     With passion's earthquake, scorch'd and wither'd up,
     Lies in its desolation,—this is love.

         What is the tale that I would tell? Not one
100 Of strange adventure, but a common tale
     Of woman's wretchedness; one to be read
     Daily in many a young and blighted heart.
     The lady whom I spake of rose again
     From the red fever's couch, to careless eyes
105 Perchance the same as she had ever been.
     But oh, how alter'd to herself! She felt
     That bird-like pining for some gentle home
     To which affection might attach itself,
     That weariness which hath but outward part
110 In what the world calls pleasure, and that chill
     Which makes life taste the bitterness of death.

         And he she loved so well,—what opiate
     Lull'd consciousness into its selfish sleep?—
     He said he loved her not; that never vow

---

2. In Eastern tales, the bird of Paradise never rests on the earth [Landon's note].

115 Or passionate pleading won her soul for him;
And that he guess'd not her deep tenderness.

Are words, then, only false? are there no looks,
Mute but most eloquent; no gentle cares
That win so much upon the fair weak things
120 They seem to guard? And had he not long read
Her heart's hush'd secret in the soft dark eye
Lighted at his approach, and on the cheek
Colouring all crimson at his lightest look?
This is the truth; his spirit wholly turn'd
125 To stern ambition's dream, to that fierce strife
Which leads to life's high places, and reck'd not
What lovely flowers might perish in his path.

And here at length is somewhat of revenge:
For man's most golden dreams of pride and power
130 Are vain as any woman-dreams of love;
Both end in weary brow and wither'd heart,
And the grave closes over those whose hopes
Have lain there long before.

1827

Revenge

Ay, gaze upon her rose-wreathed hair,
    And gaze upon her smile;
Seem as you drank the very air
    Her breath perfumed the while:

5 And wake for her the gifted line,
    That wild and witching lay,
And swear your heart is as a shrine,
    That only owns her sway.

'Tis well: I am revenged at last,—
10   Mark you that scornful cheek,—
The eye averted as you pass'd,
    Spoke more than words could speak.

Ay, now by all the bitter tears
    That I have shed for thee,—
15 The racking doubts, the burning fears,—
    Avenged they well may be—

By the nights pass'd in sleepless care,
    The days of endless woe;
All that you taught my heart to bear,
20   All that yourself will know.

I would not wish to see you laid
   Within an early tomb;
I should forget how you betray'd,
   And only weep your doom:

25 But this is fitting punishment,
   To live and love in vain,—
Oh my wrung heart, be thou content,
   And feed upon his pain.

Go thou and watch her lightest sigh,—
30   Thine own it will not be;
And bask beneath her sunny eye,—
   It will not turn on thee.

'Tis well: the rack, the chain, the wheel,
   Far better had'st thou proved;
35 Ev'n I could almost pity feel,
   For thou art not beloved.

1829

The Little Shroud

She put him on a snow-white shroud,
   A chaplet° on his head;   *wreath*
And gather'd early primroses
   To scatter o'er the dead.

5 She laid him in his little grave—
   'Twas hard to lay him there,
When spring was putting forth its flowers,
   And every thing was fair.

She had lost many children—now
10   The last of them was gone;
And day and night she sat and wept
   Beside the funeral stone.

One midnight, while her constant tears
   Were falling with the dew,
15 She heard a voice, and lo! her child
   Stood by her weeping too!

His shroud was damp, his face was white:
   He said,—"I cannot sleep,
Your tears have made my shroud so wet;
20   Oh, mother, do not weep!"

Oh, love is strong!—the mother's heart
   Was filled with tender fears;

Oh, love is strong!—and for her child
  Her grief restrained its tears.

25 One eve a light shone round her bed,
  And there she saw him stand—
Her infant, in his little shroud,
  A taper in his hand.

"Lo! mother, see my shroud is dry,
30   And I can sleep once more!"
And beautiful the parting smile
  The little infant wore.

And down within the silent grave
  He laid his weary head;
35 And soon the early violets
  Grew o'er his grassy bed.

1832

The Victorian Age
1830–1901

1832:	The First Reform Bill
1837:	Victoria becomes queen
1846:	The Corn Laws repealed
1850:	Tennyson succeeds Wordsworth as Poet Laureate
1851:	The Great Exhibition in London
1859:	Charles Darwin's *Origin of Species* published
1870–71:	Franco-Prussian War
1901:	Death of Victoria

In 1897 Mark Twain was visiting London during the Diamond Jubilee celebrations honoring the sixtieth anniversary of Queen Victoria's coming to the throne. "British history is two thousand years old," Twain observed, "and yet in a good many ways the world has moved farther ahead since the Queen was born than it moved in all the rest of the two thousand put together." And if the whole world had "moved" during that long lifetime and reign of Victoria's, it was in her own country itself that the change was most marked and dramatic, a change that brought England to its highest point of development as a world power.

In the eighteenth century the pivotal city of Western civilization had been Paris; by the second half of the nineteenth century this center of influence had shifted to London, a city that expanded from about two million inhabitants when Victoria came to the throne to six and a half million at the time of her death. The rapid growth of London is one of the many indications of the most important development of the age: the shift from a way of life based on the ownership of land to a modern urban economy based on trade and manufacturing. "We have been living, as it were, the life of three hundred years in thirty" was the impression formed by Dr. Thomas Arnold during the early stages of England's industrialization. By the end of the century—after the resources of steam power had been more fully exploited for fast railways and iron ships, for looms, printing presses, and farmers' combines, and after the introduction of the telegraph, intercontinental cable, photography, anesthetics, and universal compulsory education—a late Victorian could look back with astonishment on these developments during his or her lifetime. Walter Besant, one of these late Victorians, observed that so completely transformed were "the mind and habits of the ordinary Englishman" by 1897, "that he would not, could he see him, recognize his own grandfather."

Because England was the first country to become industrialized, its transformation was an especially painful one: it experienced a host of social and economic problems consequent to rapid and unregulated industrialization. England also experienced an enormous increase in wealth. An early start enabled England to capture markets all over the globe. Cotton and other manufactured products were exported in English ships, a merchant fleet whose size was without parallel in other countries. The profits gained from trade led also to extensive capital investments in all continents. After England had become the world's workshop, London became, from 1870 on, the world's banker. England gained particular profit from the development of its own colonies, which, by 1890, comprised more than a quarter of all the territory on the surface of the earth; one in four people was a subject of Queen Victoria. By the end of the century England was the world's foremost imperial power.

The reactions of Victorian writers to the fast-paced expansion of England were various. Thomas Babington Macaulay (1800–1859) relished the spectacle with strenuous enthusiasm. During the prosperous 1850s Macaulay's essays and histories, with their recitations of the statistics of industrial growth, constituted a Hymn to Progress as well as a celebration of the superior qualities of the English people—"the greatest and most highly civilized people that ever the world saw." Other writers felt that leadership in commerce and industry was being paid for at a terrible price in human happiness, that a so-called progress had been gained only by abandoning traditional rhythms of life and traditional patterns of human relationships. The melancholy poetry of Matthew Arnold often strikes this note:

> For what wears out the life of mortal men?
> 'Tis that from change to change their being rolls;
> 'Tis that repeated shocks, again, again,
> Exhaust the energy of strongest souls.

Although many Victorians shared a sense of satisfaction in the industrial and political preeminence of England during the period, they also suffered from an anxious sense of something lost, a sense too of being displaced persons in a world made alien by technological changes that had been exploited too quickly for the adaptive powers of the human psyche.

QUEEN VICTORIA AND THE VICTORIAN TEMPER

Queen Victoria's long reign, from 1837 to 1901, defines the historical period that bears her name. The question naturally arises whether the distinctive character of those years justifies the adjective *Victorian*. In part Victoria herself encouraged her own identification with the qualities we associate with the adjective—earnestness, moral responsibility, domestic propriety. As a young wife, as the mother of nine children, and as the black-garbed Widow of Windsor in the forty years after her husband's death in 1861, Victoria represented the domestic fidelities her citizens embraced. After her death Henry James wrote, "I mourn the safe and motherly old middle-class queen, who held the nation warm under the fold of her big, hideous Scotch-plaid shawl." Changes in the reproduction of visual images aided in making her the icon she became. She is the first British monarch of whom we have photographs. These pictures, and the ease and cheapness with which they were reproduced, facilitated her representing her country's sense of itself during her reign.

Victoria came to the throne in a decade that does seem to mark a different historical consciousness among Britain's writers. In 1831 John Stuart Mill asserts, "we are living in an age of transition." In the same year Thomas Carlyle writes, "The Old has passed away, but alas, the New appears not in its stead; the Time is still in pangs of travail with the New." Although the historical changes that created the England of the 1830s had been in progress for many decades, writers of the thirties shared a sharp new sense of modernity, of a break with the past, of historical self-consciousness. They responded to their sense of the historical moment with a strenuous call to action that they self-consciously distinguished from the attitude of the previous generation.

In 1834 Carlyle urged his contemporaries, "Close thy *Byron*; open thy *Goethe*." He was saying, in effect, to abandon the introspection of the Romantics and to turn to the higher moral purpose that he found in Goethe. The popular novelist Edward Bulwer-Lytton (1803–1873) in his *England and the English* made a similar judgment. "When Byron passed away," he wrote, " . . . we turned to the actual and practical career of life: we awoke from the morbid, the dreaming, 'the moonlight and dimness of the mind,' and by a natural reaction addressed ourselves to the active and daily objects which lay before us." This sense of historical self-consciousness, of strenuous social enterprise, and of growing national achievement led writers as early as the 1850s and 1860s to define their age as Victorian. The very fact that Victoria reigned for so long sustained the concept of a distinctive historical period that writers defined even as they lived it.

When Queen Victoria died, a reaction developed against many of the achievements of the previous century; this reinforced the sense that the Victorian age was a distinct period. In the earlier decades of the twentieth century, writers took pains to separate themselves from the Victorians. It was then the fashion for most literary critics to treat their Victorian predecessors as somewhat absurd creatures, stuffily complacent prigs with whose way of life they had little in common. Writers of the Georgian period (1911–36) took great delight in puncturing overinflated Victorian balloons, as Lytton Strachey, a member of Virginia Woolf's circle, did in *Eminent Victorians* (1918). A subtler example occurs in Woolf's *Orlando*, a fictionalized survey of English literature from Elizabethan times to 1928, in which the Victorians are presented in terms of dampness, rain, and proliferating vegetation:

> Ivy grew in unparalleled profusion. Houses that had been of bare stone were smothered in greenery. . . . And just as the ivy and the evergreen rioted in the damp earth outside, so did the same fertility show itself within. The life of the average woman was a succession of childbirths. . . . Giant cauliflowers towered deck above deck till they rivaled . . . the elm trees themselves. Hens laid incessantly eggs of no special tint. . . . The whole sky itself as it spread wide above the British Isles was nothing but a vast feather bed.

This witty description not only identifies a distinguishing quality of Victorian life and literature—a superabundant energy—but reveals the author's distaste for its smothering profusion. Woolf was the daughter of Sir Leslie Stephen (1832–1904), himself an eminent Victorian. In her later life, when assessing her father's powerful personality, Woolf recorded in her diary that she herself could never have become a writer if he had not died when he did. Growing up under such towering shadows, she and her generation mocked their predecessors to make them less intimidating. In his reminiscences *Portraits from Life,* the novelist Ford Madox Ford (1873–1939) recalled his feelings of terror when he confronted the works of Carlyle and Ruskin, which he likened to an overpowering range of high mountains. The mid-Victorians, he wrote, were "a childish nightmare to me."

The Georgian reaction against the Victorians is now only a matter of the history of taste, but its aftereffects still sometimes crop up when the term *Victorian* is employed in an exclusively pejorative sense, as prudish or old-fashioned. Contemporary historians and critics now find the Victorian period a richly complex example of a society struggling with the issues and problems we identify with modernism. But to give the period the single designation *Victorian* reduces its complexity. For a period almost seventy years in length, we can hardly expect generalizations to be uniformly applicable. It is, therefore, helpful to subdivide the age into three phases: Early Victorian (1830–48), Mid-Victorian (1848–70), and Late Victorian (1870–1901). It is also helpful to consider the final decade, the nineties, as a bridge between two centuries.

THE EARLY PERIOD (1830–48): A TIME OF TROUBLES

In the early 1830s, two historical events occurred of momentous consequence for England. In 1830 the Liverpool and Manchester Railway opened, becoming the first steam-powered, public railway line in the world. A burst of railway construction followed. By 1850, 6,621 miles of railway line connected all of England's major cities. By 1900, England had 15,195 lines of track and an underground railway system beneath London. The train transformed England's landscape, supported the growth of its commerce, and shrank the distances between its cities. The opening of England's first railway coincided with the opening of the country's Reform Parliament. The railway had increased the pressure for parliamentary reform. "Parliamentary reform must follow soon after the opening of this road," a Manchester man observed in 1830, when the railway opened. "A million of persons will pass over it in the course of this year, and see that hitherto unseen village of Newton; and they must be convinced of the absurdity of its sending two members to Parliament while Manchester sends none." Despite the growth of manufacturing cities consequent to the Industrial Revolution, England was still governed by an archaic electoral system whereby some of the new industrial cities were unrepresented in Parliament while "rotten boroughs" (communities that had become depopulated) elected the nominees of the local squire to Parliament.

By 1830 a time of economic distress had brought England close to revolution. Manufacturing interests, who refused to tolerate their exclusion from the political process any longer, led working men in agitating for reform. Fearing the kind of revolution it had seen in Europe, Parliament passed a Reform Bill in 1832 that transformed England's class structure. The Reform Bill of 1832 extended the right to vote to all males owning property worth £10 or more in annual rent. In effect the voting public thereafter included the lower middle classes but not the working classes, who did not obtain the vote until 1867, when a second reform bill was passed. Even more important than the extension of the franchise was the virtual abolition of the rotten boroughs and the redistribution of parliamentary representation. Because it broke up the monopoly of power that the conservative landowners had so long enjoyed (the Tory party had been in office almost continuously from 1783 to 1830), the Reform Bill represents the beginning of a new age, in which middle-class economic interests gained increasing power.

Yet even the newly constituted Parliament was unable to find legislative solutions to the problems facing the nation. The economic and social difficulties attendant on industrialization were so severe that the 1830s and 1840s became known as the Time of Troubles. After a period of prosperity from 1832 to 1836, a crash in 1837, followed by a series of bad harvests, produced a period of unemployment, desperate poverty, and rioting. Conditions in the new industrial and coal-mining areas were terrible. Workers and their families in the slums of such cities as Manchester lived in horribly crowded, unsanitary housing; and the conditions under which women and children toiled in mines and factories were unimaginably brutal. Elizabeth Barrett's poem *The Cry of the Children* (1843) expresses her horrified response to an official report on child labor, describing five-year-olds dragging heavy tubs of coal through low-ceilinged mine passages for sixteen hours a day.

The owners of mines and factories regarded themselves as innocent of blame for such conditions, for they were wedded to an economic theory of laissez-faire, which assumed that unregulated working conditions would ultimately benefit everyone. A sense of the seemingly hopeless complexity of the situation during the Hungry 1840s is provided by an entry for 1842 in the diary of the statesman Charles Greville, an entry written at the same time that Carlyle was making his contribution to the "Condition of England Question," *Past and Present*. Conditions in the north of England, Greville reports, were "appalling."

> There is an immense and continually increasing population, no adequate demand for labor, . . . no confidence, but a universal alarm, disquietude, and discontent. Nobody can sell anything. . . . Certainly I have never seen . . . so serious a state of things as that which now stares us in the face; and this after thirty years of uninterrupted peace, and the most ample scope afforded for the development of all our resources. . . . One remarkable feature in the present condition of affairs is that nobody can account for it, and nobody pretends to be able to point out any remedy.

In reality many remedies were proposed. One of the most striking was put forward by the Chartists, a large organization of workers. In 1838 the organization drew up a "People's Charter" advocating the extension of the right to vote, the use of secret balloting, and other legislative reforms. For ten years the Chartist leaders engaged in agitation to have their program adopted by Parliament. Their fiery speeches, delivered at conventions designed to collect signatures for petitions to Parliament, created fears of revolution. In *Locksley Hall* Tennyson seems to have had the Chartist demonstrations in mind when he wrote: "Slowly comes a hungry people, as a lion, creeping nigher, / Glares at one that nods and winks behind a slowly-dying fire." Although the Chartist movement had fallen apart by 1848, it succeeded in creating an atmosphere open to reform. One of the most important reforms was the abolition of the high tariffs on imported grains, tariffs known as the Corn Laws (the word *corn* in England refers to wheat and other grains). These high tariffs had been established to protect English farm products from having to compete with low-priced products imported from abroad. Landowners and farmers fought to keep these tariffs in force so that high prices for their wheat would be ensured; but the rest of the population suffered severely from the exorbitant price of bread or, in years of bad crops, from scarcity of food. In 1845 serious crop failures in England and the outbreak of potato blight in Ireland convinced Sir Robert Peel, the Tory prime minister, that traditional protectionism must be abandoned. In 1846 the Corn Laws were repealed by Parliament, and the way was paved for the introduction of a system of Free Trade whereby goods could be imported with the payment of only minimal tariff duties. Although Free Trade did not eradicate the slums of Manchester, it worked well for many years and helped relieve the major crisis of the Victorian economy. In 1848, when revolutions were breaking out all over Europe, England was relatively unaffected. A large Chartist demonstration in London seemed to threaten revolution, but it came to nothing. The next two decades were relatively calm and prosperous.

This Time of Troubles left its mark on some early Victorian literature. "Insurrection is a most sad necessity," Carlyle writes in his *Past and Present*, "and governors who wait for that to instruct them are surely getting into the fatalest courses." A similar refrain runs through Carlyle's history *The French Revolution* (1837). Memories of the French Reign of Terror lasted longer than memories of Trafalgar and Waterloo, memories freshened by later outbreaks of civil strife, "the red fool-fury of the Seine" as Tennyson described one of the violent overturnings of government in France. It is the novelists of the 1840s and early 1850s, however, who show the most marked response to the industrial and political scene. Vivid records of these conditions are to be found in the fiction of Charles Kingsley (1819–1875); Elizabeth Gaskell (1810–1865); and Benjamin Disraeli (1804–1881), a novelist who became prime minister. For his novel *Sybil* (1845) Disraeli chose an appropriate subtitle, *The Two Nations*—a phrase that pointed out the line dividing the England of the rich from the other nation, the England of the poor.

THE MID-VICTORIAN PERIOD (1848–70): ECONOMIC PROSPERITY, THE GROWTH OF EMPIRE, AND RELIGIOUS CONTROVERSY

In the decades following the Time of Troubles some Victorian writers, such as Dickens, continued to make critical attacks on the shortcomings of the Victorian social scene. Even more critical and indignant than Dickens was John Ruskin, who turned from a purely moral and aesthetic criticism of art during this period to denounce the evils of Victorian industry, as in his *The Stones of Venice* (1853), which combines a history of architecture with stern prophecies about the doom of technological culture, or in his attacks on laissez-faire economics in *Unto This Last* (1862). Generally speaking, however, the realistic novels of Anthony Trollope (1815–1882), with their comfortable tolerance and equanimity, are a more characteristic reflection of the mid-Victorian attitude toward the social and political scene than are Ruskin's lamentations. Overall, this second phase of the Victorian period had many harassing problems, but it was a time of prosperity. On the whole its institutions worked well. Even the badly bungled war against Russia in the Crimea (1854–56) did not seriously affect the growing sense of satisfaction that the challenging difficulties of the 1840s had been solved or would be solved by English wisdom and energy. The monarchy was proving its worth in a modern setting. The queen and her husband, Prince Albert, were themselves models of middle-class domesticity and devotion to duty. The aristocracy was discovering that Free Trade was enriching rather than impoverishing their estates; agriculture flourished together with trade and industry. And through a succession of Factory Acts in Parliament, which restricted child labor and limited hours of employment, the condition of the working classes was also being gradually improved. When we speak of Victorian complacency or stability or optimism, we are usually referring to this mid-Victorian phase—"The Age of Improvement," as the historian Asa Briggs has called it. "Of all the decades in our history," writes G. M. Young, "a wise man would choose the eighteen-fifties to be young in."

In 1851 Prince Albert opened the Great Exhibition in Hyde Park, where a gigantic glass greenhouse, the Crystal Palace, had been erected to display the exhibits of modern industry and science. The Crystal Palace was one of the first buildings constructed according to modern architectural principles in which materials such as glass and iron are employed for purely functional ends (much late Victorian furniture, on the other hand, with its fantastic and irrelevant ornamentation, was constructed according to the opposite principle). The building itself, as well as the exhibits, symbolized the triumphant feats of Victorian technology. As Benjamin Disraeli wrote to a friend in 1862: "It is a privilege to live in this age of rapid and brilliant events. What an error to consider it a utilitarian age. It is one of infinite romance."

England's technological progress, together with its prosperity, led to an enormous expansion of its influence throughout the globe. Its annual export of goods nearly trebled in value between 1850 and 1870. Not only the export of goods but that of people and capital increased. Between 1853 and 1880, 2,466,000 emigrants left Britain, many bound for British colonies. By 1870, British capitalists had invested £800 million abroad; in 1850, the total had been only £300 million. This investment, of people, money, and technology, created the British Empire. Important building blocks of the empire were put in place in the mid-Victorian period. In the 1850s and 1860s there was large-scale immigration to Australia; in 1867, Parliament unified the Canadian provinces into the Dominion of Canada. In 1857, Parliament took over the government of India from the private East India Company, which had controlled the country, and started to put in place its civil service government. In 1876, Queen Victoria was named empress of India. Although the competitive scramble for African colonies did not take place until the final decades of the century, the model of empire was created earlier, made possible by technological revolution in communication and transportation. Much as Rome had built roads through Europe in the years of the Roman Empire, Britain built railways and strung telegraph wires. It also put in place a framework for education and government that preserves British influence in former colonies even today. Britain's motives, in creating its empire, were many. It sought wealth, markets for manufactured goods, sources for raw materials, and world power and influence. Many English people also saw the expansion of empire as a moral responsibility, what Kipling termed "the White Man's burden." Queen Victoria herself stated that the imperial mission was "to protect the poor natives and advance civilization." Missionary societies flourished, spreading Christianity in India, Asia, and Africa.

At the same time that the British missionary enterprise was expanding, there was increasing debate about religious belief. By the mid-Victorian period, the Church of England had evolved into three major divisions: Evangelical, or Low Church, Broad Church, and High Church. The Evangelicals emphasized spiritual transformation of the individual by conversion and a strictly moral Christian life. Zealously dedicated to good causes (they were responsible for the emancipation of all slaves in the British Empire as early as 1833), advocates of a strict Puritan code of morality, and righteously censorious of worldliness in others, the Evangelicals became a powerful and active minority in the early part of the nineteenth century. Much of the power of the Evangelicals depended on the fact that their view of life and religion was virtually identical with that of a much larger group external to the Church of England, the Nonconformists, or Dissenters—that is, Baptists, Methodists, Congregationalists, and other Protestant denominations. The High Church was also associated with a group external to the Church of England; it was the "Catholic" side of the church, emphasizing the importance of tradition, ritual, and authority. In the 1830s, a High Church movement took shape, known both as "the Oxford movement," because it originated at Oxford University, and as "Tractarianism," because its leaders developed their arguments in a series of pamphlets or tracts. Led by John Henry Newman, who later converted to Roman Catholicism, Tractarians argued that the Church could maintain its power and authority only by resisting liberal tendencies and holding to its original traditions. The Broad Church resisted the doctrinal and ecclesiastical controversies that separated the High Church and Evangelical divisions. Open to modern advances in thought, its adherents emphasized the broadly inclusive nature of the church.

Some rationalist challenges to religious belief that developed before the Victorian period maintained their influence. The most significant was Utilitarianism, also known as Benthamism or Philosophical Radicalism. Utilitarianism derived from the thought of Jeremy Bentham (1748–1832) and his disciple James Mill (1773–1836), the father of John Stuart Mill. Bentham believed that all human beings seek to maximize pleasure and minimize pain. The criterion by which we should judge a morally correct action, therefore, is the extent to which it provides the greatest pleasure to the greatest number. Measuring religion by this moral arithmetic, Benthamites concluded that it was an outmoded superstition; it did not meet the rationalist test of value. Utilitarianism was widely influential in providing a philosophical basis for political reform, but it aroused considerable opposition on the part of those who felt it failed to recognize people's spiritual needs. Raised according to strict utilitarian principles by his father, John Stuart Mill came to be critical of them. In the mental and spiritual crisis portrayed in his *Autobiography*, Mill describes his realization that his utilitarian upbringing had left him no power to feel. In *Sartor Resartus*, Carlyle describes a similar spiritual crisis in which he struggles to rediscover the springs of religious feeling in the face of his despair at the specter of a universe governed only by utilitarian principles. Later both Dickens, in his portrayal of Thomas Gradgrind in *Hard Times*, "a man of facts and calculations," "ready to weigh and measure any parcel of human nature," and John Ruskin, in his *Unto This Last*, attack utilitarianism.

In mid-Victorian England, however, the challenge to religious belief gradually shifted from the Utilitarians to some of the leaders of science, in particular to Thomas Henry Huxley, who popularized the theories of Charles Darwin. Although many English scientists were themselves individuals of strong religious convictions, the impact of their scientific discoveries seemed consistently damaging to established faiths. Complaining in 1851 about the "flimsiness" of his own religious faith, Ruskin exclaimed: "If only the Geologists would let me alone, I could do very well, but those dreadful hammers! I hear the clink of them at the end of every cadence of the Bible verses."

The damage lamented by Ruskin was effected in two ways. First the scientific attitude of mind was applied toward a study of the Bible itself. This kind of investigation, developed especially in Germany, was known as the "Higher Criticism." Instead of treating the Bible as a sacredly infallible document, scientifically minded scholars examined it as a mere text of history and presented evidence about its composition that believers, especially in Protestant countries, found disconcerting, to say the least. A noteworthy example of such Higher Criticism studies was David Friedrich Strauss's *Das Leben Jesu,* which was translated by George Eliot in 1846 as *The Life of Jesus*. The second kind of damage was effected by the view of humanity implicit in the discoveries of geology and astronomy, the new and "Terrible Muses" of literature, as Tennyson called them in a late poem. Geology, by extending the history of the earth backward millions of years, reduced the stature of the human species in time. John Tyndall, an eminent physicist, said in an address at Belfast in 1874 that in the eighteenth century people had an "unwavering trust" in the "chronology of the Old Testament" but in Victorian times they had to become accustomed to

> the idea that not for six thousand, nor for sixty thousand, nor for six thousand thousand, but for aeons embracing untold millions of years, this earth has been the theater of life and death. The riddle of the rocks has been read by the geologist and paleontologist, from sub-Cambrian depths to the deposits thickening over the sea bottoms of today. And upon the leaves of that stone book are . . . stamped the characters, plainer and surer than those formed by the ink of history, which carry the mind back into abysses of past time.

The discoveries of astronomers, by extending a knowledge of stellar distances to dizzying expanses, were likewise disconcerting. Carlyle's friend John Sterling remarked in a letter of 1837 how geology "gives one the same sort of bewildering view of the abysmal extent of Time that Astronomy does of Space." To Tennyson's speaker in *Maud* (1855) the stars are "innumerable" tyrants of "iron skies." They are "Cold fires, yet with power to burn and brand / His nothingness into man."

In the mid-Victorian period, biology reduced humankind even further into "nothingness." Darwin's great treatise *The Origin of Species* (1859) was interpreted by the nonscientific public in a variety of ways. Some chose to assume that evolution was synonymous with progress, but most readers recognized that Darwin's theory of natural selection conflicted not only with the concept of creation derived from the Bible but also with long-established assumptions of the values attached to humanity's special role in the world. Darwin's later treatise *The Descent of Man* (1871) raised more explicitly the haunting question of our identification with the animal kingdom. If the principle of survival of the fittest was accepted as the key to conduct, there remained the inquiry: fittest for what? As John Fowles writes in his 1968 novel about Victorian England, *The French Lieutenant's Woman,* Darwin's theories made the Victorians feel "infinitely isolated." "By the 1860s the great iron structures of their philosophies, religions, and social stratifications were already beginning to look dangerously corroded to the more perspicacious."

Disputes about evolutionary science, like the disputes about religion, are a reminder that beneath the placidly prosperous surface of the mid-Victorian age there were serious conflicts and anxieties. In the same year as the Great Exhibition, with its celebration of the triumphs of trade and industry, Charles Kingsley wrote, "The young men and women of our day are fast parting from their parents and each other; the more thoughtful are wandering either towards Rome, towards sheer materialism, or towards an unchristian and unphilosophic spiritualism."

THE LATE PERIOD (1870–1901): DECAY OF VICTORIAN VALUES

The third phase of the Victorian age is more difficult to categorize. At first glance its point of view seems merely an extension of mid-Victorianism, whose golden glow lingered on through the Jubilee years of 1887 and 1897 (years celebrating the fiftieth and sixtieth anniversaries of the queen's accession) down to 1914. For many Victorians, this final phase of the century was a time of serenity and security, the age of house parties and long weekends in the country. In the amber of Henry James's prose is immortalized a sense of the comfortable pace of these pleasant, well-fed gatherings. Life in London, too, was for many an exhilarating heyday. In *My Life and Loves* the Irish-American Frank Harris (1854–1931), often a severe critic of the English scene, records his recollections of the gaiety of London in the 1880s: "London: who would give even an idea of its varied delights: London, the center of civilization, the queen city of the world without a peer in the multitude of its attractions, as superior to Paris as Paris is to New York." The exhilarating sense of London's delights reflects in part the proliferation of things: commodities, inventions, products that were changing the texture of modern life. England had become a country committed not only to continuing technological change but also to a culture of consumerism, generating new products for sale.

The wealth of England's empire provided the foundation on which its economy was built. The final decades of the century saw the apex of British imperialism, yet the cost of the empire became increasingly apparent in rebellions, massacres, and bungled wars, such as the Indian Mutiny in 1857; the Jamaica Rebellion in 1865; the massacre of General Gordon and his troops at Khartoum, in the Sudan, in 1885, where he had been sent to evacuate the British in the face of a religiously inspired revolt; and the Boer War, at the end of the century, in which England engaged in a long, bloody, and unpopular struggle to annex two independent republics in the south of Africa controlled by Dutch settlers called Boers. In addition, the "Irish Question," as it was called, became especially divisive in the 1880s when Home Rule for Ireland became a topic of heated debate—a proposed reform that was unsuccessfully advocated by Prime Minister Gladstone and other leaders. And outside of the British Empire, other developments challenged Victorian stability and security. The sudden emergence of Bismarck's Germany after the defeat of France in 1871 was progressively to confront England with powerful threats to its naval and military position and also to its preeminence in trade and industry. The recovery of the United States after the Civil War likewise provided new and serious competition not only in industry but also in agriculture. As the westward expansion of railroads in the United States and Canada opened up the vast, grain-rich prairies, the typical English farmer had to confront lower grain prices and a dramatically different scale of productivity, which England could not match. In 1873 and 1874 such severe economic depressions occurred that the rate of emigration rose to an alarming degree. Another change in the mid-Victorian balance of power was the growth of labor as a political and economic force. In 1867, under Disraeli's guidance, a second Reform Bill had been passed that extended the right to vote to sections of the working classes; and this, together with the subsequent development of trade unions, made labor a powerful political force that included a wide variety of kinds of socialism. Some labor leaders were disciples of the Tory-socialism of John Ruskin and shared his idealistic conviction that the middle-class economic and political system, with its distrust of state interference, was irresponsible and immoral. Other labor leaders had been influenced instead by the revolutionary theories of Karl Marx and Friedrich Engels as expounded in their *Communist Manifesto* of 1847 and in Marx's *Das Kapital* (1867, 1885, 1895). The first English author of note to embrace Marxism was the poet and painter William Morris, who shared with Marx a conviction that utopia could be achieved only after the working classes had, by revolution, taken control of government and industry.

In much of the literature of this final phase of Victorianism we can sense an overall change of attitudes. Some of the late Victorian writers expressed the change openly by simply attacking the major mid-Victorian idols. Samuel Butler (1835–1902), for example, set about demolishing Darwin, Tennyson, and Prime Minister Gladstone, figures whose aura of authority reminded him of his own father. For the more worldly and casual-mannered Prime Minister Disraeli, on the other hand, Butler could express considerable admiration: "Earnestness was his greatest danger, but if he did not quite overcome it (as who indeed can? it is the last enemy that shall be subdued), he managed to veil it with a fair amount of success." In his novel *The Way of All Flesh*, much of which was written in the 1870s, Butler satirized family life, in particular the tyrannical self-righteousness of a Victorian father, his own father (a clergyman) serving as his model. In a different vein Walter Pater and his followers concluded that the striving of their predecessors was ultimately pointless, that the answers to our problems are not to be found, and that our role is to enjoy the fleeting moments of beauty in "this short day of frost and sun." It is symptomatic of this shift in point of view that Edward FitzGerald's beautiful translation of the *Rubáiyát of Omar Khayyám* (1859), with its melancholy theme that life's problems are insoluble, went virtually unnoticed in the 1860s but became a popular favorite in subsequent decades.

THE NINETIES

The changes in attitude that had begun cropping up in the 1870s became much more conspicuous in the final decade of the century and give the nineties a special aura of notoriety. Of course the changes were not in evidence everywhere. Throughout the empire at its outposts in India and Africa, the English were building railways and administering governments with the same strenuous energy as in the mid-Victorian period. The stories of Kipling and Conrad variously record the struggles of such people. Also embodying the task of sustaining an empire were the soldiers and sailors who fought in various colonial wars, most notably in the war against the Boers in South Africa (1899–1902). But back in England, Victorian standards were breaking down on several fronts. One colorful embodiment of changing values was Victoria's son and heir, Edward, Prince of Wales, who was entering his fiftieth year as the nineties began. A pleasure-seeking, easygoing person, Edward was the antithesis of his father, Prince Albert, an earnest-minded intellectual who had devoted his life to hard work and to administrative responsibilities. Edward's carryings-on were a favorite topic for newspaper articles, one of which noted how this father of five children "openly maintained scandalous relations with ballet dancers and chorus singers."

Much of the writing of the decade illustrates a breakdown of a different sort. Melancholy, not gaiety, is characteristic of its spirit. Artists of the nineties, representing the Aesthetic movement, were very much aware of living at the end of a great century and often cultivated a deliberately fin de siècle ("end-of-century") pose. A studied languor, a weary sophistication, a search for new ways of titillating jaded palates can be found in both the poetry and the prose of the period. *The Yellow Book*, a periodical that ran from 1894 to 1897, is generally taken to represent the aestheticism of the nineties. The startling black-and-white drawings and designs of its art editor, Aubrey Beardsley (1872–1898), the prose of George Moore and Max Beerbohm, and the poetry of Ernest Dowson illustrate different aspects of the movement. In 1893 the Austrian critic Max Nordau summed up what seemed to him to be happening, in a book that was as sensational as its title: *Degeneration*.

From the perspective of the twentieth century, however, it is easy to see in the nineties the beginning of the modernist movement in literature; a number of the great writers of the twentieth century—Yeats, Hardy, Conrad, Shaw—were already publishing.

In Dickens's *David Copperfield* (1850) the hero affirms: "I have always been thoroughly in earnest." Forty-five years later Oscar Wilde's comedy *The Importance of Being Earnest* turns this typical mid-Victorian word *earnest* into a pun, a key joke in this comic spectacle of earlier Victorian values being turned upside down. As Richard Le Gallienne (a novelist of the nineties) remarked in *The Romantic Nineties* (1926): "Wilde made dying Victorianism laugh at itself, and it may be said to have died of the laughter."

THE ROLE OF WOMEN

Political and legal reforms in the course of the Victorian period had given citizens many rights. In 1844 Friedrich Engels observed: "England is unquestionably the freest—that is the least unfree—country in the world, North America not excepted." England had indeed done much to extend its citizens' liberties, but women did not share in these freedoms. They could not vote or hold political office. (Although petitions to Parliament advocating women's suffrage were introduced as early as the 1840s, women did not get the vote until 1918.) Until the passage of the Married Women's Property Acts (1870–1908), married women could not own or handle their own property. Although men could divorce their wives for adultery, wives could divorce their husbands only if adultery were combined with cruelty, bigamy, incest, or bestiality. Educational and employment opportunities for women were limited. These inequities stimulated a spirited debate about women's roles known as the "Woman Question." Arguments for women's rights were based on the libertarian principles that had formed the basis of extended rights for men. In Hardy's last novel, *Jude the Obscure* (1895), his heroine justifies leaving her husband by quoting a passage from Mill's *On Liberty*. She might have quoted another work by Mill, *The Subjection of Women*, which, like Mary Wollstonecraft's *A Vindication of the Rights of Women* (1792), challenges long-established assumptions about women's role in society.

The changing conditions of women's work created by the Industrial Revolution posed an equally strong challenge to traditional views of women's roles. The explosive growth of the textile industries brought hundreds of thousands of lower-class women into factory jobs with grueling working conditions, and the need for coal to fuel England's industrial development brought women into the mines. The Factory Acts (1802–78) introduced increasing regulation of the conditions of labor in mines and factories, including reduction of the sixteen-hour day. Other changes in legislation extended women's rights. The Custody Act of 1839 gave a mother the right to petition the court for access to her minor children and custody of children under seven (raised to sixteen in 1878). The Divorce and Matrimonial Causes Act of 1857 established a civil divorce court (divorce previously could be granted only by an ecclesiastical court) and provided a deserted wife the right to apply for a protection order that would allow her rights to her property. Although divorce remained so expensive as to be available only to the rich, these changes in marriage and divorce laws, together with the Married Women's Property Acts, began to establish a basis for the rights of women in marriage.

In addition to pressuring Parliament for legal reform, feminists worked to enlarge educational opportunities for women. In 1837 none of England's three universities was open to women. Tennyson's long poem *The Princess* (1847), with its fantasy of a women's college from whose precincts all males are excluded, was inspired by contemporary discussions of the need for women to obtain an education more advanced than that provided by the popular finishing schools such as Miss Pinkerton's Academy in Thackeray's *Vanity Fair*. Although by the end of the poem, Princess Ida has repented of her Amazonian scheme, she and the prince look forward to a future in which man will be "more of woman, she of man." The poem reflects a climate of opinion that led in 1848 to the establishment of the first women's college in London, an example later recommended by Thomas Henry Huxley, a strong advocate of advanced education for women. By the end of Victoria's reign, women could take degrees at twelve universities or university colleges and could study, although not earn a degree, at Oxford and Cambridge.

There was also agitation for improved employment opportunities for women. Writers as diverse as Charlotte Brontë, Elizabeth Barrett Browning, and Florence Nightingale complained that middle-class women were taught trivial accomplishments to fill up days in which there was nothing important to do. The problem of nothing to do was acute in quite a different way for what contemporary journalists called "surplus" or "redundant" women, that is, the women in the population who remained unmarried because of the imbalance in numbers between the sexes. Such women (of whom there were approximately half a million in mid-Victorian England) had few employment opportunities, none of them attractive or profitable. Emigration was frequently proposed as a solution to the problem, but the number of single female emigrants was never high enough to affect significantly the population imbalance. Bad working conditions and underemployment drove thousands of women into prostitution, which became increasingly professionalized in the nineteenth century. The only occupation at which an unmarried middle-class woman could earn a living and maintain some claim to gentility was that of a governess, but a governess could expect no security of employment, only minimal wages, and an ambiguous status, somewhere between servant and family member, that isolated her within the household. Perhaps because the governess so clearly indicated the precariousness of the unmarried middle-class woman's status in Victorian England, the governess novel, of which the most famous examples are *Jane Eyre* and *Vanity Fair*, became a popular genre through which to explore women's roles in society.

As such novels indicate, Victorian society was preoccupied not only with legal and economic limitations on women's lives but with the very nature of woman. In *The Subjection of Women* John Stuart Mill argues that "what is now called the nature of women is eminently an artificial thing—the result of forced repression in some directions, unnatural stimulation in others." In Tennyson's *The Princess* the king voices a more traditional view of woman's role:

> Man for the field and woman for the hearth:
> Man for the sword and for the needle she:
> Man with the head and woman with the heart:
> Man to command and woman to obey.

The king's relegation of women to the hearth and heart reflects an ideology that claimed that woman had a special nature peculiarly fit for her domestic role. Most aptly epitomized by the title of Coventry Patmore's immensely popular poem *The Angel in the House* (1854–62), this concept of womanhood stressed woman's purity and selflessness. Protected and enshrined within the home, her role was to create a place of peace where man could take refuge from the difficulties of modern life. In *Of Queen's Gardens* John Ruskin writes:

> This is the true nature of home—it is the place of Peace; the shelter, not only from all injury, but from all terror, doubt, and division. In so far as it is not this, it is not home; so far as the anxieties of the outer life penetrate into it, and the inconsistently-minded, unknown, unloved, or hostile society of the outer world is allowed either by husband or wife to cross the threshold, it ceases to be home; it is then only a part of that outer world which you have roofed over, and lighted fire in. But so far as it is a sacred place, a vestal temple, a temple of the hearth watched over by Household Gods, . . . so far it vindicates the name, and fulfills the praise, of home.

Such an exalted conception of home placed great pressure on the woman who ran it to be, in Ruskin's words, "enduringly, incorruptibly good; instinctively, infallibly wise—wise, not for self-development, but for self-renunciation." It is easy to recognize the oppressive aspects of this ideology. Paradoxically, however, it was used not only by antifeminists, eager to keep woman in her place, but by some feminists as well, in justifying the special contribution that woman could make to public life.

In his preface to *The Portrait of a Lady* (1881) Henry James writes: "Millions of presumptuous girls, intelligent or not intelligent, daily affront their destiny, and what is it open to their destiny to *be*, at the most, that we should make an ado about it?" Every major Victorian novelist makes the "ado" that James describes in addressing the question of woman's vocation. Ultimately, as Victorian novels illustrate, the basic problem was not only political, economic, and educational. It was how women were regarded, and regarded themselves, as members of a society.

LITERACY, PUBLICATION, AND READING

Literacy increased significantly during the Victorian period, although precise figures are difficult to calculate. In 1837 about half of the adult male population could read and write to some extent; by the end of the century, basic literacy was almost universal, the product in part of compulsory national education, required by 1880 to the age of ten. There was also an explosion of things to read. Because of technological changes in printing—presses powered by steam, paper made from wood pulp rather than rags, and, toward the end of the century, typesetting machines—publishers could bring out more printed material more cheaply than ever before. The number of newspapers, periodicals, and books increased exponentially during the Victorian period. Books remained fairly expensive, and most readers borrowed them from commercial lending libraries. (There were few public libraries until the final decades of the century.) After the repeal of the stamp tax and duties on advertisements just after midcentury, an extensive popular press developed.

The most significant development in publishing from the point of view of literary culture was the growth of the periodical. In the first thirty years of the Victorian period, 170 new periodicals were started in London alone.

There were magazines for every taste: cheap and popular magazines that published sensational tales; religious monthlys; weekly newspapers; satiric periodicals noted for their political cartoons (the most famous of these was *Punch*); women's magazines; monthly miscellanies publishing fiction, poetry, and articles on current affairs; and reviews and quarterlies, ostensibly reviewing new books but using the reviews, which were always unsigned, as occasions for essays on the subjects in question. The chief reviews and monthly magazines had a great deal of power and influence; they defined issues in public affairs, and they made and broke literary reputations. They also published the major writers of the period: the fiction of Dickens, Thackeray, Eliot, Trollope, and Gaskell; the essays of Carlyle, Mill, Arnold, and Ruskin; the poetry of Tennyson and the Brownings all appeared in monthly magazines.

The circumstances of periodical publication exerted a shaping force on literature. Novels and long works of nonfiction prose were published in serial form. Although serial publication of works began in the late eighteenth century, it was the publication of Dickens's *Pickwick Papers* (1836–37) in individual numbers that established its popularity. All of Dickens's novels and many of those of his contemporaries were published in serial form. Readers therefore read these works in relatively short, discrete installments over a period that could extend more than a year, with time for reflection and interpretation in between. Serial publication encouraged a certain kind of plotting and pacing and allowed writers to take account of their readers' reactions as they constructed subsequent installments. Writers created a continuing world, punctuated by the ends of installments, which served to stimulate the curiosity that would keep readers buying subsequent issues. Serial publication also created a distinctive sense of a community of readers, a sense encouraged by the practice of reading aloud in family gatherings.

As the family reading of novels suggests, the middle-class reading public enjoyed a common reading culture. Poets such as Tennyson and Elizabeth Barrett Browning appealed to a large body of readers; prose writers like Carlyle, Arnold, and Ruskin achieved a status as sages; and the major Victorian novelists were popular writers. Readers shared the expectation that literature would not only delight but instruct, that it would be continuous with the lived world, and that it would illuminate social problems. "Tennyson," one of his college friends warned him, "we cannot live in art." These expectations weighed more heavily on some writers than others. Tennyson wore his public mantle with considerable ambivalence; Arnold abandoned the private mode of lyric poetry in order to speak about public issues in lectures and essays.

By the 1870s the sense of a broad readership, with a shared set of social concerns, had begun to dissolve. Writers had begun to define themselves in opposition to a general public; poets like the Pre-Raphaelites pursued art for art's sake, doing exactly what Tennyson's friend had warned against; mass publication included less and less serious literature. By the end of Victoria's reign, writers could no longer assume a unified reading public.

THE NOVEL

The novel was the dominant form in Victorian literature. Initially published, for the most part, in serial form, novels subsequently appeared in three-volume editions, or "three-deckers." "Large loose baggy monsters," Henry James called them, reflecting his dissatisfaction with their sprawling, panoramic expanse. As their size suggests, Victorian novels seek to represent a large and comprehensive social world, with the variety of classes and social settings that constitute a community. They contain a multitude of characters and a number of plots, setting in motion the kinds of patterns that reveal the author's vision of the deep structures of the social world—how, in George Eliot's words, "the mysterious mixture behaves under the varying experiments of Time." They presents themselves as realistic, that is, as representing a social world that shares the features of the one we inhabit. The French novelist Stendhal (1783–1842) called the novel "a mirror wandering down a road," but the metaphor of the mirror is somewhat deceptive, since it implies that writers exert no shaping force on their material. It would be more accurate to speak not of realism but of realisms, since each novelist presents a specific vision of reality whose representational force he or she seeks to persuade us to acknowledge through a variety of techniques and conventions. The worlds of Dickens, of Trollope, of Eliot, of the Brontës hardly seem continuous with each other, but their authors share the attempt to convince us that the characters and events they imagine resemble those we experience in actual life.

The experience that Victorian novelists most frequently depict is the set of social relationships in the middle-class society developing around them. It is a society where the material conditions of life indicate social position, where money defines opportunity, where social class enforces a powerful sense of stratification, yet where chances for class mobility exist. Pip can aspire to the great expectations that provide the title for Dickens's novel; Jane Eyre can marry her employer, a landed gentleman. Most Victorian novels focus on a protagonist whose effort to define his or her place in society is the main concern of the plot. The novel thus constructs a tension between surrounding social conditions and the aspiration of the hero or heroine, whether it be for love, social position, or a life adequate to his or her imagination. This tension makes the novel the natural form to use in portraying woman's struggle for self-realization in the context of the constraints imposed upon her. For both men and women writers, the heroine is often, therefore, the representative protagonist whose search for fulfillment emblematizes the human condition. The great heroines of Victorian fiction—Jane Eyre, Maggie Tulliver, Dorothea Brooke, Isabel Archer, Tess of the d'Urbervilles, even Becky Sharp—all seem in some way to illustrate George Eliot's judgment, voiced in the Prelude to *Middlemarch*, of "a certain spiritual grandeur ill-matched with meanness of opportunity."

The novel was not only a fertile medium for the portrayal of women; women writers were, for the first time, not figures on the margins but major authors. Jane Austen, the Brontës, Elizabeth Gaskell, George Eliot—all helped define the genre. When Charlotte Brontë screwed up her courage to write to the poet laureate, Robert Southey, to ask his advice about a career as a writer, he warned her, "Literature cannot be the business of a woman's life, and it ought not to be." Charlotte Brontë put this letter, with one other from Southey, in an envelope, with the inscription "Southey's advice to be kept forever. My twenty-first birthday." Brontë's ability ultimately to depart from Southey's advice derived in part from how amenable the novel was to women writers. It concerned the domestic life that women knew well—

courtship, family relationships, marriage. It was a popular form whose market women could enter easily. It did not carry the burden of an august tradition as poetry did, nor did it build on the learning of a university education. In his essay *The Lady Novelists*, George Henry Lewes declared, "The advent of female literature promises woman's view of life, woman's experience." His common-law wife, George Eliot, together with many of her sister novelists, fulfilled his prophecy.

Whether written by women or men, the Victorian novel was extraordinarily various. It encompassed a wealth of styles and genres from the extravagant comedy of Dickens to the Gothic romances of the Brontë sisters, from the satire of Thackeray to the probing psychological fiction of Eliot, from the social and political realism of Trollope to the sensation novels of Wilkie Collins. Later in the century, a number of popular genres developed—crime, mystery, and horror novels, science fiction, detective stories. For the Victorians, the novel was both a principal form of entertainment and a spur to social sympathy. There was not a social topic that the novel did not address. Dickens, Gaskell, and many lesser novelists tried to stimulate efforts for social reform through their depiction of social problems. Writing at the beginning of the twentieth century, Joseph Conrad defined the novel in a way that could speak for the Victorians: "What is a novel if not a conviction of our fellow-men's existence strong enough to take upon itself a form of imagined life clearer than reality and whose accumulated verisimilitude of selected episodes puts to shame the pride of documentary history?"

POETRY

Victorian poetry developed in the context of the novel. As the novel emerged as the dominant form of literature, poets sought new ways of telling stories in verse; examples include Tennyson's *Maud*, Elizabeth Barrett Browning's *Aurora Leigh*, Robert Browning's *The Ring and the Book*, and Arthur Hugh Clough's *Amours de Voyage*. Poets and critics debated what the appropriate subjects of such long narrative poems should be. Some, like Matthew Arnold, held that poets should use the heroic materials of the past; others, like Elizabeth Barrett Browning, felt that poets should represent "their age, not Charlemagne's." Poets also experimented with character and perspective. *Amours de Voyage* is a long epistolary poem that tells the story of a failed romance through letters written by its various characters; *The Ring and the Book* presents its plot—an old Italian murder story—through ten different perspectives.

Victorian poetry also developed in the shadow of Romanticism. By 1837, when Victoria ascended the throne, all of the major Romantic poets, save Wordsworth, were dead, but they had died young, and many readers consequently still regarded them as their contemporaries. Not even twenty years separated the birth dates of Tennyson and Browning from that of Keats, but they lived more than three times as long as he did. All of the Victorian poets show the strong influence of the Romantics, but they cannot sustain the confidence that the Romantics felt in the power of the imagination. The Victorians often rewrite Romantic poems with a sense of belatedness and distance. When, in his poem *Resignation*, Arnold addresses his sister upon revisiting a landscape, much as Wordsworth had addressed his sister in *Tin-*

tern Abbey, he tells her the rocks and sky "seem to bear rather than rejoice." Tennyson frequently represents his muse as an embowered woman, cut off from the world and doomed to death. The speakers of Browning's poems who embrace the visions that their imaginations present are madmen. When Hardy writes *The Darkling Thrush* in December 1900, Keats's nightingale has become "an aged thrush, frail, gaunt, and small."

Victorian poets build upon this sense of belated Romanticism in a number of different ways. Some poets writing in the second half of the century, like Rossetti and Swinburne, embrace an attenuated Romanticism, art pursued for its own sake. Reacting against what he sees as the insufficiency of an allegory of the state of one's own mind as the basis of poetry, Arnold seeks an objective basis for poetic emotion and finally gives up writing poems altogether when he decides that the present age lacks the culture necessary to support great poetry. The more fruitful reaction to the subjectivity of Romantic poetry, however, was not Arnold's but Browning's. Turning from the mode of his early poetry, modeled on Shelley, Browning began writing dramatic monologues, poems, he said, which are "Lyric in expression" but "Dramatic in principle, and so many utterances of so many imaginary persons, not mine." Tennyson simultaneously developed a more lyric form of the dramatic monologue. The idea of creating a lyric poem in the voice of a speaker ironically distinct from the poet is the great achievement of Victorian poetry, one developed extensively in the twentieth century. In *Poetry and the Age* (1953), the modernist poet and critic Randall Jarrell acknowledges this fact: "The dramatic monologue, which once had depended for its effect upon being a departure from the norm of poetry, now became in one form or other the norm."

The formal experimentation of Victorian poetry, both in long narrative and in the dramatic monologue, may make it seem eclectic, but Victorian poetry shares a number of characteristics. It tends to be pictorial, to use detail to construct visual images that represent the emotion or situation the poem concerns. In his review of Tennyson's first volume of poetry, Arthur Henry Hallam defines this kind of poetry as "picturesque," as combining visual impressions in such a way that they create a picture that carries the dominant emotion of the poem. This aesthetic brings poets and painters close together. Contemporary artists frequently illustrated Victorian poems, and poems themselves often present paintings. Victorian poetry also uses sound in a distinctive way. Whether it be the mellifluousness of Tennyson or Swinburne, with its emphasis on beautiful cadences, alliteration, and vowel sounds, or the roughness of Browning or Hopkins, a roughness adopted in part in reaction against Tennyson, the sound of Victorian poetry reflects an attempt to use poetry as a medium with a presence almost independent of sense. The resulting style can become so syntactically elaborate that it is easy to parody, as in Hopkins's description of Browning as a man "bouncing up from table with his mouth full of bread and cheese" or T. S. Eliot's criticism of Swinburne's poetry, where "meaning is merely the hallucination of meaning." Yet it is important to recognize that these poets use sound to convey meaning, to quote Hallam's review of Tennyson once more, "where words would not." "The tone becomes the sign of the feeling." In all of these developments—the experimentation with narrative and perspective, the dramatic monologue, the use of visual detail and sound—Victorian poets seek to represent psychology in a different way. Their most distinctive achievement is a poetry of mood and character. They therefore sat in uneasy relationship to the public expectation that poets be sages with something to teach. Tennyson, Browning, and Arnold showed varying discomfort with this public role; poets beginning to write in the second half of the century distanced themselves from their public by embracing an identity as bohemian rebels. Women poets encountered a different set of difficulties in developing their poetic voice. When, in Barrett Browning's epic about the growth of a woman poet, Aurora Leigh's cousin Romney discourages her poetic ambitions by telling her that women are "weak for art" but "strong for life and duty," he articulates the prejudice of an age. Women poets view their vocation in the context of the constraints and expectations upon their sex. Perhaps because of this, their poems are less complicated by the experiments in perspective than those of their male contemporaries.

VICTORIAN PROSE

Although Victorian poets felt ambivalent about the didactic mission the public expected of the man of letters, writers of nonfiction prose aimed specifically to instruct. Although the term *nonfictional prose* is clumsy and not quite exact (the Victorians themselves did not use the term but instead referred to history, biography, theology, criticism), it has its uses not only to distinguish these prose writers from the novelists but to indicate the centrality of argument and persuasion to Victorian intellectual life. The growth of the periodical press, described earlier, provided the vehicle and marketplace for nonfictional prose. It reflects a vigorous sense of shared intellectual life and the public urgency of social and moral issues. On a wide range of controversial topics—religious, political, and aesthetic—writers seek to convince their readers to share their convictions and values. Such writers seem at times almost secular priests. Indeed, in the fifth lecture of *On Heroes and Hero Worship*, Carlyle defines the writer precisely in these terms: "Men of Letters are a perpetual Priesthood, from age to age, teaching all Men that God is still present in their life. . . . In the true Literary Man, there is thus ever, acknowledged or not by the world, a sacredness." The modern man of letters, Carlyle argues, differs from his earlier counterpart in that he writes for money. "Never, till about a hundred years ago, was there seen any figure of a Great Soul living apart in that anomalous manner; endeavouring to speak forth the inspiration that was in him by Printed Books, and find place and subsistence by what the world would please him for doing that." This combination, of a new market position for nonfictional writing and an exalted sense of the didactic function of the writer, produces the genre we call Victorian prose.

On behalf of nonfictional prose, Walter Pater argued in his essay *Style* (1889) that it was "the special and opportune art of the modern world." He believed not that it was superior to verse but that it more readily conveys the "chaotic variety and complexity" of modern life, the "incalculable" intellectual diversity of the "master currents of the present time." Pater's characterization of prose helps us understand what its writers were attempting to do. Despite the diversity of styles and subjects, Victorian prose writers were engaged in shaping belief in a bewilderingly complex and changing world. Their modes of persuasion differ. Mill and Huxley rely on clear reasoning, logical argument, and the kind of lucid style favored by essayists of the eighteenth century. Carlyle and Ruskin write a prose that is more Romantic in character, that seeks to move readers as well as convince them. Whatever the differences in their rhetorical techniques, however, they share an urgency of exposition. Not only by what they said but by how they said it, Victorian prose writers were claiming a place for literature in a scientific and materialistic culture. Arnold and Pater share this as an explicit aim. Each in his own way argues that culture—the intensely serious appreciation of great works of literature—provides the kind of immanence and meaning that people once found in religion. For Arnold, this is an intensely moral experience; for Pater it is aesthetic. Together they develop the basis for the claims of modern literary criticism.

VICTORIAN DRAMA AND THEATER

If the Victorian age can lay claim to greatness for its poetry, its prose, and its novels, it would be difficult to make such a high claim for its plays, at least until the final decade of the century. Here we must distinguish between play writing on the one hand and theatrical activity on the other. For the theater itself, throughout the period, was a flourishing and popular institution, in which were performed not merely conventional dramas but a rich variety of theatrical entertainments, many with lavish spectacular effects—burlesques, extravaganzas, highly scenic and altered versions of Shakespeare's plays, melodramas, pantomimes, and musicals. Robert Corrigan gives figures that suggest the extent of the popularity of such entertainment: "In the decade between 1850 and 1860 the number of theaters built throughout the country was doubled, and in the middle of the sixties, in London alone, 150,000 would be attending the theater on any given day. Only when we realize that the theatre was to Victorian England what television is to us today will we be able to comprehend both its wide appeal and its limited artistic achievement." The popularity of theatrical entertainment made theater a powerful influence in other genres. Dickens was devoted to the theater and composed many of the scenes of his novels with theatrical techniques. Thackeray represents himself as the puppetmaster of his characters in *Vanity Fair* and employs the stock gestures and expressions of melodramatic acting in his illustrations for the novel. Tennyson, Browning, and Henry James all tried their hands at writing plays, though with no commercial success. Successful plays on stage were written by the lesser lights of literature such as Dion Boucicault (1820–1890), the period's most prolific and popular dramatist. The comic operas of W. S. Gilbert and Arthur Sullivan prove the exception to this judgment. Their satire of Victorian values and institutions, what Gilbert called their "topsyturvydom," and their grave and quasi-respectful treatment of the ridiculous not only make them delightful in themselves but anticipate the techniques of Shaw and Wilde. Around 1890, when the socially controversial plays of the Norwegian dramatist Henrik Ibsen (1828–1906) became known in England, Arthur Pinero (1855–1934) and Bernard Shaw began writing "problem plays" that addressed difficult social issues. In the 1890s Shaw and Oscar Wilde transformed British theater with their comic masterpieces. Although they did not like each other's work, they both created a kind of comedy that took aim at Victorian pretense and hypocrisy.

THE VICTORIAN AGE

TEXTS	CONTEXTS
1830 Alfred Lord Tennyson, *Poems, Chiefly Lyrical*	1830 Opening of Liverpool and Manchester Railway
1832 Sir Charles Lyell, *Principles of Geology*	1832 First Reform Bill
1833 Thomas Carlyle, *Sartor Resartus*	1833 Factory Act. Beginning of Oxford Movement
1836 Charles Dickens, *Pickwick Papers*	1836 First train in London
1837 Carlyle, *The French Revolution*	1837 Victoria becomes queen
	1838 "People's Charter" issued by Chartist Movement
	1840 Queen marries Prince Albert
1842 Tennyson, *Poems*. Robert Browning, *Dramatic Lyrics*	1842 Chartist Riots. Copyright Act. Mudie's Circulating Library
1843 John Ruskin, *Modern Painters* (vol. 1)	1845–46 Potato famine in Ireland. Mass emigration to North America
1846 George Eliot, *The Life of Jesus* (translation)	1846 Repeal of Corn Laws. Browning marries Elizabeth Barrett
1847 Charlotte Brontë, *Jane Eyre*. Emily Brontë, *Wuthering Heights*	1847 Ten Hours Factory Act
1848 Elizabeth Gaskell, *Mary Barton*. William Makepeace Thackeray, *Vanity Fair*	1848 Revolution on the Continent. Second Republic established in France. Founding of Pre-Raphaelite Brotherhood
1850 Tennyson, *In Memoriam*	1850 Tennyson succeeds Wordsworth as Poet Laureate
1851 Ruskin, *Stones of Venice*	1851 Great Exhibition of science and industry at the Crystal Palace
1853 Matthew Arnold, *Poems*	
1854 Dickens, *Hard Times*	1854 Crimean War. Florence Nightingale organizes nurses to care for sick and wounded
1855 R. Browning, *Men and Women*	
1857 Elizabeth Barrett Browning, *Aurora Leigh*	1857 Indian Mutiny. Matrimonial Causes Act
1859 Charles Darwin, *The Origin of Species*. John Stuart Mill, *On Liberty*. Tennyson, *Idylls of the King* (books 1–4)	
1860 Dickens, *Great Expectations*. Eliot, *The Mill on the Floss*	1860 Italian unification
	1861 Death of Prince Albert
	1861–65 American Civil War
1862 Christina Rossetti, *Goblin Market*	
1864 R. Browning, *Dramatis Personae*	

TEXTS	CONTEXTS
1865 Lewis Carroll, *Alice's Adventures in Wonderland*	**1865** Jamaica Rebellion
1866 Algernon Charles Swinburne, *Poems and Ballads*	
1867 Karl Marx, *Das Kapital*	**1867** Second Reform Bill
	1868 Opening of Suez Canal
1869 Arnold, *Culture and Anarchy*. Mill, *The Subjection of Women*	
	1870 Married Women's Property Act. Victory in Franco-Prussian War makes Germany a world power
1871 Darwin, *Descent of Man*	**1871** Newnham College (first women's college) founded at Cambridge
1872 Eliot, *Middlemarch*	
1873 Walter Pater, *Studies in the Renaissance*	
	1877 Queen Victoria made empress of India. Gerard Manley Hopkins joins Jesuit order
	1878 Electric street lighting in London
	1882 Married Women's Property Act
1885 Gilbert and Sullivan, *The Mikado*	**1885** Massacre of General Gordon and his forces and fall of Khartoum
1886 Robert Louis Stevenson, *Doctor Jekyll and Mr. Hyde*	
1888 Rudyard Kipling, *Plain Tales from the Hills*	
1889 William Butler Yeats, *Crossways*	
	1890 First subway line in London
1891 Thomas Hardy, *Tess of the D'Urbervilles*. Bernard Shaw, *The Quintessence of Ibsenism*. Oscar Wilde, *The Picture of Dorian Grey*. Arthur Conan Doyle, *Adventures of Sherlock Holmes*	**1891** Free elementary education
1893 Shaw, *Mrs. Warren's Profession*	**1893** Independent Labour Party
1895 Wilde, *The Importance of Being Earnest*. Hardy, *Jude the Obscure*	**1895** Oscar Wilde arrested and imprisoned for homosexuality
1896 A. E. Housman, *A Shropshire Lad*	
1898 Hardy, *Wessex Poems*	**1898** Discovery of radium
	1899 Irish Literary Theater founded in Dublin
	1899–1902 Boer War
1900 Joseph Conrad, *Lord Jim*	
	1901 Death of Queen Victoria; succession of Edward VII

THOMAS CARLYLE
1795–1881

W. B. Yeats once asked William Morris which writers had inspired the socialist movement of the 1880s, and Morris replied: "Oh, Ruskin and Carlyle, but somebody should have been beside Carlyle and punched his head every five minutes." Morris's mixed feelings of admiration and exasperation are typical of the response Thomas Carlyle evokes in many readers. Anyone approaching his prose for the first time should expect to be sometimes bewildered. Like Bernard Shaw, Carlyle discovered, early in life, that exaggeration can be a highly effective way of gaining the attention of an audience. But it can also be a way of distracting an audience unfamiliar with the idiosyncrasies of his rhetoric and unprepared for the distinctive enjoyments his writings can provide.

One of the idiosyncrasies of his prose is that it is meant to be read aloud. "His paragraphs," as Emerson observes, "are all a sort of splendid conversation." As a talker Carlyle was as famous in his day as Samuel Johnson in his. Charles Darwin testified that he was "the best worth listening to of any man I know." No Boswell has adequately recorded this talk, but no Boswell was needed, for Carlyle has contrived to get the sound of his own spoken voice into his writings. It is a noisy and emphatic voice, startling on first acquaintance. To become familiar with its unusual sounds and rhythms, one can best begin by reading aloud from some of Carlyle's portraits of his contemporaries that are included in the selections printed here. Many of these colorful portraits are from his letters, and it becomes evident that the mannerisms of the author were simply the mannerisms of the man and were congenial and appropriate for the author's purposes. Writing to thank Carlyle for some letters, a friend remarked that they, "unlike other people's, have the writer's signature in every word as well as the end."

Carlyle was forty-one years old when Victoria became queen of England. He had been born in the same year as Keats, yet he is rarely grouped with his contemporaries among the Romantic writers. Instead his name is linked with younger men such as Dickens, Browning, and Ruskin, the early generation of Victorian writers, for whom he became (according to Elizabeth Barrett Browning) "the great teacher of the age." The classification is fitting, for it was Carlyle's role to foresee the problems that were to preoccupy the Victorians and early to report on his experiences in confronting these problems. After 1837 his loud voice began to attract an audience; and he soon became one of the most influential figures of the age, affecting the attitudes of scientists, statesmen, and especially of writers. His wife once complained that Ralph Waldo Emerson had no ideas (except mad ones) that he had not derived from Carlyle. " 'But pray, Mrs. Carlyle,' replied a friend, 'who has?' "

Carlyle was born in Ecclefechan, a village in Scotland, the eldest child of a large family. His mother, at the time of her marriage, was illiterate. His father, James Carlyle, a stonemason and later a farmer, was proudly characterized by his son as a peasant. The key to the character of James Carlyle was the Scottish Calvinism that he instilled into the members of his household. Frugality, hard work, a tender but undemonstrative family loyalty, and a peculiar blend of self-denial and self-righteousness were characteristic features of Carlyle's childhood home.

With his father's aid the young Carlyle was educated at Annan Academy and at Edinburgh University, the subject of his special interest being mathematics; he left without taking a degree. It was his parents' hope that their son would become a clergyman, but in this respect Thomas made a severe break with his ancestry. He was a prodigious reader; and his exposure to such skeptical writers as Hume, Voltaire, and Gibbon had undermined his faith. Gibbon's *Decline and Fall of the Roman*

Empire, he told Emerson, was "the splendid bridge from the old world to the new." By the time he was twenty-three Carlyle had crossed the bridge and had abandoned his Christian faith and his proposed career as a clergyman. During the period in which he was thinking through his religious position, he supported himself by teaching school in Scotland and, later, by tutoring private pupils; but from 1824 to the end of his life he relied exclusively on his writings for his livelihood. His early writings consisted of translations, biographies, and critical studies of Goethe and other German authors, to whose view of life he was deeply attracted. The German Romantics (loosely grouped by Carlyle under the label "Mystics") were the second most important influence on his life and character, exceeded only by his early family experiences. Aided by the writings of these German poets and philosophers, he arrived finally at a faith in life that served as a substitute for the Christian faith he had lost.

His most significant early essay, *Characteristics,* appeared in *The Edinburgh Review* in 1831. A year earlier he had begun writing *Sartor Resartus,* an account of the life and opinions of an imaginary philosopher, Professor Diogenes Teufelsdröckh, a work that he had great difficulty in persuading anyone to publish. In book form *Sartor* first appeared in America in 1836, where Carlyle's follower Emerson had prepared an enthusiastic audience for this unusual work. His American following (which was later to become a vast one) did little at first, however, to relieve the poverty in which he still found himself after fifteen years of writing. In 1837 the tide at last turned when he published *The French Revolution.* "O it has been a great success, dear," his wife assured him; but her husband, embittered by the long struggle, was incredulous that the sought-for recognition had at last come to him.

It was in character for his wife, Jane Welsh Carlyle, to be less surprised by his success than he was. That Thomas Carlyle was a genius had been an article of faith to her from her first meeting with him in 1821. A witty, intelligent, and intellectually ambitious young woman, the daughter of a doctor of good family, Jane Welsh had many suitors. When in 1826 she finally accepted Carlyle, her family and friends were shocked. This peasant's son, of no fixed employment, seemed a fantastic choice. Subsequent events seemed to confirm her family's verdict. Not long after marriage, Carlyle insisted on their retiring to a remote farm at Craigenputtock where for six years (1828–34) this sociable woman was obliged to live in isolation and loneliness. After they moved to London in 1834 and settled in a house on Cheyne Walk in Chelsea, Jane Carlyle was considerably happier and enjoyed her role at the center of the intellectual and artistic circle that surrounded her husband. Her husband, however, remained a difficult man to live with. His stomach ailments, irascible nerves, and preoccupation with his writings, as well as the lionizing to which he was subjected, left him with little inclination for domestic amenities or for encouraging his wife's considerable intellectual talents. As a young girl she had wanted to be a writer; her letters, some of the most remarkable of the century, show that she had considerable literary talent.

This marriage of the Carlyles has aroused almost as much interest as that of the Brownings. Their friend the Reverend W. H. Brookfield (whose marriage was an unhappy one) once said cynically that marrying is "dipping into a pitcher of snakes for the chance of an eel," and some biographers have argued that Jane Welsh Carlyle drew a snake instead of an eel. Yet if we study her letters, it is evident that she wanted to marry a man of genius who would change the world. Despite the years she endured of comparative poverty, ill health, and loneliness, she had the satisfaction of recognizing her husband's triumph when the peasant's son she had chosen returned to Scotland to deliver his inaugural address as lord rector of Edinburgh University. While he was away, to Carlyle's great grief, she died.

During the first thirty years of Carlyle's residence in London he wrote extensive historical works and many pamphlets concerning contemporary issues. After *The French Revolution* he edited, in 1845, the *Letters and Speeches of Oliver Cromwell,* a Puritan leader of heroic dimensions in Carlyle's eyes, and later wrote a full-length biography, *The History of Friedrich II of Prussia, Called Frederick the Great* (1858–65). Carlyle's pamphleteering is seen at its best in *Past and Present* (1843) and in its most violent phase in his *Latter-Day Pamphlets* (1850). Following the death of his wife, he wrote very little. For the remaining fifteen years of his life he confined himself to reading or to talking to the stream of visitors who called at Cheyne Walk to listen to the "Sage of Chelsea," as he came to be called. In 1874 he accepted the Prussian Order of Merit from Bismarck but declined an English baronetcy offered by Disraeli. In 1881 he died and was buried near his family in Ecclefechan churchyard.

To understand Carlyle's role as historian, biographer, and social critic, it is essential to understand his attitude toward religion. Like many Victorians, Carlyle underwent a crisis of religious belief. By the time he was twenty-three, he had been shorn of his faith in Christianity. At this stage, as Carlyle observed with dismay, many people seemed content simply to stop. A Utilitarian such as James Mill or some of his commonsensical professors at the University of Edinburgh regarded society and the universe itself as machines. To such thinkers the machines might sometimes seem complex, but they were not mysterious, for machines are subject to humankind's control and understanding through reason and observation. To Carlyle, and to many others, life without a sense of the divine was a meaningless nightmare. In the first part of *The Everlasting No*, a chapter of *Sartor Resartus*, he gives a memorable picture of the horrors of such a soulless world that drove him in 1822 to thoughts of suicide. The eighteenth-century Enlightenment had left him not in light but in darkness.

In developing his views of religion, Carlyle used the metaphor of the "Clothes Philosophy." The naked individual seeks clothing for protection. One solution, represented by Coleridge and his followers, was to repudiate the skepticism of Voltaire and Hume and to return to the protective beliefs and rituals of the Christian Church. To Carlyle such a return was pointless. The traditional Christian coverings were worn out—"Hebrew Old Clothes" he called them. His own solution, described in *The Everlasting Yea*, was to tailor a new suit of beliefs from German philosophy, shreds of Scottish Calvinism, and his own observations. The following summarizes his basic religious attitude: "Gods die with the men who have conceived them. But the godstuff roars eternally, like the sea. . . . Even the gods must be born again. We must be born again." Although this passage is from *The Plumed Serpent* (1926) by D. H. Lawrence (a writer who resembles Carlyle at many points), it might have come from any one of Carlyle's own books—most especially from *Sartor Resartus*, in which he describes his being born again—his "Fire-baptism"—into a new secular faith.

The most appropriate term to describe this faith is *vitalism*. The presence of energy in the world was, in itself, for him a sign of the godhead. Carlyle, therefore, judges everything in terms of the presence or absence of some vital spark. The minds of people, books, societies, churches, or even landscapes, are rated as alive or dead, dynamic or merely mechanical. The government of Louis XVI, for example, was obviously moribund, doomed to be swept away by the dynamic forces of the French Revolution. The government of Victorian England seemed likewise to be doomed unless infused with vital energies of leadership and an awareness of the real needs of humankind. When an editor complained that his essay *Characteristics* was "inscrutable," Carlyle remarked: "My own fear was that it might be too *scrutable*; for it indicates decisively enough that Society (in my view) is utterly condemned to destruction, and even now beginning its long travail-throes of Newbirth."

In his inquiry into the principles of government and social order, Carlyle, like many of his contemporaries, is seeking to understand a world of great social unrest and historical change. This preoccupation with revolution and the destruction of the old orders suggests that Carlyle's politics were radical, but his position is bewilderingly difficult to classify. During the Hungry 1840s he was one of the most outspoken critics of middle-class bunglings and of the economic theory of laissez-faire that, in his opinion, was ultimately responsible for these bunglings. On behalf of the millions of people suffering from the miseries attendant on a major breakdown of industry and agriculture he did strenuous work. At other times, because of his insistence on strong and heroic leadership, Carlyle appears to be a violent conservative or, as some have argued, virtually a fascist. He had no confidence that democratic institutions could work efficiently. A few individuals in every age are, in his view, leaders; the rest are followers and are happy only as followers. Society should be organized so that these gifted leaders can have scope to govern effectively. Such leaders are, for Carlyle, heroes. Bernard Shaw, who learned much from Carlyle, would call them "supermen." Liberals and democrats, however, might call them dictators. Although Carlyle was aware that the Western world was committed to a faith in a system of balloting and of legislative debate, he was confident that the system would eventually break down. The democratic assumption that all voters are equally capable of choice and the assumption that people value liberty more than they value order seemed to him nonsense. Carlyle's authoritarianism intensified as he grew older. When the governor of Jamaica violently repressed a rebellion of black plantation workers, Carlyle served as chair of his defense fund, arguing that England owed the governor honor and thanks for his defense of civilization.

Carlyle's prose style reflects the intensity of his views. At the time he began to write, the essayists of the eighteenth century, Samuel Johnson in particular, were the models of good prose. Carlyle recognized that their style, however admirable an instrument for reasoning, analysis, and generalized exposition, did not suit his purposes. Like a poet, he wanted to convey the sense of experience itself. Like a preacher or prophet, he wanted to exhort or inspire his readers rather than to develop a chain of logical argument. Like a psychoanalyst, he wanted to explore the unconscious and irrational levels of human life, the hidden nine-tenths of the iceberg rather than the conscious and rational fraction above the surface. To this end he developed his highly individual manner of writing, with its vivid imagery of fire and barnyard and zoo, its mixture of biblical rhythms and explosive talk, and its inverted and unorthodox syntax. Classicists may complain, as Landor did, that the result is not English. Carlyle would reply that it is not eighteenth-century English, but that his style was appropriate for a Victorian who reports of revolutions in society and in thought. In reply to a friend who had protested about his stylistic experiments Carlyle exclaimed: "Do you reckon this really a time for Purism of Style? I do not: with whole ragged battalions of Scott's Novel Scotch, with Irish, German, French, and even Newspaper Cockney . . . storming in on us, and the whole structure of our Johnsonian English breaking up from its foundations—revolution *there* as visible as anywhere else?" Carlyle's defense of his style can be tested by his history *The French Revolution*. One may agree or disagree with the historian's explanations of how the fire started or how it was extinguished. But the fire itself is unquestionably there before us, roaring, palpable, giving off a heat of its own.

George Eliot wrote (in an essay of 1855) that Carlyle was "more of an artist than a philosopher." As she said: "No novelist has made his creations live for us more thoroughly." Carlyle is best regarded, that is, as a man of letters, the inventor of a distinctive and extremely effective prose medium that can bring to life for us the very texture of events in scenes such as when a king confronts a guillotine, a young agnostic confronts the devil, a talker such as Coleridge stupefies an audience of admiring disciples, or a man like himself struggles to create a new spiritual and political philosophy adequate to the age in which he finds himself.

[Carlyle's Portraits of His Contemporaries][1]

[QUEEN VICTORIA AT EIGHTEEN]

Yesterday, going through one of the Parks, I saw the poor little Queen. She was in an open carriage, preceded by three or four swift red-coated troopers; all off for Windsor just as I happened to pass. Another carriage or carriages followed with maids-of-honour, etc.: the whole drove very fast. It seemed to me the poor little Queen was a bit modest, nice sonsy[2] little lassie; blue eyes, light hair, fine white skin; of extremely small stature: she looked timid, anxious, almost frightened; for the people looked at her in perfect silence; one old liveryman alone touched his hat to her: I was heartily sorry for the poor bairn,—tho' perhaps she might have said as Parson Swan did, "*Greet*[3] not for me brethren; for verily, yea verily, I greet not for mysel'." It is a strange thing to look at the fashion of this world!

[From a letter to his mother, April 12, 1838]

[SAMUEL TAYLOR COLERIDGE AT FIFTY-THREE][4]

Coleridge sat on the brow of Highgate Hill, in those years, looking down on London and its smoke-tumult, like a sage escaped from the inanity of life's battle; attracting towards him the thoughts of innumerable brave souls still engaged there. His express contributions to poetry, philosophy, or any specific province of human literature or enlightenment, had been small and sadly intermittent; but he had, especially among young inquiring men, a higher than literary, a kind of prophetic or magician character. He was thought to hold, he alone in England, the key of German and other Transcendentalisms; knew the sublime secret of believing by "the reason" what "the understanding" had been obliged to fling out as incredible; and could still, after Hume and Voltaire had done their best and worst with him, profess himself an orthodox Christian, and say and print to the Church of England, with its singular old rubrics and surplices at Allhallowtide, *Esto perpetua*.[5] A sublime man; who, alone in those dark days, had saved his crown of spiritual

---

1. Carlyle once said that "human Portraits, faithfully drawn, are of all pictures the welcomest on human walls." With his pen, rather than with brush, he himself has created a strikingly colorful gallery of his contemporaries.

  A few of the selections printed here (all of them excerpted by the present editors) were written for publication, in particular the elaborate portrait of Coleridge; the majority of them, however, are sketches from his letters, sometimes in the vein of caricature. As Charles Sanders notes, all of them—like most of the portraits by Chaucer, Robert Browning, and Yeats—are "appraisal portraits." Carlyle has been called the Victorian Rembrandt. But with his sharp eye for absurdities, he is often the Victorian Daumier or Rowlandson. This element of caricature can be partly explained in terms of difference of age. It will be noted that most of the celebrities described were older than Carlyle, and he had the customary determination of youth to make fun of the pretensions of an older and established generation. In Carlyle's case, there was

the additional urge to be irreverent in that he was a provincial in a great metropolis with the provincial's need to assert his independence of judgment.

  The portraits are not presented chronologically. The first one is a sketch of royalty; the others are of English writers. Titles for each portrait have been assigned by the editors.

2. Sweet (Scottish).
3. Weep.
4. In 1816 Coleridge moved to a London suburb as a permanent guest in the home of James Gillman. Here he received visits from admirers of his philosophy such as Carlyle's friend John Sterling, from whose biography, by Carlyle, this selection has been taken. Carlyle's visits were made during his first residence in London in 1824–25.
5. Be thou everlasting (Latin)—the last words of Paolo Sarpi (1552–1623), theologian and historian, addressed to the city of Venice. "Allhallowtide": November 1, a festival in honor of all the saints, celebrated by the Roman Catholic and Anglican churches.

manhood; escaping from the black materialisms, and revolutionary deluges, with "God, Freedom, Immortality" still his: a king of men. The practical intellects of the world did not much heed him, or carelessly reckoned him a metaphysical dreamer: but to the rising spirits of the young generation he had this dusky sublime character; and sat there as a kind of *Magus*, girt in mystery and enigma; his Dodona[6] oak-grove (Mr. Gillman's house at High-gate) whispering strange things, uncertain whether oracles or jargon.

The Gillmans did not encourage much company, or excitation of any sort, round their sage; nevertheless access to him, if a youth did reverently wish it, was not difficult. He would stroll about the pleasant garden with you, sit in the pleasant rooms of the place,—perhaps take you to his own peculiar room, high up, with a rearward view, which was the chief view of all. A really charming outlook, in fine weather. Close at hand, wide sweep of flowery leafy gardens, their few houses mostly hidden, the very chimney-pots veiled under blossomy umbrage, flowed gloriously down hill, gloriously issuing in wide-tufted undulating plain-country, rich in all charms of field and town. Waving blooming country of the brightest green; dotted all over with hand-some villas, handsome groves; crossed by roads and human traffic, here inau-dible or heard only as a musical hum: and behind all swam, under olive-tinted haze, the illimitable limitary ocean of London, with its domes and steeples definite in the sun, big Paul's and the many memories attached to it hanging high over all. Nowhere, of its kind, could you see a grander prospect on a bright summer day, with the set of the air going southward,—southward, and so draping with the city-smoke not *you* but the city. Here for hours would Coleridge talk, concerning all conceivable or inconceivable things; and liked nothing better than to have an intelligent, or failing that, even a silent and patient human listener. He distinguished himself to all that ever heard him as at least the most surprising talker extant in this world,—and to some small minority, by no means to all, as the most excellent.

The good man, he was now getting old, towards sixty perhaps; and gave you the idea of a life that had been full of sufferings; a life heavy-laden, half-vanquished, still swimming painfully in seas of manifold physical and other bewilderment. Brow and head were round, and of massive weight, but the face was flabby and irresolute. The deep eyes, of a light hazel, were as full of sorrow as of inspiration; confused pain looked mildly from them, as in a kind of mild astonishment. The whole figure and air, good and amiable other-wise, might be called flabby and irresolute; expressive of weakness under possibility of strength. He hung loosely on his limbs, with knees bent, and stooping attitude; in walking, he rather shuffled than decisively stept; and a lady once remarked, he never could fix which side of the garden walk would suit him best, but continually shifted, in corkscrew fashion, and kept trying both. A heavy-laden, high-aspiring and surely much-suffering man. His voice, naturally soft and good, had contracted itself into a plaintive snuffle and singsong; he spoke as if preaching,—you would have said, preaching earnestly and also hopelessly the weightiest things. I still recollect his "object" and "subject," terms of continual recurrence in the Kantean prov-ince; and how he sang and snuffled them into "om-m-mject" and "sum-m-

---

6. An oracle in Greece. Prophecies were voiced by priests who interpreted the rustling sounds made by oak leaves stirred by the wind. "*Magus*": an Asian magician or sorcerer.

mject," with a kind of solemn shake or quaver, as he rolled along. No talk, in his century or in any other, could be more surprising.

* * * Nothing could be more copious than his talk; and furthermore it was always, virtually or literally, of the nature of a monologue; suffering no interruption, however reverent; hastily putting aside all foreign additions, annotations, or most ingenuous desires for elucidation, as well-meant superfluities which would never do. Besides, it was talk not flowing anywhither like a river, but spreading everywhither in inextricable currents and regurgitations like a lake or sea; terribly deficient in definite goal or aim, nay often in logical intelligibility; *what* you were to believe or do, on any earthly or heavenly thing, obstinately refusing to appear from it. So that, most times, you felt logically lost; swamped near to drowning in this tide of ingenious vocables, spreading out boundless as if to submerge the world.

To sit as a passive bucket and be pumped into, whether you consent or not, can in the long-run be exhilarating to no creature; how eloquent soever the flood of utterance that is descending. But if it be withal a confused unintelligible flood of utterance, threatening to submerge all known landmarks of thought, and drown the world and you!—I have heard Coleridge talk, with eager musical energy, two stricken hours, his face radiant and moist, and communicate no meaning whatsoever to any individual of his hearers,—certain of whom, I for one, still kept eagerly listening in hope; the most had long before given up, and formed (if the room were large enough) secondary humming groups of their own. He began anywhere: you put some question to him, made some suggestive observation; instead of answering this, or decidedly setting out towards answer of it, he would accumulate formidable apparatus, logical swim-bladders, transcendental life-preservers and other precautionary and vehiculatory gear, for setting out; perhaps did at last get under way,—but was swiftly solicited, turned aside by the glance of some radiant new game on this hand or that, into new courses; and ever into new; and before long into all the Universe, where it was uncertain what game you would catch, or whether any.

His talk, alas, was distinguished, like himself, by irresolution: it disliked to be troubled with conditions, abstinences, definite fulfilments;—loved to wander at its own sweet will, and make its auditor and his claims and humble wishes a mere passive bucket for itself! He had knowledge about many things and topics, much curious reading; but generally all topics led him, after a pass or two, into the high seas of theosophic philosophy, the hazy infinitude of Kantean transcendentalism, with its "sum-m-mjects" and "om-m-mjects." Sad enough; for with such indolent impatience of the claims and ignorances of others, he had not the least talent for explaining this or anything unknown to them; and you swam and fluttered in the mistiest wide unintelligible deluge of things, for most part in a rather profitless uncomfortable manner.

Glorious islets, too, I have seen rise out of the haze; but they were few, and soon swallowed in the general element again. Balmy sunny islets, islets of the blest and the intelligible:—on which occasions those secondary humming groups would all cease humming, and hang breathless upon the eloquent words; till once your islet got wrapt in the mist again, and they could recommence humming. . . . Coleridge was not without what talkers call wit, and there were touches of prickly sarcasm in him, contemptuous enough of the world and its idols and popular dignitaries; he had traits even of poetic humour: but in general he seemed deficient in laughter; or indeed in sympathy for concrete human things either on the sunny or on the stormy side. One right peal of concrete laughter at some convicted flesh-and-blood absurdity, one burst of noble indignation at some injustice or depravity, rubbing elbows with us on this solid Earth, how strange would it have been in that Kantean haze-world, and how infinitely cheering amid its vacant air-castles and dim-melting ghosts and shadows! None such ever came. His life had been an abstract thinking and dreaming, idealistic, passed amid the ghosts of defunct bodies and of unborn ones. The meaning singsong of that theosophico-metaphysical monotony left on you, at last, a very dreary feeling.

* * *

But indeed, to the young ardent mind, instinct with pious nobleness, yet driven to the grim deserts of Radicalism for a faith, his speculations had a charm much more than literary, a charm almost religious and prophetic. The constant gist of his discourse was lamentation over the sunk condition of the world; which he recognised to be given-up to Atheism and Materialism, full of mere sordid misbeliefs, mispursuits and misresults. All Science had become mechanical; the science not of men, but of a kind of human beavers. Churches themselves had died away into a godless mechanical condition; and stood there as mere Cases of Articles, mere Forms of Churches; like the dried carcasses of once-swift camels, which you find left withering in the thirst of the universal desert,—ghastly portents for the present, beneficent ships of the desert no more. Men's souls were blinded, hebetated,[7] and sunk under the influence of Atheism and Materialism, and Hume and Voltaire: the world for the present was as an extinct world, deserted of God, and incapable of welldoing till it changed its heart and spirit. This, expressed I think with less of indignation and with more of long-drawn querulousness, was always recognisable as the ground-tone:—in which truly a pious young heart, driven into Radicalism and the opposition party, could not but recognise a too sorrowful truth; and ask of the Oracle, with all earnestness, What remedy, then?

The remedy, though Coleridge himself professed to see it as in sunbeams, could not, except by processes unspeakably difficult, be described to you at all. On the whole, those dead Churches, this dead English Church especially, must be brought to life again. Why not? It was not dead; the soul of it, in this parched-up body, was tragically asleep only. Atheistic Philosophy was true on its side, and Hume and Voltaire could on their own ground speak irrefragably for themselves against any Church: but lift the Church and them into a higher sphere of argument, *they* died into inanition, the Church revivified itself into pristine florid vigour,—became once more a living ship of the desert, and invincibly bore you over stock and stone. But how, but how! By attending to the "reason" of man, said Coleridge, and duly chaining-up the "understanding" of man: the *Vernunft* (Reason) and *Verstand* (Understanding) of the Germans, it all turned upon these, if you could well understand them,—which you couldn't. For the rest, Mr. Coleridge had on the anvil various Books, especially was about to write one grand Book *On the Logos,* which would help to bridge the chasm for us. So much appeared, however:

7. Dulled.

Churches, though proved false (as you had imagined), were still true (as you were to imagine): here was an Artist who could burn you up an old Church, root and branch; and then as the Alchymists professed to do with organic substances in general, distil you an "Astral Spirit" from the ashes, which was the very image of the old burnt article, its airdrawn counterpart,—this you still had, or might get, and draw uses from, if you could. Wait till the Book on the Logos were done;—alas, till your own terrene eyes, blind with conceit and the dust of logic, were purged, subtilised and spiritualised into the sharpness of vision requisite for discerning such an "om-m-mject."—The ingenuous young English head, of those days, stood strangely puzzled by such revelations; uncertain whether it were getting inspired, or getting infatuated into flat imbecility; and strange effulgence, of new day or else of deeper meteoric night, coloured the horizon of the future for it.

[From *Life of John Sterling*, 1851]

[WILLIAM WORDSWORTH IN HIS SEVENTIES]

On a summer morning (let us call it 1840 then) I was apprised by Taylor[8] that Wordsworth had come to town, and would meet a small party of us at a certain tavern in St. James's Street, at breakfast, to which I was invited for the given day and hour. We had a pretty little room, quiet though looking streetward (tavern's name is quite lost to me); the morning sun was pleasantly tinting the opposite houses, a balmy, calm and sunlight morning. Wordsworth, I think, arrived just along with me; we had still five minutes of sauntering and miscellaneous talking before the whole were assembled. I do not positively remember any of them, except that James Spedding[9] was there, and that the others, not above five or six in whole, were polite intelligent quiet persons, and, except Taylor and Wordsworth, not of any special distinction in the world. Breakfast was pleasant, fairly beyond the common of such things. Wordsworth seemed in good tone, and, much to Taylor's satisfaction, talked a great deal; about "poetic" correspondents of his own (i.e. correspondents for the sake of his poetry; especially one such who had sent him, from Canton, an excellent chest of tea; correspondent grinningly applauded by us all); then about ruralties and miscellanies. * * * These were the first topics. Then finally about literature, literary laws, practices, observances, at considerable length, and turning wholly on the mechanical part, including even a good deal of shallow enough etymology, from me and others, which was well received. On all this Wordsworth enlarged with evident satisfaction, and was joyfully reverent of the "wells of English undefiled";[1] though stone dumb as to the deeper rules and wells of Eternal Truth and Harmony, which you were to try and set forth by said undefiled wells of English or what other speech you had! To me a little disappointing, but not much; though it would have given me pleasure had the robust veteran man emerged a little out of vocables into things, now and then, as he never once chanced to do. For the rest, he talked well in his way; with veracity, easy brevity and force, as a wise tradesman would of his tools and workshop,— and as no unwise one could. His voice was good, frank and sonorous, though practically clear distinct and forcible rather than melodious; the tone of him

8. Henry Taylor, contemporary playwright.
9. Editor of the works of Francis Bacon.

1. Spenser, *Faerie Queene* 4.2.32, referring to Chaucer.

businesslike, sedately confident; no discourtesy, yet no anxiety about being courteous. A fine wholesome rusticity, fresh as his mountain breezes, sat well on the stalwart veteran, and on all he said and did. You would have said he was a usually taciturn man; glad to unlock himself to audience sympathetic and intelligent, when such offered itself. His face bore marks of much, not always peaceful, meditation; the look of it not bland or benevolent so much as close impregnable and hard: a man *multa tacere loquive paratus,*[2] in a world where he had experienced no lack of contradictions as he strode along! The eyes were not very brilliant, but they had a quiet clearness; there was enough of brow and well shaped; rather too much of cheek ("horse face" I have heard satirists say); face of squarish shape and decidedly longish, as I think the head itself was (its "length" going horizontal); he was large-boned, lean, but still firm-knit tall and strong-looking when he stood, a right good old steel-grey figure, with rustic simplicity and dignity about him, and a vivacious strength looking through him which might have suited one of those old steel-grey markgrafs; whom Henry the Fowler set up to ward the "marches"[3] and do battle with the intrusive heathen in a stalwart and judicious manner.

On this and other occasional visits of his, I saw Wordsworth a number of times, at dinner, in evening parties; and we grew a little more familiar, but without much increase of real intimacy or affection springing up between us. He was willing to talk with me in a corner, in noisy extensive circles, having weak eyes, and little loving the general babble current in such places. One evening, probably about this time, I got him upon the subject of great poets, who I thought might be admirable equally to us both; but was rather mistaken, as I gradually found. Pope's partial failure I was prepared for; less for the narrowish limits visible in Milton and others. I tried him with Burns, of whom he had sung tender recognition; but Burns also turned out to be a limited inferior creature, any genius he had a theme for one's pathos rather; even Shakespeare himself had his blind sides, his limitations; gradually it became apparent to me that of transcendent unlimited there was, to this critic, probably but one specimen known, Wordsworth himself! He by no means said so, or hinted so, in words; but on the whole it was all I gathered from him in this considerable *tête-à-tête*[4] of ours; and it was not an agreeable conquest. New notion as to poetry or poet I had not in the smallest degree got; but my insight into the depths of Wordsworth's pride in himself had considerably augmented; and it did not increase my love of him; though I did not in the least hate it either, so quiet was it, so fixed, unappealing, like a dim old lichened crag on the wayside, the private meaning of which, in contrast with any public meaning it had, you recognised with a kind of not wholly melancholy grin.

* * *

During the last seven or ten years of his life, Wordsworth felt himself to be a recognised lion, in certain considerable London circles, and was in the habit of coming up to town with his wife for a month or two every season, to enjoy his quiet triumph and collect his bits of tribute *tales quales.*[5] * * *

2. Prepared to speak out or to pass over much in silence (Latin).
3. Borders. "Markgrafs": governors appointed by Henry I of Germany, "the Fowler" (876–936), to guard the borders of his kingdom.
4. Private conversation between two people.
5. Of such a sort (Latin).

Wordsworth took his bit of lionism very quietly, with a smile sardonic rather that triumphant, and certainly got no harm by it, if he got or expected little good. His wife, a small, withered, puckered, winking lady, who never spoke, seemed to be more in earnest about the affair, and was visibly and sometimes ridiculously assiduous to secure her proper place of precedence at table. * * * The light was always afflictive to his eyes; he carried in his pocket something like a skeleton brass candlestick, in which, setting it on the dinner-table, between him and the most afflictive or nearest of the chief lights, he touched a little spring, and there flirted out, at the top of his brass implement, a small vertical green circle which prettily enough threw his eyes into shade, and screened him from that sorrow. In proof of his equanimity as lion I remember, in connection with this green shade, one little glimpse. * * * Dinner was large, luminous, sumptuous; I sat a long way from Wordsworth; dessert I think had come in, and certainly there reigned in all quarters a cackle as of Babel (only politer perhaps), which far up in Wordsworth's quarter (who was leftward on my side of the table) seemed to have taken a sententious, rather louder, logical and quasi-scientific turn, heartily unimportant to gods and men, so far as I could judge of it and of the other babble reigning. I looked upwards, leftwards, the coast being luckily for a moment clear; there, far off, beautifully screened in the shadow of his vertical green circle, which was on the farther side of him, sate Wordsworth, silent, slowly but steadily gnawing some portion of what I judged to be raisins, with his eye and attention placidly fixed on these and these alone. The sight of whom, and of his rock-like indifference to the babble, quasi-scientific and other, with attention turned on the small practical alone, was comfortable and amusing to me, who felt like him but could not eat raisins. This little glimpse I could still paint, so clear and bright is it, and this shall be symbolical of all.

In a few years, I forget in how many and when, these Wordsworth appearances in London ceased; we heard, not of ill-health perhaps, but of increasing love of rest; at length of the long sleep's coming; and never saw Wordsworth more. One felt his death as the extinction of a public light, but not otherwise.

[From *Reminiscences,* 1867, 1881]

[ALFRED TENNYSON AT THIRTY-FOUR]

Alfred is one of the few British or Foreign Figures (a not increasing number I think!) who are and remain beautiful to me;—a true human soul, or some authentic approximation thereto, to whom your own soul can say, Brother!— However, I doubt he will not come; he often skips me, in these brief visits to Town; skips everybody indeed; being a man solitary and sad, as certain men are, dwelling in an element of gloom,—carrying a bit of Chaos about him, in short, which he is manufacturing into Cosmos!

Alfred is the son of a Lincolnshire Gentleman Farmer, I think; indeed, you see in his verses that he is a native of "moated granges," and green, fat pastures, not of mountains and their torrents and storms. He had his breeding at Cambridge, as if for the Law or Church; being master of a small annuity on his Father's decease, he preferred clubbing with his Mother and some Sisters, to live unpromoted and write Poems. In this way he lives still, now here, now there; the family always within reach of London, never in it; he himself making rare and brief visits, lodging in some old comrade's rooms. I think he must be under forty, not much under it. One of the finest-looking men in the world. A great shock of rough dusty-dark hair; bright-laughing hazel eyes; massive aquiline face, most massive yet most delicate; of sallow-brown complexion, almost Indian-looking; clothes cynically loose, free-and-easy;—smokes infinite tobacco. His voice is musical metallic,—fit for loud laughter and piercing wail, and all that may lie between; speech and speculation free and plenteous: I do not meet, in these late decades, such company over a pipe!—We shall see what he will grow to. He is often unwell; very chaotic,—his way is through Chaos and the Bottomless and Pathless; not handy for making out many miles upon.

[From a letter to Emerson, August 5, 1844]

Sartor Resartus *Sartor Resartus* is a combination of novel, autobiography, and essay. To present some of his own experiences, Carlyle invented a hero, Professor Diogenes Teufelsdröckh of Germany, whose name itself (meaning "God-Begotten Devil's Dung") suggests the grotesque and fantastic humor that Carlyle used to expound a serious treatise. Teufelsdröckh tells the story of his unhappiness in love and of his difficulties in religion. He also airs his opinions on a variety of subjects. Interspersed between the professor's words (which are in quotation marks) are the remarks of an editor, also imaginary, who has the task of putting together the story from assorted documents written by Teufelsdröckh. The title, meaning "The Tailor Retailored," refers to the editor's role of patching the story together. The title also refers to Carlyle's so-called Clothes Philosophy, which is expounded by the hero in many chapters of *Sartor*. In effect, this Clothes Philosophy is an attempt to demonstrate the difference between the appearances of things and their reality. The appearance of an individual depends on the costume he or she wears; the reality of that individual is the body underneath the costume. By analogy, Carlyle suggests that institutions, such as churches or governments, are like clothes. They may be useful "visible emblems" of the spiritual forces that they cover, but they wear out and have to be replaced by new clothes. The Christian Church, for example, which once expressed humanity's permanent religious desires, is, in Carlyle's terms, worn out and must be discarded. But the underlying religious spirit must be recognized and kept alive at all costs. Carlyle also uses the clothes analogy to describe the relationship between the material and spiritual worlds. Clothes hide the body just as the world of nature cloaks the reality of God and as the body itself cloaks the reality of the soul. The discovery of these realities behind the appearances is, for Carlyle and for his hero, the initial stage of a solution to the dilemmas of life.

Teufelsdröckh's religious development, as described in the following chapters, may be contrasted with J. S. Mill's account of his own crisis of spirit in his *Autobiography* (p. 1166). The first three selections are chapters 7 to 9 of book 2.

From Sartor Resartus

The Everlasting No

Under the strange nebulous envelopment, wherein our Professor has now shrouded himself, no doubt but his spiritual nature is nevertheless progressive, and growing: for how can the "Son of Time," in any case, stand still? We behold him, through those dim years, in a state of crisis, of transition: his mad Pilgrimings, and general solution into aimless Discontinuity, what is all this but a mad Fermentation; wherefrom, the fiercer it is, the clearer product will one day evolve itself?

Such transitions are ever full of pain: thus the Eagle when he moults is sickly; and, to attain his new beak, must harshly dash-off the old one upon rocks. What Stoicism soever our Wanderer, in his individual acts and motions, may affect, it is clear that there is a hot fever of anarchy and misery raging within; coruscations of which flash out: as, indeed, how could there be other? Have we not seen him disappointed, bemocked of Destiny, through long years? All that the young heart might desire and pray for has been denied; nay, as in the last worst instance, offered and then snatched away. Ever an "excellent Passivity"; but of useful, reasonable Activity, essential to the former as Food to Hunger, nothing granted: till at length, in this wild Pilgrimage, he must forcibly seize for himself an Activity, though useless, unreasonable. Alas, his cup of bitterness, which had been filling drop by drop, ever since that first "ruddy morning" in the Hinterschlag Gymnasium, was at the very lip; and then with that poison-drop, of the Towgood-and-Blumine[1] business, it runs over, and even hisses over in a deluge of foam.

He himself says once, with more justice than originality: "Man is, properly speaking, based upon Hope, he has no other possession but Hope; this world of his is emphatically the Place of Hope." What, then, was our Professor's possession? We see him, for the present, quite shut-out from Hope; looking not into the golden orient, but vaguely all round into a dim copper firmament, pregnant with earthquake and tornado.

Alas, shut-out from Hope, in a deeper sense than we yet dream of! For, as he wanders wearisomely through this world, he has now lost all tidings of another and higher. Full of religion, or at least of religiosity, as our Friend has since exhibited himself, he hides not that, in those days, he was wholly irreligious: "Doubt had darkened into Unbelief," says he; "shade after shade goes grimly over your soul, till you have the fixed, starless, Tartarean black." To such readers as have reflected, what can be called reflecting, on man's life, and happily discovered, in contradiction to much Profit-and-loss Philosophy, speculative and practical, that Soul is *not* synonymous with Stomach; who understand, therefore, in our Friend's words, "that, for man's well-being, Faith is properly the one thing needful; how, with it, Martyrs, otherwise weak, can cheerfully endure the shame and the cross; and without it, Worldlings puke-up their sick existence, by suicide, in the midst of luxury": to such it will be clear that, for a pure moral nature, the loss of his religious Belief was the loss of everything. Unhappy young man! All wounds, the crush of long-continued Destitution, the stab of false Friendship and of false Love, all wounds in thy so genial heart, would have healed again, had not its life-warmth been withdrawn. Well might he exclaim, in his wild way: "Is there no God, then; but at best an absentee God, sitting idle, ever since the first Sabbath, at the outside of his Universe, and *seeing* it go? Has the word Duty no meaning; is what we call Duty no divine Messenger and Guide, but a

---

1. A woman loved by Teufelsdröckh who had married his friend Towgood. His distress is pictured in the preceding chapter, titled "Sorrows of Teufelsdröckh." "Hinterschlag Gymnasium": smite-behind grammar school (German).

false earthly Fantasm, made-up of Desire and Fear, of emanations from the Gallows and from Dr. Graham's Celestial-Bed?[2] Happiness of an approving Conscience! Did not Paul of Tarsus, whom admiring men have since named Saint, feel that *he* was 'the chief of sinners';[3] and Nero of Rome, jocund in spirit (*wohlgemuth*), spend much of his time in fiddling? Foolish Word-monger and Motive-grinder, who in thy Logic-mill hast an earthly mechanism for the Godlike itself, and wouldst fain grind me out Virtue from the husks of Pleasure,—I tell thee, Nay! To the unregenerate Prometheus Vinctus[4] of a man, it is ever the bitterest aggravation of his wretchedness that he is conscious of Virtue, that he feels himself the victim not of suffering only, but of injustice. What then? Is the heroic inspiration we name Virtue but some Passion; some bubble of the blood, bubbling in the direction others *profit* by? I know not; only this I know, If what thou namest Happiness be our true aim, then are we all astray. With Stupidity and sound Digestion man may front much. But what, in these dull unimaginative days, are the terrors of Conscience to the diseases of the Liver! Not on Morality, but on Cookery, let us build our stronghold: there brandishing our frying-pan, as censer, let us offer sweet incense to the Devil, and live at ease on the fat things *he* has provided for his Elect!"

Thus has the bewildered Wanderer to stand, as so many have done, shouting question after question into the Sibyl-cave of Destiny,[5] and receive no Answer but an Echo. It is all a grim Desert, this once-fair world of his; wherein is heard only the howling of wild-beasts, or the shrieks of despairing, hate-filled men; and no Pillar of Cloud by day, and no Pillar of Fire by night,[6] any longer guides the Pilgrim. To such length has the spirit of Inquiry carried him. "But what boots it (*was thut's*)?" cries he: "it is but the common lot in this era. Not having come to spiritual majority prior to the *Siècle de Louis Quinze*,[7] and not being born purely a Loghead (*Dummkopf*), thou hast no other outlook. The whole world is, like thee, sold to Unbelief, their old Temples of the Godhead, which for long have not been rainproof, crumble down; and men ask now: Where is the Godhead; our eyes never saw him?"

Pitiful enough were it, for all these wild utterances, to call our Diogenes wicked. Unprofitable servants as we all are, perhaps at no era of his life was he more decisively the Servant of Goodness, the Servant of God, than even now when doubting God's existence. "One circumstance I note," says he: "after all the nameless woe that Inquiry, which for me, what it is not always, was genuine Love of Truth, had wrought me, I nevertheless still loved Truth, and would bate no jot of my allegiance to her. 'Truth!' I cried, 'though the Heavens crush me for following her: no Falsehood! though a whole celestial Lubberland[8] were the price of Apostasy.' In conduct it was the same. Had a divine Messenger from the clouds, or miraculous Handwriting on the wall, convincingly proclaimed to me *This thou shalt do*, with what passionate readiness, as I often thought, would I have done it, had it been leaping into the

2. James Graham (1745–1794), a quack doctor, had invented an elaborate bed that was supposed to cure sterility in couples using it. In this passage, the bed is apparently a symbol of sexual desires.
3. Paraphrase of 1 Timothy 1.15.
4. I.e., Prometheus Bound; this is also the title of a play by Aeschylus depicting the sufferings of a hero who defied Zeus.

5. An allusion to Virgil's *Aeneid* 6.36ff., where Aeneas questions the Cumaean sibyl.
6. Exodus 13.21.
7. The Century of Louis XV (French), allusion to *Précis du Siècle de Louis XV*, Voltaire's history of the skeptical and enquiring spirit of 18th-century France during the reign of Louis XV (1715–74).
8. Land of Plenty.

infernal Fire. Thus, in spite of all Motive-grinders, and Mechanical Profit-and-Loss Philosophies, with the sick ophthalmia and hallucination they had brought on, was the Infinite nature of Duty still dimly present to me: living without God in the world, of God's light I was not utterly bereft; if my as yet sealed eyes, with their unspeakable longing, could nowhere see Him, nevertheless in my heart He was present, and His heaven-written Law still stood legible and sacred there."

Meanwhile, under all these tribulations, and temporal and spiritual destitutions, what must the Wanderer, in his silent soul, have endured! "The painfullest feeling," writes he, "is that of your own Feebleness (*Unkraft*); ever, as the English Milton says, to be weak is the true misery.[9] And yet of your Strength there is and can be no clear feeling, save by what you have prospered in, by what you have done. Between vague wavering Capability and fixed indubitable Performance, what a difference! A certain inarticulate Self-consciousness dwells dimly in us; which only our Works can render articulate and decisively discernible. Our Works are the mirror wherein the spirit first sees its natural lineaments. Hence, too, the folly of that impossible Precept, *Know thyself*;[1] till it be translated into this partially possible one, *Know what thou canst work at*.

"But for me, so strangely unprosperous had I been, the net-result of my Workings amounted as yet simply to—Nothing. How then could I believe in my Strength, when there was as yet no mirror to see it in? Ever did this agitating, yet, as I now perceive, quite frivolous question, remain to me insoluble: Hast thou a certain Faculty, a certain Worth, such even as the most have not; or art thou the completest Dullard of these modern times? Alas! the fearful Unbelief is unbelief in yourself; and how could I believe? Had not my first, last Faith in myself, when even to me the Heavens seemed laid open, and I dared to love, been all-too cruelly belied? The speculative Mystery of Life grew ever more mysterious to me: neither in the practical Mystery[2] had I made the slightest progress, but been everywhere buffeted, foiled, and contemptuously cast-out. A feeble unit in the middle of a threatening Infinitude, I seemed to have nothing given me but eyes, whereby to discern my own wretchedness. Invisible yet impenetrable walls, as of Enchantment, divided me from all living: was there, in the wide world, any true bosom I could press trustfully to mine? O Heaven, No, there was none! I kept a lock upon my lips: why should I speak much with that shifting variety of so-called Friends, in whose withered, vain and too-hungry souls Friendship was but an incredible tradition? In such cases, your resource is to talk little, and that little mostly from the Newspapers. Now when I look back, it was a strange isolation I then lived in. The men and women around me, even speaking with me, were but Figures; I had, practically, forgotten that they were alive, that they were not merely automatic. In midst of their crowded streets and assemblages, I walked solitary; and (except as it was my own heart, not another's, that I kept devouring) savage also, as the tiger in his jungle. Some comfort it would have been, could I, like a Faust,[3] have fancied myself tempted and tormented of the Devil; for a Hell, as I imagine, without Life, though only

---

9. *Paradise Lost* 1.157: "Fallen cherub, to be weak is miserable."
1. This maxim was inscribed in gold letters over the portico of the temple at Delphi.

2. A profession or practical occupation.
3. Both Christopher Marlowe and Goethe wrote plays about the temptations of Faust.

diabolic Life, were more frightful: but in our age of Down-pulling and Disbelief, the very Devil has been pulled down, you cannot so much as believe in a Devil. To me the Universe was all void of Life, of Purpose, of Volition, even of Hostility: it was one huge, dead, immeasurable Steam-engine, rolling on, in its dead indifference, to grind me limb from limb. O, the vast, gloomy, solitary Golgotha,[4] and Mill of Death! Why was the Living banished thither companionless, conscious? Why, if there is no Devil; nay, unless the Devil is your God?"

A prey incessantly to such corrosions, might not, moreover, as the worst aggravation to them, the iron constitution even of a Teufelsdröckh threaten to fail? We conjecture that he has known sickness; and, in spite of his locomotive habits, perhaps sickness of the chronic sort. Hear this, for example: "How beautiful to die of broken-heart, on Paper! Quite another thing in practice; every window of your Feeling, even of your Intellect, as it were, begrimed and mud-bespattered, so that no pure ray can enter; a whole Drug-shop in your inwards; the fordone soul drowning slowly in quagmires of Disgust!"

Putting all which external and internal miseries together, may we not find in the following sentences, quite in our Professor's still vein, significance enough? "From Suicide a certain aftershine (*Nachschein*) of Christianity withheld me: perhaps also a certain indolence of character; for, was not that a remedy I had at any time within reach? Often, however, was there a question present to me: Should some one now, at the turning of that corner, blow thee suddenly out of Space, into the other World, or other No-World, by pistol-shot,—how were it? On which ground, too, I have often, in sea-storms and sieged cities and other death-scenes, exhibited an imperturbability, which passed, falsely enough, for courage.

"So had it lasted," concludes the Wanderer, "so had it lasted, as in bitter protracted Death-agony, through long years. The heart within me, unvisited by any heavenly dewdrop, was smouldering in sulphurous, slow-consuming fire. Almost since earliest memory I had shed no tear; or once only when I, murmuring half-audibly, recited Faust's Deathsong, that wild *Selig der den er im Siegesglanze findet* (Happy whom *he* finds in Battle's splendour),[5] and thought that of this last Friend even I was not forsaken, that Destiny itself could not doom me not to die. Having no hope, neither had I any definite fear, were it of Man or of Devil: nay, I often felt as if it might be solacing, could the Arch-Devil himself, though in Tartarean terrors, but rise to me, that I might tell him a little of my mind. And yet, strangely enough, I lived in a continual, indefinite, pining fear; tremulous, pusillanimous, apprehensive of I knew not what: it seemed as if all things in the Heavens above and the Earth beneath would hurt me; as if the Heavens and the Earth were but boundless jaws of a devouring monster, wherein I, palpitating, waited to be devoured.

"Full of such humour, and perhaps the miserablest man in the whole French Capital or Suburbs, was I, one sultry Dogday, after much perambulation, toiling along the dirty little *Rue Saint-Thomas de l'Enfer*,[6] among

---

4. Calvary, the place where Christ was crucified.
5. Adapted from Goethe's *Faust* 1.4.1573–76.
6. St. Thomas-of-Hell Street (French). In later life Carlyle admitted that this incident was based on his own experience during a walk in Edinburgh (rather than in Paris). "Dogday": a hot and unwholesome summer period, coinciding with the prominence of Sirius, the Dog Star, is called the season of the dog days.

civic rubbish enough, in a close atmosphere, and over pavements hot as Nebuchadnezzar's Furnace; whereby doubtless my spirits were little cheered; when, all at once, there rose a Thought in me, and I asked myself: 'What *art* thou afraid of? Wherefore, like a coward, dost thou forever pip and whimper, and go cowering and trembling? Despicable biped! what is the sum-total of the worst that lies before thee? Death? Well, Death; and say the pangs of Tophet[7] too, and all that the Devil and Man may, will or can do against thee! Hast thou not a heart; canst thou not suffer whatsoever it be; and, as a Child of Freedom, though outcast, trample Tophet itself under thy feet, while it consumes thee? Let it come, then; I will meet it and defy it!' And as I so thought, there rushed like a stream of fire over my whole soul; and I shook base Fear away from me forever. I was strong, of unknown strength; a spirit, almost a god. Ever from that time, the temper of my misery was changed: not Fear or whining Sorrow was it, but Indignation and grim fire-eyed Defiance.

"Thus had the EVERLASTING NO[8] (*das ewige Nein*) pealed authoritatively through all the recesses of my Being, of my ME; and then was it that my whole ME stood up, in native God-created majesty, and with emphasis recorded its Protest. Such a Protest, the most important transaction in Life, may that same Indignation and Defiance, in a psychological point of view, be fitly called. The Everlasting No had said: 'Behold, thou art fatherless, outcast, and the Universe is mine (the Devil's)'; to which my whole Me now made answer: '*I am not thine, but Free, and forever hate thee!*'

"It is from this hour that I incline to date my Spiritual Newbirth, or Baphometic Fire-baptism,[9] perhaps I directly thereupon began to be a Man."

Centre of Indifference

Though, after this "Baphometic Fire-baptism" of his, our Wanderer signifies that his Unrest was but increased; as indeed, "Indignation and Defiance," especially against things in general, are not the most peaceable inmates; yet can the Psychologist surmise that it was no longer a quite hopeless Unrest; that henceforth it had at least a fixed centre to revolve round. For the fire-baptised soul, long so scathed and thunder-riven, here feels its own Freedom, which feeling is its Baphometic Baptism: the citadel of its whole kingdom it has thus gained by assault, and will keep inexpugnable; outwards from which the remaining dominions, not indeed without hard battling, will doubtless by degrees be conquered and pacificated. Under another figure, we might say, if in that great moment, in the *Rue Saint-Thomas de l'Enfer,* the old inward Satanic School was not yet thrown out of doors, it received peremptory judicial notice to quit;—whereby, for the rest, its howl-chantings, Ernulphus-cursings,[1] and rebellious gnashings of teeth, might, in the meanwhile, become only the more tumultuous, and difficult to keep secret.

---

7. Hell.
8. This phrase does not signify the hero's protest; it represents the sum of all the forces that had denied meaning to life. These negative forces, which had hitherto held the hero in bondage, are repudiated by his saying no to the "Everlasting No."
9. A transformation by a flash of spiritual illumi-

nation. The term may derive from Baphomet, an idol that inspired such spiritual experiences.
1. Curse devised by Ernulf (1040–1124), bishop of Rochester, when sentencing persons to excommunication. "Satanic School": term coined by Robert Southey (1774–1843) to characterize the self-assertive and rebellious temper of the poetry of Byron and Shelley.

Accordingly, if we scrutinise these Pilgrimings well, there is perhaps discernible henceforth a certain incipient method in their madness. Not wholly as a Spectre does Teufelsdröckh now storm through the world; at worst as a spectre-fighting Man, nay who will one day be a Spectre-queller. If pilgriming restlessly to so many "Saints' Wells,"[2] and ever without quenching of his thirst, he nevertheless finds little secular wells, whereby from time to time some alleviation is ministered. In a word, he is now, if not ceasing, yet intermitting to "eat his own heart"; and clutches round him outwardly on the NOT-ME for wholesomer food. Does not the following glimpse exhibit him in a much more natural state?

"Towns also and Cities, especially the ancient, I failed not to look upon with interest. How beautiful to see thereby, as through a long vista, into the remote Time; to have as it were, an actual section of almost the earliest Past brought safe into the Present, and set before your eyes! There, in that old City, was a live ember of Culinary Fire put down, say only two-thousand years ago; and there, burning more or less triumphantly, with such fuel as the region yielded, it has burnt, and still burns, and thou thyself seest the very smoke thereof. Ah! and the far more mysterious live ember of Vital Fire was then also put down there; and still miraculously burns and spreads; and the smoke and ashes thereof (in these Judgment-Halls and Churchyards), and its bellows-engines (in these Churches), thou still seest; and its flame, looking out from every kind countenance, and every hateful one, still warms thee or scorches thee.

"Of Man's Activity and Attainment the chief results are aeriform, mystic, and preserved in Tradition only: such are his Forms of Government, with the Authority they rest on; his Customs, or Fashions both of Cloth-habits and of Soul-habits; much more his collective stock of Handicrafts, the whole Faculty he has acquired of manipulating Nature: all these things, as indispensable and priceless as they are, cannot in any way be fixed under lock and key, but must flit, spirit-like, on impalpable vehicles, from Father to Son; if you demand sight of them, they are nowhere to be met with. Visible Plowmen and Hammermen there have been, ever from Cain and Tubalcain[3] downwards: but where does your accumulated Agricultural, Metallurgic, and other Manufacturing SKILL lie warehoused? It transmits itself on the atmospheric air, on the sun's rays (by Hearing and by Vision); it is a thing aeriform, impalpable, of quite spiritual sort. In like manner, ask me not. Where are the LAWS; where is the GOVERNMENT? In vain wilt thou go to Schönbrunn, to Downing Street, to the Palais Bourbon:[4] thou findest nothing there but brick or stone houses, and some bundles of Papers tied with tape. Where, then, is that same cunningly-devised almighty GOVERNMENT of theirs to be laid hands on? Everywhere, yet nowhere: seen only in its works, this too is a thing aeriform, invisible; or if you will, mystic and miraculous. So spiritual (geistig) is our whole daily Life: all that we do springs out of Mystery, Spirit, invisible Force; only like a little Cloud-image, or Armida's Palace,[5] air-built, does the Actual body itself forth from the great mystic Deep.

"Visible and tangible products of the Past, again, I reckon-up to the extent of three. Cities, with their Cabinets and Arsenals; then tilled Fields, to either

2. Holy fountains or wells, the waters of which were reputed to restore health.
3. Descendant of Cain, son of Adam and Eve (Genesis 4.1–22).
4. Headquarters of government in Vienna, London, and Paris, respectively.
5. The magic palace of a beautiful enchantress in Torquato Tasso's *Jerusalem Delivered*.

or to both of which divisions Roads with their Bridges, may belong; and thirdly—Books. In which third truly, the last invented, lies a worth far surpassing that of the two others. Wondrous indeed is the virtue of a true Book. Not like a dead city of stones, yearly crumbling, yearly needing repair; more like a tilled field, but then a spiritual field: like a spiritual tree, let me rather say, it stands from year to year, and from age to age (we have Books that already number some hundred-and-fifty human ages); and yearly comes its new produce of leaves (Commentaries, Deductions, Philosophical, Political Systems; or were it only Sermons, Pamphlets, Journalistic Essays), every one of which is talismanic and thaumaturgic,[6] for it can persuade men. O thou who art able to write a Book, which once in the two centuries or oftener there is a man gifted to do, envy not him whom they name City-builder, and inexpressibly pity him whom they name Conqueror or City-burner! Thou too art a Conqueror and Victor; but of the true sort, namely over the Devil: thou too hast built what will outlast all marble and metal, and be a wonder-bringing City of the Mind, a Temple and Seminary and Prophetic Mount, whereto all kindreds of the Earth will pilgrim.—Fool! why journeyest thou wearisomely, in thy antiquarian fervour, to gaze on the stone pyramids of Geeza, or the clay ones of Sacchara?[7] These stand there, as I can tell thee, idle and inert, looking over the Desert, foolishly enough, for the last three-thousand years: but canst thou not open thy Hebrew BIBLE, then, or even Luther's Version thereof?"

No less satisfactory is his sudden appearance not in Battle, yet on some Battle-field; which, we soon gather, must be that of Wagram;[8] so that here, for once, is a certain approximation to distinctiveness of date. Omitting much, let us impart what follows:

"Horrible enough! A whole Marchfeld[9] strewed with shell-splinters, cannon-shot, ruined tumbrils, and dead men and horses; stragglers still remaining not so much as buried. And those red mould heaps: ay, there lie the Shells of Men, out of which all the Life and Virtue has been blown; and now are they swept together, and crammed-down out of sight, like blown Egg-shells!—Did Nature, when she bade the Donau bring down his mould-cargoes from the Carinthian and Carpathian Heights, and spread them out here into the softest, richest level,—intend thee, O Marchfeld, for a corn-bearing Nursery, whereon her children might be nursed; or for a Cockpit, wherein they might the more commodiously be throttled and tattered? Were thy three broad Highways, meeting here from the ends of Europe, made for Ammunition-wagons, then? Were thy Wagrams and Stillfrieds[1] but so many ready-built Casemates, wherein the house of Hapsburg might batter with artillery, and with artillery be battered? König Ottokar, amid yonder hillocks, dies under Rodolf's truncheon; here Kaiser Franz falls a-swoon under Napoleon's: within which five centuries, to omit the others, how has thy breast, fair Plain, been defaced and defiled! The greensward is torn-up and trampled-down; man's fond care of it, his fruit-trees, hedge-rows, and pleas-

---

6. Miracle-working.
7. I.e., Giza and Saqqara near Cairo.
8. A village in Austria; site of Napoleon's victory over the Austrians, July 1809.
9. A fertile plain in Austria whose soil (according to Teufelsdröckh) was brought down from the Carpathian Mountains by the Danube ("Donau")

River.
1. Fortified chambers. Stillfried was the site of a battle in which Ottokar, king ("König") of Bohemia, was killed by the forces of Rudolph of Hapsburg in 1278. In 1809 the Hapsburg armies, under Emperor Francis ("Franz") I, were defeated by Napoleon at nearby Wagram.

ant dwellings, blown away with gunpowder; and the kind seedfield lies a desolate, hideous Place of Sculls.—Nevertheless, Nature is at work; neither shall these Powder-Devilkins with their utmost devilry gainsay her: but all that gore and carnage will be shrouded-in, absorbed into manure; and next year the Marchfeld will be green, nay greener. Thrifty unwearied Nature, ever out of our great waste educing some little profit of thy own,—how dost thou, from the very carcass of the Killer, bring Life for the Living!

"What, speaking in quite unofficial language, is the net-purport and upshot of war? To my own knowledge, for example, there dwell and toil, in the British village of Dumdrudge, usually some five-hundred souls. From these, by certain 'Natural Enemies'[2] of the French, there are successively selected, during the French war, say thirty able-bodied men: Dumdrudge, at her own expense, has suckled and nursed them: she has, not without difficulty and sorrow, fed them up to manhood, and even trained them to crafts, so that one can weave, another build, another hammer, and the weakest can stand under thirty stone avoirdupois. Nevertheless, amid much weeping and swearing, they are selected; all dressed in red; and shipped away, at the public charges, some two-thousand miles, or say only to the south of Spain;[3] and fed there till wanted. And now to that same spot, in the south of Spain, are thirty similar French artisans, from a French Dumdrudge, in like manner wending: till at length, after infinite effort, the two parties come into actual juxtaposition; and Thirty stands fronting Thirty, each with a gun in his hand. Straightway the word 'Fire!' is given: and they blow the souls out of one another; and in place of sixty brisk useful craftsmen, the world has sixty dead carcasses, which it must bury, and anew shed tears for. Had these men any quarrel? Busy as the Devil is, not the smallest! They lived far enough apart; were the entirest strangers; nay, in so wide a Universe, there was even, unconsciously, by Commerce, some mutual helpfulness between them. How then? Simpleton! their Governors had fallen-out; and, instead of shooting one another, had the cunning to make these poor blockheads shoot.—Alas, so is it in Deutschland, and hitherto in all other lands; still as of old, 'what devilry soever Kings do, the Greeks must pay the piper!'[4]—In that fiction of the English Smollett,[5] it is true, the final Cessation of War is perhaps prophetically shadowed forth; where the two Natural Enemies, in person, take each a Tobacco-pipe, filled with Brimstone; light the same, and smoke in one another's faces, till the weaker gives in: but from such predicted Peace-Era, what blood-filled trenches, and contentious centuries, may still divide us!"

Thus can the Professor, at least in lucid intervals, look away from his own sorrows, over the many-coloured world, and pertinently enough note what is passing there. We may remark, indeed, that for the matter of spiritual culture, if for nothing else, perhaps few periods of his life were richer than this. Internally, there is the most momentous instructive Course of Practical Philosophy, with Experiments, going on; towards the right comprehension of which his Peripatetic[6] habits, favourable to Meditation, might help him

---

2. Term often used in English newspapers to account for the frequency of wars between the English and French.
3. Where British armies fought against Napoleon (1808–14).
4. Horace's *Epistles* 1.2.14.

5. Tobias Smollett (1721–1771), *The Adventures of Ferdinand Count Fathom*, chap. 41.
6. Walking about, after the manner of Aristotle who delivered his lectures while walking in the Lyceum.

rather than hinder. Externally, again, as he wanders to and fro, there are, if for the longing heart little substance, yet for the seeing eye sights enough: in these so boundless Travels of his, granting that the Satanic School was even partially kept down, what an incredible knowledge of our Planet, and its Inhabitants and their Works, that is to say, of all knowable things, might not Teufelsdröckh acquire!

"I have read in most Public Libraries," says he, "including those of Constantinople and Samarcand: in most Colleges, except the Chinese Mandarin ones, I have studied, or seen that there was no studying. Unknown Languages have I oftenest gathered from their natural repertory, the Air, by my organ of Hearing; Statistics, Geographics, Topographics came, through the Eye, almost of their own accord. The ways of Man, how he seeks food, and warmth, and protection for himself, in most regions, are ocularly known to me. Like the great Hadrian, I meted-out much of the terraqueous Globe with a pair of Compasses[7] that belonged to myself only.

"Of great Scenes why speak? Three summer days, I lingered reflecting, and even composing (*dichtete*), by the Pine-chasms of Vaucluse; and in that clear Lakelet[8] moistened my bread. I have sat under the Palm-trees of Tadmor;[9] smoked a pipe among the ruins of Babylon. The great Wall of China I have seen; and can testify that it is of gray brick, coped and covered with granite, and shows only second-rate masonry.—Great Events, also, have not I witnessed? Kings sweated-down (*ausgemergelt*) into Berlin-and-Milan Customhouse-Officers;[1] the World well won, and the World well lost oftener than once a hundred-thousand individuals shot (by each other) in one day. All kindreds and peoples and nations dashed together, and shifted and shovelled into heaps, that they might ferment there, and in time unite. The birth-pangs of Democracy,[2] wherewith convulsed Europe was groaning in cries that reached Heaven, could not escape me.

"For great Men I have ever had the warmest predilection; and can perhaps boast that few such in this era have wholly escaped me. Great Men are the inspired (speaking and acting) Texts of that divine BOOK OF REVELATION, whereof a Chapter is completed from epoch to epoch, and by some named HISTORY; to which inspired Texts your numerous talented men, and your innumerable untalented men, are the better or worse exegetic Commentaries, and wagonload of too-stupid, heretical or orthodox, weekly Sermons. For my study, the inspired Texts themselves! Thus did not I, in very early days, having disguised me as tavern-waiter, stand behind the field-chairs, under that shady Tree at Treisnitz by the Jena Highway;[3] waiting upon the great Schiller and greater Goethe; and hearing what I have not forgotten. For—"

—But at this point the Editor recalls his principle of caution, some time ago laid down, and must suppress much. Let not the sacredness of Laurelled, still more, of Crowned Heads, be tampered with. Should we, at a future day, find circumstances altered, and the time come for Publication, then may these glimpses into the privacy of the Illustrious be conceded; which for the present were little better than treacherous, perhaps traitorous Eaves-

---

7. Legs. Hadrian (76–138), Roman emperor, who traveled extensively throughout his empire.
8. A pool at the base of a mountain in Vaucluse in southern France, one of Petrarch's favorite haunts.
9. Palmyra in Syria.
1. Napoleon reduced some of Europe's kings to

the status of mere tax collectors for his regime.
2. As manifested in the revolutionary outbreaks in France (1789 and 1830) and in the agitations in England preceding the Reform Bill of 1832.
3. Where Goethe and Schiller met during the 1790s when they were collaborating on their writings.

droppings. Of Lord Byron, therefore, of Pope Pius, Emperor Tarakwang, and the "White Water-roses"[4] (Chinese Carbonari) with their mysteries, no notice here! Of Napoleon himself we shall only, glancing from afar, remark that Teufelsdröckh's relation to him seems to have been of very varied character. At first we find our poor Professor on the point of being shot as a spy; then taken into private conversation, even pinched on the ear, yet presented with no money; at last indignantly dismissed, almost thrown out of doors, as an "Ideologist." "He himself," says the Professor, "was among the completest Ideologists, at least Ideopraxists:[5] in the Idea (*in der Idee*) he lived, moved and fought. The man was a Divine Missionary, though unconscious of it; and preached, through the cannon's throat, that great doctrine, *La carrière ouverte aux talens* (The Tools to him that can handle them), which is our ultimate Political Evangel, wherein alone can liberty lie. Madly enough he preached, it is true, as Enthusiasts[6] and first Missionaries are wont, with imperfect utterance, amid much frothy rant; yet as articulately perhaps as the case admitted. Or call him, if you will, an American Backwoodsman, who had to fell unpenetrated forests, and battle with innumerable wolves, and did not entirely forbear strong liquor, rioting, and even theft; whom, notwithstanding, the peaceful Sower will follow, and, as he cuts the boundless harvest, bless."

More legitimate and decisively authentic is Teufelsdröckh's appearance and emergence (we know not well whence) in the solitude of the North Cape, on that June Midnight. He has a "light-blue Spanish cloak" hanging round him, as his "most commodious, principal, indeed sole upper-garment"; and stands there, on the World-promontory, looking over the infinite Brine, like a little blue Belfry (as we figure), now motionless indeed, yet ready, if stirred, to ring quaintest changes.

"Silence as of death," writes he; "for Midnight, even in the Arctic latitudes, has its character: nothing but the granite cliffs ruddy-tinged, the peaceable gurgle of that slow-heaving Polar Ocean, over which in the utmost North the great Sun hangs low and lazy, as if he too were slumbering. Yet is his cloud-couch wrought of crimson and cloth-of-gold; yet does his light stream over the mirror of waters, like a tremulous fire-pillar, shooting downwards to the abyss, and hide itself under my feet. In such moments, Solitude also is invaluable; for who would speak, or be looked on, when behind him lies all Europe and Africa, fast asleep, except the watchmen; and before him the silent Immensity, and Palace of the Eternal, whereof our Sun is but a porch-lamp?

"Nevertheless, in this solemn moment comes a man, or monster, scrambling from among the rock-hollows; and, shaggy, huge as the Hyperborean[7] Bear, hails me in Russian speech: most probably, therefore, a Russian Smuggler. With courteous brevity, I signify my indifference to contraband trade, my humane intentions, yet strong wish to be private. In vain: the monster, counting doubtless on his superior stature, and minded to make sport for himself, or perhaps profit, were it with murder, continues to advance; ever assailing me with his importunate train-oil[8] breath; and now has advanced, till we stand both on the verge of the rock, the deep Sea rippling greedily

---

4. Like the Carbonari in Italy, a secret revolutionary society in China during the regime of Emperor Tarakwang (Tao Kuang, 1821–50).
5. Those who put ideas into practice.

6. Religious fanatics.
7. From the far North.
8. Whale oil.

down below. What argument will avail? On the thick Hyperborean, cherubic reasoning, seraphic eloquence were lost. Prepared for such extremity, I, deftly enough, whisk aside one step; draw out, from my interior reservoirs, a sufficient Birmingham Horse-pistol, and say, 'Be so obliging as retire, Friend (*Er ziehe sich zurück, Freund*), and with promptitude!' This logic even the Hyperborean understands: fast enough, with apologetic, petitionary growl, he sidles off; and, except for suicidal as well as homicidal purposes, need not return.

"Such I hold to be the genuine use of Gunpowder: that it makes all men alike tall. Nay, if thou be cooler, cleverer than I, if thou have more *Mind*, though all but no *Body* whatever, then canst thou kill me first, and are the taller. Hereby, at last, is the Goliath powerless, and the David resistless; savage Animalism is nothing, inventive Spiritualism is all.

"With respect to Duels, indeed, I have my own ideas. Few things, in this so surprising world, strike me with more surprise. Two little visual Spectra of men, hovering with insecure enough cohesion in the midst of the UN-FATHOMABLE, and to dissolve therein, at any rate, very soon,—make pause at the distance of twelve paces asunder; whirl round; and, simultaneously by the cunningest mechanism, explode one another into Dissolution; and off-hand become Air, and Nonextant! Deuce on it (*verdammt*), the little spit-fires!—Nay, I think with old Hugo von Trimberg:[9] 'God must needs laugh outright, could such a thing be, to see his wondrous Manikins here below.' "

But amid these specialties, let us not forget the great generality, which is our Chief guest here: How prospered the inner man of Teufelsdröckh under so much outward shifting? Does Legion[1] still lurk in him, though repressed; or has he exorcised that Devil's Brood? We can answer that the symptoms continue promising. Experience is the grand spiritual Doctor; and with him Teufelsdröckh has been long a patient, swallowing many a bitter bolus.[2] Unless our poor Friend belong to the numerous class of Incurables, which seems not likely, some cure will doubtless be effected. We should rather say that Legion, or the Satanic School, was now pretty well extirpated and cast out, but next to nothing introduced in its room; whereby the heart remains, for the while, in a quiet but no comfortable state.

"At length, after so much roasting," thus writes our Autobiographer, "I was what you might name calcined. Pray only that it be not rather, as is the more frequent issue, reduced to a *caputmortuum*![3] But in any case, by mere dint of practice, I had grown familiar with many things. Wretchedness was still wretched; but I could now partly see through it, and despise it. Which highest mortal, in this inane Existence, had I not found a Shadow-hunter, or Shadow-hunted; and, when I looked through his brave garnitures, miserable enough? Thy wishes have all been sniffed aside, thought I: but what, had they ever been all granted! Did not the Boy Alexander weep because he had not two Planets to conquer; or a whole Solar System; or after that, a whole Universe? *Ach Gott*, when I gazed into these Stars, have they not looked-down on me as if with pity, from their serene spaces; like Eyes glistening with heavenly tears over the little lot of man! Thousands of human genera-tions, all as noisy as our own, have been swallowed-up of Time, and there

---

9. Medieval poet (1260–1309).
1. Unclean spirits (Mark 5.9).
2. Large pill.
3. Death's head (Latin).

remains no wreck of them any more; and Arcturus and Orion and Sirius and the Pleiades are still shining in their courses, clear and young, as when the Shepherd first noted them in the plain of Shinar.[4] Pshaw! what is this paltry little Dog-cage[5] of an Earth; what art thou that sittest whining there? Thou art still Nothing, Nobody: true; but who, then, is Something, Somebody? For thee the Family of Man has no use; it rejects thee; thou art wholly as a dissevered limb: so be it; perhaps it is better so!"

Too-heavy-laden Teufelsdröckh! Yet surely his bands are loosening: one day he will hurl the burden far from him, and bound forth free and with a second youth.

The Everlasting Yea

"Temptations in the Wilderness!"[6] exclaims Teufelsdröckh: "Have we not all to be tried with such? Not so easily can the old Adam, lodged in us by birth, be dispossessed. Our Life is compassed round with Necessity; yet is the meaning of Life itself no other than Freedom, than Voluntary Force: thus have we a warfare; in the beginning, especially, a hard-fought battle. For the God-given mandate, *Work thou in Welldoing*, lies mysteriously written, in Promethean[7] Prophetic Characters, in our hearts; and leaves us no rest, night or day, till it be deciphered and obeyed; till it burn forth, in our conduct, a visible, acted Gospel of Freedom. And as the clay-given mandate, *Eat thou and be filled*, at the same time persuasively proclaims itself through every nerve,—must not there be a confusion, a contest, before the better Influence can become the upper?

"To me nothing seems more natural than that the Son of Man, when such God-given mandate first prophetically stirs within him, and the Clay must now be vanquished, or vanquish,—should be carried of the spirit into grim Solitudes, and there fronting the Tempter do grimmest battle with him; defiantly setting him at naught, till he yield and fly. Name it as we choose: with or without visible Devil, whether in the natural Desert of rocks and sands, or in the populous moral Desert of selfishness and baseness,—to such Temptation are we all called. Unhappy if we are not! Unhappy if we are but Halfmen, in whom that divine handwriting has never blazed forth, all-subduing, in true sun-splendour; but quivers dubiously amid meaner lights: or smoulders, in dull pain, in darkness, under earthly vapours!—Our Wilderness is the wide World in an Atheistic Century; our Forty Days are long years of suffering and fasting: nevertheless, to these also comes an end. Yes, to me also was given, if not Victory, yet the consciousness of Battle, and the resolve to persevere therein while life or faculty is left. To me also, entangled in the enchanted forests, demon-peopled, doleful of sight and of sound, it was given, after weariest wanderings, to work out my way into the higher sunlit slopes—of that Mountain which has no summit, or whose summit is in Heaven only!"

He says elsewhere, under a less ambitious figure; as figures are, once for

---

4. A plain in the Sumerian region (now in Iraq). "Shepherd": probably Abraham, who was commanded by the Lord to "tell the stars, if thou be able to number them" (Genesis 15.5).
5. A drum-shaped cage that turns when a dog runs inside the cylinder, This dog-powered device,

attached to a kitchen spit, was used for turning joints of meat during roasting.
6. Paraphrase of Matthew 4.1.
7. Fiery or fiery-spirited, an allusion to Prometheus, the defiant Titan who brought the secret of fire making to humanity.

all, natural to him: "Has not thy Life been that of most sufficient men (*tüchtigen Männer*) thou hast known in this generation? An outflush of foolish young Enthusiasm, like the first fallow-crop, wherein are as many weeds as valuable herbs: this all parched away, under the Droughts of practical and spiritual Unbelief, as Disappointment, in thought and act, often-repeated gave rise to Doubt, and Doubt gradually settled into Denial! If I have had a second-crop, and now see the perennial greensward, and sit under umbrageous[8] cedars, which defy all Drought (and Doubt); herein too, be the Heavens praised, I am not without examples, and even exemplars."

So that, for Teufelsdröckh also, there has been a "glorious revolution":[9] these mad shadow-hunting and shadow-hunted Pilgrimings of his were but some purifying "Temptation in the Wilderness," before his Apostolic work (such as it was) could begin; which Temptation is now happily over, and the Devil once more worsted! Was "that high moment in the *Rue de l'Enfer*," then, properly the turning-point of the battle; when the Fiend said, *Worship me or be torn in shreds*; and was answered valiantly with an *Apage Satana*?[1]— Singular Teufelsdröckh, would thou hadst told thy singular story in plain words! But it is fruitless to look there, in those Paper-bags,[2] for such. Nothing but innuendoes, figurative crotchets: a typical Shadow, fitfully wavering, prophetico-satiric; no clear logical Picture. "How paint to the sensual eye," asks he once, "what passes in the Holy-of-Holies of Man's Soul; in what words, known to these profane times, speak even afar-off of the unspeakable?" We ask in turn: Why perplex these times, profane as they are, with needless obscurity, by omission and by commission? Not mystical only is our Professor, but whimsical; and involves himself, now more than ever, in eye-bewildering *chiaroscuro*.[3] Successive glimpses, here faithfully imparted, our more gifted readers must endeavour to combine for their own behoof.

He says: "The hot Harmattan wind[4] had raged itself out; its howl went silent within me; and the long-deafened soul could now hear. I paused in my wild wanderings; and sat me down to wait, and consider; for it was as if the hour of change drew nigh. I seemed to surrender, to renounce utterly, and say: Fly, then, false shadows of Hope; I will chase you no more, I will believe you no more. And ye too, haggard spectres of Fear, I care not for you; ye too are all shadows and a lie. Let me rest here: for I am way-weary and life-weary; I will rest here, were it but to die: to die or to live is alike to me; alike insignificant."—And again: "Here, then, as I lay in that CENTRE of INDIFFERENCE; cast, doubtless by benignant upper Influence, into a healing sleep, the heavy dreams rolled gradually away, and I awoke to a new Heaven and a new Earth.[5] The first preliminary moral Act, Annihilation of Self (*Selbsttödtung*), had been happily accomplished; and my mind's eyes were now unsealed, and its hands ungyved."[6]

Might we not also conjecture that the following passage refers to his Locality, during this same "healing sleep"; that his Pilgrim-staff lies cast aside here, on "the high table-land"; and indeed that the repose is already taking wholesome effect on him? If it were not that the tone, in some parts, has more of riancy,[7] even of levity, than we could have expected! However, in

8. Shady.
9. The overthrow of James II of England in 1688.
1. Get thee hence, Satan (Italian; Matthew 4.8–10).
2. Bags containing documents and writings by Teufelsdröckh.

3. Light and shade (Italian).
4. A hot and dry wind in Africa.
5. Revelation 21.1.
6. Unfettered.
7. Gaiety.

Teufelsdröckh, there is always the strangest Dualism: light dancing, with guitar-music, will be going on in the fore-court, while by fits from within comes the faint whimpering of woe and wail. We transcribe the piece entire:

"Beautiful it was to sit there, as in my skyey Tent, musing and meditating; on the high table-land, in front of the Mountains; over me, as roof, the azure Dome, and around me, for walls, four azure-flowing curtains,—namely, of the Four azure winds, on whose bottom-fringes also I have seen gilding. And then to fancy the fair Castles that stood sheltered in these Mountain hollows; with their green flower-lawns, and white dames and damesels, lovely enough: or better still, the straw-roofed Cottages, wherein stood many a Mother baking bread, with her children round her:—all hidden and protectingly folded-up in the valley-folds; yet there and alive, as sure as if I beheld them. Or to see, as well as fancy, the nine Towns and Villages, that lay round my mountain-seat, which, in still weather, were wont to speak to me (by their steeple-bells) with metal tongue; and, in almost all weather, proclaimed their vitality by repeated Smoke-clouds; whereon, as on a culinary horologe,[8] I might read the hour of the day. For it was the smoke of cookery, as kind housewives at morning, midday, eventide, were boiling their husband's kettles; and ever a blue pillar rose up into the air, successively or simultaneously, from each of the nine, saying, as plainly as smoke could say: Such and such a meal is getting ready here. Not uninteresting! For you have the whole Borough, with all its love-makings and scandal-mongeries, contentions and contentments, as in miniature, and could cover it all with your hat.—If, in my wide Wayfarings, I had learned to look into the business of the World in its details, here perhaps was the place for combining it into general propositions, and deducing inferences therefrom.

"Often also could I see the black Tempest marching in anger through the Distance: round some Schreckhorn,[9] as yet grim-blue, would the eddying vapour gather, and there tumultuously eddy, and flow down like a mad witch's hair; till, after a space, it vanished, and, in the clear sunbeam, your Schreckhorn stood smiling grim-white, for the vapour had held snow. How thou fermentest and elaboratest, in thy great fermenting-vat and laboratory of an Atmosphere, of a World, O Nature!—Or what is Nature? Ha! why do I not name thee GOD? Art not thou the 'Living Garment of God'? O Heavens, is it, in very deed, HE, then, that ever speaks through thee; that lives and loves in thee, that lives and loves in me?

"Fore-shadows, call them rather fore-splendours, of that Truth, and Beginning of Truths, fell mysteriously over my soul. Sweeter than Dayspring to the Shipwrecked in Nova Zembla;[1] ah, like the mother's voice to her little child that strays bewildered, weeping, in unknown tumults; like soft streamings of celestial music to my too-exasperated heart, came that Evangel. The Universe is not dead and demoniacal, a charnel-house with spectres; but godlike, and my Father's!

"With other eyes, too, could I now look upon my fellow man; with an infinite Love, an infinite Pity. Poor, wandering, wayward man! Art thou not tired, and beaten with stripes, even as I am? Ever, whether thou bear the royal mantle or the beggar's gabardine, art thou not so weary, so heavy-laden;

8. Clock.
9. Peak of Terror (German); a mountain in Switzerland.
1. A Dutch sea captain, whose ship was wrecked off the island of Nova Zembla in the Arctic in 1596, recorded in his journal his thankfulness at the coming of daylight.

and thy Bed of Rest is but a Grave. O my Brother, my Brother, why cannot I shelter thee in my bosom, and wipe away all tears from thy eyes! Truly, the din of many-voiced Life, which, in this solitude, with the mind's organ, I could hear, was no longer a maddening discord, but a melting one; like inarticulate cries, and sobbings of a dumb creature, which in the ear of Heaven are prayers. The poor Earth, with her poor joys, was now my needy Mother, not my cruel Stepdame; man, with his so mad Wants and so mean Endeavours, had become the dearer to me; and even for his sufferings and his sins, I now first named him Brother. Thus I was standing in the porch of that 'Sanctuary of Sorrow';[2] by strange, steep ways had I too been guided thither; and ere long its sacred gates would open, and the 'Divine Depth of Sorrow' lie disclosed to me."

The Professor says, he here first got eye on the Knot that had been strangling him, and straightway could unfasten it, and was free. "A vain interminable controversy," writes he, "touching what is at present called Origin of Evil, or some such thing, arises in every soul, since the beginning of the world; and in every soul, that would pass from idle Suffering into actual Endeavouring, must first be put an end to. The most, in our time, have to go content with a simple, incomplete enough Suppression of this controversy; to a few some Solution of it is indispensable. In every new era, too, such Solution comes-out in different terms; and ever the Solution of the last era has become obsolete, and is found unserviceable. For it is man's nature to change his Dialect from century to century; he cannot help it though he would. The authentic Church-Catechism of our present century has not yet fallen into my hands: meanwhile, for my own private behoof, I attempt to elucidate the matter so. Man's Unhappiness, as I construe, comes of his Greatness; it is because there is an Infinite in him, which with all his cunning he cannot quite bury under the Finite. Will the whole Finance Ministers and Upholsterers and Confections of modern Europe undertake, in joint-stock company, to make one Shoeblack HAPPY? They cannot accomplish it, above an hour or two; for the Shoeblack also has a Soul quite other than his Stomach; and would require, if you consider it, for his permanent satisfaction and saturation, simply this allotment, no more, and no less: God's infinite Universe altogether to himself, therein to enjoy infinitely, and fill every wish as fast as it rose. Oceans of Hochheimer, a Throat like that of Ophiuchus:[3] speak not of them; to the infinite Shoeblack they are as nothing. No sooner is your ocean filled, than he grumbles that it might have been of better vintage. Try him with half of a Universe, of an Omnipotence, he sets to quarrelling with the proprietor of the other half, and declares himself the most maltreated of men.—Always there is a black spot in our sunshine: it is even as I said, the Shadow of Ourselves.

"But the whim we have of Happiness is somewhat thus. By certain valuations, and averages, of our own striking, we come upon some sort of average terrestrial lot; this we fancy belongs to us by nature, and of indefeasible right. It is simple payment of our wages, of our deserts; requires neither thanks nor complaint; only such overplus as there may be do we account Happiness; any deficit again is Misery. Now consider that we have the valuation of our

---

2. Adapted from Goethe's Wilhelm Meister.
3. The serpent in the constellation Serpentarius.

"Hochheimer": Rhine wine or hock from Hochheim.

own deserts ourselves, and what a fund of Self-conceit there is in each of us,—do you wonder that the balance should so often dip the wrong way, and many a Blockhead cry: See there, what a payment; was ever worthy gentleman so used!—I tell thee, Blockhead, it all comes of thy Vanity; of what thou *fanciest* those same deserts of thine to be. Fancy that thou deservest to be hanged (as is most likely), thou wilt feel it happiness to be only shot: fancy that thou deservest to be hanged in a hair-halter, it will be a luxury to die in hemp.

"So true is it, what I then say, that *the Fraction of Life can be increased in value not so much by increasing your Numerator as by lessening your Denominator.* Nay, unless my Algebra deceive me, *Unity* itself divided by *Zero* will give *Infinity.* Make thy claim of wages a zero, then; thou hast the world under thy feet. Well did the Wisest of our time write: 'It is only with Renunciation (*Entsagen*) that Life, properly speaking, can be said to begin.'[4]

"I asked myself: What is this that, ever since earliest years, thou hast been fretting and fuming, and lamenting and self-tormenting, on account of? Say it in a word: it is not because thou art not HAPPY? Because the THOU (sweet gentleman) is not sufficiently honoured, nourished, soft-bedded, and lovingly cared for? Foolish soul! What Act of Legislature was there that *thou* shouldst be Happy? A little while ago thou hadst no right to *be* at all. What if thou wert born and predestined not to be Happy, but to be Unhappy! Art thou nothing other than a Vulture, then, that fliest through the Universe seeking after somewhat to *eat;* and shrieking dolefully because carrion enough is not given thee? Close thy *Byron;* open thy *Goethe.*"

"*Es leuchtet mir ein,*[5] I see a glimpse of it!" cries he elsewhere: "there is in man a HIGHER than Love of Happiness: he can do without Happiness, and instead thereof find Blessedness! Was it not to preach-forth this same HIGHER that sages and martyrs, the Poet and the Priest, in all times, have spoken and suffered; bearing testimony, through life and through death, of the Godlike that is in Man, and how in the Godlike only has he Strength and Freedom? Which God-inspired Doctrine art thou also honoured to be taught; O Heavens! and broken with manifold merciful Afflictions, even till thou become contrite, and learn it! O, thank thy Destiny for these; thankfully bear what yet remain: thou hadst need of them; the Self in thee needed to be annihilated. By benignant fever-paroxysms is Life rooting out the deep-seated chronic Diseases, and triumphs over Death. On the roaring billows of Time, thou art not engulfed, but borne aloft into the azure of Eternity. Love not Pleasure; love God.[6] This is the EVERLASTING YEA wherein all contradiction is solved: wherein whoso walks and works, it is well with him."

And again: "Small is it that thou canst trample the Earth with its injuries under thy feet, as old Greek Zeno[7] trained thee: thou canst love the Earth while it injures thee, and even because it injures thee; for this a Greater than Zeno was needed, and he too was sent. Knowest thou that 'Worship of Sorrow'?[8] the Temple thereof, founded some eighteen centuries ago, now lies in ruins, overgrown with jungle, the habitation of doleful creatures: never-

---

4. Adapted from *Wilhelm Meister* by Goethe ("wisest of our time").
5. An exclamation of Wilhelm Meister's (German).
6. Adapted from 2 Timothy 3.4.
7. Stoic philosopher (3rd century B.C.E.) who,

after being injured in a fall, is reputed to have struck the earth with his hand as if the earth were responsible for his injury. Afterward he committed suicide. Hence he is said to "trample the Earth."
8. Christianity.

theless, venture forward; in a low crypt, arched out of falling fragments, thou findest the Altar still there, and its sacred Lamp perennially burning."

Without pretending to comment on which strange utterances, the Editor will only remark, that there lies beside them much of a still more questionable character; unsuited to the general apprehension; nay wherein he himself does not see his way. Nebulous disquisitions on Religion, yet not without bursts of splendour; on the "perennial continuance of Inspiration"; on Prophecy; that there are "true Priests, as well as Baal-Priests,[9] in our own day": with more of the like sort. We select some fractions, by way of finish to this farrago.

"Cease, my much-respected Herr von Voltaire," thus apostrophises the Professor: "shut thy sweet voice; for the task appointed thee seems finished. Sufficiently has thou demonstrated this proposition, considerable or otherwise: That the Mythus of the the Christian Religion looks not in the eighteenth century as it did in the eighth. Alas, were thy six-and-thirty quartos, and the six-and-thirty thousand other quartos and folios, and flying sheets or reams, printed before and since on the same subject, all needed to convince us of so little! But what next? Wilt thou help us to embody the divine Spirit of that Religion in a new Mythus, in a new vehicle and vesture, that our Souls, otherwise too like perishing, may live? What! thou hast no faculty in that kind? Only a torch for burning, no hammer for building? Take our thanks, then, and—thyself away.

"Meanwhile what are antiquated Mythuses to me? Or is the God present, felt in my own heart, a thing which Herr von Voltaire will dispute out of me; or dispute into me? To the 'Worship of Sorrow' ascribe what origin and genesis thou pleasest, *has* not that Worship originated, and been generated; is it not *here*? Feel it in thy heart, and then say whether it is of God! This is Belief; all else is Opinion,—for which latter whoso will let him worry and be worried."

"Neither," observes he elsewhere, "shall ye tear-out one another's eyes, struggling over 'Plenary Inspiration,'[1] and suchlike: try rather to get a little even Partial Inspiration, each of you for himself. One BIBLE I know, of whose Plenary Inspiration doubt is not so much as possible; nay with my own eyes I saw God's-Hand writing it: thereof all other Bibles are but leaves,—say, in Picture-Writing to assist the weaker faculty."

Or, to give the wearied reader relief, and bring it to an end, let him take the following perhaps more intelligible passage:

"To me, in this our life," says the Professor, "which is an internecine warfare with the Time-spirit, other warfare seems questionable. Hast thou in any way a Contention with thy brother, I advise thee, think well what the meaning thereof is. If thou gauge it to the bottom, it is simply this: 'Fellow, see! thou art taking more than thy share of Happiness in the world, something from *my* share: which, by the Heavens, thou shalt not; nay I will fight thee rather.'—Alas, and the whole lot to be divided is such a beggarly matter, truly a 'feast of shells,'[2] for the substance has been spilled out: not enough to quench one Appetite; and the collective human species clutching at them!—Can we not, in all such cases, rather say: 'Take it, thou too-ravenous

---

9. False priests, mentioned in 1 Kings 18.17–40.
1. Doctrine that all statements in the Bible are supernaturally inspired and authoritative. Voltaire

had sought to demonstrate that this doctrine was absurd.
2. Empty eggshells.

individual; take that pitiful additional fraction of a share, which I reckoned mine, but which thou so wantest; take it with a blessing: would to Heaven I had enough for thee!'—If Fichte's *Wissenschaftslehre*[3] be, 'to a certain extent, Applied Christianity,' surely to a still greater extent, so is this. We have here not a Whole Duty of Man,[4] yet a Half Duty, namely the Passive half: could we but do it, as we can demonstrate it!

"But indeed Conviction, were it never so excellent, is worthless till it convert itself into Conduct. Nay properly Conviction is not possible till then; inasmuch as all Speculation is by nature endless, formless, a vortex amid vortices: only by a felt indubitable certainty of Experience does it find any centre to revolve round, and so fashion itself into a system. Most true is it, as a wise man teaches us, that 'Doubt of any sort cannot be removed except by Action.' On which ground, too, let him who gropes painfully in darkness or uncertain light, and prays vehemently that the dawn may ripen into day, lay this other precept well to heart, which to me was of invaluable service: '*Do the Duty which lies nearest thee,*'[5] which thou knowest to be a Duty! Thy second Duty will already have become clearer.

"May we not say, however, that the hour of Spiritual Enfranchisement is even this: When your Ideal World, wherein the whole man has been dimly struggling and inexpressibly languishing to work, becomes revealed, and thrown open; and you discover, with amazement enough, like the Lothario in *Wilhelm Meister*, that your 'America is here or nowhere'? The Situation that has not its Duty, its Ideal, was never yet occupied by man. Yes here, in this poor, miserable, hampered, despicable Actual, wherein thou even now standest, here or nowhere is thy Ideal: work it out therefrom; and working, believe, live, be free. Fool! the Ideal is in thyself, the impediment too is in thyself: thy Condition is but the stuff thou art to shape that same Ideal out of: what matters whether such stuff be of this sort or that, so the Form thou give it be heroic, be poetic? O thou that pinest in the imprisonment of the Actual, and criest bitterly to the gods for a kingdom wherein to rule and create, know this of a truth: the thing thou seekest is already with thee, 'here or nowhere,' couldst thou only see!

"But it is with man's Soul as it was with Nature: the beginning of Creation is—Light.[6] Till the eye have vision, the whole members are in bonds.[7] Divine moment, when over the tempest-tost Soul, as once over the wild-weltering Chaos, it is spoken: Let there be Light! Ever to the greatest that has felt such moment, is it not miraculous and God-announcing; even as, under simpler figures, to the simplest and least. The mad primeval Discord is hushed; the rudely-jumbled conflicting elements bind themselves into separate Firmaments: deep silent rock-foundations are built beneath; and the skyey vault with its everlasting Luminaries above: instead of a dark wasteful Chaos, we have a blooming, fertile, heaven-encompassed World.

"I too could now say to myself: Be no longer a Chaos, but a World, or even Worldkin. Produce! Produce! Were it but the pitifullest infinitesimal fraction of a Product, produce it, in God's name! 'Tis the utmost thou hast in thee: out

---

3. The doctrine of knowledge (German); by Johann Gottlieb Fichte (1762–1814), German philosopher.
4. Title of an anonymous book of religious instruction first published in 1659.

5. This and the previous quotation are from Goethe's *Wilhelm Meister*.
6. Cf. Genesis 1.3.
7. Cf. Matthew 6.22–23.

with it, then. Up, up! Whatsoever thy hand findeth to do, do it with thy whole might. Work while it is called Today; for the Night cometh, wherein no man can work."[8]

Natural Supernaturalism[9]

It is in his stupendous Section, headed *Natural Supernaturalism*, that the Professor first becomes a Seer; and, after long effort, such as we have witnessed, finally subdues under his feet this refractory Clothes-Philosophy, and takes victorious possession thereof. Phantasms enough he has had to struggle with; "Cloth-webs and Cobwebs," of Imperial Mantles, Superannuated Symbols, and what not: yet still did he courageously pierce through. Nay, worst of all, two quite mysterious, world-embracing Phantasms, TIME and SPACE, have ever hovered round him, perplexing and bewildering: but with these also he now resolutely grapples, these also he victoriously rends asunder. In a word, he has looked fixedly on Existence, till one after the other, its earthly hulls and garnitures have all melted away; and now, to his rapt vision, the interior celestial Holy of Holies lies disclosed.

Here, therefore, properly it is that the Philosophy of Clothes attains to Transcendentalism; this last leap, can we but clear it, takes us safe into the promised land, where *Palingenesia*,[1] in all senses, may be considered as beginning. "Courage, then!" may our Diogenes exclaim, with better right than Diogenes the First[2] once did. This stupendous Section we, after long painful meditation, have found not to be unintelligible; but, on the contrary, to grow clear, nay radiant, and all-illuminating. Let the reader, turning on it what utmost force of speculative intellect is in him, do his part; as we, by judicious selection and adjustment, shall study to do ours:

"Deep has been, and is, the significance of Miracles," thus quietly begins the Professor; "far deeper perhaps than we imagine. Meanwhile, the question of questions were: What specially is a Miracle? To that Dutch King of Siam, an icicle had been a miracle; whoso had carried with him an air-pump, and vial of vitriolic ether, might have worked a miracle.[3] To my Horse, again, who unhappily is still more unscientific, do not I work a miracle, and magical

---

8. Adapted from Ecclesiastes 9.10 and John 9.4.
9. Book 3, chap. 8. The characteristically paradoxical title of this chapter can best be understood by reference to the chapter on miracles in David Hume's *An Enquiry Concerning Human Understanding* (1748), to which Carlyle makes several direct and indirect allusions in his own exposition of the nature of the miraculous. In his skeptical analysis of miracles (Christian miracles in particular), Hume asserts: "A miracle is a violation of the laws of nature.... It is no miracle that a man, seemingly in good health, should die on a sudden. ... But it is a miracle that a dead man should come to life, because that has never been observed in any age or country." The young Carlyle seems to have been impressed by Hume's arguments, as he had also been impressed (and depressed) by Gibbon's relentless exposure of traditional Christianity in *The Decline and Fall of the Roman Empire*. In his later resolution of his dilemma, he bypassed Hume's arguments. Instead of arguing whether miracles in the traditional sense (such as the resurrection of Christ) have occurred, he contends that *everything* in our experience is a miracle of a supernatural and inexplicable order, hence an appropriate cause for wonder and joy. The natural *is* supernatural.
1. Rebirth. "Transcendentalism": a term loosely used here to refer to any philosophy that opposes materialism or empiricism and that asserts the domination of the intuitive or spiritual over the material [C. F. Harrold].
2. A philosopher of the Cynic school; near the end of a dull lecture he called out to his fellow listeners: "Courage, friends! I see land."
3. In his chapter on miracles, Hume cites an incident of an Indian prince refusing to believe that water can be turned into ice. Carlyle notes that anybody could do so by treating a flask of vitriolic ether with an air pump.

'*Open sesame!*'[4] every time I please to pay twopence, and open for him an impassable *Schlagbaum,* or shut Turnpike?

" 'But is not a real Miracle simply a violation of the Laws of Nature?' ask several. Whom I answer by this new question: What are the Laws of Nature? To me perhaps the rising of one from the dead were no violation of these Laws, but a confirmation; were some far deeper Law, now first penetrated into, and by Spiritual Force, even as the rest have all been, brought to bear on us with its Material Force.

"Here too may some inquire, not without astonishment: On what ground shall one, that can make Iron swim,[5] come and declare that therefore he can teach Religion? To us, truly, of the Nineteenth Century, such declaration were inept enough; which nevertheless to our fathers, of the First Century, was full of meaning.

" 'But is it not the deepest Law of Nature that she be constant?' cries an illuminated class: 'Is not the Machine of the Universe fixed to move by unalterable rules?' Probable enough, good friends: nay I, too, must believe that the God, whom ancient inspired men assert to be 'without variableness or shadow of turning,'[6] does indeed never change; that Nature, that the Universe, which no one whom it so pleases can be prevented from calling a Machine, does move by the most unalterable rules. And now of you, too, I make the old inquiry: What those same unalterable rules, forming the complete Statute-Book of Nature, may possibly be?

"They stand written in our Works of Science, say you; in the accumulated records of Man's Experience?—Was Man with his Experience present at the Creation, then, to see how it all went on? Have any deepest scientific individuals yet dived down to the foundations of the Universe, and gauged everything there? Did the Maker take them into His counsel; that they read His ground-plan of the incomprehensible All; and can say, This stands marked therein, and no more than this? Alas, not in anywise! These scientific individuals have been nowhere but where we also are; have seen some handbreadths deeper than we see into the Deep that is infinite, without bottom as without shore.

"Laplace's[7] Book on the Stars, wherein he exhibits that certain Planets, with their Satellites, gyrate round our worthy Sun, at a rate and in a course, which, by greatest good fortune, he and the like of him have succeeded in detecting,—is to me as precious as to another. But is this what thou namest 'Mechanism of the Heavens,' and 'System of the World'; this, wherein Sirius and the Pleiades, and all Herschel's Fifteen-thousand Suns per minute, being left out, some paltry handful of Moons, and inert Balls, had been— looked at, nicknamed, and marked in the Zodiacal Way-bill;[8] so that we can now prate of their Whereabout; their How, their Why, their What, being hid from us, as in the signless Inane?

"System of Nature! To the wisest man, wide as is his vision, Nature remains of quite *infinite* depth, of quite infinite expansion; and all Experience

4. The magic password for opening a door in the cavern in the story *Ali Baba and the Forty Thieves,* in *The Arabian Nights.*
5. Elisha's miracle of causing an ax head to float in water (2 Kings 6.6).
6. Paraphrase of James 1.17.
7. Pierre Laplace (1749–1827); author of *A Trea-* tise on *Celestial Mechanics* (1799–1825) and other astronomical studies.
8. A document issued with freight shipments, providing complete information about contents and routes. Sir William Herschel (1738–1822), astronomer credited with discovering thousands of stars and other celestial bodies.

thereof limits itself to some few computed centuries and measured square-miles. The course of Nature's phases, on this our little fraction of a Planet, is partially known to us: but who knows what deeper courses these depend on; what infinitely larger Cycle (of causes) our little Epicycle[9] revolves on? To the Minnow every cranny and pebble, and quality and accident, of its little native Creek may have become familiar: but does the Minnow understand the Ocean Tides and periodic Currents, the Tradewinds, and Monsoons, and Moon's Eclipses; by all which the condition of its little Creek is regulated, and may, from time to time (*un*miraculously enough), be quite overset and reversed? Such a minnow is Man; his Creek this Planet Earth; his Ocean the immeasurable All; his Monsoons and periodic Currents the mysterious Course of Providence through Aeons of Aeons.

"We speak of the Volume of Nature: and truly a Volume it is,—whose Author and Writer is God. To read it! Dost thou, does man, so much as well know the Alphabet thereof? With its Words, Sentences, and grand descriptive Pages, poetical and philosophical, spread out through Solar Systems, and Thousands of Years, we shall not try thee. It is a Volume written in celestial hieroglyphs, in the true Sacred-writing; of which even Prophets are happy that they can read here a line and there a line. As for your Institutes, and Academies of Science, they strive bravely; and, from amid the thick-crowded, inextricably intertwisted hieroglyphic writing, pick out, by dextrous combination, some Letters in the vulgar Character, and therefrom put together this and the other economic Recipe,[1] of high avail in Practice. That Nature is more than some boundless Volume of such Recipes, or huge, well-nigh inexhaustible Domestic-Cookery Book, of which the whole secret will in this manner one day evolve itself, the fewest dream.

"Custom," continues the Professor, "doth make dotards of us all.[2] Consider well, thou wilt find that Custom is the greatest of Weavers; and weaves air raiment for all the Spirits of the Universe; whereby indeed these dwell with us visibly, as ministering servants, in our houses and workshops; but their spiritual nature becomes, to the most, forever hidden. Philosophy complains that Custom has hoodwinked us, from the first; that we do everything by Custom, even Believe by it; that our very Axioms, let us boast of Free-thinking as we may, are oftenest simply such Beliefs as we have never heard questioned. Nay, what is Philosophy throughout but a continual battle against Custom; an ever-renewed effort to *transcend* the sphere of blind Custom, and so become Transcendental?

"Innumerable are the illusions and legerdemain-tricks of Custom: but of all these, perhaps the cleverest is her knack of persuading us that the Miraculous, by simple repetition, ceases to be Miraculous. True, it is by this means we live; for man must work as well as wonder: and herein is Custom so far a kind nurse, guiding him to his true benefit. But she is a fond foolish nurse, or rather we are false foolish nurselings, when, in our resting and reflecting hours, we prolong the same deception. Am I to view the Stupendous with stupid indifference, because I have seen it twice, or two-hundred, or two-million times? There is no reason in Nature or in Art why I should: unless,

9. In Ptolemaic astronomy, a circle in which a planet moves, the center of this circle being carried round on the circumference of a larger circle (the "infinitely larger Cycle").

1. I.e., a law in economics, such as the law of supply and demand.
2. Cf. Shakespeare's *Hamlet* 1.3.83: "Thus conscience does make cowards of us all."

indeed, I am a mere Work-Machine, for whom the divine gift of Thought were no other than the terrestrial gift of Steam is to the Steam-engine; a power whereby cotton might be spun, and money and money's worth realised.

"Notable enough too, here as elsewhere, wilt thou find the potency of Names; which indeed are but one kind of such customwoven, wonder-hiding Garments. Witchcraft, and all manner of Spectre-work, and Demonology, we have now named Madness and Diseases of the Nerves. Seldom reflecting that still the new question comes upon us: What is Madness, what are Nerves? Ever, as before, does Madness remain a mysterious-terrific, altogether *infernal* boiling-up of the Nether Chaotic Deep, through this fair-painted Vision of Creation, which swims thereon, which we name the Real. Was Luther's Picture of the Devil[3] less a Reality, whether it were formed within the bodily eye, or without it? In every the wisest Soul lies a whole world of internal Madness, an authentic Demon-Empire; out of which, indeed, his world of Wisdom has been creatively built together, and now rests there, as on its dark foundations does a habitable flowery Earth-rind.

"But deepest of all illusory Appearances, for hiding Wonder, as for many other ends, are your two grand fundamental world-enveloping Appearances, SPACE and TIME. These, as spun and woven for us from before Birth itself, to clothe our celestial ME for dwelling here, and yet to blind it,—lie all-embracing, as the universal canvas, or warp and woof, whereby all minor Illusions, in this Phantasm Existence, weave and paint themselves. In vain, while here on Earth, shall you endeavour to strip them off; you can, at best, but rend them asunder for moments, and look through.

"Fortunatus had a wishing Hat, which when he put on, and wished himself Anywhere, behold he was There.[4] By this means had Fortunatus triumphed over Space, he had annihilated Space; for him there was no Where, but all was Here. Were a Hatter to establish himself, in the Wahngasse of Weiss-nichtwo, and make felts of this sort for all mankind, what a world we should have of it! Still stranger, should, on the opposite side of the street, another Hatter establish himself; and, as his fellow-craftsman made Space annihilating Hats, make Time-annihilating! Of both would I purchase, were it with my last groschen;[5] but chiefly of this latter. To clap-on your felt, and, simply by wishing that you were Any*where*, straightway to be *There*! Next to clap-on your other felt, and, simply by wishing that you were Any*when*, straightway to be *Then*! This were indeed the grander: shooting at will from the Fire-Creation of the World to its Fire-Consummation; here historically present in the First Century, conversing face to face with Paul and Seneca;[6] there prophetically in the Thirty-first, conversing also face to face with other Pauls and Senecas, who as yet stand hidden in the depth of that late Time!

"Or thinkest thou it were impossible, unimaginable? Is the Past annihilated, then, or only past; is the Future non-extant, or only future? Those mystic faculties of thine, Memory and Hope, already answer: already through

---

3. Martin Luther (1483–1546), German Reformation leader, threw his inkstand at an apparition of the devil that visited his study when he was translating the Psalms.
4. In the legend on which Thomas Dekker based his play *Old Fortunatus* (1600), a magic hat ena-

bled the owner instantaneously to be anywhere he wished.
5. Small German coin.
6. Roman philosopher (4 B.C.E.–65 C.E.) who, according to legend, conversed with St. Paul.

those mystic avenues, thou the Earth-blinded summonest both Past and Future, and communest with them, though as yet darkly, and with mute beckonings. The curtains of Yesterday drop down, the curtains of Tomorrow roll up; but Yesterday and Tomorrow both *are*. Pierce through the Time-element, glance into the Eternal. Believe what thou findest written in the sanctuaries of Man's Soul, even as all Thinkers, in all ages, have devoutly read it there: that Time and Space are not God, but creations of God; that with God as it is a universal HERE, so is it an everlasting Now.

"And seest thou therein any glimpse of IMMORTALITY?—O Heaven! Is the white Tomb of our Loved One, who died from our arms, and had to be left behind us there, which rises in the distance, like a pale, mournfully receding Milestone, to tell how many toilsome uncheered miles we have journeyed on alone,—but a pale spectral Illusion! Is the lost Friend still mysteriously Here, even as we are Here mysteriously, with God!—Know of a truth that only the Time-shadows have perished, or are perishable; that the real Being of whatever was, and whatever is, and whatever will be, *is* even now and forever. This, should it unhappily seem new, thou mayest ponder at thy leisure; for the next twenty years, or the next twenty centuries: believe it thou must; understand it thou canst not.

"That the Thought-forms, Space and Time, wherein, once for all, we are sent into this Earth to live, should condition and determine our whole Practical reasonings, conceptions, and imagings or imaginings, seems altogether fit, just, and unavoidable. But that they should, furthermore, usurp such sway over pure spiritual Meditation, and blind us to the wonder everywhere lying close on us, seems nowise so. Admit Space and Time to their due rank as Forms of Thought;[7] nay even, if thou wilt, to their quite undue rank of Realities: and consider, then, with thyself how their thin disguises hide from us the brightest God-effulgences! Thus, were it not miraculous, could I stretch forth my hand and clutch the Sun? Yet thou seest me daily stretch forth my hand and therewith clutch many a thing, and swing it hither and thither. Art thou a grown baby, then, to fancy that the Miracle lies in miles of distance, or in pounds avoirdupois of weight; and not to see that the true inexplicable God-revealing Miracle lies in this, that I can stretch forth my hand at all; that I have free Force to clutch aught therewith? Innumerable other of this sort are the deceptions, and wonder-hiding stupefactions, which Space practices on us.

"Still worse is it with regard to Time. Your grand antimagician, and universal wonder-hider, is this same lying Time. Had we but the Time-annihilating Hat, to put on for once only, we should see ourselves in a World of Miracles, wherein all fabled or authentic Thaumaturgy,[8] and feats of Magic, were outdone. But unhappily we have not such a Hat; and man, poor fool that he is, can seldom and scantily help himself without one.

"Were it not wonderful, for instance, had Orpheus, or Amphion,[9] built the walls of Thebes by the mere sound of his Lyre? Yet tell me, Who built these

---

7. The idea that time and space are modes of perception rather than realities is derived from the philosophy of Immanuel Kant (1724–1804), author of *A Critique of Pure Reason* (1781).
8. The working of miracles and magical occurrences.

9. Legendary musicians who effected miracles. Orpheus, with his lyre, could spellbind wild beasts. Amphion's playing, during the building of Thebes, caused the stones for the walls to be drawn into place.

walls of Weissnichtwo; summoning out all the sandstone rocks, to dance along from the *Steinbruch* (now a huge Troglodyte Chasm,[1] with frightful green-mantled pools), and shape themselves into Doric and Ionic pillars, squared ashlar houses[2] and noble streets? Was it not the still higher Orpheus, or Orpheuses, who, in past centuries, by the divine Music of Wisdom, succeeded in civilising Man? Our highest Orpheus walked in Judea, eighteen-hundred years ago: his sphere-melody, flowing in wild native tones, took captive the ravished souls of men; and, being of a true sphere-melody, still flows and sounds, though now with thousandfold accompaniments, and rich symphonies, through all our hearts; and modulates, and divinely leads them. Is that a wonder, which happens in two hours; and does it cease to be wonderful if happening in two million? Not only was Thebes built by the music of an Orpheus; but without the music of some inspired Orpheus was no city ever built, no work that man glories in ever done.

"Sweep away the Illusion of Time; glance, if thou have eyes, from the near moving-cause to its far-distant Mover: The stroke that came transmitted through a whole galaxy of elastic balls, was it less a stroke than if the last ball only had been struck, and sent flying? O, could I (with the Time-annihilating Hat) transport thee direct from the Beginnings to the Endings, how were thy eyesight unsealed, and thy heart set flaming in the Light-sea of celestial wonder! Then sawest thou that this fair Universe, were it in the meanest province thereof, is in very deed the star-domed City of God,[3] that through every star, through every grass-blade, and most through every Living Soul, the glory of a present God still beams. But Nature, which is the Time-vesture of God, and reveals Him to the wise, hides Him from the foolish.

"Again, could anything be more miraculous than an actual authentic Ghost? The English Johnson longed, all his life, to see one; but could not, though he went to Cock Lane,[4] and thence to the church-vaults, and tapped on coffins. Foolish Doctor! Did he never, with the mind's eye as well as with the body's, look round him into that full tide of human Life he so loved; did he never so much as look into Himself? The good Doctor was a Ghost, as actual and authentic as heart could wish; well-nigh a million of Ghosts were travelling the streets by his side. Once more I say, sweep away the illusion of Time; compress the threescore years into three minutes: what else was he, what else are we? Are we not Spirits, that are shaped into a body, into an Appearance; and that fade away again into air and Invisibility? This is no metaphor, it is a simple scientific *fact*; we start out of Nothingness, take figure, and are Apparitions; round us, as round the veriest spectre, is Eternity; and to Eternity minutes are as years and aeons. Come there not tones of Love and Faith, as from celestial harp-strings, like the Song of beatified Souls? And again, do not we squeak and jibber (in our discordant, screech-owlish debatings and recriminatings); and glide bodeful, and feeble, and fearful; or uproad (*poltern*), and revel in our mad Dance of the Dead,—till the scent of the morning air[5] summons us to our still Home; and dreamy

---

1. The emptied stone quarry of *Steinbruch* looks now like the site of primitive cave dwellers ("Troglodytes").
2. Houses made of squared blocks of hewn stone.
3. Title of St. Augustine's famous work.

4. The Cock Lane ghost in London, which proved to be a fraud, was investigated by Samuel Johnson (see Boswell for the year 1763).
5. Cf. Shakespeare's *Hamlet* 1.1.148–56 and 5.58.

Night becomes awake and Day? Where now is Alexander of Macedon: does the steel Host, that yelled in fierce battle-shouts at Issus and Arbela,[6] remain behind him; or have they all vanished utterly, even as perturbed Goblins must? Napoleon too, and his Moscow Retreats and Austerlitz Campaigns! Was it all other than the veriest Spectre-hunt; which has now, with its howling tumult that made Night hideous, flitted away?—Ghosts! There are nigh a thousand-million walking the Earth openly at noontide; some half-hundred have vanished from it, some half-hundred have arisen in it, ere thy watch ticks once.

"O Heaven, it is mysterious, it is awful to consider that we not only carry each a future Ghost within Him; but are, in very deed, Ghosts! These Limbs, whence had we them; this stormy Force; this life-blood with its burning Passion? They are dust and shadow, a Shadow-system gathered round our Me; wherein, through some moments or years, the Divine Essence is to be revealed in the Flesh. That warrior on his strong war-horse, fire flashes through his eyes; force dwells in his arm and heart: but warrior and war-horse are a vision; a revealed Force, nothing more. Stately they tread the Earth, as if it were a firm substance: fool! the Earth is but a film; it cracks in twain, and warrior and war-horse sink beyond plummet's sounding.[7] Plummet's? Fantasy herself will not follow them. A little while ago, they were not; a little while, and they are not, their very ashes are not.

"So has it been from the beginning, so will it be to the end. Generation after generation takes to itself the Form of a Body; and forth-issuing from Cimmerian[8] Night, on Heaven's mission APPEARS. What Force and Fire is in each he expends: one grinding in the mill of Industry; one hunter-like climbing the giddy Alpine heights of Science; one madly dashed in pieces on the rocks of Strife, in war with his fellow:—and then the Heaven-sent is recalled; his earthly Vesture falls away, and soon even to sense becomes a vanished Shadow. Thus, like some wild-flaming, wild-thundering train of Heaven's Artillery, does this mysterious MANKIND thunder and flame, in long-drawn, quick-succeeding grandeur, through the unknown Deep. Thus, like a God-created, fire-breathing Spirit-host, we emerge from the Inane;[9] haste stormfully across the astonished Earth; then plunge again into the Inane. Earth's mountains are levelled, and her seas filled up, in our passage: can the Earth, which is but dead and a vision, resist Spirits which have reality and are alive? On the hardest adamant some footprint of us is stamped-in; the last Rear of the host will read traces of the earliest Van. But whence?—O Heaven, whither? Sense knows not; Faith knows not; only that it is through Mystery to Mystery, from God and to God.

We *are such stuff*
As dreams are made of, and our little Life
Is rounded with a sleep!"[1]

1830–31   1833–34

---

6. Sites of two victories won by the army of Alexander the Great against the Persians under Darius (333–31 B.C.E.).
7. Shakespeare's *The Tempest* 5.1.56. "Plummet": a weight at the end of a line used to sound the depth of water under a ship.

8. A people living in perpetual darkness (cf. *Odyssey* 11.14).
9. The formless void of infinite space [NED].
1. *The Tempest* 4.1.156–58, a favorite passage for Carlyle, here slightly misquoted (Shakespeare wrote: "dreams are made on").

From The French Revolution[1]

September in Paris[2]

The tocsin is pealing its loudest, the clocks inaudibly striking *Three,* when poor Abbé Sicard, with some thirty other Nonjurant Priests,[3] in six carriages, fare along the streets, from their preliminary House of Detention at the Townhall, westward towards the Prison of the Abbaye. Carriages enough stand deserted on the streets; these six move on,—through angry multitudes, cursing as they move. Accursed Aristocrat Tartuffes,[4] this is the pass ye have brought us to! And now ye will break the Prisons, and set Capet Veto[5] on horseback to ride over us? Out upon you, Priests of Beelzebub and Moloch; of Tartuffery, Mammon and the Prussian Gallows,—which ye name Mother-Church and God!—Such reproaches have the poor Nonjurants to endure, and worse; spoken in on them by frantic Patriots, who mount even on the carriage-steps; the very Guards hardly refraining. Pull up your carriage-blinds?—No! answers Patriotism, clapping its horny paw on the carriage-blind, and crushing it down again. Patience in oppression has limits: we are close on the Abbaye, it has lasted long: a poor Nonjurant, of quicker temper, smites the horny paw with his cane; nay, finding solacement in it, smites the unkempt head, sharply and again more sharply, twice over,—seen clearly of us and of the world. It is the last that we see clearly. Alas, next moment, the carriages are locked and blocked in endless raging tumults; in yells deaf to the cry for mercy, which answer the cry for mercy with sabre-thrusts through the heart. The thirty Priests are torn out, are massacred about the Prison-Gate, one after one,—only the poor Abbé Sicard, whom one Moton a watch-maker, knowing him, heroically tried to save and secrete in the Prison, escapes to tell;—and it is Night and Orcus,[6] and Murder's snaky-sparkling head *has* risen in the murk!—

From Sunday afternoon (exclusive of intervals and pauses not final) till Thursday evening, there follow consecutively a Hundred Hours. Which hundred hours are to be reckoned with the hours of the Bartholomew Butchery, of the Armagnac Massacres, Sicilian Vespers, or whatsoever is savagest in the annals of this world. Horrible the hour when man's soul, in its paroxysm,

---

1. In telling the story of the French Revolution Carlyle composes the history as if in the midst of the action. This method of day-to-day eyewitnessing of events contributes to the effect of immediacy that Carlyle sought in what he himself called his "wild savage Book, itself a kind of French Revolution."

A second feature of his method is the device of weaving into the narrative a number of direct quotations from the sources he had consulted during the three years devoted to writing the history. Although later historians have been able to point out inaccuracies in *The French Revolution,* Carlyle did base his account on extensive research. G. M. Trevelyan has said of him that he was not only a great writer but also "in his own strange way, a great historian." Perhaps the most satisfactory comment on *The French Revolution* is J. S. Mill's statement in his 1837 review: "This is not so much a history as an epic poem, and notwithstanding . . . the truest of histories."

2. Part 3, book 1, chap. 4. In September 1792 the revolutionary party under George-Jacques Danton and Jean-Paul Marat urged desperate measures to defend Paris from the invading armies of Austria and Prussia. Hysterical fears of a counterrevolutionary "fifth column" in Paris led to the so-called September Massacres, in which fourteen hundred political prisoners were slaughtered in four days.

3. Priests who had refused to swear allegiance to the new church constitution established by the National Assembly in 1791. Sicard (d. 1822), head of a school for the deaf and dumb in Paris.

4. Hypocrites (from the title of Molière's play).

5. I.e., the king (Louis XVI). The Nonjurant Priests were accused of favoring the restoration to the king of his power to veto legislation, a power he had lost after August 10, 1792. At the same time he had been stripped of his royal titles and was thereafter referred to simply as Louis Capet, the family name of an early dynasty of French kings (Louis XVI was a Bourbon).

6. Hades, the underworld of the dead.

spurns asunder the barriers and rules; and shows what dens and depths are in it! For Night and Orcus, as we say, as was long prophesied, have burst forth, here in this Paris, from their subterranean imprisonment: hideous, dim-confused; which it is painful to look on; and yet which cannot, and indeed which should not, be forgotten.

The Reader, who looks earnestly through this dim Phantasmagory of the Pit, will discern few fixed certain objects; and yet still a few. He will observe, in this Abbaye Prison, the sudden massacre of the Priests being once over, a strange Court of Justice, or call it Court of Revenge and Wild-Justice, swiftly fashion itself, and take seat round a table, with the Prison-Registers spread before it;—Stanislas Maillard, Bastille-hero, famed Leader of the Menads,[7] presiding. O Stanislas, one hoped to meet thee elsewhere than here; thou shifty Riding-Usher, with an inkling of Law! This work also thou hadst to do; and then—to depart for ever from our eyes. At *La Force*, at the *Châtelet*, the *Conciergerie*, the like Court forms itself, with the like accompaniments: the thing that one man does, other men can do. There are some Seven Prisons in Paris, full of Aristocrats with conspiracies;—nay not even *Bicêtre* and *Salpêtrière* shall escape, with their Forgers of Assignats:[8] and there are seventy times seven hundred Patriot hearts in a state of frenzy. Scoundrel hearts also there are; as perfect, say, as the Earth holds,—if such are needed. To whom, in this mood, law is as no-law; and killing, by what name soever called, is but work to be done.

So sit these sudden Courts of Wild-Justice, with the Prison-Registers before them; unwonted wild tumult howling all round; the Prisoners in dread expectancy within. Swift: a name is called; bolts jingle, a Prisoner is there. A few questions are put; swiftly this sudden Jury decides: Royalist Plotter or not? Clearly not; in that case, Let the Prisoner be enlarged with *Vive la Nation*. Probably yea; then still, Let the Prisoner be enlarged, but without *Vive la Nation*; or else it may run. Let the Prisoner be conducted to La Force. At La Force again their formula is, Let the Prisoner be conducted to the Abbaye.—"To La Force then!" Volunteer bailiffs seize the doomed man; he is at the outer gate; "enlarged," or "conducted," not into La Force, but into a howling sea; forth, under an arch of wild sabres, axes and pikes; and sinks, hewn asunder. And another sinks, and another; and there forms itself a piled heap of corpses, and the kennels begin to run red. Fancy the yells of these men, their faces of sweat and blood; the crueller shrieks of these women, for there are women too; and a fellow-mortal hurled naked into it all! Jourgniac de Saint-Méard has seen battle, has seen an effervescent Regiment du Roi in mutiny; but the bravest heart may quail at this. The Swiss Prisoners, remnants of the Tenth of August,[9] "clasped each other spasmodically, and hung back; grey veterans crying: 'Mercy, Messieuers; ah, mercy!' But there was no mercy. Suddenly, however, one of these men steps forward. He had on a blue frock coat; he seemed about thirty, his stature was above common, his look noble and martial. 'I go first,' said he, 'since it must be so: adieu!' Then dashing his hat sharply behind him: 'Which way?' cried he to the Brig-

---

7. Frenzied women of Greece, followers of Dionysus. Maillard had led a mob of women in the march to Versailles in October 1789.
8. Paper money issued by the French revolutionary government. Royalists accused of forging such

currency were imprisoned.
9. The Swiss Guard, most of whom had been massacred on August 10, 1792, when defending the king's palace from a mob.

ands: 'Show it me, then.' They open the folding gate; he is announced to the multitude. He stands a moment motionless; then plunges forth among the pikes, and dies of a thousand wounds."

Man after man is cut down; the sabres need sharpening, the killers refresh themselves from wine-jugs. Onward and onward goes the butchery; the loud yells wearying down into bass growls. A sombre-faced shifting multitude looks on; in dull approval, or dull disapproval; in dull recognition that it is Necessity. "An *Anglais* in drab greatcoat" was seen, or seemed to be seen, serving liquor from his own drambottle;—for what purpose, "if not set on by Pitt," Satan and himself know best! Witty Dr. Moore grew sick on approaching, and turned into another street.—Quick enough goes this Jury-Court; and rigorous. The brave are not spared, nor the beautiful, nor the weak. Old M. de Montmorin, the Minister's Brother, was acquitted by the Tribunal of the Seventeenth; and conducted back, elbowed by howling galleries; but is not acquitted here. Princess de Lamballe[1] has lain down on bed: "Madame, you are to be removed to the Abbaye." "I do not wish to remove; I am well enough here." There is a need-be for removing. She will arrange her dress a little, then; rude voices answer, "You have not far to go." She too is led to the hell-gate; a manifest Queen's-Friend. She shivers back, at the sight of bloody sabres; but there is no return: Onwards! That fair hind head is cleft with the axe; the neck is severed. That fair body is cut in fragments; with indignities, and obscene horrors of moustachio *grand-lèvres*,[2] which human nature would fain find incredible,—which shall be read in the original language only. She was beautiful, she was good, she had known no happiness. Young hearts, generation after generation, will think with themselves: O worthy of worship, thou king-descended, god-descended, and poor sister-woman! why was not I there; and some Sword Balmung[3] or Thor's Hammer in my hand? Her head is fixed on a pike; paraded under the windows of the Temple; that a still more hated, a Marie Antoinette, may see. One Municipal, in the Temple with the Royal Prisoners at the moment, said, "Look out." Another eagerly whispered, "Do not look." The circuit of the Temple is guarded, in these hours, by a long stretched tricolor riband: terror enters, and the clangour of infinite tumult; hitherto not regicide, though that too may come.

But it is more edifying to note what thrillings of affection, what fragments of wild virtues turn up in this shaking asunder of man's existence; for of these too there is a proportion. Note old Marquis Cazotte: he is doomed to die; but his young Daughter clasps him in her arms, with an inspiration of eloquence, with a love which is stronger than very death: the heart of the killers themselves is touched by it; the old man is spared. Yet he was guilty, if plotting for his King is guilt: in ten days more, a Court of Law condemned him, and he had to die elsewhere; bequeathing his Daughter a lock of his old grey hair. Or note old M. de Sombreuil, who also had a Daughter:—My Father is not an Aristocrat: O good gentlemen, I will swear it, and testify it, and in all ways prove it; we are not; we hate Aristocrats! "Wilt thou drink Aristocrats' blood?" The man lifts blood (if universal Rumour can be cred-

---

1. Great-granddaughter of the king of Sardinia. She had married a Bourbon; was early widowed; and later became a close friend of Queen Marie Antoinette, with whom she had been imprisoned.

2. Thick lips (French); here a figure of speech to characterize the mob.
3. The sharp sword of Siegfried, hero of the *Nibelungenlied*.

ited); the poor maiden does drink. "This Sombreuil is innocent then!" Yes, indeed,—and now note, most of all, how the bloody pikes, at this news, do rattle to the ground; and the tiger-yells become bursts of jubilee over a brother saved; and the old man and his daughter are clasped to bloody bosoms, with hot tears; and borne home in triumph of *Vive la Nation,* the killers refusing even money! Does it seem strange, this temper of theirs? It seems very certain, well proved by Royalist testimony in other instances; and very significant.

Place de la Révolution[4]

To this conclusion, then, hast thou come, O hapless Louis! The Son of Sixty Kings is to die on the Scaffold by form of Law. Under Sixty Kings this same form of Law, form of Society, has been fashioning itself together, these thousand years; and has become, one way and other, a most strange Machine. Surely, if needful, it is also frightful, this Machine; dead, blind; not what it should be; which, with swift stroke, or by cold slow torture, has wasted the lives and souls of innumerable men. And behold now a King himself, or say rather Kinghood in his person, is to expire here in cruel tortures;—like a Phalaris[5] shut in the belly of his own red-heated Brazen Bull! It is ever so; and thou shouldst know it, O haughty tyrannous man: injustice breeds injustice; curses and falsehoods do verily return "always *home,*" wide as they may wander. Innocent Louis bears the sins of many generations: he too experiences that man's tribunal is not in this Earth; that if he had no Higher one, it were not well with him.

A King dying by such violence appeals impressively to the imagination; as the like must do, and ought to do. And yet at bottom it is not the King dying, but the man! Kingship is a coat: the grand loss is of the skin. The man from whom you take his Life, to him can the whole combined world do *more?* Lally[6] went on his hurdle; his mouth filled with a gag. Miserablest mortals, doomed for picking pockets, have a whole five-act Tragedy in them, in that dumb pain, as they go to the gallows, unregarded; they consume the cup of trembling down to the lees. For Kings and for Beggars, for the justly doomed and the unjustly, it is a hard thing to die. Pity them all: thy utmost pity, with all aids and appliances and throne-and-scaffold contrasts, how far short is it of the thing pitied!

A Confessor has come; Abbé Edgeworth, of Irish extraction, whom the King knew by good report, has come promptly on this solemn mission. Leave the Earth alone, then, thou hapless King; it with its malice will go its way, thou also canst go thine. A hard scene yet remains: the parting with our loved ones. Kind hearts, environed in the same grim peril with us; to be left *here!* Let the Reader look with the eyes of Valet Cléry,[7] through these glass-doors, where also the Municipality watches; and see the cruellest of scenes:

"At half-past eight, the door of the ante-room opened: the Queen appeared

---

4. Part 3, book 2, chap. 8. On January 20, 1793, by a small majority, the Convention of Delegates in Paris had voted for the death of the king.
5. Sicilian tyrant whose victims were roasted alive by being confined inside the brass figure of a bull under which a fire was lit.

6. French general who was accused unjustly of treachery and executed in 1766. He was gagged, presumably to prevent his protesting his innocence.
7. He attended the king during his imprisonment and later published a journal.

first, leading her Son by the hand; then Madame Royale and Madame Elizabeth:[8] they all flung themselves into the arms of the King. Silence reigned for some minutes; interrupted only by sobs. The Queen made a movement to lead his Majesty towards the inner room, where M. Edgeworth was waiting unknown to them: 'No,' said the King, 'let us go into the dining-room, it is there only that I can see you.' They entered there; I shut the door of it, which was of glass. The King sat down, the Queen on his left hand, Madame Elizabeth on his right, Madame Royale almost in front; the young Prince remained standing between his Father's legs. They all leaned towards him, and often held him embraced. This scene of woe lasted an hour and three quarters; during which we could hear nothing; we could see only that always when the King spoke, the sobbings of the Princesses redoubled, continued for some minutes; and that then the King began again to speak."—And so our meetings and our partings do now end! The sorrows we gave each other; the poor joys we faithfully shared, and all our lovings and our sufferings, and confused toilings under the earthly Sun, are over. Thou good soul, I shall never, never through all ages of Time, see thee any more!—NEVER! O Reader, knowest thou that hard word?

For nearly two hours this agony lasts; then they tear themselves asunder. "Promise that you will see us on the morrow." He promises:—Ah yes, yes; yet once; and go now, ye loved ones; cry to God for yourselves and me!—It was a hard scene, but it is over. He will not see them on the morrow. The Queen, in passing through the ante-room, glanced at the Cerberus Municipals; and, with woman's vehemence, said through her tears, *"Vous êtes tous des scélérats."*[9]

King Louis slept sound, till five in the morning, when Cléry, as he had been ordered, awoke him. Cléry dressed his hair: while this went forward, Louis took a ring from his watch, and kept trying it on his finger; it was his wedding-ring, which he is now to return to the Queen as a mute farewell. At half-past six, he took the Sacrament; and continued in devotion, and conference with Abbé Edgeworth. He will not see his Family: it were too hard to bear.

At eight, the Municipals enter: the King gives them his Will, and messages and effects; which they, at first, brutally refuse to take charge of: he gives them a roll of gold pieces, a hundred and twenty-five louis; these are to be returned to Malesherbes,[1] who had lent them. At nine, Santerre[2] says the hour is come. The King begs yet to retire for three minutes. At the end of three minutes, Santerre again says the hour is come. "Stamping on the ground with his right foot, Louis answers: *'Partons*, Let us go.'"—How the rolling of those drums comes in, through the Temple bastions and bulwarks, on the heart of a queenly wife; soon to be a widow! He is gone, then, and has not seen us? A Queen weeps bitterly; a King's Sister and Children. Over all these Four does Death also hover: all shall perish miserably save one; she, as Duchesse d'Angoulême, will live,—not happily.

---

8. The king's sister, guillotined a year later. Madame Royale (1778–1851), the king's daughter, duchesse d'Angoulême.
9. You are all scoundrels (French). "Cerberus Municipals": local officers, likened to Cerberus, the three-headed dog that guarded the entrance to

Hades.
1. A delegate who had defended the king. He was guillotined a year later.
2. Jacobin leader who commanded the troops in Paris.

At the Temple Gate were some faint cries, perhaps from voices of Pitiful women: *"Grâce!*[3] *Grâce!"* Through the rest of the streets there is silence as of the grave. No man not armed is allowed to be there: the armed, did any even pity, dare not express it, each man overawed by all his neighbors. All windows are down, none seem looking through them. All shops are shut. No wheel-carriage rolls, this morning, in these streets but one only. Eighty-thousand armed men stand ranked, like armed statues of men; cannons bristle, cannoneers with match burning, but no word or movement: it is as a city enchanted into silence and stone: one carriage with its escort, slowly rumbling, is the only sound. Louis reads, in his Book of Devotion, the Prayers of the Dying: clatter of this death-march falls sharp on the ear, in the great silence; but the thought would fain struggle heavenward, and forget the Earth.

As the clocks strike ten, behold the Place de la Révolution, once Place de Louis Quinze: the Guillotine, mounted near the old Pedestal where once stood the Statue of that Louis! Far round, all bristles with cannons and armed men: spectators crowding in the rear; D'Orléans Égalité[4] there in cabriolet. Swift messengers, *hoquetons,* speed to the Townhall, every three minutes: near by is the Convention sitting,—vengeful for Lepelletier.[5] Heedless of all, Louis reads his Prayers of the Dying; not till five minutes yet has he finished; then the Carriage opens. What temper he is in? Ten different witnesses will give ten different accounts of it. He is in the collision of all tempers; arrived now at the black Mahlstrom and descent of Death: in sorrow, in indignation, in resignation struggling to be resigned. "Take care of M. Edgeworth," he straitly charges the Lieutenant who is sitting with them: then they two descend.

The drums are beating: *"Taisez-vous,* Silence!" he cries "in a terrible voice, *d'une voix terrible."* He mounts the scaffold, not without delay; he is in puce[6] coat, breeches of grey, white stockings. He strips off the coat; stands disclosed in a sleeve-waistcoat of white flannel. The Executioners approach to bind him: he spurns, resists; Abbé Edgeworth has to remind him how the Saviour, in whom men trust, submitted to be bound. His hands are tied, his head bare; the fatal moment is come. He advances to the edge of the Scaffold, "his face very red," and says: "Frenchmen, I die innocent: it is from the Scaffold and near appearing before God that I tell you so. I pardon my enemies; I desire that France——" A General on horseback, Santerre or another, prances out, with uplifted hand: *"Tambours!"* The drums drown the voice. "Executioners, do your duty!" The Executioners, desperate lest themselves be murdered (for Santerre and his Armed Ranks will strike, if they do not), seize the hapless Louis: six of them desperate, him singly desperate, struggling there; and bind him to their plank. Abbé Edgeworth, stooping, bespeaks him: "Son of Saint Louis,[7] ascend to Heaven." The Axe clanks down; a King's Life is shorn away. It is Monday the 21st of January 1793. He was aged Thirty-eight years four months and twenty-eight days.

Executioner Samson shows the Head: fierce shout of *Vive la République*

---

3. Mercy! (French).
4. Equality (French); here the duc d'Orléans, a Royalist who had become a revolutionary leader. Despite his having voted for the king's death, he was himself executed in 1793.
5. A delegate who had voted for the king's death and was killed by a Royalist sympathizer.
6. Dull red.
7. Louis IX, king of France (reigned 1226–70).

rises, and swells; caps raised on bayonets, hats waving: students of the College of Four Nations take it up, on the far Quais; fling it over Paris. D'Orléans drives off in his cabriolet: the Townhall Councillors rub their hands, saying, "It is done, It is done." There is dipping of handkerchiefs, of pike-points in the blood. Headsman Samson, though he afterwards denied it, sells locks of the hair: fractions of the puce coat are long after worn in rings.—And so, in some half-hour it is done; and the multitude has all departed. Pastry-cooks, coffee-sellers, milkmen sing out their trivial quotidian cries: the world wags on, as if this were a common day. In the coffee-houses that evening, says Prudhomme, Patriot shook hands with Patriot in a more cordial manner than usual. Not till some days after, according to Mercier, did public men see what a grave thing it was.

From *Cause and Effect*[8]

Yes, Reader, here is the miracle. Out of that putrescent rubbish of Scepticism, Sensualism, Sentimentalism, hollow Machiavelism, such a Faith has verily risen; flaming in the heart of a People. A whole People, awakening as it were to consciousness in deep misery, believes that it is within reach of a Fraternal Heaven-on-Earth. With longing arms, it struggles to embrace the Unspeakable; cannot embrace it, owing to certain causes.—Seldom do we find that a whole People can be said to have any Faith at all; except in things which it can eat and handle. Whensoever it gets any Faith, its history becomes spirit-stirring, noteworthy. But since the time when steel Europe shook itself simultaneously at the word of Hermit Peter,[9] and rushed towards the Sepulchre where God had lain, there was no universal impulse of Faith that one could note. Since Protestantism went silent, no Luther's voice, no Zisca's drum any longer proclaiming that God's truth was *not* the Devil's Lie; and the Last of the Cameronians[1] (Renwick was the name of him; honour to the name of the brave!) sank, shot, on the Castle-hill of Edinburgh, there was no parital impulse of Faith among Nations. Till now, behold, once more, this French Nation believes! Herein, we say, in that astonishing Faith of theirs, lies the miracle.It is a Faith undoubtedly of the more prodigious sort, even among Faiths; and will embody itself in prodigies. It is the soul of that world-prodigy named French Revolution; whereat the world still gazes and shudders.

But, for the rest, let no man ask History to explain by cause and effect how the business proceeded henceforth. This battle of Mountain and Gironde,[2] and what follows, is the battle of Fanaticisms and Miracles; unsuitable for cause and effect. The sound of it, to the mind, is as a hubbub of voices in distraction; little of articulate is to be gathered by long listening

8. Part 3, book 3, chap. 1. Between the execution of the king and the advent of Napoleon, the revolutionary movement in France suffered from dissension and counterrevolutionary outbreaks that led to the Reign of Terror (1793–94). During this period most of the political leaders and thousands of their followers lost their lives. Before recommencing his narrative, Carlyle pauses, in this chapter, to consider some of the forces underlying these developments.
9. A leader of the First Crusade to Palestine in the

late 11th century.
1. A 17th-century Scottish sect. Zisca (ca. 1360–1424), successful general and leader of the Hussites, a religious sect in Bohemia.
2. The Girondists were a party of moderate revolutionaries, often of middle-class backgrounds. They were overthrown by their opponents, the Jacobins, who were more adept in controlling the populace. Because the Jacobin delegates in the National Assembly sat in the most elevated place, the party was sometimes called the Mountain.

and studying; only battle-tumult, shouts of triumph, shrieks of despair. The Mountain has left no Memoirs; the Girondins have left Memoirs, which are too often little other than long-drawn Interjections, of *Woe is me,* and *Cursed be ye.* So soon as History can philosophically delineate the conflagration of a kindled Fireship,[3] she may try this other task. Here lay the bitumen-stratum, there the brimstone one; so ran the vein of gunpowder, of nitre, terebinth[4] and foul grease: this, were she inquisitive enough, History might partly know. But how they acted and reacted below decks, one fire-stratum playing into the other, by its nature and the art of man, now when all hands ran raging, and the flames lashed high over shrouds and topmast: this let not History attempt.

The Fireship is old France, the old French Form of Life; her crew a Generation of men. Wild are their cries and their ragings there, like spirits tormented in that flame. But, on the whole, are they not *gone,* O Reader? Their Fireship and they, frightening the world, have sailed away; its flames and its thunders quite away, into the Deep of Time. One thing therefore History will do: pity them all; for it went hard with them all. Not even the seagreen Incorruptible[5] but shall have some pity, some human love, though it takes an effort. And now, so much once thoroughly attained, the rest will become easier. To the eye of equal brotherly pity, innumerable perversions dissipate themselves; exaggerations and execrations fall off, of their own accord. Standing wistfully on the safe shore, we will look, and see, what is of interest to us, what is adapted to us.

1834–37   1837

From Past and Present[1]

From *Democracy*

If the Serene Highnesses and Majesties do not take note of that,[2] then, as I perceive, *that* will take note of itself! The time for levity, insincerity, and idle babble and play-acting, in all kinds, is gone by; it is a serious, grave time. Old long-vexed questions, not yet solved in logical words or parliamentary laws, are fast solving themselves in facts, somewhat unblessed to behold! This largest of questions, this question of Work and Wages, which ought, had we heeded Heaven's voice, to have begun two generations ago or more,

3. A ship filled with combustibles (such as gunpowder and brimstone) that is set adrift among enemy ships to create havoc.
4. Turpentine.
5. Maximilien Robespierre (the Incorruptible), chief of the Jacobin Party and principal instigator of the Reign of Terror.
1. In 1845 there were reputedly one and a half million unemployed in England (out of a population of eighteen million). The closing of factories and the reduction of wages led to severe rioting in the manufacturing districts. Bread-hungry mobs (as well as the Chartist mobs who demanded political reforms) caused many observers to dread that a large-scale revolution was imminent. Carlyle was himself so appalled by the plight of the industrial workers that he postponed his research into the life and times of Cromwell to air his views on the contemporary crisis. *Past and Present,* a book written in seven weeks, was a call for heroic leadership.

Cromwell and other historic leaders are cited, but the principal example from the past is Abbot Samson, a medieval monk who established order in the monasteries under his charge. Carlyle hoped that the "Captains of Industry" might provide a comparable leadership in 1843. He was aware that the spread of democracy was inevitable, but he had little confidence in it as a method of producing leaders. Nor did he have any confidence, at this time, in the landed aristocracy, who seemed to him preoccupied with fox hunting, preserving their game, and upholding the tariffs on grain (Corn Laws). In place of a "Do nothing Aristocracy" there was need for a "Working Aristocracy." This first selection is from book 3, chap. 13.
2. The previous chapter, *Reward,* had urged that English manufacturers needed the help of everyone and that Parliament should remove the tariffs (Corn Laws) restricting the growth of trade and industry.

cannot be delayed longer without hearing Earth's voice. "Labour" will verily need to be somewhat "organized," as they say,—God knows with what difficulty. Man will actually need to have his debts and earnings a little better paid by man; which, let Parliaments speak of them, or be silent of them, are eternally his due from man, and cannot, without penalty and at length not without death-penalty,[3] be withheld. How much ought to cease among us straightway; how much ought to begin straightway, while the hours yet are!

Truly they are strange results to which this of leaving all to "Cash"; of quietly shutting up the God's Temple, and gradually opening wide-open the Mammon's Temple, with "Laissez-faire, and Every man for himself,"—have led us in these days! We have Upper, speaking Classes, who indeed do "speak" as never man spake before; the withered flimsiness, godless baseness and barrenness of whose Speech might of itself indicate what kind of Doing and practical Governing went on under it! For Speech is the gaseous element out of which most kinds of Practice and Performance, especially all kinds of moral Performance, condense themselves, and take shape; as the one is, so will the other be. Descending, accordingly, into the Dumb Class in its Stockport Cellars and Poor-Law Bastilles,[4] have we not to announce that they are hitherto unexampled in the History of Adam's Posterity?

Life was never a May-game for men: in all times the lot of the dumb millions born to toil was defaced with manifold sufferings, injustices, heavy burdens, avoidable and unavoidable; not play at all, but hard work that made the sinews sore and the heart sore. As bond-slaves, *villani, bordarii, sochemanni,* nay indeed as dukes, earls and kings, men were oftentimes made weary of their life; and had to say, in the sweat of their brow and of their soul, Behold, it is not sport, it is grim earnest, and our back can bear no more! Who knows not what massacrings and harryings there have been; grinding, long-continuing, unbearable injustices,—till the heart had to rise in madness, and some *"Eu Sachsen, nimith euer sachses,* You Saxons, out with your gully-knives, then!" You Saxons, some "arrestment," partial "arrestment of the Knaves and Dastards" has become indispensable!—The page of Dryasdust[5] is heavy with such details.

And yet I well venture to believe that in no time, since the beginnings of Society, was the lot of those same dumb millions of toilers so entirely unbearable as it is even in the days now passing over us. It is not to die, or even to die of hunger, that makes a man wretched; many men have died; all men must die,—the last exit of us all is in a Fire-Chariot of Pain.[6] But it is to live miserable we know not why; to work sore and yet gain nothing; to be heartworn, weary, yet isolated, unrelated, girt-in with a cold universal Laissez-faire: it is to die slowly all our life long, imprisoned in a deaf, dead, Infinite Injustice, as in the accursed iron belly of a Phalaris' Bull![7] This is and remains for ever intolerable to all men whom God has made. Do we wonder at French Revolutions, Chartisms, Revolts of Three Days? The times, if we will consider them, are really unexampled.

Never before did I hear of an Irish Widow reduced to "prove her sisterhood

3. I.e., by the outbreak of a revolution, as in France.
4. I.e., workhouse for the unemployed. "Stockport Cellars": in a cellar in the slum district of Stockport, an industrial town near Manchester, three children were poisoned by their starving parents, who wanted to collect insurance benefits from a burial society.
5. An imaginary author of dull histories.
6. 2 Kings 2.11.
7. Phalaris was a Sicilian tyrant whose victims were roasted alive by being confined inside the brass figure of a bull under which a fire was lit.

by dying of typhus-fever and infecting seventeen persons,"—saying in such undeniable way, "You *see*, I was your sister!"[8] Sisterhood, brotherhood, was often forgotten; but not till the rise of these ultimate Mammon and Shotbelt Gospels[9] did I ever see it so expressly denied. If no pious Lord or *Law-ward* would remember it, always some pious Lady ("*Hlaf-dig*," Benefactress, "*Loaf-giveress*," they say she is,—blessings on her beautiful heart!) was there, with mild mother-voice and hand, to remember it; some pious thoughtful *Elder*, what we now call "Prester," *Presbyter* or "Priest," was there to put all men in mind of it, in the name of the God who had made all.

Not even in Black Dahomey was it ever, I think, forgotten to the typhus-fever length. Mungo Park,[1] resourceless, had sunk down to die under the Negro Village-Tree, a horrible White object in the eyes of all. But in the poor Black Woman, and her daughter who stood aghast at him, whose earthly wealth and funded capital consisted of one small calabash of rice, there lived a heart richer than "*Laissez-faire*": they, with a royal munificence, boiled their rice for him; they sang all night to him, spinning assiduous on their cotton distaffs, as he lay to sleep: "Let us pity the poor white man; no mother has he to fetch him milk, no sister to grind him corn!" Thou poor black Noble One,—thou *Lady* too: did not a God make thee too; was there not in thee too something of a God!—

Gurth,[2] born thrall of Cedric the Saxon, has been greatly pitied by Dryasdust and others. Gurth, with the brass collar round his neck, tending Cedric's pigs in the glades of the wood, is not what I call an exemplar of human felicity: but Gurth, with the sky above him, with the free air and tinted boscage and umbrage round him, and in him at least the certainty of supper and social lodging when he came home; Gurth to me seems happy, in comparison with many a Lancashire and Buckinghamshire man, of these days, not born thrall of anybody! Gurth's brass collar did not gall him: Cedric *deserved* to be his Master. The pigs were Cedric's, but Gurth too would get his parings of them. Gurth had the inexpressible satisfaction of feeling himself related indissolubly, though in a rude brass-collar way, to his fellow-mortals in this Earth. He had superiors, inferiors, equals.—Gurth is now "emancipated" long since; has what we call "Liberty." Liberty, I am told, is a Divine thing. Liberty when it becomes the "Liberty to die by starvation" is not so divine!

Liberty? The true liberty of a man, you would say, consisted in his finding out, or being forced to find out, the right path, and to walk thereon. To learn, or to be taught, what work he actually was able for; and then by permission, persuasion, and even compulsion, to set about doing of the same! That is his true blessedness, honour, "liberty" and maximum of wellbeing: if liberty be not that, I for one have small care about liberty. You do not allow a palpable madman to leap over precipices; you violate his liberty, you that are wise; and keep him, were it in strait-waistcoats, away from the precipices! Every

---

8. An incident referred to several times in *Past and Present*. Dickens in *Bleak House* also showed how indifference to the lack of sanitation in London slums led to the spread of disease to other parts of the city.
9. The attitudes of land-owning aristocracy who were committed to preserving their exclusive right to shoot game birds and animals. "Mammon [gos-pel]": the pursuit of wealth according to the economic code of laissez-faire, whereby no one took the responsibility of caring for the starving widow.
1. Explorer and author of *Travels in the Interior of Africa* (1799); in 1806, he was killed by Africans. "Black Dahomey": a state in west Africa where human sacrifice and cannibalism persisted.
2. A swineherd described in Scott's *Ivanhoe*.

stupid, every cowardly and foolish man is but a less palpable madman: his true liberty were that a wiser man, that any and every wiser man, could, by brass collars, or in whatever milder or sharper way, lay hold of him when he was going wrong, and order and compel him to go a little righter. O, if thou really art my *Senior*, Seigneur, my *Elder*, Presbyter or Priest,—if thou art in very deed my *Wiser*, may a beneficent instinct lead and impel thee to "conquer" me, to command me! If thou do know better than I what is good and right, I conjure thee in the name of God, force me to do it; were it by never such brass collars, whips and handcuffs, leave me not to walk over precipices! That I have been called, by all the Newspapers, a "free man" will avail me little, if my pilgrimage have ended in death and wreck. O that the Newspapers had called me slave, coward, fool, or what it pleased their sweet voices to name me, and I had attained not death, but life!—Liberty requires new definitions.

A conscious abhorrence and intolerance of Folly, of Baseness, Stupidity, Poltroonery and all that brood of things, dwells deep in some men: still deeper in others an *un*conscious abhorrence and intolerance, clothed moreover by the beneficent Supreme Powers in what stout appetites, energies, egoisms so-called, are suitable to it;—these latter are your Conquerors, Romans, Normans, Russians, Indo-English; Founders of what we call Aristocracies. Which indeed have they not the most "divine right" to found;—being themselves very truly *Aristoi*, BRAVEST, BEST; and conquering generally a confused rabble of WORST, or at lowest, clearly enough, of WORSE? I think their divine right, tried, with affirmatory verdict, in the greatest Law-Court known to me, was good! A class of men who are dreadfully exclaimed against by Dryasdust; of whom nevertheless beneficent Nature has oftentimes had need; and may, alas, again have need.

When, across the hundredfold poor scepticisms, trivialisms, and constitutional cobwebberies of Dryasdust, you catch any glimpse of a William the Conqueror, a Tancred of Hauteville[3] or such like,—do you not discern veritably some rude outline of a true God-made King; whom not the Champion of England[4] cased in tin, but all Nature and the Universe were calling to the throne? It is absolutely necessary that he get thither. Nature does not mean her poor Saxon children to perish, of obesity, stupor or other malady, as yet: a stern Ruler and Line of Rulers therefore is called in,—a stern but most beneficent *perpetual House-Surgeon* is by Nature herself called in, and even the appropriate *fees* are provided for him! Dryasdust talks lamentably about Hereward and the Fen Counties; fate of earl Waltheof;[5] Yorkshire and the North reduced to ashes; all of which is undoubtedly lamentable. But even Dryasdust apprises me of one fact: "A child, in this William's reign, might have carried a purse of gold from end to end of England." My erudite friend,

---

3. Norman hero of the First Crusade. King William I of England (reigned 1066–87), surnamed *the Conqueror* after the Battle of Hastings in 1066. Being an illegitimate son, he also bore the surname of William the Bastard. Although some historians condemn William as a ruthless ruler, he is ranked by Carlyle as a hero because of his strong and efficient government. William fulfilled the requirements of the kingly hero described by Carlyle in his lectures *On Heroes*: a man fittest "to *command* over us . . . to tell us what we are to *do*."

4. An official who goes through a formality, at coronation ceremonies, of demanding whether anyone challenges the right of the monarch to ascend the throne. He wears full armor ("cased in tin"). A symbol of outworn feudal customs.

5. His execution in 1075, on a supposedly trumped-up charge, is cited as a blot on William's record as king. Hereward the Wake, an outlaw whose exploits against William the Conqueror made him seem a romantic figure like Robin Hood.

it is a fact which outweighs a thousand! Sweep away thy constitutional, sentimental, and other cobwebberies; look eye to eye, if thou still have any eye, in the face of this big burly William Bastard: thou wilt see a fellow of most flashing discernment, of most strong lion-heart;—in whom, as it were, within a frame of oak and iron, the gods have planted the soul of "a man of genius"! Dost thou call that nothing? I call it an immense thing!—Rage enough was in this Willelmus Conquaestor, rage enough for his occasions;—and yet the essential element of him, as of all such men, is not scorching *fire*, but shining illuminative *light*. Fire and light are strangely interchangeable; nay, at bottom, I have found them different forms of the same most godlike "elementary substance" in our world: a thing worth stating in these days. The essential element of this Conquaestor is, first of all, the most sun-eyed perception of what *is* really what on this God's-Earth;—which, thou wilt find, does mean at bottom "Justice," and "Virtues" not a few: *Conformity* to what the Maker has seen good to make; that, I suppose, will mean Justice and a Virtue or two?—

Dost thou think Willelmus Conquaestor would have tolerated ten years' jargon, one hour's jargon, on the propriety of killing Cotton-manufactures by partridge Corn-Laws?[6] I fancy, this was not the man to knock out of his night's-rest with nothing but a noisy bedlamism in your mouth! "Assist us still better to bush the partridges; strangle Plugson who spins the shirts?"— "*Par la Splendeur de Dieu!*"[7]—Dost thou think Willelmus Conquaestor, in this new time, with Steam-engine Captains of Industry on one hand of him, and Joe-Manton Captains of Idleness[8] on the other, would have doubted which *was* really the BEST; which did deserve strangling, and which not?

I have a certain indestructible regard for Willelmus Conquaestor. A resident House-Surgeon, provided by Nature for her beloved English People, and even furnished with the requisite fees, as I said; for he by no means felt himself doing Nature's work, this Willelmus, but his own work exclusively! And his own work withal it was; informed "*par la Splendeur de Dieu.*"—I say, it is necessary to get the work out of such a man, however harsh that be! When a world, not yet doomed for death, is rushing down to ever-deeper Baseness and Confusion, it is a dire necessity of Nature's to bring in her ARISTOCRACIES, her BEST, even by forcible methods. When their descendants or representatives cease entirely to *be* the Best, Nature's poor world will very soon rush down again to Baseness; and it becomes a dire necessity of Nature's to cast them out. Hence French Revolutions, Five-point Charters, Democracies, and a mournful list of *Etceteras*, in these our afflicted times.

✻   ✻   ✻

Democracy, the chase of Liberty in that direction, shall go its full course; unrestrained by him of Pferdefuss-Quacksalber,[9] or any of *his* household. The Toiling Millions of Mankind, in most vital need and passionate instinctive desire of Guidance, shall cast away False-Guidance; and hope, for an

---

6. See n. 1, p. 1110.
7. By the splendor of God! (French): one of William's oaths. Plugson of Undershot was Carlyle's term to describe the new class of industrial leaders.
8. The idle aristocracy who wasted time shooting partridges with guns made by Joseph Manton, a London gunsmith. This speech sums up the pleas

of the High Tariff lobby in Parliament. "Keep the Corn Laws intact so that the aristocratic landlords may continue to enjoy shooting partridges on their estates; subdue the manufacturing leaders by preventing trade."
9. Horse foot quack doctor.

hour, that No-Guidance will suffice them: but it can be for an hour only. The smallest item of human Slavery is the oppression of man by his Mock-Superiors; the palpablest, but I say at bottom the smallest. Let him shake off such oppression, trample it indignantly under his feet; I blame him not, I pity and commend him. But oppression by your Mock-Superiors well shaken off, the grand problem yet remains to solve: That of finding government by your Real-Superiors! Alas, how shall we ever learn the solution of that, benighted, bewildered, sniffing, sneering, godforgetting unfortunates as we are? It is a work for centuries; to be taught us by tribulations, confusions, insurrections, obstructions; who knows if not by conflagration and despair! It is a lesson inclusive of all other lessons; the hardest of all lessons to learn.

Captains of Industry[1]

If I believed that Mammonism with its adjuncts was to continue henceforth the one serious principle of our existence, I should reckon it idle to solicit remedial measures from any Government, the disease being insusceptible of remedy. Government can do much, but it can in no wise do all. Government, as the most conspicuous object in Society, is called upon to give signal of what shall be done; and, in many ways, to preside over further, and command the doing of it. But the Government cannot do, by all its signalling and commanding, what the Society is radically indisposed to do. In the long-run every Government is the exact symbol of its People, with their wisdom and unwisdom; we have to say, Like People like Government.— The main substance of this immense Problem of Organizing Labour, and first of all of Managing the Working Classes, will, it is very clear, have to be solved by those who stand practically in the middle of it; by those who themselves work and preside over work. Of all that can be enacted by any Parliament in regard to it, the germs must already lie potentially extant in those two Classes, who are to obey such enactment. A Human Chaos *in* which there is no light, you vainly attempt to irradiate by light shed *on* it: order never can arise there.

But it is my firm conviction that the "Hell of England" will *cease* to be that of "not making money"; that we shall get a nobler Hell and a nobler Heaven! I anticipate light *in* the Human Chaos, glimmering, shining more and more; under manifold true signals from without That light shall shine. Our deity no longer being Mammon,—O Heavens, each man will then say to himself: "Why such deadly haste to make money? I shall not go to Hell, even if I do not make money! There is another Hell, I am told!" Competition, at railway-speed, in all branches of commerce and work will then abate:—good felt-hats for the head, in every sense, instead of seven-feet lath-and-plaster hats on wheels,[2] will then be discoverable! Bubble-periods,[3] with their panics and commercial crises, will again become infrequent; steady modest industry will take the place of gambling speculation. To be a noble Master, among noble Workers, will again be the first ambition with some few; to be a rich Master only the second. How the Inventive Genius of England, with the whirr of its bobbins and billy-rollers[4] shoved somewhat into the backgrounds of the

1. From book 4, chap. 4.
2. A London hatter's mode of advertising.
3. Periods of violent fluctuation in the stock mar-

ket caused by unsound speculating.
4. Machines used to prepare cotton or wool for spinning.

brain, will contrive and devise, not cheaper produce exclusively, but fairer distribution of the produce at its present cheapness! By degrees, we shall again have a Society with something of Heroism in it, something of Heaven's Blessing on it; we shall again have, as my German friend[5] asserts, "instead of Mammon-Feudalism with unsold cotton-shirts and Preservation of the Game, noble just Industrialism and Government by the Wisest!"

It is with the hope of awakening here and there a British man to know himself for a man and divine soul, that a few words of parting admonition, to all persons to whom the Heavenly Powers have lent power of any kind in this land, may now be addressed. And first to those same Master-Workers, Leaders of Industry; who stand nearest, and in fact powerfullest, though not most prominent, being as yet in too many senses a Virtuality rather than an Actuality.

The Leaders of Industry, if Industry is ever to be led, are virtually the Captains of the World; if there be no nobleness in them, there will never be an Aristocracy more. But let the Captains of Industry consider: once again, are they born of other clay than the old Captains of Slaughter; doomed for ever to be not Chivalry, but a mere gold-plated *Doggery*,—what the French well name *Canaille*, "Doggery" with more or less gold carrion at its disposal? Captains of Industry are the true Fighters, henceforth recognizable as the only true ones: Fighters against Chaos, Necessity and the Devils and Jötuns;[6] and lead on Mankind in that great, and alone true, and universal warfare; the stars in their courses fighting for them, and all Heaven and all Earth saying audibly, Well done! Let the Captains of Industry retire into their own hearts, and ask solemnly, If there is nothing but vulturous hunger for fine wines, valet reputation and gilt carriages, discoverable there? Of hearts made by the Almighty God I will not believe such a thing. Deep-hidden under wretchedest god-forgetting Cants, Epicurisms, Dead-Sea Apisms;[7] forgotten as under foullest fat Lethe mud and weeds, there is yet, in all hearts born into this God's-World, a spark of the Godlike slumbering. Awake, O nightmare sleepers; awake, arise, or be for ever fallen! This is not playhouse poetry; it is sober fact. Our England, our world cannot live as it is. It will connect itself with a God again, or go down with nameless throes and fire-consummation to the Devils. Thou who feelest aught of such a Godlike stirring in thee, any faintest intimation of it as through heavy-laden dreams, follow *it*, I conjure thee. Arise, save thyself, be one of those that save thy country.

Bucaniers,[8] Chactaw Indians, whose supreme aim in fighting is that they may get the scalps, the money, that they may amass scalps and money; out of such came no Chivalry, and never will! Out of such came only gore and wreck, infernal rage and misery; desperation quenched in annihilation. Behold it, I bid thee, behold there, and consider! What is it that thou have a hundred thousand-pound bills laid up in thy strong-room, a hundred scalps hung up in thy wigwam? I value not them or thee. Thy scalps and thy thousand-pound bills are as yet nothing, if no nobleness from within irradiate

---

5. Teufelsdröckh, the hero of *Sartor Resartus*.
6. Giants of Scandinavian mythology.
7. A reference to a Muslim story in which a tribe living near the Dead Sea was transformed into apes because the people had ignored the prophecies of Moses.
8. Buccaneers.

them; if no Chivalry, in action, or in embryo ever struggling towards birth and action, be there.

Love of men cannot be bought by cash-payment; and without love, men cannot endure to be together. You cannot lead a Fighting World without having it regimented, chivalried: the thing, in a day, becomes impossible; all men in it, the highest at first, the very lowest at last, discern consciously, or by a noble instinct, this necessity. And can you any more continue to lead a Working World unregimented, anarchic? I answer, and the Heavens and Earth are now answering, No! The thing becomes not "in a day" impossible; but in some two generations it does. Yes, when fathers and mothers, in Stockport hunger-cellars, begin to eat their children, and Irish widows have to prove their relationship by dying of typhus-fever; and amid Governing "Corporations of the Best and Bravest," busy to preserve their game by "bushing," dark millions of God's human creatures start up in mad Chartisms, impracticable Sacred-Months, and Manchester Insurrections;[9]—and there is a virtual Industrial Aristocracy as yet only half-alive, spell-bound amid money-bags and ledgers; and an actual Idle Aristocracy seemingly near dead in somnolent delusions, in trespasses and double-barrels,[1] "sliding," as on inclined-planes, which every new year they *soap* with new Hansard's-jargon[2] under God's sky, and so are "sliding" ever faster, towards a "scale" and balance-scale whereon is written *Thou art found Wanting;*——in such days, after a generation or two, I say, it does become, even to the low and simple, very palpably impossible! No Working World, any more than a Fighting World, can be led on without a noble Chivalry of Work, and laws and fixed rules which follow out of that,—far nobler than any Chivalry of Fighting was. As an anarchic multitude on mere Supply-and-demand, it is becoming inevitable that we dwindle in horrid suicidal convulsion, and self-abrasion, frightful to the imagination, into *Chactaw* Workers. With wigwams and scalps,—with palaces and thousand-pound bills; with savagery, depopulation, chaotic desolation! Good Heavens, will not one French Revolution and Reign of Terror suffice us, but must there be two? There will be two if needed; there will be twenty if needed; there will be precisely as many as needed. The Laws of Nature will have themselves fulfilled. That is a thing certain to me.

Your gallant battle-hosts and work-hosts, as the others did, will need to be made loyally yours; they must and will be regulated, methodically secured in their just share of conquest under you;—joined with you in veritable brotherhood, sonhood, by quite other and deeper ties than those of temporary day's wages! How would mere redcoated regiments, to say nothing of chivalries, fight for you, if you could discharge them on the evening of the battle, on payment of the stipulated shillings,—and they discharge you on the morning of it! Chelsea Hospitals,[3] pensions, promotions, rigorous lasting covenant on the one side and on the other, are indispensable even for a hired fighter. The Feudal Baron, much more,—how could he subsist with mere temporary mercenaries round him, at sixpence a day; ready to go over to the other side,

---

9. In 1819 a large open-air labor meeting in Manchester was broken up by charging cavalry. Thirteen men and women were massacred, and many others were wounded.
1. I.e., the only concern of the landed aristocrats

is to keep trespassers off their game preserves and reserve shooting rights to themselves.
2. Parliamentary oratory, as in Hansard's printed record of debates in the House of Commons.
3. Home for disabled veterans.

if sevenpence were offered? He could not have subsisted;—and his noble instinct saved him from the necessity of even trying! The Feudal Baron had a Man's Soul in him; to which anarchy, mutiny, and the other fruits of temporary mercenaries, were intolerable: he had never been a Baron otherwise, but had continued a Chactaw and Bucanier. He felt it precious, and at last it became habitual, and his fruitful enlarged existence included it as a necessity, to have men round him who in heart loved him; whose life he watched over with rigour yet with love; who were prepared to give their life for him, if need came. It was beautiful; it was human! Man lives not otherwise, nor can live contented, anywhere or anywhen. Isolation is the sum-total of wretchedness to man. To be cut off, to be left solitary: to have a world alien, not your world; all a hostile camp for you; not a home at all, of hearts and faces who are yours, whose you are! It is the frightfullest enchantment; too truly a work of the Evil One. To have neither superior, nor inferior, nor equal, united manlike to you. Without father, without child, without brother. Man knows no sadder destiny. "How is each of us," exclaims Jean Paul,[4] "so lonely in the wide bosom of the All!" Encased each as in his transparent "ice-palace"; our brother visible in his, making signals and gesticulations to us;—visible, but for ever unattainable: on his bosom we shall never rest, nor he on ours. It was not a God that did this; no!

Awake, ye noble Workers, warriors in the one true war: all this must be remedied. It is you who are already half-alive, whom I will welcome into life; whom I will conjure in God's name to shake off your enchanted sleep, and live wholly! Cease to count scalps, goldpurses; not in these lies your or our salvation. Even these, if you count only these, will not be left. Let bucaniering be put far from you; alter, speedily abrogate all laws of the bucaniers, if you would gain any victory that shall endure. Let God's justice, let pity, nobleness and manly valour, with more gold-purses or with fewer, testify themselves in this your brief Life-transit to all the Eternities, the Gods and Silences. It is to you I call; for ye are not dead, ye are already half-alive: there is in you a sleepless dauntless energy, the prime-matter of all nobleness in man. Honour to you in your kind. It is to you I call: ye know at least this, That the mandate of God to His creature man is: Work! The future Epic of the World rests not with those that are near dead, but with those that are alive, and those that are coming into life.

Look around you. Your world-hosts are all in mutiny, in confusion, destitution; on the eve of fiery wreck and madness! They will not march farther for you, on the sixpence a day and supply-and-demand principle; they will not; nor ought they, nor can they. Ye shall reduce them to order, begin reducing them. To order, to just subordination; noble loyalty in return for noble guidance. Their souls are driven nigh mad; let yours be sane and ever saner. Not as a bewildered bewildering mob; but as a firm regimented mass, with real captains over them, will these men march any more. All human interests, combined human endeavours, and social growths in this world, have, at a certain stage of their development, required organizing: and Work, the grandest of human interests, does now require it.

God knows, the task will be hard: but no noble task was ever easy. This task will wear away your lives, and the lives of your sons and grandsons: but

4. Jean Paul Richter (1763–1825), German humorist.

for what purpose, if not for tasks like this, were lives given to men? Ye shall cease to count your thousand-pound scalps, the noble of you shall cease! Nay, the very scalps, as I say, will not long be left if you count on these. Ye shall cease wholly to be barbarous vulturous Chactaws, and become noble European Nineteenth-Century Men. Ye shall know that Mammon, in never such gigs[5] and flunkey "respectabilities," is not the alone God; that of himself he is but a Devil, and even a Brute-god.

Difficult? Yes, it will be difficult. The short-fibre cotton; that too was difficult. The waste cotton-shrub, long useless, disobedient, as the thistle by the wayside,—have ye not conquered it; made it into beautiful bandana webs; white woven shirts for men; bright-tinted air-garments wherein flit goddesses? Ye have shivered mountains asunder, made the hard iron pliant to you as soft putty: the Forest-giants, Marsh-jötuns bear sheaves of golden grain; Aegir the Seademon[6] himself stretches his back for a sleek highway to you, and on Firehorses and Windhorses ye career. Ye are most strong. Thor red-bearded, with his blue sun-eyes, with his cheery heart and strong thunder-hammer, he and you have prevailed. Ye are most strong, ye Sons of the icy North, of the far East,—far marching from your rugged Eastern Wildernesses, hitherward from the grey Dawn of Time! Ye are Sons of the *Jötunland*; the land of Difficulties Conquered. Difficult? You must try this thing. Once try it with the understanding that it will and shall have to be done. Try it as ye try the paltrier thing, making of money! I will bet on you once more, against all Jötuns, Tailor-gods,[7] Double-barrelled Law-wards, and Denizens of Chaos whatsoever.

1843

1843

5. Light carriages; to own one was a sign of respectable status comparable with owning certain kinds of automobiles today.

6. From Scandinavian mythology.
7. False gods.

JOHN HENRY CARDINAL NEWMAN
1801–1890

Like Carlyle, John Henry Newman powerfully affected the thinking of his contemporaries, whether they agreed or disagreed with him. Even today, according to Martin Svaglic, Newman attracts both "apotheosizers" and "calumniators" who praise or blame him "as an unusually compelling spokesman for what some consider eternal verities and others regressive myths." During his long lifetime, Newman frequently found himself at the center of some of the most intense disputes that stirred Victorian England, disputes in which he himself emerged as a controversialist of great skill—engagingly persuasive in defense of his position and devastatingly effective in disposing of opponents. Thomas Hardy, whose position was at the opposite extreme from Newman's, paid him a high compliment when he noted in his diary: "Worked at J. H. Newman's *Apologia* which we have all been talking about lately. . . . Style charming and his logic really human, being based not on syllogisms but on converging probabilities. Only—and here comes the fatal catastrophe—there is no first link to his excellent chain of reasoning, and down you come headlong."

Newman was born in London, the son (like Browning) of a banker. In his spiritual autobiography, *Apologia Pro Vita Sua* (in effect, his vindication of his life), he traces the principal stages of his religious development from the strongly Protestant period of his youth to his conversion to Roman Catholicism in 1845. Along the way, after being elected to a fellowship at Oriel College in Oxford and becoming an Anglican clergyman, he was attracted briefly into the orbit of religious liberalism. Gradually coming to realize, however, that liberalism, with its reliance on human reason, would be powerless to defend traditional religion from attack, Newman shifted over into the new High Church wing of the Anglican Church and soon was recognized as the leading figure of what was known as the Oxford movement. During the 1830s he built up a large and influential following by his sermons at Oxford and also by his writing of tracts—that is, appeals, in pamphlet form, on behalf of a cause. In these publications he developed arguments about the powers of church versus state and other issues of deep concern to his High Church colleagues—or Tractarians, as they were also called. Newman's own efforts to demonstrate the true catholicity of the Church of England provoked increasing opposition as his position grew closer to Roman Catholicism. Distressed by constant denunciations, he withdrew into isolation and silence. After much reflection, he took the final step. At the age of forty-four he entered the Roman Catholic priesthood and moved to Birmingham, where he spent the rest of his life. In 1879 he was created cardinal. In 1991, at the instigation of Pope John Paul II, his title became The Venerable John Henry Cardinal Newman, indicating the first of three stages toward sainthood.

In view of this development, Newman's response to a woman who had spoken of him as a saint is touching. In some distress he wrote to her: "Saints are not literary men, they do not love the classics, they do not write Tales."

Although the story of Newman's development seems to emphasize change, certain features remain constant. His sense of God's guidance is especially evident. Characteristic is a poem written in Italy in 1834, following a severe illness, which opens with the line "Lead, kindly light" and concludes with this stanza:

> So long Thy power hath blest me, sure it still
>   Will lead me on,
> O'er moor and fen, o'er crag and torrent, till
>   The night is gone;
> And with the morn those angel faces smile
> Which I have loved long since, and lost awhile.

Set to music, Newman's poem became one of the most popular hymns ever written.

The writing of verse, however, was a subordinate task for Newman; most of his writings are prose, and it is noteworthy that despite his mastery of prose style, Newman found the act of composition to be even more painfully difficult than most of us do. During his years at Birmingham, he was nevertheless prompted to write several books, including works of religious poetry and fiction. Most celebrated is the series of articles, published as his *Apologia* in 1864, in which he replied to an attack on his intellectual honesty made by the Reverend Charles Kingsley (1819–1875), an adherent of the Broad Church and also a popular novelist. Although parts of the *Apologia*, being devoted to fine points of theological doctrine and church history, are difficult for the ordinary reader to follow, the main argument is clearly and persuasively developed. The dignity and candor with which Newman reviewed the stages of his religious development, the repeated appeals to his fellow citizens' sense of honesty and fair play, the unobtrusively beautiful prose style, gained for his masterpiece a sympathetic audience even among those who had been least disposed to listen to his side of the dispute with Kingsley.

Seemingly less controversial than the *Apologia* are Newman's lectures on the aims of education, which were delivered in Dublin at the newly founded Catholic University of Ireland, a university of which he was for a few years the rector. These lectures, published in 1852 and later titled *The Idea of a University,* are a classic statement of the value of "the disciplined intellect" that can be developed by a liberal education rather than by a technical training. Like the later lectures of Matthew Arnold and T. H. Huxley, *The Idea of a University* shows the Victorian engagement with the role of education in society.

It should be noted that Newman's view of a liberal education is largely independent of his religious position. Such an education, he said, could form the minds of profligates and anticlericals as well as of saints and priests of the Church. In considerable measure, his view reflects his admiration for the kind of intellectual enlargement he had himself enjoyed as an undergraduate at Trinity College, Oxford. One of the most moving passages in the *Apologia* is Newman's account of his farewell to an Oxford friend, in February 1846, as he was preparing his final departure from the precincts of the university he loved:

> In him I took leave of my first College, Trinity, which was so dear to me. . . .
> There used to be much snapdragon growing on the walls opposite my freshman's
> rooms there, and I had taken it as the emblem of my perpetual residence even
> unto death in my University.
>   On the morning of the 23rd I left the Observatory. I have never seen Oxford
> since, excepting its spires, as they are seen from the railway.

From The Idea of a University
From *Discourse 5. Knowledge Its Own End*

6

Now bear with me, Gentlemen, if what I am about to say has at first sight a fanciful appearance. Philosophy, then, or Science, is related to Knowledge in this way: Knowledge is called by the name of Science or Philosophy, when it is acted upon, informed, or if I may use a strong figure, impregnated by Reason. Reason is the principle of that intrinsic fecundity of Knowledge, which, to those who possess it, is its especial value, and which dispenses with the necessity of their looking abroad for any end to rest upon external to itself. Knowledge, indeed, when thus exalted into a scientific form, is also power; not only is it excellent in itself, but whatever such excellence may be, it is something more, it has a result beyond itself. Doubtless; but that is a further consideration, with which I am not concerned. I only say that, prior to its being a power, it is a good; that it is, not only an instrument, but an end. I know well it may resolve itself into an art, and terminate in a mechanical process, and in tangible fruit; but it also may fall back upon that Reason which informs it, and resolve itself into Philosophy. In one case it is called Useful Knowledge, in the other Liberal. The same person may cultivate it in both ways at once; but this again is a matter foreign to my subject; here I do but say that there are two ways of using Knowledge, and in matter of fact those who use it in one way are not likely to use it in the other, or at least in a very limited measure. You see, then, here are two methods of Education; the end of the one is to be philosophical, of the other to be mechanical; the one rises towards general ideas, the other is exhausted upon what is particular and external. Let me not be thought to deny the necessity, or to decry the benefit, of such attention to what is particular and practical, as belongs to the useful or mechanical arts; life could not go on without them; we owe our daily welfare to them; their exercise is the duty of the many, and we owe to the many a debt of gratitude for fulfilling that duty. I only say that Knowledge, in proportion as it tends more and more to be particular, ceases to be Knowledge. It is a question whether Knowledge can in any proper sense be predicated of the brute creation; without pretending to metaphysical exactness of phraseology, which would be unsuitable to an occasion like this, I say, it seems to me improper to call that passive sensation, or perception of things, which brutes seem to possess, by the name of Knowledge. When I speak of Knowledge, I mean something intellectual, something which grasps what it perceives through the senses; something which takes a view of things; which sees more than the senses convey; which reasons upon what it sees, and while it sees; which invests it with an idea. It expresses itself, not in a mere enunciation, but by an enthymeme:[1] it is of the nature of science from the first, and in this consists its dignity. The principle of real dignity in Knowledge, its worth, its desirableness, considered irrespectively of its results, is this germ within it of a scientific or a philosophical process. This is how it comes to be an end in itself; this is why it admits of being called Liberal. Not to know the relative disposition of things is the state of slaves or children; to have mapped out the Universe is the boast, or at least the ambition, of Philosophy.

Moreover, such knowledge is not a mere extrinsic or accidental advantage, which is ours today and another's tomorrow, which may be got up from a book, and easily forgotten again, which we can command or communicate at our pleasure, which we can borrow for the occasion, carry about in our hand, and take into the market; it is an acquired illumination, it is a habit, a personal possession, and an inward endowment. And this is the reason why it is more correct, as well as more usual, to speak of a University as a place of education than of instruction, though, when knowledge is concerned, instruction would at first sight have seemed the more appropriate work. We are instructed, for instance, in manual exercises, in the fine and useful arts, in trades, and in ways of business; for these are methods, which have little or no effect upon the mind itself, are contained in rules committed to memory, to tradition, or to use, and bear upon an end external to themselves. But education is a higher word; it implies an action upon our mental nature, and the formation of a character; it is something individual and permanent, and is commonly spoken of in connection with religion and virtue. When, then, we speak of the communication of Knowledge as being Education, we thereby really imply that that Knowledge is a state or condition of mind; and since cultivation of mind is surely worth seeking for its own sake, we are thus brought once more to the conclusion, which the word "Liberal" and the word "Philosophy" have already suggested, that there is a Knowledge, which is desirable, though nothing come of it, as being of itself a treasure, and a sufficient remuneration of years of labor.

1. A syllogism in which one of the premises is understood but not stated.

From *Discourse 7. Knowledge Viewed in Relation to Professional Skill*

1

I have been insisting, in my two preceding Discourses, first, on the cultivation of the intellect, as an end which may reasonably be pursued for its own sake; and next, on the nature of that cultivation, or what that cultivation consists in. Truth of whatever kind is the proper object of the intellect; its cultivation then lies in fitting it to apprehend and contemplate truth. Now the intellect in its present state, with exceptions which need not here be specified, does not discern truth intuitively, or as a whole. We know, not by a direct and simple vision, not at a glance, but, as it were, by piecemeal and accumulation, by a mental process, by going round an object, by the comparison, the combination, the mutual correction, the continual adaptation, of many partial notions, by the employment, concentration, and joint action of many faculties and exercises of mind. Such a union and concert of the intellectual powers, such an enlargement and development, such a comprehensiveness, is necessarily a matter of training. And again, such a training is a matter of rule; it is not mere application, however exemplary, which introduces the mind to truth, nor the reading many books, nor the getting up many subjects, nor the witnessing many experiments, nor the attending many lectures. All this is short of enough; a man may have done it all, yet be lingering in the vestibule of knowledge: he may not realize what his mouth utters; he may not see with his mental eye what confronts him; he may have no grasp of things as they are; or at least he may have no power at all of advancing one step forward of himself, in consequence of what he has already acquired, no power of discriminating between truth and falsehood, of sifting out the grains of truth from the mass, of arranging things according to their real value, and, if I may use the phrase, of building up ideas. Such a power is the result of a scientific formation of mind; it is an acquired faculty of judgment, of clearsightedness, of sagacity, of wisdom, of philosophical reach of mind, and of intellectual self-possession and repose—qualities which do not come of mere acquirement. The bodily eye, the organ for apprehending material objects, is provided by nature; the eye of the mind, of which the object is truth, is the work of discipline and habit.

This process of training, by which the intellect, instead of being formed or sacrificed to some particular or accidental purpose, some specific trade or profession, or study or science, is disciplined for its own sake, for the perception of its own proper object, and for its own highest culture, is called Liberal Education; and though there is no one in whom it is carried as far as is conceivable, or whose intellect would be a pattern of what intellects should be made, yet there is scarcely anyone but may gain an idea of what real training is, and at least look towards it, and make its true scope and result, not something else, his standard of excellence; and numbers there are who may submit themselves to it, and secure it to themselves in good measure. And to set forth the right standard, and to train according to it, and to help forward all students toward it according to their various capacities, this I conceive to be the business of a University.

2

Now this is what some great men are very slow to allow; they insist that Education should be confined to some particular and narrow end, and should issue in some definite work, which can be weighed and measured. They argue as if every thing, as well as every person, had its price; and that where there has been a great outlay, they have a right to expect a return in kind. This they call making Education and Instruction "useful," and "Utility" becomes their watchword. With a fundamental principle of this nature, they very naturally go on to ask what there is to show for the expense of a University; what is the real worth in the market of the article called "a Liberal Education," on the supposition that it does not teach us definitely how to advance our manufactures, or to improve our lands, or to better our civil economy; or again, if it does not at once make this man a lawyer, that an engineer, and that a surgeon; or at least if it does not lead to discoveries in chemistry, astronomy, geology, magnetism, and science of every kind.

* * *

5

* * *

This is the obvious answer which may be made to those who urge upon us the claims of Utility in our plans of Education;[2] but I am not going to leave the subject here: I mean to take a wider view of it. Let us take "useful," as Locke[3] takes it, in its proper and popular sense, and then we enter upon a large field of thought, to which I cannot do justice in one Discourse, though today's is all the space that I can give to it. I say, let us take "useful" to mean, not what is simply good, but what *tends* to good, or is the *instrument* of good; and in this sense also, Gentlemen, I will show you how a liberal education is truly and fully a useful, though it be not a professional, education. "Good" indeed means one thing, and "useful" means another; but I lay it down as a principle, which will save us a great deal of anxiety, that, though the useful is not always good, the good is always useful. Good is not only good, but reproductive of good; this is one of its attributes; nothing is excellent, beautiful, perfect, desirable for its own sake, but it overflows, and spreads the likeness of itself all around it. Good is prolific; it is not only good to the eye, but to the taste; it not only attracts us, but it communicates itself; it excites first our admiration and love, then our desire and our gratitude, and that, in proportion to its intenseness and fullness in particular instances. A great good will impart great good. If then the intellect is so excellent a portion of us, and its cultivation so excellent, it is not only beautiful, perfect, admirable, and noble in itself, but in a true and high sense it must be useful to the possessor and to all around him; not useful in any low, mechanical, mercantile sense, but as diffusing good, or as a blessing, or a gift, or power, or a

2. The Utilitarians argued that a useful education would be one that trained the mind in the "habit of pushing things up to their first principles." Newman had earlier pointed out that a liberal educa-

tion does exactly that and is hence useful.
3. John Locke (1632–1704), whose treatise *Of Education* advocated a utilitarian concept of education.

treasure, first to the owner, then through him to the world. I say then, if a liberal education be good, it must necessarily be useful too.

6

You will see what I mean by the parallel of bodily health. Health is a good in itself, though nothing came of it, and is especially worth seeking and cherishing; yet, after all, the blessings which attend its presence are so great, while they are so close to it and so redound back upon it and encircle it, that we never think of it except as useful as well as good, and praise and prize it for what it does, as well as for what it is, though at the same time we cannot point out any definite and distinct work or production which it can be said to effect. And so as regards intellectual culture, I am far from denying utility in this large sense as the end of Education, when I lay it down that the culture of the intellect is a good in itself and its own end; I do not exclude from the idea of intellectual culture what it cannot but be, from the very nature of things; I only deny that we must be able to point out, before we have any right to call it useful, some art, or business, or profession, or trade, or work, as resulting from it, and as its real and complete end. The parallel is exact: As the body may be sacrificed to some manual or other toil, whether moderate or oppressive, so may the intellect be devoted to some specific profession; and I do not call *this* the culture of the intellect. Again, as some member or organ of the body may be inordinately used and developed, so may memory, or imagination, or the reasoning faculty; and *this* again is not intellectual culture. On the other hand, as the body may be tended, cherished, and exercised with a simple view to its general health, so may the intellect also be generally exercised in order to its perfect state; and this *is* its cultivation.

Again, as health ought to precede labor of the body, and as a man in health can do what an unhealthy man cannot do, and as of this health the properties are strength, energy, agility, graceful carriage and action, manual dexterity, and endurance of fatigue, so in like manner general culture of mind is the best aid to professional and scientific study, and educated men can do what illiterate cannot; and the man who has learned to think and to reason and to compare and to discriminate and to analyze, who has refined his taste, and formed his judgment, and sharpened his mental vision, will not indeed at once be a lawyer, or a pleader, or an orator, or a statesman, or a physician, or a good landlord, or a man of business, or a soldier, or an engineer, or a chemist, or a geologist, or an antiquarian, but he will be placed in that state of intellect in which he can take up any one of the sciences or callings I have referred to, or any other for which he has a taste or special talent, with an ease, a grace, a versatility, and a success, to which another is a stranger. In this sense then, and as yet I have said but a very few words on a large subject, mental culture is emphatically *useful.*

If then I am arguing, and shall argue, against Professional or Scientific knowledge as the sufficient end of a University Education, let me not be supposed, Gentlemen, to be disrespectful towards particular studies, or arts, or vocations, and those who are engaged in them. In saying that Law or Medicine is not the end of a University course, I do not mean to imply that the University does not teach Law or Medicine. What indeed can it teach at all, if it does not teach something particular? It teaches *all* knowledge by teaching all *branches* of knowledge, and in no other way. I do but say that there will be this distinction as regards a Professor of Law, or of Medicine, or of Geology, or of Political Economy, in a University and out of it, that out of a University he is in danger of being absorbed and narrowed by his pursuit, and of giving Lectures which are the Lectures of nothing more than a lawyer, physician, geologist, or political economist; whereas in a University he will just know where he and his science stand, he has come to it, as it were, from a height, he has taken a survey of all knowledge, he is kept from extravagance by the very rivalry of other studies, he has gained from them a special illumination and largeness of mind and freedom and self-possession, and he treats his own in consequence with a philosophy and a resource, which belongs not to the study itself, but to his liberal education.

This then is how I should solve the fallacy, for so I must call it, by which Locke and his disciples would frighten us from cultivating the intellect, under the notion that no education is useful which does not teach us some temporal calling, or some mechanical art, or some physical secret. I say that a cultivated intellect, because it is a good in itself, brings with it a power and a grace to every work and occupation which it undertakes, and enables us to be more useful, and to a greater number. There is a duty we owe to human society as such, to the state to which we belong, to the sphere in which we move, to the individuals towards whom we are variously related, and whom we successively encounter in life; and that philosophical or liberal education, as I have called it, which is the proper function of a University, if it refuses the foremost place to professional interest, does but postpone them to the formation of the citizen, and, while it subserves the larger interests of philanthropy, prepares also for the successful prosecution of those merely personal objects which at first sight it seems to disparage.

* * *

10

But I must bring these extracts[4] to an end. Today I have confined myself to saying that that training of the intellect, which is best for the individual himself, best enables him to discharge his duties to society. The Philosopher, indeed, and the man of the world differ in their very notion, but the methods, by which they are respectively formed, are pretty much the same. The Philosopher has the same command of matters of thought, which the true citizen and gentleman has of matters of business and conduct. If then a practical end must be assigned to a University course, I say it is that of training good members of society. Its art is the art of social life, and its end is fitness for the world. It neither confines its views to particular professions on the one hand, nor creates heroes or inspires genius on the other. Works indeed of genius fall under no art; heroic minds come under no rule; a University is not a birthplace of poets or of immortal authors, of founders of schools, leaders of colonies, or conquerors of nations. It does not promise a generation of Aristotles or Newtons, of Napoleons or Washingtons, or Raphaels or Shakespeares, though such miracles of nature it has before now contained

---

4. Quotations cited from other authorities on education.

within its precincts. Nor is it content on the other hand with forming the critic or the experimentalist, the economist or the engineer, though such too it includes within its scope. But a University training is the great ordinary means to a great but ordinary end; it aims at raising the intellectual tone of society, at cultivating the public mind, at purifying the national taste, at supplying true principles to popular enthusiasm and fixed aims to popular aspiration, at giving enlargement and sobriety to the ideas of the age, at facilitating the exercise of political power, and refining the intercourse of private life. It is the education which gives a man a clear conscious view of his own opinions and judgments, a truth in developing them, an eloquence in expressing them, and a force in urging them. It teaches him to see things as they are, to go right to the point, to disentangle a skein of thought, to detect what is sophistical, and to discard what is irrelevant. It prepares him to fill any post with credit, and to master any subject with facility. It shows him how to accommodate himself to others, how to throw himself into their state of mind, how to bring before them his own, how to influence them, how to come to an understanding with them, how to bear with them. He is at home in any society, he has common ground with every class; he knows when to speak and when to be silent; he is able to converse, he is able to listen; he can ask a question pertinently, and gain a lesson seasonably, when he has nothing to impart himself; he is ever ready, yet never in the way; he is a pleasant companion, and a comrade you can depend upon; he knows when to be serious and when to trifle, and he has a sure tact which enables him to trifle with gracefulness and to be serious with effect. He has the repose of a mind which lives in itself, while it lives in the world, and which has resources for its happiness at home when it cannot go abroad. He has a gift which serves him in public, and supports him in retirement,[5] without which good fortune is but vulgar, and with which failure and disappointment have a charm. The art which tends to make a man all this is in the object which it pursues as useful as the art of wealth or the art of health, though it is less susceptible of method, and less tangible, less certain, less complete in its result.

1852, 1873

---

5. In a later work, *The Grammar of Assent* (1870), Newman enlarges on this aspect of his subject in a passage describing the impact that classical literature may have on us at different ages of our lives, a passage admired by James Joyce. "Let us consider, too, how differently young and old are affected by the words of some classic author, such as Homer or Horace. Passages, which to a boy are but rhetorical commonplaces, neither better nor worse than a hundred others which any clever writer might supply, which he gets by heart and thinks very fine, and imitates, as he thinks, successfully, in his own flowing versification, at length come home to him, when long years have passed, and he has had experience of life, and pierce him, as if he had never before known them, with their sad earnestness and vivid exactness. Then he comes to understand how it is that lines, the birth of some chance morning or evening at an Ionian festival, or among the Sabine hills, have lasted generation after generation, for thousands of years, with a power over the mind, and a charm, which the current literature of his own day, with all its obvious advantages, is utterly unable to rival. Perhaps this is the reason of the medieval opinion about Virgil, as if a prophet or magician; his single words and phrases, his pathetic half lines, giving utterance, as the voice of Nature herself, to that pain and weariness, yet hope of better things, which is the experience of her children in every time."

From Apologia Pro Vita Sua

From *Chapter 1. History of My Religious Opinions to the Year 1833*

It may easily be conceived how great a trial it is to me to write the following history of myself; but I must not shrink from the task. The words, "Secretum meum mihi,"[1] keep ringing in my ears; but as men draw towards their end, they care less for disclosures. Nor is it the least part of my trial, to anticipate that, upon first reading what I have written, my friends may consider much in it irrelevant to my purpose; yet I cannot help thinking that, viewed as a whole, it will effect what I propose to myself in giving it to the public.

I was brought up from a child to take great delight in reading the Bible; but I had no formed religious convictions till I was fifteen. Of course I had a perfect knowledge of my Catechism.

After I was grown up, I put on paper my recollections of the thoughts and feelings on religious subjects, which I had at the time that I was a child and a boy,—such as had remained on my mind with sufficient prominence to make me then consider them worth recording. Out of these, written in the Long Vacation of 1820, and transcribed with additions in 1823, I select two, which are at once the most definite among them, and also have a bearing on my later convictions.

1. "I used to wish the Arabian Tales were true: my imagination ran on unknown influences, on magical powers, and talismans. . . . .I thought life might be a dream, or I an Angel, and all this world a deception, my fellow-angels by a playful device concealing themselves from me, and deceiving me with the semblance of a material world."

Again: "Reading in the Spring of 1816 a sentence from [Dr. Watt's] 'Remnants of Time,'[2] entitled 'the Saints unknown to the world,' to the effect, that 'there is nothing in their figure or countenance to distinguish them,' &c., &c., I supposed he spoke of Angels who lived in the world, as it were disguised."

2. The other remark is this: "I was very superstitious, and for some time previous to my conversion" [when I was fifteen] "used constantly to cross myself on going into the dark."

Of course I must have got this practice from some external source or other; but I can make no sort of conjecture whence; and certainly no one had ever spoken to me on the subject of the Catholic religion, which I only knew by name. The French master was an *émigré* Priest, but he was simply made a butt, as French masters too commonly were in that day, and spoke English very imperfectly. There was a Catholic family in the village, old maiden ladies we used to think; but I knew nothing about them. I have of late years heard that there were one or two Catholic boys in the school; but either we were carefully kept from knowing this, or the knowledge of it made simply no impression on our minds. My brother will bear witness how free the school was from Catholic ideas.

---

1. My secret is my own (Latin).
2. *The Improvement of the Mind, with a discourse on Education, and the Remnants of Time, employed*

in prose and verse, by Isaac Watts (1674–1748), a Nonconformist clergyman. All text in brackets was added by Newman.

I had once been into Warwick Street Chapel, with my father, who, I believe, wanted to hear some piece of music; all that I bore away from it was the recollection of a pulpit and a preacher, and a boy swinging a censer.

When I was at Littlemore,[3] I was looking over old copybooks of my school days, and I found among them my first Latin verse-book; and in the first page of it there was a device which almost took my breath away with surprise. I have the book before me now, and have just been showing it to others. I have written in the first page, in my school-boy hand, "John H. Newman, February 11th, 1811, Verse Book;" then follow my first Verses. Between "Verse" and "Book" I have drawn the figure of a solid cross upright, and next to it is, what may indeed be meant for a necklace, but what I cannot make out to be any thing else than a set of beads suspended, with a little cross attached. At this time I was not quite ten years old. I suppose I got these ideas from some romance, Mrs. Radcliffe's or Miss Porter's;[4] or from some religious picture; but the strange thing is, how, among the thousand objects which meet a boy's eyes, these in particular should so have fixed themselves in my mind, that I made them thus practically my own. I am certain there was nothing in the churches I attended, or the prayer books I read, to suggest them. It must be recollected that Anglican churches and prayer books were not decorated in those days as I believe they are now.

When I was fourteen, I read Paine's Tracts against the Old Testament,[5] and found pleasure in thinking of the objections which were contained in them. Also, I read some of Hume's[6] Essays; and perhaps that on Miracles. So at least I gave my Father to understand; but perhaps it was a brag. Also, I recollect copying out some French verses, perhaps Voltaire's,[7] in denial of the immortality of the soul, and saying to myself something like "How dreadful, but how plausible!"

When I was fifteen, (in the autumn of 1816,) a great change of thought took place in me. I fell under the influences of a definite Creed, and received into my intellect impressions of dogma, which, through God's mercy, have never been effaced or obscured. Above and beyond the conversations and sermons of the excellent man, long dead, the Rev. Walter Mayers, of Pembroke College, Oxford, who was the human means of this beginning of divine faith in me, was the effect of the books which he put into my hands, all of the school of Calvin.[8] One of the first books I read was a work of Romaine's;[9] I neither recollect the title nor the contents, except one doctrine, which of course I do not include among those which I believe to have come from a divine source, viz. the doctrine of final perseverance.[1] I received it at once, and believed that the inward conversion of which I was conscious, (and of which I still am more certain than that I have hands and feet,) would last into the next life, and that I was elected to eternal glory. I have no consciousness that this belief had any tendency whatever to lead me to be careless about pleasing God. I retained it till the age of twenty-one, when it

3. A village near Oxford, whose parish was under Newman's care.
4. Ann Radcliffe (1764–1823) and Jane Porter (1776–1850), writers of romances.
5. Probably *The Age of Reason* by Thomas Paine (1737–1809), an attack on Christianity and the Bible from a Deist point of view.
6. David Hume (1711–1776), Scottish philosopher.

7. French satirist and philosopher (1694–1778).
8. John Calvin (1509–1564), Protestant reformer who stressed predestination, the sinfulness of humankind, and the power of grace. Mayers was one of Newman's schoolmasters.
9. William Romaine (1714–1795), Anglican clergyman and writer, of the Calvinist school.
1. The Calvinist view that God will not let His chosen fall away from Him.

gradually faded away; but I believe that it had some influence on my opinions, in the direction of those childish imaginations which I have already mentioned, viz. in isolating me from the objects which surrounded me, in confirming me in my mistrust of the reality of material phenomena, and making me rest in the thought of two and two only absolute and luminously self-evident beings, myself and my Creator;—for while I considered myself predestined to salvation, my mind did not dwell upon others, as fancying them simply passed over, not predestined to eternal death. I only thought of the mercy to myself.

* * *

There is one remaining source of my opinions to be mentioned, and that far from the least important. In proportion as I moved out of the shadow of that liberalism which had hung over my course, my early devotion towards the Fathers returned; and in the Long Vacation of 1828 I set about to read them chronologically, beginning with St. Ignatius and St. Justin.[2] About 1830 a proposal was made to me by Mr. Hugh Rose, who with Mr. Lyall[3] (afterwards Dean of Canterbury) was providing writers for a Theological Library, to furnish them with a History of the Principal Councils. I accepted it, and at once set to work on the Council of Nicæa.[4] It was to launch myself on an ocean with currents innumerable; and I was drifted back first to the ante-Nicene history, and then to the Church of Alexandria. The work at last appeared under the title of "The Arians of the Fourth Century;" and of its 422 pages, the first 117 consisted of introductory matter, and the Council of Nicæa did not appear till the 254th, and then occupied at most twenty pages.

I do not know when I first learnt to consider that Antiquity was the true exponent of the doctrines of Christianity and the basis of the Church of England; but I take it for granted that the works of Bishop Bull,[5] which at this time I read, were my chief introduction to this principle. The course of reading, which I pursued in the composition of my volume, was directly adapted to develop it in my mind. What principally attracted me in the ante-Nicene period was the great Church of Alexandria, the historical center of teaching in those times. Of Rome for some centuries comparatively little is known. The battle of Arianism was first fought in Alexandria; Athanasius, the champion of the truth, was Bishop of Alexandria; and in his writings he refers to the great religious names of an earlier date, to Origen, Dionysius,[6] and others, who were the glory of its see, or of its school. The broad philosophy of Clement[7] and Origen carried me away; the philosophy, not the theological doctrine; and I have drawn out some features of it in my volume, with the zeal and freshness, but with the partiality, of a neophyte. Some portions of their teaching, magnificent in themselves, came like music to my inward ear, as if the response to ideas, which, with little external to encourage

2. St. Ignatius of Antioch (ca. 35–ca. 107) and St. Justin Martyr (ca. 100–ca. 165), fathers of the church and early theological writers whose authority on doctrinal matters carried special weight.
3. Hugh James Rose (1795–1838) and William Rowe Lyall (1788–1857), contemporary theologians.
4. Convened by the emperor Constantine in 325 to deal with Arianism, a heresy that denied the full

divinity of Christ. The Church of Alexandria was a center of Christian thought in the 3rd–5th centuries.
5. George Bull (1634–1710), Anglican theologian.
6. Alexandrian theologians of the 1st and 2nd centuries. St. Athanasius (ca. 296–373), an anti-Arian leader at the Council of Nicaea.
7. Another early Alexandrian theologian.

them, I had cherished so long. These were based on the mystical or sacramental principle, and spoke of the various Economies or Dispensations of the Eternal. I understood these passages to mean that the exterior world, physical and historical, was but the manifestation to our senses of realities greater than itself.[8] Nature was a parable: Scripture was an allegory: pagan literature, philosophy, and mythology, properly understood, were but a preparation for the Gospel. The Greek poets and sages were in a certain sense prophets; for "thoughts beyond their thought to those high bards were given."[9] There had been a directly divine dispensation granted to the Jews; but there had been in some sense a dispensation carried on in favour of the Gentiles. He who had taken the seed of Jacob for His elect people had not therefore cast the rest of mankind out of His sight. In the fulness of time both Judaism and Paganism had come to nought; the outward framework, which concealed yet suggested the Living Truth, had never been intended to last, and it was dissolving under the beams of the Sun of Justice which shone behind it and through it. The process of change had been slow; it had been done not rashly, but by rule and measure, "at sundry times and in divers manners,"[1] first one disclosure and then another, till the whole evangelical doctrine was brought into full manifestation. And thus room was made for the anticipation of further and deeper disclosures, of truths still under the veil of the letter, and in their season to be revealed. The visible world still remains without its divine interpretation; Holy Church in her sacraments and her hierarchical appointments, will remain, even to the end of the world, after all but a symbol of those heavenly facts which fill eternity. Her mysteries are but the expressions in human language of truths to which the human mind is unequal. It is evident how much there was in all this in correspondence with the thoughts which had attracted me when I was young, and with the doctrine which I have already associated with the Analogy and the Christian Year.[2]

It was, I suppose, to the Alexandrian school and to the early Church, that I owe in particular what I definitely held about the Angels. I viewed them, not only as the ministers employed by the Creator in the Jewish and Christian dispensations, as we find on the face of Scripture, but as carrying on, as Scripture also implies, the Economy of the Visible World. I considered them as the real causes of motion, light, and life, and of those elementary principles of the physical universe, which, when offered in their developments to our senses, suggest to us the notion of cause and effect, and of what are called the laws of nature. This doctrine I have drawn out in my Sermon for Michaelmas day, written in 1831. I say of the Angels, "Every breath of air and ray of light and heat, every beautiful prospect, is, as it were, the skirts of their garments, the waving of the robes of those whose faces see God." Again, I ask what would be the thoughts of a man who, "when examining a flower, or a herb, or a pebble, or a ray of light, which he treats as something so beneath him in the scale of existence, suddenly discovered that he was in the presence of some powerful being who was hidden behind the visible

8. Cf. Carlyle's Clothes Philosophy in *Sartor Resartus* (p. 1077).
9. John Keble's *The Christian Year* (1827), a collection of poems for the Christian calendar.
1. Hebrews 1.1.

2. Joseph Butler's *The Analogy of Religion* (1736), a theological work, and Keble's *The Christian Year.* Newman had previously discussed the influence both works had on him.

things he was inspecting,—who, though concealing his wise hand, was giving them their beauty, grace, and perfection, as being God's instrument for the purpose,—nay, whose robe and ornaments those objects were, which he was so eager to analyze?" and I therefore remark that "we may say with grateful and simple hearts with the Three Holy Children, 'O all ye works of the Lord, &c., &c., bless ye the Lord, praise Him, and magnify Him for ever.' "

* * *

While I was engaged in writing my work upon the Arians, great events were happening at home and abroad, which brought out into form and passionate expression the various beliefs which had so gradually been winning their way into my mind. Shortly before, there had been a Revolution in France;[3] the Bourbons had been dismissed: and I held that it was unchristian for nations to cast off their governors, and, much more, sovereigns who had the divine right of inheritance. Again, the great Reform Agitation was going on around me as I wrote. The Whigs had come into power; Lord Grey[4] had told the Bishops to set their house in order, and some of the Prelates had been insulted and threatened in the streets of London. The vital question was, how were we to keep the Church from being liberalized? there was such apathy on the subject in some quarters, such imbecile alarm in others; the true principles of Churchmanship seemed so radically decayed, and there was such distraction in the councils of the Clergy. Blomfield,[5] the Bishop of London of the day, an active and open-hearted man, had been for years engaged in diluting the high orthodoxy of the Church by the introduction of members of the Evangelical body into places of influence and trust. He had deeply offended men who agreed in opinion with myself, by an off-hand saying (as it was reported) to the effect that belief in the Apostolical succession had gone out with the Non-jurors.[6] "We can count you," he said to some of the gravest and most venerated persons of the old school. And the Evangelical party itself, with their late successes, seemed to have lost that simplicity and unworldliness which I admired so much in Milner and Scott.[7] It was not that I did not venerate such men as Ryder,[8] the then Bishop of Lichfield, and others of similar sentiments, who were not yet promoted out of the ranks of the Clergy, but I thought little of the Evangelicals as a class. I thought they played into the hands of the Liberals. With the Establishment thus divided and threatened, thus ignorant of its true strength, I compared that fresh vigorous Power of which I was reading in the first centuries. In her triumphant zeal on behalf of that Primeval Mystery, to which I had had so great a devotion from my youth, I recognized the movement of my Spiritual Mother. "Incessu patuit Dea."[9] The self-conquest of her Ascetics, the patience of her Martyrs, the irresistible determination of her Bishops, the joyous swing of her advance, both exalted and abashed me. I said to myself,

3. The July Revolution of 1830.
4. Earl Grey (1764–1845), prime minister (1830–34) during the "Agitation" leading to the passage of the Reform Bill of 1832. There were also growing demands for reform of ecclesiastical abuses.
5. Charles James Blomfield (1786–1857).
6. English and Scottish clergymen who refused to take the oath of allegiance to William and Mary when they succeeded James II. "Apostolical suc-

cession": the doctrine whereby the ministry of the Church is understood to be derived from the apostles by continuous succession.
7. Joseph Milner (1744–1797) and Thomas Scott (1747–1821), Evangelical theologians.
8. Henry Ryder (1777–1836), a prominent Evangelical.
9. The goddess stood revealed by her walk (Latin; Aeneid 1.405).

"Look on this picture and on that;"[1] I felt affection for my own Church, but not tenderness; I felt dismay at her prospects, anger and scorn at her do-nothing perplexity. I thought that if Liberalism once got a footing within her, it was sure of the victory in the event. I saw that Reformation principles were powerless to rescue her. As to leaving her, the thought never crossed my imagination; still I ever kept before me that there was something greater than the Established Church, and that that was the Church Catholic and Apostolic, set up from the beginning, of which she was but the local presence and the organ. She was nothing, unless she was this. She must be dealt with strongly, or she would be lost. There was need of a second reformation.

At this time I was disengaged from College duties, and my health had suffered from the labour involved in the composition of my Volume. It was ready for the Press in July, 1832, though not published till the end of 1833. I was easily persuaded to join Hurrell Froude[2] and his Father, who were going to the south of Europe for the health of the former.

We set out in December, 1832. It was during this expedition that my Verses which are in the Lyra Apostolica were written;—a few indeed before it, but not more than one or two of them after it. Exchanging, as I was, definite Tutorial work, and the literary quiet and pleasant friendships of the last six years, for foreign countries and an unknown future, I naturally was led to think that some inward changes, as well as some larger course of action, were coming upon me. At Whitchurch, while waiting for the down mail to Falmouth, I wrote the verses about my Guardian Angel, which begin with these words: "Are these the tracks of some unearthly Friend?" and which go on to speak of "the vision" which haunted me:—that vision is more or less brought out in the whole series of these compositions.

I went to various coasts of the Mediterranean; parted with my friends at Rome; went down for the second time to Sicily without companion, at the end of April; and got back to England by Palermo in the early part of July. The strangeness of foreign life threw me back into myself; I found pleasure in historical sites and beautiful scenes, not in men and manners. We kept clear of Catholics throughout our tour. I had a conversation with the Dean of Malta, a most pleasant man, lately dead; but it was about the Fathers, and the Library of the great church. I knew the Abbate Santini, at Rome, who did no more than copy for me the Gregorian tones. Froude and I made two calls upon Monsignore (now Cardinal) Wiseman[3] at the Collegio Inglese, shortly before we left Rome. Once we heard him preach at a church in the Corso. I do not recollect being in a room with any other ecclesiastics, except a Priest at Castro-Giovanni in Sicily, who called on me when I was ill, and with whom I wished to hold a controversy. As to Church Services, we attended the Tenebræ, at the Sestine, for the sake of the Miserere;[4] and that was all. My general feeling was, "All, save the spirit of man, is divine." I saw nothing but what was external; of the hidden life of Catholics I knew nothing. I was still more driven back into myself, and felt my isolation. England was in my thoughts solely, and the news from England came rarely and imper-

1. Hamlet's words, when he compares the picture of his father to that of his uncle (Shakespeare's *Hamlet* 3.4.53).
2. Richard Hurrell Froude (1803–1836), close friend of Newman's and fellow Tractarian.

3. Nicholas Patrick Stephen Wiseman (1802–1865), who did much to advance Roman Catholicism in England.
4. Psalm 51, part of the "Tenebrae" service, which is for the last three days of Holy Week.

fectly. The Bill for the Suppression of the Irish Sees[5] was in progress, and filled my mind. I had fierce thoughts against the Liberals.

It was the success of the Liberal cause which fretted me inwardly. I became fierce against its instruments and its manifestations. A French vessel was at Algiers; I would not even look at the tricolour.[6] On my return, though forced to stop twenty-four hours at Paris, I kept indoors the whole time, and all that I saw of that beautiful city was what I saw from the Diligence.[7] The Bishop of London had already sounded me as to my filling one of the White-hall preacherships, which he had just then put on a new footing; but I was indignant at the line which he was taking, and from my Steamer I had sent home a letter declining the appointment by anticipation, should it be offered to me. At this time I was specially annoyed with Dr. Arnold,[8] though it did not last into later years. Some one, I think, asked, in conversation at Rome, whether a certain interpretation of Scripture was Christian? it was answered that Dr. Arnold took it; I interposed, "But is *he* a Christian?" The subject went out of my head at once; when afterwards I was taxed with it, I could say no more in explanation, than (what I believe was the fact) that I must have had in mind some free views of Dr. Arnold about the Old Testament:—I thought I must have meant, "Arnold answers for the interpretation, but who is to answer for Arnold?" It was at Rome, too, that we began the Lyra Apostolica which appeared monthly in the British Magazine. The motto shows the feeling of both Froude and myself at the time: we borrowed from M. Bunsen a Homer, and Froude chose the words in which Achilles, on returning to the battle, says, "You shall know the difference, now that I am back again."[9]

Especially when I was left by myself, the thought came upon me that deliverance is wrought, not by the many but by the few, not by bodies but by persons. Now it was, I think, that I repeated to myself the words, which had ever been dear to me from my school days, "Exoriare aliquis!"[1]—now too, that Southey's beautiful poem of Thalaba,[2] for which I had an immense liking, came forcibly to my mind. I began to think that I had a mission. There are sentences of my letters to my friends to this effect, if they are not destroyed. When we took leave of Monsignore Wiseman, he had courteously expressed a wish that we might make a second visit to Rome; I said with great gravity, "We have a work to do in England." I went down at once to Sicily, and the presentiment grew stronger. I struck into the middle of the island, and fell ill of a fever at Leonforte. My servant thought that I was dying, and begged for my last directions. I gave them, as he wished; but I said, "I shall not die." I repeated, "I shall not die, for I have not sinned against light, I have not sinned against light." I never have been able quite to make out what I meant.

I got to Castro-Giovanni, and was laid up there for nearly three weeks. Towards the end of May I left for Palermo, taking three days for the journey. Before starting from my inn in the morning of May 26th or 27th, I sat down

5. For suppressing ten of the twenty-two bishoprics of the Church of Ireland, introduced in 1833.
6. The French flag.
7. The stagecoach.
8. Thomas Arnold (1795–1842), an educational and religious reformer of liberal views; father of Matthew Arnold.

9. *Iliad* 18.125. C. J. K. Bunsen (1791–1860), Prussian minister to the Vatican.
1. May someone arise! (Latin; *Aeneid* 4.265).
2. Robert Southey's 1801 poem tells the story of a young Arab, appointed to destroy a race of sorcerers.

on my bed, and began to sob violently. My servant, who had acted as my nurse, asked what ailed me. I could only answer him, "I have a work to do in England."

I was aching to get home; yet for want of a vessel I was kept at Palermo for three weeks. I began to visit the Churches, and they calmed my impatience, though I did not attend any services. I knew nothing of the Presence of the Blessed Sacrament there. At last I got off in an orange boat, bound for Marseilles. Then it was that I wrote the lines, "Lead, kindly light," which have since become well known. We were becalmed a whole week in the Straits of Bonifacio. I was writing verses the whole time of my passage. At length I got to Marseilles, and set off for England. The fatigue of travelling was too much for me, and I was laid up for several days at Lyons. At last I got off again, and did not stop night or day, (except a compulsory delay at Paris,) till I reached England, and my mother's house. My brother had arrived from Persia only a few hours before. This was on the Tuesday. The following Sunday, July 14th, Mr. Keble preached the Assize Sermon[3] in the University Pulpit. It was published under the title of "National Apostasy." I have ever considered and kept the day, as the start of the religious movement of 1833.

* * *

From *Liberalism*

I have been asked to explain more fully what it is I mean by "Liberalism," because merely to call it the Antidogmatic Principle is to tell very little about it.

* * *

Now by Liberalism I mean false liberty of thought, or the exercise of thought upon matters, in which, from the constitution of the human mind, thought cannot be brought to any successful issue, and therefore is out of place. Among such matters are first principles of whatever kind; and of these the most sacred and momentous are especially to be reckoned the truths of Revelation. Liberalism then is the mistake of subjecting to human judgment those revealed doctrines which are in their nature beyond and independent of it, and of claiming to determine on intrinsic grounds the truth and value of propositions which rest for their reception simply on the external authority of the Divine Word.

* * *

I conclude this notice of Liberalism in Oxford, and the party which was antagonistic to it,[4] with some propositions in detail, which, as a member of the latter, and together with the High Church, I earnestly denounced and abjured.

1. No religious tenet is important, unless reason shows it to be so.

Therefore, e.g., the doctrine of the Athanasian Creed[5] is not to be insisted on, unless it tends to convert the soul; and the doctrine of the Atonement is to be insisted on, if it does convert the soul.

---

3. In which Keble used the doctrine of apostolic succession to condemn the bill to suppress the Irish bishops as an apostasy.

4. I.e., the Tractarians.
5. Belief in the Trinity.

2. No one can believe what he does not understand.

Therefore, e.g., there are no mysteries in true religion.

3. No theological doctrine is anything more than an opinion which happens to be held by bodies of men.

Therefore, e.g., no creed, as such, is necessary for salvation.

4. It is dishonest in a man to make an act of faith in what he has not had brought home to him by actual proof.

Therefore, e.g., the mass of men ought not absolutely to believe in the divine authority of the Bible.

5. It is immoral in a man to believe more than he can spontaneously receive as being congenial to his moral and mental nature.

Therefore, e.g., a given individual is not bound to believe in eternal punishment.

6. No revealed doctrines or precepts may reasonably stand in the way of scientific conclusions.

Therefore, e.g., Political Economy may reverse our Lord's declarations about poverty and riches, or a system of Ethics may teach that the highest condition of body is ordinarily essential to the highest state of mind.

7. Christianity is necessarily modified by the growth of civilization, and the exigencies of times.

Therefore, e.g., the Catholic priesthood, though necessary in the Middle Ages, may be superseded now.

8. There is a system of religion more simply true than Christianity as it has ever been received.

Therefore, e.g., we may advance that Christianity is the "corn of wheat" which has been dead for 1800 years, but at length will bear fruit; and that Mahometanism is the manly religion, and existing Christianity the womanish.

9. There is a right of Private Judgment: that is, there is no existing authority on earth competent to interfere with the liberty of individuals in reasoning and judging for themselves about the Bible and its contents, as they severally please.

Therefore, e.g., religious establishments requiring subscription are Antichristian.

10. There are rights of conscience such that everyone may lawfully advance a claim to profess and teach what is false and wrong in matters, religious, social, and moral, provided that to his private conscience it seems absolutely true and right.

Therefore, e.g., individuals have a right to preach and practice fornication and polygamy.

11. There is no such thing as a national or state conscience.

Therefore, e.g., no judgments can fall upon a sinful or infidel nation.

12. The civil power has no positive duty, in a normal state of things, to maintain religious truth.

Therefore, e.g., blasphemy and sabbath-breaking are not rightly punishable by law.

13. Utility and expedience are the measure of political duty.

Therefore, e.g., no punishment may be enacted, on the ground that God commands it: e.g., on the text, "Whoso sheddeth man's blood, by man shall his blood be shed."[6]

---

6. Genesis 9.6.

14. The Civil Power may dispose of Church property without sacrilege.

Therefore, e.g., Henry VIII committed no sin in his spoliations.[7]

15. The Civil Power has the right of ecclesiastical jurisdiction and administration.

Therefore, e.g., Parliament may impose articles of faith on the Church or suppress Dioceses.[8]

16. It is lawful to rise in arms against legitimate princes.

Therefore, e.g., the Puritans in the seventeenth century, and the French in the eighteenth, were justified in their Rebellion and Revolution respectively.

17. The people are the legitimate source of power.

Therefore, e.g., Universal Suffrage is among the natural rights of man.

18. Virtue is the child of knowledge, and vice of ignorance.

Therefore, e.g., education, periodical literature, railroad traveling, ventilation, drainage, and the arts of life, when fully carried out, serve to make a population moral and happy.

All of these propositions, and many others too, were familiar to me thirty years ago, as in the number of the tenets of Liberalism, and, while I gave in to none of them except No. 12, and perhaps No. 11, and partly No. 1, before I began to publish, so afterwards I wrote against most of them in some part or other of my Anglican works.

* * *

I need hardly say that the above Note is mainly historical. How far the Liberal party of 1830–40 really held the above eighteen Theses, which I attributed to them, and how far and in what sense I should oppose those Theses now, could scarcely be explained without a separate Dissertation.

1864–65

7. The dissolution of the monasteries by Henry VIII.
8. An allusion to the abolishing of ten Irish bishoprics by liberal reformers in Parliament in 1833.

This instance of interference by the state in affairs of the Church had prompted Newman and his associates into organizing what became the Oxford movement.

JOHN STUART MILL
1806–1873

In many American colleges the writings of J. S. Mill are studied in courses in government or in philosophy, and it may therefore be asked why they should also have a place in the study of literature. It may seem that Mill is less literary than other Victorian prose writers. His analytic mind, preoccupied with abstractions rather than with the concrete details that are the concern of the more typical writer; his self-effacing manner and his relatively transparent style are the marks of an author whose value lies in generalizations from personal experience rather than in the rendering of particular experiences for their own sake. Yet a knowledge of Mill's writings is essential to our understanding of Victorian literature. He is one of the leading figures in the intellectual history of his century, a thinker whose honest grappling with the political and religious problems of his age was to have a profound influence on writers as diverse as Arnold, Swinburne, and Hardy.

Mill was educated at home in London under the direction of his father, James Mill, a leader of the Utilitarians. James Mill believed that ordinary schooling fails to develop our intellectual capacities early enough, and he demonstrated his point by the extraordinary results he achieved in training his son. As a child, John Stuart Mill read Greek and Latin; and as a boy, he could carry on intelligent discussions of problems in mathematics, philosophy, and economics. By the time he was fourteen, as he reports in his *Autobiography*, his intensive education enabled him to start his career "with an advantage of a quarter of a century" over his contemporaries.

Mill worked in the office of the East India Company for many years and also served a term in Parliament in the 1860s; but his principal energies were devoted to his writings on such subjects as logic and philosophy, political principles, and economics. He began as a disciple of the Utilitarian theories of his father and of Jeremy Bentham but became gradually dissatisfied with the narrowness of their conception of human motives. His honesty and open-mindedness enabled him to appreciate the values of such anti-Utilitarians as Coleridge and Carlyle and, whenever possible, to incorporate some of these values into the Utilitarian system. In part, this sympathy was gained by the lesson he learned through experiencing a nervous breakdown during his early twenties. This painful event, described in a chapter of his *Autobiography*, taught him that the lack of concern for people's affections and emotions characteristic of the Utilitarian system of thought (and typified by his own education) was a fatal flaw in that system. His tribute to the therapeutic value of art (because of its effect on human emotions), both in his *Autobiography* and in his early essay *What Is Poetry?* would have astonished Mill's master, Bentham, who had equated poetry with pushpin, a trifling game.

Mill's emotional life was also broadened by his love for Harriet Taylor, a married woman who shared his intellectual interests and eventually became his wife, in 1851, after the death of her husband. Mill later described her as "the inspirer, and in part the author, of all that is best in my writings." They shared a commitment to the cause of female emancipation, one of several unpopular movements to which Mill was dedicated. Throughout human history, as he saw it, the role of a husband has always been legally that of a tyrant, and the object of his far-seeing essay *The Subjection of Women* (1869) was to change law and public opinion so that half the human race might be liberated from slavery into the status of individuals. The subjection of women was, however, only one aspect of the tyranny against which he fought. His fundamental concern was to prevent the subjection of individuals in a democracy. His classic treatise *On Liberty* (1859) is not a traditional liberal attack against tyrannical kings or dictators; it is an attack against tyrannical majorities. Mill foresaw that in democracies such as the United States the pressure toward conformity might crush all individualists (intellectual individualists in particular) to the level of what he called a "collective mediocrity." Throughout all of his writings, even in his discussions of the advantages of socialism, Mill is concerned with demonstrating that the individual is more important than institutions such as church or state. In *On Liberty* we find a characteristic example of the process of his reasoning; but here, where the theme of individualism is central, his logic is charged with eloquence.

A similar eloquence is evident in a passage from his *Principles of Political Economy* (1848), a prophetic comment on the fate of the individual in an overpopulated world:

> There is room in the world, no doubt, and even in old countries, for a great increase of population, supposing the arts of life go on improving, and capital to increase. But even if innocuous, I confess I see very little reason for desiring it. . . . It is not good for a man to be kept perforce at all times in the presence of his species. A world from which solitude is extirpated, is a very poor ideal. Solitude, in the sense of being often alone, is essential to any depth of meditation

or of character: and solitude in the presence of natural beauty and grandeur, is the cradle of thoughts and aspirations which are not only good for the individual, but which society could ill do without. Nor is there much satisfaction in contemplating the world with nothing left to the spontaneous activity of nature; with every rood of land brought into cultivation, which is capable of growing food for human beings; every flowery waste or natural pasture ploughed up, all quadrupeds or birds which are not domesticated for man's use exterminated as his rivals for food, every hedgerow or superfluous tree rooted out, and scarcely a place left where a wild shrub or flower could grow without being eradicated as a weed in the name of improved agriculture. If the earth must lose that great portion of its pleasantness which it owes to things that the unlimited increase of wealth and population would extirpate from it, for the mere purpose of enabling it to support a larger, but not a better or happier population, I sincerely hope, for the sake of posterity, that they will be content to be stationary, long before necessity compels them to it.

What Is Poetry?

It has often been asked, What Is Poetry? And many and various are the answers which have been returned. The vulgarest of all—one with which no person possessed of the faculties to which poetry addresses itself can ever have been satisfied—is that which confounds poetry with metrical composition; yet to this wretched mockery of a definition many have been led back by the failure of all their attempts to find any other that would distinguish what they have been accustomed to call poetry from much which they have known only under other names.

That, however, the word "poetry" imports something quite peculiar in its nature; something which may exist in what is called prose as well as in verse; something which does not even require the instrument of words, but can speak through the other audible symbols called musical sounds, and even through the visible ones which are the language of sculpture, painting, and architecture—all this, we believe, is and must be felt, though perhaps indistinctly, by all upon whom poetry in any of its shapes produces any impression beyond that of tickling the ear. The distinction between poetry and what is not poetry, whether explained or not, is felt to be fundamental; and, where every one feels a difference, a difference there must be. All other appearances may be fallacious; but the appearance of a difference is a real difference. Appearances too, like other things, must have a cause; and that which can cause anything, even an illusion, must be a reality. And hence, while a half-philosophy disdains the classifications and distinctions indicated by popular language, philosophy carried to its highest point frames new ones, but rarely sets aside the old, content with correcting and regularizing them. It cuts fresh channels for thought, but does not fill up such as it finds ready-made: it traces, on the contrary, more deeply, broadly, and distinctly, those into which the current has spontaneously flowed.

Let us then attempt, in the way of modest inquiry, not to coerce and confine Nature within the bounds of an arbitrary definition, but rather to find the boundaries which she herself has set, and erect a barrier round them; not calling mankind to account for having misapplied the word "poetry," but attempting to clear up the conception which they already attach to it, and to bring forward as a distinct principle that which, as a vague feeling, has really guided them in their employment of the term.

The object of poetry is confessedly to act upon the emotions; and therein is poetry sufficiently distinguished from what Wordsworth affirms to be its logical opposite;[1] namely, not prose but matter of fact, or science. The one addresses itself to the belief; the other, to the feelings. The one does its work by convincing or persuading; the other, by moving. The one acts by presenting a proposition to the understanding; the other, by offering interesting objects of contemplation to the sensibilities.

This, however, leaves us very far from a definition of poetry. This distinguishes it from one thing; but we are bound to distinguish it from everything. To bring thoughts or images before the mind, for the purpose of acting upon the emotions, does not belong to poetry alone. It is equally the province (for example) of the novelist: and yet the faculty of the poet and that of the novelist are as distinct as any other two faculties; as the faculties of the novelist and of the orator, or of the poet and the metaphysician. The two characters may be united, as characters the most disparate may; but they have no natural connection.

Many of the greatest poems are in the form of fictitious narratives; and, in almost all good serious fictions, there is true poetry. But there is a radical distinction between the interest felt in a story as such, and the interest excited by poetry; for the one is derived from incident, the other from the representation of feeling. In one, the source of the emotion excited is the exhibition of a state or states of human sensibility; in the other, of a series of states of mere outward circumstances. Now, all minds are capable of being affected more or less by representations of the latter kind, and all, or almost all, by those of the former; yet the two sources of interest correspond to two distinct and (as respects their greatest development) mutually exclusive characters of mind.

At what age is the passion for a story, for almost any kind of story, merely as a story, the most intense? In childhood. But that also is the age at which poetry, even of the simplest description, is least relished and least understood; because the feelings with which it is especially conversant are yet undeveloped, and, not having been even in the slightest degree experienced, cannot be sympathized with. In what stage of the progress of society, again, is storytelling most valued, and the storyteller in greatest request and honor? In a rude state like that of the Tartars and Arabs at this day, and of almost all nations in the earliest ages. But, in this state of society, there is little poetry except ballads, which are mostly narrative—that is, essentially stories—and derive their principal interest from the incidents. Considered as poetry, they are of the lowest and most elementary kind: the feelings depicted, or rather indicated, are the simplest our nature has; such joys and griefs as the immediate pressure of some outward event excites in rude minds, which live wholly immersed in outward things, and have never, either from choice or a force they could not resist, turned themselves to the contemplation of the world within. Passing now from childhood, and from the childhood of society, to the grown-up men and women of this most grown-up and unchildlike age, the minds and hearts of greatest depth and elevation

---

1. In his "Preface" to *Lyrical Ballads*.

are commonly those which take greatest delight in poetry: the shallowest and emptiest, on the contrary, are, at all events, not those least addicted to novel-reading. This accords, too, with all analogous experience of human nature. The sort of persons whom not merely in books, but in their lives, we find perpetually engaged in hunting for excitement from without, are invariably those who do not possess, either in the vigor of their intellectual powers or in the depth of their sensibilities, that which would enable them to find ample excitement nearer home. The most idle and frivolous persons take a natural delight in fictitious narrative: the excitement it affords is of the kind which comes from without. Such persons are rarely lovers of poetry, though they may fancy themselves so because they relish novels in verse. But poetry, which is the delineation of the deeper and more secret workings of human emotion, is interesting only to those to whom it recalls what they have felt, or whose imagination it stirs up to conceive what they could feel, or what they might have been able to feel, had their outward circumstances been different.

Poetry, when it is really such, is truth; and fiction also, if it is good for anything, is truth: but they are different truths. The truth of poetry is to paint the human soul truly: the truth of fiction is to give a true picture of life. The two kinds of knowledge are different, and come by different ways, come mostly to different persons. Great poets are often proverbially ignorant of life. What they know has come by observation of themselves: they have found within them one highly delicate and sensitive specimen of human nature, on which the laws of emotion are written in large characters, such as can be read off without much study. Other knowledge of mankind, such as comes to men of the world by outward experience, is not indispensable to them as poets: but, to the novelist, such knowledge is all in all; he has to describe outward things, not the inward man; actions and events, not feelings; and it will not do for him to be numbered among those, who, as Madame Roland said of Brissot,[2] know man, but not *men*.

All this is no bar to the possibility of combining both elements, poetry and narrative or incident, in the same work, and calling it either a novel or a poem; but so may red and white combine on the same human features or on the same canvas. There is one order of composition which requires the union of poetry and incident, each in its highest kind—the dramatic. Even there, the two elements are perfectly distinguishable, and may exist of unequal quality and in the most various proportion. The incidents of a dramatic poem may be scanty and ineffective, though the delineation of passion and character may be of the highest order, as in Goethe's admirable "Torquato Tasso"; or, again, the story as a mere story may be well got up for effect, as is the case with some of the most trashy productions of the Minerva Press:[3] it may even be, what those are not, a coherent and probable series of events, though there be scarcely a feeling exhibited which is not represented falsely, or in a manner absolutely commonplace. The combination of the two excellences is what renders Shakespeare so generally acceptable, each sort of readers finding in him what is suitable to their faculties. To the many, he is great as a storyteller; to the few, as a poet.

In limiting poetry to the delineation of states of feeling, and denying the

2. Jacques-Pierre Brissot (1754–1793), a leading reformer during the French Revolution, is characterized in the *Mémoires* of Jeanne-Manon Roland (1754–1793).

3. An early-19th-century publishing house that fostered the production of sentimental novels.

name where nothing is delineated but outward objects, we may be thought to have done what we promised to avoid—to have not found, but made, a definition in opposition to the usage of language, since it is established by common consent that there is a poetry called descriptive. We deny the charge. Description is not poetry because there is descriptive poetry, no more than science is poetry because there is such a thing as a didactic poem. But an object which admits of being described, or a truth which may fill a place in a scientific treatise, may also furnish an occasion for the generation of poetry, which we thereupon choose to call descriptive or didactic. The poetry is not in the object itself, nor in the scientific truth itself, but in the state of mind in which the one and the other may be contemplated. The mere delineation of the dimensions and colors of external objects is not poetry, no more than a geometrical ground-plan of St. Peter's or Westminster Abbey is painting. Descriptive poetry consists, no doubt, in description, but in description of things as they appear, not as they are; and it paints them, not in their bare and natural lineaments, but seen through the medium and arrayed in the colors of the imagination set in action by the feelings. If a poet describes a lion, he does not describe him as a naturalist would, nor even as a traveler would, who was intent upon stating the truth, the whole truth, and nothing but the truth. He describes him by imagery, that is, by suggesting the most striking likenesses and contrasts which might occur to a mind contemplating a lion, in the state of awe, wonder, or terror, which the spectacle naturally excites, or is, on the occasion, supposed to excite. Now, this is describing the lion professedly, but the state of excitement of the spectator really. The lion may be described falsely or with exaggeration and the poetry be all the better: but, if the human emotion be not painted with scrupulous truth, the poetry is bad poetry, i.e., is not poetry at all, but a failure.

Thus far, our progress towards a clear view of the essentials of poetry has brought us very close to the last two attempts at a definition of poetry which we happen to have seen in print, both of them by poets, and men of genius. The one is by Ebenezer Elliott, the author of "Corn-law Rhymes," and other poems of still greater merit. "Poetry," says he, "is impassioned truth."[4] The other is by a writer in "Blackwood's Magazine," and comes, we think, still nearer the mark. He defines poetry, "man's thoughts tinged by his feelings." There is in either definition a near approximation to what we are in search of. Every truth which a human being can enunciate, every thought, even every outward impression, which can enter into his consciousness, may become poetry, when shown through any impassioned medium; when invested with the coloring of joy, or grief, or pity, or affection, or admiration, or reverence, or awe, or even hatred or terror; and, unless so colored, nothing, be it as interesting as it may, is poetry. But both these definitions fail to discriminate between poetry and eloquence. Eloquence, as well as poetry, is impassioned truth; eloquence, as well as poetry, is thoughts colored by the feelings. Yet common apprehension and philosophic criticism alike recognize a distinction between the two: there is much that everyone would call eloquence, which no one would think of classing as poetry. A question will sometimes arise, whether some particular author is a poet; and those who maintain the negative commonly allow, that, though not a poet, he is a highly

4. In the "Preface" to *Corn-Law Rhymes* (1828) by Ebenezer Elliott (1781–1849).

eloquent writer. The distinction between poetry and eloquence appears to us to be equally fundamental with the distinction between poetry and narrative, or between poetry and description, while it is still farther from having been satisfactorily cleared up than either of the others.

Poetry and eloquence are both alike the expression or utterance of feeling: but, if we may be excused the antithesis, we should say that eloquence is *heard*; poetry is *over*heard. Eloquence supposes an audience. The peculiarity of poetry appears to us to lie in the poet's utter unconsciousness of a listener. Poetry is feeling confessing itself to itself in moments of solitude, and embodying itself in symbols which are the nearest possible representations of the feeling in the exact shape in which it exists in the poet's mind. Eloquence is feeling pouring itself out to other minds, courting their sympathy, or endeavoring to influence their belief, or move them to passion or to action.

All poetry is of the nature of soliloquy. It may be said that poetry which is printed on hot-pressed paper, and sold at a bookseller's shop, is a soliloquy in full dress and on the stage. It is so; but there is nothing absurd in the idea of such a mode of soliloquizing. What we have said to ourselves we may tell to others afterwards; what we have said or done in solitude we may voluntarily reproduce when we know that other eyes are upon us. But no trace of consciousness that any eyes are upon us must be visible in the work itself. The actor knows that there is an audience present: but, if he act as though he knew it, he acts ill. A poet may write poetry, not only with the intention of printing it, but for the express purpose of being paid for it. That it should *be* poetry, being written under such influences, is less probable, not, however, impossible; but no otherwise possible than if he can succeed in excluding from his work every vestige of such lookings-forth into the outward and every-day world, and can express his emotions exactly as he has felt them in solitude, or as he is conscious that he should feel them, though they were to remain for ever unuttered, or (at the lowest) as he knows that others feel them in similar circumstances of solitude. But when he turns round, and addresses himself to another person; when the act of utterance is not itself the end, but a means to an end—viz., by the feelings he himself expresses, to work upon the feelings, or upon the belief or the will of another; when the expression of his emotions, or of his thoughts tinged by his emotions, is tinged also by that purpose, by that desire of making an impression upon another mind—then it ceases to be poetry, and becomes eloquence.

Poetry, accordingly, is the natural fruit of solitude and meditation; eloquence, of intercourse with the world. The persons who have most feeling of their own, if intellectual culture has given them a language in which to express it, have the highest faculty of poetry: those who best understand the feelings of others are the most eloquent. The persons and the nations who commonly excel in poetry are those whose character and tastes render them least dependent upon the applause or sympathy or concurrence of the world in general. Those to whom that applause, that sympathy, that concurrence, are most necessary, generally excel most in eloquence. And hence, perhaps, the French, who are the least poetical of all great and intellectual nations, are among the most eloquent; the French also being the most sociable, the vainest, and the least self-dependent.

If the above be, as we believe, the true theory of the distinction commonly admitted between eloquence and poetry, or even though it be not so, yet if, as we cannot doubt, the distinction above stated be a real bona fide distinction, it will be found to hold, not merely in the language of words, but in all other language, and to intersect the whole domain of art.

Take, for example, music. We shall find in that art, so peculiarly the expression of passion, two perfectly distinct styles—one of which may be called the poetry, the other the oratory, of music. This difference, being seized, would put an end to much musical sectarianism. There has been much contention whether the music of the modern Italian school, that of Rossini,[5] and his successors, be impassioned or not. Without doubt, the passion it expresses is not the musing, meditative tenderness or pathos or grief of Mozart or Beethoven; yet it is passion, but garrulous passion, the passion which pours itself into other ears, and therein the better calculated for dramatic effect, having a natural adaptation for dialogue. Mozart also is great in musical oratory; but his most touching compositions are in the opposite style, that of soliloquy. Who can imagine "Dove sono"[6] heard? We imagine it overheard.

Purely pathetic music commonly partakes of soliloquy. The soul is absorbed in its distress and, though there may be bystanders, it is not thinking of them. When the mind is looking within, and not without, its state does not often or rapidly vary; and hence the even, uninterrupted flow, approaching almost to monotony, which a good reader or a good singer will give to words or music of a pensive or melancholy cast. But grief, taking the form of a prayer or of a complaint, becomes oratorical: no longer low and even and subdued, it assumes a more emphatic rhythm, a more rapidly returning accent; instead of a few slow, equal notes, following one after another at regular intervals, it crowds note upon note, and often assumes a hurry and bustle like joy. Those who are familiar with some of the best of Rossini's serious compositions, such as the air "Tu che i miseri conforti,"[7] in the opera of "Tancredi," or the duet "Ebben per mia memoria,"[8] in "La Gazza Ladra," will at once understand and feel our meaning. Both are highly tragic and passionate: the passion of both is that of oratory, not poetry. The like may be said of that most moving invocation in Beethoven's "Fidelio,"

> "Komm, Hoffnung, lass das letzte Stern
> Der Müde nicht erbleichen"—[9]

in which Madame Schröder Devrient exhibited such consummate powers of pathetic expression. How different from Winter's beautiful "Paga fui,"[1] the very soul of melancholy exhaling itself in solitude! fuller of meaning, and therefore more profoundly poetical, than the words for which it was composed; for it seems to express, not simple melancholy, but the melancholy of remorse.

If from vocal music we now pass to instrumental, we may have a specimen

5. Gioacchino Rossini (1792–1868), composer of operas.
6. Where are fled [the lovely moments?] (Italian); soprano aria from Mozart's *The Marriage of Figaro*, act 3 (1786).
7. You, who give comfort to the wretched (Italian); soprano aria from Rossini's *Tancredi* (1813).
8. Indeed according to my memory (Italian); soprano aria from Rossini's *La gazza Ladra* (1817).

9. Come, Hope, let not the weary person's last star fade out (German); aria from Beethoven's *Fidelio* (1805). Mill seems to be quoting from memory. The passage should read: "Komm, Hoffnung, lass den letzten Stern / Der Müden nicht erbleichen."
1. I have been contented (Italian); aria from the once-popular opera *Il ratto di Proserpina* by Peter Winter (1754–1825), first performed in London in 1804.

of musical oratory in any fine military symphony or march; while the poetry of music seems to have attained its consummation in Beethoven's "Overture to Egmont," so wonderful in its mixed expression of grandeur and melancholy.

In the arts which speak to the eye, the same distinctions will be found to hold, not only between poetry and oratory, but between poetry, oratory, narrative, and simple imitation or description.

Pure description is exemplified in a mere portrait or a mere landscape, productions of art, it is true, but of the mechanical rather than of the fine arts; being works of simple imitation, not creation. We say, a mere portrait or a mere landscape; because it is possible for a portrait or a landscape, without ceasing to be such, to be also a picture, like Turner's[2] landscapes, and the great portraits by Titian or Vandyke.

Whatever in painting or sculpture expresses human feeling—or character, which is only a certain state of feeling grown habitual—may be called, according to circumstances, the poetry or the eloquence of the painter's or the sculptor's art: the poetry, if the feeling declares itself by such signs as escape from us when we are unconscious of being seen; the oratory, if the signs are those we use for the purpose of voluntary communication.

The narrative style answers to what is called historical painting, which it is the fashion among connoisseurs to treat as the climax of the pictorial art. That it is the most difficult branch of the art, we do not doubt, because, in its perfection, it includes the perfection of all the other branches; as, in like manner, an epic poem, though, in so far as it is epic (i.e. narrative), it is not poetry at all, is yet esteemed the greatest effort of poetic genius, because there is no kind whatever of poetry which may not appropriately find a place in it. But an historical picture as such, that is, as the representation of an incident, must necessarily, as it seems to us, be poor and ineffective. The narrative powers of painting are extremely limited. Scarcely any picture, scarcely even any series of pictures, tells its own story without the aid of an interpreter. But it is the single figures, which, to us, are the great charm even of an historical picture. It is in these that the power of the art is really seen. In the attempt to narrate, visible and permanent signs are too far behind the fugitive audible ones, which follow so fast one after another; while the faces and figures in a narrative picture, even though they be Titian's, stand still. Who would not prefer one "Virgin and Child" of Raphael to all the pictures which Rubens, with his fat, frouzy Dutch Venuses, ever painted?—though Rubens, besides excelling almost everyone in his mastery over the mechanical parts of his art, often shows real genius in *grouping* his figures, the peculiar problem of historical painting. But then, who, except a mere student of drawing and coloring, ever cared to look twice at any of the figures themselves? The power of painting lies in poetry, of which Rubens had not the slightest tincture, not in narrative, wherein he might have excelled.

The single figures, however, in an historical picture, are rather the eloquence of painting than the poetry. They mostly (unless they are quite out of place in the picture) express the feelings of one person as modified by the presence of others. Accordingly, the minds whose bent leads them

2. J. M. W. Turner (1775–1851), English landscape painter.

rather to eloquence than to poetry rush to historical painting. The French painters, for instance, seldom attempt, because they could make nothing of, single heads, like those glorious ones of the Italian masters with which they might feed themselves day after day in their own Louvre. They must all be historical; and they are, almost to a man, attitudinizers. If we wished to give any young artist the most impressive warning our imagination could devise against that kind of vice in the pictorial which corresponds to rant in the histrionic art, we would advise him to walk once up and once down the gallery of the Luxembourg.[3] Every figure in French painting or statuary seems to be showing itself off before spectators. They are not poetical, but in the worst style of corrupted eloquence.

1833, 1859

From On Liberty

From Chapter 3. Of Individuality as One of the Elements of Well-Being

* * *

Few persons, out of Germany, even comprehend the meaning of the doctrine which Wilhelm von Humboldt, so eminent both as a savant and as a politician, made the text of a treatise—that "the end of man, or that which is prescribed by the eternal or immutable dictates of reason, and not suggested by vague and transient desires, is the highest and most harmonious development of his powers to a complete and consistent whole"; that, therefore, the object "towards which every human being must ceaselessly direct his efforts, and on which especially those who design to influence their fellow men must ever keep their eyes, is the individuality of power and development"; that for this there are two requisites, "freedom, and variety of situations"; and that from the union of these arise "individual vigor and manifold diversity," which combine themselves in "originality."[1]

Little, however, as people are accustomed to a doctrine like that of Von Humboldt, and surprising as it may be to them to find so high a value attached to individuality, the question, one must nevertheless think, can only be one of degree. No one's idea of excellence in conduct is that people should do absolutely nothing but copy one another. No one would assert that people ought not to put into their mode of life, and into the conduct of their concerns, any impress whatever of their own judgment, or of their own individual character. On the other hand, it would be absurd to pretend that people ought to live as if nothing whatever had been known in the world before they came into it; as if experience had as yet done nothing towards showing that one mode of existence, or conduct, is preferable to another. Nobody denies that people should be so taught and trained in youth, as to know and benefit by the ascertained results of human experience. But it is the privilege and proper condition of a human being, arrived at the maturity of his faculties,

3. A palace in Paris, where paintings of scenes from French history were exhibited.
1. From The Sphere and Duties of Government, by Baron Wilhelm von Humboldt (1767–1835), Prus-sian statesman and man of letters. Originally written in 1791, the treatise was first published in Germany in 1852 and was translated into English in 1854.

to use and interpret experience in his own way. It is for him to find out what part of recorded experience is properly applicable to his own circumstances and character. The traditions and customs of other people are, to a certain extent, evidence of what their experience has taught *them;* presumptive evidence, and as such, have a claim to his deference: but, in the first place, their experience may be too narrow; or they may not have interpreted it rightly. Secondly, their interpretation of experience may be correct, but unsuitable to him. Customs are made for customary circumstances, and customary characters; and his circumstances or his character may be uncustomary. Thirdly, though the customs be both good as customs, and suitable to him, yet to conform to custom, merely *as* custom, does not educate or develop in him any of the qualities which are the distinctive endowment of a human being. The human faculties of perception, judgment, discriminative feeling, mental activity, and even moral preference are exercised only in making a choice. He who does anything because it is the custom makes no choice. He gains no practice either in discerning or in desiring what is best. The mental and moral, like the muscular powers, are improved only by being used. The faculties are called into no exercise by doing a thing merely because others do it, no more than by believing a thing only because others believe it. If the grounds of an opinion are not conclusive to the person's own reason, his reason cannot be strengthened, but is likely to be weakened, by his adopting it: and if the inducements to an act are not such as are consentaneous[2] to his own feelings and character (where affection, or the rights of others, are not concerned) it is so much done towards rendering his feelings and character inert and torpid, instead of active and energetic.

He who lets the world, or his own portion of it, choose his plan of life for him has no need of any other faculty than the apelike one of imitation. He who chooses his plan for himself employs all his faculties. He must use observation to see, reasoning and judgment to foresee, activity to gather materials for decision, discrimination to decide, and when he has decided, firmness and self-control to hold to his deliberate decision. And these qualities he requires and exercises exactly in proportion as the part of his conduct which he determines according to his own judgment and feelings is a large one. It is possible that he might be guided in some good path, and kept out of harm's way, without any of these things. But what will be his comparative worth as a human being? It really is of importance, not only what men do, but also what manner of men they are that do it. Among the works of man, which human life is rightly employed in perfecting and beautifying, the first in importance surely is man himself. Supposing it were possible to get houses built, corn grown, battles fought, causes tried, and even churches erected and prayers said, by machinery—by automatons in human form—it would be a considerable loss to exchange for these automatons even the men and women who at present inhabit the more civilized parts of the world, and who assuredly are but starved specimens of what nature can and will produce. Human nature is not a machine to be built after a model, and set to do exactly the work prescribed for it, but a tree, which requires to grow and develop itself on all sides, according to the tendency of the inward forces which make it a living thing.

2. Agreeable.

It will probably be conceded that it is desirable people should exercise their understandings, and that an intelligent following of custom, or even occasionally an intelligent deviation from custom, is better than a blind and simply mechanical adhesion to it. To a certain extent it is admitted that our understanding should be our own: but there is not the same willingness to admit that our desires and impulses should be our own likewise; or that to possess impulses of our own, and of any strength, is anything but a peril and a snare. Yet desires and impulses are as much a part of a perfect human being, as beliefs and restraints: and strong impulses are only perilous when not properly balanced; when one set of aims and inclinations is developed into strength, while others, which ought to coexist with them, remain weak and inactive. It is not because men's desires are strong that they act ill; it is because their consciences are weak. There is no natural connection between strong impulses and a weak conscience. The natural connection is the other way. To say that one person's desires and feelings are stronger and more various than those of another is merely to say that he has more of the raw material of human nature, and is therefore capable, perhaps of more evil, but certainly of more good. Strong impulses are but another name for energy. Energy may be turned to bad uses; but more good may always be made of an energetic nature than of an indolent and impassive one. Those who have most natural feeling are always those whose cultivated feelings may be made the strongest. The same strong susceptibilities which make the personal impulses vivid and powerful are also the source from whence are generated the most passionate love of virtue, and the sternest self-control. It is through the cultivation of these that society both does its duty and protects its interests: not by rejecting the stuff of which heroes are made, because it knows not how to make them. A person whose desires and impulses are his own—are the expression of his own nature, as it has been developed and modified by his own culture—is said to have a character. One whose desires and impulses are not his own, has no character, no more than a steam engine has a character. If, in addition to being his own, his impulses are strong, and are under the government of a strong will, he has an energetic character. Whoever thinks that individuality of desires and impulses should not be encouraged to unfold itself must maintain that society has no need of strong natures—is not the better for containing many persons who have much character—and that a high general average of energy is not desirable.

In some early states of society, these forces might be, and were, too much ahead of the power which society then possessed of disciplining and controlling them. There has been a time when the element of spontaneity and individuality was in excess, and the social principle had a hard struggle with it. The difficulty then was to induce men of strong bodies or minds to pay obedience to any rules which require them to control their impulses. To overcome this difficulty, law and discipline, like the Popes struggling against the Emperors, asserted a power over the whole man, claiming to control all his life in order to control his character—which society had not found any other sufficient means of binding. But society has now fairly got the better of individuality; and the danger which threatens human nature is not the excess, but the deficiency, of personal impulses and preferences. Things are vastly changed, since the passions of those who were strong by station or by personal endowment were in a state of habitual rebellion against laws and ordinances, and required to be rigorously chained up to enable the persons within their reach to enjoy any particle of security. In our times, from the highest class of society down to the lowest, everyone lives as under the eye of a hostile and dreaded censorship. Not only in what concerns others, but in what concerns only themselves, the individual or the family do not ask themselves—what do I prefer? or, what would suit my character and disposition? or, what would allow the best and highest in me to have fair play, and enable it to grow and thrive? They ask themselves, what is suitable to my position? what is usually done by persons of my station and pecuniary circumstances? or (worse still) what is usually done by persons of a station and circumstances superior to mine? I do not mean that they choose what is customary, in preference to what suits their own inclination. It does not occur to them to have any inclination, except for what is customary. Thus the mind itself is bowed to the yoke: even in what people do for pleasure, conformity is the first thing thought of; they like in crowds; they exercise choice only among things commonly done: peculiarity of taste, eccentricity of conduct, are shunned equally with crimes: until by dint of not following their own nature, they have no nature to follow: their human capacities are withered and starved: they become incapable of any strong wishes or native pleasures, and are generally without either opinions or feelings of home growth, or properly their own. Now is this, or is it not, the desirable condition of human nature?

It is so, on the Calvinistic theory. According to that, the one great offense of man is self-will. All the good of which humanity is capable is comprised in obedience. You have no choice; thus you must do, and no otherwise: "whatever is not a duty is a sin." Human nature being radically corrupt, there is no redemption for anyone until human nature is killed within him. To one holding this theory of life, crushing out any of the human faculties, capacities, and susceptibilities is no evil: man needs no capacity but that of surrendering himself to the will of God: and if he uses any of his faculties for any other purpose but to do that supposed will more effectually, he is better without them. This is the theory of Calvinism; and it is held, in a mitigated form, by many who do not consider themselves Calvinists; the mitigation consisting in giving a less ascetic interpretation to the alleged will of God; asserting it to be his will that mankind should gratify some of their inclinations; of course not in the manner they themselves prefer, but in the way of obedience, that is, in a way prescribed to them by authority; and, therefore, by the necessary conditions of the case, the same for all.

In some such insidious form there is at present a strong tendency to this narrow theory of life, and to the pinched and hidebound type of human character which it patronizes. Many persons, no doubt, sincerely think that human beings thus cramped and dwarfed are as their Maker designed them to be; just as many have thought that trees are a much finer thing when clipped into pollards,[3] or cut out into figures of animals, than as nature made them. But if it be any part of religion to believe that man was made by a good Being, it is more consistent with that faith to believe that this Being gave all human faculties that they might be cultivated and unfolded, not rooted out and consumed, and that he takes delight in every nearer approach

---

3. Trees that acquire an artificial shape by being cut back to produce a mass of dense foliage.

made by his creatures to the ideal conception embodied in them, every increase in any of their capabilities of comprehension, of action, or of enjoyment. There is a different type of human excellence from the Calvinistic; a conception of humanity as having its nature bestowed on it for other purposes than merely to be abnegated. "Pagan self-assertion" is one of the elements of human worth, as well as "Christian self-denial."[4] There is a Greek ideal of self-development, which the Platonic and Christian ideal of self-government blends with, but does not supersede. It may be better to be a John Knox than an Alcibiades, but it is better to be a Pericles[5] than either, nor would a Pericles, if we had one in these days, be without anything good which belonged to John Knox.

It is not by wearing down into uniformity all that is individual in themselves, but by cultivating it and calling it forth, within the limits imposed by the rights and interests of others, that human beings become a noble and beautiful object of contemplation; and as the works partake the character of those who do them, by the same process human life also becomes rich, diversified, and animating, furnishing more abundant aliment to high thoughts and elevating feelings, and strengthening the tie which binds every individual to the race, by making the race infinitely better worth belonging to. In proportion to the development of his individuality, each person becomes more valuable to himself, and is therefore capable of being more valuable to others. There is a greater fullness of life about his own existence, and when there is more life in the units there is more in the mass which is composed of them. As much compression as is necessary to prevent the stronger specimens of human nature from encroaching on the rights of others cannot be dispensed with; but for this there is ample compensation even in the point of view of human development. The means of development which the individual loses by being prevented from gratifying his inclinations to the injury of others are chiefly obtained at the expense of the development of other people. And even to himself there is a full equivalent in the better development of the social part of his nature, rendered possible by the restraint put upon the selfish part. To be held to rigid rules of justice for the sake of others develops the feelings and capacities which have the good of others for their object. But to be restrained in things not affecting their good, by their mere displeasure, develops nothing valuable, except such force of character as may unfold itself in resisting the restraint. If acquiesced in, it dulls and blunts the whole nature. To give any fair play to the nature of each, it is essential that different persons should be allowed to lead different lives. In proportion as this latitude has been exercised in any age, has that age been noteworthy to posterity. Even despotism does not produce its worst effects, so long as individuality exists under it; and whatever crushes individuality is despotism, by whatever name it may be called, and whether it professes to be enforcing the will of God or the injunctions of men.

Having said that Individuality is the same thing with development, and that it is only the cultivation of individuality which produces, or can produce, well-developed human beings, I might here close the argument: for what more or better can be said of any condition of human affairs than that it

---

4. From the *Essays* (1848) of John Sterling, a minor writer and friend of Carlyle's.
5. A model statesman in Athens (495–429 B.C.E.).

Knox (1514–1572), a stern Scottish Calvinist reformer. Alcibiades (450–404 B.C.E.), a dissolute Athenian commander.

brings human beings themselves nearer to the best thing they can be? or what worse can be said of any obstruction to good than that it prevents this? Doubtless, however, these considerations will not suffice to convince those who most need convincing; and it is necessary further to show that these developed human beings are of some use to the undeveloped—to point out to those who do not desire liberty, and would not avail themselves of it, that they may be in some intelligible manner rewarded for allowing other people to make use of it without hindrance.

In the first place, then, I would suggest that they might possibly learn something from them. It will not be denied by anybody, that originality is a valuable element in human affairs. There is always need of persons not only to discover new truths, and point out when what were once truths are true no longer, but also to commence new practices, and set the example of more enlightened conduct, and better taste and sense in human life. This cannot well be gainsaid by anybody who does not believe that the world has already attained perfection in all its ways and practices. It is true that this benefit is not capable of being rendered by everybody alike: there are but few persons, in comparison with the whole of mankind, whose experiments, if adopted by others, would be likely to be any improvement on established practice. But these few are the salt of the earth; without them, human life would become a stagnant pool. Not only is it they who introduce good things which did not before exist; it is they who keep the life in those which already existed. If there were nothing new to be done, would human intellect cease to be necessary? Would it be a reason why those who do the old things should forget why they are done, and do them like cattle, not like human beings? There is only too great a tendency in the best beliefs and practices to degenerate into the mechanical; and unless there were a succession of persons whose ever-recurring originality prevents the grounds of those beliefs and practices from becoming merely traditional, such dead matter would not resist the smallest shock from anything really alive, and there would be no reason why civilization should not die out, as in the Byzantine Empire. Persons of genius, it is true, are, and are always likely to be, a small minority; but in order to have them, it is necessary to preserve the soil in which they grow. Genius can only breathe freely in an *atmosphere* of freedom. Persons of genius are, *ex vi termini*,[6] *more* individual than any other people—less capable, consequently, of fitting themselves, without hurtful compression, into any of the small number of molds which society provides in order to save its members the trouble of forming their own character. If from timidity they consent to be forced into one of these molds, and to let all that part of themselves which cannot expand under the pressure remain unexpanded, society will be little the better for their genius. If they are of a strong character, and break their fetters, they become a mark for the society which has not succeeded in reducing them to commonplace, to point at with solemn warning as "wild," "erratic," and the like; much as if one should complain of the Niagara River for not flowing smoothly between its banks like a Dutch canal.

I insist thus emphatically on the importance of genius, and the necessity of allowing it to unfold itself freely both in thought and in practice, being well aware that no one will deny the position in theory, but knowing also

---

6. By force of the term (Latin); i.e., by definition.

that almost everyone, in reality, is totally indifferent to it. People think genius a fine thing if it enables a man to write an exciting poem, or paint a picture. But in its true sense, that of originality in thought and action, though no one says that it is not a thing to be admired, nearly all, at heart, think that they can do very well without it. Unhappily this is too natural to be wondered at. Originality is the one thing which unoriginal minds cannot feel the use of. They cannot see what it is to do for them: how should they? If they could see what it would do for them, it would not be originality. The first service which originality has to render them is that of opening their eyes: which being once fully done, they would have a chance of being themselves original. Meanwhile, recollecting that nothing was ever yet done which someone was not the first to do, and that all good things which exist are the fruits of originality, let them be modest enough to believe that there is something still left for it to accomplish, and assure themselves that they are more in need of originality, the less they are conscious of the want.

In sober truth, whatever homage may be professed, or even paid, to real or supposed mental superiority, the general tendency of things throughout the world is to render mediocrity the ascendant power among mankind. In ancient history, in the middle ages, and in a diminishing degree through the long transition from feudality to the present time, the individual was power in himself; and if he had either great talents or a high social position, he was a considerable power. At present individuals are lost in the crowd. In politics it is almost a triviality to say that public opinion now rules the world. The only power deserving the name is that of masses, and of governments while they make themselves the organ of the tendencies and instincts of masses. This is as true in the moral and social relations of private life as in public transactions. Those whose opinions go by the name of public opinion, are not always the same sort of public: in America they are the whole white population; in England, chiefly the middle class. But they are always a mass, that is to say, collective mediocrity. And what is a still greater novelty, the mass do not now take their opinions from dignitaries in Church or State, from ostensible leaders, or from books. Their thinking is done for them by men much like themselves, addressing them or speaking in their name, on the spur of the moment, through the newspapers. I am not complaining of all this. I do not assert that anything better is compatible, as a general rule, with the present low state of the human mind. But that does not hinder the government of mediocrity from being mediocre government. No government by a democracy or a numerous aristocracy, either in its political acts or in the opinions, qualities, and tone of mind which it fosters, ever did or could rise above mediocrity, except in so far as the sovereign Many have let themselves be guided (which in their best times they always have done) by the counsels and influence of a more highly gifted and instructed One or Few. The initiation of all wise or noble things, comes and must come from individuals; generally at first from some one individual. The honor and glory of the average man is that he is capable of following that initiative; that he can respond internally to wise and noble things, and be led to them with his eyes open. I am not countenancing the sort of "hero worship" which applauds the strong man of genius for forcibly seizing on the government of the world and making it do his bidding in spite of itself. All he can claim is freedom to point out the way. The power of compelling others into it is not only inconsistent with the freedom and development of all the rest, but corrupting to the strong man himself. It does seem, however, that when the opinions of masses of merely average men are everywhere become or becoming the dominant power, the counterpoise and corrective to that tendency would be the more and more pronounced individuality of those who stand on the higher eminences of thought. It is in these circumstances most especially that exceptional individuals, instead of being deterred, should be encouraged in acting differently from the mass. In other times there was no advantage in their doing so, unless they acted not only differently, but better. In this age, the mere example of nonconformity, the mere refusal to bend the knee to custom, is itself a service. Precisely because the tyranny of opinion is such as to make eccentricity a reproach, it is desirable, in order to break through that tyranny, that people should be eccentric. Eccentricity has always abounded when and where strength of character has abounded; and the amount of eccentricity in a society has generally been proportional to the amount of genius, mental vigor, and moral courage which it contained. That so few now dare to be eccentric marks the chief danger of the time.

* * *

There is one characteristic of the present direction of public opinion, peculiarly calculated to make it intolerant of any marked demonstration of individuality. The general average of mankind are not only moderate in intellect, but also moderate in inclinations: they have no tastes or wishes strong enough to incline them to do anything unusual, and they consequently do not understand those who have, and class all such with the wild and intemperate whom they are accustomed to look down upon. Now, in addition to this fact which is general, we have only to suppose that a strong movement has set in towards the improvement of morals, and it is evident what we have to expect. In these days such a movement has set in; much has actually been effected in the way of increased regularity of conduct, and discouragement of excesses; and there is a philanthropic spirit abroad, for the exercise of which there is no more inviting field than the moral and prudential improvement of our fellow creatures. These tendencies of the times cause the public to be more disposed than at most former periods to prescribe general rules of conduct, and endeavor to make everyone conform to the approved standard. And that standard, express or tacit, is to desire nothing strongly. Its ideal of character is to be without any marked character; to maim by compression, like a Chinese lady's foot, every part of human nature which stands out prominently, and tends to make the person markedly dissimilar in outline to commonplace humanity.

As is usually the case with ideals which exclude one half of what is desirable, the present standard of approbation produces only an inferior imitation of the other half. Instead of great energies guided by vigorous reason, and strong feelings strongly controlled by a conscientious will, its result is weak feelings and weak energies, which therefore can be kept in outward conformity to rule without any strength either of will or reason. Already energetic characters on any large scale are becoming merely traditional. There is now scarcely any outlet for energy in this country except business. The energy expended in this may still be regarded as considerable. What little is left from that employment, is expended on some hobby; which may be a useful, even a philanthropic hobby, but is always some one thing, and generally a thing of small dimensions. The greatness of England is now all collective: individually small, we only appear capable of anything great by our habit of combining; and with this our moral and religious philanthropies are perfectly contented. But it was men of another stamp than this that made England what it has been; and men of another stamp will be needed to prevent its decline.

The despotism of custom is everywhere the standing hindrance to human advancement, being in unceasing antagonism to that disposition to aim at something better than customary, which is called, according to circumstances, the spirit of liberty, or that of progress or improvement. The spirit of improvement is not always a spirit of liberty, for it may aim at forcing improvements on an unwilling people; and the spirit of liberty, in so far as it resists such attempts, may ally itself locally and temporarily with the opponents of improvement; but the only unfailing and permanent source of improvement is liberty, since by it there are as many possible independent centers of improvement as there are individuals. The progressive principle, however, in either shape, whether as the love of liberty or of improvement, is antagonistic to the sway of Custom, involving at least emancipation from that yoke; and the contest between the two constitutes the chief interest of the history of mankind. The greater part of the world has, properly speaking, no history, because the depotism of Custom is complete. This is the case over the whole East. Custom is there, in all things, the final appeal; justice and right mean conformity to custom; the argument of custom no one, unless some tyrant intoxicated with power, thinks of resisting. And we see the result. Those nations must once have had originality; they did not start out of the ground populous, lettered, and versed in many of the arts of life; they made themselves all this, and were then the greatest and most powerful nations of the world. What are they now? The subjects or dependants of tribes whose forefathers wandered in the forests when theirs had magnificent palaces and gorgeous temples, but over whom custom exercised only a divided rule with liberty and progress. A people, it appears, may be progressive for a certain length of time, and then stop: when does it stop? When it ceases to possess individuality. If a similar change should befall the nations of Europe, it will not be in exactly the same shape: the despotism of custom with which these nations are threatened is not precisely stationariness. It proscribes singularity, but it does not preclude change, provided all change together. We have discarded the fixed costumes of our forefathers; everyone must still dress like other people, but the fashion may change once or twice a year. We thus take care that when there is change it shall be for change's sake, and not from any idea of beauty or convenience; for the same idea of beauty or convenience would not strike all the world at the same moment, and be simultaneously thrown aside by all at another moment. But we are progressive as well as changeable: we continually make new inventions in mechanical things, and keep them until they are again superseded by better; we are eager for improvement in politics, in education, even in morals, though in this last our idea of improvement chiefly consists in persuading or forcing other people to be as good as ourselves. It is not progress that we object to; on the contrary, we flatter ourselves that we are the most progressive people who ever lived. It is individuality that we war against: we should think we had done wonders if we had made ourselves all alike; forgetting that the unlikeness of one person to another is generally the first thing which draws the attention of either to the imperfection of his own type, and the superiority of another, or the possibility, by combining the advantages of both, of producing something better than either. We have a warning example in China— a nation of much talent, and, in some respects, even wisdom, owing to the rare good fortune of having been provided at an early period with a particularly good set of customs, the work, in some measure, of men to whom even the most enlightened European must accord, under certain limitations, the title of sages and philosophers. They are remarkable, too, in the excellence of their apparatus for impressing, as far as possible, the best wisdom they possess upon every mind in the community, and securing that those who have appropriated most of it shall occupy the posts of honor and power. Surely the people who did this have discovered the secret of human progressiveness, and must have kept themselves steadily at the head of the movement of the world. On the contrary, they have become stationary—have remained so for thousands of years; and if they are ever to be farther improved, it must be by foreigners. They have succeeded beyond all hope in what English philanthropists are so industriously working at—in making a people all alike, all governing their thoughts and conduct by the same maxims and rules; and these are the fruits. The modern regime of public opinion is, in an unorganized form, what the Chinese educational and political systems are in an organized; and unless individuality shall be able successfully to assert itself against this yoke, Europe, notwithstanding its noble antecedents and its professed Christianity, will tend to become another China. . . .

1859

The Subjection of Women

After its 1869 publication in England and America, Mill's *The Subjection of Women* was quickly adopted by the leaders of the suffrage movement as the definitive analysis of the position of women in society. American suffragists sold copies of the book at their conventions; at the age of seventy-nine, American reformer Sarah Grimké went door to door in her hometown to sell one hundred copies.

The book had its roots in a tradition of libertarian thought and writing dating from the late eighteenth century. Out of this context came the first major work of feminist theory, Mary Wollstonecraft's *A Vindication of the Rights of Women* (1792). (Wollstonecraft's reputation was so scandalous, Mill avoided referring to her work.) In the early decades of the century, there was much discussion of women's rights in the Unitarian and radical circles inhabited by Mill and his wife, Harriet Taylor, who wrote her own essay on women's suffrage. By the middle of the century, "the woman question," as the Victorians called it, had become a frequent subject of writing and debate; and an organized feminist movement had begun to develop. Early reform efforts focused on the conditions of women's work, particularly in mines and factories; access to better jobs and to higher education; and married women's property rights. Women's suffrage started attracting support in the 1860s. Mill himself introduced the first parliamentary motion extending the franchise to women in 1866.

From The Subjection of Women

From *Chapter 1*

The object of this Essay is to explain as clearly as I am able, the grounds of an opinion which I have held from the very earliest period when I had formed any opinions at all on social or political matters, and which, instead of being weakened or modified, has been constantly growing stronger by the progress of reflection and the experience of life: That the principle which regulates the existing social relations between the two sexes—the legal sub-ordination of one sex to the other—is wrong in itself, and now one of the chief hindrances to human improvement; and that it ought to be replaced by a principle of perfect equality, admitting no power or privilege on the one side, nor disability on the other.

* * *

Some will object, that a comparison cannot fairly be made between the government of the male sex and the forms of unjust power[1] which I have adduced in illustration of it, since these are arbitrary, and the effect of mere usurpation, while it on the contrary is natural. But was there ever any dom-ination which did not appear natural to those who possessed it? There was a time when the division of mankind into two classes, a small one of masters and a numerous one of slaves, appeared, even to the most cultivated minds, to be a natural, and the only natural, condition of the human race. No less an intellect, and one which contributed no less to the progress of human thought, than Aristotle, held this opinion without doubt or misgiving; and rested it on the same premises on which the same assertion in regard to the dominion of men over women is usually based, namely that there are differ-ent natures among mankind, free natures, and slave natures; that the Greeks were of a free nature, the barbarian races of Thracians and Asiatics of a slave nature. But why need I go back to Aristotle? Did not the slaveowners of the Southern United States maintain the same doctrine, with all the fanaticism with which men cling to the theories that justify their passions and legitimate their personal interests? Did they not call heaven and earth to witness that the dominion of the white man over the black is natural, that the black race is by nature incapable of freedom, and marked out for slavery? some even going so far as to say that the freedom of manual laborers is an unnatural order of things anywhere. Again, the theorists of absolute monarchy have always affirmed it to be the only natural form of government; issuing from the patriarchal, which was the primitive and spontaneous form of society, framed on the model of the paternal, which is anterior to society itself, and, as they contend, the most natural authority of all. Nay, for that matter, the law of force itself, to those who could not plead any other, has always seemed the most natural of all grounds for the exercise of authority. Conquering races hold it to be Nature's own dictate that the conquered should obey the conquerors, or, as they euphoniously paraphrase it, that the feebler and more unwarlike races should submit to the braver and manlier. The smallest

---

1. As examples of unjust power Mill had cited the forceful control of slaves by slave owners or of nations by military despots.

acquaintance with human life in the middle ages, shows how supremely natural the dominion of the feudal nobility over men of low condition appeared to the nobility themselves, and how unnatural the conception seemed, of a person of the inferior class claiming equality with them, or exercising authority over them. It hardly seemed less so to the class held in subjection. The emancipated serfs and burgesses, even in their most vigorous struggles, never made any pretension to a share of authority; they only demanded more or less of limitation to the power of tyrannizing over them. So true is it that unnatural generally means only uncustomary, and that everything which is usual appears natural. The subjection of women to men being a universal custom, any departure from it quite naturally appears unnatural. But how entirely, even in this case, the feeling is dependent on custom, appears by ample experience. Nothing so much astonishes the people of distant parts of the world, when they first learn anything about England, as to be told that it is under a queen: the thing seems to them so unnatural as to be almost incredible. To Englishmen this does not seem in the least degree unnatural, because they are used to it; but they do feel it unnatural that women should be soldiers or members of Parliament. In the feudal ages, on the contrary, war and politics were not thought unnatural to women, because not unusual; it seemed natural that women of the privileged classes should be of manly character, inferior in nothing but bodily strength to their husbands and fathers. The independence of women seemed rather less unnatural to the Greeks than to other ancients, on account of the fabulous Amazons (whom they believed to be historical), and the partial example afforded by the Spartan women; who, though no less subordinate by law than in other Greek states, were more free in fact, and being trained to bodily exercises in the same manner with men, gave ample proof that they were not naturally disqualified for them. There can be little doubt that Spartan experience suggested to Plato, among many other of his doctrines, that of the social and political equality of the two sexes.[2]

But, it will be said, the rule of men over women differs from all these others in not being a rule of force: it is accepted voluntarily; women make no complaint, and are consenting parties to it. In the first place, a great number of women do not accept it. Ever since there have been women able to make their sentiments known by their writings (the only mode of publicity which society permits to them), an increasing number of them have recorded protests against their present social condition: and recently many thousands of them, headed by the most eminent women known to the public, have petitioned Parliament for their admission to the Parliamentary Suffrage.[3] The claim of women to be educated as solidly, and in the same branches of knowledge, as men, is urged with growing intensity, and with a great prospect of success; while the demand for their admission into professions and occupations hitherto closed against them, becomes every year more urgent. Though there are not in this country, as there are in the United States, periodical Conventions and an organized party to agitate for the Rights of Women,[4] there is a numerous and active Society organized and managed by

2. Plato's *The Republic* 5.
3. As a member of the House of Commons, Mill had introduced a petition for women's suffrage in 1866.

4. Such as the Women's Rights Convention held at Worcester, Massachusetts, in October 1850, which had occasioned an essay by Mill's wife titled *Enfranchisement of Women* (1851).

women, for the more limited object of obtaining the political franchise. Nor is it only in our own country and in America that women are beginning to protest, more or less collectively, against the disabilities under which they labor. France, and Italy, and Switzerland, and Russia now afford examples of the same thing. How many more women there are who silently cherish similar aspirations, no one can possibly know; but there are abundant tokens how many *would* cherish them, were they not so strenuously taught to repress them as contrary to the proprieties of their sex. It must be remembered, also, that no enslaved class ever asked for complete liberty at once. When Simon de Montfort[5] called the deputies of the commons to sit for the first time in Parliament, did any of them dream of demanding that an assembly, elected by their constituents, should make and destroy ministries, and dictate to the king in affairs of state? No such thought entered into the imagination of the most ambitious of them. The nobility had already these pretensions; the commons pretended to nothing but to be exempt from arbitrary taxation, and from the gross individual oppression of the king's officers. It is a political law of nature that those who are under any power of ancient origin, never begin by complaining of the power itself, but only of its oppressive exercise. There is never any want of women who complain of ill usage by their husbands. There would be infinitely more, if complaint were not the greatest of all provocatives to a repetition and increase of the ill usage. It is this which frustrates all attempts to maintain the power but protect the woman against its abuses. In no other case (except that of a child) is the person who has been proved judicially to have suffered an injury, replaced under the physical power of the culprit who inflicted it. Accordingly wives, even in the most extreme and protracted cases of bodily ill usage, hardly ever dare avail themselves of the laws made for their protection: and if, in a moment of irrepressible indignation, or by the interference of neighbors, they are induced to do so, their whole effort afterward is to disclose as little as they can, and to beg off their tyrant from his merited chastisement.

All causes, social and natural, combine to make it unlikely that women should be collectively rebellious to the power of men. They are so far in a position different from all other subject classes, that their masters require something more from them than actual service. Men do not want solely the obedience of women, they want their sentiments. All men, except the most brutish, desire to have, in the woman most nearly connected with them, not a forced slave but a willing one, not a slave merely, but a favorite. They have therefore put everything in practice to enslave their minds. The masters of all other slaves rely, for maintaining obedience, on fear; either fear of themselves, or religious fears. The masters of women wanted more than simple obedience, and they turned the whole force of education to effect their purpose. All women are brought up from the very earliest years in the belief that their ideal of character is the very opposite to that of men; not self-will, and government by self-control, but submission, and yielding to the control of others. All the moralities tell them that it is the duty of women, and all the current sentimentalities that it is their nature, to live for others; to make complete abnegation of themselves, and to have no life but in their affec-

---

5. English nobleman and statesman (ca. 1208–1265), who assembled a parliament in 1265 that has been called the basis of the modern House of Commons.

tions. And by their affections are meant the only ones they are allowed to have—those to the men with whom they are connected, or to the children who constitute an additional and indefeasible tie between them and a man. When we put together three things—first, the natural attraction between opposite sexes; secondly, the wife's entire dependence on the husband, every privilege or pleasure she has being either his gift, or depending entirely on his will; and lastly, that the principal object of human pursuit, consideration, and all objects of social ambition, can in general be sought or obtained by her only through him, it would be a miracle if the object of being attractive to men had not become the polar star of feminine education and formation of character. And, this great means of influence over the minds of women having been acquired, an instinct of selfishness made men avail themselves of it to the utmost as a means of holding women in subjection, by representing to them meekness, submissiveness, and resignation of all individual will into the hands of a man, as an essential part of sexual attractiveness. Can it be doubted that any of the other yokes which mankind have succeeded in breaking, would have subsisted till now if the same means had existed, and had been as sedulously used, to bow down their minds to it? If it had been made the object of the life of every young plebeian to find personal favor in the eyes of some patrician, of every young serf with some seigneur; if domestication with him, and a share of his personal affections, had been held out as the prize which they all should look out for, the most gifted and aspiring being able to reckon on the most desirable prizes; and if, when this prize had been obtained, they had been shut out by a wall of brass from all interests not centering in him, all feelings and desires but those which he shared or inculcated; would not serfs and seigneurs, plebeians and patricians, have been as broadly distinguished at this day as men and women are? and would not all but a thinker here and there, have believed the distinction to be a fundamental and unalterable fact in human nature?

The preceding considerations are amply sufficient to show that custom, however universal it may be, affords in this case no presumption, and ought not to create any prejudice, in favor of the arrangements which place women in social and political subjection to men. But I may go farther, and maintain that the course of history, and the tendencies of progressive human society, afford not only no presumption in favor of this system of inequality of rights, but a strong one against it; and that, so far as the whole course of human improvement up to this time, the whole stream of modern tendencies, warrants any inference on the subject, it is, that this relic of the past is discordant with the future, and must necessarily disappear.

For, what is the peculiar character of the modern world—the difference which chiefly distinguishes modern institutions, modern social ideas, modern life itself, from those of times long past? It is, that human beings are no longer born to their place in life, and chained down by an inexorable bond to the place they are born to, but are free to employ their faculties, and such favourable chances as offer, to achieve the lot which may appear to them most desirable.

* * *

The social subordination of women thus stands out an isolated fact in modern social institutions; a solitary breach of what has become their fundamental law; a single relic of an old world of thought and practice exploded in everything else, but retained in the one thing of most universal interest; as if a gigantic dolmen,[6] or a vast temple of Jupiter Olympius, occupied the site of St. Paul's and received daily worship, while the surrounding Christian churches were only resorted to on fasts and festivals. This entire discrepancy between one social fact and all those which accompany it, and the radical opposition between its nature and the progressive movement which is the boast of the modern world, and which has successively swept away everything else of an analogous character, surely affords, to a conscientious observer of human tendencies, serious matter for reflection. It raises a *primâ facie* presumption on the unfavorable side, far outweighing any which custom and usage could in such circumstances create on the favorable; and should at least suffice to make this, like the choice between republicanism and royalty, a balanced question.

The least that can be demanded is, that the question should not be considered as prejudged by existing fact and existing opinion, but open to discussion on its merits, as a question of justice and expediency: the decision on this, as on any of the other social arrangements of mankind, depending on what an enlightened estimate of tendencies and consequences may show to be most advantageous to humanity in general, without distinction of sex. And the discussion must be a real discussion, descending to foundations, and not resting satisfied with vague and general assertions. It will not do, for instance, to assert in general terms, that the experience of mankind has pronounced in favor of the existing system. Experience cannot possibly have decided between two courses, so long as there has only been experience of one. If it be said that the doctrine of the equality of the sexes rests only on theory, it must be remembered that the contrary doctrine also has only theory to rest upon. All that is proved in its favor by direct experience, is that mankind have been able to exist under it, and to attain the degree of improvement and prosperity which we now see; but whether that prosperity has been attained sooner, or is now greater, than it would have been under the other system, experience does not say. On the other hand, experience does say, that every step in improvement has been so invariably accompanied by a step made in raising the social position of women, that historians and philosophers have been led to adopt their elevation or debasement as on the whole the surest test and most correct measure of the civilization of a people or an age. Through all the progressive period of human history, the condition of women has been approaching nearer to equality with men. This does not of itself prove that the assimilation must go on to complete equality; but it assuredly affords some presumption that such is the case.

Neither does it avail anything to say that the *nature* of the two sexes adapts them to their present functions and position, and renders these appropriate to them. Standing on the ground of common sense and the constitution of the human mind, I deny that any one knows, or can know, the nature of the two sexes, as long as they have only been seen in their present relation to one another. If men had ever been found in society without women, or women without men, or if there had been a society of men and women in which the women were not under the control of the men, something might

6. Prehistoric stone monument; here associated with pagan religious rites.

have been positively known about the mental and moral differences which may be inherent in the nature of each. What is now called the nature of women is an eminently artificial thing—the result of forced repression in some directions, unnatural stimulation in others. It may be asserted without scruple, that no other class of dependents have had their character so entirely distorted from its natural proportions by their relation with their masters; for, if conquered and slave races have been, in some respects, more forcibly repressed, whatever in them has not been crushed down by an iron heel has generally been let alone, and if left with any liberty of development, it has developed itself according to its own laws; but in the case of women, a hot-house and stove cultivation has always been carried on of some of the capabilities of their nature, for the benefit and pleasure of their masters. Then, because certain products of the general vital force sprout luxuriantly and reach a great development in this heated atmosphere and under this active nurture and watering, while other shoots from the same root, which are left outside in the wintry air, with ice purposely heaped all round them, have a stunted growth, and some are burnt off with fire and disappear; men, with that inability to recognize their own work which distinguishes the unanalytic mind, indolently believe that the tree grows of itself in the way they have made it grow, and that it would die if one half of it were not kept in a vapour bath and the other half in the snow.

Of all difficulties which impede the progress of thought, and the formation of well-grounded opinions on life and social arrangements, the greatest is now the unspeakable ignorance and inattention of mankind in respect to the influences which form human character. Whatever any portion of the human species now are, or seem to be, such, it is supposed, they have a natural tendency to be: even when the most elementary knowledge of the circumstances in which they have been placed, clearly points out the causes that made them what they are. Because a cottier[7] deeply in arrears to his landlord is not industrious, there are people who think that the Irish are naturally idle. Because constitutions can be overthrown when the authorities appointed to execute them turn their arms against them, there are people who think the French incapable of free government. Because the Greeks cheated the Turks, and the Turks only plundered the Greeks, there are persons who think that the Turks are naturally more sincere: and because women, as is often said, care nothing about politics except their personalities, it is supposed that the general good is naturally less interesting to women than to men. History, which is now so much better understood than formerly, teaches another lesson: if only by showing the extraordinary susceptibility of human nature to external influences, and the extreme variableness of those of its manifestations which are supposed to be most universal and uniform. But in history, as in traveling, men usually see only what they already had in their own minds; and few learn much from history, who do not bring much with them to its study.

Hence, in regard to that most difficult question, what are the natural differences between the two sexes—a subject on which it is impossible in the present state of society to obtain complete and correct knowledge—while almost everybody dogmatizes upon it, almost all neglect and make light of

7. Tenant cottager on a small Irish farm.

the only means by which any partial insight can be obtained into it. This is, an analytic study of the most important department of psychology, the laws of the influence of circumstances on character. For, however great and apparently ineradicable the moral and intellectual differences between men and women might be, the evidence of their being natural differences could only be negative. Those only could be inferred to be natural which could not possibly be artificial—the residuum, after deducting every characteristic of either sex which can admit of being explained from education or external circumstances. The profoundest knowledge of the laws of the formation of character is indispensable to entitle any one to affirm even that there is any difference, much more what the difference is, between the two sexes considered as moral and rational beings; and since no one, as yet, has that knowledge (for there is hardly any subject which, in proportion to its importance, has been so little studied), no one is thus far entitled to any positive opinion on the subject. Conjectures are all that can at present be made; conjectures more or less probable, according as more or less authorized by such knowledge as we yet have of the laws of psychology, as applied to the formation of character.

Even the preliminary knowledge, what the differences between the sexes now are, apart from all question as to how they are made what they are, is still in the crudest and most incomplete state. Medical practitioners and physiologists have ascertained, to some extent, the differences in bodily constitution; and this is an important element to the psychologist: but hardly any medical practitioner is a psychologist. Respecting the mental characteristics of women; their observations are of no more worth than those of common men. It is a subject on which nothing final can be known, so long as those who alone can really know it, women themselves, have given but little testimony, and that little, mostly suborned. It is easy to know stupid women. Stupidity is much the same all the world over. A stupid person's notions and feelings may confidently be inferred from those which prevail in the circle by which the person is surrounded. Not so with those whose opinions and feelings are an emanation from their own nature and faculties. It is only a man here and there who has any tolerable knowledge of the character even of the women of his own family. I do not mean, of their capabilities; these nobody knows, not even themselves, because most of them have never been called out. I mean their actually existing thoughts and feelings. Many a man thinks he perfectly understands women, because he has had amatory relations with several, perhaps with many of them. If he is a good observer, and his experience extends to quality as well as quantity, he may have learnt something of one narrow department of their nature—an important department, no doubt. But of all the rest of it, few persons are generally more ignorant, because there are few from whom it is so carefully hidden. The most favorable case which a man can generally have for studying the character of a woman, is that of his own wife: for the opportunities are greater, and the cases of complete sympathy not so unspeakably rare. And in fact, this is the source from which any knowledge worth having on the subject has, I believe, generally come. But most men have not had the opportunity of studying in this way more than a single case: accordingly one can, to an almost laughable degree, infer what a man's wife is like, from his opinions about women in general. To make even this one case yield any result, the woman must be worth knowing, and the man not only a competent judge, but of a character so sympathetic in itself, and so well adapted to hers, that he can either read her mind by sympathetic intuition, or has nothing in himself which makes her shy of disclosing it. Hardly anything, I believe, can be more rare than this conjunction. It often happens that there is the most complete unity of feeling and community of interests as to all external things, yet the one has as little admission into the internal life of the other as if they were common acquaintance. Even with true affection, authority on the one side and subordination on the other prevent perfect confidence. Though nothing may be intentionally withheld, much is not shown. In the analogous relation of parent and child, the corresponding phenomenon must have been in the observation of every one. As between father and son, how many are the cases in which the father, in spite of real affection on both sides, obviously to all the world does not know, nor suspect, parts of the son's character familiar to his companions and equals. The truth is, that the position of looking up to another is extremely unpropitious to complete sincerity and openness with him. The fear of losing ground in his opinion or in his feelings is so strong, that even in an upright character, there is an unconscious tendency to show only the best side, or the side which, though not the best, is that which he most likes to see: and it may be confidently said that thorough knowledge of one another hardly ever exists, but between persons who, besides being intimates, are equals. How much more true, then, must all this be, when the one is not only under the authority of the other, but has it inculcated on her as a duty to reckon everything else subordinate to his comfort and pleasure, and to let him neither see nor feel anything coming from her, except what is agreeable to him. All these difficulties stand in the way of a man's obtaining any thorough knowledge even of the one woman whom alone, in general, he has sufficient opportunity of studying. When we further consider that to understand one woman is not necessarily to understand any other woman; that even if he could study many women of one rank, or of one country, he would not thereby understand women of other ranks or countries; and even if he did, they are still only the women of a single period of history; we may safely assert that the knowledge which men can acquire of women, even as they have been and are, without reference to what they might be, is wretchedly imperfect and superficial, and always will be so, until women themselves have told all that they have to tell.

And this time has not come; nor will it come otherwise than gradually. It is but of yesterday that women have either been qualified by literary accomplishments, or permitted by society, to tell anything to the general public. As yet very few of them dare tell anything, which men, on whom their literary success depends, are unwilling to hear. Let us remember in what manner, up to a very recent time, the expression, even by a male author, of uncustomary opinions, or what are deemed eccentric feelings, usually was, and in some degree still is, received; and we may form some faint conception under what impediments a woman, who is brought up to think custom and opinion her sovereign rule, attempts to express in books anything drawn from the depths of her own nature. The greatest woman who has left writings behind her sufficient to give her an eminent rank in the literature of her country, thought it necessary to prefix as a motto to her boldest work, "Un homme peut braver l'opinion; une femme doit s'y soumettre."[8] The greater part of what women write about women is mere sycophancy to men. In the case of unmarried women, much of it seems only intended to increase their chance of a husband. Many, both married and unmarried, overstep the mark, and inculcate a servility beyond what is desired or relished by any man, except the very vulgarest. But this is not so often the case as, even at a quite late period, it still was. Literary women are becoming more freespoken, and more willing to express their real sentiments. Unfortunately, in this country especially, they are themselves such artificial products, that their sentiments are compounded of a small element of individual observation and consciousness, and a very large one of acquired associations. This will be less and less the case, but it will remain true to a great extent, as long as social institutions do not admit the same free development of originality in women which is possible to men. When that time comes, and not before, we shall see, and not merely hear, as much as it is necessary to know of the nature of women, and the adaptation of other things to it.

* * *

One thing we may be certain of—that what is contrary to women's nature to do, they never will be made to do by simply giving their nature free play. The anxiety of mankind to interfere in behalf of nature, for fear lest nature should not succeed in effecting its purpose, is an altogether unnecessary solicitude. What women by nature cannot do, it is quite superfluous to forbid them from doing. What they can do, but not so well as the men who are their competitors, competition suffices to exclude them from; since nobody asks for protective duties and bounties in favor of women; it is only asked that the present bounties and protective duties in favor of men should be recalled. If women have a greater natural inclination for some things than for others, there is no need of laws or social inculcation to make the majority of them do the former in preference to the latter. Whatever women's services are most wanted for, the free play of competition will hold out the strongest inducements to them to undertake. And, as the words imply, they are most wanted for the things for which they are most fit; by the apportionment of which to them, the collective faculties of the two sexes can be applied on the whole with the greatest sum of valuable result.

The general opinion of men is supposed to be, that the natural vocation of a woman is that of a wife and mother. I say, is supposed to be, because, judging from acts—from the whole of the present constitution of society— one might infer that their opinion was the direct contrary. They might be supposed to think that the alleged natural vocation of women was of all things the most repugnant to their nature; insomuch that if they are free to do anything else—if any other means of living, or occupation of their time and faculties, is open, which has any chance of appearing desirable to them—there will not be enough of them who will be willing to accept the condition said to be natural to them. If this is the real opinion of men in general, it would be well that it should be spoken out. I should like to hear somebody openly enunciating the doctrine (it is already implied in much that

8. A man can defy what is thought; a woman must submit to it (French); the epigraph to Mme. de Staël's *Delphine*.

is written on the subject)—"It is necessary to society that women should marry and produce children. They will not do so unless they are compelled. Therefore it is necessary to compel them." The merits of the case would then be clearly defined. It would be exactly that of the slaveholders of South Carolina and Louisiana. "It is necessary that cotton and sugar should be grown. White men cannot produce them. Negroes will not, for any wages which we choose to give. *Ergo*[9] they must be compelled." An illustration still closer to the point is that of impressment.[1] Sailors must absolutely be had to defend the country. It often happens that they will not voluntarily enlist. Therefore there must be the power of forcing them. How often has this logic been used! and, but for one flaw in it, without doubt it would have been successful up to this day. But it is open to the retort—First pay the sailors the honest value of their labor. When you have made it as well worth their while to serve you, as to work for other employers, you will have no more difficulty than others have in obtaining their services. To this there is no logical answer except "I will not:" and as people are now not only ashamed, but are not desirous, to rob the laborer of his hire, impressment is no longer advocated. Those who attempt to force women into marriage by closing all other doors against them, lay themselves open to a similar retort. If they mean what they say, their opinion must evidently be, that men do not render the married condition so desirable to women, as to induce them to accept it for its own recommendations. It is not a sign of one's thinking the boon one offers very attractive, when one allows only Hobson's choice,[2] "that or none." And here, I believe, is the clue to the feelings of those men, who have a real antipathy to the equal freedom of women. I believe they are afraid, not lest women should be unwilling to marry, for I do not think that any one in reality has that apprehension; but lest they should insist that marriage should be on equal conditions; lest all women of spirit and capacity should prefer doing almost anything else, not in their own eyes degrading, rather than marry, when marrying is giving themselves a master, and a master too of all their earthly possessions. And truly, if this consequence were necessarily incident to marriage, I think that the apprehension would be very well founded. I agree in thinking it probable that few women, capable of anything else, would, unless under an irresistible *entrainement*,[3] rendering them for the time insensible to anything but itself, choose such a lot, when any other means were open to them of filling a conventionally honorable place in life: and if men are determined that the law of marriage shall be a law of despotism, they are quite right, in point of mere policy, in leaving to women only Hobson's choice. But, in that case, all that has been done in the modern world to relax the chain on the minds of women, has been a mistake. They never should have been allowed to receive a literary education. Women who read, much more women who write, are, in the existing constitution of things, a contradiction and a disturbing element: and it was wrong to bring women up with any acquirements but those of an odalisque, or of a domestic servant.

1860   1869

---

9. Therefore (Latin).
1. The practice of seizing men and forcing them into service as sailors.
2. A choice without an alternative, so called in ref-

erence to the practice of Thomas Hobson, who rented out horses and required every customer to take the horse nearest the door.
3. Rapture.

From Autobiography

From *Chapter 5. A Crisis in My Mental History.*
One Stage Onward

For some years after this time[1] I wrote very little, and nothing regularly, for publication: and great were the advantages which I derived from the intermission. It was of no common importance to me, at this period, to be able to digest and mature my thoughts for my own mind only, without any immediate call for giving them out in print. Had I gone on writing, it would have much disturbed the important transformation in my opinions and character, which took place during those years. The origin of this transformation, or at least the process by which I was prepared for it, can only be explained by turning some distance back.

From the winter of 1821, when I first read Bentham, and especially from the commencement of the *Westminster Review,* I had what might truly be called an object in life; to be a reformer of the world. My conception of my own happiness was entirely identified with this object. The personal sympathies I wished for were those of fellow laborers in this enterprise. I endeavored to pick up as many followers as I could by the way; but as a serious and permanent personal satisfaction to rest upon, my whole reliance was placed on this; and I was accustomed to felicitate myself on the certainty of a happy life which I enjoyed, through placing my happiness in something durable and distant, in which some progress might be always making, while it could never be exhausted by complete attainment. This did very well for several years, during which the general improvement going on in the world and the idea of myself as engaged with others in struggling to promote it, seemed enough to fill up an interesting and animated existence. But the time came when I awakened from this as from a dream. It was in the autumn of 1826. I was in a dull state of nerves, such as everybody is occasionally liable to; unsusceptible to enjoyment or pleasurable excitement; one of those moods when what is pleasure at other times becomes insipid or indifferent; the state, I should think, in which converts to Methodism usually are, when smitten by their first "conviction of sin." In this frame of mind it occurred to me to put the question directly to myself: "Suppose that all your objects in life were realized; that all the changes in institutions and opinions which you are looking forward to could be completely effected at this very instant: would this be a great joy and happiness to you?" And an irrepressible self-consciousness distinctly answered, "No!" At this my heart sank within me: the whole foundation on which my life was constructed fell down. All my happiness was to have been found in the continual pursuit of this end. The end had ceased to charm, and how could there ever again be any interest in the means? I seemed to have nothing left to live for.

At first I hoped that the cloud would pass away of itself; but it did not. A night's sleep, the sovereign remedy for the smaller vexations of life, had no effect on it. I awoke to a renewed consciousness of the woeful fact. I carried it with me into all companies, into all occupations. Hardly anything had power to cause me even a few minutes' oblivion of it. For some months the

---

1. I.e., 1828. Mill had been contributing articles to the *Westminster Review.*

cloud seemed to grow thicker and thicker. The lines in Coleridge's *Dejection*—I was not then acquainted with them—exactly describe my case:

A grief without a pang, void, dark and drear,
A drowsy, stifled, unimpassioned grief,
Which finds no natural outlet or relief
In word, or sigh, or tear.[2]

In vain I sought relief from my favorite books; those memorials of past nobleness and greatness from which I had always hitherto drawn strength and animation. I read them now without feeling, or with the accustomed feeling minus all its charm; and I became persuaded that my love of mankind, and of excellence for its own sake, had worn itself out. I sought no comfort by speaking to others of what I felt. If I had loved anyone sufficiently to make confiding my griefs a necessity, I should not have been in the condition I was. I felt, too, that mine was not an interesting, or in any way respectable distress. There was nothing in it to attract sympathy. Advice, if I had known where to seek it, would have been most precious. The words of Macbeth to the physician[3] often occurred to my thoughts. But there was no one on whom I could build the faintest hope of such assistance. My father, to whom it would have been natural to me to have recourse in any practical difficulties, was the last person to whom, in such a case as this, I looked for help. Everything convinced me that he had no knowledge of any such mental state as I was suffering from, and that even if he could be made to understand it, he was not the physician who could heal it. My education, which was wholly his work, had been conducted without any regard to the possibility of its ending in this result; and I saw no use in giving him the pain of thinking that his plans had failed, when the failure was probably irremediable, and, at all events, beyond the power of *his* remedies. Of other friends, I had at that time none to whom I had any hope of making my condition intelligible. It was however abundantly intelligible to myself; and the more I dwelt upon it, the more hopeless it appeared.

My course of study had led me to believe that all mental and moral feelings and qualities, whether of a good or of a bad kind, were the results of association; that we love one thing, and hate another, take pleasure in one sort of action or contemplation, and pain in another sort, through the clinging of pleasurable or painful ideas to those things, from the effect of education or of experience. As a corollary from this, I had always heard it maintained by my father, and was myself convinced, that the object of education should be to form the strongest possible associations of the salutary class; associations of pleasure with all things beneficial to the great whole, and of pain with all things hurtful to it. This doctrine appeared inexpugnable; but it now seemed to me, on retrospect, that my teachers had occupied themselves but superficially with the means of forming and keeping up these salutary associations. They seemed to have trusted altogether to the old familiar instruments, praise and blame, reward and punishment. Now, I did not doubt that by these means, begun early, and applied unremittingly, intense associations of pain and pleasure, especially of pain, might be created, and might produce

2. *Dejection: An Ode* 21–24.
3. Shakespeare's *Macbeth* 5.3.40–44: "Canst thou not minister to a mind diseas'd?"

desires and aversions capable of lasting undiminished to the end of life. But there must always be something artificial and casual in associations thus produced. The pains and pleasures thus forcibly associated with things are not connected with them by any natural tie; and it is therefore, I thought, essential to the durability of these associations that they should have become so intense and inveterate as to be practically indissoluble, before the habitual exercise of the power of analysis had commenced. For I now saw, or thought I saw, what I had always before received with incredulity—that the habit of analysis has a tendency to wear away the feelings: as indeed it has, when no other mental habit is cultivated, and the analyzing spirit remains without its natural complements and correctives. The very excellence of analysis (I argued) is that it tends to weaken and undermine whatever is the result of prejudice; that it enables us mentally to separate ideas which have only casually clung together: and no associations whatever could ultimately resist this dissolving force, were it not that we owe to analysis our clearest knowledge of the permanent sequences in nature; the real connections between Things, not dependent on our will and feelings; natural laws, by virtue of which, in many cases, one thing is inseparable from another in fact; which laws, in proportion as they are clearly perceived and imaginatively realized, cause our ideas of things which are always joined together in Nature to cohere more and more closely in our thoughts. Analytic habits may thus even strengthen the associations between causes and effects, means and ends, but tend altogether to weaken those which are, to speak familiarly, a *mere* matter of feeling. They are therefore (I thought) favorable to prudence and clearsightedness, but a perpetual worm at the root both of the passions and of the virtues; and, above all, fearfully undermine all desires, and all pleasures, which are the effects of association, that is, according to the theory I held, all except the purely physical and organic; of the entire insufficiency of which to make life desirable, no one had a stronger conviction than I had. These were the laws of human nature, by which, as it seemed to me, I had been brought to my present state. All those to whom I looked up were of opinion that the pleasure of sympathy with human beings, and the feelings which made the good of others, and especially of mankind on a large scale, the object of existence, were the greatest and surest sources of happiness. Of the truth of this I was convinced, but to know that a feeling would make me happy if I had it, did not give me the feeling. My education, I thought, had failed to create these feelings in sufficient strength to resist the dissolving influence of analysis, while the whole course of my intellectual cultivation had made precocious and premature analysis the inveterate habit of my mind. I was thus, as I said to myself, left stranded at the commencement of my voyage, with a well-equipped ship and a rudder, but no sail; without any real desire for the ends which I had been so carefully fitted out to work for: no delight in virtue, or the general good, but also just as little in anything else. The fountains of vanity and ambition seemed to have dried up within me, as completely as those of benevolence. I had had (as I reflected) some gratification of vanity at too early an age: I had obtained some distinction, and felt myself of some importance, before the desire of distinction and of importance had grown into a passion: and little as it was which I had attained, yet having been attained too early, like all pleasures enjoyed too soon, it had made me *blasé* and indifferent to the pursuit. Thus neither selfish nor unselfish pleasures were pleasures to me. And there seemed no power in nature sufficient to begin the formation of my character anew, and create in a mind now irretrievably analytic, fresh associations of pleasure with any of the objects of human desire.

These were the thoughts which mingled with the dry heavy dejection of the melancholy winter of 1826–7. During this time I was not incapable of my usual occupations. I went on with them mechanically, by the mere force of habit. I had been so drilled in a certain sort of mental exercise that I could still carry it on when all the spirit had gone out of it. I even composed and spoke several speeches at the debating society, how, or with what degree of success, I know not. Of four years continual speaking at that society, this is the only year of which I remember next to nothing. Two lines of Coleridge, in whom alone of all writers I have found a true description of what I felt, were often in my thoughts, not at this time (for I had never read them), but in a later period of the same mental malady:

> Work without hope draws nectar in a sieve,
> And hope without an object cannot live.[4]

In all probability my case was by no means so peculiar as I fancied it, and I doubt not that many others have passed through a similar state; but the idiosyncrasies of my education had given to the general phenomenon a special character, which made it seem the natural effect of causes that it was hardly possible for time to remove. I frequently asked myself if I could, or if I was bound to go on living, when life must be passed in this manner. I generally answered to myself, that I did not think I could possibly bear it beyond a year. When, however, not more than half that duration of time had elapsed, a small ray of light broke in upon my gloom. I was reading, accidentally, Marmontel's *Mémoires*,[5] and came to the passage which relates his father's death, the distressed position of the family, and the sudden inspiration by which he, then a mere boy, felt and made them feel that he would be everything to them—would supply the place of all that they had lost. A vivid conception of that scene and its feelings came over me, and I was moved to tears. From this moment my burden grew lighter. The oppression of the thought that all feeling was dead within me was gone. I was no longer hopeless: I was not a stock or a stone. I had still, it seemed, some of the material out of which all worth of character, and all capacity for happiness, are made. Relieved from my ever present sense of irremediable wretchedness, I gradually found that the ordinary incidents of life could again give me some pleasure; that I could again find enjoyment, not intense, but sufficient for cheerfulness, in sunshine and sky, in books, in conversation, in public affairs; and that there was, once more, excitement, though of a moderate kind, in exerting myself for my opinions, and for the public good. Thus the cloud gradually drew off, and I again enjoyed life: and though I had several relapses, some of which lasted many months, I never again was as miserable as I had been.

The experiences of this period had two very marked effects on my opinions and character. In the first place, they led me to adopt a theory of life, very

---

4. The last two lines of Coleridge's short poem *Work without Hope*.

5. J. F. Marmontel (1723–1799), whose *Mémoires* were published in 1804.

unlike that on which I had before acted, and having much in common with what at that time I certainly had never heard of, the anti-self-consciousness theory of Carlyle.[6] I never, indeed, wavered in the conviction that happiness is the test of all rules of conduct, and the end of life. But I now thought that this end was only to be attained by not making it the direct end. Those only are happy (I thought) who have their minds fixed on some object other than their own happiness; on the happiness of others, on the improvement of mankind, even on some art or pursuit, followed not as a means, but as itself an ideal end. Aiming thus at something else, they find happiness by the way. The enjoyments of life (such was now my theory) are sufficient to make it a pleasant thing, when they are taken *en passant*,[7] without being made a principal object. Once make them so, and they are immediately felt to be insufficient. They will not bear a scrutinizing examination. Ask yourself whether you are happy, and you cease to be so. The only chance is to treat, not happiness, but some end external to it, as the purpose of life. Let your self-consciousness, your scrutiny, your self-interrogation exhaust themselves on that; and if otherwise fortunately circumstanced you will inhale happiness with the air you breathe, without dwelling on it or thinking about it, without either forestalling it in imagination, or putting it to flight by fatal questioning. This theory now became the basis of my philosophy of life. And I still hold to it as the best theory for all those who have but a moderate degree of sensibility and of capacity for enjoyment, that is, for the great majority of mankind.

The other important change which my opinions at this time underwent was that I, for the first time, gave its proper place, among the prime necessities of human well-being, to the internal culture of the individual. I ceased to attach almost exclusive importance to the ordering of outward circumstances, and the training of the human being for speculation and for action.

I had now learnt by experience that the passive susceptibilities needed to be cultivated as well as the active capacities, and required to be nourished and enriched as well as guided. I did not, for an instant, lose sight of, or undervalue, that part of the truth which I had seen before; I never turned recreant to intellectual culture, or ceased to consider the power and practice of analysis as an essential condition both of individual and of social improvement. But I thought that it had consequences which required to be corrected, by joining other kinds of cultivation with it. The maintenance of a due balance among the faculties now seemed to me of primary importance. The cultivation of the feelings became one of the cardinal points in my ethical and philosophical creed. And my thoughts and inclinations turned in an increasing degree toward whatever seemed capable of being instrumental to that object.

I now began to find meaning in the things which I had read or heard about the importance of poetry and art as instruments of human culture. But it was some time longer before I began to know this by personal experience. The only one of the imaginative arts in which I had from childhood taken great pleasure was music; the best effect of which (and in this it surpasses perhaps every other art) consists in exciting enthusiasm; in winding up to a

---

6. See *The Everlasting Yea* (p. 1089), of Carlyle's *Sartor Resartus*.

7. In passing (Latin).

high pitch those feelings of an elevated kind which are already in the character, but to which this excitement gives a glow and a fervor, which, though transitory at its utmost height, is precious for sustaining them at other times. This effect of music I had often experienced; but like all my pleasurable susceptibilities it was suspended during the gloomy period. I had sought relief again and again from this quarter, but found none. After the tide had turned, and I was in process of recovery, I had been helped forward by music, but in a much less elevated manner. I at this time first became acquainted with Weber's *Oberon*,[8] and the extreme pleasure which I drew from its delicious melodies did me good, by showing me a source of pleasure to which I was as susceptible as ever. The good, however, was much impaired by the thought that the pleasure of music (as is quite true of such pleasure as this was, that of mere tune) fades with familiarity, and requires either to be revived by intermittence, or fed by continual novelty. And it is very characteristic both of my then state, and of the general tone of my mind at this period of my life, that I was seriously tormented by the thought of the exhaustibility of musical combinations. The octave consists only of five tones and two semitones, which can be put together in only a limited number of ways, of which but a small proportion are beautiful: most of these, it seemed to me, must have been already discovered, and there could not be room for a long succession of Mozarts and Webers, to strike out, as these had done, entirely new and surpassingly rich veins of musical beauty. This source of anxiety may, perhaps, be thought to resemble that of the philosophers of Laputa,[9] who feared lest the sun should be burnt out. It was, however, connected with the best feature in my character, and the only good point to be found in my very unromantic and in no way honorable distress. For though my dejection, honestly looked at, could not be called other than egotistical, produced by the ruin, as I thought, of my fabric of happiness, yet the destiny of mankind in general was ever in my thoughts, and could not be separated from my own. I felt that the flaw in my life must be a flaw in life itself; that the question was whether, if the reformers of society and government could succeed in their objects, and every person in the community were free and in a state of physical comfort, the pleasures of life, being no longer kept up by struggle and privation, would cease to be pleasures. And I felt that unless I could see my way to some better hope than this for human happiness in general, my dejection must continue; but that if I could see such an outlet, I should then look on the world with pleasure; content as far as I was myself concerned, with any fair share of the general lot.

This state of my thoughts and feelings made the fact of my reading Wordsworth for the first time (in the autumn of 1828), an important event in my life. I took up the collection of his poems from curiosity, with no expectation of mental relief from it, though I had before resorted to poetry with that hope. In the worst period of my depression, I had read through the whole of Byron (then new to me), to try whether a poet, whose peculiar department was supposed to be that of the intenser feelings, could rouse any feeling in me. As might be expected, I got no good from this reading, but the reverse. The poet's state of mind was too like my own. His was the lament of a man

---

8. A romantic opera composed by Carl Maria von Weber (1786–1826).

9. In part 3 of Swift's *Gulliver's Travels*.

who had worn out all pleasures, and who seemed to think that life, to all who possess the good things of it, must necessarily be the vapid, uninteresting thing which I found it. His Harold and Manfred had the same burden on them which I had; and I was not in a frame of mind to derive any comfort from the vehement sensual passion of his Giaours, or the sullenness of his Laras.[1] But while Byron was exactly what did not suit my condition, Wordsworth was exactly what did. I had looked into *The Excursion*[2] two or three years before, and found little in it; and I should probably have found as little had I read it at this time. But the miscellaneous poems, in the two-volume edition of 1815 (to which little of value was added in the latter part of the author's life), proved to be the precise thing for my mental wants at that particular juncture.

In the first place, these poems addressed themselves powerfully to one of the strongest of my pleasurable susceptibilities, the love of rural objects and natural scenery; to which I had been indebted not only for much of the pleasure of my life, but quite recently for relief from one of my longest relapses into depression. In this power of rural beauty over me, there was a foundation laid for taking pleasure in Wordsworth's poetry; the more so, as his scenery lies mostly among mountains, which, owing to my early Pyrenean excursion,[3] were my ideal of natural beauty. But Wordsworth would never have had any great effect on me, if he had merely placed before me beautiful pictures of natural scenery. Scott does this still better than Wordsworth, and a very second-rate landscape does it more effectually than any poet. What made Wordsworth's poems a medicine for my state of mind, was that they expressed, not mere outward beauty, but states of feeling, and of thought colored by feeling, under the excitement of beauty. They seemed to be the very culture of the feelings, which I was in quest of. In them I seemed to draw from a source of inward joy, of sympathetic and imaginative pleasure, which could be shared in by all human beings; which had no connection with struggle or imperfection, but would be made richer by every improvement in the physical or social condition of mankind. From them I seemed to learn what would be the perennial sources of happiness, when all the greater evils of life shall have been removed. And I felt myself at once better and happier as I came under their influence. There have certainly been, even in our own age, greater poets than Wordsworth; but poetry of deeper and loftier feeling could not have done for me at that time what his did. I needed to be made to feel that there was real, permanent happiness in tranquil contemplation. Wordsworth taught me this, not only without turning away from, but with a greatly increased interest in the common feelings and common destiny of human beings. And the delight which these poems gave me proved that with culture of this sort, there was nothing to dread from the most confirmed habit of analysis. At the conclusion of the Poems came the famous *Ode*, falsely called Platonic, *Intimations of Immortality*: in which, along with more than his usual sweetness of melody and rhythm, and along with the two passages of grand imagery but bad philosophy so often quoted,

---

1. The heroes of some of Byron's early poems were usually gloomy and self-preoccupied. Mill refers here to *Childe Harold's Pilgrimage* (1812–18), *Manfred* (1817), *The Giaour* (1813), and *Lara* (1814).
2. A long meditative poem by Wordsworth, pub-
lished in 1814.
3. At fifteen, Mill had been deeply affected by the landscape of the Pyrenees in Spain, a mountainous region that also made a strong impression on Tennyson.

I found that he too had had similar experience to mine; that he also had felt that the first freshness of youthful enjoyment of life was not lasting; but that he had sought for compensation, and found it, in the way in which he was now teaching me to find it. The result was that I gradually, but completely, emerged from my habitual depression, and was never again subject to it. I long continued to value Wordsworth less according to his intrinsic merits than by the measure of what he had done for me. Compared with the greatest poets, he may be said to be the poet of unpoetical natures, possessed of quiet and contemplative tastes. But unpoetical natures are precisely those which require poetic cultivation. This cultivation Wordsworth is much more fitted to give than poets who are intrinsically far more poets than he.

* * *

1873

ELIZABETH BARRETT BROWNING
1806–1861

During her lifetime, Elizabeth Barrett Browning was England's most famous woman poet. Passionately admired by contemporaries as diverse as Ruskin, Swinburne, and Emily Dickinson for her moral and emotional ardor and her energetic engagement with the issues of her day, she was more famous than her husband, Robert Browning, at the time of her death. Her work fell into disrepute with the modernist reaction against what was seen as the inappropriate didacticism and rhetorical excess of Victorian poetry; but recently scholars interested in her exploration of what it means to be a woman poet have restored her status as a major writer.

Barrett Browning received an unusual education for a woman of her time. Availing herself of her brother's tutor, she studied Latin and Greek. She read voraciously in history, philosophy, and literature and began to write poetry from an early age—her first volume of poetry was published when she was thirteen. But as her intellectual and literary powers matured, her personal life became increasingly circumscribed both by ill health and by a tyrannically protective father, who had forbidden any of his eleven children to marry. By the age of thirty-nine, Elizabeth Barrett was a prominent woman of letters who lived in semiseclusion as an invalid in her father's house, where she occasionally received visitors in her room. One of these visitors was Robert Browning, who, moved by his admiration of her poetry, wrote to tell her "I do as I say, love these books with all my heart—and I love you too." He thereby initiated a courtship that culminated in 1846 in their secret marriage and elopement to Italy, for which her father never forgave her. Once in Italy, she regained much health and strength, bearing and raising a son, Pen, to whom she was ardently devoted, and becoming deeply involved in Italian nationalist politics. She and her husband made their home in Florence, at the house called Casa Guidi, where she died in 1861.

Barrett Browning's poetry is characterized by a fervent moral sensibility. In her early work, she tended to use the visionary modes of Romantic narrative poetry, but she turned increasingly to contemporary topics, particularly liberal causes of her day. For example, in 1843, when government investigations had exposed the exploitation of children employed in coal mines and factories, she wrote *The Cry of the Children*, a powerful indictment of the appalling use of child labor. Like Harriet Beecher Stowe in *Uncle Tom's Cabin*, Barrett Browning uses literature as a tool of social protest and reform. In later poems she took up the cause of the *risorgimento*, the movement to unify Italy as a nation-state, in which Italy's struggle for freedom and identity found resonance with her own.

For many years Elizabeth Barrett Browning was best known for her *Sonnets from the Portuguese*, a sequence of forty-four sonnets presented under the guise of a translation from the Portuguese language, in which she recorded the stages of her love for Robert Browning. But increasingly, her verse novel *Aurora Leigh* (1857) has attracted critical attention. The poem depicts the growth of a woman poet and is thus, as Cora Kaplan observes, the first work in English by a woman writer in which the heroine herself is an author. When Barrett Browning first envisioned the poem, she wrote, "My chief *intention* just now is the writing of a sort of novel-poem . . . running into the midst of our conventions, and rushing into drawing-rooms and the like 'where angels fear to tread'; and so, meeting face to face and without mask the Humanity of the age, and speaking the truth as I conceive of it out plainly." The poem is a female *Prelude* (cf. Wordsworth's *The Prelude*), a portrait of the artist as a young woman committed to a socially inclusive realist art. It is a daring work both in its presentation of social issues concerning women and in its claims for Aurora's poetic vocation; on her twentieth birthday, to pursue her career as a poet, Aurora refuses a proposal of marriage from her cousin Romney, who wants her to be his helpmate in the liberal causes he has embraced. Later in the poem, she rescues a fallen woman and takes her to Italy, where they settle together and confront a chastened Romney.

Immensely popular in its own day, *Aurora Leigh* had extravagant admirers (like Ruskin, who asserted that it was the greatest poem written in English) and critics who found fault with both its poetry and its morality. With its crowded canvas and melodramatic plot, it seems closer to the novel than to poetry, but it is important to view the poem in the context of the debate about appropriate poetic subject that engaged other Victorian poets. Unlike Arnold, who believed that the present age had not produced actions heroic enough to be the subjects of a great poetry, and unlike Tennyson, who used Arthurian legend to represent contemporary concerns, Barrett Browning felt that the present age contained the materials for an epic poetry. Virginia Woolf writes that "Elizabeth Barrett was inspired by a flash of true genius when she rushed into the drawing-room and said that here, where we live and work, is the true place for the poet." And whatever its faults, *Aurora Leigh* succeeds in giving us what Woolf describes as "a sense of life in general, of people who are unmistakably Victorian, wrestling with the problems of their own time, all brightened, intensified, and compacted by the fire of poetry. . . . Aurora Leigh, with her passionate interest in social questions, her conflict as artist and woman, her longing for knowledge and freedom, is the true daughter of her age."

The Cry of the Children[1]

"Φεῦ, φεῦ, τί προσδέρκεσθέ μ' ὄμμασιν, τέκνα;"
—*Medea*[2]

Do ye hear the children weeping, O my brothers,
　　Ere the sorrow comes with years?

---

1. Barrett Browning wrote *The Cry of the Children* in response to the report of a parliamentary commission written by her friend R. H. Horne on the labor of children in mines and factories. Many of the details of Barrett Browning's poem derive from the report.

2. Alas, my children, why do you look at me? (Greek), from Euripides' tragedy *Medea*. Medea speaks these lines when she kills her children in vengeance.

They are leaning their young heads against their mothers,
    And *that* cannot stop their tears.
5   The young lambs are bleating in the meadows,
    The young birds are chirping in the nest,
The young fawns are playing with the shadows,
    The young flowers are blowing toward the west—
But the young, young children, O my brothers,
10   They are weeping bitterly!
They are weeping in the playtime of the others,
    In the country of the free.

Do you question the young children in the sorrow
    Why their tears are falling so?
15 The old man may weep for his to-morrow
    Which is lost in Long Ago;
The old tree is leafless in the forest,
    The old year is ending in the frost,
The old wound, if stricken, is the sorest,
20   The old hope is hardest to be lost:
But the young, young children, O my brothers,
    Do you ask them why they stand
Weeping sore before the bosoms of their mothers,
    In our happy Fatherland?

25 They look up with their pale and sunken faces,
    And their looks are sad to see,
For the man's hoary anguish draws and presses
    Down the cheeks of infancy;
"Your old earth," they say, "is very dreary,"
30   "Our young feet," they say, "are very weak;
Few paces have we taken, yet are weary—
    Our grave-rest is very far to seek:
Ask the aged why they weep, and not the children,
    For the outside earth is cold,
35 And we young ones stand without, in our bewildering,
    And the graves are for the old."

"True," say the children, "it may happen
    That we die before our time:
Little Alice died last year, her grave is shapen
40   Like a snowball, in the rime.
We looked into the pit prepared to take her:
    Was no room for any work in the close clay!
From the sleep wherein she lieth none will wake her,
    Crying, 'Get up, little Alice! it is day.'
45 If you listen by that grave, in sun and shower,
    With your ear down, little Alice never cries;
Could we see her face, be sure we should not know her,
    For the smile has time for growing in her eyes:
And merry go her moments, lulled and stilled in
50   The shroud by the kirk° chime.   *church*

It is good when it happens," say the children,
    "That we die before our time."

Alas, alas, the children! they are seeking
    Death in life, as best to have:
55 They are binding up their hearts away from breaking,
    With a ceremen° from the grave.   *shroud*
Go out, children, from the mine and from the city,
    Sing out, children, as the little thrushes do;
Pluck your handfuls of the meadow-cowslips pretty,
60   Laugh aloud, to feel your fingers let them through!
But they answer, "Are your cowslips of the meadows
    Like our weeds anear the mine?
Leave us quiet in the dark of the coal-shadows,
    From your pleasures fair and fine!

65 "For oh," say the children, "we are weary,
    And we cannot run or leap;
If we cared for any meadows, it were merely
    To drop down in them and sleep.
Our knees tremble sorely in the stooping,
70   We fall upon our faces, trying to go;
And, underneath our heavy eyelids drooping,
    The reddest flower would look as pale as snow.
For, all day, we drag our burden tiring
    Through the coal-dark, underground;
75 Or, all day, we drive the wheels of iron
    In the factories, round and round.

"For, all day, the wheels are droning, turning;
    Their wind comes in our faces,
Till our hearts turn, our heads with pulses burning,
80   And the walls turn in their places:
Turns the sky in the high window blank and reeling,
    Turns the long light that drops adown the wall,
Turn the black flies that crawl along the ceiling,
    All are turning, all the day, and we with all.
85 And all day, the iron wheels are droning,
    And sometimes we could pray,
'O ye wheels,' (breaking out in a mad moaning)
    'Stop! be silent for to-day!' "

Ay, be silent! Let them hear each other breathing
90   For a moment, mouth to mouth!
Let them touch each other's hands, in a fresh wreathing
    Of their tender human youth!
Let them feel that this cold metallic motion
    Is not all the life God fashions or reveals:
95 Let them prove their living souls against the notion
    That they live in you, or under you, O wheels!
Still, all day, the iron wheels go onward,
    Grinding life down from its mark;

And the children's souls, which God is calling sunward,
100   Spin on blindly in the dark.

Now tell the poor young children; O my brothers,
        To look up to Him and pray;
So the blessed One who blesseth all the others,
        Will bless them another day.
105 They answer, "Who is God that He should hear us,
    While the rushing of the iron wheels is stirred?
When we sob aloud, the human creatures near us
    Pass by, hearing not, or answer not a word.
And *we* hear not (for the wheels in their resounding)
110   Strangers speaking at the door:
Is it likely God, with angels singing round Him,
        Hears our weeping any more?

Two words, indeed, of praying we remember,
        And at midnight's hour of harm,
115 'Our Father,' looking upward in the chamber,
        We say softly for a charm.
We know no other words except 'Our Father.'
    And we think that, in some pause of angels' song,
God may pluck them with the silence sweet to gather,
120   And hold both within His right hand which is strong.
'Our Father!' If He heard us, He would surely
        (For they call Him good and mild)
Answer, smiling down the steep world very purely,
        'Come and rest with me, my child.'

125 "But, no!" say the children, weeping faster,
        "He is speechless as a stone:
And they tell us, of His image is the master
        Who commands us to work on.
Go to!" say the children,— "up in Heaven,
130   Dark, wheel-like, turning clouds are all we find.
Do not mock us; grief has made us unbelieving:
We look up for God, but tears have made us blind."
Do you hear the children weeping and disproving,
        O my brothers, what ye preach?
135 For God's possible is taught by His world's loving,
        And the children doubt of each.

And well may the children weep before you!
        They are weary ere they run;
They have never seen the sunshine, nor the glory
140   Which is brighter than the sun.
They know the grief of man, without its wisdom;
    They sink in man's despair, without its calm;
Are slaves, without the liberty in Christdom,
    Are martyrs, by the pang without the palm:
145 Are worn as if with age, yet unretrievingly
        The harvest of its memories cannot reap,—

Are orphans of the earthly love and heavenly.
　　　Let them weep! let them weep!

They look up with their pale and sunken faces,
150　　And their look is dread to see,
For they mind you of their angels in high places,
　　　With eyes turned on Deity.
"How long," they say, "how long, O cruel nation,
　　　Will you stand, to move the world, on a child's heart,—
155　Stifle down with a mailed heel its palpitation,
　　　And tread onward to your throne amid the mart?
Our blood splashes upward, O gold-heaper,
　　　And your purple shows your path!
But the child's sob in the silence curses deeper
160　　Than the strong man in his wrath."

　　　　　　　　　　　　　　　　　　　1843

To George Sand[1]

A Desire

Thou large-brained woman and large-hearted man,
Self-called George Sand! whose soul, amid the lions
Of thy tumultuous senses, moans defiance
And answers roar for roar, as spirits can:
5　I would some mild miraculous thunder ran
Above the applauded circus,[2] in appliance
Of thine own nobler nature's strength and science,
Drawing two pinions, white as wings of swan,
From thy strong shoulders, to amaze the place
10　With holier light! that thou to woman's claim
And man's, mightst join beside the angel's grace
Of a pure genius sanctified from blame,
Till child and maiden pressed to thine embrace
To kiss upon thy lips a stainless fame.

　　　　　　　　　　　　　　　　　　　1844

To George Sand

A Recognition

True genius, but true woman! dost deny
The woman's nature with a manly scorn,

---

1. French Romantic novelist (1804–1876), famous for her unconventional ideas and behavior. Barrett Browning discovered her writing when she was an invalid, "a prisoner," and asserts that Sand, together with Balzac, "kept the color in my life." Barrett Browning defended Sand's genius to her less-sympathetic friends, who were critical of Sand's morality; she writes to her friend Mary Rus-sell Mitford, a contemporary novelist and dramatist, "She is eloquent as a fallen angel. . . . A true woman of genius!—but of a womanhood tired of itself, and scorned by her, while she bears it burning above her head."
2. A Roman spectacle that might include such things as combats with lions.

And break away the gauds° and armlets worn ornaments
By weaker women in captivity?
5 Ah, vain denial! that revolted cry
Is sobbed in by a woman's voice forlorn,—
Thy woman's hair, my sister, all unshorn
Floats back dishevelled strength in agony,
Disproving thy man's name: and while before
10 The world thou burnest in a poet-fire,
We see thy woman-heart beat evermore
Through the large flame. Beat purer, heart, and higher,
Till God unsex thee on the heavenly shore
Where unincarnate spirits purely aspire!

1844

From Sonnets from the Portuguese

21

Say over again, and yet once over again,
That thou dost love me. Though the word repeated
Should seem "a cuckoo song,"[1] as thou dost treat it,
Remember, never to the hill or plain,
5 Valley and wood, without her cuckoo strain
Comes the fresh Spring in all her green completed.
Belovèd, I, amid the darkness greeted
By a doubtful spirit voice, in that doubt's pain
Cry, "Speak once more—thou lovest!" Who can fear
10 Too many stars, though each in heaven shall roll,
Too many flowers, though each shall crown the year?
Say thou dost love me, love me, love me—toll
The silver iterance!°—only minding, Dear, repetition
To love me also in silence with thy soul.

22

When our two souls stand up erect and strong,
Face to face, silent, drawing nigh and nigher,
Until the lengthening wings break into fire
At either curvèd point—what bitter wrong
5 Can the earth do to us, that we should not long
Be here contented? Think. In mounting higher,
The angels would press on us and aspire
To drop some golden orb of perfect song
Into our deep, dear silence. Let us stay
10 Rather on earth, Belovèd,—where the unfit
Contrarious moods of men recoil away
And isolate pure spirits, and permit
A place to stand and love in for a day,
With darkness and the death-hour rounding it.

1. The cuckoo has a repeating call.

32

The first time that the sun rose on thine oath
To love me, I looked forward to the moon
To slacken all those bonds which seemed too soon
And quickly tied to make a lasting troth.
5 Quick-loving hearts, I thought, may quickly loathe;
And, looking on myself, I seemed not one
For such man's love!—more like an out-of-tune
Worn viol, a good singer would be wroth
To spoil his song with, and which, snatched in haste,
10 Is laid down at the first ill-sounding note.
I did not wrong myself so, but I placed
A wrong on *thee*. For perfect strains may float
'Neath master-hands, from instruments defaced—
And great souls, at one stroke, may do and dote.

43

How do I love thee? Let me count the ways.
I love thee to the depth and breadth and height
My soul can reach, when feeling out of sight
For the ends of Being and ideal Grace.
5 I love thee to the level of everyday's
Most quiet need, by sun and candlelight.
I love thee freely, as men strive for Right;
I love thee purely, as they turn from Praise.
I love thee with the passion put to use
10 In my old griefs, and with my childhood's faith.
I love thee with a love I seemed to lose
With my lost saints—I love thee with the breath,
Smiles, tears, of all my life!—and, if God choose,
I shall but love thee better after death.

1845–47   1850

From Aurora Leigh

From *Book 1*

[THE FEMININE EDUCATION OF AURORA LEIGH][1]

Then, land!—then, England! oh, the frosty cliffs[2]
Looked cold upon me. Could I find a home
Among those mean red houses through the fog?
And when I heard my father's language first
255 From alien lips which had no kiss for mine

---

1. Aurora Leigh, the only child of an Italian mother and an English father, was raised in Italy by her father since her mother's death when Aurora was four years old. When she was thirteen her father also died, and the orphaned girl has been sent to England to live with her father's maiden sister, who is to be responsible for the girl's education.
2. The white chalk cliffs at Dover.

I wept aloud, then laughed, then wept, then wept,
And some one near me said the child was mad
Through much sea-sickness. The train swept us on:
Was this my father's England? the great isle?
260 The ground seemed cut up from the fellowship
Of verdure, field from field,[3] as man from man;
The skies themselves looked low and positive,
As almost you could touch them with a hand,
And dared to do it they were so far off
265 From God's celestial crystals;[4] all things blurred
And dull and vague. Did Shakespeare and his mates
Absorb the light here?—not a hill or stone
With heart to strike a radiant colour up
Or active outline on the indifferent air.

270 I think I see my father's sister stand
Upon the hall-step of her country-house
To give me welcome. She stood straight and calm,
Her somewhat narrow forehead braided tight
As if for taming accidental thoughts
275 From possible pulses;[5] brown hair pricked with gray
By frigid use of life (she was not old,
Although my father's elder by a year),
A nose drawn sharply, yet in delicate lines;
A close mild mouth, a little soured about
280 The ends, through speaking unrequited loves
Or peradventure niggardly half-truths;
Eyes of no colour,—once they might have smiled,
But never, never have forgot themselves
In smiling; cheeks, in which was yet a rose
285 Of perished summers, like a rose in a book,
Kept more for ruth° than pleasure,—if past bloom,   *remorse*
Past fading also.
            She had lived, we'll say,
A harmless life, she called a virtuous life,
A quiet life, which was not life at all
290 (But that, she had not lived enough to know),
Between the vicar and the county squires,
The lord-lieutenant[6] looking down sometimes
From the empyrean to assure their souls
Against chance vulgarisms, and, in the abyss,
295 The apothecary,[7] looked on once a year
To prove their soundness of humility.
The poor-club[8] exercised her Christian gifts
Of knitting stockings, stitching petticoats,
Because we are of one flesh, after all,
300 And need one flannel[9] (with a proper sense

---

3. English fields were separated from each other by hedgerows.
4. Perhaps a reference to the ancient notion that the sky was composed of several crystalline spheres orbiting around the earth.
5. I.e., pulsation in her temples from excitement.

6. Governor of the county.
7. Pharmacist, who in England at the time could prescribe as well as sell medicine.
8. Club devoted to making things for the poor.
9. I.e., flannel petticoat.

Of difference in the quality)—and still
The book-club, guarded from your modern trick
Of shaking dangerous questions from the crease,[1]
Preserved her intellectual. She had lived
305   A sort of cage-bird life, born in a cage,
Accounting that to leap from perch to perch
Was act and joy enough for any bird.
Dear heaven, how silly are the things that live
In thickets, and eat berries!
                   I, alas,
310   A wild bird scarcely fledged, was brought to her cage,
And she was there to meet me. Very kind.
Bring the clean water, give out the fresh seed.

She stood upon the steps to welcome me,
Calm, in black garb. I clung about her neck,—
315   Young babes, who catch at every shred of wool
To draw the new light closer, catch and cling
Less blindly. In my ears my father's word
Hummed ignorantly, as the sea in shells,
"Love, love, my child." She, black there with my grief,
320   Might feel my love— she was his sister once—
I clung to her. A moment she seemed moved,
Kissed me with cold lips, suffered me to cling,
And drew me feebly through the hall into
The room she sat in.
               There, with some strange spasm
325   Of pain and passion, she wrung loose my hands
Imperiously, and held me at arm's length,
And with two grey-steel naked-bladed eyes
Searched through my face,—ay, stabbed it through and through,
Through brows and cheeks and chin, as if to find
330   A wicked murderer in my innocent face,
If not here, there perhaps. Then, drawing breath,
She struggled for her ordinary calm—
And missed it rather,—told me not to shrink,
As if she had told me not to lie or swear,—
335   "She loved my father and would love me too
As long as I deserved it." Very kind.

I understood her meaning afterward;
She thought to find my mother in my face,
And questioned it for that. For she, my aunt,
340   Had loved my father truly, as she could,
And hated, with the gall of gentle souls,
My Tuscan[2] mother who had fooled away
A wise man from wise courses, a good man
From obvious duties, and, depriving her,
345   His sister, of the household precedence,

1. The fold between two pages of a book, which had to be cut to open the pages. Presumably more modern books revealed more dangerous material when the crease was cut.
2. From Tuscany, a region in central Italy.

Had wronged his tenants, robbed his native land,
And made him mad, alike by life and death,
In love and sorrow. She had pored° for years   *pored over*
What sort of woman could be suitable
350 To her sort of hate, to entertain it with,
And so, her very curiosity
Became hate too, and all the idealism
She ever used in life was used for hate,
Till hate, so nourished, did exceed at last
355 The love from which it grew, in strength and heat,
And wrinkled her smooth conscience with a sense
Of disputable virtue (say not, sin)
When Christian doctrine was enforced at church.

And thus my father's sister was to me
360 My mother's hater. From that day she did
Her duty to me (I appreciate it
In her own word as spoken to herself),
Her duty, in large measure, well pressed out
But measured always. She was generous, bland,
365 More courteous than was tender, gave me still
The first place,—as if fearful that God's saints
Would look down suddenly and say "Herein
You missed a point, I think, through lack of love."
Alas, a mother never is afraid
370 Of speaking angerly to any child,
Since love, she knows, is justified of love.
And I, I was a good child on the whole,
A meek and manageable child. Why not?
I did not live, to have the faults of life:
375 There seemed more true life in my father's grave
Than in all England. Since *that* threw me off
Who fain would cleave (his latest will, they say,
Consigned me to his land), I only thought
Of lying quiet there where I was thrown
380 Like sea-weed on the rocks, and suffering her
To prick me to a pattern with her pin,³
Fibre from fibre, delicate leaf from leaf,
And dry out from my drowned anatomy
The last sea-salt left in me.
                                        So it was.
385 I broke the copious curls upon my head
In braids, because she liked smooth-ordered hair.
I left off saying my sweet Tuscan words
Which still at any stirring of the heart
Came up to float across the English phrase
390 As lilies (*Bene* or *Che che*⁴), because
She liked my father's child to speak his tongue.
I learnt the collects⁵ and the catechism,

---

3. As in embroidery.
4. No, no, indeed (Italian). *"Bene"*: it is well (Italian).

5. Seasonal opening prayers in the Anglican Church service.

The creeds,[6] from Athanasius back to Nice,
The Articles, the Tracts *against* the times[7]
395 (By no means Buonaventure's "Prick of Love"[8]),
And various popular synopses of
Inhuman doctrines never taught by John,[9]
Because she liked instructed piety.
I learnt my complement of classic French
400 (Kept pure of Balzac and neologism[1])
And German also, since she liked a range
Of liberal education,—tongues,° not books.   languages
I learnt a little algebra, a little
Of the mathematics,—brushed with extreme flounce
405 The circle of the sciences, because
She misliked women who are frivolous.
I learnt the royal genealogies
Of Oviedo,[2] the internal laws
Of the Burmese empire,—by how many feet
410 Mount Chimborazo outsoars Teneriffe,
What navigable river joins itself
To Lara,[3] and what census of the year five
Was taken at Klagenfurt,[4]—because she liked
A general insight into useful facts.
415 I learnt much music,—such as would have been
As quite impossible in Johnson's day[5]
As still it might be wished—fine sleights of hand
And unimagined fingering, shuffling off
The hearer's soul through hurricanes of notes
420 To a noisy Tophet;° and I drew . . . costumes   Hell
From French engravings, nereids° neatly draped   sea nymphs
(With smirks of simmering godship): I washed in[6]
Landscapes from nature (rather say, washed out).
I danced the polka and Cellarius,[7]
425 Spun glass, stuffed birds, and modeled flowers in wax,
Because she liked accomplishments in girls.
I read a score of books on womanhood
To prove, if women do not think at all,
They may teach thinking (to a maiden aunt
430 Or else the author),—books that boldly assert
Their right of comprehending husband's talk
When not too deep, and even of answering

---

6. Articles of Christian faith such as those proclaimed at the early church council held at Nicaea.
7. In the 1830s leaders of the conservative High Church party, such as John Henry Newman, had published *Tracts for the Times*, which expounded arguments against efforts by liberals to modernize the Anglican Church. Aurora's version of the title is hence ironic. "Articles": the thirty-nine articles are the principles of faith of the Church of England.
8. St. Bonaventure's doctrine that the power of the heart to love leads to higher illumination than the power of the mind to reason.
9. I.e., the author of the Gospel.
1. A new word or expression. Balzac (1799–1850),

a French novelist whose realism made him improper reading for a young lady.
2. Spanish historian (16th century), who wrote a book on the genealogies of the grandees of Spain.
3. A town in Spain on the river Arlanza. Mount Chimborazo is one of the highest peaks of the Andes. Teneriffe is a mountain in the Canary Islands.
4. A town in Austria.
5. Allusion to the story about Samuel Johnson, who, when told how difficult a piece of music was that a young lady was playing, replied, "I would it had been impossible."
6. As in painting with watercolors.
7. A kind of waltz.

With pretty "may it please you," or "so it is,"—
Their rapid insight and fine aptitude,
435 Particular worth and general missionariness,
As long as they keep quiet by the fire
And never say "no" when the world says "ay,"
For that is fatal,—their angelic reach
Of virtue, chiefly used to sit and darn,
440 And fatten household sinners,—their, in brief,
Potential faculty in everything
Of abdicating power in it: she owned
She liked a woman to be womanly,
And English women, she thanked God and sighed
445 (Some people always sigh in thanking God),
Were models to the universe. And last
I learnt cross-stitch,[8] because she did not like
To see me wear the night with empty hands
A-doing nothing. So, my shepherdess
450 Was something after all (the pastoral saints
Be praised for't), leaning lovelorn with pink eyes
To match her shoes, when I mistook the silks;
Her head uncrushed by that round weight of hat
So strangely similar to the tortoise shell
Which slew the tragic poet.[9]
455   By the way,
The works of women are symbolical.
We sew, sew, prick our fingers, dull our sight,
Producing what? A pair of slippers, sir,
To put on when you're weary—or a stool
460 To stumble over and vex you . . . "curse that stool!"
Or else at best, a cushion, where you lean
And sleep, and dream of something we are not
But would be for your sake. Alas, alas!
This hurts most, this—that, after all, we are paid
The worth of our work, perhaps.
465   In looking down
Those years of education (to return)
I wonder if Brinvilliers suffered more
In the water-torture[1] . . . flood succeeding flood
To drench the incapable throat and split the veins . . .
470 Than I did. Certain of your feebler souls
Go out in such a process; many pine
To a sick, inodorous light; my own endured:
I had relations in the Unseen, and drew
The elemental nutriment and heat
475 From nature, as earth feels the sun at nights,
Or as a babe sucks surely in the dark.
I kept the life thrust on me, on the outside

---

8. I.e., embroidery.
9. According to tradition, the Greek playwright
Aeschylus was killed by an eagle, who, mistaking
his bald head for a stone, dropped a tortoise on it
to break the shell.

1. Marie Marguerite, Marquise de Brinvilliers, a
celebrated criminal who was beheaded in 1676,
was tortured by having water forced down her
throat.

Of the inner life with all its ample room
For heart and lungs, for will and intellect,
480 Inviolable by conventions. God,
I thank thee for that grace of thine!
                                        At first
I felt no life which was not patience,—did
The thing she bade me, without heed to a thing
Beyond it, sat in just the chair she placed,
485 With back against the window, to exclude
The sight of the great lime-tree on the lawn,[2]
Which seemed to have come on purpose from the woods
To bring the house a message,—ay, and walked
Demurely in her carpeted low rooms,
490 As if I should not, harkening my own steps,
Misdoubt I was alive. I read her books,
Was civil to her cousin, Romney Leigh,
Gave ear to her vicar, tea to her visitors,
And heard them whisper, when I changed a cup
495 (I blushed for joy at that),—"The Italian child,
For all her blue eyes and her quiet ways,
Thrives ill in England: she is paler yet
Than when we came the last time; she will die."

From *Book 2*

[AURORA'S ASPIRATIONS][3]

Times followed one another. Came a morn
I stood upon the brink of twenty years,
And looked before and after, as I stood
Woman and artist,—either incomplete,
5 Both credulous of completion. There I held
The whole creation in my little cup,
And smiled with thirsty lips before I drank
"Good health to you and me, sweet neighbour mine,
And all these peoples."
                                    I was glad, that day;
10 The June was in me, with its multitudes
Of nightingales all singing in the dark,
And rosebuds reddening where the calyx[4] split.
I felt so young, so strong, so sure of God!
So glad, I could not choose be very wise!
15 And, old at twenty, was inclined to pull
My childhood backward in a childish jest
To see the face of't once more, and farewell!

---

2. Cf. Coleridge's *This Lime-Tree Bower My Prison*, in which the lime tree becomes the vehicle of a realization that Nature never deserts the wise and pure even when they seem to be cut off from her most beautiful vistas.
3. Stifled by her aunt's oppressive conventionality, Aurora has found three sources of comfort and inspiration: poetic aspirations, fostered by the dis-
covery of her father's library; the beauty of the natural world; and the intellectual companionship of her cousin Romney Leigh, an idealistic young man troubled by the misery of the poor and inspired by contemporary notions of social reform.
4. The protective outer leaves covering a flower or bud.

In which fantastic mood I bounded forth
At early morning,—would not wait so long
20 As even to snatch my bonnet by the strings,
But, brushing a green trail across the lawn
With my gown in the dew, took will and away
Among the acacias of the shrubberies,
To fly my fancies in the open air
25 And keep my birthday, till my aunt awoke
To stop good dreams. Meanwhile I murmured on
As honeyed bees keep humming to themselves,
"The worthiest poets have remained uncrowned
Till death has bleached their foreheads to the bone;
30 And so with me it must be unless I prove
Unworthy of the grand adversity,
And certainly I would not fail so much.
What, therefore, if I crown myself to-day
In sport, not pride, to learn the feel of it,
35 Before my brows be numbed as Dante's own
To all the tender pricking of such leaves?
Such leaves! what leaves?"
                      I pulled the branches down
To choose from.
                "Not the bay!⁵ I choose no bay
(The fates deny us if we are overbold),
40 Nor myrtle—which means chiefly love; and love
Is something awful which one dares not touch
So early o' mornings. This verbena strains
The point of passionate fragrance; and hard by,
This guelder-rose,° at far too slight a beck   *cranberry bush*
45 Of the wind; will toss about her flower-apples.
Ah—there's my choice,—that ivy on the wall,
That headlong ivy! not a leaf will grow
But thinking of a wreath. Large leaves, smooth leaves,
Serrated like my vines, and half as green.
50 I like such ivy, bold to leap a height
'Twas strong to climb; as good to grow on graves
As twist about a thyrsus;⁶ pretty too
(And that's not ill) when twisted round a comb."
Thus speaking to myself, half singing it,
55 Because some thoughts are fashioned like a bell
To ring with once being touched, I drew a wreath
Drenched, blinding me with dew, across my brow,
And fastening it behind so, turning faced
. . . My public!—cousin Romney—with a mouth
Twice graver than his eyes.
60   I stood there fixed,—
My arms up, like the caryatid,⁷ sole
Of some abolished temple, helplessly

---

5. A type of laurel tree whose leaves the ancient Greeks used to honor athletic champions; subsequently, a symbol of poetic achievement.
6. Staff twined with ivy, carried by Dionysus in Greek myth.
7. Classical column in the form of a draped female figure.

Persistent in a gesture which derides
A former purpose. Yet my blush was flame,
As if from flax, not stone.
                              "Aurora Leigh,
65 The earliest of Auroras!"[8]
                              Hand stretched out
I clasped, as shipwrecked men will clasp a hand,
Indifferent to the sort of palm. The tide
Had caught me at my pastime, writing down
70 My foolish name too near upon the sea
Which drowned me with a blush as foolish. "You,
My cousin!"
              The smile died out in his eyes
And dropped upon his lips, a cold dead weight,
For just a moment, "Here's a book I found!
75 No name writ on it—poems, by the form;
Some Greek upon the margin,—lady's Greek
Without the accents. Read it? Not a word.
I saw at once the thing had witchcraft in't,
Whereof the reading calls up dangerous spirits:
I rather bring it to the witch."
80   "My book.
You found it" . . .
                    "In the hollow by the stream
That beech leans down into—of which you said
The Oread in it has a Naiad's[9] heart
And pines for waters."
                        "Thank you."
                                      "Thanks to *you*
85 My cousin! that I have seen you not too much
Witch, scholar, poet, dreamer, and the rest,
To be a woman also."
                      With a glance
The smile rose in his eyes again and touched
The ivy on my forehead, light as air.
90 I answered gravely "Poets needs must be
Or men or women—more's the pity."
                                    "Ah,
But men, and still less women, happily,
Scarce need be poets. Keep to the green wreath,
Since even dreaming of the stone and bronze
95 Brings headaches, pretty cousin, and defiles
The clean white morning dresses."
                                    "So you judge!
Because I love the beautiful I must
Love pleasure chiefly, and be overcharged
For ease and whiteness! well, you know the world,
100 And only miss your cousin, 'tis not much.
But learn this; I would rather take my part

8. Dawns; from Aurora, Roman goddess of the   9. Water nymph's. "Oread": tree nymph.
dawn.

With God's Dead, who afford to walk in white
Yet spread His glory, than keep quiet here
And gather up my feet from even a step
105 For fear to soil my gown in so much dust.
I choose to walk at all risks.—Here, if heads
That hold a rhythmic thought, must ache perforce,
For my part I choose headaches,—and to-day's
My birthday,"
             "Dear Aurora, choose instead
To cure them. You have balsams."°   *balms*
110   "I perceive.
The headache is too noble for my sex.
You think the heartache would sound decenter,
Since that's the woman's special, proper ache,
And altogether tolerable, except
115 To a woman."

[AURORA'S REJECTION OF ROMNEY][1]

                  There he glowed on me
With all his face and eyes. "No other help?"
Said he—"no more than so?"
345   "What help?" I asked.
"You'd scorn my help,—as Nature's self, you say,
Has scorned to put her music in my mouth
Because a woman's. Do you now turn round
And ask for what a woman cannot give?"

350 "For what she only can, I turn and ask,"
He answered, catching up my hands in his,
And dropping on me from his high-eaved brow
The full weight of his soul,—"I ask for love,
And that, she can; for life in fellowship
355 Through bitter duties—that, I know she can;
For wifehood—will she?"
                      "Now," I said, "may God
Be witness 'twixt us two!" and with the word,
Meseemed[2] I floated into a sudden light
Above his stature,—"am I proved too weak
360 To stand alone, yet strong enough to bear
Such leaners on my shoulder? poor to think,
Yet rich enough to sympathise with thought?
Incompetent to sing, as blackbirds can,
Yet competent to love, like HIM?"
                          I paused;
365 Perhaps I darkened, as the lighthouse will

---

1. Romney and Aurora have been arguing about whether art, particularly a young woman's poetry, is useful in a world that, according to Romney, is full of human suffering. Romney claims that women have no faculty of generalizing and are, therefore, doomed to be trivial poets and ineffectual social reformers. Aurora is quick to agree that to be merely a poetaster would be intolerable to her, but while she admires Romney's lofty concern for humanity, she remains untempted to join forces with him.
2. It seemed to me.

That turns upon the sea. "It's always so.
Anything does for a wife."
                              "Aurora, dear,
And dearly honoured,"—he pressed in at once
With eager utterance,—"you translate me ill.
370   I do not contradict my thought of you
Which is most reverent, with another thought
Found less so. If your sex is weak for art
(And I, who said so, did but honour you
By using truth in courtship), it is strong
375   For life and duty. Place your fecund heart
In mine, and let us blossom for the world
That wants love's colour in the grey of time.
My talk, meanwhile, is arid to you, ay,
Since all my talk can only set you where
380   You look down coldly on the arena-heaps
Of headless bodies, shapeless, indistinct!
The Judgment-Angel scarce would find his way
Through such a heap of generalised distress
To the individual man with lips and eyes,
385   Much less Aurora. Ah, my sweet, come down,
And hand in hand we'll go where yours shall touch
These victims, one by one! till, one by one,
The formless, nameless trunk of every man
Shall seem to wear a head with hair you know,
390   And every woman catch your mother's face
To melt you into passion."
                              "I am a girl,"
I answered slowly; "you do well to name
My mother's face. Though far too early, alas,
God's hand did interpose 'twixt it and me,
395   I know so much of love as used to shine
In that face and another. Just so much;
No more indeed at all. I have not seen
So much love since, I pray you pardon me,
As answers even to make a marriage with
400   In this cold land of England. What you love
Is not a woman, Romney, but a cause:
You want a helpmate, not a mistress, sir,
A wife to help your ends,—in her no end.
Your cause is noble, your ends excellent,
405   But I, being most unworthy of these and that,
Do otherwise conceive of love. Farewell."

"Farewell, Aurora? you reject me thus?"
He said.
              "Sir, you were married long ago.
You have a wife already whom you love,
410   Your social theory. Bless you both, I say.
For my part, I am scarcely meek enough
To be the handmaid of a lawful spouse.

Do I look a Hagar,[3] think you?"

"So you jest."

"Nay, so, I speak in earnest," I replied.
415 "You treat of marriage too much like, at least,
A chief apostle: you would bear with you
A wife . . . a sister . . . shall we speak it out?
A sister of charity."

"Then, must it be
Indeed farewell? And was I so far wrong
420 In hope and in illusion, when I took
The woman to be nobler than the man,
Yourself the noblest woman, in the use
And comprehension of what love is,—love,
That generates the likeness of itself
425 Through all heroic duties? so far wrong,
In saying bluntly, venturing truth on love,
'Come, human creature, love and work with me,'—
Instead of 'Lady, thou art wondrous fair,
'And, where the Graces walk before, the Muse
430 'Will follow at the lightning of their eyes,
'And where the Muse walks, lovers need to creep:
'Turn round and love me, or I die of love.' "

With quiet indignation I broke in.
"You misconceive the question like a man,
435 Who sees a woman as the complement
Of his sex merely. You forget too much
That every creature, female as the male,
Stands single in responsible act and thought
As also in birth and death. Whoever says
440 To a loyal woman, 'Love and work with me,'
Will get fair answers if the work and love,
Being good themselves, are good for her—the best
She was born for. Women of a softer mood,
Surprised by men when scarcely awake to life,
445 Will sometimes only hear the first word, love,
And catch up with it any kind of work,
Indifferent, so that dear love go with it.
I do not blame such women, though, for love,
They pick much oakum;[4] earth's fanatics make
450 Too frequently heaven's saints. But *me* your work
Is not the best for,—nor your love the best,
Nor able to commend the kind of work
For love's sake merely. Ah, you force me, sir,
To be overbold in speaking of myself:
455 I too have my vocation,—work to do,
The heavens and earth have set me since I changed

---

3. In Genesis 16, Sarah's maidservant, who bore a child, Ishmael, by Sarah's husband, Abraham.

4. Fiber derived by untwisting (picking) old rope, a task frequently assigned to workhouse inmates.

My father's face for theirs, and, though your world
Were twice as wretched as you represent,
Most serious work, most necessary work
460 As any of the economists'. Reform,
Make trade a Christian possibility,
And individual right no general wrong;
Wipe out earth's furrows of the Thine and Mine,
And leave one green for men to play at bowls,[5]
465 With innings for them all! . . . What then, indeed,
If mortals are not greater by the head
Than any of their prosperities? what then,
Unless the artist keep up open roads
Betwixt the seen and unseen,—bursting through
470 The best of your conventions with his best,
The speakable, imaginable best
God bids him speak, to prove what lies beyond
Both speech and imagination? A starved man
Exceeds a fat beast: we'll not barter, sir,
475 The beautiful for barley.—And, even so,
I hold you will not compass your poor ends
Of barley-feeding and material ease,
Without a poet's individualism
To work your universal. It takes a soul,
480 To move a body: it takes a high-souled man,
To move the masses, even to a cleaner stye:
It takes the ideal, to blow a hair's-breadth off
The dust of the actual.—Ah, your Fouriers[6] failed,
Because not poets enough to understand
485 That life develops from within.——For me,
Perhaps I am not worthy, as you say,
Of work like this: perhaps a woman's soul
Aspires, and not creates: yet we aspire,
And yet I'll try out your perhapses, sir,
490 And if I fail . . . why, burn me up my straw[7]
Like other false works—I'll not ask for grace;
Your scorn is better, cousin Romney. I
Who love my art, would never wish it lower
To suit my stature. I may love my art.
495 You'll grant that even a woman may love art,
Seeing that to waste true love on anything
Is womanly, past question."

From *Book 5*

[POETS AND THE PRESENT AGE]

The critics say that epics have died out
140 With Agamemnon and the goat-nursed gods;[8]

5. A game of skill played on a smooth lawn with weighted wooden balls.
6. François-Marie-Charles Fourier (1772–1837), a French political theorist who advocated com-

munal property as a basis for social harmony.
7. I.e., destroy my poetry (a deliberate archaism).
8. Zeus was nursed by a goat.

I'll not believe it. I could never deem,
As Payne Knight[9] did (the mythic mountaineer
Who travelled higher than he was born to live,
And showed sometimes the goitre[1] in his throat
145 Discoursing of an image seen through fog),
That Homer's heroes measured twelve feet high.
They were but men:—his Helen's hair turned grey
Like any plain Miss Smith's who wears a front;[2]
And Hector's infant whimpered at a plume[3]
150 As yours last Friday at a turkey-cock.
All actual heroes are essential men,
And all men possible heroes: every age,
Heroic in proportions, double-faced,
Looks backward and before, expects a morn
And claims an epos.°   *epic poem*
155   Ay, but every age
Appears to souls who live in 't (ask Carlyle)[4]
Most unheroic. Ours, for instance, ours:
The thinkers scout it, and the poets abound
Who scorn to touch it with a finger-tip:
160 A pewter age,[5]—mixed metal, silver-washed;
An age of scum, spooned off the richer past,
An age of patches for old gaberdines,°   *coats*
An age of mere transition,[6] meaning nought
Except that what succeeds must shame it quite
165 If God please. That's wrong thinking, to my mind,
And wrong thoughts make poor poems.
                                        Every age,
Through being beheld too close, is ill-discerned
By those who have not lived past it. We'll suppose
Mount Athos carved, as Alexander schemed,
170 To some colossal statue of a man.[7]
The peasants, gathering brushwood in his ear,
Had guessed as little as the browsing goats
Of form or feature of humanity
Up there,—in fact, had travelled five miles off
175 Or ere the giant image broke on them,
Full human profile, nose and chin distinct,
Mouth, muttering rhythms of silence up the sky

---

9. Richard Payne Knight (1750–1824), a classical philologist, who, upon England's acquisition of the Parthenon marbles, claimed that Lord Elgin had wasted his labor because they were not all Greek.
1. A disease often contracted in high mountain areas because of the low iodine content of the water.
2. A piece of false hair worn over the forehead by women.
3. In an episode in the *Iliad*, Hector tries to take his infant son in his arms; but the child clings to his nurse, frightened of his father's helmet and crest.
4. In *Heroes and Hero-Worship* (1841), Carlyle argues that the present age needs a renewed per-
ception of the heroic.
5. Allusion to the convention, which originates in Hesiod, of describing civilization's decline through a succession of ages named for increasingly less precious materials, i.e., the Golden Age, the Silver Age, the Bronze Age.
6. In *The Spirit of the Age* (1831) John Stuart Mill calls the present age "an age of transition."
7. Dionocrates, a sculptor, is said to have suggested to Alexander that Mount Athos be carved into the statue of a conqueror with a city in his left hand and a basin in his right, where all the waters of the region could be collected and used to water the pasture lands below.

And fed at evening with the blood of suns;
Grand torso,—hand, that flung perpetually
180 The largesse of a silver river down
To all the country pastures. 'Tis even thus
With times we live in,—evermore too great
To be apprehended near.
　　　　　　　　　But poets should
Exert a double vision; should have eyes
185 To see near things as comprehensively
As if afar they took their point of sight,
And distant things as intimately deep
As if they touched them. Let us strive for this.
I do distrust the poet who discerns
190 No character or glory in his times,
And trundles back his soul five hundred years,
Past moat and drawbridge, into a castle-court,
To sing—oh, not of lizard or of toad
Alive i' the ditch there,—'twere excusable,
195 But of some black chief, half knight, half sheep-lifter,
Some beauteous dame, half chattel and half queen,
As dead as must be, for the greater part,
The poems made on their chivalric bones;
And that's no wonder: death inherits death.

200 Nay, if there's room for poets in this world
A little overgrown (I think there is),
Their sole work is to represent the age,
Their age, not Charlemagne's,[8]—this live, throbbing age,
That brawls, cheats, maddens, calculates, aspires,
205 And spends more passion, more heroic heat,
Betwixt the mirrors of its drawing-rooms,
Than Roland[9] with his knights at Roncesvalles.
To flinch from modern varnish, coat or flounce,
Cry out for togas and the picturesque,
210 Is fatal,—foolish too. King Arthur's self
Was commonplace to Lady Guenever;
And Camelot to minstrels seemed as flat
As Fleet Street[1] to our poets.
　　　　　　　　　Never flinch,
But still, unscrupulously epic, catch
215 Upon the burning lava of a song
The full-veined, heaving, double-breasted Age:
That, when the next shall come, the men of that
May touch the impress with reverent hand, and say
"Behold,—behold the paps° we all have sucked!"　　　　breasts
220 This bosom seems to beat still, or at least
It sets ours beating: this is living art,
Which thus presents and thus records true life."

1853–56　　　　　　　　　　　　　　　　　　　　　1857

---

8. Frankish conqueror (742–814), who created a
European empire.
9. Legendary medieval hero, whose adventures

are told in the epic poem *Chanson de Roland*.
1. A center for book shops and newspaper and
publishing offices in London.

Mother and Poet[1]

(Turin, After News from Gaeta, 1861)

1

DEAD! One of them shot by the sea in the east,
  And one of them shot in the west by the sea.
Dead! both my boys! When you sit at the feast
  And are wanting a great song for Italy free,
5   Let none look at *me*!

2

Yet I was a poetess only last year,
  And good at my art, for a woman, men said;
But *this* woman, *this*, who is agonised here,
  —The east sea and west sea rhyme on in her head
10   For ever instead.

3

What art can a woman be good at? Oh, vain!
  What art *is* she good at, but hurting her breast
With the milk-teeth of babes, and a smile at the pain?
  Ah boys, how you hurt! you were strong as you pressed,
15   And I proud, by that test.

4

What art's for a woman? To hold on her knees
  Both darlings! to feel all their arms round her throat,
Cling, strangle a little! to sew by degrees
  And 'broider the long-clothes and neat little coat;
20   To dream and to doat.

5

To teach them . . . It stings there! *I* made them indeed
  Speak plain the word *country*. *I* taught them, no doubt,
That a country's a thing men should die for at need.
  I prated of liberty, rights, and about
25   The tyrant cast out.

6

And when their eyes flashed . . . O my beautiful eyes! . . .
  I exulted; nay, let them go forth at the wheels
Of the guns, and denied not. But then the surprise
  When one sits quite alone! Then one weeps, then one kneels!
30   God, how the house feels!

1. The speaker is the Italian poet and patriot
Laura Savio of Turin, both of whose sons were
killed in the struggle for the unification of Italy,
one in the attack on the fortress at Ancona, the
other at the siege of Gaeta, the last stronghold of
the Neapolitan government.

7

At first, happy news came, in gay letters moiled°   moistened
  With my kisses,—of camp-life and glory, and how
They both loved me; and, soon coming home to be spoiled
  In return would fan off every fly from my brow
35   With their green laurel-bough.[2]

8

Then was triumph at Turin: "Ancona was free!"
  And some one came out of the cheers in the street,
With a face pale as stone, to say something to me.
  My Guido was dead! I fell down at his feet,
40   While they cheered in the street.

9

I bore it; friends soothed me; my grief looked sublime
  As the ransom of Italy. One boy remained
To be leant on and walked with, recalling the time
  When the first grew immortal, while both of us strained
45   To the height he had gained.

10

And letters still came, shorter, sadder, more strong,
  Writ now but in one hand, "I was not to faint,—
One loved me for two—would be with me ere long:
  And *Viva l'Italia!—he* died for, our saint,
50   Who forbids our complaint."

11

My Nanni would add, "he was safe, and aware
  Of a presence that turned off the balls,°—was imprest   cannonballs
It was Guido himself, who knew what I could bear,
  And how 'twas impossible, quite dispossessed
55   To live on for the rest."

12

On which, without pause, up the telegraph line
  Swept smoothly the next news from Gaeta:—*Shot.*
Tell his mother. Ah, ah, "his," "their" mother,—not "mine,"
  No voice says *"My* mother" again to me. What!
60   You think Guido forgot?

13

Are souls straight so happy that, dizzy with Heaven,
  They drop earth's affections, conceive not of woe?
I think not. Themselves were too lately forgiven
  Through THAT Love and Sorrow which reconciled so
65   The Above and Below.

2. A laurel crown is the conventional mark of a poet's fame.

14

O Christ of the five wounds, who look'dst through the dark
   To the face of thy mother! consider, I pray,
How we common mothers stand desolate, mark,
    Whose sons, not being Christs, die with eyes turned away
70   And no last word to say!

15

Both boys dead? but that's out of nature. We all
   Have been patriots, yet each house must always keep one.
'Twere imbecile, hewing out roads to a wall;
   And, when Italy's made, for what end is it done
75   If we have not a son?

16

Ah, ah, ah! when Gaeta's taken, what then?
   When the fair wicked queen sits no more at her sport
Of the fire-balls of death crashing souls out of men?
   When the guns of Cavalli[3] with final retort
80   Have cut the game short?

17

When Venice and Rome keep their new jubilee,[4]
   When your flag takes all heaven for its white, green, and red,
When *you* have your country from mountain to sea,
   When King Victor has Italy's crown on his head,
85   (And *I* have my Dead)—

18

What then? Do not mock me. Ah, ring your bells low,
   And burn your lights faintly! *My* country is *there,*
Above the star pricked by the last peak of snow:
   My Italy's THERE, with my brave civic Pair,
90   To disfranchise despair!

19

Forgive me. Some women bear children in strength,
   And bite back the cry of their pain in self-scorn;
But the birth-pangs of nations will wring us at length
   Into wail such as this—and we sit on forlorn
95   When the man-child is born.

20

Dead! One of them shot by the sea in the east,
   And one of them shot in the west by the sea.
Both! both my boys! If in keeping the feast

---

3. The general commanding the siege of Gaeta. "The fair wicked queen": Maria, wife of Francis II, the last ruler of the Neapolitan government, who retreated to Gaeta.
4. The celebration when they too will have been united with the rest of Italy under King Victor Emmanuel. In 1861, when the poem was written, they were the two cities that were still independent of the new state.

You want a great song for your Italy free,
100 Let none look at *me*!

1861 1862

ALFRED, LORD TENNYSON
1809–1892

Whether or not Alfred Tennyson was the greatest of the Victorian poets, as affirmed by many critics today, there is no doubt that in his own lifetime he was the most popular of poets. On the bookshelves of almost every family of readers in England and the United States, from 1850 onward, were the works of a man who had incontestably gained the title that Walt Whitman longed for: "The Poet of the People" (Whitman, in fact, called Tennyson, colorfully, "the Boss"). Popularity inevitably provided provocation for a reaction in the decades following his death. In the course of repudiating their Victorian predecessors, the Edwardians and Georgians established the fashion of making fun of Tennyson's great achievements. Samuel Butler (1835–1902), who anticipated early twentieth-century tastes, has a characteristic entry in his *Notebooks:* "Talking it over, we agreed that Blake was no good because he learnt Italian at sixty in order to study Dante, and we knew Dante was no good because he was so fond of Virgil, and Virgil was no good because Tennyson ran him, and as for Tennyson—well, Tennyson goes without saying." In the second half of the twentieth century, Butler's flippant dismissal of Tennyson expresses an attitude that is no longer fashionable. The delights to be found in this superb "lord of language"—as Tennyson himself addresses his favorite predecessor, Virgil—have been rediscovered, and Tennyson's stature as one of the major poets of any age has been reestablished.

Like his poetry, Tennyson's life and character have been reassessed in the twentieth century. To many of his contemporaries he seemed a remote wizard, secure in his laureate's robes, a man whose life had been sheltered, marred only by the loss of his best friend in youth. During much of his career Tennyson may have been isolated, but his was not a sheltered life in the real sense of the word. Although he grew up in a parsonage, it was not the kind of parsonage one encounters in the novels of Jane Austen. It was a household dominated by frictions and loyalties and broodings over ancestral inheritances, in which the children showed marked strains of instability and eccentricity.

Alfred was the fourth son in a family of twelve children. One of his brothers had to be confined to an insane asylum for life; another was long addicted to opium; another had violent quarrels with his father, the Reverend Dr. George Tennyson. This father, a man of considerable learning, had himself been born the eldest son of a wealthy landowner and had, therefore, expected to be heir to his family's estates. Instead he was disinherited in favor of his younger brother and had to make his own livelihood by joining the clergy, a profession that he disliked. After George Tennyson had settled in a small rectory in Somersby, his brooding sense of dissatisfaction led to increasingly violent bouts of drunkenness, despite which he was able to serve as tutor for his sons in classical and modern languages to prepare them for entering the university.

Before leaving this strange household for Cambridge, Alfred had already demonstrated a flair for writing verse—precocious exercises in the manner of Milton or Byron or the Elizabethan dramatists. He had even published a volume in 1827, in collaboration with his brother Charles, *Poems by Two Brothers*. This feat drew him to the attention of a group of gifted undergraduates at Cambridge, "the Apostles," who encouraged him to devote his life to poetry. Up until that time, the young man had known scarcely anyone outside the circle of his own family. Despite his massive frame and powerful physique, he was painfully shy; and the friendships he found at Cambridge as well as the intellectual and political discussions in which he participated served to give him confidence and to widen his horizons as a poet. The most important of these friendships was with Arthur Hallam, a leader of the Apostles, who later became engaged to Tennyson's sister. Hallam's sudden death, in 1833, seemed an overwhelming calamity to his friend. Not only the long elegy *In Memoriam* but many of Tennyson's other poems are tributes to this early friendship.

Alfred's career at Cambridge was interrupted and finally broken off in 1831 by family dissensions and financial need, and he returned home to study and practice the craft of poetry. His early volumes (1830 and 1832) were attacked as "obscure" or "affected" by some of the reviewers. Tennyson suffered acutely under hostile criticism, but he also profited from it. His volume of 1842 demonstrated a remarkable advance in taste and technical excellence, and in 1850 he at last attained fame and full critical recognition with *In Memoriam*. In the same year, he became poet laureate in succession to Wordsworth. The struggle during the previous twenty years had been made especially painful by the long postponement of his marriage to Emily Sellwood, whom he had loved since 1836 but could not marry, because of poverty, until 1850.

His life thereafter was a comfortable one. He was as popular as Byron had been. The earnings from his poetry (sometimes exceeding £10,000 a year) enabled him to purchase a house in the country and to enjoy the kind of seclusion he liked. His notoriety was enhanced, like that of Bernard Shaw and Walt Whitman, by his colorful appearance. Huge and shaggy, in cloak and broad-brimmed hat, gruff in manner as a farmer, he impressed everyone as what is called a "character." The pioneering photographer Julia Cameron, who took magnificent portraits of him, called him "the most beautiful old man on earth." Like Dylan Thomas in the twentieth century, he had a booming voice that electrified listeners when he read his poetry, "mouthing out his hollow o's and a's, / Deep-chested music." Moreover, for many Victorian readers, he seemed not only a great poetical phrase maker and a striking individual but also a wise man whose occasional pronouncements on politics or world affairs represented the national voice itself. In 1884 he accepted a peerage. In 1892 he died and was buried in Westminster Abbey.

It is often said that success was bad for Tennyson and that after *In Memoriam* his poetic power seriously declined. That in his last forty-two years certain of his mannerisms became accentuated is true. One of the difficulties of his dignified blank verse was, as he said himself, that it is hard to describe commonplace objects and "at the same time to retain poetical elevation." This difficulty is evident, for example, in *Enoch Arden* (1864), a long blank verse narrative of everyday life in a fishing village, in which a basketful of fish is ornately described as "Enoch's ocean spoil / In ocean-smelling osier." In others of his later poems, those dealing with national affairs, there is also an increased shrillness of tone—a mannerism accentuated by Tennyson's realizing that like Dickens he had a vast public behind him to back up his pronouncements.

It is foolish, however, to try to shelve all of Tennyson's later productions. In 1855 he published his experimental monologue *Maud*, perhaps his finest long poem, in which he displays the bitterness and despair its alienated hero feels toward society. In 1859 he published four books of his *Idylls of the King*, a large-scale epic that occupied most of his energies in the second half of his career. The *Idylls* uses the body of Arthurian legend to construct a vision of the rise and fall of civilization. In this civilization, women at once inspire men's highest efforts and sow the seeds of their destruction. The *Idylls* provides Tennyson's most extensive social vision, one whose concern with medieval ideals of social community, heroism, and courtly love and whose despairing sense of the cycles of historical change typifies much social thought of the age.

W. H. Auden stated that Tennyson had "the finest ear, perhaps, of any English poet." The interesting point is that Tennyson did not "have" such an ear: he developed it. Studies of the original versions of his poems in the 1830 and 1832 volumes demonstrate how hard he worked at his craftsmanship. Like Chaucer or Keats or Pope, Tennyson studied his predecessors assiduously to perfect his technique. Anyone wanting to learn the traditional craft of English verse can study with profit the various stages of revision that such poems as *The Lotos-Eaters* were subjected to by this painstaking and artful poet. Some lines of 1988 by the American poet Karl Shapiro effectively characterize Tennyson's accomplishments in these areas:

> Long-lived, the very image of English Poet,
> Whose songs still break out tears in the generations,
> Whose poetry for practitioners still astounds,
> Who crafted his life and letters like a watch.

Tennyson's early poetry shows other skills as well. One of these was a capacity for linking scenery to states of mind. As early as 1835, J. S. Mill identified the special kind of scene painting to be found in early poems such as *Mariana*: "not the power of producing that rather vapid species of composition usually termed descriptive poetry . . . but the power of *creating* scenery, in keeping with some state of human feeling so fitted to it as to be the embodied symbol of it, and to summon up the state of feeling itself, with a force not to be surpassed by anything but reality."

The state of feeling to which Tennyson was most intensely drawn was a melancholy isolation, often portrayed through the consciousness of an abandoned woman, as in *Mariana*. Tennyson's absorption with such emotions in his early poetry evoked considerable criticism. His friend R. C. Trench warned him, "Tennyson, we cannot live in Art," and Mill urged him to "cultivate, and with no half devotion, philosophy as well as poetry." Advice of this kind Tennyson was already predisposed to heed. The death of Hallam, the religious uncertainties that he had himself experienced, together with his own extensive study of writings by geologists, astronomers, and biologists, led him to confront many of the religious issues that bewildered his and later generations. The result was *In Memoriam* (1850), a long elegy written over a period of seventeen years, embodying the poet's reflections on our relation to God and to nature.

Was Tennyson intellectually equipped to deal with the great questions raised in *In Memoriam*? The answer may depend on a reader's religious and philosophical presuppositions. Some, such as T. H. Huxley, considered Tennyson an intellectual giant, a thinker who had mastered the scientific thought of his century and fully confronted the issues it raised. Others dismissed Tennyson, in this phase, as a lightweight. Auden went so far as to call him the "stupidest" of English poets. He went on to say, "There was little about melancholia that he didn't know; there was little else that he did." Perhaps T. S. Eliot's evaluation of *In Memoriam* is the more accurate: the poem, he wrote, is remarkable not "because of the quality of its faith but because of the quality of its doubt." Tennyson's mind was slow, ponderous, brooding; for the composition of *In Memoriam* such qualities of mind were assets, not liabilities. In these terms we can understand when Tennyson's poetry really fails to measure up: it is when he writes of events of the moment over which his thoughts and feelings have had no time to brood. Several of his poems are what he himself called "newspaper verse." They are letters to the editor, in effect, with the ephemeral heat and simplicity we expect of such productions. *The Charge of the Light Brigade*, inspired by a report in the *Times* of a cavalry charge at Balaclava during the Crimean War, is one of the best of his productions in this category.

Tennyson's poems of contemporary events were inevitably popular in his own day. So too were those poems in which, as in *Locksley Hall*, he dipped into the future.

The technological changes wrought by Victorian inventors and engineers fascinated him. Sometimes they gave him an assurance of human progress as swaggeringly exultant as that of Macaulay. At other times the horrors of industrialism's by-products in the slums, the persistence of barbarity and bloodshed, the greed of the newly rich, destroyed his hopes that humanity was evolving upward. Such a late poem as *The Dawn* embodies an attitude that he found in Virgil: "Thou majestic in thy sadness at the doubtful doom of human kind."

For despite Tennyson's fascination with technological developments, he was essentially a poet of the countryside, a man whose whole being was conditioned by the recurring rhythms of rural rather than urban life. He had the country dweller's awareness of traditional roots and sense of the past. It is appropriate that most of his best poems are about the past, not about the present or future. Even in his childhood, Tennyson said that "the words 'far, far away' had always a strange charm for me"; he was haunted by what he called "the passion of the past." The past became his great theme, whether it be his own past (as in *In the Valley of Cauteretz*), his country's past (as in *The Idylls of the King*), the past of humankind, the past of the world itself:

> There rolls the deep where grew the tree.
> O earth, what changes hast thou seen!
> There where the long street roars hath been
> The stillness of the central sea.

Tennyson is the first major writer to express this awareness of the vast extent of geological time that has haunted human consciousness since Victorian scientists exposed the history of the earth's crust. In his more usual vein, however, it is the recorded past of humankind that inspires him, the classical past in particular. Classical themes, as Douglas Bush has noted, "generally banished from his mind what was timid, parochial, sentimental . . . and evoked his special gifts and most authentic emotions, his rich and wistful sense of the past, his love of nature, and his power of style."

One returns, finally, to the question of language. At the time of his death, a critic complained that Tennyson was merely "a discoverer of words rather than of ideas." The same complaint has been made by Bernard Shaw and others—not about Tennyson but about Shakespeare.

The Kraken[1]

Below the thunders of the upper deep,
Far, far beneath in the abysmal sea,
His ancient, dreamless, uninvaded sleep
The Kraken sleepeth: faintest sunlights flee

5 About his shadowy sides; above him swell
Huge sponges of millennial growth and height;
And far away into the sickly light,
From many a wondrous grot and secret cell
Unnumbered and enormous polypi°   octopuses

10 Winnow with giant arms the slumbering green.
There hath he lain for ages, and will lie
Battening upon huge sea worms in his sleep,
Until the latter fire[2] shall heat the deep;

---

1. A mythical sea beast of gigantic size.
2. Fire that would finally consume the world (Revelation 16.8–9).

Then once by man and angels to be seen,
15 In roaring he shall rise and on the surface die.

1830

Mariana[1]

"Mariana in the moated grange."
Measure for Measure

With blackest moss the flower-plots
Were thickly crusted, one and all;
The rusted nails fell from the knots
That held the pear to the gable wall.
5   The broken sheds looked sad and strange:
Unlifted was the clinking latch;
Weeded and worn the ancient thatch
Upon the lonely moated grange.
    She only said, "My life is dreary,
10   He cometh not," she said;
    She said, "I am aweary, aweary,
    I would that I were dead!"

Her tears fell with the dews at even;
Her tears fell ere the dews were dried;
15 She could not look on the sweet heaven,
Either at morn or eventide.
After the flitting of the bats,
When thickest dark did trance° the sky,   cross
She drew her casement curtain by,
20 And glanced athwart the glooming flats.
    She only said, "The night is dreary,
        He cometh not," she said;
    She said, "I am aweary, aweary,
    I would that I were dead!"

25 Upon the middle of the night,
Waking she heard the nightfowl crow;
The cock sung out an hour ere light;
From the dark fen the oxen's low
Came to her; without hope of change,
30   In sleep she seemed to walk forlorn,
Till cold winds woke the gray-eyed morn
About the lonely moated grange.
    She only said, "The day is dreary,
        He cometh not," she said;
35   She said, "I am aweary, aweary,
    I would that I were dead!"

1. Mariana, in Shakespeare's *Measure for Measure* 3.1.277, waits in a grange (an outlying farmhouse) for her lover, who has deserted her.

About a stonecast from the wall
A sluice with blackened waters slept,
And o'er it many, round and small,
40   The clustered marish-mosses[2] crept.
Hard by a poplar shook alway,
All silver-green with gnarlèd bark:
For leagues no other tree did mark
The level waste, the rounding gray.
45   She only said, "My life is dreary,
He cometh not," she said;
She said, "I am aweary, aweary,
I would that I were dead!"

And ever when the moon was low,
50   And the shrill winds were up and away,
In the white curtain, to and fro,
She saw the gusty shadow sway.
But when the moon was very low,
And wild winds bound within their cell,[3]
55   The shadow of the poplar fell
Upon her bed, across her brow.
She only said, "The night is dreary,
He cometh not," she said;
She said, "I am aweary, aweary,
60   I would that I were dead!"

All day within the dreamy house,
The doors upon their hinges creaked;
The blue fly sung in the pane; the mouse
Behind the moldering wainscot shrieked,
65   Or from the crevice peered about.
Old faces glimmered through the doors,
Old footsteps trod the upper floors,
Old voices called her from without.
She only said, "My life is dreary,
70   He cometh not," she said;
She said, "I am aweary, aweary,
I would that I were dead!"

The sparrow's chirrup on the roof,
The slow clock ticking, and the sound
75 Which to the wooing wind aloof
The poplar made, did all confound
Her sense; but most she loathed the hour
When the thick-moted sunbeam lay
Athwart the chambers, and the day
80 Was sloping toward his western bower.
Then, said she, "I am very dreary,
He will not come," she said;

---

2. The little marsh-moss lumps that float on the surface of water [Tennyson's note].

3. According to Virgil, Aeolus, god of winds, kept the winds imprisoned in a cave (*Aeneid* 1.50–59).

> She wept, "I am aweary, aweary,
> Oh God, that I were dead!"

1830

The Lady of Shalott[1]

Part 1

On either side the river lie
Long fields of barley and of rye,
That clothe the wold° and meet the sky;   *rolling plain*
And through the field the road runs by
5   To many-towered Camelot;
And up and down the people go,
Gazing where the lilies blow°   *bloom*
Round an island there below,
     The island of Shalott.

10 Willows whiten, aspens quiver,
Little breezes dusk and shiver
Through the wave that runs forever
By the island in the river
     Flowing down to Camelot.
15 Four gray walls, and four gray towers,
Overlook a space of flowers,
And the silent isle imbowers
     The Lady of Shalott.

By the margin, willow-veiled,
20 Slide the heavy barges trailed
By slow horses; and unhailed
The shallop° flitteth silken-sailed   *light open boat*
     Skimming down to Camelot:
But who hath seen her wave her hand?
25 Or at the casement seen her stand?
Or is she known in all the land,
     The Lady of Shalott?

Only reapers, reaping early
In among the bearded barley,
30 Hear a song that echoes cheerly
From the river winding clearly,
     Down to towered Camelot;
And by the moon the reaper weary,
Piling sheaves in uplands airy,
35 Listening, whispers " 'Tis the fairy
     Lady of Shalott."

---

1. For the author's revisions while composing this poem, see "Poems in Process," in the appendices to this volume.

Part 2

There she weaves by night and day
A magic web with colors gay.
She has heard a whisper say,
40   A curse is on her if she stay
        To look down to Camelot.
She knows not what the curse may be,
And so she weaveth steadily,
And little other care hath she,
45   The Lady of Shalott.

And moving through a mirror clear²
That hangs before her all the year,
Shadows of the world appear.
There she sees the highway near
50   Winding down to Camelot;
There the river eddy whirls,
And there the surly village churls,
And the red cloaks of market girls,
        Pass onward from Shalott.

55   Sometimes a troop of damsels glad,
An abbot on an ambling pad,°   *easy-paced horse*
Sometimes a curly shepherd lad,
Or long-haired page in crimson clad,
        Goes by to towered Camelot;
60   And sometimes through the mirror blue
The knights come riding two and two:
She hath no loyal knight and true,
        The Lady of Shalott.

But in her web she still delights
65   To weave the mirror's magic sights,
For often through the silent nights
A funeral, with plumes and lights
        And music, went to Camelot;
Or when the moon was overhead,
70   Came two young lovers lately wed:
"I am half sick of shadows," said
        The Lady of Shalott.

Part 3

A bowshot from her bower eaves,
He rode between the barley sheaves,
75   The sun came dazzling through the leaves,
And flamed upon the brazen greaves³
        Of bold Sir Lancelot.

---

2. Weavers used mirrors, placed facing their looms, to see the progress of their work.   3. Armor protecting the leg below the knee.

A red-cross knight[4] forever kneeled
To a lady in his shield,
80   That sparkled on the yellow field,
      Beside remote Shalott.

The gemmy bridle glittered free,
Like to some branch of stars we see
Hung in the golden Galaxy.
85   The bridle bells rang merrily
      As he rode down to Camelot;
And from his blazoned baldric[5] slung
A mighty silver bugle hung,
And as he rode his armor rung,
90   Beside remote Shalott.

All in the blue unclouded weather
Thick-jeweled shone the saddle leather,
The helmet and the helmet-feather
Burned like one burning flame together,
95   As he rode down to Camelot;
As often through the purple night,
Below the starry clusters bright,
Some bearded meteor, trailing light,
      Moves over still Shalott.

100 His broad clear brow in sunlight glowed;
On burnished hooves his war horse trode;
From underneath his helmet flowed
His coal-black curls as on he rode,
      As he rode down to Camelot.
105 From the bank and from the river
He flashed into the crystal mirror,
"Tirra lirra," by the river
      Sang Sir Lancelot.

She left the web, she left the loom,
110 She made three paces through the room,
She saw the water lily bloom,
She saw the helmet and the plume,
      She looked down to Camelot.
Out flew the web and floated wide;
115 The mirror cracked from side to side;
"The curse is come upon me," cried
      The Lady of Shalott.

Part 4

In the stormy east wind straining,
The pale yellow woods were waning,
120 The broad stream in his banks complaining,

---

4. Cf. *The Faerie Queene* 1 and 3.2.17–25.
5. A belt worn diagonally from one shoulder to the opposite hip; it supported a sword, bugle, etc.

Heavily the low sky raining
    Over towered Camelot;
Down she came and found a boat
Beneath a willow left afloat,
125 And round about the prow she wrote
    The Lady of Shalott.

And down the river's dim expanse
Like some bold seër in a trance,
Seeing all his own mischance—
130 With a glassy countenance
    Did she look to Camelot.
And at the closing of the day
She loosed the chain, and down she lay;
The broad steam bore her far away,
135   The Lady of Shalott.

Lying, robed in snowy white
That loosely flew to left and right—
The leaves upon her falling light—
Through the noises of the night
140   She floated down to Camelot;
And as the boat-head wound along
The willowy hills and fields among,
They heard her singing her last song,
    The Lady of Shalott.

145 Heard a carol, mournful, holy,
Chanted loudly, chanted lowly,
Till her blood was frozen slowly,
And her eyes were darkened wholly,[6]
    Turned to towered Camelot.
150 For ere she reached upon the tide
The first house by the waterside,
Singing in her song she died,
    The Lady of Shalott.

Under tower and balcony,
155 By garden wall and gallery,
A gleaming shape she floated by,
Dead-pale between the houses high,
    Silent into Camelot.
Out upon the wharfs they came,
160 Knight and burgher, lord and dame,
And round the prow they read her name,
    The Lady of Shalott.

Who is this? and what is here?
And in the lighted palace near
165 Died the sound of royal cheer;

---

6. In the 1832 version (reproduced in "Poems in Process") this line read: "And her smooth face sharpened slowly." George Eliot informed Tennyson that she preferred the earlier version.

And they crossed themselves for fear,
    All the knights at Camelot:
But Lancelot mused a little space;
    He said, "She has a lovely face;
170 God in his mercy lend her grace,
      The Lady of Shalott."

shallow oo what!

1831–32   1832, 1842

Dante Gabriel Rossetti's 1857 engraving for publisher Edward Moxon's illustrated collection of Tennyson's poetry shows Lancelot musing "a little space" on the Lady of Shalott in her boat.

The Lotos-Eaters[1]

"Courage!" he[2] said, and pointed toward the land,
"This mounting wave will roll us shoreward soon."

1. Based on a short episode from the *Odyssey* (9.82–97) in which the weary Greek veterans of the Trojan War are tempted by a desire to abandon their long voyage homeward. As Odysseus later reported: "On the tenth day we set foot on the land of the lotos-eaters who eat a flowering food. . . . I sent forth certain of my company [who] . . . mixed with the men of the lotos-eaters who gave . . . them of the lotos to taste. Now whosoever of them did eat the honey-sweet fruit of the lotos had no more wish to bring tidings nor to come back, but there he chose to abide . . . forgetful of his homeward way."

    Tennyson expands Homer's brief account into an elaborate picture of weariness and the desire for rest and death. The descriptions in the first stanzas are similar to *Faerie Queene* 2.6 and employ the same stanza form. The final section derives, in part, from Lucretius's conception of the gods in *De rerum natura*.

2. Odysseus (or Ulysses).

In the afternoon they came unto a land[3]
In which it seemèd always afternoon.
5 All round the coast the languid air did swoon,
Breathing like one that hath a weary dream.
Full-faced above the valley stood the moon;
And, like a downward smoke, the slender stream
Along the cliff to fall and pause and fall did seem.

10 A land of streams! some, like a downward smoke,
Slow-dropping veils of thinnest lawn,° did go;   *fine, thin linen*
And some through wavering lights and shadows broke,
Rolling a slumbrous sheet of foam below.
They saw the gleaming river seaward flow
15 From the inner land; far off, three mountaintops
Three silent pinnacles of aged snow,
Stood sunset-flushed; and, dewed with showery drops,
Up-clomb the shadowy pine above the woven copse.

The charmèd sunset lingered low adown
20 In the red West; through mountain clefts the dale
Was seen far inland, and the yellow down[4]
Bordered with palm, and many a winding vale
And meadow, set with slender galingale;[5]
A land where all things always seemed the same!
25 And round about the keel with faces pale,
Dark faces pale against that rosy flame,
The mild-eyed melancholy Lotos-eaters came.

Branches they bore of that enchanted stem,
Laden with flower and fruit, whereof they gave
30 To each, but whoso did receive of them
And taste, to him the gushing of the wave
Far far away did seem to mourn and rave
On alien shores; and if his fellow spake,
His voice was thin, as voices from the grave;
35 And deep-asleep he seemed, yet all awake,
And music in his ears his beating heart did make.

They sat them down upon the yellow sand,
Between the sun and moon upon the shore;
And sweet it was to dream of Fatherland,
40 Of child, and wife, and slave; but evermore
Most weary seemed the sea, weary the oar,
Weary the wandering fields of barren foam,
Then some one said, "We will return no more";
And all at once they sang, "Our island home°   *Ithaca*
45 Is far beyond the wave; we will no longer roam."

3. The repetition of "land" from line 1 was deliberate; Tennyson said that this "no rhyme" was
"lazier" in its effect. Cf. "afternoon" (lines 3–4) and
the rhyming of "adown" and "down" (lines 19 and

21).
4. An open plain on high ground.
5. A plant resembling tall coarse grass.

Choric Song[6]

1

There is sweet music here that softer falls
Than petals from blown roses on the grass,
Or night-dews on still waters between walls
Of shadowy granite, in a gleaming pass;
50 Music that gentlier on the spirit lies,
Than tired[7] eyelids upon tired eyes;
Music that brings sweet sleep down from the blissful skies.
Here are cool mosses deep,
And through the moss the ivies creep,
55 And in the stream the long-leaved flowers weep,
And from the craggy ledge the poppy hangs in sleep.

2

Why are we weighed upon with heaviness,
And utterly consumed with sharp distress,
While all things else have rest from weariness?
60 All things have rest: why should we toil alone,
We only toil, who are the first of things,
And make perpetual moan,
Still from one sorrow to another thrown;
Nor ever fold our wings,
65 And cease from wanderings,
Nor steep our brows in slumber's holy balm;
Nor harken what the inner spirit sings,
"There is no joy but calm!"—
Why should we only toil, the roof and crown of things?[8]

3

70 Lo! in the middle of the wood,
The folded leaf is wooed from out the bud
With winds upon the branch, and there
Grows green and broad, and takes no care,
Sun-steeped at noon, and in the moon
75 Nightly dew-fed; and turning yellow
Falls, and floats adown the air.
Lo! sweetened with summer light,
The full-juiced apple, waxing over-mellow,
Drops in a silent autumn night.
80 All its allotted length of days
The flower ripens in its place,
Ripens and fades, and falls, and hath no toil,
Fast-rooted in the fruitful soil.

---

6. Sung by the mariners.
7. Tennyson wanted the word to be pronounced as *tie-yerd* rather than *tier'd* or *tire-èd*, thus "making the word neither monosyllable or disyllabic, but a dreamy child of the two."

8. Cf. *Faerie Queene* 2.6.17: "Why then dost thou, O man, that of them all / Art Lord, and eke of nature Sovereaine, / Wilfully . . . wast thy joyous houres in needlesse paine?"

4

Hateful is the dark blue sky,
85 Vaulted o'er the dark blue sea.
Death is the end of life; ah, why
Should life all labor be?
Let us alone. Time driveth onward fast,
And in a little while our lips are dumb.
90 Let us alone. What is it that will last?
All things are taken from us, and become
Portions and parcels of the dreadful past.
Let us alone. What pleasure can we have
To war with evil? Is there any peace
95 In ever climbing up the climbing wave?
All things have rest, and ripen toward the grave
In silence—ripen, fall, and cease:
Give us long rest or death, dark death, or dreamful ease.[9]

5

How sweet it were, hearing the downward stream,
100 With half-shut eyes ever to seem
Falling asleep in a half-dream!
To dream and dream, like yonder amber light,
Which will not leave the myrrh-bush on the height;
To hear each other's whispered speech;
105 Eating the Lotos day by day,
To watch the crisping° ripples on the beach,   *curling*
And tender curving lines of creamy spray;
To lend our hearts and spirits wholly
To the influence of mild-minded melancholy;
110 To muse and brood and live again in memory,
With those old faces of our infancy
Heaped over with a mound of grass,
Two handfuls of white dust, shut in an urn of brass!

6

Dear is the memory of our wedded lives,
115 And dear the last embraces of our wives
And their warm tears; but all hath suffered change;
For surely now our household hearths are cold,
Our sons inherit us, our looks are strange,
And we should come like ghosts to trouble joy.
120 Or else the island princes° overbold   *Penelope's suitors*
Have eat our substance, and the minstrel sings
Before them of the ten years' war in Troy,
And our great deeds, as half-forgotten things.
Is there confusion in the little isle?
125 Let what is broken so remain.
The Gods are hard to reconcile;

---

9. Cf. *Faerie Queen* 1.9.40: "Sleepe after toyle, port after stormie seas, / Ease after warre, death after life does greatly please."

'Tis hard to settle order once again.
There *is* confusion worse than death,
Trouble on trouble, pain on pain,
130   Long labor unto aged breath,
Sore tasks to hearts worn out by many wars
And eyes grown dim with gazing on the pilot-stars.

7

But, propped on beds of amaranth and moly,[1]
How sweet—while warm airs lull us, blowing lowly—
135   With half-dropped eyelid still,
Beneath a heaven dark and holy,
To watch the long bright river drawing slowly
His waters from the purple hill—
To hear the dewy echoes calling
140   From cave to cave through the thick-twined vine—
To watch the emerald-colored water falling
Through many a woven acanthus[2] wreath divine!
Only to hear and see the far-off sparkling brine,
Only to hear were sweet, stretched out beneath the pine.

8

145   The Lotos blooms below the barren peak,
The Lotos blows by every winding creek;
All day the wind breathes low with mellower tone;
Through every hollow cave and alley lone
Round and round the spicy downs the yellow Lotos dust is blown.
150   We have had enough of action, and of motion we,
Rolled to starboard, rolled to larboard, when the surge was seething free,
Where the wallowing monster spouted his foam-fountains in the sea.
Let us swear an oath, and keep it with an equal mind,
In the hollow Lotos land to live and lie reclined
155   On the hills like Gods together, careless of mankind.
For they lie beside their nectar, and the bolts° are hurled   *thunderbolts*
Far below them in the valleys, and the clouds are lightly curled
Round their golden houses, girdled with the gleaming world;
Where they smile in secret, looking over wasted lands,
160   Blight and famine, plague and earthquake, roaring deeps and fiery sands,
Clanging fights, and flaming towns, and sinking ships, and praying hands.
But they smile, they find a music centered in a doleful song
Steaming up, a lamentation and an ancient tale of wrong,
Like a tale of little meaning though the words are strong;
165   Chanted from an ill-used race of men that cleave the soil,
Sow the seed, and reap the harvest with enduring toil,
Storing yearly little dues of wheat, and wine and oil;
Till they perish and they suffer—some, 'tis whispered—down in hell
Suffer endless anguish, others in Elysian valleys dwell,
170   Resting weary limbs at last on beds of asphodel.[3]

---

1. A flower with magical properties mentioned by
Homer. "Amaranth": a legendary unfading flower.
2. A plant resembling a thistle. Its leaves were the
model for ornaments on Corinthian columns.
3. A yellow lilylike flower supposed to grow in the
Elysian valleys.

Surely, surely, slumber is more sweet than toil, the shore
Than labor in the deep mid-ocean, wind and wave and oar;
O, rest ye, brother mariners, we will not wander more.

1832, 1842

Ulysses[1]

It little profits that an idle king,
By this still hearth, among these barren crags,
Matched with an aged wife, I mete and dole
Unequal laws[2] unto a savage race,
5 That hoard, and sleep, and feed,[3] and know not me.
    I cannot rest from travel; I will drink
Life to the lees. All times I have enjoyed
Greatly, have suffered greatly, both with those
That loved me, and alone; on shore, and when
10 Through scudding drifts the rainy Hyades[4]
Vexed the dim sea. I am become a name;
For always roaming with a hungry heart
Much have I seen and known—cities of men
And manners, climates, councils, governments,
15 Myself not least, but honored of them all—
And drunk delight of battle with my peers,
Far on the ringing plains of windy Troy,
I am a part of all that I have met;
Yet all experience is an arch wherethrough
20 Gleams that untraveled world whose margin fades
Forever and forever when I move.
How dull it is to pause, to make an end,
To rust unburnished, not to shine in use!⁵
As though to breathe were life! Life piled on life
25 Were all too little, and of one to me
Little remains; but every hour is saved
From that eternal silence, something more,
A bringer of new things; and vile it were
For some three suns to store and hoard myself,
30 And this gray spirit yearning in desire

---

1. According to Dante, after the fall of Troy, Ulysses never returned to his island home of Ithaca. Instead he persuaded some of his followers to seek new experiences by a voyage of exploration westward out beyond the Strait of Gibraltar. In his inspiring speech to his aging crew he said: "Consider your origin: you were not made to live as brutes, but to pursue virtue and knowledge" (*Inferno* 26). Tennyson modified Dante's version by combining it with Homer's account (*Odyssey* 19–24). Thus Tennyson has Ulysses make his speech in Ithaca some time after his return home to his reunion with his wife, Penelope, and his son, Telemachus, and, presumably, his resumption of administrative responsibilities involved in governing his kingdom.

Tennyson himself stated that this poem expressed his own "need of going forward and braving the struggle of life" after the death of Hallam.
2. Measure out rewards and punishments.
3. Cf. *Hamlet* 4.4.33–35: "What is a man, / If his chief good . . . / Be but to sleep and feed? a beast, no more."
4. A group of stars whose rising was assumed to be followed by rain. "Scudding drifts": driving showers of spray and rain.
5. Cf. Ulysses' speech in *Troilus and Cressida* 3.3.150–53: "Perseverance, dear my lord, / Keeps honour bright; to have done, is to hang / Quite out of fashion, like a rusty mail / in monumental mockery."

To follow knowledge like a sinking star,
Beyond the utmost bound of human thought.

This is my son, mine own Telemachus,
To whom I leave the scepter and the isle—
35 Well-loved of me, discerning to fulfill
This labor, by slow prudence to make mild
A rugged people, and through soft degrees
Subdue them to the useful and the good.
Most blameless is he, centered in the sphere
40 Of common duties, decent not to fail
In offices of tenderness, and pay
Meet adoration to my household gods,
When I am gone. He works his work, I mine.

There lies the port; the vessel puffs her sail;
45 There gloom the dark, broad seas. My mariners,
Souls that have toiled, and wrought, and thought with me—
That ever with a frolic welcome took
The thunder and the sunshine, and opposed
Free hearts, free foreheads—you and I are old;
50 Old age hath yet his honor and his toil.
Death closes all; but something ere the end,
Some work of noble note, may yet be done,
Not unbecoming men that strove with Gods.
The lights begin to twinkle from the rocks;
55 The long day wanes; the slow moon climbs; the deep
Moans round with many voices. Come, my friends,
'Tis not too late to seek a newer world.
Push off, and sitting well in order smite
The sounding furrows; for my purpose holds
60 To sail beyond the sunset, and the baths
Of all the western stars,[6] until I die.
It may be that the gulfs will wash us down;
It may be we shall touch the Happy Isles,[7]
And see the great Achilles, whom we knew.
65 Though much is taken, much abides; and though
We are not now that strength which in old days
Moved earth and heaven, that which we are, we are—
One equal temper of heroic hearts,
Made weak by time and fate, but strong in will
70 To strive, to seek, to find, and not to yield.

1833   1842

---

6. The outer ocean or river that, in Greek cosmology, surrounded the flat circle of the earth and into which the stars descended.
7. In Greek myth the Islands of the Blessed, a paradise of perpetual summer, located in the far-western ocean. They were peopled by great heroes who, without having died, had been translated there by the gods and made immortal.

Tithonus[1]

The woods decay, the woods decay and fall,
The vapors weep their burthen to the ground,
Man comes and tills the field and lies beneath,
And after many a summer dies the swan.[2]
5   Me only cruel immortality
Consumes; I wither slowly in thine arms,[3]
Here at the quiet limit of the world,
A white-haired shadow roaming like a dream
The ever-silent spaces of the East,
10   Far-folded mists, and gleaming halls of morn.
    Alas! for this gray shadow, once a man—
So glorious in his beauty and thy choice,
Who madest him thy chosen, that he seemed
To his great heart none other than a God!
15   I asked thee, "Give me immortality."
Then didst thou grant mine asking with a smile,
Like wealthy men who care not how they give.
But thy strong Hours indignant worked their wills,
And beat me down and marred and wasted me,
20   And though they could not end me, left me maimed
To dwell in presence of immortal youth,
Immortal age beside immortal youth,
And all I was in ashes. Can thy love,
Thy beauty, make amends, though even now,
25   Close over us, the silver star,[4] thy guide,
Shines in those tremulous eyes that fill with tears
To hear me? Let me go; take back thy gift.
Why should a man desire in any way
To vary from the kindly race of men,
30   Or pass beyond the goal of ordinance[5]
Where all should pause, as is most meet for all?
    A soft air fans the cloud apart; there comes
A glimpse of that dark world where I was born.
Once more the old mysterious glimmer steals
35   From thy pure brows, and from thy shoulders pure,
And bosom beating with a heart renewed.
Thy cheek begins to redden through the gloom,
Thy sweet eyes brighten slowly close to mine,
Ere yet they blind the stars, and the wild team[6]
40   Which love thee, yearning for thy yoke, arise,
And shake the darkness from their loosened manes,
And beat the twilight into flakes of fire.
    Lo! ever thus thou growest beautiful

---

1. A Trojan prince loved by the goddess of the dawn, Eos or Aurora, who obtained for him the gift of living forever but neglected to obtain for him the gift of everlasting youth. For the author's revisions while composing this poem, see "Poems in Process," in the appendices to this volume.
2. Some species of swans live for at least fifty years.
3. The arms of Aurora.
4. The morning star that precedes the dawn.
5. What is decreed or ordained as human destiny.
6. The horses that draw Aurora's chariot into the sky at daybreak.

In silence, then before thine answer given
45 Departest, and thy tears are on my cheek.
　　Why wilt thou ever scare me with thy tears,
And make me tremble lest a saying learnt,
In days far-off, on that dark earth, be true?
"The Gods themselves cannot recall their gifts."
50 　　Ay me! ay me! with what another heart
In days far-off, and with what other eyes
I used to watch—if I be he that watched—
The lucid outline forming round thee; saw
The dim curls kindle into sunny rings;
55 Changed with thy mystic change, and felt my blood
Glow with the glow that slowly crimsoned all
Thy presence and thy portals, while I lay,
Mouth, forehead, eyelids, growing dewy-warm
With kisses balmier than half-opening buds
60 Of April, and could hear the lips that kissed
Whispering I knew not what of wild and sweet,
Like that strange song I heard Apollo sing,
While Ilion like a mist rose into towers.[7]
　　Yet hold me not forever in thine East;
65 How can my nature longer mix with thine?
Coldly thy rosy shadows bathe me, cold
Are all thy lights, and cold my wrinkled feet
Upon thy glimmering thresholds, when the steam
Floats up from those dim fields about the homes
70 Of happy men that have the power to die,
And grassy barrows of the happier dead.
Release me, and restore me to the ground.
Thou seest all things, thou wilt see my grave;
Thou wilt renew thy beauty morn by morn,
75 I earth in earth forget these empty courts,
And thee returning on thy silver wheels.

1833, 1859　　　　　　　　　　　　　　　　　　　　　　1860

Break, Break, Break

Break, break, break,
　　On thy cold gray stones, O Sea!
And I would that my tongue could utter
　　The thoughts that arise in me.

5 　O, well for the fisherman's boy,
　　That he shouts with his sister at play!
O, well for the sailor lad,
　　That he sings in his boat on the bay!

And the stately ships go on
10 　　To their haven under the hill;

---

7. The walls of Troy ("Ilion") were supposed to have been built to the strains of Apollo's music.

But O for the touch of a vanished hand,
And the sound of a voice that is still!

Break, break, break,
At the foot of thy crags, O Sea!
15   But the tender grace of a day that is dead
Will never come back to me.

1834   1842

The Epic [Morte d'Arthur][1]

At Francis Allen's on the Christmas eve—
The game of forfeits done—the girls all kissed
Beneath the sacred bush° and passed away—   mistletoe
The parson Holmes, the poet Everard Hall,
5   The host, and I sat round the wassail-bowl,
Then halfway ebbed; and there we held a talk,
How all the old honor had from Christmas gone,
Or gone or dwindled down to some odd games
In some odd nooks like this; till I, tired out
10   With cutting eights that day upon the pond,
Where, three times slipping from the outer edge,
I bumped the ice into three several stars,
Fell in a doze; and half-awake I heard
The parson taking wide and wider sweeps,
15   Now harping on the church-commissioners,[2]
Now hawking at geology and schism;
Until I woke, and found him settled down
Upon the general decay of faith
Right through the world: "at home was little left,
20   And none abroad; there was no anchor, none,
To hold by." Francis, laughing, clapped his hand
On Everard's shoulder, with "I hold by him."
"And I," quoth Everard, "by the wassail-bowl."
"Why yes," I said, "we knew your gift that way
25   At college; but another which you had—
I mean of verse (for so we held it then),
What came of that?" "You know," said Frank, "he burnt
His epic, his King Arthur, some twelve books"—
And then to me demanding why: "O, sir,
30   He thought that nothing new was said, or else

---

1. At age twenty-four, Tennyson proposed to write a long epic on King Arthur. Five years later he had completed one book of the twelve, the story of Arthur's death, which he published in 1842 under the title Morte d'Arthur. In this early version the story is given a framework titled The Epic, which consists of a short introductory section (fifty-one lines) and an epilogue (thirty lines), describing a party on Christmas Eve in modern times, at which the poet reads Morte d'Arthur to his friends. In 1869, Tennyson incorporated Morte d'Arthur into his long narrative poem Idylls of the King; it appears there as the twelfth book, under the new title, The Passing of Arthur. At that time The Epic framework was discarded and some lines added. The 1842 version can be reconstructed (only two lines are modified) by reading The Passing of Arthur, lines 170–440.

2. Commissioners appointed by the government in 1835 to regulate finances of the Anglican Church.

Something so said 'twas nothing—that a truth
Looks freshest in the fashion of the day;
God knows; he has a mint of reasons; ask.
It pleased *me* well enough." "Nay, nay," said Hall,
35 "Why take the style of those heroic times?
For nature brings not back the mastodon,
Nor we those times; and why should any man
Remodel models? these twelve books of mine
Were faint Homeric echoes,[3] nothing-worth,
40 Mere chaff and draff, much better burnt." "But I,"
Said Francis, "picked the eleventh from this hearth,
And have it; keep a thing, its use will come.
I hoard it as a sugarplum for Holmes."
He laughed, and I, though sleepy, like a horse
45 That hears the corn-bin open, pricked my ears;
For I remembered Everard's college fame
When we were Freshmen. Then at my request
He brought it; and the poet, little urged,
But with some prelude of disparagement,
50 Read, mouthing out his hollow o's and a's,
Deep-chested music, and to this result.[4]

          *   *   *

Here ended Hall, and our last light, that long
325 Had winked and threatened darkness, flared and fell;
At which the parson, sent to sleep with sound,
And waked with silence, grunted "Good!" but we
Sat rapt: it was the tone with which he read—
Perhaps some modern touches here and there
330 Redeemed it from the charge of nothingness—
Or else we loved the man, and prized his work;
I know not; but we sitting, as I said,
The cock crew loud, as at that time of year
The lusty bird takes every hour for dawn.[5]
335 Then Francis, muttering like a man ill-used,
"There now—that's nothing!" drew a little back,
And drove his heel into the smoldered log,
That sent a blast of sparkles up the flue.
And so to bed, where yet in sleep I seemed
340 To sail with Arthur under looming shores,
Point after point; till on to dawn, when dreams
Begin to feel the truth and stir of day,
To me, methought, who waited with the crowd,
There came a bark that, blowing forward, bore
345 King Arthur, like a modern gentleman
Of stateliest port; and all the people cried,
"Arthur is come again: he cannot die."

---

3. After reading *Morte d'Arthur* in manuscript, Walter Savage Landor commented: "It is more Homeric than any poem of our time, and rivals some of the noblest parts of the Odyssey."
4. Here followed the 271 lines of *Morte d'Arthur* in 1842 (see *The Passing of Arthur*, lines 170–440,

pp. 1297–1303). *The Epic* then continued as follows.
5. See Shakespeare's *Hamlet* 1.1.157–60 on the legend of the cock's crowing "all night long" on Christmas Eve.

Then those that stood upon the hills behind
Repeated—"Come again, and thrice as fair";
350 And, further inland, voices echoed—"Come
With all good things, and war shall be no more."
At this a hundred bells began to peal,
That with the sound I woke, and heard indeed
The clear church bells ring in the Christmas morn.

1833–38   1842

The Eagle: A Fragment

He clasps the crag with crooked hands;
Close to the sun in lonely lands,
Ringed with the azure world, he stands.

The wrinkled sea beneath him crawls:
5   He watches from his mountain walls,
And like a thunderbolt he falls.

1851

Locksley Hall[1]

Comrades, leave me here a little, while as yet 'tis early morn;
Leave me here, and when you want me, sound upon the bugle horn.

'Tis the place, and all around it, as of old, the curlews call,
Dreary gleams[2] about the moorland flying over Locksley Hall;

5   Locksley Hall, that in the distance overlooks the sandy tracts,
And the hollow ocean-ridges roaring into cataracts.

Many a night from yonder ivied casement, ere I went to rest,
Did I look on great Orion sloping slowly to the west.

Many a night I saw the Pleiads,[3] rising through the mellow shade,
10   Glitter like a swarm of fireflies tangled in a silver braid.

Here about the beach I wandered, nourishing a youth sublime
With the fairy tales of science, and the long result of time;

1. The situation in this poem—of a young man's being jilted by a woman who chose to marry a wealthy landowner—may have been suggested to Tennyson by the experience of his brother Frederick, a hot-tempered man who had fallen in love with his cousin Julia Tennyson and who was similarly unsuccessful. It may also have been inspired by Tennyson's own frustrated courtship of Rosa Baring, who rejected the young poet in favor of a wealthy suitor. Concerning the ranting tone of the speaker (a tone accentuated by the heavily marked trochaic meter), Tennyson said: "The whole poem represents young life, its good side, its deficiencies, and its yearnings."
2. Tennyson stated that "gleams" does not refer to "curlews" flying but to streaks of light.
3. Or the Pleiades, a seven-starred constellation.

When the centuries behind me like a fruitful land reposed;
When I clung to all the present for the promise that it closed°   *enclosed*

15   When I dipped into the future far as human eye could see,
Saw the vision of the world and all the wonder that would be.—

In the spring a fuller crimson comes upon the robin's breast;
In the spring the wanton lapwing gets himself another crest;

In the spring a livelier iris changes on the burnished dove;[4]
20   In the spring a young man's fancy lightly turns to thoughts of love.

Then her cheek was pale and thinner than should be for one so young,
And her eyes on all my motions with a mute observance hung.

And I said, "My cousin Amy, speak, and speak the truth to me,
Trust me, cousin, all the current of my being sets to thee."

25   On her pallid cheek and forehead came a color and a light,
As I have seen the rosy red flushing in the northern night.

And she turned—her bosom shaken with a sudden storm of sighs—
All the spirit deeply dawning in the dark of hazel eyes—

Saying, "I have hid my feelings, fearing they should do me wrong";
30   Saying, "Dost thou love me, cousin?" weeping, "I have loved thee long."

Love took up the glass of Time, and turned it in his glowing hands;
Every moment, lightly shaken, ran itself in golden sands.

Love took up the harp of Life, and smote on all the chords with might;
Smote the chord of Self, that, trembling, passed in music out of sight.

35   Many a morning on the moorland did we hear the copses ring,
And her whisper thronged my pulses with the fullness of the spring.

Many an evening by the waters did we watch the stately ships,
And our spirits rushed together at the touching of the lips.

O my cousin, shallow-hearted! O my Amy, mine no more!
40   O the dreary, dreary moorland! O the barren, barren shore!

Falser than all fancy fathoms, falser than all songs have sung,
Puppet to a father's threat, and servile to a shrewish tongue!

Is it well to wish thee happy?—having known me—to decline
On a range of lower feelings and a narrower heart than mine!

45   Yet it shall be; thou shalt lower to his level day by day,
What is fine within thee growing coarse to sympathize with clay.

---

4. The rainbowlike colors of a dove's throat plumage are intensified in the mating season.

As the husband is, the wife is; thou art mated with a clown,°   *boor*
And the grossness of his nature will have weight to drag thee down.

He will hold thee, when his passion shall have spent its novel force,
50   Something better than his dog, a little dearer than his horse.

What is this? his eyes are heavy; think not they are glazed with wine.
Go to him, it is thy duty; kiss him, take his hand in thine.

It may be my lord is weary, that his brain is overwrought;
Soothe him with thy finer fancies, touch him with thy lighter thought.

55   He will answer to the purpose, easy things to understand—
Better thou wert dead before me, though I slew thee with my hand!

Better thou and I were lying, hidden from the heart's disgrace,
Rolled in one another's arms, and silent in a last embrace.

Cursed be the social wants that sin against the strength of youth!
60   Cursed be the social lies that warp us from the living truth!

Cursed be the sickly forms that err from honest Nature's rule!
Cursed be the gold that gilds the straitened° forehead of the fool!   *narrowed*

Well—'tis well that I should bluster!—Hadst thou less unworthy proved—
Would to God—for I had loved thee more than ever wife was loved.

65   Am I mad, that I should cherish that which bears but bitter fruit?
I will pluck it from my bosom, though my heart be at the root.

Never, though my mortal summers to such length of years should come
As the many-wintered crow⁵ that leads the clanging rookery home.

Where is comfort? in division of the records of the mind?
70   Can I part her from herself, and love her, as I knew her, kind?

I remember one that perished; sweetly did she speak and move;
Such a one do I remember, whom to look at was to love.

Can I think of her as dead, and love her for the love she bore?
No—she never loved me truly; love is love for evermore.

75   Comfort? comfort scorned of devils! this is truth the poet⁶ sings,
That a sorrow's crown of sorrow is remembering happier things.

Drug thy memories, lest thou learn it, lest thy heart be put to proof,
In the dead unhappy night, and when the rain is on the roof.

Like a dog, he hunts in dreams, and thou art staring at the wall,
80   Where the dying night-lamp flickers, and the shadows rise and fall.

---

5. A rook, a long-lived bird.   6. Dante's *Inferno* 5.121–23.

Then a hand shall pass before thee, pointing to his drunken sleep,
To thy widowed[7] marriage-pillows, to the tears that thou wilt weep.

Thou shalt hear the "Never, never," whispered by the phantom years.
And a song from out the distance in the ringing of thine ears;

85 And an eye shall vex thee, looking ancient kindness on thy pain.
Turn thee, turn thee on thy pillow; get thee to thy rest again.

Nay, but Nature brings thee solace; for a tender voice will cry.
'Tis a purer life than thine, a lip to drain thy trouble dry.

Baby lips will laugh me down; my latest rival brings thee rest.
90 Baby fingers, waxen touches, press me from the mother's breast.

O, the child too clothes the father with a dearness not his due.
Half is thine and half is his; it will be worthy of the two.

O, I see thee old and formal, fitted to thy petty part,
With a little hoard of maxims preaching down a daughter's heart.

95 "They were dangerous guides the feelings—she herself was not exempt—
Truly, she herself had suffered"—Perish in thy self-contempt!

Overlive it—lower yet—be happy! wherefore should I care?
I myself must mix with action, lest I wither by despair.

What is that which I should turn to, lighting upon days like these?
100 Every door is barred with gold, and opens but to golden keys.

Every gate is thronged with suitors, all the markets overflow.
I have but an angry fancy; what is that which I should do?

I had been content to perish, falling on the foeman's ground,
When the ranks are rolled in vapor, and the winds are laid with sound.[8]

105 But the jingling of the guinea helps the hurt that Honor feels,
And the nations do but murmur, snarling at each other's heels.

Can I but relive in sadness? I will turn that earlier page.
Hide me from my deep emotion, O thou wondrous Mother-Age![9]

Make me feel the wild pulsation that I felt before the strife,
110 When I heard my days before me, and the tumult of my life;

Yearning for the large excitement that the coming years would yield,
Eager-hearted as a boy when first he leaves his father's field,

---

7. Presumably figurative. Her marriage having
become a mockery, she is widowed.
8. It was once believed that the firing of artillery
stilled the winds.

9. A happier past at life's beginning, which generated a more confident anticipation of the future
(see also line 185).

And at night along the dusky highway near and nearer drawn,
Sees in heaven the light of London flaring like a dreary dawn;

115 And his spirit leaps within him to be gone before him then,
Underneath the light he looks at, in among the throngs of men;

Men, my brothers, men the workers, ever reaping something new;
That which they have done but earnest° of the things that they   *pledge*
    shall do.

For I dipped into the future, far as human eye could see,
120 Saw the Vision of the world, and all the wonder that would be;

Saw the heavens fill with commerce, argosies of magic sails,[1]
Pilots of the purple twilight, dropping down with costly bales;

Heard the heavens fill with shouting, and there rained a ghastly dew
From the nations' airy navies grappling in the central blue;

125 Far along the world-wide whisper of the south wind rushing warm,
With the standards of the peoples plunging through the thunderstorm;

Till the war drum throbbed no longer, and the battle flags were furled
In the Parliament of man, the Federation of the world.

There the common sense of most shall hold a fretful realm in awe,
130 And the kindly earth shall slumber, lapped in universal law.

So I triumphed ere my passion sweeping through me left me dry,
Left me with the palsied heart, and left me with the jaundiced eye;

Eye, to which all order festers, all things here are out of joint.
Science moves, but slowly, slowly, creeping on from point to point;

135 Slowly comes a hungry people, as a lion, creeping nigher,
Glares at one that nods and winks behind a slowly-dying fire.

Yet I doubt not through the ages one increasing purpose runs,
And the thoughts of men are widened with the process of the suns.

What is that to him that reaps not harvest of his youthful joys,
140 Though the deep heart of existence beat forever like a boy's?

Knowledge comes, but wisdom lingers, and I linger on the shore,
And the individual withers, and the world is more and more.

Knowledge comes, but wisdom lingers, and he bears a laden breast,
Full of sad experience, moving toward the stillness of his rest.

1. Probably airships, such as balloons.

145 Hark, my merry comrades call me, sounding on the bugle horn,
They to whom my foolish passion were a target for their scorn.

Shall it not be scorn to me to harp on such a moldered string?
I am shamed through all my nature to have loved so slight a thing.

Weakness to be wroth with weakness! woman's pleasure, woman's pain—
150 Nature made them blinder motions bounded in a shallower brain.

Woman is the lesser man, and all thy passions, matched with mine,
Are as moonlight unto sunlight, and as water unto wine—

Here at least, where nature sickens, nothing. Ah, for some retreat
Deep in yonder shining Orient, where my life began to beat.

155 Where in wild Mahratta-battle[2] fell my father evil-starred—
I was left a trampled orphan, and a selfish uncle's ward.

Or to burst all links of habit—there to wander far away,
On from island unto island at the gateways of the day.

Larger constellations burning, mellow moons and happy skies,
160 Breadths of tropic shade and palms in cluster, knots of Paradise.

Never comes the trader, never floats an European flag,
Slides the bird o'er lustrous woodland, swings the trailer° from   *vine*
    the crag;

Droops the heavy-blossomed bower, hangs the heavy-fruited tree—
Summer isles of Eden lying in dark purple spheres of sea.

165 There methinks would be enjoyment more than in this march of mind,
In the steamship, in the railway, in the thoughts that shake mankind.

There the passions cramped no longer shall have scope and breathing space;
I will take some savage woman, she shall rear my dusky race.

Iron-jointed, supple-sinewed, they shall dive, and they shall run,
170 Catch the wild goat by the hair, and hurl their lances in the sun;

Whistle back the parrot's call, and leap the rainbows of the brooks,
Not with blinded eyesight poring over miserable books—

Fool, again the dream, the fancy! but I *know* my words are wild,
But I count the gray barbarian lower than the Christian child.

175 I, to herd with narrow foreheads, vacant of our glorious gains,
Like a beast with lower pleasures, like a beast with lower pains!

2. Reference to wars waged by a Hindu people against the British forces in India (1803 and 1817).

Mated with a squalid savage—what to me were sun or clime?
I the heir of all the ages, in the foremost files of time—

I that rather held it better men should perish one by one,
180   Than that earth should stand at gaze like Joshua's moon in Ajalon![3]

Not in vain the distance beacons. Forward, forward let us range,
Let the great world spin forever down the ringing grooves[4] of change.

Through the shadow of the globe we sweep into the younger day;
Better fifty years of Europe than a cycle of Cathay.[5]

185   Mother-Age—for mine I knew not—help me as when life begun;
Rift the hills, and roll the waters, flash the lightnings, weigh the sun.

O, I see the crescent promise of my spirit hath not set.
Ancient founts of inspiration well through all my fancy yet.

Howsoever these things be, a long farewell to Locksley Hall!
190   Now for me the woods may wither, now for me the roof-tree fall.

Comes a vapor from the margin, blackening over heath and holt,
Cramming all the blast before it, in its breast a thunderbolt.

Let it fall on Locksley Hall, with rain or hail, or fire or snow;
For the mighty wind arises, roaring seaward, and I go.

1837–38   1842

FROM THE PRINCESS[1]

Sweet and Low

Sweet and low, sweet and low,
  Wind of the western sea,
Low, low, breathe and blow,
  Wind of the western sea!
5   Over the rolling waters go,
Come from the dying moon, and blow,
  Blow him again to me;
While my little one, while my pretty one, sleeps.

Sleep and rest, sleep and rest,
10   Father will come to thee soon;

3. At the command of Joshua, the sun and moon
stood still while the Israelites completed the
slaughter of their enemies in the valley of Ajalon
(Joshua 10.12–13).
4. Railroad tracks. Tennyson at one time had the
impression that train wheels ran in grooved rails.
5. China, regarded in the 19th century as a static,
unprogressive country.

1. *The Princess* (1847), a long narrative poem,
contains interludes in which occasional songs are
sung. The six songs printed here, some of which
first appeared in later editions of the poem, rank
among the finest of Tennyson's lyrics, and various
19th- and 20th-century composers have set them
to music.

Rest, rest, on mother's breast,
    Father will come to thee soon;
Father will come to his babe in the nest,
    Silver sails all out of the west
15   Under the silver moon;
Sleep, my little one, sleep, my pretty one, sleep.

1849   1850

The Splendor Falls

The splendor falls on castle walls
    And snowy summits old in story;
The long light shakes across the lakes,
    And the wild cataract leaps in glory.
5   Blow, bugle, blow, set the wild echoes flying,
Blow, bugle; answer, echoes, dying, dying, dying.

O, hark, O, hear! how thin and clear,
    And thinner, clearer, farther going!
O, sweet and far from cliff and scar°   mountainside
10   The horns of Elfland faintly blowing!
Blow, let us hear the purple glens replying,
Blow, bugle; answer, echoes, dying, dying, dying.

O love, they die in yon rich sky,
    They faint on hill or field or river;
15 Our echoes roll from soul to soul,
    And grow forever and forever.
Blow, bugle, blow, set the wild echoes flying,
And answer, echoes, answer, dying, dying, dying.

                                                                        1850

Tears, Idle Tears[1]

Tears, idle tears, I know not what they mean,
Tears from the depth of some divine despair
Rise in the heart, and gather to the eyes,
In looking on the happy autumn-fields,
5   And thinking of the days that are no more.

Fresh as the first beam glittering on a sail,
That brings our friends up from the underworld,
Sad as the last which reddens over one
That sinks with all we love below the verge;
10 So sad, so fresh, the days that are no more.

1. Tennyson commented: "This song came to me on the yellowing autumn-tide at Tintern Abbey, full for me of its bygone memories." This locale would be for him associated both with Wordsworth's *Tintern Abbey* and with memories of Hallam, who was buried across the Bristol Channel in this area. "It is what I have always felt even from a boy, and what as a boy I called the 'passion of the past.' And it is so always with me now; it is the distance that charms me in the landscape, the picture and the past, and not the immediate today in which I move."

Ah, sad and strange as in dark summer dawns
The earliest pipe of half-awakened birds
To dying ears, when unto dying eyes
The casement slowly grows a glimmering square;
15   So sad, so strange, the days that are no more.

Dear as remembered kisses after death,
And sweet as those by hopeless fancy feigned
On lips that are for others; deep as love,
Deep as first love, and wild with all regret;
20   O Death in Life, the days that are no more!

1847

Ask Me No More

Ask me no more: the moon may draw the sea;
The cloud may stoop from heaven and take the shape,
With fold to fold, of mountain or of cape;
But O too fond, when have I answered thee?
5   Ask me no more.

Ask me no more: what answer should I give?
I love not hollow cheek or faded eye:
Yet, O my friend, I will not have thee die!
Ask me no more, lest I should bid thee live;
10   Ask me no more.

Ask me no more: thy fate and mine are sealed;
I strove against the stream and all in vain;
Let the great river take me to the main.
No more, dear love, for at a touch I yield;
15   Ask me no more.

1849   1850

Now Sleeps the Crimson Petal

Now sleeps the crimson petal, now the white;
Nor waves the cypress in the palace walk;
Nor winks the gold fin in the porphyry font.
The firefly wakens; waken thou with me.

5   Now droops the milk-white peacock like a ghost,
And like a ghost she glimmers on to me.

Now lies the Earth all Danaë[1] to the stars,
And all thy heart lies open unto me.

1. A Greek princess, who was confined in a metal tower by her father to prevent suitors from coming near her. Zeus, however, succeeded in visiting her in the form of a shower of gold. Their offspring was the hero Perseus.

Now slides the silent meteor on, and leaves
10   A shining furrow, as thy thoughts in me.

Now folds the lily all her sweetness up,
And slips into the bosom of the lake.
So fold thyself, my dearest, thou, and slip
Into my bosom and be lost in me.

1847

Come Down, O Maid[1]

Come down, O maid, from yonder mountain height.
What pleasure lives in height (the shepherd sang),
In height and cold, the splendor of the hills?
But cease to move so near the heavens, and cease
5   To glide a sunbeam by the blasted pine,
To sit a star upon the sparkling spire;
And come, for Love is of the valley, come,
For Love is of the valley, come thou down
And find him; by the happy threshold, he,
10   Or hand in hand with Plenty in the maize,
Or red with spirted purple of the vats,
Or foxlike in the vine; nor cares to walk
With Death and Morning on the Silver Horns,°   *mountain peaks*
Nor wilt thou snare him in the white ravine,
15   Nor find him dropped upon the firths of ice,°   *glaciers*
That huddling slant in furrow-cloven falls
To roll the torrent out of dusky doors.
But follow; let the torrent dance thee down
To find him in the valley; let the wild
20   Lean-headed eagles yelp alone, and leave
The monstrous ledges there to slope, and spill
Their thousand wreaths of dangling water-smoke,
That like a broken purpose waste in air.
So waste not thou, but come; for all the vales
25   Await thee; azure pillars of the hearth[2]
Arise to thee; the children call, and I
Thy shepherd pipe, and sweet is every sound,
Sweeter thy voice, but every sound is sweet;
Myriads of rivulets hurrying through the lawn,
30   The moan of doves in immemorial elms,
And murmuring of innumerable bees.

1847

---

1. Written during Tennyson's visit to the Swiss
Alps in 1846, after he had seen Mount Jungfrau
("The Maiden").

2. Columns of smoke from the houses in the valley.

["The Woman's Cause Is Man's"][1]

"Blame not thyself too much," I said, "nor blame
240   Too much the sons of men and barbarous laws;
These were the rough ways of the world till now.
Henceforth thou hast a helper, me, that know
The woman's cause is man's: they rise or sink
Together, dwarfed or godlike, bond or free:
245   For she that out of Lethe scales with man
The shining steps of Nature, shares with man
His nights, his days, moves with him to one goal,
Stays all the fair young planet in her hands—
If she be small, slight-natured, miserable,
250   How shall men grow? but work no more alone!
Our place is much: as far as in us lies
We two will serve them both in aiding her—
Will clear away the parasitic forms
That seem to keep her up but drag her down—
255   Will leave her space to burgeon out of all
Within her—let her make herself her own
To give or keep, to live and learn and be
All that not harms distinctive womanhood.
For woman is not undevelopt man,
260   But diverse: could we make her as the man,
Sweet Love were slain: his dearest bond is this,
Not like to like, but like in difference.
Yet in the long years liker must they grow;
The man be more of woman, she of man;
265   He gain in sweetness and in moral height,
Nor lose the wrestling thews that throw the world;
She mental breadth, nor fail in childward care,
Nor lose the childlike in the larger mind;
Till at the last she set herself to man,
270   Like perfect music unto noble words;
And so these twain, upon the skirts of Time,
Sit side by side, full-summed in all their powers,
Dispensing harvest, sowing the To-be,
Self-reverent each and reverencing each,
275   Distinct in individualities,
But like each other even as those who love.
Then comes the statelier Eden back to men:
Then reign the world's great bridals, chaste and calm:
Then springs the crowning race of humankind.

1. *The Princess* was Tennyson's attempt to address the contemporary debate over woman's proper role. It tells the story of a prince who courts the young and beautiful Princess Ida. She has vowed she will never marry and has established a women's university from which men are excluded. The prince and his two companions dress themselves up in women's clothes to gain entrance to the university. When a battle ensues—in which King Gama, the prince's father, invades the university to rescue his son and force Ida to marry him—the university is turned into a hospital and the princess is persuaded of the error of her ways. The prince's final vision, from book 7 (reprinted here), in which he imagines a future of gradual change, by which men and women adopt the strengths of the other while maintaining their distinct natures, has been a key text in discussing Victorian patriarchy. In the operetta *Princess Ida,* Gilbert and Sullivan use Tennyson's story to satirize feminism.

May these things be!"
280   Sighing she spoke "I fear
They will not."
              Dear, but let us type them now
In our own lives, and this proud watchword rest
Of equal; seeing either sex alone
Is half itself, and in true marriage lies
285 Nor equal, nor unequal: each fulfils
Defect in each, and always thought in thought,
Purpose in purpose, will in will, they grow,
The single pure and perfect animal,
The two-celled heart beating, with one full stroke,
Life."
290   And again sighing she spoke: "A dream
That once was mine! what woman taught you this?"

1839–47   1847

In Memoriam A. H. H.   When Arthur Hallam died suddenly at the age of twenty-two, Tennyson felt that his life had been shattered. Hallam was not only Tennyson's closest friend, and his sister's fiancé, but a critic and champion of his poetry. Widely regarded as the most promising young man of his generation, Hallam had written a review of Tennyson's first book of poetry that is still one of the best assessments of it. When Tennyson lost Hallam's love and support, he was overwhelmed with doubts about his own life and vocation and about the meaning of the universe and humankind's place in it, doubts reinforced by his study of geology and other sciences. To express the variety of his feelings and reflections, he began to compose a series of lyrics. Tennyson later arranged these "short swallow-flights of song," as he called them, written at intervals over a period of seventeen years, into one long elegy. Although the resulting poem has many affinities with traditional elegies like Milton's *Lycidas* and Shelley's *Adonais,* its structure is strikingly different. It is made up of individual lyric units that are seemingly self-contained but take their full meaning from their place in the whole. As T. S. Eliot has written, "It is unique: it is a long poem made by putting together lyrics, which have only the unity and continuity of a diary, the concentrated diary of a man confessing himself." Though intensely personal, it expressed the religious doubts of his age. Eliot continues, "It is not religious because of the quality of its faith but because of the quality of its doubt. . . . *In Memoriam* is a poem of despair." It is also a love poem. Like Shakespeare's sonnets, to which the poem alludes, *In Memoriam* vests its most intense emotion in male friendship.

The sections of the poem record a progressive development from despair to some sort of hope. Some of the early sections of the poem resemble traditional pastoral elegies, including those portraying the voyage during which Hallam's body was brought to England for burial (sections 9 to 15 and 19). Other early sections portraying the speaker's loneliness, in which even Christmas festivities seem joyless (sections 28 to 30), are more distinctive. With the passage of time, indicated by anniversaries and by recurring changes of the seasons, the speaker comes to accept the loss and to assert his belief in life and in an afterlife. In particular the recurring Christmases (sections 28, 78, 104) indicate the stages of his development, yet the pattern of progress in the poem is not a simple unimpeded movement upward. Dramatic conflicts recur throughout. Thus the most intense expression of doubt occurs not at the beginning of *In Memoriam* but as late as sections 54, 55, and 56.

The quatrain form in which the whole poem is written is usually called the "*In Memoriam* stanza," although it had been occasionally used by earlier poets. So rigid a form taxed Tennyson's ingenuity in achieving variety, but it is one of several means by which the diverse parts of the poem are knitted together.

The introductory section, consisting of eleven stanzas, is commonly referred to as the "Prologue," although Tennyson did not assign a title to it. It was written in 1849 after the rest of the poem was complete.

FROM IN MEMORIAM A. H. H.

OBIIT MDCCCXXXIII[1]

Strong Son of God, immortal Love,
    Whom we, that have not seen thy face,
    By faith, and faith alone, embrace,
Believing where we cannot prove;[2]

5   Thine are these orbs[3] of light and shade;
    Thou madest Life in man and brute;
    Thou madest Death; and lo, thy foot
Is on the skull which thou hast made.

Thou wilt not leave us in the dust:
10   Thou madest man, he knows not why,
    He thinks he was not made to die;
And thou hast made him: thou art just.

Thou seemest human and divine,
    The highest, holiest manhood, thou.
15   Our wills are ours, we know not how;
Our wills are ours, to make them thine.

Our little systems[4] have their day;
    They have their day and cease to be;
    They are but broken lights of thee,
20 And thou, O Lord, art more than they.

We have but faith: we cannot know,
    For knowledge is of things we see;
    And yet we trust it comes from thee,
A beam in darkness: let it grow.

25   Let knowledge grow from more to more,
    But more of reverence in us dwell;
    That mind and soul, according well,
May make one music as before,[5]

1. Died 1833.
2. Cf. John 20.24–29, in which Jesus rebukes Thomas for his doubts concerning the Resurrection: "Blessed are they that have not seen, and yet have believed."
3. The sun and moon (according to Tennyson's note).
4. Of religion and philosophy.
5. As in the days of fixed religious faith.

But vaster. We are fools and slight;
30   We mock thee when we do not fear:
     But help thy foolish ones to bear;
Help thy vain worlds to bear thy light.

Forgive what seemed my sin in me,
     What seemed my worth since I began;
35   For merit lives from man to man,
And not from man, O Lord, to thee.

Forgive my grief for one removed,
     Thy creature, whom I found so fair.
     I trust he lives in thee, and there
40   I find him worthier to be loved.

Forgive these wild and wandering cries,
     Confusions of a wasted° youth;   *desolated*
     Forgive them where they fail in truth,
And in thy wisdom make me wise.

1849

1

I held it truth, with him who sings
     To one clear harp in divers tones,[6]
     That men may rise on stepping stones
Of their dead selves to higher things.

5   But who shall so forecast the years
     And find in loss a gain to match?
     Or reach a hand through time to catch
The far-off interest of tears?

Let Love clasp Grief lest both be drowned,
10   Let darkness keep her raven gloss.
     Ah, sweeter to be drunk with loss,
To dance with Death, to beat the ground,

Than that the victor Hours should scorn
     The long result of love, and boast,
15   "Behold the man that loved and lost,
But all he was is overworn."

2

Old yew, which graspest at the stones
     That name the underlying dead,

---

6. Identified by Tennyson as Goethe.

Thy fibers net the dreamless head,
Thy roots are wrapped about the bones.

5   The seasons bring the flower again,
     And bring the firstling to the flock;
     And in the dusk of thee the clock
Beats out the little lives of men.

O, not for thee the glow, the bloom,
10   Who changest not in any gale,
     Nor branding summer suns avail
To touch thy thousand years of gloom[7]

And gazing on thee, sullen tree,
     Sick for° thy stubborn hardihood,   *envying*
15   I seem to fail from out my blood
And grow incorporate into thee.

3

O Sorrow, cruel fellowship,
     O Priestess in the vaults of Death,
     O sweet and bitter in a breath,
What whispers from thy lying lip?

5   "The stars," she whispers, "blindly run;
     A web is woven across the sky;
     From out waste places comes a cry,
And murmurs from the dying sun;

"And all the phantom, Nature, stands—
10   With all the music in her tone,
     A hollow echo of my own—
A hollow form with empty hands."

And shall I take a thing so blind,
     Embrace her° as my natural good;   *Sorrow*
15   Or crush her, like a vice of blood,
Upon the threshold of the mind?

4

To Sleep I give my powers away;
     My will is bondsman to the dark;
     I sit within a helmless bark,
And with my heart I muse and say:

---

7. The ancient yew tree, growing in the grounds near the clock tower and church where Hallam was to be buried, seems neither to blossom in spring nor to change from its dark mournful color in summer. "Thousand years": cf. Book of Common Prayer Psalm 90: "For a thousand years in Thy sight are but as yesterday when it is past, and as a watch in the night."

5   O heart, how fares it with thee now,
       That thou should fail from thy desire,
       Who scarcely darest to inquire,
    "What is it makes me beat so low?"

    Something it is which thou hast lost,
10   Some pleasure from thine early years.
       Break thou deep vase of chilling tears,
    That grief hath shaken into frost![8]

    Such clouds of nameless trouble cross
       All night below the darkened eyes;
15   With morning wakes the will, and cries,
    "Thou shalt not be the fool of loss."

5

    I sometimes hold it half a sin
       To put in words the grief I feel;
       For words, like Nature, half reveal
    And half conceal the Soul within.

5   But, for the unquiet heart and brain,
       A use in measured language lies;
       The sad mechanic exercise,
    Like dull narcotics, numbing pain.

    In words, like weeds,° I'll wrap me o'er,   *garments*
10   Like coarsest clothes against the cold;
       But that large grief which these enfold
    Is given in outline and no more.

6

    One writes, that "Other friends remain,"
       That "Loss is common to the race"—
       And common is the commonplace,
    And vacant chaff well meant for grain.

5   That loss is common would not make
       My own less bitter, rather more:
       Too common! Never morning wore
    To evening, but some heart did break.

    O father, wheresoe'er thou be,
10   Who pledgest° now thy gallant son;   *toasts*
       A shot, ere half thy draft be done,
    Hath stilled the life that beat from thee.

---

8. Water can be brought below freezing-point and not turn into ice—if it be kept still; but if it be moved suddenly it turns into ice and may break a vase [Tennyson's note].

O mother, praying God will save
  Thy sailor—while thy head is bowed,
15   His heavy-shotted hammock-shroud
Drops in his vast and wandering grave.

Ye know no more than I who wrought
  At that last hour to please him well;[9]
  Who mused on all I had to tell,
20 And something written, something thought;

Expecting still his advent home;
  And ever met him on his way
  With wishes, thinking, "here today,"
Or "here tomorrow will he come."

25 O somewhere, meek, the unconscious dove,
  That sittest ranging° golden hair;   *arranging*
  And glad to find thyself so fair,
Poor child, that waitest for thy love!

For now her father's chimney glows
30 In expectation of a guest;
  And thinking "this will please him best,"
She takes a riband or a rose;

For he will see them on tonight;
  And with the thought her color burns;
35 And, having left the glass, she turns
Once more to set a ringlet right;

And, even when she turned, the curse
  Had fallen, and her future Lord
  Was drowned in passing through the ford,
40 Or killed in falling from his horse.

O what to her shall be the end?
  And what to me remains of good?
  To her, perpetual maidenhood,
And unto me no second friend.

7

Dark house,[1] by which once more I stand
  Here in the long unlovely street,
  Doors, where my heart was used to beat
So quickly, waiting for a hand,

9. According to Tennyson's son, his father had discovered that he had been writing a letter to Hallam
during the very hour when his friend died.

1. The house on Wimpole Street, in London,
where Hallam had lived.

5 A hand that can be clasped no more—
    Behold me, for I cannot sleep,
    And like a guilty thing I creep
At earliest morning to the door.

He is not here; but far away
10   The noise of life begins again,
    And ghastly through the drizzling rain
On the bald street breaks the blank day.

8

A happy lover who has come
    To look on her that loves him well,
    Who 'lights and rings the gateway bell,
And learns her gone and far from home;

5 He saddens, all the magic light
    Dies off at once from bower and hall,
    And all the place is dark, and all
The chambers emptied of delight:

So find I every pleasant spot
10   In which we two were wont to meet,
    The field, the chamber, and the street,
For all is dark where thou art not.

Yet as that other, wandering there
    In those deserted walks, may find
15   A flower beat with rain and wind,
Which once she fostered up with care;

So seems it in my deep regret,
    O my forsaken heart, with thee
    And this poor flower of poesy
20 Which little cared for fades not yet.

But since it pleased a vanished eye,[2]
    I go to plant it on his tomb,
    That if it can it there may bloom,
Or dying, there at least may die.

9

Fair ship, that from the Italian shore
    Sailest the placid ocean-plains
    With my lost Arthur's loved remains,
Spread thy full wings, and waft him o'er.

---

2. Hallam expressed enthusiasm for Tennyson's early poetry in a review written in 1831.

5   So draw him home to those that mourn
     In vain; a favorable speed
     Ruffle thy mirrored mast, and lead
Through prosperous floods his holy urn.

All night no ruder air perplex
10   Thy sliding keel, till Phosphor,° bright   *morning star*
     As our pure love, through early light
Shall glimmer on the dewey decks.

Sphere all your lights around, above;
     Sleep, gentle heavens, before the prow;
15   Sleep, gentle winds, as he sleeps now,
My friend, the brother of my love;

My Arthur, whom I shall not see
     Till all my widowed race be run;
     Dear as the mother to the son,
20   More than my brothers are to me.

10

I hear the noise about thy keel;
     I hear the bell struck in the night;
     I see the cabin window bright;
I see the sailor at the wheel.

5   Thou bring'st the sailor to his wife,
     And traveled men from foreign lands;
     And letters unto trembling hands;
And, thy dark freight, a vanished life.

So bring him; we have idle dreams;
10   This look of quiet flatters thus
     Our home-bred fancies. O, to us,
The fools of habit, sweeter seems

To rest beneath the clover sod,
     That takes the sunshine and the rains,
15   Or where the kneeling hamlet drains
The chalice of the grapes of God;[3]

Than if with thee the roaring wells
     Should gulf him fathom-deep in brine,
     And hands so often clasped in mine,
20   Should toss with tangle° and with shells.   *seaweed*

3. Reference to a burial inside a church building rather than in the churchyard.

11

Calm is the morn without a sound,
  Calm as to suit a calmer grief,
  And only through the faded leaf
The chestnut pattering to the ground;

5   Calm and deep peace on this high wold,°   *open countryside*
  And on these dews that drench the furze,
  And all the silvery gossamers
That twinkle into green and gold;

Calm and still light on yon great plain
10   That sweeps with all its autumn bowers,
  And crowded farms and lessening towers,
To mingle with the bounding main;

Calm and deep peace in this wide air,
  These leaves that redden to the fall,
15   And in my heart, if calm at all,
If any calm, a calm despair;

Calm on the seas, and silver sleep,
  And waves that sway themselves in rest,
  And dead calm in that noble breast
20   Which heaves but with the heaving deep.[4]

12

Lo, as a dove when up she springs
  To bear through Heaven a tale of woe,
  Some dolorous message knit below
The wild pulsation of her wings;

5   Like her I go; I cannot stay;
  I leave this mortal ark behind,
  A weight of nerves without a mind,
And leave the cliffs, and haste away

O'er ocean-mirrors rounded large,
10   And reach the glow of southern skies,
  And see the sails at distance rise,
And linger weeping on the marge,

And saying; "Comes he thus, my friend?
  Is this the end of all my care?"
15   And circle moaning in the air:
"Is this the end? Is this the end?"

4. It is now the autumn of 1833, and the poet imagines that Hallam's body was already being brought back by ship to England. The date of the actual voyage seems to have been later in the year.

> And forward dart again, and play
>   About the prow, and back return
>   To where the body sits, and learn
> 20 That I have been an hour away.

13

> Tears of the widower, when he sees
>   A late-lost form that sleep reveals,
>   And moves his doubtful arms, and feels
> Her place is empty, fall like these;
>
> 5   Which weep a loss forever new,
>   A void where heart on heart reposed;
>   And, where warm hands have pressed and closed,
> Silence, till I be silent too;
>
> Which weep the comrade of my choice,
> 10   An awful thought, a life removed,
>   The human-hearted man I loved,
> A Spirit, not a breathing voice.
>
> Come, Time, and teach me, many years,
>   I do not suffer in a dream;
> 15   For now so strange do these things seem,
> Mine eyes have leisure for their tears,
>
> My fancies time to rise on wing,
>   And glance about the approaching sails,
>   As though they brought but merchants' bales,
> 20 And not the burthen that they bring.[5]

14

> If one should bring me this report,
>   That thou° hadst touched the land today,   *the ship*
>   And I went down unto the quay;[6]
> And found thee lying in the port;
>
> 5   And standing, muffled round with woe,
>   Should see thy passengers in rank
>   Come stepping lightly down the plank
> And beckoning unto those they know;
>
> And if along with these should come
> 10   The man I held as half divine,

---

5. The poet asks Time to teach him to confront the "awful" fact of what has happened (line 10) so that he will not delude himself by fancying the ship is bearing only merchandise and not the body of his friend.

6. By 1850 the accepted pronunciation of "quay" would rhyme with *key*, but Tennyson reverts to an earlier pronunciation, *kay*.

Should strike a sudden hand in mine,
   And ask a thousand things of home;

And I should tell him all my pain,
   And how my life had drooped of late,
15   And he should sorrow o'er my state
And marvel what possessed my brain;

And I perceived no touch of change,
   No hint of death in all his frame,
   But found him all in all the same,
20 I should not feel it to be strange.

15

Tonight the winds begin to rise
   And roar from yonder dropping day;
   The last red leaf is whirled away,
The rooks are blown about the skies;

5 The forest cracked, the waters curled,
   The cattle huddled on the lea;
   And wildly dashed on tower and tree
The sunbeam strikes along the world:

And but for fancies, which aver
10   That all thy motions gently pass
   Athwart a plane of molten glass,
I scarce could brook the strain and stir

That makes the barren branches loud;
   And but for fear it is not so,
15   The wild unrest that lives in woe
Would dote and pore on yonder cloud

That rises upward always higher,
   And onward drags a laboring breast,
   And topples round the dreary west,
20 A looming bastion fringed with fire.

*   *   *

19

The Danube to the Severn[7] gave
   The darkened heart that beat no more;

---

7. Hallam died at Vienna on the Danube. His burial place is on the banks of the Severn, a tidal river in the southwest of England.

They laid him by the pleasant shore,
    And in the hearing of the wave.

5   There twice a day the Severn fills;
        The salt sea water passes by,
        And hushes half the babbling Wye,[8]
    And makes a silence in the hills.

    The Wye is hushed nor moved along,
10   And hushed my deepest grief of all,
        When filled with tears that cannot fall,
    I brim with sorrow drowning song.

    The tide flows down, the wave again
        Is vocal in its wooded walls;
15   My deeper anguish also falls,
    And I can speak a little then.

                *   *   *

21

I sing to him that rests below,
    And, since the grasses round me wave,
    I take the grasses of the grave,[9]
And make them pipes whereon to blow.

5   The traveler hears me now and then,
        And sometimes harshly will he speak:
        "This fellow would make weakness weak,
    And melt the waxen hearts of men."

    Another answers: "Let him be,
10   He loves to make parade of pain,
        That with his piping he may gain
    The praise that comes to constancy."

    A third is wroth: "Is this an hour
        For private sorrow's barren song,
15   When more and more the people throng
    The chairs and thrones of civil power?

    "A time to sicken and to swoon,
        When Science reaches forth her arms[1]
        To feel from world to world, and charms
20 Her secret from the latest moon?"[2]

---

8. The water of the Wye River, a tributary of the Severn, is dammed up as the tide flows in, and its sound is silenced until, with the turn of the tide, its "wave" once more becomes "vocal" (lines 13–14); these stanzas were written at Tintern Abbey in the Wye River country.
9. The poet assumes that the burial was in the churchyard; in fact, Hallam's body was interred in a vault inside St. Andrews church at Clevedon, Somersetshire, on January 3, 1834 (see section 10, lines 11–16).
1. Astronomical instruments such as telescopes.
2. Probably alluding to the discovery in 1846 of the planet Neptune and one of its moons.

Behold, ye speak an idle thing;
　　Ye never knew the sacred dust.
　　I do but sing because I must,
And pipe but as the linnets sing:

25　And one is glad; her note is gay,
　　For now her little ones have ranged;
　　And one is sad; her note is changed,
Because her brood is stolen away.

22

The path by which we twain did go,
　　Which led by tracts that pleased us well,
　　Through four sweet years arose and fell,
From flower to flower, from snow to snow;

5　And we with singing cheered the way,
　　And, crowned with all the season lent,
　　From April on to April went,
And glad at heart from May to May.

But where the path we walked began
10　　To slant the fifth autumnal slope,[3]
　　As we descended following Hope,
There sat the Shadow feared of man;

Who broke our fair companionship,
　　And spread his mantle dark and cold,
15　　And wrapped thee formless in the fold,
And dulled the murmur on thy lip,

And bore thee where I could not see
　　Nor follow, though I walk in haste,
　　And think that somewhere in the waste
20　The Shadow sits and waits for me.

23

Now, sometimes in my sorrow shut,
　　Or breaking into song by fits,
　　Alone, alone, to where he sits,
The Shadow cloaked from head to foot,

5　Who keeps the keys of all the creeds,
　　I wander, often falling lame,
　　And looking back to whence I came,
Or on to where the pathway leads;

3. Hallam died just before the beginning of autumn (September 15, 1833) in the fifth year of the friendship.

And crying, How changed from where it ran
10   Through lands where not a leaf was dumb,
But all the lavish hills would hum
The murmur of a happy Pan;

When each by turns was guide to each,
And Fancy light from Fancy caught,
15   And Thought leapt out to wed with Thought
Ere Thought could wed itself with Speech;

And all we met was fair and good,
And all was good that Time could bring,
And all the secret of the Spring
20 Moved in the chambers of the blood;

And many an old philosophy
On Argive heights[4] divinely sang,
And round us all the thicket rang
To many a flute of Arcady.[5]

24

And was the day of my delight
As pure and perfect as I say?
The very source and fount of day
Is dashed with wandering isles of night.[6]

5   If all was good and fair we met,
This earth had been the Paradise
It never looked to human eyes
Since our first sun arose and set.

And is it that the haze of grief
10   Makes former gladness loom so great?
The lowness of the present state,
That sets the past in this relief?

Or that the past will always win
A glory from its being far,
15   And orb into the perfect star
We saw not when we moved therein?[7]

25

I know that this was Life—the track
Whereon with equal feet we fared;

4. Argos, a Greek city renowned for its music.
5. A sheep-raising region in Greece associated with pastoral poetry.
6. Moving spots on the sun.
7. The poet speculates whether past experiences seem so much more "pure and perfect" (line 2)
than present ones because they are far distant from us in time, just as our planet earth would have the deceptive appearance of being a perfect orb if we viewed it from a great distance in space, as from another planet (cf. *Locksley Hall Sixty Years After*, lines 187–92).

1244 / Alfred, Lord Tennyson

And then, as now, the day prepared
The daily burden for the back.

5   But this it was that made me move
        As light as carrier birds in air;
        I loved the weight I had to bear,
      Because it needed help of Love;

      Nor could I weary, heart or limb,
10   When mighty Love would cleave in twain
        The lading° of a single pain,   *burden*
      And part it, giving half to him.

26

      Still onward winds the dreary way;
        I with it, for I long to prove
        No lapse of moons can canker Love,
      Whatever fickle tongues may say.

5   And if that eye which watches guilt
        And goodness, and hath power to see
        Within the green the mouldered tree,
      And towers fallen as soon as built—

      O, if indeed that eye foresee
10   Or see—in Him is no before—
        In more of life true life no more
      And Love the indifference to be,

      Then might I find, ere yet the morn
        Breaks hither over Indian seas,
15   That Shadow waiting with the keys,
      To shroud me from my proper scorn.[8]

27

      I envy not in any moods
        The captive void of noble rage,
        The linnet born within the cage,
      That never knew the summer woods;

5   I envy not the beast that takes
        His license in the field of time,
        Unfettered by the sense of crime,
      To whom a conscience never wakes;

8. The Deity, being outside time, sees (rather than foresees) whether or not the rest of life ("more of life," line 11) will be pointless. If pointless, then the way for the speaker to deal with his self-scorn ("proper scorn") might be to seek death.

Nor, what may count itself as blest,
10   The heart that never plighted troth
But stagnates in the weeds of sloth;
Nor any want-begotten rest.[9]

I hold it true, whate'er befall;
I feel it, when I sorrow most;
15   'Tis better to have loved and lost
Than never to have loved at all.

28

The time draws near the birth of Christ.[1]
The moon is hid, the night is still;
The Christmas bells from hill to hill
Answer each other in the mist.

5   Four voices of four hamlets round,
From far and near, on mead and moor,
Swell out and fail, as if a door
Were shut between me and the sound;

Each voice four changes[2] on the wind,
10   That now dilate, and now decrease,
Peace and goodwill, goodwill and peace,
Peace and goodwill, to all mankind.

This year I slept and woke with pain,
I almost wished no more to wake,
15   And that my hold on life would break
Before I heard those bells again;

But they my troubled spirit rule,
For they controlled me when a boy;
They bring me sorrow touched with joy,
20   The merry, merry bells of Yule.

29

With such compelling cause to grieve
As daily vexes household peace,
And chains regret to his decease,
How dare we keep our Christmas eve;

5   Which brings no more a welcome guest
To enrich the threshold of the night

9. Complacency resulting from some deficiency
("want").
1. The first Christmas after Hallam's death
(1833); the setting is Tennyson's family home in
Lincolnshire.
2. Different sequences in which church bells are
pealed.

With showered largess of delight
In dance and song and game and jest?

Yet go, and while the holly boughs
10   Entwine the cold baptismal font,
        Make one wreath more for Use and Wont,[3]
That guard the portals of the house;

Old sisters of a day gone by,
        Gray nurses, loving nothing new;
15   Why should they miss their yearly due
Before their time? They too will die.

30

With trembling fingers did we weave
        The holly round the Christmas hearth;
        A rainy cloud possessed the earth,
And sadly fell our Christmas eve.

5   At our old pastimes in the hall
        We gamboled, making vain pretense
        Of gladness, with an awful sense
Of one mute Shadow watching all.

We paused: the winds were in the beech;
10   We heard them sweep the winter land;
        And in a circle hand-in-hand
Sat silent, looking each at each.

Then echo-like our voices rang;
        We sung, though every eye was dim,
15   A merry song we sang with him
Last year; impetuously we sang.

We ceased; a gentler feeling crept
        Upon us: surely rest is meet.[4]
        "They rest," we said, "their sleep is sweet,"
20   And silence followed, and we wept.

Our voices took a higher range;
        Once more we sang: "They do not die
        Nor lose their mortal sympathy,
Nor change to us, although they change;

25   "Rapt[5] from the fickle and the frail
        With gathered power, yet the same,
        Pierces the keen seraphic flame
From orb to orb,[6] from veil to veil."

3. Personifying the spirits who expect customary
observances of the Christmas season to be followed.
4. Proper or appropriate.

5. Carried away from.
6. The angelic spirit ("flame") of the dead moves
from star to star.

Rise, happy morn, rise, holy morn,
30   Draw forth the cheerful day from night:
O Father, touch the east, and light
The light that shone when Hope was born.

*   *   *

34

My own dim life should teach me this,
That life shall live forevermore,
Else earth is darkness at the core,
And dust and ashes all that is;

5 This round of green, this orb of flame,
Fantastic beauty; such as lurks
In some wild poet, when he works
Without a conscience or an aim.

What then were God to such as I?
10   'Twere hardly worth my while to choose
Of things all mortal, or to use
A little patience ere I die;

'Twere best at once to sink to peace,
Like birds the charming serpent[7] draws,
15   To drop head-foremost in the jaws
Of vacant darkness and to cease.

35

Yet if some voice that man could trust
Should murmur from the narrow house,
"The cheeks drop in, the body bows;
Man dies, nor is there hope in dust";

5 Might I not say? "Yet even here,
But for one hour, O Love, I strive
To keep so sweet a thing alive."
But I should turn mine ears and hear

The moanings of the homeless sea,
10 The sound of streams that swift or slow
Draw down Aeonian[8] hills, and sow
The dust of continents to be;

And Love would answer with a sigh,
"The sound of that forgetful shore

7. Some snakes are reputed to capture their prey by casting a charm.

8. Eons old, seemingly everlasting.

15 Will change my sweetness more and more,
　　Half-dead to know that I shall die."

O me, what profits it to put
　　An idle case? If Death were seen
　　At first as Death, Love had not been,
20 Or been in narrowest working shut,

Mere fellowship of sluggish moods,
　　Or in his coarsest Satyr-shape
　　Had bruised the herb and crushed the grape,
And basked and battened in the woods.[9]

*　*　*

39

Old warder of these buried bones,
　　And answering now my random stroke
　　With fruitful cloud and living smoke,
Dark yew, that graspest at the stones

5 And dippest toward the dreamless head,
　　To thee too comes the golden hour
　　When flower is feeling after flower;[1]
But Sorrow—fixed upon the dead,

And darkening the dark graves of men—
10 　　What whispered from her lying lips?
　　Thy gloom is kindled at the tips,[2]
And passes into gloom again.

*　*　*

47

That each, who seems a separate whole,
　　Should move his rounds,[3] and fusing all
　　The skirts[4] of self again, should fall
Remerging in the general Soul,

5 Is faith as vague as all unsweet.
　　Eternal form shall still divide

---

9. Lines 18ff. may be paraphrased: if we knew
death to be final and that no afterlife were possible,
love could not exist except on a primitive or bestial
level.
1. The ancient yew tree in the graveyard was
described in section 2 as never changing. Now the

poet discovers that in the flowering season, if the
tree is struck ("my random stroke"), it gives off a
cloud of golden pollen.
2. Only the tips of the yew branches are in flower.
3. I.e., go through the customary circuit of life.
4. Outer edges or fringes.

The eternal soul from all beside;
And I shall know him when we meet;

And we shall sit at endless feast,
10 Enjoying each the other's good.
What vaster dream can hit the mood
Of Love on earth? He seeks at least

Upon the last and sharpest height,
Before the spirits fade away,
15 Some landing place, to clasp and say,
"Farewell! We lose ourselves in light."

48

If these brief lays, of Sorrow born,
Were taken to be such as closed
Grave doubts and answers here proposed,
Then these were such as men might scorn.

5 Her care is not to part and prove;
She takes, when harsher moods remit,
What slender shade of doubt may flit,
And makes it vassal unto love;

And hence, indeed, she sports with words,
10 But better serves a wholesome law,
And holds it sin and shame to draw
The deepest measure from the chords;

Nor dare she trust a larger lay,
But rather loosens from the lip
15 Short swallow-flights of song, that dip
Their wings in tears, and skim away.

50

Be near me when my light is low,
When the blood creeps, and the nerves prick
And tingle; and the heart is sick,
And all the wheels of being slow.

5 Be near me when the sensuous frame
Is racked with pangs that conquer trust;
And Time, a maniac scattering dust,
And Life, a Fury slinging flame.

Be near me when my faith is dry,
10 And men the flies of latter spring,

That lay their eggs, and sting and sing
And weave their petty cells and die.

Be near me when I fade away,
    To point the term of human strife,
15   And on the low dark verge of life
The twilight of eternal day.

*   *   *

54

O, yet we trust that somehow good
    Will be the final goal of ill,
    To pangs of nature, sins of will,
Defects of doubt, and taints of blood;

5   That nothing walks with aimless feet;
    That not one life shall be destroyed,
    Or cast as rubbish to the void,
When God hath made the pile complete;

That not a worm is cloven in vain;
10   That not a moth with vain desire
    Is shriveled in a fruitless fire,
Or but subserves another's gain.

Behold, we know not anything;
    I can but trust that good shall fall
15   At last—far off—at last, to all,
And every winter change to spring.

So runs my dream; but what am I?
    An infant crying in the night;
    An infant crying for the light,
20 And with no language but a cry.

55

The wish, that of the living whole
    No life may fail beyond the grave,
    Derives it not from what we have
The likest God within the soul?

5   Are God and Nature then at strife,
    That Nature lends such evil dreams?
    So careful of the type she seems,
So careless of the single life,

That I, considering everywhere
10   Her secret meaning in her deeds,
        And finding that of fifty seeds
She often brings but one to bear,

I falter where I firmly trod,
        And falling with my weight of cares
15   Upon the great world's altar-stairs
That slope through darkness up to God,

I stretch lame hands of faith, and grope,
        And gather dust and chaff, and call
        To what I feel is Lord of all,
20   And faintly trust the larger hope.[5]

56

"So careful of the type?" but no.
        From scarpèd[6] cliff and quarried stone
        She° cries, "A thousand types are gone;   *i.e., Nature*
I care for nothing, all shall go.

5   "Thou makest thine appeal to me:
        I bring to life, I bring to death;
        The spirit does but mean the breath:
I know no more." And he, shall he,

Man, her last work, who seemed so fair,
10   Such splendid purpose in his eyes,
        Who rolled the psalm to wintry skies,
Who built him fanes° of fruitless prayer,   *temples*

Who trusted God was love indeed
        And love Creation's final law—
15   Though Nature, red in tooth and claw
With ravine, shrieked against his creed—

Who loved, who suffered countless ills,
        Who battled for the True, the Just,
        Be blown about the desert dust,
20   Or sealed within the iron hills?[7]

No more? A monster then, a dream,
        A discord. Dragons of the prime,
        That tare° each other in their slime,   *tore (archaic)*
Were mellow music matched with° him.   *compared to*

---

5. As expressed in lines 1 and 2.   7. Preserved like fossils in rock.
6. Cut away so that the strata are exposed.

25   O life as futile, then, as frail!
      O for thy voice to soothe and bless!
      What hope of answer, or redress?
   Behind the veil, behind the veil.

57

   Peace; come away: the song of woe
      Is after all an earthly song.
      Peace; come away: we do him wrong
   To sing so wildly: let us go.

5   Come; let us go: your cheeks are pale;
      Methinks my friend is richly shrined;
      But half my life I leave behind.
   But I shall pass, my work will fail.

   Yet in these ears, till hearing dies,
10   One set slow bell will seem to toll
      The passing of the sweetest soul
   That ever looked with human eyes.

   I hear it now, and o'er and o'er,
      Eternal greetings to the dead;
15   And "Ave,° Ave, Ave," said,   *Hail (Latin)*
   "Adieu, adieu," forevermore.

58

In those sad words I took farewell.
   Like echoes in sepulchral halls,
   As drop by drop the water falls
In vaults and catacombs, they fell;

5   And, falling, idly broke the peace
   Of hearts that beat from day to day,
   Half-conscious of their dying clay,
And those cold crypts where they shall cease.

The high Muse answered: "Wherefore grieve
10   Thy brethren with a fruitless tear?
   Abide a little longer here,
And thou shalt take a nobler leave."

59

   O Sorrow, wilt thou live with me
      No casual mistress, but a wife,

My bosom friend and half of life;
    As I confess it needs must be?

5   O Sorrow, wilt thou rule my blood,
        Be sometimes lovely like a bride,
        And put thy harsher moods aside,
    If thou wilt have me wise and good?

    My centered passion cannot move,
10   Nor will it lessen from today;
        But I'll have leave at times to play
    As with the creature of my love;

    And set thee forth, for thou art mine,
        With so much hope for years to come,
15   That, howsoe'er I know thee, some
    Could hardly tell what name were thine.

                    *   *   *

64

Dost thou look back on what hath been,
    As some divinely gifted man,
    Whose life in low estate began
And on a simple village green;

5   Who breaks his birth's invidious bar,
        And grasps the skirts of happy chance,
        And breasts the blows of circumstance,
    And grapples with his evil star;

    Who makes by force his merit known
10   And lives to clutch the golden keys,[8]
        To mold a mighty state's decrees,
    And shape the whisper of the throne;

    And moving up from high to higher,
        Becomes on Fortune's crowning slope
15   The pillar of a people's hope,
    The center of a world's desire;

    Yet feels, as in a pensive dream,
        When all his active powers are still,
        A distant dearness in the hill,
20   A secret sweetness in the stream,

    The limit of his narrower fate,
        While yet beside its vocal springs

8. Badges of high public office.

He played at counselors and kings,
With one that was his earliest mate;

25 Who plows with pain his native lea
And reaps the labor of his hands,
Or in the furrow musing stands:
"Does my old friend remember me?"

※   ※   ※

67

When on my bed the moonlight falls,
I know that in thy place of rest
By that broad water[9] of the west
There comes a glory on the walls:

5   Thy marble bright in dark appears,
As slowly steals a silver flame
Along the letters of thy name,
And o'er the number of thy years.

The mystic glory swims away,
10   From off my bed the moonlight dies;
And closing eaves of wearied eyes
I sleep till dusk is dipped in gray;

And then I know the mist is drawn
A lucid veil from coast to coast,
15   And in the dark church like a ghost
Thy tablet glimmers to the dawn.

※   ※   ※

70

I cannot see the features right,
When on the gloom I strive to paint
The face I know; the hues are faint
And mix with hollow masks of night;

5   Cloud-towers by ghostly masons wrought,
A gulf that ever shuts and gapes,
A hand that points, and pallèd shapes
In shadowy thoroughfares of thought;

And crowds that stream from yawning doors,
10   And shoals of puckered faces drive;

9. The Severn River.

Dark bulks that tumble half alive,
And lazy lengths on boundless shores;

Till all at once beyond the will
I hear a wizard music roll,
15   And through a lattice on the soul
Looks thy fair face and makes it still.

71

Sleep, kinsman thou to death and trance
And madness, thou has forged at last
A night-long present of the past
In which we went through summer France.[1]

5   Hadst thou such credit with the soul?
Then bring an opiate trebly strong,
Drug down the blindfold sense of wrong,
That so my pleasure may be whole;

While now we talk as once we talked
10   Of men and minds, the dust of change,
The days that grow to something strange,
In walking as of old we walked

Beside the river's wooded reach,
The fortress, and the mountain ridge,
15   The cataract flashing from the bridge,
The breaker breaking on the beach.

72

Risest thou thus, dim dawn, again,[2]
And howlest, issuing out of night,
With blasts that blow the poplar white,
And lash with storm the streaming pane?

5   Day, when my crowned estate[3] begun
To pine in that reverse of doom,[4]
Which sickened every living bloom,
And blurred the splendor of the sun;

Who usherest in the dolorous hour
10   With thy quick tears that make the rose
Pull sideways, and the daisy close
Her crimson fringes to the shower;

1. In the summer of 1830 Hallam and Tennyson
went through southern France en route to Spain.
2. September 15, 1834, the first anniversary of
Hallam's death.

3. State of happiness.
4. The reversal or disaster that doom brought
upon him when Hallam died.

Who mightst have heaved a windless flame
   Up the deep East, or, whispering, played
15   A checker-work of beam and shade
Along the hills, yet looked the same,

As wan, as chill, as wild as now;
   Day, marked as with some hideous crime,
   When the dark hand struck down through time,
20   And canceled nature's best: but thou,

Lift as thou mayst thy burthened brows
   Through clouds that drench the morning star,
   And whirl the ungarnered sheaf afar,
And sow the sky with flying boughs,

25   And up thy vault with roaring sound
   Climb thy thick noon, disastrous day;
   Touch thy dull goal of joyless gray,
And hide thy shame beneath the ground.

*   *   *

75

I leave thy praises unexpressed
   In verse that brings myself relief,
   And by the measure of my grief
I leave thy greatness to be guessed.

5   What practice howsoe'er expert
   In fitting aptest words to things,
   Or voice the richest-toned that sings,
Hath power to give thee as thou wert?

I care not in these fading days
10   To raise a cry that lasts not long,
   And round thee with the breeze of song
To stir a little dust of praise.

Thy leaf has perished in the green,
   And, while we breathe beneath the sun,
15   The world which credits what is done
Is cold to all that might have been.

So here shall silence guard thy fame;
   But somewhere, out of human view,
   Whate'er thy hands are set to do
20   Is wrought with tumult of acclaim.

*   *   *

78

Again at Christmas[5] did we weave
  The holly round the Christmas hearth;
  The silent snow possessed the earth,
And calmly fell our Christmas eve.

5 The yule clog° sparkled keen with frost,   *log*
  No wing of wind the region swept,
  But over all things brooding slept
The quiet sense of something lost.

As in the winters left behind,
10 Again our ancient games had place,
  The mimic picture's[6] breathing grace,
And dance and song and hoodman-blind.[7]

Who showed a token of distress?
  No single tear, no mark of pain—
15 O sorrow, then can sorrow wane?
O grief, can grief be changed to less?

O last regret, regret can die!
  No—mixed with all this mystic frame,
  Her deep relations are the same,
20 But with long use her tears are dry.

＊　＊　＊

82

I wage not any feud with Death
  For changes wrought on form and face;
  No lower life that earth's embrace
May breed with him can fright my faith.

5 Eternal process moving on,
  From state to state the spirit walks;
  And these are but the shattered stalks,
Or ruined chrysalis of one.

Nor blame I Death, because he bare
10 The use of virtue out of earth;
  I know transplanted human worth
Will bloom to profit, otherwhere.

5. The second Christmas (1834) after Hallam's death.
6. A game in which the participants pose in the manner of some famous statue or painting and the spectators try to guess what work of art is being portrayed.
7. The player in the game of blindman's buff who wears a blindfold or hood.

For this alone on Death I wreak
　　The wrath that garners in my heart:
15　　He put our lives so far apart
　　We cannot hear each other speak.

83

Dip down upon the northern shore,
　　O sweet new-year° delaying long;　　　　　　*spring 1835*
　　Thou doest expectant Nature wrong;
Delaying long, delay no more.

5　What stays thee from the clouded noons,
　　Thy sweetness from its proper place?
　　Can trouble live with April days,
Or sadness in the summer moons?

Bring orchis, bring the foxglove spire,
10　　The little speedwell's° darling blue,　　　　　*spring flower*
　　Deep tulips dashed with fiery dew,
Laburnums, dropping-wells of fire.

O thou, new-year, delaying long,
　　Delayest the sorrow in my blood,
15　　That longs to burst a frozen bud
And flood a fresher throat with song.

84

When I contemplate all alone
　　The life that had been thine below,
　　And fix my thoughts on all the glow
To which thy crescent would have grown,

5　I see thee sitting crowned with good,
　　A central warmth diffusing bliss
　　In glance and smile, and clasp and kiss,
On all the branches of thy blood;

Thy blood, my friend, and partly mine;
10　　For now the day was drawing on,
　　When thou shouldst link thy life with one
Of mine own house, and boys of thine

Had babbled "Uncle" on my knee;
　　But that remorseless iron hour
15　　Made cypress of her orange flower,[8]
Despair of hope, and earth of thee.

---

8. Orange blossoms are associated with brides—here the poet's sister Emily Tennyson, to whom Hallam had been engaged.

I seem to meet their least desire,
    To clap their cheeks, to call them mine.
    I see their unborn faces shine
20 Beside the never-lighted fire.

I see myself an honored guest,
    Thy partner in the flowery walk
    Of letters, genial table talk,
Or deep dispute, and graceful jest;

25 While now thy prosperous labor fills
    The lips of men with honest praise,
    And sun by sun the happy days
Descend below the golden hills

With promise of a morn as fair;
30   And all the train of bounteous hours
    Conduct, by paths of growing powers,
To reverence and the silver hair;

Till slowly worn her earthly robe,
    Her lavish mission richly wrought,
35   Leaving great legacies of thought,
Thy spirit should fail from off the globe;

What time mine own might also flee,
    As linked with thine in love and fate,
    And, hovering o'er the dolorous strait
40 To the other shore, involved in thee,

Arrive at last the blessed goal,
    And He that died in Holy Land
    Would reach us out the shining hand,
And take us as a single soul.

45 What reed was that on which I leant?
    Ah, backward fancy, wherefore wake
    The old bitterness again, and break
The low beginnings of content?

*   *   *

86

Sweet after showers, ambrosial air,
    That rollest from the gorgeous gloom
    Of evening over brake and bloom
And meadow, slowly breathing bare

5 The round of space,[9] and rapt below
    Through all the dewy-tasseled wood,

9. Air that is slowly clearing the clouds from the sky.

And shadowing down the hornèd flood[1]
In ripples, fan my brows and blow

The fever from my cheek, and sigh
10   The full new life that feeds thy breath
Throughout my frame, till Doubt and Death,
Ill brethren, let the fancy fly

From belt to belt of crimson seas
On leagues of odor streaming far,
15   To where in yonder orient star
A hundred spirits whisper "Peace."

87

I passed beside the reverend walls[2]
In which of old I wore the gown;
I roved at random through the town,
And saw the tumult of the halls;

5   And heard once more in college fanes
The storm their high-built organs make,
And thunder-music, rolling, shake
The prophet blazoned on the panes;

And caught once more the distant shout,
10   The measured pulse of racing oars
Among the willows; paced the shores
And many a bridge, and all about

The same gray flats again, and felt
The same, but not the same; and last
15   Up that long walk of limes I passed
To see the rooms in which he dwelt.

Another name was on the door.
I lingered; all within was noise
Of songs, and clapping hands, and boys
20   That crashed the glass and beat the floor;

Where once we held debate, a band
Of youthful friends,[3] on mind and art,
And labor, and the changing mart,
And all the framework of the land;

25   When one would aim an arrow fair,
But send it slackly from the string;

1. Between two promontories [Tennyson's note].
2. Of Trinity College, Cambridge University.
3. "The Apostles," an undergraduate club to which Tennyson and Hallam had belonged.

And one would pierce an outer ring,
And one an inner, here and there;

And last the master bowman, he,
30   Would cleave the mark. A willing ear
We lent him. Who but hung to hear
The rapt oration flowing free

From point to point, with power and grace
And music in the bounds of law,[4]
35   To those conclusions when we saw
The God within him light his face,

And seem to lift the form, and glow
In azure orbits heavenly-wise;
And over those ethereal eyes
40   The bar of Michael Angelo?[5]

88

Wild bird,[6] whose warble, liquid sweet,
Rings Eden through the budded quicks,[7]
O tell me where the senses mix,
O tell me where the passions meet,

5   Whence radiate: fierce extremes employ
Thy spirits in the darkening leaf,
And in the midmost heart of grief
Thy passion clasps a secret joy;

And I—my harp would prelude woe—
10   I cannot all command the strings;
The glory of the sum of things
Will flash along the chords and go.

89

Witch elms that counterchange the floor
Of this flat lawn with dusk and bright;[8]
And thou, with all thy breadth and height
Of foliage, towering sycamore;

5   How often, hither wandering down,
My Arthur found your shadows fair,

4. An essay presented by Hallam at Cambridge in 1831 provides an example of his skill while still an undergraduate in theological argument (cf. *The Writings of Arthur Hallam,* edited by T. H. V. Motter, 1943, pp. 198–213).
5. Hallam, like Michelangelo, had a prominent ridge of bone above his eyes.
6. Probably a nightingale.
7. Hawthorn hedges.
8. Shadows of the elm tree checker the lawn at Somersby, the Tennysons' country home.

And shook to all the liberal air
The dust and din and steam of town!

He brought an eye for all he saw;
10   He mixed in all our simple sports;
     They pleased him, fresh from brawling courts
And dusty purlieus of the law.[9]

O joy to him in this retreat,
     Immantled in ambrosial dark,
15   To drink the cooler air, and mark
The landscape winking through the heat!

O sound to rout the brood of cares,
     The sweep of scythe in morning dew,
     The gust that round the garden flew,
20   And tumbled half the mellowing pears!

O bliss, when all in circle drawn
     About him, heart and ear were fed
     To hear him, as he lay and read
The Tuscan poets on the lawn!

25   Or in the all-golden afternoon
     A guest, or happy sister, sung,
     Or here she brought the harp and flung
A ballad to the brightening moon.

Nor less it pleased in livelier moods,
30   Beyond the bounding hill to stray,
     And break the livelong summer day
With banquet in the distant woods;

Whereat we glanced from theme to theme,
     Discussed the books to love or hate,
35   Or touched the changes of the state,
Or threaded some Socratic dream;[1]

But if I praised the busy town,
     He loved to rail against it still,
     For "ground in yonder social mill
40   We rub each other's angles down,

"And merge," he said, "in form and gloss
     The picturesque of man and man."
     We talked: the stream beneath us ran,
The wine-flask lying couched in moss,

---

9. Hallam became a law student in London after leaving Cambridge.

1. I.e., worked our way through some discourse of Socrates (as recorded by Plato).

45   Or cooled within the glooming wave;
    And last, returning from afar,
    Before the crimson-circled star[2]
Had fallen into her father's[3] grave,

    And brushing ankle-deep in flowers,
50   We heard behind the woodbine veil
    The milk that bubbled in° the pail,   *into*
And buzzings of the honeyed hours.

*   *   *

91

    When rosy plumelets tuft the larch,
    And rarely° pipes the mounted thrush,   *exquisitely*
    Or underneath the barren bush
Flits by the sea-blue bird° of March;   *kingfisher*

5   Come, wear the form by which I know
    Thy spirit in time among thy peers;
    The hope of unaccomplished years
Be large and lucid round thy brow.

    When summer's hourly-mellowing change
10   May breathe, with many roses sweet,
    Upon the thousand waves of wheat
That ripple round the lowly grange,

    Come; not in watches of the night,
    But where the sunbeam broodeth warm,
15   Come, beauteous in thine after form,
And like a finer light in light.

*   *   *

93

I shall not see thee. Dare I say
    No spirit ever brake the band
    That stays him from the native land
Where first he walked when clasped in clay?[4]

5   No visual shade of someone lost,
    But he, the Spirit himself, may come
    Where all the nerve of sense is numb,
Spirit to Spirit, Ghost to Ghost.

2. Venus, which will sink into the west as the sun has done.
3. According to the nebular hypothesis, planets condensed out of the sun's atmosphere; in this sense the sun is the "father" of planets.
4. I.e., when he was alive and clothed in flesh.

Oh, therefore from thy sightless° range   *invisible*
10   With gods in unconjectured bliss,
Oh, from the distance of the abyss
Of tenfold-complicated change,

Descend, and touch, and enter; hear
The wish too strong for words to name,
15   That in this blindness of the frame°   *living frame*
My Ghost may feel that thine is near.

94

How pure at heart and sound in head,
With what divine affections bold
Should be the man whose thought would hold
An hour's communion with the dead.

5   In vain shalt thou, or any, call
The spirits from their golden day,
Except, like them, thou too canst say,
My spirit is at peace with all.

They haunt the silence of the breast,
10   Imaginations calm and fair,
The memory like a cloudless air,
The conscience as a sea at rest;

But when the heart is full of din,
And doubt beside the portal waits,
15   They can but listen at the gates,
And hear the household jar within.

95

By night we lingered on the lawn,
For underfoot the herb was dry;
And genial warmth; and o'er the sky
The silvery haze of summer drawn;

5   And calm that let the tapers burn
Unwavering: not a cricket chirred;
The brook alone far off was heard,
And on the board the fluttering urn.[5]

And bats went round in fragrant skies,
10   And wheeled or lit the filmy shapes[6]
That haunt the dusk, with ermine capes
And woolly breasts and beaded eyes;

---

5. For boiling water for tea or coffee, heated by a fluttering flame.

6. The white-winged night moths called ermine moths.

While now we sang old songs that pealed
   From knoll to knoll, where, couched at ease,
15   The white kine° glimmered, and the trees   *cows*
   Laid their dark arms[7] about the field.

But when those others, one by one,
   Withdrew themselves from me and night,
   And in the house light after light
20 Went out, and I was all alone,

A hunger seized my heart; I read
   Of that glad year which once had been,
   In those fallen leaves which kept their green,
   The noble letters of the dead.

25 And strangely on the silence broke
   The silent-speaking words, and strange
   Was love's dumb cry defying change
   To test his worth; and strangely spoke

The faith, the vigor, bold to dwell
30   On doubts that drive the coward back,
   And keen through wordy snares to track
   Suggestion to her inmost cell.

So word by word, and line by line,
   The dead man touched me from the past,
35   And all at once it seemed at last
   The[8] living soul was flashed on mine.

And mine in this was wound, and whirled
   About empyreal heights of thought,
   And came on that which is, and caught
40 The deep pulsations of the world,

Aeonian music[9] measuring out
   The steps of Time—the shocks of Chance—
   The blows of Death. At length my trance
   Was canceled, stricken through with doubt.[1]

45 Vague words! but ah, how hard to frame
   In matter-molded forms of speech,

7. Cast the shadows of their branches.
8. It was "His" in the 1st edition, and also in the 1st edition, line 37 read, "And mine in his was wound."
9. Of the universe, which has pulsated for eons.
1. In a letter of 1874, replying to an inquiry about his experience of mystical trances, Tennyson wrote: "A kind of waking trance I have frequently had, quite up from boyhood, when I have been all alone. This has generally come upon me through repeating my own name two or three times to myself silently, till all at once, as it were out of the intensity of the consciousness of individuality, the individuality itself seemed to dissolve and fade away into boundless being, and this not a confused state, but the clearest of the clearest, the surest of the surest, the weirdest of the weirdest, utterly beyond words, where death was an almost laughable impossibility, the loss of personality (if so it were) seeming no extinction but the only true life. . . . This might . . . be the state which St. Paul describes, 'Whether in the body I cannot tell, or whether out of the body I cannot tell.' . . . I am ashamed of my feeble description. Have I not said the state is utterly beyond words? But in a moment, when I come back to my normal state of 'sanity,' I am ready to fight for *mein liebes Ich* [my dear self], and hold that it will last for aeons of aeons" (*Alfred Lord Tennyson, A Memoir*, 1897, vol. 1, 320).

Or even for intellect to reach
Through memory that which I became.

Till now the doubtful dusk revealed
50   The knolls once more where, couched at ease,
        The white kine glimmered, and the trees
Laid their dark arms about the field;

And sucked from out the distant gloom
        A breeze began to tremble o'er
55   The large leaves of the sycamore,
And fluctuate all the still perfume,

And gathering freshlier overhead,
        Rocked the full-foliaged elms, and swung
        The heavy-folded rose, and flung
60 The lilies to and fro, and said,

"The dawn, the dawn," and died away;
        And East and West, without a breath,
        Mixed their dim lights, like life and death,
To broaden into boundless day.

96

You say, but with no touch of scorn,
        Sweet-hearted, you,[2] whose light blue eyes
        Are tender over drowning flies,
You tell me, doubt is Devil-born.

5   I know not: one indeed I knew
        In many a subtle question versed,
        Who touched a jarring lyre at first,
But ever strove to make it true;

Perplexed in faith, but pure in deeds,
10   At last he beat his music out.
        There lives more faith in honest doubt,
Believe me, than in half the creeds.

He fought his doubts and gathered strength,
        He would not make his judgment blind,
15   He faced the specters of the mind
And laid them; thus he came at length

To find a stronger faith his own,
        And Power was with him in the night,
        Which makes the darkness and the light,
20   And dwells not in the light alone,

---

2. A woman of simple faith.

But in the darkness and the cloud,
  As over Sinaï's peaks of old,[3]
  While Israel made their gods of gold,
Although the trumpet blew so loud.

*   *   *

99

Risest thou thus, dim dawn, again,[4]
  So loud with voices of the birds,
  So thick with lowings of the herds,
Day, when I lost the flower of men;

5 Who tremblest through thy darkling red
  On yon swollen brook that bubbles fast[5]
  By meadows breathing of the past,
And woodlands holy to the dead;

Who murmurest in the foliage eaves
10 A song that slights the coming care,[6]
  And Autumn laying here and there
A fiery finger on the leaves;

Who wakenest with thy balmy breath
  To myriads on the genial earth,
15 Memories of bridal, or of birth,[7]
And unto myriads more, of death.

Oh, wheresoever those[8] may be,
  Betwixt the slumber of the poles,
  Today they count as kindred souls;
20 They know me not, but mourn with me.

*   *   *

103

On that last night before we went
  From out the doors where I was bred,[9]
  I dreamed a vision of the dead,
Which left my after-morn content.

---

3. Cf. Exodus 19.16–25. After veiling Mount Sinai in a "cloud" of smoke, God addressed Moses from the darkness.
4. September 15, 1835, the second anniversary of Hallam's death.
5. I.e., reflections of the clouded red light of dawn quiver on the surface of the fast-moving water.
6. I.e., disregards future events such as death or the coming of autumn.

7. Cf. *Epilogue*, lines 117–28 (pp. 1279–80).
8. I.e., the many who remember death.
9. In 1837 Tennyson and his family moved away from their home in Lincolnshire, which had been closely associated with his friendship with Hallam. In section 104 the move seems to occur in 1835, the year of the third Christmas after Hallam's death.

5 Methought I dwelt within a hall,
     And maidens with me; distant hills
     From hidden summits fed with rills
  A river sliding by the wall.

  The hall with harp and carol rang.
10   They sang of what is wise and good
     And graceful. In the center stood
  A statue veiled, to which they sang;

  And which, though veiled, was known to me,
     The shape of him I loved, and love
15   Forever. Then flew in a dove
  And brought a summons from the sea;

  And when they learnt that I must go,
     They wept and wailed, but led the way
     To where the little shallop° lay   *light open boat*
20 At anchor in the flood below;

  And on by many a level mead,
     And shadowing bluff that made the banks,
     We glided winding under ranks
  Of iris and the golden reed;

25 And still as vaster grew the shore
     And rolled the floods in grander space,
     The maidens gathered strength and grace
  And presence, lordlier than before;

  And I myself, who sat apart
30   And watched them, waxed in every limb;
     I felt the thews of Anakim,[1]
  The pulses of a Titan's[2] heart;

  As one would sing the death of war,
     And one would chant the history
35   Of that great race which is to be,[3]
  And one the shaping of a star;

  Until the forward-creeping tides
     Began to foam, and we to draw
     From deep to deep, to where we saw
40 A great ship lift her shining sides.[4]

1. Plural of *Anak;* a reference to the giant sons of
Anak (cf. Numbers 13.33).
2. Giant of Greek mythology.
3. See the account of the "crowning race" in *Epilogue,* lines 128–44.
4. Cf. *Morte d'Arthur,* lines 255–322, in which
Bedivere is left behind as Arthur's barge, the ship

of death, sails away. In the present dream vision
not only is the speaker taken aboard but also his
companions, who represent the creative arts of this
world—"all the human powers and talents that do
not pass with life but go along with it," as Tennyson
said of this passage.

The man we loved was there on deck,
   But thrice as large as man he bent
   To greet us. Up the side I went,
And fell in silence on his neck;

45 Whereat those maidens with one mind
   Bewailed their lot; I did them wrong:
   "We served thee here," they said, "so long,
And wilt thou leave us now behind?"

So rapt° I was, they could not win   *entranced*
50 An answer from my lips, but he
   Replying, "Enter likewise ye
And go with us:" they entered in.

And while the wind began to sweep
   A music out of sheet and shroud,
55 We steered her toward a crimson cloud
That landlike slept along the deep.

104

The time draws near the birth of Christ;[5]
   The moon is hid, the night is still;
   A single church below the hill
Is pealing, folded in the mist.

5 A single peal of bells below,
   That wakens at this hour of rest
   A single murmur in the breast,
That these are not the bells I know.

Like strangers' voices here they sound,
10 In lands where not a memory strays,
   Nor landmark breathes of other days,
But all is new unhallowed ground.

105

Tonight ungathered let us leave
   This laurel, let this holly stand:[6]
   We live within the stranger's land,
And strangely falls our Christmas eve.

5 Our father's dust is left alone
   And silent under other snows:

5. See n. 1, p. 1245.
6. Cf. section 29, in which the family in their former home still continued to gather holly. In the
new home, the customary observances lapse.

There in due time the woodbine blows,
The violet comes, but we are gone.

No more shall wayward grief abuse
10   The genial hour with mask and mime;
For change of place, like growth of time,
Has broke the bond of dying use.

Let cares that petty shadows cast,
By which our lives are chiefly proved,
15   A little spare the night I loved,
And hold it solemn to the past.

But let no footstep beat the floor,
Nor bowl of wassail mantle warm;[7]
For who would keep an ancient form
20   Through which the spirit breathes no more?

Be neither song, nor game, nor feast;
Nor harp be touched, nor flute be blown;
No dance, no motion, save alone
What lightens in the lucid east

25   Of rising worlds[8] by yonder wood.
Long sleeps the summer in the seed;
Run out your measured arcs, and lead
The closing cycle rich in good.

106

Ring out, wild bells, to the wild sky,
The flying cloud, the frosty light:
The year is dying in the night;
Ring out, wild bells, and let him die.

5   Ring out the old, ring in the new,
Ring, happy bells, across the snow:
The year is going, let him go;
Ring out the false, ring in the true.

Ring out the grief that saps the mind,
10   For those that here we see no more;
Ring out the feud of rich and poor,
Ring in redress to all mankind.

Ring out a slowly dying cause,
And ancient forms of party strife;

---

7. I.e., no bowl of hot punch warms the mantel-piece.

8. The scintillating motion of the stars that rise [Tennyson's note].

15   Ring in the nobler modes of life,
     With sweeter manners, purer laws.

     Ring out the want, the care, the sin,
        The faithless coldness of the times:
        Ring out, ring out my mournful rhymes,
20   But ring the fuller minstrel in.

     Ring out false pride in place and blood,
        The civic slander and the spite;
        Ring in the love of truth and right,
     Ring in the common love of good.

25   Ring out old shapes of foul disease;
        Ring out the narrowing lust of gold;
        Ring out the thousand wars of old,
     Ring in the thousand years of peace.

     Ring in the valiant man and free,
30   The larger heart, the kindlier hand;
        Ring out the darkness of the land,
     Ring in the Christ that is to be.[9]

107

     It is the day when he was born.°   *February 1*
        A bitter day that early sank
        Behind a purple-frosty bank
     Of vapor, leaving night forlorn.

5   The time admits not flowers or leaves
        To deck the banquet. Fiercely flies
        The blast of North and East, and ice
     Makes daggers at the sharpened eaves,

     And bristles all the brakes and thorns
10   To yon hard crescent, as she hangs
        Above the wood which grides[1] and clangs
     Its leafless ribs and iron horns

     Together, in the drifts[2] that pass
        To darken on the rolling brine
15   That breaks the coast. But fetch the wine,
     Arrange the board and brim the glass;

---

9. These allusions to the second coming of Christ and to the millennium are derived from Revelation 20, but Tennyson has interpreted the biblical account in his own way. He once told his son of his conviction that "the forms of Christian religion would alter; but that the spirit of Christ would still grow from more to more."
1. Clashes with a strident noise.
2. Either cloud-drifts or clouds of snow.

Bring in great logs and let them lie,
　　To make a solid core of heat;
　　Be cheerful-minded, talk and treat
20　Of all things even as he were by;

We keep the day. With festal cheer,
　　With books and music, surely we
　　Will drink to him, whate'er he be,
And sing the songs he loved to hear.

108

I will not shut me from my kind,
　　And, lest I stiffen into stone,
　　I will not eat my heart alone,
Nor feed with sighs a passing wind:

5　What profit lies in barren faith,
　　And vacant yearning, though with might
　　To scale the heaven's highest height,
Or dive below the wells of Death?

What find I in the highest place,
10　But mine own phantom chanting hymns?
　　And on the depths of death there swims
The reflex of a human face.°　　　　　　　　　　　　　*his own face*

I'll rather take what fruit may be
　　Of sorrow under human skies:
15　'Tis held that sorrow makes us wise,
Whatever wisdom sleep with thee.°　　　　　　　　　　　*Hallam*

109

Heart-affluence in discursive talk
　　From household fountains never dry;
　　The critic clearness of an eye
That saw through all the Muses' walk;[3]

5　Seraphic intellect and force
　　To seize and throw the doubts of man;
　　Impassioned logic, which outran
The hearer in its fiery course;

High nature amorous of the good,
10　But touched with no ascetic gloom;
　　And passion pure in snowy bloom
Through all the years of April blood;

---

3. The realm of art and literature.

A love of freedom rarely felt,
   Of freedom in her regal seat
15   Of England; not the schoolboy heat,
The blind hysterics of the Celt;[4]

And manhood fused with female grace
   In such a sort, the child would twine
   A trustful hand, unasked, in thine,
20 And find his comfort in thy face;

All these have been, and thee mine eyes
   Have looked on: if they looked in vain,
   My shame is greater who remain,
Nor let thy wisdom make me wise.

*   *   *

115

Now fades the last long streak of snow,
   Now burgeons every maze of quick°   *hawthorn hedges*
   About the flowering squares,° and thick   *fields*
By ashen roots the violets blow.

5   Now rings the woodland loud and long,
   The distance takes a lovelier hue,
   And drowned in yonder living blue
The lark becomes a sightless song.

Now dance the lights on lawn and lea,
10   The flocks are whiter down the vale,
   And milkier every milky sail
On winding stream or distant sea;

Where now the seamew pipes, or dives
   In yonder greening gleam, and fly
15   The happy birds, that change their sky
To build and brood, that live their lives

From land to land; and in my breast
   Spring wakens too, and my regret
   Becomes an April violet,
20 And buds and blossoms like the rest.

*   *   *

4. A member of one of the groups of peoples populating ancient Britain; i.e., a less-civilized people.

118

Contèmplate all this work of Time,
    The giant laboring in his youth;
    Nor dream of human love and truth,
As dying Nature's earth and lime;[5]

5   But trust that those we call the dead
    Are breathers of an ampler day
    For ever nobler ends. They[6] say,
The solid earth whereon we tread

In tracts of fluent heat began,
10   And grew to seeming-random forms,
    The seeming prey of cyclic storms,
Till at the last arose the man;

Who throve and branched from clime to clime,
    The herald of a higher race,
15   And of himself in higher place
If so he type[7] this work of time

Within himself, from more to more;
    Or, crowned with attributes of woe
    Like glories, move his course, and show
20 That life is not as idle ore,

But iron dug from central gloom,
    And heated hot with burning fears,
    And dipped in baths of hissing tears,
And battered with the shocks of doom

25 To shape and use. Arise and fly
    The reeling Faun, the sensual feast;
    Move upward, working out the beast,
And let the ape and tiger die.

119

Doors, where my heart was used to beat
    So quickly, not as one that weeps
    I come once more; the city sleeps;
I smell the meadow in the street;

5   I hear a chirp of birds; I see
    Betwixt the black fronts long-withdrawn
    A light blue lane of early dawn,
And think of early days and thee,

---

5. Alluding to the materialistic analysis of living
matter into chemicals and simpler compounds
[cited by Susan Shatto].

6. Geologists and astronomers.
7. Emulate, prefigure as a type.

And bless thee, for thy lips are bland,
10   And bright the friendship of thine eye;
And in my thoughts with scarce a sigh
I take the pressure of thine hand.

120

I trust I have not wasted breath:
I think we are not wholly brain,
Magnetic mockeries;[8] not in vain,
Like Paul[9] with beasts, I fought with Death;

5   Not only cunning casts in clay:
Let Science prove we are, and then
What matters Science unto men,
At least to me? I would not stay.

Let him, the wiser man who springs
10   Hereafter, up from childhood shape
His action like the greater ape,
But I was *born* to other things.

121

Sad Hesper° o'er the buried sun   *evening star*
And ready, thou, to die with him,
Thou watchest all things ever dim
And dimmer, and a glory done.

5   The team is loosened from the wain,°   *hay wagon*
The boat is drawn upon the shore;
Thou listenest to the closing door,
And life is darkened in the brain.

Bright Phosphor,° fresher for the night,   *morning star*
10   By thee the world's great work is heard
Beginning, and the wakeful bird;
Behind thee comes the greater light.[1]

The market boat is on the stream,
And voices hail it from the brink;
15   Thou hear'st the village hammer clink,
And see'st the moving of the team.

Sweet Hesper-Phosphor, double name[2]
For what is one, the first, the last,

8. Mechanisms operated by responses to electrical forces.
9. 1 Corinthians 15.32.
1. Cf. Genesis 1.16: "The greater light to rule the day."
2. The planet Venus is both evening star and morning star.

Thou, like my present and my past,
20   Thy place is changed; thou art the same.

*   *   *

123

There rolls the deep where grew the tree.
    O earth, what changes hast thou seen!
    There where the long street roars hath been
The stillness of the central sea.[3]

5   The hills are shadows, and they flow
    From form to form, and nothing stands;
    They melt like mist, the solid lands,
Like clouds they shape themselves and go.

But in my spirit will I dwell,
10   And dream my dream, and hold it true;
    For though my lips may breathe adieu,
I cannot think the thing farewell.

124

That which we dare invoke to bless;
    Our dearest faith; our ghastliest doubt;
    He, They, One, All; within, without;
The Power in darkness whom we guess—

5   I found Him not in world or sun,
    Or eagle's wing, or insect's eye,[4]
    Nor through the questions men may try,
The petty cobwebs we have spun.

If e'er when faith had fallen asleep,
10   I heard a voice, "believe no more,"
    And heard an ever-breaking shore
That tumbled in the Godless deep,

A warmth within the breast would melt
    The freezing reason's colder part,
15   And like a man in wrath the heart
Stood up and answered, "I have felt."[5]

3. Cf. a passage from Sir Charles Lyell's *The Principles of Geology* (1832), a book well known to Tennyson. In discussing the "interchange of sea and land" that has occurred "on the surface of our globe" Lyell remarks: "In the Mediterranean alone, many flourishing inland towns and a still greater number of ports now stand where the sea rolled its waves since the era when civilized nations first grew in Europe."
4. He does not discover satisfactory proof of God's existence in the 18th-century argument that because objects in nature are designed there must exist a designer.
5. Cf. Carlyle's *Sartor Resartus, The Everlasting No* (p. 1077).

No, like a child in doubt and fear:
  But that blind clamor made me wise;
  Then was I as a child that cries,
20 But, crying, knows his father near;

And what I am beheld again
  What is, and no man understands;
  And out of darkness came the hands
That reach through nature, molding men.

*   *   *

126

Love is and was my lord and king,
  And in his presence I attend
  To hear the tidings of my friend,
Which every hour his couriers bring.

5 Love is and was my king and lord,
  And will be, though as yet I keep
  Within the court on earth, and sleep
Encompassed by his faithful guard,

And hear at times a sentinel
10 Who moves about from place to place,
  And whispers to the worlds of space,
In the deep night, that all is well.

127

And all is well, though faith and form[6]
  Be sundered in the night of fear;
  Well roars the storm to those that hear
A deeper voice across the storm,

5 Proclaiming social truth shall spread,
  And justice, even though thrice again
  The red fool-fury of the Seine
Should pile her barricades with dead.[7]

But ill for him that wears a crown,
10 And him, the lazar,[8] in his rags!
  They tremble, the sustaining crags;
The spires of ice are toppled down,

6. Traditional institutions through which faith was formerly expressed, such as the church.
7. Revolutionary uprisings in France, in each of which a king lost his throne (line 9): in 1789 against Louis XVI, in 1830 against Charles X, and in 1848 against Louis-Philippe. The third (line 6) would have been a prophecy if, as Tennyson recollected, section 127 were finished at a date earlier than 1848.
8. Pauper suffering from disease.

And molten up, and roar in flood;
   The fortress crashes from on high,
15   The brute earth lightens[9] to the sky,
And the great Aeon[1] sinks in blood,

And compassed by the fires of hell,
   While thou, dear spirit, happy star,
   O'erlook'st the tumult from afar,
20   And smilest, knowing all is well.

             � *   *   *

129

Dear friend, far off, my lost desire,
   So far, so near in woe and weal,
   O loved the most, when most I feel
There is a lower and a higher;

5 Known and unknown, human, divine;
   Sweet human hand and lips and eye;
   Dear heavenly friend that canst not die,
Mine, mine, forever, ever mine;

Strange friend, past, present, and to be;
10   Loved deeplier, darklier understood;
   Behold, I dream a dream of good,
And mingle all the world with thee.

130

Thy voice is on the rolling air
   I hear thee where the waters run;
   Thou standest in the rising sun,
And in the setting thou art fair.

5 What art thou then? I cannot guess;
   But though I seem in star and flower
   To feel thee some diffusive power,
I do not therefore love thee less.

My love involves the love before;
10   My love is vaster passion now;
   Tho' mix'd with God and Nature thou,
I seem to love thee more and more.

Far off thou art, but ever nigh;
   I have thee still, and I rejoice;

9. Is lit up by fire.
1. A vast tract of time, here perhaps modern Western civilization.

15   I prosper, circled with thy voice;
      I shall not lose thee tho' I die.

131

O living will² that shalt endure
    When all that seems shall suffer shock,
    Rise in the spiritual rock,°   *Christ*
Flow through our deeds and make them pure,

5   That we may lift from out of dust
    A voice as unto him that hears,
    A cry above the conquered years
To one that with us works, and trust,

With faith that comes of self-control,
10   The truths that never can be proved
    Until we close with all we loved,
And all we flow from, soul in soul.

From Epilogue³

✧   ✧   ✧

And rise, O moon, from yonder down,
110   Till over down and over dale
    All night the shining vapor sail
And pass the silent-lighted town,

The white-faced halls, the glancing rills,
    And catch at every mountain head,
115   And o'er the friths° that branch and spread   *inlets of the sea*
Their sleeping silver through the hills;

And touch with shade the bridal doors,
    With tender gloom the roof, the wall;
    And breaking let the splendor fall
120   To spangle all the happy shores

By which they rest, and ocean sounds,
    And, star and system rolling past,
    A soul shall draw from out the vast
And strike his being into bounds,

125   And, moved through life of lower phase,
    Result in man,⁴ be born and think,

2. Tennyson later commented that he meant here the moral will of humankind.
3. The *Epilogue* describes the wedding day of Tennyson's sister Cecilia to Edmund Lushington. At the conclusion (printed here) the speaker reflects on the moonlit wedding night and the kind of offspring that will result from their union.
4. A child will be conceived and will develop in embryo through various stages. This development is similar to human evolution from the animal to

And act and love, a closer link
Betwixt us and the crowning race

Of those that, eye to eye, shall look
130   On knowledge; under whose command
Is Earth and Earth's, and in their hand
Is Nature like an open book;

No longer half-akin to brute,
For all we thought and loved and did,
135   And hoped, and suffered, is but seed
Of what in them is flower and fruit;

Whereof the man that with me trod
This planet was a noble type
Appearing ere the times were ripe,
140   That friend of mine who lives in God,

That God, which ever lives and loves,
One God, one law, one element,
And one far-off divine event,
To which the whole creation moves.

1833–50   1850

The Charge of the Light Brigade[1]

1

Half a league, half a league,
Half a league onward,
All in the valley of Death
        Rode the six hundred.
5   "Forward the Light Brigade!
Charge for the guns!" he said.
Into the valley of Death
        Rode the six hundred.[2]

2

"Forward, the Light Brigade!"
10   Was there a man dismayed?
Not though the soldier knew
        Someone had blundered.
Theirs not to make reply,
Theirs not to reason why,
15   Theirs but to do and die.

---

the human level and perhaps to a future higher
stage of development.
1. During the Crimean War, owing to confusion
of orders, a brigade of British cavalry charged some
entrenched batteries of Russian artillery. This
blunder cost the lives of three-quarters of the six
hundred horsemen engaged (see Cecil Woodham-

Smith, *The Reason Why,* 1954). Tennyson rapidly
composed his "ballad" (as he called the poem) after
reading an account of the battle in a newspaper.
2. In the recording Tennyson made of this poem,
"hundred" sounds like "hunderd"—a Lincolnshire
pronunciation that reinforces the rhyme with
"thundered," etc.

Into the valley of Death
        Rode the six hundred.

3

Cannon to right of them,
Cannon to left of them,
20   Cannon in front of them
        Volleyed and thundered;
Stormed at with shot and shell,
Boldly they rode and well,
Into the jaws of Death,
25   Into the mouth of hell
        Rode the six hundred.

4

Flashed all their sabers bare,
Flashed as they turned in air
Sab'ring the gunners there,
30   Charging an army, while
        All the world wondered.
Plunged in the battery smoke
Right through the line they broke;
Cossack and Russian
35   Reeled from the saber stroke
        Shattered and sundered.
Then they rode back, but not,
        Not the six hundred.

5

Cannon to right of them,
40   Cannon to left of them,
Cannon behind them
        Volleyed and thundered;
Stormed at with shot and shell,
While horse and hero fell.
45   They that had fought so well
Came through the jaws of Death,
Back from the mouth of hell,
All that was left of them,
        Left of six hundred.

6

50   When can their glory fade?
O the wild charge they made!
        All the world wondered.
Honor the charge they made!
Honor the Light Brigade,
55   Noble six hundred!

1854   1854

Idylls of the King   When John Milton was considering subjects suitable for an epic poem, one of those he entertained was the story of the Christian British king Arthur, a semilegendary leader of about 500 who fought off the heathen Saxon invaders who had swarmed into Britain after the withdrawal of the Roman legions. Tennyson likewise saw that the Arthurian story had epic potential and selected it for his lifework as "the greatest of all poetical subjects." At intervals, during a period of fifty years, he labored over the twelve books that make up his *Idylls of the King,* completing the work in 1888.

The principal source of Tennyson's stories of Arthur and his knights was Sir Thomas Malory's *Morte Darthur,* a version that Malory translated into English prose from French sources in 1470. As Talbot Donaldson has suggested, one basis of the appeal of the Arthurian stories, like the legends of Robin Hood and stories of the American West, is that all three represent the struggle of individuals to restore order in situations of chaos and anarchy, a task performed in the face of seemingly overwhelming odds. The individual stories in Tennyson's *Idylls* have the same basic appeal, but the overall design of the whole poem is more ambitious and impressive. The *Idylls of the King* represent the rise and fall of a civilization. They imply that after two thousand years of Christianity, Western civilization may be going through a cycle in which it must confront the possibilities of a renewal in the future or an apocalyptic extinction. The first book, *The Coming of Arthur,* introduces the basic myth of a springtime hero transforming a wasteland and inspiring faith and hope in the highest values of civilized life among his devoted followers. Succeeding books move through summer and autumn and culminate in the bleak wintry scene of Arthur's last battle in which his order perishes in a civil war; the leader of the enemy forces is his own nephew, Sir Modred.

Throughout the later books of the *Idylls* the forces of opposition grow in strength, and disaffections infect leading figures of the Round Table itself. The most glaring example is the adulterous relationship between Guinevere, Arthur's "sumptuous" queen (as Tennyson once described her), and the king's chief lieutenant and friend, Sir Lancelot. Many other fallings away subsequently come to light, such as the perfidious betrayal by Sir Gawain in the ninth book, *Pelleas and Ettarre,* and the cynical conduct of Sir Tristram, whose story is told in the bitter tenth book, *The Last Tournament.* Even Merlin, Arthur's trusted magician and counselor, becomes corrupted and can perform no further offices for the king (*Merlin and Vivien*). *The Passing of Arthur* depicts the apocalyptic end of this long process of disintegration and decay.

FROM IDYLLS OF THE KING

The Coming of Arthur

> Leodogran, the King of Cameliard,
> Had one fair daughter, and none other child;
> And she was fairest of all flesh on earth,
> Guinevere, and in her his one delight.
>
> 5   For many a petty king ere Arthur came
> Ruled in this isle, and ever waging war
> Each upon other, wasted all the land;
> And still from time to time the heathen host
> Swarm'd overseas, and harried° what was left.   ravaged
> 10 And so there grew great tracts of wilderness,
> Wherein the beast was ever more and more,

But man was less and less, till Arthur came.
For first Aurelius[1] lived and fought and died,
And after him King Uther fought and died,
15   But either fail'd to make the kingdom one.
And after these King Arthur for a space,
And thro' the puissance° of his Table Round,   *power*
Drew all their petty princedoms under him,
Their king and head, and made a realm, and reign'd.

20   And thus the land of Cameliard was waste,
Thick with wet woods, and many a beast therein,
And none or few to scare or chase the beast;
So that wild dog, and wolf and boar and bear
Came night and day, and rooted[2] in the fields,
25   And wallow'd in the gardens of the King.
And ever and anon the wolf would steal
The children and devour, but now and then,
Her own brood lost or dead, lent her fierce teat
To human sucklings; and the children, housed
30   In her foul den, there at their meat would growl,
And mock their foster-mother on four feet,
Till, straighten'd, they grew up to wolf-like men,
Worse than the wolves. And King Leodogran
Groan'd for the Roman legions here again,
35   And Caesar's eagle:[3] then his brother king,
Urien, assail'd him: last a heathen horde,
Reddening the sun with smoke and earth with blood,
And on the spike that split the mother's heart
Spitting° the child, brake on him, till, amazed,   *impaling*
40   He knew not whither he should turn for aid.

But—for he heard of Arthur newly crown'd,
Tho' not without an uproar made by those
Who cried, "He is not Uther's son"—the King
Sent to him, saying, "Arise, and help us thou!
45   For here between the man and beast we die."

And Arthur yet had done no deed of arms,
But heard the call, and came: and Guinevere
Stood by the castle walls to watch him pass;
But since he neither wore on helm or shield
50   The golden symbol of his kinglihood,[4]
But rode a simple knight among his knights,
And many of these in richer arms than he,
She saw him not, or mark'd not, if she saw,
One among many, tho' his face was bare.
55   But Arthur, looking downward as he past,
Felt the light of her eyes into his life
Smite on the sudden, yet rode on, and pitch'd

---

1. Brother of King Uther.
2. Tore up the earth.
3. Imperial protection.
4. The golden dragon [Tennyson's note].

His tents beside the forest. Then he drave°   *drove*
The heathen; after, slew the beast, and fell'd
60   The forest, letting in the sun, and made
Broad pathways for the hunter and the knight
And so return'd.

        For while he linger'd there,
A doubt that ever smoulder'd in the hearts
Of those great Lords and Barons of his realm
65   Flash'd forth and into war: for most of these,
Colleaguing with a score of petty kings,
Made head against him, crying, 'Who is he
That he should rule us? who hath proven him
King Uther's son? for lo! we look at him,
70   And find nor face nor bearing, limbs nor voice,
Are like to those of Uther whom we knew.
This is the son of Gorloïs, not the King;
This is the son of Anton, not the King.'

      And Arthur, passing thence to battle, felt
75   Travail, and throes and agonies of the life,
Desiring to be join'd with Guinevere;
And thinking as he rode, "Her father said
That there between the man and beast they die.
Shall I not lift her from this land of beasts
80   Up to my throne, and side by side with me?
What happiness to reign a lonely king,
Vext—O ye stars that shudder over me,
O earth that soundest hollow under me,
Vext with waste dreams? for saving I be join'd
85   To her that is the fairest under heaven,
I seem as nothing in the mighty world,
And cannot will my will, nor work my work
Wholly, nor make myself in mine own realm
Victor and lord. But were I join'd with her,
90   Then might we live together as one life,
And reigning with one will in everything
Have power on this dark land to lighten it,
And power on this dead world to make it live."

      Thereafter—as he speaks who tells the tale—
95   When Arthur reach'd a field-of-battle bright
With pitch'd pavilions of his foe, the world
Was all so clear about him, that he saw
The smallest rock far on the faintest hill,
And even in high day the morning star.
100   So when the King had set his banner broad,
At once from either side, with trumpet-blast,
And shouts, and clarions shrilling unto blood,
The long-lanced battle let their horses run.
And now the Barons and the kings prevail'd,
105   And now the King, as here and there that war

Went swaying; but the Powers who walk the world
Made lightnings and great thunders over him,
And dazed all eyes, till Arthur by main might,
And mightier of his hands with every blow,
110 And leading all his knighthood threw the kings
Carádos, Urien, Cradlemont of Wales,
Claudias, and Clariance of Northumberland,
The King Brandagoras of Latangor,
With Anguisant of Erin, Morganore,
115 And Lot of Orkney.[5] Then, before a voice
As dreadful as the shout of one who sees
To one who sins, and deems himself alone
And all the world asleep, they swerved and brake
Flying, and Arthur call'd to stay the brands
120 That hack'd among the flyers, "Ho! they yield!"
So like a painted battle the war stood
Silenced, the living quiet as the dead,
And in the heart of Arthur joy was lord.
He laugh'd upon his warrior° whom he loved   *Lancelot*
125 And honour'd most. "Thou dost not doubt me King,
So well thine arm hath wrought for me to-day."
"Sir and my liege," he cried, "the fire of God
Descends upon thee in the battle-field:
I know thee for my King!" Whereat the two,
130 For each had warded° either in the fight,   *guarded*
Sware on the field of death a deathless love.
And Arthur said, "Man's word is God in man:
Let chance what will, I trust thee to the death."

Then quickly from the foughten field he sent
135 Ulfius, and Brastias, and Bedivere,
His new-made knights, to King Leodogran,
Saying, "If I in aught have served thee well,
Give me thy daughter Guinevere to wife."

Whom when he heard, Leodogran in heart
140 Debating—"How should I that am a king,
However much he holp me at my need,
Give my one daughter saving to a king,
And a king's son?"—lifted his voice, and call'd
A hoary man, his chamberlain, to whom
145 He trusted all things, and of him required
His counsel: "Knowest thou aught of Arthur's birth?"

Then spake the hoary chamberlain and said,
"Sir King, there be but two old men that know:
And each is twice as old as I; and one
150 Is Merlin, the wise man that ever served
King Uther thro' his magic art; and one
Is Merlin's master (so they call him) Bleys,

5. Islands north of Scotland. These kings opposed Arthur in Malory's version.

Who taught him magic; but the scholar ran
Before the master, and so far, that Bleys
155 Laid magic by, and sat him down, and wrote
All things and whatsoever Merlin did
In one great annal-book, where after-years
Will learn the secret of our Arthur's birth."

To whom the King Leodogran replied,
160 "O friend, had I been holpen half as well
By this King Arthur as by thee to-day,
Then beast and man had had their share of me:
But summon here before us yet once more
Ulfius, and Brastias, and Bedivere."

165 Then, when they came before him, the King said,
"I have seen the cuckoo chased by lesser fowl,
And reason in the chase: but wherefore now
Do these your lords stir up the heat of war,
Some calling Arthur born of Gorloïs,
170 Others of Anton? Tell me, ye yourselves,
Hold ye this Arthur for King Uther's son?"

And Ulfius and Brastias answer'd, "Ay."
Then Bedivere, the first of all his knights
Knighted by Arthur at his crowning, spake—
175 For bold in heart and act and word was he,
Whenever slander breathed against the King—

"Sir, there be many rumours on this head:
For there be those who hate him in their hearts,
Call him baseborn, and since his ways are sweet,
180 And theirs are bestial, hold him less than man:
And there be those who deem him more than man,
And dream he dropt from heaven: but my belief
In all this matter—so ye care to learn—
Sir, for ye know that in King Uther's time
185 The prince and warrior Gorloïs, he that held
Tintagil castle by the Cornish sea,
Was wedded with a winsome wife, Ygerne:
And daughters had she borne him,—one whereof,
Lot's wife, the Queen of Orkney, Bellicent,
190 Hath ever like a loyal sister cleaved
To Arthur,—but a son she had not borne.
And Uther cast upon her eyes of love:
But she, a stainless wife to Gorloïs,
So loathed the bright dishonour of his love,
195 That Gorloïs and King Uther went to war:
And overthrown was Gorloïs and slain.
Then Uther in his wrath and heat besieged
Ygerne within Tintagil, where her men,
Seeing the mighty swarm about their walls,
200 Left her and fled, and Uther enter'd in,

And there was none to call to but himself.
So, compass'd by the power of the King,
Enforced she was to wed him in her tears,
And with a shameful swiftness: afterward,
205 Not many moons, King Uther died himself,
Moaning and wailing for an heir to rule
After him, lest the realm should go to wrack.
And that same night, the night of the new year,
By reason of the bitterness and grief
210 That vext his mother, all before his time
Was Arthur born, and all as soon as born
Deliver'd at a secret postern-gate
To Merlin, to be holden far apart
Until his hour should come; because the lords
215 Of that fierce day were as the lords of this,
Wild beasts, and surely would have torn the child
Piecemeal among them, had they known; for each
But sought to rule for his own self and hand,
And many hated Uther for the sake
220 Of Gorloïs. Wherefore Merlin took the child,
And gave him to Sir Anton, an old knight
And ancient friend of Uther; and his wife
Nursed the young prince, and rear'd him with her own;
And no man knew. And ever since the lords
225 Have foughten like wild beasts among themselves,
So that the realm has gone to wrack: but now,
This year, when Merlin (for his hour had come)
Brought Arthur forth, and set him in the hall,
Proclaiming, 'Here is Uther's heir, your king,'
230 A hundred voices cried, 'Away with him!
No king of ours! a son of Gorloïs he,
Or else the child of Anton, and no king,
Or else baseborn.' Yet Merlin thro' his craft,
And while the people clamour'd for a king,
235 Had Arthur crown'd; but after, the great lords
Banded, and so brake out in open war."

Then while the King debated with himself
If Arthur were the child of shamefulness,
Or born the son of Gorloïs, after death,
240 Or Uther's son, and born before his time,
Or whether there were truth in anything
Said by these three, there came to Cameliard,
With Gawain and young Modred, her two sons,
Lot's wife, the Queen of Orkney, Bellicent;
245 Whom as he could, not as he would, the King
Made feast for, saying, as they sat at meat,

"A doubtful throne is ice on summer seas.
Ye come from Arthur's court. Victor his men
Report him! Yea, but ye—think ye this king—
250 So many those that hate him, and so strong,

So few his knights, however brave they be—
Hath body enow to hold his foemen down?"

"O King," she cried, "and I will tell thee: few,
Few, but all brave, all of one mind with him;
255 For I was near him when the savage yells
Of Uther's peerage died, and Arthur sat
Crown'd on the daïs, and his warriors cried,
'Be thou the king, and we will work thy will
Who love thee.' Then the King in low deep tones,
260 And simple words of great authority,
Bound them by so strait vows to his own self,
That when they rose, knighted from kneeling, some
Were pale as at the passing of a ghost,
Some flush'd, and others dazed, as one who wakes
265 Half-blinded at the coming of a light.

"But when he spake and cheer'd his Table Round
With large, divine, and comfortable words,
Beyond my tongue to tell thee—I beheld
From eye to eye thro' all their Order flash
270 A momentary likeness of the King:
And ere it left their faces, thro' the cross
And those around it and the Crucified,
Down from the casement over Arthur, smote
Flame-colour, vert° and azure, in three rays,   green
275 One falling upon each of three fair queens,
Who stood in silence near his throne, the friends
Of Arthur, gazing on him, tall, with bright
Sweet faces, who will help him at his need.

"And there I saw mage° Merlin, whose vast wit   magician
280 And hundred winters are but as the hands
Of loyal vassals toiling for their liege.

"And near him stood the Lady of the Lake,[6]
Who knows a subtler magic than his own—
Clothed in white samite,[7] mystic, wonderful.
285 She gave the King his huge cross-hilted sword,
Whereby to drive the heathen out: a mist
Of incense curl'd about her, and her face
Wellnigh was hidden in the minister gloom;
But there was heard among the holy hymns
290 A voice as of the waters,[8] for she dwells
Down in a deep; calm, whatsoever storms
May shake the world, and when the surface rolls,
Hath power to walk the waters like our Lord.

"There likewise I beheld Excalibur
295 Before him at his crowning borne, the sword

---

6. The Lady of the Lake in the old legends is the
Church [Tennyson's note].
7. A rich silk fabric.

8. Cf. Revelation 14.2: "And I heard a voice from
Heaven, as the voice of many waters."

That rose from out the bosom of the lake,
And Arthur row'd across and took it—rich
With jewels, elfin Urim,[9] on the hilt,
Bewildering heart and eye—the blade so bright
300 That men are blinded by it—on one side,
Graven in the oldest tongue of all this world,
'Take me,' but turn the blade and ye shall see,
And written in the speech ye speak yourself,
'Cast me away!' And sad was Arthur's face
305 Taking it, but old Merlin counsell'd him,
'Take thou and strike! the time to cast away
Is yet far-off.' So this great brand° the king   *sword*
Took, and by this will beat his foemen down."

Thereat Leodogran rejoiced, but thought
310 To sift his doubtings to the last, and ask'd,
Fixing full eyes of question on her face,
"The swallow and the swift are near akin,
But thou art closer to this noble prince,
Being his own dear sister;" and she said,
315 "Daughter of Gorloïs and Ygerne am I;"
"And therefore Arthur's sister?" ask'd the King
She answer'd, "These be secret things," and sign'd
To those two sons to pass, and let them be.
And Gawain went, and breaking into song
320 Sprang out, and follow'd by his flying hair
Ran like a colt, and leapt at all he saw:
But Modred laid his ear beside the doors,
And there half-heard; the same that afterward
Struck for the throne, and striking found his doom.

325 And then the Queen made answer, "What know I?
For dark my mother was in eyes and hair,
And dark in hair and eyes am I; and dark
Was Gorloïs, yea and dark was Uther too,
Wellnigh to blackness; but this King is fair
330 Beyond the race of Britons and of men.
Moreover, always in my mind I hear
A cry from out the dawning of my life,
A mother weeping, and I hear her say,
'O that ye had some brother, pretty one,
335 To guard thee on the rough ways of the world.'

"Ay," said the King, "and hear ye such a cry?
But when did Arthur chance upon thee first?"

"O King!" she cried, "and I will tell thee true:
He found me first when yet a little maid:
340 Beaten I had been for a little fault
Whereof I was not guilty; and out I ran
And flung myself down on a bank of heath,

9. Gems used for divination.

And hated this fair world and all therein,
And wept, and wish'd that I were dead; and he—
345   I know not whether of himself he came,
Or brought by Merlin, who, they say, can walk
Unseen at pleasure—he was at my side,
And spake sweet words, and comforted my heart,
And dried my tears, being a child with me.
350   And many a time he came, and evermore
As I grew greater grew with me; and sad
At times he seem'd, and sad with him was I,
Stern too at times, and then I loved him not,
But sweet again, and then I loved him well.
355   And now of late I see him less and less,
But those first days had golden hours for me,
For then I surely thought he would be king.

"But let me tell thee now another tale:
For Bleys, our Merlin's master, as they say,
360   Died but of late, and sent his cry to me,
To hear him speak before he left his life.
Shrunk like a fairy changeling[1] lay the mage;
And when I enter'd told me that himself
And Merlin ever served about the King,
365   Uther, before he died; and on the night
When Uther in Tintagil past away
Moaning and wailing for an heir, the two
Left the still King, and passing forth to breathe,
Then from the castle gateway by the chasm
370   Descending thro' the dismal night—a night
In which the bounds of heaven and earth were lost—
Beheld, so high upon the dreary deeps
It seem'd in heaven, a ship, the shape thereof
A dragon wing'd, and all from stem to stern
375   Bright with a shining people on the decks,
And gone as soon as seen. And then the two
Dropt to the cove, and watch'd the great sea fall,
Wave after wave, each mightier than the last,
Till last, a ninth one, gathering half the deep
380   And full of voices, slowly rose and plunged
Roaring, and all the wave was in a flame:
And down the wave and in the flame was borne
A naked babe, and rode to Merlin's feet,
Who stoopt and caught the babe, and cried 'The King!
385   Here is an heir for Uther!' And the fringe
Of that great breaker, sweeping up the strand,
Lash'd at the wizard as he spake the word,
And all at once all round him rose in fire,
So that the child and he were clothed in fire.
390   And presently thereafter follow'd calm,
Free sky and stars: 'And this same child,' he said,

---

1. Child secretly substituted for another.

'Is he who reigns; nor could I part in peace
Till this were told.' And saying this the seer
Went thro' the strait and dreadful pass of death,
395 Not ever to be question'd any more
Save on the further side; but when I met
Merlin, and ask'd him if these things were truth—
The shining dragon and the naked child
Descending in the glory of the seas—
400 He laugh'd as is his wont, and answer'd me
In riddling triplets of old time, and said:

' "Rain, rain, and sun! a rainbow in the sky!
A young man will be wiser by and by;
An old man's wit may wander ere he die.
405 Rain, rain, and sun! a rainbow on the lea!
And truth is this to me, and that to thee;
And truth or clothed or naked let it be.
Rain, sun, and rain! and the free blossom blows:
Sun, rain, and sun! and where is he who knows?
410 From the great deep to the great deep he goes.'

"So Merlin riddling anger'd me; but thou
Fear not to give this King thine only child,
Guinevere: so great bards of him will sing
Hereafter; and dark sayings from of old
415 Ranging and ringing thro' the minds of men,
And echo'd by old folk beside their fires
For comfort after their wage-work is done,
Speak of the King; and Merlin in our time
Hath spoken also, not in jest, and sworn
420 Tho' men may wound him that he will not die,
But pass, again to come; and then or now
Utterly smite the heathen underfoot,
Till these and all men hail him for their king."

She spake and King Leodogran rejoiced,
425 But musing "Shall I answer yea or nay?"
Doubted, and drowsed, nodded and slept, and saw,
Dreaming, a slope of land that ever grew,
Field after field, up to a height, the peak
Haze-hidden, and thereon a phantom king,
430 Now looming, and now lost; and on the slope
The sword rose, the hind° fell, the herd was driven,   *servant*
Fire glimpsed;° and all the land from roof and rick,[2]   *glimmered*
In drifts of smoke before a rolling wind,
Stream'd to the peak, and mingled with the haze
435 And made it thicker; while the phantom king
Sent out at times a voice; and here or there
Stood one who pointed toward the voice, the rest
Slew on and burnt, crying, "No king of ours,

---

2. Stacks of grain.

No son of Uther, and no king of ours;"
440 Till with a wink his dream was changed, the haze
Descended, and the solid earth became
As nothing, but the King stood out in heaven,
Crown'd. And Leodogran awoke, and sent
Ulfius, and Brastias and Bedivere,
445 Back to the court of Arthur answering yea.

Then Arthur charged his warrior whom he loved
And honour'd most, Sir Lancelot, to ride forth
And bring the Queen;—and watch'd him from the gates:
And Lancelot past away among the flowers,
450 (For then was latter April) and return'd
Among the flowers, in May, with Guinevere.
To whom arrived, by Dubric the high saint,
Chief of the church in Britain, and before
The stateliest of her altar-shrines, the King
455 That morn was married, while in stainless white,
The fair beginners of a nobler time,
And glorying in their vows and him, his knights
Stood round him, and rejoicing in his joy.
Far shone the fields of May thro' open door,
460 The sacred altar blossom'd white with May,
The Sun of May descended on their King,
They gazed on all earth's beauty in their Queen,
Roll'd incense, and there past along the hymns
A voice as of the waters, while the two
465 Sware at the shrine of Christ a deathless love:
And Arthur said, "Behold, thy doom is mine.
Let chance what will, I love thee to the death!"
To whom the Queen replied with drooping eyes,
"King and my lord, I love thee to the death!"
470 And holy Dubric spread his hands and spake,
"Reign ye, and live and love, and make the world
Other, and may thy Queen be one with thee,
And all this Order of thy Table Round
Fulfil the boundless purpose of their King!"
475 So Dubric said; but when they left the shrine
Great Lords from Rome before the portal stood,
In scornful stillness gazing as they past;
Then while they paced a city all on fire
With sun and cloth of gold, the trumpets blew,
480 And Arthur's knighthood sang before the King:—

"Blow trumpet, for the world is white with May;
Blow trumpet, the long night hath roll'd away!
Blow thro' the living world—'Let the King reign.'

"Shall Rome or Heathen rule in Arthur's realm?
485 Flash brand and lance, fall battleaxe upon helm,
Fall battleaxe, and flash brand! Let the King reign.

"Strike for the King and live! his knights have heard.
That God hath told the King a secret word.
Fall battleaxe, and flash brand! Let the King reign.

490   "Blow trumpet! he will lift us from the dust.
Blow trumpet! live the strength and die the lust!
Clang battleaxe, and clash brand! Let the King reign.

"Strike for the King and die! and if thou diest,
The King is King, and ever wills the highest.
495   Clang battleaxe, and clash brand! Let the King reign.

"Blow, for our Sun is mighty in his May!
Blow, for our Sun is mightier day by day!
Clang battleaxe, and clash brand! Let the King reign.

"The King will follow Christ, and we the King
500   In whom high God hath breathed a secret thing.
Fall battleaxe, and flash brand! Let the King reign."

So sang the knighthood, moving to their hall.
There at the banquet those great Lords from Rome,
The slowly-fading mistress of the world,
505   Strode in, and claim'd their tribute as of yore.
But Arthur spake, "Behold, for these have sworn
To wage my wars, and worship me their King;
The old order changeth, yielding place to new;
And we that fight for our fair father Christ,
510   Seeing that ye be grown too weak and old
To drive the heathen from your Roman wall,
No tribute will we pay:" so those great lords
Drew back in wrath, and Arthur strove with Rome.

And Arthur and his knighthood for a space
515   Were all one will, and thro' that strength the King
Drew in the petty princedoms under him,
Fought, and in twelve great battles overcame
The heathen hordes, and made a realm and reign'd.

1869   1869

The Passing of Arthur[1]

That story which the bold Sir Bedivere,[2]
First made and latest left of all the knights,
Told, when the man was no more than a voice

1. On the composition of this final idyll and its relation to his *Morte d'Arthur* of 1842, see n. 1, p. 1217. The principal source was Malory's *Morte Darthur* 21.4–5. Preceding the action of this idyll, Arthur had been in France with his nephew Gawain fighting against the forces of Lancelot. Learning at that time of the gathering of an army against him in England, under the leadership of his nephew, Modred, Arthur returned there to engage in his last battle. Upon landing at Dover, Gawain was slain.
2. A knight who had long been close to the king, described in *The Coming of Arthur*: "Bedivere, the first of all his knights / Knighted by Arthur at his crowning."

In the white winter of his age, to those
5   With whom he dwelt, new faces, other minds.

For on their march to westward, Bedivere,
Who slowly paced among the slumbering host,
Heard in his tent the moanings of the King:

"I found Him in the shining of the stars,
10 I marked Him in the flowering of His fields,
But in His ways with men I find Him not.
I waged His wars, and now I pass and die.
O me! for why is all around us here
As if some lesser god had made the world,
15 But had not force to shape it as he would,
Till the High God behold it from beyond,
And enter it, and make it beautiful?
Or else as if the world were wholly fair,
But that these eyes of men are dense and dim,
20 And have not power to see it as it is:
Perchance, because we see not to the close;—
For I, being simple, thought to work His will,
And have but stricken with the sword in vain;
And all whereon I leaned in wife and friend
25 Is traitor to my peace, and all my realm
Reels back into the beast, and is no more.
My God, thou hast forgotten me in my death:[3]
Nay—God my Christ—I pass but shall not die."

Then, ere that last weird battle in the west,
30 There came on Arthur sleeping, Gawain killed
In Lancelot's war, the ghost of Gawain blown
Along a wandering wind, and past his ear
Went shrilling. "Hollow, hollow all delight!
Hail, King! tomorrow thou shalt pass away.
35 Farewell! there is an isle of rest for thee.
And I am blown along a wandering wind,
And hollow, hollow, hollow all delight."
And fainter onward, like wild birds that change
Their season in the night and wail their way
40 From cloud to cloud, down the long wind the dream
Shrilled; but in going mingled with dim cries
Far in the moonlit haze among the hills,
As of some lonely city sacked by night,
When all is lost, and wife and child with wail
45 Pass to new lords; and Arthur woke and called,
"Who spake? A dream. O light upon the wind,
Thine, Gawain, was the voice—are these dim cries
Thine? or doth all that haunts the waste and wild
Mourn, knowing it will go along with me?"

50   This heard the bold Sir Bedivere and spake:
"O me, my King, let pass whatever will,

---

3. Cf. Matthew 27.46: "My God, my God, why hast thou forsaken me?"

Elves, and the harmless glamor of the field;[4]
But in their stead thy name and glory cling
To all high places like a golden cloud
55   Forever: but as yet thou shalt not pass.
Light was Gawain in life, and light in death
Is Gawain, for the ghost is as the man;
And care not thou for dreams from him, but rise—
I hear the steps of Modred in the west,
60   And with him many of thy people, and knights
Once thine, whom thou hast loved, but grosser grown
Than heathen, spitting at their vows and thee.
Right well in heart they know thee for the King.
Arise, go forth and conquer as of old."

65   Then spake King Arthur to Sir Bedivere:
"Far other is this battle in the west
Whereto we move, than when we strove in youth,
And brake the petty kings, and fought with Rome,
Or thrust the heathen from the Roman wall,
70   And shook him through the north. Ill doom is mine
To war against my people and my knights.
The king who fights his people fights himself.
And they thy knights, who loved me once, the stroke
That strikes them dead is as my death to me.
75   Yet let us hence, and find or feel a way
Through this blind haze, which ever since I saw
One lying in the dust at Almesbury,[5]
Hath folded in the passes of the world."

        Then rose the King and moved his host by night,
80   And ever pushed Sir Modred, league by league,
Back to the sunset bound of Lyonnesse[6]—
A land of old upheaven from the abyss
By fire, to sink into the abyss again;
Where fragments of forgotten peoples dwelled,
85   And the long mountains ended in a coast
Of ever-shifting sand, and far away
The phantom circle of a moaning sea.
There the pursuer could pursue no more,
And he that fled no further fly the King;
90   And there, that day when the great light of heaven
Burned at his lowest in the rolling year,
On the waste sand by the waste sea they closed.
Nor ever yet had Arthur fought a fight
Like this last, dim, weird battle of the west.
95   A deathwhite mist slept over sand and sea:
Whereof the chill, to him who breathed it, drew
Down with his blood, till all his heart was cold

4. Tennyson said the reference is to "the legends
which cluster round the King's name." One legend
told of the elves' bestowing gifts on Arthur as a
child.
5. The convent to which Guinevere had with-

drawn; during the king's farewell visit to her there,
she had lain in the dust at his feet.
6. Legendary land, extending west from Cornwall,
which sank into the sea.

With formless fear; and even on Arthur fell
Confusion, since he saw not whom he fought.
100 For friend and foe were shadows in the mist,
And friend slew friend not knowing whom he slew;
And some had visions out of golden youth,
And some beheld the faces of old ghosts
Look in upon the battle; and in the mist
105 Was many a noble deed, many a base,
And chance and craft and strength in single fights,
And ever and anon with host to host
Shocks, and the splintering spear, the hard mail hewn,
Shield-breakings, and the clash of brands, the crash
110 Of battleaxes on shattered helms, and shrieks
After the Christ, of those who falling down
Looked up for heaven, and only saw the mist;
And shouts of heathen and the traitor knights,
Oaths, insult, filth, and monstrous blasphemies,
115 Sweat, writhings, anguish, laboring of the lungs
In that close mist, and cryings for the light,
Moans of the dying, and voices of the dead.

    Last, as by some one deathbed after wail
Of suffering, silence follows, or through death
120 Or deathlike swoon, thus over all that shore,
Save for some whisper of the seething seas,
A dead hush fell; but when the dolorous day
Grew drearier toward twilight falling, came
A bitter wind, clear from the North, and blew
125 The mist aside, and with that wind the tide
Rose, and the pale King glanced across the field
Of battle: but no man was moving there;
Nor any cry of Christian heard thereon,
Nor yet of heathen; only the wan wave
130 Brake in among dead faces, to and fro
Swaying the helpless hands, and up and down
Tumbling the hollow helmets of the fallen,
And shivered brands that once had fought with Rome,
And rolling far along the gloomy shores
135 The voice of days of old and days to be.

    Then spake King Arthur to Sir Bedivere,
And whiter than the mist that all day long
Had held the field of battle was the King:

    "Hearest thou this great voice that shakes the world,
140 And wastes the narrow realm whereon we move,
And beats upon the faces of the dead,
My dead, as though they had not died for me?—
O Bedivere, for on my heart hath fallen
Confusion, till I know not what I am,
145 Nor whence I am, nor whether I be King.
Behold, I seem but King among the dead."

Then spake the bold Sir Bedivere: "My King,
King everywhere! and so the dead have kings,
There also will I worship thee as King.
150 Yet still thy life is whole, and still I live
Who love thee; but who hates thee, he that brought
The heathen back among us, yonder stands,
Modred, unharmed, the traitor of thine house."

Then spake the King: "My house hath been my doom.
155 But call not thou this traitor of my house
Who hath but dwelled beneath one roof with me.
My house are rather they who sware my vows,
Yea, even while they brake them, owned me King.
And well for thee, saying in my dark hour,
160 When all the purport of my throne hath failed,
That quick or dead thou holdest me for King.
King am I, whatsoever be their cry;
And one last act of kinghood shalt thou see
Yet, ere I pass." And uttering this the King
165 Made at the man: then Modred smote his liege
Hard on that helm which many a heathen sword
Had beaten thin; while Arthur at one blow,
Striking the last stroke with Excalibur,
Slew him, and all but slain himself, he fell.

170 So all day long the noise of battle rolled
Among the mountains by the winter sea;
Until King Arthur's Table, man by man,
Had fallen in Lyonnesse about their lord,
King Arthur. Then, because his wound was deep,
175 The bold Sir Bedivere uplifted him,
And bore him to a chapel nigh the field,
A broken chancel with a broken cross,
That stood on a dark strait of barren land:
On one side lay the Ocean, and on one
180 Lay a great water, and the moon was full.

Then spake King Arthur to Sir Bedivere:
"The sequel of today unsolders all
The goodliest fellowship of famous knights
Whereof this world holds record. Such a sleep
185 They sleep—the men I loved. I think that we
Shall never more, at any future time,
Delight our souls with talk of knightly deeds,
Walking about the gardens and the halls
Of Camelot, as in the days that were.
190 I perish by this people which I made,—
Though Merlin sware that I should come again
To rule once more;[7] but, let what will be, be,

---

7. Cf. Malory, *Morte Darthur* 21.7: "Some men yet say in many parts of England that King Arthur is not dead, but by the will of our Lord in another place. And men say that he will come again."

I am so deeply smitten through the helm
That without help I cannot last til morn.
195   Thou therefore take my brand Excalibur,
Which was my pride: for thou rememberest how
In those old days, one summer noon, an arm
Rose up from out the bosom of the lake,
Clothed in white samite, mystic, wonderful,
200   Holding the sword—and how I rowed across
And took it, and have worn it, like a king;
And, wheresoever I am sung or told
In aftertime, this also shall be known:
But now delay not: take Excalibur,
205   And fling him far into the middle mere:[8]
Watch what thou seëst, and lightly° bring me word."   *quickly*

    To him replied the bold Sir Bedivere:
"It is not meet, Sir King, to leave thee thus,
Aidless, alone, and smitten through the helm—
210   A little thing may harm a wounded man;
Yet I thy hest° will all perform at full,   *command*
Watch what I see, and lightly bring thee word."

    So saying, from the ruined shrine he stepped,
And in the moon athwart the place of tombs,
215   Where lay the mighty bones of ancient men,
Old knights, and over them the sea-wind sang
Shrill, chill, with flakes of foam. He, stepping down
By zigzag paths, and juts of pointed rock,
Came on the shining levels of the lake.

220   There drew he forth the brand Excalibur,
And o'er him, drawing it, the winter moon,
Brightening the skirts of a long cloud, ran forth
And sparkled keen with frost against the hilt:
For all the haft twinkled with diamond sparks,
225   Myriads of topaz-lights, and jacinth°-work   *red gem*
Of subtlest jewelry. He gazed so long
That both his eyes were dazzled as he stood,
This way and that dividing the swift mind,
In act to throw: but at the last it seemed
230   Better to leave Excalibur concealed
There in the many-knotted waterflags,
That whistled stiff and dry about the marge.
So strode he back slow to the wounded King.

    Then spake King Arthur to Sir Bedivere:
235   "Hast thou performed my mission which I gave?
What is it thou hast seen? or what hast heard?"
    And answer made the bold Sir Bedivere:
"I heard the ripple washing in the reeds,
And the wild water lapping on the crag."

8. Middle of the lake.

240　To whom replied King Arthur, faint and pale:
　　　"Thou hast betrayed thy nature and thy name.
　　　Not rendering true answer, as beseemed
　　　Thy fëalty, nor like a noble knight:
　　　For surer sign had followed, either hand,
245　Or voice, or else a motion of the mere.
　　　This is a shameful thing for men to lie.
　　　Yet now, I charge thee, quickly go again,
　　　As thou art lief° and dear, and do the thing　　　　　　　　　*beloved*
　　　I bade thee, watch, and lightly bring me word."

250　Then went Sir Bedivere the second time
　　　Across the ridge, and paced beside the mere,
　　　Counting the dewy pebbles, fixed in thought;
　　　But when he saw the wonder of the hilt,
　　　How curiously and strangely chased,[9] he smote
255　His palms together, and he cried aloud:

　　　　"And if indeed I cast the brand away,
　　　Surely a precious thing, one worthy note,
　　　Should thus be lost forever from the earth,
　　　Which might have pleased the eyes of many men.
260　What good should follow this, if this were done?
　　　What harm, undone? Deep harm to disobey,
　　　Seeing obedience is the bond of rule.
　　　Were it well to obey then, if a king demand
　　　An act unprofitable, against himself?
265　The King is sick, and knows not what he does.
　　　What record, or what relic of my lord
　　　Should be to aftertime, but empty breath
　　　And rumors of a doubt? But were this kept,
　　　Stored in some treasure-house of mighty kings,
270　Some one might show it at a joust of arms,
　　　Saying, 'King Arthur's sword, Excalibur,
　　　Wrought by the lonely maiden of the Lake.
　　　Nine years she wrought it, sitting in the deeps
　　　Upon the hidden bases of the hills.'
275　So might some old man speak in the aftertime
　　　To all the people, winning reverence.
　　　But now much honor and much fame were lost."

　　　　So spake he, clouded with his own conceit,[1]
　　　And hid Excalibur the second time,
280　And so strode back slow to the wounded king.

　　　　Then spoke King Arthur, breathing heavily:
　　　"What is it thou hast seen? or what hast heard?"

　　　　And answer made the bold Sir Bedivere:
　　　"I heard the water lapping on the crag,
285　And the long ripple washing in the reeds."

---

9. Adorned. "Curiously": skillfully.　　　　　　　1. Vain and foolish fancies.

   To whom replied King Arthur, much in wrath:
"Ah, miserable and unkind, untrue,
Unknightly, traitor-hearted! Woe is me!
Authority forgets a dying king,
290 Laid widowed of the power in his eye
That bowed the will. I see thee what thou art,
For thou, the latest-left of all my knights,
In whom should meet the offices of all,
Thou wouldst betray me for the precious hilt;
295 Either from lust of gold, or like a girl
Valuing the giddy pleasure of the eyes.
Yet, for a man may fail in duty twice,
And the third time may prosper, get thee hence:
But, if thou spare to fling Excalibur,
300 I will arise and slay thee with my hands."

   Then quickly rose Sir Bedivere, and ran,
And, leaping down the ridges lightly, plunged
Among the bullrush beds, and clutched the sword,
And strongly wheeled and threw it. The great brand
305 Made lightnings in the splendor of the moon,
And flashing round and round and whirled in an arch,
Shot like a streamer of the northern morn,[2]
Seen where the moving isles of winter shock[3]
By night, with noises of the Northern Sea.
310 So flashed and fell the brand Excalibur:
But ere he dipped the surface, rose an arm
Clothed in white samite, mystic, wonderful,
And caught him by the hilt, and brandished him
Three times, and drew him under in the mere.
315 And lightly went the other to the King.

   Then spoke King Arthur, drawing thicker breath:
"Now see I by thine eyes that this is done.
Speak out: what is it thou hast heard, or seen?"

   And answer made the bold Sir Bedivere:
320 "Sir King, I closed mine eyelids, lest the gems
Should blind my purpose, for I never saw,
Nor shall see, here or elsewhere, till I die,
Not though I live three lives of mortal men,
So great a miracle as yonder hilt.
325 Then with both hands I flung him, wheeling him;
But when I looked again, behold an arm,
Clothed in white samite, mystic, wonderful,
That caught him by the hilt, and brandished him
Three times, and drew him under in the mere."

330   And answer made King Arthur, breathing hard:
"My end draws nigh; 'tis time that I were gone.

---

2. The northern lights.   3. Where the icebergs collide.

Make broad thy shoulders to receive my weight,
And bear me to the margin; yet I fear
My wound hath taken cold, and I shall die."

335   So saying, from the pavement he half rose,
Slowly, with pain, reclining on his arm,
And looking wistfully with wide blue eyes
As in a picture. Him Sir Bedivere
Remorsefully regarded through his tears,
340 And would have spoken, but he found not words;
Then took with care, and kneeling on one knee,
O'er both his shoulders drew the languid hands,
And rising bore him through the place of tombs.

    But, as he walked, King Arthur panted hard,
345 Like one that feels a nightmare on his bed
When all the house is mute. So sighed the King,
Muttering and murmuring at his ear, "Quick, quick!
I fear it is too late, and I shall die."
But the other swiftly strode from ridge to ridge,
350 Clothed with his breath, and looking, as he walked,
Larger than human on the frozen hills.
He heard the deep behind him, and a cry
Before. His own thought drove him like a goad.
Dry clashed his harness in the icy caves
355 And barren chasms, and all to left and right
The bare black cliff clanged round him, as he based
His feet on juts of slippery crag that rang
Sharp-smitten with the dint of armèd heels—
And on a sudden, lo! the level lake,
360 And the long glories of the winter moon.

    Then saw they how there hove a dusky barge,
Dark as a funeral scarf from stem to stern,
Beneath them; and descending they were ware
That all the decks were dense with stately forms,
365 Black-stoled, black-hooded, like a dream—by these
Three Queens with crowns of gold: and from them rose
A cry that shivered to the tingling stars,
And, as it were one voice, an agony
Of lamentation, like a wind that shrills
370 All night in a waste land, where no one comes,
Or hath come, since the making of the world.

    Then murmured Arthur, "Place me in the barge."
So to the barge they came. There those three Queens
Put forth their hands, and took the King, and wept.
375 But she, that rose the tallest of them all
And fairest, laid his head upon her lap,
And loosed the shattered casque,° and chafed his hands,   *helmet*
And called him by his name, complaining loud,
And dropping bitter tears against a brow

380 Striped with dark blood: for all his face was white
And colorless, and like the withered moon
Smote by the fresh beam of the springing east;
And all his greaves and cuisses⁴ dashed with drops
Of onset;⁵ and the light and lustrous curls—
385 That made his forehead like a rising sun
High from the daïs-throne—were parched with dust;
Or, clotted into points and hanging loose,
Mixed with the knightly growth that fringed his lips.
So like a shattered column lay the King;
390 Not like that Arthur who, with lance in rest,
From spur to plume a star of tournament,
Shot through the lists at Camelot, and charged
Before the eyes of ladies and of kings.

Then loudly cried the bold Sir Bedivere:
395 "Ah! my Lord Arthur, whither shall I go?
Where shall I hide my forehead and my eyes?
For now I see the true old times are dead,
When every morning brought a noble chance,
And every chance brought out a noble knight.
400 Such times have been not since the light that led
The holy Elders⁶ with the gift of myrrh.
But now the whole Round Table is dissolved
Which was an image of the mighty world,
And I, the last, go forth companionless,
405 And the days darken round me, and the years,
Among new men, strange faces, other minds."

And slowly answered Arthur from the barge:
"The old order changeth, yielding place to new,
And God fulfills himself in many ways,
410 Lest one good custom should corrupt the world.
Comfort thyself: what comfort is in me?
I have lived my life, and that which I have done
May He within himself make pure! but thou,
If thou shouldst never see my face again,
415 Pray for my soul. More things are wrought by prayer
Than this world dreams of. Wherefore, let thy voice
Rise like a fountain for me night and day.
For what are men better than sheep or goats
That nourish a blind life within the brain,
420 If, knowing God, they lift not hands of prayer
Both for themselves and those who call them friend?
For so the whole round earth is every way
Bound by gold chains about the feet of God.
But now farewell. I am going a long way
425 With these thou seëst—if indeed I go
(For all my mind is clouded with a doubt)—

4. Armor to protect the front of the thighs.
"Greaves": armor to protect the leg below the knee.
5. Blood from battle.
6. I.e., the star that guided the three kings
("Elders") to the Christ child at Bethlehem.

To the island-valley of Avilion;[7]
Where falls not hail, or rain, or any snow,
Nor ever wind blows loudly: but it lies
430   Deep-meadowed, happy, fair with orchard lawns
And bowery hollows crowned with summer sea,
Where I will heal me of my grievous wound."

    So said he, and the barge with oar and sail
Moved from the brink, like some full-breasted swan
435   That, fluting a wild carol ere her death,
Ruffles her pure cold plume, and takes the flood
With swarthy webs. Long stood Sir Bedivere
Revolving many memories, till the hull
Looked one black dot against the verge of dawn,
440   And on the mere the wailing died away.

    But when that moan had passed for evermore,
The stillness of the dead world's winter dawn
Amazed him, and he groaned, "The King is gone."
And therewithal came on him the weird rhyme,[8]
445   "From the great deep to the great deep he goes."

    Whereat he slowly turned and slowly clomb
The last hard footstep of that iron crag;
Thence marked the black hull moving yet, and cried,
"He passes to be King among the dead,
450   And after healing of his grievous wound
He comes again; but—if he come no more—
O me, be yon dark Queens in yon black boat,
Who shrieked and wailed, the three whereat we gazed
On that high day, when, clothed with living light,
455   They stood before his throne in silence, friends
Of Arthur, who should help him at his need?"

    Then from the dawn it seemed there came, but faint
As from beyond the limit of the world,
Like the last echo born of a great cry,
460   Sounds, as if some fair city were one voice
Around a king returning from his wars.

    Thereat once more he moved about, and clomb
Even to the highest he could climb, and saw,
Straining his eyes beneath an arch of hand,
465   Or thought he saw, the speck that bare the King,
Down that long water opening on the deep
Somewhere far off, pass on and on, and go
From less to less and vanish into light.
And the new sun rose bringing the new year.

1833–69   1869

7. Or Avalon, in Celtic mythology and medieval romance, the Vale of the Blessed where heroes enjoyed life after death.

8. A mysterious prophecy in verse had been spoken by Merlin concerning Arthur's birth; see *The Coming of Arthur*, lines 409–10, p. 1291.

Flower in the Crannied Wall

Flower in the crannied wall,
I pluck you out of the crannies,
I hold you here, root and all, in my hand,
Little flower—but if I could understand
5 What you are, root and all, and all in all,
I should know what God and man is.

1869

Crossing the Bar[1]

Sunset and evening star,
    And one clear call for me!
And may there be no moaning of the bar,[2]
    When I put out to sea,

5 But such a tide as moving seems asleep,
    Too full for sound and foam,
When that which drew from out the boundless deep
    Turns again home.

Twilight and evening bell,
10   And after that the dark!
And may there be no sadness of farewell,
    When I embark;

For though from out our bourne° of Time and Place   boundary
    The flood may bear me far,
15 I hope to see my Pilot face to face[3]
    When I have crossed the bar.

1889   1889

1. Although not the last poem written by Tenny-son, *Crossing the Bar* appears, at his request, as the final poem in all collections of his work.
2. Mournful sound of the ocean beating on a sand bar at the mouth of a harbor.

3. The expression "face to face" also occurs in two lines of section 131 of *In Memoriam* not used but left in manuscript: "And come to look on those we loved / And That which made us, face to face."

EDWARD FITZGERALD
1809–1883

Omar Khayyám was a twelfth-century mathematician, astronomer, and teacher from Nishapur in Persia. He was also the author of numerous rhymed quatrains, a verse form called *rubā'i* in Persian. Omar's four-lined epigrams were subsequently brought together in collections called *Rubáiyát* and recorded in various manuscripts.

More than seven hundred years later, in 1857, one such Omar manuscript came into the hands of Edward FitzGerald, who made from it one of the most popular poems in the English language. FitzGerald was a scholar of comfortable means who lived in the country reading the classics and cultivating his garden. He also cultivated his friendships with writers like Tennyson, Thackeray, and Carlyle, to whom he wrote charming letters. His translations from Greek and Latin were largely ignored and so too, at first, was his translation of Omar's Persian verses, which he published anonymously. In 1859, only two reviewers noticed the appearance of the *Rubáiyát of Omar Khayyám*, and the edition was soon remaindered. Two years later the volume was discovered by D. G. Rossetti, and enthusiasm for it gradually spread, until edition after edition was called for. The demand for the poem led FitzGerald to revise his translation considerably by further polishing his already finely polished stanzas (the fifth version of these revisions is printed here).

Experts have argued at great length whether FitzGerald's adaptation of Omar's poem is a faithful translation, but no one argues its beauty. One reader said of Fitz-Gerald's witty and melancholy masterpiece: "It reads like the latest and freshest expression of the perplexity and of the doubt of the generation to which we ourselves belong." This comment was made by the American Charles Eliot Norton writing in 1869. Norton's favorable opinion has been endorsed by later generations as well. The *Rubáiyát* has much in common with another late Victorian volume, *A Shropshire Lad* by A. E. Housman, and the remarkable popularity of these two collections of nostalgic lyrics is a reminder that to be popular, especially among young readers, poetry does not have to offer optimistic edification. As George Moore said, "The sadness of life is the joy of art."

The Rubáiyát of Omar Khayyám

1

Wake! For the Sun, who scattered into flight
The Stars before him from the Field of Night,
    Drives Night along with them from Heav'n and strikes
The Sultán's Turret with a Shaft of Light.

2

5   Before the phantom of False morning[1] died,
Methought a Voice within the Tavern cried,
    "When all the Temple is prepared within,
Why nods the drowsy Worshiper outside?"

3

And, as the Cock crew, those who stood before
10 The Tavern shouted—"Open, then, the Door!
    You know how little while we have to stay,
And, once departed, may return no more."

4

Now the New Year[2] reviving old Desires,
The thoughtful Soul to Solitude retires,

1. A transient Light on the Horizon about an hour before the . . . True Dawn [FitzGerald's note].

2. In Persia, the beginning of spring.

15   Where the WHITE HAND OF MOSES on the Bough
       Puts out, and Jesus from the Ground suspires.[3]

                         5

       Iram[4] indeed is gone with all his Rose,
       And Jamshyd's° Sev'n-ringed Cup where no one knows;   *legendary king*
           But still a Ruby kindles in the Vine,
20   And many a Garden by the Water blows.

                         6

       And David's lips are locked; but in divine
       High-piping Pehleví,[5] with "Wine! Wine! Wine!
           Red Wine!"—the Nightingale cries to the Rose
       That sallow cheek of hers to incarnadine.

                         7

25   Come, fill the Cup, and in the fire of Spring
       Your Winter-garment of Repentance fling;
           The Bird of Time has but a little way
       To flutter—and the Bird is on the Wing.

                         8

       Whether at Naishápur or Babylon,
30   Whether the Cup with sweet or bitter run,
           The Wine of Life keeps oozing drop by drop,
       The Leaves of Life keep falling one by one.

                         9

       Each Morn a thousand Roses brings, you say;
       Yes, but where leaves the Rose of Yesterday?
35   And this first Summer month that brings the Rose
       Shall take Jamshyd and Kaikobád[6] away.

                        10

       Well, let it take them! What have we to do
       With Kaikobád the Great, or Kaikhosrú?°   *king*
           Let Zál and Rustum[7] bluster as they will,
40   Or Hátim[8] call to Supper—heed not you.

                        11

       With me along the strip of Herbage strown
       That just divides the desert from the sown,
           Where name of Slave and Sultán is forgot—
       And Peace to Mahmúd[9] on his golden Throne!

---

3. Breathes. "Moses" and "Jesus": plants named in honor of prophets who came before Mohammed. The Persians believed that the healing power of Jesus was in his breath.
4. A royal Garden now sunk somewhere in the Sands of Arabia [FitzGerald's note].

5. The classical language of Persia.
6. Founder of a line of Persian kings.
7. Son and father who were warriors.
8. A generous host.
9. A sultan who conquered India.

12

45 A Book of Verses underneath the Bough,
A Jug of Wine, a Loaf of Bread—and Thou
 Beside me singing in the Wilderness—
Oh, Wilderness were Paradise enow!

13

Some for the Glories of This World; and some
50 Sigh for the Prophet's° Paradise to come;   *Mohammed's*
 Ah, take the Cash, and let the Credit go,
Nor heed the rumble of a distant Drum!

14

Look to the blowing Rose about us—"Lo,
Laughing," she says, "into the world I blow,
55 At once the silken tassel of my Purse
Tear, and its Treasure on the Garden throw."

15

And those who husbanded the Golden Grain,
And those who flung it to the winds like Rain,
 Alike to no such aureate Earth are turned
60 As, buried once, Men want dug up again.

16

The Worldly Hope men set their Hearts upon
Turns Ashes—or it prospers; and anon,
 Like Snow upon the Desert's dusty Face,
Lighting a little hour or two—is gone.

17

65 Think, in this battered Caravanserai°   *inn*
Whose Portals are alternate Night and Day,
 How Sultán after Sultán with his Pomp
Abode his destined Hour, and went his way.

18

They say the Lion and the Lizard keep
70 The Courts where Jamshyd gloried and drank deep;
 And Bahrám,[1] that great Hunter—the Wild Ass
Stamps o'er his Head, but cannot break his Sleep.

19

I sometimes think that never blows so red
The Rose as where some buried Caesar bled;
75 That every Hyacinth[2] the Garden wears
Dropped in her Lap from some once lovely Head.

1. A king who was lost while hunting a wild ass.
2. In classical myth the hyacinth had associations
of sadness because the plant was supposed to have
sprung from the blood of Hyacinthus, a beautiful
youth who was killed in an accident. Its petals were
marked AI, meaning "alas." FitzGerald, however,
seems to be referring more particularly to the
shape of the flower, as in *Odyssey* 6.231, where
locks of hair are likened to hyacinth clusters.

20

And this reviving Herb whose tender Green
Fledges the River-Lip on which we lean—
    Ah, lean upon it lightly! for who knows
80 From what once lovely Lip it springs unseen!

21

Ah, my Belovèd, fill the Cup that clears
TODAY of past Regrets and future Fears:
    Tomorrow!—Why, Tomorrow I may be
Myself with Yesterday's Sev'n thousand Years.

22

85 For some we loved, the loveliest and the best
That from his Vintage rolling Time hath pressed,
    Have drunk their Cup a Round or two before,
And one by one crept silently to rest.

23

And we, that now make merry in the Room
90 They left, and Summer dresses in new bloom,
    Ourselves must we beneath the Couch of Earth
Descend—ourselves to make a Couch—for whom?

24

Ah, make the most of what we yet may spend,
Before we too into the Dust descend;
95   Dust into Dust, and under Dust to lie,
Sans Wine, sans Song, sans Singer, and—sans End!

25

Alike for those who for TODAY prepare,
And those that after some TOMORROW stare,
    A Muezzín[3] from the Tower of Darkness cries,
100 "Fools, your Reward is neither Here nor There."

26

Why, all the Saints and Sages who discussed
Of the Two Worlds so wisely—they are thrust
    Like foolish Prophets forth; their Words to Scorn
Are scattered, and their Mouths are stopped with Dust.

27

105 Myself when young did eagerly frequent
Doctor and Saint, and heard great argument
    About it and about; but evermore
Came out by the same door where in I went.

---

3. One who calls the hour of prayer from the tower of a mosque.

28

With them the seed of Wisdom did I sow,
110 And with mine own hand wrought to make it grow;
  And this was all the Harvest that I reaped—
"I came like Water, and like Wind I go."

29

Into this Universe, and *Why* not knowing
Nor *Whence*, like Water willy-nilly flowing;
115 And out of it, as Wind along the Waste,
I know not *Whither*, willy-nilly blowing.

30

What, without asking, hither hurried *Whence?*
And, without asking, *Whither* hurried hence!
  Oh, many a Cup of this forbidden Wine⁴
120 Must drown the memory of that insolence!

31

Up from the Earth's Center through the Seventh Gate
I rose, and on the Throne of Saturn⁵ sate,
  And many a Knot unraveled by the Road;
But not the Master-knot of Human Fate.

32

125 There was the Door to which I found no Key;
There was the Veil through which I might not see;
  Some little talk awhile of ME and THEE
There was—and then no more of THEE and ME.

33

Earth could not answer; nor the Seas that mourn
130 In flowing Purple, of their Lord forlorn;
  Nor rolling Heaven, with all his Signs° revealed   *of the zodiac*
And hidden by the sleeve of Night and Morn.

34

Then of the THEE IN ME who works behind
The Veil, I lifted up my hands to find
135 A lamp amid the Darkness; and I heard,
As from Without—"THE ME WITHIN THEE BLIND!"

35

Then to the Lip of this poor earthen Urn
I leaned, the Secret of my Life to learn;
  And Lip to Lip it murmured—"While you live,
140 Drink!—for, once dead, you never shall return."

4. Alcohol is forbidden to strict Muslims.
5. The seat of knowledge. According to a note by FitzGerald, Saturn was lord of the seventh heaven.

36

I think the Vessel, that with fugitive
Articulation answered, once did live,
    And drink; and Ah! the passive Lip I kissed,
How many Kisses might it take—and give!

37

145 For I remember stopping by the way
To watch a Potter thumping his wet Clay;
    And with its all-obliterated Tongue
It murmured—"Gently, Brother, gently, pray!"

38

And has not such a Story from of Old
150 Down Man's successive generations rolled
    Of such a clod of saturated Earth
Cast by the Maker into Human mold?

39

And not a drop that from our Cups we throw
For Earth to drink of,[6] but may steal below
155   To quench the fire of Anguish in some Eye
There hidden—far beneath, and long ago.

40

As then the Tulip, for her morning sup
Of Heav'nly Vintage, from the soil looks up,
    Do you devoutly do the like, till Heav'n
160 To Earth invert you—like an empty Cup.

41

Perplexed no more with Human or Divine,
Tomorrow's tangle to the winds resign,
    And lose your fingers in the tresses of
The Cypress-slender Minister of Wine.[7]

42

165 And if the Wine you drink, the Lip you press,
End in what All begins and ends in—Yes;
    Think then you are TODAY what YESTERDAY
You were—TOMORROW you shall not be less.

43

So when that Angel of the darker Drink
170 At last shall find you by the river brink,
    And offering his Cup, invite your Soul
Forth to your Lips to quaff—you shall not shrink.

---

6. A reference to the custom of pouring some wine on the ground before drinking to refresh some dead and buried wine drinker.
7. Maiden who serves the wine.

44

Why, if the Soul can fling the Dust aside,
And naked on the Air of Heaven ride,
175   Were 't not a Shame—were 't not a Shame for him
In this clay carcass crippled to abide?

45

'Tis but a Tent where takes his one day's rest
A Sultán to the realm of Death addressed;
    The Sultán rises, and the dark Ferrásh[8]
180 Strikes, and prepares it for another Guest.

46

And fear not lest Existence closing your
Account, and mine, should know the like no more;
    The Eternal Sákí[9] from that Bowl has poured
Millions of Bubbles like us, and will pour.

47

185 When You and I behind the Veil are past,
Oh, but the long, long while the World shall last,
    Which of our Coming and Departure heeds
As the Sea's self should heed a pebble-cast.

48

A Moment's Halt—a momentary taste
190 Of BEING from the Well amid the Waste—
    And Lo!—the phantom Caravan has reached
The NOTHING it set out from—Oh, make haste!

49

Would you that spangle of Existence spend
About THE SECRET—quick about it, Friend!
195   A Hair perhaps divides the False and True—
And upon what, prithee, may life depend?

50

A Hair perhaps divides the False and True—
Yes; and a single Alif[1] were the clue—
    Could you but find it—to the Treasure-house,
200 And peradventure to THE MASTER too;

51

Whose secret Presence, through Creation's veins
Running Quicksilver-like, eludes your pains;
    Taking all shapes from Máh to Máhi;[2] and
They change and perish all—but He remains;

---

8. Servant who takes down ("strikes") a tent.
9. Servant who passes the wine.
1. The first letter of the Arabic alphabet, represented by a single vertical line.
2. From lowest to highest.

52

205 A moment guessed—then back behind the Fold
Immersed of Darkness round the Drama rolled
   Which, for the Pastime of Eternity,
He doth Himself contrive, enact, behold.

53

But if in vain, down on the stubborn floor
210 Of Earth, and up to Heav'n's unopening Door,
   You gaze TODAY, while You are You—how then
TOMORROW, You when shall be You no more?

54

Waste not your Hour, nor in the vain pursuit
Of This and That endeavor and dispute;
215   Better be jocund with the fruitful Grape
Than sadden after none, or bitter, Fruit.

55

You know, my Friends, with what a brave Carouse
I made a Second Marriage in my house;
   Divorced old barren Reason from my Bed,
220 And took the Daughter of the Vine to Spouse.

56

For "Is" and "IS-NOT" though with Rule and Line,
And "UP-AND-DOWN" by Logic, I define,
   Of all that one should care to fathom, I
Was never deep in anything but—Wine.

57

225 Ah, but my Computations, People say,
Reduced the Year to better reckoning?[3]—Nay,
   'Twas only striking from the Calendar
Unborn Tomorrow, and dead Yesterday.

58

And lately, by the Tavern Door agape,
230 Came shining through the Dusk an Angel Shape
   Bearing a Vessel on his Shoulder; and
He bid me taste of it; and 'twas—the Grape!

59

The Grape that can with Logic absolute
The Two-and-Seventy jarring Sects[4] confute;
235   The sovereign Alchemist that in a trice
Life's leaden metal into Gold transmute;

---

3. As a mathematician, Omar had devised an improved calendar.

4. The 72 religions supposed to divide the world [FitzGerald's note].

60

The mighty Mahmúd, Allah-breathing Lord,
That all the misbelieving and black Horde[5]
   Of Fears and Sorrows that infest the Soul
240 Scatters before him with his whirlwind Sword.

61

Why, be this Juice the growth of God, who dare
Blaspheme the twisted tendril as a Snare?
   A Blessing, we should use it, should we not?
And if a Curse—why, then, Who set it there?

62

245 I must abjure the Balm of Life, I must,
Scared by some After-reckoning ta'en on trust
   Or lured with Hope of some Diviner Drink,
To fill the Cup—when crumbled into Dust!

63

Oh threats of Hell and Hopes of Paradise!
250 One thing at least is certain—*This* Life flies;
   One thing is certain and the rest is Lies—
The Flower that once has blown forever dies.

64

Strange, is it not? that of the myriads who
Before us passed the door of Darkness through,
255   Not one returns to tell us of the Road,
Which to discover we must travel too.

65

The Revelations of Devout and Learn'd
Who rose before us, and as Prophets burned,[6]
   Are all but Stories, which, awoke from Sleep,
260 They told their comrades, and to Sleep returned.

66

I sent my Soul through the Invisible,
Some letter of that After-life to spell;
   And by and by my Soul returned to me,
And answered, "I Myself am Heav'n and Hell"—

67

265 Heaven but the Vision of fulfilled Desire,
And Hell the Shadow from a Soul on fire
   Cast on the Darkness into which Ourselves,
So late emerged from, shall so soon expire.

---

5. Alluding to Sultan Mahmúd's Conquest of India and its dark people [FitzGerald's note].

6. I.e., inspired by burning zeal to spread their prophecies.

68

We are no other than a moving row
270 Of Magic Shadow-shapes that come and go
    Round with the Sun-illumined Lantern held
In Midnight by the Master of the Show;

69

But helpless Pieces of the Game He plays
Upon this Checkerboard of Nights and Days;
275   Hither and thither moves, and checks, and slays,
And one by one back in the Closet lays.

70

The Ball no question makes of Ayes and Noes,
But Here or There as strikes the Player° goes;   *polo player*
    And He that tossed you down into the Field,
280 *He* knows about it all—HE knows—HE knows!

71

The Moving Finger writes, and, having writ,
Moves on; nor all your Piety nor Wit
    Shall lure it back to cancel half a Line,
Nor all your Tears wash out a Word of it.

72

285 And that inverted Bowl they call the Sky,
Whereunder crawling cooped we live and die,
    Lift not your hands to *It* for help—for It
As impotently moves as you or I.

73

With Earth's first Clay They did the Last Man knead,
290 And there of the Last Harvest sowed the Seed;
    And the first Morning of Creation wrote
What the Last Dawn of Reckoning shall read.

74

YESTERDAY *This* Day's Madness did prepare;
TOMORROW'S Silence, Triumph, or Despair.
295   Drink! for you know not whence you came, nor why;
Drink, for you know not why you go, nor where.

75

I tell you this—When, started from the Goal,
Over the flaming shoulders of the Foal
    Of Heav'n Parwín and Mushtarí they flung,
300 In my predestined Plot of Dust and Soul[7]

---

7. The speaker asserts that his fate was predestined in accordance with the relationship of the
stars and planets at the moment of his birth when

he "started from the Goal." In his horoscope the
particular relationship involved the Pleiades ("Par-
wín") and the planet Jupiter ("Mushtarí") that were

76

The Vine had struck a fiber; which about
If clings my Being—let the Dervish[8] flout;
    Of my Base metal may be filed a Key,
That shall unlock the Door he howls without.

77

305 And this I know: whether the one True Light
Kindle to Love, or Wrath—consume me quite,
    One Flash of It within the Tavern caught
Better than in the Temple lost outright.

78

What! out of senseless Nothing to provoke
310 A conscious Something to resent the yoke
    Of unpermitted Pleasure, under pain
Of Everlasting Penalties, if broke!

79

What! from his helpless Creature be repaid
Pure Gold for what he lent him dross-allayed—
315 Sue for a Debt he never did contract,
And cannot answer—Oh, the sorry trade!

80

O Thou, who didst with pitfall and with gin°   trap
Beset the Road I was to wander in,
    Thou wilt not with Predestined Evil round
320 Enmesh, and then impute my Fall to Sin!

81

O Thou, who Man of Baser Earth didst make,
And ev'n with Paradise devise the Snake,
    For all the Sin wherewith the Face of Man
Is blackened—Man's forgiveness give—and take!

82

325 As under cover of departing Day
Slunk hunger-stricken Ramazán[9] away,
    Once more within the Potter's house alone
I stood, surrounded by the Shapes of Clay—

83

Shapes of all Sorts and Sizes, great and small
330 That stood along the floor and by the wall;

"flung" by the gods into a special position in relation to the place in the sky of the constellation
Equuleus ("the Foal" or Colt).
8. Ascetic, who would despise ("flout") wine as a

means of discovering truth.
9. The month of fasting, during which no food is
eaten from sunrise to sunset.

And some loquacious Vessels were; and some
Listened perhaps, but never talked at all.

84

Said one among them—"Surely not in vain
My substance of the common Earth was ta'en
335   And to this Figure molded, to be broke,
Or trampled back to shapeless Earth again."

85

Then said a Second—"Ne'er a peevish Boy
Would break the Bowl from which he drank in joy;
And He that with his hand the Vessel made
340   Will surely not in after Wrath destroy."

86

After a momentary silence spake
Some Vessel of a more ungainly Make:
"They sneer at me for leaning all awry;
What! did the Hand, then, of the Potter shake?"

87

345   Whereat someone of the loquacious Lot—
I think a Súfi° pipkin—waxing hot—   *mystic*
"All this of Pot and Potter—Tell me then,
Who is the Potter, pray, and who the Pot?"

88

"Why," said another, "Some there are who tell
350   Of one who threatens he will toss to Hell
The luckless Pots he marred in making—Pish!
He's a Good Fellow, and 'twill all be well."

89

"Well," murmured one, "Let whoso make or buy,
My Clay with long Oblivion is gone dry;
355   But fill me with the old familiar Juice,
Methinks I might recover by and by."

90

So while the Vessels one by one were speaking
The little Moon looked in that all were seeking;[1]
And then they jogged each other, "Brother! Brother!
360   Now for the Porter's shoulder-knot[2] a-creaking!"

---

1. At the close of the Fasting Month, Ramazán . . . the first Glimpse of the new Moon . . . is looked for with the utmost Anxiety and hailed with all Acclamation [FitzGerald's note].
2. The rope or strap on which were hung the wine jars carried by the porter.

91

Ah, with the Grape my fading Life provide,
And wash the Body whence the Life has died,
    And lay me, shrouded in the living Leaf,
By some not unfrequented Garden-side—

92

365 That ev'n my buried Ashes such a snare
Of Vintage shall fling up into the Air
    As not a True-believer passing by
But shall be overtaken unaware.

93

Indeed the Idols I have loved so long
370 Have done my credit in this World much wrong,
    Have drowned my Glory in a shallow Cup,
And sold my Reputation for a Song.

94

Indeed, indeed, Repentance oft before
I swore—but was I sober when I swore?
375   And then and then came Spring, and Rose-in-hand
My threadbare Penitence apieces tore.

95

And much as Wine has played the Infidel,
And robbed me of my Robe of Honor—Well,
    I wonder often what the Vintners buy
380 One-half so precious as the stuff they sell.

96

Yet Ah, that Spring should vanish with the Rose!
That Youth's sweet-scented manuscript should close!
    The Nightingale that in the branches sang,
Ah whence, and whither flown again, who knows!

97

385 Would but the Desert of the Fountain yield
One glimpse—if dimly, yet indeed, revealed,
    To which the fainting Traveler might spring,
As springs the trampled herbage of the field.

98

Would but some wingèd Angel ere too late
390 Arrest the yet unfolded Roll of Fate,
    And make the stern Recorder otherwise
Enregister, or quite obliterate!

99

Ah, Love! could you and I with Him conspire
To grasp this sorry Scheme of Things entire,

395   Would not we shatter it to bits—and then
     Remold it nearer to the Heart's Desire!

100

     Yon rising Moon that looks for us again—
     How oft hereafter will she wax and wane;
       How oft hereafter rising look for us
400   Through this same Garden—and for *one* in vain!

101

     And when like her, O Sákí, you shall pass
     Among the Guests Star-scattered on the Grass,
       And in your joyous errand reach the spot
     Where I made One—turn down an empty Glass!

TAMÁM[3]

1857   1859, 1889

3. It is ended.

ELIZABETH GASKELL
1810–1865

It is ironic that the writer whom contemporaries and future generations knew as "Mrs. Gaskell" once instructed her sister-in-law that it was "a silly piece of bride-like affectation not to sign yourself by your proper name." Despite the wifely identity that the name Mrs. Gaskell connotes, Elizabeth Gaskell, as she always signed herself, wrote fiction on contemporary social topics that stimulated considerable controversy. Her first novel, *Mary Barton* (1848), presents a sympathetic picture of the hardships and the grievances of the working class. Another early novel, *Ruth* (1853), portrays the seduction and rehabilitation of an unwed mother.

Elizabeth Cleghorn Gaskell was born in 1810 in Chelsea, on the outskirts of London, to a Unitarian family. Her mother died when Gaskell was one, and the girl was sent to rural Knutsford, in Cheshire, to be raised by her aunt. At the age of twenty-one, she met and married William Gaskell, a Unitarian minister whose chapel was in the industrial city of Manchester. For the first ten years of her marriage, she led the life of a minister's wife, bearing five children, keeping a house, and helping her husband serve his congregation. When her fourth child and only son, William, died at the age of one year, Gaskell grew despondent. Her husband encouraged her to write as a way of allaying her grief, and so she produced *Mary Barton*, subtitled *A Tale of Manchester Life*. In the preface to the novel she wrote that she was inspired by thinking "how deep might be the romance in the lives of some of those who elbowed me daily in the busy streets of the town in which I resided. I had always felt a deep sympathy with the careworn men, who looked as if doomed to struggle through their lives in strange alternations between work and want." She observes the bitterness of their resentment against the rich and sets herself the task of creating understanding and sympathy for them.

Anonymously published, the novel was widely reviewed and discussed. Elizabeth Gaskell was soon identified as the author; she subsequently developed a wide acquaintance in literary circles. She wrote five more novels and about thirty short stories, many of which were published in Dickens's journal *Household Words*, later titled *All the Year Round*. The contrasting experiences Gaskell's life had given her of the south and the north, of rural Knutsford and industrial Manchester, defined the poles of her fiction. Her second novel, *Cranford* (1853), presents a delicate picture of the small events of country village life, a subject to which she returns with greater range and psychological depth in her last novel, *Wives and Daughters* (1866). In *North and South* (1855), Gaskell brings together the two worlds of her fiction in the story of Margaret Hale, a young woman from the south who moves to a factory town in the north.

One of the writers her literary fame led her to know was Charlotte Brontë, with whom she became friends. When Brontë died in 1855, Gaskell was approached by Patrick Brontë to write the story of his daughter's life. Gaskell's *Life of Charlotte Brontë* (1857) is a masterpiece of English biography and one of Gaskell's finest portrayals of character. Her focus in the *Life* on the relationship between Brontë's identity as a writer and her role as daughter, sister, and wife reflects the balance Gaskell herself sought between the stories she wove and the people she tended. "My dear Scheherazade," Dickens called her, words of praise and affection in which future readers have joined.

The Old Nurse's Story[1]

You know, my dears, that your mother was an orphan, and an only child; and I dare say you have heard that your grandfather was a clergyman up in Westmoreland, where I come from. I was just a girl in the village school, when, one day, your grandmother came in to ask the mistress if there was any scholar there who would do for a nurse-maid; and mighty proud I was, I can tell ye, when the mistress called me up, and spoke to my being a good girl at my needle, and a steady honest girl, and one whose parents were very respectable, though they might be poor. I thought I should like nothing better than to serve the pretty young lady, who was blushing as deep as I was, as she spoke of the coming baby, and what I should have to do with it. However, I see you don't care so much for this part of my story, as for what you think is to come, so I'll tell you at once I was engaged, and settled at the parsonage before Miss Rosamond (that was the baby, who is now your mother) was born. To be sure, I had little enough to do with her when she came, for she was never out of her mother's arms, and slept by her all night long; and proud enough was I sometimes when missis trusted her to me. There never was such a baby before or since, though you've all of you been fine enough in your turns; but for sweet winning ways, you've none of you come up to your mother. She took after her mother, who was a real lady born; a Miss Furnivall, a granddaughter of Lord Furnivall's in Northumberland. I believe she had neither brother nor sister, and had been brought up in my lord's family till she had married your grandfather, who was just a curate, son to a shopkeeper in Carlisle—but a clever fine gentleman as ever was—and one who was a right-down hard worker in his parish, which was very wide, and scattered all abroad over the Westmoreland Fells. When your mother, little Miss

1. Originally published anonymously in the 1852 Christmas number of Dickens's journal *Household Words*; it was later republished in Gaskell's *Lizzie Leigh, and Other Tales* (1855).

Rosamond, was about four or five years old, both her parents died in a fort-night—one after the other. Ah! that was a sad time. My pretty young mistress and me was looking for another baby, when my master came home from one of his long rides, wet and tired, and took the fever he died of; and then she never held up her head again, but just lived to see her dead baby, and have it laid on her breast before she sighed away her life. My mistress had asked me, on her death-bed, never to leave Miss Rosamond; but if she had never spoken a word, I would have gone with the little child to the end of the world.

The next thing, and before we had well stilled our sobs, the executors and guardians came to settle the affairs. They were my poor young mistress's own cousin, Lord Furnivall, and Mr. Esthwaite, my master's brother, a shop-keeper in Manchester; not so well to do then, as he was afterwards, and with a large family rising about him. Well! I don't know if it were their settling, or because of a letter my mistress wrote on her death-bed to her cousin, my lord; but somehow it was settled that Miss Rosamond and me were to go to Furnivall Manor House, in Northumberland, and my lord spoke as if it had been her mother's wish that she should live with his family, and as if he had no objections, for that one or two more or less could make no difference in so grand a household. So, though that was not the way in which I should have wished the coming of my bright and pretty pet to have been looked at— who was like a sunbeam in any family, be it never so grand—I was well pleased that all the folks in the Dale should stare and admire, when they heard I was going to be young lady's maid at my Lord Furnivall's at Furnivall Manor.

But I made a mistake in thinking we were to go and live where my lord did. It turned out that the family had left Furnivall Manor House fifty years or more. I could not hear that my poor young mistress had ever been there, though she had been brought up in the family; and I was sorry for that, for I should have liked Miss Rosamond's youth to have passed where her mother's had been.

My lord's gentleman, from whom I asked as many questions as I durst, said that the Manor House was at the foot of the Cumberland Fells, and a very grand place; that an old Miss Furnivall, a great-aunt of my lord's, lived there, with only a few servants; but that it was a very healthy place, and my lord had thought that it would suit Miss Rosamond very well for a few years, and that her being there might perhaps amuse his old aunt.

I was bidden by my lord to have Miss Rosamond's things ready by a certain day. He was a stern, proud man, as they say all the Lord Furnivalls were; and he never spoke a word more than was necessary. Folk did say he had loved my young mistress; but that, because she knew that his father would object, she would never listen to him, and married Mr. Esthwaite; but I don't know. He never married at any rate. But he never took much notice of Miss Rosamond; which I thought he might have done if he had cared for her dead mother. He sent his gentleman with us to the Manor House, telling him to join him at Newcastle that same evening; so there was no great length of time for him to make us known to all the strangers before he, too, shook us off; and we were left, two lonely young things (I was not eighteen), in the great old Manor House. It seems like yesterday that we drove there. We had left our own dear parsonage very early, and we had both cried as if our hearts would break, though we were travelling in my lord's carriage, which I had thought so much of once. And now it was long past noon on a September day, and we stopped to change horses for the last time at a little smoky town, all full of colliers and miners. Miss Rosamond had fallen asleep, but Mr. Henry told me to waken her, that she might see the park and the Manor House as we drove up. I thought it rather a pity; but I did what he bade me, for fear he should complain of me to my lord. We had left all signs of a town or even a village, and were then inside the gates of a large wild park—not like the parks here in the south, but with rocks, and the noise of running water, and gnarled thorn-trees, and old oaks, all white and peeled with age.

The road went up about two miles, and then we saw a great and stately house, with many trees close around it, so close that in some places their branches dragged against the walls when the wind blew; and some hung broken down; for no one seemed to take much charge of the place;—to lop the wood, or to keep the moss-covered carriage-way in order. Only in front of the house all was clear. The great oval drive was without a weed; and neither tree nor creeper was allowed to grow over the long, many-windowed front; at both sides of which a wing projected, which were each the ends of other side fronts; for the house, although it was so desolate, was even grander than I expected. Behind it rose the Fells, which seemed unenclosed and bare enough; and on the left hand of the house as you stood facing it, was a little old-fashioned flower-garden, as I found out afterwards. A door opened out upon it from the west front; it had been scooped out of the thick dark wood for some old Lady Furnivall; but the branches of the great forest trees had grown and overshadowed it again, and there were very few flowers that would live there at that time.

When we drove up to the great front entrance, and went into the hall I thought we should be lost—it was so large, and vast, and grand. There was a chandelier all of bronze, hung down from the middle of the ceiling; and I had never seen one before, and looked at it all in amaze. Then, at one end of the hall, was a great fire-place, as large as the sides of the houses in my country, with massy andirons and dogs to hold the wood; and by it were heavy old-fashioned sofas. At the opposite end of the hall, to the left as you went in—on the western side—was an organ built into the wall, and so large that it filled up the best part of that end. Beyond it, on the same side, was a door; and opposite, on each side of the fire-place, were also doors leading to the east front; but those I never went through as long as I stayed in the house, so I can't tell you what lay beyond.

The afternoon was closing in, and the hall, which had no fire lighted in it, looked dark and gloomy; but we did not stay there a moment. The old servant who had opened the door for us bowed to Mr. Henry, and took us in through the door at the further side of the great organ, and led us through several smaller halls and passages into the west drawing-room, where he said that Miss Furnivall was sitting. Poor little Miss Rosamond held very tight to me, as if she were scared and lost in that great place, and, as for myself, I was not much better. The west drawing-room was very cheerful-looking, with a warm fire in it, and plenty of good comfortable furniture about. Miss Furnivall was an old lady not far from eighty, I should think, but I do not know. She was thin and tall, and had a face as full of fine wrinkles as if they had been drawn all over it with a needle's point. Her eyes were very watchful, to make up, I suppose, for her being so deaf as to be obliged to use a trumpet.[2]

2. A horn-shaped device used by the hard of hearing to amplify sound.

Sitting with her, working at the same great piece of tapestry, was Mrs. Stark, her maid and companion, and almost as old as she was. She had lived with Miss Furnivall ever since they both were young, and now she seemed more like a friend than a servant; she looked so cold and grey, and stony, as if she had never loved or cared for any one; and I don't suppose she did care for any one, except her mistress; and, owing to the great deafness of the latter, Mrs. Stark treated her very much as if she were a child. Mr. Henry gave some message from my lord, and then he bowed good-bye to us all,—taking no notice of my sweet little Miss Rosamond's out-stretched hand—and left us standing there, being looked at by the two old ladies through their spectacles.

I was right glad when they rung for the old footman who had shown us in at first, and told him to take us to our rooms. So we went out of that great drawing-room, and into another sitting-room, and out of that, and then up a great flight of stairs, and along a broad gallery—which was something like a library, having books all down one side, and windows and writing-tables all down the other—till we came to our rooms, which I was not sorry to hear were just over the kitchens; for I began to think I should be lost in that wilderness of a house. There was an old nursery, that had been used for all the little lords and ladies long ago, with a pleasant fire burning in the grate, and the kettle boiling on the hob, and tea things spread out on the table; and out of that room was the night-nursery, with a little crib for Miss Rosamond close to my bed. And old James called up Dorothy, his wife, to bid us welcome; and both he and she were so hospitable and kind, that by-and-by Miss Rosamond and me felt quite at home; and by the time tea was over, she was sitting on Dorothy's knee, and chattering away as fast as her little tongue could go. I soon found out that Dorothy was from Westmoreland, and that bound her and me together, as it were; and I would never wish to meet with kinder people than were old James and his wife. James had lived pretty nearly all his life in my lord's family, and thought there was no one so grand as they. He even looked down a little on his wife; because, till he had married her, she had never lived in any but a farmer's household. But he was very fond of her, as well he might be. They had one servant under them, to do all the rough work. Agnes they called her; and she and me, and James and Dorothy, with Miss Furnivall and Mrs. Stark, made up the family; always remembering my sweet little Miss Rosamond! I used to wonder what they had done before she came, they thought so much of her now. Kitchen and drawing-room, it was all the same. The hard, sad Miss Furnivall, and the cold Mrs. Stark, looked pleased when she came fluttering in like a bird, playing and pranking hither and thither, with a continual murmur, and pretty prattle of gladness. I am sure, they were sorry many a time when she flitted away into the kitchen, though they were too proud to ask her to stay with them, and were a little surprised at her taste; though, to be sure, as Mrs. Stark said, it was not to be wondered at, remembering what stock her father had come of. The great, old rambling house, was a famous place for little Miss Rosamond. She made expeditions all over it, with me at her heels; all, except the east wing, which was never opened, and whither we never thought of going. But in the western and northern part was many a pleasant room; full of things that were curiosities to us, though they might not have been to people who had seen more. The windows were darkened by the sweeping boughs of the trees, and the ivy which had overgrown them: but, in the green gloom, we could manage to see old China jars and carved ivory boxes, and great heavy books, and, above all, the old pictures!

Once, I remember, my darling would have Dorothy go with us to tell us who they all were; for they were all portraits of some of my lord's family, though Dorothy could not tell us the names of every one. We had gone through most of the rooms, when we came to the old state drawing-room over the hall, and there was a picture of Miss Furnivall; or, as she was called in those days, Miss Grace, for she was the younger sister. Such a beauty she must have been! but with such a set, proud look, and such scorn looking out of her handsome eyes, with her eyebrows just a little raised, as if she wondered how any one could have the impertinence to look at her; and her lip curled at us, as we stood there gazing. She had a dress on, the like of which I had never seen before, but it was all the fashion when she was young; a hat of some soft white stuff like beaver, pulled a little over her brows, and a beautiful plume of feathers sweeping round it on one side; and her gown of blue satin was open in front to a quilted white stomacher.[3]

"Well, to be sure!" said I, when I had gazed my fill. "Flesh is grass, they do say; but who would have thought that Miss Furnivall had been such an out-and-out beauty, to see her now?"

"Yes," said Dorothy. "Folks change sadly. But if what my master's father used to say was true, Miss Furnivall, the elder sister, was handsomer than Miss Grace. Her picture is here somewhere; but, if I show it you, you must never let on, even to James, that you have seen it. Can the little lady hold her tongue, think you?" asked she.

I was not so sure, for she was such a little sweet, bold, open-spoken child, so I set her to hide herself; and then I helped Dorothy to turn a great picture, that leaned with its face towards the wall, and was not hung up as the others were. To be sure, it beat Miss Grace for beauty; and, I think, for scornful pride, too, though in that matter it might be hard to choose. I could have looked at it an hour, but Dorothy seemed half frightened of having shown it to me, and hurried it back again, and bade me run and find Miss Rosamond, for that there were some ugly places about the house, where she should like ill for the child to go. I was a brave, high-spirited girl, and thought little of what the old woman said, for I liked hide-and-seek as well as any child in the parish; so off I ran to find my little one.

As winter drew on, and the days grew shorter, I was sometimes almost certain that I heard a noise as if some one was playing on the great organ in the hall. I did not hear it every evening; but, certainly, I did very often; usually when I was sitting with Miss Rosamond, after I had put her to bed, and keeping quite still and silent in the bedroom. Then I used to hear it booming and swelling away in the distance. The first night, when I went down to my supper, I asked Dorothy who had been playing music, and James said very shortly that I was a gowk to take the wind soughing[4] among the trees for music; but I saw Dorothy look at him very fearfully, and Bessy, the kitchen-maid, said something beneath her breath, and went quite white. I saw they did not like my question, so I held my peace till I was with Dorothy alone,

3. Ornamental covering for the front of the body. "Beaver": felted wool.   4. Moaning.

when I knew I could get a good deal out of her. So, the next day, I watched my time, and I coaxed and asked her who it was that played the organ; for I knew that it was the organ and not the wind well enough, for all I had kept silence before James. But Dorothy had had her lesson, I'll warrant, and never a word could I get from her. So then I tried Bessy, though I had always held my head rather above her, as I was evened to James and Dorothy, and she was little better than their servant. So she said I must never, never tell; and, if I ever told, I was never to say *she* had told me; but it was a very strange noise, and she had heard it many a time, but most of all on winter nights, and before storms; and folks did say, it was the old lord playing on the great organ in the hall, just as he used to do when he was alive; but who the old lord was, or why he played, and why he played on stormy winter evenings in particular, she either could not or would not tell me. Well! I told you I had a brave heart; and I thought it was rather pleasant to have that grand music rolling about the house, let who would be the player; for now it rose above the great gusts of wind, and wailed and triumphed just like a living creature, and then it fell to a softness most complete; only it was always music and tunes, so it was nonsense to call it the wind. I thought, at first, it might be Miss Furnivall who played, unknown to Bessy; but, one day when I was in the hall by myself, I opened the organ and peeped all about it, and around it, as I had done to the organ in Crosthwaite Church once before, and I saw it was all broken and destroyed inside, though it looked so brave and fine; and then, though it was noon-day, my flesh began to creep a little, and I shut it up, and ran away pretty quickly to my own bright nursery; and I did not like hearing the music for some time after that, any more than James and Dorothy did. All this time Miss Rosamond was making herself more and more beloved. The old ladies liked her to dine with them at their early dinner; James stood behind Miss Furnivall's chair, and I behind Miss Rosamond's, all in state; and, after dinner, she would play about in a corner of the great drawing-room, as still as any mouse, while Miss Furnivall slept, and I had my dinner in the kitchen. But she was glad enough to come to me in the nursery afterwards; for, as she said, Miss Furnivall was so sad, and Mrs. Stark so dull; but she and I were merry enough; and, by-and-by, I got not to care for that weird rolling music, which did one no harm, if we did not know where it came from.

That winter was very cold. In the middle of October the frosts began, and lasted many, many weeks. I remember, one day at dinner, Miss Furnivall lifted up her sad, heavy eyes, and said to Mrs. Stark, "I am afraid we shall have a terrible winter," in a strange kind of meaning way. But Mrs. Stark pretended not to hear, and talked very loud of something else. My little lady and I did not care for the frost;—not we! As long as it was dry we climbed up the steep brows, behind the house, and went up on the Fells, which were bleak and bare enough, and there we ran races in the fresh, sharp air; and once we came down by a new path that took us past the two old gnarled holly-trees, which grew about half-way down by the east side of the house. But the days grew shorter and shorter; and the old lord, if it was he, played away more and more stormily and sadly on the great organ. One Sunday afternoon,—it must have been towards the end of November—I asked Dorothy to take charge of little Missey when she came out of the drawing-room, after Miss Furnivall had had her nap; for it was too cold to take her with me to church, and yet I wanted to go. And Dorothy was glad enough to promise, and was so fond of the child that all seemed well; and Bessy and I set off very briskly, though the sky hung heavy and black over the white earth, as if the night had never fully gone away; and the air, though still, was very biting and keen.

"We shall have a fall of snow," said Bessy to me. And sure enough, even while we were in church, it came down thick, in great large flakes, so thick it almost darkened the windows. It had stopped snowing before we came out, but it lay soft, thick and deep beneath our feet, as we tramped home. Before we got to the hall the moon rose, and I think it was lighter then,—what with the moon, and what with the white dazzling snow—than it had been when we went to church, between two and three o'clock. I have not told you that Miss Furnivall and Mrs. Stark never went to church: they used to read the prayers together, in their quiet gloomy way; they seemed to feel the Sunday very long without their tapestry-work to be busy at. So when I went to Dorothy in the kitchen, to fetch Miss Rosamond and take her up-stairs with me, I did not much wonder when the old woman told me that the ladies had kept the child with them, and that she had never come to the kitchen, as I had bidden her, when she was tired of behaving pretty in the drawing-room. So I took off my things and went to find her, and bring her to her supper in the nursery. But when I went into the best drawing-room, there sat the two old ladies, very still and quiet, dropping out a word now and then, but looking as if nothing so bright and merry as Miss Rosamond had ever been near them. Still I thought she might be hiding from me; it was one of her pretty ways; and that she had persuaded them to look as if they knew nothing about her; so I went softly peeping under this sofa, and behind that chair, making believe I was sadly frightened at not finding her.

"What's the matter, Hester?" said Mrs. Stark sharply. I don't know if Miss Furnivall had seen me, for, as I told you, she was very deaf, and she sat quite still, idly staring into the fire, with her hopeless face. "I'm only looking for my little Rosy-Posy," replied I, still thinking that the child was there, and near me, though I could not see her.

"Miss Rosamond is not here," said Mrs. Stark. "She went away more than an hour ago to find Dorothy." And she too turned and went on looking into the fire.

My heart sank at this, and I began to wish I had never left my darling. I went back to Dorothy and told her. James was gone out for the day, but she and me and Bessy took lights, and went up into the nursery first and then we roamed over the great large house, calling and entreating Miss Rosamond to come out of her hiding place, and not frighten us to death in that way. But there was no answer; no sound.

"Oh!" said I at last, "Can she have got into the east wing and hidden there?"

But Dorothy said it was not possible, for that she herself had never been in there; that the doors were always locked, and my lord's steward had the keys, she believed; at any rate, neither she nor James had ever seen them: so, I said I would go back and see it, after all, she was not hidden in the drawing-room, unknown to the old ladies; and if I found her there, I said, I would whip her well for the fright she had given me; but I never meant to do it. Well, I went back to the west drawing-room, and I told Mrs. Stark we could not find her anywhere, and asked for leave to look all about the fur-

niture there, for I thought now, that she might have fallen asleep in some
warm hidden corner; but no! we looked, Miss Furnivall got up and looked,
trembling all over, and she was no where there; then we set off again, every
one in the house, and looked in all the places we had searched before, but
we could not find her. Miss Furnivall shivered and shook so much, that Mrs.
Stark took her back into the warm drawing-room; but not before they had
made me promise to bring her to them when she was found. Well-a-day! I
began to think she never would be found, when I bethought me to look out
into the great front court, all covered with snow. I was up-stairs when I
looked out; but, it was such clear moonlight, I could see quite plain two little
footprints, which might be traced from the hall door, and round the corner
of the east wing. I don't know how I got down, but I tugged open the great,
stiff hall door; and, throwing the skirt of my gown over my head for a cloak,
I ran out. I turned the east corner, and there a black shadow fell on the snow;
but when I came again into the moonlight, there were the little footmarks
going up—up to the Fells. It was bitter cold; so cold that the air almost took
the skin off my face as I ran, but I ran on, crying to think how my poor little
darling must be perished and frightened. I was within sight of the holly-trees,
when I saw a shepherd coming down the hill, bearing something in his arms
wrapped in his maud.[5] He shouted to me, and asked me if I had lost a bairn;[6]
and, when I could not speak for crying, he bore towards me, and I saw my
wee bairnie lying still, and white, and stiff, in his arms, as if she had been
dead. He told me he had been up the Fells to gather in his sheep, before the
deep cold of night came on, and that under the holly-trees (black marks on
the hill-side, where no other bush was for miles around) he had found my
little lady—my lamb—my queen—my darling—stiff and cold, in the terrible
sleep which is frost-begotten. Oh! the joy, and the tears of having her in my
arms once again! for I would not let him carry her; but took her, maud and
all, into my own arms, and held her near my own warm neck and heart, and
felt the life stealing slowly back again into her little gentle limbs. But she
was still insensible when we reached the hall, and I had no breath for speech.
We went in by the kitchen door.

"Bring the warming-pan," said I; and I carried her up-stairs and began
undressing her by the nursery fire, which Bessy had kept up. I called my
little lammie all the sweet and playful names I could think of,—even while
my eyes were blinded by my tears; and at last, oh! at length she opened her
large blue eyes. Then I put her into her warm bed, and sent Dorothy down
to tell Miss Furnivall that all was well; and I made up my mind to sit by my
darling's bedside the live-long night. She fell away into a soft sleep as soon
as her pretty head had touched the pillow, and I watched by her till morning
light; when she wakened up bright and clear—or so I thought at first—and,
my dears, so I think now.

She said, that she had fancied that she should like to go to Dorothy, for
that both the old ladies were asleep, and it was very dull in the drawing-
room; and that, as she was going through the west lobby, she saw the snow
through the high window falling—falling—soft and steady; but she wanted
to see it lying pretty and white on the ground; so she made her way into the

---

5. Shawl of gray plaid used by shepherds in the   6. Child.
region.

great hall; and then, going to the window, she saw it bright and soft upon the drive; but while she stood there, she saw a little girl, not so old as she was, "but so pretty," said my darling, "and this little girl beckoned to me to come out; and oh, she was so pretty and so sweet, I could not choose but go." And then this other little girl had taken her by the hand, and side by side the two had gone round the east corner.

"Now you are a naughty little girl, and telling stories," said I. "What would your good mamma, that is in heaven, and never told a story in her life, say to her little Rosamond, if she heard her—and I dare say she does—telling stories!"

"Indeed, Hester," sobbed out my child; "I'm telling you true. Indeed I am."

"Don't tell me!" said I, very stern. "I tracked you by your foot-marks through the snow; there were only yours to be seen: and if you had had a little girl to go hand-in-hand with you up the hill, don't you think the foot-prints would have gone along with yours?"

"I can't help it, dear, dear Hester," said she, crying, "if they did not; I never looked at her feet, but she held my hand fast and tight in her little one, and it was very, very cold. She took me up the Fell-path, up to the holly trees; and there I saw a lady weeping and crying; but when she saw me, she hushed her weeping, and smiled very proud and grand, and took me on her knees, and began to lull me to sleep; and that's all, Hester—but that is true; and my dear mamma knows it is," said she, crying. So I thought the child was in a fever, and pretended to believe her, as she went over her story—over and over again, and always the same. At last Dorothy knocked at the door with Miss Rosamond's breakfast; and she told me the old ladies were down in the eating-parlour, and that they wanted to speak to me. They had both been into the night-nursery the evening before, but it was after Miss Rosamond was asleep; so they had only looked at her—not asked me any questions.

"I shall catch it," thought I to myself, as I went along the north gallery. "And yet," I thought, taking courage, "it was in their charge I left her; and it's they that's to blame for letting her steal away unknown and unwatched." So I went in boldly, and told my story. I told it all to Miss Furnivall, shouting it close to her ear; but when I came to the mention of the other little girl out in the snow, coaxing and tempting her out, and willing her up to the grand and beautiful lady by the Holly-tree, she threw her arms up—her old and withered arms—and cried aloud, "Oh! Heaven, forgive! Have mercy!"

Mrs. Stark took hold of her; roughly enough, I thought; but she was past Mrs. Stark's management, and spoke to me, in a kind of wild warning and authority.

"Hester! keep her from that child! It will lure her to her death! That evil child! Tell her it is a wicked, naughty child." Then, Mrs. Stark hurried me out of the room; where, indeed, I was glad enough to go; but Miss Furnivall kept shrieking out, "Oh! have mercy! Wilt Thou never forgive! It is many a long year ago——"

I was very uneasy in my mind after that. I durst never leave Miss Rosamond, night or day, for fear lest she might slip off again, after some fancy or other; and all the more, because I thought I could make out that Miss Furnivall was crazy, from their odd ways about her; and I was afraid lest something of the same kind (which might be in the family, you know) hung over my darling. And the great frost never ceased all this time; and, whenever it was a more stormy night than usual, between the gusts, and through the wind, we heard the old lord playing on the great organ. But, old lord, or not, wherever Miss Rosamond went, there I followed; for my love for her, pretty helpless orphan, was stronger than my fear for the grand and terrible sound. Besides, it rested with me to keep her cheerful and merry, as beseemed her age. So we played together, and wandered together, here and there, and everywhere; for I never dared to lose sight of her again in that large and rambling house. And so it happened, that one afternoon, not long before Christmas day, we were playing together on the billiard-table in the great hall (not that we knew the right way of playing, but she liked to roll the smooth ivory balls with her pretty hands, and I liked to do whatever she did); and, by-and-bye, without our noticing it, it grew dusk indoors, though it was still light in the open air, and I was thinking of taking her back into the nursery, when, all of a sudden, she cried out:

"Look, Hester! look! there is my poor little girl out in the snow!"

I turned towards the long narrow windows, and there, sure enough, I saw a little girl, less than my Miss Rosamond—dressed all unfit to be out-of-doors such a bitter night—crying, and beating against the window-panes, as if, she wanted to be let in. She seemed to sob and wail, till Miss Rosamond could bear it no longer, and was flying to the door to open it, when, all of a sudden, and close upon us, the great organ pealed out so loud and thundering, it fairly made me tremble; and all the more, when I remembered me that, even in the stillness of that dead-cold weather, I had heard no sound of little battering hands upon the window-glass, although the Phantom Child had seemed to put forth all its force; and, although I had seen it wail and cry, no faintest touch of sound had fallen upon my ears. Whether I remembered all this at the very moment, I do not know; the great organ sound had so stunned me into terror; but this I know, I caught up Miss Rosamond before she got the hall-door opened, and clutched her, and carried her away, kicking and screaming, into the large bright kitchen, where Dorothy and Agnes were busy with their mince-pies.

"What is the matter with my sweet one?" cried Dorothy, as I bore in Miss Rosamond, who was sobbing as if her heart would break.

"She won't let me open the door for my little girl to come in; and she'll die if she is out on the Fells all night. Cruel, naughty Hester," she said, slapping me; but she might have struck harder, for I had seen a look of ghastly terror on Dorothy's face, which made my very blood run cold.

"Shut the back kitchen door fast, and bolt it well," said she to Agnes. She said no more; she gave me raisins and almonds to quiet Miss Rosamond: but she sobbed about the little girl in the snow, and would not touch any of the good things. I was thankful when she cried herself to sleep in bed. Then I stole down to the kitchen, and told Dorothy I had made up my mind. I would carry my darling back to my father's house in Applethwaite; where, if we lived humbly, we lived at peace. I said I had been frightened enough with the old lord's organ-playing; but now, that I had seen for myself this little moaning child, all decked out as no child in the neighborhood could be, beating and battering to get in, yet always without any sound or noise—with the dark wound on its right shoulder; and that Miss Rosamond had known it again for the phantom that had nearly lured her to her death (which Dorothy knew was true); I would stand it no longer.

I saw Dorothy change color once or twice. When I had done, she told me she did not think I could take Miss Rosamond with me, for that she was my lord's ward, and I had no right over her; and she asked me, would I leave the child that I was so fond of, just for sounds and sights that could do me no harm; and that they had all had to get used to in their turns? I was all in a hot, trembling passion; and I said it was very well for her to talk, that knew what these sights and noises betokened, and that had, perhaps, had something to do with the Spectre-child while it was alive. And I taunted her so, that she told me all she knew, at last; and then I wished I had never been told, for it only made me more afraid than ever.

She said she had heard the tale from old neighbors, that were alive when she was first married; when folks used to come to the hall sometimes, before it had got such a bad name on the country side: it might not be true, or it might, what she had been told.

The old lord was Miss Furnivall's father—Miss Grace, as Dorothy called her, for Miss Maude was the elder, and Miss Furnivall by rights. The old lord was eaten up with pride. Such a proud man was never seen or heard of; and his daughters were like him. No one was good enough to wed them, although they had choice enough; for they were the great beauties of their day, as I had seen by their portraits, where they hung in the state drawing-room. But, as the old saying is, "Pride will have a fall;" and these two haughty beauties fell in love with the same man, and he no better than a foreign musician, whom their father had down from London to play music with him at the Manor House. For, above all things, next to his pride, the old lord loved music. He could play on nearly every instrument that ever was heard of; and it was a strange thing it did not soften him; but he was a fierce dour old man, and had broken his poor wife's heart with his cruelty, they said. He was mad after music, and would pay any money for it. So he got this foreigner to come; who made such beautiful music, that they said the very birds on the trees stopped their singing to listen. And, by degrees, this foreign gentleman got such a hold over the old lord, that nothing would serve him but that he must come every year; and it was he that had the great organ brought from Holland and built up in the hall, where it stood now. He taught the old lord to play on it; but many and many a time, when Lord Furnivall was thinking of nothing but his fine organ, and his finer music, the dark foreigner was walking abroad in the woods with one of the young ladies; now Miss Maude, and then Miss Grace.

Miss Maude won the day and carried off the prize, such as it was; and he and she were married, all unknown to any one; and before he made his next yearly visit, she had been confined of a little girl at a farm-house on the Moors, while her father and Miss Grace thought she was away at Doncaster Races. But though she was a wife and a mother, she was not a bit softened, but as haughty and as passionate as ever; and perhaps more so, for she was jealous of Miss Grace, to whom her foreign husband paid a deal of court—by way of blinding her—as he told his wife. But Miss Grace triumphed over Miss Maude, and Miss Maude grew fiercer and fiercer, both with her husband and with her sister; and the former—who could easily shake off what was disagreeable, and hide himself in foreign countries—went away a month before his usual time that summer, and half threatened that he would never come back again. Meanwhile, the little girl was left at the farm-house, and her mother used to have her horse saddled and gallop wildly over the hills to see her once every week, at the very least—for where she loved, she loved; and where she hated, she hated. And the old lord went on playing—playing on his organ; and the servants thought the sweet music he made had soothed down his awful temper, of which (Dorothy said) some terrible tales could be told. He grew infirm too, and had to walk with a crutch; and his son—that was the present Lord Furnivall's father—was with the army in America, and the other son at sea; so Miss Maude had it pretty much her own way, and she and Miss Grace grew colder and bitterer to each other every day; till at last they hardly ever spoke, except when the old lord was by. The foreign musician came again the next summer, but it was for the last time; for they led him such a life with their jealously and their passions, that he grew weary, and went away, and never was heard of again. And Miss Maude, who had always meant to have her marriage acknowledged when her father should be dead, was left now a deserted wife—whom nobody knew to have been married—with a child that she dared not own, although she loved it to distraction; living with a father whom she feared, and a sister whom she hated. When the next summer passed over and the dark foreigner never came, both Miss Maude and Miss Grace grew gloomy and sad; they had a haggard look about them, though they looked handsome as ever. But by and by Miss Maude brightened; for her father grew more and more infirm, and more than ever carried away by his music; and she and Miss Grace lived almost entirely apart, having separate rooms, the one on the west side—Miss Maude on the east—those very rooms which were now shut up. So she thought she might have her little girl with her, and no one need ever know except those who dared not speak about it, and were bound to believe that it was, as she said, a cottager's child she had taken a fancy to. All this, Dorothy said, was pretty well known; but what came afterwards no one knew, except Miss Grace, and Mrs. Stark, who was even then her maid, and much more of a friend to her than ever her sister had been. But the servants supposed, from words that were dropped, that Miss Maude had triumphed over Miss Grace, and told her that all the time the dark foreigner had been mocking her with pretended love—he was her own husband; the color left Miss Grace's cheek and lips that very day for ever, and she was heard to say many a time that sooner or later she would have her revenge; and Mrs. Stark was for ever spying about the east rooms.

One fearful night, just after the New Year had come in, when the snow was lying thick and deep, and the flakes were still falling—fast enough to blind any one who might be out and abroad—there was a great and violent noise heard, and the old lord's voice above all, cursing and swearing awfully,—and the cries of a little child,—and the proud defiance of a fierce woman,—and the sound of a blow,—and a dead stillness,—and moans and wailings dying away on the hill-side! Then the old lord summoned all his servants, and told them, with terrible oaths, and words more terrible, that his daughter had disgraced herself, and that he had turned her out of doors,—her, and her child,—and that if ever they gave her help,—or food— or shelter,—he prayed that they might never enter Heaven. And, all the while, Miss Grace stood by him, white and still as any stone; and when he had ended she heaved a great sigh, as much as to say her work was done, and her end was accomplished. But the old lord never touched his organ again, and died within the year; and no wonder! for, on the morrow of that wild and fearful night, the shepherds, coming down the Fell side, found Miss Maude sitting, all crazy and smiling, under the holly-trees, nursing a dead child,—with a terrible mark on its right shoulder. "But that was not what killed it," said Dorothy; "it was the frost and the cold—every wild creature was in its hole, and every beast in its fold,—while the child and its mother were turned out to wander on the Fells! And now you know all! and I wonder if you are less frightened now?"

I was more frightened than ever; but I said I was not. I wished Miss Rosamond and myself well out of that dreadful house for ever; but I would not leave her, and I dared not take her away. But oh! how I watched her, and guarded her! We bolted the doors, and shut the window-shutters fast, an hour or more before dark, rather than leave them open five minutes too late. But my little lady still heard the weird child crying and mourning; and not all we could do or say, could keep her from wanting to go to her, and let her in from the cruel wind and the snow. All this time, I kept away from Miss Furnivall and Mrs. Stark, as much as ever I could; for I feared them—I knew no good could be about them, with their grey hard faces, and their dreamy eyes, looking back into the ghastly years that were gone. But, even in my fear, I had a kind of pity—for Miss Furnivall, at least. Those gone down to the pit can hardly have a more hopeless look than that which was ever on her face. At last I even got so sorry for her—who never said a word but what was quite forced from her—that I prayed for her; and I taught Miss Rosamond to pray for one who had done a deadly sin; but often when she came to those words, she would listen, and start up from her knees, and say, "I hear my little girl plaining and crying very sad—Oh! let her in, or she will die!"

One night—just after New Year's Day had come at last, and the long winter had taken a turn as I hoped—I heard the west drawing-room bell ring three times, which was the signal for me. I would not leave Miss Rosamond alone, for all she was asleep—for the old lord had been playing wilder than ever—and I feared lest my darling should waken to hear the spectre child; see her I knew she could not, I had fastened the windows too well for that. So, I took her out of her bed and wrapped her up in such outer clothes as were most handy, and carried her down to the drawing-room, where the old ladies sat at their tapestry work as usual. They looked up when I came in, and Mrs. Stark asked, quite astounded, "Why did I bring Miss Rosamond there, out of her warm bed?" I had begun to whisper, "Because I was afraid of her being tempted out while I was away, by the wild child in the snow," when she stopped me short (with a glance at Miss Furnivall) and said Miss Furnivall wanted me to undo some work she had done wrong, and which neither of them could see to unpick. So, I laid my pretty dear on the sofa, and sat down on a stool by them, and hardened my heart against them as I heard the wind rising and howling.

Miss Rosamond slept on sound, for all the wind blew so; and Miss Furnivall said never a word, nor looked round when the gusts shook the windows. All at once she started up to her full height, and put up one hand as if to bid us listen.

"I hear voices!" said she. "I hear terrible screams—I hear my father's voice!"

Just at that moment, my darling wakened with a sudden start: "My little girl is crying, oh, how she is crying!" and she tried to get up and go to her, but she got her feet entangled in the blanket, and I caught her up; for my flesh had begun to creep at these noises, which they heard while we could catch no sound. In a minute or two the noises came, and gathered fast, and filled our ears; we, too, heard voices and screams, and no longer heard the winter's wind that raged abroad. Mrs. Stark looked at me, and I at her, but we dared not speak. Suddenly Miss Furnivall went towards the door, out into the ante-room, through the west lobby, and opened the door into the great hall. Mrs. Stark followed, and I durst not be left, though my heart almost stopped beating for fear. I wrapped my darling tight in my arms, and went out with them. In the hall the screams were louder than ever; they sounded to come from the east wing—nearer and nearer—close on the other side of the locked-up doors—close behind them. Then I noticed that the great bronze chandelier seemed all alight, though the hall was dim, and that a fire was blazing in the vast hearth-place, though it gave no heat; and I shuddered up with terror, and folded my darling closer to me. But as I did so, the east door shook, and she, suddenly struggling to get free from me, cried, "Hester! I must go! My little girl is there; I hear her; she is coming! Hester, I must go!"

I held her tight with all my strength; with a set will, I held her. If I had died, my hands would have grasped her still; I was so resolved in my mind. Miss Furnivall stood listening, and paid no regard to my darling, who had got down to the ground, and whom I, upon my knees now, was holding with both my arms clasped round her neck; she still striving and crying to get free.

All at once, the east door gave way with a thundering crash, as if torn open in a violent passion, and there came into that broad and mysterious light, the figure of a tall old man, with grey hair and gleaming eyes. He drove before him, with many a relentless gesture of abhorrence, a stern and beautiful woman, with a little child clinging to her dress.

"Oh Hester! Hester!" cried Miss Rosamond. "It's the lady! the lady below the holly-trees; and my little girl is with her. Hester! Hester! let me go to her; they are drawing me to them. I feel them—I feel them. I must go!"

Again she was almost convulsed by her efforts to get away; but I held her tighter and tighter; till I feared I should do her a hurt; but rather that than let her go towards those terrible phantoms. They passed along towards the great hall-door, where the winds howled and ravened for their prey; but before they reached that, the lady turned; and I could see that she defied the old man with a fierce and proud defiance; but then she quailed—and then she threw up her arms wildly and piteously to save her child—her little child—from a blow from his uplifted crutch.

And Miss Rosamond was torn as by a power stronger than mine, and writhed in my arms, and sobbed (for by this time the poor darling was growing faint).

"They want me to go with them on to the Fells—they are drawing me to them. Oh, my little girl! I would come, but cruel, wicked Hester holds me very tight." But when she saw the uplifted crutch she swooned away, and I thanked God for it. Just at this moment—when the tall old man, his hair streaming as in the blast of a furnace, was going to strike the little shrinking child—Miss Furnivall, the old woman by my side, cried out, "Oh, father! father! spare the little innocent child!" But just then I saw—we all saw— another phantom shape itself, and grow clear out of the blue and misty light that filled the hall; we had not seen her till now, for it was another lady who stood by the old man, with a look of relentless hate and triumphant scorn. That figure was very beautiful to look upon, with a soft white hat drawn down over the proud brows, and a red and curling lip. It was dressed in an open robe of blue satin. I had seen that figure before. It was the likeness of Miss Furnivall in her youth; and the terrible phantoms moved on, regardless of old Miss Furnivall's wild entreaty,—and the uplifted crutch fell on the right shoulder of the little child, and the younger sister looked on, stony and deadly serene. But at that moment, the dim lights, and the fire that gave no heat, went out of themselves, and Miss Furnivall lay at our feet stricken down by the palsy—death-stricken.

Yes! she was carried to her bed that night never to rise again. She lay with her face to the wall, muttering low but muttering alway: "Alas! alas! what is done in youth can never be undone in age! What is done in youth can never be undone in age!"

1852

CHARLES DICKENS
1812–1870

Charles Dickens was Victorian England's most beloved and distinctive novelist. In the words of the eulogy that the classicist Benjamin Jowett spoke at his funeral service, Dickens "occupied a greater space than any other writer during the last thirty-five years. We read him, talked about him, acted him; we laughed with him, we were roused by him to a consciousness of the misery of others, and to a pathetic interest in human life."

Charles Dickens was born the second of eight children in the coastal town of Portsmouth in southern England. His father, a clerk in the Naval Pay Office, found it difficult to keep his family out of debt. Plagued by financial insecurity, the family moved from place to place, to increasingly poorer lodgings, finally ending up in London. In an effort to help the family out, a friend of his father's offered Charles a job in a shoe-blacking factory. Two days before his twelfth birthday, he began work, labeling bottles for six shillings a week. Two weeks later his father was arrested and sent to the Marshalsea Prison for debt. His family went to live in prison with him, as was the custom; but they decided that Charles should remain outside, boarding with a woman who took in young lodgers and continuing to work.

The months in which Charles lived alone and worked in the blacking warehouse were traumatic, and the intense feeling Dickens had of injury and abandonment shaped his fiction in profound ways. The sense he had of himself as "a child of singular abilities: quick, eager, delicate, and soon hurt, bodily or mentally," who had been cast away to suffer unjustly, formed the basis for characters such as Oliver Twist, the young David Copperfield, and Pip in *Great Expectations*, whose mistreatment represents Dickens's harshest indictment of society.

Dickens's father was able to leave debtors prison after three months, upon receipt of a legacy from his mother. He removed Charles from the factory and sent him to school. At fifteen Dickens began work as a junior clerk at a law office; eighteen months later he became a freelance newspaper reporter, first reporting court proceedings and later debates in the House of Commons. Reporting led him to fiction. He began publishing literary sketches, at first anonymously and then under the pseudonym Boz. In 1836, on his twenty-fourth birthday, he published the collection *Sketches by Boz*. The success of the volume led to a commission from the publishers Chapman & Hall to publish a book in serial installments with companion illustrations. The result, *Pickwick Papers* (1836–37), brought Dickens fame and prosperity. This picaresque novel, relating the adventures of Mr. Pickwick and his friends as they travel around England, set the pattern of illustrated serial publication that was to define Dickens's writing career and to shape the reading habits of his generation. Families would wait in suspense for the next installment of a novel to be issued, which they would read aloud as an evening's entertainment. Successes followed quickly: *Oliver Twist* (1838), *Nicholas Nickleby* (1838–39), and *The Old Curiosity Shop* (1840–41).

By the time of *Pickwick*'s completion, Dickens had married Catherine Hogarth, the daughter of a fellow journalist, and had begun a family; they eventually had ten children, and household chaos would come increasingly to frustrate him. Dickens's portrayal of women, both as unreachable ideals and as inadequate keepers of domestic order, was influenced by two other women. Maria Beadnell, the daughter of a banker, was his first love; but his courtship was discouraged by her family, who felt he was beneath her. He was left with a painful sense that he had lost his ideal love. Dickens experienced another traumatic loss when Mary, his seventeen-year-old sister-in-law to whom he had become devoted, died in his arms.

Through the 1840s and 1850s Dickens continued to write novels at an intense pace, producing *Barnaby Rudge* (1841), *Martin Chuzzlewit* (1843–44), *Dombey and Son* (1846–48), *David Copperfield* (1849–50), *Bleak House* (1852–53), *Hard Times* (1854), *Little Dorrit* (1855–57), and *A Tale of Two Cities* (1859). He also became deeply involved in a number of other activities, including traveling, working for charities, and acting. During this time he founded and edited the weekly magazine *Household Words* (incorporated in 1859 into *All the Year Round*), which published fiction by Elizabeth Gaskell, Wilkie Collins, Dickens himself, and other novelists as well as opinion pieces about political and social issues. And he began a series of Christmas books, the first of which was *A Christmas Carol* (1843).

In 1858 when Dickens separated from his wife, his life and work changed. He became involved with the actress Ellen Ternan, and he took up residence at Gad's Hill, a gentleman's house in Kent. Abandoning amateur theatricals, he embarked on a series of lucrative professional readings, which were so emotionally and physically exhausting his doctor finally instructed him to stop. He slowed the pace of his writing, publishing only two novels in the 1860s: *Great Expectations* (1860–61) and *Our Mutual Friend* (1864–65). He died suddenly in 1870, leaving his last novel, *The Mystery of Edwin Drood* (1870), unfinished.

Dickens's early fiction is remarkable for its extravagance, which Franz Kafka calls "Dickens' opulence and great, careless prodigality." It marks many elements of his novels—their baggy plots, filled with incident; the constant metaphorical invention of their language; and the multitude of their characters. Anthony Trollope observed that no other writer except Shakespeare has left so many "characters which are known by their names familiarly as household words, and which bring to our minds vividly and at once, a certain well-understood set of ideas, habits, phrases and costumes, making together a man, or woman, or child, whom we know at a glance and recognize at a sound, as we do our own intimate friends."

Dickens builds character from a repeated set of gestures, phrases, and metaphors. For example, whenever Mrs. Micawber enters the story of *David Copperfield*, she repeats, "I will never desert Mr. Micawber." Dickens identifies Wemmick in *Great Expectations* with his post office mouth and Mr. Gradgrind in *Hard Times* with the squareness of each of his physical attributes. This way of creating character led the novelist E. M. Forster to use Dickens to illustrate what he means by a flat, as opposed to a round, character. Such a reductive technique of characterization might seem to have little to offer by way of depth of insight, yet such is not the case. In particular, as Dickens's fiction becomes more complex in the course of his career, the repeated tics that identify his characters come to represent emotional fixations and social distortions. Dickens's early fiction exults in a comedy of humors. In his later fiction, that comedy becomes grotesque, as the distortions of caricature reflect failures of humanity in his increasingly dark social vision.

Bernard Shaw wrote that "Dickens never regarded himself as a revolutionist, though he certainly was one." Dickens's early novels often concern social abuses— the workhouses in which pauper children were confined in *Oliver Twist*, abusive and fraudulent schools in *Nicholas Nickleby*. As his career progressed, Dickens felt an increasing urgency about the social criticism his novels made. He gave *Hard Times* the subtitle *For These Times* and dedicated the book to Thomas Carlyle, indicating his ambition to write a work in the tradition of Carlyle's social indictment, *Signs of the Times*. In his middle novels, Dickens's criticism of society becomes increasingly systemic, and he begins to use organizing metaphors to express his social vision. *Bleak House*, for example, concerns the failings of the legal system, but the obfuscation and self-interest of the law is symptomatic of a larger social ill, symbolized in the smothering fog whose description begins the novel.

Despite the bleakness of Dickens's view of society and the fierceness of his criticism of it, his novels always end with a sentimental assertion of the virtues of home and heart. A number of critics have thought this sentimentality blunts his social analysis. Whatever the claims Dickens makes for fellow feeling, however, his sentimental endings are never completely consistent with his social analysis. Although Dickens tries to use fiction to stir the human heart and evoke humanitarian feelings, the domestic refuges of his novels never change the world outside. The modern novelist Graham Greene has written that Dickens's inability to believe in his own good characters creates the real tension of his fiction. Without sharing Greene's incredulity, one can see the novels as polyphonic, as giving expression to many voices that together create a structural sense not only of Victorian society but also of the values that give shape to its perceptions, including its sentimentality.

The distinctive character of Dickens's fiction is so pronounced that critics often talk of his world as if the individual worlds of all of his novels were continuous. In part, Dickens's tendency to return repeatedly to the subjects that possessed his imagination supports this impression. One of those subjects is prisons. *A Visit to Newgate* is his earliest piece about prisons; but he returns to the subject many times, as in *Great Expectations, Oliver Twist, Pickwick Papers,* and *Little Dorrit*. Prison for Dickens is a particular social abuse, the most harrowing setting in which to contemplate criminality and guilt, a metaphor for the psychological captivity his characters create for themselves, and the system through which society enforces its discipline. In the many layers of significance that the main elements of Victorian society take on in his fiction, Dickens's creative vision, as the critic J. Hillis Miller observes, in part determines the Victorian spirit itself.

A Visit to Newgate[1]

"The force of habit" is a trite phrase in everybody's mouth; and it is not a little remarkable that those who use it most as applied to others, uncon-

---

1. First published in *Sketches by Boz* (1836). Newgate was London's main criminal prison.

sciously afford in their own persons singular examples of the power which habit and custom exercise over the minds of men, and of the little reflection they are apt to bestow on subjects with which every day's experience has rendered them familiar. If Bedlam could be suddenly removed like another Aladdin's palace,[2] and set down on the space now occupied by Newgate, scarcely one man out of a hundred, whose road to business every morning lies through Newgate-street, or the Old Bailey,[3] would pass the building without bestowing a hasty glance on its small, grated windows, and a transient thought upon the condition of the unhappy beings immured in its dismal cells; and yet these same men, day by day, and hour by hour, pass and repass this gloomy depository of the guilt and misery of London, in one perpetual stream of life and bustle, utterly unmindful of the throng of wretched creatures pent up within it—nay, not even knowing, or if they do, not heeding, the fact, that as they pass one particular angle of the massive wall with a light laugh or a merry whistle, they stand within one yard of a fellow-creature, bound and helpless, whose hours are numbered, from whom the last feeble ray of hope has fled for ever, and whose miserable career will shortly terminate in a violent and shameful death. Contact with death even in its least terrible shape, is solemn and appalling. How much more awful is it to reflect on this near vicinity to the dying—to men in full health and vigour, in the flower of youth or the prime of life, with all their faculties and perceptions as acute and perfect as your own; but dying, nevertheless—dying as surely—with the hand of death imprinted upon them as indelibly—as if mortal disease had wasted their frames to shadows, and corruption had already begun!

It was with some such thoughts as these that we determined, not many weeks since, to visit the interior of Newgate—in an amateur capacity, of course; and, having carried our intention into effect, we proceed to lay its results before our readers, in the hope—founded more upon the nature of the subject, than on any presumptuous confidence in our own descriptive powers—that this paper may not be found wholly devoid of interest. We have only to premise, that we do not intend to fatigue the reader with any statistical accounts of the prison; they will be found at length in numerous reports of numerous committees, and a variety of authorities of equal weight. We took no notes, made no memoranda, measured none of the yards, ascertained the exact number of inches in no particular room, are unable even to report of how many apartments the gaol is composed.

We saw the prison, and saw the prisoners; and what we did see, and what we thought, we will tell at once in our own way.

Having delivered our credentials to the servant who answered our knock at the door of the governor's[4] house, we were ushered into the "office;" a little room, on the right-hand side as you enter, with two windows looking into the Old Bailey: fitted up like an ordinary attorney's office, or merchant's counting-house, with the usual fixtures—a wainscoted partition, a shelf or two, a desk, a couple of stools, a pair of clerks, an almanack, a clock, and a few maps. After a little delay, occasioned by sending into the interior of the

---

2. In *Tales of the Arabian Nights*, an evil magician temporarily gets control of Aladdin's magic lamp and transports his palace to Africa. "Bedlam": a London hospital for the insane.

3. London's criminal court, which is located on the street of the same name.
4. The head of the prison.

prison for the officer whose duty it was to conduct us, that functionary arrived; a respectable-looking man of about two or three and fifty, in a broad-brimmed hat, and full suit of black, who, but for his keys, would have looked quite as much like a clergyman as a turnkey. We were disappointed; he had not even top-boots on. Following our conductor by a door opposite to that at which we had entered, we arrived at a small room, without any other furniture than a little desk, with a book for visitors' autographs, and a shelf, on which were a few boxes for papers, and casts of the heads and faces of the two notorious murderers, Bishop and Williams;[5] the former, in particular, exhibiting a style of head and set of features, which might have afforded sufficient moral grounds for his instant execution at any time, even had there been no other evidence against him. Leaving this room also, by an opposite door, we found ourself in the lodge which opens on the Old Bailey; one side of which is plentifully garnished with a choice collection of heavy sets of irons, including those worn by the redoubtable Jack Sheppard—genuine; and those *said* to have been graced by the sturdy limbs of the no less celebrated Dick Turpin[6]—doubtful. From this lodge, a heavy oaken gate, bound with iron, studded with nails of the same material, and guarded by another turn-key, opens on a few steps, if we remember right, which terminate in a narrow and dismal stone passage, running parallel with the Old Bailey, and leading to the different yards, through a number of tortuous and intricate windings, guarded in their turn by huge gates and gratings, whose appearance is sufficient to dispel at once the slightest hope of escape that any new comer may have entertained; and the very recollection of which, on eventually traversing the place again, involves one in a maze of confusion.

It is necessary to explain here, that the buildings in the prison, or in other words the different wards—form a square, of which the four sides abut respectively on the Old Bailey, the old College of Physicians (now forming a part of Newgate-market), the Sessions-house, and Newgate-street. The intermediate space is divided into several paved yards, in which the prisoners take such air and exercise as can be had in such a place. These yards, with the exception of that in which prisoners under sentence of death are confined (of which we shall presently give a more detailed description), run parallel with Newgate-street, and consequently from the Old Bailey, as it were, to Newgate-market. The women's side is in the right wing of the prison nearest the Sessions-house. As we were introduced into this part of the building first, we will adopt the same order, and introduce our readers to it also.

Turning to the right, then, down the passage to which we just now adverted, omitting any mention of intervening gates—for if we noticed every gate that was unlocked for us to pass through, and locked again as soon as we had passed, we should require a gate at every comma—we came to a door composed of thick bars of wood, through which were discernible, passing to and fro in a narrow yard, some twenty women: the majority of whom, however, as soon as they were aware of the presence of strangers, retreated to their wards. One side of this yard is railed off at a considerable distance, and formed into a kind of iron cage, about five feet ten inches in height, roofed at the top, and defended in front by iron bars, from which the friends of the

5. John Bishop and Thomas Head (aka "Williams"), notorious body snatchers who were hanged for murdering a young boy in 1831.

6. Notorious 18th-century thieves and highwaymen. "Irons": shackles.

female prisoners communicate with them. In one corner of this singular-looking den, was a yellow, haggard, decrepit old woman, in a tattered gown that had once been black, and the remains of an old straw bonnet, with faded ribbon of the same hue, in earnest conversation with a young girl—a prisoner, of course—of about two-and-twenty. It is impossible to imagine a more poverty-stricken object, or a creature so borne down in soul and body, by excess of misery and destitution as the old woman. The girl was a good-looking robust female, with a profusion of hair streaming about in the wind—for she had no bonnet on—and a man's silk pocket-handkerchief loosely thrown over a most ample pair of shoulders. The old woman was talking in that low, stifled tone of voice which tells so forcibly of mental anguish; and every now and then burst into an irrepressible sharp, abrupt cry of grief, the most distressing sound that ears can hear. The girl was perfectly unmoved. Hardened beyond all hope of redemption, she listened doggedly to her mother's entreaties, whatever they were: and, beyond inquiring after "Jem," and eagerly catching at the few halfpence her miserable parent had brought her, took no more apparent interest in the conversation than the most unconcerned spectators. Heaven knows there were enough of them, in the persons of the other prisoners in the yard, who were no more concerned by what was passing before their eyes, and within their hearing, than if they were blind and deaf. Why should they be? Inside the prison, and out, such scenes were too familiar to them, to excite even a passing thought, unless of ridicule or contempt for feelings which they had long since forgotten.

A little farther on, a squalid-looking woman in a slovenly, thick-bordered cap, with her arms muffled in a large red shawl, the fringed ends of which straggled nearly to the bottom of a dirty white apron, was communicating some instructions to *her* visitor—her daughter evidently. The girl was thinly clad, and shaking with the cold. Some ordinary word of recognition passed between her and her mother when she appeared at the grating, but neither hope, condolence, regret, nor affection was expressed on either side. The mother whispered her instructions, and the girl received them with her pinched-up half-starved features twisted into an expression of careful cunning. It was some scheme for the woman's defence that she was disclosing, perhaps; and a sullen smile came over the girl's face for an instant, as if she were pleased: not so much at the probability of her mother's liberation, as at the chance of her "getting off" in spite of her prosecutors. The dialogue was soon concluded; and with the same careless indifference with which they had approached each other, the mother turned towards the inner end of the yard, and the girl to the gate at which she had entered.

The girl belonged to a class—unhappily but too extensive—the very existence of which, should make men's hearts bleed. Barely past her childhood, it required but a glance to discover that she was one of those children, born and bred in neglect and vice, who have never known what childhood is: who have never been taught to love and court a parent's smile, or to dread a parent's frown. The thousand nameless endearments of childhood, its gaiety and its innocence, are alike unknown to them. They have entered at once upon the stern realities and miseries of life, and to their better nature it is almost hopeless to appeal in aftertimes, by any of the references which will awaken, if it be only for a moment, some good feeling in ordinary bosoms, however corrupt they may have become. Talk to *them* of parental solicitude, the happy days of childhood, and the merry games of infancy! Tell them of hunger and the streets, beggary and stripes, the gin-shop, the station-house, and the pawnbroker's, and they will understand you.

Two or three women were standing at different parts of the grating, conversing with their friends, but a very large proportion of the prisoners appeared to have no friends at all, beyond such of their old companions as might happen to be within the walls. So, passing hastily down the yard, and pausing only for an instant to notice the little incidents we have just recorded, we were conducted up a clean and well-lighted flight of stone stairs to one of the wards. There are several in this part of the building, but a description of one is a description of the whole.

It was a spacious, bare, whitewashed apartment, lighted of course, by windows looking into the interior of the prison, but far more light and airy than one could reasonably expect to find in such a situation. There was a large fire with a deal table before it, round which ten or a dozen women were seated on wooden forms at dinner. Along both sides of the room ran a shelf; below it, at regular intervals, a row of large hooks were fixed in the wall, on each of which was hung the sleeping mat of a prisoner: her rug and blanket being folded up, and placed on the shelf above. At night, these mats are placed on the floor, each beneath the hook on which it hangs during the day; and the ward is thus made to answer the purposes both of a day-room and sleeping apartment. Over the fireplace, was a large sheet of pasteboard, on which were displayed a variety of texts from Scripture, which were also scattered about the room in scraps about the size and shape of the copy-slips which are used in schools. On the table was a sufficient provision of a kind of stewed beef and brown bread, in pewter dishes, which are kept perfectly bright, and displayed on shelves in great order and regularity when they are not in use.

The women rose hastily, on our entrance, and retired in a hurried manner to either side of the fireplace. They were all cleanly—many of them decently—attired, and there was nothing peculiar, either in their appearance or demeanour. One or two resumed the needlework which they had probably laid aside at the commencement of their meal; others gazed at the visitors with listless curiosity; and a few retired behind their companions to the very end of the room, as if desirous to avoid even the casual observation of the strangers. Some old Irish women, both in this and other wards, to whom the thing was no novelty, appeared perfectly indifferent to our presence, and remained standing close to the seats from which they had just risen; but the general feeling among the females seemed to be one of uneasiness during the period of our stay among them: which was very brief. Not a word was uttered during the time of our remaining, unless, indeed, by the wardswoman in reply to some question which we put to the turnkey who accompanied us. In every ward on the female side, a wardswoman is appointed to preserve order, and a similar regulation is adopted among the males. The wardsmen and wardswomen are all prisoners, selected for good conduct. They alone are allowed the privilege of sleeping on bedsteads; a small stump bedstead[7] being placed in every ward for that purpose. On both sides of the gaol, is a small receiving-room, to which prisoners are conducted on their first recep-

---

7. Bedframe that ends at the level of the mattress.

tion, and whence they cannot be removed until they have been examined by the surgeon of the prison.[8]

Retracing our steps to the dismal passage in which we found ourselves at first (and which, by-the-bye, contains three or four dark cells for the accommodation of refractory prisoners), we were led through a narrow yard to the "school"—a portion of the prison set apart for boys under fourteen years of age. In a tolerable-sized room, in which were writing-materials and some copy-books, was the school-master, with a couple of his pupils; the remainder having been fetched from an adjoining apartment, the whole were drawn up in line for our inspection. There were fourteen of them in all, some with shoes, some without; some in pinafores[9] without jackets, others in jackets without pinafores, and one in scarce anything at all. The whole number, without an exception we believe, had been committed for trial on charges of pocket-picking; and fourteen such terrible little faces we never beheld.— There was not one redeeming feature among them—not a glance of honesty—not a wink expressive of anything but the gallows and the hulks,[1] in the whole collection. As to anything like shame or contrition, that was entirely out of the question. They were evidently quite gratified at being thought worth the trouble of looking at; their idea appeared to be, that we had come to see Newgate as a grand affair, and that they were an indispensable part of the show; and every boy as he "fell in" to the line, actually seemed as pleased and important as if he had done something excessively meritorious in getting there at all. We never looked upon a more disagreeable sight, because we never saw fourteen such hopeless creatures of neglect, before.

On either side of the school-yard is a yard for men, in one of which—that towards Newgate-street—prisoners of the more respectable class are confined. Of the other, we have little description to offer, as the different wards necessarily partake of the same character. They are provided, like the wards on the women's side, with mats and rugs, which are disposed of in the same manner during the day; the only very striking difference between their appearance and that of the wards inhabited by the females, is the utter absence of any employment. Huddled together on two opposite forms, by the fireside, sit twenty men perhaps; here, a boy in livery; there, a man in a rough great-coat and top-boots; farther on, a desperate-looking fellow in his shirt sleeves, with an old Scotch cap[2] upon his shaggy head; near him again, a tall ruffian, in a smock-frock; next to him, a miserable being of distressed appearance, with his head resting on his hand;—all alike in one respect, all idle and listless. When they do leave the fire, sauntering moodily about, lounging in the window, or leaning against the wall, vacantly swinging their bodies to and fro. With the exception of a man reading an old newspaper, in two or three instances, this was the case in every ward we entered.

The only communication these men have with their friends, is through two close iron gratings, with an intermediate space of about a yard in width between the two, so that nothing can be handed across, nor can the prisoner

---

8. The regulations of the prison relative to the confinement of prisoners during the day, their sleeping at night, their taking their meals, and other matters of gaol economy, have been all altered—greatly for the better—since this sketch was published. Even the construction of the prison itself has been changed [Dickens's note].
9. Aprons.
1. Prison ships.
2. Brimless woolen hat with two tails.

have any communication by touch with the person who visits him. The married men have a separate grating, at which to see their wives, but its construction is the same.

The prison chapel is situated at the back of the governor's house: the latter having no windows looking into the interior of the prison. Whether the associations connected with the place—the knowledge that here a portion of the burial service is, on some dreadful occasions, performed over the quick[3] and not upon the dead—cast over it a still more gloomy and sombre air than art has imparted to it, we know not, but its appearance is very striking. There is something in a silent and deserted place of worship, solemn and impressive at any time; and the very dissimilarity of this one from any we have been accustomed to, only enhances the impression. The meanness of its appointments—the bare and scanty pulpit, with the paltry painted pillars on either side—the women's gallery with its great heavy curtain—the men's with its unpainted benches and dingy front—the tottering little table at the altar, with the commandments on the wall above it, scarcely legible through lack of paint, and dust and damp—so unlike the velvet and gilding, the marble and wood, of a modern church—are strange and striking. There is one object, too, which rivets the attention and fascinates the gaze, and from which we may turn horror-stricken in vain, for the recollection of it will haunt us, waking and sleeping, for a long time afterwards. Immediately below the reading-desk, on the floor of the chapel, and forming the most conspicuous object in its little area, is *the condemned pew*; a huge black pen, in which the wretched people, who are singled out for death, are placed on the Sunday preceding their execution, in sight of all their fellow-prisoners, from many of whom they may have been separated but a week before, to hear prayers for their own souls, to join in the responses of their own burial service, and to listen to an address, warning their recent companions to take example by their fate, and urging themselves, while there is yet time—nearly four-and-twenty hours—to "turn, and flee from the wrath to come!"[4] Imagine what have been the feelings of the men whom that fearful pew has enclosed, and of whom, between the gallows and the knife, no mortal remnant may now remain! Think of the hopeless clinging to life to the last, and the wild despair, far exceeding in anguish the felon's death itself, by which they have heard the certainty of their speedy transmission to another world, with all their crimes upon their heads, rung into their ears by the officiating clergyman!

At one time—and at no distant period either—the coffins of the men about to be executed, were placed in that pew, upon the seat by their side, during the whole service. It may seem incredible, but it is true. Let us hope that the increased spirit of civilization and humanity which abolished this frightful and degrading custom, may extend itself to other usages equally barbarous; usages which have not even the plea of utility in their defense, as every year's experience has shown them to be more and more inefficacious.

Leaving the chapel, descending to the passage so frequently alluded to, and crossing the yard before noticed as being allotted to prisoners of a more respectable description than the generality of men confined here, the visitor arrives at a thick iron gate of great size and strength. Having been admitted

3. Living.
4. Cf. Matthew 3.7 and Luke 3.7: "O generation of vipers, who hath warned you to flee from the wrath to come?"

through it by the turnkey on duty, he turns sharp round to the left, and pauses before another gate; and, having passed this last barrier, he stands in the most terrible part of this gloomy building—the condemned ward.

The press-yard,[5] well known by name to newspaper readers, from its frequent mention in accounts of executions, is at the corner of the building, and next to the ordinary's[6] house, in Newgate-street: running from Newgate-street, towards the centre of the prison, parallel with Newgate-market. It is a long, narrow court, of which a portion of the wall in Newgate-street forms one end, and the gate the other. At the upper end, on the left-hand—that is, adjoining the wall in Newgate-street—is a cistern of water, and at the bottom a double grating (of which the gate itself forms a part) similar to that before described. Through these grates the prisoners are allowed to see their friends; a turnkey always remaining in the vacant space between, during the whole interview. Immediately on the right as you enter, is a building containing the press-room, day-room, and cells; the yard is on every side surrounded by lofty walls guarded by *chevaux de frise*;[7] and the whole is under the constant inspection of vigilant and experienced turnkeys.

In the first apartment into which we were conducted—which was at the top of a staircase, and immediately over the press-room—were five-and-twenty or thirty prisoners, all under sentence of death, awaiting the result of the recorder's report—men of all ages and appearances, from a hardened old offender with swarthy face and grizzly beard of three days' growth, to a handsome boy, not fourteen years old, and of singularly youthful appearance even for that age, who had been condemned for burglary. There was nothing remarkable in the appearance of these prisoners. One or two decently-dressed men were brooding with a dejected air over the fire; several little groups of two or three had been engaged in conversation at the upper end of the room, or in the windows; and the remainder were crowded round a young man seated at a table, who appeared to be engaged in teaching the younger ones to write. The room was large, airy, and clean. There was very little anxiety or mental suffering depicted in the countenance of any of the men;—they had all been sentenced to death, it is true, and the recorder's report had not yet been made; but, we question whether there was a man among them, notwithstanding, who did not *know* that although he had undergone the ceremony, it never was intended that his life should be sacrificed. On the table lay a Testament, but there were no tokens of its having been in recent use.

In the press-room below, were three men, the nature of whose offence rendered it necessary to separate them, even from their companions in guilt. It is a long, sombre room, with two windows sunk into the stone wall, and here the wretched men are pinioned on the morning of their execution, before moving towards the scaffold. The fate of one of these prisoners was uncertain; some mitigatory circumstances having come to light since his trial, which had been humanely represented in the proper quarter. The other two had nothing to expect from the mercy of the crown; their doom was sealed; no plea could be urged in extenuation of their crime, and they well knew that for them there was no hope in this world. "The two short ones," the turnkey whispered, "were dead men."

5. Area from which criminals condemned to death started for the place of execution.
6. Clergyman appointed to prepare criminals for execution.
7. Line of spikes (French).

The man to whom we have alluded as entertaining some hopes of escape, was lounging, at the greatest distance he could place between himself and his companions, in the window nearest to the door. He was probably aware of our approach, and had assumed an air of courageous indifference; his face was purposely averted towards the window, and he stirred not an inch while we were present. The other two men were at the upper end of the room. One of them, who was imperfectly seen in the dim light, had his back towards us, and was stooping over the fire, with his right arm on the mantel-piece, and his head sunk upon it. The other, was leaning on the sill of the farthest window. The light fell full upon him, and communicated to his pale, haggard face, and disordered hair, an appearance which, at that distance, was ghastly. His cheek rested upon his hand; and, with his face a little raised, and his eyes wildly staring before him, he seemed to be unconsciously intent on counting the chinks in the opposite wall. We passed this room again afterwards. The first man was pacing up and down the court with a firm military step—he had been a soldier in the foot-guards—and a cloth cap jauntily thrown on one side of his head. He bowed respectfully to our conductor, and the salute was returned. The other two still remained in the positions we have described, and were as motionless as statues.[8]

A few paces up the yard, and forming a continuation of the building, in which are the two rooms we have just quitted, lie the condemned cells. The entrance is by a narrow and obscure staircase leading to a dark passage, in which a charcoal stove casts a lurid tint over the objects in its immediate vicinity, and diffuses something like warmth around. From the left-hand side of this passage, the massive door of every cell on the story opens; and from it alone can they be approached. There are three of these passages, and three of these ranges of cells, one above the other; but in size, furniture and appearance, they are all precisely alike. Prior to the recorder's report being made, all the prisoners under sentence of death are removed from the day-room at five o'clock in the afternoon, and locked up in these cells, where they are allowed a candle until ten o'clock; and here they remain until seven next morning. When the warrant for a prisoner's execution arrives, he is removed to the cells and confined in one of them until he leaves it for the scaffold. He is at liberty to walk in the yard; but, both in his walks and in his cell, he is constantly attended by a turnkey who never leaves him on any pretence.

We entered the first cell. It was a stone dungeon, eight feet long by six wide, with a bench at the upper end, under which were a common rug, a bible, and prayer-book. An iron candlestick was fixed into the wall at the side; and a small high window in the back admitted as much air and light as could struggle in between a double row of heavy, crossed iron bars. It contained no other furniture of any description.

Conceive the situation of a man, spending his last night on earth in this cell. Buoyed up with some vague and undefined hope of reprieve, he knew not why—indulging in some wild and visionary idea of escaping, he knew not how—hour after hour of the three preceding days allowed him for preparation, has fled with a speed which no man living would deem possible, for none but this dying man can know. He has wearied his friends with entreaties, exhausted the attendants with importunities, neglected in his feverish

8. These two men were executed shortly afterwards. The other was respited during his Majesty's pleasure [Dickens's note].

restlessness the timely warnings of his spiritual consoler; and, now that the illusion is at last dispelled, now that eternity is before him and guilt behind, now that his fears of death amount almost to madness, and an overwhelming sense of his helpless, hopeless state rushes upon him, he is lost and stupified, and has neither thoughts to turn to, nor power to call upon, the Almighty Being, from whom alone he can seek mercy and forgiveness, and before whom his repentance can alone avail.

Hours have glided by, and still he sits upon the same stone bench with folded arms, heedless alike of the fast decreasing time before him, and the urgent entreaties of the good man at his side. The feeble light is wasting gradually, and the deathlike stillness of the street without, broken only by the rumbling of some passing vehicle which echoes mournfully through the empty yards, warns him that the night is waning fast away. The deep bell of St. Paul's strikes—one! He heard it; it has roused him. Seven hours left! He paces the narrow limits of his cell with rapid strides, cold drops of terror starting on his forehead, and every muscle of his frame quivering with agony. Seven hours! He suffers himself to be led to his seat, mechanically takes the bible which is placed in his hand, and tries to read and listen. No: his thoughts will wander. The book is torn and soiled by use—and like the book he read his lessons in, at school, just forty years ago! He has never bestowed a thought upon it, perhaps, since he left it as a child: and yet the place, the time, the room—nay, the very boys he played with, crowd as vividly before him as if they were scenes of yesterday; and some forgotten phrase, some childish word, rings in his ears like the echo of one uttered but a minute since. The voice of the clergyman recalls him to himself. He is reading from the sacred book its solemn promises of pardon for repentance, and its awful denunciation of obdurate men. He falls upon his knees and clasps his hands to pray. Hush! what sound was that? He starts upon his feet. It cannot be two yet. Hark! Two quarters have struck;—the third—the fourth. It is! Six hours left. Tell him not of repentance! Six hours' repentance for eight times six years of guilt and sin! He buries his face in his hands, and throws himself on the bench.

Worn with watching and excitement, he sleeps, and the same unsettled state of mind pursues him in his dreams. An insupportable load is taken from his breast; he is walking with his wife in a pleasant field, with the bright sky above them, and a fresh and boundless prospect on every side—how different from the stone walls of Newgate! She is looking—not as she did when he saw her for the last time in that dreadful place, but as she used when he loved her—long, long ago, before misery and ill-treatment had altered her looks, and vice had changed his nature, and she is leaning upon his arm, and looking up into his face with tenderness and affection—and he does *not* strike her now, nor rudely shake her from him. And oh! how glad he is to tell her all he had forgotten in that last hurried interview, and to fall on his knees before her and fervently beseech her pardon for all the unkindness and cruelty that wasted her form and broke her heart! The scene suddenly changes. He is on his trial again: there are the judge and jury, and prosecutors, and witnesses, just as they were before. How full the court is—what a sea of heads—with a gallows, too, and a scaffold—and how all those people stare at *him*! Verdict, "Guilty." No matter; he will escape.

The night is dark and cold, the gates have been left open, and in an instant he is in the street, flying from the scene of his imprisonment like the wind. The streets are cleared, the open fields are gained and the broad wide country lies before him. Onward he dashes in the midst of darkness, over hedge and ditch, through mud and pool, bounding from spot to spot with a speed and lightness, astonishing even to himself. At length he pauses; he must be safe from pursuit now; he will stretch himself on that bank and sleep till sunrise.

A period of unconsciousness succeeds. He wakes, cold and wretched. The dull gray light of morning is stealing into the cell, and falls upon the form of the attendant turnkey. Confused by his dreams, he starts from his uneasy bed in momentary uncertainty. It is but momentary. Every object in the narrow cell is too frightfully real to admit of doubt or mistake. He is the condemned felon again, guilty and despairing; and in two hours more will be dead.

1835   1836

ROBERT BROWNING
1812–1889

During the years of his marriage Robert Browning was sometimes referred to as "Mrs. Browning's husband." Elizabeth Barrett was at that time a famous poet, whereas her husband was a relatively unknown experimenter whose poems were greeted with misunderstanding or indifference. Not until the 1860s did he at last gain a public and become recognized as the rival or equal of Tennyson. In the twentieth century his reputation has persisted but in an unusual way: his poetry is admired by two groups of readers widely different in tastes. To one group, among whom are the Browning societies that have flourished in England and America, Browning is a wise philosopher and religious teacher who resolved the doubts that had troubled Arnold and Tennyson.

The second group of readers enjoy Browning less for his attempt to solve problems of religious doubt than for his attempt to solve the problems of how poetry should be written. Such poets as Ezra Pound and Robert Lowell have recognized that more than any other nineteenth-century poet, it was Browning who energetically hacked through a trail that has subsequently become the main road of twentieth-century poetry. In *Poetry and the Age* (1953) Randall Jarrell remarked how "the dramatic monologue, which once had depended for its effect upon being a departure from the norm of poetry, now became in one form or another the norm."

The dramatic monologue, as Browning uses it, separates the speaker from the poet in such a way that the reader must work through the words of the speaker to discover the meaning of the poet. For example, in the well-known early monologue *My Last Duchess,* we listen to the duke as he speaks of his dead wife. From his one-sided conversation we piece together the situation, both past and present, and we infer what sort of woman the duchess really was and what sort of man the duke is. Ultimately, we may also infer what the poet himself thinks of the speaker he has created. In this poem, it is fairly easy to reach such a judgment, although the pleasure of the poem results from our reconstruction of a story quite different from the one the duke thinks he is telling. Many of Browning's poems are far less stable, and it is difficult to discern the relationship of the poet to his speaker. In reading *A Gram-*

marian's Funeral, for example, can we be sure that the central character is a hero? Or is he merely a fool? In *"Childe Roland to the Dark Tower Came"* is the speaker describing a phantasmagoric landscape of his own paranoid imagining or is the poem a fable of courage and defiance in a modern wasteland?

In addition to his experiments with the dramatic monologue, Browning also experimented with language and syntax. The grotesque rhymes and jaw-breaking diction that he often employs have been repugnant to some critics; George Santayana, for instance, dismissed him as a clumsy barbarian. But to those who appreciate Browning, the incongruities of language are a humorous and appropriate counterpart to an imperfect world. Ezra Pound's tribute to "Old Hippety-Hop o' the accents," as he addresses Browning, is both affectionate and memorable:

> Heart that was big as the bowels of Vesuvius
> Words that were winged as her sparks in eruption,
> Eagled and thundered as Jupiter Pluvius
> Sound in your wind past all signs o' corruption.

Robert Browning was born in Camberwell, a London suburb. His father, a bank clerk, was a learned man with an extensive library. His mother was a kindly, religious-minded woman, interested in music, whose love for her brilliant son was warmly reciprocated. Until the time of his marriage, at the age of thirty-four, Browning was rarely absent from his parents' home. He attended a boarding school near Camberwell, traveled a little (to Russia and Italy), and was a student at the University of London for a short period, but he preferred to pursue his education at home, where he was tutored in foreign languages, music, boxing, and horsemanship and where he read omnivorously. From this unusual education he acquired a store of knowledge on which to draw for the background of his poems.

The "obscurity" of which his contemporaries complained in his earlier poetry may be partly accounted for by the circumstances of Browning's education, but it also reflects his anxious desire to avoid exposing himself too explicitly before his readers. His first poem, *Pauline,* published when he was twenty-one, had been modeled on the example of Shelley, the most personal of poets. When an otherwise admiring review by John Stuart Mill noted that the young author was afflicted with an "intense and morbid self-consciousness," Browning was overwhelmed with embarrassment. He resolved to avoid confessional writings thereafter.

One way of reducing the personal element in his poetry was to write plays instead of soul-searching narratives or lyrics. In 1836, encouraged by the actor W. C. Macready, Browning began work on his first play, *Strafford,* a historical tragedy that lasted only four nights when it was produced in London in 1837. For ten years, the young writer struggled to write for the theater, but all his stage productions remained failures. Nevertheless, writing dialogue for actors led him to explore another form more congenial to his genius, the dramatic monologue, a form that enabled him through imaginary speakers to avoid explicit autobiography. His first collection of such monologues, *Dramatic Lyrics,* appeared in 1842; but it received no more critical enthusiasm than did his plays.

Browning's resolution to avoid the subjective manner of Shelley did not preclude his being influenced by the earlier poet in other ways. At fourteen, when he first discovered Shelley's works, he became an atheist and liberal. Although he grew away from the atheism, after a struggle, and also the extreme phases of his liberalism, he retained from Shelley's influence something permanent and more difficult to define: an ardent dedication to ideals (often undefined ideals) and an energetic striving toward goals (often undefined goals).

Browning's ardent romanticism also found expression in his love affair with Elizabeth Barrett, which had the dramatic ingredients of Browning's own favorite story of St. George rescuing the maiden from the dragon. Almost everything seemed unpropitious when Browning met Elizabeth Barrett in 1845. She was six years older than he was, a semi-invalid, jealously guarded by her possessively tyrannical father. But love, as the poet was to say later, is best; and love swept aside all obstacles. After their elopement to Italy, the former semi-invalid was soon enjoying good health and a full life. The husband likewise seemed to thrive during the years of this remarkable marriage. His most memorable volume of poems, *Men and Women* (1855), reflects his enjoyment of Italy: its picturesque landscapes and lively street scenes as well as its monuments from the past—its Renaissance past in particular.

The happy fifteen-year sojourn in Italy ended in 1861 with Elizabeth's death. The widower returned to London with his son. During the twenty-eight years remaining to him, the quantity of verse he produced did not diminish. Nor, during the first decade, did it decrease in quality. *Dramatis Personae* (1864) is a volume containing some of his finest monologues, such as *Caliban upon Setebos.* And in 1868 he published his greatest single poem, *The Ring and the Book,* which was inspired by his discovery of an old book of legal records concerning a murder trial in seventeenth-century Rome. His poem tells the story of a brutally sadistic husband, Count Guido Franceschini. The middle-aged Guido grows dissatisfied with his young wife, Pompilia, and accuses her of having adulterous relations with a handsome priest who, like St. George, had tried to rescue her from the dragon's den in which her husband confined her. Eventually Guido stabs his wife to death and is himself executed. In a series of twelve books, Browning retells this tale of violence, presenting it from the contrasting points of view of participants and spectators. Because of its vast scale, *The Ring and the Book* is like a Victorian novel, but in its experiments with multiple points of view it anticipates later novels such as Conrad's *Lord Jim* (1900).

After *The Ring and the Book* several more volumes appeared. In general, Browning's writings during the last two decades of his life suffer from a certain mechanical repetition of mannerism and an excess of argumentation—faults into which he may have been led by the unqualified enthusiasm of his admirers, for it was during this period that he gained his great following. When he died, in 1889, he was buried in Westminster Abbey.

During the London years, Browning became abundantly fond of social life. He dined at the homes of friends and at clubs, where he enjoyed port wine and conversation. He would talk loudly and emphatically about many topics—except his own poetry, about which he was usually reticent.

Despite his bursts of outspokenness, Browning's character seemed, in Hardy's words, "*the* literary puzzle of the nineteenth century." Like Yeats, he was a poet preoccupied with masks. On the occasion of his burial, his friend Henry James reflected that many oddities and many great writers have been buried in Westminster Abbey, "but none of the odd ones have been so great and none of the great ones been so odd."

Just as Browning's character is hard to identify so also are his poems difficult to relate to the age in which they were written. Bishops and painters of the Renaissance, physicians of the Roman Empire, musicians of eighteenth-century Germany—as we explore this gallery of talking portraits we seem to be in a world of time long past, remote from the world of steam engines and disputes about human beings' descent from the ape.

Yet our first impression is misleading. Many of these portraits explore problems that confronted Browning's contemporaries, especially problems of faith and doubt, good and evil, and problems of the function of the artist in modern life. *Caliban upon Setebos,* for example, is a highly topical critique of Darwinism and of natural (as opposed to supernatural) religions. Browning's own attitude toward these topics is partially concealed because of his use of speakers and of settings from earlier ages, yet we do encounter certain recurrent religious assumptions that we can safely assign to the poet himself. The most recurrent is that God has created an imperfect world as a kind of testing ground, a "vale of soul-making," as Keats had said. It followed, for Browning's purposes, that the human soul must be immortal and that heaven itself be perfect. As Abt Vogler affirms: "On the earth the broken arcs; in the heaven, a perfect round." Armed with such a faith, Browning sometimes gives the impression that he was himself untroubled by the doubts that gnawed at the hearts of Arnold and Clough and Tennyson. Yet Browning's apparent optimism is consistently being tested by his bringing to light the evils of human nature. His gallery of villains— murderers, sadistic husbands, mean and petty manipulators—is an extraordinary one. Few writers, in fact, seem to have been more aware of the existence of evil.

A second aspect of Browning's poetry that separates it from the Victorian age is its style. The most representative Victorian poets such as Tennyson and Dante Gabriel Rossetti write in the manner of Keats, Milton, Spenser, and of classical poets such as Virgil. Theirs is the central stylistic tradition in English poetry, one that favors smoothly polished texture, elevated diction and subjects, and pleasing liquidity of sound. Browning draws from a different tradition, more colloquial and discordant, a tradition that includes the poetry of John Donne, the soliloquies of Shakespeare, and certain features of the narrative style of Chaucer. Of most significance are Browning's affinities with Donne. Both poets sacrifice, on occasion, the pleasures of harmony and of a consistent elevation of tone by using a harshly discordant style and unexpected juxtapositions that startle us into an awareness of a world of everyday realities and trivialities. Readers who dislike this kind of poetry in Browning or in Donne argue that it suffers from prosiness. Oscar Wilde once described the novelist George Meredith as "a prose Browning." And so, he added, was Browning. Wilde's joke may help us to relate Browning to his contemporaries. For if Browning seems out of step with other Victorian poets, he is by no means out of step with his contemporaries in prose. The grotesque, which plays such a prominent role in the style and subject matter of Carlyle and Dickens and in the aesthetic theories of John Ruskin, is equally prominent in Browning's verse:

> Fee, faw, fum! bubble and squeak!
> Blessedest Thursday's the fat of the week.
> Rumble and tumble, sleek and rough,
> Stinking and savory, smug and gruff.

Like Carlyle's *Sartor Resartus* these lines from *Holy-Cross Day* present a situation of grave seriousness with noisy jocularity. It was fitting that Browning and Carlyle remained good friends, even though the elder writer kept urging Browning to give up verse in favor of prose.

The link between Browning and the Victorian prose writers is not limited to style. With the later generation of Victorian novelists, George Eliot, George Meredith, and Henry James, Browning shares a central preoccupation. Like Eliot in particular, he was interested in exposing the devious ways in which our minds work and the complexity of our motives. "My stress lay on incidents in the development of a human soul," he wrote; "little else is worth study." His psychological insights can be illustrated in such poems as *The Bishop Orders His Tomb* and *Andrea del Sarto*. Although these are spoken monologues, not inner monologues in the manner of James Joyce, the insight into the workings of the mind is similarly acute. As in reading Joyce, we must be on our guard to follow the rapid shifts of the speakers' mental processes as jumps are made from one cluster of associations to another. A further challenge for the reader of Browning is to identify what has been left out. As was remarked in a letter by the 1890s poet Ernest Dowson, Browning's "masterpieces in verse" demonstrate both "subtlety" and "the tact of omission." *My Last Duchess*, he added, "is pure Henry James."

But Browning's role as a forerunner of twentieth-century literature should not blind us to his essential Victorianism. Energy is the most characteristic aspect of his writing and of the man (Turgenev compared Browning's handshake to an electric shock). Gerard Manley Hopkins described Browning as "a man bouncing up from table with his mouth full of bread and cheese and saying that he meant to stand no blasted nonsense." This buoyancy imparts a creative vitality to all of Browning's writings.

Porphyria's Lover[1]

The rain set early in tonight,
    The sullen wind was soon awake,
It tore the elm-tops down for spite,
    And did its worst to vex the lake:
5   I listened with heart fit to break.
When glided in Porphyria; straight
    She shut the cold out and the storm,
And kneeled and made the cheerless grate
    Blaze up, and all the cottage warm;
10   Which done, she rose, and from her form
Withdrew the dripping cloak and shawl,
    And laid her soiled gloves by, untied
Her hat and let the damp hair fall,
    And, last, she sat down by my side
15   And called me. When no voice replied,
She put my arm about her waist,
    And made her smooth white shoulder bare,
And all her yellow hair displaced,
    And, stooping, made my cheek lie there,
20   And spread, o'er all, her yellow hair,
Murmuring how she loved me—she
    Too weak, for all her heart's endeavor,
To set its struggling passion free
    From pride, and vainer ties dissever,
25   And give herself to me forever.
But passion sometimes would prevail,
    Nor could tonight's gay feast restrain
A sudden thought of one so pale
    For love of her, and all in vain:
30   So, she was come through wind and rain.
Be sure I looked up at her eyes
    Happy and proud; at last I knew
Porphyria worshiped me: surprise
    Made my heart swell, and still it grew
35   While I debated what to do.
That moment she was mine, mine, fair,
    Perfectly pure and good: I found
A thing to do, and all her hair
    In one long yellow string I wound
40   Three times her little throat around,
And strangled her. No pain felt she;
    I am quite sure she felt no pain.

1. One of a pair of monologues originally published under the title *Madhouse Cells*, a title that emphasized the abnormal state of mind of the speaker.

As a shut bud that holds a bee,
　　I warily oped her lids: again
45　　Laughed the blue eyes without a stain.
And I untightened next the tress
　　About her neck; her cheek once more
Blushed bright beneath my burning kiss:
　　I propped her head up as before,
50　　Only, this time my shoulder bore
Her head, which droops upon it still:
　　The smiling rosy little head,
So glad it has its utmost will,
　　That all it scorned at once is fled,
55　　And I, its love, am gained instead!
Porphyria's love: she guessed not how
　　Her darling one wish would be heard.
And thus we sit together now,
　　And all night long we have not stirred,
60　　And yet God has not said a word!

1834   1836, 1842

Soliloquy of the Spanish Cloister

1

Gr-r-r—there go, my heart's abhorrence!
　　Water your damned flowerpots, do!
If hate killed men, Brother Lawrence,
　　God's blood, would not mine kill you!
5　What? your myrtle bush wants trimming?
　　Oh, that rose has prior claims—
Needs its leaden vase filled brimming?
　　Hell dry you up with its flames!

2

At the meal we sit together:
10　　*Salve tibi!*[1] I must hear
Wise talk of the kind of weather,
　　Sort of season, time of year:
Not a plenteous cork crop: scarcely
　　Dare we hope oak-galls,[2] *I doubt:*
15　*What's the Latin name for "parsley"?*
　　What's the Greek name for Swine's Snout?[3]

3

Whew! We'll have our platter burnished,
　　Laid with care on our own shelf!
With a fire-new spoon we're furnished,

20 And a goblet for ourself,
  Rinsed like something sacrificial
   Ere 'tis fit to touch our chaps°   *jaws*
  Marked with L. for our initial!
   (He-he! There his lily snaps!)

4

25 *Saint,* forsooth! While brown Dolores
   Squats outside the Convent bank
  With Sanchicha, telling stories,
   Steeping tresses in the tank,
  Blue-black, lustrous, thick like horsehairs,
30   —Can't I see his dead eye glow,
  Bright as 'twere a Barbary corsair's?[4]
   (That is, if he'd let it show!)

5

  When he finishes refection,°   *dinner*
   Knife and fork he never lays
35 Cross-wise, to my recollection,
   As do I, in Jesu's praise.
  I the Trinity illustrate,
   Drinking watered orange pulp—
  In three sips the Arian[5] frustrate;
40   While he drains his at one gulp.

6

  Oh, those melons? If he's able
   We're to have a feast! so nice!
  One goes to the Abbot's table,
   All of us get each a slice.
45 How go on your flowers? None double?
   Not one fruit-sort can you spy?
  Strange!—And I, too, at such trouble,
   Keep them close-nipped on the sly!

7

  There's a great text in Galatians,[6]
50   Once you trip on it, entails
  Twenty-nine distinct damnations,
   One sure, if another fails:
  If I trip him just a-dying,
   Sure of heaven as sure can be,
55 Spin him round and send him flying
   Off to hell, a Manichee?[7]

4. Pirate of the Barbary Coast of northern Africa, renowned for fierceness and lechery.
5. Heretical follower of Arius (256–336), who denied the doctrine of the Trinity.
6. The speaker hopes to obtain Lawrence's damnation by luring him into a heresy, this to be accomplished by exposing him to the difficult task of interpreting "Galatians" in an unswervingly orthodox way. In Galatians 5.15–23, St. Paul specifies an assortment of "works of the flesh" that lead to damnation, which could make up a total of "twenty-nine" (line 51).
7. A heretic, a follower of Mani (3rd century), Persian prophet.

8

Or, my scrofulous French novel
On gray paper with blunt type!
Simply glance at it, you grovel
60   Hand and foot in Belial's gripe:
If I double down its pages
At the woeful sixteenth print,
When he gathers his greengages,
Ope a sieve and slip it in't?

9

65 Or, there's Satan!—one might venture
Pledge one's soul to him, yet leave
Such a flaw in the indenture
As he'd miss till, past retrieve,
Blasted lay that rose-acacia[8]
70   We're so proud of! *Hy, Zy, Hine*[9]
'St, there's Vespers! *Plena gratiâ
Ave, Virgo!*[1] Gr-r-r—you swine!

ca. 1839   1842

My Last Duchess[1]

Ferrara

That's my last Duchess painted on the wall,
Looking as if she were alive. I call
That piece a wonder, now: Frà Pandolf's[2] hands
Worked busily a day, and there she stands.
5 Will 't please you sit and look at her? I said
"Frà Pandolf" by design, for never read
Strangers like you that pictured countenance,
The depth and passion of its earnest glance,
But to myself they turned (since none puts by
10 The curtain I have drawn for you, but I)
And seemed as they would ask me, if they durst,
How such a glance came there; so, not the first
Are you to turn and ask thus. Sir, 'twas not
Her husband's presence only, called that spot
15 Of joy into the Duchess' cheek: perhaps
Frà Pandolf chanced to say "Her mantle laps
Over my lady's wrist too much," or "Paint
Must never hope to reproduce the faint

---

8. The speaker would pledge his own soul to Satan in return for blasting Lawrence and his "rose-acacia," but the pledge would be so cleverly worded that the speaker himself would not have to pay his debt to Satan. There would be an escape clause ("flaw in the indenture") for himself.
9. Perhaps the opening of a mysterious curse against Lawrence.
1. Full of grace, Hail, Virgin! (Latin). The speaker's twisted state of mind may be reflected in

his mixed-up version of the prayer to Mary: "Ave, Maria, gratia plena."
1. The poem is based on incidents in the life of Alfonso II, duke of Ferrara in Italy, whose first wife, Lucrezia, a young woman, died in 1561 after three years of marriage. Following her death, the duke negotiated through an agent to marry a niece of the count of Tyrol. Browning represents the duke as addressing this agent.
2. Brother Pandolf, an imaginary painter.

Half-flush that dies along her throat": such stuff
20 Was courtesy, she thought, and cause enough
For calling up that spot of joy. She had
A heart—how shall I say?—too soon made glad,
Too easily impressed; she liked whate'er
She looked on, and her looks went everywhere.
25 Sir, 'twas all one! My favor at her breast,
The dropping of the daylight in the West,
The bough of cherries some officious fool
Broke in the orchard for her, the white mule
She rode with round the terrace—all and each
30 Would draw from her alike the approving speech,
Or blush, at least. She thanked men—good! but thanked
Somehow—I know not how—as if she ranked
My gift of a nine-hundred-years-old name
With anybody's gift. Who'd stoop to blame
35 This sort of trifling? Even had you skill
In speech—(which I have not)—to make your will
Quite clear to such an one, and say, "Just this
Or that in you disgusts me; here you miss,
Or there exceed the mark"—and if she let
40 Herself be lessoned so, nor plainly set
Her wits to yours, forsooth, and made excuse
—E'en then would be some stooping; and I choose
Never to stoop. Oh sir, she smiled, no doubt,
Whene'er I passed her; but who passed without
45 Much the same smile? This grew; I gave commands;
Then all smiles stopped together. There she stands
As if alive. Will 't please you rise? We'll meet
The company below, then. I repeat,
The Count your master's known munificence
50 Is ample warrant that no just pretense
Of mine for dowry will be disallowed;
Though his fair daughter's self, as I avowed
At starting, is my object. Nay, we'll go
Together down, sir. Notice Neptune, though,
55 Taming a sea horse, thought a rarity,
Which Claus of Innsbruck[3] cast in bronze for me!

1842   1842

The Laboratory

Ancien Régime[1]

I

Now that I, tying thy glass mask tightly,
May gaze thro' these faint smokes curling whitely,

---

3. An unidentified or imaginary sculptor. The count of Tyrol had his capital at Innsbruck.

1. The regime in France before the Revolution of 1789.

As thou pliest thy trade in this devil's-smithy—
Which is the poison to poison her, prithee?

2

5   He is with her, and they know that I know
Where they are, what they do: they believe my tears flow
While they laugh, laugh at me, at me fled to the drear
Empty church, to pray God in, for them!—I am here.

3

Grind away, moisten and mash up thy paste,
10   Pound at thy powder—I am not in haste!
Better sit thus, and observe thy strange things,
Than go where men wait me and dance at the King's.

4

That in the mortar—you call it a gum?
Ah, the brave tree whence such gold oozings come!
15   And yonder soft phial, the exquisite blue,
Sure to taste sweetly, is that poison too?

5

Had I but all of them, thee and thy treasures,
What a wild crowd of invisible pleasures!
To carry pure death in an earring, a casket,
20   A signet, a fan-mount, a filigree basket!

6

Soon, at the King's,[2] a mere lozenge to give,
And Pauline should have just thirty minutes to live!
But to light a pastile, and Elise, with her head
And her breast and her arms and her hands, should drop dead!

7

25   Quick—is it finished? The color's too grim!
Why not soft like the phial's, enticing and dim?
Let it brighten her drink, let her turn it and stir,
And try it and taste, ere she fix and prefer!

8

What a drop! She's not little, no minion[3] like me!
30   That's why she ensnared him: this never will free
The soul from those masculine eyes—say, "no!"
To that pulse's magnificent come-and-go.

---

2. Probably King Louis XIV of France (1643–
1715). In the 1670s, a police investigation disclosed that an extraordinary number of women and
men attached to the king's court had been disposing of rivals and enemies by poisonings. Some
thirty-six of the accused courtiers and the dealers
from whom they had purchased poisons were punished by torture and burned to death.
3. A dainty and delicate person.

9

For only last night, as they whispered, I brought
My own eyes to bear on her so, that I thought
35 Could I keep them one half minute fixed, she would fall
Shriveled; she fell not; yet this does it all!

10

Not that I bid you spare her the pain;
Let death be felt and the proof remain:
Brand, burn up, bite into its grace—
40 He is sure to remember her dying face!

11

Is it done? Take my mask off! Nay, be not morose;
It kills her, and this prevents seeing it close:
The delicate droplet, my whole fortune's fee!
If it hurts her, beside, can it ever hurt me?

12

45 Now, take all my jewels, gorge gold to your fill,
You may kiss me, old man, on my mouth if you will!
But brush this dust off me, lest horror it brings
Ere I know it—next moment I dance at the King's!

ca. 1844   1844

The Lost Leader[1]

I

Just for a handful of silver he left us,
    Just for a riband[2] to stick in his coat—
Found the one gift of which fortune bereft us,
    Lost all the others she lets us devote;
5 They, with the gold to give, doled him out silver,
    So much was theirs who so little allowed:
How all our copper had gone for his service!
    Rags—were they purple, his heart had been proud!
We that had loved him so, followed him, honored him,
10   Lived in his mild and magnificent eye,
Learned his great language, caught his clear accents,
    Made him our pattern to live and to die!
Shakespeare was of us, Milton was for us,
    Burns, Shelley, were with us—they watch from their graves!
15 He alone breaks from the van[3] and the freemen
    —He alone sinks to the rear and the slaves!

---

1. William Wordsworth, who had been an ardent liberal in his youth, had become a political conservative in later years. In old age, when he accepted a grant of money from the government and the office of poet laureate, he alienated some of his young admirers such as Browning, whose liberalism was then as ardent as Wordsworth's had once been.
2. Symbol of the office of poet laureate.
3. Vanguard of the army of liberalism.

2

We shall march prospering—not through his presence;
    Songs may inspirit us—not from his lyre;
Deeds will be done—while he boasts his quiescence,
20   Still bidding crouch whom the rest bade aspire:
  Blot out his name, then, record one lost soul more,
    One task more declined, one more footpath untrod,
One more devils'-triumph and sorrow for angels,
    One wrong more to man, one more insult to God!
25 Life's night begins: let him never come back to us!
    There would be doubt, hesitation and pain,
Forced praise on our part—the glimmer of twilight,
    Never glad confident morning again!
Best fight on well, for we taught him—strike gallantly,
30   Menace our heart ere we master his own;
Then let him receive the new knowledge and wait us,
    Pardoned in heaven, the first by the throne!

1843   1845

How They Brought the Good News
from Ghent to Aix[1]

(16—)

1

I sprang to the stirrup, and Joris, and he;
I galloped, Dirck galloped, we galloped all three;
"Good speed!" cried the watch, as the gate-bolts undrew;
"Speed!" echoed the wall to us galloping through;
5 Behind shut the postern, the lights sank to rest,
And into the midnight we galloped abreast.

2

Not a word to each other; we kept the great pace
Neck by neck, stride by stride, never changing our place;
I turned in my saddle and made its girths tight,
10 Then shortened each stirrup, and set the pique° right,   *spur or pommel*
Rebuckled the cheek-strap, chained slacker the bit,
Nor galloped less steadily Roland a whit.

3

'Twas moonset at starting; but while we drew near
Lokeren, the cocks crew and twilight dawned clear;
15 At Boom, a great yellow star came out to see;
At Düffeld, 'twas morning as plain as could be;
And from Mecheln church-steeple we heard the half-chime,
So, Joris broke silence with, "Yet there is time!"

---

1. The distance between Ghent, in Flanders, and Aix-la-Chapelle is about one hundred miles. Browning said that the incident, occurring during the wars between Flanders and Spain, was an imaginary one. In 1889, Thomas Edison prepared a cylinder recording of Browning's reciting of the opening lines of this poem.

4

At Aershot, up leaped of a sudden the sun,
20 And against him the cattle stood black every one,
To stare through the mist at us galloping past,
And I saw my stout galloper Roland at last,
With resolute shoulders, each butting away
The haze, as some bluff river headland its spray:

5

25 And his low head and crest, just one sharp ear bent back
For my voice, and the other pricked out on his track;
And one eye's black intelligence—ever that glance
O'er its white edge at me, his own master, askance!
And the thick heavy spume-flakes which ay and anon
30 His fierce lips shook upwards in galloping on.

6

By Hasselt, Dirck groaned; and cried Joris, "Stay spur!
Your Roos galloped bravely, the fault's not in her,
We'll remember at Aix"—for one heard the quick wheeze
Of her chest, saw the stretched neck and staggering knees,
35 And sunk tail, and horrible heave of the flank
As down on her haunches she shuddered and sank.

7

So, we were left galloping, Joris and I,
Past Looz and past Tongres, no cloud in the sky;
The broad sun above laughed a pitiless laugh,
40 'Neath our feet broke the brittle bright stubble like chaff;
Till over by Dalhem a dome-spire sprang white,
And "Gallop," gasped Joris, "for Aix is in sight!"

8

"How they'll greet us!"—and all in a moment his roan
Rolled neck and croup over, lay dead as a stone;
45 And there was my Roland to bear the whole weight
Of the news which alone could save Aix from her fate,
With his nostrils like pits full of blood to the brim,
And with circles of red for his eye-sockets' rim.

9

Then I cast loose my buffcoat, each holster let fall,
50 Shook off both my jack boots, let go belt and all,
Stood up in the stirrup, leaned, patted his ear,
Called my Roland his pet name, my horse without peer;
Clapped my hands, laughed and sang, any noise, bad or good,
Till at length into Aix Roland galloped and stood.

10

55 And all I remember is—friends flocking round
As I sat with his head 'twixt my knees on the ground;

And no voice but was praising this Roland of mine,
As I poured down his throat our last measure of wine,
Which (the burgesses voted by common consent)
60   Was no more than his due who brought good news from Ghent.

ca. 1844   1845

Home-Thoughts, from Abroad

1

Oh, to be in England
Now that April's there,
And whoever wakes in England
Sees, some morning, unaware,
5   That the lowest boughs and the brushwood sheaf
Round the elm-tree bole are in tiny leaf,
While the chaffinch sings on the orchard bough
In England—now!

2

And after April, when May follows,
10   And the whitethroat builds, and all the swallows!
Hark, where my blossomed peartree in the hedge
Leans to the field and scatters on the clover
Blossoms and dewdrops—at the bent spray's edge—
That's the wise thrush; he sings each song twice over,
15   Lest you should think he never could recapture
The first fine careless rapture!
And though the fields look rough with hoary dew,
All will be gay when noontide wakes anew
The buttercups, the little children's dower
20   —Far brighter than this gaudy melon-flower!

ca. 1845   1845

Home-Thoughts, from the Sea

Nobly, nobly Cape Saint Vincent[1] to the northwest died away;
Sunset ran, one glorious blood-red, reeking into Cadiz Bay;
Bluish 'mid the burning water, full in face Trafalgar[2] lay;
In the dimmest northeast distance dawned Gibraltar grand and gray;
5   "Here and here did England help me: how can I help England?"—say,
Whoso turns as I, this evening, turn to God to praise and pray,
While Jove's planet° rises yonder, silent over Africa.   *Jupiter*

1844   1845

1. Off the coast of Portugal, scene of British naval   2. A cape in Spain, where Nelson won his great
victory under Commodore Nelson (1797).   victory over Napoleon's fleets (1805).

The Bishop Orders His Tomb at Saint Praxed's Church[1]

Rome, 15—

Vanity, saith the preacher, vanity![2]
Draw round my bed: is Anselm keeping back?
Nephews—sons mine . . . ah God, I know not! Well—
She, men would have to be your mother once,
5   Old Gandolf envied me, so fair she was!
What's done is done, and she is dead beside,
Dead long ago, and I am Bishop since,
And as she died so must we die ourselves,
And thence ye may perceive the world's a dream.
10 Life, how and what is it? As here I lie
In this state chamber, dying by degrees,
Hours and long hours in the dead night, I ask
"Do I live, am I dead?" Peace, peace seems all.
Saint Praxed's ever was the church for peace;
15 And so, about this tomb of mine. I fought
With tooth and nail to save my niche, ye know:
—Old Gandolf cozened° me, despite my care;   *cheated*
Shrewd was that snatch from out the corner south
He graced his carrion with, God curse the same!
20 Yet still my niche is not so cramped but thence
One sees the pulpit o' the epistle side,[3]
And somewhat of the choir, those silent seats,
And up into the aery dome where live
The angels, and a sunbeam's sure to lurk:
25 And I shall fill my slab of basalt[4] there,
And 'neath my tabernacle[5] take my rest,
With those nine columns round me, two and two,
The odd one at my feet where Anselm stands:
Peach-blossom marble all, the rare, the ripe
30 As fresh-poured red wine of a mighty pulse.[6]
—Old Gandolf with his paltry onion-stone,[7]

---

1. In *Fra Lippo Lippi*, Browning represents the dawn of the Renaissance in Italy, with its fresh zest for human experiences in this world. In this monologue, he portrays a later stage of the Renaissance when such worldliness, full-blown, had infected some of the leading clergy of Italy. Browning's portrait of the dying bishop is, however, not primarily a satire against corruption in the church. It is a brilliant exposition of the workings of a mind, a mind that has been conditioned by special historical circumstances. The Victorian historian of art John Ruskin said of this poem:

> I know of no other piece of modern English, prose or poetry, in which there is so much told, as in these lines, of the Renaissance spirit—its worldliness, inconsistency, pride, hypocrisy, ignorance of itself, love of art, of luxury, and of good Latin. It is nearly all that I have said of the central Renaissance in thirty pages of the *Stones of Venice*, put into as many lines, Browning's

also being the antecedent work.

St. Praxed's Church was named in honor of St. Praxedes, a Roman virgin of the 2nd century who gave her riches to poor Christians. Both the bishop and his predecessor, Gandolf, are imaginary persons.
2. Cf. Ecclesiastes 1.2.
3. The Epistles of the New Testament are read from the right-hand side of the altar (as one faces it).
4. Dark-colored igneous rock.
5. Stone canopy or tentlike roof, presumably supported by the "nine columns" under which the sculptured effigy of the bishop would lie on the "slab of basalt."
6. Browning uses "pulse" in the special sense of a pulpy mash of fermented grapes from which a strong wine might be poured off.
7. An inferior marble that peels in layers.

Put me where I may look at him! True peach,
Rosy and flawless: how I earned the prize!
Draw close: that conflagration of my church
35 —What then? So much was saved if aught were missed!
My sons, ye would not be my death? Go dig
The white-grape vineyard where the oil-press stood,
Drop water gently till the surface sink,
And if ye find . . . Ah God, I know not, I! . . .
40 Bedded in store of rotten fig leaves soft,
And corded up in a tight olive-frail,[8]
Some lump, ah God, of *lapis lazuli*,[9]
Big as a jew's head cut off at the nape,[1]
Blue as a vein o'er the Madonna's breast . . .
45 Sons, all have I bequeathed you, villas, all,
That brave Frascati[2] villa with its bath,
So, let the blue lump poise between my knees,
Like God the Father's globe on both his hands
Ye worship in the Jesu Church[3] so gay,
50 For Gandolf shall not choose but see and burst!
Swift as a weaver's shuttle fleet our years:[4]
Man goeth to the grave, and where is he?
Did I say basalt for my slab, sons? Black[5]—
'Twas ever antique-black I meant! How else
55 Shall ye contrast my frieze[6] to come beneath?
The bas-relief[7] in bronze ye promised me,
Those Pans and Nymphs ye wot of, and perchance
Some tripod, thyrsus, with a vase or so,
The Saviour at his sermon on the mount,
60 Saint Praxed in a glory, and one Pan
Ready to twitch the Nymph's last garment off,
And Moses with the tables[8] . . . but I know
Ye mark me not! What do they whisper thee,
Child of my bowels, Anselm? Ah, ye hope
65 To revel down my villas while I gasp
Bricked o'er with beggar's moldy travertine°   *Italian limestone*
Which Gandolf from his tomb-top chuckles at!
Nay, boys, ye love me—all of jasper, then!
'Tis jasper ye stand pledged to, lest I grieve
70 My bath must needs be left behind, alas!
One block, pure green as a pistachio nut,
There's plenty jasper somewhere in the world—
And have I not Saint Praxed's ear to pray

---

8. Basket for holding olives.
9. Valuable bright blue stone.
1. Perhaps a reference to the head of John the Baptist, cut off at the request of Salomé.
2. Suburb of Rome, used as a resort by wealthy Italians.
3. Il Gesù, a Jesuit church in Rome. In a chapel in this church the figure of an angel (rather than God) holds a huge lump of lapis lazuli in his hands.
4. Cf. Job 7.6.
5. I.e., black marble.
6. Continuous band of sculpture.
7. Sculpture in which the figures do not project

far from the background surface.
8. Sculpture in which the figures do not project far from the background surface. The sculpture would consist of a mixture of pagan and Christian iconography. "Tripod": seat on which the Oracle of Delphi made prophecies. "Thyrsus": a long staff carried in processions in honor of Bacchus, the god of wine. "Glory": halo. "Tables": the stone tablets on which the Ten Commandments were written. Such intermingling of pagan and Christian traditions, characteristic of the Renaissance, had been attacked in 1841 in *Contrasts*, a book on architecture by A. W. Pugin, a Roman Catholic.

Horses for ye, and brown Greek manuscripts,
75 And mistresses with great smooth marbly limbs?
—That's if ye carve my epitaph aright,
Choice Latin, picked phrase, Tully's[9] every word,
No gaudy ware like Gandolf's second line—
Tully, my masters? Ulpian[1] serves his need!
80 And then how I shall lie through centuries,
And hear the blessed mutter of the mass,
And see God made and eaten all day long,[2]
And feel the steady candle flame, and taste
Good strong thick stupefying incense-smoke!
85 For as I lie here, hours of the dead night,
Dying in state and by such slow degrees,
I fold my arms as if they clasped a crook,°   *bishop's staff*
And stretch my feet forth straight as stone can point,
And let the bedclothes, for a mortcloth,[3] drop
90 Into great laps and folds of sculptor's-work:
And as yon tapers dwindle, and strange thoughts
Grow, with a certain humming in my ears,
About the life before I lived this life,
And this life too, popes, cardinals, and priests,
95 Saint Praxed at his sermon on the mount,[4]
Your tall pale mother with her talking eyes,
And new-found agate urns as fresh as day,
And marble's language, Latin pure, discreet
—Aha, ELUCESCEBAT[5] quoth our friend?
100 No Tully, said I, Ulpian at the best!
Evil and brief hath been my pilgrimage.[6]
All *lapis,* all, sons! Else I give the Pope
My villas! Will ye ever eat my heart?
Ever your eyes were as a lizard's quick,
105 They glitter like your mother's for my soul,
Or ye would heighten my impoverished frieze,
Piece out its starved design, and fill my vase
With grapes, and add a vizor and a Term,[7]
And to the tripod ye would tie a lynx
110 That in his struggle throws the thyrsus down,
To comfort me on my entablature[8]
Whereon I am to lie till I must ask
"Do I live, am I dead?" There, leave me, there!
For ye have stabbed me with ingratitude
115 To death—ye wish it—God, ye wish it! Stone—
Gritstone,[9] a-crumble! Clammy squares which sweat

9. I.e., Marcus Tullius Cicero, whose writing was the model, during the Renaissance, of classical Latin prose.
1. Late Latin prose writer, not a model of good style.
2. Reference to the doctrine of transubstantiation.
3. Rich cloth spread over a dead body or coffin.
4. The bishop is confusing St. Praxed (a woman) with Christ—an indication that his mind is wandering.
5. He was illustrious (Latin); word from Gandolf's

epitaph. The bishop considers the form of the verb to be in "gaudy" bad taste (line 78). If the epitaph had been copied from Cicero instead of from Ulpian, the word would have been *elucebat.*
6. Cf. Genesis 47.9.
7. Statue of Terminus, the Roman god of boundaries, usually represented without arms. "Vizor": part of a helmet, often represented in sculpture.
8. Horizontal platform supporting a statue or effigy.
9. Coarse sandstone.

As if the corpse they keep were oozing through—
And no more *lapis* to delight the world!
Well go! I bless ye. Fewer tapers there,
120 But in a row: and, going, turn your backs
—Aye, like departing altar-ministrants,
And leave me in my church, the church for peace,
That I may watch at leisure if he leers—
Old Gandolf, at me, from his onion-stone,
125 As still he envied me, so fair she was!

1844   1845

Meeting at Night[1]

1

The gray sea and the long black land;
And the yellow half-moon large and low;
And the startled little waves that leap
In fiery ringlets from their sleep,
5 As I gain the cove with pushing prow,
And quench its speed i' the slushy sand.

2

Then a mile of warm sea-scented beach;
Three fields to cross till a farm appears;
A tap at the pane, the quick sharp scratch
10 And blue spurt of a lighted match,
And a voice less loud, through its joys and fears,
Than the two hearts beating each to each!

1845

Parting at Morning

Round the cape of a sudden came the sea,
And the sun looked over the mountain's rim:
And straight was a path of gold for him,°   *the sun*
And the need of a world of men for me.

1845

---

1. This poem and the one that follows it appeared originally under the single title *Night and Morning*. The speaker in both is a man.

A Toccata of Galuppi's[1]

1

Oh, Galuppi, Baldassaro, this is very sad to find!
I can hardly misconceive you; it would prove me deaf and blind;
But although I take your meaning, 'tis with such a heavy mind!

2

Here you come with your old music, and here's all the good it brings.
5 What, they lived once thus at Venice where the merchants were the kings,
Where Saint Mark's is, where the Doges used to wed the sea with rings?[2]

3

Aye, because the sea's the street there; and 'tis arched by . . . what you call
. . . Shylock's bridge[3] with houses on it, where they kept the carnival:
I was never out of England—it's as if I saw it all.

4

10 Did young people take their pleasure when the sea was warm in May?
Balls and masks° begun at midnight, burning ever to midday,   masquerades
When they made up fresh adventures for the morrow, do you say?

5

Was a lady such a lady, cheeks so round and lips so red—
On her neck the small face buoyant, like a bellflower on its bed,
15 O'er the breast's superb abundance where a man might base his head?

6

Well, and it was graceful of them—they'd break talk off and afford
—She, to bite her mask's black velvet—he, to finger on his sword,
While you sat and played toccatas, stately at the clavichord?[4]

7

What? Those lesser thirds so plaintive, sixths diminished, sigh on sigh,
20 Told them something? Those suspensions, those solutions—"Must we die?"
Those commiserating sevenths—"Life might last! we can but try!"

1. There are three speakers in this short poem. The first is a 19th-century scientist in England who is listening to a musical composition by Baldassaro Galuppi (1706–1785), a Venetian. The music evokes for this scientist the voice of the dead composer (the third speaker) who comments on the pointless and butterfly-like frivolity of his 18th-century contemporaries. The second group of voices is made up of comments by members of Galuppi's audience as they respond to the different moods of his clavichord playing during a party that the scientist imagines to have taken place in Venice. "Toccata": according to *Grove's Dictionary of Music*, a "touch-piece, or a composition intended

to exhibit the touch and execution of the performer." The same authority states that "no particular composition was taken as the basis of the poem."
2. An annual ceremony in which the doge, the Venetian chief magistrate, threw a ring into the water to symbolize the bond between his city, with its maritime empire, and the sea.
3. The Rialto, a bridge over the Grand Canal.
4. A keyboard instrument in which the strings are struck by metal hammers. As a mechanism, it resembles a piano, but the sound is more like that of a harpsichord.

8

"Were you happy?"—"Yes."—"And are you still as happy?"—"Yes. And you?"
—"Then, more kisses!"—"Did *I* stop them, when a million seemed so few?"
Hark, the dominant's persistence till it must be answered to!

9

25 So, an octave struck the answer.[5] Oh, they praised you, I dare say!
"Brave Galuppi! that was music; good alike at grave and gay!
I can always leave off talking when I hear a master play!"

10

Then they left you for their pleasure: till in due time, one by one,
Some with lives that came to nothing, some with deeds as well undone,
30 Death stepped tacitly and took them where they never see the sun.

11

But when I sit down to reason, think to take my stand nor swerve,
While I triumph o'er a secret wrung from nature's close reserve,
In you come with your cold music till I creep through every nerve.

12

Yes, you, like a ghostly cricket, creaking where a house was burned:
35 "Dust and ashes, dead and done with, Venice spent what Venice earned.
The soul, doubtless, is immortal—where a soul can be discerned.

13

"Yours for instance: you know physics, something of geology,
Mathematics are your pastime; souls shall rise in their degree;
Butterflies may dread extinction—you'll not die, it cannot be!

14

40 "As for Venice and her people, merely born to bloom and drop,
Here on earth they bore their fruitage, mirth and folly were the crop:
What of soul was left, I wonder, when the kissing had to stop?

15

"Dust and ashes!" So you creak it, and I want° the heart to scold.   lack
Dear dead women, with such hair, too—what's become of all the gold
45 Used to hang and brush their bosoms? I feel chilly and grown old.

ca. 1847   1855

5. The terms in these lines refer to the technical
devices used by Galuppi to produce alternating
moods in his music, conflict in each instance being
resolved into harmony. Thus the "dominant" (the
fifth note of the scale), after being persistently
sounded, is answered by a resolving chord (lines
24–25).

Memorabilia[1]

1

Ah, did you once see Shelley plain,
    And did he stop and speak to you
And did you speak to him again?
    How strange it seems and new!

2

5   But you were living before that,
    And also you are living after;
And the memory I started at—
    My starting moves your laughter.

3

I crossed a moor, with a name of its own
10   And a certain use in the world no doubt,
Yet a hand's-breadth of it shines alone
    'Mid the blank miles round about:

4

For there I picked up on the heather
    And there I put inside my breast
15   A molted feather, an eagle feather!
    Well, I forget the rest.

ca. 1851   1855

Love among the Ruins[1]

1

Where the quiet-colored end of evening smiles,
    Miles and miles
On the solitary pastures where our sheep
    Half-asleep
5   Tinkle homeward through the twilight, stray or stop
    As they crop—
Was the site once of a city great and gay
    (So they say),
Of our country's very capital, its prince
10   Ages since
Held his court in, gathered councils, wielding far
    Peace or war.

1. Things worth remembering. Browning reports that he once met a stranger in a bookstore who mentioned having talked with Shelley. "Suddenly the stranger paused, and burst into laughter as he observed me staring at him with blanched face. . . . I still vividly remember how strangely the presence of a man who had seen and spoken with Shelley affected me."

1. The ruins may be those of such cities as Babylon and Nineveh or the site of the Circus Maximus in Rome. The unusual stanza used in this poem was invented by Browning. The contrast between past and present, which is the core of the poem, is reinforced by devoting one half of each stanza to the past and the other half to the present.

2

Now—the country does not even boast a tree,
    As you see,
15 To distinguish slopes of verdure, certain rills
    From the hills
Intersect and give a name to (else they run
    Into one),
Where the domed and daring palace shot its spires
20   Up like fires
O'er the hundred-gated circuit of a wall
    Bounding all,
Made of marble, men might march on nor be pressed,
    Twelve abreast.

3

25 And such plenty and perfection, see, of grass
    Never was!
Such a carpet as, this summertime, o'erspreads
    And embeds
Every vestige of the city, guessed alone,
30   Stock or stone—
Where a multitude of men breathed joy and woe
    Long ago;
Lust of glory pricked their hearts up, dread of shame
    Struck them tame;
35 And that glory and that shame alike, the gold
    Bought and sold.

4

Now—the single little turret that remains
    On the plains,
By the caper overrooted, by the gourd
40   Overscored,
While the patching houseleek's[2] head of blossom winks
    Through the chinks—
Marks the basement whence a tower in ancient time
    Sprang sublime,
45 And a burning ring, all round, the chariots traced
    As they raced,
And the monarch and his minions and his dames
    Viewed the games.

5

And I know, while thus the quiet-colored eve
50   Smiles to leave
To their folding, all our many-tinkling fleece
    In such peace,
And the slopes and rills in undistinguished gray
    Melt away—
55 That a girl with eager eyes and yellow hair
    Waits me there

2. Common European plant, with petals clustered in the shape of rosettes.

In the turret whence the charioteers caught soul
    For the goal,
When the king looked, where she looks now, breathless, dumb
60   Till I come.

6

But he looked upon the city, every side,
    Far and wide,
All the mountains topped with temples, all the glades'
    Colonnades,
65 All the causeys,³ bridges, aqueducts—and then,
    All the men!
When I do come, she will speak not, she will stand,
    Either hand
On my shoulder, give her eyes the first embrace
70   Of my face,
Ere we rush, ere we extinguish sight and speech
    Each on each.

7

In one year they sent a million fighters forth
    South and north,
75 And they built their gods a brazen pillar high
    As the sky,
Yet reserved a thousand chariots in full force—
    Gold, of course.
Oh heart! oh blood that freezes, blood that burns!
80   Earth's returns
For whole centuries of folly, noise, and sin!
    Shut them in,
With their triumphs and their glories and the rest!
    Love is best.

1853   1855

"Childe Roland to the Dark Tower Came"¹

(See Edgar's Song in "Lear")

I

My first thought was, he lied in every word,
   That hoary cripple, with malicious eye

---

3. Causeways or roads raised above low ground.
1. Browning stated that this poem "came upon me as a kind of dream," and that it was written in one day. Although the poem was among those of his own writings that pleased him most, he was reluctant to explain what the dream (or nightmare) signified. He once agreed with a friend's suggestion that the meaning might be expressed in the statement: "He that endureth to the end shall be saved." Most readers have responded to the poem in this way, finding in the story of Roland's quest an inspiring expression of defiance and courage. Other readers find the poem to be more expressive of despair than of enduring hope, and it is at least true that the landscape is as grim and nightmare-

like as in such 20th-century writings as T. S. Eliot's *Hollow Men* or Franz Kafka's *Penal Colony*. It has been said of *"Childe Roland"* that every reader can be his own allegorist.

The lines from Shakespeare's *King Lear* 3.4 (lines 163–65), from which the title is taken, are spoken when Lear is about to enter a hovel on the heath, and Edgar, feigning madness, chants the fragment of a song reminiscent of quests and challenges in fairy tales: "Child Rowland to the dark tower came, / His word was still,—Fie, foh, and fum, / I smell the blood of a British man." "Childe": a youth of gentle birth, usually a candidate for knighthood.

Askance° to watch the working of his lie   *squinting sidewise*
On mine, and mouth scarce able to afford
5   Suppression of the glee, that pursed and scored
     Its edge, at one more victim gained thereby.

2

What else should he be set for, with his staff?
     What, save to waylay with his lies, ensnare
     All travelers who might find him posted there,
10 And ask the road? I guessed what skull-like laugh
Would break, what crutch 'gin write my epitaph
     For pastime in the dusty thoroughfare,

3

If at his counsel I should turn aside
     Into that ominous tract which, all agree,
15   Hides the Dark Tower. Yet acquiescingly
I did turn as he pointed: neither pride
Nor hope rekindling at the end descried,
     So much as gladness that some end might be.

4

For, what with my whole world-wide wandering,
20   What with my search drawn out through years, my hope
     Dwindled into a ghost not fit to cope
With that obstreperous joy success would bring,
I hardly tried now to rebuke the spring
     My heart made, finding failure in its scope.

5

25 As when a sick man very near to death
     Seems dead indeed, and feels begin and end
     The tears and takes the farewell of each friend,
And hears one bid the other go, draw breath
Freelier outside ("since all is o'er," he saith,
30   "And the blow fallen no grieving can amend"),

6

While some discuss if near the other graves
     Be room enough for this, and when a day
     Suits best for carrying the corpse away,
With care about the banners, scarves and staves:
35 And still the man hears all, and only craves
     He may not shame such tender love and stay.

7

Thus, I had so long suffered in this quest,
     Heard failure prophesied so oft, been writ
     So many times among "The Band"—to wit,
40 The knights who to the Dark Tower's search addressed

Their steps—that just to fail as they, seemed best,
    And all the doubt was now—should I be fit?

8

So, quiet as despair, I turned from him,
    That hateful cripple, out of his highway
45   Into the path he pointed. All the day
Had been a dreary one at best, and dim
Was settling to its close, yet shot one grim
    Red leer to see the plain catch its estray.[2]

9

For mark! no sooner was I fairly found
50   Pledged to the plain, after a pace or two,
    Than, pausing to throw backward a last view
O'er the safe road, 'twas gone; gray plain all round:
Nothing but plain to the horizon's bound.
    I might go on; naught else remained to do.

10

55 So, on I went. I think I never saw
    Such starved ignoble nature; nothing throve:
    For flowers—as well expect a cedar grove!
But, cockle, spurge,[3] according to their law
Might propagate their kind, with none to awe,
60   You'd think; a burr had been a treasure trove.

11

No! penury, inertness and grimace,
    In some strange sort, were the land's portion. "See
    Or shut your eyes," said Nature peevishly,
"It nothing skills: I cannot help my case;
65 'Tis the Last Judgment's fire must cure this place,
    Calcine[4] its clods and set my prisoners free."

12

If there pushed any ragged thistle stalk
    Above its mates, the head was chopped; the bents[5]
    Were jealous else. What made those holes and rents
70 In the dock's° harsh swarth leaves, bruised as to balk   *coarse plant*
All hope of greenness? 'tis a brute must walk
    Pashing their life out, with a brute's intents.

13

As for the grass, it grew as scant as hair
    In leprosy; thin dry blades pricked the mud

2. Literally, a domestic animal that has strayed away from its home.
3. A bitter-juiced weed. "Cockle": a weed that bears burrs.
4. Turn to powder by heat.
5. Coarse, stiff grasses.

75   Which underneath looked kneaded up with blood.
One stiff blind horse, his every bone a-stare,
Stood stupefied, however he came there:
    Thrust out past service from the devil's stud!

14

Alive? he might be dead for aught I know,
80   With that red gaunt and colloped° neck a-strain,   *ridged*
    And shut eyes underneath the rusty mane;
Seldom went such grotesqueness with such woe;
I never saw a brute I hated so;
    He must be wicked to deserve such pain.

15

85 I shut my eyes and turned them on my heart.
    As a man calls for wine before he fights,
    I asked one draught of earlier, happier sights,
Ere fitly I could hope to play my part.
Think first, fight afterwards—the soldier's art:
90   One taste of the old time sets all to rights.

16

Not it! I fancied Cuthbert's reddening face
    Beneath its garniture of curly gold,
    Dear fellow, till I almost felt him fold
An arm in mine to fix me to the place,
95 That way he used. Alas, one night's disgrace!
    Out went my heart's new fire and left it cold.

17

Giles then, the soul of honor—there he stands
    Frank as ten years ago when knighted first.
    What honest man should dare (he said) he durst.
100 Good—but the scene shifts—faugh! what hangman hands
Pin to his breast a parchment? His own bands
    Read it. Poor traitor, spit upon and cursed!

18

Better this present than a past like that;
    Back therefore to my darkening path again!
105   No sound, no sight as far as eye could strain.
Will the night send a howlet° or a bat?   *owl*
I asked: when something on the dismal flat
    Came to arrest my thoughts and change their train.

19

A sudden little river crossed my path
110   As unexpected as a serpent comes.
    No sluggish tide congenial to the glooms;
This, as it frothed by, might have been a bath

For the fiend's glowing hoof—to see the wrath
    Of its black eddy bespate° with flakes and spumes.   *bespattered*

20

115 So petty yet so spiteful! All along,
    Low scrubby alders kneeled down over it;
    Drenched willows flung them headlong in a fit
Of mute despair, a suicidal throng:
The river which had done them all the wrong,
120   Whate'er that was, rolled by, deterred no whit.

21

Which, while I forded—good saints, how I feared
    To set my foot upon a dead man's cheek,
    Each step, or feel the spear I thrust to seek
For hollows, tangled in his hair or beard!
125 —It may have been a water rat I speared,
    But, ugh! it sounded like a baby's shriek.

22

Glad was I when I reached the other bank.
    Now for a better country. Vain presage!
    Who were the strugglers, what war did they wage,
130 Whose savage trample thus could pad the dank
Soil to a plash? Toads in a poisoned tank,
    Or wild cats in a red-hot iron cage—

23

The fight must so have seemed in that fell cirque.°   *dreadful arena*
    What penned them there, with all the plain to choose?
135   No footprint leading to that horrid mews,[6]
None out of it. Mad brewage set to work
Their brains, no doubt, like galley slaves the Turk
    Pits for his pastime, Christians against Jews.

24

And more than that—a furlong on—why, there!
140   What bad use was that engine for, that wheel,
    Or brake,[7] not wheel—that harrow fit to reel
Men's bodies out like silk? with all the air
Of Tophet's° tool, on earth left unaware,   *Hell's*
    Or brought to sharpen its rusty teeth of steel.

25

145 Then came a bit of stubbed ground, once a wood,
    Next a marsh, it would seem, and now mere earth
    Desperate and done with; (so a fool finds mirth,

6. Enclosed stable yard.
7. A toothed machine used for separating the

fibers of flax or hemp; here an instrument of torture.

Makes a thing and then mars it, till his mood
Changes and off he goes!) within a rood[8]
150   Bog, clay and rubble, sand and stark black dearth.

26

Now blotches rankling, colored gay and grim,
    Now patches where some leanness of the soil's
    Broke into moss or substances like boils;
Then came some palsied oak, a cleft in him
155 Like a distorted mouth that splits its rim
    Gaping at death, and dies while it recoils.

27

And just as far as ever from the end!
    Naught in the distance but the evening, naught
    To point my footstep further! At the thought,
160 A great black bird, Apollyon's[9] bosom friend,
Sailed past, nor beat his wide wing dragon-penned[1]
    That brushed my cap—perchance the guide I sought.

28

For, looking up, aware I somehow grew,
    'Spite of the dusk, the plain had given place
165   All round to mountains—with such name to grace
Mere ugly heights and heaps now stolen in view.
How thus they had surprised me—solve it, you!
How to get from them was no clearer case.

29

Yet half I seemed to recognize some trick
170   Of mischief happened to me, God knows when—
    In a bad dream perhaps. Here ended, then,
Progress this way. When, in the very nick
Of giving up, one time more, came a click
    As when a trap shuts—you're inside the den!

30

175 Burningly it came on me all at once,
    This was the place! those two hills on the right,
    Crouched like two bulls locked horn in horn in fight;
While to the left, a tall scalped mountain . . . Dunce,
Dotard, a-dozing at the very nonce,°   *moment*
180   After a life spent training for the sight!

31

What in the midst lay but the Tower itself?
    The round squat turret, blind as the fool's heart,[2]

---

8. Quarter acre of land.
9. In Revelation 9.11 Apollyon is "the angel of the bottomless pit." In Bunyan's *Pilgrim's Progress*, he is a hideous "monster"; "he had wings like a dragon."
1. With wings or pinions like those of a dragon.
2. Cf. Psalm 14.1: "The fool hath said in his heart, There is no God."

Built of brown stone, without a counterpart
In the whole world. The tempest's mocking elf
185 Points to the shipman thus the unseen shelf
He strikes on, only when the timbers start.

32

Not see? because of night perhaps?—why, day
Came back again for that! before it left,
The dying sunset kindled through a cleft:
190 The hills, like giants at a hunting, lay,
Chin upon hand, to see the game at bay—
"Now stab and end the creature—to the heft!"[3]

33

Not hear? when noise was everywhere! it tolled
Increasing like a bell. Names in my ears
195 Of all the lost adventurers my peers—
How such a one was strong, and such was bold,
And such was fortunate, yet each of old
Lost, lost! one moment knelled the woe of years.

34

There they stood, ranged along the hillsides, met
200 To view the last of me, a living frame
For one more picture! in a sheet of flame
I saw them and I knew them all. And yet
Dauntless the slug-horn[4] to my lips I set,
And blew. *"Childe Roland to the Dark Tower came."*

1852   1855

Fra Lippo Lippi[1]

I am poor brother Lippo, by your leave!
You need not clap your torches to my face.
Zooks,[2] what's to blame? you think you see a monk!
What, 'tis past midnight, and you go the rounds,
5 And here you catch me at an alley's end
Where sportive ladies leave their doors ajar?
The Carmine's[3] my cloister: hunt it up,
Do—harry out, if you must show your zeal,

3. Handle of dagger or sword.
4. The war cry or slogan of a clan about to engage
in battle (Scottish). In 1770, however, the poet
Chatterton was misled into using it to mean a kind
of trumpet or horn. Browning followed Chatterton's example, although the original meaning
would also be relevant here.
1. This monologue portrays the dawn of the
Renaissance in Italy at a point when the medieval
attitude toward life and art was about to be displaced by a fresh appreciation of earthly pleasures.
It was from Giorgio Vasari's *Lives of the Painters*

that Browning derived most of his information
about the life of the Florentine painter and friar
Lippo Lippi (1406–1469), but the theory of art
propounded by Lippi in the poem was developed
by the poet himself.
2. A shortened version of *Gadzooks*, a mild oath
now obscure in meaning but perhaps resembling a
phrase still in use: "God's truth."
3. Santa Maria del Carmine, a church and cloister
of the Carmelite order of friars to which Lippi
belonged.

Whatever rat, there, haps on his wrong hole,
10 And nip each softling of a wee white mouse,
Weke, weke, that's crept to keep him company!
Aha, you know your betters! Then, you'll take
Your hand away that's fiddling on my throat,
And please to know me likewise. Who am I?
15 Why, one, sir, who is lodging with a friend
Three streets off—he's a certain . . . how d'ye call?
Master—a . . . Cosimo of the Medici,⁴
I' the house that caps the corner. Boh! you were best!
Remember and tell me, the day you're hanged,
20 How you affected such a gullet's gripe!⁵
But you,⁶ sir, it concerns you that your knaves
Pick up a manner nor discredit you:
Zooks, are we pilchards,° that they sweep the streets   *small fish*
And count fair prize what comes into this net?
25 He's Judas to a tittle, that man is!⁷
Just such a face! Why, sir, you make amends.
Lord, I'm not angry! Bid your hangdogs go
Drink out this quarter-florin to the health
Of the munificent House that harbors me
30 (And many more beside, lads! more beside!)
And all's come square again. I'd like his face—
His, elbowing on his comrade in the door
With the pike and lantern—for the slave that holds
John Baptist's head a-dangle by the hair
35 With one hand ("Look you, now," as who should say)
And his weapon in the other, yet unwiped!
It's not your chance to have a bit of chalk,
A wood-coal or the like? or you should see!
Yes, I'm the painter, since you style me so.
40 What, brother Lippo's doings, up and down,
You know them and they take you? like enough!
I saw the proper twinkle in your eye—
'Tell you, I liked your looks at very first.
Let's sit and set things straight now, hip to haunch.
45 Here's spring come, and the nights one makes up bands
To roam the town and sing out carnival,⁸
And I've been three weeks shut within my mew,°   *private den*
A-painting for the great man, saints and saints
And saints again. I could not paint all night—
50 Ouf! I leaned out of window for fresh air.
There came a hurry of feet and little feet,
A sweep of lute-strings, laughs, and whifts of song—
Flower o' the broom,
Take away love, and our earth is a tomb!
55 *Flower o' the quince,*
*I let Lisa go, and what good in life since?*⁹

Flower o' the thyme—and so on. Round they went.
Scarce had they turned the corner when a titter
Like the skipping of rabbits by moonlight—three slim shapes,
60　And a face that looked up . . . zooks, sir, flesh and blood,
That's all I'm made of! Into shreds it went,
Curtain and counterpane and coverlet,
All the bed-furniture—a dozen knots,
There was a ladder! Down I let myself,
65　Hands and feet, scrambling somehow, and so dropped,
And after them. I came up with the fun
Hard by Saint Laurence,[1] hail fellow, well met—
Flower o' the rose,
If I've been merry, what matter who knows!
70　And so as I was stealing back again
To get to bed and have a bit of sleep
Ere I rise up tomorrow and go work
On Jerome knocking at his poor old breast
With his great round stone to subdue the flesh,[2]
75　You snap me of the sudden. Ah, I see!
Though your eye twinkles still, you shake your head—
Mine's shaved—a monk, you say—the sting's in that!
If Master Cosimo announced himself,
Mum's the word naturally; but a monk!
80　Come, what am I a beast for? tell us, now!
I was a baby when my mother died
And father died and left me in the street.
I starved there, God knows how, a year or two
On fig skins, melon parings, rinds and shucks,
85　Refuse and rubbish. One fine frosty day,
My stomach being empty as your hat,
The wind doubled me up and down I went.
Old Aunt Lapaccia trussed me with one hand
(Its fellow was a stinger as I knew),
90　And so along the wall, over the bridge,
By the straight cut to the convent. Six words there,
While I stood munching my first bread that month:
"So, boy, you're minded," quoth the good fat father
Wiping his own mouth, 'twas refection time°—　　　　　　　mealtime
95　"To quit this very miserable world?
Will you renounce" . . . "the mouthful of bread?" thought I;
By no means! Brief, they made a monk of me;
I did renounce the world, its pride and greed,
Palace, farm, villa, shop, and banking house,
100　Trash, such as these poor devils of Medici
Have given their hearts to—all at eight years old.
Well, sir, I found in time, you may be sure,
'Twas not for nothing—the good bellyful,
The warm serge and the rope that goes all round,
105　And day-long blessed idleness beside!
"Let's see what the urchin's fit for"—that came next.

1. San Lorenzo, a church in Florence.
2. A picture of Saint Jerome (ca. 340–420), whose
ascetic observances were hardly a congenial subject for such a painter as Lippi.

Not overmuch their way, I must confess.
Such a to-do! They tried me with their books:
Lord, they'd have taught me Latin in pure waste!
110 *Flower o' the clove,*
All the Latin I construe is "amo," I love!
But, mind you, when a boy starves in the streets
Eight years together, as my fortune was,
Watching folk's faces to know who will fling
115 The bit of half-stripped grape bunch he desires,
And who will curse or kick him for his pains—
Which gentleman processional and fine,
Holding a candle to the Sacrament,
Will wink and let him lift a plate and catch
120 The droppings of the wax to sell again,
Or holla for the Eight° and have him whipped—   *Florentine magistrates*
How say I?—nay, which dog bites, which lets drop
His bone from the heap of offal in the street—
Why, soul and sense of him grow sharp alike,
125 He learns the look of things, and none the less
For admonition from the hunger-pinch.
I had a store of such remarks, be sure,
Which, after I found leisure, turned to use.
I drew men's faces on my copybooks,
130 Scrawled them within the antiphonary's marge,[3]
Joined legs and arms to the long music-notes,
Found eyes and nose and chin for A's and B's,
And made a string of pictures of the world
Betwixt the ins and outs of verb and noun,
135 On the wall, the bench, the door. The monks looked black.
"Nay," quoth the Prior,[4] "turn him out, d' ye say?
In no wise. Lose a crow and catch a lark.
What if at last we get our man of parts,
We Carmelites, like those Camaldolese
140 And Preaching Friars,[5] to do our church up fine
And put the front on it that ought to be!"
And hereupon he bade me daub away.
Thank you! my head being crammed, the walls a blank,
Never was such prompt disemburdening.
145 First, every sort of monk, the black and white,
I drew them, fat and lean: then, folk at church,
From good old gossips waiting to confess
Their cribs of barrel droppings, candle ends—
To the breathless fellow at the altar-foot,
150 Fresh from his murder, safe and sitting there
With the little children round him in a row
Of admiration, half for his beard and half
For that white anger of his victim's son
Shaking a fist at him with one fierce arm,
155 Signing himself with the other because of Christ

---

3. Margin of music book used for choral singing.
4. Head of a Carmelite convent.

5. Benedictine and Dominican religious orders, respectively.

(Whose sad face on the cross sees only this
After the passion° of a thousand years)   *sufferings*
Till some poor girl, her apron o'er her head
(Which the intense eyes looked through), came at eve
160   On tiptoe, said a word, dropped in a loaf,
Her pair of earrings and a bunch of flowers
(The brute took growling), prayed, and so was gone.
I painted all, then cried " 'Tis ask and have;
Choose, for more's ready!"—laid the ladder flat,
165   And showed my covered bit of cloister wall.
The monks closed in a circle and praised loud
Till checked, taught what to see and not to see,
Being simple bodies—"That's the very man!
Look at the boy who stoops to pat the dog!
170   That woman's like the Prior's niece who comes
To care about his asthma: it's the life!"
But there my triumph's straw-fire flared and funked;[6]
Their betters took their turn to see and say:
The Prior and the learned pulled a face
175   And stopped all that in no time. "How? what's here?
Quite from the mark of painting, bless us all!
Faces, arms, legs and bodies like the true
As much as pea and pea! it's devil's game!
Your business is not to catch men with show,
180   With homage to the perishable clay,
But lift them over it, ignore it all,
Make them forget there's such a thing as flesh.
Your business is to paint the souls of men—
Man's soul, and it's a fire, smoke . . . no, it's not . . .
185   It's vapor done up like a newborn babe—
(In that shape when you die it leaves your mouth)
It's . . . well, what matters talking, it's the soul!
Give us no more of body than shows soul!
Here's Giotto,[7] with his Saint a-praising God,
190   That sets us praising—why not stop with him?
Why put all thoughts of praise out of our head
With wonder at lines, colors, and what not?
Paint the soul, never mind the legs and arms!
Rub all out, try at it a second time.
195   Oh, that white smallish female with the breasts,
She's just my niece . . . Herodias,[8] I would say—
Who went and danced and got men's heads cut off!
Have it all out!" Now, is this sense, I ask?
A fine way to paint soul, by painting body
200   So ill, the eye can't stop there, must go further
And can't fare worse! Thus, yellow does for white
When what you put for yellow's simply black,

6. Went up in smoke.
7. Great Florentine painter (1276–1337), whose stylized pictures of religious subjects were admired as models of pre-Renaissance art.
8. Also called Salomé, had the same name as her mother (Herodias), sister-in-law of King Herod. The daughter's dance coincided with the beheading of John the Baptist, who had aroused her mother's displeasure (Matthew 14.6–11).

And any sort of meaning looks intense
When all beside itself means and looks naught.
205   Why can't a painter lift each foot in turn,
Left foot and right foot, go a double step,
Make his flesh liker and his soul more like,
Both in their order? Take the prettiest face,
The Prior's niece . . . patron-saint—is it so pretty
210   You can't discover if it means hope, fear,
Sorrow or joy? won't beauty go with these?
Suppose I've made her eyes all right and blue,
Can't I take breath and try to add life's flash,
And then add soul and heighten them threefold?
215   Or say there's beauty with no soul at all—
(I never saw it—put the case the same—)
If you get simple beauty and naught else,
You get about the best thing God invents:
That's somewhat: and you'll find the soul you have missed,
220   Within yourself, when you return him thanks.
"Rub all out!" Well, well, there's my life, in short,
And so the thing has gone on ever since.
I'm grown a man no doubt, I've broken bounds:
You should not take a fellow eight years old
225   And make him swear to never kiss the girls.
I'm my own master, paint now as I please—
Having a friend, you see, in the Corner-house!⁹
Lord, it's fast holding by the rings in front—
Those great rings serve more purposes than just
230   To plant a flag in, or tie up a horse!
And yet the old schooling sticks, the old grave eyes
Are peeping o'er my shoulder as I work,
The heads shake still—"It's art's decline, my son!
You're not of the true painters, great and old;
235   Brother Angelico's the man, you'll find;
Brother Lorenzo¹ stands his single peer:
Fag on at flesh, you'll never make the third!"
Flower o' the pine,
You keep your mistr . . . manners, and I'll stick to mine!
240   I'm not the third, then: bless us, they must know!
Don't you think they're the likeliest to know,
They with their Latin? So, I swallow my rage,
Clench my teeth, suck my lips in tight, and paint
To please them—sometimes do and sometimes don't;
245   For, doing most, there's pretty sure to come
A turn, some warm eve finds me at my saints—
A laugh, a cry, the business of the world—
(Flower o' the peach,
Death for us all, and his own life for each!)
250   And my whole soul revolves, the cup runs over,

---

9. The Medici palace.
1. Fra Angelico (1387–1455) and Lorenzo Mon-
aco (1370–1425), whose paintings were in the
approved traditional manner.

The world and life's too big to pass for a dream,
And I do these wild things in sheer despite,
And play the fooleries you catch me at,
In pure rage! The old mill-horse, out at grass
255 After hard years, throws up his stiff heels so,
Although the miller does not preach to him
The only good of grass is to make chaff.°   straw
What would men have? Do they like grass or no—
May they or mayn't they? all I want's the thing
260 Settled forever one way. As it is,
You tell too many lies and hurt yourself:
You don't like what you only like too much,
You do like what, if given you at your word,
You find abundantly detestable.
265 For me, I think I speak as I was taught;
I always see the garden and God there
A-making man's wife: and, my lesson learned,
The value and significance of flesh,
I can't unlearn ten minutes afterwards.

270   You understand me: I'm a beast, I know.
But see, now—why, I see as certainly
As that the morning star's about to shine,
What will hap some day. We've a youngster here
Comes to our convent, studies what I do,
275 Slouches and stares and lets no atom drop:
His name is Guidi²—he'll not mind the monks—
They call him Hulking Tom, he lets them talk—
He picks my practice up—he'll paint apace,
I hope so—though I never live so long,
280 I know what's sure to follow. You be judge!
You speak no Latin more than I, belike;
However, you're my man, you've seen the world
—The beauty and the wonder and the power,
The shapes of things, their colors, lights and shades,
285 Changes, surprises—and God made it all!
—For what? Do you feel thankful, aye or no,
For this fair town's face, yonder river's line,
The mountain round it and the sky above,
Much more the figures of man, woman, child,
290 These are the frame to? What's it all about?
To be passed over, despised? or dwelt upon,
Wondered at? oh, this last of course!—you say.
But why not do as well as say—paint these
Just as they are, careless what comes of it?
295 God's works—paint any one, and count it crime
To let a truth slip. Don't object, "His works

2. Guidi or Masaccio (1401–1428), a painter who may have been Lippi's master rather than his pupil, although Browning, in a letter to the press in 1870, argued that Lippi had been born earlier. Like Lippi, Masaccio was in revolt against the medieval theory of art. His frescoes in the chapel of Santa Maria del Carmine are considered his masterpiece.

Are here already; nature is complete:
Suppose you reproduce her—(which you can't)
There's no advantage! You must beat her, then."
300 For, don't you mark? we're made so that we love
First when we see them painted, things we have passed
Perhaps a hundred times nor cared to see;
And so they are better, painted—better to us,
Which is the same thing. Art was given for that;
305 God uses us to help each other so,
Lending our minds out. Have you noticed, now,
Your cullion's° hanging face? A bit of chalk,   rascal's
And trust me but you should, though! How much more,
If I drew higher things with the same truth!
310 That were to take the Prior's pulpit-place,
Interpret God to all of you! Oh, oh,
It makes me mad to see what men shall do
And we in our graves! This world's no blot for us,
Nor blank; it means intensely, and means good:
315 To find its meaning is my meat and drink.
"Aye, but you don't so instigate to prayer!"
Strikes in the Prior: "when your meaning's plain
It does not say to folk—remember matins,
Or, mind you fast next Friday!" Why, for this
320 What need of art at all? A skull and bones,
Two bits of stick nailed crosswise, or, what's best,
A bell to chime the hour with, does as well.
I painted a Saint Laurence[3] six months since
At Prato, splashed the fresco[4] in fine style:
325 "How looks my painting, now the scaffold's down?"
I ask a brother: "Hugely," he returns—
"Already not one phiz of your three slaves
Who turn the Deacon off his toasted side,
But it's scratched and prodded to our heart's content,
330 The pious people have so eased their own
With coming to say prayers there in a rage:
We get on fast to see the bricks beneath.
Expect another job this time next year,
For pity and religion grow i' the crowd—
335 Your painting serves its purpose!" Hang the fools!

      —That is—you'll not mistake an idle word
Spoke in a huff by a poor monk, God wot,
Tasting the air this spicy night which turns
The unaccustomed head like Chianti wine!
340 Oh, the church knows! don't misreport me, now!
It's natural a poor monk out of bounds
Should have his apt word to excuse himself:
And hearken how I plot to make amends.

3. A scene representing the fiery martyrdom of
Saint Laurence.
4. Painted on a freshly plastered surface. It must

be painted quickly before the plaster dries. Prato
is a town near Florence

I have bethought me: I shall paint a piece
345 . . . There's for you! Give me six months, then go, see
Something in Sant' Ambrogio's![5] Bless the nuns!
They want a cast o' my office.[6] I shall paint
God in the midst, Madonna and her babe,
Ringed by a bowery flowery angel brood,
350 Lilies and vestments and white faces, sweet
As puff on puff of grated orris-root[7]
When ladies crowd to Church at midsummer.
And then i' the front, of course a saint or two—
Saint John, because he saves the Florentines,
355 Saint Ambrose, who puts down in black and white
The convent's friends and gives them a long day,
And Job, I must have him there past mistake,
The man of Uz (and Us without the z,
Painters who need his patience). Well, all these
360 Secured at their devotion, up shall come
Out of a corner when you least expect,
As one by a dark stair into a great light,
Music and talking, who but Lippo! I!—
Mazed, motionless and moonstruck—I'm the man!
365 Back I shrink—what is this I see and hear?
I, caught up with my monk's things by mistake,
My old serge gown and rope that goes all round,
I, in this presence, this pure company!
Where's a hole, where's a corner for escape?
370 Then steps a sweet angelic slip of a thing
Forward, puts out a soft palm—"Not so fast!"
—Addresses the celestial presence, "nay—
He made you and devised you, after all,
Though he's none of you! Could Saint John there draw—
375 His camel-hair[8] make up a painting-brush?
We come to brother Lippo for all that,
Iste perfecit opus!"[9] So, all smile—
I shuffle sideways with my blushing face
Under the cover of a hundred wings
380 Thrown like a spread of kirtles° when you're gay   *skirts*
And play hot cockles,[1] all the doors being shut,
Till, wholly unexpected, in there pops
The hothead husband! Thus I scuttle off
To some safe bench behind, not letting go
385 The palm of her, the little lily thing
That spoke the good word for me in the nick,
Like the Prior's niece . . . Saint Lucy, I would say.
And so all's saved for me, and for the church

---

5. A convent church in Florence.
6. Sample of my work. The completed painting, which Browning saw in Florence, is Lippi's *Coronation of the Virgin*.
7. Powder (like talcum) made from sweet-smelling roots of a flower.
8. Cf. Mark 1.6: "And John was clothed with camel's hair."
9. This man made the work! (Latin). In this painting, as later completed, these words appear beside a figure that Browning took to be Lippi's self-portrait.
1. A game in which a player wears a blindfold.

A pretty picture gained. Go, six months hence!
390 Your hand, sir, and good-by: no lights, no lights!
The street's hushed, and I know my own way back,
Don't fear me! There's the gray beginning. Zooks!

ca. 1853   1855

The Last Ride Together

1

I said—Then, dearest, since 'tis so,
Since now at length my fate I know,
Since nothing all my love avails,
Since all, my life seemed meant for, fails,
5   Since this was written and needs must be—
My whole heart rises up to bless
Your name in pride and thankfulness!
Take back the hope you gave—I claim
Only a memory of the same,
10 —And this beside, if you will not blame,
Your leave for one more last ride with me.

2

My mistress bent that brow of hers;
Those deep dark eyes where pride demurs
When pity would be softening through,
15 Fixed me a breathing-while or two
With life or death in the balance: right!
The blood replenished me again;
My last thought was at least not vain:
I and my mistress, side by side
20 Shall be together, breathe and ride,
So, one day more am I deified.
Who knows but the world may end tonight?

3

Hush! if you saw some western cloud
All billowy-bosomed, over-bowed
25 By many benedictions—sun's
And moon's and evening star's at once—
And so, you, looking and loving best,
Conscious grew, your passion drew
Cloud, sunset, moonrise, star-shine too,
30 Down on you, near and yet more near,
Till flesh must fade for heaven was here!—
Thus leant she and lingered[1]—joy and fear!
Thus lay she a moment on my breast.

---

1. Before she mounted her horse.

4

Then we began to ride. My soul
35 Smoothed itself out, a long-cramped scroll
Freshening and fluttering in the wind.
Past hopes already lay behind.
        What need to strive with a life awry?
Had I said that, had I done this,
40 So might I gain, so might I miss.
Might she have loved me? just as well
She might have hated, who can tell!
Where had I been now if the worst befell?
        And here we are riding, she and I.

5

45 Fail I alone, in words and deeds?
Why, all men strive and who succeeds?
We rode; it seemed my spirit flew,
Saw other regions, cities new,
        As the world rushed by on either side.
50 I thought—All labor, yet no less
Bear up beneath their unsuccess.
Look at the end of work, contrast
The petty done, the undone vast,
This present of theirs with the hopeful past!
55   I hoped she would love me; here we ride.

6

What hand and brain went ever paired?
What heart alike conceived and dared?
What act proved all its thought had been?
What will but felt the fleshly screen?
60   We ride and I see her bosom heave.
There's many a crown for who can reach.
Ten lines, a statesman's life in each![2]
The flag stuck on a heap of bones,
A soldier's doing! what atones?
65 They scratch his name on the Abbey stones.[3]
        My riding is better, by their leave.

7

What does it all mean, poet? Well,
Your brains beat into rhythm, you tell
What we felt only; you expressed
70 You hold things beautiful the best,
        And pace them in rhyme so, side by side.
'Tis something, nay 'tis much: but then,

---

2. If a man tries hard enough, he may be crowned
with what seems to be success. He might become,
for example, an eminent "statesman." Yet his only
memorial would be a short sketch of his career

("ten lines") in some history or biographical
dictionary.
3. I.e., he is honored by burial in Westminster
Abbey.

Have you yourself what's best for men?
Are you—poor, sick, old ere your time—
75   Nearer one whit your own sublime
Than we who never have turned a rhyme?
      Sing, riding's a joy! For me, I ride.

8

And you, great sculptor—so, you gave
A score of years to Art, her slave,
80   And that's your Venus, whence we turn
To yonder girl that fords the burn![4]
      You acquiesce, and shall I repine?
What, man of music, you grown gray
With notes and nothing else to say,
85   Is this your sole praise from a friend,
"Greatly his opera's strains intend,
But in music we know how fashions end!"
      I gave my youth; but we ride, in fine.°   *in short*

9

Who knows what's fit for us? Had fate
90   Proposed bliss here should sublimate
My being—had I signed the bond—
Still one must lead some life beyond,
      Have a bliss to die with, dim-descried.
This foot once planted on the goal,
95   This glory-garland round my soul,
Could I descry such? Try and test!
I sink back shuddering from the quest.
Earth being so good, would Heaven seem best?[5]
      Now, Heaven and she are beyond this ride.

10

100   And yet—she has not spoke so long!
What if heaven be that, fair and strong
At life's best, with our eyes upturned
Whither life's flower is first discerned,
      We, fixed so, ever should so abide?
105   What if we still ride on, we two
With life forever old yet new,
Changed not in kind but in degree,
The instant made eternity—
      And heaven just prove that I and she
110   Ride, ride together, forever ride?

1855

4. Crosses the brook.
5. If fate had decreed that he could possess his mistress fully, life on earth would have been so blissful that heaven could offer nothing for him to look forward to after death. Hence (he argues) to preserve "a bliss to die with" (line 93), it is better that she never really became his on earth.

Andrea del Sarto[1]

(*called "The Faultless Painter"*)

But do not let us quarrel any more,
No, my Lucrezia; bear with me for once:
Sit down and all shall happen as you wish.
You turn your face, but does it bring your heart?
5   I'll work then for your friend's friend, never fear,
Treat his own subject after his own way,
Fix his own time, accept too his own price,
And shut the money into this small hand
When next it takes mine. Will it? tenderly?
10   Oh, I'll content him—but tomorrow, Love!
I often am much wearier than you think,
This evening more than usual, and it seems
As if—forgive now—should you let me sit
Here by the window with your hand in mine
15   And look a half-hour forth on Fiesole,[2]
Both of one mind, as married people use,
Quietly, quietly the evening through,
I might get up tomorrow to my work
Cheerful and fresh as ever. Let us try.
20   Tomorrow, how you shall be glad for this!
Your soft hand is a woman of itself,
And mine the man's bared breast she curls inside.
Don't count the time lost, neither; you must serve
For each of the five pictures we require:
25   It saves a model. So! keep looking so—
My serpentining beauty, rounds on rounds![3]
—How could you ever prick those perfect ears,
Even to put the pearl there! oh, so sweet—
My face, my moon, my everybody's moon,
30   Which everybody looks on and calls his,
And, I suppose, is looked on by in turn,
While she looks—no one's: very dear, no less.[4]
You smile? why, there's my picture ready made,
There's what we painters call our harmony!

---

1. This portrait of Andrea del Sarto (1486–1531) was derived from a biography written by his pupil Giorgio Vasari, author of *The Lives of the Painters*. Vasari's account seeks to explain why his Florentine master, one of the most skillful painters of the Renaissance, never altogether fulfilled the promise he had shown early in his career and why he had never arrived (in Vasari's opinion) at the level of such artists as Raphael. Vasari noted that Andrea suffered from "a certain timidity of mind . . . which rendered it impossible that those evidences of ardor and animation, which are proper to the more exalted character, should ever appear in him." Browning also follows Vasari's account of Andrea's marriage to a beautiful widow, Lucrezia, "an artful woman who made him do as she pleased in all things." Vasari reports that Andrea's "immoderate love for her soon caused him to neglect the studies demanded by his art" and that this infatuation had "more influence over him than the glory and honor towards which he had begun to make such hopeful advances."

Browning's poem has often been praised for its exposition of a paradoxical theory of success and failure, but it has other qualities as well. Its slow-paced, enervated blank verse, its setting of a quiet evening in autumn, its comparative lack of the movement and noise that we expect in Browning's energetic verse create a unity of impression that is unobtrusive yet effective.
2. A suburb on the hills overlooking Florence.
3. Coils of hair like the coils of a serpent.
4. Her affections are centered on no one person, not even on her husband, yet she is nevertheless dear to him.

35 A common grayness silvers everything[5]—
    All in a twilight, you and I alike
    —You, at the point of your first pride in me
    (That's gone you know)—but I, at every point;
    My youth, my hope, my art, being all toned down
40 To yonder sober pleasant Fiesole.
    There's the bell clinking from the chapel top;
    That length of convent wall across the way
    Holds the trees safer, huddled more inside;
    The last monk leaves the garden; days decrease,
45 And autumn grows, autumn in everything.
    Eh? the whole seems to fall into a shape
    As if I saw alike my work and self
    And all that I was born to be and do,
    A twilight-piece. Love, we are in God's hand.
50 How strange now, looks the life he makes us lead;
    So free we seem, so fettered fast we are!
    I feel he laid the fetter: let it lie!
    This chamber for example—turn your head—
    All that's behind us! You don't understand
55 Nor care to understand about my art,
    But you can hear at least when people speak:
    And that cartoon,° the second from the door   *drawing*
    —It is the thing, Love! so such things should be—
    Behold Madonna!—I am bold to say.
60 I can do with my pencil what I know,
    What I see, what at bottom of my heart
    I wish for, if I ever wish so deep—
    Do easily, too—when I say, perfectly,
    I do not boast, perhaps: yourself are judge,
65 Who listened to the Legate's[6] talk last week,
    And just as much they used to say in France.
    At any rate 'tis easy, all of it!
    No sketches first, no studies, that's long past:
    I do what many dream of, all their lives,
70 —Dream? strive to do, and agonize to do,
    And fail in doing. I could count twenty such
    On twice your fingers, and not leave this town,
    Who strive—you don't know how the others strive
    To paint a little thing like that you smeared
75 Carelessly passing with your robes afloat—
    Yet do much less, so much less, Someone[7] says
    (I know his name, no matter)—so much less!
    Well, less is more, Lucrezia: I am judged.
    There burns a truer light of God in them,
80 In their vexed beating stuffed and stopped-up brain,
    Heart, or whate'er else, than goes on to prompt
    This low-pulsed forthright craftsman's hand of mine.
    Their works drop groundward, but themselves, I know,

5. The predominant color in many of Andrea's
paintings is silver gray.

6. A deputy of the pope.
7. Probably Michelangelo (1475–1564).

Reach many a time a heaven that's shut to me,
85 Enter and take their place there sure enough,
Though they come back and cannot tell the world.
My works are nearer heaven, but I sit here.
The sudden blood of these men! at a word—
Praise them, it boils, or blame them, it boils too.
90 I, painting from myself and to myself,
Know what I do, am unmoved by men's blame
Or their praise either. Somebody remarks
Morello's⁸ outline there is wrongly traced,
His hue mistaken; what of that? or else,
95 Rightly traced and well ordered; what of that?
Speak as they please, what does the mountain care?
Ah, but a man's reach should exceed his grasp,
Or what's a heaven for? All is silver-gray
Placid and perfect with my art: the worse!
100 I know both what I want and what might gain,
And yet how profitless to know, to sigh
"Had I been two, another and myself,
Our head would have o'erlooked the world!" No doubt.
Yonder's a work now, of that famous youth
105 The Urbinate⁹ who died five years ago.
('Tis copied,¹ George Vasari sent it me.)
Well, I can fancy how he did it all,
Pouring his soul, with kings and popes to see,
Reaching, that heaven might so replenish him,
110 Above and through his art—for it gives way;
That arm is wrongly put—and there again—
A fault to pardon in the drawing's lines,
Its body, so to speak: its soul is right,
He means right—that, a child may understand.
115 Still, what an arm! and I could alter it:
But all the play, the insight and the stretch—
Out of me, out of me! And wherefore out?
Had you enjoined them on me, given me soul,
We might have risen to Rafael, I and you!
120 Nay, Love, you did give all I asked, I think—
More than I merit, yes, by many times.
But had you—oh, with the same perfect brow,
And perfect eyes, and more than perfect mouth,
And the low voice my soul hears, as a bird
125 The fowler's pipe,² and follows to the snare—
Had you, with these the same, but brought a mind!
Some women do so. Had the mouth there urged
"God and the glory! never care for gain.
The present by the future, what is that?
130 Live for fame, side by side with Agnolo!°   *Michelangelo*
Rafael is waiting: up to God, all three!"

---

8. A mountain peak outside Florence.
9. Raphael (1483–1520), born at Urbino.
1. In saying that the painting is a copy, Andrea
may perhaps be concerned to prevent Lucrezia
from selling it.
2. Whistle or call used by hunters to lure wild fowl
into range.

I might have done it for you. So it seems:
Perhaps not. All is as God overrules.
Beside, incentives come from the soul's self;
135   The rest avail not. Why do I need you?
What wife had Rafael, or has Agnolo?
In this world, who can do a thing, will not;
And who would do it, cannot, I perceive:
Yet the will's somewhat—somewhat, too, the power—
140   And thus we half-men struggle. At the end,
God, I conclude, compensates, punishes.
'Tis safer for me, if the award be strict,
That I am something underrated here.
Poor this long while, despised, to speak the truth.
145   I dared not, do you know, leave home all day,
For fear of chancing on the Paris lords.
The best is when they pass and look aside;
But they speak sometimes; I must bear it all.
Well may they speak! That Francis,[3] that first time,
150   And that long festal year at Fontainebleau!
I surely then could sometimes leave the ground,
Put on the glory, Rafael's daily wear,
In that humane great monarch's golden look—
One finger in his beard or twisted curl
155   Over his mouth's good mark that made the smile,
One arm about my shoulder, round my neck,
The jingle of his gold chain in my ear,
I painting proudly with his breath on me,
All his court round him, seeing with his eyes,
160   Such frank French eyes, and such a fire of souls
Profuse, my hand kept plying by those hearts—
And, best of all, this, this, this face beyond,
This in the background, waiting on my work,
To crown the issue with a last reward!
165   A good time, was it not, my kingly days?
And had you not grown restless . . . but I know—
'Tis done and past; 'twas right, my instinct said;
Too live the life grew, golden and not gray,
And I'm the weak-eyed bat no sun should tempt
170   Out of the grange whose four walls make his world.
How could it end in any other way?
You called me, and I came home to your heart.
The triumph was—to reach and stay there; since
I reached it ere the triumph, what is lost?
175   Let my hands frame your face in your hair's gold,
You beautiful Lucrezia that are mine!
"Rafael did this, Andrea painted that;
The Roman's is the better when you pray,
But still the other's Virgin was his wife—"
180   Men will excuse me. I am glad to judge

---

3. King Francis I of France had invited Andrea to his court at Fontainebleau and warmly encouraged him in his painting. On returning to Florence, however, Andrea is reputed to have stolen some funds entrusted to him by Francis; and to please Lucrezia he built a house with the money. Now he is afraid of being insulted by "Paris lords" on the streets.

Both pictures in your presence; clearer grows
My better fortune, I resolve to think.
For, do you know, Lucrezia, as God lives,
Said one day Agnolo, his very self,
185   To Rafael . . . I have known it all these years . . .
(When the young man was flaming out his thoughts
Upon a palace wall for Rome to see,
Too lifted up in heart because of it)
"Friend, there's a certain sorry little scrub
190   Goes up and down our Florence, none cares how,
Who, were he set to plan and execute
As you are, pricked on by your popes and kings,
Would bring the sweat into that brow of yours!"
To Rafael's—And indeed the arm is wrong.
195   I hardly dare . . . yet, only you to see,
Give the chalk here—quick, thus the line should go!
Aye, but the soul! he's Rafael! rub it out!
Still, all I care for, if he spoke the truth,
(What he? why, who but Michel Agnolo?
200   Do you forget already words like those?)
If really there was such a chance, so lost—
Is, whether you're—not grateful—but more pleased.
Well, let me think so. And you smile indeed!
This hour has been an hour! Another smile?
205   If you would sit thus by me every night
I should work better, do you comprehend?
I mean that I should earn more, give you more.
See, it is settled dusk now; there's a star;
Morello's gone, the watch-lights show the wall,
210   The cue-owls[4] speak the name we call them by.
Come from the window, love—come in, at last,
Inside the melancholy little house
We built to be so gay with. God is just.
King Francis may forgive me: oft at nights
215   When I look up from painting, eyes tired out,
The walls become illumined, brick from brick
Distinct, instead of mortar, fierce bright gold,
That gold of his I did cement them with!
Let us but love each other. Must you go?
220   That Cousin here again? he waits outside?
Must see you—you, and not with me? Those loans?
More gaming debts to pay?[5] you smiled for that?
Well, let smiles buy me! have you more to spend?
While hand and eye and something of a heart
225   Are left me, work's my ware, and what's it worth?
I'll pay my fancy. Only let me sit
The gray remainder of the evening out,
Idle, you call it, and muse perfectly
How I could paint, were I but back in France,

---

4. A kind of owl named for its cry, which sounds
like *cue*.
5. Lucrezia's "Cousin" (or lover or friend) owes
gambling debts to a creditor. Andrea has already
contracted (lines 5–10) to pay off these debts by
painting some pictures according to the creditor's
specifications. Now he agrees to pay off further
debts.

230 One picture, just one more—the Virgin's face,
     Not yours this time! I want you at my side
     To hear them—that is, Michel Agnolo—
     Judge all I do and tell you of its worth.
     Will you? Tomorrow, satisfy your friend.
235 I take the subjects for his corridor,
     Finish the portrait out of hand—there, there,
     And throw him in another thing or two
     If he demurs; the whole should prove enough
     To pay for this same Cousin's freak. Beside,
240 What's better and what's all I care about,
     Get you the thirteen scudi° for the ruff!   *Italian coins*
     Love, does that please you? Ah, but what does he,
     The Cousin! What does he to please you more?

     I am grown peaceful as old age tonight.
245 I regret little, I would change still less.
     Since there my past life lies, why alter it?
     The very wrong to Francis!—it is true
     I took his coin, was tempted and complied,
     And built this house and sinned, and all is said.
250 My father and my mother died of want.[6]
     Well, had I riches of my own? you see
     How one gets rich! Let each one bear his lot.
     They were born poor, lived poor, and poor they died:
     And I have labored somewhat in my time
255 And not been paid profusely. Some good son
     Paint my two hundred pictures—let him try!
     No doubt, there's something strikes a balance. Yes,
     You loved me quite enough, it seems tonight.
     This must suffice me here. What would one have?
260 In heaven, perhaps, new chances, one more chance—
     Four great walls in the New Jerusalem,[7]
     Meted on each side by the angel's reed,°   *measuring rod*
     For Leonard,[8] Rafael, Agnolo and me
     To cover—the three first without a wife,
265 While I have mine! So—still they overcome
     Because there's still Lucrezia—as I choose.

     Again the Cousin's whistle! Go, my Love.

ca. 1853   1855

Two in the Campagna[1]

I

I wonder do you feel today
As I have felt since, hand in hand,

---

6. According to Vasari, Andrea's infatuation for Lucrezia prompted him to stop supporting his poverty-stricken parents.
7. Cf. Revelation 21.10–21.

8. Leonardo da Vinci (1452–1519).
1. The level plains and pasture lands near Rome where the ruins of ancient cities are overrun with wildflowers.

We sat down on the grass, to stray
    In spirit better through the land,
5 This morn of Rome and May?

2

For me, I touched a thought, I know,
    Has tantalized me many times,
(Like turns of thread the spiders throw
    Mocking across our path) for rhymes
10 To catch at and let go.

3

Help me to hold it! First it left
    The yellowing fennel,[2] run to seed
There, branching from the brickwork's cleft,
    Some old tomb's ruin: yonder weed
15 Took up the floating weft,[3]

4

Where one small orange cup amassed
    Five beetles—blind and green they grope
Among the honey-meal: and last,
    Everywhere on the grassy slope
20 I traced it. Hold it fast!

5

The champaign° with its endless fleece   *the Campagna*
    Of feathery grasses everywhere!
Silence and passion, joy and peace,
    An everlasting wash of air—
25 Rome's ghost since her decease.

6

Such life here, through such lengths of hours,
    Such miracles performed in play,
Such primal naked forms of flowers,
    Such letting nature have her way
30 While heaven looks from its towers!

7

How say you? Let us, O my dove,
    Let us be unashamed of soul,
As earth lies bare to heaven above!
    How is it under our control
35 To love or not to love?

8

I would that you were all to me,
    You that are just so much, no more.

---

2. A yellow-flowered plant from which a pungent
spice is derived.   3. Threads crossing from side to side of a web.

Nor yours nor mine, nor slave nor free!
 Where does the fault lie? What the core
40 O' the wound, since wound must be?

9

I would I could adopt your will,
 See with your eyes, and set my heart
Beating by yours, and drink my fill
 At your soul's springs—your part my part
45 In life, for good and ill.

10

No. I yearn upward, touch you close,
 Then stand away. I kiss your cheek,
Catch your soul's warmth—I pluck the rose
 And love it more than tongue can speak—
50 Then the good minute goes.

11

Already how am I so far
 Out of that minute? Must I go
Still like the thistle-ball, no bar,
 Onward, whenever light winds blow,
55 Fixed by no friendly star?[4]

12

Just when I seemed about to learn!
 Where is the thread now? Off again!
The old trick! Only I discern—
 Infinite passion, and the pain
60 Of finite hearts that yearn.

1854   1855

A Grammarian's Funeral[1]

Shortly after the Revival of Learning in Europe

Let us begin and carry up this corpse,
 Singing together.
Leave we the common crofts,[2] the vulgar thorpes°   *villages*
 Each in its tether[3]
5 Sleeping safe on the bosom of the plain,
 Cared for till cock-crow:

---

4. Cf. Shakespeare's Sonnet 116.

1. The speaker is one of the students who are bearing the body of their scholarly master to the mountaintop for burial. The student's defense of the dead grammarian's idealistic dedication to knowledge and faith in a future life is expressed in some of the harshest-sounding and most laborious verse ever written by Browning. It is this grotesque combination of opposites (soaring idealism in conjunction with harsh or petty realities) that gives *A*

Grammarian's Funeral its distinctive tone.

No model for the grammarian has been specifically identified. Browning seems to have had in mind the kind of early Renaissance scholar whose devotion to the Greek language made it possible for others to enjoy the more recognizably significant aspects of the revival of learning.

2. Small tracts of land farmed by peasants.

3. Restricted to a narrow sphere like an animal tied to a stake.

Look out if yonder be not day again
    Rimming the rock-row!
That's the appropriate country; there, man's thought,
10   Rarer, intenser,
Self-gathered for an outbreak, as it ought,
    Chafes in the censer.
Leave we the unlettered plain[4] its herd and crop;
    Seek we sepulture°   *burial place*
15 On a tall mountain, citied to the top,
    Crowded with culture!
All the peaks soar, but one the rest excels;
    Clouds overcome it;
No! yonder sparkle is the citadel's
20   Circling its summit.
Thither our path lies; wind we up the heights:
    Wait ye the warning?
Our low life was the level's and the night's;
    He's for the morning.
25 Step to a tune, square chests, erect each head,
    'Ware° the beholders!   *beware*
This is our master, famous, calm, and dead,
    Borne on our shoulders.

Sleep, crop and herd! sleep, darkling thorpe and croft,
30   Safe from the weather!
He, whom we convoy to his grave aloft,
    Singing together,
He was a man born with thy face and throat,
    Lyric Apollo![5]
35 Long he lived nameless: how should spring take note
    Winter would follow?
Till lo, the little touch, and youth was gone!
    Cramped and diminished,
Moaned he, "New measures, other feet anon!
40   My dance is finished?"
No, that's the world's way: (keep the mountain-side,
    Make for the city!)
He knew the signal, and stepped on with pride
    Over men's pity;
45 Left play for work, and grappled with the world
    Bent on escaping:
"What's in the scroll," quoth he, "thou keepest furled?
    Show me their shaping,
Theirs who most studied man, the bard and sage—
50   Give!"—So, he gowned him,[6]
Straight got by heart that book to its last page:
    Learned, we found him.
Yea, but we found him bald too, eyes like lead,
    Accents uncertain:
55 "Time to taste life," another would have said,
    "Up with the curtain!"

---

4. Flatlands at the base of the mountain that are populated by illiterate shepherds and peasants.

5. God of music and embodiment of male beauty.

6. Dressed in academic gown; became a scholar.

This man said rather, "Actual life comes next?
    Patience a moment!
Grant I have mastered learning's crabbed text,
60   Still there's the comment.[7]
Let me know all! Prate not of most or least,
    Painful or easy!
Even to the crumbs I'd fain eat up the feast,
    Aye, nor feel queasy."
65 Oh, such a life as he resolved to live,
    When he had learned it,
When he had gathered all books had to give!
    Sooner, he spurned it.
Image the whole, then execute the parts—
70   Fancy the fabric
Quite, ere you build, ere steel strike fire from quartz,
    Ere mortar dab brick!

(Here's the town gate reached: there's the market place
    Gaping before us.)
75 Yea, this in him was the peculiar grace
    (Hearten our chorus!)
That before living he'd learn how to live—
    No end to learning:
Earn the means first—God surely will contrive
80   Use for our earning.
Others mistrust and say, "But time escapes:
    Live now or never!"
He said, "What's time? Leave Now for dogs and apes!
    Man has Forever."
85 Back to his book then: deeper drooped his head:
    Calculus[8] racked him:
Leaden before, his eyes grew dross of lead:
    Tussis° attacked him.   *a cough*
"Now, master, take a little rest!"—not he!
90   (Caution redoubled,
Step two abreast, the way winds narrowly!)
    Not a whit troubled
Back to his studies, fresher than at first,
    Fierce as a dragon
95 He (soul-hydroptic[9] with a sacred thirst)
    Sucked at the flagon.
Oh, if we draw a circle premature,
    Heedless of far gain,
Greedy for quick returns of profit, sure
100   Bad is our bargain!
Was it not great? did not he throw on God
    (He loves the burthen)—
God's task to make the heavenly period
    Perfect the earthen?

7. Commentaries or annotations on a text.   9. Insatiably soul thirsty.
8. A stone such as a gallstone.

105 Did not he magnify the mind, show clear
        Just what it all meant?
    He would not discount life, as fools do here,
        Paid by installment.
    He ventured neck or nothing—heaven's success
110   Found, or earth's failure:
    "Wilt thou trust death or not?" He answered "Yes:
        Hence with life's pale lure!"
    That low man seeks a little thing to do,
        Sees it and does it:
115 This high man, with a great thing to pursue,
        Dies ere he knows it.
    That low man goes on adding one to one,
        His hundred's soon hit:
    This high man, aiming at a million,
120   Misses an unit.[1]
    That, has the world here—should he need the next,
        Let the world mind him!
    This, throws himself on God, and unperplexed
        Seeking shall find him.
125 So, with the throttling hands of death at strife,
        Ground he at grammar;
    Still, through the rattle, parts of speech were rife:
        While he could stammer
    He settled *Hoti's* business—let it be!—
130   Properly based *Oun*—
    Gave us the doctrine of the enclitic *De*,[2]
        Dead from the waist down.
    Well, here's the platform, here's the proper place:
        Hail to your purlieus,
135 All ye highfliers of the feathered race,
        Swallows and curlews!
    Here's the top peak; the multitude below
        Live, for they can, there:
    This man decided not to Live but Know—
140   Bury this man there?
    Here—here's his place, where meteors shoot, clouds form,
        Lightnings are loosened,
    Stars come and go! Let joy break with the storm,
        Peace let the dew send!
145 Lofty designs must close in like effects:
        Loftily lying,
    Leave him—still loftier than the world suspects,
        Living and dying.

ca. 1854   1855

---

1. A small item such as some trifling worldly pleasure.
2. "*Hoti*," "*Oun*," and "*De*": Greek particles meaning "that," "then," and "toward." An unaccented
word such as *de* is "enclitic" when it affects the
accentuation of a word adjacent to it. In a letter of
1863, Browning commented to Tennyson that he
wanted his grammarian to have been working on
"the biggest of the littlenesses."

An Epistle Containing the Strange Medical Experience of Karshish, the Arab Physician[1]

Karshish, the picker-up of learning's crumbs,
The not-incurious in God's handiwork
(This man's-flesh he hath admirably made,
Blown like a bubble, kneaded like a paste,
5   To coop up and keep down on earth a space
That puff of vapor from his mouth, man's soul)[2]
—To Abib, all-sagacious in our art,
Breeder in me of what poor skill I boast,
Like me inquisitive how pricks and cracks
10 Befall the flesh through too much stress and strain,
Whereby the wily vapor fain would slip
Back and rejoin its source before the term,—
And aptest in contrivance (under God)
To baffle it by deftly stopping such:—
15 The vagrant° Scholar to his Sage at home   *wandering*
Sends greeting (health and knowledge, fame with peace)
Three samples of true snakestone[3]—rarer still,
One of the other sort, the melon-shaped,
(But fitter, pounded fine, for charms than drugs)
20 And writeth now the twenty-second time.

My journeyings were brought to Jericho:
Thus I resume. Who studious in our art
Shall count a little labor unrepaid?
I have shed sweat enough, left flesh and bone
25 On many a flinty furlong of this land.
Also, the country-side is all on fire
With rumors of a marching hitherward:
Some say Vespasian[4] cometh, some, his son.
A black lynx snarled and pricked a tufted ear;
30 Lust of my blood inflamed his yellow balls:°   *eyeballs*
I cried and threw my staff and he was gone.
Twice have the robbers stripped and beaten me,
And once a town declared me for a spy;
But at the end, I reach Jerusalem,
35 Since this poor covert where I pass the night,
This Bethany,[5] lies scarce the distance thence
A man with plague-sores at the third degree

1. The letter is written in 66 C.E., when the Romans, under Vespasian, were to invade Palestine. During a journey across the country, Karshish, whose name in Arabic means "one who gathers" (or roughly, "the picker-up of learning's crumbs"), has been collecting information on medical and scientific developments he has encountered. The "case" that has intrigued him most recently is that of Lazarus, a Jew who is reputed to have died and been miraculously brought back to life by a "Nazarene physician" many years earlier (cf. John 11.1–46). Karshish's letter is addressed from Bethlehem to Abib, formerly his science teacher and now his colleague and friend. Both scientists are imaginary characters.
2. Karshish is referring to the old belief that the soul leaves the body with the last breath in the form of a vapor.
3. A stone used to treat snake bites.
4. The Roman commander (and later emperor) who invaded Palestine in 66 C.E. His son Titus destroyed Jerusalem four years later.
5. The small village where Lazarus lives, located two miles south of Jerusalem.

Runs till he drops down dead. Thou laughest here!
'Sooth,[6] it elates me, thus reposed and safe,
40   To void the stuffing of my travel-scrip°   *small bag*
And share with thee whatever Jewry yields.
A viscid choler is observable
In tertians,[7] I was nearly bold to say;
And falling-sickness° hath a happier cure   *epilepsy*
45   Than our school wots° of: there's a spider here   *knows*
Weaves no web, watches on the ledge of tombs,
Sprinkled with mottles on an ash-gray back;
Take five and drop them . . . but who knows his mind,
The Syrian runagate° I trust this to?   *renegade*
50   His service payeth me a sublimate[8]
Blown up his nose to help the ailing eye.
Best wait: I reach Jerusalem at morn,
There set in order my experiences,
Gather what most deserves, and give thee all—
55   Or I might add, Judea's gum-tragacanth[9]
Scales off in purer flakes, shines clearer-grained,
Cracks 'twixt the pestle and the porphyry,[1]
In fine exceeds our produce. Scalp-disease
Confounds me, crossing so with leprosy—
60   Thou hadst admired one sort I gained at Zoar[2]
But zeal outruns discretion. Here I end.

     Yet stay: my Syrian blinketh gratefully,
Protesteth his devotion is my price—
Suppose I write what harms not, though he steal?
65   I half resolve to tell thee, yet I blush,
What set me off a-writing first of all.
An itch I had, a sting to write, a tang!
For, be it this town's barrenness—or else
The Man° had something in the look of him—   *Lazarus*
70   His case has struck me far more than 'tis worth.
So, pardon if—(lest presently I lose
In the great press of novelty at hand
The care and pains this somehow stole from me)
I bid thee take the thing while fresh in mind,
75   Almost in sight—for, wilt thou have the truth?
The very man is gone from me but now,
Whose ailment is the subject of discourse.
Thus then, and let thy better wit help all!

     'Tis but a case of mania—subinduced[3]
80   By epilepsy, at the turning-point
Of trance prolonged unduly some three days:

---

6. Forsooth; in truth.
7. A sticky bile is observable in fevers occurring
every other day.
8. I.e., pays me for a medicine.
9. A salve derived from a plant.

1. A hard rock against which the substance is
pounded with a pestle.
2. Town north of the Dead Sea.
3. Brought about as a result of something else.

When, by the exhibition° of some drug   *administration*
Or spell, exorcization, stroke of art
Unknown to me and which 'twere well to know,
85   The evil thing out-breaking all at once
Left the man whole and sound of body indeed,—
But, flinging (so to speak) life's gates too wide,
Making a clear house of it too suddenly,
The first conceit° that entered might inscribe   *idea*
90   Whatever it was minded on the wall
So plainly at that vantage, as it were,
(First come, first served) that nothing subsequent
Attaineth to erase those fancy-scrawls
The just-returned and new-established soul
95   Hath gotten now so thoroughly by heart
That henceforth she will read or these or none.
And first—the man's own firm conviction rests
That he was dead (in fact they buried him)
—That he was dead and then restored to life
100 By a Nazarene physician of his tribe:
—'Sayeth, the same bade "Rise," and he did rise.
"Such cases are diurnal,"[4] thou wilt cry.
Not so this figment!—not, that such a fume,[5]
Instead of giving way to time and health,
105 Should eat itself into the life of life,
As saffron[6] tingeth flesh, blood, bones and all!
For see, how he takes up the after-life.
The man—it is one Lazarus a Jew,
Sanguine,° proportioned, fifty years of age,   *robust*
110 The body's habit wholly laudable,°   *healthy*
As much, indeed, beyond the common health
As he were made and put aside to show.
Think, could we penetrate by any drug
And bathe the wearied soul and worried flesh,
115 And bring it clear and fair, by three days' sleep!
Whence has the man the balm that brightens all?
This grown man eyes the world now like a child.
Some elders of his tribe, I should premise,[7]
Led in their friend, obedient as a sheep,
120 To bear my inquisition. While they spoke,
Now sharply, now with sorrow,—told the case,—
He listened not except I spoke to him,
But folded his two hands and let them talk,
Watching the flies that buzzed: and yet no fool.
125 And that's a sample how his years must go.
Look, if a beggar, in fixed middle-life,
Should find a treasure,—can he use the same
With straitened habits and with tastes starved small,
And take at once to his impoverished brain
130 The sudden element that changes things,

4. Occur every day.
5. A vapor standing for a hallucinated belief.
6. Yellow-colored dye made from the plant of the
same name, also used as a spice.
7. Set forth beforehand.

That sets the undreamed-of rapture at his hand
And puts the cheap old joy in the scorned dust?
Is he not such an one as moves to mirth—
Warily parsimonious, when no need,
135 Wasteful as drunkenness at undue times?
All prudent counsel as to what befits
The golden mean, is lost on such an one:
The man's fantastic will is the man's law.
So here—we call the treasure knowledge, say,
140 Increased beyond the fleshly faculty—
Heaven opened to a soul while yet on earth,
Earth forced on a soul's use while seeing heaven:
The man is witless of the size, the sum,
The value in proportion of all things,
145 Or whether it be little or be much.
Discourse to him of prodigious armaments
Assembled to besiege his city now,
And of the passing of a mule with gourds—
'Tis one! Then take it on the other side,
150 Speak of some trifling fact,—he will gaze rapt
With stupor at its very littleness
(Far as I see), as if in that indeed
He caught prodigious import, whole results;
And so will turn to us the bystanders
155 In ever the same stupor (note this point)
That we too see not with his opened eyes.
Wonder and doubt come wrongly into play,
Preposterously, at cross-purposes.
Should his child sicken unto death,—why, look
160 For scarce abatement of his cheerfulness,
Or pretermission° of the daily craft!   *interruption*
While a word, gesture, glance from that same child
At play or in the school or laid asleep,
Will startle him to an agony of fear,
165 Exasperation, just as like. Demand
The reason why—" 'tis but a word," object—
"A gesture"—he regards thee as our lord[8]
Who lived there in the pyramid alone,
Looked at us (dost thou mind?) when, being young,
170 We both would unadvisedly recite
Some charm's beginning, from that book of his,
Able to bid the sun throb wide and burst
All into stars, as suns grown old are wont.
Thou and the child have each a veil alike
175 Thrown o'er your heads, from under which ye both
Stretch your blind hands and trifle with a match
Over a mine of Greek fire,[9] did ye know!
He holds on firmly to some thread of life—
(It is the life to lead perforcedly)

8. A magician or wise man under whom Karshish   9. Weapon made of sulfur, naphtha, and saltpeter.
and Abib had studied.

180 Which runs across some vast distracting orb
Of glory on either side that meager thread,
Which, conscious of, he must not enter yet—
The spiritual life around the earthly life:
The law of that is known to him as this,[1]
185 His heart and brain move there, his feet stay here.
So is the man perplexed with impulses
Sudden to start off crosswise, not straight on,
Proclaiming what is right and wrong across,
And not along, this black thread through the blaze—
190 "It should be" balked by "here it cannot be."
And oft the man's soul springs into his face
As if he saw again and heard again
His sage that bade him "Rise" and he did rise.
Something, a word, a tick o' the blood° within   *pulse beat*
195 Admonishes: then back he sinks at once
To ashes, who was very fire before,
In sedulous recurrence to his trade
Whereby he earneth him the daily bread;
And studiously the humbler for that pride,
200 Professedly the faultier that he knows
God's secret, while he holds the thread of life.
Indeed the especial marking of the man
Is prone submission to the heavenly will—
Seeing it, what it is, and why it is.
205 'Sayeth,° he will wait patient to the last   *he says*
For that same death which must restore his being
To equilibrium, body loosening soul
Divorced even now by premature full growth:
He will live, nay, it pleaseth him to live
210 So long as God please, and just how God please.
He even seeketh not to please God more
(Which meaneth, otherwise) than as God please.
Hence, I perceive not he affects° to preach   *aspires*
The doctrine of his sect whate'er it be,
215 Make proselytes as madmen thirst to do:
How can he give his neighbor the real ground,
His own conviction? Ardent as he is—
Call his great truth a lie, why, still the old
"Be it as God please" reassureth him.
220 I probed the sore[2] as thy disciple should:
"How, beast," said I, "this stolid carelessness
Sufficeth thee, when Rome is on her march
To stamp out like a little spark thy town,
Thy tribe, thy crazy tale and thee at once?"
225 He merely looked with his large eyes on me.
The man is apathetic, you deduce?
Contrariwise, he loves both old and young,
Able and weak, affects[3] the very brutes

---

1. I.e., he knows the law of the spiritual life as well
as that of the earthly life.

2. Investigated the case.
3. Has affection for.

And birds—how say I? flowers of the field—
230 As a wise workman recognizes tools
In a master's workshop, loving what they make.
Thus is the man, as harmless as a lamb:
Only impatient, let him do his best,
At ignorance and carelessness and sin—
235 An indignation which is promptly curbed:
As when in certain travels I have feigned
To be an ignoramus in our art
According to some preconceived design,
And happed to hear the land's practitioners
240 Steeped in conceit sublimed[4] by ignorance,
Prattle fantastically on disease,
Its cause and cure—and I must hold my peace!

Thou wilt object—Why have I not ere this
Sought out the sage himself, the Nazarene
245 Who wrought this cure, inquiring at the source,
Conferring with the frankness that befits?
Alas! it grieveth me, the learnèd leech°   doctor
Perished in a tumult many years ago,
Accused,—our learning's fate,—of wizardry,
250 Rebellion, to the setting up a rule
And creed prodigious as described to me.
His death, which happened when the earthquake fell[5]
(Prefiguring, as soon appeared, the loss
To occult learning in our lord the sage
255 Who lived there in the pyramid alone)
Was wrought by the mad people—that's their wont!
On vain recourse, as I conjecture it,
To his tried virtue, for miraculous help—
How could he stop the earthquake? That's their way!
260 The other imputations must be lies:
But take one, though I loathe to give it thee,
In mere respect for any good man's fame.
(And after all, our patient Lazarus
Is stark mad; should we count on what he says?
265 Perhaps not: though in writing to a leech
'Tis well to keep back nothing of a case.)
This man so cured regards the curer, then,
As—God forgive me! who but God himself,
Creator and sustainer of the world,
270 That came and dwelt in flesh on it awhile!
—'Sayeth that such an one was born and lived,
Taught, healed the sick, broke bread at his own house,
Then died, with Lazarus by, for aught I know,
And yet was . . . what I said nor choose repeat,
275 And must have so avouched himself, in fact,
In hearing of this very Lazarus

4. Exalted. "Conceit": foolish fancy.
5. The earthquake at the time of Christ's crucifixion reported in Matthew 27.51.

Who saith—but why all this of what he saith?
Why write of trivial matters, things of price
Calling at every moment for remark?
280 I noticed on the margin of a pool
Blue-flowering borage, the Aleppo[6] sort,
Aboundeth, very nitrous. It is strange!

Thy pardon for this long and tedious case,
Which, now that I review it, needs must seem
285 Unduly dwelt on, prolixly set forth!
Nor I myself discern in what is writ
Good cause for the peculiar interest
And awe indeed this man has touched me with.
Perhaps the journey's end, the weariness
290 Had wrought upon me first. I met him thus:
I crossed a ridge of short sharp broken hills
Like an old lion's cheek teeth. Out there came
A moon made like a face with certain spots
Multiform, manifold and menacing:
295 Then a wind rose behind me. So we met
In this old sleepy town at unaware,
The man and I. I send thee what is writ.
Regard it as a chance, a matter risked
To this ambiguous Syrian—he may lose,
300 Or steal, or give it thee with equal good,
Jerusalem's repose shall make amends
For time this letter wastes, thy time and mine;
Till when, once more thy pardon and farewell!

The very God! think, Abib; dost thou think?
305 So, the All-Great, were the All-Loving too—
So, through the thunder comes a human voice
Saying, "O heart I made, a heart beats here!
Face, my hands fashioned, see it in myself!
Thou hast no power nor mayst conceive of mine,
310 But love I gave thee, with myself to love,
And thou must love me who have died for thee!"
The madman saith He said so: it is strange.

1855

Caliban upon Setebos

Two closely related controversies of the Victorian period led Browning to write this poem (the title of which means "Caliban's thoughts about Setebos"). The first, stimulated by Darwin, was concerned with humanity's origins and our relation to other animals (the poem teems with animal life; in 295 lines, as Park Honan has shown, there are sixty-three references to animals). Caliban, the half-man and half-monster of Shakespeare's *Tempest*, provided the poet with a model of how the mind of a primitive creature may operate. The second controversy

---

6. Town in northern Syria. "Borage": herb used medicinally that contains niter.

concerned the nature of God and God's responsibility for the existence of suffering in the world. Like many humans, Caliban thinks of God's nature as similar to his own. His anthropomorphic conception of the deity, whom he calls Setebos, is confined to what he has observed of life on his island and to what he has observed of himself. From the former derives his "natural theology," that is, his identifying the character of God from evidences provided by nature rather than from the evidence of supernatural revelation. From the latter, his observation of his own character, derives Caliban's conception of God's willful power. Caliban himself admires power and thinks of God in Calvinistic terms as a being who selects at random some creatures who are to be saved and others who are to be condemned to suffer.

An obstacle for the reader is Caliban's use of the third-person pronoun to refer to himself. Thus " 'Will sprawl" means "Caliban will sprawl" (an apostrophe before the verb usually indicates that Caliban himself is the implied subject). The deity is also referred to in the third person but with an initial capital letter ("He").

Caliban upon Setebos

Or Natural Theology in the Island

"Thou thoughtest that I was altogether such a one as thyself."[1]

['Will sprawl, now that the heat of day is best,
Flat on his belly in the pit's much mire,
With elbows wide, fists clenched to prop his chin.
And, while he kicks both feet in the cool slush,
5   And feels about his spine small eft-things° course,   *water lizards*
Run in and out each arm, and make him laugh:
And while above his head a pompion° plant,   *pumpkin*
Coating the cave-top as a brow its eye,
Creeps down to touch and tickle hair and beard,
10   And now a flower drops with a bee inside,
And now a fruit to snap at, catch and crunch—
He looks out o'er yon sea which sunbeams cross
And recross till they weave a spider web
(Meshes of fire, some great fish breaks at times)
15   And talks to his own self, howe'er he please,
Touching that other, whom his dam[2] called God.
Because to talk about Him, vexes—ha,
Could He but know! and time to vex is now,
When talk is safer than in wintertime.
20   Moreover Prosper and Miranda[3] sleep
In confidence he drudges at their task,
And it is good to cheat the pair, and gibe,
Letting the rank tongue blossom into speech.]

Setebos, Setebos, and Setebos!
25   'Thinketh, He dwelleth i' the cold o' the moon.

'Thinketh He made it, with the sun to match,
But not the stars; the stars came otherwise;

1. Psalm 50.21. The speaker is God.
2. Caliban's mother, Sycorax.

3. The daughter of Prospero, the magician, who is Caliban's master in *The Tempest*.

Only made clouds, winds, meteors, such as that:
Also this isle, what lives and grows thereon,
30　And snaky sea which rounds and ends the same.

'Thinketh, it came of being ill at ease:
He hated that He cannot change His cold,
Nor cure its ache. 'Hath spied an icy fish
That longed to 'scape the rock-stream where she lived,
35　And thaw herself within the lukewarm brine
O' the lazy sea her stream thrusts far amid,
A crystal spike 'twixt two warm walls of wave;[4]
Only, she ever sickened, found repulse
At the other kind of water, not her life,
40　(Green-dense and dim-delicious, bred o' the sun)
Flounced back from bliss she was not born to breathe,
And in her old bounds buried her despair,
Hating and loving warmth alike: so He.

'Thinketh, He made thereat the sun, this isle,
45　Trees and the fowls here, beast and creeping thing.
Yon otter, sleek-wet, black, lithe as a leech;
Yon auk,° one fire-eye in a ball of foam,　　　　　　　*sea bird*
That floats and feeds; a certain badger brown
He hath watched hunt with that slant white-wedge eye
50　By moonlight; and the pie° with the long tongue　　*magpie*
That pricks deep into oakwarts for a worm,
And says a plain word when she finds her prize,
But will not eat the ants; the ants themselves
That build a wall of seeds and settled stalks
55　About their hole—He made all these and more,
Made all we see, and us, in spite: how else?
He could not, Himself, make a second self
To be His mate; as well have made Himself:
He would not make what he mislikes or slights,
60　An eyesore to Him, or not worth His pains:
But did, in envy, listlessness, or sport,
Make what Himself would fain, in a manner, be—
Weaker in most points, stronger in a few,
Worthy, and yet mere playthings all the while,
65　Things He admires and mocks too—that is it.
Because, so brave, so better though they be,
It nothing skills if He begin to plague.[5]
Look now, I melt a gourd-fruit into mash,
Add honeycomb and pods, I have perceived,
70　Which bite like finches when they bill and kiss—
Then, when froth rises bladdery,° drink up all,　　　*bubbly*
Quick, quick, till maggots scamper through my brain;
Last, throw me on my back i' the seeded thyme,
And wanton, wishing I were born a bird.

---

4. I.e., the thin stream of cold water that is driven into the warm ocean like a spike between walls.

5. I.e., our superior virtues are of no help to us if God elects to inflict plagues on us.

75   Put case, unable to be what I wish,
      I yet could make a live bird out of clay:
      Would not I take clay, pinch my Caliban
      Able to fly?—for, there, see, he hath wings,
      And great comb like the hoopoe's[6] to admire,
80   And there, a sting to do his foes offense,
      There, and I will that he begin to live,
      Fly to yon rock-top, nip me off the horns
      Of griggs° high up that make the merry din,   *grasshoppers*
      Saucy through their veined wings, and mind me not.
85   In which feat, if his leg snapped, brittle clay,
      And he lay stupid-like—why, I should laugh;
      And if he, spying me, should fall to weep,
      Beseech me to be good, repair his wrong,
      Bid his poor leg smart less or grow again—
90   Well, as the chance were, this might take or else
      Not take my fancy: I might hear his cry,
      And give the mankin three sound legs for one,
      Or pluck the other off, leave him like an egg,
      And lessoned he was mine and merely clay.
95   Were this no pleasure, lying in the thyme,
      Drinking the mash, with brain become alive,
      Making and marring clay at will? So He.
      'Thinketh, such shows nor right nor wrong in Him,
      Nor kind, nor cruel: He is strong and Lord.
100   'Am strong myself compared to yonder crabs
      That march now from the mountain to the sea;
      'Let twenty pass, and stone the twenty-first,
      Loving not, hating not, just choosing so.
      'Say, the first straggler that boasts purple spots
105   Shall join the file, one pincer twisted off;
      'Say, this bruised fellow shall receive a worm,
      And two worms he whose nippers end in red;
      As it likes me each time, I do: so He.

      Well then, 'supposeth He is good i' the main,
110   Placable if His mind and ways were guessed,
      But rougher than His handiwork, be sure!
      Oh, He hath made things worthier than Himself,
      And envieth that, so helped, such things do more
      Than He who made them! What consoles but this?
115   That they, unless through Him, do naught at all,
      And must submit: what other use in things?
      'Hath cut a pipe of pithless elder-joint
      That, blown through, gives exact the scream o' the jay
      When from her wing you twitch the feathers blue:
120   Sound this, and little birds that hate the jay
      Flock within stone's throw, glad their foe is hurt:
      Put case such pipe could prattle and boast forsooth,
      "I catch the birds, I am the crafty thing,

6. Bird with bright plumage.

I make the cry my maker cannot make
125   With his great round mouth; he must blow through mine!"
Would not I smash it with my foot? So He.

But wherefore rough, why cold and ill at ease?
Aha, that is a question! Ask, for that,
What knows—the something over Setebos
130   That made Him, or He, may be, found and fought,
Worsted, drove off and did to nothing,° perchance.   *completely overcame*
There may be something quiet o'er His head,
Out of His reach, that feels nor joy nor grief,
Since both derive from weakness in some way.
135   I joy because the quails come; would not joy
Could I bring quails here when I have a mind:
This Quiet, all it hath a mind to, doth.
'Esteemeth stars the outposts of its couch,
But never spends much thought nor care that way.
140   It may look up, work up—the worse for those
It works on! 'Careth but for Setebos[7]
The many-handed as a cuttlefish,
Who, making Himself feared through what He does,
Looks up, first, and perceives he cannot soar
145   To what is quiet and hath happy life;
Next looks down here, and out of very spite
Makes this a bauble-world to ape yon real,
These good things to match those as hips[8] do grapes.
'Tis solace making baubles, aye, and sport.
150   Himself peeped late, eyed Prosper at his books
Careless and lofty, lord now of the isle:
Vexed, 'stitched a book of broad leaves, arrow-shaped,
Wrote thereon, he knows what, prodigious words;
Has peeled a wand and called it by a name;
155   Weareth at whiles for an enchanter's robe
The eyed skin of a supple oncelot;[9]
And hath an ounce[1] sleeker than youngling mole,
A four-legged serpent he makes cower and couch,
Now snarl, now hold its breath and mind his eye,
160   And saith she is Miranda and my wife:
'Keeps for his Ariel[2] a tall pouch-bill crane
He bids go wade for fish and straight disgorge;
Also a sea beast, lumpish, which he snared,
Blinded the eyes of, and brought somewhat tame,
165   And split its toe-webs, and now pens the drudge
In a hole o' the rock and calls him Caliban;
A bitter heart that bides its time and bites.
'Plays thus at being Prosper in a way,
Taketh his mirth with make-believes: so He.

---

7. Caliban's concern is to appease only Setebos, not the other deity—the Quiet.
8. Hard fruits produced by wild roses.
9. Browning may have invented this term from the Spanish *oncela* or from the French *ocelot*. Both words signify a leopard or spotted wildcat.
1. A large, ferocious leopard, six or seven feet in length.
2. In *The Tempest*, a spirit who serves Prospero.

170   His dam held that the Quiet made all things
     Which Setebos vexed only: 'holds not so.
     Who made them weak, meant weakness He might vex.
     Had He meant other, while His hand was in,
     Why not make horny eyes no thorn could prick,
175   Or plate my scalp with bone against the snow,
     Or overscale my flesh 'neath joint and joint,
     Like an orc's° armor? Aye—so spoil His sport!   *sea monster's*
     He is the One now: only He doth all.

     'Saith, He may like, perchance, what profits Him.
180   Aye, himself loves what does him good; but why?
     'Gets good no otherwise. This blinded beast
     Loves whoso places flesh-meat on his nose,
     But, had he eyes, would want no help, but hate
     Or love, just as it liked him: He hath eyes.
185   Also it pleaseth Setebos to work,
     Use all His hands, and exercise much craft,
     By no means for the love of what is worked.
     'Tasteth, himself, no finer good i' the world
     When all goes right, in this safe summertime,
190   And he wants little, hungers, aches not much,
     Than trying what to do with wit and strength.
     'Falls to make something: 'piled yon pile of turfs,
     And squared and stuck there squares of soft white chalk,
     And, with a fish-tooth, scratched a moon on each,
195   And set up endwise certain spikes of tree,
     And crowned the whole with a sloth's skull a-top,
     Found dead i' the woods, too hard for one to kill.
     No use at all i' the work, for work's sole sake;
     'Shall some day knock it down again: so He.

200   'Saith He is terrible: watch His feats in proof!
     One hurricane will spoil six good months' hope.
     He hath a spite against me, that I know,
     Just as He favors Prosper, who knows why?
     So it is, all the same, as well I find.
205   'Wove wattles half the winter, fenced them firm
     With stone and stake to stop she-tortoises
     Crawling to lay their eggs here: well, one wave,
     Feeling the foot of Him upon its neck,
     Gaped as a snake does, lolled out its large tongue,
210   And licked the whole labor flat; so much for spite.
     'Saw a ball° flame down late (yonder it lies)   *meteorite*
     Where, half an hour before, I slept i' the shade:
     Often they scatter sparkles: there is force!
     'Dug up a newt He may have envied once
215   And turned to stone, shut up inside a stone.
     Please Him and hinder this?—What Prosper does?[3]

---

3. I.e., shall I please Setebos, as Prospero does, and thus prevent my being punished as the newt was punished?

Aha, if He would tell me how! Not He!
There is the sport: discover how or die!
All need not die, for of the things o' the isle
220 Some flee afar, some dive, some run up trees;
Those at His mercy—why, they please Him most
When . . . when . . . well, never try the same way twice!
Repeat what act has pleased, He may grow wroth.
You must not know His ways, and play Him off,
225 Sure of the issue. 'Doth the like himself:
'Spareth a squirrel that it nothing fears
But steals the nut from underneath my thumb,
And when I threat, bites stoutly in defense:
'Spareth an urchin° that contrariwise   *hedgehog*
230 Curls up into a ball, pretending death
For fright at my approach: the two ways please.
But what would move my choler more than this,
That either creature counted on its life
Tomorrow and next day and all days to come,
235 Saying, forsooth, in the inmost of its heart,
"Because he did so yesterday with me,
And otherwise with such another brute,
So must he do henceforth and always."—Aye?
Would teach the reasoning couple what "must" means!
240 'Doth as he likes, or wherefore Lord? So He.

'Conceiveth all things will continue thus,
And we shall have to live in fear of Him
So long as He lives, keeps His strength: no change,
If He have done His best, make no new world
245 To please Him more, so leave off watching this—
If He surprise not even the Quiet's self
Some strange day—or, suppose, grow into it
As grubs grow butterflies: else, here are we,
And there is He, and nowhere help at all.
250 'Believeth with the life, the pain shall stop.
His dam held different, that after death
He both plagued enemies and feasted friends:
Idly![4] He doth His worst in this our life,
Giving just respite lest we die through pain,
255 Saving last pain for worst—with which, an end.
Meanwhile, the best way to escape His ire
Is, not to seem too happy. 'Sees, himself,
Yonder two flies, with purple films and pink,
Bask on the pompion-bell above: kills both.
260 'Sees two black painful beetles roll their ball
On head and tail as if to save their lives:
Moves them the stick away they strive to clear.

Even so, 'would have Him misconceive, suppose
This Caliban strives hard and ails no less,

---

4. I.e., Caliban thinks his mother's opinion was wrong or idle. God's sport with humankind is confined to this world: there is no afterlife.

265　And always, above all else, envies Him;
　　　Wherefore he mainly dances on dark nights,
　　　Moans in the sun, gets under holes to laugh,
　　　And never speaks his mind save housed as now:
　　　Outside, 'groans, curses. If He caught me here,
270　O'erheard this speech, and asked "What chucklest at?"
　　　'Would, to appease Him, cut a finger off,
　　　Or of my three kid yearlings burn the best,
　　　Or let the toothsome apples rot on tree,
　　　Or push my tame beast for the orc to taste:
275　While myself lit a fire, and made a song
　　　And sung it, *"What I hate, be consecrate*
　　　To celebrate Thee and Thy state, no mate
　　　For Thee; what see for envy in poor me?"
　　　Hoping the while, since evils sometimes mend,
280　Warts rub away and sores are cured with slime,
　　　That some strange day, will either the Quiet catch
　　　And conquer Setebos, or likelier He
　　　Decrepit may doze, doze, as good as die.

　　　[What, what? A curtain o'er the world at once!
285　Crickets stop hissing; not a bird—or, yes,
　　　There scuds His raven that has told Him all!
　　　It was fool's play this prattling! Ha! The wind
　　　Shoulders the pillared dust, death's house o' the move,[5]
　　　And fast invading fires begin! White blaze—
290　A tree's head snaps—and there, there, there, there, there,
　　　His thunder follows! Fool to gibe at Him!
　　　Lo! 'Lieth flat and loveth Setebos!
　　　'Maketh his teeth meet through his upper lip,
　　　Will let those quails fly, will not eat this month
295　One little mess of whelks,° so he may 'scape!]　　　　*shellfish*

ca. 1860　　　　　　　　　　　　　　　　　　　　　　　　1864

Prospice[1]

　　　Fear death?—to feel the fog in my throat,
　　　　　The mist in my face,
　　　When the snows begin, and the blasts denote
　　　　　I am nearing the place,
5　　　The power of the night, the press of the storm,
　　　　　The post of the foe;
　　　Where he stands, the Arch Fear in a visible form,
　　　　　Yet the strong man must go:
　　　For the journey is done and the summit attained,
10　　　　And the barriers fall,
　　　Though a battle's to fight ere the guerdon be gained,
　　　　　The reward of it all.

5. The whirlwind stirs up a column of dust that
Caliban associates with a house of death.

1. The title means "Look forward."

I was ever a fighter, so—one fight more,
    The best and the last!
15 I would hate that death bandaged my eyes, and forbore,
    And bade me creep past.
No! let me taste the whole of it, fare like my peers
    The heroes of old,
Bear the brunt, in a minute pay glad life's arrears
20   Of pain, darkness, and cold.
For sudden the worst turns the best to the brave,
    The black minute's at end,
And the elements' rage, the fiend-voices that rave,
    Shall dwindle, shall blend,
25 Shall change, shall become first a peace out of pain,
    Then a light, then thy breast,
O thou soul of my soul![2] I shall clasp thee again,
    And with God be the rest!

ca. 1861   1864

Abt Vogler[1]

(*After He has Been Extemporizing Upon the Musical Instrument of His Invention*[2])

I

Would that the structure brave, the manifold music I build,
    Bidding my organ obey, calling its keys to their work,
Claiming each slave of the sound, at a touch, as when Solomon willed
    Armies of angels that soar, legions of demons that lurk,
5 Man, brute, reptile, fly—alien of end and of aim,
    Adverse, each from the other heaven-high, hell-deep removed—
Should rush into sight at once as he named the ineffable Name,[3]
    And pile him a palace straight, to pleasure the princess[4] he loved!

2

Would it might tarry like his, the beautiful building of mine,
10   This which my keys in a crowd pressed and importuned to raise!
Ah, one and all, how they helped, would dispart now and now combine,
    Zealous to hasten the work, heighten their master his praise!
And one would bury his brow with a blind plunge down to hell,

2. Browning's wife.
1. Georg Joseph Vogler (1749–1814), a German priest and musician, held the honorary title of *Abbé* or *Abt*. As a composer, teacher, and designer of musical instruments he was well known in his own day, but he was most famous as an extemporizer at the organ. Browning's soliloquy represents Vogler at the organ joyfully improvising a piece of music and then reflecting on the ephemeral existence of such a unique work of art and of its possible relation to God's purposes in heaven and on earth.
    A characteristic feature of *Abt Vogler* is the use

of exceptionally long sentences, densely packed with details, which may evoke for us the effects of rolling organ music. The resulting movement is markedly different from the brisk staccato rhythms of *A Toccata of Galuppi's*.
2. A compact organ called the orchestrion.
3. According to Jewish legend King Solomon (because he possessed a seal inscribed with the "ineffable Name" of God) had the power of compelling the demons of earth and air to perform his bidding.
4. Pharaoh's daughter (1 Kings 7.8).

Burrow awhile and build, broad on the roots of things,
15   Then up again swim into sight, having based me my palace well,
      Founded it, fearless of flame, flat on the nether springs.

3

And another would mount and march, like the excellent minion he was,
      Aye, another and yet another, one crowd but with many a crest,
Raising my rampired walls of gold as transparent as glass,
20   Eager to do and die, yield each his place to the rest:
For higher still and higher (as a runner tips with fire,
      When a great illumination surprises a festal night—
Outlining round and round Rome's dome from space to spire)[5]
      Up, the pinnacled glory reached, and the pride of my soul was in sight.

4

25 In sight? Not half! for it seemed, it was certain, to match man's birth,
      Nature in turn conceived, obeying an impulse as I;
And the emulous heaven yearned down, made effort to reach the earth,
      As the earth had done her best, in my passion, to scale the sky:
Novel splendors burst forth, grew familiar and dwelt with mine,
30   Not a point nor peak but found and fixed its wandering star;
Meteor-moons, balls of blaze: and they did not pale nor pine,
      For earth had attained to heaven, there was no more near nor far.

5

Nay more; for there wanted not who walked in the glare and glow,
      Presences plain in the place; or, fresh from the Protoplast,[6]
35 Furnished for ages to come, when a kindlier wind should blow,
      Lured now to begin and live, in a house to their liking at last;
Or else the wonderful Dead who have passed through the body and gone,
      But were back once more to breathe in an old world worth their new:
What never had been, was now; what was, as it shall be anon;
40   And what is—shall I say, matched both? for I was made perfect too.

6

All through my keys that gave their sounds to a wish of my soul,
      All through my soul that praised as its wish flowed visibly forth,
All through music and me! For think, had I painted the whole,
      Why, there it had stood, to see, nor the process so wonderworth:
45 Had I written the same, made verse—still, effect proceeds from cause,
      Ye know why the forms are fair, ye hear how the tale is told;
It is all triumphant art, but art in obedience to laws,
      Painter and poet are proud in the artist-list enrolled—

7

But here is the finger of God, a flash of the will that can,
50   Existent behind all laws, that made them and, lo, they are!

---

5. On festival nights the dome of Saint Peter's in Rome is illuminated by a series of lights ignited by a torch-bearer.

6. The original or archetypal form of a species. "Presences": beings of the future, not yet existing, who are "lured" into life by the music (line 36).

And I know not if, save in this, such gift be allowed to man,
 That out of three sounds he frame, not a fourth sound, but a star.[7]
Consider it well: each tone of our scale in itself is naught;
 It is everywhere in the world—loud, soft, and all is said:
55 Give it to me to use! I mix it with two in my thought:
 And, there! Ye have heard and seen: consider and bow the head!

8

Well, it is gone at last, the palace of music I reared;
 Gone! and the good tears start, the praises that come too slow;
For one is assured at first, one scarce can say that he feared,
60 That he even gave it a thought, the gone thing was to go.
Never to be again! But many more of the kind
 As good, nay, better perchance: is this your comfort to me?
To me, who must be saved because I cling with my mind
 To the same, same self, same love, same God: aye, what was, shall be.

9

65 Therefore to whom turn I but to thee, the ineffable Name?
 Builder and maker, thou, of houses not made with hands![8]
What, have fear of change from thee who art ever the same?
 Doubt that thy power can fill the heart that thy power expands?
There shall never be one lost good! What was, shall live as before;
70 The evil is null, is naught, is silence implying sound;
What was good shall be good, with, for evil, so much good more;
 On the earth the broken arcs; in the heaven, a perfect round.

10

All we have willed or hoped or dreamed of good shall exist;
 Not its semblance, but itself; no beauty, nor good, nor power
75 Whose voice has gone forth, but each survives for the melodist
 When eternity affirms the conception of an hour.
The high that proved too high, the heroic for earth too hard,
 The passion that left the ground to lose itself in the sky,
Are music sent up to God by the lover and the bard;
80 Enough that he heard it once: we shall hear it by-and-by.

11

And what is our failure here but a triumph's evidence
 For the fullness of the days? Have we withered or agonized?
Why else was the pause prolonged but that singing might issue thence?
 Why rushed the discords in but that harmony should be prized?
85 Sorrow is hard to bear, and doubt is slow to clear,
 Each sufferer says his say, his scheme of the weal and woe:
But God has a few of us whom he whispers in the ear;
 The rest may reason and welcome: 'tis we musicians know.

---

7. I.e., the musician's combining of three notes into a new harmonic unit is a creative act as miraculous as the creation of a star.

8. Cf. 2 Corinthians 5.1, in which Saint Paul speaks of "a building of God, a house not made with hands, eternal in the heavens."

12

Well, it is earth with me; silence resumes her reign:
90   I will be patient and proud, and soberly acquiesce.
Give me the keys. I feel for the common chord again,
     Sliding by semitones, till I sink to the minor—yes,
And I blunt it into a ninth,[9] and I stand on alien ground,
     Surveying awhile the heights I rolled from into the deep;
95 Which, hark, I have dared and done, for my resting place is found,
     The C Major[1] of this life: so, now I will try to sleep.

1864

Rabbi Ben Ezra[1]

1

    Grow old along with me!
    The best is yet to be,
The last of life, for which the first was made:
     Our times are in His hand
5   Who saith, "A whole I planned,
Youth shows but half; trust God: see all nor be afraid!"

2

    Not that, amassing flowers,
    Youth sighed, "Which rose make ours,
Which lily leave and then as best recall?"
10   Not that, admiring stars,
    It yearned, "Nor Jove, nor Mars;
Mine be some figured flame which blends, transcends them all!"

3

    Not for such hopes and fears
    Annulling youth's brief years,
15 Do I remonstrate: folly wide the mark!
    Rather I prize the doubt
    Low kinds exist without,
Finished and finite clods, untroubled by a spark.

4

    Poor vaunt of life indeed,
20   Were man but formed to feed
On joy, to solely seek and find and feast:
    Such feasting ended, then

9. A discord that requires resolution.
1. A key without sharps or flats, representing the plane of ordinary life.
1. The speaker, Abraham Ibn Ezra (ca. 1092–1167), was an eminent biblical scholar of Spain, but Browning makes little attempt to present him as a distinct individual or to relate him to the age in which he lived. Unlike the more characteristic monologues, *Rabbi Ben Ezra* is not dramatic but declamatory.

As sure an end to men;
Irks care the crop-full bird? Frets doubt the maw-crammed beast?[2]

5

25   Rejoice we are allied
    To That which doth provide
And not partake, effect and not receive!
    A spark disturbs our clod;
    Nearer we hold of God
30 Who gives, than of His tribes that take, I must believe.

6

    Then, welcome each rebuff
    That turns earth's smoothness rough,
Each sting that bids nor sit nor stand but go!
    Be our joys three parts pain!
35   Strive, and hold cheap the strain;
Learn, nor account the pang; dare, never grudge the throe!°   *anguish*

7

    For thence—a paradox
    Which comforts while it mocks—
Shall life succeed in that it seems to fail:
40   What I aspired to be,
    And was not, comforts me:
A brute I might have been, but would not sink i' the scale.

8

    What is he but a brute
    Whose flesh has soul to suit,
45 Whose spirit works lest arms and legs want play?
    To man, propose this test—
    Thy body at its best,
How far can that project thy soul on its lone way?

9

    Yet gifts should prove their use:
50   I own the Past profuse
Of power each side, perfection every turn:
    Eyes, ears took in their dole,
    Brain treasured up the whole;
Should not the heart beat once, "How good to live and learn"?

10

55   Not once beat, "Praise be Thine!
    I see the whole design,
I, who saw power, see now love perfect too:
    Perfect I call Thy plan:

---

2. I.e., does care disturb a bird whose gullet ("crop") is full of food? Does doubt trouble an animal whose stomach ("maw") is full?

Thanks that I was a man!
60 Maker, remake, complete—I trust what Thou shalt do!"

11

For pleasant is this flesh;
Our soul, in its rose-mesh[3]
Pulled ever to the earth, still yearns for rest;
Would we some prize might hold
65 To match those manifold
Possessions of the brute—gain most, as we did best!

12

Let us not always say,
"Spite of this flesh today
I strove, made head, gained ground upon the whole!"
70 As the bird wings and sings,
Let us cry, "All good things
Are ours, nor soul helps flesh more, now, than flesh helps soul!"

13

Therefore I summon age
To grant youth's heritage,
75 Life's struggle having so far reached its term:
Thence shall I pass, approved
A man, for aye removed
From the developed brute; a god though in the germ.

14

And I shall thereupon
80 Take rest, ere I be gone
Once more on my adventure brave and new;[4]
Fearless and unperplexed,
When I wage battle next,
What weapons to select, what armor to indue.°   *put on*

15

85 Youth ended, I shall try
My gain or loss thereby;
Leave the fire ashes,[5] what survives is gold:
And I shall weigh the same,
Give life its praise or blame:
90 Young, all lay in dispute; I shall know, being old.

16

For note, when evening shuts,
A certain moment cuts
The deed off, calls the glory from the gray:
A whisper from the west

---

3. The body, which holds the soul in its net.   5. If the fire leaves ashes.
4. In the next life.

95 Shoots—"Add this to the rest,
Take it and try its worth: here dies another day."

17

So, still within this life,
Though lifted o'er its strife,
Let me discern, compare, pronounce at last,
100 "This rage was right i' the main,
That acquiescence vain:
The Future I may face now I have proved the Past."

18

For more is not reserved
To man, with soul just nerved
105 To act tomorrow what he learns today:
Here, work enough to watch
The Master work, and catch
Hints of the proper craft, tricks of the tool's true play.

19

As it was better, youth
110 Should strive, through acts uncouth,
Toward making, than repose on aught found made:
So, better, age, exempt
From strife, should know, than tempt°   *attempt*
Further. Thou waitedst age: wait death nor be afraid!

20

115 Enough now, if the Right
And Good and Infinite
Be named here, as thou callest thy hand thine own,
With knowledge absolute,
Subject to no dispute
120 From fools that crowded youth, nor let thee feel alone.

21

Be there, for once and all,
Severed great minds from small,
Announced to each his station in the Past!
Was I, the world arraigned,[6]
125 Were they, my soul disdained,
Right? Let age speak the truth and give us peace at last![7]

22

Now, who shall arbitrate?
Ten men love what I hate,
Shun what I follow, slight what I receive;
130 Ten, who in ears and eyes

6. I.e., was I, whom the world arraigned.
7. Stanzas 20 and 21 affirm that in age we can more readily think independently than in youth.

Maturity enables us to ignore the pressure of having to conform to the thinking of the crowd of small-minded people.

Match me: we all surmise,
They this thing, and I that: whom shall my soul believe?

23

    Not on the vulgar mass
    Called "work," must sentence pass,
135   Things done, that took the eye and had the price;
      O'er which, from level stand,
      The low world laid its hand,
Found straightway to its mind, could value in a trice:

24

    But all, the world's coarse thumb
140   And finger failed to plumb,
So passed in making up the main account;
      All instincts immature,
      All purposes unsure,
That weighed not as his work, yet swelled the man's amount:

25

145   Thoughts hardly to be packed
    Into a narrow act,
Fancies that broke through language and escaped;
      All I could never be,
      All, men ignored in me,
150 This, I was worth to God, whose wheel the pitcher shaped.[8]

26

    Aye, note that Potter's wheel,
    That metaphor! and feel
Why time spins fast, why passive lies our clay—
      Thou, to whom fools propound,[9]
155   When the wine makes its round,
"Since life fleets, all is change; the Past gone, seize today!"

27

    Fool! All that is, at all,
    Lasts ever, past recall;
Earth changes, but thy soul and God stand sure:
160   What entered into thee,
      That was, is, and shall be:
Time's wheel runs back or stops: Potter and clay endure.

28

    He fixed thee 'mid this dance
    Of plastic circumstance,
165 This Present, thou, forsooth, wouldst fain arrest:[1]

---

8. The speaker's highest qualities of soul were shaped on a potting wheel into an enduring "pitcher" by God. Cf. Isaiah 64.8.
9. Perhaps addressed to Omar Khayyám, whose poem, *The Rubáiyát*, urged men to eat, drink, and be merry. Edward FitzGerald's translation of Omar's poem had appeared in 1859.
1. I.e., you would be glad to stop ("arrest") time at this present point of your life.

Machinery just meant
To give thy soul its bent,
Try thee and turn thee forth, sufficiently impressed.

29

What though the earlier grooves
170   Which ran the laughing loves
Around thy base,[2] no longer pause and press?
    What though, about thy rim,
    Skull-things in order grim
Grow out, in graver mood, obey the sterner stress?

30

175   Look not thou down but up!
    To uses of a cup,
The festal board, lamp's flash, and trumpet's peal,
    The new wine's foaming flow,
    The Master's lips a-glow!
180 Thou, heaven's consummate cup, what need'st thou with earth's wheel?

31

    But I need, now as then,
    Thee, God, who moldest men;
And since, not even while the whirl was worst,
    Did I—to the wheel of life
185   With shapes and colors rife,
Bound dizzily—mistake my end, to slake Thy thirst:

32

    So, take and use Thy work:
    Amend what flaws may lurk,
What strain o' the stuff, what warpings past the aim!
190   My times be in Thy hand!
    Perfect the cup as planned!
Let age approve of youth, and death complete the same!

ca. 1862   1864

2. Of the clay pitcher.

EMILY BRONTË
1818–1848

Emily Brontë spent most of her life in a stone parsonage in the small village of Haworth on the wild and bleak Yorkshire moors. She was the fifth of Patrick and Maria Brontë's six children. Her father was a clergyman; her mother died when she was two. At the age of six, she was sent away to a school for the daughters of poor clergy with her three elder sisters; within a year, the two oldest girls had died, in part the result of the school's harsh and unhealthful conditions, which Charlotte Brontë was later to portray in *Jane Eyre*. Mr. Brontë brought his two remaining daughters home, where, together with their brother and younger sister, he educated them himself. Emily was the most reclusive and private of the children; she shunned the company of those outside her family and suffered acutely from homesickness in her few short stays away from the parsonage.

Despite the isolation of Haworth, the Brontë family shared a rich literary life. Mr. Brontë discussed poetry, history, and politics with his children, and the children themselves created an extraordinary fantasy world together. When Mr. Brontë gave his son a box of wooden soldiers, each child excitedly seized one and named it. The soldiers became for them the centers of an increasingly elaborate set of stories that they first acted out in plays and later recorded in a series of book-length manuscripts, composed for the most part by Charlotte and her brother, Branwell. The two younger children, Emily and Anne, later started a separate series, a chronicle about an imaginary island called Gondal.

In Charlotte Brontë's preface to the second edition of *Wuthering Heights,* she tells the story of how she and her sister came to write for publication. One day when she accidentally came upon a manuscript volume of verse in Emily's handwriting, she was struck by the conviction "that these were not common effusions, nor at all like the poetry women generally write." With some difficulty, Charlotte persuaded her intensely private sister to publish some of her poems in a selection of poetry by all three Brontë sisters. Averse to personal publicity and afraid that "authoresses are liable to be looked on with prejudice," Charlotte, Emily, and Anne adopted the pseudonyms of Currer, Ellis, and Acton Bell. Although the book sold only two copies, its publication inspired each of the Brontë sisters to begin work on a novel; Emily's, of course, was *Wuthering Heights*. She began work on a second novel, but a year after the publication of *Wuthering Heights,* she died of consumption.

Many of Emily's poems—*Remembrance* and *The Prisoner,* for example—were written for the Gondal saga and express its preoccupation with political intrigue, passionate love, rebellion, war, imprisonment, and exile. Brontë also wrote personal lyrics unconnected with the Gondal stories; but both groups of poems share a drive to break through the constrictions of ordinary life, whether by the transfigurative power of the imagination, by union with another, or by death itself. Like Catherine and Heathcliff in *Wuthering Heights,* the speakers of Brontë's poems yearn for a fuller, freer world of spirit, transcending the forms and limits of mortal life. Her concern with a visionary world links her to the Romantic poets, particularly to Byron and Shelley; but her hymnlike stanzas have a haunting quality that distinguishes her individual voice.

The texts printed here are from the edition of *Poems* published by the Brontë sisters for the poems it includes and C. W. Hatfield's edition of Brontë's manuscripts for the poems she did not publish during her life.

I'm Happiest When Most Away

I'm happiest when most away
I can bear my soul from its home of clay
On a windy night when the moon is bright
And the eye can wander through worlds of light—

5   When I am not and none beside—
Nor earth nor sea nor cloudless sky—
But only spirit wandering wide
Through infinite immensity.

1838   1910

The Night-Wind

In summer's mellow midnight,
A cloudless moon shone through
Our open parlour window
And rosetrees wet with dew.

5 I sat in silent musing,
The soft wind waved my hair:
It told me Heaven was glorious.
And sleeping Earth was fair.

I needed not its breathing
10 To bring such thoughts to me,
But still it whispered lowly,
"How dark the woods will be!

"The thick leaves in my murmur
Are rustling like a dream,
15 And all their myriad voices
Instinct with spirit seem."

I said, "Go, gentle singer,
Thy wooing voice is kind,
But do not think its music
20 Has power to reach my mind.

"Play with the scented flower,
The young tree's supple bough,
And leave my human feelings
In their own course to flow."

25 The wanderer would not leave me;
Its kiss grew warmer still—
"O come," it sighed so sweetly,
"I'll win thee 'gainst thy will.

"Have we not been from childhood friends?
30 Have I not loved thee long?
As long as thou hast loved the night
Whose silence wakes my song.

"And when thy heart is laid at rest
Beneath the church-yard stone
35 I shall have time enough to mourn
And thou to be alone."

1840   1850

Remembrance[1]

Cold in the earth, and the deep snow piled above thee!
Far, far removed, cold in the dreary grave!
Have I forgot, my Only Love, to love thee,
Severed at last by Time's all-wearing wave?

5   Now, when alone, do my thoughts no longer hover
Over the mountains, on that northern shore;
Resting their wings where heath and fern-leaves cover
Thy noble heart for ever, ever more?

Cold in the earth, and fifteen wild Decembers
10 From those brown hills have melted into spring—
Faithful indeed is the spirit that remembers
After such years of change and suffering!

Sweet Love of youth, forgive if I forget thee
While the World's tide is bearing me along:
15 Other desires and other hopes beset me,
Hopes which obscure but cannot do thee wrong.

No later light has lightened up my heaven,
No second morn has ever shone for me:
All my life's bliss from thy dear life was given—
20 All my life's bliss is in the grave with thee.

But when the days of golden dreams had perished
And even Despair was powerless to destroy,
Then did I learn how existence could be cherished,
Strengthened and fed without the aid of joy;

25 Then did I check the tears of useless passion,
Weaned my young soul from yearning after thine;
Sternly denied its burning wish to hasten
Down to that tomb already more than mine!

And even yet, I dare not let it languish,
30 Dare not indulge in Memory's rapturous pain;
Once drinking deep of that divinest anguish,
How could I seek the empty world again?

1845   1846

Stars

Ah! why, because the dazzling sun
Restored our earth to joy

---

1. Titled in manuscript *R. Alcona to J. Breznaida,* this poem was originally composed as a lament by the heroine of the Gondal saga for the hero's death.

Have you departed, every one,
And left a desert sky?

5   All through the night, your glorious eyes
Were gazing down in mine,
And with a full heart's thankful sighs
I blessed that watch divine!

I was at peace, and drank your beams
10   As they were life to me
And revelled in my changeful dreams
Like petrel° on the sea.   *small dark seabirds*

Thought followed thought—star followed star
Through boundless regions on,
15   While one sweet influence, near and far,
Thrilled through and proved us one.

Why did the morning dawn to break
So great, so pure a spell,
And scorch with fire the tranquil cheek
20   Where your cool radiance fell?

Blood-red he rose, and arrow-straight
His fierce beams struck my brow:
The soul of Nature sprang elate,
But mine sank sad and low!

25   My lids closed down—yet through their veil
I saw him blazing still;
And steep in gold the misty dale
And flash upon the hill.

I turned me to the pillow then
30   To call back Night, and see
Your worlds of solemn light, again
Throb with my heart and me!

It would not do—the pillow glowed
And glowed both roof and floor,
35   And birds sang loudly in the wood,
And fresh winds shook the door.

The curtains waved, the wakened flies
Were murmuring round my room,
Imprisoned there, till I should rise
40   And give them leave to roam.

O Stars and Dreams and Gentle Night;
O Night and Stars return!
And hide me from the hostile light
That does not warm, but burn—

⁴⁵ That drains the blood of suffering men;
Drinks tears, instead of dew:
Let me sleep through his blinding reign,
And only wake with you!

1845   1846

The Prisoner. A Fragment[1]

In the dungeon crypts idly did I stray,
Reckless of the lives wasting there away;
"Draw the ponderous bars; open, Warder stern!"
He dare not say me nay—the hinges harshly turn.

5   "Our guests are darkly lodged," I whispered, gazing through
The vault whose grated eye showed heaven more grey than blue.
(This was when glad spring laughed in awaking pride.)
"Aye, darkly lodged enough!" returned my sullen guide.

Then, God forgive my youth, forgive my careless tongue!
10 I scoffed, as the chill chains on the damp flagstones rung;
"Confined in triple walls, art thou so much to fear,
That we must bind thee down and clench thy fetters here?"

The captive raised her face; it was as soft and mild
As sculptured marble saint or slumbering, unweaned child;
15 It was so soft and mild, it was so sweet and fair,
Pain could not trace a line nor grief a shadow there!

The captive raised her hand and pressed it to her brow:
"I have been struck," she said, "and I am suffering now;
Yet these are little worth, your bolts and irons strong;
20 And were they forged in steel they could not hold me long."

Hoarse laughed the jailor grim: "Shall I be won to hear;
Dost think, fond° dreaming wretch, that *I* shall grant thy prayer?   *foolish*
Or, better still, wilt melt my master's heart with groans?
Ah, sooner might the sun thaw down these granite stones!

25 "My master's voice is low, his aspect bland and kind,
But hard as hardest flint the soul that lurks behind;
And I am rough and rude, yet not more rough to see
Than is the hidden ghost which has its home in me!

About her lips there played a smile of almost scorn:
30 "My friend," she gently said, "you have not heard me mourn;
When you my kindred's lives—*my* lost life, can restore
Then may I weep and sue—but *never*, Friend, before!"

1. An excerpt from a poem in the Gondal manuscript, *Julian M. and A. G. Rochelle*, describing an
event unplaced in the story, this poem was printed
as *The Prisoner: A Fragment* in *Poems* by the
Brontë sisters. The speaker, a man, is visiting a
dungeon in his father's castle.

"Still, let my tyrants know, I am not doomed to wear
Year after year in gloom and desolate despair;
35 A messenger of Hope comes every night to me,
And offers, for short life, eternal liberty.

He comes with western winds, with evening's wandering airs,
With that clear dusk of heaven that brings the thickest stars;
Winds take a pensive tone, and stars a tender fire,
40 And visions rise and change that kill me with desire—

"Desire for nothing known in my maturer years
When joy grew mad with awe at counting future tears;
When, if my spirit's sky was full of flashes warm,
I knew not whence they came, from sun or thunderstorm;

45 "But first a hush of peace, a soundless calm descends;
The struggle of distress and fierce impatience ends;
Mute music soothes my breast—unuttered harmony
That I could never dream till earth was lost to me.

"Then dawns the Invisible, the Unseen its truth reveals;
50 My outward sense is gone, my inward essence feels—
Its wings are almost free, its home, its harbour found;
Measuring the gulf it stoops and dares the final bound!

"Oh, dreadful is the check—intense the agony
When the ear begins to hear and the eye begins to see;
55 When the pulse begins to throb, the brain to think again,
The soul to feel the flesh and the flesh to feel the chain!

"Yet I would lose no sting, would wish no torture less;
The more that anguish racks the earlier it will bless;
And robed in fires of Hell, or bright with heavenly shine,
60 If it but herald Death, the vision is divine."[2]

She ceased to speak, and we, unanswering turned to go—
We had no further power to work the captive woe;
Her cheek, her gleaming eye, declared that man had given
A sentence unapproved, and overruled by Heaven.

1845   1846

No Coward Soul Is Mine[1]

No coward soul is mine
No trembler in the world's storm-troubled sphere

2. Cf. the words of the dying Catherine in *Wuthering Heights*: "The thing that irks me most is this shattered prison [my body]. . . . I'm tired, tired of being enclosed here. I'm wearying to escape into that glorious world, and to be always there. . . . I shall be incomparably beyond and above you all."
1. According to Charlotte Brontë, these are the last lines written by her sister.

I see Heaven's glories shine
And Faith shines equal arming me from Fear

5   O God within my breast
Almighty ever-present Deity
Life, that in me hast rest
As I Undying Life, have power in Thee

Vain are the thousand creeds
10   That move men's hearts, unutterably vain,
Worthless as withered weeds
Or idlest froth amid the boundless main

To waken doubt in one
Holding so fast by thy infinity
15   So surely anchored on
The steadfast rock of Immortality

With wide-embracing love
Thy spirit animates eternal years
Pervades and broods above,
20   Changes, sustains, dissolves, creates and rears

Though Earth and moon were gone
And suns and universes ceased to be
And thou wert left alone
Every Existence would exist in thee

25   There is not room for Death
Nor atom that his might could render void
Since thou art Being and Breath
And what thou art may never be destroyed.

1846   1850

JOHN RUSKIN
1819–1900

John Ruskin was both the leading Victorian critic of art and an important critic of society. These two roles can be traced back to two important influences of his childhood. His father, a wealthy wine merchant, was fond of travel, and on tours of the Continent he introduced his son to landscape, architecture, and art. From this exposure Ruskin acquired a zest for beauty that animates even the most theoretical of his discussions of aesthetics. In his autobiography he describes his first view of the Swiss Alps at sunset: "the seen walls of lost Eden could not have been more beautiful" (he was fourteen at the time):

It is not possible to imagine, in any time of the world, a more blessed entrance into life, for a child of such a temperament as mine. True, the temperament belonged to the age: a very few years,—within the hundred,—before that, no child could have been born to care for mountains, or for the men that lived among them, in that way. Till Rousseau's time, there had been no "sentimental" love of nature; and till Scott's, no such apprehensive love of "all sorts and conditions of men," not in the soul merely, but in the flesh . . . I went down that evening from the garden-terrace of Schaffhausen with my destiny fixed in all of it that was to be sacred and useful.

Such a rapturous response to the beauties of nature was later to be duplicated by his response to the beauties of architecture and art. During a tour of "this Holy Land of Italy" (as he called it), he visited Venice and recorded in his diary (May 6, 1841) his response to Saint Mark's cathedral square in that city: "Thank God I am here! It is the Paradise of cities and there is moon enough to make herself the sanities of earth lunatic, striking its pure flashes of light against the grey water before the window; and I am happier than I have been these five years. . . . I feel fresh and young when my foot is on these pavements."

Ruskin's choice of phrase in these accounts of how beauty affected him reflects the second influence in his life, often at variance with the first: his daily Bible readings under the direction of his mother. From this biblical indoctrination, Ruskin derived some elements of his lush and highly rhythmical prose style but more especially his sense of prophecy and mission as a critic of modern society.

Ruskin's life was spent in traveling, lecturing, and writing. His prodigious literary output can be roughly divided into three phases. At first he was preoccupied with problems of art. *Modern Painters,* which he began writing at the age of twenty-three after his graduation from Oxford, was a defense of the English landscape painter J. M. W. Turner (1775–1851). This defense (which was to extend to five volumes) involved Ruskin in problems of truth in art (as in his chapter "Pathetic Fallacy") and in the ultimate importance of imagination (as in his discussion of Turner's painting *The Slave Ship*).

During the 1850s Ruskin's principal interest shifted from art to architecture, especially to the problem of determining what kind of society is capable of producing great buildings. His enthusiasm for Gothic architecture was infectious, and he has sometimes been blamed for the prevalence of Gothic buildings on college campuses in America. A study of *The Stones of Venice* (1851–53), however (especially the chapter printed here), will show that merely to revive the Gothic style was not his concern. What he wanted to revive was the kind of society that had produced such architecture, a society in which the individual workers could express themselves and enjoy what Ruskin's disciple William Morris called "work-pleasure." A mechanized production-line society, such as Ruskin's or our own, could not produce Gothic architecture but only imitations of its mannerisms. Ruskin's concern was to change industrial society not to decorate concrete towers with gargoyles.

This interest in the stultifying effects of industrialism led Ruskin gradually into economics. After 1860 the critic of art became (like his master, Carlyle) an outspoken critic of laissez-faire economics. His conception of the responsibilities of employers toward their workers, as expounded in *Unto This Last* (1860), was dismissed by his contemporaries as an absurdity. What he was laboring to show was that self-seeking business relationships might be made over on the principle of dedicated service, taking as a model the learned professions and also the military. The soldier, however crude, is more highly regarded by society than the capitalist, Ruskin said, "for the soldier's trade . . . is not slaying, but being slain." Although his position was essentially conservative in the proper sense of the word (he styled himself "a violent Tory of the old school;—Walter Scott's school"), he was regarded as a radical eccentric. It was many years before his social criticism gained a following among writers as diverse as William Morris, Bernard Shaw, and D. H. Lawrence; and in particular among the founders of the British Labour Party, his influence was to be profound and lasting.

Ruskin's realization, after 1860, that despite his fame he was becoming isolated and that the world was continuing to move in directions opposite from those to which he pointed may have contributed to the recurrent mental breakdowns from which he suffered between 1870 and 1900. As he reports in *Fors Clavigera* (1880): "The doctors said I went mad, this time two years ago, from overwork," but he had not then been working harder than usual. "I went mad because nothing came of my work . . . because after I got [my manuscripts] published, nobody believed a word of them." Also contributing to his breakdowns may have been his unhappiness in his relations with women. His marriage to Effie Gray in 1848 was a disaster. After six years of living together an annulment was arranged on the grounds that the marriage had not been consummated. Ruskin testified that he had not found his wife's person physically attractive, although by others she was considered a great beauty. One of these admirers was the Pre-Raphaelite painter John Millais, who fell in love with her at a time when he was painting her husband's portrait; shortly after the annulment he married her. In later years Ruskin fell pathetically in love with a young Irish girl, Rose La Touche, whom he first met when he was nearly forty and she was a child of nine. They were divided not only by the gap of age but by religious differences. She was an intensely pious believer; and for several years after Ruskin proposed marriage to her, when she was eighteen, she tried unsuccessfully to persuade him to return to the Evangelical faith that he had abandoned. In 1875, after herself suffering attacks of mental illness, La Touche died at the age of twenty-five. In his autobiography Ruskin commented: "I wonder mightily what sort of creature I should have turned out, if instead of the distracting and useless pain, I had had the joy of approved love, and the untellable, incalculable motive of its sympathy and praise. It seems to me such things are not allowed in the world. The men capable of the highest imaginative passion are always tossed on fiery waves by it." Despite both the despair that he suffered following La Touche's death and the recurring attacks of mental illness that blighted the last thirty-five years of his life, Ruskin remained active and productive up until his final silent decade of the 1890s. His publications during his active period included six volumes of his lectures on art that he had delivered as Slade Professor of Fine Arts at Oxford and his letters to laborers, *Fors Clavigera* (1871–84). One topic that becomes especially prominent in these later writings is pollution of air and water—an ideal subject for Ruskin's eloquence. In discussing it he combines his lifelong love for beautiful landscape and landscape painting with his later acquired conviction that modern industrial leadership was woefully irresponsible. A letter of A. E. Housman, who was an undergraduate at Oxford in 1877, provides a vivid record of how effective Ruskin could be:

> This afternoon Ruskin gave us a great outburst against modern times. He had got a picture of Turner's, framed and glassed, representing Leicester and the Abbey in the distance at sunset, over a river. He read the account of Wolsey's death out of *Henry VIII.* Then he pointed to the picture as representing Leicester when Turner had drawn it. Then he said, "You, if you like, may go to Leicester to see what it is like now. I never shall. But I can make a pretty good guess." Then he caught up a paintbrush. "These stepping-stones of course have been done away with, and are replaced by a be-au-ti-ful iron bridge." Then he dashed in the iron bridge on the glass of the picture. "The color of the stream is supplied on one side by the indigo factory." Forthwith one side of the stream became indigo. "On the other side by the soap factory." Soap dashed in. "They mix in the middle—like curds," he said, working them together with a sort of malicious deliberation. "This field, over which you see the sun setting behind the abbey, is

now occupied in a *proper* manner." Then there went a flame of scarlet across the picture, which developed itself into windows and roofs and red brick, and rushed up into a chimney. "The atmosphere is supplied—thus!" A puff and cloud of smoke all over Turner's sky: and then the brush thrown down, and Ruskin confronting modern civilization amidst a tempest of applause, which he always elicits now, as he has this term become immensely popular, his lectures being crowded, whereas of old he used to prophesy to empty benches.

Among Ruskin's publications that illustrate this crusade against pollution is his tirade of 1884, *The Storm-Cloud of the Nineteenth Century*. And finally, following this awesome vision of the future, Ruskin concluded his long writing career with a dramatic shift of focus from time future to time past—in his delightful autobiography, *Praeterita* (meaning "the past"), written from 1885 to 1889.

From Modern Painters

[A DEFINITION OF GREATNESS IN ART][1]

Painting, or art generally, as such, with all its technicalities, difficulties, and particular ends, is nothing but a noble and expressive language, invaluable as the vehicle of thought, but by itself nothing. He who has learned what is commonly considered the whole art of painting, that is, the art of representing any natural object faithfully, has as yet only learned the language by which his thoughts are to be expressed. He has done just as much towards being that which we ought to respect as a great painter, as a man who has learnt how to express himself grammatically and melodiously has towards being a great poet. The language is, indeed, more difficult of acquirement in the one case than in the other, and possesses more power of delighting the sense, while it speaks to the intellect; but it is, nevertheless, nothing more than language, and all those excellences which are peculiar to the painter as such, are merely what rhythm, melody, precision, and force are in the words of the orator and the poet, necessary to their greatness, but not the tests of their greatness. It is not by the mode of representing and saying, but by what is represented and said, that the respective greatness either of the painter or the writer is to be finally determined.

*   *   *

* * * So that, if I say that the greatest picture is that which conveys to the mind of the spectator the greatest number of the greatest ideas, I have a definition which will include as subjects of comparison every pleasure which art is capable of conveying. If I were to say, on the contrary, that the best picture was that which most closely imitated nature, I should assume that art could only please by imitating nature; and I should cast out of the pale of criticism those parts of works of art which are not imitative, that is to say, intrinsic beauties of color and form, and those works of art wholly, which, like the Arabesques of Raffaelle in the Loggias,[2] are not imitative at all. Now, I want a definition of art wide enough to include all its varieties of aim. I do not say, therefore, that the art is greatest which gives most pleasure, because

---

1. From vol. 1, part 1, section 1, chap. 2.
2. The arabesques in the Loggia of the Vatican, designed by Raphael, were decorative wall paint- ings that feature a complex pattern of leaves, animals, and human figures.

perhaps there is some art whose end is to teach, and not to please. I do not say that the art is greatest which teaches us most, because perhaps there is some art whose end is to please, and not to teach. I do not say that the art is greatest which imitates best, because perhaps there is some art whose end is to create and not to imitate. But I say that the art is greatest which conveys to the mind of the spectator, by any means whatsoever, the greatest number of the greatest ideas; and I call an idea great in proportion as it is received by a higher faculty of the mind, and as it more fully occupies, and in occupying, exercises and exalts, the faculty by which it is received.

If this, then, be the definition of great art, that of a great artist naturally follows. He is the greatest artist who has embodied, in the sum of his works, the greatest number of the greatest ideas.

["THE SLAVE SHIP"][3]

But I think the noblest sea that Turner has ever painted, and, if so, the noblest certainly ever painted by man, is that of "The Slave Ship," the chief Academy[4] picture of the exhibition of 1840. It is a sunset on the Atlantic after prolonged storm; but the storm is partially lulled, and the torn and streaming rain clouds are moving in scarlet lines to lose themselves in the hollow of the night. The whole surface of sea included in the picture is divided into two ridges of enormous swell, not high, nor local, but a low, broad heaving of the whole ocean, like the lifting of its bosom by deep-drawn breath after the torture of the storm. Between these two ridges the fire of the sunset falls along the trough of the sea, dyeing it with an awful but glorious light, the intense and lurid splendor which burns like gold and bathes like blood. Along this fiery path and valley the tossing waves by which the swell of the sea is restlessly divided lift themselves in dark, indefinite, fantastic forms, each casting a faint and ghastly shadow behind it along the illumined foam. They do not rise everywhere, but three or four together in wild groups, fitfully and furiously, as the under-strength of the swell compels or permits them; leaving between them treacherous spaces of level and whirling water, now lighted with green and lamplike fire, now flashing back the gold of the declining sun, now fearfully shed from above with the indistinguishable images of the burning clouds, which fall upon them in flakes of crimson and scarlet and give to the reckless waves the added motion of their own fiery being. Purple and blue, the lurid shadows of the hollow breakers are cast upon the mist of night, which gathers cold and low, advancing like the shadow of death upon the guilty ship as it labors amidst the lightning of the sea, its thin masts written upon the sky in lines of blood, girded with condemnation in that fearful hue which signs the sky with horror, and mixes its flaming flood with the sunlight, and, cast far along the desolate heave of the sepulchral waves, incarnadines the multitudinous sea.[5]

I believe, if I were reduced to rest Turner's immortality upon any single

3. From vol. 1, part 2, section 5, chap. 3. The painting is of a ship in which slaves are being transported. Victims who have died during the passage are being thrown overboard at sunset; as Ruskin noted, "the near sea is encumbered with corpses." 4. The Royal Academy of Arts, founded in London in 1768. The painting was given to Ruskin by his father as a New Year's present in 1844 and hung in the Ruskin household for a number of years until Ruskin decided to sell it because he found its subject "too painful to live with." The painting now hangs in the Museum of Fine Arts in Boston. 5. Shakespeare's *Macbeth* 2.2.60.

work, I should choose this. Its daring conception—ideal in the highest sense of the word—is based on the purest truth, and wrought out with the concentrated knowledge of a life; its color is absolutely perfect, not one false or morbid hue in any part or line, and so modulated that every square inch of canvas is a perfect composition; its drawing as accurate as fearless; the ship buoyant, bending, and full of motion; its tones as true as they are wonderful; and the whole picture dedicated to the most sublime of subjects and impressions—completing thus the perfect system of all truth which we have shown to be formed by Turner's works—the power, majesty, and deathfulness of the open, deep, illimitable Sea.

1843

From *Of the Pathetic Fallacy*[6]

* * *

Now therefore, putting these tiresome and absurd words[7] quite out of our way, we may go on at our ease to examine the point in question—namely, the difference between the ordinary, proper, and true appearances of things to us; and the extraordinary, or false appearances, when we are under the influence of emotion, or contemplative fancy; false appearances, I say, as being entirely unconnected with any real power of character in the object, and only imputed to it by us.

For instance—

The spendthrift crocus, bursting through the mold
Naked and shivering, with his cup of gold.[8]

This is very beautiful, and yet very untrue. The crocus is not a spendthrift, but a hardy plant; its yellow is not gold, but saffron. How is it that we enjoy so much the having it put into our heads that it is anything else than a plain crocus?

It is an important question. For, throughout our past reasonings about art, we have always found that nothing could be good or useful, or ultimately pleasurable, which was untrue. But here is something pleasurable in written poetry, which is nevertheless *un*true. And what is more, if we think over our favorite poetry, we shall find it full of this kind of fallacy, and that we like it all the more for being so.

It will appear also, on consideration of the matter, that this fallacy is of two principal kinds. Either, as in this case of the crocus, it is the fallacy of willful fancy, which involves no real expectation that it will be believed; or else it is a fallacy caused by an excited state of the feelings, making us, for the time, more or less irrational. Of the cheating of the fancy we shall have to speak presently; but, in this chapter, I want to examine the nature of the

6. From vol. 3, part 4, chap. 12. In this celebrated chapter, Ruskin shifts from discussing problems of truth and realism in art to the same problems in literature. The term *pathetic* refers not to something feebly ineffective but to the emotion (pathos) with which a writer invests descriptions of objects and of the distortion (fallacy) that may result. Poets such as Tennyson protested that Ruskin was being unfairly rigorous in pointing up the fallacy, and it may be noted that Ruskin himself falls into it often. See, e.g., his reference to the "guilty ship" in his discussion of Turner's *The Slave Ship*, p. 1429.

7. The metaphysical terms *objective* and *subjective* as applied to kinds of truth.

8. From a poem by Oliver Wendell Holmes.

other error, that which the mind admits when affected strongly by emotion. Thus, for instance, in *Alton Locke*—

> They rowed her in across the rolling foam—
> The cruel, crawling foam.[9]

The foam is not cruel, neither does it crawl. The state of mind which attributes to it these characters of a living creature is one in which the reason is unhinged by grief. All violent feelings have the same effect. They produce in us a falseness in all our impressions of external things, which I would generally characterize as the "pathetic fallacy."

Now we are in the habit of considering this fallacy as eminently a character of poetical description, and the temper of mind in which we allow it, as one eminently poetical, because passionate. But, I believe, if we look well into the matter, that we shall find the greatest poets do not often admit this kind of falseness—that it is only the second order of poets who much delight in it.

Thus, when Dante describes the spirits falling from the bank of Acheron "as dead leaves flutter from a bough,"[1] he gives the most perfect image possible of their utter lightness, feebleness, passiveness, and scattering agony of despair, without, however, for an instant losing his own clear perception that *these* are souls, and *those* are leaves: he makes no confusion of one with the other. But when Coleridge speaks of

> The one red leaf, the last of its clan,
> That dances as often as dance it can,[2]

he has a morbid, that is to say, a so far false, idea about the leaf: he fancies a life in it, and will, which there are not; confuses its powerlessness with choice, its fading death with merriment, and the wind that shakes it with music. Here, however, there is some beauty, even in the morbid passage; but take an instance in Homer and Pope. Without the knowledge of Ulysses, Elpenor, his youngest follower, has fallen from an upper chamber in the Circean palace, and has been left dead, unmissed by his leader or companions, in the haste of their departure. They cross the sea to the Cimmerian land; and Ulysses summons the shades from Tartarus. The first which appears is that of the lost Elpenor. Ulysses, amazed, and in exactly the spirit of bitter and terrified lightness which is seen in Hamlet, addresses the spirit with the simple, startled words: "Elpenor! How camest thou under the shadowy darkness? Hast thou come faster on foot than I in my black ship?"[3] Which Pope renders thus:

> O, say, what angry power Elpenor led
> To glide in shades, and wander with the dead?
> How could thy soul, by realms and seas disjoined,
> Outfly the nimble sail, and leave the lagging wind?

I sincerely hope the reader finds no pleasure here, either in the nimbleness of the sail, or the laziness of the wind! And yet how is it that these conceits are so painful now, when they have been pleasant to us in the other instances?

For a very simple reason. They are not a *pathetic* fallacy at all, for they are

9. From chap. 26 of Charles Kingsley's novel *Alton Locke* (1850).
1. *Inferno* 3.112.

2. *Christabel* 49–50.
3. *Odyssey* 11.51.

put into the mouth of the wrong passion—a passion which never could possibly have spoken them—agonized curiosity. Ulysses wants to know the facts of the matter; and the very last thing his mind could do at the moment would be to pause, or suggest in anywise what was *not* a fact. The delay in the first three lines, and conceit in the last, jar upon us instantly, like the most frightful discord in music. No poet of true imaginative power would possibly have written the passage.

Therefore, we see that the spirit of truth must guide us in some sort, even in our enjoyment of fallacy. Coleridge's fallacy has no discord in it, but Pope's has set our teeth on edge. * * *

1856

From The Stones of Venice

[THE SAVAGENESS OF GOTHIC ARCHITECTURE][1]

I am not sure when the word "Gothic" was first generically applied to the architecture of the North; but I presume that, whatever the date of its original usage, it was intended to imply reproach, and express the barbaric character of the nations among whom that architecture arose. It never implied that they were literally of Gothic lineage, far less that their architecture had been originally invented by the Goths themselves; but it did imply that they and their buildings together exhibited a degree of sternness and rudeness, which, in contradistinction to the character of Southern and Eastern nations, appeared like a perpetual reflection of the contrast between the Goth and the Roman in their first encounter. And when that fallen Roman, in the utmost impotence of his luxury, and insolence of his guilt, became the model for the imitation of civilized Europe,[2] at the close of the so-called Dark Ages, the word Gothic became a term of unmitigated contempt, not unmixed with aversion. From that contempt, by the exertion of the antiquaries and architects of this century, Gothic architecture has been sufficiently vindicated; and perhaps some among us, in our admiration of the magnificent science of its structure, and sacredness of its expression, might desire that the term of ancient reproach should be withdrawn, and some other, of more apparent honorableness, adopted in its place. There is no chance, as there is no need, of such a substitution. As far as the epithet was used scornfully, it was used falsely; but there is no reproach in the word, rightly understood; on the contrary, there is a profound truth, which the instinct of mankind almost unconsciously recognizes. It is true, greatly and deeply true, that the architecture of the North is rude and wild; but it is not true that, for this reason, we are to condemn it, or despise. Far otherwise: I believe it is in this very character that it deserves our profoundest reverence.

The charts of the world which have been drawn up by modern science have thrown into a narrow space the expression of a vast amount of knowledge, but I have never yet seen any one pictorial enough to enable the spec-

1. From vol. 2, chap. 6.
2. Renaissance architecture, based on imitating classical buildings, was distasteful to Ruskin. He later stated that his aim in *The Stones of Venice* had been "to show that the Gothic architecture of

Venice had risen out of . . . a state of pure national faith and domestic virtue; and that its Renaissance architecture had arisen out of . . . a state of concealed national infidelity and domestic corruption."

tator to imagine the kind of contrast in physical character which exists between Northern and Southern countries. We know the differences in detail, but we have not that broad glance and grasp which would enable us to feel them in their fullness. We know that gentians grow on the Alps, and olives on the Apennines; but we do not enough conceive for ourselves that variegated mosaic of the world's surface which a bird sees in its migration, that difference between the district of the gentian and of the olive which the stork and the swallow see far off, as they lean upon the sirocco wind.[3] Let us, for a moment, try to raise ourselves even above the level of their flight, and imagine the Mediterranean lying beneath us like an irregular lake, and all its ancient promontories sleeping in the sun: here and there an angry spot of thunder, a gray stain of storm, moving upon the burning field; and here and there a fixed wreath of white volcano smoke, surrounded by its circle of ashes; but for the most part a great peacefulness of light, Syria and Greece, Italy and Spain, laid like pieces of a golden pavement into the sea-blue, chased, as we stoop nearer to them, with bossy beaten work of mountain chains, and glowing softly with terraced gardens, and flowers heavy with frankincense, mixed among masses of laurel, and orange, and plumy palm, that abate with their gray-green shadows the burning of the marble rocks, and of the ledges of porphyry sloping under lucent sand. Then let us pass farther towards the north, until we see the orient colors change gradually into a vast belt of rainy green, where the pastures of Switzerland, and poplar valleys of France, and dark forests of the Danube and Carpathians stretch from the mouths of the Loire to those of the Volga, seen through clefts in gray swirls of rain cloud and flaky veils of the mist of the brooks, spreading low along the pasture lands: and then, farther north still, to see the earth heave into mighty masses of leaden rock and heathy moor, bordering with a broad waste of gloomy purple that belt of field and wood, and splintering into irregular and grisly islands amidst the northern seas, beaten by storm, and chilled by ice drift, and tormented by furious pulses of contending tide, until the roots of the last forests fail from among the hill ravines, and the hunger of the north wind bites their peaks into barrenness; and, at last, the wall of ice, durable like iron, sets, deathlike, its white teeth against us out of the polar twilight. And, having once traversed in thought this gradation of the zoned iris of the earth in all its material vastness, let us go down nearer to it, and watch the parallel change in the belt of animal life: the multitudes of swift and brilliant creatures that glance in the air and sea, or tread the sands of the southern zone; striped zebras and spotted leopards, glistening serpents, and birds arrayed in purple and scarlet. Let us contrast their delicacy and brilliancy of color, and swiftness of motion, with the frost-cramped strength, and shaggy covering, and dusky plumage of the northern tribes; contrast the Arabian horse with the Shetland, the tiger and leopard with the wolf and bear, the antelope with the elk, the bird of paradise with the osprey: and then, submissively acknowledging the great laws by which the earth and all that it bears are ruled throughout their being, let us not condemn, but rejoice in the expression by man of his own rest in the statutes of the lands that gave him birth. Let us watch him with reverence as he sets side by side the burning gems, and smooths with soft sculpture the jasper pillars, that

---

3. Hot wind from the southern Mediterranean.

are to reflect a ceaseless sunshine, and rise into a cloudless sky: but not with less reverence let us stand by him, when, with rough strength and hurried stroke, he smites an uncouth animation out of the rocks which he has torn from among the moss of the moorland, and heaves into the darkened air the pile of iron buttress and rugged wall, instinct with work of an imagination as wild and wayward as the northern sea; creations of ungainly shape and rigid limb, but full of wolfish life; fierce as the winds that beat, and changeful as the clouds that shade them.

There is, I repeat, no degradation, no reproach in this, but all dignity and honorableness: and we should err grievously in refusing either to recognize as an essential character of the existing architecture of the North, or to admit as a desirable character in that which it yet may be, this wildness of thought, and roughness of work; this look of mountain brotherhood between the cathedral and the Alp; this magnificence of sturdy power, put forth only the more energetically because the fine finger-touch was chilled away by the frosty wind, and the eye dimmed by the moor mist, or blinded by the hail; this outspeaking of the strong spirit of men who may not gather redundant fruitage from the earth, nor bask in dreamy benignity of sunshine, but must break the rock for bread, and cleave the forest for fire, and show, even in what they did for their delight, some of the hard habits of the arm and heart that grew on them as they swung the ax or pressed the plow.

If, however, the savageness of Gothic architecture, merely as an expression of its origin among Northern nations, may be considered, in some sort, a noble character, it possesses a higher nobility still, when considered as an index, not of climate, but of religious principle.

In the 13th and 14th paragraphs of Chapter XXI of the first volume of this work, it was noticed that the systems of architectural ornament, properly so called, might be divided into three: (1) Servile ornament, in which the execution or power of the inferior workman is entirely subjected to the intellect of the higher; (2) Constitutional ornament, in which the executive inferior power is, to a certain point, emancipated and independent, having a will of its own, yet confessing its inferiority and rendering obedience to higher powers; and (3) Revolutionary ornament, in which no executive inferiority is admitted at all. I must here explain the nature of these divisions at somewhat greater length.

Of Servile ornament, the principal schools are the Greek, Ninevite, and Egyptian; but their servility is of different kinds. The Greek master-workman was far advanced in knowledge and power above the Assyrian or Egyptian. Neither he nor those for whom he worked could endure the appearance of imperfection in anything; and, therefore, what ornament he appointed to be done by those beneath him was composed of mere geometrical forms—balls, ridges, and perfectly symmetrical foliage—which could be executed with absolute precision by line and rule, and were as perfect in their way, when completed, as his own figure sculpture. The Assyrian and Egyptian, on the contrary, less cognizant of accurate form in anything, were content to allow their figure sculpture to be executed by inferior workmen, but lowered the method of its treatment to a standard which every workman could reach, and then trained him by discipline so rigid that there was no chance of his falling beneath the standard appointed. The Greek gave to the lower workman no subject which he could not perfectly execute. The Assyrian gave him subjects which he could only execute imperfectly, but fixed a legal standard for his imperfection. The workman was, in both systems, a slave.

But in the medieval, or especially Christian, system of ornament, this slavery is done away with altogether; Christianity having recognized, in small things as well as great, the individual value of every soul. But it not only recognizes its value; it confesses its imperfection, in only bestowing dignity upon the acknowledgment of unworthiness. That admission of lost power and fallen nature, which the Greek or Ninevite felt to be intensely painful, and, as far as might be, altogether refused, the Christian makes daily and hourly, contemplating the fact of it without fear, as tending, in the end, to God's greater glory. Therefore, to every spirit which Christianity summons to her service, her exhortation is: Do what you can, and confess frankly what you are unable to do; neither let your effort be shortened for fear of failure, nor your confession silenced for fear of shame. And it is, perhaps, the principal admirableness of the Gothic schools of architecture, that they thus receive the results of the labor of inferior minds; and out of fragments full of imperfection, and betraying that imperfection in every touch, indulgently raise up a stately and unaccusable whole.

But the modern English mind has this much in common with that of the Greek, that it intensely desires, in all things, the utmost completion or perfection compatible with their nature. This is a noble character in the abstract, but becomes ignoble when it causes us to forget the relative dignities of that nature itself, and to prefer the perfectness of the lower nature to the imperfection of the higher; not considering that as, judged by such a rule, all the brute animals would be preferable to man, because more perfect in their functions and kind, and yet are always held inferior to him, so also in the works of man, those which are more perfect in their kind are always inferior to those which are, in their nature, liable to more faults and shortcomings. For the finer the nature, the more flaws it will show through the clearness of it; and it is a law of this universe that the best things shall be seldomest seen in their best form. The wild grass grows well and strongly, one year with another; but the wheat is, according to the greater nobleness of its nature, liable to the bitterer blight. And therefore, while in all things that we see, or do, we are to desire perfection, and strive for it, we are nevertheless not to set the meaner thing, in its narrow accomplishment, above the nobler thing, in its mighty progress; not to esteem smooth minuteness above shattered majesty; not to prefer mean victory to honorable defeat; not to lower the level of our aim, that we may the more surely enjoy the complacency of success. But above all, in our dealings with the souls of other men, we are to take care how we check, by severe requirement or narrow caution, efforts which might otherwise lead to a noble issue; and, still more, how we withhold our admiration from great excellencies, because they are mingled with rough faults. Now, in the make and nature of every man, however rude or simple, whom we employ in manual labor, there are some powers for better things: some tardy imagination, torpid capacity of emotion, tottering steps of thought, there are, even at the worst; and in most cases it is all our own fault that they *are* tardy or torpid. But they cannot be strengthened, unless we are content to take them in their feebleness, and unless we prize and honor them in their imperfection above the best and most perfect manual skill. And this is what we have to do with all our laborers; to look for the *thoughtful* part of them, and get that out of them, whatever we lose for it, whatever faults and errors we are obliged to take with it. For the best that is in them cannot manifest itself, but in company with much error. Understand this clearly: You can teach a man to draw a straight line, and to cut one; to strike a curved line, and to carve it; and to copy and carve any number of given lines or forms, with admirable speed and perfect precision; and you find his work perfect of its kind: but if you ask him to think about any of those forms, to consider if he cannot find any better in his own head, he stops; his execution becomes hesitating; he thinks, and ten to one he thinks wrong; ten to one he makes a mistake in the first touch he gives to his work as a thinking being. But you have made a man of him for all that. He was only a machine before, an animated tool.

And observe, you are put to stern choice in this matter. You must either make a tool of the creature, or a man of him. You cannot make both. Men were not intended to work with the accuracy of tools, to be precise and perfect in all their actions. If you will have that precision out of them, and make their fingers measure degrees like cogwheels, and their arms strike curves like compasses, you must unhumanize them. All the energy of their spirits must be given to make cogs and compasses of themselves. All their attention and strength must go to the accomplishment of the mean act. The eye of the soul must be bent upon the finger point, and the soul's force must fill all the invisible nerves that guide it, ten hours a day, that it may not err from its steely precision, and so soul and sight be worn away, and the whole human being be lost at last—a heap of sawdust, so far as its intellectual work in this world is concerned; saved only by its Heart, which cannot go into the form of cogs and compasses, but expands, after the ten hours are over, into fireside humanity. On the other hand, if you will make a man of the working creature, you cannot make a tool. Let him but begin to imagine, to think, to try to do anything worth doing; and the engine-turned precision is lost at once. Out come all his roughness, all his dullness, all his incapability; shame upon shame, failure upon failure, pause after pause: but out comes the whole majesty of him also; and we know the height of it only, when we see the clouds settling upon him. And, whether the clouds be bright or dark, there will be transfiguration behind and within them.

And now, reader, look around this English room of yours, about which you have been proud so often, because the work of it was so good and strong, and the ornaments of it so finished. Examine again all those accurate moldings, and perfect polishings, and unerring adjustments of the seasoned wood and tempered steel. Many a time you have exulted over them, and thought how great England was, because her slightest work was done so thoroughly. Alas! if read rightly, these perfectnesses are signs of a slavery in our England a thousand times more bitter and more degrading than that of the scourged African, or helot[4] Greek. Men may be beaten, chained, tormented, yoked like cattle, slaughtered like summer flies, and yet remain in one sense, and the best sense, free. But to smother their souls within them, to blight and hew into rotting pollards[5] the suckling branches of their human intelligence, to make the flesh and skin which, after the worm's work on it, is to see God, into leathern thongs to yoke machinery with—this it is to be slave-masters

---

4. A class of serfs in Sparta.   5. Trees with top branches cut back to the trunk.

indeed; and there might be more freedom in England, though her feudal lords' lightest words were worth men's lives, and though the blood of the vexed husbandman dropped in the furrows of her fields, than there is while the animation of her multitudes is sent like fuel to feed the factory smoke, and the strength of them is given daily to be wasted into the fineness of a web, or racked into the exactness of a line.

And, on the other hand, go forth again to gaze upon the old cathedral front, where you have smiled so often at the fantastic ignorance of the old sculptors: examine once more those ugly goblins, and formless monsters, and stern statues, anatomiless[6] and rigid; but do not mock at them, for they are signs of the life and liberty of every workman who struck the stone; a freedom of thought, and rank in scale of being, such as no laws, no charters, no charities can secure; but which it must be the first aim of all Europe at this day to regain for her children.

Let me not be thought to speak wildly or extravagantly. It is verily this degradation of the operative into a machine, which, more than any other evil of the times, is leading the mass of the nations everywhere into vain, incoherent, destructive struggling for a freedom of which they cannot explain the nature to themselves. Their universal outcry against wealth, and against nobility, is not forced from them either by the pressure of famine, or the sting of mortified pride. These do much, and have done much in all ages; but the foundations of society were never yet shaken as they are at this day. It is not that men are ill fed, but that they have no pleasure in the work by which they make their bread, and therefore look to wealth as the only means of pleasure. It is not that men are pained by the scorn of the upper classes, but they cannot endure their own; for they feel that the kind of labor to which they are condemned is verily a degrading one, and makes them less than men. Never had the upper classes so much sympathy with the lower, or charity for them, as they have at this day, and yet never were they so much hated by them: for, of old, the separation between the noble and the poor was merely a wall built by law; now it is a veritable difference in level of standing, a precipice between upper and lower grounds in the field of humanity, and there is pestilential air at the bottom of it. I know not if a day is ever to come when the nature of right freedom will be understood, and when men will see that to obey another man, to labor for him, yield reverence to him or to his place, is not slavery. It is often the best kind of liberty—liberty from care. The man who says to one, Go, and he goeth, and to another, Come, and he cometh,[7] has, in most cases, more sense of restraint and difficulty than the man who obeys him. The movements of the one are hindered by the burden on his shoulder; of the other, by the bridle on his lips: there is no way by which the burden may be lightened; but we need not suffer from the bridle if we do not champ at it. To yield reverence to another, to hold ourselves and our lives at his disposal, is not slavery; often, it is the noblest state in which a man can live in this world. There is, indeed, a reverence which is servile, that is to say irrational or selfish: but there is also noble reverence, that is to say, reasonable and loving; and a man is never so noble as when he is reverent in this kind; nay, even if the feeling pass the bounds

---

6. A coinage by Ruskin meaning devoid of anatomy.   7. Matthew 8.9.

of mere reason, so that it be loving, a man is raised by it. Which had, in reality, most of the serf nature in him—the Irish peasant who was lying in wait yesterday for his landlord, with his musket muzzle thrust through the ragged hedge; or that old mountain servant, who, 200 years ago, at Inverkeithing, gave up his own life and the lives of his seven sons for his chief?[8]— as each fell, calling forth his brother to the death, "Another for Hector!" And therefore, in all ages and all countries, reverence has been paid and sacrifice made by men to each other, not only without complaint, but rejoicingly; and famine, and peril, and sword, and all evil, and all shame, have been borne willingly in the causes of masters and kings; for all these gifts of the heart ennobled the men who gave not less than the men who received them, and nature prompted, and God rewarded the sacrifice. But to feel their souls withering within them, unthanked, to find their whole being sunk into an unrecognized abyss, to be counted off into a heap of mechanism, numbered with its wheels, and weighed with its hammer strokes—this nature bade not—this God blesses not—this humanity for no long time is able to endure.

We have much studied and much perfected, of late, the great civilized invention of the division of labor; only we give it a false name. It is not, truly speaking, the labor that is divided; but the men: Divided into mere segments of men—broken into small fragments and crumbs of life; so that all the little piece of intelligence that is left in a man is not enough to make a pin, or a nail, but exhausts itself in making the point of a pin, or the head of a nail. Now it is a good and desirable thing, truly, to make many pins in a day; but if we could only see with what crystal sand their points were polished—sand of human soul, much to be magnified before it can be discerned for what it is—we should think there might be some loss in it also. And the great cry that rises from all our manufacturing cities, louder than their furnace blast, is all in very deed for this—that we manufacture everything there except men; we blanch cotton, and strengthen steel, and refine sugar, and shape pottery; but to brighten, to strengthen, to refine, or to form a single living spirit, never enters into our estimate of advantages. And all the evil to which that cry is urging our myriads can be met only in one way: not by teaching nor preaching, for to teach them is but to show them their misery, and to preach to them, if we do nothing more than preach, is to mock at it. It can be met only by a right understanding, on the part of all classes, of what kinds of labor are good for men, raising them, and making them happy; by a determined sacrifice of such convenience, or beauty, or cheapness as is to be got only by the degradation of the workman; and by equally determined demand for the products and results of healthy and ennobling labor.

And how, it will be asked, are these products to be recognized, and this demand to be regulated? Easily: by the observance of three broad and simple rules:

1. Never encourage the manufacture of any article not absolutely necessary, in the production of which *Invention* has no share.

2. Never demand an exact finish for its own sake, but only for some practical or noble end.

---

8. An incident described in the preface to Walter Scott's novel *The Fair Maid of Perth*.

3. Never encourage imitation or copying of any kind, except for the sake of preserving record of great works.

The second of these principles is the only one which directly rises out of the consideration of our immediate subject; but I shall briefly explain the meaning and extent of the first also, reserving the enforcement of the third for another place.

1. Never encourage the manufacture of anything not necessary, in the production of which invention has no share.

For instance. Glass beads are utterly unnecessary, and there is no design or thought employed in their manufacture. They are formed by first drawing out the glass into rods; these rods are chopped up into fragments of the size of beads by the human hand, and the fragments are then rounded in the furnace. The men who chop up the rods sit at their work all day, their hands vibrating with a perpetual and exquisitely timed palsy, and the beads dropping beneath their vibration like hail. Neither they, nor the men who draw out the rods or fuse the fragments, have the smallest occasion for the use of any single humanfaculty; and every young lady, therefore, who buys glass beads is engaged in the slave trade, and in a much more cruel one than that which we have so long been endeavoring to put down.

But glass cups and vessels may become the subjects of exquisite invention; and if in buying these we pay for the invention, that is to say for the beautiful form, or color, or engraving, and not for mere finish of execution, we are doing good to humanity.

So, again, the cutting of precious stones, in all ordinary cases, requires little exertion of any mental faculty; some tact and judgment in avoiding flaws, and so on, but nothing to bring out the whole mind. Every person who wears cut jewels merely for the sake of their value is, therefore, a slave driver.

But the working of the goldsmith, and the various designing of grouped jewelry and enamel-work, may become the subject of the most noble human intelligence. Therefore, money spent in the purchase of well-designed plate, of precious engraved vases, cameos, or enamels, does good to humanity; and, in work of this kind, jewels may be employed to heighten its splendor; and their cutting is then a price paid for the attainment of a noble end, and thus perfectly allowable.

I shall perhaps press this law farther elsewhere, but our immediate concern is chiefly with the second, namely, never to demand an exact finish, when it does not lead to a noble end. For observe, I have only dwelt upon the rudeness of Gothic, or any other kind of imperfectness, as admirable, where it was impossible to get design or thought without it. If you are to have the thought of a rough and untaught man, you must have it in a rough and untaught way; but from an educated man, who can without effort express his thoughts in an educated way, take the graceful expression, and be thankful. Only *get* the thought, and do not silence the peasant because he cannot speak good grammar, or until you have taught him his grammar. Grammar and refinement are good things, both, only be sure of the better thing first. And thus in art, delicate finish is desirable from the greatest masters, and is always given by them. In some places Michael Angelo, Leonardo, Phidias, Perugino, Turner all finished with the most exquisite care; and the finish they give always leads to the fuller accomplishment of their noble purposes.

But lower men than these cannot finish, for it requires consummate knowledge to finish consummately, and then we must take their thoughts as they are able to give them. So the rule is simple: Always look for invention first, and after that, for such execution as will help the invention, and as the inventor is capable of without painful effort, and *no more*. Above all, demand no refinement of execution where there is no thought, for that is slaves' work, unredeemed. Rather choose rough work than smooth work, so only that the practical purpose be answered, and never imagine there is reason to be proud of anything that may be accomplished by patience and sandpaper.

I shall only give one example, which however will show the reader what I mean, from the manufacture already alluded to, that of glass. Our modern glass is exquisitely clear in its substance, true in its form, accurate in its cutting. We are proud of this. We ought to be ashamed of it. The old Venice glass was muddy, inaccurate in all its forms, and clumsily cut, if at all. And the old Venetian was justly proud of it. For there is this difference between the English and Venetian workman, that the former thinks only of accurately matching his patterns, and getting his curves perfectly true and his edges perfectly sharp, and becomes a mere machine for rounding curves and sharpening edges, while the old Venetian cared not a whit whether his edges were sharp or not, but he invented a new design for every glass that he made, and never molded a handle or a lip without a new fancy in it. And therefore, though some Venetian glass is ugly and clumsy enough, when made by clumsy and uninventive workmen, other Venetian glass is so lovely in its forms that no price is too great for it; and we never see the same form in it twice. Now you cannot have the finish and the varied form too. If the workman is thinking about his edges, he cannot be thinking of his design; if of his design, he cannot think of his edges. Choose whether you will pay for the lovely form or the perfect finish, and choose at the same moment whether you will make the worker a man or a grindstone.

Nay, but the reader interrupts me—"If the workman can design beautifully, I would not have him kept at the furnace. Let him be taken away and made a gentleman, and have a studio, and design his glass there, and I will have it blown and cut for him by common workmen, and so I will have my design and my finish too."

All ideas of this kind are founded upon two mistaken suppositions: the first, that one man's thoughts can be, or ought to be, executed by another man's hands; the second, that manual labor is a degradation, when it is governed by intellect.

On a large scale, and in work determinable by line and rule, it is indeed both possible and necessary that the thoughts of one man should be carried out by the labor of others; in this sense I have already defined the best architecture to be the expression of the mind of manhood by the hands of childhood. But on a smaller scale, and in a design which cannot be mathematically defined, one man's thoughts can never be expressed by another: and the difference between the spirit of touch of the man who is inventing, and of the man who is obeying directions, is often all the difference between a great and a common work of art. How wide the separation is between original and secondhand execution, I shall endeavor to show elsewhere; it is not so much to our purpose here as to mark the other and more fatal error of despising manual labor when governed by intellect; for it is no less fatal an error to despise it when thus regulated by intellect, than to value it for its own sake. We are always in these days endeavoring to separate the two; we want one man to be always thinking, and another to be always working, and we call one a gentleman, and the other an operative; whereas the workman ought often to be thinking, and the thinker often to be working, and both should be gentlemen, in the best sense. As it is, we make both ungentle, the one envying, the other despising, his brother; and the mass of society is made up of morbid thinkers, and miserable workers. Now it is only by labor that thought can be made healthy, and only by thought that labor can be made happy, and the two cannot be separated with impunity. It would be well if all of us were good handicraftsmen in some kind, and the dishonor of manual labor done away with altogether; so that though there should still be a trenchant distinction of race between nobles and commoners, there should not, among the latter, be a trenchant distinction of employment, as between idle and working men, or between men of liberal and illiberal professions. All professions should be liberal, and there should be less pride felt in peculiarity of employment, and more in excellence of achievement. And yet more, in each several profession, no master should be too proud to do its hardest work. The painter should grind his own colors; the architect work in the mason's yard with his men; the master manufacturer be himself a more skillful operative than any man in his mills; and the distinction between one man and another be only in experience and skill, and the authority and wealth which these must naturally and justly obtain.

I should be led far from the matter in hand, if I were to pursue this interesting subject. Enough, I trust, has been said to show the reader that the rudeness or imperfection which at first rendered the term "Gothic" one of reproach is indeed, when rightly understood, one ot the most noble characters of Christian architecture, and not only a noble but an *essential* one. It seems a fantastic paradox, but it is nevertheless a most important truth, that no architecture can be truly noble which is *not* imperfect. And this is easily demonstrable. For since the architect, whom we will suppose capable of doing all in perfection, cannot execute the whole with his own hands, he must either make slaves of his workmen in the old Greek, and present English fashion, and level his work to a slave's capacities, which is to degrade it; or else he must take his workmen as he finds them, and let them show their weaknesses together with their strength, which will involve the Gothic imperfection, but render the whole work as noble as the the intellect of the age can make it.

But the principle may be stated more broadly still. I have confined the illustration of it to architecture, but I must not leave it as if true of architecture only. Hitherto I have used the words imperfect and perfect merely to distinguish between work grossly unskillful, and work executed with average precision and science; and I have been pleading that any degree of unskillfulness should be admitted, so only that the laborer's mind had room for expression. But, accurately speaking, no good work whatever can be perfect, and *the demand for perfection is always a sign of a misunderstanding of the ends of art.*

This for two reasons, both based on everlasting laws. The first, that no great man ever stops working till he has reached his point of failure; that is to say, his mind is always far in advance of his powers of execution, and the latter will now and then give way in trying to follow it; besides that he will always give to the inferior portions of his work only such inferior attention as they require; and according to his greatness he becomes so accustomed to the feeling of dissatisfaction with the best he can do, that in moments of lassitude or anger with himself he will not care though the beholder be dissatisfied also. I believe there has only been one man who would not acknowledge this necessity, and strove always to reach perfection, Leonardo; the end of his vain effort being merely that he would take ten years to a picture, and leave it unfinished. And therefore, if we are to have great men working at all, or less men doing their best, the work will be imperfect, however beautiful. Of human work none but what is bad can be perfect, in its own bad way.[9]

The second reason is that imperfection is in some sort essential to all that we know of life. It is the sign of life in a mortal body, that is to say, of a state of progress and change. Nothing that lives is, or can be, rigidly perfect; part of it is decaying, part nascent. The foxglove blossom—a third part bud, a third part past, a third part in full bloom—is a type of the life of this world. And in all things that live there are certain irregularities and deficiencies which are not only signs of life, but sources of beauty. No human face is exactly the same in its lines on each side, no leaf perfect in its lobes, no branch in its symmetry. All admit irregularity as they imply change; and to banish imperfection is to destroy expression, to check exertion, to paralyze vitality. All things are literally better, lovelier, and more beloved for the imperfections which have been divinely appointed, that the law of human life may be Effort, and the law of human judgment, Mercy.

Accept this then for a universal law, that neither architecture nor any other noble work of man can be good unless it be imperfect; and let us be prepared for the otherwise strange fact, which we shall discern clearly as we approach the period of the Renaissance, that the first cause of the fall of the arts of Europe was a relentless requirement of perfection, incapable alike either of being silenced by veneration for greatness, or softened into forgiveness of simplicity.

Thus far then of the Rudeness or Savageness, which is the first mental element of Gothic architecture. It is an element in many other healthy architectures also, as in Byzantine and Romanesque; but true Gothic cannot exist without it.

1851–53

---

9. "The Elgin marbles are supposed by many persons to be 'perfect.' In the most important portions they indeed approach perfection, but only there. The draperies are unfinished, the hair and wool of the animals are unfinished, and the entire bas-reliefs of the frieze are roughly cut" [Ruskin's note]. Ruskin is referring to the collection of statues brought from Athens to England by Lord Elgin, statues that were considered models of perfect realism. Cf. Keats, *On Seeing the Elgin Marbles*, p. 828.

The Storm-Cloud of the Nineteenth Century

Lecture 1[1]

Let me first assure my audience that I have no *arrière pensée*[2] in the title chosen for this lecture. I might, indeed, have meant, and it would have been only too like me to mean, any number of things by such a title;—but, tonight, I mean simply what I have said, and propose to bring to your notice a series of cloud phenomena, which, so far as I can weigh existing evidence, are peculiar to our own times; yet which have not hitherto received any special notice or description from meteorologists.

So far as the existing evidence, I say, of former literature can be interpreted, the storm-cloud—or more accurately plague-cloud, for it is not alway stormy—which I am about to describe to you, never was seen but by now living, or *lately* living eyes. It is not yet twenty years that this—I may well call it, wonderful—cloud has been, in its essence, recognizable. There is no description of it, so far as I have read, or by any ancient observer. Neither Homer nor Virgil, neither Aristophanes nor Horace, acknowledge any such clouds among those compelled by Jove. Chaucer has no word of them, nor Dante; Milton none, nor Thomson. In modern times, Scott, Wordsworth, and Byron are alike unconscious of them; and the most observant and descriptive of scientific men, De Saussure,[3] is utterly silent concerning them. Taking up the traditions of air from the year before Scott's death, I am able, by my own constant and close observation, to certify you that in the forty following years (1831 to 1871 approximately—for the phenomena in question came on gradually)—no such clouds as these are, and are now often for months without intermission, were ever seen in the skies of England, France or Italy.

In those old days, when weather was fine, it was luxuriously fine; when it was bad—it was often abominably bad, but it had its fit of temper and was done with it—it didn't sulk for three months without letting you see the sun,—nor send you one cyclone inside out, every Saturday afternoon, and another outside in, every Monday morning.

In fine weather the sky was either blue or clear in its light; the clouds, either white or golden, adding to, not abating, the luster of the sky. In wet weather, there were two different species of clouds,—those of beneficent rain, which for distinction's sake I will call the non-electric rain-cloud, and

1. Delivered February 4, 1884, at the London Institution. Some newspapers complained that the lecture seemed merely to blame air pollution on the devil; however, what Ruskin was blaming was the devil of industrialism, the source of the "Manchester devil's darkness" and of the "dense manufacturing mist." As E. T. Cook noted:

industrial statistics fully bear out the date which Ruskin fixes for the growth of the phenomena in question: the storm-cloud thickened just when the consumption of coal went up by leaps and bounds, both in this country [England] and in the industrialized parts of central Europe.

Much of the evidence cited in the lecture derives from diaries and sketchbooks in which, over a period of fifty years, Ruskin had recorded observations of sunsets and storms, a record that enabled him to point out the changes. As he stated in

his second lecture:

Had the weather when I was young been such as it is now, no book such as *Modern Painters* ever would or *could* have been written; for every argument, and every sentiment in that book, was founded on the personal experience of the beauty and blessing of nature, all spring and summer long; and on the then demonstrable fact that over a great portion of the world's surface the air and the earth were fitted to the education of the spirit of man as closely as a schoolboy's primer is to his labor, and as gloriously as a lover's mistress is to his eyes.

That harmony is now broken and broken the world round.

2. Afterthought or hidden meaning (French).
3. Horace Bénédict de Saussure (1740–1799), Swiss geologist and alpinist.

those of storm, usually charged highly with electricity. The beneficent rain-cloud was indeed often extremely dull and gray for days together, but gracious nevertheless, felt to be doing good, and often to be delightful after drought; capable also of the most exquisite coloring, under certain conditions; and continually traversed in clearing by the rainbow:—and, secondly, the storm-cloud, always majestic, often dazzlingly beautiful, and felt also to be beneficent in its own way, affecting the mass of the air with vital agitation, and purging it from the impurity of all morbific elements.

In the entire system of the Firmament, thus seen and understood, there appeared to be, to all the thinkers of those ages, the incontrovertible and unmistakable evidence of a Divine Power in creation, which had fitted, as the air for human breath, so the clouds for human sight and nourishment;—the Father who was in heaven feeding day by day the souls of His children with marvels, and satisfying them with bread, and so filling their hearts with food and gladness.[4]

* * *

Thus far then of clouds that were once familiar; now at last, entering on my immediate subject, I shall best introduce it to you by reading an entry in my diary which gives progressive description of the most gentle aspect of the modern plague-cloud.

Bolton Abbey, 4th July, 1875.

Half-past eight, morning; the first bright morning for the last fortnight.

At half-past five it was entirely clear, and entirely calm; the moorlands glowing, and the Wharfe[5] glittering in sacred light, and even the thin-stemmed field-flowers quiet as stars, in the peace in which—

> All trees and simples, great and small,
> That balmy leaf do bear,
> Than they were painted on a wall,
> No more do move, no steir.[6]

But, an hour ago, the leaves at my window first shook slightly. They are now trembling *continuously,* as those of all the trees, under a gradually rising wind, of which the tremulous action scarcely permits the direction to be defined,—but which falls and returns in fits of varying force, like those which precede a thunderstorm—never wholly ceasing: the direction of its upper current is shown by a few ragged white clouds, moving fast from the north, which rose, at the time of the first leaf-shaking, behind the edge of the moors in the east.

This wind is the plague-wind of the eighth decade of years in the nineteenth century; a period which will assuredly be recognized in future meteorological history as one of phenomena hitherto unrecorded in the courses of nature, and characterized preeminently by the almost ceaseless action of this calamitous wind. While I have been writing these sentences, the white clouds above specified have increased to twice the size they had when I began to write; and in about two hours from this time—say by eleven o'clock, if the wind continue,—the whole sky will be dark with them, as it was yesterday, and has been through prolonged periods during the last five years. I first noticed the definite character of this wind, and of the clouds it brings with it, in the year 1871, describing it then in the July number of *Fors Clavigera*; but little, at the time, apprehending either its universality, or any probability of its annual continuance. I am able now to state positively that its range of power extends from the North of England to Sicily; and that it blows more or less during the whole of the year, except the early autumn. This autumnal abdication is, I hope, beginning: it blew but feebly yesterday, though without intermission, from the north, making every shady place cold, while the sun was burning; its effect on the sky being only to dim the blue of it between masses of ragged cumulus. Today it has entirely fallen; and there seems hope of bright weather, the first for me since the end of May, when I had two fine days at Aylesbury; the third, May 28th, being black again from morning to evening. There seems to be some reference to the blackness caused by the prevalence of this wind in the old French name of Bise, "*grey* wind"; and, indeed, one of the darkest and bitterest days of it I ever saw was at Vevay in 1872.

The first time I recognized the clouds brought by the plague-wind as distinct in character was in walking back from Oxford, after a hard day's work, to Abingdon, in the early spring of 1871: it would take too long to give you any account this evening of the particulars which drew my attention to them; but during the following months I had too frequent opportunities of verifying my first thoughts of them, and on the first of July in that year wrote the description of them which begins the *Fors Clavigera* of August, thus:—

It is the first of July, and I sit down to write by the dismalest light that ever yet I wrote by; namely, the light of this midsummer morning, in mid-England (Matlock, Derbyshire), in the year 1871.

For the sky is covered with gray cloud;—not rain-cloud, but a dry black veil which no ray of sunshine can pierce; partly diffused in mist, feeble mist, enough to make distant objects unintelligible, yet without any substance, or wreathing, or color of its own. And everywhere the leaves of the trees are shaking fitfully, as they do before a thunderstorm; only not violently, but enough to show the passing to and fro of a strange, bitter, blighting wind. Dismal enough, had it been the first morning of its kind that summer had sent. But during all this spring, in London, and at Oxford, through meager March, through changelessly sullen April, through despondent May, and darkened June, morning after morning has come gray-shrouded thus.

And it is a new thing to me, and a very dreadful one. I am fifty years old, and more; and since I was five, have gleaned the best hours of my life in the sun of spring and summer mornings; and I never saw such as these, till now.

And the scientific men are busy as ants, examining the sun and the moon, and the seven stars, and can tell me all about *them*, I believe, by this time; and how they move, and what they are made of.

And I do not care, for my part, two copper spangles how they move, nor what they are made of. I can't move them any other way than they go, nor make them of anything else, better than they are made. But I would care much and give much, if I could be told where this bitter wind comes from, and what *it* is made of.

For, perhaps, with forethought, and fine laboratory science, one might make it of something else.

It looks partly as if it were made of poisonous smoke; very possibly it may be: there are at least two hundred furnace chimneys in a square of two miles on every side of me. But mere smoke would not blow to and fro in that wild way. It looks more to me as if it were made of dead men's souls—such of them as are not gone yet where they have to go, and may be flitting hither and thither, doubting, themselves, of the fittest place for them.

You know, if there *are* such things as souls, and if ever any of them haunt places where they have been hurt, there must be many above us, just now, displeased enough!

The last sentence refers of course to the battles of the Franco-German campaign, which was especially horrible to me, in its digging, as the Germans should have known, a moat flooded with waters of death between the two nations for a century to come.

Since that Midsummer day, my attention, however otherwise occupied, has never relaxed in its record of the phenomena characteristic of the plague-wind; and I now define for you, as briefly as possible, the essential signs of it.

(1.) It is a wind of darkness,—all the former conditions of tormenting winds, whether from the north or east, were more or less capable of co-existing with sunlight, and often with steady and bright sunlight; but whenever, and wherever the plague-wind blows, be it but for ten minutes, the sky is darkened instantly.

(2.) It is a malignant *quality* of wind, unconnected with any one quarter of the compass; it blows indifferently from all, attaching its own bitterness and malice to the worst characters of the proper winds of each quarter. It will blow either with drenching rain, or dry rage, from the south,—with ruinous blasts from the west,—with bitterest chills from the north,—and with venomous blight from the east.

Its own favorite quarter, however, is the southwest, so that it is distinguished in its malignity equally from the Bise of Provence, which is a north wind always, and from our own old friend, the east.

(3.) It always blows *tremulously*, making the leaves of the trees shudder as if they were all aspens, but with a peculiar fitfulness which gives them—and I watch them this moment as I write—an expression of anger as well as of fear and distress. You may see the kind of quivering, and hear the ominous whimpering, in the gusts that precede a great thunderstorm; but plague-wind is more panic-struck, and feverish; and its sound is a hiss instead of a wail.

When I was last at Avallon, in South France, I went to see *Faust*[7] played at the little country theater: it was done with scarcely any means of pictorial effect, except a few old curtains, and a blue light or two. But the night on the Brocken was nevertheless extremely appalling to me,—a strange ghastliness being obtained in some of the witch scenes merely by fine management of gesture and drapery; and in the phantom scenes, by the half-palsied, half-furious, faltering or fluttering past of phantoms stumbling as into graves; as if of not only soulless, but senseless, Dead, moving with the very action, the rage, the decrepitude, and the trembling of the plague-wind.

---

7. Goethe's drama, which Ruskin saw in 1882.

(4.) Not only tremulous at every moment, it is also *intermittent* with a rapidity quite unexampled in former weather. There are, indeed, days—and weeks, on which it blows without cessation, and is as inevitable as the Gulf Stream; but also there are days when it is contending with healthy weather, and on such days it will remit for half an hour, and the sun will begin to show itself, and then the wind will come back and cover the whole sky with clouds in ten minutes; and so on, every half-hour, through the whole day; so that it is often impossible to go on with any kind of drawing in color, the light being never for two seconds the same from morning till evening.

(5.) It degrades, while it intensifies, ordinary storm; but before I read you any description of its efforts in this kind, I must correct an impression which has got abroad through the papers, that I speak as if the plague-wind blew now always, and there were no more any natural weather. On the contrary, the winter of 1878–9 was one of the most healthy and lovely I ever saw ice in;—Coniston lake[8] shone under the calm clear frost in one marble field, as strong as the floor of Milan Cathedral, half a mile across and four miles down; and the first entries in my diary which I read you shall be from the 22nd to 26th June, 1876, of perfectly lovely and natural weather:—

Sunday, 25th June, 1876.

Yesterday, an entirely glorious sunset, unmatched in beauty since that at Abbeville,[9]—deep scarlet, and purest rose, on purple gray, in bars; and stationary, plumy, sweeping filaments above in upper sky, like *"using up the brush,"* said Joanie; remaining in glory, every moment best, changing from one good into another, (but only in color or light—*form steady,*) for half an hour full, and the clouds afterwards fading into the gray against amber twilight, *stationary in the same form for about two hours,* at least. The darkening rose tint remained till half-past ten, the grand time being at nine.

The day had been fine,—exquisite green light on afternoon hills.

Monday, 26th June, 1876.

Yesterday an entirely perfect summer light on the Old Man;[1] Lancaster Bay all clear; Ingleborough and the great Pennine fault as on a map. Divine beauty of western color on thyme and rose,—then twilight of clearest *warm* amber far into night, of *pale* amber all night long; hills dark-clear against it.

And so it continued, only growing more intense in blue and sunlight, all day. After breakfast, I came in from the well under strawberry bed, to say I had never seen anything like it, so pure or intense, in Italy; and so it went glowing on, cloudless, with soft north wind, all day.

16th July.

The sunset almost too bright *through the blinds* for me to read Humboldt at tea by,—finally, new moon like a lime-light, reflected on breeze-struck water; traces, across dark calm, of reflected hills.

---

8. In the Lake District of north Lancashire, where Ruskin's house, Brantwood, was located.
9. Ruskin had made a sketch of this sunset, in October 1868, and described it as "a beautiful example of what . . . a sunset could then be, in the districts of Kent and Picardy unaffected by smoke."
1. Mountain near Ruskin's home.

These extracts are, I hope, enough to guard you against the absurdity of supposing that it all only means that I am myself soured, or doting, in my old age, and always in an ill humor. Depend upon it, when old men are worth anything, they are better-humored than young ones; and have learned to see what good there is, and pleasantness, in the world they are likely so soon to have orders to quit.

Now then—take the following sequences of accurate description of thunderstorm, *with* plague-wind.

22nd June, 1876.

Thunderstorm; pitch dark, with no *blackness*,—but deep, high, *filthiness* of lurid, yet not sublimely lurid, smoke-cloud; dense manufacturing mist; fearful squalls of shivery wind, making Mr. Severn's sails[2] quiver like a man in a fever fit—all about four, afternoon—but only two or three claps of thunder, and feeble, though near, flashes. I never saw such a dirty, weak, foul storm. It cleared suddenly after raining all afternoon, at half-past eight to nine, into pure, natural weather,—low rain-clouds on quite clear, green, wet hills.

Brantwood, 13th August, 1879.

The most terrific and horrible thunderstorm, this morning, I ever remember. It waked me at six, or a little before—then rolling incessantly, like railway luggage trains, quite ghastly in its mockery of them—the air one loathsome mass of sultry and foul fog, like smoke; scarcely raining at all, but increasing to heavier rollings, with flashes quivering vaguely through all the air, and at last terrific double streams of reddish-violet fire, not forked or zigzag, but rippled rivulets—two at the same instant some twenty to thirty degrees apart, and lasting on the eye at least half a second, with grand artillery-peals following; not rattling crashes, or irregular cracklings, but delivered volleys. It lasted an hour, then passed off, clearing a little, without rain to speak of,—not a glimpse of blue,—and now, half-past seven, seems settling down again into Manchester devil's darkness.

Quarter to eight, morning.—Thunder returned, all the air collapsed into one black fog, the hills invisible, and scarcely visible the opposite shore; heavy rain in short fits, and frequent, though less formidable, flashes, and shorter thunder. While I have written this sentence the cloud has again dissolved itself, like a nasty solution in a bottle, with miraculous and unnatural rapidity, and the hills are in sight again; a double-forked flash—rippled, I mean, like the others—starts into its frightful ladder of light between me and Wetherlam, as I raise my eyes. All black above, a rugged spray cloud on the Eaglet. The "Eaglet" is my own name for the bold and elevated crag to the west of the little lake above Coniston mines. It had no name among the country people, and is one of the most conspicuous features of the mountain chain, as seen from Brantwood.

Half-past eight.—Three times light and three times dark since last I wrote, and the darkness seeming each time as it settles more loathsome,

---

2. A neighbor's sailboat on Coniston Lake.

at last stopping my reading in mere blindness. One lurid gleam of white cumulus in upper lead-blue sky, seen for half a minute through the sulphurous chimney-pot vomit of blackguardly cloud beneath, where its rags were thinnest.

Thursday, 22nd Feb. 1883.

Yesterday a fearfully dark mist all afternoon, with steady, south plague-wind of the bitterest, nastiest, poisonous blight, and fretful flutter. I could scarcely stay in the wood for the horror of it. Today, really rather bright blue, and bright semi-cumuli, with the frantic Old Man blowing sheaves of lancets and chisels across the lake—not in strength enough, or whirl enough, to raise it in spray, but tracing every squall's outline in black on the silver grey waves, and whistling meanly, and as if on a flute made of a file.

Sunday, 17th August, 1879.

Raining in foul drizzle, slow and steady; sky pitch-dark, and I just get a little light by sitting in the bow-window; diabolic clouds over everything: and looking over my kitchen garden yesterday, I found it one miserable mass of weeds gone to seed, the roses in the higher garden putrefied into brown sponges, feeling like dead snails; and the half-ripe strawberries all rotten at the stalks.

And now I come to the most important sign of the plague-wind and the plague-cloud: that in bringing on their peculiar darkness, they *blanch* the sun instead of reddening it. And here I must note briefly to you the uselessness of observation by instruments, or machines, instead of eyes. In the first year when I had begun to notice the specialty of the plague-wind, I went of course to the Oxford observatory to consult its registrars. They have their anemometer always on the twirl, and can tell you the force, or at least the pace, of a gale, by day or night. But the anemometer can only record for you how often it has been driven round, not at all whether it went round *steadily,* or went round *trembling.* And on that point depends the entire question whether it is a plague breeze or a healthy one: and what's the use of telling you whether the wind's strong or not, when it can't tell you whether it's a strong medicine, or a strong poison?

But again—you have your *sun*-measure, and can tell exactly at any moment how strong, or how weak, or how wanting, the sun is. But the sun-measurer can't tell you whether the rays are stopped by a dense *shallow* cloud, or a thin *deep* one. In healthy weather, the sun is hidden behind a cloud, as it is behind a tree; and, when the cloud is past, it comes out again, as bright as before. But in plague-wind, the sun is choked out of the whole heaven, all day long, by a cloud which may be a thousand miles square and five miles deep.

And yet observe: that thin, scraggy, filthy, mangy, miserable cloud, for all the depth of it, can't turn the sun red, as a good, business-like fog does with a hundred feet or so of itself. By the plague-wind every breath of air you draw is polluted, half round the world; in a London fog the air itself is pure, though you choose to mix up dirt with it, and choke yourself with your own nastiness.

Now I'm going to show you a diagram of a sunset in entirely pure weather, above London smoke.[3] I saw it and sketched it from my old post of observation—the top garret of my father's house at Herne Hill. There, when the wind is south, we are outside of the smoke and above it; and this diagram, admirably enlarged from my own drawing by my, now in all things best aide-de-camp, Mr. Collingwood, shows you an old-fashioned sunset—the sort of thing Turner and I used to have to look at,—(nobody else ever would) constantly. Every sunset and every dawn, in fine weather, had something of the sort to show us. This is one of the last pure sunsets I ever saw, about the year 1876,—and the point I want you to note in it is, that the air being pure, the smoke on the horizon, though at last it hides the sun, yet hides it through gold and vermilion. Now, don't go away fancying there's any exaggeration in that study. The *prismatic* colors, I told you, were simply impossible to paint; these, which are transmitted colors, can indeed be suggested, but no more. The brightest pigment we have would look dim beside the truth.

I should have liked to have blotted down for you a bit of plague-cloud to put beside this; but Heaven knows, you can see enough of it nowadays without any trouble of mine; and if you want, in a hurry, to see what the sun looks like through it, you've only to throw a bad half-crown into a basin of soap and water.

Blanched Sun,—blighted grass,—blinded man.—If, in conclusion, you ask me for any conceivable cause or meaning of these things—I can tell you none, according to your modern beliefs; but I can tell you what meaning it would have borne to the men of old time. Remember, for the last twenty years, England, and all foreign nations, either tempting her, or following her, have blasphemed[4] the name of God deliberately and openly; and have done iniquity by proclamation, every man doing as much injustice to his brother as it is in his power to do. Of states in such moral gloom every seer of old predicted the physical gloom, saying, "The light shall be darkened in the heavens thereof, and the stars shall withdraw their shining."[5] All Greek, all Christian, all Jewish prophecy insists on the same truth through a thousand myths; but of all the chief, to former thought, was the fable of the Jewish warrior and prophet, for whom the sun hasted not to go down,[6] with which I leave you to compare at leisure the physical result of your own wars and prophecies, as declared by your own elect journal not fourteen days ago,— that the Empire of England, on which formerly the sun never set, has become one on which he never rises.[7]

What is best to be done, do you ask me? The answer is plain. Whether you can affect the signs of the sky or not, you *can* the signs of the times. Whether you can bring the *sun* back or not, you can assuredly bring back your own cheerfulness, and your own honesty. You may not be able to say to the winds, "Peace; be still,"[8] but you can cease from the insolence of your

---

3. The illustration shown at the lecture was titled *An Old-Fashioned Sunset, 1876.*
4. Ruskin defined blasphemy as

"harmful speaking"—not against God only, but against man, and against all the good works and purposes of Nature. The word is accurately opposed to "Euphemy," the right or well-speaking of God and His world . . . And the universal instinct of blasphemy in the modern scientific mind is above all manifested in its love

of what is ugly, and natural enthrallment by the abominable.
5. Cf. Joel 2.10.
6. On Joshua's commanding the sun to stand still, see Joshua 10.13.
7. In January 1884, after weeks of sunless weather, the *Pall Mall Gazette* had made joking references to the popular boast about the sun never setting on the British dominions, for the good reason that it never rises.
8. Mark 4.39.

own lips, and the troubling of your own passions. And all *that* it would be extremely well to do, even though the day *were* coming when the sun should be as darkness, and the moon as blood.[9] But, the paths of rectitude and piety once regained, who shall say that the promise of old time would not be found to hold for us also?—"Bring ye all the tithes into my storehouse, and prove me now herewith, saith the Lord God, if I will not open you the windows of heaven, and pour you out a blessing, that there shall not be room enough to receive it."[1]

1884

9. Cf. the prophecy in Revelation 6.12: "the sun became black as sackcloth of hair, and the moon became as blood." 1. Malachi 3.10.

ARTHUR HUGH CLOUGH
1819–1861

The writings of Arthur Hugh Clough (whose name is pronounced so as to rhyme with *rough*) are usually treated as a kind of footnote to those of his friend Matthew Arnold. Read in this way they can indeed add to our understanding of Arnold's early poems written during the phase of religious stress shared by both young men. Some of Clough's admirers argue, however, that such a reading is to be deplored because Clough, despite his frequent clumsiness in versification, is a poet of considerable stature in his own right. What is beyond dispute is that he provides exceptional insights into the intellectual history of his century.

Like many Victorians (including John Ruskin, his exact contemporary), Clough was permanently influenced by his mother's pious religious convictions, her influence being reinforced by his years at Rugby School, where he was the prize pupil of Dr. Thomas Arnold. Later, at Oxford, his earnest preoccupation with religious duty was undermined by a number of different intellectual developments. He was forced to think through questions of High Church authoritarianism and traditionalism—provoked by John Henry Newman's presence at Oxford—and to confront the evidence of scientific critics who challenged the authority and authenticity of the Scriptures. Clough emerged as a skeptic in the real sense of the word. In a letter to his sister in 1847, speaking of the Atonement as an article of Christian faith, he remarks: "I think others are more right who say boldly, we don't understand it, and therefore we won't fall down and worship it. Though there is no occasion for adding—'there *is* nothing in it'—I should say, until I know, I will wait, and if I am not born with the power to discover, I will do what I can . . . and neither pretend to know, nor, without knowing, pretend to embrace: nor yet oppose those who, by whatever means, are increasing or trying to increase knowledge." A year later, reflections of this kind led Clough to resign his fellowship at Oxford where he was expected to subscribe to the doctrines of the Church of England. For the rest of his life he held various educational posts. On one occasion, his application for a chair of classics in Australia was unsuccessful. His failure may be attributed to the refusal of his principal referee at Oxford to write a recommendation for him on the grounds that "no one ought to be appointed to such a situation who is at all in a state of doubt or difficulty as to his religious beliefs." Such obstacles did not prevent Clough's obtaining other employments in London and, in 1852–53 (under the auspices of Emerson), in America, where he had spent his early childhood. Clough was fond of travel, especially in Italy, which served as the setting for several of his poems, including *Amours de Voyage,* the most modern of his poems, an epistolary narrative about a young intellectual whose ironic self-conscoiusness causes him the loss of his love.

Much of Clough's poetry was published posthumously. His first volume, *The Bothie of Tober-na-Vuolich* (1848), is a delightful novel in verse, an undergraduate love story exhibiting aspects of his character omitted in Arnold's picture of him in *Thyrsis*. For despite his painful exposure to religious uncertainties, Clough had a strain of high spirits and fun that gives flavor to his best poems. In his later poems, including *Dipsychus* (1850), a series of debates between idealism and worldliness, the strains of earnestness, uncertainty, and humor are blended into an ironic point of view different from Matthew Arnold's and, in fact, different from the characteristic tone of most of his contemporaries. Perhaps one of the reasons that Clough's poetry has been inadequately appreciated is that this distinctive tone of his is most evident in his full-length poems rather than in the short hymnlike verses by which he is usually represented in anthologies.

Epi-strauss-ium[1]

Matthew and Mark and Luke and holy John
Evanished all and gone!
Yea, he[2] that erst, his dusky curtains quitting,
Through Eastern pictured panes his level beams transmitting,
5 With gorgeous portraits blent,
On them his glories intercepted spent,
Southwestering now, through windows plainly glassed,
On the inside face his radiance keen hath cast,
And in the luster lost, invisible, and gone,
10 Are, say you, Matthew, Mark, and Luke and holy John?
Lost, is it? lost, to be recovered never?
However,
The place of worship the meantime with light
Is, if less richly, more sincerely bright,
15 And in blue skies the Orb is manifest to sight.

1847   1869

The Latest Decalogue

Thou shalt have one God only; who
Would be at the expense of two?
No graven images may be
Worshiped, except the currency.
5 Swear not at all; for, for thy curse
Thine enemy is none the worse.
At church on Sunday to attend

1. The title is a play on *epi-thalamium*, which means "concerning the bridal chamber." The word usually refers to a song in honor of a bride and bridegroom (as in Spenser's poem). Clough's title means "concerning Strauss-ism," a reference to D. F. Strauss, a German biblical scholar whose

Life of Jesus was translated into English by George Eliot in 1846. The "light" of Strauss's analysis reputedly showed up the historical inaccuracy of parts of the Gospels in the Bible.
2. The sun. Cf. lines 13–16 of *Say Not the Struggle Nought Availeth* (p. 1453).

Will serve to keep the world thy friend.
Honor thy parents; that is, all
10   From whom advancement may befall.
Thou shalt not kill; but need'st not strive
Officiously to keep alive.
Do not adultery commit;
Advantage rarely comes of it.
15   Thou shalt not steal; an empty feat,
When it's so lucrative to cheat.
Bear not false witness; let the lie
Have time on its own wings to fly.
Thou shalt not covet, but tradition
20   Approves all forms of competition.

The sum of all is, thou shalt love,
If anybody, God above:
At any rate shall never labor
More than thyself to love thy neighbor.[1]

1862

Say Not the Struggle Nought Availeth

Say not the struggle nought availeth,
    The labor and the wounds are vain,
The enemy faints not, nor faileth,
    And as things have been they remain.

5   If hopes were dupes, fears may be liars;
    It may be, in yon smoke concealed,
Your comrades chase e'en now the fliers,
    And, but for you, possess the field.

For while the tired waves, vainly breaking,
10   Seem here no painful inch to gain,
Far back, through creeks and inlets making,
    Comes silent, flooding in, the main.

And not by eastern windows only,
    When daylight comes, comes in the light,
15   In front, the sun climbs slow, how slowly,
    But westward, look, the land is bright.

1849   1862

---

1. Lines 21–24 were discovered in one of Clough's manuscripts and were not originally included in published versions of the poem.

GEORGE ELIOT
1819–1880

Like many English novelists (Dickens being an exception) George Eliot came to novel writing relatively late in life. She was forty when her first novel, *Adam Bede,* an outstandingly popular work, was published. The lives of her characters are, therefore, viewed from the vantage point of maturity and extensive experience; and this perspective is accentuated by her practice of setting her stories back in time to the period of her own childhood, or even earlier. In most of her novels, she evokes a preindustrial rural scene or the small-town life of the English Midlands, which she views with a combination of nostalgia and candid awareness of their limitations.

The place Eliot looks back on is usually the Warwickshire countryside, where, under her real name, Marian Evans, she spent her childhood at Arbury Farm, of which her father, Robert Evans, was supervisor and land agent. The time was the 1820s and 1830s (1819, the year of her birth, was an *annus mirabilis* for the nineteenth century, for in the same year were born John Ruskin, Herman Melville, Walt Whitman, Arthur Hugh Clough, and Queen Victoria). During these decades, Evans read widely in and out of school and was also strongly affected by Evangelicism; she even advocated, at one point in her girlhood, giving up novelists such as Scott (who was later to influence her own novel writing) on the grounds that fiction was frivolous and time wasting. Her mother's death led to her leaving school at sixteen, and in the next four or five years she seems to have experienced bouts of depression and self-doubt. In a letter of 1871, looking back to the period, she likened her state of mind to that of Mary Wollstonecraft at the time of her attempted suicide: "Hopelessness has been to me, all through my life, but especially in the painful years of my youth, the chief source of wasted energy with all the consequent bitterness of regret. Remember, it has happened to many to be glad they did not commit suicide, though they once ran for the final leap, or as Mary Wollstonecraft did, wetted their garments well in the rain hoping to sink the better when they plunged."

At the age of twenty-one Evans moved with her father to the town of Coventry, and in this new setting, her intellectual horizons were extensively widened. As the result of her association with a group of freethinking intellectuals, and her own studies of theology, she reluctantly decided that she could no longer believe in the Christian religion. Her decision created a painful break with her father, finally resolved when she agreed to observe the formality of attending church with him and he agreed, tacitly at least, that while there she could think what she liked.

These preoccupations with theological issues led to her first book, a translation of *The Life of Jesus* by D. F. Strauss, one of the leading figures of the Higher Criticism in Germany. This criticism was the work of a group of scholars dedicated to testing the historical authenticity of biblical narratives in the light of modern methods of research. For the rest of her life, Evans continued to read extensively in English and Continental philosophy; and when she moved to London in 1851, after her father's death, her impressive intellectual credentials led to her appointment as an assistant editor of the *Westminster Review,* a learned journal formerly edited by John Stuart Mill. In the years in which she served as editor, she wrote a number of essays, including *Margaret Fuller and Mary Wollstonecraft* and *Silly Novels by Lady Novelists,* which she contributed to various periodicals, in addition to the *Westminster Review.*

Her work at the *Review* brought her into contact with many important writers and thinkers. Among them was George Henry Lewes, a brilliant critic of literature and philosophy, with whom she fell in love. Lewes, a married man and father of three children, could not obtain a divorce. Evans, therefore, elected to live with him as a common-law wife, and what they called their "marriage" lasted happily until his death in 1878. In the last year of her life, she married an admirer and friend, J. W. Cross, who became her biographer.

Her earlier decision to live with Lewes was painfully made: "Light and easily broken ties are what I neither desire theoretically nor could live for practically. Women who are satisfied with such ties do *not* act as I have done—they obtain what they desire and are still invited to dinner." Mrs. Lewes, as she called herself, was not invited to dinner; instead, those who wanted to visit with her had themselves to seek her company at the house that she shared with Lewes, where she received visitors on Sunday afternoons. These Sunday afternoons became legendary occasions, over which she presided almost like a sibyl. However, her decision to live with Lewes cost her a number of social and family ties, including her relationship with her brother, Isaac, to whom she had been deeply attached since childhood. Isaac never spoke to her again after her elopement. It is reasonable to conjecture that this experience affects the stress, in all of her novels, on incidents involving choice. All of her characters are tested by situations in which they must choose, and the choices, as in *The Mill on the Floss,* are often agonizingly painful.

Although she had occasionally tried her hand at fiction earlier in life, it was only after her relationship with Lewes became established that she turned her full attention to this form. *Scenes from Clerical Life* appeared in magazine installments in 1857 under the pen name that misled most of her readers (Dickens excepted) into believing the author to be a man—a "university man," it was commonly said, to Eliot's amusement and satisfaction. This work was followed by seven full-length novels in the 1860s and 1870s, most of which repeated the success of *Adam Bede* with the Victorian reading public and which, after a period of being out of favor earlier in our century, are now once more deeply admired by readers and critics. Virginia Woolf praised *Middlemarch* as "one of the few English novels written for grown-up people," and later readers have found a similar maturity combined with a powerful creative energy in other novels by Eliot such as *The Mill on the Floss* and *Daniel Deronda* (1876).

When Eliot began writing fiction, she and Lewes were reading to each other the novels of Jane Austen. Eliot's fiction owes much to Austen's with its concern with provincial society, its satire of human motives, its focus on courtship. But Eliot brings to these subjects a philosophical and psychological depth very different in character from that of the novel of manners. Eliot's fiction typically combines expansive philosophic meditation with an acute dissection of her characters' motives and feelings.

In a famous passage from *Middlemarch,* Eliot compares herself with the great eighteenth-century novelist Henry Fielding:

> A great historian, as he insisted on calling himself, who had the happiness to be dead a hundred and twenty years ago, and so to take his place among the colossi whose huge legs our living pettiness is observed to walk under, glories in his copious remarks and digressions as the least imitable part of his work. . . . But Fielding lived when the days were longer. . . . We belated historians must not linger after his example; I at least have so much to do in unravelling certain human lots, and seeing how they were woven and interwoven, that all the light I can command must be concentrated on this particular web, and not dispersed over that tempting range of relevancies called the universe.

Despite her ironic disclaimer Eliot too prides herself on her remarks and digressions— as this passage, itself a digression, suggests. As a "belated historian," however, she focuses on the intersection of a few human lives at a particular time and place in her country's history. She frequently likened herself not only to a historian but to a scientist, who, with a microscope, observes and analyzes the tangled web of character and circumstance that determines human history. As both comparisons imply, Eliot strives to present her fiction as a mirror that reflects without distortion our experience of life. But her insistence on art's transparency is often troubled both by her consciousness of its fictions and by her sense of the way in which the egoism we all share distorts our perceptions. Hence she portrays this egoism with a combination of acuity and compassion. It is this distinctive compounding of realism and sympathy that makes her, according to the French critic Brunetiere, a better realist than her famous French contemporary Flaubert, author of *Madame Bovary.* Often compared with Tolstoy, she is, perhaps, the greatest English realist.

Eliot's definition of herself as a historian leads us to expect her novels to offer considerable insight into contemporary issues. The Woman Question, as her essay *Margaret Fuller and Mary Wollstonecraft* suggests, held particular interest for her. She typically chooses for her heroine a young woman, like Maggie Tulliver of *The Mill on the Floss* or Dorothea Brooke of *Middlemarch,* of powerful imagination and of yearning to be more than her society allows her to be. The prelude to *Middlemarch* speaks of the modern-day Saint Teresa, with the ardor and vision to found a religious order, caught at a historical moment that gives no outlet for her ambition. In her portrayal of the frustrations and yearnings of such a heroine, Eliot seems sympathetic to a feminist point of view. Yet her stress on the values of loyalty to one's past; of adherence to duty, despite personal desire; and of what Wordsworth calls "little, nameless, unremembered acts of kindness and of love" suggests that her attitude toward the Woman Question is complex.

George Eliot wrote, "My function is that of the *aesthetic* not the doctrinal teacher." The largeness of vision through which Eliot enters into the consciousness of all her characters makes the perspective of her novels on many issues a complex one, for it is finally issues as they are refracted through the lens of human character that interest her.

Margaret Fuller and Mary Wollstonecraft[1]

The dearth of new books just now gives us time to recur to less recent ones which we have hitherto noticed but slightly; and among these we choose the late edition of Margaret Fuller's *Woman in the Nineteenth Century,* because we think it has been unduly thrust into the background by less comprehensive and candid productions on the same subject. Notwithstanding certain defects of taste and a sort of vague spiritualism and grandiloquence which belong to all but the very best American writers, the book is a valuable one; it has the enthusiasm of a noble and sympathetic nature, with the moderation and breadth and large allowance of a vigorous and cultivated understanding. There is no exaggeration of woman's moral excellence or intellectual capabilities; no injudicious insistence on her fitness for this or that function hitherto engrossed by men; but a calm plea for the removal of unjust laws and artificial restrictions, so that the possibilities of her nature may have room for full development, a wisely stated demand to disencumber her of the

> Parasitic forms
> That seem to keep her up, but drag her down—
> And leave her field to burgeon and to bloom

1. Published in *The Leader* in 1855, this essay is a retrospective book review of two important feminist publications—*A Vindication of the Rights of Woman* (1792) by Mary Wollstonecraft and *Woman in the Nineteenth Century* (1855; published originally as *The Great Lawsuit,* 1843), by Margaret Fuller (1810–1850), an American essayist and editor whom Eliot warmly admired.

As Barbara Hardy notes, despite "her generous sympathy with Victorian feminism," George Eliot "played no active part in the movement." Eliot seems to have shared the view of women's relation to men expressed by the Prince in Tennyson's *Princess,* whose speeches she cites in this essay. As she herself wrote in 1854, in another essay, *Women in France:*

Women became superior in France by being admitted to a common fund of ideas, to common objects of interest with men; and this must ever be the essential condition at once of true womanly culture and of true social well-being. . . . Let the whole field of reality be laid open to woman as well as to man, and then that which is peculiar in the mental modification, instead of being, as it is now, a source of discord and repulsion between the sexes, will be found to be a necessary complement to the truth and beauty of life.

> From all within her, make herself her own
> To give or keep, to live and learn and be
> All that not harms distinctive womanhood.[2]

It is interesting to compare this essay of Margaret Fuller's published in its earliest form in 1843,[3] with a work on the position of woman, written between sixty and seventy years ago—we mean Mary Wollstonecraft's *Rights of Woman*. The latter work was not continued beyond the first volume; but so far as this carries the subject, the comparison, at least in relation to strong sense and loftiness of moral tone, is not at all disadvantageous to the woman of the last century. There is in some quarters a vague prejudice against the *Rights of Woman* as in some way or other a reprehensible book, but readers who go to it with this impression will be surprised to find it eminently serious, severely moral, and withal rather heavy—the true reason, perhaps, that no edition has been published since 1796, and that it is now rather scarce. There are several points of resemblance, as well as of striking difference, between the two books. A strong understanding is present in both; but Margaret Fuller's mind was like some regions of her own American continent, where you are constantly stepping from the sunny "clearings" into the mysterious twilight of the tangled forest—she often passes in one breath from forcible reasoning to dreamy vagueness; moreover, her unusually varied culture gives her great command of illustration. Mary Wollstonecraft, on the other hand, is nothing if not rational; she has no erudition, and her grave pages are lit up by no ray of fancy. In both writers we discern, under the brave bearing of a strong and truthful nature, the beating of a loving woman's heart, which teaches them not to undervalue the smallest offices of domestic care or kindliness. But Margaret Fuller, with all her passionate sensibility, is more of the literary woman, who would not have been satisfied without intellectual production; Mary Wollstonecraft, we imagine, wrote not at all for writing's sake, but from the pressure of other motives. So far as the difference of date allows, there is a striking coincidence in their trains of thought; indeed, every important idea in the *Rights of Woman*, except the combination of home education with a common day-school for boys and girls, reappears in Margaret Fuller's essay.

One point on which they both write forcibly is the fact that, while men have a horror of such faculty or culture in the other sex as tends to place it on a level with their own, they are really in a state of subjection to ignorant and feeble-minded women. Margaret Fuller says:

> Wherever man is sufficiently raised above extreme poverty or brutal stupidity, to care for the comforts of the fireside, or the bloom and ornament of life, woman has always power enough, if she chooses to exert it, and is usually disposed to do so, in proportion to her ignorance and childish vanity. Unacquainted with the importance of life and its purposes, trained to a selfish coquetry and love of petty power, she does not look beyond the pleasure of making herself felt at the moment, and governments are shaken and commerce broken up to gratify the pique

---

2. Tennyson's *The Princess* 7.253–258. As noted by Thomas Pinney, the quotation, slightly inaccurate, is from the unrevised 1847 text of the poem. See the passage containing these lines ["*The*

Woman's Cause Is Man's"], p. 1229.
3. I.e., the original version published in *The Dial*; revised and expanded in 1855.

of a female favorite. The English shopkeeper's wife does not vote, but it is for her interest that the politician canvasses by the coarsest flattery.

Again:

> All wives, bad or good, loved or unloved, inevitably influence their husbands from the power their position not merely gives, but necessitates of coloring evidence and infusing feelings in hours when the— patient, shall I call him?—is off his guard.

Hear now what Mary Wollstonecraft says on the same subject:

> Women have been allowed to remain in ignorance and slavish dependence many, very many years, and still we hear of nothing but their fondness of pleasure and sway, their preference of rakes and soldiers, their childish attachment to toys, and the vanity that makes them value accomplishments more than virtues. History brings forward a fearful catalogue of the crimes which their cunning has produced, when the weak slaves have had sufficient address to overreach their masters. . . . When, therefore, I call women slaves, I mean in a political and civil sense; for indirectly they obtain too much power, and are debased by their exertions to obtain illicit sway. . . . The libertinism, and even the virtues of superior men, will always give women of some description great power over them; and these weak women, under the influence of childish passions and selfish vanity, *will throw a false light over the objects which the very men view with their eyes who ought to enlighten their judgment.* Men of fancy, and those sanguine characters who mostly hold the helm of human affairs in general, relax in the society of women; and surely I need not cite to the most superficial reader of history the numerous examples of vice and oppression which the private intrigues of female favorites have produced; not to dwell on the mischief that naturally arises from the blundering interposition of well-meaning folly. *For in the transactions of business it is much better to have to deal with a knave than a fool, because a knave adheres to some plan, and any plan of reason may be seen through sooner than a sudden flight of folly.* The power which vile and foolish women have had over wise men who possessed sensibility is notorious.

There is a notion commonly entertained among men that an instructed woman, capable of having opinions, is likely to prove an unpracticable yokefellow, always pulling one way when her husband wants to go the other, oracular in tone, and prone to give curtain lectures[4] on metaphysics. But surely, so far as obstinacy is concerned, your unreasoning animal is the most unmanageable of creatures, where you are not allowed to settle the question by a cudgel, a whip and bridle, or even a string to the leg. For our own parts, we see no consistent or commodious medium between the old plan of corporal discipline and that thorough education of women which will make them rational beings in the highest sense of the word. Wherever weakness is not harshly controlled it must *govern*, as you may see when a strong man holds a little child by the hand, how he is pulled hither and thither, and

---

4. See Douglas Jerrold's comic sketches of a wife who delivers nightly lectures to her husband from behind their bed curtains, *Mrs. Caudle's Curtain Lectures* (1846).

wearied in his walk by his submission to the whims and feeble movements of his companion. A really cultured woman, like a really cultured man, will be ready to yield in trifles. So far as we see, there is no indissoluble connection between infirmity of logic and infirmity of will, and a woman quite innocent of an opinion in philosophy, is as likely as not to have an indomitable opinion about the kitchen. As to airs of superiority, no woman ever had them in consequence of true culture, but only because her culture was shallow or unreal, only as a result of what Mrs. Malaprop well calls "the ineffectual qualities in a woman"[5]—mere acquisitions carried about, and not knowledge thoroughly assimilated so as to enter into the growth of the character.

To return to Margaret Fuller, some of the best things she says are on the folly of absolute definitions of woman's nature and absolute demarcations of woman's mission. "Nature," she says, "seems to delight in varying the arrangements, as if to show that she will be fettered by no rule; and we must admit the same varieties that she admits." Again: "If nature is never bound down, nor the voice of inspiration stifled, that is enough. We are pleased that women should write and speak, if they feel need of it, from having something to tell; but silence for ages would be no misfortune, if that silence be from divine command, and not from man's tradition." And here is a passage, the beginning of which has been often quoted:

> If you ask me what offices they [women] may fill, I reply—any. I do
> not care what case you put; let them be sea-captains if you will. I do not
> doubt there are women well fitted for such an office, and, if so, I should
> be as glad as to welcome the Maid of Saragossa, or the Maid of Misso-
> longhi, or the Suliote heroine, or Emily Plater.[6] I think women need,
> especially at this juncture, a much greater range of occupation than they
> have, to rouse their latent powers. . . . In families that I know, some little
> girls like to saw wood, others to use carpenter's tools. Where these tastes
> are indulged, cheerfulness and good-humor are promoted. Where they
> are forbidden, because "such things are not proper for girls," they grow
> sullen and mischievous. Fourier had observed these wants of women, as
> no one can fail to do who watches the desires of little girls, or knows the
> *ennui* that haunts grown women, except where they make to themselves
> a serene little world by art of some kind. He, therefore, in proposing a
> great variety of employments, in manufactures or the care of plants and
> animals, allows for one-third of women as likely to have a taste for mas-
> culine pursuits, one-third of men for feminine.[7] . . . I have no doubt,
> however, that a large proportion of women would give themselves to the
> same employments as now, because there are circumstances that must
> lead them. Mothers will delight to make the nest soft and warm. Nature

5. In response to compliments about her "intellectual accomplishments," Mrs. Malaprop exclaims: "Ah! few gentlemen, nowadays, know how to value the ineffectual qualities in a woman!" Richard Brinsley Sheridan, *The Rivals* 3.2 (1775).
6. A Polish patriot, who became a captain in command of a company in the insurgent army fighting the Russians in 1831. "Maid of Saragossa": Maria Agustin, who fought against the French at the siege of Saragossa, in Spain, in 1808 (see Byron, *Childe Harold's Pilgrimage* 1.54–56). "Maid of

Missolonghi": an unidentified Greek, who must have made some heroic exploit during the Turkish sieges of that town in 1822 or 1826. "The Suliote heroine": probably Moscha, who led a band of three hundred women to rout the Turks during the siege of Souli, in Albania, in 1803.
7. Charles Fourier (1772–1837), in his utopian treatise *The New Industrial World* (1829–30), develops these theories in his discussion of "the Little Hordes."

would take care of that; no need to clip the wings of any bird that wants to soar and sing, or finds in itself the strength of pinion for a migratory flight unusual to its kind. The difference would be that *all* need not be constrained to employments for which *some* are unfit.

Apropos of the same subject, we find Mary Wollstonecraft offering a suggestion which the women of the United States have already begun to carry out. She says:

> Women, in particular, all want to be ladies, which is simply to have nothing to do, but listlessly to go they scarcely care where, for they cannot tell what. But what have women to do in society? I may be asked, but to loiter with easy grace; surely you would not condemn them all to suckle fools and chronicle small beer.[8] No. *Women might certainly study the art of healing, and be physicians as well as nurses. . . .* Business of various kinds they might likewise pursue, if they were educated in a more orderly manner. . . . Women would not then marry for a support, as men accept of places under government, and neglect the implied duties.

Men pay a heavy price for their reluctance to encourage self-help and independent resources in women. The precious meridian years of many a man of genius have to be spent in the toil of routine, that an "establishment" may be kept up for a woman who can understand none of his secret yearnings,[9] who is fit for nothing but to sit in her drawing-room like a doll-Madonna in her shrine. No matter. Anything is more endurable than to change our established formulae about women, or to run the risk of looking up to our wives instead of looking down on them. *Sit divus, dummodo non sit vivus* (let him be a god, provided he be not living), said the Roman magnates of Romulus;[1] and so men say of women, let them be idols, useless absorbents of previous things, provided we are not obliged to admit them to be strictly fellow-beings, to be treated, one and all, with justice and sober reverence.

On one side we hear that woman's position can never be improved until women themselves are better; and, on the other, that women can never become better until their position is improved—until the laws are made more just, and a wider field opened to feminine activity. But we constantly hear the same difficulty stated about the human race in general. There is a perpetual action and reaction between individuals and institutions; we must try and mend both by little and little—the only way in which human things can be mended. Unfortunately, many over-zealous champions of women assert their actual equality with men—nay, even their moral superiority to men—as a ground for their release from oppressive laws and restrictions. They lose strength immensely by this false position. If it were true, then there would be a case in which slavery and ignorance nourished virtue, and so far we should have an argument for the continuance of bondage. But we want freedom and culture for woman, because subjection and ignorance have debased her, and with her, Man; for—

---

8. Iago on the role of women, Shakespeare's *Othello* 2.1.160.
9. Cf. Eliot's fictional representation of such a situation in her account of Dr. Lydgate's married life in *Middlemarch*.
1. Cf. *Historia Augusta, Geta* 2, in which the same cynical comment is made on a proposal to have a man deified.

> If she be small, slight-natured, miserable,
> How shall men grow?[2]

Both Margaret Fuller and Mary Wollstonecraft have too much sagacity to fall into this sentimental exaggeration. Their ardent hopes of what women may become do not prevent them from seeing and painting women as they are. On the relative moral excellence of men and women Mary Wollstonecraft speaks with the most decision:

> Women are supposed to possess more sensibility, and even humanity, than men, and their strong attachments and instantaneous emotions of compassion are given as proofs; but the clinging affection of ignorance has seldom anything noble in it, and may mostly be resolved into self-ishness, as well as the affection of children and brutes. I have known many weak women whose sensibility was entirely engrossed by their hus-bands; and as for their humanity, it was very faint indeed, or rather it was only a transient emotion of compassion. Humanity does not consist "in a squeamish ear," says an eminent orator.[3] "It belongs to the mind as well as to the nerves." But this kind of exclusive affection, though it degrades the individual, should not be brought forward as a proof of the inferiority of the sex, because it is the natural consequence of confined views; for even women of superior sense, having their attention turned to little employments and private plans, rarely rise to heroism, unless when spurred on by love! and love, as an heroic passion, like genius, appears but once in an age. I therefore agree with the moralist who asserts "that women have seldom so much generosity as men"; and that their narrow affections, to which justice and humanity are often sacri-ficed, render the sex apparently inferior, especially as they are commonly inspired by men; but I contend that the heart would expand as the under-standing gained strength, if women were not depressed from their cradles.

We had marked several other passages of Margaret Fuller's for extract, but as we do not aim at an exhaustive treatment of our subject, and are only touching a few of its points, we have, perhaps, already claimed as much of the reader's attention as he will be willing to give to such desultory material.

1855

Silly Novels by Lady Novelists[1]

Silly Novels by Lady Novelists are a genus with many species, determined by the particular quality of silliness that predominates in them—the frothy, the prosy, the pious, or the pedantic. But it is a mixture of all these—a composite order of feminine fatuity, that produces the largest class of such novels, which we shall distinguish as the *mind-and-millinery* species. The

2. Tennyson's *The Princess* 7.249–50.
3. Perhaps Edmund Burke (1729–1797).
1. Published anonymously in the *Westminster Review*, this review essay, satirizing a number of contemporary novels, provides a good indication of Eliot's ideas about fiction at the time she was beginning her first story, *The Sad Fortunes of the Rev. Amos Barton*.

heroine is usually an heiress, probably a peeress in her own right, with perhaps a vicious baronet, an amiable duke, and an irresistible younger son of a marquis as lovers in the foreground, a clergyman and a poet sighing for her in the middle distance, and a crowd of undefined adorers dimly indicated beyond. Her eyes and her wit are both dazzling; her nose and her morals are alike free from any tendency to irregularity; she has a superb *contralto* and a superb intellect; she is perfectly well-dressed and perfectly religious; she dances like a sylph, and reads the Bible in the original tongues. Or it may be that the heroine is not an heiress—that rank and wealth are the only things in which she is deficient; but she infallibly gets into high society, she has the triumph of refusing many matches and securing the best, and she wears some family jewels or other as a sort of crown of righteousness at the end. Rakish men either bite their lips in impotent confusion at her repartees, or are touched to penitence by her reproofs, which, on appropriate occasions, rise to a lofty strain of rhetoric; indeed, there is a general propensity in her to make speeches, and to rhapsodize at some length when she retires to her bedroom. In her recorded conversations she is amazingly eloquent, and in her unrecorded conversations, amazingly witty. She is understood to have a depth of insight that looks through and through the shallow theories of philosophers, and her superior instincts are a sort of dial by which men have only to set their clocks and watches, and all will go well. The men play a very subordinate part by her side. You are consoled now and then by a hint that they have affairs, which keeps you in mind that the working-day business of the world is somehow being carried on, but ostensibly the final cause of their existence is that they may accompany the heroine on her "starring" expedition through life. They see her at a ball, and are dazzled; at a flower-show, and they are fascinated; on a riding excursion, and they are witched[2] by her noble horsemanship; at church, and they are awed by the sweet solemnity of her demeanour. She is the ideal woman in feelings, faculties, and flounces. For all this, she as often as not marries the wrong person to begin with, and she suffers terribly from the plots and intrigues of the vicious baronet; but even death has a soft place in his heart for such a paragon, and remedies all mistakes for her just at the right moment. The vicious baronet is sure to be killed in a duel, and the tedious husband dies in his bed requesting his wife, as a particular favour to him, to marry the man she loves best, and having already dispatched a note to the lover informing him of the comfortable arrangement. Before matters arrive at this desirable issue our feelings are tried by seeing the noble, lovely, and gifted heroine pass through many *mauvais*[3] *moments*, but we have the satisfaction of knowing that her sorrows are wept into embroidered pocket-handkerchiefs, that her fainting form reclines on the very best upholstery, and that whatever vicissitudes she may undergo, from being dashed out of her carriage to having her head shaved in a fever, she comes out of them all with a complexion more blooming and locks more redundant than ever.

We may remark, by the way, that we have been relieved from a serious scruple by discovering that silly novels by lady novelists rarely introduce us into any other than very lofty and fashionable society. We had imagined that destitute women turned novelists, as they turned governesses, because they

---

2. Bewitched.   3. Bad (French).

had no other "lady-like" means of getting their bread. On this supposition, vacillating syntax and improbable incident had a certain pathos for us, like the extremely supererogatory pincushions and ill-devised nightcaps that are offered for sale by a blind man. We felt the commodity to be a nuisance, but we were glad to think that the money went to relieve the necessitous, and we pictured to ourselves lonely women struggling for a maintenance, or wives and daughters devoting themselves to the production of "copy" out of pure heroism,—perhaps to pay their husband's debts, or to purchase luxuries for a sick father. Under these impressions we shrank from criticising a lady's novel: her English might be faulty, but, we said to ourselves, her motives are irreproachable; her imagination may be uninventive, but her patience is untiring. Empty writing was excused by an empty stomach, and twaddle was consecrated by tears. But no! This theory of ours, like many other pretty theories, has had to give way before observation. Women's silly novels, we are now convinced, are written under totally different circumstances. The fair writers have evidently never talked to a tradesman except from a carriage window; they have no notion of the working-classes except as "dependents; " they think five hundred a-year a miserable pittance; Belgravia[4] and "baronial halls" are their primary truths; and they have no idea of feeling interest in any man who is not at least a great landed proprietor, if not a prime minister. It is clear that they write in elegant boudoirs, with violet-colored ink and a ruby pen; that they must be entirely indifferent to publishers' accounts, and inexperienced in every form of poverty except poverty of brains. It is true that we are constantly struck with the want of verisimilitude in their representations of the high society in which they seem to live; but then they betray no closer acquaintance with any other form of life. If their peers and peeresses are improbable, their literary men, tradespeople, and cottagers are impossible; and their intellect seems to have the peculiar impartiality of reproducing both what they *have* seen and heard, and what they have *not* seen and heard, with equal unfaithfulness.

* * *

Writers of the mind-and-millinery school are remarkably unanimous in their choice of diction. In their novels, there is usually a lady or gentleman who is more or less of a upas tree:[5] the lover has a manly breast; minds are redolent of various things; hearts are hollow; events are utilized; friends are consigned to the tomb; infancy is an engaging period; the sun is a luminary that goes to his western couch, or gathers the rain-drops into his refulgent bosom; life is a melancholy boon; Albion and Scotia[6] are conversational epithets. There is a striking resemblance, too, in the character of their moral comments, such, for instance, as that "It is a fact, no less true than melancholy, that all people, more or less, richer or poorer, are swayed by bad example;" that "Books, however trivial, contain some subjects from which useful information may be drawn;" that "Vice can too often borrow the language of virtue;" that "Merit and nobility of nature must exist, to be accepted, for clamour and pretension cannot impose upon those too well read in human nature to be easily deceived;" and that, "In order to forgive, we must

4. A wealthy district of London.
5. A Javanese tree from which an arrow poison is derived; here, a figurative cliché meaning "a poi-

sonous influence."
6. Poetic clichés for England and Scotland, respectively.

have been injured." There is, doubtless, a class of readers to whom these remarks appear peculiarly pointed and pungent; for we often find them doubly and trebly scored with the pencil, and delicate hands giving in their determined adhesion to these hardy novelties by a distinct *très vrai*,[7] emphasized by many notes of exclamation. The colloquial style of these novels is often marked by much ingenious inversion, and a careful avoidance of such cheap phraseology as can be heard every day. Angry young gentlemen exclaim—" 'Tis ever thus, methinks;" and in the half-hour before dinner a young lady informs her next neighbour that the first day she read Shakspeare she "stole away into the park, and beneath the shadow of the greenwood tree, devoured with rapture the inspired page of the great magician." But the most remarkable efforts of the mind-and-millinery writers lie in their philosophic reflections. The authoress of "Laura Gay,"[8] for example, having married her hero and heroine, improves the event by observing that "if those sceptics, whose eyes have so long gazed on matter that they can no longer see aught else in man, could once enter with heart and soul into such bliss as this, they would come to say that the soul of man and the polypus are not of common origin, or of the same texture." Lady novelists, it appears, can see something else besides matter; they are not limited to phenomena, but can relieve their eyesight by occasional glimpses of the *noumenon*,[9] and are, therefore, naturally better able than any one else to confound sceptics, even of that remarkable, but to us unknown school, which maintains that the soul of man is of the same texture as the polypus.[1]

The most pitiable of all silly novels by lady novelists are what we may call the *oracular* species—novels intended to expound the writer's religious, philosophical, or moral theories. There seems to be a notion abroad among women, rather akin to the superstition that the speech and actions of idiots are inspired, and that the human being most entirely exhausted of common sense is the fittest vehicle of revelation. To judge from their writings, there are certain ladies who think that an amazing ignorance, both of science and of life, is the best possible qualification for forming an opinion on the knottiest moral and speculative questions. Apparently, their recipe for solving all such difficulties is something like this:—Take a woman's head, stuff it with a smattering of philosophy and literature chopped small, and with false notions of society baked hard, let it hang over a desk a few hours every day, and serve up hot in feeble English, when not required. You will rarely meet with a lady novelist of the oracular class who is diffident of her ability to decide on theological questions,—who has any suspicion that she is not capable of discriminating with the nicest accuracy between the good and evil in all church parties,—who does not see precisely how it is that men have gone wrong hitherto,—and pity philosophers in general that they have not had the opportunity of consulting her. Great writers, who have modestly contented themselves with putting their experience into fiction, and have thought it quite a sufficient task to exhibit men and things as they are, she sighs over as deplorably deficient in the application of their powers. "They have solved no great questions"—and she is ready to remedy their omission by setting before you a complete theory of life and manual of divinity, in a

7. Very true (French).
8. The novel Eliot has just satirized in the preceding section.
9. An object of purely rational, as opposed to sensual, perception.
1. Polyp.

love story, where ladies and gentlemen of good family go through genteel vicissitudes, to the utter confusion of Deists, Puseyites,[2] and ultra-Protestants, and to the perfect establishment of that particular view of Christianity which either condenses itself into a sentence of small caps, or explodes into a cluster of stars on the three hundred and thirtieth page. It is true, the ladies and gentlemen will probably seem to you remarkably little like any you have had the fortune or misfortune to meet with, for, as a general rule, the ability of a lady novelist to describe actual life and her fellow-men, is in inverse proportion to her confident eloquence about God and the other world, and the means by which she usually chooses to conduct you to true ideas of the invisible is a totally false picture of the visible.

* * *

The epithet "silly" may seem impertinent, applied to a novel which indicates so much reading and intellectual activity as "The Enigma;"[3] but we use this epithet advisedly. If, as the world has long agreed, a very great amount of instruction will not make a wise man, still less will a very mediocre amount of instruction make a wise woman. And the most mischievous form of feminine silliness is the literary form, because it tends to confirm the popular prejudice against the more solid education of women. When men see girls wasting their time in consultations about bonnets and ball dresses, and in giggling or sentimental love-confidences, or middle-aged women mismanaging their children, and solacing themselves with acrid gossip, they can hardly help saying, "For Heaven's sake, let girls be better educated; let them have some better objects of thought—some more solid occupations." But after a few hours' conversation with an oracular literary woman, or a few hours' reading of her books, they are likely enough to say, "After all, when a woman gets some knowledge, see what use she makes of it! Her knowledge remains acquisition, instead of passing into culture; instead of being subdued into modesty and simplicity by a larger acquaintance with thought and fact, she has a feverish consciousness of her attainments; she keeps a sort of mental pocket-mirror, and is continually looking in it at her own 'intellectuality;' she spoils the taste of one's muffin by questions of metaphysics; 'puts down' men at a dinner table with her superior information; and seizes the opportunity of a *soirée* to catechise us on the vital question of the relation between mind and matter. And then, look at her writings! She mistakes vagueness for depth, bombast for eloquence, and affectation for originality; she struts on one page, rolls her eyes on another, grimaces in a third, and is hysterical in a fourth. She may have read many writings of great men, and a few writings of great women; but she is as unable to discern the difference between her own style and theirs as a Yorkshireman is to discern the difference between his own English and a Londoner's: rhodomontade[4] is the native accent of her intellect. No—the average nature of women is too shallow and feeble a soil to bear much tillage; it is only fit for the very lightest crops."

It is true that the men who come to such a decision on such very superficial

---

2. Protestants who believed in the importance of liturgical sacraments. "Deists": Protestants who believed in a personal God who created the universe but who was completely beyond human experience.

3. The novel Eliot has just satirized in the preceding section.

4. Inflated diction. It is assumed a Yorkshireman cannot discern the difference between his provincial northern dialect and the sophisticated speech of a Londoner.

and imperfect observation may not be among the wisest in the world; but we have not now to contest their opinion—we are only pointing out how it is unconsciously encouraged by many women who have volunteered themselves as representatives of the feminine intellect. We do not believe that a man was ever strengthened in such an opinion by associating with a woman of true culture, whose mind had absorbed her knowledge instead of being absorbed by it. A really cultured woman, like a really cultured man, is all the simpler and the less obtrusive for her knowledge; it has made her see herself and her opinions in something like just proportions; she does not make it a pedestal from which she flatters herself that she commands a complete view of men and things, but makes it a point of observation from which to form a right estimate of herself. She neither spouts poetry nor quotes Cicero[5] on slight provocation; not because she thinks that a sacrifice must be made to the prejudices of men, but because that mode of exhibiting her memory and Latinity does not present itself to her as edifying or graceful. She does not write books to confound philosophers, perhaps because she is able to write books that delight them. In conversation she is the least formidable of women, because she understands you, without wanting to make you aware that you *can't* understand her. She does not give you information, which is the raw material of culture,—she gives you sympathy, which is its subtlest essence.

A more numerous class of silly novels than the oracular, (which are generally inspired by some form of High Church, or transcendental Christianity,) is what we may call the *white neck-cloth* species, which represent the tone of thought and feeling in the Evangelical party. This species is a kind of genteel tract on a large scale, intended as a sort of medicinal sweetmeat for Low Church young ladies; an Evangelical substitute for the fashionable novel, as the May Meetings[6] are a substitute for the Opera. Even Quaker children, one would think, can hardly have been denied the indulgence of a doll; but it must be a doll dressed in a drab gown and a coal-scuttle bonnet— not a worldly doll, in gauze and spangles. And there are no young ladies, we imagine,—unless they belong to the Church of the United Brethren, in which people are married without any love-making—who can dispense with love stories. Thus, for Evangelical young ladies there are Evangelical love stories, in which the vicissitudes of the tender passion are sanctified by saving views of Regeneration and the Atonement. These novels differ from the oracular ones, as a Low Churchwoman often differs from a High Churchwoman: they are a little less supercilious, and a great deal more ignorant, a little less correct in their syntax, and a great deal more vulgar.

The Orlando[7] of Evangelical literature is the young curate, looked at from the point of view of the middle class, where cambric bands are understood to have as thrilling an effect on the hearts of young ladies as epaulettes have in the classes above and below it. In the ordinary type of these novels, the hero is almost sure to be a young curate, frowned upon, perhaps, by worldly mammas, but carrying captive the hearts of their daughters, who can "never forget *that* sermon;" tender glances are seized from the pulpit stairs instead of the opera-box; *tête-à-têtes* are seasoned with quotations from Scripture, instead of quotations from the poets; and questions as to the state of the

---

5. Roman statesman and orator (106–43 B.C.E.).
6. The Church of England's Missionary Society's annual spring meetings.

7. The romantic hero (in allusion to the hero of Shakespeare's *As You Like It*).

heroine's affections are mingled with anxieties as to the state of her soul. The young curate always has a background of well-dressed and wealthy, if not fashionable society;—for Evangelical silliness is as snobbish as any other kind of silliness; and the Evangelical lady novelist, while she explains to you the type of the scapegoat on one page, is ambitious on another to represent the manners and conversation of aristocratic people. Her pictures of fashionable society are often curious studies considered as efforts of the Evangelical imagination; but in one particular the novels of the White Neck-cloth School are meritoriously realistic,—their favourite hero, the Evangelical young curate is always rather an insipid personage.

* * *

But, perhaps, the least readable of silly women's novels, are the *modern-antique* species, which unfold to us the domestic life of Jannes and Jambres, the private love affairs of Sennacherib, or the mental struggles and ultimate conversion of Demetrius the silversmith.[8] From most silly novels we can at least extract a laugh; but those of the modern antique school have a ponderous, a leaden kind of fatuity, under which we groan. What can be more demonstrative of the inability of literary women to measure their own powers, than their frequent assumption of a task which can only be justified by the rarest concurrence of acquirement with genius? The finest effort to reanimate the past is of course only approximative—is always more or less an infusion of the modern spirit into the ancient form,—

> Was ihr den Geist der Zeiten heisst,
> Das ist im Grund der Herren eigner Geist,
> In dem die Zeiten sich bespiegeln.[9]

Admitting that genius which has familiarized itself with all the relics of an ancient period can sometimes, by the force of its sympathetic divination, restore the missing notes in the "music of humanity," and reconstruct the fragments into a whole which will really bring the remote past nearer to us, and interpret it to our duller apprehension,—this form of imaginative power must always be among the very rarest, because it demands as much accurate and minute knowledge as creative vigour. Yet we find ladies constantly choosing to make their mental mediocrity more conspicuous, by clothing it in a masquerade of ancient names; by putting their feeble sentimentality into the mouths of Roman vestals or Egyptian princesses, and attributing their rhetorical arguments to Jewish high-priests and Greek philosophers. * * *

"Be not a baker if your head be made of butter," says a homely proverb, which, being interpreted, may mean, let no woman rush into print who is not prepared for the consequences. We are aware that our remarks are in a very different tone from that of the reviewers who, with a perennial recurrence of precisely similar emotions, only paralleled, we imagine, in the experience of monthly nurses,[1] tell one lady novelist after another that they "hail"

8. In Acts 19.24–27 he makes statues of the Roman goddess Diana and denounces Paul for taking business away from him and his fellow craftsmen by converting people to Christianity. Jannes and Jambres were Egyptian magicians who opposed Moses at Pharaoh's court (2 Timothy 3.8). Sennacherib was an Assyrian king who ruled from

705 to 681 B.C.E.
9. What they call the spirit of the age / is at the base the gentlemen's own spirit, / in which the ages are reflected (German; Goethe's *Faust I, Nacht,* lines 577–79).
1. Women hired to nurse infants.

her productions "with delight." We are aware that the ladies at whom our criticism is pointed are accustomed to be told, in the choicest phraseology of puffery, that their pictures of life are brilliant, their characters well drawn, their style fascinating, and their sentiments lofty. But if they are inclined to resent our plainness of speech, we ask them to reflect for a moment on the chary praise, and often captious blame, which their panegyrists give to writers whose works are on the way to become classics. No sooner does a woman show that she has genius or effective talent, than she receives the tribute of being moderately praised and severely criticised. By a peculiar thermometric adjustment, when a woman's talent is at zero, journalistic approbation is at the boiling pitch; when she attains mediocrity, it is already at no more than summer heat; and if ever she reaches excellence, critical enthusiasm drops to the freezing point. Harriet Martineau, Currer Bell,[2] and Mrs. Gaskell have been treated as cavalierly as if they had been men. And every critic who forms a high estimate of the share women may ultimately take in literature, will, on principle, abstain from any exceptional indulgence towards the productions of literary women. For it must be plain to every one who looks impartially and extensively into feminine literature, that its greatest deficiencies are due hardly more to the want of intellectual power than to the want of those moral qualities that contribute to literary excellence—patient diligence, a sense of the responsibility involved in publication, and an appreciation of the sacredness of the writer's art. In the majority of women's books you see that kind of facility which springs from the absence of any high standard; that fertility in imbecile combination or feeble imitation which a little self-criticism would check and reduce to barrenness; just as with a total want of musical ear people will sing out of tune, while a degree more melodic sensibility would suffice to render them silent. The foolish vanity of wishing to appear in print, instead of being counterbalanced by any consciousness of the intellectual or moral derogation implied in futile authorship, seems to be encouraged by the extremely false impression that to write *at all* is a proof of superiority in a woman. On this ground, we believe that the average intellect of women is unfairly represented by the mass of feminine literature, and that while the few women who write well are very far above the ordinary intellectual level of their sex, the many women who write ill are very far below it. So that, after all, the severer critics are fulfilling a chivalrous duty in depriving the mere fact of feminine authorship of any false prestige which may give it a delusive attraction, and in recommending women of mediocre faculties—as at least a negative service they can render their sex—to abstain from writing.

The standing apology for women who become writers without any special qualification is, that society shuts them out from other spheres of occupation. Society is a very culpable entity, and has to answer for the manufacture of many unwholesome commodities, from bad pickles to bad poetry. But society, like "matter," and Her Majesty's Government, and other lofty abstractions, has its share of excessive blame as well as excessive praise. Where there is one woman who writes from necessity, we believe there are three women who write from vanity; and, besides, there is something so antiseptic in the mere healthy fact of working for one's bread, that the most

2. Pseudonym of Charlotte Brontë.

trashy and rotten kind of feminine literature is not likely to have been produced under such circumstances. "In all labour there is profit;" but ladies' silly novels, we imagine, are less the result of labour than of busy idleness.

Happily, we are not dependent on argument to prove that Fiction is a department of literature in which women can, after their kind, fully equal men. A cluster of great names, both living and dead, rush to our memories in evidence that women can produce novels not only fine, but among the very finest;—novels, too, that have a precious speciality, lying quite apart from masculine aptitudes and experience. No educational restrictions can shut women out from the materials of fiction, and there is no species of art which is so free from rigid requirements. Like crystalline masses, it may take any form, and yet be beautiful; we have only to pour in the right elements—genuine observation, humour, and passion. But it is precisely this absence of rigid requirement which constitutes the fatal seduction of novel-writing to incompetent women. Ladies are not wont to be very grossly deceived as to their power of playing on the piano; here certain positive difficulties of execution have to be conquered, and incompetence inevitably breaks down. Every art which has its absolute *technique* is, to a certain extent, guarded from the intrusions of mere left-handed imbecility. But in novel-writing there are no barriers for incapacity to stumble against, no external criteria to prevent a writer from mistaking foolish facility for mastery. And so we have again and again the old story of La Fontaine's ass, who puts his nose to the flute, and, finding that he elicits some sound, exclaims, "Moi, aussi, je joue de la flute;"[3]—a fable which we commend, at parting, to the consideration of any feminine reader who is in danger of adding to the number of "silly novels by lady novelists."

1856   1856

From The Mill on the Floss[1]

From *Book First. Boy and Girl*

CHAPTER 1. OUTSIDE DORLCOTE MILL

A wide plain, where the broadening Floss hurries on between its green banks to the sea, and the loving tide, rushing to meet it, checks its passage with an impetuous embrace. On this mighty tide the black ships—laden with the fresh-scented fir-planks, with rounded sacks of oil-bearing seed, or with the dark glitter of coal—are borne along to the town of St. Ogg's, which shows its aged, fluted red roofs and the broad gables of its wharves between the low wooded hill and the river brink, tinging the water with a soft purple hue under the transient glance of this February sun. Far away on each hand stretch the rich pastures, and the patches of dark earth, made ready for the

3. I also play the flute (French). Jean de La Fontaine (1621–1695), French author of beast fables.
1. Published in 1860, *The Mill on the Floss* draws on George Eliot's Warwickshire childhood. Beginning in 1829, when its heroine, Maggie, is ten years old (as Eliot was in that year), the novel represents in idealized form Eliot's relationship with her brother, Isaac, in Maggie and Tom Tulliver. Like many of Eliot's novels, *The Mill on the Floss*

portrays a passionate, rapidly developing consciousness in conflict with a conservative social order. It is also, however, a panoramic depiction, at once nostalgic and critical, of a rural middle class whose values were undergoing transformation. Printed here is the first chapter of *The Mill on the Floss*, Eliot's retrospective meditation on the scene of the novel that Marcel Proust claimed reduced him to tears.

seed of broad-leaved green crops, or touched already with the tint of the tender-bladed autumn-sown corn.[2] There is a remnant still of the last year's golden clusters of beehive ricks rising at intervals beyond the hedgerows; and everywhere the hedgerows are studded with trees: the distant ships seem to be lifting their masts and stretching their red-brown sails close among the branches of the spreading ash. Just by the red-roofed town the tributary Ripple flows with a lively current into the Floss. How lovely the little river is, with its dark, changing wavelets! It seems to me like a living companion while I wander along the bank and listen to its low placid voice, as to the voice of one who is deaf and loving. I remember those large dipping willows. I remember the stone bridge.

And this is Dorlcote Mill. I must stand a minute or two here on the bridge and look at it, though the clouds are threatening, and it is far on in the afternoon. Even in this leafless time of departing February it is pleasant to look at—perhaps the chill damp season adds a charm to the trimly-kept, comfortable dwelling-house, as old as the elms and chestnuts that shelter it from the northern blast. The stream is brimful now, and lies high in this little withy plantation, and half drowns the grassy fringe of the croft[3] in front of the house. As I look at the full stream, the vivid grass, the delicate bright-green powder softening the outline of the great trunks and branches that gleam from under the bare purple boughs, I am in love with moistness, and envy the white ducks that are dipping their heads far into the water here among the withes, unmindful of the awkward appearance they make in the drier world above.

The rush of the water, and the booming of the mill, bring a dreamy deaf-ness, which seems to heighten the peacefulness of the scene. They are like a great curtain of sound, shutting one out from the world beyond. And now there is the thunder of the huge covered waggon coming home with sacks of grain. That honest waggoner is thinking of his dinner, getting sadly dry in the oven at this late hour; but he will not touch it till he has fed his horses,— the strong, submissive, meek-eyed beasts, who, I fancy, are looking mild reproach at him from between their blinkers, that he should crack his whip at them in that awful manner as if they needed that hint! See how they stretch their shoulders up the slope towards the bridge, with all the more energy because they are so near home. Look at their grand shaggy feet that seem to grasp the firm earth, at the patient strength of their necks, bowed under the heavy collar, at the mighty muscles of their struggling haunches! I should like well to hear them neigh over their hardly-earned feed of corn, and see them, with their moist necks freed from the harness, dipping their eager nostrils into the muddy pond. Now they are on the bridge, and down they go again at a swifter pace, and the arch of the covered waggon disappears at the turning behind the trees.

Now I can turn my eyes towards the mill again, and watch the unresting wheel sending out its diamond jets of water. That little girl[4] is watching it too: she has been standing on just the same spot at the edge of the water ever since I paused on the bridge. And that queer white cur with the brown ear seems to be leaping and barking in ineffectual remonstrance with the

---

2. Wheat.
3. A patch of farmland adjacent to a house or cottage. "Withy": willow.
4. Maggie Tulliver, the heroine.

wheel; perhaps he is jealous, because his playfellow in the beaver bonnet is so rapt in its movement. It is time the little playfellow went in, I think; and there is a very bright fire to tempt her: the red light shines out under the deepening grey of the sky. It is time, too, for me to leave off resting my arms on the cold stone of this bridge. . . .

Ah, my arms are really benumbed. I have been pressing my elbows on the arms of my chair, and dreaming that I was standing on the bridge in front of Dorlcote Mill, as it looked one February afternoon many years ago. Before I dozed off, I was going to tell you what Mr. and Mrs. Tulliver were talking about, as they sat by the bright fire in the left-hand parlour, on that very afternoon I have been dreaming of.

1860

MATTHEW ARNOLD
1822–1888

How is a full and enjoyable life to be lived in a modern industrial society? This was the recurrent topic in the poetry and prose of Matthew Arnold. In his poetry the question itself is raised; in his prose some answers are attempted. "The misapprehensiveness of his age is exactly what a poet is sent to remedy," wrote Browning. Oddly enough it is to Arnold's work rather than to Browning's that the statement seems more appropriate. And its applicability to Arnold has persisted from Victorian times to ours, in part because the "misapprehensiveness" has also persisted.

Matthew Arnold was born in Laleham, a village in the valley of the Thames. That his childhood was spent in the vicinity of a river seems appropriate, for clear-flowing streams were later to appear in his poems as symbols of serenity. At six, Arnold was moved to Rugby School, where his father, Dr. Thomas Arnold, had become headmaster. As a clergyman Dr. Arnold was a leader of the liberal or Broad Church and hence one of the principal opponents of John Henry Newman. As a headmaster he became famous as an educational reformer, a teacher who instilled into his pupils an earnest preoccupation with moral and social issues and also an awareness of the connection between liberal studies and modern life. At Rugby his eldest son, Matthew, was directly exposed to the powerful force of the father's mind and character. The son's attitude toward this force was a mixture of attraction and repulsion. That he was permanently influenced by his father is evident in his poems and in his writings on religion and politics, but like many sons of clergymen, he made a determined effort in his youth to be different. At Oxford he behaved like a character from one of Evelyn Waugh's early novels. Elegantly and colorfully dressed, alternately languid or merry in manner, he attracted attention as a dandy whose irreverent jokes irritated his more solemn undergraduate friends and acquaintances. "His manner displeases, from its seeming foppery," wrote Charlotte Brontë after talking with the young man. "The shade of Dr. Arnold," she added, "seemed to me to frown on his young representative." Thus with Rugby School's standards of earnestness the son of Dr. Arnold appeared to have no connection. Even his studies did not seem to occupy him seriously. By a session of cramming, he managed to earn second-class honors in his final examinations, a near disaster that was redeemed by his election to a fellowship at Oriel College.

Arnold's biographers usually dismiss his youthful frivolity of spirit as a temporary pose or mask, but it was more. It remained to color his prose style, brightening his most serious criticism with geniality and wit. For most readers the jauntiness of his prose is a virtue, although for others it is offensive. Anyone suspicious of urbanity and irony would applaud Whitman's sour comment that Arnold is "one of the dudes of literature." A more appropriate estimate of his manner is provided by Arnold's own description of Sainte-Beuve as a critic: "a critic of measure, not exuberant; of the center, not provincial . . . with gay and amiable temper, his manner as good as his matter—the '*critique souriant*' [smiling critic]."

Unlike Tennyson or Carlyle, Arnold had to confine his writing and reading to his spare time. In 1847 he took the post of private secretary to Lord Lansdowne, and in 1851, the year of his marriage, he became an inspector of schools, a position that he held for thirty-five years. Although his work as an inspector may have reduced his output as a writer, it had several advantages. His extensive traveling in England took him to the homes of the more ardently Protestant middle classes, and when he criticized the dullness of middle-class life (as he often did), Arnold knew his subject intimately. His position also led to travel on the Continent to study the schools of Europe. As a critic of English education, he was thus able to make helpful comparisons and to draw on a stock of fresh ideas in the same way as in his literary criticism he used his knowledge of French, German, Italian, and classical literatures to measure the achievements of English writers. Despite the monotony of much of his work as an inspector, Arnold became convinced of its importance. It was work that contributed to what he regarded as the most important need of his century: the development of a satisfactory system of education for the middle classes.

In 1849, Arnold published *The Strayed Reveler*, the first of his volumes of poetry. Eight years later, as a tribute to his poetic achievement, he was elected to the professorship of poetry at Oxford, a part-time position that he held for ten years. Later, like Dickens and Thackeray before him, Arnold toured America to make money by lecturing. The reception accorded his lectures was varied. Sometimes his audiences were indifferent, but it is of interest to learn from the *Washington Post* of his stunning success in that city, where, following a two-hour address, the great African American leader Frederick Douglass "moved that a tremendous vote of thanks be tendered to the speaker." For his two visits (1883 and 1886), there was the further inducement of seeing his daughter Lucy, who had married an American. Two years after his second visit to the United States, Arnold died of a sudden heart attack.

Arnold's career as a writer can be divided roughly into four periods. In the 1850s most of his poems appeared; in the 1860s, his literary criticism and social criticism; in the 1870s, his religious and educational writings; and in the 1880s, his second set of essays in literary criticism.

About his career as a poet, two questions are repeatedly asked. The first is whether his poetry is as effective as or better than his prose; the second is why he virtually stopped writing poetry after 1860. The first has, of course, been variously answered. Many would endorse Tennyson's request in a letter: "Tell Mat not to write any more of those prose things like *Literature and Dogma*, but to give us something like his *Thyrsis, Scholar Gypsy,* or *Forsaken Merman.*" At the opposite extreme is a recent critic, J. D. Jump, who has a high regard for Arnold's prose but considers only one of the poems (*Dover Beach*) to have merit. Such readers complain, and with good cause, of Arnold's bad habits as a poet: for example, his excessive reliance on italics instead of on meter as a method of emphasizing the meaning of a line. Or they cite the prosy flatness of some of his lines. Contrariwise, when Arnold leaves the flat plane of versified reflections and attempts to scale the heights of what he called "the grand style," there is a different kind of uncertainty that becomes evident, as in *Sohrab and Rustum*, in the overelaborated similes. Yet the success of such lovely poems as *Thyrsis* is more than enough to overcome the indictments of the critics. Often, as in *Thyrsis*, he is at his best as a poet of nature. Settings of seashore or river or mountaintop provide something more than picturesque backdrops for these poems; they function to draw the meaning together. A concern for rendering outdoor nature may seem a curious accomplishment for so sophisticated a writer, but as his contemporaries noted, Arnold is in this respect, as in several others, similar to Thomas Gray.

Arnold's own verdict on the qualities of his poetry is a reasonable one. In a letter to his mother, in 1869, he writes:

> My poems represent, on the whole, the main movement of mind of the last quarter of a century, and thus they will probably have their day as people become conscious to themselves of what that movement of mind is, and interested in the literary productions which reflect it. It might be fairly urged that I have less poetical sentiment than Tennyson, and less intellectual vigor and abundance than Browning; yet, because I have perhaps more of a fusion of the two than either of them, and have more regularly applied that fusion to the main line of modern development, I am likely enough to have my turn, as they have had theirs.

The emphasis in the letter on "movement of mind" suggests that Arnold's poetry and prose should be studied together. Such an approach can be fruitful provided that it does not obscure the important difference between Arnold the poet and Arnold the critic. T. S. Eliot once said of his own writings that "in one's prose reflections one may be legitimately occupied with ideals, whereas in the writing of verse, one can deal only with actuality." Arnold's writings provide a nice verification of Eliot's seeming paradox. As a poet he usually records his own experiences, his own feelings of loneliness and isolation as a lover, his longing for a serenity that he cannot find, his melancholy sense of the passing of youth (more than for many men, Arnold's thirtieth birthday was an awesome landmark after which he felt, he said, "three parts iced over"). Above all he records his despair in a universe in which humanity's role seemed as incongruous as it was later to seem to Thomas Hardy. In a memorable passage of his *Stanzas from the Grande Chartreuse,* he describes himself as "wandering between two worlds, one dead, / The other powerless to be born." And addressing the representatives of a faith that seems to him dead, he cries: "Take me, cowled forms, and fence me round, / Till I possess my soul again."

As a poet, then, like T. S. Eliot and W. H. Auden, Arnold provides a record of a sick individual in a sick society. This was "actuality" as he experienced it—an actuality, like Eliot's and Auden's, representative of his era. As a prose writer, a formulator of "ideals," he seeks a different role. It is the role of what Auden calls the "healer" of a sick society, or as he himself called Goethe, the "Physician of the iron age." And in this difference we have a clue to the question previously raised: why did Arnold virtually abandon the writing of poetry and shift into criticism? Among other reasons, he abandoned it because he was dissatisfied with the kind of poetry he himself was writing.

In one of his excellent letters to his friend Arthur Hugh Clough in the 1850s (letters that provide the best insight we have into Arnold's mind and tastes) this note of dissatisfaction is struck: "I am glad you like the *Gypsy Scholar*—but what does it *do* for you? Homer *animates*—Shakespeare *animates*—in its poor way I think *Sohrab and Rustum animates*—the *Gypsy Scholar* at best awakens a pleasing melancholy. But this is not what we want." It is evident that early in his career Arnold had evolved a theory of what poetry should do for its readers, a theory based, in part, on his impression of what classical poetry had achieved. To help make life bearable, poetry, in Arnold's view, must bring joy. As he says in the preface to his *Poems* in 1853, it must "inspirit and rejoice the reader"; it must "convey a charm, and infuse delight." Such a demand does not exclude tragic poetry but does exclude works "in which suffering finds no vent in action; in which a continual state of mental distress is prolonged." Of Charlotte Brontë's novel *Villette* he says witheringly: "The writer's mind contains nothing but hunger, rebellion, and rage. . . . No fine writing can hide this thoroughly, and it will be fatal to her in the long run." Judged by such a standard, most nineteenth-century poems, including *Empedocles on Etna* and others by Arnold, were unsatisfactory. And when Arnold tried himself to write poems that would meet his own requirements—*Sohrab and Rustum* or *Balder Dead*—he was not at his best. By the late 1850s he thus found himself at a dead end. By turning aside to literary criticism he was able partially to escape the dilemma. In his prose his melancholy and "morbid" personality was subordinated to the resolutely cheerful and purposeful character he had created for himself by an effort of will.

Arnold's two volumes of *Essays in Criticism* (1865 and 1888) repeatedly show how authors as different as Marcus Aurelius, Tolstoy, Homer, and Wordsworth provide the virtues he sought in his reading. Among these virtues was plainness of style. Although he could on occasion recommend the richness of language of such poets as Keats or Tennyson—their "natural magic" as he himself called it—Arnold's usual preference was for literature that was unadorned. And beyond stylistic excellences the principal virtue he admired as a critic was what he called the quality of "high seriousness." Given a world in which formal religion appeared to be of subordinate importance, it became increasingly important to Arnold that the poet must be a serious thinker who could offer guidance for his readers. Arnold's attitude toward religion helps to account for his finally asking perhaps too much from literature. Excessive expectations underlie his most glaring blunder as a critic: his solemnly inadequate discussion of Chaucer's lack of high seriousness in *The Study of Poetry.*

In *The Function of Criticism,* it is apparent that Arnold regarded good literary criticism, as he regarded literature itself, as a potent force in producing what he conceived as a civilized society. From a close study of this basic essay one could forecast the third stage of his career: his excursion into the criticism of society that was to culminate in *Culture and Anarchy* (1869) and *Friendship's Garland* (1871).

Arnold's starting point as a critic of society is different from that of Carlyle and John Ruskin. The older prophets attacked the Victorian middle classes on the grounds of their materialism, their selfish indifference to the sufferings of the poor—their immorality, in effect. Arnold argued instead that the "Philistines," as he called them, were not so much wicked as ignorant, narrow-minded, and suffering from the dullness of their private lives. This novel analysis was reinforced by Arnold's conviction that the world of the future, both in England and America, would be a middle-class world, a world dominated therefore by a class inadequately equipped for leadership and inadequately equipped to enjoy civilized living.

To establish this point, Arnold employed cajolery, satire, and even quotations from the newspapers with considerable effect. He also employed memorable catchwords (such as "sweetness and light") that sometimes pose an obstacle to understanding the complexities of his position. His view of civilization, for example, was pared down to a four-point formula of the four "powers": conduct, intellect and knowledge, beauty, social life and manners. The formula was simple and workable. Applying it to French or American civilizations, he had a scale by which to show up the virtues of different countries as well as their inadequacies. Applying the formula to his own country, Arnold usually awarded the Victorian middle classes an A in the first category (of conduct) but a failing grade in the other three categories.

Arnold's relentless exposure of middle-class narrow-mindedness eventually led him into the arena of religious controversy. As a critic of religious institutions he was arguing, in effect, that just as the middle classes did not know how to lead full lives, so also did they not know how to read the Bible intelligently or attend church intelligently. Of the Christian religion, he remarked that there are two things "that surely must be clear to anybody with eyes in his head. One is, that men cannot do without it; the other that they cannot do with it as it is." His three full-length studies of the Bible, including *Literature and Dogma* (1873), are best considered in this way as a postscript to his social criticism. The Bible, to Arnold, was a great work of literature like the *Odyssey,* and the Church of England was a great national institution like Parliament. Both Bible and church must be preserved not because historical Christianity was credible but because both, when properly understood, were agents of what he called "culture"—they contributed to making humanity more civilized.

The term *culture* is perhaps Arnold's most familiar catchword, although what he meant by it has sometimes been misunderstood. For him the term connotes the qualities of an open-minded intelligence (as described in *The Function of Criticism*)—a refusal to take things on authority. In this respect, Arnold appears close to T. H. Huxley and J. S. Mill. But the word also connotes a full awareness of humanity's past and a capacity to enjoy the best works of art, literature, history, and philosophy that have come down to us from that past. As a way of viewing life in all its aspects, including the social, political, and religious, culture represents for Arnold the most effective way of curing the ills of a sick society. It is his principal prescription.

To attempt to define culture brings one to a final aspect of Arnold's career as a critic: his writings on education, in which he sought to make cultural values, as he said, "prevail." Most obviously these writings comprise his reply to Huxley in his admirably reasoned essay *Literature and Science,* and his volumes of official reports written as an inspector of schools. Less obviously, they comprise all his prose. At the core of these writings is his belief that good education is *the* crucial need. Arnold was essentially a great teacher. He has the faults of a teacher: a tendency to repeat himself, to lean too hard on formulated phrases, and he displays something of the lectern manner at times. He also has the great teacher's virtues, in particular the virtue of skillfully conveying to us the conviction on which all his arguments are based. This conviction is that the humanist tradition of which he is the expositor can enable the individual man or woman to live life more fully and to change the course of society. He believes that a democratic society can thrive only if its citizens become educated in what he saw as the great Western tradition, "the best that is known and thought." These values, which some readers find elitist, make Arnold both timely and controversial. It is for these values Arnold fought. He boxed with the gloves on—kid gloves, his opponents used to say—and he provided a lively exhibition of footwork that is a pleasure in itself for us to witness. Yet the gracefulness of the display should not obscure the fact that he is landing hard blows squarely on his opponents.

Although his lifelong attacks against the inadequacies of puritanism make Arnold one of the most anti-Victorian figures of the Victorian age, there is an assumption behind his attacks that is itself characteristically Victorian. This assumption is that the puritan middle classes *can* be changed, that they are, as we would more clumsily say, educable. In 1852, writing to Clough on the subject of equality (a political objective in which he believed by conviction if not by instinct), he observed: "I am more and more convinced that the world tends to become more comfortable for the mass, and more uncomfortable for those of any natural gift or distinction—and it is as well perhaps that it should be so—for hitherto the gifted have astonished and delighted the world, but not trained or inspired or in any real way changed it." Arnold's gifts as a poet and critic enabled him to do both: to delight the world and also to change it.

The Forsaken Merman

Come, dear children, let us away;
Down and away below!
Now my brothers call from the bay,
Now the great winds shoreward blow,
5   Now the salt tides seaward flow;
Now the wild white horses play,
Champ and chafe and toss in the spray.
Children dear, let us away!
This way, this way!

10   Call her once before you go—
Call once yet!

In a voice that she will know:
"Margaret! Margaret!"
Children's voices should be dear
15   (Call once more) to a mother's ear;
Children's voices, wild with pain—
Surely she will come again!
Call her once and come away;
This way, this way!
20   "Mother dear, we cannot stay!
The wild white horses foam and fret."
Margaret! Margaret!

Come, dear children, come away down;
Call no more!
25   One last look at the white-walled town,
And the little gray church on the windy shore,
Then come down!
She will not come though you call all day;
Come away, come away!

30   Children dear, was it yesterday
We heard the sweet bells over the bay?
In the caverns where we lay,
Through the surf and through the swell,
The far-off sound of a silver bell?
35   Sand-strewn caverns, cool and deep,
Where the winds are all asleep;
Where the spent lights quiver and gleam,
Where the salt weed sways in the stream,
Where the sea beasts, ranged all round,
40   Feed in the ooze of their pasture ground;
Where the sea snakes coil and twine,
Dry their mail and bask in the brine;
Where great whales come sailing by,
Sail and sail, with unshut eye,
45   Round the world for ever and aye?
When did music come this way?
Children dear, was it yesterday?

Children dear, was it yesterday
(Call yet once) that she went away?
50   Once she sate with you and me,
On a red gold throne in the heart of the sea,
And the youngest sate on her knee.
She combed its bright hair, and she tended it well,
When down swung the sound of a far-off bell.
55   She sighed, she looked up through the clear green sea;
She said: "I must go, for my kinsfolk pray
In the little gray church on the shore today.
'Twill be Easter time in the world—ah me!
And I lose my poor soul, Merman! here with thee."
60   I said: "Go up, dear heart, through the waves;

Say thy prayer, and come back to the kind sea-caves!"
She smiled, she went up through the surf in the bay.
Children dear, was it yesterday?

Children dear, were we long alone?
65 "The sea grows stormy, the little ones moan;
Long prayers," I said, "in the world they say;
Come!" I said; and we rose through the surf in the bay.
We went up the beach, by the sandy down
Where the sea-stocks bloom, to the white-walled town;
70 Through the narrow paved streets, where all was still,
To the little gray church on the windy hill.
From the church came a murmur of folk at their prayers,
But we stood without in the cold blowing airs.
We climbed on the graves, on the stones worn with rains,
75 And we gazed up the aisle through the small leaded panes.
She sate by the pillar; we saw her clear:
"Margaret, hist! come quick, we are here!
Dear heart," I said, "we are long alone;
The sea grows stormy, the little ones moan."
80 But, ah, she gave me never a look,
For her eyes were sealed to the holy book!
Loud prays the priest; shut stands the door.
Come away, children, call no more!
Come away, come down, call no more!

85   Down, down, down!
Down to the depths of the sea!
She sits at her wheel in the humming town,
Singing most joyfully.
Hark what she sings: "O joy, O joy,
90 For the humming street, and the child with its toy!
For the priest, and the bell, and the holy well;
For the wheel where I spun,
And the blessed light of the sun!"
And so she sings her fill,
95 Singing most joyfully,
Till the spindle drops from her hand,
And the whizzing wheel stands still.
She steals to the window, and looks at the sand,
And over the sand at the sea;
100 And her eyes are set in a stare;
And anon there breaks a sigh,
And anon there drops a tear,
From a sorrow-clouded eye,
And a heart sorrow-laden,
105 A long, long sigh;
For the cold strange eyes of a little Mermaiden
And the gleam of her golden hair.

    Come away, away children;
Come children, come down!

110 The hoarse wind blows coldly;
    Lights shine in the town.
    She will start from her slumber
    When gusts shake the door;
    She will hear the winds howling,
115 Will hear the waves roar.
    We shall see, while above us
    The waves roar and whirl,
    A ceiling of amber,
    A pavement of pearl.
120 Singing: "Here came a mortal,
    But faithless was she!
    And alone dwell forever
    The kings of the sea."

    But, children, at midnight,
125 When soft the winds blow,
    When clear falls the moonlight,
    When spring tides are low;
    When sweet airs come seaward
    From heaths starred with broom,
130 And high rocks throw mildly
    On the blanched sands a gloom;
    Up the still, glistening beaches,
    Up the creek we will hie,
    Over banks of bright seaweed
135 The ebb-tide leaves dry.
    We will gaze, from the sand-hills,
    At the white, sleeping town;
    At the church on the hillside—
    And then come back down.
140 Singing: "There dwells a loved one,
    But cruel is she!
    She left lonely forever
    The kings of the sea."

1849

Isolation. To Marguerite[1]

We were apart; yet, day by day,
I bade my heart more constant be.
I bade it keep the world away,
And grow a home for only thee;
5 Nor feared but thy love likewise grew,
Like mine, each day, more tried, more true.

The fault was grave! I might have known,
What far too soon, alas! I learned—

1. Addressed to a woman Arnold is reputed to
have met in Switzerland in the 1840s. It has been
commonly assumed that she was French or Swiss;
but some recent biographies speculate she might
have been Mary Claude, a woman Arnold knew in
England at this same period, who, although
English, had connections with Germany and had
translated German prose and verse.

The heart can bind itself alone,
10   And faith may oft be unreturned.
Self-swayed our feelings ebb and swell—
Thou lov'st no more—Farewell! Farewell!

Farewell!—and thou, thou lonely heart,[2]
Which never yet without remorse
15   Even for a moment didst depart
From thy remote and spherèd course
To haunt the place where passions reign—
Back to thy solitude again!

Back with the conscious thrill of shame
20   Which Luna felt, that summer night,
Flash through her pure immortal frame,
When she forsook the starry height
To hang over Endymion's sleep
Upon the pine-grown Latmian steep.[3]
25   Yet she, chaste queen, had never proved
How vain a thing is mortal love,
Wandering in Heaven, far removed.
But thou hast long had place to prove
This truth—to prove, and make thine own:
30   "Thou hast been, shalt be, art, alone."

Or, if not quite alone, yet they
Which touch thee are unmating things—
Ocean and clouds and night and day;
Lorn autumns and triumphant springs;
35   And life, and others' joy and pain,
And love, if love, of happier men.

Of happier men—for they, at least,
Have *dreamed* two human hearts might blend
In one, and were through faith released
40   From isolation without end
Prolonged; nor knew, although not less
Alone than thou, their loneliness.

1849   1857

To Marguerite—Continued

Yes! in the sea of life enisled,
With echoing straits between us thrown,
Dotting the shoreless watery wild,
We mortal millions live *alone*.
5   The islands feel the enclasping flow,
And then their endless bounds they know.
But when the moon their hollows lights,

2. Presumably the speaker's heart, not Marguerite's.
3. Luna (or Diana), goddess of chastity and the
moon, fell in love with Endymion, a handsome
shepherd, whom she discovered asleep on Mount
Latmos.

And they are swept by balms of spring,
And in their glens, on starry nights,
10   The nightingales divinely sing;
And lovely notes, from shore to shore,
Across the sounds and channels pour—

Oh! then a longing like despair
Is to their farthest caverns sent;
15   For surely once, they feel, we were
Parts of a single continent!
Now round us spreads the watery plain—
Oh might our marges meet again!

Who ordered that their longing's fire
20   Should be, as soon as kindled, cooled?
Who renders vain their deep desire?—
A God, a God their severance ruled!
And bade betwixt their shores to be
The unplumbed, salt, estranging sea.

1849   1852

The Buried Life

Light flows our war of mocking words, and yet,
Behold, with tears mine eyes are wet!
I feel a nameless sadness o'er me roll.
Yes, yes, we know that we can jest,
5   We know, we know that we can smile!
But there's a something in this breast,
To which thy light words bring no rest,
And thy gay smiles no anodyne.
Give me thy hand, and hush awhile,
10   And turn those limpid eyes on mine,
And let me read there, love! thy inmost soul.

Alas! is even love too weak
To unlock the heart, and let it speak?
Are even lovers powerless to reveal
15   To one another what indeed they feel?
I knew the mass of men concealed
Their thoughts, for fear that if revealed
They would by other men be met
With blank indifference, or with blame reproved;
20   I knew they lived and moved
Tricked in disguises, alien to the rest
Of men, and alien to themselves—and yet
The same heart beats in every human breast!

But we, my love!—doth a like spell benumb
25   Our hearts, our voices?—must we too be dumb?

Ah! well for us, if even we,
Even for a moment, can get free
Our heart, and have our lips unchained;
For that which seals them hath been deep-ordained!

30   Fate, which foresaw
How frivolous a baby man would be—
By what distractions he would be possessed,
How he would pour himself in every strife,
And well-nigh change his own identity—
35   That it might keep from his capricious play
His genuine self, and force him to obey
Even in his own despite his being's law,
Bade through the deep recesses of our breast
The unregarded river of our life
40   Pursue with indiscernible flow its way;
And that we should not see
The buried stream, and seem to be
Eddying at large in blind uncertainty,
Though driving on with it eternally.

45   But often, in the world's most crowded streets,[1]
But often, in the din of strife,
There rises an unspeakable desire
After the knowledge of our buried life;
A thirst to spend our fire and restless force
50   In tracking out our true, original course;
A longing to inquire
Into the mystery of this heart which beats
So wild, so deep in us—to know
Whence our lives come and where they go.
55   And many a man in his own breast then delves,
But deep enough, alas! none ever mines.
And we have been on many thousand lines,
And we have shown, on each, spirit and power;
But hardly have we, for one little hour,
60   Been on our own line, have we been ourselves—
Hardly had skill to utter one of all
The nameless feelings that course through our breast,
But they course on forever unexpressed.
And long we try in vain to speak and act
65   Our hidden self, and what we say and do
Is eloquent, is well—but 'tis not true!
And then we will no more be racked
With inward striving, and demand
Of all the thousand nothings of the hour
70   Their stupefying power;
Ah yes, and they benumb us at our call!
Yet still, from time to time, vague and forlorn,

---

1. This passage, like many others in Arnold's poetry, illustrates Wordsworth's effect on his writings. In this instance cf. Wordsworth's *Tintern*
Abbey 25–27: "But oft, in lonely rooms, and 'mid the din / Of towns and cities, I have owed to them, / In hours of weariness, sensations sweet."

From the soul's subterranean depth upborne
As from an infinitely distant land,
75 Come airs, and floating echoes, and convey
A melancholy into all our day.[2]

Only—but this is rare—
When a beloved hand is laid in ours,
When, jaded with the rush and glare
80 Of the interminable hours,
Our eyes can in another's eyes read clear,
When our world-deafened ear
Is by the tones of a loved voice caressed—
A bolt is shot back somewhere in our breast,
85 And a lost pulse of feeling stirs again.
The eye sinks inward, and the heart lies plain,
And what we mean, we say, and what we would, we know.
A man becomes aware of his life's flow,
And hears its winding murmur; and he sees
90 The meadows where it glides, the sun, the breeze.

And there arrives a lull in the hot race
Wherein he doth forever chase
That flying and elusive shadow, rest.
An air of coolness plays upon his face,
95 And an unwonted calm pervades his breast.
And then he thinks he knows
The hills where his life rose,
And the sea where it goes.

1852

Memorial Verses[1]

April 1850

Goethe in Weimar sleeps, and Greece,
Long since, saw Byron's struggle cease.
But one such death remained to come;
The last poetic voice is dumb—
5 We stand today by Wordsworth's tomb.

When Byron's eyes were shut in death,
We bowed our head and held our breath.
He taught us little; but our soul
Had *felt* him like the thunder's roll.
10 With shivering heart the strife we saw

---

2. Cf. Wordsworth's *Ode: Intimations of Immortality*, lines 149–51: "Those shadowy recollections, / Which, be they what they may, / Are yet the fountain light of all our day."
1. This elegy was written shortly after Wordsworth had died in April 1850, at the age of eighty. Arnold had known the poet as a man and deeply admired his writings—as is evident not only in this poem but in his late essay *Wordsworth*. Byron, who died in Greece in 1824, had affected Arnold profoundly in his youth, but later that strenuous "Titanic" (line 14) poetry seemed to him less satisfactory, its value limited by its lack of serenity. His final verdict on Byron can be encountered in his essay in *Essays in Criticism: Second Series*. Goethe, who died in 1832, was regarded by Arnold as a great philosophical poet and the most significant man of letters of the early 19th century.

Of passion with eternal law;
And yet with reverential awe
We watched the fount of fiery life
Which served for that Titanic strife.
15 When Goethe's death was told, we said:
Sunk, then, is Europe's sagest head.
Physician of the iron age,
Goethe has done his pilgrimage.
He took the suffering human race,
20 He read each wound, each weakness clear;
And struck his finger on the place,
And said: *Thou ailest here, and here!*
He looked on Europe's dying hour
Of fitful dream and feverish power;
25 His eye plunged down the weltering strife,
The turmoil of expiring life—
He said: *The end is everywhere,*
Art still has truth, take refuge there!
And he was happy, if to know
30 Causes of things, and far below
His feet to see the lurid flow
Of terror, and insane distress,
And headlong fate, be happiness.

And Wordsworth!—Ah, pale ghosts, rejoice!
35 For never has such soothing voice
Been to your shadowy world conveyed,
Since erst, at morn, some wandering shade
Heard the clear song of Orpheus[2] come
Through Hades, and the mournful gloom.
40 Wordsworth has gone from us—and ye,
Ah, may ye feel his voice as we!
He too upon a wintry clime
Had fallen—on this iron time
Of doubts, disputes, distractions, fears.
45 He found us when the age had bound
Our souls in its benumbing round;
He spoke, and loosed our heart in tears.
He laid us as we lay at birth
On the cool flowery lap of earth,
50 Smiles broke from us and we had ease;
The hills were round us, and the breeze
Went o'er the sunlit fields again;
Our foreheads felt the wind and rain.
Our youth returned; for there was shed
55 On spirits that had long been dead,
Spirits dried up and closely furled,
The freshness of the early world.

Ah! since dark days still bring to light
Man's prudence and man's fiery might,

2. By means of his beautiful music, Orpheus won his way through Hades in his search for the "shade" of his dead wife, Eurydice.

60   Time may restore us in his course
Goethe's sage mind and Byron's force;
But where will Europe's latter hour
Again find Wordsworth's healing power?
Others will teach us how to dare,
65   And against fear our breast to steel;
Others will strengthen us to bear—
But who, ah! who, will make us feel?
The cloud of mortal destiny,
Others will front it fearlessly—
70   But who, like him, will put it by?

Keep fresh the grass upon his grave
O Rotha,[3] with thy living wave!
Sing him thy best! for few or none
Hears thy voice right, now he is gone.

1850   1850

Lines Written in Kensington Gardens[1]

In this lone, open glade I lie,
Screened by deep boughs on either hand;
And at its end, to stay the eye,
Those black-crowned, red-boled pine trees stand!

5   Birds here make song, each bird has his,
Across the girdling city's hum.
How green under the boughs it is!
How thick the tremulous sheep-cries come![2]

Sometimes a child will cross the glade
10   To take his nurse his broken toy;
Sometimes a thrush flit overhead
Deep in her unknown day's employ.

Here at my feet what wonders pass,
What endless, active life is here!
15   What blowing daisies, fragrant grass!
An air-stirred forest, fresh and clear.

Scarce fresher is the mountain sod
Where the tired angler lies, stretched out,
And, eased of basket and of rod,
20   Counts his day's spoil, the spotted trout.

In the huge world, which roars hard by,
Be others happy if they can!

3. A river near Wordsworth's burial place.   2. Sheep sometimes grazed in London parks.
1. A park in the heart of London.

But in my helpless cradle I
Was breathed on by the rural Pan.

25 I, on men's impious uproar hurled,
Think often, as I hear them rave,
That peace has left the upper world
And now keeps only in the grave.

Yet here is peace forever new!
30 When I who watch them am away,
Still all things in this glade go through
The changes of their quiet day.

Then to their happy rest they pass!
The flowers upclose, the birds are fed,
35 The night comes down upon the grass,
The child sleeps warmly in his bed.

Calm soul of all things! make it mine
To feel, amid the city's jar,
That there abides a peace of thine,
40 Man did not make, and cannot mar.

The will to neither strive nor cry,
The power to feel with others give!
Calm, calm me more! nor let me die
Before I have begun to live.

1852

The Scholar Gypsy

The Scholar Gypsy   The story of a seventeenth-century student who left Oxford and joined a band of gypsies had made a strong impression on Arnold. In the poem he wistfully imagines that the spirit of this scholar is still to be encountered in the Cumner countryside near Oxford, having achieved immortality by a serene pursuit of the secret of human existence. Like Keats's nightingale, the scholar has escaped "the weariness, the fever, and the fret" of modern life.

At the outset, the poet addresses a shepherd who has been helping him in his search for traces of the scholar. The shepherd is addressed as *you*. After line 61, with the shift to *thou* and *thy*, the person addressed is the scholar himself, and the poet thereafter sometimes uses the pronoun *we* to indicate he is speaking for all humanity of later generations.

About the setting Arnold wrote to his brother Tom on May 15, 1857: "You alone of my brothers are associated with that life at Oxford, the *freest* and most delightful part, perhaps, of my life, when with you and Clough and Walrond I shook off all the bonds and formalities of the place, and enjoyed the spring of life and that unforgotten Oxfordshire and Berkshire country. Do you remember a poem of mine called 'The Scholar Gipsy'? It was meant to fix the remembrance of those delightful wanderings of ours in the Cumner Hills."

The passage from Joseph Glanvill's *Vanity of Dogmatizing* (1661) that inspired the poem was included by Arnold as a note:

There was very lately a lad in the University of Oxford, who was by his poverty forced to leave his studies there; and at last to join himself to a company of vagabond gypsies. Among these extravagant people, by the insinuating subtilty of his carriage, he quickly got so much of their love and esteem as that they discovered to him their mystery. After he had been a pretty while exercised in the trade, there chanced to ride by a couple of scholars, who had formerly been of his acquaintance. They quickly spied out their old friend among the gypsies; and he gave them an account of the necessity which drove him to that kind of life, and told them that the people he went with were not such imposters as they were taken for, but that they had a traditional kind of learning among them, and could do wonders by the power of imagination, their fancy binding that of others: that himself had learned much of their art, and when he had compassed the whole secret, he intended, he said, to leave their company, and give the world an account of what he had learned.

The Scholar Gypsy

Go, for they call you, shepherd, from the hill;
  Go, shepherd, and untie the wattled cotes!¹
  No longer leave thy wistful flock unfed,
  Nor let thy bawling fellows rack their throats,
5   Nor the cropped herbage shoot another head.
      But when the fields are still,
  And the tired men and dogs all gone to rest,
    And only the white sheep are sometimes seen
    Cross and recross the strips of moon-blanched green,
10 Come, shepherd, and again begin the quest!

Here, where the reaper was at work of late—
  In this high field's dark corner, where he leaves
    His coat, his basket, and his earthen cruse,²
  And in the sun all morning binds the sheaves,
15   Then here, at noon, comes back his stores to use—
      Here will I sit and wait,
  While to my ear from uplands far away
    The bleating of the folded° flocks is borne,   *penned up*
    With distant cries of reapers in the corn³—
20 All the live murmur of a summer's day.

Screened is this nook o'er the high, half-reaped field,
  And here till sundown, shepherd! will I be.
    Through the thick corn the scarlet poppies peep,
  And round green roots and yellowing stalks I see
25   Pale pink convolvulus in tendrils creep;
      And air-swept lindens yield
  Their scent, and rustle down their perfumed showers
    Of bloom on the bent grass⁴ where I am laid,
    And bower me from the August sun with shade;
30 And the eye travels down to Oxford's towers.

---

1. Sheepfolds woven from sticks.   3. Grain or wheat.
2. Pot or jug for carrying his drink.   4. A stiff kind of grass.

And near me on the grass lies Glanvill's book—
    Come, let me read the oft-read tale again!
    The story of the Oxford scholar poor,
    Of pregnant parts[5] and quick inventive brain,
35   Who, tired of knocking at preferment's door,
        One summer morn forsook
His friends, and went to learn the gypsy lore,
    And roamed the world with that wild brotherhood,
    And came, as most men deemed, to little good,
40   But came to Oxford and his friends no more.

But once, years after, in the country lanes,
    Two scholars, whom at college erst he knew,
    Met him, and of his way of life inquired;
    Whereat he answered, that the gypsy crew,
45   His mates, had arts to rule as they desired
        The workings of men's brains,
And they can bind them to what thoughts they will.
    "And I," he said, "the secret of their art,
    When fully learned, will to the world impart;
50   But it needs heaven-sent moments for this skill."

This said, he left them, and returned no more.—
    But rumors hung about the countryside,
    That the lost Scholar long was seen to stray,
    Seen by rare glimpses, pensive and tongue-tied,
55   In hat of antique shape, and cloak of grey,
        The same the gypsies wore.
Shepherds had met him on the Hurst[6] in spring;
    At some lone alehouse in the Berkshire moors,
    On the warm ingle-bench, the smock-frocked boors[7]
60   Had found him seated at their entering,

But, 'mid their drink and clatter, he would fly.
    And I myself seem half to know thy looks,
    And put the shepherds, wanderer! on thy trace;
    And boys who in lone wheatfields scare the rooks[8]
65   I ask if thou hast passed their quiet place;
        Or in my boat I lie
Moored to the cool bank in the summer heats,
    'Mid wide grass meadows which the sunshine fills,
    And watch the warm, green-muffled Cumner hills,
70   And wonder if thou haunt'st their shy retreats.

For most, I know, thou lov'st retired ground!
    Thee at the ferry Oxford riders blithe,
    Returning home on summer nights, have met
    Crossing the stripling Thames[9] at Bab-lock-hithe,

5. Teeming with ideas.
6. A hill near Oxford. All the place names in the poem (except those in the final two stanzas) refer to the countryside near Oxford.
7. Rustics. "Ingle-bench": fireside bench.

8. Boys hired to frighten crows away from eating wheat grains.
9. The narrow upper reaches of the river before it broadens out to its full width.

75   Trailing in the cool stream thy fingers wet,
       As the punt's rope chops round;[1]
And leaning backward in a pensive dream,
   And fostering in thy lap a heap of flowers
   Plucked in shy fields and distant Wychwood bowers,
80   And thine eyes resting on the moonlit stream.

And then they land, and thou art seen no more!—
   Maidens, who from the distant hamlets come
     To dance around the Fyfield elm in May,
   Oft through the darkening fields have seen thee roam,
85   Or cross a stile into the public way.
      Oft thou hast given them store
   Of flowers—the frail-leafed, white anemone,
    Dark bluebells drenched with dews of summer eves,
    And purple orchises with spotted leaves—
90   But none hath words she can report of thee.

And, above Godstow Bridge, when hay time's here
   In June, and many a scythe in sunshine flames,
    Men who through those wide fields of breezy grass
   Where black-winged swallows haunt the glittering Thames,
95   To bathe in the abandoned lasher pass,[2]
      Have often passed thee near
   Sitting upon the river bank o'ergrown;
    Marked thine outlandish garb, thy figure spare,
    Thy dark vague eyes, and soft abstracted air—
100   But, when they came from bathing, thou wast gone!

At some lone homestead in the Cumner hills,
   Where at her open door the housewife darns,
    Thou hast been seen, or hanging on a gate
   To watch the threshers in the mossy barns.
105   Children, who early range these slopes and late
      For cresses from the rills,
   Have known thee eying, all an April day,
    The springing pastures and the feeding kine;
    And marked thee, when the stars come out and shine,
110   Through the long dewy grass move slow away.

In autumn, on the skirts of Bagley Wood—
   Where most the gypsies by the turf-edged way
    Pitch their smoked tents, and every bush you see
   With scarlet patches tagged and shreds of grey,
115   Above the forest ground called Thessaly—
      The blackbird, picking food,
   Sees thee, nor stops his meal, nor fears at all;
    So often has he known thee past him stray,
    Rapt, twirling in thy hand a withered spray,
120   And waiting for the spark from heaven to fall.

---

1. The scholar's flat-bottomed boat ("punt") is tied up by a rope at the riverbank near the ferry crossing like the speaker's boat (in the previous stanza), which was "moored to the cool bank." The motion of the boat as it is stirred by the current of the river causes the chopping sound of the rope in the water.

2. Water that spills over a dam or weir.

And once, in winter, on the causeway chill
  Where home through flooded fields foot-travelers go,
    Have I not passed thee on the wooden bridge,
  Wrapped in thy cloak and battling with the snow,
125   Thy face tow'rd Hinksey and its wintry ridge?
      And thou hast climbed the hill,
  And gained the white brow of the Cumner range;
    Turned once to watch, while thick the snowflakes fall,
    The line of festal light in Christ Church hall[3]—
130 Then sought thy straw in some sequestered grange.

But what—I dream! Two hundred years are flown
  Since first thy story ran through Oxford halls,
    And the grave Glanvill did the tale inscribe
  That thou wert wandered from the studious walls
135   To learn strange arts, and join a gypsy tribe;
      And thou from earth art gone
  Long since, and in some quiet churchyard laid—
    Some country nook, where o'er thy unknown grave
    Tall grasses and white flowering nettles wave,
140 Under a dark, red-fruited yew tree's shade.

—No, no, thou hast not felt the lapse of hours!
  For what wears out the life of mortal men?
    'Tis that from change to change their being rolls;
  'Tis that repeated shocks, again, again,
145   Exhaust the energy of strongest souls
      And numb the elastic powers.
  Till having used our nerves with bliss and teen,°   *vexation*
    And tired upon a thousand schemes our wit,
    To the just-pausing Genius[4] we remit
150 Our worn-out life, and are—what we have been.

Thou hast not lived, why should'st thou perish, so?
  Thou hadst *one* aim, *one* business, *one* desire;
    Else wert thou long since numbered with the dead!
  Else hadst thou spent, like other men, thy fire!
155   The generations of thy peers are fled,
      And we ourselves shall go;
  But thou possessest an immortal lot,
    And we imagine thee exempt from age
    And living as thou liv'st on Glanvill's page,
160 Because thou hadst—what we, alas! have not.

For early didst thou leave the world, with powers
  Fresh, undiverted to the world without,
    Firm to their mark, not spent on other things;
  Free from the sick fatigue, the languid doubt,
165   Which much to have tried, in much been baffled, brings.
      O life unlike to ours!

3. The dining hall of an Oxford college.
4. Perhaps the spirit of the universe, which pauses briefly to receive back the life given to us.

Who fluctuate idly without term or scope,
 Of whom each strives, nor knows for what he strives,
  And each half[5] lives a hundred different lives;
170 Who wait like thee, but not, like thee, in hope.

Thou waitest for the spark from heaven! and we,
 Light half-believers of our casual creeds,
  Who never deeply felt, nor clearly willed,
  Whose insight never has borne fruit in deeds,
175 Whose vague resolves never have been fulfilled;
  For whom each year we see
 Breeds new beginnings, disappointments new;
  Who hesitate and falter life away,
  And lose tomorrow the ground won today—
180 Ah! do not we, wanderer! await it too?

Yes, we await it!—but it still delays,
 And then we suffer! and amongst us one,[6]
  Who most has suffered, takes dejectedly
  His seat upon the intellectual throne;
185 And all his store of sad experience he
  Lays bare of wretched days;
 Tells us his misery's birth and growth and signs,
  And how the dying spark of hope was fed,
  And how the breast was soothed, and how the head,
190 And all his hourly varied anodynes.

This for our wisest! and we others pine,
 And wish the long unhappy dream would end,
  And waive all claim to bliss, and try to bear;
  With close-lipped patience for our only friend,
195 Sad patience, too near neighbor to despair—
  But none has hope like thine!
 Thou through the fields and through the woods dost stray,
  Roaming the countryside, a truant boy,
  Nursing thy project in unclouded joy,
200 And every doubt long blown by time away.

O born in days when wits were fresh and clear,
 And life ran gaily as the sparkling Thames;
  Before this strange disease of modern life,
  With its sick hurry, its divided aims,
205 Its heads o'ertaxed, its palsied hearts, was rife—
  Fly hence, our contact fear!
 Still fly, plunge deeper in the bowering wood!
  Averse, as Dido did with gesture stern
  From her false friend's approach in Hades turn,[7]
210 Wave us away, and keep thy solitude!

---

5. An adverb modifying "lives."
6. Probably Goethe, although possibly referring to Tennyson, whose *In Memoriam* had appeared in 1850.

7. Dido committed suicide after her lover, Aeneas, deserted her. When he later encountered her in Hades, she turned sternly away from him.

Still nursing the unconquerable hope,
    Still clutching the inviolable shade,
      With a free, onward impulse brushing through,
    By night, the silvered branches of the glade—
215   Far on the forest skirts, where none pursue.
        On some mild pastoral slope
    Emerge, and resting on the moonlit pales
      Freshen thy flowers as in former years
      With dew, or listen with enchanted ears,
220   From the dark dingles,° to the nightingales!   *small deep valleys*

But fly our paths, our feverish contact fly!
    For strong the infection of our mental strife,
      Which, though it gives no bliss, yet spoils for rest;
    And we should win thee from thy own fair life,
225   Like us distracted, and like us unblest.
        Soon, soon thy cheer would die,
    Thy hopes grow timorous, and unfixed thy powers,
    And thy clear aims be cross and shifting made;
    And then thy glad perennial youth would fade,
230   Fade, and grow old at last, and die like ours.

Then fly our greetings, fly our speech and smiles!
    —As some grave Tyrian trader, from the sea,
      Descried at sunrise an emerging prow
    Lifting the cool-haired creepers stealthily,
235   The fringes of a southward-facing brow
        Among the Aegean isles;
    And saw the merry Grecian coaster come,
      Freighted with amber grapes, and Chian wine,
      Green, bursting figs, and tunnies° steeped in brine—   *tuna fish*
240   And knew the intruders on his ancient home,

The young lighthearted masters of the waves—
    And snatched his rudder, and shook out more sail;
      And day and night held on indignantly
    O'er the blue Midland waters with the gale,
245   Betwixt the Syrtes[8] and soft Sicily,
        To where the Atlantic raves
    Outside the western straits; and unbent sails
      There, where down cloudy cliffs, through sheets of foam,
      Shy traffickers, the dark Iberians[9] come;
250   And on the beach undid his corded bales.[1]

1853

8. Shoals off the coast of North Africa.
9. Dark inhabitants of Spain and Portugal—perhaps associated with gypsies.
1. The elaborate simile of the final two stanzas has been variously interpreted. The trader from Tyre is disconcerted when, peering out through the foliage ("fringes," line 235) that screens his hiding place, he sees noisy intruders entering his harbor. Like the Scholar Gypsy, when similarly intruded on by hearty extroverts, he resolves to flee and seek a new home.

The reference (line 249) to the Iberians as "*shy traffickers*" (traders) is explained by Kenneth Allott as having been derived from Herodotus's *History* (4.196). Herodotus describes a distinctive method of selling goods established by Carthaginian merchants who used to sail through the Strait of Gibraltar to trade with the inhabitants of the coast of West Africa. The Carthaginians would leave bales of their merchandise on display along the beaches and, without having seen their prospective customers, would return to their ships. The shy natives

Dover Beach

The sea is calm tonight.
The tide is full, the moon lies fair
Upon the straits—on the French coast the light
Gleams and is gone; the cliffs of England stand,
5   Glimmering and vast, out in the tranquil bay.
Come to the window, sweet is the night air!
Only, from the long line of spray
Where the sea meets the moon-blanched land,
Listen! you hear the grating roar[1]
10   Of pebbles which the waves draw back, and fling,
At their return, up the high strand,
Begin, and cease, and then again begin,
With tremulous cadence slow, and bring
The eternal note of sadness in.

15   Sophocles long ago
Heard it on the Aegean, and it brought
Into his mind the turbid ebb and flow
Of human misery;[2] we
Find also in the sound a thought,
20   Hearing it by this distant northern sea.

The Sea of Faith
Was once, too, at the full, and round earth's shore
Lay like the folds of a bright girdle furled.[3]
But now I only hear
25   Its melancholy, long, withdrawing roar,
Retreating, to the breath
Of the night wind, down the vast edges drear
And naked shingles[4] of the world.

Ah, love, let us be true
30   To one another! for the world, which seems
To lie before us like a land of dreams,
So various, so beautiful, so new,
Hath really neither joy, nor love, nor light,
Nor certitude, nor peace, nor help for pain;

would then come down from their inland hiding places and set gold beside the bales they wished to buy. When the natives withdrew in their turn, the Carthaginians would return to the beach and decide whether payments were adequate, a process repeated until agreement was reached. On the Atlantic coasts this method of bargaining persisted into the 19th century. As William Beloe, a translator of Herodotus, noted in 1844: "In this manner they transact their exchange without seeing one another, or without the least instance of dishonesty . . . on either side." For the solitary Tyrian trader such a procedure, with its avoidance of "contact" (line 221), would have been especially appropriate.
1. Cf. Wordsworth's *It Is a Beauteous Evening*, lines 6–8: "Listen! the mighty Being is awake, / And

doth with his eternal motion make / A sound like thunder—everlastingly."
2. A reference to a chorus in *Antigone*, which compares human sorrow to the sound of the waves moving the sand beneath them (lines 585–91).
3. This difficult line means, in general, that at high tide the sea envelops the land closely. Its forces are "gathered" up (to use Wordsworth's term for it) like the "folds" of bright clothing ("girdle") that have been compressed ("furled"). At ebb tide, as the sea retreats, it is unfurled and spread out. It still surrounds the shoreline but not as an "enclasping flow" (as in *To Marguerite—Continued*).
4. Beaches covered with pebbles.

35　And we are here as on a darkling plain
　　Swept with confused alarms of struggle and flight,
　　Where ignorant armies[5] clash by night.

ca. 1851　　　　　　　　　　　　　　　　　　　　　　　　　1867

Stanzas from the Grande Chartreuse[1]

　　Through Alpine meadows soft-suffused
　　With rain, where thick the crocus blows,
　　Past the dark forges long disused,
　　The mule track from Saint Laurent goes.
5　The bridge is crossed, and slow we ride,
　　Through forest, up the mountainside.

　　The autumnal evening darkens round,
　　The wind is up, and drives the rain;
　　While, hark! far down, with strangled sound
10　Doth the Dead Guier's[2] stream complain,
　　Where that wet smoke, among the woods,
　　Over his boiling cauldron broods.

　　Swift rush the spectral vapors white
　　Past limestone scars° with ragged pines,　　　　　　　*precipices*
15　Showing—then blotting from our sight!—
　　Halt—through the cloud-drift something shines!
　　High in the valley, wet and drear,
　　The huts of Courrerie appear.

　　Strike leftward! cries our guide; and higher
20　Mounts up the stony forest way.
　　At last the encircling trees retire;
　　Look! through the showery twilight grey
　　What pointed roofs are these advance?—
　　A palace of the Kings of France?

25　Approach, for what we seek is here!
　　Alight, and sparely sup, and wait
　　For rest in this outbuilding near;
　　Then cross the sward and reach that gate.

5. Perhaps alluding to conflicts in Arnold's own time such as occurred during the revolutions of 1848 in Europe, or at the Siege of Rome by the French in 1849 (the date of composition of the poem is unknown, although generally assumed to be 1851.) But the passage also refers back to another battle, one that occurred more than two thousand years earlier when an Athenian army was attempting an invasion of Sicily at nighttime. As this "night battle" was described by Thucydides in his *History of the Peloponnesian War* (7, chap.44), the invaders became confused by darkness and slaughtered many of their own men. Hence "ignorant armies."

1. A monastery situated high in the French Alps. It was established in 1084 by Saint Bruno, founder of the Carthusians (line 30), whose austere regimen of solitary contemplation, fasting, and religious exercises (lines 37–44) had remained virtually unchanged for centuries. Arnold visited the site on September 7, 1851, accompanied by his bride. His account may be compared with that by Wordsworth (*Prelude* 6.416–88), who had made a similar visit in 1790.
2. The Guiers Mort River flows down from the monastery and joins the Guiers Vif in the valley below. Wordsworth speaks of the two rivers as "the sister streams of Life and Death."

Knock; pass the wicket! Thou art come
30 To the Carthusians' world-famed home.

The silent courts, where night and day
Into their stone-carved basins cold
The splashing icy fountains play—
The humid corridors behold!
35 Where, ghostlike in the deepening night,
Cowled forms brush by in gleaming white.

The chapel, where no organ's peal
Invests the stern and naked prayer—
With penitential cries they kneel
40 And wrestle; rising then, with bare
And white uplifted faces stand,
Passing the Host from hand to hand;[3]

Each takes, and then his visage wan
Is buried in his cowl once more.
45 The cells!—the suffering Son of Man
Upon the wall—the knee-worn floor—
And where they sleep, that wooden bed,
Which shall their coffin be, when dead![4]

The library, where tract and tome
50 Not to feed priestly pride are there,
To hymn the conquering march of Rome,
Nor yet to amuse, as ours are!
They paint of souls the inner strife,
Their drops of blood, their death in life.

55 The garden, overgrown—yet mild,
See, fragrant herbs[5] are flowering there!
Strong children of the Alpine wild
Whose culture is the brethren's care;
Of human tasks their only one,
60 And cheerful works beneath the sun.

Those halls, too, destined to contain
Each its own pilgrim-host of old,
From England, Germany, or Spain—
All are before me! I behold
65 The House, the Brotherhood austere!
—And what am I, that I am here?

For rigorous teachers seized my youth,
And purged its faith, and trimmed its fire,

---

3. Arnold, during his short visit, may not actually
have witnessed the service of the Mass in the monastery. The consecrated wafer ("the Host") is not
passed from the hand of the officiating priest to
the hands of the communicant (as is the practice
in Arnold's own Anglican Church) but placed,
instead, on the tongue of the communicant (who

kneels rather than stands).
4. A Carthusian is buried on a wooden plank but
does not sleep in a coffin.
5. From which the liqueur Chartreuse is manufactured. Sales of this liqueur provide the principal
revenues for upkeep of the monastery.

Showed me the high, white star of Truth,
70 There bade me gaze, and there aspire.
Even now their whispers pierce the gloom:
What dost thou in this living tomb?

Forgive me, masters of the mind![6]
At whose behest I long ago
75 So much unlearnt, so much resigned—
I come not here to be your foe!
I seek these anchorites, not in ruth,[7]
To curse and to deny your truth;

Not as their friend, or child, I speak!
80 But as, on some far northern strand,
Thinking of his own Gods, a Greek
In pity and mournful awe might stand
Before some fallen Runic stone[8]—
For both were faiths, and both are gone.

85 Wandering between two worlds, one dead,
The other powerless to be born,
With nowhere yet to rest my head,
Like these, on earth I wait forlorn.
Their faith, my tears, the world deride—
90 I come to shed them at their side.

Oh, hide me in your gloom profound,
Ye solemn seats of holy pain!
Take me, cowled forms, and fence me round,
Till I possess my soul again;
95 Till free my thoughts before me roll,
Not chafed by hourly false control!

For the world cries your faith is now
But a dead time's exploded dream;
My melancholy, sciolists[9] say,
100 Is a passed mode, an outworn theme—
As if the world had ever had
A faith, or sciolists been sad!

Ah, if it *be* passed, take away,
At least, the restlessness, the pain;
105 Be man henceforth no more a prey
To these out-dated stings again!

6. Writers whose insistence on testing religious beliefs in the light of fact and reason persuaded Arnold that faith in Christianity (especially in the Roman Catholic or Anglo Catholic forms) was no longer tenable in the modern world.
7. Remorse for having adopted the rationalist view of Christianity.
8. A monument inscribed in Teutonic letters (runes), emblematic of a Nordic religion that has become extinct. The relic reminds the Greek that his own religion is likewise dying and will soon be extinct (see *Preface to Poems* [1853], p. 1504, para. 2).
9. Superficial-minded persons who pretend to know the answers to all questions.

The nobleness of grief is gone—
Ah, leave us not the fret alone!

But—if you[1] cannot give us ease—
110 Last of the race of them who grieve
Here leave us to die out with these
Last of the people who believe!
Silent, while years engrave the brow;
Silent—the best are silent now.

115 Achilles[2] ponders in his tent,
The kings of modern thought[3] are dumb;
Silent they are, though not content,
And wait to see the future come.
They have the grief men had of yore,
120 But they contend and cry no more.

Our fathers[4] watered with their tears
This sea of time whereon we sail,
Their voices were in all men's ears
Who passed within their puissant hail.
125 Still the same ocean round us raves,
But we stand mute, and watch the waves.

For what availed it, all the noise
And outcry of the former men?—
Say, have their sons achieved more joys,
130 Say, is life lighter now than then?
The sufferers died, they left their pain—
The pangs which tortured them remain.

What helps it now, that Byron bore,
With haughty scorn which mocked the smart,
135 Through Europe to the Aetolian shore[5]
The pageant of his bleeding heart?
That thousands counted every groan,
And Europe made his woe her own?

What boots it, Shelley! that the breeze
140 Carried thy lovely wail away,
Musical through Italian trees
Which fringe thy soft blue Spezzian bay?[6]
Inheritors of thy distress
Have restless hearts one throb the less?

---

1. It is not clear whether the speaker has resumed addressing his "rigorous teachers" (line 67) or (as would seem more likely) a combination of the sciolists, who scorn the speaker's melancholy, and the worldly, who scorn the faith of the monks. See his address to the "sons of the world" (lines 161–68).
2. Until the death of Patroclus, he refused to participate in the Trojan war, hence similar to modern intellectual leaders who refuse to speak out about their frustrated sense of alienation.

3. Variously but never satisfactorily identified as Newman or Carlyle (the latter was said to have preached the gospel of silence in forty volumes). Another advocate of stoical silence was the French poet Alfred de Vigny (1797–1863).
4. Predecessors among the Romantic writers such as Byron.
5. Region in Greece where Byron died.
6. The Gulf of Spezia in Italy, where Shelley was drowned.

145 Or are we easier, to have read,
O Obermann![7] the sad, stern page,
Which tells us how thou hidd'st thy head
From the fierce tempest of thine age
In the lone brakes of Fontainebleau,
150 Or chalets near the Alpine snow?

Ye slumber in your silent grave!
The world, which for an idle day
Grace to your mood of sadness gave,
Long since hath flung her weeds° away.   *mourning clothes*
155 The eternal trifler[8] breaks your spell;
But we—we learnt your lore too well!

Years hence, perhaps, may dawn an age,
More fortunate, alas! than we,
Which without hardness will be sage,
160 And gay without frivolity.
Sons of the world, oh, speed those years;
But, while we wait, allow our tears!

Allow them! We admire with awe
The exulting thunder of your race;
165 You give the universe your law,
You triumph over time and space!
Your pride of life, your tireless powers,
We laud them, but they are not ours.

We are like children reared in shade
170 Beneath some old-world abbey wall,
Forgotten in a forest glade,
And secret from the eyes of all.
Deep, deep the greenwood round them waves,
Their abbey, and its close° of graves!   *enclosure*

175 But, where the road runs near the stream,
Oft through the trees they catch a glance
Of passing troops in the sun's beam—
Pennon, and plume, and flashing lance!
Forth to the world those soldiers fare,
180 To life, to cities, and to war!

And through the wood, another way,
Faint bugle notes from far are borne,
Where hunters gather, staghounds bay,[9]
Round some fair forest-lodge at morn.
185 Gay dames are there, in sylvan green;
Laughter and cries—those notes between!

7. Melancholy hero of *Obermann* (1804), a novel
by the French writer Senancour.
8. The sciolist, as in line 99.

9. Cf. the contrast between recluses and hunters
in *The Scholar Gypsy*, lines 71–81 (pp. 1487–
88).

The banners flashing through the trees
Make their blood dance and chain their eyes;
That bugle music on the breeze
190   Arrests them with a charmed surprise.
Banner by turns and bugle woo:
Ye shy recluses, follow too!

O children, what do ye reply?—
"Action and pleasure, will ye roam
195   Through these secluded dells to cry
And call us?—but too late ye come!
Too late for us your call ye blow,
Whose bent was taken long ago.

"Long since we pace this shadowed nave;
200   We watch those yellow tapers shine,
Emblems of hope over the grave,
In the high altar's depth divine;
The organ carries to our ear
Its accents of another sphere.[1]

205   "Fenced early in this cloistral round
Of reverie, of shade, of prayer,
How should we grow in other ground?
How can we flower in foreign air?
—Pass, banners, pass, and bugles, cease;
210   And leave our desert to its peace!"

1852(?)   1855

Thyrsis[1]

*A Monody, to Commemorate the Author's Friend, Arthur Hugh Clough,
Who Died at Florence, 1861*

How changed is here each spot man makes or fills!
    In the two Hinkseys[2] nothing keeps the same;
    The village street its haunted mansion lacks,
    And from the sign is gone Sibylla's[3] name,
5   And from the roofs the twisted chimney stacks—

1. The organ music is from the abbey in the green-wood (line 174), as contrasted with the monastery on the mountaintop in which there is no organ (line 37).
1. In the 1840s, at Oxford, Clough had been one of Arnold's closest friends. After the death of this fellow poet twenty years later, Arnold revisited the Thames valley countryside that they had explored together. The familiar scenes prompted him to review the changes wrought by time on the ideals shared in his Oxford days with Clough, ideals symbolized, in part, by a distant elm and by the story of the Scholar Gypsy. The survival of these ideals in the face of the difficulties of modern life is the subject of this elegy. Unlike Tennyson in such elegies as *In Memoriam*, Arnold rarely touches here

on other kinds of immortality.
    As a framework for his elegy, Arnold draws on the same Greek and Latin pastoral tradition from which Milton's *Lycidas* and Shelley's *Adonais* were derived. Hence Clough is referred to by one of the traditional names for a shepherd poet, Thyrsis, and Arnold himself as Corydon. The sense of distancing that results from this traditional elegiac mode is reduced considerably by the realism of the setting with its bleak wintry landscape at twilight, a landscape that is brightened, in turn, by evocations of the return of hopeful springtime.
2. The villages of North Hinksey and South Hinksey.
3. Sibylla Kerr had been the proprietress of a tavern in South Hinksey.

Are ye too changed, ye hills?
See, 'tis no foot of unfamiliar men
   Tonight from Oxford up your pathway strays!
Here came I often, often, in old days—
10   Thyrsis and I; we still had Thyrsis then.

Runs it not here, the track by Childsworth Farm,
   Past the high wood, to where the elm tree crowns
   The hill behind whose ridge the sunset flames?
The signal-elm, that looks on Ilsley Downs,
15   The Vale, the three lone weirs, the youthful Thames?—
     This winter eve is warm,
Humid the air! leafless, yet soft as spring,
   The tender purple spray on copse and briers!
And that sweet city with her dreaming spires,
20   She needs not June for beauty's heightening,

Lovely all times she lies, lovely tonight!—
   Only, methinks, some loss of habit's power
   Befalls me wandering through this upland dim.
Once passed I blindfold here, at any hour;
25   Now seldom come I, since I came with him.
     That single elm tree bright
Against the west—I miss it! is it gone?
   We prized it dearly; while it stood, we said,
   Our friend, the Gypsy Scholar, was not dead;
30   While the tree lived, he in these fields lived on.

Too rare, too rare, grow now my visits here,
   But once I knew each field, each flower, each stick;
   And with the countryfolk acquaintance made
By barn in threshing time, by new-built rick.
35   Here, too, our shepherd pipes we first assayed.
     Ah me! this many a year
My pipe is lost, my shepherd's holiday!
   Needs must I lose them, needs with heavy heart
   Into the world and wave of men depart;
40   But Thyrsis of his own will went away.[4]

It irked him to be here, he could not rest.
   He loved each simple joy the country yields,
   He loved his mates; but yet he could not keep,°   *stay*
For that a shadow loured on the fields,
45   Here with the shepherds and the silly° sheep.   *innocent*
     Some life of men unblest
He knew, which made him droop, and filled his head.
   He went; his piping took a troubled sound
   Of storms[5] that rage outside our happy ground;
50   He could not wait their passing, he is dead.

4. Arnold left Oxford out of the necessity for earning a living; Clough left as a matter of principle when in 1848 he resigned a fellowship rather than subscribe to the doctrines of the Church of England.
5. Religious and political controversies.

So, some tempestuous morn in early June,
  When the year's primal burst of bloom is o'er,
    Before the roses and the longest day—
  When garden walks and all the grassy floor
55   With blossoms red and white of fallen May
      And chestnut flowers are strewn—
  So have I heard the cuckoo's parting cry,
    From the wet field, through the vexed garden trees,
    Come with the volleying rain and tossing breeze:
60   *The bloom is gone, and with the bloom go I!*

Too quick despairer, wherefore wilt thou go?
  Soon will the high Midsummer pomps come on,
    Soon will the musk carnations break and swell,
  Soon shall we have gold-dusted snapdragon,
65   Sweet-William with his homely cottage-smell,
      And stocks in fragrant blow;
  Roses that down the alleys shine afar,
    And open, jasmine-muffled lattices,
    And groups under the dreaming garden trees,
70 And the full moon, and the white evening star.

He hearkens not! light comer, he is flown!
  What matters it? next year he will return,
    And we shall have him in the sweet spring days,
  With whitening hedges, and uncrumpling fern,
75   And bluebells trembling by the forest ways,
      And scent of hay new-mown.
  But Thyrsis never more we swains shall see,
    See him come back, and cut a smoother reed,
    And blow a strain the world at last shall heed—
80 For Time, not Corydon, hath conquered thee!

Alack, for Corydon no rival now!—
  But when Sicilian shepherds lost a mate,
    Some good survivor with his flute would go,
  Piping a ditty sad for Bion's fate;[6]
85   And cross the unpermitted ferry's flow,[7]
      And relax Pluto's brow,
  And make leap up with joy the beauteous head
    Of Proserpine, among whose crownèd hair
    Are flowers first opened on Sicilian air,[8]
90 And flute his friend, like Orpheus,[9] from the dead.

O easy access to the hearer's grace
  When Dorian shepherds[1] sang to Proserpine!

6. Moschus, a Greek poet, composed a pastoral
elegy upon the death of the poet Bion in Sicily.
7. The river Styx across which the dead were fer-
ried to the underworld.
8. Pluto ruled the underworld with his queen,
Proserpine. In spring, Proserpine's returning above
ground in Sicily would cause the flowers to blossom.
9. His music enabled him to enter the "unpermitted" realms of the dead and to bring his wife,
Eurydice, back with him to the land of the living.
1. Greeks who colonized Sicily, the home of pastoral poetry.

For she herself had trod Sicilian fields,
She knew the Dorian water's gush divine,
95   She knew each lily white which Enna² yields,
           Each rose with blushing face;
She loved the Dorian pipe, the Dorian strain.
But ah, of our poor Thames she never heard!
Her foot the Cumner cowslips never stirred;
100   And we should tease her with our plaint in vain!

Well! wind-dispersed and vain the words will be,
Yet, Thyrsis, let me give my grief its hour
           In the old haunt, and find our tree-topped hill!
Who, if not I, for questing here hath power?
105   I know the wood which hides the daffodil,
           I know the Fyfield tree,
I know what white, what purple fritillaries³
           The grassy harvest of the river fields,
           Above by Ensham, down by Sandford, yields,
110   And what sedged brooks are Thames's tributaries;

I know these slopes; who knows them if not I?—
But many a dingle⁴ on the loved hillside,
           With thorns once studded, old, white-blossomed trees,
Where thick the cowslips grew, and far descried
115   High towered the spikes of purple orchises,
           Hath since our day put by
The coronals of that forgotten time;
           Down each green bank hath gone the plowboy's team,
           And only in the hidden brookside gleam
120   Primroses, orphans of the flowery prime.

Where is the girl, who by the boatman's door,
Above the locks, above the boating throng,
           Unmoored our skiff when through the Wytham flats,
Red loosestrife⁵ and blond meadowsweet among
125   And darting swallows and light water-gnats,
           We tracked the shy Thames shore?
Where are the mowers, who, as the tiny swell
           Of our boat passing heaved the river grass,
           Stood with suspended scythe to see us pass?—
130   They all are gone, and thou art gone as well!

Yes, thou art gone! and round me too the night
In ever-nearing circle weaves her shade.
           I see her veil draw soft across the day,
I feel her slowly chilling breath invade
135   The cheek grown thin, the brown hair sprent° with grey;   *sprinkled*
           I feel her finger light
Laid pausefully upon life's headlong train;

---

2. From a meadow near the Sicilian town of Enna,
Proserpine had been carried off to the underworld
by Pluto (or Dis).

3. Flowers commonly found in moist meadows.
4. Small deep valley.
5. Flowers that grow on banks of streams.

The foot less prompt to meet the morning dew,
The heart less bounding at emotion new,
140   And hope, once crushed, less quick to spring again.

And long the way appears, which seemed so short
To the less practiced eye of sanguine youth;
And high the mountaintops, in cloudy air,
The mountaintops where is the throne of Truth,
145   Tops in life's morning sun so bright and bare!
Unbreachable the fort
Of the long-battered world uplifts its wall;
And strange and vain the earthly turmoil grows,
And near and real the charm of thy repose,
150   And night as welcome as a friend would fall.

But hush! the upland hath a sudden loss
Of quiet!—Look, adown the dusk hillside,
A troop of Oxford hunters going home,
As in old days, jovial and talking, ride!
155   From hunting with the Berkshire hounds they come.
Quick! let me fly, and cross
Into yon farther field!—'Tis done; and see,
Backed by the sunset, which doth glorify
The orange and pale violet evening sky,
160   Bare on its lonely ridge, the Tree! the Tree!

I take the omen! Eve lets down her veil,
The white fog creeps from bush to bush about,
The west unflushes, the high stars grow bright,
And in the scattered farms the lights come out.
165   I cannot reach the signal-tree tonight,
Yet, happy omen, hail!
Hear it from thy broad lucent Arno vale[6]
(For there thine earth-forgetting eyelids keep
The morningless and unawakening sleep
170   Under the flowery oleanders pale),

Hear it, O Thyrsis, still our tree is there!—
Ah, vain! These English fields, this upland dim,
These brambles pale with mist engarlanded,
That lone, sky-pointing tree, are not for him;
175   To a boon southern country he is fled,
And now in happier air,
Wandering with the great Mother's train divine[7]
(And purer or more subtle soul than thee,
I trow, the mighty Mother doth not see)
180   Within a folding of the Apennine,[8]

Thou hearest the immortal chants[9] of old!—
Putting his sickle to the perilous grain

6. Clough was buried in Florence, which is situated in the valley of the Arno River.
7. Followers of Demeter (whose name may mean Earth Mother), who was worshiped as the goddess of agriculture.
8. Mountains near Florence.
9. Sung in Demeter's honor.

In the hot cornfield of the Phrygian king,[1]
For thee the Lityerses song again
185   Young Daphnis with his silver voice doth sing;
      Sings his Sicilian fold,
His sheep, his hapless love, his blinded eyes—
And how a call celestial round him rang,
And heavenward from the fountain brink he sprang,
190   And all the marvel of the golden skies.

There thou art gone, and me thou leavest here
Sole in these fields! yet will I not despair.
    Despair I will not, while I yet descry
    'Neath the mild canopy of English air
195   That lonely tree against the western sky.
      Still, still these slopes, 'tis clear,
Our Gypsy Scholar haunts, outliving thee!
Fields where soft sheep from cages pull the hay,
Woods with anemones in flower till May,
200   Know him a wanderer still; then why not me?

A fugitive and gracious light he seeks,
Shy to illumine; and I seek it too.
    This does not come with houses or with gold,
    With place, with honor, and a flattering crew;
205   'Tis not in the world's market bought and sold—
      But the smooth-slipping weeks
Drop by, and leave its seeker still untired;
Out of the heed of mortals he is gone,
He wends unfollowed, he must house alone;
210   Yet on he fares, by his own heart inspired.

Thou too, O Thyrsis, on like quest wast bound;
Thou wanderedst with me for a little hour!
    Men gave thee nothing; but this happy quest,
    If men esteemed thee feeble, gave thee power,
215   If men procured thee trouble, gave thee rest.
      And this rude Cumner ground,
Its fir-topped Hurst, its farms, its quiet fields,
Here cam'st thou in thy jocund youthful time,
Here was thine height of strength, thy golden prime!
220   And still the haunt beloved a virtue yields.

What though the music of thy rustic flute
Kept not for long its happy, country tone;
    Lost it too soon, and learnt a stormy note[2]

---

1. Daphnis, the ideal Sicilian shepherd of Greek pastoral poetry, was said to have followed into Phrygia his mistress Piplea, who had been carried off by robbers, and to have found her in the power of the king of Phrygia, Lityerses. Lityerses used to make strangers try a contest with him in reaping corn, and to put them to death if he overcame them. Hercules arrived in time to save Daphnis, took upon himself the reaping contest with Lityerses, overcame him, and slew him. The Lityerses song connected with this tradition was, like the Linus song, one of the early plaintive strains of Greek popular poetry, and used to be sung by corn reapers. Other traditions represented Daphnis as beloved by a nymph who exacted from him an oath to love no one else. He fell in love with a princess, and was struck blind by the jealous nymph. Mercury, who was his father, raised him to heaven, and made a fountain spring up in the place from which he ascended. At this fountain the Sicilians offered yearly sacrifices [from Servius's commentary on Virgil's *Ecologues*; Arnold's note].
2. Clough's poetry often dealt with contemporary religious problems.

Of men contention-tossed, of men who groan,
225   Which tasked thy pipe too sore, and tired thy throat—
      It failed, and thou wast mute!
Yet hadst thou always visions of our light,
    And long with men of care thou couldst not stay,
    And soon thy foot resumed its wandering way,
230   Left human haunt, and on alone till night.

Too rare, too rare, grow now my visits here!
    'Mid city noise, not, as with thee of yore,
      Thyrsis! in reach of sheep-bells is my home.
—Then through the great town's harsh, heart-wearying roar,
235   Let in thy voice a whisper often come,
      To chase fatigue and fear:
Why faintest thou? I wandered till I died.
Roam on! The light we sought is shining still.
Dost thou ask proof? Our tree yet crowns the hill,
240 *Our Scholar travels yet the loved hillside.*

1866

Preface to *Poems* (1853)

In two small volumes of poems, published anonymously, one in 1849, the other in 1852, many of the poems which compose the present volume have already appeared. The rest are now published for the first time.

I have, in the present collection, omitted the poem from which the volume published in 1852 took its title.[1] I have done so, not because the subject of it was a Sicilian Greek born between two and three thousand years ago, although many persons would think this a sufficient reason. Neither have I done so because I had, in my own opinion, failed in the delineation which I intended to effect. I intended to delineate the feelings of one of the last of the Greek religious philosophers, one of the family of Orpheus and Musaeus,[2] having survived his fellows, living on into a time when the habits of Greek thought and feeling had begun fast to change, character to dwindle, the influence of the Sophists[3] to prevail. Into the feelings of a man so situated there entered much that we are accustomed to consider as exclusively modern; how much, the fragments of Empedocles[4] himself which remain to us

1. *Empedocles on Etna,* the long poem that supplied the title for Arnold's second collection of poems, portrays the disillusioned reflections of the Greek philosopher and scientist Empedocles and culminates in the speaker's suicide on Mount Etna in Sicily, in the 5th century B.C.E. Because of his dissatisfaction with what he calls the "morbid" tone of *Empedocles on Etna,* Arnold continued to exclude it from his volumes of poetry until 1867 when he reprinted it at the request, he said, "of a man of genius, whom it had the honor and good fortune to interest—Mr. Robert Browning." It should be noted that in the arguments developed in the Preface against his own poem (and against 19th-century poetry in general), Arnold is exclusively concerned with narrative and dramatic poetry. The Preface, as he himself remarked in 1854, "leaves . . . untouched the question, how far, and in what manner, the opinions there expressed respecting the choice of subjects apply to lyric poetry; that region of the poetical field which is chiefly cultivated at present."

2. Pupil of the poet and musician Orpheus. The latter was the legendary founder of the Orphic religion that flourished in 6th-century Greece and later declined.

3. Greek rhetoricians, often criticized because of their reputed concern for niceties of expression over substance of knowledge.

4. Empedocles' writings (medical and scientific treatises in verse) have survived only in fragments.

are sufficient at least to indicate. What those who are familiar only with the great monuments of early Greek genius suppose to be its exclusive characteristics, have disappeared; the calm, the cheerfulness, the disinterested objectivity have disappeared; the dialogue of the mind with itself has commenced; modern problems have presented themselves, we hear already the doubts, we witness the discouragement, of Hamlet and of Faust.

The representation of such a man's feelings must be interesting, if consistently drawn. We all naturally take pleasure, says Aristotle, in any imitation or representation whatever;[5] this is the basis of our love of poetry; and we take pleasure in them, he adds, because all knowledge is naturally agreeable to us; not to the philosopher only, but to mankind at large. Every representation therefore which is consistently drawn may be supposed to be interesting, inasmuch as it gratifies this natural interest in knowledge of all kinds. What is *not* interesting is that which does not add to our knowledge of any kind; that which is vaguely conceived and loosely drawn; a representation which is general, indeterminate, and faint, instead of being particular, precise, and firm.

Any accurate representation may therefore be expected to be interesting; but, if the representation be a poetical one, more than this is demanded. It is demanded, not only that it shall interest, but also that it shall inspirit and rejoice the reader; that it shall convey a charm, and infuse delight. For the muses, as Hesiod says, were born that they might be "a forgetfulness of evils, and a truce from cares":[6] and it is not enough that the poet should add to the knowledge of men, it is required of him also that he should add to their happiness. "All art," says Schiller, "is dedicated to Joy, and there is no higher and no more serious problem, than how to make men happy. The right art is that alone, which creates the highest enjoyment."[7]

A poetical work, therefore, is not yet justified when it has been shown to be an accurate, and therefore interesting representation; it has to be shown also that it is a representation from which men can derive enjoyment. In presence of the most tragic circumstances, represented in a work of Art, the feeling of enjoyment, as is well known, may still subsist; the representation of the most utter calamity, of the liveliest anguish, is not sufficient to destroy it; the more tragic the situation, the deeper becomes the enjoyment; and the situation is more tragic in proportion as it becomes more terrible.

What then are the situations, from the representation of which, though accurate, no poetical enjoyment can be derived? They are those in which the suffering finds no vent in action; in which a continuous state of mental distress is prolonged, unrelieved by incident, hope, or resistance; in which there is everything to be endured, nothing to be done. In such situations there is inevitably something morbid, in the description of them something monotonous. When they occur in actual life, they are painful, not tragic; the representation of them in poetry is painful also.

To this class of situations, poetically faulty as it appears to me, that of Empedocles, as I have endeavored to represent him, belongs; and I have therefore excluded the poem from the present collection.

---

5. See Aristotle's *Poetics*, especially 1, 2, 4, 7, 14.
6. From *Theogony* 52–56, by Hesiod, early Greek poet.
7. J. C. F. von Schiller's *On the Use of the Chorus*

in *Tragedy*, prefatory essay to *The Bride of Messina* (1803). See *Friedrich Schiller's Works* (1903) 8.224.

And why, it may be asked, have I entered into this explanation respecting a matter so unimportant as the admission or exclusion of the poem in question? I have done so, because I was anxious to avow that the sole reason for its exclusion was that which has been stated above; and that it has not been excluded in deference to the opinion which many critics of the present day appear to entertain against subjects chosen from distant times and countries: against the choice, in short, of any subjects but modern ones.

"The poet," it is said, and by an intelligent critic, "the poet who would really fix the public attention must leave the exhausted past, and draw his subjects from matters of present import, and *therefore* both of interest and novelty."[8]

Now this view I believe to be completely false. It is worth examining, inasmuch as it is a fair sample of a class of critical dicta everywhere current at the present day, having a philosophical form and air, but no real basis in fact; and which are calculated to vitiate the judgment of readers of poetry, while they exert, so far as they are adopted, a misleading influence on the practice of those who write it.

What are the eternal objects of poetry, among all nations and at all times? They are actions; human actions; possessing an inherent interest in themselves, and which are to be communicated in an interesting manner by the art of the poet.[9] Vainly will the latter imagine that he has everything in his own power; that he can make an intrinsically inferior action equally delightful with a more excellent one by his treatment of it; he may indeed compel us to admire his skill, but his work will possess, within itself, an incurable defect.

The poet, then, has in the first place to select an excellent action; and what actions are the most excellent? Those, certainly, which most powerfully appeal to the great primary human affections: to those elementary feelings which subsist permanently in the race, and which are independent of time. These feelings are permanent and the same; that which interests them is permanent and the same also. The modernness or antiquity of an action, therefore, has nothing to do with its fitness for poetical representation; this depends upon its inherent qualities. To the elementary part of our nature, to our passions, that which is great and passionate is eternally interesting; and interesting solely in proportion to its greatness and to its passion. A great human action of a thousand years ago is more interesting to it than a smaller human action of today, even though upon the representation of this last the most consummate skill may have been expended, and though it has the advantage of appealing by its modern language, familiar manners, and contemporary allusions, to all our transient feelings and interests. These, however, have no right to demand of a poetical work that it shall satisfy them; their claims are to be directed elsewhere. Poetical works belong to the domain of our permanent passions; let them interest these, and the voice of all subordinate claims upon them is at once silenced.

Achilles, Prometheus, Clytemnestra, Dido—what modern poem presents personages as interesting, even to us moderns, as these personages of an

8. In the *Spectator* of April 2nd, 1853. The words quoted were not used with reference to poems of mine [Arnold's note]. According to Arnold the "intelligent critic" was R. S. Rintoul, editor of the *Spectator*.
9. Cf. Aristotle's *Poetics* 6.

"exhausted past"? We have the domestic epic dealing with the details of modern life which pass daily under our eyes;[1] we have poems representing modern personages in contact with the problems of modern life, moral, intellectual, and social; these works have been produced by poets the most distinguished of their nation and time; yet I fearlessly assert that *Hermann and Dorothea, Childe Harold, Jocelyn, The Excursion*,[2] leave the reader cold in comparison with the effect produced upon him by the latter books of the *Iliad*, by the *Oresteia*, or by the episode of Dido.[3] And why is this? Simply because in the three last-named cases the action is greater, the personages nobler, the situations more intense: and this is the true basis of the interest in a poetical work, and this alone.

It may be urged, however, that past actions may be interesting in themselves, but that they are not to be adopted by the modern poet, because it is impossible for him to have them clearly present to his own mind, and he cannot therefore feel them deeply, nor represent them forcibly. But this is not necessarily the case. The externals of a past action, indeed, he cannot know with the precision of a contemporary; but his business is with its essentials. The outward man of Oedipus or of Macbeth, the houses in which they lived, the ceremonies of their courts, he cannot accurately figure to himself; but neither do they essentially concern him. His business is with their inward man; with their feelings and behavior in certain tragic situations, which engage their passions as men; these have in them nothing local and casual; they are as accessible to the modern poet as to a contemporary.

The date of an action, then, signifies nothing: the action itself, its selection and construction, this is what is all-important. This the Greeks understood far more clearly than we do. The radical difference between their poetical theory and ours consists, as it appears to me, in this: that, with them, the poetical character of the action in itself, and the conduct of it, was the first consideration; with us, attention is fixed mainly on the value of the separate thoughts and images which occur in the treatment of an action. They regarded the whole; we regard the parts. With them, the action predominated over the expression of it; with us, the expression predominates over the action. Not that they failed in expression, or were inattentive to it; on the contrary, they are the highest models of expression, the unapproached masters of the *grand style*: but their expression is so excellent because it is so admirably kept in its right degree of prominence; because it is so simple and so well subordinated; because it draws its force directly from the pregnancy of the matter which it conveys. For what reason was the Greek tragic poet confined to so limited a range of subjects? Because there are so few actions which unite in themselves, in the highest degree, the conditions of excellence: and it was not thought that on any but an excellent subject could an excellent poem be constructed. A few actions, therefore, eminently adapted for tragedy, maintained almost exclusive possession of the Greek tragic stage; their significance appeared inexhaustible; they were as permanent problems,

---

1. Perhaps alluding to such poems as Tennyson's *The Princess* (1847) and Alexander Smith's *Life Drama* (1853) or to the modern novel.
2. Long poems by Goethe (1797), Byron (1818), Lamartine (1836), and Wordsworth (1814),

respectively.
3. See Virgil's *Aeneid* 4. "*Oresteia*": a trilogy of plays by Aeschylus concerned with the stories of Agamemnon, Clytemnestra, and their son, Orestes.

perpetually offered to the genius of every fresh poet. This too is the reason of what appears to us moderns a certain baldness of expression in Greek tragedy; of the triviality with which we often reproach the remarks of the chorus, where it takes part in the dialogue: that the action itself, the situation of Orestes, or Merope, or Alcmaeon,[4] was to stand the central point of interest, unforgotten, absorbing, principal; that no accessories were for a moment to distract the spectator's attention from this; that the tone of the parts was to be perpetually kept down, in order not to impair the grandiose effect of the whole. The terrible old mythic story on which the drama was founded stood, before he entered the theater, traced in its bare outlines upon the spectator's mind; it stood in his memory, as a group of statuary, faintly seen, at the end of a long and dark vista: then came the poet, embodying outlines, developing situations, not a word wasted, not a sentiment capriciously thrown in: stroke upon stroke, the drama proceeded: the light deepened upon the group; more and more it revealed itself to the riveted gaze of the spectator: until at last, when the final words were spoken, it stood before him in broad sunlight, a model of immortal beauty.

This was what a Greek critic demanded; this was what a Greek poet endeavored to effect. It signified nothing to what time an action belonged; we do not find that the *Persae* occupied a particularly high rank among the dramas of Aeschylus, because it represented a matter of contemporary interest:[5] this was not what a cultivated Athenian required, he required that the permanent elements of his nature should be moved; and dramas of which the action, though taken from a long-distant mythic time, yet was calculated to accomplish this in a higher degree than that of the *Persae,* stood higher in his estimation accordingly. The Greeks felt, no doubt, with their exquisite sagacity of taste, that an action of present times was too near them, too much mixed up with what was accidental and passing, to form a sufficiently grand, detached, and self-subsistent object for a tragic poem: such objects belonged to the domain of the comic poet, and of the lighter kinds of poetry. For the more serious kinds, for *pragmatic* poetry, to use an excellent expression of Polybius,[6] they were more difficult and severe in the range of subjects which they permitted. Their theory and practice alike, the admirable treatise of Aristotle, and the unrivaled works of their poets, exclaim with a thousand tongues—"All depends upon the subject; choose a fitting action, penetrate yourself with the feeling of its situations; this done, everything else will follow."

But for all kinds of poetry alike there was one point on which they were rigidly exacting; the adaptability of the subject to the kind of poetry selected, and the careful construction of the poem.

How different a way of thinking from this is ours! We can hardly at the present day understand what Menander[7] meant when he told a man who inquired as to the progress of his comedy that he had finished it, not having yet written a single line, because he had constructed the action of it in his mind. A modern critic would have assured him that the merit of his piece

---

4. The son of a legendary Greek hero, who, like Orestes, avenged his father's death by killing his mother. He was the subject of several Greek plays now lost. Merope, queen of Messene in Greece, appears in plays by Euripides and in Arnold's own play *Merope* (1858).

5. Aeschylus's *Persians* (472 B.C.E.) portrays the Greek victory over the Persian invaders, which had occurred only a few years before the play was produced.

6. Greek historian (202–120 B.C.E.).

7. Greek writer of comedies (342–292 B.C.E.).

depended on the brilliant things which arose under his pen as he went along. We have poems which seem to exist merely for the sake of single lines and passages; not for the sake of producing any total impression. We have critics who seem to direct their attention merely to detached expressions, to the language about the action, not to the action itself, I verily think that the majority of them do not in their hearts believe that there is such a thing as a total impression to be derived from a poem at all, or to be demanded from a poet; they think the term a commonplace of metaphysical criticism. They will permit the poet to select any action he pleases, and to suffer that action to go as it will, provided he gratifies them with occasional bursts of fine writing, and with a shower of isolated thoughts and images. That is, they permit him to leave their poetical sense ungratified, provided that he gratifies their rhetorical sense and their curiosity. Of his neglecting to gratify these, there is little danger. He needs rather to be warned against the danger of attempting to gratify these alone; he needs rather to be perpetually reminded to prefer his action to everything else; so to treat this, as to permit its inherent excellences to develop themselves, without interruption from the intrusion of his personal peculiarities; most fortunate, when he most entirely succeeds in effacing himself, and in enabling a noble action to subsist as it did in nature.

But the modern critic not only permits a false practice; he absolutely prescribes false aims.—"A true allegory of the state of one's own mind in a representative history," the poet is told, "is perhaps the highest thing that one can attempt in the way of poetry."[8] And accordingly he attempts it. An allegory of the state of one's own mind, the highest problem of an art which imitates actions! No assuredly, it is not, it never can be so: no great poetical work has ever been produced with such an aim. *Faust* itself, in which something of the kind is attempted, wonderful passages as it contains, and in spite of the unsurpassed beauty of the scenes which relate to Margaret, *Faust* itself, judged as a whole, and judged strictly as a poetical work, is defective: its illustrious author, the greatest poet of modern times, the greatest critic of all times, would have been the first to acknowledge it; he only defended his work, indeed, by asserting it to be "something incommensurable."[9]

The confusion of the present times is great, the multitude of voices counseling different things bewildering, the number of existing works capable of attracting a young writer's attention and of becoming his models, immense. What he wants is a hand to guide him through the confusion, a voice to prescribe to him the aim which he should keep in view, and to explain to him that the value of the literary works which offer themselves to his attention is relative to their power of helping him forward on his road towards this aim. Such a guide the English writer at the present day will nowhere find. Failing this, all that can be looked for, all indeed that can be desired is, that his attention should be fixed on excellent models; that he may reproduce, at any rate, something of their excellence, by penetrating himself with their works and by catching their spirit, if he cannot be taught to produce what is excellent independently.

8. *North British Review* 19 (Aug. 1853): 180 (U.S. edition). Arnold seems not to have noticed that Goethe (a critic he revered) had been cited earlier in the article as the authority for this critical generalization.
9. J. Eckermann's *Conversations with Goethe*, Jan. 3, 1830.

Foremost among these models for the English writer stands Shakespeare: a name the greatest perhaps of all poetical names; a name never to be mentioned without reverence. I will venture, however, to express a doubt, whether the influence of his works, excellent and fruitful for the readers of poetry, for the great majority, has been of unmixed advantage to the writers of it. Shakespeare indeed chose excellent subjects; the world could afford no better than Macbeth, or Romeo and Juliet, or Othello: he had no theory respecting the necessity of choosing subjects of present import, or the paramount interest attaching to allegories of the state of one's own mind; like all great poets, he knew well what constituted a poetical action; like them, wherever he found such an action, he took it; like them, too, he found his best in past times. But to these general characteristics of all great poets he added a special one of his own; a gift, namely, of happy, abundant, and ingenious expression, eminent and unrivaled: so eminent as irresistibly to strike the attention first in him, and even to throw into comparative shade his other excellences as a poet. Here has been the mischief. These other excellences were his fundamental excellences *as a poet;* what distinguishes the artist from the mere amateur, says Goethe, is *Architectonicè* in the highest sense;[1] that power of execution, which creates, forms, and constitutes: not the profoundness of single thoughts, not the richness of imagery, not the abundance of illustration. But these attractive accessories of a poetical work being more easily seized than the spirit of the whole, and these accessories being possessed by Shakespeare in an unequaled degree, a young writer having recourse to Shakespeare as his model runs great risk of being vanquished and absorbed by them, and, in consequence, of reproducing, according to the measure of his power, these, and these alone.[2] Of this preponderating quality of Shakespeare's genius, accordingly almost the whole of modern English poetry has, it appears to me, felt the influence. To the exclusive attention on the part of his imitators to this it is in a great degree owing, that of the majority of modern poetical works the details alone are valuable, the composition worthless. In reading them one is perpetually reminded of that terrible sentence on a modern French poet: *Il dit tout ce qu'il veut, mais malheureusement il n'a rien à dire.*[3]

Let me give an instance of what I mean. I will take it from the works of the very chief among those who seem to have been formed in the school of Shakespeare: of one whose exquisite genius and pathetic death render him forever interesting. I will take the poem of *Isabella, or the Pot of Basil*, by Keats. I choose this rather than the *Endymion*, because the latter work (which a modern critic has classed with the *Fairy Queen!*)[4] although undoubtedly there blows through it the breath of genius, is yet as a whole so utterly incoherent, as not strictly to merit the name of a poem at all. The poem of *Isabella*, then, is a perfect treasure house of graceful and felicitous

1. In the essay *Concerning the So-called Dilettantism* (1799) in his *Werke* (1851) 25.322.
2. Cf. Arnold's letter to Clough (Oct. 28, 1852):

> More and more I feel that the difference between a mature and a youthful age of the world compels the poetry of the former to use great plainness of speech . . . and that Keats and Shelley were on a false track when they set themselves to reproduce the exuberance of expression, the charm, the richness of images,

and the felicity, of the Elizabethan poets.
3. He says everything he wishes to, but unfortunately he has nothing to say (French). A comment on Théophile Gautier (1811–1872), whose emphasis on style was severely criticized by Arnold in his late essay *Wordsworth*.
4. In the *North British Review* 19 (Aug. 1853): 172–74, Keats's *Endymion* is twice linked with Spenser's *Faerie Queene* as "leisurely compositions of the sweet sensuous order."

words and images: almost in every stanza there occurs one of those vivid and picturesque turns of expression, by which the object is made to flash upon the eye of the mind, and which thrill the reader with a sudden delight. This one short poem contains, perhaps, a greater number of happy single expressions which one could quote than all the extant tragedies of Sophocles. But the action, the story? The action in itself is an excellent one; but so feebly is it conceived by the poet, so loosely constructed, that the effect produced by it, in and for itself, is absolutely null. Let the reader, after he has finished the poem of Keats, turn to the same story in the *Decameron*:[5] he will then feel how pregnant and interesting the same action has become in the hands of a great artist, who above all things delineates his object; who subordinates expression to that which it is designed to express.

I have said that the imitators of Shakespeare, fixing their attention on his wonderful gift of expression, have directed their imitation to this, neglecting his other excellences. These excellences, the fundamental excellences of poetical art, Shakespeare no doubt possessed them—possessed many of them in a splendid degree; but it may perhaps be doubted whether even he himself did not sometimes give scope to his faculty of expression to the prejudice of a higher poetical duty. For we must never forget that Shakespeare is the great poet he is from his skill in discerning and firmly conceiving an excellent action, from his power of intensely feeling a situation, of intimately associating himself with a character; not from his gift of expression, which rather even leads him astray, degenerating sometimes into a fondness for curiosity of expression, into an irritability of fancy, which seems to make it impossible for him to say a thing plainly, even when the press of the action demands the very direct language, or its level character the very simplest. Mr. Hallam, than whom it is impossible to find a saner and more judicious critic, has had the courage (for at the present day it needs courage) to remark, how extremely and faultily difficult Shakespeare's language often is.[6] It is so: you may find main scenes in some of his greatest tragedies, *King Lear* for instance, where the language is so artificial, so curiously tortured, and so difficult, that every speech has to be read two or three times before its meaning can be comprehended. This overcuriousness of expression is indeed but the excessive employment of a wonderful gift—of the power of saying a thing in a happier way than any other man; nevertheless, it is carried so far that one understands what M. Guizot meant, when he said that Shakespeare appears in his language to have tried all styles except that of simplicity.[7] He has not the severe and scrupulous self-restraint of the ancients, partly no doubt, because he had a far less cultivated and exacting audience. He has indeed a far wider range than they had, a far richer fertility of thought; in this respect he rises above them. In his strong conception of his subject, in the genuine way in which he is penetrated with it, he resembles them, and is unlike the moderns. But in the accurate limitation of it, the conscientious rejection of superfluities, the simple and rigorous development of it from the first line of his work to the last, he falls below them, and comes nearer to the moderns. In his chief works, besides what he has of his own, he has the

5. By Boccaccio: fourth day, fifth story.
6. *Introduction to the Literature of Europe* (1838–39), chap. 23, by Henry Hallam (1779–1859), historian.

7. F. P. G. Guizot (1787–1874), French historian discussing Shakespeare's sonnets in his *Shakespeare et son temps* (1852), 114.

elementary soundness of the ancients; he has their important action and their large and broad manner; but he has not their purity of method. He is therefore a less safe model; for what he has of his own is personal, and inseparable from his own rich nature; it may be imitated and exaggerated, it cannot be learned or applied as an art. He is above all suggestive; more valuable, therefore, to young writers as men than as artists. But clearness of arrangement, rigor of development, simplicity of style—these may to a certain extent be learned; and these may, I am convinced, be learned best from the ancients, who although infinitely less suggestive than Shakespeare, are thus, to the artist, more instructive.

What, then, it will be asked, are the ancients to be our sole models? the ancients with their comparatively narrow range of experience, and their widely different circumstances? Not, certainly, that which is narrow in the ancients, nor that in which we can no longer sympathize. An action like the action of the *Antigone* of Sophocles, which turns upon the conflict between the heroine's duty to her brother's corpse and that to the laws of her country, is no longer one in which it is possible that we should feel a deep interest. I am speaking too, it will be remembered, not of the best sources of intellectual stimulus for the general reader, but of the best models of instruction for the individual writer. This last may certainly learn of the ancients, better than anywhere else, three things which it is vitally important for him to know: the all-importance of the choice of a subject; the necessity of accurate construction; and the subordinate character of expression. He will learn from them how unspeakably superior is the effect of the one moral impression left by a great action treated as a whole, to the effect produced by the most striking single thought or by the happiest image. As he penetrates into the spirit of the great classical works, as he becomes gradually aware of their intense significance, their noble simplicity, and their calm pathos, he will be convinced that it is this effect, unity and profoundness of moral impression, at which the ancient poets aimed; that it is this which constitutes the grandeur of their works, and which makes them immortal. He will desire to direct his own efforts towards producing the same effect. Above all, he will deliver himself from the jargon of modern criticism, and escape the danger of producing poetical works conceived in the spirit of the passing time, and which partake of its transitoriness.

The present age makes great claims upon us; we owe it service, it will not be satisfied without our admiration. I know not how it is, but their commerce with the ancients appears to me to produce, in those who constantly practice it, a steadying and composing effect upon their judgment, not of literary works only, but of men and events in general. They are like persons who have had a very weighty and impressive experience; they are more truly than others under the empire of facts, and more independent of the language current among those with whom they live. They wish neither to applaud nor to revile their age; they wish to know what it is, what it can give them, and whether this is what they want. What they want, they know very well; they want to educe and cultivate what is best and noblest in themselves; they know, too, that this is no easy task—χαλεπόν, as Pittacus said, χαλεπόν ἐσθλὸν ἔμμεναι[8]—and they ask themselves sincerely whether their age and its literature can assist them in the attempt. If they are endeavoring to prac-

8. It is hard to be good (Greek); an aphorism of Pittacus (7th century B.C.E.).

tice any art, they remember the plain and simple proceedings of the old artists, who attained their grand results by penetrating themselves with some noble and significant action, not by inflating themselves with a belief in the pre-eminent importance and greatness of their own times. They do not talk of their mission, nor of interpreting their age, nor of the coming poet; all this, they know, is the mere delirium of vanity; their business is not to praise their age, but to afford to the men who live in it the highest pleasure which they are capable of feeling. If asked to afford this by means of subjects drawn from the age itself, they ask what special fitness the present age has for supplying them. They are told that it is an era of progress, an age commissioned to carry out the great ideas of industrial development and social amelioration. They reply that with all this they can do nothing; that the elements they need for the exercise of their art are great actions, calculated powerfully and delightfully to affect what is permanent in the human soul; that so far as the present age can supply such actions, they will gladly make use of them; but that an age wanting in moral grandeur can with difficulty supply such, and an age of spiritual discomfort with difficulty be powerfully and delightfully affected by them.

A host of voices will indignantly rejoin that the present age is inferior to the past neither in moral grandeur nor in spiritual health. He who possesses the discipline I speak of will content himself with remembering the judgments passed upon the present age, in this respect, by the two men, the one of strongest head, the other of widest culture, whom it has produced; by Goethe and by Niebuhr.[9] It will be sufficient for him that he knows the opinions held by these two great men respecting the present age and its literature; and that he feels assured in his own mind that their aims and demands upon life were such as he would wish, at any rate, his own to be; and their judgment as to what is impeding and disabling such as he may safely follow. He will not, however, maintain a hostile attitude towards the false pretensions of his age: he will content himself with not being overwhelmed by them. He will esteem himself fortunate if he can succeed in banishing from his mind all feelings of contradiction, and irritation, and impatience; in order to delight himself with the contemplation of some noble action of a heroic time, and to enable others, through his representation of it, to delight in it also.

I am far indeed from making any claim, for myself, that I possess this discipline; or for the following poems, that they breathe its spirit. But I say, that in the sincere endeavor to learn and practice, amid the bewildering confusion of our times, what is sound and true in poetical art, I seemed to myself to find the only sure guidance, the only solid footing, among the ancients. They, at any rate, knew what they wanted in art, and we do not. It is this uncertainty which is disheartening, and not hostile criticism. How often have I felt this when reading words of disparagement or of cavil: that it is the uncertainty as to what is really to be aimed at which makes our difficulty, not the dissatisfaction of the critic, who himself suffers from the same uncertainty. *Non me tua fervida terrent Dicta; . . . Dii me terrent, et Jupiter hostis.*[1]

---

9. B. G. Niebuhr (1776–1831), German historian.
1. Your fiery speeches do not frighten me; . . . it is the gods and the enmity of Jupiter that frighten me

(Latin); from Virgil's *Aeneid* 12.894–95. Turnus, a warrior abandoned by the gods, is replying to Aeneas, who has taunted him with being afraid.

Two kinds of *dilettanti,* says Goethe, there are in poetry: he who neglects the indispensable mechanical part, and thinks he has done enough if he shows spirituality and feeling; and he who seeks to arrive at poetry merely by mechanism, in which he can acquire an artisan's readiness, and is without soul and matter. And he adds, that the first does most harm to art, and the last to himself. If we must be *dilettanti;* if it is impossible for us, under the circumstances amidst which we live, to think clearly, to feel nobly, and to delineate firmly; if we cannot attain to the mastery of the great artists; let us, at least, have so much respect for our art as to prefer it to ourselves. Let us not bewilder our successors; let us transmit to them the practice of poetry, with its boundaries and wholesome regulative laws, under which excellent works may again, perhaps, at some future time, be produced, not yet fallen into oblivion through our neglect, not yet condemned and canceled by the influence of their eternal enemy, caprice.

From The Function of Criticism at the Present Time[1]

Many objections have been made to a proposition which, in some remarks of mine on translating Homer,[2] I ventured to put forth; a proposition about criticism, and its importance at the present day. I said: "Of the literature of France and Germany, as of the intellect of Europe in general, the main effort, for now many years, has been a critical effort; the endeavor, in all branches of knowledge, theology, philosophy, history, art, science, to see the object as in itself it really is." I added, that owing to the operation in English literature of certain causes, "almost the last thing for which one would come to English literature is just that very thing which now Europe most desires—criticism"; and that the power and value of English literature was thereby impaired. More than one rejoinder declared that the importance I here assigned to criticism was excessive, and asserted the inherent superiority of the creative effort of the human spirit over its critical effort. And the other day, having been led by a Mr. Shairp's excellent notice of Wordsworth[3] to turn again to his biography, I found, in the words of this great man, whom I, for one, must always listen to with the profoundest respect, a sentence passed on the critic's business, which seems to justify every possible disparagement of it. Wordsworth says in one of his letters:

1. This essay served as an introduction to *Essays in Criticism* (1865). As a declaration of intentions it can serve as a standard for measuring his total accomplishment in criticism. The essay makes us aware that criticism, for Arnold, meant a great deal more than casual book reviewing or mere censoriousness. He was not a Utilitarian, yet his object in this essay is to show that good criticism is useful. Creative writers, he argues, can profit in a special way from good criticism, but all of us can also derive from it benefits of the greatest value. In particular, we may develop a civilized attitude of mind in which to examine the social, political, aesthetic, and religious problems that confront us.
2. *On Translating Homer* (1861).
3. J. C. Shairp's essay *Wordsworth: The Man and the Poet* was published in 1864. Arnold comments

in a footnote:

I cannot help thinking that a practice, common in England during the last century, and still followed in France, of printing a notice of this kind—a notice by a competent critic—to serve as an introduction to an eminent author's works, might be revived among us with advantage. To introduce all succeeding editions of Wordsworth, Mr. Shairp's notice might, it seems to me, excellently serve; it is written from the point of view of an admirer, nay, of a disciple, and that is right; but then the disciple must be also, as in this case he is, a critic, a man of letters, not, as too often happens, some relation or friend with no qualification for his task except affection for his author.

The writers in these publications (the Reviews), while they prosecute their inglorious employment, cannot be supposed to be in a state of mind very favorable for being affected by the finer influences of a thing so pure as genuine poetry.

And a trustworthy reporter of his conversation quotes a more elaborate judgment to the same effect:

> Wordsworth holds the critical power very low, infinitely lower than the inventive; and he said today that if the quantity of time consumed in writing critiques on the works of others were given to original composition, of whatever kind it might be, it would be much better employed; it would make a man find out sooner his own level, and it would do infinitely less mischief. A false or malicious criticism may do much injury to the minds of others; a stupid invention, either in prose or verse, is quite harmless.

It is almost too much to expect of poor human nature, that a man capable of producing some effect in one line of literature, should, for the greater good of society, voluntarily doom himself to impotence and obscurity in another. Still less is this to be expected from men addicted to the composition of the "false or malicious criticism" of which Wordsworth speaks. However, everybody would admit that a false or malicious criticism had better never have been written. Everybody, too, would be willing to admit, as a general proposition, that the critical faculty is lower than the inventive. But is it true that criticism is really, in itself, a baneful and injurious employment; is it true that all time given to writing critiques on the works of others would be much better employed if it were given to original composition, of whatever kind this may be? Is it true that Johnson had better have gone on producing more Irenes[4] instead of writing his Lives of the Poets; nay, is it certain that Wordsworth himself was better employed in making his Ecclesiastical Sonnets than when he made his celebrated Preface[5] so full of criticism, and criticism of the works of others? Wordsworth was himself a great critic, and it is to be sincerely regretted that he has not left us more criticism; Goethe was one of the greatest of critics, and we may sincerely congratulate ourselves that he has left us so much criticism. Without wasting time over the exaggeration which Wordsworth's judgment on criticism clearly contains, or over an attempt to trace the causes—not difficult, I think, to be traced—which may have led Wordsworth to this exaggeration, a critic may with advantage seize an occasion for trying his own conscience, and for asking himself of what real service, at any given moment, the practice of criticism either is or may be made to his own mind and spirit, and to the minds and spirits of others.

The critical power is of lower rank than the creative. True; but in assenting to this proposition, one or two things are to be kept in mind. It is undeniable that the exercise of a creative power, that a free creative activity, is the highest function of man; it is proved to be so by man's finding in it his true happiness. But it is undeniable, also, that men may have the sense of exer-

---

4. *Irene* is the name of a clumsy play by Samuel Johnson.
5. To *Lyrical Ballads* (1800). "Ecclesiastical Son-

nets": a sonnet sequence by Wordsworth, usually regarded as minor verse.

cising this free creative activity in other ways than in producing great works of literature or art; if it were not so, all but a very few men would be shut out from the true happiness of all men. They may have it in well-doing, they may have it in learning, they may have it even in criticizing. This is one thing to be kept in mind. Another is, that the exercise of the creative power in the production of great works of literature or art, however high this exercise of it may rank, is not at all epochs and under all conditions possible; and that therefore labor may be vainly spent in attempting it, which might with more fruit be used in preparing for it, in rendering it possible. This creative power works with elements, with materials; what if it has not those materials, those elements, ready for its use? In that case it must surely wait till they are ready. Now, in literature—I will limit myself to literature, for it is about literature that the question arises—the elements with which the creative power works are ideas; the best ideas on every matter which literature touches, current at the time. At any rate we may lay it down as certain that in modern literature no manifestation of the creative power not working with these can be very important or fruitful. And I say *current* at the time, not merely accessible at the time; for creative literary genius does not principally show itself in discovering new ideas, that is rather the business of the philosopher. The grand work of literary genius is a work of synthesis and exposition, not of analysis and discovery; its gift lies in the faculty of being happily inspired by a certain intellectual and spiritual atmosphere, by a certain order of ideas, when it finds itself in them; of dealing divinely with these ideas, presenting them in the most effective and attractive combinations—making beautiful works with them, in short. But it must have the atmosphere, it must find itself amidst the order of ideas, in order to work freely; and these it is not so easy to command. This is why great creative epochs in literature are so rare, this is why there is so much that is unsatisfactory in the productions of many men of real genius; because, for the creation of a masterwork of literature two powers must concur, the power of the man and the power of the moment, and the man is not enough without the moment; the creative power has, for its happy exercise, appointed elements, and those elements are not in its own control.

Nay, they are more within the control of the critical power. It is the business of the critical power, as I said in the words already quoted, "in all branches of knowledge, theology, philosophy, history, art, science, to see the object as in itself it really is." Thus it tends, at last, to make an intellectual situation of which the creative power can profitably avail itself. It tends to establish an order of ideas, if not absolutely true, yet true by comparison with that which it displaces; to make the best ideas prevail. Presently these new ideas reach society, the touch of truth is the touch of life, and there is a stir and growth everywhere; out of this stir and growth come the creative epochs of literature.

Or, to narrow our range, and quit these considerations of the general march of genius and of society—considerations which are apt to become too abstract and impalpable—everyone can see that a poet, for instance, ought to know life and the world before dealing with them in poetry; and life and the world being in modern times very complex things, the creation of a modern poet, to be worth much, implies a great critical effort behind it; else it must be a comparatively poor, barren, and short-lived affair. This is why Byron's poetry had so little endurance in it, and Goethe's so much; both

Byron and Goethe had a great productive power, but Goethe's was nourished by a great critical effort providing the true materials for it, and Byron's was not; Goethe knew life and the world, the poet's necessary subjects, much more comprehensively and thoroughly than Byron. He knew a great deal more of them, and he knew them much more as they really are.

It has long seemed to me that the burst of creative activity in our literature, through the first quarter of this century, had about it in fact something premature; and that from this cause its productions are doomed, most of them, in spite of the sanguine hopes which accompanied and do still accompany them, to prove hardly more lasting than the productions of far less splendid epochs. And this prematureness comes from its having proceeded without having its proper data, without sufficient materials to work with. In other words, the English poetry of the first quarter of this century, with plenty of energy, plenty of creative force, did not know enough. This makes Byron so empty of matter, Shelley so incoherent, Wordsworth even, profound as he is, yet so wanting in completeness and variety. Wordsworth cared little for books, and disparaged Goethe. I admire Wordsworth, as he is, so much that I cannot wish him different; and it is vain, no doubt, to imagine such a man different from what he is, to suppose that he *could* have been different. But surely the one thing wanting to make Wordsworth an even greater poet than he is—his thought richer, and his influence of wider application—was that he should have read more books, among them, no doubt, those of that Goethe whom he disparaged without reading him.

But to speak of books and reading may easily lead to a misunderstanding here. It was not really books and reading that lacked to our poetry at this epoch: Shelley had plenty of reading, Coleridge had immense reading. Pindar and Sophocles—as we all say so glibly, and often with so little discernment of the real import of what we are saying—had not many books; Shakespeare was no deep reader. True; but in the Greece of Pindar and Sophocles, in the England of Shakespeare, the poet lived in a current of ideas in the highest degree animating and nourishing to the creative power; society was, in the fullest measure, permeated by fresh thought, intelligent and alive. And this state of things is the true basis for the creative power's exercise, in this it finds its data, its materials, truly ready for its hand; all the books and reading in the world are only valuable as they are helps to this. Even when this does not actually exist, books and reading may enable a man to construct a kind of semblance of it in his own mind, a world of knowledge and intelligence in which he may live and work. This is by no means an equivalent to the artist for the nationally diffused life and thought of the epochs of Sophocles or Shakespeare; but, besides that it may be a means of preparation for such epochs, it does really constitute, if many share in it, a quickening and sustaining atmosphere of great value. Such an atmosphere the many-sided learning and the long and widely combined critical effort of Germany formed for Goethe, when he lived and worked. There was no national glow of life and thought there as in the Athens of Pericles[6] or the England of Elizabeth. That was the poet's weakness. But there was a sort of equivalent for it in the complete culture and unfettered thinking of a large body of Germans. That

---

6. The leading statesman of Athens (d. 429 B.C.E.) during a period of the city's most outstanding achievements in art, literature, and politics.

was his strength. In the England of the first quarter of this century there was neither a national glow of life and thought, such as we had in the age of Elizabeth, nor yet a culture and a force of learning and criticism such as were to be found in Germany. Therefore the creative power of poetry wanted, for success in the highest sense, materials and a basis; a thorough interpretation of the world was necessarily denied to it.

At first sight it seems strange that out of the immense stir of the French Revolution and its age should not have come a crop of works of genius equal to that which came out of the stir of the great productive time of Greece, or out of that of the Renascence, with its powerful episode the Reformation. But the truth is that the stir of the French Revolution took a character which essentially distinguished it from such movements as these. These were, in the main, disinterestedly intellectual and spiritual movements; movements in which the human spirit looked for its satisfaction in itself and in the increased play of its own activity. The French Revolution took a political, practical character. The movement, which went on in France under the old *régime,* from 1700 to 1789, was far more really akin than that of the Revolution itself to the movement of the Renascence; the France of Voltaire and Rousseau told far more powerfully upon the mind of Europe than the France of the Revolution. Goethe reproached this last expressly with having "thrown quiet culture back." Nay, and the true key to how much in our Byron, even in our Wordsworth, is this!—that they had their source in a great movement of feeling, not in a great movement of mind. The French Revolution, however— that object of so much blind love and so much blind hatred—found undoubtedly its motive power in the intelligence of men, and not in their practical sense; this is what distinguishes it from the English Revolution of Charles the First's time. This is what makes it a more spiritual event than our Revolution, an event of much more powerful and worldwide interest, though practically less successful; it appeals to an order of ideas which are universal, certain, permanent. 1789 asked of a thing, Is it rational? 1642 asked of a thing, Is it legal? or, when it went furthest, Is it according to conscience? This is the English fashion, a fashion to be treated, within its own sphere, with the highest respect; for its success, within its own sphere, has been prodigious. But what is law in one place is not law in another; what is law here today is not law even here tomorrow; and as for conscience, what is binding on one man's conscience is not binding on another's. The old woman who threw her stool at the head of the surpliced minister in St. Giles's Church at Edinburgh[7] obeyed an impulse to which millions of the human race may be permitted to remain strangers. But the prescriptions of reason are absolute, unchanging, of universal validity; *to count by tens is the easiest way of counting*—that is a proposition of which everyone, from here to the Antipodes, feels the force; at least I should say so if we did not live in a country where it is not impossible that any morning we may find a letter in the *Times* declaring that a decimal coinage is an absurdity.[8] That a whole nation should have been penetrated with an enthusiasm for pure reason, and with an ardent zeal for making its prescriptions triumph, is a very remarkable thing, when we consider how lit-

---

7. In 1637 rioting broke out in Scotland against a new kind of church service prescribed by Charles I. The riot was started by an old woman hurling a stool at a clergyman.
8. In 1863 a proposal in Parliament to introduce the French decimal system for weights and measures had provoked articles in the *Times* defending the English system (of ounces and pounds or inches and feet) as more practical.

tle of mind, or anything so worthy and quickening as mind, comes into the motives which alone, in general, impel great masses of men. In spite of the extravagant direction given to this enthusiasm, in spite of the crimes and follies in which it lost itself, the French Revolution derives from the force, truth, and universality of the ideas which it took for its law, and from the passion with which it could inspire a multitude for these ideas, a unique and still living power; it is—it will probably long remain—the greatest, the most animating event in history. And as no sincere passion for the things of the mind, even though it turn out in many respects an unfortunate passion, is ever quite thrown away and quite barren of good, France has reaped from hers one fruit—the natural and legitimate fruit though not precisely the grand fruit she expected: she is the country in Europe where *the people* is most alive.

But the mania for giving an immediate political and practical application to all these fine ideas of the reason was fatal. Here an Englishman is in his element: on this theme we can all go on for hours. And all we are in the habit of saying on it has undoubtedly a great deal of truth. Ideas cannot be too much prized in and for themselves, cannot be too much lived with; but to transport them abruptly into the world of politics and practice, violently to revolutionize this world to their bidding—that is quite another thing. There is the world of ideas and there is the world of practice; the French are often for suppressing the one and the English the other; but neither is to be suppressed. A member of the House of Commons said to me the other day: "That a thing is an anomaly, I consider to be no objection to it whatever." I venture to think he was wrong; that a thing is an anomaly *is* an objection to it, but absolutely and in the sphere of ideas: it is not necessarily, under such and such circumstances, or at such and such a moment, an objection to it in the sphere of politics and practice. Joubert[9] has said beautifully: "*C'est la force et le droit qui règlent toutes choses dans le monde; la force en attendant le droit.*"—"*Force and right are the governors of this world; force till right is ready.*" *Force till right is ready;* and till right is ready, force, the existing order of things, is justified, is the legitimate ruler. But right is something moral, and implies inward recognition, free assent of the will; we are not ready for right—*right,* so far as we are concerned, is *not ready*—until we have attained this sense of seeing it and willing it. The way in which for us it may change and transform force, the existing order of things, and become, in its turn, the legitimate ruler of the world, should depend on the way in which, when our time comes, we see it and will it. Therefore for other people enamored of their own newly discerned right, to attempt to impose it upon us as ours, and violently to substitute their right for our force, is an act of tyranny, and to be resisted. It sets at nought the second great half of our maxim, *force till right is ready.* This was the grand error of the French Revolution; and its movement of ideas, by quitting the intellectual sphere and rushing furiously into the political sphere, ran, indeed a prodigious and memorable course, but produced no such intellectual fruit as the movement of ideas of the Renascence, and created, in opposition to itself, what I may call an *epoch of concentration.* The great force of that epoch of concentration was England; and the great voice of that epoch of concentration was Burke.[1] It is the

---

9. Joseph Joubert (1754–1824), French moralist about whom Arnold wrote one of his *Essays in Criticism.*

1. Edmund Burke (1729–1797), prominent statesman and author of *Reflections on the French Revolution* (1790), which expressed the conservative opposition to revolutionary theories.

fashion to treat Burke's writings on the French Revolution as superannuated and conquered by the event; as the eloquent but unphilosophical tirades of bigotry and prejudice. I will not deny that they are often disfigured by the violence and passion of the moment, and that in some directions Burke's view was bounded, and his observation therefore at fault. But on the whole, and for those who can make the needful corrections, what distinguishes these writings is their profound, permanent, fruitful, philosophical truth, They contain the true philosophy of an epoch of concentration, dissipate the heavy atmosphere which its own nature is apt to engender round it, and make its resistance rational instead of mechanical.

But Burke is so great because, almost alone in England, he brings thought to bear upon politics, he saturates politics with thought. It is his accident that his ideas were at the service of an epoch of concentration, not of an epoch of expansion; it is his characteristic that he so lived by ideas, and had such a source of them welling up within him, that he could float even an epoch of concentration and English Tory politics with them. It does not hurt him that Dr. Price[2] and the Liberals were enraged with him; it does not even hurt him that George the Third and the Tories were enchanted with him. His greatness is that he lived in a world which neither English Liberalism nor English Toryism is apt to enter—the world of ideas, not the world of catchwords and party habits. So far is it from being really true of him that he "to party gave up what was meant for mankind,"[3] that at the very end of his fierce struggle with the French Revolution, after all his invectives against its false pretensions, hollowness, and madness, with his sincere convictions of its mischievousness, he can close a memorandum on the best means of combating it, some of the last pages he ever wrote[4]—the *Thoughts on French Affairs*, in December 1791—with these striking words:

> The evil is stated, in my opinion, as it exists. The remedy must be where power, wisdom, and information, I hope, are more united with good intentions than they can be with me. I have done with this subject, I believe, forever. It has given me many anxious moments for the last two years. *If a great change is to be made in human affairs, the minds of men will be fitted to it; the general opinions and feelings will draw that way. Every fear, every hope will forward it; and then they who persist in opposing this mighty current in human affairs, will appear rather to resist the decrees of Providence itself, than the mere designs of men. They will not be resolute and firm, but perverse and obstinate.*

That return of Burke upon himself has always seemed to me one of the finest things in English literature, or indeed in any literature. That is what I call living by ideas: when one side of a question has long had your earnest support, when all your feelings are engaged, when you hear all round you no language but one, when your party talks this language like a steam engine and can imagine no other—still to be able to think, still to be irresistibly carried, if so it be, by the current of thought to the opposite side of the

---

2. Richard Price (1723–1791), a prorevolutionary clergyman who was an opponent of Burke's.
3. From Oliver Goldsmith's poem *Retaliation* (1774).
4. Arnold was mistaken; Burke continued to write

for another six years after 1791. According to Arnold's editor, R. H. Super, the mistake was caused by misunderstanding a passage in one of Burke's letters.

question, and, like Balaam, to be unable to speak anything *but what the Lord has put in your mouth.*[5] I know nothing more striking, and I must add that I know nothing more un-English.

For the Englishman in general is like my friend the Member of Parliament, and believes, point-blank, that for a thing to be an anomaly is absolutely no objection to it whatever. He is like the Lord Auckland of Burke's day, who, in a memorandum on the French Revolution, talks of certain "miscreants, assuming the name of philosophers, who have presumed themselves capable of establishing a new system of society." The Englishman has been called a political animal, and he values what is political and practical so much that ideas easily become objects of dislike in his eyes, and thinkers, "miscreants," because ideas and thinkers have rashly meddled with politics and practice. This would be all very well if the dislike and neglect confined themselves to ideas transported out of their own sphere, and meddling rashly with practice; but they are inevitably extended to ideas as such, and to the whole life of intelligence; practice is everything, a free play of the mind is nothing. The notion of the free play of the mind upon all subjects being a pleasure in itself, being an object of desire, being an essential provider of elements without which a nation's spirit, whatever compensations it may have for them, must, in the long run, die of inanition, hardly enters into an Englishman's thoughts. It is noticeable that the word *curiosity,* which in other languages is used in a good sense, to mean, as a high and fine quality of man's nature, just this disinterested love of a free play of the mind on all subjects, for its own sake— it is noticeable, I say, that this word has in our language no sense of the kind, no sense but a rather bad and disparaging one. But criticism, real criticism, is essentially the exercise of this very quality. It obeys an instinct prompting it to try to know the best that is known and thought in the world, irrespectively of practice, politics, and everything of the kind; and to value knowledge and thought as they approach this best, without the intrusion of any other considerations whatever. This is an instinct for which there is, I think, little original sympathy in the practical English nature, and what there was of it has undergone a long benumbing period of blight and suppression in the epoch of concentration which followed the French Revolution.

But epochs of concentration cannot well endure forever; epochs of expansion, in the due course of things, follow them. Such an epoch of expansion seems to be opening in this country. In the first place all danger of a hostile forcible pressure of foreign ideas upon our practice has long disappeared; like the traveler in the fable, therefore, we begin to wear our cloak a little more loosely.[6] Then, with a long peace, the ideas of Europe steal gradually and amicably in, and mingle, though in infinitesimally small quantities at a time, with our own notions. Then, too, in spite of all that is said about the absorbing and brutalizing influence of our passionate material progress, it seems to me indisputable that this progress is likely, though not certain, to lead in the end to an apparition of intellectual life; and that man, after he has made himself perfectly comfortable and has now to determine what to do with himself next, may begin to remember that he has a mind, and that the mind may be made the source of great pleasure. I grant it is mainly the

5. Cf. Numbers 22.38.
6. See Aesop's fable of the wind and the sun, in which the wind and the sun compete to see who is more powerful. The sun wins because he causes the traveler to take off his coat, whereas the wind makes him hold it closely.

privilege of faith, at present, to discern this end to our railways, our business, and our fortune-making; but we shall see if, here as elsewhere, faith is not in the end the true prophet. Our ease, our traveling, and our unbounded liberty to hold just as hard and securely as we please to the practice to which our notions have given birth, all tend to beget an inclination to deal a little more freely with these notions themselves, to canvass them a little, to penetrate a little into their real nature. Flutterings of curiosity, in the foreign sense of the word, appear amongst us, and it is in these that criticism must look to find its account. Criticism first; a time of true creative activity, perhaps—which, as I have said, must inevitably be preceded amongst us by a time of criticism—hereafter, when criticism has done its work.

It is of the last importance that English criticism should clearly discern what rule for its course, in order to avail itself of the field now opening to it, and to produce fruit for the future, it ought to take. The rule may be summed up in one word—*disinterestedness*.[7] And how is criticism to show disinterestedness? By keeping aloof from what is called "the practical view of things"; by resolutely following the law of its own nature, which is to be a free play of the mind on all subjects which it touches. By steadily refusing to lend itself to any of those ulterior, political, practical considerations about ideas, which plenty of people will be sure to attach to them, which perhaps ought often to be attached to them, which in this country at any rate are certain to be attached to them quite sufficiently, but which criticism has really nothing to do with. Its business is, as I have said, simply to know the best that is known and thought in the world, and by in its turn making this known, to create a current of true and fresh ideas. Its business is to do this with inflexible honesty, with due ability; but its business is to do no more, and to leave alone all questions of practical consequences and applications, questions which will never fail to have due prominence given to them. Else criticism, besides being really false to its own nature, merely continues in the old rut which it has hitherto followed in this country, and will certainly miss the chance now given to it. For what is at present the bane of criticism in this country? It is that practical considerations cling to it and stifle it. It subserves interests not its own. Our organs of criticism are organs of men and parties having practical ends to serve, and with them those practical ends are the first thing and the play of mind the second; so much play of mind as is compatible with the prosecution of those practical ends is all that is wanted. An organ like the *Revue des Deux Mondes*,[8] having for its main function to understand and utter the best that is known and thought in the world, existing, it may be said, as just an organ for a free play of the mind, we have not. But we have the *Edinburgh Review*, existing as an organ of the old Whigs, and for as much play of mind as may suit its being that; we have the *Quarterly Review*, existing as an organ of the Tories, and for as much play of mind as may suit its being that; we have the *British Quarterly Review*, existing as an organ of the political Dissenters, and for as much play of mind as may suit its being that; we have the *Times*, existing as an organ of the common, satisfied, well-to-do Englishman, and for as much play of mind as may suit its being that. And so on through all the various fractions, political and religious, of our society; every fraction has, as such, its organ of criticism, but the

7. This key word in Arnold's argument connotes independence and objectivity of mind. It means not having an interest, in the sense of an ax to grind. It does not mean lack of interest.
8. An international magazine of exceptionally high quality, founded in Paris in 1829.

notion of combining all fractions in the common pleasure of a free disinterested play of mind meets with no favor. Directly this play of mind wants to have more scope, and to forget the pressure of practical considerations a little, it is checked, it is made to feel the chain. We saw this the other day in the extinction, so much to be regretted, of the *Home and Foreign Review*.[9] Perhaps in no organ of criticism in this country was there so much knowledge, so much play of mind; but these could not save it. The *Dublin Review* subordinates play of mind to the practical business of English and Irish Catholicism, and lives. It must needs be that men should act in sects and parties, that each of these sects and parties should have its organ, and should make this organ subserve the interests of its action; but it would be well, too, that there should be a criticism, not the minister of these interests, not their enemy, but absolutely and entirely independent of them. No other criticism will ever attain any real authority or make any real way towards its end—the creating a current of true and fresh ideas.

It is because criticism has so little kept in the pure intellectual sphere, has so little detached itself from practice, has been so directly polemical and controversial, that it has so ill accomplished, in this country, its best spiritual work, which is to keep man from a self-satisfaction which is retarding and vulgarizing, to lead him towards perfection, by making his mind dwell upon what is excellent in itself, and the absolute beauty and fitness of things. A polemical practical criticism makes men blind even to the ideal imperfection of their practice, makes them willingly assert its ideal perfection, in order the better to secure it against attack; and clearly this is narrowing and baneful for them. If they were reassured on the practical side, speculative considerations of ideal perfection they might be brought to entertain, and their spiritual horizon would thus gradually widen. Sir Charles Adderley[1] says to the Warwickshire farmers:

> Talk of the improvement of breed! Why, the race we ourselves represent, the men and women, the old Anglo-Saxon race, are the best breed in the whole world. . . . The absence of a too enervating climate, too unclouded skies, and a too luxurious nature, has produced so vigorous a race of people, and has rendered us so superior to all the world.

Mr. Roebuck[2] says to the Sheffield cutlers:

> I look around me and ask what is the state of England? Is not property safe? Is not every man able to say what he likes? Can you not walk from one end of England to the other in perfect security? I ask you whether, the world over or in past history, there is anything like it? Nothing. I pray that our unrivaled happiness may last.

Now obviously there is a peril for poor human nature in words and thoughts of such exuberant self-satisfaction, until we find ourselves safe in the streets of the Celestial City.

> *Das wenige verschwindet leicht dem Blicke*
> *Der vorwärts sieht, wie viel noch übrig bleibt—*[3]

---

9. A liberal Catholic periodical, founded in 1862, which ceased publication in 1864.
1. Conservative politician and wealthy landowner (1814–1905).

2. John Arthur Roebuck (1801–1879), radical politician and representative in Parliament for the industrial city of Sheffield.
3. Goethe's *Iphigenie auf Tauris* 1.2.91–92.

says Goethe; "the little that is done seems nothing when we look forward and see how much we have yet to do." Clearly this is a better line of reflection for weak humanity, so long as it remains on this earthly field of labor and trial.

But neither Sir Charles Adderley nor Mr. Roebuck is by nature inaccessible to considerations of this sort. They only lose sight of them owing to the controversial life we all lead, and the practical form which all speculation takes with us. They have in view opponents whose aim is not ideal, but practical; and in their zeal to uphold their own practice against these innovators, they go so far as even to attribute to this practice an ideal perfection. Somebody has been wanting to introduce a six-pound franchise, or to abolish church-rates,[4] or to collect agricultural statistics by force, or to diminish local self-government. How natural, in reply to such proposals, very likely improper or ill-timed, to go a little beyond the mark and to say stoutly, "Such a race of people as we stand, so superior to all the world! The old Anglo-Saxon race, the best breed in the whole world! I pray that our unrivaled happiness may last! I ask you whether, the world over or in past history, there is anything like it?" And so long as criticism answers this dithyramb by insisting that the old Anglo-Saxon race would be still more superior to all others if it had no church-rates, or that our unrivaled happiness would last yet longer with a six-pound franchise, so long will the strain, "The best breed in the whole world!" swell louder and louder, everything ideal and refining will be lost out of sight, and both the assailed and their critics will remain in a sphere, to say the truth, perfectly unvital, a sphere in which spiritual progression is impossible. But let criticism leave church-rates and the franchise alone, and in the most candid spirit, without a single lurking thought of practical innovation, confront with our dithyramb this paragraph on which I stumbled in a newspaper immediately after reading Mr. Roebuck:

> A shocking child murder has just been committed at Nottingham. A girl named Wragg left the workhouse there on Saturday morning with her young illegitimate child. The child was soon afterwards found dead on Mapperly Hills, having been strangled. Wragg is in custody.

Nothing but that; but, in juxtaposition with the absolute eulogies of Sir Charles Adderley and Mr. Roebuck, how eloquent, how suggestive are those few lines! "Our old Anglo-Saxon breed, the best in the whole world!"—how much that is harsh and ill-favored there is in this best! *Wragg!* If we are to talk of ideal perfection, of "the best in the whole world," has anyone reflected what a touch of grossness in our race, what an original shortcoming in the more delicate spiritual perceptions, is shown by the natural growth amongst us of such hideous names—Higginbottom, Stiggins, Bugg! In Ionia and Attica they were luckier in this respect than "the best race in the world"; by the Ilissus[5] there was no Wragg, poor thing! And "our unrivaled happiness"— what an element of grimness, bareness, and hideousness mixes with it and blurs it; the workhouse, the dismal Mapperly Hills[6]—how dismal those who have seen them will remember—the gloom, the smoke, the cold, the stran-

---

4. Taxes supporting the Church of England. "Six-pound franchise": a radical proposal to extend the right to vote to anyone owning land worth £6 annual rent.

5. A stream in Attica, Greece.
6. Adjacent to the coal-mining and industrial area of Nottingham (later associated with the writings of D. H. Lawrence).

gled illegitimate child! "I ask you whether, the world over or in past history, there is anything like it?" Perhaps not, one is inclined to answer; but at any rate, in that case, the world is very much to be pitied. And the final touch—short, bleak and inhuman: *Wragg is in custody.* The sex lost in the confusion of our unrivaled happiness; or (shall I say?) the superfluous Christian name lopped off by the straightforward vigor of our old Anglo-Saxon breed! There is profit for the spirit in such contrasts as this; criticism serves the cause of perfection by establishing them. By eluding sterile conflict, by refusing to remain in the sphere where alone narrow and relative conceptions have any worth and validity, criticism may diminish its momentary importance, but only in this way has it a chance of gaining admittance for those wider and more perfect conceptions to which all its duty is really owed. Mr. Roebuck will have a poor opinion of an adversary who replies to his defiant songs of triumph only by murmuring under his breath, *Wragg is in custody;* but in no other way will these songs of triumph be induced gradually to moderate themselves, to get rid of what in them is excessive and offensive, and to fall into a softer and truer key.

It will be said that it is a very subtle and indirect action which I am thus prescribing for criticism, and that, by embracing in this manner the Indian virtue of detachment and abandoning the sphere of practical life, it condemns itself to a slow and obscure work. Slow and obscure it may be, but it is the only proper work of criticism. The mass of mankind will never have any ardent zeal for seeing things as they are; very inadequate ideas will always satisfy them. On these inadequate ideas reposes, and must repose, the general practice of the world. That is as much as saying that whoever sets himself to see things as they are will find himself one of a very small circle; but it is only by this small circle resolutely doing its own work that adequate ideas will ever get current at all. The rush and roar of practical life will always have a dizzying and attracting effect upon the most collected spectator, and tend to draw him into its vortex; most of all will this be the case where that life is so powerful as it is in England. But it is only by remaining collected, and refusing to lend himself to the point of view of the practical man, that the critic can do the practical man any service, and it is only by the greatest sincerity in pursuing his own course, and by at last convincing even the practical man of his sincerity, that he can escape misunderstandings which perpetually threaten him.

For the practical man is not apt for fine distinctions, and yet in these distinctions truth and the highest culture greatly find their account. But it is not easy to lead a practical man—unless you reassure him as to your practical intentions, you have no chance of leading him—to see that a thing which he has always been used to look at from one side only, which he greatly values, and which, looked at from that side, quite deserves, perhaps, all the prizing and admiring which he bestows upon it—that this thing, looked at from another side, may appear much less beneficent and beautiful, and yet retain all its claims to our practical allegiance. Where shall we find language innocent enough, how shall we make the spotless purity of our intentions evident enough, to enable us to say to the political Englishman that the British Constitution itself, which, seen from the practical side, looks such a magnificent organ of progress and virtue, seen from the speculative side—with its compromises, its love of facts, its horror of theory, its studied avoidance of clear thoughts—that, seen from this side, our august Constitution sometimes looks—forgive me, shade of Lord Somers!—a colossal machine for the manufacture of Philistines?[7] How is Cobbett[8] to say this and not be misunderstood, blackened as he is with the smoke of a lifelong conflict in the field of political practice? how is Mr. Carlyle to say it and not be misunderstood, after his furious raid into this field with his *Latter-day Pamphlets*? how is Mr. Ruskin, after his pugnacious political economy?[9] I say, the critic must keep out of the region of immediate practice in the political, social, humanitarian sphere if he wants to make a beginning for that more free speculative treatment of things, which may perhaps one day make its benefits felt even in this sphere, but in a natural and thence irresistible manner.

* * *

If I have insisted so much on the course which criticism must take where politics and religion are concerned, it is because, where these burning matters are in question, it is most likely to go astray. I have wished, above all, to insist on the attitude which criticism should adopt towards things in general; on its right tone and temper of mind. But then comes another question as to the subject matter which literary criticism should most seek. Here, in general, its course is determined for it by the idea which is the law of its being; the idea of a disinterested endeavor to learn and propagate the best that is known and thought in the world, and thus to establish a current of fresh and true ideas. By the very nature of things, as England is not all the world, much of the best that is known and thought in the world cannot be of English growth, must be foreign; by the nature of things, again, it is just this that we are least likely to know, while English thought is streaming in upon us from all sides, and takes excellent care that we shall not be ignorant of its existence. The English critic of literature, therefore, must dwell much on foreign thought, and with particular heed on any part of it, which, while significant and fruitful in itself, is for any reason specially likely to escape him. Again, judging is often spoken of as the critic's one business, and so in some sense it is; but the judgment which almost insensibly forms itself in a fair and clear mind, along with fresh knowledge, is the valuable one; and thus knowledge, and ever fresh knowledge, must be the critic's great concern for himself. And it is by communicating fresh knowledge, and letting his own judgment pass along with it—but insensibly, and in the second place, not the first, as a sort of companion and clue, not as an abstract lawgiver—that the critic will generally do most good to his readers. Sometimes, no doubt, for the sake of establishing an author's place in literature, and his relation to a central standard (and if this is not done, how are we to get at our *best in the world*?) criticism may have to deal with a subject matter so familiar that fresh knowledge is out of the question, and then it must be all judgment; an enunciation and detailed application of principles. Here the great safe-

---

7. The unenlightened middle classes, whose opposition to the defenders of culture is parallel to the biblical tribe that fought against the people of Israel, "the children of light." Arnold's repeated use of this parallel has established the term in our language. John Somers (1651–1716), statesman responsible for formulating the Declaration of Rights.

8. William Cobbett (1762–1835), vehement reformer whose political position anticipated that of Dickens.

9. Reference to *Unto This Last* (1862), in which Ruskin shifted from art criticism to an attack on traditional theories of economics.

guard is never to let oneself become abstract, always to retain an intimate and lively consciousness of the truth of what one is saying, and, the moment this fails us, to be sure that something is wrong. Still under all circumstances, this mere judgment and application of principles is, in itself, not the most satisfactory work to the critic; like mathematics, it is tautological, and cannot well give us, like fresh learning, the sense of creative activity.

But stop, some one will say; all this talk is of no practical use to us whatever; this criticism of yours is not what we have in our minds when we speak of criticism; when we speak of critics and criticism, we mean critics and criticism of the current English literature of the day; when you offer to tell criticism its function, it is to this criticism that we expect you to address yourself. I am sorry for it, for I am afraid I must disappoint these expectations. I am bound by my own definition of criticism: *a disinterested endeavor to learn and propagate the best that is known and thought in the world.* How much of current English literature comes into this "best that is known and thought in the world"? Not very much I fear; certainly less, at this moment, than of the current literature of France or Germany. Well, then, am I to alter my definition of criticism, in order to meet the requirements of a number of practicing English critics, who, after all, are free in their choice of a business? That would be making criticism lend itself just to one of those alien practical considerations, which, I have said, are so fatal to it. One may say, indeed, to those who have to deal with the mass—so much better disregarded—of current English literature, that they may at all events endeavor, in dealing with this, to try it, so far as they can, by the standard of the best that is known and thought in the world; one may say, that to get anywhere near this standard, every critic should try and possess one great literature, at least, besides his own; and the more unlike his own, the better. But, after all, the criticism I am really concerned with—the criticism which alone can much help us for the future, the criticism which, throughout Europe, is at the present day meant, when so much stress is laid on the importance of criticism and the critical spirit—is a criticism which regards Europe as being, for intellectual and spiritual purposes, one great confederation, bound to a joint action and working to a common result, and whose members have, for their proper outfit, a knowledge of Greek, Roman, and Eastern antiquity, and of one another. Special, local, and temporary advantages being put out of account, that modern nation will in the intellectual and spiritual sphere make most progress, which most thoroughly carries out this program. And what is that but saying that we too, all of us, as individuals, the more thoroughly we carry it out, shall make the more progress?

There is so much inviting us!—what are we to take? what will nourish us in growth towards perfection? That is the question which, with the immense field of life and of literature lying before him, the critic has to answer; for himself first, and afterwards for others. In this idea of the critic's business the essays brought together in the following pages have had their origin; in this idea, widely different as are their subjects, they have, perhaps, their unity.

I conclude with what I said at the beginning: to have the sense of creative activity is the great happiness and the great proof of being alive, and it is not denied to criticism to have it; but then criticism must be sincere, simple, flexible, ardent, ever widening its knowledge. Then it may have, in no contemptible measure, a joyful sense of creative activity; a sense which a man of insight and conscience will prefer to what he might derive from a poor, starved, fragmentary, inadequate creation. And at some epochs no other creation is possible.

Still, in full measure, the sense of creative activity belongs only to genuine creation; in literature we must never forget that. But what true man of letters ever can forget it? It is no such common matter for a gifted nature to come into possession of a current of true and living ideas, and to produce amidst the inspiration of them, that we are likely to underrate it. The epochs of Aeschylus and Shakespeare make us feel their pre-eminence. In an epoch like those is, no doubt, the true life of literature; there is the promised land, towards which criticism can only beckon. That promised land it will not be ours to enter, and we shall die in the wilderness: but to have desired to enter it, to have saluted it from afar, is already, perhaps, the best distinction among contemporaries; it will certainly be the best title to esteem with posterity.

1864, 1865

From Culture and Anarchy[1]

From Chapter 1. Sweetness and Light

The impulse of the English race towards moral development and self-conquest has nowhere so powerfully manifested itself as in Puritanism. Nowhere has Puritanism found so adequate an expression as in the religious organization of the Independents.[2] The modern Independents have a newspaper, the Nonconformist, written with great sincerity and ability. The motto, the standard, the profession of faith which this organ of theirs carries aloft, is: "The Dissidence of Dissent and the Protestantism of the Protestant religion." There is sweetness and light, and an ideal of complete harmonious human perfection! One need not go to culture and poetry to find language to judge it. Religion, with its instinct for perfection, supplies language to judge it, language, too, which is in our mouths every day. "Finally, be of one mind, united in feeling," says St. Peter.[3] There is an ideal which judges the Puritan ideal: "The Dissidence of Dissent and the Protestantism of the Protestant religion!" And religious organizations like this are what people believe

---

1. Arnold began Culture and Anarchy in the context of the turbulent political debate that preceded the passage of the second Reform Bill in 1867. The political climate seemed to some to threaten anarchy, to which Arnold opposed culture. A characteristic quality of the cultured state of mind is summed up, for his purposes, in his formula "sweetness and light," a phrase suggesting reasonableness of temper and intellectual insight. Arnold derived the phrase from a fable contrasting the spider with the bee in Swift's Battle of the Books. The spider (representing a narrow, self-centered, and uncultured mind) spins out of itself "nothing at all but flybane and cobweb." The bee (representing a cultured mind that has drawn nourishment from the humanist tradition) ranges far and wide and brings to its hive honey and also wax out of which candles may be made. Therefore, the bee, Swift says, furnishes humankind "with the two noblest

of things, which are sweetness and light."

The selections printed here illustrate aspects of Arnold's indictment of the middle classes for their lack of sweetness and light. The first and third expose the narrowness and dullness of middle-class Puritan religious institutions in both the 17th and 19th centuries. The second, Doing As One Likes, shows the limitations of the middle-class political bias and the irresponsibility of laissez-faire. Here Arnold is most close to Carlyle and Ruskin. These three extracts indicate why it has been said that Matthew Arnold discovered the foibles of Main Street fifty years before Sinclair Lewis exposed them in his novels of American life.

2. A 17th-century Puritan group (of which Cromwell was an adherent), allied with the Congregationalists.

3. Cf. 1 Peter 3.8.

in, rest in, would give their lives for! Such, I say, is the wonderful virtue of even the beginnings of perfection, of having conquered even the plain faults of our animality, that the religious organization which has helped us to do it can seem to us something precious, salutary, and to be propagated, even when it wears such a brand of imperfection on its forehead as this. And men have got such a habit of giving to the language of religion a special application, of making it a mere jargon, that for the condemnation which religion itself passes on the shortcomings of their religious organizations they have no ear; they are sure to cheat themselves and to explain this condemnation away. They can only be reached by the criticism which culture, like poetry, speaking of language not to be sophisticated, and resolutely testing these organizations by the ideal of a human perfection complete on all sides, applies to them.

But men of culture and poetry, it will be said, are again and again failing, and failing conspicuously, in the necessary first stage to a harmonious perfection, in the subduing of the great obvious faults of our animality, which it is the glory of these religious organizations to have helped us to subdue. True, they do often so fail. They have often been without the virtues as well as the faults of the Puritan; it has been one of their dangers that they so felt the Puritan's faults that they too much neglected the practice of his virtues. I will not, however, exculpate them at the Puritan's expense. They have often failed in morality, and morality is indispensable. And they have been punished for their failure, as the Puritan has been rewarded for his performance. They have been punished wherein they erred; but their ideal of beauty, of sweetness and light, and a human nature complete on all its sides, remains the true ideal of perfection still; just as the Puritan's ideal of perfection remains narrow and inadequate, although for what he did well he has been richly rewarded. Notwithstanding the mighty results of the Pilgrim Fathers' voyage, they and their standard of perfection are rightly judged when we figure to ourselves Shakespeare or Virgil—souls in whom sweetness and light, and all that in human nature is most humane, were eminent—accompanying them on their voyage, and think what intolerable company Shakespeare and Virgil would have found them! In the same way let us judge the religious organizations which we see all around us. Do not let us deny the good and the happiness which they have accomplished; but do not let us fail to see clearly that their idea of human perfection is narrow and inadequate, and that the Dissidence of Dissent and the Protestantism of the Protestant religion will never bring humanity to its true goal. As I said with regard to wealth: Let us look at the life of those who live in and for it—so I say with regard to the religious organizations. Look at the life imaged in such a newspaper as the *Nonconformist*—a life of jealousy of the Establishment,[4] disputes, tea-meetings, openings of chapels, sermons; and then think of it as an ideal of a human life completing itself on all sides, and aspiring with all its organs after sweetness, light, and perfection!

---

4. The Church of England or the Established Church.

From *Chapter 2. Doing As One Likes*

* * *

When I began to speak of culture, I insisted on our bondage to machinery, on our proneness to value machinery as an end in itself, without looking beyond it to the end for which alone, in truth, it is valuable. Freedom, I said, was one of those things which we thus worshiped in itself, without enough regarding the ends for which freedom is to be desired. In our common notions and talk about freedom, we eminently show our idolatry of machinery. Our prevalent notion is—and I quoted a number of instances to prove it—that it is a most happy and important thing for a man merely to be able to do as he likes. On what he is to do when he is thus free to do as he likes, we do not lay so much stress. Our familiar praise of the British Constitution under which we live, is that it is a system of checks—a system which stops and paralyzes any power in interfering with the free action of individuals. To this effect Mr. Bright,[5] who loves to walk in the old ways of the Constitution, said forcibly in one of his great speeches, what many other people are every day saying less forcibly, that the central idea of English life and politics is *the assertion of personal liberty.* Evidently this is so; but evidently, also, as feudalism, which with its ideas, and habits of subordination was for many centuries silently behind the British Constitution, dies out, and we are left with nothing but our system of checks, and our notion of its being the great right and happiness of an Englishman to do as far as possible what he likes, we are in danger of drifting towards anarchy. We have not the notion, so familiar on the Continent and to antiquity, of *the State*—the nation in its collective and corporate character, entrusted with stringent powers for the general advantage, and controlling individual wills in the name of an interest wider than that of individuals. We say, what is very true, that this notion is often made instrumental to tyranny; we say that a State is in reality made up of the individuals who compose it, and that every individual is the best judge of his own interests. Our leading class is an aristocracy, and no aristocracy likes the notion of a State-authority greater than itself, with a stringent administrative machinery superseding the decorative inutilities of lord-lieutenancy, deputy-lieutenancy, and the *posse comitatus,*[6] which are all in its own hands. Our middle class, the great representative of trade and Dissent, with its maxims of every man for himself in business, every man for himself in religion, dreads a powerful administration which might somehow interfere with it; and besides, it has its own decorative inutilities of vestry-manship and guardianship, which are to this class what lord-lieutenancy and the county magistracy are to the aristocratic class, and a stringent administration might either take these functions out of its hands, or prevent its exercising them in its own comfortable, independent manner, as at present.

Then as to our working class. This class, pressed constantly by the hard daily compulsion of material wants, is naturally the very center and stronghold of our national idea, that it is man's ideal right and felicity to do as he likes. I think I have somewhere related how M. Michelet[7] said to me of the

5. John Bright (19th century), orator and reformer.
6. Power of the county (Latin); a feudal method of enforcing law by local authorities instead of by agencies of the central government.
7. Jules Michelet (1798–1874), French historian.

people of France, that it was "a nation of barbarians civilized by the conscription." He meant that through their military service the idea of public duty and of discipline was brought to the mind of these masses, in other respects so raw and uncultivated. Our masses are quite as raw and uncultivated as the French; and so far from their having the idea of public duty and of discipline, superior to the individual's self-will, brought to their mind by a universal obligation of military service, such as that of the conscription—so far from their having this, the very idea of a conscription is so at variance with our English notion of the prime right and blessedness of doing as one likes, that I remember the manager of the Clay Cross works in Derbyshire told me during the Crimean war, when our want of soldiers was much felt and some people were talking of a conscription, that sooner than submit to a conscription the population of that district would flee to the mines, and lead a sort of Robin Hood life underground.

For a long time, as I have said, the strong feudal habits of subordination and deference continued to tell upon the working class. The modern spirit has now almost entirely dissolved those habits, and the anarchical tendency of our worship of freedom in and for itself, of our superstitious faith, as I say, in machinery, is becoming very manifest. More and more, because of this our blind faith in machinery, because of our want of light to enable us to look beyond machinery to the end for which machinery is valuable, this and that man, and this and that body of men, all over the country, are beginning to assert and put in practice an Englishman's right to do what he likes; his right to march where he likes, meet where he likes, enter where he likes, hoot as he likes, threaten as he likes, smash as he likes.[8] All this, I say, tends to anarchy; and though a number of excellent people, and particularly my friends of the Liberal or progressive party, as they call themselves, are kind enough to reassure us by saying that these are trifles, that a few transient outbreaks of rowdyism signify nothing, that our system of liberty is one which itself cures all the evils which it works, that the educated and intelligent classes stand in overwhelming strength and majestic repose, ready, like our military force in riots, to act at a moment's notice—yet one finds that one's Liberal friends generally say this because they have such faith in themselves and their nostrums, when they shall return, as the public welfare requires, to place and power. But this faith of theirs one cannot exactly share, when one has so long had them and their nostrums at work, and see that they have not prevented our coming to our present embarrassed condition. And one finds, also, that the outbreaks of rowdyism tend to become less and less of trifles, to become more frequent rather than less frequent; and that meanwhile our educated and intelligent classes remain in their majestic repose, and somehow or other, whatever happens, their overwhelming strength, like our military force in riots, never does act.

How indeed, *should* their overwhelming strength act, when the man who gives an inflammatory lecture, or breaks down the park railings, or invades a Secretary of State's office, is only following an Englishman's impulse to do as he likes; and our own conscience tells us that we ourselves have always regarded this impulse as something primary and sacred? Mr. Murphy[9] lec-

8. A reference to the riots of 1866 in which a London mob demolished the iron railings enclosing Hyde Park.

9. An orator whose inflammatory anti-Catholic public speech *The Errors of the Roman Church* led to rioting in Birmingham and other cities in 1867.

tures at Birmingham, and showers on the Catholic population of that town "words," says the Home Secretary, "only fit to be addressed to thieves or murderers." What then? Mr. Murphy has his own reasons of several kinds. He suspects the Roman Catholic Church of designs upon Mrs. Murphy; and he says if mayors and magistrates do not care for their wives and daughters, he does. But, above all, he is doing as he likes; or, in worthier language, asserting his personal liberty. "I will carry out my lectures if they walk over my body as a dead corpse, and I say to the Mayor of Birmingham that he is my servant while I am in Birmingham, and as my servant he must do his duty and protect me." Touching and beautiful words, which find a sympathetic chord in every British bosom! The moment it is plainly put before us that a man is asserting his personal liberty, we are half disarmed; because we are believers in freedom, and not in some dream of a right reason to which the assertion of our freedom is to be subordinated. Accordingly, the Secretary of State had to say that although the lecturer's language was "only fit to be addressed to thieves or murderers," yet, "I do not think he is to be deprived, I do not think that anything I have said could justify the inference that he is to be deprived, of the right of protection in a place built by him for the purpose of these lectures; because the language was not language which afforded grounds for a criminal prosecution." No, nor to be silenced by Mayor, or Home Secretary, or any administrative authority on earth, simply on their notion of what is discreet and reasonable! This is in perfect consonance with our public opinion, and with our national love for the assertion of personal liberty.

* * *

From *Chapter 5.* Porro Unum Est Necessarium[1]

* * *

* * * Sweetness and light evidently have to do with the bent or side in humanity which we call Hellenic. Greek intelligence has obviously for its essence the instinct for what Plato calls the true, firm, intelligible law of things; the law of light, of seeing things as they are. Even in the natural sciences, where the Greeks had not time and means adequately to apply this instinct, and where we have gone a great deal further than they did, it is this instinct which is the root of the whole matter and the ground of all our success; and this instinct the world has mainly learnt of the Greeks, inasmuch as they are humanity's most signal manifestation of it. Greek art, again, Greek beauty, have their root in the same impulse to see things as they really are, inasmuch as Greek art and beauty rest on fidelity to nature—the *best* nature—and on a delicate discrimination of what this best nature is. To say we work for sweetness and light, then, is only another way of saying that we work for Hellenism. But, oh! cry many people, sweetness and light are not enough; you must put strength or energy along with them, and make a kind of trinity of strength, sweetness and light, and then, perhaps, you may do some good. That is to say, we are to join Hebraism, strictness of the moral

---

conscience, and manful walking by the best light we have, together with Hellenism, inculcate both, and rehearse the praises of both.

Or, rather, we may praise both in conjunction, but we must be careful to praise Hebraism most. "Culture," says an acute, though somewhat rigid critic, Mr. Sidgwick,[2] "diffuses sweetness and light. I do not undervalue these blessings, but religion gives fire and strength, and the world wants fire and strength even more than sweetness and light." By religion, let me explain, Mr. Sidgwick here means particularly that Puritanism on the insufficiency of which I have been commenting and to which he says I am unfair. Now, no doubt, it is possible to be a fanatical partisan of light and the instincts which push us to it, a fanatical enemy of strictness of moral conscience and the instincts which push us to it. A fanaticism of this sort deforms and vulgarizes the well-known work, in some respects so remarkable, of the late Mr. Buckle.[3] Such a fanaticism carries its own mark with it, in lacking sweetness; and its own penalty, in that, lacking sweetness, it comes in the end to lack light too. And the Greeks—the great exponents of humanity's bent for sweetness and light united, of its perception that the truth of things must be at the same time beauty—singularly escaped the fanaticism which we moderns, whether we Hellenize or whether we Hebraize, are so apt to show. They arrived—though failing, as has been said, to give adequate practical satisfaction to the claims of man's moral side—at the idea of a comprehensive adjustment of the claims of both the sides in man, the moral as well as the intellectual, of a full estimate of both, and of a reconciliation of both; an idea which is philosophically of the greatest value, and the best of lessons for us moderns. So we ought to have no difficulty in conceding to Mr. Sidgwick that manful walking by the best light one has—fire and strength as he calls it—has its high value as well as culture, the endeavor to see things in their truth and beauty, the pursuit of sweetness and light. But whether at this or that time, and to this or that set of persons, one ought to insist most on the praises of fire and strength, or on the praises of sweetness and light, must depend, one would think, on the circumstances and needs of that particular time and those particular persons. And all that we have been saying, and indeed any glance at the world around us, shows that with us, with the most respectable and strongest part of us, the ruling force is now, and long has been, a Puritan force—the care for fire and strength, strictness of conscience, Hebraism, rather than the care for sweetness and light, spontaneity of consciousness, Hellenism.

Well, then, what is the good of our now rehearsing the praises of fire and strength to ourselves, who dwell too exclusively on them already? When Mr. Sidgwick says so broadly, that the world wants fire and strength even more than sweetness and light, is he not carried away by a turn for broad generalization? does he not forget that the world is not all of one piece, and every piece with the same needs at the same time? It may be true that the Roman world at the beginning of our era, or Leo the Tenth's Court at the time of the Reformation, or French society in the eighteenth century,[4] needed fire

---

2. Henry Sidgwick (1838–1900), philosopher, whose article on Arnold appeared in *Macmillan's Magazine* (Aug. 1867).
3. Henry Thomas Buckle (1821–1862), author of *A History of Civilization*.

4. Societies representing an excess of sophisticated worldliness as at the courts of such a Roman emperor as Nero (54–68 C.E.) or Pope Leo X (1513–1521) or Louis XV (1715–1774), respectively.

and strength even more than sweetness and light. But can it be said that the Barbarians who overran the empire needed fire and strength even more than sweetness and light; or that the Puritans needed them more; or that Mr. Murphy, the Birmingham lecturer, and the Rev. W. Cattle[5] and his friends, need them more?

The Puritan's great danger is that he imagines himself in possession of a rule telling him the *unum necessarium,* or one thing needful, and that he then remains satisfied with a very crude conception of what this rule really is and what it tells him, thinks he has now knowledge and henceforth needs only to act, and, in this dangerous state of assurance and self-satisfaction, proceeds to give full swing to a number of the instincts of his ordinary self. Some of the instincts of his ordinary self he has, by the help of his rule of life, conquered; but others which he has not conquered by this help he is so far from perceiving to need subjugation, and to be instincts of an inferior self, that he even fancies it to be his right and duty, in virtue of having conquered a limited part of himself, to give unchecked swing to the remainder. He is, I say, a victim of Hebraism, of the tendency to cultivate strictness of conscience rather than spontaneity of consciousness. And what he wants is a larger conception of human nature, showing him the number of other points at which his nature must come to its best, besides the points which he himself knows and thinks of. There is no *unum necessarium,* or one thing needful, which can free human nature from the obligation of trying to come to its best at all these points. The real *unum necessarium* for us is to come to our best at all points. Instead of our "one thing needful," justifying in us vulgarity, hideousness, ignorance, violence—our vulgarity, hideousness, ignorance, violence, are really so many touchstones which try our one thing needful, and which prove that in the state, at any rate, in which we ourselves have it, it is not all we want. And as the force which encourages us to stand staunch and fast by the rule and ground we have is Hebraism, so the force which encourages us to go back upon this rule, and to try the very ground on which we appear to stand, is Hellenism—a turn for giving our consciousness free play and enlarging its range. And what I say is, not that Hellenism is always for everybody more wanted than Hebraism, but that for the Rev. W. Cattle at this particular moment, and for the great majority of us his fellow countrymen, it is more wanted.

*   *   *

1868, 1869

From The Study of Poetry[1]

"The future of poetry is immense, because in poetry, where it is worthy of its high destinies, our race, as time goes on, will find an ever surer

---

5. A Nonconformist clergyman who was chairman of the anti-Catholic meeting addressed by Murphy in 1867 (see *Chapter 2. Doing As One Likes,* p. 1530).

1. Aside from its vindication of the importance of literature, this essay is an interesting example of the variety of Arnold's own reading. To know literature in only one language seemed to him not to know literature. His personal *Notebooks* show that throughout his active life he continued to read books in French, German, Italian, Latin, and Greek. His favorite authors in these languages are used by him as a means of testing English poetry.

The testing is sometimes a severe one. Readers may also protest that despite Arnold's own wit, his essay is limited by an incomplete recognition of the values of comic literature, a shortcoming abundantly evident in the discussion of Chaucer. Nevertheless, whether we agree or disagree with some of Arnold's verdicts, we can be attracted by the combination of traditionalism and impressionism on which these verdicts are based, and we can enjoy the memorable phrasemaking in which the verdicts are expressed. *The Study of Poetry* has been extraordinarily potent in shaping literary tastes in England and in America.

and surer stay. There is not a creed which is not shaken, not an accredited dogma which is not shown to be questionable, not a received tradition which does not threaten to dissolve. Our religion has materialized itself in the fact, in the supposed fact; it has attached its emotion to the fact, and now the fact is failing it. But for poetry the idea is everything; the rest is a world of illusion, of divine illusion. Poetry attaches its emotion to the idea; the idea *is* the fact. The strongest part of our religion today is its unconscious poetry."

Let me be permitted to quote these words of my own, as uttering the thought which should, in my opinion, go with us and govern us in all our study of poetry. In the present work[2] it is the course of one great contributory stream to the world-river of poetry that we are invited to follow. We are here invited to trace the stream of English poetry. But whether we set ourselves, as here, to follow only one of the several streams that make the mighty river of poetry, or whether we seek to know them all, our governing thought should be the same. We should conceive of poetry worthily, and more highly than it has been the custom to conceive of it. We should conceive of it as capable of higher uses, and called to higher destinies, than those which in general men have assigned to it hitherto. More and more mankind will discover that we have to turn to poetry to interpret life for us, to console us, to sustain us. Without poetry, our science will appear incomplete; and most of what now passes with us for religion and philosophy will be replaced by poetry. Science, I say, will appear incomplete without it. For finely and truly does Wordsworth call poetry "the impassioned expression which is in the countenance of all science";[3] and what is a countenance without its expression? Again, Wordsworth finely and truly calls poetry "the breath and finer spirit of all knowledge": our religion, parading evidences such as those on which the popular mind relies now; our philosophy, pluming itself on its reasonings about causation and finite and infinite being; what are they but the shadows and dreams and false shows of knowledge? The day will come when we shall wonder at ourselves for having trusted to them, for having taken them seriously; and the more we perceive their hollowness, the more we shall prize "the breath and finer spirit of knowledge" offered to us by poetry.

But if we conceive thus highly of the destinies of poetry, we must also set our standard for poetry high, since poetry, to be capable of fulfilling such high destinies, must be poetry of a high order of excellence. We must accustom ourselves to a high standard and to a strict judgment. * * *

The best poetry is what we want; the best poetry will be found to have a power of forming, sustaining, and delighting us, as nothing else can. A clearer, deeper sense of the best in poetry, and of the strength and joy to be drawn from it, is the most precious benefit which we can gather from a poetical collection such as the present. And yet in the very nature and conduct of such a collection there is inevitably something which tends to obscure in us the consciousness of what our benefit should be, and to distract us from the pursuit of it. We should therefore steadily set it before our minds at the outset, and should compel ourselves to revert constantly to the thought of it as we proceed.

Yes; constantly in reading poetry, a sense for the best, the really excellent,

2. An anthology of English poetry for which this essay served as the introduction.

3. Preface to *Lyrical Ballads*.

and of the strength and joy to be drawn from it, should be present in our minds and should govern our estimate of what we read. But this real estimate, the only true one, is liable to be superseded, if we are not watchful, by two other kinds of estimate, the historic estimate and the personal estimate, both of which are fallacious. A poet or a poem may count to us historically, they may count to us on grounds personal to ourselves, and they may count to us really. They may count to us historically. The course of development of a nation's language, thought, and poetry, is profoundly interesting; and by regarding a poet's work as a stage in this course of development we may easily bring ourselves to make it of more importance as poetry than in itself it really is, we may come to use a language of quite exaggerated praise in criticizing it; in short, to overrate it. So arises in our poetic judgments the fallacy caused by the estimate which we may call historic. Then, again, a poet or a poem may count to us on grounds personal to ourselves. Our personal affinities, likings, and circumstances, have great power to sway our estimate of this or that poet's work, and to make us attach more importance to it as poetry than in itself it really possesses, because to us it is, or has been, of high importance. Here also we overrate the object of our interest, and apply to it a language of praise which is quite exaggerated. And thus we get the source of a second fallacy in our poetic judgments—the fallacy caused by an estimate which we may call personal.

* * *

* * * The historic estimate is likely in especial to affect our judgment and our language when we are dealing with ancient poets; the personal estimate when we are dealing with poets our contemporaries, or at any rate modern. The exaggerations due to the historic estimate are not in themselves, perhaps, of very much gravity. Their report hardly enters the general ear; probably they do not always impose even on the literary men who adopt them. But they lead to a dangerous abuse of language. So we hear Caedmon,[4] amongst our own poets, compared to Milton. I have already noticed the enthusiasm of one accomplished French critic for "historic origins."[5] Another eminent French critic, M. Vitet, comments upon that famous document of the early poetry of his nation, the *Chanson de Roland*.[6] It is indeed a most interesting document. The *joculator* or *jongleur*[7] Taillefer, who was with William the Conqueror's army at Hastings, marched before the Norman troops, so said the tradition, singing "of Charlemagne and of Roland and of Oliver, and of the vassals who died at Roncevaux"; and it is suggested that in the *Chanson de Roland* by one Turoldus or *Theroulde*, a poem preserved in a manuscript of the twelfth century in the Bodleian Library at Oxford, we have certainly the matter, perhaps even some of the words, of the chant which Taillefer sang. The poem has vigor and freshness; it is not without pathos. But M. Vitet is not satisfied with seeing in it a document of some poetic value, and of very high historic and linguistic value; he sees in it a grand and beautiful work, a monument of epic genius. In its general design he finds the grandiose conception, in its details he finds the constant union

4. A 7th-century Old English poet.
5. Charles d'Héricault, a critic cited earlier in a passage omitted here. Arnold had mildly reprimanded him for his "historical" bias in praising a 15th-century poet, Clément Marot, at the expense of such classical 17th-century poets as Racine.

6. An 11th-century epic poem in Old French that tells of the wars of Charlemagne against the Moors in Spain and of the bravery of the French leaders Roland and Oliver.
7. Minstrel.

of simplicity with greatness, which are the marks, he truly says, of the genuine epic, and distinguish it from the artificial epic of literary ages. One thinks of Homer; this is the sort of praise which is given to Homer, and justly given. Higher praise there cannot well be, and it is the praise due to epic poetry of the highest order only, and to no other. Let us try, then, the *Chanson de Roland* at its best. Roland, mortally wounded, lays himself down under a pine tree, with his face turned towards Spain and the enemy—

> De plusurs choses à remembrer li prist,
> De tantes teres cume li bers cunquist,
> De dulce France, des humes de sun lign,
> De Carlemagne sun seignor ki l'nurrit.[8]

That is primitive work, I repeat, with an undeniable poetic quality of its own. It deserves such praise, and such praise is sufficient for it. But now turn to Homer—

> Ὥς φάτο τούς δ' ἤδη κάτεχεν φυσίζοος αἶα
> ἐν Λἀκεδαίμονι ἀνθι, φίλη ἐν πατρίδι γαίη.[9]

We are here in another world, another order of poetry altogether; here is rightly due such supreme praise as that which M. Vitet gives to the *Chanson de Roland*. If our words are to have any meaning, if our judgments are to have any solidity, we must not heap that supreme praise upon poetry of an order immeasurably inferior.

Indeed there can be no more useful help for discovering what poetry belongs to the class of the truly excellent, and can therefore do us most good, than to have always in one's mind lines and expressions of the great masters, and to apply them as a touchstone to other poetry. Of course we are not to require this other poetry to resemble them; it may be very dissimilar. But if we have any tact we shall find them, when we have lodged them well in our minds, an infallible touchstone for detecting the presence or absence of high poetic quality, and also the degree of this quality, in all other poetry which we may place beside them. Short passages, even single lines, will serve our turn quite sufficiently. Take the two lines which I have just quoted from Homer, the poet's comment on Helen's mention of her brothers—or take his

> Ἆ δειλώ, τί σφωϊ δόμεν Πηληΐ ἄνακτι
> θνητῷ; ὑμεῖς δ' ἐστὸν ἀγήρω τ' ἀθανάτω τε.
> ἦ ἵνα δυστήνοισι μετ' ἀνδράσιν ἄλγε' ἔχητον;[1]

the address of Zeus to the horses of Peleus—or take finally his

> Καί σέ, γέρον, τὸ πρὶν μὲν ἀκούομεν ὄλβιον εἶναι·[2]

the words of Achilles to Priam, a suppliant before him. Take that incomparable line and a half of Dante, Ugolino's tremendous words—

> Io no piangeva; sì dentro impietrai.
> Piangevan elli . . .[3]

8. "Then began he to call many things to remembrance—all the lands which his valor conquered and pleasant France, and the men of his lineage, and Charlemagne his liege lord who nourished him." *Chanson de Roland* 3.939–42 [Arnold's note].

9. "So said she; they long since in Earth's soft arms were reposing, / There, in their own dear land, their fatherland, Lacedaemon." *Iliad* 3.243–44 (translated by Dr. Hawtrey) [Arnold's note].

1. "Ah, unhappy pair, why gave we you to King Peleus, to a mortal? but ye are without old age, and immortal. Was it that with men born to misery ye might have sorrow?" *Iliad* 17.443–45 [Arnold's note].

2. "Nay, and thou too, old man, in former days wast, as we hear, happy." *Iliad* 14.543 [Arnold's note].

3. "I wailed not, so of stone I grew within; *they* wailed." *Inferno* 33.49–50 [Arnold's note].

take the lovely words of Beatrice to Virgil—

> *Io son fatta da Dio, sua mercè, tale,*
> *Che la vostra miseria non mi tange,*
> *Nè fiamma d'esto incendio non m'assale . . .* [4]

take the simple, but perfect, single line—

> *In la sua volontade è nostra pace.* [5]

Take of Shakespeare a line or two of Henry the Fourth's expostulation with sleep—

> Wilt thou upon the high and giddy mast
> Seal up the shipboy's eyes, and rock his brains
> In cradle of the rude imperious surge . . . [6]

and take, as well, Hamlet's dying request to Horatio—

> If thou didst ever hold me in thy heart,
> Absent thee from felicity awhile,
> And in this harsh world draw thy breath in pain,
> To tell my story . . . [7]

Take of Milton that Miltonic passage—

> Darkened so, yet shone
> Above them all the archangel; but his face
> Deep scars of thunder had intrenched, and care
> Sat on his faded cheek . . . [8]

add two such lines as—

> And courage never to submit or yield
> And what is else not to be overcome . . . [9]

and finish with the exquisite close to the loss of Proserpine, the loss

> . . . which cost Ceres all that pain
> To seek her through the world. [1]

These few lines, if we have tact and can use them, are enough even of themselves to keep clear and sound our judgments about poetry, to save us from fallacious estimates of it, to conduct us to a real estimate.

The specimens I have quoted differ widely from one another, but they have in common this: the possession of the very highest poetical quality. If we are thoroughly penetrated by their power, we shall find that we have acquired a sense enabling us, whatever poetry may be laid before us, to feel the degree in which a high poetical quality is present or wanting there. Critics give themselves great labor to draw out what in the abstract constitutes the characters of a high quality of poetry. It is much better simply to have recourse to concrete examples—to take specimens of poetry of the high, the

---

4. "Of such sort hath God, thanked be His mercy, made me, that your misery toucheth me not, neither doth the flame of this fire strike me." *Inferno* 2.91–93 [Arnold's note].
5. "In His will is our peace." *Paradiso* 3.85 [Arnold's note].

6. *2 Henry IV* 3.1.18–20.
7. *Hamlet* 5.2.357–60.
8. *Paradise Lost* 1.599–602.
9. *Paradise Lost* 1.108–9.
1. *Paradise Lost* 4.271–72.

very highest quality, and to say: The characters of a high quality of poetry are what is expressed *there*. They are far better recognized by being felt in the verse of the master, than by being perused in the prose of the critic. Nevertheless if we are urgently pressed to give some critical account of them, we may safely, perhaps, venture on laying down, not indeed how and why the characters arise, but where and in what they arise. They are in the matter and substance of the poetry, and they are in its manner and style. Both of these, the substance and matter on the one hand, the style and manner on the other, have a mark, an accent, of high beauty, worth, and power. But if we are asked to define this mark and accent in the abstract, our answer must be: No, for we should thereby be darkening the question, not clearing it. The mark and accent are as given by the substance and matter of that poetry, by the style and manner of that poetry, and of all other poetry which is akin to it in quality.

Only one thing we may add as to the substance and matter of poetry, guiding ourselves by Aristotle's profound observation that the superiority of poetry over history consists in its possessing a higher truth and a higher seriousness (φιλοσοφώτερον καὶ σπουδαιότερον).[2] Let us add, therefore, to what we have said, this: that the substance and matter of the best poetry acquire their special character from possessing, in an eminent degree, truth and seriousness. We may add yet further, what is in itself evident, that to the style and manner of the best poetry their special character, their accent, is given by their diction, and, even yet more, by their movement. And though we distinguish between the two characters, the two accents, of superiority, yet they are nevertheless vitally connected one with the other. The superior character of truth and seriousness, in the matter and substance of the best poetry, is inseparable from the superiority of diction and movement marking its style and manner. The two superiorities are closely related, and are in steadfast proportion one to the other. So far as high poetic truth and seriousness are wanting to a poet's matter and substance, so far also, we may be sure, will a high poetic stamp of diction and movement be wanting to his style and manner. In proportion as this high stamp of diction and movement, again, is absent from a poet's style and manner, we shall find, also, that high poetic truth and seriousness are absent from his substance and matter.

So stated, these are but dry generalities; their whole force lies in their application. And I could wish every student of poetry to make the application of them for himself. Made by himself, the application would impress itself upon his mind far more deeply than made by me. Neither will my limits allow me to make any full application of the generalities above propounded; but in the hope of bringing out, at any rate, some significance in them, and of establishing an important principle more firmly by their means, I will, in the space which remains to me, follow rapidly from the commencement the course of our English poetry with them in my view.

* * *

Chaucer's * * * poetical importance does not need the assistance of the historic estimate; it is real. He is a genuine source of joy and strength, which is flowing still for us and will flow always. He will be read, as time goes on,

2. Aristotle's *Poetics* 9.

far more generally than he is read now. His language is a cause of difficulty for us; but so also, and I think in quite as great a degree, is the language of Burns. In Chaucer's case, as in that of Burns, it is a difficulty to be unhesitatingly accepted and overcome.

If we ask ourselves wherein consists the immense superiority of Chaucer's poetry over the romance poetry—why it is that in passing from this to Chaucer we suddenly feel ourselves to be in another world, we shall find that his superiority is both in the substance of his poetry and in the style of his poetry. His superiority in substance is given by his large, free, simple, clear yet kindly view of human life—so unlike the total want, in the romance poets, of all intelligent command of it. Chaucer has not their helplessness; he has gained the power to survey the world from a central, a truly human point of view. We have only to call to mind the Prologue to *The Canterbury Tales*. The right comment upon it is Dryden's: "It is sufficient to say, according to the proverb, that *here is God's plenty*." And again: "He is a perpetual fountain of good sense."[3] It is by a large, free, sound representation of things, that poetry, this high criticism of life, has truth of substance; and Chaucer's poetry has truth of substance.

Of his style and manner, if we think first of the romance poetry and then of Chaucer's divine liquidness of diction, his divine fluidity of movement, it is difficult to speak temperately. They are irresistible, and justify all the rapture with which his successors speak of his "gold dewdrops of speech."[4] Johnson misses the point entirely when he finds fault with Dryden for ascribing to Chaucer the first refinement of our numbers, and says that Gower[5] also can show smooth numbers and easy rhymes. The refinement of our numbers means something far more than this. A nation may have versifiers with smooth numbers and easy rhymes, and yet may have no real poetry at all. Chaucer is the father of our splendid English poetry; he is our "well of English undefiled,"[6] because by the lovely charm of his diction, the lovely charm of his movement, he makes an epoch and founds a tradition. In Spenser, Shakespeare, Milton, Keats, we can follow the tradition of the liquid diction, the fluid movement, of Chaucer; at one time it is his liquid diction of which in these poets we feel the virtue, and at another time it is his fluid movement. And the virtue is irresistible.

Bounded as is my space, I must yet find room for an example of Chaucer's virtue, as I have given examples to show the virtue of the great classics. I feel disposed to say that a single line is enough to show the charm of Chaucer's verse; that merely one line like this—

O martyr souded[7] in virginitee!

has a virtue of manner and movement such as we shall not find in all the verse of romance poetry—but this is saying nothing. The virtue is such as we shall not find, perhaps, in all English poetry, outside the poets whom I have named as the special inheritors of Chaucer's tradition. A single line,

3. Both quotations are from Dryden's preface to his *Fables Ancient and Modern* (1700).
4. *The Life of Our Lady*, a poem by John Lydgate (ca. 1370–ca.1451).
5. John Gower (ca. 1325–1408), friend of Chaucer and author of the *Confessio Amantis*, a long poem in octosyllabic couplets.

6. Said of Chaucer by Spenser in *Faerie Queene* 4.2.32.
7. The French *soudé*: soldered, fixed fast [Arnold's note]. From *The Canterbury Tales*, *The Prioress's Tale* (line 127); Chaucer wrote "souded to" rather than "souded in."

however, is too little if we have not the strain of Chaucer's verse well in our memory; let us take a stanza. It is from *The Prioress's Tale,* the story of the Christian child murdered in a Jewry—

> My throte is cut unto my nekke-bone
> Saidè this child, and as by way of kinde
> I should have deyd, yea, longè time agone;
> But Jesu Christ, as ye in bookès finde,
> Will that his glory last and be in minde,
> And for the worship of his mother dere
> Yet may I sing O *Alma* loud and clere.

Wordsworth has modernized this Tale, and to feel how delicate and evanescent is the charm of verse, we have only to read Wordsworth's first three lines of this stanza after Chaucer's—

> My throat is cut unto the bone, I trow,
> Said this young child, and by the law of kind
> I should have died, yea, many hours ago.

The charm is departed. It is often said that the power of liquidness and fluidity in Chaucer's verse was dependent upon a free, a licentious dealing with language, such as is now impossible; upon a liberty, such as Burns too enjoyed, of making words like *neck, bird,* into a dissyllable by adding to them, and words like *cause, rhyme,* into a dissyllable by sounding the *e* mute. It is true that Chaucer's fluidity is conjoined with this liberty, and is admirably served by it; but we ought not to say that it was dependent upon it. It was dependent upon his talent. Other poets with a like liberty do not attain to the fluidity of Chaucer; Burns himself does not attain to it. Poets, again, who have a talent akin to Chaucer's, such as Shakespeare or Keats, have known how to attain to his fluidity without the like liberty.

And yet Chaucer is not one of the great classics. His poetry transcends and effaces, easily and without effort, all the romance poetry of Catholic Christendom; it transcends and effaces all the English poetry contemporary with it, it transcends and effaces all the English poetry subsequent to it down to the age of Elizabeth. Of such avail is poetic truth of substance, in its natural and necessary union with poetic truth of style. And yet, I say, Chaucer is not one of the great classics. He has not their accent. What is wanting to him is suggested by the mere mention of the name of the first great classic of Christendom, the immortal poet who died eighty years before Chaucer—Dante. The accent of such verse as

> *In la sua volontade è nostra pace . . .*

is altogether beyond Chaucer's reach; we praise him, but we feel that this accent is out of the question for him. It may be said that it was necessarily out of the reach of any poet in the England of that stage of growth. Possibly; but we are to adopt a real, not a historic, estimate of poetry. However we may account for its absence, something is wanting, then, to the poetry of Chaucer, which poetry must have before it can be placed in the glorious class of the best. And there is no doubt what that something is. It is the spoudaiotes, the high and excellent seriousness, which Aristotle assigns as one of the grand virtues of poetry. The substance of Chaucer's poetry, his view of things and his criticism of life, has largeness, freedom, shrewdness, benignity; but it has not this high seriousness. Homer's criticism of life has it, Dante's has it, Shakespeare's has it. It is this chiefly which gives to our spirits what they can rest upon; and with the increasing demands of our modern ages upon poetry, this virtue of giving us what we can rest upon will be more and more highly esteemed. A voice from the slums of Paris, fifty or sixty years after Chaucer, the voice of poor Villon[8] out of his life of riot and crime, has at its happy moments (as, for instance, in the last stanza of *La Belle Heaulmière*)[9] more of this important poetic virtue of seriousness than all the productions of Chaucer. But its apparition in Villon, and in men like Villon, is fitful; the greatness of the great poets, the power of their criticism of life, is that their virtue is sustained.

To our praise, therefore, of Chaucer as a poet there must be this limitation: he lacks the high seriousness of the great classics, and therewith an important part of their virtue. Still, the main fact for us to bear in mind about Chaucer is his sterling value according to that real estimate which we firmly adopt for all poets. He has poetic truth of substance, though he has not high poetic seriousness, and corresponding to his truth of substance he has an exquisite virtue of style and manner. With him is born our real poetry.

For my present purpose I need not dwell on our Elizabethan poetry, or on the continuation and close of this poetry in Milton. We all of us profess to be agreed in the estimate of this poetry; we all of us recognize it as great poetry, our greatest, and Shakespeare and Milton as our poetical classics. The real estimate, here, has universal currency. With the next age of our poetry divergency and difficulty begin. An historic estimate of that poetry has established itself; and the question is, whether it will be found to coincide with the real estimate.

The age of Dryden, together with our whole eighteenth century which followed it, sincerely believed itself to have produced poetical classics of its own, and even to have made advance, in poetry, beyond all its predecessors. Dryden regards as not seriously disputable the opinion "that the sweetness of English verse was never understood or practiced by our fathers."[1] Cowley[2] could see nothing at all in Chaucer's poetry. Dryden heartily admired it, and, as we have seen, praised its matter admirably; but of its exquisite manner and movement all he can find to say is that "there is the rude sweetness of a Scotch tune in it, which is natural and pleasing, though not perfect."[3] Addison, wishing to praise Chaucer's numbers, compares them with Dryden's own. And all through the eighteenth century, and down even into our own times, the stereotyped phrase of approbation for good verse found in our early poetry has been, that it even approached the verse of Dryden, Addison, Pope, and Johnson.

---

8. François Villon (1431–1484), French poet and vagabond.
9. The name *Heaulmière* is said to be derived from a headdress (helm) worn as a mask by courtesans. In Villon's ballad, a poor old creature of this class laments her days of youth and beauty. The last stanza of the ballad runs thus—"*Ainsi le bon temps regretons / Entrenous, pauvres vieilles sottes, / Assises bas, à croppetons, / Tout en ung tas comme pelottes; / A petit feu de chenevottes / Tost allumeés, tost estaincles, / Et jadis fusmes si mignottes! / Ainsi*

en prend à maintz et maintes." [It may be translated:] "Thus amongst ourselves we regret the good time, poor silly old things, low-seated on our heels, all in a heap like so many balls; by a little fire of hemp stalks, soon lighted, soon spent. And once we were such darlings! So fares it with many and many a one" [Arnold's note].
1. *Essay on Dramatic Poesy.*
2. Abraham Cowley (1618–1667), English poet.
3. Preface to his *Fables.*

Are Dryden and Pope poetical classics? Is the historic estimate, which represents them as such, and which has been so long established that it cannot easily give way, the real estimate? Wordsworth and Coleridge, as is well known, denied it; but the authority of Wordsworth and Coleridge does not weigh much with the young generation, and there are many signs to show that the eighteenth century and its judgments are coming into favor again. Are the favorite poets of the eighteenth century classics?

It is impossible within my present limits to discuss the question fully. And what man of letters would not shrink from seeming to dispose dictatorially of the claims of two men who are, at any rate, such masters in letters as Dryden and Pope; two men of such admirable talent, both of them, and one of them, Dryden, a man, on all sides, of such energetic and genial power? And yet, if we are to gain the full benefit from poetry, we must have the real estimate of it. I cast about for some mode of arriving, in the present case, at such an estimate without offense. And perhaps the best way is to begin, as it is easy to begin, with cordial praise.

When we find Chapman, the Elizabethan translator of Homer, expressing himself in his preface thus: "Though truth in her very nakedness sits in so deep a pit, that from Gades to Aurora and Ganges few eyes can sound her, I hope yet those few here will so discover and confirm that, the date being out of her darkness in this morning of our poet, he shall now gird his temples with the sun," we pronounce that such a prose is intolerable. When we find Milton writing: "And long it was not after, when I was confirmed in this opinion, that he, who would not be frustrate of his hope to write well hereafter in laudable things, ought himself to be a true poem"[4]—we pronounce that such a prose has its own grandeur, but that it is obsolete and inconvenient. But when we find Dryden telling us: "What Virgil wrote in the vigor of his age, in plenty and at ease, I have undertaken to translate in my declining years; struggling with wants, oppressed with sickness, curbed in my genius, liable to be misconstrued in all I write"[5]—then we exclaim that here at last we have the true English prose, a prose such as we would all gladly use if we only knew how. Yet Dryden was Milton's contemporary.

But after the Restoration the time had come when our nation felt the imperious need of a fit prose. So, too, the time had likewise come when our nation felt the imperious need of freeing itself from the absorbing preoccupation which religion in the Puritan age had exercised. It was impossible that this freedom should be brought about without some negative excess, without some neglect and impairment of the religious life of the soul; and the spiritual history of the eighteenth century shows us that the freedom was not achieved without them. Still, the freedom was achieved; the preoccupation, an undoubtedly baneful and retarding one if it had continued, was got rid of. And as with religion amongst us at that period, so it was also with letters. A fit prose was a necessity; but it was impossible that a fit prose should establish itself amongst us without some touch of frost to the imaginative life of the soul. The needful qualities for a fit prose are regularity, uniformity, precision, balance. The men of letters, whose destiny it may be to bring their nation to the attainment of a fit prose, must of necessity, whether they work

4. *Apology for Smectymnuus.*
5. *Postscript to the Reader* in his translation of Virgil.

in prose or in verse, give a predominating, an almost exclusive attention to the qualities of regularity, uniformity, precision, balance. But an almost exclusive attention to these qualities involves some repression and silencing of poetry.

We are to regard Dryden as the puissant and glorious founder, Pope as the splendid high priest, of our age of prose and reason, of our excellent and indispensable eighteenth century. For the purposes of their mission and destiny their poetry, like their prose, is admirable. Do you ask me whether Dryden's verse, take it almost where you will, is not good?

> A milk-white Hind, immortal and unchanged,
> Fed on the lawns and in the forest ranged.[6]

I answer: Admirable for the purposes of the inaugurator of an age of prose and reason. Do you ask me whether Pope's verse, take it almost where you will, is not good?

> To Hounslow Heath I point, and Banstead Down;
> Thence comes your mutton, and these chicks my own.[7]

I answer: Admirable for the purposes of the high priest of an age of prose and reason. But do you ask me whether such verse proceeds from men with an adequate poetic criticism of life, from men whose criticism of life has a high seriousness, or even, without that high seriousness, has poetic largeness, freedom, insight, benignity? Do you ask me whether the application of ideas to life in the verse of these men, often a powerful application, no doubt, is a powerful *poetic* application? Do you ask me whether the poetry of these men has either the matter or the inseparable manner of such an adequate poetic criticism; whether it has the accent of

> Absent thee from felicity awhile . . .

or of

> And what is else not to be overcome . . .

or of

> O martyr souded in virginitee!

I answer: It has not and cannot have them; it is the poetry of the builders of an age of prose and reason. Though they may write in verse, though they may in a certain sense be masters of the art of versification, Dryden and Pope are not classics of our poetry, they are classics of our prose.

Gray is our poetical classic of that literature and age; the position of Gray is singular, and demands a word of notice here. He has not the volume or the power of poets who, coming in times more favorable, have attained to an independent criticism of life. But he lived with the great poets, he lived, above all, with the Greeks, through perpetually studying and enjoying them; and he caught their poetic point of view for regarding life, caught their poetic manner. The point of view and the manner are not self-sprung in him, he caught them of others; and he had not the free and abundant use of them. But whereas Addison and Pope never had the use of them, Gray had the use

---

6. *The Hind and the Panther* 1.1–2.   7. *Imitations of Horace,* Satire 2.2.143–144.

of them at times. He is the scantiest and frailest of classics in our poetry, but he is a classic.[8]

* * *

At any rate the end to which the method and the estimate are designed to lead, and from leading to which, if they do lead to it, they get their whole value—the benefit of being able clearly to feel and deeply to enjoy the best, the truly classic, in poetry—is an end, let me say it once more at parting, of supreme importance. We are often told that an era is opening in which we are to see multitudes of a common sort of readers, and masses of a common sort of literature; that such readers do not want and could not relish anything better than such literature, and that to provide it is becoming a vast and profitable industry. Even if good literature entirely lost currency with the world, it would still be abundantly worth while to continue to enjoy it by oneself. But it never will lose currency with the world, in spite of momentary appearances; it never will lose supremacy. Currency and supremacy are insured to it, not indeed by the world's deliberate and conscious choice, but by something far deeper—by the instinct of self-preservation in humanity.

1880

Literature and Science[1]

Practical people talk with a smile of Plato and of his absolute ideas: and it is impossible to deny that Plato's ideas do often seem unpractical and unpracticable, and especially when one views them in connection with the life of a great work-a-day world like the United States. The necessary staple of the life of such a world Plato regards with disdain; handicraft and trade and the working professions he regards with disdain; but what becomes of the life of an industrial modern community if you take handicraft and trade and the working professions out of it? The base mechanic arts and handicrafts, says Plato, bring about a natural weakness in the principle of excellence in a man, so that he cannot govern the ignoble growths in him, but nurses them, and cannot understand fostering any other. Those who exercise such arts and trades, as they have their bodies, he says, marred by their vulgar businesses, so they have their souls, too, bowed and broken by them. And if one of these uncomely people has a mind to seek self-culture and philosophy, Plato compares him to a bald little tinker, who has scraped together money, and has got his release from service, and has had a bath, and bought a new coat, and is rigged out like a bridegroom about to marry the daughter of his master who has fallen into poor and helpless estate.

Nor do the working professions fare any better than trade at the hands of Plato. He draws for us an inimitable picture of the working lawyer, and of

8. After Gray, the only other poet discussed by Arnold is Burns (not printed here). Arnold concludes that "Burns, like Chaucer, comes short of the high seriousness of the great classics."
1. Delivered as a lecture during Arnold's tour of the United States in 1883 and published in *Discourses in America* (1885), this essay has become a classic contribution to a subject endlessly debated. Its main argument was summed up by Stuart P. Sherman: "If Arnold had said outright that the study of letters helps us to *bear* the grand results of science, he would not have been guilty of a superficial epigram; he would have spoken from the depths of his experience."

his life of bondage; he shows how this bondage from his youth up has stunted and warped him, and made him small and crooked of soul, encompassing him with difficulties which he is not man enough to rely on justice and truth as means to encounter, but has recourse, for help out of them, to falsehood and wrong. And so, says Plato, this poor creature is bent and broken, and grows up from boy to man without a particle of soundness in him, although exceedingly smart and clever in his own esteem.

One cannot refuse to admire the artist who draws these pictures. But we say to ourselves that his ideas show the influence of a primitive and obsolete order of things, when the warrior caste and the priestly caste were alone in honor, and the humble work of the world was done by slaves. We have now changed all that; the modern majesty consists in work, as Emerson declares; and in work, we may add, principally of such plain and dusty kind as the work of cultivators of the ground, handicraftsmen, men of trade and business, men of the working professions. Above all is this true in a great industrious community such as that of the United States.

Now education, many people go on to say, is still mainly governed by the ideas of men like Plato, who lived when the warrior caste and the priestly or philosophical class were alone in honor, and the really useful part of the community were slaves. It is an education fitted for persons of leisure in such a community. This education passed from Greece and Rome to the feudal communities of Europe, where also the warrior caste and the priestly caste were alone held in honor, and where the really useful and working part of the community, though not nominally slaves as in the pagan world, were practically not much better off than slaves, and not more seriously regarded. And how absurd it is, people end by saying, to inflict this education upon an industrious modern community, where very few indeed are persons of leisure, and the mass to be considered has not leisure, but is bound, for its own great good, and for the great good of the world at large, to plain labor and to industrial pursuits, and the education in question tends necessarily to make men dissatisfied with these pursuits and unfitted for them!

That is what is said. So far I must defend Plato, as to plead that his view of education and studies is in the general, as it seems to me, sound enough, and fitted for all sorts and conditions of men, whatever their pursuits may be. "An intelligent man," says Plato, "will prize those studies which result in his soul getting soberness, righteousness, and wisdom, and will less value the others."[2] I cannot consider *that* a bad description of the aim of education, and of the motives which should govern us in the choice of studies, whether we are preparing ourselves for a hereditary seat in the English House of Lords or for the pork trade in Chicago.

Still I admit that Plato's world was not ours, that his scorn of trade and handicraft is fantastic, that he had no conception of a great industrial community such as that of the United States, and that such a community must and will shape its education to suit its own needs. If the usual education handed down to it from the past does not suit it, it will certainly before long drop this and try another. The usual education in the past has been mainly literary. The question is whether the studies which were long supposed to be the best for all of us are practically the best now; whether others are not

2. *Republic* 9.591.

better. The tyranny of the past, many think, weighs on us injuriously in the predominance given to letters in education. The question is raised whether, to meet the needs of our modern life, the predominance ought not now to pass from letters to science; and naturally the question is nowhere raised with more energy than here in the United States. The design of abasing what is called "mere literary instruction and education," and of exalting what is called "sound, extensive, and practical scientific knowledge," is, in this intensely modern world of the United States, even more perhaps than in Europe, a very popular design, and makes great and rapid progress.

I am going to ask whether the present movement for ousting letters from their old predominance in education, and for transferring the predominance in education to the natural sciences, whether this brisk and flourishing movement ought to prevail, and whether it is likely that in the end it really will prevail. An objection may be raised which I will anticipate. My own studies have been almost wholly in letters, and my visits to the field of the natural sciences have been very slight and inadequate, although those sciences have always strongly moved my curiosity. A man of letters, it will perhaps be said, is not competent to discuss the comparative merits of letters and natural science as means of education. To this objection I reply, first of all, that his incompetence, if he attempts the discussion but is really incompetent for it, will be abundantly visible; nobody will be taken in; he will have plenty of sharp observers and critics to save mankind from that danger. But the line I am going to follow is, as you will soon discover, so extremely simple, that perhaps it may be followed without failure even by one who for a more ambitious line of discussion would be quite incompetent.

Some of you may possibly remember a phrase of mine which has been the object of a good deal of comment; an observation to the effect that in our culture, the aim being *to know ourselves and the world*, we have, as the means to this end, *to know the best which has been thought and said in the world*.[3] A man of science, who is also an excellent writer and the very prince of debaters, Professor Huxley, in a discourse at the opening of Sir Josiah Mason's college at Birmingham,[4] laying hold of this phrase, expanded it by quoting some more words of mine, which are these: "The civilized world is to be regarded as now being, for intellectual and spiritual purposes, one great confederation, bound to a joint action and working to a common result; and whose members have for their proper outfit a knowledge of Greek, Roman, and Eastern antiquity, and of one another. Special local and temporary advantages being put out of account, that modern nation will in the intellectual and spiritual sphere make most progress, which most thoroughly carries out this program."

Now on my phrase, thus enlarged, Professor Huxley remarks that when I speak of the above-mentioned knowledge as enabling us to know ourselves and the world, I assert *literature* to contain the materials which suffice for thus making us know ourselves and the world. But it is not by any means clear, says he, that after having learnt all which ancient and modern literatures have to tell us, we have laid a sufficiently broad and deep foundation for that criticism of life, that knowledge of ourselves and the world, which

---

3. See *The Function of Criticism at the Present Time* (p. 1514). 4. See *Science and Culture* (p. 1559).

constitutes culture. On the contrary, Professor Huxley declares that he finds himself "wholly unable to admit that either nations or individuals will really advance, if their outfit draws nothing from the stores of physical science. An army without weapons of precision, and with no particular base of operations, might more hopefully enter upon a campaign on the Rhine, than a man, devoid of a knowledge of what physical science has done in the last century, upon a criticism of life."

This shows how needful it is for those who are to discuss any matter together, to have a common understanding as to the sense of the terms they employ—how needful, and how difficult. What Professor Huxley says, implies just the reproach which is so often brought against the study of belles-lettres, as they are called: that the study is an elegant one, but slight and ineffectual; a smattering of Greek and Latin and other ornamental things, of little use for anyone whose object is to get at truth, and to be a practical man. So, too, M. Renan[5] talks of the "superficial humanism" of a school course which treats us as if we were all going to be poets, writers, preachers, orators, and he opposes this humanism to positive science, or the critical search after truth. And there is always a tendency in those who are remonstrating against the predominance of letters in education, to understand by letters belles-lettres, and by belles-lettres a superficial humanism, the opposite of science or true knowledge.

But when we talk of knowing Greek and Roman antiquity, for instance, which is the knowledge people have called the humanities, I for my part mean a knowledge which is something more than a superficial humanism, mainly decorative. "I call all teaching *scientific*," says Wolf,[6] the critic of Homer, "which is systematically laid out and followed up to its original sources. For example: a knowledge of classical antiquity is scientific when the remains of classical antiquity are correctly studied in the original languages." There can be no doubt that Wolf is perfectly right; that all learning is scientific which is systematically laid out and followed up to its original sources, and that a genuine humanism is scientific.

When I speak of knowing Greek and Roman antiquity, therefore, as a help to knowing ourselves and the world, I mean more than a knowledge of so much vocabulary, so much grammar, so many portions of authors in the Greek and Latin languages, I mean knowing the Greeks and Romans, and their life and genius, and what they were and did in the world; what we get from them, and what is its value. That, at least, is the ideal; and when we talk of endeavoring to know Greek and Roman antiquity, as a help to knowing ourselves and the world, we mean endeavoring so to know them as to satisfy this ideal, however much we may still fall short of it.

The same also as to knowing our own and other modern nations, with the like aim of getting to understand ourselves and the world. To know the best that has been thought and said by the modern nations, is to know, says Professor Huxley, "only what modern *literatures* have to tell us; it is the criticism of life contained in modern literature." And yet "the distinctive character of our times," he urges, "lies in the vast and constantly increasing part which is played by natural knowledge." And how, therefore, can a man,

5. Ernest Renan (1823–1892), French religious philosopher and author of *The Life of Jesus*.

6. Friedrich August Wolf (1759–1824), German scholar.

devoid of knowledge of what physical science has done in the last century, enter hopefully upon a criticism of modern life?

Let us, I say, be agreed about the meaning of the terms we are using. I talk of knowing the best which has been thought and uttered in the world; Professor Huxley says this means knowing *literature*. Literature is a large word; it may mean everything written with letters or printed in a book. Euclid's *Elements* and Newton's *Principia* are thus literature. All knowledge that reaches us through books is literature. But by literature Professor Huxley means belles-lettres. He means to make me say, that knowing the best which has been thought and said by the modern nations is knowing their belles-lettres and no more. And this is no sufficient equipment, he argues, for a criticism of modern life. But as I do not mean, by knowing ancient Rome, knowing merely more or less of Latin belles-lettres, and taking no account of Rome's military, and political, and legal, and administrative work in the world; and as, by knowing ancient Greece, I understand knowing her as the giver of Greek art, and the guide to a free and right use of reason and to scientific method, and the founder of our mathematics and physics and astronomy and biology—I understand knowing her as all this, and not merely knowing certain Greek poems, and histories, and treatises, and speeches— so as to the knowledge of modern nations also. By knowing modern nations, I mean not merely knowing their belles-lettres, but knowing also what has been done by such men as Copernicus, Galileo, Newton, Darwin. "Our ancestors learned," says Professor Huxley, "that the earth is the center of the visible universe, and that man is the cynosure of things terrestrial; and more especially was it inculcated that the course of nature had no fixed order, but that it could be, and constantly was, altered." "But for us now," continues Professor Huxley, "the notions of the beginning and the end of the world entertained by our forefathers are no longer credible. It is very certain that the earth is not the chief body in the material universe, and that the world is not subordinated to man's use. It is even more certain that nature is the expression of a definite order, with which nothing interferes." "And yet," he cries, "the purely classical education advocated by the representatives of the humanists in our day gives no inkling of all this."

In due place and time I will just touch upon that vexed question of classical education; but at present the question is as to what is meant by knowing the best which modern nations have thought and said. It is not knowing their belles-lettres merely which is meant. To know Italian belles-lettres is not to know Italy, and to know English belles-lettres is not to know England. Into knowing Italy and England there comes a great deal more, Galileo and Newton amongst it. The reproach of being a superficial humanism, a tincture of belles-lettres, may attach rightly enough to some other disciplines; but to the particular discipline recommended when I proposed knowing the best that has been thought and said in the world, it does not apply. In that best I certainly include what in modern times has been thought and said by the great observers and knowers of nature.

There is, therefore, really no question between Professor Huxley and me as to whether knowing the great results of the modern scientific study of nature is not required as a part of our culture, as well as knowing the products of literature and art. But to follow the processes by which those results are reached, ought, say the friends of physical science, to be made the staple of education for the bulk of mankind. And here there does arise a question between those whom Professor Huxley calls with playful sarcasm "the Levites of culture," and those whom the poor humanist is sometimes apt to regard as its Nebuchadnezzars.[7]

The great results of the scientific investigation of nature we are agreed upon knowing, but how much of our study are we bound to give to the processes by which those results are reached? The results have their visible bearing on human life. But all the processes, too, all the items of fact, by which those results are reached and established, are interesting. All knowledge is interesting to a wise man, and the knowledge of nature is interesting to all men. It is very interesting to know, that, from the albuminous white of the egg, the chick in the egg gets the materials for its flesh, bones, blood, and feathers; while, from the fatty yolk of the egg, it gets the heat and energy which enable it at length to break its shell and begin the world. It is less interesting, perhaps, but still it is interesting, to know that when a taper burns, the wax is converted into carbonic acid and water. Moreover, it is quite true that the habit of dealing with facts, which is given by the study of nature, is, as the friends of physical science praise it for being, an excellent discipline. The appeal, in the study of nature, is constantly to observation and experiment; not only is it said that the thing is so, but we can be made to see that it is so. Not only does a man tell us that when a taper burns the wax is converted into carbonic acid and water, as a man may tell us, if he likes, that Charon[8] is punting his ferry boat on the river Styx, or that Victor Hugo is a sublime poet, or Mr. Gladstone the most admirable of statesmen; but we are made to see that the conversion into carbonic acid and water does actually happen. This reality of natural knowledge it is, which makes the friends of physical science contrast it, as a knowledge of things, with the humanist's knowledge, which is, say they, a knowledge of words. And hence Professor Huxley is moved to lay it down that, "for the purpose of attaining real culture, an exclusively scientific education is at least as effectual as an exclusively literary education." And a certain President of the Section for Mechanical Science in the British Association is, in Scripture phrase, "very bold," and declares that if a man, in his mental training, "has substituted literature and history for natural science, he has chosen the less useful alternative." But whether we go these lengths or not, we must all admit that in natural science the habit gained of dealing with facts is a most valuable discipline, and that everyone should have some experience of it.

More than this, however, is demanded by the reformers. It is proposed to make the training in natural science the main part of education, for the great majority of mankind at any rate. And here, I confess, I part company with the friends of physical science, with whom up to this point I have been agreeing. In differing from them, however, I wish to proceed with the utmost caution and diffidence. The smallness of my own acquaintance with the disciplines of natural science is ever before my mind, and I am fearful of doing these disciplines an injustice. The ability and pugnacity of the partisans of natural science make them formidable persons to contradict. The tone of tentative inquiry, which befits a being of dim faculties and bounded knowl-

---

7. Huxley implied that the humanists are hidebound conservatives like the Levites, priests who were preoccupied with traditional ritual observances. Arnold implies that the scientists may be like Nebuchadnezzar, a Babylonian king who destroyed the temple of Jerusalem.
8. In Greek mythology, the boatman who conducted the souls of the dead across the river Styx.

edge, is the tone I would wish to take and not to depart from. At present it seems to me, that those who are for giving to natural knowledge, as they call it, the chief place in the education of the majority of mankind, leave one important thing out of their account: the constitution of human nature. But I put this forward on the strength of some facts not at all recondite, very far from it; facts capable of being stated in the simplest possible fashion, and to which, if I so state them, the man of science will, I am sure, be willing to allow their due weight.

Deny the facts altogether, I think, he hardly can. He can hardly deny, that when we set ourselves to enumerate the powers which go to the building up of human life, and say that they are the power of conduct, the power of intellect and knowledge, the power of beauty, and the power of social life and manners—he can hardly deny that this scheme, though drawn in rough and plain lines enough, and not pretending to scientific exactness, does yet give a fairly true representation of the matter. Human nature is built up by these powers; we have the need for them all. When we have rightly met and adjusted the claims of them all, we shall then be in a fair way for getting soberness and righteousness, with wisdom. This is evident enough, and the friends of physical science would admit it.

But perhaps they may not have sufficiently observed another thing: namely, that the several powers just mentioned are not isolated, but there is, in the generality of mankind, a perpetual tendency to relate them one to another in divers ways. With one such way of relating them I am particularly concerned now. Following our instinct for intellect and knowledge, we acquire pieces of knowledge; and presently, in the generality of men, there arises the desire to relate these pieces of knowledge to our sense for conduct, to our sense for beauty—and there is weariness and dissatisfaction if the desire is balked. Now in this desire lies, I think, the strength of that hold which letters have upon us.

All knowledge is, as I said just now, interesting; and even items of knowledge which from the nature of the case cannot well be related, but must stand isolated in our thoughts, have their interest. Even lists of exceptions have their interest. If we are studying Greek accents, it is interesting to know that *pais* and *pas,* and some other monosyllables of the same form of declension, do not take the circumflex upon the last syllable of the genitive plural, but vary, in this respect, from the common rule. If we are studying physiology, it is interesting to know that the pulmonary artery carries dark blood and the pulmonary vein carries bright blood, departing in this respect from the common rule for the division of labor between the veins and the arteries. But everyone knows how we seek naturally to combine the pieces of our knowledge together, to bring them under general rules, to relate them to principles; and how unsatisfactory and tiresome it would be to go on forever learning lists of exceptions, or accumulating items of fact which must stand isolated.

Well, that same need of relating our knowledge, which operates here within the sphere of our knowledge itself, we shall find operating, also, outside that sphere. We experience, as we go on learning and knowing—the vast majority of us experience—the need of relating what we have learnt and known to the sense which we have in us for conduct, to the sense which we have in us for beauty.

A certain Greek prophetess of Mantineia in Arcadia, Diotima by name, once explained to the philosopher Socrates that love, and impulse, and bent of all kinds, is, in fact, nothing else but the desire in men that good should forever be present to them. This desire for good, Diotima assured Socrates, is our fundamental desire, of which fundamental desire every impulse in us is only some one particular form.[9] And therefore this fundamental desire it is, I suppose—this desire in men that good should be forever present to them—which acts in us when we feel the impulse for relating our knowledge to our sense for conduct and to our sense for beauty. At any rate, with men in general the instinct exists. Such is human nature. And the instinct, it will be admitted, is innocent, and human nature is preserved by our following the lead of its innocent instincts. Therefore, in seeking to gratify this instinct in question, we are following the instinct of self-preservation in humanity.

But, no doubt, some kinds of knowledge cannot be made to directly serve the instinct in question, cannot be directly related to the sense for beauty, to the sense for conduct. These are instrument knowledges; they lead on to other knowledges, which can. A man who passes his life in instrument knowledges is a specialist. They may be invaluable as instruments to something beyond, for those who have the gift thus to employ them; and they may be disciplines in themselves wherein it is useful for everyone to have some schooling. But it is inconceivable that the generality of men should pass all their mental life with Greek accents or with formal logic. My friend Professor Sylvester,[1] who is one of the first mathematicians in the world, holds transcendental doctrines as to the virtue of mathematics, but those doctrines are not for common men. In the very Senate House and heart of our English Cambridge[2] I once ventured, though not without an apology for my profaneness, to hazard the opinion that for the majority of mankind a little of mathematics, even, goes a long way. Of course this is quite consistent with their being of immense importance as an instrument to something else; but it is the few who have the aptitude for thus using them, not the bulk of mankind.

The natural sciences do not, however, stand on the same footing with these instrument knowledges. Experience shows us that the generality of men will find more interest in learning that, when a taper burns, the wax is converted into carbonic acid and water, or in learning the explanation of the phenomenon of dew, or in learning how the circulation of the blood is carried on, than they find in learning that the genitive plural of *pais* and *pas* does not take the circumflex on the termination. And one piece of natural knowledge is added to another, and others are added to that, and at last we come to propositions so interesting as Mr. Darwin's famous proposition that "our ancestor was a hairy quadruped furnished with a tail and pointed ears, probably arboreal in his habits." Or we come to propositions of such reach and magnitude as those which Professor Huxley delivers, when he says that the notions of our forefathers about the beginning and the end of the world were all wrong, and that nature is the expression of a definite order with which nothing interferes.

Interesting, indeed, these results of science are, important they are, and

9. Plato's *Symposium* 201–07.
1. James T. Sylvester, professor of mathematics at Johns Hopkins University.
2. At Cambridge University mathematics has been

traditionally emphasized. In its original form *Literature and Science* had been delivered as a lecture at Cambridge.

we should all of us be acquainted with them. But what I now wish you to mark is, that we are still, when they are propounded to us and we receive them, we are still in the sphere of intellect and knowledge. And for the generality of men there will be found, I say, to arise, when they have duly taken in the proposition that their ancestor was "a hairy quadruped furnished with a tail and pointed ears, probably arboreal in his habits," there will be found to arise an invincible desire to relate this proposition to the sense in us for conduct, and to the sense in us for beauty. But this the men of science will not do for us, and will hardly even profess to do. They will give us other pieces of knowledge, other facts, about other animals and their ancestors, or about plants, or about stones, or about stars; and they may finally bring us to those great "general conceptions of the universe, which are forced upon us all," says Professor Huxley, "by the progress of physical science." But still it will be *knowledge* only which they give us; knowledge not put for us into relation with our sense for conduct, our sense for beauty, and touched with emotion by being so put; not thus put for us, and therefore, to the majority of mankind, after a certain while, unsatisfying, wearying.

Not to the born naturalist, I admit. But what do we mean by a born naturalist? We mean a man in whom the zeal for observing nature is so uncommonly strong and eminent, that it marks him off from the bulk of mankind. Such a man will pass his life happily in collecting natural knowledge and reasoning upon it, and will ask for nothing, or hardly anything, more. I have heard it said that the sagacious and admirable naturalist whom we lost not very long ago, Mr. Darwin, once owned to a friend that for his part he did not experience the necessity for two things which most men find so necessary to them—religion and poetry; science and the domestic affections, he thought, were enough. To a born naturalist, I can well understand that this should seem so. So absorbing is his occupation with nature, so strong his love for his occupation, that he goes on acquiring natural knowledge and reasoning upon it, and has little time or inclination for thinking about getting it related to the desire in man for conduct, the desire in man for beauty. He relates it to them for himself as he goes along, so far as he feels the need; and he draws from the domestic affections all the additional solace necessary. But then Darwins are extremely rare. Another great and admirable master of natural knowledge, Faraday,[3] was a Sandemanian. That is to say, he related his knowledge to his instinct for conduct and to his instinct for beauty, by the aid of that respectable Scottish sectary, Robert Sandeman.[4] And so strong, in general, is the demand of religion and poetry to have their share in a man, to associate themselves with his knowing, and to relieve and rejoice it, that, probably, for one man amongst us with the disposition to do as Darwin did in this respect, there are at least fifty with the disposition to do as Faraday.

Education lays hold upon us, in fact, by satisfying this demand. Professor Huxley holds up to scorn medieval education, with its neglect of the knowledge of nature, its poverty even of literary studies, its formal logic devoted to "showing how and why that which the Church said was true must be true." But the great medieval Universities were not brought into being, we

---

3. Michael Faraday (1791–1867), chemist.
4. Founder of a Scottish sect bearing his name (1718–1771). "Sectary": zealous member of a sect.

may be sure, by the zeal for giving a jejune and contemptible education. Kings have been their nursing fathers, and queens have been their nursing mothers, but not for this. The medieval Universities came into being, because the supposed knowledge, delivered by Scripture and the Church, so deeply engaged men's hearts, by so simply, easily, and powerfully relating itself to their desire for conduct, their desire for beauty. All other knowledge was dominated by this supposed knowledge and was subordinated to it, because of the surpassing strength of the hold which it gained upon the affections of men, by allying itself profoundly with their sense for conduct, their sense for beauty.

But now, says Professor Huxley, conceptions of the universe fatal to the notions held by our forefathers have been forced upon us by physical science. Grant to him that they are thus fatal, that the new conceptions must and will soon become current everywhere, and that everyone will finally perceive them to be fatal to the beliefs of our forefathers. The need of humane letters, as they are truly called, because they serve the paramount desire in men that good should be forever present to them—the need of humane letters, to establish a relation between the new conceptions, and our instinct for beauty, our instinct for conduct, is only the more visible. The Middle Age could do without humane letters, as it could do without the study of nature, because its supposed knowledge was made to engage its emotions so powerfully. Grant that the supposed knowledge disappears, its power of being made to engage the emotions will of course disappear along with it—but the emotions themselves, and their claim to be engaged and satisfied, will remain. Now if we find by experience that humane letters have an undeniable power of engaging the emotions, the importance of humane letters in a man's training becomes not less, but greater, in proportion to the success of modern science in extirpating what it calls "medieval thinking."

Have humane letters, then, have poetry and eloquence, the power here attributed to them of engaging the emotions, and do they exercise it? And if they have it and exercise it, *how* do they exercise it, so as to exert an influence upon man's sense for conduct, his sense for beauty? Finally, even if they both can and do exert an influence upon the senses in question, how are they to relate to them the results—the modern results—of natural science? All these questions may be asked. First, have poetry and eloquence the power of calling out the emotions? The appeal is to experience. Experience shows that for the vast majority of men, for mankind in general, they have the power. Next, do they exercise it? They do. But then, *how* do they exercise it so as to affect man's sense for conduct, his sense for beauty? And this is perhaps a case for applying the Preacher's words: "Though a man labor to seek it out, yet he shall not find it; yea, father, though a wise man think to know it, yet shall he not be able to find it."[5] Why should it be one thing, in its effect upon the emotions, to say, "Patience is a virtue," and quite another thing, in its effect upon the emotions, to say with Homer,

$$τλητὸν\ γὰρ\ Μοῖραι\ θυμὸν\ θέσαν\ ἀνθρώποισιν^6—$$

"for an enduring heart have the destinies appointed to the children of men"? Why should it be one thing, in its effect upon the emotions, to say with the

---

5. Ecclesiastes 8.17 [Arnold's note].   6. *Iliad* 24.49 [Arnold's note].

philosopher Spinoza, *Felicitas in eo consistit quod homo suum esse conservare potest*—"Man's happiness consists in his being able to preserve his own essence,"[7] and quite another thing, in its effect upon the emotions, to say with the Gospel, "What is a man advantaged, if he gain the whole world, and lose himself, forfeit himself?"[8] How does this difference of effect arise? I cannot tell, and I am not much concerned to know; the important thing is that it does arise, and that we can profit by it. But how, finally, are poetry and eloquence to exercise the power of relating the modern results of natural science to man's instinct for conduct, his instinct for beauty? And here again I answer that I do not know *how* they will exercise it, but that they can and will exercise it I am sure. I do not mean that modern philosophical poets and modern philosophical moralists are to come and relate for us, in express terms, the results of modern scientific research to our instinct for conduct, our instinct for beauty. But I mean that we shall find, as a matter of experience, if we know the best that has been thought and uttered in the world, we shall find that the art and poetry and eloquence of men who lived, perhaps, long ago, who had the most limited natural knowledge, who had the most erroneous conceptions about many important matters, we shall find that this art, and poetry, and eloquence, have in fact not only the power of refreshing and delighting us, they have also the power—such is the strength and worth, in essentials, of their authors' criticism of life—they have a fortifying, and elevating, and quickening, and suggestive power, capable of wonderfully helping us to relate the results of modern science to our need for conduct, our need for beauty. Homer's conceptions of the physical universe were, I imagine, grotesque; but really, under the shock of hearing from modern science that "the world is not subordinated to man's use, and that man is not the cynosure of things terrestrial," I could, for my own part, desire no better comfort than Homer's line which I quoted just now,

τλητὸν γὰρ Μοῖραι θυμὸν θέσαν ἀνθρώποισιν—

"for an enduring heart have the destinies appointed to the children of men"!

And the more that men's minds are cleared, the more that the results of science are frankly accepted, the more that poetry and eloquence come to be received and studied as what in truth they really are—the criticism of life by gifted men, alive and active with extraordinary power at an unusual number of points—so much the more will the value of humane letters, and of art also, which is an utterance having a like kind of power with theirs, be felt and acknowledged, and their place in education be secured.

Let us therefore, all of us, avoid indeed as much as possible any invidious comparison between the merits of humane letters, as means of education, and the merits of the natural sciences. But when some President of a Section for Mechanical Science insists on making the comparison, and tells us that "he who in his training has substituted literature and history for natural science has chosen the less useful alternative," let us make answer to him that the student of humane letters only, will, at least, know also the great general conceptions brought in by modern physical science; for science, as Professor Huxley says, forces them upon us all. But the student of the natural sciences only, will, by our very hypothesis, know nothing of humane letters;

---

7. *Ethics* 4.18. 8. Cf. Luke 9.25.

not to mention that in setting himself to be perpetually accumulating natural knowledge, he sets himself to do what only specialists have in general the gift for doing genially. And so he will probably be unsatisfied, or at any rate incomplete, and even more incomplete than the student of humane letters only.

I once mentioned in a school report, how a young man in one of our English training colleges having to paraphrase the passage in *Macbeth* beginning,

Can'st thou not minister to a mind diseased?[9]

turned this line into, "Can you not wait upon the lunatic?" And I remarked what a curious state of things it would be, if every pupil of our national schools knew, let us say, that the moon is two thousand one hundred and sixty miles in diameter, and thought at the same time that a good paraphrase for

Can'st thou not minister to a mind diseased?

was, "Can you not wait upon the lunatic?" If one is driven to choose, I think I would rather have a young person ignorant about the moon's diameter, but aware that "Can you not wait upon the lunatic?" is bad, than a young person whose education had been such as to manage things the other way.

Or to go higher than the pupils of our national schools. I have in my mind's eye a member of our British Parliament who comes to travel here in America, who afterwards relates his travels, and who shows a really masterly knowledge of the geology of this great country and of its mining capabilities, but who ends by gravely suggesting that the United States should borrow a prince from our Royal Family, and should make him their king, and should create a House of Lords of great landed proprietors after the pattern of ours; and then America, he thinks, would have her future happily and perfectly secured. Surely, in this case, the President of the Section for Mechanical Science would himself hardly say that our member of Parliament, by concentrating himself upon geology and mineralogy, and so on, and not attending to literature and history, had "chosen the more useful alternative."

If then there is to be separation and option between humane letters on the one hand, and the natural sciences on the other, the great majority of mankind, all who have not exceptional and overpowering aptitudes for the study of nature, would do well, I cannot but think, to chose to be educated in humane letters rather than in the natural sciences. Letters will call out their being at more points, will make them live more.

I said that before I ended I would just touch on the question of classical education, and I will keep my word. Even if literature is to retain a large place in our education, yet Latin and Greek, say the friends of progress, will certainly have to go. Greek is the grand offender in the eyes of these gentlemen. The attackers of the established course of study think that against Greek, at any rate, they have irresistible arguments. Literature may perhaps be needed in education, they say; but why on earth should it be Greek literature? Why not French or German? Nay, "has not an Englishman models in his own literature of every kind of excellence?"[1] As before, it is not on any weak pleadings of my own that I rely for convincing the gainsayers; it is on

9. *Macbeth* 5.3.40.   1. *Science and Culture.*

the constitution of human nature itself, and on the instinct of self-preservation in humanity. The instinct for beauty is set in human nature, as surely as the instinct for knowledge is set there, or the instinct for conduct. If the instinct for beauty is served by Greek literature and art as it is served by no other literature and art, we may trust to the instinct of self-preservation in humanity for keeping Greek as part of our culture. We may trust to it for even making the study of Greek more prevalent than it is now. Greek will come, I hope, some day to be studied more rationally than at present; but it will be increasingly studied as men increasingly feel the need in them for beauty, and how powerfully Greek art and Greek literature can serve this need. Women will again study Greek, as Lady Jane Grey[2] did; I believe that in that chain of forts, with which the fair host of the Amazons are now engirdling our English universities,[3] I find that here in America, in colleges like Smith College in Massachusetts, and Vassar College in the State of New York, and in the happy families of the mixed universities out West, they are studying it already.

Defuit una mihi symmetria prisca—"The antique symmetry was the one thing wanting to me," said Leonardo da Vinci; and he was an Italian. I will not presume to speak for the Americans, but I am sure that, in the Englishman, the want of this admirable symmetry of the Greeks is a thousand times more great and crying than in any Italian. The results of the want show themselves most glaringly, perhaps, in our architecture, but they show themselves, also, in all our art. *Fit details strictly combined, in view of a large general result nobly conceived*; that is just the beautiful *symmetria prisca* of the Greeks, and it is just where we English fail, where all our art fails. Striking ideas we have, and well-executed details we have; but that high symmetry which, with satisfying and delightful effect, combines them, we seldom or never have. The glorious beauty of the Acropolis at Athens did not come from single fine things stuck about on that hill, a statue here, a gateway there—no, it arose from all things being perfectly combined for a supreme total effect. What must not an Englishman feel about our deficiencies in this respect, as the sense for beauty, whereof this symmetry is an essential element, awakens and strengthens within him! what will not one day be his respect and desire for Greece and its *symmetria prisca,* when the scales drop from his eyes as he walks the London streets, and he sees such a lesson in meanness as the Strand, for instance, in its true deformity! But here we are coming to our friend Mr. Ruskin's province,[4] and I will not intrude upon it, for he is its very sufficient guardian.

And so we at last find, it seems, we find flowing in favor of the humanities the natural and necessary stream of things, which seemed against them when we started. The "hairy quadruped furnished with a tail and pointed ears, probably arboreal in his habits," this good fellow carried hidden in his nature, apparently, something destined to develop into a necessity for humane letters. Nay, more; we seem finally to be even led to the further conclusion that our hairy ancestor carried in his nature, also, a necessity for Greek.

And therefore, to say the truth, I cannot really think that humane letters

2. Reputed to be a learned scholar in Greek. Grey (1537–1554) was proclaimed queen of England in 1553 but was forced to abdicate the throne nine days later. She was executed by order of Queen Mary.

3. Colleges for women at Oxford and Cambridge.
4. In such books as *The Stones of Venice,* Ruskin had criticized the "meanness" of Victorian architecture.

are in much actual danger of being thrust out from their leading place in education, in spite of the array of authorities against them at this moment. So long as human nature is what it is, their attractions will remain irresistible. As with Greek, so with letters generally: they will some day come, we may hope, to be studied more rationally, but they will not lose their place. What will happen will rather be that there will be crowded into education other matters besides, far too many; there will be, perhaps, a period of unsettlement and confusion and false tendency; but letters will not in the end lose their leading place. If they lose it for a time, they will get it back again. We shall be brought back to them by our wants and aspirations. And a poor humanist may possess his soul in patience, neither strive nor cry, admit the energy and brilliancy of the partisans of physical science, and their present favor with the public, to be far greater than his own, and still have a happy faith that the nature of things works silently on behalf of the studies which he loves, and that, while we shall all have to acquaint ourselves with the great results reached by modern science, and to give ourselves as much training in its disciplines as we can conveniently carry, yet the majority of men will always require humane letters; and so much the more, as they have the more and the greater results of science to relate to the need in man for conduct, and to the need in him for beauty.

1882, 1885

THOMAS HENRY HUXLEY
1825–1895

In Victorian controversies over religion and education, one of the most distinctive participants was Thomas Henry Huxley, a scientist who wrote clear, readable, and very persuasive English prose. Huxley's literary skill was responsible for his being lured out of his laboratory onto the platforms of public debate where his role was to champion, as he said, "the application of scientific methods of investigation to all the problems of life."

Huxley, a schoolmaster's son, was born in a London suburb. Until beginning the study of medicine, at seventeen, he had had little formal education, having taught himself classical and modern languages and the rudiments of scientific theory. In 1846, after receiving his degree in medicine, he embarked on a long voyage to the South Seas during which he studied the marine life of the tropical oceans and established a considerable reputation as a zoologist. Later he made investigations in geology and physiology, completing a total of 250 research papers during his lifetime. He also held teaching positions and served on public committees, but it was as a popularizer of science that he made his real mark. His popularizing was of two kinds. The first was to make the results of scientific investigations intelligible to a large audience. Such lectures as *On a Piece of Chalk* (not included here) are models of clear, vivid exposition that can be studied with profit by anyone interested in the art of teaching. His second kind of popularizing consisted of expounding the values of scientific education or of the application of scientific thinking to problems in religion. Here Huxley excels not so much as a teacher as a debater. In 1860 he demonstrated his argumentative skill when, as Darwin's defender or "bulldog," he demolished Bishop Wilberforce in a battle over *The Origin of Species*. In the 1870s, in such lectures as *Science and Culture*, he engaged in more genial fencing with Matthew Arnold concerning the relative importance of the study of science or the humanities in education. And in the 1880s he debated with William Gladstone on the topic of interpreting the Bible. His essay *Agnosticism and Christianity* indicates his premises in this controversy.

Summing up his own career in his *Autobiography*, Huxley noted that he had subordinated his ambition for scientific fame to other ends: "to the popularization of science; to the development and organization of scientific education; to the endless series of battles and skirmishes over evolution; and to untiring opposition to that ecclesiastical spirit, that clericalism, which . . . to whatever denomination it may belong, is the deadly enemy of science." In fighting these "battles" Huxley operated from different bases. Most of the time he wrote as a biologist engaged in assessing all assumptions by the tests of laboratory science. In this role he argued that humans are merely animals and that traditional religion is a tissue of superstitions and lies. At other times, however, Huxley wrote as a humanist and even as a follower of Carlyle. As he stated in a letter: "*Sartor Resartus* led me to know that a deep sense of religion was compatible with the entire absence of theology." In this second role he argued that humans are a very special kind of animal whose great distinction is that they are endowed with a moral sense and with freedom of the will; creatures who are admirable not for following nature but for departing from nature. The humanistic streak muddies the seemingly clear current of Huxley's thinking yet makes him a more interesting figure than he might otherwise have been. It is noteworthy that in the writings of his grandsons, Julian Huxley, the biologist, and Aldous Huxley, the novelist, a similar division of mind can once more be detected.

Even in his dying, T. H. Huxley continued his role as controversialist. The words he asked to be engraved on his tomb are typical of his view of life and typical, also, in the effect they had on his contemporaries, some of whom found the epitaph to be shocking:

> Be not afraid, ye waiting hearts that weep
> For still he giveth His beloved sleep,
> And if an endless sleep He wills, so best.

From Science and Culture[1]

[THE VALUES OF EDUCATION IN THE SCIENCES]

From the time that the first suggestion to introduce physical science into ordinary education was timidly whispered, until now, the advocates of scientific education have met with opposition of two kinds. On the one hand, they have been pooh-poohed by the men of business who pride themselves on being the representatives of practicality; while, on the other hand, they have been excommunicated by the classical scholars, in their capacity of Levites in charge of the ark of culture[2] and monopolists of liberal education.

The practical men believed that the idol whom they worship—rule of thumb—has been the source of the past prosperity, and will suffice for the future welfare of the arts and manufactures. They are of opinion that science is speculative rubbish; that theory and practice have nothing to do with one

---

1. This essay was first delivered as an address in 1880. The occasion had been the opening of a new Scientific College at Birmingham, which had been endowed by Sir Josiah Mason (1795–1881), a self-made businessman. For Matthew Arnold's reply to Huxley's argument see his essay *Literature and Science* (p. 1545).

2. In the Old Testament, the Levites were the priests preoccupied with traditional ritual observances (cf. Joshua 6).

another; and that the scientific habit of mind is an impediment, rather than an aid, in the conduct of ordinary affairs.

I have used the past tense in speaking of the practical men—for although they were very formidable thirty years ago, I am not sure that the pure species has not been extirpated. In fact, so far as mere argument goes, they have been subjected to such a *feu d'enfer*[3] that it is a miracle if any have escaped. But I have remarked that your typical practical man has an unexpected resemblance to one of Milton's angels. His spiritual wounds, such as are inflicted by logical weapons, may be as deep as a well and as wide as a church door,[4] but beyond shedding a few drops of ichor,[5] celestial or otherwise, he is no whit the worse. So, if any of these opponents be left, I will not waste time in vain repetition of the demonstrative evidence of the practical value of science; but knowing that a parable will sometimes penetrate where syllogisms fail to effect an entrance, I will offer a story for their consideration.

Once upon a time, a boy, with nothing to depend upon but his own vigorous nature, was thrown into the thick of the struggle for existence in the midst of a great manufacturing population. He seems to have had a hard fight, inasmuch as, by the time he was thirty years of age, his total disposable funds amounted to twenty pounds. Nevertheless, middle life found him giving proof of his comprehension of the practical problems he had been roughly called upon to solve, by a career of remarkable prosperity.

Finally, having reached old age with its well-earned surroundings of "honor, troops of friends,"[6] the hero of my story bethought himself of those who were making a like start in life, and how he could stretch out a helping hand to them.

After long and anxious reflection this successful practical man of business could devise nothing better than to provide them with the means of obtaining "sound, extensive, and practical scientific knowledge." And he devoted a large part of his wealth and five years of incessant work to this end.

I need not point the moral of a tale which, as the solid and spacious fabric of the Scientific College assures us, is no fable, nor can anything which I could say intensify the force of this practical answer to practical objections.

We may take it for granted then, that, in the opinion of those best qualified to judge, the diffusion of thorough scientific education is an absolutely essential condition of industrial progress; and that the College which has been opened today will confer an inestimable boon upon those whose livelihood is to be gained by the practice of the arts and manufactures of the district.

The only question worth discussion is whether the conditions under which the work of the College is to be carried out are such as to give it the best possible chance of achieving permanent success.

Sir Josiah Mason, without doubt most wisely, has left very large freedom of action to the trustees, to whom he proposes ultimately to commit the administration of the College, so that they may be able to adjust its arrangements in accordance with the changing conditions of the future. But, with respect to three points, he has laid most explicit injunctions upon both administrators and teachers.

---

3. Hellfire (French).
4. Shakespeare's *Romeo and Juliet* 3.1.99–100.
5. Ethereal fluid that supposedly flows through

the veins of the gods.
6. Cf. Shakespeare's *Macbeth* 5.3.25.

Party politics are forbidden to enter into the minds of either, so far as the work of the College is concerned; theology is as sternly banished from its precincts; and finally, it is especially declared that the College shall make no provision for "mere literary instruction and education."

It does not concern me at present to dwell upon the first two injunctions any longer than may be needful to express my full conviction of their wisdom. But the third prohibition brings us face to face with those other opponents of scientific education, who are by no means in the moribund condition of the practical man, but alive, alert, and formidable.

It is not impossible that we shall hear this express exclusion of "literary instruction and education" from a College which, nevertheless, professes to give a high and efficient education, sharply criticized. Certainly the time was that the Levites of culture would have sounded their trumpets against its walls as against an educational Jericho.[7]

How often have we not been told that the study of physical science is incompetent to confer culture; that it touches none of the higher problems of life; and, what is worse, that the continual devotion to scientific studies tends to generate a narrow and bigoted belief in the applicability of scientific methods to the search after truth of all kinds? How frequently one has reason to observe that no reply to a troublesome argument tells so well as calling its author a "mere scientific specialist." And, as I am afraid it is not permissible to speak of this form of opposition to scientific education in the past tense; may we not expect to be told that this, not only omission, but prohibition, of "mere literary instruction and education" is a patent example of scientific narrow-mindedness?

I am not acquainted with Sir Josiah Mason's reasons for the action which he has taken; but if, as I apprehend is the case, he refers to the ordinary classical course of our schools and universities by the name of "mere literary instruction and education," I venture to offer sundry reasons of my own in support of that action.

For I hold very strongly by two convictions: The first is that neither the discipline nor the subject matter of classical education is of such direct value to the student of physical science as to justify the expenditure of valuable time upon either; and the second is that for the purpose of attaining real culture, an exclusively scientific education is at least as effectual as an exclusively literary education.

I need hardly point out to you that these opinions, especially the latter, are diametrically opposed to those of the great majority of educated Englishmen, influenced as they are by school and university traditions. In their belief, culture is obtainable only by a liberal education; and a liberal education is synonymous, not merely with education and instruction in literature, but in one particular form of literature, namely, that of Greek and Roman antiquity. They hold that the man who has learned Latin and Greek, however little, is educated; while he who is versed in other branches of knowledge, however deeply, is a more or less respectable specialist, not admissible into the cultured caste. The stamp of the educated man, the University degree, is not for him.

I am too well acquainted with the generous catholicity of spirit, the true

7. The Levites blew their trumpets before the city walls of Jericho to bring them down (Joshua 6).

sympathy with scientific thought, which pervades the writings of our chief apostle of culture[8] to identify him with these opinions; and yet one may cull from one and another of those epistles to the Philistines, which so much delight all who do not answer to that name, sentences which lend them some support.

Mr. Arnold tells us that the meaning of culture is "to know the best that has been thought and said in the world." It is the criticism of life contained in literature. That criticism regards "Europe as being, for intellectual and spiritual purposes, one great confederation, bound to a joint action and working to a common result; and whose members have, for their common outfit, a knowledge of Greek, Roman, and Eastern antiquity, and of one another. Special, local, and temporary advantages being put out of account, that modern nation will in the intellectual and spiritual sphere make most progress, which most thoroughly carries out this program. And what is that but saying that we too, all of us, as individuals, the more thoroughly we carry it out, shall make the more progress?"[9]

We have here to deal with two distinct propositions. The first, that a criticism of life is the essence of culture; the second, that literature contains the materials which suffice for the construction of such criticism.

I think that we must all assent to the first proposition. For culture certainly means something quite different from learning or technical skill. It implies the possession of an ideal, and the habit of critically estimating the value of things by comparison with a theoretic standard. Perfect culture should supply a complete theory of life, based upon a clear knowledge alike of its possibilities and of its limitations.

But we may agree to all this, and yet strongly dissent from the assumption that literature alone is competent to supply this knowledge. After having learnt all that Greek, Roman, and Eastern antiquity have thought and said, and all that modern literature have to tell us, it is not self-evident that we have laid a sufficiently broad and deep foundation for that criticism of life which constitutes culture.

Indeed, to anyone acquainted with the scope of physical science, it is not at all evident. Considering progress only in the "intellectual and spiritual sphere," I find myself wholly unable to admit that either nations or individuals will really advance, if their common outfit draws nothing from the stores of physical science. I should say that an army, without weapons of precision and with no particular base of operations, might more hopefully enter upon a campaign on the Rhine than a man, devoid of a knowledge of what physical science has done in the last century, upon a criticism of life.

When a biologist meets with an anomaly, he instinctively turns to the study of development to clear it up. The rationale of contradictory opinions may with equal confidence be sought in history.

It is, happily, no new thing that Englishmen should employ their wealth in building and endowing institutions for educational purposes. But, five or six hundred years ago, deeds of foundation expressed or implied conditions as nearly as possible contrary to those which have been thought expedient

---

8. I.e., Matthew Arnold. For his discussion of the Philistines, see *Culture and Anarchy* (p. 1528).

9. Arnold, *The Function of Criticism at the Present Time*, para. 4 from the end.

by Sir Josiah Mason. That is to say, physical science was practically ignored, while a certain literary training was enjoined as a means to the acquirement of knowledge which was essentially theological.

The reason of this singular contradiction between the actions of men alike animated by a strong and disinterested desire to promote the welfare of their fellows, is easily discovered.

At that time, in fact, if anyone desired knowledge beyond such as could be obtained by his own observation, or by common conversation, his first necessity was to learn the Latin language, inasmuch as all the higher knowledge of the western world was contained in words written in that language. Hence, Latin grammar, with logic and rhetoric, studied through Latin, were the fundamentals of education. With respect to the substance of the knowledge imparted through this channel, the Jewish and Christian Scriptures, as interpreted and supplemented by the Romish Church, were held to contain a complete and infallibly true body of information.

Theological dicta were, to the thinkers of those days, that which the axioms and definitions of Euclid are to the geometers of these. The business of the philosophers of the Middle Ages was to deduce from the data furnished by the theologians, conclusions in accordance with ecclesiastical decrees. They were allowed the high privilege of showing, by logical process, how and why that which the Church said was true, must be true. And if their demonstrations fell short of or exceeded this limit, the Church was maternally ready to check their aberrations; if need were, by the help of the secular arm.

Between the two, our ancestors were furnished with a compact and complete criticism of life. They were told how the world began and how it would end; they learned that all material existence was but a base and insignificant blot upon the fair face of the spiritual world, and that nature was, to all intents and purposes, the playground of the devil; they learned that the earth is the center of the visible universe, and that man is the cynosure of things terrestrial, and more especially was it inculcated that the course of nature had no fixed order, but that it could be, and constantly was, altered by the agency of innumerable spiritual beings, good and bad, according as they were moved by the deeds and prayers of men. The sum and substance of the whole doctrine was to produce the conviction that the only thing really worth knowing in this world was how to secure that place in a better which, under certain conditions, the Church promised.

Our ancestors had a living belief in this theory of life, and acted upon it in their dealings with education, as in all other matters. Culture meant saintliness—after the fashion of the saints of those days; the education that led to it was, of necessity, theological; and the way to theology lay through Latin.

That the study of nature—further than was requisite for the satisfaction of everyday wants—should have any bearing on human life was far from the thoughts of men thus trained. Indeed, as nature had been cursed for man's sake, it was an obvious conclusion that those who meddled with nature were likely to come into pretty close contact with Satan. And, if any born scientific investigator followed his instincts, he might safely reckon upon earning the reputation, and probably upon suffering the fate, of a sorcerer.

Had the western world been left to itself in Chinese isolation, there is no saying how long this state of things might have endured. But, happily, it was not left to itself. Even earlier than the thirteenth century, the development of Moorish civilization in Spain and the great movement of the Crusades had introduced the leaven which, from that day to this, has never ceased to work. At first, through the intermediation of Arabic translations, afterwards by the study of the originals, the western nations of Europe became acquainted with the writings of the ancient philosophers and poets, and, in time, with the whole of the vast literature of antiquity.

Whatever there was of high intellectual aspiration or dominant capacity in Italy, France, Germany, and England, spent itself for centuries in taking possession of the rich inheritance left by the dead civilizations of Greece and Rome. Marvelously aided by the invention of printing,[1] classical learning spread and flourished. Those who possessed it prided themselves on having attained the highest culture then within the reach of mankind.

And justly. For, saving Dante on his solitary pinnacle, there was no figure in modern literature at the time of the Renaissance to compare with the men of antiquity; there was no art to compete with their sculpture; there was no physical science but that which Greece had created. Above all, there was no other example of perfect intellectual freedom—of the unhesitating acceptance of reason as the sole guide to truth and the supreme arbiter of conduct.

The new learning necessarily soon exerted a profound influence upon education. The language of the monks and schoolmen[2] seemed little better than gibberish to scholars fresh from Virgil and Cicero, and the study of Latin was placed upon a new foundation. Moreover, Latin itself ceased to afford the sole key to knowledge. The student who sought the highest thought of antiquity found only a secondhand reflection of it in Roman literature, and turned his face to the full light of the Greeks. And after a battle, not altogether dissimilar to that which is at present being fought over the teaching of physical science, the study of Greek was recognized as an essential element of all higher education.

Then the Humanists, as they were called, won the day; and the great reform which they effected was of incalculable service to mankind. But the nemesis of all reformers is finality; and the reformers of education, like those of religion, fell into the profound, however common, error of mistaking the beginning for the end of the work of reformation.

The representatives of the Humanists, in the nineteenth century, take their stand upon classical education as the sole avenue to culture as firmly as if we were still in the age of Renaissance. Yet, surely, the present intellectual relations of the modern and the ancient worlds are profoundly different from those which obtained three centuries ago. Leaving aside the existence of a great and characteristically modern literature, of modern painting, and, especially, of modern music, there is one feature of the present state of the civilized world which separates it more widely from the Renaissance than the Renaissance was separated from the Middle Ages.

This distinctive character of our own times lies in the vast and constantly increasing part which is played by natural knowledge. Not only is our daily life shaped by it; not only does the prosperity of millions of men depend upon it, but our whole theory of life has long been influenced, consciously or unconsciously, by the general conceptions of the universe which have been forced upon us by physical science.

1. In the mid-15th century.
2. Exponents of the theology, philosophy, and logic of the medieval period in Europe.

In fact, the most elementary acquaintance with the results of scientific investigation shows us that they offer a broad and striking contradiction to the opinion so implicitly credited and taught in the Middle Ages.

The notions of the beginning and the end of the world entertained by our forefathers are no longer credible. It is very certain that the earth is not the chief body in the material universe, and that the world is not subordinated to man's use. It is even more certain that nature is the expression of a definite order with which nothing interferes, and that the chief business of mankind is to learn that order and govern themselves accordingly. Moreover this scientific "criticism of life" presents itself to us with different credentials from any other. It appeals not to authority, nor to what anybody may have thought or said, but to nature. It admits that all our interpretations of natural fact are more or less imperfect and symbolic, and bids the learner seek for truth not among words but among things. It warns us that the assertion which outstrips evidence is not only a blunder but a crime.

The purely classical education advocated by the representatives of the Humanists in our day gives no inkling of all this. A man may be a better scholar than Erasmus,[3] and know no more of the chief causes of the present intellectual fermentation than Erasmus did. Scholarly and pious persons, worthy of all respect, favor us with allocutions upon the sadness of the antagonism of science to their medieval way of thinking, which betray an ignorance of the first principles of scientific investigation, an incapacity for understanding what a man of science means by veracity, and an unconsciousness of the weight of established scientific truths, which is almost comical.

*   *   *

Thus I venture to think that the pretensions of our modern Humanists to the possession of the monopoly of culture and to the exclusive inheritance of the spirit of antiquity must be abated, if not abandoned. But I should be very sorry that anything I have said should be taken to imply a desire on my part to depreciate the value of classical education, as it might be and as it sometimes is. The native capacities of mankind vary no less than their opportunities; and while culture is one, the road by which one man may best reach it is widely different from that which is most advantageous to another. Again, while scientific education is yet inchoate and tentative, classical education is thoroughly well organized upon the practical experience of generations of teachers. So that, given ample time for learning and estimation for ordinary life, or for a literary career, I do not think that a young Englishman in search of culture can do better than follow the course usually marked out for him, supplementing its deficiencies by his own efforts.

But for those who mean to make science their serious occupation; or who intend to follow the profession of medicine; or who have to enter early upon the business of life; for all these, in my opinion, classical education is a mistake; and it is for this reason that I am glad to see "mere literary education and instruction" shut out from the curriculum of Sir Josiah Mason's College, seeing that its inclusion would probably lead to the introduction of the ordinary smattering of Latin and Greek.

Nevertheless, I am the last person to question the importance of genuine

3. Eminent Dutch humanist and scholar (1466–1536).

literary education, or to suppose that intellectual culture can be complete without it. An exclusively scientific training will bring about a mental twist as surely as an exclusively literary training. The value of the cargo does not compensate for a ship's being out of trim; and I should be very sorry to think that the Scientific College would turn out none but lopsided men.

There is no need, however, that such a catastrophe should happen. Instruction in English, French, and German is provided, and thus the three greatest literatures of the modern world are made accessible to the student.

French and German, and especially the latter language, are absolutely indispensable to those who desire full knowledge in any department of science. But even supposing that the knowledge of these languages acquired is not more than sufficient for purely scientific purposes, every Englishman has, in his native tongue, an almost perfect instrument of literary expression; and, in his own literature, models of every kind of literary excellence. If an Englishman cannot get literary culture out of his Bible, his Shakespeare, his Milton, neither, in my belief, will the profoundest study of Homer and Sophocles, Virgil and Horace, give it to him.

Thus, since the constitution of the College makes sufficient provision for literary as well as for scientific education, and since artistic instruction is also contemplated, it seems to me that a fairly complete culture is offered to all who are willing to take advantage of it.

1880, 1881

From Agnosticism and Christianity[1]

[AGNOSTICISM DEFINED]

Nemo ergo ex me scire quaerat, quod me nescire scio, nisi forte ut nescire discat.

—AUGUSTINUS, *De Civ. Dei*, XII.7.[2]

The present discussion has arisen out of the use, which has become general in the last few years, of the terms "Agnostic"[3] and "Agnosticism."

The people who call themselves "Agnostics" have been charged with doing so because they have not the courage to declare themselves "Infidels." It has been insinuated that they have adopted a new name in order to escape the unpleasantness which attaches to their proper denomination. To this wholly erroneous imputation I have replied by showing that the term "Agnostic" did, as a matter of fact, arise in a manner which negatives it; and my statement has not been, and cannot be, refuted. Moreover, speaking for myself, and without impugning the right of any other person to use the term in another sense, I further say that Agnosticism is not properly described as a "negative" creed, nor indeed as a creed of any kind, except in so far as it expresses absolute faith in the validity of a principle, which is as much ethical as intellectual. This principle may be stated in various ways, but they all amount

1. This essay appeared in a magazine in 1889 as a reply to critics who had argued that agnostics were simply infidels under a new name. It was later included in Huxley's volume *Essays on Some Controverted Questions* (1892).

2. No one, therefore, should seek to learn knowledge from me, for I know that I do not know— unless indeed he wishes to learn that he does not know (Latin; Saint Augustine, *City of God* 12.7).

3. The term *agnostic* was coined by Huxley.

to this: that it is wrong for a man to say that he is certain of the objective truth of any proposition unless he can produce evidence which logically justifies that certainty. This is what Agnosticism asserts; and, in my opinion, it is all that is essential to Agnosticism. That which Agnostics deny and repudiate, as immoral, is the contrary doctrine, that there are propositions which men ought to believe, without logically satisfactory evidence; and that reprobation ought to attach to the profession of disbelief in such inadequately supported propositions. The justification of the Agnostic principles lies in the success which follows upon its application, whether in the field of natural, or in that of civil, history; and in the fact that, so far as these topics are concerned, no sane man thinks of denying its validity.

Still speaking for myself, I add that though Agnosticism is not, and cannot be, a creed, except in so far as its general principle is concerned; yet that the application of that principle results in the denial of, or the suspension of judgment concerning, a number of propositions respecting which our contemporary ecclesiastical "gnostics" profess entire certainty. And, in so far as these eccelesiastical persons can be justified in their old-established custom (which many nowadays think more honored in the breach than the observance) of using opprobrious names to those who differ from them, I fully admit their right to call me and those who think with me "Infidels"; all I have ventured to urge is that they must not expect us to speak of ourselves by that title.

The extent of the region of the uncertain, the number of the problems the investigation of which ends in a verdict of not proven, will vary according to the knowledge and the intellectual habits of the individual Agnostic. I do not very much care to speak of anything as "unknowable." What I am sure about is that there are many topics about which I know nothing; and which, so far as I can see, are out of reach of my faculties. But whether these things are knowable by anyone else is exactly one of those matters which is beyond my knowledge, though I may have a tolerably strong opinion as to the probabilities of the case. Relatively to myself, I am quite sure that the region of uncertainty—the nebulous country in which words play the part of realities—is far more extensive than I could wish. Materialism and Idealism; Theism and Atheism; the doctrine of the soul and its mortality or immortality—appear in the history of philosophy like the shades of Scandinavian heroes, eternally slaying one another and eternally coming to life again in a metaphysical "Nifelheim."[4] It is getting on for twenty-five centuries, at least, since mankind began seriously to give their minds to these topics. Generation after generation, philosophy has been doomed to roll the stone uphill; and, just as all the world swore it was at the top, down it has rolled to the bottom again.[5] All this is written in innumerable books; and he who will toil through them will discover that the stone is just where it was when the work began. Hume saw this; Kant saw it; since their time, more and more eyes have been cleansed of the films which prevented them from seeing it; until now the weight and number of those who refuse to be the prey of verbal mystifications has begun to tell in practical life.

It was inevitable that a conflict should arise between Agnosticism and

4. In Norse mythology, realms of cold and darkness.
5. Cf. the Greek story of Sisyphus in Hades, who was condemned to keep rolling a stone uphill, which always rolled downhill again before it reached the summit.

Theology; or rather, I ought to say, between Agnosticism and Ecclesiasticism. For Theology, the science, is one thing; and Ecclesiasticism, the championship of a foregone conclusion[6] as to the truth of a particular form of Theology, is another. With scientific Theology, Agnosticism has no quarrel. On the contrary, the Agnostic, knowing too well the influence of prejudice and idiosyncrasy, even on those who desire most earnestly to be impartial, can wish for nothing more urgently than that the scientific theologian should not only be at perfect liberty to thresh out the matter in his own fashion; but that he should, if he can, find flaws in the Agnostic position; and, even if demonstration is not to be had, that he should put, in their full force, the grounds of the conclusions he thinks probable. The scientific theologian admits the Agnostic principle, however widely his results may differ from those reached by the majority of Agnostics.

But, as between Agnosticism and Ecclesiasticism, or, as our neighbors across the Channel call it, Clericalism, there can be neither peace nor truce. The Cleric asserts that it is morally wrong not to believe certain propositions, whatever the results of a strict scientific investigation of the evidence of these propositions. He tells us "that religious error is, in itself, of an immoral nature."[7] He declares that he has prejudged certain conclusions, and looks upon those who show cause for arrest of judgment as emissaries of Satan. It necessarily follows that, for him, the attainment of faith, not the ascertainment of truth, is the highest aim of mental life. And, on careful analysis of the nature of this faith, it will too often be found to be, not the mystic process of unity with the Divine, understood by the religious enthusiast; but that which the candid simplicity of a Sunday scholar once defined it to be. "Faith," said this unconscious plagiarist of Tertullian,[8] "is the power of saying you believe things which are incredible."

Now I, and many other Agnostics, believe that faith, in this sense, is an abomination; and though we do not indulge in the luxury of self-righteousness so far as to call those who are not of our way of thinking hard names, we do feel that the disagreement between ourselves and those who hold this doctrine is even more moral than intellectual. It is desirable there should be an end of any mistakes on this topic. If our clerical opponents were clearly aware of the real state of the case, there would be an end of the curious delusion, which often appears between the lines of their writings, that those whom they are so fond of calling "Infidels" are people who not only ought to be, but in their hearts are, ashamed of themselves. It would be discourteous to do more than hint the antipodal opposition of this pleasant dream of theirs to facts.

The clerics and their lay allies commonly tell us that if we refuse to admit that there is good ground for expressing definite convictions about certain topics, the bonds of human society will dissolve and mankind lapse into savagery. There are several answers to this assertion. One is that the bonds of human society were formed without the aid of their theology; and, in the opinion of not a few competent judges, have been weakened rather than strengthened by a good deal of it. Greek science, Greek art, the ethics of old

6. Let us maintain, before we have proved. This seeming paradox is the secret of happiness. (Dr. Newman, Tract 85) [Huxley's note].
7. Dr. Newman, Essay on Development [Huxley's note].
8. Roman author and church father (ca. 155–ca. 222).

Israel, the social organization of old Rome, contrived to come into being, without the help of anyone who believed in a single distinctive article of the simplest of the Christian creeds. The science, the art, the jurisprudence, the chief political and social theories, of the modern world have grown out of those of Greece and Rome—not by favor of, but in the teeth of, the fundamental teachings of early Christianity, to which science, art, and any serious occupation with the things of this world, were alike despicable.

Again, all that is best in the ethics of the modern world, in so far as it has not grown out of Greek thought, or Barbarian manhood, is the direct development of the ethics of old Israel. There is no code of legislation, ancient or modern, at once so just and so merciful, so tender to the weak and poor, as the Jewish law; and, if the Gospels are to be trusted, Jesus of Nazareth himself declared that he taught nothing but that which lay implicitly, or explicitly, in the religious and ethical system of his people.

> And the scribe said unto him, Of a truth, Teacher, thou hast well said that he is one; and there is none other but he and to love him with all the heart, and with all the understanding, and with all the strength, and to love his neighbour as himself, is much more than all whole burnt offerings and sacrifices. (Mark xii.32–33)

Here is the briefest of summaries of the teaching of the prophets of Israel of the eighth century; does the Teacher, whose doctrine is thus set forth in his presence, repudiate the exposition? Nay; we are told, on the contrary, that Jesus saw that he "answered discreetly," and replied, "Thou are not far from the kingdom of God."

So that I think that even if the creeds,[9] from the so-called "Apostles' " to the so-called "Athanasian," were swept into oblivion; and even if the human race should arrive at the conclusion that, whether a bishop washes a cup or leaves it unwashed, is not a matter of the least consequence, it will get on very well. The causes which have led to the development of morality in mankind, which have guided or impelled us all the way from the savage to the civilized state, will not cease to operate because a number of ecclesiastical hypotheses turn out to be baseless. And, even if the absurd notion that morality is more the child of speculation than of practical necessity and inherited instinct, had any foundation; if all the world is going to thieve, murder, and otherwise misconduct itself as soon as it discovers that certain portions of ancient history are mythical; what is the relevance of such arguments to any one who holds by the Agnostic principle?

Surely, the attempt to cast out Beelzebub by the aid of Beelzebub is a hopeful procedure as compared to that of preserving morality by the aid of immorality. For I suppose it is admitted that an Agnostic may be perfectly sincere, may be competent, and may have studied the question at issue with as much care as his clerical opponents. But, if the Agnostic really believes what he says, the "dreadful consequence" argufier (consistently, I admit, with his own principles) virtually asks him to abstain from telling the truth, or to say what he believes to be untrue, because of the supposed injurious consequences to morality. "Beloved brethren, that we may be spotlessly moral, before all things let us lie," is the sum total of many an exhortation addressed

9. Summaries of Christian doctrine.

to the "Infidel." Now, as I have already pointed out, we cannot oblige our exhorters. We leave the practical application of the convenient doctrines of "Reserve" and "Non-natural interpretation" to those who invented them.

I trust that I have now made amends for any ambiguity, or want of fullness, in my previous exposition of that which I hold to be the essence of the Agnostic doctrine. Henceforward, I might hope to hear no more of the assertion that we are necessarily Materialists, Idealists, Atheists, Theists, or any other ists, if experience had led me to think that the proved falsity of a statement was any guarantee against its repetition. And those who appreciate the nature of our position will see, at once, that when Ecclesiasticism declares that we ought to believe this, that, and the other, and are very wicked if we don't, it is impossible for us to give any answer but this: We have not the slightest objection to believe anything you like, if you will give us good grounds for belief; but, if you cannot, we must respectfully refuse, even if that refusal should wreck morality and insure our own damnation several times over. We are quite content to leave that to the decision of the future. The course of the past has impressed us with the firm conviction that no good ever comes of falsehood, and we feel warranted in refusing even to experiment in that direction. * * *

1889, 1892

GEORGE MEREDITH
1828–1909

Like Thomas Hardy, George Meredith preferred writing poetry to writing novels, but it was as the author of *The Ordeal of Richard Feverel* (1859), *The Egoist* (1879), and other novels that he made his mark. His poems nevertheless deserve more attention than they have yet received, especially *Modern Love* (1862), a brilliant narrative poem that was greeted by the *Saturday Review* as "a grave moral mistake." This sequence of fifty 16-line sonnets is a kind of novel in verse that analyzes the sufferings of a husband and wife whose marriage is breaking up. The story is told, for the most part, by the husband speaking in the first person, but the opening and closing sections are in third person. *Modern Love* was probably derived, in part, from Meredith's own experiences. At twenty-one, at the outset of his career as a writer in London, he married a daughter of the satirist Thomas Love Peacock. Nine years later, after a series of quarrels, his wife eloped to Europe with another artist. The Merediths were never reconciled, and in 1861 she died.

From Modern Love

1

By this he knew she wept with waking eyes:
That, at his hand's light quiver by her head,
The strange low sobs that shook their common bed
Were called into her with a sharp surprise,
5   And strangled mute, like little gaping snakes,

Dreadfully venomous to him. She lay
Stone-still, and the long darkness flowed away
With muffled pulses. Then, as midnight makes
Her giant heart of Memory and Tears
10   Drink the pale drug of silence, and so beat
Sleep's heavy measure, they from head to feet
Were moveless, looking through their dead black years
By vain regret scrawled over the blank wall.
Like sculptured effigies they might be seen
15   Upon their marriage tomb, the sword between;[1]
Each wishing for the sword that severs all.

2

It ended, and the morrow brought the task.
Her eyes were guilty gates, that let him in
By shutting all too zealous for their sin:
Each sucked a secret, and each wore a mask.
5   But, oh, the bitter taste her beauty had!
He sickened as at breath of poison-flowers:
A languid humor stole among the hours,
And if their smiles encountered, he went mad,
And raged deep inward, till the light was brown
10   Before his vision, and the world, forgot,
Looked wicked as some old dull murder spot.
A star with lurid beams, she seemed to crown
The pit of infamy: and then again
He fainted on his vengefulness, and strove
15   To ape the magnanimity of love,
And smote himself, a shuddering heap of pain.

17

At dinner, she is hostess, I am host.
Went the feast ever cheerfuller? She keeps
The Topic over intellectual deeps
In buoyancy afloat. They see no ghost.
5   With sparkling surface-eyes we ply the ball:
It is in truth a most contagious game:
HIDING THE SKELETON, shall be its name.
Such play as this the devils might appall!
But here's the greater wonder: in that we,
10   Enamored of an acting naught can tire.
Each other, like true hypocrites, admire;
Warm-lighted looks, Love's ephemeridae,[2]
Shoot gayly o'er the dishes and the wine.
We waken envy of our happy lot.
15   Fast, sweet, and golden, shows the marriage knot.
Dear guests, you now have seen Love's corpse-light[3] shine.

---

1. The now silent couple are as motionless as
recumbent stone statues on top of a tomb. In medieval legend, a naked sword between lovers ensured
chastity.

2. Insects that live for one day only.
3. Phosphorescent light such as seen in marshes.
When appearing in a cemetery it was believed to
portend a funeral.

49

He found her by the ocean's moaning verge,
Nor any wicked change in her discerned;
And she believed his old love had returned,
Which was her exultation, and her scourge.
5 She took his hand, and walked with him, and seemed
The wife he sought, though shadowlike and dry.
She had one terror, lest her heart should sigh,
And tell her loudly she no longer dreamed.
She dared not say, "This is my breast: look in."
10 But there's a strength to help the desperate weak.
That night he learned how silence best can speak
The awful things when Pity pleads for Sin.
About the middle of the night her call
Was heard, and he came wondering to the bed.
15 "Now kiss me, dear! it may be, now!" she said.
Lethe[4] had passed those lips, and he knew all.

50

Thus piteously Love closed what he begat:
The union of this ever diverse pair!
These two were rapid falcons in a snare,
Condemned to do the flitting of the bat.
5 Lovers beneath the singing sky of May,
They wandered once; clear as the dew on flowers:
But they fed not on the advancing hours:
Their hearts held cravings for the buried day.
Then each applied to each that fatal knife,
10 Deep questioning, which probes to endless dole.
Ah, what a dusty answer gets the soul
When hot for certainties in this our life!—
In tragic hints here see what evermore
Moves dark as yonder midnight ocean's force,
15 Thundering like ramping hosts of warrior horse,
To throw that faint thin line upon the shore!

1862

Lucifer in Starlight

On a starred night Prince Lucifer uprose.
Tired of his dark dominion, swung the fiend
Above the rolling ball, in cloud part screened,
Where sinners hugged their specter of repose.
5 Poor prey to his hot fit of pride were those.
And now upon his western wing he leaned,
Now his huge bulk o'er Afric's sands careened,
Now the black planet shadowed Arctic snows.

---

4. River of forgetfulness in Hades, the Greek underworld.

Soaring through wider zones that pricked his scars[1]
10 With memory of the old revolt from Awe,
He reached a middle height, and at the stars,
Which are the brain of heaven, he looked, and sank.
Around the ancient track marched, rank on rank,
The army of unalterable law.

1883

1. The vast expanse of sky reminds Satan of the wounds he suffered when his revolt against God was crushed and he was hurled from heaven to hell.

DANTE GABRIEL ROSSETTI
1828–1882

Dante Gabriel Rossetti was the son of an Italian patriot whose political activities had led to his being exiled to England. The Rossetti household in London was one in which liberal politics and artistic topics were hotly debated; all three children—Dante Gabriel, William Michael, and Christina—wrote and drew from an early age. Displaying extraordinary early promise both as a painter and as a poet, Rossetti valued the beauty of colors and textures, above all the beauty of a woman's face and figure. His view of life and art, derived in part from his close study of Keats's poems and letters, anticipated by many years the aesthetic movement later to be represented by such men as Walter Pater, Oscar Wilde, and the painter James McNeill Whistler, who were to insist that art must be exclusively concerned with the beautiful, not with the useful or didactic.

The beauty that Rossetti admired in the faces of women was of a distinctive kind. In at least two of his models he found what he sought. The first was his wife, Elizabeth Siddal, whose suicide in 1862 haunted him with a sense of guilt for the rest of his life. The other was Jane Morris, the wife of his friend William Morris. In Rossetti's paintings both of these models are shown with dreamy stares, as if they were breathless from visions of heaven, but counteracting this impression is an emphasis on parted lips and voluptuous curves suggesting a more earthly kind of ecstasy. A similar combination is to be found in Rossetti's poems. *The Blessed Damozel,* first written when he was eighteen, portrays a heaven that is warm with physical bodies. And *The House of Life* (1870), his sonnet sequence, undertakes to explore the relationship of spirit to body in love. Some Victorian readers saw no Dante-like spirituality in *The House of Life.* Robert Buchanan saw in the poem nothing but lewd sensuality, and in 1871 he published a pamphlet, *The Fleshly School of Poetry,* that treated Rossetti's poetry to the most severe abuse. Buchanan's attack hurt the poet profoundly and contributed to the recurring seizures of nervous depression from which he suffered in the remaining years of his life.

Rossetti and his artist friends used to call such women as Jane Morris "stunners." The epithet can also be applied to Rossetti's own poetry, especially his later writings. In his maturity he used stunning polysyllabic diction to give an effect of opulence and density to his lines. His earlier poems such as *My Sister's Sleep* are usually much less elaborate in manner and can be related to the Pre-Raphaelite movement of which, in 1848, he became a founder and energetic leader.

This Pre-Raphaelite Brotherhood, as it was called, was a group of young artists and writers. The most prominent members were painters such as John Everett Millais,

William Holman Hunt, and Rossetti himself. Their principal object was to reform English painting by repudiating the established academic style in favor of a revival of the simplicity and pure colors of pre-Renaissance art. Because each artist preferred to develop his own individual manner, the Brotherhood did not cohere for more than a few years. Rossetti himself grew away from the Pre-Raphaelite manner and cultivated a more richly ornate style of painting. In both the early and late phases of his writing and painting, however, it can be said that he remained a poet in his painting and a painter in his poetry. "Color and meter," he once said, "these are the true patents of nobility in painting and poetry, taking precedence of all intellectual claims."

The Blessed Damozel[1]

The blessed damozel leaned out
  From the gold bar of heaven;
Her eyes were deeper than the depth
  Of waters stilled at even;
5 She had three lilies in her hand,
  And the stars in her hair were seven.

Her robe, ungirt from clasp to hem,
  No wrought flowers did adorn,
But a white rose of Mary's gift,
10 For service meetly worn;
Her hair that lay along her back
  Was yellow like ripe corn.°   *grain*

Herseemed[2] she scarce had been a day
  One of God's choristers;
15 The wonder was not yet quite gone
  From that still look of hers;
Albeit, to them she left, her day
  Had counted as ten years.

(To one it is ten years of years.
20 . . . Yet now, and in this place,
Surely she leaned o'er me—her hair
  Fell all about my face. . . .
Nothing: the autumn-fall of leaves.
  The whole year sets apace.)

25 It was the rampart of God's house
  That she was standing on;
By God built over the sheer depth
  The which is Space begun;
So high, that looking downward thence
30 She scarce could see the sun.

1. A poetic version of "damsel," signifying a young unmarried lady. Rossetti once explained that *The Blessed Damozel* is related to Poe's *Raven*, a poem that he admired. "I saw that Poe had done the utmost it was possible to do with the grief of the lover on earth, and so I determined to reverse the conditions, and give utterance to the yearning of the loved one in heaven."
2. It seemed to her.

The Blessed Damozel (1875–78). In the second phase of his painting career, Rossetti turned from the flat, intricately patterned illustrations of literary subjects that had characterized his early work (a good example is his drawing for *The Lady of Shalott*, p. 1208) to huge, sensual portraits of women, often designed as companion pieces to his poems.

It lies in heaven, across the flood
   Of ether, as a bridge.
Beneath the tides of day and night
   With flame and darkness ridge
35 The void, as low as where this earth
   Spins like a fretful midge.

Around her, lovers, newly met
   'Mid deathless love's acclaims,
Spoke evermore among themselves
40 Their heart-remembered names;
And the souls mounting up to God
   Went by her like thin flames.

And still she bowed herself and stooped
   Out of the circling charm;
45 Until her bosom must have made
   The bar she leaned on warm,
And the lilies lay as if asleep
   Along her bended arm.

From the fixed place of heaven she saw
50 Time like a pulse shake fierce
Through all the worlds. Her gaze still strove
   Within the gulf to pierce
Its path; and now she spoke as when
   The stars sang in their spheres.

55   The sun was gone now; the curled moon
        Was like a little feather
    Fluttering far down the gulf; and now
        She spoke through the still weather.
    Her voice was like the voice the stars
60   Had when they sang together.

    (Ah, sweet! Even now, in that bird's song,
        Strove not her accents there,
    Fain to be harkened? When those bells
        Possessed the midday air,
65   Strove not her steps to reach my side
        Down all the echoing stair?)

    "I wish that he were come to me,
        For he will come," she said.
    "Have I not prayed in heaven?—on earth,
70   Lord, Lord, has he not prayed?
    Are not two prayers a perfect strength?
        And shall I feel afraid?

    "When round his head the aureole clings,
        And he is clothed in white,
75   I'll take his hand and go with him
        To the deep wells of light;
    As unto a stream we will step down,
        And bathe there in God's sight.

    "We two will stand beside that shrine,
80   Occult, withheld, untrod,
    Whose lamps are stirred continually
        With prayer sent up to God;
    And see our old prayers, granted, melt
        Each like a little cloud.

85   "We two will lie i' the shadow of
        That living mystic tree[3]
    Within whose secret growth the Dove
        Is sometimes felt to be,
    While every leaf that His plumes touch
90   Saith His Name audibly.

    "And I myself will teach to him,
        I myself, lying so,
    The songs I sing here; which his voice
        Shall pause in, hushed and slow,
95   And find some knowledge at each pause,
        Or some new thing to know."

    (Alas! We two, we two, thou say'st!
        Yea, one wast thou with me

---

3. Cf. Revelation 22.2.

That once of old. But shall God lift
100   To endless unity
The soul whose likeness with thy soul
   Was but its love for thee?)

"We two," she said, "will seek the groves
   Where the lady Mary is,
105 With her five handmaidens, whose names
   Are five sweet symphonies,
Cecily, Gertrude, Magdalen,
   Margaret, and Rosalys.

"Circlewise sit they, with bound locks
110   And foreheads garlanded;
Into the fine cloth white like flame
   Weaving the golden thread,
To fashion the birth-robes for them
   Who are just born, being dead.

115 "He shall fear, haply, and be dumb;
   Then will I lay my cheek
To his, and tell about our love,
   Not once abashed or weak;
And the dear Mother will approve
120   My pride, and let me speak.

"Herself shall bring us, hand in hand,
   To Him round whom all souls
Kneel, the clear-ranged unnumbered heads
   Bowed with their aureoles;
125 And angels meeting us shall sing
   To their citherns and citoles.[4]

"There will I ask of Christ the Lord
   Thus much for him and me—
Only to live as once on earth
130   With Love—only to be,
As then awhile, forever now,
   Together, I and he."

She gazed and listened and then said,
   Less sad of speech than mild—
135 "All this is when he comes." She ceased.
   The light thrilled toward her, filled
With angels in strong, level flight.
   Her eyes prayed, and she smiled.

(I saw her smile.) But soon their path
140   Was vague in distant spheres;
And then she cast her arms along

4. Guitarlike instruments.

> The golden barriers,
> And laid her face between her hands,
> And wept. (I heard her tears.)

1846   1850

My Sister's Sleep[1]

She fell asleep on Christmas Eve.
  At length the long-ungranted shade
  Of weary eyelids overweighed
The pain nought else might yet relieve.

5 Our mother, who had leaned all day
  Over the bed from chime to chime,
  Then raised herself for the first time,
And as she sat her down, did pray.

Her little worktable was spread
10 With work to finish. For the glare
  Made by her candle, she had care
To work some distance from the bed.

Without, there was a cold moon up,
  Of winter radiance sheer and thin;
15 The hollow halo it was in
Was like an icy crystal cup.

Through the small room, with subtle sound
  Of flame, by vents the fireshine drove
  And reddened. In its dim alcove
20 The mirror shed a clearness round.

I had been sitting up some nights,
  And my tired mind felt weak and blank;
  Like a sharp strengthening wine it drank
The stillness and the broken lights.

25 Twelve struck. That sound, by dwindling years
  Heard in each hour, crept off; and then
  The ruffled silence spread again,
Like water that a pebble stirs.

Our mother rose from where she sat;
30 Her needles, as she laid them down,
  Met lightly, and her silken gown
Settled—no other noise than that.

---

1. The incident in this poem is imaginary, not autobiographical.

"Glory unto the Newly Born!"
   So, as said angels, she did say,
35   Because we were in Christmas Day,
Though it would still be long till morn.

Just then in the room over us
   There was a pushing back of chairs,
   As some who had sat unawares
40 So late, now heard the hour, and rose.

With anxious softly-stepping haste
   Our mother went where Margaret lay,
   Fearing the sounds o'erhead—should they
Have broken her long watched-for rest!

45 She stooped an instant, calm, and turned,
   But suddenly turned back again;
   And all her features seemed in pain
With woe, and her eyes gazed and yearned.

For my part, I but hid my face,
50   And held my breath, and spoke no word.
   There was none spoken; but I heard
The silence for a little space.

Our mother bowed herself and wept;
   And both my arms fell, and I said,
55   "God knows I knew that she was dead."
And there, all white, my sister slept.

Then kneeling, upon Christmas morn
   A little after twelve o'clock,
   We said, ere the first quarter struck,
60 "Christ's blessing on the newly born!"

1847   1850

The Woodspurge

The wind flapped loose, the wind was still,
Shaken out dead from tree and hill;
I had walked on at the wind's will—
I sat now, for the wind was still.

5 Between my knees my forehead was—
My lips, drawn in, said not Alas!
My hair was over in the grass,
My naked ears heard the day pass.

My eyes, wide open, had the run
10 Of some ten weeds to fix upon;

Among those few, out of the sun,
The woodspurge flowered, three cups in one.

From perfect grief there need not be
Wisdom or even memory;
One thing then learned remains to me—
The woodspurge has a cup of three.

1856   1870

From The House of Life

The Sonnet

A Sonnet is a moment's monument—
 Memorial from the Soul's eternity
 To one dead deathless hour. Look that it be,
Whether for lustral° rite or dire portent,   purification
 Of its own arduous fullness reverent;
  Carve it in ivory or in ebony,
  As Day or Night may rule; and let Time see
Its flowering crest impearled and orient.

A Sonnet is a coin; its face reveals
 The soul—its converse, to what Power 'tis due—
Whether for tribute to the august appeals
  Of Life, or dower in Love's high retinue,
It serve; or, 'mid the dark wharf's cavernous breath,
In Charon's[1] palm it pay the toll to Death.

Nuptial Sleep[2]

At length their long kiss severed, with sweet smart:
 And as the last slow sudden drops are shed
 From sparkling eaves when all the storm has fled,
So singly flagged the pulses of each heart.
 Their bosoms sundered, with the opening start
  Of married flowers to either side outspread
  From the knit stem; yet still their mouths, burnt red,
Fawned on each other where they lay apart.

Sleep sank them lower than the tide of dreams,
 And their dreams watched them sink, and slid away.
Slowly their souls swam up again, through gleams
  Of watered light and dull drowned waifs of day;
Till from some wonder of new woods and streams
 He woke, and wondered more: for there she lay.

1. The ferryman who, for a fee, rowed the souls of the dead across the river Styx.
2. In *The Fleshly School of Poetry*, Robert Buchanan made this poem the focus of his attack on what he felt was Rossetti's lewd sensuality in the 1870 volume *Poems*. In 1881, when Rossetti published his next collection of poems, he omitted this sonnet from *The House of Life*.

19. Silent Noon

Your hands lie open in the long fresh grass—
   The finger-points look through like rosy blooms;
   Your eyes smile peace. The pasture gleams and glooms
'Neath billowing skies that scatter and amass.
5 All round our nest, far as the eye can pass,
   Are golden kingcup-fields with silver edge
   Where the cow-parsley skirts the hawthorn hedge.
'Tis visible silence, still as the hourglass.

Deep in the sun-searched growths the dragonfly
10 Hangs like a blue thread loosened from the sky—
   So this winged hour is dropped to us from above.
Oh! clasp we to our hearts, for deathless dower,
This close-companioned inarticulate hour
   When twofold silence was the song of love.

77. Soul's Beauty[3]

Under the arch of Life, where love and death,
   Terror and mystery, guard her shrine, I saw
   Beauty enthroned; and though her gaze struck awe,
I drew it in as simply as my breath.
5 Hers are the eyes which, over and beneath,
   The sky and sea bend on thee,—which can draw,
   By sea or sky or woman, to one law,
The allotted bondman of her palm and wreath.

This is that Lady Beauty, in whose praise
10 Thy voice and hand shake still,—long known to thee
   By flying hair and fluttering hem,—the beat
   Following her daily of thy heart and feet,
   How passionately and irretrievably,
In what fond flight, how many ways and days!

78. Body's Beauty

Of Adams's first wife, Lilith, it is told
   (The witch he loved before the gift of Eve,)
   That, ere the snake's, her sweet tongue could deceive,
And her enchanted hair was the first gold.
5 And still she sits, young while the earth is old,
   And subtly of herself contemplative,
   Draws men to watch the bright web she can weave,
Till heart and body and life are in its hold.

3. This sonnet and the next were not originally part of *The House of Life,* but were composed to accompany paintings with the same names as the sonnets' original titles. The original title of *Soul's Beauty* was "Sibylla Palmifera," or "palm-bearing sibyl." Sibyls are prophetesses; one of them, the Sibyl of Cumae, wrote her prophecies on palm leaves. The original title of *Body's Beauty* was "Lilith," in Talmudic legend, the first wife of Adam, who ran away from him to become a witch.

The rose and poppy are her flowers; for where
10   Is he not found, O Lilith, whom shed scent
And soft-shed kisses and soft sleep shall snare?
     Lo! as that youth's eyes burned at thine, so went
     Thy spell through him, and left his straight neck bent
And round his heart one strangling golden hair

97. A Superscription

Look in my face; my name is Might-have-been;
     I am also called No-more, Too-late, Farewell;
     Unto thine ear I hold the dead-sea shell
Cast up thy Life's foam-fretted feet between;
5   Unto thine eyes the glass° where that is seen   *mirror*
     Which had Life's form and Love's, but by my spell
     Is now a shaken shadow intolerable,
Of ultimate things unuttered the frail screen.

Mark me, how still I am! But should there dart
10   One moment through thy soul the soft surprise
     Of that winged Peace which lulls the breath of sighs—
Then shalt thou see me smile, and turn apart
Thy visage to mine ambush at thy heart
     Sleepless with cold commemorative eyes.

101. The One Hope

When vain desire at last and vain regret
     Go hand in hand to death, and all is vain,
     What shall assuage the unforgotten pain
And teach the unforgetful to forget?
5   Shall Peace be still a sunk stream long unmet—
     Or may the soul at once in a green plain
     Stoop through the spray of some sweet life-fountain
And cull the dew-drenched flowering amulet?[4]

Ah! when the wan soul in that golden air
10   Between the scriptured petals softly blown
     Peers breathless for the gift of grace unknown,
Ah! let none other alien spell soe'er
But only the one Hope's one name be there—
     Not less nor more, but even that word alone.

1848–80   1870, 1881

---

4. A charm to protect the wearer from harm.

CHRISTINA ROSSETTI
1830–1894

Referring to the title of George Gissing's novel about women who choose not to marry, the critic Jerome McGann calls Christina Rossetti "one of nineteenth-century England's greatest 'Odd Women.' " Her life had little apparent incident. She was the youngest child in the Rossetti family. Her father was an exiled Italian patriot who wrote poetry and commentaries on Dante that tried to show evidence in his poems of mysterious ancient conspiracies; her mother was an Anglo-Italian who had worked as a governess. Their household was a lively gathering place for Italian exiles, full of conversation of politics and culture, which encouraged Christina, like her brothers Dante Gabriel and William Michael, to develop an early love for art and literature and to draw and write poetry from a very early age. When she was an adolescent, her life changed dramatically: her father became a permanent invalid, the family's economic situation worsened, and her own health deteriorated. At this point, she, her mother, and her sister became intensely involved with the Anglo-Catholic movement within the Church of England. For the rest of her life, Christina Rossetti governed herself by strict religious principles, giving up theater, opera, and chess; on two occasions, she canceled plans for marriage because of religious scruples, breaking her first engagement when her fiancé reverted to Roman Catholicism and ultimately refusing to marry a second suitor because he seemed insufficiently concerned with religion. She lived a quiet life, occupying herself with charitable work—including ten years of volunteer service at a penitentiary for fallen women—with caring for her family, and with writing poetry.

Christina Rossetti's first volume of poetry, *Goblin Market and Other Poems* (1862), contains all the different poetic modes that mark her achievement—pure lyric, narrative fable, ballad, and the devotional verse to which she increasingly turned in her later years. The most remarkable poem in the book is the title piece, which early established its popularity as a seemingly simple moral fable for children. Later readers have likened it to Coleridge's *Rime of the Ancient Mariner* and have detected in it a complex representation of the religious themes of temptation and sin, and of redemption by vicarious suffering; the fruit that tempts Laura, however, is clearly not from the Tree of Knowledge but from an orchard of sensual delights. In its deceptively simple style, *Goblin Market*, like many of her poems, demonstrates her affinity with the early aims of the Pre-Raphaelite group, but her work as a whole resists this classification. A consciousness of gender often leads her to criticize the conventional representation of women in Pre-Raphaelite art, as in her sonnet *In An Artist's Studio*, and a stern religious vision controls the sensuous impulses typical of Pre-Raphaelite poetry and painting. Virginia Woolf has described the distinctive combination of sensuousness and religious severity in Rossetti's work.

> Your poems are full of gold dust and "sweet geraniums' varied brightness"; your eye noted incessantly how rushes are "velvet headed," and lizards have a "strange metallic mail"—your eye, indeed, observed with a sensual pre-Raphaelite intensity that must have surprised Christina the Anglo-Catholic. But to her you owed perhaps the fixity and sadness of your muse. . . . No sooner have you feasted on beauty with your eyes than your mind tells you that beauty is vain and beauty passes. Death, oblivion, and rest lap round your songs with their dark wave.

William Michael Rossetti wrote of his sister, "She was replete with the spirit of self-postponement." Christina Rossetti was a poet who created, in Sandra M. Gilbert and Susan Gubar's term, "an aesthetics of renunciation." She writes a poetry of deferral, of deflection, of negation, whose very denials and constraints give her a powerful way to articulate a poetic self in critical relationship to the little that the world offers.

Like Emily Dickinson, she often, as in *Winter: My Secret,* uses a coy playfulness and sardonic wit to reduce the self but at the same time to preserve for it a secret inner space. And like Dickinson, she wrote many poems of an extraordinarily pure lyric beauty that made Virginia Woolf remark, "Your instinct was so sure, so direct, so intense that it produced poems that sing like music in one's ears—like a melody by Mozart or an air by Gluck."

Song

She sat and sang alway
  By the green margin of a stream,
Watching the fishes leap and play
  Beneath the glad sunbeam.

5 I sat and wept alway
  Beneath the moon's most shadowy beam,
Watching the blossoms of the May
  Weep leaves into the stream.

I wept for memory;
10 She sang for hope that is so fair:
My tears were swallowed by the sea;
  Her songs died on the air.

1848   1862

Song

When I am dead, my dearest,
  Sing no sad songs for me;
Plant thou no roses at my head,
  Nor shady cypress tree:
5 Be the green grass above me
  With showers and dewdrops wet;
And if thou wilt, remember,
  And if thou wilt, forget.

I shall not see the shadows,
10 I shall not feel the rain;
I shall not hear the nightingale
  Sing on, as if in pain:
And dreaming through the twilight
  That doth not rise nor set,
15 Haply I may remember,
  And haply may forget.

1848   1862

After Death

The curtains were half drawn, the floor was swept
    And strewn with rushes, rosemary and may[1]
Lay thick upon the bed on which I lay,
Where thro' the lattice ivy-shadows crept.
5   He leaned above me, thinking that I slept
    And could not hear him; but I heard him say:
    "Poor child, poor child": and as he turned away
Came a deep silence, and I knew he wept.
He did not touch the shroud, or raise the fold
10   That hid my face, or take my hand in his,
    Or ruffle the smooth pillows for my head:
    He did not love me living; but once dead
He pitied me; and very sweet it is
To know he still is warm tho' I am cold.

1849   1862

Dead before Death

Ah! changed and cold, how changed and very cold!
    With stiffened smiling lips and cold calm eyes:
    Changed, yet the same; much knowing, little wise;
This was the promise of the days of old!
5   Grown hard and stubborn in the ancient mould,
    Grown rigid in the sham of lifelong lies:
    We hoped for better things as years would rise,
But it is over as a tale once told.
All fallen the blossom that no fruitage bore,
10   All lost the present and the future time,
All lost, all lost, the lapse that went before:
So lost till death shut-to the opened door,
    So lost from chime to everlasting chime,
So cold and lost for ever evermore.

1854   1862

Cobwebs

It is a land with neither night nor day,
    Nor heat nor cold, nor any wind, nor rain,
    Nor hills nor valleys; but one even plain
Stretches thro' long unbroken miles away:
5   While thro' the sluggish air a twilight grey
    Broodeth; no moons or seasons wax and wane,
    No ebb and flow are there along the main,

---

1. Flowers associated with death.

No bud-time no leaf-falling, there for aye:—
No ripple on the sea, no shifting sand,
10   No beat of wings to stir the stagnant space,
No pulse of life thro' all the loveless land:
And loveless sea; no trace of days before,
    No guarded home, no toil-won resting place,
No future hope no fear for evermore.

1855   1896

A Triad

Three sang of love together: one with lips
    Crimson, with cheeks and bosom in a glow,
Flushed to the yellow hair and finger tips;
    And one there sang who soft and smooth as snow
5   Bloomed like a tinted hyacinth at a show;
And one was blue with famine after love,
    Who like a harpstring snapped rang harsh and low
The burden of what those were singing of.
One shamed herself in love; one temperately
10   Grew gross in soulless love, a sluggish wife;
One famished died for love. Thus two of three
    Took death for love and won him after strife;
One droned in sweetness like a fattened bee:
    All on the threshold, yet all short of life.

1856   1862

In an Artist's Studio[1]

One face looks out from all his canvases,
    One selfsame figure sits or walks or leans;
    We found her hidden just behind those screens,
That mirror gave back all her loveliness.
5   A queen in opal or in ruby dress,
    A nameless girl in freshest summer-greens,
    A saint, an angel;—every canvass means
The same one meaning, neither more nor less.
He feeds upon her face by day and night,
10   And she with true kind eyes looks back on him
Fair as the moon and joyful as the light:
    Not wan with waiting, not with sorrow dim;
Not as she is, but was when hope shone bright;
    Not as she is, but as she fills his dream.

1856   1896

1. William Michael Rossetti, the younger of Christina's older brothers, noted, "The reference is apparently to our brother's studio, and to his con- stantly repeated heads of the lady whom he after- wards married, Miss Siddal."

A Birthday

My heart is like a singing bird
   Whose nest is in a watered shoot;
My heart is like an apple tree
   Whose boughs are bent with thickset fruit;
5 My heart is like a rainbow shell
   That paddles in a halcyon° sea;   *tranquil*
My heart is gladder than all these
   Because my love is come to me.

Raise me a dais of silk and down;
10   Hang it with vair° and purple dyes;   *squirrel fur*
Carve it in doves and pomegranates,
   And peacocks with a hundred eyes;
Work it in gold and silver grapes,
   In leaves and silver fleurs-de-lys;
15 Because the birthday of my life
   Is come, my love is come to me.

1857   1862

An Apple-Gathering

I plucked pink blossoms from mine apple tree
   And wore them all that evening in my hair:
Then in due season when I went to see
   I found no apples there.

5 With dangling basket all along the grass
   As I had come I went the selfsame track:
My neighbours mocked me while they saw me pass
   So empty-handed back.

Lilian and Lilias smiled in trudging by,
10   Their heaped-up basket teazed me like a jeer;
Sweet-voiced they sang beneath the sunset sky,
   Their mother's home was near.

Plump Gertrude passed me with her basket full,
   A stronger hand than hers helped it along;
15 A voice talked with her thro' the shadows cool
   More sweet to me than song.

Ah Willie, Willie, was my love less worth
   Than apples with their green leaves piled above?
I counted rosiest apples on the earth
20   Of far less worth than love.

So once it was with me you stooped to talk
   Laughing and listening in this very lane:

To think that by this way we used to walk
    We shall not walk again!

25 I let my neighbours pass me, ones and twos
        And groups; the latest said the night grew chill,
    And hastened: but I loitered, while the dews
        Fell fast I loitered still.

1857   1862

Winter: My Secret

I tell my secret? No indeed, not I:
Perhaps some day, who knows?
But not today; it froze, and blows, and snows,
And you're too curious: fie!
5   You want to hear it? well:
Only, my secret's mine, and I won't tell.

Or, after all, perhaps there's none:
Suppose there is no secret after all,
But only just my fun.
10 Today's a nipping day, a biting day;
In which one wants a shawl,
A veil, a cloak, and other wraps:
I cannot ope to every one who taps,
And let the draughts come whistling thro' my hall;
15 Come bounding and surrounding me,
Come buffeting, astounding me,
Nipping and clipping thro' my wraps and all.
I wear my mask for warmth: who ever shows
His nose to Russian snows
20 To be pecked at by every wind that blows?
You would not peck? I thank you for good will,
Believe, but leave that truth untested still.

Spring's an expansive time: yet I don't trust
March with its peck of dust,
25 Nor April with its rainbow-crowned brief showers,
Nor even May, whose flowers
One frost may wither thro' the sunless hours.

Perhaps some languid summer day,
When drowsy birds sing less and less,
30 And golden fruit is ripening to excess,
If there's not too much sun nor too much cloud,
And the warm wind is neither still nor loud,
Perhaps my secret I may say,
Or you may guess.

1857   1862

Up-Hill

Does the road wind up-hill all the way?
   Yes, to the very end.
Will the day's journey take the whole long day?
   From morn to night, my friend.

5 But is there for the night a resting-place?
   A roof for when the slow dark hours begin.
May not the darkness hide it from my face?
   You cannot miss that inn.

Shall I meet other wayfarers at night?
10   Those who have gone before.
Then must I knock, or call when just in sight?
   They will not keep you standing at that door.

Shall I find comfort, travel-sore and weak?
   Of labour you shall find the sum.
15 Will there be beds for me and all who seek?
   Yea, beds for all who come.

1858   1862

Goblin Market

Morning and evening
Maids heard the goblins cry:
"Come buy our orchard fruits,
Come buy, come buy:
5 Apples and quinces,
Lemons and oranges,
Plump unpecked cherries,
Melons and raspberries,
Bloom-down-cheeked peaches,
10 Swart-headed mulberries,
Wild free-born cranberries,
Crab-apples, dewberries,
Pine-apples, blackberries,
Apricots, strawberries;—
15 All ripe together
In summer weather,—
Morns that pass by,
Fair eves that fly;
Come buy, come buy:
20 Our grapes fresh from the vine,
Pomegranates full and fine,
Dates and sharp bullaces,
Rare pears and greengages,
Damsons[1] and bilberries,

---

1. "Bullaces," "greengages," and "damsons" are varieties of plums.

25   Taste them and try:
Currants and gooseberries,
Bright-fire-like barberries,
Figs to fill your mouth,
Citrons from the South,
30   Sweet to tongue and sound to eye;
Come buy, come buy."

Evening by evening
Among the brookside rushes,
Laura bowed her head to hear,
35   Lizzie veiled her blushes:
Crouching close together
In the cooling weather,
With clasping arms and cautioning lips,
With tingling cheeks and finger tips.
40   "Lie close," Laura said,
Pricking up her golden head:
"We must not look at goblin men,
We must not buy their fruits:
Who knows upon what soil they fed
45   Their hungry thirsty roots?"
"Come buy," call the goblins
Hobbling down the glen.
"Oh," cried Lizzie, "Laura, Laura,
You should not peep at goblin men."
50   Lizzie covered up her eyes,
Covered close lest they should look;
Laura reared her glossy head,
And whispered like the restless brook:
"Look, Lizzie, look, Lizzie,
55   Down the glen tramp little men.
One hauls a basket,
One bears a plate,
One lugs a golden dish
Of many pounds weight.
60   How fair the vine must grow
Whose grapes are so luscious;
How warm the wind must blow
Thro' those fruit bushes."
"No," said Lizzie: "No, no, no;
65   Their offers should not charm us,
Their evil gifts would harm us."
She thrust a dimpled finger
In each ear, shut eyes and ran:
Curious Laura chose to linger
70   Wondering at each merchant man.
One had a cat's face,
One whisked a tail,
One tramped at a rat's pace,
One crawled like a snail,
75   One like a wombat prowled obtuse and furry,

One like a ratel[2] tumbled hurry skurry.
She heard a voice like voice of doves
Cooing all together:
They sounded kind and full of loves
80 In the pleasant weather.

Laura stretched her gleaming neck
Like a rush-imbedded swan,
Like a lily from the beck,°   *small brook*
Like a moonlit poplar branch,
85 Like a vessel at the launch
When its last restraint is gone.

Backwards up the mossy glen
Turned and trooped the goblin men,
With their shrill repeated cry,
90 "Come buy, come buy."
When they reached where Laura was
They stood stock still upon the moss,
Leering at each other,
Brother with queer brother;
95 Signalling each other,
Brother with sly brother.
One set his basket down,
One reared his plate;
One began to weave a crown
100 Of tendrils, leaves and rough nuts brown
(Men sell not such in any town);
One heaved the golden weight
Of dish and fruit to offer her:
"Come buy, come buy," was still their cry.
105 Laura stared but did not stir,
Longed but had no money:
The whisk-tailed merchant bade her taste
In tones as smooth as honey,
The cat-faced purr'd,
110 The rat-paced spoke a word
Of welcome, and the snail-paced even was heard;
One parrot-voiced and jolly
Cried "Pretty Goblin" still for "Pretty Polly;"—
One whistled like a bird.

115 But sweet-tooth Laura spoke in haste:
"Good folk, I have no coin;
To take were to purloin:
I have no copper in my purse,
I have no silver either,
120 And all my gold is on the furze
That shakes in windy weather
Above the rusty heather."

2. South African mammal resembling a badger (pronounced *ray-tell*).

"You have much gold upon your head,"
They answered all together:
125 "Buy from us with a golden curl."
She clipped a precious golden lock,
She dropped a tear more rare than pearl,
Then sucked their fruit globes fair or red:
Sweeter than honey from the rock.
130 Stronger than man-rejoicing wine,
Clearer than water flowed that juice;
She never tasted such before,
How should it cloy with length of use?
She sucked and sucked and sucked the more
135 Fruits which that unknown orchard bore;
She sucked until her lips were sore;
Then flung the emptied rinds away
But gathered up one kernel-stone,
And knew not was it night or day
140 As she turned home alone.

Lizzie met her at the gate
Full of wise upbraidings:
"Dear, you should not stay so late,
Twilight is not good for maidens;
145 Should not loiter in the glen
In the haunts of goblin men.
Do you not remember Jeanie,
How she met them in the moonlight,
Took their gifts both choice and many,
150 Ate their fruits and wore their flowers
Plucked from bowers
Where summer ripens at all hours?
But ever in the noonlight
She pined and pined away;
155 Sought them by night and day,
Found them no more but dwindled and grew grey;
Then fell with the first snow,
While to this day no grass will grow
Where she lies low:
160 I planted daisies there a year ago
That never blow.
You should not loiter so."
"Nay, hush," said Laura:
"Nay, hush, my sister:
165 I ate and ate my fill,
Yet my mouth waters still;
Tomorrow night I will
Buy more:" and kissed her:
"Have done with sorrow;
170 I'll bring you plums tomorrow
Fresh on their mother twigs,
Cherries worth getting;

You cannot think what figs
My teeth have met in,
175 What melons icy-cold
Piled on a dish of gold
Too huge for me to hold,
What peaches with a velvet nap,
Pellucid grapes without one seed:
180 Odorous indeed must be the mead
Whereon they grow, and pure the wave they drink
With lilies at the brink,
And sugar-sweet their sap."

Golden head by golden head,
185 Like two pigeons in one nest
Folded in each other's wings,
They lay down in their curtained bed:
Like two blossoms on one stem,
Like two flakes of new-fall'n snow,
190 Like two wands of ivory
Tipped with gold for awful° kings.   *awe-inspiring*
Moon and stars gazed in at them,

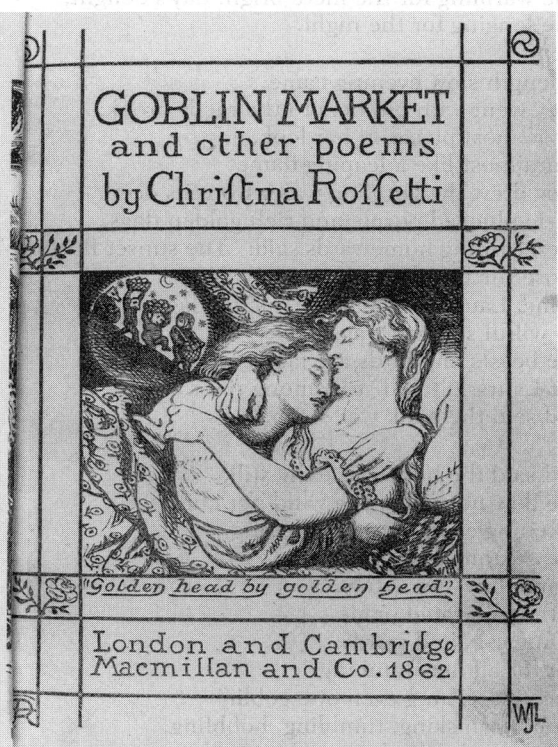

This frontispiece is one of the two illustrations that Dante Gabriel Rossetti provided for his sister's first volume of poetry in 1862.

Wind sang to them lullaby,
Lumbering owls forbore to fly,
195   Not a bat flapped to and fro
Round their rest:
Cheek to cheek and breast to breast
Locked together in one nest.

Early in the morning
200   When the first cock crowed his warning,
Neat like bees, as sweet and busy,
Laura rose with Lizzie:
Fetched in honey, milked the cows,
Aired and set to rights the house,
205   Kneaded cakes of whitest wheat,
Cakes for dainty mouths to eat,
Next churned butter, whipped up cream,
Fed their poultry, sat and sewed;
Talked as modest maidens should:
210   Lizzie with an open heart,
Laura in an absent dream,
One content, one sick in part;
One warbling for the mere bright day's delight,
One longing for the night.

215   At length slow evening came:
They went with pitchers to the reedy brook;
Lizzie most placid in her look,
Laura most like a leaping flame.
They drew the gurgling water from its deep;
220   Lizzie plucked purple and rich golden flags,
Then turning homewards said: "The sunset flushes
Those furthest loftiest crags;
Come, Laura, not another maiden lags,
No wilful squirrel wags,
225   The beasts and birds are fast asleep."
But Laura loitered still among the rushes
And said the bank was steep.

And said the hour was early still,
The dew not fall'n, the wind not chill:
230   Listening ever, but not catching
The customary cry,
"Come buy, come buy,"
With its iterated jingle
Of sugar-baited words:
235   Not for all her watching
Once discerning even one goblin
Racing, whisking, tumbling, hobbling;
Let alone the herds
That used to tramp along the glen,
240   In groups or single,
Of brisk fruit-merchant men.

Till Lizzie urged, "O Laura, come;
I hear the fruit-call but I dare not look:
You should not loiter longer at this brook:
245   Come with me home.
The stars rise, the moon bends her arc,
Each glowworm winks her spark,
Let us get home before the night grows dark:
For clouds may gather
250   Tho' this is summer weather,
Put out the lights and drench us thro';
Then if we lost our way what should we do?"

Laura turned cold as stone
To find her sister heard that cry alone,
255   That goblin cry,
"Come buy our fruits, come buy."
Must she then buy no more such dainty fruit?
Must she no more such succous° pasture find,   *juicy, succulent*
Gone deaf and blind?
260   Her tree of life drooped from the root:
She said not one word in her heart's sore ache;
But peering thro' the dimness, nought discerning,
Trudged home, her pitcher dripping all the way;
So crept to bed, and lay
265   Silent till Lizzie slept;
Then sat up in a passionate yearning,
And gnashed her teeth for baulked desire, and wept
As if her heart would break.

Day after day, night after night,
270   Laura kept watch in vain
In sullen silence of exceeding pain.
She never caught again the goblin cry:
"Come buy, come buy;"—
She never spied the goblin men
275   Hawking their fruits along the glen:
But when the noon waxed bright
Her hair grew thin and gray;
She dwindled, as the fair full moon doth turn
To swift decay and burn
280   Her fire away.

One day remembering her kernel-stone
She set it by a wall that faced the south;
Dewed it with tears, hoped for a root,
Watched for a waxing shoot,
285   But there came none;
It never saw the sun,
It never felt the trickling moisture run:
While with sunk eyes and faded mouth
She dreamed of melons, as a traveller sees
290   False waves in desert drouth

With shade of leaf-crowned trees,
And burns the thirstier in the sandful breeze.

She no more swept the house,
Tended the fowls or cows,
295 Fetched honey, kneaded cakes of wheat,
Brought water from the brook:
But sat down listless in the chimney-nook
And would not eat.

Tender Lizzie could not bear
300 To watch her sister's cankerous care
Yet not to share.
She night and morning
Caught the goblins' cry:
"Come buy our orchard fruits,
305 Come buy, come buy:"—
Beside the brook, along the glen,
She heard the tramp of goblin men,
The voice and stir
Poor Laura could not hear;
310 Longed to buy fruit to comfort her,
But feared to pay too dear.
She thought of Jeanie in her grave,
Who should have been a bride;
But who for joys brides hope to have
315 Fell sick and died
In her gay prime,
In earliest Winter time,
With the first glazing rime,
With the first snow-fall of crisp Winter time.

320 Till Laura dwindling
Seemed knocking at Death's door:
Then Lizzie weighed no more
Better and worse;
But put a silver penny in her purse,
325 Kissed Laura, crossed the heath with clumps of furze
At twilight, halted by the brook:
And for the first time in her life
Began to listen and look.

Laughed every goblin
330 When they spied her peeping:
Came towards her hobbling,
Flying, running, leaping,
Puffing and blowing,
Chuckling, clapping, crowing,
335 Clucking and gobbling,
Mopping and mowing,
Full of airs and graces,
Pulling wry faces,

Demure grimaces,
340 Cat-like and rat-like,
Ratel- and wombat-like,
Snail-paced in a hurry,
Parrot-voiced and whistler,
Helter skelter, hurry skurry,
345 Chattering like magpies,
Fluttering like pigeons,
Gliding like fishes,—
Hugged her and kissed her,
Squeezed and caressed her:
350 Stretched up their dishes,
Panniers, and plates:
"Look at our apples
Russet and dun,
Bob at our cherries,
355 Bite at our peaches,
Citrons and dates,
Grapes for the asking,
Pears red with basking
Out in the sun,
360 Plums on their twigs;
Pluck them and suck them,
Pomegranates, figs."—

"Good folk," said Lizzie,
Mindful of Jeanie:
365 "Give me much and many:"—
Held out her apron,
Tossed them her penny.
"Nay, take a seat with us,
Honour and eat with us,"
370 They answered grinning:
"Our feast is but beginning.
Night yet is early,
Warm and dew-pearly,
Wakeful and starry:
375 Such fruits as these
No man can carry;
Half their bloom would fly,
Half their dew would dry,
Half their flavour would pass by.
380 Sit down and feast with us,
Be welcome guest with us,
Cheer you and rest with us."—
"Thank you," said Lizzie: "But one waits
At home alone for me:
385 So without further parleying,
If you will not sell me any
Of your fruits tho' much and many,
Give me back my silver penny
I tossed you for a fee."—

390   They began to scratch their pates,
No longer wagging, purring,
But visibly demurring,
Grunting and snarling.
One called her proud,
395   Cross-grained, uncivil;
Their tones waxed loud,
Their looks were evil.
Lashing their tails
They trod and hustled her,
400   Elbowed and jostled her,
Clawed with their nails,
Barking, mewing, hissing, mocking,
Tore her gown and soiled her stocking,
Twitched her hair out by the roots,
405   Stamped upon her tender feet,
Held her hands and squeezed their fruits
Against her mouth to make her eat.

White and golden Lizzie stood,
Like a lily in a flood,—
410   Like a rock of blue-veined stone
Lashed by tides obstreperously,—
Like a beacon left alone
In a hoary roaring sea,
Sending up a golden fire,—
415   Like a fruit-crowned orange-tree
White with blossoms honey-sweet
Sore beset by wasp and bee,—
Like a royal virgin town
Topped with gilded dome and spire
420   Close beleaguerred by a fleet
Mad to tug her standard down.

One may lead a horse to water,
Twenty cannot make him drink.
Tho' the goblins cuffed and caught her,
425   Coaxed and fought her,
Bullied and besought her,
Scratched her, pinched her black as ink,
Kicked and knocked her,
Mauled and mocked her,
430   Lizzie uttered not a word;
Would not open lip from lip
Lest they should cram a mouthful in:
But laughed in heart to feel the drip
Of juice that syruped all her face,
435   And lodged in dimples of her chin,
And streaked her neck which quaked like curd.
At last the evil people
Worn out by her resistance
Flung back her penny, kicked their fruit

440 Along whichever road they took,
  Not leaving root or stone or shoot;
  Some writhed into the ground,
  Some dived into the brook
  With ring and ripple,
445 Some scudded on the gale without a sound,
  Some vanished in the distance.

  In a smart, ache, tingle,
  Lizzie went her way;
  Knew not was it night or day;
450 Sprang up the bank, tore thro' the furze,
  Threaded copse and dingle,
  And heard her penny jingle
  Bouncing in her purse,
  Its bounce was music to her ear.
455 She ran and ran
  As if she feared some goblin man
  Dogged her with gibe or curse
  Or something worse:
  But not one goblin skurried after,
460 Nor was she pricked by fear;
  The kind heart made her windy-paced
  That urged her home quite out of breath with haste
  And inward laughter.

  She cried "Laura," up the garden,
465 "Did you miss me?
  Come and kiss me.
  Never mind my bruises,
  Hug me, kiss me, suck my juices
  Squeezed from goblin fruits for you,
470 Goblin pulp and goblin dew.
  Eat me, drink me, love me;
  Laura, make much of me:
  For your sake I have braved the glen
  And had to do with goblin merchant men."

475 Laura started from her chair,
  Flung her arms up in the air,
  Clutched her hair:
  "Lizzie, Lizzie, have you tasted
  For my sake the fruit forbidden?
480 Must your light like mine be hidden,
  Your young life like mine be wasted,
  Undone in mine undoing
  And ruined in my ruin,
  Thirsty, cankered, goblin-ridden?"—
485 She clung about her sister,
  Kissed and kissed and kissed her:
  Tears once again
  Refreshed her shrunken eyes,

Dropping like rain
490   After long sultry drouth;
Shaking with aguish fear, and pain,
She kissed and kissed her with a hungry mouth.

Her lips began to scorch,
That juice was wormwood to her tongue,
495   She loathed the feast:
Writhing as one possessed she leaped and sung,
Rent all her robe, and wrung
Her hands in lamentable haste,
And beat her breast.
500   Her locks streamed like the torch
Borne by a racer at full speed,
Or like the mane of horses in their flight,
Or like an eagle when she stems[3] the light
Straight toward the sun,
505   Or like a caged thing freed,
Or like a flying flag when armies run.

Swift fire spread thro' her veins, knocked at her heart,
Met the fire smouldering there
And overbore its lesser flame;
510   She gorged on bitterness without a name:
Ah! fool, to choose such part
Of soul-consuming care!
Sense failed in the mortal strife:
Like the watch-tower of a town
515   Which an earthquake shatters down,
Like a lightning-stricken mast,
Like a wind-uprooted tree
Spun about,
Like a foam-topped waterspout
520   Cast down headlong in the sea,
She fell at last;
Pleasure past and anguish past,
Is it death or is it life?

Life out of death.
525   That night long Lizzie watched by her,
Counted her pulse's flagging stir,
Felt for her breath,
Held water to her lips, and cooled her face
With tears and fanning leaves:
530   But when the first birds chirped about their eaves,
And early reapers plodded to the place
Of golden sheaves,
And dew-wet grass
Bowed in the morning winds so brisk to pass,
535   And new buds with new day
Opened of cup-like lilies on the stream,

---

3. Makes headway against.

Laura awoke as from a dream,
Laughed in the innocent old way,
Hugged Lizzie but not twice or thrice;
540 Her gleaming locks showed not one thread of grey,
Her breath was sweet as May
And light danced in her eyes.

Days, weeks, months, years
Afterwards, when both were wives
545 With children of their own;
Their mother-hearts beset with fears,
Their lives bound up in tender lives;
Laura would call the little ones
And tell them of her early prime,
550 Those pleasant days long gone
Of not-returning time:
Would talk about the haunted glen,
The wicked, quaint fruit-merchant men,
Their fruits like honey to the throat
555 But poison in the blood;
(Men sell not such in any town:)
Would tell them how her sister stood
In deadly peril to do her good,
And win the fiery antidote:
560 Then joining hands to little hands
Would bid them cling together,
"For there is no friend like a sister
In calm or stormy weather;
To cheer one on the tedious way,
565 To fetch one if one goes astray,
To lift one if one totters down,
To strengthen whilst one stands."

1859   1862

"No, Thank You, John"

I never said I loved you, John:
    Why will you teaze me day by day,
And wax a weariness to think upon
    With always "do" and "pray"?

5   You know I never loved you, John;
    No fault of mine made me your toast:
Why will you haunt me with a face as wan
    As shows an hour-old ghost?

I dare say Meg or Moll would take
10   Pity upon you, if you'd ask:
And pray don't remain single for my sake
    Who can't perform that task.

I have no heart?—Perhaps I have not;
    But then you're mad to take offence

15 That I don't give you what I have not got:
  Use your own common sense.

Let bygones be bygones:
 Don't call me false, who owed not to be true:
I'd rather answer "No" to fifty Johns
20 Than answer "Yes" to you.

Let's mar our pleasant days no more,
 Song-birds of passage, days of youth:
Catch at today, forget the days before:
 I'll wink at your untruth.

25 Let us strike hands as hearty friends;
 No more, no less; and friendship's good:
Only don't keep in view ulterior ends,
  And points not understood

In open treaty. Rise above
30 Quibbles and shuffling off and on:
Here's friendship for you if you like; but love,—
 No, thank you, John.

1860   1862

Promises Like Pie-Crust

Promise me no promises,
 So will I not promise you:
Keep we both our liberties,
 Never false and never true:
5 Let us hold the die uncast,
 Free to come as free to go:
For I cannot know your past,
 And of mine what can you know?

You, so warm, may once have been
10 Warmer towards another one:
I, so cold, may once have seen
 Sunlight, once have felt the sun:
Who shall show us if it was
 Thus indeed in time of old?
15 Fades the image from the glass,
 And the fortune is not told.

If you promised, you might grieve
 For lost liberty again:
If I promised, I believe
20 I should fret to break the chain.
Let us be the friends we were,
 Nothing more but nothing less:

Many thrive on frugal fare
Who would perish of excess.

1861   1896

In Progress

Ten years ago it seemed impossible
    That she should ever grow so calm as this,
    With self-remembrance in her warmest kiss
And dim dried eyes like an exhausted well.
5   Slow-speaking when she has some fact to tell,
    Silent with long-unbroken silences,
    Centred in self yet not unpleased to please,
Gravely monotonous like a passing bell.
Mindful of drudging daily common things,
10   Patient at pastime, patient at her work,
    Wearied perhaps but strenuous certainly.
    Sometimes I fancy we may one day see
Her head shoot forth seven stars from where they lurk
And her eyes lightnings and her shoulders wings.

1862   1896

A Life's Parallels

Never on this side of the grave again,
    On this side of the river,
On this side of the garner of the grain,
    Never,—

5   Ever while time flows on and on and on,
    That narrow noiseless river,
Ever while corn bows heavy-headed, wan,
    Ever,—

Never despairing, often fainting, rueing,
10   But looking back, ah never!
Faint yet pursuing, faint yet still pursuing
    Ever.

1881

From Later Life

17

Something this foggy day, a something which
    Is neither of this fog nor of today,
    Has set me dreaming of the winds that play
Past certain cliffs, along one certain beach,

5   And turn the topmost edge of waves to spray:
      Ah pleasant pebbly strand so far away,
So out of reach while quite within my reach,
      As out of reach as India or Cathay!
I am sick of where I am and where I am not,
10   I am sick of foresight and of memory,
      I am sick of all I have and all I see,
        I am sick of self, and there is nothing new;
    Oh weary impatient patience of my lot!—
        Thus with myself: how fares it, Friends, with you?

                                                   1881

Cardinal Newman[1]

In the grave, whither thou goest[2]

O weary Champion of the Cross, lie still:
    Sleep thou at length the all-embracing sleep:
    Long was thy sowing-day, rest now and reap:
Thy fast was long, feast now thy spirit's fill.
5   Yea, take thy fill of love, because thy will
    Chose love not in the shallows but the deep:
    Thy tides were springtides, set against the neap[3]
Of calmer souls: thy flood rebuked their rill.
Now night has come to thee—please God, of rest:
10   So some time must it come to every man;
    To first and last, where many last are first.
Now fixed and finished thine eternal plan,
    Thy best has done its best, thy worst its worst:
Thy best its best, Please God, thy best its best.

                                                   1890

Sleeping at Last

Sleeping at last, the trouble & tumult over,
    Sleeping at last, the struggle & horror past,
Cold & white out of sight of friend & of lover
    Sleeping at last.

5   No more a tired heart downcast or overcast,
No more pangs that wring or shifting fears that hover,
    Sleeping at last in a dreamless sleep locked fast.

Fast asleep.   Singing birds in their leafy cover
    Cannot wake her, nor shake her the gusty blast.

1. Written on the occasion of the death of John Henry Newman.
2. Ecclesiastes 9.10.

3. Tides that do not rise to the high-water mark of the spring tides.

10   Under the purple thyme and the purple clover
                Sleeping at last.

                                                    1896

WILLIAM MORRIS
1834–1896

In his autobiography William Butler Yeats observes that if some angel offered him the choice, he would rather live William Morris's life than his own or any other man's. Morris's career was more multifaceted than that of any other Victorian writer. He was a poet, a writer of prose romances, a painter, a designer of furniture, a businessman, a printer, and a leader of the British socialist movement.

Born of wealthy parents and brought up in the Essex countryside, he went to Oxford with the intention of becoming a clergyman. However, art for him soon displaced religion. At Oxford he discovered the work of John Ruskin, which was, in his words, "a revelation." Later in life he wrote, "It was through him that I learned to give form to my discontent. . . . Apart from the desire to produce beautiful things, the leading passion of my life has been and is hatred of modern civilization." Morris's career in many ways realizes Ruskin's views. In 1861 Morris and several friends founded a company to design and produce furniture, wallpaper, textiles, stained glass, tapestries, and carpets, objects still prized today as masterpieces of decorative art. Morris's aim was not only to make beautiful things but, much as Ruskin had urged in *The Nature of Gothic,* to restore creativity to modern manufacture. The minor arts, he believed, were in a state of complete degradation; through his firm he wanted to restore beauty of design and individual craftsmanship.

In his design work, Morris developed close ties with the Pre-Raphaelites. In 1858, he published a remarkable book of poetry, *The Defense of Guenevere,* which some critics regard as the finest book of Pre-Raphaelite verse. Using medieval materials, the poems plunge the reader into the middle of dramatic situations with little sense of larger narrative context or even right and wrong, where little is clear but the vividness of the characters' perceptions. After *The Defense of Guenevere,* Morris turned from lyric to narrative, publishing *The Life and Death of Jason* (1867) and *The Earthly Paradise* (1868–70), a series of twenty-four classical and medieval tales. He then discovered the Icelandic sagas. He co-translated the *Volsunga Saga* and wrote a poem based on it, *The Story of Sigurd the Volsung* (1876). In 1877, he founded the Society for the Protection of Ancient Buildings.

In the late 1870s, after Morris came to the conclusion that art could not have real life and growth under the commercialism of modern society, he turned to socialism. In 1883 he joined the Socialist Democratic Federation; the next year he led the secession of a large faction to found the Socialist League. He was at the center of socialist activity in England through the rest of the decade. At the famous debates held on Sunday evenings at Morris's house, political and literary figures regularly gathered, including Yeats and Bernard Shaw. Morris lectured and wrote tirelessly for the cause, producing essays, columns, and a series of socialist literary works including *A Dream of John Ball* (1887) and *News from Nowhere* (1890), a utopian vision of life under communism in twenty-first-century England.

In 1890, Morris's health failed and factionalism brought his leadership of the Socialist League to an end. In 1891, he co-founded the Kelmscott Press, the first fine art press in England, whose masterpiece was the Kelmscott Chaucer, an edition of *The Canterbury Tales* with illustrations by the Pre-Raphaelite painter Edward Burne Jones and designs by Morris himself.

In the obituary he published after Morris's death, Shaw wrote, "He was ultra-modern—not merely up-to-date, but far ahead of it: his wall papers, his hangings, his tapestries, and his printed books have the twentieth century in every touch of them." Not only did Morris develop design principles that remained important in the twentieth century but he had a radical vision of the relationship of aesthetics to politics. He was, as Shaw said, "a complete artist."

The Defense of Guenevere   Several episodes in Thomas Malory's *Morte Darthur* (1470), one of Morris's favorite books, provided the materials on which he based this poem, although how he presents them is strikingly original. In Malory's narrative, Arthur's kingdom is eventually destroyed by dissensions among his followers; one chief focus of dissension concerned rumors of an adulterous relation between Queen Guenevere and Arthur's chief knight, Launcelot. On two occasions Guenevere had been discovered in apparently compromising circumstances, both of which led to public accusations of adultery. On the first occasion (lines 167–220), her accuser, Sir Mellyagraunce, was challenged by Launcelot to a trial by battle, in which Mellyagraunce was slain. The queen's honor was thereby restored, although, in the poem, the Mellyagraunce scandal is revived by Sir Gauwaine in his accusations against her. The second occasion, which occurred just before the poem opens, was more seriously incriminating. A band of thirteen knights had plotted to trap Launcelot when he was enjoying a visit at night in the queen's chamber, at her invitation (lines 242–77). In making his escape, Launcelot killed all but one of the knights—an event that would later lead to civil war. In Malory's version there is no formal trial of the queen after this event; she is simply told of her sentence, which is to be burned to death at the stake, and is thereafter rescued by Launcelot who takes her away to safety in his castle. Morris's trial scene is hence his own invention, although he probably drew from another episode, in chapter 18 of Malory, which shows Guenevere being accused of treason by Sir Gauwaine in the presence of twenty-four of his knights.

According to Morris's daughter, this poem originally opened with a long introductory passage of description and background, which Morris wisely decided to omit. As a result we are plunged at once into a dramatic scene reminiscent of the openings of some of the dramatic monologues of Robert Browning (the Victorian poet whom Morris most admired). Also like Browning is the way Guenevere's speech keeps shifting back and forth from present to past events such as her recalling the spring day, early in her marriage to Arthur, when Launcelot first kissed her.

During the same year in which Morris's poem appeared, one of Tennyson's *Idylls of the King,* also focused on Guenevere, was published. It is interesting to compare the two portraits of the queen, especially in terms of their pictorial qualities, although Morris's seductively eloquent Guenevere is very different from Tennyson's subdued representation of a guilt-ridden wife.

The Defense of Guenevere

> But, knowing now that they would have her speak,
> She threw her wet hair backward from her brow,
> Her hand close to her mouth touching her cheek,

As though she had had there a shameful blow,
5 And feeling it shameful to feel aught but shame
All through her heart, yet felt her cheek burned so,

She must a little touch it; like one lame
She walked away from Gauwaine, with her head
Still lifted up; and on her cheek of flame

10 The tears dried quick; she stopped at last and said:
"O knights and lords, it seems but little skill°   *use*
To talk of well-known things past now and dead.

"God wot° I ought to say, I have done ill,   *knows*
And pray you all forgiveness heartily!
15 Because you must be right such great lords—still

"Listen, suppose your time were come to die,
And you were quite alone and very weak;
Yea, laid a dying while very mightily

"The wind was ruffling up the narrow streak
20 Of river through your broad lands running well:
Suppose a hush should come, then someone speak:

" 'One of these cloths is heaven, and one is hell,
Now choose one cloth forever, which they be,
I will not tell you, you must somehow tell

25 " 'Of your own strength and mightiness; here, see!'
Yea, yea, my lord, and you to ope your eyes,
At foot of your familiar bed to see

"A great God's angel standing, with such dyes,
Not known on earth, on his great wings, and hands,
30 Held out two ways, light from the inner skies

"Showing him well, and making his commands
Seem to be God's commands, moreover, too,
Holding within his hands the cloths on wands;

"And one of these strange choosing cloths was blue,
35 Wavy and long, and one cut short and red;
No man could tell the better of the two.

"After a shivering half hour you said,
'God help! heaven's color, the blue'; and he said, 'hell.'
Perhaps you then would roll upon your bed,

40 "And cry to all good men that loved you well,
'Ah Christ! if only I had known, known, known';
Launcelot went away, then I could tell,

"Like wisest man how all things would be, moan,
And roll and hurt myself, and long to die,
45   And yet fear much to die for what was sown.

"Nevertheless you, O Sir Gauwaine, lie,
Whatever may have happened through these years,
God knows I speak truth, saying that you lie."

Her voice was low at first, being full of tears,
50   But as it cleared, it grew full loud and shrill,
Growing a windy shriek in all men's ears,

A ringing in their startled brains, until
She said that Gauwaine lied, then her voice sunk,
And her great eyes began again to fill,

55   Though still she stood right up, and never shrunk,
But spoke on bravely, glorious lady fair!
Whatever tears her full lips may have drunk,

She stood, and seemed to think, and wrung her hair,
Spoke out at last with no more trace of shame,
60   With passionate twisting of her body there:

"It chanced upon a day that Launcelot came
To dwell at Arthur's court: at Christmas time
This happened; when the heralds sung his name,

" 'Son of King Ban[1] of Benwick,' seemed to chime
65   Along with all the bells that rang that day,
O'er the white roofs, with little change of rhyme.

"Christmas and whitened winter passed away,
And over me the April sunshine came,
Made very awful with black hail-clouds, yea.

70   "And in Summer I grew white with flame,
And bowed my head down—Autumn, and the sick
Sure knowledge things would never be the same,

"However often Spring might be most thick
Of blossoms and buds, smote on me, and I grew
75   Careless of most things, let the clock tick, tick,

"To my unhappy pulse, that beat right through
My eager body; while I laughed out loud,
And let my lips curl up at false or true,

---

1. Launcelot's father, a king of Brittany.

"Seemed cold and shallow without any cloud.
80   Behold my judges, then the cloths were brought:
While I was dizzied thus, old thoughts would crowd,

"Belonging to the time ere I was bought
By Arthur's great name and his little love,
Must I give up forever then, I thought,

85   "That which I deemed would ever round me move
Glorifying all things; for a little word,[2]
Scarce ever meant at all, must I now prove

"Stone-cold for ever? Pray you, does the Lord
Will that all folks should be quite happy and good?
90   I love God now a little, if this cord[3]

"Were broken, once for all what striving could
Make me love anything in earth or heaven.
So day by day it grew, as if one should

"Slip slowly down some path worn smooth and even,
95   Down to a cool sea on a summer day;
Yet still in slipping there was some small leaven

"Of stretched hands catching small stones by the way,
Until one surely reached the sea at last,
And felt strange new joy as the worn head lay

100   "Back, with the hair like seaweed; yea all past
Sweat of the forehead, dryness of the lips,
Washed utterly out by the dear waves o'ercast,

"In the lone sea, far off from any ships!
Do I not know now of a day in Spring?
105   No minute of that wild day ever slips

"From out my memory; I hear thrushes sing,
And wheresoever I may be, straightway
Thoughts of it all come up with most fresh sting:

"I was half mad with beauty on that day,
110   And went without my ladies all alone,
In a quiet garden walled round every way;

"I was right joyful of that wall of stone,
That shut the flowers and trees up with the sky,
And trebled all the beauty: to the bone,

---

2. Her marriage vow.   3. Her ties with Launcelot.

115 "Yea right through to my heart, grown very shy
With weary thoughts, it pierced, and made me glad;
Exceedingly glad, and I knew verily,

"A little thing just then had made me mad;
I dared not think, as I was wont to do,
120 Sometimes, upon my beauty; If I had

"Held out my long hand up against the blue,
And, looking on the tenderly darkened fingers,
Thought that by rights one ought to see quite through,

"There, see you, where the soft still light yet lingers,
125 Round by the edges; what should I have done,
If this had joined with yellow spotted singers,

"And startling green drawn upward by the sun?
But shouting, loosed out, see now! all my hair,
And trancedly stood watching the west wind run

130 "With faintest half-heard breathing sound—why there
I lose my head e'en now in doing this;
But shortly listen—In that garden fair

"Came Launcelot walking; this is true, the kiss
Wherewith we kissed in meeting that spring day,
135 I scarce dare talk of the remembered bliss,

"When both our mouths went wandering in one way,
And aching sorely, met among the leaves;
Our hands being left behind strained far away.

"Never within a yard of my bright sleeves
140 Had Launcelot come before—and now, so nigh!
After that day why is it Guenevere grieves?

"Nevertheless you, O Sir Gauwaine, lie,
Whatever happened on through all those years,
God knows I speak truth, saying that you lie.

145 "Being such a lady could I weep these tears
If this were true? A great queen such as I
Having sinned this way, straight her conscience sears;

"And afterwards she liveth hatefully,
Slaying and poisoning, certes° never weeps—   certainly
150 Gauwaine be friends now, speak me lovingly.

"Do I not see how God's dear pity creeps
All through your frame, and trembles in your mouth?
Remember in what grave your mother sleeps,

"Buried in some place far down in the south,
155   Men are forgetting as I speak to you;
By her head severed in that awful drouth

"Of pity that drew Agravaine's fell blow,[4]
I pray your pity! let me not scream out
Forever after, when the shrill winds blow

160   "Through half your castle-locks! let me not shout
Forever after in the winter night
When you ride out alone! in battle rout

"Let not my rusting tears make your sword light!°   *weak*
Ah! God of mercy how he turns away!
165   So, ever must I dress me to the fight,

"So—let God's justice work! Gauwaine, I say,
See me hew down your proofs: yea all men know
Even as you said how Mellyagraunce one day,

"One bitter day in *la Fausse Garde*,[5] for so
170   All good knights held it after, saw—
Yea, sirs, by cursed unknightly outrage; though

"You, Gauwaine, held his word without a flaw,
This Mellyagraunce saw blood upon my bed[6]—
Whose blood then pray you? is there any law

175   "To make a queen say why some spots of red
Lie on her coverlet? or will you say,
'Your hands are white, lady, as when you wed,

" 'Where did you bleed?' and must I stammer out—'Nay,
I blush indeed, fair lord, only to rend
180   My sleeve up to my shoulder, where there lay

" 'A knife-point last night': so must I defend
The honor of the lady Guenevere?
Not so, fair lords, even if the world should end

"This very day, and you were judges here
185   Instead of God. Did you see Mellyagraunce
When Launcelot stood by him? what white fear

"Curdled his blood, and how his teeth did dance,
His side sink in? as my knight cried and said,
'Slayer of unarmed men, here is a chance!

---

4. Gauwaine's brother, Agravaine, had beheaded their mother after she had been accused of adultery.
5. The False Castle (French); a term expressing her contempt.
6. Guenevere and some of her young knights who had been wounded in a skirmish were confined for a night in a room in Mellyagraunce's castle. Discovering bloodstains on her bedclothes the following morning, Mellyagraunce accused her of adulterous relations with one of the wounded knights. Actually her visiting bedfellow had been Launcelot, who had cut his hand on the window bars as he climbed into her room.

190 " 'Setter of traps,[7] I pray you guard your head,
By God I am so glad to fight with you,
Stripper of ladies, that my hand feels lead

" 'For driving weight; hurrah now! draw and do,
For all my wounds are moving in my breast,
195 And I am getting mad with waiting so.'

"He struck his hands together o'er the beast,
Who fell down flat, and groveled at his feet,
And groaned at being slain so young—'at least.'

"My knight said, 'Rise you, sir, who are so fleet
200 At catching ladies, half-armed will I fight,
My left side all uncovered!' then I weet,°   know

"Up sprang Sir Mellyagraunce with great delight
Upon his knave's face; not until just then
Did I quite hate him, as I saw my knight

205 "Along the lists look to my stake and pen
With such a joyous smile, it made me sigh
From agony beneath my waist-chain,[8] when

"The fight began, and to me they drew nigh;
Ever Sir Launcelot kept him on the right,
210 And traversed warily, and ever high

"And fast leaped caitiff's sword, until my knight
Sudden threw up his sword to his left hand,
Caught it, and swung it; that was all the fight.

"Except a spout of blood on the hot land;
215 For it was hottest summer; and I know
I wondered how the fire, while I should stand,

"And burn, against the heat, would quiver so,
Yards above my head; thus these matters went:
Which things were only warnings of the woe

220 "That fell on me. Yet Mellyagraunce was shent,°   destroyed
For Mellyagraunce had fought against the Lord;
Therefore, my lords, take heed lest you be blent°   blinded

"With all this wickedness; say no rash word
Against me, being so beautiful; my eyes,
225 Wept all away to gray, may bring some sword

---

7. Mellyagraunce had tried to prevent Launcelot
from coming to defend the queen's honor by making him fall through a trapdoor into a dungeon.

8. She is chained to a stake, at which she will be
burned if Launcelot fails to overcome her accuser.

"To drown you in your blood; see my breast rise,
Like waves of purple sea, as here I stand;
And how my arms are moved in wonderful wise,

"Yea also at my full heart's strong command,
230   See through my long throat how the words go up
In ripples to my mouth; how in my hand

"The shadow lies like wine within a cup
Of marvelously colored gold; yea now
This little wind is rising, look you up,

235   "And wonder how the light is falling so
Within my moving tresses: will you dare,
When you have looked a little on my brow,

"To say this thing is vile? or will you care
For any plausible lies of cunning woof,
240   When you can see my face with no lie there

"Forever? am I not a gracious proof—
'But in your chamber Launcelot was found'—
Is there a good knight then would stand aloof,

"When a queen says with gentle queenly sound:
245   'O true as steel come now and talk with me,
I love to see your step upon the ground

" 'Unwavering, also well I love to see
That gracious smile light up your face, and hear
Your wonderful words, that all mean verily

250   " 'The thing they seem to mean: good friend, so dear
To me in everything, come here tonight,
Or else the hours will pass most dull and drear;

" 'If you come not, I fear this time I might
Get thinking over much of times gone by,
255   When I was young, and green hope was in sight:

" 'For no man cares now to know why I sigh;
And no man comes to sing me pleasant songs,
Nor any brings me the sweet flowers that lie

" 'So thick in the gardens; therefore one so longs
260   To see you, Launcelot; that we may be
Like children once again, free from all wrongs

" 'Just for one night.' Did he not come to me?
What thing could keep true Launcelot away
If I said 'Come?' there was one less than three

265 "In my quiet room that night, and we were gay;
Till sudden I rose up, weak, pale, and sick,
Because a bawling broke our dream up, yea

"I looked at Launcelot's face and could not speak,
For he looked helpless too, for a little while;
270 Then I remember how I tried to shriek,

"And could not, but fell down; from tile to tile
The stones they threw up rattled o'er my head
And made me dizzier; till within a while

"My maids were all about me, and my head
275 On Launcelot's breast was being soothed away
From its white chattering, until Launcelot said—

"By God! I will not tell you more today,
Judge any way you will—what matters it?
You know quite well the story of that fray,

280 "How Launcelot stilled their bawling, the mad fit
That caught up Gauwaine—all, all, verily,
But just that which would save me; these things flit.

"Nevertheless you, O Sir Gauwaine, lie,
Whatever may have happened these long years,
285 God knows I speak truth, saying that you lie!

"All I have said is truth, by Christ's dear tears."
She would not speak another word, but stood.
Turned sideways; listening, like a man who hears

His brother's trumpet sounding through the wood
290 Of his foes' lances. She leaned eagerly,
And gave a slight spring sometimes, as she could

At last hear something really; joyfully
Her cheek grew crimson, as the headlong speed
Of the roan charger drew all men to see,
295 The knight who came was Launcelot at good need.

1859

The Haystack in the Floods[1]

Had she come all the way for this,
To part at last without a kiss?
Yea, had she borne the dirt and rain

---

1. After the defeat of the French at Poitiers in 1356, an English knight, Sir Robert de Marny, is riding with Jehane, his mistress, to reach the frontier of Gascony, which was in English hands.

That her own eyes might see him slain
5   Beside the haystack in the floods?

Along the dripping leafless woods,
The stirrup touching either shoe,
She rode astride as troopers do;
With kirtle° kilted to her knee,   *long skirt*
10   To which the mud splashed wretchedly;
And the wet dripped from every tree
Upon her head and heavy hair,
And on her eyelids broad and fair;
The tears and rain ran down her face.
15   By fits and starts they rode apace,
And very often was his place
Far off from her; he had to ride
Ahead, to see what might betide
When the roads crossed; and sometimes, when
20   There rose a murmuring from his men,
Had to turn back with promises.
Ah me! she had but little ease;
And often for pure doubt and dread
She sobbed, made giddy in the head
25   By the swift riding; while, for cold,
Her slender fingers scarce could hold
The wet reins; yea, and scarcely, too,
She felt the foot within her shoe
Against the stirrup: all for this,
30   To part at last without a kiss
Beside the haystack in the floods.

For when they neared that old soaked hay,
They saw across the only way
That Judas, Godmar, and the three
35   Red running lions dismally
Grinned from his pennon, under which
In one straight line along the ditch,
They counted thirty heads.

               So then
While Robert turned round to his men,
40   She saw at once the wretched end,
And, stooping down, tried hard to rend
Her coif the wrong way from her head,
And hid her eyes; while Robert said:
"Nay, love, 'tis scarcely two to one;
45   At Poitiers where we made them run
So fast—why, sweet my love, good cheer,
The Gascon frontier is so near,
Nought after this."

               But: "O!" she said,
"My God! my God! I have to tread

50 The long way back without you; then
The court at Paris; those six men,°   *the judges*
The gratings of the Chatelet°   *Paris prison*
The swift Seine on some rainy day
Like this, and people standing by,
55 And laughing, while my weak hands try
To recollect how strong men swim.[2]
All this, or else a life with him,
For which I should be damned at last,
Would God that this next hour were past!"

60 He answered not, but cried his cry,
"St. George for Marny!" cheerily;
And laid his hand upon her rein.
Alas! no man of all this train
Gave back that cheery cry again;
65 And, while for rage his thumb beat fast
Upon his sword hilt, someone cast
About his neck a kerchief long,
And bound him.

           Then they went along
To Godmar; who said: "Now, Jehane,
70 Your lover's life is on the wane
So fast, that, if this very hour
You yield not as my paramour,
He will not see the rain leave off:
Nay, keep your tongue from gibe and scoff,
75 Sir Robert, or I slay you now."

She laid her hand upon her brow,
Then gazed upon the palm, as though
She thought her forehead bled, and: "No!"
She said, and turned her head away,
80 As there was nothing else to say,
And everything were settled: red
Grew Godmar's face from chin to head:
"Jehane, on yonder hill there stands
My castle, guarding well my lands;
85 What hinders me from taking you,
And doing that I list to do
To your fair willful body, while
Your knight lies dead?"

           A wicked smile
Wrinkled her face, her lips grew thin,
90 A long way out she thrust her chin:

---

2. In trial by water a woman accused of witchcraft or other crimes was thrown into the river to determine her guilt or innocence. For this ordeal the accused would customarily have her hands tied. If she sank she was deemed innocent and thereafter spared by being hauled from the water. If she floated she was guilty and thereafter burned. In Morris's version Jehane would have no chance of escaping death; if she swam she would be burned, and if she sank she would be drowned (line 108).

"You know that I should strangle you
While you were sleeping; or bite through
Your throat, by God's help: ah!" she said,
"Lord Jesus, pity your poor maid!
95   For in such wise they hem me in,
I cannot choose but sin and sin,
Whatever happens: yet I think
They could not make me eat or drink,
And so should I just reach my rest."
100 "Nay, if you do not my behest,
O Jehane! though I love you well,"
Said Godmar, "would I fail to tell
All that I know?" "Foul lies," she said.
"Eh? lies, my Jehane? by God's head,
105 At Paris folks would deem them true!
Do you know, Jehane, they cry for you:
'Jehane the brown! Jehane the brown!
Give us Jehane to burn or drown!'
Eh!—gag me Robert!—sweet my friend,
110 This were indeed a piteous end
For those long fingers, and long feet,
And long neck, and smooth shoulders sweet;
An end that few men would forget
That saw it. So, an hour yet:
115 Consider, Jehane, which to take
Of life or death!"

                    So, scarce awake,
Dismounting, did she leave that place,
And totter some yards: with her face
Turned upward to the sky she lay,
120 Her head on a wet heap of hay,
And fell asleep: and while she slept,
And did not dream, the minutes crept
Round to the twelve again; but she,
Being waked at last, sighed quietly,
125 And strangely childlike came, and said:
"I will not." Straightway Godmar's head,
As though it hung on strong wires, turned
Most sharply round, and his face burned.

For Robert, both his eyes were dry,
130 He could not weep, but gloomily
He seemed to watch the rain; yea, too,
His lips were firm; he tried once more
To touch her lips; she reached out, sore
And vain desire so tortured them,
135 The poor gray lips, and now the hem
Of his sleeve brushed them.

                    With a start
Up Godmar rose, thrust them apart;

From Robert's throat he loosed the bands
Of silk and mail; with empty hands
140 Held out, she stood and gazed, and saw,
The long bright blade without a flaw
Glide out from Godmar's sheath, his hand
In Robert's hair; she saw him bend
Back Robert's head; she saw him send
145 The thin steel down; the blow told well,
Right backward the knight Robert fell,
And moaned as dogs do, being half dead,
Unwitting, as I deem: so then
Godmar turned grinning to his men,
150 Who ran, some five or six, and beat
His head to pieces at their feet.

Then Godmar turned again and said:
"So, Jehane, the first fitte³ is read!
Take note, my lady, that your way
155 Lies backward to the Chatelet!"
She shook her head and gazed awhile
At her cold hands with a rueful smile,
As though this thing had made her mad.

This was the parting that they had
160 Beside the haystack in the floods.

1858

How I Became a Socialist¹

I am asked by the Editor to give some sort of a history of the above conversion, and I feel that it may be of some use to do so, if my readers will look
upon me as a type of a certain group of people, but not so easy to do clearly,
briefly and truly. Let me, however, try. But first, I will say what I mean by
being a Socialist, since I am told that the word no longer expresses definitely
and with certainty what it did ten years ago. Well, what I mean by Socialism
is a condition of society in which there should be neither rich nor poor,
neither master nor master's man, neither idle nor overworked, neither brain-
sick brain workers, nor heart-sick hand workers, in a word, in which all men
would be living in equality of condition, and would manage their affairs
unwastefully, and with the full consciousness that harm to one would mean
harm to all—the realization at last of the meaning of the word COMMON-
WEALTH.

Now this view of Socialism which I hold to-day, and hope to die holding,
is what I began with; I had no transitional period, unless you may call such
a brief period of political radicalism during which I saw my ideal clear

3. Canto of a poem.
1. Written for the socialist magazine *Justice* in 1894.

enough, but had no hope of any realization of it. That came to an end some months before I joined the (then) Democratic Federation,[2] and the meaning of my joining that body was that I had conceived a hope of the realization of my ideal. If you ask me how much of a hope, or what I thought we Socialists then living and working would accomplish towards it, or when there would be effected any change in the face of society, I must say, I do not know. I can only say that I did not measure my hope, nor the joy that it brought me at the time. For the rest, when I took that step I was blankly ignorant of economics; I had never so much as opened Adam Smith, or heard of Ricardo, or of Karl Marx.[3] Oddly enough, I *had* read some of Mill,[4] to wit, those posthumous papers of his (published, was it in the *Westminster Review* or the *Fortnightly?*) in which he attacks Socialism in its Fourierist[5] guise. In those papers he put the arguments, as far as they go, clearly and honestly, and the result, so far as I was concerned, was to convince me that Socialism was a necessary change, and that it was possible to bring it about in our own days. Those papers put the finishing touch to my conversion to Socialism. Well, having joined a Socialist body (for the Federation soon became definitely Socialist), I put some conscience into trying to learn the economical side of Socialism, and even tackled Marx, though I must confess that, whereas I thoroughly enjoyed the historical part of "Capital," I suffered agonies of confusion of the brain over reading the pure economics of that great work. Anyhow, I read what I could, and will hope that some information stuck to me from my reading; but more, I must think, from continuous conversation with such friends as Bax and Hyndman and Scheu,[6] and the brisk course of propaganda meetings which were going on at the time, and in which I took my share. Such finish to what of education in practical Socialism as I am capable of I received afterwards from some of my Anarchist friends, from whom I learned, quite against their intention, that Anarchism was impossible, much as I learned from Mill against *his* intention that Socialism was necessary.

But in this telling how I fell into *practical* Socialism I have begun, as I perceive, in the middle, for in my position of a well-to-do man, not suffering from the disabilities which oppress a working-man at every step, I feel that I might never have been drawn into the practical side of the question if an ideal had not forced me to seek towards it. For politics as politics, *i.e.*, not regarded as a necessary if cumbersome and disgustful means to an end, would never have attracted me, nor when I had become conscious of the wrongs of society as it now is, and the oppression of poor people, could I have ever believed in the possibility of a *partial* setting right of those wrongs. In other words, I could never have been such a fool as to believe in the happy and "respectable" poor.

If, therefore, my ideal forced me to look for practical Socialism, what was

2. The first socialist organization in London, founded in 1881.
3. Political philosopher (1818–1883), who developed the concept of communism. Smith (1723–1790), Scottish economist whose argument that natural laws of production and exchange govern economies and produce wealth was an important justification of capitalism. David Ricardo (1772–1823), English economist.

4. James Mill (1773–1836), father of John Stuart Mill, philosopher and political economist.
5. Political philosophy, developed by Charles Fourier (1772–1837), that advocated a social reorganization that equalized wealth.
6. Ernest Belfort Bax, H. M. Hyndman, and Andreas Sheu, leaders in the early English socialist movement.

it that forced me to conceive of an ideal? Now, here comes in what I said (in this paper) of my being a type of a certain group of mind.

Before the uprising of *modern* Socialism almost all intelligent people either were, or professed themselves to be, quite contented with the civilization of this century. Again, almost all of these really were thus contented, and saw nothing to do but to perfect the said civilization by getting rid of a few ridiculous survivals of the barbarous ages. To be short, this was the *Whig*[7] frame of mind, natural to the modern prosperous middle-class men, who, in fact, as far as mechanical progress is concerned, have nothing to ask for, if only Socialism would leave them alone to enjoy their plentiful style.

But besides these contented ones there were others who were not really contented, but had a vague sentiment of repulsion to the triumph of civilization, but were coerced into silence by the measureless power of Whiggery. Lastly, there were a few who were in open rebellion against the said Whiggery—a few, say two, Carlyle and Ruskin. The latter, before my days of practical Socialism, was my master towards the ideal aforesaid, and, looking backward, I cannot help saying, by the way, how deadly dull the world would have been twenty years ago but for Ruskin! It was through him that I learned to give form to my discontent, which I must say was not by any means vague. Apart from the desire to produce beautiful things, the leading passion of my life has been and is hatred of modern civilization. What shall I say of it now, when the words are put into my mouth, my hope of its destruction—what shall I say of its supplanting by Socialism?

What shall I say concerning its mastery of and its waste of mechanical power, its commonwealth so poor, its enemies of the commonwealth so rich, its stupendous organization—for the misery of life! Its contempt of simple pleasures which everyone could enjoy but for its folly? Its eyeless vulgarity which has destroyed art, the one certain solace of labour? All this I felt then as now, but I did not know why it was so. The hope of the past times was gone, the struggles of mankind for many ages had produced nothing but this sordid, aimless, ugly confusion; the immediate future seemed to me likely to intensify all the present evils by sweeping away the last survivals of the days before the dull squalor of civilization had settled down on the world. This was a bad look-out indeed, and, if I may mention myself as a personality and not as a mere type, especially so to a man of my disposition, careless of metaphysics and religion, as well as of scientific analysis, but with a deep love of the earth and the life on it, and a passion for the history of the past of mankind. Think of it! Was it all to end in a counting-house on the top of a cinder-heap, with Podsnap's[8] drawing-room in the offing, and a Whig committee dealing out champagne to the rich and margarine to the poor in such convenient proportions as would make all men contented together, though the pleasure of the eyes was gone from the world, and the place of Homer was to be taken by Huxley?[9] Yet, believe me, in my heart, when I really forced myself to look towards the future, that is what I saw in it, and, as far as I could tell, scarce anyone seemed to think it worth while to struggle against such a consummation of civilization. So there I was in for a fine pessimistic

7. Political party largely identified with industry and with parliamentary and social reform; became part of the Liberal party in the early 1840s.
8. Character in Dickens's *Our Mutual Friend*, the epitome of pretentious middle-class respectability.
9. T. H. Huxley (1825–1895), writer on science and philosophy.

end of life, if it had not somehow dawned on me that amidst all this filth of civilization the seeds of a great chance, what we others call Social-Revolution, were beginning to germinate. The whole face of things was changed to me by that discovery, and all I had to do then in order to become a Socialist was to hook myself on to the practical movement, which, as before said, I have tried to do as well as I could.

To sum up, then, the study of history and the love and practice of art forced me into a hatred of the civilization which, if things were to stop as they are, would turn history into inconsequent nonsense, and make art a collection of the curiosities of the past which would have no serious relation to the life of the present.

But the consciousness of revolution stirring amidst our hateful modern society prevented me, luckier than many others of artistic perceptions, from crystallizing into a mere railer against "progress" on the one hand, and on the other from wasting time and energy in any of the numerous schemes by which the quasi-artistic of the middle classes hope to make art grow when it has no longer any root, and thus I became a practical Socialist.

A last word or two. Perhaps some of our friends will say, what have we to do with these matters of history and art? We want by means of Social-Democracy to win a decent livelihood, we want in some sort to live, and that at once. Surely any one who professes to think that the question of art and cultivation must go before that of the knife and fork (and there are some who do propose that) does not understand what art means, or how that its roots must have a soil of a thriving and unanxious life. Yet it must be remembered that civilization has reduced the workman to such a skinny and pitiful existence, that he scarcely knows how to frame a desire for any life much better than that which he now endures perforce. It is the province of art to set the true ideal of a full and reasonable life before him, a life to which the perception and creation of beauty, the enjoyment of real pleasure that is, shall be felt to be as necessary to man as his daily bread, and that no man, and no set of men, can be deprived of this except by mere opposition, which should be resisted to the utmost.

1894   1894

ALGERNON CHARLES SWINBURNE
1837–1909

In a review of Baudelaire's *Fleurs du Mal* Algernon Charles Swinburne remarked that "the mass of readers seem actually to think that a poem is the better for containing a moral lesson." He goes on to praise the courage and sense of a man who acts on the conviction "that the art of poetry has nothing to do with didactic matter at all." Certainly Swinburne's poems are not didactic in the sense of containing traditional moral values. As John Morley commented in a review of Swinburne's first volume of poems, "He is so firmly and avowedly fixed in an attitude of revolt against the current notions of decency and dignity and social duty that to beg of him to be a little more decent, to fly a little less persistently and gleefully to the animal side of human nature, is simply to beg him to be something different from Mr. Swinburne." Like the fat boy in *Pickwick Papers* who terrified the old lady by announcing, "I wants to make your flesh creep," Swinburne set about shocking his elders by a variety of rebellious gestures. In religion he appeared to be a pagan; in politics, a liberal republican dedicated to the overthrow of established governments. And on the subject of love he was often preoccupied with the pleasures of the lover who inflicts pain or accepts pain, pleasures of which he had read in the writings of the Marquis de Sade. As Arnold Bennett said of *Anactoria,* a dramatic monologue in which the poet Sappho addresses a woman with whom she is madly in love, Swinburne played "a rare trick" on England by "enshrining in the topmost heights of its literature a lovely poem that cannot be discussed."

To a more limited extent, Swinburne also expressed his rebellion against established codes by his personal behavior. He came from a distinguished family and attended Eton and Oxford, but sought the company of the bohemians of Paris and of London, where he became temporarily associated with Dante Gabriel Rossetti and other Pre-Raphaelites. By 1879 his alcoholism had profoundly affected his frail physique, and he was obliged to put himself into the protective custody of a friend, Theodore Watts-Dunton, who removed him to the countryside and kept him alive although sobered and tamed.

Swinburne continued to write voluminously and sometimes memorably, but most of his best poetry is in his early publications. His early play *Atalanta in Calydon* (1865) was described by Swinburne himself as "pure Greek," and his command of classical allusions here, as well as in other poems, is indeed impressive. Yet the kind of spirit that he found in Greek literature was not the traditional quality of classic serenity admired by Matthew Arnold. Like Shelley (the poet he most closely resembles), Swinburne loved Greece as a land of liberty in which men had expressed themselves with the most complete unrestraint. To call such an ardently romantic poet "classical" requires a series of qualifying clauses that makes the term meaningless.

In his play and in the volume that followed it, *Poems and Ballads* (1866), Swinburne demonstrated a metrical virtuosity that dazzled his early readers and is still dazzling. Those who demand that poetry should make sense, first and foremost, may find that much of his poetry is not to their taste. What he offers, instead, are heady rhythmical patterns in which words are relished as much for their sound as for their sense.

> There lived a singer in France of old
> By the tideless dolorous midland sea.
> In a land of sand and ruin and gold
> There shone one woman, and none but she.

These lines from *The Triumph of Time* have often been cited to illustrate Swinburne's qualities. Like some of the poems of the later French symbolists, such passages defy traditional kinds of critical analysis and oblige us to reconsider the variety of ways in which poetry may achieve its effects.

Another noteworthy aspect of these poems is their recurring preoccupation with death, as in the memorable re-creations of the underworld garden of Proserpine, frozen in timelessness. And as the critic Jerome McGann notes: "No English poet has composed more elegies than Swinburne." The death of any prominent figure, such as Browning, almost always prompted Swinburne to compose a poem for the occasion. Some of these are merely competent editorials in verse; others, especially his moving *Ave Atque Vale* in honor of Charles Baudelaire, are of a different dimension. Swinburne modestly hoped that *Ave Atque Vale* might find its niche as a fourth in line among the major elegies in English, following Milton's *Lycidas,* Shelley's *Adonais,* and Arnold's *Thyrsis.* McGann argues that the "elusive beauty and enigmatic greatness" of Swinburne's elegy make his poem clearly superior to *Thyrsis* and assure *Ave Atque Vale* the third place (at least) in this distinguished quartet.

Choruses from Atalanta in Calydon
When the Hounds of Spring[1]

When the hounds of spring are on winter's traces,
    The mother of months in meadow or plain
Fills the shadows and windy places
    With lisp of leaves and ripple of rain;
5 And the brown bright nightingale[2] amorous
    Is half assuaged for Itylus,
For the Thracian ships and the foreign faces,
    The tongueless vigil and all the pain.

Come with bows bent and with emptying of quivers,
10   Maiden most perfect, lady of light,
With a noise of winds and many rivers,
    With a clamor of waters, and with might;
Bind on thy sandals, O thou most fleet,
    Over the splendor and speed of thy feet;
15 For the faint east quickens, the wan west shivers,
    Round the feet of the day and the feet of the night.

Where shall we find her, how shall we sing to her,
    Fold our hands round her knees, and cling?
O that man's heart were as fire and could spring to her,
20   Fire, or the strength of the streams that spring!
For the stars and the winds are unto her
    As raiment, as songs of the harp player;
For the risen stars and the fallen cling to her,
    And the southwest wind and the west wind sing.

25 For winter's rains and ruins are over,
    And all the season of snows and sins;
The days dividing lover and lover,
    The light that loses, the night that wins;
And time remembered is grief forgotten,
30 And frosts are slain and flowers begotten,
    And in green underwood and cover
      Blossom by blossom the spring begins.

The full streams feed on flower of rushes,
    Ripe grasses trammel a traveling foot,

1. This choral hymn, with which Swinburne's tragedy opens, is addressed to Artemis (or Diana), virgin goddess and huntress. Artemis was also goddess of the moon and hence, as affecting the seasons, the "mother of months" (line 2).
2. Philomela, after being raped by her brother-in-law and having her tongue cut out, was changed into a nightingale. To obtain revenge, her sister, Procne, killed her own son, Itylus, and fed the child's body to her husband, Tereus, a Thracian king.

35   The faint fresh flame of the young year flushes
       From leaf to flower and flower to fruit;
    And fruit and leaf are as gold and fire,
    And the oat[3] is heard above the lyre,
    And the hoofèd heel of a satyr crushes
40   The chestnut husk at the chestnut root.

    And Pan by noon and Bacchus by night,
       Fleeter of foot than the fleet-foot kid,
    Follows with dancing and fills with delight
       The Maenad and the Bassarid;[4]
45   And soft as lips that laugh and hide,
    The laughing leaves of the trees divide,
    And screen from seeing and leave in sight
       The god pursuing, the maiden hid.

    The ivy falls with the Bacchanal's hair
50   Over her eyebrows hiding her eyes;
    The wild vine slipping down leaves bare
       Her bright breast shortening into sighs;
    The wild vine slips with the weight of its leaves,
    But the berried ivy catches and cleaves
55   To the limbs that glitter, the feet that scare
       The wolf that follows, the fawn that flies.

Before the Beginning of Years

    Before the beginning of years
       There came to the making of man
    Time, with a gift of tears;
       Grief, with a glass that ran;
5   Pleasure, with pain for leaven;
       Summer, with flowers that fell;
    Remembrance fallen from heaven,
       And madness risen from hell;
    Strength without hands to smite;
10   Love that endures for a breath;
    Night, the shadow of light,
       And life, the shadow of death.

    And the high gods took in hand
       Fire, and the falling of tears,
15   And a measure of sliding sand
       From under the feet of the years;
    And froth and drift of the sea;
       And dust of the laboring earth;
    And bodies of things to be
20   In the houses of death and of birth;
    And wrought with weeping and laughter,

3. Musical pipe made from an oaten straw.
4. Participants in the spring festival honoring Dio-nysus (or Bacchus). Such festivals sometimes developed into frenzied sexual orgies.

And fashioned with loathing and love,
With life before and after
And death beneath and above,
25   For a day and a night and a morrow,
That his strength might endure for a span
With travail and heavy sorrow,
The holy spirit of man.

From the winds of the north and the south
30   They gathered as unto strife;
They breathed upon his mouth,
They filled his body with life;
Eyesight and speech they wrought
For the veils of the soul therein,
35   A time for labor and thought,
A time to serve and to sin;
They gave him light in his ways,
And love, and a space for delight,
And beauty and length of days,
40   And night, and sleep in the night.
His speech is a burning fire;
With his lips he travaileth;
In his heart is a blind desire,
In his eyes foreknowledge of death;
45   He weaves, and is clothed with derision;
Sows, and he shall not reap;
His life is a watch or a vision
Between a sleep and a sleep.

1865

Hymn to Proserpine

(After the Proclamation in Rome of the Christian Faith)

Vicisti, Galilaee[1]

I have lived long enough, having seen one thing, that love hath an end;
Goddess and maiden and queen, be near me now and befriend.
Thou art more than the day or the morrow, the seasons that laugh or
    that weep;
For these give joy and sorrow; but thou, Proserpina, sleep.
5 Sweet is the treading of wine, and sweet the feet of the dove;

---

1. Thou hast conquered, O Galilean (Latin); words supposedly addressed to Christ by the Roman emperor Julian the Apostate, on his death-bed in 363. Julian had tried to revive paganism and to discourage Christianity, which, after a procla-mation in 313, had been tolerated in Rome. His efforts, however, were unsuccessful. The speaker of the poem, a Roman patrician and also a poet (line 9), is like Emperor Julian: he prefers the old order of pagan gods. His hymn is addressed to the goddess Proserpine, who was carried off by Hades (or Pluto) to be queen of the lower world. In this role, she is addressed in the poem as goddess of death and of sleep. The speaker also associates her with the earth itself (line 93) because she was the daughter of Demeter (or Ceres), goddess of agri-culture, whose name means "Earth Mother." Swinburne may have derived some details here from the 4th-century Latin poet Claudian, whose long narrative The Rape of Proserpine provides helpful background for this hymn.

But a goodlier gift is thine than foam of the grapes or love.
Yea, is not even Apollo, with hair and harpstring of gold,
A bitter god to follow, a beautiful god to behold?
I am sick of singing; the bays[2] burn deep and chafe. I am fain
10   To rest a little from praise and grievous pleasure and pain.
For the gods we know not of, who give us our daily breath,
We know they are cruel as love or life, and lovely as death.

O gods dethroned and deceased, cast forth, wiped out in a day!
From your wrath is the world released, redeemed from your chains, men
          say.
15   New gods are crowned in the city; their flowers have broken your rods;
They are merciful, clothed with pity, the young compassionate gods.
But for me their new device is barren, the days are bare;
Things long past over suffice, and men forgotten that were.
Time and the gods are at strife; ye dwell in the midst thereof,
20   Draining a little life from the barren breasts of love.
I say to you, cease, take rest; yea, I say to you all, be at peace,
Till the bitter milk of her breast and the barren bosom shall cease.
Wilt thou yet take all, Galilean? But these thou shalt not take—
The laurel, the palms, and the paean, the breasts of the nymphs in the
          brake,
25   Breasts more soft than a dove's, that tremble with tenderer breath;
And all the wings of the Loves, and all the joy before death;
All the feet of the hours that sound as a single lyre,
Dropped and deep in the flowers, with strings that flicker like fire.
More than these wilt thou give, things fairer than all these things?
30   Nay, for a little we live, and life hath mutable wings.
A little while and we die; shall life not thrive as it may?
For no man under the sky lives twice, outliving his day.
And grief is a grievous thing, and a man hath enough of his tears;
Why should he labor, and bring fresh grief to blacken his years?

35   Thou hast conquered, O pale Galilean; the world has grown gray from
          thy breath;
We have drunken of things Lethean,[3] and fed on the fullness of death.
Laurel is green for a season, and love is sweet for a day;
But love grows bitter with treason, and laurel outlives not May.
Sleep, shall we sleep after all? for the world is not sweet in the end;
40   For the old faiths loosen and fall, the new years ruin and rend.
Fate is a sea without shore, and the soul is a rock that abides;
But her ears are vexed with the roar and her face with the foam of the
          tides.
O lips that the live blood faints in, the leavings of racks and rods!
O ghastly glories of saints, dead limbs of gibbeted gods!
45   Though all men abase them before you in spirit, and all knees bend,
I kneel not, neither adore you, but standing look to the end.

All delicate days and pleasant, all spirits and sorrows are cast
Far out with the foam of the present that sweeps to the surf of the past;

2. Laurel leaves of a poet's crown.
3. I.e., of Lethe, a river in the lower world. By drinking its waters the dead forgot the past.

Where beyond the extreme sea wall, and between the remote sea gates,
50　Waste water washes, and tall ships founder, and deep death waits;
Where, mighty with deepening sides, clad about with the seas as with
　　wings,
And impelled of invisible tides, and fulfilled of unspeakable things,
White-eyed and poisonous-finned, shark-toothed and serpentinecurled,
Rolls, under the whitening wind of the future, the wave of the world.
55　The depths stand naked in sunder behind it, the storms flee away;
In the hollow before it the thunder is taken and snared as a prey;
In its sides is the north wind bound; and its salt is of all men's tears,
With light of ruin, and sound of changes, and pulse of years;
With travail of day after day, and with trouble of hour upon hour.
60　And bitter as blood is the spray; and the crests are as fangs that devour;
And its vapor and storm of its steam as the sighing of spirits to be;
And its noise as the noise in a dream; and its depths as the roots of the
　　sea;
And the height of its heads as the height of the utmost stars of the air;
And the ends of the earth at the might thereof tremble, and time is
　　made bare.
65　Will ye bridle the deep sea with reins, will ye chasten the high sea with
　　rods?
Will ye take her to chain her with chains, who is older than all ye gods?
All ye as a wind shall go by, as a fire shall ye pass and be past;
Ye are gods, and behold, ye shall die, and the waves be upon you at last.
In the darkness of time, in the deeps of the years, in the changes of
　　things,
70　Ye shall sleep as a slain man sleeps, and the world shall forget you or
　　kings.
Though the feet of thine high priests tread where thy lords and our
　　forefathers trod,
Though these that were gods are dead, and thou being dead art a god,
Though before thee the throned Cytherean[4] be fallen, and hidden her
　　head,
Yet thy kingdom shall pass, Galilean, thy dead shall go down to thee
　　dead.

75　Of the maiden thy mother men sing as a goddess with grace clad around;
Thou art throned where another was king; where another was queen
　　she is crowned.
Yea, once we had sight of another; but now she is queen, say these.
Not as thine, not as thine was our mother, a blossom of flowering seas,
Clothed round with the world's desire as with raiment, and fair as the
　　foam.
80　And fleeter than kindled fire, and a goddess, and mother of Rome.[5]
For thine came pale and a maiden, and sister to sorrow; but ours,
Her deep hair heavily laden with odor and color of flowers,
White rose of the rose-white water, a silver splendor, a flame,
Bent down unto us that besought her, and earth grew sweet with her
　　name.

---

4. Aphrodite (or Venus), who was born from the
waves near the island of Cythera.

5. Aeneas, the founder of Rome, was said to have
been the son of Aphrodite.

85 For thine came weeping, a slave among slaves, and rejected; but she
    Came flushed from the full-flushed wave, and imperial, her foot on the
       sea.
    And the wonderful waters knew her, the winds and the viewless ways,
    And the roses grew rosier, and bluer the sea-blue stream of the bays.

    Ye are fallen, our lords, by what token? we wist that ye should not fall.
90 Ye were all so fair that are broken; and one more fair than ye all.
    But I turn to her° still, having seen she shall surely abide in   *Proserpine*
       the end.
    Goddess and maiden and queen, be near me now and befriend.
    O daughter of earth, of my mother, her crown and blossom of birth,
    I am also, I also, thy brother; I go as I came unto earth.
95 In the night where thine eyes are as moons are in heaven, the night
       where thou art,
    Where the silence is more than all tunes, where sleep overflows from
       the heart,
    Where the poppies are sweet as the rose in our world, and the red rose
       is white,
    And the wind falls faint as it blows with the fume of the flowers of the
       night,
    And the murmur of spirits that sleep in the shadow of gods from afar
100 Grows dim in thine ears and deep as the deep dim soul of a star,
    In the sweet low light of thy face, under heavens untrod by the sun,
    Let my soul with their souls find place, and forget what is done and
       undone.
    Thou art more than the gods who number the days of our temporal
       breath;
    For these give labor and slumber; but thou, Proserpina, death.
105 Therefore now at thy feet I abide for a season in silence. I know
    I shall die as my fathers died, and sleep as they sleep; even so.
    For the glass of the years is brittle wherein we gaze for a span.
    A little soul for a little bears up this corpse which is man.
    So long I endure, no longer; and laugh not again, neither weep.
110 For there is no god found stronger than death; and death is a sleep.

                                                                   1866

The Garden of Proserpine[1]

       Here, where the world is quiet;
       Here, where all trouble seems
       Dead winds' and spent waves' riot
       In doubtful dreams of dreams;
5   I watch the green field growing

---

1. Or Proserpina, the goddess who was carried off by Hades (or Pluto) to be queen of the lower world. According to some accounts, she had there a garden of ever-blooming flowers. The Greek and Roman festivals honoring her and her mother, Ceres, emphasized Proserpine's return to the upper world in spring. In Swinburne's poems, however, the emphasis is on her role as goddess of death and eternal sleep. Swinburne also associates her with the sea, which he usually represents as eternally unchanging despite its surface changefulness.

For reaping folk and sowing,
For harvest time and mowing,
   A sleepy world of streams.

I am tired of tears and laughter,
10   And men that laugh and weep;
Of what may come hereafter
   For men that sow to reap;
I am weary of days and hours,
Blown buds of barren flowers,
15 Desires and dreams and powers
   And everything but sleep.

Here life has death for neighbor,
   And far from eye or ear
Wan waves and wet winds labor,
20   Weak ships and spirits steer;
They drive adrift, and whither
They wot not who make thither;
But no such winds blow hither,
   And no such things grow here.

25 No growth of moor or coppice,
   No heather flower or vine,
But bloomless buds of poppies,
   Green grapes of Proserpine,
Pale beds of blowing rushes,
30 Where no leaf blooms or blushes
Save this whereout she crushes
   For dead men deadly wine.

Pale, without name or number,
   In fruitless fields of corn,°   *wheat*
35 They bow themselves and slumber
   All night till light is born;
And like a soul belated,
In hell and heaven unmated,
By cloud and mist abated
40   Comes out of darkness morn.

Though one were strong as seven,
   He too with death shall dwell,
Nor wake with wings in heaven,
   Nor weep for pains in hell;
45 Though one were fair as roses,
His beauty clouds and closes;
And well though love reposes,
   In the end it is not well.

Pale, beyond porch and portal,
50   Crowned with calm leaves, she stands
Who gathers all things mortal

With cold immortal hands;
Her languid lips are sweeter
Than love's who fears to greet her
55 To men that mix and meet her
From many times and lands.

She waits for each and other,
She waits for all men born;
Forgets the earth her mother,
60 The life of fruits and corn;
And spring and seed and swallow
Take wing for her and follow
Where summer song rings hollow
And flowers are put to scorn.

65 There go the loves that wither,
The old loves with wearier wings;
And all dead years draw thither,
And all disastrous things;
Dead dreams of days forsaken,
70 Blind buds that snows have shaken,
Wild leaves that winds have taken,
Red strays of ruined springs.

We are not sure of sorrow,
And joy was never sure;
75 Today will die tomorrow;
Time stoops to no man's lure;
And love, grown faint and fretful,
With lips but half regretful
Sighs, and with eyes forgetful
80 Weeps that no loves endure.

From too much love of living,
From hope and fear set free,
We thank with brief thanksgiving
Whatever gods may be
85 That no life lives forever;
That dead men rise up never;
That even the weariest river
Winds somewhere safe to sea.

Then star nor sun shall waken,
90 Nor any change of light:
Nor sound of waters shaken,
Nor any sound or sight:
Nor wintry leaves nor vernal,
Nor days nor things diurnal;
95 Only the sleep eternal
In an eternal night.

1866

Ave Atque Vale[1]

In Memory of Charles Baudelaire

Nous devrions pourtant lui porter quelques fleurs;
Les morts, les pauvres morts, ont de grandes douleurs,
Et quand Octobre souffle, émondeur des vieux arbres,
Son vent mélancolique à l'entour de leurs marbres,
Certe, ils doivent trouver les vivants bien ingrats.
—*"Les Fleurs du Mal."*[2]

1

    Shall I strew on thee rose or rue or laurel,[3]
      Brother, on this that was the veil[4] of thee?
    Or quiet sea-flower molded by the sea,
    Or simplest growth of meadow-sweet or sorrel,
5   Such as the summer-sleepy Dryads° weave,   *wood nymphs*
      Waked up by snow-soft sudden rains at eve?
    Or wilt thou rather, as on earth before,
      Half-faded fiery blossoms, pale with heat
      And full of bitter summer, but more sweet
10   To thee than gleanings of a northern shore
      Trod by no tropic feet?[5]

2

    For always thee the fervid languid glories
      Allured of heavier suns in mightier skies;
    Thine ears knew all the wandering watery sighs
15   Where the sea sobs round Lesbian promontories,
      The barren kiss of piteous wave to wave
      That knows not where is that Leucadian grave[6]
    Which hides too deep the supreme head of song.
      Ah, salt and sterile as her kisses were,
20   The wild sea winds her and the green gulfs bear
    Hither and thither, and vex and work her wrong,
      Blind gods that cannot spare.

1. Hail and farewell (Latin); a line from an elegy by Catullus occasioned by a farewell visit to the grave of his brother, to whom he brought gifts, a situation closely echoed in Swinburne's final stanza. Swinburne's elegy likewise begins with a visit to the grave of a man whom the poet regards as a brother but had never met. Charles Baudelaire (1821–1867) had impressed Swinburne as one of the "most perfect poets of the century." In 1861, in an essay on the 2nd edition of Baudelaire's collection *Les Fleurs du Mal* (Flowers of evil, 1857), Swinburne had commented on the French poet's preoccupation with "sad and strange things"—"the sharp and cruel enjoyments of pain, the acrid relish of suffering felt or inflicted"; "it has the languid, lurid beauty of close and threatening weather—a heavy, heated temperature, with dangerous hot-house scents in it." These qualities are also celebrated in Swinburne's elegy, into which are woven many allusions to Baudelaire's poems, especially

his *Litanies de Satan*, which Swinburne regarded as the keynote poem of *Les Fleurs du Mal*.
2. From *La servante au grand coeur* (The great-hearted servant): We must nevertheless bring some flowers to her [or him]. / The dead, the poor dead, have great sadnesses, / And when October, the pruner of old trees, blows, / Its melancholy wind in the vicinity of their marble tombs, / Then indeed they must find the living highly ungrateful (French).
3. Respectively, symbols of love, mourning, and poetic fame.
4. I.e., the body as a veil for the soul.
5. A voyage to the tropics in Baudelaire's youth made a lasting impact on his poetry.
6. According to legend, the poetess Sappho, who was born on the island of Lesbos, destroyed herself by leaping from the rock of Leucas into the Ionian Sea. In this section Swinburne makes allusions to Baudelaire's *Lesbos*.

3

Thou sawest, in thine old singing season, brother,
    Secrets and sorrows unbeheld of us:
25   Fierce loves, and lovely leaf-buds poisonous,
Bare to thy subtler eye, but for none other
        Blowing by night in some unbreathed-in clime;
        The hidden harvest of luxurious time,
Sin without shape, and pleasure without speech;
30   And where strange dreams in a tumultuous sleep
        Make the shut eyes of stricken spirits weep;
And with each face thou sawest the shadow on each,
        Seeing as men sow men reap.[7]

4

O sleepless heart and somber soul unsleeping,
35   That were athirst for sleep and no more life
        And no more love, for peace and no more strife!
Now the dim gods of death have in their keeping
        Spirit and body and all the springs of song,
        Is it well now where love can do no wrong,
40   Where stingless pleasure has no foam or fang
        Behind the unopening closure of her lips?
        Is it not well where soul from body slips
And flesh from bone divides without a pang
        As dew from flower-bell drips?

5

45 It is enough; the end and the beginning
        Are one thing to thee, who art past the end.
        O hand unclasped of unbeholden friend,
For thee no fruits to pluck, no palms for winning,
        No triumph and no labor and no lust,
50   Only dead yew-leaves and a little dust.
O quiet eyes wherein the light saith naught,
        Whereto the day is dumb, nor any night
        With obscure finger silences your sight,
Nor in your speech the sudden soul speaks thought,
55   Sleep, and have sleep for light.

6

Now all strange hours and all strange loves are over,
        Dreams and desires and somber songs and sweet,
        Hast thou found place at the great knees and feet
Of some pale Titan-woman like a lover,
60   Such as thy vision here solicited,[8]
        Under the shadow of her fair vast head,
The deep division of prodigious breasts,
        The solemn slope of mighty limbs asleep,

---

7. Cf. Galatians 6.7: "Whatsoever a man soweth, that shall he also reap."

8. An allusion to Baudelaire's *La Géante* (The giantess).

The weight of awful tresses that still keep
65   The savor and shade of old-world pine forests
        Where the wet hill-winds weep?

7

Hast thou found any likeness for thy vision?
        O gardener of strange flowers, what bud, what bloom,
        Hast thou found sown, what gathered in the gloom?
70   What of despair, of rapture, of derision,
        What of life is there, what of ill or good?
        Are the fruits gray like dust or bright like blood?
Does the dim ground grow any seed of ours,
        The faint fields quicken any terrene root,
75   In low lands where the sun and moon are mute
And all the stars keep silence? Are there flowers
        At all, or any fruit?

8

Alas, but though my flying song flies after,
        O sweet strange elder singer, thy more fleet
80   Singing, and footprints of thy fleeter feet,
Some dim derision of mysterious laughter
        From the blind tongueless warders of the dead,
        Some gainless glimpse of Proserpine's[9] veiled head,
Some little sound of unregarded tears
85   Wept by effaced unprofitable eyes,
        And from pale mouths some cadence of dead sighs—
These only, these the hearkening spirit hears,
        Sees only such things rise.

9

Thou art far too far for wings of words to follow,
90   Far too far off for thought or any prayer.
        What ails us with thee, who are wind and air?
What ails us gazing where all seen is hollow?
        Yet with some fancy, yet with some desire,
        Dreams pursue death as winds a flying fire,
95   Our dreams pursue our dead and do not find.
        Still, and more swift than they, the thin flame flies,
        The low light fails us in elusive skies,
Still the foiled earnest ear is deaf, and blind
        Are still the eluded eyes.

10

100   Not thee, O never thee, in all time's changes,
        Not thee, but this the sound of thy sad soul,
        The shadow of thy swift spirit, this shut scroll
I lay my hand on, and not death estranges

9. Queen of the underworld.

My spirit from communion of thy song—
105   These memories and these melodies that throng
Veiled porches of a Muse funereal[1]—
    These I salute, these touch, these clasp and fold
    As though a hand were in my hand to hold,
Or through mine ears a mourning musical
110   Of many mourners rolled.

11

I among these, I also, in such station
    As when the pyre was charred, and piled the sods,
    And offering to the dead made, and their gods,
The old mourners had, standing to make libation,
115   I stand, and to the gods and to the dead
    Do reverence without prayer or praise, and shed
Offering to these unknown, the gods of gloom,
    And what of honey and spice my seedlands bear,
    And what I may of fruits in this chilled air,
120 And lay, Orestes-like, across the tomb
    A curl of severed hair.

12

But by no hand nor any treason stricken,
    Not like the low-lying head of Him, the King,
    The flame that made of Troy a ruinous thing,
125 Thou liest, and on this dust no tears could quicken
    There fall no tears like theirs[2] that all men hear
    Fall tear by sweet imperishable tear
Down the opening leaves of holy poets' pages.
    Thee not Orestes, not Electra mourns;[3]
130   But bending us-ward with memorial urns
The most high Muses that fulfill all ages
    Weep, and our God's heart yearns.

13

For, sparing of his sacred strength, not often
    Among us darkling here the lord of light[4]
135   Makes manifest his music and his might
In hearts that open and in lips that soften
    With the soft flame and heat of songs that shine.
    Thy lips indeed he touched with bitter wine,
And nourished them indeed with bitter bread;
140   Yet surely from his hand thy soul's food came;
    The fire that scarred thy spirit at his flame

1. According to Jerome McGann, Swinburne associates Baudelaire's distinctive kind of poetry with a tenth muse, one who inspires songs of lamentation ("funereal"). What is meant by this muse's "veiled porches" seems tantalizingly obscure.
2. Referring to the muses and holy poets, not to Orestes and Electra [noted by Jerome McGann].
3. For lines 120–29, see Aeschylus's *Choëphoroe*

4–8. King Agamemnon, after returning from Troy, had been treacherously slain, an event that made "a ruinous thing" of the Greek victory. His son, Orestes, visits Agamemnon's grave and dedicates on it a lock of his own hair, which is later discovered by his sister, Electra, who mournfully visits her father's grave to offer libations.
4. Apollo, god of light and poetry.

Was lighted, and thine hungering heart he fed
Who feeds our hearts with fame.

14

145 Therefore he too now at thy soul's sunsetting,
God of all suns and songs he too bends down
To mix his laurel with thy cypress[5] crown.
And save thy dust from blame and from forgetting,
Therefore he too, seeing all thou wert and art,
Compassionate, with sad and sacred heart,
150 Mourns thee of many his children the last dead,
And hallows with strange tears and alien sighs
Thine unmelodious mouth and sunless eyes,
And over thine irrevocable head
Sheds light from the under skies.[6]

15

155 And one weeps with him in the ways Lethean,[7]
And stains with tears her changing bosom chill;
That obscure Venus of the hollow hill,
That thing transformed which was the Cytherean,
With lips that lost their Grecian laugh divine
160 Long since, and face no more called Erycine;[8]
A ghost, a bitter and luxurious god.
Thee also with fair flesh and singing spell
Did she, a sad and second prey,[9] compel
Into the footless places once more trod,
165 And shadows hot from hell.

16

And now no sacred staff shall break in blossom,[1]
No choral salutation lure to light
A spirit sick with perfume and sweet night
And love's tired eyes and hands and barren bosom.
170 There is no help for these things; none to mend
And none to mar; not all our songs, O friend,
Will make death clear or make life durable.
Howbeit with rose and ivy and wild vine
And with wild notes about this dust of thine
175 At least I fill the place where white dreams dwell[2]
And wreathe an unseen shrine.

5. Associated with mourning. "Laurel": the crown of Apollo, a wreath honoring poets.
6. I.e., flickering flaming light of the underworld.
7. Lethe was the river of oblivion in Hades.
8. The Venus of medieval legends held her court inside a mountain in Germany (the Hörselberg). This later Venus is a transformed version of the joyous foam-born goddess associated with the island of Cythera and also worshiped in Sicily at a shrine on Mount Eryx (hence "Erycine"). Horace described her as "blithe goddess of Eryx, about whom hover mirth and desire" (Odes 1.2.33–34).

9. The first "prey" of Venus had been Tannhäuser, whom she had lured into the "footless places" of her cave. Baudelaire is her "second prey." Swinburne, after reading Baudelaire's pamphlet on Wagner's *Tannhäuser*, described this Venus as "the queen of evil, the lady of lust."
1. After Tannhäuser's pilgrimage to Rome to seek absolution for having lived in sin with Venus, a miraculous event occurred: the pope having denied such absolution until his staff should bloom, it burst into blossom.
2. Presumably the abode of the ghosts of the dead.

17

Sleep; and if life was bitter to thee, pardon,
　　If sweet, give thanks; thou hast no more to live;
　　And to give thanks is good, and to forgive.
180　Out of the mystic and the mournful garden
　　Where all day through thine hands in barren braid
　　Wove the sick flowers of secrecy and shade,
　　Green buds of sorrow and sin, and remnants grey,
　　　Sweet-smelling, pale with poison, sanguine-hearted,
185　　Passions that sprang from sleep and thoughts that started,
　　Shall death not bring us all as thee one day
　　　Among the days departed?

18

For thee, O now a silent soul, my brother,
　　Take at my hands this garland, and farewell.
190　Thin is the leaf, and chill the wintry smell,
　　And chill the solemn earth, a fatal mother,
　　　With sadder than the Niobean womb,[3]
　　And in the hollow of her breasts a tomb.
　　Content thee, howsoe'er, whose days are done;
195　　There lies not any troublous thing before,
　　　Nor sight nor sound to war against thee more,
　　For whom all winds are quiet as the sun,
　　　All waters as the shore.

1866–67　　　　　　　　　　　　　　　　　　　　　　1868

3. Niobe's fourteen children were slain by Apollo and Artemis.

WALTER PATER
1839–1894

Studies in the History of the Renaissance, a collection of essays published in 1873, was the first of several volumes that established Walter Pater as the most important critical writer of the late Victorian period. His flair for critical writing may have first been sparked when he was an undergraduate at Oxford (1858–62), where he heard and enjoyed the lectures of Matthew Arnold, who was then professor of poetry. After graduation, Pater remained at Oxford, a shy bachelor who spent his life as a tutor of classics (for the story of his earlier years see *The Child in the House,* an autobiographical sketch that provides a helpful introduction to all of his writings). In view of his retiring disposition Pater was surprised and even alarmed by the impact made by his books on young readers of the 1870s and 1880s. Some of his younger followers such as Oscar Wilde and George Moore may have misread him. As T. S. Eliot wrote somewhat primly, "[Pater's] view of art, as expressed in *The Renaissance,* impressed itself upon a number of writers in the nineties, and propagated some confusion between life and art which is not wholly irresponsible for some untidy lives." It can be demonstrated that Pater's writings (especially his historical novel *Marius the Epicurean*, 1885) have much in common with his earnest-minded mid-Victorian predecessors, but his disciples overlooked these similarities. To them, his work seemed strikingly different and, in its quiet way, more subversive than the head-on attacks against traditional Victorianism made by Swinburne or Samuel Butler. Instead of recommending a continuation of the painful quest for Truth that had dominated Oxford in the days of Newman, Pater assured his readers that the quest was pointless. Truth, he said, is relative. And instead of echoing Carlyle's call to duty and social responsibilities, Pater reminded his readers that life passes quickly and that our only responsibility is to enjoy fully "this short day of frost and sun," to relish its sensations, especially those sensations provoked by works of art.

This epicurean gospel was conveyed in a highly wrought prose style that baffles anyone who likes to read quickly. Pater believed that prose was as difficult an art as poetry, and he expected his own elaborate sentences to be savored. Like Gustave Flaubert (1821–1880), the French novelist whom he admired, Pater painstakingly revised his sentences with special attention to their rhythms, seeking always the right word, *le mot juste*, as Flaubert had called it. For many years, Pater's day would begin with his making a careful study of a dictionary. What Pater said of Dante is an apt description of his own polished style: "He is one of those artists whose general effect largely depends on vocabulary, on the minute particles of which his work is wrought, on the color and outline of single words and phrases." An additional characteristic of his highly wrought style is its relative absence of humor. Pater was valued among his friends for his flashes of wit in conversation and for his lively and irreverent sallies. In his writings such traits are suppressed. As Michael Levey observed in *The Case of Walter Pater*, "Even for irony the mood of his writing is almost too intense."

In addition to being a key figure in the transition from mid-Victorianism to the "decadence" of the 1890s, Pater commands our attention as the writer of exemplary impressionistic criticism. In each of his essays he seeks to communicate what he called the "special unique impression of pleasure" made on him by the works of some artist or writer. His range of subjects included the dialogues of Plato, the paintings of Leonardo da Vinci, the plays of Shakespeare, and the writings of the French Romantic school of the nineteenth century. Of particular value to students of English literature are his discriminating studies of Wordsworth, Coleridge, Lamb, and Sir Thomas Browne in his volume of *Appreciations* (1889) and his essay on the poetry of William Morris titled *Aesthetic Poetry* (1868). These and other essays by Pater were praised by Oscar Wilde in a review in 1890 as "absolutely modern, in the true meaning of the term modernity. For he to whom the present is the only thing that is present, knows nothing of the age in which he lives. . . . The true critic is he who bears within himself the dreams and ideas and feelings of myriad generations, and to whom no form of thought is alien, no emotional impulse obscure."

The final sentences of his *Appreciations* volume are a revealing indication of Pater's critical position. After having attempted to show the differences between the classical and romantic schools of art, he concludes that most great artists combine the qualities of both. "To discriminate schools, of art, of literature," he writes, "is, of course, part of the obvious business of literary criticism: but, in the work of literary production, it is easy to be overmuch occupied concerning them. For, in truth, the legitimate contention is, not of one age or school of literary art against another, but of all successive schools alike, against the stupidity which is dead to the substance, and the vulgarity which is dead to form."

From The Renaissance

Preface

Many attempts have been made by writers on art and poetry to define beauty in the abstract, to express it in the most general terms, to find some universal formula for it. The value of these attempts has most often been in the suggestive and penetrating things said by the way. Such discussions help us very little to enjoy what has been well done in art or poetry, to discriminate between what is more and what is less excellent in them, or to use words like beauty, excellence, art, poetry, with a more precise meaning than they would otherwise have. Beauty, like all other qualities presented to human experience, is relative; and the definition of it becomes unmeaning and use-less in proportion to its abstractness. To define beauty, not in the most abstract but in the most concrete terms possible, to find not its universal formula, but the formula which expresses most adequately this or that special manifestation of it, is the aim of the true student of aesthetics.

"To see the object as in itself it really is,"[1] has been justly said to be the aim of all true criticism whatever; and in aesthetic criticism the first step towards seeing one's object as it really is, is to know one's own impression as it really is, to discriminate it, to realize it distinctly. The objects with which aesthetic criticism deals—music, poetry, artistic and accomplished forms of human life—are indeed receptacles of so many powers or forces: they pos-sess, like the products of nature, so many virtues or qualities. What is this song or picture, this engaging personality presented in life or in a book, to *me*? What effect does it really produce on me? Does it give me pleasure? and if so, what sort or degree of pleasure? How is my nature modified by its presence, and under its influence? The answers to these questions are the original facts with which the aesthetic critic has to do; and, as in the study of light, of morals, of number, one must realize such primary data for one's self, or not at all. And he who experiences these impressions strongly, and drives directly at the discrimination and analysis of them, has no need to trouble himself with the abstract question what beauty is in itself, or what its exact relation to truth or experience—metaphysical questions, as unprof-itable as metaphysical questions elsewhere. He may pass them all by as being, answerable or not, of no interest to him.

The aesthetic critic, then, regards all the objects with which he has to do, all works of art, and the fairer forms of nature and human life, as powers or forces producing pleasurable sensations, each of a more or less peculiar or unique kind. This influence he feels, and wishes to explain, by analyzing and reducing it to its elements. To him, the picture, the landscape, the engaging personality in life or in a book, "La Gioconda," the hills of Carrara, Pico of Mirandola,[2] are valuable for their virtues, as we say, in speaking of a herb, a wine, a gem; for the property each has of affecting one with a special, a unique, impression of pleasure. Our education becomes complete in pro-portion as our susceptibility to these impressions increases in depth and

---

1. Cf. Matthew Arnold, *The Function of Criticism at the Present Time*, para. 1.
2. Pico della Mirandola (1463–1494), Italian phi-losopher and classical scholar, subject of an essay

by Pater that was included in *The Renaissance*. "La Gioconda": Leonardo da Vinci's famous painting, the *Mona Lisa*. "The hills of Carrara": marble quar-ries in Italy.

variety. And the function of the aesthetic critic is to distinguish, to analyze, and separate from its adjuncts, the virtue by which a picture, a landscape, a fair personality in life or in a book, produces this special impression of beauty or pleasure, to indicate what the source of that impression is, and under what conditions it is experienced. His end is reached when he has disengaged that virtue, and noted it, as a chemist notes some natural element, for himself and others; and the rule for those who would reach this end is stated with great exactness in the words of a recent critic of Sainte-Beuve: *De se borner à connaître de près les belles choses, et à s'en nourrir en exquis amateurs, en humanistes accomplis.*[3]

What is important, then, is not that the critic should possess a correct abstract definition of beauty for the intellect, but a certain kind of temperament, the power of being deeply moved by the presence of beautiful objects. He will remember always that beauty exists in many forms. To him all periods, types, schools of taste, are in themselves equal. In all ages there have been some excellent workmen, and some excellent work done. The question he asks is always: In whom did the stir, the genius, the sentiment of the period find itself? where was the receptacle of its refinement, its elevation, its taste? "The ages are all equal," says William Blake, "but genius is always above its age."[4]

Often it will require great nicety to disengage this virtue from the commoner elements with which it may be found in combination. Few artists, not Goethe or Byron even, work quite cleanly, casting off all debris, and leaving us only what the heat of their imagination has wholly fused and transformed. Take, for instance, the writings of Wordsworth. The heat of his genius, entering into the substance of his work, has crystallized a part, but only a part, of it; and in that great mass of verse there is much which might well be forgotten. But scattered up and down it, sometimes fusing and transforming entire compositions, like the stanzas on *Resolution and Independence,* or the *Ode on the Recollections of Childhood,*[5] sometimes, as if at random, depositing a fine crystal here or there, in a matter it does not wholly search through and transmute, we trace the action of his unique, incommunicable faculty, that strange, mystical sense of a life in natural things, and of man's life as a part of nature, drawing strength and color and character from local influences, from the hills and streams, and from natural sights and sounds. Well! that is the *virtue,* the active principle in Wordsworth's poetry; and then the function of the critic of Wordsworth is to follow up that active principle, to disengage it, to mark the degree in which it penetrates his verse.

The subjects of the following studies are taken from the history of the *Renaissance,* and touch what I think the chief points in that complex, many-sided movement. I have explained in the first of them what I understand by the word, giving it a much wider scope than was intended by those who originally used it to denote that revival of classical antiquity in the fifteenth century which was only one of many results of a general excitement and

3. To confine themselves to knowing beautiful things intimately, and to sustain themselves by these, as sensitive amateurs and accomplished humanists do (French). In 1980 editor Donald J. Hill discovered that this quotation is *by* Sainte-Beuve rather than about him; therefore, Hill conjectures that "a recent critic" ought to be "a recent critique."

4. From Blake's annotations to *The Works of Sir Joshua Reynolds.* The "genius" was the German painter Albrecht Dürer (1471–1528).

5. Wordsworth's ode was titled *Intimations of Immortality from Recollections of Early Childhood.*

enlightening of the human mind, but of which the great aim and achievements of what, as Christian art, is often falsely opposed to the Renaissance, were another result. This outbreak of the human spirit may be traced far into the Middle Age itself, with its motives already clearly pronounced, the care for physical beauty, the worship of the body, the breaking down of those limits which the religious system of the Middle Age imposed on the heart and the imagination. I have taken as an example of this movement, this earlier Renaissance within the Middle Age itself, and as an expression of its qualities, two little compositions in early French; not because they constitute the best possible expression of them, but because they help the unity of my series, inasmuch as the Renaissance ends also in France, in French poetry, in a phase of which the writings of Joachim du Bellay[6] are in many ways the most perfect illustration. The Renaissance, in truth, put forth in France an aftermath, a wonderful later growth, the products of which have to the full that subtle and delicate sweetness which belongs to a refined and comely decadence, just as its earliest phases have the freshness which belongs to all periods of growth in art, the charm of _ascêsis_,[7] of the austere and serious girding of the loins in youth.

But it is in Italy, in the fifteenth century, that the interest of the Renaissance mainly lies—in that solemn fifteenth century which can hardly be studied too much, not merely for its positive results in the things of the intellect and the imagination, its concrete works of art, its special and prominent personalities, with their profound aesthetic charm, but for its general spirit and character, for the ethical qualities of which it is a consummate type.

The various forms of intellectual activity which together make up the culture of an age, move for the most part from different starting points, and by unconnected roads. As products of the same generation they partake indeed of a common character, and unconsciously illustrate each other; but of the producers themselves, each group is solitary, gaining what advantage or disadvantage there may be in intellectual isolation. Art and poetry, philosophy and the religious life, and that other life of refined pleasure and action in the conspicuous places of the world, are each of them confined to its own circle of ideas, and those who prosecute either of them are generally little curious of the thoughts of others. There come, however, from time to time, eras of more favorable conditions, in which the thoughts of men draw nearer together than is their wont, and the many interests of the intellectual world combine in one complete type of general culture. The fifteenth century in Italy is one of these happier eras, and what is sometimes said of the age of Pericles is true of that of Lorenzo: it is an age productive in personalities, many-sided, centralized, complete. Here, artists and philosophers and those whom the action of the world has elevated and made keen, do not live in isolation, but breathe a common air, and catch light and heat from each other's thoughts. There is a spirit of general elevation and enlightenment in which all alike communicate. The unity of this spirit gives unity to all the various products of the Renaissance; and it is to this intimate alliance with mind, this participation in the best thoughts which that age produced, that

6. French poet and critic (ca.1522–1560); subject
of another essay in _The Renaissance_.

7. Asceticism.

the art of Italy in the fifteenth century owes much of its grave dignity and influence.

I have added an essay on Winckelmann,[8] as not incongruous with the studies which precede it, because Winckelmann, coming in the eighteenth century, really belongs in spirit to an earlier age. By his enthusiasm for the things of the intellect and the imagination for their own sake, by his Hellenism, his lifelong struggle to attain to the Greek spirit, he is in sympathy with the humanists of a previous century. He is the last fruit of the Renaissance, and explains in a striking way its motive and tendencies.

["LA GIOCONDA"][9]

"La Gioconda" is, in the truest sense, Leonardo's masterpiece, the revealing instance of his mode of thought and work. In suggestiveness, only the "Melancholia" of Dürer is comparable to it; and no crude symbolism disturbs the effect of its subdued and graceful mystery. We all know the face and hands of the figure, set in its marble chair, in that circle of fantastic rocks, as in some faint light under sea. Perhaps of all ancient pictures time has chilled it least. As often happens with works in which invention seems to reach its limit, there is an element in it given to, not invented by, the master. In that inestimable folio of drawings, once in the possession of Vasari, were certain designs by Verrocchio,[1] faces of such impressive beauty that Leonardo in his boyhood copied them many times. It is hard not to connect with these designs of the elder, by-past master, as with its germinal principle, the unfathomable smile, always with a touch of something sinister in it, which plays over all Leonardo's work. Besides, the picture is a portrait. From childhood we see this image defining itself on the fabric of his dreams, and but for express historical testimony, we might fancy that this was but his ideal lady, embodied and beheld at last. What was the relationship of a living Florentine to this creature of his thought? By what strange affinities had the dream and the person grown up thus apart, and yet so closely together? Present from the first incorporeally in Leonardo's brain, dimly traced in the designs of Verrocchio, she is found present at last in Il Giocondo's house. That there is much of mere portraiture in the picture is attested by the legend that by artificial means, the presence of mimes[2] and flute-players, that subtle expression was protracted on the face. Again, was it in four years and by renewed labor never really completed, or in four months and as by stroke of magic, that the image was projected?

The presence that rose thus so strangely beside the waters, is expressive of what in the ways of a thousand years men had come to desire. Hers is the head upon which all "the ends of the world are come,"[3] and the eyelids are a little weary. It is a beauty wrought out from within upon the flesh, the deposit, little cell by cell, of strange thoughts and fantastic reveries and

8. Johann Joachim Winckelmann (1717–1768), German classicist.

9. Or *Mona Lisa*, the famous painting by Leonardo da Vinci that now hangs in the Louvre in Paris. The sitter for the portrait may have been Lisa, the third wife of the Florentine Francesco del Giocondo (to whom Pater refers as "Il Giocondo")— hence her title, La Gioconda. *Mona* (more cor-

rectly *Monna*) *Lisa* means "Madonna Lisa" or "My Lady Lisa." This selection is drawn from the essay on Leonardo da Vinci.

1. Andrea del Verrocchio (1435–1488), Florentine painter and sculptor. Giorgio Vasari, author of *Lives of the Most Excellent Italian Painters* (1550).

2. Mimics or clowns.

3. 1 Corinthians 10.11.

exquisite passions. Set it for a moment beside one of those white Greek goddesses or beautiful women of antiquity, and how would they be troubled by this beauty, into which the soul with all its maladies has passed! All the thoughts and experience of the world have etched and molded there, in that which they have of power to refine and make expressive the outward form, the animalism of Greece, the lust of Rome, the mysticism of the Middle Age with its spiritual ambition and imaginative loves, the return of the Pagan world, the sins of the Borgias.[4] She is older than the rocks among which she sits; like the vampire, she has been dead many times, and learned the secrets of the grave; and has been a diver in deep seas, and keeps their fallen day about her; and trafficked for strange webs with Eastern merchants, and, as Leda, was the mother of Helen of Troy,[5] and, as Saint Anne, the mother of Mary; and all this has been to her but as the sound of lyres and flutes, and lives only in the delicacy with which it has molded the changing lineaments, and tinged the eyelids and the hands. The fancy of a perpetual life, sweeping together ten thousand experiences, is an old one; and modern philosophy has conceived the idea of humanity as wrought upon by, and summing up in itself, all modes of thought and life. Certainly Lady Lisa might stand as the embodiment of the old fancy, the symbol of the modern idea.

Conclusion[6]

Λέγει που Ἡράκλειτος ὅτι πάντα χωρεῖ καὶ οὐδὲν μένει[7]

To regard all things and principles of things as inconstant modes or fashions has more and more become the tendency of modern thought. Let us begin with that which is without—our physical life. Fix upon it in one of its more exquisite intervals, the moment, for instance, of delicious recoil from the flood of water in summer heat. What is the whole physical life in that moment but a combination of natural elements to which science gives their names? But those elements, phosphorus and lime and delicate fibers, are present not in the human body alone: we detect them in places most remote from it. Our physical life is a perpetual motion of them—the passage of the blood, the waste and repairing of the lenses of the eye, the modification of the tissues of the brain under every ray of light and sound—processes which science reduces to simpler and more elementary forces. Like the elements of which we are composed, the action of these forces extends beyond us: it rusts iron and ripens corn. Far out on every side of us those elements are broadcast, driven in many currents; and birth and gesture and death and the springing of violets from the grave are but a few out of ten thousand resultant combinations. That clear, perpetual outline of face and limb is but an image of ours, under which we group them—a design in a web, the actual threads of which pass out beyond it. This at least of flamelike our life has, that it is

4. An Italian family during the Renaissance whose reputation for scandalous conduct was notorious.
5. Her father was Zeus (who approached Leda in the form of a swan).
6. This brief "Conclusion" was omitted in the second edition of this book, as I conceived it might possibly mislead some of those young men into whose hands it might fall. On the whole, I have

thought it best to reprint it here, with some slight changes which bring it closer to my original meaning. I have dealt more fully in *Marius the Epicurean* with the thoughts suggested by it [Pater's note to the 3rd edition, 1888].
7. Heraclitus says, "All things give way; nothing remaineth" [Pater's translation].

but the concurrence, renewed from moment to moment, of forces parting sooner or later on their ways.

Or, if we begin with the inward world of thought and feeling, the whirlpool is still more rapid, the flame more eager and devouring. There it is no longer the gradual darkening of the eye, the gradual fading of color from the wall—movements of the shore-side, where the water flows down indeed, though in apparent rest—but the race of the midstream, a drift of momentary acts of sight and passion and thought. At first sight experience seems to bury us under a flood of external objects, pressing upon us with a sharp and importunate reality, calling us out of ourselves in a thousand forms of action. But when reflection begins to play upon those objects they are dissipated under its influence; the cohesive force seems suspended like some trick of magic; each object is loosed into a group of impressions—color, odor, texture—in the mind of the observer. And if we continue to dwell in thought on this world, not of objects in the solidity with which language invests them, but of impressions, unstable, flickering, inconsistent, which burn and are extinguished with our consciousness of them, it contracts still further: the whole scope of observation is dwarfed into the narrow chamber of the individual mind. Experience, already reduced to a group of impressions, is ringed round for each one of us by that thick wall of personality through which no real voice has ever pierced on its way to us, or from us to that which we can only conjecture to be without. Every one of those impressions is the impression of the individual in his isolation, each mind keeping as a solitary prisoner its own dream of a world. Analysis goes a step farther still, and assures us that those impressions of the individual mind to which, for each one of us, experience dwindles down, are in perpetual flight; that each of them is limited by time, and that as time is infinitely divisible, each of them is infinitely divisible also; all that is actual in it being a single moment, gone while we try to apprehend it, of which it may ever be more truly said that it has ceased to be than that it is. To such a tremulous wisp constantly reforming itself on the stream, to a single sharp impression, with a sense in it, a relic more or less fleeting, of such moments gone by, what is real in our life fines itself down. It is with this movement, with the passage and dissolution of impressions, images, sensations, that analysis leaves off—that continual vanishing away, that strange, perpetual weaving and unweaving of ourselves.

Philosophiren, says Novalis, *ist dephlegmatisiren, vivificiren.*[8] The service of philosophy, of speculative culture, towards the human spirit is to rouse, to startle it to a life of constant and eager observation. Every moment some form grows perfect in hand or face; some tone on the hills or the sea is choicer than the rest; some mood of passion or insight or intellectual excitement is irresistibly real and attractive to us—for that moment only. Not the fruit of experience, but experience itself, is the end. A counted number of pulses only is given to us of a variegated, dramatic life. How may we see in them all that is to be seen in them by the finest senses? How shall we pass most swiftly from point to point, and be present always at the focus where the greatest number of vital forces unite in their purest energy?

To burn always with this hard, gemlike flame, to maintain this ecstasy, is

8. To philosophize is to cast off inertia, to make oneself alive (German). "Novalis" was the pseudonym of Friedrich von Hardenberg (1772–1801), German Romantic writer.

success in life. In a sense it might even be said that our failure is to form habits: for, after all, habit is relative to a stereotyped world, and meantime it is only the roughness of the eye that makes any two persons, things, situations, seem alike. While all melts under our feet, we may well grasp at any exquisite passion, or any contribution to knowledge that seems by a lifted horizon to set the spirit free for a moment, or any stirring of the senses, strange dyes, strange colors, and curious odors, or work of the artist's hands, or the face of one's friend. Not to discriminate every moment some passionate attitude in those about us, and in the very brilliancy of their gifts some tragic dividing of forces on their ways, is, on this short day of frost and sun, to sleep before evening. With this sense of the splendor of our experience and of its awful brevity, gathering all we are into one desperate effort to see and touch, we shall hardly have time to make theories about the things we see and touch. What we have to do is to be forever curiously testing new opinions and courting new impressions, never acquiescing in a facile orthodoxy of Comte, or of Hegel,[9] or of our own. Philosophical theories or ideas, as points of view, instruments of criticism, may help us to gather up what might otherwise pass unregarded by us. "Philosophy is the microscope of thought." The theory or idea or system which requires of us the sacrifice of any part of this experience, in consideration of some interest into which we cannot enter, or some abstract theory we have not identified with ourselves, or of what is only conventional, has no real claim upon us.

One of the most beautiful passages of Rousseau is that in the sixth book of the *Confessions*, where he describes the awakening in him of the literary sense. An undefinable taint of death had clung always about him, and now in early manhood he believed himself smitten by mortal disease. He asked himself how he might make as much as possible of the interval that remained; and he was not biased by anything in his previous life when he decided that it must be by intellectual excitement, which he found just then in the clear, fresh writings of Voltaire. Well! we are all *condamnés* as Victor Hugo says: we are all under sentence of death but with a sort of indefinite reprieve—*les hommes sont tous condamnés à mort avec des sursis indéfinis:* we have an interval, and then our place knows us no more. Some spend this interval in listlessness, some in high passions, the wisest, at least among "the children of this world,"[1] in art and song. For our one chance lies in expanding that interval, in getting as many pulsations as possible into the given time. Great passions may give us this quickened sense of life, ecstasy and sorrow of love, the various forms of enthusiastic activity, disinterested or otherwise, which come naturally to many of us. Only be sure it is passion—that it does yield you this fruit of a quickened, multiplied consciousness. Of such wisdom, the poetic passion, the desire of beauty, the love of art for its own sake, has most. For art comes to you proposing frankly to give nothing but the highest quality to your moments as they pass, and simply for those moments' sake.

1868   1873

9. Georg W. F. Hegel (1770–1831), German idealistic philosopher. Auguste Comte (1798–1857),

French founder of positivism.
1. Luke 16.8.

From Appreciations

From *Style*

Since all progress of mind consists for the most part in differentiation, in the resolution of an obscure and complex object into its component aspects, it is surely the stupidest of losses to confuse things which right reason has put asunder, to lose the sense of achieved distinctions, the distinction between poetry and prose, for instance, or, to speak more exactly, between the laws and characteristic excellences of verse and prose composition. On the other hand, those who have dwelt most emphatically on the distinction between prose and verse, prose and poetry, may sometimes have been tempted to limit the proper functions of prose too narrowly; and this again is at least false economy, as being, in effect, the renunciation of a certain means or faculty, in a world where after all we must needs make the most of things. Critical efforts to limit art *a priori*,[1] by anticipations regarding the natural incapacity of the material with which this or that artist works, as the sculptor with solid form, or the prose-writer with the ordinary language of men, are always liable to be discredited by the facts of artistic production; and while prose is actually found to be a colored thing with Bacon, picturesque with Livy and Carlyle, musical with Cicero and Newman, mystical and intimate with Plato and Michelet and Sir Thomas Browne, exalted or florid, it may be, with Milton and Taylor,[2] it will be useless to protest that it can be nothing at all, except something very tamely and narrowly confined to mainly practical ends—a kind of "good round hand"; as useless as the protest that poetry might not touch prosaic subjects as with Wordsworth, or an abstruse matter as with Browning, or treat contemporary life nobly as with Tennyson. In subordination to one essential beauty in all good literary style, in all literature as a fine art, as there are many beauties of poetry so the beauties of prose are many, and it is the business of criticism to estimate them as such; as it is good in the criticism of verse to look for those hard, logical, and quasi-prosaic excellences which that too has, or needs. To find in the poem, amid the flowers, the allusions, the mixed perspectives, of *Lycidas* for instance, the thought, the logical structure: how wholesome! how delightful! as to identify in prose what we call the poetry, the imaginative power, not treating it as out of place and a kind of vagrant intruder, but by way of an estimate of its rights, that is, of its achieved powers, there.

Dryden, with the characteristic instinct of his age, loved to emphasize the distinction between poetry and prose, the protest against their confusion with each other, coming with somewhat diminished effect from one whose poetry was so prosaic. In truth, his sense of prosaic excellence affected his verse rather than his prose, which is not only fervid, richly figured, poetic, as we say, but vitiated, all unconsciously, by many a scanning line. Setting up correctness, that humble merit of prose, as the central literary excellence, he is really a less correct writer than he may seem, still with an imperfect mastery of the relative pronoun. It might have been foreseen that, in the

---

1. Prior to experience (Latin).
2. Jeremy Taylor (1613–1667), famous for the elaborate style of his sermons. Jules Michelet (1798–1874), French historian.

rotations of mind, the province of poetry in prose would find its assertor; and, a century after Dryden, amid very different intellectual needs, and with the need therefore of great modifications in literary form, the range of the poetic force in literature was effectively enlarged by Wordsworth. The true distinction between prose and poetry he regarded as the almost technical or accidental one of the absence or presence of metrical beauty, or, say! metrical restraint; and for him the opposition came to be between verse and prose of course; but, as the essential dichotomy in this matter, between imaginative and unimaginative writing, parallel to De Quincey's distinction between "the literature of power and the literature of knowledge,"[3] in the former of which the composer gives us not fact, but his peculiar sense of fact, whether past or present.

Dismissing then, under sanction of Wordsworth, that harsher opposition of poetry to prose, as savoring in fact of the arbitrary psychology of the last century, and with it the prejudice that there can be but one only beauty of prose style, I propose here to point out certain qualities of all literature as a fine art, which, if they apply to the literature of fact, apply still more to the literature of the imaginative sense of fact, while they apply indifferently to verse and prose, so far as either is really imaginative—certain conditions of true art in both alike, which conditions may also contain in them the secret of the proper discrimination and guardianship of the peculiar excellences of either.

The line between fact and something quite different from external fact is, indeed, hard to draw. In Pascal,[4] for instance, in the persuasive writers generally, how difficult to define the point where, from time to time, argument which, if it is to be worth anything at all, must consist of facts or groups of facts, becomes a pleading—a theorem no longer, but essentially an appeal to the reader to catch the writer's spirit, to think with him, if one can or will— an expression no longer of fact but of his sense of it, his peculiar intuition of a world, prospective, or discerned below the faulty conditions of the present, in either case changed somewhat from the actual world. In science, on the other hand, in history so far as it conforms to scientific rule, we have a literary domain where the imagination may be thought to be always an intruder. And as, in all science, the functions of literature reduce themselves eventually to the transcribing of fact, so all the excellences of literary form in regard to science are reducible to various kinds of painstaking; this good quality being involved in all "skilled work" whatever, in the drafting of an act of parliament, as in sewing. Yet here again, the writer's sense of fact, in history especially, and in all those complex subjects which do but lie on the borders of science, will still take the place of fact, in various degrees. Your historian, for instance, with absolutely truthful intention, amid the multitude of facts presented to him must needs select, and in selecting assert something of his own humor, something that comes not of the world without but of a vision within. So Gibbon molds his unwieldy material to a preconceived view. Livy, Tacitus, Michelet, moving full of poignant sensibility amid the records of the past, each, after his own sense, modifies—who can tell where and to what degree?—and becomes something else than a transcriber; each, as he thus modifies, passing into the domain of art proper. For just in proportion as the

3. De Quincey's essay on this topic appeared in 1848.

4. Blaise Pascal (1623–1662), French scientist, philosopher, and theologian.

writer's aim, consciously or unconsciously, comes to be the transcribing, not of the world, not of mere fact, but of his sense of it, he becomes an artist, his work *fine* art; and good art (as I hope ultimately to show) in proportion to the truth of his presentment of that sense; as in those humbler or plainer functions of literature also, truth—truth to bare fact, there—is the essence of such artistic quality as they may have. Truth! there can be no merit, no craft at all, without that. And further, all beauty is in the long run only *fineness* of truth, or what we call expression, the finer accommodation of speech to that vision within.

—The transcript of his sense of fact rather than the fact, as being preferable, pleasanter, more beautiful to the writer himself. In literature, as in every other product of human skill, in the molding of a bell or a platter for instance, wherever this sense asserts itself, wherever the producer so modifies his work as, over and above its primary use or intention, to make it pleasing (to himself, of course, in the first instance) there, "fine" as opposed to merely serviceable art, exists. Literary art, that is, like all art which is in any way imitative or reproductive of fact—form, or color, or incident—is the representation of such fact as connected with soul, of a specific personality, in its preferences, its volition and power.

Such is the matter of imaginative or artistic literature—this transcript, not of mere fact, but of fact in its infinite variety, as modified by human preference in all its infinitely varied forms. It will be good literary art not because it is brilliant or sober, or rich, or impulsive, or severe, but just in proportion as its representation of that sense, that soul-fact, is true, verse being only one department of such literature, and imaginative prose, it may be thought, being the special art of the modern world. That imaginative prose should be the special and opportune art of the modern world results from two important facts about the latter: first, the chaotic variety and complexity of its interests, making the intellectual issue, the really master currents of the present time incalculable—a condition of mind little susceptible of the restraint proper to verse form, so that the most characteristic verse of the nineteenth century has been lawless verse; and secondly, an all-pervading naturalism, a curiosity about everything whatever as it really is, involving a certain humility of attitude, cognate to what must, after all, be the less ambitious form of literature. And prose thus asserting itself as the special and privileged artistic faculty of the present day, will be, however critics may try to narrow its scope, as varied in its excellence as humanity itself reflecting on the facts of its latest experience—an instrument of many stops, meditative, observant, descriptive, eloquent, analytic, plaintive, fervid. Its beauties will not be exclusively "pedestrian": it will exert, in due measure, all the varied charms of poetry, down to the rhythm which, as in Cicero, or Michelet, or Newman, at their best, gives its musical value to every syllable.

* * *

If the style be the man, in all the color and intensity of a veritable apprehension, it will be in a real sense "impersonal."

I said, thinking of books like Victor Hugo's *Les Misérables*, that prose literature was the characteristic art of the nineteenth century, as others, thinking of its triumphs since the youth of Bach, have assigned that place to music. Music and prose literature are, in one sense, the opposite terms of art; the art of literature presenting to the imagination, through the intelligence, a range of interests, as free and various as those which music presents to it through sense. And certainly the tendency of what has been here said is to bring literature too under those conditions, by conformity to which music takes rank as the typically perfect art. If music be the ideal of all art whatever, precisely because in music it is impossible to distinguish the form from the substance or matter, the subject from the expression, then, literature, by finding its specific excellence in the absolute correspondence of the term to its import, will be but fulfilling the condition of all artistic quality in things everywhere, of all good art.

Good art, but not necessarily great art; the distinction between great art and good art depending immediately, as regards literature at all events, not on its form, but on the matter. Thackeray's *Esmond,* surely, is greater art than *Vanity Fair,* by the greater dignity of its interests. It is on the quality of the matter it informs or controls, its compass, its variety, its alliance to great ends, or the depth of the note of revolt, or the largeness of hope in it, that the greatness of literary art depends, as *The Divine Comedy, Paradise Lost, Les Misérables,* the English Bible, are great art. Given the conditions I have tried to explain as constituting good art—then, if it be devoted further to the increase of men's happiness, to the redemption of the oppressed, or the enlargement of our sympathies with each other, or to such presentment of new or old truth about ourselves and our relation to the world as may ennoble and fortify us in our sojourn here, or immediately, as with Dante, to the glory of God, it will be also great art; if, over and above those qualities I summed up as mind and soul—that color and mystic perfume, and that reasonable structure, it has something of the soul of humanity in it, and finds its logical, architectural place, in the great structure of human life.

1889

GERARD MANLEY HOPKINS
1844–1889

It has been said that the most important date in Gerard Manley Hopkins's career was 1918, twenty-nine years after his death, for it was then that the first publication of his poems made them accessible to the world of readers. During his lifetime, these remarkable poems, most of them celebrating the wonders of God's creation, had been known only to a small circle of friends, including his literary executor, the poet Robert Bridges, who waited until 1918 before releasing them to a publisher. Partly because his work was first made public in a twentieth-century volume, but especially because of his striking experiments in meter and diction, Hopkins was widely hailed as a pioneering figure of "modern" literature, miraculously unconnected with his fellow Victorian poets (who during the 1920s and 1930s were largely out of fashion among critical readers). And this way of classifying and evaluating his writings has long persisted. In 1936 a substantial selection of his poems led off *The Faber Book of Modern Verse,* one of the most influential anthologies of the century, featuring poets such as W. H. Auden, Dylan Thomas, and T. S. Eliot (the only one whose selections occupy more pages than those allotted to Hopkins). And the first four editions of *The Norton Anthology of English Literature* (1962–79) grouped Hopkins with these same twentieth-century poets. To reclassify him is not to repudiate his earlier reputation as a "modern" but rather to suggest that his work can be better understood and appreciated if it is restored to the Victorian world out of which it developed.

Hopkins was born near London into a large and cultivated family in comfortable circumstances. After a brilliant career at Highgate School, he entered Oxford in 1863, where he was exposed to a variety of Victorian ways of thinking, both secular and religious. Among influential leaders at Oxford was Matthew Arnold, professor of poetry, but more important for Hopkins was his tutor, Walter Pater, an aesthetician whose emphasis on the intense apprehension of sensuous beauty struck a responsive chord in Hopkins. At Oxford he was also exposed to the Broad Church theology of one of the tutors at his college (Balliol), Benjamin Jowett. But Hopkins became increasingly attracted first to the High Church movement represented at Oxford by Edward Pusey, and then to Roman Catholicism. Profoundly influenced by John Henry Newman's conversion to Rome and by subsequent conversations with Newman himself, Hopkins entered the Roman Catholic Church in 1866. The estrangement from his family that resulted from his conversion was very painful for him; his parents' letters to him were so "terrible" (he reported to Newman) that he could not bear to "read them twice." And this alienation was heightened by his decision not only to become a Roman Catholic but to become a priest and, in particular, a Jesuit priest, for in the eyes of many Victorian Protestants, the Jesuit order was regarded with a special distrust. For the rest of his life, Hopkins served as a priest and teacher in various places, among them Oxford, Liverpool, and Lancashire. In 1884 he was appointed professor of classics at University College in Dublin, where Newman had served as rector in the 1850s and where James Joyce would be enrolled as a student at the turn of the century.

At school and at Oxford in the early 1860s, Hopkins had written poems in the vein of Keats. He burned most of these early writings after his conversion (although drafts survive), for he believed that his vocation must require renouncing such personal satisfactions as the writing of poems. Only after his superiors in the church encouraged him to do so did he resume writing poetry, but during the seven years of silence, as his letters show, he had been thinking about experimenting with what he called a "new rhythm." The result, in 1876, was his rhapsodic lyric-narrative, *The Wreck of the Deutschland,* a long ode about the wreck of a ship in which five Franciscan nuns were drowned. The style of the poem was so distinctive that the editor of the Jesuit magazine to which he had submitted it "dared not print it," as Hopkins himself reported. During the remaining fourteen years of his life, Hopkins continued to write poems but seldom submitted them for publication, partly because he was convinced that poetic fame was incompatible with his religious vocation but also because of a fear that readers would be discouraged by the eccentricity of his work.

Hopkins's sense of his own singularity gives us an indication of the organizing structure of his poetry. Drawing on the theology of Duns Scotus, a medieval philosopher, he felt that everything in the universe was characterized by what he called *inscape,* the distinctive design that constitutes individual identity. This identity is not static but dynamic. Each being in the universe "selves," that is, enacts its identity. And the human being, the most highly selved, the most individually distinctive being in the universe, recognizes the inscape of other beings in an act that Hopkins calls *instress,* the apprehension of an object in an intense thrust of energy toward it that enables one to realize its specific distinctiveness. Ultimately, the instress of inscape leads one to Christ, for the individual identity of any object is the stamp of divine creation on it. In the act of instress, therefore, the human being becomes a celebrant of the divine, at once recognizing God's creation and enacting his or her own God-given identity within it.

Poetry for Hopkins enacts this celebration. It is instress, and it realizes the inscape of its subject in its own distinctive design. Hopkins wrote, "But as air, melody, is what strikes me most of all in music and design in painting, so design, pattern or what I am in the habit of calling 'inscape' is what I above all aim at in poetry." To create inscape, Hopkins seeks to give each poem a unique design that captures the initial inspiration when he is "caught" by his subject. Many of the characteristics of Hopkins's style—his disruption of conventional syntax, his coining and compounding of words, his use of ellipsis and repetition—can be understood as ways of representing the stress and action of the brain in moments of inspiration. He creates compounds to represent the unique interlocking of the characteristics of an object—"piece-bright," "dapple-dawn-drawn," "blue-bleak." He omits syntactical connections to fuse qualities more intensely—"the dearest freshness deep down things." He creates puns to suggest how God's creation rhymes and chimes in a divine patterning. He violates conventional syntactic order to represent the shape of mental experience. In the act of imaginative apprehension, a language particular to the moment generates itself.

Hopkins also uses a new rhythm to give each poem its distinctive design. In the new metric system he created, which he called *sprung rhythm,* lines have a given number of stresses, but the number and placement of unstressed syllables is highly variable. Hopkins rarely marks all the intended stresses, only those that readers might not anticipate. To indicate stressed syllables, Hopkins often uses both the stress (´) and the "great stress" (˝). A curved line marks an "outride"—one or more syllables added to a foot but not counted in the scansion of the line; they indicate a stronger stress on the preceding syllable and a short pause after the outride. Here, for example, is the scansion for the first three lines of *The Windhover*:

> I caúght this mórning mórning's mínion, kíng-
> dom of dáylight's daúphin, dapple-dawn-drawn Fálcon, in his ríding
> Of the rólling level underneáth him steady aír, and stríding

Hopkins argued that sprung rhythm was the natural rhythm of common speech and written prose, as well as of music. He found a model for it in Old English poetry and in nursery rhymes, but he claimed that it had not been used in English poetry since the Elizabethan Age.

The density and difficulty that result from Hopkins's unconventional rhythm and syntax make his poetry seem modern, but his concern with the imagination's shaping of the natural world puts him very much in the Romantic tradition, and his creation of a rough and difficult style, designed to capture the mind's own motion, resembles the style of Browning. "A horrible thing has happened to me," Hopkins wrote in 1864, "I have begun to *doubt* Tennyson." He goes on to criticize Tennyson for using the grand style as a smooth and habitual poetic speech. Like Swinburne, Pater, and Henry James as well as Browning, Hopkins displays a new mannerism, characteristic of the latter part of the nineteenth century, which paradoxically combines an elaborate aestheticism with a more complex representation of consciousness.

In Hopkins's early poetry, his singular apprehension of the beauty of individual objects always brings him to an ecstatic illumination of the presence of God. But in his late poems, the so-called terrible sonnets, his distinctive individuality comes to isolate him from the God who made him thus. Hopkins wrote, "To me there is no resemblance: searching nature, I taste *self* but at one tankard, that of my own being." In the terrible sonnets, Hopkins confronts the solipsism to which his own stress on individuality seems to lead him. Like the mad speakers of so many Victorian dramatic monologues, he cannot escape a world solely of his own imagining. Yet even these poems of despair, which seem so distinctively modern, reflect a traditional religious vision, the dark night of the soul as described by the Spanish mystic Saint John of the Cross.

In his introduction to *The Oxford Book of Modern Verse,* Yeats calls Hopkins's poetry "a last development of poetical diction." Yeats's remark indicates the anomaly that Hopkins's work poses. Perhaps it is only appropriate for a writer who stressed the uniqueness of inscape to strike us with the individuality of his achievement.

God's Grandeur

The world is charged with the grandeur of God.
   It will flame out, like shining from shook foil;[1]
   It gathers to a greatness, like the ooze of oil
Crushed.[2] Why do men then now not reck his rod?
5 Generations have trod, have trod, have trod;
   And all is seared with trade; bleared, smeared with toil;
   And wears man's smudge and shares man's smell: the soil
Is bare now, nor can foot feel, being shod.

And for° all this, nature is never spent;   *despite*
10 There lives the dearest freshness deep down things;
   And though the last lights off the black West went
   Oh, morning, at the brown brink eastward, springs—
Because the Holy Ghost over the bent
   World broods with warm breast and with ah! bright wings.

1877   1918

The Starlight Night

Look at the stars! look, look up at the skies!
   O look at all the fire-folk sitting in the air!
   The bright boroughs, the circle-citadels there!
Down in dim woods the diamond delves!° the elves'-eyes!   *quarries*
5 The grey lawns cold where gold, where quickgold;[1] lies!
   Wind-beat whitebeam! airy abeles° set on a flare!   *white poplars*
   Flake-doves sent floating forth at a farmyard scare!—
Ah well! it is all a purchase, all is a prize.

Buy then! bid then!—What?—Prayer, patience, alms, vows.
10 Look, look: a May-mess,[2] like on orchard boughs!
   Look! March-bloom, like on mealed-with-yellow sallows![3]
These are indeed the barn; withindoors house
   The shocks. This piece-bright paling[4] shuts the spouse
   Christ home, Christ and his mother and all his hallows.°   *saints*

1877   1918

1. Hopkins explained this image in a letter: "I mean foil in its sense of leaf or tinsel. . . . Shaken goldfoil gives off broad glares like sheet lightning and also, and this is true of nothing else, owing to its zigzag dints and creasings and network of small many cornered facets, a sort of fork lightning too."
2. I.e., from the crushing of olives.

1. Coined by analogy with quicksilver. The starlight night resembles the lawns below it where the dew, reflecting the starlight, looks like gold.
2. A profusion of growing things such as May blossoms.
3. Willows, here with yellow spots like meal.
4. Picket fence. "Shocks": sheaves of grain.

As Kingfishers Catch Fire

As kingfishers catch fire, dragonflies draw flame;
    As tumbled over rim in roundy wells
    Stones ring; like each tucked° string tells, each hung bell's   *plucked*
Bow swung finds tongue to fling out broad its name;
5 Each mortal thing does one thing and the same:
    Deals out that being indoors° each one dwells;   *within*
    Selves[1]—goes itself; *myself* it speaks and spells,
Crying *What I do is me: for that I came.*

I say more: the just man justices;[2]
10   Keeps gráce: thát keeps all his goings graces;
Acts in God's eye what in God's eye he is—
    Chríst. For Christ plays in ten thousand places,
Lovely in limbs, and lovely in eyes not his
    To the Father through the features of men's faces.

1877   1918

Spring

Nothing is so beautiful as Spring—
    When weeds, in wheels, shoot long and lovely and lush;
    Thrush's eggs look little low heavens, and thrush
Through the echoing timber does so rinse and wring
5 The ear, it strikes like lightnings to hear him sing;
    The glassy peartree leaves and blooms, they brush
    The descending blue; that blue is all in a rush
With richness; the racing lambs too have fair their fling.

What is all this juice and all this joy?
10   A strain of the earth's sweet being in the beginning
In Eden garden.—Have, get, before it cloy,
    Before it cloud, Christ, lord, and sour with sinning,
Innocent mind and Mayday in girl and boy,
    Most, O maid's child,[1] thy choice and worthy the winning.

1877   1918

The Windhover[1]

To Christ our Lord

I caught this morning morning's minion,° king-   *darling*
  dom of daylight's dauphin,[2] dapple-dawn-drawn Falcon, in his riding

---

1. Fulfills its individuality.
2. Acts in a just manner.
1. Jesus, son of the Virgin Mary.

1. Kestrel, a small falcon noted for hovering in the air.
2. A prince who is heir to the French throne.

Of the rolling level underneath him steady air, and striding
High there, how he rung upon the rein of a wimpling[3] wing
5   In his ecstasy! then off, off forth on swing,
      As a skate's heel sweeps smooth on a bow-bend: the hurl and gliding
Rebuffed the big wind. My heart in hiding
Stirred for a bird,—the achieve of, the mastery of the thing!

Brute beauty and valour and act, oh, air, pride, plume, here
10   Buckle![4] AND the fire that breaks from thee then, a billion
Times told lovelier, more dangerous, O my chevalier!°   *knight*

No wonder of it: shéer plód makes plough down sillion[5]
Shine, and blue-bleak embers, ah my dear,
Fall, gall[6] themselves, and gash gold-vermilion.

1877   1918

Pied[1] Beauty

Glory be to God for dappled things—
      For skies of couple-colour as a brinded[2] cow;
          For rose-moles all in stipple upon trout that swim;
Fresh-firecoal chestnut-falls,[3] finches' wings;
5   Landscape plotted and pieced—fold, fallow, and plough;[4]
          And áll trádes, their gear and tackle and trim.°   *equipment*

All things counter, original, spare,[5] strange;
      Whatever is fickle, freckled (who knows how?)
          With swift, slow; sweet, sour; adazzle, dim;
10   He fathers-forth whose beauty is past change:
                      Praise him.

1877   1918

Hurrahing in Harvest

Summer ends now; now, barbarous in beauty, the stooks[1] rise
Around; up above, what wind-walks! what lovely behavior
Of silk-sack clouds! has wilder, wilful-wavier
Meal-drift moulded ever and melted across skies?

5   I walk, I lift up, I lift up heart, eyes,
      Down all that glory in the heavens to glean our Saviour;

3. Rippling. "Rung upon the rein": circled at the end of a rein.
4. The verb can be read as imperative or indicative. All three meanings are relevant: to prepare for action, to fasten together, to collapse.
5. The ridge between two furrows of a plowed field.
6. Break the surface of.

1. Of two or more colors in blotches, variegated.
2. Brownish orange in color with streaks of gray.
3. I.e., freshly fallen chestnuts, bright as coals.
4. Divided into fields used as pastures ("fold"), lying fallow, or plowed for cultivation. The landscape thus appears like patches of different colors.
5. Rare. "Counter": contrary.
1. Sheaves of grain.

And, éyes, heárt, what looks, what lips yet gave you a
Rapturous love's greeting of realer, of rounder replies?

And the azurous hung hills are his world-wielding shoulder
10 Majestic—as a stallion stalwart, very-violet-sweet!—
These things, these things were here and but the beholder
Wanting; which two when they once meet,
The heart rears wings bold and bolder
And hurls for him, O half hurls earth for him off under his feet.

1877   1918

Binsey Poplars

felled 1879

My aspens dear, whose airy cages quelled,
Quelled or quenched in leaves the leaping sun,
All felled, felled, are all felled;
    Of a fresh and following folded rank
5   Not spared, not one
            That dandled a sandalled
        Shadow that swam or sank
On meadow and river and wind-wandering
        weed-winding bank.

10   O if we but knew what we do
        When we delve° or hew—   dig
    Hack and rack° the growing green!   torture
        Since country is so tender
        To touch, her being só slender,
15   That, like this sleek and seeing ball°   the eye
    But a prick will make no eye at all,

        Where we, even where we mean
            To mend her we end her,
            When we hew or delve:
20   After-comers cannot guess the beauty been.
        Ten or twelve, only ten or twelve
            Strokes of havoc únselve[1]
            The sweet especial scene,
            Rural scene, a rural scene,
25   Sweet especial rural scene.

1879   1918

Duns Scotus's Oxford[1]

Towery city and branchy between towers;
Cuckoo-echoing, bell-swarmèd, lark-charmèd, rook-racked, river-rounded;

---

1. Rob it of self.
1. Duns Scotus, the medieval theologian, lectured at Oxford about 1301. His idea that individuality is the final perfection of any creature influenced Hopkins's conception of inscape. When Hopkins

came on two of Scotus's commentaries in 1872, he wrote that he was immediately "flush with a new stroke of enthusiasm . . . when I took in any inscape of the sky or sea I thought of Scotus."

The dapple-eared lily below thee; that country and town did
Once encounter in, here coped[2] and poisèd powers;

5 Thou hast a base and brickish skirt[3] there, sours
That neighbour-nature thy grey beauty is grounded
Best in; graceless growth, thou hast confounded
Rural rural keeping[4]—folk, flocks, and flowers.

Yet ah! this air I gather and I release
10 He lived on; these weeds and waters, these walls are what
He haunted who of all men most sways my spirits to peace;

Of realty° the rarest-veinèd unraveller; a not   *reality*
Rivalled insight, be rival Italy or Greece;
Who fired France for Mary without spot.[5]

1879   1918

Felix Randal

Felix Randal the farrier,° O is he dead then? my duty   *blacksmith*
    all ended,
Who have watched his mould of man, big-boned and hardy-handsome
Pining, pining, till time when reason rambled in it and some
Fatal four disorders, fleshed there, all contended?

5 Sickness broke him. Impatient, he cursed at first, but mended
Being anointed[1] and all; though a heavenlier heart began some
Months earlier, since I had our sweet reprieve and ransom[2]
Tendered to him. Ah well, God rest him all road ever[3] he offended!

This seeing the sick endears them to us, us too it endears.
10 My tongue had taught thee comfort, touch had quenched thy tears,
Thy tears that touched my heart, child, Felix, poor Felix Randal;
How far from then forethought of, all thy more boisterous years,
When thou at the random[4] grim forge, powerful amidst peers,
Didst fettle° for the great grey drayhorse his bright and battering   *prepare*
    sandal!

1880   1918

Spring and Fall:

to a young child

Márgarét, áre you gríeving
Over Goldengrove unleaving?

---

2. Set off against one another.
3. Redbrick housing developments and industrial complexes, built in the 19th century on the north edge of Oxford, are in marked contrast with the "gray" stone buildings of the medieval city.
4. The "brickish skirt" has destroyed the way in which the rural landscape and the old city have tended and preserved each other.
5. In Paris, Scotus was the first to defend the doc-

trine of the Immaculate Conception, that Mary was born without original sin.
1. In Extreme Unction, the sacrament for the dying.
2. Holy Communion preceded by confession and absolution.
3. In whatever way.
4. Built with stones of irregular size and shape.

Leáves, líke the things of man, you
With your fresh thoughts care for, can you?
5   Áh! ás the heart grows older
It will come to such sights colder
By and by, nor spare a sigh
Though worlds of wanwood leafmeal[1] lie;
And yet you *will* weep and know why.
10   Now no matter, child, the name:
Sórrow's spríngs áre the same.
Nor mouth had, no nor mind, expressed
What heart heard of, ghost° guessed: *spirit*
It ís the blight man was born for,
15   It is Margaret you mourn for.

1880   1918

[Carrion Comfort][1]

Not, I'll not, carrion comfort, Despair, not feast on thee,[2]
Not untwist—slack they may be—these last strands of man
In me ór, most weary, cry *I can no more.* I can;
Can something, hope, wish day come, not choose not to be.

5   But ah, but O thou terrible, why wouldst thou rude on me
Thy wring-world right foot rock?[3] lay a lionlimb against me?
     scan
With darksome devouring eyes my bruisèd bones? and fan,
O in turns of tempest, me heaped there; me frantic to avoid
     thee and flee?

Why? That my chaff might fly; my grain lie, sheer and clear.
10   Nay in all that toil, that coil,° since (seems) I kissed the rod,   *tumult*
Hand rather,[4] my heart lo! lapped strength, stole joy, would
     laugh, chéer.
Cheer whom though? The Hero whose heaven-handling
     flung me, fóot tród
Me? or me that fought him? O which one? is it each one?
     That night, that year
Of now done darkness I wretch lay wrestling with (my God!)
     my God.

1885   1918

---

1. Coined by analogy with piecemeal. "Wanwood": pale or dim; the forest may be pale because
of light-colored autumn leaves or dim because light
is filtered through the leaves.
1. The title of this poem was supplied by Bridges.
It is one of the "terrible sonnets," as are the three
following poems.

2. The satisfaction of giving in to despair as a kind
of "comfort" is implicitly likened to a vulture's satisfaction in feasting on dead flesh.
3. I.e., why wouldst thou roughly against me rock
thy right foot that wrings the world?
4. I.e., the hand that wields the rod.

No Worst, There Is None

No worst, there is none. Pitched past pitch of grief,
More pangs will, schooled at forepangs, wilder wring.
Comforter, where, where is your comforting?
Mary, mother of us, where is your relief?

5 My cries heave, herds-long;[1] huddle in a main, a chief-
woe, world-sorrow; on an age-old anvil wince and sing—
Then lull, then leave off. Fury had shrieked "No ling-
ering! Let me be fell: force[2] I must be brief."
O the mind, mind has mountains; cliffs of fall
10 Frightful, sheer, no-man-fathomed. Hold them cheap
May who ne'er hung there. Nor does long our small
Durance° deal with that steep or deep. Here! creep,   *endurance*
Wretch, under a comfort serves in a whirlwind: all
Life death does end and each day dies with sleep.

1885   1918

I Wake and Feel the Fell of Dark, Not Day

I wake and feel the fell° of dark, not day.   *bitterness*
What hours, O what black hoürs we have spent
This night! what sights you, heart, saw; ways you went!
And more must, in yet longer light's delay.

5 With witness I speak this. But where I say
Hours I mean years, mean life. And my lament
Is cries countless, cries like dead letters[1] sent
To dearest him that lives alas! away.

I am gall, I am heartburn. God's most deep decree
10 Bitter would have me taste: my taste was me;
Bones built in me, flesh filled, blood brimmed the curse.

Selfyeast of spirit a dull dough sours. I see
The lost are like this, and their scourge to be
As I am mine, their sweating selves; but worse.

1885   1918

1. Like the succession of cries made by cattle that
have been following one another in a long line.
2. Perforce. "Fell": fierce.

1. Letters undelivered or returned to the sender
by the post office.

That Nature Is a Heraclitean Fire[1] and of the Comfort of the Resurrection

Cloud-puffball, torn tufts, tossed pillows | flaunt forth, then chevy°   *race*
   on an air-
built thoroughfare: heaven-roysterers,° in gay-gangs | they   *swaggerers*
   throng; they glitter in marches.
Down roughcast, down dazzling whitewash, | wherever an elm arches.
Shivelights and shadowtackle[2] in long | lashes lace, lance, and pair.
5   Delightfully the bright wind boisterous | ropes, wrestles, beats earth bare
Of yestertempest's creases; in pool and rut peel parches[3]
Squandering ooze to squeezed | dough, crust, dust; stanches, starches
Squadroned masks and manmarks[4] | treadmire toil there
Footfretted in it. Million-fuelèd, | nature's bonfire burns on.
10   But quench her bonniest, dearest | to her, her clearest-selvèd°   *most individual*
   spark
Man, how fast his firedint | his mark on mind, is gone!
Both are in an unfathomable, all is in an enormous dark
Drowned. O pity and indig | nation! Manshape, that shone
Sheer off, disseveral,° a star, | death blots black out; nor mark   *separate*
15   Is any of him at all so stark
But vastness blurs and time | beats level. Enough! the Resurrection,
A heart's-clarion! Away grief's gasping, | joyless days, dejection.
      Across my foundering deck shone
A beacon, an eternal beam. | Flesh fade, and mortal trash
20   Fall to the residuary worm; | world's wildfire, leave but ash:
      In a flash, at a trumpet crash,
I am all at once what Christ is, | since he was what I am, and
This Jack, joke, poor potsherd, | patch, matchwood,[5] immortal diamond,
      Is immortal diamond.

1888   1918

Thou Art Indeed Just, Lord

*Justus quidem tu es, Domine, si disputem tecum; verumtamen
justa loquar ad te: Quare via impiorum prosperatur? &c.[1]*

    Thou art indeed just, Lord, if I contend
    With thee; but, sir, so what I plead is just.
    Why do sinners' ways prosper? and why must
    Disappointment all I endeavour end?

5   Wert thou my enemy, O thou my friend,
    How wouldst thou worse, I wonder, than thou dost

1. Heraclitus (ca. 535–ca. 475 B.C.E.) taught that all things are in flux and that they ultimately return to the basic principle of fire.
2. Branches imagined as the shadows of a ship's rigging. "Shivelights": strips of light.
3. Ruts described as peeled places. "Parches" is a verb whose subject is *wind*.

4. The marks that people have made on the earth by walking ("Footfretted") on it.
5. Kindling. "Jack": ordinary man.
1. "Righteous art thou, O Lord, when I plead with thee: yet let me talk with thee of thy judgments: Wherefore doth the way of the wicked prosper?" (Jeremiah 12.1). The Latin was Hopkins's title.

Defeat, thwart me? Oh, the sots and thralls of lust
Do in spare hours more thrive than I that spend,

      Sir, life upon thy cause. See, banks and brakes°   *thickets*
10 Now, leavèd how thick! lacèd they are again
      With fretty chervil,² look, and fresh wind shakes

      Them; birds build—but not I build; no, but strain,
      Time's eunuch, and not breed one work that wakes.
      Mine, O thou lord of life, send my roots rain.

1889   1918

From Journal¹

May 3 [1866]. Cold. Morning raw and wet, afternoon fine. Walked then with Addis, crossing Bablock Hythe, round by Skinner's Weir² through many fields into the Witney road. Sky sleepy blue without liquidity. From Cumnor Hill saw St. Philip's and the other spires through blue haze rising pale in a pink light. On further side of the Witney road hills, just fleeced with grain or other green growth, by their dips and waves foreshortened here and there and so differenced in brightness and opacity the green on them, with delicate effect. On left, brow of the near hill glistening with very bright newly turned sods and a scarf of vivid green slanting away beyond the skyline, against which the clouds shewed the slightest tinge of rose or purple. Copses in grey-red or grey-yellow—the tinges immediately forerunning the opening of full leaf. Meadows skirting Seven-bridge road voluptuous green. Some oaks are out in small leaf. Ashes not out, only tufted with their fringy blooms. Hedges springing richly. Elms in small leaf, with more or less opacity. White poplars most beautiful in small grey crisp spray-like leaf. Cowslips capriciously colouring meadows in creamy drifts. Bluebells, purple orchis. Over the green water of the river passing the slums of the town and under its bridges swallows shooting, blue and purple above and shewing their amber-tinged breasts reflected in the water, their flight unsteady with wagging wings and leaning first to one side then the other. Peewits flying. Towards sunset the sky partly swept, as often, with moist white cloud, tailing off across which are morsels of grey-black woolly clouds. Sun seemed to make a bright liquid hole in this, its texture had an upward northerly sweep or drift from the W, marked softly in grey. Dog violets. Eastward after sunset range of clouds rising in bulky heads moulded softly in tufts or bunches of snow—so it looks—and membered somewhat elaborately, rose-coloured. Notice often imperfect fairy rings. Apple and other fruit trees blossomed beautifully.

*   *   *

2. A kind of herb, related to parsley.
1. With the exception of one year, Hopkins kept a journal from May 1866 to Feb. 1875. Its most interesting entries are minutely observed descriptions of natural phenomena, which reveal the character of his imagination. The brackets and abbreviations are Hopkins's own.
2. Dam. William E. Addis (1844–1917), friend of Hopkins at Oxford; like him he became a Catholic convert and priest. The places mentioned are around Oxford. "Hythe": landing place on a river.

Feb.—1870. One day in the Long Retreat (which ended on Xmas Day) they were reading in the refectory Sister Emmerich's[3] account of the Agony in the Garden and I suddenly began to cry and sob and could not stop. I put it down for this reason, that if I had been asked a minute beforehand I should have said that nothing of the sort was going to happen and even when it did I stood in a manner wondering at myself not seeing in my reason the traces of an adequate cause for such strong emotion—the traces of it I say because of course the cause in itself is adequate for the sorrow of a lifetime. I remember much the same thing on Maundy Thursday when the presanctified Host[4] was carried to the sacristy. But neither the weight nor the stress of sorrow, that is to say of the thing which should cause sorrow, by themselves move us or bring the tears as a sharp knife does not cut for being pressed as long as it is pressed without any shaking of the hand but there is always one touch, something striking sideways and unlooked for, which in both cases undoes resistance and pierces, and this may be so delicate that the pathos seems to have gone directly to the body and cleared the understanding in its passage. On the other hand the pathetic touch by itself, as in dramatic pathos, will only draw slight tears if its matter is not important or not of import to us, the strong emotion coming from a force which was gathered before it was discharged: in this way a knife may pierce the flesh which it had happened only to graze and only grazing will go no deeper.

* * *

May 18 [1870]. —Great brilliancy and projection: the eye seemed to fall perpendicular from level to level along our trees, the nearer and further Park; all things hitting the sense with double but direct instress. * * *

This was later. One day when the bluebells were in bloom I wrote the following. I do not think I have ever seen anything more beautiful than the bluebell I have been looking at. I know the beauty of our Lord by it. It[s inscape] is [mixed of] strength and grace, like an ash [tree]. The head is strongly drawn over [backwards] and arched down like a cutwater [drawing itself back from the line of the keel.] The lines of the bells strike and overlie this, rayed but not symmetrically, some lie parallel. They look steely against [the] paper, the shades lying between the bells and behind the cockled petal-ends and nursing up the precision of their distinctness, the petal-ends themselves being delicately lit. Then there is the straightness of the trumpets in the bells softened by the slight entasis and [by] the square splay of the mouth. One bell, the lowest, some way detached and carried on a longer footstalk, touched out with the tips of the petals on oval / not like the rest in a plane perpendicular of the axis of the bell but a little atilt, and so with [the] square-in-rounding turns of the petals

* * *

Aug. 10 [1872]. —I was looking at high waves. The breakers always are parallel to the coast and shape themselves to it except where the curve is sharp however the wind blows. They are rolled out by the shallowing shore just as a piece of putty between the palms whatever its shape runs into a

3. *The Dolorous Passion of Our Lord Jesus Christ;*
from the Meditations of Anne Catherine Emmerich,
an Augustinian nun (1774–1824).

4. The bread wafer sanctified for Holy Communion. "Maundy Thursday": the Thursday before Easter, day of the Last Supper.

long roll. The slant ruck[5] or crease one sees in them shows the way of the wind. The regularity of the barrels surprised and charmed the eye; the edge behind the comb or crest was as smooth and bright as glass. It may be noticed to be green behind and silver white in front: the silver marks where the air begins, the pure white is foam, the green / solid water. Then looked at to the right or left they are scrolled over like mouldboards[6] or feathers or jibsails seen by the edge. It is pretty to see the hollow of the barrel disappearing as the white combs on each side run along the wave gaining ground till the two meet at a pitch and crush and overlap each other.

About all the turns of the scaping from the break and flooding of wave to its run out again I have not yet satisfied myself. The shores are swimming and the eyes have before them a region of milky surf but it is hard for them to unpack the huddling and gnarls of the water and law out the shapes and the sequence of the running: I catch however the looped or forked wisp made by every big pebble the backwater runs over—if it were clear and smooth there would be a network from their overlapping, such as can in fact be seen on smooth sand after the tide is out—; then I saw it run browner, the foam dwindling and twitched into long chains of suds, while the strength of the back-draught shrugged the stones together and clocked them one against another

1959

---

5. Fold or crease.

6. Curved iron plates attached to plowshares.

Light Verse

Despite its later reputation as an age of solemnity, the Victorian age produced a remarkable outburst of humorous prose and verse from the time of Dickens's *Pickwick Papers* at the beginning of the period to the operas of Gilbert and Sullivan near the end. The following selections provide examples of two varieties of Victorian light verse. One, represented by W. S. Gilbert, makes playful mockery of institutions such as the Court of Chancery and marriage. Gilbert's burlesque mode is also to be found, though managed by less inspired writers, in many pages of *Punch,* a humorous and satirical magazine that began publication in 1841. Although exaggeration and absurdities are important ingredients in these writings, the world of Gilbert is still recognizably related to the ordinary world.

The other variety is a more distinctive Victorian specialty—nonsense writing—represented here by the verse of Edward Lear and Lewis Carroll. Nonsense writing was occasionally used by Shakespeare and, in the twentieth century, by James Joyce and James Thurber, but the period in which this genre had its finest flowering was, without question, the Victorian age. Freudian explanations can be devised to account for its appearance during this particular period; and indeed, if nonsense writing does originate in a writer's repressions, we may have a clue to the undertone of melancholy that some readers detect in the verses of Lear and Carroll. The best nonsense writing, however, raises its own less solemn problems. Lear and Carroll created a zany upside-down world full of puzzles; the attempt to solve such puzzles, even when they cannot be solved, is in itself a perennial satisfaction.

EDWARD LEAR
1812–1888

Edward Lear was a landscape painter who spent much of his life in Mediterranean countries. In 1846 he published his first *Book of Nonsense,* a collection of limericks for children. The form of the limerick was not invented by Lear, but his use of it served to establish its popularity. In later volumes of the *Book of Nonsense,* he used other forms of verse, some of them modeled on rhythms that had been developed by his close friend Tennyson. All of his own poems were characteristically classified by Lear as "nonsense pure and absolute," yet it is as the author of *The Owl and the Pussy-Cat, The Jumblies,* and other poems that Lear is remembered. Evidently pure and absolute nonsense is a rare art.

Limerick

There was an Old Man who supposed
That the street door was partially closed;
But some very large rats ate his coats and his hats,
While that futile old gentleman dozed.

1846

How Pleasant to Know Mr. Lear

"How pleasant to know Mr. Lear!"
   Who has written such volumes of stuff!
Some think him ill-tempered and queer,
   But a few think him pleasant enough.

5 His mind is concrete and fastidious,
   His nose is remarkably big;
His visage is more or less hideous,
   His beard it resembles a wig.

He has ears, and two eyes, and ten fingers,
10   Leastways if you reckon two thumbs;
Long ago he was one of the singers,
   But now he is one of the dumbs.

He sits in a beautiful parlor,
   With hundreds of books on the wall;
15 He drinks a great deal of Marsala,
   But never gets tipsy at all.

He has many friends, lay men and clerical,
   Old Foss is the name of his cat;
His body is perfectly spherical,
20   He weareth a runcible[1] hat.

When he walks in waterproof white,
   The children run after him so!
Calling out, "He's come out in his night-
   Gown, that crazy old Englishman, oh!"

25 He weeps by the side of the ocean,
   He weeps on the top of the hill;
He purchases pancakes and lotion,
   And chocolate shrimps from the mill.

He reads, but he cannot speak, Spanish,
30   He cannot abide ginger beer:

---

1. A runcible spoon is a spoon-shaped fork with a cutting edge.

Ere the days of his pilgrimage vanish,
How pleasant to know Mr. Lear!

1871

The Jumblies

They went to sea in a sieve, they did;
   In a sieve they went to sea;
In spite of all their friends could say,
On a winter's morn, on a stormy day,
5   In a sieve they went to sea.
And when the sieve turned round and round,
And everyone cried, "You'll be drowned!"
They called aloud, "Our sieve ain't big,
But we don't care a button; we don't care a fig—
10   In a sieve we'll go to sea!"
     Far and few, far and few,
      Are the lands where the Jumblies live.
     Their heads are green, and their hands are blue;
     And they went to sea in a sieve.

15 They sailed away in a sieve, they did,
   In a sieve they sailed so fast,
With only a beautiful pea-green veil
Tied with a ribbon, by way of a sail,
   To a small tobacco-pipe mast.
20 And everyone said who saw them go,
"Oh! won't they be soon upset, you know,
For the sky is dark, and the voyage is long;
And, happen what may, it's extremely wrong
   In a sieve to sail so fast."

25 The water it soon came in, it did;
   The water it soon came in.
So, to keep them dry, they wrapped their feet
In a pinky paper all folded neat;
   And they fastened it down with a pin.
30 And they passed the night in a crockery-jar;
And each of them said, "How wise we are!
Though the sky be dark, and the voyage be long,
Yet we never can think we were rash or wrong,
   While round in our sieve we spin."

35 And all night long they sailed away;
   And, when the sun went down,
They whistled and warbled a moony song
To the echoing sound of a coppery gong,
   In the shade of the mountains brown,
40   "O Timballoo! how happy we are
When we live in a sieve and a crockery-jar!

And all night long, in the moonlight pale,
We sail away with a pea-green sail
   In the shade of the mountains brown."

45 They sailed to the Western Sea, they did—
   To a land all covered with trees;
And they bought an owl, and a useful cart,
And a pound of rice, and a cranberry tart,
   And a hive of silvery bees;
50 And they bought a pig, and some green jackdaws,
And a lovely monkey with lollipop paws,
And seventeen bags of edelweiss tea,
   And forty bottles of ring-bo-ree,
     And no end of Stilton cheese.

55 And in twenty years they all came back—
   In twenty years or more;
And everyone said, "How tall they've grown!
For they've been to the Lakes, and the Torrible Zone,
   And the hills of the Chankly Bore."
60 And they drank their health, and gave them a feast
Of dumplings made of beautiful yeast;
And everyone said, "If we only live,
We, too, will go to sea in a sieve,
   To the hills of the Chankly Bore."
65   Far and few, far and few,
     Are the lands where the Jumblies live.
     Their heads are green, and their hands are blue;
     And they went to sea in a sieve.

                                     1871

Cold Are the Crabs

Cold are the crabs that crawl on yonder hills,
Colder the cucumbers that grow beneath,
And colder still the brazen chops that wreathe
   The tedious gloom of philosophic pills!
5 For when the tardy film of nectar fills
The ample bowls of demons and of men,
There lurks the feeble mouse, the homely hen,
   And there the porcupine with all her quills.
Yet much remains—to weave a solemn strain
10 That lingering sadly—slowly dies away,
Daily departing with departing day.
A pea-green gamut on a distant plain
When wily walruses in congress meet—
   Such such is life—

                                     1953

LEWIS CARROLL
1832–1898

Charles Lutwidge Dodgson was a deacon in the Anglican Church and a lecturer in mathematics at Oxford as well as a pioneer in the art of portrait photography. Most of his publications were mathematical treatises, but his fame rests on the strange pair of books he wrote for children: *Alice in Wonderland* (1865) and *Through the Looking-Glass* (1871), both published under the pseudonym Lewis Carroll. Like *Gulliver's Travels*, these narratives have long been enjoyed, at different levels, by both children and adults. The various songs scattered through the stories are sometimes parodies, as, for example, *The White Knight's Song*, but more often they are classic examples of nonsense verse. Poems such as *Jabberwocky* exhibit a mathematician's fondness for puzzles combined with a literary person's fondness for word games. At this level, *Jabberwocky* can be enjoyed as a small-scale *Finnegans Wake.*

Carroll's art has obviously many affinities with that of another eccentric Victorian, Edward Lear, although the two men never met and (so far as we know) never referred to each other. Despite these affinities, Carroll's nonsense, often on the brink of satire, is more pointed than Lear's.

Jabberwocky[1]

'Twas brillig, and the slithy toves
    Did gyre and gimble in the wabe;
All mimsy were the borogoves,
    And the mome raths outgrabe.

5 "Beware the Jabberwock, my son!
    The jaws that bite, the claws that catch!
Beware the Jubjub bird, and shun
    The frumious Bandersnatch!"

He took his vorpal sword in hand;
10   Long time the manxome foe he sought—
So rested he by the Tumtum tree,
    And stood awhile in thought.

And, as in uffish thought he stood,
    The Jabberwock, with eyes of flame,
15 Came whiffling through the tulgey wood,
    And burbled as it came!

One, two! One, two! And through and through
    The vorpal blade went snicker-snack!
He left it dead, and with its head
20   He went galumphing back.

"And hast thou slain the Jabberwock?
    Come to my arms, my beamish boy!

---

1. From *Through the Looking-Glass,* chap. 1.

O frabjous day! Callooh! Callay!"
   He chortled in his joy.

25   'Twas brillig, and the slithy toves
     Did gyre and gimble in the wabe;
   All mimsy were the borogoves,
     And the mome raths outgrabe.

1855   1871

[Humpty Dumpty's Explication of *Jabberwocky*][1]

"You seem very clever at explaining words, Sir," said Alice. "Would you kindly tell me the meaning of the poem *Jabberwocky*?"

"Let's hear it," said Humpty Dumpty. "I can explain all the poems that ever were invented—and a good many that haven't been invented just yet."

This sounded very hopeful, so Alice repeated the first verse:

" 'Twas brillig, and the slithy toves
     Did gyre and gimble in the wabe;
   All mimsy were the borogoves,
     And the mome raths outgrabe."

"That's enough to begin with," Humpty Dumpty interrupted: "there are plenty of hard words there. 'Brillig' means four o'clock in the afternoon— the time when you begin *broiling* things for dinner."

"That'll do very well," said Alice: "and 'slithy'?"[2]

"Well, 'slithy' means 'lithe and slimy.' 'Lithe' is the same as 'active.' You see it's like a portmanteau[3]—there are two meanings packed up into one word."

"I see it now," Alice remarked thoughtfully: "and what are 'toves'?"

"Well, 'toves' are something like badgers—they're something like lizards— and they're something like corkscrews."

"They must be very curious creatures."

"They are that," said Humpty Dumpty: "also they make their nests under sundials—also they live on cheese."

"And what's to 'gyre' and to 'gimble'?"

"To 'gyre' is to go round and round like a gyroscope. To 'gimble' is to make holes like a gimlet."

"And the 'wabe' is the grass plot round a sundial, I suppose?" said Alice, surprised at her own ingenuity.

"Of course it is. It's called 'wabe,' you know, because it goes a long way before it, and a long way behind it——"

"And a long way beyond it on each side," Alice added.

"Exactly so. Well then, 'mimsy' is 'flimsy and miserable' (there's another

---

1. From *Through the Looking-Glass,* chap. 6.
2. Concerning the pronunciation of these words, Carroll later said: "The 'i' in 'slithy' is long, as in 'writhe'; and 'toves' is pronounced so as to rhyme with 'groves.' Again, the first 'o' in 'borogroves' is

pronounced like the 'o' in 'borrow.' I have heard people try to give it the sound of the 'o' in 'worry.' Such is Human Perversity."
3. Large suitcase.

portmanteau for you). And a 'borogove' is a thin shabby-looking bird with its feathers sticking out all round—something like a live mop."

"And then 'mome raths'?" said Alice. "If I'm not giving you too much trouble."

"Well, a 'rath' is a sort of green pig: but 'mome' I'm not certain about. I think it's short for 'from home'—meaning that they'd lost their way, you know."

"And what does 'outgrabe' mean?"

"Well, 'outgribing' is something between bellowing and whistling, with a kind of sneeze in the middle: however, you'll hear it done, maybe—down in the wood yonder—and when you've once heard it you'll be *quite* content. Who's been repeating all that hard stuff to you?"

"I read it in a book," said Alice.

1871

The White Knight's Song[1]

I'll tell thee everything I can;
　　There's little to relate.
I saw an aged, aged man,
　　A-sitting on a gate.
5　"Who are you, aged man?" I said.
　　"And how is it you live?"
And his answer trickled through my head
　　Like water through a sieve.

He said "I look for butterflies
10　That sleep among the wheat;
I make them into mutton-pies,
　　And sell them in the street.
I sell them unto men," he said,
　　"Who sail on stormy seas;
15　And that's the way I get my bread—
　　A trifle, if you please."

But I was thinking of a plan
　　To dye one's whiskers green,
And always use so large a fan
20　That they could not be seen.
So, having no reply to give
　　To what the old man said,
I cried, "Come, tell me how you live!"
　　And thumped him on the head.

25　His accents mild took up the tale;
　　He said, "I go my ways,
And when I find a mountain-rill,

---

1. From *Through the Looking-Glass*, chap. 8. Cf. Wordsworth's poem concerning the aged leech gatherer: *Resolution and Independence.*

I set it in a blaze;
And thence they make a stuff they call
30   Rowland's Macassar Oil—
Yet twopence-halfpenny is all
    They give me for my toil."

But I was thinking of a way
    To feed oneself on batter,
35   And so go on from day to day
    Getting a little fatter.
I shook him well from side to side,
    Until his face was blue;
"Come, tell me how you live," I cried
40   "And what it is you do!"

He said, "I hunt for haddocks' eyes
    Among the heather bright,
And work them into waistcoat-buttons
    In the silent night.
45   And these I do not sell for gold
    Or coin of silvery shine,
But for a copper halfpenny,
    And that will purchase nine.

"I sometimes dig for buttered rolls,
50   Or set limed twigs for crabs;
I sometimes search the grassy knolls
    For wheels of hansom-cabs.
And that's the way" (he gave a wink)
    "By which I get my wealth—
55   And very gladly will I drink
    Your Honor's noble health."

I heard him then, for I had just
    Completed my design
To keep the Menai bridge[2] from rust
60   By boiling it in wine.
I thanked him much for telling me
    The way he got his wealth,
But chiefly for his wish that he
    Might drink my noble health.

65   And now, if e'er by chance I put
    My fingers into glue,
Or madly squeeze a right-hand foot
    Into a left-hand shoe,
Or if I drop upon my toe
70   A very heavy weight,
I weep, for it reminds me so
Of that old man I used to know—

2. Railway bridge in Wales (completed in 1850).

Whose look was mild, whose speech was slow,
Whose hair was whiter than the snow,
75   Whose face was very like a crow,
With eyes, like cinders, all aglow,
Who seemed distracted with his woe.
Who rocked his body to and fro,
And muttered mumblingly and low,
80   As if his mouth were full of dough,
Who snorted like a buffalo—
That summer evening long ago
   A-sitting on a gate.

1856   1871

The Walrus and the Carpenter[1]

The sun was shining on the sea,
   Shining with all his might;
He did his very best to make
   The billows smooth and bright—
5   And this was odd, because it was
   The middle of the night.

The moon was shining sulkily,
   Because she thought the sun
Had got no business to be there
10   After the day was done—
"It's very rude of him," she said,
   "To come and spoil the fun!"

The sea was wet as wet could be,
   The sands were dry as dry.
15   You could not see a cloud, because
   No cloud was in the sky;
No birds were flying overhead—
   There were no birds to fly.

The Walrus and the Carpenter
20   Were walking close at hand;
They wept like anything to see
   Such quantities of sand.
"If this were only cleared away,"
   They said, "it *would* be grand!"

25   "If seven maids with seven mops
   Swept it for half a year,
Do you suppose," the Walrus said,
   "That they could get it clear?"

1. Recited by Tweedledee in chap. 4 of *Through the Looking-Glass*.

"I doubt it," said the Carpenter,
30   And shed a bitter tear.

"O Oysters, come and walk with us!"
    The Walrus did beseech.
"A pleasant walk, a pleasant talk,
    Along the briny beach;
35   We cannot do with more than four,
    To give a hand to each."

The eldest Oyster looked at him,
    But never a word he said;
The eldest Oyster winked his eye,
40   And shook his heavy head—
Meaning to say he did not choose
    To leave the oyster-bed.

But four young Oysters hurried up,
    All eager for the treat;
45   Their coats were brushed, their faces washed,
    Their shoes were clean and neat—
And this was odd, because, you know,
    They hadn't any feet.

Four other Oysters followed them,
50   And yet another four;
And thick and fast they came at last,
    And more, and more, and more—
All hopping through the frothy waves,
    And scrambling to the shore.

55   The Walrus and the Carpenter
    Walked on a mile or so,
And then they rested on a rock
    Conveniently low;
And all the little Oysters stood
60   And waited in a row.

"The time has come," the Walrus said,
    "To talk of many things:
Of shoes—and ships—and sealing-wax—
    Of cabbages—and kings—
65   And why the sea is boiling hot—
    And whether pigs have wings."

"But wait a bit," the Oysters cried,
    "Before we have our chat;
For some of us are out of breath,
70   And all of us are fat!"
"No hurry!" said the Carpenter.
    They thanked him much for that.

"A loaf of bread," the Walrus said,
  "Is what we chiefly need;
75 Pepper and vinegar besides
  Are very good indeed—
Now, if you're ready, Oysters dear,
  We can begin to feed."

"But not on us!" the Oysters cried,
80   Turning a little blue.
"After such kindness, that would be
  A dismal thing to do!"
"The night is fine," the Walrus said,
  "Do you admire the view?

85 "It was so kind of you to come!
  And you are very nice!"
The Carpenter said nothing but
  "Cut us another slice.
I wish you were not quite so deaf—
90   I've had to ask you twice!"

"It seems a shame," the Walrus said,
  "To play them such a trick,
After we've brought them out so far,
  And made them trot so quick!"
95 The Carpenter said nothing but
  "The butter's spread too thick!"

"I weep for you," the Walrus said;
  "I deeply sympathize."
With sobs and tears he sorted out
100   Those of the largest size,
Holding his pocket-handkerchief
  Before his streaming eyes.

"O Oysters," said the Carpenter,
  "You've had a pleasant run!
105 Shall we be trotting home again?"
  But answer came there none—
And this was scarcely odd, because
  They'd eaten every one.

1871

From The Hunting of the Snark

The Baker's Tale

They roused him[1] with muffins—they roused him with ice—
  They roused him with mustard and cress—

1. I.e., the Baker, a member of the Snark-hunting expedition. He had fainted when the leader of the crew, the Bellman, had mentioned that one species of Snark is called Boojum. The nameless Baker's fear of Boojums turns out later to have been well founded: at the end of the poem he encounters a Boojum and is never seen again.

They roused him with jam and judicious advice—
    They set him conundrums to guess.

5   When at length he sat up and was able to speak,
    His sad story he offered to tell;
And the Bellman cried, "Silence! Not even a shriek!"
    And excitedly tingled his bell.[2]

There was silence supreme! Not a shriek, not a scream,
10   Scarcely even a howl or a groan,
As the man they called "Ho!" told his story of woe
    In an antediluvian tone.

"My father and mother were honest though poor—"
    "Skip all that!" cried the Bellman in haste.
15   "If it once becomes dark, there's no chance of a Snark—
    We have hardly a minute to waste!"

"I skip forty years," said the Baker, in tears,
    "And proceed without further remark
To the day when you took me aboard of your ship
20   To help you in hunting the Snark.

"A dear uncle of mine (after whom I was named)
    Remarked, when I bade him farewell—"
"Oh, skip your dear uncle!" the Bellman exclaimed,
    As he angrily tingled his bell.

25   "He remarked to me then," said that mildest of men,
    " 'If your Snark be a Snark, that is right;
Fetch it home by all means—you may serve it with greens,
    And it's handy for striking a light.

" 'You may seek it with thimbles—and seek it with care;
30   You may hunt it with forks and hope;
You may threaten its life with a railway-share;
    You may charm it with smiles and soap—' "

("That's exactly the method," the Bellman bold
    In a hasty parenthesis cried,
35   "That's exactly the way I have always been told
    That the capture of Snarks should be tried!")

" 'But oh, beamish[3] nephew, beware of the day,
    If your Snark be a Boojum! For then
You will softly and suddenly vanish away,
40   And never be met with again!'

"It is this, it is this that oppresses my soul,
    When I think of my uncle's last words;

2. A Bellman sold muffins (carried on a tray) on city streets. He would announce his wares by "tin-gling" a bell.
3. See *Jabberwocky*, line 22 (p. 1666).

And my heart is like nothing so much as a bowl
    Brimming over with quivering curds!

45 "It is this, it is this—" "We have had that before!"
    The Bellman indignantly said.
And the Baker replied, "Let me say it once more.
    It is this, it is this that I dread!

"I engage with the Snark—every night after dark—
50   In a dreamy, delirious fight;
I serve it with greens in those shadowy scenes,
    And I use it for striking a light;

"But if ever I meet with a Boojum, that day,
    In a moment (of this I am sure),
55 I shall softly and suddenly vanish away—
    And the notion I cannot endure!"

1874–76   1876

W. S. GILBERT
1836–1911

Before becoming a full-time writer William Schwenck Gilbert had worked in the civil service and as a lawyer. In 1869, he published *Bab Ballads,* a collection of narrative verses he had contributed to a magazine called *Fun.* These ballads are indeed funny but also curiously macabre in their imperturbable accounts of disasters, cannibalism, and murders. Gilbert's skills as a writer of light verse, together with his experience in devising plays for the London theater, were responsible for his triumphant success as a librettist in a series of light operas that he composed in collaboration with the eminent musician Sir Arthur Sullivan. For twenty-five years (1871–96) Gilbert and Sullivan captivated audiences in London and New York with such delightfully entertaining productions as *H.M.S. Pinafore* and *The Mikado.* Most of these operas exhibit Gilbert's satirical flair; good-hearted fun is made of the pretentious ineffectuality of the House of Lords and of corner-cutting lawyers and politicians as well as of bumbling admirals and generals. The good-hearted quality is especially evident in the happy endings of the operas: the satire is usually blunted in the finales by a jovial-spirited acceptance of characters who in earlier scenes were exposed as foolish or inept.

    Gilbert was knighted in 1907 (some twenty-five years after Sullivan had received the same honor in token of Queen Victoria's interest in his "serious" music). He died on May 29, 1911, while attempting to save a young woman from drowning.

When I, Good Friends, Was Called to the Bar[1]

When I, good friends, was called to the bar,
    I'd an appetite fresh and hearty,
But I was, as many young barristers are,
    An impecunious party.
5   I'd a swallow-tail coat of a beautiful blue—
    A brief which I bought of a booby[2]—
A couple of shirts and a collar or two,
    And a ring that looked like a ruby!

CHORUS.   A couple of shirts, etc.

In Westminster Hall[3] I danced a dance,
10   Like a semidespondent fury;
For I thought I should never hit on a chance
    Of addressing a British jury—
But I soon got tired of third-class journeys,
    And dinners of bread and water;
15   So I fell in love with a rich attorney's
    Elderly, ugly daughter.

CHORUS.   So he fell in love, etc.

The rich attorney, he jumped with joy,
    And replied to my fond professions:
"You shall reap the reward of your pluck, my boy
20   At the Bailey and Middlesex Sessions.[4]
You'll soon get used to her looks," said he,
    "And a very nice girl you'll find her!
She may very well pass for forty-three
    In the dusk, with a light behind her!"

CHORUS.   She may very well, etc.

25   The rich attorney was good as his word;
    The briefs came trooping gaily,
And every day my voice was heard
    At the Sessions or Ancient Bailey.
All thieves who could my fees afford
30   Relied on my orations,
And many a burglar I've restored
    To his friends and his relations.

CHORUS.   And many a burglar, etc.

1. Before a breach of promise suit begins in *Trial by Jury*, the judge in this song tells the court "how I came to be a Judge."
2. A fool or dunce. "Brief": a summary of the facts of a case that is prepared (usually by a solicitor) to assist a barrister in presenting the case in court.
3. Courtrooms of the Court of Chancery in London.
4. Meetings of the county court of Middlesex (which includes London). "Bailey": the Old Bailey was a court where criminals were tried.

At length I became as rich as the Gurneys[5]—
    An incubus[6] then I thought her,
35 So I threw over that rich attorney's
    Elderly, ugly daughter.
The rich attorney my character high
    Tried vainly to disparage—
And now, if you please, I'm ready to try
40   This Breach of Promise of Marriage!

1875

If You're Anxious for to Shine in the High Aesthetic Line[1]

Am I alone,
    And unobserved? I am!
Then let me own
    I'm an aesthetic sham!

5 This air severe
    Is but a mere
        Veneer!

This cynic smile
    Is but a wile
10   Of guile!

This costume chaste
    Is but good taste
        Misplaced!

    Let me confess!
15 A languid love for lilies does *not* blight me!
Lank limbs and haggard cheeks do *not* delight me!
    I do *not* care for dirty greens
        By any means.
    I do *not* long for all one sees
20   That's Japanese.[2]
    I am *not* fond of uttering platitudes
        In stained-glass attitudes.
    In short, my medievalism's affectation,
    Born of a morbid love of admiration!

5. A wealthy banking family.
6. Oppressive demon as encountered in a nightmare.
1. Sung in *Patience* (act 1) by Reginald Bunthorne, a caricature of such poets of the "aesthetic school" as Oscar Wilde.
2. To admire Japanese vases and paintings had become a cult among aesthetes like the painter

James McNeill Whistler (1834–1903). Bunthorne's other references are probably to Pre-Raphaelite paintings such as Rossetti's portraits of languidly gazing women (sometimes in green dresses) in which the subject might be posed in a cramped posture like a figure in a stained-glass window.

25 If you're anxious for to shine in the high aesthetic line as a man of
culture rare,
You must get up all the germs of the transcendental terms, and plant
them everywhere.
You must lie upon the daisies and discourse in novel phrases of your
complicated state of mind,
The meaning doesn't matter if it's only idle chatter of a transcendental
kind.
             And everyone will say,
30   As you walk your mystic way,
"If this young man expresses himself in terms too deep for *me,*
Why, what a very singularly deep young man this deep young man
must be!"

Be eloquent in praise of the very dull old days which have long since
passed away,
And convince 'em, if you can, that the reign of good Queen Anne was
Culture's palmiest day.
35 Of course you will pooh-pooh whatever's fresh and new, and declare
it's crude and mean,
For Art stopped short in the cultivated court of the Empress Josephine.[3]
             And everyone will say,
             As you walk your mystic way,
"If that's not good enough for him which is good enough for *me,*
40 Why, what a very cultivated kind of youth this kind of youth must
be!"

Then a sentimental passion of a vegetable fashion must excite your
languid spleen,
An attachment *à la* Plato[4] for a bashful young potato, or a not-too-
French French bean!
Though the Philistines[5] may jostle, you will rank as an apostle in the
high aesthetic band,
If you walk down Piccadilly with a poppy or a lily in your medieval
hand.
45   And everyone will say,
             As you walk your flowery way,
"If he's content with a vegetable love which would certainly not suit
me,
Why, what a most particularly pure young man this pure young man
must be!"

1881

---

3. Napoleon's wife and empress of France from
1804 to 1811.
4. Platonic love denotes a spiritual relationship,
devoid of sexual desire.

5. A term used by Matthew Arnold to describe the
respectable middle classes, who predictably disapproved of the aesthetes' flamboyant behavior.

When Britain Really Ruled the Waves[1]

When Britain really ruled the waves
   (In good Queen Bess's time)—
The House of Peers made no pretense
To intellectual eminence,
5   Or scholarship sublime;
Yet Britain won her proudest bays°   *honors*
In good Queen Bess's glorious days!

CHORUS.   Yes, Britain won, etc.

When Wellington thrashed Bonaparte,
   As every child can tell,
10 The House of Peers, throughout the war,
Did nothing in particular,
   And did it very well:
Yet Britain set the world ablaze
In good King George's glorious days![2]

CHORUS.   Yes, Britain set, etc.

15 And while the House of Peers withholds
   Its legislative hand,
And noble statesmen do not itch
To interfere with matters which
   They do not understand,
20 As bright will shine Great Britain's rays
As in King George's glorious days!

CHORUS.   As bright will shine, etc.

1882

---

1. From *Iolanthe* (act 2), sung by Lord Mount-ararat, following a discussion about whether or not members of the House of Lords should obtain their titles by competitive examination instead of by inheritance. His Lordship prefaces his song by affirming "that if there is any institution in Great Britain which is not susceptible of any improvement at all, it is the House of Peers!"
2. At the time of the Battle of Waterloo (1815), Britain's king was George III (1760–1820).

Victorian Issues

EVOLUTION

One of the most dramatic controversies in the Victorian age concerned theories of evolution. This controversy exploded into prominence in 1859 when Charles Darwin's *Origin of Species* was published, but it had been rumbling for many years previously. Sir Charles Lyell's *Principles of Geology* (1830) and Robert Chambers's popular book *Vestiges of Creation* (1843–46) had already raised issues that Tennyson aired in his *In Memoriam* (1850). It was Darwin, however, with his monumental marshaling of evidence to establish his theory of natural selection, who finally brought the topic fully into the open, and the public, as well as the experts, took sides.

The opposition aroused by Darwin's treatise came from two different quarters. The first consisted of some of his fellow scientists, who affirmed that his theory was unsound. The second consisted of religious leaders who attacked his theory because it seemed to contradict a literal interpretation of the Bible. Sometimes the two kinds of opposition combined forces, as in 1860 when his scientific opponents selected Bishop Wilberforce to be their spokesman in spearheading their attack on *The Origin of Species.* In replying to such attacks, Darwin had the good fortune to be supported by two of the ablest popularizers of science in his day, T. H. Huxley and John Tyndall. Moreover, although shy by temperament, Darwin was himself (as Tyndall affirms and the selections printed here will illustrate) an exceptionally effective expositor of his own theories.

CHARLES DARWIN

Charles Darwin (1809–1882) developed an interest in geology and biology at Cambridge, where he was studying to become a clergyman. Aided by a private income, he resolved to devote the rest of his life to scientific research. The observations he made during a long voyage to the South Seas on the HMS *Beagle* (on which he served as a naturalist) led Darwin to construct hypotheses about evolution. In 1858, more than twenty years after his return to England from his voyage, he ventured to submit a paper developing his theory of the origin of species. A year later, when his theory appeared in book form, as *The Origin of Species*, Darwin emerged as a famous and controversial figure.

From The Origin of Species

Struggle for Existence

We will now discuss in a little more detail the struggle for existence. . . . Nothing is easier than to admit in words the truth of the universal struggle for life, or more difficult—at least I have found it so—than constantly to bear this conclusion in mind. Yet unless it be thoroughly engrained in the mind, the whole economy of nature, with every fact on distribution, rarity, abundance, extinction, and variation, will be dimly seen or quite misunderstood. We behold the face of nature bright with gladness, we often see superabundance of food; we do not see or we forget, that the birds which are idly singing round us mostly live on insects or seeds, and are thus constantly destroying life; or we forget how largely these songsters, or their eggs, or their nestlings, are destroyed by birds and beasts of prey; we do not always bear in mind, that, though food may be now superabundant, it is not so at all seasons of each recurring year.

THE TERM, STRUGGLE FOR EXISTENCE, USED IN A LARGE SENSE

I should premise that I use this term in a large and metaphorical sense including dependence of one being on another, and including (which is more important) not only the life of the individual, but success in leaving progeny. Two canine animals, in a time of dearth, may be truly said to struggle with each other which shall get food and live. But a plant on the edge of a desert is said to struggle for life against the drought, though more properly it should be said to be dependent on the moisture. A plant which annually produces a thousand seeds, of which only one of an average comes to maturity, may be more truly said to struggle with the plants of the same and other kinds which already clothe the ground. The mistletoe is dependent on the apple and a few other trees, but can only in a farfetched sense be said to struggle with these trees, for, if too many of these parasites grow on the same tree, it languishes and dies. But several seedling mistletoes, growing close together on the same branch, may more truly be said to struggle with each other. As the mistletoe is disseminated by birds, its existence depends on them; and it may methodically be said to struggle with other fruit-bearing plants, in tempting the birds to devour and thus disseminate its seeds. In these several senses, which pass into each other, I use for convenience' sake the general term of Struggle for Existence.

GEOMETRICAL RATIO OF INCREASE

A struggle for existence inevitably follows from the high rate at which all organic beings tend to increase. Every being, which during its natural lifetime produces several eggs or seeds, must suffer destruction during some period of its life, and during some season or occasional year, otherwise, on the principle of geometrical increase, its numbers would quickly become so inordinately great that no country could support the product. Hence, as more individuals are produced than can possibly survive, there must in every case be a struggle for existence, either one individual with another of the same species, or with the individuals of distinct species, or with the physical conditions of life. It is the doctrine of Malthus[1] applied with manifold force to the whole animal and vegetable kingdoms; for in this case there can be no artificial increase of food, and no prudential restraint from marriage.

1. Thomas Robert Malthus (1766–1834), British social theorist who argued that because the population, increasing geometrically, would grow beyond the means of subsistence, which increased arithmetically, poverty, disease, and starvation were necessary natural checks.

Although some species may be now increasing, more or less rapidly, in numbers, all cannot do so, for the world would not hold them.

There is no exception to the rule that every organic being naturally increases at so high a rate, that, if not destroyed, the earth would soon be covered by the progeny of a single pair. Even slow-breeding man has doubled in twenty-five years, and at this rate, in less than a thousand years, there would literally not be standing-room for his progeny. Linnæus[2] has calculated that if an annual plant produced only two seeds—and there is no plant so unproductive as this—and their seedlings next year produced two, and so on, then in twenty years there should be a million plants. The elephant is reckoned the slowest breeder of all known animals, and I have taken some pains to estimate its probable minimum rate of natural increase; it will be safest to assume that it begins breeding when thirty years old, and goes on breeding till ninety years old, bringing forth six young in the interval, and surviving till one hundred years old; if this be so, after a period of from 740 to 750 years there would be nearly nineteen million elephants alive, descended from the first pair.

* * *

COMPLEX RELATIONS OF ALL ANIMALS AND PLANTS TO EACH OTHER IN THE STRUGGLE FOR EXISTENCE

Many cases are on record showing how complex and unexpected are the checks and relations between organic beings, which have to struggle together in the same country.

* * *

Nearly all our orchidaceous plants absolutely require the visits of insects to remove their pollen-masses and thus to fertilise them. I find from experiments that humble-bees are almost indispensable to the fertilisation of the heartsease (Viola tricolor), for other bees do not visit this flower. I have also found that the visits of bees are necessary for the fertilisation of some kinds of clover; for instance, 20 heads of Dutch clover (Trifolium repens) yielded 2,290 seeds, but 20 other heads protected from bees produced not one. Again, 100 heads of red clover (T. pratense) produced 2,700 seeds, but the same number of protected heads produced not a single seed. Humble-bees alone visit red clover, as other bees cannot reach the nectar. It has been suggested that moths may fertilise the clovers; but I doubt whether they could do so in the case of the red clover, from their weight not being sufficient to depress the wing petals. Hence we may infer as highly probable that, if the whole genus of humble-bees became extinct or very rare in England, the heartsease and red clover would become very rare, or wholly disappear. The number of humble-bees in any district depends in a great measure upon the number of field-mice, which destroy their combs and nests; and Col. Newman, who has long attended to the habits of humble-bees, believes that "more than two-thirds of them are thus destroyed all over England." Now the number of mice is largely dependent, as every one knows, on the number of cats; and Col. Newman says, "Near villages and small towns I have found

2. Carl Linnaeus (1707–1778), Swedish naturalist who developed the binomial system for naming plants and animals.

the nests of humble-bees more numerous than elsewhere, which I attribute to the number of cats that destroy the mice." Hence it is quite credible that the presence of a feline animal in large numbers in a district might determine, through the intervention first of mice and then of bees, the frequency of certain flowers in that district!

In the case of every species, many different checks, acting at different periods of life, and during different seasons or years, probably come into play; some one check or some few being generally the most potent; but all will concur in determining the average number or even the existence of the species. In some cases it can be shown that widely-different checks act on the same species in different districts. When we look at the plants and bushes clothing an entangled bank, we are tempted to attribute their proportional numbers and kinds to what we call chance. But how false a view is this! Every one has heard that when an American forest is cut down a very different vegetation springs up; but it has been observed that ancient Indian ruins in the Southern United States, which must formerly have been cleared of trees, now display the same beautiful diversity and proportion of kinds as in the surrounding virgin forest. What a struggle must have gone on during long centuries between the several kinds of trees each annually scattering its seeds by the thousand; what war between insect and insect—between insects, snails, and other animals with birds and beasts of prey—all striving to increase, all feeding on each other, or on the trees, their seeds and seedlings, or on the other plants which first clothed the ground and thus checked the growth of the trees! Throw up a handful of feathers, and all fall to the ground according to definite laws; but how simple is the problem where each shall fall compared to that of the action and reaction of the innumerable plants and animals which have determined, in the course of centuries, the proportional numbers and kinds of trees now growing on the old Indian ruins!

Recapitulation and Conclusion[3]

I see no good reason why the views given in this volume should shock the religious feelings of any one. It is satisfactory, as showing how transient such impressions are, to remember that the greatest discovery ever made by man, namely, the law of the attraction of gravity, was also attacked by Leibnitz,[4] "as subversive of natural, and inferentially of revealed, religion." A celebrated author and divine has written to me that "he has gradually learnt to see that it is just as noble a conception of the Deity to believe that He created a few original forms capable of self-development into other and needful forms, as to believe that He required a fresh act of creation to supply the voids caused by the action of His laws."

Why, it may be asked, until recently did nearly all the most eminent living naturalists and geologists disbelieve in the mutability of species? It cannot be asserted that organic beings in a state of nature are subject to no variation; it cannot be proved that the amount of variation in the course of long ages is a limited quality; no clear distinction has been, or can be, drawn between species and well-marked varieties. It cannot be maintained that species when

3. From chap. 15.
4. Gottfried Wilhelm Leibniz (1646–1716),

German philosopher and mathematician, contemporary of Isaac Newton.

intercrossed are invariably sterile, and varieties invariably fertile; or that sterility is a special endowment and sign of creation. The belief that species were immutable productions was almost unavoidable as long as the history of the world was thought to be of short duration; and now that we have acquired some idea of the lapse of time, we are too apt to assume, without proof, that the geological record is so perfect that it would have afforded us plain evidence of the mutation of species, if they had undergone mutation.

But the chief cause of our natural unwillingness to admit that one species has given birth to clear and distinct species, is that we are always slow in admitting great changes of which we do not see the steps. The difficulty is the same as that felt by so many geologists, when Lyell[5] first insisted that long lines of inland cliffs had been formed, and great valleys excavated, by the agencies which we see still at work. The mind cannot possibly grasp the full meaning of the term of even a million years; it cannot add up and perceive the full effects of many slight variations, accumulated during an almost infinite number of generations.

Although I am fully convinced of the truth of the views given in this volume under the form of an abstract, I by no means expect to convince experienced naturalists whose minds are stocked with a multitude of facts all viewed, during a long course of years, from a point of view directly opposite to mine. It is so easy to hide our ignorance under such expressions as the "plan of creation," "unity of design," &c., and to think that we give an explanation when we only re-state a fact. Any one whose disposition leads him to attach more weight to unexplained difficulties than to the explanation of a certain number of facts will certainly reject the theory. A few naturalists, endowed with much flexibility of mind, and who have already begun to doubt the immutability of species, may be influenced by this volume; but I look with confidence to the future,—to young and rising naturalists, who will be able to view both sides of the question with impartiality. Whoever is led to believe that species are mutable will do good service by conscientiously expressing his conviction; for thus only can the load of prejudice by which this subject is overwhelmed be removed.

* * *

It may be asked how far I extend the doctrine of the modification of species. The question is difficult to answer, because the more distinct the forms are which we consider, by so much the arguments in favour of community of descent become fewer in number and less in force. But some arguments of the greatest weight extend very far. All the members of whole classes are connected together by a chain of affinities, and all can be classed on the same principle, in groups subordinate to groups. Fossil remains sometimes tend to fill up very wide intervals between existing orders.

Organs in a rudimentary condition plainly show that an early progenitor had the organ in a fully developed condition; and this in some cases implies an enormous amount of modification in the descendants. Throughout whole classes various structures are formed on the same pattern, and at a very early

5. Charles Lyell (1797–1875), geologist whose book *Principles of Geology* (1830–33) was important in dissociating geological theory from the Bible and in establishing nature as the record of the earth's history, which he saw as a record of lengthy and gradual change rather than swift catastrophic events.

age the embryos closely resemble each other. Therefore I cannot doubt that the theory of descent with modification embraces all the members of the same great class or kingdom. I believe that animals are descended from at most only four or five progenitors, and plants from an equal or lesser number.

Analogy would lead me one step farther, namely, to the belief that all animals and plants are descended from some one prototype. But analogy may be a deceitful guide. Nevertheless all living things have much in common, in their chemical composition, their cellular structure, their laws of growth, and their liability to injurious influences. We see this even in so trifling a fact as that the same poison often similarly affects plants and animals; or that the poison secreted by the gall-fly produces monstrous growths on the wild rose or oak-tree. With all organic beings excepting perhaps some of the very lowest, sexual production seems to be essentially similar. With all, as far as is at present known the germinal vesicle is the same; so that all organisms start from a common origin. If we look even to the two main divisions—namely, to the animal and vegetable kingdoms—certain low forms are so far intermediate in character that naturalists have disputed to which kingdom they should be referred. As Professor Asa Gray[6] has remarked, "the spores and other reproductive bodies of many of the lower algae may claim to have first a characteristically animal, and then an unequivocally vegetable existence." Therefore, on the principle of natural selection with divergence of character, it does not seem incredible that, from such low and intermediate form, both animals and plants may have been developed; and, if we admit this, we must likewise admit that all the organic beings which have ever lived on this earth may be descended from some one primordial form.

* * *

When we feel assured that all the individuals of the same species, and all the closely allied species of most genera, have within a not very remote period descended from one parent, and have migrated from some one birth-place; and when we better know the many means of migration, then, by the light which geology now throws, and will continue to throw, on former changes of climate and of the level of the land, we shall surely be enabled to trace in an admirable manner the former migrations of the inhabitants of the whole world. Even at present, by comparing the differences between the inhabitants of the sea on the opposite sides of a continent, and the nature of the various inhabitants on that continent, in relation to their apparent means of immigration, some light can be thrown on ancient geography.

The noble science of Geology loses glory from the extreme imperfection of the record. The crust of the earth with its imbedded remains must not be looked at as a well-filled museum, but as a poor collection made at hazard and at rare intervals. The accumulation of each great fossiliferous formation will be recognised as having depended on an unusual concurrence of favourable circumstances, and the blank intervals between the successive stages as having been of vast duration. But we shall be able to gauge with some security the duration of these intervals by a comparison of the preceding and succeeding organic forms. We must be cautious in attempting to correlate

6. American botanist (1810–1888).

as strictly contemporaneous two formations, which do not include many identical species, by the general succession of the forms of life. As species are produced and exterminated by slowly acting and still existing causes, and not by miraculous acts of creation; and as the most important of all causes of organic change is one which is almost independent of altered and perhaps suddenly altered physical conditions, namely, the mutual relation of organism to organism,—the improvement of one organism entailing the improvement or the extermination of others; it follows, that the amount of organic change in the fossils of consecutive formations probably serves as a fair measure of the relative though not actual lapse of time. A number of species, however, keeping in a body might remain for a long period unchanged, whilst within the same period several of these species by migrating into new countries and coming into competition with foreign associates, might become modified; so that we must not overrate the accuracy of organic change as a measure of time.

In the future I see open fields for far more important researches. Psychology will be securely based on the foundation already well laid by Mr. Herbert Spencer,[7] that of the necessary acquirement of each mental power and capacity by gradation. Much light will be thrown on the origin of man and his history.

Authors of the highest eminence seem to be fully satisfied with the view that each species has been independently created. To my mind it accords better with what we know of the laws impressed on matter by the Creator, that the production and extinction of the past and present inhabitants of the world should have been due to secondary causes, like those determining the birth and death of the individual. When I view all beings not as special creations, but as the lineal descendants of some few beings which lived long before the first bed of the Cambrian system was deposited, they seem to me to become ennobled. Judging from the past, we may safely infer that not one living species will transmit its unaltered likeness to a distant futurity. And of the species now living very few will transmit progeny of any kind to a far distant futurity; for the manner in which all organic beings are grouped, shows that the greater number of species in each genus, and all the species in many genera, have left no descendants, but have become utterly extinct. We can so far take a prophetic glance into futurity as to foretell that it will be the common and widely-spread species, belonging to the larger and dominant groups within each class, which will ultimately prevail and procreate new and dominant species. As all the living forms of life are the lineal descendants of those which lived long before the Cambrian epoch, we may feel certain that the ordinary succession by generation has never once been broken, and that no cataclysm has desolated the whole world. Hence we may look with some confidence to a secure future of great length. And as natural selection works solely by and for the good of each being, all corporeal and mental endowments will tend to progress towards perfection.

It is interesting to contemplate a tangled bank, clothed with many plants of many kinds, with birds singing on the bushes, with various insects flitting about, and with worms crawling through the damp earth, and to reflect that these elaborately constructed forms, so different from each other, and

7. Social theorist (1820–1903), who developed the concept of social Darwinism.

dependent upon each other in so complex a manner, have all been produced by laws acting around us. These laws, taken in the largest sense, being Growth with Reproduction; Inheritance which is almost implied by reproduction; Variability from the indirect and direct action of the conditions of life, and from use and disuse: a Ratio of Increase so high as to lead to a Struggle for Life, and as a consequence to Natural Selection, entailing Divergence of Character and the Extinction of less-improved forms. Thus, from the war of nature, from famine and death, the most exalted object which we are capable of conceiving, namely, the production of the higher animals, directly follows. There is grandeur in this view of life, with its several powers, having been originally breathed by the Creator into a few forms or into one; and that, whilst this planet has gone cycling on according to the fixed law of gravity, from so simple a beginning endless forms most beautiful and most wonderful have been, and are being evolved.

1859

CHARLES DARWIN

After he published *The Origin of Species*, Darwin wrote several treatises, some of which develop and clarify the theory of *The Origin of Species*. One of these works, *The Descent of Man* (1871), was especially provocative in its stress on the similarities between humans and animals and in its naturalistic explanations of the beautiful colorings of birds, insects, and flowers.

From The Descent of Man

[NATURAL SELECTION AND SEXUAL SELECTION][1]

A brief summary will here be sufficient to recall to the reader's mind the more salient points in this work. Many of the views which have been advanced are highly speculative, and some no doubt will prove erroneous; but I have in every case given the reasons which have led me to one view rather than to another. It seemed worth while to try how far the principle of evolution would throw light on some of the more complex problems in the natural history of man. False facts are highly injurious to the progress of science, for they often long endure; but false views, if supported by some evidence, do little harm, as everyone takes a salutary pleasure in proving their falseness; and when this is done, one path towards error is closed and the road to truth is often at the same time opened.

The main conclusion arrived at in this work, and now held by many naturalists who are well competent to form a sound judgment, is that man is descended from some less highly organized form. The grounds upon which

1. From chap. 21.

this conclusion rests will never be shaken, for the close similarity between man and the lower animals in embryonic development, as well as in innumerable points of structure and constitution, both of high and of the most trifling importance—the rudiments which he retains, and the abnormal reversions to which he is occasionally liable—are facts which cannot be disputed. They have long been known, but until recently they told us nothing with respect to the origin of man. Now when viewed by the light of our knowledge of the whole organic world, their meaning is unmistakable. The great principle of evolution stands up clear and firm, when these groups of facts are considered in connection with others, such as the mutual affinities of the members of the same group, their geographical distribution in past and present times, and their geological succession. It is incredible that all these facts should speak falsely. He who is not content to look, like a savage, at the phenomena of nature as disconnected cannot any longer believe that man is the work of a separate act of creation. He will be forced to admit that the close resemblance of the embryo of man to that, for instance, of a dog—the construction of his skull, limbs, and whole frame, independently of the uses to which the parts may be put, on the same plan with that of other mammals—the occasional reappearance of various structures, for instance of several distinct muscles, which man does not normally possess, but which are common to the Quadrumana[2]—and a crowd of analogous facts—all point in the plainest manner to the conclusion that man is the codescendant with other mammals of a common progenitor.

* * *

By considering the embryological structure of man—the homologies which he presents with the lower animals, the rudiments which he retains, and the reversions to which he is liable—we can partly recall in imagination the former condition of our early progenitors; and can approximately place them in their proper position in the zoological series. We thus learn that man is descended from a hairy quadruped, furnished with a tail and pointed ears, probably arboreal in its habits, and an inhabitant of the Old World. This creature, if its whole structure had been examined by a naturalist, would have been classed amongst the Quadrumana, as surely as would the common and still more ancient progenitor of the Old and New World monkeys. The Quadrumana and all the higher mammals are probably derived from an ancient marsupial animal, and this through a long line of diversified forms, either from some reptile-like or some amphibianlike creature, and this again from some fishlike animal. In the dim obscurity of the past we can see that the early progenitor of all the Vertebrata must have been an aquatic animal, provided with branchae, with the two sexes united in the same individual, and with the most important organs of the body (such as the brain and heart) imperfectly developed. This animal seems to have been more like the larvae of our existing marine ascidians[3] than any other known form.

* * *

2. Animals, such as monkeys, whose hind feet and forefeet can be used as hands—hence "four-handed."

3. Part of a group of marine animals called tunicata, or popularly "sea squirts," sometimes assumed to be ancestors of the vertebrate animals.

Sexual selection has been treated at great length in these volumes; for, as I have attempted to show, it has played an important part in the history of the organic world.

* * *

The belief in the power of sexual selection rests chiefly on the following considerations. The characters which we have the best reason for supposing to have been thus acquired are confined to one sex; and this alone renders it probable that they are in some way connected with the act of reproduction. These characters in innumerable instances are fully developed only at maturity; and often during only a part of the year, which is always the breeding season. The males (passing over a few exceptional cases) are the most active in courtship; they are the best armed, and are rendered the most attractive in various ways. It is to be especially observed that the males display their attractions with elaborate care in the presence of the females; and that they rarely or never display them excepting during the season of love. It is incredible that all this display should be purposeless. Lastly we have distinct evidence with some quadrupeds and birds that the individuals of the one sex are capable of feeling a strong antipathy or preference for certain individuals of the opposite sex.

Bearing these facts in mind, and not forgetting the marked results of man's unconscious selection, it seems to me almost certain that if the individuals of one sex were during a long series of generations to prefer pairing with certain individuals of the other sex, characterized in some peculiar manner, the offspring would slowly but surely become modified in this same manner. I have not attempted to conceal that, excepting when the males are more numerous than the females, or when polygamy prevails, it is doubtful how the more attractive males succeed in leaving a larger number of offspring to inherit their superiority in ornaments or other charms than the less attractive males; but I have shown that this would probably follow from the females—especially the more vigorous females which would be the first to breed, preferring not only the more attractive but at the same time the more vigorous and victorious males.

Although we have some positive evidence that birds appreciate bright and beautiful objects, as with the bowerbirds of Australia, and although they certainly appreciate the power of song, yet I fully admit that it is an astonishing fact that the females of many birds and some mammals should be endowed with sufficient taste for what has apparently been effected through sexual selection; and this is even more astonishing in the case of reptiles, fish, and insects. But we really know very little about the minds of the lower animals. It cannot be supposed that male birds of paradise or peacocks, for instance, should take so much pains in erecting, spreading, and vibrating their beautiful plumes before the females for no purpose. We should remember the fact given on excellent authority in a former chapter, namely that several peahens, when debarred from an admired male, remained widows during a whole season rather than pair with another bird.

Nevertheless I know of no fact in natural history more wonderful than that the female argus pheasant should be able to appreciate the exquisite shading of the ball-and-socket ornaments and the elegant patterns on the wing feathers of the male. He who thinks that the male was created as he now exists must admit that the great plumes, which prevent the wings from being used for flight, and which, as well as the primary feathers, are displayed in a manner quite peculiar to this one species during the act of courtship, and at no other time, were given to him as an ornament. If so, he must likewise admit that the female was created and endowed with the capacity of appreciating such ornaments. I differ only in the conviction that the male argus pheasant acquired his beauty gradually, through the females having preferred during many generations the more highly ornamented males; the aesthetic capacity of the females having been advanced through exercise or habit in the same manner as our own taste is gradually improved. In the male, through the fortunate chance of a few feathers not having been modified, we can distinctly see how simple spots with a little fulvous[4] shading on one side might have been developed by small and graduated steps into the wonderful ball-and-socket ornaments; and it is probable that they were actually thus developed.

* * *

He who admits the principle of sexual selection will be led to the remarkable conclusion that the cerebral system not only regulates most of the existing functions of the body, but has indirectly influenced the progressive development of various bodily structures and of certain mental qualities. Courage, pugnacity, perseverance, strength and size of body, weapons of all kinds, musical organs, both vocal and instrumental, bright colors, stripes and marks, and ornamental appendages have all been indirectly gained by the one sex or the other, through the influence of love and jealousy, through the appreciation of the beautiful in sound, color or form, and through the exertion of a choice; and these powers of the mind manifestly depend on the development of the cerebral system.

* * *

The main conclusion arrived at in this work, namely that man is descended from some lowly-organized form, will, I regret to think, be highly distasteful to many persons. But there can hardly be a doubt that we are descended from barbarians. The astonishment which I felt on first seeing a party of Fuegians[5] on a wild and broken shore will never be forgotten by me, for the reflection at once rushed into my mind—such were our ancestors. These men were absolutely naked and bedaubed with paint, their long hair was tangled, their mouths frothed with excitement, and their expression was wild, startled, and distrustful. They possessed hardly any arts, and like wild animals lived on what they could catch; they had no government, and were merciless to everyone not of their own small tribe. He who has seen a savage in his native land will not feel much shame, if forced to acknowledge that the blood of some more humble creature flows in his veins. For my own part I would as soon be descended from that heroic little monkey, who braved his dreaded enemy in order to save the life of his keeper; or from that old baboon, who, descending from the mountains, carried away in triumph his

4. Dull yellow.
5. Natives inhabiting the islands off the southern tip of South America, Tierra del Fuego, which Dar- win had visited in 1832. See his *Voyage of the Beagle*, chap. 10.

young comrade from a crowd of astonished dogs[6]—as from a savage who delights to torture his enemies, offers up bloody sacrifices, practices infanticide without remorse, treats his wives like slaves, knows no decency, and is haunted by the grossest superstitions.

Man may be excused for feeling some pride at having risen, though not through his own exertions, to the very summit of the organic scale; and the fact of his having thus risen, instead of having been aboriginally placed there, may give him hopes for a still higher destiny in the distant future. But we are not here concerned with hopes or fears, only with the truth as far as our reason allows us to discover it. I have given the evidence to the best of my ability; and we must acknowledge, as it seems to me, that man with all his noble qualities, with sympathy which feels for the most debased, with benevolence which extends not only to other men but to the humblest living creature, with his godlike intellect which has penetrated into the movements and constitution of the solar system—with all these exalted powers—Man still bears in his bodily frame the indelible stamp of his lowly origin.

1871

6. Incidents described in chap. 4 to demonstrate that animals may be endowed with a moral sense.

LEONARD HUXLEY

At meetings of the British Association for the Advancement of Science, the reading of a paper is followed by a discussion. In 1860, at Oxford, this discussion developed into a debate between Thomas Henry Huxley (1825–1895), a defender of Darwin's theories, and Bishop Samuel Wilberforce (1805–1873). Although he had majored in mathematics as an undergraduate, Wilberforce could hardly lay claim to be a scientist. He was willing, nevertheless, to serve as a spokesperson for those scientists who disagreed with *The Origin of Species,* and he reportedly came to the meeting ready to "smash Darwin." The bishop's principal qualifications for this role were his great powers as a smoothly persuasive orator (he was commonly known by his detractors as "Soapy Sam"), but he met more than his match in Huxley.

Because no complete transcript of this celebrated debate was made at the time, Huxley's son Leonard (1860–1933), in writing his father's biography, had to reconstruct the scene by combining quotations from reports made by magazine writers and other witnesses. The account given here is from chapter 14.

From The Life and Letters
of Thomas Henry Huxley

[THE HUXLEY-WILBERFORCE DEBATE AT OXFORD]

The famous Oxford Meeting of 1860 was of no small importance in Huxley's career. It was not merely that he helped to save a great cause from being stifled under misrepresentation and ridicule—that he helped to extort for it a fair hearing; it was now that he first made himself known in popular estimation as a dangerous adversary in debate—a personal force in the world of science which could not be neglected. From this moment he entered the front fighting line in the most exposed quarter of the field. * * *

It was the merest chance, as I have already said, that Huxley attended the meeting of the section that morning. Dr. Draper of New York was to read a paper on the *Intellectual Development of Europe considered with reference to the views of Mr. Darwin.* "I can still hear," writes one who was present, "the American accents of Dr. Draper's opening address when he asked 'Air we a fortuitous concourse of atoms?' " However, it was not to hear him, but the eloquence of the Bishop, that the members of the Association crowded in such numbers into the Lecture Room of the Museum, that this, the appointed meeting place of the section, had to be abandoned for the long west room, since cut in two by a partition for the purposes of the library. It was not term time, nor were the general public admitted; nevertheless the room was crowded to suffocation long before the protagonists appeared on the scene, 700 persons or more managing to find places. The very windows by which the room was lighted down the length of its west side were packed with ladies, whose white handkerchiefs, waving and fluttering in the air at the end of the Bishop's speech, were an unforgettable factor in the acclamation of the crowd.

On the east side between the two doors was the platform. Professor Henslow, the President of the section, took his seat in the center; upon his right was the Bishop, and beyond him again Dr. Draper; on his extreme left was Mr. Dingle, a clergyman from Lanchester, near Durham, with Sir J. Hooker and Sir J. Lubbock in front of him, and nearer the center, Professor Beale of King's College, London, and Huxley.

The clergy, who shouted lustily for the Bishop, were massed in the middle of the room; behind them in the northwest corner a knot of undergraduates (one of these was T. H. Green, who listened but took no part in the cheering) had gathered together beside Professor Brodie, ready to lift their voices, poor minority though they were, for the opposite party. Close to them stood one of the few men among the audience already in Holy orders, who joined in— and indeed led—the cheers for the Darwinians.

So "Dr. Draper droned out his paper, turning first to the right hand and then to the left, of course bringing in a reference to the *Origin of Species* which set the ball rolling."

An hour or more that paper lasted, and then discussion began. The President "wisely announced *in limine*[1] that none who had not valid arguments to bring forward on one side or the other would be allowed to address the meeting; a caution that proved necessary, for no fewer than four combatants had their utterances burked by him, because of their indulgence in vague declamation."

> First spoke (writes Professor Farrar) a layman from Brompton, who gave his name as being one of the Committee of the (newly formed) Economic section of the Association. He, in a stentorian voice, let off his theological venom. Then jumped up Richard Greswell with a thin voice, saying much the same, but speaking as a scholar; but we did not merely want any theological discussion, so we shouted them down. Then

1. As a starting point (Latin).

a Mr. Dingle got up and tried to show that Darwin would have done much better if he had taken him into consultation. He used the blackboard and began a mathematical demonstration on the question—"Let this point A be man, and let that point B be the mawnkey." He got no further; he was shouted down with cries of "mawnkey." None of these had spoken more than three minutes. It was when these were shouted down that Henslow said he must demand that the discussion should rest on *scientific* grounds only.

Then there were calls for the Bishop, but he rose and said he understood his friend Professor Beale had something to say first. Beale, who was an excellent histologist,[2] spoke to the effect that the new theory ought to meet with fair discussion, but added, with great modesty, that he himself had not sufficient knowledge to discuss the subject adequately. Then the Bishop spoke the speech that you know, and the question about his mother being an ape, or his grandmother.

From the scientific point of view, the speech was of small value. It was evident from his mode of handling the subject that he had been "crammed up to the throat," and knew nothing at first hand; he used no argument beyond those to be found in his *Quarterly* article, which appeared a few days later, and is now admitted to have been inspired by Owen.[3] "He ridiculed Darwin badly and Huxley savagely; but," confesses one of his strongest opponents, "all in such dulcet tones, so persuasive a manner, and in such well turned periods, that I who had been inclined to blame the President for allowing a discussion that could serve no scientific purpose, now forgave him from the bottom of my heart."

The Bishop spoke thus "for full half an hour with inimitable spirit, emptiness and unfairness." "In a light, scoffing tone, florid and fluent, he assured us there was nothing in the idea of evolution; rock pigeons were what rock pigeons had always been. Then, turning to his antagonist with a smiling insolence, he begged to know, was it through his grandfather or his grandmother that he claimed his descent from a monkey?"

This was the fatal mistake of his speech. Huxley instantly grasped the tactical advantage which the descent to personalities gave him. He turned to Sir Benjamin Brodie, who was sitting beside him, and emphatically striking his hand upon his knee, exclaimed, "The Lord hath delivered him into mine hands." The bearing of the exclamation did not dawn upon Sir Benjamin until after Huxley had completed his "forcible and eloquent" answer to the scientific part of the Bishop's argument, and proceeded to make his famous retort.

On this (continues the writer in *Macmillan's Magazine*) Mr. Huxley slowly and deliberately arose. A slight tall figure, stern and pale, very quiet and very grave, he stood before us and spoke those tremendous words—words which no one seems sure of now, nor, I think, could remember just after they were spoken, for their meaning took away our breath, though it left us in no doubt as to what it was. He was not

---

2. A biologist specializing in the study of the minute structure of the tissues of plants and animals.
3. Sir Richard Owen (1804–1892), a leading zoologist and paleontologist who was opposed to Darwin's theories.

ashamed to have a monkey for his ancestor; but he would be ashamed to be connected with a man who used great gifts to obscure the truth. No one doubted his meaning, and the effect was tremendous. One lady fainted and had to be carried out; I, for one, jumped out of my seat.

The fullest and probably most accurate account of these concluding words is the following, from a letter of the late John Richard Green, then an undergraduate, to his friend, afterwards Professor Boyd Dawkins:

> I asserted—and I repeat—that a man has no reason to be ashamed of having an ape for his grandfather. If there were an ancestor whom I should feel shame in recalling it would rather be a man—a man of restless and versatile intellect—who, not content with an equivocal success in his own sphere of activity, plunges into scientific questions with which he has no real acquaintance, only to obscure them by an aimless rhetoric, and distract the attention of his hearers from the real point at issue by eloquent digressions and skilled appeals to religious prejudice.

The result of this encounter, though a check to the other side, cannot, of course, be represented as an immediate and complete triumph for evolutionary doctrine. This was precluded by the character and temper of the audience, most of whom were less capable of being convinced by the arguments than shocked by the boldness of the retort, although, being gentlefolk, as Professor Farrar remarks, they were disposed to admit on reflection that the Bishop had erred on the score of taste and good manners. Nevertheless, it was a noticeable feature of the occasion, Sir M. Foster tells me, that when Huxley rose he was received coldly, just a cheer of encouragement from his friends, the audience as a whole not joining in it. But as he made his points the applause grew and widened, until, when he sat down, the cheering was not very much less than that given to the Bishop. To that extent he carried an unwilling audience with him by the force of his speech. The debate on the ape question, however, was continued elsewhere during the next two years, and the evidence was completed by the unanswerable demonstrations of Sir W. H. Flower at the Cambridge meeting of the Association in 1862.

The importance of the Oxford meeting lay in the open resistance that was made to authority, at a moment when even a drawn battle was hardly less effectual than acknowledged victory. Instead of being crushed under ridicule, the new theories secured a hearing, all the wider, indeed, for the startling nature of their defense.

1901

SIR EDMUND GOSSE

Philip Henry Gosse (1810–1888) was a zoologist of some repute and also an ardent adherent of a strict Protestant sect, the Plymouth Brethren. To reconcile his scientific knowledge with his fundamentalist position in religion, Gosse published a book called *Omphalos,* which pleased no one. His dilemma is described by his son, the literary critic Sir Edmund Gosse (1849–1928), in an autobiography published in 1907. This selection is from chapter 5.

From Father and Son

[THE DILEMMA OF THE FUNDAMENTALIST AND SCIENTIST]

So, through my Father's brain, in that year of scientific crisis, 1857, there rushed two kinds of thought, each absorbing, each convincing, yet totally irreconcilable. There is a peculiar agony in the paradox that truth has two forms, each of them indisputable, yet each antagonistic to the other. It was this discovery, that there were two theories of physical life, each of which was true, but the truth of each incompatible with the truth of the other, which shook the spirit of my Father with perturbation. It was not, really, a paradox, it was a fallacy, if he could only have known it, but he allowed the turbid volume of superstition to drown the delicate stream of reason. He took one step in the service of truth, and then he drew back in an agony, and accepted the servitude of error.

This was the great moment in the history of thought when the theory of the mutability of species was preparing to throw a flood of light upon all departments of human speculation and action. It was becoming necessary to stand emphatically in one army or the other. Lyell was surrounding himself with disciples, who were making strides in the direction of discovery. Darwin had long been collecting facts with regard to the variation of animals and plants. Hooker and Wallace, Asa Gray and even Agassiz, each in his own sphere, were coming closer and closer to a perception of that secret which was first to reveal itself clearly to the patient and humble genius of Darwin. In the year before, in 1856, Darwin, under pressure from Lyell, had begun that modest statement of the new revelation, that "abstract of an essay," which developed so mightily into *The Origin of Species.* Wollaston's *Variation of Species* had just appeared, and had been a nine days' wonder in the wilderness.

On the other side, the reactionaries, although never dreaming of the fate which hung over them, had not been idle. In 1857 the astounding question had for the first time been propounded with contumely, "What, then, did we come from orangoutang?" The famous *Vestiges of Creation* had been supplying a sugar-and-water panacea for those who could not escape from the trend of evidence, and who yet clung to revelation. Owen was encouraging reaction by resisting, with all the strength of his prestige, the theory of the mutability of species.

In this period of intellectual ferment, as when a great political revolution is being planned, many possible adherents were confidentially tested with hints and encouraged to reveal their bias in a whisper. It was the notion of Lyell, himself a great mover of men, that, before the doctrine of natural selection was given to a world which would be sure to lift up at it a howl of execration, a certain bodyguard of sound and experienced naturalists, expert in the description of species, should be privately made aware of its tenor. Among those who were thus initiated, or approached with a view towards possible illumination, was my Father. He was spoken to by Hooker, and later on by Darwin, after meetings of the Royal Society in the summer of 1857.

My Father's attitude towards the theory of natural selection was critical in his career, and oddly enough, it exercised an immense influence on my own experience as a child. Let it be admitted at once, mournful as the admission is, that every instinct in his intelligence went out at first to greet the new light. It had hardly done so, when a recollection of the opening chapter of Genesis checked it at the outset. He consulted with Carpenter, a great investigator, but one who was fully as incapable as himself of remodeling his ideas with regard to the old, accepted hypotheses. They both determined, on various grounds, to have nothing to do with the terrible theory, but to hold steadily to the law of the fixity of species. * * *

My Father had never admired Sir Charles Lyell. I think that the famous Lord Chancellor manner of the geologist intimidated him, and we undervalue the intelligence of those whose conversation puts us at a disadvantage. For Darwin and Hooker, on the other hand, he had a profound esteem, and I know not whether this had anything to do with the fact that he chose, for his impetuous experiment in reaction, the field of geology, rather than that of zoology or botany. Lyell had been threatening to publish a book on the geological history of Man, which was to be a bombshell flung into the camp of the catastrophists. My Father, after long reflection, prepared a theory of his own, which, as he fondly hoped, would take the wind out of Lyell's sails, and justify geology to godly readers of Genesis. It was, very briefly, that there had been no gradual modification of the surface of the earth, or slow development of organic forms, but that when the catastrophic act of creation took place, the world presented, instantly, the structural appearance of a planet on which life had long existed.

The theory, coarsely enough, and to my Father's great indignation, was defined by a hasty press as being this—that God hid the fossils in the rocks in order to tempt geologists into infidelity. In truth, it was the logical and inevitable conclusion of accepting, literally, the doctrine of a sudden act of creation; it emphasized the fact that any breach in the circular course of nature could be conceived only on the supposition that the object created bore false witness to past processes, which had never taken place.

Never was a book cast upon the waters with greater anticipations of success than was this curious, this obstinate, this fanatical volume. My Father lived in a fever of suspense, waiting for the tremendous issue. This *Omphalos* of his, he thought, was to bring all the turmoil of scientific speculation to a close, fling geology into the arms of Scripture, and make the lion eat grass with the lamb. It was not surprising, he admitted, that there had been experienced an ever-increasing discord between the facts which geology brings to light and the direct statements of the early chapters of Genesis. Nobody was to blame for that. My Father, and my Father alone, possessed the secret of the enigma; he alone held the key which could smoothly open the lock of geological mystery. He offered it, with a glowing gesture, to atheists and Christians alike. This was to be the universal panacea; this the system of intellectual therapeutics which could not but heal all the maladies of the age. But, alas! atheists and Christians alike looked at it, and laughed, and threw it away.

In the course of that dismal winter, as the post began to bring in private letters, few and chilly, and public reviews, many and scornful, my Father looked in vain for the approval of the churches, and in vain for the acquiescence of the scientific societies, and in vain for the gratitude of those "thousands of thinking persons," which he had rashly assured himself of receiving. As his reconciliation of Scripture statements and geological deductions was welcomed nowhere; as Darwin continued silent, and the youthful Huxley was scornful, and even Charles Kingsley,[1] from whom my Father had expected the most instant appreciation, wrote that he could not "give up the painful and slow conclusion of five and twenty years' study of geology, and believe that God has written on the rocks one enormous and superfluous lie"—as all this happened or failed to happen, a gloom, cold and dismal, descended upon our morning teacups. * * *

1907

1. Clergyman and novelist (1819–1875).

INDUSTRIALISM: PROGRESS OR DECLINE?

In 1835, the French statesman and author Alexis de Tocqueville wrote of Manchester: "From this foul drain, the greatest stream of human industry flows out to fertilize the whole world. From this filthy sewer pure gold flows. Here humanity attains its most complete development and its most brutish, here civilization works its miracles and civilized man is turned almost into a savage." De Tocqueville's graphic sense of the wealth and the wretchedness that the Industrial Revolution created epitomized contemporary responses to the way in which manufacturing had transformed nineteenth-century England. Victorians debated whether the machine age was a blessing or a curse, whether the middle-class economic system was making humanity happier or more miserable. Did the Industrial Revolution represent progress, and how, in fact, was progress to be defined?

The Industrial Revolution began with a set of inventions for spinning and weaving developed in England in the eighteenth century. At first this new machinery was operated by workers in their homes, but in the 1780s the introduction of the steam engine to drive these new machines led manufacturers to install them in large buildings called at first mills and later factories. Mill towns, producing cotton cloth for the world's markets, quickly grew in central and northern England; the population of the city of Manchester, for example, increased by ten times in the years between 1760 and 1830. The development of the railways in the 1830s initiated a new phase in industrial development, marked by an enormous expansion in the production of iron and coal. By the beginning of the Victorian period, the Industrial Revolution had created profound economic and social changes. Hundreds of thousands of workers had migrated to industrial towns, where they lived in horribly crowded, unsanitary housing and worked very long hours—fourteen a day or even more—at very low wages. Employers often preferred to hire women and children, who worked for even less than men.

Moved by the terrible suffering of the workers, which was intensified by a severe depression in the early 1840s, writers and legislators drew increasingly urgent attention to the condition of the working class. A number of parliamentary committees and commissions in the 1830s and 1840s introduced testimony about working conditions in mines and factories that led to the beginning of government regulation and inspection, particularly of the working conditions of women and children. Other eye-witness accounts created a growing consciousness of the plight of the workers. In *The Condition of the Working Class* (1845), Friedrich Engels described the conclusions he drew in the twenty months he spent observing industrial conditions in Manchester. In a series of interviews written for the *Morning Chronicle* (1849–52), later published as *London Labour and the London Poor* (1861–62), the journalist Henry Mayhew created a portrait of working London by collecting scores of interviews in the voices of the workers. Novels began to appear, such as Elizabeth Gaskell's *Mary Barton* (1848) and *North and South* (1855) and Charles Dickens's *Hard Times* (1854), portraying the painful consequences of industrialism.

The terrible living and working conditions of industrial laborers led a number of writers to see the Industrial Revolution as an appalling retrogression. Carlyle and Ruskin both lamented the changed conditions of labor, the loss of craftsmanship and individual creativity, and the disappearance of what Karl Marx called the "feudal, patriarchal, idyllic relations" between employer and employee that they believed had existed in earlier economies. They criticized industrial manufacture not only for the misery of the conditions it created but also for its regimentation of minds and hearts as well as bodies and resources. In works like *Past and Present* and *Unto This Last*, Carlyle and Ruskin advocated a nostalgic and conservative ideal, in which employers and workers returned to a medieval relationship to craft and to authority and responsibility. Other writers drew more radical conclusions. William Morris's perception of the workers' plight led him to socialism, though a socialism with a medieval ideal, and Marx, in collaboration with Engels, based *The Communist Manifesto* of 1848 in part on Engels's observation of Manchester in *The Condition of the Working Class*. All of these writers seem very distant from the satisfaction the historian Thomas Babington Macaulay voiced in the progress industrialism had enabled.

It is instructive to compare the selections in this section with Carlyle's chapter *Captains of Industry* from *Past and Present*; Elizabeth Barrett Browning's poem about child labor, *The Cry of the Children*; John Ruskin's arguments about manufacture in *The Stones of Venice*; his apocalyptic vision of industrial pollution in *The Storm Cloud of the Nineteenth Century*; and William Morris's explanation in *How I Became a Socialist*.

THOMAS BABINGTON MACAULAY

In a book titled *Colloquies on the Progress and Prospects of Society* (1829), the poet Robert Southey (1774–1843) had sought to expose the evils of industrialism and to assert the superiority of the traditional feudal and agricultural way of life of England's past. His romantic Toryism provoked Macaulay (1800–1859) to review the book in a long and characteristic essay, published in the *Edinburgh Review* (1830). As in his popular *History of England* (1849–61), Macaulay seeks here to demolish his opponent with a bombardment of facts and figures, demonstrating that industrialism and middle-class government have resulted in progress and increased comforts for humankind.

From A Review of Southey's *Colloquies*

[EVIDENCE OF PROGRESS]

* * * Perhaps we could not select a better instance of the spirit which pervades the whole book than the passages in which Mr. Southey gives his opinion of the manufacturing system. There is nothing which he hates so bitterly. It is, according to him, a system more tyrannical than that of the feudal ages, a system of actual servitude, a system which destroys the bodies and degrades the minds of those who are engaged in it. He expresses a hope that the competition of other nations may drive us out of the field; that our foreign trade may decline; and that we may thus enjoy a restoration of national sanity and strength. But he seems to think that the extermination of the whole manufacturing population would be a blessing, if the evil could be removed in no other way.

Mr. Southey does not bring forward a single fact in support of these views; and, as it seems to us, there are facts which lead to a very different conclusion. In the first place, the poor rate[1] is very decidedly lower in the manufacturing than in the agricultural districts. If Mr. Southey will look over the Parliamentary returns on this subject, he will find that the amount of parochial relief required by the laborers in the different counties of England is almost exactly in inverse proportion to the degree in which the manufacturing system has been introduced into those counties. The returns for the years ending in March, 1825, and in March, 1828, are now before us. In the former year we find the poor rate highest in Sussex,[2] about twenty shillings to every inhabitant. Then come Buckinghamshire, Essex, Suffolk, Bedfordshire, Huntingdonshire, Kent, and Norfolk. In all these the rate is above fifteen shillings a head. We will not go through the whole. Even in Westmoreland and the North Riding of Yorkshire, the rate is at more than eight shillings. In Cumberland and Monmouthshire, the most fortunate of all the agricultural districts, it is at six shillings. But in the West Riding of Yorkshire,[3] it is as low as five shillings: and when we come to Lancashire, we find it at four shillings, one-fifth of what it is in Sussex. The returns of the year ending in March, 1828, are a little, and but a little, more unfavorable to the manufacturing districts. Lancashire, even in that season of distress, required a smaller poor rate than any other district, and little more than one-fourth of the poor rate raised in Sussex. Cumberland alone, of the agricultural districts, was as well off as the West Riding of Yorkshire. These facts seem to indicate that the manufacturer is both in a more comfortable and in a less dependent situation than the agricultural laborer.

As to the effect of the manufacturing system on the bodily health, we must beg leave to estimate it by a standard far too low and vulgar for a mind so imaginative as that of Mr. Southey, the proportion of births and deaths. We know that, during the growth of this atrocious system, this new misery, to use the phrases of Mr. Southey, this new enormity, this birth of a portentous age, this pest which no man can approve whose heart is not seared or whose understanding has not been darkened, there has been a great diminution of mortality, and that this diminution has been greater in the manufacturing towns than anywhere else. The mortality still is, as it always was, greater in towns than in the country. But the difference has diminished in an extraordinary degree. There is the best reason to believe that the annual mortality of Manchester, about the middle of the last century, was one in twenty-eight.

1. Taxes on property, to provide food and lodging for the unemployed or unemployable. The amount or rate of such taxes varied from district to district in England, depending on local conditions of unemployment.
2. A predominantly agricultural district.
3. A manufacturing district.

It is now reckoned at one in forty-five. In Glasgow and Leeds a similar improvement has taken place. Nay, the rate of mortality in those three great capitals of the manufacturing districts is now considerably less than it was, fifty years ago, over England and Wales, taken together, open country and all. We might with some plausibility maintain that the people live longer because they are better fed, better lodged, better clothed, and better attended in sickness, and that these improvements are owing to that increase of national wealth which the manufacturing system has produced.

Much more might be said on this subject. But to what end? It is not from bills of mortality and statistical tables that Mr. Southey has learned his political creed. He cannot stoop to study the history of the system which he abuses, to strike the balance between the good and evil which it has produced, to compare district with district, or generation with generation. We will give his own reason for his opinion, the only reason which he gives for it, in his own words:

> We remained a while in silence looking upon the assemblage of dwellings below. Here, and in the adjoining hamlet of Millbeck, the effects of manufacturer and of agriculture may be seen and compared. The old cottages are such as the poet and the painter equally delight in beholding. Substantially built of the native stone without mortar, dirtied with no white lime, and their long low roofs covered with slate, if they had been raised by the magic of some indigenous Amphion's[4] music, the materials could not have adjusted themselves more beautifully in accord with the surrounding scene; and time has still further harmonized them with weather stains, lichens, and moss, short grasses, and short fern, and stoneplants of various kinds. The ornamented chimneys, round or square, less adorned than those which, like little turrets, crest the houses of the Portuguese peasantry, and yet not less happily suited to their place; the hedge of clipped box beneath the windows, the rose bushes beside the door, the little patch of flower ground, with its tall hollyhocks in front; the garden beside, the beehives, and the orchard with its bank of daffodils and snowdrops, the earliest and the profusest in these parts, indicate in the owners some portion of ease and leisure, some regard to neatness and comfort, some sense of natural, and innocent, and healthful enjoyment. The new cottages of the manufacturers are upon the manufacturing pattern—naked, and in a row.
>
> "How is it," said I, "that everything which is connected with manufactures presents such features of unqualified deformity? From the largest of Mammon's temples down to the poorest hovel in which his helotry are stalled, these edifices have all one character. Time will not mellow them; nature will neither clothe nor conceal them; and they will remain always as offensive to the eye as to the mind."

Here is wisdom. Here are the principles on which nations are to be governed. Rosebushes and poor rates, rather than steam engines and independence. Mortality and cottages with weather stains, rather than health and long life with edifices which time cannot mellow. We are told that our age

4. According to Greek mythology, Amphion's magical skill as a harp player caused the walls of Thebes to be erected without human aid.

has invented atrocities beyond the imagination of our fathers; that society has been brought into a state compared with which extermination would be a blessing; and all because the dwellings of cotton-spinners are naked and rectangular. Mr. Southey has found out a way, he tells us, in which the effects of manufactures and agriculture may be compared. And what is this way? To stand on a hill, to look at a cottage and a factory, and to see which is the prettier. Does Mr. Southey think that the body of the English peasantry live, or ever lived, in substantial or ornamented cottages, with boxhedges, flower gardens, beehives, and orchards? If not, what is his parallel worth? We despise those mock philosophers,[5] who think that they serve the cause of science by depreciating literature and the fine arts. But if anything could excuse their narrowness of mind, it would be such a book as this. It is not strange that, when one enthusiast makes the picturesque the test of political good, another should feel inclined to proscribe altogether the pleasures of taste and imagination.

*　*　*

It is not strange that, differing so widely from Mr. Southey as to the past progress of society, we should differ from him also as to its probable destiny. He thinks, that to all outward appearance, the country is hastening to destruction; but he relies firmly on the goodness of God. We do not see either the piety or the rationality of thus confidently expecting that the Supreme Being will interfere to disturb the common succession of causes and effects. We, too, rely on his goodness, on his goodness as manifested, not in extraordinary interpositions, but in those general laws which it has pleased him to establish in the physical and in the moral world. We rely on the natural tendency of the human intellect to truth, and on the natural tendency of society to improvement. We know no well-authenticated instance of a people which has decidedly retrograded in civilization and prosperity, except from the influence of violent and terrible calamities, such as those which laid the Roman Empire in ruins, or those which, about the beginning of the sixteenth century, desolated Italy. We know of no country which, at the end of fifty years of peace and tolerably good government, has been less prosperous than at the beginning of that period. The political importance of a state may decline, as the balance of power is disturbed by the introduction of new forces. Thus the influence of Holland and of Spain is much diminished. But are Holland and Spain poorer than formerly? We doubt it. Other countries have outrun them. But we suspect that they have been positively, though not relatively, advancing. We suspect that Holland is richer than when she sent her navies up the Thames,[6] that Spain is richer than when a French king was brought captive to the footstool of Charles the Fifth.[7]

History is full of the signs of this natural progress of society. We see in almost every part of the annals of mankind how the industry of individuals, struggling up against wars, taxes, famines, conflagrations, mischievous pro-

5. Presumably such Utilitarian philosophers as Jeremy Bentham, who had equated poetry with pushpin, a trifling game. It should be noted, however, that although Macaulay often attacked the Utilitarians for their narrow preoccupation with theory, his own position had much in common with theirs.
6. In 1667 a Dutch fleet displayed its power by sailing up the river Thames without being challenged by the English navy.
7. The Spanish king Charles V captured the king of France, Francis I, in the battle of Pavia (1525).

hibitions, and more mischievous protections, creates faster than governments can squander, and repairs whatever invaders can destroy. We see the wealth of nations increasing, and all the arts of life approaching nearer and nearer to perfection, in spite of the grossest corruption and the wildest profusion on the part of rulers.

The present moment is one of great distress. But how small will that distress appear when we think over the history of the last forty years; a war,[8] compared with which all other wars sink into insignificance; taxation, such as the most heavily taxed people of former times could not have conceived; a debt larger than all the public debts that ever existed in the world added together; the food of the people studiously rendered dear; the currency imprudently debased, and imprudently restored. Yet is the country poorer than in 1790? We firmly believe that, in spite of all the misgovernment of her rulers, she has been almost constantly becoming richer and richer. Now and then there has been a stoppage, now and then a short retrogression; but as to the general tendency there can be no doubt. A single breaker may recede; but the tide is evidently coming in.

If we were to prophesy that in the year 1930 a population of fifty millions, better fed, clad, and lodged than the English of our time, will cover these islands, that Sussex and Huntingdonshire will be wealthier than the wealthiest parts of the West Riding of Yorkshire now are, that cultivation, rich as that of a flower garden, will be carried up to the very tops of Ben Nevis and Helvellyn,[9] that machines constructed on principles yet undiscovered will be in every house, that there will be no highways but railroads, no traveling but by steam, that our debt, vast as it seems to us, will appear to our great-grandchildren a trifling encumbrance, which might easily be paid off in a year or two, many people would think us insane. We prophesy nothing; but this we say: If any person had told the Parliament which met in perplexity and terror after the crash in 1720 that in 1830 the wealth of England would surpass all their wildest dreams, that the annual revenue would equal the principal of that debt which they considered as an intolerable burden, that for one man of ten thousand pounds then living there would be five men of fifty thousand pounds, that London would be twice as large and twice as populous, and that nevertheless the rate of mortality would have diminished to one-half of what it then was, that the post office would bring more into the exchequer than the excise and customs had brought in together under Charles the Second, that stage coaches would run from London to York in twenty-four hours, that men would be in the habit of sailing without wind, and would be beginning to ride without horses, our ancestors would have given as much credit to the prediction as they gave to *Gulliver's Travels*. Yet the prediction would have been true; and they would have perceived that it was not altogether absurd, if they had considered that the country was then raising every year a sum which would have purchased the fee-simple of the revenue of the Plantagenets,[1] ten times what supported the Government of Elizabeth, three times what, in the time of Cromwell, had been thought intolerably oppressive. To almost all men the state of things under which

---

8. The wars against France and Napoleon, extending, with some interruptions, from 1792 to 1815.
9. Mountains, in Scotland and in the English Lake District, respectively.

1. The Plantagenet family provided the monarchs of England from 1145 to 1485. "Fee-simple": absolute ownership of their estates.

they have been used to live seems to be the necessary state of things. We have heard it said that five per cent is the natural interest of money, that twelve is the natural number of a jury, that forty shillings is the natural qualification of a county voter. Hence it is that, though in every age everybody knows that up to his own time progressive improvement has been taking place, nobody seems to reckon on any improvement during the next generation. We cannot absolutely prove that those are in error who tell us that society has reached a turning point, that we have seen our best days. But so said all who came before us, and with just as much apparent reason. "A million a year will beggar us," said the patriots of 1640. "Two millions a year will grind the country to powder," was the cry in 1660. "Six millions a year, and a debt of fifty millions!" exclaimed Swift, "the high allies have been the ruin of us." "A hundred and forty millions of debt!" said Junius;[2] "well may we say that we owe Lord Chatham more than we shall ever pay, if we owe him such a load as this." "Two hundred and forty millions of debt!" cried all the statesmen of 1783 in chorus; "what abilities, or what economy on the part of a minister, can save a country so burdened?" We know that if, since 1783, no fresh debt had been incurred, the increased resources of the country would have enabled us to defray that debt at which Pitt, Fox, and Burke stood aghast, nay, to defray it over and over again, and that with much lighter taxation than what we have actually borne. On what principle is it that, when we see nothing but improvement behind us, we are to expect nothing but deterioration before us?

It is not by the intermeddling of Mr. Southey's idol, the omniscient and omnipotent State, but by the prudence and energy of the people, that England has hitherto been carried forward in civilization; and it is to the same prudence and the same energy that we now look with comfort and good hope. Our rulers will best promote the improvement of the nation by strictly confining themselves to their own legitimate duties, by leaving capital to find its most lucrative course, commodities their fair price, industry and intelligence their natural reward, idleness and folly their natural punishment, by maintaining peace, by defending property, by diminishing the price of law, and by observing strict economy in every department of the State. Let the Government do this: the People will assuredly do the rest.

1830

2. Pseudonym of a political commentator whose letters (1769–72) usually praised William Pitt, earl of Chatham. Pitt, as leader of the war against France, which gained Canada for England, could have been blamed for running his country into debt.

FRIEDRICH ENGELS

These eyewitness accounts from *The Condition of the Working Class* (1845) describe conditions of 1844, when Engels (1820–1895) had been living in England, chiefly in Manchester. The book was first translated from the German into English in 1892; this translation is by W. O. Henderson and W. H. Chaloner (1958). The first two paragraphs are the conclusion of chapter 2, *The Industrial Proletariat*; the balance is from chapter 3.

From The Great Towns

Industry and commerce attain their highest stage of development in the big towns, so that it is here that the effects of industrialization on the wage earners can be most clearly seen. It is in these big towns that the concentration of property has reached its highest point. Here the manners and customs of the good old days have been most effectively destroyed. Here the very name of "Merry England" has long since been forgotten, because the inhabitants of the great manufacturing centers have never even heard from their grandparents what life was like in those days. In these towns there are only rich and poor, because the lower middle classes are fast disappearing. At one time this section of the middle classes was the most stable social group, but now it has become the least stable. It is represented in the big factory towns today partly by a few survivors from a bygone age and partly by a group of people who are anxious to get rich as quickly as possible. Of these shady speculators and dubious traders one becomes rich while ninety-nine go bankrupt. Indeed, for more than half of those who have failed, bankruptcy has become a habit.

The vast majority of the inhabitants of these towns are the workers. We propose to discuss their condition and to discover how they have been influenced by life and work in the great factory towns.

* * *

London is unique, because it is a city in which one can roam for hours without leaving the built-up area and without seeing the slightest sign of the approach of open country. This enormous agglomeration of population on a single spot has multiplied a hundred-fold the economic strength of the two and a half million inhabitants concentrated there. This great population has made London the commercial capital of the world and has created the gigantic docks in which are assembled the thousands of ships which always cover the River Thames. I know nothing more imposing than the view one obtains of the river when sailing from the sea up to London Bridge. Especially above Woolwich the houses and docks are packed tightly together on both banks of the river. The further one goes up the river the thicker becomes the concentration of ships lying at anchor, so that eventually only a narrow shipping lane is left free in midstream. Here hundreds of steamships dart rapidly to and fro. All this is so magnificent and impressive that one is lost in admiration. The traveler has good reason to marvel at England's greatness even before he steps on English soil.

It is only later that the traveler appreciates the human suffering which has made all this possible. He can only realize the price that has been paid for all this magnificence after he has tramped the pavements of the main streets of London for some days and has tired himself out by jostling his way through the crowds and dodging the endless stream of coaches and carts which fills the streets. It is only when he has visited the slums of this great city that it dawns upon him that the inhabitants of modern London have had to sacrifice so much that is best in human nature in order to create those wonders of civilization with which their city teems. The vast majority of Londoners have had to let so many of their potential creative faculties lie dormant, stunted and unused in order that a small, closely-knit group of their fellow citizens could develop to the full the qualities with which nature has endowed them. The restless and noisy activity of the crowded streets is highly distasteful, and it is surely abhorrent to human nature itself. Hundreds of thousands of men and women drawn from all classes and ranks of society pack the streets of London. Are they not all human beings with the same innate characteristics and potentialities? Are they not all equally interested in the pursuit of happiness? And do they not all aim at happiness by following similar methods? Yet they rush past each other as if they had nothing in common. They are tacitly agreed on one thing only—that everyone should keep to the right of the pavement so as not to collide with the stream of people moving in the opposite direction. No one even thinks of sparing a glance for his neighbor in the streets. The more that Londoners are packed into a tiny space, the more repulsive and disgraceful becomes the brutal indifference with which they ignore their neighbors and selfishly concentrate upon their private affairs. We know well enough that this isolation of the individual—this narrow-minded egotism—is everywhere the fundamental principle of modern society. But nowhere is this selfish egotism so blatantly evident as in the frantic bustle of the great city. The disintegration of society into individuals, each guided by his private principles and each pursuing his own aims has been pushed to its furthest limits in London. Here indeed human society has been split into its component atoms.

From this it follows that the social conflict—the war of all against all—is fought in the open. * * * Here men regard their fellows not as human beings, but as pawns in the struggle for existence. Everyone exploits his neighbor with the result that the stronger tramples the weaker under foot. The strongest of all, a tiny group of capitalists, monopolize everything, while the weakest, who are in the vast majority, succumb to the most abject poverty.

What is true of London is true also of all the great towns, such as Manchester, Birmingham, and Leeds. Everywhere one finds on the one hand the most barbarous indifference and selfish egotism and on the other the most distressing scenes of misery and poverty. Signs of social conflict are to be found everywhere. Everyone turns his house into a fortress to defend himself—under the protection of the law—from the depredations of his neighbors. Class warfare is so open and shameless that it has to be seen to be believed. The observer of such an appalling state of affairs must shudder at the consequences of such feverish activity and can only marvel that so crazy a social and economic structure should survive at all.

* * *

Every great town has one or more slum areas into which the working classes are packed. Sometimes, of course, poverty is to be found hidden away in alleys close to the stately homes of the wealthy. Generally, however, the workers are segregated in separate districts where they struggle through life as best they can out of sight of the more fortunate classes of society. The slums of the English towns have much in common—the worst houses in a town being found in the worst districts. They are generally unplanned wildernesses of one- or two-storied terrace houses built of brick. Wherever possible these have cellars which are also used as dwellings. These little houses of three or four rooms and a kitchen are called cottages, and throughout England, except for some parts of London, are where the working classes normally live. These streets themselves are usually unpaved and full of holes. They are filthy and strewn with animal and vegetable refuse. Since they have neither gutters nor drains the refuse accumulates in stagnant, stinking puddles. Ventilation in the slums is inadequate owing to the hopelessly unplanned nature of these areas. A great many people live huddled together in a very small area, and so it is easy to imagine the nature of the air in these workers' quarters. However, in fine weather the streets are used for the drying of washing, and clothes lines are stretched across the streets from house to house and wet garments are hung out on them.

We propose to describe some of these slums in detail.

* * *

If we cross Blackstone Edge on foot or take the train we reach Manchester, the regional capital of South Lancashire, and enter the classic home of English industry. This is the masterpiece of the Industrial Revolution and at the same time the mainspring of all the workers' movements. Once more we are in a beautiful hilly countryside. The land slopes gently down toward the Irish Sea, intersected by the charming green valleys of the Ribble, the Irwell, the Mersey, and their tributaries. A hundred years ago this region was to a great extent thinly populated marshland. Now it is covered with towns and villages and is the most densely populated part of England. In Lancashire— particularly in Manchester—is to be found not only the origin but the heart of the industry of the United Kingdom. Manchester Exchange is the thermometer which records all the fluctuations of industrial and commercial activity. The evolution of the modern system of manufacture has reached its climax in Manchester. It was in the South Lancashire cotton industry that water and steam power first replaced hand machines. It was here that such machines as the power-loom and the self-acting mule replaced the old handloom and spinning wheel. It is here that the division of labor has been pushed to its furthest limits. These three factors are the essence of modern industry. In all three of them the cotton industry was the pioneer and remains ahead in all branches of industry. In the circumstances it is to be expected that it is in this region that the inevitable consequences of industrialization in so far as they affect the working classes are most strikingly evident. Nowhere else can the life and conditions of the industrial proletariat be studied in all their aspects as in South Lancashire. Here can be seen most clearly the degradation into which the worker sinks owing to the introduction of steam power, machinery, and the division of labor. Here, too, can be seen most the strenuous efforts of the proletariat to raise themselves from their degraded situation. I propose to examine conditions in Manchester in greater detail for two reasons. In the first place, Manchester is the classic type of modern industrial town. Secondly, I know Manchester as well as I know my native town and I know more about it than most of its inhabitants.

* * *

* * * Owing to the curious lay-out of the town it is quite possible for someone to live for years in Manchester and to travel daily to and from his work without ever seeing a working-class quarter or coming into contact with an artisan. He who visits Manchester simply on business or for pleasure need never see the slums, mainly because the working-class districts and the middle-class districts are quite distinct. This division is due partly to deliberate policy and partly to instinctive and tacit agreement between the two social groups. In those areas where the two social groups happen to come into contact with each other the middle classes sanctimoniously ignore the existence of their less fortunate neighbors. In the center of Manchester there is a fairly large commercial district, which is about half a mile long and half a mile broad. This district is almost entirely given over to offices and warehouses. Nearly the whole of this district has no permanent residents and is deserted at night, when only policemen patrol its dark, narrow thoroughfares with their bull's-eye lanterns. This district is intersected by certain main streets which carry an enormous volume of traffic. The lower floors of the buildings are occupied by shops of dazzling splendor. A few of the upper stories on these premises are used as dwellings and the streets present a relatively busy appearance until late in the evening. Around this commercial quarter there is a belt of built-up areas on the average one and a half miles in width, which is occupied entirely by working-class dwellings. This area of workers' houses includes all Manchester proper, except the center, all Salford and Hulme, an important part of Pendleton and Chorlton, two-thirds of Ardwick, and certain small areas of Cheetham Hill and Broughton. Beyond this belt of working-class houses or dwellings lie the districts inhabited by the middle classes and the upper classes. The former are to be found in regularly laid out streets near the working-class districts—in Chorlton and in the remoter parts of Cheetham Hill. The villas of the upper classes are surrounded by gardens and lie in the higher and remoter parts of Chorlton and Ardwick or on the breezy heights of Cheetham Hill, Broughton, and Pendleton. The upper class enjoy healthy country air and live in luxurious and comfortable dwellings which are linked to the center of Manchester by omnibuses which run every fifteen or thirty minutes. To such an extent has the convenience of the rich been considered in the planning of Manchester that these plutocrats can travel from their houses to their places of business in the center of the town by the shortest routes, which run entirely through working-class districts, without even realizing how close they are to the misery and filth which lie on both sides of the road.

* * *

* * * I will now give a description of the working-class districts of Manchester. The first of them is the Old Town, which lies between the northern limit of the commercial quarter and the River Irk. Here even the better streets, such Todd Street, Long Millgate, Withy Grove, and Shudehill are narrow and tortuous. The houses are dirty, old, and tumble-down. The side-streets have been built in a disgraceful fashion. If one enters the district near the "Old Church" and goes down Long Millgate, one sees immediately on the right hand side a row of antiquated houses where not a single front wall is standing upright. This is a remnant of the old Manchester of the days before the town became industrialized. The original inhabitants and their children have left for better houses in other districts, while the houses in Long Millgate, which no longer satisfied them, were left to a tribe of workers containing a strong Irish element. Here one is really and truly in a district which is quite obviously given over entirely to the working classes, because even the shopkeepers and the publicans of Long Millgate make no effort to give their establishments a semblance of cleanliness. The condition of this street may be deplorable, but it is by no means as bad as the alleys and courts which lie behind it, and which can be approached only by covered passages so narrow that two people cannot pass. Anyone who has never visited these courts and alleys can have no idea of the fantastic way in which the houses have been packed together in disorderly confusion in impudent defiance of all reasonable principles of town planning. And the fault lies not merely in the survival of old property from earlier periods in Manchester's history. Only in quite modern times has the policy of cramming as many houses as possible on to such space as was not utilized in earlier periods reached its climax. The result is that today not an inch of space remains between the houses and any further building is now physically impossible. To prove my point I reproduce a small section of a plan of Manchester.[1] It is by no means the worst slum in Manchester and it does not cover one-tenth of the area of Manchester.

This sketch will be sufficient to illustrate the crazy layout of the whole district lying near the River Irk. There is a very sharp drop of some 15 to 30 feet down to the south bank of the Irk at this point. As many as three rows of houses have generally been squeezed onto this precipitous slope. The lowest row of houses stands directly on the bank of the river while the front walls of the highest row stand on the crest of the ridge in Long Millgate. Moreover, factory buildings are also to be found on the banks of the river. In short the layout of the upper part of Long Millgate at the top of the rise is just as disorderly and congested as the lower part of the street. To the right and left a number of covered passages from Long Millgate give access to several courts. On reaching them one meets with a degree of dirt and revolting filth the like of which is not to be found elsewhere. The worst courts are those leading down to the Irk, which contain unquestionably the most dreadful dwellings I have ever seen. In one of these courts, just at the entrance where the covered passage ends, there is a privy without a door. This privy is so dirty that the inhabitants of the court can only enter or leave the court if they are prepared to wade through puddles of stale urine and excrement. Anyone who wishes to confirm this description should go to the first court on the bank of the Irk above Ducie Bridge. Several tanneries are situated on the bank of the river and they fill the neighborhood with the stench of animal putrefaction. The only way of getting to the courts below Ducie Bridge is by going down flights of narrow dirty steps and one can only reach the houses by treading over heaps of dirt and filth. The first court below Ducie Bridge is called Allen's Court. At the time of the cholera [1832] this court was in such a disgraceful state that the sanitary inspectors [of the local Board of Health] evacuated the inhabitants. The court was then swept and fumigated with chlorine. In his pamphlet Dr. Kay gives a horrifying description of conditions in this court at that time. Since Kay wrote this pamphlet, this court appears to have been at any rate partly demolished and rebuilt. If one looks down the river from Ducie Bridge one does at least see several ruined walls

---

1. Not reprinted here.

and high piles of rubble, side by side with some recently built houses. The view from this bridge, which is mercifully concealed by a high parapet from all but the tallest mortals, is quite characteristic of the whole district. At the bottom the Irk flows, or rather, stagnates. It is a narrow, coal-black, stinking river full of filth and rubbish which it deposits on the more low-lying right bank. In dry weather this bank presents the spectacle of a series of the most revolting blackish-green puddles of slime from the depths of which bubbles of miasmatic gases constantly rise and create a stench which is unbearable even to those standing on the bridge forty or fifty feet above the level of the water. Moreover, the flow of the river is continually interrupted by numerous high weirs, behind which large quantities of slime and refuse collect and putrefy. Above Ducie Bridge there are some tall tannery buildings, and further up there are dye-works, bone mills, and gasworks. All the filth, both liquid and solid, discharged by these works finds its way into the River Irk, which also receives the contents of the adjacent sewers and privies. The nature of the filth deposited by this river may well be imagined. If one looks at the heaps of garbage below Ducie Bridge one can gauge the extent to which accumulated dirt, filth, and decay permeate the courts on the steep left bank of the river. The houses are packed very closely together and since the bank of the river is very steep it is possible to see a part of every house. All of them have been blackened by soot, all of them are crumbling with age and all have broken window panes and window frames. In the background there are old factory buildings which look like barracks. On the opposite, low-lying bank of the river, one sees a long row of houses and factories. The second house is a roofless ruin, filled with refuse, and the third is built in such a low situation that the ground floor is uninhabitable and has neither doors nor windows. In the background one sees the paupers' cemetery, and the stations of the railways to Liverpool and Leeds. Behind these buildings is situated the workhouse, Manchester's "Poor Law Bastille."[2] The workhouse is built on a hill and from behind its high walls and battlements seems to threaten the whole adjacent working-class quarter like a fortress.

Above Ducie Bridge the left bank of the Irk becomes flatter and the right bank of the Irk becomes steeper and so the condition of the houses on both sides of the river becomes worse rather than better. Turning left from the main street which is still Long Millgate, the visitor can easily lose his way. He wanders aimlessly from one court to another. He turns one corner after another through innumerable narrow dirty alleyways and passages, and in only a few minutes he has lost all sense of direction and does not know which way to turn. The area is full of ruined or half-ruined buildings. Some of them are actually uninhabited and that means a great deal in this quarter of the town. In the houses one seldom sees a wooden or a stone floor, while the doors and windows are nearly always broken and badly fitting. And as for the dirt! Everywhere one sees heaps of refuse, garbage, and filth. There are stagnant pools instead of gutters and the stench alone is so overpowering that no human being, even partially civilized, would find it bearable to live in such

---

2. The workhouses established by the Poor Laws of the 1830s, because of the strict regimens enforced on inmates, were commonly likened to prisons such as the Bastille in Paris.

a district.[3] The recently constructed extension of the Leeds railway which crosses the Irk at this point has swept away some of these courts and alleys, but it has thrown open to public gaze some of the others. So it comes about that there is to be found immediately under the railway bridge a court which is even filthier and more revolting than all the others. This is simply because it was formerly so hidden and secluded that it could only be reached with considerable difficulty, [but is now exposed to the human eye]. I thought I knew this district well, but even I would never have found it had not the railway viaduct made a breach in the slums at this point. One walks along a very rough path on the river bank, in between clothes-posts and washing lines to reach a chaotic group of little, one-storied, one-roomed cabins. Most of them have earth floors, and working, living, and sleeping all take place in the one room. In such a hole, barely six feet long and five feet wide, I saw two beds—and what beds and bedding!—which filled the room, except for the fireplace and the doorstep. Several of these huts, as far as I could see, were completely empty, although the door was open and the inhabitants were leaning against the door posts. In front of the doors filth and garbage abounded. I could not see the pavement, but from time to time, I felt it was there because my feet scraped it. This whole collection of cattle sheds for human beings was surrounded on two sides by houses and a factory and on a third side by the river. [It was possible to get to this slum by only two routes]. One was the narrow path along the river bank, while the other was a narrow gateway which led to another human rabbit warren which was nearly as badly built and was nearly in such a bad condition as the one I have just described.

Enough of this! All along the Irk slums of this type abound. There is an unplanned and chaotic conglomeration of houses, most of which are more or less unhabitable. The dirtiness of the interiors of these premises is fully in keeping with the filth that surrounds them. How can people dwelling in such places keep clean! There are not even adequate facilities for satisfying the most natural daily needs. There are so few privies that they are either filled up everyday or are too far away for those who need to use them. How can these people wash when all that is available is the dirty water of the Irk? Pumps and piped water are to be found only in the better-class districts of the town. Indeed no one can blame these helots of modern civilization if their homes are no cleaner than the occasional pigsties which are a feature of these slums. There are actually some property owners who are not ashamed to let dwellings such as those which are to be found below Scotland Bridge. Here on the quayside a mere six feet from the water's edge is to be found a row of six or seven cellars, the bottoms of which are at least two feet

---

3. Cf. another account of Manchester slums of the same decade in Elizabeth Gaskell's novel *Mary Barton* (1848), chap. 6:

Women from their doors tossed household slops of *every* description into the gutter; they ran into the next pool, which overflowed and stagnated. Heaps of ashes were stepping-stones, on which the passer-by, who cared in the least for cleanliness, took care not to put his foot. Our friends [two factory workers] were not dainty, but even they picked their way, till they got to some steps leading down . . . into the cellar in which a fam-

ily of human beings lived. . . . After the account I have given of the state of the street, no one can be surprised that on going into the cellar inhabited by Davenport, the smell was so foetid as almost to knock the two men down. Quickly recovering themselves, as those inured to such things do, they began to penetrate the thick darkness of the place, and to see three or four children rolling on the damp, nay wet brick floor, through which the stagnant, filthy moisture of the street oozed up; the fireplace was empty and black; the wife sat on her husband's lair [couch], and cried in the dank loneliness.

beneath the low-water level of the Irk. [What can one say of the owner of] the corner house—situated on the opposite bank of the river above Scotland Bridge—who actually lets the upper floor although the premises downstairs are quite uninhabitable and no attempt has been made to board up the gaps left by the disappearance of doors and windows? This sort of thing is by no means uncommon in this part of Manchester, where, owing to the lack of conveniences, such deserted ground floors are often used by the whole neighborhood as privies.

*　*　*

1845

CHARLES KINGSLEY

The following selection is from chapter 8 of *Alton Locke*, a novel by Charles Kingsley (1819–1875). Under the influence of Carlyle's writings and also as a result of his own observations, Kingsley, a clergyman, became deeply concerned with the sufferings of the working classes. The speaker here is a young tailor who is accompanied by an elderly Scottish bookseller, Sandy Mackaye.

From Alton Locke

[A LONDON SLUM]

It was a foul, chilly, foggy Saturday night. From the butchers' and greengrocers' shops the gaslights flared and flickered, wild and ghastly, over haggard groups of slipshod dirty women, bargaining for scraps of stale meat and frostbitten vegetables, wrangling about short weight and bad quality. Fish stalls and fruit stalls lined the edge of the greasy pavement, sending up odors as foul as the language of sellers and buyers. Blood and sewer water crawled from under doors and out of spouts, and reeked down the gutters among offal, animal and vegetable, in every stage of putrefaction. Foul vapors rose from cow sheds and slaughterhouses, and the doorways of undrained alleys, where the inhabitants carried the filth out on their shoes from the backyard into the court, and from the court up into the main street; while above, hanging like cliffs over the streets—those narrow, brawling torrents of filth, and poverty, and sin—the houses with their teeming load of life were piled up into the dingy, choking night. A ghastly, deafening, sickening sight it was. Go, scented Belgravian![1] and see what London is! and then go to the library which God has given thee—one often fears in vain—and see what science says this London might be!

*　*　*

We went on through a back street or two, and then into a huge, miserable house, which, a hundred years ago, perhaps, had witnessed the luxury, and

---

1. Inhabitant of Belgravia, a wealthy residential district of London.

rung to the laughter of some one great fashionable family, alone there in their glory. Now every room of it held its family, or its group of families—a phalanstery[2] of all the fiends—its grand staircase, with the carved balustrades rotting and crumbling away piecemeal, converted into a common sewer for all its inmates. Up stair after stair we went, while wails of children, and curses of men, steamed out upon the hot stifling rush of air from every doorway, till, at the topmost story, we knocked at a garret door. We entered. Bare it was of furniture, comfortless, and freezing cold; but, with the exception of the plaster dropping from the roof, and the broken windows, patched with rags and paper, there was a scrupulous neatness about the whole, which contrasted strangely with the filth and slovenliness outside. There was no bed in the room—no table. On a broken chair by the chimney sat a miserable old woman, fancying that she was warming her hands over embers which had long been cold, shaking her head, and muttering to herself, with palsied lips, about the guardians and the workhouse; while upon a few rags on the floor lay a girl, ugly, small-pox-marked, hollow-eyed, emaciated, her only bedclothes the skirt of a large handsome new riding habit, at which two other girls, wan and tawdry, were stitching busily, as they sat right and left of her on the floor. The old woman took no notice of us as we entered; but one of the girls looked up, and, with a pleased gesture of recognition, put her finger up to her lips, and whispered, "Ellen's asleep."

"I'm not asleep, dears," answered a faint unearthly voice; "I was only praying. Is that Mr. Mackaye?"

"Aye, my lassies; but ha' ye gotten na fire the nicht?"

"No," said one of them, bitterly, "we've earned no fire tonight, by fair trade or foul either."

1850

2. A kind of model housing development proposed by the French socialist Charles Fourier (1772–1837).

CHARLES DICKENS

The following selection is from chapter 5 of *Hard Times*, a novel by Charles Dickens (1812–1870). The picture of Coketown was based on Dickens's impressions of the raw industrial towns of central and northern England such as Manchester and, in particular, Preston, a cotton-manufacturing center in Lancashire.

From Hard Times

[COKETOWN]

It was a town of red brick, or of brick that would have been red if the smoke and ashes had allowed it; but as matters stood it was a town of unnatural red and black like the painted face of a savage. It was a town of machinery and tall chimneys, out of which interminable serpents of smoke trailed themselves forever and ever, and never got uncoiled. It had a black canal in it, and a river that ran purple with ill-smelling dye, and vast piles of buildings full of windows where there was a rattling and a trembling all day long, and where the piston of the steam engine worked monotonously up and down like the head of an elephant in a state of melancholy madness. It contained several large streets all very like one another, and many small streets still more like one another, inhabited by people equally like one another, who all went in and out at the same hours, with the same sound upon the same pavements, to do the same work, and to whom every day was the same as yesterday and tomorrow, and every year the counterpart of the last and the next.

These attributes of Coketown were in the main inseparable from the work by which it was sustained; against them were to be set off, comforts of life which found their way all over the world, and elegancies of life which made, we will not ask how much of the fine lady, who could scarcely bear to hear the place mentioned. The rest of its features were voluntary, and they were these.

You saw nothing in Coketown but what was severely workful. If the members of a religious persuasion built a chapel there—as the members of eighteen religious persuasions had done—they made it a pious warehouse of red brick, with sometimes (but this is only in highly ornamented examples) a bell in a birdcage on the top of it. The solitary exception was the New Church; a stuccoed edifice with a square steeple over the door terminating in four short pinnacles like florid wooden legs. All the public inscriptions in the town were painted alike, in severe characters of black and white. The jail might have been the infirmary, the infirmary might have been the jail, the town hall might have been either, or both, or anything else, for anything that appeared to the contrary in the graces of their construction. Fact, fact, fact, everywhere in the material aspect of the town; fact, fact, fact, everywhere in the immaterial. The M'Choakumchild school was all fact, and the school of design was all fact, and the relations between master and man were all fact, and everything was fact between the lying-in hospital and the cemetery, and what you couldn't state in figures, or show to be purchasable in the cheapest market and salable in the dearest, was not, and never should be, world without end, Amen.

1854

ANONYMOUS

A. L. Lloyd, a collector of British folk songs, heard *Poverty Knock* from a weaver in 1965, who had learned it sixty years earlier. The song certainly dates from before that.

Poverty Knock[1]

REFRAIN[2]

Poverty, poverty knock!
Me loom is a-sayin' all day.
Poverty, poverty knock!
Gaffer's too skinny[3] to pay.
Poverty, poverty knock!
Keepin' one eye on the clock.
Ah know ah can guttle°   *eat*
When ah hear me shuttle
Go: Poverty, poverty knock!

Up every mornin' at five.
Ah wonder that we keep alive.
Tired an' yawnin' on the cold mornin',
It's back to the dreary old drive.

5   Oh dear, we're goin' to be late.
Gaffer is stood at the gate.
We're out o' pocket, our wages they're docket°   *docked*
We'll 'a' to buy grub on the slate.[4]

An' when our wages they'll bring,
10   We're often short of a string.[5]
While we are fratchin' wi' gaffer for snatchin',[6]
We know to his brass° he will cling.   *money*

We've got to wet our own yarn
By dippin' it into the tarn.°   *pool*
15   It's wet an' soggy an' makes us feel groggy,
An' there's mice in that dirty old barn.

Oh dear, me poor 'ead it sings.
Ah should have woven three strings,
But threads are breakin' and my back is achin'.
20   Oh dear, ah wish ah had wings.

Sometimes a shuttle flies out,
Gives some poor woman a clout.
Ther she lies bleedin', but nobody's 'eedin'.
Who's goin' t'carry her out?

25   Tuner[7] should tackle me loom.
'E'd rather sit on his bum.
'E's far too busy a-courtin' our Lizzie,
An' ah cannat get 'im to come.

---

1. The sound of a 19th-century loom.
2. Repeated after each stanza.
3. Stingy. "Gaffer's": the foreman's.
4. On credit, as recorded on a piece of slate.

5. Short payment for a piece of cloth.
6. Cheating. "Fratchin' ": quarreling.
7. Man who maintains the loom.

Lizzie is so easy led.
30   Ah think that 'e teks her to bed.
She allus was skinny, now look at her pinny.°   *pinafore*
It's just about time they was wed.

1967

HENRY MAYHEW

In 1849, Henry Mayhew (1812–1887) was asked by the *Morning Chronicle* to be the metropolitan correspondent for its series "Labour and the Poor." His interviews of workers and of street folk, later published as a book, convey a vivid sense of the lives of London's poor.

From London Labour and the London Poor

[BOY INMATE OF THE CASUAL WARDS[1]]

I am now seventeen, My father was a cotton-spinner in Manchester, but has been dead ten years; and soon after that my mother went into the workhouse, leaving me with an aunt; and I had to work in a cotton factory. As young as I was, I earned 2*s.* 2*d.*[2] a-week at first. I can read well, and write a little. I worked at the factory two years, and was then earning 7*s.* a-week. I then ran away, for I had always a roving mind; but I should have stayed if my master hadn't knocked me about so. I thought I should make my fortune in London—I'd heard it was such a grand place. I had read in novels and romances,—halfpenny and penny books,—about such things, but I've met with nothing of the kind. I started without money, and begged my way from Manchester to London, saying I was going up to look for work. I wanted to see the place more than anything else. I suffered very much on the road, having to be out all night often; and the nights were cold, though it was summer. When I got to London all my hopes were blighted. I could get no further. I never tried for work in London, for I believe there are no cotton factories in it; besides, I wanted to see life. I begged, and slept in the unions.[3] I got acquainted with plenty of boys like myself. We met at the casual wards, both in London and the country. I have now been five years at this life. We were merry enough in the wards, we boys, singing and telling stories.

*   *   *

I live a roving life, at first, being my own master. I was fond of going to plays, and such-like, when I got money; but now I'm getting tired of it, and wish for something else. I have tried for work at cotton factories in Lancashire and Yorkshire, but never could get any. I'm sure I could settle now. I couldn't have done that two years ago, the roving spirit was so strong upon me and the company I kept got a strong hold on me. Two winters back, there

---

1. Short-term poor shelters.
2. Two shillings, two pence.

3. Shelters for the poor maintained by two or more parishes

was a regular gang of us boys in London. After sleeping at a union, we would fix where to meet at night to get into another union to sleep. There were thirty of us that way, all boys; besides forty young men, and thirty young women. Sometimes we walked the streets all night. We didn't rob, at least I never saw any robbing. We had pleasure in chaffing[4] the policemen, and some of us got taken up. I always escaped. We got broken up in time,— some's dead, some's gone to sea, some into the country, some home, and some lagged.[5] Among them were many young lads very expert in reading, writing, and arithmetic. One young man—he was only twenty-five—could speak several languages: he had been to sea. He was then begging, though a strong young man. I suppose he liked that life: some soon got tired of it.

I often have suffered from cold and hunger. I never made more than 3*d*. a-day in money, take the year round, by begging; some make more than 6*d* . . . but then, I've had meat and bread given besides. I say nothing when I beg, but that I am a poor boy out of work and starving. I never stole anything in my life. I've often been asked to do so by my mates. I never would. The young women steal the most. I know, least, I did know, two that kept young men, their partners, going about the country with them, chiefly by their stealing. Some do so by their prostitution. Those go as partners are all prostitutes. There is a great deal of sickness among the young men and women, but I never was ill these last seven years. Fevers, colds, and venereal diseases, are very common.

1851

4. Making fun of.   5. Fell behind.

ANNIE BESANT

In 1873 Annie Besant (1847–1933) left the church and her marriage to an Anglican clergyman to become active in feminist and socialist causes. When she heard about the high dividends and low wages at the match factory of Bryant and May, she wrote a series of articles, including this one published in the magazine *Link*, that led to a public boycott and a strike of fourteen hundred match workers.

The "White Slavery" of London Match Workers

Bryant and May, now a limited liability company, paid last year a dividend of 23 per cent to its shareholders; two years ago it paid a dividend of 25 per cent, and the original £5 shares were then quoted for sale at £18 7s. 6d.[1] The highest dividend paid has been 38 per cent.

Let us see how the money is made with which these monstrous dividends are paid. . . .

1. Eighteen pounds, seven shillings, six pence.

The hour for commencing work is 6.30 in summer and 8 in winter; work concludes at 6 P.M. Half-an-hour is allowed for breakfast and an hour for dinner. This long day of work is performed by young girls, who have to stand the whole of the time. A typical case is that of a girl of 16, a piece-worker; she earns 4s. a week, and lives with a sister, employed by the same firm, who "earns good money, as much as 8s. or 9s. per week." Out of the earnings 2s. is paid for the rent of one room; the child lives on only bread-and-butter and tea, alike for breakfast and dinner, but related with dancing eyes that once a month she went to a meal where "you get coffee, and bread and butter, and jam, and marmalade, and lots of it." . . . The splendid salary of 4s. is subject to deductions in the shape of fines; if the feet are dirty, or the ground under the bench is left untidy, a fine of 3d. is inflicted; for putting "burnts"— matches that have caught fire during the work—on the bench 1s. has been forfeited, and one unhappy girl was once fined 2s. 6d. for some unknown crime. If a girl leaves four or five matches on her bench when she goes for a fresh "frame" she is fined 3d., and in some departments a fine of 3d. is inflicted for talking. If a girl is late she is shut out for "half the day," that is for the morning six hours, and 5d. is deducted out of her day's 8d. One girl was fined 1s. for letting the web twist around a machine in the endeavor to save her fingers from being cut, and was sharply told to take care of the machine, "never mind your fingers." Another, who carried out the instructions and lost a finger thereby, was left unsupported while she was helpless. The wage covers the duty of submitting to an occasional blow from a foreman; one, who appears to be a gentleman of variable temper, "clouts" them "when he is mad."

One department of the work consists in taking matches out of a frame and putting them into boxes; about three frames can be done in an hour, and ½d. is paid for each frame emptied; only one frame is given out at a time, and the girls have to run downstairs and upstairs each time to fetch the frame, thus much increasing their fatigue. One of the delights of the frame work is the accidental firing of the matches: when this happens the worker loses the work, and if the frame is injured she is fined or "sacked." 5s. a week had been earned at this by one girl I talked to.

The "fillers" get ¾d. a gross for filling boxes; at "boxing," i.e. wrapping papers round the boxes, they can earn from 4s 6d. to 5s. a week. A very rapid "filler" has been known to earn once "as much as 9s." in a week, and 6s. a week "sometimes." The making of boxes is not done in the factory; for these 2 ¼d. a gross is paid to people who work in their own homes, and "find your own paste." Daywork is a little better paid than piecework, and is done chiefly by married women, who earn as much sometimes as 10s. a week, the piecework falling to the girls. Four women day workers, spoken of with reverent awe, earn—13s. a week.

A very bitter memory survives in the factory. Mr. Theodore Bryant, to show his admiration of Mr. Gladstone[2] and the greatness of his own public spirit, bethought him to erect a statue to that eminent statesman. In order that his workgirls might have the privilege of contributing, he stopped 1s. each out of their wages, and further deprived them of half-a-day's work by closing the

2. William Ewart Gladstone (1809–1898), leader of the Liberal Party from 1868 to 1875 and 1880 to 1894 and prime minister on four occasions.

factory, "giving them a holiday." ("We don't want no holidays," said one of the girls pathetically, for—needless to say—the poorer employees of such a firm lose their wages when a holiday is "given.") So furious were the girls at this cruel plundering, that many went to the unveiling of the statue with stones and bricks in their pockets, and I was conscious of a wish that some of those bricks had made an impression on Mr. Bryant's conscience. Later on they surrounded the statue—"we paid for it" they cried savagely—shouting and yelling, and a gruesome story is told that some cut their arms and let their blood trickle on the marble paid for, in very truth, by their blood. . . .

Such is a bald account of one form of white slavery as it exists in London. With chattel slaves Mr. Bryant could not have made his huge fortune, for he could not have fed, clothed, and housed them for 4s. a week each, and they would have had a definite money value which would have served as a protection. But who cares for the fate of these white wage slaves? Born in slums, driven to work while still children, undersized because underfed, oppressed because helpless, flung aside as soon as worked out, who cares if they die or go on the streets, provided only that the Bryant and May shareholders get their 23 per cent, and Mr. Theodore Bryant can erect statues and buy parks? Oh if we had but a people's Dante, to make a special circle in the Inferno for those who live on this misery, and suck wealth out of the starvation of helpless girls.

Failing a poet to hold up their conduct to the execration of posterity, enshrined in deathless verse, let us strive to touch their consciences, *i.e.* their pockets, and let us at least avoid being "partakers of their sins," by abstaining from using their commodities.

1888

ADA NIELD CHEW

Born on a farm in North Staffordshire, Ada Nield Chew (1870–1945) left school at the age of eleven to help her mother with taking care of house and family. In her early twenties, she worked as a tailor in a factory in Crewe. She wrote a series of letters to the *Crewe Chronicle* about working conditions in the factory. When her identity was discovered, an uproar ensued, and she was fired. She became active in politics and continued to write for political causes.

A Living Wage for Factory Girls at Crewe, 5 May 1894

Sir,

—Will you grant me space in your sensible and widely read paper to complain of a great grievance of the class—that of tailoresses in some of the Crewe factories—to which I belong? I have hoped against hope that some influential man (or woman) would take up our cause and put us in the right way to remedy—for of course there is a remedy—for the evils we are suffering from. But although one cannot open a newspaper without seeing what all sorts and conditions of men are constantly agitating for and slowly but surely obtaining—as in the miners' eight hour bill[1]— only very vague mention is ever made of the under-paid, over-worked "Factory Girl." And I have come to the conclusion, sir, that as long as we are silent ourselves and apparently content with our lot, so long shall we be left in the enjoyment [?] of that lot.

The rates paid for the work done by us are so fearfully low as to be totally inadequate to—I had almost said keep body and soul together. Well, sir, it is a fact which I could prove, if necessary, that we are compelled, not by our employers, but by stern necessity, in order to keep ourselves in independence, which self-respecting girls even in our class of life like to do, to work so many hours—I would rather not say how many—that life loses its savour, and our toil, which in moderation and at a fair rate of remuneration would be pleasurable, becomes drudgery of the most wearisome kind.

To take what may be considered a good week's wage the work has to be so close and unremitting that we cannot be said to "live"—we merely exist. We eat, we sleep, we work, endlessly, ceaselessly work, from Monday morning till Saturday night, without remission. Cultivation of the mind? How is it possible? Reading? Those of us who are determined to live like human beings and require food for mind as well as body are obliged to take time which is necessary for sleep to gratify this desire. As for recreation and enjoying the beauties of nature, the seasons come and go, and we have barely time to notice whether it is spring or summer.

Certainly we have Sundays: but Sunday is to many of us, after our week of slavery, a day of exhaustion. It has frequently been so in my case, and I am not delicate. This, you will understand, sir, is when work is plentiful. Of course we have slack times, of which the present is one (otherwise I should not have time to write to you). It may be said that we should utilise these slack times for recruiting our bodies and cultivating our minds. Many of us do so, as far as is possible in the anxious state we are necessarily in, knowing that we are not earning our "keep," for it is not possible, absolutely not possible, for the average ordinary "hand" to earn enough in busy seasons, even with the overtime I have mentioned, to make up for slack ones.

"A living wage!" Ours is a lingering, dying wage. Who reaps the benefit of our toil? I read sometimes of a different state of things in other factories, and if in others, why not those in Crewe? I have just read the report of the Royal Commission on Labour. Very good, but while Royal Commissions are enquiring and reporting and making suggestions, some of the workers are being hurried to their graves.

I am afraid I am trespassing a great deal on your space, sir, but my subject has such serious interest for me—I sometimes wax very warm as I sit stitching and thinking over our wrongs—that they, and the knowledge that your columns are always open to the needy, however humble, must be my excuse.

I am, sir, yours sincerely,
A CREWE FACTORY GIRL
Crewe, 1 May 1894

1. Bill limiting miners' workshifts to eight hours.

Editor's note: Our correspondent writes a most intelligent letter; and if she is a specimen of the factory girl, then Crewe factory proprietors should be proud of their "hands." We shall be glad to hear further from our correspondent as to the wages paid, the numbers of hours worked, and the conditions of their employment. *Crewe Chronicle*, 5 May 1894

1894

THE "WOMAN QUESTION":
THE VICTORIAN DEBATE ABOUT GENDER

"The greatest social difficulty in England today is the relationship between men and women. The principal difference between ourselves and our ancestors is that they took society as they found it while we are self-conscious and perplexed. The institution of marriage might almost seem just now to be upon trial." This assertion by Justin M'Carthy (1830–1912), appearing in an essay on novels in the *Westminster Review* (July 1864), could be further extended, for on trial throughout the Victorian period was not only the institution of marriage but the family itself, and, most particularly, the traditional roles of women as wives, mothers, and daughters. The "Woman Question," as it was called, engaged many Victorians, both male and female.

As indicated in a section of the introduction to the Victorian age, "The Role of Women" (p. 1055), the Woman Question was not one but many. The mixed opinions of Queen Victoria herself make an interesting illustration of some of its different aspects. Believing in education for her sex, she gave support and encouragement to the founding of a college for women in 1847. On the other hand, she opposed the movement to give women the right to vote, which she described in a letter as "this mad folly." But most interesting, for our purposes, is another letter in which she comments on women and marriage. In 1858, writing to her recently married daughter, Victoria remarks: "There is great happiness . . . in devoting oneself to another who is worthy of one's affection; still, men are very selfish and the woman's devotion is always one of submission which makes our poor sex so very unenviable. This you will feel hereafter—I know; though it cannot be otherwise as God has willed it so."

Many of the queen's female subjects shared her assumptions that woman's role was to be accepted as divinely willed—as illustrated in the selections from Sarah Ellis's popular guidebook, *The Women of England* (1839). The required "submission" of which the queen wrote was justified in many quarters on the grounds of the supposed intellectual inferiority of women. As popularly accepted lore expressed it: "Average Weight of Man's Brain 3½ lbs; Woman's 2 lbs, 11 ozs." Such inferiority justified woman's dependent role. Another early Victorian guidebook, *The Female Instructor*, in reminding wives of their dependent roles, recommended always wearing one's wedding ring so that whenever a wife felt "ruffled," she might "cast [her] eyes upon it, and call to mind who gave it to [her]." In such quarters it would follow that a woman who tried to cultivate her intellect beyond drawing-room accomplishments was violating the order of Nature and of religious tradition. Woman was to be valued, instead, for other qualities considered to be especially characteristic of her sex: tenderness of understanding, unworldliness and innocence, domestic affection, and, in various degrees, submissiveness. By virtue of these qualities, woman became an object to be worshiped—an "angel in the house," as Coventry Patmore describes her in the title of his popular poem. Although a number of feminists as well as more traditional thinkers held this ideal view of woman's character, the exalted pedestal on which women were placed, as George Eliot argued in her essay on Mary Wollstonecraft, was one of the principal obstacles to their achieving any change of status.

It is commonly said that, as a result, Victorian women, married or unmarried, suffered painfully from boredom, as the experiences of Caroline Helstone in Charlotte Brontë's *Shirley* (1849) illustrate. Living in the home of her uncle, a clergyman, she finds no outlet for her energies, and her boredom becomes so intense that she longs for death. A reviewer of *Shirley* commented:

> The author is very bitter against *men* . . . she speaks as one outraged and aggrieved by their contemptuous treatment of her sex. We discern symptoms of a bitterness . . . almost a fierceness—for which there is probably some good cause. But there are few women of strong powers of mind, such as the author of this book unquestionably is, who do not feel that the social position of women is not at all what it should be, and hence she speaks in her angry and indignant tone.

Yet generalizations about bored Victorian females need to be severely qualified; by the year in which *Shirley* appeared, one-quarter of England's female population had jobs, most of them onerous and low paying. Although the millions of women employed as domestics, seamstresses, factory workers, or farm laborers had many problems, excessive leisure was not one of them. To be bored was the privilege of wives and daughters in upper- and middle-class families in which feminine idleness was treasured as a status symbol. It was only among this small and important segment of the population, as the novelist Dinah Maria Mulock emphasizes, that there was "nothing to do" for these comfortably well-off wives and daughters, because in such households the servants ran everything, even taking over the principal role in the rearing of children. Another group in which frustration was common consisted of women from the same classes whose families had lost their fortunes, thereby obliging their daughters to seek employment as governesses. Charlotte Brontë's governess-heroine Jane Eyre, reflecting that among both men and women, "millions are in silent revolt against their lot," adds:

> Women are supposed to be very calm generally: but women feel just as men feel; they need exercise for their faculties and a field for their efforts as much as their brothers do; they suffer from too rigid a restraint, too absolute a stagnation, precisely as men would suffer; and it is narrow-minded in their more privileged fellow-creatures to say that they ought to confine themselves to making puddings and knitting stockings, to playing on the piano and embroidering bags. It is thoughtless to condemn them, or laugh at them, if they seek to do more or learn more than custom has pronounced necessary for their sex.

George Meredith, in his *Essay on Comedy* (1873), develops the same argument; the test of a civilization, he writes, is whether men "consent to talk on equal terms with their women, and to listen to them." Yet at least two reviewers of *Jane Eyre*, both women, regarded such proposals as virtually seditious. Margaret Oliphant called the novel "A wild declaration of the 'Rights of Women' in a new aspect." And Elizabeth Rigby attacked its "pervading tone of ungodly discontent."

In some households such discontent, whether godly or ungodly, led to a daughter's open rebellion. A remarkable instance was Florence Nightingale, who found family life in the 1850s intolerably pointless and, despite parental opposition, cut loose from home to carve out a career for herself in nursing and hospital administration.

According to Sir Walter Besant, similar drives for independence produced an extraordinary change in the status of women during the late Victorian period, opening up for them a wide variety of professional opportunities. Many women became successful novelists, but embarking on such a career was no easy choice. The selections from Harriet Martineau's autobiography included here suggest some of the obstacles, internal and external, against which the aspiring woman writer struggled. Inevitably, some women writers were hacks, of whom Eliot made fun in her essay *Silly Novels by Lady Novelists* (1855). Nonetheless, women emerge as major literary artists during the period, as illustrated in the careers of the Brontë sisters and of George Eliot, one of the great novelists of the language.

It is instructive to compare the selections in this section with Eliot's judicious essay on the Woman Question, inspired by her rereading of Mary Wollstonecraft (p. 1456). It should be noted, however, that it was not only as an essayist but as a novelist that the Woman Question engaged her attention, as in her highly complex portrait of the frustrations of Maggie Tulliver, the bookish early-Victorian heroine of *The Mill on the Floss*. And her portraits of women were not restricted to the frustrated and discontented. As a realist, Eliot recognized that many upper- and middle-class women apparently found their leisurely lives fully enjoyable. In *Middlemarch,* for example, she portrays one of these in Celia Brooke Chetham, who rejoices in her comfortable life as wife and mother on a country estate. Her sister Dorothea, however (whom Celia regards with affectionate indulgence as an eccentric misfit), finds the traditional womanly dispensation as painfully frustrating as Florence Nightingale had found it. And it was on behalf of such women as Dorothea that Mill developed his argument in *The Subjection of Women* (1869; p. 1155), a classic essay that should be read in conjunction with the selections in this section. It is also interesting to compare these discussions of the Woman Question with Elizabeth Barrett Browning's *Aurora Leigh* (p. 1180), a novel in verse that represents the life of a woman poet; the *Anthology* includes a selection portraying the way the typical girl's education constricts her mind and one portraying Aurora's defense of her vocation as a poet.

SARAH STICKNEY ELLIS

Sarah Stickney (d. 1872), an essayist, married in 1837 William Ellis, a missionary, and worked with him for the temperance movement and other evangelical causes. Ellis's book on women's education and domestic roles (1839) became a best-seller and went through sixteen editions in two years. In the 1840s, she founded a school for girls that sought to inculcate her theories that feminine education should cultivate what she called "the heart" rather than the intellectual faculties of her pupils.

From The Women of England: Their Social Duties and Domestic Habits

[DISINTERESTED KINDNESS]

To men belongs the potent—(I had almost said the *omnipotent*) consideration of worldly aggrandizement; and it is constantly misleading their steps, closing their ears against the voice of conscience, and beguiling them with the promise of peace, where peace was never found.

* * *

How often has man returned to his home with a mind confused by the many voices, which in the mart, the exchange, or the public assembly, have addressed themselves to his inborn selfishness, or his worldly pride; and while his integrity was shaken, and his resolution gave way beneath the pressure of apparent necessity, or the insidious pretenses of expediency, he has stood corrected before the clear eye of woman, as it looked directly to the naked truth, and detected the lurking evil of the specious act he was about to commit. Nay, so potent may have become this secret influence, that he may have borne it about with him like a kind of second conscience, for mental reference, and spiritual counsel, in moments of trial; and when the snares of the world were around him, and temptations from within and without have bribed over the witness in his own bosom, he has thought of the humble monitress who sat alone, guarding the fireside comforts of his distant home; and the remembrance of her character, clothed in moral beauty, has scattered the clouds before his mental vision, and sent him back to that beloved home, a wiser and a better man.

The women of England, possessing the grand privilege of being better instructed than those of any other country, in the minutiae of domestic comfort, have obtained a degree of importance in society far beyond what their unobtrusive virtues would appear to claim. The long-established customs of their country have placed in their hands the high and holy duty of cherishing and protecting the minor morals of life, from whence springs all that is elevated in purpose, and glorious in action. The sphere of their direct personal influence is central, and consequently small; but its extreme operations are as widely extended as the range of human feeling. They may be less striking in society than some of the women of other countries, and may feel themselves, on brilliant and stirring occasions, as simple, rude, and unsophisticated in the popular science of excitement; but as far as the noble daring of Britain has sent forth her adventurous sons, and that is to every point of danger on the habitable globe, they have borne along with them a generosity, a disinterestedness, and a moral courage, derived in no small measure from the female influence of their native country.

It is a fact well worthy of our serious attention, and one which bears immediately upon the subject under consideration, that the present state of our national affairs is such as to indicate that the influence of woman in counteracting the growing evils of society is about to be more needed than ever.

* * *

In order to ascertain what kind of education is most effective in making woman what she ought to be, the best method is to inquire into the character, station, and peculiar duties of woman throughout the largest portion of her earthly career; and then ask, for what she is most valued, admired, and beloved?

In answer to this, I have little hesitation in saying—for her disinterested kindness. Look at all the heroines, whether of romance or reality—at all the female characters that are held up to universal admiration—at all who have gone down to honored graves, amongst the tears and lamentations of their survivors. Have these been the learned, the accomplished women; the women who could solve problems, and elucidate systems of philosophy? No: or if they have, they have also been women who were dignified with the majesty of moral greatness.

* * *

Let us single out from any particular seminary a child who has been there from the years of ten to fifteen, and reckon, if it can be reckoned, the pains that have been spent in making that child proficient in Latin. Have the same pains been spent in making her disinterestedly kind? And yet what man is there in existence who would not rather his wife should be free from selfishness, than be able to read Virgil without the use of a dictionary?

* * *

I still cling fondly to the hope that some system of female instruction will be discovered, by which the young women of England may be sent from school to the homes of their parents, habituated to be on the watch for every opportunity of doing good to others; making it the first and the last inquiry of every day, "What can I do to make my parents, my brothers, or my sisters, more happy? I am but a feeble instrument in the hands of Providence, but as He will give me strength, I hope to pursue the plan to which I have been accustomed, of seeking my own happiness only in the happiness of others."

1839

COVENTRY PATMORE

First published in 1854–62, this long poem about courtship and marriage became a best-seller first in the United States and later in Britain. Dedicated to Patmore's first wife, Emily Augusta Andrews, the poem celebrated their fifteen years of married life. (She died in 1862, and Patmore, who lived from 1823 to 1896, twice remarried.) The popularity of the poem among Patmore's contemporaries (including Hopkins and Ruskin) plummeted in later years. Feminist critics, such as Virginia Woolf, criticized *The Angel in the House* both for the sentimentality of its ideal of woman and for the oppressive effect of this ideal on women's lives. Since Woolf, the phrase "the angel in the house" has often been used to characterize a patronizing Victorian sentimentality toward women, with the implication that, if the woman is the angel in the house, her husband is its lord.

From The Angel in the House

The Paragon

When I behold the skies aloft
   Passing the pageantry of dreams,
The cloud whose bosom, cygnet-soft,
   A couch for nuptial Juno seems,
5 The ocean broad, the mountains bright,
   The shadowy vales with feeding herds,
I from my lyre the music smite,
   Nor want for justly matching words.
All forces of the sea and air,
10   All interests of hill and plain,
I so can sing, in seasons fair,
   That who hath felt may feel again.
Elated oft by such free songs,

I think with utterance free to raise
15 That hymn for which the whole world longs,
A worthy hymn in woman's praise;
A hymn bright-noted like a bird's,
Arousing these song-sleepy times
With rhapsodies of perfect words,
20 Ruled by returning kiss of rhymes.
But when I look on her and hope
To tell with joy what I admire,
My thoughts lie cramp'd in narrow scope,
Or in the feeble birth expire;
25 No mystery of well-woven speech,
No simplest phrase of tenderest fall,
No liken'd excellence can reach
Her, the most excellent of all,
The best half of creation's best,
30 Its heart to feel, its eye to see,
The crown and complex of the rest,
Its aim and its epitome.
Nay, might I utter my conceit,
'Twere after all a vulgar song,
35 For she's so simply, subtly sweet,
My deepest rapture does her wrong.
Yet is it now my chosen task
To sing her worth as Maid and Wife;
Nor happier post than this I ask,
40 To live her laureate all my life.
On wings of love uplifted free,
And by her gentleness made great,
I'll teach how noble man should be
To match with such a lovely mate;
45 And then in her may move the more
The woman's wish to be desired,
(By praise increased,) till both shall soar,
With blissful emulations fired.
And, as geranium, pink, or rose
50 Is thrice itself through power of art,
So may my happy skill disclose
New fairness even in her fair heart;
Until that churl shall nowhere be
Who bends not, awed, before the throne
55 Of her affecting majesty,
So meek, so far unlike our own;
Until (for who may hope too much
From her who wields the powers of love?)
Our lifted lives at last shall touch
60 That happy goal to which they move;
Until we find, as darkness rolls
Away, and evil mists dissolve,
The nuptial contrasts are the poles
On which the heavenly spheres revolve.

1854–62

HARRIET MARTINEAU

Harriet Martineau (1802–1876), who grew up in the town of Norwich, suffered a painfully unhappy childhood and adolescence both because of recurring illnesses and because of the strict and narrow lifestyle of her middle-class Unitarian family. She was a prolific author, who produced many kinds of books—history, political and economic theory, travel narratives, fiction, translation. She was best known for her collection of instructive stories, *Illustrations of Political Economy* (1832 and later); but she also dealt with a wide variety of other issues, such as slavery in the United States (she was an early supporter of the Abolitionists). Her *Autobiography*, written in 1855, was published in 1877. In the first selection, she is eighteen years old.

From Autobiography

When I was young, it was not thought proper for young ladies to study very conspicuously; and especially with pen in hand. Young ladies (at least in provincial towns) were expected to sit down in the parlour to sew,—during which reading aloud was permitted,—or to practice their music; but so as to be fit to receive callers, without any signs of bluestockingism which could be reported abroad. Jane Austen herself, the Queen of novelists, the immortal creator of Anne Elliott, Mr. Knightley, and a score or two more of unrivalled intimate friends of the whole public, was compelled by the feelings of her family to cover up her manuscripts with a large piece of muslin work, kept on the table for the purpose, whenever any genteel people came in. So it was with other young ladies, for some time after Jane Austen was in her grave; and thus my first studies in philosophy were carried on with great care and reserve. I was at the work table regularly after breakfast,—making my own clothes, or the shirts of the household, or about some fancy work: I went out walking with the rest,—before dinner in winter, and after tea in summer: and if ever I shut myself into my own room for an hour of solitude, I knew it was at the risk of being sent for to join the sewing-circle, or to read aloud,— I being the reader, on account of my growing deafness. But I won time for what my heart was set upon, nevertheless,—either in the early morning, or late at night. I had a strange passion for translating, in those days; and a good preparation it proved for the subsequent work of my life. Now, it was meeting James at seven in the morning to read Lowth's Prelections[1] in the Latin, after having been busy since five about something else, in my own room. Now it was translating Tacitus,[2] in order to try what was the utmost compression of style that I could attain.—About this I may mention an incident while it occurs. We had all grown up with a great reverence for Mrs. Barbauld[3] (which she fully deserved from much wiser people than ourselves) and, reflectively, for Dr. Aikin,[4] her brother,—also able in his way, and far more industrious, but without her genius. Among a multitude of other

---

1. *Praelectiones de Sacra Poesi Herbraeorum (Lectures on Hebrew Poetry*, 1753–70), by Robert Lowth (1710–1787), an English bishop and scholar. "James": James Martineau (1805–1900), her younger brother, who later became a renowned Unitarian preacher and moral philosopher.

2. Roman historian (ca. 55–ca. 118).
3. Anna Laetitia Barbauld (1743–1825), poet and writer of prose for children.
4. John Aikin (1747–1822), English physician, author, and biographer.

labours, Dr. Aikin had translated the Agricola[5] of Tacitus. I went into such an enthusiasm over the original, and especially over the celebrated concluding passage, that I thought I would translate it, and correct it by Dr. Aikin's, which I could procure from our public library. I did it, and found my own translation unquestionably the best of the two. I had spent an infinity of pains over it,—word by word; and I am confident I was not wrong in my judgment. I stood pained and mortified before my desk, I remember, thinking how strange and small a matter was human achievement, if Dr. Aikin's fame was to be taken as a testimony of literary desert. I had beaten him whom I had taken for my master. I need not point out that, in the first place, Dr. Aikin's fame did not hang on this particular work; nor that, in the second place, I had exaggerated his fame by our sectarian estimate of him. I give the incident as a curious little piece of personal experience, and one which helped to make me like literary labour more for its own sake, and less for its rewards, than I might otherwise have done.—Well: to return to my translating propensities. Our cousin J. M. L., then studying for his profession in Norwich, used to read Italian with Rachel[6] and me,—also before breakfast. We made some considerable progress, through the usual course of prose authors and poets; and out of this grew a fit which Rachel and I at one time took, in concert with our companions and neighbours, the C.'s, to translate Petrarch.[7] Nothing could be better as an exercise in composition than translating Petrarch's sonnets into English of the same limits. It was putting ourselves under compulsion to do with the Italian what I had set myself voluntarily to do with the Latin author. I believe we really succeeded pretty well; and I am sure that all these exercises were a singularly apt preparation for my after work. At the same time, I went on studying Blair's Rhetoric[8] (for want of a better guide) and inclining mightily to every kind of book or process which could improve my literary skill,—really as if I had foreseen how I was to spend my life.

* * *

At this time,—(I think it must have been in 1821,) was my first appearance in print. * * * My brother James, then my idolized companion, discovered how wretched I was when he left me for his college, after the vacation; and he told me that I must not permit myself to be so miserable. He advised me to take refuge, on each occasion, in a new pursuit; and on that particular occasion, in an attempt at authorship. I said, as usual, that I would if he would: to which he answered that it would never do for him, a young student, to rush into print before the eyes of his tutors; but he desired me to write something that was in my head, and try my chance with it in the "Monthly Repository,"—the poor little Unitarian periodical in which I have mentioned that Talfourd[9] tried his young powers. What James desired, I always did, as of course; and after he had left me to my widowhood soon after six o'clock, one bright September morning, I was at my desk before seven, beginning a letter to the Editor of the "Monthly Repository,"—that editor being the formidable prime minister of his sect,—Rev. Robert Aspland.[1] I suppose I must

---

5. A biography of Julius Agricola (40–93), Tacitus's father-in-law and a Roman senator and general.
6. Martineau's sister.
7. Italian poet (1304–1374).
8. *Lectures on Rhetoric and Belles Lettres* (1784)

by Hugh Blair (1718–1800), a Scottish divine and professor of rhetoric, which expressed 18th-century ideals of prose style.
9. Sir Thomas Noon Talfourd (1795–1854), English lawyer and author.
1. A Unitarian divine (1782–1845).

tell what that first paper was, though I had much rather not; for I am so heartily ashamed of the whole business as never to have looked at the article since the first flutter of it went off. It was on Female Writers on Practical Divinity. I wrote away, in my abominable scrawl of those days, on foolscap paper,[2] feeling mightily like a fool all the time. I told no one, and carried my expensive packet to the post-office myself, to pay the postage. I took the letter V for my signature,—I cannot at all remember why. The time was very near the end of the month: I had no definite expectation that I should ever hear any thing of my paper; and certainly did not suppose it could be in the forthcoming number. That number was sent in before service-time on a Sunday morning. My heart may have been beating when I laid hands on it; but it thumped prodigiously when I saw my article there, and, in the Notices to Correspondents, a request to hear more from V. of Norwich. There is certainly something entirely peculiar in the sensation of seeing oneself in print for the first time:—the lines burn themselves in upon the brain in a way of which black ink is incapable, in any other mode. So I felt that day, when I went about with my secret.—I have said what my eldest brother was to us,— in what reverence we held him. He was just married, and he and his bride asked me to return from chapel with them to tea. After tea he said, "Come now, we have had plenty of talk; I will read you something;" and he held out his hand for the new "Repository." After glancing at it, he exclaimed, "They have got a new hand here. Listen." After a paragraph, he repeated, "Ah! this is a new hand; they have had nothing so good as this for a long while." (It would be impossible to convey to any who do not know the "Monthly Repository" of that day, how very small a compliment this was.) I was silent, of course. At the end of the first column, he exclaimed about the style, looking at me in some wonder at my being as still as a mouse. Next (and well I remember his tone, and thrill to it still) his words were—"What a fine sentence that is! Why, do you not think so?" I mumbled out, sillily enough, that it did not seem any thing particular. "Then," said he, "you were not listening. I will read it again. There now!" As he still got nothing out of me, he turned round upon me, as we sat side by side on the sofa, with "Harriet, what is the matter with you? I never knew you so slow to praise any thing before." I replied, in utter confusion,—"I never could baffle any body. The truth is, that paper is mine." He made no reply; read on in silence, and spoke no more till I was on my feet to come away. He then laid his hand on my shoulder, and said gravely (calling me 'dear' for the first time) "Now, dear, leave it to other women to make shirts and darn stockings; and do you devote yourself to this." I went home in a sort of dream, so that the squares of the pavement seemed to float before my eyes. That evening made me an authoress.

* * *

While I was at Newcastle [1829], a change, which turned out a very happy one, was made in our domestic arrangements. * * * I call it a misfortune, because in common parlance it would be so treated; but I believe that my mother and all her other daughters would have joined heartily, if asked, in my conviction that it was one of the best things that ever happened to us. My mother and her daughters lost, at a stroke, nearly all they had in the world by the failure of the house,—the old manufactory,—in which their

---

2. A thirteen-by-sixteen-inch sheet of paper.

money was placed. We never recovered more than the merest pittance; and at the time, I, for one, was left destitute;—that is to say, with precisely one shilling in my purse. The effect upon me of this new "calamity," as people called it, was like that of a blister upon a dull, weary pain, or series of pains. I rather enjoyed it, even at the time; for there was scope for action; whereas, in the long, dreary series of preceding trials, there was nothing possible but endurance. In a very short time, my two sisters at home and I began to feel the blessing of a wholly new freedom. I, who had been obliged to write before breakfast, or in some private way, had henceforth liberty to do my own work in my own way; for we had lost our gentility. Many and many a time since have we said that, but for that loss of money, we might have lived on in the ordinary provincial method of ladies with small means, sewing, and economizing, and growing narrower every year; whereas, by being thrown, while it was yet time, on our own resources, we have worked hard and usefully, won friends, reputation and independence, seen the world abundantly, abroad and at home, and, in short, have truly lived instead of vegetated.

1855   1877

ANONYMOUS

In early January 1858 a prostitute, signing herself "One More Unfortunate," wrote a letter to *The Times*, describing her respectable upbringing and her experience as a governess, lamenting her disgrace, and calling on men to be compassionate in their reform efforts. "The Great Social Evil," another letter from a prostitute, published on February 24, 1858, responds in part to the first.

The Great Social Evil
To the Editor of the Times

Sir,—another "Unfortunate," but of a class entirely different from the one who has already instructed the public in your columns, presumes to address you.

I am a stranger to all the fine sentiments which still linger in the bosom of your correspondent. I have none of those youthful recollections which, contrasting her early days with her present life, aggravate the misery of the latter. My parents did not give me any education; they did not instil into my mind virtuous precepts nor set me a good example. All my experiences in early life were gleaned among associates who knew nothing of the laws of God but by dim tradition and faint report, and whose chiefest triumphs of wisdom consisted in picking their way through the paths of destitution in which they were cast by cunning evasion or in open defiance of the laws of man.

*   *   *

Let me tell you something of my parents. My father's most profitable occupation was brickmaking. When not employed at this he did anything he could get to do. My mother worked with him in the brickfield, and so did I and a progeny of brothers and sisters; for, somehow or other, although my parents occupied a very unimportant space in the world, it pleased God to make them fruitful. We all slept in the same room. There were few privacies, few family secrets in our house.

*   *   *

I was a very pretty child, and had a sweet voice; of course I used to sing. Most London boys and girls of the lower classes sing. "My face is my fortune, kind Sir, she said" was the ditty on which I bestowed most pains, and my father and mother would wink knowingly as I sang it. The latter would also tell me how pretty she was when young, and how she sang, and what a fool she had been, and how well she might have done had she been wise.

Frequently we had quite a stir in our colony. Some young lady who had quitted the paternal restraints, or perhaps, been started off, none knew whither or how, to seek her fortune, would reappear among us with a profusion of ribands, fine clothes, and lots of cash. Visiting the neighbors, treating indiscriminately, was the order of the day on such occasions, without any more definite information of the means by which the dazzling transformation had been effected than could be conveyed by knowing winks and the words "luck" and "friends." Then she would disappear and leave us in our dirt, penury, and obscurity. You cannot conceive, Sir, how our young ambition was stirred by these visitations.

Now commences an important era in my life. I was a fine, robust, healthy girl, 13 years of age. I had larked with the boys of my own age. I had huddled with them, boys and girls together, all night long in our common haunts. I had seen much and heard abundantly of the mysteries of the sexes. To me such things had been matters of common sight and common talk. For some time I had trembled and coquetted on the verge of a strong curiosity, and a natural desire, and without a particle of affection, scarce a partiality, I lost what? not my virtue, for I never had any. That which is commonly, but untruly called virtue, I gave away.

You reverend Mr. Philanthropist—what call you virtue? Is it not the principle, the essence, which keeps watch and ward over the conduct, over the substance, the materiality? No such principle ever kept watch and ward over me, and I repeat that I never lost that which I never had—my virtue.

According to my own ideas at the time I only extended my rightful enjoyments. Opportunity was not long wanting to put my newly-acquired knowledge to profitable use. In the commencement of my fifteenth year one of our be-ribanded visitors took me off, and introduced me to the great world, and thus commenced my career as what you better classes call a prostitute. I cannot say that I felt any other shame than the bashfulness of a noviciate introduced to strange society. Remarkable for good looks, and no less so for good temper, I gained money, dressed gaily, and soon agreeably astonished my parents and old neighbors by making a descent upon them.

Passing over the vicissitudes of my course, alternating between reckless gaiety and extreme destitution, I improved myself greatly; and at the age of 18 was living partly under the protection of one who thought he discovered that I had talent, and some good qualities as well as beauty, who treated me more kindly and considerately than I had ever before been treated, and thus drew from me something like a feeling of regard, but not sufficiently strong to lift me to that sense of my position which the so-called virtuous and respectable members of society seem to entertain. Under the protection of this gentleman, and encouraged by him, I commenced the work of my education; that portion of education which is comprised in some knowledge of my own language and the ordinary accomplishments of my sex;—moral science, as I believe it is called, has always been an enigma to me, and is so to this day

* * *

Now, what if I am a prostitute, what business has society to abuse me? Have I received any favours at the hands of society? If I am a hideous cancer in society, are not the causes of the disease to be sought in the rottenness of the carcass? Am I not its legitimate child; no bastard, Sir? Why does my unnatural parent repudiate me, and what has society ever done for me, that I should do anything for it, and what have I ever done against society that it should drive me into a corner and crush me to the earth? I have neither stolen (at least not since I was a child), nor murdered, nor defrauded. I earn my money and pay my way, and try to do good with it, according to my ideas of good. I do not get drunk, nor fight, nor create uproar in the streets or out of them. I do not use bad language. I do not offend the public eye by open indecencies. I go to the Opera, I go to Almack's,[1] I go to the theatres, I go to quiet, well-conducted casinos, I go to all places of public amusement, behaving myself with as much propriety as society can exact. I pay business visits to my tradespeople, the most fashionable of the West-end.[2] My milliners, my silk-mercers,[3] my bootmaker know, all of them, who I am and how I live, and they solicit my patronage as earnestly and cringingly as if I were Madam, the lady of the right rev. patron of the Society for the Suppression of Vice. They find my money as good and my pay better (for we are robbed on every hand) than that of Madam, my Lady; and, if all the circumstances and conditions of our lives had been reversed, would Madam, my Lady, have done better or been better than I?

I speak for others as well as for myself, for the very great majority, nearly all of the real undisguised prostitutes in London, spring from my class, and are made by and under pretty much such conditions of life as I have narrated, and particularly by untutored and unrestrained intercourse of the sexes in early life. We come from the dregs of society, as our so-called betters term it. What business has society to have dregs—such dregs as we? You railers of the Society for the Suppression of Vice, you the pious, the moral, the respectable, as you call yourselves, who stand on your smooth and pleasant side of the great gulf you have dug and keep between yourselves and the dregs, why don't you bridge it over, or fill it up, and by some humane and generous process absorb us into your leavened mass, until we become interpenetrated with goodness like yourselves? Why stand on your eminence

1. Assembly rooms, the scene of social functions.   3. Dealers in textiles.
2. A fashionable shopping district in London.

shouting that we should be ashamed of ourselves? What have we to be ashamed of, we who do not know what shame is—the shame you mean? I conduct myself prudently, and defy you and your policemen too. Why stand you there mouthing with sleek face about morality? What is morality? Will you make us responsible for what we never knew? Teach us what is right and tutor us in good before you punish us for doing wrong. We who are the real prostitutes of the true natural growth of society, and no impostors, will not be judged by "One more Unfortunate," nor measured by any standard of her setting up. She is a mere chance intruder in our ranks, and has no business there.

* * *

Hurling big figures at us, it is said that there are 80,000 of us in London alone—which is a monstrous falsehood—and of this 80,000, poor hard-working sewing girls, sewing women, are numbered in by thousands and called indiscriminately prostitutes; writing, preaching, speechifying, that they have lost their virtue too.

It is a cruel calumny to call them in mass prostitutes; and, as for their virtue, they lose it as one loses his watch who is robbed by the highway thief. Their virtue is the watch, and society is the thief. These poor women toiling on starvation wages, while penury, misery, and famine clutch them by the throat and say, "Render up your body or die."

* * *

Admire this magnificent shop in this fashionable street; its front, fittings, and decorations cost not less than a thousand pounds. The respectable master of the establishment keeps his carriage, and lives in his countryhouse. He has daughters too; his patronesses are fine ladies, the choicest impersonations of society. Do they think, as they admire the taste and elegance of that tradesman's show, of the poor creatures who wrought it, and of what they were paid for it? Do they reflect on the weary toiling fingers, on the eyes dim with watching, on the bowels yearning with hunger, on the bended frames, on the broken constitutions, on poor human nature driven to its coldest corner and reduced to its narrowest means in the production of these luxuries and adornments? This is an old story! Would it not be truer and more charitable to call these poor souls "victims?"—some gentler, some more humane name than prostitute—to soften by some Christian expression, if you cannot better the un-Christian system, the oppobrium of a fate to which society has itself driven them by the direst straits? What business has society to point its finger in scorn, and to raise its voice in reprobation of them? Are they not its children, born of its cold indifference, of its callous selfishness, of its cruel pride?

Sir, I have trespassed on your patience beyond limit, and yet much remains to be said, which I leave for further communication if you think proper to insert this. The difficulty of dealing with the evil is not so great as society considers it. Setting aside "the sin," we are not so bad as we are thought to be. The difficulty is for society to set itself, with the necessary earnestness, self-humiliation, and self-denial to the work. But of this hereafter. To deprive us of proper and harmless amusements, to subject us in mass to the pressure of force—of force wielded, for the most part, by ignorant, and often by brutal men—is only to add the cruelty of active persecution to the cruelty of the passive indifference which made us as we are.

I remain your humble servant,
ANOTHER UNFORTUNATE

1858

DINAH MARIA MULOCK

In 1857, a year earlier than her book on women, Dinah Mulock (1826–1887) had published her best-known novel, a Victorian best-seller, *John Halifax, Gentleman*. In 1864, she married George Craik.

From A Woman's Thoughts about Women

[SOMETHING TO DO]

Man and woman were made for, and not like one another. Only one "right" we have to assert in common with mankind—and that is as much in our hands as theirs—the right of having something to do.

* * *

But how few parents ever consider this! Tom, Dick, and Harry, aforesaid, leave school and plunge into life; "the girls" likewise finish their education, come home, and stay at home. That is enough. Nobody thinks it needful to waste a care upon them. Bless them, pretty dears, how sweet they are! papa's nosegay of beauty to adorn his drawing-room. He delights to give them all they can desire—clothes, amusements, society; he and mamma together take every domestic care off their hands; they have abundance of time and nothing to occupy it; plenty of money, and little use for it; pleasure without end, but not one definite object of interest or employment; flattery and flummery enough, but no solid food whatever to satisfy mind or heart—if they happen to possess either—at the very emptiest and most craving season of both. They have literally nothing whatever to do. * * *

* * *

And so their whole energies are devoted to the massacre of old Time. They prick him to death with crochet and embroidery needles; strum him deaf with piano and harp playing—*not* music; cut him up with morning visitors, or leave his carcass in ten-minute parcels at every "friend's" house they can think of. Finally, they dance him defunct at all sort of unnatural hours; and then, rejoicing in the excellent excuse, smother him in sleep for a third of the following day. Thus he dies, a slow, inoffensive, perfectly natural death; and they will never recognize his murder till, on the confines of this world, or from the unknown shores of the next, the question meets them: "What have you done with Time?"—Time, the only mortal gift bestowed equally on every living soul, and excepting the soul, the only mortal loss which is totally irretrievable.

* * *

But "what am I to do with my life?" as once asked me one girl out of the numbers who begin to feel aware that, whether marrying or not, each possesses an individual life, to spend, to use, or to lose. And herein lies the momentous question.

* * *

A definite answer to this question is simply impossible. Generally—and this is the best and safest guide—she will find her work lying very near at hand: some desultory tastes to condense into regular studies, some faulty household quietly to remodel, some child to teach, or parent to watch over. All these being needless or unattainable, she may extend her service out of the home into the world, which perhaps never at any time so much needed the help of us women. And hardly one of its charities and duties can be done so thoroughly as by a wise and tender woman's hand.

* * *

These are they who are little spoken of in the world at large. * * * They have made for themselves a place in the world: the harsh, practical, yet no ill-meaning world, where all find their level soon or late, and where a frivolous young maid sunk into a helpless old one, can no more expect to keep her pristine position than a last year's leaf to flutter upon a spring bough. But an old maid who deserves well of this same world, by her ceaseless work therein, having won her position, keeps it to the end.

Not an ill position either, or unkindly; often higher and more honorable than that of many a mother of ten sons. In households, where "Auntie" is the universal referee, nurse, playmate, comforter, and counselor: in society, where "that nice Miss So-and-so," though neither clever, handsome, nor young, is yet such a person as can neither be omitted nor overlooked: in charitable works, where she is "such a practical body—always knows exactly what to do, and how to do it": or perhaps, in her own house, solitary indeed, as every single woman's home must be, yet neither dull nor unhappy in itself, and the nucleus of cheerfulness and happiness to many another home besides.

* * *

Published or unpublished, this woman's life is a goodly chronicle, the title page of which you may read in her quiet countenance; her manner, settled, cheerful, and at ease; her unfailing interest in all things and all people. You will rarely find she thinks much about herself; she has never had time for it. And this her life-chronicle, which, out of its very fullness, has taught her that the more one does, the more one finds to do—she will never flourish in your face, or the face of Heaven, as something uncommonly virtuous and extraordinary. She knows that, after all, she has simply done what it was her duty to do.

But—and when her place is vacant on earth, this will be said of her assuredly, both here and Otherwhere—"*She hath done what she could.*"

1858

FLORENCE NIGHTINGALE

Florence Nightingale (1820–1910) was in 1854 to become world famous for organizing a contingent of nurses to take care of sick and wounded soldiers in the Crimean War, an event that provided an outlet for her passionate desire to change the world of hospital treatments. At the time she was writing *Cassandra*, however, she had not yet been able to realize her aims; at thirty-two she was still living at home, unmarried (having declined several proposals), with her well-to-do family. Some members of her family, in particular her mother, strongly opposed her nursing ambitions and kept pressure on her to remain at home. In 1852, so bored with family and social life that she had thoughts of suicide, she began writing *Cassandra*, which she called her "family manuscript"; it is a record of her frustrations before she escaped into a professional world where there was "something to do." In 1859 she revised the manuscript, and a few copies were privately printed that year, but it was not published until 1928. The title refers to the Trojan princess whose true prophecies went unheeded by those around her.

From Cassandra

[NOTHING TO DO]

Why have women passion, intellect, moral activity—these three—and a place in society where no one of the three can be exercised? Men say that God punishes for complaining. No, but men are angry with misery. They are irritated with women for not being happy. They take it as a personal offense. To God alone may women complain without insulting Him!

* * *

Is discontent a privilege?

Yes, it is a privilege for you to suffer for your race—a privilege not reserved to the Redeemer, and the martyrs alone, but one enjoyed by numbers in every age.

The commonplace life of thousands; and in that is its only interest—its only merit as a history; viz., that it *is* the type of common sufferings—the story of one who has not the courage to resist nor to submit to the civilization of her time—is this.

Poetry and imagination begin life. A child will fall on its knees on the gravel walk at the sight of a pink hawthorn in full flower, when it is by itself, to praise God for it.

Then comes intellect. It wishes to satisfy the wants which intellect creates for it. But there is a physical, not moral, impossibility of supplying the wants of the intellect in the state of civilization at which we have arrived. The stimulus, the training, the time, are all three wanting to us; or, in other words, the means and inducements are not there.

Look at the poor lives we lead. It is a wonder that we are so good as we are, not that we are so bad. In looking round we are struck with the power of the organizations we see, not with their want of power. Now and then, it is true, we are conscious that *there* is an inferior organization, but, in general, just the contrary. Mrs A. has the imagination, the poetry of a Murillo,[1] and has sufficient power of execution to show that she might have had a great deal more. Why is she not a Murillo? From a material difficulty, not a mental one. If she has a knife and fork in her hands for three hours of the day, she cannot have a pencil or brush. Dinner is the great sacred ceremony of this day, the great sacrament. To be absent from dinner is equivalent to being ill. Nothing else will excuse us from it. Bodily incapacity is the only apology valid. If she has a pen and ink in her hands during other three hours, writing answers for the penny post, again, she cannot have her pencil, and so *ad infinitum* through life. People have no type before them in their lives, neither fathers nor mothers, nor the children themselves. They look at things in detail. They say, "It is very desirable that A., my daughter, should go to such a party, should know such a lady, should sit by such a person." It is true. But what standard have they before them of the nature and destination of man? The very words are rejected as pedantic. But might they not, at least, have a type in their minds that such an one might be a discoverer through her intellect, such another through her art, a third through her moral power?

Women often try one branch of intellect after another in their youth, e.g., mathematics. But that, least of all, is compatible with the life of "society." It is impossible to follow up anything systematically. Women often long to enter some man's profession where they would find direction, competition (or rather opportunity of measuring the intellect with others) and, above all, time.

In those wise institutions, mixed as they are with many follies, which will last as long as the human race lasts, because they are adapted to the wants of the human race; those institutions which we call monasteries, and which, embracing much that is contrary to the laws of nature, are yet better adapted to the union of the life of action and that of thought than any other mode of life with which we are acquainted; in many such, four and a half hours, at least, are daily set aside for thought, rules are given for thought, training and opportunity afforded. Among us there is *no* time appointed for this purpose, and the difficulty is that, in our social life, we must be always doubtful whether we ought not to be with somebody else or be doing something else.

Are men better off than women in this?

If one calls upon a friend in London and sees her son in the drawing room, it strikes one as odd to find a young man sitting idle in his mother's drawing room in the morning. For men, who are seen much in those haunts, there is no end of the epithets we have: "knights of the carpet," "drawing-room heroes," "ladies' men." But suppose we were to see a number of men in the morning sitting round a table in the drawing-room, looking at prints, doing worsted work, and reading little books, how we should laugh! A member of the House of Commons was once known to do worsted work. Of another

1. Bartolomé Murillo (1617–1682), Spanish painter.

man was said, "His only fault is that he is too good; he drives out with his mother every day in the carriage, and if he is asked anywhere he answers that he must dine with his mother, but, if she can spare him, he will come in to tea, and he does not come."

Now, why is it more ridiculous for a man than for a woman to do worsted work and drive out every day in the carriage? Why should we laugh if we were to see a parcel of men sitting round a drawing room table in the morning, and think it all right if they were women?

Is man's time more valuable than woman's? or is the difference between man and woman this, that woman has confessedly nothing to do?

Women are never supposed to have any occupation of sufficient importance *not* to be interrupted, except "suckling their fools";[2] and women themselves have accepted this, have written books to support it, and have trained themselves so as to consider whatever they do as *not* of such value to the world or to others, but that they can throw it up at the first "claim of social life." They have accustomed themselves to consider intellectual occupation as a merely selfish amusement, which it is their "duty" to give up for every trifler more selfish than themselves.

* * *

Women have no means given them, whereby they *can* resist the "claims of social life." They are taught from their infancy upwards that it is a wrong, ill-tempered, and a misunderstanding of "woman's mission" (with a great M) if they do not allow themselves *willingly* to be interrupted at all hours. If a woman has once put in a claim to be treated as a man by some work of science or art or literature, which she can *show* as the "fruit of her leisure," then she will be considered justified in *having* leisure (hardly, perhaps, even then). But if not, not. If she has nothing to show, she must resign herself to her fate.

"I like riding about this beautiful place, why don't you? I like walking about the garden, why don't you?" is the common expostulation—as if we were children, whose spirits rise during a fortnight's holiday, who think that they will last forever—and look neither backwards nor forwards.

Society triumphs over many. They wish to regenerate the world with their institutions, with their moral philosophy, with their love. Then they sink to living from breakfast till dinner, from dinner till tea, with a little worsted work, and to looking forward to nothing but bed.

When shall we see a life full of steady enthusiasm, walking straight to its aim, flying home, as that bird is now, against the wind—with the calmness and the confidence of one who knows the laws of God and can apply them?

* * *

When shall we see a woman making a *study* of what she does? Married women cannot; for a man would think, if his wife undertook any great work with the intention of carrying it out—of making anything but a sham of it— that she would "suckle his fools and chronicle his small beer" less well for

---

2. See Iago's cynical comments on the role of women, *Othello* 2.1.160: "To suckle fools, and chronicle small beer."

it—that he would not have so good a dinner—that she would destroy, as it is called, his domestic life.

The intercourse of man and woman—how frivolous, how unworthy it is! Can we call *that* the true vocation of woman—her high career? Look round at the marriages which you know. The true marriage—that noble union, by which a man and woman become together the one perfect being—probably does not exist at present upon earth.

It is not surprising that husbands and wives seem so little part of one another. It is surprising that there is so much love as there is. For there is no food for it. What does it live upon—what nourishes it? Husbands and wives never seem to have anything to say to one another. What do they talk about? Not about any great religious, social, political questions or feelings. They talk about who shall come to dinner, who is to live in this lodge and who in that, about the improvement of the place, or when they shall go to London. If there are children, they form a common subject of some nourishment. But, even then, the case is oftenest thus—the husband is to think of how they are to get on in life; the wife of bringing them up at home.

But any real communion between husband and wife—any descending into the depths of their being, and drawing out thence what they find and comparing it—do we ever dream of such a thing? Yes, we may dream of it during the season of "passion," but we shall not find it afterwards. We even expect it to go off, and lay our account that it will. If the husband has, by chance, gone into the depths of *his* being, and found there anything unorthodox, he, oftenest, conceals it carefully from his wife—he is afraid of "unsettling her opinions."

* * *

* * * For a woman is "by birth a Tory"—has often been said—by education a "Tory," we mean.

Women dream till they have no longer the strength to dream; those dreams against which they so struggle, so honestly, vigorously, and conscientiously, and so in vain, yet which are their life, without which they could not have lived; those dreams go at last. All their plans and visions seem vanished, and they know not where; gone, and they cannot recall them. They do not even remember them. And they are left without the food of reality or of hope.

Later in life, they neither desire nor dream, neither of activity, nor of love, nor of intellect. The last often survives the longest. They wish, if their experiences would benefit anybody, to give them to someone. But they never find an hour free in which to collect their thoughts, and so discouragement becomes ever deeper and deeper, and they less and less capable of undertaking anything.

It seems as if the female spirit of the world were mourning everlastingly over blessings, not *lost,* but which she has never had, and which, in her discouragement she feels that she never will have, they are so far off.

The more complete a woman's organization, the more she will feel it, till at last there shall arise a woman, who will resume, in her own soul, all the sufferings of her race, and that woman will be the Saviour of her race.

1852–59   1928

WALTER BESANT

Walter Besant (1836–1901) was a literary critic, historian, and novelist. His history *The Queen's Reign* (1897) celebrated the improvements that he thought had occurred during his lifetime.

From The Queen's Reign

[THE TRANSFORMATION OF WOMEN'S STATUS BETWEEN 1837 AND 1897]

Let me present to you, first, an early Victorian girl, born about the Waterloo year; next, her granddaughter, born about 1875. * * *

The young lady of 1837 * * * cannot reason on any subject whatever because of her ignorance—as she herself would say, because she is a woman. In her presence, and indeed in the presence of ladies generally, men talk trivialities. * * * It has often been charged against Thackeray[1] that his good women were insipid. Thackeray, like most artists, could only draw the women of his own time, and at that time they were undoubtedly insipid. Men, I suppose, liked them so. To be childishly ignorant; to carry shrinking modesty so far as to find the point of a shoe projecting beyond the folds of a frock indelicate; to confess that serious subjects were beyond a woman's grasp; never even to pretend to form an independent judgment; to know nothing of Art, History, Science, Literature, Politics, Sociology, Manners—men liked these things; women yielded to please the men; her very ignorance formed a subject of laudable pride with the Englishwoman of the Forties. * * * There was something Oriental in the seclusion of women in the home, and their exclusion from active and practical life.

* * *

Let us turn to the Englishwoman—the young Englishwoman—of 1897. She is educated. Whatever things are taught to the young man are taught to the young woman. If she wants to explore the wickedness of the world she can do so, for it is all in the books. The secrets of Nature are not closed to her; she can learn the structure of the body if she wishes. At school, at college, she studies just as the young man studies, but harder and with greater concentration. * * * She has invaded the professions. She cannot become a priest, because the Oriental prejudice against women still prevails, so that women in High Church places are not allowed to sing in the choir, or to play the organ, not to speak of preaching. * * * In the same way she cannot enter the Law. Some day she will get over this restriction, but not yet. For a long time she was kept out of medicine. That restriction is now removed; she can, and she does, practice as a physician or a surgeon, generally the former. I believe that she has shown in this profession, as in her university studies, she can stand, *inter pares*,[2] among her equals and her peers, not her superiors. There is no branch of literature in which women have not distinguished themselves. * * * In music they compose, but not

---

1. William Makepeace Thackeray (1811–1863), novelist. The character of Amelia Sedley, in his novel *Vanity Fair* (1848), is cited by Besant as typ-ical of the "insipid" women of the 1840s.
2. Between equals (Latin).

greatly; they play and sing divinely. The acting of the best among them is equal to that of any living man. They have become journalists, in some cases of remarkable ability; in fact, there are thousands of women who now make their livelihood by writing in all its branches. As for the less common professions—the accountants, architects, actuaries, agents—they are rapidly being taken over by women.

It is no longer a question of necessity; women do not ask themselves whether they must earn their own bread, or live a life of dependence. Necessity or no necessity they demand work, with independence and personal liberty. Whether they will take upon them the duties and responsibilities of marriage, they postpone for further consideration. I believe that, although in the first eager running there are many who profess to despise marriage, the voice of nature and the instinctive yearning for love will prevail.

Personal independence: that is the keynote of the situation. Mothers no longer attempt the old control over their daughters: they would find it impossible. The girls go off by themselves on their bicycles; they go about as they please; they neither compromise themselves nor get talked about. For the first time in man's history it is regarded as a right and proper thing to trust a girl as a boy insists upon being trusted. Out of this personal freedom will come, I daresay, a change in the old feelings of young man to maiden. He will not see in her a frail, tender plant which must be protected from cold winds; she can protect herself perfectly well. He will not see in her any longer a creature of sweet emotions and pure aspirations, coupled with a complete ignorance of the world, because she already knows all that she wants to know. Nor will he see in her a companion whose mind is a blank, and whose conversation is insipid, because she already knows as much as he knows himself. Nor, again, will he see in her a housewife whose whole time will be occupied in superintending servants or in making, brewing, confecting things with her own hand.

1897

The Nineties

The state of mind prevailing during the final decade of the nineteenth century was characterized previously (in the introduction to the Victorian age) as typical neither of the earlier Victorians nor of the twentieth century. As a result of their between-centuries role, writers of the 1890s are sometimes styled "Late Victorians"—a perfectly legitimate label in chronological terms—and sometimes (more ambiguously) "the first of the 'Moderns.' " In the *Anthology,* we retain as "Late Victorians" those writers who made their chief contribution before 1900. And we reserve for the twentieth century a number of writers—already on the scene in the 1890s—whose work achieved particular prominence in the twentieth century: these are William Butler Yeats, Joseph Conrad, A. E. Housman, and Thomas Hardy. Hardy's writings offer an example of the principle. He was born fifteen to twenty years before most of the writers of the nineties, and his last two great novels, *Tess of the D'Urbervilles* and *Jude the Obscure,* were published during that decade. But since it was only after 1900 that Hardy made his name as a poet, we include him in the twentieth century, even though many of the attitudes toward life and literature in his poetry are recognizably Victorian and his writings can be considered as having contributed, in part, to the overall accomplishments of Victorian literature. (The same generalizations may be made about Gerard Manley Hopkins, whom we include in the Victorian section because he wrote during the Victorian period but whose work was not published until 1918, when it had a great effect on modernist poets and critics.) The problem of placing Hardy or Hopkins in one age or another is a striking reminder that literary history, as is sometimes said of all history, is a seamless web, resistant to the divisive time categories that we set up for ease of reference.

The writers most closely identified with the decade of the nineties, epitomized by the career of Oscar Wilde, were proponents of "art for art's sake": they believed that art should be unconcerned with controversial issues, such as politics, and that it should be restricted to celebrating beauty in a highly polished style. The "aesthetes," as these writers and artists were called, included in their group painters such as James McNeill Whistler, critics such as Arthur Symons, and the young Yeats. In 1936, when Yeats in old age was compiling an anthology of "modern verse," he looked back, as he often did, to the group of poets of the 1890s to which he himself had once been attached, a group styling itself The Rhymers' Club, whose members used to meet at a restaurant to read their poems aloud to each other. Among this coterie, an admiration for the writings of Walter Pater was, according to Yeats, a badge of membership. Indeed the first "poem" in Yeats's anthology is a passage of Pater's prose that Yeats prints as verse—the passage about the Mona Lisa in *The Renaissance* that begins: "She is older than the rocks among which she sits."

The Rhymers' Club poets liked to think of themselves as anti-Victorians, and they had some cause to do so in view of their revolt against the moral earnestness of such early Victorian prophets as Thomas Carlyle and against a whole set of middle-class opinions that they enjoyed mocking. Even Matthew Arnold, although appreciated for his ridicule of middle-class Philistines, was suspect in the eyes of the aesthetes because he had attacked, in his essay on Wordsworth, the French poet Théophile Gautier, who was regarded as a chief progenitor of the aesthetic movement. What Tennyson called in 1873 "poisonous honey stolen from France" was, in the 1890s, favored fare. Nevertheless it can be shown that the aesthetes' credo of art for art's sake was also rooted in the writings of some of their nineteenth-century predecessors in England. The poets of the aesthetic movement were in a sense the last heirs of the Romantics; the appeal to sensation in their imagery goes back through Rossetti and Tennyson to Keats. They developed this sensationalism, however, much more histrionically than their predecessors, seeking compensation for the drabness of ordinary life in melancholy suggestiveness, antibourgeois sensationalism, heady ritualism, world weariness, or mere emotional debauchery, qualities that led some critics to denounce the nineties as a time of decadence and degeneration. What makes the nineties important as a period of English literary history is not, however, its writers' sensationalism and desire to shock. It is their strongly held belief in the independence of art, their view that a work of art has its own unique kind of value—that, in T. S. Eliot's phrase, poetry must be judged "as poetry and not another thing"—which has most strongly influenced later generations. Not only did the aesthetic movement nurse the young Yeats and provide him with his lifelong belief in poetry as poetry rather than as a means to some moral or other end; it is also provided some of the principal schools of modern criticism with their basic assumptions. "Art for art's sake" was in the nineties a provocative slogan; in the modern period, many leading critics have been largely concerned with demonstrating the uniqueness of the literary use of language and with training us to see works of literary art as possessing their special kind of form, their special kind of meaning, and hence their special kind of value. In this these critics are the heir of the nineties, however much they may have modified or enriched the legacy. It was the poets of the 1890s, too, who first absorbed the influence of the French *symboliste* poets, an influence that has proved pervasive in the twentieth century and is especially strong (although in different ways) in the poetry of Yeats and Eliot.

Despite the characterization of the nineties as the Decadence, the poetry of the period was more various than this label suggests. Much as Wilde and Beardsley expanded the range of male literary identity through their dandyism and effeminacy, women writers of the aesthetic movement such as the pseudonymous Michael Field (Katherine Harris Bradley and her niece Edith Emma Cooper) and Mary Elizabeth Coleridge made equally untraditional claims for women's experience, Field translating and elaborating on Sappho's poems and Coleridge taking on the voice of the witch. There were also poets, such as William Earnest Henley and Rudyard Kipling, whose tone, in contrast to the aesthetes, was strenuously masculine. They embraced the values not of languid contemplation but of a life of action, and they shared a belief in the civilizing mission of British imperial power and the responsibilities called for in exercising that power—what Kipling called "The White Man's Burden." They also shared a commitment to realism that links them to naturalist novelists of the decade like George Gissing and George Moore. Henley's realism appears in his grim sketches of hospital experiences, and Kipling's in his distinctive recreation of the lives of common soldiers in the British army in India and Africa.

Ironically, perhaps, it was Kipling who in 1897 wrote, in his hymn *Recessional,* not a jingoistic celebration of sixty years of Victoria's reign but, instead, a haunting elegy that evokes the achievement of his country and his century but also, from the vaster perspectives of human history, the fragility of that achievement.

MICHAEL FIELD
Katherine Bradley (1846–1914)
Edith Cooper (1862–1913)

Michael Field was the pseudonym adopted by Katherine Bradley and her niece Edith Cooper, who together published twenty-seven verse plays and eight volumes of poems. When Robert Browning wrote to Michael Field to praise a volume of plays, Edith Cooper responded, "My Aunt and I work together after the fashion of Beaumont and Fletcher. She is my senior, by but fifteen years. She has lived with me, taught me, encouraged me and joined me to her poetic life." When Browning let slip the secret of their authorship, Katherine Bradley begged him to maintain the disguise. The revelation of their secret, she pleaded, "would indeed be utter ruin to us," adding, "We have many things to say that the world will not tolerate from a woman's lips."

Katherine Bradley, lost her father, a tobacco manufacturer, when she was two and her mother when she was twenty-two. After her mother's death, she attended Newnham College, Cambridge, and the Collège de France in Paris. When she returned home, she joined John Ruskin's Guild of Saint George, a small utopian society. When Katherine wrote to Ruskin telling him that she had lost God and found a Skye terrier, he angrily ended their friendship. Shortly thereafter she began attending classes at Bristol University with her niece, Edith Cooper, whom she had adopted and raised after Edith's mother became ill. The two became lovers and began a life of writing and traveling together. Their first joint volume of poetry, *Long Ago* (1889), was inspired by Henry Wharton's edition of Sappho (1885), which was the first English translation to represent the object of Sappho's love poems as a woman. The preface to *Long Ago* explains their attempt to create poems elaborating on Sappho's fragments: "Devoutly as the fiery-bosomed Greek turned in her anguish to Aphrodite to accomplish her heart's desires, I have turned to the one woman who has dared to speak unfalteringly of the fearful mastery of love."

Bradley and Cooper knew most of the literary figures of the nineties, including Pater, Wilde, and Yeats, although their relationship to the decadent movement was complex. The eroticism of their early poetry, with its frank expression of love between women, seems consistent with the spirit of the decade; but Bradley and Cooper sharply criticized the work of Beardsley for its depravity and withdrew one of their poems from publication in *The Yellow Book* in protest against its style. In 1906, they converted to Roman Catholicism when their beloved chow dog died, thus reversing the substitution of dog for God Katherine had flippantly described to Ruskin three decades earlier. In 1911, Edith was diagnosed with cancer. Suffering too from cancer, which she kept a secret from Edith to spare her pain, Katherine survived her by only eight months.

[Maids, not to you my mind doth change]

Ταῖς κάλαις ἴμμιν [τὸ] νόημα τῶμον οὐ διάμειπτον.[1]

Maids, not to you my mind doth change;
Men I defy, allure, estrange,
Prostrate, make bond or free:
Soft as the stream beneath the plane

---

1. A fragment from the works of the Greek poet Sappho (mid-7th century B.C.E.), which is translated in the first line of the poem.

5   To you I sing my love's refrain;
Between us is no thought of pain,
        Peril, satiety.

    Soon doth a lover's patience tire,
    But ye to manifold desire
10   Can yield response, ye know
When for long, museful days I pine,
The presage at my heart divine;
To you I never breathe a sign
    Of inward want or woe.

15   When injuries my spirit bruise,
    Allaying virtue ye infuse
    With unobtrusive skill:
And if care frets ye come to me
As fresh as nymph from stream or tree,
20   And with your soft vitality
        My weary bosom fill.

                            1889

[A girl]

    A girl,
    Her soul a deep-wave pearl
Dim, lucent of all lovely mysteries;
    A face flowered for heart's ease,
5   A brow's grace soft as seas
    Seen through faint forest-trees:
    A mouth, the lips apart,
Like aspen-leaflets trembling in the breeze
From her tempestuous heart.
10 Such: and our souls so knit,
    I leave a page half-writ—
        The work begun
Will be to heaven's conception done,
        If she come to it.

                            1893

Unbosoming

The love that breeds
In my heart for thee!
As the iris is full, brimful of seeds,
And all that it flowered for among the reeds
5 Is packed in a thousand vermilion-beads
That push, and riot, and squeeze, and clip,
Till they burst the sides of the silver scrip,

And at last we see
What the bloom, with its tremulous, bowery fold
10   Of zephyr-petal at heart did hold:
So my breast is rent
With the burthen and strain of its great content;
For the summer of fragrance and sighs is dead,
The harvest-secret is burning red,
15   And I would give thee, after my kind,
The final issues of heart and mind.

1893

[It was deep April, and the morn]

It was deep April, and the morn
   Shakspere was born;
The world was on us, pressing sore;
My Love and I took hands and swore,
5   Against the world, to be
Poets and lovers evermore,
To laugh and dream on Lethe's[1] shore,
To sing to Charon[2] in his boat,
Heartening the timid souls afloat;
10   Of judgment never to take heed,
But to those fast-locked souls to speed,
Who never from Apollo fled,
Who spent no hour among the dead;
   Continually
15   With them to dwell,
Indifferent to heaven and hell.

1893

To Christina Rossetti

Lady, we would behold thee moving bright
As Beatrice or Matilda[1] mid the trees,
Alas! thy moan was as a moan for ease
And passage through cool shadows to the night:
5   Fleeing from love, hadst thou not poet's right
To slip into the universe? The seas
Are fathomless to rivers drowned in these,
And sorrow is secure in leafy light.
Ah, had this secret touched thee, in a tomb
10   Thou hadst not buried thy enchanting self,
As happy Syrinx[2] murmuring with the wind,
Or Daphne,[3] thrilled through all her mystic bloom,

---

1. The river of forgetfulness in the underworld.
2. The ferryman who rows the dead across the river Styx to the underworld.
1. An idealized virgin in Dante's *Purgatorio* (28. 30), who explains to the poet that he's in the Garden of Eden. Beatrice, Dante's idealized beloved, appears to the poet in the Earthly Paradise at the top of the mountain of Purgatory.
2. A nymph who, when pursued by Pan, fled into the river Ladon, where she was transformed into a reed, from which Pan made his flute.
3. A nymph who, to escape Apollo's pursuit, was transformed into a laurel tree.

From safe recess as genius or as elf,
Thou hadst breathed joy in earth and in thy kind.

1896

Nests in Elms

The rooks are cawing up and down the trees!
Among their nests they caw. O sound I treasure,
Ripe as old music is, the summer's measure,
Sleep at her gossip, sylvan mysteries,
5   With prate and clamour to give zest of these—
In rune I trace the ancient law of pleasure,
Of love, of all the busy-ness of leisure,
With dream on dream of never-thwarted ease.
O homely birds, whose cry is harbinger
10   Of nothing sad, who know not anything
Of sea-birds' loneliness, of Procne's[1] strife,
Rock round me when I die! So sweet it were
To die by open doors, with you on wing
Humming the deep security of life.

1908

Eros

O Eros of the mountains, of the earth,
One thing I know of thee that thou art old,
Far, sovereign, lonesome tyrant of the dearth
Of chaos, ruler of the primal cold!
5   None gave thee nurture: chaos' icy rings
Pressed on thy plenitude. O fostering power,
Thine the first voice, first warmth, first golden wings,
First blowing zephyr, earliest opened flower,
Thine the first smile of Time: thou hast no mate,
10   Thou art alone forever, giving all:
After thine image, Love, thou did'st create
Man to be poor, man to be prodigal;
And thus, O awful god, he is endued
With the raw hungers of thy solitude.

1908

1. In Greek myth her husband, King Tereus, raped her sister, Philomela. Tereus then ripped out Philomela's tongue to keep her from revealing the crime, but she wove the story into a tapestry. Procne in revenge killed her son and served him to Tereus in a stew. When the sisters fled Tereus, Procne was changed into a swallow and Philomela, into a nightingale.

WILLIAM ERNEST HENLEY
1849–1903

During the 1880s and 1890s William Ernest Henley edited the *National Observer* and other periodicals in London, where he became a powerful figure in literary circles. The affectionate regard in which he was held by his contemporaries was enhanced by his courageous confrontation of long years of crippling physical pain caused by tuberculosis of the bone. Yeats said of him: "I disagreed with him about everything, but I admired him beyond words."

Most of Henley's poems, such as his vivid accounts of his hospital experiences, are realistic sketches of city life, often in free verse. Also characteristic, but in a different vein, are his hearty affirmations of faith in the indomitable human spirit, as in *Invictus,* and his patriotic verses expressing his pride in England's imperial role and her shouldering the responsibility for a world order. In *England, My England* he writes

> They call you proud and hard,
>> England, my England:
> You with worlds to watch and ward,
>> England, my own!
> You whose mailed hand keeps the keys
>> Of such teeming destinies
> You could know nor dread nor ease
>> Were the Song on your bugles blown,
>> England
> Round the Pit on your bugles blown!

The spirit in poems such as these links Henley's writings to the poetry of his friend Rudyard Kipling.

In Hospital

Waiting

A square, squat room (a cellar on promotion),
Drab to the soul, drab to the very daylight;
Plasters astray in unnatural-looking tinware;
Scissors and lint and apothecary's jars.

5   Here, on a bench a skeleton would writhe from,
Angry and sore, I wait to be admitted;
Wait till my heart is lead upon my stomach,
While at their ease two dressers do their chores.

One has a probe—it feels to me a crowbar.
10 A small boy sniffs and shudders after bluestone.[1]
A poor old tramp explains his poor old ulcers.
Life is (I think) a blunder and a shame.

1875

---

1. Or hydrated copper sulfate, commonly used in emergency wards as an emetic for patients who have taken poison.

Invictus[1]

Out of the night that covers me,
   Black as the Pit from pole to pole,
I thank whatever gods may be
   For my unconquerable soul.

5 In the fell clutch of circumstance
   I have not winced nor cried aloud.
Under the bludgeonings of chance
   My head is bloody, but unbowed.

Beyond this place of wrath and tears
10   Looms but the Horror of the shade,
And yet the menace of the years
   Finds, and shall find, me unafraid.

It matters not how strait the gate,
   How charged with punishments the scroll,
15 I am the master of my fate;
   I am the captain of my soul.

1875   1888

1. Unconquered (Latin).

OSCAR WILDE
1854–1900

In Oscar Wilde's comedy *The Importance of Being Earnest* (1895) there is an account of a rakish character, Ernest Worthing, whose death in a Paris hotel is reported by the manager. Five years later, Wilde himself died in Paris (where he was living in exile) attended by a hotel manager. The coincidence seems a curious paradigm of Wilde's whole career, for with him the connections between his life and his art were unusually close. Indeed, in his last years, he told André Gide that he seemed to have put his genius into his life and only his talent into his writings.

His father, Sir William, was a distinguished surgeon in Dublin, where Wilde was born and grew up. After majoring in classical studies at Trinity College, Dublin, he won a scholarship to Oxford and there established a brilliant academic record. At Oxford he came under the influence of the aesthetic theories of John Ruskin (who was at the time professor of fine arts) and, more important, of Walter Pater. With characteristic hyperbole, Wilde affirmed of Pater's *Renaissance*: "It is my golden book; I never travel anywhere without it. But it is the very flower of decadence; the last trumpet should have sounded the moment it was written."

After graduating in 1878, Wilde settled in London, where his fellow Irishmen, Bernard Shaw and William Butler Yeats, were also to settle. Here Wilde quickly established himself both as a writer and as a spokesperson for the school of "art for art's sake." In Wilde's view this school included not only French poets and critics but also a line of English poets going back through Rossetti and the Pre-Raphaelites to Keats. In 1882 he visited America for a lengthy (and successful) lecture tour during which he startled audiences by airing the gospel of the "aesthetic movement." In one of these lectures, he asserted that "to disagree with three fourths of all England on all points of view is one of the first elements of sanity."

For his role as a spokesperson for aestheticism, Wilde had many gifts. From all accounts he was a dazzling conversationalist. Yeats reported, after first listening to him: "I never before heard a man talking with perfect sentences, as if he had written them all overnight with labor and yet all spontaneous." Wilde delighted his listeners not only by his polished wordplay but also by uttering opinions that were both outrageous and incongruous, as for example, his solemn affirmation that Queen Victoria was one of the three women he most admired and whom he would have married "with pleasure" (the other two were Sarah Bernhardt, the actress, and Lillie Langtry, reputedly a mistress of Victoria's son Edward, prince of Wales).

In addition to his mastery of witty conversation, Wilde had the gifts of an actor who delights in gaining attention. Pater had been a most shy and reticent man, but there was nothing reticent about his disciple who had discovered, early, that a flamboyant style of dress was one of the most effective means of gaining attention. Like the dandies of the earlier decades of the nineteenth century (including Benjamin Disraeli and Charles Dickens), Wilde favored colorful costumes in marked contrast to the sober black suits of the late-Victorian middle classes. A green carnation in his buttonhole and velvet knee breeches became for Wilde badges of his youthful iconoclasm, and even when he approached middle age, he continued to emphasize the gap between generations. In a letter written when he was forty-two years old, he remarks: "The opinions of the old on matters of Art are, of course, of no value whatever."

Wilde's campaign early prompted an amused response from middle-class quarters. In 1881, Gilbert and Sullivan staged their comic opera *Patience*, which mocked the affectations of the aesthetes in the character of Bunthorne, especially in his song, "If You're Anxious for to Shine in the High Aesthetic Line."

Wilde's successes for seventeen years in England and America were, of course, not limited to his self-advertising stunts as a dandy. In his writings, he excelled in a variety of genres: as a critic of literature and of society (*The Decay of Lying*, 1889, and *The Soul of Man under Socialism*, 1891) and also as a novelist, poet, and dramatist. Much of his prose, including *The Critic as Artist*, develops Pater's aestheticism, particularly its sense of the superiority of art to life and its lack of obligation to any standards of mimesis. His novel *The Picture of Dorian Gray*, which created a sensation when it was published in 1891, takes a somewhat different perspective. The novel is a strikingly ingenious story of a handsome young man and his selfish pursuit of sensual pleasures. Until the end of the book he himself remains fresh and healthy in appearance while his portrait mysteriously changes into a horrible image of his corrupted soul. Although the preface to the novel (reprinted here) emphasizes that art and morality are totally separate, in the novel itself, at least in its later chapters, Wilde seems to be portraying the evils of self-regarding hedonism.

As a poet Wilde felt overshadowed by the Victorian predecessors whom he admired—Robert Browning, D. G. Rossetti, and Swinburne—and had trouble finding his own voice. Many of the poems in his first volume (1881) are highly derivative, but such pieces as *The Harlot's House* and *Impression du Matin* offer a distinctive perspective on city streets that seems to anticipate early poems by T. S. Eliot. His most outstanding success, however, was as a writer of comedies, which were staged in London and New York from 1892 through 1895, including *Lady Windermere's Fan*, *A Woman of No Importance*, *An Ideal Husband*, and *The Importance of Being Earnest*.

By the spring of 1895 this triumphant success suddenly crumbled when Wilde was arrested and sentenced to jail, with hard labor, for two years. Although Wilde was married and the father of two children, he did not hide his homosexual relationships. When he began a romance (in 1891) with the handsome young poet Lord Alfred Douglas, he set in motion the events that brought about his ruin. In 1895, Lord Alfred's father, the marquis of Queensberry, accused Wilde of homosexuality; Wilde recklessly sued for libel, lost the case, and was thereupon arrested and convicted for what was then on the statute books a serious criminal offense. The revulsion of feeling against him in England and in America was violent, and the aesthetic movement itself suffered a severe setback not only with the public but among writers as well.

His two years in jail led Wilde to write two sober and emotionally high-pitched works, his poem *The Ballad of Reading Gaol* (1898) and his prose confession *De Profundis* (1905). After leaving jail, Wilde, a ruined man, emigrated to France, where he lived out the last three years of his life under an assumed name. Before his departure from England he had been divorced and declared a bankrupt, and in France he had to rely on friends for financial support. Wilde is buried in Paris in the Père Lachaise cemetery.

Impression du Matin[1]

The Thames nocturne of blue and gold[2]
    Changed to a harmony in gray;
    A barge with ocher-colored hay
Dropped from the wharf:[3] and chill and cold

5   The yellow fog came creeping down
      The bridges, till the houses' walls
      Seemed changed to shadows, and St. Paul's
    Loomed like a bubble o'er the town.

    Then suddenly arose the clang
10   Of waking life; the streets were stirred
      With country wagons; and a bird
    Flew to the glistening roofs and sang.

    But one pale woman all alone,
      The daylight kissing her wan hair,
15   Loitered beneath the gas lamps' flare,
    With lips of flame and heart of stone.

1881

Hélas[1]

To drift with every passion till my soul
Is a stringed lute on which all winds can play,
Is it for this that I have given away

---

1. Impression of the morning (French).
2. Cf. the "Nocturnes" (paintings of nighttime scenes) by James McNeill Whistler in the 1870s. *Nocturne in Blue and Gold: Old Battersea Bridge* was one of this series; it was painted by 1875 but given its present title in 1892. An earlier painting by Whistler, *Harmony in Gray*, may be referred to in the next line.
3. I.e., left the wharf and went down river with the ebb tide.
1. "Alas!"

Mine ancient wisdom, and austere control?
Methinks my life is a twice-written scroll
Scrawled over on some boyish holiday
With idle songs for pipe and virelay,[2]
Which do but mar the secret of the whole.
Surely there was a time I might have trod
The sunlit heights, and from life's dissonance
Struck one clear chord to reach the ears of God.
Is that time dead? lo! with a little rod
I did but touch the honey of romance—
And must I lose a soul's inheritance?[3]

1881

E Tenebris[1]

Come down, O Christ, and help me! reach thy hand,
For I am drowning in a stormier sea
Than Simon on thy lake of Galilee:[2]
The wine of life is spilt upon the sand,
My heart is as some famine-murdered land
Whence all good things have perished utterly,
And well I know my soul in Hell must lie
If I this night before God's throne should stand.
"He sleeps perchance, or rideth to the chase,
Like Baal, when his prophets howled that name
From morn to noon on Carmel's smitten height."[3]
Nay, peace, I shall behold, before the night,
The feet of brass,[4] the robe more white than flame,
The wounded hands, the weary human face.

1881

The Harlot's House

We caught the tread of dancing feet,
We loitered down the moonlit street,
And stopped beneath the Harlot's house.

Inside, above the din and fray,
We heard the loud musicians play
The "Treues Liebes Herz" of Strauss.[1]

---

2. A song or short lyric in stanzas.
3. Perhaps referring to Numbers 20.10–13. After Moses had obtained water for his people by striking a rock with his rod, he was denied the privilege of entering the Promised Land.
1. Out of darkness (Latin).
2. Simon Peter, one of the twelve apostles, came close to drowning in a storm until rescued by Christ (Matthew 14.28–31).
3. The poet imagines an ironic voice discouraging

him; it uses the language of Elijah when he mocked the priests of Baal for their god's impotence by suggesting that perhaps Baal was on a journey or asleep (1 Kings 18.19–40).
4. Cf. Revelation 1.13–16, where the "Son of man" is seen in a vision, "his feet like unto fine brass, as if they burned in a furnace."
1. *Heart of True Love*, a waltz by the Austrian composer and "Waltz King" Johann Strauss (1825–1899).

Like strange mechanical grotesques,
Making fantastic arabesques,
The shadows raced across the blind.

10 We watched the ghostly dancers spin
To sound of horn and violin,
Like black leaves wheeling in the wind.

Like wire-pulled automatons,
Slim silhouetted skeletons
15 Went sidling through the slow quadrille,[2]

Then took each other by the hand,
And danced a stately saraband;[3]
Their laughter echoed thin and shrill.

Sometimes a clockwork puppet pressed
20 A phantom lover to her breast,
Sometimes they seemed to try to sing,

Sometimes a horrible marionette
Came out, and smoked its cigarette
Upon the steps like a live thing.[4]

25 Then turning to my love I said,
"The dead are dancing with the dead,
The dust is whirling with the dust."

But she, she heard the violin,
And left my side, and entered in;
30 Love passed into the house of Lust.

Then suddenly the tune went false,
The dancers wearied of the waltz,
The shadows ceased to wheel and whirl,

And down the long and silent street,
35 The dawn, with silver-sandaled feet,
Crept like a frightened girl.

1885, 1908

2. Intricate dance involving four couples facing
each other in a square.
3. A slow and stately dance, originating in Spain.

4. In an illustration for the poem by Althea Gyles
(approved by Wilde), the marionette is pictured as
a man in evening dress.

From The Critic as Artist[1]

[CRITICISM ITSELF AN ART]

ERNEST   Gilbert, you sound too harsh a note. Let us go back to the more
gracious fields of literature. What was it you said? That it was more
difficult to talk about a thing than to do it?

GILBERT   [*after a pause*] Yes: I believe I ventured upon that simple truth.
Surely you see now that I am right? When man acts he is a puppet. When
he describes he is a poet. The whole secret lies in that. It was easy enough
on the sandy plains by windy Ilion[2] to send the notched arrow from the
painted bow, or to hurl against the shield of hide and flamelike brass the
long ash-handled spear. It was easy for the adulterous queen[3] to spread
the Tyrian carpets for her lord, and then, as he lay couched in the marble
bath, to throw over his head the purple net, and call to her smooth-faced
lover to stab through the meshes at the heart that should have broken
at Aulis.[4] For Antigone[5] even, with Death waiting for her as her bridegroom, it was easy to pass through the tainted air at noon, and climb the
hill, and strew with kindly earth the wretched naked corse that had no
tomb. But what of those who wrote about these things? What of those
who gave them reality, and made them live forever? Are they not greater
than the men and women they sing of? "Hector that sweet knight is
dead."[6] And Lucian[7] tells us how in the dim underworld Menippus saw
the bleaching skull of Helen, and marveled that it was for so grim a favor
that all those horned ships were launched, those beautiful mailed men
laid low, those towered cities brought to dust. Yet, every day the swanlike
daughter of Leda comes out on the battlements, and looks down at the
tide of war. The graybeards wonder at her loveliness, and she stands by
the side of the king.[8] In his chamber of stained ivory lies her leman.[9] He
is polishing his dainty armor, and combing the scarlet plume. With squire
and page, her husband passes from tent to tent. She can see his bright
hair, and hears, or fancies that she hears, that clear cold voice. In the
courtyard below, the son of Priam is buckling on his brazen cuirass. The
white arms of Andromache[1] are around his neck. He sets his helmet on
the ground, lest their babe should be frightened. Behind the embroidered
curtains of his pavilion sits Achilles,[2] in perfumed raiment, while in har-

---

1. In "the library of a house in Piccadilly," Gilbert
and Ernest, two sophisticated young men, are talking about the use and function of criticism. Earlier
in the dialogue, Ernest had complained that criticism is officious and useless: "Why should the artist be troubled by the shrill clamor of criticism?
Why should those who cannot create take upon
themselves to estimate the value of creative work?"
Gilbert, in his reply, argues that criticism is creative in its own right. He digresses to compare the
life of action unfavorably with the life of art:
actions are dangerous and their results unpredictable; "if we lived long enough to see the results of
our actions it may be that those who call themselves good would be sickened by a dull remorse,
and those whom the world calls evil stirred by a
noble joy." The excerpt printed here begins immediately following this digression.
2. Troy. Gilbert is referring to Homer's *Iliad*.
3. Clytemnestra, whose murder of her husband,
Agamemnon, provides the plot for Aeschylus's

tragedy of that name.
4. Where Agamemnon sacrificed his daughter
Iphigenia, thus incurring Clytemnestra's wrath.
5. Antigone defied Creon, king of Thebes, by burying the body of her brother, an act that Creon had
forbidden, and was punished by death; see Sophocles' play *Antigone*.
6. Cf. Shakespeare's *Love's Labour's Lost* 5.2.663:
"The sweet war-man [Hector] is dead and rotten."
7. Late Greek satirical writer, influenced by the
earlier Greek seriocomic writer Menippus.
8. Priam. Homer in the *Iliad* describes the old
men of Troy admiring the beauty of Helen, "swanlike daughter of Leda" and of Zeus (Zeus came to
Leda in the form of a swan).
9. Lover (i.e., Paris).
1. Wife of Hector, one of the sons of Priam.
2. Son of Peleus and of the sea nymph Thetis;
Achilles was the Greek hero, opposite of Hector,
the Trojan hero, in the Trojan war. The scene set
here is a tissue of recollections from the *Iliad*.

ness of gilt and silver the friend of his soul[3] arrays himself to go forth to fight. From a curiously carven chest that his mother Thetis had brought to his shipside, the Lord of the Myrmidons takes out that mystic chalice that the lip of man had never touched, and cleanses it with brimstone, and with fresh water cools it, and, having washed his hands, fills with black wine its burnished hollow, and spills the thick grape-blood upon the ground in honor of Him whom at Dodona[4] barefooted prophets worshiped, and prays to Him, and knows not that he prays in vain, and that by the hands of two knights from Troy, Panthous' son, Euphorbus, whose love-locks were looped with gold, and the Priamid,[5] the lion-hearted, Patroclus, the comrade of comrades, must meet his doom. Phantoms, are they? Heroes of mist and mountain? Shadows in a song? No: they are real. Action! What is action? It dies at the moment of its energy. It is a base concession to fact. The world is made by the singer for the dreamer.

ERNEST   While you talk it seems to me to be so.

GILBERT   It is so in truth. On the moldering citadel of Troy lies the lizard like a thing of green bronze. The owl has built her nest in the palace of Priam. Over the empty plain wander shepherd and goatherd with their flocks, and where, on the wine-surfaced, oily sea, οἶνοψ πόντος,[6] as Homer calls it, copper-prowed and streaked with vermilion, the great galleys of the Danaoi[7] came in their gleaming crescent, the lonely tunny-fisher sits in his little boat and watches the bobbing corks of his net. Yet, every morning the doors of the city are thrown open, and on foot, or in horse-drawn chariot, the warriors go forth to battle, and mock their enemies from behind their iron masks. All day long the fight rages, and when night comes the torches gleam by the tents, and the cresset[8] burns in the hall. Those who live in marble or on painted panel know of life but a single exquisite instant, eternal indeed in its beauty, but limited to one note of passion or one mood of calm. Those whom the poet makes live have their myriad emotions of joy and terror, of courage and despair, of pleasure and of suffering. The seasons come and go in glad or saddening pageant, and with winged or leaden feet the years pass by before them. They have their youth and their manhood, they are children, and they grow old. It is always dawn for St. Helena, as Veronese saw her at the window.[9] Through the still morning air the angels bring her the symbol of God's pain. The cool breezes of the morning lift the gilt threads from her brow. On that little hill by the city of Florence, where the lovers of Giorgione[1] are lying, it is always the solstice of noon, made so languorous by summer suns that hardly can the slim naked girl dip into the marble tank the round bubble of clear glass, and the long fingers of the lute player rest idly upon the chords. It is twilight always for the dancing nymphs whom Corot[2] set free among the silver poplars of France. In eternal twilight they move, those frail diaphanous figures, whose trem-

3. I.e., Patroclus.
4. Seat of a very ancient oracle of Zeus.
5. "Son of Priam," i.e., Hector. With the help of Euphorbus, one of the bravest of the Trojans, he slew Patroclus and was in turn slain by Achilles.
6. Wine-dark sea (Greek).
7. Greeks.
8. Metal basket holding fuel burned for illumina-

tion, often hung from the ceiling.
9. One of the best-known paintings of the 16th-century Italian Paolo Veronese is *Helena's Vision*.
1. Italian painter (ca. 1477–1511), the most brilliant colorist of his time.
2. Jean-Baptiste-Camille Corot, 19th-century French painter, best-known for his shimmering trees.

ulous white feet seem not to touch the dew-drenched grass they tread on. But those who walk in epos,[3] drama, or romance, see through the laboring months the young moons wax and wane, and watch the night from evening unto morning star, and from sunrise unto sunsetting can note the shifting day with all its gold and shadow. For them, as for us, the flowers bloom and wither, and the Earth, that Green-tressed Goddess as Coleridge calls her, alters her raiment for their pleasure. The statue is concentrated to one moment of perfection. The image stained upon the canvas possesses no spiritual element of growth or change. If they know nothing of death, it is because they know little of life, for the secrets of life and death belong to those, and those only, whom the sequence of time affects, and who possess not merely the present but the future, and can rise or fall from a past of glory or of shame. Movement, that problem of the visible arts, can be truly realized by Literature alone. It is Literature that shows us the body in its swiftness and the soul in its unrest.

ERNEST   Yes; I see now what you mean. But, surely, the higher you place the creative artist, the lower must the critic rank.

GILBERT   Why so?

ERNEST   Because the best that he can give us will be but an echo of rich music, a dim shadow of clear-outlined form. It may, indeed, be that life is chaos, as you tell me that it is; that its martyrdoms are mean and its heroisms ignoble; and that it is the function of Literature to create, from the rough material of actual existence, a new world that will be more marvelous, more enduring, and more true than the world that common eyes look upon, and through which common natures seek to realize their perfection. But surely, if this new world has been made by the spirit and touch of a great artist, it will be a thing so complete and perfect that there will be nothing left for the critic to do. I quite understand now, and indeed admit most readily, that it is far more difficult to talk about a thing than to do it. But it seems to me that this sound and sensible maxim, which is really extremely soothing to one's feelings, and should be adopted as its motto by every Academy of Literature all over the world, applies only to the relations that exist between Art and Life, and not to any relations that there may be between Art and Criticism.

GILBERT   But, surely, Criticism is itself an art. And just as artistic creation implies the working of the critical faculty, and, indeed, without it cannot be said to exist at all, so Criticism is really creative in the highest sense of the word. Criticism is, in fact, both creative and independent.

ERNEST   Independent?

GILBERT   Yes; independent. Criticism is no more to be judged by any low standard of imitation or resemblance than is the work of poet or sculptor. The critic occupies the same relation to the work of art that he criticizes as the artist does to the visible world of form and color, or the unseen world of passion and of thought. He does not even require for the perfection of his art the finest materials. Anything will serve his purpose. And just as out of the sordid and sentimental amours of the silly wife of a small country doctor in the squalid village of Yonville-l'Abbaye, near

3. Epic poetry.

Rouen, Gustave Flaubert[4] was able to create a classic, and make a masterpiece of style, so, from subjects of little or of no importance, such as the pictures in this year's Royal Academy, or in any year's Royal Academy for that matter, Mr. Lewis Morris's poems, M. Ohnet's novels, or the plays of Mr. Henry Arthur Jones,[5] the true critic can, if it be his pleasure so to direct or waste his faculty of contemplation, produce work that will be flawless in beauty and instinct with intellectual subtlety. Why not? Dullness is always an irresistible temptation for brilliancy, and stupidity is the permanent *Bestia Trionfans*[6] that calls wisdom from its cave. To an artist so creative as the critic, what does subject matter signify? No more and no less than it does to the novelist and the painter. Like them, he can find his motives everywhere. Treatment is the test. There is nothing that has not in it suggestion or challenge.

ERNEST   But is Criticism really a creative art?

GILBERT   Why should it not be? It works with materials, and puts them into a form that is at once new and delightful. What more can one say of poetry? Indeed, I would call criticism a creation within a creation. For just as the great artists, from Homer and Aeschylus, down to Shakespeare and Keats, did not go directly to life for their subject matter, but sought for it in myth, and legend, and ancient tale, so the critic deals with materials that others have, as it were, purified for him, and to which imaginative form and color have been already added. Nay, more, I would say that the highest Criticism, being the purest form of personal impression, is in its way more creative than creation, as it has least reference to any standard external to itself, and is, in fact, its own reason for existing, and, as the Greeks would put it, in itself, and to itself, an end. Certainly, it is never trammeled by any shackles of verisimilitude. No ignoble considerations of probability, that cowardly concession to the tedious repetitions of domestic or public life, affect it ever. One may appeal from fiction unto fact. But from the soul there is no appeal.

ERNEST   From the soul?

GILBERT   Yes, from the soul. That is what the highest criticism really is, the record of one's own soul. It is more fascinating than history, as it is concerned simply with oneself. It is more delightful than philosophy, as its subject is concrete and not abstract, real and not vague. It is the only civilized form of autobiography, as it deals not with the events, but with the thoughts of one's life, not with life's physical accidents of deed or circumstance, but with the spiritual moods and imaginative passions of the mind. I am always amused by the silly vanity of those writers and artists of our day who seem to imagine that the primary function of the critic is to chatter about their second-rate work. The best that one can say of most modern creative art is that it is just a little less vulgar than reality, and so the critic, with his fine sense of distinction and sure instinct of delicate refinement, will prefer to look into the silver mirror or through the woven veil, and will turn his eyes away from the chaos

---

4. French novelist (1821–1880); the reference is to his novel *Madame Bovary* (1857).
5. Wilde is mischievously suggesting his low opinion of the contemporary writers just named. Morris was a Welsh poet and essayist often ridiculed by the critics. Georges Ohnet was a French novelist

and dramatist. Jones was one of the leading English playwrights of his time.
6. Triumphant beast (Latin). A reference to *Spaccio della Bestia Trionfante* (Expulsion of the triumphant beast, 1584), a philosophical allegory by the Italian philosopher Giordano Bruno.

and clamor of actual existence, though the mirror be tarnished and the veil be torn. His sole aim is to chronicle his own impressions. It is for him that pictures are painted, books written, and marble hewn into form.

ERNEST   I seem to have heard another theory of Criticism.

GILBERT   Yes: it has been said by one whose gracious memory we all revere,[7] and the music of whose pipe once lured Proserpina from her Sicilian fields, and made those white feet stir, and not in vain, the Cumnor cowslips, that the proper aim of Criticism is to see the object as in itself it really is. But this is a very serious error, and takes no cognizance of Criticism's most perfect form, which is in its essence purely subjective, and seeks to reveal its own secret and not the secret of another. For the highest Criticism deals with art not as expressive but as impressive purely.

ERNEST   But is that really so?

GILBERT   Of course it is. Who cares whether Mr. Ruskin's views on Turner[8] are sound or not? What does it matter? That mighty and majestic prose of his, so fervid and so fiery-colored in its noble eloquence, so rich in its elaborate symphonic music, so sure and certain, at its best, in subtle choice of word and epithet, is at least as great a work of art as any of those wonderful sunsets that bleach or rot on their corrupted canvases in England's Gallery; greater indeed, one is apt to think at times, not merely because its equal beauty is more enduring, but on account of the fuller variety of its appeal, soul speaking to soul in those long-cadenced lines, not through form and color alone, though through these, indeed, completely and without loss, but with intellectual and emotional utterance, with lofty passion and with loftier thought, with imaginative insight, and with poetic aim; greater, I always think, even as Literature is the greater art. Who, again, cares whether Mr. Pater has put into the portrait of Mona Lisa[9] something that Leonardo never dreamed of? The painter may have been merely the slave of an archaic smile, as some have fancied, but whenever I pass into the cool galleries of the Palace of the Louvre, and stand before that strange figure "set in its marble chair in that cirque of fantastic rocks, as in some faint light under sea," I murmur to myself, "She is older than the rocks among which she sits; like the vampire, she has been dead many times, and learned the secrets of the grave; and has been a diver in deep seas, and keeps their fallen day about her: and trafficked for strange webs with Eastern merchants; and, as Leda, was the mother of Helen of Troy, and, as St. Anne, the mother of Mary; and all this has been to her but as the sound of lyres and flutes, and lives only in the delicacy with which it has molded the changing lineaments, and tinged the eyelids and the hands." And I say to my friend, "The presence that thus so strangely rose beside the waters is expressive of what in the ways of a thousand years man had come to desire"; and

---

7. I.e., Matthew Arnold, whose poem *Thyrsis* (lines 91–100) evokes the legend of Proserpina, a goddess associated with the pastoral landscapes of Sicily. Arnold believed that it would be "in vain" to summon Proserpina to visit the Cumnor hills landscape (near Oxford), but Wilde's speaker here flatters Arnold that the summons was so beautiful that it was "not in vain." For the prose passage about

the "aim of Criticism," see Arnold's *The Function of Criticism at the Present Time* (para. 1, p. 1514).
8. For Ruskin's defense of the paintings of Turner, see *Modern Painters*, especially his praise of Turner's *The Slave Ship* (p. 1429).
9. All remaining references in this paragraph are to Pater's essay *La Gioconda* (p. 1641).

he answers me, "Hers is the head upon which all 'the ends of the world are come,' and the eyelids are a little weary."

And so the picture becomes more wonderful to us than it really is, and reveals to us a secret of which, in truth, it knows nothing, and the music of the mystical prose is as sweet in our ears as was that flute-player's music that lent to the lips of La Gioconda[1] those subtle and poisonous curves. Do you ask me what Leonardo would have said had any one told him of this picture that "all the thoughts and experience of the world had etched and molded therein that which they had of power to refine and make expressive the outward form, the animalism of Greece, the lust of Rome, the reverie of the Middle Age with its spiritual ambition and imaginative loves, the return of the Pagan world, the sins of the Borgias?" He would probably have answered that he had contemplated none of these things, but had concerned himself simply with certain arrangements of lines and masses, and with new and curious color-harmonies of blue and green. And it is for this very reason that the criticism which I have quoted is criticism of the highest kind. It treats the work of art simply as a starting point for a new creation. It does not confine itself— let us at least suppose so for the moment—to discovering the real intention of the artist and accepting that as final. And in this it is right, for the meaning of any beautiful created thing is, at least, as much in the soul of him who looks at it, as it was in his soul who wrought it. Nay, it is rather the beholder who lends to the beautiful thing its myriad meanings, and makes it marvelous for us, and sets it in some new relation to the age, so that it becomes a vital portion of our lives, and symbol of what we pray for, or perhaps of what, having prayed for, we fear that we may receive. The longer I study, Ernest, the more clearly I see that the beauty of the visible arts is, as the beauty of music, impressive[2] primarily, and that it may be marred, and indeed often is so, by any excess of intellectual intention on the part of the artist. For when the work is finished it has, as it were, an independent life of its own, and may deliver a message far other than that which was put into its lips to say. Sometimes, when I listen to the overture to *Tannhäuser*,[3] I seem indeed to see that comely knight treading delicately on the flower-strewn grass, and to hear the voice of Venus calling to him from the caverned hill. But at other times it speaks to me of a thousand different things, of myself, it may be, and my own life, or of the lives of others whom one has loved and grown weary of loving, or of the passions that man has known, or of the passions that man has not known, and so has sought for. Tonight it may fill one with that ΕΡΩΣ ΤΩΝ ΑΔΥΝΑΤΩΝ, that *amour de l'impossible*,[4] which falls like a madness on many who think they live securely and out of reach of harm, so that they sicken suddenly with the poison of unlimited desire, and, in the infinite pursuit of what they may not obtain, grow faint and swoon or stumble. Tomorrow, like the music of which Aristotle and Plato tell us, the noble Dorian music of the Greek, it may perform

1. I.e., the *Mona Lisa* (she was the wife of Francesco del Gioconda—hence "La Gioconda").
2. I.e., designed to create an impression of the senses.
3. An opera by Richard Wagner (1845) based on the legend of a 14th-century German poet who fell

under the spell of Venus and lived with her in the Venusberg.
4. Love of the impossible, in Greek (in capital letters, perhaps to give the effect of an inscription) and in French.

the office of a physician, and give us an anodyne against pain, and heal the spirit that is wounded, and "bring the soul into harmony with all right things." And what is true about music is true about all the arts. Beauty has as many meanings as man has moods. Beauty is the symbol of symbols. Beauty reveals everything, because it expresses nothing. When it shows us itself, it shows us the whole fiery-colored world.

ERNEST   But is such work as you have talked about really criticism?

GILBERT   It is the highest Criticism, for it criticizes not merely the individual work of art, but Beauty itself, and fills with wonder a form which the artist may have left void, or not understood, or understood incompletely.

ERNEST   The highest Criticism, then, is more creative than creation, and the primary aim of the critic is to see the object as in itself it really is not; that is your theory, I believe?

GILBERT   Yes, that is my theory. To the critic the work of art is simply a suggestion for a new work of his own, that need not necessarily bear any obvious resemblance to the thing it criticizes. The one characteristic of a beautiful form is that one can put into it whatever one wishes, and see in it whatever one chooses to see; and the Beauty, that gives to creation its universal and aesthetic element, makes the critic a creator in his turn, and whispers of a thousand different things which were not present in the mind of him who carved the statue or painted the panel or graved the gem.

   It is sometimes said by those who understand neither the nature of the highest Criticism nor the charm of the highest Art, that the pictures that the critic loves most to write about are those that belong to the anecdotage of painting, and that deal with scenes taken out of literature or history. But this is not so. Indeed, pictures of this kind are far too intelligible. As a class, they rank with illustrations, and even considered from this point of view are failures, as they do not stir the imagination, but set definite bounds to it. For the domain of the painter is, as I suggested before, widely different from that of the poet. To the latter belongs life in its full and absolute entirety; not merely the beauty that men look at, but the beauty that men listen to also; not merely the momentary grace of form or the transient gladness of color, but the whole sphere of feeling, the perfect cycle of thought. The painter is so far limited that it is only through the mask of the body that he can show us the mystery of the soul; only through conventional images that he can handle ideas; only through its physical equivalents that he can deal with psychology. And how inadequately does he do it then, asking us to accept the torn turban of the Moor for the noble rage of Othello, or a dotard in a storm for the wild madness of Lear! Yet it seems as if nothing could stop him. Most of our elderly English painters spend their wicked and wasted lives in poaching upon the domain of the poets, marring their motives by clumsy treatment, and striving to render, by visible form or color, the marvel of what is invisible, the splendor of what is not seen. Their picures are, as a natural consequence, insufferably tedious. They have degraded the invisible arts into the obvious arts, and the one thing not worth looking at is the obvious. I do not say that poet and painter may not treat of the same subject. They have always done so, and will always do so. But while the poet can be pictorial or not, as he chooses, the painter must be pictorial always. For a painter is limited, not to what he sees in nature, but to what upon canvas may be seen.

And so, my dear Ernest, pictures of this kind will not really fascinate the critic. He will turn from them to such works as make him brood and dream and fancy, to works that possess the subtle quality of suggestion, and seem to tell one that even from them there is an escape into a wider world. It is sometimes said that the tragedy of an artist's life is that he cannot realize his ideal. But the true tragedy that dogs the steps of most artists is that they realize their ideal too absolutely. For, when the ideal is realized, it is robbed of its wonder and its mystery, and becomes simply a new starting point for an ideal that is other than itself. This is the reason why music is the perfect type of art. Music can never reveal its ultimate secret. This, also, is the explanation of the value of limitations in art. The sculptor gladly surrenders imitative color, and the painter the actual dimensions of form, because by such renunciations they are able to avoid too definite a presentation of the Real, which would be mere imitation, and too definite a realization of the Ideal, which would be too purely intellectual. It is through its very incompleteness that Art becomes complete in beauty, and so addresses itself, not to the faculty of recognition nor to the faculty of reason, but to the aesthetic sense alone, which, while accepting both reason and recognition as stages of apprehension, subordinates them both to a pure synthetic impression of the work of art as a whole, and, taking whatever alien emotional elements the work may possess, uses their very complexity as a means by which a richer unity may be added to the ultimate impression itself. You see, then, how it is that the aesthetic critic rejects these obvious modes of art that have but one message to deliver, and having delivered it become dumb and sterile, and seeks rather for such modes as suggest reverie and mood, and by their imaginative beauty make all interpretations true, and no interpretation final. Some resemblance, no doubt, the creative work of the critic will have to the work that has stirred him to creation, but it will be such resemblance as exists, not between Nature and the mirror that the painter of landscape or figure may be supposed to hold up to her, but between Nature and the work of the decorative artist. Just as on the flowerless carpets of Persia, tulip and rose blossom indeed and are lovely to look on, though they are not reproduced in visible shape or line; just as the pearl and purple of the sea shell is echoed in the church of St. Mark at Venice; just as the vaulted ceiling of the wondrous chapel at Ravenna is made gorgeous by the gold and green and sapphire of the peacock's tail, though the birds of Juno fly not across it; so the critic reproduces the work that he criticizes in a mode that is never imitative, and part of whose charm may really consist in the rejection of resemblance, and shows us in this way not merely the meaning but also the mystery of Beauty, and, by transforming each art into literature, solves once for all the problem of Art's unity.

But I see it is time for supper. After we have discussed some Chambertin and a few ortolans,[5] we will pass on to the question of the critic considered in the light of the interpreter.

ERNEST   Ah! you admit, then, that the critic may occasionally be allowed to see the object as in itself it really is.

GILBERT   I am not quite sure. Perhaps I may admit it after supper. There is a subtle influence in supper.

1890, 1891

Preface to *The Picture of Dorian Gray*

The artist is the creator of beautiful things.
To reveal art and conceal the artist is art's aim.
The critic is he who can translate into another manner or a new material his impression of beautiful things.
    The highest, as the lowest, form of criticism is a mode of autobiography.
Those who find ugly meanings in beautiful things are corrupt without being charming. This is a fault.
    Those who find beautiful meanings in beautiful things are the cultivated. For these there is hope.
    They are the elect to whom beautiful things mean only Beauty.
    There is no such thing as a moral or an immoral book.
    Books are well written, or badly written. That is all.
The nineteenth-century dislike of Realism is the rage of Caliban[1] seeing his own face in a glass.
    The nineteenth-century dislike of Romanticism is the rage of Caliban not seeing his own face in a glass.
The moral life of man forms part of the subject matter of the artist, but the morality of art consists in the perfect use of an imperfect medium. No artist desires to prove anything. Even things that are true can be proved.
    No artist has ethical sympathies. An ethical sympathy in an artist is an unpardonable mannerism of style.
    No artist is ever morbid. The artist can express everything.
Thought and language are to the artist instruments of an art.
    Vice and Virtue are to the artist materials for an art.
From the point of view of form, the type of all the arts is the art of the musician. From the point of view of feeling, the actor's craft is the type.
    All art is at once surface and symbol.
    Those who go beneath the surface do so at their peril.
    Those who read the symbol do so at their peril.
It is the spectator, and not life, that art really mirrors.
    Diversity of opinion about a work of art shows that the work is new, complex, and vital.
    When critics disagree the artist is in accord with himself. We can forgive a man for making a useful thing as long as he does not admire

5. Birds esteemed by epicures for their delicate flavor. "Chambertin": one of the finest wines of Burgundy.

1. The character in Shakespeare's *Tempest* is half-human, half-monster.

it. The only excuse for making a useless thing is that one admires it intensely.

   All art is quite useless.

                             1891

The Importance of Being Earnest   Of the four stage comedies by Wilde,

his last, *The Importance of Being Earnest,* is generally regarded as his masterpiece. It was first staged in February 1895 and was an immediate hit. Only one critic failed to find it delightful; curiously, this was Wilde's fellow playwright from Ireland, Bernard Shaw, who, though amused, found Wilde's wit "hateful" and "sinister," and thought the play exhibited "real degeneracy." Despite Shaw's complaints, the first London production ran for eighty-six performances, but when Wilde was sentenced to prison, production ceased for several years. Shortly before his death it was revived in London and New York, and has subsequently become a classic of the theater.

In its original version, the play was in four acts. At the request of the stage producer, Wilde reduced it to three acts—the version almost always used in performances and therefore the version reprinted here. A few of the notes in the text cite passages from the four-act version.

The play was first published in 1899. Earlier, in an interview, Wilde had described his overall aim in writing it: "It has as its philosophy . . . that we should treat all the trivial things of life seriously, and all the serious things of life with sincere and studied triviality." Just before his death he remarked that although he was pleased with the "bright and happy" tone and temper of his play, he wished it might have had a "higher seriousness of intent." Later critics have found this seriousness of intent in the play's deconstruction of Victorian moral and social values. Like another Victorian masterpiece of the absurd, *Alice's Adventures in Wonderland, The Importance of Being Earnest* empties manners and morals of their underlying sense to create a nominalist world where earnest is not a quality of character but a name, where words, to paraphrase Humpty Dumpty in *Through the Looking-Glass,* mean what you choose them to mean, neither more nor less.

The literary ancestry of Wilde's play has been variously identified. In its witty wordplay and worldly attitudes it has been likened to comedies of the Restoration period such as Congreve's *Love for Love.* In its genial and lighthearted tone, it has some affinities with the festive comedies of Shakespeare, such as *Twelfth Night,* and with Goldsmith's *She Stoops to Conquer.* A more immediate predecessor was *Engaged* (1877), a comic play by W. S. Gilbert that anticipated some of the burlesque effects exploited by Wilde, such as the interrupting of sentimental scenes by the consumption of food, and the inviolable imperturbability of the speakers. Gilbert's advice to the actors who were putting on his *Engaged* is worth citing as a clue to how *The Importance of Being Earnest* may be most effectively imagined as a stage representation:

> It is absolutely essential to the success of this piece that it should be played with the most perfect earnestness and gravity throughout. . . . Directly the actors show that they are conscious of the absurdity of their utterances the piece begins to drag.

The Importance of Being Earnest

First Act

SCENE—*Morning room in* ALGERNON's *flat in Half-Moon Street.*[1]

The room is luxuriously and artistically furnished. The sound of a piano is heard in the adjoining room.

[LANE *is arranging afternoon tea on the table, and after the music has ceased,* ALGERNON *enters.*]

ALGERNON Did you hear what I was playing, Lane?

LANE I didn't think it polite to listen, sir.

ALGERNON I'm sorry for that, for your sake. I don't play accurately—anyone can play accurately—but I play with wonderful expression. As far as the piano is concerned, sentiment is my forte. I keep science for Life.

LANE Yes, sir.

ALGERNON And, speaking of the science of Life, have you got the cucumber sandwiches cut for Lady Bracknell?[2]

LANE Yes, sir. [*Hands them on a salver.*]

ALGERNON [*Inspects them, takes two, and sits down on the sofa.*] Oh! . . . by the way, Lane, I see from your book[3] that on Thursday night, when Lord Shoreham and Mr. Worthing were dining with me, eight bottles of champagne are entered as having been consumed.

LANE Yes, sir; eight bottles and a pint.

ALGERNON Why is it that at a bachelor's establishment the servants invariably drink the champagne? I ask merely for information.

LANE I attribute it to the superior quality of the wine, sir. I have often observed that in married households the champagne is rarely of a first-rate brand.

ALGERNON Good Heavens! Is marriage so demoralizing as that?

LANE I believe it *is* a very pleasant state, sir. I have had very little experience of it myself up to the present. I have only been married once. That was in consequence of a misunderstanding between myself and a young person.

ALGERNON [*Languidly.*] I don't know that I am much interested in your family life, Lane.

LANE No, sir; it is not a very interesting subject. I never think of it myself.

ALGERNON Very natural, I am sure. That will do, Lane, thank you.

LANE Thank you, sir.   [LANE *goes out.*]

ALGERNON Lane's views on marriage seem somewhat lax. Really, if the lower orders don't set us a good example, what on earth is the use of them? They seem, as a class, to have absolutely no sense of moral responsibility.

[*Enter* LANE.]

LANE Mr. Ernest Worthing.

---

1. A highly fashionable location (at the time of the play) in the West End of London.
2. The name of a place in Berkshire where the mother of Lord Alfred Douglas had her summer home, which Wilde had visited.
3. Cellar book, in which records were kept of wines.

[*Enter* JACK.]   [LANE *goes out.*]

ALGERNON   How are you, my dear Ernest? What brings you up to town?

JACK   Oh, pleasure, pleasure! What else should bring one anywhere? Eating as usual, I see, Algy!

ALGERNON [*Stiffly.*]   I believe it is customary in good society to take some slight refreshment at five o'clock. Where have you been since last Thursday?

JACK [*Sitting down on the sofa.*]   In the country.

ALGERNON   What on earth do you do there?

JACK [*Pulling off his gloves.*]   When one is in town one amuses oneself. When one is in the country one amuses other people. It is excessively boring.

ALGERNON   And who are the people you amuse?

JACK [*Airily.*]   Oh, neighbors, neighbors.

ALGERNON   Got nice neighbors in your part of Shropshire?

JACK   Perfectly horrid! Never speak to one of them.

ALGERNON   How immensely you must amuse them! [*Goes over and takes sandwich.*] By the way, Shropshire is your county, is it not?

JACK   Eh? Shropshire?⁴ Yes, of course. Hallo! Why all these cups? Why cucumber sandwiches? Why such reckless extravagance in one so young? Who is coming to tea?

ALGERNON   Oh! merely Aunt Augusta and Gwendolen.

JACK   How perfectly delightful!

ALGERNON   Yes, that is all very well; but I am afraid Aunt Augusta won't quite approve of your being here.

JACK   May I ask why?

ALGERNON   My dear fellow, the way you flirt with Gwendolen is perfectly disgraceful. It is almost as bad as the way Gwendolen flirts with you.

JACK   I am in love with Gwendolen. I have come up to town expressly to propose to her.

ALGERNON   I thought you had come up for pleasure? . . . I call that business.

JACK   How utterly unromantic you are!

ALGERNON   I really don't see anything romantic in proposing. It is very romantic to be in love. But there is nothing romantic about a definite proposal. Why, one may be accepted. One usually is, I believe. Then the excitement is all over. The very essence of romance is uncertainty. If ever I get married, I'll certainly try to forget the fact.

JACK   I have no doubt about that, dear Algy. The Divorce Court was specially invented for people whose memories are so curiously constituted.

ALGERNON   Oh! there is no use speculating on that subject. Divorces are made in Heaven—[JACK *puts out his hand to take a sandwich.* ALGERNON *at once interferes.*] Please don't touch the cucumber sandwiches. They are ordered specially for Aunt Augusta. [*Takes one and eats it.*]

JACK   Well, you have been eating them all the time.

---

4. As we learn later, the estate is in Hertfordshire, a very long distance from Shropshire. In the four-act version of the play, when this discrepancy is pointed out by Algernon, Jack replies: "My dear fellow! Surely you don't expect me to be accurate about geography? No gentleman is accurate about geography. Why, I got a prize for geography when I was at school. I can't be expected to know anything about it now."

ALGERNON   That is quite a different matter. She is my aunt. [*Takes plate from below.*] Have some bread and butter. The bread and butter is for Gwendolen. Gwendolen is devoted to bread and butter.

JACK [*Advancing to table and helping himself.*]   And very good bread and butter it is too.

ALGERNON   Well, my dear fellow, you need not eat as if you were going to eat it all. You behave as if you were married to her already. You are not married to her already, and I don't think you ever will be.

JACK   Why on earth do you say that?

ALGERNON   Well, in the first place, girls never marry the men they flirt with. Girls don't think it right.

JACK   Oh, that is nonsense!

ALGERNON   It isn't. It is a great truth. It accounts for the extraordinary number of bachelors that one sees all over the place. In the second place, I don't give my consent.

JACK   Your consent!

ALGERNON   My dear fellow, Gwendolen is my first cousin. And before I allow you to marry her, you will have to clear up the whole question of Cecily. [*Rings bell.*]

JACK   Cecily! What on earth do you mean? What do you mean, Algy, by Cecily? I don't know anyone of the name of Cecily.

[*Enter* LANE.]

ALGERNON   Bring me that cigarette case Mr. Worthing left in the smoking-room the last time he dined here.

LANE   Yes, sir.   [LANE *goes out.*]

JACK   Do you mean to say you have had my cigarette case all this time? I wish to goodness you had let me know. I have been writing frantic letters to Scotland Yard[5] about it. I was very nearly offering a large reward.

ALGERNON   Well, I wish you would offer one. I happen to be more than usually hard up.

JACK   There is no good offering a large reward now that the thing is found.

[*Enter* LANE *with the cigarette case on a salver.* ALGERNON *takes it at once.* LANE *goes out.*]

ALGERNON   I think that is rather mean of you, Ernest, I must say. [*Opens case and examines it.*] However, it makes no matter, for, now that I look at the inscription inside, I find that the thing isn't yours after all.

JACK   Of course it's mine. [*Moving to him.*] You have seen me with it a hundred times, and you have no right whatsoever to read what is written inside. It is a very ungentlemanly thing to read a private cigarette case.

ALGERNON   Oh! it is absurd to have a hard-and-fast rule about what one should read and what one shouldn't. More than half of modern culture depends on what one shouldn't read.

JACK   I am quite aware of the fact, and I don't propose to discuss modern culture. It isn't the sort of thing one should talk of in private. I simply want my cigarette case back.

ALGERNON   Yes; but this isn't your cigarette case. This cigarette case is a present from someone of the name of Cecily, and you said you didn't know anyone of that name.

5. Police headquarters in London.

JACK   Well, if you want to know, Cecily happens to be my aunt.

ALGERNON   Your aunt!

JACK   Yes. Charming old lady she is, too. Lives at Tunbridge Wells.[6] Just give it back to me, Algy.

ALGERNON [*retreating to back of sofa.*]   But why does she call herself little Cecily if she is your aunt and lives at Tunbridge Wells? [*Reading.*] "From little Cecily with her fondest love."

JACK [*Moving to sofa and kneeling upon it.*]   My dear fellow, what on earth is there in that? Some aunts are tall, some aunts are not tall. That is a matter that surely an aunt may be allowed to decide for herself. You seem to think that every aunt should be exactly like your aunt! That is absurd! For Heaven's sake give me back my cigarette case. [*Follows Algy round the room.*]

ALGERNON   Yes. But why does your aunt call you her uncle? "From little Cecily, with her fondest love to her dear Uncle Jack." There is no objection, I admit, to an aunt being a small aunt, but why an aunt, no matter what her size may be, should call her own nephew her uncle, I can't quite make out. Besides, your name isn't Jack at all; it is Ernest.

JACK   It isn't Ernest; it's Jack.

ALGERNON   You have always told me it was Ernest. I have introduced you to everyone as Ernest. You answer to the name of Ernest. You look as if your name was Ernest. You are the most earnest looking person I ever saw in my life. It is perfectly absurd your saying that your name isn't Ernest. It's on your cards. Here is one of them. [*Taking it from case.*] "Mr. Ernest Worthing, B. 4, The Albany."[7] I'll keep this as a proof that your name is Ernest if ever you attempt to deny it to me, or to Gwendolen, or to anyone else. [*Puts the card in his pocket.*]

JACK   Well, my name is Ernest in town and Jack in the country, and the cigarette case was given to me in the country.

ALGERNON   Yes, but that does not account for the fact that your small Aunt Cecily, who lives at Tunbridge Wells, calls you her dear uncle. Come, old boy, you had much better have the thing out at once.

JACK   My dear Algy, you talk exactly as if you were a dentist. It is very vulgar to talk like a dentist when one isn't a dentist. It produces a false impression.

ALGERNON   Well, that is exactly what dentists always do. Now, go on! Tell me the whole thing. I may mention that I have always suspected you of being a confirmed and secret Bunburyist; and I am quite sure of it now.

JACK   Bunburyist? What on earth do you mean by a Bunburyist?

ALGERNON   I'll reveal to you the meaning of that incomparable expression as soon as you are kind enough to inform me why you are Ernest in town and Jack in the country.

JACK   Well, produce my cigarette case first.

ALGERNON   Here it is. [*Hands cigarette case.*] Now produce your explanation, and pray make it improbable. [*Sits on sofa.*]

JACK   My dear fellow, there is nothing improbable about my explanation at all. In fact it's perfectly ordinary. Old Mr. Thomas Cardew, who

6. A fashionable resort town south of London.
7. A former residence of the duke of Albany (brother of George IV) near Piccadilly that had been converted into elegant apartments often rented by country gentry for visits to London.

1766 / Oscar Wilde

adopted me when I was a little boy, made me in his will guardian to his granddaughter, Miss Cecily Cardew. Cecily, who addresses me as her uncle from motives of respect that you could not possibly appreciate, lives at my place in the country under the charge of her admirable governess, Miss Prism.

ALGERNON Where is that place in the country, by the way?

JACK That is nothing to you, dear boy. You are not going to be invited. . . . I may tell you candidly that the place is not in Shropshire.

ALGERNON I suspected that, my dear fellow! I have Bunburyed all over Shropshire on two separate occasions. Now, go on. Why are you Ernest in town and Jack in the country?

JACK My dear Algy, I don't know whether you will be able to understand my real motives. You are hardly serious enough. When one is placed in the position of guardian, one has to adopt a very high moral tone on all subjects. It's one's duty to do so. And as a high moral tone can hardly be said to conduce very much to either one's health or one's happiness, in order to get up to town I have always pretended to have a younger brother of the name of Ernest, who lives in the Albany, and gets into the most dreadful scrapes. That, my dear Algy, is the whole truth pure and simple.

ALGERNON The truth is rarely pure and never simple. Modern life would be very tedious if it were either, and modern literature a complete impossibility!

JACK That wouldn't be at all a bad thing.

ALGERNON Literary criticism is not your forte, my dear fellow. Don't try it. You should leave that to people who haven't been at a University. They do it so well in the daily papers. What you really are is a Bunburyist. I was quite right in saying you were a Bunburyist. You are one of the most advanced Bunburyists I know.

JACK What on earth do you mean?

ALGERNON You have invented a very useful young brother called Ernest, in order that you may be able to come up to town as often as you like. I have invented an invaluable permanent invalid called Bunbury, in order that I may be able to go down into the country whenever I choose. Bunbury is perfectly invaluable. If it wasn't for Bunbury's extraordinary bad health, for instance, I wouldn't be able to dine with you at Willis's tonight, for I have been really engaged[8] to Aunt Augusta for more than a week.

JACK I haven't asked you to dine with me anywhere tonight.

ALGERNON I know. You are absurdly careless about sending out invitations. It is very foolish of you. Nothing annoys people so much as not receiving invitations.

JACK You had much better dine with your Aunt Augusta.

ALGERNON I haven't the smallest intention of doing anything of the kind. To begin with, I dined there on Monday, and once a week is quite enough to dine with one's own relations. In the second place, whenever I do dine there I am always treated as a member of the family, and sent down with[9] either no woman at all, or two. In the third place, I know perfectly well whom she will place me next to, tonight. She will place me next Mary

---

8. I.e., committed to attend her dinner party. "Willis's": a first-class restaurant in the vicinity of St. James's Street.

9. I.e., required to escort, as a dinner partner.

Farquhar, who always flirts with her own husband across the dinner table. That is not very pleasant. Indeed, it is not even decent . . . and that sort of thing is enormously on the increase. The amount of women in London who flirt with their own husbands is perfectly scandalous. It looks so bad. It is simply washing one's clean linen in public. Besides, now that I know you to be a confirmed Bunburyist, I naturally want to talk to you about Bunburying. I want to tell you the rules.

JACK   I'm not a Bunburyist at all. If Gwendolen accepts me, I am going to kill my brother, indeed I think I'll kill him in any case. Cecily is a little too much interested in him. It is rather a bore. So I am going to get rid of Ernest. And I strongly advise you to do the same with Mr. . . . with your invalid friend who has the absurd name.

ALGERNON   Nothing will induce me to part with Bunbury, and if you ever get married, which seems to me extremely problematic, you will be very glad to know Bunbury. A man who marries without knowing Bunbury has a very tedious time of it.

JACK   That is nonsense. If I marry a charming girl like Gwendolen, and she is the only girl I ever saw in my life that I would marry, I certainly won't want to know Bunbury.

ALGERNON   Then your wife will. You don't seem to realize, that in married life three is company and two is none.

JACK   [Sententiously.]   That, my dear young friend, is the theory that the corrupt French Drama has been propounding for the last fifty years.[1]

ALGERNON   Yes; and that the happy English home has proved in half the time.

JACK   For heaven's sake, don't try to be cynical. It's perfectly easy to be cynical.

ALGERNON   My dear fellow, it isn't easy to be anything nowadays. There's such a lot of beastly competition about. [The sound of an electric bell is heard.] Ah! that must be Aunt Augusta. Only relatives, or creditors, ever ring in that Wagnerian manner.[2] Now, if I get her out of the way for ten minutes, so that you can have an opportunity for proposing to Gwendolen, may I dine with you tonight at Willis's?

JACK   I suppose so, if you want to.

ALGERNON   Yes, but you must be serious about it. I hate people who are not serious about meals. It is so shallow of them.
         [Enter LANE.]

LANE   Lady Bracknell and Miss Fairfax.
         [ALGERNON goes forward to meet them. Enter LADY BRACKNELL and
         GWENDOLEN.]

LADY BRACKNELL   Good afternoon, dear Algernon, I hope you are behaving very well.

ALGERNON   I'm feeling very well, Aunt Augusta.

LADY BRACKNELL   That's not quite the same thing. In fact the two things rarely go together. [Sees JACK and bows to him with icy coldness.]

ALGERNON [To GWENDOLEN.]   Dear me, you are smart![3]

---

1. Almost all the plays by the leading French playwrights of the second half of the 19th century (Alexandre Dumas *fils*, Émile Augier, and Victorien Sardou) focus on the topic of marital infidelity. As Brander Matthews, an American critic, noted in 1882, "the trio—husband, wife, and lover" had become "almost universal" in the French theater.
2. Insistently loud, like some of the music in Richard Wagner's large-scale operas.
3. Elegantly fashionable.

GWENDOLEN   I am always smart! Aren't I, Mr. Worthing?

JACK   You're quite perfect, Miss Fairfax.

GWENDOLEN   Oh! I hope I am not that. It would leave no room for developments, and I intend to develop in many directions. [GWENDOLEN *and* JACK *sit down together in the corner.*]

LADY BRACKNELL   I'm sorry if we are a little late, Algernon, but I was obliged to call on dear Lady Harbury. I hadn't been there since her poor husband's death. I never saw a woman so altered; she looks quite twenty years younger. And now I'll have a cup of tea, and one of those nice cucumber sandwiches you promised me.

ALGERNON   Certainly, Aunt Augusta. [*Goes over to teatable.*]

LADY BRACKNELL   Won't you come and sit here, Gwendolen?

GWENDOLEN   Thanks, mamma,[4] I'm quite comfortable where I am.

ALGERNON [*Picking up empty plate in horror.*]   Good heavens! Lane! Why are there no cucumber sandwiches? I ordered them specially.

LANE [*Gravely.*]   There were no cucumbers in the market this morning, sir. I went down twice.

ALGERNON   No cucumbers!

LANE   No, sir. Not even for ready money.

ALGERNON   That will do, Lane, thank you.

LANE   Thank you, sir.

ALGERNON   I am greatly distressed, Aunt Augusta, about there being no cucumbers, not even for ready money.

LADY BRACKNELL   It really makes no matter, Algernon. I had some crumpets[5] with Lady Harbury, who seems to me to be living entirely for pleasure now.

ALGERNON   I hear her hair has turned quite gold from grief.

LADY BRACKNELL   It certainly has changed its color. From what cause I, of course, cannot say. [ALGERNON *crosses and hands tea.*] Thank you. I've quite a treat for you tonight, Algernon. I am going to send you down with Mary Farquhar. She is such a nice woman, and so attentive to her husband. It's delightful to watch them.

ALGERNON   I am afraid, Aunt Augusta, I shall have to give up the pleasure of dining with you tonight after all.

LADY BRACKNELL [*Frowning.*]   I hope not, Algernon. It would put my table completely out. Your uncle would have to dine upstairs. Fortunately he is accustomed to that.

ALGERNON   It is a great bore, and, I need hardly say, a terrible disappointment to me, but the fact is I have just had a telegram to say that my poor friend Bunbury is very ill again. [*Exchanges glances with* JACK.] They seem to think I should be with him.

LADY BRACKNELL   It is very strange. This Mr. Bunbury seems to suffer from curiously bad health.

ALGERNON   Yes; poor Bunbury is a dreadful invalid.

LADY BRACKNELL   Well, I must say, Algernon, that I think it is high time that Mr. Bunbury made up his mind whether he was going to live or to die. This shilly-shallying with the question is absurd. Nor do I in any way

---

4. Pronounced with the accent on the second syllable.

5. A kind of toasted muffin.

approve of the modern sympathy with invalids. I consider it morbid. Illness of any kind is hardly a thing to be encouraged in others. Health is the primary duty of life. I am always telling that to your poor uncle, but he never seems to take much notice . . . as far as any improvement in his ailments goes. I should be obliged if you would ask Mr. Bunbury, from me, to be kind enough not to have a relapse on Saturday, for I rely on you to arrange my music for me. It is my last reception, and one wants something that will encourage conversation, particularly at the end of the season[6] when everyone has practically said whatever they had to say, which, in most cases, was probably not much.

ALGERNON   I'll speak to Bunbury, Aunt Augusta, if he is still conscious, and I think I can promise you he'll be all right by Saturday. Of course the music is a great difficulty. You see, if one plays good music, people don't listen, and if one plays bad music, people don't talk. But I'll run over the program I've drawn out, if you will kindly come into the next room for a moment.

LADY BRACKNELL   Thank you, Algernon. It is very thoughtful of you. [*Rising, and following* ALGERNON.] I'm sure the program will be delightful, after a few expurgations. French songs I cannot possibly allow. People always seem to think that they are improper, and either look shocked, which is vulgar, or laugh, which is worse. But German sounds a thoroughly respectable language, and indeed, I believe is so. Gwendolen, you will accompany me.

GWENDOLEN   Certainly, mamma.

[LADY BRACKNELL *and* ALGERNON *go into the music room,* GWENDOLEN *remains behind.*]

JACK   Charming day it has been, Miss Fairfax.

GWENDOLEN   Pray don't talk to me about the weather, Mr. Worthing. Whenever people talk to me about the weather, I always feel quite certain that they mean something else. And that makes me so nervous.

JACK   I do mean something else.

GWENDOLEN   I thought so. In fact, I am never wrong.

JACK   And I would like to be allowed to take advantage of Lady Bracknell's temporary absence . . .

GWENDOLEN   I would certainly advise you to do so. Mamma has a way of coming back suddenly into a room that I have often had to speak to her about.

JACK [*Nervously.*]   Miss Fairfax, ever since I met you I have admired you more than any girl . . . I have ever met since . . . I met you.

GWENDOLEN   Yes, I am quite aware of the fact. And I often wish that in public, at any rate, you had been more demonstrative. For me you have always had an irresistible fascination. Even before I met you I was far from indifferent to you. [JACK *looks at her in amazement.*] We live, as I hope you know, Mr. Worthing, in an age of ideals. The fact is constantly mentioned in the more expensive monthly magazines, and has reached the provincial pulpits, I am told: and my ideal has always been to love someone of the name of Ernest. There is something in that name that

---

6. The social season, extending from May through July, when people of fashion came into London from their country estates for entertainments and parties.

inspires absolute confidence. The moment Algernon first mentioned to me that he had a friend called Ernest, I knew I was destined to love you.

JACK You really love me, Gwendolen?

GWENDOLEN Passionately!

JACK Darling! You don't know how happy you've made me.

GWENDOLEN My own Ernest!

JACK But you don't really mean to say that you couldn't love me if my name wasn't Ernest?

GWENDOLEN But your name is Ernest.

JACK Yes, I know it is. But supposing it was something else? Do you mean to say you couldn't love me then?

GWENDOLEN [Glibly.] Ah! that is clearly a metaphysical speculation, and like most metaphysical speculations has very little reference at all to the actual facts of real life, as we know them.

JACK Personally, darling, to speak quite candidly, I don't much care about the name of Ernest . . . I don't think the name suits me at all.

GWENDOLEN It suits you perfectly. It is a divine name. It has a music of its own. It produces vibrations.

JACK Well, really, Gwendolen, I must say that I think there are lots of other much nicer names. I think Jack, for instance, a charming name.

GWENDOLEN Jack? . . . No, there is very little music in the name Jack, if any at all, indeed. It does not thrill. It produces absolutely no vibrations. . . . I have known several Jacks, and they all, without exception, were more than usually plain. Besides, Jack is a notorious domesticity for John! And I pity any woman who is married to a man called John. She would probably never be allowed to know the entrancing pleasure of a single moment's solitude. The only really safe name is Ernest.

JACK Gwendolen, I must get christened at once—I mean we must get married at once. There is no time to be lost.

GWENDOLEN Married, Mr. Worthing?

JACK [Astounded.] Well . . . surely. You know that I love you, and you led me to believe, Miss Fairfax, that you were not absolutely indifferent to me.

GWENDOLEN I adore you. But you haven't proposed to me yet. Nothing has been said at all about marriage. The subject has not even been touched on.

JACK Well . . . may I propose to you now?

GWENDOLEN I think it would be an admirable opportunity. And to spare you any possible disappointment, Mr. Worthing, I think it only fair to tell you quite frankly beforehand that I am fully determined to accept you.

JACK Gwendolen!

GWENDOLEN Yes, Mr. Worthing, what have you got to say to me?

JACK You know what I have got to say to you.

GWENDOLEN Yes, but you don't say it.

JACK Gwendolen, will you marry me? [Goes on his knees.]

GWENDOLEN Of course I will, darling. How long you have been about it! I am afraid you have had very little experience in how to propose.

JACK My own one, I have never loved anyone in the world but you.

GWENDOLEN Yes, but men often propose for practice. I know my brother Gerald does. All my girlfriends tell me so. What wonderfully blue eyes you have, Ernest! They are quite, quite blue. I hope you will always look at me just like that, especially when there are other people present.

[*Enter* LADY BRACKNELL.]

LADY BRACKNELL   Mr. Worthing! Rise, sir, from this semi-recumbent posture. It is most indecorous.

GWENDOLEN   Mamma! [*He tries to rise; she restrains him.*] I must beg you to retire. This is no place for you. Besides, Mr. Worthing has not quite finished yet.

LADY BRACKNELL   Finished what, may I ask?

GWENDOLEN   I am engaged to Mr. Worthing, mamma.

[*They rise together.*]

LADY BRACKNELL   Pardon me, you are not engaged to anyone. When you do become engaged to someone, I, or your father, should his health permit him, will inform you of the fact. An engagement should come on a young girl as a surprise, pleasant or unpleasant, as the case may be. It is hardly a matter that she could be allowed to arrange for herself. . . . And now I have a few questions to put to you, Mr. Worthing. While I am making these inquiries, you, Gwendolen, will wait for me below in the carriage.

GWENDOLEN [*Reproachfully.*]   Mamma!

LADY BRACKNELL   In the carriage, Gwendolen! [GWENDOLEN *goes to the door. She and* JACK *blow kisses to each other behind* LADY BRACKNELL's *back.* LADY BRACKNELL *looks vaguely about as if she could not understand what the noise was. Finally turns round.*] Gwendolen, the carriage!

GWENDOLEN   Yes, mamma. [*Goes out, looking back at* JACK.]

LADY BRACKNELL [*Sitting down.*]   You can take a seat, Mr. Worthing.

[*Looks in her pocket for notebook and pencil.*]

JACK   Thank you, Lady Bracknell, I prefer standing.

LADY BRACKNELL [*Pencil and notebook in hand.*]   I feel bound to tell you that you are not down on my list of eligible young men, although I have the same list as the dear Duchess of Bolton has. We work together, in fact. However, I am quite ready to enter your name, should your answers be what a really affectionate mother requires. Do you smoke?

JACK   Well, yes, I must admit I smoke.

LADY BRACKNELL   I am glad to hear it. A man should always have an occupation of some kind. There are far too many idle men in London as it is. How old are you?

JACK   Twenty-nine.

LADY BRACKNELL   A very good age to be married at. I have always been of opinion that a man who desires to get married should know either everything or nothing. Which do you know?

JACK [*After some hesitation.*]   I know nothing, Lady Bracknell.

LADY BRACKNELL   I am pleased to hear it. I do not approve of anything that tampers with natural ignorance. Ignorance is like a delicate exotic fruit; touch it and the bloom is gone. The whole theory of modern education is radically unsound. Fortunately in England, at any rate, education produces no effect whatsoever. If it did, it would prove a serious danger to the upper classes, and probably lead to acts of violence in Grosvenor Square.[7] What is your income?

---

7. A fashionable residential area in the West End of London.

JACK Between seven and eight thousand a year.

LADY BRACKNELL [*Makes a note in her book.*] In land, or in investments?

JACK In investments, chiefly.

LADY BRACKNELL That is satisfactory. What between the duties expected of one during one's lifetime, and the duties exacted from one after one's death,[8] land has ceased to be either a profit or a pleasure. It gives one position, and prevents one from keeping it up. That's all that can be said about land.

JACK I have a country house with some land, of course, attached to it, about fifteen hundred acres, I believe; but I don't depend on that for my real income. In fact, as far as I can make out, the poachers are the only people who make anything out of it.

LADY BRACKNELL A country house! How many bedrooms? Well, that point can be cleared up afterwards. You have a town house, I hope? A girl with a simple, unspoiled nature, like Gwendolen, could hardly be expected to reside in the country.

JACK Well, I own a house in Belgrave Square,[9] but it is let by the year to Lady Bloxham. Of course, I can get it back whenever I like, at six months' notice.

LADY BRACKNELL Lady Bloxham? I don't know her.

JACK Oh, she goes about very little. She is a lady considerably advanced in years.

LADY BRACKNELL Ah, nowadays that is no guarantee of respectability of character. What number in Belgrave Square?

JACK 149.

LADY BRACKNELL [*Shaking her head.*] The unfashionable side. I thought there was something. However, that could easily be altered.

JACK Do you mean the fashion, or the side?

LADY BRACKNELL [*Sternly.*] Both, if necessary, I presume. What are your politics?

JACK Well, I am afraid I really have none. I am a Liberal Unionist.[1]

LADY BRACKNELL Oh, they count as Tories. They dine with us. Or come in the evening, at any rate. Now to minor matters. Are your parents living?

JACK I have lost both my parents.

LADY BRACKNELL Both? To lose one parent may be regarded as a misfortune—to lose *both* seems like carelessness. Who was your father? He was evidently a man of some wealth. Was he born in what the Radical papers call the purple of commerce, or did he rise from the ranks of aristocracy?

JACK I am afraid I really don't know. The fact is, Lady Bracknell, I said I had lost my parents. It would be nearer the truth to say that my parents seem to have lost me. . . . I don't actually know who I am by birth. I was . . . well, I was found.

LADY BRACKNELL Found!

JACK The late Mr. Thomas Cardew, an old gentleman of a very charitable

8. The wordplay is on "death duties"—i.e., inheritance taxes.
9. Another fashionable residential area in the West End known as Belgravia.

1. A splinter group of members of the Liberal Party who, in 1886, led by Joseph Chamberlain, joined forces with the Conservative Party (the "Tories") in opposing Home Rule for Ireland.

and kindly disposition, found me, and gave me the name of Worthing, because he happened to have a first-class ticket for Worthing in his pocket at the time. Worthing is a place in Sussex. It is a seaside resort.

LADY BRACKNELL   Where did the charitable gentleman who had a first-class ticket for this seaside resort find you?

JACK [*Gravely.*]   In a handbag.

LADY BRACKNELL   A handbag?

JACK. [*Very seriously.*] Yes, Lady Bracknell. I was in a handbag—a somewhat large, black leather handbag, with handles to it—an ordinary handbag, in fact.

LADY BRACKNELL   In what locality did this Mr. James, or Thomas, Cardew come across this ordinary handbag?

JACK   In the cloak room at Victoria Station. It was given to him in mistake for his own.[2]

LADY BRACKNELL   The cloak room at Victoria Station?

JACK   Yes. The Brighton line.

LADY BRACKNELL   The line is immaterial. Mr. Worthing, I confess I feel somewhat bewildered by what you have just told me. To be born, or at any rate, bred in a handbag, whether it had handles or not, seems to me to display a contempt for the ordinary decencies of family life that reminds one of the worst excesses of the French Revolution. And I presume you know what that unfortunate movement led to? As for the particular locality in which the handbag was found, a cloak room at a railway station might serve to conceal a social indiscretion—has probably, indeed, been used for that purpose before now—but it could hardly be regarded as an assured basis for a recognized position in good society.

JACK   May I ask you then what you would advise me to do? I need hardly say I would do anything in the world to ensure Gwendolen's happiness.

LADY BRACKNELL   I would strongly advise you, Mr. Worthing, to try and acquire some relations as soon as possible, and to make a definite effort to produce at any rate one parent, of either sex, before the season is quite over.[3]

JACK   Well, I don't see how I could possibly manage to do that. I can produce the handbag at any moment, it is in my dressing room at home. I really think that should satisfy you, Lady Bracknell.

LADY BRACKNELL   Me, sir! What has it to do with me? You can hardly imagine that I and Lord Bracknell would dream of allowing our only daughter—a girl brought up with the utmost care—to marry into a cloak room, and form an alliance with a parcel? Good morning, Mr. Worthing!

[LADY BRACKNELL *sweeps out in majestic indignation.*]

JACK   Good morning! [ALGERNON, *from the other room, strikes up the Wedding March.* JACK *looks perfectly furious, and goes to the door.*] For goodness' sake don't play that ghastly tune, Algy! How idiotic you are!

[*The music stops, and* ALGERNON *enters cheerily.*]

2. In the four-act version of the play, Jack explains further what happened to Mr. Cardew: "He did not discover the error till he arrived at his own house. All subsequent efforts to ascertain who I was were unavailing."
3. In the four-act version of the play, Jack later comments to Algernon about Lady Bracknell's demands about locating parents: "After all what does it matter whether a man has ever had a father and mother or not? Mothers, of course, are all right. They pay a chap's bills and don't bother him. But fathers bother a chap and never pay his bills. I don't know a single chap at the club who speaks to his father." And Algernon remarks: "Yes. Fathers are certainly not popular just at present. . . . They are like these chaps, the minor poets. They are never quoted."

ALGERNON   Didn't it go off all right, old boy? You don't mean to say Gwendolen refused you? I know it is a way she has. She is always refusing people. I think it is most ill-natured of her.

JACK   Oh, Gwendolen is as right as a trivet.[4] As far as she is concerned, we are engaged. Her mother is perfectly unbearable. Never met such a Gorgon[5] . . . I don't really know what a Gorgon is like, but I am quite sure that Lady Bracknell is one. In any case, she is a monster, without being a myth, which is rather unfair . . . I beg your pardon, Algy, I suppose I shouldn't talk about your own aunt in that way before you.

ALGERNON   My dear boy, I love hearing my relations abused. It is the only thing that makes me put up with them at all. Relations are simply a tedious pack of people who haven't got the remotest knowledge of how to live, nor the smallest instinct about when to die.

JACK   Oh, that is nonsense!

ALGERNON   It isn't!

JACK   Well, I won't argue about the matter. You always want to argue about things.

ALGERNON   That is exactly what things were originally made for.

JACK   Upon my word, if I thought that, I'd shoot myself . . . [*A pause.*] You don't think there is any chance of Gwendolen becoming like her mother in about a hundred and fifty years, do you, Algy?

ALGERNON   All women become like their mothers. That is their tragedy. No man does. That's his.

JACK   Is that clever?

ALGERNON   It is perfectly phrased! and quite as true as any observation in civilized life should be.

JACK   I am sick to death of cleverness. Everybody is clever nowadays. You can't go anywhere without meeting clever people. The thing has become an absolute public nuisance. I wish to goodness we had a few fools left.

ALGERNON   We have.

JACK   I should extremely like to meet them. What do they talk about?

ALGERNON   The fools? Oh! about the clever people, of course.

JACK   What fools!

ALGERNON   By the way, did you tell Gwendolen the truth about your being Ernest in town, and Jack in the country?

JACK   [*In a very patronizing manner.*]   My dear fellow, the truth isn't quite the sort of thing one tells to a nice sweet refined girl. What extraordinary ideas you have about the way to behave to a woman!

ALGERNON   The only way to behave to a woman is to make love to her, if she is pretty, and to someone else if she is plain.

JACK   Oh, that is nonsense.

ALGERNON   What about your brother? What about the profligate Ernest?

JACK   Oh, before the end of the week I shall have got rid of him. I'll say he died in Paris of apoplexy. Lots of people die of apoplexy, quite suddenly, don't they?

ALGERNON   Yes, but it's hereditary, my dear fellow. It's a sort of thing that runs in families. You had much better say a severe chill.

---

4. Proverbial expression meaning reliably steady, like a tripod ("trivet") used to support pots over a fire.

5. A mythical female creature, like Medusa, whose look turned into stone anyone beholding her.

JACK   You are sure a severe chill isn't hereditary, or anything of that kind?

ALGERNON   Of course it isn't!

JACK   Very well, then. My poor brother Ernest is carried off suddenly in Paris, by a severe chill. That gets rid of him.[6]

ALGERNON   But I thought you said that . . . Miss Cardew was a little too much interested in your poor brother Ernest? Won't she feel his loss a good deal?

JACK   Oh, that is all right. Cecily is not a silly romantic girl, I am glad to say. She has got a capital appetite, goes on long walks, and pays no attention at all to her lessons.

ALGERNON   I would rather like to see Cecily.

JACK   I will take very good care you never do. She is excessively pretty, and she is only just eighteen.

ALGERNON   Have you told Gwendolen yet that you have an excessively pretty ward who is only just eighteen?

JACK   Oh! one doesn't blurt these things out to people. Cecily and Gwendolen are perfectly certain to be extremely great friends. I'll bet you anything you like that half an hour after they have met, they will be calling each other sister.

ALGERNON   Women only do that when they have called each other a lot of other things first. Now, my dear boy, if we want to get a good table at Willis's, we really must go and dress. Do you know it is nearly seven?

JACK   [Irritably.] Oh! it always is nearly seven.

ALGERNON   Well, I'm hungry.

JACK   I never knew you when you weren't. . . .

ALGERNON   What shall we do after dinner? Go to the theater?

JACK   Oh no! I loathe listening.

ALGERNON   Well, let us go to the club?

JACK   Oh, no! I hate talking.

ALGERNON   Well, we might trot around to the Empire[7] at ten?

JACK   Oh no! I can't bear looking at things. It is so silly.

ALGERNON   Well, what shall we do?

JACK   Nothing!

ALGERNON   It is awfully hard work doing nothing. However, I don't mind hard work where there is no definite object of any kind.

   [Enter LANE.]

LANE   Miss Fairfax.

   [Enter GWENDOLEN. LANE goes out.]

ALGERNON   Gwendolen, upon my word!

GWENDOLEN   Algy, kindly turn your back. I have something very particular to say to Mr. Worthing.

ALGERNON   Really, Gwendolen, I don't think I can allow this at all.

GWENDOLEN   Algy, you always adopt a strictly immoral attitude towards life. You are not quite old enough to do that. [ALGERNON retires to the fireplace.]

JACK   My own darling!

---

6. In the four-act version of the play Jack explains further: "I'll wear mourning for him, of course; that would be only decent. I don't at all mind wearing mourning. I think that all black, with a good pearl pin, rather smart. Then I'll go down home and break the news to my household."

7. A music hall in Leicester Square that featured light entertainment.

GWENDOLEN   Ernest, we may never be married. From the expression on mamma's face I fear we never shall. Few parents nowadays pay any regard to what their children say to them. The old-fashioned respect for the young is fast dying out. Whatever influence I ever had over mamma, I lost at the age of three. But although she may prevent us from becoming man and wife, and I may marry someone else, and marry often, nothing that she can possibly do can alter my eternal devotion to you.

JACK   Dear Gwendolen!

GWENDOLEN   The story of your romantic origin, as related to me by mamma, with unpleasing comments, has naturally stirred the deeper fibers of my nature. Your Christian name has an irresistible fascination. The simplicity of your character makes you exquisitely incomprehensible to me. Your town address at the Albany I have. What is your address in the country?

JACK   The Manor House, Woolton, Hertfordshire.

[ALGERNON, *who has been carefully listening, smiles to himself, and writes the address on his shirt-cuff.*[8] *Then picks up the Railway Guide.*]

GWENDOLEN   There is a good postal service, I suppose? It may be necessary to do something desperate. That of course will require serious consideration. I will communicate with you daily.

JACK   My own one!

GWENDOLEN   How long do you remain in town?

JACK   Till Monday.

GWENDOLEN   Good! Algy, you may turn round now.

ALGERNON   Thanks, I've turned round already.

GWENDOLEN   You may also ring the bell.

JACK   You will let me see you to your carriage, my own darling?

GWENDOLEN   Certainly.

JACK [*To* LANE, *who now enters.*]   I will see Miss Fairfax out.

LANE   Yes, sir. [JACK *and* GWENDOLEN *go off.*]

[LANE *presents several letters on a salver to* ALGERNON. *It is to be surmised that they are bills, as* ALGERNON *after looking at the envelopes, tears them up.*]

ALGERNON   A glass of sherry, Lane.

LANE   Yes, sir.

ALGERNON   Tomorrow, Lane, I'm going Bunburying.

LANE   Yes, sir.

ALGERNON   I shall probably not be back till Monday. You can put up my dress clothes, my smoking jacket,[9] and all the Bunbury suits . . .

LANE   Yes, sir. [*Handing sherry.*]

ALGERNON   I hope tomorrow will be a fine day, Lane.

LANE   It never is, sir.

ALGERNON   Lane, you're a perfect pessimist.

LANE   I do my best to give satisfaction, sir.

[*Enter* JACK. LANE *goes off.*]

JACK   There's a sensible, intellectual girl! the only girl I ever cared for in

---

8. Because shirt cuffs were heavily starched they provided a good surface on which to make notes.
9. Coat worn when gentlemen assembled in a room designated for smoking. The object was to avoid contaminating their regular clothing with the smell of cigars or pipes, which was considered offensive to ladies.

my life. [ALGERNON *is laughing immoderately.*] What on earth are you so amused at?

ALGERNON   Oh, I'm a little anxious about poor Bunbury, that is all.

JACK   If you don't take care, your friend Bunbury will get you into a serious scrape some day.

ALGERNON   I love scrapes. They are the only things that are never serious.

JACK   Oh, that's nonsense, Algy. You never talk anything but nonsense.

ALGERNON   Nobody ever does.

> [JACK *looks indignantly at him, and leaves the room.* ALGERNON *lights a cigarette, reads his shirt-cuff, and smiles.*]

ACT-DROP[1]

Second Act

> SCENE—*Garden at the Manor House. A flight of gray stone steps leads up to the house. The garden, an old-fashioned one, full of roses. Time of year, July. Basket chairs, and a table covered with books, are set under a large yew tree.*

> [MISS PRISM[2] *discovered seated at the table.* CECILY *is at the back watering flowers.*]

MISS PRISM [*Calling.*]   Cecily, Cecily! Surely such a utilitarian occupation as the watering of flowers is rather Moulton's duty than yours? Especially at a moment when intellectual pleasures await you. Your German grammar is on the table. Pray open it at page fifteen. We will repeat yesterday's lesson.

CECILY [*Coming over very slowly.*]   But I don't like German. It isn't at all a becoming language. I know perfectly well that I look quite plain after my German lesson.

MISS PRISM   Child, you know how anxious your guardian is that you should improve yourself in every way. He laid particular stress on your German, as he was leaving for town yesterday. Indeed, he always lays stress on your German when he is leaving for town.

CECILY   Dear Uncle Jack is so very serious! Sometime he is so serious that I think he cannot be quite well.

MISS PRISM [*Drawing herself up.*]   Your guardian enjoys the best of health, and his gravity of demeanor is especially to be commended in one so comparatively young as he is. I know no one who has a higher sense of duty and responsibility.

CECILY   I suppose that is why he often looks a little bored when we three are together.

MISS PRISM   Cecily! I am surprised at you. Mr. Worthing has many troubles in his life. Idle merriment and triviality would be out of place in his conversation. You must remember his constant anxiety about that unfortunate young man his brother.

CECILY   I wish Uncle Jack would allow that unfortunate young man, his

1. A special curtain lowered during theatrical performances to denote intervals between acts or scenes.
2. The name has connotations with the expression "prunes and prism" from Dickens's *Little Dorrit*, in which Mrs. General, a prim and proper teacher of manners for young ladies, trains them to repeat "prunes and prism" aloud because this exercise "gives a pretty form to the lips."

brother, to come down here sometimes. We might have a good influence over him, Miss Prism. I am sure you certainly would. You know German, and geology, and things of that kind influence a man very much. [CECILY *begins to write in her diary.*]

MISS PRISM [*Shaking her head.*]   I do not think that even I could produce any effect on a character that according to his own brother's admission is irretrievably weak and vacillating. Indeed I am not sure that I would desire to reclaim him. I am not in favor of this modern mania for turning bad people into good people at a moment's notice. As a man sows so let him reap.[3] You must put away your diary, Cecily. I really don't see why you should keep a diary at all.

CECILY   I keep a diary in order to enter the wonderful secrets of my life. If I didn't write them down I should probably forget all about them.

MISS PRISM   Memory, my dear Cecily, is the diary that we all carry about with us.

CECILY   Yes, but it usually chronicles the things that have never happened, and couldn't possibly have happened. I believe that Memory is responsible for nearly all the three-volume novels that Mudie[4] sends us.

MISS PRISM   Do not speak slightingly of the three-volume novel, Cecily. I wrote one myself in earlier days.

CECILY   Did you really, Miss Prism? How wonderfully clever you are! I hope it did not end happily? I don't like novels that end happily. They depress me so much.

MISS PRISM   The good ended happily, and the bad unhappily. That is what Fiction means.

CECILY   I suppose so. But it seems very unfair. And was your novel ever published?

MISS PRISM   Alas! no. The manuscript unfortunately was abandoned. I use the word in the sense of lost or mislaid. To your work, child, these speculations are profitless.

CECILY [*Smiling.*]   But I see dear Dr. Chasuble coming up through the garden.

MISS PRISM [*Rising and advancing.*]   Dr. Chasuble! This is indeed a pleasure.

[*Enter* CANON CHASUBLE.]

CHASUBLE   And how are we this morning? Miss Prism, you are, I trust, well?

CECILY   Miss Prism has just been complaining of a slight headache. I think it would do her so much good to have a short stroll with you in the Park, Dr. Chasuble.

MISS PRISM   Cecily, I have not mentioned anything about a headache.

CECILY   No, dear Miss Prism, I know that, but I felt instinctively that you had a headache. Indeed I was thinking about that, and not about my German lesson, when the Rector came in.

CHASUBLE   I hope, Cecily, you are not inattentive.

CECILY   Oh, I am afraid I am.

---

3. Cf. Galatians 6.7.
4. Mudie's Circulating Library lent copies of new three-volume novels (usually sentimental tales) to subscribers for a moderate fee. Mudie's power in controlling the book market, especially for novels, was on the wane by 1895.

CHASUBLE   That is strange. Were I fortunate enough to be Miss Prism's pupil, I would hang upon her lips. [MISS PRISM *glares*.] I spoke metaphorically.—My metaphor was drawn from bees. Ahem! Mr. Worthing, I suppose, has not returned from town yet?

MISS PRISM   We do not expect him till Monday afternoon.

CHASUBLE   Ah yes, he usually likes to spend his Sunday in London. He is not one of those whose sole aim is enjoyment, as, by all accounts, that unfortunate young man his brother seems to be. But I must not disturb Egeria[5] and her pupil any longer.

MISS PRISM   Egeria? My name is Laetitia, Doctor.

CHASUBLE   [*Bowing*.]   A classical allusion merely, drawn from the Pagan authors. I shall see you both no doubt at Evensong?[6]

MISS PRISM   I think, dear Doctor, I will have a stroll with you. I find I have a headache after all, and a walk might do it good.

CHASUBLE   With pleasure, Miss Prism, with pleasure. We might go as far as the schools and back.

MISS PRISM   That would be delightful. Cecily, you will read your Political Economy[7] in my absence. The chapter on the Fall of the Rupee[8] you may omit. It is somewhat too sensational. Even these metallic problems have their melodramatic side. [*Goes down the garden with* DR. CHASUBLE.]

CECILY   [*Picks up books and throws them back on table*.]   Horrid Political Economy! Horrid Geography! Horrid, horrid German!

[*Enter* MERRIMAN *with a card on a salver*.]

MERRIMAN   Mr. Ernest Worthing has just driven over from the station. He has brought his luggage with him.

CECILY   [*Takes the card and reads it*.]   "Mr. Ernest Worthing, B. 4, The Albany, W." Uncle Jack's brother! Did you tell him Mr. Worthing was in town?

MERRIMAN   Yes, Miss. He seemed very much disappointed. I mentioned that you and Miss Prism were in the garden. He said he was anxious to speak to you privately for a moment.

CECILY.   Ask Mr. Ernest Worthing to come here. I suppose you had better talk to the housekeeper about a room for him.

MERRIMAN   Yes, Miss. [MERRIMAN *goes off*.]

CECILY   I have never met any really wicked person before. I feel rather frightened. I am so afraid he will look just like everyone else. [*Enter* ALGERNON, *very gay and debonair*.] He does!

ALGERNON   [*Raising his hat*.]   You are my little cousin Cecily, I'm sure.

CECILY   You are under some strange mistake. I am not little. In fact, I believe I am more than usually tall for my age. [ALGERNON *is rather taken aback*.] But I am your cousin Cecily. You, I see from your card, are Uncle Jack's brother, my cousin Ernest, my wicked cousin Ernest.

ALGERNON   Oh! I am not really wicked at all, cousin Cecily. You mustn't think that I am wicked.

CECILY   If you are not, then you have certainly been deceiving us all in a

5. Roman goddess of fountains. Her name was also used as an epithet for a woman who provides guidance for other women.
6. Evening church services.

7. I.e., book about economics.
8. The basic unit of currency in India. British civil servants who worked in India were paid in rupees and would suffer from its fall in value.

very inexcusable manner. I hope you have not been leading a double life, pretending to be wicked and being really good all the time. That would be hypocrisy.

ALGERNON [*Looks at her in amazement.*]   Oh! Of course I have been rather reckless.

CECILY   I am glad to hear it.

ALGERNON   In fact, now you mention the subject, I have been very bad in my own small way.

CECILY   I don't think you should be so proud of that, though I am sure it must have been very pleasant.

ALGERNON   It is much pleasanter being here with you.

CECILY   I can't understand how you are here at all. Uncle Jack won't be back till Monday afternoon.

ALGERNON   That is a great disappointment. I am obliged to go up by the first train on Monday morning. I have a business appointment that I am anxious . . . to miss.

CECILY   Couldn't you miss it anywhere but in London?

ALGERNON   No: the appointment is in London.

CECILY   Well, I know, of course, how important it is not to keep a business engagement, if one wants to retain any sense of the beauty of life, but still I think you had better wait till Uncle Jack arrives. I know he wants to speak to you about your emigrating.

ALGERNON   About my what?

CECILY   Your emigrating. He has gone up to buy your outfit.

ALGERNON   I certainly wouldn't let Jack buy my outfit. He has no taste in neckties at all.

CECILY   I don't think you will require neckties. Uncle Jack is sending you to Australia.[9]

ALGERNON   Australia? I'd sooner die.

CECILY   Well, he said at dinner on Wednesday night, that you would have to choose between this world, the next world, and Australia.

ALGERNON   Oh, well! The accounts I have received of Australia and the next world are not particularly encouraging. This world is good enough for me, cousin Cecily.

CECILY   Yes, but are you good enough for it?

ALGERNON   I'm afraid I'm not that. That is why I want you to reform me. You might make that your mission, if you don't mind, cousin Cecily.

CECILY   I'm afraid I've no time, this afternoon.

ALGERNON   Well, would you mind my reforming myself this afternoon?

CECILY   It is rather Quixotic of you. But I think you should try.

ALGERNON   I will. I feel better already.

CECILY   You are looking a little worse.

ALGERNON   That is because I am hungry.

CECILY   How thoughtless of me. I should have remembered that when one is going to lead an entirely new life, one requires regular and wholesome meals. Won't you come in?

---

9. Although Australia had originally been a place to which criminals were banished, it was, by this time, like Canada, a place to which families might send harmless but useless members, who would be paid an allowance to remain abroad.

ALGERNON   Thank you. Might I have a buttonhole[1] first? I never have any appetite unless I have a buttonhole first.

CECILY   A Maréchal Niel?[2] [*Picks up scissors.*]

ALGERNON   No, I'd sooner have a pink rose.

CECILY   Why? [*Cuts a flower.*]

ALGERNON   Because you are like a pink rose, cousin Cecily.

CECILY   I don't think it can be right for you to talk to me like that. Miss Prism never says such things to me.

ALGERNON   Then Miss Prism is a shortsighted old lady. [CECILY *puts the rose in his buttonhole.*] You are the prettiest girl I ever saw.

CECILY   Miss Prism says that all good looks are a snare.

ALGERNON   They are a snare that every sensible man would like to be caught in.

CECILY   Oh! I don't think I would care to catch a sensible man. I shouldn't know what to talk to him about.

[*They pass into the house.* MISS PRISM *and* DR. CHASUBLE *return.*]

MISS PRISM   You are too much alone, dear Dr. Chasuble. You should get married. A misanthrope I can understand—a womanthrope, never!

CHASUBLE [*With a scholar's shudder.*][3]   Believe me, I do not deserve so neologistic a phrase. The precept as well as the practice of the Primitive Church was distinctly against matrimony.

MISS PRISM [*Sententiously.*]   That is obviously the reason why the Primitive Church has not lasted up to the present day. And you do not seem to realize, dear Doctor, that by persistently remaining single, a man converts himself into a permanent public temptation. Men should be more careful; this very celibacy leads weaker vessels astray.

CHASUBLE   But is a man not equally attractive when married?

MISS PRISM   No married man is ever attractive except to his wife.

CHASUBLE   And often, I've been told, not even to her.

MISS PRISM   That depends on the intellectual sympathies of the woman. Maturity can always be depended on. Ripeness can be trusted. Young women are green. [DR. CHASUBLE *starts.*] I spoke horticulturally. My metaphor was drawn from fruits. But where is Cecily?

CHASUBLE   Perhaps she followed us to the schools.

[*Enter* JACK *slowly from the back of the garden. He is dressed in the deepest mourning, with crape hat-band and black gloves.*]

MISS PRISM   Mr. Worthing!

CHASUBLE   Mr. Worthing?

MISS PRISM   This is indeed a surprise. We did not look for you till Monday afternoon.

JACK [*Shakes* MISS PRISM's *hand in a tragic manner.*]   I have returned sooner than I expected. Dr. Chasuble, I hope you are well?

CHASUBLE   Dear Mr. Worthing, I trust this garb of woe does not betoken some terrible calamity?

JACK   My brother.

MISS PRISM   More shameful debts and extravagance?

---

1. I.e., a flower worn in the buttonhole of a man's coat lapel.
2. A chrome yellow variety of rose named after one of the generals of Napoleon III.

3. He shudders because instead of using the correct word for woman hater, *misogynist*, she has coined her own expression.

CHASUBLE   Still leading his life of pleasure?

JACK [*Shaking his head.*]   Dead!

CHASUBLE   Your brother Ernest dead?

JACK   Quite dead.

MISS PRISM   What a lesson for him! I trust he will profit by it.

CHASUBLE   Mr. Worthing, I offer you my sincere condolence. You have at least the consolation of knowing that you were always the most generous and forgiving of brothers.

JACK   Poor Ernest! He had many faults, but it is a sad, sad blow.

CHASUBLE   Very sad indeed. Were you with him at the end?

JACK   No. He died abroad; in Paris, in fact. I had a telegram last night from the manager of the Grand Hotel.

CHASUBLE   Was the cause of death mentioned?

JACK   A severe chill, it seems.

MISS PRISM   As a man sows, so shall he reap.

CHASUBLE [*Raising his hand.*]   Charity, dear Miss Prism, charity! None of us are perfect. I myself am peculiarly susceptible to drafts. Will the interment take place here?

JACK   No. He seemed to have expressed a desire to be buried in Paris.

CHASUBLE   In Paris! [*Shakes his head.*] I fear that hardly points to any very serious state of mind at the last. You would no doubt wish me to make some slight allusion to this tragic domestic affliction next Sunday. [JACK *presses his hand convulsively.*] My sermon on the meaning of the manna in the wilderness can be adapted to almost any occasion, joyful, or, as in the present case, distressing. [*All sigh.*] I have preached it at harvest celebrations, christenings, confirmations, on days of humiliation and festal days. The last time I delivered it was in the Cathedral, as a charity sermon on behalf of the Society for the Prevention of Discontent among the Upper Orders. The Bishop, who was present, was much struck by some of the analogies I drew.

JACK   Ah! That reminds me, you mentioned christenings, I think, Dr. Chasuble? I suppose you know how to christen all right? [DR. CHASUBLE *looks astounded.*] I mean, of course, you are continually christening, aren't you?

MISS PRISM   It is, I regret to say, one of the Rector's most constant duties in this parish. I have often spoken to the poorer classes on the subject. But they don't seem to know what thrift is.

CHASUBLE   But is there any particular infant in whom you are interested, Mr. Worthing? Your brother was, I believe, unmarried, was he not?

JACK   Oh yes.

MISS PRISM [*Bitterly.*]   People who live entirely for pleasure usually are.

JACK   But it is not for any child, dear Doctor. I am very fond of children. No! the fact is, I would like to be christened myself, this afternoon, if you have nothing better to do.

CHASUBLE   But surely, Mr. Worthing, you have been christened already?

JACK   I don't remember anything about it.

CHASUBLE   But have you any grave doubts on the subject?

JACK   I certainly intend to have. Of course I don't know if the thing would bother you in any way, or if you think I am a little too old now.

CHASUBLE   Not at all. The sprinkling, and, indeed, the immersion of adults is a perfectly canonical practice.

JACK   Immersion!

CHASUBLE   You need have no apprehensions. Sprinkling is all that is necessary, or indeed I think advisable. Our weather is so changeable. At what hour would you wish the ceremony performed?

JACK   Oh, I might trot round about five if that would suit you.

CHASUBLE   Perfectly, perfectly! In fact I have two similar ceremonies to perform at that time. A case of twins that occurred recently in one of the outlying cottages on your own estate. Poor Jenkins the carter, a most hard-working man.

JACK   Oh! I don't see much fun in being christened along with other babies. It would be childish. Would half-past five do?

CHASUBLE   Admirably! Admirably! [*Takes out watch.*] And now, dear Mr. Worthing, I will not intrude any longer into a house of sorrow. I would merely beg you not to be too much bowed down by grief. What seem to us bitter trials are often blessings in disguise.

MISS PRISM   This seems to me a blessing of an extremely obvious kind.

[*Enter* CECILY *from the house.*]

CECILY   Uncle Jack! Oh, I am pleased to see you back. But what horrid clothes you have got on! Do go and change them.

MISS PRISM   Cecily!

CHASUBLE   My child! my child! [CECILY *goes towards* JACK; *he kisses her brow in a melancholy manner.*]

CECILY   What is the matter, Uncle Jack? Do look happy! You look as if you had toothache, and I have got such a surprise for you. Who do you think is in the dining room? Your brother!

JACK   Who?

CECILY   Your brother Ernest. He arrived about half an hour ago.

JACK   What nonsense! I haven't got a brother!

CECILY   Oh, don't say that. However badly he may have behaved to you in the past he is still your brother. You couldn't be so heartless as to disown him. I'll tell him to come out. And you will shake hands with him, won't you, Uncle Jack? [*Runs back into the house.*]

CHASUBLE   These are very joyful tidings.

MISS PRISM   After we had all been resigned to his loss, his sudden return seems to me peculiarly distressing.

JACK   My brother is in the dining room? I don't know what it all means. I think it is perfectly absurd.

[*Enter* ALGERNON *and* CECILY *hand in hand. They come slowly up to* JACK.]

JACK   Good heavens! [*Motions* ALGERNON *away.*]

ALGERNON   Brother John, I have come down from town to tell you that I am very sorry for all the trouble I have given you, and that I intend to lead a better life in the future. [JACK *glares at him and does not take his hand.*]

CECILY   Uncle Jack, you are not going to refuse your own brother's hand?

JACK   Nothing will induce me to take his hand. I think his coming down here disgraceful. He knows perfectly well why.

CECILY   Uncle Jack, do be nice. There is some good in everyone. Ernest has just been telling me about his poor invalid friend Mr. Bunbury whom he goes to visit so often. And surely there must be much good in one who is kind to an invalid, and leaves the pleasures of London to sit by a bed of pain.

JACK Oh! he has been talking about Bunbury, has he?

CECILY Yes, he has told me all about poor Mr. Bunbury, and his terrible state of health.

JACK Bunbury! Well, I won't have him talk to you about Bunbury or about anything else. It is enough to drive one perfectly frantic.

ALGERNON Of course I admit that the faults were all on my side. But I must say that I think that Brother John's coldness to me is peculiarly painful. I expected a more enthusiastic welcome, especially considering it is the first time I have come here.

CECILY Uncle Jack, if you don't shake hands with Ernest, I will never forgive you.

JACK Never forgive me?

CECILY Never, never, never!

JACK Well, this is the last time I shall ever do it. [Shakes hands with ALGERNON and glares.]

CHASUBLE It's pleasant, is it not, to see so perfect a reconciliation? I think we might leave the two brothers together.

MISS PRISM Cecily, you will come with us.

CECILY Certainly, Miss Prism. My little task of reconciliation is over.

CHASUBLE You have done a beautiful action today, dear child.

MISS PRISM We must not be premature in our judgments.

CECILY I feel very happy. [They all go off.]

JACK You young scoundrel, Algy, you must get out of this place as soon as possible. I don't allow any Bunburying here.

[Enter MERRIMAN.]

MERRIMAN I have put Mr. Ernest's things in the room next to yours, sir. I suppose that is all right?

JACK What?

MERRIMAN Mr. Ernest's luggage, sir. I have unpacked it and put it in the room next to your own.

JACK His luggage?

MERRIMAN Yes, sir. Three portmanteaus, a dressing case, two hat-boxes, and a large luncheon basket.[4]

ALGERNON I am afraid I can't stay more than a week this time.

JACK Merriman, order the dogcart[5] at once. Mr. Ernest has been suddenly called back to town.

MERRIMAN Yes, sir.   [Goes back into the house.]

ALGERNON What a fearful liar you are, Jack. I have not been called back to town at all.

JACK Yes, you have.

4. According to *Cassell's Domestic Dictionary*, "a convenient little receptacle in which gentlemen who are going out shooting for the day, or artists who wish to sketch, can carry their luncheon with them." "Portmanteaus": large leather suitcases. A "dressing case" (also according to *Cassell's*) was "ordinarily made of rosewood, mahogany or cormandel wood." It was supposed to include "scent bottles, jars for pomade and tooth-powders, hair brushes and combs, shaving, nail and tooth brushes, razors and strop, nail scissors, button-hook, tweezer, nail file and penknife" [noted by Russell Jackson].
5. A horse-drawn cart with seats, originally designed to carry hunters and their hunting dogs.

ALGERNON   I haven't heard anyone call me.

JACK   Your duty as a gentleman calls you back.

ALGERNON   My duty as a gentleman has never interfered with my pleasures in the smallest degree.

JACK   I can quite understand that.

ALGERNON   Well, Cecily is a darling.

JACK   You are not to talk of Miss Cardew like that. I don't like it.

ALGERNON   Well, I don't like your clothes. You look perfectly ridiculous in them. Why on earth don't you go up and change? It is perfectly childish to be in deep mourning for a man who is actually staying for a whole week with you in your house as a guest. I call it grotesque.

JACK   You are certainly not staying with me for a whole week as a guest or anything else. You have got to leave . . . by the four-five train.

ALGERNON   I certainly won't leave you so long as you are in mourning. It would be most unfriendly. If I were in mourning you would stay with me, I suppose. I should think it very unkind if you didn't.

JACK   Well, will you go if I change my clothes?

ALGERNON   Yes, if you are not too long. I never saw anybody take so long to dress, and with such little result.

JACK   Well, at any rate, that is better than being always overdressed as you are.

ALGERNON   If I am occasionally a little overdressed, I make up for it by being always immensely overeducated.

JACK   Your vanity is ridiculous, your conduct an outrage, and your presence in my garden utterly absurd. However, you have got to catch the four-five, and I hope you will have a pleasant journey back to town. This Bunburying, as you call it, has not been a great success for you. [*Goes into the house.*]

ALGERNON   I think it has been a great success. I'm in love with Cecily, and that is everything.

[*Enter* CECILY *at the back of the garden. She picks up the can and begins to water the flowers.*]

But I must see her before I go, and make arrangements for another Bunbury. Ah, there she is.

CECILY   Oh, I merely came back to water the roses. I thought you were with Uncle Jack.

ALGERNON   He's gone to order the dogcart for me.

CECILY   Oh, is he going to take you for a nice drive?

ALGERNON   He's going to send me away.

CECILY   Then have we got to part?

ALGERNON   I am afraid so. It's very painful parting.

CECILY   It is always painful to part from people whom one has known for a very brief space of time. The absence of old friends one can endure with equanimity. But even a momentary separation from anyone to whom one has just been introduced is almost unbearable.

ALGERNON   Thank you.

[*Enter* MERRIMAN.]

MERRIMAN   The dogcart is at the door, sir. [ALGERNON *looks appealingly at* CECILY.]

CECILY   It can wait, Merriman . . . for . . . five minutes.

MERRIMAN   Yes, Miss.   [*Exit* MERRIMAN.]

ALGERNON   I hope, Cecily, I shall not offend you if I state quite frankly and openly that you seem to me to be in every way the visible personification of absolute perfection.

CECILY   I think your frankness does you great credit, Ernest. If you will allow me I will copy your remarks into my diary. [*Goes over to table and begins writing in diary.*]

ALGERNON   Do you really keep a diary? I'd give anything to look at it. May I?

CECILY   Oh no. [*Puts her hand over it.*] You see, it is simply a very young girl's record of her own thoughts and impressions, and consequently meant for publication. When it appears in volume form I hope you will order a copy. But pray, Ernest, don't stop. I delight in taking down from dictation. I have reached "absolute perfection." You can go on. I am quite ready for more.

ALGERNON   [*Somewhat taken aback.*]   Ahem! Ahem!

CECILY   Oh, don't cough, Ernest. When one is dictating one should speak fluently and not cough. Besides, I don't know how to spell a cough. [*Writes as* ALGERNON *speaks.*]

ALGERNON   [*Speaking very rapidly.*]   Cecily, ever since I first looked upon your wonderful and incomparable beauty, I have dared to love you wildly, passionately, devotedly, hopelessly.

CECILY   I don't think that you should tell me that you love me wildly, passionately, devotedly, hopelessly. Hopelessly doesn't seem to make much sense, does it?

ALGERNON   Cecily!
   [*Enter* MERRIMAN.]

MERRIMAN   The dogcart is waiting, sir.

ALGERNON   Tell it to come round next week, at the same hour.

MERRIMAN   [*Looks at* CECILY, *who makes no sign.*]   Yes, sir.
   [MERRIMAN *retires.*]

CECILY   Uncle Jack would be very much annoyed if he knew you were staying on till next week, at the same hour.

ALGERNON   Oh, I don't care about Jack. I don't care for anybody in the whole world but you. I love you, Cecily. You will marry me, won't you?

CECILY   You silly boy! Of course. Why, we have been engaged for the last three months.

ALGERNON   For the last three months?

CECILY   Yes, it will be exactly three months on Thursday.

ALGERNON   But how did we become engaged?

CECILY   Well, ever since dear Uncle Jack first confessed to us that he had a younger brother who was very wicked and bad, you of course have formed the chief topic of conversation between myself and Miss Prism. And of course a man who is much talked about is always very attractive. One feels there must be something in him after all. I daresay it was foolish of me, but I fell in love with you, Ernest.

ALGERNON   Darling! And when was the engagement actually settled?

CECILY   On the 14th of February last. Worn out by your entire ignorance of my existence, I determined to end the matter one way or the other, and after a long struggle with myself I accepted you under this dear old tree here. The next day I bought this little ring in your name, and this is the little bangle with the true lovers' knot I promised you always to wear.

ALGERNON   Did I give you this? It's very pretty, isn't it?

CECILY   Yes, you've wonderfully good taste, Ernest. It's the excuse I've always given for your leading such a bad life. And this is the box in which I keep all your dear letters. [*Kneels at table, opens box, and produces letters tied up with blue ribbon.*]

ALGERNON   My letters! But my own sweet Cecily, I have never written you any letters.

CECILY   You need hardly remind me of that, Ernest. I remember only too well that I was forced to write your letters for you. I always wrote three times a week, and sometimes oftener.

ALGERNON   Oh, do let me read them, Cecily?

CECILY   Oh, I couldn't possibly. They would make you far too conceited. [*Replaces box.*] The three you wrote me after I had broken off the engagement are so beautiful, and so badly spelled, that even now I can hardly read them without crying a little.

ALGERNON   But was our engagement ever broken off?

CECILY   Of course it was. On the 22nd of last March. You can see the entry if you like. [*Shows diary.*] "Today I broke off my engagement with Ernest. I feel it is better to do so. The weather still continues charming."

ALGERNON   But why on earth did you break if off? What had I done? I had done nothing at all. Cecily, I am very much hurt indeed to hear you broke it off. Particularly when the weather was so charming.

CECILY   It would hardly have been a really serious engagement if it hadn't been broken off at least once. But I forgave you before the week was out.

ALGERNON [*Crossing to her, and kneeling.*]   What a perfect angel you are, Cecily.

CECILY   You dear romantic boy. [*He kisses her, she puts her fingers through his hair.*] I hope your hair curls naturally, does it?

ALGERNON   Yes, darling, with a little help from others.

CECILY   I am so glad.

ALGERNON   You'll never break off our engagement again, Cecily?

CECILY   I don't think I could break it off now that I have actually met you. Besides, of course, there is the question of your name.

ALGERNON   Yes, of course. [*Nervously.*]

CECILY   You must not laugh at me, darling, but it had always been a girlish dream of mine to love someone whose name was Ernest. [ALGERNON rises, CECILY also.] There is something in that name that seems to inspire absolute confidence. I pity any poor married woman whose husband is not called Ernest.

ALGERNON   But, my dear child, do you mean to say you could not love me if I had some other name?

CECILY   But what name?

ALGERNON   Oh, any name you like—Algernon—for instance . . .

CECILY   But I don't like the name of Algernon.

ALGERNON   Well, my own dear, sweet, loving little darling, I really can't see why you should object to the name of Algernon. It is not at all a bad name. In fact, it is rather an aristocratic name. Half of the chaps who get into the Bankruptcy Court are called Algernon. But seriously, Cecily . . . [*Moving to her.*] . . . if my name was Algy, couldn't you love me?

CECILY [*Rising.*]   I might respect you, Ernest, I might admire your character, but I fear that I should not be able to give you my undivided attention.

ALGERNON   Ahem! Cecily! [*Picking up hat.*] Your Rector here is, I suppose, thoroughly experienced in the practice of all the rites and ceremonials of the Church?

CECILY   Oh, yes. Dr. Chasuble is a most learned man. He has never written a single book, so you can imagine how much he knows.

ALGERNON   I must see him at once on a most important christening—I mean on most important business.

CECILY   Oh!

ALGERNON   I shan't be away more than half an hour.

CECILY   Considering that we have been engaged since February the 14th, and that I only met you today for the first time, I think it is rather hard that you should leave me for so long a period as half an hour. Couldn't you make it twenty minutes?

ALGERNON   I'll be back in no time. [*Kisses her and rushes down the garden.*]

CECILY   What an impetuous boy he is! I like his hair so much. I must enter his proposal in my diary.

[*Enter* MERRIMAN.]

MERRIMAN   A Miss Fairfax has just called to see Mr. Worthing. On very important business, Miss Fairfax states.

CECILY   Isn't Mr. Worthing in his library?

MERRIMAN   Mr. Worthing went over in the direction of the Rectory some time ago.

CECILY   Pray ask the lady to come out here; Mr. Worthing is sure to be back soon. And you can bring tea.

MERRIMAN   Yes, Miss.   [*Goes out.*]

CECILY   Miss Fairfax! I suppose one of the many good elderly women who are associated with Uncle Jack in some of his philanthropic work in London. I don't quite like women who are interested in philanthropic work. I think it is so forward of them.

[*Enter* MERRIMAN.]

MERRIMAN   Miss Fairfax.

[*Enter* GWENDOLEN.]   [*Exit* MERRIMAN.]

CECILY [*Advancing to meet her.*]   Pray let me introduce myself to you. My name is Cecily Cardew.

GWENDOLEN   Cecily Cardew? [*Moving to her and shaking hands.*] What a very sweet name! Something tells me that we are going to be great friends. I like you already more than I can say. My first impressions of people are never wrong.

CECILY   How nice of you to like me so much after we have known each other such a comparatively short time. Pray sit down.

GWENDOLEN [*Still standing up.*]   I may call you Cecily, may I not?

CECILY   With pleasure!

GWENDOLEN   And you will always call me Gwendolen, won't you?

CECILY   If you wish.

GWENDOLEN   Then that is all quite settled, is it not?

CECILY   I hope so. [*A pause. They both sit down together.*]

GWENDOLEN   Perhaps this might be a favorable opportunity for my mentioning who I am. My father is Lord Bracknell. You have never heard of papa, I suppose?

CECILY I don't think so.

GWENDOLEN Outside the family circle, papa, I am glad to say, is entirely unknown. I think that is quite as it should be. The home seems to me to be the proper sphere for the man. And certainly once a man begins to neglect his domestic duties he becomes painfully effeminate, does he not? And I don't like that. It makes men so very attractive. Cecily, mamma, whose views on education are remarkably strict, has brought me up to be extremely shortsighted; it is part of her system; so do you mind my looking at you through my glasses?

CECILY Oh! not at all, Gwendolen. I am very fond of being looked at.

GWENDOLEN [After examining CECILY carefully through a lorgnette.] You are here on a short visit, I suppose.

CECILY Oh no! I live here.

GWENDOLEN [Severely.] Really? Your mother, no doubt, or some female relative of advanced years, resides here also?

CECILY Oh no! I have no mother, nor, in fact, any relations.

GWENDOLEN Indeed?

CECILY My dear guardian, with the assistance of Miss Prism, has the arduous task of looking after me.

GWENDOLEN Your guardian?

CECILY Yes, I am Mr. Worthing's ward.

GWENDOLEN Oh! It is strange he never mentioned to me that he had a ward. How secretive of him! He grows more interesting hourly. I am not sure, however, that the news inspires me with feelings of unmixed delight. [Rising and going to her.] I am very fond of you, Cecily; I have liked you ever since I met you! But I am bound to state that now that I know that you are Mr. Worthing's ward, I cannot help expressing a wish you were—well just a little older than you seem to be—and not quite so very alluring in appearance. In fact, if I may speak candidly——

CECILY Pray do! I think that whenever one has anything unpleasant to say, one should always be quite candid.

GWENDOLEN Well, to speak with perfect candor, Cecily, I wish that you were fully forty-two, and more than usually plain for your age. Ernest has a strong upright nature. He is the very soul of truth and honor. Disloyalty would be as impossible to him as deception. But even men of the noblest possible moral character are extremely susceptible to the influence of the physical charms of others. Modern, no less than Ancient History, supplies us with many most painful examples of what I refer to. If it were not so, indeed, History would be quite unreadable.

CECILY I beg your pardon, Gwendolen, did you say Ernest?

GWENDOLEN Yes.

CECILY Oh, but it is not Mr. Ernest Worthing who is my guardian. It is his brother—his elder brother.

GWENDOLEN [Sitting down again.] Ernest never mentioned to me that he had a brother.

CECILY I am sorry to say they have not been on good terms for a long time.

GWENDOLEN Ah! that accounts for it. And now that I think of it I have never heard any man mention his brother. The subject seems distasteful to most men. Cecily, you have lifted a load from my mind. I was growing almost anxious. It would have been terrible if any cloud had come across a friendship like ours, would it not? Of course you are quite, quite sure that it is not Mr. Ernest Worthing who is your guardian?

CECILY   Quite sure. [*A pause.*] In fact, I am going to be his.

GWENDOLEN [*Inquiringly.*]   I beg your pardon?

CECILY [*Rather shy and confidingly.*]   Dearest Gwendolen, there is no reason why I should make a secret of it to you. Our little county newspaper is sure to chronicle the fact next week. Mr. Ernest Worthing and I are engaged to be married.

GWENDOLEN [*Quite politely, rising.*]   My darling Cecily, I think there must be some slight error. Mr. Ernest Worthing is engaged to me. The announcement will appear in the *Morning Post*[6] on Saturday at the latest.

CECILY [*Very politely, rising.*]   I am afraid you must be under some misconception. Ernest proposed to me exactly ten minutes ago. [*Shows diary.*]

GWENDOLEN [*Examines diary through her lorgnette carefully.*]   It is certainly very curious, for he asked me to be his wife yesterday afternoon at 5:30. If you would care to verify the incident, pray do so. [*Produces diary of her own.*] I never travel without my diary. One should always have something sensational to read in the train. I am so sorry, dear Cecily, if it is any disappointment to you, but I am afraid *I* have the prior claim.

CECILY   It would distress me more than I can tell you, dear Gwendolen, if it caused you any mental or physical anguish, but I feel bound to point out that since Ernest proposed to you he clearly has changed his mind.

GWENDOLEN [*Meditatively.*]   If the poor fellow has been entrapped into any foolish promise I shall consider it my duty to rescue him at once, and with a firm hand.

CECILY [*Thoughtfully and sadly.*]   Whatever unfortunate entanglement my dear boy may have got into, I will never reproach him with it after we are married.

GWENDOLEN   Do you allude to me, Miss Cardew, as an entanglement? You are presumptuous. On an occasion of this kind it becomes more than a moral duty to speak one's mind. It becomes a pleasure.

CECILY   Do you suggest, Miss Fairfax, that I entrapped Ernest into an engagement? How dare you? This is no time for wearing the shallow mask of manners. When I see a spade I call it a spade.

GWENDOLEN [*Satirically.*]   I am glad to say that I have never seen a spade. It is obvious that our social spheres have been widely different.

[*Enter* MERRIMAN, *followed by the footman. He carries a salver, tablecloth, and plate stand.* CECILY *is about to retort. The presence of the servants exercises a restraining influence, under which both girls chafe.*]

MERRIMAN   Shall I lay tea here as usual, Miss?

CECILY [*Sternly, in a calm voice.*]   Yes, as usual.

[MERRIMAN *begins to clear table and lay cloth. A long pause.* CECILY *and* GWENDOLEN *glare at each other.*]

GWENDOLEN   Are there many interesting walks in the vicinity, Miss Cardew?

CECILY   Oh! yes! a great many. From the top of one of the hills quite close one can see five counties.

---

6. A popular journal featuring society gossip and also announcements of engagements and marriages.

GWENDOLEN   Five counties! I don't think I should like that. I hate crowds.

CECILY [*Sweetly.*]   I suppose that is why you live in town?

> [GWENDOLEN *bites her lip, and beats her foot nervously with her parasol.*]

GWENDOLEN [*Looking round.*]   Quite a well-kept garden this is, Miss Cardew.

CECILY   So glad you like it, Miss Fairfax.

GWENDOLEN   I had no idea there were any flowers in the country.

CECILY   Oh, flowers are as common here, Miss Fairfax, as people are in London.

GWENDOLEN   Personally I cannot understand how anybody manages to exist in the country, if anybody who is anybody does. The country always bores me to death.

CECILY   Ah! This is what the newspapers call agricultural depression, is it not? I believe the aristocracy are suffering very much from it just at present.[7] It is almost an epidemic amongst them, I have been told. May I offer you some tea, Miss Fairfax?

GWENDOLEN [*With elaborate politeness.*]   Thank you. [*Aside.*] Detestable girl! But I require tea!

CECILY [*Sweetly.*]   Sugar?

GWENDOLEN [*Superciliously.*]   No, thank you. Sugar is not fashionable any more. [CECILY *looks angrily at her, takes up the tongs and puts four lumps of sugar into the cup.*]

CECILY [*Severely.*]   Cake or bread and butter?

GWENDOLEN [*In a bored manner.*]   Bread and butter, please. Cake is rarely seen at the best houses nowadays.

CECILY [*Cuts a very large slice of cake, and puts it on the tray.*]   Hand that to Miss Fairfax.

> [MERRIMAN *does so, and goes out with footman.* GWENDOLEN *drinks the tea and makes a grimace. Puts down cup at once, reaches out her hand to the bread and butter, looks at it, and finds it is cake. Rises in indignation.*]

GWENDOLEN   You have filled my tea with lumps of sugar, and though I asked most distinctly for bread and butter, you have given me cake. I am known for the gentleness of my disposition, and the extraordinary sweetness of my nature, but I warn you, Miss Cardew, you may go too far.

CECILY [*Rising.*]   To save my poor, innocent, trusting boy from the machinations of any other girl there are no lengths to which I would not go.

GWENDOLEN   From the moment I saw you I distrusted you. I felt that you were false and deceitful. I am never deceived in such matters. My first impressions of people are invariably right.

CECILY   It seems to me, Miss Fairfax, that I am trespassing on your valuable time. No doubt you have many other calls of a similar character to make in the neighborhood.

> [*Enter* JACK.]

GWENDOLEN [*Catching sight of him.*]   Ernest! My own Ernest!

JACK   Gwendolen! Darling! [*Offers to kiss her.*]

---

7. From the 1870s on, landowners (including aristocrats) had been suffering severe losses because of adverse economic conditions.

GWENDOLEN [*Drawing back.*]   A moment! May I ask if you are engaged to be married to this young lady? [*Points to* CECILY.]

JACK [*Laughing.*]   To dear little Cecily! Of course not! What could have put such an idea into your pretty little head?

GWENDOLEN   Thank you. You may! [*Offers her cheek.*]

CECILY [*Very sweetly.*]   I knew there must be some misunderstanding, Miss Fairfax. The gentleman whose arm is at present round your waist is my dear guardian, Mr. John Worthing.

GWENDOLEN   I beg your pardon?

CECILY   This is Uncle Jack.

GWENDOLEN [*Receding.*]   Jack! Oh!

[*Enter* ALGERNON.]

CECILY   Here is Ernest.

ALGERNON [*Goes straight over to* CECILY *without noticing anyone else.*]   My own love! [*Offers to kiss her.*]

CECILY [*Drawing back.*]   A moment, Ernest! May I ask you—are you engaged to be married to this young lady?

ALGERNON [*Looking round.*]   To what young lady? Good heavens! Gwendolen!

CECILY   Yes! to good heavens, Gwendolen, I mean to Gwendolen.

ALGERNON [*Laughing.*]   Of course not! What could have put such an idea into your pretty little head?

CECILY   Thank you. [*Presenting her cheek to be kissed.*] You may. [ALGERNON *kisses her.*]

GWENDOLEN   I felt there was some slight error, Miss Cardew. The gentleman who is now embracing you is my cousin, Mr. Algernon Moncrieff.

CECILY. [*Breaking away from* ALGERNON.] Algernon Moncrieff! Oh! [*The two girls move towards each other and put their arms round each other's waists as if for protection.*]

CECILY   Are you called Algernon?

ALGERNON   I cannot deny it.

CECILY   Oh!

GWENDOLEN   Is your name really John?

JACK [*Standing rather proudly.*]   I could deny it if I liked, I could deny anything if I liked. But my name certainly is John. It has been John for years.

CECILY [*To* GWENDOLEN.]   A gross deception has been practiced on both of us.

GWENDOLEN   My poor wounded Cecily!

CECILY   My sweet wronged Gwendolen!

GWENDOLEN [*Slowly and seriously.*]   You will call me sister, will you not? [*They embrace.* JACK *and* ALGERNON *groan and walk up and down.*]

CECILY [*Rather brightly.*]   There is just one question I would like to be allowed to ask my guardian.

GWENDOLEN   An admirable idea! Mr. Worthing, there is just one question I would like to be permitted to put to you. Where is your brother Ernest? We are both engaged to be married to your brother Ernest, so it is a matter of some importance to us to know where your brother Ernest is at present.

JACK [*Slowly and hesitatingly.*] Gwendolen—Cecily—it is very painful for me to be forced to speak the truth. It is the first time in my life that I have ever been reduced to such a painful position, and I am really quite inexperienced in doing anything of the kind. However I will tell you quite frankly that I have no brother Ernest. I have no brother at all. I never had a brother in my life, and I certainly have not the smallest intention of ever having one in the future.

CECILY [*Surprised.*] No brother at all?

JACK [*Cheerily.*] None!

GWENDOLEN [*Severely.*] Had you never a brother of any kind?

JACK [*Pleasantly.*] Never. Not even of any kind.

GWENDOLEN I am afraid it is quite clear, Cecily, that neither of us is engaged to be married to anyone.

CECILY It is not a very pleasant position for a young girl suddenly to find herself in. Is it?

GWENDOLEN Let us go into the house. They will hardly venture to come after us there.

CECILY No, men are so cowardly, aren't they?

[*They retire into the house with scornful looks.*]

JACK This ghastly state of things is what you call Bunburying, I suppose?

ALGERNON Yes, and a perfectly wonderful Bunbury it is. The most wonderful Bunbury I have ever had in my life.

JACK Well, you've no right whatsoever to Bunbury here.

ALGERNON That is absurd. One has a right to Bunbury anywhere one chooses. Every serious Bunburyist knows that.

JACK Serious Bunburyist! Good heavens!

ALGERNON Well, one must be serious about something, if one wants to have any amusement in life. I happen to be serious about Bunburying. What on earth you are serious about I haven't got the remotest idea. About everything, I should fancy. You have such an absolutely trivial nature.

JACK Well, the only small satisfaction I have in the whole of this wretched business is that your friend Bunbury is quite exploded. You won't be able to run down to the country quite so often as you used to do, dear Algy. And a very good thing too.

ALGERNON Your brother is a little off-color, isn't he, dear Jack? You won't be able to disappear to London quite so frequently as your wicked custom was. And not a bad thing either.

JACK As for your conduct towards Miss Cardew, I must say that your taking in a sweet, simple, innocent girl like that is quite inexcusable. To say nothing of the fact that she is my ward.

ALGERNON I can see no possible defense at all for your deceiving a brilliant, clever, thoroughly experienced young lady like Miss Fairfax. To say nothing of the fact that she is my cousin.

JACK I wanted to be engaged to Gwendolen, that is all. I love her.

ALGERNON Well, I simply wanted to be engaged to Cecily. I adore her.

JACK There is certainly no chance of your marrying Miss Cardew.

ALGERNON I don't think there is much likelihood, Jack, of you and Miss Fairfax being united.

JACK   Well, that is no business of yours.

ALGERNON   If it was my business, I wouldn't talk about it. [*Begins to eat muffins.*] It is very vulgar to talk about one's business. Only people like stockbrokers do that, and then merely at dinner parties.

JACK   How can you sit there, calmly eating muffins when we are in this horrible trouble, I can't make out. You seem to me to be perfectly heartless.

ALGERNON   Well, I can't eat muffins in an agitated manner. The butter would probably get on my cuffs. One should always eat muffins quite calmly. It is the only way to eat them.

JACK   I say it's perfectly heartless your eating muffins at all, under the circumstances.

ALGERNON   When I am in trouble, eating is the only thing that consoles me. Indeed, when I am in really great trouble, as anyone who knows me intimately will tell you, I refuse everything except food and drink. At the present moment I am eating muffins because I am unhappy. Besides, I am particularly fond of muffins. [*Rising.*]

JACK [*Rising.*]   Well, that is no reason why you should eat them all in that greedy way. [*Takes muffins from* ALGERNON.]

ALGERNON [*Offering tea cake.*]   I wish you would have tea cake instead. I don't like tea cake.

JACK   Good heavens! I suppose a man may eat his own muffins in his own garden.

ALGERNON   But you have just said it was perfectly heartless to eat muffins.

JACK   I said it was perfectly heartless of you, under the circumstances. That is a very different thing.

ALGERNON   That may be. But the muffins are the same. [*He seizes the muffin dish from* JACK.]

JACK   Algy, I wish to goodness you would go.

ALGERNON   You can't possibly ask me to go without having some dinner. It's absurd. I never go without my dinner. No one ever does, except vegetarians and people like that. Besides I have just made arrangements with Dr. Chasuble to be christened at a quarter to six under the name of Ernest.

JACK   My dear fellow, the sooner you give up that nonsense the better. I made arrangements this morning with Dr. Chasuble to be christened myself at 5:30, and I naturally will take the name of Ernest. Gwendolen would wish it. We can't both be christened Ernest. It's absurd. Besides, I have a perfect right to be christened if I like. There is no evidence at all that I ever have been christened by anybody. I should think it extremely probable I never was, and so does Dr. Chasuble. It is entirely different in your case. You have been christened already.

ALGERNON   Yes, but I have not been christened for years.

JACK   Yes, but you have been christened. That is the important thing.

ALGERNON   Quite so. So I know my constitution can stand it. If you are not quite sure about your ever having been christened, I must say I think it rather dangerous your venturing on it now. It might make you very unwell. You can hardly have forgotten that someone very closely connected with you was very nearly carried off this week in Paris by a severe chill.

JACK   Yes, but you said yourself that a severe chill was not hereditary.

ALGERNON   It usen't to be, I know—but I daresay it is now. Science is always making wonderful improvements in things.

JACK [*Picking up the muffin dish.*]   Oh, that is nonsense; you are always talking nonsense.

ALGERNON   Jack, you are at the muffins again! I wish you wouldn't. There are only two left. [*Takes them.*] I told you I was particularly fond of muffins.

JACK   But I hate tea cake.

ALGERNON   Why on earth then do you allow tea cake to be served up for your guests? What ideas you have of hospitality!

JACK   Algernon! I have already told you to go. I don't want you here. Why don't you go!

ALGERNON   I haven't quite finished my tea yet! and there is still one muffin left. [*Jack groans, and sinks into a chair.* ALGERNON *still continues eating.*]

ACT-DROP

Third Act

SCENE—*Morning room*[8] *at the Manor House.*

[GWENDOLEN *and* CECILY *are at the window, looking out into the garden.*]

GWENDOLEN   The fact that they did not follow us at once into the house, as anyone else would have done, seems to me to show that they have some sense of shame left.

CECILY   They have been eating muffins. That looks like repentance.

GWENDOLEN [*After a pause.*]   They don't seem to notice us at all. Couldn't you cough?

CECILY   But I haven't got a cough.

GWENDOLEN   They're looking at us. What effrontery!

CECILY   They're approaching. That's very forward of them.

GWENDOLEN   Let us preserve a dignified silence.

CECILY   Certainly. It's the only thing to do now.

[*Enter* JACK *followed by* ALGERNON. *They whistle some dreadful popular air from a British Opera.*[9]]

GWENDOLEN   This dignified silence seems to produce an unpleasant effect.

CECILY   A most distasteful one.

GWENDOLEN   But we will not be the first to speak.

CECILY   Certainly not.

GWENDOLEN   Mr. Worthing, I have something very particular to ask you. Much depends on your reply.

CECILY   Gwendolen, your common sense is invaluable. Mr. Moncrieff, kindly answer me the following question. Why did you pretend to be my guardian's brother?

8. A relatively informally furnished room for receiving visitors making morning calls (usually close friends of the host or hostess). Afternoon visitors, on the other hand, would be received in the drawing room, a much more formal and elegant setting.

9. Probably a reference to one of the operas of Gilbert and Sullivan.

ALGERNON   In order that I might have an opportunity of meeting you.

CECILY [*To* GWENDOLEN.]   That certainly seems a satisfactory explanation, does it not?

GWENDOLEN   Yes, dear, if you can believe him.

CECILY   I don't. But that does not affect the wonderful beauty of his answer.

GWENDOLEN   True. In matters of grave importance, style, not sincerity is the vital thing. Mr. Worthing, what explanation can you offer to me for pretending to have a brother? Was it in order that you might have an opportunity of coming up to town to see me as often as possible?

JACK   Can you doubt it, Miss Fairfax?

GWENDOLEN   I have the gravest doubts upon the subject. But I intend to crush them. This is not the moment for German skepticism.[1] [*Moving to* CECILY.] Their explanations appear to be quite satisfactory, especially Mr. Worthing's. That seems to me to have the stamp of truth upon it.

CECILY   I am more than content with what Mr. Moncrieff said. His voice alone inspires one with absolute credulity.

GWENDOLEN   Then you think we should forgive them?

CECILY   Yes. I mean no.

GWENDOLEN   True! I had forgotten. There are principles at stake that one cannot surrender. Which of us should tell them? The task is not a pleasant one.

CECILY   Could we not both speak at the same time?

GWENDOLEN   An excellent idea! I nearly always speak at the same time as other people. Will you take the time from me?

CECILY   Certainly. [GWENDOLEN *beats time with uplifted finger.*]

GWENDOLEN AND CECILY [*Speaking together.*]   Your Christian names are still an insuperable barrier. That is all!

JACK AND ALGERNON [*Speaking together.*]   Our Christian names! Is that all? But we are going to be christened this afternoon.

GWENDOLEN [*To* JACK.]   For my sake you are prepared to do this terrible thing?

JACK   I am.

CECILY [*To* ALGERNON.]   To please me you are ready to face this fearful ordeal?

ALGERNON   I am!

GWENDOLEN   How absurd to talk of the equality of the sexes! Where questions of self-sacrifice are concerned, men are infinitely beyond us.

JACK   We are. [*Clasps hands with* ALGERNON.]

CECILY   They have moments of physical courage of which we women know absolutely nothing.

GWENDOLEN [*To* JACK.]   Darling!

ALGERNON [*To* CECILY.]   Darling. [*They fall into each other's arms.*]
   [*Enter* MERRIMAN. *When he enters he coughs loudly, seeing the situation.*]

MERRIMAN   Ahem! Ahem! Lady Bracknell!

JACK   Good heavens!

---

1. Many 19th-century German scholars (e.g., D. F. Strauss) seemed, in England, to be notoriously skeptical in their analyses of religious texts.

[*Enter* LADY BRACKNELL. *The couples separate in alarm. Exit* MERRI-
MAN.]

LADY BRACKNELL   Gwendolen! What does this mean?

GWENDOLEN   Merely that I am engaged to be married to Mr. Worthing,
mamma.

LADY BRACKNELL   Come here. Sit down. Sit down immediately. Hesitation of any kind is a sign of mental decay in the young, of physical weakness in the old. [*Turns to* JACK.] Apprised, sir, of my daughter's sudden
flight by her trusty maid, whose confidence I purchased by means of
a small coin, I followed her at once by a luggage train. Her unhappy
father is, I am glad to say, under the impression that she is attending a
more than usually lengthy lecture by the University Extension Scheme
on the Influence of a Permanent Income on Thought. I do not propose
to undeceive him. Indeed I have never undeceived him on any question.
I would consider it wrong. But of course, you will clearly understand that
all communication between yourself and my daughter must cease immediately from this moment. On this point, as indeed on all points, I am
firm.

JACK   I am engaged to be married to Gwendolen, Lady Bracknell!

LADY BRACKNELL   You are nothing of the kind, sir. And now, as regards
Algernon! . . . Algernon!

ALGERNON   Yes, Aunt Augusta.

LADY BRACKNELL   May I ask if it is in this house that your invalid friend
Mr. Bunbury resides?

ALGERNON [*Stammering.*]   Oh! No! Bunbury doesn't live here. Bunbury is
somewhere else at present. In fact, Bunbury is dead.

LADY BRACKNELL   Dead! When did Mr. Bunbury die? His death must have
been extremely sudden.

ALGERNON [*Airily.*]   Oh! I killed Bunbury this afternoon. I mean poor Bunbury died this afternoon.

LADY BRACKNELL   What did he die of?

ALGERNON   Bunbury? Oh, he was quite exploded.

LADY BRACKNELL   Exploded! Was he the victim of a revolutionary outrage?
I was not aware that Mr. Bunbury was interested in social legislation. If
so, he is well punished for his morbidity.

ALGERNON   My dear Aunt Augusta, I mean he was found out! The doctors
found out that Bunbury could not live, that is what I mean—so Bunbury
died.

LADY BRACKNELL   He seems to have had great confidence in the opinion
of his physicians. I am glad, however, that he made up his mind at the
last to some definite course of action, and acted under proper medical
advice. And now that we have finally got rid of this Mr. Bunbury, may I
ask, Mr. Worthing, who is that young person whose hand my nephew
Algernon is now holding in what seems to me a peculiarly unnecessary
manner?

JACK   That lady is Miss Cecily Cardew, my ward.

[LADY BRACKNELL *bows coldly to* CECILY.]

ALGERNON   I am engaged to be married to Cecily, Aunt Augusta.

LADY BRACKNELL   I beg your pardon?

CECILY   Mr. Moncrieff and I are engaged to be married, Lady Bracknell.

LADY BRACKNELL [*With a shiver, crossing to the sofa and sitting down.*] I do not know whether there is anything peculiarly exciting in the air of this particular part of Hertfordshire, but the number of engagements that go on seems to me considerably above the proper average that statistics have laid down for our guidance. I think some preliminary inquiry on my part would not be out of place. Mr. Worthing, is Miss Cardew at all connected with any of the larger railway stations in London? I merely desire information. Until yesterday I had no idea that there were any families or persons whose origin was a Terminus.[2] [JACK *looks perfectly furious, but restrains himself.*]

JACK [*In a clear, cold voice.*] Miss Cardew is the granddaughter of the late Mr. Thomas Cardew of 149, Belgrave Square, S.W.; Gervase Park, Dorking, Surrey; and the Sporran, Fifeshire, N.B.[3]

LADY BRACKNELL That sounds not unsatisfactory. Three addresses always inspire confidence, even in tradesmen. But what proof have I of their authenticity?

JACK I have carefully preserved the Court Guides of the period. They are open to your inspection, Lady Bracknell.

LADY BRACKNELL [*Grimly.*] I have known strange errors in that publication.

JACK Miss Cardew's family solicitors are Messrs. Markby, Markby, and Markby.

LADY BRACKNELL Markby, Markby, and Markby? A firm of the very highest position in their profession. Indeed I am told that one of the Mr. Markbys is occasionally to be seen at dinner parties. So far I am satisfied.

JACK [*Very irritably.*] How extremely kind of you, Lady Bracknell! I have also in my possession, you will be pleased to hear, certificates of Miss Cardew's birth, baptism, whooping cough, registration, vaccination, confirmation, and the measles; both the German and the English variety.

LADY BRACKNELL Ah! A life crowded with incident, I see; though perhaps somewhat too exciting for a young girl. I am not myself in favor of premature experiences. [*Rises, looks at her watch.*] Gwendolen! the time approaches for our departure. We have not a moment to lose. As a matter of form, Mr. Worthing, I had better ask you if Miss Cardew has any little fortune?

JACK Oh! about a hundred and thirty thousand pounds in the Funds.[4] That is all. Good-bye, Lady Bracknell. So pleased to have seen you.

LADY BRACKNELL [*Sitting down again.*] A moment, Mr. Worthing. A hundred and thirty thousand pounds! And in the Funds! Miss Cardew seems to me a most attractive young lady, now that I look at her. Few girls of the present day have any really solid qualities, any of the qualities that last, and improve with time. We live, I regret to say, in an age of surfaces. [*To* CECILY.] Come over here, dear. [CECILY *goes across.*] Pretty child! your dress is sadly simple, and your hair seems almost as Nature might have left it. But we can soon alter all that. A thoroughly experienced French maid produces a really marvelous result in a very brief space of

---

2. Station at the end of a railway line.

3. Presumably North Britain, i.e., Scotland.

4. Interest-bearing government bonds.

time. I remember recommending one to young Lady Lancing, and after three months her own husband did not know her.

JACK [*Aside.*]   And after six months nobody knew her.

LADY BRACKNELL [*Glares at* JACK *for a few moments. Then bends, with a practiced smile, to* CECILY.]   Kindly turn round, sweet child. [CECILY *turns completely round.*] No, the side view is what I want. [CECILY *presents her profile.*] Yes, quite as I expected. There are distinct social possibilities in your profile. The two weak points in our age are its want of principle and its want of profile. The chin a little higher, dear. Style largely depends on the way the chin is worn. They are worn very high, just at present. Algernon!

ALGERNON   Yes, Aunt Augusta!

LADY BRACKNELL   There are distinct social possibilities in Miss Cardew's profile.

ALGERNON   Cecily is the sweetest, dearest, prettiest girl in the whole world. And I don't care twopence about social possibilities.

LADY BRACKNELL   Never speak disrespectfully of Society, Algernon. Only people who can't get into it do that. [*To* CECILY.] Dear child, of course you know that Algernon has nothing but his debts to depend upon. But I do not approve of mercenary marriages. When I married Lord Bracknell I had no fortune of any kind. But I never dreamed for a moment of allowing that to stand in my way. Well, I suppose I must give my consent.

ALGERNON   Thank you, Aunt Augusta.

LADY BRACKNELL   Cecily, you may kiss me!

CECILY [*Kisses her.*]   Thank you, Lady Bracknell.

LADY BRACKNELL. You may also address me as Aunt Augusta for the future.

CECILY   Thank you, Aunt Augusta.

LADY BRACKNELL   The marriage, I think, had better take place quite soon.

ALGERNON   Thank you, Aunt Augusta.

CECILY   Thank you, Aunt Augusta.

LADY BRACKNELL   To speak frankly, I am not in favor of long engagements. They give people the opportunity of finding out each other's character before marriage, which I think is never advisable.

JACK   I beg your pardon for interrupting you, Lady Bracknell, but this engagement is quite out of the question. I am Miss Cardew's guardian, and she cannot marry without my consent until she comes of age. That consent I absolutely decline to give.

LADY BRACKNELL   Upon what grounds may I ask? Algernon is an extremely, I may almost say an ostentatiously, eligible young man. He has nothing, but he looks everything. What more can one desire?

JACK   It pains me very much to have to speak frankly to you, Lady Bracknell, about your nephew, but the fact is that I do not approve at all of his moral character. I suspect him of being untruthful. [ALGERNON *and* CECILY *look at him in indignant amazement.*]

LADY BRACKNELL   Untruthful! My nephew Algernon? Impossible! He is an Oxonian.[5]

JACK   I fear there can be no possible doubt about the matter. This afternoon, during my temporary absence in London on an important question

---

5. I.e., he had been a student at Oxford (originally spelled *Oxenford*).

of romance, he obtained admission to my house by means of the false pretense of being my brother. Under an assumed name he drank, I've just been informed by my butler, an entire pint bottle of my Perrier-Jouet, Brut, '89;[6] a wine I was specially reserving for myself. Continuing his disgraceful deception, he succeeded in the course of the afternoon in alienating the affections of my only ward. He subsequently stayed to tea, and devoured every single muffin. And what makes his conduct all the more heartless is, that he was perfectly well aware from the first that I have no brother, that I never had a brother, and that I don't intend to have a brother, not even of any kind. I distinctly told him so myself yesterday afternoon.

LADY BRACKNELL   Ahem! Mr. Worthing, after careful consideration I have decided entirely to overlook my nephew's conduct to you.

JACK   That is very generous of you, Lady Bracknell. My own decision, however, is unalterable. I decline to give my consent.

LADY BRACKNELL [*To* CECILY.]   Come here, sweet child. [CECILY *goes over.*] How old are you, dear?

CECILY   Well, I am really only eighteen, but I always admit to twenty when I go to evening parties.

LADY BRACKNELL   You are perfectly right in making some slight alteration. Indeed, no woman should ever be quite accurate about her age. It looks so calculating. . . . [*In a meditative manner.*] Eighteen, but admitting to twenty at evening parties. Well, it will not be very long before you are of age and free from the restraints of tutelage. So I don't think your guardian's consent is, after all, a matter of any importance.

JACK   Pray excuse me, Lady Bracknell, for interrupting you again, but it is only fair to tell you that according to the terms of her grandfather's will Miss Cardew does not come legally of age till she is thirty-five.

LADY BRACKNELL   That does not seem to me to be a grave objection. Thirty-five is a very attractive age. London society is full of women of the very highest birth who have, of their own free choice, remained thirty-five for years. Lady Dumbleton is an instance in point. To my own knowledge she has been thirty-five ever since she arrived at the age of forty, which was many years ago now. I see no reason why our dear Cecily should not be even still more attractive at the age you mention than she is at present. There will be a large accumulation of property.

CECILY   Algy, could you wait for me till I was thirty-five?

ALGERNON   Of course I could, Cecily. You know I could.

CECILY   Yes, I felt it instinctively, but I couldn't wait all that time. I hate waiting even five minutes for anybody. It always makes me rather cross. I am not punctual myself, I know, but I do like punctuality in others, and waiting, even to be married, is quite out of the question.

ALGERNON   Then what is to be done, Cecily?

CECILY   I don't know, Mr. Moncrieff.

LADY BRACKNELL   My dear Mr. Worthing, as Miss Cardew states positively that she cannot wait till she is thirty-five—a remark which I am bound to say seems to me to show a somewhat impatient nature—I would beg of you to reconsider your decision.

---

6. An outstanding brand and year of dry champagne.

JACK   But my dear Lady Bracknell, the matter is entirely in your own hands. The moment you consent to my marriage with Gwendolen, I will most gladly allow your nephew to form an alliance with my ward.

LADY BRACKNELL [*Rising and drawing herself up.*]   You must be quite aware that what you propose is out of the question.

JACK   Then a passionate celibacy is all that any of us can look forward to.

LADY BRACKNELL   This is not the destiny I propose for Gwendolen. Algernon, of course, can choose for himself. [*Pulls out her watch.*] Come, dear; [GWENDOLEN *rises.*] we have already missed five, if not six, trains. To miss any more might expose us to comment on the platform.

    [*Enter* DR. CHASUBLE.]

CHASUBLE   Everything is quite ready for the christenings.

LADY BRACKNELL   The christenings, sir! Is not that somewhat premature!

CHASUBLE [*Looking rather puzzled, and pointing to* JACK *and* ALGERNON.]   Both these gentlemen have expressed a desire for immediate baptism.

LADY BRACKNELL   At their age? The idea is grotesque and irreligious! Algernon, I forbid you to be baptized. I will not hear of such excesses. Lord Bracknell would be highly displeased if he learned that that was the way in which you wasted your time and money.

CHASUBLE   Am I to understand then that there are to be no christenings at all this afternoon?

JACK   I don't think that, as things are now, it would be of much practical value to either of us, Dr. Chasuble.

CHASUBLE   I am grieved to hear such sentiments from you, Mr. Worthing. They savor of the heretical views of the Anabaptists,[7] views that I have completely refuted in four of my unpublished sermons. However, as your present mood seems to be one peculiarly secular, I will return to the church at once. Indeed, I have just been informed by the pew-opener[8] that for the last hour and a half Miss Prism has been waiting for me in the vestry.

LADY BRACKNELL [*Starting.*]   Miss Prism! Did I hear you mention a Miss Prism?

CHASUBLE   Yes, Lady Bracknell. I am on my way to join her.

LADY BRACKNELL   Pray allow me to detain you for a moment. This matter may prove to be one of vital importance to Lord Bracknell and myself. Is this Miss Prism a female of repellent aspect, remotely connected with education?

CHASUBLE [*Somewhat indignantly.*]   She is the most cultivated of ladies, and the very picture of respectability.

LADY BRACKNELL   It is obviously the same person. May I ask what position she holds in your household?

CHASUBLE [*Severely.*]   I am a celibate, madam.

JACK [*Interposing.*]   Miss Prism, Lady Bracknell, has been for the last three years Miss Cardew's esteemed governess and valued companion.

LADY BRACKNELL   In spite of what I hear of her, I must see her at once. Let her be sent for.

---

7. A radical Protestant sect of the 17th century, whose views about baptism were regarded as heretical by Anglicans.

8. A person employed at church services to usher worshipers to their pews and open the doors for them.

CHASUBLE [*Looking off.*]   She approaches; she is nigh.

[*Enter* MISS PRISM *hurriedly.*]

MISS PRISM   I was told you expected me in the vestry, dear Canon. I have been waiting for you there for an hour and three quarters. [*Catches sight of* LADY BRACKNELL *who has fixed her with a stony glare.* MISS PRISM *grows pale and quails. She looks anxiously round as if desirous to escape.*]

LADY BRACKNELL [*In a severe, judicial voice.*]   Prism! [MISS PRISM *bows her head in shame.*] Come here, Prism! [MISS PRISM *approaches in a humble manner.*] Prism! Where is that baby? [*General consternation.* THE CANON *starts back in horror.* ALGERNON *and* JACK *pretend to be anxious to shield* CECILY *and* GWENDOLEN *from hearing the details of a terrible public scandal.*] Twenty-eight years ago, Prism, you left Lord Bracknell's house, Number 104, Upper Grosvenor Street, in charge of a perambulator that contained a baby, of the male sex. You never returned. A few weeks later, through the elaborate investigations of the Metropolitan police, the perambulator was discovered at midnight, standing by itself in a remote corner of Bayswater.[9] It contained the manuscript of a three-volume novel of more than usually revolting sentimentality. [MISS PRISM *starts in involuntary indignation.*] But the baby was not there! [*Everyone looks at* MISS PRISM.] Prism! Where is that baby? [*A pause.*]

MISS PRISM   Lady Bracknell, I admit with shame that I do not know. I only wish I did. The plain facts of the case are these. On the morning of the day you mention, a day that is forever branded on my memory, I prepared as usual to take the baby out in its perambulator. I had also with me a somewhat old, but capacious handbag, in which I had intended to place the manuscript of a work of fiction that I had written during my few unoccupied hours. In a moment of mental abstraction, for which I never can forgive myself, I deposited the manuscript in the bassinette, and placed the baby in the handbag.

JACK   [*Who has been listening attentively.*] But where did you deposit the handbag?

MISS PRISM.   Do not ask me, Mr. Worthing.

JACK   Miss Prism, this is a matter of no small importance to me. I insist on knowing where you deposited the handbag that contained that infant.

MISS PRISM   I left it in the cloak room of one of the larger railway stations in London.

JACK   What railway station?

MISS PRISM [*Quite crushed.*]   Victoria. The Brighton line. [*Sinks into a chair.*]

JACK   I must retire to my room for a moment. Gwendolen, wait here for me.

GWENDOLEN   If you are not too long, I will wait here for you all my life.

[*Exit* JACK *in great excitement.*]

CHASUBLE   What do you think this means, Lady Bracknell?

LADY BRACKNELL   I dare not even suspect, Dr. Chasuble. I need hardly tell you that in families of high position strange coincidences are not supposed to occur. They are hardly considered the thing.

---

9. A once fashionable locality in the West End near Kensington Gardens.

[*Noises heard overhead as if someone was throwing trunks about. Everyone looks up.*]

CECILY Uncle Jack seems strangely agitated.

CHASUBLE Your guardian has a very emotional nature.

LADY BRACKNELL This noise is extremely unpleasant. It sounds as if he was having an argument. I dislike arguments of any kind. They are always vulgar, and often convincing.

CHASUBLE [*Looking up.*] It has stopped now. [*The noise is redoubled.*]

LADY BRACKNELL I wish he would arrive at some conclusion.

GWENDOLEN This suspense is terrible. I hope it will last.

[*Enter* JACK *with a handbag of black leather in his hand.*]

JACK [*Rushing over to* MISS PRISM.] Is this the handbag, Miss Prism? Examine it carefully before you speak. The happiness of more than one life depends on your answer.

MISS PRISM [*Calmly.*] It seems to be mine. Yes, here is the injury it received through the upsetting of a Gower Street omnibus in younger and happier days. Here is the stain on the lining caused by the explosion of a temperance beverage, an incident that occurred at Leamington. And here, on the lock, are my initials. I had forgotten that in an extravagant mood I had had them placed there. The bag is undoubtedly mine. I am delighted to have it so unexpectedly restored to me. It has been a great inconvenience being without it all these years.

JACK [*In a pathetic voice.*] Miss Prism, more is restored to you than this handbag. I was the baby you placed in it.

MISS PRISM [*Amazed.*] You!

JACK [*Embracing her.*] Yes . . . mother!

MISS PRISM [*Recoiling in indignant astonishment.*] Mr. Worthing! I am unmarried!

JACK Unmarried! I do not deny that is a serious blow. But after all, who has the right to cast a stone against one who has suffered? Cannot repentance wipe out an act of folly? Why should there be one law for men, and another for women? Mother, I forgive you. [*Tries to embrace her again.*]

MISS PRISM [*Still more indignant.*] Mr. Worthing, there is some error. [*Pointing to* LADY BRACKNELL.] There is the lady who can tell you who you really are.

JACK [*After a pause.*] Lady Bracknell, I hate to seem inquisitive, but would you kindly inform me who I am?

LADY BRACKNELL I am afraid that the news I have to give you will not altogether please you. You are the son of my poor sister, Mrs. Moncrieff, and consequently Algernon's elder brother.

JACK Algy's elder brother! Then I have a brother after all. I knew I had a brother! I always said I had a brother! Cecily—how could you have ever doubted that I had a brother? [*Seizes hold of* ALGERNON.] Dr. Chasuble, my unfortunate brother. Miss Prism, my unfortunate brother. Gwendolen, my unfortunate brother. Algy, you young scoundrel, you will have to treat me with more respect in the future. You have never behaved to me like a brother in all your life.

ALGERNON Well, not till today, old boy, I admit. I did my best, however, though I was out of practice. [*Shakes hands.*]

GWENDOLEN [*To* JACK.]   My own! But what own are you? What is your Christian name, now that you have become someone else?

JACK   Good heavens! . . . I had quite forgotten that point. Your decision on the subject of my name is irrevocable, I suppose?

GWENDOLEN   I never change, except in my affections.

CECILY   What a noble nature you have, Gwendolen!

JACK   Then the question had better be cleared up at once. Aunt Augusta, a moment. At the time when Miss Prism left me in the handbag, had I been christened already?

LADY BRACKNELL   Every luxury that money could buy, including christening, had been lavished on you by your fond and doting parents.

JACK   Then I was christened! That is settled. Now, what name was I given? Let me know the worst.

LADY BRACKNELL   Being the eldest son you were naturally christened after your father.

JACK [*Irritably.*]   Yes, but what was my father's Christian name?

LADY BRACKNELL [*Meditatively.*]   I cannot at the present moment recall what the General's Christian name was. But I have no doubt he had one. He was eccentric, I admit. But only in later years. And that was the result of the Indian climate, and marriage, and indigestion, and other things of that kind.

JACK   Algy! Can't you recollect what our father's Christian name was?

ALGERNON   My dear boy, we were never even on speaking terms. He died before I was a year old.

JACK   His name would appear in the Army Lists of the period, I suppose, Aunt Augusta?

LADY BRACKNELL   The General was essentially a man of peace, except in his domestic life. But I have no doubt his name would appear in any military directory.

JACK   The Army Lists of the last forty years are here. These delightful records should have been my constant study. [*Rushes to bookcase and tears the books out.*] M. Generals . . . Mallam, Maxbohm,[1] Magley, what ghastly names they have—Markby, Migsby, Mobbs, Moncrieff! Lieutenant 1840, Captain, Lieutenant Colonel, Colonel, General 1869, Christian names, Ernest John. [*Puts book very quietly down and speaks quite calmly.*] I always told you, Gwendolen, my name was Ernest, didn't I? Well it is Ernest after all. I mean it naturally is Ernest.

LADY BRACKNELL   Yes, I remember now that the General was called Ernest. I knew I had some particular reason for disliking the name.

GWENDOLEN   Ernest! My own Ernest! I felt from the first that you could have no other name!

JACK   Gwendolen, it is a terrible thing for a man to find out suddenly that all his life he has been speaking nothing but the truth. Can you forgive me?

GWENDOLEN   I can. For I feel that you are sure to change.

JACK   My own one!

CHASUBLE [*To* MISS PRISM.]   Laetitia! [*Embraces her.*]

MISS PRISM [*Enthusiastically.*]   Frederick! At last!

---

1. A play on the name of Max Beerbohm (1872–1956), English essayist, caricaturist, and parodist.

ALGERNON   Cecily! [*Embraces her.*] At last!
JACK   Gwendolen! [*Embraces her.*] At last!
LADY BRACKNELL   My nephew, you seem to be displaying signs of triviality.
JACK   On the contrary, Aunt Augusta, I've now realized for the first time in my life the vital Importance of Being Earnest.

CURTAIN

performed 1895   1899

From De Profundis[1]

*   *   *

And the end of it all is that I have got to forgive you. I must do so. I don't write this letter to put bitterness into your heart, but to pluck it out of mine. For my own sake I must forgive you. One cannot always keep an adder in one's breast to feed on one, nor rise up every night to sow thorns in the garden of one's soul. It will not be difficult at all for me to do so, if you help me a little. Whatever you did to me in old days I always readily forgave. It did you no good then. Only one whose life is without stain of any kind can forgive sins. But now when I sit in humiliation and disgrace it is different. My forgiveness should mean a great deal to you now. Some day you will realise it. Whether you do so early or late, soon or not at all, my way is clear before me. I cannot allow you to go through life bearing in your heart the burden of having ruined a man like me. The thought might make you callously indifferent, or morbidly sad. I must take the burden from you and put it on my own shoulders.

I must say to myself that neither you nor your father, multiplied a thousand times over, could possibly have ruined a man like me: that I ruined myself: and that nobody, great or small, can be ruined except by his own hand. I am quite ready to do so. I am trying to do so, though you may not think it at the present moment. If I have brought this pitiless indictment against you, think what an indictment I bring without pity against myself. Terrible as what you did to me was, what I did to myself was far more terrible still.

I was a man who stood in symbolic relations to the art and culture of my age. I had realized this for myself at the very dawn of my manhood, and had forced my age to realize it afterwards. Few men hold such a position in their own lifetime and have it so acknowledged. It is usually discerned, if discerned at all, by the historian, or the critic, long after both the man and his age have passed away. With me it was different. I felt it myself, and made others feel it. Byron[2] was a symbolic figure, but his relations were to the passion of his

---

1. Out of the depths (Latin); Psalm 130.1: "Out of the depths have I cried unto thee, O Lord." While in prison in Reading Gaol, Wilde was allowed a pen and paper only to write letters. Given one sheet of paper at a time, which was taken away after it was filled, Wilde wrote this work as a letter to Lord Alfred Douglas, or Bosie. Wilde titled it *Epistola: In Carcere et Vinculis* (Letter: in prison and in chains). He was given the manuscript on

his release and turned it over to a friend, Robert Ross, who gave it its current title and published it in an abridged version in 1905, after Wilde's death. After Douglas's death in 1945 a fuller text was published by Wilde's son, Vyvyan Holland; but only in 1962, when scholars could consult the original manuscript, did a complete version appear.
2. George Gordon, Lord Byron (1788–1824), the Romantic poet.

age and its weariness of passion. Mine were to something more noble, more permanent, of more vital issue, of larger scope.

The gods had given me almost everything. I had genius, a distinguished name, high social position, brilliancy, intellectual daring: I made art a philosophy, and philosophy an art: I altered the minds of men and the colors of things: there was nothing I said or did that did not make people wonder: I took the drama, the most objective form known to art, and made it as personal a mode of expression as the lyric or the sonnet, at the same time that I widened its range and enriched its characterization: drama, novel, poem in rhyme, poem in prose, subtle or fantastic dialogue, whatever I touched I made beautiful in a new mode of beauty: to truth itself I gave what is false no less than what is true as its rightful province, and showed that the false and the true are merely forms of intellectual existence. I treated Art as the supreme reality, and life as a mere mode of fiction: I awoke the imagination of my century so that it created myth and legend around me: I summed up all systems in a phrase, and all existence in an epigram.

Along with these things, I had things that were different. I let myself be lured into long spells of senseless and sensual ease. I amused myself with being a *flâneur*,[3] a dandy, a man of fashion. I surrounded myself with the smaller natures and the meaner minds. I became the spendthrift of my own genius, and to waste an eternal youth gave me a curious joy. Tired of being on the heights I deliberately went to the depths in the search for new sensations. What the paradox was to me in the sphere of thought, perversity became to me in the sphere of passion. Desire, at the end, was a malady, or a madness, or both. I grew careless of the lives of others. I took pleasure where it pleased me and passed on. I forgot that every little action of the common day makes or unmakes character, and that therefore what one has done in the secret chamber one has some day to cry aloud on the housetops. I ceased to be Lord over myself. I was no longer the Captain of my Soul, and did not know it. I allowed you to dominate me, and your father to frighten me. I ended in horrible disgrace. There is only one thing for me now, absolute Humility: just as there is only one thing for you, absolute Humility also. You had better come down into the dust and learn it beside me.

I have lain in prison for nearly two years. Out of my nature has come wild despair; an abandonment to grief that was piteous even to look at: terrible and impotent rage: bitterness and scorn: anguish that wept aloud: misery that could find no voice: sorrow that was dumb. I have passed through every possible mood of suffering. Better than Wordsworth himself I know what Wordsworth meant when he said:

> Suffering is permanent, obscure, and dark
> And has the nature of Infinity.[4]

But while there were times when I rejoiced in the idea that my sufferings were to be endless, I could not bear them to be without meaning. Now I find hidden away in my nature something that tells me that nothing in the whole world is meaningless, and suffering least of all. That something hidden away in my nature, like a treasure in a field, is Humility.

It is the last thing left in me, and the best: the ultimate discovery at which

---

3. Idle stroller (French).　　　　　　　4. From *The Borderers*, lines 1543–44.

I have arrived: the starting-point for a fresh development. It has come to me right out of myself, so I know that it has come at the proper time. It could not have come before, nor later. Had anyone told me of it, I would have rejected it. Had it been brought to me, I would have refused it. As I found it, I want to keep it. I must do so. It is the one thing that has in it the elements of life, of a new life, a *Vita Nuova*[5] for me.

* * *

Morality does not help me. I am a born antinomian.[6] I am one of those who are made for exceptions, not for laws. But while I see that there is nothing wrong in what one does, I see that there is something wrong in what one becomes. It is well to have learned that.

Religion does not help me. The faith that others give to what is unseen, I give to what one can touch, and look at. My Gods dwell in temples made with hands, and within the circle of actual experience is my creed made perfect and complete: too complete it may be, for like many or all of those who have placed their Heaven in this earth, I have found in it not merely the beauty of Heaven, but the horror of Hell also. When I think about Religion at all, I feel as if I would like to found an order for those who cannot believe: the Confraternity of the Fatherless one might call it, where on an altar, on which no taper burned, a priest, in whose heart peace had no dwelling, might celebrate with unblessed bread and a chalice empty of wine. Everything to be true must become a religion. And agnosticism should have its ritual no less than faith. It has sown its martyrs, it should reap its saints, and praise God daily for having hidden Himself from man. But whether it be faith or agnosticism, it must be nothing external to me. Its symbols must be of my own creating. Only that is spiritual which makes its own form. If I may not find its secret within myself, I shall never find it. If I have not got it already, it will never come to me.

Reason does not help me. It tells me that the laws under which I am convicted are wrong and unjust laws, and the system under which I have suffered a wrong and unjust system. But, somehow, I have got to make both of these things just and right to me. And exactly as in Art one is only concerned with what a particular thing is at a particular moment to oneself, so it is also in the ethical evolution of one's character. I have got to make everything that has happened to me good for me. The plank-bed, the loathsome food, the hard ropes shredded into oakum[7] till one's fingertips grow dull with pain, the menial offices with which each day begins and finishes, the harsh orders that routine seems to necessitate, the dreadful dress that makes sorrow grotesque to look at, the silence, the solitude, the shame—each and all of these things I have to transform into a spiritual experience. There is not a single degradation of the body which I must not try and make into a spiritualizing of the soul.

I want to get to the point when I shall be able to say, quite simply and without affection, that the two great turning-points of my life were when my father sent me to Oxford, and when society sent me to prison. I will not say that it is the best thing that could have happened to me, for that phrase

---

5. New life (Italian); here Dante's earliest work (1292–94) about his love for Beatrice.
6. One who believes that faith alone, and not obe-

dience of the moral law, is necessary for salvation.
7. Loose fiber from old hemp ropes, which prisoners were often made to shred.

would savour of too great bitterness towards myself. I would sooner say, or hear it said of me, that I was so typical a child of my age that in my perversity, and for that perversity's sake, I turned the good things of my life to evil, and the evil things of my life to good. What is said, however, by myself or by others matters little. The important thing, the thing that lies before me, the thing that I have to do, or be for the brief remainder of my days one maimed, marred, and incomplete, is to absorb into my nature all that has been done to me, to make it part of me, to accept it without complaint, fear, or reluctance. The supreme vice is shallowness. Whatever is realized is right.

1897   1962

BERNARD SHAW
1856–1950

Winston Churchill described Bernard Shaw as a "bright, nimble, fierce, and comprehending being, Jack Frost dancing bespangled in the sunshine." Churchill's words not only name essential qualities of the man but also suggest how long his life and historical reach were. Born and raised in the Victorian period, Shaw continued an important public figure until his death in 1950. His experience encompassed the momentous historical changes of the last half of the nineteenth century and the first half of the twentieth. Shaw made it his business to pronounce on them all in the witty epigrammatic style that characterizes his plays. He was an engaged public intellectual, who created himself as a remarkable public character.

Like Oscar Wilde, the other playwright whose work changed the course of British drama, Shaw was an Irishman. He was born in Dublin, in Shaw's own words, "the fruit of an unsuitable marriage between two quite amiable people who finally separated in the friendliest fashion." His mother, an aspiring singer, went to London to pursue her musical career; Shaw followed five years later, in 1876, quitting the job he had held since the age of fifteen at a land agent's office. His intention was to become a novelist. He spent much of his time in the Reading Room of the British Museum, where a young journalist named William Archer introduced himself because he was so intrigued by the combination of things Shaw was studying—Marx's *Das Kapital* and the score of Wagner's opera, *Tristan and Isolde*.

These two works indicate the main involvements of Shaw's life in London. *Das Kapital* convinced him that socialism was the answer to society's problems. With the socialist economist Sidney Webb and his wife, also a socialist economist, Beatrice Webb, Shaw joined the Fabian Society, a socialist organization that had committed itself to gradual reform rather than revolution. Shaw quickly became a leader in the group and its principal spokesman. His pronouncements and tracts had a wit absent from most political writing. In *Fabian Tract No. 2,* for example, he argued that nineteenth-century capitalism had divided society "into hostile classes, with large appetites and no dinners at one extreme and large dinners and no appetites at the other." Though painfully shy, he disciplined himself to become an accomplished public speaker. Accepting fees from no one, he spoke everywhere, stipulating only that he could speak on whatever subject he liked.

Meanwhile, his acquaintance with William Archer led him to journalism. He worked first as an art critic, then as a music critic, championing the operas of Richard Wagner and introducing a new standard of wit and judgment to music reviewing, writing of a hapless soprano who "fell fearlessly on Mozart and was defeated with heavy loss to the hearers," a corps de ballet, that "wandered about in the prompt corner as if some vivisector had removed from their heads that portion of the brain which enables us to find our way out the door," or Schubert's "Death and the Maiden" quartet, which makes one "reconciled to Death and indifferent to the Maiden." Shaw then turned to drama criticism, where he later described his work as "a siege laid to the theater of the XIXth Century by an author who had to cut his own way into it at the point of the pen, and throw some of its defenders into the moat." Just as he championed the music of Wagner, he now championed the plays of the Norwegian dramatist, Henrik Ibsen. In 1891 he published *The Quintessence of Ibsenism*, in which, in setting out the reasons for his admiration of Ibsen, he defined the kind of drama he wanted to write.

In the first ten years of his life in London, Shaw had written five unsuccessful novels. When he turned to drama in the 1890s, he found his medium. Shaw's first play, *Widowers' Houses* (1892), dealt with the problem of slum landlords. Though it ran only two performances, Shaw's career as a dramatist was launched. In the course of his career he wrote more than fifty plays. Among the most famous are *Mrs. Warren's Profession* (1893), *Arms and the Man* (1894), *Candida* (1894), *The Devil's Disciple* (1896), *Caesar and Cleopatra* (1898), *Man and Superman* (1903), *Major Barbara* (1905), *Androcles and the Lion* (1912), *Pygmalion* (1912; later the basis of the musical *My Fair Lady*), *Heartbreak House* (1919), *Back to Methuselah* (1920), and *Saint Joan* (1923). (Because the production and publication history of Shaw's plays is so complex, this list gives the date of composition.) Shaw at first had difficulty getting his plays performed. Therefore, in 1898 he decided to publish them in book form as *Plays Pleasant and Unpleasant*, for which he wrote a didactic preface, the first of many that he provided his plays. Then in 1904, the producer and Shakespearean Harley Granville-Barker put on *Candida* at the Royal Court Theater, which he was managing. The play was a success, and Shaw went on to work with Barker in making the Royal Court the center for avant-garde drama in London.

In *The Quintessence of Ibsenism*, Shaw defines the elements of the kind of theater he aspired to create:

> first, the introduction of the discussion and its development until it so overspreads and interpenetrates the action that it finally assimilates it, making play and discussion practically identical; and second, as a consequence of making the spectators themselves the persons of the drama, and the incidents of their own lives its incidents, the disuse of the old stage tricks by which audiences had to be induced to take an interest in unreal people and improbable circumstances, and the substitution of a forensic technique of recrimination, disillusion, and penetration through ideals to the truth, with a free use of all the rhetorical and lyrical arts of the orator, the preacher, the pleader, and the rhapsodist.

Shaw created a drama of ideas, in which his characters strenuously argue points of view that justify their social positions—the prostitute in *Mrs. Warren's Profession*, the munitions manufacturer in *Major Barbara*. His object is to attack the complacencies and conventional moralism of his audience. By the rhetorical brilliance of his dialogue and by surprising reversals of plot conventions, Shaw manipulates his audience into a position of uncomfortable sympathy with points of view and characters that violate traditional assumptions.

By the end of the first decade of the twentieth century, as a result of the success of his plays at the Royal Court Theater, Shaw had become a literary celebrity. Like Oscar Wilde, he had worked to develop a public persona, but with a substantial difference in aim. Whereas Wilde used his public image to define an aesthetic point of view, Shaw used his public personality—iconoclastic, clownish, argumentative—to advocate social ideas. He was radical in many respects. He was a vegetarian, a nonsmoker, and a nondrinker. He was courageous enough to be a pacifist in World War I. He championed the reform of English spelling and punctuation. He believed in women's rights and the abolition of private property. He also believed in the Life Force and progressive evolution, driven by the power of the human will, a point of view that led to sympathy with Mussolini and other dictators before World War II. Shaw's insistent rationality made some of his contemporaries view him as bloodless. After seeing *Arms and the Man*, Yeats described a nightmare in which he was haunted by a sewing machine, "that clicked and shone, but the incredible thing was that the machine smiled, smiled perpetually." However, Yeats goes on to say, "Yet I delighted in Shaw the formidable man. He could hit my enemies and the enemies of all I loved, as I could never hit, as no living author that was dear to me could ever hit."

Shaw wrote *Mrs. Warren's Profession* in 1893, but though it was published in *Plays Pleasant and Unpleasant* in 1898, public performance was long prohibited by British censors. In 1902, the Stage Society, technically a private club and so not under the jurisdiction of the censors, gave performances for its own members. The play was produced in New York in 1905; but it was closed down by the police, and the producer and his company were arrested. They were eventually acquitted, and the play was allowed to continue. Legal public performance in England did not take place until 1926, the year after Shaw won the Nobel Prize.

Shaw's preface to the play attacks the confusions and contradictions involved in the censorship of plays and contains an eloquent plea for the recognition of the seriousness and morality of *Mrs. Warren's Profession*. The play was written, he tells us, "to draw attention to the truth that prostitution is caused, not by female depravity and male licentiousness, but simply by underpaying, undervaluing, and overworking women so shamefully that the poorest of them are forced to resort to prostitution to keep body and soul together. He argues that Mrs. Warren's defense of herself in the play is "valid and unanswerable." (It is interesting to compare Mrs. Warren's defense with that of the prostitute who wrote *The Great Social Evil* [p. 1728] as a letter to the *Times*.) Shaw's discussion of Mrs. Warren's self-justification continues:

> But it is no defense at all of the vice which she organizes. It is no defense of an immoral life to say that the alternative offered by society collectively to poor women is a miserable life, starved, overworked, fetid, ailing, ugly. Though it is quite natural and *right* for Mrs. Warren to choose what is, according to her lights, the least immoral alternative, it is none the less infamous of society to offer such alternatives. For the alternatives offered are not morality and immorality but two sorts of immorality. The man who cannot see that starvation, overwork, dirt, and disease are as anti-social as prostitution—that they are the vices and crimes of a nation, and not merely its misfortunes—is (to put it as politely as possible) a hopelessly Private Person.

This is Shaw's way of saying that such a man is a hopeless idiot; the word *idiot* comes from the Greek *idiotes*, "a private person," as distinct from one interested in public affairs.

Shaw's belief in spelling reform led him to introduce simplifications in his own texts that he insisted on his publishers retaining. These simplifications (omission of the apostrophe in a number of contractions, and the use of widely spaced letters rather than italics to indicate emphasis, for example) are retained in the selection reprinted here.

Mrs. Warren's Profession

Act 1

Summer afternoon in a cottage garden on the eastern slope of a hill a little south of Haslemere in Surrey. Looking up the hill, the cottage is seen in the left hand corner of the garden, with its thatched roof and porch, and a large latticed window to the left of the porch. A paling completely shuts in the gar-

den, except for a gate on the right. The common rises uphill beyond the paling to the sky line. Some folded canvas garden chairs are leaning against the side bench in the porch. A lady's bicycle is propped against the wall, under the window. A little to the right of the porch a hammock is slung from two posts. A big canvas umbrella, stuck in the ground, keeps the sun off the hammock, in which a young lady lies reading and making notes, her head towards the cottage and her feet towards the gate. In front of the hammock, and within reach of her hand, is a common kitchen chair, with a pile of serious-looking books and a supply of writing paper on it.

A gentleman walking on the common comes into sight from behind the cottage. He is hardly past middle age, with something of the artist about him, unconventionally but carefully dressed, and clean-shaven except for a moustache, with an eager susceptible face and very amiable and considerate manners. He has silky black hair, with waves of grey and white in it. His eyebrows are white, his moustache black. He seems not certain of his way. He looks over the paling; takes stock of the place; and sees the young lady.

THE GENTLEMAN [*Taking off his hat.*] I beg your pardon. Can you direct me to Hindhead View—Mrs Alison's?

THE YOUNG LADY [*Glancing up from her book.*] This is Mrs Alison's. [*She resumes her work.*]

THE GENTLEMAN Indeed! Perhaps—may I ask are you Miss Vivie Warren?

THE YOUNG LADY [*Sharply, as she turns on her elbow to get a good look at him.*] Yes.

THE GENTLEMAN [*Daunted and conciliatory.*] I'm afraid I appear intrusive. My name is Praed. [VIVIE *at once throws her books upon the chair, and gets out of the hammock.*] Oh, pray dont let me disturb you.

VIVIE [*Striding to the gate and opening it for him.*] Come in, Mr Praed. [*He comes in.*] Glad to see you. [*She proffers her hand and takes his with a resolute and hearty grip. She is an attractive specimen of the sensible, able, highly-educated young middle-class Englishwoman. Age 22. Prompt, strong, confident, self-possessed. Plain business-like dress, but not dowdy. She wears a chatelaine[1] at her belt, with a fountain pen and a paper knife among its pendants.*]

PRAED Very kind of you indeed, Miss Warren. [*She shuts the gate with a vigorous slam. He passes in to the middle of the garden, exercising his fingers, which are slightly numbed by her greeting.*] Has your mother arrived?

VIVIE [*Quickly, evidently scenting aggression.*] Is she coming?

PRAED [*Surprised.*] Didnt you expect us?

VIVIE No.

PRAED Now, goodness me, I hope Ive not mistaken the day. That would be just like me, you know. Your mother arranged that she was to come down from London and that I was to come over from Horsham to be introduced to you.

VIVIE [*Not at all pleased.*] Did she? Hm! My mother has rather a trick of taking me by surprise—to see how I behave myself when she's away, I suppose. I fancy I shall take my mother very much by surprise one of

1. Clasp or hook.

these days, if she makes arrangements that concern me without consulting me beforehand. She hasnt come.

PRAED [*Embarrassed.*] I'm really very sorry.

VIVIE [*Throwing off her displeasure.*] It's not your fault, Mr Praed, is it?
And I'm very glad youve come. You are the only one of my mother's
friends I have ever asked her to bring to see me.

PRAED [*Relieved and delighted.*] Oh, now this is really very good of you,
Miss Warren!

VIVIE Will you come indoors; or would you rather sit out here and
talk?

PRAED It will be nicer out here, dont you think?

VIVIE Then I'll go and get you a chair. [*She goes to the porch for a garden
chair.*]

PRAED [*Following her.*] Oh, pray, pray! Allow me. [*He lays hands on the
chair.*]

VIVIE [*Letting him take it.*] Take care of your fingers: theyre rather dodgy
things, those chairs. [*She goes across to the chair with the books on it;
pitches them into the hammock; and brings the chair forward with one
swing.*]

PRAED [*Who has just unfolded his chair.*] Oh, now d o let me take that
hard chair. I like hard chairs.

VIVIE So do I. Sit down, Mr Praed. [*This invitation she gives with genial
peremptoriness, his anxiety to please her clearly striking her as a sign of
weakness of character on his part. But he does not immediately obey.*]

PRAED By the way, though, hadnt we better go to the station to meet your
mother?

VIVIE [*Coolly.*] Why? She knows the way.

PRAED [*Disconcerted.*] Er—I suppose she does. [*He sits down.*]

VIVIE Do you know, you are just like what I expected. I hope you are
disposed to be friends with me.

PRAED [*Again beaming.*] Thank you, my d e a r Miss Warren: thank you.
Dear me! I'm glad your mother hasnt spoilt you!

VIVIE How?

PRAED Well, in making you too conventional. You know, my dear Miss
Warren, I am a born anarchist. I hate authority. It spoils the relations
between parent and child: even between mother and daughter. Now I
was always afraid that your mother would strain her authority to make
you very conventional. It's such a relief to find that she hasnt.

VIVIE Oh! have I been behaving unconventionally?

PRAED Oh no; oh dear no. At least not conventionally unconventionally,
you understand. [*She nods and sits down. He goes on, with a cordial outburst.*] But it was so charming of you to say that you were disposed to be
friends with me! You modern young ladies are splendid: perfectly splendid!

VIVIE [*Dubiously.*] Eh? [*Watching him with dawning disappointment as to
the quality of his brains and character.*]

PRAED When I was your age, young men and women were afraid of each
other: there was no good fellowship. Nothing real. Only gallantry copied
out of novels, and as vulgar and affected as it could be. Maidenly reserve!
gentlemanly chivalry! always saying no when you meant yes! simple purgatory for shy and sincere souls.

VIVIE   Yes, I imagine there must have been a frightful waste of time. Especially women's time.

PRAED   Oh, waste of life, waste of everything. But things are improving. Do you know, I have been in a positive state of excitement about meeting you ever since your magnificent achievements at Cambridge: a thing unheard of in my day. It was perfectly splendid, you tieing with the third wrangler.[2] Just the right place, you know. The first wrangler is always a dreamy, morbid fellow, in whom the thing is pushed to the length of a disease.

VIVIE   It doesnt pay. I wouldnt do it again for the same money.

PRAED   [Aghast.]   The same money!

VIVIE   I did it for £50.

PRAED   Fifty pounds!

VIVIE   Yes. Fifty pounds. Perhaps you dont know how it was. Mrs. Latham, my tutor at Newnham,[3] told my mother that I could distinguish myself in the mathematical tripos if I went in for it in earnest. The papers were full just then of Phillipa Summers beating the senior wrangler. You remember about it, of course.

PRAED   [Shakes his head energetically.]!!!

VIVIE   Well anyhow she did; and nothing would please my mother but that I should do the same thing. I said flatly it was not worth my while to face the grind since I was not going in for teaching; but I offered to try for fourth wrangler, or thereabouts, for £50. She closed with me at that, after a little grumbling; and I was better than my bargain. But I wouldn't do it again for that. Two hundred pounds would have been nearer the mark.

PRAED   [Much damped.]   Lord bless me! Thats a very practical way of looking at it.

VIVIE   Did you expect to find me an unpractical person?

PRAED   But surely it's practical to consider not only the work these honors cost, but also the culture they bring.

VIVIE   Culture! My dear Mr Praed: do you know what the mathematical tripos means? It means grind, grind, grind for six to eight hours a day at mathematics, and nothing but mathematics. I'm supposed to know something about science; but I know nothing except the mathematics it involves. I can make calculations for engineers, electricians, insurance companies, and so on; but I know next to nothing about engineering or electricity or insurance. I dont even know arithmetic well. Outside mathematics, lawn-tennis, eating, sleeping, cycling, and walking, I'm a more ignorant barbarian than any woman could possibly be who hadnt gone in for the tripos.

PRAED   [Revolted.]   What a monstrous, wicked, rascally system! I knew it! I felt at once that it meant destroying all that makes womanhood beautiful.

VIVIE   I dont object to it on that score in the least. I shall turn it to very good account, I assure you.

PRAED   Pooh! In what way?

---

2. A unique Cambridge term denoting distinction in the final honors examination (known as the tripos) leading to an A.B. in mathematics. The person who achieved the top mark was the senior wran-gler; then came the junior wrangler, and then the third wrangler.

3. Women's college at Cambridge University.

VIVIE   I shall set up in chambers in the City, and work at actuarial calculations and conveyancing. Under cover of that I shall do some law,
with one eye on the Stock Exchange all the time. Ive come down here
by myself to read law: not for a holiday, as my mother imagines. I hate
holidays.

PRAED   You make my blood run cold. Are you to have no romance, no
beauty in your life?

VIVIE   I don't care for either, I assure you.

PRAED   You cant mean that.

VIVIE   Oh yes I do. I like working and getting paid for it. When I'm tired
of working, I like a comfortable chair, a cigar, a little whisky, and a novel
with a good detective story in it.

PRAED [Rising in a frenzy of repudiation.]   I dont believe it. I am an artist;
and I cant believe it: I refuse to believe it. It's only that you havnt discovered yet what a wonderful world art can open up to you.

VIVIE   Yes I have. Last May I spent six weeks in London with Honoria
Fraser. Mamma thought we were doing a round of sightseeing together;
but I was really at Honoria's chambers in Chancery Lane[4] every day,
working away at actuarial calculations for her, and helping her as well
as a greenhorn could. In the evenings we smoked and talked, and never
dreamt of going out except for exercise. And I never enjoyed myself more
in my life. I cleared all my expenses, and got initiated into the business
without a fee into the bargain.

PRAED   But bless my heart and soul, Miss Warren, do you call that discovering art?

VIVIE   Wait a bit. That wasnt the beginning. I went up to town on an
invitation from some artistic people in Fitzjohn's Avenue: one of the girls
was a Newnham chum. They took me to the National Gallery—

PRAED [Approving.]   Ah!! [He sits down, much relieved.]

VIVIE [Continuing.]—to the Opera—

PRAED [Still more pleased.]   Good!

VIVIE—and to a concert where the band played all the evening: Beethoven
and Wagner and so on. I wouldnt go through that experience again for
anything you could offer me. I held out for civility's sake until the third
day; and then I said, plump out, that I couldnt stand any more of it, and
went off to Chancery Lane. N o w you know the sort of perfectly splendid
modern young lady I am. How do you think I shall get on with my
mother?

PRAED [Startled.]   Well, I hope—er—

VIVIE   It's not so much what you hope as what you believe, that I want to
know.

PRAED   Well, frankly, I am afraid your mother will be a little disappointed.
Not from any shortcoming on your part, you know: I dont mean that.
But you are so different from her ideal.

VIVIE   Her what?!

PRAED   Her ideal.

VIVIE   Do you mean her ideal of ME?

PRAED   Yes.

---

4. I.e., office in the legal quarter of London.

VIVIE   What on earth is it like?

PRAED   Well, you must have observed, Miss Warren, that people who are dissatisfied with their own bringing-up generally think that the world would be all right if everybody were to be brought up quite differently. Now your mother's life has been—er—I suppose you know—

VIVIE   Dont suppose anything, Mr Praed. I hardly know my mother. Since I was a child I have lived in England, at school or college, or with people paid to take charge of me. I have been boarded out all my life. My mother has lived in Brussels or Vienna and never let me go to her. I only see her when she visits England for a few days. I dont complain: it's been very pleasant; for people have been very good to me; and there has always been plenty of money to make things smooth. But dont imagine I know anything about my mother. I know far less than you do.

PRAED   [*Very ill at ease.*]   In that case—[*He stops, quite at a loss. Then, with a forced attempt at gaiety*] But what nonsense we are talking! Of course you and your mother will get on capitally. [*He rises, and looks abroad at the view.*] What a charming little place you have here!

VIVIE   [*Unmoved.*]   Rather a violent change of subject, Mr Praed. Why wont my mother's life bear being talked about?

PRAED   Oh, you really mustnt say that. Isnt it natural that I should have a certain delicacy in talking to my old friend's daughter about her behind her back? You and she will have plenty of opportunity of talking about it when she comes.

VIVIE   No: s h e wont talk about it either. [*Rising.*] However, I daresay you have good reasons for telling me nothing. Only, mind this, Mr Praed. I expect there will be a battle royal when my mother hears of my Chancery Lane project.

PRAED   [*Ruefully.*]   I'm afraid there will.

VIVIE   Well, I shall win, because I want nothing but my fare to London to start there to-morrow earning my own living by devilling[5] for Honoria. Besides, I have no mysteries to keep up; and it seems she has. I shall use that advantage over her if necessary.

PRAED   [*Greatly shocked.*]   Oh no! No, pray. Youd not do such a thing.

VIVIE   Then tell me why not.

PRAED   I really cannot. I appeal to your good feeling. [*She smiles at his sentimentality.*] Besides you may be too bold. Your mother is not to be trifled with when she's angry.

VIVIE   You cant frighten me, Mr Praed. In that month at Chancery Lane I had opportunities of taking the measure of one or two women v e r y like my mother. You may back me to win. But if I hit harder in my ignorance than I need, remember that it is you who refuse to enlighten me. Now, let us drop the subject. [*She takes her chair and replaces it near the hammock with the same vigorous swing as before.*]

PRAED   [*Taking a desperate resolution.*]   One word, Miss Warren. I had better tell you. It's very difficult; but—

[MRS WARREN *and* SIR GEORGE CROFTS *arrive at the gate.* MRS WARREN *is between 40 and 50, formerly pretty, showily dressed in a brilliant hat and a gay blouse fitting tightly over her bust and flanked by fashionable*

---

5. Acting as assistant to a barrister (trial lawyer) as a way of gaining legal experience.

sleeves, Rather spoilt and domineering, and decidedly vulgar, but, on the whole, a genial and fairly presentable old blackguard of a woman.

CROFTS *is a tall powerfully-built man of about 50, fashionably dressed in the style of a young man. Nasal voice, reedier than might be expected from his strong frame. Clean-shaven bulldog jaws, large flat ears, and thick neck: gentlemanly combination of the most brutal types of city man, sporting man, and man about town.*]

VIVIE   Here they are. [*Coming to them as they enter the garden.*] How do, mater? Mr Praed's been here this half hour waiting for you.

MRS WARREN   Well, if youve been waiting, Praddy, it's your own fault: I thought youd have the gumption to know I was coming by the 3.10 train. Vivie: put your hat on, dear: youll get sunburnt. Oh, I forgot to introduce you. Sir George Crofts: my little Vivie.

    [CROFTS *advances to* VIVIE *with his most courtly manner. She nods, but makes no motion to shake hands.*]

CROFTS   May I shake hands with a young lady whom I have known by reputation very long as the daughter of one of my oldest friends?

VIVIE [*Who has been looking him up and down sharply.*]   If you like. [*She takes his tenderly proffered hand and gives it a squeeze that makes him open his eyes; then turns away, and says to her mother*] Will you come in, or shall I get a couple more chairs? [*She goes into the porch for the chairs.*]

MRS WARREN   Well George, what do you think of her?

CROFTS [*Ruefully.*]   She has a powerful fist. Did you shake hands with her, Praed?

PRAED   Yes: it will pass off presently.

CROFTS   I hope so. [VIVIE *reappears with two more chairs. He hurries to her assistance.*] Allow me.

MRS WARREN [*Patronizingly.*]   Let Sir George help you with the chairs, dear.

VIVIE [*Pitching them into his arms.*]   Here you are. [*She dusts her hands and turns to* MRS WARREN.] Youd like some tea, wouldnt you?

MRS WARREN [*Sitting in* PRAED's *chair and fanning herself.*]   I'm dying for a drop to drink.

VIVIE   I'll see about it. [*She goes into the cottage.*]

    [SIR GEORGE *has by this time managed to unfold a chair and plant it beside* MRS WARREN, *on her left. He throws the other on the grass and sits down, looking dejected and rather foolish, with the handle of his stick in his mouth.* PRAED, *still very uneasy, fidgets about the garden on their right.*]

MRS WARREN [*To* PRAED, *looking at* CROFTS.]   Just look at him, Praddy: he looks cheerful, dont he? He's been worrying my life out these three years to have that little girl of mine shewn to him; and now that Ive done it, he's quite out of countenance. [*Briskly.*] Come! sit up, George; and take your stick out of your mouth. [CROFTS *sulkily obeys.*]

PRAED   I think, you know—if you dont mind my saying so—that we had better get out of the habit of thinking of her as a little girl. You see she has really distinguished herself; and I'm not sure, from what I have seen of her, that she is not older than any of us.

MRS WARREN [*Greatly amused.*]   Only listen to him, George! Older than any of us! Well, she has been stuffing you nicely with her importance.

PRAED But young people are particularly sensitive about being treated in that way.

MRS WARREN Yes; and young people have to get all that nonsense taken out of them, and a good deal more besides. Dont you interfere, Praddy: I know how to treat my own child as well as you do. [PRAED, *with a grave shake of his head, walks up the garden with his hands behind his back.* MRS WARREN *pretends to laugh, but looks after him with perceptible concern. Then she whispers to* CROFTS] Whats the matter with him? What does he take it like that for?

CROFTS [*Morosely.*] Youre afraid of Praed.

MRS WARREN What! Me! Afraid of dear old Praddy! Why, a fly wouldnt be afraid of him.

CROFTS Y o u r e afraid of him.

MRS WARREN [*Angry.*] I'll trouble you to mind your own business, and not try any of your sulks on me. I'm not afraid of y o u, anyhow. If you cant make yourself agreeable, youd better go home. [*She gets up, and turning her back on him, finds herself face to face with* PRAED.] Come, Praddy, I know it was only your tender-heartedness. Youre afraid I'll bully her.

PRAED My dear Kitty: you think I'm offended. Dont imagine that: pray dont. But you know I often notice things that escape you; and though you never take my advice, you sometimes admit afterwards that you ought to have taken it.

MRS WARREN Well, what do you notice now?

PRAED Only that Vivie is a grown woman. Pray, Kitty, treat her with every respect.

MRS WARREN [*With genuine amazement.*] Respect! Treat my own daughter with respect! What next, pray!

VIVIE [*Appearing at the cottage door and calling to* MRS WARREN.] Mother: will you come to my room before tea?

MRS WARREN Yes, dearie. [*She laughs indulgently at* PRAED's *gravity, and pats him on the cheek as she passes him on her way to the porch.*] Dont be cross, Praddy. [*She follows* VIVIE *into the cottage.*]

CROFTS [*Furtively.*] I say, Praed.

PRAED Yes.

CROFTS I want to ask you a rather particular question.

PRAED Certainly. [*He takes* MRS WARREN's *chair and sits close to* CROFTS.]

CROFTS Thats right: they might hear us from the window. Look here: did Kitty ever tell you who that girl's father is?

PRAED Never.

CROFTS Have you any suspicion of who it might be?

PRAED None.

CROFTS [*Not believing him.*] I know, of course, that you perhaps might feel bound not to tell if she had said anything to you. But it's very awkward to be uncertain about it now that we shall be meeting the girl every day. We dont exactly know how we ought to feel towards her.

PRAED What difference can that make? We take her on her own merits. What does it matter who her father was?

CROFTS [*Suspiciously.*] Then you know who he was?

PRAED [*With a touch of temper.*] I said no just now. Did you not hear me?

CROFTS Look here, Praed. I ask you as a particular favor. If you do know

[*Movement of protest from* PRAED.]—I only say, if you know you might at least set my mind at rest about her. The fact is, I feel attracted.

PRAED [*Sternly.*]   What do you mean?

CROFTS   Oh, dont be alarmed: it's quite an innocent feeling. Thats what puzzles me about it. Why, for all I know, *I* might be her father.

PRAED   You! Impossible!

CROFTS [*Catching him up cunningly.*]   You know for certain that I'm not?

PRAED   I know nothing about it, I tell you, any more than you. But really, Crofts—oh no, it's out of the question. Theres not the least resemblance.

CROFTS   As to that, theres no resemblance between her and her mother that I can see. I suppose she's not y o u r daughter, is she?

PRAED [*Rising indignantly.*]   Really, Crofts—!

CROFTS   No offence, Praed. Quite allowable as between two men of the world.

PRAED [*Recovering himself with an effort and speaking gently and gravely.*]   Now listen to me, my dear Crofts. [*He sits down again.*] I have nothing to do with that side of Mrs Warren's life, and never had. She has never spoken to me about it; and of course I have never spoken to her about it. Your delicacy will tell you that a handsome woman needs s o m e friends who are not—well, not on that footing with her. The effect of her own beauty would become a torment to her if she could not escape from it occasionally. You are probably on much more confidential terms with Kitty than I am. Surely you can ask her the question yourself.

CROFTS   I have asked her, often enough. But she's so determined to keep the child all to herself that she would deny that it ever had a father if she could. [*Rising.*] I'm thoroughly uncomfortable about it, Praed.

PRAED [*Rising also.*]   Well, as you are, at all events, old enough to be her father, I dont mind agreeing that we both regard Miss Vivie in a parental way, as a young girl whom we are bound to protect and help. What do you say?

CROFTS [*Aggressively.*]   I'm no older than you, if you come to that.

PRAED   Yes you are, my dear fellow: you were born old. I was born a boy: Ive never been able to feel the assurance of a grown-up man in my life. [*He folds his chair and carries it to the porch.*]

MRS WARREN [*Calling from within the cottage.*]   Prad-dee! George! Tea-ea-ea-ea!

CROFTS [*Hastily.*]   She's calling us. [*He hurries in.*]

[PRAED *shakes his head bodingly, and is following* CROFTS *when he is hailed by a young gentleman who has just appeared on the common, and is making for the gate. He is pleasant, pretty, smartly dressed, cleverly good-for-nothing, not long turned 20, with a charming voice and agreeably disrespectful manners. He carries a light sporting magazine rifle.*]

THE YOUNG GENTLEMAN   Hallo! Praed!

PRAED   Why, Frank Gardner! [FRANK *comes in and shakes hands cordially.*] What on earth are you doing here?

FRANK   Staying with my father.

PRAED   The Roman father?[6]

---

6. Not "Roman Catholic" (he is a Church of England priest) but a father with a Roman sense of duty. The word is used ironically.

FRANK   He's rector here. I'm living with my people this autumn for the sake of economy. Things came to a crisis in July: the Roman father had to pay my debts. He's stony broke in consequence; and so am I. What are you up to in these parts? Do you know the people here?

PRAED   Yes: I'm spending the day with a Miss Warren.

FRANK [*Enthusiastically.*]   What! Do you know Vivie? Isnt she a jolly girl? I'm teaching her to shoot with this. [*Putting down the rifle.*] I'm so glad she knows you: youre just the sort of fellow she ought to know. [*He smiles, and raises the charming voice almost to a singing tone as he exclaims*] It's e v e r so jolly to find you here, Praed.

PRAED   I'm an old friend of her mother. Mrs Warren brought me over to make her daughter's acquaintance.

FRANK   The mother! Is s h e here?

PRAED   Yes: inside, at tea.

MRS WARREN [*Calling from within.*]   Prad-dee-ee-ee-eee! The tea-cake'll be cold.

PRAED [*Calling.*]   Yes, Mrs Warren. In a moment. Ive just met a friend here.

MRS WARREN   A what?

PRAED [*Louder.*]   A friend.

MRS WARREN   Bring him in.

PRAED   All right. [*to FRANK*] Will you accept the invitation?

FRANK [*Incredulous, but immensely amused.*]   Is that Vivie's mother?

PRAED   Yes.

FRANK   By jove! What a lark! Do you think she'll like me?

PRAED   Ive no doubt youll make yourself popular, as usual. Come in and try. [*Moving towards the house.*]

FRANK   Stop a bit. [*Seriously.*] I want to take you into my confidence.

PRAED   Pray dont. It's only some fresh folly, like the barmaid at Redhill.

FRANK   It's ever so much more serious than that. You say youve only just met Vivie for the first time?

PRAED   Yes.

FRANK [*Rhapsodically.*]   Then you can have no idea what a girl she is. Such character! Such sense! And her cleverness! Oh, my eye, Praed, but I can tell you she is clever! And—need I add?—she loves me.

CROFTS [*Putting his head out of the window.*]   I say, Praed: what are you about? D o come along. [*He disappears.*]

FRANK   Hallo! Sort of chap that would take a prize at a dog show, aint he? Who's he?

PRAED   Sir George Crofts, an old friend of Mrs Warren's. I think we had better come in.

> [*On their way to the porch they are interrupted by a call from the gate. Turning, they see an elderly clergyman looking over it.*]

THE CLERGYMAN [*Calling.*]   Frank!

FRANK   Hallo! [*To PRAED.*] The Roman father. [*To the clergyman.*] Yes, gov'nor: all right: presently. [*To PRAED.*] Look here, Praed: youd better go in to tea. I'll join you directly.

PRAED   Very good. [*He goes into the cottage.*]

> [*The clergyman remains outside the gate, with his hands on the top of it. The* REV. SAMUEL GARDNER, *a beneficed clergyman of the Established*

*Church, is over 50. Externally he is pretentious, booming, noisy, impor-
tant. Really he is that obsolescent social phenomenon the fool of the
family dumped on the Church by his father, the patron, clamorously
asserting himself as father and clergyman without being able to command
respect in either capacity.*]

REV. SAMUEL   Well, sir. Who are your friends here, if I may ask?

FRANK   Oh, it's all right, gov'nor! Come in.

REV. SAMUEL   No sir; not until I know whose garden I am entering.

FRANK   It's all right. It's Miss Warren's.

REV. SAMUEL   I have not seen her at church since she came.

FRANK   Of course not: she's a third wrangler. Ever so intellectual. Took a
higher degree than you did; so why should she go to hear you preach?

REV. SAMUEL   Dont be disrespectful, sir.

FRANK   Oh, it dont matter: nobody hears us. Come in. [*He opens the gate,
unceremoniously pulling his father with it into the garden.*] I want to
introduce you to her. Do you remember the advice you gave me last July,
gov'nor?

REV. SAMUEL [*Severely.*]   Yes, I advised you to conquer your idleness and
flippancy, and to work your way into an honorable profession and live on
it and not upon me.

FRANK   No; thats what you thought of afterwards. What you actually said
was that since I had neither brains nor money, I'd better turn my good
looks to account by marrying somebody with both. Well, look here. Miss
Warren has brains: you cant deny that.

REV. SAMUEL   Brains are not everything.

FRANK   No, of course not: theres the money—

REV. SAMUEL [*Interrupting him austerely.*]   I was not thinking of money,
sir. I was speaking of higher things. Social position, for instance.

FRANK   I dont care a rap about that.

REV. SAMUEL   But I do, sir.

FRANK   Well, nobody wants you to marry her. Anyhow, she has what
amounts to a high Cambridge degree; and she seems to have as much
money as she wants.

REV. SAMUEL [*Sinking into a feeble vein of humor.*]   I greatly doubt
whether she has as much money as y o u will want.

FRANK   Oh, come; I havnt been so very extravagant. I live ever so quietly;
I dont drink; I dont bet much; and I never go regularly on the razzle-
dazzle as you did when you were my age.

REV. SAMUEL [*Booming hollowly.*]   Silence, sir.

FRANK   Well, you told me yourself, when I was making ever such an ass
of myself about the barmaid at Redhill, that you once offered a woman
£50 for the letters you wrote to her when—

REV. SAMUEL [*Terrified.*]   Sh-sh-sh, Frank, for heaven's sake! [*He looks
round apprehensively. Seeing no one within earshot he plucks up courage
to boom again, but more subduedly.*] You are taking an ungentlemanly
advantage of what I confided to you for your own good, to save you from
an error you would have repented all your life long. Take warning by your
father's follies, sir; and dont make them an excuse for your own.

FRANK   Did you ever hear the story of the Duke of Wellington and his
letters?

REV. SAMUEL   No, sir; and I dont want to hear it.

FRANK   The old Iron Duke didnt throw away £50: not he. He just wrote: "Dear Jenny: publish and be damned! Yours affectionately, Wellington." Thats what you should have done.

REV. SAMUEL [*Piteously.*]   Frank, my boy: when I wrote those letters I put myself into that woman's power. When I told you about them I put myself, to some extent, I am sorry to say, in your power. She refused my money with these words, which I shall never forget. "Knowledge is power" she said; "and I never sell power." Thats more than twenty years ago; and she has never made use of her power or caused me a moment's uneasiness. You are behaving worse to me than she did, Frank.

FRANK   Oh yes I dare say! Did you ever preach at her the way you preach at me every day?

REV. SAMUEL [*Wounded almost to tears.*]   I leave you sir. You are incorrigible. [*He turns towards the gate.*]

FRANK [*Utterly unmoved.*]   Tell them I shant be home to tea, will you, gov'nor, like a good fellow? [*He moves towards the cottage door and is met by* PRAED *and* VIVIE *coming out.*]

VIVIE. [*To* FRANK.] Is that your father, Frank? I do so want to meet him.

FRANK   Certainly. [*Calling after his father.*] Gov'nor. Youre wanted. [*The parson turns at the gate, fumbling nervously at his hat.* PRAED *crosses the garden to the opposite side, beaming in anticipation of civilities.*] My father: Miss Warren.

VIVIE [*Going to the clergyman and shaking his hand.*]   Very glad to see you here, Mr Gardner. [*Calling to the cottage.*] Mother: come along: youre wanted.

> [MRS WARREN *appears on the threshold, and is immediately transfixed recognizing the clergyman.*]

VIVIE [*Continuing.*]   Let me introduce—

MRS WARREN [*Swooping on the* REVEREND SAMUEL.]   Why, it's Sam Gardner, gone into the Church! Well, I never! Dont you know us, Sam? This is George Crofts, as large as life and twice as natural. Dont you remember me?

REV. SAMUEL [*Very red.*]   I really—er—

MRS WARREN   Of course you do. Why, I have a whole album of your letters still: I came across them only the other day.

REV. SAMUEL [*Miserably confused.*]   Miss Vavasour, I believe.

MRS WARREN [*Correcting him quickly in a loud whisper.*]   Tch! Nonsense! Mrs Warren: dont you see my daughter there?

Act 2

Inside the cottage after nightfall. Looking eastward from within instead of westward from without, the latticed window, with its curtains drawn, is now seen in the middle of the front wall of the cottage, with the porch door to the left of it. In the left-hand side wall is the door leading to the kitchen. Farther back against the same wall is a dresser with a candle and matches on it, and FRANK's *rifle standing beside them, with the barrel resting in the plate-rack. In the centre a table stands with a lighted lamp on it.* VIVIE's *books and writing materials are on a table to the right of the window, against the wall. The fireplace is on the right, with a settle: there is no fire. Two of the chairs are set right and left of the table. The cottage door opens, shewing a fine starlit night without; and* MRS WARREN, *her shoulders wrapped in a shawl borrowed from* VIVIE, *enters, followed by* FRANK, *who throws his cap on the window seat. She has had enough of walking, and gives a gasp of relief as she unpins her hat; takes it off; sticks the pin through the crown; and puts it on the table.*

MRS WARREN   O Lord! I dont know which is the worst of the country, the walking or the sitting at home with nothing to do. I could do with a whisky and soda now very well, if only they had such a thing in this place.

FRANK   Perhaps Vivie's got some.

MRS WARREN   Nonsense! What would a young girl like her be doing with such things! Never mind: it dont matter. I wonder how she passes her time here! I'd a good deal rather be in Vienna.

FRANK   Let me take you there. [*He helps her to take off her shawl, gallantly giving her shoulders a very perceptible squeeze as he does so.*]

MRS WARREN   Ah! would you? I'm beginning to think youre a chip of the old block.

FRANK   Like the gov'nor, eh? [*He hangs the shawl on the nearest chair, and sits down.*]

MRS WARREN   Never you mind. What do you know about such things? Youre only a boy. [*She goes to the hearth, to be farther from temptation.*]

FRANK   Do come to Vienna with me? It'd be ever such larks.

MRS WARREN   No, thank you. Vienna is no place for you—at least not until youre a little older. [*She nods at him to emphasize this piece of advice. He makes a mock-piteous face, belied by his laughing eyes. She looks at him; then comes back to him.*] Now, look here, little boy [*taking his face in her hands and turning it up to her*]; I know you through and through by your likeness to your father, better than you know yourself. Dont you go taking any silly ideas into your head about me. Do you hear?

FRANK [*Gallantly wooing her with his voice.*]   Cant help it, my dear Mrs Warren: it runs in the family.

[*She pretends to box his ears; then looks at the pretty laughing upturned face for a moment, tempted. At last she kisses him, and immediately turns away, out of patience with herself.*]

MRS WARREN   There! I shouldnt have done that. I am wicked. Never you mind, my dear: it's only a motherly kiss. Go and make love to Vivie.

FRANK   So I have.

MRS WARREN [*Turning on him with a sharp note of alarm in her voice.*]   What!

FRANK   Vivie and I are ever such chums.

MRS WARREN   What do you mean? Now see here: I wont have any young scamp tampering with my little girl. Do you hear? I wont have it.

FRANK [*Quite unabashed.*]   My dear Mrs Warren: dont you be alarmed. My intentions are honorable: ever so honorable; and your little girl is jolly well able to take care of herself. She dont need looking after half so much as her mother. She aint so handsome, you know.

MRS WARREN [*Taken aback by his assurance.*]   Well, you have got a nice healthy two inches thick of cheek all over you. I dont know where you got it. Not from your father, anyhow.

CROFTS [*In the garden.*]   The gipsies, I suppose?

REV. SAMUEL [*Replying.*]   The broomsquires[7] are far worse.

MRS WARREN [*To* FRANK.]   S-sh! Remember! youve had your warning.

[CROFTS *and the* REVEREND SAMUEL *come in from the garden, the clergyman continuing his conversation as he enters.*]

REV. SAMUEL   The perjury at the Winchester assizes[8] is deplorable.

MRS WARREN   Well? What became of you two? And wheres Praddy and Vivie?

CROFTS [*Putting his hat on the settle and his stick in the chimney corner.*]   They went up the hill. We went to the village. I wanted a drink. [*He sits down on the settle, putting his legs up along the seat.*]

MRS WARREN   Well, she oughtnt to go off like that without telling me. [*To* FRANK.] Get your father a chair, Frank: where are your manners? [FRANK *springs up and gracefully offers his father his chair; and then takes another from the wall and sits down at the table, in the middle, with his father on his right and* MRS WARREN *on his left.*] George: where are you going to stay to-night? You cant stay here. And whats Praddy going to do?

CROFTS   Gardner'll put me up.

MRS WARREN   Oh no doubt youve taken care of yourself! But what about Praddy?

CROFTS   Dont know. I suppose he can sleep at the inn.

MRS WARREN   Havnt you room for him, Sam?

REV. SAMUEL   Well—er—you see, as rector here, I am not free to do as I like. Er—what is Mr Praed's social position?

MRS. WARREN   Oh, he's all right: he's an architect. What an old stick-in-the-mud you are, Sam!

FRANK   Yes, it's all right, gov'nor. He built that place down in Wales for the Duke. Caernarvon Castle they call it. You must have heard of it. [*He winks with lightning smartness at* MRS WARREN, *and regards his father blandly.*]

REV. SAMUEL   Oh, in that case, of course we shall only be too happy. I suppose he knows the Duke personally.

FRANK   Oh, ever so intimately! We can stick him in Georgina's old room.

MRS WARREN   Well, thats settled. Now if those two would only come in and let us have supper. Theyve no right to stay out after dark like this.

CROFTS [*Aggressively.*]   What harm are they doing you?

MRS WARREN   Well, harm or not, I dont like it.

FRANK   Better not wait for them, Mrs Warren. Praed will stay out as long as possible. He has never known before what it is to stray over the heath on a summer night with my Vivie.

CROFTS [*Sitting up in some consternation.*]   I say, you know! Come!

REV. SAMUEL [*Rising, startled out of his professional manner into real force and sincerity.*]   Frank, once for all, it's out of the question. Mrs Warren will tell you that it's not to be thought of.

CROFTS   Of course not.

FRANK [*With enchanting placidity.*]   Is that so, Mrs Warren?

---

7. Small country landowners.   8. Law courts.

MRS WARREN [*Reflectively.*]   Well, Sam, I dont know. If the girl wants to get married, no good can come of keeping her unmarried.

REV. SAMUEL [*Astounded.*]   But married to him!—your daughter to my son! Only think: it's impossible.

CROFTS   Of course it's impossible. Dont be a fool, Kitty.

MRS WARREN [*Nettled.*]   Why not? Isnt my daughter good enough for your son?

REV. SAMUEL   But surely, my dear Mrs Warren, you know the reasons—

MRS WARREN [*Defiantly.*]   I know no reasons. If you know any, you can tell them to the lad, or to the girl, or to your congregation, if you like.

REV. SAMUEL [*Collapsing helplessly into his chair.*]   You know very well that I couldnt tell anyone the reasons. But my boy will believe me when I tell him there a r e reasons.

FRANK   Quite right, Dad: he will. But has your boy's conduct ever been influenced by your reasons?

CROFTS   You cant marry her: and thats all about it. [*He gets up and stands on the hearth, with his back to the fireplace, frowning determinedly.*]

MRS WARREN [*Turning on him sharply.*]   What have you got to do with it, pray?

FRANK [*With his prettiest lyrical cadence.*]   Precisely what I was going to ask, myself, in my own graceful fashion.

CROFTS [*To* MRS WARREN.]   I suppose you dont want to marry the girl to a man younger than herself and without either a profession or twopence to keep her on. Ask Sam, if you dont believe me. [*To the parson.*] How much more money are you going to give him?

REV. SAMUEL   Not another penny. He has had his patrimony; and he spent the last of it in July. [MRS WARREN's *face falls.*]

CROFTS [*Watching her.*]   There! I told you. [*He resumes his place on the settle and puts up his legs on the seat again, as if the matter were finally disposed of.*]

FRANK [*Plaintively.*]   This is ever so mercenary. Do you suppose Miss Warren's going to marry for money? If we love one another—

MRS WARREN   Thank you. Your love's a pretty cheap commodity, my lad. If you have no means of keeping a wife, that settles it: you cant have Vivie.

FRANK [*Much amused.*]   What do y o u say, gov'nor, eh?

REV. SAMUEL   I agree with Mrs Warren.

FRANK   And good old Crofts has already expressed his opinion.

CROFTS [*Turning angrily on his elbow.*]   Look here: I want none of y o u r cheek.

FRANK [*Pointedly.*]   I'm ever so sorry to surprise you, Crofts, but you allowed yourself the liberty of speaking to me like a father a moment ago. One father is enough, thank you.

CROFTS [*Contemptuously.*]   Yah! [*He turns away again.*]

FRANK [*Rising.*]   Mrs Warren: I cannot give my Vivie up, even for your sake.

MRS WARREN [*Muttering.*]   Young scamp!

FRANK [*Continuing.*]   And as you no doubt intend to hold out other prospects to her, I shall lose no time in placing my case before her. [*They stare at him; and he begins to declaim gracefully*]

He either fears his fate too much,
Or his deserts are small,
That dares not put it to the touch
To gain or lose it all.[9]

[*The cottage door opens whilst he is reciting; and* VIVIE *and* PRAED *come in. He breaks off.* PRAED *puts his hat on the dresser. There is an immediate improvement in the company's behavior.* CROFTS *takes down his legs from the settle and pulls himself together as* PRAED *joins him at the fireplace.* MRS WARREN *loses her ease of manner and takes refuge in querulousness.*]

MRS WARREN   Wherever have you been, Vivie?

VIVIE [*Taking off her hat and throwing it carelessly on the table.*]   On the hill.

MRS WARREN   Well, you shouldnt go off like that without letting me know. How could I tell what had become of you? And night coming on too!

VIVIE [*Going to the door of the kitchen and opening it, ignoring her mother.*]   Now, about supper? [*All rise except* MRS WARREN.] We shall be rather crowded in here, I'm afraid.

MRS WARREN   Did you hear what I said, Vivie?

VIVIE [*Quietly.*]   Yes, mother. [*Reverting to the supper difficulty.*] How many are we? [*Counting.*] One, two, three, four, five, six. Well, two will have to wait until the rest are done: Mrs Alison has only plates and knives for four.

PRAED   Oh, it doesnt matter about me. I—

VIVIE   You have had a long walk and are hungry, Mr Praed: you shall have your supper at once. I can wait myself. I want one person to wait with me. Frank: are you hungry?

FRANK   Not the least in the world. Completely off my peck, in fact.

MRS WARREN [*To* CROFTS.]   Neither are you, George. You can wait.

CROFTS   Oh, hang it. Ive eaten nothing since tea-time. Cant Sam do it?

FRANK   Would you starve my poor father?

REV. SAMUEL [*Testily.*]   Allow me to speak for myself, sir. I am perfectly willing to wait.

VIVIE [*Decisively.*]   Theres no need. Only two are wanted. [*She opens the door of the kitchen.*] Will you take my mother in, Mr Gardner. [*The parson takes* MRS WARREN; *and they pass into the kitchen.* PRAED *and* CROFTS *follow. All except* PRAED *clearly disapprove of the arrangement, but do not know how to resist it.* VIVIE *stands at the door looking in at them.*] Can you squeeze past to that corner, Mr Praed: it's rather a tight fit. Take care of your coat against the white-wash: thats right. Now, are you all comfortable?

PRAED [*Within.*]   Quite, thank you.

MRS WARREN [*Within.*]   Leave the door open, dearie. [VIVIE *frowns; but* FRANK *checks her with a gesture, and steals to the cottage door, which he softly sets wide open.*] Oh Lor, what a draught! Youd better shut it, dear.

[VIVIE *shuts it with a slam, and then, noting with disgust that her mother's hat and shawl are lying about, takes them tidily to the window seat, whilst* FRANK *noiselessly shuts the cottage door.*]

---

9. From the poem *My Dear and Only Love,* by the marquis of Montrose (1612–1650).

FRANK [*Exulting.*] Aha! Got rid of em. Well, Vivvums: what do you think
of my guvernor?

VIVIE [*Preoccupied and serious.*] Ive hardly spoken to him. He doesnt
strike me as being a particularly able person.

FRANK Well, you know, the old man is not altogether such a fool as he
looks. You see, he was shoved into the Church rather; and in trying to
live up to it he makes a much bigger ass of himself than he really is. I
dont dislike him as much as you might expect. He means well. How do
you think youll get on with him?

VIVIE [*Rather grimly.*] I dont think my future life will be much concerned
with him, or with any of that old circle of my mother's, except perhaps
Praed. [*She sits down on the settle.*] What do you think of my mother?

FRANK Really and truly?

VIVIE Yes, really and truly.

FRANK Well, she's ever so jolly. But she's rather a caution, isn't she? And
Crofts! Oh my eye, Crofts! [*He sits beside her.*]

VIVIE What a lot, Frank!

FRANK What a crew!

VIVIE [*With intense contempt for them.*] If I thought that *I* was like that—
that I was going to be a waster, shifting along from one meal to another
with no purpose, and no character, and no grit in me, I'd open an artery
and bleed to death without one moment's hesitation.

FRANK Oh no, you wouldnt. Why should they take any grind when they
can afford not to? I wish I had their luck. No: what I object to is their
form. It isnt the thing: it's slovenly, ever so slovenly.

VIVIE Do you think your form will be any better when youre as old as
Crofts, if you dont work?

FRANK Of course I do. Ever so much better. Vivvums mustnt lecture: her
little boy's incorrigible. [*He attempts to take her face caressingly in his
hands.*]

VIVIE [*Striking his hands down sharply.*] Off with you: Vivvums is not in
a humor for petting her little boy this evening. [*She rises and comes forward to the other side of the room.*]

FRANK [*Following her.*] How unkind!

VIVIE [*Stamping at him.*] Be serious. I'm serious.

FRANK Good. Let us talk learnedly. Miss Warren: do you know that
all the most advanced thinkers are agreed that half the diseases of modern civilization are due to starvation of the affections in the young. Now,
I—

VIVIE [*Cutting him short.*] You are very tiresome. [*She opens the inner
door.*] Have you room for Frank there? He's complaining of starvation.

MRS WARREN [*Within.*] Of course there is. [*Clatter of knives and glasses
as she moves the things on the table.*] Here! theres room now beside me.
Come along, Mr Frank.

FRANK Her little boy will be ever so even with his Vivvums for this. [*He
passes into the kitchen.*]

MRS WARREN [*Within.*] Here, Vivie: come on you too, child. You must be
famished. [*She enters, followed by* CROFTS, *who holds the door open for*
VIVIE *with marked deference. She goes out without looking at him; and he
shuts the door after her.*] Why, George, you cant be done: youve eaten
nothing. Is there anything wrong with you?

CROFTS   Oh, all I wanted was a drink. [*He thrusts his hands in his pockets, and begins prowling about the room, restless and sulky.*]

MRS WARREN   Well, I like enough to eat. But a little of that cold beef and cheese and lettuce goes a long way. [*With a sigh of only half repletion she sits down lazily on the settle.*]

CROFTS   What do you go encouraging that young pup for?

MRS WARREN [*On the alert at once.*]   Now see here, George: what are you up to about that girl? Ive been watching your way of looking at her. Remember: I know you and what your looks mean.

CROFTS   Theres no harm in looking at her, is there?

MRS WARREN   I'd put you out and pack you back to London pretty soon if I saw any of your nonsense. My girl's little finger is more to me than your whole body and soul. [CROFTS *receives this with a sneering grin.* MRS WARREN, *flushing a little at her failure to impose on him in the character of a theatrically devoted mother, adds in a lower key*] Make your mind easy: the young pup has no more chance than you have.

CROFTS   Maynt a man take an interest in a girl?

MRS WARREN   Not a man like you.

CROFTS   How old is she?

MRS WARREN   Never you mind how old she is.

CROFTS   Why do you make such a secret of it?

MRS WARREN   Because I choose.

CROFTS   Well, I'm not fifty yet; and my property is as good as ever it was—

MRS WARREN [*Interrupting him.*]   Yes; because youre as stingy as youre vicious.

CROFTS [*Continuing.*]   And a baronet isnt to be picked up every day. No other man in my position would put up with you for a mother-in-law. Why shouldnt she marry me?

MRS WARREN   You!

CROFTS   We three could live together quite comfortably. I'd die before her and leave her a bouncing widow with plenty of money. Why not? It's been growing in my mind all the time Ive been walking with that fool inside there.

MRS WARREN [*Revolted.*]   Yes; it's the sort of thing that would grow in your mind.

[*He halts in his prowling; and the two look at one another, she steadfastly, with a sort of awe behind her contemptuous disgust: he stealthily, with a carnal gleam in his eye and a loose grin.*]

CROFTS [*Suddenly becoming anxious and urgent as he sees no sign of sympathy in her.*]   Look here, Kitty: youre a sensible woman: you neednt put on any moral airs. I'll ask no more questions; and you need answer none. I'll settle the whole property on her; and if you want a cheque for yourself on the wedding day, you can name any figure you like—in reason.

MRS WARREN   So it's come to that with you, George, like all the other worn-out old creatures!

CROFTS [*Savagely.*]   Damn you!

[*Before she can retort the door of the kitchen is opened; and the voices of the others are heard returning.* CROFTS, *unable to recover his presence of mind, hurries out of the cottage. The clergyman appears at the kitchen door.*]

REV. SAMUEL [*Looking around.*]   Where is Sir George?

MRS WARREN   Gone out to have a pipe. [*The clergyman takes his hat from the table, and joins* MRS WARREN *at the fireside. Meanwhile* VIVIE *comes in, followed by* FRANK, *who collapses into the nearest chair with an air of extreme exhaustion.* MRS WARREN *looks round at* VIVIE *and says, with her affectation of maternal patronage even more forced than usual*] Well, dearie: have you had a good supper?

VIVIE   You know what Mrs Alison's suppers are. [*She turns to* FRANK *and pets him.*] Poor Frank! was all the beef gone? did it get nothing but bread and cheese and ginger beer? [*Seriously, as if she had done quite enough trifling for one evening.*] Her butter is really awful. I must get some down from the stores.

FRANK   Do, in heaven's name!

[VIVIE *goes to the writing-table and makes a memorandum to order the butter.* PRAED *comes in from the kitchen, putting up his handkerchief, which he has been using as a napkin.*]

REV. SAMUEL   Frank, my boy: it is time for us to be thinking of home. Your mother does not know yet that we have visitors.

PRAED   I'm afraid we're giving trouble.

FRANK [*Rising.*]   Not the least in the world; my mother will be delighted to see you. She's a genuinely intellectual artistic woman; and she sees nobody here from one year's end to another except the gov'nor; so you can imagine how jolly dull it pans out for her. [*To his father.*] Y o u r e not intellectual or artistic are you, pater? So take Praed home at once; and I'll stay here and entertain Mrs Warren. Youll pick up Crofts in the garden. He'll be excellent company for the bull-pup.

PRAED [*Taking his hat from the dresser, and coming close to* FRANK.]   Come with us, Frank. Mrs Warren has not seen Miss Vivie for a long time; and we have prevented them from having a moment together yet.

FRANK [*Quite softened, and looking at* PRAED *with romantic admiration.*]   Of course. I forgot. Ever so thanks for reminding me. Perfect gentleman, Praddy. Always were. My ideal through life. [*He rises to go, but pauses a moment between the two older men, and puts his hand on* PRAED'*s shoulder.*] Ah, if you had only been my father instead of this unworthy old man! [*He puts his other hand on his father's shoulder.*]

REV. SAMUEL [*Blustering.*]   Silence, sir, silence; you are profane.

MRS WARREN [*Laughing heartily.*]   You should keep him in better order, Sam. Goodnight. Here: take George his hat and stick with my compliments.

REV. SAMUEL [*Taking them.*]   Goodnight. [*They shake hands. As he passes* VIVIE *he shakes hands with her also and bids her goodnight. Then, in booming command, to* FRANK.] Come along, sir, at once. [*He goes out.*]

MRS WARREN   Byebye, Praddy.

PRAED   Byebye, Kitty.

[*They shake hands affectionately and go out together, she accompanying him to the garden gate.*]

FRANK [*To* VIVIE.]   Kissums?

VIVIE [*Fiercely.*]   No. I hate you. [*She takes a couple of books and some paper from the writing-table, and sits down with them at the middle table, at the end next the fireplace.*]

FRANK [*Grimacing.*]   Sorry. [*He goes for his cap and rifle.* MRS WARREN *returns. He takes her hand.*] Goodnight, d e a r Mrs Warren. [*He kisses her hand. She snatches it away, her lips tightening, and looks more than half disposed to box his ears. He laughs mischievously and runs off, clapping-to the door behind him.*]

MRS WARREN [*Resigning herself to an evening of boredom now that the men are gone.*]   Did you ever in your life hear anyone rattle on so? Isnt he a tease? [*She sits at the table.*] Now that I think of it, dearie, dont you go on encouraging him. I'm sure he's a regular good-for-nothing.

VIVIE [*Rising to fetch more books.*]   I'm afraid so. Poor Frank! I shall have to get rid of him; but I shall feel sorry for him, though he's not worth it. That man Crofts does not seem to me to be good for much either: is he? [*She throws the books on the table rather roughly.*]

MRS WARREN [*Galled by* VIVIE'*s indifference.*]   What do you know of men, child, to talk that way about them? Youll have to make up your mind to see a good deal of Sir George Crofts, as he's a friend of mine.

VIVIE [*Quite unmoved.*]   Why? [*She sits down and opens a book.*] Do you expect that we shall be much together? You and I, I mean?

MRS WARREN [*Staring at her.*]   Of course: until youre married. Youre not going back to college again.

VIVIE   Do you think my way of life would suit you? I doubt it.

MRS WARREN   Y o u r way of life! What do you mean?

VIVIE [*Cutting a page of her book with the paper knife on her chatelaine.*]   Has it really never occurred to you, mother, that I have a way of life like other people?

MRS WARREN   What nonsense is this youre trying to talk? Do you want to shew your independence, now that youre a great little person at school? Dont be a fool, child.

VIVIE [*Indulgently.*]   Thats all you have to say on the subject, is it, mother?

MRS WARREN [*Puzzled, then angry.*]   Dont you keep on asking me questions like that. [*Violently.*] Hold your tongue. [VIVIE *works on, losing no time, and saying nothing.*] You and your way of life, indeed! What next? [*She looks at* VIVIE *again. No reply.*] Your way of life will be what I please, so it will. [*Another pause.*] Ive been noticing these airs in you ever since you got that tripos or whatever you call it. If you think I'm going to put up with them youre mistaken; and the sooner you find it out, the better. [*Muttering.*] All I have to say on the subject, indeed! [*Again raising her voice angrily.*] Do you know who youre speaking to, Miss?

VIVIE [*Looking across at her without raising her head from her book.*]   No. Who are you? What are you?

MRS WARREN [*Rising breathless.*]   You young imp!

VIVIE   Everybody knows my reputation, my social standing, and the profession I intend to pursue. I know nothing about you. What is that way of life which you invite me to share with you and Sir George Crofts, pray?

MRS WARREN   Take care. I shall do something I'll be sorry for after, and you too.

VIVIE [*Putting aside her books with cool decision.*]   Well, let us drop the subject until you are better able to face it. [*Looking critically at her mother.*] You want some good walks and a little lawn tennis to set you up. You are shockingly out of condition: you were not able to manage twenty yards uphill today without stopping to pant; and your wrists are mere rolls of fat. Look at mine. [*She holds out her wrists.*]

MRS WARREN [*After looking at her helplessly, begins to whimper.*] Vivie—

VIVIE [*Springing up sharply.*] Now pray dont begin to cry. Anything but that. I really cannot stand whimpering. I will go out of the room if you do.

MRS WARREN [*Piteously.*] Oh, my darling, how can you be so hard on me? Have I no rights over you as your mother?

VIVIE Are you my mother?

MRS WARREN [*Appalled.*] Am I your mother! Oh, Vivie!

VIVIE Then where are our relatives? my father? our family friends? You claim the rights of a mother: the right to call me fool and child; to speak to me as no woman in authority over me at college dare speak to me; to dictate my way of life; and to force on me the acquaintance of a brute whom anyone can see to be the most vicious sort of London man about town. Before I give myself the trouble to resist such claims, I may as well find out whether they have any real existence.

MRS WARREN [*Distracted, throwing herself on her knees.*] Oh no, no. Stop, stop. I am your mother: I swear it. Oh, you cant mean to turn on me— my own child! It's not natural. You believe me, dont you? Say you believe me.

VIVIE Who was my father?

MRS WARREN You dont know what youre asking. I cant tell you.

VIVIE [*Determinedly.*] Oh yes you can, if you like. I have a right to know; and you know very well that I have that right. You can refuse to tell me, if you please; but if you do, you will see the last of me tomorrow morning.

MRS WARREN Oh, it's too horrible to hear you talk like that. You wouldnt—you c o u l d n t leave me.

VIVIE [*Ruthlessly.*] Yes, without a moment's hesitation, if you trifle with me about this. [*Shivering with disgust.*] How can I feel sure that I may not have the contaminated blood of that brutal waster in my veins?

MRS WARREN No, no. On my oath it's not he, nor any of the rest that you have ever met. I'm certain of that, at least.

[VIVIE*'s eyes fasten sternly on her mother as the significance of this flashes on her.*]

VIVIE [*Slowly.*] You are certain of that, a t l e a s t. Ah! You mean that that is all you are certain of. [*Thoughtfully.*] I see. [MRS WARREN *buries her face in her hands.*] Dont do that, mother: you know you dont feel it a bit. [MRS WARREN *takes down her hands and looks up deplorably at* VIVIE, *who takes out her watch and says*] Well, that is enough for tonight. At what hour would you like breakfast? Is half-past eight too early for you?

MRS WARREN [*Wildly.*] My God, what sort of woman are you?

VIVIE [*Coolly.*] The sort the world is mostly made of, I should hope. Otherwise I dont understand how it gets its business done. Come [*taking her mother by the wrist, and pulling her up pretty resolutely*]: pull yourself together. Thats right.

MRS WARREN [*Querulously.*] Youre very rough with me, Vivie.

VIVIE Nonsense. What about bed? It's past ten.

MRS WARREN [*Passionately.*] Whats the use of my going to bed? Do you think I could sleep?

VIVIE   Why not? I shall.

MRS WARREN   You! youve no heart. [*She suddenly breaks out vehemently in her natural tongue—the dialect of a woman of the people—with all her affectations of maternal authority and conventional manners gone, and an overwhelming inspiration of true conviction and scorn in her.*] Oh, I wont bear it: I wont put up with the injustice of it. What right have you to set yourself up above me like this? You boast of what you are to me—to m e, who gave you the chance of being what you are. What chance had I! Shame on you for a bad daughter and a stuck-up prude!

VIVIE   [*Sitting down with a shrug, no longer confident; for her replies, which have sounded sensible and strong to her so far, now begin to ring rather woodenly and even priggishly against the new tone of her mother.*]   Dont think for a moment I set myself above you in any way. You attacked me with the conventional authority of a mother: I defended myself with the conventional superiority of a respectable woman. Frankly, I am not going to stand any of your nonsense; and when you drop it I shall not expect you to stand any of mine. I shall always respect your right to your own opinions and your own way of life.

MRS WARREN   My own opinions and my own way of life! Listen to her talking! Do you think I was brought up like you? able to pick and choose my own way of life? Do you think I did what I did because I liked it, or thought it right, or wouldnt rather have gone to college and been a lady if I'd had the chance?

VIVIE   Everybody has some choice, mother. The poorest girl alive may not be able to choose between being Queen of England or Principal of Newnham; but she can choose between ragpicking and flower-selling, according to her taste. People are always blaming their circumstances for what they are. I dont believe in circumstances. The people who get on in this world are the people who get up and look for the circumstances they want, and, if they cant find them, make them.

MRS WARREN   Oh, it's easy to talk, very easy, isnt it? Here! would you like to know what my circumstances were?

VIVIE   Yes: you had better tell me. Wont you sit down?

MRS WARREN   Oh, I'll sit down: dont you be afraid. [*She plants her chair farther forward with brazen energy, and sits down.* VIVIE *is impressed in spite of herself.*] D'you know what your gran'mother was?

VIVIE   No.

MRS WARREN   No you dont. I do. She called herself a widow and had a fried-fish shop down by the Mint, and kept herself and four daughters out of it. Two of us were sisters: that was me and Liz; and we were both good-looking and well made. I suppose our father was a well-fed man: mother pretended he was a gentleman; but I dont know. The other two were only half sisters: undersized, ugly, starved looking, hard working, honest poor creatures: Liz and I would have half-murdered them if mother hadnt half-murdered us to keep our hands off them. They were the respectable ones. Well, what did they get by their respectability? I'll tell you. One of them worked in a whitelead factory twelve hours a day for nine shillings a week until she died of lead poisoning. She only expected to get her hands a little paralyzed; but she died. The other was always held up to us as a model because she married a Government laborer in the Deptford victualling yard, and kept his room and the three children neat and tidy on eighteen shillings a week—until he took to drink. That was worth being respectable for, wasnt it?

VIVIE [*Now thoughtfully attentive.*]   Did you and your sister think so?

MRS WARREN   Liz didnt, I can tell you: she had more spirit. We both went to a church school—that was part of the ladylike airs we gave ourselves to be superior to the children that knew nothing and went nowhere— and we stayed there until Liz went out one night and never came back. I know the school-mistress thought I'd soon follow her example; for the clergyman was always warning me that Lizzie'd end by jumping off Waterloo Bridge. Poor fool: that was all he knew about it! But I was more afraid of the whitelead factory than I was of the river; and so would you have been in my place. That clergyman got me a situation as a scullery maid in a temperance restaurant where they sent out for anything you liked. Then I was waitress; and then I went to the bar at Waterloo station: fourteen hours a day serving drinks and washing glasses for four shillings a week and my board. That was considered a great promotion for me. Well, one cold, wretched night, when I was so tired I could hardly keep myself awake, who should come up for a half of Scotch but Lizzie, in a long fur cloak, elegant and comfortable, with a lot of sovereigns in her purse.

VIVIE [*Grimly.*]   My aunt Lizzie!

MRS WARREN.   Yes; and a very good aunt to have, too. She's living down at Winchester now, close to the cathedral, one of the most respectable ladies there. Chaperones girls at the county ball, if you please. No river for Liz, thank you! You remind me of Liz a little: she was a first-rate business woman—saved money from the beginning—never let herself look too like what she was—never lost her head or threw away a chance. When she saw I'd grown up good-looking she said to me across the bar "What are you doing there, you little fool? wearing out your health and your appearance for other people's profit!" Liz was saving money then to take a house for herself in Brussels; and she thought we two could save faster than one. So she lent me some money and gave me a start; and I saved steadily and first paid her back, and then went into business with her as her partner. Why shouldnt I have done it? The house in Brussels was real high class: a much better place for a woman to be in than the factory where Anne Jane got poisoned. None of our girls were ever treated as I was treated in the scullery of that temperance place, or at the Waterloo bar, or at home. Would you have had me stay in them and become a worn out old drudge before I was forty?

VIVIE [*Intensely interested by this time.*]   No; but why did you choose that business? Saving money and good management will succeed in any business.

MRS WARREN   Yes, saving money. But where can a woman get the money to save in any other business? Could you save out of four shillings a week and keep yourself dressed as well? Not you. Of course, if youre a plain woman and cant earn anything more; or if you have a turn for music, or the stage, or newspaper writing; thats different. But neither Liz nor I had any turn for such things: all we had was our appearance and our turn for pleasing men. Do you think we were such fools as to let other people trade in our good looks by employing us as shopgirls, or barmaids, or waitresses, when we could trade in them ourselves and get all the profits instead of starvation wages? Not likely.

VIVIE   You were certainly quite justified—from the business point of view.

MRS WARREN   Yes; or any other point of view. What is any respectable girl brought up to do but to catch some rich man's fancy and get the benefit of his money by marrying him?—as if a marriage ceremony could make any difference in the right or wrong of the thing! Oh! the hypocrisy of the world makes me sick! Liz and I had to work and save and calculate just like other people; elseways we should be as poor as any good-for-nothing drunken waster of a woman that thinks her luck will last for ever. [*With great energy.*] I despise such people: theyve no character; and if theres a thing I hate in a woman, it's want of character.

VIVIE   Come now, mother: frankly! Isnt it part of what you call character in a woman that she should greatly dislike such a way of making money?

MRS WARREN   Why, of course. Everybody dislikes having to work and make money; but they have to do it all the same. I'm sure Ive often pitied a poor girl; tired out and in low spirits, having to try to please some man that she doesnt care two straws for—some half-drunken fool that thinks he's making himself agreeable when he's teasing and worrying and disgusting a woman so that hardly any money could pay her for putting up with it. But she has to bear with disagreeables and take the rough with the smooth, just like a nurse in a hospital or anyone else. It's not work that any woman would do for pleasure, goodness knows; though to hear the pious people talk you would suppose it was a bed of roses.

VIVIE   Still, you consider it worth while. It pays.

MRS WARREN   Of course it's worth while to a poor girl, if she can resist temptation and is good-looking and well conducted and sensible. It's far better than any other employment open to her. I always thought that oughtnt to be. It c a n t be right, Vivie, that there shouldnt be better opportunities for women. I stick to that: it's wrong. But it's so, right or wrong; and a girl must make the best of it. But of course it's not worth while for a lady. If you took to it youd be a fool; but I should have been a fool if I'd taken to anything else.

VIVIE   [*More and more deeply moved.*]   Mother; suppose we were both as poor as you were in those wretched old days, are you quite sure that you wouldnt advise me to try the Waterloo bar, or marry a laborer, or even go into the factory?

MRS WARREN   [*Indignantly.*]   Of course not. What sort of mother do you take me for! How could you keep your self-respect in such starvation and slavery? And whats a woman worth? whats life worth? without self-respect! Why am I independent and able to give my daughter a first-rate education, when other women that had just as good opportunities are in the gutter? Because I always knew how to respect myself and control myself. Why is Liz looked up to in a cathedral town? The same reason. Where would we be now if we'd minded the clergyman's foolishness? Scrubbing floors for one and sixpence a day and nothing to look forward to but the workhouse infirmary. Dont you be led astray by people who dont know the world, my girl. The only way for a woman to provide for herself decently is for her to be good to some man that can afford to be good to her. If she's in his own station of life, let her make him marry her; but if she's far beneath him she cant expect it: why should she? it wouldn't be for her own happiness. Ask any lady in London society that has daughters; and she'll tell you the same, except that I tell you straight and she'll tell you crooked. Thats all the difference.

VIVIE [*Fascinated, gazing at her.*] My dear mother; you are a wonderful woman: you are stronger than all England. And are you really and truly not one wee bit doubtful—or—or—ashamed?

MRS WARREN Well, of course, dearie, it's only good manners to be ashamed of it; it's expected from a woman. Women have to pretend to feel a great deal that they dont feel. Liz used to be angry with me for plumping out the truth about it. She used to say that when every woman could learn enough from what was going on in the world before her eyes, there was no need to talk about it to her. But then Liz was such a perfect lady! She had the true instinct of it; while I was always a bit of a vulgarian. I used to be so pleased when you sent me your photos to see that you were growing up like Liz: youve just her ladylike, determined way. But I cant stand saying one thing when everyone knows I mean another. Whats the use in such hypocrisy? If people arrange the world that way for women, theres no good pretending it's arranged the other way. No: I never was a bit ashamed really. I consider I had a right to be proud of how we managed everything so respectably, and never had a word against us, and how the girls were so well taken care of. Some of them did very well: one of them married an ambassador. But of course now I darent talk about such things: whatever would they think of us! [*She yawns.*] Oh dear! I do believe I'm getting sleepy after all. [*She stretches herself lazily, thoroughly relieved by her explosion, and placidly ready for her night's rest.*]

VIVIE I believe it is I who will not be able to sleep now. [*She goes to the dresser and lights the candle. Then she extinguishes the lamp, darkening the room a good deal.*] Better let in some fresh air before locking up. [*She opens the cottage door, and finds that it is broad moonlight.*] What a beautiful night! Look! [*She draws aside the curtains of the window. The landscape is seen bathed in the radiance of the harvest moon rising over Blackdown.*]

MRS WARREN [*With a perfunctory glance at the scene.*] Yes, dear; but take care you dont catch your death of cold from the night air.

VIVIE [*Contemptuously.*] Nonsense.

MRS WARREN [*Querulously.*] Oh yes: everything I say is nonsense, according to you.

VIVIE [*Turning to her quickly.*] No: really that is not so, mother. You have got completely the better of me tonight, though I intended it to be the other way. Let us be good friends now.

MRS WARREN [*Shaking her head a little ruefully.*] So it has been the other way. But I suppose I must give in to it. I always got the worst of it from Liz; and now I suppose it'll be the same with you.

VIVIE Well, never mind. Come: goodnight, dear old mother. [*She takes her mother in her arms.*]

MRS WARREN [*Fondly.*] I brought you up well, didnt I, dearie?

VIVIE You did.

MRS WARREN And youll be good to your poor old mother for it, wont you?

VIVIE   I will, dear. [*Kissing her.*] Goodnight.

MRS WARREN [*With unction.*]   Blessings on my own dearie darling! a mother's blessing!

> [*She embraces her daughter protectingly, instinctively looking upward for divine sanction.*]

Act 3

In the Rectory garden next morning, with the sun shining from a cloudless sky. The garden wall has a five-barred wooden gate, wide enough to admit a carriage, in the middle. Beside the gate hangs a bell on a coiled spring, communicating with a pull outside. The carriage drive comes down the middle of the garden and then swerves to its left, where it ends in a little gravelled circus opposite the Rectory porch. Beyond the gate is seen the dusty high road, parallel with the wall, bounded on the farther side by a strip of turf and an unfenced pine wood. On the lawn, between the house and the drive, is a clipped yew tree, with a garden bench in its shade. On the opposite side the garden is shut in by a box hedge; and there is a sundial on the turf, with an iron chair near it. A little path leads off through the box hedge, behind the sundial.

FRANK, *seated on the chair near the sundial, on which he has placed the morning papers, is reading* The Standard. *His father comes from the house, red-eyed and shivery, and meets* FRANK's *eye with misgiving.*

FRANK [*Looking at his watch.*]   Half-past eleven. Nice hour for a rector to come down to breakfast!

REV. SAMUEL   Dont mock, Frank: dont mock. I am a little—er—[*Shivering.*]—

FRANK   Off color?

REV. SAMUEL [*Repudiating the expression.*]   No, sir: u n w e l l this morning. Wheres your mother?

FRANK   Dont be alarmed: she's not here. Gone to town by the 11.13 with Bessie. She left several messages for you. Do you feel equal to receiving them now, or shall I wait til youve breakfasted?

REV. SAMUEL   I h a v e breakfasted, sir. I am surprised at your mother going to town when we have people staying with us. Theyll think it very strange.

FRANK   Possibly she has considered that. At all events, if Crofts is going to stay here, and you are going to sit up every night with him until four, recalling the incidents of your fiery youth, it is clearly my mother's duty, as a prudent housekeeper, to go up to the stores and order a barrel of whisky and few hundred siphons.

REV. SAMUEL   I did not observe that Sir George drank excessively.

FRANK   You were not in a condition to, gov'nor.

REV. SAMUEL   Do you mean to say that I—?

FRANK [*Calmly.*]   I never saw a beneficed clergyman less sober. The anecdotes you told about your past career were so awful that I really dont think Praed would have passed the night under your roof if it hadnt been for the way my mother and he took to one another.

REV. SAMUEL   Nonsense, sir. I am Sir George Crofts' host. I must talk to him about something; and he has only one subject. Where is Mr Praed now?

FRANK   He is driving my mother and Bessie to the station.

REV. SAMUEL   Is Crofts up yet?

FRANK   Oh, long ago. He hasnt turned a hair: he's in much better practice than you. Has kept it up ever since, probably. He's taken himself off somewhere to smoke.

> [FRANK *resumes his paper. The parson turns disconsolately towards the gate; then comes back irresolutely.*]

REV. SAMUEL   Er—Frank.

FRANK   Yes.

REV. SAMUEL   Do you think the Warrens will expect to be asked here after yesterday afternoon?

FRANK   Theyve been asked already.

REV. SAMUEL [*Appalled.*]   What!!!

FRANK   Crofts informed us at breakfast that you told him to bring Mrs Warren and Vivie over here today, and to invite them to make this house their home. My mother then found she must go to town by the 11.13 train.

REV. SAMUEL [*With despairing vehemence.*]   I never gave any such invitation. I never thought of such a thing.

FRANK [*Compassionately.*]   How do you know, gov'nor, what you said and thought last night?

PRAED [*Coming in through the hedge.*]   Good morning.

REV. SAMUEL   Good morning. I must apologize for not having met you at breakfast. I have a touch of—of—

FRANK   Clergyman's sore throat, Praed. Fortunately not chronic.

PRAED [*Changing the subject.*]   Well, I must say your house is in a charming spot here. Really most charming.

REV. SAMUEL   Yes: it is indeed. Frank will take you for a walk, Mr Praed, if you like. I'll ask you to excuse me: I must take the opportunity to write my sermon while Mrs Gardner is away and you are all amusing yourselves. You wont mind, will you?

PRAED   Certainly not. Dont stand on the slightest ceremony with me.

REV. SAMUEL   Thank you. I'll—er—er—[*He stammers his way to the porch and vanishes into the house.*]

PRAED   Curious thing it must be writing a sermon every week.

FRANK   Ever so curious, if he did it. He buys em. He's gone for some soda water.

PRAED   My dear boy: I wish you would be more respectful to your father. You know you can be so nice when you like.

FRANK   My dear Praddy: you forget that I have to live with the governor. When two people live together—it doesnt matter whether theyre father and son or husband and wife or brother and sister—they cant keep up the polite humbug thats so easy for ten minutes on an afternoon call. Now the governor, who unites to many admirable domestic qualities the irresoluteness of a sheep and the pompousness and aggressiveness of a jackass—

PRAED   No, pray, pray, my dear Frank, remember! He is your father.

FRANK   I give him due credit for that. [*Rising and flinging down his paper.*] But just imagine his telling Crofts to bring the Warrens over here! He must have been ever so drunk. You know, my dear Praddy, my mother wouldnt stand Mrs Warren for a moment. Vivie mustnt come here until she's gone back to town.

PRAED   But your mother doesnt know anything about Mrs Warren, does she? [*He picks up the paper and sits down to read it.*]

FRANK   I don't know. Her journey to town looks as if she did. Not that my mother would mind in the ordinary way: she has stuck like a brick to lots of women who had got into trouble. But they were all nice women. Thats what makes the real difference. Mrs Warren, no doubt, has her merits; but she's ever so rowdy; and my mother simply wouldnt put up with her. So—hallo! [*This exclamation is provoked by the reappearance of the clergyman, who comes out of the house in haste and dismay.*]

REV. SAMUEL   Frank: Mrs Warren and her daughter are coming across the heath with Crofts: I saw them from the study windows. What am I to say about your mother?

FRANK   Stick on your hat and go out and say how delighted you are to see them; and that Frank's in the garden; and that mother and Bessie have been called to the bedside of a sick relative, and were ever so sorry they couldnt stop; and that you hope Mrs Warren slept well; and—and—say any blessed thing except the truth, and leave the rest to Providence.

REV. SAMUEL   But how are we to get rid of them afterwards?

FRANK   Theres no time to think of that now. Here! [*He bounds into the house.*]

REV. SAMUEL   He's so impetuous. I dont know what to do with him, Mr Praed.

FRANK [*Returning with clerical felt hat, which he claps on his father's head.*]   Now: off with you. [*Rushing him through the gate.*] Praed and I'll wait here, to give the thing an unpremeditated air. [*The clergyman, dazed but obedient, hurries off.*]

FRANK   We must get the old girl back to town somehow, Praed. Come! Honestly, dear Praddy, do you like seeing them together?

PRAED   Oh, why not?

FRANK [*His teeth on edge.*]   Dont it make your flesh creep ever so little? that wicked old devil, up to every villainy under the sun, I'll swear, and Vivie—ugh!

PRAED   Hush, pray. Theyre coming.

[*The clergyman and* CROFTS *are seen coming along the road, followed by* MRS WARREN *and* VIVIE *walking affectionately together.*]

FRANK   Look: she actually has her arm round the old woman's waist. It's her right arm: she began it. She's gone sentimental, by God! Ugh! ugh! Now do you feel the creeps? [*The clergyman opens the gate; and* MRS WARREN *and* VIVIE *pass him and stand in the middle of the garden looking at the house.* FRANK, *in an ecstasy of dissimulation, turns gaily to* MRS WARREN, *exclaiming*] Ever so delighted to see you, Mrs Warren. This quiet old rectory garden becomes you perfectly.

MRS WARREN   Well, I never! Did you hear that, George? He says I look well in a quiet old rectory garden.

REV. SAMUEL [*Still holding the gate for* CROFTS, *who loafs through it, heavily bored.*]   You look well everywhere, Mrs Warren.

FRANK   Bravo, gov'nor! Now look here: lets have a treat before lunch. First lets see the church. Everyone has to do that. It's a regular old thirteenth century church, you know: the gov'nor's ever so fond of it, because he got up a restoration fund and had it completely rebuilt six years ago. Praed will be able to shew its points.

PRAED [*Rising.*] Certainly, if the restoration has left any to shew.

REV. SAMUEL [*Mooning hospitably at them.*] I shall be pleased, I'm sure, if Sir George and Mrs Warren really care about it.

MRS WARREN Oh, come along and get it over.

CROFTS [*Turning back towards the gate.*] Ive no objection.

REV. SAMUEL Not that way. We go through the fields, if you dont mind. Round here. [*He leads the way by the little path through the box hedge.*]

CROFTS Oh, all right. [*He goes with the parson.*]

> [PRAED *follows with* MRS WARREN. VIVIE *does not stir: she watches them until they have gone, with all the lines of purpose in her face marking it strongly.*]

FRANK Aint you coming?

VIVIE No. I want to give you a warning, Frank. You were making fun of my mother just now when you said that about the rectory garden. That is barred in future. Please treat my mother with as much respect as you treat your own.

FRANK My dear Viv: she wouldnt appreciate it: the two cases require different treatment. But what on earth has happened to you? Last night we were perfectly agreed as to your mother and her set. This morning I find you attitudinizing sentimentally with your arm round your parent's waist.

VIVIE [*Flushing.*] Attitudinizing!

FRANK That was how it struck me. First time I ever saw you do a second-rate thing.

VIVIE [*Controlling herself.*] Yes, Frank: there has been a change; but I dont think it a change for the worse. Yesterday I was a little prig.

FRANK And today?

VIVIE [*Wincing; then looking at him steadily.*] Today I know my mother better than you do.

FRANK Heaven forbid!

VIVIE What do you mean?

FRANK Viv: theres a freemasonry among thoroughly immoral people that you know nothing of. Youve too much character. T h a t s the bond between your mother and me: thats why I know her better than youll ever know her.

VIVIE You are wrong: you know nothing about her. If you knew the circumstances against which my mother had to struggle—

FRANK [*Adroitly finishing the sentence for her.*] I should know why she is what she is, shouldnt I? What difference would that make? Circumstances or no circumstances, Viv, you wont be able to stand your mother.

VIVIE [*Very angrily.*] Why not?

FRANK Because she's an old wretch, Viv. If you ever put your arm round her waist in my presence again, I'll shoot myself there and then as a protest against an exhibition which revolts me.

VIVIE Must I choose between dropping your acquaintance and dropping my mother's?

FRANK [*Gracefully.*] That would put the old lady at ever such a disadvantage. No, Viv: your infatuated little boy will have to stick to you in any case. But he's all the more anxious that you shouldnt make mistakes. It's no use, Viv: your mother's impossible. She may be a good sort; but she's a bad lot, a very bad lot.

VIVIE [*Hotly.*]   Frank—! [*He stands his ground. She turns away and sits down on the bench under the yew tree, struggling to recover her self-command. Then she says*] Is she to be deserted by all the world because she's what you call a bad lot? Has she no right to live?

FRANK   No fear of that, Viv: s h e wont ever be deserted. [*He sits on the bench beside her.*]

VIVIE   But I am to desert her, I suppose.

FRANK [*Babyishly, lulling her and making love to her with his voice.*] Mustnt go live with her. Little family group of mother and daughter wouldnt be a success. Spoil our little group.

VIVIE [*Falling under the spell.*]   What little group?

FRANK   The babes in the wood: Vivie and little Frank. [*He nestles against her like a weary child.*] Lets go and get covered up with leaves.

VIVIE [*Rhythmically, rocking him like a nurse.*]   Fast asleep, hand in hand, under the trees.

FRANK   The wise little girl with her silly little boy.

VIVIE   The dear little boy with his dowdy little girl.

FRANK   Ever so peaceful, and relieved from the imbecility of the little boy's father and the questionableness of the little girl's—

VIVIE [*Smothering the word against her breast.*]   Sh-sh-sh-sh! little girl wants to forget all about her mother. [*They are silent for some moments, rocking one another. Then* VIVIE *wakes up with a shock, exclaiming*] What a pair of fools we are! Come: sit up. Gracious! your hair. [*She smoothes it.*] I wonder do all grown up people play in that childish way when nobody is looking. I never did it when I was a child.

FRANK   Neither did I. You are my first playmate. [*He catches her hand to kiss it, but checks himself to look round first. Very unexpectedly, he sees* CROFTS *emerging from the box hedge.*] Oh damn!

VIVIE   Why damn, dear?

FRANK [*Whispering.*]   Sh! Here's this brute Crofts. [*He sits farther away from her with an unconcerned air.*]

CROFTS.   Could I have a few words with you, Miss Vivie?

VIVIE   Certainly.

CROFTS [*To* FRANK.]   Youll excuse me, Gardner. Theyre waiting for you in the church, if you don't mind.

FRANK [*Rising.*]   Anything to oblige you, Crofts—except church. If you should happen to want me, Vivvums, ring the gate bell. [*He goes into the house with unruffled suavity.*]

CROFTS [*Watching him with a crafty air as he disappears, and speaking to* VIVIE *with an assumption of being on privileged terms with her.*]   Pleasant young fellow that, Miss Vivie. Pity he has no money, isnt it?

VIVIE   Do you think so?

CROFTS   Well, whats he to do? No profession. No property. Whats he good for?

VIVIE   I realize his disadvantages, Sir George.

CROFTS [*A little taken aback at being so precisely interpreted.*]   Oh, it's not that. But while we're in this world we're in it; and money's money. [*Vivie does not answer.*] Nice day, isnt it?

VIVIE [*With scarcely veiled contempt for this effort at conversation.*]   Very.

CROFTS [*With brutal good humor, as if he liked her pluck.*]   Well, thats not

what I came to say. [*Sitting down beside her.*] Now listen, Miss Vivie. I'm
quite aware that I'm not a young lady's man.

VIVIE   Indeed, Sir George?

CROFTS   No; and to tell you the honest truth I dont want to be either. But
when I say a thing I mean it; when I feel a sentiment I feel it in earnest;
and what I value I pay hard money for. Thats the sort of man I am.

VIVIE   It does you great credit, I'm sure.

CROFTS   Oh, I dont mean to praise myself. I have my faults, Heaven
knows: no man is more sensible of that than I am. I know I'm not perfect:
thats one of the disadvantages of being a middle-aged man; for I'm not
a young man, and I know it. But my code is a simple one, and, I think,
a good one. Honor between man and man; fidelity between man and
woman; and no cant about this religion or that religion, but an honest
belief that things are making for good on the whole.

VIVIE   [*With biting irony.*]   "A power, not ourselves, that makes for righteousness," eh?

CROFTS   [*Taking her seriously.*]   Oh certainly. Not ourselves, of course. You
understand what I mean. Well, now as to practical matters. You may
have an idea that Ive flung my money about; but I havnt: I'm richer today
than when I first came into the property. Ive used my knowledge of the
world to invest my money in ways that other men have overlooked; and
whatever else I may be, I'm a safe man from the money point of view.

VIVIE   It's very kind of you to tell me all this.

CROFTS   Oh well, come, Miss Vivie: you neednt pretend you dont see what
I'm driving at. I want to settle down with a Lady Crofts. I suppose you
think me very blunt, eh?

VIVIE   Not at all: I am much obliged to you for being so definite and business-like. I quite appreciate the offer: the money, the position, L a d y
C r o f t s, and so on. But I think I will say no, if you don't mind. I'd
rather not. [*She rises, and strolls across to the sundial to get out of his
immediate neighborhood.*]

CROFTS   [*Not at all discouraged, and taking advantage of the additional room
left him on the seat to spread himself comfortably, as if a few preliminary
refusals were part of the inevitable routine of courtship.*]   I'm in no hurry.
It was only just to let you know in case young Gardner should try to trap
you. Leave the question open.

VIVIE   [*Sharply.*]   My no is final. I wont go back from it.

   [CROFTS *is not impressed. He grins; leans forward with his elbows on his
   knees to prod with his stick at some unfortunate insect in the grass; and
   looks cunningly at her. She turns away impatiently.*]

CROFTS   I'm a good deal older than you. Twenty-five years; quarter of a
century. I shant live for ever; and I'll take care that you shall be well off
when I'm gone.

VIVIE   I am proof against even that inducement, Sir George. Dont you
think youd better take your answer? There is not the slightest chance of
my altering it.

CROFTS   [*Rising after a final slash at a daisy, and coming nearer to her.*]
Well, no matter. I could tell you some things that would change your
mind fast enough; but I wont, because I'd rather win you by honest
affection. I was a good friend to your mother: ask her whether I wasnt.

She'd never have made the money that paid for your education if it hadnt been for my advice and help, not to mention the money I advanced her. There are not many men would have stood by her as I have. I put not less than £40,000 into it, from first to last.

VIVIE [*Staring at him.*]   Do you mean to say you were my mother's business partner?

CROFTS   Yes. Now just think of all the trouble and the explanations it would save if we were to keep the whole thing in the family, so to speak. Ask your mother whether she'd like to have to explain all her affairs to a perfect stranger.

VIVIE   I see no difficulty, since I understand that the business is wound up, and the money invested.

CROFTS [*Stopping short, amazed.*]   Wound up! Wind up a business thats paying 35 per cent in the worst years! Not likely. Who told you that?

VIVIE [*Her color quite gone.*]   Do you mean that it is still—? [*She stops abruptly, and puts her hand on the sundial to support herself. Then she gets quickly to the iron chair and sits down.*] What business are you talking about?

CROFTS   Well, the fact is it's not what would be considered exactly a high-class business in my set—the county set, you know—our set it will be if you think better of my offer. Not that theres any mystery about it: dont think that. Of course you know by your mother's being in it that it's perfectly straight and honest. Ive known her for many years; and I can say of her that she'd cut off her hands sooner than touch anything that was not what it ought to be. I'll tell you all about it if you like. I dont know whether youve found in travelling how hard it is to find a really comfortable private hotel.

VIVIE [*Sickened, averting her face.*]   Yes: go on.

CROFTS   Well, thats all it is. Your mother has a genius for managing such things. We've got two in Brussels, one in Ostend, one in Vienna, and two in Budapest. Of course there are others besides ourselves in it; but we hold most of the capital; and your mother's indispensable as managing director. Youve noticed, I daresay, that she travels a good deal. But you see you cant mention such things in society. Once let out the word hotel and everybody says you keep a public-house. You wouldnt like people to say that of your mother, would you? Thats why we're so reserved about it. By the way, youll keep it to yourself, wont you? Since it's been a secret so long, it had better remain so.

VIVIE   And this is the business you invite me to join you in?

CROFTS   Oh, no. My wife shant be troubled with business. Youll not be in it more than youve always been.

VIVIE   I always been! What do you mean?

CROFTS   Only that youve always lived on it. It paid for your education and the dress you have on your back. Dont turn up your nose at business, Miss Vivie: where would your Newnhams and Girtons[1] be without it?

VIVIE [*Rising, almost beside herself.*]   Take care. I know what this business is.

CROFTS [*Staring, with a suppressed oath.*]   Who told you?

1. Girton, like Newnham, is a women's college at Cambridge University.

VIVIE   Your partner. My mother.

CROFTS [Black with rage.]   The old—

VIVIE   Just so.

[He swallows the epithet and stands for a moment swearing and raging foully to himself. But he knows that his cue is to be sympathetic. He takes refuge in generous indignation.]

CROFTS   She ought to have had more consideration for you. I'd never have told you.

VIVIE   I think you would probably have told me when we were married; it would have been a convenient weapon to break me in with.

CROFTS [Quite sincerely.]   I never intended that. On my word as a gentleman I didnt.

[VIVIE wonders at him. Her sense of the irony of his protest cools and braces her. She replies with contemptuous self-possession.]

VIVIE   It does not matter. I suppose you understand that when we leave here today our acquaintance ceases.

CROFTS   Why? Is it for helping your mother?

VIVIE   My mother was a very poor woman who had no reasonable choice but to do as she did. You were a rich gentleman; and you did the same for the sake of 35 per cent. You are a pretty common sort of scoundrel, I think. That is my opinion of you.

CROFTS [After a stare: not at all displeased, and much more at ease on these frank terms than on their former ceremonious ones.]   Ha! ha! ha! ha! Go it, little missie, go it: it doesnt hurt me and it amuses you. Why the devil shouldnt I invest my money that way? I take the interest on my capital like other people: I hope you dont think I dirty my own hands with the work. Come! you wouldnt refuse the acquaintance of my mother's cousin the Duke of Belgravia because some of the rents he gets are earned in queer ways. You wouldnt cut the Archbishop of Canterbury, I suppose, because the Ecclesiastical Commissioners have a few publicans and sinners among their tenants. Do you remember your Crofts scholarship at Newnham? Well, that was founded by my brother the M.P.[2] He gets his 22 per cent out of a factory with 600 girls in it, and not one of them getting wages enough to live on. How d'ye suppose they manage when they have no family to fall back on? Ask your mother. And do you expect me to turn my back on 35 per cent when all the rest are pocketing what they can, like sensible men? No such fool! If youre going to pick and choose your acquaintances on moral principles, youd better clear out of this country, unless you want to cut yourself out of all decent society.

VIVIE [Conscience stricken.]   You might go on to point out that I myself never asked where the money I spent came from. I believe I am just as bad as you.

CROFTS [Greatly reassured.]   Of course you are; and a very good thing too! What harm does it do after all? [Rallying her jocularly.] So you dont think me such a scoundrel now you come to think it over. Eh?

VIVIE   I have shared profits with you; and I admitted you just now to the familiarity of knowing what I think of you.

CROFTS [With serious friendliness.]   To be sure you did. You wont find me

2. Member of Parliament.

a bad sort: I dont go in for being superfine intellectually; but Ive plenty of honest human feeling; and the old Crofts breed comes out in a sort of instinctive hatred of anything low, in which I'm sure youll sympathize with me. Believe me, Miss Vivie, the world isnt such a bad place as the croakers make out. As long as you dont fly openly in the face of society, society doesnt ask any inconvenient questions; and it makes precious short work of the cads who do. There are no secrets better kept than the secrets everybody guesses. In the class of people I can introduce you to, no lady or gentleman would so far forget themselves as to discuss my business affairs or your mother's. No man can offer you a safer position.

VIVIE [*Studying him curiously.*]   I suppose you really think youre getting on famously with me.

CROFTS   Well, I hope I may flatter myself that you think better of me than you did at first.

VIVIE [*Quietly.*]   I hardly find you worth thinking about at all now. When I think of the society that tolerates you, and the laws that protect you! when I think of how helpless nine out of ten young girls would be in the hands of you and my mother! the unmentionable woman and her capitalist bully—

CROFTS [*Livid.*]   Damn you!

VIVIE   You need not. I feel among the damned already.

[*She raises the latch of the gate to open it and go out. He follows her and puts his hand heavily on the top bar to prevent its opening.*]

CROFTS [*Panting with fury.*]   Do you think I'll put up with this from you, you young devil?

VIVIE [*Unmoved.*]   Be quiet. Some one will answer the bell. [*Without flinching a step she strikes the bell with the back of her hand. It clangs harshly; and he starts back involuntarily. Almost immediately* FRANK *appears at the porch with his rifle.*]

FRANK [*With cheerful politeness.*]   Will you have the rifle, Viv; or shall I operate?

VIVIE   Frank: have you been listening?

FRANK [*Coming down into the garden.*]   Only for the bell, I assure you; so that you shouldn't have to wait. I think I shewed great insight into your character Crofts.

CROFTS   For two pins I'd take that gun from you and break it across your head.

FRANK [*Stalking him cautiously.*]   Pray dont. I'm ever so careless in handling firearms. Sure to be a fatal accident, with a reprimand from the coroner's jury for my negligence.

VIVIE   Put the rifle away, Frank: it's quite unnecessary.

FRANK   Quite right, Viv. Much more sportsmanlike to catch him in a trap. [CROFTS, *understanding the insult, makes a threatening movement.*] Crofts: there are fifteen cartridges in the magazine here; and I am a dead shot at the present distance and at an object of your size.

CROFTS   Oh, you neednt be afraid. I'm not going to touch you.

FRANK   Ever so magnanimous of you under the circumstances! Thank you!

CROFTS   I'll tell you this before I go. It may interest you, since youre so fond of one another. Allow me, Mister Frank, to introduce you to your half-sister, the eldest daughter of the Reverend Samuel Gardner. Miss

Vivie: your half-brother. Good morning. [*He goes out through the gate and along the road.*]

FRANK [*After a pause of stupefaction, raising the rifle.*]   Youll testify before the coroner that it's an accident, Viv. [*He takes aim at the retreating figure of* CROFTS. VIVIE *seizes the muzzle and pulls it round against her breast.*]

VIVIE   Fire now. You may.

FRANK [*Dropping his end of the rifle hastily.*]   Stop! take care. [*She lets go. It falls on the turf.*] Oh, youve given your little boy such a turn. Suppose it had gone off! ugh! [*He sinks on the garden seat, overcome.*]

VIVIE   Suppose it had: do you think it would not have been a relief to have some sharp physical pain tearing through me?

FRANK [*Coaxingly.*]   Take it ever so easy, dear Viv. Remember; even if the rifle scared that fellow into telling the truth for the first time in his life, that only makes us the babes in the wood in earnest. [*He holds out his arms to her.*] Come and be covered up with leaves again.

VIVIE [*With a cry of disgust.*]   Ah, not that, not that. You make all my flesh creep.

FRANK   Why, whats the matter?

VIVIE   Goodbye. [*She makes for the gate.*]

FRANK [*Jumping up.*]   Hallo! Stop! Viv! Viv! [*She turns in the gateway.*] Where are you going to? Where shall we find you?

VIVIE   At Honoria Fraser's chambers, 67 Chancery Lane, for the rest of my life. [*She goes off quickly in the opposite direction to that taken by* CROFTS.]

FRANK   But I say—wait—dash it! [*He runs after her.*]

Act 4

HONORIA FRASER's *chambers in Chancery Lane. An office at the top of New Stone Buildings, with a plate-glass window, distempered walls, electric light, and a patent stove. Saturday afternoon. The chimneys of Lincoln's Inn[3] and the western sky beyond are seen through the window. There is a double writing table in the middle of the room, with a cigar box, ash pans, and a portable electric reading lamp almost snowed up in heaps of papers and books. This table has knee holes and chairs right and left and is very untidy. The clerk's desk, closed and tidy, with its high stool, is against the wall, near a door communicating with the inner rooms. In the opposite wall is the door leading to the public corridor. Its upper panel is of opaque glass, lettered in black on the outside,* FRASER AND WARREN. *A baize screen hides the corner between this door and the window.*

FRANK, *in a fashionable light-colored coaching suit, with his stick, gloves, and white hat in his hands, is pacing up and down the office. Somebody tries the door with a key.*

FRANK [*Calling.*]   Come in. It's not locked.

[VIVIE *comes in, in her hat and jacket. She stops and stares at him.*]

VIVIE [*Sternly.*]   What are you doing here?

FRANK   Waiting to see you. Ive been here for hours. Is this the way you attend to your business? [*He puts his hat and stick on the table, and*

---

3. One of the four legal societies in London collectively known as the Inns of Court.

perches himself with a vault on the clerk's stool, looking at her with every appearance of being in a specially restless, teasing flippant mood.]

VIVIE   Ive been away exactly twenty minutes for a cup of tea. [*She takes off her hat and jacket and hangs them up behind the screen.*] How did you get in?

FRANK   The staff had not left when I arrived. He's gone to play cricket on Primrose Hill.[4] Why dont you employ a woman, and give your sex a chance?

VIVIE   What have you come for?

FRANK [*Springing off the stool and coming close to her.*]   Viv: lets go and enjoy the Saturday half-holiday somewhere, like the staff. What do you say to Richmond,[5] and then a music hall, and a jolly supper?

VIVIE   Cant afford it. I shall put in another six hours work before I go to bed.

FRANK   Cant afford it, cant we? Aha! Look here. [*He takes out a handful of sovereigns and makes them chink.*] Gold, Viv: gold!

VIVIE   Where did you get it?

FRANK   Gambling, Viv: gambling. Poker.

VIVIE   Pah! It's meaner than stealing it. No: I'm not coming. [*She sits down to work at the table, with her back to the glass door, and begins turning over the papers.*]

FRANK [*Remonstrating piteously.*]   But, my dear Viv, I want to talk to you ever so seriously.

VIVIE   Very well: sit down in Honoria's chair and talk here. I like ten minutes chat after tea. [*He murmurs.*] No use groaning: I'm inexorable. [*He takes the opposite seat disconsolately.*] Pass that cigar box, will you?

FRANK [*Pushing the cigar box across.*]   Nasty womanly habit. Nice men dont do it any longer.

VIVIE   Yes: they object to the smell in the office; and weve had to take to cigarets. See! [*She opens the box and takes out a cigaret, which she lights. She offers him one; but he shakes his head with a wry face. She settles herself comfortably in her chair, smoking.*] Go ahead.

FRANK   Well, I want to know what youve done—what arrangements youve made.

VIVIE   Everything was settled twenty minutes after I arrived here. Honoria has found the business too much for her this year; and she was on the point of sending for me and proposing a partnership when I walked in and told her I hadnt a farthing in the world. So I installed myself and packed her off for a fortnight's holiday. What happened at Haslemere when I left?

FRANK   Nothing at all. I said youd gone to town on particular business.

VIVIE   Well?

FRANK   Well, either they were too flabbergasted to say anything, or else Crofts had prepared your mother. Anyhow, she didnt say anything; and Crofts didnt say anything; and Praddy only stared. After tea they got up and went; and Ive not seen them since.

VIVIE [*Nodding placidly with one eye on a wreath of smoke.*]   Thats all right.

4. A park in northwest London.   5. A residential suburb in southwest London.

FRANK [*Looking round disparagingly.*]   Do you intend to stick in this confounded place?

VIVIE [*Blowing the wreath decisively away, and sitting straight up.*]   Yes.
These two days have given me back all my strength and self-possession.
I will never take a holiday again as long as I live.

FRANK [*With a very wry face.*]   Mps! You look quite happy. And as hard as
nails.

VIVIE [*Grimly.*]   Well for me that I am!

FRANK [*Rising.*]   Look here, Viv: we must have an explanation. We parted
the other day under a complete misunderstanding. [*He sits on the table,
close to her.*]

VIVIE [*Putting away the cigaret.*]   Well: clear it up.

FRANK   You remember what Crofts said?

VIVIE   Yes.

FRANK   That revelation was supposed to bring about a complete change
in the nature of our feeling for one another. It placed us on the footing
of brother and sister.

VIVIE   Yes.

FRANK   Have you ever had a brother?

VIVIE   No.

FRANK   Then you dont know what being brother and sister feels like? Now
I have lots of sisters; and the fraternal feeling is quite familiar to me. I
assure you my feeling for you is not the least in the world like it. The
girls will go their way; I will go mine; and we shant care if we never see
one another again. Thats brother and sister. But as to you, I cant be easy
if I have to pass a week without seeing you. Thats not brother and sister.
It's exactly what I felt an hour before Crofts made his revelation. In short,
dear Viv, it's love's young dream.

VIVIE [*Bitingly.*]   The same feeling, Frank, that brought your father to my
mother's feet. Is that it?

FRANK [*So revolted that he slips off the table for a moment.*]   I very strongly
object, Viv, to have my feelings compared to any which the Reverend
Samuel is capable of harboring; and I object still more to a comparison
of you to your mother. [*Resuming his perch.*] Besides, I dont believe the
story. I have taxed my father with it, and obtained from him what I
consider tantamount to a denial.

VIVIE   What did he say?

FRANK   He said he was sure there must be some mistake.

VIVIE   Do you believe him?

FRANK   I am prepared to take his word as against Crofts'.

VIVIE   Does it make any difference? I mean in your imagination or conscience; for of course it makes no real difference.

FRANK [*Shaking his head.*]   None whatever to m e.

VIVIE   Nor to me.

FRANK [*Staring.*]   But this is ever so surprising! [*He goes back to his chair.*]
I thought our whole relations were altered in your imagination and conscience, as you put it, the moment those words were out of the brute's
muzzle.

VIVIE   No: it was not that. I didnt believe him. I only wish I could.

FRANK   Eh?

VIVIE   I think brother and sister would be a very suitable relation for us.

FRANK   You really mean that?

VIVIE   Yes. It's the only relation I care for, even if we could afford any other. I mean that.

FRANK [*Raising his eyebrows like one on whom a new light has dawned, and rising with quite an effusion of chivalrous sentiment.*]   My dear Viv: why didnt you say so before? I am ever so sorry for persecuting you. I understand, of course.

VIVIE [*Puzzled.*]   Understand what?

FRANK   Oh, I'm not a fool in the ordinary sense: only in the Scriptural sense of doing all the things the wise man declared to be folly, after trying them himself on the most extensive scale. I see I am no longer Vivvum's little boy. Dont be alarmed: I shall never call you Vivvums again—at least unless you get tired of your new little boy, whoever he may be.

VIVIE   My new little boy!

FRANK [*With conviction.*]   Must be a new little boy. Always happens that way. No other way, in fact.

VIVIE   None that you know of, fortunately for you.

[*Someone knocks at the door.*]

FRANK   My curse upon yon caller, whoe'er he be!

VIVIE   It's Praed. He's going to Italy and wants to say goodbye. I asked him to call this afternoon. Go and let him in.

FRANK   We can continue our conversation after his departure for Italy. I'll stay him out. [*He goes to the door and opens it.*] How are you, Praddy? Delighted to see you. Come in.

[PRAED, *dressed for travelling, comes in, in high spirits.*]

PRAED   How do you do, Miss Warren? [*She presses his hand cordially, though a certain sentimentality in his high spirits jars on her.*] I start in an hour from Holborn Viaduct.[6] I wish I could persuade you to try Italy.

VIVIE   What for?

PRAED   Why, to saturate yourself with beauty and romance, of course.

[VIVIE, *with a shudder, turns her chair to the table, as if the work waiting for her were a support to her.* PRAED *sits opposite to her.* FRANK *places a chair near* VIVIE, *and drops lazily and carelessly into it, talking at her over his shoulder.*]

FRANK   No use, Praddy. Viv is a little Philistine. She is indifferent to my romance, and insensible to my beauty.

VIVIE   Mr Praed: once for all, there is no beauty and no romance in life for me. Life is what it is; and I am prepared to take it as it is.

PRAED [*Enthusiastically.*]   You will not say that if you come with me to Verona and on to Venice. You will cry with delight at living in such a beautiful world.

FRANK   This is most eloquent, Praddy. Keep it up.

PRAED   Oh, I assure you *I* have cried—I shall cry again, I hope—at fifty! At your age, Miss Warren, you would not need to go so far as Verona. Your spirits would absolutely fly up at the mere sight of Ostend. You would be charmed with the gaiety, the vivacity, the happy air of Brussels.

VIVIE [*Springing up with an exclamation of loathing.*]   Agh!

6. A road bridge in the City of London.

PRAED [*Rising.*] Whats the matter?

FRANK [*Rising.*] Hallo, Viv!

VIVIE [*To* PRAED, *with deep reproach.*] Can you find no better example of your beauty and romance than Brussels to talk to me about?

PRAED [*Puzzled.*] Of course it's very different from Verona. I dont suggest for a moment that—

VIVIE [*Bitterly.*] Probably the beauty and romance come to much the same in both places.

PRAED [*Completely sobered and much concerned.*] My dear Miss Warren: I—[*Looking inquiringly at* FRANK.] Is anything the matter?

FRANK She thinks your enthusiasm frivolous, Praddy. She's had ever such a serious call.

VIVIE [*Sharply.*] Hold your tongue, Frank. Dont be silly.

FRANK [*Sitting down.*] Do you call this good manners, Praed?

PRAED [*Anxious and considerate.*] Shall I take him away, Miss Warren? I feel sure we have disturbed you at your work.

VIVIE Sit down: I'm not ready to go back to work yet. [PRAED *sits.*] You both think I have an attack of nerves. Not a bit of it. But there are two subjects I want dropped, if you dont mind. One of them [*To* FRANK.] is love's young dream in any shape or form: the other [*To* PRAED.] is the romance and beauty of life, especially Ostend and the gaiety of Brussels. You are welcome to any illusions you may have left on these subjects: I have none. If we three are to remain friends, I must be treated as a woman of business, permanently single [*To* FRANK.] and permanently unromantic [*to* PRAED].

FRANK I also shall remain permanently single until you change your mind. Praddy: change the subject. Be eloquent about something else.

PRAED [*Diffidently.*] I'm afraid theres nothing else in the world that I c a n talk about. The Gospel of Art is the only one I can preach. I know Miss Warren is a great devotee of the Gospel of Getting On; but we cant discuss that without hurting your feelings, Frank, since you are determined not to get on.

FRANK Oh, dont mind my feelings. Give me some improving advice by all means: it does me ever so much good. Have another try to make a successful man of me, Viv. Come; lets have it all: energy, thrift, foresight, self-respect, character. Dont you hate people who have no character, Viv?

VIVIE [*Wincing.*] Oh, stop, stop: let us have no more of that horrible cant. Mr Praed: if there are really only those two gospels in the world, we had better all kill ourselves; for the same taint is in both, through and through.

FRANK [*Looking critically at her.*] There is a touch of poetry about you today, Viv, which has hitherto been lacking.

PRAED [*Remonstrating.*] My dear Frank: arnt you a little unsympathetic?

VIVIE [*Merciless to herself.*] No: it's good for me. It keeps me from being sentimental.

FRANK [*Bantering her.*] Checks your strong natural propensity that way, dont it?

VIVIE [*Almost hysterically.*] Oh yes; go on: dont spare me. I was sentimental for one moment in my life—beautifully sentimental—by moonlight; and now—

FRANK [*Quickly.*]   I say, Viv: take care. Dont give yourself away.

VIVIE   Oh, do you think Mr Praed does not know all about my mother? [*Turning on* PRAED.] You had better have told me that morning, Mr Praed. You are very old fashioned in your delicacies, after all.

PRAED   Surely it is you who are a little old fashioned in your prejudices, Miss Warren, I feel bound to tell you, speaking as an artist, and believing that the most intimate human relationships are far beyond and above the scope of the law, that though I know that your mother is an unmarried woman, I do not respect her the less on that account. I respect her more.

FRANK [*Airily.*]   Hear! Hear!

VIVIE [*Staring at him.*]   Is that a l l you know?

PRAED   Certainly that is all.

VIVIE   Then you neither of you know anything. Your guesses are innocence itself compared to the truth.

PRAED [*Rising, startled and indignant, and preserving his politeness with an effort.*]   I hope not. [*More emphatically.*] I hope not, Miss Warren.

FRANK [*Whistles.*]   Whew!

VIVIE   You are not making it easy for me to tell you, Mr Praed.

PRAED [*His chivalry drooping before their conviction.*]   If there is anything worse—that is, anything else—are you sure you are right to tell us, Miss Warren?

VIVIE   I am sure that if I had the courage I should spend the rest of my life in telling everybody—stamping and branding it into them until they all felt their part in its abomination as I feel mine. There is nothing I despise more than the wicked convention that protects these things by forbidding a woman to mention them. And yet I cant tell you. The two infamous words that describe what my mother is are ringing in my ears and struggling on my tongue; but I cant utter them: the shame of them is too horrible for me. [*She buries her face in her hands. The two men, astonished, stare at one another and then at her. She raises her head again desperately and snatches a sheet of paper and a pen.*] Here: let me draft you a prospectus.

FRANK   Oh, she's mad. Do you hear, Viv? mad. Come! pull yourself together.

VIVIE   You shall see. [*She writes.*] "Paid up capital: not less than £40,000 standing in the name of Sir George Crofts, Baronet, the chief shareholder. Premises at Brussels, Ostend, Vienna and Budapest. Managing director: Mrs Warren"; and now dont let us forget her qualifications: the two words. [*She writes the words and pushes the paper to them.*] There! Oh no: dont read it: dont! [*She snatches it back and tears it to pieces; then seizes her head in her hands and hides her face on the table.*]

     [FRANK, *who has watched the writing over his shoulder, and opened his eyes very widely at it, takes a card from his pocket; scribbles the two words on it; and silently hands it to* PRAED, *who reads it with amazement, and hides it hastily in his pocket.*]

FRANK [*Whispering tenderly.*]   Viv, dear: thats all right. I read what you wrote: so did Praddy. We understand. And we remain, as this leaves us at present, yours ever so devotedly.

PRAED   We do indeed, Miss Warren. I declare you are the most splendidly courageous woman I ever met.

[*This sentimental compliment braces* VIVIE. *She throws it away from her with an impatient shake, and forces herself to stand up, though not without some support from the table.*]

FRANK   Dont stir, Viv, if you dont want to. Take it easy.

VIVIE   Thank you. You can always depend on me for two things: not to cry and not to faint. [*She moves a few steps towards the door of the inner room, and stops close to* PRAED *to say.*] I shall need much more courage than that when I tell my mother that we have come to the parting of the ways. Now I must go into the next room for a moment to make myself neat again, if you dont mind.

PRAED   Shall we go away?

VIVIE   No; I shall be back presently. Only for a moment. [*She goes into the other room,* PRAED *opening the door for her.*]

PRAED   What an amazing revelation! I'm extremely disappointed in Crofts: I am indeed.

FRANK   I'm not in the least. I feel he's perfectly accounted for at last. But what a facer for me, Praddy! I cant marry her now.

PRAED   [*Sternly.*]   Frank! [*The two look at one another,* FRANK *unruffled,* PRAED *deeply indignant.*] Let me tell you, Gardner, that if you desert her now you will behave very despicably.

FRANK   Good old Praddy! Ever chivalrous! But you mistake: it's not the moral aspect of the case: it's the money aspect. I really cant bring myself to touch the old woman's money now.

PRAED   And was that what you were going to marry on?

FRANK   What else? *I* havnt any money, nor the smallest turn for making it. If I married Viv now she would have to support me; and I should cost her more than I am worth.

PRAED   But surely a clever bright fellow like you can make something by your own brains.

FRANK   Oh yes, a little. [*He takes out his money again.*] I made all that yesterday in an hour and a half. But I made it in a highly speculative business. No, dear Praddy: even if Bessie and Georgina marry million-aires and the governor dies after cutting them off with a shilling, I shall have only four hundred a year. And he wont die until he's three score and ten: he hasnt originality enough. I shall be on short allowance for the next twenty years. No short allowance for Viv, if I can help it. I withdraw gracefully and leave the field to the gilded youth of England. So thats settled. I shant worry her about it: I'll just send her a little note after we're gone. She'll understand.

PRAED   [*Grasping his hand.*]   Good fellow, Frank! I heartily beg your pardon. But must you never see her again?

FRANK   Never see her again! Hang it all, be reasonable. I shall come along as often as possible, and be her brother. I can n o t understand the absurd consequences you romantic people expect from the most ordinary transactions. [*A knock at the door.*] I wonder who this is. Would you mind opening the door? If it's a client it will look more respectable than if I appeared.

PRAED   Certainly. [*He goes to the door and opens it.* FRANK *sits down in* VIVIE's *chair to scribble a note.*] My dear Kitty: come in: come in.

[MRS WARREN *comes in, looking apprehensively round for* VIVIE. *She has*

*done her best to make herself matronly and dignified. The brilliant hat
is replaced by a sober bonnet, and the gay blouse covered by a costly black
silk mantle. She is pitiably anxious and ill at ease: evidently panic-
stricken.*]

MRS WARREN [*To* FRANK.] What! Y o u r e here, are you?

FRANK [*Turning in his chair from his writing, but not rising.*] Here, and
charmed to see you. You come like a breath of spring.

MRS WARREN Oh, get out with your nonsense. [*In a low voice.*] Wheres
Vivie?

[FRANK *points expressively to the door of the inner room, but says nothing.*]

MRS WARREN [*Sitting down suddenly and almost beginning to cry.*] Praddy:
wont she see me, dont you think?

PRAED My dear Kitty: dont distress yourself. Why should she not?

MRS WARREN Oh, you never can see why not: youre too innocent. Mr
Frank: did she say anything to you?

FRANK [*Folding his note.*] She m u s t see you, if [*very expressively*] you
wait til she comes in.

MRS WARREN [*Frightened.*] Why shouldnt I wait?

[FRANK *looks quizzically at her; puts his note carefully on the inkbottle,
so that* VIVIE *cannot fail to find it when next she dips her pen; then rises
and devotes his attention entirely to her.*]

FRANK My dear Mrs Warren: suppose you were a sparrow—ever so tiny
and pretty a sparrow hopping in the roadway—and you saw a steam roller
coming in your direction, would you wait for it?

MRS WARREN Oh, dont bother me with your sparrows. What did she run
away from Haslemere like that for?

FRANK I'm afraid she'll tell you if you rashly await her return.

MRS WARREN Do you want me to go away?

FRANK No: I always want you to stay. But I a d v i s e you to go away.

MRS WARREN What! and never see her again!

FRANK Precisely.

MRS WARREN [*Crying again.*] Praddy: dont let him be cruel to me. [*She
hastily checks her tears and wipes her eyes.*] She'll be so angry if she sees
Ive been crying.

FRANK [*With a touch of real compassion in his airy tenderness.*] You know
that Praddy is the soul of kindness, Mrs Warren. Praddy: what do y o u
say? Go or stay?

PRAED [*To* MRS WARREN.] I really should be very sorry to cause you unnecessary pain; but I think perhaps you had better not wait. The fact is—
[VIVIE *is heard at the inner door.*]

FRANK Sh! Too late. She's coming.

MRS WARREN Dont tell her I was crying. [VIVIE *comes in. She stops gravely
on seeing* MRS WARREN, *who greets her with hysterical cheerfulness.*] Well,
dearie. So here you are at last.

VIVIE I am glad you have come: I want to speak to you. You said you were
going, Frank, I think.

FRANK Yes. Will you come with me, Mrs Warren? What do you say to a
trip to Richmond, and the theatre in the evening? There is safety in
Richmond. No steam roller there.

VIVIE   Nonsense, Frank. My mother will stay here.

MRS WARREN [*Scared.*]   I dont know: perhaps I'd better go. We're disturbing you at your work.

VIVIE [*With quiet decision.*]   Mr. Praed: please take Frank away. Sit down, mother. [MRS WARREN *obeys helplessly.*]

PRAED   Come, Frank. Goodbye, Miss Vivie.

VIVIE [*Shaking hands.*]   Goodbye. A pleasant trip.

PRAED   Thank you: thank you. I hope so.

FRANK [*To* MRS WARREN.]   Goodbye: youd ever so much better have taken my advice. [*He shakes hands with her. Then airily to* VIVIE] Byebye, Viv.

VIVIE   Goodbye. [*He goes out gaily without shaking hands with her.*]

PRAED [*Sadly.*]   Goodbye, Kitty.

MRS WARREN [*Sniveling.*]   —oobye!

> [PRAED *goes.* VIVIE, *composed and extremely grave, sits down in Honoria's chair, and waits for her mother to speak.* MRS WARREN, *dreading a pause, loses no time in beginning.*]

MRS WARREN   Well, Vivie, what did you go away like that for without saying a word to me? How could you do such a thing! And what have you done to poor George? I wanted him to come with me; but he shuffled out of it. I could see that he was quite afraid of you. Only fancy: he wanted me not to come. As if [*Trembling.*] I should be afraid of you, dearie. [VIVIE's *gravity deepens.*] But of course I told him it was all settled and comfortable between us, and that we were on the best of terms. [*She breaks down.*] Vivie: whats the meaning of this? [*She produces a commercial envelope, and fumbles at the enclosure with trembling fingers.*] I got it from the bank this morning.

VIVIE   It is my month's allowance. They sent it to me as usual the other day. I simply sent it back to be placed to your credit, and asked them to send you the lodgment receipt. In future I shall support myself.

MRS WARREN [*Not daring to understand.*]   Wasnt it enough? Why didnt you tell me? [*With a cunning gleam in her eye.*] I'll double it: I was intending to double it. Only let me know how much you want.

VIVIE   You know very well that that has nothing to do with it. From this time I go my own way in my own business and among my own friends. And you will go yours. [*She rises.*] Goodbye.

MRS WARREN [*Rising, appalled.*]   Goodbye?

VIVIE   Yes: Goodbye. Come: dont let us make a useless scene: you understand perfectly well. Sir George Crofts has told me the whole business.

MRS WARREN [*Angrily.*]   Silly old— [*She swallows an epithet, and turns white at the narrowness of her escape from uttering it.*]

VIVIE   Just so.

MRS WARREN   He ought to have his tongue cut out. But I thought it was ended: you said you didnt mind.

VIVIE [*Steadfastly.*]   Excuse me: I d o mind.

MRS WARREN   But I explained—

VIVIE   You explained how it came about. You did not tell me that it is still going on. [*She sits.*]

> [MRS WARREN, *silenced for a moment, looks forlornly at* VIVIE, *who waits, secretly hoping that the combat is over. But the cunning expression comes back into* MRS WARREN's *face; and she bends across the table, sly and urgent, half whispering.*]

MRS WARREN   Vivie: do you know how rich I am?

VIVIE   I have no doubt you are very rich.

MRS WARREN   But you dont know all that that means: youre too young. It means a new dress every day; it means theatres and balls every night; it means having the pick of all the gentlemen in Europe at your feet; it means a lovely house and plenty of servants; it means the choicest of eating and drinking; it means everything you like, everything you want, everything you can think of. And what are you here? A mere drudge, toiling and moiling early and late for your bare living and two cheap dresses a year. Think over it. [*Soothingly.*] Youre shocked, I know. I can enter into your feelings; and I think they do you credit; but trust me, nobody will blame you: you may take my word for that. I know what young girls are; and I know youll think better of it when youve turned it over in your mind.

VIVIE   So thats how it's done, is it? You must have said all that to many a woman, mother, to have it so pat.

MRS WARREN   [*Passionately.*]   What harm am I asking you to do? [VIVIE *turns away contemptuously.* MRS WARREN *continues desperately.*] Vivie: listen to me: you dont understand: youve been taught wrong on purpose: you dont know what the world is really like.

VIVIE   [*Arrested.*]   Taught wrong on purpose! What do you mean?

MRS WARREN   I mean that youre throwing away all your chances for nothing. You think that people are what they pretend to be: that the way you were taught at school and college to think right and proper is the way things really are. But it's not: it's all only a pretence, to keep the cowardly slavish common run of people quiet. Do you want to find that out, like other women, at forty, when youve thrown yourself away and lost your chances; or wont you take it in good time now from your own mother, that loves you and swears to you that it's truth: gospel truth? [*urgently*] Vivie: the big people, the clever people, the managing people, all know it. They do as I do, and think what I think. I know plenty of them. I know them to speak to, to introduce you to, to make friends of for you. I dont mean anything wrong; thats what you dont understand: your head is full of ignorant ideas about me. What do the people that taught you know about life or about people like me? When did they ever meet me, or speak to me, or let anyone tell them about me? the fools! Would they ever have done anything for you if I hadnt paid them? Havnt I told you that I want you to be respectable? Havnt I brought you up to be respectable? And how can you keep it up without my money and my influence and Lizzie's friends? Cant you see that youre cutting your own throat as well as breaking my heart in turning your back on me?

VIVIE   I recognize the Crofts philosophy of life, mother. I heard it all from him that day at the Gardners'.

MRS WARREN   You think I want to force that played-out old sot on you! I dont, Vivie: on my oath I dont.

VIVIE   It would not matter if you did: you would not succeed. [MRS WARREN *winces, deeply hurt by the implied indifference towards her affectionate intention.* VIVIE, *neither understanding this nor concerning herself about it, goes on calmly.*] Mother: you dont at all know the sort of person I am. I dont object to Crofts more than to any other coarsely built man of his class. To tell you the truth, I rather admire him for being strong-minded enough to enjoy himself in his own way and make plenty of money instead of living the usual shooting, hunting, dining-out, tailoring, loafing life of his set merely because all the rest do it. And I'm perfectly aware that if I'd been in the same circumstances as my aunt Liz, I'd have done exactly what she did. I dont think I'm more prejudiced or straitlaced than you: I think I'm less. I'm certain I'm less sentimental. I know very well that fashionable morality is all a pretence, and that if I took your money and devoted the rest of my life to spending it fashionably, I might be as worthless and vicious as the silliest woman could possibly want to be without having a word said to me about it. But I dont want to be worthless. I shouldnt enjoy trotting about the park to advertize my dressmaker and carriage builder, or being bored at the opera to shew off a shopwindowful of diamonds.

MRS WARREN [*Bewildered.*]   But—

VIVIE   Wait a moment: Ive not done. Tell me why you continue your business now that you are independent of it. Your sister, you told me, has left all that behind her. Why dont you do the same?

MRS WARREN   Oh, it's all very easy for Liz: she likes good society, and has the air of being a lady. Imagine me in a cathedral town! Why, the very rooks in the trees would find me out even if I could stand the dulness of it. I must have work and excitement, or I should go melancholy mad. And what else is there for me to do? The life suits me: I'm fit for it and not for anything else. If I didnt do it somebody else would; so I dont do any real harm by it. And then it brings in money; and I like making money. No; it's no use: I cant give it up—not for anybody. But what need you know about it? I'll never mention it. I'll keep Crofts away. I'll not trouble you much: you see I have to be constantly running about from one place to another. Youll be quit of me altogether when I die.

VIVIE   No: I am my mother's daughter. I am like you: I must have work, and must make more money than I spend. But my work is not your work, and my way not your way. We must part. It will not make much difference to us: instead of meeting one another for perhaps a few months in twenty years we shall never meet: thats all.

MRS WARREN [*Her voice stifled in tears.*]   Vivie: I meant to have been more with you: I did indeed.

VIVIE   It's no use, mother: I am not to be changed by a few cheap tears and entreaties any more than you are, I daresay.

MRS WARREN [*Wildly.*]   Oh, you call a mother's tears cheap.

VIVIE   They cost you nothing; and you ask me to give you the peace and quietness of my whole life in exchange for them. What use would my company be to you if you could get it? What have we two in common that could make either of us happy together?

MRS WARREN [*Lapsing recklessly into her dialect.*]   We're mother and daughter. I want my daughter. Ive a right to you. Who is to care for me when I'm old? Plenty of girls have taken to me like daughters and cried at leaving me; but I let them all go because I had you to look forward to. I kept myself lonely for you. Youve no right to turn on me now and refuse to do your duty as a daughter.

VIVIE [*Jarred and antagonized by the echo of the slums in her mother's voice.*]   My duty as a daughter! I thought we should come to that presently. Now once for all, mother, you want a daughter and Frank wants a wife. I dont want a mother; and I dont want a husband. I have spared neither Frank nor myself in sending him about his business. Do you think I will spare y o u ?

MRS WARREN [*Violently.*]   Oh, I know the sort you are: no mercy for yourself or anyone else. *I* know. My experience has done that for me anyhow: I can tell the pious, canting, hard, selfish woman when I meet her. Well, keep yourself to yourself: *I* dont want you. But listen to this. Do you know what I would do with you if you were a baby again? aye, as sure as there's a Heaven above us.

VIVIE   Strangle me, perhaps.

MRS WARREN   No: I'd bring you up to be a real daughter to me, and not what you are now, with your pride and your prejudices and the college education you stole from me: yes, stole: deny it if you can: what was it but stealing? I'd bring you up in my own house, I would.

VIVIE [*Quietly.*]   In one of your own houses.

MRS WARREN [*Screaming.*]   Listen to her! listen to how she spits on her mother's grey hairs! Oh, may you live to have your own daughter tear and trample on you as you have trampled on me. And you will: you will. No woman ever had luck with a mother's curse on her.

VIVIE   I wish you wouldnt rant, mother. It only hardens me. Come: I suppose I am the only young woman you ever had in your power that you did good to. Dont spoil it all now.

MRS WARREN   Yes, Heaven forgive me, it's true; and you are the only one that ever turned on me. Oh, the injustice of it! the injustice! the injustice! I always wanted to be a good woman. I tried honest work; and I was slave-driven until I cursed the day I ever heard of honest work. I was a good mother; and because I made my daughter a good woman she turns me out as if I was a leper. Oh, if I only had my life to live over again! I'd talk to that lying clergyman in the school. From this time forth, so help me Heaven in my last hour, I'll do wrong and nothing but wrong. And I'll prosper on it.

VIVIE   Yes: it's better to choose your line and go through with it. If I had been you, mother, I might have done as you did; but I should not have lived one life and believed in another. You are a conventional woman at heart. That is why I am bidding you goodbye now. I am right, am I not?

MRS WARREN [*Taken aback.*]   Right to throw away all my money?

VIVIE   No: right to get rid of you? I should be a fool not to! Isnt that so?

MRS WARREN [*Sulkily.*]   Oh well, yes, if you come to that, I suppose you are. But Lord help the world if everybody took to doing the right thing! And now I'd better go than stay where I'm not wanted. [*She turns to the door.*]

VIVIE [*Kindly.*]   Wont you shake hands?

MRS WARREN [*After looking at her fiercely for a moment with a savage impulse to strike her.*]   No, thank you. Goodbye.

VIVIE [*Matter-of-factly.*]   Goodbye. [MRS WARREN *goes out, slamming the door behind her. The strain on* VIVIE's *face relaxes; her grave expression breaks up into one of joyous content; her breath goes out in a half sob, half laugh of intense relief. She goes buoyantly to her place at the writing-table; pushes the electric lamp out of the way; pulls over a great sheaf of papers;*

and is in the act of dipping her pen in the ink when she finds FRANK's *note. She opens it unconcernedly and reads it quickly, giving a little laugh at some quaint turn of expression in it.*] And goodbye, Frank. [*She tears the note up and tosses the pieces into the wastepaper basket without a second thought. Then she goes at her work with a plunge, and soon becomes absorbed in its figures.*]

1893   1898

FRANCIS THOMPSON
1859–1907

Much of the poetry of the 1890s was written by members of groups such as The Rhymers' Club, of which Ernest Dowson and the young Yeats were members. Henley, too, had a band of writers associated with him who shared his views on life and poetry. Although Francis Thompson preferred to work more independently (he declined an invitation to join The Rhymers'), his poetry does have affinities with the writings of other poets of the time, in particular because of his Roman Catholicism, a religion that had attracted several converts during the nineties, including Dowson, Lionel Johnson (1867–1902), and the artist Aubrey Beardsley (1872–1898).

Thompson's career seems like a tale from one of the novels of Graham Greene. The son of Roman Catholic converts, he was anxious to enter the priesthood but was not considered an eligible candidate. Later, after an unsuccessful attempt to complete medical school, he moved to London. Here he lived for several years as a tramp, suffering painfully not only from poverty but from an addiction to opium: when in his poems Thompson speaks of being an outcast, he speaks with the authority of experience. In 1888 he was rescued by magazine editor Wilfred Meynell, who recognized his literary talents and encouraged him to publish his poems. Owing to shattered health and to a marked streak of indolence, Thompson's output in poetry was not extensive; but in his few best poems his achievement is impressive and distinctive. As his friend Coventry Patmore noted, *The Hound of Heaven* is one of the finest odes in English literature. In its fast-paced passages it reminds us of the odes of Shelley, about whom Thompson wrote an appreciative essay. An even more important influence than Shelley on Thompson was that of the seventeenth-century Metaphysical poets, particularly the Roman Catholic poet Richard Crashaw. The Crashaw-like blending of religious fervor and striking conceits (such as "traitorous trueness"), evident in the very title of *The Hound of Heaven,* seemed merely fantastic to some of Thompson's readers in the 1890s. To later readers, accustomed to the metaphysical devices of much twentieth-century poetry, it has seemed less bizarre. Interesting comparisons may also be made between Thompson and Gerard Manley Hopkins, another Roman Catholic writer who likewise demonstrated, as the nineteenth century drew to its close, the remarkable variety in the poetry of the Victorian age.

The Hound of Heaven

I fled Him,[1] down the nights and down the days;
  I fled Him, down the arches of the years;
  I fled Him, down the labyrinthine ways
    Of my own mind; and in the mist of tears
5 I hid from Him, and under running laughter.
          Up vistaed hopes I sped;
          And shot, precipitated,
Adown Titanic glooms of chasmèd fears,
  From those strong Feet that followed, followed after.
10   But with unhurrying chase,
          And unperturbèd pace,
      Deliberate speed, majestic instancy,°   *urgency*
          They beat—and a Voice beat
          More instant than the Feet—
15   "All things betray thee, who betrayest Me."

          I pleaded, outlaw-wise,
By many a hearted casement, curtained red,
  Trellised with intertwining charities
(For, though I knew His love Who followed,
20   Yet was I sore adread
Lest, having Him, I must have naught beside);[2]
But, if one little casement parted wide,
  The gust of His approach would clash it to.
  Fear wist not to evade, as Love wist to pursue.[3]
25 Across the margent° of the world I fled,   *boundary*
  And troubled the gold gateways of the stars,
Smiting for shelter on their clangèd bars;
          Fretted to dulcet jars
And silvern chatter the pale ports o' the moon.[4]
30 I said to dawn, Be sudden; to eve, Be soon;
  With thy young skyey blossoms heap me over
          From this tremendous Lover!
Float thy vague veil about me, lest He see!
      I tempted all His servitors, but to find
35 My own betrayal in their constancy,
In faith to Him their fickleness to me,
  Their traitorous trueness, and their loyal deceit.
To all swift things for swiftness did I sue;
  Clung to the whistling mane of every wind.
40   But whether they swept, smoothly fleet,
          The long savannahs° of the blue;   *plains*

1. Cf. Saint Augustine's *Confessions* 4.4.7: "And lo, Thou wert close on the heels of those fleeing from Thee, God of vengeance and fountain of mercies, both at the same time, who turnest us to Thyself by most wonderful means."
2. The speaker, afraid that love of God will exclude other kinds of love, is seeking shelter in one of the warm dwellings associated with human love. But his pursuer cuts off his escape, forcing him to remain outside, an outcast (lines 22–23).
3. This line apparently means that Fear did not know how to escape so effectively as Love knew how to pursue.
4. I.e., shook the gates of the moon until they gave forth soft and silvery sounds.

Or whether, Thunder-driven,
They clanged his chariot 'thwart a heaven
Plashy with flying lightnings round the spurn o' their feet—
45   Fear wist not to evade as Love wist to pursue.
Still with unhurrying chase,
And unperturbèd pace,
Deliberate speed, majestic instancy,
Came on the following Feet,
50   And a Voice above their beat—
"Naught shelters thee, who wilt not shelter Me."

I sought no more that after which I strayed
In face of man or maid;
But still within the little children's eyes
55   Seems something, something that replies;
They at least are for me, surely for me!
I turned me to them very wistfully;
But, just as their young eyes grew sudden fair
With dawning answers there,
60   Their angel plucked them from me by the hair.
"Come then, ye other children, Nature's—share
With me," said I, "your delicate fellowship;
Let me greet you lip to lip,
Let me twine with you caresses,
65   Wantoning
With our Lady-Mother's[5] vagrant tresses,
Banqueting
With her in her wind-walled palace,
Underneath her azured daïs,[6]
70   Quaffing, as your taintless way is,
From a chalice
Lucent-weeping out of the dayspring."[7]
So it was done;
I in their delicate fellowship was one—
75   Drew the bolt of Nature's secrecies.
I knew all the swift importings°   *meanings*
On the willful face of skies;
I knew how the clouds arise
Spumèd of the wild sea-snortings;
80   All that's born or dies
Rose and drooped with—made them shapers
Of mine own moods, or wailful or divine—
With them joyed and was bereaven.
I was heavy with the even,
85   When she lit her glimmering tapers
Round the day's dead sanctities.
I laughed in the morning's eyes.
I triumphed and I saddened with all weather,
Heaven and I wept together,
90   And its sweet tears were salt with mortal mine;
Against the red throb of its sunset-heart

5. I.e., Mother Nature's.
6. Blue canopy of the sky.

7. Overflowing with shining light from the sun (i.e., the children of Nature drink the sunshine).

I laid my own to beat,
And share commingling heat;
But not by that, by that, was eased my human smart.
95   In vain my tears were wet on Heaven's gray cheek.
For ah! we know not what each other says,
These things and I; in sound *I* speak—
Their sound is but their stir, they speak by silences.
Nature, poor stepdame, cannot slake my drouth;
100   Let her, if she would owe° me,   *own*
Drop yon blue bosom-veil of sky, and show me
The breasts o' her tenderness;
Never did any milk of hers once bless
My thirsting mouth.
105   Nigh and nigh draws the chase,
With unperturbèd pace,
Deliberate speed, majestic instancy;
And past those noisèd Feet
A voice comes yet more fleet—
110   "Lo naught contents thee, who content'st not Me."

Naked I wait Thy love's uplifted stroke!
My harness° piece by piece Thou hast hewn from me,   *armor*
And smitten me to my knee;
I am defenseless utterly.
115   I slept, methinks, and woke,
And, slowly gazing, find me stripped in sleep.
In the rash lustihead of my young powers,
I shook the pillaring hours
And pulled my life upon me;[8] grimed with smears,
120   I stand amid the dust o' the mounded years—
My mangled youth lies dead beneath the heap.
My days have crackled and gone up in smoke,
Have puffed and burst as sun-starts° on a stream.   *bubbles*
Yea, faileth now even dream
125   The dreamer, and the lute the lutanist;
Even the linked fantasies, in whose blossomy twist
I swung the earth a trinket at my wrist,
Are yielding;[9] cords of all too weak account
For earth with heavy griefs so overplussed.
130   Ah! is Thy love indeed
A weed, albeit an amaranthine[1] weed,
Suffering no flowers except its own to mount?
Ah! must—
Designer infinite!—
135   Ah! must Thou char the wood ere Thou canst limn[2] with it?
My freshness spent its wavering shower i' the dust;
And now my heart is as a broken fount,
Wherein tear-drippings stagnate, spilt down ever
From the dank thoughts that shiver

8. Like Samson when he shook the pillars of the temple of Dagon and pulled down the roof on his head (Judges 16).
9. I.e., even his power of creating an imaginary world by poetry and song ("linked fantasies") is now inadequate.
1. Unfading and immortal.
2. Draw, as with charcoal.

140　Upon the sightful branches of my mind.
　　　　　　Such is; what is to be?
　　The pulp so bitter, how shall taste the rind?
　　I dimly guess what Time in mists confounds;
　　Yet ever and anon a trumpet sounds
145　From the hid battlements of Eternity;
　　Those shaken mists a space unsettle, then
　　Round the half-glimpsèd turrets slowly wash again.
　　　　　　But not ere him who summoneth
　　　　　　I first have seen, enwound
150　With blooming robes, purpureal, cypress-crowned;
　　His name I know, and what his trumpet saith.
　　Whether man's heart or life it be which yields
　　　　　　Thee harvest, must Thy harvest fields
　　　　　　Be dunged with rotten death?

155　　　　　　　　Now of that long pursuit
　　　　　　　　Comes on at hand the bruit;°　　　　　　　　*noise*
　　　　　　That Voice is round me like a bursting sea:
　　　　　　　"And is thy earth so marred,
　　　　　　　Shattered in shard[3] on shard?
160　　　　　Lo, all things fly thee, for thou fliest Me!
　　　　　　Strange, piteous, futile thing,
　　Wherefore should any set thee love apart?
　　Seeing none but I makes much of naught," He said,
　　"And human love needs human meriting,
165　　　　　How hast thou merited—
　　Of all man's clotted clay the dingiest clot?
　　　　　　Alack, thou knowest not
　　How little worthy of any love thou art!
　　Whom wilt thou find to love ignoble thee
170　　　　　Save Me, save only Me?
　　All which I took from thee I did but take,
　　　　　　Not for thy harms,
　　But just that thou might'st seek it in My arms.
　　　　　　All which thy child's mistake
175　Fancies as lost, I have stored for thee at home;
　　　　　　Rise, clasp My hand, and come!"

　　　　Halts by me that footfall;
　　　　Is my gloom, after all,
　　Shade of His hand, outstretched caressingly?
180　　"Ah, fondest,° blindest, weakest,　　　　　　　*most foolish*
　　I am He Whom thou seekest!
　　Thou dravest love from thee, who dravest Me."

1890–92　　　　　　　　　　　　　　　　　　　　　　1893

---

3. Fragment, as of broken pottery.

MARY ELIZABETH COLERIDGE
1861–1907

The great-great niece of Samuel Taylor Coleridge, Mary Elizabeth Coleridge once wrote, "I have no fairy god-mother, but lay claim to a fairy great-great uncle, which is perhaps the reason that I am condemned to wander restlessly around the Gates of Fairyland, although I have never yet passed them." Born in London to a literary and musical family that regularly entertained guests such as Tennyson and Browning, Coleridge lived her whole life at home with her parents and one sister. She was unusually well educated, under the supervision of a tutor, William Cory, a scholar and poet, who had been forced by scandal to leave his teaching position at Eton. Mary Coleridge thus received an education usually reserved for boys. She knew six languages, including Greek, and she studied philosophy. In the 1890s she began giving lessons in English literature to working girls; in 1895, she started to teach at the Working Woman's College, an activity she continued for the rest of her life. She died suddenly of appendicitis at the age of forty-six.

Mary Coleridge's tutor, Cory, encouraged her to write poetry and short stories. When Henry Newbolt, a poet and family friend, joined her reading group of women friends, The Quintette, he urged her to publish her first two novels. She later published three more, in addition to a number of stories and essays. Although she wrote poetry continuously, she published little of it during her life. When a manuscript of her poems was given to Robert Bridges, a family friend who was also a friend of Gerard Manley Hopkins and responsible for the posthumous publication of Hopkins's poetry, Bridges recognized her talent. He made suggestions for revisions and encouraged her to publish a volume. She allowed two small volumes to be privately printed in the nineties, under the pseudonym *Anodos*, or the wanderer; most of her poetry was published after her death.

Although Mary Coleridge did not participate in the feminist debates of her time, her poems contain a subversive sense of anarchic feminine energy. She believed women had a spiritual identity distinct from men's; she wrote, "I don't think we are separate only in body and in mind, I think we are separate in soul too." Some of her poems rewrite earlier texts. Sandra Gilbert and Susan Gubar have speculated that *The Other Side of a Mirror* portrays the mad Bertha Mason from Charlotte Brontë's *Jane Eyre*; Angela Leighton and Margaret Reynolds have argued that *The Witch* reimagines Samuel Taylor Coleridge's visionary poem *Christabel*. Both of these poems demonstrate another characteristic of her writing—presentation of a luminous narrative fragment with little sense of surrounding context. The effect in the words of Henry Newbolt, the first friend who had encouraged her to publish, is one of "very deep shadows filled with strange shapes."

The Other Side of a Mirror

I sat before my glass one day,
  And conjured up a vision bare,
Unlike the aspects glad and gay,
  That erst were found reflected there—
5 The vision of a woman, wild
  With more than womanly despair.

Her hair stood back on either side
A face bereft of loveliness.

It had no envy now to hide
10   What once no man on earth could guess.
It formed the thorny aureole
   Of hard unsanctified distress.

Her lips were open—not a sound
   Came through the parted lines of red.
15 Whate'er it was, the hideous wound
   In silence and in secret bled.
No sigh relieved her speechless woe,
   She had no voice to speak her dread.

And in her lurid eyes there shone
20   The dying flame of life's desire,
Made mad because its hope was gone,
   And kindled at the leaping fire
Of jealousy, and fierce revenge,
   And strength that could not change nor tire.

25 Shade of a shadow in the glass,
   O set the crystal surface free!
Pass—as the fairer visions pass—
   Nor ever more return, to be
The ghost of a distracted hour,
30   That heard me whisper, "I am she!"

1882   1896

The Witch

I have walked a great while over the snow,
And I am not tall nor strong.
My clothes are wet, and my teeth are set,
And the way was hard and long.
5 I have wandered over the fruitful earth,
But I never came here before.
Oh, lift me over the threshold, and let me in at the door!

The cutting wind is a cruel foe.
I dare not stand in the blast.
10 My hands are stone, and my voice a groan,
And the worst of death is past.
I am but a little maiden still,
My little white feet are sore.
Oh, lift me over the threshold, and let me in at the door!

15 Her voice was the voice that women have,
Who plead for their heart's desire.
She came—she came—and the quivering flame
Sank and died in the fire.
It never was lit again on my hearth

20 Since I hurried across the floor,
    To lift her over the threshold, and let her in at the door.

1892   1907

RUDYARD KIPLING
1865–1936

Rudyard Kipling shares with an earlier Victorian, William Makepeace Thackeray, the distinction of having been born in India and, at the age of six, having been sent home to England for his education. For his first six years in England, he was desperately unhappy; his parents had made the disastrous choice of a rigidly Calvinistic foster home in which to board him, where he was treated with considerable cruelty. His parents finally removed him from the home when he was twelve and sent him to a private school, where his experience was far better. His views in later life were deeply affected by the English schoolboy code of honor and duty, especially when it involved loyalty to a group or team. At seventeen he rejoined his parents in India, where his father was a teacher of sculpture at the Bombay School of Art. For seven years he worked in India as a newspaper reporter and a part-time writer before returning to England, where his poems and stories (published while he was abroad) had brought him early fame. In 1892, after his marriage to an American woman, he lived for a five-year interval in Brattleboro, Vermont, until driven out in consequence of a quarrel with his wife's relatives. So violent was the quarrel that in later trips to North America, the Kiplings restricted their travels to Canada. Upon returning to England from Vermont, Kipling settled on a country estate and purchased, at the turn of the century, an expensive early-model automobile. He seems to have been the first English author to own an automobile, which was appropriate because of his keen interest in all kinds of machinery and feats of engineering—one of many tastes in which he differed markedly from his contemporaries in the nineties, the aesthetes. He was also the first English author to receive the Nobel Prize for Literature (1907).

In the final decades of the nineteenth century, India was the most important colony of Britain's empire. English people were consequently curious about the world of India, a world that Kipling's stories and poems helped them to envision. Indeed, Leonard Woolf, Virginia Woolf's husband, wrote the following about his experience in India in the early years of this century: "I could never make up my mind whether Kipling had molded his characters accurately in the image of Anglo-Indian society or whether we were molding our characters accurately in the image of a Kipling story." During his seven years in India in the 1880s, Kipling gained a rich experience of colonial life, which he presented in his stories and poems. His first volume of stories, *Plain Tales from the Hills* (1888), explores some of the psychological and moral problems of the Anglo-Indians and their relationship with the people they had colonized. In his two *Jungle Books* (1894, 1895) he ingeniously draws on the Indian scene to create a world of jungle animals. And although Kipling never professed to fully understand the way of life of the Indians themselves, or their religions, he was fascinated by them and tried to portray them with understanding. This effort is especially evident in his narrative *Kim* (1901), in which the contemplative and religious way of life of Indians is treated with no less sympathy than the active and worldly way of life of the Victorian English governing classes. It is usually said that Kipling, one of the great masters of the short story, and a superb craftsman, was not as a rule successful with long narratives, but *Kim* disproves the rule.

In his poems, Kipling also draws on the Indian scene, most commonly as it is viewed through the eyes of private soldiers of the regular army, men who had been sent out from England to garrison the country and fight off invaders on the northwest frontiers. Kipling is usually thought of as the poet of British imperialism, as indeed he often was, but in these poems about ordinary British soldiers in India, there is little by way of flag-waving celebrations of the triumph of empire. The soldier who speaks in *The Widow at Windsor* is simply bewildered by the events in which he has taken part. As one of the soldiers of the queen (one of "Missis Victorier's sons"), he has done his duty, but he does not see the course of the empire as a divine design to which he has been a contributor. In presenting India through the eyes of the common soldier, Kipling frequently reflects racist attitudes, such as those in *The Ladies*, which readers today may find offensive. Nonetheless, Kipling can be credited with developing a new subject in the working-class soldier, which proved an effective way to portray modern social experience.

This fresh perspective of the common individual on events, expressed in the accent of the London cockney, was one of the qualities that gained Kipling an immediate audience for his *Barrack-Room Ballads* (1890, 1892). For many years Kipling was exceedingly popular. What attracted his vast audience was not just the freshness of his subjects but his mastery of swinging verse rhythms. Aside from his genius, Kipling's literary ancestry helps explain his success. In part he learned his craft as a poet from traditional sources. He was not unsophisticated or unlearned; in his own family he had connections with the Pre-Raphaelites, and he was considerably influenced by such immediate literary predecessors as Swinburne and Browning. But the special influences on his style and rhythms were not traditional. One was the Protestant hymn. Both of his parents were children of Methodist clergymen, and hymn singing, as well as preaching, affected him profoundly: "Three generations of Wesleyan ministers . . . lie behind me," he noted. The second influence came from what seems an antithetical secular quarter, the songs of the music hall. As a teenager in London, Kipling had enjoyed music-hall entertainments, which were to reach their peak of popularity in the 1890s. According to his biographer Sir Angus Wilson, even though Kipling was, like Tennyson, the "most unmusical" of writers, he knew how to make poems that call to be set to music, such as *The Road to Mandalay* or *Gentlemen Rankers*, with its memorable refrain (still popular in America): "We're poor little lambs who've lost our way, Baa! Baa! Baa!" Such a poem as *The Ladies* is ideal fare for a music-hall number and gains immeasurably by being sung.

Today Kipling's stories are more valued than his poems. In his portrayal of the British community in India and their relationship with the people they ruled, Kipling created a rich and various fictional world that reflects profoundly upon England's imperialism as lived in all its peculiar social relationships by the officers of the empire. After returning from India, he gradually turned to English subjects in his short stories, which he continued to write until his death in 1936. In their representation of new subjects, their wonderful ear for dialect, their economy of style, and their complex irony, Kipling's short stories provide some of the best examples of the genre.

The Man Who Would Be King[1]

"Brother to a Prince and fellow to a beggar if he be found worthy."[2]

The law, as quoted, lays down a fair conduct of life, and one not easy to follow. I have been fellow to a beggar again and again under circumstances which prevented either of us finding out whether the other was worthy. I have still to be brother to a Prince, though I once came near to kinship with what might have been a veritable King and was promised the reversion of a Kingdom—army, law-courts, revenue and policy all complete. But, to-day, I greatly fear that my King is dead, and if I want a crown I must go and hunt it for myself.

The beginning of everything was in a railway train upon the road to Mhow from Ajmir. There had been a Deficit in the Budget, which necessitated traveling, not Second-class, which is only half as dear as First-class, but by Intermediate, which is very awful indeed. There are no cushions in the Intermediate class, and the population are either Intermediate, which is Eurasian, or native, which for a long night journey is nasty, or Loafer,[3] which is amusing though intoxicated. Intermediates do not patronize refreshment-rooms. They carry their food in bundles and pots, and buy sweets from the native sweetmeat-sellers, and drink the roadside water. That is why in the hot weather Intermediates are taken out of the carriages dead, and in all weathers are most properly looked down upon.

My particular Intermediate happened to be empty till I reached Nasirabad, when a huge gentleman in shirt-sleeves entered, and, following the custom of Intermediates, passed the time of day. He was a wanderer and a vagabond like myself, but with an educated taste for whiskey. He told tales of things he had seen and done, of out-of-the-way corners of the Empire into which he had penetrated, and of adventures in which he risked his life for a few days' food. "If India was filled with men like you and me, not knowing more than the crows where they'd get their next day's rations, it isn't seventy millions of revenue the land would be paying—it's seven hundred millions," said he; and as I looked at his mouth and chin I was disposed to agree with him. We talked politics—the politics of Loaferdom that sees things from the underside where the lath and plaster is not smoothed off—and we talked postal arrangements because my friend wanted to send a telegram back from the next station to Ajmir, which is the turning-off place from the Bombay to the Mhow line as you travel westward. My friend had no money beyond eight annas which he wanted for dinner, and I had no money at all, owing to the hitch in the Budget before mentioned. Further, I was going into a wilderness where, though I should resume touch with the Treasury, there were no telegraph offices. I was, therefore, unable to help him in any way.

"We might threaten a Station-master, and make him send a wire on tick,"[4] said my friend, "but that'd mean inquiries for you and for me, and I've got

---

1. Originally published in December 1888.
2. Meant to suggest the principles of Freemasonry, a secret fraternal society that developed from the masons' guild in medieval Britain. By Victorian times it had grown to a prominent national organization, whose members were bound to help each other in times of distress. The places mentioned in the beginning of the story are in northern India.
3. A European in India with no official attachment or position.
4. On credit.

my hands full these days. Did you say you are traveling back along this line within any days?"

"Within ten," I said.

"Can't you make it eight?" said he. "Mine is rather urgent business."

"I can send your telegram within ten days if that will serve you," I said.

"I couldn't trust the wire to fetch him now I think of it. It's this way. He leaves Delhi on the 23d for Bombay. That means he'll be running through Ajmir about the night of the 23d."

"But I'm going into the Indian Desert," I explained.

"Well *and* good," said he. "You'll be changing at Marwar Junction to get into Jodhpore territory—you must do that—and he'll be coming through Marwar Junction in the early morning of the 24th by the Bombay Mail. Can you be at Marwar Junction on that time? 'Twon't be inconveniencing you because I know that there's precious few pickings to be got out of these Central India States—even though you pretend to be correspondent of the *Backwoodsman*."[5]

"Have you ever tried that trick?" I asked.

"Again and again, but the Residents[6] find you out, and then you get escorted to the Border before you've time to get your knife into them. But about my friend here. I *must* give him a word o' mouth to tell him what's come to me or else he won't know where to go. I would take it more than kind of you if you was to come out of Central India in time to catch him at Marwar Junction, and say to him:—'He has gone South for the week.' He'll know what that means. He's a big man with a red beard, and a great swell[7] he is. You'll find him sleeping like a gentleman with all his luggage round him in a Second-class compartment. But don't you be afraid. Slip down the window, and say:—'He has gone South for the week,' and he'll tumble.[8] It's only cutting your time of stay in those parts by two days. I ask you as a stranger—going to the West,"[9] he said, with emphasis.

"Where have *you* come from?" said I.

"From the East," said he, "and I am hoping that you will give him the message on the Square[1]—for the sake of my Mother as well as your own."

Englishmen are not usually softened by appeals to the memory of their mothers, but for certain reasons, which will be fully apparent, I saw fit to agree.

"It's more than a little matter," said he, "and that's why I ask you to do it—and now I know that I can depend on you doing it. A Second-class carriage at Marwar Junction, and a red-haired man asleep in it. You'll be sure to remember. I get out at the next station, and I must hold on there till he comes or sends me what I want."

"I'll give the message if I catch him," I said, "and for the sake of your Mother as well as mine I'll give you a word of advice. Don't try to run the Central India States just now as the correspondent of the *Backwoodsman*. There's a real one knocking about here, and it might lead to trouble."

"Thank you," said he, simply, "and when will the swine be gone? I can't

---

5. The Allahabad *Pioneer*, which employed Kipling as a roving correspondent.
6. British political officers appointed to oversee doings at the court of one of the quasi-independent Native States.

7. Fashionable fellow.
8. Catch on, understand.
9. This, and the following phrase, are from the code of the Freemasons.
1. Honestly.

starve because he's ruining my work. I wanted to get hold of the Degumber Rajah down here about his father's widow, and give him a jump."

"What did he do to his father's widow, then?"

"Filled her up with red pepper and slippered her to death as she hung from a beam. I found that out myself, and I'm the only man that would dare going into the State to get hush-money for it. They'll try to poison me, same as they did in Chortumna when I went on the loot there. But you'll give the man at Marwar Junction my message?"

He got out at a little roadside station, and I reflected. I had heard, more than once, of men personating correspondents of newspapers and bleeding small Native States with threats of exposure, but I had never met any of the caste before. They lead a hard life, and generally die with great suddenness. The Native States have a wholesome horror of English newspapers, which may throw light on their peculiar methods of government, and do their best to choke correspondents with champagne, or drive them out of their mind with four-in-hand barouches.[2] They do not understand that nobody cares a straw for the internal administration of Native States so long as oppression and crime are kept within decent limits, and the ruler is not drugged, drunk, or diseased from one end of the year to the other. Native States were created by Providence in order to supply picturesque scenery, tigers, and tall-writing. They are the dark places of the earth, full of unimaginable cruelty, touching the Railway and the Telegraph on one side, and, on the other, the days of Harun-al-Raschid.[3] When I left the train I did business with divers Kings, and in eight days passed through many changes of life. Sometimes I wore dress-clothes and consorted with Princes and Politicals,[4] drinking from crystal and eating from silver. Sometimes I lay out upon the ground and devoured what I could get, from a plate made of a flapjack, and drank the running water, and slept under the same rug as my servant. It was all in the day's work.

Then I headed for the Great Indian Desert upon the proper date, as I had promised, and the night Mail set me down at Marwar Junction, where a funny little, happy-go-lucky, native-managed railway runs to Jodhpore. The Bombay Mail from Delhi makes a short halt at Marwar. She arrived as I got in, and I had just time to hurry to her platform and go down the carriages. There was only one Second-class on the train. I slipped the window, and looked down upon a flaming red beard, half covered by a railway rug. That was my man, fast asleep, and I dug him gently in the ribs. He woke with a grunt, and I saw his face in the light of the lamps. It was a great and shining face.

"Tickets again?" said he.

"No," said I. "I am to tell you that he is gone South for the week. He is gone South for the week!"

The train had begun to move out. The red man rubbed his eyes. "He has gone South for the week," he repeated. "Now that's just like his impidence. Did he say that I was to give you anything?—'Cause I won't."

"He didn't," I said, and dropped away, and watched the red lights die out in the dark. It was horribly cold, because the wind was blowing off the sands.

2. Fashionable four-wheeled carriages.
3. Caliph of Baghdad (763–809), who figures in
many tales of the *Arabian Nights*.
4. I.e., residents.

I climbed into my own train—not an Intermediate Carriage this time—and went to sleep.

If the man with the beard had given me a rupee I should have kept it as a memento of a rather curious affair. But the consciousness of having done my duty was my only reward.

Later on I reflected that two gentlemen like my friends could not do any good if they foregathered and personated correspondents of newspapers, and might, if they "stuck up"[5] one of the little rat-trap states of Central India or Southern Rajputana, get themselves into serious difficulties. I therefore took some trouble to describe them as accurately as I could remember to people who would be interested in deporting them; and succeeded, so I was later informed, in having them headed back from Degumber borders.

Then I became respectable, and returned to an Office where there were no Kings and no incidents except the daily manufacture of a newspaper. A newspaper office seems to attract every conceivable sort of person, to the prejudice of discipline. Zenana-mission ladies[6] arrive, and beg that the Editor will instantly abandon all his duties to describe a Christian prize-giving in a back-slum of a perfectly inaccessible village; Colonels who have been over-passed for commands sit down and sketch the outline of a series of ten, twelve, or twenty-four leading articles on Seniority *versus* Selection; mission-aries wish to know why they have not been permitted to escape from their regular vehicles of abuse and swear at a brother missionary under special patronage of the editorial We; stranded theatrical companies troop up to explain that they cannot pay for their advertisements, but on their return from New Zealand or Tahiti will do so with interest; inventors of patent punkah[7]-pulling machines, carriage couplings and unbreakable swords and axle-trees call with specifications in their pockets and hours at their disposal; tea-companies enter and elaborate their prospectuses with the office pens; secretaries of ball-committees clamor to have the glories of their last dance more fully expounded; strange ladies rustle in and say:—"I want a hundred lady's cards printed *at once*, please," which is manifestly part of an Editor's duty; and every dissolute ruffian that ever tramped the Grand Trunk Road makes it his business to ask for employment as a proof-reader. And, all the time, the telephone-bell is ringing madly, and Kings are being killed on the Continent, and Empires are saying—"You're another," and Mister Glad-stone[8] is calling down brimstone upon the British Dominions, and the little black copy-boys are whining, "*kaa-pi chay-ha-yeh*" (copy wanted) like tired bees, and most of the paper is as blank as Modred's shield.[9]

But that is the amusing part of the year. There are other six months wherein none ever come to call, and the thermometer walks inch by inch up to the top of the glass, and the office is darkened to just above reading-light, and the press machines are red-hot of touch, and nobody writes anything but accounts of amusements in the Hill-stations[1] or obituary notices. Then the telephone becomes a tinkling terror, because it tells you of the sudden deaths of men and women that you knew intimately, and the prickly-heat

---

5. Fraudulently extorted money from. "Foregath-ered": met.
6. Female missionaries doing work among Indian women.
7. Large swinging fan, usually worked by hand.
8. William Ewart Gladstone (1809–1898), leader

of the Liberal Party from 1868 to 1875 and 1880 to 1894, opposed to overseas expansion.
9. The shield of King Arthur's traitorous nephew was blank because he had done no deeds of valor.
1. Official outposts in the northern hills.

covers you as with a garment, and you sit down and write:—"A slight increase of sickness is reported from the Khuda Janta Khan[2] District. The outbreak is purely sporadic in its nature, and, thanks to the energetic efforts of the District authorities, is now almost at an end. It is, however, with deep regret we record the death, etc."

Then the sickness really breaks out, and the less recording and reporting the better for the peace of the subscribers. But the Empires and the Kings continue to divert themselves as selfishly as before, and the Foreman thinks that a daily paper really ought to come out once in twenty-four hours, and all the people at the Hill-stations in the middle of their amusements say:— "Good gracious! Why can't the paper be sparkling? I'm sure there's plenty going on up here."

That is the dark half of the moon, and, as the advertisements say, "must be experienced to be appreciated."

It was in that season, and a remarkably evil season, that the paper began running the last issue of the week on Saturday night, which is to say, Sunday morning, after the custom of a London paper. This was a great convenience, for immediately after the paper was put to bed, the dawn would lower the thermometer from 96° to almost 84° for half an hour, and in that chill—you have no idea how cold is 84° on the grass until you begin to pray for it—a very tired man could set off to sleep ere the heat roused him.

One Saturday night it was my pleasant duty to put the paper to bed alone. A King or courtier or a courtesan or a community was going to die or get a new Constitution, or do something that was important on the other side of the world, and the paper was to be held open till the latest possible minute in order to catch the telegram. It was a pitchy black night, as stifling as a June night can be, and the *loo*, the red-hot wind from the westward, was booming among the tinder-dry trees and pretending that the rain was on its heels. Now and again a spot of almost boiling water would fall on the dust with the flop of a frog, but all our weary world knew that was only pretence. It was a shade cooler in the press-room than the office, so I sat there, while the type clicked and clicked and the night-jars hooted at the windows, and the all but naked compositors wiped the sweat from their foreheads and called for water. The thing that was keeping us back, whatever it was, would not come off, though the *loo* dropped and the last type was set, and the whole round earth stood still in the choking heat, with its finger on its lip, to wait the event. I drowsed, and wondered whether the telegraph was a blessing, and whether this dying man, or struggling people, was aware of the inconvenience the delay was causing. There was no special reason beyond the heat and worry to make tension, but, as the clock hands crept up to three o'clock and the machines spun their fly-wheels two and three times to see that all was in order, before I said the word that would set them off, I could have shrieked aloud.

Then the roar and rattle of the wheels shivered the quiet into little bits. I rose to go away, but two men in white clothes stood in front of me. The first one said:—"It's him!" The second said:—"So it is!" And they both laughed almost as loudly as the machinery roared, and mopped their foreheads. "We see there was a light burning across the road and we were sleeping in that

---

2. God knows town; i.e., nowheresville.

ditch there for coolness, and I said to my friend here, 'The office is open. Let's come along and speak to him as turned us back from the Degumber State,' " said the smaller of the two. He was the man I had met in the Mhow train, and his fellow was the red-bearded man of Marwar Junction. There was no mistaking the eyebrows of the one or the beard of the other.

I was not pleased, because I wished to go to sleep, not to squabble with loafers. "What do you want?" I asked.

"Half an hour's talk with you cool and comfortable, in the office," said the red-bearded man. "We'd *like* some drink—the Contrack doesn't begin yet, Peachey, so you needn't look—but what we really want is advice. We don't want money. We ask you as a favor, because you did us a bad turn about Degumber."

I led from the press-room to the stifling office with the maps on the walls, and the red-haired man rubbed his hands. "That's something like," said he. "This was the proper shop to come to. Now, Sir, let me introduce to you Brother[3] Peachey Carnehan, that's him, and Brother Daniel Dravot, that is *me*, and the less said about our professions the better, for we have been most things in our time. Soldier, sailor, compositor, photographer, proof-reader, street-preacher, and correspondents of the *Backwoodsman* when we thought the paper wanted one. Carnehan is sober, and so am I. Look at us first and see that's sure. It will save you cutting into my talk. We'll take one of your cigars apiece, and you shall see us light."

I watched the test. The men were absolutely sober, so I gave them each a tepid peg.[4]

"Well *and* good," said Carnehan of the eyebrows, wiping the froth from his moustache. "Let me talk now, Dan. We have been all over India, mostly on foot. We have been boiler-fitters, engine-drivers, petty contractors, and all that, and we have decided that India isn't big enough for such as us."

They certainly were too big for the office. Dravot's beard seemed to fill half the room and Carnehan's shoulders the other half, as they sat on the big table. Carnehan continued: "The country isn't half worked out because they that governs it won't let you touch it. They spend all their blessed time in governing it, and you can't lift a spade, nor chip a rock, nor look for oil, nor anything like that without all the Government saying—'Leave it alone and let us govern.' Therefore, such as it is, we will let it alone, and go away to some other place where a man isn't crowded and can come to his own. We are not little men, and there is nothing that we are afraid of except Drink, and we have signed a Contrack on that. *Therefore*, we are going away to be Kings."

"Kings in our own right," muttered Dravot.

"Yes, of course," I said. "You've been tramping in the sun, and it's a very warm night, and hadn't you better sleep over the notion? Come to-morrow."

"Neither drunk nor sunstruck," said Dravot. "We have slept over the notion half a year, and require to see Books and Atlases, and we have decided that there is only one place now in the world that two strong men can Sar-a-*whack*.[5] They call it Kafiristan. By my reckoning it's the top right-hand

3. Meant to recall the Freemason connection.
4. A drink.
5. A reference to Sir James Brooke (1803–1868), "the White Rajah of Sarawak," who in return for

helping the raja of Sarawak, in Borneo, put down a rebellion, succeeded him after his death and established a dynasty.

corner of Afghanistan, not more than three hundred miles from Pesha-wur. They have two and thirty heathen idols there, and we'll be the thirty-third. It's a mountainous country, and the women of those parts are very beautiful."

"But that is provided against in the Contrack," said Carnehan. "Neither Women nor Liquor, Daniel."

"And that's all we know, except that no one has gone there, and they fight, and in any place where they fight, a man who knows how to drill men can always be a King. We shall go to those parts and say to any King we find— 'D'you want to vanquish your foes?' and we will show him how to drill men; for that we know better than anything else. Then we will subvert that King and seize his Throne and establish a Dy-nasty."

"You'll be cut to pieces before you're fifty miles across the Border," I said. "You have to travel through Afghanistan to get to that country. It's one mass of mountains and peaks and glaciers, and no Englishman has been through it. The people are utter brutes, and even if you reached them you couldn't do anything."

"That's more like," said Carnehan: "If you could think us a little more mad we would be more pleased. We have come to you to know about this country, to read a book about it, and to be shown maps. We want you to tell us that we are fools and to show us your books." He turned to the bookcases.

"Are you at all in earnest?" I said.

"A little," said Dravot, sweetly. "As big a map as you have got, even if it's all blank where Kafiristan is, and any books you've got. We can read, though we aren't very educated."

I uncased the big thirty-two-miles-to-the-inch map of India, and two smaller Frontier maps, hauled down volume INF-KAN of the *Encyclopaedia Britannica*, and the men consulted them.

"See here!" said Dravot, his thumb on the map. "Up to Jagdallak, Peachey and me know the road. We was there with Roberts's Army.[6] We'll have to turn off to the right at Jagdallak through Laghmann territory. Then we get among the hills—fourteen thousand feet—fifteen thousand—it will be cold work there, but it don't look very far on the map."

I handed him Wood on the *Sources of the Oxus*.[7] Carnehan was deep in the *Encyclopaedia*.

"They're a mixed lot," said Dravot, reflectively; "and it won't help us to know the names of their tribes. The more tribes the more they'll fight, and the better for us. From Jagdallak to Ashang. H'mm!"

"But all the information about the country is as sketchy and inaccurate as can be," I protested. "No one knows anything about it really. Here's the file of the *United Services' Institute*. Read what Bellew says."

"Blow Bellew!" said Carnehan. "Dan, they're an all-fired lot of heathens, but this book here says they think they're related to us English."

I smoked while the men pored over *Raverty*, *Wood*, the maps, and the *Encyclopaedia*.

"There is no use your waiting," said Dravot, politely. "It's about four o'clock now. We'll go before six o'clock if you want to sleep, and we won't steal any

6. In the Second Afghan War (1878–80), a force under the command of General Frederick Roberts made a three-hundred-mile forced march through the area.

7. The Oxus is a river whose sources are in the area.

of the papers. Don't you sit up. We're two harmless lunatics and if you come, to-morrow evening, down to the Serai[8] we'll say good-bye to you."

"You *are* two fools," I answered. "You'll be turned back at the Frontier or cut up the minute you set foot in Afghanistan. Do you want any money or a recommendation downcountry? I can help you to the chance of work next week."

"Next week we shall be hard at work ourselves, thank you," said Dravot. "It isn't so easy being a King as it looks. When we've got our Kingdom in going order we'll let you know, and you can come up and help us to govern it."

"Would two lunatics make a Contrack like that?" said Carnehan, with subdued pride, showing me a greasy half-sheet of note-paper on which was written the following. I copied it, then and there, as a curiosity:

This Contract between me and you persuing witnesseth in the name of God—Amen and so forth.

(One) *That me and you will settle this matter together: i. e., to be Kings of Kafiristan.*

(Two) *That you and me will not, while this matter is being settled, look at any Liquor, nor any Woman, black, white or brown, so as to get mixed up with one or the other harmful.*

(Three) *That we conduct ourselves with dignity and discretion and if one of us gets into trouble the other will stay by him.*

   Signed by you and me this day.
   Peachey Taliaferro Carnehan.
   Daniel Dravot.
   Both Gentlemen at Large.

"There was no need for the last article," said Carnehan, blushing modestly; "but it looks regular. Now you know the sort of men that loafers are—we *are* loafers, Dan, until we get out of India—and *do* you think that we would sign a Contrack like that unless we was in earnest? We have kept away from the two things that make life worth having."

"You won't enjoy your lives much longer if you are going to try this idiotic adventure. Don't set the office on fire," I said, "and go away before nine o'clock."

I left them still poring over the maps and making notes on the back of the "Contrack." "Be sure to come down to the Serai to-morrow," were their parting words.

The Kumharsen Serai is the great foursquare sink of humanity where the strings of camels and horses from the North load and unload. All the nationalities of Central Asia may be found there, and most of the folk of India proper. Balkh and Bokhara there meet Bengal and Bombay, and try to draw eye-teeth. You can buy ponies, turquoises, Persian pussy-cats, saddle-bags, fat-tailed sheep and musk in the Kumharsen Serai, and get many strange things for nothing. In the afternoon I went down there to see whether my friends intended to keep their word or were lying about drunk.

A priest attired in fragments of ribbons and rags stalked up to me, gravely twisting a child's paper whirligig.[9] Behind was his servant bending under the

8. Place or building for the accommodation of   9. Pinwheel.
travelers and their pack animals.

load of a crate of mud toys. The two were loading up two camels, and the inhabitants of the Serai watched them with shrieks of laughter.

"The priest is mad," said a horse-dealer to me. "He is going up to Kabul to sell toys to the Amir.[1] He will either be raised to honor or have his head cut off. He came in here this morning and has been behaving madly ever since."

"The witless are under the protection of God," stammered a flat-cheeked Usbeg[2] in broken Hindi. "They foretell future events."

"Would they could have foretold that my caravan would have been cut up by the Shinwaris almost within shadow of the Pass!" grunted the Eusufzai agent of a Rajputana trading-house whose goods had been feloniously diverted into the hands of other robbers just across the Border, and whose misfortunes were the laughing-stock of the bazar. "Ohé, priest, whence come you and whither do you go?"

"From Roum[3] have I come," shouted the priest, waving his whirligig; "from Roum, blown by the breath of a hundred devils across the sea! O thieves, robbers, liars, the blessing of Pir Khan on pigs, dogs, and perjurers! Who will take the Protected of God to the North to sell charms that are never still to the Amir? The camels shall not gall,[4] the sons shall not fall sick, and the wives shall remain faithful while they are away, of the men who give me place in their caravan. Who will assist me to slipper the King of the Roos[5] with a golden slipper with a silver heel? The protection of Pir Khan be upon his labors!" He spread out the skirts of his gaberdine and pirouetted between the lines of tethered horses.

"There starts a caravan from Peshawur to Kabul in twenty days, *Huzrut*,"[6] said the Eusufzai trader. "My camels go therewith. Do thou also go and bring us good-luck."

"I will go even now!" shouted the priest. "I will depart upon my winged camels, and be at Peshawur in a day! Ho! Hazar[7] Mir Khan," he yelled to his servant, "drive out the camels, but let me first mount my own."

He leaped on the back of his beast as it knelt, and, turning round to me, cried:—"Come thou also, Sahib, a little along the road, and I will sell thee a charm—an amulet that shall make thee King of Kafiristan."

Then the light broke upon me, and I followed the two camels out of the Serai till we reached open road and the priest halted.

"What d' you think o' that?" said he in English. "Carnehan can't talk their patter, so I've made him my servant. He makes a handsome servant. 'Tisn't for nothing that I've been knocking about the country for fourteen years. Didn't I do that talk neat? We'll hitch on to a caravan at Peshawur till we get to Jagdallak, and then we'll see if we can get donkeys for our camels, and strike into Kafiristan. Whirligigs for the Amir, O Lor! Put your hand under the camel-bags and tell me what you feel."

I felt the butt of a Martini,[8] and another and another.

"Twenty of 'em," said Dravot, placidly. "Twenty of 'em, and ammunition to correspond, under the whirligigs and the mud dolls."

---

1. The ruler of Afghanistan. Kabul is in Afghanistan.
2. Person from Uzbekistan.
3. Turkey.
4. Become sore.

5. Czar of Russia.
6. Presence; an honorary form of address.
7. Get ready.
8. Rifle issued to British infantry.

"Heaven help you if you are caught with those things!" I said. "A Martini is worth her weight in silver among the Pathans."[9]

"Fifteen hundred rupees of capital—every rupee we could beg, borrow, or steal—are invested on these two camels," said Dravot. "We won't get caught. We're going through the Khaiber with a regular caravan. Who'd touch a poor mad priest?"

"Have you got everything you want?" I asked, overcome with astonishment.

"Not yet, but we shall soon. Give us a memento of your kindness, *Brother.* You did me a service yesterday, and that time in Marwar. Half my Kingdom shall you have, as the saying is." I slipped a small charm compass from my watch-chain and handed it up to the priest.

"Good-bye," said Dravot, giving me hand cautiously. "It's the last time we'll shake hands with an Englishman these many days. Shake hands with him, Carnehan," he cried, as the second camel passed me.

Carnehan leaned down and shook hands. Then the camels passed away along the dusty road, and I was left alone to wonder. My eye could detect no failure in the disguises. The scene in Serai attested that they were complete to the native mind. There was just the chance, therefore, that Carnehan and Dravot would be able to wander through Afghanistan without detection. But, beyond, they would find death, certain and awful death.

Ten days later a native friend of mine, giving me the news of the day from Peshawur, wound up his letter with:—"There has been much laughter here on account of a certain mad priest who is going in his estimation to sell petty gauds and insignificant trinkets which he ascribes as great charms to H. H. the Amir of Bokhara. He passed through Peshawur and associated himself to the Second Summer caravan that goes to Kabul. The merchants are pleased, because through superstition they imagine that such mad fellows bring good-fortune."

The two, then, were beyond the Border. I would have prayed for them, but, that night, a real King died in Europe, and demanded an obituary notice.

The wheel of the world swings through the same phases again and again. Summer passed and winter thereafter, and came and passed again. The daily paper continued and I with it, and upon the third summer there fell a hot night, a night-issue, and a strained waiting for something to be telegraphed from the other side of the world, exactly as had happened before. A few great men had died in the past two years, the machines worked with more clatter, and some of the trees in the Office garden were a few feet taller. But that was all the difference.

I passed over to the press-room, and went through just such a scene as I have already described. The nervous tension was stronger than it had been two years before, and I felt the heat more acutely. At three o'clock I cried, "Print off," and turned to go, when there crept to my chair what was left of a man. He was bent into a circle, his head was sunk between his shoulders, and he moved his feet one over the other like a bear. I could hardly see whether he walked or crawled—this rag-wrapped, whining cripple who addressed me by name, crying that he was come back. "Can you give me a drink?" he whimpered. "For the Lord's sake, give me a drink!"

9. The principal tribe in Afghanistan.

I went back to the office, the man following with groans of pain, and I turned up the lamp.

"Don't you know me?" he gasped, dropping into a chair, and he turned his drawn face, surmounted by a shock of grey hair, to the light.

I looked at him intently. Once before had I seen eyebrows that met over the nose in an inch-broad black band, but for the life of me I could not tell where.

"I don't know you," I said, handing him the whiskey. "What can I do for you?"

He took a gulp of the spirit raw, and shivered in spite of the suffocating heat.

"I've come back," he repeated; "and I was the King of Kafiristan—me and Dravot—crowned Kings we was! In this office we settled it—you setting there and giving us the books. I am Peachey—Peachey Taliaferro Carnehan, and you've been setting here ever since—O Lord!"

I was more than a little astonished, and expressed my feelings accordingly.

"It's true," said Carnehan, with a dry cackle, nursing his feet, which were wrapped in rags. "True as gospel. Kings we were, with crowns upon our heads—me and Dravot—poor Dan—oh, poor, poor Dan, that would never take advice, not though I begged of him!"

"Take the whiskey," I said, "and take your own time. Tell me all you can recollect of everything from beginning to end. You got across the border on your camels, Dravot dressed as a mad priest and you his servant. Do you remember that?"

"I ain't mad—yet, but I shall be that way soon. Of course I remember. Keep looking at me, or maybe my words will go all to pieces. Keep looking at me in my eyes and don't say anything."

I leaned forward and looked into his face as steadily as I could. He dropped one hand upon the table and I grasped it by the wrist. It was twisted like a bird's claw, and upon the back was a ragged, red, diamond-shaped scar.

"No, don't look there. Look at *me*," said Carnehan.

"That comes afterward, but for the Lord's sake don't distrack me. We left with that caravan, me and Dravot playing all sorts of antics to amuse the people we were with. Dravot used to make us laugh in the evenings when all the people was cooking their dinners—cooking their dinners, and . . . what did they do then? They lit little fires with sparks that went into Dravot's beard, and we all laughed—fit to die. Little red fires they was, going into Dravot's big red beard—so funny." His eyes left mine and he smiled foolishly.

"You went as far as Jagdallak with that caravan," I said, at a venture, "after you had lit those fires. To Jagdallak, where you turned off to try to get into Kafiristan."

"No, we didn't neither. What are you talking about? We turned off before Jagdallak, because we heard the roads was good. But they wasn't good enough for our two camels—mine and Dravot's. When we left the caravan, Dravot took off all his clothes and mine too, and said we would be heathen, because the Kafirs[1] didn't allow Mohammedans to talk to them. So we dressed betwixt and between, and such a sight as Daniel Dravot I never saw yet nor expect to see again. He burned half his beard, and slung a sheep-

---

1. Non-Muslims.

skin over his shoulder, and shaved his head into patterns. He shaved mine, too, and made me wear outrageous things to look like a heathen. That was in a most mountaineous country, and our camels couldn't go along any more because of the mountains. They were tall and black, and coming home I saw them fight like wild goats—there are lots of goats in Kafiristan. And these mountains, they never keep still, no more than goats. Always fighting they are, and don't let you sleep at night."

"Take some more whiskey," I said, very slowly. "What did you and Daniel Dravot do when the camels could go no further because of the rough roads that led into Kafiristan?"

"What did which do? There was a party called Peachey Taliaferro Carnehan that was with Dravot. Shall I tell you about him? He died out there in the cold. Slap from the bridge fell old Peachey, turning and twisting in the air like a penny whirligig that you can sell to the Amir—No; they was two for three ha'pence, those whirligigs, or I am much mistaken and woful sore. And then these camels were no use, and Peachey said to Dravot—'For the Lord's sake, let's get out of this before our heads are chopped off,' and with that they killed the camels all among the mountains, not having anything in particular to eat, but first they took off the boxes with the guns and the ammunition, till two men came along driving four mules. Dravot up and dances in front of them, singing,—'Sell me four mules.' Says the first man,— 'If you are rich enough to buy, you are rich enough to rob;' but before ever he could put his hand to his knife, Dravot breaks his neck over his knee, and the other party runs away. So Carnehan loaded the mules with the rifles that was taken off the camels, and together we starts forward into those bitter cold mountaineous parts, and never a road broader than the back of your hand."

He paused for a moment, while I asked him if he could remember the nature of the country through which he had journeyed.

"I am telling you as straight as I can, but my head isn't as good as it might be. They drove nails through it to make me hear better how Dravot died. The country was mountaineous and the mules were most contrary, and the inhabitants was dispersed and solitary. They went up and up, and down and down, and that other party, Carnehan, was imploring of Dravot not to sing and whistle so loud, for fear of bringing down the tremenjus avalanches. But Dravot says that if a King couldn't sing it wasn't worth being King, and whacked the mules over the rump, and never took no heed for ten cold days. We came to a big level valley all among the mountains, and the mules were near dead, so we killed them, not having anything in special for them or us to eat. We sat upon the boxes, and played odd and even with the cartridges that was jolted out.

"Then ten men with bows and arrows ran down that valley, chasing twenty men with bows and arrows, and the row was tremenjus. They was fair men— fairer than you or me—with yellow hair and remarkable well built.[2] Says Dravot, unpacking the guns—'This is the beginning of the business. We'll fight for the ten men,' and with that he fires two rifles at the twenty men, and drops one of them at two hundred yards from the rock where we was sitting. The other men began to run, but Carnehan and Dravot sits on the

---

2. There was a legend that Alexander the Great left a Greek colony in the area.

boxes picking them off at all ranges, up and down the valley. Then we goes up to the ten men that had run across the snow too, and they fires a footy little arrow at us. Dravot he shoots above their heads and they all falls down flat. Then he walks over and kicks them, and then he lifts them up and shakes hands all round to make them friendly like. He calls them and gives them the boxes to carry, and waves his hand for all the world as though he was King already. They takes the boxes and him across the valley and up the hill into a pine wood on the top, where there was half a dozen big stone idols. Dravot he goes to the biggest—a fellow they call Imbra—and lays a rifle and a cartridge at his feet, rubbing his nose respectful with his own nose, patting him on the head, and saluting in front of it. He turns round to the men and nods his head, and says,—'That's all right. I'm in the know too, and all these old jim-jams are my friends.' Then he opens his mouth and points down it, and when the first man brings him food, he says—'No;' and when the second man brings him food, he says—'No;' but when one of the old priests and the boss of the village brings him food, he says—'Yes;' very haughty, and eats it slow. That was how we came to our first village, without any trouble, just as though we had tumbled from the skies. But we tumbled from one of those damned rope-bridges, you see, and you couldn't expect a man to laugh much after that."

"Take some more whiskey and go on," I said. "That was the first village you came into. How did you get to be King?"

"I wasn't King," said Carnehan. "Dravot he was the King, and a handsome man he looked with the gold crown on his head and all. Him and the other party stayed in that village, and every morning Dravot sat by the side of old Imbra, and the people came and worshipped. That was Dravot's order. Then a lot of men came into the valley, and Carnehan and Dravot picks them off with the rifles before they knew where they was, and runs down into the valley and up again the other side, and finds another village, same as the first one, and the people all falls down flat on their faces, and Dravot says,—'Now what is the trouble between you two villages?' and the people points to a woman, as fair as you or me, that was carried off, and Dravot takes her back to the first village and counts up the dead—eight there was. For each dead man Dravot pours a little milk on the ground and waves his arms like a whirligig and 'That's all right,' says he. Then he and Carnehan takes the big boss of each village by the arm and walks them down into the valley, and shows them how to scratch a line with a spear right down the valley, and gives each a sod of turf from both sides o' the line. Then all the people comes down and shouts like the devil and all, and Dravot says,—'Go and dig the land, and be fruitful and multiply,'[3] which they did, though they didn't under-stand. Then we asks the names of things in their lingo—bread and water and fire and idols and such, and Dravot leads the priest of each village up to the idol, and says he must sit there and judge the people, and if anything goes wrong he is to be shot.

"Next week they was all turning up the land in the valley as quiet as bees and much prettier, and the priests heard all the complaints and told Dravot in dumb show what it was about. 'That's just the beginning,' says Dravot. 'They think we're Gods.' He and Carnehan picks out twenty good men and

---

3. God's command to Adam and Eve (Genesis 1.28).

shows them how to click off a rifle, and form fours, and advance in line, and they was very pleased to do so, and clever to see the hang of it. Then he takes out his pipe and his baccy-pouch and leaves one at one village and one at the other, and off we two goes to see what was to be done in the next valley. That was all rock, and there was a little village there, and Carnehan says,— 'Send 'em to the old valley to plant,' and takes 'em there and gives 'em some land that wasn't took before. They were a poor lot, and we blooded 'em with a kid[4] before letting 'em into the new Kingdom. That was to impress the people, and then they settled down quiet, and Carnehan went back to Dravot, who had got into another valley, all snow and ice and most mountaineous. There was no people there, and the Army got afraid, so Dravot shoots one of them, and goes on till he finds some people in a village, and the Army explains that unless the people wants to be killed they had better not shoot their little matchlocks;[5] for they had matchlocks. We makes friends with the priest and I stays there alone with two of the Army, teaching the men how to drill, and a thundering big Chief comes across the snow with kettle-drums and horns twanging, because he heard there was a new God kicking about. Carnehan sights for the brown[6] of the men half a mile across the snow and wings one of them. Then he sends a message to the Chief that, unless he wished to be killed, he must come and shake hands with me and leave his arms behind. The Chief comes alone first, and Carnehan shakes hands with him and whirls his arms about, same as Dravot used, and very much surprised that Chief was, and strokes my eyebrows. Then Carnehan goes alone to the Chief, and asks him in dumb show if he had an enemy he hated. 'I have,' says the Chief. So Carnehan weeds out the pick of his men, and sets the two of the Army to show them drill, and at the end of two weeks the men can manoeuvre about as well as Volunteers. So he marches with the Chief to a great big plain on the top of a mountain, and the Chief's men rushes into a village and takes it; we three Martinis firing into the brown of the enemy. So we took that village too, and I gives the Chief a rag from my coat and says, 'Occupy till I come;'[7] which was scriptural. By way of a reminder, when me and the Army was eighteen hundred yards away, I drops a bullet near him standing on the snow, and all the people falls flat on their faces. Then I sends a letter to Dravot, wherever he be by land or by sea."

At the risk of throwing the creature out of train I interrupted,—"How could you write a letter up yonder?"

"The letter?—Oh!—The letter! Keep looking at me between the eyes, please. It was a string-talk letter, that we'd learned the way of it from a blind beggar in the Punjab."

I remember that there had once come to the office a blind man with a knotted twig and a piece of string which he wound round the twig according to some cipher of his own. He could, after the lapse of days or hours, repeat the sentence which he had reeled up. He had reduced the alphabet to eleven primitive sounds; and tried to teach me his method, but failed.

"I sent that letter to Dravot," said Carnehan; "and told him to come back because this Kingdom was growing too big for me to handle, and then I struck

---

4. I.e., a kid goat, a fake religious ritual.
5. Primitive kind of musket.
6. Fires into the middle of a group of game birds rather than aiming at a particular one (a hunting term).
7. In Jesus' parable of the talents, a nobleman gives each of his servants a coin to invest with those instructions (Luke 19.13).

for the first valley, to see how the priests were working. They called the village we took along with the Chief, Bashkai, and the first village we took, Er-Heb. The priests at Er-Heb was doing all right, but they had a lot of pending cases about land to show me, and some men from another village had been firing arrows at night. I went out and looked for that village and fired four rounds at it from a thousand yards. That used all the cartridges I cared to spend, and I waited for Dravot, who had been away two or three months, and I kept my people quiet.

"One morning I heard the devil's own noise of drums and horns, and Dan Dravot marches down the hill with his Army and a tail of hundreds of men, and, which was the most amazing—a great gold crown on his head. 'My Gord, Carnehan,' says Daniel, 'this is a tremenjus business, and we've got the whole country as far as it's worth having. I am the son of Alexander by Queen Semiramis,[8] and you're my younger brother and a God too! It's the biggest thing we've ever seen. I've been marching and fighting for six weeks with the Army, and every footy little village for fifty miles has come in rejoiceful; and more than that, I've got the key of the whole show, as you'll see, and I've got a crown for you! I told 'em to make two of 'em at a place called Shu, where the gold lies in the rock like suet in mutton. Gold I've seen, and turquoise I've kicked out of the cliffs, and there's garnets in the sands of the river, and here's a chunk of amber that a man brought me. Call up all the priests and, here, take your crown.'

"One of the men opens a black hair bag and I slips the crown on. It was too small and too heavy, but I wore it for the glory. Hammered gold it was— five pound weight, like a hoop of a barrel.

" 'Peachey,' says Dravot, 'we don't want to fight no more. The Craft's[9] the trick, so help me!' and he brings forward that same Chief that I left at Bash-kai—Billy Fish we called him afterward, because he was so like Billy Fish that drove the big tank-engine at Mach on the Bolan in the old days. 'Shake hands with him,' says Dravot, and I shook hands and nearly dropped, for Billy Fish gave me the Grip.[1] I said nothing, but tried him with the Fellow Craft Grip. He answers, all right, and I tried the Master's Grip, but that was a slip. 'A Fellow Craft he is!' I says to Dan. 'Does he know the word?' 'He does,' says Dan, 'and all the priests know. It's a miracle! The Chiefs and the priests can work a Fellow Craft Lodge in a way that's very like ours, and they've cut the marks on the rocks, but they don't know the Third Degree, and they've come to find out. It's Gord's Truth. I've known these long years that the Afghans knew up to the Fellow Craft Degree, but this is a miracle. A God and a Grand-Master of the Craft am I, and a Lodge in the Third Degree I will open, and we'll raise the head priests and the Chiefs of the villages.'

" 'It's against all the law,' I says, 'holding a Lodge without warrant from any one; and we never held office in any Lodge.'

" 'It's a master-stroke of policy,' says Dravot. 'It means running the country as easy as a four-wheeled bogy[2] on a down grade. We can't stop to inquire now, or they'll turn against us. I've forty Chiefs at my heel, and passed and raised according to their merit they shall be. Billet these men on the villages

8. Legendary Assyrian queen.
9. Freemasonry.

1. Freemason handshake.
2. Railway truck.

and see that we run up a Lodge of some kind. The temple of Imbra will do for the Lodge-room. The women must make aprons as you show them. I'll hold a levee[3] of Chiefs to-night and Lodge to-morrow.'

"I was fair run off my legs, but I wasn't such a fool as not to see what a pull this Craft business gave us. I showed the priests' families how to make aprons of the degrees, but for Dravot's apron the blue border and marks was made of turquoise lumps on white hide, not cloth. We took a great square stone in the temple for the Master's chair, and little stones for the officers' chairs, and painted the black pavement with white squares, and did what we could to make things regular.

"At the levee which was held that night on the hillside with big bonfires, Dravot gives out that him and me were Gods and sons of Alexander, and Past Grand-Masters in the Craft, and was come to make Kafiristan a country where every man should eat in peace and drink in quiet, and specially obey us. Then the Chiefs come round to shake hands, and they was so hairy and white and fair it was just shaking hands with old friends. We gave them names according as they was like men we had known in India—Billy Fish, Holly Wilworth, Pikky Kergan that was Bazar-master when I was at Mhow, and so on and so on.

"*The* most amazing miracle was at Lodge next night. One of the old priests was watching us continuous, and I felt uneasy, for I knew we'd have to fudge the Ritual, and I didn't know what the men knew. The old priest was a stranger come in from beyond the village of Bashkai. The minute Dravot puts on the Master's apron that the girls had made for him, the priest fetches a whoop and a howl, and tries to overturn the stone that Dravot was sitting on. 'It's all up now,' I says. 'That comes of meddling with the Craft without warrant!' Dravot never winked an eye, not when ten priests took and tilted over the Grand-Master's chair—which was to say the stone of Imbra. The priest begins rubbing the bottom end of it to clear away the black dirt, and presently he shows all the other priests the Master's Mark, same as was on Dravot's apron, cut into the stone. Not even the priests of the temple of Imbra knew it was there. The old chap falls flat on his face at Dravot's feet and kisses 'em. 'Luck again,' says Dravot, across the Lodge to me, 'they say it's the missing Mark that no one could understand the why of. We're more than safe now.' Then he bangs the butt of his gun for a gavel and says:—'By virtue of the authority vested in me by my own right hand and the help of Peachey, I declare myself Grand-Master of all Freemasonry in Kafiristan in this the Mother Lodge o' the country, and King of Kafiristan equally with Peachey!' At that he puts on his crown and I puts on mine—I was doing Senior Warden—and we opens the Lodge in most ample form. It was a amazing miracle! The priests moved in Lodge through the first two degrees almost without telling, as if the memory was coming back to them. After that, Peachey and Dravot raised such as was worthy—high priests and Chiefs of far-off villages. Billy Fish was the first, and I can tell you we scared the soul out of him. It was not in any way according to Ritual, but it served our turn. We didn't raise more than ten of the biggest men, because we didn't want to make the Degree common. And they was clamoring to be raised.

" 'In another six months,' says Dravot, 'we'll hold another Communication

---

3. Gathering.

and see how you are working.' Then he asks them about their villages, and learns that they was fighting one against the other and were fair sick and tired of it. And when they wasn't doing that they was fighting with the Mohammedans. 'You can fight those when they come into our country,' says Dravot. 'Tell off every tenth man of your tribes for a Frontier guard, and send two hundred at a time to this valley to be drilled. Nobody is going to be shot or speared any more so long as he does well, and I know that you won't cheat me because you're white people—sons of Alexander—and not like common, black Mohammedans. You are *my* people and by God,' says he, running off into English at the end—'I'll make a damned fine Nation of you, or I'll die in the making!'

"I can't tell all we did for the next six months because Dravot did a lot I couldn't see the hang off, and he learned their lingo in a way I never could. My work was to help the people plough, and now and again go out with some of the Army and see what the other villages were doing, and make 'em throw rope-bridges across the ravines which cut up the country horrid. Dravot was very kind to me, but when he walked up and down in the pine wood pulling that bloody red beard of his with both fists I knew he was thinking plans I could not advise him about, and I just waited for orders.

"But Dravot never showed me disrespect before the people. They were afraid of me and the Army, but they loved Dan. He was the best of friends with the priests and the Chiefs; but any one could come across the hills with a complaint and Dravot would hear him out fair, and call four priests together and say what was to be done. He used to call in Billy Fish from Bashkai, and Pikky Kergan from Shu, and an old Chief we called Kafuzelum—it was like enough to his real name—and hold councils with 'em when there was any fighting to be done in small villages. That was his Council of War, and the four priests of Bashkai, Shu, Khawak, and Madora was his Privy Council. Between the lot of 'em they sent me, with forty men and twenty rifles, and sixty men carrying turquoises, into the Ghorband country to buy those hand-made Martini rifles, that come out of the Amir's workshops at Kabul, from one of the Amir's Herati regiments that would have sold the very teeth out of their mouths for turquoises.

"I stayed in Ghorband a month, and gave the Governor there the pick of my baskets for hush-money, and bribed the Colonel of the regiment some more, and, between the two and the tribes-people, we got more than a hundred hand-made Martinis, a hundred good Kohat Jezails[4] that'll throw to six hundred yards, and forty man-loads of very bad ammunition for the rifles. I came back with what I had, and distributed 'em among the men that the Chiefs sent to me to drill. Dravot was too busy to attend to those things, but the old Army that we first made helped me, and we turned out five hundred men that could drill, and two hundred that knew how to hold arms pretty straight. Even those cork-screwed, hand-made guns was a miracle to them. Dravot talked big about powder-shops and factories, walking up and down in the pine wood when the winter was coming on.

" 'I won't make a Nation,' says he. 'I'll make an Empire! These men aren't niggers; they're English! Look at their eyes—look at their mouths. Look at the way they stand up. They sit, on chairs in their own houses. They're the

---

4. Afghan muskets.

Lost Tribes, or something like it, and they've grown to be English. I'll take a census in the spring if the priests don't get frightened. There must be a fair two million of 'em in these hills. The villages are full o' little children. Two million people—two hundred and fifty thousand fighting men—and all English! They only want the rifles and a little drilling. Two hundred and fifty thousand men, ready to cut in on Russia's right flank when she tries for India! Peachey, man,' he says, chewing his beard in great hunks, 'we shall be Emperors—Emperors of the Earth! Rajah Brooke[5] will be a suckling to us. I'll treat with the Viceroy on equal terms. I'll ask him to send me twelve picked English—twelve that I know of—to help us govern a bit. There's Mackray, Sergeant-pensioner at Segowli—many's the good dinner he's given me, and his wife a pair of trousers. There's Donkin, the Warder of Tounghoo Jail; there's hundreds that I could lay my hand on if I was in India. The Viceroy shall do it for me. I'll send a man through in the spring for those men, and I'll write for a dispensation from the Grand-Lodge for what I've done as Grand-Master. That—and all the Sniders[6] that'll be thrown out when the native troops in India take up the Martini. They'll be worn smooth, but they'll do for fighting in these hills. Twelve English, a hundred thousand Sniders run through the Amir's country in driblets—I'd be content with twenty thousand in one year—and we'd be an Empire. When everything was shipshape, I'd hand over the crown—this crown I'm wearing now—to Queen Victoria on my knees, and she'd say: "Rise up, Sir Daniel Dravot." Oh, it's big! It's big, I tell you! But there's so much to be done in every place—Bashkai, Khawak, Shu, and everywhere else.'

" 'What is it?' I says. 'There are no more men coming in to be drilled this autumn. Look at those fat, black clouds. They're bringing the snow.'

" 'It isn't that,' says Daniel, putting his hand very hard on my shoulder; 'and I don't wish to say anything that's against you, for no other living man would have followed me and made me what I am as you have done. You're a first-class Commander-in-Chief, and the people know you; but—it's a big country, and somehow you can't help me, Peachey, in the way I want to be helped.'

" 'Go to your blasted priests, then!' I said, and I was sorry when I made that remark, but it did hurt me sore to find Daniel talking so superior when I'd drilled all the men, and done all he told me.

" 'Don't let's quarrel, Peachey,' says Daniel, without cursing. 'You're a King, too, and the half of this Kingdom is yours; but can't you see, Peachey, we want cleverer men than us now—three or four of 'em, that we can scatter about for our Deputies. It's a hugeous great State, and I can't always tell the right thing to do, and I haven't time for all I want to do, and here's the winter coming on and all.' He put half his beard into his mouth, and it was as red as the gold of his crown.

" 'I'm sorry, Daniel,' says I. 'I've done all I could. I've drilled the men and shown the people how to stack their oats better; and I've brought in those tinware rifles from Ghorband—but I know what you're driving at. I take it Kings always feel oppressed that way.'

" 'There's another thing too,' says Dravot, walking up and down. 'The winter's coming and these people won't be giving much trouble and if they do we can't move about. I want a wife.'

---

5. See n. 5, p. 1870.   6. Older rifles being replaced by Martinis.

" 'For Gord's sake leave the women alone!' I says. 'We've both got all the work we can, though I *am* a fool. Remember the Contrack, and keep clear o' women.'

" 'The Contrack only lasted till such time as we was Kings; and Kings we have been these months past,' says Dravot, weighing his crown in his hand. 'You go get a wife too, Peachey—a nice, strappin', plump girl that'll keep you warm in the winter. They're prettier than English girls, and we can take the pick of 'em. Boil 'em once or twice in hot water, and they'll come as fair as chicken and ham.'

" 'Don't tempt me!' I says. 'I will not have any dealings with a woman not till we are a dam' side more settled than we are now. I've been doing the work o' two men, and you've been doing the work o' three. Let's lie off a bit, and see if we can get some better tobacco from Afghan country and run in some good liquor; but no women.'

" 'Who's talking o' *women?*' says Dravot. 'I said *wife*—a Queen to breed a King's son for the King. A Queen out of the strongest tribe, that'll make them your blood-brothers, and that'll lie by your side and tell you all the people thinks about you and their own affairs. That's what I want.'

" 'Do you remember that Bengali woman I kept at Mogul Serai when I was a plate-layer?'[7] says I. 'A fat lot o' good she was to me. She taught me the lingo and one or two other things; but what happened? She ran away with the Station-master's servant and half my month's pay. Then she turned up at Dadur Junction in tow of a half-caste, and had the impidence to say I was her husband—all among the drivers in the running-shed!'

" 'We've done with that,' says Dravot. 'These women are whiter than you or me, and a Queen I will have for the winter months.'

" 'For the last time o' asking, Dan, do *not*,' I says. 'It'll only bring us harm. The Bible says that Kings ain't to waste their strength on women, 'specially when they've got a new raw Kingdom to work over.'[8]

" 'For the last time of answering, I will,' said Dravot, and he went away through the pine-trees looking like a big red devil. The low sun hit his crown and beard on one side and the two blazed like hot coals.

"But getting a wife was not as easy as Dan thought. He put it before the Council, and there was no answer till Billy Fish said that he'd better ask the girls. Dravot damned them all round. 'What's wrong with me?' he shouts, standing by the idol Imbra. 'Am I a dog or am I not enough of a man for your wenches? Haven't I put the shadow of my hand over this country? Who stopped the last Afghan raid?' It was me really, but Dravot was too angry to remember. 'Who brought your guns? Who repaired the bridges? Who's the Grand-Master of the sign cut in the stone?' and he thumped his hand on the block that he used to sit on in Lodge, and at Council, which opened like Lodge always. Billy Fish said nothing, and no more did the others. 'Keep your hair on, Dan,' said I; 'and ask the girls. That's how it's done at Home, and these people are quite English.'

" 'The marriage of the King is a matter of State,' says Dan, in a white-hot rage, for he could feel, I hope, that he was going against his better mind. He walked out of the Council-room, and the others sat still, looking at the ground.

7. Layer of railway track.
8. "Give not thy strength unto women, nor thy ways to that which destroyeth kings" (Proverbs 31.3).

" 'Billy Fish,' says I to the Chief of Bashkai, 'what's the difficulty here? A straight answer to a true friend,' 'You know,' says Billy Fish. 'How should a man tell you who know everything? How can daughters of men marry Gods or Devils? It's not proper.'

"I remembered something like that in the Bible;[9] but if, after seeing us as long as they had, they still believed we were Gods, it wasn't for me to undeceive them.

" 'A God can do anything,' says I. 'If the King is fond of a girl he'll not let her die.' 'She'll have to,' said Billy Fish. 'There are all sorts of Gods and Devils in these mountains, and now and again a girl marries one of them and isn't seen any more. Besides, you two know the Mark cut in the stone. Only the Gods know that. We thought you were men till you showed the sign of the Master.'

"I wished then that we had explained about the loss of the genuine secrets of a Master-Mason at the first go-off; but I said nothing. All that night there was a blowing of horns in a little dark temple half-way down the hill, and I heard a girl crying fit to die. One of the priests told us that she was being prepared to marry the King.

" 'I'll have no nonsense of that kind,' says Dan. 'I don't want to interfere with your customs, but I'll take my own wife.' 'The girl's a little bit afraid,' says the priest. 'She thinks she's going to die, and they are a-heartening of her up down in the temple.'

" 'Hearten her very tender, then,' says Dravot, 'or I'll hearten you with the butt of a gun so that you'll never want to be heartened again.' He licked his lips, did Dan, and stayed up walking about more than half the night, thinking of the wife that he was going to get in the morning. I wasn't any means comfortable, for I knew that dealings with a woman in foreign parts, though you was a crowned King twenty times over, could not but be risky. I got up very early in the morning while Dravot was asleep, and I saw the priests talking together in whispers, and the Chiefs talking together too, and they looked at me out of the corners of their eyes.

" 'What is up, Fish?' I says to the Bashkai man, who was wrapped up in his furs and looking splendid to behold.

" 'I can't rightly say,' says he; 'but if you can induce the King to drop all this nonsense about marriage, you'll be doing him and me and yourself a great service.'

" 'That I do believe,' says I. 'But sure, you know, Billy, as well as me, having fought against and for us, that the King and me are nothing more than two of the finest men that God Almighty ever made. Nothing more, I do assure you.'

" 'That may be,' says Billy Fish, 'and yet I should be sorry if it was.' He sinks his head upon his great fur cloak for a minute and thinks. 'King,' says he, 'be you man or God or Devil, I'll stick by you to-day. I have twenty of my men with me, and they will follow me. We'll go to Bashkai until the storm blows over.'

"A little snow had fallen in the night, and everything was white except the greasy fat clouds that blew down and down from the north. Dravot came out

---

9. "That the sons of God saw the daughters of men that they were fair; and they took them wives of all which they chose" (Genesis 6.2).

with his crown on his head, swinging his arms and stamping his feet, and looking more pleased than Punch.

" 'For the last time, drop it, Dan,' says I, in a whisper. 'Billy Fish here says that there will be a row.'

" 'A row among my people!' says Dravot. 'Not much. Peachey, you're a fool not to get a wife too. Where's the girl?' says he, with a voice as loud as the braying of a jackass. 'Call up all the Chiefs and priests, and let the Emperor see if his wife suits him.'

"There was no need to call any one. They were all there leaning on their guns and spears round the clearing in the centre of the pine wood. A deputation of priests went down to the little temple to bring up the girl, and the horns blew up fit to wake the dead. Billy Fish saunters round and gets as close to Daniel as he could, and behind him stood his twenty men with matchlocks. Not a man of them under six feet. I was next to Dravot, and behind me was twenty men of the regular Army. Up comes the girl, and a strapping wench she was, covered with silver and turquoises, but white as death, and looking back every minute at the priests.

" 'She'll do,' said Dan, looking her over. 'What's to be afraid of, lass? Come and kiss me.' He puts his arm round her. She shuts her eyes, gives a bit of a squeak, and down goes her face in the side of Dan's flaming red beard.

" 'The slut's bitten me!' says he, clapping his hand to his neck, and, sure enough, his hand was red with blood. Billy Fish and two of his matchlock-men catches hold of Dan by the shoulders and drags him into the Bashkai lot, while the priests howl in their lingo,—'Neither God nor Devil, but a man!' I was all taken aback, for a priest cut at me in front, and the Army behind began firing into the Bashkai men.

" 'God A-mighty!' says Dan. 'What is the meaning o' this?'

" 'Come back! Come away!' says Billy Fish. 'Ruin and Mutiny is the matter. We'll break for Bashkai if we can.'

"I tried to give some sort of orders to my men—the men o' the regular Army—but it was no use, so I fired into the brown of 'em with an English Martini and drilled three beggars in a line. The valley was full of shouting, howling creatures, and every soul was shrieking, 'Not a God nor a Devil, but only a man!' The Bashkai troops stuck to Billy Fish all they were worth, but their matchlocks wasn't half as good as the Kabul breech-loaders, and four of them dropped. Dan was bellowing like a bull, for he was very wrathy; and Billy Fish had a hard job to prevent him running out at the crowd.

" 'We can't stand,' says Billy Fish. 'Make a run for it down the valley! The whole place is against us.' The matchlock-men ran, and we went down the valley in spite of Dravot's protestations. He was swearing horribly and crying out that he was a King. The priests rolled great stones on us, and the regular Army fired hard, and there wasn't more than six men, not counting Dan, Billy Fish, and Me, that came down to the bottom of the valley alive.

"Then they stopped firing and the horns in the temple blew again. 'Come away—for Gord's sake come away!' says Billy Fish. 'They'll send runners out to all the villages before ever we get to Bashkai. I can protect you there, but I can't do anything now.'

"My own notion is that Dan began to go mad in his head from that hour. He stared up and down like a stuck pig. Then he was all for walking back alone and killing the priests with his bare hands; which he could have done.

'An Emperor am I,' says Daniel, 'and next year I shall be a Knight of the Queen.'

" 'All right, Dan,' says I; 'but come along now while there's time.'

" 'It's your fault,' says he, 'for not looking after your Army better. There was mutiny in the midst and you didn't know—you damned engine-driving, plate-laying, missionary's-pass-hunting hound!' He sat upon a rock and called me every foul name he could lay tongue to. I was too heart-sick to care, though it was all his foolishness that brought the smash.

" 'I'm sorry, Dan,' says I, 'but there's no accounting for natives. This business is our Fifty-Seven.[1] Maybe we'll make something out of it yet, when we've got to Bashkai.'

" 'Let's get to Bashkai, then,' says Dan, 'and, by God, when I come back here again I'll sweep the valley so there isn't a bug in a blanket left!'

"We walked all that day, and all that night Dan was stumping up and down on the snow, chewing his beard and muttering to himself.

" 'There's no hope o' getting clear,' said Billy Fish. 'The priests will have sent runners to the villages to say that you are only men. Why didn't you stick on as Gods till things was more settled? I'm a dead man,' says Billy Fish, and he throws himself down on the snow and begins to pray to his Gods.

"Next morning we was in a cruel bad country—all up and down, no level ground at all, and no food either. The six Bashkai men looked at Billy Fish hungry-wise as if they wanted to ask something, but they said never a word. At noon we came to the top of a flat mountain all covered with snow, and when we climbed up into it, behold, there was an Army in position waiting in the middle!

" 'The runners have been very quick,' says Billy Fish, with a little bit of a laugh. 'They are waiting for us.'

"Three or four men began to fire from the enemy's side, and a chance shot took Daniel in the calf of the leg. That brought him to his senses. He looks across the snow at the Army, and sees the rifles that we had brought into the country.

" 'We're done for,' says he. 'They are Englishmen, these people,—and it's my blasted nonsense that has brought you to this. Get back, Billy Fish, and take your men away; you've done what you could, and now cut for it. Carnehan,' says he, 'shake hands with me and go along with Billy. Maybe they won't kill you. I'll go and meet 'em alone. It's me that did it. Me, the King!'

" 'Go!' says I. 'Go to Hell, Dan. I'm with you here. Billy Fish, you clear out, and we two will meet those folk.'

" 'I'm a Chief,' says Billy Fish, quite quiet. 'I stay with you. My men can go.'

"The Bashkai fellows didn't wait for a second word, but ran off, and Dan and me and Billy Fish walked across to where the drums were drumming and the horns were horning. It was cold—awful cold. I've got that cold in the back of my head now. There's a lump of it there."

The punkah-coolies had gone to sleep. Two kerosene lamps were blazing in the office, and the perspiration poured down my face and splashed on the blotter as I leaned forward. Carnehan was shivering, and I feared that his

---

1. Mutiny of 1857, when the Bengal Army rebelled against their British officers.

mind might go. I wiped my face, took a fresh grip of the piteously mangled hands, and said: "What happened after that?"

The momentary shift of my eyes had broken the clear current.

"What was you pleased to say?" whined Carnehan. "They took them without any sound. Not a little whisper all along the snow, not though the King knocked down the first man that set hand on him—not though old Peachey fired his last cartridge into the brown of 'em. Not a single solitary sound did those swines make. They just closed up tight, and I tell you their furs stunk. There was a man called Billy Fish, a good friend of us all, and they cut his throat, Sir, then and there, like a pig; and the King kicks up the bloody snow and says:—'We've had a dashed fine run for our money. What's coming next?' But Peachey, Peachey Taliaferro, I tell you, Sir, in confidence as betwixt two friends, he lost his head, Sir. No, he didn't neither. The King lost his head, so he did, all along o' one of those cunning rope-bridges. Kindly let me have the paper-cutter, Sir. It tilted this way. They marched him a mile across that snow to a rope-bridge over a ravine with a river at the bottom. You may have seen such. They prodded him behind like an ox. 'Damn your eyes!' says the King. 'D'you suppose I can't die like a gentleman?' He turns to Peachey—Peachey that was crying like a child. 'I've brought you to this, Peachey,' says he. 'Brought you out of your happy life to be killed in Kafiristan, where you was late Commander-in-Chief of the Emperor's forces. Say you forgive me, Peachey.' 'I do,' says Peachey. 'Fully and freely do I forgive you, Dan.' 'Shake hands, Peachey,' says he. 'I'm going now. Out he goes, looking neither right nor left, and when he was plumb in the middle of those dizzy dancing ropes, 'Cut, you beggars,' he shouts; and they cut, and old Dan fell, turning round and round and round twenty thousand miles, for he took half an hour to fall till he struck the water, and I could see his body caught on a rock with the gold crown close beside.

"But do you know what they did to Peachey between two pine trees? They crucified him, Sir, as Peachey's hand will show. They used wooden pegs for his hands and his feet; and he didn't die. He hung there and screamed, and they took him down next day, and said it was a miracle that he wasn't dead. They took him down—poor old Peachey that hadn't done them any harm—that hadn't done them any . . . "

He rocked to and fro and wept bitterly, wiping his eyes with the back of his scarred hands and moaning like a child for some ten minutes.

"They was cruel enough to feed him up in the temple, because they said he was more of a God than old Daniel that was a man. Then they turned him out on the snow, and told him to go home, and Peachey came home in about a year, begging along the roads quite safe; for Daniel Dravot he walked before and said:—'Come along, Peachey. It's a big thing we're doing.' The mountains they danced at night, and the mountains they tried to fall on Peachey's head, but Dan he held up his hand, and Peachey came along bent double. He never let go of Dan's hand, and he never let go of Dan's head. They gave it to him as a present in the temple, to remind him not to come again, and though the crown was pure gold, and Peachey was starving, never would Peachey sell the same. You knew Dravot, Sir! You knew Right Worshipful Brother Dravot! Look at him now!"

He fumbled in the mass of rags round his bent waist; brought out a black horsehair bag embroidered with silver thread; and shook therefrom on to my table—the dried, withered head of Daniel Dravot! The morning sun that had long been paling the lamps struck the red beard and blind, sunken eyes; struck, too, a heavy circlet of gold studded with raw turquoises, that Carnehan placed tenderly on the battered temples.

"You behold now," said Carnehan, "the Emperor in his habit as he lived[2]—the King of Kafiristan with his crown upon his head. Poor old Daniel that was a monarch once!"

I shuddered, for, in spite of defacements manifold, I recognized the head of the man of Marwar Junction. Carnehan rose to go. I attempted to stop him. He was not fit to walk abroad. "Let me take away the whiskey, and give me a little money," he gasped. "I was a King once. I'll go to the Deputy Commissioner and ask to set in the Poorhouse till I get my health. No, thank you, I can't wait till you get a carriage for me. I've urgent private affairs—in the south—at Marwar."

He shambled out of the office and departed in the direction of the Deputy Commissioner's house. That day at noon I had occasion to go down the blinding hot Mall, and I saw a crooked man crawling along the white dust of the roadside, his hat in his hand, quavering dolorously after the fashion of street-singers at Home. There was not a soul in sight, and he was out of all possible earshot of the houses. And he sang through his nose, turning his head from right to left:

> "The Son of Man goes forth to war,
> A golden crown to gain;
> His blood-red banner streams afar—
> Who follows in his train?"[3]

I waited to hear no more, but put the poor wretch into my carriage and drove him off to the nearest missionary for eventual transfer to the Asylum. He repeated the hymn twice while he was with me, whom he did not in the least recognize, and I left him singing it to the missionary.

Two days later I inquired after his welfare of the Superintendent of the Asylum.

"He was admitted suffering from sunstroke. He died early yesterday morning," said the Superintendent. "Is it true that he was half an hour bareheaded in the sun at midday?"

"Yes," said I, "but do you happen to know if he had anything upon him by any chance when he died?"

"Not to my knowledge," said the Superintendent.

And there the matter rests.

1888

Danny Deever

"What are the bugles blowin' for?" said Files-on-Parade.°   *army private*
"To turn you out, to turn you out," the Color-Sergeant[1] said.

---

2. Allusion to Hamlet's description of his father's ghost, "My father, in his habit as he lived" (*Hamlet* 3.4.135).
3. A well-known hymn, corrected in later editions

to the actual words of the first line: "The Son of God goes forth to war."
1. High-ranking noncommissioned officer.

"What makes you look so white, so white?" said Files-on-Parade.
"I'm dreadin' what I've got to watch," the Color-Sergeant said.
5   For they're hangin' Danny Deever, you can hear the Dead March play,
The regiment's in 'ollow square²—they're hangin' him today;
They've taken of his buttons off an' cut his stripes³ away,
An they're hangin' Danny Deever in the mornin'.

"What makes the rear rank breathe so 'ard?" said Files-on-Parade.
10   "It's bitter cold, it's bitter cold," the Color-Sergeant said.
"What makes that front-rank man fall down?" said Files-on-Parade.
"A touch o' sun, a touch o' sun," the Color-Sergeant said.
They are hangin' Danny Deever, they are marchin' of 'im round,
They 'ave 'alted Danny Deever by 'is coffin on the ground;
15   An' 'e'll swing in 'arf a minute for a sneakin' shootin' hound—
O they're hangin' Danny Deever in the mornin'!

" 'Is cot was right-'and cot to mine," said Files-on-Parade.
" 'E's sleepin' out an' far tonight," the Color-Sergeant said.
"I've drunk 'is beer a score o' times," said Files-on-Parade.
20   " 'E's drinkin bitter beer⁴ alone," the Color-Sergeant said.
They are hangin' Danny Deever, you must mark 'im to 'is place,
For 'e shot a comrade sleepin'—you must look 'im in the face;
Nine 'undred of 'is county⁵ an' the Regiment's disgrace,
While they're hangin' Danny Deever in the mornin'.

25   "What's that so black agin the sun?" said Files-on-Parade.
"It's Danny fightin' 'ard for life," the Color-Sergeant said.
"What's that that whimpers over'ead?" said Files-on-Parade.
"It's Danny's soul that's passin' now," the Color-Sergeant said.
For they're done with Danny Deever, you can 'ear the quickstep play,
30   The regiment's in column, an' they're marchin' us away;
Ho! the young recruits are shakin', an' they'll want their beer today,
After hangin' Danny Deever in the mornin'.

1890

The Widow at Windsor

'Ave you 'eard o' the Widow at Windsor
    With a hairy gold crown on 'er 'ead?
She 'as ships on the foam—she 'as millions at 'ome,
    An' she pays us poor beggars in red.
5   (Ow, poor beggars in red!)
There's 'er nick¹ on the cavalry 'orses,
    There's 'er mark² on the medical stores—

2. Ceremonial formation: the troops line four
sides of a parade square, facing inward.
3. Chevrons denoting rank, worn by corporals and
sergeants on the sleeves of their tunics.
4. Or simply "bitter," a favorite variety of beer
drunk in English pubs. The word *bitter* thus
becomes a grim pun.

5. English regiments often bear the name of a particular county from which most of its men have
been recruited (e.g., the Lancashire Fusiliers).
1. A nick on one of their hoofs identified army
horses as property of the Crown.
2. The queen's mark: "V.R.I." (*Victoria Regina et
Imperatrix*, "Victoria Queen and Empress").

An' 'er troopers° you'll find with a fair wind be'ind   *troopships*
   That takes us to various wars.
10   (Poor beggars!—barbarious wars!)
        Then 'ere's to the Widow at Windsor,
          An' 'ere's to the stores an' the guns,
        The men an' the 'orses what makes up the forces
          O' Missis Victorier's sons.
15   (Poor beggars! Victorier's sons!)

Walk wide o' the Widow at Windsor,
   For 'alf o' Creation she owns:
We 'ave bought 'er the same with the sword an' the flame,
   An' we've salted it down with our bones.
20   (Poor beggars!—it's blue with our bones!)
Hands off o' the sons o' the widow,
   Hands off o' the goods in 'er shop,
For the kings must come down an' the emperors frown
   When the Widow at Windsor says "Stop!"
25   (Poor beggars!—we're sent to say "Stop!")
        Then 'ere's to the Lodge o' the Widow,[3]
          From the Pole to the Tropics it runs—
        To the Lodge that we tile with the rank an' the file,
          An' open in form with the guns.
30   (Poor beggars!—it's always they guns!)

We 'ave 'eard o' the Widow at Windsor,
   It's safest to leave 'er alone:
For 'er sentries we stand by the sea an' the land
   Wherever the bugles are blown.
35   (Poor beggars!—an' don't we get blown!)
Take 'old o' the Wings o' the Mornin',
   An' flop round the earth till you're dead;
But you won't get away from the tune that they play
   To the bloomin' old rag over'ead.
40   (Poor beggars!—it's 'ot over'ead!)
        Then 'ere's to the sons o' the Widow,
          Wherever, 'owever they roam.
        'Ere's all they desire, an' if they require
          A speedy return to their 'ome.
45   (Poor beggars!—they'll never see 'ome!)

1892

The Ladies

I've taken my fun where I've found it;
   I've rogued an' I've ranged in my time;
I've 'ad my pickin' o' sweethearts,
   An' four o' the lot was prime.

---

3. One of the lodges in the forest surrounding Windsor Castle where the queen and her family could relax in seclusion.

5   One was an 'arf-caste widow,
            One was a woman at Prome,[1]
        One was the wife of a *jemadar-sais*,°   head groom
            An' one is a girl at 'ome.

        Now I aren't no 'and with the ladies,
10   *For, takin' 'em all along,*
        You never can say till you've tried 'em,
            An' then you are like to be wrong.
        There's times when you'll think that you mightn't,
            There's times when you'll know that you might;
15   *But the things you will learn from the Yellow an' Brown,*
            They'll 'elp you a lot with the White!

        I was a young un at 'Oogli,[2]
            Shy as a girl to begin;
        Aggie de Castrer she made me,
20   An' Aggie was clever as sin;
        Older than me, but my first un—
            More like a mother she were—
        Showed me the way to promotion an' pay,
            An' I learned about women from 'er!

25   Then I was ordered to Burma,
            Actin' in charge o' Bazar,[3]
        An' I got me a tiddy° live 'eathen   tiny
            Through buyin' supplies off 'er pa.
        Funny an' yellow an' faithful—
30   Doll in a teacup she were—
        But we lived on the square, like a true-married pair,
            An' I learned about women from 'er!

        Then we was shifted to Neemuch[4]
            (Or I might ha' been keepin' 'er now),
35   An' I took with a shiny she-devil,
            The wife of a nigger at Mhow;
        'Taught me the gypsy-folks' *bolee*;[5]
            Kind o' volcano she were,
        For she knifed me one night 'cause I wished she was white,
40   And I learned about women from 'er!

        Then I come 'ome in a trooper,
            'Long of a kid o' sixteen—
        'Girl from a convent at Meerut,
            The straightest I ever 'ave seen.
45   Love at first sight was 'er trouble,
            She didn't know what it were;
        An' I wouldn't do such, 'cause I liked 'er too much,
            But—I learned about women from 'er!

---

1. Town in Burma.   4. Nimach, Mhow (line 36), and Meerut (line 43)
2. Hoogli, a town near Calcutta.   are towns in India.
3. Shop selling provisions to troops.   5. Slang.

I've taken my fun where I've found it,
50   An' now I must pay for my fun,
For the more you 'ave known o' the others
    The less will you settle to one;
An' the end of it's sittin' and thinkin',
    An' dreamin' Hell-fires to see;
55 So be warned by my lot (which I know you will not),
    An' learn about women from me!

What did the Colonel's Lady think?
    Nobody never knew.
Somebody asked the Sergeant's Wife,
60   *An' she told 'em true!*
When you get to a man in the case,
    They're like as a row of pins—
For the Colonel's Lady an' Judy O'Grady
    Are sisters under their skins!

1896

Recessional[1]

1897

God of our fathers, known of old—
    Lord of our far-flung battle-line—
Beneath whose awful Hand we hold
    Dominion over palm and pine—
5 Lord God of Hosts, be with us yet
Lest we forget—lest we forget!

The tumult and the shouting dies—
    The Captains and the Kings depart—
Still stands Thine ancient Sacrifice,
10   An humble and a contrite heart.[2]
Lord God of Hosts, be with us yet,
    Lest we forget—lest we forget!

Far-called, our navies melt away—
    On dune and headland sinks the fire[3]—
15 Lo, all our pomp of yesterday
    Is one with Nineveh and Tyre![4]
Judge of the Nations, spare us yet,
    Lest we forget—lest we forget!

1. A hymn sung as the clergy and choir leave a church in procession at the end of a service. Kipling's hymn was written on the occasion of the Jubilee celebrations honoring the sixtieth anniversary of Queen Victoria's reign, celebrations that had prompted a good deal of boasting in the press about the greatness of her empire. *Recessional* was first published in the *Times,* and Kipling refused to accept any payment for its publication, then or later.

2. Cf. Psalm 51.17: "The sacrifices of God are a broken spirit: a broken and a contrite heart, O God, thou wilt not despise."
3. Bonfires were lit on high ground all over Britain on the night of the Jubilee.
4. Once capitals of great empires. The ruins of Nineveh, in Assyria, were discovered buried in desert sands by British archaeologists in the 1850s. Tyre, in Phoenicia, had dwindled into a small Lebanese town.

If, drunk with sight of power, we loose
20   Wild tongues that have not Thee in awe—
Such boasting as the Gentiles use
    Or lesser breeds without the Law[5]—
Lord God of Hosts, be with us yet,
Lest we forget—lest we forget!

25   For heathen heart that puts her trust
    In reeking tube and iron shard—
All valiant dust that builds on dust,
    And guarding calls not Thee to guard—
For frantic boast and foolish word,
30   Thy mercy on Thy People, Lord!

1897   1897, 1899

The Hyenas

After the burial-parties leave
    And the baffled kites[1] have fled;
The wise hyenas come out at eve
    To take account of our dead.

5   How he died and why he died
    Troubles them not a whit.
They snout the bushes and stones aside
    And dig till they come to it.

They are only resolute they shall eat
10   That they and their mates may thrive,
And they know that the dead are safer meat
    Than the weakest thing alive.

(For a goat may butt, and a worm may sting,
    And a child will sometimes stand;
15   But a poor dead soldier of the king
    Can never lift a hand.)

They whoop and halloo and scatter the dirt
    Until their tushes° white   *canine teeth*
Take good hold in the army shirt,
20   And tug the corpse to light,

And the pitiful face is shown again
    For an instant ere they close;
But it is not discovered to living men—
    Only to God and to those

5. Cf. Romans 2.14: "For when the Gentiles, which have not the law, do by nature the things contained in the law, these, having not the law, are a law unto themselves."
1. Birds of prey that feed on dead bodies.

25   Who, being soulless, are free from shame,
       Whatever meat they may find.
       Nor do they defile the dead man's name—
       That is reserved for his kind.

1918, 1919

ERNEST DOWSON
1867–1900

Ernest Christopher Dowson spent much of his childhood traveling with his father on the Continent, mostly in France. His education was thus irregular and informal, but he acquired a thorough knowledge of French and of his favorite French writers— Gustave Flaubert, Honoré de Balzac, and Paul Verlaine—and a good knowledge of Latin poetry, especially Catullus, Propertius, and Horace. Dowson went to Oxford in 1886, but he did not take to regular academic instruction and left after a year. Though nominally assisting his father to manage a dock in the London district of Limehouse, Dowson spent most of his time writing poetry, stories, and essays and talking with Lionel Johnson, W. B. Yeats, and other members of The Rhymers' Club, in which he played a prominent part. Between 1890 and 1894 Dowson, though leading the irregular life of so many of the nineties poets, produced his best work, and his volume *Verses* came out in 1896. Late nights and excessive drinking impaired a constitution already threatened by tuberculosis. He moved to France in 1894, making a living by translating from the French for an English publisher but growing steadily worse in health. After his return to England, he was discovered in a dying condition by a friend, who took him to his home and nursed him until his death six weeks later.

    Dowson was a member of what Yeats called "the tragic generation" of poets in the nineties who seemed to be driven by their own restless energies to dissipation and premature death. As a poet, he was considerably influenced by Swinburne (whose feverish emotional tone he often captures very skillfully). He experimented with a variety of meters, and in *Cynara* used the alexandrine as the normal line of a six-line stanza in a manner more common in French than in English poetry. He was also especially interested in the work of the French symbolist poets and in their theories of verbal suggestiveness and of poetry as incantation: he believed (as he once wrote in a letter) that a finer poetry could sometimes be achieved by "mere sound and music, with just a suggestion of sense."

Cynara

Non sum qualis eram bonae sub regno Cynarae[1]

Last night, ah, yesternight, betwixt her lips and mine
There fell thy shadow, Cynara! thy breath was shed

---

1. I am not as I was under the reign of the good Cynara (Latin). This is the third line and part of the fourth of an ode of Horace (4.1) in which the poet pleads with Venus to stop tormenting him with love, since he is growing old and is no longer what he was when under the sway of Cynara (*Sin-ah-rah*), the girl he used to love. Of Dowson's "Cynara" Yeats later wrote: "Dowson, who seemed to drink so little and had so much dignity and reserve, was breaking his heart for the daughter of the keeper of an Italian eating house, in dissipation and drink." Dowson's "Cynara" was, in fact, a Polish woman by the name of Adelaide Foltino-wicz.

Upon my soul between the kisses and the wine;
And I was desolate and sick of an old passion,
5   Yea, I was desolate and bowed my head:
I have been faithful to thee, Cynara! in my fashion.

All night upon mine heart I felt her warm heart beat,
Night-long within mine arms in love and sleep she lay;
Surely the kisses of her bought red mouth were sweet;
10   But I was desolate and sick of an old passion,
     When I awoke and found the dawn was gray:
I have been faithful to thee, Cynara! in my fashion.

I have forgot much, Cynara! gone with the wind,
Flung roses, roses riotously with the throng,
15   Dancing, to put thy pale, lost lilies out of mind;
But I was desolate and sick of an old passion,
     Yea, all the time, because the dance was long:
I have been faithful to thee, Cynara! in my fashion.

I cried for madder music and for stronger wine,
20   But when the feast is finished and the lamps expire,
Then falls thy shadow, Cynara! the night is thine;
And I am desolate and sick of an old passion,
     Yea, hungry for the lips of my desire:
I have been faithful to thee, Cynara! in my fashion.

                                          1891, 1896

They Are Not Long

Vitae summa brevis spem nos vetat incohare longam.[1]

They are not long, the weeping and the laughter,
     Love and desire and hate:
I think they have no portion in us after
     We pass the gate.

5   They are not long, the days of wine and roses:
     Out of a misty dream
Our path emerges for a while, then closes
     Within a dream.

                                                  1896

Carthusians[1]

Through what long heaviness, assayed in what strange fire,
     Have these white monks been brought into the way of peace,

---

1. The shortness of life prevents us from entertaining far-off hopes (Latin; Horace, *Odes* 1.4).
1. A monastic order founded in 1084 at Chartreuse in the French Alps. The Carthusian regimen is stringently ascetic; each white-robed monk is a silent solitary except when participating in services of worship. Cf. Arnold, *Stanzas from the Grande Chartreuse* (p. 1493).

Despising the world's wisdom and the world's desire,
　　Which from the body of this death bring no release?

5　Within their austere walls no voices penetrate;
　　A sacred silence only, as of death, obtains;
Nothing finds entry here of loud or passionate;
　　This quiet is the exceeding profit of their pains.

From many lands they came, in divers fiery ways;
10　Each knew at last the vanity of earthly joys;
And one was crowned with thorns, and one was crowned with bays,[2]
　　And each was tired at last of the world's foolish noise.

It was not theirs with Dominic to preach God's holy wrath,
　　They were too stern to bear sweet Francis'[3] gentle sway;
15　Theirs was a higher calling and a steeper path,
　　To dwell alone with Christ, to meditate and pray.

A cloistered company, they are companionless,
　　None knoweth here the secret of his brother's heart:
They are but come together for more loneliness,
20　Whose bond is solitude and silence all their part.

O beatific life! Who is there shall gainsay,
　　Your great refusal's victory, your little loss,
Deserting vanity for the more perfect way,
　　The sweeter service of the most dolorous Cross.

25　Ye shall prevail at last! Surely ye shall prevail!
　　Your silence and austerity shall win at last:
Desire and mirth, the world's ephemeral lights shall fail,
　　The sweet star of your queen is never overcast.

We fling up flowers and laugh, we laugh across the wine,
30　With wine we dull our souls and careful strains of art;
Our cups are polished skulls round which the roses twine:
　　None dares to look at Death who leers and lurks apart.

Move on, white company, whom that has not sufficed!
　　Our viols cease, our wine is death, our roses fail:
35　Pray for our heedlessness, O dwellers with the Christ!
　　Though the world fall apart, surely ye shall prevail.

1891   1899

---

2. A crown of bay leaves (or laurel) was awarded
to poets whose work was admired.
3. Saint Francis of Assisi, founder of the Franciscan order of friars in 1209, was a gentle and
tender-spirited leader who worked and preached
among the poor. Saint Dominic, founder of the
Dominican order of friars (1215), whose preaching
was especially directed to converting heathens to
Christianity.

The Twentieth Century

1914–18:	World War I
1918:	Gerard Manley Hopkins's poetry published
1922:	T. S. Eliot's *The Waste Land*; James Joyce's *Ulysses*
1930:	Period of depression and unemployment begins
1939–45:	World War II
1947:	India and Pakistan become independent nations
1952:	George VI dies; accession of Elizabeth II
1955:	Samuel Beckett, *Waiting for Godot*
1991:	Collapse of the Soviet Union
1994:	Democracy comes to South Africa

HISTORICAL BACKGROUND

The modern period, which for convenience we call "the twentieth century," begins really with the late nineteenth, when the sense of the passing of a major phase of English history was already in the air. Queen Victoria's Jubilee in 1887 and, even more, her Diamond Jubilee in 1897 were felt even by contemporaries to mark the end of an era. As the nineteenth century drew to a close, there were many manifestations of a weakening of traditional stabilities. The aesthetic movement, with its insistence on "art for art's sake," assaulted the assumptions about the nature and function of art held by ordinary middle-class readers, deliberately, provocatively. It helped to widen the breach between artists and writers on the one hand and the "Philistine" public on the other—a breach an earlier symptom of which was Matthew Arnold's war on the Philistines in *Culture and Anarchy* and that was later to result in the "alienation of the artist," which has since become a commonplace of criticism. This breach was more than a purely English matter. From France came the tradition of the bohemian life that scorned the limits imposed by conventional ideas of respectability, together with other notions of the artist as rejecting and rejected by ordinary society, which in different ways fostered the view of the alienated artist. The life and work of the French symbolist poets and James Joyce's *Portrait of the Artist as a Young Man* (1916) show some of the very different ways in which this attitude revealed itself in literature all over Europe. In England, the growth of popular education as a result of the Education Act of 1870, which finally made elementary education compulsory and universal, led to the rapid emergence of a large, unsophisticated literary public at whom new kinds of journalism, in particular the cheap "yellow press," were directed. A public that was literate increased steadily throughout the nineteenth century, and one result of this was the splitting up of the audience for literature into "highbrows," "lowbrows," and "middlebrows." Although in earlier periods there had been different kinds of audience for different kinds of writing, the split now developed with unprec-

edented speed and to an unprecedented degree because of the mass production of popular literature for the newly literate. The fragmentation of the
reading public now merged with the artist's war on the Philistine (and indeed
was one of the causes of that war in the first place) to widen the gap between
popular art and art esteemed only by the sophisticated and the expert.

Another manifestation—or at least accompaniment—of the end of the
Victorian Age was the rise of various kinds of pessimism and stoicism. The
novels and poetry of Thomas Hardy show one kind of pessimism (and it *was*
pessimism, even if Hardy himself repudiated the term), and the poems of
A. E. Housman show another variety, while a real or affected stoicism is to
be found not only in these writers but also in many minor writers of the last
decade of the nineteenth century and the first decade of the twentieth.
Examples of this stoicism—the determination to stand for human dignity by
enduring bravely, with a stiff upper lip, whatever fate may bring—range from
Robert Louis Stevenson's essays and the rhetorically assertive poems of the
editor and journalist W. E. Henley, to Rudyard Kipling's *Jungle Books* and
many of his short stories, and the last stanza of Housman's *The Chestnut
Casts His Flambeaux* ("Bear them we can, and if we can we must").

Although the high tide of anti-Victorianism was marked by the publication
in 1918 of that classic of ironic debunking, *Eminent Victorians* by Lytton
Strachey (1880–1932), the criticism of the normal attitudes and preconceptions of the Victorian middle classes first became really violent in the last
two decades of the nineteenth century. No one could have been more savage
in attacks on the Victorian conceptions of the family, education, and religion
than Samuel Butler, whose novel *The Way of All Flesh* (completed in 1884,
posthumously published in 1903) is still the bitterest indictment in English
literature of the Victorian way of life. The chorus of those calling in question
Victorian assumptions grew ever louder as the century drew to an end;
sounding prominently in it was the voice of the young Bernard Shaw, one of
Butler's greatest admirers. The position of women, too, was rapidly changing
during this period. The Married Woman's Property Act of 1882, which
allowed married women to own property in their own right; the admission
of women to the universities at different times during the latter part of the
century; the fight for women's suffrage, which was not won until 1918 (and
not fully won until 1928)—these events marked a change in the attitude
toward women and in the part they played in the national life as well as in
the relation between the sexes, which is reflected in a variety of ways in the
literature of the period.

The Boer War (1899–1902), fought by the British to establish political
and economic control over the Boer republics (self-governing states) of
South Africa, marked both the high point of and the reaction against British
imperialism. It was a war against which many British intellectuals protested
and one that the British in the end were slightly ashamed of having won.
The development of the British Empire into the British Commonwealth (an
association of self-governing countries) continued in fits and starts throughout the first half of the twentieth century, with imperialist and anti-
imperialist sentiment often meeting head on in Parliament and the press;
writers as far apart as Kipling and E. M. Forster occupied themselves with
the problem. The Irish question also caused a great deal of excitement from
the beginning of the period until well into the 1920s. A steadily rising Irish

nationalism protested with increasing violence against the cultural, economic, and political subordination of Ireland to the British Crown and government. In World War I some Irish nationalists sought German help in
rebelling against Britain, and this exacerbated feelings on both sides. No one
can fully understand Yeats or Joyce without some awareness of the Irish
struggle for independence, the feelings of Anglo-Irish literary people on this
burning topic, and the way in which the Irish literary revival of the late
nineteenth and early twentieth centuries (with which Yeats was much concerned) reflected a determination to achieve a vigorous national life culturally even if the road seemed blocked politically.

Edwardian England (1901–10) was very conscious of being no longer Victorian. Edward VII stamped his extrovert and self-indulgent character on the
decade in which he reigned. It was a vulgar age of conspicuous enjoyment
by those who could afford it, and writers and artists kept well away from
involvement in high society (although there were some important exceptions): in general, there was no equivalent in this period to Queen Victoria's
interest in Tennyson. The alienation of artists and intellectuals was proceeding apace. From 1910 (when George V came to the throne) until war
broke out in August 1914, Britain achieved a temporary equilibrium between
Victorian earnestness and Edwardian flashiness; in retrospect that Georgian
period seems peculiarly golden, the last phase of assurance and stability
before the old order throughout Europe broke up in violence with results
that are still with us. Yet even then, under the surface, there was restlessness
and experimentation. If this was the age of Rupert Brooke, it was also the
age of T. S. Eliot's first experiments in a radically new kind of poetry.

Edwardian as a term applied to English cultural history suggests a period
in which the social and economic stabilities of the Victorian age—country
houses with numerous servants, a flourishing and confident middle class, a
strict hierarchy of social classes—remained unimpaired, though on the level
of ideas there was a sense of change and liberation. _Georgian_ refers largely
to the lull before the storm of World War I. That war, as the anthology's
selection of the war poets makes clear, produced some major shifts in attitude.

The postwar disillusion of the 1920s was, it might be said, a spiritual
matter, just as Eliot's Waste Land was a spiritual and not a literal wasteland.
Depression and unemployment in the early 1930s, followed by the rise of
Hitler and the cruel shadow of Fascism and Nazism over Europe, with its
threat of another war, represented another sort of wasteland that produced
another sort of effect on poets and novelists. While Eliot, Lawrence, Wyndham Lewis, Yeats, and others of the older generation turned to the political
right, the impotence of capitalist governments in the face of Hitlerism combined with economic dislocation to turn the majority of young intellectuals
(and not only intellectuals) in the 1930s to the political Left. The 1930s were
the red decade, because only the Left seemed to offer any solution. The early
poetry of W. H. Auden and his contemporaries cried out for "the death of
the old gang" (in Auden's phrase)and a clean sweep politically and econom-
ically, while the right-wing army's rebellion against the left-wing republican
government in Spain, which started in the summer of 1936 and soon led to
full-scale civil war, was regarded as a rehearsal for an inevitable second world
war and thus further emphasized the inadequacy of politicians. Yet though

all this is reflected passionately in the literature of the period, particularly in the poetry, it was not accompanied by any interesting developments in technique; many younger writers were more anxious to express their attitudes than to construct new kinds of works of art. The outbreak of World War II in September 1939, following very shortly on Hitler's pact with the Soviet Union, which shocked and disillusioned so many of the young left-wing writers, marked the sudden end of the red decade; the concern of writers in Britain now was to maintain their integrity and indeed their existence in what was from the beginning expected to be a long and destructive war. This they did surprisingly well, but nevertheless the struggle brought inevitable exhaustion, and winning a war, Great Britain lost an empire. India, long the jewel in the imperial Crown, came to independence in 1947 and, although India and the newly formed Muslim state of Pakistan elected to remain within the British Commonwealth, other former dominions did not. The Irish Republic withdrew from the Commonwealth in 1949, and the Republic of South Africa in 1961. While Britain was engaged in a painful reappraisal of its place in the world, countries that had lost the war—West Germany and Japan—were, in economic terms, winning the peace that followed.

Less obvious, but no less significant for English literature, were changes on the national scene. London, as the capital of the empire, had long dominated the culture as well as the politics and the economy of the British Isles. London spoke for Britain in the impeccable southern English intonations of the radio announcers of the state-owned British Broadcasting Corporation (known as the BBC), but from the 1960s this changed. Regional dialects and, then, multicultural accents were admitted to the airwaves. Regional radio and television stations sprang up. The Arts Council, which had subsidized the nation's drama, literature, music, painting, and plastic arts from London, delegated much of its grant-giving responsibility to regional arts councils. This gave a new confidence to writers and artists outside London—the Beatles were launched from Liverpool—and has since contributed to a notable renaissance of regional literature. At its best, this builds on the native tradition of Hardy and Yeats, transcending the narrowly provincial to achieve a true universality. These decentralizing developments also encouraged the efflorescence of black British and postcolonial writing, a different vision of the destiny and cultural significance of English literature, that would add such names as Wole Soyinka and Derek Walcott (both Nobel Prize winners), Chinua Achebe, Anita Desai, Hanif Kureishi, and V. S. Naipaul to the annals of that literature.

From the 1960s, London ceased to be essentially the sole cultural stage of the United Kingdom, and though its Parliament remained the sole political stage, successive governments came under increasing pressure from the regions and the wider world. The Labour government of Harold Wilson (1964–70) so capitulated to the demands of powerful labor unions that inflation spiraled out of control and the Labour Party lost the next election. Wilson's government was succeeded by that of the Conservative Edward Heath (1970–74), who negotiated Britain's entry into the European Common Market but, trying to break a militant miners' strike, called a general election and was defeated. The following Labour government, elected with the crucial support of the unions, again tried to resist their demands and again failed. In the general election of 1979, Margaret Thatcher led the

Conservatives to power, becoming thereby the country's first woman to hold the office of prime minister, an office she was to hold for an unprecedented twelve years. Pursuing a vision of a "new," more productive Britain, she curbed the power of the unions and began to dismantle the "welfare state," privatizing nationalized industries and utilities in the interests of an aggressive free-market economy. Initially, her policies had a bracing effect on a nation still sunk in postwar, postimperial torpor, but increasingly they widened the gap between rich and poor, black and white, north and south (in both England and Ireland), and between the constituent parts of the United Kingdom.

Thatcher was deposed by her own party in 1990, but the Conservatives had run out of energy and ideas, and they were routed in the election of 1997. The electorate's message was clear, and Tony Blair, the new Labour prime minister, moved at once to restore the rundown Health Service and system of state education. Honoring other of his campaign pledges, he offered Scotland its own parliament and Wales its own assembly, each with tax-raising powers and a substantial budget for the operation of its social services.

The Labour government also made significant progress toward solving the bitter and bloody problems of Northern Ireland. Since the mid-1980s, it had been clear that neither the British Army nor the Provisional IRA could achieve a decisive military victory. Within both the IRA and its political wing, Sinn Fein (Ourselves Alone), recognition of this fact led to internal discussion about achieving an alternative to a purely militarist approach to securing a united Ireland. This internal dialogue ultimately resulted in the declaration of a first ceasefire in 1994, which was broken, and a second in 1997. Though Sinn Fein still cannot be described as a wholly constitutional party, available evidence seems to show that politics have now taken precedence over violent struggle in the republican movement. Since the outbreak of the present troubles in the late 1960s, there have been many peace initiatives, none of them successful, but with the Labour victory of 1997, the most significant opportunity for peace has arisen from a redirection of IRA/Sinn Fein policy toward abandoning armed struggle. This shift in direction should also be seen in the light of greater London-Dublin cooperation, which culminated in the Downing Street Declaration of December 1993. The declaration attempted to create a framework for political cooperation within the context of the European Community and greater North-South cooperation on the island of Ireland. This most promising initiative culminated in elections to a Northern Ireland Assembly, which met for the first time in July 1998. That October, John Hume, leader of the (Roman Catholic) Social Democratic and Labour Party, and David Trimble, leader of the (Protestant) Ulster Unionist Party, were jointly awarded the Nobel Peace Prize, and the business of politics, after an absence of nearly three decades, returned from the streets to the floor of a parliament in Northern Ireland.

POETRY

The years leading up to World War I saw the start of a poetic revolution. The imagist movement, influenced by the philosopher-poet T. E. Hulme's insistence on hard, clear, precise images and encouraged by the modernist American poet Ezra Pound, who was then living in London, fought against romantic fuzziness and facile emotionalism in poetry. The movement developed simultaneously on both sides of the Atlantic, and its early members included Amy Lowell, Richard Aldington, H. D. (Hilda Doolittle), John Gould Fletcher, and F. S. Flint. As Flint explained in an article in March 1913, imagists insisted on "direct treatment of the 'thing,' whether subjective or objective," on the avoidance of all words "that did not contribute to the presentation," and on a freer metrical movement than a strict adherence to "the sequence of a metronome" could allow. All this encouraged precision in imagery and freedom of rhythmic movement, but more was required for the production of poetry of any real scope and interest. Imagism went in for the short, sharply etched, descriptive lyric, but it had no technique for the production of longer and more complex poems. Other new ideas about poetry helped to provide this technique. Sir Herbert Grierson's great edition of the poems of John Donne in 1912 both reflected and helped to encourage a new enthusiasm for seventeenth-century Metaphysical poetry. The revival of interest in Metaphysical wit brought with it a desire on the part of some pioneering poets to introduce into their poetry a much higher degree of intellectual complexity than had been found among the Victorians or the Georgians. The full subtlety of French symbolist poetry also now came to be appreciated; it had been admired in the 1890s, but for its dreamy suggestiveness rather than for its imagistic precision and complexity. At the same time a need was felt to bring poetic language and rhythms closer to those of conversation or at least to spice the formalities of poetic utterance with echoes of the colloquial and even the slangy. Irony, which made possible several levels of discourse simultaneously, and wit, with the use of puns (banished from serious poetry for more than two hundred years), helped to achieve that union of thought and passion that T. S. Eliot, in his review of Grierson's anthology of Metaphysical poetry (1921), saw as characteristic of the Metaphysicals and wished to bring back into modern poetry. A new critical and a new creative movement in poetry went hand in hand, with Eliot the high priest of both. It was Eliot who extended the scope of Imagism by bringing the English Metaphysicals and the French symbolists (as well as the English Jacobean dramatists) to the rescue, thus adding new criteria of complexity and allusiveness to the criteria of concreteness and precision stressed by the Imagists. It was Eliot, too, who introduced into modern English and American poetry the kind of irony achieved by shifting suddenly from the formal to the colloquial or by oblique allusions to objects or ideas that contrasted sharply with those carried by the surface meaning of the poem. Thus between, say, 1911 (the first year of the Georgian poets) and 1922 (the year of the publication of The Waste Land) a major revolution occurred in English—and for that matter American—poetic theory and practice, one that determined the way in which most serious poets and critics now think about their art. This revolution was by no means an isolated literary phenomenon. Writers on both sides of the English Channel were influenced by the French impressionist, postimpressionist, and cubist painters' radical reexamination of the nature of reality. Pound wrote books about the French sculptor Henri Gaudier-Brzeska and the American composer George Antheil. Wilfred Owen wrote in 1918: "I suppose I am doing in poetry what the advanced composers are doing in music"; and Eliot, while writing *The Waste Land* three years later, was so impressed by a performance of the composer Igor Stravinsky's *Le Sacre du Printemps* (The Rite of Spring) that he stood up at the end and cheered.

The posthumous publication by Robert Bridges in 1918 of the poetry of Gerard Manley Hopkins encouraged experimentation in language and rhythms. Hopkins combined absolute precision of the individual image with a complex ordering of images and a new kind of metrical patterning. The young poets of the early 1930s—Auden, Stephen Spender, C. Day Lewis— were much influenced by Hopkins as well as by Eliot (then the presiding genius of modern English and American poetry) and by a variety of other poets from the sixteenth-century John Skelton to Wilfred Owen.

Meanwhile the remarkable career of Yeats, stretching across the whole modern period, showed how a truly great poet can reflect the varying developments of his or her age yet maintain an unmistakably individual accent. Beginning among the aesthetes of the 1890s, turning later to a more tough and spare ironic language without losing his characteristic verbal magic, working out his own notions of symbolism and bringing them in different ways into his poetry, developing in his full maturity a rich symbolic and Metaphysical poetry with its own curiously haunting cadences and its imagery both shockingly realistic and movingly suggestive, Yeats's work is itself a history of English poetry between 1890 and 1939. Yet he is always Yeats, unique and inimitable—without doubt the greatest English-speaking poet of his age.

In his poem *Remembering the Thirties*, Donald Davie declared: "A neutral tone is nowadays preferred." That tone—the coolly clinical tone of Auden— dominated the poetry of the decade, but as it ended and World War II began, a neutral tone gave way to the vehemence of what came to be known as the New Apocalypse. The poets of this movement, the most notable of whom was Dylan Thomas, owed something of their audacity and violence to the example of the French surrealist poets and painters, who sought to express, often by free association, the operation of the subconscious mind. Many of these, such as Salvador Dali and Pablo Picasso, were both poets and painters, whose poetry was introduced to English readers in translations and in *A Short History of Surrealism* (1936) by David Gascoyne, one of the poets of the New Apocalypse. With the coming of the 1950s, however, the pendulum swung back again. A new generation of poets that included Donald Davie, Thom Gunn, and Philip Larkin reacted against what seemed to them the verbal excesses of Dylan Thomas, Edith Sitwell, and others. "The Movement," as this new group came to be called, aimed once again for a neutral tone, a purity of diction, in which to render an unpretentious fidelity to experience. Larkin, its most notable exponent, explicitly rejected the imported modernism of Pound and Eliot in favor of a native tradition represented in this century by Hardy. That tradition now flourishes in the work of Tony Harrison. Other poets, following the example of Craig Raine and taking their name—the Martian School—from his poem *A Martian Sends a Postcard Home* once again look to the painters for their inspiration. *Look* is the operative word, for the eye is paramount in their poetry, an eye that sees the world with the freshness of a child or a painter or a visitor from Mars and records what it sees with an often exuberant wit.

The last quarter century has seen no poetic movement or school of comparable originality and importance, but such groupings—and "isms" (modernism, symbolism, surrealism) in the arts generally—have never flourished on British soil as they have in France and America. In 1994, the New Generation Poets were launched by their publishers but, though individually lively, they lacked any unifying program, and the marketing of their work belongs (as F. R. Leavis famously said of the Sitwells) "to the history of publicity rather than of poetry." Public relations, however, have had a measurable impact on what has long—at least since the Middle Ages—been thought of as an essentially private art. An expanding poetry industry, with a network of well-publicized, well-attended public readings, has encouraged the development of "performance poetry." Written for the stage, these poems tend to be more accessible, informal, loosely textured, loosely structured, and lighter in tone than those written for the page. The future of such poems, which do not always "work" on the page (any more than those written for the page always work on the stage), may well lie with electronic media rather than with what Craig Raine's Martian calls "Caxtons . . . mechanical birds with many wings."

A century that began with a springtime of poetic innovation drew to its close with the full flowering of such older poets as Heaney, Hill, Hughes, and Walcott, and welcome signs of new growth wherever English is spoken.

FICTION

Novels—Henry James's "loose baggy monsters"—can be and do and include anything at all. The form defies prescriptions and limits. But its variety can be thought of as always converging energetically on the main and normal focuses of western literary endeavor, namely, constructing the self, reproducing what appears to be the nature of the real, and wrestling with the difficulties and intransigencies of the words one is compelled to use in these writing struggles. What characterizes twentieth-century fiction making is that these ancient problems of literary idea and practice become matters of intense reflection and debate as never before: for all writers, of course, but especially for novelists.

The century's novels may be divided roughly into three main strata: the period of high modernism through the 1920s, celebrating personal and textual inwardness; the reaction against modernism, involving a return to social realism and assorted documentary endeavors, which particularly characterizes the 1930s; the messy half century or so after World War II, in which the fictional claims of various realisms—urban, proletarian, provincial English, regional (especially Scottish and Irish), immigrant, postcolonial, feminist, gay—are asserted alongside, but also through, a continuing self-consciousness about language and form and meaning which is, in effect, the enduring legacy of modernism. By the end of the century, the modernist impulse had turned thus, amidst the vast array of possible subjects and styles, into the striking pluralism of postmodernism: a challenging mix of possibilities oddly reminiscent of the early part of the century when a Pole, Joseph Conrad, an Irishman, James Joyce, and an American, Henry James, were the most instrumental inventors of the modernist "English" novel.

The high modernists—the later James, Conrad, Joyce, plus the home-produced D. H. Lawrence and Virginia Woolf—wrote in the wake of the shattering of confidence in the great old certainties about the deity and the Christian faith, about the person, knowledge, materialism, history, the old Grand Narratives, which had, more or less, sustained the western novel through the nineteenth century. Into this general shaking of belief in the novel's founding assumptions—that the world, things, selves, were knowable, that language was a usefully revelatory instrument created under the aegis of the Divine Word, that the Divine Author and His story gave history meaning and moral shape and sanctioned the ordering of narratives into morally telling beginnings, middles, and endings—the modernists bravely ventured, trying all at once to be true to the new skepticisms and hesitations, and also to construct credible new alternatives to the old belief systems.

The once-prevailing nineteenth-century notions of ordinary reality came under serious attack. Virginia Woolf's explicit assault (in her famous 1919 essay *Modern Fiction*) on the "materialism" of the realistic Edwardian heirs of Victorian naturalist confidence, Arnold Bennett, H. G. Wells, and John Galsworthy, set the current tone. What was knowable, and thus writable, was not out there as some given, fixed, transcribable essence. Reality existed, rather, only as it was perceived. Hence the introduction of the impressionistic, flawed, even utterly unreliable narration, represented very commonly in some not-to-be-relied-on narrator ("reflectors" James called them)—a substitute for the classic nineteenth-century authoritative narrating voice (usually the voice of the author or some close substitute for that). Conrad's Marlow, the main narrating voice of *Heart of Darkness* as of other central Conrad fictions, with his large rhetoric of the invisible, inaudible, impossible, unintelligible, and so unsayable, came to seem foundational. The real was offered, thus, only, or mainly, as refracted and reflected in the novel's representative consciousnesses. "Look within," Virginia Woolf urged the novelist. Reality and its truth had gone inward.

Woolf's subject would be "an ordinary mind on an ordinary day." The life that mattered most would now be mental life. And so the modernist novel turned resolutely inward, its large concern being now with consciousness—a flow of reflections, momentary impressions, disjunctive bits of recall and half-memory, simultaneously revealing both the past and the way the past is repressed, though who can tell how much exactly? This concentration was mightily assisted by the great contemporary drive of the psychoanalytic movement led by Sigmund Freud, to narrate the reality of persons as the life primarily of the mind in all its expanding dimensions of investigation—consciousness, subconsciousness, unconsciousness, id, libido, and so on. And the apparent truths of this inward life were, of course, utterly tricky, scattered, fragmentary, spotty, now illuminated, now twilit, now quite occluded. Virginia Woolf was right to perceive Joyce's *Ulysses* as a prime expression of this desired impressionistic agenda ("he is concerned at all costs to reveal the flickerings of that innermost flame which flashes its messages through the brain").

The characters of Joyce and Woolf are caught, then, as they are immersed in the so-called "stream of consciousness"; and some version of an interior flow of thought becomes the main modernist access to "character." The reader overhears the characters speaking, so to say, from within their particular consciousnesses, but not always directly. The modernists felt free also to enter their characters' minds to speak as it were on their behalf in the technique known as *free indirect style* (*style indirect libre* in French).

A marked feature of the new fictional selfhood was a fraught condition of existential loneliness. Conrad's Lord Jim, Joyce's Leopold Bloom and Stephen Dedalus, Lawrence's Paul Morel or his Birkin, and Woolf's Mrs. Dalloway were people on their own, choosing individuals, but bereft of the old props, Church, Bible, ideological consensus, and so doomed to make their own puzzled way through life's labyrinths without much confidence in teleology or ontology, in means and ends, in the knowable solidity of the world, above all in language as a tool of knowledge about self and other. Epistemological confidence leaked dramatically away from the novel. Jacob of Woolf's *Jacob's Room* remains stubbornly unknowable to his closest friends and loved ones, above all to his novelist. The walls and cupboards of Rhoda's room in *The Waves* bend disconcertingly around her bed; she tries in vain to restore her sense of the solidity of things by touching the bottom bed rail with her toes; her mind "pours" out of her; the very boundaries of her self soften, slip, dissolve. The old conclusive tendency of plots (everything resolved on the novel's last page, on the model of the detective story) gave place to irresolute open endings—the unending vista of the last paragraph of D. H. Lawrence's *Sons and Lovers*, the circularity by which the last sentence of James Joyce's *Finnegans Wake* hooks back to be completed in the novel's own first word, so that reading simply starts all over again.

Not surprisingly, novelists became central to the building of modern myths on the dry bones of the old Christian ones. In his review of *Ulysses* ("*Ulysses*, Order, and Myth," 1921), T. S. Eliot famously praised the novel for replacing old "narrative method" by a new "mythical method" (he meant particularly the way Joyce's Irish Jew Bloom is mythicized as a modern Ulysses, his life's odyssey a revival of old episodes from the Homeric *Odyssey*). This manipulation of "a continuous parallel between contemporaneity and antiquity" was, Eliot thought, "a step toward making the modern world possible for art," much in keeping with the new anthropology and psychology as well as with what Yeats was doing in verse. Such private myth-making could, of course, take worrying turns. The "religion of the blood" that D. H. Lawrence celebrated led directly to the fascist sympathies of his *Aaron's Rod* and the revived Aztec blood-cult of *The Plumed Serpent*. And the new centrality of the linguistic and textual subject, the now central business of reading and writing in these highly metafictional novels (all about writers and artists, and surrogates for artists, such as Woolf's Mrs. Ramsay with her dinners and Mrs. Dalloway with her party, all those producers of what Woolf called the "unpublished works of women"), was not necessarily more consoling either. Mrs. Flanders's vision blurs and an inkblot spreads across the postcard we find her writing in the opening page of *Jacob's Room*: "Accidents were awful things." "How like Jacob his letters are," people say; but his writing is full of fibs. And the greatest modernist example of linguisticity rampant as such, *Finnegans Wake*, verges on unreadability.

And, of course, though the skeptical modernist linguistic turn, the rejection of materialist externality and of the realist project of the Victorians, did leave ineradicable traces on twentieth-century fiction, its revolutions never became absolute or permanent. *Ulysses* was simply unrepeatable and *Fin-*

negans Wake a monumental dead end. But even within the greatest modernist fictions the worldly subject, politics, moral questions, never quite dried
up. Woolf and Joyce are, for example, great celebrators of the perplexities of
urban life in London and Dublin. (Modernist fiction is everywhere an art of
the great city.) Lawrence was greatly preoccupied with the condition
of England, industrialism, provincial life. Satire was one of modernism's
recurrent notes. So it was not odd for the novelists who came through in the
1920s—for instance, the right-wing Wyndham Lewis and Evelyn Waugh—
to resort to the social subject and the satiric stance, nor for their left-leaning
contemporaries who developed alongside them and came to be seen as even
more characteristic of the 1930s Red Decade—Graham Greene, it might be,
or George Orwell—to engage with the *condition humaine* in ways that Dickens or Balzac, let alone Bennett-Wells-Galsworthy, would have recognized
as not all that distant from their own spirit. (Woolf's denigrated trio all lived
on into the 1930s; Wells, whose *Time Machine* and *War of the Worlds* helped
pioneer the SciFi genre at the end of the nineteenth century, was still producing scary prognostications of apocalyptic war in the 1930s, for instance
The Shape of Things to Come, and did not die until 1946.)

Linguistic self-consciousness would remain high on the novel's agenda—
the modernist lessons ran deep—but the documentarists who dominated the
1930s indicated just how much the linguistic subject would rely on politi-
cization for its survival: the estranging grammar of Henry Green's *Living* is
a part of his proletarian people's West Midland's discourse; the lexicography
of Walter Greenwood's *Love on the Dole* is a key part of his radical protest
on behalf of Manchester's unemployed; the comically chaotic meeting of
English and German languages in Christopher Isherwood's Berlin stories is
central to a fiction of dire warning about Anglo-German politics; George
Orwell's Newspeak in *Nineteen-Eighty-Four* is the culmination of nearly two
decades of politically motivated engagement with the ways of English speakers at home and abroad. In this politicized aftermath of the modernist experiment, Huxley's *Eyeless in Gaza,* say, is as much a matter of satirical
engagement with the socio-politico-moral matter of the 1930s as are the
reflections on modern linguistic corruptions in the Year of Our Ford in Huxley's even more obviously satirical *Brave New World.*

Where World War I was a great engine of modernism, a prime endorser
of the chaos of belief and the fragility of language and the human subject,
the impact of the Spanish Civil War and then World War II was to confirm
the English novel in its return to registering the social scene and the historical event. World War II provoked whole series of more or less realist fictions:
Evelyn Waugh's *Sword of Honour* trilogy, Anthony Powell's *A Dance to the
Music of Time* sequence, Olivia Manning's *Balkan Trilogy,* as well as powerful singletons such as Greene's *The Ministry of Fear,* Waugh's *Brideshead
Revisited,* and H. E. Bates's *Fair Stood the Wind for France.* C. P. Snow's
long *Strangers and Brothers* sequence is central to the English novel's mid-
century role as concerned assessor of the War and its human aftermaths.

The new fictions of the post–World War II period speak with the satirical
energies of the young demobilized officer class (Kingsley Amis's *Lucky Jim*
set the tone of a whole generation of disgruntled awkward-squad jokers), and
of the ordinary provincial citizen finding a fictional voice yet again in the
new Welfare State atmosphere of the 1950s (as Alan Sillitoe's proletarian

Nottingham novel *Saturday Night and Sunday Morning*, for instance, or John Wain's graduating scholarship-boy's protest against the educational posh-ocracy, *Hurry on Down*).

Two undoubtedly major careers were launched in 1954 in this atmosphere of questing for new moral bases for the post-Holocaust nuclear age—William Golding, with *The Lord of the Flies*, and Iris Murdoch, with *Under the Net*. Both writers produced large numbers of novels carrying on where their first novels began: intense post-Christian moral fables in Golding's case, moral philosophy in Murdoch's. In her many fine theoretical texts, Murdoch spelled out her lifelong fictional espousal of the "sovereignty of good" and the importance of the novel's loving devotion to "the otherness of the other person." Murdoch and Golding were consciously retrospective (as were the important group of contemporary Roman Catholics—Greene, Waugh, and Muriel Spark) in their investment in moral form. But such conscious retro-determinations were not enough to hold back or calm the anxiety that all belatedness inevitably entails. And as the century drew on, British fiction's main effort was a coming to terms with the many palpably disconcerting features of a pervasive sense of posteriority—postwar flatness; postimperial diminutions of power and influence; and the sense of the Grand Narratives really now losing their force as never before.

Younger novelists, such as Anita Brookner, Martin Amis, Michele Roberts, Graham Swift, Sebastian Faulks, and Ian McEwan, became massively obsessed with Germany (the now accusingly prosperous old foe), and with the still haunting ghosts of the *Hitlerzeit*—and not least after 1989, when the Berlin Wall came down and wartime European horrors stirred once more into vivid focus. Meanwhile, the postimperial dereliction of the once-grand center of London became a main topic of the later Kingsley Amis, of ex-Rhodesian Doris Lessing, of Ian McEwan, as well as of Kingsley Amis's son Martin (especially in his greatly important *London Fields* and *The Information*). Where earlier in the century Conrad and E. M. Forster (*A Passage to India*) and Jean Rhys (*Wide Sargasso Sea*) had been harshly accusatory about Britain's overseas behavior, now it was nostalgia for old imperial days that energized the pages of Lawrence Durrell's *Alexandrian Quartet*, Paul Scott's *Raj Quartet* and *Staying On*, and J. G. Farrell's *The Siege of Krishnapur* and *Singapore Grip*. At the same time, there was a widespread sense that what was mainly left now for English fiction was merely a rehashing of old stories (critics often accuse the late-century English novel of being far too obsessed with the past, much too content with the historical subject). The modernist, Joycean notion that resurrecting ancient narratives was a way of revitalizing present consciousness had given way to a fear that the postmodern present was under condemnation to a rather disabled career of simply parroting old stuff (*on est parle*, "one is spoken," rather than speaking for oneself, thinks the main character of Julian Barnes's *Flaubert's Parrot*, reflecting in some dismay on this dilemma). Ventriloquial reproduction of old voices became Peter Ackroyd's trademark. Like the subject of A. S. Byatt's *Possession*, which is about the magnetism of past (Victorian) writers and writings, all this comes to seem central to late-century times. And being merely possessed by the past revives all the old orthodox worries about mediumistic, even demonic, possession, which Yeats managed to avoid and which Peter Ackroyd's encounters with London mediums (as in his *English Music*) and A. S. Byatt's stories about raising the dead in seances, in *Angels and Insects,* do not.

Of course there are many energetic new end-of-century voices, particularly ones from assorted margins, eager to fight off and against prevalent moods of enervation at the English center. Women's voices (like Beryl Bainbridge, dark historicizer of male as well as female plights; Jeanette Winterson, great word-mongering celebrator of women's arts and bodiliness; Michele Roberts, lusty reviver of repressed female stories; above all, Angela Carter, feminist neomythographer, reviser of fairy tales, rewriter of Sade, espouser of raucously bad-mouthing girls). And regional voices (especially Irish ones, as Brian Moore, John Banville, Bernard MacLaverty; and Scottish ones, not least the so-called Glasgow School of Alasdair Gray, A. L. Kennedy, and James Kelman). And "genre" voices (that is, novelists pushing their way into the mainstream from the generic edge, especially of science fiction—a movement fathered, or grandfathered, by J. G. Ballard, author of the influential *Crash* and *The Atrocity Exhibition,* and guru of Martin Amis and Will Self). And male-gay voices (Alan Hollinghurst, pioneer of the openly male-homosexual literary novel of the post–World War II period; Adam Mars-Jones, short-story chronicler of the AIDS crisis among gay men). And, of course, immigrant, postcolonial voices. Where once Jean Rhys, V. S. Naipaul, and Doris Lessing led a distinct but limited phalanx of old Commonwealth novelists residing in Britain, late-century English fiction would look startlingly thin and poverty-stricken indeed were it not for the huge presence of writers of overseas, mainly Commonwealth, origin—the likes of Wilson Harris, Fred d'Aguiar, David Dabydeen, Alice Munro, Christopher Hope, Caryl Phillips, Adam Zameenzad, Abdulrazak Gurnah, Hanif Kureishi, Kazuo Ishiguro, and, above all, Salman Rushdie, Indian-born importer of South American and German (Gunther Grass–type) magic realism, many-voiced satirist of Indian, Pakistani, and British life (the latter especially in his masterpiece, *The Satanic Verses*). Among such novelists, and in particular Rushdie, the English novel deploys its postmodernistic energies with little anxiety about belatedness, no fright over parroting, and no neomodernist worries about attempting realistic encounters with the world.

Energetic such postcolonialist writings undoubtedly are. They do not, however, manage to keep quite at bay the prevailing sense of strain infecting end-of-century (and end-of-millennium) British fiction—the rather desperate attempt by the best of the younger novelists to ward off a general failure of British cultural nerve and particular fears about the British novel's contemporary sterility, that is to be witnessed in their rather hectic investment in what Martin Amis has called the gimmick, and J. G. Ballard for his part has welcomed as "ransacking the library of extreme metaphors": efforts, important in their way, but tellingly overdone, such as Angela Carter's sadomasochistic female heroics; Martin Amis's stylistic and formal extremes (including the backward narration of his Holocaust novel, *Time's Arrow*); Julian Barnes's persistent risky investment in the essayistic; Patrick McGrath's dark revival of the gothic; Will Self's showy parade of urban criminals and degenerates. Grimly attractive as these are, they are desperate measures nonetheless.

DRAMA

Modern drama begins in a sense with the witty drawing-room comedies of Oscar Wilde; yet Wilde founded no dramatic school. His wit was combative and generative of paradoxes, but beneath the glitter of his verbal play it is possible to see serious—if heavily coded—reflections on social, political, and even feminist issues. Bernard Shaw brought still another kind of wit into drama—not Wilde's lighthearted sparkle but the provocative paradox that was meant to tease and disturb, to challenge the complacency of the audience. Shaw's discussion plays were given dramatic life through the mastery of theatrical techniques, which he learned during his years as a drama critic.

Wilde and Shaw were both born in Ireland, and it was in Dublin that the century's first major theatrical movement originated. The Irish Literary Theatre was founded in 1899, with Yeats's early play *The Countess Cathleen* as its first production. The founders—Yeats, Lady Gregory, George Moore, and Edward Martyn—wanted to make a contribution to an Irish literary revival, but they were influenced also by the Independent Theatre in London, founded in 1891 by J. T. Grein in order to encourage new developments in the drama. In 1902 the Irish Literary Theatre was able to maintain a permanent all-Irish company and changed its name to the Irish National Theatre, which moved in 1904 to the Abbey Theatre, by which name it has since been known. J. M. Synge's use of the speech and imagination of Irish country people, Yeats's powerful symbolic use of themes from old Irish legend, and Sean O'Casey's use of the Irish civil war as a background for plays combining tragic melodrama, humor of character, and irony of circumstance brought new kinds of vitality to the theater. In England, T. S. Eliot attempted with considerable success to revive a ritual poetic drama with his *Murder in the Cathedral* (1935). His later attempts to combine religious symbolism with the box-office appeal of an entertaining society comedy (as in *The Cocktail Party*, 1950), although impressive technical achievements, were not wholly successful: the combination of contemporary social chatter with profound religious symbolism produces both an unevenness of tone and disturbing shifts in levels of realism.

In spite of the achievements of Shaw, Yeats, and Eliot, it cannot be said of the drama, as it can of poetry and fiction in the first half of the century, that a technical revolution occurred that changed the whole course of literary history with respect to that particular literary form. The reformers of the 1890s invoked the name of the Norwegian playwright Ibsen: like Shaw they saw him as essentially a critic of middle-class society rather than (as critics tend to see him today) as an essentially poetic dramatist experimenting with symbolic modes of expression. This may be the reason why the influence of Ibsen soon petered out in run-of-the-mill plays of humanitarian social concern. The staple of the London West End theater remained social comedy stiffened by occasional irony and sweetened by sentimentality (Noel Coward [1899–1973] was one of the best, as well as most successful, purveyors of this sort of fare though his work was often underpinned by a frisson of sexual innuendo). The cleverly contrived sentimentalities of J. M. Barrie (1860–1937) were highly popular in their day; Barrie's plays showed a great theatrical skill and a determined cunning in the exploitation of the audience's reaction.

The course of British and Irish drama during the first half of the century may have been less revolutionary than developments in poetry and fiction over the same period, but its revolution was to come in the decade following the end of World War II. Wartime verse plays, commissioned by the BBC and written for radio by Louis MacNeice and other poets, helped prepare the audience that in the late 1940s and early 1950s rapturously received the verse plays of Christopher Fry. It seemed that these were about to bring a new kind of poetic life into English drama. But Fry's exuberant use of metaphor—often more pyrotechnic than functional—soon lost its appeal, and by the late 1950s a very different kind of drama brought vitality to the British theater.

While Brecht, Ionesco, and Sartre straddled the stages of Europe in the postwar years, and English followers of "absurd" drama like N. F. Simpson presented a rather anemic version of European existentialism, Samuel Beckett changed the history of drama with his first play, written in French in 1948 and translated by the author himself as *Waiting for Godot* (1953). *Godot*'s apparent lack of plot ("nothing happens—twice") throws the theatrical focus onto its language, which George Steiner has described as "the main instrument of man's refusal to accept the world as it is." The theatrical tremors caused by *Godot* and such of Beckett's later plays as *Not I* (1973) and *That Time* (1976) gave impetus to a seismic shift in British writing for the theater.

The epicenter of this new movement was the Royal Court Theatre, symbolically located a little away from London's West End "theater land." From 1956, the Royal Court was the home of the English Stage Company. Together they provided a venue and a vision that provoked and enabled a new wave of writers, many of whom had learned their stagecraft as actors in provincial repertory theaters and touring companies throughout Britain and Ireland. John Osborne's *Look Back in Anger* (1956) was the hit of the ESCs first season (significantly helped by its broadcast on television in the autumn of 1956). Osborne offered his audience what he called "lessons in feeling" through his searing depiction of the emotional cruelty and directionless angst of Jimmy Porter, described by one puzzled contemporary critic as a "Wolverhampton Hamlet." *Look Back in Anger* is technically a rather traditional play, but its novelty lay in its nonmetropolitan setting and in the arias of discontent of its very English rebel without a cause. Osborne explored issues and injustices with a tone of savage indignation, and his later plays, *The Entertainer* (1957) and *Luther* (1960), are technically more adventurous. The former explores the changes in English society through the elegant and challenging allegory of Archie Rice's declining fortunes as a music-hall artist, while the latter studies a historical rebel with a very tangible cause (and chronic constipation).

The changes in British theater in the 1950s and 1960s were in part a response to the new challenges of technicolor cinema and increasing public access to television. Many landmark social dramas of the 1950s were subsequently filmed (often under the imaginative direction of Tony Richardson). Theater had to rediscover and redefine what was distinctive about the experience it offered in the face of the large budgets and technical resources of the new media. Indeed, in the middle to late 1960s (generally considered a dry period in British theater) a generation of talented writers, such as David Mercer and David Rudkin, worked almost exclusively for television, where the stand-alone single play became a hallmark of high-class scheduling. But they built on the foundations laid by the naturalism of the so-called "kitchen sink" dramatists of the 1950s, like Arnold Wesker, a would-be English Arthur Miller, whose trilogy *Chicken Soup with Barley* (1958) showed that the personal was the political by confronting social, cultural, and psychological issues in the family arena. While naturalistic plays were one response to social and cultural changes of the postwar period, another group of Royal Court writers was refocusing theater on language and symbolism. Harold Pinter's "comedies of menace" map out a social trajectory from his early study of working-class stress and inarticulate anxiety, *The Room* (1957), through the film-noirish black farce of *The Dumb Waiter* (1960) and the emotional power plays of *The Caretaker* (1960), to the savagely comic study of middle-class escape from working-class mores in *The Homecoming* (1965). Later plays reflect on patrician suspicion and betrayal, though in the 1980s his work acquired a more overtly political voice.

The political was always close to the surface of John Arden. His *Sergeant Musgrave's Dance* (1959) explores colonial oppression, communal guilt for wartime atrocities, and pacifism in the stylized setting of an isolated mining town. Using songs, ballads, dance, and proverbs, Arden makes a dramatic and vivid synthesis of popular cultural forms to highlight the universality of his political and social analyses, a process he later applied in developing community drama on aspects of Irish history. More experimentally, Joan Littlewood's Theatre Workshop pioneered the use of improvisation and group work to develop shows made up of filmlike collage of numerous small scenes: distinctive examples are Shelagh Delaney's *A Taste of Honey* (1958) and *O, What a Lovely War* (1963), both subsequently filmed.

In the theater of the 1960s, the black comedies of Joe Orton shocked bourgeois sentiment in a series of classically precise and sexually ambiguous parodies of other forms of theater: his farce *What the Butler Saw* (1969) even ends with a *deus ex machina*. The cerebral fireworks of Tom Stoppard were supported by an unusually high degree of technical virtuosity in his stagecraft. While Orton reads like Pinter on fast-forward, early Stoppard pays parodic homage to the verbal texture and theatrical technique of Beckett: *Rosencrantz and Guildenstern Are Dead* (1966) is *Godot* for English graduates. His *The Real Inspector Hound* (1968) is a virtuoso pastiche of the creaky prewar murder mystery which blurs the gap between proscenium and audience. This enjoyment and exploitation of self-conscious theatricality arises partly out of the desire to show theater as different from film and television and is everywhere apparent in the drama of the 1970s. The liturgical stylization of Peter Shaffer's *Equus* (1973) and the bleak mental landscape of his Salieri in *Amadeus* emphasize the stage as battleground and site of struggle (an effect lost in their naturalistic film versions), while Stoppard's time-slips and memory lapses in *Travesties* (1974) allow a nonnaturalistic study of the role of memory and imagination in the creative process, a theme he returns to more recently in *Arcadia* (1995), a stunning double-exposure account of a Romantic poet and his modern critical commentators occupying the same physical space but never reaching intellectual common ground. Alan Ayckbourn's work at Scarborough has explored and extended the technical possibilities of "theater in the round" in a prolific and highly successful series of social tragicomedies.

The Lord Chamberlain's abolition in 1968 of state censorship of plays permitted mainstream theaters to commission and perform for the first time work that addressed and presented controversial political, social, and sexual issues. Challenging studies of violence, social deprivation, and political and sexual aggression have characterized the work of Howard Brenton, Howard Barker, and Edward Bond. They often use mythical settings and epic stories to construct austerely sweeping critiques and striking tableaux of power and oppression. Bond's *Lear* (1971) typifies his ambitious combination of soaring lyrical language and alienatingly realistic violence. The post-1968 liberalization coincided with the collapse of the postwar liberal humanist consensus and encouraged the emergence of new theater groups addressing specific political agendas. Companies such as John McGrath's 7:84; Monstrous Regiment; Gay Sweatshop and Joint Stock worked collaboratively with dramatists who were invited in to help devise and develop shows. Increasingly in the 1970s, published plays are either transcriptions of the first production or "blueprints for the alchemy of live performance" (Micheline Wandor). In Ireland, the foundation of the Field Day Theatre Company in 1980 by the well-established playwright Brian Friel and actor Stephen Rea had similar motives of collaborative cultural catalysis. Their first production, Friel's *Translations* (1980), exploring linguistic colonialism and the fragility of cultural identity in nineteenth-century Ireland, achieved huge international success.

It may not be accidental that this ethos of collaboration and group development produced the first major cohort of women dramatists to break through onto mainstream stages. Caryl Churchill, whose *Top Girls* (1982) and *Serious Money* (1987) anatomize the market-driven ethos of the 1980s, explores modern society with the wit and detachment of Restoration comedy. Like David Mamet in the United States, she carefully transcribes and overlaps the speech of her characters to create a seamlessly interlocking web of discourse that aspires to reproduce a streamlined version of the ebb and flow of normal speech. Pam Gems studies the social and sexual politics of misogyny and feminism in her campy theatrical explorations of strong women— *Queen Cristina* (1977), *Piaf* (1978), *Camille* (1984)—while Sarah Daniels reinterprets the naturalism of kitchen-sink drama by adding to it the linguistic stylization of Churchill.

In retrospect, the opening of the new National Theatre complex on London's South Bank in 1976 may represent the high-water mark in postwar British theater. The 1980s and 1990s have seen recession and shrinking subsidy close companies and theaters. As in the 1920s and 1930s, musical theater has offered an escapist perspective, while the globalization of television has seen a retreat from new and challenging work into the synthetic world of soap opera, costume drama, and the classic serial.

THE TWENTIETH CENTURY

TEXTS	CONTEXTS
	1901–10 Reign of Edward VII
1902 Joseph Conrad, *Heart of Darkness*	**1902** End of the Anglo-Boer War
	1903 Henry Ford founds Ford Motor Company. Wright Brothers make the first successful airplane flight
	1905 Albert Einstein, theory of special relativity. Impressionist exhibition, London
	1910 Post-Impressionist exhibition, London
	1910–36 Reign of George V
1910 Bernard Shaw, *Pygmalion*	
1914 James Joyce, *Dubliners*. Thomas Hardy, *Satires of Circumstance*	**1914–18** World War I
1916 Joyce, *A Portrait of the Artist as a Young Man*	**1916** Easter Uprising in Dublin
1917 T. S. Eliot, *The Love Song of J. Alfred Prufrock*	
1918 Gerard Manley Hopkins, *Poems*	**1918** Armistice. Franchise Act grants vote to women over thirty
1920 D. H. Lawrence, *Women in Love*	**1920** Treaty of Versailles. League of Nations formed
1921 William Butler Yeats, *Michael Robartes and the Dancer*	**1921** Formation of Irish Free State with Northern Ireland (Ulster) remaining part of Great Britain
1922 Katherine Mansfield, *The Garden Party and Other Stories*. Joyce, *Ulysses*. Eliot, *The Waste Land*.	
1924 Forster, *A Passage to India*	
1927 Virginia Woolf, *To the Lighthouse*	
1928 Yeats, *The Tower*	
1929 Woolf, *A Room of One's Own*. Robert Graves, *Goodbye to All That*	**1929** Stock market crash; the Great Depression begins
1930 Siegfried Sassoon, *Memoirs of an Infantry Officer*	
	1933 Hitler comes to power in Germany
1935 Eliot, *Murder in the Cathedral*	**1936–39** Spanish Civil War
	1936 Edward VIII succeeds George V but abdicates in favor of his brother, crowned as George VI
1937 David Jones, *In Parenthesis*	
1939 Joyce, *Finnegans Wake*. Yeats, *Last Poems and Two Plays*	**1939–45** World War II
	1940 Fall of France. Battle of Britain
	1941–45 The Holocaust

TEXTS	CONTEXTS
1944 Eliot, *Four Quartets*	
1945 W. H. Auden, *Collected Poems.* George Orwell, *Animal Farm*	**1945** First atomic bombs dropped, on Japan
1946 Dylan Thomas, *Deaths and Entrances*	
	1947 India and Pakistan become independent nations
1949 Orwell, *Nineteen Eighty-Four*	**1950** Apartheid laws passed in South Africa
1955 Samuel Beckett, *Waiting for Godot*	
	1956 Suez Crisis
	1961 Berlin Wall erected
1962 Doris Lessing, *The Golden Notebook*	**1962** Cuban missile crisis
1964 Philip Larkin, *The Whitsun Weddings*	
	1965 U.S. troops land in South Vietnam
1966 Nadine Gordimer, *The Late Bourgeois World*. Tom Stoppard, *Rosencrantz and Guildenstern Are Dead*	
1969 Jean Rhys, *Wide Sargasso Sea*	**1969** Apollo moon landing
1971 V. S. Naipaul, *In a Free State*	**1971** Indo-Pakistan War, leading to creation of Bangladesh
1972 Seamus Heaney, *North*	**1972** Britain enters European Common Market
	1973 U.S. troops leave Vietnam
1979 Craig Raine, *A Martian Sends a Postcard Home*	**1979** Islamic Revolution in Iran; the Shah flees. Soviets invade Afghanistan
1980 J. M. Coetzee, *Waiting for the Barbarians*	**1980–88** Iran-Iraq War
1981 Salman Rushdie, *Midnight's Children*	
	1982 Falklands War
1988 Rushdie, *The Satanic Verses*	
	1989 Fall of the Berlin Wall. Tieneman Square, Beijing, demonstration and massacre
1991 Derek Walcott, *Omeros*	**1991** Collapse of the Soviet Union
1992 Thom Gunn, *The Man with Night Sweats*	
	1994 Democracy comes to South Africa
	1997 Labour Party victory in the UK ends eighteen years of Conservative government
1998 Ted Hughes, *Birthday Letters*	**1998** Anglo-American bombing of Iraq. British handover of Hong Kong to China. Northern Ireland Assembly established

THOMAS HARDY
1840–1928

Thomas Hardy was born near Dorchester, in that area of southwest England that he was to make the "Wessex" of his novels. He attended local schools until the age of fifteen, when he was apprenticed to a Dorchester architect with whom he worked for six years. In 1861 he went to London to continue his studies and to practice as an architect. Meanwhile he was completing his general education informally through his own erratic reading and was becoming more and more interested in both fiction and poetry. After some early attempts at writing both short stories and poems, he decided to concentrate on fiction. His first novel was rejected by the publishers in 1868 on the recommendation of George Meredith, who nevertheless advised Hardy to write another. The result was *Desperate Remedies*, published anonymously in 1871, followed the next year by his first real success (also published anonymously), *Under the Greenwood Tree*. Hardy's career as a novelist was now well launched; he gave up his architectural work and produced a series of novels that ended with *Jude the Obscure* in 1896. The hostile reception of this novel sent him back to poetry. His remarkable epic-drama of the Napoleonic Wars, *The Dynasts*, came out in three parts between 1903 and 1908; after this he wrote mostly lyric poetry.

Hardy's novels, set in a predominantly rural "Wessex," show the forces of nature outside and inside individuals combining to shape human destiny. Against a background of immemorial agricultural labor, with ancient monuments such as Stonehenge or an old Roman amphitheater reminding us of the human past, he presents characters at the mercy of their own passions or finding temporary salvation in the age-old rhythms of rural work or rural recreation. Men and women in Hardy's fiction are not masters of their fates; they are at the mercy of the indifferent forces that manipulate their behavior and their relations with others, but they can achieve dignity through endurance and heroism through simple strength of character. The characteristic Victorian novelist—e.g., Dickens or Thackeray—was concerned with the behavior and problems of people in a given social milieu, which were described in detail; Hardy preferred to go directly for the elemental in human behavior with a minimum of contemporary social detail. Most of Hardy's novels are tragic, although *Under the Greenwood Tree* has an idyllic character possessed by no other of his novels. But even here the happy ending is achieved only by ending the story with the marriage of the hero and heroine and refusing to go further; the texture of the narrative, for all its moments of gaiety and charm, has already suggested the bitter ironies of which life is capable. His later work explores those ironies with sometimes an almost malevolent staging of coincidence to emphasize the disparity between human desire and ambition on the one hand and what fate has in store for the characters on the other. But fate is not a wholly external force. Men and women are driven by the demands of their own nature as much as by anything from outside them. *Tess of the D'Urbervilles* (1891) is the story of an intelligent and sensitive girl, daughter of a poor family, driven to murder and so to death by hanging, by a concatenation of events and circumstances so bitterly ironic that many readers find it the darkest of Hardy's novels. Published in the same year as *Tess*, the story anthologized here, *On the Western Circuit*, similarly has at its center a country girl seduced by a sophisticated city man; her "ruin" (see also Hardy's poem *The Ruined Maid*) leads—contrary to the good intentions of the three protagonists, and again as the result of bitter irony—to *his* ruin and a lifetime of misery for all concerned.

Hardy himself denied that he was a pessimist, calling himself a "meliorist," that is, one who believes that the world may be made better by human effort. But there is little sign of meliorism in either his most important novels or his lyric poetry. In the poems, many of his characteristic attitudes and ideas and many of his favorite situations can be found. A number of his poems are verse anecdotes illustrating the perversity of fate, the disastrous or ironic coincidence. But his best poems go beyond this mood to present with quiet gravity and a carefully controlled elegiac feeling some aspect of human sorrow or loss or frustration or regret, always projected through a particular, fully realized situation. *Hap* shows Hardy in the characteristic mood of complaining about the irony of human destiny in a universe ruled by chance, but a poem such as *The Walk* (one of a group of poems written after the death of his first wife in 1912) gives, with remarkable power, concrete embodiment to a sense of loss. That power—we see it also in *A Broken Appointment* and *She Hears the Storm*—is achieved through a kind of verbal as well as an emotional integrity. Hardy's poetry, like his prose, often has a self-taught air about it; both can seem odd or, on first reading, clumsy. But at their best both his poetry and his prose have an air of persuasive authenticity. The association of a given emotion with particular visual memories in *Neutral Tones,* for example, is impressive because it carries such extraordinary conviction, and it carries that conviction because the rhythms and rhymes are handled so as to suggest the kind of utterance actually wrung from the poet (consider, e.g., the curious dead fall of "They had fallen from an ash, and were gray"). At the same time, Hardy will use an antique or a poetic word or phrase ("thereby," "a-wing") if it fits in with the movement of the poem and keeps him from having to stop and search for something more deft: the result is an effect not of artificiality but of spontaneity. Hardy's use of ballad rhythms often helps to give an elemental quality to his poetry, suggesting that this incident or situation, carefully particularized though it is, nevertheless stands for some profound and recurring themes in human experience.

The sadness in Hardy—his inability to believe in the government of the world by a benevolent God, his sense of the waste and frustration involved in human life, his insistent irony when faced with moral or metaphysical questions—is part of the late Victorian mood. We can see something like it in A. E. Housman, and there is an earlier version of Victorian pessimism in Edward FitzGerald's *Rubáiyát of Omar Khayyám,* published when Hardy was nineteen. What has been termed "the disappearance of God" affected him more deeply than many of his contemporaries, because until he was twenty-five he seriously considered entering the church. Yet his characteristic themes and attitudes cannot be related simply to the reaction to new scientific and philosophical ideas (Darwin's theory of evolution, for example) that we see in so many forms in late-nineteenth-century literature. The favorite poetic mood of both Tennyson and Arnold was also an elegiac one (e.g., in Tennyson's *Break, Break, Break* and Arnold's *Dover Beach*), but this is not Hardy's mood. The sad-sweet cadences of Victorian self-pity are not to be found in Hardy's poetry, which is sterner, as though braced by a long look at the worst. It is this sternness—sometimes amounting to ruggedness—together with his verbal and emotional integrity, his refusal ever to surrender to mere poetic fashion, his quietly searching individual accent, that has helped to bring about the steady rise in Hardy's poetic reputation, so that today he is regarded not only as a distinguished novelist but also as a great English poet. He appears as the major figure—with more poems than either Yeats or Eliot—in Philip Larkin's influential *Oxford Book of Twentieth-Century English Verse* (1973).

On the Western Circuit[1]

I

The man who played the disturbing part in the two quiet feminine lives hereunder depicted—no great man, in any sense, by the way—first had knowledge of them on an October evening, in the city of Melchester. He had been standing in the Close,[2] vainly endeavouring to gain amid the darkness a glimpse of the most homogeneous pile of mediæval architecture in England, which towered and tapered from the damp and level sward[3] in front of him. While he stood the presence of the Cathedral walls was revealed rather by the ear than by the eyes; he could not see them, but they reflected sharply a roar of sound which entered the Close by a street leading from the city square, and, falling upon the building, was flung back upon him.

He postponed till the morrow his attempt to examine the deserted edifice, and turned his attention to the noise. It was compounded of steam barrel-organs, the clanging of gongs, the ringing of hand-bells, the clack of rattles, and the undistinguishable shouts of men. A lurid light hung in the air in the direction of the tumult. Thitherward he went, passing under the arched gate-way, along a straight street, and into the square.

He might have searched Europe over for a greater contrast between jux-taposed scenes. The spectacle was that of the eighth chasm of the Inferno as to colour and flame, and, as to mirth, a development of the Homeric heaven. A smoky glare, of the complexion of brass-filings, ascended from the fiery tongues of innumerable naphtha lamps affixed to booths, stalls, and other temporary erections which crowded the spacious market-square. In front of this irradiation scores of human figures, more or less in profile, were darting athwart and across, up, down, and around, like gnats against a sunset.

Their motions were so rhythmical that they seemed to be moved by machinery. And it presently appeared that they were moved by machinery indeed; the figures being those of the patrons of swings, see-saws, flying-leaps, above all of the three steam roundabouts[4] which occupied the centre of the position. It was from the latter that the din of steam-organs came.

Throbbing humanity in full light was, on second thoughts, better than architecture in the dark. The young man, lighting a short pipe, and putting his hat on one side and one hand in his pocket, to throw himself into har-mony with his new environment, drew near to the largest and most patron-ized of the steam circuses, as the roundabouts were called by their owners. This was one of brilliant finish, and it was now in full revolution. The musical instrument around which and to whose tones the riders revolved, directed its trumpet-mouths of brass upon the young man, and the long plate-glass mirrors set at angles, which revolved with the machine, flashed the gyrating personages and hobby-horses kaleidoscopically into his eyes.

1. When first published in magazine form in England and America in 1891, *On the Western Circuit* was altered to minimize its illicit sexuality. References to Anna's seduction and pregnancy were eliminated, and Mrs. Harnham was made a widow rather than a wife. When Hardy published the story in his collection *Life's Little Ironies* (1894), he restored it to its original form. The

Western Circuit was the subdivision of England's High Court of Justice with jurisdiction over the southwestern counties. In Hardy's literary landscape, Melchester is Salisbury, which has a particularly beautiful cathedral.
2. Closed yard surrounding a church.
3. Grassy surface of ground.
4. Carousels.

It could now be seen that he was unlike the majority of the crowd. A gentlemanly young fellow, one of the species found in large towns only, and London particularly, built on delicate lines, well, though not fashionably dressed, he appeared to belong to the professional class; he had nothing square or practical about his look, much that was curvilinear and sensuous. Indeed, some would have called him a man not altogether typical of the middle-class male of a century wherein sordid ambition is the master-passion that seems to be taking the time-honoured place of love.

The revolving figures passed before his eyes with an unexpected and quiet grace in a throng whose natural movements did not suggest gracefulness or quietude as a rule. By some contrivance there was imparted to each of the hobby-horses a motion which was really the triumph and perfection of round-about inventiveness—a galloping rise and fall, so timed that, of each pair of steeds, one was on the spring while the other was on the pitch. The riders were quite fascinated by these equine undulations in this most delightful holiday-game of our times. There were riders as young as six, and as old as sixty years, with every age between. At first it was difficult to catch a personality, but by and by the observer's eyes centred on the prettiest girl out of the several pretty ones revolving.

It was not that one with the light frock and light hat whom he had been at first attracted by; no, it was the one with the black cape, grey skirt, light gloves and—no, not even she, but the one behind her; she with the crimson skirt, dark jacket, brown hat and brown gloves. Unmistakably that was the prettiest girl.

Having finally selected her, this idle spectator studied her as well as he was able during each of her brief transits across his visual field. She was absolutely unconscious of everything save the act of riding: her features were rapt in an ecstatic dreaminess; for the moment she did not know her age or her history or her lineaments, much less her troubles. He himself was full of vague latter-day glooms and popular melancholies, and it was a refreshing sensation to behold this young thing then and there, absolutely as happy as if she were in a Paradise.

Dreading the moment when the inexorable stoker, grimily lurking behind the glittering rococo-work,[5] should decide that this set of riders had had their pennyworth, and bring the whole concern of steam-engine, horses, mirrors, trumpets, drums, cymbals, and such-like to pause and silence, he waited for her every reappearance, glancing indifferently over the intervening forms, including the two plainer girls, the old woman and child, the two youngsters, the newly-married couple, the old man with a clay pipe, the sparkish youth with a ring, the young ladies in the chariot, the pair of journeyman[6]-carpenters, and others, till his select country beauty followed on again in her place. He had never seen a fairer product of nature, and at each round she made a deeper mark in his sentiments. The stoppage then came, and the sighs of the riders were audible.

He moved round to the place at which he reckoned she would alight; but she retained her seat. The empty saddles began to refill, and she plainly was

5. Florid ornamentation. "Stoker": man who stokes the furnace powering the "steam circus."
6. Craftsman who has completed an apprentice-ship but not yet attained mastership of his craft or guild.

deciding to have another turn. The young man drew up to the side of her steed, and pleasantly asked her if she had enjoyed her ride.

'O yes!' she said, with dancing eyes. 'It has been quite unlike anything I have ever felt in my life before!'

It was not difficult to fall into conversation with her. Unreserved—too unreserved—by nature, she was not experienced enough to be reserved by art, and after a little coaxing she answered his remarks readily. She had come to live in Melchester from a village on the Great Plain[7], and this was the first time that she had ever seen a steam-circus; she could not understand how such wonderful machines were made. She had come to the city on the invitation of Mrs Harnham, who had taken her into her household to train her as a servant, if she showed any aptitude. Mrs Harnham was a young lady who before she married had been Miss Edith White, living in the country near the speaker's cottage; she was now very kind to her through knowing her in childhood so well. She was even taking the trouble to educate her. Mrs Harnham was the only friend she had in the world, and being without children had wished to have her near her in preference to anybody else, though she had only lately come; allowed her to do almost as she liked, and to have a holiday whenever she asked for it. The husband of this kind young lady was a rich wine-merchant of the town, but Mrs Harnham did not care much about him. In the daytime you could see the house from where they were talking. She, the speaker, liked Melchester better than the lonely country, and she was going to have a new hat for next Sunday that was to cost fifteen and ninepence.[8]

Then she inquired of her acquaintance where he lived, and he told her in London, that ancient and smoky city, where everybody lived who lived at all, and died because they could not live there. He came into Wessex two or three times a year for professional reasons; he had arrived from Wintoncester yesterday, and was going on into the next county in a day or two. For one thing he did like the country better than the town, and it was because it contained such girls as herself.

Then the pleasure-machine started again, and, to the light-hearted girl, the figure of the handsome young man, the market-square with its lights and crowd, the houses beyond, and the world at large, began moving round as before, countermoving in the revolving mirrors on her right hand, she being as it were the fixed point in an undulating, dazzling, lurid universe, in which loomed forward most prominently of all the form of her late interlocutor. Each time that she approached the half of her orbit that lay nearest him they gazed at each other with smiles, and with that unmistakable expression which means so little at the moment, yet so often leads up to passion, heart-ache, union, disunion, devotion, overpopulation, drudgery, content, resignation, despair.

When the horses slowed anew he stepped to her side and proposed another heat. 'Hang the expense for once,' he said. 'I'll pay!'

She laughed till the tears came.

'Why do you laugh, dear?' said he.

'Because—you are so genteel that you must have plenty of money, and only say that for fun!' she returned.

---

7. In Hardy's Wessex, the Salisbury Plain, a large plateau on which stands Stonehenge.

8. Approximately one dollar.

'Ha-ha!' laughed the young man in unison, and gallantly producing his money she was enabled to whirl on again.

As he stood smiling there in the motley crowd, with his pipe in his hand, and clad in the rough pea-jacket and wideawake[9] that he had put on for his stroll, who would have supposed him to be Charles Bradford Raye, Esquire, stuff-gownsman,[1] educated at Wintoncester, called to the Bar at Lincoln's-Inn,[2] now going the Western Circuit, merely detained in Melchester by a small arbitration after his brethren had moved on to the next county-town?

II

The square was overlooked from its remoter corner by the house of which the young girl had spoken, a dignified residence of considerable size, having several windows on each floor. Inside one of these, on the first floor, the apartment being a large drawing-room, sat a lady, in appearance from twenty-eight to thirty years of age. The blinds were still undrawn, and the lady was absently surveying the weird scene without, her cheek resting on her hand. The room was unlit from within, but enough of the glare from the market-place entered it to reveal the lady's face. She was what is called an interesting creature rather than a handsome woman; dark-eyed, thoughtful, and with sensitive lips.

A man sauntered into the room from behind and came forward.

'O, Edith, I didn't see you,' he said. 'Why are you sitting here in the dark?'

'I am looking at the fair,' replied the lady in a languid voice.

'Oh? Horrid nuisance every year! I wish it could be put a stop to.'

'I like it.'

'H'm. There's no accounting for taste.'

For a moment he gazed from the window with her, for politeness sake, and then went out again.

In a few minutes she rang.

'Hasn't Anna come in?' asked Mrs Harnham.

'No m'm.'

'She ought to be in by this time. I meant her to go for ten minutes only.'

'Shall I go and look for her, m'm?' said the house-maid alertly.

'No. It is not necessary: she is a good girl and will come soon.'

However, when the servant had gone Mrs Harnham arose, went up to her room, cloaked and bonneted herself, and proceeded downstairs, where she found her husband.

'I want to see the fair,' she said; 'and I am going to look for Anna. I have made myself responsible for her, and must see she comes to no harm. She ought to be indoors. Will you come with me?'

'Oh, she's all right. I saw her on one of those whirligig things, talking to her young man as I came in. But I'll go if you wish, though I'd rather go a hundred miles the other way.'

'Then please do so. I shall come to no harm alone.'

She left the house and entered the crowd which thronged the market-

9. Soft felt hat.
1. A junior counsel, who wears a gown of "stuff" rather than silk; qualified to plead cases in court but not appointed to a senior position.
2. One of the four London Inns of Court, at which lawyers must be trained in order to qualify for the bar and to which they afterward must belong in order to practice law. "Wintoncester": Winchester College, the oldest English public school (the equivalent in the American system of an elite private secondary boarding school).

place, where she soon discovered Anna, seated on the revolving horse. As soon as it stopped Mrs Harnham advanced and said severely, 'Anna, how can you be such a wild girl? You were only to be out for ten minutes.'

Anna looked blank, and the young man, who had dropped into the background, came to help her alight.

'Please don't blame her,' he said politely. 'It is my fault that she has stayed. She looked so graceful on the horse that I induced her to go round again. I assure you that she has been quite safe.'

'In that case I'll leave her in your hands,' said Mrs Harnham, turning to retrace her steps.

But this for the moment it was not so easy to do. Something had attracted the crowd to a spot in their rear, and the wine-merchant's wife, caught by its sway, found herself pressed against Anna's acquaintance without power to move away. Their faces were within a few inches of each other, his breath fanned her cheek as well as Anna's. They could do no other than smile at the accident; but neither spoke, and each waited passively. Mrs Harnham then felt a man's hand clasping her fingers, and from the look of consciousness on the young fellow's face she knew the hand to be his: she also knew that from the position of the girl he had no other thought than that the imprisoned hand was Anna's. What prompted her to refrain from undeceiving him she could hardly tell. Not content with holding the hand, he playfully slipped two of his fingers inside her glove, against her palm. Thus matters continued till the pressure lessened; but several minutes passed before the crowd thinned sufficiently to allow Mrs Harnham to withdraw.

'How did they get to know each other, I wonder?' she mused as she retreated. 'Anna is really very forward—and he very wicked and nice.'

She was so gently stirred with the stranger's manner and voice, with the tenderness of his idle touch, that instead of re-entering the house she turned back again and observed the pair from a screened nook. Really she argued (being little less impulsive than Anna herself) it was very excusable in Anna to encourage him, however she might have contrived to make his acquaintance; he was so gentlemanly, so fascinating, had such beautiful eyes. The thought that he was several years her junior produced a reasonless sigh.

At length the couple turned from the roundabout towards the door of Mrs Harnham's house, and the young man could be heard saying that he would accompany her home. Anna, then, had found a lover, apparently a very devoted one. Mrs Harnham was quite interested in him. When they drew near the door of the wine-merchant's house, a comparatively deserted spot by this time, they stood invisible for a little while in the shadow of a wall, where they separated, Anna going on to the entrance, and her acquaintance returning across the square.

'Anna,' said Mrs Harnham, coming up. 'I've been looking at you! That young man kissed you at parting, I am almost sure.'

'Well,' stammered Anna; 'he said, if I didn't mind—it would do me no harm, and, and, him a great deal of good!'

'Ah, I thought so! And he was a stranger till tonight?'

'Yes ma'am.'

'Yet I warrant you told him your name and everything about yourself?'

'He asked me.'

'But he didn't tell you his?'

'Yes ma'am, he did!' cried Anna victoriously. 'It is Charles Bradford, of London.'

'Well, if he's respectable, of course I've nothing to say against your knowing him,' remarked her mistress, prepossessed, in spite of general principles, in the young man's favour. 'But I must reconsider all that, if he attempts to renew your acquaintance. A country-bred girl like you, who has never lived in Melchester till this month, who had hardly ever seen a black-coated man till you came here, to be so sharp as to capture a young Londoner like him!'

'I didn't capture him. I didn't do anything,' said Anna, in confusion.

When she was indoors and alone Mrs Harnham thought what a well-bred and chivalrous young man Anna's companion had seemed. There had been a magic in his wooing touch of her hand; and she wondered how he had come to be attracted by the girl.

The next morning the emotional Edith Harnham went to the usual week-day service in Melchester cathedral. In crossing the Close through the fog she again perceived him who had interested her the previous evening, gazing up thoughtfully at the high-piled architecture of the nave: and as soon as she had taken her seat he entered and sat down in a stall opposite hers.

He did not particularly heed her; but Mrs Harnham was continually occupying her eyes with him, and wondered more than ever what had attracted him in her unfledged maid-servant. The mistress was almost as unaccustomed as the maiden herself to the end-of-the-age young man, or she might have wondered less. Raye, having looked about him awhile, left abruptly, without regard to the service that was proceeding; and Mrs Harnham— lonely, impressionable creature that she was—took no further interest in praising the Lord. She wished she had married a London man who knew the subtleties of love-making as they were evidently known to him who had mistakenly caressed her hand.

III

The calendar at Melchester had been light, occupying the court only a few hours; and the assizes[3] at Casterbridge, the next county-town on the Western Circuit, having no business for Raye, he had not gone thither. At the next town after that they did not open till the following Monday, trials to begin on Tuesday morning. In the natural order of things Raye would have arrived at the latter place on Monday afternoon; but it was not till the middle of Wednesday that his gown and grey wig, curled in tiers, in the best fashion of Assyrian bas-reliefs, were seen blowing and bobbing behind him as he hastily walked up the High Street from his lodgings. But though he entered the assize building there was nothing for him to do, and sitting at the blue baize table in the well of the court, he mended pens with a mind far away from the case in progress. Thoughts of unpremeditated conduct, of which a week earlier he would not have believed himself capable, threw him into a mood of dissatisfied depression.

He had contrived to see again the pretty rural maiden Anna, the day after the fair, had walked out of the city with her to the earthworks[4] of Old Mel-

---

3. Sessions of the superior court. "Calendar": list of cases to be tried.

4. Banks of earth constructed as fortifications in ancient times.

chester, and feeling a violent fancy for her, had remained in Melchester all Sunday, Monday, and Tuesday; by persuasion obtaining walks and meetings with the girl six or seven times during the interval; had in brief won her, body and soul.

He supposed it must have been owing to the seclusion in which he had lived of late in town that he had given way so unrestrainedly to a passion for an artless creature whose inexperience had, from the first, led her to place herself unreservedly in his hands. Much he deplored trifling with her feelings for the sake of a passing desire; and he could only hope that she might not live to suffer on his account.

She had begged him to come to her again; entreated him; wept. He had promised that he would do so, and he meant to carry out that promise. He could not desert her now. Awkward as such unintentional connections were, the interspace of a hundred miles—which to a girl of her limited capabilities was like a thousand—would effectually hinder this summer fancy from greatly encumbering his life; while thought of her simple love might do him the negative good of keeping him from idle pleasures in town when he wished to work hard. His circuit journeys would take him to Melchester three or four times a year; and then he could always see her.

The pseudonym, or rather partial name, that he had given her as his before knowing how far the acquaintance was going to carry him, had been spoken on the spur of the moment, without any ulterior intention whatever. He had not afterwards disturbed Anna's error, but on leaving her he had felt bound to give her an address at a stationer's not far from his chambers, at which she might write to him under the initials 'C. B'.

In due time Raye returned to his London abode, having called at Melchester on his way and spent a few additional hours with his fascinating child of nature. In town he lived monotonously every day. Often he and his rooms were enclosed by a tawny fog from all the world besides, and when he lighted the gas to read or write by, his situation seemed so unnatural that he would look into the fire and think of that trusting girl at Melchester again and again. Often, oppressed by absurd fondness for her, he would enter the dim religious nave of the Law Courts by the north door, elbow other juniors habited like himself, and like him unretained; edge himself into this or that crowded court where a sensational case was going on, just as if he were in it, though the police officers at the door knew as well as he knew himself that he had no more concern with the business in hand than the patient idlers at the gallery-door outside, who had waited to enter since eight in the morning because, like him, they belonged to the classes that live on expectation. But he would do these things to no purpose, and think how greatly the characters in such scenes contrasted with the pink and breezy Anna.

An unexpected feature in that peasant maiden's conduct was that she had not as yet written to him, though he had told her she might do so if she wished. Surely a young creature had never before been so reticent in such circumstances. At length he sent her a brief line, positively requesting her to write. There was no answer by the return post, but the day after a letter in a neat feminine hand, and bearing the Melchester post-mark, was handed to him by the stationer.

The fact alone of its arrival was sufficient to satisfy his imaginative sentiment. He was not anxious to open the epistle, and in truth did not begin to read it for nearly half-an-hour, anticipating readily its terms of passionate retrospect and tender adjuration. When at last he turned his feet to the fireplace and unfolded the sheet, he was surprised and pleased to find that neither extravagance nor vulgarity was there. It was the most charming little missive he had ever received from woman. To be sure the language was simple and the ideas were slight; but it was so self-possessed; so purely that of a young girl who felt her womanhood to be enough for her dignity that he read it twice. Four sides were filled, and a few lines written across, after the fashion of former days; the paper, too, was common, and not of the latest shade and surface. But what of those things? He had received letters from women who were fairly called ladies, but never so sensible, so human a letter as this. He could not single out any one sentence and say it was at all remarkable or clever; the *ensemble* of the letter it was which won him; and beyond the one request that he would write or come to her again soon there was nothing to show her sense of a claim upon him.

To write again and develop a correspondence was the last thing Raye would have preconceived as his conduct in such a situation; yet he did send a short, encouraging line or two, signed with his pseudonym, in which he asked for another letter, and cheeringly promised that he would try to see her again on some near day, and would never forget how much they had been to each other during their short acquaintance.

IV

To return now to the moment at which Anna, at Melchester, had received Raye's letter.

It had been put into her own hand by the postman on his morning rounds. She flushed down to her neck on receipt of it, and turned it over and over. 'It is mine?' she said.

'Why, yes, can't you see it is?' said the postman, smiling as he guessed the nature of the document and the cause of the confusion.

'O yes, of course!' replied Anna, looking at the letter, forcedly tittering, and blushing still more.

Her look of embarrassment did not leave her with the postman's departure. She opened the envelope, kissed its contents, put away the letter in her pocket, and remained musing till her eyes filled with tears.

A few minutes later she carried up a cup of tea to Mrs Harnham in her bed-chamber. Anna's mistress looked at her, and said: 'How dismal you seem this morning, Anna. What's the matter?'

'I'm not dismal, I'm glad; only I—' She stopped to stifle a sob.

'Well?'

'I've got a letter—and what good is it to me, if I can't read a word in it!'

'Why, I'll read it, child, if necessary.'

'But this is from somebody—I don't want anybody to read it but myself!' Anna murmured.

'I shall not tell anybody. Is it from that young man?'

'I think so.' Anna slowly produced the letter, saying: 'Then will you read it to me, ma'am?'

This was the secret of Anna's embarrassment and flutterings. She could neither read nor write. She had grown up under the care of an aunt by marriage, at one of the lonely hamlets on the Great Mid-Wessex Plain where, even in days of national education, there had been no school within a distance of two miles. Her aunt was an ignorant woman; there had been nobody to investigate Anna's circumstances, nobody to care about her learning the rudiments; though, as often in such cases, she had been well fed and clothed and not unkindly treated. Since she had come to live at Melchester with Mrs Harnham, the latter, who took a kindly interest in the girl, had taught her to speak correctly, in which accomplishment Anna showed considerable readiness, as is not unusual with the illiterate; and soon became quite fluent in the use of her mistress's phraseology. Mrs Harnham also insisted upon her getting a spelling and copy book, and beginning to practise in these. Anna was slower in this branch of her education, and meanwhile here was the letter.

Edith Harnham's large dark eyes expressed some interest in the contents, though, in her character of mere interpreter, she threw into her tone as much as she could of mechanical passiveness. She read the short epistle on to its concluding sentence, which idly requested Anna to send him a tender answer.

'Now—you'll do it for me, won't you, dear mistress?' said Anna eagerly. 'And you'll do it as well as ever you can, please? Because I couldn't bear him to think I am not able to do it myself. I should sink into the earth with shame if he knew that!'

From some words in the letter Mrs Harnham was led to ask questions, and the answers she received confirmed her suspicions. Deep concern filled Edith's heart at perceiving how the girl had committed her happiness to the issue of this new-sprung attachment. She blamed herself for not interfering in a flirtation which had resulted so seriously for the poor little creature in her charge; though at the time of seeing the pair together she had a feeling that it was hardly within her province to nip young affection in the bud. However, what was done could not be undone, and it behoved her now, as Anna's only protector, to help her as much as she could. To Anna's eager request that she, Mrs Harnham, should compose and write the answer to this young London man's letter, she felt bound to accede, to keep alive his attachment to the girl if possible; though in other circumstances she might have suggested the cook as an amanuensis.[5]

A tender reply was thereupon concocted, and set down in Edith Harnham's hand. This letter it had been which Raye had received and delighted in. Written in the presence of Anna it certainly was, and on Anna's humble note-paper, and in a measure indited by the young girl; but the life, the spirit, the individuality, were Edith Harnham's.

'Won't you at least put your name yourself?' she said. 'You can manage to write that by this time?'

'No, no,' said Anna, shrinking back. 'I should do it so bad. He'd be ashamed of me, and never see me again!'

The note, so prettily requesting another from him, had, as we have seen, power enough in its pages to bring one. He declared it to be such a pleasure to hear from her that she must write every week. The same process of manufacture was accordingly repeated by Anna and her mistress, and continued

5. Secretary.

for several weeks in succession; each letter being penned and suggested by Edith, the girl standing by; the answer read and commented on by Edith, Anna standing by and listening again.

Late on a winter evening, after the dispatch of the sixth letter, Mrs Harnham was sitting alone by the remains of her fire. Her husband had retired to bed, and she had fallen into that fixity of musing which takes no count of hour or temperature. The state of mind had been brought about in Edith by a strange thing which she had done that day. For the first time since Raye's visit Anna had gone to stay over a night or two with her cottage friends on the Plain, and in her absence had arrived, out of its time, a letter from Raye. To this Edith had replied on her own responsibility, from the depths of her own heart, without waiting for her maid's collaboration. The luxury of writing to him what would be known to no consciousness but his was great, and she had indulged herself therein.

Why was it a luxury?

Edith Harnham led a lonely life. Influenced by the belief of the British parent that a bad marriage with its aversions is better than free womanhood with its interests, dignity, and leisure, she had consented to marry the elderly wine-merchant as a *pis aller,*[6] at the age of seven-and-twenty—some three years before this date—to find afterwards that she had made a mistake. That contract had left her still a woman whose deeper nature had never been stirred.

She was now clearly realising that she had become possessed to the bottom of her soul with the image of a man to whom she was hardly so much as a name. From the first he had attracted her by his looks and voice; by his tender touch; and, with these as generators, the writing of letter after letter and the reading of their soft answers had insensibly developed on her side an emotion which fanned his; till there had resulted a magnetic reciprocity between the correspondents, notwithstanding that one of them wrote in a character not her own. That he had been able to seduce another woman in two days was his crowning though unrecognised fascination for her as the she-animal.

They were her own impassioned and pent-up ideas—lowered to monosyllabic phraseology in order to keep up the disguise—that Edith put into letters signed with another name, much to the shallow Anna's delight, who, unassisted, could not for the world have conceived such pretty fancies for winning him, even had she been able to write them. Edith found that it was these, her own foisted-in sentiments, to which the young barrister mainly responded. The few sentences occasionally added from Anna's own lips made apparently no impression upon him.

The letter-writing in her absence Anna never discovered; but on her return the next morning she declared she wished to see her lover about something at once, and begged Mrs Harnham to ask him to come.

There was a strange anxiety in her manner which did not escape Mrs Harnham, and ultimately resolved itself into a flood of tears. Sinking down at Edith's knees, she made confession that the result of her relations with her lover it would soon become necessary to disclose.

Edith Harnham was generous enough to be very far from inclined to cast

6. Last resort (French).

Anna adrift at this conjuncture. No true woman ever is so inclined from her own personal point of view, however prompt she may be in taking such steps to safeguard those dear to her. Although she had written to Raye so short a time previously, she instantly penned another Anna-note hinting clearly though delicately the state of affairs.

Raye replied by a hasty line to say how much he was concerned at her news: he felt that he must run down to see her almost immediately.

But a week later the girl came to her mistress's room with another note, which on being read informed her that after all he could not find time for the journey. Anna was broken with grief; but by Mrs Harnham's counsel strictly refrained from hurling at him the reproaches and bitterness customary from young women so situated. One thing was imperative: to keep the young man's romantic interest in her alive. Rather therefore did Edith, in the name of her *protégée*, request him on no account to be distressed about the looming event, and not to inconvenience himself to hasten down. She desired above everything to be no weight upon him in his career, no clog upon his high activities. She had wished him to know what had befallen: he was to dismiss it again from his mind. Only he must write tenderly as ever, and when he should come again on the spring circuit it would be soon enough to discuss what had better be done.

It may well be supposed that Anna's own feelings had not been quite in accord with these generous expressions; but the mistress's judgment had ruled, and Anna had acquiesced. 'All I want is that *niceness* you can so well put into your letters, my dear, dear mistress, and that I can't for the life o' me make up out of my own head; though I mean the same thing and feel it exactly when you've written it down!'

When the letter had been sent off, and Edith Harnham was left alone, she bowed herself on the back of her chair and wept.

'I wish his child was mine—I wish it was!' she murmured. 'Yet how can I say such a wicked thing!'

V

The letter moved Raye considerably when it reached him. The intelligence itself had affected him less than her unexpected manner of treating him in relation to it. The absence of any word of reproach, the devotion to his interests, the self-sacrifice apparent in every line, all made up a nobility of character that he had never dreamt of finding in womankind.

'God forgive me!' he said tremulously. 'I have been a wicked wretch. I did not know she was such a treasure as this!'

He reassured her instantly; declaring that he would not of course desert her, that he would provide a home for her somewhere. Meanwhile she was to stay where she was as long as her mistress would allow her.

But a misfortune supervened in this direction. Whether an inkling of Anna's circumstances reached the knowledge of Mrs Harnham's husband or not cannot be said, but the girl was compelled, in spite of Edith's entreaties, to leave the house. By her own choice she decided to go back for a while to the cottage on the Plain. This arrangement led to a consultation as to how the correspondence should be carried on; and in the girl's inability to continue personally what had been begun in her name, and in the difficulty of their acting in concert as heretofore, she requested Mrs Harnham—the only well-to-do friend she had in the world—to receive the letters and reply to them off-hand, sending them on afterwards to herself on the Plain, where she might at least get some neighbour to read them to her, if a trustworthy one could be met with. Anna and her box then departed for the Plain.

Thus it befell that Edith Harnham found herself in the strange position of having to correspond, under no supervision by the real woman, with a man not her husband, in terms which were virtually those of a wife, concerning a corporeal condition that was not Edith's at all; the man being one for whom, mainly through the sympathies involved in playing this part, she secretly cherished a predilection, subtle and imaginative truly, but strong and absorbing. She opened each letter, read it as if intended for herself, and replied from the promptings of her own heart and no other.

Throughout this correspondence, carried on in the girl's absence, the high-strung Edith Harnham lived in the ecstasy of fancy; the vicarious intimacy engendered such a flow of passionateness as was never exceeded. For conscience' sake Edith at first sent on each of his letters to Anna, and even rough copies of her replies; but later on these so-called copies were much abridged, and many letters on both sides were not sent on at all.

Though sensuous, and, superficially at least, infested with the self-indulgent vices of artificial society, there was a substratum of honesty and fairness in Raye's character. He had really a tender regard for the country girl, and it grew more tender than ever when he found her apparently capable of expressing the deepest sensibilities in the simplest words. He meditated, he wavered; and finally resolved to consult his sister, a maiden lady much older than himself, of lively sympathies and good intent. In making this confidence he showed her some of the letters.

'She seems fairly educated,' Miss Raye observed. 'And bright in ideas. She expresses herself with a taste that must be innate.'

'Yes. She writes very prettily, doesn't she, thanks to these elementary schools?'

'One is drawn out towards her, in spite of one's self, poor thing.'

The upshot of the discussion was that though he had not been directly advised to do it, Raye wrote, in his real name, what he would never have decided to write on his own responsibility; namely that he could not live without her, and would come down in the spring and shelve her looming difficulty by marrying her.

This bold acceptance of the situation was made known to Anna by Mrs Harnham driving out immediately to the cottage on the Plain. Anna jumped for joy like a little child. And poor, crude directions for answering appropriately were given to Edith Harnham, who on her return to the city carried them out with warm intensifications.

'O!' she groaned, as she threw down the pen. 'Anna—poor good little fool—hasn't intelligence enough to appreciate him! How should she? While I—don't bear his child!'

It was now February. The correspondence had continued altogether for four months; and the next letter from Raye contained incidentally a statement of his position and prospects. He said that in offering to wed her he had, at first, contemplated the step of retiring from a profession which hitherto had brought him very slight emolument, and which, to speak plainly, he had thought might be difficult of practice after his union with her. But the unexpected mines of brightness and warmth that her letters had disclosed to be lurking in her sweet nature had led him to abandon that somewhat sad prospect. He felt sure that, with her powers of development, after a little private training in the social forms of London under his supervision, and a little help from a governess if necessary, she would make as good a professional man's wife as could be desired, even if he should rise to the woolsack.[7] Many a Lord Chancellor's wife had been less intuitively a lady than she had shown herself to be in her lines to him.

'O—poor fellow, poor fellow!' mourned Edith Harnham.

Her distress now raged as high as her infatuation. It was she who had wrought him to this pitch—to a marriage which meant his ruin; yet she could not, in mercy to her maid, do anything to hinder his plan. Anna was coming to Melchester that week, but she could hardly show the girl this last reply from the young man; it told too much of the second individuality that had usurped the place of the first.

Anna came, and her mistress took her into her own room for privacy. Anna began by saying with some anxiety that she was glad the wedding was so near.

'O Anna!' replied Mrs Harnham. 'I think we must tell him all—that I have been doing your writing for you?—lest he should not know it till after you become his wife, and it might lead to dissension and recriminations—'

'O mis'ess, dear mis'ess—please don't tell him now!' cried Anna in distress. 'If you were to do it, perhaps he would not marry me; and what should I do then? It would be terrible what would come to me! And I am getting on with my writing, too. I have brought with me the copybook you were so good as to give me, and I practise every day, and though it is so, so hard, I shall do it well at last, I believe, if I keep on trying.'

Edith looked at the copybook. The copies had been set by herself, and such progress as the girl had made was in the way of grotesque facsimile of her mistress's hand. But even if Edith's flowing calligraphy were reproduced the inspiration would be another thing.

'You do it so beautifully,' continued Anna, 'and say all that I want to say so much better than I could say it, that I do hope you won't leave me in the lurch just now!'

'Very well,' replied the other. 'But I—but I thought I ought not to go on!' 'Why?'

Her strong desire to confide her sentiments led Edith to answer truly:

'Because of its effect upon me.'

'But it can't have any!'

'Why, child?'

'Because you are married already!' said Anna with lucid simplicity.

'Of course it can't,' said her mistress hastily; yet glad, despite her conscience, that two or three out-pourings still remained to her. 'But you must concentrate your attention on writing your name as I write it here.'

---

7. Seat of the Lord Chancellor in the House of Lords, formerly made of a sack of wool.

VI

Soon Raye wrote about the wedding. Having decided to make the best of what he feared was a piece of romantic folly, he had acquired more zest for the grand experiment. He wished the ceremony to be in London, for greater privacy. Edith Harnham would have preferred it at Melchester; Anna was passive. His reasoning prevailed, and Mrs Harnham threw herself with mournful zeal into the preparations for Anna's departure. In a last desperate feeling that she must at every hazard be in at the death of her dream, and see once again the man who by a species of telepathy had exercised such an influence on her, she offered to go up with Anna and be with her through the ceremony—'to see the end of her,' as her mistress put it with forced gaiety; an offer which the girl gratefully accepted; for she had no other friend capable of playing the part of companion and witness, in the presence of a gentlemanly bridegroom, in such a way as not to hasten an opinion that he had made an irremediable social blunder.

It was a muddy morning in March when Raye alighted from a four-wheel cab at the door of a registry-office in the S.W. district of London, and carefully handed down Anna and her companion Mrs Harnham. Anna looked attractive in the somewhat fashionable clothes which Mrs Harnham had helped her to buy, though not quite so attractive as, an innocent child, she had appeared in her country gown on the back of the wooden horse at Melchester Fair.

Mrs Harnham had come up this morning by an early train, and a young man—a friend of Raye's—having met them at the door, all four entered the registry-office together. Till an hour before this time Raye had never known the wine-merchant's wife, except at that first casual encounter, and in the flutter of the performance before them he had little opportunity for more than a brief acquaintance. The contract of marriage at a registry is soon got through; but somehow, during its progress, Raye discovered a strange and secret gravitation between himself and Anna's friend.

The formalities of the wedding—or rather ratification of a previous union—being concluded, the four went in one cab to Raye's lodgings, newly taken in a new suburb in preference to a house, the rent of which he could ill afford just then. Here Anna cut the little cake which Raye had bought at a pastrycook's on his way home from Lincoln's Inn the night before. But she did not do much besides. Raye's friend was obliged to depart almost immediately, and when he had left the only ones virtually present were Edith and Raye, who exchanged ideas with much animation. The conversation was indeed theirs only, Anna being as a domestic animal who humbly heard but understood not. Raye seemed startled in awakening to this fact, and began to feel dissatisfied with her inadequacy.

At last, more disappointed than he cared to own, he said, 'Mrs Harnham, my darling is so flurried that she doesn't know what she is doing or saying. I see that after this event a little quietude will be necessary before she gives tongue to that tender philosophy which she used to treat me to in her letters.'

They had planned to start early that afternoon for Knollsea, to spend the few opening days of their married life there, and as the hour for departure was drawing near Raye asked his wife if she would go to the writing-desk in the next room and scribble a little note to his sister, who had been unable to attend through indisposition, informing her that the ceremony was over, thanking her for her little present, and hoping to know her well now that she was the writer's sister as well as Charles's.

'Say it in the pretty poetical way you know so well how to adopt,' he added, 'for I want you particularly to win her, and both of you to be dear friends.'

Anna looked uneasy, but departed to her task, Raye remaining to talk to their guest. Anna was a long while absent, and her husband suddenly rose and went to her.

He found her still bending over the writing-table, with tears brimming up in her eyes; and he looked down upon the sheet of note-paper with some interest, to discover with what tact she had expressed her good-will in the delicate circumstances. To his surprise she had progressed but a few lines, in the characters and spelling of a child of eight, and with the ideas of a goose.

'Anna,' he said, staring; 'what's this?'

'It only means—that I can't do it any better!' she answered, through her tears.

'Eh? Nonsense!'

'I can't!' she insisted, with miserable, sobbing hardihood. 'I—I—didn't write those letters, Charles! I only told *her* what to write! And not always that! But I am learning, O so fast, my dear, dear husband! And you'll forgive me, won't you, for not telling you before?' She slid to her knees, abjectly clasped his waist and laid her face against him.

He stood a few moments, raised her, abruptly turned, and shut the door upon her, rejoining Edith in the drawing-room. She saw that something untoward had been discovered, and their eyes remained fixed on each other.

'Do I guess rightly?' he asked, with wan quietude. '*You* were her scribe through all this?'

'It was necessary,' said Edith.

'Did she dictate every word you ever wrote to me?'

'Not every word.'

'In fact, very little?'

'Very little.'

'You wrote a great part of those pages every week from your own conceptions, though in her name!'

'Yes.'

'Perhaps you wrote many of the letters when you were alone, without communication with her?'

'I did.'

He turned to the bookcase, and leant with his hand over his face; and Edith, seeing his distress, became white as a sheet.

'You have deceived me—ruined me!' he murmured.

'O, don't say it!' she cried in her anguish, jumping up and putting her hand on his shoulder. 'I can't bear that!'

'Delighting me deceptively! Why did you do it—*why* did you!'

'I began doing it in kindness to her! How could I do otherwise than try to save such a simple girl from misery? But I admit that I continued it for pleasure to myself.'

Raye looked up. 'Why did it give you pleasure?' he asked.

'I must not tell,' said she.

He continued to regard her, and saw that her lips suddenly began to quiver under his scrutiny, and her eyes to fill and droop. She started aside, and said that she must go to the station to catch the return train: could a cab be called immediately?

But Raye went up to her, and took her unresisting hand. 'Well, to think of such a thing as this!' he said. 'Why, you and I are friends—lovers—devoted lovers—by correspondence!'

'Yes; I suppose.'

'More.'

'More?'

'Plainly more. It is no use blinking that. Legally I have married her—God help us both!—in soul and spirit I have married you, and no other woman in the world!'

'Hush!'

'But I will not hush! Why should you try to disguise the full truth, when you have already owned half of it? Yes, it is between you and me that the bond is—not between me and her! Now I'll say no more. But, O my cruel one, I think I have one claim upon you!'

She did not say what, and he drew her towards him, and bent over her. 'If it was all pure invention in those letters,' he said emphatically, 'give me your cheek only. If you meant what you said, let it be lips. It is for the first and last time, remember!'

She put up her mouth, and he kissed her long. 'You forgive me?' she said, crying.

'Yes.'

'But you are ruined!'

'What matter!' he said, shrugging his shoulders. 'It serves me right!'

She withdrew, wiped her eyes, entered and bade good-bye to Anna, who had not expected her to go so soon, and was still wrestling with the letter. Raye followed Edith downstairs, and in three minutes she was in a hansom driving to the Waterloo station.

He went back to his wife. 'Never mind the letter, Anna, to-day,' he said gently. 'Put on your things. We, too, must be off shortly.'

The simple girl, upheld by the sense that she was indeed married, showed her delight at finding that he was as kind as ever after the disclosure. She did not know that before his eyes he beheld as it were a galley, in which he, the fastidious urban, was chained to work for the remainder of his life, with her, the unlettered peasant, chained to his side.

Edith travelled back to Melchester that day with a face that showed the very stupor of grief, her lips still tingling from the desperate pressure of his kiss. The end of her impassioned dream had come. When at dusk she reached the Melchester station her husband was there to meet her, but in his perfunctoriness and her preoccupation they did not see each other, and she went out of the station alone.

She walked mechanically homewards without calling a fly.[8] Entering, she could not bear the silence of the house, and went up in the dark to where

8. Carriage.

Anna had slept, where she remained thinking awhile. She then returned to the drawing-room, and not knowing what she did, crouched down upon the floor.

'I have ruined him!' she kept repeating. 'I have ruined him; because I would not deal treacherously towards her!'

In the course of half an hour a figure opened the door of the apartment. 'Ah—who's that?' she said, starting up, for it was dark.

'Your husband—who should it be?' said the worthy merchant.

'Ah—my husband!—I forgot I had a husband!' she whispered to herself.

'I missed you at the station,' he continued. 'Did you see Anna safely tied up? I hope so, for 'twas time.'

'Yes—Anna is married.'

Simultaneously with Edith's journey home Anna and her husband were sitting at the opposite windows of a second-class carriage which sped along to Knollsea. In his hand was a pocket-book full of creased sheets closely written over. Unfolding them one after another he read them in silence, and sighed.

'What are you doing, dear Charles?' she said timidly from the other window, and drew nearer to him as if he were a god.

'Reading over all those sweet letters to me signed "Anna," ' he replied with dreary resignation.

1891

Hap[1]

<blockquote>

If but some vengeful god would call to me
From up the sky, and laugh: "Thou suffering thing,
Know that thy sorrow is my ecstasy,
That thy love's loss is my hate's profiting!"

⁵ Then would I bear it, clench myself, and die,
Steeled by the sense of ire° unmerited;   *anger*
Half-eased in that a Powerfuller than I
Had willed and meted° me the tears I shed.   *allotted, given*

But not so. How arrives it joy lies slain,
¹⁰ And why unblooms the best hope ever sown?
—Crass Casualty obstructs the sun and rain,
And dicing Time for gladness casts a moan . . . .
These purblind Doomsters[2] had as readily strown
Blisses about my pilgrimage as pain.

</blockquote>

<table>
<tr><td>1866</td><td align="right">1898</td></tr>
</table>

---

1. I.e., chance (as also "Casualty," line 11).   2. Half-blind judges.

The Impercipient[1]

(At a Cathedral Service)

That with this bright believing band
 I have no claim to be,
That faiths by which my comrades stand
 Seem fantasies to me,
5 And mirage-mists their Shining Land,
 Is a strange destiny.

Why thus my soul should be consigned
 To infelicity,
Why always I must feel as blind
10 To sights my brethren see,
Why joys they have found I cannot find,
 Abides a mystery.

Since heart of mine knows not that ease
 Which they know; since it be
15 That He who breathes All's Well to these
 Breathes no All's-Well to me,
My lack might move their sympathies
 And Christian charity!

I am like a gazer who should mark
20 An inland company
Standing upfingered, with, "Hark! hark!
 The glorious distant sea!"
And feel, "Alas, 'tis but yon dark
 And wind-swept pine to me!"

25 Yet I would bear my shortcomings
 With meet tranquillity,
But for the charge that blessed things
 I'd liefer[2] not have be.
O, doth a bird beshorn of wings
30 Go earth-bound wilfully!

• • •

Enough. As yet disquiet clings
 About us. Rest shall we.

1898

Neutral Tones

We stood by a pond that winter day,
And the sun was white, as though chidden of° God, *rebuked by*

---

1. An unperceiving person.   2. I would prefer.

And a few leaves lay on the starving sod°   *turf*
    —They had fallen from an ash, and were grey.

5   Your eyes on me were as eyes that rove
    Over tedious riddles of years ago;
    And some words played between us to and fro
        On which lost the more by our love.

    The smile on your mouth was the deadest thing
10 Alive enough to have strength to die;
    And a grin of bitterness swept thereby
        Like an ominous bird a-wing . . .

    Since then, keen lessons that love deceives,
    And wrings with wrong, have shaped to me
15 Your face, and the God-curst sun, and a tree,
        And a pond edged with greyish leaves.

1867   1898

I Look into My Glass[1]

    I look into my glass,
    And view my wasting skin,
    And say, "Would God it came to pass
    My heart had shrunk as thin!"

5   For then, I, undistrest
    By hearts grown cold to me,
    Could lonely wait my endless rest
    With equanimity.

    But Time, to make me grieve,
10 Part steals, lets part abide;
    And shakes this fragile frame at eve
    With throbbings of noontide.

                                                                                1898

A Broken Appointment

    You did not come.
    And marching Time drew on, and wore me numb.—
    Yet less for loss of your dear presence there
    Than that I thus found lacking in your make
5   That high compassion which can overbear
    Reluctance for pure lovingkindness' sake
    Grieved I, when, as the hope-hour stroked its sum,
        You did not come.

1. Mirror.

You love not me,
10   And love alone can lend you loyalty;
     —I know and knew it. But, unto the store
     Of human deeds divine in all but name,
     Was it not worth a little hour or more
     To add yet this: Once you, a woman, came
15   To soothe a time-torn man; even though it be
          You love not me?

1902

Drummer Hodge

I

     They throw in Drummer Hodge, to rest
          Uncoffined—just as found:
     His landmark is a kopje-crest
          That breaks the veldt¹ around;
5   And foreign constellations² west°   set
          Each night above his mound.

2

     Young Hodge the Drummer never knew—
          Fresh from his Wessex home—
     The meaning of the broad Karoo,³
10   The Bush,⁴ the dusty loam,
     And why uprose to nightly view
          Strange stars amid the gloam.

3

     Yet portion of that unknown plain
          Will Hodge for ever be;
15   His homely Northern breast and brain
          Grow to some Southern tree,
     And strange-eyed constellations reign
          His stars eternally.

1899   1902

The Darkling¹ Thrush

     I leant upon a coppice gate²
          When Frost was spectre-grey,
     And Winter's dregs made desolate
          The weakening eye of day.

1. South African Dutch (Afrikaans) word for a plain or prairie. "Kopje-crest": Afrikaans for a small hill. The poem is a lament for an English soldier killed in the Boer War (1899–1902).
2. Those visible only in the Southern Hemisphere.
3. A dry tableland region in South Africa (usually spelled "Karroo").
4. British colonial word for an uncleared area of land.
1. In the dark.
2. Gate leading to a small wood or thicket.

5 The tangled bine-stems[3] scored the sky
   Like strings of broken lyres,
And all mankind that haunted nigh°   *near*
   Had sought their household fires.

The land's sharp features seemed to be
10   The Century's corpse outleant,[4]
His crypt the cloudy canopy,
   The wind his death-lament.
The ancient pulse of germ and birth
   Was shrunken hard and dry,
15 And every spirit upon earth
   Seemed fervourless as I.

At once a voice arose among
   The bleak twigs overhead
In a full-hearted evensong
20   Of joy illimited;
An aged thrush, frail, gaunt, and small,
   In blast-beruffled plume,
Had chosen thus to fling his soul
   Upon the growing gloom.

25 So little cause for carolings
   Of such ecstatic sound
Was written on terrestrial things
   Afar or nigh around,
That I could think there trembled through
30   His happy good-night air
Some blessed Hope, whereof he knew
   And I was unaware.

1900   1901

The Ruined Maid

"O 'Melia,[1] my dear, this does everything crown!
Who could have supposed I should meet you in Town?
And whence such fair garments, such prosperi-ty?"—
"O didn't you know I'd been ruined?" said she.

5 —"You left us in tatters, without shoes or socks,
Tired of digging potatoes, and spudding up docks;[2]
And now you've gay bracelets and bright feathers three!"—
"Yes: that's how we dress when we're ruined," said she.

—"At home in the barton° you said 'thee' and 'thou,'   *farmyard*
10 And 'thik oon,' and 'theäs oon,' and 't'other'; but now

---

3. Twining stems of shrubs.
4. Leaning out (of its coffin); i.e., the 19th century
was dead. This poem was written on December 31,

1900.
1. Diminutive form of Amelia.
2. Digging up a species of thick-rooted weed.

Your talking quite fits 'ee for high compa-ny!"—
"Some polish is gained with one's ruin," said she.

—"Your hands were like paws then, your face blue and bleak
But now I'm bewitched by your delicate cheek,
15   And your little gloves fit as on any la-dy!"—
"We never do work when we're ruined," said she.

—"You used to call home-life a hag-ridden dream,
And you'd sigh, and you'd sock;° but at present you seem   *sigh*
To know not of megrims° or melancho-ly!"—   *low spirits*
20   "True. One's pretty lively when ruined," said she.

—"I wish I had feathers, a fine sweeping gown,
And a delicate face, and could strut about Town!"—
"My dear—a raw country girl, such as you be,
Cannot quite expect that. You ain't ruined," said she.

1866   1901

A Trampwoman's Tragedy

(182–)

1

From Wynyard's Gap[1] the livelong day,
        The livelong day,
We beat afoot the northward way
        We had travelled times before.
5   The sun-blaze burning on our backs,
Our shoulders sticking to our packs,
By fosseway,[2] fields, and turnpike tracks
        We skirted sad Sedge-Moor.[3]

2

Full twenty miles we jaunted on,
10   We jaunted on,—
My fancy-man, and jeering John,
        And Mother Lee, and I.
And, as the sun drew down to west,
We climbed the toilsome Poldon crest,
15   And saw, of landskip° sights the best,   *landscape*
        The inn that beamed thereby.

3

For months we had padded side by side,
        Ay, side by side

1. The places named are in Somerset, in south-west England on the northern edge of the area that Hardy called "Wessex" and of which his native Dorset, the county south and southwest of Somerset, reaching to the English Channel, was the major part.

2. Path running along a ditch.
3. Sad because of the Battle of Sedgemoor (1685), when the rebellion of the duke of Monmouth against James II was crushed with excessive cruelty.

Through the Great Forest, Blackmoor wide,
20   And where the Parret ran,
We'd faced the gusts on Mendip ridge,
Had crossed the Yeo unhelped by bridge,
Been stung by every Marshwood midge,
    I and my fancy-man.

4

25 Lone inns we loved, my man and I,
    My man and I;
"King's Stag," "Windwhistle"⁴ high and dry,
    "The Horse" on Hintock Green,
The cozy house at Wynyard's Gap,
30 "The Hut" renowned on Bredy Knap,
And many another wayside tap°   *taproom, inn*
    Where folk might sit unseen.

5

Now as we trudged—O deadly day,
    O deadly day!—
35 I teased my fancy-man in play
    And wanton idleness.
I walked alongside jeering John,
I laid his hand my waist upon;
I would not bend my glances on
40   My lover's dark distress.

6

Thus Poldon top at last we won,
    At last we won,
And gained the inn at sink of sun
    Far-famed as "Marshal's Elm."⁵
45 Beneath us figured tor and lea,⁶
From Mendip to the western sea—
I doubt if finer sight there be
    Within this royal realm.

7

Inside the settle all a-row—
50   All four a-row
We sat, I next to John, to show
    That he had wooed and won.
And then he took me on his knee,
And swore it was his turn to be

4. The highness and dryness of Windwhistle Inn was impressed upon the writer two or three years ago, when, after climbing on a hot afternoon to the beautiful spot near which it stands and entering the inn for tea, he was informed by the landlady that none could be had, unless he would fetch water from a valley half a mile off, the house containing not a drop, owing to its situation. However, a tantalizing row of full barrels behind her back testified to a wetness of a certain sort, which was not at that time desired [Hardy's note].

5. "Marshal's Elm," so picturesquely situated, is no longer an inn, though the house, or part of it, still remains. It used to exhibit a fine old swinging sign [Hardy's note].

6. Rocky hill and tract of open ground.

55   My favoured mate, and Mother Lee
                Passed to my former one.

                        8

        Then in a voice I had never heard,
                I had never heard,
        My only Love to me: "One word,
60   My lady, if you please!
        Whose is the child you are like to bear?—
                His? After all my months o' care?"
        God knows 'twas not! But, O despair!
                I nodded—still to tease.

                        9

65   Then up he sprung, and with his knife—
                And with his knife
        He let out jeering Johnny's life,
                Yes; there, at set of sun.
        The slant ray through the window nigh
70   Gilded John's blood and glazing eye,
        Ere scarcely Mother Lee and I
                Knew that the deed was done.

                        10

        The taverns tell the gloomy tale,
                The gloomy tale,
75   How that at Ivel-chester jail
                My Love, my sweetheart swung;
        Though stained till now by no misdeed
        Save one horse ta'en in time o' need;
        (Blue Jimmy stole right many a steed
80   Ere his last fling he flung).[7]

                        11

        Thereaft I walked the world alone,
                Alone, alone!
        On his death-day I gave my groan
                And dropt his dead-born child.
85   'Twas nigh° the jail, beneath a tree,   *near*
        None tending me; for Mother Lee
        Had died at Glaston, leaving me
                Unfriended on the wild.

                        12

        And in the night as I lay weak,
90   As I lay weak,

7. "Blue Jimmy" was a notorious horse stealer of Wessex in those days, who appropriated more than a hundred horses before he was caught, among others one belonging to a neighbor of the writer's grandfather. He was hanged at the now demolished Ivel-chester or Ilchester jail above mentioned—that building formerly of so many sinister associations in the minds of the local peasantry, and the continual haunt of fever, which at last led to its condemnation. Its site is now an innocent-looking green meadow [Hardy's note].

The leaves a-falling on my cheek,
      The red moon low declined—
The ghost of him I'd die to kiss
      Rose up and said: "Ah, tell me this!
95   Was the child mine, or was it his?
      Speak, that I rest may find!"

13

O doubt not but I told him then,
      I told him then,
That I had kept me from all men
100   Since we joined lips and swore.
Whereat he smiled, and thinned away
      As the wind stirred to call up day . . .
—'Tis past! And here alone I stray
      Haunting the Western Moor.

Apr. 1902   1909

One We Knew

(M. H.[1] 1772–1857)

She told how they used to form for the country dances—
      "The Triumph," "The New-rigged Ship"—
To the light of the guttering wax in the panelled manses,
      And in cots to the blink of a dip.[2]

5   She spoke of the wild "poussetting" and "allemanding"[3]
      On carpet, on oak, and on sod;°   turf
And the two long rows of ladies and gentlemen standing,
      And the figures the couples trod.

She showed us the spot where the maypole was yearly planted,
10   And where the bandsmen stood
While breeched and kerchiefed partners whirled, and panted
      To choose each other for good.[4]

She told of that far-back day when they learnt astounded
      Of the death of the King of France:
15   Of the Terror; and then of Bonaparte's unbounded
      Ambition and arrogance.

Of how his threats woke warlike preparations
      Along the southern strand,

---

1. Hardy's grandmother.
2. I.e., in cottages by the light of a candle.
3. Allemande is the name of a dance originating in Germany. To pousette is to dance round with hands joined.

4. A tall pole, gaily painted and decorated with flowers and ribbons ("the maypole"), was danced around on May 1 by men (wearing "breeches," or trousers) and women (wearing "kerchiefs," or headscarves).

And how each night brought tremors and trepidations
20   Lest morning should see him land.

She said she had often heard the gibbet creaking
    As it swayed in the lightning flash,
Had caught from the neighbouring town a small child's shrieking
    At the cart-tail under the lash. . . .

25 With cap-framed face and long gaze into the embers—
    We seated around her knees—
She would dwell on such dead themes, not as one who remembers,
    But rather as one who sees.

She seemed one left behind of a band gone distant
30   So far that no tongue could hail:
Past things retold were to her as things existent,
    Things present but as a tale.

May 20, 1902   1909

She Hears the Storm

There was a time in former years—
    While my roof-tree was his—
When I should have been distressed by fears
    At such a night as this.

5 I should have murmured anxiously,
    "The pricking rain strikes cold;
His road is bare of hedge or tree,
    And he is getting old."

But now the fitful chimney-roar,
10   The drone of Thorncombe trees,
The Froom in flood upon the moor,
    The mud of Mellstock Leaze,[1]

The candle slanting sooty wick'd,
    The thuds upon the thatch,
15 The eaves-drops on the window flicked,
    The clacking garden-hatch,°   *gate*

And what they mean to wayfarers,
    I scarcely heed or mind;
He has won that storm-tight roof of hers
20   Which Earth grants all her kind.

                                    1909

1. The place names in Hardy's fictional "Wessex" were often invented ("Thorncombe," "Mellstock Leaze"), but he also used the names of real loca- tions, as in *A Trampwoman's Tragedy*. "The Froom" is presumably the river Frome, flowing through Dorset and Somerset.

Channel Firing[1]

That night your great guns, unawares,
Shook all our coffins as we lay,
And broke the chancel[2] window-squares,
We thought it was the Judgement-day

5 And sat upright. While drearisome
Arose the howl of wakened hounds:
The mouse let fall the altar-crumb,
The worms drew back into the mounds,

The glebe cow[3] drooled. Till God called, "No;
10 It's gunnery practise out at sea
Just as before you went below;
The world is as it used to be:

"All nations striving strong to make
Red war yet redder. Mad as hatters[4]
15 They do no more for Christès[5] sake
Than you who are helpless in such matters.

"That this is not the judgement-hour
For some of them's a blessed thing,
For if it were they'd have to scour
20 Hell's floor for so much threatening. . . .

"Ha, ha. It will be warmer when
I blow the trumpet (if indeed
I ever do; for you are men,
And rest eternal sorely need)."

25 So down we lay again. "I wonder,
Will the world ever saner be,"
Said one, "than when He sent us under
In our indifferent century!"

And many a skeleton shook his head.
30 "Instead of preaching forty year,"
My neighbour Parson Thirdly said,
"I wish I had stuck to pipes and beer."

Again the guns disturbed the hour,
Roaring their readiness to avenge,

1. Written in April 1914, when Anglo-German naval rivalry was growing steadily more acute; the title refers to gunnery practice in the English Channel. Four months later (August 4), World War I broke out.
2. Part of church nearest to the altar.
3. I.e., cow on a small plot of land belonging to a church (a "glebe" is a small field).
4. Cf. the Mad Hatter in Lewis Carroll's *Alice's Adventures in Wonderland* (1865).
5. The archaic spelling and pronunciation suggest a ballad note of doom.

35 As far inland as Stourton Tower,
And Camelot, and starlit Stonehenge.[6]

1914   1914

The Convergence of the Twain

(*Lines on the Loss of the* Titanic)[1]

I

In a solitude of the sea
Deep from human vanity,
And the Pride of Life that planned her, stilly couches she.

2

Steel chambers, late the pyres
5   Of her salamandrine fires,[2]
Cold currents thrid,[3] and turn to rhythmic tidal lyres.

3

Over the mirrors meant
To glass the opulent
The sea-worm crawls—grotesque, slimed, dumb, indifferent.

4

10   Jewels in joy designed
To ravish the sensuous mind
Lie lightless, all their sparkles bleared and black and blind.

5

Dim moon-eyed fishes near
Gaze at the gilded gear
15 And query: "What does this vaingloriousness down here?" . . .

6

Well: while was fashioning
This creature of cleaving wing,
The Immanent Will[4] that stirs and urges everything

6. The sound of guns preparing for war across the Channel reaches Alfred's ("Stourten") Tower (near Stourton in Dorset), commemorating King Alfred's defeat of a Danish invasion in 879; also the site of King Arthur's court at Camelot (supposedly near Glastonbury) and the famous prehistoric stone circle of Stonehenge on Salisbury Plain.

1. The *Titanic* was the largest and most luxurious ocean liner of the day. Considered unsinkable, it sank with great loss of life on April 15, 1912, on the ship's maiden voyage, from Southampton to the United States, after colliding with an iceberg. Twain: two.

2. Probably "fires in which nothing could survive" (although, since the salamander is a lizardlike animal supposed to be able to live in fire, "salamandrine" usually means "able to resist or to live in fire").

3. A variant form of the verb *thread*.

4. The force (blind, but slowly gaining consciousness throughout history) that drives the world, according to Hardy's philosophy.

7

Prepared a sinister mate
20   For her—so gaily great—
A Shape of Ice, for the time far and dissociate.

8

And as the smart ship grew
In stature, grace, and hue,
In shadowy silent distance grew the Iceberg too.

9

25   Alien they seemed to be:
No mortal eye could see
The intimate welding of their later history,

10

Or sign that they were bent
By paths coincident
30   On being anon° twin halves of one august° event,   *soon / important*

11

Till the Spinner of the Years
Said "Now!" And each one hears,
And consummation comes, and jars two hemispheres.

1912   1912, 1914

Ah, Are You Digging on My Grave?

"Ah, are you digging on my grave
            My loved one?—planting rue?"[1]
—"No: yesterday he went to wed
One of the brightest wealth has bred.
5   'It cannot hurt her now,' he said,
            'That I should not be true.' "

"Then who is digging on my grave?
            My nearest dearest kin?"
—"Ah, no; they sit and think, 'What use!
10   What good will planting flowers produce?
No tendance of her mound can loose
            Her spirit from Death's gin.' "°   *trap*

"But some one digs upon my grave?
            My enemy?—prodding sly?"
15   —"Nay: when she heard you had passed the Gate
            That shuts on all flesh soon or late,

---

1. A yellow-flowered herb, traditionally an emblem of sorrow (*rue* is also an archaic word for "sorrow").

She thought you no more worth her hate,
    And cares not where you lie."

"Then, who is digging on my grave?
20   Say—since I have not guessed!"
—"O it is I, my mistress dear,
Your little dog, who still lives near,
And much I hope my movements here
    Have not disturbed your rest?"

25   "Ah, yes! *You* dig upon my grave . . .
    Why flashed it not on me
That one true heart was left behind!
What feeling do we ever find
To equal among human kind
30   A dog's fidelity!"

"Mistress, I dug upon your grave
    To bury a bone, in case
I should be hungry near this spot
When passing on my daily trot.
35   I am sorry, but I quite forgot
    It was your resting-place."

1914

Under the Waterfall

"Whenever I plunge my arm, like this,
In a basin of water, I never miss
The sweet sharp sense of a fugitive day
Fetched back from its thickening shroud of grey.
5   Hence the only prime
      And real love-rhyme
      That I know by heart,
      And that leaves no smart,
Is the purl° of a little valley fall   *rippling flow*
10 About three spans wide and two spans tall
Over a table of solid rock,
And into a scoop of the self-same block;
The purl of a runlet that never ceases
In stir of kingdoms, in wars, in peaces;
15 With a hollow boiling voice it speaks
And has spoken since hills were turfless peaks."

"And why gives this the only prime
Idea to you of a real love-rhyme?
And why does plunging your arm in a bowl
20 Full of spring water, bring throbs to your soul?"

"Well, under the fall, in a crease of the stone,
Though where precisely none ever has known,

Jammed darkly, nothing to show how prized,
And by now with its smoothness opalised,
25   Is a drinking-glass:
             For, down that pass
             My lover and I
             Walked under a sky
Of blue with a leaf-wove awning of green,
30   In the burn of August, to paint the scene,
And we placed our basket of fruit and wine
By the runlet's rim, where we sat to dine;
And when we had drunk from the glass together,
Arched by the oak-copse from the weather,
35   I held the vessel to rinse in the fall,
Where it slipped, and sank, and was past recall,
Though we stooped and plumbed the little abyss
With long bared arms. There the glass still is.
And, as said, if I thrust my arm below
40   Cold water in basin or bowl, a throe°   *violent pang*
From the past awakens a sense of that time,
And the glass we used, and the cascade's rhyme.
The basin seems the pool, and its edge
The hard smooth face of the brook-side ledge,
45   And the leafy pattern of china-ware
The hanging plants that were bathing there.

"By night, by day, when it shines or lours,
There lies intact that chalice of ours,
And its presence adds to the rhyme of love
50   Persistently sung by the fall above.
No lip has touched it since his and mine
In turns therefrom sipped lovers' wine."

                                                        1914

The Walk

      You did not walk with me
      Of late to the hill-top tree
            By the gated ways,
            As in earlier days;
5   You were weak and lame,
            So you never came,
      And I went alone, and I did not mind,
      Not thinking of you as left behind.

            I walked up there to-day
10   Just in the former way:
            Surveyed around
            The familiar ground
            By myself again:
            What difference, then?

15 Only that underlying sense
  Of the look of a room on returning thence.

1912–13   1914

The Voice

Woman much missed, how you call to me, call to me,
Saying that now you are not as you were
When you had changed from the one who was all to me,
But as at first, when our day was fair.

5 Can it be you that I hear? Let me view you, then,
 Standing as when I drew near to the town
Where you would wait for me: yes, as I knew you then,
 Even to the original air-blue gown!

Or is it only the breeze, in its listlessness
10 Travelling across the wet mead° to me here,   *meadow*
You being ever dissolved to wan wistlessness,°   *inattention*
 Heard no more again far or near?

  Thus I; faltering forward,
  Leaves around me falling,
15 Wind oozing thin through the thorn from norward,° *northward*
  And the woman calling.

Dec. 1912   1914

The Workbox

"See, here's the workbox, little wife,
 That I made of polished oak."
He was a joiner,° of village life;   *carpenter*
 She came of borough folk.°   *townspeople*

5 He holds the present up to her
  As with a smile she nears
And answers to the profferer,
 " 'Twill last all my sewing years!"

"I warrant it will. And longer too.
10 'Tis a scantling[1] that I got
Off poor John Wayward's coffin, who
 Died of they knew not what.

"The shingled pattern that seems to cease
 Against your box's rim

1. Small piece of wood.

15   Continues right on in the piece
      That's underground with him.

    "And while I worked it made me think
      Of timber's varied doom;
    One inch where people eat and drink,
20   The next inch in a tomb.

    "But why do you look so white, my dear,
      And turn aside your face?
    You knew not that good lad, I fear,
      Though he came from your native place?"

25   "How could I know that good young man,
      Though he came from my native town,
    When he must have left far earlier than
      I was a woman grown?"

    "Ah, no. I should have understood!
30   It shocked you that I gave
    To you one end of a piece of wood
      Whose other is in a grave?"

    "Don't, dear, despise my intellect,
      Mere accidental things
35   Of that sort never have effect
      On my imaginings."

    Yet still her lips were limp and wan,
      Her face still held aside,
    As if she had known not only John,
40   But known of what he died.

                       1914

During Wind and Rain

    They sing their dearest songs—
    He, she, all of them—yea,
    Treble and tenor and bass,
      And one to play;
5   With the candles mooning each face. . . .
      Ah, no; the years O!
How the sick leaves reel down in throngs!

    They clear the creeping moss—
    Elders and juniors—aye,
10   Making the pathways neat
      And the garden gay;
    And they build a shady seat. . . .
      Ah, no; the years, the years;
See, the white storm-birds wing across.

15 They are blithely breakfasting all—
   Men and maidens—yea,
   Under the summer tree,
      With a glimpse of the bay,
   While pet fowl come to the knee. . . .
20   Ah, no; the years O!
   And the rotten rose is ript from the wall.

   They change to a high new house,
   He, she, all of them—aye,
   Clocks and carpets and chairs
25   On the lawn all day,
   And brightest things that are theirs. . . .
      Ah, no; the years, the years;
   Down their carved names the rain-drop ploughs.

                                                    1917

In Time of "The Breaking of Nations"[1]

1

Only a man harrowing clods
   In a slow silent walk
With an old horse that stumbles and nods
   Half asleep as they stalk.

2

5 Only thin smoke without flame
   From the heaps of couch-grass;
Yet this will go onward the same
   Though Dynasties pass.

3

Yonder a maid and her wight°   man
10   Come whispering by:
War's annals will cloud into night
   Ere their story die.

1915   1916

He Never Expected Much

[or]
A Consideration
[A reflection] on My Eighty-Sixth Birthday

Well, World, you have kept faith with me,
   Kept faith with me;

1. Cf. "Thou art my battle axe and weapon of war: for with thee will I break in pieces the nations" (Jeremiah 51.20). The poem was written during World War I.

Upon the whole you have proved to be
   Much as you said you were.
5 Since as a child I used to lie
Upon the leaze° and watch the sky,   *pasture*
Never, I own, expected I
   That life would all be fair.

'Twas then you said, and since have said,
10   Times since have said,
In that mysterious voice you shed
   From clouds and hills around:
"Many have loved me desperately,
Many with smooth serenity,
15 While some have shown contempt of me
   Till they dropped underground.

"I do not promise overmuch,
       Child; overmuch;
Just neutral-tinted haps° and such,"   *happenings*
20   You said to minds like mine.
Wise warning for your credit's sake!
Which I for one failed not to take,
And hence could stem such strain and ache
   As each year might assign.

1926   1928

JOSEPH CONRAD
1857–1924

Joseph Conrad was born Jozef Teodor Konrad Nalecz Korzeniowski in Poland (then under Russian rule), son of a Polish patriot who suffered exile in Russia for his Polish nationalist activities and died in 1869, leaving Conrad to be brought up by a maternal uncle. At the age of fifteen he amazed his family and friends by announcing his passionate desire to go to sea; he was eventually allowed to go to Marseilles in 1874, and from there he made a number of voyages on French merchant ships to Martinique and the West Indies. In 1878 he signed on an English ship that brought him to the east coast English port of Lowestoft, where (still as an ordinary seaman) he joined the crew of a small coasting vessel plying between Lowestoft and Newcastle. In six voyages between these two ports he learned English. Thus launched on a career in the British merchant service, Conrad sailed on a variety of British ships to the East and elsewhere and eventually gained his master's certificate in 1886, the year when he became a naturalized British subject. He received his first command in 1888, and in 1890 took a steamboat up the Congo River in nightmarish circumstances (described in *Heart of Darkness*) that produced severe illness and permanently haunted his imagination. In the early 1890s he was already thinking of turning some of his Malayan experiences into English fiction, and in 1892–93, when serving as first mate on the *Torrens* sailing from London to Adelaide, he revealed to a sympathetic passenger that he had begun a novel (*Almayer's Folly*), while on the return journey he impressed the young John Galsworthy, who was on board, with his conversation. Although possessed of a master's certificate, Conrad found it difficult to get the kind of job as master that he wished, and occasionally he had to serve in lesser capacities. His difficulty in obtaining a command, together with the interest aroused by *Almayer's Folly* when it was published in 1895, helped to turn him away from the sea to a career as a writer. He settled in London and in 1896 married an English woman; this son of a Polish patriot turned merchant seaman turned writer was henceforth an English novelist.

Conrad was for a long time regarded as a sea writer whose exotic descriptions of eastern landscapes and exploitation of the romantic atmosphere of Malaya and other unfamiliar regions gave his work a special kind of richness and splendor. But this is only one, and not in the last analysis the most important, aspect of his work. More and more Conrad used the sea and the circumstances of life on shipboard or in remote eastern settlements as means of exploring certain profound moral ambiguities in human experience. In *The Nigger of the "Narcissus"* (1897) he shows how a dying black seaman corrupts the morale of a ship's crew by the very fact that his plight produces sympathy, thus symbolically presenting one of his commonest themes—the necessity and at the same time the dangers of human contact. In *Lord Jim* (1900), using the device of an intermediate narrator, he probes the meaning of a gross failure of duty on the part of a romantic and idealistic young sailor, and by presenting the hero's history from a series of different points of view keeps the moral questioning continuing to the end. The use of intermediate narrators and multiple points of view is common in Conrad; it is his favorite way of suggesting the complexity of experience and the difficulty of judging human actions.

This notion of the difficulty of true communion, coupled with the idea that communion can be unexpectedly forced on us—sometimes with someone who may be on the surface our moral opposite, so that we can at times be compelled into a mysterious recognition of our opposite as our true self—is found in many of Conrad's works; it provides one of the underlying themes of *The Secret Sharer* (1912). This story can be enjoyed for the clarity and power with which Conrad renders the atmosphere of the Gulf of Siam as felt by a young sea captain on taking on his first command, but it also uses situation and incident symbolically to suggest some of the paradoxes of identity and sympathy.

Other stories and novels explore the ways in which the codes we live by are tested in moments of crisis, revealing either their inadequacy or our own. Imagination can corrupt (as with Lord Jim) or save (as in *The Shadow-Line*, 1917), and there are times when total lack of it can see a man through (Captain MacWhirr in *Typhoon*, 1902), though a similar lack in other circumstances can render a man comically ridiculous (Captain Mitchell in *Nostromo*, 1904).

Nostromo, a profound and subtle study of the corrupting effects of politics and "material interests" on personal relationships (set in an imaginary Latin American republic), is often regarded as Conrad's greatest work. He wrote two other political novels—*The Secret Agent* (1906) and *Under Western Eyes* (1911). The latter is the story of a Russian student who becomes involuntarily associated with antigovernment violence in czarist Russia and is irresistibly maneuvered by circumstances into a position where, although a government spy, he has to pretend to be a revolutionary among revolutionaries. This is the ultimate in human loneliness and incommunicability—when you must consistently pretend to be the opposite of what you are. It is a story of Dostoyevskian power, and shows a very different Conrad from the picturesque sea-dreamer portrayed by the earlier critics. Conrad was as much a pessimist as Hardy, but he projected his pessimism in subtler ways. He was also a great master of English prose, an astonishing fact when we realize that he was twenty-one before he learned any English, and that to the end of his life he spoke English with a thick foreign accent.

Preface to *The Nigger of the "Narcissus"*[1]

[THE TASK OF THE ARTIST]

A work that aspires, however humbly, to the condition of art should carry its justification in every line. And art itself may be defined as a single-minded attempt to render the highest kind of justice to the visible universe, by bringing to light the truth, manifold and one, underlying its every aspect. It is an attempt to find in its forms, in its colours, in its light, in its shadows, in the aspects of matter and in the facts of life what of each is fundamental, what is enduring and essential—their one illuminating and convincing quality— the very truth of their existence. The artist, then, like the thinker or the scientist, seeks the truth and makes his appeal. Impressed by the aspect of the world the thinker plunges into ideas, the scientist into facts—whence, presently, emerging they make their appeal to those qualities of our being that fit us best for the hazardous enterprise of living. They speak authoritatively to our common-sense, to our intelligence, to our desire of peace or to our desire of unrest; not seldom to our prejudices, sometimes to our fears, often to our egoism—but always to our credulity. And their words are heard with reverence, for their concern is with weighty matters: with the cultivation of our minds and the proper care of our bodies, with the attainment of our ambitions, with the perfection of the means and the glorification of our precious aims.

It is otherwise with the artist.

Confronted by the same enigmatical spectacle the artist descends within himself, and in that lonely region of stress and strife, if he be deserving and fortunate, he finds the terms of his appeal. His appeal is made to our less obvious capacities: to that part of our nature which, because of the warlike conditions of existence, is necessarily kept out of sight within the more resisting and hard qualities—like the vulnerable body within a steel armour. His appeal is less loud, more profound, less distinct, more stirring—and sooner forgotten. Yet its effect endures forever. The changing wisdom of successive generations discards ideas, questions facts, demolishes theories. But the artist appeals to that part of our being which is not dependent on wisdom; to that in us which is a gift and not an acquisition—and, therefore, more permanently enduring. He speaks to our capacity for delight and wonder, to the sense of mystery surrounding our lives; to our sense of pity, and beauty, and pain; to the latent feeling of fellowship with all creation—and to the subtle but invincible conviction of solidarity that knits together the loneliness of innumerable hearts, to the solidarity in dreams, in joy, in sorrow, in aspirations, in illusions, in hope, in fear, which binds men to each other, which binds together all humanity—the dead to the living and the living to the unborn.

---

1. Conrad wrote *The Nigger of the "Narcissus"* in 1896–97, shortly after his marriage; it was published first in *The New Review*, August–December 1897, and then in book form in 1898. The novel, in the words of Jocelyn Baines, a Conrad biographer, "is the culmination of Conrad's apprenticeship as a novelist." Conrad took particular pleasure in writing the book and later called it "the story by which, as a creative artist, I stand or fall." It was with the feeling that he was now wholly dedicated to writing and had finally (in his own words) "done with the sea" that, a few months after finishing the novel, he wrote the preface in which he defined his aims as an artist. The preface first appeared in the 1898 edition.

It is only some such train of thought, or rather of feeling, that can in a measure explain the aim of the attempt, made in the tale which follows,[2] to present an unrestful episode in the obscure lives of a few individuals out of all the disregarded multitude of the bewildered, the simple and the voiceless. For, if any part of truth dwells in the belief confessed above, it becomes evident that there is not a place of splendour or a dark corner of the earth that does not deserve, if only a passing glance of wonder and pity. The motive then, may be held to justify the matter of the work; but this preface, which is simply an avowal of endeavour, cannot end here—for the avowal is not yet complete.

Fiction—if it at all aspires to be art—appeals to temperament. And in truth it must be, like painting, like music, like all art, the appeal of one temperament to all the other innumerable temperaments whose subtle and resistless power endows passing events with their true meaning, and creates the moral, the emotional atmosphere of the place and time. Such an appeal to be effective must be an impression conveyed through the senses; and, in fact, it cannot be made in any other way, because temperament, whether individual or collective, is not amenable to persuasion. All art, therefore, appeals primarily to the senses, and the artistic aim when expressing itself in written words must also make its appeal through the senses, if its high desire is to reach the secret spring of responsive emotions. It must strenuously aspire to the plasticity of sculpture, to the colour of painting, and to the magic suggestiveness of music—which is the art of arts. And it is only through complete, unswerving devotion to the perfect blending of form and substance; it is only through an unremitting never-discouraged care for the shape and ring of sentences that an approach can be made to plasticity, to colour, and that the light of magic suggestiveness may be brought to play for an evanescent instant over the commonplace surface of words: of the old, old words, worn thin, defaced by ages of careless usage.

The sincere endeavour to accomplish that creative task, to go as far on that road as his strength will carry him, to go undeterred by faltering, weariness or reproach, is the only valid justification for the worker in prose. And if his conscience is clear, his answer to those who in the fulness of a wisdom which looks for immediate profit, demand specifically to be edified, consoled, amused; who demand to be promptly improved, or encouraged, or frightened, or shocked, or charmed, must run thus:—My task which I am trying to achieve is, by the power of the written word to make you hear, to make you feel—it is, before all, to make you *see*. That—and no more, and it is everything. If I succeed, you shall find there according to your deserts: encouragement, consolation, fear, charm—all you demand—and, perhaps, also that glimpse of truth for which you have forgotten to ask.

To snatch in a moment of courage, from the remorseless rush of time, a passing phase of life, is only the beginning of the task. The task approached in tenderness and faith is to hold up unquestioningly, without choice and without fear, the rescued fragment before all eyes in the light of a sincere mood. It is to show its vibration, its colour, its form; and through its movement, its form, and its colour, reveal the substance of its truth—disclose its inspiring secret: the stress and passion within the core of each convincing

2. *The Nigger of the "Narcissus."*

moment. In a single-minded attempt of that kind, if one be deserving and fortunate, one may perchance attain to such clearness of sincerity that at last the presented vision of regret or pity, of terror or mirth, shall awaken in the hearts of the beholders that feeling of unavoidable solidarity; of the solidarity in mysterious origin, in toil, in joy, in hope, in uncertain fate, which binds men to each other and all mankind to the visible world.

It is evident that he who, rightly or wrongly, holds by the convictions expressed above cannot be faithful to any one of the temporary formulas of his craft. The enduring part of them—the truth which each only imperfectly veils—should abide with him as the most precious of his possessions, but they all: Realism, Romanticism, Naturalism, even the unofficial sentimentalism (which like the poor, is exceedingly difficult to get rid of),[3] all these gods must, after a short period of fellowship, abandon him—even on the very threshold of the temple—to the stammerings of his conscience and to the outspoken consciousness of the difficulties of his work. In that uneasy solitude the supreme cry of Art for Art itself, loses the exciting ring of its apparent immorality. It sounds far off. It has ceased to be a cry, and is heard only as a whisper, often incomprehensible, but at times and faintly encouraging.

Sometimes, stretched at ease in the shade of a roadside tree, we watch the motions of a labourer in a distant field, and after a time, begin to wonder languidly as to what the fellow may be at. We watch the movements of his body, the waving of his arms, we see him bend down, stand up, hesitate, begin again. It may add to the charm of an idle hour to be told the purpose of his exertions. If we know he is trying to lift a stone, to dig a ditch, to uproot a stump, we look with a more real interest at his efforts; we are disposed to condone the jar of his agitation upon the restfulness of the landscape; and even, if in a brotherly frame of mind, we may bring ourselves to forgive his failure. We understood his object, and, after all, the fellow has tried, and perhaps he had not the strength—and perhaps he had not the knowledge. We forgive, go on our way—and forget.

And so it is with the workman of art. Art is long and life is short,[4] and success is very far off. And thus, doubtful of strength to travel so far, we talk a little about the aim—the aim of art, which, like life itself, is inspiring, difficult—obscured by mists. It is not in the clear logic of a triumphant conclusion; it is not in the unveiling of one of those heartless secrets which are called the Laws of Nature. It is not less great, but only more difficult.

To arrest, for the space of a breath, the hands busy about the work of the earth, and compel men entranced by the sight of distant goals to glance for a moment at the surrounding vision of form and colour, of sunshine and shadows; to make them pause for a look, for a sigh, for a smile—such is the aim, difficult and evanescent, and reserved only for a very few to achieve. But sometimes, by the deserving and the fortunate, even that task is accomplished. And when it is accomplished—behold!—all the truth of life is there: a moment of vision, a sigh, a smile—and the return to an eternal rest.

1897   1898

---

3. For the poor always ye have with you (John 12.8).
4. A Latin proverb (deriving from a dictum of the Greek physician Hippocrates): *ars longa, vita brevis.*

Heart of Darkness   This story is derived from Conrad's personal experience in the Congo in 1890. Like Marlow, the narrator of the story, Conrad had as a child determined one day to visit the heart of Africa. "It was in 1868, when nine years old or thereabouts, that while looking at a map of Africa at the time and putting my finger on the blank space then representing the unsolved mystery of that continent, I said to myself with absolute assurance and an amazing audacity which are no longer in my character now: 'When I grow up I shall go *there*' " (*A Personal Record*, 1912).

Conrad was promised a job as a Congo River pilot through the influence of his distant cousin Marguerite Poradowska, who lived in Brussels and knew important officials of the Belgian company that exploited the Congo. At this time the Congo, although nominally an independent state, the Congo Free State (État Indépendent du Congo), was virtually the personal property of Leopold II, king of the Belgians, who made a fortune out of it. Later, the appalling abuses involved in the naked colonial exploitation that went on in the Congo were exposed to public view, and international criticism compelled the setting up of a committee of inquiry in 1904. What Conrad saw in 1890 shocked him profoundly and shook his view of the moral basis of all exploring and trading in newly discovered countries and indeed of civilization in general. "*Heart of Darkness* is experience, too," Conrad wrote in his 1917 "Author's Note," "but it is experience pushed a little (and only very little) beyond the actual facts of the case for the perfectly legitimate, I believe, purpose of bringing it home to the minds and bosoms of the readers." And later he told Edward Garnett: "Before the Congo I was just a mere animal."

Conrad arrived in Africa in May 1890 and made his way up the Congo River very much as described in *Heart of Darkness*. At Kinshasa (which Conrad spells Kinchassa) on Stanley Pool, which he reached after an exhausting two-hundred-mile trek from Matadi, near the mouth of the river, Conrad was much taken aback to learn that the steamer of which he was to be captain had been damaged and was undergoing repairs. He was sent as supernumerary on another steamer to learn the river. This other steamer was sent to Stanley Falls to collect and bring back to Kinshasa one Georges Antoine Klein, an agent of the company who had fallen gravely ill and who in fact died on board. Klein was the original of Kurtz. Conrad himself then fell seriously ill and eventually returned to London in January 1891 without ever having actually served as a Congo River pilot, the job for which he went out to Africa. The Congo experience permanently impaired his health; it also permanently haunted his imagination. The nightmare atmosphere of *Heart of Darkness* is an accurate reflection of Conrad's own response to his traumatic experience.

The theme of the story is partly the "choice of nightmares" facing the white man in the Congo—either to become like the wholly commercially minded manager, who sees Africa, its people, and its resources solely as instruments of financial gain, or to become like Kurtz, the self-tortured and corrupted idealist. The manager is a "hollow man" (T. S. Eliot quoted from this story in his poem of that title); his only objections to Kurtz are commercial, not moral; Kurtz's methods are "unsound" and would therefore lose the company money. At the last, he seems to recognize the moral horror of his having succumbed to the dark temptations that African life posed for the white man. "He had summed up—he had judged." But the story also has other levels of meaning, and the counterpointing of Western civilization in Europe with what that civilization has done in Africa (see the concluding interview between Marlow and Kurtz's "intended"—based on a real interview between Conrad and the dead Klein's fiancée) throws out several of these. See also the extract from Chinua Achebe's essay, "An Image of Africa: Racism in Joseph Conrad's *Heart of Darkness*," on p. 2035.

Heart of Darkness

1

The *Nellie,* a cruising yawl,[1] swung to her anchor without a flutter of the sails, and was at rest. The flood had made, the wind was nearly calm, and being bound down the river, the only thing for it was to come to and wait for the turn of the tide.

The sea-reach of the Thames stretched before us like the beginning of an interminable waterway. In the offing the sea and the sky were welded together without a joint, and in the luminous space the tanned sails of the barges drifting up with the tide seemed to stand still in red clusters of canvas sharply peaked, with gleams of varnished sprits. A haze rested on the low shores that ran out to sea in vanishing flatness. The air was dark above Gravesend,[2] and farther back still seemed condensed into a mournful gloom, brooding motionless over the biggest, and the greatest, town on earth.

The Director of Companies was our captain and our host. We four affectionately watched his back as he stood in the bows looking to seaward. On the whole river there was nothing that looked half so nautical. He resembled a pilot, which to a seaman is trustworthiness personified. It was difficult to realise his work was not out there in the luminous estuary, but behind him, within the brooding gloom.

Between us there was, as I have already said somewhere, the bond of the sea. Besides holding our hearts together through long periods of separation, it had the effect of making us tolerant of each other's yarns—and even convictions. The Lawyer—the best of old fellows—had, because of his many years and many virtues, the only cushion on deck, and was lying on the only rug. The Accountant had brought out already a box of dominoes, and was toying architecturally with the bones. Marlow sat cross-legged right aft, leaning against the mizzenmast. He had sunken cheeks, a yellow complexion, a straight back, an ascetic aspect, and, with his arms dropped, the palms of hands outwards, resembled an idol. The Director, satisfied the anchor had good hold, made his way aft and sat down amongst us. We exchanged a few words lazily. Afterwards there was silence on board the yacht. For some reason or other we did not begin that game of dominoes. We felt meditative, and fit for nothing but placid staring. The day was ending in a serenity of still and exquisite brilliance. The water shone pacifically; the sky, without a speck, was a benign immensity of unstained light; the very mist on the Essex marshes was like a gauzy and radiant fabric, hung from the wooded rises inland, and draping the low shores in diaphanous folds. Only the gloom to the west, brooding over the upper reaches, became more sombre every minute, as if angered by the approach of the sun.

And at last, in its curved and imperceptible fall, the sun sank low, and from glowing white changed to a dull red without rays and without heat, as if about to go out suddenly, stricken to death by the touch of that gloom brooding over a crowd of men.

Forthwith a change came over the waters, and the serenity became less brilliant but more profound. The old river in its broad reach rested unruffled

---

1. Two-masted boat.
2. River port on the south bank of the Thames twenty-four miles east (downriver) of London.

at the decline of day, after ages of good service done to the race that peopled its banks, spread out in the tranquil dignity of a waterway leading to the uttermost ends of the earth. We looked at the venerable stream not in the vivid flush of a short day that comes and departs for ever, but in the august light of abiding memories. And indeed nothing is easier for a man who has, as the phrase goes, "followed the sea" with reverence and affection, than to evoke the great spirit of the past upon the lower reaches of the Thames. The tidal current runs to and fro in its unceasing service, crowded with memories of men and ships it has borne to the rest of home or to the battles of the sea. It had known and served all the men of whom the nation is proud, from Sir Francis Drake to Sir John Franklin,[3] knights all, titled and untitled—the great knights-errant of the sea. It had borne all the ships whose names are like jewels flashing in the night of time, from the *Golden Hind* returning with her round flanks full of treasure, to be visited by the Queen's Highness and thus pass out of the gigantic tale, to the *Erebus* and *Terror,* bound on other conquests—and that never returned. It had known the ships and the men. They had sailed from Deptford, from Greenwich, from Erith—the adventurers and the settlers; kings' ships and the ships of men on 'Change; captains, admirals, the dark "interlopers"[4] of the Eastern trade, and the commissioned "generals" of East India fleets. Hunters for gold or pursuers of fame, they all had gone out on that stream, bearing the sword, and often the torch, messengers of the might within the land, bearers of a spark from the sacred fire. What greatness had not floated on the ebb of that river into the mystery of an unknown earth! . . . The dreams of men, the seed of commonwealths, the germs of empires.

The sun set; the dusk fell on the stream, and lights began to appear along the shore. The Chapman lighthouse, a three-legged thing erect on a mudflat, shone strongly. Lights of ships moved in the fairway[5]—a great stir of lights going up and going down. And farther west on the upper reaches the place of the monstrous town was still marked ominously on the sky, a brooding gloom in sunshine, a lurid glare under the stars.

"And this also," said Marlow suddenly, "has been one of the dark places of the earth."

He was the only man of us who still "followed the sea." The worst that could be said of him was that he did not represent his class. He was a seaman, but he was a wanderer too, while most seamen lead, if one may so express it, a sedentary life. Their minds are of the stay-at-home order, and their home is always with them—the ship; and so is their country—the sea. One ship is very much like another, and the sea is always the same. In the immutability of their surroundings the foreign shores, the foreign faces, the changing immensity of life, glide past, veiled not by a sense of mystery but by a slightly

---

3. Sir John Franklin (1786–1847), Arctic explorer who in 1845 commanded an expedition consisting of the ships *Erebus* and *Terror* in search of the Northwest Passage. The ships never returned. Sir Francis Drake (ca. 1540–1596), Elizabethan naval hero and explorer, sailed around the world on his ship *The Golden Hind*. Queen Elizabeth knighted Drake on board his ship, loaded with captured Spanish treasure, on his return.

4. Private ships muscling in on the monopoly of the East India Company, which was founded in 1600, lost its trading monopoly in 1813, and transferred its governmental functions to the Crown in 1858. Deptford, on the south bank of the Thames, on the eastern edge of London, was once an important dockyard. Greenwich is on the south bank of the Thames immediately east of Deptford. Erith is eight miles farther east. " 'Change": the Stock Exchange.

5. Navigable part of a river, through which ships enter and depart.

disdainful ignorance; for there is nothing mysterious to a seaman unless it be the sea itself, which is the mistress of his existence and as inscrutable as Destiny. For the rest, after his hours of work, a casual stroll or a casual spree on shore suffices to unfold for him the secret of a whole continent, and generally he finds the secret not worth knowing. The yarns of seamen have a direct simplicity, the whole meaning of which lies within the shell of a cracked nut. But Marlow was not typical (if his propensity to spin yarns be excepted), and to him the meaning of an episode was not inside like a kernel but outside, enveloping the tale which brought it out only as a glow brings out a haze, in the likeness of one of these misty halos that sometimes are made visible by the spectral illumination of moonshine.

His remark did not seem at all surprising. It was just like Marlow. It was accepted in silence. No one took the trouble to grunt even; and presently he said, very slow:

"I was thinking of very old times, when the Romans first came here, nineteen hundred years ago—the other day. . . . Light came out of this river since—you say Knights? Yes; but it is like a running blaze on a plain, like a flash of lightning in the clouds. We live in the flicker—may it last as long as the old earth keeps rolling! But darkness was here yesterday. Imagine the feelings of a commander of a fine—what d'ye call 'em?—trireme[6] in the Mediterranean, ordered suddenly to the north; run overland across the Gauls in a hurry; put in charge of one of these craft the legionaries—a wonderful lot of handy men they must have been too—used to build, apparently by the hundred, in a month or two, if we may believe what we read. Imagine him here—the very end of the world, a sea the colour of lead, a sky the colour of smoke, a kind of ship about as rigid as a concertina—and going up this river with stores, or orders, or what you like. Sandbanks, marshes, forests, savages—precious little to eat fit for a civilised man, nothing but Thames water to drink. No Falernian wine[7] here, no going ashore. Here and there a military camp lost in a wilderness, like a needle in a bundle of hay—cold, fog, tempests, disease, exile, and death—death skulking in the air, in the water, in the bush. They must have been dying like flies here. Oh yes—he did it. Did it very well, too, no doubt, and without thinking much about it either, except afterwards to brag of what he had gone through in his time, perhaps. They were men enough to face the darkness. And perhaps he was cheered by keeping his eye on a chance of promotion to the fleet at Ravenna[8] by and by, if he had good friends in Rome and survived the awful climate. Or think of a decent young citizen in a toga—perhaps too much dice, you know—coming out here in the train of some prefect, or tax-gatherer, or trader, even, to mend his fortunes. Land in a swamp, march through the woods, and in some inland post feel the savagery, the utter savagery, had closed round him—all that mysterious life of the wilderness that stirs in the forest, in the jungles, in the hearts of wild men. There's no initiation either into such mysteries. He has to live in the midst of the incomprehensible, which is also detestable. And it has a fascination, too, that goes to work upon him. The fascination of the abomination—you know. Imagine the growing regrets, the longing to escape, the powerless disgust, the surrender, the hate."

---

6. Ancient Greek and Roman galley with three ranks of oars.

7. Wine from a famed wine-making district in Campania (Italy).

8. A city in northern Italy once directly on the Adriatic Sea and an important naval station in Roman times. It is now about six miles from the sea, connected with it by a canal.

He paused.

"Mind," he began again, lifting one arm from the elbow, the palm of the hand outwards, so that, with his legs folded before him, he had the pose of a Buddha preaching in European clothes and without a lotus-flower—"Mind, none of us would feel exactly like this. What saves us is efficiency—the devotion to efficiency. But these chaps were not much account, really. They were no colonists; their administration was merely a squeeze, and nothing more, I suspect. They were conquerors, and for that you want only brute force—nothing to boast of, when you have it, since your strength is just an accident arising from the weakness of others. They grabbed what they could get for the sake of what was to be got. It was just robbery with violence, aggravated murder on a great scale, and men going at it blind—as is very proper for those who tackle a darkness. The conquest of the earth, which mostly means the taking it away from those who have a different complexion or slightly flatter noses than ourselves, is not a pretty thing when you look into it too much. What redeems it is the idea only. An idea at the back of it; not a sentimental pretence but an idea; and an unselfish belief in the idea— something you can set up, and bow down before, and offer a sacrifice to. . . ."

He broke off. Flames glided in the river, small green flames, red flames, white flames, pursuing, overtaking, joining, crossing each other—then separating slowly or hastily. The traffic of the great city went on in the deepening night upon the sleepless river. We looked on, waiting patiently—there was nothing else to do till the end of the flood; but it was only after a long silence, when he said, in a hesitating voice, "I suppose you fellows remember I did once turn fresh-water sailor for a bit," that we knew we were fated, before the ebb began to run, to hear about one of Marlow's inconclusive experiences.

"I don't want to bother you much with what happened to me personally," he began, showing in this remark the weakness of many tellers of tales who seem so often unaware of what their audience would best like to hear; "yet to understand the effect of it on me you ought to know how I got out there, what I saw, how I went up that river to the place where I first met the poor chap. It was the farthest point of navigation and the culminating point of my experience. It seemed somehow to throw a kind of light on everything about me—and into my thoughts. It was sombre enough too—and pitiful— not extraordinary in any way—not very clear either. No, not very clear. And yet it seemed to throw a kind of light.

"I had then, as you remember, just returned to London after a lot of Indian Ocean, Pacific, China Seas—a regular dose of the East—six years or so, and I was loafing about, hindering you fellows in your work and invading your homes, just as though I had got a heavenly mission to civilise you. It was very fine for a time, but after a bit I did get tired of resting. Then I began to look for a ship—I should think the hardest work on earth. But the ships wouldn't even look at me. And I got tired of that game too.

"Now when I was a little chap I had a passion for maps. I would look for hours at South America, or Africa, or Australia, and lose myself in all the glories of exploration. At that time there were many blank spaces on the earth, and when I saw one that looked particularly inviting on a map (but they all look that) I would put my finger on it and say, When I grow up I will go there. The North Pole was one of these places, I remember. Well, I haven't been there yet, and shall not try now. The glamour's off. Other places were scattered about the Equator, and in every sort of latitude all over the two hemispheres. I have been in some of them, and . . . well, we won't talk about that. But there was one yet—the biggest, the most blank, so to speak—that I had a hankering after.

"True, by this time it was not a blank space any more. It had got filled since my boyhood with rivers and lakes and names. It had ceased to be a blank space of delightful mystery—a white patch for a boy to dream gloriously over. It had become a place of darkness. But there was in it one river especially, a mighty big river, that you could see on the map, resembling an immense snake uncoiled, with its head in the sea, its body at rest curving afar over a vast country, and its tail lost in the depths of the land. And as I looked at the map of it in a shop-window, it fascinated me as a snake would a bird—a silly little bird. Then I remembered there was a big concern, a Company for trade on that river. Dash it all! I thought to myself, they can't trade without using some kind of craft on that lot of fresh water—steamboats! Why shouldn't I try to get charge of one? I went on along Fleet Street, but could not shake off the idea. The snake had charmed me.

"You understand it was a Continental concern, that Trading Society; but I have a lot of relations living on the Continent, because it's cheap and not so nasty as it looks, they say.

"I am sorry to own I began to worry them. This was already a fresh departure for me. I was not used to get things that way, you know. I always went my own road and on my own legs where I had a mind to go. I wouldn't have believed it of myself; but, then—you see—I felt somehow I must get there by hook or by crook. So I worried them. The men said, 'My dear fellow,' and did nothing. Then—would you believe it?—I tried the women. I, Charlie Marlow, set the women to work—to get a job. Heavens! Well, you see, the notion drove me. I had an aunt, a dear enthusiastic soul. She wrote: 'It will be delightful. I am ready to do anything, anything for you. It is a glorious idea. I know the wife of a very high personage in the Administration, and also a man who has lots of influence with,' etc. etc. She was determined to make no end of fuss to get me appointed skipper of a river steamboat, if such was my fancy.

"I got my appointment—of course; and I got it very quick. It appears the Company had received news that one of their captains had been killed in a scuffle with the natives. This was my chance, and it made me the more anxious to go. It was only months and months afterwards, when I made the attempt to recover what was left of the body, that I heard the original quarrel arose from a misunderstanding about some hens. Yes, two black hens. Fresleven—that was the fellow's name, a Dane—thought himself wronged somehow in the bargain, so he went ashore and started to hammer the chief of the village with a stick. Oh, it didn't surprise me in the least to hear this, and at the same time to be told that Fresleven was the gentlest, quietest creature that ever walked on two legs. No doubt he was; but he had been a couple of years already out there engaged in the noble cause, you know, and he probably felt the need at last of asserting his self-respect in some way. Therefore he whacked the old nigger mercilessly, while a big crowd of his people watched him, thunderstruck, till some man—I was told the chief's son—in desperation at hearing the old chap yell, made a tentative jab with a spear at the white man—and of course it went quite easy between the shoulder-blades. Then the whole population cleared into the forest, expecting all kinds of calamities to happen, while, on the other hand, the steamer Fresleven commanded left also in a bad panic, in charge of the engineer, I believe. Afterwards nobody seemed to trouble much about Fresleven's remains, till I got out and stepped into his shoes. I couldn't let it rest, though; but when an opportunity offered at last to meet my predecessor, the grass growing through his ribs was tall enough to hide his bones. They were all there. The supernatural being had not been touched after he fell. And the village was deserted, the huts gaped black, rotting, all askew within the fallen enclosures. A calamity had come to it, sure enough. The people had vanished. Mad terror had scattered them, men, women, and children, through the bush, and they had never returned. What became of the hens I don't know either. I should think the cause of progress got them, anyhow. However, through this glorious affair I got my appointment, before I had fairly begun to hope for it.

"I flew around like mad to get ready, and before forty-eight hours I was crossing the Channel to show myself to my employers, and sign the contract. In a very few hours I arrived in a city that always makes me think of a whited sepulchre. Prejudice no doubt. I had no difficulty in finding the Company's offices. It was the biggest thing in the town, and everybody I met was full of it. They were going to run an oversea empire, and make no end of coin by trade.

"A narrow and deserted street in deep shadow, high houses, innumerable windows with venetian blinds, a dead silence, grass sprouting between the stones, imposing carriage archways right and left, immense double doors standing ponderously ajar. I slipped through one of these cracks, went up a swept and ungarnished staircase, as arid as a desert, and opened the first door I came to. Two women, one fat and the other slim, sat on straw-bottomed chairs, knitting black wool. The slim one got up and walked straight at me—still knitting with downcast eyes—and only just as I began to think of getting out of her way, as you would for a somnambulist, stood still, and looked up. Her dress was as plain as an umbrella-cover, and she turned round without a word and preceded me into a waiting-room. I gave my name, and looked about. Deal table in the middle, plain chairs all round the walls, on one end a large shining map, marked with all the colours of a rainbow. There was a vast amount of red—good to see at any time, because one knows that some real work is done in there, a deuce of a lot of blue, a little green, smears of orange, and, on the East Coast, a purple patch, to show where the jolly pioneers of progress drink the jolly lager-beer. However, I wasn't going into any of these. I was going into the yellow. Dead in the centre. And the river was there—fascinating—deadly—like a snake. Ough! A door opened, a white-haired secretarial head, but wearing a compassionate expression, appeared, and a skinny forefinger beckoned me into the sanctuary. Its light was dim, and a heavy writing desk squatted in the middle. From behind that structure came out an impression of pale plumpness in a frockcoat. The great man himself. He was five feet six, I should judge, and had his grip on the handle-end of ever so many millions. He shook hands, I fancy, murmured vaguely, was satisfied with my French. *Bon voyage.*

"In about forty-five seconds I found myself again in the waiting-room with the compassionate secretary, who, full of desolation and sympathy, made me sign some document. I believe I undertook amongst other things not to disclose any trade secrets. Well, I am not going to.

"I began to feel slightly uneasy. You know I am not used to such ceremonies, and there was something ominous in the atmosphere. It was just as though I had been let into some conspiracy—I don't know—something not quite right; and I was glad to get out. In the outer room the two women knitted black wool feverishly. People were arriving, and the younger one was walking back and forth introducing them. The old one sat on her chair. Her flat cloth slippers were propped up on a foot-warmer, and a cat reposed on her lap. She wore a starched white affair on her head, had a wart on one cheek, and silver-rimmed spectacles hung on the tip of her nose. She glanced at me above the glasses. The swift and indifferent placidity of that look troubled me. Two youths with foolish and cheery countenances were being piloted over, and she threw at them the same quick glance of unconcerned wisdom. She seemed to know all about them and about me too. An eerie feeling came over me. She seemed uncanny and fateful. Often far away there I thought of these two, guarding the door of Darkness, knitting black wool as for a warm pall, one introducing, introducing continuously to the unknown, the other scrutinising the cheery and foolish faces with unconcerned old eyes. *Ave!* Old knitter of black wool. *Morituri te salutant.*[9] Not many of those she looked at ever saw her again—not half, by a long way.

"There was yet a visit to the doctor. 'A simple formality,' assured me the secretary, with an air of taking an immense part in all my sorrows. Accordingly a young chap wearing his hat over the left eyebrow, some clerk I suppose—there must have been clerks in the business, though the house was as still as a house in a city of the dead—came from somewhere upstairs, and led me forth. He was shabby and careless, with ink-stains on the sleeves of his jacket, and his cravat was large and billowy, under a chin shaped like the toe of an old boot. It was a little too early for the doctor, so I proposed a drink, and thereupon he developed a vein of joviality. As we sat over our vermuths he glorified the Company's business, and by and by I expressed casually my surprise at him not going out there. He became very cool and collected all at once. 'I am not such a fool as I look, quoth Plato to his disciples,' he said sententiously, emptied his glass with great resolution, and we rose.

"The old doctor felt my pulse, evidently thinking of something else the while. 'Good, good for there,' he mumbled, and then with a certain eagerness asked me whether I would let him measure my head. Rather surprised, I said Yes, when he produced a thing like callipers and got the dimensions back and front and every way, taking notes carefully. He was an unshaven little man in a threadbare coat like a gaberdine, with his feet in slippers, and I thought him a harmless fool. 'I always ask leave, in the interests of science, to measure the crania of those going out there,' he said. 'And when they come back too?' I asked. 'Oh, I never see them,' he remarked; 'and, moreover, the changes take place inside, you know.' He smiled, as if at some quiet joke. 'So you are going out there. Famous. Interesting too.' He gave me a searching glance, and made another note. 'Ever any madness in your family?' he asked, in a matter-of-fact tone. I felt very annoyed. 'Is that question in the interests

9. "Hail! . . . Those who are about to die salute you" (Latin). The Roman gladiators' salute to the emperor on entering the arena.

of science too?' 'It would be,' he said, without taking notice of my irritation, 'interesting for science to watch the mental changes of individuals, on the spot, but . . . ' 'Are you an alienist?'[1] I interrupted. 'Every doctor should be—a little,' answered that original[2] imperturbably. 'I have a little theory which you Messieurs who go out there must help me to prove. This is my share in the advantages my country shall reap from the possession of such a magnificent dependency. The mere wealth I leave to others. Pardon my questions, but you are the first Englishman coming under my observation . . . ' I hastened to assure him I was not in the least typical. 'If I were,' said I, 'I wouldn't be talking like this with you.' 'What you say is rather profound, and probably erroneous,' he said, with a laugh. 'Avoid irritation more than exposure to the sun. Adieu. How do you English say, eh? Good-bye. Ah! Good-bye. Adieu. In the tropics one must before everything keep calm.' . . . . He lifted a warning forefinger. . . . 'Du calme, du calme. Adieu.'

"One thing more remained to do—say good-bye to my excellent aunt. I found her triumphant. I had a cup of tea—the last decent cup of tea for many days—and in a room that most soothingly looked just as you would expect a lady's drawing-room to look, we had a long quiet chat by the fireside. In the course of these confidences it became quite plain to me I had been represented to the wife of the high dignitary, and goodness knows to how many more people besides, as an exceptional and gifted creature—a piece of good fortune for the Company—a man you don't get hold of every day. Good heavens! and I was going to take charge of a two-penny-halfpenny river-steamboat with a penny whistle attached! It appeared, however, I was also one of the Workers, with a capital—you know. Something like an emissary of light, something like a lower sort of apostle. There had been a lot of such rot let loose in print and talk just about that time, and the excellent woman, living right in the rush of all that humbug, got carried off her feet. She talked about 'weaning those ignorant millions from their horrid ways,' till, upon my word, she made me quite uncomfortable. I ventured to hint that the Company was run for profit.

" 'You forget, dear Charlie, that the labourer is worthy of his hire,' she said brightly. It's queer how out of touch with truth women are. They live in a world of their own, and there had never been anything like it, and never can be. It is too beautiful altogether, and if they were to set it up it would go to pieces before the first sunset. Some confounded fact we men have been living contentedly with ever since the day of creation would start up and knock the whole thing over.

"After this I got embraced, told to wear flannel, be sure to write often, and so on—and I left. In the street—I don't know why—a queer feeling came to me that I was an impostor. Odd thing that I, who used to clear out for any part of the world at twenty-four hours' notice, with less thought than most men give to the crossing of a street, had a moment—I won't say of hesitation, but of startled pause, before this commonplace affair. The best way I can explain it to you is by saying that, for a second or two, I felt as though, instead of going to the centre of a continent, I were about to set off for the centre of the earth.

"I left in a French steamer, and she called in every blamed port they have

1. Doctor who treats mental diseases. (The term   2. Eccentric person.
has now been replaced by *psychiatrist*.)

out there, for, as far as I could see, the sole purpose of landing soldiers and custom-house officers. I watched the coast. Watching a coast as it slips by the ship is like thinking about an enigma. There it is before you—smiling, frowning, inviting, grand, mean, insipid, or savage, and always mute with an air of whispering, Come and find out. This one was almost featureless, as if still in the making, with an aspect of monotonous grimness. The edge of a colossal jungle, so dark green as to be almost black, fringed with white surf, ran straight, like a ruled line, far, far away along a blue sea whose glitter was blurred by a creeping mist. The sun was fierce, the land seemed to glisten and drip with steam. Here and there greyish-whitish specks showed up clustered inside the white surf, with a flag flying above them perhaps—settlements some centuries old, and still no bigger than pin-heads on the untouched expanse of their background. We pounded along, stopped, landed soldiers; went on, landed custom-house clerks to levy toll in what looked like a God-forsaken wilderness, with a tin shed and a flag-pole lost in it; landed more soldiers—to take care of the custom-house clerks presumably. Some, I heard, got drowned in the surf; but whether they did or not, nobody seemed particularly to care. They were just flung out there, and on we went. Every day the coast looked the same, as though we had not moved; but we passed various places—trading places—with names like Gran' Bassam, Little Popo; names that seemed to belong to some sordid farce acted in front of a sinister back-cloth. The idleness of a passenger, my isolation amongst all these men with whom I had no point of contact, the oily and languid sea, the uniform sombreness of the coast, seemed to keep me away from the truth of things, within the toil of a mournful and senseless delusion. The voice of the surf heard now and then was a positive pleasure, like the speech of a brother. It was something natural, that had its reason, that had a meaning. Now and then a boat from the shore gave one a momentary contact with reality. It was paddled by black fellows. You could see from afar the white of their eyeballs glistening. They shouted, sang; their bodies streamed with perspiration; they had faces like grotesque masks—these chaps; but they had bone, muscle, a wild vitality, an intense energy of movement, that was as natural and true as the surf along their coast. They wanted no excuse for being there. They were a great comfort to look at. For a time I would feel I belonged still to a world of straightforward facts; but the feeling would not last long. Something would turn up to scare it away. Once, I remember, we came upon a man-of-war anchored off the coast. There wasn't even a shed there, and she was shelling the bush. It appears the French had one of their wars going on thereabouts. Her ensign dropped limp like a rag; the muzzles of the long six-inch guns stuck out all over the low hull; the greasy, slimy swell swung her up lazily and let her down, swaying her thin masts. In the empty immensity of earth, sky, and water, there she was, incomprehensible, firing into a continent. Pop, would go one of the six-inch guns; a small flame would dart and vanish, a little white smoke would disappear, a tiny projectile would give a feeble screech—and nothing happened. Nothing could happen. There was a touch of insanity in the proceeding, a sense of lugubrious drollery in the sight; and it was not dissipated by somebody on board assuring me earnestly there was a camp of natives—he called them enemies!—hidden out of sight somewhere.

"We gave her her letters (I heard the men in that lonely ship were dying of fever at the rate of three a day) and went on. We called at some more places with farcical names, where the merry dance of death and trade goes on in a still and earthy atmosphere as of an overheated catacomb; all along the formless coast bordered by dangerous surf, as if Nature herself had tried to ward off intruders; in and out of rivers, streams of death in life, whose banks were rotting into mud, whose waters, thickened into slime, invaded the contorted mangroves, that seemed to writhe at us in the extremity of an impotent despair. Nowhere did we stop long enough to get a particularised impression, but the general sense of vague and oppressive wonder grew upon me. It was like a weary pilgrimage amongst hints for nightmares.

"It was upward of thirty days before I saw the mouth of the big river. We anchored off the seat of the government. But my work would not begin till some two hundred miles farther on. So as soon as I could I made a start for a place thirty miles higher up.

"I had my passage on a little sea-going steamer. Her captain was a Swede, and knowing me for a seaman, invited me on the bridge. He was a young man, lean, fair, and morose, with lanky hair and a shuffling gait. As we left the miserable little wharf, he tossed his head contemptuously at the shore. 'Been living there?' he asked. I said, 'Yes.' 'Fine lot these government chaps—are they not?' he went on, speaking English with great precision and considerable bitterness. 'It is funny what some people will do for a few francs a month. I wonder what becomes of that kind when it goes up country?' I said to him I expected to see that soon. 'So-o-o!' he exclaimed. He shuffled athwart, keeping one eye ahead vigilantly. 'Don't be too sure,' he continued. 'The other day I took up a man who hanged himself on the road. He was a Swede, too.' 'Hanged himself! Why, in God's name?' I cried. He kept on looking out watchfully. 'Who knows? The sun too much for him, or the country perhaps.'

"At last we opened a reach. A rocky cliff appeared, mounds of turned-up earth by the shore, houses on a hill, others with iron roofs, amongst a waste of excavations, or hanging to the declivity. A continuous noise of the rapids above hovered over this scene of inhabited devastation. A lot of people, mostly black and naked, moved about like ants. A jetty projected into the river. A blinding sunlight drowned all this at times in a sudden recrudescence of glare. 'There's your Company's station,' said the Swede, pointing to three wooden barrack-like structures on the rocky slope. 'I will send your things up. Four boxes did you say? So. Farewell.'

"I came upon a boiler wallowing in the grass, then found a path leading up the hill. It turned aside for the boulders, and also for an undersized railway truck lying there on its back with its wheels in the air. One was off. The thing looked as dead as the carcass of some animal. I came upon more pieces of decaying machinery, a stack of rusty nails. To the left a clump of trees made a shady spot, where dark things seemed to stir feebly. I blinked, the path was steep. A horn tooted to the right, and I saw the black people run. A heavy and dull detonation shook the ground, a puff of smoke came out of the cliff, and that was all. No change appeared on the face of the rock. They were building a railway. The cliff was not in the way or anything; but this objectless blasting was all the work going on.

"A slight clinking behind me made me turn my head. Six black men advanced in a file, toiling up the path. They walked erect and slow, balancing small baskets full of earth on their heads, and the clink kept time with their footsteps. Black rags were wound round their loins, and the short ends behind waggled to and fro like tails. I could see every rib, the joints of their limbs were like knots in a rope; each had an iron collar on his neck, and all were connected together with a chain whose bights swung between them, rhythmically clinking. Another report from the cliff made me think suddenly of that ship of war I had seen firing into a continent. It was the same kind of ominous voice; but these men could by no stretch of imagination be called enemies. They were called criminals, and the outraged law, like the bursting shells, had come to them, an insoluble mystery from the sea. All their meagre breasts panted together, the violently dilated nostrils quivered, the eyes stared stonily uphill. They passed me within six inches, without a glance, with that complete, deathlike indifference of unhappy savages. Behind this raw matter one of the reclaimed, the product of the new forces at work, strolled despondently, carrying a rifle by its middle. He had a uniform jacket with one button off, and seeing a white man on the path, hoisted his weapon to his shoulder with alacrity. This was simple prudence, white men being so much alike at a distance that he could not tell who I might be. He was speedily reassured, and with a large, white, rascally grin, and a glance at his charge, seemed to take me into partnership in his exalted trust. After all, I also was a part of the great cause of these high and just proceedings.

"Instead of going up, I turned and descended to the left. My idea was to let that chain-gang get out of sight before I climbed the hill. You know I am not particularly tender; I've had to strike and to fend off. I've had to resist and to attack sometimes—that's only one way of resisting—without counting the exact cost, according to the demands of such sort of life as I had blundered into. I've seen the devil of violence, and the devil of greed, and the devil of hot desire; but, by all the stars! these were strong, lusty, red-eyed devils, that swayed and drove men—men, I tell you. But as I stood on this hillside, I foresaw that in the blinding sunshine of that land I would become acquainted with a flabby, pretending, weak-eyed devil of a rapacious and pitiless folly. How insidious he could be, too, I was only to find out several months later and a thousand miles farther. For a moment I stood appalled, as though by a warning. Finally I descended the hill, obliquely, towards the trees I had seen.

"I avoided a vast artificial hole somebody had been digging on the slope, the purpose of which I found it impossible to divine. It wasn't a quarry or a sandpit, anyhow. It was just a hole. It might have been connected with the philanthropic desire of giving the criminals something to do. I don't know. Then I nearly fell into a very narrow ravine, almost no more than a scar in the hillside. I discovered that a lot of imported drainage-pipes for the settlement had been tumbled in there. There wasn't one that was not broken. It was a wanton smash-up. At last I got under the trees. My purpose was to stroll into the shade for a moment; but no sooner within than it seemed to me I had stepped into the gloomy circle of some Inferno. The rapids were near, and an uninterrupted, uniform, headlong, rushing noise filled the mournful stillness of the grove, where not a breath stirred, not a leaf moved, with a mysterious sound—as though the tearing pace of the launched earth had suddenly become audible.

"Black shapes crouched, lay, sat between the trees, leaning against the trunks, clinging to the earth, half coming out, half effaced within the dim light, in all the attitudes of pain, abandonment, and despair. Another mine on the cliff went off, followed by a slight shudder of the soil under my feet. The work was going on. The work! And this was the place where some of the helpers had withdrawn to die.

"They were dying slowly—it was very clear. They were not enemies, they were not criminals, they were nothing earthly now—nothing but black shadows of disease and starvation, lying confusedly in the greenish gloom. Brought from all the recesses of the coast in all the legality of time contracts, lost in uncongenial surroundings, fed on unfamiliar food, they sickened, became inefficient, and were then allowed to crawl away and rest. These moribund shapes were free as air—and nearly as thin. I began to distinguish the gleam of eyes under the trees. Then, glancing down, I saw a face near my hand. The black bones reclined at full length with one shoulder against the tree, and slowly the eyelids rose and the sunken eyes looked up at me, enormous and vacant, a kind of blind, white flicker in the depths of the orbs, which died out slowly. The man seemed young—almost a boy—but you know with them it's hard to tell. I found nothing else to do but to offer him one of my good Swede's ship's biscuits I had in my pocket. The fingers closed slowly on it and held—there was no other movement and no other glance. He had tied a bit of white worsted[3] round his neck—Why? Where did he get it? Was it a badge—an ornament—a charm—a propitiatory act? Was there any idea at all connected with it? It looked startling round his black neck, this bit of white thread from beyond the seas.

"Near the same tree two more bundles of acute angles sat with their legs drawn up. One, with his chin propped on his knees, stared at nothing, in an intolerable and appalling manner: his brother phantom rested its forehead, as if overcome with a great weariness; and all about others were scattered in every pose of contorted collapse, as in some picture of a massacre or a pestilence. While I stood horror-struck, one of these creatures rose to his hands and knees, and went off on all-fours towards the river to drink. He lapped out of his hand, then sat up in the sunlight, crossing his shins in front of him, and after a time let his woolly head fall on his breastbone.

"I didn't want any more loitering in the shade, and I made haste towards the station. When near the buildings I met a white man, in such an unexpected elegance of get-up that in the first moment I took him for a sort of vision. I saw a high starched collar, white cuffs, a light alpaca[4] jacket, snowy trousers, a clear necktie, and varnished boots. No hat. Hair parted, brushed, oiled, under a green-lined parasol held in a big white hand. He was amazing, and had a penholder behind his ear.

"I shook hands with this miracle, and I learned he was the Company's chief accountant, and that all the book-keeping was done at this station. He had come out for a moment, he said, 'to get a breath of fresh air.' The expression sounded wonderfully odd, with its suggestion of sedentary desk-life. I wouldn't have mentioned the fellow to you at all, only it was from his lips that I first heard the name of the man who is so indissolubly connected with the memories of that time. Moreover, I respected the fellow. Yes; I

---

3. Fine wool fabric.
4. Made from the wool of a South American animal.

respected his collars, his vast cuffs, his brushed hair. His appearance was certainly that of a hairdresser's dummy; but in the great demoralisation of the land he kept up his appearance. That's backbone. His starched collars and got-up shirt-fronts were achievements of character. He had been out nearly three years; and, later, I could not help asking him how he managed to sport such linen. He had just the faintest blush, and said modestly, 'I've been teaching one of the native women about the station. It was difficult. She had a distaste for the work.' Thus this man had verily accomplished something. And he was devoted to his books, which were in apple-pie order.

"Everything else in the station was in a muddle,—heads, things, buildings. Strings of dusty niggers with splay feet arrived and departed; a stream of manufactured goods, rubbishy cottons, beads, and brass-wire sent into the depths of darkness, and in return came a precious trickle of ivory.

"I had to wait in the station for ten days—an eternity. I lived in a hut in the yard, but to be out of the chaos I would sometimes get into the account-ant's office. It was built of horizontal planks, and so badly put together that, as he bent over his high desk, he was barred from neck to heels with narrow strips of sunlight. There was no need to open the big shutter to see. It was hot there too; big flies buzzed fiendishly, and did not sting, but stabbed. I sat generally on the floor, while, of faultless appearance (and even slightly scented), perching on a high stool, he wrote, he wrote. Sometimes he stood up for exercise. When a truckle-bed with a sick man (some invalided agent from up country) was put in there, he exhibited a gentle annoyance. 'The groans of this sick person' he said, 'distract my attention. And without that it is extremely difficult to guard against clerical errors in this climate.'

"One day he remarked, without lifting his head, 'In the interior you will no doubt meet Mr Kurtz.' On my asking who Mr Kurtz was, he said he was a first-class agent; and seeing my disappointment at this information, he added slowly, laying down his pen, 'He is a very remarkable person.' Further questions elicited from him that Mr Kurtz was at present in charge of a trading-post, a very important one, in the true ivory-country, at 'the very bottom of there. Sends in as much ivory as all the others put together . . .' He began to write again. The sick man was too ill to groan. The flies buzzed in a great peace.

"Suddenly there was a growing murmur of voices and a great tramping of feet. A caravan had come in. A violent babble of uncouth sounds burst out on the other side of the planks. All the carriers were speaking together, and in the midst of the uproar the lamentable voice of the chief agent was heard 'giving it up' tearfully for the twentieth time that day. . . . He rose slowly. 'What a frightful row,' he said. He crossed the room gently to look at the sick man, and returning, said to me, 'He does not hear.' 'What! Dead?' I asked, startled. 'No, not yet,' he answered, with great composure. Then, alluding with a toss of the head to the tumult in the station-yard, 'When one has got to make correct entries, one comes to hate those savages—hate them to the death.' He remained thoughtful for a moment. 'When you see Mr Kurtz,' he went on, 'tell him from me that everything here'—he glanced at the desk—'is very satisfactory. I don't like to write to him—with those messengers of ours you never know who may get hold of your letter—at that Central Sta-tion.' He stared at me for a moment with his mild, bulging eyes. 'Oh, he will go far, very far,' he began again. 'He will be a somebody in the Administration before long. They, above—the Council in Europe, you know—mean him to be.'

"He turned to his work. The noise outside had ceased, and presently in going out I stopped at the door. In the steady buzz of flies the homeward-bound agent was lying flushed and insensible; the other, bent over his books, was making correct entries of perfectly correct transactions; and fifty feet below the doorstep I could see the still tree-tops of the grove of death.

"Next day I left that station at last, with a caravan of sixty men, for a two-hundred-mile tramp.

"No use telling you much about that. Paths, paths, everywhere; a stamped-in network of paths spreading over the empty land, through long grass, through burnt grass, through thickets, down and up chilly ravines, up and down stony hills ablaze with heat; and a solitude, a solitude, nobody, not a hut. The population had cleared out a long time ago. Well, if a lot of mysterious niggers armed with all kinds of fearful weapons suddenly took to travelling on the road between Deal and Gravesend, catching the yokels right and left to carry heavy loads for them, I fancy every farm and cottage thereabouts would get empty very soon. Only here the dwellings were gone too. Still, I passed through several abandoned villages. There's something pathetically childish in the ruins of grass walls. Day after day, with the stamp and shuffle of sixty pair of bare feet behind me, each pair under a 60-lb. load. Camp, cook, sleep, strike camp, march. Now and then a carrier dead in harness, at rest in the long grass near the path, with an empty water-gourd and his long staff lying by his side. A great silence around and above. Perhaps on some quiet night the tremor of far-off drums, sinking, swelling, a tremor vast, faint; a sound weird, appealing, suggestive, and wild—and perhaps with as profound a meaning as the sound of bells in a Christian country. Once a white man in an unbuttoned uniform, camping on the path with an armed escort of lank Zanzibaris,[5] very hospitable and festive—not to say drunk. Was looking after the upkeep of the road, he declared. Can't say I saw any road or any upkeep, unless the body of a middle-aged negro, with a bullet-hole in the forehead, upon which I absolutely stumbled three miles farther on, may be considered as a permanent improvement. I had a white companion too, not a bad chap, but rather too fleshy and with the exasperating habit of fainting on the hot hillsides, miles away from the least bit of shade and water. Annoying, you know, to hold your own coat like a parasol over a man's head while he is coming-to. I couldn't help asking him once what he meant by coming there at all. 'To make money, of course. What do you think?' he said scornfully. Then he got fever, and had to be carried in a hammock slung under a pole. As he weighed sixteen stone[6] I had no end of rows with the carriers. They jibbed, ran away, sneaked off with their loads in the night—quite a mutiny. So, one evening, I made a speech in English with gestures, not one of which was lost to the sixty pairs of eyes before me, and the next morning I started the hammock off in front all right. An hour afterwards I came upon the whole concern wrecked in a bush—man, hammock, groans, blankets, horrors. The heavy pole had skinned his poor nose. He was very

5. Natives of Zanzibar, an island off the east coast of Africa, once part of the sultanate of Zanzibar and a British protectorate, now part of the independent state of Tanzania. Zanzibaris were used as mercenaries throughout Africa.

6. One stone equals 14 pounds. The man weighed 224 pounds.

anxious for me to kill somebody, but there wasn't the shadow of a carrier near. I remembered the old doctor—'It would be interesting for science to watch the mental changes of individuals, on the spot.' I felt I was becoming scientifically interesting. However, all that is to no purpose. On the fifteenth day I came in sight of the big river again, and hobbled into the Central Station. It was on a back water surrounded by scrub and forest, with a pretty border of smelly mud on one side, and on the three others enclosed by a crazy fence of rushes. A neglected gap was all the gate it had, and the first glance at the place was enough to let you see the flabby devil was running that show. White men with long staves in their hands appeared languidly from amongst the buildings, strolling up to take a look at me, and then retired out of sight somewhere. One of them, a stout, excitable chap with black moustaches, informed me with great volubility and many digressions, as soon as I told him who I was, that my steamer was at the bottom of the river. I was thunderstruck. What, how, why? Oh, it was 'all right.' The 'manager himself' was there. All quite correct. 'Everybody had behaved splendidly! splendidly!'—'You must,' he said in agitation, 'go and see the general manager at once. He is waiting!'

"I did not see the real significance of that wreck at once. I fancy I see it now, but I am not sure—not at all. Certainly the affair was too stupid—when I think of it—to be altogether natural. Still . . . But at the moment it presented itself simply as a confounded nuisance. The steamer was sunk. They had started two days before in a sudden hurry up the river with the manager on board, in charge of some volunteer skipper, and before they had been out three hours they tore the bottom out of her on stones, and she sank near the south bank. I asked myself what I was to do there, now my boat was lost. As a matter of fact, I had plenty to do in fishing my command out of the river. I had to set about it the very next day. That, and the repairs when I brought the pieces to the station, took some months.

"My first interview with the manager was curious. He did not ask me to sit down after my twenty-mile walk that morning. He was commonplace in complexion, in feature, in manners, and in voice. He was of middle size and of ordinary build. His eyes, of the usual blue, were perhaps remarkably cold, and he certainly could make his glance fall on one as trenchant and heavy as an axe. But even at these times the rest of his person seemed to disclaim the intention. Otherwise there was only an indefinable, faint expression of his lips, something stealthy—a smile—not a smile—I remember it, but I can't explain. It was unconscious, this smile was, though just after he had said something it got intensified for an instant. It came at the end of his speeches like a seal applied on the words to make the meaning of the commonest phrase appear absolutely inscrutable. He was a common trader, from his youth up employed in these parts—nothing more. He was obeyed, yet he inspired neither love nor fear, nor even respect. He inspired uneasiness. That was it! Uneasiness. Not a definite mistrust—just uneasiness—nothing more. You have no idea how effective such a . . . a . . . faculty can be. He had no genius for organising, for initiative, or for order even. That was evident in such things as the deplorable state of the station. He had no learning, and no intelligence. His position had come to him—why? Perhaps because he was never ill . . . He had served three terms of three years out there . . . Because triumphant health in the general rout of constitutions is a kind of power in itself. When he went home on leave he rioted on a large scale—pompously. Jack ashore—with a difference—in externals only. This one could gather from his casual talk. He originated nothing, he could keep the routine going—that's all. But he was great. He was great by this little thing that it was impossible to tell what could control such a man. He never gave that secret away. Perhaps there was nothing within him. Such a suspicion made one pause—for out there there were no external checks. Once when various tropical diseases had laid low almost every 'agent' in the station, he was heard to say, 'Men who come out here should have no entrails.' He sealed the utterance with that smile of his, as though it had been a door opening into a darkness he had in his keeping. You fancied you had seen things—but the seal was on. When annoyed at meal-times by the constant quarrels of the white men about precedence, he ordered an immense round table to be made, for which a special house had to be built. This was the station's mess-room. Where he sat was the first place—the rest were nowhere. One felt this to be his unalterable conviction. He was neither civil nor uncivil. He was quiet. He allowed his 'boy'—an overfed young negro from the coast—to treat the white men, under his very eyes, with provoking insolence.

"He began to speak as soon as he saw me. I had been very long on the road. He could not wait. Had to start without me. The up-river stations had to be relieved. There had been so many delays already that he did not know who was dead and who was alive, and how they got on—and so on, and so on. He paid no attention to my explanations, and, playing with a stick of sealing-wax, repeated several times that the situation was 'very grave, very grave.' There were rumours that a very important station was in jeopardy, and its chief, Mr Kurtz, was ill. Hoped it was not true. Mr Kurtz was . . . I felt weary and irritable. Hang Kurtz, I thought. I interrupted him by saying I had heard of Mr Kurtz on the coast. 'Ah! So they talk of him down there,' he murmured to himself. Then he began again, assuring me Mr Kurtz was the best agent he had, an exceptional man, of the greatest importance to the Company; therefore I could understand his anxiety. He was, he said, 'very, very uneasy.' Certainly he fidgeted on his chair a good deal, exclaimed, 'Ah, Mr Kurtz!' broke the stick of sealing-wax and seemed dumbfounded by the accident. Next thing he wanted to know 'how long it would take to' . . . I interrupted him again. Being hungry, you know, and kept on my feet too, I was getting savage. 'How can I tell?' I said, 'I haven't even seen the wreck yet—some months, no doubt.' All this talk seemed to me so futile. 'Some months,' he said. 'Well, let us say three months before we can make a start. Yes. That ought to do the affair.' I flung out of his hut (he lived all alone in a clay hut with a sort of verandah) muttering to myself my opinion of him. He was a chattering idiot. Afterwards I took it back when it was borne in upon me startlingly with what extreme nicety he had estimated the time requisite for the 'affair.'

"I went to work the next day, turning, so to speak, my back on that station. In that way only it seemed to me I could keep my hold on the redeeming facts of life. Still, one must look about sometimes; and then I saw this station, these men strolling aimlessly about in the sunshine of the yard. I asked myself sometimes what it all meant. They wandered here and there with their absurd long staves in their hands, like a lot of faithless pilgrims bewitched inside a rotten fence. The word 'ivory' rang in the air, was whispered, was sighed. You would think they were praying to it. A taint of imbecile rapacity blew through it all, like a whiff from some corpse. By Jove! I've never seen anything so unreal in my life. And outside, the silent wilderness surrounding this cleared speck on the earth struck me as something great and invincible, like evil or truth, waiting patiently for the passing away of this fantastic invasion.

"Oh, these months! Well, never mind. Various things happened. One evening a grass shed full of calico, cotton prints, beads, and I don't know what else, burst into a blaze so suddenly that you would have thought the earth had opened to let an avenging fire consume all that trash. I was smoking my pipe quietly by my dismantled steamer, and saw them all cutting capers in the light, with their arms lifted high, when the stout man with moustaches came tearing down to the river, a tin pail in his hand, assured me that everybody was 'behaving splendidly, splendidly,' dipped about a quart of water and tore back again. I noticed there was a hole in the bottom of his pail.

"I strolled up. There was no hurry. You see the thing had gone off like a box of matches. It had been hopeless from the very first. The flame had leaped high, driven everybody back, lighted up everything—and collapsed. The shed was already a heap of embers glowing fiercely. A nigger was being beaten near by. They said he had caused the fire in some way; be that as it may, he was screeching most horribly. I saw him, later, for several days, sitting in a bit of shade looking very sick and trying to recover himself: afterwards he arose and went out—and the wilderness without a sound took him into its bosom again. As I approached the glow from the dark I found myself at the back of two men, talking. I heard the name of Kurtz pronounced, then the words, 'take advantage of this unfortunate accident.' One of the men was the manager. I wished him a good evening. 'Did you ever see anything like it—eh? it is incredible,' he said, and walked off. The other man remained. He was a first-class agent, young, gentlemanly, a bit reserved, with a forked little beard and a hooked nose. He was standoffish with the other agents, and they on their side said he was the manager's spy upon them. As to me, I had hardly ever spoken to him before. We got into talk, and by and by we strolled away from the hissing ruins. Then he asked me to his room, which was in the main building of the station. He struck a match, and I perceived that this young aristocrat had not only a silver-mounted dressing-case but also a whole candle all to himself. Just at that time the manager was the only man supposed to have any right to candles. Native mats covered the clay walls; a collection of spears, assegais,[7] shields, knives, was hung up in trophies. The business entrusted to this fellow was the making of bricks—so I had been informed; but there wasn't a fragment of a brick anywhere in the station, and he had been there more than a year—waiting. It seems he could not make bricks without something, I don't know what—straw maybe. Anyway, it could not be found there, and as it was not likely to be sent from Europe, it did not appear clear to me what he was waiting for. An act of special creation perhaps. However, they were all waiting—all the sixteen or twenty pilgrims of them—for something; and upon my word it did not seem an uncongenial occupation, from the way they took it, though the only thing that ever came to them was disease—as far as I could see. They beguiled the

---

7. Slender iron-tipped spears.

time by backbiting and intriguing against each other in a foolish kind of way. There was an air of plotting about that station, but nothing came of it, of course. It was as unreal as everything else—as the philanthropic pretence of the whole concern, as their talk, as their government, as their show of work. The only real feeling was a desire to get appointed to a trading-post where ivory was to be had, so that they could earn percentages. They intrigued and slandered and hated each other only on that account—but as to effectually lifting a little finger—oh no. By heavens! there is something after all in the world allowing one man to steal a horse while another must not look at a halter. Steal a horse straight out. Very well. He has done it. Perhaps he can ride. But there is a way of looking at a halter that would provoke the most charitable of saints into a kick.

"I had no idea why he wanted to be sociable, but as we chatted in there it suddenly occurred to me the fellow was trying to get at something—in fact, pumping me. He alluded constantly to Europe, to the people I was supposed to know there—putting leading questions as to my acquaintances in the sepulchral city, and so on. His little eyes glittered like mica[8] discs—with curiosity—though he tried to keep up a bit of superciliousness. At first I was astonished, but very soon I became awfully curious to see what he would find out from me. I couldn't possibly imagine what I had in me to make it worth his while. It was very pretty to see how he baffled himself, for in truth my body was full only of chills, and my head had nothing in it but that wretched steamboat business. It was evident he took me for a perfectly shameless prevaricator. At last he got angry, and, to conceal a movement of furious annoyance, he yawned. I rose. Then I noticed a small sketch in oils, on a panel, representing a woman, draped and blindfolded, carrying a lighted torch. The background was sombre—almost black. The movement of the woman was stately, and the effect of the torchlight on the face was sinister.

"It arrested me, and he stood by civilly, holding an empty half-pint champagne bottle (medical comforts) with the candle stuck in it. To my question he said Mr Kurtz had painted this—in this very station more than a year ago—while waiting for means to go to his trading-post. 'Tell me, pray,' said I, 'who is this Mr Kurtz?'

" 'The chief of the Inner Station,' he answered in a short tone, looking away. 'Much obliged,' I said, laughing. 'And you are the brickmaker of the Central Station. Every one knows that.' He was silent for a while. 'He is a prodigy,' he said at last. 'He is an emissary of pity, and science, and progress, and devil knows what else. We want,' he began to declaim suddenly, 'for the guidance of the cause entrusted to us by Europe, so to speak, higher intelligence, wide sympathies, a singleness of purpose.' 'Who says that?' I asked. 'Lots of them,' he replied. 'Some even write that; and so *he* comes here, a special being, as you ought to know.' 'Why ought I to know?' I interrupted, really surprised. He paid no attention. 'Yes. To-day he is chief of the best station, next year he will be assistant-manager, two years more and . . . but I daresay you know what he will be in two years' time. You are of the new gang—the gang of virtue. The same people who sent him specially also recommended you. Oh, don't say no. I've my own eyes to trust.' Light dawned upon me. My dear aunt's influential acquaintances were producing an unex-

8. Glassy mineral.

pected effect upon that young man. I nearly burst into a laugh. 'Do you read the Company's confidential correspondence?' I asked. He hadn't a word to say. It was great fun. 'When Mr Kurtz,' I continued severely, 'is General Manager, you won't have the opportunity.'

"He blew the candle out suddenly, and we went outside. The moon had risen. Black figures strolled about listlessly, pouring water on the glow, whence proceeded a sound of hissing; steam ascended in the moonlight; the beaten nigger groaned somewhere. 'What a row the brute makes!' said the indefatigable man with the moustaches, appearing near us. 'Serve him right. Transgression—punishment—bang! Pitiless, pitiless. That's the only way. This will prevent all conflagrations for the future. I was just telling the manager . . . ' He noticed my companion, and became crestfallen all at once. 'Not in bed yet,' he said, with a kind of servile heartiness; 'it's so natural. Ha! Danger—agitation.' He vanished. I went on to the river-side, and the other followed me. I heard a scathing murmur at my ear, 'Heap of muffs—go to.' The pilgrims could be seen in knots gesticulating, discussing. Several had still their staves in their hands. I verily believe they took these sticks to bed with them. Beyond the fence the forest stood up spectrally in the moonlight, and through the dim stir, through the faint sounds of that lamentable court-yard, the silence of the land went home to one's very heart—its mystery, its greatness, the amazing reality of its concealed life. The hurt nigger moaned feebly somewhere near by, and then fetched a deep sigh that made me mend my pace away from there. I felt a hand introducing itself under my arm. 'My dear sir,' said the fellow, 'I don't want to be misunderstood, and especially by you, who will see Mr Kurtz long before I can have that pleasure. I wouldn't like him to get a false idea of my disposition. . . . '

"I let him run on, this papier-mâché Mephistopheles, and it seemed to me that if I tried I could poke my forefinger through him, and would find nothing inside but a little loose dirt, maybe. He, don't you see, had been planning to be assistant-manager by and by under the present man, and I could see that the coming of that Kurtz had upset them both not a little. He talked precipitately, and I did not try to stop him. I had my shoulders against the wreck of my steamer, hauled up on the slope like a carcass of some big river animal. The smell of mud, of primeval mud, by Jove! was in my nostrils, the high stillness of primeval forest was before my eyes; there were shiny patches on the black creek. The moon had spread over everything a thin layer of silver—over the rank grass, over the mud, upon the wall of matted vegetation standing higher than the wall of a temple, over the great river I could see through a sombre gap glittering, glittering, as it flowed broadly by without a murmur. All this was great, expectant, mute, while the man jabbered about himself. I wondered whether the stillness on the face of the immensity looking at us two were meant as an appeal or as a menace. What were we who had strayed in here? Could we handle that dumb thing, or would it handle us? I felt how big, how confoundedly big, was that thing that couldn't talk and perhaps was deaf as well. What was in there? I could see a little ivory coming out from there, and I had heard Mr Kurtz was in there. I had heard enough about it too—God knows! Yet somehow it didn't bring any image with it—no more than if I had been told an angel or a fiend was in there. I believed it in the same way one of you might believe there are inhabitants in the planet Mars. I knew once a Scotch sailmaker who was certain, dead sure, there were people in Mars. If you asked him for some idea how they looked and behaved, he would get shy and mutter something about 'walking on all-fours.' If you as much as smiled, he would—though a man of sixty—offer to fight you. I would not have gone so far as to fight for Kurtz, but I went for him near enough to a lie. You know I hate, detest, and can't bear a lie, not because I am straighter than the rest of us, but simply because it appals me. There is a taint of death, a flavour of mortality in lies—which is exactly what I hate and detest in the world—what I want to forget. It makes me miserable and sick, like biting something rotten would do. Temperament, I suppose. Well, I went near enough to it by letting the young fool there believe anything he liked to imagine as to my influence in Europe. I became in an instant as much of a pretence as the rest of the bewitched pilgrims. This simply because I had a notion it somehow would be of help to that Kurtz whom at the time I did not see—you understand. He was just a word for me. I did not see the man in the name any more than you do. Do you see him? Do you see the story? Do you see anything? It seems to me I am trying to tell you a dream—making a vain attempt, because no relation of a dream can convey the dream-sensation, that commingling of absurdity, surprise, and bewilderment in a tremor of struggling revolt, that notion of being captured by the incredible which is of the very essence of dreams. . . ."

He was silent for a while.

". . . No, it is impossible; it is impossible to convey the life-sensation of any given epoch of one's existence—that which makes its truth, its meaning—its subtle and penetrating essence. It is impossible. We live, as we dream—alone. . . ."

He paused again as if reflecting, then added:

"Of course in this you fellows see more than I could then. You see me, whom you know. . . ."

It had become so pitch dark that we listeners could hardly see one another. For a long time already he, sitting apart, had been no more to us than a voice. There was not a word from anybody. The others might have been asleep, but I was awake. I listened, I listened on the watch for the sentence, for the word, that would give me the clue to the faint uneasiness inspired by this narrative that seemed to shape itself without human lips in the heavy night-air of the river.

". . . Yes—I let him run on," Marlow began again, "and think what he pleased about the powers that were behind me. I did! And there was nothing behind me! There was nothing but that wretched, old, mangled steamboat I was leaning against, while he talked fluently about 'the necessity for every man to get on.' 'And when one comes out here, you conceive, it is not to gaze at the moon.' Mr Kurtz was a 'universal genius,' but even a genius would find it easier to work with 'adequate tools—intelligent men.' He did not make bricks—why, there was a physical impossibility in the way—as I was well aware; and if he did secretarial work for the manager, it was because 'no sensible man rejects wantonly the confidence of his superiors.' Did I see it? I saw it. What more did I want? What I really wanted was rivets, by heaven! Rivets. To get on with the work—to stop the hole. Rivets I wanted. There were cases of them down at the coast—cases—piled up—burst—split! You kicked a loose rivet at every second step in that station yard on the hillside. Rivets had rolled into the grove of death. You could fill your pockets with rivets for the trouble of stooping down—and there wasn't one rivet to be found where it was wanted. We had plates that would do, but nothing to fasten them with. And every week the messenger, a lone negro, letter-bag on shoulder and staff in hand, left our station for the coast. And several times a week a coast caravan came in with trade goods—ghastly glazed calico that made you shudder only to look at it, glass beads value about a penny a quart, confounded spotted cotton handkerchiefs. And no rivets. Three carriers could have brought all that was wanted to set that steamboat afloat.

"He was becoming confidential now, but I fancy my unresponsive attitude must have exasperated him at last, for he judged it necessary to inform me he feared neither God nor devil, let alone any mere man. I said I could see that very well, but what I wanted was a certain quantity of rivets—and rivets were what really Mr Kurtz wanted, if he had only known it. Now letters went to the coast every week. . . . 'My dear sir,' he cried, 'I write from dictation.' I demanded rivets. There was a way—for an intelligent man. He changed his manner; became very cold, and suddenly began to talk about a hippopotamus; wondered whether sleeping on board the steamer (I stuck to my salvage night and day) I wasn't disturbed. There was an old hippo that had the bad habit of getting out on the bank and roaming at night over the station grounds. The pilgrims used to turn out in a body and empty every rifle they could lay hands on at him. Some even had sat up o' nights for him. All this energy was wasted, though. 'That animal has a charmed life,' he said; 'but you can say this only of brutes in this country. No man—you apprehend me?—no man here bears a charmed life.' He stood there for a moment in the moonlight with his delicate hooked nose set a little askew, and his mica eyes glittering without a wink, then, with a curt Good-night, he strode off. I could see he was disturbed and considerably puzzled, which made me feel more hopeful than I had been for days. It was a great comfort to turn from that chap to my influential friend, the battered, twisted, ruined, tinpot steamboat. I clambered on board. She rang under my feet like an empty Huntley & Palmer biscuit-tin kicked along a gutter; she was nothing so solid in make, and rather less pretty in shape, but I had expended enough hard work on her to make me love her. No influential friend would have served me better. She had given me a chance to come out a bit—to find out what I could do. No, I don't like work. I had rather laze about and think of all the fine things that can be done. I don't like work—no man does—but I like what is in the work— the chance to find yourself. Your own reality—for yourself, not for others— what no other man can ever know. They can only see the mere show, and never can tell what it really means.

"I was not surprised to see somebody sitting aft, on the deck, with his legs dangling over the mud. You see I rather chummed with the few mechanics there were in that station, whom the other pilgrims naturally despised—on account of their imperfect manners, I suppose. This was the foreman—a boiler-maker by trade—a good worker. He was a lank, bony, yellow-faced man, with big intense eyes. His aspect was worried, and his head was as bald as the palm of my hand; but his hair in falling seemed to have stuck to his chin, and had prospered in the new locality, for his beard hung down to his waist. He was a widower with six young children (he had left them in charge of a sister of his to come out there), and the passion of his life was pigeon-flying. He was an enthusiast and a connoisseur. He would rave about pigeons. After work hours he used sometimes to come over from his hut for a talk about his children and his pigeons; at work, when he had to crawl in the mud under the bottom of the steamboat, he would tie up that beard of his in a kind of white serviette[9] he brought for the purpose. It had loops to go over his ears. In the evening he could be seen squatted on the bank rinsing that wrapper in the creek with great care, then spreading it solemnly on a bush to dry.

"I slapped him on the back and shouted 'We shall have rivets!' He scrambled to his feet exclaiming 'No! Rivets!' as though he couldn't believe his ears. Then in a low voice, 'You . . . eh?' I don't know why we behaved like lunatics. I put my finger to the side of my nose and nodded mysteriously. 'Good for you!' he cried, snapped his fingers above his head, lifting one foot. I tried a jig. We capered on the iron deck. A frightful clatter came out of that hulk, and the virgin forest on the other bank of the creek sent it back in a thundering roll upon the sleeping station. It must have made some of the pilgrims sit up in their hovels. A dark figure obscured the lighted doorway of the manager's hut, vanished, then, a second or so after, the doorway itself vanished too. We stopped, and the silence driven away by the stamping of our feet flowed back again from the recesses of the land. The great wall of vegetation, an exuberant and entangled mass of trunks, branches, leaves, boughs, festoons, motionless in the moonlight, was like a rioting invasion of soundless life, a rolling wave of plants, piled up, crested, ready to topple over the creek, to sweep every little man of us out of his little existence. And it moved not. A deadened burst of mighty splashes and snorts reached us from afar, as though an ichthyosaurus[1] had been taking a bath of glitter in the great river. 'After all,' said the boiler-maker in a reasonable tone, 'why shouldn't we get the rivets?' Why not, indeed! I did not know of any reason why we shouldn't. 'They'll come in three weeks,' I said confidently.

"But they didn't. Instead of rivets there came an invasion, an infliction, a visitation. It came in sections during the next three weeks, each section headed by a donkey carrying a white man in new clothes and tan shoes, bowing from that elevation right and left to the impressed pilgrims. A quarrelsome band of footsore sulky niggers trod on the heels of the donkey; a lot of tents, camp-stools, tin boxes, white cases, brown bales would be shot down in the courtyard, and the air of mystery would deepen a little over the muddle of the station. Five such instalments came, with their absurd air of disorderly flight with the loot of innumerable outfit shops and provision stores, that, one would think, they were lugging, after a raid, into the wilderness for equitable division. It was an inextricable mess of things decent in themselves but that human folly made look like the spoils of thieving.

"This devoted band called itself the Eldorado[2] Exploring Expedition, and I believe they were sworn to secrecy. Their talk, however, was the talk of sordid buccaneers: it was reckless without hardihood, greedy without audacity, and cruel without courage; there was not an atom of foresight or of serious intention in the whole batch of them, and they did not seem aware these things are wanted for the work of the world. To tear treasure out of the bowels of the land was their desire, with no more moral purpose at the

9. Table napkin.
1. Large prehistoric marine creature.
2. Fabled laud of gold (*el dorado*, Spanish for "the

gilded") imagined by the Spanish conquistadors to exist in South America.

back of it than there is in burglars breaking into a safe. Who paid the expenses of the noble enterprise I don't know; but the uncle of our manager was leader of that lot.

"In exterior he resembled a butcher in a poor neighbourhood, and his eyes had a look of sleepy cunning. He carried his fat paunch with ostentation on his short legs, and during the time his gang infested the station spoke to no one but his nephew. You could see these two roaming about all day long with their heads close together in an everlasting confab.[3]

"I had given up worrying myself about the rivets. One's capacity for that kind of folly is more limited than you would suppose. I said Hang!—and let things slide. I had plenty of time for meditation, and now and then I would give some thought to Kurtz. I wasn't very interested in him. No. Still, I was curious to see whether this man, who had come out equipped with moral ideas of some sort, would climb to the top after all, and how he would set about his work when there."

2

"One evening as I was lying flat on the deck of my steamboat, I heard voices approaching—and there were the nephew and the uncle strolling along the bank. I laid my head on my arm again, and had nearly lost myself in a doze, when somebody said in my ear, as it were: 'I am as harmless as a little child, but I don't like to be dictated to. Am I the manager—or am I not? I was ordered to send him there. It's incredible.' . . . I became aware that the two were standing on the shore alongside the forepart of the steamboat, just below my head. I did not move; it did not occur to me to move: I was sleepy. 'It *is* unpleasant,' grunted the uncle. 'He has asked the Administration to be sent there,' said the other, 'with the idea of showing what he could do; and I was instructed accordingly. Look at the influence that man must have. Is it not frightful?' They both agreed it was frightful, then made several bizarre remarks: 'Make rain and fine weather—one man—the Council—by the nose'—bits of absurd sentences that got the better of my drowsiness, so that I had pretty near the whole of my wits about me when the uncle said, 'The climate may do away with this difficulty for you. Is he alone there?' 'Yes,' answered the manager; 'he sent his assistant down the river with a note to me in these terms: "Clear this poor devil out of the country, and don't bother sending more of that sort. I had rather be alone than have the kind of men you can dispose of with me." It was more than a year ago. Can you imagine such impudence?' 'Anything since then?' asked the other hoarsely. 'Ivory,' jerked the nephew; 'lots of it—prime sort—lots—most annoying, from him.' 'And with that?' questioned the heavy rumble. 'Invoice,' was the reply fired out, so to speak. Then silence. They had been talking about Kurtz.

"I was broad awake by this time, but, lying perfectly at ease, remained still, having no inducement to change my position. 'How did that ivory come all this way?' growled the elder man, who seemed very vexed. The other explained that it had come with a fleet of canoes in charge of an English half-caste clerk Kurtz had with him; that Kurtz had apparently intended to

3. Confabulation, talk.

return himself, the station being by that time bare of goods and stores, but after coming three hundred miles, had suddenly decided to go back, which he started to do alone in a small dugout with four paddlers, leaving the half-caste to continue down the river with the ivory. The two fellows there seemed astounded at anybody attempting such a thing. They were at a loss for an adequate motive. As for me, I seemed to see Kurtz for the first time. It was a distinct glimpse: the dugout, four paddling savages, and the lone white man turning his back suddenly on the headquarters, on relief, on thoughts of home—perhaps; setting his face towards the depths of the wilderness, towards his empty and desolate station. I did not know the motive. Perhaps he was just simply a fine fellow who stuck to his work for its own sake. His name, you understand, had not been pronounced once. He was 'that man.' The half-caste, who, as far as I could see, had conducted a difficult trip with great prudence and pluck, was invariably alluded to as 'that scoundrel.' The 'scoundrel' had reported that the 'man' had been very ill—had recovered imperfectly. . . . The two below me moved away then a few paces, and strolled back and forth at some little distance. I heard: 'Military post—doctor—two hundred miles—quite alone now—unavoidable delays—nine months—no news—strange rumours.' They approached again, just as the manager was saying, 'No one, as far as I know, unless a species of wandering trader—a pestilential fellow, snapping ivory from the natives.' Who was it they were talking about now? I gathered in snatches that this was some man supposed to be in Kurtz's district, and of whom the manager did not approve. 'We will not be free from unfair competition till one of these fellows is hanged for an example,' he said. 'Certainly,' grunted the other; 'get him hanged! Why not? Anything—anything can be done in this country. That's what I say; nobody here, you understand, *here*, can endanger your position. And why? You stand the climate—you outlast them all. The danger is in Europe; but there before I left I took care to—' They moved off and whispered, then their voices rose again. 'The extraordinary series of delays is not my fault. I did my possible.'[4] The fat man sighed, 'Very sad.' 'And the pestiferous absurdity of his talk,' continued the other; 'he bothered me enough when he was here. "Each station should be like a beacon on the road towards better things, a centre for trade of course, but also for humanising, improving, instructing." Conceive you—that ass! And he wants to be manager! No, it's—' Here he got choked by excessive indignation, and I lifted my head the least bit. I was surprised to see how near they were—right under me. I could have spat upon their hats. They were looking on the ground, absorbed in thought. The manager was switching his leg with a slender twig: his sagacious relative lifted his head. 'You have been well since you came out this time?' he asked. The other gave a start. 'Who? I? Oh! Like a charm—like a charm. But the rest—oh, my goodness! All sick. They die so quick, too, that I haven't the time to send them out of the country—it's incredible!' 'H'm. Just so,' grunted the uncle. 'Ah! my boy, trust to this—I say, trust to this.' I saw him extend his short flipper of an arm for a gesture that took in the forest, the creek, the mud, the river—seemed to beckon with a dishonouring flourish

---

4. Literal rendering of the French *J'ai fait mon possible* (I have done all I could). Conrad sprinkles the conversation of his Belgian characters with Gallicisms to remind us that their words, though reported in English, were spoken in French. Other examples are "a species of wandering trader" (above), "Conceive you" (below), "I would be desolated" (p. 1989).

before the sunlit face of the land a treacherous appeal to the lurking death, to the hidden evil, to the profound darkness of its heart. It was so startling that I leaped to my feet and looked back at the edge of the forest, as though I had expected an answer of some sort to that black display of confidence. You know the foolish notions that come to one sometimes. The high stillness confronted these two figures with its ominous patience, waiting for the passing away of a fantastic invasion.

"They swore aloud together—out of sheer fright, I believe—then, pretending not to know anything of my existence, turned back to the station. The sun was low; and leaning forward side by side, they seemed to be tugging painfully uphill their two ridiculous shadows of unequal length, that trailed behind them slowly over the tall grass without bending a single blade.

"In a few days the Eldorado Expedition went into the patient wilderness, that closed upon it as the sea closes over a diver. Long afterwards the news came that all the donkeys were dead. I know nothing as to the fate of the less valuable animals. They, no doubt, like the rest of us, found what they deserved. I did not inquire. I was then rather excited at the prospect of meeting Kurtz very soon. When I say very soon I mean it comparatively. It was just two months from the day we left the creek when we came to the bank below Kurtz's station.

"Going up that river was like travelling back to the earliest beginnings of the world, when vegetation rioted on the earth and the big trees were kings. An empty stream, a great silence, an impenetrable forest. The air was warm, thick, heavy, sluggish. There was no joy in the brilliance of sunshine. The long stretches of the waterway ran on, deserted, into the gloom of overshadowed distances. On silvery sandbanks hippos and alligators sunned themselves side by side. The broadening waters flowed through a mob of wooded islands; you lost your way on that river as you would in a desert, and butted all day long against shoals, trying to find the channel, till you thought yourself bewitched and cut off for ever from everything you had known once—somewhere—far away—in another existence perhaps. There were moments when one's past came back to one, as it will sometimes when you have not a moment to spare to yourself; but it came in the shape of an unrestful and noisy dream, remembered with wonder amongst the overwhelming realities of this strange world of plants, and water, and silence. And this stillness of life did not in the least resemble a peace. It was the stillness of an implacable force brooding over an inscrutable intention. It looked at you with a vengeful aspect. I got used to it afterwards; I did not see it any more; I had no time. I had to keep guessing at the channel; I had to discern, mostly by inspiration, the signs of hidden banks; I watched for sunken stones; I was learning to clap my teeth smartly before my heart flew out, when I shaved by a fluke some infernal sly old snag that would have ripped the life out of the tin-pot steamboat and drowned all the pilgrims; I had to keep a look-out for the signs of dead wood we could cut up in the night for next day's steaming. When you have to attend to things of that sort, to the mere incidents of the surface, the reality—the reality, I tell you— fades. The inner truth is hidden—luckily, luckily. But I felt it all the same; I felt often its mysterious stillness watching me at my monkey tricks, just as it watches you fellows performing on your respective tight-ropes for—what is it? half a crown a tumble—"

"Try to be civil, Marlow," growled a voice, and I knew there was at least one listener awake besides myself.

"I beg your pardon. I forgot the heartache which makes up the rest of the price. And indeed what does the price matter, if the trick be well done? You do your tricks very well. And I didn't do badly either, since I managed not to sink that steamboat on my first trip. It's a wonder to me yet. Imagine a blindfolded man set to drive a van over a bad road. I sweated and shivered over that business considerably, I can tell you. After all, for a seaman, to scrape the bottom of the thing that's supposed to float all the time under his care is the unpardonable sin. No one may know of it, but you never forget the thump—eh? A blow on the very heart. You remember it, you dream of it, you wake up at night and think of it—years after—and go hot and cold all over. I don't pretend to say that steamboat floated all the time. More than once she had to wade for a bit, with twenty cannibals splashing around and pushing. We had enlisted some of these chaps on the way for a crew. Fine fellows—cannibals—in their place. They were men one could work with, and I am grateful to them. And, after all, they did not eat each other before my face: they had brought along a provision of hippo-meat which went rotten, and made the mystery of the wilderness stink in my nostrils. Phoo! I can sniff it now. I had the manager on board and three or four pilgrims with their staves—all complete. Sometimes we came upon a station close by the bank, clinging to the skirts of the unknown, and the white men rushing out of a tumble-down hovel, with great gestures of joy and surprise and welcome, seemed very strange—had the appearance of being held there captive by a spell. The word 'ivory' would ring in the air for a while—and on we went again into the silence, along empty reaches, round the still bends, between the high walls of our winding way, reverberating in hollow claps the ponderous beat of the stern-wheel. Trees, trees, millions of trees, massive, immense, running up high; and at their foot, hugging the bank against the stream, crept the little begrimed steamboat, like a sluggish beetle crawling on the floor of a lofty portico. It made you feel very small, very lost, and yet it was not altogether depressing, that feeling. After all, if you were small, the grimy beetle crawled on—which was just what you wanted it to do. Where the pilgrims imagined it crawled to I don't know. To some place where they expected to get something, I bet! For me it crawled towards Kurtz—exclusively; but when the steam-pipes started leaking we crawled very slow. The reaches opened before us and closed behind, as if the forest had stepped leisurely across the water to bar the way for our return. We penetrated deeper and deeper into the heart of darkness. It was very quiet there. At night sometimes the roll of drums behind the curtain of trees would run up the river and remain sustained faintly, as if hovering in the air high over our heads, till the first break of day. Whether it meant war, peace, or prayer we could not tell. The dawns were heralded by the descent of a chill stillness; the woodcutters slept, their fires burned low; the snapping of a twig would make you start. We were wanderers on a prehistoric earth, on an earth that wore the aspect of an unknown planet. We could have fancied ourselves the first of men taking possession of an accursed inheritance, to be subdued at the cost of profound anguish and of excessive toil. But suddenly, as we struggled round a bend, there would be a glimpse of rush walls, of peaked grass-roofs, a burst of yells, a whirl of black limbs, a mass of hands clapping, of feet stamping, of bodies swaying, of eyes rolling, under the droop of heavy and motionless foliage. The steamer toiled along slowly on the edge of a black and incomprehensible frenzy. The prehistoric man was cursing us, praying to us, welcoming us—who could tell? We were cut off from the comprehension of our surroundings; we glided past like phantoms, wondering and secretly appalled, as sane men would be before an enthusiastic outbreak in a madhouse. We could not understand because we were too far and could not remember, because we were travelling in the night of first ages, of those ages that are gone, leaving hardly a sign—and no memories.

"The earth seemed unearthly. We are accustomed to look upon the shackled form of a conquered monster, but there—there you could look at a thing monstrous and free. It was unearthly, and the men were— No, they were not inhuman. Well, you know, that was the worst of it—this suspicion of their not being inhuman. It would come slowly to one. They howled and leaped, and spun, and made horrid faces; but what thrilled you was just the thought of their humanity—like yours—the thought of your remote kinship with this wild and passionate uproar. Ugly. Yes, it was ugly enough; but if you were man enough you would admit to yourself that there was in you just the faintest trace of a response to the terrible frankness of that noise, a dim suspicion of there being a meaning in it which you—you so remote from the night of first ages—could comprehend. And why not? The mind of man is capable of anything—because everything is in it, all the past as well as all the future. What was there after all? Joy, fear, sorrow, devotion, valour, rage—who can tell?—but truth—truth stripped of its cloak of time. Let the fool gape and shudder—the man knows, and can look on without a wink. But he must at least be as much of a man as these on the shore. He must meet that truth with his own true stuff—with his own inborn strength. Principles? Principles won't do. Acquisitions, clothes, pretty rags—rags that would fly off at the first good shake. No; you want a deliberate belief. An appeal to me in this fiendish row—is there? Very well; I hear; I admit, but I have a voice too, and for good or evil mine is the speech that cannot be silenced. Of course, a fool, what with sheer fright and fine sentiments, is always safe. Who's that grunting? You wonder I didn't go ashore for a howl and a dance? Well, no—I didn't. Fine sentiments, you say? Fine sentiments be hanged! I had no time. I had to mess about with white-lead and strips of woollen blanket helping to put bandages on those leaky steam-pipes—I tell you. I had to watch the steering, and circumvent those snags, and get the tin-pot along by hook or by crook. There was surface-truth enough in these things to save a wiser man. And between whiles I had to look after the savage who was fireman. He was an improved specimen; he could fire up a vertical boiler. He was there below me, and, upon my word, to look at him was as edifying as seeing a dog in a parody of breeches and a feather hat, walking on his hind legs. A few months of training had done for that really fine chap. He squinted at the steam-gauge and at the water-gauge with an evident effort of intrepidity—and he had filed teeth too, the poor devil, and the wool of his pate shaved into queer patterns, and three ornamental scars on each of his cheeks. He ought to have been clapping his hands and stamping his feet on the bank, instead of which he was hard at work, a thrall to strange witchcraft, full of improving knowledge. He was useful because he had been instructed; and what he knew was this—that should the water in that transparent thing disappear, the evil spirit inside the boiler would get angry through the greatness of his thirst, and take a terrible vengeance. So he sweated and fired up and watched the glass fearfully (with an impromptu charm, made of rags, tied to his arm, and a piece of polished bone, as big as a watch, stuck flatways through his lower lip), while the wooded banks slipped past us slowly, the short noise was left behind, the interminable miles of silence—and we crept on, towards Kurtz. But the snags were thick, the water was treacherous and shallow, the boiler seemed indeed to have a sulky devil in it, and thus neither that fireman nor I had any time to peer into our creepy thoughts.

"Some fifty miles below the Inner Station we came upon a hut of reeds, an inclined and melancholy pole, with the unrecognisable tatters of what had been a flag of some sort flying from it, and a neatly stacked wood-pile. This was unexpected. We came to the bank, and on the stack of firewood found a flat piece of board with some faded pencil-writing on it. When deciphered it said: 'Wood for you. Hurry up. Approach cautiously.' There was a signature, but it was illegible—not Kurtz—a much longer word. Hurry up. Where? Up the river? 'Approach cautiously.' We had not done so. But the warning could not have been meant for the place where it could be only found after approach. Something was wrong above. But what—and how much? That was the question. We commented adversely upon the imbecility of that telegraphic style. The bush around said nothing, and would not let us look very far, either. A torn curtain of red twill hung in the doorway of the hut, and flapped sadly in our faces. The dwelling was dismantled; but we could see a white man had lived there not very long ago. There remained a rude table—a plank on two posts; a heap of rubbish reposed in a dark corner, and by the door I picked up a book. It had lost its covers, and the pages had been thumbed into a state of extremely dirty softness; but the back had been lovingly stitched afresh with white cotton thread, which looked clean yet. It was an extraordinary find. Its title was, *An Inquiry into some Points of Seamanship*, by a man Towser, Towson—some such name—Master in His Majesty's Navy. The matter looked dreary reading enough, with illustrative diagrams and repulsive tables of figures, and the copy was sixty years old. I handled this amazing antiquity with the greatest possible tenderness, lest it should dissolve in my hands. Within, Towson or Towser was inquiring earnestly into the breaking strain of ships' chains and tackle, and other such matters. Not a very enthralling book; but at the first glance you could see there a singleness of intention, an honest concern for the right way of going to work, which made these humble pages, thought out so many years ago, luminous with another than a professional light. The simple old sailor, with his talk of chains and purchases, made me forget the jungle and the pilgrims in a delicious sensation of having come upon something unmistakably real. Such a book being there was wonderful enough; but still more astounding were the notes pencilled in the margin, and plainly referring to the text. I couldn't believe my eyes! They were in cipher! Yes, it looked like cipher. Fancy a man lugging with him a book of that description into this nowhere and studying it—and making notes—in cipher at that! It was an extravagant mystery.

"I had been dimly aware for some time of a worrying noise, and when I lifted my eyes I saw the wood-pile was gone, and the manager, aided by all the pilgrims, was shouting at me from the river-side. I slipped the book into my pocket. I assure you to leave off reading was like tearing myself away from the shelter of an old and solid friendship.

"I started the lame engine ahead. 'It must be this miserable trader—this intruder,' exclaimed the manager, looking back malevolently at the place we had left. 'He must be English,' I said. 'It will not save him from getting into trouble if he is not careful,' muttered the manager darkly. I observed with assumed innocence that no man was safe from trouble in this world.

"The current was more rapid now, the steamer seemed at her last gasp, the stern-wheel flopped languidly, and I caught myself listening on tiptoe for the next beat of the float,[5] for in sober truth I expected the wretched thing to give up every moment. It was like watching the last flickers of a life. But still we crawled. Sometimes I would pick out a tree a little way ahead to measure our progress towards Kurtz by, but I lost it invariably before we got abreast. To keep the eyes so long on one thing was too much for human patience. The manager displayed a beautiful resignation. I fretted and fumed and took to arguing with myself whether or no I would talk openly with Kurtz; but before I could come to any conclusion it occurred to me that my speech or my silence, indeed any action of mine, would be a mere futility. What did it matter what any one knew or ignored? What did it matter who was manager? One gets sometimes such a flash of insight. The essentials of this affair lay deep under the surface, beyond my reach, and beyond my power of meddling.

"Towards the evening of the second day we judged ourselves about eight miles from Kurtz's station. I wanted to push on; but the manager looked grave, and told me the navigation up there was so dangerous that it would be advisable, the sun being very low already, to wait where we were till next morning. Moreover, he pointed out that if the warning to approach cautiously were to be followed, we must approach in daylight—not at dusk, or in the dark. This was sensible enough. Eight miles meant nearly three hours' steaming for us, and I could also see suspicious ripples at the upper end of the reach. Nevertheless, I was annoyed beyond expression at the delay, and most unreasonably too, since one night more could not matter much after so many months. As we had plenty of wood, and caution was the word, I brought up in the middle of the stream. The reach was narrow, straight, with high sides like a railway cutting. The dusk came gliding into it long before the sun had set. The current ran smooth and swift, but a dumb immobility sat on the banks. The living trees, lashed together by the creepers and every living bush of the undergrowth, might have been changed into stone, even to the slenderest twig, to the lightest leaf. It was not sleep—it seemed unnatural, like a state of trance. Not the faintest sound of any kind could be heard. You looked on amazed, and began to suspect yourself of being deaf—then the night came suddenly, and struck you blind as well. About three in the morning some large fish leaped, and the loud splash made me jump as though a gun had been fired. When the sun rose there was a white fog, very warm and clammy, and more blinding than the night. It did not shift or drive; it was just there, standing all round you like something solid. At eight or nine, perhaps, it lifted as a shutter lifts. We had a glimpse of the towering multitude of trees, of the immense matted jungle, with the blazing little ball of

5. Automatic water-level regulator opening and closing a water-supply valve.

the sun hanging over it—all perfectly still—and then the white shutter came down again, smoothly, as if sliding in greased grooves. I ordered the chain, which we had begun to heave in, to be paid out again. Before it stopped running with a muffled rattle, a cry, a very loud cry, as of infinite desolation, soared slowly in the opaque air. It ceased. A complaining clamour, modulated in savage discords, filled our ears. The sheer unexpectedness of it made my hair stir under my cap. I don't know how it struck the others: to me it seemed as though the mist itself had screamed, so suddenly, and apparently from all sides at once, did this tumultuous and mournful uproar arise. It culminated in a hurried outbreak of almost intolerably excessive shrieking, which stopped short, leaving us stiffened in a variety of silly attitudes, and obstinately listening to the nearly as appalling and excessive silence. 'Good God! What is the meaning—?' stammered at my elbow one of the pilgrims—a little fat man, with sandy hair and red whiskers, who wore side-spring boots, and pink pyjamas tucked into his socks. Two others remained open-mouthed a whole minute, then dashed into the little cabin, to rush out incontinently and stand darting scared glances, with Winchesters at 'ready' in their hands. What we could see was just the steamer we were on, her outlines blurred as though she had been on the point of dissolving, and a misty strip of water, perhaps two feet broad, around her—and that was all. The rest of the world was nowhere, as far as our eyes and ears were concerned. Just nowhere. Gone, disappeared; swept off without leaving a whisper or a shadow behind.

"I went forward, and ordered the chain to be hauled in short, so as to be ready to trip the anchor and move the steamboat at once if necessary. 'Will they attack?' whispered an awed voice. 'We will all be butchered in this fog,' murmured another. The faces twitched with the strain, the hands trembled slightly, the eyes forgot to wink. It was very curious to see the contrast of expressions of the white men and of the black fellows of our crew, who were as much strangers to that part of the river as we, though their homes were only eight hundred miles away. The whites, of course greatly discomposed, had besides a curious look of being painfully shocked by such an outrageous row. The others had an alert, naturally interested expression; but their faces were essentially quiet, even those of the one or two who grinned as they hauled at the chain. Several exchanged short, grunting phrases, which seemed to settle the matter to their satisfaction. Their headman, a young, broad-chested black, severely draped in dark-blue fringed cloths, with fierce nostrils and his hair all done up artfully in oily ringlets, stood near me. 'Aha!' I said, just for good fellowship's sake. 'Catch 'im,' he snapped, with a blood-shot widening of his eyes and a flash of sharp teeth—'catch 'im. Give 'im to us.' 'To you, eh?' I asked; 'what would you do with them?' 'Eat 'im!' he said curtly, and, leaning his elbow on the rail, looked out into the fog in a dignified and profoundly pensive attitude. I would no doubt have been properly horrified, had it not occurred to me that he and his chaps must be very hungry: that they must have been growing increasingly hungry for at least this month past. They had been engaged for six months (I don't think a single one of them had any clear idea of time, as we at the end of countless ages have. They still belonged to the beginnings of time—had no inherited experience to teach them, as it were), and of course, as long as there was a piece of paper written over in accordance with some farcical law or other made down the river, it didn't enter anybody's head to trouble how they would live. Certainly they had brought with them some rotten hippo-meat, which couldn't have lasted very long, anyway, even if the pilgrims hadn't, in the midst of a shocking hullabaloo, thrown a considerable quantity of it overboard. It looked like a high-handed proceeding; but it was really a case of legitimate self-defence. You can't breathe dead hippo waking, sleeping, and eating, and at the same time keep your precarious grip on existence. Besides that, they had given them every week three pieces of brass wire, each about nine inches long; and the theory was they were to buy their provisions with that currency in river-side villages. You can see how *that* worked. There were either no villages, or the people were hostile, or the director, who like the rest of us fed out of tins, with an occasional old he-goat thrown in, didn't want to stop the steamer for some more or less recondite reasons. So, unless they swallowed the wire itself, or made loops of it to snare the fishes with, I don't see what good their extravagant salary could be to them. I must say it was paid with a regularity worthy of a large and honourable trading company. For the rest, the only thing to eat—though it didn't look eatable in the least—I saw in their possession was a few lumps of some stuff like half-cooked dough, of a dirty lavender colour, they kept wrapped in leaves, and now and then swallowed a piece of, but so small that it seemed done more for the look of the thing than for any serious purpose of sustenance. Why in the name of all the gnawing devils of hunger they didn't go for us—they were thirty to five—and have a good tuck-in for once, amazes me now when I think of it. They were big powerful men, with not much capacity to weigh the consequences, with courage, with strength, even yet, though their skins were no longer glossy and their muscles no longer hard. And I saw that something restraining, one of those human secrets that baffle probability, had come into play there. I looked at them with a swift quickening of interest—not because it occurred to me I might be eaten by them before very long, though I own to you that just then I perceived—in a new light, as it were—how unwholesome the pilgrims looked, and I hoped, yes, I positively hoped, that my aspect was not so—what shall I say?—so—unappetising: a touch of fantastic vanity which fitted well with the dream-sensation that pervaded all my days at that time. Perhaps I had a little fever too. One can't live with one's finger everlastingly on one's pulse. I had often 'a little fever,' or a little touch of other things—the playful paw-strokes of the wilderness, the preliminary trifling before the more serious onslaught which came in due course. Yes; I looked at them as you would on any human being, with a curiosity of their impulses, motives, capacities, weaknesses, when brought to the test of an inexorable physical necessity. Restraint! What possible restraint? Was it superstition, disgust, patience, fear—or some kind of primitive honour? No fear can stand up to hunger, no patience can wear it out, disgust simply does not exist where hunger is; and as to superstition, beliefs, and what you may call principles, they are less than chaff in a breeze. Don't you know the devilry of lingering starvation, its exasperating torment, its black thoughts, its sombre and brooding ferocity? Well, I do. It takes a man all his inborn strength to fight hunger properly. It's really easier to face bereavement, dishonour, and the perdition of one's soul—than this kind of prolonged hunger. Sad, but true. And these chaps too had no earthly reason for any kind of scruple. Restraint! I would just as soon have expected restraint from a hyena prowling amongst the corpses of a battlefield. But there was the fact facing me—the fact dazzling, to be seen, like the foam on the depths of the sea, like a ripple on an unfathomable enigma, a mystery greater—when I thought of it—than the curious, inexplicable note of desperate grief in this savage clamour that had swept by us on the river-bank, behind the blind whiteness of the fog.

"Two pilgrims were quarrelling in hurried whispers as to which bank. 'Left.' 'No, no; how can you? Right, right, of course.' 'It is very serious,' said the manager's voice behind me; 'I would be desolated if anything should happen to Mr. Kurtz before we came up.' I looked at him, and had not the slightest doubt he was sincere. He was just the kind of man who would wish to preserve appearances. That was his restraint. But when he muttered something about going on at once, I did not even take the trouble to answer him. I knew, and he knew, that it was impossible. Were we to let go our hold of the bottom, we would be absolutely in the air—in space. We wouldn't be able to tell where we were going to—whether up or down stream, or across—till we fetched against one bank or the other—and then we wouldn't know at first which it was. Of course I made no move. I had no mind for a smashup. You couldn't imagine a more deadly place for a shipwreck. Whether drowned at once or not, we were sure to perish speedily in one way or another. 'I authorise you to take all the risks,' he said, after a short silence. 'I refuse to take any,' I said shortly; which was just the answer he expected, though its tone might have surprised him. 'Well, I must defer to your judgment. You are captain,' he said, with marked civility. I turned my shoulder to him in sign of my appreciation, and looked into the fog. How long would it last? It was the most hopeless look-out. The approach to this Kurtz grubbing for ivory in the wretched bush was beset by as many dangers as though he had been an enchanted princess sleeping in a fabulous castle. 'Will they attack, do you think?' asked the manager, in a confidential tone.

"I did not think they would attack, for several obvious reasons. The thick fog was one. If they left the bank in their canoes they would get lost in it, as we would be if we attempted to move. Still, I had also judged the jungle of both banks quite impenetrable—and yet eyes were in it, eyes that had seen us. The river-side bushes were certainly very thick; but the undergrowth behind was evidently penetrable. However, during the short lift I had seen no canoes anywhere in the reach—certainly not abreast of the steamer. But what made the idea of attack inconceivable to me was the nature of the noise—of the cries we had heard. They had not the fierce character boding of immediate hostile intention. Unexpected, wild, and violent as they had been, they had given me an irresistible impression of sorrow. The glimpse of the steamboat had for some reason filled those savages with unrestrained grief. The danger, if any, I expounded, was from our proximity to a great human passion let loose. Even extreme grief may ultimately vent itself in violence—but more generally takes the form of apathy. . . .

"You should have seen the pilgrims stare! They had no heart to grin, or even to revile me; but I believe they thought me gone mad—with fright, maybe. I delivered a regular lecture. My dear boys, it was no good bothering. Keep a look-out? Well, you may guess I watched the fog for the signs of lifting as a cat watches a mouse; but for anything else our eyes were of no more use to us than if we had been buried miles deep in a heap of cotton-wool. It felt like it too—choking, warm, stifling. Besides, all I said, though it sounded extravagant, was absolutely true to fact. What we afterwards alluded to as an attack was really an attempt at repulse. The action was very far from being aggressive—it was not even defensive, in the usual sense: it was undertaken under the stress of desperation, and in its essence was purely protective.

"It developed itself, I should say, two hours after the fog lifted, and its commencement was at a spot, roughly speaking, about a mile and a half below Kurtz's station. We had just floundered and flopped round a bend, when I saw an islet, a mere grassy hummock of bright green, in the middle of the stream. It was the only thing of the kind; but as we opened the reach more, I perceived it was the head of a long sandbank, or rather of a chain of shallow patches stretching down the middle of the river. They were discoloured, just awash, and the whole lot was seen just under the water, exactly as a man's backbone is seen running down the middle of his back under the skin. Now, as far as I did see, I could go to the right or to the left of this. I didn't know either channel, of course. The banks looked pretty well alike, the depth appeared the same; but as I had been informed the station was on the west side, I naturally headed for the western passage.

"No sooner had we fairly entered it than I became aware it was much narrower than I had supposed. To the left of us there was the long uninterrupted shoal, and to the right a high steep bank heavily overgrown with bushes. Above the bush the trees stood in serried ranks. The twigs overhung the current thickly, and from distance to distance a large limb of some tree projected rigidly over the stream. It was then well on in the afternoon, the face of the forest was gloomy, and a broad strip of shadow had already fallen on the water. In this shadow we steamed up—very slowly, as you may imagine. I sheered her well inshore—the water being deepest near the bank, as the sounding-pole informed me.

"One of my hungry and forbearing friends was sounding in the bows just below me. This steamboat was exactly like a decked scow. On the deck there were two little teak-wood houses, with doors and windows. The boiler was in the fore-end, and the machinery right astern. Over the whole there was a light roof, supported on stanchions. The funnel projected through that roof, and in front of the funnel a small cabin built of light planks served for a pilot-house. It contained a couch, two camp-stools, a loaded Martini-Henry[6] leaning in one corner, a tiny table, and the steering-wheel. It had a wide door in front and a broad shutter at each side. All these were always thrown open, of course. I spent my days perched up there on the extreme fore-end of that roof, before the door. At night I slept, or tried to, on the couch. An athletic black belonging to some coast tribe, and educated by my poor predecessor, was the helmsman. He sported a pair of brass earrings, wore a blue cloth wrapper from the waist to the ankles, and thought all the world of himself. He was the most unstable kind of fool I had ever seen. He steered with no end of a swagger while you were by; but if he lost sight of you, he became instantly the prey of an abject funk, and would let that cripple of a steamboat get the upper hand of him in a minute.

"I was looking down at the sounding-pole, and feeling much annoyed to see at each try a little more of it stick out of that river, when I saw my poleman

6. Rifle combining the seven-grooved barrel of the Scottish gunmaker A. Henry with the block-action breech mechanism introduced by the Swiss inventor F. Martini.

give up the business suddenly, and stretch himself flat on the deck, without even taking the trouble to haul his pole in. He kept hold on it though, and it trailed in the water. At the same time the fireman, whom I could also see below me, sat down abruptly before his furnace and ducked his head. I was amazed. Then I had to look at the river mighty quick, because there was a snag in the fairway. Sticks, little sticks, were flying about—thick; they were whizzing before my nose, dropping below me, striking behind me against my pilot-house. All this time the river, the shore, the woods, were very quiet—perfectly quiet. I could only hear the heavy splashing thump of the stern-wheel and the patter of these things. We cleared the snag clumsily. Arrows, by Jove! We were being shot at! I stepped in quickly to close the shutter on the land-side. That fool-helmsman, his hands on the spokes, was lifting his knees high, stamping his feet, champing his mouth, like a reined-in horse. Confound him! And we were staggering within ten feet of the bank. I had to lean right out to swing the heavy shutter, and I saw a face amongst the leaves on the level with my own, looking at me very fierce and steady; and then suddenly, as though a veil had been removed from my eyes, I made out, deep in the tangled gloom, naked breasts, arms, legs, glaring eyes—the bush was swarming with human limbs in movement, glistening, of bronze colour. The twigs shook, swayed, and rustled, the arrows flew out of them, and then the shutter came to. 'Steer her straight,' I said to the helmsman. He held his head rigid, face forward; but his eyes rolled, he kept on lifting and setting down his feet gently, his mouth foamed a little. 'Keep quiet!' I said in a fury. I might just as well have ordered a tree not to sway in the wind. I darted out. Below me there was a great scuffle of feet on the iron deck; confused exclamations; a voice screamed, 'Can you turn back?' I caught sight of a V-shaped ripple on the water ahead. What? Another snag! A fusillade burst out under my feet. The pilgrims had opened with their Winchesters, and were simply squirting lead into that bush. A deuce of a lot of smoke came up and drove slowly forward. I swore at it. Now I couldn't see the ripple or the snag either. I stood in the doorway, peering, and the arrows came in swarms. They might have been poisoned, but they looked as though they wouldn't kill a cat. The bush began to howl. Our wood-cutters raised a warlike whoop; the report of a rifle just at my back deafened me. I glanced over my shoulder, and the pilot-house was yet full of noise and smoke when I made a dash at the wheel. The fool-nigger had dropped everything, to throw the shutter open and let off that Martini-Henry. He stood before the wide opening, glaring, and I yelled at him to come back, while I straightened the sudden twist out of that steamboat. There was no room to turn even if I had wanted to, the snag was somewhere very near ahead in that confounded smoke, there was no time to lose, so I just crowded her into the bank—right into the bank, where I knew the water was deep.

"We tore slowly along the overhanging bushes in a whirl of broken twigs and flying leaves. The fusillade below stopped short, as I had foreseen it would when the squirts got empty. I threw my head back to a glinting whizz that traversed the pilot-house, in at one shutter-hole and out at the other. Looking past that mad helmsman, who was shaking the empty rifle and yelling at the shore, I saw vague forms of men running bent double, leaping, gliding, distinct, incomplete, evanescent. Something big appeared in the air before the shutter, the rifle went overboard, and the man stepped back swiftly, looked at me over his shoulder in an extraordinary, profound, familiar manner, and fell upon my feet. The side of his head hit the wheel twice, and the end of what appeared a long cane clattered round and knocked over a little camp-stool. It looked as though after wrenching that thing from somebody ashore he had lost his balance in the effort. The thin smoke had blown away, we were clear of the snag, and looking ahead I could see that in another hundred yards or so I would be free to sheer off, away from the bank; but my feet felt so very warm and wet that I had to look down. The man had rolled on his back and stared straight up at me; both his hands clutched that cane. It was the shaft of a spear that, either thrown or lunged through the opening, had caught him in the side just below the ribs; the blade had gone in out of sight, after making a frightful gash; my shoes were full; a pool of blood lay very still, gleaming dark-red under the wheel; his eyes shone with an amazing lustre. The fusillade burst out again. He looked at me anxiously, gripping the spear like something precious, with an air of being afraid I would try to take it away from him. I had to make an effort to free my eyes from his gaze and attend to the steering. With one hand I felt above my head for the line of the steam whistle, and jerked out screech after screech hurriedly. The tumult of angry and warlike yells was checked instantly, and then from the depths of the woods went out such a tremulous and prolonged wail of mournful fear and utter despair as may be imagined to follow the flight of the last hope from the earth. There was a great commotion in the bush; the shower of arrows stopped, a few dropping shots rang out sharply—then silence, in which the languid beat of the stern-wheel came plainly to my ears. I put the helm hard a-starboard at the moment when the pilgrim in pink pyjamas, very hot and agitated, appeared in the doorway. 'The manager sends me—' he began in an official tone, and stopped short. 'Good God!' he said, glaring at the wounded man.

"We two whites stood over him, and his lustrous and inquiring glance enveloped us both. I declare it looked as though he would presently put to us some question in an understandable language; but he died without uttering a sound, without moving a limb, without twitching a muscle. Only in the very last moment, as though in response to some sign we could not see, to some whisper we could not hear, he frowned heavily, and that frown gave to his black death-mask an inconceivably sombre, brooding, and menacing expression. The lustre of inquiring glance faded swiftly into vacant glassiness. 'Can you steer?' I asked the agent eagerly. He looked very dubious; but I made a grab at his arm, and he understood at once I meant him to steer whether or no. To tell you the truth, I was morbidly anxious to change my shoes and socks. 'He is dead,' murmured the fellow, immensely impressed. 'No doubt about it,' said I, tugging like mad at the shoe-laces. 'And by the way, I suppose Mr Kurtz is dead as well by this time.'

"For the moment that was the dominant thought. There was a sense of extreme disappointment, as though I had found out I had been striving after something altogether without a substance. I couldn't have been more disgusted if I had travelled all this way for the sole purpose of talking with Mr Kurtz. Talking with . . . I flung one shoe overboard, and became aware that that was exactly what I had been looking forward to—a talk with Kurtz. I made the strange discovery that I had never imagined him as doing, you know, but as discoursing. I didn't say to myself, 'Now I will never see him,' or 'Now I will never shake him by the hand,' but, 'Now I will never hear him.' The man presented himself as a voice. Not of course that I did not connect him with some sort of action. Hadn't I been told in all the tones of jealousy and admiration that he had collected, bartered, swindled, or stolen more ivory than all the other agents together? That was not the point. The point was in his being a gifted creature, and that of all his gifts the one that stood out pre-eminently, that carried with it a sense of real presence, was his ability to talk, his words—the gift of expression, the bewildering, the illuminating, the most exalted and the most contemptible, the pulsating stream of light, or the deceitful flow from the heart of an impenetrable darkness.

"The other shoe went flying unto the devil-god of that river. I thought, By Jove! it's all over. We are too late; he has vanished—the gift has vanished, by means of some spear, arrow, or club. I will never hear that chap speak after all—and my sorrow had a startling extravagance of emotion, even such as I had noticed in the howling sorrow of these savages in the bush. I couldn't have felt more of lonely desolation somehow, had I been robbed of a belief or had missed my destiny in life. . . . Why do you sigh in this beastly way, somebody? Absurd? Well, absurd. Good Lord! mustn't a man ever— Here, give me some tobacco." . . .

There was a pause of profound stillness, then a match flared, and Marlow's lean face appeared, worn, hollow, with downward folds and dropped eyelids, with an aspect of concentrated attention; and as he took vigorous draws at his pipe, it seemed to retreat and advance out of the night in the regular flicker of the tiny flame. The match went out.

"Absurd!" he cried. "This is the worst of trying to tell . . . Here you all are, each moored with two good addresses, like a hulk with two anchors, a butcher round one corner, a policeman round another, excellent appetites, and temperature normal—you hear—normal from year's end to year's end. And you say, Absurd! Absurd be—exploded! Absurd! My dear boys, what can you expect from a man who out of sheer nervousness had just flung overboard a pair of new shoes? Now I think of it, it is amazing I did not shed tears. I am, upon the whole, proud of my fortitude. I was cut to the quick at the idea of having lost the inestimable privilege of listening to the gifted Kurtz. Of course I was wrong. The privilege was waiting for me. Oh yes, I heard more than enough. And I was right, too. A voice. He was very little more than a voice. And I heard—him—it—this voice—other voices—all of them were so little more than voices—and the memory of that time itself lingers around me, impalpable, like a dying vibration of one immense jabber, silly, atrocious, sordid, savage, or simply mean, without any kind of sense. Voices, voices— even the girl herself—now—"

He was silent for a long time.

"I laid the ghost of his gifts at last with a lie," he began suddenly. "Girl! What? Did I mention a girl? Oh, she is out of it—completely. They—the women I mean—are out of it—should be out of it. We must help them to stay in that beautiful world of their own, lest ours gets worse. Oh, she had to be out of it. You should have heard the disinterred body of Mr Kurtz saying, 'My Intended.' You would have perceived directly then how completely she was out of it. And the lofty frontal bone of Mr Kurtz! They say the hair goes on growing sometimes, but this—ah—specimen was impressively bald. The wilderness had patted him on the head, and, behold, it was like a ball—an

ivory ball; it had caressed him, and—lo!—he had withered; it had taken him,
loved him, embraced him, got into his veins, consumed his flesh, and sealed
his soul to its own by the inconceivable ceremonies of some devilish initiation. He was its spoiled and pampered favourite. Ivory? I should think so.
Heaps of it, stacks of it. The old mud shanty was bursting with it. You would
think there was not a single tusk left either above or below the ground in the
whole country. 'Mostly fossil,' the manager had remarked disparagingly. It
was no more fossil than I am; but they call it fossil when it is dug up. It
appears these niggers do bury the tusks sometimes—but evidently they
couldn't bury this parcel deep enough to save the gifted Mr Kurtz from his
fate. We filled the steamboat with it, and had to pile a lot on the deck. Thus
he could see and enjoy as long as he could see, because the appreciation of
this favour had remained with him to the last. You should have heard him
say, 'My ivory.' Oh yes, I heard him. 'My Intended, my ivory, my station, my
river, my—' everything belonged to him. It made me hold my breath in expectation of hearing the wilderness burst into a prodigious peal of laughter that
would shake the fixed stars in their places. Everything belonged to him—but
that was a trifle. The thing was to know what he belonged to, how many
powers of darkness claimed him for their own. That was the reflection that
made you creepy all over. It was impossible—it was not good for one either—
trying to imagine. He had taken a high seat amongst the devils of the land—I
mean literally. You can't understand. How could you?—with solid pavement
under your feet, surrounded by kind neighbours ready to cheer you or to fall
on you, stepping delicately between the butcher and the policeman, in the
holy terror of scandal and gallows and lunatic asylums—how can you imagine what particular region of the first ages a man's untrammelled feet may
take him into by the way of solitude—utter solitude without a policeman—
by the way of silence—utter silence, where no warning voice of a kind neighbour can be heard whispering of public opinion? These little things make all
the great difference. When they are gone you must fall back upon your own
innate strength, upon your own capacity for faithfulness. Of course you may
be too much of a fool to go wrong—too dull even to know you are being
assaulted by the powers of darkness. I take it, no fool ever made a bargain
for his soul with the devil: the fool is too much of a fool, or the devil too
much of a devil—I don't know which. Or you may be such a thunderingly
exalted creature as to be altogether deaf and blind to anything but heavenly
sights and sounds. Then the earth for you is only a standing place—and
whether to be like this is your loss or your gain I won't pretend to say. But
most of us are neither one nor the other. The earth for us is a place to live
in, where we must put up with sights, with sounds, with smells, too, by
Jove!—breathe dead hippo, so to speak, and not be contaminated. And there,
don't you see? your strength comes in, the faith in your ability for the digging
of unostentatious holes to bury the stuff in—your power of devotion, not to
yourself, but to an obscure, back-breaking business. And that's difficult
enough. Mind, I am not trying to excuse or even explain—I am trying to
account to myself for—for—Mr Kurtz—for the shade of Mr Kurtz. This
initiated wraith from the back of Nowhere honoured me with its amazing
confidence before it vanished altogether. This was because it could speak
English to me. The original Kurtz had been educated partly in England,
and—as he was good enough to say himself—his sympathies were in the

right place. His mother was half-English, his father was half-French. All Europe contributed to the making of Kurtz; and by and by I learned that, most appropriately, the International Society for the Suppression of Savage Customs had entrusted him with the making of a report, for its future guidance. And he had written it too. I've seen it. I've read it. It was eloquent, vibrating with eloquence, but too high-strung, I think. Seventeen pages of close writing he had found time for! But this must have been before his— let us say—nerves went wrong, and caused him to preside at certain midnight dances ending with unspeakable rites, which—as far as I reluctantly gathered from what I heard at various times—were offered up to him—do you understand?—to Mr Kurtz himself. But it was a beautiful piece of writing. The opening paragraph, however, in the light of later information, strikes me now as ominous. He began with the argument that we whites, from the point of development we had arrived at, 'must necessarily appear to them [savages] in the nature of supernatural beings—we approach them with the might as of a deity,' and so on, and so on. 'By the simple exercise of our will we can exert a power for good practically unbounded,' etc. etc. From that point he soared and took me with him. The peroration was magnificent, though difficult to remember, you know. It gave me the notion of an exotic Immensity ruled by an august Benevolence. It made me tingle with enthusiasm. This was the unbounded power of eloquence—of words—of burning noble words. There were no practical hints to interrupt the magic current of phrases, unless a kind of note at the foot of the last page, scrawled evidently much later, in an unsteady hand, may be regarded as the exposition of a method. It was very simple, and at the end of that moving appeal to every altruistic sentiment it blazed at you, luminous and terrifying, like a flash of lightning in a serene sky: 'Exterminate all the brutes!' The curious part was that he had apparently forgotten all about that valuable postscriptum, because, later on, when he in a sense came to himself, he repeatedly entreated me to take good care of 'my pamphlet' (he called it), as it was sure to have in the future a good influence upon his career. I had full information about all these things, and, besides, as it turned out, I was to have the care of his memory. I've done enough for it to give me the indisputable right to lay it, if I choose, for an everlasting rest in the dust-bin of progress, amongst all the sweepings and, figuratively speaking, all the dead cats of civilisation. But then, you see, I can't choose. He won't be forgotten. Whatever he was, he was not common. He had the power to charm or frighten rudimentary souls into an aggravated witchdance in his honour; he could also fill the small souls of the pilgrims with bitter misgivings: he had one devoted friend at least, and he had conquered one soul in the world that was neither rudimentary nor tainted with self-seeking. No; I can't forget him, though I am not prepared to affirm the fellow was exactly worth the life we lost in getting to him. I missed my late helmsman awfully—I missed him even while his body was still lying in the pilot-house. Perhaps you will think it passing strange this regret for a savage who was no more account than a grain of sand in a black Sahara. Well, don't you see, he had done something, he had steered; for months I had him at my back—a help—an instrument. It was a kind of partnership. He steered for me—I had to look after him, I worried about his deficiencies, and thus a subtle bond had been created, of which I only became aware when it was suddenly broken. And the intimate profundity of that look he gave me when he received his hurt remains to this day in my memory—like a claim of distant kinship affirmed in a supreme moment.

"Poor fool! If he had only left that shutter alone. He had no restraint, no restraint—just like Kurtz—a tree swayed by the wind. As soon as I had put on a dry pair of slippers, I dragged him out, after first jerking the spear out of his side, which operation I confess I performed with my eyes shut tight. His heels leaped together over the little doorstep; his shoulders were pressed to my breast; I hugged him from behind desperately. Oh! he was heavy, heavy; heavier than any man on earth, I should imagine. Then without more ado I tipped him overboard. The current snatched him as though he had been a wisp of grass, and I saw the body roll over twice before I lost sight of it for ever. All the pilgrims and the manager were then congregated on the awning-deck about the pilot-house, chattering at each other like a flock of excited magpies, and there was a scandalised murmur at my heartless promptitude. What they wanted to keep that body hanging about for I can't guess. Embalm it, maybe. But I had also heard another, and a very ominous, murmur on the deck below. My friends the wood-cutters were likewise scandalised, and with a better show of reason—though I admit that the reason itself was quite inadmissible. Oh, quite! I had made up my mind that if my late helmsman was to be eaten, the fishes alone should have him. He had been a very second-rate helmsman while alive, but now he was dead he might have become a first-class temptation, and possibly cause some startling trouble. Besides, I was anxious to take the wheel, the man in pink pyjamas showing himself a hopeless duffer at the business.

"This I did directly the simple funeral was over. We were going half-speed, keeping right in the middle of the stream, and I listened to the talk about me. They had given up Kurtz, they had given up the station; Kurtz was dead, and the station had been burnt—and so on—and so on. The red-haired pilgrim was beside himself with the thought that at least this poor Kurtz had been properly revenged. 'Say! We must have made a glorious slaughter of them in the bush. Eh? What do you think? Say?' He positively danced, the bloodthirsty little gingery beggar.[7] And he had nearly fainted when he saw the wounded man! I could not help saying, 'You made a glorious lot of smoke, anyhow.' I had seen, from the way the tops of the bushes rustled and flew, that almost all the shots had gone too high. You can't hit anything unless you take aim and fire from the shoulder; but these chaps fired from the hip with their eyes shut. The retreat, I maintained—and I was right—was caused by the screeching of the steam-whistle. Upon this they forgot Kurtz, and began to howl at me with indignant protests.

"The manager stood by the wheel murmuring confidentially about the necessity of getting well away down the river before dark at all events, when I saw in the distance a clearing on the river-side and the outlines of some sort of building. 'What's this?' I asked. He clapped his hands in wonder. 'The station!' he cried. I edged in at once, still going half-speed.

"Through my glasses I saw the slope of a hill interspersed with rare trees and perfectly free from undergrowth. A long decaying building on the summit was half buried in the high grass; the large holes in the peaked roof gaped black from afar; the jungle and the woods made a background. There was

---

7. Redheaded rascal.

no enclosure or fence of any kind; but there had been one apparently, for near the house half a dozen slim posts remained in a row, roughly trimmed, and with their upper ends ornamented with round carved balls. The rails, or whatever there had been between, had disappeared. Of course the forest surrounded all that. The river-bank was clear, and on the water side I saw a white man under a hat like a cart-wheel beckoning persistently with his whole arm. Examining the edge of the forest above and below, I was almost certain I could see movements—human forms gliding here and there. I steamed past prudently, then stopped the engines and let her drift down. The man on the shore began to shout, urging us to land. 'We have been attacked,' screamed the manager. 'I know—I know. It's all right,' yelled back the other, as cheerful as you please. 'Come along. It's all right. I am glad.'

"His aspect reminded me of something I had seen—something funny I had seen somewhere. As I manœuvred to get alongside, I was asking myself, 'What does this fellow look like?' Suddenly I got it. He looked like a harlequin.[8] His clothes had been made of some stuff that was brown holland[9] probably, but it was covered with patches all over, with bright patches, blue, red, and yellow—patches on the back, patches on the front, patches on elbows, on knees; coloured binding round his jacket, scarlet edging at the bottom of his trousers; and the sunshine made him look extremely gay and wonderfully neat withal, because you could see how beautifully all this patching had been done. A beardless, boyish face, very fair, no features to speak of, nose peeling, little blue eyes, smiles and frowns chasing each other over that open countenance like sunshine and shadow on a wind-swept plain. 'Look out, captain!' he cried; 'there's a snag lodged in here last night.' What! Another snag? I confess I swore shamefully. I had nearly holed my cripple, to finish off that charming trip. The harlequin on the bank turned his little pug nose up to me. 'You English?' he asked, all smiles. 'Are you?' I shouted from the wheel. The smiles vanished, and he shook his head as if sorry for my disappointment. Then he brightened up. 'Never mind!' he cried encouragingly. 'Are we in time?' I asked. 'He is up there,' he replied, with a toss of the head up the hill, and becoming gloomy all of a sudden. His face was like the autumn sky, overcast one moment and bright the next.

"When the manager, escorted by the pilgrims, all of them armed to the teeth, had gone to the house, this chap came on board. 'I say, I don't like this. These natives are in the bush,' I said. He assured me earnestly it was all right. 'They are simple people,' he added; 'well, I am glad you came. It took me all my time to keep them off.' 'But you said it was all right,' I cried. 'Oh, they meant no harm,' he said; and as I stared he corrected himself, 'Not exactly.' Then vivaciously, 'My faith, your pilot-house wants a clean up!' In the next breath he advised me to keep enough steam on the boiler to blow the whistle in case of any trouble. 'One good screech will do more for you than all your rifles. They are simple people,' he repeated. He rattled away at such a rate he quite overwhelmed me. He seemed to be trying to make up for lots of silence, and actually hinted, laughing, that such was the case. 'Don't you talk with Mr Kurtz?' I said. 'You don't talk with that man—you listen to him,' he exclaimed with severe exaltation. 'But now—' He waved

8. Character from Italian comedy traditionally dressed in multicolored clothes.

9. Coarse linen fabric.

his arm, and in the twinkling of an eye was in the uttermost depths of despondency. In a moment he came up again with a jump, possessed himself of both my hands, shook them continuously, while he gabbled: 'Brother sailor . . . honour . . . pleasure . . . delight . . . introduce myself . . . Russian . . . son of an arch-priest . . . Government of Tambov . . . What? Tobacco! English tobacco; the excellent English tobacco! Now, that's brotherly. Smoke? Where's a sailor that does not smoke?'

"The pipe soothed him, and gradually I made out he had run away from school, had gone to sea in a Russian ship; ran away again; served some time in English ships; was now reconciled with the arch-priest. He made a point of that. 'But when one is young one must see things, gather experience, ideas; enlarge the mind.' 'Here!' I interrupted. 'You can never tell! Here I met Mr Kurtz,' he said, youthfully solemn and reproachful. I held my tongue after that. It appears he had persuaded a Dutch trading-house on the coast to fit him out with stores and goods, and had started for the interior with a light heart, and no more idea of what would happen to him than a baby. He had been wandering about that river for nearly two years alone, cut off from everybody and everything. 'I am not so young as I look. I am twenty-five,' he said. 'At first old Van Shuyten would tell me to go to the devil,' he narrated with keen enjoyment; 'but I stuck to him, and talked and talked, till at last he got afraid I would talk the hind-leg off his favourite dog, so he gave me some cheap things and a few guns, and told me he hoped he would never see my face again. Good old Dutchman, Van Shuyten. I sent him one small lot of ivory a year ago, so that he can't call me a little thief when I get back. I hope he got it. And for the rest I don't care. I had some wood stacked for you. That was my old house. Did you see?'

"I gave him Towson's book. He made as though he would kiss me, but restrained himself. 'The only book I had left, and I thought I had lost it,' he said, looking at it ecstatically. 'So many accidents happen to a man going about alone, you know. Canoes get upset sometimes—and sometimes you've got to clear out so quick when the people get angry.' He thumbed the pages. 'You made notes in Russian?' I asked. He nodded. 'I thought they were written in cipher,' I said. He laughed, then became serious. 'I had lots of trouble to keep these people off,' he said. 'Did they want to kill you?' I asked. 'Oh no!' he cried, and checked himself. 'Why did they attack us?' I pursued. He hesitated, then said shamefacedly, 'They don't want him to go.' 'Don't they?' I said curiously. He nodded a nod full of mystery and wisdom. 'I tell you,' he cried, 'this man has enlarged my mind.' He opened his arms wide, staring at me with his little blue eyes that were perfectly round."

3

"I looked at him, lost in astonishment. There he was before me, in motley, as though he had absconded from a troupe of mimes, enthusiastic, fabulous. His very existence was improbable, inexplicable, and altogether bewildering. He was an insoluble problem. It was inconceivable how he had existed, how he had succeeded in getting so far, how he had managed to remain—why he did not instantly disappear. 'I went a little farther,' he said, 'then still a little farther—till I had gone so far that I don't know how I'll ever get back. Never mind. Plenty time. I can manage. You take Kurtz away quick—quick—

I tell you.' The glamour of youth enveloped his particoloured rags, his destitution, his loneliness, the essential desolation of his futile wanderings. For months—for years—his life hadn't been worth a day's purchase; and there he was gallantly, thoughtlessly alive, to all appearance indestructible solely by the virtue of his few years and of his unreflecting audacity. I was seduced into something like admiration—like envy. Glamour urged him on, glamour kept him unscathed. He surely wanted nothing from the wilderness but space to breathe in and to push on through. His need was to exist, and to move onwards at the greatest possible risk, and with a maximum of privation. If the absolutely pure, uncalculating, unpractical spirit of adventure had ever ruled a human being, it ruled this be-patched youth. I almost envied him the possession of this modest and clear flame. It seemed to have consumed all thought of self so completely, that, even while he was talking to you, you forgot that it was he—the man before your eyes—who had gone through these things. I did not envy him his devotion to Kurtz, though. He had not meditated over it. It came to him, and he accepted it with a sort of eager fatalism. I must say that to me it appeared about the most dangerous thing in every way he had come upon so far.

"They had come together unavoidably, like two ships becalmed near each other, and lay rubbing sides at last. I suppose Kurtz wanted an audience, because on a certain occasion, when encamped in the forest, they had talked all night, or more probably Kurtz had talked. 'We talked of everything,' he said, quite transported at the recollection. 'I forgot there was such a thing as sleep. The night did not seem to last an hour. Everything! Everything! . . . Of love too.' 'Ah, he talked to you of love!' I said, much amused. 'It isn't what you think,' he cried, almost passionately. 'It was in general. He made me see things—things.'

"He threw his arms up. We were on deck at the time, and the head-man of my wood-cutters, lounging near by, turned upon him his heavy and glittering eyes. I looked around, and I don't know why, but I assure you that never, never before, did this land, this river, this jungle, the very arch of this blazing sky, appear to me so hopeless and so dark, so impenetrable to human thought, so pitiless to human weakness. 'And, ever since, you have been with him, of course?' I said.

"On the contrary. It appears their intercourse had been very much broken by various causes. He had, as he informed me proudly, managed to nurse Kurtz through two illnesses (he alluded to it as you would to some risky feat), but as a rule Kurtz wandered alone, far in the depths of the forest. 'Very often coming to this station, I had to wait days and days before he would turn up,' he said. 'Ah, it was worth waiting for!—sometimes.' 'What was he doing? exploring or what?' I asked. 'Oh yes, of course'; he had discovered lots of villages, a lake too—he did not know exactly in what direction; it was dangerous to inquire too much—but mostly his expeditions had been for ivory. 'But he had no goods to trade with by that time,' I objected. 'There's a good lot of cartridges left even yet,' he answered, looking away. 'To speak plainly, he raided the country,' I said. He nodded. 'Not alone, surely!' He muttered something about the villages round that lake. 'Kurtz got the tribe to follow him, did he?' I suggested. He fidgeted a little. 'They adored him,' he said. The tone of these words was so extraordinary that I looked at him searchingly. It was curious to see his mingled eagerness and reluctance to speak of Kurtz. The man filled his life, occupied his thoughts, swayed his emotions. 'What can you expect?' he burst out; 'he came to them with thunder and lightning, you know—and they had never seen anything like it—and very terrible. He could be very terrible. You can't judge Mr Kurtz as you would an ordinary man. No, no, no! Now—just to give you an idea—I don't mind telling you, he wanted to shoot me too one day—but I don't judge him.' 'Shoot you!' I cried. 'What for?' 'Well, I had a small lot of ivory the chief of that village near my house gave me. You see I used to shoot game for them. Well, he wanted it, and wouldn't hear reason. He declared he would shoot me unless I gave him the ivory and then cleared out of the country, because he could do so, and had a fancy for it, and there was nothing on earth to prevent him killing whom he jolly well pleased. And it was true too. I gave him the ivory. What did I care! But I didn't clear out. No, no. I couldn't leave him. I had to be careful, of course, till we got friendly again for a time. He had his second illness then. Afterwards I had to keep out of the way; but I didn't mind. He was living for the most part in those villages on the lake. When he came down to the river, sometimes he would take to me, and sometimes it was better for me to be careful. This man suffered too much. He hated all this, and somehow he couldn't get away. When I had a chance I begged him to try and leave while there was time; I offered to go back with him. And he would say yes, and then he would remain; go off on another ivory hunt; disappear for weeks; forget himself amongst these people—forget himself—you know.' 'Why! he's mad,' I said. He protested indignantly. Mr Kurtz couldn't be mad. If I had heard him talk, only two days ago, I wouldn't dare hint at such a thing. . . . I had taken up my binoculars while we talked, and was looking at the shore, sweeping the limit of the forest at each side and at the back of the house. The consciousness of there being people in that bush, so silent, so quiet—as silent and quiet as the ruined house on the hill—made me uneasy. There was no sign on the face of nature of this amazing tale that was not so much told as suggested to me in desolate exclamations, completed by shrugs, in interrupted phrases, in hints ending in deep sighs. The woods were unmoved, like a mask—heavy, like the closed door of a prison—they looked with their air of hidden knowledge, of patient expectation, of unapproachable silence. The Russian was explaining to me that it was only lately that Mr Kurtz had come down to the river, bringing along with him all the fighting men of that lake tribe. He had been absent for several months—getting himself adored, I suppose—and had come down unexpectedly, with the intention to all appearance of making a raid either across the river or down stream. Evidently the appetite for more ivory had got the better of the—what shall I say?—less material aspirations. However, he had got much worse suddenly. 'I heard he was lying helpless, and so I came up—took my chance,' said the Russian. 'Oh, he is bad, very bad.' I directed my glass to the house. There were no signs of life, but there was the ruined roof, the long mud wall peeping above the grass, with three little square window-holes, no two of the same size; all this brought within reach of my hand, as it were. And then I made a brusque movement, and one of the remaining posts of that vanished fence leaped up in the field of my glass. You remember I told you I had been struck at the distance by certain attempts at ornamentation, rather remarkable in the ruinous aspect of the place. Now I had suddenly a nearer view, and its first result was to make me throw my head back as if before a blow. Then I went carefully from post to post with my glass, and I saw my mistake. These round knobs were not ornamental but symbolic; they were expressive and puzzling, striking and disturbing—food for thought and also for the vultures if there had been any looking down from the sky; but at all events for such ants as were industrious enough to ascend the pole. They would have been even more impressive, those heads on the stakes, if their faces had not been turned to the house. Only one, the first I had made out, was facing my way. I was not so shocked as you may think. The start back I had given was really nothing but a movement of surprise. I had expected to see a knob of wood there, you know. I returned deliberately to the first I had seen—and there it was, black, dried, sunken, with closed eyelids—a head that seemed to sleep at the top of that pole, and, with the shrunken dry lips showing a narrow white line of the teeth, was smiling too, smiling continuously at some endless and jocose dream of that eternal slumber.

"I am not disclosing any trade secrets. In fact the manager said afterwards that Mr Kurtz's methods had ruined the district. I have no opinion on that point, but I want you clearly to understand that there was nothing exactly profitable in these heads being there. They only show that Mr Kurtz lacked restraint in the gratification of his various lusts, that there was something wanting in him—some small matter which, when the pressing need arose, could not be found under his magnificent eloquence. Whether he knew of this deficiency himself I can't say. I think the knowledge came to him at last—only at the very last. But the wilderness had found him out early, and had taken on him a terrible vengeance for the fantastic invasion. I think it had whispered to him things about himself which he did not know, things of which he had no conception till he took counsel with this great solitude—and the whisper had proved irresistibly fascinating. It echoed loudly within him because he was hollow at the core. . . . I put down the glass, and the head that had appeared near enough to be spoken to seemed at once to have leaped away from me into inaccessible distance.

"The admirer of Mr Kurtz was a bit crestfallen. In a hurried, indistinct voice he began to assure me he had not dared to take these—say, symbols— down. He was not afraid of the natives; they would not stir till Mr Kurtz gave the word. His ascendancy was extraordinary. The camps of these people surrounded the place, and the chiefs came every day to see him. They would crawl . . . 'I don't want to know anything of the ceremonies used when approaching Mr Kurtz,' I shouted. Curious, this feeling that came over me that such details would be more intolerable than those heads drying on the stakes under Mr Kurtz's windows. After all, that was only a savage sight, while I seemed at one bound to have been transported into some lightless region of subtle horrors, where pure, uncomplicated savagery was a positive relief, being something that had a right to exist—obviously—in the sunshine. The young man looked at me with surprise. I suppose it did not occur to him that Mr Kurtz was no idol of mine. He forgot I hadn't heard any of these splendid monologues on, what was it? on love, justice, conduct of life—or what not. If it had come to crawling before Mr Kurtz, he crawled as much as the veriest savage of them all. I had no idea of the conditions, he said: these heads were the heads of rebels. I shocked him excessively by laughing. Rebels! What would be the next definition I was to hear? There had been enemies, criminals, workers—and these were rebels. Those rebellious heads looked very subdued to me on their sticks. 'You don't know how such a life tries a man like Kurtz,' cried Kurtz's last disciple. 'Well, and you?' I said. 'I! I! I am a simple man. I have no great thoughts. I want nothing from anybody. How can you compare me to . . . ?' His feelings were too much for speech, and suddenly he broke down. 'I don't understand,' he groaned. 'I've been doing my best to keep him alive, and that's enough. I had no hand in all this. I have no abilities. There hasn't been a drop of medicine or a mouthful of invalid food for months here. He was shamefully abandoned. A man like this, with such ideas. Shamefully! Shamefully! I—I—haven't slept for the last ten nights. . . .'

"His voice lost itself in the calm of the evening. The long shadows of the forest had slipped down hill while we talked, had gone far beyond the ruined hovel, beyond the symbolic row of stakes. All this was in the gloom, while we down there were yet in the sunshine, and the stretch of the river abreast of the clearing glittered in a still and dazzling splendour, with a murky and overshadowed bend above and below. Not a living soul was seen on the shore. The bushes did not rustle.

"Suddenly round the corner of the house a group of men appeared, as though they had come up from the ground. They waded waist-deep in the grass, in a compact body, bearing an improvised stretcher in their midst. Instantly, in the emptiness of the landscape, a cry arose whose shrillness pierced the still air like a sharp arrow flying straight to the very heart of the land; and, as if by enchantment, streams of human beings—of naked human beings—with spears in their hands, with bows, with shields, with wild glances and savage movements, were poured into the clearing by the dark-faced and pensive forest. The bushes shook, the grass swayed for a time, and then everything stood still in attentive immobility.

" 'Now, if he does not say the right thing to them we are all done for,' said the Russian at my elbow. The knot of men with the stretcher had stopped too, half-way to the steamer, as if petrified. I saw the man on the stretcher sit up, lank and with an uplifted arm, above the shoulders of the bearers. 'Let us hope that the man who can talk so well of love in general will find some particular reason to spare us this time,' I said. I resented bitterly the absurd danger of our situation, as if to be at the mercy of that atrocious phantom had been a dishonouring necessity. I could not hear a sound, but through my glasses I saw the thin arm extended commandingly, the lower jaw moving, the eyes of that apparition shining darkly far in its bony head that nodded with grotesque jerks. Kurtz—Kurtz—that means 'short' in German—don't it? Well, the name was as true as everything else in his life—and death. He looked at least seven feet long. His covering had fallen off, and his body emerged from it pitiful and appalling as from a winding-sheet. I could see the cage of his ribs all astir, the bones of his arm waving. It was as though an animated image of death carved out of old ivory had been shaking its hand with menaces at a motionless crowd of men made of dark and glittering bronze. I saw him open his mouth wide—it gave him a weirdly voracious aspect, as though he had wanted to swallow all the air, all the earth, all the men before him. A deep voice reached me faintly. He must have been shouting. He fell back suddenly. The stretcher shook as the bearers staggered forward again, and almost at the same time I noticed that the crowd of savages was vanishing without any perceptible movement of retreat, as if the forest that had ejected these beings so suddenly had drawn them in again as the breath is drawn in a long aspiration.

"Some of the pilgrims behind the stretcher carried his arms—two shot-guns, a heavy rifle, and a light revolver-carbine—the thunderbolts of that pitiful Jupiter. The manager bent over him murmuring as he walked beside his head. They laid him down in one of the little cabins—just a room for a bedplace and a camp-stool or two, you know. We had brought his belated correspondence, and a lot of torn envelopes and open letters littered his bed. His hand roamed feebly amongst these papers. I was struck by the fire of his eyes and the composed languor of his expression. It was not so much the exhaustion of disease. He did not seem in pain. This shadow looked satiated and calm, as though for the moment it had had its fill of all the emotions.

"He rustled one of the letters, and looking straight in my face said, 'I am glad.' Somebody had been writing to him about me. These special recom-mendations were turning up again. The volume of tone he emitted without effort, almost without the trouble of moving his lips, amazed me. A voice! a voice! It was grave, profound, vibrating, while the man did not seem capable of a whisper. However, he had enough strength in him—factitious no doubt—to very nearly make an end of us, as you shall hear directly.

"The manager appeared silently in the doorway; I stepped out at once and he drew the curtain after me. The Russian, eyed curiously by the pilgrims, was staring at the shore. I followed the direction of his glance.

"Dark human shapes could be made out in the distance, flitting indistinctly against the gloomy border of the forest, and near the river two bronze figures, leaning on tall spears, stood in the sunlight under fantastic head-dresses of spotted skins, warlike and still in statuesque repose. And from right to left along the lighted shore moved a wild and gorgeous apparition of a woman.

"She walked with measured steps, draped in striped and fringed cloths, treading the earth proudly, with a slight jingle and flash of barbarous orna-ments. She carried her head high; her hair was done in the shape of a helmet; she had brass leggings to the knee, brass wire gauntlets to the elbow, a crimson spot on her tawny cheek, innumerable necklaces of glass beads on her neck; bizarre things, charms, gifts of witch-men, that hung about her, glittered and trembled at every step. She must have had the value of several elephant tusks upon her. She was savage and superb, wild-eyed and magnif-icent; there was something ominous and stately in her deliberate progress. And in the hush that had fallen suddenly upon the whole sorrowful land, the immense wilderness, the colossal body of the fecund and mysterious life seemed to look at her, pensive, as though it had been looking at the image of its own tenebrous and passionate soul.

"She came abreast of the steamer, stood still, and faced us. Her long shadow fell to the water's edge. Her face had a tragic and fierce aspect of wild sorrow and of dumb pain mingled with the fear of some struggling, half-shaped resolve. She stood looking at us without a stir, and like the wilderness itself, with an air of brooding over an inscrutable purpose. A whole minute passed, and then she made a step forward. There was a low jingle, a glint of yellow metal, a sway of fringed draperies, and she stopped as if her heart had failed her. The young fellow by my side growled. The pilgrims murmured at my back. She looked at us all as if her life had depended upon the unswerving steadiness of her glance. Suddenly she opened her bared arms and threw them up rigid above her head, as though in an uncontrollable desire to touch the sky, and at the same time the swift shadows darted out on the earth, swept around on the river, gathering the steamer into a shadowy embrace. A formidable silence hung over the scene.

"She turned away slowly, walked on, following the bank, and passed into the bushes to the left. Once only her eyes gleamed back at us in the dusk of the thickets before she disappeared.

" 'If she had offered to come aboard I really think I would have tried to shoot her,' said the man of patches nervously. 'I had been risking my life every day for the last fortnight to keep her out of the house. She got in one day and kicked up a row about those miserable rags I picked up in the store-room to mend my clothes with. I wasn't decent. At least it must have been that, for she talked like a fury to Kurtz for an hour, pointing at me now and then. I don't understand the dialect of this tribe. Luckily for me, I fancy Kurtz felt too ill that day to care, or there would have been mischief. I don't understand. . . . No—it's too much for me. Ah, well, it's all over now.'

"At this moment I heard Kurtz's deep voice behind the curtain: 'Save me!—save the ivory, you mean. Don't tell me. Save *me*! Why, I've had to save you. You are interrupting my plans now. Sick! Sick! Not so sick as you would like to believe. Never mind. I'll carry my ideas out yet—I will return. I'll show you what can be done. You with your little peddling notions—you are interfering with me. I will return. I . . .'

"The manager came out. He did me the honour to take me under the arm and lead me aside. 'He is very low, very low,' he said. He considered it necessary to sigh, but neglected to be consistently sorrowful. 'We have done all we could for him—haven't we? But there is no disguising the fact, Mr Kurtz has done more harm than good to the Company. He did not see the time was not ripe for vigorous action. Cautiously, cautiously—that's my principle. We must be cautious yet. The district is closed to us for a time. Deplorable! Upon the whole, the trade will suffer. I don't deny there is a remarkable quantity of ivory—mostly fossil. We must save it, at all events—but look how precarious the position is—and why? Because the method is unsound.' 'Do you,' said I, looking at the shore, 'call it "unsound method"?' 'Without doubt,' he exclaimed hotly, 'Don't you?' . . . 'No method at all,' I murmured after a while. 'Exactly,' he exulted. 'I anticipated this. Shows a complete want of judgment. It is my duty to point it out in the proper quarter.' 'Oh,' said I, 'that fellow—what's his name?—the brickmaker, will make a readable report for you.' He appeared confounded for a moment. It seemed to me I had never breathed an atmosphere so vile, and I turned mentally to Kurtz for relief—positively for relief. 'Nevertheless, I think Mr Kurtz is a remarkable man,' I said with emphasis. He started, dropped on me a cold heavy glance, said very quietly, 'He *was*,' and turned his back on me. My hour of favour was over; I found myself lumped along with Kurtz as a partisan of methods for which the time was not ripe: I was unsound! Ah! but it was something to have at least a choice of nightmares.

"I had turned to the wilderness really, not to Mr Kurtz, who, I was ready to admit, was as good as buried. And for a moment it seemed to me as if I also were buried in a vast grave full of unspeakable secrets. I felt an intolerable weight oppressing my breast, the smell of the damp earth, the unseen presence of victorious corruption, the darkness of an impenetrable night. . . . The Russian tapped me on the shoulder. I heard him mumbling and stammering something about 'brother seaman—couldn't conceal—knowledge of matters that would affect Mr Kurtz's reputation.' I waited. For him evidently Mr Kurtz was not in his grave; I suspect that for him Mr Kurtz was one of the immortals. 'Well!' said I at last, 'speak out. As it happens, I am Mr Kurtz's friend—in a way.'

"He stated with a good deal of formality that had we not been 'of the same profession,' he would have kept the matter to himself without regard to consequences. He suspected 'there was an active ill-will towards him on the part of these white men that—' 'You are right,' I said, remembering a certain conversation I had overheard. 'The manager thinks you ought to be hanged.' He showed a concern at this intelligence which amused me at first. 'I had better get out of the way quietly,' he said earnestly. 'I can do no more for Kurtz now, and they would soon find some excuse. What's to stop them? There's a military post three hundred miles from here.' 'Well, upon my word,' said I, 'perhaps you had better go if you have any friends amongst the savages near by.' 'Plenty,' he said. 'They are simple people—and I want nothing, you know.' He stood biting his lip, then: 'I don't want any harm to happen to these whites here, but of course I was thinking of Mr Kurtz's reputation—but you are a brother seaman and—' 'All right,' said I, after a time. 'Mr Kurtz's reputation is safe with me.' I did not know how truly I spoke.

"He informed me, lowering his voice, that it was Kurtz who had ordered the attack to be made on the steamer. 'He hated sometimes the idea of being taken away—and then again . . . But I don't understand these matters. I am a simple man. He thought it would scare you away—that you would give it up, thinking him dead. I could not stop him. Oh, I had an awful time of it this last month.' 'Very well,' I said. 'He is all right now.' 'Ye-e-es,' he muttered, not very convinced apparently. 'Thanks,' said I; 'I shall keep my eyes open.' 'But quiet—eh?' he urged anxiously. 'It would be awful for his reputation if anybody here—' I promised a complete discretion with great gravity. 'I have a canoe and three black fellows waiting not very far. I am off. Could you give me a few Martini-Henry cartridges?' I could, and did, with proper secrecy. He helped himself, with a wink at me, to a handful of my tobacco. 'Between sailors—you know—good English tobacco.' At the door of the pilot-house he turned round—'I say, haven't you a pair of shoes you could spare?' He raised one leg. 'Look.' The soles were tied with knotted strings sandal-wise under his bare feet. I rooted out an old pair, at which he looked with admiration before tucking it under his left arm. One of his pockets (bright red) was bulging with cartridges, from the other (dark blue) peeped 'Towson's Inquiry,' etc. etc. He seemed to think himself excellently well equipped for a renewed encounter with the wilderness. 'Ah! I'll never, never meet such a man again. You ought to have heard him recite poetry—his own too it was, he told me. Poetry!' He rolled his eyes at the recollection of these delights. 'Oh, he enlarged my mind!' 'Good-bye,' said I. He shook hands and vanished in the night. Sometimes I ask myself whether I had ever really seen him—whether it was possible to meet such a phenomenon! . . .

"When I woke up shortly after midnight his warning came to my mind with its hint of danger that seemed, in the starred darkness, real enough to make me get up for the purpose of having a look round. On the hill a big fire burned, illuminating fitfully a crooked corner of the station-house. One of the agents with a picket of a few of our blacks, armed for the purpose, was keeping guard over the ivory; but deep within the forest, red gleams that wavered, that seemed to sink and rise from the ground amongst confused columnar shapes of intense blackness, showed the exact position of the camp where Mr Kurtz's adorers were keeping their uneasy vigil. The monotonous beating of a big drum filled the air with muffled shocks and a lingering vibration. A steady droning sound of many men chanting each to himself some weird incantation came out from the black, flat wall of the woods as the humming of bees comes out of a hive, and had a strange narcotic effect upon my half-awake senses. I believe I dozed off leaning over the rail, till an abrupt burst of yells, an overwhelming outbreak of a pent-up and mysterious frenzy, woke me up in a bewildered wonder. It was cut short all at once, and the low droning went on with an effect of audible and soothing silence. I glanced casually into the little cabin. A light was burning within, but Mr Kurtz was not there.

"I think I would have raised an outcry if I had believed my eyes. But I didn't believe them at first—the thing seemed so impossible. The fact is I was completely unnerved by a sheer blank fright, pure abstract terror, unconnected with any distinct shape of physical danger. What made this emotion so overpowering was—how shall I define it?—the moral shock I received, as if something altogether monstrous, intolerable to thought and odious to the soul, had been thrust upon me unexpectedly. This lasted of course the merest fraction of a second, and then the usual sense of commonplace, deadly danger, the possibility of a sudden onslaught and massacre, or something of the kind, which I saw impending, was positively welcome and composing. It pacified me, in fact, so much, that I did not raise an alarm.

"There was an agent buttoned up inside an ulster[1] and sleeping on a chair on deck within three feet of me. The yells had not awakened him; he snored very slightly; I left him to his slumbers and leaped ashore. I did not betray Mr Kurtz—it was ordered I should never betray him—it was written I should be loyal to the nightmare of my choice. I was anxious to deal with this shadow by myself alone—and to this day I don't know why I was so jealous of sharing with any one the peculiar blackness of that experience.

"As soon as I got on the bank I saw a trail—a broad trail through the grass. I remember the exultation with which I said to myself, 'He can't walk—he is crawling on all-fours—I've got him.' The grass was wet with dew. I strode rapidly with clenched fists. I fancy I had some vague notion of falling upon him and giving him a drubbing. I don't know. I had some imbecile thoughts. The knitting old woman with the cat obtruded herself upon my memory as a most improper person to be sitting at the other end of such an affair. I saw a row of pilgrims squirting lead in the air out of Winchesters held to the hip. I thought I would never get back to the steamer, and imagined myself living alone and unarmed in the woods to an advanced age. Such silly things—you know. And I remember I confounded the beat of the drum with the beating of my heart, and was pleased at its calm regularity.

"I kept to the track though—then stopped to listen. The night was very clear; a dark blue space, sparkling with dew and starlight, in which black

---

1. Long overcoat.

things stood very still. I thought I could see a kind of motion ahead of me. I was strangely cocksure of everything that night. I actually left the track and ran in a wide semicircle (I verily believe chuckling to myself) so as to get in front of that stir, of that motion I had seen—if indeed I had seen anything. I was circumventing Kurtz as though it had been a boyish game.

"I came upon him, and, if he had not heard me coming, I would have fallen over him too, but he got up in time. He rose, unsteady, long, pale, indistinct, like a vapour exhaled by the earth, and swayed slightly, misty and silent before me; while at my back the fires loomed between the trees, and the murmur of many voices issued from the forest. I had cut him off cleverly; but when actually confronting him I seemed to come to my senses, I saw the danger in its right proportion. It was by no means over yet. Suppose he began to shout? Though he could hardly stand, there was still plenty of vigour in his voice. 'Go away—hide yourself,' he said, in that profound tone. It was very awful. I glanced back. We were within thirty yards of the nearest fire. A black figure stood up, strode on long black legs, waving long black arms, across the glow. It had horns—antelope horns, I think—on its head. Some sorcerer, some witch-man no doubt: it looked fiend-like enough. 'Do you know what you are doing?' I whispered. 'Perfectly,' he answered, raising his voice for that single word: it sounded to me far off and yet loud, like a hail through a speaking-trumpet. If he makes a row we are lost, I thought to myself. This clearly was not a case for fisticuffs, even apart from the very natural aversion I had to beat that Shadow—this wandering and tormented thing. 'You will be lost,' I said—'utterly lost.' One gets sometimes such a flash of inspiration, you know. I did say the right thing, though indeed he could not have been more irretrievably lost than he was at this very moment, when the foundations of our intimacy were being laid—to endure—to endure—even to the end—even beyond.

" 'I had immense plans,' he muttered irresolutely. 'Yes,' said I; 'but if you try to shout I'll smash your head with—' There was not a stick or a stone near. 'I will throttle you for good,' I corrected myself. 'I was on the threshold of great things,' he pleaded, in a voice of longing, with a wistfulness of tone that made my blood run cold. 'And now for this stupid scoundrel—' 'Your success in Europe is assured in any case,' I affirmed steadily. I did not want to have the throttling of him, you understand—and indeed it would have been very little use for any practical purpose. I tried to break the spell—the heavy, mute spell of the wilderness—that seemed to draw him to its pitiless breast by the awakening of forgotten and brutal instincts, by the memory of gratified and monstrous passions. This alone, I was convinced, had driven him out to the edge of the forest, to the bush, towards the gleam of fires, the throb of drums, the drone of weird incantations; this alone had beguiled his unlawful soul beyond the bounds of permitted aspirations. And, don't you see, the terror of the position was not in being knocked on the head—though I had a very lively sense of that danger too—but in this, that I had to deal with a being to whom I could not appeal in the name of anything high or low. I had, even like the niggers, to invoke him—himself—his own exalted and incredible degradation. There was nothing either above or below him, and I knew it. He had kicked himself loose of the earth. Confound the man! he had kicked the very earth to pieces. He was alone, and I before him did not know whether I stood on the ground or floated in the air. I've been telling you what we said—repeating the phrases we pronounced—but what's the good? They were common everyday words—the familiar, vague sounds exchanged on every waking day of life. But what of that? They had behind them, to my mind, the terrific suggestiveness of words heard in dreams, of phrases spoken in nightmares. Soul! If anybody had ever struggled with a soul, I am the man. And I wasn't arguing with a lunatic either. Believe me or not, his intelligence was perfectly clear—concentrated, it is true, upon himself with horrible intensity, yet clear; and therein was my only chance—barring, of course, the killing him there and then, which wasn't so good, on account of unavoidable noise. But his soul was mad. Being alone in the wilderness, it had looked within itself, and, by heavens! I tell you, it had gone mad. I had—for my sins, I suppose, to go through the ordeal of looking into it myself. No eloquence could have been so withering to one's belief in mankind as his final burst of sincerity. He struggled with himself too. I saw it—I heard it. I saw the inconceivable mystery of a soul that knew no restraint, no faith, and no fear, yet struggling blindly with itself. I kept my head pretty well; but when I had him at last stretched on the couch, I wiped my forehead, while my legs shook under me as though I had carried half a ton on my back down that hill. And yet I had only supported him, his bony arm clasped round my neck—and he was not much heavier than a child.

"When next day we left at noon, the crowd, of whose presence behind the curtain of trees I had been acutely conscious all the time, flowed out of the woods again, filled the clearing, covered the slope with a mass of naked, breathing, quivering, bronze bodies. I steamed up a bit, then swung downstream, and two thousand eyes followed the evolutions of the splashing, thumping, fierce river-demon beating the water with its terrible tail and breathing black smoke into the air. In front of the first rank, along the river, three men, plastered with bright red earth from head to foot, strutted to and fro restlessly. When we came abreast again, they faced the river, stamped their feet, nodded their horned heads, swayed their scarlet bodies; they shook towards the fierce river-demon a bunch of black feathers, a mangy skin with a pendent tail—something that looked like a dried gourd; they shouted periodically together strings of amazing words that resembled no sounds of human language; and the deep murmurs of the crowd, interrupted suddenly, were like the responses of some satanic litany.

"We had carried Kurtz into the pilot-house: there was more air there. Lying on the couch, he stared through the open shutter. There was an eddy in the mass of human bodies, and the woman with helmeted head and tawny cheeks rushed out to the very brink of the stream. She put out her hands, shouted something, and all that wild mob took up the shout in a roaring chorus of articulated, rapid, breathless utterance.

" 'Do you understand this?' I asked.

"He kept on looking out past me with fiery, longing eyes, with a mingled expression of wistfulness and hate. He made no answer, but I saw a smile, a smile of indefinable meaning, appear on his colourless lips that a moment after twitched convulsively. 'Do I not?' he said slowly, gasping, as if the words had been torn out of him by a supernatural power.

"I pulled the string of the whistle, and I did this because I saw the pilgrims on deck getting out their rifles with an air of anticipating a jolly lark. At the sudden screech there was a movement of abject terror through that wedged mass of bodies. 'Don't! don't you frighten them away,' cried some one on deck disconsolately. I pulled the string time after time. They broke and ran, they leaped, they crouched, they swerved, they dodged the flying terror of the sound. The three red chaps had fallen flat, face down on the shore, as though they had been shot dead. Only the barbarous and superb woman did not so much as flinch, and stretched tragically her bare arms after us over the sombre and glittering river.

"And then that imbecile crowd down on the deck started their little fun, and I could see nothing more for smoke.

"The brown current ran swiftly out of the heart of darkness, bearing us down towards the sea with twice the speed of our upward progress; and Kurtz's life was running swiftly too, ebbing, ebbing out of his heart into the sea of inexorable time. The manager was very placid, he had no vital anxieties now, he took us both in with a comprehensive and satisfied glance: the 'affair' had come off as well as could be wished. I saw the time approaching when I would be left alone of the party of 'unsound method.' The pilgrims looked upon me with disfavour. I was, so to speak, numbered with the dead. It is strange how I accepted this unforeseen partnership, this choice of night-mares forced upon me in the tenebrous land invaded by these mean and greedy phantoms.

"Kurtz discoursed. A voice! a voice! It rang deep to the very last. It survived his strength to hide in the magnificent folds of eloquence the barren darkness of his heart. Oh, he struggled! he struggled! The wastes of his weary brain were haunted by shadowy images now—images of wealth and fame revolving obsequiously round his unextinguishable gift of noble and lofty expression. My Intended, my station, my career, my ideas—these were the subjects for the occasional utterances of elevated sentiments. The shade of the original Kurtz frequented the bedside of the hollow sham, whose fate it was to be buried presently in the mould of primeval earth. But both the diabolic love and the unearthly hate of the mysteries it had penetrated fought for the possession of that soul satiated with primitive emotions, avid of lying fame, of sham distinction, of all the appearances of success and power.

"Sometimes he was contemptibly childish. He desired to have kings meet him at railway stations on his return from some ghastly Nowhere, where he intended to accomplish great things. 'You show them you have in you some-thing that is really profitable, and then there will be no limits to the recog-nition of your ability,' he would say. 'Of course you must take care of the motives—right motives—always.' The long reaches that were like one and the same reach, monotonous bends that were exactly alike, slipped past the steamer with their multitude of secular[2] trees looking patiently after this grimy fragment of another world, the forerunner of change, of conquest, of trade, of massacres, of blessings. I looked ahead—piloting. 'Close the shut-ter,' said Kurtz suddenly one day; 'I can't bear to look at this.' I did so. There was a silence. 'Oh, but I will wring your heart yet!' he cried at the invisible wilderness.

"We broke down—as I had expected—and had to lie up for repairs at the head of an island. This delay was the first thing that shook Kurtz's confi-dence. One morning he gave me a packet of papers and a photograph—the

2. Centuries old.

lot tied together with a shoe-string. 'Keep this for me,' he said. 'This noxious fool' (meaning the manager) 'is capable of prying into my boxes when I am not looking.' In the afternoon I saw him. He was lying on his back with closed eyes, and I withdrew quietly, but I heard him mutter, 'Live rightly, die, die . . . ' I listened. There was nothing more. Was he rehearsing some speech in his sleep, or was it a fragment of a phrase from some newspaper article? He had been writing for the papers and meant to do so again, 'for the furthering of my ideas. It's a duty.'

"His was an impenetrable darkness. I looked at him as you peer down at a man who is lying at the bottom of a precipice where the sun never shines. But I had not much time to give him, because I was helping the engine-driver to take to pieces the leaky cylinders, to straighten a bent connecting-rod, and in other such matters. I lived in an infernal mess of rust, filings, nuts, bolts, spanners, hammers, ratchet-drills—things I abominate, because I don't get on with them. I tended the little forge we fortunately had aboard; I toiled wearily in a wretched scrap-heap—unless I had the shakes too bad to stand.

"One evening coming in with a candle I was startled to hear him say a little tremulously, 'I am lying here in the dark waiting for death.' The light was within a foot of his eyes. I forced myself to murmur, 'Oh, nonsense!' and stood over him as if transfixed.

"Anything approaching the change that came over his features I have never seen before, and hope never to see again. Oh, I wasn't touched. I was fascinated. It was as though a veil had been rent. I saw on that ivory face the expression of sombre pride, of ruthless power, of craven terror—of an intense and hopeless despair. Did he live his life again in every detail of desire, temptation, and surrender during that supreme moment of complete knowledge? He cried in a whisper at some image, at some vision—he cried out twice, a cry that was no more than a breath:

" 'The horror! The horror!'

"I blew the candle out and left the cabin. The pilgrims were dining in the mess-room, and I took my place opposite the manager, who lifted his eyes to give me a questioning glance, which I successfully ignored. He leaned back, serene, with that peculiar smile of his sealing the unexpressed depths of his meanness. A continuous shower of small flies streamed upon the lamp, upon the cloth, upon our hands and faces. Suddenly the manager's boy put his insolent black head in the doorway, and said in a tone of scathing contempt:

" 'Mistah Kurtz—he dead.'

"All the pilgrims rushed out to see. I remained, and went on with my dinner. I believe I was considered brutally callous. However, I did not eat much. There was a lamp in there—light, don't you know—and outside it was so beastly, beastly dark. I went no more near the remarkable man who had pronounced a judgement upon the adventures of his soul on this earth. The voice was gone. What else had been there? But I am of course aware that next day the pilgrims buried something in a muddy hole.

"And then they very nearly buried me.

"However, as you see, I did not go to join Kurtz there and then. I did not. I remained to dream the nightmare out to the end, and to show my loyalty to Kurtz once more. Destiny. My destiny! Droll thing life is—that mysterious arrangement of merciless logic for a futile purpose. The most you can hope from it is some knowledge of yourself—that comes too late—a crop of unextinguishable regrets. I have wrestled with death. It is the most unexciting contest you can imagine. It takes place in an impalpable greyness, with nothing underfoot, with nothing around, without spectators, without clamour, without glory, without the great desire of victory, without the great fear of defeat, in a sickly atmosphere of tepid scepticism, without much belief in your own right, and still less in that of your adversary. If such is the form of ultimate wisdom, then life is a greater riddle than some of us think it to be. I was within a hair's-breadth of the last opportunity for pronouncement, and I found with humiliation that probably I would have nothing to say. This is the reason why I affirm that Kurtz was a remarkable man. He had something to say. He said it. Since I had peeped over the edge myself, I understand better the meaning of his stare, that could not see the flame of the candle, but was wide enough to embrace the whole universe, piercing enough to penetrate all the hearts that beat in the darkness. He had summed up—he had judged. 'The horror!' He was a remarkable man. After all, this was the expression of some sort of belief; it had candour, it had conviction, it had a vibrating note of revolt in its whisper, it had the appalling face of a glimpsed truth—the strange commingling of desire and hate. And it is not my own extremity I remember best—a vision of greyness without form filled with physical pain, and a careless contempt for the evanescence of all things— even of this pain itself. No! It is his extremity that I seem to have lived through. True, he had made that last stride, he had stepped over the edge, while I had been permitted to draw back my hesitating foot. And perhaps in this is the whole difference; perhaps all the wisdom, and all truth, and all sincerity, are just compressed into that inappreciable moment of time in which we step over the threshold of the invisible. Perhaps! I like to think my summing-up would not have been a word of careless contempt. Better his cry—much better. It was an affirmation, a moral victory paid for by innumerable defeats, by abominable terrors, by abominable satisfactions. But it was a victory! That is why I have remained loyal to Kurtz to the last, and even beyond, when a long time after I heard once more, not his own voice, but the echo of his magnificent eloquence thrown to me from a soul as translucently pure as a cliff of crystal.

"No, they did not bury me, though there is a period of time which I remember mistily, with a shuddering wonder, like a passage through some inconceivable world that had no hope in it and no desire. I found myself back in the sepulchral city resenting the sight of people hurrying through the streets to filch a little money from each other, to devour their infamous cookery, to gulp their unwholesome beer, to dream their insignificant and silly dreams. They trespassed upon my thoughts. They were intruders whose knowledge of life was to me an irritating pretence, because I felt so sure they could not possibly know the things I knew. Their bearing, which was simply the bearing of commonplace individuals going about their business in the assurance of perfect safety, was offensive to me like the outrageous flauntings of folly in the face of a danger it is unable to comprehend. I had no particular desire to enlighten them, but I had some difficulty in restraining myself from laughing in their faces, so full of stupid importance. I daresay I was not very well at that time. I tottered about the streets—there were various affairs to settle—grinning bitterly at perfectly respectable persons. I admit my behaviour was inexcusable, but then my temperature was seldom normal in these days. My dear aunt's endeavours to 'nurse up my strength' seemed altogether beside the mark. It was not my strength that wanted nursing, it was my imagination that wanted soothing. I kept the bundle of papers given me by Kurtz, not knowing exactly what to do with it. His mother had died lately, watched over, as I was told, by his Intended. A clean-shaven man, with an official manner and wearing gold-rimmed spectacles, called on me one day and made inquiries, at first circuitous, afterwards suavely pressing, about what he was pleased to denominate certain 'documents.' I was not surprised, because I had had two rows with the manager on the subject out there. I had refused to give up the smallest scrap out of that package, and I took the same attitude with the spectacled man. He became darkly menacing at last, and with much heat argued that the Company had the right to every bit of information about its 'territories.' And, said he, 'Mr Kurtz's knowledge of unexplored regions must have been necessarily extensive and peculiar— owing to his great abilities and to the deplorable circumstances in which he had been placed: therefore—' I assured him Mr Kurtz's knowledge, however extensive, did not bear upon the problems of commerce or administration. He invoked then the name of science. 'It would be an incalculable loss if,' etc. etc. I offered him the report on the 'Suppression of Savage Customs,' with the postscriptum torn off. He took it up eagerly, but ended by sniffing at it with an air of contempt. 'This is not what we had a right to expect,' he remarked. 'Expect nothing else,' I said. 'There are only private letters.' He withdrew upon some threat of legal proceedings, and I saw him no more; but another fellow, calling himself Kurtz's cousin, appeared two days later, and was anxious to hear all the details about his dear relative's last moments. Incidentally he gave me to understand that Kurtz had been essentially a great musician. 'There was the making of an immense success,' said the man, who was an organist, I believe, with lank grey hair flowing over a greasy coat-collar. I had no reason to doubt his statement; and to this day I am unable to say what was Kurtz's profession, whether he ever had any—which was the greatest of his talents. I had taken him for a painter who wrote for the papers, or else for a journalist who could paint—but even the cousin (who took snuff during the interview) could not tell me what he had been—exactly. He was a universal genius—on that point I agreed with the old chap, who thereupon blew his nose noisily into a large cotton handkerchief and withdrew in senile agitation, bearing off some family letters and memoranda without impor-tance. Ultimately a journalist anxious to know something of the fate of his 'dear colleague' turned up. This visitor informed me Kurtz's proper sphere ought to have been politics 'on the popular side.' He had furry straight eye-brows, bristly hair cropped short, an eyeglass on a broad ribbon, and, becom-ing expansive, confessed his opinion that Kurtz really couldn't write a bit— 'but heavens! how that man could talk! He electrified large meetings. He had faith—don't you see?—he had the faith. He could get himself to believe anything—anything. He would have been a splendid leader of an extreme party.' 'What party?' I asked. 'Any party,' answered the other. 'He was an— an—extremist.' Did I not think so? I assented. Did I know, he asked, with a sudden flash of curiosity, 'what it was that had induced him to go out there?' 'Yes,' said I, and forthwith handed him the famous Report for publication, if he thought fit. He glanced through it hurriedly, mumbling all the time, judged 'it would do,' and took himself off with this plunder.

"Thus I was left at last with a slim packet of letters and the girl's portrait. She struck me as beautiful—I mean she had a beautiful expression. I know that the sunlight can be made to lie too, yet one felt that no manipulation of light and pose could have conveyed the delicate shade of truthfulness upon those features. She seemed ready to listen without mental reservation, without suspicion, without a thought for herself. I concluded I would go and give her back her portrait and those letters myself. Curiosity? Yes; and also some other feeling perhaps. All that had been Kurtz's had passed out of my hands: his soul, his body, his station, his plans, his ivory, his career. There remained only his memory and his Intended—and I wanted to give that up too to the past, in a way—to surrender personally all that remained of him with me to that oblivion which is the last word of our common fate. I don't defend myself. I had no clear perception of what it was I really wanted. Perhaps it was an impulse of unconscious loyalty, or the fulfilment of one of those ironic necessities that lurk in the facts of human existence. I don't know. I can't tell. But I went.

"I thought his memory was like the other memories of the dead that accumulate in every man's life—a vague impress on the brain of shadows that had fallen on it in their swift and final passage; but before the high and ponderous door, between the tall houses of a street as still and decorous as a well-kept alley in a cemetery, I had a vision of him on the stretcher, opening his mouth voraciously, as if to devour all the earth with all its mankind. He lived then before me; he lived as much as he had ever lived—a shadow insatiable of splendid appearances, of frightful realities; a shadow darker than the shadow of the night, and draped nobly in the folds of a gorgeous eloquence. The vision seemed to enter the house with me—the stretcher, the phantom-bearers, the wild crowd of obedient worshippers, the gloom of the forests, the glitter of the reach between the murky bends, the beat of the drum, regular and muffled like the beating of a heart—the heart of a conquering darkness. It was a moment of triumph for the wilderness, an invading and vengeful rush which, it seemed to me, I would have to keep back alone for the salvation of another soul. And the memory of what I had heard him say afar there, with the horned shapes stirring at my back, in the glow of fires, within the patient woods, those broken phrases came back to me, were heard again in their ominous and terrifying simplicity. I remembered his abject pleading, his abject threats, the colossal scale of his vile desires, the meanness, the torment, the tempestuous anguish of his soul. And later on I seemed to see his collected languid manner, when he said one day, 'This lot of ivory now is really mine. The Company did not pay for it. I collected it myself at a very great personal risk. I am afraid they will try to claim it as theirs though. H'm. It is a difficult case. What do you think I ought to do—resist? Eh? I want no more than justice.' . . . He wanted no more than justice—no more than justice. I rang the bell before a mahogany door on the first floor, and while I waited he seemed to stare at me out of the glossy panel—stare with that wide and immense stare embracing, condemning, loathing all the universe. I seemed to hear the whispered cry, 'The horror! The horror!'

"The dusk was falling. I had to wait in a lofty drawing-room with three long windows from floor to ceiling that were like three luminous and be-draped columns. The bent gilt legs and backs of the furniture shone in indistinct curves. The tall marble fireplace had a cold and monumental whiteness. A grand piano stood massively in a corner; with dark gleams on the flat surfaces like a sombre and polished sarcophagus. A high door opened—closed. I rose.

"She came forward, all in black, with a pale head, floating towards me in the dusk. She was in mourning. It was more than a year since his death, more than a year since the news came; she seemed as though she would remember and mourn for ever. She took both my hands in hers and murmured, 'I had heard you were coming.' I noticed she was not very young—I mean not girlish. She had a mature capacity for fidelity, for belief, for suffering. The room seemed to have grown darker, as if all the sad light of the cloudy evening had taken refuge on her forehead. This fair hair, this pale visage, this pure brow, seemed surrounded by an ashy halo from which the dark eyes looked out at me. Their glance was guileless, profound, confident, and trustful. She carried her sorrowful head as though she were proud of that sorrow, as though she would say, I—I alone know how to mourn for him as he deserves. But while we were still shaking hands, such a look of awful desolation came upon her face that I perceived she was one of those creatures that are not the playthings of Time. For her he had died only yesterday. And, by Jove! the impression was so powerful that for me too he seemed to have died only yesterday—nay, this very minute. I saw her and him in the same instant of time—his death and her sorrow—I saw her sorrow in the very moment of his death. Do you understand? I saw them together—I heard them together. She had said, with a deep catch of the breath, 'I have survived'; while my strained ears seemed to hear distinctly, mingled with her tone of despairing regret, the summing-up whisper of his eternal condemnation. I asked myself what I was doing there, with a sensation of panic in my heart as though I had blundered into a place of cruel and absurd mysteries not fit for a human being to behold. She motioned me to a chair. We sat down. I laid the packet gently on the little table, and she put her hand over it. . . . 'You knew him well,' she murmured, after a moment of mourning silence.

" 'Intimacy grows quickly out there,' I said. 'I knew him as well as it is possible for one man to know another.'

" 'And you admired him,' she said. 'It was impossible to know him and not to admire him. Was it?'

" 'He was a remarkable man,' I said unsteadily. Then before the appealing fixity of her gaze, that seemed to watch for more words on my lips, I went on, 'It was impossible not to—'

" 'Love him,' she finished eagerly, silencing me into an appalled dumbness. 'How true! how true! But when you think that no one knew him so well as I! I had all his noble confidence. I knew him best.'

" 'You knew him best,' I repeated. And perhaps she did. But with every word spoken the room was growing darker, and only her forehead, smooth and white, remained illumined by the unextinguishable light of belief and love.

" 'You were his friend,' she went on. 'His friend,' she repeated, a little louder. 'You must have been, if he had given you this, and sent you to me. I feel I can speak to you—and oh! I must speak. I want you—you who have heard his last words—to know I have been worthy of him. . . . It is not pride. . . . Yes! I am proud to know I understood him better than any one on earth— he told me so himself. And since his mother died I have had no one—no one—to—to—'

"I listened. The darkness deepened. I was not even sure whether he had given me the right bundle. I rather suspect he wanted me to take care of another batch of his papers which, after his death, I saw the manager examining under the lamp. And the girl talked, easing her pain in the certitude of my sympathy; she talked as thirsty men drink. I had heard that her engagement with Kurtz had been disapproved by her people. He wasn't rich enough or something. And indeed I don't know whether he had not been a pauper all his life. He had given me some reason to infer that it was his impatience of comparative poverty that drove him out there.

" ' . . . Who was not his friend who had heard him speak once?' she was saying. 'He drew men towards him by what was best in them.' She looked at me with intensity. 'It is the gift of the great,' she went on, and the sound of her low voice seemed to have the accompaniment of all the other sounds, full of mystery, desolation, and sorrow, I had ever heard—the ripple of the river, the soughing of the trees swayed by the wind, the murmurs of the crowds, the faint ring of incomprehensible words cried from afar, the whisper of a voice speaking from beyond the threshold of an eternal darkness. 'But you have heard him! You know!' she cried.

" 'Yes, I know,' I said with something like despair in my heart, but bowing my head before the faith that was in her, before that great and saving illusion that shone with an unearthly glow in the darkness, in the triumphant darkness from which I could not have defended her—from which I could not even defend myself.

" 'What a loss to me—to us!'—she corrected herself with beautiful generosity; then added in a murmur, 'To the world.' By the last gleams of twilight I could see the glitter of her eyes, full of tears—of tears that would not fall.

" 'I have been very happy—very fortunate—very proud,' she went on. 'Too fortunate. Too happy for a little while. And now I am unhappy for—for life.'

"She stood up; her fair hair seemed to catch all the remaining light in a glimmer of gold. I rose too.

" 'And of all this,' she went on mournfully, 'of all his promise, and of all his greatness, of his generous mind, of his noble heart, nothing remains— nothing but a memory. You and I—'

" 'We shall always remember him,' I said hastily.

" 'No!' she cried. 'It is impossible that all this should be lost—that such a life should be sacrificed to leave nothing—but sorrow. You know what vast plans he had. I knew of them too—I could not perhaps understand—but others knew of them. Something must remain. His words, at least, have not died.'

" 'His words will remain,' I said.

" 'And his example,' she whispered to herself. 'Men looked up to him—his goodness shone in every act. His example—'

" 'True,' I said; 'his example too. Yes, his example. I forgot that.'

" 'But I do not. I cannot—I cannot believe—not yet. I cannot believe that

I shall never see him again, that nobody will see him again, never, never, never.'

"She put out her arms as if after a retreating figure, stretching them black and with clasped pale hands across the fading and narrow sheen of the window. Never see him! I saw him clearly enough then. I shall see this eloquent phantom as long as I live, and I shall see her too, a tragic and familiar Shade, resembling in this gesture another one, tragic also, and bedecked with powerless charms, stretching bare brown arms over the glitter of the infernal stream, the stream of darkness. She said suddenly very low, 'He died as he lived.'

" 'His end,' said I, with dull anger stirring in me, 'was in every way worthy of his life.'

" 'And I was not with him,' she murmured. My anger subsided before a feeling of infinite pity.

" 'Everything that could be done—' I mumbled.

" 'Ah, but I believed in him more than any one on earth—more than his own mother, more than—himself. He needed me! Me! I would have treasured every sigh, every word, every sign, every glance.'

"I felt like a chill grip on my chest. 'Don't,' I said, in a muffled voice.

" 'Forgive me. I—I—have mourned so long in silence—in silence. . . . You were with him—to the last? I think of his loneliness. Nobody near to understand him as I would have understood. Perhaps no one to hear. . . .'

" 'To the very end,' I said shakily. 'I heard his very last words. . . .' I stopped in a fright.

" 'Repeat them,' she murmured in a heart-broken tone. 'I want—I want—something—something—to—to live with.'

"I was on the point of crying at her, 'Don't you hear them?' The dusk was repeating them in a persistent whisper all around us, in a whisper that seemed to swell menacingly like the first whisper of a rising wind. 'The horror! The horror!'

" 'His last word—to live with,' she insisted. 'Don't you understand I loved him—I loved him—I loved him!'

"I pulled myself together and spoke slowly.

" 'The last word he pronounced was—your name.'

"I heard a light sigh and then my heart stood still, stopped dead short by an exulting and terrible cry, by the cry of inconceivable triumph and of unspeakable pain. 'I knew it—I was sure!' . . . She knew. She was sure. I heard her weeping; she had hidden her face in her hands. It seemed to me that the house would collapse before I could escape, that the heavens would fall upon my head. But nothing happened. The heavens do not fall for such a trifle. Would they have fallen, I wonder, if I had rendered Kurtz that justice which was his due? Hadn't he said he wanted only justice? But I couldn't. I could not tell her. It would have been too dark—too dark altogether. . . ."[3]

Marlow ceased, and sat apart, indistinct and silent, in the pose of a meditating Buddha. Nobody moved for a time. "We have lost the first of the ebb," said the Director suddenly. I raised my head. The offing was barred by a

---

3. Writing to William Blackwood (editor of *Blackwood's Magazine*, where the story first appeared) in May 1902, Conrad referred to "the last pages of Heart of Darkness where the interview of the man and the girl locks in—as it were—the whole 30,000 words of narrative description into one suggestive view of a whole phase of life, and makes of that story something quite on another plane than an anecdote of a man who went mad in the Centre of Africa" (Joseph Conrad, *Letters to William Blackwood and David S. Meldrum*, ed. William Blackburn, 1958).

black bank of clouds, and the tranquil waterway leading to the uttermost ends of the earth flowed sombre under an overcast sky—seemed to lead into the heart of an immense darkness.

1899   1902

The Rise and Fall of Empire

In theory, *imperialism*, the principle, spirit, or system of empire, is driven by ideology, whereas *colonialism*, the principle, spirit, or system of establishing colonies, is driven by commerce. In practice, it is often difficult to distinguish where one ends and the other begins.

Historians make a distinction between two British Empires, dating the first from the seventeenth century, when the European demand for sugar and tobacco led to the development of plantations on the islands of the Caribbean and in southeast North America. These colonies, and those settled by religious dissenters in northeast North America, attracted increasing numbers of British and European colonists. The late seventeenth and early eighteenth centuries saw the first British Empire expanding into areas formerly controlled by the Dutch and Spanish Empires (then in decline) and coming into conflict with French colonial aspirations in Africa, Canada, and India. With the Treaty of Paris in 1763, the British effectively took control of Canada and India, but the American Revolution brought their first empire to an end.

Captain James Cook's voyages to Australia and New Zealand in the 1770s initiated a further phase of territorial expansion that led to the second British Empire. This reached its widest point during the reign of Queen Victoria (1837–1901). At no time in the first half of her reign was empire a central preoccupation of her or her governments, but this was to change in the wake of the Franco-Prussian War (1870–71), which altered the balance of power in Europe. During the next decades, two great statesmen brought the issue of imperialism to the top of the nation's political agenda: the flamboyant Benjamin Disraeli (1804–1881), who had a romantic vision of empire that the graver William Ewart Gladstone (1809–1898) distrusted and rejected. Disraeli's expansionist vision prevailed and was transmitted by newspapers and novels to a reading public dramatically expanded by the Education Act of 1870.

Symbolically, the British Empire reached its highest point on June 22, 1897, the occasion of Queen Victoria's Diamond Jubilee, which the British celebrated (in the words of the historian James Morris)[1]

> as a festival of Empire. They were in possession that day of the largest Empire ever known to history, and since a large part of it had been acquired during the sixty years of Victoria's reign, it seemed proper to honour the one with the other. It would mark this moment of British history as an Imperial moment, a Roman moment. It would proclaim to the world, flamboyantly, that England was far more than England: that beneath the Queen's dominion lay a quarter of the earth's land surface, and nearly a quarter of its people—literally, as Christopher North the poet had long before declared it, an Empire on which the sun never set.

1. James Morris, *Farewell the Trumpets: An Imperial Retreat* (1978), pp. 1–2.

It was "a Roman moment." The analogy of the Roman Empire was endlessly invoked in discussions of the British Empire. It figures, for example, at the start of Conrad's novel *Heart of Darkness,* and in *Embarkation,* the first of Thomas Hardy's (Anglo-Boer) "War Poems."

The Roman Empire, at its height, comprised perhaps 120 million people in an area of 2.5 million square miles. The British Empire, in 1897, comprised some 372 million people in 11 million square miles. An interesting aspect of the analogy is that the Roman Empire was long held—by the descendants of the defeated and oppressed peoples of the British Isles, which was part of that empire—to be generally a Good Thing. Children in the United Kingdom are still taught that the Roman legions brought laws and roads and civilization rather than oppression, and in the second half of the nineteenth century, the Roman era was the precedent invoked to sanction the *Pax Britannica* (Latin for "British Peace").

In 1897 the Empire seemed invincible, but only two years later British confidence was shaken by the news of defeats at Magersfontein and Spion Kop in the Anglo-Boer War in South Africa. Those and other battles were lost, but eventually the war was won, and it took two world wars to bring the British Empire to its end. Those wars also were won, with the loyal help of troops from the overseas empire (more than two hundred thousand of whom were killed in the 1914–18 war alone). In return, however, the countries of the overseas empire wanted a greater measure of self-government, and, in 1931, the British Parliament recognized the independent and equal status under the Crown of its former dominions within a British Commonwealth of Nations. Following World War II, most of the remaining imperial possessions were granted independence; and fifty years after Queen Victoria's Diamond Jubilee, India, "the Jewel in the Crown" (Disraeli's phrase), was cut in two to become the Commonwealth countries of India and Pakistan. So, one by one, the subject peoples of the British Empire entered what is often termed a Postcolonial era, in which they would reassess their national identity, their history and literature, their relationship with the land, language, cultural and literary traditions of their former colonizers.

In the second half of our century, that process has been reflected in a dramatic efflorescence of creativity in these new nations. Initial doubts about the political propriety of conveying the experience of empire in English, the imperialists' language, rather than in an indigenous language, seem largely to have been dispelled by the recognition that the English language is no longer a possession of the English nation but, rather, the rightful inheritance of all English-speaking peoples. And just as that language has been enriched over many centuries by loan words from other languages (*moccasin* from Powhatan, *veranda* from Hindu), so English literature has been enriched—and in some areas transformed—by the writings of Chinua Achebe, J. M. Coetzee, Anita Desai, Seamus Heaney, Katherine Mansfield, V. S. Naipaul, Jean Rhys, Salman Rushdie, and Derek Walcott—to mention only some of those represented in this anthology.

JOHN RUSKIN

John Ruskin (1819–1900) was both the leading Victorian critic of art and an influential critic of society (p. 1425). In 1870, he was appointed Slade Professor of Fine Art at Oxford. "There clung to his person, as to his reputation, the charisma of a prophet," writes James Morris. "He spoke, we are told, 'in mediaeval way,' his pronunciation archaic, his Rs peculiarly rolled, and his words remained in the memory like music. Ruskin talked much nonsense in his time, but when he struck one of his grand themes the effect was unforgettable." Imperial duty was the subject of his inaugural lecture at Oxford, delivered to a packed audience on February 8, 1870, and its effects would be felt far beyond the shores of the British Isles. The lecture was published in Ruskin's *Lectures on Art* (1894).

From Lectures on Art

[IMPERIAL DUTY]

There is a destiny now possible to us—the highest ever set before a nation to be accepted or refused. We are still undergenerate in race; a race mingled of the best northern blood. We are not yet dissolute in temper, but still have the firmness to govern, and the grace to obey. We have been taught a religion of pure mercy, which we must either now betray, or learn to defend by fulfilling. And we are rich in an inheritance of honour, bequeathed to us through a thousand years of noble history, which it should be our daily thirst to increase with splendid avarice, so that Englishmen, if it be a sin to covet honour, should be the most offending souls alive.[1] Within the last few years we have had the laws of natural science opened to us with a rapidity which has been blinding by its brightness; and means of transit and communication given to us, which have made but one kingdom of the habitable globe. One kingdom;—but who is to be its king? Is there to be no king in it, think you, and every man to do that which is right in his own eyes? Or only kings of terror, and the obscene empires of Mammon and Belial?[2] Or will you, youths of England, make your country again a royal throne of kings; a sceptred isle,[3] for all the world a source of light, a centre of peace; mistress of Learning and of the Arts;—faithful guardian of great memories in the midst of irreverent and ephemeral visions;—faithful servant of time-tried principles, under temptation from fond experiments and licentious desires; and amidst the cruel and clamorous jealousies of the nations, worshipped in her strange valour of goodwill towards men?

'Vexilla regis prodeunt.'[4] Yes, but of which king? There are the two oriflammes;[5] which shall we plant on the farthest islands,—the one that floats in heavenly fire, or that hangs heavy with foul tissue of terrestrial gold? There is indeed a course of beneficent glory open to us, such as never was yet offered to any poor group of mortal souls. But it must be—it *is* with us, now, 'Reign or Die.' And if it shall be said of this country, 'Fece per viltate, il gran rifiuto;'[6] that refusal of the crown will be, of all yet recorded in history, the shamefullest and most untimely.

And this is what she must either do, or perish: she must found colonies as fast and as far as she is able, formed of her most energetic and worthiest men;—seizing every piece of fruitful waste ground she can set her foot on,

---

1. "But if it be a sin to covet honour,/ I am the most offending soul alive" (Shakespeare, *Henry V* 4.3.28–29).
2. Medieval writers took Mammon (Aramaic for "riches"), as the proper name of the devil of covetousness and Belial (adapted from the Hebrew for "worthlessness" and "destruction") as a name for the devil or one of the fallen angels.

3. "This royal throne of kings, this sceptred isle" (Shakespeare, *Richard II* 2.1.40).
4. The royal banners forward go (Venantius Fortunatus).
5. Sacred banners of the early French kings.
6. Who from cowardice made the great refusal (Dante Alighieri, *Inferno* 3.60).

and there teaching these her colonists that their chief virtue is to be fidelity to their country, and that their first aim is to be to advance the power of England by land and sea: and that, though they live on a distant plot of ground, they are no more to consider themselves therefore disfranchised from their native land, than the sailors of her fleets do, because they float on distant waves. So that literally, these colonies must be fastened fleets; and every man of them must be under authority of captains and officers, whose better command is to be over fields and streets instead of ships of the line; and England, in these her motionless navies (or, in the true and mightiest sense, motionless *churches*, ruled by pilots on the Galilean lake[7] of all the world), is to 'expect every man to do his duty;'[8] recognising that duty is indeed possible no less in peace than war; and that if we can get men, for little pay, to cast themselves against cannon-mouths for love of England, we may find men also who will plough and sow for her, who will behave kindly and righteously for her, who will bring up their children to love her, and who will gladden themselves in the brightness of her glory, more than in all the light of tropic skies.

But that they may be able to do this, she must make her own majesty stainless; she must give them thoughts of their home of which they can be proud. The England who is to be mistress of half the earth, cannot remain herself a heap of cinders, trampled by contending and miserable crowds; she must yet again become the England she was once, and in all beautiful ways,—more: so happy, so secluded, and so pure, that in her sky—polluted by no unholy clouds—she may be able to spell rightly of every star that heaven doth show; and in her fields, ordered and wide and fair, of every herb that sips the dew; and under the green avenues of her enchanted garden, a sacred Circe,[9] true Daughter of the Sun, she must guide the human arts, and gather the divine knowledge, of distant nations, transformed from savageness to manhood, and redeemed from despairing into peace.

You think that an impossible ideal. Be it so; refuse to accept it if you will; but see that you form your own in its stead. All that I ask of you is to have a fixed purpose of some kind for your country and yourselves; no matter how restricted, so that it be fixed and unselfish.

1870   1894

7. "The pilot of the Galilean lake" is St. Peter in Milton's *Lycidas*, line 109.
8. "England expects every man will do his duty" was Admiral Horatio Nelson's signal before the

Battle of Trafalgar (1805).
9. Enchantress (in Homer's *Odyssey*) celebrated for her knowledge of magic and herbs.

JOHN ATKINSON HOBSON

J. A. Hobson (1858–1940), the distinguished Liberal economist and writer, was educated at Oxford University and worked, first, as a schoolmaster, teaching classics; then as a lecturer in English literature and economics for the Oxford University Extension Delegacy and the London Society for the Extension of University Teaching; before becoming a freelance writer. His many books include *Problems of Poverty*

(1891), *The Evolution of Modern Capitalism* (1894), *The Problem of the Unemployed* (1896), and *John Ruskin, Social Reformer* (1898).

The view of imperialism to emerge from the searching analysis of his influential *Imperialism: A Study* (1902)—from which the following extract is taken—was diametrically opposed to that of Ruskin's inaugural lecture.

The Political Significance of Imperialism

The curious ignorance which prevails regarding the political character and tendencies of Imperialism cannot be better illustrated than by the following passage from a learned work upon "The History of Colonisation":[1] "The extent of British dominion may perhaps be better imagined than described, when the fact is appreciated that, of the entire land surface of the globe, approximately one-fifth is actually or theoretically under that flag, while more than one-sixth of all the human beings living in this planet reside under one or the other type of English colonisation. The names by which authority is exerted are numerous, and processes are distinct, but the goals to which this manifold mechanism is working are very similar. According to the climate, the natural conditions and the inhabitants of the regions affected, procedure and practice differ. The means are adapted to the situation; there is not any irrevocable, immutable line of policy; from time to time, from decade to decade, English statesmen have applied different treatments to the same territory. Only one fixed rule of action seems to exist; it is to promote the interests of the colony to the utmost, to develop its scheme of government as rapidly as possible, and eventually to elevate it from the position of inferiority to that of association. Under the charm of this beneficent spirit the chief colonial establishments of Great Britain have already achieved substantial freedom, without dissolving nominal ties; the other subordinate possessions are aspiring to it, while, on the other hand, this privilege of local independence has enabled England to assimilate with ease many feudatory States[2] into the body politic of her system." Here then is the theory that Britons are a race endowed, like the Romans, with a genius for government, that our colonial and imperial policy is animated by a resolve to spread throughout the world the arts of free self-government which we enjoy at home,[3] and that in truth we are accomplishing this work.

Now, without discussing here the excellencies or the defects of the British theory and practice of representative self-government, to assert that our "fixed rule of action" has been to educate our dependencies in this theory and practice is quite the largest misstatement of the facts of our colonial and imperial policy that is possible. Upon the vast majority of the populations throughout our Empire we have bestowed no real powers of self-government, nor have we any serious intention of doing so, or any serious belief that it is possible for us to do so.

Of the three hundred and sixty-seven millions of British subjects outside these isles, not more than ten millions, or one in thirty-seven, have any real self-government for purposes of legislation and administration.

---

1. H. C. Morris, *The History of Colonization*, 1900, vol. 2, p. 80 [Hobson's note].

2. Feudally subject states.

3. "The British Empire is a galaxy of free States," said Sir W. Laurier in a speech, 8 July 1902 [Hobson's note].

Political freedom, and civil freedom, so far as it rests upon the other, are simply non-existent for the over-whelming majority of British subjects. In the self-governing colonies of Australasia and North America alone is responsible representative government a reality, and even there considerable populations of outlanders, as in West Australia, or servile labour, as in Queensland, temper the genuineness of democracy. In Cape Colony and Natal recent events testify how feebly the forms and even the spirit of the free British institutions have taken root in States where the great majority of the population were always excluded from political rights. The franchise and the rights it carries will remain virtually a white monopoly in so-called self-governing colonies, where the coloured population is to the white as four to one and ten to one respectively.

In certain of our older Crown colonies there exists a representative element in the government. While the administration is entirely vested in a governor appointed by the Crown, assisted by a council nominated by him, the colonists elect a portion of the legislative assembly. The following colonies belong to this order: Jamaica, Barbados, Trinidad, Bahamas, British Guiana, Windward Islands, Bermudas, Malta, Mauritius, Ceylon.

The representative element differs considerably in size and influence in these colonies, but nowhere does it outnumber the non-elected element. It thus becomes an advisory rather than a really legislative factor. Not merely is the elected always dominated in numbers by the non-elected element, but in all cases the veto of the Colonial Office is freely exercised upon measures passed by the assemblies. To this it should be added that in nearly all cases a fairly high property qualification is attached to the franchise, precluding the coloured people from exercising an elective power proportionate to their numbers and their stake in the country.

The entire population of these modified Crown colonies amounted to 5,700,000 in 1898.[4]

The overwhelming majority of the subjects of the British Empire are under Crown colony government, or under protectorates. In neither case do they enjoy any of the important political rights of British citizens; in neither case are they being trained in the arts of free British institutions. In the Crown colony the population exercises no political privileges. The governor, appointed by the Colonial Office, is absolute, alike for legislation and administration; he is aided by a council of local residents usually chosen by himself or by home authority, but its function is merely advisory, and its advice can be and frequently is ignored. In the vast protectorates we have assumed in Africa and Asia there is no tincture of British representative government; the British factor consists in arbitrary acts of irregular interference with native government. Exceptions to this exist in the case of districts assigned to Chartered Companies, where business men, animated avowedly by business ends, are permitted to exercise arbitrary powers of government over native populations under the imperfect check of some British Imperial Commissioner.

Again, in certain native and feudatory States of India our Empire is virtually confined to government of foreign relations, military protection, and a veto upon grave internal disorder, the real administration of the countries being left in the hands of native princes or headmen. However excellent this

---

4. In all essential features, India and Egypt are to be classed as Crown colonies [Hobson's note].

arrangement may be, it lends little support to the general theory of the British Empire as an educator of free political institutions.

Where British government is real, it does not carry freedom or self-government; where it does carry a certain amount of freedom and self-government, it is not real. Not five per cent. of the population of our Empire are possessed of any appreciable portion of the political and civil liberties which are the basis of British civilisation. Outside the ten millions of British subjects in Canada, Australia, and New Zealand, no considerable body is endowed with full self-government in the more vital matters, or is being "elevated from the position of inferiority to that of association."

This is the most important of all facts for students of the present and probable future of the British Empire. We have taken upon ourselves in these little islands the responsibility of governing huge aggregations of lower races in all parts of the world by methods which are antithetic to the methods of government which we most value for ourselves.

1902

ANONYMOUS

In 1886, it seemed as if the long night of Irish history might be ending. A bill granting Home Rule to Ireland, promoted by the charismatic leader of the Irish parliamentary party, Charles Stewart Parnell, and the Liberal prime minister, William Gladstone, came before the British Parliament, but was defeated. A Second Home Rule Bill was put forward in 1892, but it too was defeated. A third was passed by the House of Commons (the Lower House) in 1912, only to be rejected by the House of Lords (the Upper House); but such a rejection simply defers a bill passed by the Lower House for a year, so the Irish people could look forward to ruling themselves from 1914. This, however, proved another false dawn, as in 1915 the House of Commons was preoccupied with wartime legislation, and Home Rule for Ireland was deferred until the end of the war.

In 1916, members of the Irish Republican Brotherhood (forerunners of the Irish Republican Army) decided they would wait no longer, and a force of at most sixteen hundred mounted what would come to be known as the Dublin Easter Rising. They took over key buildings, centered on the General Post Office in O'Connell Street, where Padraic Pearse, head of a Provisional Government of the Irish Republic, read out the following proclamation that he and his colleagues had written.

Easter 1916 Proclamation of an Irish Republic

Poblacht Na h-Eireann
The Provisional Government
of the
Irish Republic
To the People of Ireland

IRISHMEN AND IRISHWOMEN: In the name of God and of the dead generations from which she receives her old tradition of nationhood, Ireland, through us, summons her children to her flag and strikes for her freedom.

Having organised and trained her manhood through her secret revolutionary organisation, the Irish Republican Brotherhood, and through her open military organisations, the Irish Volunteers and the Irish Citizen Army, having patiently perfected her discipline, having resolutely waited for the right moment to reveal itself, she now seizes that moment, and supported by her exiled children in America and by gallant allies in Europe,[1] but relying in the first on her own strength, she strikes in full confidence of victory.

We declare the right of the people of Ireland to the ownership of Ireland and to the unfettered control of Irish destinies, to be sovereign and indefeasible. The long usurpation of that right by a foreign people and government has not extinguished the right, nor can it ever be extinguished except by the destruction of the Irish people. In every generation the Irish people have asserted their right to national freedom and sovereignty; six times during the past three hundred years they have asserted it in arms. Standing on that fundamental right and again asserting it in arms in the face of the world, we hereby proclaim the Irish Republic as a Sovereign Independent State, and we pledge our lives and the lives of our comrades in arms to the cause of its freedom, of its welfare, and of its exaltation among the nations.

The Irish Republic is entitled to, and hereby claims, the allegiance of every Irishman and Irishwoman. The Republic guarantees religious and civil liberty, equal rights and equal opportunities to all its citizens, and declares its resolve to pursue the happiness and prosperity of the whole nation and of all its parts, cherishing all of the children of the nation equally, and oblivious of the differences carefully fostered by an alien Government, which have divided a minority from the majority in the past.

Until our arms have brought the opportune moment for the establishment of a permanent National Government, representative of the whole people of Ireland and elected by the suffrages of all her men and women, the Provisional Government, hereby constituted, will administer the civil and military affairs of the Republic in trust for the people.

We place the cause of the Irish Republic under the protection of the Most High God, Whose blessing we invoke upon our arms, and we pray that no one who serves that cause will dishonour it by cowardice, inhumanity, or rapine. In this supreme hour the Irish nation must, by its valour and discipline, and by the readiness of its children to sacrifice themselves for the common good, prove itself worthy of the august destiny to which it is called.

Signed on behalf of the Provisional Government:

THOMAS J. CLARKE

SEAN Mac DIARMADA	THOMAS MacDONAGH
P. H. PEARSE	EAMONN CEANNT
JAMES CONNOLLY	JOSEPH PLUNKETT

---

1. German contacts of the Irish Republican Brotherhood had undertaken to send twenty thousand rifles and ten machine guns to County Kerry by Easter Sunday, but the arms-steamer was captured by the British and sunk.

RICHARD MULCAHY

Mulcahy (1886–1971), a post office clerk, had joined the Irish Volunteers in 1913 and fought in the 1916 Easter Rising. After the insurgents' surrender and the execution of their leaders (see Yeats's *Easter 1916* on p. 2104), Mulcahy was interned until the general amnesty of 1917 and, in the savage guerrilla war that followed, rose to be the chief of staff of the Irish Republican Army (IRA).

In December 1920, the British Parliament's Government of Ireland Act partitioned the country, incorporating the six (predominantly Protestant) counties of the north in the United Kingdom of Great Britain. The following July, a truce was called between the British forces and the IRA, and the British government offered the twenty-six (predominantly Roman Catholic) counties of the south a treaty and dominion status—the status of Australia, Canada, and New Zealand—under the British Crown. The offer was accepted by sixty-four votes to fifty-eight in Dáil Eireann (Sinn Fein's revolutionary assembly) on January 7, 1922. In the course of the debate on the treaty, Mulcahy, who was also a Member of Parliament, made a speech from which the following extract is taken.

[On the Treaty between Great Britain and Ireland]

* * * None of us want this Treaty. None of us want the Crown. None of us want the representative of the Crown. None of us want our harbours occupied by enemy forces; and none of us want what is said to be partition; and we want no arguments against any of these things. But we want an alternative. * * * I, personally, see no alternative to the acceptance of this Treaty. I see no solid spot of ground upon which the Irish people can put its political feet but upon that Treaty. * * * I can realise the difficulties of those who can put their finger upon the line and letter of the document which says that, in Ireland, all power of the Executive and otherwise comes from the King,[1] and will, under the circumstances that will be created by the acceptance of that Treaty, come from the King. I can understand the difficulties of that person. But the feeling of my mind, and the instinct of my bones was, that the power of the Executive Government to control and discharge the resources of this county lies in the people. The 17th, 18th, and 19th centuries, as far as we can hear, have brought us constitutional usage and practice, and I take it that the arrangement has been that when people took away their power from their princes, in order to leave their princes down lightly, they said: "This is constitutional usage." And if these centuries have provided us with constitutional usage and practice, and if the constitutional outlook of the King in Ireland at the present moment is to be that Executive power and control come from him, I think it won't be very long, under whatever arrangement is set up in Ireland—Treaty or otherwise—until the Irish people show, both for the benefit of themselves and perhaps for the benefit of others, that sovereign rights in this county lie in the people, and that the sovereign rights in every other country do and will be the same. With my understanding leading me in that I can see no other road to go but the road of this Treaty, with the appreciation that this Treaty distinctly states that it does secure to

1. Of England.

Ireland the control in Ireland with full executive and administrative powers, and the Executive in Ireland responsible to that control. I am not afraid of the influence of the King, or the influence of the King exerted through some supposedly corrupt court of his representative here. I am not afraid of that power interfering with the power of the Irish people; because, if we have control, it is full control over legislation, over order, over peace, over the whole internal life and resources of the country, and if we have executive responsibility to that Parliament I don't see the way or in what way pernicious to the Irish people, the King or his representative could interfere with them. As to our ports, we are not in a position of force, either military or otherwise, to drive the enemy from our ports. We have not—those to whom the responsibility has been for doing such things—we have not been able to drive the enemy from anything but from a fairly good-sized police barracks. We have not that power; and with regard to the ports, I doubt if anybody in this assembly at the present moment—visualising the necessity for coastal and external defence—who, visualising the financial aspect of these things, would be able to point to the mark we are aiming at as regards the necessity for defence and the financial aspect of it. When we have established a police force that will do the internal work of the country, and when we have established such small internal defence force as is necessary, we shall probably—both intellectually and from the ordinary, common understanding—we will be coming to a point of intelligence at which we can decide what our external defences should be like. With regard to partition, I don't look upon the clause with regard to Ulster in this Treaty as prejudicing the Ulster position in any way. I see no solution of the Ulster difficulty or of the Six County difficulty at the present moment. On the other hand the Treaty leaves the Irish people that they will be in absolute possession of their country's resources, and, in my opinion, with full executive power and control over them; and—if in order to bring the Irish people to the goal that they have always aimed at, and that we have always aimed at with them—if we were given on one side this Treaty, and I on the other such military power that we might reasonably equate with the enemy's power, and left to decide by which of these two instruments we would bring Ireland definitely to a status of equality with our old enemy, and if the responsibility of deciding between these two instruments were placed in the hands of any one particular person here, I think there would be very great searchings of heart and mind and conscience before taking the alternative of the two instruments—the instrument of war on one side, and on the other the instrument of this particular Treaty of the Irish people battling upon their own powers, upon their own resources, to bring the nation in power and equality with the enemy. We have before us today in Europe the spectacle of France and Germany striving for supremacy over each other with military force, and we see the internal unhappiness, the waste of human life, sorrow, misery, and the degradation it all involved. The fact that these two countries had elected to struggle for supremacy with one another, involved, not only these two countries, but disturbed the peace of the whole world, by the weapon of war we see what it has brought these two countries to—not only these two countries, but the peace of the whole world was disturbed—and we now stand at a time when we have it in our power to take our choice. Shall we grow to equality of status with our old enemy by taking complete control of our own internal resources? And, if at the present moment there are disabilities with regard to ourselves in this particular Treaty, whether we shall endeavour to outgrow these by taking our own resources, or rather by taking the chances of war—not with anything like adequate military forces, but with very small forces, sufficient to make our country resist force for years, but certainly not able to win even a war of internal liberation? That is one outstanding aspect of the situation at the present time. Are we going to choose in the next onward march of this nation the weapons which will give us dead in our country the Crompton-Smiths of England and the Potters of Ireland;[2] or, are we going to take our own resources and grow to manhood, in friendliness and with some chance of avoiding that polarisation of mind and polarisation in antagonisms with the English people that are have been forced into at the present time?

* * * We have suffered a defeat. But even in that defeat we have got for the Irish people, at any rate, powers that I believe—if this Dáil passes away, if every bit of organisation that is in the country as its result at the present moment passed away with it—I believe that the Irish people would rise upon their resources, if left untrammelled and unfettered in their hands, to the full height of their aspirations and to the full vigour which has been so long lying undeveloped in our people; and with the responsibility of peace, the responsibility of taking their own materials and living their own lives and delving for their own materials of subsistence, they would find in that work all those high influences which in our war have developed—the character and manliness and their valuable characteristics that our period of warfare has developed in the country.[3]

1922

2. Crompton-Smith was a British major in the Royal Welsh Fusiliers executed after capture by the IRA in reprisal for the execution of IRA prisoners. Potter was a Royal Irish Constabulary inspector in country Tipperary executed for the same reason. Both were shot in April 1921.
3. Although the Dáil approved the treaty conclud-

ing the Anglo-Irish War, the Republican wing of the IRA (led by Eamon de Valera) rejected it. Some two thousand lives were lost in the ensuing Civil War before, in 1923, de Valera ordered the "Rearguard of the Republic" to cease hostilities. (See Yeats's *Meditations in Time of Civil War*.)

JAMES MORRIS

James (now Jan) Morris (b. 1926), historian, traveler, and travel writer, was educated at Oxford University and worked on the editorial staff of *The Guardian* newspaper from 1957 to 1962. Her many books include *Coronation Everest* (1958), an account of the first successful ascent of that mountain, which Morris covered as a journalist; *Venice* (1960); and *Conundrum* (1987), a courageous and moving account of the sex-change operation by which James became Jan. Her masterpiece may prove to be the three-volume history of the British Empire: *Pax Britannica: The Climax of an Empire* (1968), *Heaven's Command: An Imperial Progress* (1973), and *Farewell the Trumpets: An Imperial Retreat* (1978).

[The Partition of India]

Attlee,[1] the Prime Minister of the new Labour Government, had firm views about India. He had gone there on a Parliamentary mission as long before as 1928, and had concerned himself with the subject ever since. He had long ago reached the conclusion that only the Indians themselves could solve their own problems, freed of all British constitutional restraints, and even before the war he had argued that India should be given Dominion status within a fixed period of years. By 1946 he was sure that the transfer of power must be made as soon as possible—peaceably if possible, with the rights of minorities protected if they could be, but above all quickly, and absolutely. The first necessity, he thought, was to be rid of poor Wavell,[2] whom he considered defeatist and ineffectual, 'a curious silent bird'. It did not take him long to find a successor. 'I thought very hard,' he wrote, 'and looked all around. And suddenly I had what I now think was an inspiration. I thought of Mountbatten.'[3]

Mountbatten! The perfect, the allegorical last Viceroy! Royal himself, great-grandson of the original Queen-Empress, second cousin of George VI, though by blood he was almost as German as he was English he seemed nevertheless the last epitome of the English aristocrat. He was a world figure in his own right, too, for as Supreme Commander in South-East Asia he had commanded forces of all the allied nations—one of the four supremos who, in the last year of the war, had disposed the vast fleets and armies of the western alliance. Moreover he was a recognised progressive, sympathetic to the ideals of Labour, anything but a reactionary on the meaning of Empire, and with a cosmopolitan contempt for the petty prejudices of race and class.

'What is different about you from your predecessors?' Nehru[4] asked Mountbatten soon after his arrival in India. 'Can it be that you have been given plenipotentiary[5] powers? In that case you will succeed where all others have failed.' The Viceroy had in fact *demanded* such powers, enabling him to reach swift decisions on the spot. He had also committed Attlee to a date for the end of British rule in India, with no escape clauses. The Raj[6] was to end not later than June, 1948, when complete power would be handed to Indian successors.

This renunciation meant that Britain had no bargaining power any more: she was genuinely disinterested at last, and was concerned only to see that India was left a workable State, preferably a member of the Commonwealth, at least friendly to Great Britain. She had nothing much to offer in return, now that liberty was so firmly pledged, but nevertheless Mountbatten was marvellously, some thought overweeningly, self-confident. As he said himself, he thought he could do anything, and sure enough the combination of prestige, assurance and clear intention made him a much more formidable

---

1. Clement Richard Attlee (1883–1967), Labour (socialist) prime minister of Great Britain (1945–51).
2. Archibald Percival Wavell (1883–1950), British field marshal and viceroy of India (1943–47).
3. Louis Francis Albert Victor Nicholas, Earl

Mountbatten of Burma (1900–79), British admiral, viceroy of India in 1947, and chief of the British Defence Staff (1959–65).
4. See headnote, p. 2034.
5. Absolute.
6. British rule (Hindu for "reign").

negotiator than the aloof Linlithgow[7] or the despondent Wavell. It meant that he was arguing, if not from strength, at least from style.

The Mountbattens brought to the viceregal office an element of *brio*[8] absent since the days of Curzon.[9] They sustained the swagger of it all, the thousands of servants, the white viceregal train, the bodyguards, the curt-seying and the royal emblems, but they made it contemporary. Gone were the ancient shibboleths[1] of the court. The only royal Viceroy was the least grandiose of them all. At viceregal dinners now half the guests were always Indian, and earlier incumbents might have been horrified to observe how frankly the Mountbattens talked to natives of all ranks. It was an abdication in itself, for it was the very negation of imperial technique, but it was proper for the times and the purpose.

Mountbatten hoped to leave behind a federal united India, Hindus, Muslims and Princely States constitutionally linked. As second-best, he aimed at a peacefully divided one. He was adamant from the start that there would be no reservations or hidden clauses. 'All this is yours', he said to Gandhi[2] one day, when the Mahatma asked if he might walk around the viceregal gardens. 'We are only trustees. We have come to make it over to you.' No Viceroy had ever talked like that before, and no Viceroy had ever ventured into such intimate political relationships. During his first two months in India Mountbatten had 133 recorded interviews with Indian political leaders, conducted always in an atmosphere of candid urgency—if the Indians wished to inherit a peaceful India, they must decide fast how to arrange it. He talked to scores of politicians, but the fate of the country was really decided by four men: the Viceroy himself, Gandhi, Nehru and Mohammed Ali Jinnah.[3]

Mountbatten recognized the force of these men. Day after day he received them, usually together, sometimes separately, in the sunny and fresh-painted study at his palace. Times had greatly changed, since the half-naked fakir[4] had first penetrated this imperial sanctum to negotiate with the austere Lord Irwin,[5] while the palace servants gaped to see a political agitator exchanging badinage with the Viceroy. Now the negotiators met on an equal footing, like distant relatives assembling to divide an inheritance. The talks were seldom easy, for the issues were colossal and Indian passions ran high, but they were not generally rancorous, for at last it was patent that the British interest was not in keeping India, but in honourably getting rid of it.

Mountbatten's relations with the three leaders greatly differed. Gandhi, past the peak of his career, he recognized as a kind of constitutional mon-arch: he was baffled by him, charmed by him, often, like all Englishmen, irritated by him—'judge of my delight', he reported once, 'when Gandhi

---

7. Victor Alexander John Hope, marquess of Lin-lithgow (1887–1952), statesman and longest serv-ing viceroy of India (1936–43).
8. Vivacity (Italian).
9. George Nathaniel Curzon, marquess of Kedles-ton (1859–1925), flamboyant viceroy of India (1896–1905).
1. Old-fashioned behavior or doctrine.
2. Mohandas Karamchand Gandhi (1869–1948), lawyer, political, and (Hindu) spiritual leader, a major figure in the Indian independence move-

ment, was popularly known as "the Mahatma" (Hindu for "Great Soul").
3. Muhammad Ali Jinnah (1876–1948), lawyer, leader of the Muslim League, governor general of Pakistan, and first president of its constituent assembly.
4. Religious ascetic.
5. Edward Frederick Lindley Wood, Baron Irwin (1881–1959), statesman and viceroy of India (1925–31).

arrived for a crucial meeting holding his finger to his lips—it was his day of silence!' Alone among the senior British officials of India, though, he became a friend of the Mahatma, and Gandhi in return gave him his affection. He was, as always, free with his advice—'Have the courage to see the truth, and act by it!'—but he was attracted by the soigné[6] youthfulness of the Mountbattens, their combination of the simple and the very urbane. Though he was never reconciled to the idea of a divided India, still by making his friendship publicly clear, by appearing often in happy companionship with the Viceroy and his wife, Gandhi gave his *imprimatur*[7] to the course of events.

Jinnah was a very different negotiator. He was dying of cancer, but nobody knew it: he was as decisive as Mountbatten himself, and as confident too—since the date of independence had already been decreed, he knew that he had only to keep arguing to ensure that Pakistan came into being. His lawyer's brain was sharper than the Viceroy's, his purpose more dogmatic, and as the months passed towards independence day he became ever more adamant that the only solution was the partition of India and the establishment of Pakistan under the government of the Muslim League. Though a Muslim only in theory—he was the grandson of converts, and could speak no Urdu, the language of Islam in India—rather than submit to Hindu rule, he said, he would have a Pakistan consisting only of the Sind desert. A gaunt, wintry, rather alarming-looking man, wearing a monocle said to have been inspired by Joe Chamberlain's,[8] and suits of irreproachable cut, Jinnah was very Anglicised: he had a house in London, and had spent much of his life in England. He was, though, impervious to the Mountbatten charm, and noticeably resistant to logic or sweet reason. Mountbatten thought him the evil genius of the drama, the wrecker, and called him a haughty megalomaniac.

It was Nehru who became closest to the Mountbattens, and this was not surprising. Nehru was an agnostic intellectual, but of a sensual, emotional kind, a patrician like Mountbatten himself, a charmer and a lover of women—the Nehrus were famous philanderers. He was a Kashmiri Brahmin,[9] with much of the Kashmiri melancholy and introspection, and though he had spent his life fighting in the patriotic cause, he was highly susceptible to personal magnetisms. He needed a cause, a love, a leader. He was the devoted subject of Gandhi, and in a subtle, tacit way he was the passive collaborator of Mountbatten. The two men were of an age and of a taste, in many ways complementary to one another: through all their tortuous talks an understanding ran, an acceptance perhaps that they had more in common as men than they were at variance as statesmen.

Getting to know these three men, consulting many others, weighing the opinions of his administrators, nevertheless Mountbatten soon made up his mind about the fate of India—too soon, his critics were to say, and there was something impetuous to his solution, something inherited perhaps from his experiences of war. As the months passed so the British grip on security weakened, until the army could no longer guarantee order, the police were helplessly over-strained, the intelligence services had disastrously decayed and even the last Britons of the administration were demoralized. The con-

6. Elegant.
7. Official sanction, authorization.
8. Sir Joseph Austen Chamberlain (1863–1937),

British foreign secretary (1924–29).
9. Member of Hindu priestly caste.

viction had gone, and as the country slid towards anarchy few Britons in India would now argue the case for Empire—Field Marshal Claude Auchlinleck, the Commander-in-Chief, said of his own army that any Indian officer worth his salt was now a nationalist, 'and so he should be'.

Mountbatten's press attaché, Alan Campbell-Johnson, likened India in 1947 to a ship on fire in mid-ocean with a hold full of ammunition. The Viceroy himself, finding the parties irreconcilable, decided that partition was inevitable, and the sooner the better. 'There was in fact no option', Campbell-Johnson thought. Two Dominions would be created at once, with immediate independence. There would be no interim Government of any kind, no gradual transfer of power. Punjab and Bengal, with almost equal numbers of Muslims and Hindus, would be bisected. The Princely States would be urged to join one Dominion or the other. Everything would be partitioned, the Indian Army, the National Debt, the railway system, down to the stocks of stationery at the New Delhi secretariat, and the staff cars of GHQ.[1]

Mountbatten flew to London to get the Government's approval, and persuaded Churchill,[2] in Opposition, not to delay the process. Then, in an enormous hurry to prevent the whole administration falling apart in communal violence, he set the plan in motion. Congress[3] and the Muslim League both accepted the proposals, and together their leaders announced it to the nation on All-India Radio—Jinnah in English, his speech being then translated into Urdu. Mountbatten himself gave a press conference to announce that the British could not wait until the following year after all—independence had to come before the end of 1947. Pressed by reporters to name a date, he decided there and then upon the anniversary of the surrender of the Japanese in 1945. They would withdraw from India, he said, completely and irrevocably, by August 15, 1947, and sovereignty would then be surrendered. After 250 years on Indian soil, the British had given themselves seventy-three days to retire.

'Plan Balkan', the precipitate partitioning of India, was hardly a dignified process, but it was decisive. It was, like Dunkirk,[4] a failure dashingly achieved, with a touch of sleight of hand. The unity of India, the proudest achievement of British rule, was to be deliberately sundered. The great institutions of British India were to be split down the middle. The Indian Princes,[5] who had lost their own independence in return for the protection of the Crown, were to be betrayed. A sub-continent on the brink of civil war was to be subjected to an enormous social and governmental upheaval, millions of people to assume new nationalities, Ministries to be shuffled here and there, loyalties to be suddenly jettisoned or invented. Mountbatten himself called it 'sheer madness, fantastic communal madness'.

But it was final. Gone were the old fumblings and second thoughts which had, for forty years, alternately delayed, hastened and obfuscated the transfer

---

1. General Headquarters.
2. Sir Winston Leonard Spencer Churchill (1874–1965), British statesman, soldier, and author; conservative prime minister (1940–45), and leader of the opposition (1945–55).
3. The Indian National Congress was a political party that, in the 1946 elections, won the Hindu vote, but lost the Muslim vote to the Muslim League.
4. French port from which, in 1940, 300,000 Allied troops, retreating from the Germans, were evacuated by sea in small boats, many manned by civilian volunteers.
5. Rulers of the Princely States.

of power in India. Seventy-three days! In London the India Independence Bill ran through all its Parliamentary stages in a single week, ending at a stroke all British claims to sovereignty in India, and abrogating[6] all the hundreds of treaties concluded between the Crown and the Princely States. Mountbatten kept a large calendar on his desk, to mark off the days, like the count-down of a space launching, and with hectic resolution the British in India prepared the obsequies of their paramountcy.[7] It had taken them centuries to pacify and survey the immense expanses of their Indian territories, father succeeding son in the great task: now in a matter of weeks a boundary commission sliced the edifice into parts, laying new frontiers like string on a building-site, under the dispassionate instructions of an English barrister, Sir Cyril Radcliffe, who had never set foot in India before. The Indian Army was bisected, regiments split by squadrons, companies that had served together for a century suddenly distributed among alien battalions. The white Viceregal train chuffed away from Delhi for the last time, for it was allotted to Pakistan: the officials of the Kennel Club were relieved to be told that its assets would remain in India.

All went! All the dreams of the Empire-builders long before, all the Curzonian[8] splendour of imperial function, and as the British relentlessly cleared their office desks, India subsided into anarchy. Eleven million people abandoned their homes and moved in hordes across the countryside, hastening to the right side of the new communal frontiers. The roads were crammed with refugees, people clung to the steps of trains, or crowded upon their roofs, and the old gypsy confusion of India, the crowding and the clutter, the always familiar scenes of exhaustion, bewilderment and deprivation, were multiplied a thousand times. Violence erupted on a scale never known in British India before, even in the Mutiny.[9] It was like a gigantic boil bursting, an enormous eruption of frustrations and resentments suppressed for so long by the authority of Empire. Whole communities were massacred. Entire train-loads of refugees died on the tracks, to the last child in arms. In the Punjab gangs of armed men roamed the countryside, slaughtering columns of refugees, and thousands of people died unremarked in the streets of Amritsar,[1] where the death of 400 had horrified the world twenty-five years before.

The Viceroy was not deterred. Working day and night the last British officials of the Indian Civil Service established administrations for the two new Dominions, one with its capital at New Delhi, the other at Karachi. A Boundary Force, commanded by a Welshman with Hindu and Muslim advisers, was hastily put together to try to keep the peace, and the British Army was steadily and unostentatiously withdrawn: one by one the regiments left the soil of India, embarking on their troopships at Bombay while the bands on the Apollo Bunder played 'Auld Lang Syne', and the old hands of the Royal Bombay Yacht Club looked on sadly from their verandah.

The last days passed. The last of the wavering Princely States opted for one Dominion or the other, leaving only Kashmir, Hyderabad and Junagadh with their futures unresolved. The last of the British imperialists desperately

---

6. Canceling.
7. Funeral rites of their supremacy.
8. Grand, in the manner of George Nathaniel Curzon (see n. 9, p. 2029).

9. Indian uprising (1857) against the British, suppressed with great savagery on both sides.
1. City in eastern central India, scene of a massacre of Indian civilians by British troops in 1919.

worked against the clock, creating at least rudimentary Governments to succeed themselves. As the bloodshed and the turmoil continued, as the migratory masses laboured this way and that across the Indian plains, in the midst of it all the British Empire came to an end in India. At 8.30 a.m. on the appointed day, August 15, 1947, the Union Jack was hauled down all over the sub-continent, from frontier fort and Governor's palace, from law court and town hall, from the water-front at Surat where it all began, from the Viceroy's crowning palace, from the ruined Residency at Lucknow where the flag had flown night and day since the Indian Mutiny—

> Shot thro' the staff or the halyard, but ever we raised thee anew,
> And ever upon the topmost roof our banner of England blew[2]

In Karachi Jinnah was sworn in as Governor-General of the Dominion of Pakistan.[3] In Delhi Lord Mountbatten gave up the Viceroyalty, with its almost despotic power, and became the Governor-General of the Dominion of India, with no power at all.

Incalculable crowds celebrated the event in Delhi—the largest crowds anybody could remember seeing, in a country of multitudes. The grand military parade planned for that evening was cancelled, the military being so engulfed in the crowd that only the coloured tips of their puggarees[4] were visible from the grandstands. When the Mountbattens returned in their State coach to the palace, thronged all about by hysterically happy crowds, Nehru sat on top of the hood, 'like a schoolboy', Mountbatten reported, four Indian ladies with their children clambered up the sides, a Polish woman and an Indian newspaperman hung on behind. Thus queerly loaded, and accompanied by several thousand running, cheering people, the last of the Viceroys clattered the long mile up Kingsway to his great house, while fireworks sprayed the evening sky above him, and the thunder of a million people echoed across Delhi.

It was done. The flags of the new Dominions, the Indian decorated with the Wheel of Ashoka,[5] the Pakistani with Islam's star and crescent, flew all over the sub-continent, and all the paraphernalia of authority was handed over to the successor States. King George VI, Emperor no longer, sent his somewhat stilted greetings. Mountbatten proclaimed it 'a parting between friends, who have learned to honour and respect one another, even in disagreement'. Attlee said it was not the abdication, but the fulfilment of Britain's mission to India. The British Press was self-congratulatory, the British public, casting a cursory eye over the reportage, thought that on the whole they were well out of it. Some 200,000 Indians had died.

1978

---

2. Said to have been the 200th in the line of succession from the original mutiny flag, the Lucknow Union Jack was sent to King George, at his own request, to be kept at Windsor Castle [Morris's note].

3. A conception first devised by Indian students at Cambridge in 1932. P stood for Punjab, A for the Afghan areas of the North-West Frontier, K for Kashmir and S for Sind, while PAK handily meant "pure," in a religious sense [Morris's note].

4. Indian turbans.

5. Buddhist symbol associated with Ashoka (ca. 273–ca. 232 B.C.E.), Indian emperor of the Mauryan Dynasty.

JAWAHARLAL NEHRU

Jawaharlal Nehru (1889–1964), first president of postpartition India, was an aristocratic Kashmiri Brahmin. Educated in England at Harrow School and Cambridge University, he was admitted to the English bar and practiced law in India for several years. After the Amritsar Massacre of 1919, he devoted himself to the struggle for Indian freedom, working closely with Mahatma ("Great Soul") Gandhi. Four times president of the Indian National Congress, he spent much of the years 1930–36 in prison for conducting civil disobedience campaigns against the British. He and Gandhi opposed the participation of Indian troops in support of the British during World War II—unless India were granted immediate independence—and for his opposition was again imprisoned, from 1942 to 1945. Released after the Allied victory, he became the principal negotiator of the Indian independence movement, a role for which he was uniquely fitted by his English education, long experience of the imperial cast of mind, legal training, and an aristocratic background that gave him much in common with the aristocratic Mountbatten. The two of them tried, with Gandhi, to preserve a united India, but, after 1946, Jinnah became the first governor general of the new dominion of Pakistan, and Nehru the first prime minister of the new India. Printed here is his first speech in that role.

Tryst with Destiny[1]

Long years ago we made a tryst with destiny, and now the time comes when we shall redeem our pledge, not wholly or in full measure, but very substantially. At the stroke of the midnight hour, when the world sleeps, India will awake to life and freedom. A moment comes, which comes but rarely in history, when we step out from the old to the new, when an age ends, and when the soul of a nation, long suppressed, finds utterance. It is fitting that at this solemn moment we take the pledge of dedication to the service of India and her people and to the still larger cause of humanity.

At the dawn of history India started on her unending quest, and trackless centuries are filled with her striving and the grandeur of her success and her failures. Through good and ill fortune alike she has never lost sight of that quest or forgotten the ideals which gave her strength. We end today a period of ill fortune and India discovers herself again. The achievement we celebrate today is but a step, an opening of opportunity, to the greater triumphs and achievements that await us. Are we brave enough and wise enough to grasp this opportunity and accept the challenge of the future?

Freedom and power bring responsibility. The responsibility rests upon this Assembly, a sovereign body representing the sovereign people of India. Before the birth of freedom we have endured all the pains of labour and our hearts are heavy with the memory of this sorrow. Some of those pains continue even now. Nevertheless, the past is over and it is the future that beckons to us now.

That future is not one of ease or resting but of incessant striving so that we may fulfil the pledges we have so often taken and the one we shall take

1. Speech delivered in the Constituent Assembly, New Delhi, August 14, 1947, on the eve of the attainment of independence.

today. The service of India means the service of the millions who suffer. It means the ending of poverty and ignorance and disease and inequality of opportunity. The ambition of the greatest man of our generation[2] has been to wipe every tear from every eye. That may be beyond us, but as long as there are tears and suffering, so long our work will not be over.

And so we have to labour and to work, and work hard, to give reality to our dreams. Those dreams are for India, but they are also for the world, for all the nations and peoples are too closely knit together today for any one of them to imagine that it can live apart. Peace has been said to be indivisible; so is freedom, so is prosperity now, and so also is disaster in this One World that can no longer be split into isolated fragments.

To the people of India, whose representatives we are, we make an appeal to join us with faith and confidence in this great adventure. This is no time for petty and destructive criticism, no time for ill will or blaming others. We have to build the noble mansion of free India where all her children may dwell.

1947

2. Mahatma Gandhi (see n. 2, p. 2029).

CHINUA ACHEBE

Chinua Achebe (b. 1930; see headnote on p. 2616) has written poems and short stories but is best known for his novels. These demonstrate his belief in the duty of the writer to help change the way the colonized world is seen, to wage "a battle of the mind with colonialism" by "re-educating" readers. Nowhere does he do this more dramatically than in the essay from which the following extract is taken. Like a brilliant courtroom lawyer, Achebe sets Conrad in the dock and indicts him for racism. But just as he interrogates the text of *Heart of Darkness* in his passionate polemic, *his* text also must be submitted to interrogation. Is Achebe making Conrad a scapegoat for the offenses of others? Does he make sufficient allowance for the fact that Conrad was writing a dramatic fiction rather than a documentary denunciation of the great evils of racist colonialism? Is he even, influenced by what Harold Bloom has called "the Anxiety of Influence," trying to "kill the father" (discredit the precursor) whose work helped engender his own? Readers of Achebe and Conrad will want to answer these questions themselves.

From An Image of Africa: Racism in Conrad's *Heart of Darkness*

Heart of Darkness projects the image of Africa as 'the other world', the antithesis of Europe and therefore of civilization, a place where man's vaunted intelligence and refinement are finally mocked by triumphant bestiality. The book opens on the River Thames, tranquil, resting peacefully 'at the decline of day after ages of good service done to the race that peopled its banks' (1958–59).[1] But the actual story will take place on the River Congo, the very antithesis of the Thames. The River Congo is quite decidedly not a River Emeritus.[2] It has rendered no service and enjoys no old-age pension. We are told that 'going up that river was like travelling back to the earliest beginning of the world'.

Is Conrad saying then that these two rivers are very different, one good, the other bad? Yes, but that is not the real point. It is not the differentness that worries Conrad but the lurking hint of kinship, of common ancestry. For the Thames too 'has been one of the dark places of the earth'. It conquered its darkness, of course, and is now in daylight and at peace. But if it were to visit its primordial relative, the Congo, it would run the terrible risk of hearing grotesque echoes of its own forgotten darkness, and falling victim to an avenging recrudescence of the mindless frenzy of the first beginnings.

These suggestive echoes comprise Conrad's famed evocation of the African atmosphere in *Heart of Darkness*. In the final consideration his method amounts to no more than a steady, ponderous, fake-ritualistic repetition of two antithetical sentences, one about silence and the other about frenzy. We can inspect samples of this on pages 1982 and 1984: (a) 'It was the stillness of an implacable force brooding over an inscrutable intention' and (b) 'The steamer toiled along slowly on the edge of a black and incomprehensible frenzy.' Of course there is a judicious change of adjective from time to time, so that instead of inscrutable', for example, you might have 'unspeakable', even plain 'mysterious', etc., etc.

The eagle-eyed English critic F. R. Leavis[3] drew attention long ago to Conrad's 'adjectival insistence upon inexpressible and incomprehensible mystery'. That insistence must not be dismissed lightly, as many Conrad critics have tended to do, as a mere stylistic flaw; for it raises serious questions of artistic good faith. When a writer while pretending to record scenes, incidents and their impact is in reality engaged in inducing hypnotic stupor in his readers through a bombardment of emotive words and other forms of trickery, much more has to be at stake than stylistic felicity. Generally normal readers are well armed to detect and resist such underhand activity. But Conrad chose his subject well—one which was guaranteed not to put him in conflict with the psychological predisposition of his readers or raise the need for him to contend with their resistance. He chose the role of purveyor of comforting myths.

The most interesting and revealing passages in *Heart of Darkness* are, however, about people. I must crave the indulgence of my reader to quote almost a whole page from about the middle of the story when representatives of Europe in a steamer going down the Congo encounter the denizens of Africa:

> We were wanderers on a prehistoric earth, on an earth that wore the aspect of an unknown planet. We could have fancied ourselves the first of men taking possession of an accursed inheritance, to be subdued at the cost of profound anguish and of excessive toil. But suddenly, as we

1. Page numbers refer to this volume of *The Norton Anthology of English Literature*.
2. Honorably discharged from service.

3. Frank Raymond Leavis (1895–1978), famous English literary critic and Cambridge University academic.

struggled round a bend, there would be a glimpse of rush walls, of peaked grass-roofs, a burst of yells, a whirl of black limbs, a mass of hands clapping, of feet stamping, of bodies swaying, of eyes rolling, under the droop of heavy and motionless foliage. The steamer toiled along slowly on the edge of the black and incomprehensible frenzy. The prehistoric man was cursing us, praying to us, welcoming us—who could tell? We were cut off from the comprehension of our surroundings; we glided past like phantoms, wondering and secretly appalled, as sane men would be before an enthusiastic outbreak in a madhouse. We could not understand because we were too far and could not remember because we were travelling in the night of first ages, of those ages that are gone, leaving hardly a sign—and no memories.

The earth seemed unearthly. We are accustomed to look upon the shackled form of a conquered monster, but there—there you could look at a thing monstrous and free. It was unearthly, and the men were— No, they were not inhuman. Well, you know, that was the worst of it— this suspicion of their not being inhuman. It would come slowly to one. They howled and leaped, and spun, and made horrid faces; but what thrilled you was just the thought of their humanity—like yours—the thought of your remote kinship with this wild and passionate uproar. Ugly. Yes, it was ugly enough; but if you were man enough you would admit to yourself that there was in you just the faintest trace of a response to the terrible frankness of that noise, a dim suspicion of there being a meaning in it which you—you so remote from the night of first ages—could comprehend. (1983–84)

Herein lies the meaning of *Heart of Darkness* and the fascination it holds over the Western mind: 'What thrilled you was just the thought of their humanity—like yours . . . Ugly.'

Having shown us Africa in the mass, Conrad then zeros in, half a page later, on a specific example, giving us one of his rare descriptions of an African who is not just limbs or rolling eyes:

And between whiles I had to look after the savage who was fireman. He was an improved specimen; he could fire up a vertical boiler. He was there below me, and, upon my word, to look at him was as edifying as seeing a dog in a parody of breeches and a feather hat, walking on his hind legs. A few months of training had done for that really fine chap. He squinted at the steam gauge and at the water gauge with an evident effort of intrepidity—and he had filed his teeth, too, the poor devil, and the wool of his pate shaved into queer patterns, and three ornamental scars on each of his cheeks. He ought to have been clapping his hands and stamping his feet on the bank, instead of which he was hard at work, a thrall to strange witchcraft, full of improving knowledge. (1984)

As everybody knows, Conrad is a romantic on the side. He might not exactly admire savages clapping their hands and stamping their feet but they have at least the merit of being in their place, unlike this dog in a parody of breeches. For Conrad things being in their place is of the utmost importance. 'Fine fellows—cannibals—in their place,' he tells us pointedly. Tragedy begins when things leave their accustomed place, like Europe leaving its safe stronghold between the policeman and the baker to take a peep into the heart of darkness.

Before the story takes us into the Congo basin proper we are given this nice little vignette as an example of things in their place:

> Now and then a boat from the shore gave one a momentary contact with reality. It was paddled by black fellows. You could see from afar the white of their eyeballs glistening. They shouted, sang; their bodies streamed with perspiration; they had faces like grotesque masks—these chaps; but they had bone, muscle, a wild vitality, an intense energy of movement, that was as natural and true as the surf along their coast. They wanted no excuse for being there. They were a great comfort to look at. (1966)

Towards the end of the story Conrad lavishes a whole page quite unexpectedly on an African woman who has obviously been some kind of mistress to Mr Kurtz and now presides (if I may be permitted a little liberty) like a formidable mystery over the inexorable imminence of his departure:

> She was savage and superb, wild-eyed and magnificent . . . She stood looking at us without a stir and like the wilderness itself, with an air of brooding over an inscrutable purpose. (2003)

This Amazon is drawn in considerable detail, albeit of a predictable nature, for two reasons. First, she is in her place and so can win Conrad's special brand of approval; and second, she fulfils a structural requirement of the story: a savage counterpart to the refined, European woman who will step forth to end the story:

> She came forward, all in black with a pale head, floating toward me in the dusk. She was in mourning . . . She took both my hands in hers and murmured, 'I had heard you were coming' . . . She had a mature capacity for fidelity, for belief, for suffering. (2014)

The difference in the attitude of the novelist to these two women is conveyed in too many direct and subtle ways to need elaboration. But perhaps the most significant difference is the one implied in the author's bestowal of human expression to the one and the withholding of it from the other. It is clearly not part of Conrad's purpose to confer language on the 'rudimentary souls' of Africa. In place of speech they made 'a violent babble of uncouth sounds'. They 'exchanged short grunting phrases' even among themselves. But most of the time they were too busy with their frenzy. There are two occasions in the book, however, when Conrad departs somewhat from his practice and confers speech, even English speech, on the savages. The first occurs when cannibalism gets the better of them:

> 'Catch 'im,' he snapped, with a bloodshot widening of his eyes and a flash of sharp white teeth—'catch 'im. Give 'im to us.' 'To you, eh?' I asked; 'what would you do with them?' 'Eat 'im!' he said curtly. (1987)

The other occasion was the famous announcement: 'Mistah Kurtz—he dead' (2010).

At first sight these instances might be mistaken for unexpected acts of generosity from Conrad. In reality they constitute some of his best assaults.

In the case of the cannibals the incomprehensible grunts that had thus far served them for speech suddenly proved inadequate for Conrad's purpose of letting the European glimpse the unspeakable craving in their hearts. Weighing the necessity for consistency in the portrayal of the dumb brutes against the sensational advantages of securing their conviction by clear, unambiguous evidence issuing out of their own mouth Conrad chose the latter. As for the announcement of Mr Kurtz's death by the 'insolent black head in the doorway', what better or more appropriate *finis* could be written to the horror story of that wayward child of civilization who wilfully had given his soul to the powers of darkness and 'taken a high seat amongst the devils of the land' than the proclamation of his physical death by the forces he had joined?

It might be contended, of course, that the attitude to the African in *Heart of Darkness* is not Conrad's but that of his fictional narrator, Marlow, and that far from endorsing it Conrad might indeed be holding it up to irony and criticism. Certainly Conrad appears to go to considerable pains to set up layers of insulation between himself and the moral universe of his story. He has, for example, a narrator behind a narrator. The primary narrator is Marlow but his account is given to us through the filter of a second, shadowy person. But if Conrad's intention is to draw a cordon sanitaire[4] between himself and the moral and psychological *malaise* of his narrator his care seems to me totally wasted because he neglects to hint, clearly and adequately, at an alternative frame of reference by which we may judge the actions and opinions of his characters. It would not have been beyond Conrad's power to make that provision if he had thought it necessary. Conrad seems to me to approve of Marlow, with only minor reservations—a fact reinforced by the similarities between their two careers.

Marlow comes through to us not only as a witness of truth, but one holding those advanced and humane views appropriate to the English liberal tradition which required all Englishmen of decency to be deeply shocked by atrocities in Bulgaria or the Congo of King Leopold of the Belgians[5] or wherever.

Thus Marlow is able to toss out such bleeding-heart sentiments as these:

> They were all dying slowly—it was very clear. They were not enemies, they were not criminals, they were nothing earthly now—nothing but black shadows of disease and starvation, lying confusedly in the greenish gloom. Brought from all the recesses of the coast in all the legality of time contracts, lost in uncongenial surroundings, fed on unfamiliar food, they sickened, became inefficient, and were then allowed to crawl away and rest. (1969)

The kind of liberalism espoused here by Marlow/Conrad touched all the best minds of the age in England, Europe and America. It took different forms in the minds of different people but almost always managed to sidestep the ultimate question of equality between white people and black people. That extraordinary missionary, Albert Schweitzer,[6] who sacrificed brilliant careers in music and theology in Europe for a life of service to Africans in much the

4. A guarded line between infected and uninfected areas.
5. Leopold II (1835–1909) satisfied a lust for personal wealth by the brutal exploitation of the people of the Belgian Congo.

6. Medical missionary (1875–1965), who established a hospital at Lambaréné, Gabon (then in French Equatorial Africa), famous for its treatment of lepers.

same area as Conrad writes about, epitomizes the ambivalence. In a comment which has often been quoted Schweitzer says: 'The African is indeed my brother but my junior brother.' And so he proceeded to build a hospital appropriate to the needs of junior brothers with standards of hygiene reminiscent of medical practice in the days before the germ theory of disease came into being. Naturally he became a sensation in Europe and America. Pilgrims flocked, and I believe still flock even after he has passed on, to witness the prodigious miracle in Lamberene, on the edge of the primeval forest.

Conrad's liberalism would not take him quite as far as Schweitzer's, though. He would not use the word 'brother' however qualified; the farthest he would go was 'kinship'. When Marlow's African helmsman falls down with a spear in his heart he gives his white master one final disquieting look:

> And the intimate profundity of that look he gave me when he received his hurt remains to this day in my memory—like a claim of distant kinship affirmed in a supreme moment.

It is important to note that Conrad, careful as ever with his words, is concerned not so much about 'distant kinship' as about someone *laying a claim* on it. The black man lays a claim on the white man which is well-nigh intolerable. It is the laying of this claim which frightens and at the same time fascinates Conrad, 'the thought of their humanity—like yours . . . Ugly.'

The point of my observations should be quite clear by now, namely that Joseph Conrad was a thoroughgoing racist. That this simple truth is glossed over in criticisms of his work is due to the fact that white racism against Africa is such a normal way of thinking that its manifestations go completely unremarked. Students of *Heart of Darkness* will often tell you that Conrad is concerned not so much with Africa as with the deterioration of one European mind caused by solitude and sickness. They will point out to you that Conrad is, if anything, less charitable to the Europeans in the story than he is to the natives, that the point of the story is to ridicule Europe's civilizing mission in Africa. A Conrad student informed me in Scotland that Africa is merely a setting for the disintegration of the mind of Mr Kurtz.

Which is partly the point. Africa as setting and backdrop which eliminates the African as human factor. Africa as a metaphysical battlefield devoid of all recognizable humanity, into which the wandering European enters at his peril. Can nobody see the preposterous and perverse arrogance in thus reducing Africa to the role of props for the break-up of one petty European mind? But that is not even the point. The real question is the dehumanization of Africa and Africans which this age-long attitude has fostered and continues to foster in the world. And the question is whether a novel which celebrates this dehumanization, which depersonalizes a portion of the human race, can be called a great work of art. My answer is: No, it cannot.

1975   1977

A. E. HOUSMAN
1859–1936

Alfred Edward Housman was born in Fockbury, Worcestershire (close to the Shropshire border). After attending school at the nearby town of Bromsgrove he proceeded to Oxford, where he studied classics and philosophy and in 1881 shocked his friends and teachers by failing his final examinations (he was at the time in a state of psychological turmoil resulting from his suppressed homosexual love for a fellow student). He obtained a civil service job and pursued his classical studies alone, gradually building up a reputation as a great textual critic of Latin literature by his contributions to learned periodicals. In 1892 he was appointed to the chair of Latin at University College, London, and from 1911 until his death he was professor of Latin at Cambridge.

It was characteristic of Housman that his classical studies consisted of meticulous, impersonal textual investigations; there was something reserved and solitary about his life as there was about his scholarship, in which he allowed no trace of his feeling for literature to appear. That feeling nevertheless ran strong and deep, and in his lecture *The Name and Nature of Poetry* (1933) he expressed the view that poetry cannot be explained or analyzed but is recognized by its almost physical effects on the reader as he reads. His own poetry was limited both in quantity and in range. Two "slim volumes"—*A Shropshire Lad* (1896) and *Last Poems* (1922)—were all that appeared during his lifetime, and after his death his brother Laurence Housman, playwright and poet, brought out another small book of *More Poems* (1936), on the whole inferior in quality to the first two.

Housman's writings on classical subjects consisted of articles and reviews marked by bitterly sarcastic exposure of the work of inferior editors punctuated by gloomy remarks about life. He was a very great textual critic of Latin poetry, but his remarks on the folly and incompetence of other textual critics go far beyond anything normally expected of superior scholarship talking of inferior. "If a man will comprehend the richness and variety of the universe, and inspire his mind with a due measure of wonder and of awe, he must contemplate the human intellect not only on its heights of genius but in its abysses of ineptitude. . . . Elias Stoeber['s] reprint . . . saw the light in 1767 at Strasburg, a city still famous for its geese. . . . Stoeber's mind, though that is no name to call it by, was one which turned as unswervingly to the false, the meaningless, the unmetrical, and the ungrammatical, as the needle to the pole" (preface to *Manilius*, 1903).

Housman's aim as a poet was not to expand or develop the resources of English poetry but by limitation and concentration to achieve an utterance both compact and moving. He was influenced by Greek and Latin lyric poetry, by the traditional ballad, and by the lyrics of the early nineteenth-century German poet Heinrich Heine. His favorite theme is that of the doomed youth acting out the tragedy of his brief life in a context of agricultural activity and against a specific English background containing visual reminders of humanity's long history there. Nature is beautiful but indifferent and is to be enjoyed while we are still able to enjoy it. Love, friendship, and conviviality cannot last and may well result in betrayal or death, but are likewise to be relished while there is time. The wryly ironic tone sometimes degenerates into melodrama, and the stoicism seems at times histrionic, but at his best Housman's control of cadence enabled him to sound the note of resigned wisdom with quiet poignancy. He avoids self-pity by projecting the emotion through an imagined character, notably the "Shropshire lad," so that even the first-person poems seem to be distanced in some degree. At the same time the poems are distinguished sharply from the "gather ye rosebuds" tradition by the undertones of fatalism and even of doom.

Loveliest of Trees

Loveliest of trees, the cherry now
Is hung with bloom along the bough,
And stands about the woodland ride
Wearing white for Eastertide.

5   Now, of my threescore years and ten,
Twenty will not come again,
And take from seventy springs a score,
It only leaves me fifty more.

And since to look at things in bloom
10 Fifty springs are little room,
About the woodlands I will go
To see the cherry hung with snow.

1896

When I Was One-and-Twenty

When I was one-and-twenty
I heard a wise man say,
"Give crowns and pounds and guineas
But not your heart away;
5   Give pearls away and rubies
But keep your fancy free."
But I was one-and-twenty,
No use to talk to me.

When I was one-and-twenty
10 I heard him say again,
"The heart out of the bosom
Was never given in vain;
'Tis paid with sighs a plenty
And sold for endless rue."°   repentance
15 And I am two-and-twenty,
And oh, 'tis true, 'tis true.

1896

To an Athlete Dying Young

The time you won your town the race
We chaired you through the market-place;

Man and boy stood cheering by,
And home we brought you shoulder-high.

5 Today, the road all runners come,
Shoulder-high we bring you home,
And set you at your threshold down,
Townsman of a stiller town.

Smart lad, to slip betimes away
10 From fields where glory does not stay,
And early though the laurel[1] grows
It withers quicker than the rose.

Eyes the shady night has shut
Cannot see the record cut,°   *broken*
15 And silence sounds no worse than cheers
After earth has stopped the ears:

Now you will not swell the rout°   *crowd*
Of lads that wore their honours out,
Runners whom renown outran
20 And the name died before the man.

So set, before its echoes fade,
The fleet foot on the sill of shade,
And hold to the low lintel up
The still-defended challenge-cup.

25 And round that early laurelled head
Will flock to gaze the strengthless dead
And find unwithered on its curls
The garland briefer than a girl's.

1896

On Wenlock Edge[1]

On Wenlock Edge the wood's in trouble;
His forest fleece the Wrekin[2] heaves;
The gale, it plies the saplings double,
And thick on Severn[3] snow the leaves.

---

1. In ancient Greece and Rome, victorious athletes were crowned with laurel wreaths.
1. A sharp ridge, twenty miles long, in southeastern Shropshire.

2. A prominent hill at the northeast end of the
Caradoc Hills in Shropshire.
3. The Severn River flows through Shropshire past
the Wrekin into Wales.

5 'Twould blow like this through holt and hanger[4]
   When Uricon[5] the city stood:
'Tis the old wind in the old anger,
   But then it threshed another wood.

Then, 'twas before my time, the Roman
10   At yonder heaving hill would stare:
The blood that warms an English yeoman,
   The thoughts that hurt him, they were there.

There, like the wind through woods in riot,
   Through him the gale of life blew high;
15 The tree of man was never quiet:
   Then 'twas the Roman, now 'tis I.

The gale, it plies the saplings double,
   It blows so hard, 'twill soon be gone:
Today the Roman and his trouble
20   Are ashes under Uricon.

                                        1896

With Rue My Heart Is Laden

With rue my heart is laden
   For golden friends I had,
For many a rose-lipt maiden
   And many a lightfoot lad.

5   By brooks too broad for leaping
   The lightfoot boys are laid;
The rose-lipt girls are sleeping
   In fields where roses fade.

                                        1896

Terence,[1] This Is Stupid Stuff

"Terence, this is stupid stuff:
You eat your victuals fast enough;
There can't be much amiss, 'tis clear,
To see the rate you drink your beer.
5   But oh, good Lord, the verse you make,
It gives a chap the belly-ache.
The cow, the old cow, she is dead;
It sleeps well, the hornèd head:
We poor lads, 'tis our turn now

---

4. Wood on the side of a steep hill. "Holt": wooded
hill.
5. The Roman city of Uriconium (whose site is
near Shrewsbury, the county seat of Shropshire).
1. *The Poems of Terence Hearsay* was Housman's
intended title for *The Shropshire Lad*.

10 To hear such tunes as killed the cow.
Pretty friendship 'tis to rhyme
Your friends to death before their time
Moping melancholy mad:
Come, pipe a tune to dance to, lad."

15   Why, if 'tis dancing you would be,
There's brisker pipes than poetry.
Say, for what were hop-yards meant,
Or why was Burton built on Trent?[2]
Oh many a peer[3] of England brews
20 Livelier liquor than the Muse,
And malt does more than Milton can
To justify God's ways to man.
Ale, man, ale's the stuff to drink
For fellows whom it hurts to think:
25 Look into the pewter pot
To see the world as the world's not.
And faith, 'tis pleasant till 'tis past:
The mischief is that 'twill not last.
Oh I have been to Ludlow[4] fair
30 And left my necktie God knows where,
And carried half-way home, or near,
Pints and quarts of Ludlow beer:
Then the world seemed none so bad,
And I myself a sterling lad;
35 And down in lovely muck I've lain,
Happy till I woke again.
Then I saw the morning sky:
Heigho, the tale was all a lie;
The world, it was the old world yet,
40 I was I, my things were wet,
And nothing now remained to do
But begin the game anew.

    Therefore, since the world has still
Much good, but much less good than ill,
45 And while the sun and moon endure
Luck's a chance, but trouble's sure,
I'd face it as a wise man would,
And train for ill and not for good.
'Tis true the stuff I bring for sale
50 Is not so brisk a brew as ale:
Out of a stem that scored° the hand   cut
I wrung it in a weary land.
But take it: if the smack is sour,
The better for the embittered hour;
55 It should do good to heart and head
When your soul is in my soul's stead;

2. Burton-on-Trent is the most famous of all   nates raised to the peerage.
English brewing towns.   4. A market town in Shropshire.
3. A reference to the "beer barons," brewery mag-

And I will friend you, if I may,
In the dark and cloudy day.

There was a king reigned in the East:
60   There, when kings will sit to feast,
They get their fill before they think
With poisoned meat and poisoned drink.
He gathered all that springs to birth
From the many-venomed earth;
65   First a little, thence to more,
He sampled all her killing store;
And easy, smiling, seasoned sound,
Sate the king when healths went round.
They put arsenic in his meat
70   And stared aghast to watch him eat;
They poured strychnine in his cup
And shook to see him drink it up:
They shook, they stared as white's their shirt:
Them it was their poison hurt.
75   —I tell the tale that I heard told.
Mithridates, he died old.[5]

1896

The Chestnut Casts His Flambeaux[1]

The chestnut casts his flambeaux, and the flowers
Stream from the hawthorn in the wind away,
The doors clap to, the pane is blind with showers.
Pass me the can,° lad; there's an end of May.   tankard

5   There's one spoilt spring to scant our mortal lot,
One season ruined of our little store.
May will be fine next year as like as not:
Oh ay, but then we shall be twenty-four.

We for a certainty are not the first
10   Have sat in taverns while the tempest hurled
Their hopeful plans to emptiness, and cursed
Whatever brute and blackguard made the world.

It is in truth iniquity on high
To cheat our sentenced souls of aught they crave,
15   And mar the merriment as you and I
Fare on our long fool's-errand to the grave.

5. The story of Mithridates, king of Pontus, who made himself immune to poison by taking small doses daily, is told in Pliny's *Natural History*.

1. Literally, torches. Housman is here referring to the erect flower clusters (white, dashed with red and yellow) of the horse chestnut tree.

Iniquity it is; but pass the can.
   My lad, no pair of kings our mothers bore;
Our only portion is the estate of man:
20   We want the moon, but we shall get no more.

If here today the cloud of thunder lours°   *looks threatening*
   Tomorrow it will hie° on far behests;°   *go quickly / commands*
The flesh will grieve on other bones than ours
   Soon, and the soul will mourn in other breasts.

25   The troubles of our proud and angry dust
   Are from eternity, and shall not fail.
Bear them we can, and if we can we must.
   Shoulder the sky, my lad, and drink your ale.

1922

Epitaph on an Army of Mercenaries[1]

These, in the day when heaven was falling,
   The hour when earth's foundations fled,
Followed their mercenary calling
   And took their wages and are dead.

5   Their shoulders held the sky suspended;
   They stood, and earth's foundations stay;
What God abandoned, these defended,
   And saved the sum of things for pay.

1922

1. To honor the heroism of the professional soldiers of the British Regular Army in the First Battle of Ypres (1914), Housman published this poem in *The Times* on the third anniversary of the turning point of that battle, October 31, 1917. See Hugh MacDiarmid's angry response, *Another Epitaph on an Army of Mercenaries* (p. 2437).

Voices from World War I

Britain declared war on Germany on August 4, 1914, after Germany had ignored Britain's appeal to refrain from violating Belgium's neutrality in its attack on France. The original spark that set off what proved to be the bloodiest and most widespread war that had yet been fought was the murder of the Archduke Ferdinand of Austria in the Balkan state of Serbia on June 28. Austria, supported by Germany, used the murder as a reason for declaring war on Serbia, which in turn was supported by its fellow-Slav country Russia. Because Russia was bound by a treaty obligation to both France and Britain, Russia and France were soon at war with Germany and Austria. The most effective way of attacking France was for Germany to go through Belgium, though all the powers had guaranteed Belgian neutrality. Although it was the attack on Belgium that brought Britain into the conflict, rival imperialisms, an international armaments race, French desire to regain Alsace-Lorraine, which it had lost to Germany in 1870, and German and Austrian ambitions in the Balkans were some of the many other factors that helped to bring about the four-year struggle, a struggle that shook the world and seemed to mark the end of a whole phase of European civilization. Other countries joined in. Turkey sided with Germany and Austria in October 1914, and Bulgaria allied itself with them the following year. Britain and France were joined by Japan late in August 1914, by Italy (although Italy had in 1882 joined the "Triple Alliance" with Germany and Austria directed against France and Russia) in May 1915, and by the United States in April 1917.

Before the collapse of Germany followed by the armistice of November 11, 1918, some 8,700,000 lives had been lost (including 780,000 British) and the prolonged horrors of trench warfare had seared themselves into the minds of the survivors. For three years the battle line, "the Western Front," was stabilized between northwest France and Switzerland, with both sides dug in and making repeated, costly, and generally useless attempts to advance. The German use of poison gas at the second battle of Ypres in 1915, the massive German attack at Verdun in 1916, and the British introduction of tanks on the Somme in the same year failed to produce the breakthrough each side desired. Desolate, war-scarred landscapes with blasted trees and mud everywhere, trenches half-filled with water and infested with rats, miles of protective barbed wire strung out requiring to be cut by individual "volunteers" crawling through machine-gun fire to reach it before any advance could begin, long-continued massive bombardments by heavy artillery, and a sense of permanent stalemate that suggested to the soldiers involved that this living hell could go on forever—all this was long kept from the knowledge of the civilians at home, who continued to use the old patriotic slogans and write in old-fashioned romantic terms of the glories of war. But those poets who were involved on the front, however romantically they may have felt about the war when they first joined up, soon realized its full horror, and this realization affected both their imaginations and their poetic techniques. They had to find a way of expressing the terrible truths they had experienced, and even when they did not express them directly, the underlying knowledge affected the way they wrote.

We must remember not only that the battle casualties of World War I were many times greater than those of World War II, wiping out virtually a whole generation of young men and shattering so many illusions and ideals, but also that people were wholly unprepared for the horrors of modern trench warfare. World War I broke out on a largely innocent world, a world that still associated warfare with glorious cavalry charges and the noble pursuit of heroic ideals. That is why the poets of that war who spoke for the trauma of their generation were "war poets" of a special kind and why it is reasonable to break our chronological arrangement and discuss them as a group.

The "Georgian" poetry that was in vogue when war broke out, and that some poets continued to write for some years afterward, was so named in honor of the reign of King George V, who had succeeded Edward VII in 1910. The term was first used of poets when Edward Marsh brought out in 1912 the first of a series of five anthologies called *Georgian Poetry*. Their work represented an attempt to wall in the garden of English poetry against the disruptive forces of modern civilization. Cultured meditations of the English countryside ("I love the mossy quietness / That grows upon the great stone flags") alternated with self-conscious exercises in the exotic ("When I was but thirteen or so / I went into a golden land, / Chimporazo, Cotopaxi / Took me by the hand"). Sometimes the magical note was authentic, as in many of Walter de la Mare's poems, and sometimes the meditative strain was original and impressive, as in the poetry of Edward Thomas (although his style was toughened and tightened as a result of his war experiences). But as World War I went on, with more and more poets killed and the survivors increasingly disillusioned, the whole world on which the Georgian imagination rested came to appear unreal. A patriotic poem such as Rupert Brooke's *The Soldier* became a ridiculous anachronism in the face of the realities of trench warfare, and the even more blatantly patriotic note sounded by other Georgian poems (as in John Freeman's *Happy Is England Now,* which claimed that "there's not a nobleness of heart, hand, brain / But shines the purer; happiest is England now / In those that fight") came to seem positively obscene. The savage ironies of Siegfried Sassoon's war poems and the combination of pity and irony of those of Wilfred Owen portrayed a world undreamed of in the golden years from 1910 to 1914.

World War I left throughout Europe a sense that the bases of civilization had been destroyed, that all traditional values had been wiped out, and we see this sense reflected in the years immediately after the war in different ways in *The Waste Land* of T. S. Eliot and the early novels and stories of Aldous Huxley. But it was the poets who wrote during the war who most directly reflected the impact of the war experience.

RUPERT BROOKE
1887–1915

Rupert Brooke was educated at Rugby School and at King's College, Cambridge. After an unhappy love affair, he traveled extensively in Europe, the United States, Canada, and the South Seas, writing poems and essays. When World War I broke out, he was commissioned as an officer into the Royal Naval Division and took part in its brief and abortive expedition to Antwerp. On leave in December 1914, he wrote the "war sonnets" that were to make him famous and, five months later, died of dysentery and blood poisoning on a troopship destined for Gallipoli. He was buried on the Greek island of Skyros.

Brooke is often, and with considerable justice, taken as representative of the golden world of liberal culture shattered by the Great War. His early death was symbolic of the death of a whole generation of patriotic Englishmen—brilliant and beautiful young men as they seemed in retrospect—for, like Byron, Brooke was strikingly handsome, athletic, intelligent, and witty. Shortly before the poet's death, the dean of St. Paul's read *The Soldier* in a sermon from the Cathedral pulpit, and a Valediction in the London *Times,* written by Winston Churchill in 1915, sounded a note that was to swell over the months and years that followed: "The thoughts to which he gave expression in the very few incomparable war sonnets which he has left behind will be shared by many thousands of young men moving resolutely and blithely forward into this, the hardest, the cruellest, and the least-rewarded of all the wars that men have fought. They are a whole history and revelation of Rupert Brooke himself. Joyous, fearless, versatile, deeply instructed, with classic symmetry of mind and body, he was all that one would wish England's noblest sons to be in days when no sacrifice but the most precious is acceptable, and the most precious is that which is most freely proffered." Brooke's *1914 and Other Poems* was published in June 1915 and over the next decade this and his *Collected Poems* sold three hundred thousand copies.

He has been criticized for not responding to the horrors of war, but it should be remembered that in 1914 Wilfred Owen was himself writing:

> O meet it is and passing sweet
>   To live in peace with others,
> But sweeter still and far more meet,
>   To die in war for brothers.

Brooke may have been a Georgian poet, but he considered his "masters" to be the Elizabethans, Donne, and Browning. His *Poems* (1911) were criticized by reviewers for their blunt diction and, had he lived to experience the Gallipoli landings, it is hard to believe that Brooke would not have responded as Owen to the horrors of the Western Front.

The Soldier

If I should die, think only this of me:
   That there's some corner of a foreign field
That is forever England. There shall be
   In that rich earth a richer dust concealed;
5 A dust whom England bore, shaped, made aware,
   Gave, once, her flowers to love, her ways to roam,
A body of England's, breathing English air,
   Washed by the rivers, blest by suns of home.

And think, this heart, all evil shed away,
10   A pulse in the Eternal mind, no less
      Gives somewhere back the thoughts by England given,
Her sights and sounds; dreams happy as her day;
   And laughter, learnt of friends; and gentleness,
      In hearts at peace, under an English heaven.

1914   1915

EDWARD THOMAS
1878–1917

Edward Thomas was born in London and was educated there and at Lincoln College, Oxford, which he left with a wife, a baby, and high literary ambitions, but a melancholy disposition, inherited from his mother, became more marked over the difficult years that followed. He was reviewing up to fifteen books a week and, although he hated the drudgery, was reviewing them conscientiously and with discernment. The meager income from this he supplemented by selling his review copies and writing one book after another. Thirty were published between 1897 and 1917, and during those twenty years he also edited sixteen anthologies and editions. Everything was done hurriedly, but nothing was slovenly, and he was able to find delight—and communicate it with freshness and charm—even in many unpromising hack assignments. His great gifts as a literary critic appeared to best advantage in his reviewing of poetry, and he was the first to salute such new stars in the literary firmament as W. H. Davies the "Super-Tramp," Robert Frost, and Ezra Pound.

Although he had been reviewing poetry, which he regarded as the highest form of literature, for years, he apparently made no serious attempt to write poems himself until the autumn of 1914. Then, under the stress of deciding whether or not to enlist, poems suddenly began to pour out of him: five between December 3 and 7, and ten more before the end of the month. His friend Frost offered to find him work in the United States, but feelings of patriotism, and the attraction of a salary that would support his growing family, led him to enlist in July 1915. He was still writing poems, and many of them (such as *Rain*) owe a curious debt to his earlier writings. His deepest loyalties and preoccupations, his love of England and its seasons that he had celebrated so long in prose, are distilled to a purer form in his poems. His awareness of the natural world, its richness and beauty, is now intensified by a sense of impending loss and the certainty of death—his own and others'. Thomas's "war poems" are those of a countryman perceiving the violence done by a distant conflict to the natural order of things. In January 1917, he was sent to the Western Front and, on Easter Monday, was killed by the blast of a shell.

Adlestrop[1]

Yes, I remember Adlestrop—
The name, because one afternoon
Of heat the express-train drew up there
Unwontedly. It was late June.

5 The steam hissed. Someone cleared his throat.
No one left and no one came
On the bare platform. What I saw
Was Adlestrop—only the name

And willows, willow-herb, and grass,
10 And meadowsweet, and haycocks dry,
No whit less still and lonely fair
Than the high cloudlets in the sky.

And for that minute a blackbird sang
Close by, and round him, mistier,

---

1. A village in Gloucestershire.

15   Farther and farther, all the birds
     Of Oxfordshire and Gloucestershire.

Jan. 1915   1917

Tears

It seems I have no tears left. They should have fallen—
Their ghosts, if tears have ghosts, did fall—that day
When twenty hounds streamed by me, not yet combed out
But still all equals in their rage of gladness
5 Upon the scent, made one, like a great dragon
In Blooming Meadow that bends towards the sun
And once bore hops: and on that other day
When I stepped out from the double-shadowed Tower
Into an April morning, stirring and sweet
10 And warm. Strange solitude was there and silence.
A mightier charm than any in the Tower
Possessed the courtyard. They were changing guard,
Soldiers in line, young English countrymen,
Fair-haired and ruddy, in white tunics. Drums
15 And fifes were playing "The British Grenadiers."[1]
The men, the music piercing that solitude
And silence, told me truths I had not dreamed,
And have forgotten since their beauty passed.

Jan. 1915   1917

The Owl

Downhill I came, hungry, and yet not starved;
Cold, yet had heat within me that was proof
Against the North wind; tired, yet so that rest
Had seemed the sweetest thing under a roof.

5 Then at the inn I had food, fire, and rest,
Knowing how hungry, cold, and tired was I.
All of the night was quite barred out except
An owl's cry, a most melancholy cry

Shaken out long and clear upon the hill,
10 No merry note, nor cause of merriment,
But one telling me plain what I escaped
And others could not, that night, as in I went.

And salted° was my food, and my repose,   *flavored (as with salt)*
Salted and sobered, too, by the bird's voice

---

1. Famous British marching song about the Brigade of Guards, an elite infantry unit.

15 Speaking for all who lay under the stars,
Soldiers and poor, unable to rejoice.

Feb. 1915   1917

Rain[1]

Rain, midnight rain, nothing but the wild rain
On this bleak hut, and solitude, and me
Remembering again that I shall die
And neither hear the rain nor give it thanks
5 For washing me cleaner than I have been
Since I was born into this solitude.
Blessed are the dead that the rain rains upon:
But here I pray that none whom once I loved
Is dying tonight or lying still awake
10 Solitary, listening to the rain,
Either in pain or thus in sympathy
Helpless among the living and the dead,
Like a cold water among broken reeds,
Myriads of broken reeds all still and stiff,
15 Like me who have no love which this wild rain
Has not dissolved except the love of death,
If love it be towards what is perfect and
Cannot, the tempest tells me, disappoint.

Jan. 1916   1917

The Cherry Trees

The cherry trees bend over and are shedding
On the old road where all that passed are dead,
Their petals, strewing the grass as for a wedding
This early May morn when there is none to wed.

May 1916   1917

As the Team's Head Brass[1]

As the team's head brass flashed out on the turn
The lovers disappeared into the wood.
I sat among the boughs of the fallen elm
That strewed an angle of the fallow,[2] and

1. Cf. Thomas's account of an English walking tour, *The Icknield Way* (1913): "In the heavy, black rain falling straight from invisible, dark sky to invisible, dark earth the heat of summer is annihilated, the splendour is dead, the summer is gone. The midnight rain buries it away where it has buried all sound but its own. I am alone in the dark still night, and my ear listens to the rain piping in the gutters and roaring softly in the trees of the world. Even so will the rain fall darkly upon the grass over the grave when my ears can hear it no more. . . . Black and monotonously sounding is the midnight and solitude of the rain. In a little while or in an age— for it is all one—I shall know the full truth of the words I used to love, I knew not why, in my days of nature, in the days before the rain: 'Blessed are the dead that the rain rains on.' "
1. Also known as horse brass: a decorative brass medallion or emblem attached to a horse's harness.
2. Ground plowed and harrowed but left uncropped for a year or more.

5   Watched the plough narrowing a yellow square
   Of charlock.° Every time the horses turned   *wild mustard*
   Instead of treading me down, the ploughman leaned
   Upon the handles to say or ask a word,
   About the weather, next about the war.
10   Scraping the share he faced towards the wood,
   And screwed along the furrow till the brass flashed
   Once more.
            The blizzard felled the elm whose crest
   I sat in, by a woodpecker's round hole,
   The ploughman said. "When will they take it away?"
15   "When the war's over." So the talk began—
   One minute and an interval of ten,
   A minute more and the same interval.
   "Have you been out?" "No." "And don't want to, perhaps?"
   "If I could only come back again, I should.
20   I could spare an arm. I shouldn't want to lose
   A leg. If I should lose my head, why, so,
   I should want nothing more. . . . Have many gone
   From here?" "Yes." "Many lost?" "Yes, a good few.
   Only two teams work on the farm this year.
25   One of my mates is dead. The second day
   In France they killed him. It was back in March,
   The very night of the blizzard, too. Now if
   He had stayed here we should have moved the tree."
   "And I should not have sat here. Everything
30   Would have been different. For it would have been
   Another world." "Ay, and a better, though
   If we could see all all might seem good." Then
   The lovers came out of the wood again:
   The horses started and for the last time
35   I watched the clods crumble and topple over
   After the ploughshare and the stumbling team.

May 1916   1917

SIEGFRIED SASSOON
1886–1967

Educated at Marlborough College and Clare College, Cambridge (which he left without taking a degree), Siegfried Sassoon came from a rich Jewish family and had a private income that enabled him, as a young man, to divide his time between the world of literary London and that of the country gentleman. These and the brutally different world of the trenches, in which he found himself in 1914, are memorably described in his classic *Memoirs of a Fox-Hunting Man* (1928) and its sequel, *Memoirs of an Infantry Officer* (1930).

He fought at Mametz Wood and in the Somme Offensive of July 1916 with such conspicuous courage that he acquired the Military Cross and the nickname Mad Jack.

However, invalided back to England at the beginning of April 1917, with a sniper's bullet through his chest, he began to take a different view of the war and eventually, with courage equal to any he had shown in action, made public a statement sent to his commanding officer:

> I am making this statement as an act of wilful defiance of military authority, because I believe that the war is being deliberately prolonged by those who have the power to end it.
>
> I am a soldier, convinced that I am acting on behalf of soldiers. I believe that this war, upon which I entered as a war of defence and liberation, has now become a war of aggression and conquest. I believe that the purposes for which I and my fellow-soldiers entered upon this war should have been so clearly stated as to have made it impossible to change them, and that, had this been done, the objects which actuated us would now be attainable by negotiation.

Rather than make a martyr of him, the military authorities announced that he was suffering from shell shock and sent him to an Edinburgh hospital where he met and befriended Wilfred Owen.

Sassoon's public protest may have been smothered, but his poems, with their shock tactics, bitter irony, and masterly use of direct speech (learned from Thomas Hardy), continued to attack the old men of the army, church, and government whom he held responsible for the miseries and murder of the young.

He returned to the Western Front in 1918, was wounded again, and again invalided home. After the war, living the life of an increasingly reclusive country gentleman, he continued to write poetry, but his style changed. At times, as in his *Satirical Poems* (1926) attacking society, his work still displayed a cutting edge, but never again did he achieve the pungency of the "war poems" that made him famous. In 1957 he was received into the Roman Catholic church, and until he died in 1967 he wrote mainly devotional poems.

"They"

The Bishop tells us: "When the boys come back
They will not be the same; for they'll have fought
In a just cause: they lead the last attack
On Anti-Christ; their comrades' blood has bought
5   New right to breed an honourable race,
They have challenged Death and dared him face to face."

"We're none of us the same!" the boys reply.
"For George lost both his legs; and Bill's stone blind;
Poor Jim's shot through the lungs and like to die;
10   And Bert's gone syphilitic: you'll not find
A chap who's served that hasn't found *some* change."
And the Bishop said: "The ways of God are strange!"

Oct. 31, 1916   1917

The Rear-Guard

(Hindenburg Line, April 1917)[1]

Groping along the tunnel, step by step,
He winked his prying torch with patching glare
From side to side, and sniffed the unwholesome air.
Tins, boxes, bottles, shapes too vague to know;
5   A mirror smashed, the mattress from a bed;
And he, exploring fifty feet below
The rosy gloom of battle overhead.

Tripping, he grabbed the wall; saw some one lie
Humped at his feet, half-hidden by a rug,
10 And stooped to give the sleeper's arm a tug.
"I'm looking for headquarters." No reply.
"God blast your neck!" (For days he'd had no sleep)
"Get up and guide me through this stinking place."
Savage, he kicked a soft unanswering heap,
15 And flashed his beam across the livid face
Terribly glaring up, whose eyes yet wore
Agony dying hard ten days before;
And fists of fingers clutched a blackening wound.

Alone he staggered on until he found
20 Dawn's ghost that filtered down a shafted stair
To the dazed, muttering creatures underground
Who hear the boom of shells in muffled sound.
At last, with sweat of horror in his hair,
He climbed through darkness to the twilight air,
25 Unloading hell behind him step by step.

Apr. 22, 1917   1918

The General

"Good-morning; good-morning!" the General said
When we met him last week on our way to the line.
Now the soldiers he smiled at are most of 'em dead,
And we're cursing his staff for incompetent swine.
5 "He's a cheery old card," grunted Harry to Jack
As they slogged up to Arras[1] with rifle and pack.

                      • • •

But he did for them both by his plan of attack.

Apr. 1917   1918

1. In 1916, Field Marshal Paul von Hindenburg
(1847–1934) became commander in chief of the
German armies and, for a time, blocked the Allied
advance in western France with the massive defensive "line" named after him. Its barbed-wire entanglements, deep trenches, and gun emplacements
ran from Lens to Rheims.
1. A city in northern France, in the front line
throughout much of the war. The British assault
on the Western Front that began on April 9, 1917,
was known as the Battle of Arras. The British suffered casualties of 84,000 troops, inflicted casualties of 75,000 on the Germans, and took 13,000
prisoners. Canadian troops captured Vimy Ridge,
which proved an invaluable defensive position
against the German offensive of March 1918.

Glory of Women

You love us when we're heroes, home on leave,
Or wounded in a mentionable place.
You worship decorations; you believe
That chivalry redeems the war's disgrace.
5 You make us shells.[1] You listen with delight,
By tales of dirt and danger fondly thrilled.
You crown our distant ardours while we fight,
And mourn our laurelled memories when we're killed.
You can't believe that British troops "retire"
10 When hell's last horror breaks them, and they run,
Trampling the terrible corpses—blind with blood.
    O German mother dreaming by the fire,
While you are knitting socks to send your son
His face is trodden deeper in the mud.

1917   1918

Everyone Sang

Everyone suddenly burst out singing;
And I was filled with such delight
As prisoned birds must find in freedom,
Winging wildly across the white
5 Orchards and dark-green fields; on—on—and out of sight.

Everyone's voice was suddenly lifted;
And beauty came like the setting sun:
My heart was shaken with tears; and horror
Drifted away . . . O, but Everyone
10 Was a bird; and the song was wordless; the singing will never be done.

Apr. 1919   1919

On Passing the New Menin Gate[1]

Who will remember, passing through this Gate,
The unheroic Dead who fed the guns?
Who shall absolve the foulness of their fate,—
Those doomed, conscripted, unvictorious ones?
5 Crudely renewed, the Salient[2] holds its own.
Paid are its dim defenders by this pomp;
Paid, with a pile of peace-complacent stone,
The armies who endured that sullen swamp.

---

1. Many women were recruited into munitions
factories during the war.
1. The names of 54,889 men are engraved on this
war memorial outside Brussels.

2. Protruding part of fortifications or, as here, line
of defensive trenches. Salients are particularly vulnerable, being exposed to enemy fire from the front
and both sides.

Here was the world's worst wound. And here with pride
10   "Their name liveth for ever," the Gateway claims.
Was ever an immolation so belied
As these intolerably nameless names?
Well might the Dead who struggled in the slime
Rise and deride this sepulchre° of crime.   *tomb*

1927–28   1928

From Memoirs of an Infantry Officer

[THE OPENING OF THE BATTLE OF THE SOMME]

On July [1916] the first the weather, after an early morning mist, was of
the kind commonly called heavenly. Down in our frowsty cellar we breakfasted at six, unwashed and apprehensive. Our table, appropriately enough,
was an empty ammunition box. At six-forty-five the final bombardment
began, and there was nothing for us to do except sit round our candle until
the tornado ended. For more than forty minutes the air vibrated and the
earth rocked and shuddered. Through the sustained uproar the tap and rattle
of machine-guns could be identified; but except for the whistle of bullets no
retaliation came our way until a few 5.9 shells[1] shook the roof of our dug-
out. Barton and I sat speechless, deafened and stupefied by the seismic state
of affairs, and when he lit a cigarette the match flame staggered crazily.
Afterwards I asked him what he had been thinking about. His reply was
'Carpet slippers and Kettle-holders'. My own mind had been working in
much the same style, for during that cannonading cataclysm the following
refrain was running in my head:

> *They come as a boon and a blessing to men,*
> *The Something, the Owl, and the Waverley Pen.*

For the life of me I couldn't remember what the first one was called. Was
it the Shakespeare? Was it the Dickens? Anyhow it was an advertisement
which I'd often seen in smoky railway stations. Then the bombardment lifted
and lessened, our vertigo abated, and we looked at one another in dazed
relief. Two Brigades of our Division were now going over the top on our
right. Our Brigade was to attack 'when the main assault had reached its final
objective'. In our fortunate rôle of privileged spectators Barton and I went
up the stairs to see what we could from Kingston Road Trench. We left
Jenkins crouching in a corner, where he remained most of the day. His
haggard blinking face haunts my memory. He was an example of the para-
lysing effect which such an experience could produce on a nervous system
sensitive to noise, for he was a good officer both before and afterwards. I felt
no sympathy for him at the time, but I do now. From the support-trench,
which Barton called 'our opera box', I observed as much of the battle as the
formation of the country allowed, the rising ground on the right making it
impossible to see anything of the attack towards Mametz. A small shiny black
note-book contains my pencilled particulars, and nothing will be gained by

---

1. I.e., 5.9-caliber shells.

embroidering them with afterthoughts. I cannot turn my field-glasses on to the past.[2]

7.45.   The barrage is now working to the right of Fricourt and beyond. I can see the 21st Division advancing about three-quarters of a mile away on the left and a few Germans coming to meet them, apparently surrendering. Our men in small parties (not extended in line) go steadily on to the German front-line. Brilliant sunshine and a haze of smoke drifting along the land-scape. Some Yorkshires[3] a little way below on the left, watching the show and cheering as if at a football match. The noise almost as bad as ever.

9.30.   Came back to dug-out and had a shave. 21st Division still going across the open, apparently without casualties. The sunlight flashes on bay-onets as the tiny figures move quietly forward and disappear beyond mounds of trench debris. A few runners come back and ammunition parties go across. Trench-mortars are knocking hell out of Sunken Road trench and the ground where the Manchesters[4] will attack soon. Noise not so bad now and very little retaliation.

9.50.   Fricourt half-hidden by clouds of drifting smoke, blue, pinkish and grey. Shrapnel bursting in small bluish-white puffs with tiny flashes. The birds seem bewildered; a lark begins to go up and then flies feebly along, thinking better of it. Others flutter above the trench with querulous cries, weak on the wing. I can see seven of our balloons,[5] on the right. On the left our men still filing across in twenties and thirties. Another huge explosion in Fricourt and a cloud of brown-pink smoke. Some bursts are yellowish.

10.5.   I can see the Manchesters down in New Trench, getting ready to go over. Figures filing down the trench. Two of them have gone out to look at our wire gaps![6] Have just eaten my last orange. . . . I am staring at a sunlit picture of Hell, and still the breeze shakes the yellow weeds, and the poppies glow under Crawley Ridge where some shells fell a few minutes ago. Man-chesters are sending forward some scouts. A bayonet glitters. A runner comes back across the open to their Battalion Headquarters, close here on the right. 21st Division still trotting along the sky line toward La Boisselle. Barrage going strong to the right of Contalmaison Ridge. Heavy shelling toward Mametz.

1916   1930

---

2. The extracts that follow are edited versions of the actual entries in Sassoon's diary. (See *Siegfried Sassoon: Diaries 1915–1918*, ed. Rupert Hart-Davis, 1983, pp. 82–83.)
3. Men of a Yorkshire regiment.

4. Men of the Manchester regiment.
5. Long cables, tethering such balloons, prevented attacks by low-flying aircraft.
6. Holes, made by shell fire, in the long coils of barbed wire protecting the trenches.

IVOR GURNEY
1890–1937

Ivor Bertie Gurney was born at Gloucester and showed an early aptitude for music. After five years at the King's School, Gloucester, he won a scholarship to the Royal College of Music. His chief interest was now composing song music, and it was as a composer rather than as a poet that he first acquired a modest reputation. After war broke out in August 1914, he enlisted; his battalion was sent to France the following year, and Gurney experienced all the horrors of the Western Front. He was wounded in April 1917, and when in the hospital in Rouen, he sent some of his poems to friends in London. The result was a volume published under the title *Severn and Somme* in 1917. (The Severn is the English river at the head of whose estuary Gloucester is situated; it appears often in his poetry. The Somme is the river in northern France that was the scene of some of the most murderous fighting in the war during the costly British and French offensive of July to October 1916.)

Gurney was returned to the front in time to take part in the grim Paschendale offensive of the summer of 1917. He suffered the effects of a poison-gas attack on August 22 and was sent to a mental hospital at Warrington and then to another at St. Albans, but he recovered sufficiently to be released before the end of the war. He returned to the Royal College of Music to study under the composer Ralph Vaughan Williams (1872–1958), and continued also to write poetry. His second book of poems, *War's Emblems,* appeared in 1919.

By September 1922, it was clear that Gurney's experiences of the war had been so working on him that he suffered periodically from delusions. He was confined at Barnwood House, a home for the mentally ill in Gloucester, and later, when the prospect of recovery seemed hopeless, to the City of London Mental Hospital at Dartford, Kent, where he died on December 26, 1937. He continued to write poetry during his fifteen-year confinement—like the nineteenth-century poet John Clare, some of whose poems he set to music.

Gurney was one of the first English poets to feel the influence of Gerard Manley Hopkins, and some of his poems of despair written in confinement are reminiscent in tone and movement of Hopkins's "terrible" sonnets. A greater influence on him was Edward Thomas, with whom he shares a limpid directness of utterance. His poems, descriptive of his experiences in the war, avoid all histrionics and attitudinizing but with a painful quietness recapture particular scenes and moments.

To His Love

He's gone, and all our plans
    Are useless indeed.
We'll walk no more on Cotswold[1]
    Where the sheep feed
5   Quietly and take no heed.

His body that was so quick
    Is not as you
Knew it, on Severn river
    Under the blue
10   Driving our small boat through.

---

1. Range of hills in Gloucestershire, in western England.

You would not know him now . . .
But still he died
Nobly, so cover him over
With violets of pride
15   Purple from Severn side.

Cover him, cover him soon!
And with thick-set
Masses of memoried flowers—
Hide that red wet
20   Thing I must somehow forget.

1919

The Silent One

Who died on the wires,[1] and hung there, one of two—
Who for his hours of life had chattered through
Infinite lovely chatter of Bucks[2] accent:
Yet faced unbroken wires; stepped over, and went
5   A noble fool, faithful to his stripes—and ended.
But I weak, hungry, and willing only for the chance
Of line—to fight in the line, lay down under unbroken
Wires, and saw the flashes and kept unshaken,
Till the politest voice—a finicking accent, said:
10   "Do you think you might crawl through there: there's a hole."
Darkness, shot at: I smiled, as politely replied—
"I'm afraid not, Sir." There was no hole no way to be seen
Nothing but chance of death, after tearing of clothes.
Kept flat, and watched the darkness, hearing bullets whizzing—
15   And thought of music—and swore deep heart's deep oaths
(Polite to God) and retreated and came on again,
Again retreated—and a second time faced the screen.

1954

1. The barbed wire protecting the front from   2. Buckinghamshire, in southern England.
infantry attack.

ISAAC ROSENBERG
1890–1918

Isaac Rosenberg was born in Bristol of a humble Anglo-Jewish family that moved to
London in 1897. There, at Stepney, Rosenberg attended elementary schools until the
age of fourteen, when he became apprenticed as an engraver in a firm of art publishers
and attended evening classes at the Art School of Birkbeck College. His first ambition
was to be a painter, and in 1911, when his apprenticeship was over, a group of three

Jewish women provided the means for his studying at the Slade School of Art. His interest in writing poetry steadily developed, and with the encouragement of his married sister he circulated copies of his poems among members of London's literary set and gained a certain reputation, though neither his poetry nor his painting won him any material success. In 1912 he published the first of three pamphlets of poetry at his own expense, *Night and Day*. The other two were *Youth* (1915) and *Moses, A Play* (1916).

In 1914 Rosenberg went to South Africa for his health, and lived there with another of his sisters. He returned to England in 1915, enlisted in the army, and was killed in action on April 1, 1918. After his death his reputation steadily grew as an unusually interesting and original poet, who, although he did not live to reach maturity, nevertheless produced some poetry that broke new ground in imagery, rhythms, and the handling of dramatic effects. The fierce apprehension of the physical reality of war, the exclamatory directness of the language, and the vivid sense of involvement distinguish his poems from those of other war poets. Perhaps Rosenberg's working-class background had something to do with this vividness: like Ivor Gurney and David Jones, he served in the ranks.

Break of Day in the Trenches

The darkness crumbles away.
It is the same old druid[1] Time as ever,
Only a live thing leaps my hand,
A queer sardonic rat,
5 As I pull the parapet's[2] poppy
To stick behind my ear.
Droll rat, they would shoot you if they knew
Your cosmopolitan sympathies.
Now you have touched this English hand
10 You will do the same to a German
Soon, no doubt, if it be your pleasure
To cross the sleeping green between.
It seems you inwardly grin as you pass
Strong eyes, fine limbs, haughty athletes,
15 Less chanced than you for life,
Bonds to the whims of murder,
Sprawled in the bowels of the earth,
The torn fields of France.
What do you see in our eyes
20 At the shrieking iron and flame
Hurled through still heavens?
What quaver—what heart aghast?
Poppies whose roots are in man's veins
Drop, and are ever dropping;
25 But mine in my ear is safe—
Just a little white with the dust.

June 1916   1922

---

1. Member of a Celtic religious order found in ancient Gaul, Britain, and Ireland.   2. Wall protecting a trench.

Louse Hunting

Nudes—stark and glistening,
Yelling in lurid glee.   Grinning faces
And raging limbs
Whirl over the floor one fire.
5   For a shirt verminously busy
Yon soldier tore from his throat, with oaths
Godhead might shrink at, but not the lice.
And soon the shirt was aflare
Over the candle he'd lit while we lay.

10   Then we all sprang up and stript
To hunt the verminous brood.
Soon like a demons' pantomime
The place was raging.
See the silhouettes agape,
15   See the gibbering shadows
Mixed with the battled arms on the wall.
See gargantuan hooked fingers
Pluck in supreme flesh
To smutch supreme littleness.
20   See the merry limbs in hot Highland fling[1]
Because some wizard vermin
Charmed from the quiet this revel
When our ears were half lulled
By the dark music
25   Blown from Sleep's trumpet.

1917   1922

Returning, We Hear the Larks

Sombre the night is.
And though we have our lives, we know
What sinister threat lurks there.

Dragging these anguished limbs, we only know
5   This poison-blasted track opens on our camp—
On a little safe sleep.

But hark! joy—joy—strange joy.
Lo! heights of night ringing with unseen larks.
Music showering on our upturned list'ning faces.

10   Death could drop from the dark
As easily as song—
But song only dropped,
Like a blind man's dreams on the sand

1. Wild Scottish dance.

By dangerous tides,
15 Like a girl's dark hair for she dreams no ruin lies there,
Or her kisses where a serpent hides.

1917   1922

Dead Man's Dump

The plunging limbers[1] over the shattered track
Racketed with their rusty freight,
Stuck out like many crowns of thorns,
And the rusty stakes like sceptres old
5 To stay the flood of brutish men
Upon our brothers dear.

The wheels lurched over sprawled dead
But pained them not, though their bones crunched,
Their shut mouths made no moan.
10 They lie there huddled, friend and foeman,
Man born of man, and born of woman,
And shells go crying over them
From night till night and now.

Earth has waited for them,
15 All the time of their growth
Fretting for their decay:
Now she has them at last!
In the strength of their strength
Suspended—stopped and held.

20 What fierce imaginings their dark souls lit?
Earth! have they gone into you?
Somewhere they must have gone,
And flung on your hard back
Is their soul's sack,
25 Emptied of God-ancestralled essences.
Who hurled them out?   Who hurled?

None saw their spirits' shadow shake the grass,
Or stood aside for the half-used life to pass
Out of those doomed nostrils and the doomed mouth,
30 When the swift iron burning bee
Drained the wild honey of their youth.

What of us who, flung on the shrieking pyre,
Walk, our usual thoughts untouched,
Our lucky limbs as on ichor[2] fed,
35 Immortal seeming ever?
Perhaps when the flames beat loud on us,

---

1. Two-wheeled vehicles for pulling guns or caissons (ammunition wagons).

2. In Greek mythology, the ethereal fluid that flowed in the veins of the gods.

A fear may choke in our veins
And the startled blood may stop.

The air is loud with death,
40   The dark air spurts with fire,
The explosions ceaseless are.
Timelessly now, some minutes past,
These dead strode time with vigorous life,
Till the shrapnel called "An end!"
45   But not to all.   In bleeding pangs
Some borne on stretchers dreamed of home,
Dear things, war-blotted from their hearts.

A man's brains splattered on
A stretcher-bearer's face;
50   His shook shoulders slipped their load,
But when they bent to look again
The drowning soul was sunk too deep
For human tenderness.

They left this dead with the older dead,
55   Stretched at the crossroads.

Burnt black by strange decay
Their sinister faces lie;
The lid over each eye,
The grass and coloured clay
60   More motion have than they,
Joined to the great sunk silences.

Here is one not long dead;
His dark hearing caught our far wheels,
And the choked soul stretched weak hands
65   To reach the living word the far wheels said,
The blood-dazed intelligence beating for light,
Crying through the suspense of the far torturing wheels
Swift for the end to break,
Or the wheels to break,
70   Cried as the tide of the world broke over his sight.

Will they come?   Will they ever come?
Even as the mixed hoofs of the mules,
The quivering-bellied mules,
And the rushing wheels all mixed
75   With his tortured upturned sight.
So we crashed round the bend,
We heard his weak scream,
We heard his very last sound,
And our wheels grazed his dead face.

1917   1922

WILFRED OWEN
1893–1918

Wilfred Owen was brought up in the back streets of Birkenhead and Shrewsbury, and on leaving school, he took up a post as lay assistant to a country vicar. Removed from the influence of a devout mother, he became increasingly critical of the role of the church in society. His letters and poems of this period show an increasing awareness of the sufferings of the poor and the first stirrings of the compassion that was to characterize his later poems about the Western Front. In 1913, he broke with the vicar and went to teach English in France.

For more than a year after the outbreak of war, Owen could not decide whether—as both a poet and a firm believer in Christian teaching (as distinct from church practice)—he ought to enlist. Finally he did, and from January to May 1917 he fought as an officer in the Battle of the Somme. Then, invalided out of the Front Line with shell shock, he was sent to an Edinburgh hospital, where he had the good fortune to meet Sassoon, whose first fiercely realistic "war poems" had just appeared. Under their influence, and with the encouragement and expert guidance of the older man, Owen was soon producing poems purged of his earlier sub-Keatsian luxuriance and far superior to any he had written before. Throughout his months in the hospital he suffered from the horrendous nightmares symptomatic of shell shock. The experience of battle, banished from his waking mind, erupted into his dreams and then into poems haunted with obsessive images of blinded eyes (*Dulce et Decorum Est*) and the mouth of hell (*Miners* and *Strange Meeting*). The distinctive music of such later poems owes much of its power to Owen's mastery of alliteration, onomatopoeia, assonance, half-rhyme, and the pararhyme that he pioneered. This last, the rhyming of two words with identical or similar consonants but differing, stressed vowels (as *hall/hell*), of which the second is usually the lower in pitch, produces effects of dissonance, failure, and unfulfillment that subtly reinforce his themes.

In the year of life left to him after leaving the hospital in November 1917, Owen matured rapidly. Success as a soldier, marked by the award of the Military Cross, and as a poet, which had won him the recognition of his peers, gave him a new confidence. He wrote eloquently of the tragedy of young men killed in battle. In his later elegies, a disciplined sensuality and a passionate intelligence find their fullest, most moving, and most memorable expression.

Owen was killed in action a week before the war ended.

Anthem for Doomed Youth

What passing-bells for these who die as cattle?[1]
  —Only the monstrous anger of the guns.
  Only the stuttering rifles' rapid rattle
Can patter out their hasty orisons.

---

1. Owen was probably responding to the anonymous Prefatory Note to *Poems of Today* (1916), of which he possessed a copy: "This book has been compiled in order that boys and girls, already perhaps familiar with the great classics of the English speech, may also know something of the newer poetry of their own day. Most of the writers are living, and the rest are still vivid memories among us, while one of the youngest, almost as these words are written, has gone singing to lay down his life for his country's cause. . . . There is no arbitrary isolation of one theme from another; they mingle and interpenetrate throughout, to the music of Pan's flute, and of Love's viol, and the bugle-call of Endeavour, and the passing-bells of Death."

5   No mockeries now for them; no prayers nor bells;
      Nor any voice of mourning save the choirs,—
   The shrill, demented choirs of wailing shells;
      And bugles calling for them from sad shires.°   *counties*

   What candles may be held to speed them all?
10   Not in the hands of boys but in their eyes
   Shall shine the holy glimmers of goodbyes.
      The pallor of girls' brows shall be their pall;
   Their flowers the tenderness of patient minds,
   And each slow dusk a drawing-down of blinds.

Sept.–Oct. 1917   1920

Apologia Pro Poemate Meo[1]

I, too, saw God through mud,—
   The mud that cracked on cheeks when wretches smiled.
War brought more glory to their eyes than blood,
   And gave their laughs more glee than shakes a child.

5   Merry it was to laugh there—
   Where death becomes absurd and life absurder.
For power was on us as we slashed bones bare
   Not to feel sickness or remorse of murder.

I, too, have dropped off Fear—
10   Behind the barrage, dead as my platoon,
And sailed my spirit surging light and clear
   Past the entanglement where hopes lay strewn;

And witnessed exultation[2]—
   Faces that used to curse me, scowl for scowl,
15   Shine and lift up with passion of oblation,[3]
   Seraphic° for an hour; though they were foul.   *ecstatic*

I have made fellowships—
   Untold of happy lovers in old song.
For love is not the binding of fair lips
20   With the soft silk of eyes that look and long,

By Joy, whose ribbon slips,—
   But wound with war's hard wire whose stakes are strong;

1. This Latin title, meaning "Apology for My Poem," may have been prompted by that of Cardinal Newman's *Apologia Pro Vita Sua*, "Apology for His Life." Here, an apology is a written vindication rather than remorseful account.
2. Cf. Shelley, *A Defence of Poetry*: "Poetry is a mirror which makes beautiful that which is distorted. . . . It exalts the beauty of that which is most beautiful, and it adds beauty to that which is most deformed; it marries exultation and horror."
3. Sacrifice offered to God.

Bound with the bandage of the arm that drips;
Knit in the webbing of the rifle-thong.

25 I have perceived much beauty
In the hoarse oaths that kept our courage straight;
Heard music in the silentness of duty;
Found peace where shell-storms spouted reddest spate.

Nevertheless, except you share
30 With them in hell the sorrowful dark of hell,
Whose world is but the trembling of a flare
And heaven but as the highway for a shell,

You shall not hear their mirth:
You shall not come to think them well content
35 By any jest of mine. These men are worth
Your tears. You are not worth their merriment.

Nov.–Dec. 1917   1920

Miners[1]

There was a whispering in my hearth,
    A sigh of the coal,
Grown wistful of a former earth
    It might recall.

5 I listened for a tale of leaves
    And smothered ferns,
Frond-forests, and the low sly lives
    Before the fauns.

My fire might show steam-phantoms simmer
10   From Time's old cauldron,
Before the birds made nests in summer,
    Or men had children.

But the coals were murmuring of their mine,
    And moans down there
15 Of boys that slept wry sleep, and men
    Writhing for air.

And I saw white bones in the cinder-shard,
    Bones without number.
Many the muscled bodies charred,
20   And few remember.

I thought of all that worked dark pits
    Of war, and died[2]

1. Wrote a poem on the Colliery Disaster [of Jan. 12, 1918, at Halmerend]: but I get mixed up with the War at the end. It is short, but oh! sour [Jan. 14 letter of Owen to his mother].

2. Miners who dug tunnels under no-man's-land in which to detonate mines beneath the enemy trenches.

Digging the rock where Death reputes
　　Peace lies indeed.

25　Comforted years will sit soft-chaired,
　　In rooms of amber;
The years will stretch their hands, well-cheered
　　By our life's ember;

The centuries will burn rich loads
30　　With which we groaned,
Whose warmth shall lull their dreaming lids,
　　While songs are crooned;
But they will not dream of us poor lads,
　　Left in the ground.

Jan. 1918　　　　　　　　　　　　　　　　　　　　　　1931

Dulce Et Decorum Est[1]

Bent double, like old beggars under sacks,
Knock-kneed, coughing like hags, we cursed through sludge,
Till on the haunting flares we turned our backs
And towards our distant rest began to trudge.
5　Men marched asleep. Many had lost their boots
But limped on, blood-shod. All went lame; all blind;
Drunk with fatigue; deaf even to the hoots
Of tired, outstripped Five-Nines[2] that dropped behind.

Gas! GAS! Quick, boys!—An ecstasy of fumbling,
10　Fitting the clumsy helmets just in time;
But someone still was yelling out and stumbling,
And flound'ring like a man in fire or lime . . .
Dim, through the misty panes[3] and thick green light,
As under a green sea, I saw him drowning.

15　In all my dreams, before my helpless sight,
He plunges at me, guttering, choking, drowning.

If in some smothering dreams you too could pace
Behind the wagon that we flung him in,
And watch the white eyes writhing in his face,
20　His hanging face, like a devil's sick of sin;
If you could hear, at every jolt, the blood
Come gargling from the froth-corrupted lungs,
Obscene as cancer, bitter as the cud
Of vile, incurable sores on innocent tongues,—
25　My friend,[4] you would not tell with such high zest

---

1. The famous Latin tag [from Horace, *Odes* 3.2.13] means, of course, *It is sweet and meet to die for one's country. Sweet! And decorum!* [Oct. 16, 1917, letter of Owen to his mother].
2. I.e., 5.9-caliber shells.

3. Of the gas mask's celluloid window.
4. Jessie Pope, to whom the poem was originally to have been dedicated, was the author of numerous prewar children's books as well as *Jessie Pope's War Poems* (1915).

To children ardent for some desperate glory,
The old Lie: Dulce et decorum est
Pro patria mori.

Oct. 1917–Mar. 1918   1920

Strange Meeting[1]

It seemed that out of battle I escaped
Down some profound dull tunnel,[2] long since scooped
Through granites which titanic wars had groined.°   *grooved*

Yet also there encumbered sleepers groaned,
5   Too fast in thought or death to be bestirred.
Then, as I probed them, one sprang up, and stared
With piteous recognition in fixed eyes,
Lifting distressful hands, as if to bless.
And by his smile, I knew that sullen hall,—
10   By his dead smile I knew we stood in Hell.

With a thousand pains that vision's face was grained;
Yet no blood reached there from the upper ground,
And no guns thumped, or down the flues made moan.
"Strange friend," I said, "here is no cause to mourn."
15   "None," said that other, "save the undone years,
The hopelessness. Whatever hope is yours,
Was my life also; I went hunting wild
After the wildest beauty in the world,
Which lies not calm in eyes, or braided hair,
20   But mocks the steady running of the hour,
And if it grieves, grieves richlier than here.
For by my glee might many men have laughed,
And of my weeping something had been left,
Which must die now. I mean the truth untold,
25   The pity of war, the pity war distilled.[3]
Now men will go content with what we spoiled,
Or, discontent, boil bloody, and be spilled.
They will be swift with swiftness of the tigress.
None will break ranks, though nations trek from progress.
30   Courage was mine, and I had mystery,
Wisdom was mine, and I had mastery:
To miss the march of this retreating world
Into vain citadels that are not walled.
Then, when much blood had clogged their chariot-wheels,
35   I would go up and wash them from sweet wells,
Even with truths that lie too deep for taint.

1. Cf. Shelley, *The Revolt of Islam*, lines 1828–32:

    And one whose spear had pierced me, leaned beside,
      With quivering lips and humid eyes;—and all
    Seemed like some brothers on a journey wide
      Gone forth, whom now strange meeting did befall
      In a strange land.

The speaker of Owen's poem imagines his victim a poet like himself.

2. Cf. Sassoon's *The Rear-Guard* (p. 2056).
3. My subject is War, and the pity of War. The Poetry is in the pity [Owen's draft preface to his poems].

I would have poured my spirit without stint
But not through wounds; not on the cess[4] of war.
Foreheads of men have bled where no wounds were.

40 "I am the enemy you killed, my friend.
I knew you in this dark: for so you frowned
Yesterday through me as you jabbed and killed.
I parried; but my hands were loath and cold.
Let us sleep now . . . ."

May [?] 1918   1920

Futility

Move him into the sun—
Gently its touch awoke him once,
At home, whispering of fields half-sown.
Always it woke him, even in France,
5   Until this morning and this snow.
If anything might rouse him now
The kind old sun will know.

Think how it wakes the seeds—
Woke once the clays of a cold star.
10   Are limbs, so dear achieved, are sides
Full-nerved, still warm, too hard to stir?
Was it for this the clay grew tall?
—O what made fatuous sunbeams toil
To break earth's sleep at all?

May 1918   1920

Disabled

He sat in a wheeled chair, waiting for dark,
And shivered in his ghastly suit of grey,
Legless, sewn short at elbow. Through the park
Voices of boys rang saddening like a hymn,
5   Voices of play and pleasure after day,
Till gathering sleep had mothered them from him.

About this time Town used to swing so gay
When glow-lamps budded in the light blue trees,
And girls glanced lovelier as the air grew dim,—
10   In the old times, before he threw away his knees.
Now he will never feel again how slim
Girls' waists are, or how warm their subtle hands.
All of them touch him like some queer disease.

4. Luck, as in the phrase *bad cess to you* (may evil befall you), and muck or excrement, as in the word
cesspool.

• • •

    There was an artist silly for his face,
15   For it was younger than his youth, last year.
    Now, he is old; his back will never brace;
    He's lost his colour very far from here,
    Poured it down shell-holes till the veins ran dry,
    And half his lifetime lapsed in the hot race
20   And leap of purple spurted from his thigh.

• • •

    One time he liked a blood-smear down his leg,
    After the matches, carried shoulder-high.[1]
    It was after football, when he'd drunk a peg,[2]
    He thought he'd better join.—He wonders why.
25   Someone had said he'd look a god in kilts,
    That's why; and maybe, too, to please his Meg,
    Aye, that was it, to please the giddy jilts[3]
    He asked to join. He didn't have to beg;
    Smiling they wrote his lie: aged nineteen years.[4]
30   Germans he scarcely thought of; all their guilt,
    And Austria's, did not move him. And no fears
    Of Fear came yet. He thought of jewelled hilts
    For daggers in plaid socks; of smart salutes;
    And care of arms; and leave; and pay arrears;
35   Esprit de corps;[5] and hints for young recruits.
    And soon, he was drafted out with drums and cheers.

• • •

    Some cheered him home, but not as crowds cheer Goal.
    Only a solemn man who brought him fruits
    Thanked him; and then enquired about his soul.

• • •

40   Now, he will spend a few sick years in institutes,
    And do what things the rules consider wise,
    And take whatever pity they may dole.
    Tonight he noticed how the women's eyes
    Passed from him to the strong men that were whole.
45   How cold and late it is! Why don't they come
    And put him into bed? Why don't they come?

Oct. 1917–July 1918   1920

From Owen's Letters to His Mother

16 January 1917

*   *   *

    I can see no excuse for deceiving you about these last 4 days. I have suffered seventh hell.

---

1. Cf. Housman's *To an Athlete Dying Young* (p. 2042, lines 1–4).
2. Slang for a drink, usually brandy and soda.
3. Capricious women.
4. The recruiting officers entered on his enlist-

ment form his lie that he was nineteen years old and, therefore, above the minimum age for military service.
5. Regard for the honor and interests of an organization or, as here, a military unit.

I have not been at the front.

I have been in front of it.

I held an advanced post, that is, a 'dug-out' in the middle of No Man's Land.

We had a march of 3 miles over shelled road then nearly 3 along a flooded trench. After that we came to where the trenches had been blown flat out and had to go over the top. It was of course dark, too dark, and the ground was not mud, not sloppy mud, but an octopus of sucking clay, 3, 4, and 5 feet deep, relieved only by craters full of water. Men have been known to drown in them. Many stuck in the mud & only got on by leaving their waders, equipment, and in some cases their clothes.

High explosives were dropping all around out, and machine guns spluttered every few minutes. But it was so dark that even the German flares did not reveal us.

Three quarters dead, I mean each of us ¾ dead, we reached the dug-out, and relieved the wretches therein. I then had to go forth and find another dug-out for a still more advanced post where I left 18 bombers. I was responsible for other posts on the left but there was a junior officer in charge.

My dug-out held 25 men tight packed. Water filled it to a depth of 1 or 2 feet, leaving say 4 feet of air.

One entrance had been blown in & blocked.

So far, the other remained.

The Germans knew we were staying there and decided we shouldn't.

Those fifty hours were the agony of my happy life.

Every ten minutes on Sunday afternoon seemed an hour.

I nearly broke down and let myself drown in the water that was now slowly rising over my knees.

Towards 6 o'clock, when, I suppose, you would be going to church, the shelling grew less intense and less accurate: so that I was mercifully helped to do my duty and crawl, wade, climb and flounder over No Man's Land to visit my other post. It took me half an hour to move about 150 yards.

I was chiefly annoyed by our own machine guns from behind. The seeng-seeng-seeng of the bullets reminded me of Mary's[1] canary. On the whole I can support the canary better.

In the Platoon on my left the sentries over the dug-out were blown to nothing. One of these poor fellows was my first servant whom I rejected. If I had kept him he would have lived, for servants don't do Sentry Duty. I kept my own sentries half way down the stairs during the more terrific bombardment. In spite of this one lad was blown down and, I am afraid, blinded.[2]

31 December 1917

Last year, at this time, (it is just midnight, and now is the intolerable instant of the Change) last year I lay awake in a windy tent in the middle of a vast, dreadful encampment. It seemed neither France nor England, but a kind of paddock where the beasts are kept a few days before the shambles. I heard the revelling of the Scotch troops, who are now dead, and who knew they would be dead. I thought of this present night, and whether I should

---

1. Owen's sister.
2. This incident prompted Owen's poem *The Sentry*.

indeed—whether we should indeed—whether you would indeed—but I thought neither long nor deeply, for I am a master of elision.

But chiefly I thought of the very strange look on all faces in that camp; an incomprehensible look, which a man will never see in England, though wars should be in England; nor can it be seen in any battle. But only in Étaples.[3]

It was not despair, or terror, it was more terrible than terror, for it was a blindfold look, and without expression, like a dead rabbit's.

It will never be painted, and no actor will ever seize it. And to describe it, I think I must go back and be with them.

3. Until 1914, a fishing port of 5,800 inhabitants, Étaples and its surrounding hills housed 100,000 soldiers on their way to and from the front in 1917.

MAY WEDDERBURN CANNAN
1893–1973

Born and educated in Oxford, May Wedderburn Cannan was the daughter of the secretary to the delegates (or chief executive officer) of the Oxford University Press. At eighteen, she joined the Red Cross Voluntary Aid Detachment and, when England entered the war three years later, was active in the Red Cross mobilization, setting up a hospital in a local school. During the early part of the war she worked at Oxford University Press, continued her volunteer nursing, and spent a month as a volunteer worker in a soldiers' canteen in Rouen, France. In 1918 she joined the War Office in Paris to work in intelligence. Her fiancé, Bevil Quiller-Couch, survived the devastating Battle of the Somme and the remainder of the war, only to die of pneumonia several months after the armistice. She later worked at King's College, London, and at the Athenaeum Club as assistant librarian. She married Brigadier P. J. Slater. Cannan wrote three books of poems, *In War Time* (1917), *The Splendid Days* (1919), and *The House of Hope* (1923), and a novel, *The Lonely Generation* (1934). Her unfinished autobiography, *Grey Ghosts and Voices*, was posthumously published in 1976.

Rouen, with its echoes of G. K. Chesterton's incantatory *Tarantella* (beginning "Do you remember an Inn, / Miranda?"), voices emotions closer to those of Rupert Brooke's *The Soldier* than to any given expression by the other soldier poets in this section. In 1917, however, Cannan and Brooke spoke for what was then the majority. As she wrote in her autobiography: "Siegfried Sassoon wrote to the Press from France saying that the war was now a war of conquest and without justification, and declared himself to be a conscientious objector. . . . A saying went round, 'Went to the war with Rupert Brooke and came home with Siegfried Sassoon.' " Her own poems pose an alternative to protest and despair: "I had much admired some of Sassoon's verse but I was not coming home with him. Someone must go on writing for those who were still convinced of the right of the cause for which they had taken up arms."

Rouen

26 April–25 May 1915

Early morning over Rouen, hopeful, high, courageous morning,
And the laughter of adventure and the steepness of the stair,

And the dawn across the river, and the wind across the bridges,
And the empty littered station and the tired people there.

5   Can you recall those mornings and the hurry of awakening,
And the long-forgotten wonder if we should miss the way,
And the unfamiliar faces, and the coming of provisions,
And the freshness and the glory of the labour of the day?

Hot noontide over Rouen, and the sun upon the city,
10   Sun and dust unceasing, and the glare of cloudless skies,
And the voices of the Indians and the endless stream of soldiers,
And the clicking of the tatties,[1] and the buzzing of the flies.

Can you recall those noontides and the reek of steam and coffee,
Heavy-laden noontides with the evening's peace to win,
15   And the little piles of Woodbines,[2] and the sticky soda bottles,
And the crushes[3] in the "Parlour," and the letters coming in?

Quiet night-time over Rouen, and the station full of soldiers,
All the youth and pride of England from the ends of all the earth;
And the rifles piled together, and the creaking of the sword-belts,
20   And the faces bent above them, and the gay, heart-breaking mirth.

Can I forget the passage from the cool white-bedded Aid Post
Past the long sun-blistered coaches of the khaki Red Cross train
To the truck train full of wounded, and the weariness and laughter,
And "Good-bye, and thank-you, Sister,"[4] and the empty yards again?

25   Can you recall the parcels that we made them for the railroad,
Crammed and bulging parcels held together by their string,
And the voices of the sergeants who called the Drafts together,
And the agony and splendour when they stood to save the King?

Can you forget their passing, the cheering and the waving,
30   The little group of people at the doorway of the shed,
The sudden awful silence when the last train swung to darkness,
And the lonely desolation, and the mocking stars o'erhead?

Can you recall the midnights, and the footsteps of night watchers,
Men who came from darkness and went back to dark again,
35   And the shadows on the rail-lines and the all-inglorious labour,
And the promise of the daylight firing blue the window-pane?

Can you recall the passing through the kitchen door to morning,
Morning very still and solemn breaking slowly on the town,
And the early coastways engines that had met the ships at daybreak,
40   And the Drafts just out from England, and the day shift coming down?

1. Screens or mats, usually made of the roots of the fragrant cuscus grass, which are hung in a doorway and kept wet, in order to cool and freshen the air of a room.   2. Popular brand of cheap cigarette. 3. Crowded social gatherings. 4. Nurse.

Can you forget returning slowly, stumbling on the cobbles,
And the white-decked Red Cross barges dropping seawards for the tide,
And the search for English papers, and the blessed cool of water,
And the peace of half-closed shutters that shut out the world outside?

45 Can I forget the evenings and the sunsets on the island,
And the tall black ships at anchor far below our balcony,
And the distant call of bugles, and the white wine in the glasses,
And the long line of the street lamps, stretching Eastwards to the sea?

. . . When the world slips slow to darkness, when the office fire burns
    lower,
50 My heart goes out to Rouen, Rouen all the world away;
When other men remember I remember our Adventure
And the trains that go from Rouen at the ending of the day.

1916

From Grey Ghosts and Voices

I suppose it is difficult for anyone to realise now what "France" meant to us. In the second war I met a young man of the Left who assured me that Rupert Brooke's verse was of no account, phoney, because it was "impossible that anyone should have thought like that." I turned and rent him, saying that he was entitled to his own opinion of Rupert Brooke's verse, but *not* entitled to say that no one could have thought like that. How could he know how we had thought?—All our hopes and all our loves, and God knew, all our fears, were in France; to get to France, if only to stand on her soil, was something; to share, in however small a way, in what was done there was Heart's Desire.

I asked my Father[1] could I take all my holidays in one and go for four weeks to France—I did not want holidays, I said, but I did want France. It was dark and we were walking home through the confines of Little Clarendon Street; my voice, I knew, shook; he took his pipe out of his mouth, halted his step for a moment and looked down at me. "Ah! France," he said, "France, yes I think you should go. We'll manage." I stammered thanks and we walked home in silence, understanding each other.

The Canteen was started at Rouen because Lord Brassey's yacht, *The Sunbeam*, had made two or three journeys there during the shortage of hospital ships bringing wounded home. Lady Mabelle Egerton, his daughter, looking round the desolate railway yards beyond the quays asked the R[ail]. T[ransport]. O[fficer]. if there was anything that could be done for the troops; drafts going up the line to Railhead, who had to spend a long day there, and sometimes a long night.

He said that the men brought their rations, including tea, but that there

---

1. Chief executive of the Oxford University Press, for which his daughter was then also working.

was no means of making hot water. (It was long before the days of another war when motorised infantry "brewed up" with their petrol cans)—Could she find some philanthropic person to take on the job? She could find no one—and decided to do it herself, and so the canteen, later known affectionately to thousands of the B[ritish]. E[xpeditionary]. F[orce]. and the New Armies, as "the Coffee Shop" was born.

I had a passport. I packed. Left as little urgent work behind me as I could, and met Lucie, who I adored, in London. We travelled to Southampton and Hilary, who after sick leave had been posted to a home battalion of his regiment in Hampshire, came to dinner and we sat far into the night talking. He had been in France; I was going, and generously he treated me as if I was one of the fraternity. . . .

I had done nothing about a berth, and there was none to be had so I spent the night curled up, blissfully happy, on a coil of rope in the bow where no one noticed me, and woke in the early morning as we came into Le Havre. There were English soldiers in the streets, and in the cold spring sunshine a battery clattered by. We went up by train to Rouen. Someone had got us a couple of rooms in a small hotel with a restaurant below that overlooked the quays; those same broad quays where Bevil had disembarked. I fell into bed too happy to worry or to dream and went on duty after breakfast next morning.

Along the length of railway line ran a row of sheds with huge sliding doors. In the first, and smaller one, was established a boiler room where enormous vats of hot water forever boiled. * * *

When the big trains were due in we opened the sliding doors of the sheds, the train doors banged and banged down the long line of the corridors and some 2,000 men would surge in. Barricaded behind our heavy table, and thankful for it when the pressure was heavy or a draft[2] had somehow got hold of some drink, we handed out bowls of coffee and sandwiches, washed dirty bowls till the water in the tall vats was chocolate brown, and served again.

Someone would play the piano; Annie Laurie; Loch Lomond.[3] Blurred lanterns lit the scene as best they might when it rained and our candles in the tills under the tables guttered in the wind. One was hot or horrid cold, harried, dirty, and one's feet ached with the stone floors. When the smaller drafts came one could distinguish faces, and regimental badges; have a word or two. * * *

When the whistle blew they stood to save the King[4] and the roof came off the sheds. Two thousand men, maybe, singing—it was the most moving thing I knew. Then there'd be the thunder of seats pushed back, the stamp of army boots on the pavé, and as the train went out they sang Tipperary.[5]

1976

---

2. Group of soldiers.
3. Two Scottish songs.
4. I.e., to sing the British National Anthem, "God

Save the King."
5. Irish song: "It's a long way to Tipperary."

DAVID JONES
1895–1974

David Jones was born in Brockley, Kent, son of a Welsh father and an English mother, and studied at the Camberwell School of Art before joining the army in January 1915 to serve as a private soldier until the end of World War I. It is his experiences during the earlier part of this service that provided the material for his modern epic of war, *In Parenthesis*. He attended Westminster Art School after the war and subsequently made a name for himself as an illustrator, engraver, and water colorist. In 1924 he worked with Eric Gill, the stone carver and engraver whose strong Roman Catholic feeling and belief are reflected in his work, and under Gill's influence he also joined the Roman Catholic church. Jones's joint Welsh and English origins, his visual sensitivity as an artist, and his interest in Catholic liturgy and ritual can be seen in his literary work, which includes the obscure but powerful long religious poem *The Anathémata* (1952) and *The Sleeping Lord and Other Fragments* (1973), as well as *In Parenthesis,* which combines prose and poetry with remarkable effect.

In Parenthesis, Jones's first literary work, was published in 1937 and won the Hawthornden Prize. It is an evocation in forty thousand words of the activities of members of a British infantry unit from its period of training in England to its participation in the murderous Somme offensive of July 1916. The book is epic in scope and tone, echoing in carefully patterned moments themes from English and Welsh history and literature—especially the sixth-century heroic Welsh poem by Aneirin, *Y Gododdin,* which tells of an expedition of three hundred Celtic warriors from Dineidyn (Edinburgh) against a vastly superior force of Saxons at Catraeth (Catterick) to perish except for three survivors, among them the bard himself. *In Parenthesis* avoids the traditional heroic poet's concentration on high-ranking heroes to build the narrative around very ordinary characters, both English and Welsh, who are presented in vivid silhouettes and sudden stabs of personal memory or reflections of them in the eyes of their fellow soldiers—Mr. Jenkins, Sergeant Snell, Corporal Quilter, Lance-Corporal Lewis, and (in a sense the central figure, suggesting the poet himself, the sole if wounded survivor of his unit at the end of the work) Private John Ball. Other characters flit in and out, some real, some legendary, some—like *Dai de la Cote male taille*—both real and legendary.

In a note to *Dai de la Cote male taille* Jones refers us to the *Morte Darthur* of Sir Thomas Malory, book 9, chapter 1, where we find the story of the knight called La Cote Male Tayle, which Malory renders as "The Evyll-Shapyn Cote." *Dai* is the familiar Welsh form of "David"; the addition of heroic echoes from Malory gives this Welsh soldier of World War I another dimension, which the author exploits some pages further on in putting into his mouth an epic boast that is derived from both early Welsh and Anglo-Saxon poetry. He is the same character as Dai Great-coat whom we see among the dead in the concluding section, below.

In Parenthesis is in seven parts, beginning with a battalion parade in England before embarkation for France and moving in later sections ever nearer to the front lines, with a great number of incidental episodes and widenings of reference, until (after a break in time from Christmas Day 1915, to June 1916) we reach the preparations for the offensive, with the battalion moving up ready to attack, the terrible moments before zero hour, and the final action in which John Ball's platoon is destroyed and he himself crawls wounded away from the action. Yet though the work has a chronological sequence, it is far from being a straightforward narrative; there are multiple identifications of present characters with historical or mythological figures; echoes of Christian liturgy and ritual, suggesting that the soldiers are in some way acting out a ritual sacrifice, which contrast with or at least are modified by echoes of Old English and Welsh epic poetry, suggesting that the suffering is to some extent redeemed by willed heroic action.

This war poem (if poem it can be called) could not have been written when Wilfred Owen and Siegfried Sassoon wrote their war poems. For Jones is writing after James Joyce's *Ulysses* and T. S. Eliot's *Waste Land* and is able to profit by the ways in which Joyce and Eliot brought mythology and ritual into narrative to give it a new kind of depth and scope. Eliot himself, in an introduction to a newer edition of the work (New York, 1961), pointed this out. Jones has brought together the committed pity and irony of the serving soldier that we see in Owen with the distanced, more elaborately illustrated, less immediately personal, more completely textured style of Eliot's long poem, and like Eliot, he introduces notes to help the reader in following the mythological and literary references. Another significant difference between Jones and Owen is that Jones's is essentially a religious work. There is a meaning in all this suffering and killing, and in spite of ironies, comic or sardonic reference to popular soldiers' songs, follies and vices and vanities and every kind of trivial behavior that goes to make up the texture of experience for a group of men serving in an army (and here again we can see parallels with similar aspects of *The Waste Land*), the notes of ritual and mystery on the one hand and of history and heroic myth on the other combine to suggest that, although the experience of war was "in parenthesis," bracketed outside normal living, it had its own secret meaning.

The extracts printed here are, first, from Jones's "Preface," in which he explains his intention and method, and, second, from part 7, describing events during and after the attack. At the beginning of the last section quoted, Private John Ball, wounded, is crawling painfully toward the rear through the mingled bodies of British and German soldiers: in his fevered imagination he sees the queen of the Woods distributing flowers to the dead. He then wonders whether he is able to continue carrying his rifle. (At the end of the *Chanson de Roland* the dying Roland tries in vain to shatter his sword, Durendal, to prevent it from being taken as a trophy by the Saracens; he finally puts it under his body. John Ball finally leaves his rifle under an oak tree.) In the end he lies still under the oak beside a dead German and a dead Englishman, hearing the reserves coming forward to continue the battle.

From In Parenthesis

From *Preface*

This writing has to do with some things I saw, felt, & was part of. The period covered begins early in December 1915 and ends early in July 1916. The first date corresponds to my going to France. The latter roughly marks a change in the character of our lives in the Infantry on the West Front. From then onward things hardened into a more relentless, mechanical affair, took on a more sinister aspect. The wholesale slaughter of the later years, the conscripted levies filling the gaps in every file of four, knocked the bottom out of the intimate, continuing, domestic life of small contingents of men, within whose structure Roland could find, and, for a reasonable while, enjoy, his Oliver.[1] In the earlier months there was a certain attractive amateurishness, and elbow-room for idiosyncrasy that connected one with a less exacting past. The period of the individual rifle-man, of the "old sweat" of the Boer campaign, the "Bairns-father"[2] war, seemed to terminate with the

---

1. Roland's close friend and companion-at-arms in the Old French epic *Chanson de Roland* (The song of Roland).

2. Bruce Bairnsfather (1888–1959), English cartoonist and journalist, best known for his sketches of life in the trenches during World War I.

Somme battle. There were, of course, glimpses of it long after—all through in fact—but it seemed never quite the same. * * *

My companions in the war were mostly Londoners with an admixture of Welshmen, so that the mind and folk-life of those two differing racial groups are an essential ingredient to my theme. Nothing could be more representative. These came from London. Those from Wales. Together they bore in their bodies the genuine tradition of the Island of Britain, from Bendigeid Vran to Jingle and Marie Lloyd. These were the children of Doll Tearsheet. Those are before Caractacus[3] was. Both speak in parables, the wit of both is quick, both are natural poets; yet no two groups could well be more dissimilar. It was curious to know them harnessed together, and together caught in the toils of "good order and military discipline"; to see them shape together to the remains of an antique regimental tradition, to see them react to the few things that united us—the same jargon, the same prejudice against "other arms" and against the Staff, the same discomforts, the same grievances, the same maims, the same deep fears, the same pathetic jokes; to watch them, oneself part of them, respond to the war landscape; for I think the day by day in the Waste Land, the sudden violences and the long stillnesses, the sharp contours and unformed voids of that mysterious existence, profoundly affected the imaginations of those who suffered it. It was a place of enchantment. It is perhaps best described in Malory,[4] book iv, chapter 15—that landscape spoke "with a grimly voice."

I suppose at no time did one so much live with a consciousness of the past, the very remote, and the more immediate and trivial past, both superficially and more subtly. No one, I suppose, however much not given to association, could see infantry in tin-hats, with ground-sheets over their shoulders, with sharpened pine-stakes in their hands, and not recall

> . . . or may we cram,
> Within this wooden O . . .[5]

But there were deeper complexities of sight and sound to make ever present

> the pibble pabble in Pompey's camp.[6]

Every man's speech and habit of mind were a perpetual showing: now of Napier's expedition, now of the Legions at the Wall, now of "train-band captain," now of Jack Cade, of John Ball, of the commons in arms. Now of *High Germany*, of *Dolly Gray*, of Bullcalf, Wart and Poins; of Jingo largenesses, of things as small as the Kingdom of Elmet; of Wellington's raw shire recruits, of ancient border antipathies, of our contemporary, less intimate, larger unities, of *John Barleycorn*, of "sweet Sally Frampton." Now of Coel Hên—of the Celtic cycle that lies, a subterranean influence as a deep water

---

3. Caractacus or Caradoc, king of the Silures in the west of Britain during the reign of Roman emperor Claudius. He was taken to Rome as a prisoner in 51 C.E. but was pardoned by Claudius, who was impressed by his nobility of spirit. Bendigeid Vran, hero in Welsh heroic legend. Alfred Jingle, character in Dickens's *Pickwick Papers*. Marie

Lloyd (real name Matilda Alice Victoria Wood), English music-hall comedienne. Doll Tearsheet, prostitute in 2 *Henry IV*.
4. Sir Thomas Malory, author of *Morte Darthur*.
5. *Henry V*, prologue. The "wooden O" is the stage of the theater.
6. *Henry V* 4.1.

troubling, under every tump[7] in this Island, like Merlin[8] complaining under his big rock.[9] * * *

* * *

This writing is called *In Parenthesis* because I have written it in a kind of space between—I don't know between quite what—but as you turn aside to do something; and because for us amateur soldiers (and especially for the writer, who was not only amateur, but grotesquely incompetent, a knocker-over of piles, a parade's despair) the war itself was a parenthesis—how glad we thought we were to step outside its brackets at the end of '18—and also because our curious type of existence here is altogether in parenthesis.

D. J.

From *Part 7: The Five Unmistakeable Marks*[1]

Gododdin I demand thy support.
It is our duty to sing: a meeting
place has been found.[2]

* * *

The gentle slopes are green to remind you
of South English places, only far wider and flatter spread and grooved and
harrowed criss-cross whitely and the disturbed subsoil heaped up albescent.[3]

Across upon this undulated board of verdure[4] chequered bright
when you look to left and right
small, drab, bundled pawns severally make effort
moved in tenuous line
and if you looked behind—the next wave came slowly, as successive surfs
creep in to dissipate on flat shore;
and to your front, stretched long laterally,
and receded deeply,
the dark wood.

And now the gradient runs more flatly toward the separate scarred saplings,
where they make fringe for the interior thicket and you take notice.

---

7. Mound or tumulus.
8. The powerful enchanter of the Arthurian legends.
9. The mass of references here provide a wide area of historical and literary association, beginning with *Henry V* and going on to refer to Sir William Napier, who fought in the Peninsular War and later wrote a famous history of that campaign; to the Roman legions who manned the Great Wall built by the Romans in Britain; to Jack Cade, who led an unsuccessful popular revolt against the misrule of Henry VI in 1450, and John Ball, a leader of the Peasants' Revolt of 1381; to a number of English ballads and popular songs and to characters in *Henry IV*; to the ancient British kingdom of Elmet in southwest Yorkshire, finally overthrown by Anglo-Saxon invaders early in the 7th century; to Wellington's "raw shire recruits" who helped to win the Battle of Waterloo; and concluding with a reference to the old Celtic British myths that lie beneath everything.

1. Carroll's *Hunting of the Snark,* Fit the 2nd verse 15 [Jones's note]. Lewis Carroll's mock-heroic nonsense poem concerns the hunting of the elusive animal Snark, which may be known by "five unmistakable marks." A reference to the five wounds of the crucified Christ may also be intended.
2. From *Y Gododdin,* early Welsh epical poem attributed to Aneirin (6th century); commemorates raid of 300 Welsh of Gododdin (the territory of the Otadini located near the Firth of Forth) into English kingdom of Deira. Describes the ruin of this 300 in battle at Catraeth (perhaps Catterick in Yorkshire). Three men alone escaped death, including the poet, who laments his friends [Jones's note].
3. Becoming white.
4. Green vegetation.

There between the thinning uprights
at the margin
straggle tangled oak and flayed sheeny beech-bole, and fragile birch
 whose silver queenery is draggled and ungraced
and June shoots lopt
and fresh stalks bled
   runs the Jerry[5] trench.
And cork-screw stapled trip-wire
to snare among the briars
and iron warp with bramble weft[6]
with meadow-sweet and lady-smock
for a fair camouflage.

Mr Jenkins half inclined his head to them—he walked just barely in advance
of his platoon and immediately to the left of Private Ball.
 He makes the conventional sign
and there is the deeply inward effort of spent men who would make response
for him,
and take it at the double.
He sinks on one knee
and now on the other,
his upper body tilts in rigid inclination
this way and back;
weighted lanyard[7] runs out to full tether,
   swings like a pendulum
   and the clock run down.
Lurched over, jerked iron saucer over tilted brow,
clampt unkindly over lip and chin
nor no ventaille[8] to this darkening
   and masked face lifts to grope the air
and so disconsolate;
enfeebled fingering at a paltry strap—
buckle holds,
holds him blind against the morning.
 Then stretch still where weeds pattern the chalk predella[9]—
where it rises to his wire[1]—and Sergeant T. Quilter takes over.

     * * *

It's difficult with the weight of the rifle.
Leave it—under the oak.
Leave it for a salvage-bloke[2]
let it lie bruised for a monument
dispense the authenticated fragments to the faithful.
It's the thunder-besom for us
it's the bright bough borne

---

5. British army slang for "German" in both world
wars.
6. Warp and weft are the horizontal and vertical
threads of woven cloth.
7. Short cord (here "weighted" by a whistle).

8. Hinged visor of a helmet.
9. A platform or shelf below or behind an altar.
1. The approach to the German trenches here
rose slightly, in low chalk ridges [Jones's note].
2. Man (slang).

it's the tensioned yew for a Genoese jammed arbalest[3] and a scarlet square for a mounted *mareschal*,[4] it's that county-mob back to back.[5] Majuba mountain and Mons Cherubim[6] and spreaded mats for Sydney Street East,[7] and come to Bisley for a Silver Dish.[8] It's R. S. M. O'Grady[9] says, it's the soldier's best friend if you care for the working parts and let us be 'aving those springs released smartly in Company billets on wet forenoons and clickerty-click and one up the spout and you men must really cultivate the habit of treating this weapon with the very greatest care and there should be a healthy rivalry among you—it should be a matter of very proper pride and

Marry it man! Marry it!
Cherish her, she's your very own.

Coax it man coax it—it's delicately and ingeniously made—it's an instrument of precision—it costs us tax-payers, money—I want you men to remember that.

Fondle it like a granny—talk to it—consider it as you would a friend—and when you ground these arms she's not a rooky's gas-pipe for greenhorns to tarnish.[1]

You've known her hot and cold.
You would choose her from among many.
You know her by her bias, and by her exact error at 300, and by the deep scar at the small, by the fair flaw in the grain, above the lower sling-swivel—but leave it under the oak.

* * *

The secret princes between the leaning trees have diadems given them.

Life the leveller hugs her impudent equality—she may proceed at once to less discriminating zones.

The Queen of the Woods has cut bright boughs of various flowering.

These knew her influential eyes. Her awarding hands can pluck for each their fragile prize.

She speaks to them according to precedence. She knows what's due to this elect society. She can choose twelve gentle-men. She knows who is most lord between the high trees and on the open down.

Some she gives white berries
    some she gives brown

---

3. A powerful medieval crossbow.
4. Marshal (French).
5. The Gloucestershire Regiment, during an action near Alexandria, in 1801, about-turned their rear rank and engaged the enemy back to back [Jones's note].
6. The British were defeated by the Boers on Majuba Hill on February 27, 1881. The "Angels of Mons" were angels (varying in number from two to a platoon) widely believed to have assisted the British to repel an attack at Mons by superior German forces on August 23, 1914.
7. In what became known as the Siege or Battle of Sydney Street, Winston Churchill, when he was home secretary in 1911, directed military operations in London against a group of anarchists. "It

is said that in 'The Battle of Sydney Street' under Mr. Churchill's Home Secretaryship mats were spread on the pavement for troops firing from the prone position" [Jones's note].
8. At Bisley marksmen compete annually in rifle shooting for such trophies as "a Silver Dish."
9. "R.S.M.": Regimental sergeant major. "R.S.M. O'Grady," according to Jones's note, "refers to mythological personage figuring in Army exercises, the precise describing of which would be tedious. Anyway these exercises were supposed to foster alertness in dull minds—and were a curious blend of the parlour game and military drill."
1. I have employed here only such ideas as were common to the form of speech affected by Instructors in Musketry [Jones's note].

Emil has a curious crown it's
   made of golden saxifrage.
Fatty wears sweet-briar,
he will reign with her for a thousand years.
For Balder she reaches high to fetch his.
Ulrich smiles for his myrtle wand.
That swine Lillywhite has daisies to his chain—you'd hardly credit it.
She plaits torques[2] of equal splendour for Mr Jenkins and Billy Crower.
Hansel with Gronwy share dog-violets for a palm, where they lie in serious embrace beneath the twisted tripod.
Siôn gets St John's Wort—that's fair enough.
Dai Great-coat,[3] she can't find him anywhere—she calls both high and low, she had a very special one for him.
Among this July noblesse she is mindful of December wood—when the trees of the forest beat against each other because of him.
She carries to Aneirin-in-the-nullah[4] a rowan[5] sprig, or the glory of Guenedota.[6] You couldn't hear what she said to him, because she was careful for the Disciplines of the Wars.

At the gate of the wood you try a last adjustment, but slung so, it's an impediment, it's of detriment to your hopes, you had best be rid of it—the sagging webbing and all and what's left of your two fifty[7]—but it were wise to hold on to your mask.

You're clumsy in your feebleness, you implicate your tin-hat rim with the slack sling of it.
   Let it lie for the dews to rust it, or ought you to decently cover the working parts.
   Its dark barrel, where you leave it under the oak, reflects the solemn star that rises urgently from Cliff Trench.
   It's a beautiful doll for us
it's the Last Reputable Arm.
   But leave it—under the oak.
leave it for a Cook's tourist to the Devastated Areas and crawl as far
   as you can and wait for the bearers.[8]

1937

---

2. Collars, like those of gold worn by warriors of *Y Gododdin*.
3. See headnote (p. 2078).
4. A river, stream, or riverbed.
5. Also called mountain ash, a tree with magical properties in Celtic folklore.
6. The northwest parts of Wales. The last king of Wales, Llywelyn, was killed there in 1282. Jones refers to his death in another note on this part of Wales. He adds: "His [Llywelyn's] contemporary, Gruffydd ap yr Ynad Côch, sang of his death: 'The voice of lamentation is heard in every place . . . the course of nature is changed . . . the trees of the for-est furiously rush against each other.' "
7. Two hundred and fifty rounds of ammunition.
8. This may appear to be an anachronism, but I remember in 1917 discussing with a friend the possibilities of tourist activity if peace ever came. I remember we went into details and wondered if the unexploded projectile lying near us would go up under a holiday-maker, and how people would stand to up to be photographed on our parapets. I recall feeling very angry about this, as you do if you think of strangers ever occupying a house you live in, and which has, for you, particular associations [Jones's note].

WILLIAM BUTLER YEATS
1865–1939

William Butler Yeats was born in Sandymount, Dublin. His father's family, of English stock, had been in Ireland for at least two hundred years; his mother's, the Pollexfens, hailing originally from Devon, had been for some generations in Sligo, in the west of Ireland. J. B. Yeats, his father, had abandoned law to take up painting, at which he made a somewhat precarious living. The Yeatses were in London from 1874 until 1883, when they returned to Ireland—to Howth, a few miles from Dublin. On leaving high school in Dublin in 1883 Yeats decided to be an artist, with poetry as his avocation, and attended art school; but he soon left, to concentrate on poetry. His first published poems appeared in the *Dublin University Review* in 1885.

Yeats's father was a religious skeptic, but he believed in the "religion of art." Yeats himself, religious by temperament but unable to believe in Christian orthodoxy, sought all his life for traditions of esoteric thought that would compensate for a lost religion. This search led him to various kinds of mysticism, to folklore, theosophy, spiritualism, and neoplatonism—not in any strict chronological order, for he kept returning to and reworking earlier aspects of his thought. In middle life he elaborated a symbolic system of his own, based on a variety of sources, that enabled him to strengthen the pattern and coherence of his poetic imagery. The student of Yeats is constantly coming up against this willful and sometimes baffling esotericism that he cultivated sometimes playfully, sometimes earnestly, sometimes treating it as though it were a body of truths and sometimes as though it were a convenient language of symbols. Modern scholarship has traced most of Yeats's mystical and quasi-mystical ideas to sources that were common to William Blake and Percy Shelley and that sometimes go far back into pre-Platonic beliefs and traditions. But his greatness as a poet lies in his ability to communicate the power and significance of his symbols, by the way he expresses and organizes them, even to readers who know nothing of his system.

Yeats's childhood and young manhood were spent between Dublin, London, and Sligo; and each of these places contributed something to his poetic development. In London in the 1890s he met the important poets of the day; and in 1891 was one of the founders of the Rhymers' Club, whose members included Lionel Johnson, Ernest Dowson, and many other characteristic figures of the 1890s. Here he acquired ideas of poetry that were vaguely Pre-Raphaelite: he believed, in this early stage of his career, that a poet's language should be dreamy, evocative, and ethereal. From the countryside around Sligo he got something much more vigorous and earthy—a knowledge of the life of the peasantry and of their folklore. In Dublin he was influenced by the currents of Irish nationalism and, although often in disagreement with those who wished to use literature for crude political ends, he nevertheless learned to see his poetry as a contribution to a rejuvenated Irish culture. The three influences of Dublin, London, and Sligo did not develop in chronological order—he was going to and fro among these places throughout his early life—and we sometimes find a poem based on Sligo folklore in the midst of a group of dreamy poems written under the influence of the Rhymers' Club or an echo of Irish nationalist feeling in a lyric otherwise wholly Pre-Raphaelite in tone.

We can distinguish quite clearly, however, the main periods into which Yeats's poetic career falls. He began in the tradition of self-conscious Romanticism, which he learned from the London poets of the 1890s. Edmund Spenser and Shelley, and a little later Blake, were also important influences. One of his early verse plays ends with a song:

> The woods of Arcady are dead
> And over is their antique joy;

Of old the world on dreaming fed;
Grey Truth is now her painted toy.

About the same time he was writing poems (e.g., *The Stolen Child*) deriving from his Sligo experience, with a quiet precision of natural imagery, country place names, and themes from folklore. A little later—i.e., in the latter part of his first period—Dublin literary circles sent him to Standish O'Grady's *History of Ireland: Heroic Period*, where he found the great stories of the heroic age of Irish history, and to George Sigerson's and Douglas Hyde's translations of Gaelic poetry into "that dialect which gets from Gaelic its syntax and keeps its still partly Tudor vocabulary." Even when he plays with Neoplatonic ideas, as in *The Rose of the World* (also the product of the latter part of his early period), he can link them with Irish heroic themes and so give a dignity and a *style* to his imagery not normally associated with this sort of poetic dreaminess. Thus the heroic legends of old Ireland and the folk traditions of the modern Irish countryside provided Yeats with a stiffening for his early dreamlike imagery, which is why even his first, "nineties" phase is productive of interesting poems. *The Lake Isle of Innisfree*, spoiled for some by overanthologizing, is nevertheless a fine poem of its kind: it is the clarity and control shown in the handling of the imagery that keeps all romantic fuzziness out of it and gives it its haunting quality. In *The Man Who Dreamed of Faeryland* he makes something peculiarly effective out of the contrast between human activities and the strangeness of nature. In *The Madness of King Goll* the disturbing sense of the *otherness* of the natural world drives the king mad. (Such contrasts are common in the early Yeats; in his later poetry he tries to resolve what he called these "antinomies" in inclusive symbols; e.g., *Crazy Jane Talks with the Bishop*.)

It is important to realize that Yeats had a habit of revising his earlier poems in later printings, tightening up the language and getting rid of the more self-indulgent romantic imagery. The revised versions are found in his *Collected Poems*, which, therefore, present a somewhat muted picture of his poetic development. For the complete picture one should consult *The Variorum Edition* edited by Peter Allt and Russell K. Alspach (1957).

It was Irish nationalism that first sent Yeats in search of a consistently simpler and more popular style. He tells in one of his autobiographical essays how he sought for a style in which to express the elemental facts about Irish life and aspirations. This led him to the concrete image, as did Hyde's translations from Gaelic folk songs, in which "nothing . . . was abstract, nothing worn-out." But other forces were also working on him. In 1902 a friend gave him the works of the German philosopher Friedrich Nietzsche, to which he responded with great excitement, and it would seem that, in persuading Yeats, the passive love-poet, to get off his knees, Nietzsche's books prompted his search for a more active stance, a more masculine style. Looking back in 1906, he found that he had mistaken the poetic ideal. "Without knowing it, I had come to care for nothing but impersonal beauty. . . . We should ascend out of common interests, the thoughts of the newspapers, of the market place, but only so far as we can carry the normal, passionate, reasoning self, the personality as a whole." The result of the abandonment of "impersonal beauty," and of the desire to "carry the normal, passionate, reasoning self" into his poetry, is seen in the volumes of collected poems, *In the Seven Woods* (1903) and *The Green Helmet and Other Poems* (1910). *The Folly of Being Comforted* and *Adam's Curse* are from the former of these, and one can see immediately how Yeats here combines the colloquial with the formal. This is characteristic of his "second period."

By this time Yeats had met the beautiful actress and violent Irish nationalist Maud Gonne, with whom he was desperately in love for many years, but who persistently refused to marry him. The affair is reflected in many of the poems of his second period, notably *No Second Troy*, published in *The Green Helmet*. He had also met Lady Gregory, Irish writer and promoter of Irish literature, in 1896, and she invited him to spend the following summer at her country house, Coole Park, in Galway. Yeats spent many holidays with Lady Gregory and discovered the attractiveness of the "country house ideal," seeing in an aristocratic life of elegance and leisure in a great house a method of imposing order on chaos and a symbol of the Neoplatonic dance of life. He expresses this view many times in his poetry—e.g., at the end of *A Prayer for My Daughter*—and it became an important part of his complex of attitudes. The middle classes, with their Philistine money grubbing, he detested, and for his ideal characters he looked either below them, to peasants and beggars, or above them, to the aristocracy, for each of these had their own traditions and lived according to them.

It was under Lady Gregory's influence that Yeats became involved in the founding of the Irish National Theatre in 1899. This led to his active participation in problems of play production, which included political problems of censorship, economic problems of paying carpenters and actors, and other aspects of "theater business, management of men." All this had an effect on his style. The reactions of Dublin audiences did not encourage Yeats's trust in popular judgment, and his bitterness with the "Paudeens," middle-class shopkeepers—who seemed to him to be without any dignity, or understanding, or nobility of spirit—produced some of the most effective poems of his third or middle period. He was now becoming more and more of a national figure. Three public controversies had moved him to anger and to poetry; the first over the hounding of Parnell (*To a Shade*), the second over Synge's play *The Playboy of the Western World* in 1907, and the third over the Lane pictures (*September 1913*). In each, the cause for which he fought was defeated by representatives of the Roman Catholic middle class, and at last, bitterly turning his back on Ireland, Yeats moved to England. Then came the Easter Rising (*Easter 1916*), mounted by members of the class and religion that had so long opposed him. Persuaded by Gonne (whose estranged husband was one of the executed leaders of the rising) that "tragic dignity had returned to Ireland," Yeats himself returned. To mark his new commitment, he refurbished, occupied, and renamed "Thoor Ballylee" the Norman tower on Lady Gregory's land that was to become one of the central symbols of his later poetry. In 1922 he was appointed a senator of the recently established Irish Free State and served until 1928, playing an active part not only in promoting the arts but also in general political affairs, in which he supported the views of the Protestant landed class.

Meanwhile Yeats was responding in his own way to the change in poetic taste represented in the poetry and criticism of Ezra Pound and T. S. Eliot immediately before World War I. A gift for epigram had already begun to emerge in his poetry; in the volume titled *The Wild Swans at Coole* (1919) he has a poem citing Walter Savage Landor (the nineteenth-century poet who wrote some fine lapidary verse) and John Donne as masters. To the precision, and the combination of colloquial and formal, that he had achieved early in the century, he now added a metaphysical as well as an epigrammatic element, and this is seen in the later poems of his third period. He also continued his experiments with different kinds of rhythm. At the same time he was continuing his search for a language of symbols and pursuing his esoteric studies. Yeats married in 1917, and his wife proved so sympathetic to his imaginative needs that the automatic writing which for several years she produced (believed by Yeats to have been dictated by spirits) gave him the elements of a symbolic system that he later worked out in his book *A Vision* (1925, 1937) and that he used in all sorts of ways in much of his later poetry. The system was both a theory of the movements of history and a theory of the different types of personality, each movement and type being related in various complicated ways to a different phase of the moon. Some of Yeats's poetry is unintelligible without a knowledge of *A Vision*, but the better poems, such as the two on Byzantium, can be appreciated without such knowledge by the experienced reader who responds sensitively to the patterning of the imagery reinforced by the incantatory effect of the rhythms. Some criticism decries attempts by those who are not experts in the background of Yeats's esoteric thought to discuss his poetry and insists that only a detailed knowledge of Yeats's sources can yield his poetic meaning; but while it is true that some particular images do not yield all their significance to those who are ignorant of the background, it is also true that too literal a paraphrase of the symbolism in the light of the sources robs the poems of their power by reducing them to mere exercises in the use of a code.

The Tower (1928) and *The Winding Stair* (1933), from which the poems from *Sailing to Byzantium* through *After Long Silence* have been here selected, represent the mature Yeats at his very best—a realist-symbolist-Metaphysical poet with an uncanny power over words. These volumes represent his fourth and greatest period. Here, in his poems of the 1920s and 1930s, winding stairs, spinning tops, "gyres," spirals of all kinds, are important symbols; not only are they connected with Yeats's philosophy of history and of personality but they also serve as a means of resolving some of those contraries that had arrested him from the beginning. Life is a journey up a spiral staircase; as we grow older we cover the ground we have covered before, only higher up; as we look down the winding stair below us we measure our progress by the number of places where we were but no longer are. The journey is both repetitious and progressive; we go both round and upward. Through symbolic images of this kind Yeats explores the paradoxes of time and change, of growth and identity, of love and age, of life and art, of madness and wisdom.

The Byzantium poems show him trying to escape from the turbulence of life to the calm eternity of art. But in his fifth and final period he returned to the turbulence after (if only partly as a result of) undergoing the Steinach operation to increase his sexual potency in 1934, and his last poems have a controlled yet startling wildness. Yeats's return to life, to "the foul rag-and-bone shop of the heart," is one of the most impressive final phases of any poet's career. "I shall be a sinful man to the end, and think upon my deathbed of all the nights I wasted in my youth," he wrote in old age to a correspondent, and in one of his last letters he wrote: "When I try to put all into a phrase I say, 'Man can embody truth but he cannot know it.' . . . The abstract is not life and everywhere draws out its contradictions. You can refute Hegel but not the Saint or the Song of Sixpence." When he died in January 1939, he left a body of verse that, in variety and power, makes him beyond question the greatest twentieth-century poet of the English language.

The Madness of King Goll[1]

I sat on cushioned otter-skin:
My word was law from Ith to Emain,[2]
And shook at Inver Amergin
The hearts of the world-troubling seamen,
5 And drove tumult and war away
From girl and boy and man and beast;
The fields grew fatter day by day,
The wild fowl of the air increased;
And every ancient Ollave° said,   *learned man, bard*
10 While he bent down his fading head,

---

1. Originally titled *King Goll, An Irish Legend*, this poem was much revised, and it is the revised version that is printed here. (In all cases of revision, we print the version revised by Yeats for his *Collected Poems*.) The legend tells of an ancient Irish king, who went mad and hid himself in a valley near Cork, where all the madmen of Ireland were believed to wish to gather if they were free. Yeats's father painted his son (in the latter's words) "as

King Goll, tearing the strings out of a harp, being insane with youth."
2. The ancient Irish place names evoke the old heroic legends of Ireland. "Emain," said to have been founded by Queen Macha of the Golden Hair (3rd or 4th century B.C.E.), was in County Armagh (Armagh-Ard-macha, hill of Macha); it is now Navan Rath.

"He drives away the Northern cold."
They will not hush, the leaves a-flutter round me,
the beech leaves old.

I sat and mused and drank sweet wine;
A herdsman came from inland valleys,
15   Crying, the pirates drove his swine
To fill their dark-beaked hollow galleys.
I called my battle-breaking men
And my loud brazen battle-cars
From rolling vale and rivery glen;
20   And under the blinking of the stars
Fell on the pirates by the deep,
And hurled them in the gulph of sleep:
These hands won many a torque° of gold.   *collar*
They will not hush, the leaves a-flutter round me,
the beech leaves old.

25   But slowly, as I shouting slew
And trampled in the bubbling mire,
In my most secret spirit grew
A whirling and a wandering fire:
I stood: keen stars above me shone,
30   Around me shone keen eyes of men:
I laughed aloud and hurried on
By rocky shore and rushy fen;
I laughed because birds fluttered by,
And starlight gleamed, and clouds flew high,
35   And rushes waved and waters rolled.
They will not hush, the leaves a-flutter round me,
the beech leaves old.

And now I wander in the woods
When summer gluts the golden bees,
Or in autumnal solitudes
40   Arise the leopard-coloured trees;
Or when along the wintry strands
The cormorants shiver on their rocks;
I wander on, and wave my hands,
And sing, and shake my heavy locks.
45   The grey wolf knows me; by one ear
I lead along the woodland deer;
The hares run by me growing bold.
They will not hush, the leaves a-flutter round me,
the beech leaves old.

I came upon a little town
50   That slumbered in the harvest moon,
And passed a-tiptoe up and down,
Murmuring, to a fitful tune,
How I have followed, night and day,
A tramping of tremendous feet,

55   And saw where this old tympan[3] lay
     Deserted on a doorway seat,
     And bore it to the woods with me;
     Of some inhuman misery
     Our married voices wildly trolled.
60   *They will not hush, the leaves a-flutter round me,*
         the beech leaves old.

     I sang how, when day's toil is done,
     Orchil shakes out her long dark hair
     That hides away the dying sun
     And sheds faint odours through the air:
65   When my hand passed from wire to wire
     It quenched, with sound like falling dew,
     The whirling and the wandering fire;
     But lift a mournful ulalu,
     For the kind wires are torn and still,
70   And I must wander wood and hill
     Through summer's heat and winter's cold.
     They will not hush, the leaves a-flutter round me,
         the beech leaves old.

1884   1887, 1888

The Stolen Child

     Where dips the rocky highland
     Of Sleuth Wood[1] in the lake,
     There lies a leafy island
     Where flapping herons wake
5   The drowsy water-rats;
     There we've hid our faery vats,
     Full of berries
     And of reddest stolen cherries.
     Come away, O human child!
10   *To the waters and the wild*
     With a faery, hand in hand,
     For the world's more full of weeping than you can understand.

     Where the wave of moonlight glosses
     The dim grey sands with light,
15   Far off by furthest Rosses
     We foot it all the night,
     Weaving olden dances,
     Mingling hands and mingling glances
     Till the moon has taken flight;
20   To and fro we leap

---

3. Ancient Irish stringed instrument played with a bow.
1. This and other places mentioned in the poem are in County Sligo, in northwestern Ireland, where Yeats spent much of his childhood.

And chase the frothy bubbles,
While the world is full of troubles
And is anxious in its sleep.
Come away, O human child!
25 *To the waters and the wild*
With a faery, hand in hand,
For the world's more full of weeping than you can understand.

Where the wandering water gushes
From the hills above Glen-Car,
30 In pools among the rushes
That scarce could bathe a star,
We seek for slumbering trout
And whispering in their ears
Give them unquiet dreams;
35 Leaning softly out
From ferns that drop their tears
Over the young streams.
Come away, O human child!
To the waters and the wild
40 *With a faery, hand in hand,*
For the world's more full of weeping than you can understand.

Away with us he's going,
The solemn-eyed:
He'll hear no more the lowing
45 Of the calves on the warm hillside
Or the kettle on the hob
Sing peace into his breast,
Or see the brown mice bob
Round and round the oatmeal-chest.
50 *For he comes, the human child,*
To the waters and the wild
With a faery, hand in hand,
From a world more full of weeping than he can understand.

1886, 1889

Down by the Salley Gardens[1]

Down by the salley gardens my love and I did meet;
She passed the salley gardens with little snow-white feet.
She bid me take love easy, as the leaves grow on the tree;
But I being young and foolish, with her would not agree.

5 In a field by the river my love and I did stand,
And on my leaning shoulder she laid her snow-white hand.

1. Originally titled *An Old Song Resung,* with Yeats's footnote: "This is an attempt to reconstruct an old song from three lines imperfectly remembered by an old peasant woman in the village of Ballysodare, Sligo, who often sings them to herself." "Salley": a variant of *sallow,* a species of willow tree.

She bid me take life easy, as the grass grows on the weirs;
But I was young and foolish, and now am full of tears.

1889

The Rose of the World[1]

Who dreamed that beauty passes like a dream?
For these red lips, with all their mournful pride,
Mournful that no new wonder may betide,
Troy passed away in one high funeral gleam,
5   And Usna's children died.[2]

We and the labouring world are passing by:
Amid men's souls, that waver and give place
Like the pale waters in their wintry race,
Under the passing stars, foam of the sky,
10 Lives on this lonely face.

Bow down, archangels, in your dim abode:
Before you were, or any hearts to beat,
Weary and kind one lingered by His seat;
He made the world to be a grassy road
15 Before her wandering feet.

1892

The Lake Isle of Innisfree[1]

I will arise and go now, and go to Innisfree,
And a small cabin build there, of clay and wattles[2] made;
Nine bean-rows will I have there, a hive for the honey-bee,
And live alone in the bee-loud glade.

5   And I shall have some peace there, for peace comes dropping slow,
Dropping from the veils of the morning to where the cricket sings;
There midnight's all a glimmer, and noon a purple glow,
And evening full of the linnet's wings.

I will arise and go now, for always night and day
10 I hear lake water lapping with low sounds by the shore;

---

1. The platonic idea of eternal beauty. "I notice upon reading these poems for the first time for several years that the quality symbolized as The Rose differs from the Intellectual Beauty of Shelley and of Spenser in that I have imagined it as suffering with man and not as something pursued and seen from afar" [Yeats, in 1925].

2. In Old Irish legend the Ulster warrior Naoise, son of Usna or Usnach (pronounced Úskna) carried off the beautiful Deirdre, whom King Con-

chubar of Ulster had intended to marry, and with his two brothers took her to Scotland. Eventually Conchubar lured the four of them back to Ireland and killed the three brothers.

1. Island in Lough Gill, County Sligo. "My father had read to me some passage out of [Thoreau's] *Walden*, and I planned to live some day in a cottage on a little island called Innisfree." For the origin of this poem, see p. 2130.

2. Stakes interwoven with twigs or branches.

While I stand on the roadway, or on the pavements grey,
I hear it in the deep heart's core.

1890   1890, 1892

The Sorrow of Love[1]

The brawling of a sparrow in the eaves,
The brilliant moon and all the milky sky,
And all that famous harmony of leaves,
Had blotted out man's image and his cry.

5   A girl arose that had red mournful lips
And seemed the greatness of the world in tears,
Doomed like Odysseus and the labouring ships
And proud as Priam murdered with his peers;[2]

Arose, and on the instant clamorous eaves,
10 A climbing moon upon an empty sky,
And all that lamentation of the leaves,
Could but compose man's image and his cry.

1891   1892, 1925

When You Are Old[1]

When you are old and grey and full of sleep,
And nodding by the fire, take down this book,
And slowly read, and dream of the soft look
Your eyes had once, and of their shadows deep;

5   How many loved your moments of glad grace,
And loved your beauty with love false or true,
But one man loved the pilgrim soul in you,
And loved the sorrows of your changing face;

And bending down beside the glowing bars,[2]
10 Murmur, a little sadly, how Love fled
And paced upon the mountains overhead
And hid his face amid a crowd of stars.

1891   1892

---

1. For the author's revisions while composing this poem, see "Poems in Process," in the appendices to this volume.
2. Odysseus (whom the Romans called Ulysses), hero of Homer's *Odyssey*, which describes how, after having fought in the siege of Troy, he wandered for ten years before reaching his home, the Greek island of Ithaca. Priam was king of Troy at the time of the siege and was killed when the

Greeks captured the city.
1. A poem suggested by a sonnet of the 16th-century French poet Pierre de Ronsard; it begins *"Quand vous serez bien vieille, au soir, à la chandelle"* ("When you are old, sitting at evening by candle light") but ends very differently from Yeats's poem.
2. I.e., of the grate.

Who Goes with Fergus?[1]

Who will go drive with Fergus now,
And pierce the deep wood's woven shade,
And dance upon the level shore?
Young man, lift up your russet brow,
5 And lift your tender eyelids, maid,
And brood on hopes and fear no more.

And no more turn aside and brood
Upon love's bitter mystery;
For Fergus rules the brazen cars,°   *bronze chariots*
10 And rules the shadows of the wood,
And the white breast of the dim sea
And all dishevelled wandering stars.

1893

The Man Who Dreamed of Faeryland

He stood among a crowd at Dromahair;[1]
His heart hung all upon a silken dress,
And he had known at last some tenderness,
Before earth took him to her stony care;
5 But when a man poured fish into a pile,
It seemed they raised their little silver heads,
And sang what gold morning or evening sheds
Upon a woven world-forgotten isle
Where people love beside the ravelled[2] seas;
10 That Time can never mar a lover's vows
Under that woven changeless roof of boughs:
The singing shook him out of his new ease.

He wandered by the sands of Lissadell;
His mind ran all on money cares and fears,
15 And he had known at last some prudent years
Before they heaped his grave under the hill;
But while he passed before a plashy place,
A lug-worm with its grey and muddy mouth
Sang that somewhere to north or west or south
20 There dwelt a gay, exulting, gentle race
Under the golden or the silver skies;
That if a dancer stayed his hungry foot
It seemed the sun and moon were in the fruit:
And at that singing he was no more wise.

---

1. In a late version of this Irish heroic legend, Fergus, "king of the proud Red Branch Kings," gave up his throne voluntarily to King Conchubar of Ulster to learn by dreaming and meditating the bitter wisdom of the poet and philosopher.
1. This and other place names in the poem refer to places in County Sligo.
2. Tangled; here turbulent.

25   He mused beside the well of Scanavin,
       He mused upon his mockers: without fail
       His sudden vengeance were a country tale,
       When earthy night had drunk his body in;
       But one small knot-grass growing by the pool
30   Sang where—unnecessary cruel voice—
       Old silence bids its chosen race rejoice,
       Whatever ravelled waters rise and fall
       Or stormy silver fret the gold of day,
       And midnight there enfold them like a fleece
35   And lover there by lover be at peace.
       The tale drove his fine angry mood away.

       He slept under the hill of Lugnagall;
       And might have known at last unhaunted sleep
       Under that cold and vapour-turbaned steep,
40   Now that the earth had taken man and all:
       Did not the worms that spired about his bones
       Proclaim with that unwearied, reedy cry
       That God has laid His fingers on the sky,
       That from those fingers glittering summer runs
45   Upon the dancer by the dreamless wave.
       Why should those lovers that no lovers miss
       Dream, until God burn Nature with a kiss?
       The man has found no comfort in the grave.

                         1891, 1892

The Secret Rose[1]

    Far-off, most secret, and inviolate Rose,
    Enfold me in my hour of hours; where those
    Who sought thee in the Holy Sepulchre,
    Or in the wine-vat, dwell beyond the stir
5   And tumult of defeated dreams; and deep
    Among pale eyelids, heavy with the sleep

1. The Rose is a symbol of beauty (see *The Rose of the World*, p. 2092). Yeats reveals in an interesting note how he used his sources: "I find that I have unintentionally changed the old story of Conchubar's death. He did not see the Crucifixion in a vision but was told of it . . . I have imagined Cuchulain meeting Fand 'walking among the flaming dew,' because, I think, of something in Mr. Standish O'Grady's books. [See headnote, p. 2086.] I have founded the man 'who drove the gods out of their liss,' or fort, upon something I have read about Caoilte after the battle of Gabhra, when almost all his companions were killed, driving the gods out of their liss, . . . I have founded 'the proud dreaming kind' upon Fergus, the son of Rogh, but when I wrote my poem here, and in the song in my early book, 'Who will drive with Fergus now?' I only knew him in Mr. Standish O'Grady, . . . I have founded 'him who sold tillage, and house, and goods,' upon something in 'The Red Pony,' a folktale in Mr. Larminie's *West Irish Folk Tales.* A young man 'saw a light before him on the high-road. When he came as far, there was an open box on the road, and a light coming up out of it. He took up the box. There was a lock of hair in it. Presently he had to go to become the servant of a king for his living. There were eleven boys. When they were going out into the stable at ten o'clock, each of them took a light but he. He took no candle at all with him. Each of them went into his own stable. When he went into his stable he opened the box. He left it in a hole in the wall. The light was great. It was twice as much as in the other stables.' The king hears of it, and makes him show him the box. The king says, 'You must go and bring me the woman to whom the hair belongs.' In the end the young man, and not the king, marries the woman."

Men have named beauty. Thy great leaves enfold
The ancient beards, the helms of ruby and gold
Of the crowned Magi;[2] and the king whose eyes
10 Saw the Pierced Hands and Rood° of elder rise   *the Cross*
In Druid vapour and make the torches dim;
Till vain frenzy awoke and he died;[3] and him
Who met Fand walking among flaming dew
By a grey shore where the wind never blew,
15 And lost the world and Emer for a kiss;[4]
And him[5] who drove the gods out of their liss,°   *fort*
And till a hundred morns had flowered red
Feasted, and wept the barrows of his dead;
And the proud dreaming king[6] who flung the crown
20 And sorrow away, and calling bard and clown
Dwelt among wine-stained wanderers in deep woods;
And him who sold tillage, and house, and goods,
And sought through lands and islands numberless years,
Until he found, with laughter and with tears,
25 A woman of so shining loveliness
That men threshed corn at midnight by a tress,
A little stolen tress.[7] I, too, await
The hour of thy great wind of love and hate.
When shall the stars be blown about the sky,
30 Like the sparks blown out of a smithy, and die?
Surely thine hour has come, thy great wind blows,
Far-off, most secret, and inviolate Rose?

                                                          1896, 1897

The Folly of Being Comforted

One that is ever kind said yesterday:
"Your well-belovèd's hair has threads of grey,
And little shadows come about her eyes;
Time can but make it easier to be wise
5 Though now it seem impossible, and so
All that you need is patience."

                               Heart cries, "No,
I have not a crumb of comfort, not a grain.
Time can but make her beauty over again:
Because of that great nobleness of hers
10 The fire that stirs about her, when she stirs,
When all the wild summer was in her gaze."

---

2. The wise men from the east who came to do
homage to the infant Jesus.
3. King Conchubar, in early Christian legend, is
said to have died on the day of Christ's crucifixion
in a fit of rage at hearing the news. Yeats makes
Conchubar see the crucifixion in a vision raised by
the magic of the ancient Celtic priests, or Druids

(see n. 1). "Pierced Hands": Christ's.
4. The ancient Irish hero Cuchulain was seduced
by Fand away from his wife, Emer.
5. Legendary Irish hero and companion of Oisin,
son of Finn, poet and warrior.
6. I.e., Fergus (see n. 1, p. 2094).
7. See n. 1, p. 2095.

O heart! O heart! if she'd but turn her head,
You'd know the folly of being comforted.

1902, 1903

Adam's Curse[1]

We sat together at one summer's end,
That beautiful mild woman, your close friend,
And you and I, and talked of poetry.
I said: "A line will take us hours maybe;
5 Yet if it does not seem a moment's thought,
Our stitching and unstitching has been naught.
Better go down upon your marrow-bones
And scrub a kitchen pavement, or break stones
Like an old pauper, in all kinds of weather;
10 For to articulate sweet sounds together
Is to work harder than all these, and yet
Be thought an idler by the noisy set
Of bankers, schoolmasters, and clergymen
The martyrs call the world."

                And thereupon
15 That beautiful mild woman for whose sake
There's many a one shall find out all heartache
On finding that her voice is sweet and low
Replied: "To be born woman is to know—
Although they do not talk of it at school—
20 That we must labour to be beautiful."

I said: "It's certain there is no fine thing
Since Adam's fall but needs much labouring.
There have been lovers who thought love should be
So much compounded of high courtesy
25 That they would sigh and quote with learned looks
Precedents out of beautiful old books;
Yet now it seems an idle trade enough."

We sat grown quiet at the name of love;
We saw the last embers of daylight die,
30 And in the trembling blue-green of the sky
A moon, worn as if it had been a shell
Washed by time's waters as they rose and fell
About the stars and broke in days and years.

I had a thought for no one's but your ears:
35 That you were beautiful, and that I strove

---

1. To work for a living was the curse imposed by
God on Adam after the Fall (Genesis 3.17–19).
The poem reflects an incident in Yeats's passionate
but hopeless love for the beautiful revolutionary
Maud Gonne (see A. N. Jeffares, *W. B. Yeats: Man
and Poet*, 1949, pp. 128–29).

To love you in the old high way of love;
That it had all seemed happy, and yet we'd grown
As weary-hearted as that hollow moon.

Nov. 1902   1902, 1903

No Second Troy

Why should I blame her[1] that she filled my days
With misery, or that she would of late
Have taught to ignorant men most violent ways,
Or hurled the little streets upon the great,
5   Had they but courage equal to desire?
What could have made her peaceful with a mind
That nobleness made simple as a fire,
With beauty like a tightened bow, a kind
That is not natural in an age like this,
10   Being high and solitary and most stern?
Why, what could she have done, being what she is?
Was there another Troy for her to burn?[2]

Dec. 1908   1910

The Fascination of What's Difficult[1]

The fascination of what's difficult
Has dried the sap out of my veins, and rent
Spontaneous joy and natural content
Out of my heart. There's something ails our colt
5   That must, as if it had not holy blood
Nor on Olympus leaped from cloud to cloud,
Shiver under the lash, strain, sweat and jolt
As though it dragged road-metal. My curse on plays
That have to be set up in fifty ways,
10   On the day's war with every knave and dolt,
Theatre business, management of men.
I swear before the dawn comes round again
I'll find the stable and pull out the bolt.

Sept. 1909–Mar. 1910   1910

---

1. Maud Gonne.
2. Helen of Troy was the cause of the destruction of the first Troy.
1. Written when Yeats was director-manager of the Abbey Theatre. "Subject. To complain of the fascination of what's difficult. It spoils spontaneity and pleasure, and wastes time. Repeat the line ending difficult three times and rhyme on bolt, exalt, colt, jolt" [Yeats's diary for September 1909].

September 1913[1]

What need you,[2] being come to sense,
But fumble in a greasy till
And add the halfpence to the pence
And prayer to shivering prayer, until
₅   You have dried the marrow from the bone?
For men were born to pray and save:
Romantic Ireland's dead and gone,
It's with O'Leary[3] in the grave.

Yet they were of a different kind,
₁₀   The names that stilled your childish play,
They have gone about the world like wind,
But little time had they to pray
For whom the hangman's rope was spun,
And what, God help us, could they save?
₁₅   Romantic Ireland's dead and gone,
It's with O'Leary in the grave.

Was it for this the wild geese[4] spread
The grey wing upon every tide;
For this that all that blood was shed,
₂₀   For this Edward Fitzgerald died,
And Robert Emmet and Wolfe Tone,[5]
All that delirium of the brave?
Romantic Ireland's dead and gone,
It's with O'Leary in the grave.

₂₅   Yet could we turn the years again,
And call those exiles as they were
In all their loneliness and pain,
You'd cry, "Some woman's yellow hair
Has maddened every mother's son":
₃₀   They weighed so lightly what they gave.
But let them be, they're dead and gone,
They're with O'Leary in the grave.

Sept. 1913   1913

---

1. Originally titled *Romance in Ireland (On Reading Much of the Correspondence against the Art Gallery)* and published in the *Irish Times* of Sept. 8, 1913. Sir Hugh Lane, Lady Gregory's nephew, had offered his collection of French impressionist paintings to the city of Dublin, provided they were permanently housed in a suitable gallery. Fierce abuse of the paintings and of the proposed design of the gallery in the Dublin nationalist press caused Lane to send the pictures to the London National Gallery. (Lane was drowned in the *Lusitania* in 1915; after years of bitter court dispute over an unwitnessed codicil to his will bequeathing the paintings to Dublin, an arrangement was reached in 1959 for the pictures to hang first in Dublin and then in London, for five years at a time.)
2. I.e., members of the new and predominantly Roman Catholic middle class.
3. John O'Leary (1830–1907), Irish nationalist of great courage and integrity who, returning to Dublin in 1885 after five years' imprisonment and fifteen years' exile, drew Yeats and others to the nationalist cause.
4. Popular name for the Irishmen who, because of the penal laws against Catholics, were forced to flee to the Continent from 1691 until Catholic Emancipation in 1829. One hundred and twenty thousand fought in the armies of France, Spain, and Austria.
5. Theobald Wolfe Tone (1763–1798), one of the chief founders of the United Irishmen (an Irish nationalist organization), committed suicide in prison in Dublin. Lord Edward Fitzgerald (1763–1798), British officer who, after being dismissed from the army for disloyal activities, joined the United Irishmen, was arrested, and died in prison. Emmet (1778–1803), also an Irish patriot, was executed for treason after a heroic career.

To a Shade[1]

If you have revisited the town, thin Shade,
Whether to look upon your monument
(I wonder if the builder has been paid)
Or happier-thoughted when the day is spent
5   To drink of that salt breath out of the sea
When grey gulls flit about instead of men,
And the gaunt houses put on majesty:
Let these content you and be gone again;
For they are at their old tricks yet.
                       A man[2]
10 Of your own passionate serving kind who had brought
In his full hands what, had they only known,
Had given their children's children loftier thought,
Sweeter emotion, working in their veins
Like gentle blood, has been driven from the place,
15 And insult heaped upon him for his pains,
And for his open-handedness, disgrace;
Your enemy, an old foul mouth, had set
The pack upon him.[3]
              Go, unquiet wanderer,
And gather the Glasnevin[4] coverlet
20 About your head till the dust stops your ear,
The time for you to taste of that salt breath
And listen at the corners has not come;
You had enough of sorrow before death—
Away, away! You are safer in the tomb.

Sept. 1913   1913

A Coat

I made my song a coat
Covered with embroideries
Out of old mythologies[1]
From heel to throat;
5 But the fools caught it,[2]
Wore it in the world's eyes
As though they'd wrought it.
Song, let them take it,
For there's more enterprise
10 In walking naked.

1912   1914

1. The spirit of the great Irish nationalist leader Charles Stewart Parnell (1846–1891).
2. Sir Hugh Lane (see n. 1, p. 2099).
3. William Martin Murphy, proprietor of the *Irish Independent* and *Evening Herald*. He had opposed the Lane benefaction and had earlier supported those who led the attack on Parnell.
4. The cemetery where Parnell is buried.

1. Gaelic legends, which Yeats had read in such translations as those of Standish O'Grady and James Clarence Mangan.
2. Probably a reference to the protégés of Æ [George William Russell], among them Seamus O'Sullivan. Cf. *To a poet who would have me Praise certain Bad Poets, Imitators of His and Mine.*

The Wild Swans at Coole[1]

The trees are in their autumn beauty,
The woodland paths are dry,
Under the October twilight the water
Mirrors a still sky;
5   Upon the brimming water among the stones
Are nine-and-fifty swans.

The nineteenth autumn has come upon me
Since I first made my count;[2]
I saw, before I had well finished,
10   All suddenly mount
And scatter wheeling in great broken rings
Upon their clamorous wings.

I have looked upon those brilliant creatures,
And now my heart is sore.
15   All's changed since I, hearing at twilight,
The first time on this shore,
The bell-beat of their wings above my head,
Trod with a lighter tread.

Unwearied still, lover by lover,[3]
20   They paddle in the cold
Companionable streams or climb the air;
Their hearts have not grown old;
Passion or conquest, wander where they will,
Attend upon them still.

25   But now they drift on the still water,
Mysterious, beautiful;
Among what rushes will they build,
By what lake's edge or pool
Delight men's eyes when I awake some day
30   To find they have flown away?

Oct. 1916   1917

---

1. Coole Park, Lady Gregory's country estate, where Yeats was a frequent guest.
2. His first visit had been in 1897 (nineteen years earlier).

3. In Irish legend, the lovers Baile and Aillinn had been changed into swans; also, the subject of Yeats's poem *Baile and Aillinn* (1903).

In Memory of Major Robert Gregory[1]

1

Now that we're almost settled in our house[2]
I'll name the friends that cannot sup with us
Beside a fire of turf° in th' ancient tower,   peat
And having talked to some late hour
5   Climb up the narrow winding stair to bed:
Discoverers of forgotten truth[3]
Or mere companions of my youth,
All, all are in my thoughts to-night being dead.

2

Always we'd have the new friend meet the old
10   And we are hurt if either friend seem cold,
And there is salt to lengthen out the smart
In the affections of our heart,
And quarrels are blown up upon that head;
But not a friend that I would bring
15   This night can set us quarrelling,
For all that come into my mind are dead.

3

Lionel Johnson[4] comes the first to mind,
That loved his learning better than mankind,
Though courteous to the worst; much falling he
20   Brooded upon sanctity
Till all his Greek and Latin learning seemed
A long blast upon the horn that brought
A little nearer to his thought
A measureless consummation that he dreamed.

4

25   And that enquiring man John Synge[5] comes next,
That dying chose the living world for text
And never could have rested in the tomb
But that, long travelling, he had come
Towards nightfall upon certain set apart
30   In a most desolate stony place,[6]
Towards nightfall upon a race
Passionate and simple like his heart.

---

1. Robert Gregory (1881–1918), the only child of
Lady Gregory, Yeats's friend, patron, and codirector of the Abbey Theatre. At its first printing, this
elegy carried the following note: "(Major Robert
Gregory, R.F.C. [Royal Flying Corps], M.C. [Mil-
itary Cross], Legion of Honour, was killed in action
on the Italian Front, January 23, 1918)."
2. Thoor Ballylee, the Norman tower and adjoining cottages Yeats had purchased for himself and
his wife.
3. Those interested in the occult tradition.
4. English poet and scholar (1867–1902).
5. Irish poet and playwright (1871–1909), who
was codirector—with Yeats and Lady Gregory—of
the Abbey Theatre.
6. The Aran Islands off the west coast of Ireland,
the setting of such Synge plays as The Playboy of
the Western World (1907).

5

And then I think of old George Pollexfen,[7]
In muscular youth well known to Mayo[8] men
35   For horsemanship at meets or at racecourses,
That could have shown how pure-bred horses
And solid men, for all their passion, live
But as the outrageous stars incline
By opposition, square and trine;[9]
40   Having grown sluggish and contemplative.

6

They were my close companions many a year,
A portion of my mind and life, as it were,
And now their breathless faces seem to look
Out of some old picture-book;
45   I am accustomed to their lack of breath,
But not that my dear friend's dear son,
Our Sidney[1] and our perfect man,
Could share in that discourtesy of death.

7

For all things the delighted eye now sees
50   Were loved by him;[2] the old storm-broken trees
That cast their shadows upon road and bridge;
The tower set on the stream's edge;
The ford where drinking cattle make a stir
Nightly, and startled by that sound
55   The water-hen must change her ground;
He might have been your heartiest welcomer.

8

When with the Galway foxhounds he would ride
From Castle Taylor to the Roxborough side[3]
Or Esserkelly plain, few kept his pace;
60   At Mooneen he had leaped a place
So perilous that half the astonished meet
Had shut their eyes; and where was it
He rode a race without a bit?
And yet his mind outran the horses' feet.

9

65   We dreamed that a great painter had been born[4]
To cold Clare[5] rock and Galway rock and thorn,

---

7. Yeats's maternal uncle (1839–1910), with whom he had spent holidays in Sligo as a young man.
8. Irish county north of Galway.
9. Terms from astrology, a pseudoscience in which both Pollexfen and Yeats were interested.
1. Robert Gregory had an Elizabethan versatility like that of Sir Philip Sidney (1554–1586), poet, scholar, and soldier, who died young and in battle overseas. Yeats's admiration for Gregory was more qualified than his elegy suggests (see n. 7, p.

2104).
2. Thoor Ballylee had formerly been owned by the Gregory family.
3. Big country houses in County Galway. Roxborough was Lady Gregory's childhood home.
4. "Robert Gregory painted the Burren Hills and thereby found what promised to grow into a great style, but he had hardly found it before he was killed" (Yeats, *Essays and Introductions*, p. 209).
5. A county south of County Galway.

To that stern colour and that delicate line
That are our secret discipline
Wherein the gazing heart doubles her might.
70 Soldier, scholar, horseman, he,
And yet he had the intensity
To have published all to be a world's delight.

10

What other could so well have counselled us
In all lovely intricacies of a house
75 As he that practised or that understood
All work in metal or in wood,
In moulded plaster or in carven stone?
Soldier, scholar, horseman, he,
And all he did done perfectly
80 As though he had but that one trade alone.

11

Some burn damp faggots,[6] others may consume
The entire combustible world in one small room
As though dried straw, and if we turn about
The bare chimney is gone black out
85 Because the work had finished in that flare.
Soldier, scholar, horseman, he,
As 'twere all life's epitome,[7]
What made us dream that he could comb grey hair?

12

I had thought, seeing how bitter is that wind
90 That shakes the shutter, to have brought to mind
All those that manhood tried, or childhood loved
Or boyish intellect approved,
With some appropriate commentary on each;
Until imagination brought
95 A fitter welcome; but a thought
Of that late death took all my heart for speech.

June 1918   1918

Easter 1916[1]

I have met them at close of day
Coming with vivid faces

6. Bundle of sticks or small branches used for fuel.
7. Cf. Dryden's scathingly satirical portrait of
George Villiers (1628–1687), second duke of
Buckingham, *Absalom and Achitophel: A Poem*,
lines 544–52.
1. This title, with its resemblance to *September
1913*, suggests that the poem is a palinode (one in
which the author retracts something said in a former poem). On Easter Monday of 1916, Irish

nationalists launched a heroic but unsuccessful
revolt against the British government; the week of
street fighting that followed is known as the Easter
Rebellion. As a result, a number of the nationalists
were executed; Britain, at war with Germany, was
in no mood to tolerate Irish agitation for independence—which was supported, for obvious reasons,
by Germany. Yeats knew the chief rebels personally.

From counter or desk among grey
Eighteenth-century houses.
5 I have passed with a nod of the head
Or polite meaningless words,
Or have lingered awhile and said
Polite meaningless words,
And thought before I had done
10 Of a mocking tale or a gibe
To please a companion
Around the fire at the club,
Being certain that they and I
But lived where motley[2] is worn:
15 All changed, changed utterly:
A terrible beauty is born.

That woman's days were spent
In ignorant good-will,
Her nights in argument
20 Until her voice grew shrill.
What voice more sweet than hers
When, young and beautiful,
She rode to harriers?[3]
This man had kept a school
25 And rode our wingèd horse;[4]
This other his helper and friend[5]
Was coming into his force;
He might have won fame in the end,
So sensitive his nature seemed,
30 So daring and sweet his thought.
This other man I had dreamed
A drunken, vainglorious lout.[6]
He had done most bitter wrong
To some who are near my heart,
35 Yet I number him in the song;
He, too, has resigned his part
In the casual comedy;
He, too, has been changed in his turn,
Transformed utterly:
40 A terrible beauty is born.

Hearts with one purpose alone
Through summer and winter seem
Enchanted to a stone
To trouble the living stream.
45 The horse that comes from the road,
The rider, the birds that range

2. Jester's parti-colored costume.
3. Constance Gore-Booth (afterward Countess Markiewicz), a member of the Sligo county aristocracy. A gay and beautiful woman, she had annoyed Yeats by becoming an embittered nationalist.
4. Padraic Pearse, a schoolmaster, a leader in the movement to restore the Gaelic language in Ireland, and a poet (hence the reference to "our wingèd horse"—Pegasus, the horse of the Muses).
5. Thomas MacDonagh.
6. Major John MacBride. Gonne, to Yeats's great disgust, had married MacBride in 1903, only to be separated from him after two years.

From cloud to tumbling cloud,
Minute by minute they change;
A shadow of cloud on the stream
50 Changes minute by minute;
A horse-hoof slides on the brim,
And a horse plashes within it;
The long-legged moor-hens dive,
And hens to moor-cocks call;
55 Minute by minute they live:
The stone's in the midst of all.

Too long a sacrifice
Can make a stone of the heart.
O when may it suffice?
60 That is Heaven's part, our part
To murmur name upon name,
As a mother names her child
When sleep at last has come
On limbs that had run wild.
65 What is it but nightfall?
No, no, not night but death;
Was it needless death after all?
For England may keep faith
For all that is done and said.
70 We know their dream; enough
To know they dreamed and are dead;
And what if excess of love
Bewildered them till they died?
I write it out in a verse—
75 MacDonagh and MacBride
And Connolly[7] and Pearse
Now and in time to be,
Wherever green is worn,
Are changed, changed utterly:
80 A terrible beauty is born.

May–Sept. 1916   1916, 1920

The Second Coming[1]

Turning and turning in the widening gyre
The falcon cannot hear the falconer;
Things fall apart; the center cannot hold;
Mere anarchy is loosed upon the world,

7. James Connolly, Pearse's partner in leading the insurrection. Like the other rebels named here, he was executed by firing squad.
1. This poem expresses Yeats's sense of the dissolution of the civilization of his time, the end of one cycle of history and the approach of another. He called each cycle of history a "gyre" (line 1)—literally a circular or spiral turn (Yeats pronounced it with a hard g). The birth of Christ brought to an end the cycle that had lasted from what Yeats called the "Babylonian mathematical starlight" (2000 B.C.E.) to the dissolution of Greco-Roman culture. "What if the irrational return?" Yeats asked in his prose work A Vision. "What if the circle begin again?" He speculates that "we may be about to accept the most implacable authority the world has known."

5   The blood-dimmed tide is loosed, and everywhere
    The ceremony of innocence is drowned;
    The best lack all conviction, while the worst
    Are full of passionate intensity.[2]
    Surely some revelation is at hand;
10   Surely the Second Coming is at hand.
    The Second Coming! Hardly are those words out
    When a vast image out of *Spiritus Mundi*[3]
    Troubles my sight: somewhere in sands of the desert
    A shape with lion body and the head of a man,
15   A gaze blank and pitiless as the sun,
    Is moving its slow thighs, while all about it
    Reel shadows of the indignant desert birds.
    The darkness drops again; but now I know
    That twenty centuries of stony sleep
20   Were vexed to nightmare by a rocking cradle,[4]
    And what rough beast, its hour come round at last,
    Slouches towards Bethlehem to be born?

Jan. 1919   1920, 1921

A Prayer for My Daughter[1]

Once more the storm is howling, and half hid
Under this cradle-hood and coverlid
My child sleeps on. There is no obstacle
But Gregory's wood[2] and one bare hill
5   Whereby the haystack- and roof-levelling wind,
Bred on the Atlantic, can be stayed;
And for an hour I have walked and prayed
Because of the great gloom that is in my mind.

I have walked and prayed for this young child an hour
10   And heard the sea-wind scream upon the tower,
And under the arches of the bridge, and scream
In the elms above the flooded stream;
Imagining in excited reverie
That the future years had come,
15   Dancing to a frenzied drum,
Out of the murderous innocence of the sea.[3]

May she be granted beauty and yet not
Beauty to make a stranger's eye distraught,

2. Lines 4–8 refer to the Russian Revolution of 1917. "The ceremony of innocence" suggests Yeats's view of ritual as the basis of civilized living. Cf. the last stanza of *A Prayer for My Daughter* (p. 2109).
3. The spirit or soul of the universe, with which all individual souls are connected through the "Great Memory," which Yeats held to be a universal subconscious in which the human race preserves its past memories. It is thus a source of symbolic images for the poet.

4. I.e., the cradle of the infant Christ.
1. Yeats's daughter, Anne Butler, was born on February 26, 1919, in Dublin and brought home to the refitted Norman tower of Thoor Ballylee (Ballylee Castle) in Galway, where Yeats lived; it is not far from Coole Park.
2. Originally part of the Gregory estate, which had once also included Thoor Ballylee.
3. A reference to Yeats's visions of the future (cf. *The Second Coming*, p. 2106).

Or hers before a looking-glass, for such,
20   Being made beautiful overmuch,
Consider beauty a sufficient end,
Lose natural kindness and maybe
The heart-revealing intimacy
That chooses right, and never find a friend.

25   Helen being chosen found life flat and dull
And later had much trouble from a fool,[4]
While that great Queen, that rose out of the spray,[5]
Being fatherless could have her way
Yet chose a bandy-leggèd smith for man.
30   It's certain that fine women eat
A crazy salad with their meat
Whereby the Horn of Plenty is undone.

In courtesy I'd have her chiefly learned;
Hearts are not had as a gift but hearts are earned
35   By those that are not entirely beautiful;
Yet many, that have played the fool
For beauty's very self, has charm made wise,
And many a poor man that has roved,
Loved and thought himself beloved,
40   From a glad kindness cannot take his eyes.

May she become a flourishing hidden tree
That all her thoughts may like the linnet° be,   *songbird*
And have no business but dispensing round
Their magnanimities of sound,
45   Not but in merriment begin a chase,
Nor but in merriment a quarrel.
O may she live like some green laurel
Rooted in one dear perpetual place.

My mind, because the minds that I have loved,
50   The sort of beauty that I have approved,
Prosper but little, has dried up of late,
Yet knows that to be choked with hate
May well be of all evil chances chief.
If there's no hatred in a mind
55   Assault and battery of the wind
Can never tear the linnet from the leaf.

An intellectual hatred is the worst,
So let her think opinions are accursed.
Have I not seen the loveliest woman[6] born
60   Out of the mouth of Plenty's horn,
Because of her opinionated mind
Barter that horn and every good

---

4. Menelaus, the husband of Helen, whom she deserted in favor of Paris.
5. Venus, wife (in the *Odyssey* and later accounts) of Vulcan, "bandy-leggèd" god of fire and forge (line 29).
6. Maud Gonne.

By quiet natures understood
For an old bellows full of angry wind?

65 Considering that, all hatred driven hence,
The soul recovers radical innocence
And learns at last that it is self-delighting,
Self-appeasing, self-affrighting,
And that its own sweet will is Heaven's will;
70 She can, though every face should scowl
And every windy quarter howl
Or every bellows burst, be happy still.

And may her bridegroom bring her to a house
Where all's accustomed, ceremonious;
75 For arrogance and hatred are the wares
Peddled in the thoroughfares.
How but in custom and in ceremony
Are innocence and beauty born?
Ceremony's a name for the rich horn,
80 And custom for the spreading laurel tree.

Feb.–June 1919   1919, 1921

Sailing to Byzantium[1]

I

That is no country for old men. The young
In one another's arms, birds in the trees
—Those dying generations—at their song,
The salmon-falls, the mackerel-crowded seas,
5 Fish, flesh, or fowl, commend all summer long
Whatever is begotten, born, and dies.
Caught in that sensual music all neglect
Monuments of unageing intellect.

2

An aged man is but a paltry thing,
10 A tattered coat upon a stick, unless
Soul clap its hands and sing, and louder sing
For every tatter in its mortal dress,
Nor is there singing school but studying
Monuments of its own magnificence;
15 And therefore I have sailed the seas and come
To the holy city of Byzantium.

1. Yeats wrote in *A Vision:* "I think that if I could be given a month of antiquity and leave to spend it where I chose, I would spend it in Byzantium [modern Istanbul] a little before Justinian opened St. Sophia and closed the Academy of Plato [i.e., ca. 535 C.E.]. . . . I think that in early Byzantium, maybe never before or since in recorded history, religious, aesthetic, and practical life were one, that architects and artificers . . . spoke to the multitude in gold and silver. The painter, the mosaic worker, the worker in gold and silver, the illuminator of sacred books were almost impersonal, almost perhaps without the consciousness of individual design, absorbed in their subject matter and that the vision of a whole people."

3

O sages standing in God's holy fire
As in the gold mosaic of a wall,[2]
Come from the holy fire, perne in a gyre,[3]
20 And be the singing-masters of my soul.
Consume my heart away; sick with desire
And fastened to a dying animal
It knows not what it is; and gather me
Into the artifice of eternity.

4

25 Once out of nature I shall never take
My bodily form from any natural thing,
But such a form as Grecian goldsmiths make
Of hammered gold and gold enamelling
To keep a drowsy Emperor awake;[4]
30 Or set upon a golden bough to sing
To lords and ladies of Byzantium
Of what is past, or passing, or to come.

Sept. 1926   1927

Leda and the Swan[1]

A sudden blow: the great wings beating still
Above the staggering girl, her thighs caressed
By the dark webs, her nape caught in his bill,
He holds her helpless breast upon his breast.

5   How can those terrified vague fingers push
The feathered glory from her loosening thighs?
And how can body, laid in that white rush,
But feel the strange heart beating where it lies?

A shudder in the loins engenders there
10   The broken wall, the burning roof and tower[2]

2. Yeats had in mind the mosaic frieze of the holy martyrs in the church of San Apollinare Nuovo at Ravenna, which he had visited in 1907.
3. I.e., whirl round in a spiral motion. "Perne": or pirn; literally a bobbin, reel, or spool, on which something is wound. It became a favorite word of Yeats's, used as a verb meaning "to spin round"; he associated the spinning with the spinning of fate.
4. "I have read somewhere," Yeats wrote, "that in the Emperor's palace at Byzantium was a tree made of gold and silver, and artificial birds that sang." Cf. also Hans Christian Andersen's *Emperor's Nightingale,* which may have been in Yeats's mind at the time.
1. In Greek mythology Zeus visited Leda in the form of a swan. As a result of the union Leda gave birth to Helen and to Clytemnestra (wife of Agamemnon). Yeats saw Zeus's visit to Leda as an "annunciation," marking the beginning of Greek civilization: "I imagine the annunciation that founded Greece as made to Leda, remembering that they showed in a Spartan temple, strung up

to the roof as a holy relic, an unhatched egg of hers, and that from one of her eggs came love and from the other war" (*A Vision*). In the original Cuala Press edition Yeats noted: "I wrote *Leda and the Swan* because the editor of a political review asked me for a poem. I thought, 'After the individualist, demagogic movement, founded by Hobbes and popularized by the Encyclopedists and the French Revolution, we have a soil so exhausted that it cannot grow that crop again for centuries.' Then I thought, 'Nothing is now possible but some movement from above preceded by some violent annunciation.' My fancy began to play with Leda and the Swan for metaphor, and I began this poem; but as I wrote, bird and lady took such possession of the scene that all politics went out of it, and my friend tells me that his 'conservative readers would misunderstand the poem.' " For the author's revisions while composing this poem, see "Poems in Process," in the appendices to this volume.
2. I.e., the destruction of Troy, caused by Helen's elopement with the Trojan Paris. Agamemnon was

And Agamemnon dead.
                              Being so caught up,
So mastered by the brute blood of the air,
Did she put on his knowledge with his power
Before the indifferent beak could let her drop?

Sept. 1923   1924, 1928

Among School Children

1

I walk through the long schoolroom questioning;
A kind old nun in a white hood replies;
The children learn to cipher and to sing,
To study reading-books and history,
5   To cut and sew, be neat in everything
In the best modern way—the children's eyes
In momentary wonder stare upon
A sixty-year-old smiling public man.

2

I dream of a Ledaean[1] body, bent
10   Above a sinking fire, a tale that she
Told of a harsh reproof, or trivial event
That changed some childish day to tragedy—
Told, and it seemed that our two natures blent
Into a sphere from youthful sympathy,
15   Or else, to alter Plato's parable,
Into the yolk and white of the one shell.[2]

3

And thinking of that fit of grief or rage
I look upon one child or t'other there
And wonder if she stood so at that age—
20   For even daughters of the swan can share
Something of every paddler's heritage—
And had that colour upon cheek or hair,
And thereupon my heart is driven wild:
She stands before me as a living child.

4

25   Her present image floats into the mind—
Did Quattrocento[3] finger fashion it
Hollow of cheek as though it drank the wind

---

murdered by his wife, Clytemnestra, the other daughter of Leda and the Swan.
1. Adjective from "Leda," meaning "like Helen of Troy" (Leda's daughter). The reference is to Maud Gonne (as also in lines 19–28).
2. In Plato's *Symposium* Aristophanes explains love by supposing that "the primeval man was round and had four hands and four feet, back and sides forming a circle, one head with two faces,"

and was subsequently divided into two. "After the division, the two parts of man, each desiring his other half, came together, and threw their arms about one another eager to grow into one." The fact that Helen was born from an egg (as the daughter of Leda and the Swan) suggests Yeats's image for such a union.
3. I.e., 15th century; a reference to Italian painters the period.

And took a mess of shadows for its meat?
And I though never of Ledaean kind
30 Had pretty plumage once—enough of that,
Better to smile on all that smile, and show
There is a comfortable kind of old scarecrow.

5

What youthful mother, a shape upon her lap
Honey of generation had betrayed,
35 And that must sleep, shriek, struggle to escape
As recollection or the drug decide,[4]
Would think her son, did she but see that shape
With sixty or more winters on its head,
A compensation for the pang of his birth,
40 Or the uncertainty of his setting forth?

6

Plato thought nature but a spume that plays
Upon a ghostly paradigm of things;
Solider Aristotle played the taws
Upon the bottom of a king of kings;[5]
45 World-famous golden-thighed Pythagoras[6]
Fingered upon a fiddle-stick or strings
What a star sang and careless Muses heard:
Old clothes upon old sticks to scare a bird.[7]

7

Both nuns and mothers worship images,[8]
50 But those the candles light are not as those
That animate a mother's reveries,
But keep a marble or a bronze repose.
And yet they too break hearts—O Presences
That passion, piety or affection knows,
55 And that all heavenly glory symbolise—
O self-born mockers of man's enterprise;

8

Labour is blossoming or dancing where
The body is not bruised to pleasure soul,

---

4. I have taken the 'honey of generation' from Porphyry's essay on 'The Cave of the Nymphs,' but
find no warrant in Porphyry for considering it the
'drug' that destroys the 'recollection' of prenatal
freedom [Yeats's note]. Porphyry was a Neoplatonic philosopher of the 3rd century C.E. "Honey
of generation," by blotting out the memory of prenatal happiness, "betrays" an infant to be born into
this world. The infant will either "sleep" or "struggle to escape" (from this world), depending on
whether the drug works or the recollection of blissful prenatal life overcomes the oblivion caused by
the drug.
5. I.e., Plato thought nature was a mere appearance ("spume") veiling the ultimate spiritual and
mathematical reality ("ghostly paradigm"). Aristotle was "solider" in that he believed that form
really inhered in the matter of nature and thus that

nature itself had reality. Aristotle was tutor to Alexander the Great and disciplined him by applying
the "taws" or strap.
6. Greek philosopher (early 6th century B.C.E.),
interested in mathematics and the mathematical
study of acoustics and music. His disciples, the
Pythagoreans, developed a mystical philosophy of
numerical relations and united the notions of
astronomical and mathematical relations in the
theory of the music of the spheres. Pythagoreans
regarded their master with veneration as a god with
a golden thigh.
7. A contemptuous description of the philosophies of Plato, Aristotle, and Pythagoras.
8. Nuns worship images of Christ or the Virgin;
mothers worship their own inward images of their
children.

Nor beauty born out of its own despair,
60 Nor blear-eyed wisdom out of midnight oil.
O chestnut tree, great-rooted blossomer,
Are you the leaf, the blossom, or the bole?
O body swayed to music, O brightening glance,
How can we know the dancer from the dance?

June 1926   1927

A Dialogue of Self and Soul[1]

1

MY SOUL. I summon to the winding ancient stair;
Set all your mind upon the steep ascent,
Upon the broken, crumbling battlement,
Upon the breathless starlit air,
5   Upon the star that marks the hidden pole;
Fix every wandering thought upon
That quarter where all thought is done:
Who can distinguish darkness from the soul?

MY SELF. The consecrated blade upon my knees
10   Is Sato's ancient blade, still as it was,
Still razor-keen, still like a looking-glass
Unspotted by the centuries;
That flowering, silken, old embroidery, torn
From some court-lady's dress and round
15   The wooden scabbard bound and wound,
Can, tattered, still protect, faded adorn.

MY SOUL. Why should the imagination of a man
Long past his prime remember things that are
Emblematical of love and war?
20   Think of ancestral night that can,
If but imagination scorn the earth
And intellect its wandering
To this and that and t'other thing,
Deliver from the crime of death and birth.

25   MY SELF. Montashigi, third of his family, fashioned it
Five hundred years ago, about it lie
Flowers from I know not what embroidery—
Heart's purple—and all these I set
For emblems of the day against the tower
30   Emblematical of the night,
And claim as by a soldier's right
A charter to commit the crime once more.

---

1. In a letter of Oct. 2, 1923, Yeats wrote, "I am writing a new tower poem 'Sword and Tower,' which is a choice of rebirth rather than deliverance from birth. I make the Japanese sword and its silk covering my symbol of life." The sword was a present from a friend, Junzo Sato.

MY SOUL. Such fullness in that quarter overflows
  And falls into the basin of the mind
35 That man is stricken deaf and dumb and blind,
  For intellect no longer knows
  Is from *Ought,* or *Knower* from the *Known—*
  That is to say, ascends to Heaven;
  Only the dead can be forgiven;
40 But when I think of that my tongue's a stone.

2

MY SELF. A living man is blind and drinks his drop.
  What matter if the ditches are impure?
  What matter if I live it all once more?
  Endure that toil of growing up;
45 The ignominy of boyhood; the distress
  Of boyhood changing into man;
  The unfinished man and his pain
  Brought face to face with his own clumsiness;

  The finished man among his enemies?—
50 How in the name of Heaven can he escape
  That defiling and disfigured shape
  The mirror of malicious eyes
  Casts upon his eyes until at last
  He thinks that shape must be his shape?
55 And what's the good of an escape
  If honour find him in the wintry blast?

  I am content to live it all again
  And yet again, if it be life to pitch
  Into the frog-spawn of a blind man's ditch,
60 A blind man battering blind men;
  Or into that most fecund ditch of all,
  The folly that man does
  Or must suffer, if he woos
  A proud woman not kindred of his soul.

65 I am content to follow to its source
  Every event in action or in thought;
  Measure the lot; forgive myself the lot!
  When such as I cast out remorse
  So great a sweetness flows into the breast
70 We must laugh and we must sing,
  We are blest by everything,
  Everything we look upon is blest.

July–Dec. 1927   1929

For Anne Gregory

"Never shall a young man,
Thrown into despair
By those great honey-coloured
Ramparts at your ear,
5   Love you for yourself alone
And not your yellow hair."

"But I can get a hair-dye
And set such colour there,
Brown, or black, or carrot,
10   That young men in despair
May love me for myself alone
And not my yellow hair."

"I heard an old religious man
But yesternight declare
15   That he had found a text to prove
That only God, my dear,
Could love you for yourself alone
And not your yellow hair."

Sept. 1930   1931, 1932

Byzantium[1]

The unpurged images of day recede;
The Emperor's drunken soldiery are abed;
Night resonance recedes, night-walkers' song
After great cathedral gong;
5   A starlit or a moonlit dome[2] disdains
All that man is,
All mere complexities,
The fury and the mire° of human veins.   *deep mud*

Before me floats an image, man or shade,
10   Shade more than man, more image than a shade;
For Hades'[3] bobbin bound in mummy-cloth
May unwind the winding path;[4]
A mouth that has no moisture and no breath

---

1. On October 4, 1930, Yeats sent his friend Sturge Moore a copy of *Byzantium*, saying, "The poem originates from a criticism of yours. You objected to the last verse of 'Sailing to Byzantium' because a bird made by a goldsmith was just as natural as anything else. That showed me that the idea needed exposition." The previous April, Yeats had noted in his diary: "Subject for a poem / Describe Byzantium as it is in the system towards the end of the first Christian millennium. A walking mummy; flames at the street corners where the soul is purified. Birds of hammered gold singing in the golden trees. In the harbour [dolphins] offering their backs to the wailing dead that they may carry them to paradise."
2. Of the great church of St. Sophia.
3. Hell in Greek mythology.
4. The spool of people's fate, which spins their destiny and which is symbolized by the wrappings around a mummy, may lead people, as it unwinds, to the realm of pure spirit.

Breathless mouths may summon;
15   I hail the superhuman;
I call it death-in-life and life-in-death.[5]

Miracle, bird or golden handiwork,
More miracle than bird or handiwork,
Planted on the star-lit golden bough,[6]
20   Can like the cocks of Hades crow,
Or, by the moon embittered, scorn aloud
In glory of changeless metal
Common bird or petal
And all complexities of mire or blood.

25   At midnight on the Emperor's pavement flit
Flames that no faggot feeds, nor steel has lit,
Nor storm disturbs, flames begotten of flame,
Where blood-begotten spirits come
And all complexities of fury leave,
30   Dying into a dance,
An agony of trance,
An agony of flame[7] that cannot singe a sleeve.

Astraddle on the dolphin's mire and blood,[8]
Spirit after spirit! The smithies break the flood,
35   The golden smithies of the Emperor!
Marbles of the dancing floor
Break bitter furies of complexity,
Those images that yet
Fresh images beget,
40   That dolphin-torn, that gong-tormented sea.

Sept. 1930   1932

Crazy Jane Talks with the Bishop[1]

I met the Bishop on the road
And much said he and I.
"Those breasts are flat and fallen now,
Those veins must soon be dry;
5   Live in a heavenly mansion,
Not in some foul sty."

---

5. Cf. Coleridge's *The Rime of the Ancient Mariner*, line 193: "The Night-mare LIFE-IN-DEATH was she."
6. Part of the death-world of artifice and eternity; it is opposed to a real, living bough, which would be lighted by the sun or the moon. Reminiscent of the golden bough that guides Aeneas through the underworld in Virgil's *Aeneid*, it is also associated with the mystical tree of the esoteric Hebrew doctrine of the cabala, in whose branches "the birds lodge and build their nests; that is, the souls or angels have their place." The cock, that crows at dawn, appears on Roman tombstones as a herald of rebirth (line 20).

7. This phrase was suggested to Yeats by a Japanese Nō play, *Motomezuka*, wherein a young girl suffers from perpetual burning, which is a sense of her own guilt. A priest tells her that the flames will cease if she no longer believes in their reality; she finds herself incapable of disbelief, however, and the play ends in "the dance of her agony."
8. The dolphin, in ancient art, was a symbol of the soul in transit from one state to another.
1. One of a series of poems dealing with the paradox that wisdom may reside with fools and beggars (such as Jane) rather than with the respectable representatives of orthodoxy (such as the bishop).

"Fair and foul are near of kin,
And fair needs foul," I cried.[2]
"My friends are gone, but that's a truth
10 Nor grave nor bed denied,
Learned in bodily lowliness
And in the heart's pride.

"A woman can be proud and stiff
When on love intent;
15 But Love has pitched his mansion in
The place of excrement;
For nothing can be sole or whole
That has not been rent."

Nov. 1931   1932

After Long Silence[1]

Speech after long silence; it is right,
All other lovers being estranged or dead,
Unfriendly lamplight hid under its shade,
The curtains drawn upon unfriendly night,
5 That we descant and yet again descant
Upon the supreme theme of Art and Song:
Bodily decrepitude is wisdom; young
We loved each other and were ignorant.

Nov. 1929   1932

Lapis Lazuli[1]

(For Harry Clifton)

I have heard that hysterical women say
They are sick of the palette and fiddle-bow,
Of poets that are always gay,
For everybody knows or else should know
5 That if nothing drastic is done
Aeroplane and Zeppelin will come out,
Pitch like King Billy[2] bomb-balls in
Until the town lie beaten flat.

---

2. Cf. Shakespeare's Macbeth 1.1.10: "Fair is foul, and foul is fair."
1. For the author's revisions while composing this poem, see "Poems in Process," in the appendices to this volume.
1. A deep blue stone. "I notice that you have much lapis lazuli; someone has sent me a present of a great piece carved by some Chinese sculptor into the semblance of a mountain with temple, trees, paths, and an ascetic and pupil about to climb the mountain. Ascetic, pupil, hard stone, eternal

theme of the sensual east. The heroic cry in the midst of despair. But no, I am wrong, the east has its solutions always and therefore knows nothing of tragedy. It is we, not the east, that must raise the heroic cry" [Yeats to Dorothy Wellesley, July 6, 1935].
2. King William III (William of Orange), who defeated the army of King James II at the Battle of the Boyne in 1690. "Zeppelin": a cigar-shaped airship invented by a German, Count F. von Zeppelin.

All perform their tragic play,
10 There struts Hamlet, there is Lear,
That's Ophelia, that Cordelia;
Yet they, should the last scene be there,
The great stage curtain about to drop,
If worthy their prominent part in the play,
15 Do not break up their lines to weep.
They know that Hamlet and Lear are gay;
Gaiety transfiguring all that dread.
All men have aimed at, found and lost;
Black out; Heaven blazing into the head:
20 Tragedy wrought to its uttermost.
Though Hamlet rambles and Lear rages,
And all the drop-scenes drop at once
Upon a hundred thousand stages,
It cannot grow by an inch or an ounce.

25 On their own feet they came, or on shipboard,
Camel-back, horse-back, ass-back, mule-back,
Old civilisations put to the sword.
Then they and their wisdom went to rack:
No handiwork of Callimachus,[3]
30 Who handled marble as if it were bronze,
Made draperies that seemed to rise
When sea-wind swept the corner, stands;
His long lamp-chimney shaped like the stem
Of a slender palm, stood but a day;
35 All things fall and are built again,
And those that build them again are gay.

Two Chinamen, behind them a third,
Are carved in lapis lazuli,
Over them flies a long-legged bird,
40 A symbol of longevity;
The third, doubtless a serving-man,
Carries a musical instrument.

Every discolouration of the stone,
Every accidental crack or dent,
45 Seems a water-course or an avalanche,
Or lofty slope where it still snows
Though doubtless plum or cherry-branch
Sweetens the little half-way house
Those Chinamen climb towards, and I
50 Delight to imagine them seated there;
There, on the mountain and the sky,
On all the tragic scene they stare.

3. Greek sculptor (5th century B.C.E.), supposedly the originator of the Corinthian column and of the use of the running drill to imitate folds in drapery in statues. Yeats wrote of him: "With Callimachus pure Ionic revives again . . . and upon the only example of his work known to us, a marble chair, a Persian is represented, and may one not discover a Persian symbol in that bronze lamp, shaped like a palm . . . ? But he was an archaistic workman, and those who set him to work brought back public life to an older form" (A Vision).

One asks for mournful melodies;
Accomplished fingers begin to play.
55 Their eyes mid many wrinkles, their eyes,
Their ancient, glittering eyes, are gay.

July 1936   1938

Long-Legged Fly

That civilisation may not sink,
Its great battle lost,
Quiet the dog, tether the pony
To a distant post;
5 Our master Caesar[1] is in the tent
Where the maps are spread,
His eye fixed upon nothing,
A hand under his head.
Like a long-legged fly upon the stream
10 *His mind moves upon silence.*

That the topless towers be burnt
And men recall that face,
Move most gently if move you must
In this lonely place.
15 She[2] thinks, part woman, three parts a child,
That nobody looks; her feet
Practice a tinker shuffle
Picked up on a street.
Like a long-legged fly upon the stream
20 *Her mind moves upon silence.*

That girls at puberty may find
The first Adam in their thought,
Shut the door of the Pope's chapel,
Keep those children out.
25 There on that scaffolding reclines
Michael Angelo.[3]
With no more sound than the mice make
His hand moves to and fro.
Like a long-legged fly upon the stream
30 *His mind moves upon silence.*

Nov. 1937   1939

---

1. Emperor of Rome.
2. Helen of Troy, who precipitated the Trojan War. Cf. Marlowe, *Dr. Faustus:* "Was this the face that launched a thousand ships / And burnt the topless towers of Ilium?"

3. Michelangelo (1475–1564) is painting *The Creation of Man* on the Sistine Chapel ceiling in the Vatican. Cf. *Under Ben Bulben* (p. 2121).

2120 / William Butler Yeats

The Circus Animals' Desertion

1

I sought a theme and sought for it in vain,
I sought it daily for six weeks or so.
Maybe at last, being but a broken man,
I must be satisfied with my heart, although
5   Winter and summer till old age began
My circus animals were all on show,
Those stilted boys, that burnished chariot,
Lion and woman and the Lord knows what.[1]

2

What can I but enumerate old themes?
10   First that sea-rider Oisin[2] led by the nose
Through three enchanted islands, allegorical dreams,
Vain gaiety, vain battle, vain repose,
Themes of the embittered heart, or so it seems,
That might adorn old songs or courtly shows;
15   But what cared I that set him on to ride,
I, starved for the bosom of his faery bride?

And then a counter-truth filled out its play,
The Countess Cathleen[3] was the name I gave it;
She, pity-crazed, had given her soul away,
20   But masterful Heaven had intervened to save it.
I thought my dear must her own soul destroy,
So did fanaticism and hate enslave it,
And this brought forth a dream and soon enough
This dream itself had all my thought and love.

25   And when the Fool and Blind Man stole the bread
Cuchulain fought the ungovernable sea;[4]
Heart-mysteries there, and yet when all is said
It was the dream itself enchanted me:
Character isolated by a deed
30   To engross the present and dominate memory.
Players and painted stage took all my love,
And not those things that they were emblems of.

---

1. Yeats refers to the ancient Irish heroes of his early work ("those stilted boys"), the gilded carriage of his play *The Unicorn from the Stars* (1908), and "A Sphinx with woman breast and lion paw" in his poem *The Double Vision of Michael Robartes*.
2. In the long title-poem of Yeats's first book, *The Wanderings of Oisin and Other Poems* (1889), the legendary poet-warrior Oisin (pronounced *Ushēēn*) is bewitched by the beautiful fairy woman Niamh (pronounced *Neeve*). He returns 150 years later to

find his friends dead and Ireland Christian.
3. A play (1892) about an Irish countess who sells her soul to the devil to buy food for the starving peasantry but is taken up to heaven (for God "Looks always on the motive, not the deed"). It was dedicated to Maud Gonne ("my dear," line 21) and inspired by her work on behalf of evicted peasants in the West of Ireland.
4. In Yeats's play *On Baile's Strand* (1904).

3

Those masterful images because complete
Grew in pure mind, but out of what began?
35 A mound of refuse or the sweepings of a street,
Old kettles, old bottles, and a broken can,
Old iron, old bones, old rags, that raving slut
Who keeps the till. Now that my ladder's gone,
I must lie down where all the ladders start,
40 In the foul rag-and-bone shop of the heart.

1939

Under Ben Bulben[1]

1

Swear by what the sages spoke
Round the Mareotic Lake[2]
That the Witch of Atlas knew,
Spoke and set the cocks a-crow.

5 Swear by those horsemen, by those women
Complexion and form prove superhuman,[3]
That pale, long-visaged company
That air in immortality
Completeness of their passions won;
10 Now they ride the wintry dawn
Where Ben Bulben sets the scene.

Here's the gist of what they mean.

2

Many times man lives and dies
Between his two eternities,
15 That of race and that of soul,
And ancient Ireland knew it all.
Whether man die in his bed
Or the rifle knocks him dead,
A brief parting from those dear
20 Is the worst man has to fear.
Though grave-diggers' toil is long,
Sharp their spades, their muscles strong,

1. Mountain in Country Sligo that Yeats had often climbed as a boy. Nine years after he died in the south of France, his body was brought home to Ireland and buried in Drumcliff churchyard at the foot of Ben Bulben.
2. Lake Mareotis, bordering the city of Alexandria, Egypt, where a school of neo-Pythagorean philosophers flourished in the 1st century C.E. By Lake Mareotis also flourished (3rd century C.E.) the Christian Neoplatonists, in whom Yeats was much interested. The lake is mentioned in Shelley's poem *The Witch of Atlas*, a poem that Yeats admired and interpreted in his own way, seeing the witch as a symbol of timeless, absolute beauty; hence what she "knew" and "spoke" and what "set the cocks a-crow" can be related to the "miracle" that "can like the cocks of Hades crow" in *Byzantium* (lines 17–20, p. 2116).
3. The *sidhe*, or fairy folk, who were believed to ride through the countryside near Ben Bulben.

They but thrust their buried men
Back in the human mind again.

3

25 You that Mitchel's prayer have heard,
"Send war in our time, O Lord!"[4]
Know that when all words are said
And a man is fighting mad,
Something drops from eyes long blind,
30 He completes his partial mind,
For an instant stands at ease,
Laughs aloud, his heart at peace.
Even the wisest man grows tense
With some sort of violence
35 Before he can accomplish fate,
Know his work or choose his mate.

4

Poet and sculptor, do the work,
Nor let the modish painter shirk
What his great forefathers did,
40 Bring the soul of man to God.
Make him fill the cradles right.

Measurement began our might:
Forms a stark Egyptian thought,
Forms that gentler Phidias[5] wrought
45 Michael Angelo left a proof
On the Sistine Chapel roof,
Where but half-awakened Adam
Can disturb globe-trotting Madam
Till her bowels are in heat,[6]
50 Proof that there's a purpose set
Before the secret working mind:
Profane perfection of mankind.

Quattrocento[7] put in paint
On backgrounds for a God or Saint
55 Gardens where a soul's at ease;
Where everything that meets the eye,
Flowers and grass and cloudless sky,
Resemble forms that are or seem
When sleepers wake and yet still dream,
60 And when it's vanished still declare,
With only bed and bedstead there,

---

4. John Mitchel (1815–1875), an Irish patriot
imprisoned for his activities, wrote in his *Jail Journal*: "Give us war in our time, O Lord!"
5. Greek sculptor (5th century B.C.), generally
thought to have raised the classical ideal in art to
its highest culmination. Yeats here itemizes steps
in his history of knowledge and the arts, beginning
with Babylonian mathematics ("measurement"),
through "stark Egyptian thought," to the Renaissance of Michelangelo. Each of these steps is
related to Yeats's cyclical theory of history.
6. Cf. *Long-Legged Fly*, stanza 3, p. 2119.
7. 15th-century Italian art.

That heavens had opened.
                    Gyres[8] run on;
When that greater dream had gone
Calvert and Wilson, Blake and Claude,[9]
65 Prepared a rest for the people of God,
Palmer's phrase, but after that
Confusion fell upon our thought.

5

Irish poets, learn your trade,
Sing whatever is well made,
70 Scorn the sort now growing up
All out of shape from toe to top,
Their unremembering hearts and heads
Base-born products of base beds.
Sing the peasantry, and then
75 Hard-riding country gentlemen,
The holiness of monks, and after
Porter-drinkers'[1] randy laughter;
Sing the lords and ladies gay
That were beaten into the clay
80 Through seven heroic centuries;
Cast your mind on other days
That we in coming days may be
Still the indomitable Irishry.

6

Under bare Ben Bulben's head
85 In Drumcliff churchyard Yeats is laid.
An ancestor was rector there[2]
Long years ago, a church stands near,
By the road an ancient cross.
No marble, no conventional phrase;
90 On limestone quarried near the spot
By his command these words are cut:
        Cast a cold eye
        On life, on death.
        Horseman, pass by!

Sept. 1938   1939

---

8. See n. 1, p. 2106.
9. Works by the five artists all provided images for Yeats's poetry. Edward Calvert, 19th-century wood engraver. Richard Wilson, 18th-century landscape painter. William Blake, "one of the great myth-makers and mask-makers." Claude Lorrain, 17th-century landscape painter. Samuel Palmer (line

66), 19th-century landscape painter and etcher, one of whose works was *The Lonely Tower*. Calvert, Blake, and Palmer knew one another and shared a view of the holiness of art.
1. Drinkers of dark brown bitter beer.
2. The Reverend John Yeats (1774–1847) was rector of Drumcliff from 1805.

From Reveries over Childhood and Youth[1]

[THE YEATS FAMILY]

Some six miles off towards Ben Bulben and beyond the Channel,[2] as we call the tidal river between Sligo and the Rosses, and on top of a hill there was a little square two-storied house covered with creepers and looking out upon a garden where the box borders were larger than any I had ever seen, and where I saw for the first time the crimson streak of the gladiolus and awaited its blossom with excitement. Under one gable a dark thicket of small trees made a shut-in mysterious place, where one played and believed that something was going to happen. My great-aunt Micky lived there. Micky was not her right name for she was Mary Yeats and her father had been my great-grandfather, John Yeats, who had been Rector of Drumcliffe, a few miles further off, and died in 1847. She was a spare, high-coloured, elderly woman and had the oldest-looking cat I had ever seen, for its hair had grown into matted locks of yellowy white. She farmed and had one old man-servant, but could not have farmed at all, had not neighbouring farmers helped to gather in the crops, in return for the loan of her farm implements and "out of respect for the family," for as Johnny MacGurk, the Sligo barber said to me, "The Yeats's were always very respectable." She was full of family history; all her dinner-knives were pointed like daggers through much cleaning, and there was a little James the First cream-jug with the Yeats motto and crest, and on her dining-room mantel-piece a beautiful silver cup that had belonged to my great-great-grandfather, who had married a certain Mary Butler. It had upon it the Butler crest and had been already old at the date 1534, when the initials of some bride and bridegroom were engraved under the lip. All its history for generations was rolled up inside it upon a piece of paper yellow with age, until some caller took the paper to light his pipe.

Another family of Yeats, a widow and her two children on whom I called sometimes with my grandmother, lived near in a long low cottage, and owned a very fierce turkey-cock that did battle with their visitors; and some miles away lived the secretary to the Grand Jury and Land Agent, my great-uncle Mat Yeats and his big family of boys and girls; but I think it was only in later years that I came to know them well. I do not think any of these liked the Pollexfens, who were well off and seemed to them purse-proud, whereas they themselves had come down in the world. I remember them as very well-bred and very religious in the Evangelical way and thinking a good deal of Aunt Micky's old histories. There had been among our ancestors a King's County soldier, one of Marlborough's[3] generals, and when his nephew came to dine he gave him boiled pork, and when the nephew said he disliked boiled pork he had asked him to dine again and promised him something he would like better. However, he gave him boiled pork again and the nephew took the hint in silence. The other day as I was coming home from America, I met

---

1. Yeats wrote a variety of autobiographical essays between 1914 and 1928; these were originally published separately and later collected as *The Autobiography of W. B. Yeats* (1936, 1953). The selections given here are from *Reveries over Childhood and Youth*, first published in 1915, and *The*

Trembling of the Veil, first published in 1922.
2. Yeats's favorite County Sligo landscape. Cf. the places named in *The Stolen Child* (p. 2090).
3. John Churchill, duke of Marlborough (1650–1722) English general in the War of the Spanish Succession (1702–13).

one of his descendants whose family has not another discoverable link with ours, and he too knew the boiled pork story and nothing else. We have the General's portrait, and he looks very fine in his armour and his long curly wig, and underneath it, after his name, are many honours that have left no tradition among us. Were we country people, we could have summarised his life in a legend. Other ancestors or great-uncles bore a part in Irish history; one saved the life of Sarsfield[4] at the battle of Sedgmoor; another, taken prisoner by King James's army, owed his to Sarsfield's gratitude; another, a century later, roused the gentlemen of Meath[5] against some local Jacquerie,[6] and was shot dead upon a country road, and yet another "chased the United Irishmen[7] for a fortnight, fell into their hands and was hanged." The notorious Major Sirr, who arrested Lord Edward Fitzgerald[8] and gave him the bullet wound he died of in the jail, was godfather to several of my great-great-grandfather's children; while to make a balance, my great-grandfather had been Robert Emmett's[9] friend and was suspected and imprisoned though but for a few hours. One great-uncle fell at New Orleans in 1813, while another, who became Governor of Penang, led the forlorn hope at the taking of Rangoon,[1] and even in the last generation of all there had been lives of some power and pleasure. An old man who had entertained many famous people, in his eighteenth-century house, where battlement and tower showed the influence of Horace Walpole,[2] had but lately, after losing all his money, drowned himself, first taking off his rings and chain and watch as became a collector of many beautiful things; and once to remind us of more passionate life, a gunboat put into Rosses, commanded by the illegitimate son of some great-uncle or other. Now that I can look at their miniatures, turning them over to find the name of soldier, or lawyer, or Castle official,[3] and wondering if they cared for good books or good music, I am delighted with all that joins my life to those who had power in Ireland or with those anywhere that were good servants and poor bargainers, but I cared nothing as a child for Micky's tales. I could see my grandfather's ships come up the bay or the river, and his sailors treated me with deference, and a ship's carpenter made and mended my toy boats and I thought that nobody could be so important as my grandfather. Perhaps, too, it is only now that I can value those more gentle natures so unlike his passion and violence. An old Sligo priest has told me how my great-grandfather John Yeats always went into his kitchen rattling the keys, so much did he fear finding some one doing wrong, and of a speech of his when the agent of the great landowner of his parish brought him from cottage to cottage to bid the women send their children to the Protestant

---

4. Patrick Sarsfield (d. 1693), Irish Jacobite general who served in the battle of Sedgemoor (1685) when the duke of Monmouth, illegitimate son of Charles II who was claiming the throne from his uncle James II, was defeated and captured.
5. Maritime county in province of Leinster, in the east of Ireland.
6. Peasant revolutionary. The "Jacquerie" was a peasants' revolt (1358) against the nobles in northern France (the term derived from *Jacques Bonhomme*, the nobility's contemptuous name for a peasant).
7. The Irish society founded in 1791 by Theobald Wolfe Tone that later was influential in causing the Irish rebellion of 1798.
8. A British officer (1763–1798), who, after dis-

missal from the army for disloyal activities, joined the United Irishmen. Cf. *September 1913*, lines 19–22 (p. 2099).
9. An Irish patriot, (1778–1803), hanged at Dublin for treason.
1. Capital of Burma, which was taken by the British in 1824. Penang is an island in Malaya.
2. The 18th-century English author whose pseudo-Gothic house, Strawberry Hill, much influenced subsequent Gothic architecture in England and elsewhere.
3. Official at Dublin Castle, where the viceroy (representing the British Crown) lived with his staff before Irish independence was achieved in 1922.

school. All promised till they came to one who cried, "Child of mine will never darken your door." "Thank you, my woman," he said, "you are the first honest woman I have met to-day." My uncle, Mat Yeats, the Land Agent, had once waited up every night for a week to catch some boys who stole his apples and when he caught them had given them six-pence and told them not to do it again. Perhaps it is only fancy or the softening touch of the miniaturist that makes me discover in their faces some courtesy and much gentleness. Two eighteenth-century faces interest me the most, one that of a great-great-grandfather, for both have under their powdered curling wigs a half-feminine charm, and as I look at them I discover a something clumsy and heavy in myself. Yet it was a Yeats who spoke the only eulogy that turns my head: "We have ideas and no passions, but by marriage with a Pollexfen we have given a tongue to the sea cliffs."

Among the miniatures there is a larger picture, an admirable drawing by I know not what master, that is too harsh and merry for its company. He was a connection and close friend of my great-grandmother Corbet, and though we spoke of him as "Uncle Beattie" in our childhood, no blood relation. My great-grandmother who died at ninety-three had many memories of him. He was the friend of Goldsmith and was accustomed to boast, clergyman though he was, that he belonged to a hunt-club of which every member but himself had been hanged or transported for treason, and that it was not possible to ask him a question he could not reply to with a perfectly appropriate blasphemy or indecency.

[AN IRISH LITERATURE]

From these debates, from O'Leary's[4] conversation, and from the Irish books he lent or gave me has come all I have set my hand to since. I had begun to know a great deal about the Irish poets who had written in English. I read with excitement books I should find unreadable to-day, and found romance in lives that had neither wit nor adventure. I did not deceive myself, I knew how often they wrote a cold and abstract language, and yet I who had never wanted to see the houses where Keats and Shelley lived would ask everybody what sort of place Inchedony was, because Callanan had named after it a bad poem in the manner of *Childe Harold*.[5] Walking home from a debate, I remember saying to some college student, "Ireland cannot put from her the habits learned from her old military civilisation and from a church that prays in Latin. Those popular poets have not touched her heart, her poetry when it comes will be distinguished and lonely." O'Leary had once said to me, "Neither Ireland nor England knows the good from the bad in any art, but Ireland unlike England does not hate the good when it is pointed out to her." I began to plot and scheme how one might seal with the right image the soft wax before it began to harden. I had noticed that Irish Catholics among whom had been born so many political martyrs had not the good taste, the household courtesy and decency of the Protestant Ireland I had known, yet Protestant Ireland seemed to think of nothing but getting on in

---

4. John O'Leary (d. 1907), an Irish nationalist, for whom Yeats had great respect. Cf. *September 1913* (p. 2099), lines 7–8: "Romantic Ireland's dead and gone, / It's with O'Leary in the grave."

5. *Childe Harold's Pilgrimage*. Jeremiah John Callanan, Anglo-Irish poet, published *The Recluse of Inchedony and Other Poems* in 1830.

the world. I thought we might bring the halves together if we had a national literature that made Ireland beautiful in the memory, and yet had been freed from provincialism by an exacting criticism, an European pose.

1915

From The Trembling of the Veil

[LONDON AND PRE-RAPHAELITISM]

At the end of the eighties my father and mother, my brother and sisters and myself, all newly arrived from Dublin, were settled in Bedford Park in a red-brick house with several mantelpieces of wood, copied from marble mantelpieces designed by the brothers Adam,[1] a balcony and a little garden shadowed by a great horse-chestnut tree. Years before we had lived there, when the crooked ostentatiously picturesque streets with great trees casting great shadows had been a new enthusiasm: the pre-Raphaelite movement at last affecting life. But now exaggerated criticism had taken the place of enthusiasm, the tiled roofs, the first in modern London, were said to leak, which they did not, and the drains to be bad, though that was no longer true; and I imagine that houses were cheap. I remember feeling disappointed because the co-operative stores, with their little seventeenth-century panes, had lost the romance I saw there when I passed them still unfinished on my way to school; and because the public-house, called The Tabard after Chaucer's Inn, was so plainly a common public-house; and because the great sign of a trumpeter designed by Rooke, the pre-Raphaelite artist, had been freshened by some inferior hand. The big red-brick church had never pleased me, and I was accustomed, when I saw the wooden balustrade that ran along the slanting edge of the roof where nobody ever walked or could walk, to remember the opinion of some architect friend of my father's, that it had been put there to keep the birds from falling off. Still, however, it had some village characters and helped us to feel not wholly lost in the metropolis. I no longer went to church as a regular habit, but go I sometimes did, for one Sunday morning I saw these words painted on a board in the porch: "The congregation are requested to kneel during prayers; the kneelers are afterwards to be hung upon pegs provided for the purpose." In front of every seat hung a little cushion and these cushions were called "kneelers." Presently the joke ran through the community, where there were many artists who considered religion at best an unimportant accessory to good architecture and who disliked that particular church.

I could not understand where the charm had gone that I had felt, when as a schoolboy of twelve or thirteen I had played among the unfinished houses, once leaving the marks of my two hands, blacked by a fall among some paint, upon a white balustrade.

Yet I was in all things pre-Raphaelite. When I was fifteen or sixteen my father had told me about Rossetti and Blake and given me their poetry to read; and once at Liverpool on my way to Sligo I had seen Dante's *Dream* in the gallery there, a picture painted when Rossetti had lost his dramatic power

---

1. James and Robert, 18th-century Scottish architects and furniture designers who successfully adapted ancient Roman style in their work in England and Scotland.

and to-day not very pleasing to me, and its colour, its people, its romantic architecture had blotted all other pictures away. It was a perpetual bewilderment that when my father, moved perhaps by some memory of his youth, chose some theme from poetic tradition, he would soon weary and leave it unfinished. I had seen the change coming bit by bit and its defence elaborated by young men fresh from the Paris art-schools. "We must paint what is in front of us," or "A man must be of his own time," they would say, and if I spoke of Blake or Rossetti they would point out his bad drawing and tell me to admire Carolus Duran and Bastien-Lepage.[2] Then, too, they were very ignorant men; they read nothing, for nothing mattered but "knowing how to paint," being in reaction against a generation that seemed to have wasted its time upon so many things. I thought myself alone in hating these young men, their contempt for the past, their monopoly of the future, but in a few months I was to discover others of my own age, who thought as I did, for it is not true that youth looks before it with the mechanical gaze of a well-drilled soldier. Its quarrel is not with the past, but with the present, where its elders are so obviously powerful and no cause seems lost if it seem to threaten that power. Does cultivated youth ever really love the future, where the eye can discover no persecuted Royalty hidden among oak leaves,[3] though from it certainly does come so much proletarian rhetoric?

I was unlike others of my generation in one thing only. I am very religious, and deprived by Huxley and Tyndall,[4] whom I detested, of the simple-minded religion of my childhood. I had made a new religion, almost an infallible church of poetic tradition, of a fardel[5] of stories, and of personages, and of emotions, inseparable from their first expression, passed on from generation to generation by poets and painters with some help from philosophers and theologians. I wished for a world, where I could discover this tradition perpetually, and not in pictures and in poems only, but in tiles round the chimney-piece and in the hangings that kept out the draft. I had even created a dogma: "Because those imaginary people are created out of the deepest instinct of man, to be his measure and his norm, whatever I can imagine those mouths speaking may be the nearest I can go to truth." When I listened they seemed always to speak of one thing only: they, their loves, every incident of their lives, were steeped in the supernatural. Could even Titian's "Ariosto"[6] that I loved beyond other portraits have its grave look, as if waiting for some perfect final event, if the painters before Titian had not learned portraiture, while painting into the corner of compositions full of saints and Madonnas, their kneeling patrons? At seventeen years old I was already an old-fashioned brass cannon full of shot, and nothing had kept me from going off but a doubt as to my capacity to shoot straight.

2. Jules Bastien-Lepage (1848–1884) and Duran (1837–1917) were French painters.
3. Charles II, after the decisive defeat of his father, Charles I, by the Parliamentarians at Naseby in 1645, hid in an oak tree before escaping abroad.
4. John Tyndall (1820–1893), physicist and active propagandist for science and materialism. Thomas Henry Huxley (1825–1895), biologist and popu-larizer of Darwin's ideas.
5. Bundle. This archaic word suggests Yeats's poetic attitude at the stage in his life that he is describing.
6. Titian (ca. 1477–1576), a Venetian painter, was thought to have painted a portrait of Lodovico Ariosto, the Italian poet and author of *Orlando Furioso*. The painting is now described simply as *Portrait of a Man*.

[OSCAR WILDE]

My first meeting with Oscar Wilde was an astonishment. I never before heard a man talking with perfect sentences, as if he had written them all over night with labour and yet all spontaneous. There was present that night at Henley's,[7] by right of propinquity or of accident, a man full of the secret spite of dullness, who interrupted from time to time, and always to check or disorder thought; and I noticed with what mastery he was foiled and thrown. I noticed, too, that the impression of artificiality that I think all Wilde's listeners have recorded came from the perfect rounding of the sentences and from the deliberation that made it possible. That very impression helped him, as the effect of metre, or of the antithetical prose of the seventeenth century, which is itself a true metre, helped its writers, for he could pass without incongruity from some unforeseen, swift stroke of wit to elaborate reverie. I heard him say a few nights later: "Give me *The Winter's Tale*, 'Daffodils that come before the swallow dare' but not *King Lear*. What is *King Lear* but poor life staggering in the fog?" and the slow, carefully modulated cadence sounded natural to my ears. That first night he praised Walter Pater's *Studies in the History of the Renaissance*: "It is my golden book; I never travel anywhere without it; but it is the very flower of decadence: the last trumpet should have sounded the moment it was written." "But," said the dull man, "would you not have given us time to read it?" "Oh no," was the retort, "there would have been plenty of time afterwards—in either world." I think he seemed to us, baffled as we were by youth, or by infirmity, a triumphant figure, and to some of us a figure from another age, an audacious Italian fifteenth-century figure. A few weeks before I had heard one of my father's friends, an official in a publishing firm that had employed both Wilde and Henley as editors, blaming Henley who was "no use except under control" and praising Wilde, "so indolent but such a genius"; and now the firm became the topic of our talk. "How often do you go to the office?" said Henley. "I used to go three times a week," said Wilde, "for an hour a day but I have since struck off one of the days." "My God," said Henley, "I went five times a week for five hours a day and when I wanted to strike off a day they had a special committee meeting." "Furthermore," was Wilde's answer, "I never answered their letters. I have known men come to London full of bright prospects and seen them complete wrecks in a few months through a habit of answering letters." He too knew how to keep our elders in their place, and his method was plainly the more successful, for Henley had been dismissed. "No he is not an aesthete," Henley commented later, being somewhat embarrassed by Wilde's pre-Raphaelite entanglement; "one soon finds that he is a scholar and a gentleman." And when I dined with Wilde a few days afterwards he began at once, "I had to strain every nerve to equal that man at all"; and I was too loyal to speak my thought: "You and not he said all the brilliant things." He like the rest of us had felt the strain of an intensity that seemed to hold life at the point of drama. He had said on that first meeting "The basis of literary friendship is mixing the poisoned bowl"; and for a few weeks Henley and he became close friends till, the astonishment of their meeting over, diversity of character and ambition pushed them apart, and,

---

7. William Ernest Henley (1849–1903), poet, critic, and editor.

with half the cavern helping, Henley began mixing the poisoned bowl for Wilde. Yet Henley never wholly lost that first admiration, for after Wilde's downfall he said to me: "Why did he do it? I told my lads to attack him and yet we might have fought under his banner."

[THE ORIGIN OF THE LAKE ISLE OF INNISFREE]

I had various women friends on whom I would call towards five o'clock mainly to discuss my thoughts that I could not bring to a man without meeting some competing thought, but partly because their tea and toast saved my pennies for the 'bus ride home; but with women, apart from their intimate exchanges of thought, I was timid and abashed. I was sitting on a seat in front of the British Museum feeding pigeons when a couple of girls sat near and began enticing my pigeons away, laughing and whispering to one another, and I looked straight in front of me, very indignant, and presently went into the Museum without turning my head towards them. Since then I have often wondered if they were pretty or merely very young. Sometimes I told myself very adventurous love-stories with myself for hero, and at other times I planned out a life of lonely austerity, and at other times mixed the ideals and planned a life of lonely austerity mitigated by periodical lapses. I had still the ambition, formed in Sligo in my teens, of living in imitation of Thoreau on Innisfree, a little island in Lough Gill,[8] and when walking through Fleet Street very homesick I heard a little tinkle of water and saw a fountain in a shop-window which balanced a little ball upon its jet, and began to remember lake water. From the sudden remembrance came my poem Innisfree, my first lyric with anything in its rhythm of my own music. I had begun to loosen rhythm as an escape from rhetoric and from that emotion of the crowd that rhetoric brings, but I only understood vaguely and occasionally that I must for my special purpose use nothing but the common syntax. A couple of years later I would not have written that first line with its conventional archaism—"Arise and go"—nor the inversion in the last stanza.

*   *   *

[THE RHYMERS' CLUB]

I had already met most of the poets of my generation. I had said, soon after the publication of The Wanderings of Usheen,[9] to the editor of a series of shilling reprints, who had set me to compile tales of the Irish fairies, "I am growing jealous of other poets and we will all grow jealous of each other unless we know each other and so feel a share in each other's triumph." He was a Welshman, lately a mining engineer, Ernest Rhys,[1] a writer of Welsh translations and original poems, that have often moved me greatly though I can think of no one else who has read them. He was perhaps a dozen years older than myself and through his work as editor knew everybody who would compile a book for seven or eight pounds. Between us we founded The Rhymers' Club, which for some years was to meet every night in an upper

---

8. See The Lake Isle of Innisfree (n. 1, p. 2092).
9. An early long poem by Yeats (1889). He later spelled the name of the hero "Oisin."

1. A Welsh writer and editor (1859–1946); original editor of Everyman's Library.

room with a sanded floor in an ancient eating-house in the Strand called The Cheshire Cheese. Lionel Johnson, Ernest Dowson, Victor Plarr, Ernest Radford, John Davidson, Richard le Gallienne, T. W. Rolleston, Selwyn Image, Edwin Ellis, and John Todhunter came constantly for a time, Arthur Symons and Herbert Horne, less constantly, while William Watson joined but never came and Francis Thompson[2] came once but never joined; and sometimes if we met in a private house, which we did occasionally, Oscar Wilde came. It had been useless to invite him to The Cheshire Cheese for he hated Bohemia. "Olive Schreiner,"[3] he said once to me, "is staying in the East End because that is the only place where people do not wear masks upon their faces, but I have told her that I live in the West End because nothing in life interests me but the mask."

We read our poems to one another and talked criticism and drank a little wine. I sometimes say when I speak of the club, "We had such and such ideas, such and such a quarrel with the great Victorians, we set before us such and such aims," as though we had many philosophical ideas. I say this because I am ashamed to admit that I had these ideas and that whenever I began to talk of them a gloomy silence fell upon the room. A young Irish poet, who wrote excellently but had the worst manners, was to say a few years later, "You do not talk like a poet, you talk like a man of letters," and if all the Rhymers had not been polite, if most of them had not been to Oxford or Cambridge, the greater number would have said the same thing. I was full of thought, often very abstract thought, longing all the while to be full of images, because I had gone to the art school instead of a university. Yet even if I had gone to a university, and learned all the classical foundations of English literature and English culture, all that great erudition which once accepted frees the mind from restlessness, I should have had to give up my Irish subject-matter, or attempt to found a new tradition. Lacking sufficient recognised precedent I must needs find out some reason for all I did.

* * *

1922

2. The names here are of poets and writers of the 1890s who were fellow members with Yeats of the Rhymers' Club. Thompson (1859–1907), who "never joined," was the author of The Hound of

Heaven.
3. South Africa novelist, author of The Story of an African Farm (1883).

E. M. FORSTER
1879–1970

Edward Morgan Forster was born in London; his father was an architect of Welsh extraction and his mother, a member of a family distinguished during several generations for its evangelical religion and its philanthropic activities. He was educated at Tonbridge School (the "Sawston" of The Longest Journey), where he suffered the tribulations of a day boy at a boarding school, and at King's College, Cambridge. The friends he made and the intellectual companionship he found at Cambridge influenced his entire life. He visited Greece and spent some time in Italy in 1901, and this experience also had a permanent influence on him; throughout his life he tended to set Greek and Italian peasant life in symbolic contrast to the stuffy and repressed life of middle-class England. Both Greek mythology and Italian Renaissance art opened up to him a world of what Matthew Arnold called "spontaneity of consciousness," and most of his work is concerned with ways of discovering such a quality in personal relationships amid the complexities and distortions of modern life. He began writing as a contributor to the newly founded liberal *Independent Review* in 1903, and in 1905 published his first novel, *Where Angels Fear to Tread*, a tragicomic projection of conflicts between refined English gentility and coarse Italian vitality.

English tutoring in Germany; an extended visit to India in 1912 and a shorter one in 1922; continuous intellectual companionship with a lively circle of friends; and in 1946 an honorary fellowship at King's College, Cambridge, where he mostly lived afterward, though with a good deal of traveling abroad—all this added up to a civilized and humane existence and (as Forster himself insisted) an unusually happy one. His main interest was always in personal relations, the "little society" we make for ourselves with our friends. He was a member of the "Bloomsbury Group"—so called because some of its more prominent figures lived in the Bloomsbury district of London—that included such writers as Lytton Strachey and Virginia Woolf, the art historians Clive Bell and Roger Fry, and the economist John Maynard Keynes. Looking beyond that "little society," he cast a critical and reforming eye on the abuses of the world, his point of view being always that of the independent liberal, suspicious of all political slogans and catchwords.

Forster's second novel, *The Longest Journey* (1907), examines the differences between living and dead relationships with much incidental satire of English public-school education and English notions of respectability. *A Room with a View* (1908) explores the nature of love with a great deal of subtlety, using (as with his first novel) Italy as a liberating agent. *Howards End* (1910) probes the relation between inward feeling and outward action, between the kinds of reality in which people get involved in living. "Only connect!" exclaims one of the characters. "Only connect the prose and the passion, and both will be exalted, and human love will soon be at its height." But no one knew better than Forster that this is more easily said than done and that false or premature connections, connections made by rule and not achieved through total realization of the personality, can destroy and corrupt. The halfway house to salvation is often grimmer than the starting point. In his last novel (for Forster wrote no more fiction), *A Passage to India* (1924), he takes the relations between British and Indians in the subcontinent as a background for the most searching and complex of all his explorations of the possibilities and limitations, the promises and pitfalls, of human relationships. Between his two visits to India lay the Great War, which, eroding the manpower and confidence of the upper and middle classes in England, eroded also the confidence of the British Raj (Hindu for "reign"). Worsening relations between British and Indians had culminated in what came to be known as the Amritsar Massacre of 1919, when Gurka troops under a British general opened fire on a crowd of protesters, killing almost four hundred.

Faced with the problem of whether to set the novel he had begun in 1912 in the prewar or the postwar period, Forster set it "out of time" and deliberately free from specific political reference. Its theme is the question three Indians debate in the second chapter, *Mosque*—"whether or not it is possible to be friends with an Englishman"—a debate followed by a practical demonstration of the difficulties of establishing such a friendship. Forster told the Indian friend to whom he dedicated it: "When I began the book I thought of it as a little bridge between East and West, but this conception has had to go, my sense of truth forbids anything so comfortable." When in the last chapter the question is asked again, "Why can't we be friends now?" the answer is "No, not yet," an answer seen by some as a prophecy of the improved relations between India and Great Britain, independent members of today's Commonwealth.

A Passage to India remains Forster's best-known novel, as well as his best. Published posthumously was another novel, Maurice, written more than fifty years before, in which he tried to define and do justice to the homosexual love that had played an important part in his life. It was a brave attempt but, as a work of art, not a success. He also wrote short stories, as well as critical, autobiographical, and descriptive prose, notably Aspects of the Novel (1927), which, as a discussion of the techniques of fiction by a practicing novelist, has become a minor classic of criticism.

From A Passage to India[1]

Chapter 2. Mosque

Abandoning his bicycle, which fell before a servant could catch it, the young man sprang up onto the veranda. He was all animation. "Hamidullah, Hamidullah! Am I late?" he cried.

"Do not apologize," said his host. "You are always late."

"Kindly answer my question. Am I late? Has Mahmoud Ali eaten all the food? If so I go elsewhere. Mr Mahmoud Ali, how are you?"

"Thank you, Dr Aziz, I am dying."

"Dying before your dinner? Oh, poor Mahmoud Ali!"

"Hamidullah here is actually dead. He passed away just as you rode up on your bike."

"Yes, that is so," said the other. "Imagine us both as addressing you from another and a happier world."

"Does there happen to be such a thing as a hookah[2] in that happier world of yours?"

"Aziz, don't chatter. We are having a very sad talk."

The hookah had been packed too tight, as was usual in his friend's house, and bubbled sulkily. He coaxed it. Yielding at last, the tobacco jetted up into his lungs and nostrils, driving out the smoke of burning cow-dung that had filled them as he rode through the bazaar. It was delicious. He lay in a trance, sensuous but healthy, through which the talk of the two others did not seem particularly sad—they were discussing as to whether or no it is possible to be friends with an Englishman. Mahmoud Ali argued that it was not, Hamidullah disagreed, but with so many reservations that there was no friction between them. Delicious indeed to lie on the broad veranda with the moon rising in front and the servants preparing dinner behind, and no trouble happening.

"Well, look at my own experience this morning."

"I only contend that it is possible in England," replied Hamidullah, who had been to that country long ago, before the big rush, and had received a cordial welcome at Cambridge.

"It is impossible here. Aziz! The red-nosed boy[3] has again insulted me in court. I do not blame him. He was told that he ought to insult me. Until lately he was quite a nice boy, but the others have got hold of him."

1. Muslim place of worship.
2. Eastern tobacco pipe with a long tube; smoke is drawn through water in a vase to which tube and bowl are attached.
3. Ronnie Heaslop, city magistrate of Chandrapore, newly arrived from England.

"Yes, they have no chance here, that is my point. They come out intending to be gentlemen, and are told it will not do. Look at Lesley, look at Blakiston, now it is your red-nosed boy, and Fielding will go next. Why, I remember when Turton came out first. It was in another part of the Province. You fellows will not believe me, but I have driven with Turton in his carriage— Turton! Oh yes, we were once quite intimate. He has shown me his stamp collection."

"He would expect you to steal it now. Turton! But red-nosed boy will be far worse than Turton!"

"I do not think so. They all become exactly the same—not worse, not better. I give any Englishman two years, be he Turton or Burton. It is only the difference of a letter. And I give any Englishwoman six months. All are exactly alike. Do you not agree with me?"

"I do not," replied Mahmoud Ali, entering into the bitter fun, and feeling both pain and amusement at each word that was uttered. "For my own part I find such profound differences among our rulers. Red-nose mumbles, Turton talks distinctly, Mrs Turton takes bribes, Mrs Red-nose does not and cannot, because so far there is no Mrs Red-nose."

"Bribes?"

"Did you not know that when they were lent to Central India over a canal scheme some rajah or other gave her a sewing machine in solid gold so that the water should run through his state?"

"And does it?"

"No, that is where Mrs Turton is so skilful. When we poor blacks take bribes, we perform what we are bribed to perform, and the law discovers us in consequence. The English take and do nothing. I admire them."

"We all admire them. Aziz, please pass me the hookah."

"Oh, not yet—hookah is so jolly now."

"You are a very selfish boy." He raised his voice suddenly, and shouted for dinner. Servants shouted back that it was ready. They meant that they wished it was ready, and were so understood, for nobody moved. Then Hamidullah continued, but with changed manner and evident emotion.

"But take my case—the case of young Hugh Bannister. Here is the son of my dear, my dead friends, the Reverend and Mrs Bannister, whose goodness to me in England I shall never forget or describe. They were father and mother to me, I talked to them as I do now. In the vacations their rectory became my home. They entrusted all their children to me—I often carried little Hugh about—I took him up to the funeral of Queen Victoria, and held him in my arms above the crowd."

"Queen Victoria was different," murmured Mahmoud Ali.

"I learn now that this boy is in business as a leather merchant at Cawnpore. Imagine how I long to see him and to pay his fare that this house may be his home. But it is useless. The other Anglo-Indians[4] will have got hold of him long ago. He will probably think that I want something, and I cannot face that from the son of my old friends. Oh, what in this country has gone wrong with everything, Vakil Sahib? I ask you."

Aziz joined in. "Why talk about the English? Brrrr . . . ! Why be either friends with the fellows or not friends? Let us shut them out and be jolly.

4. People of British birth living in India.

Queen Victoria and Mrs Bannister were the only exceptions, and they're dead."

"No, no, I do not admit that, I have met others."

"So have I," said Mahmoud Ali, unexpectedly veering. "All ladies are far from alike." Their mood was changed, and they recalled little kindnesses and courtesies. "She said 'Thank you so much' in the most natural way." "She offered me a lozenge when the dust irritated my throat." Hamidullah could remember more important examples of angelic ministration, but the other, who only knew Anglo-India, had to ransack his memory for scraps, and it was not surprising that he should return to "But of course all this is exceptional. The exception does not prove the rule. The average woman is like Mrs Turton, and, Aziz, you know what she is." Aziz did not know, but said he did. He too generalized from his disappointments—it is difficult for members of a subject race to do otherwise. Granted the exceptions, he agreed that all Englishwomen are haughty and venal. The gleam passed from the conversation, whose wintry surface unrolled and expanded interminably.

A servant announced dinner. They ignored him. The elder men had reached their eternal politics, Aziz drifted into the garden. The trees smelt sweet—green-blossomed champak[5]—and scraps of Persian poetry came into his head. Dinner, dinner, dinner . . . but when he returned to the house for it Mahmoud Ali had drifted away in his turn, to speak to his sais.[6] "Come and see my wife a little then," said Hamidullah, and they spent twenty minutes behind the purdah.[7] Hamidullah Begum[8] was a distant aunt of Aziz, and the only female relative he had in Chandrapore, and she had much to say to him on this occasion about a family circumcision that had been celebrated with imperfect pomp. It was difficult to get away, because until they had had their dinner she would not begin hers, and consequently prolonged her remarks in case they should suppose she was impatient. Having censured the circumcision, she bethought her of kindred topics, and asked Aziz when he was going to be married.

Respectful but irritated, he answered, "Once is enough."

"Yes, he has done his duty," said Hamidullah. "Do not tease him so. He carries on his family, two boys and their sister."

"Aunt, they live most comfortably with my wife's mother, where she was living when she died. I can see them whenever I like. They are such very, very small children."

"And he sends them the whole of his salary and lives like a low-grade clerk, and tells no one the reason. What more do you require him to do?"

But this was not Hamidullah Begum's point, and having courteously changed the conversation for a few moments she returned and made it. She said: "What is to become of all our daughters if men refuse to marry? They will marry beneath them, or—" And she began the oft-told tale of a lady of imperial descent who could find no husband in the narrow circle where her pride permitted her to mate, and had lived on unwed, her age now thirty, and would die unwed, for no one would have her now. While the tale was in

5. The blossoms of this tree, much featured in poetry, turn into fragrant yellow-white flowers.
6. Groom (Arabic).
7. Curtain (Urdu and Persian) screening Muslim

or Hindu women from the sight of strangers.
8. Married Indian Muslim lady of high rank (Urdu).

progress, it convinced the two men, the tragedy seemed a slur on the whole community; better polygamy almost, than that a woman should die without the joys God has intended her to receive. Wedlock, motherhood, power in the house—for what else is she born, and how can the man who has denied them to her stand up to face her creator and his own at the last day? Aziz took his leave saying "Perhaps . . . but later . . ."—his invariable reply to such an appeal.

"You mustn't put off what you think right," said Hamidullah. "That is why India is in such a plight, because we put off things." But seeing that his young relative looked worried he added a few soothing words, and thus wiped out any impression that his wife might have made.

During their absence, Mahmoud Ali had gone off in his carriage, leaving a message that he should be back in five minutes, but they were on no account to wait. They sat down to meat with a distant cousin of the house, Mohammed Latif, who lived on Hamidullah's bounty and who occupied the position neither of a servant nor of an equal. He did not speak unless spoken to, and since no one spoke kept unoffended silence. Now and then he belched, in compliment to the richness of the food. A gentle, happy and dishonest old man; all his life he had never done a stroke of work. So long as someone of his relatives had a house he was sure of a home, and it was unlikely that so large a family would all go bankrupt. His wife led a similar existence some hundreds of miles away—he did not visit her, owing to the expense of the railway ticket. Presently Aziz chaffed him, also the servants, and then began quoting poetry: Persian, Urdu, a little Arabic. His memory was good, and for so young a man he had read largely; the themes he preferred were the decay of Islam and the brevity of love. They listened delighted, for they took the public view of poetry, not the private which obtains in England. It never bored them to hear words, words; they breathed them with the cool night air, never stopping to analyse; the name of the poet, Hafiz, Hali, Iqbal,[9] was sufficient guarantee. India—a hundred Indias—whispered outside beneath the indifferent moon, but for the time India seemed one and their own, and they regained their departed greatness by hearing its departure lamented, they felt young again because reminded that youth must fly. A servant in scarlet interrupted him; he was the chuprassy[1] of the Civil Surgeon, and he handed Aziz a note.

"Old Callendar wants to see me at his bungalow," he said, not rising. "He might have the politeness to say why."

"Some case, I dare say."

"I dare say not, I dare say nothing. He has found out our dinner-hour, that's all, and chooses to interrupt us every time, in order to show his power."

"On the one hand he always does this, on the other it may be a serious case, and you cannot know," said Hamidullah, considerately paving the way towards obedience. "Had you not better clean your teeth after pan?"[2]

"If my teeth are to be cleaned, I don't go at all. I am an Indian, it is an Indian habit to take pan. The Civil Surgeon must put up with it. Mohammed Latif, my bike, please."

The poor relation got up. Slightly immersed in the realms of matter, he

---

9. Muhammad Iqbal (1876–1938), Indian poet and philosopher. Mohammad Shams Od-Din Hafiz (1325/26–1389/90), Persian lyric poet. Altaf Husain "Hali" (1837–1914), Urdu poet and founder of literary criticism in Urdu.
1. Official messenger (Hindi).
2. Leaf of the betel nut, chewed, as a delicacy, by southern Asians.

laid his hand on the bicycle's saddle, while a servant did the actual wheeling. Between them they took it over a tin-tack. Aziz held his hands under the ewer,[3] dried them, fitted on his green felt hat, and then with unexpected energy whizzed out of Hamidullah's compound.

"Aziz, Aziz, imprudent boy. . . ." But he was far down the bazaar, riding furiously. He had neither light nor bell nor had he a brake, but what use are such adjuncts in a land where the cyclist's only hope is to coast from face to face, and just before he collides with each it vanishes? And the city was fairly empty at this hour. When his tyre went flat, he leapt off and shouted for a tonga.[4]

He did not at first find one, and he had also to dispose of his bicycle at a friend's house. He dallied furthermore to clean his teeth. But at last he was rattling towards the Civil Lines,[5] with a vivid sense of speed. As he entered their arid tidiness, depression suddenly seized him. The roads, named after victorious generals and intersecting at right angles, were symbolic of the net Great Britain had thrown over India. He felt caught in their meshes. When he turned into Major Callendar's compound he could with difficulty restrain himself from getting down from the tonga and approaching the bungalow on foot, and this not because his soul was servile but because his feelings—the sensitive edges of him—feared a gross snub. There had been a "case" last year—an Indian gentleman had driven up to an official's house and been turned back by the servants and told to approach more suitably—only one case among thousands of visits to hundreds of officials, but its fame spread wide. The young man shrank from a repetition of it. He compromised, and stopped the driver just outside the flood of light that fell across the veranda.

The Civil Surgeon was out.

"But the sahib has left me some message?"

The servant returned an indifferent "No". Aziz was in despair. It was a servant whom he had forgotten to tip, and he could do nothing now because there were people in the hall. He was convinced that there was a message, and that the man was withholding it out of revenge. While they argued, the people came out. Both were ladies. Aziz lifted his hat. The first, who was in evening dress, glanced at the Indian and turned instinctively away.

"Mrs Lesley, it *is* a tonga," she cried.

"Ours?" inquired the second, also seeing Aziz, and doing likewise.

"Take the gifts the gods provide, anyhow," she screeched, and both jumped in. "O tonga-wallah, Club, Club.[6] Why doesn't the fool go?"

"Go, I will pay you tomorrow," said Aziz to the driver, and as they went off he called courteously, "You are most welcome, ladies." They did not reply, being full of their own affairs.

So it had come, the usual thing—just as Mahmoud Ali said. The inevitable snub—his bow ignored, his carriage taken. It might have been worse, for it comforted him somehow that Mesdames[7] Callendar and Lesley should both be fat and weigh the tonga down behind. Beautiful women would have pained him. He turned to the servant, gave him a couple of rupees,[8] and

---

3. Water jug with a wide mouth.
4. Light two-wheeled, horse-drawn vehicle (Hindi).
5. Civilian (as distinct from military) residential area.

6. European Club, membership of which was only open to Europeans. "Wallah": man (Hindi).
7. Mrs. (French; pl.).
8. Small silver coins.

asked again whether there was a message. The man, now very civil, returned the same answer. Major Callendar had driven away half an hour before.

"Saying nothing?"

He had as a matter of fact said, "Damn Aziz"—words that the servant understood, but was too polite to repeat. One can tip too much as well as too little, indeed the coin that buys the exact truth has not yet been minted.

"Then I will write him a letter."

He was offered the use of the house, but was too dignified to enter it. Paper and ink were brought onto the veranda. He began: "Dear Sir,—At your express command I have hastened as a subordinate should—" and then stopped. "Tell him I have called, that is sufficient," he said, tearing the protest up. "Here is my card. Call me a tonga."

"Huzoor,[9] all are at the Club."

"Then telephone for one down to the railway station." And since the man hastened to do this he said, "Enough, enough, I prefer to walk." He commandeered a match and lit a cigarette. These attentions, though purchased, soothed him. They would last as long as he had rupees, which is something. But to shake the dust of Anglo-India off his feet! To escape from the net and be back among manners and gestures that he knew! He began to walk, an unwonted exercise.

He was an athletic little man, daintily put together, but really very strong. Nevertheless walking fatigued him, as it fatigues everyone in India except the newcomer. There is something hostile in that soil. It either yields, and the foot sinks into a depression, or else it is unexpectedly rigid and sharp, pressing stones or crystals against the tread. A series of these little surprises exhausts; and he was wearing pumps, a poor preparation for any country. At the edge of the Civil Station[1] he turned into a mosque to rest.

He had always liked this mosque. It was gracious, and the arrangement pleased him. The courtyard—entered through a ruined gate—contained an ablution-tank of fresh clear water, which was always in motion, being indeed part of a conduit that supplied the city. The courtyard was paved with broken slabs. The covered part of the mosque was deeper than is usual; its effect was that of an English parish church whose side has been taken out. Where he sat, he looked into three arcades whose darkness was illuminated by a small hanging lamp and by the moon. The front—in full moonlight—had the appearance of marble, and the ninety-nine names of God on the frieze stood out black, as the frieze stood out white against the sky. The contrast between this dualism and the contention of shadows within pleased Aziz, and he tried to symbolize the whole into some truth of religion or love. A mosque by winning his approval let loose his imagination. The temple of another creed, Hindu, Christian or Greek, would have bored him and failed to awaken his sense of beauty. Here was Islam, his own country, more than a Faith, more than a battle-cry, more, much more . . . Islam, an attitude towards life both exquisite and durable, where his body and his thoughts found their home.

His seat was the low wall that bounded the courtyard on the left. The ground fell away beneath him towards the city, visible as a blur of trees, and in the stillness he heard many small sounds. On the right, over in the Club,

9. Title of respect (Arabic).
1. Civilian (as distinct from military) residential area. "Pumps": light shoes.

the English community contributed an amateur orchestra. Elsewhere some Hindus were drumming—he knew they were Hindus, because the rhythm was uncongenial to him—and others were bewailing a corpse—he knew whose, having certified it in the afternoon. There were owls, the Punjab mail[2] . . . and flowers smelt deliciously in the station-master's garden. But the mosque—that alone signified, and he returned to it from the complex appeal of the night, and decked it with meanings the builder had never intended. Some day he too would build a mosque, smaller than this but in perfect taste, so that all who passed by should experience the happiness he felt now. And near it, under a low dome, should be his tomb, with a Persian inscription:

> Alas, without me for thousands of years
> The Rose will blossom and the Spring will bloom,
> But those who have secretly understood my heart—
> They will approach and visit the grave where I lie.

He had seen the quatrain on the tomb of a Deccan[3] king and regarded it as profound philosophy—he always held pathos to be profound. The secret understanding of the heart! He repeated the phrase with tears in his eyes, and as he did so one of the pillars of the mosque seemed to quiver. It swayed in the gloom and detached itself. Belief in ghosts ran in his blood, but he sat firm. Another pillar moved, a third, and then an Englishwoman stepped out into the moonlight. Suddenly he was furiously angry and shouted: "Madam! Madam! Madam!"

"Oh! Oh!" the woman gasped.

"Madam, this is a mosque, you have no right here at all; you should have taken off your shoes; this is a holy place for Moslems."

"I have taken them off."

"You have?"

"I left them at the entrance."

"Then I ask your pardon."

Still startled, the woman moved out, keeping the ablution-tank between them. He called after her, "I am truly sorry for speaking."

"Yes, I was right, was I not? If I remove my shoes, I am allowed?"

"Of course, but so few ladies take the trouble, especially if thinking no one is there to see."

"That makes no difference. God is here."

"Madam!"

"Please let me go."

"Oh, can I do you some service now or at any time?"

"No, thank you, really none—good night."

"May I know your name?"

She was now in the shadow of the gateway, so that he could not see her face, but she saw his, and she said with a change of voice, "Mrs Moore."

"Mrs—" Advancing, he found that she was old. A fabric bigger than the mosque fell to pieces, and he did not know whether he was glad or sorry. She was older than Hamidullah Begum, with a red face and white hair. Her voice had deceived him.

"Mrs Moore, I am afraid I startled you. I shall tell our community—my

---

2. Mail train serving northwest India. 3. High triangular tableland of central south India.

friends—about you. That God is here—very good, very fine indeed. I think you are newly arrived in India."

"Yes—how did you know?"

"By the way you address me. No, but can I call you a carriage?"

"I have only come from the Club. They are doing a play that I have seen in London, and it was so hot."

"What was the name of the play?"

"*Cousin Kate*."[4]

"I think you ought not to walk at night alone, Mrs Moore. There are bad characters about and leopards may come across from the Marabar Hills. Snakes also."

She exclaimed; she had forgotten the snakes.

"For example, a six-spot beetle," he continued. "You pick it up, it bites, you die."

"But you walk alone yourself."

"Oh, I am used to it."

"Used to snakes?"

They both laughed. "I'm a doctor," he said. "Snakes don't dare bite me." They sat down side by side in the entrance, and slipped on their evening shoes. "Please may I ask you a question now? Why do you come to India at this time of year, just as the cold weather is ending?"

"I intended to start earlier, but there was an unavoidable delay."

"It will soon be so unhealthy for you! And why ever do you come to Chandrapore?"

"To visit my son. He is the City Magistrate here."

"Oh no, excuse me, that is quite impossible. Our City Magistrate's name is Mr Heaslop. I know him intimately."

"He's my son all the same," she said, smiling.

"But, Mrs Moore, how can he be?"

"I was married twice."

"Yes, now I see, and your first husband died."

"He did, and so did my second husband."

"Then we are in the same box," he said cryptically.

"Then is the City Magistrate the entire of your family now?"

"No, there are the younger ones—Ralph and Stella in England."

"And the gentleman here, is he Ralph and Stella's half-brother?"

"Quite right."

"Mrs Moore, this is all extremely strange, because like yourself I have also two sons and a daughter. Is not this the same box with a vengeance?"

"What are their names? Not also Ronny, Ralph and Stella, surely?"

The suggestion delighted him. "No, indeed. How funny it sounds! Their names are quite different and will surprise you. Listen, please. I am about to tell you my children's names. The first is called Ahmed, the second is called Karim, the third—she is the eldest—Jamila. Three children are enough. Do not you agree with me?"

"I do."

They were both silent for a little, thinking of their respective families. She sighed and rose to go.

---

4. *Cousin Kate: A New Comedy in Three Acts,* by Hubert Henry Davies (1869–1917), was published in 1910.

"Would you care to see over the Minto Hospital one morning?" he inquired. "I have nothing else to offer at Chandrapore."

"Thank you, I have seen it already, or I should have liked to come with you very much."

"I suppose the Civil Surgeon took you."

"Yes, and Mrs Callendar."

His voice altered. "Ah! A very charming lady."

"Possibly, when one knows her better."

"What? What? You didn't like her?"

"She was certainly intending to be kind, but I did not find her exactly charming."

He burst out with: "She has just taken my tonga without my permission— do you call that being charming?—and Major Callendar interrupts me night after night from where I am dining with my friends and I go at once, breaking up a most pleasant entertainment, and he is not there and not even a message. Is this charming, pray? But what does it matter? I can do nothing and he knows it. I am just a subordinate, my time is of no value, the veranda is good enough for an Indian, yes, yes, let him stand, and Mrs Callendar takes my carriage and cuts me dead. . . ."

She listened.

He was excited partly by his wrongs, but much more by the knowledge that someone sympathized with them. It was this that led him to repeat, exaggerate, contradict. She had proved her sympathy by criticizing her fellow countrywoman to him, but even earlier he had known. The flame that not even beauty can nourish was springing up, and though his words were querulous his heart began to glow secretly. Presently it burst into speech.

"You understand me, you know what I feel. Oh, if others resembled you!"

Rather surprised, she replied: "I don't think I understand people very well. I only know whether I like or dislike them."

"Then you are an Oriental."

She accepted his escort back to the Club, and said at the gate that she wished she was a member, so that she could have asked him in.

"Indians are not allowed into the Chandrapore Club even as guests," he said simply. He did not expatiate on his wrongs now, being happy. As he strolled downhill beneath the lovely moon, and again saw the lovely mosque, he seemed to own the land as much as anyone owned it. What did it matter if a few flabby Hindus had preceded him there, and a few chilly English succeeded?

1924

VIRGINIA WOOLF
1882–1941

Virginia Woolf was born in London, daughter of Leslie (later Sir Leslie) Stephen, the Victorian critic, philosopher, biographer, and scholar. She grew up as a member of a large and talented family, educating herself in her father's magnificent library, meeting in childhood many eminent Victorians, learning Greek from Walter Pater's sister. After her father's death in 1904 she settled with her sister and two brothers in Bloomsbury, that district of London which later was to become associated with her and the group among whom she moved. The "Bloomsbury Group" included Lytton Strachey, the biographer; J. M. Keynes, the celebrated economist; Roger Fry, an art critic; and E. M. Forster. When her sister, Vanessa, a notable painter, married Clive Bell, an art critic, in 1907, she and her brother took together another house in Bloomsbury, and there they entertained their literary and artistic friends at evening gatherings where the conversation sparkled. Their intelligence was equaled by their frankness, notably on sexual topics, and the sexual life of Bloomsbury provided ample material for discussion. The painter Duncan Grant, for example, was at different times the lover of Maynard Keynes, Virginia Woolf's brother Adrian, and her sister, Vanessa, and he was the father of Vanessa's daughter, Angelica. Virginia was herself bisexual; and thirteen years after her marriage to the journalist and essayist Leonard Woolf, she fell passionately in love with the poet Vita [Victoria] Sackville-West, wife of the bisexual diplomat and author Harold Nicolson. Woolf's relationship with this aristocratic lesbian was to produce the most lighthearted and scintillating of her books, *Orlando* (1928). She was fortunate to have a husband as supportive emotionally as he was intellectually, and their marriage withstood this and other strains. Together they founded the Hogarth Press in 1917—a press that published some of the most interesting literature of our time, including Eliot's *Poems* (1919) and *Homage to John Dryden* (1924), the English translations of Freud, as well as her own novels. Her suicide in March 1941, resulting from her dread of World War II and her fear that she was about to lose her mind and become a burden on her husband, first revealed to the public that she had been subject to periods of nervous depression, particularly after finishing a book, and that underneath the liveliness and wit so well known among the Bloomsbury Group lay disturbing pyschological tensions.

Woolf came naturally into the profession of writing. She moved among writers and artists, and her world was from the beginning the cultured world of the middle-class and upper-middle-class London intelligentsia. She rebelled against what she called the "materialism" of such novelists as Arnold Bennett and John Galsworthy and sought a more delicate rendering of those aspects of consciousness in which she felt that the truth of human experience really lay (see her essay *Modern Fiction,* printed here). After two novels cast in traditional form, she developed her own style, which handled the stream of consciousness with a carefully modulated poetic flow and brought into prose fiction something of the rhythms and the imagery of lyric poetry. The sketches in which she explored the possibilities of moving between action and contemplation, between specific external events in time and delicate tracings of the flow of consciousness where the mind moves between retrospect and anticipation, were collected in *Monday or Tuesday* (1921). These were technical experiments, and they made possible those later novels in which her characteristic method is fully developed—*Jacob's Room* (1922); *Mrs. Dalloway* (1925), the first completely successful novel in her "new" style; *To the Lighthouse* (1927); *The Waves* (1931), the most stylized of her novels; and *Between the Acts* (1941), published after her death. She was a skilled exponent of the stream of consciousness technique in her novels, exploring with great subtlety problems of personal identity and personal relationships as well as the significance of time, change, and memory for human personality.

Woolf was increasingly concerned with the position of women, especially professional women, and the constrictions they suffered under. She wrote several cogent essays on the subject, notably in *A Room of One's Own* (1929) and *Three Guineas* (1938). Her novel *The Years* (1937) was originally to have included reflections on the position of women interspersed amid the action, but she later decided to publish them as a separate book, which became *Three Guineas*.

She also wrote a great many reviews and critical essays, collected in *The Common Reader* (1925) and *The Second Common Reader* (1932); informal and personal in tone, her criticism is suggestive rather than authoritative and has an engaging air of spontaneity. She is equally concerned with her own craft as a writer and with what it was like to be a quite different person living in a different age. At once more informal and more revealing are the six volumes of her *Letters* (1975–80) and five volumes of her *Diary* (1977–84). These, with their running commentary on her life and work, resemble the sketchbooks of a great painter and serve as a reminder that her writings, for all their variety, have the coherence found only in the work of the greatest writers.

The Mark on the Wall

Perhaps it was the middle of January in the present year that I first looked up and saw the mark on the wall. In order to fix a date it is necessary to remember what one saw. So now I think of the fire; the steady film of yellow light upon the page of my book; the three chrysanthemums in the round glass bowl on the mantelpiece. Yes, it must have been the winter time, and we had just finished our tea, for I remember that I was smoking a cigarette when I looked up and saw the mark on the wall for the first time. I looked up through the smoke of my cigarette and my eye lodged for a moment upon the burning coals, and that old fancy of the crimson flag flapping from the castle tower came into my mind, and I thought of the cavalcade of red knights riding up the side of the black rock. Rather to my relief the sight of the mark interrupted the fancy, for it is an old fancy, an automatic fancy, made as a child perhaps. The mark was a small round mark, black upon the white wall, about six or seven inches above the mantelpiece.

How readily our thoughts swarm upon a new object, lifting it a little way, as ants carry a blade of straw so feverishly, and then leave it. . . . If that mark was made by a nail, it can't have been for a picture, it must have been for a miniature—the miniature of a lady with white powdered curls, powder-dusted cheeks, and lips like red carnations. A fraud of course, for the people who had this house before us would have chosen pictures in that way—an old picture for an old room. That is the sort of people they were—very interesting people, and I think of them so often, in such queer places, because one will never see them again, never know what happened next. They wanted to leave this house because they wanted to change their style of furniture, so he said, and he was in process of saying that in his opinion art should have ideas behind it when we were torn asunder, as one is torn from the old lady about to pour out tea and the young man about to hit the tennis ball in the back garden of the suburban villa as one rushes past in the train.

But for that mark, I'm not sure about it; I don't believe it was made by a nail after all; it's too big, too round, for that. I might get up, but if I got up and looked at it, ten to one I shouldn't be able to say for certain; because once a thing's done, no one ever knows how it happened. Oh! dear me, the mystery of life; the inaccuracy of thought! The ignorance of humanity! To show how very little control of our possessions we have—what an accidental affair this living is after all our civilisation—let me just count over a few of the things lost in one lifetime, beginning, for that seems always the most mysterious of losses—what cat would gnaw, what rat would nibble—three pale blue canisters of book-binding tools? Then there were the bird cages, the iron hoops, the steel skates, the Queen Anne coal-scuttle, the bagatelle board, the hand organ—all gone, and jewels, too. Opals and emeralds, they lie about the roots of turnips. What a scraping paring affair it is to be sure! The wonder is that I've any clothes on my back, that I sit surrounded by solid furniture at this moment. Why, if one wants to compare life to anything, one must liken it to being blown through the Tube[1] at fifty miles an hour— landing at the other end without a single hairpin in one's hair! Shot out at the feet of God entirely naked! Tumbling head over heels in the asphodel meadows[2] like brown paper parcels pitched down a shoot in the post office! With one's hair flying back like the tail of a race-horse. Yes, that seems to express the rapidity of life, the perpetual waste and repair; all so casual, all so haphazard. . . .

But after life. The slow pulling down of thick green stalks so that the cup of the flower, as it turns over, deluges one with purple and red light. Why, after all, should one not be born there as one is born here, helpless, speech-less, unable to focus one's eyesight, groping at the roots of the grass, at the toes of the Giants? As for saying which are trees, and which are men and women, or whether there are such things, that one won't be in a condition to do for fifty years or so. There will be nothing but spaces of light and dark, intersected by thick stalks, and rather higher up perhaps, rose-shaped blots of an indistinct colour—dim pinks and blues—which will, as time goes on, become more definite, become—I don't know what. . . .

And yet that mark on the wall is not a hole at all. It may even be caused by some round black substance, such as a small rose leaf, left over from the summer, and I, not being a very vigilant housekeeper—look at the dust on the mantelpiece, for example, the dust which, so they say, buried Troy three times over, only fragments of pots utterly refusing annihilation, as one can believe.

The tree outside the window taps very gently on the pane. . . . I want to think quietly, calmly, spaciously, never to be interrupted, never to have to rise from my chair, to slip easily from one thing to another, without any sense of hostility, or obstacle. I want to sink deeper and deeper, away from the surface, with its hard separate facts. To steady myself, let me catch hold of the first idea that passes . . . Shakespeare. . . . Well, he will do as well as another. A man who sat himself solidly in an arm-chair, and looked into the fire, so— A shower of ideas fell perpetually from some very high Heaven down through his mind. He leant his forehead on his hand, and people, looking in through the open door—for this scene is supposed to take place on a summer's evening— But how dull this is, this historical fiction! It doesn't interest me at all. I wish I could hit upon a pleasant track of thought, a track indirectly reflecting credit upon myself, for those are the pleasantest thoughts, and very frequent even in the minds of modest mouse-coloured people, who believe genuinely that they dislike to hear their own praises. They are not thoughts directly praising oneself; that is the beauty of them; they are thoughts like this:

"And then I came into the room. They were discussing botany. I said how I'd seen a flower growing on a dust heap on the site of an old house in Kingsway.[3] The seed, I said, must have been sown in the reign of Charles

---

1. The London underground railway, or subway.
2. I.e., heaven, the next world (in Greek mythology, asphodel flowers grow in the Elysian fields).
3. Street in London.

the First. What flowers grew in the reign of Charles the First?" I asked—(But I don't remember the answer.) Tall flowers with purple tassels to them perhaps. And so it goes on. All the time I'm dressing up the figure of myself in my own mind, lovingly, stealthily, not openly adoring it, for if I did that, I should catch myself out, and stretch my hand at once for a book in self-protection. Indeed, it is curious how instinctively one protects the image of oneself from idolatry or any other handling that could make it ridiculous, or too unlike the original to be believed in any longer. Or is it not so very curious after all? It is a matter of great importance. Suppose the looking-glass smashes, the image disappears, and the romantic figure with the green of forest depths all about it is there no longer, but only that shell of a person which is seen by other people—what an airless, shallow, bald, prominent world it becomes! A world not to be lived in. As we face each other in omnibuses and underground railways we are looking into the mirror; that accounts for the vagueness, the gleam of glassiness, in our eyes. And the novelists in future will realise more and more the importance of these reflections, for of course there is not one reflection but an almost infinite number; those are the depths they will explore, those the phantoms they will pursue, leaving the description of reality more and more out of their stories, taking a knowledge of it for granted, as the Greeks did and Shakespeare perhaps—but these generalisations are very worthless. The military sound of the word is enough. It recalls leading articles, cabinet ministers—a whole class of things indeed which, as a child, one thought the thing itself, the standard thing, the real thing, from which one could not depart save at the risk of nameless damnation. Generalisations bring back somehow Sunday in London, Sunday afternoon walks, Sunday luncheons, and also ways of speaking of the dead, clothes, and habits—like the habit of sitting all together in one room until a certain hour, although nobody liked it. There was a rule for everything. The rule for tablecloths at that particular period was that they should be made of tapestry with little yellow compartments marked upon them, such as you may see in photographs of the carpets in the corridors of the royal palaces. Tablecloths of a different kind were not real tablecloths. How shocking, and yet how wonderful it was to discover that these real things, Sunday luncheons, Sunday walks, country houses, and tablecloths were not entirely real, were indeed half phantoms, and the damnation which visited the disbeliever in them was only a sense of illegitimate freedom. What now takes the place of those things I wonder, those real standard things? Men perhaps, should you be a woman; the masculine point of view which governs our lives, which sets the standard, which establishes Whitaker's Table of Precedency,[4] which has become, I suppose, since the war, half a phantom to many men and women, which soon, one may hope, will be laughed into the dustbin where the phantoms go, the mahogany sideboards and the Landseer[5] prints, Gods and Devils, Hell and so forth, leaving us all with an intoxicating sense of illegitimate freedom—if freedom exists. . . .

In certain lights that mark on the wall seems actually to project from the wall. Nor is it entirely circular. I cannot be sure, but it seems to cast a

4. *Whitaker's Almanack,* an annual compendium of information, prints a "Table of Precedency," which shows the order in which the various ranks in public life and society proceed on formal occasions.

5. Edwin Henry Landseer, 19th-century animal painter, reproductions of whose *Stag at Bay, Monarch of the Glen,* and similar paintings were often found in Victorian homes.

perceptible shadow, suggesting that if I ran my finger down that strip of the wall it would, at a certain point, mount and descend a small tumulus, a smooth tumulus like those barrows on the South Downs[6] which are, they say, either tombs or camps. Of the two I should prefer them to be tombs, desiring melancholy like most English people, and finding it natural at the end of a walk to think of the bones stretched beneath the turf. . . . There must be some book about it. Some antiquary must have dug up those bones and given them a name. . . . What sort of a man is an antiquary, I wonder? Retired Colonels for the most part, I daresay, leading parties of aged labourers to the top here, examining clods of earth and stone, and getting into correspondence with the neighbouring clergy, which, being opened at breakfast time, gives them a feeling of importance, and the comparison of arrowheads necessitates cross-country journeys to the country towns, an agreeable necessity both to them and to their elderly wives, who wish to make plum jam or to clean out the study, and have every reason for keeping that great question of the camp or the tomb in perpetual suspension, while the Colonel himself feels agreeably philosophic in accumulating evidence on both sides of the question. It is true that he does finally incline to believe in the camp; and, being opposed, indites a pamphlet which he is about to read at the quarterly meeting of the local society when a stroke lays him low, and his last conscious thoughts are not of wife or child, but of the camp and that arrow-head there, which is now in the case at the local museum, together with the foot of a Chinese murderess, a handful of Elizabethan nails, a great many Tudor clay pipes, a piece of Roman pottery, and the wineglass that Nelson drank out of—proving I really don't know what.

No, no, nothing is proved, nothing is known. And if I were to get up at this very moment and ascertain that the mark on the wall is really—what shall we say?—the head of a gigantic old nail, driven in two hundred years ago, which has now, owing to the patient attrition of many generations of housemaids, revealed its head above the coat of paint, and is taking its first view of modern life in the sight of a white-walled fire-lit room, what should I gain?—Knowledge? Matter for further speculation? I can think sitting still as well as standing up. And what is knowledge? What are our learned men save the descendants of witches and hermits who crouched in caves and in woods brewing herbs, interrogating shrew-mice and writing down the language of the stars? And the less we honour them as our superstitions dwindle and our respect for beauty and health of mind increases. . . . Yes, one could imagine a very pleasant world. A quiet, spacious world, with the flowers so red and blue in the open fields. A world without professors or specialists or house-keepers with the profiles of policemen, a world which one could slice with one's thought as a fish slices the water with his fin, grazing the stems of the water-lilies, hanging suspended over nests of white sea eggs. . . . How peaceful it is down here, rooted in the centre of the world and gazing up through the grey waters, with their sudden gleams of light, and their reflections—if it were not for Whitaker's Almanack—if it were not for the Table of Precedency!

I must jump up and see for myself what that mark on the wall really is—a nail, a rose-leaf, a crack in the wood?

---

6. A range of low hills in southeastern England. "Barrows": mounds of earth or stones erected by prehistoric peoples, usually as burial places.

Here is nature once more at her old game of self-preservation. This train of thought, she perceives, is threatening mere waste of energy, even some collision with reality, for who will ever be able to lift a finger against Whitaker's Table of Precedency? The Archbishop of Canterbury is followed by the Lord High Chancellor; the Lord High Chancellor is followed by the Archbishop of York. Everybody follows somebody, such is the philosophy of Whitaker; and the great thing is to know who follows whom. Whitaker knows, and let that, so Nature counsels, comfort you, instead of enraging you; and if you can't be comforted, if you must shatter this hour of peace, think of the mark on the wall.

I understand Nature's game—her prompting to take action as a way of ending any thought that threatens to excite or to pain. Hence, I suppose, comes our slight contempt for men of action—men, we assume, who don't think. Still, there's no harm in putting a full stop to one's disagreeable thoughts by looking at a mark on the wall.

Indeed, now that I have fixed my eyes upon it, I feel that I have grasped a plank in the sea; I feel a satisfying sense of reality which at once turns the two Archbishops and the Lord High Chancellor to the shadows of shades. Here is something definite, something real. Thus, waking from a midnight dream of horror, one hastily turns on the light and lies quiescent, worshipping the chest of drawers, worshipping solidity, worshipping reality, worshipping the impersonal world which is a proof of some existence other than ours. That is what one wants to be sure of. . . . Wood is a pleasant thing to think about. It comes from a tree; and trees grow, and we don't know how they grow. For years and years they grow, without paying any attention to us, in meadows, in forests, and by the side of rivers—all things one likes to think about. The cows swish their tails beneath them on hot afternoons; they paint rivers so green that when a moorhen dives one expects to see its feathers all green when it comes up again. I like to think of the fish balanced against the stream like flags blown out; and of water-beetles slowly raising domes of mud upon the bed of the river. I like to think of the tree itself: first of the close dry sensation of being wood; then the grinding of the storm; then the slow, delicious ooze of sap; I like to think of it, too, on winter's nights standing in the empty field with all leaves close-furled, nothing tender exposed to the iron bullets of the moon, a naked mast upon an earth that goes tumbling, tumbling, all night long. The song of birds must sound very loud and strange in June; and how cold the feet of insects must feel upon it, as they make laborious progresses up the creases of the bark, or sun themselves upon the thin green awning of the leaves, and look straight in front of them with diamond-cut red eyes. . . . One by one the fibres snap beneath the immense cold pressure of the earth, then the last storm comes and, falling, the highest branches drive deep into the ground again. Even so, life isn't done with; there are a million patient, watchful lives still for a tree, all over the world, in bedrooms, in ships, on the pavement, living rooms, where men and women sit after tea, smoking cigarettes. It is full of peaceful thoughts, happy thoughts, this tree. I should like to take each one separately—but something is getting in the way. . . . Where was I? What has it all been about? A tree? A river? The Downs? Whitaker's Almanack? The fields of asphodel? I can't remember a thing. Everything's moving, falling, slipping, vanishing. . . . There is a vast upheaval of matter. Someone is standing over me and saying:

"I'm going out to buy a newspaper."

"Yes?"

"Though it's no good buying newspapers. . . . Nothing ever happens. Curse this war; God damn this war! . . . All the same, I don't see why we should have a snail on our wall."

Ah, the mark on the wall! It was a snail.

1921

Modern Fiction

In making any survey, even the freest and loosest, of modern fiction, it is difficult not to take it for granted that the modern practice of the art is somehow an improvement upon the old. With their simple tools and primitive materials, it might be said, Fielding[1] did well and Jane Austen even better, but compare their opportunities with ours! Their masterpieces certainly have a strange air of simplicity. And yet the analogy between literature and the process, to choose an example, of making motor cars scarcely holds good beyond the first glance. It is doubtful whether in the course of the centuries, though we have learnt much about making machines, we have learnt anything about making literature. We do not come to write better; all that we can be said to do is to keep moving, now a little in this direction, now in that, but with a circular tendency should the whole course of the track be viewed from a sufficiently lofty pinnacle. It need scarcely be said that we make no claim to stand, even momentarily, upon that vantage-ground. On the flat, in the crowd, half blind with dust, we look back with envy to those happier warriors, whose battle is won and whose achievements wear so serene an air of accomplishment that we can scarcely refrain from whispering that the fight was not so fierce for them as for us. It is for the historian of literature to decide; for him to say if we are now beginning or ending or standing in the middle of a great period of prose fiction, for down in the plain little is visible. We only know that certain gratitudes and hostilities inspire us; that certain paths seem to lead to fertile land, others to the dust and the desert; and of this perhaps it may be worth while to attempt some account.

Our quarrel, then, is not with the classics, and if we speak of quarrelling with Mr Wells, Mr Bennett, and Mr Galsworthy;[2] it is partly that by the mere fact of their existence in the flesh their work has a living, breathing, everyday imperfection which bids us take what liberties with it we choose. But it is also true, that, while we thank them for a thousand gifts, we reserve our unconditional gratitude for Mr Hardy, for Mr Conrad, and in much lesser degree for the Mr Hudson of *The Purple Land, Green Mansions,* and *Far Away and Long Ago.*[3] Mr Wells, Mr Bennett, and Mr Galsworthy have excited so many hopes and disappointed them so persistently that our gratitude

---

1. Henry Fielding (1707–1754), novelist.

2. H. G. Wells (1866–1946), Arnold Bennett (1867–1931), John Galsworthy (1867–1933), novelists.

3. W. H. Hudson (1841–1922), naturalist and

writer, was born in Argentina, although he later lived in London. *The Purple Land* (1885) is about South America; *Green Mansions* (1904), a novel set in South America, was his first real success.

largely takes the form of thanking them for having shown us what they might have done but have not done; what we certainly could not do, but as certainly, perhaps, do not wish to do. No single phrase will sum up the charge or grievance which we have to bring against a mass of work so large in its volume and embodying so many qualities, both admirable and the reverse. If we tried to formulate our meaning in one word we should say that these three writers are materialists. It is because they are concerned not with the spirit but with the body that they have disappointed us, and left us with the feeling that the sooner English fiction turns its back upon them, as politely as may be, and marches, if only into the desert, the better for its soul. Naturally, no single word reaches the centre of three separate targets. In the case of Mr Wells it falls notably wide of the mark. And yet even with him it indicates to our thinking the fatal alloy in his genius, the great clod of clay that has got itself mixed up with the purity of his inspiration. But Mr Bennett is perhaps the worst culprit of the three, inasmuch as he is by far the best workman. He can make a book so well constructed and solid in its craftsmanship that it is difficult for the most exacting of critics to see through what chink or crevice decay can creep in. There is not so much as a draught between the frames of the windows, or a crack in the boards. And yet—if life should refuse to live there? That is a risk which the creator of *The Old Wives' Tale,* George Cannon, Edwin Clayhanger,[4] and hosts of other figures, may well claim to have surmounted. His characters live abundantly, even unexpectedly, but it remains to ask how do they live, and what do they live for? More and more they seem to us, deserting even the well-built villa in the Five Towns,[5] to spend their time in some softly padded first-class railway carriage, pressing bells and buttons innumerable; and the destiny to which they travel so luxuriously becomes more and more unquestionably an eternity of bliss spent in the very best hotel in Brighton.[6] It can scarcely be said of Mr Wells that he is a materialist in the sense that he takes too much delight in the solidity of his fabric. His mind is too generous in its sympathies to allow him to spend much time in making things shipshape and substantial. He is a materialist from sheer goodness of heart, taking upon his shoulders the work that ought to have been discharged by Government officials, and in the plethora of his ideas and facts scarcely having leisure to realize, or forgetting to think important, the crudity and coarseness of his human beings. Yet what more damaging criticism can there be both of his earth and of his Heaven than that they are to be inhabited here and hereafter by his Joans and his Peters? Does not the inferiority of their natures tarnish whatever institutions and ideals may be provided for them by the generosity of their creator? Nor, profoundly though we respect the integrity and humanity of Mr Galsworthy, shall we find what we seek in his pages.

If we fasten, then, one label on all these books, on which is one word, materialists, we mean by it that they write of unimportant things; that they spend immense skill and immense industry making the trivial and the transitory appear the true and the enduring.

We have to admit that we are exacting, and, further, that we find it difficult to justify our discontent by explaining what it is that we exact. We frame our

---

4. Characters in Arnold Bennett's novels; *The Old Wives' Tale* (1908) is the best known.
5. The pottery towns of Staffordshire in which many of Bennett's novels and stories were set.
6. One-time fashionable seaside resort on the southwest coast of England.

question differently at different times. But it reappears most persistently as we drop the finished novel on the crest of a sigh—Is it worth while? What is the point of it all? Can it be that, owing to one of those little deviations which the human spirit seems to make from time to time, Mr Bennett has come down with his magnificent apparatus for catching life just an inch or two on the wrong side? Life escapes; and perhaps without life nothing else is worth while. It is a confession of vagueness to have to make use of such a figure as this, but we scarcely better the matter by speaking, as critics are prone to do, of reality. Admitting the vagueness which afflicts all criticism of novels, let us hazard the opinion that for us at this moment the form of fiction most in vogue more often misses than secures the thing we seek. Whether we call it life or spirit, truth or reality, this, the essential thing, has moved off, or on, and refuses to be contained any longer in such ill-fitting vestments as we provide. Nevertheless, we go on perseveringly, conscientiously, constructing our two and thirty chapters after a design which more and more ceases to resemble the vision in our minds. So much of the enormous labour of proving the solidity, the likeness to life, of the story is not merely labour thrown away but labour misplaced to the extent of obscuring and blotting out the light of the conception. The writer seems constrained, not by his own free will but by some powerful and unscrupulous tyrant who has him in thrall, to provide a plot, to provide comedy, tragedy, love interest, and an air of probability embalming the whole so impeccable that if all his figures were to come to life they would find themselves dressed down to the last button of their coats in the fashion of the hour. The tyrant is obeyed; the novel is done to a turn. But sometimes, more and more often as time goes by, we suspect a momentary doubt, a spasm of rebellion, as the pages fill themselves in the customary way. Is life like this? Must novels be like this?

Look within and life, it seems, is very far from being "like this." Examine for a moment an ordinary mind on an ordinary day. The mind receives a myriad impressions—trivial, fantastic, evanescent, or engraved with the sharpness of steel. From all sides they come, an incessant shower of innumerable atoms; and as they fall, as they shape themselves into the life of Monday or Tuesday,[7] the accent falls differently from of old; the moment of importance came not here but there; so that, if a writer were a free man and not a slave, if he could write what he chose, not what he must, if he could base his work upon his own feeling and not upon convention, there would be no plot, no comedy, no tragedy, no love interest or catastrophe in the accepted style, and perhaps not a single button sewn on as the Bond Street[8] tailors would have it. Life is not a series of gig-lamps[9] symmetrically arranged; life is a luminous halo, a semi-transparent envelope surrounding us from the beginning of consciousness to the end. Is it not the task of the novelist to convey this varying, this unknown and uncircumscribed spirit, whatever aberration or complexity it may display, with as little mixture of the alien and external as possible? We are not pleading merely for courage and sincerity; we are suggesting that the proper stuff of fiction is a little other than custom would have us believe it.

---

7. *Monday or Tuesday* was the title of the collection of experimental stories and sketches that Woolf brought out in 1921.

8. Fashionable shopping street in London.
9. Carriage lamps.

It is, at any rate, in some such fashion as this that we seek to define the quality which distinguishes the work of several young writers, among whom Mr James Joyce is the most notable, from that of their predecessors. They attempt to come closer to life, and to preserve more sincerely and exactly what interests and moves them, even if to do so they must discard most of the conventions which are commonly observed by the novelist. Let us record the atoms as they fall upon the mind in the order in which they fall, let us trace the pattern, however disconnected and incoherent in appearance, which each sight or incident scores upon the consciousness. Let us not take it for granted that life exists more fully in what is commonly thought big than in what is commonly thought small. Anyone who has read *The Portrait of the Artist as a Young Man* or, what promises to be a far more interesting work, *Ulysses*,[1] now appearing in the *Little Review,* will have hazarded some theory of this nature as to Mr Joyce's intention. On our part, with such a fragment before us, it is hazarded rather than affirmed; but whatever the intention of the whole, there can be no question but that it is of the utmost sincerity and that the result, difficult or unpleasant as we may judge it, is undeniably important. In contrast with those whom we have called materialists, Mr Joyce is spiritual; he is concerned at all costs to reveal the flickerings of that innermost flame which flashes its messages through the brain, and in order to preserve it he disregards with complete courage whatever seems to him adventitious, whether it be probability, or coherence, or any other of these signposts which for generations have served to support the imagination of a reader when called upon to imagine what he can neither touch nor see. The scene in the cemetery,[2] for instance, with its brilliancy, its sordidity, its incoherence, its sudden lightning flashes of significance, does undoubtedly come so close to the quick of the mind that, on a first reading at any rate, it is difficult not to acclaim a masterpiece. If we want life itself, here surely we have it. Indeed, we find ourselves fumbling rather awkwardly if we try to say what else we wish, and for what reason a work of such originality yet fails to compare, for we must take high examples, with *Youth* or *The Mayor of Casterbridge.*[3] It fails because of the comparative poverty of the writer's mind, we might say simply and have done with it. But it is possible to press a little further and wonder whether we may not refer our sense of being in a bright yet narrow room, confined and shut in, rather than enlarged and set free, to some limitation imposed by the method as well as by the mind. Is it the method that inhibits the creative power? Is it due to the method that we feel neither jovial nor magnanimous, but centred in a self which, in spite of its tremor of susceptibility, never embraces or creates what is outside itself and beyond? Does the emphasis laid, perhaps didactically, upon indecency contribute to the effect of something angular and isolated? Or is it merely that in any effort of such originality it is much easier, for contemporaries especially, to feel what it lacks than to name what it gives? In any case it is a mistake to stand outside examining "methods". Any method is right, every method is right, that expresses what we wish to express, if we are writers; that brings us closer to the novelist's intention if we are readers. This method has the merit of bringing us closer to what we were prepared

1. Written April, 1919 [Woolf's note].
2. The sixth episode ("Hades") of *Ulysses,* where Bloom goes to Paddy Dignam's funeral.

3. Stories by, respectively, Joseph Conrad and Thomas Hardy.

to call life itself; did not the reading of *Ulysses* suggest how much of life is excluded or ignored, and did it not come with a shock to open *Tristram Shandy* or even *Pendennis*[4] and be by them convinced that there are not only other aspects of life, but more important ones into the bargain.

However this may be, the problem before the novelist at present, as we suppose it to have been in the past, is to contrive means of being free to set down what he chooses. He has to have the courage to say that what interests him is no longer "this" but "that": out of "that" alone must he construct his work. For the moderns "that", the point of interest, lies very likely in the dark places of psychology. At once, therefore, the accent falls a little differently; the emphasis is upon something hitherto ignored; at once a different outline of form becomes necessary, difficult for us to grasp, incomprehensible to our predecessors. No one but a modern, no one perhaps but a Russian, would have felt the interest of the situation which Tchekov[5] has made into the short story which he calls "Gusev." Some Russian soldiers lie ill on board a ship which is taking them back to Russia. We are given a few scraps of their talk and some of their thoughts; then one of them dies and is carried away; the talk goes on among the others for a time, until Gusev himself dies, and looking "like a carrot or a radish" is thrown overboard. The emphasis is laid upon such unexpected places that at first it seems as if there were no emphasis at all; and then, as the eyes accustom themselves to twilight and discern the shapes of things in a room we see how complete the story is, how profound, and how truly in obedience to his vision Tchekov has chosen this, that, and the other, and placed them together to compose something new. But it is impossible to say "this is comic," or "that is tragic," nor are we certain, since short stories, we have been taught, should be brief and conclusive, whether this, which is vague and inconclusive, should be called a short story at all.

The most elementary remarks upon modern English fiction can hardly avoid some mention of the Russian influence, and if the Russians are mentioned one runs the risk of feeling that to write of any fiction save theirs is waste of time. If we want understanding of the soul and heart where else shall we find it of comparable profundity? If we are sick of our own materialism the least considerable of their novelists has by right of birth a natural reverence for the human spirit. "Learn to make yourself akin to people. . . . But let this sympathy be not with the mind—for it is easy with the mind— but with the heart, with love towards them." In every great Russian writer we seem to discern the features of a saint, if sympathy for the sufferings of others, love towards them, endeavour to reach some goal worthy of the most exacting demands of the spirit constitute saintliness. It is the saint in them which confounds us with a feeling of our own irreligious triviality, and turns so many of our famous novels to tinsel and trickery. The conclusions of the Russian mind, thus comprehensive and compassionate, are inevitably, perhaps, of the utmost sadness. More accurately indeed we might speak of the inconclusiveness of the Russian mind. It is the sense that there is no answer, that if honestly examined life presents question after question which must be left to sound on and on after the story is over in hopeless interrogation

---

4. Novels by, respectively, Laurence Sterne (1713–1768) and William Makepeace Thackeray

(1811–1863).
5. Anton Pavlovich Chekhov (1860–1904).

that fills us with a deep, and finally it may be with a resentful, despair. They are right perhaps; unquestionably they see further than we do and without our gross impediments of vision. But perhaps we see something that escapes them, or why should this voice of protest mix itself with our gloom? The voice of protest is the voice of another and an ancient civilisation which seems to have bred in us the instinct to enjoy and fight rather than to suffer and understand. English fiction from Sterne to Meredith[6] bears witness to our natural delight in humour and comedy, in the beauty of earth, in the activities of the intellect, and in the splendour of the body. But any deductions that we may draw from the comparison of two fictions so immeasurably far apart are futile save indeed as they flood us with a view of the infinite possibilities of the art and remind us that there is no limit to the horizon, and that nothing—no "method," no experiment, even of the wildest—is forbidden, but only falsity and pretence. "The proper stuff of fiction" does not exist; everything is the proper stuff of fiction, every feeling, every thought; every quality of brain and spirit is drawn upon; no perception comes amiss. And if we can imagine the art of fiction come alive and standing in our midst, she would undoubtedly bid us break her and bully her, as well as honour and love her, for so her youth is renewed and her sovereignty assured.

1925

A Room of One's Own[1]

Chapter One

But, you may say, we asked you to speak about women and fiction—what has that got to do with a room of one's own? I will try to explain. When you asked me to speak about women and fiction I sat down on the banks of a river and began to wonder what the words meant. They might mean simply a few remarks about Fanny Burney; a few more about Jane Austen; a tribute to the Brontës and a sketch of Haworth Parsonage under snow; some witticisms if possible about Miss Mitford; a respectful allusion to George Eliot; a reference to Mrs. Gaskell[2] and one would have done. But at second sight the words seemed not so simple. The title women and fiction might mean, and you may have meant it to mean, women and what they are like; or it might mean women and the fiction that they write; or it might mean women and the fiction that is written about them; or it might mean that somehow all three are inextricably mixed together and you want me to consider them in that light. But when I began to consider the subject in this last way, which seemed the most interesting, I soon saw that it had one fatal drawback. I should never be able to come to a conclusion. I should never be able to fulfil what is, I understand, the first duty of a lecturer—to hand you after an hour's discourse a nugget of pure truth to wrap up between the pages of your note-

6. George Meredith (1828–1909), novelist.
1. This essay is based upon two papers read to the Arts Society at Newnham and the Odtaa at Girton in October 1928. The papers were too long to be read in full, and have since been altered and expanded [Woolf's note]. Newnham and Girton are women's colleges at Cambridge. Odtaa, or "One Damn Thing After Another," was an elite literary society.

2. All British writers: Frances Burney (1752–1840); Jane Austen (1775–1817); Charlotte (1816–1855), Emily (1818–1848), and Anne (1820–1849) Brontë, who grew up in the parsonage in Haworth (Yorkshire), where their father was curate; Mary Russell Mitford (1787–1855); George Eliot (pseudonym of Marian Evans, 1819–1880); and Elizabeth Gaskell (1810–1865).

books and keep on the mantelpiece for ever. All I could do was to offer you an opinion upon one minor point—a woman must have money and a room of her own if she is to write fiction; and that, as you will see, leaves the great problem of the true nature of woman and the true nature of fiction unsolved. I have shirked the duty of coming to a conclusion upon these two questions— women and fiction remain, so far as I am concerned, unsolved problems. But in order to make some amends I am going to do what I can to show you how I arrived at this opinion about the room and the money. I am going to develop in your presence as fully and freely as I can the train of thought which led me to think this. Perhaps if I lay bare the ideas, the prejudices, that lie behind this statement you will find that they have some bearing upon women and some upon fiction. At any rate, when a subject is highly contro- versial—and any question about sex is that—one cannot hope to tell the truth. One can only show how one came to hold whatever opinion one does hold. One can only give one's audience the chance of drawing their own conclusions as they observe the limitations, the prejudices, the idiosyncrasies of the speaker. Fiction here is likely to contain more truth than fact. Therefore I propose, making use of all the liberties and licences of a novelist, to tell you the story of the two days that preceded my coming here—how, bowed down by the weight of the subject which you have laid upon my shoulders, I pondered it, and made it work in and out of my daily life. I need not say that what I am about to describe has no existence; Oxbridge[3] is an invention; so is Fernham; "I" is only a convenient term for somebody who has no real being. Lies will flow from my lips, but there may perhaps be some truth mixed up with them; it is for you to seek out this truth and to decide whether any part of it is worth keeping. If not, you will of course throw the whole of it into the wastepaper basket and forget all about it.

Here then was I (call me Mary Beton, Mary Seton, Mary Carmichael or by any name you please—it is not a matter of any importance) sitting on the banks of a river a week or two ago in fine October weather, lost in thought. That collar I have spoken of, women and fiction, the need of coming to some conclusion on a subject that raises all sorts of prejudices and passions, bowed my head to the ground. To the right and left bushes of some sort, golden and crimson, glowed with the colour, even it seemed burnt with the heat, of fire. On the further bank the willows wept in perpetual lamentation, their hair about their shoulders. The river reflected whatever it chose of sky and bridge and burning tree, and when the undergraduate had oared his boat through the reflections they closed again, completely, as if he had never been. There one might have sat the clock round lost in thought. Thought—to call it by a prouder name than it deserved—had let its line down into the stream. It swayed, minute after minute, hither and thither among the reflec- tions and the weeds, letting the water lift it and sink it, until—you know the little tug—the sudden conglomeration of an idea at the end of one's line: and then the cautious hauling of it in, and the careful laying of it out? Alas, laid on the grass how small, how insignificant this thought of mine looked; the sort of fish that a good fisherman puts back into the water so that it may grow fatter and be one day worth cooking and eating. I will not trouble you with that thought now, though if you look carefully you may find it for your- selves in the course of what I am going to say.

---

3. A common term blending Oxford and Cambridge.

But however small it was, it had, nevertheless, the mysterious property of its kind—put back into the mind, it became at once very exciting, and important; and as it darted and sank, and flashed hither and thither, set up such a wash and tumult of ideas that it was impossible to sit still. It was thus that I found myself walking with extreme rapidity across a grass plot. Instantly a man's figure rose to intercept me. Nor did I at first understand that the gesticulations of a curious-looking object, in a cut-away coat and evening shirt, were aimed at me. His face expressed horror and indignation. Instinct rather than reason came to my help; he was a Beadle; I was a woman. This was the turf; there was the path. Only the Fellows and Scholars are allowed here; the gravel is the place for me. Such thoughts were the work of a moment. As I regained the path the arms of the Beadle sank, his face assumed its usual repose, and though turf is better walking than gravel, no very great harm was done. The only charge I could bring against the Fellows and Scholars of whatever the college might happen to be was that in protection of their turf, which has been rolled for 300 years in succession, they had sent my little fish into hiding.

What idea it had been that had sent me so audaciously trespassing I could not now remember. The spirit of peace descended like a cloud from heaven, for if the spirit of peace dwells anywhere, it is in the courts and quadrangles of Oxbridge on a fine October morning. Strolling through those colleges past those ancient halls the roughness of the present seemed smoothed away; the body seemed contained in a miraculous glass cabinet through which no sound could penetrate, and the mind, freed from any contact with facts (unless one trespassed on the turf again), was at liberty to settle down upon whatever meditation was in harmony with the moment. As chance would have it, some stray memory of some old essay about revisiting Oxbridge in the long vacation brought Charles Lamb to mind—Saint Charles, said Thackeray,[4] putting a letter of Lamb's to his forehead. Indeed, among all the dead (I give you my thoughts as they came to me), Lamb is one of the most congenial; one to whom one would have liked to say, Tell me then how you wrote your essays? For his essays are superior even to Max Beerbohm's,[5] I thought, with all their perfection, because of that wild flash of imagination, that lightning crack of genius in the middle of them which leaves them flawed and imperfect, but starred with poetry. Lamb then came to Oxbridge perhaps a hundred years ago. Certainly he wrote an essay—the name escapes me[6]— about the manuscript of one of Milton's poems which he saw here. It was *Lycidas* perhaps, and Lamb wrote how it shocked him to think it possible that any word in *Lycidas* could have been different from what it is. To think of Milton changing the words in that poem seemed to him a sort of sacrilege. This led me to remember what I could of *Lycidas* and to amuse myself with guessing which word it could have been that Milton had altered, and why. It then occurred to me that the very manuscript itself which Lamb had looked at was only a few hundred yards away, so that one could follow Lamb's footsteps across the quadrangle to that famous library[7] where the treasure is kept. Moreover, I recollected, as I put this plan into execution, it is in this famous library that the manuscript of Thackeray's *Esmond* is also preserved.

4. William Makepeace Thackeray (1811–1863), English novelist, was author of *The History of Henry Esmond, Esquire* (1852), mentioned later. Charles Lamb (1775–1834), English writer.

5. Beerbohm (1872–1956), English essayist and parodist.
6. *Oxford in the Vacation.*
7. The library at Trinity College, Cambridge.

The critics often say that *Esmond* is Thackeray's most perfect novel. But the affectation of the style, with its imitation of the eighteenth century, hampers one, so far as I remember; unless indeed the eighteenth-century style was natural to Thackeray—a fact that one might prove by looking at the manuscript and seeing whether the alterations were for the benefit of the style or of the sense. But then one would have to decide what is style and what is meaning, a question which—but here I was actually at the door which leads into the library itself. I must have opened it, for instantly there issued, like a guardian angel barring the way with a flutter of black gown instead of white wings, a deprecating, silvery, kindly gentleman, who regretted in a low voice as he waved me back that ladies are only admitted to the library if accompanied by a Fellow of the College or furnished with a letter of introduction.

That a famous library has been cursed by a woman is a matter of complete indifference to a famous library. Venerable and calm, with all its treasures safe locked within its breast, it sleeps complacently and will, so far as I am concerned, so sleep for ever. Never will I wake those echoes, never will I ask for that hospitality again, I vowed as I descended the steps in anger. Still an hour remained before luncheon, and what was one to do? Stroll on the meadows? sit by the river? Certainly it was a lovely autumn morning; the leaves were fluttering red to the ground; there was no great hardship in doing either. But the sound of music reached my ear. Some service or celebration was going forward. The organ complained magnificently as I passed the chapel door. Even the sorrow of Christianity sounded in that serene air more like the recollection of sorrow than sorrow itself; even the groanings of the ancient organ seemed lapped in peace. I had no wish to enter had I the right, and this time the verger might have stopped me, demanding perhaps my baptismal certificate, or a letter of introduction from the Dean. But the outside of these magnificent buildings is often as beautiful as the inside. Moreover, it was amusing enough to watch the congregation assembling, coming in and going out again, busying themselves at the door of the chapel like bees at the mouth of a hive. Many were in cap and gown; some had tufts of fur on their shoulders; others were wheeled in bath-chairs; others, though not past middle age, seemed creased and crushed into shapes so singular that one was reminded of those giant crabs and crayfish who heave with difficulty across the sand of an aquarium. As I leant against the wall the University indeed seemed a sanctuary in which are preserved rare types which would soon be obsolete if left to fight for existence on the pavement of the Strand.[8] Old stories of old deans and old dons came back to mind, but before I had summoned up courage to whistle—it used to be said that at the sound of a whistle old Professor ——— instantly broke into a gallop—the venerable congregation had gone inside. The outside of the chapel remained. As you know, its high domes and pinnacles can be seen, like a sailing-ship always voyaging never arriving, lit up at night and visible for miles, far away across the hills. Once, presumably, this quadrangle with its smooth lawns, its massive buildings, and the chapel itself was marsh too, where the grasses waved and the swine rooted. Teams of horses and oxen, I thought, must have hauled the stone in wagons from far countries, and then with infinite labour the grey blocks in whose shade I was now standing were poised in

8. A busy thoroughfare in London.

order one on top of another, and then the painters brought their glass for the windows, and the masons were busy for centuries up on that roof with putty and cement, spade and trowel.[9] Every Saturday somebody must have poured gold and silver out of a leathern purse into their ancient fists, for they had their beer and skittles presumably of an evening. An unending stream of gold and silver, I thought, must have flowed into this court perpetually to keep the stones coming and the masons working; to level, to ditch, to dig and to drain. But it was then the age of faith, and money was poured liberally to set these stones on a deep foundation, and when the stones were raised, still more money was poured in from the coffers of kings and queens and great nobles to ensure that hymns should be sung here and scholars taught. Lands were granted; tithes were paid. And when the age of faith was over and the age of reason had come, still the same flow of gold and silver went on; fellowships were founded; lectureships endowed; only the gold and silver flowed now, not from the coffers of the king, but from the chests of merchants and manufacturers, from the purses of men who had made, say, a fortune from industry, and returned, in their wills, a bounteous share of it to endow more chairs, more lectureships, more fellowships in the university where they had learnt their craft. Hence the libraries and laboratories; the observatories; the splendid equipment of costly and delicate instruments which now stands on glass shelves, where centuries ago the grasses waved and the swine rootled. Certainly, as I strolled round the court, the foundation of gold and silver seemed deep enough; the pavement laid solidly over the wild grasses. Men with trays on their heads went busily from staircase to staircase. Gaudy blossoms flowered in window-boxes. The strains of the gramophone blared out from the rooms within. It was impossible not to reflect—the reflection whatever it may have been was cut short. The clock struck. It was time to find one's way to luncheon.

It is a curious fact that novelists have a way of making us believe that luncheon parties are invariably memorable for something very witty that was said, or for something very wise that was done. But they seldom spare a word for what was eaten. It is part of the novelist's convention not to mention soup and salmon and ducklings, as if soup and salmon and ducklings were of no importance whatsoever, as if nobody ever smoked a cigar or drank a glass of wine. Here, however, I shall take the liberty to defy that convention and to tell you that the lunch on this occasion began with soles, sunk in a deep dish, over which the college cook had spread a counterpane of the whitest cream, save that it was branded here and there with brown spots like the spots on the flanks of a doe. After that came the partridges, but if this suggests a couple of bald, brown birds on a plate you are mistaken. The partridges, many and various, came with all their retinue of sauces and salads, the sharp and the sweet, each in its order; their potatoes, thin as coins but not so hard; their sprouts, foliated as rosebuds but more succulent. And no sooner had the roast and its retinue been done with than the silent serving-man, the Beadle himself perhaps in a milder manifestation, set before us, wreathed in napkins, a confection which rose all sugar from the waves. To call it pudding and so relate it to rice and tapioca would be an insult. Meanwhile the wineglasses had flushed yellow and flushed crimson; had

9. King's College Chapel, Cambridge, was built from 1446 to 1547.

been emptied; had been filled. And thus by degrees was lit, halfway down the spine, which is the seat of the soul, not that hard little electric light which we call brilliance, as it pops in and out upon our lips, but the more profound, subtle and subterranean glow, which is the rich yellow flame of rational intercourse. No need to hurry. No need to sparkle. No need to be anybody but oneself. We are all going to heaven and Vandyck[1] is of the company—in other words, how good life seemed, how sweet its rewards, how trivial this grudge or that grievance, how admirable friendship and the society of one's kind, as, lighting a good cigarette, one sunk among the cushions in the window-seat.

If by good luck there had been an ash-tray handy, if one had not knocked the ash out of the window in default, if things had been a little different from what they were, one would not have seen, presumably, a cat without a tail. The sight of that abrupt and truncated animal padding softly across the quadrangle changed by some fluke of the subconscious intelligence the emotional light for me. It was as if some one had let fall a shade. Perhaps the excellent hock was relinquishing its hold. Certainly, as I watched the Manx cat pause in the middle of the lawn as if it too questioned the universe, something seemed lacking, something seemed different. But what was lacking, what was different, I asked myself, listening to the talk. And to answer that question I had to think myself out of the room, back into the past, before the war indeed, and to set before my eyes the model of another luncheon party held in rooms not very far distant from these; but different. Everything was different. Meanwhile the talk went on among the guests, who were many and young, some of this sex, some of that; it went on swimmingly, it went on agreeably, freely, amusingly. And as it went on I set it against the background of that other talk, and as I matched the two together I had no doubt that one was the descendant, the legitimate heir of the other. Nothing was changed; nothing was different save only—here I listened with all my ears not entirely to what was being said, but to the murmur or current behind it. Yes, that was it—the change was there. Before the war at a luncheon party like this people would have said precisely the same things but they would have sounded different, because in those days they were accompanied by a sort of humming noise, not articulate, but musical, exciting, which changed the value of the words themselves. Could one set that humming noise to words? Perhaps with the help of the poets one could. A book lay beside me and, opening it, I turned casually enough to Tennyson. And here I found Tennyson was singing:

> There has fallen a splendid tear
> From the passion-flower at the gate.
> She is coming, my dove, my dear;
> She is coming, my life, my fate;
> The red rose cries, "She is near, she is near";
> And the white rose weeps, "She is late";
> The larkspur listens, "I hear, I hear";
> And the lily whispers, "I wait."[2]

Was that what men hummed at luncheon parties before the war? And the women?

---

1. Sir Anthony Van Dyck (1599–1641), born in Antwerp but lived for some years in England. He painted many grand portraits of the English royal family and court.
2. *Maud* 1.22.10.

> *My heart is like a singing bird*
> *Whose nest is in a water'd shoot;*
> *My heart is like an apple tree*
> *Whose boughs are bent with thick-set fruit;*
> *My heart is like a rainbow shell*
> *That paddles in a halcyon sea;*
> *My heart is gladder than all these*
> *Because my love is come to me.*[3]

Was that what women hummed at luncheon parties before the war?

There was something so ludicrous in thinking of people humming such things even under their breath at luncheon parties before the war that I burst out laughing, and had to explain my laughter by pointing at the Manx cat, who did look a little absurd, poor beast, without a tail, in the middle of the lawn. Was he really born so, or had he lost his tail in an accident? The tailless cat, though some are said to exist in the Isle of Man, is rarer than one thinks. It is a queer animal, quaint rather than beautiful. It is strange what a difference a tail makes—you know the sort of things one says as a lunch party breaks up and people are finding their coats and hats.

This one, thanks to the hospitality of the host, had lasted far into the afternoon. The beautiful October day was fading and the leaves were falling from the trees in the avenue as I walked through it. Gate after gate seemed to close with gentle finality behind me. Innumerable beadles were fitting innumerable keys into well-oiled locks; the treasure-house was being made secure for another night. After the avenue one comes out upon a road—I forget its name—which leads you, if you take the right turning, along to Fernham. But there was plenty of time. Dinner was not till half-past seven. One could almost do without dinner after such a luncheon. It is strange how a scrap of poetry works in the mind and makes the legs move in time to it along the road. Those words—

> *There has fallen a splendid tear*
> *From the passion-flower at the gate.*
> *She is coming, my dove, my dear—*

sang in my blood as I stepped quickly along towards Headingley. And then, switching off into the other measure, I sang, where the waters are churned up by the weir:

> *My heart is like a singing bird*
> *Whose nest is in a water'd shoot;*
> *My heart is like an apple tree . . .*

What poets, I cried aloud, as one does in the dusk, what poets they were!

In a sort of jealousy, I suppose, for our own age, silly and absurd though these comparisons are, I went on to wonder if honestly one could name two living poets now as great as Tennyson and Christina Rossetti were then. Obviously it is impossible, I thought, looking into those foaming waters, to compare them. The very reason why the poetry excites one to such abandonment, such rapture, is that it celebrates some feeling that one used to have (at luncheon parties before the war perhaps), so that one responds easily, familiarly, without troubling to check the feeling, or to compare it

3. Christina Rossetti's *A Birthday,* first stanza.

with any that one has now. But the living poets express a feeling that is actually being made and torn out of us at the moment. One does not recognize it in the first place; often for some reason one fears it; one watches it with keenness and compares it jealously and suspiciously with the old feeling that one knew. Hence the difficulty of modern poetry; and it is because of this difficulty that one cannot remember more than two consecutive lines of any good modern poet. For this reason—that my memory failed me—the argument flagged for want of material. But why, I continued, moving on towards Headingley, have we stopped humming under our breath at luncheon parties? Why has Alfred ceased to sing

> She is coming, my dove, my dear?

Why has Christina ceased to respond

> My heart is gladder than all these
> Because my love is come to me?

Shall we lay the blame on the war? When the guns fired in August 1914, did the faces of men and women show so plain in each other's eyes that romance was killed? Certainly it was a shock (to women in particular with their illusions about education, and so on) to see the faces of our rulers in the light of the shell-fire. So ugly they looked—German, English, French—so stupid. But lay the blame where one will, on whom one will, the illusion which inspired Tennyson and Christina Rossetti to sing so passionately about the coming of their loves is far rarer now than then. One has only to read, to look, to listen, to remember. But why say "blame"? Why, if it was an illusion, not praise the catastrophe, whatever it was, that destroyed illusion and put truth in its place? For truth . . . those dots mark the spot where, in search of truth, I missed the turning up to Fernham. Yes indeed, which was truth and which was illusion, I asked myself. What was the truth about these houses, for example, dim and festive now with their red windows in the dusk, but raw and red and squalid, with their sweets and their boot-laces, at nine o'clock in the morning? And the willows and the river and the gardens that run down to the river, vague now with the mist stealing over them, but gold and red in the sunlight—which was the truth, which was the illusion about them? I spare you the twists and turns of my cogitations, for no conclusion was found on the road to Headingley, and I ask you to suppose that I soon found out my mistake about the turning and retraced my steps to Fernham.

As I have said already that it was an October day, I dare not forfeit your respect and imperil the fair name of fiction by changing the season and describing lilacs hanging over garden walls, crocuses, tulips and other flowers of spring. Fiction must stick to facts, and the truer the facts the better the fiction—so we are told. Therefore it was still autumn and the leaves were still yellow and falling, if anything, a little faster than before, because it was now evening (seven twenty-three to be precise) and a breeze (from the southwest to be exact) had risen. But for all that there was something odd at work:

> My heart is like a singing bird
>   Whose nest is in a water'd shoot;
> My heart is like an apple tree
>   Whose boughs are bent with thick-set fruit—

perhaps the words of Christina Rossetti were partly responsible for the folly of the fancy—it was nothing of course but a fancy—that the lilac was shaking its flowers over the garden walls, and the brimstone butterflies were scudding hither and thither, and the dust of the pollen was in the air. A wind blew, from what quarter I know not, but it lifted the half-grown leaves so that there was a flash of silver grey in the air. It was the time between the lights when colours undergo their intensification and purples and golds burn in window-panes like the beat of an excitable heart; when for some reason the beauty of the world revealed and yet soon to perish (here I pushed into the garden, for, unwisely, the door was left open and no beadles seemed about), the beauty of the world which is so soon to perish, has two edges, one of laughter, one of anguish, cutting the heart asunder. The gardens of Fernham lay before me in the spring twilight, wild and open, and in the long grass, sprinkled and carelessly flung, were daffodils and bluebells, not orderly perhaps at the best of times, and now wind-blown and waving as they tugged at their roots. The windows of the building, curved like ships' windows among generous waves of red brick, changed from lemon to silver under the flight of the quick spring clouds. Somebody was in a hammock, somebody, but in this light they were phantoms only, half guessed, half seen, raced across the grass—would no one stop her?—and then on the terrace, as if popping out to breathe the air, to glance at the garden, came a bent figure, formidable yet humble, with her great forehead and her shabby dress—could it be the famous scholar, could it be J—— H—— herself?[4] All was dim, yet intense too, as if the scarf which the dusk had flung over the garden were torn asunder by star or sword—the flash of some terrible reality leaping, as its way is, out of the heart of the spring. For youth——

Here was my soup. Dinner was being served in the great dining-hall. Far from being spring it was in fact an evening in October. Everybody was assembled in the big dining-room. Dinner was ready. Here was the soup. It was a plain gravy soup. There was nothing to stir the fancy in that. One could have seen through the transparent liquid any pattern that there might have been on the plate itself. But there was no pattern. The plate was plain. Next came beef with its attendant greens and potatoes—a homely trinity, suggesting the rumps of cattle in a muddy market, and sprouts curled and yellowed at the edge, and bargaining and cheapening, and women with string bags on Monday morning. There was no reason to complain of human nature's daily food, seeing that the supply was sufficient and coal-miners doubtless were sitting down to less. Prunes and custard followed. And if any one complains that prunes, even when mitigated by custard, are an uncharitable vegetable (fruit they are not), stringy as a miser's heart and exuding a fluid such as might run in misers' veins who have denied themselves wine and warmth for eighty years and yet not given to the poor, he should reflect that there are people whose charity embraces even the prune. Biscuits and cheese came next, and here the water-jug was liberally passed round, for it is the nature of biscuits to be dry, and these were biscuits to the core. That was all. The meal was over. Everybody scraped their chairs back; the swing-doors swung violently to and fro; soon the hall was emptied of every sign of food and made ready

---

4. Jane Harrison (1850–1928), fellow and lecturer in classical archaeology at Newnham College, Cambridge; author of *Ancient Art and Ritual* (1913) and other influential books.

no doubt for breakfast next morning. Down corridors and up staircases the youth of England went banging and singing. And was it for a guest, a stranger (for I had no more right here in Fernham than in Trinity or Somerville or Girton or Newnham or Christchurch), to say, "The dinner was not good," or to say (we were now, Mary Seton and I, in her sitting-room), "Could we not have dined up here alone?" for if I had said anything of the kind I should have been prying and searching into the secret economies of a house which to the stranger wears so fine a front of gaiety and courage. No, one could say nothing of the sort. Indeed, conversation for a moment flagged. The human frame being what it is, heart, body and brain all mixed together, and not contained in separate compartments as they will be no doubt in another million years, a good dinner is of great importance to good talk. One cannot think well, love well, sleep well, if one has not dined well. The lamp in the spine does not light on beef and prunes. We are all *probably* going to heaven, and Vandyck is, we *hope,* to meet us round the next corner—that is the dubious and qualifying state of mind that beef and prunes at the end of the day's work breed between them. Happily my friend, who taught science, had a cupboard where there was a squat bottle and little glasses—(but there should have been sole and partridge to begin with)—so that we were able to draw up to the fire and repair some of the damages of the day's living. In a minute or so we were slipping freely in and out among all those objects of curiosity and interest which form in the mind in the absence of a particular person, and are naturally to be discussed on coming together again—how somebody has married, another has not; one thinks this, another that; one has improved out of all knowledge, the other most amazingly gone to the bad—with all those speculations upon human nature and the character of the amazing world we live in which spring naturally from such beginnings. While these things were being said, however, I became shamefacedly aware of a current setting in of its own accord and carrying everything forward to an end of its own. One might be talking of Spain or Portugal, of book or racehorse, but the real interest of whatever was said was none of those things, but a scene of masons on a high roof some five centuries ago. Kings and nobles brought treasure in huge sacks and poured it under the earth. This scene was for ever coming alive in my mind and placing itself by another of lean cows and a muddy market and withered greens and the stringy hearts of old men—these two pictures, disjointed and disconnected and nonsensical as they were, were for ever coming together and combating each other and had me entirely at their mercy. The best course, unless the whole talk was to be distorted, was to expose what was in my mind to the air, when with good luck it would fade and crumble like the head of the dead king when they opened the coffin at Windsor. Briefly, then, I told Miss Seton about the masons who had been all those years on the roof of the chapel, and about the kings and queens and nobles bearing sacks of gold and silver on their shoulders, which they shovelled into the earth; and then how the great financial magnates of our own time came and laid cheques and bonds, I suppose, where the others had laid ingots and rough lumps of gold. All that lies beneath the colleges down there, I said; but this college, where we are now sitting, what lies beneath its gallant red brick and the wild unkempt grasses of the garden? What force is behind the plain china off which we dined, and (here it popped out of my mouth before I could stop it) the beef, the custard and the prunes?

Well, said Mary Seton, about the year 1860—Oh, but you know the story, she said, bored, I suppose, by the recital. And she told me—rooms were hired. Committees met. Envelopes were addressed. Circulars were drawn up. Meetings were held; letters were read out; so-and-so has promised so much; on the contrary, Mr ——— won't give a penny. The *Saturday Review* has been very rude. How can we raise a fund to pay for offices? Shall we hold a bazaar? Can't we find a pretty girl to sit in the front row? Let us look up what John Stuart Mill said on the subject. Can any one persuade the editor of the ——— to print a letter? Can we get Lady ——— to sign it? Lady ——— is out of town. That was the way it was done, presumably, sixty years ago, and it was a prodigious effort, and a great deal of time was spent on it. And it was only after a long struggle and with the utmost difficulty that they got thirty thousand pounds together.[5] So obviously we cannot have wine and partridges and servants carrying tin dishes on their heads, she said. We cannot have sofas and separate rooms. "The amenities," she said, quoting from some book or other, "will have to wait."[6]

At the thought of all those women working year after year and finding it hard to get two thousand pounds together, and as much as they could do to get thirty thousand pounds, we burst out in scorn at the reprehensible poverty of our sex. What had our mothers been doing then that they had no wealth to leave us? Powdering their noses? Looking in at shop windows? Flaunting in the sun at Monte Carlo? There were some photographs on the mantel-piece. Mary's mother—if that was her picture—may have been a wastrel in her spare time (she had thirteen children by a minister of the church), but if so her gay and dissipated life had left too few traces of its pleasures on her face. She was a homely body; an old lady in a plaid shawl which was fastened by a large cameo; and she sat in a basket-chair, encouraging a spaniel to look at the camera, with the amused, yet strained expression of one who is sure that the dog will move directly the bulb is pressed. Now if she had gone into business; had become a manufacturer of artificial silk or a magnate on the Stock Exchange; if she had left two or three hundred thousand pounds to Fernham, we could have been sitting at our ease tonight and the subject of our talk might have been archaeology, botany, anthropology, physics, the nature of the atom, mathematics, astronomy, relativity, geography. If only Mrs Seton and her mother and her mother before her had learnt the great art of making money and had left their money, like their fathers and their grandfathers before them, to found fellowships and lectureships and prizes and scholarships appropriated to the use of their own sex, we might have dined very tolerably up here alone off a bird and a bottle of wine; we might have looked forward without undue confidence to a pleasant and honourable lifetime spent in the shelter of one of the liberally endowed professions. We might have been exploring or writing; mooning about the venerable places of the earth; sitting contemplative on the steps of the Parthenon, or going at ten to an office and coming home comfortably at half-past four to write a little poetry. Only, if Mrs Seton and her like had

5. "We are told that we ought to ask for £30,000 at least. . . . It is not a large sum, considering that there is to be but one college of this sort for Great Britain, Ireland and the Colonies, and considering how easy it is to raise immense sums for boys' schools. But considering how few people really wish women to be educated, it is a good deal."— Lady Stephen, *Life of Miss Emily Davies* [Woolf's note].

6. "Every penny which could be scraped together was set aside for building, and the amenities had to be postponed."—R. Strachey, *The Cause* [Woolf's note].

gone into business at the age of fifteen, there would have been—that was the snag in the argument—no Mary. What, I asked, did Mary think of that? There between the curtains was the October night, calm and lovely, with a star or two caught in the yellowing trees. Was she ready to resign her share of it and her memories (for they had been a happy family, though a large one) of games and quarrels up in Scotland, which she is never tired of praising for the fineness of its air and the quality of its cakes, in order that Fernham might have been endowed with fifty thousand pounds or so by a stroke of the pen? For, to endow a college would necessitate the suppression of families altogether. Making a fortune and bearing thirteen children—no human being could stand it. Consider the facts, we said. First there are nine months before the baby is born. Then the baby is born. Then there are three or four months spent in feeding the baby. After the baby is fed there are certainly five years spent in playing with the baby. You cannot, it seems, let children run about the streets. People who have seen them running wild in Russia say that the sight is not a pleasant one. People say, too, that human nature takes its shape in the years between one and five. If Mrs Seton, I said, had been making money, what sort of memories would you have had of games and quarrels? What would you have known of Scotland, and its fine air and cakes and all the rest of it? But it is useless to ask these questions, because you would never have come into existence at all. Moreover, it is equally useless to ask what might have happened if Mrs Seton and her mother and her mother before her had amassed great wealth and laid it under the foundations of college and library, because, in the first place, to earn money was impossible for them, and in the second, had it been possible, the law denied them the right to possess what money they earned. It is only for the last forty-eight years that Mrs Seton has had a penny of her own. For all the centuries before that it would have been her husband's property—a thought which, perhaps, may have had its share in keeping Mrs Seton and her mothers off the Stock Exchange. Every penny I earn, they may have said, will be taken from me and disposed of according to my husband's wisdom—perhaps to found a scholarship or to endow a fellowship in Balliol or Kings,[7] so that to earn money, even if I could earn money, is not a matter that interests me very greatly. I had better leave it to my husband.

At any rate, whether or not the blame rested on the old lady who was looking at the spaniel, there could be no doubt that for some reason or other our mothers had mismanaged their affairs very gravely. Not a penny could be spared for "amenities"; for partridges and wine, beadles and turf, books and cigars, libraries and leisure. To raise bare walls out of the bare earth was the utmost they could do.

So we talked standing at the window and looking, as so many thousands look every night, down on the domes and towers of the famous city beneath us. It was very beautiful, very mysterious in the autumn moonlight. The old stone looked very white and venerable. One thought of all the books that were assembled down there; of the pictures of old prelates and worthies hanging in the panelled rooms; of the painted windows that would be throwing strange globes and crescents on the pavement; of the tablets and memo-

---

7. Colleges at Oxford and Cambridge, respectively.

rials and inscriptions; of the fountains and the grass; of the quiet rooms looking across the quiet quadrangles. And (pardon me the thought) I thought, too, of the admirable smoke and drink and the deep armchairs and the pleasant carpets: of the urbanity, the geniality, the dignity which are the offspring of luxury and privacy and space. Certainly our mothers had not provided us with anything comparable to all this—our mothers who found it difficult to scrape together thirty thousand pounds, our mothers who bore thirteen children to ministers of religion at St Andrews.[8]

So I went back to my inn, and as I walked through the dark streets I pondered this and that, as one does at the end of the day's work. I pondered why it was that Mrs Seton had no money to leave us; and what effect poverty has on the mind; and what effect wealth has on the mind; and I thought of the queer old gentlemen I had seen that morning with tufts of fur upon their shoulders; and I remembered how if one whistled one of them ran; and I thought of the organ booming in the chapel and of the shut doors of the library; and I thought how unpleasant it is to be locked out; and I thought how it is worse perhaps to be locked in; and, thinking of the safety and prosperity of the one sex and of the poverty and insecurity of the other and of the effect of tradition and of the lack of tradition upon the mind of a writer, I thought at last that it was time to roll up the crumpled skin of the day, with its arguments and its impressions and its anger and its laughter, and cast it into the hedge. A thousand stars were flashing across the blue wastes of the sky. One seemed alone with an inscrutable society. All human beings were laid asleep—prone, horizontal, dumb. Nobody seemed stirring in the streets of Oxbridge. Even the door of the hotel sprang open at the touch of an invisible hand—not a boots was sitting up to light me to bed, it was so late.

Chapter Two

The scene, if I may ask you to follow me, was now changed. The leaves were still falling, but in London now, not Oxbridge; and I must ask you to imagine a room, like many thousands, with a window looking across people's hats and vans and motor-cars to other windows, and on the table inside the room a blank sheet of paper on which was written in large letters WOMEN AND FICTION, but no more. The inevitable sequel to lunching and dining at Oxbridge seemed, unfortunately, to be a visit to the British Museum. One must strain off what was personal and accidental in all these impressions and so reach the pure fluid, the essential oil of truth. For that visit to Oxbridge and the luncheon and the dinner had started a swarm of questions. Why did men drink wine and women water? Why was one sex so prosperous and the other so poor? What effect has poverty on fiction? What conditions are necessary for the creation of works of art?—a thousand questions at once suggested themselves. But one needed answers, not questions; and an answer was only to be had by consulting the learned and the unprejudiced, who have removed themselves above the strife of tongue and the confusion of body and issued the result of their reasoning and research in books which are to be found in the British Museum. If truth is not to be found on the shelves

8. Perhaps St. Andrew Holborn, a church in London designed by Sir Christopher Wren (1632–1723).

of the British Museum, where, I asked myself, picking up a notebook and a pencil, is truth?

Thus provided, thus confident and enquiring, I set out in the pursuit of truth. The day, though not actually wet, was dismal, and the streets in the neighbourhood of the Museum were full of open coal-holes, down which sacks were showering; four-wheeled cabs were drawing up and depositing on the pavement corded boxes containing, presumably, the entire wardrobe of some Swiss or Italian family seeking fortune or refuge or some other desirable commodity which is to be found in the boarding-houses of Bloomsbury in the winter. The usual hoarse-voiced men paraded the streets with plants on barrows. Some shouted; others sang. London was like a workshop. London was like a machine. We were all being shot backwards and forwards on this plain foundation to make some pattern. The British Museum was another department of the factory. The swing-doors swung open; and there one stood under the vast dome, as if one were a thought in the huge bald forehead which is so splendidly encircled by a band of famous names. One went to the counter; one took a slip of paper; one opened a volume of the catalogue, and . . . . . the five dots here indicate five separate minutes of stupefaction, wonder and bewilderment. Have you any notion how many books are written about women in the course of one year? Have you any notion how many are written by men? Are you aware that you are, perhaps, the most discussed animal in the universe? Here had I come with a notebook and a pencil proposing to spend a morning reading, supposing that at the end of the morning I should have transferred the truth to my notebook. But I should need to be a herd of elephants, I thought, and a wilderness of spiders, desperately referring to the animals that are reputed longest lived and most multitudinously eyed, to cope with all this. I should need claws of steel and beak of brass even to penetrate the husk. How shall I ever find the grains of truth embedded in all this mass of paper, I asked myself, and in despair began running my eye up and down the long list of titles. Even the names of the books gave me food for thought. Sex and its nature might well attract doctors and biologists; but what was surprising and difficult of explanation was the fact that sex—woman, that is to say—also attracts agreeable essayists, light-fingered novelists, young men who have taken the M.A. degree; men who have taken no degree; men who have no apparent qualification save that they are not women. Some of these books were, on the face of it, frivolous and facetious; but many, on the other hand, were serious and prophetic, moral and hortatory. Merely to read the titles suggested innumerable schoolmasters, innumerable clergymen mounting their platforms and pulpits and holding forth with a loquacity which far exceeded the hour usually allotted to such discourse on this one subject. It was a most strange phenomenon; and apparently—here I consulted the letter M—one confined to male sex. Women do not write books about men—a fact that I could not help welcoming with relief, for if I had first to read all that men have written about women, then all that women have written about men, the aloe that flowers once in a hundred years would flower twice before I could set pen to paper. So, making a perfectly arbitrary choice of a dozen volumes or so, I sent my slips of paper to lie in the wire tray, and waited in my stall, among the other seekers for the essential oil of truth.

What could be the reason, then, of this curious disparity, I wondered, drawing cart-wheels on the slips of paper provided by the British taxpayer for other purposes. Why are women, judging from this catalogue, so much more interesting to men than men are to women? A very curious fact it seemed, and my mind wandered to picture the lives of men who spend their time in writing books about women; whether they were old or young, married or unmarried, red-nosed or hump-backed—anyhow, it was flattering, vaguely, to feel oneself the object of such attention, provided that it was not entirely bestowed by the crippled and the infirm—so I pondered until all such frivolous thoughts were ended by an avalanche of books sliding down on to the desk in front of me. Now the trouble began. The student who has been trained in research at Oxbridge has no doubt some method of shepherding his question past all distractions till it runs into its answer as a sheep runs into its pen. The student by my side, for instance, who was copying assiduously from a scientific manual was, I felt sure, extracting pure nuggets of the essential ore every ten minutes or so. His little grunts of satisfaction indicated so much. But if, unfortunately, one has had no training in a university, the question far from being shepherded to its pen flies like a frightened flock hither and thither, helter-skelter, pursued by a whole pack of hounds. Professors, schoolmasters, sociologists, clergymen, novelists, essayists, journalists, men who had no qualification save that they were not women, chased my simple and single question— Why are women poor?—until it became fifty questions; until the fifty questions leapt frantically into mid-stream and were carried away. Every page in my notebook was scribbled over with notes. To show the state of mind I was in, I will read you a few of them, explaining that the page was headed quite simply, WOMEN AND POVERTY, in block letters; but what followed was something like this:

Condition in Middle Ages of,
Habits in the Fiji Islands of,
Worshipped as goddesses by,
Weaker in moral sense than,
Idealism of,
Greater conscientiousness of,
South Sea Islanders, age of puberty among,
Attractiveness of,
Offered as sacrifice to,
Small size of brain of,
Profounder sub-consciousness of,
Less hair on the body of,
Mental, moral and physical inferiority of,
Love of children of,
Greater length of life of,
Weaker muscles of,
Strength of affections of,
Vanity of,
Higher education of,
Shakespeare's opinion of,
Lord Birkenhead's opinion of,

> Dean Inge's opinion of,
> La Bruyère's opinion of,
> Dr Johnson's opinion of,
> Mr Oscar Browning's[9] opinion of, . . .

Here I drew breath and added, indeed, in the margin, Why does Samuel Butler[1] say, "Wise men never say what they think of women"? Wise men never say anything else apparently. But, I continued, leaning back in my chair and looking at the vast dome in which I was a single but by now somewhat harassed thought, what is so unfortunate is that wise men never think the same thing about women. Here is Pope:

> Most women have no character at all.

And here is La Bruyère:

> Les femmes sont extrêmes; elles sont meilleures ou pires que les hommes—[2]

a direct contradiction by keen observers who were contemporary. Are they capable of education or incapable? Napoleon thought them incapable. Dr Johnson thought the opposite.[3] Have they souls or have they not souls? Some savages say they have none. Others, on the contrary, maintain that women are half divine and worship them on that account.[4] Some sages hold that they are shallower in the brain; others that they are deeper in the consciousness. Goethe honoured them; Mussolini[5] despises them. Wherever one looked men thought about women and thought differently. It was impossible to make head or tail of it all, I decided, glancing with envy at the reader next door who was making the neatest abstracts, headed often with an A or a B or a C, while my own notebook rioted with the wildest scribble of contradictory jottings. It was distressing, it was bewildering, it was humiliating. Truth had run through my fingers. Every drop had escaped.

I could not possibly go home, I reflected, and add as a serious contribution to the study of women and fiction that women have less hair on their bodies than men, or that the age of puberty among the South Sea Islanders is nine— or is it ninety?—even the handwriting had become in its distraction indecipherable. It was disgraceful to have nothing more weighty or respectable to show after a whole morning's work. And if I could not grasp the truth about W. (as for brevity's sake I had come to call her) in the past, why bother about W. in the future? It seemed pure waste of time to consult all those gentlemen

9. F. E. Smith, earl of Birkenhead (1872–1930), was lord chancellor (1919–22) and an opponent of women's suffrage. William Ralph Inge (1860–1954), dean of St. Paul's Cathedral in London (1911–34). Woolf quotes the opinions of the French moralist Jean de La Bruyère (1645–1696) and of the English writer Samuel Johnson (1609–1784) below. Oscar Browning (1837–1923) was a famous history lecturer at King's College, Cambridge.
1. British writer (1835–1902).
2. Women are extreme: they are better or worse than men (French).
3. " 'Men know that women are an overmatch for them, and therefore they choose the weakest or the

most ignorant. If they did not think so, they never could be afraid of women knowing as much as themselves.' . . . In justice to the sex, I think it but candid to acknowledge that, in a subsequent conversation, he told me that he was serious in what he said."—Boswell, *The Journal of a Tour to the Hebrides* [Woolf's note].
4. "The ancient Germans believed that there was something holy in women, and accordingly consulted them as oracles."—Frazer, *Golden Bough* [Woolf's note].
5. Italian Fascist dictator (1883–1945). Johann Wolfgang von Goethe (1749–1832), German poet, novelist, and playwright.

who specialise in woman and her effect on whatever it may be—politics, children, wages, morality—numerous and learned as they are. One might as well leave their books unopened.

But while I pondered I had unconsciously, in my listlessness, in my desperation, been drawing a picture where I should, like my neighbour, have been writing a conclusion. I had been drawing a face, a figure. It was the face and the figure of Professor von X. engaged in writing his monumental work entitled *The Mental, Moral, and Physical Inferiority of the Female Sex*. He was not in my picture a man attractive to women. He was heavily built; he had a great jowl; to balance that he had very small eyes; he was very red in the face. His expression suggested that he was labouring under some emotion that made him jab his pen on the paper as if he were killing some noxious insect as he wrote, but even when he had killed it that did not satisfy him; he must go on killing it; and even so, some cause for anger and irritation remained. Could it be his wife, I asked, looking at my picture. Was she in love with a cavalry officer? Was the cavalry officer slim and elegant and dressed in astrachan? Had he been laughed at, to adopt the Freudian theory, in his cradle by a pretty girl? For even in his cradle the professor, I thought, could not have been an attractive child. Whatever the reason, the professor was made to look very angry and very ugly in my sketch, as he wrote his great book upon the mental, moral and physical inferiority of women. Drawing pictures was an idle way of finishing an unprofitable morning's work. Yet it is in our idleness, in our dreams, that the submerged truth sometimes comes to the top. A very elementary exercise in psychology, not to be dignified by the name of psycho-analysis, showed me, on looking at my notebook, that the sketch of the angry professor had been made in anger. Anger had snatched my pencil while I dreamt. But what was anger doing there? Interest, confusion, amusement, boredom—all these emotions I could trace and name as they succeeded each other throughout the morning. Had anger, the black snake, been lurking among them? Yes, said the sketch, anger had. It referred me unmistakably to the one book, to the one phrase, which had roused the demon; it was the professor's statement about the mental, moral and physical inferiority of women. My heart had leapt. My cheeks had burnt. I had flushed with anger. There was nothing specially remarkable, however foolish, in that. One does not like to be told that one is naturally the inferior of a little man—I looked at the student next me—who breathes hard, wears a ready-made tie, and has not shaved this fortnight. One has certain foolish vanities. It is only human nature, I reflected, and began drawing cartwheels and circles over the angry professor's face till he looked like a burning bush or a flaming comet—anyhow, an apparition without human semblance or significance. The professor was nothing now but a faggot burning on the top of Hampstead Heath.[6] Soon my own anger was explained and done with; but curiosity remained. How explain the anger of the professors? Why were they angry? For when it came to analysing the impression left by these books there was always an element of heat. This heat took many forms; it showed itself in satire, in sentiment, in curiosity, in reprobation. But there was another element which was often present and could not immediately be identified.

6. An extensive area of open land on a hill overlooking London. "Faggot": a bundle of sticks.

Anger, I called it. But it was anger that had gone underground and mixed itself with all kinds of other emotions. To judge from its odd effects, it was anger disguised and complex, not anger simple and open.

Whatever the reason, all these books, I thought, surveying the pile on the desk, are worthless for my purposes. They were worthless scientifically, that is to say, though humanly they were full of instruction, interest, boredom, and very queer facts about the habits of the Fiji Islanders. They had been written in the red light of emotion and not in the white light of truth. Therefore they must be returned to the central desk and restored each to his own cell in the enormous honeycomb. All that I had retrieved from that morning's work had been the one fact of anger. The professors—I lumped them together thus—were angry. But why, I asked myself, having returned the books, why, I repeated, standing under the colonnade among the pigeons and the prehistoric canoes, why are they angry? And, asking myself this question, I strolled off to find a place for luncheon. What is the real nature of what I call for the moment their anger? I asked. Here was a puzzle that would last all the time that it takes to be served with food in a small restaurant somewhere near the British Museum. Some previous luncher had left the lunch edition of the evening paper on a chair, and, waiting to be served, I began idly reading the headlines. A ribbon of very large letters ran across the page. Somebody had made a big score in South Africa. Lesser ribbons announced that Sir Austen Chamberlain was at Geneva.[7] A meat axe with human hair on it had been found in a cellar. Mr Justice ——— commented in the Divorce Courts upon the Shamelessness of Women. Sprinkled about the paper were other pieces of news. A film actress had been lowered from a peak in California and hung suspended in mid-air. The weather was going to be foggy. The most transient visitor to this planet, I thought, who picked up this paper could not fail to be aware, even from this scattered testimony, that England is under the rule of a patriarchy. Nobody in their senses could fail to detect the dominance of the professor. His was the power and the money and the influence. He was the proprietor of the paper and its editor and sub-editor. He was the Foreign Secretary and the Judge. He was the cricketer; he owned the racehorses and the yachts. He was the director of the company that pays two hundred per cent to its shareholders. He left millions to charities and colleges that were ruled by himself. He suspended the film actress in mid-air. He will decide if the hair on the meat axe is human; he it is who will acquit or convict the murderer, and hang him, or let him go free. With the exception of the fog he seemed to control everything. Yet he was angry. I knew that he was angry by this token. When I read what he wrote about women I thought, not of what he was saying, but of himself. When an arguer argues dispassionately he thinks only of the argument; and the reader cannot help thinking of the argument too. If he had written dispassionately about women, had used indisputable proofs to establish his argument and had shown no trace of wishing that the result should be one thing rather than another, one would not have been angry either. One would have accepted the fact, as one accepts the fact that a pea is green or a canary yellow. So be it, I should have said. But I had been angry because

7. Headquarters of the League of Nations. Chamberlain (1863–1937) was a British statesman and brother of Neville Chamberlain, British prime minister (1937–40).

he was angry. Yet it seemed absurd, I thought, turning over the evening paper, that a man with all this power should be angry. Or is anger, I wondered, somehow, the familiar, the attendant sprite on power? Rich people, for example, are often angry because they suspect that the poor want to seize their wealth. The professors, or patriarchs, as it might be more accurate to call them, might be angry for that reason partly, but partly for one that lies a little less obviously on the surface. Possibly they were not "angry" at all; often, indeed, they were admiring, devoted, exemplary in the relations of private life. Possibly when the professor insisted a little too emphatically upon the inferiority of women, he was concerned not with their inferiority, but with his own superiority. That was what he was protecting rather hotheadedly and with too much emphasis, because it was a jewel to him of the rarest price. Life for both sexes—and I looked at them, shouldering their way along the pavement—is arduous, difficult, a perpetual struggle. It calls for gigantic courage and strength. More than anything, perhaps, creatures of illusion as we are, it calls for confidence in oneself. Without self-confidence we are as babes in the cradle. And how can we generate this imponderable quality, which is yet so invaluable, most quickly? By thinking that other people are inferior to oneself. By feeling that one has some innate superiority—it may be wealth, or rank, a straight nose, or the portrait of a grandfather by Romney[8]—for there is no end to the pathetic devices of the human imagination—over other people. Hence the enormous importance to a patriarch who has to conquer, who has to rule, of feeling that great numbers of people, half the human race indeed, are by nature inferior to himself. It must indeed be one of the chief sources of his power. But let me turn the light of this observation on to real life, I thought. Does it help to explain some of those psychological puzzles that one notes in the margin of daily life? Does it explain my astonishment the other day when Z, most humane, most modest of men, taking up some book by Rebecca West[9] and reading a passage in it, exclaimed, "The arrant feminist! She says that men are snobs!" The exclamation, to me so surprising—for why was Miss West an arrant feminist for making a possibly true if uncomplimentary statement about the other sex?—was not merely the cry of wounded vanity; it was a protest against some infringement of his power to believe in himself. Women have served all these centuries as looking-glasses possessing the magic and delicious power of reflecting the figure of man at twice its natural size. Without that power probably the earth would still be swamp and jungle. The glories of all our wars would be unknown. We should still be scratching the outlines of deer on the remains of mutton bones and bartering flints for sheepskins or whatever simple ornament took our unsophisticated taste. Supermen and Fingers of Destiny would never have existed. The Czar and the Kaiser[1] would never have worn their crowns or lost them. Whatever may be their use in civilised societies, mirrors are essential to all violent and heroic action. That is why Napoleon and Mussolini[2] both insist so emphatically upon the inferiority of women, for if they were not inferior, they would cease to enlarge. That serves to explain in part the necessity that women so often are to men. And it serves to explain how restless they are under her criticism; how impos-

---

8. George Romney (1734–1802), fashionable portrait painter.
9. Adopted name of Cecily Isabel Fairfield (1892–

1983), feminist, journalist, and novelist.
1. Rulers of Russia and Germany, respectively.
2. I.e., dictators.

sible it is for her to say to them this book is bad, this picture is feeble, or whatever it may be, without giving far more pain and rousing far more anger than a man would do who gave the same criticism. For if she begins to tell the truth, the figure in the looking-glass shrinks; his fitness for life is diminished. How is he to go on giving judgement, civilising natives, making laws, writing books, dressing up and speechifying at banquets, unless he can see himself at breakfast and at dinner at least twice the size he really is? So I reflected, crumbling my bread and stirring my coffee and now and again looking at the people in the street. The looking-glass vision is of supreme importance because it charges the vitality; it stimulates the nervous system. Take it away and man may die, like the drug fiend deprived of his cocaine. Under the spell of that illusion, I thought, looking out of the window, half the people on the pavement are striding to work. They put on their hats and coats in the morning under its agreeable rays. They start the day confident, braced, believing themselves desired at Miss Smith's tea party; they say to themselves as they go into the room, I am the superior of half the people here, and it is thus that they speak with that self-confidence, that self-assurance, which have had such profound consequences in public life and lead to such curious notes in the margin of the private mind.

But these contributions to the dangerous and fascinating subject of the psychology of the other sex—it is one, I hope, that you will investigate when you have five hundred a year of your own—were interrupted by the necessity of paying the bill. It came to five shillings and ninepence. I gave the waiter a ten-shilling note and he went to bring me change. There was another ten-shilling note in my purse; I noticed it, because it is a fact that still takes my breath away—the power of my purse to breed ten-shillings notes automatically. I open it and there they are. Society gives me chicken and coffee, bed and lodging, in return for a certain number of pieces of paper which were left me by an aunt, for no other reason than that I share her name.

My aunt, Mary Beton, I must tell you, died by a fall from her horse when she was riding out to take the air in Bombay. The news of my legacy reached me one night about the same time that the act was passed that gave votes to women. A solicitor's letter fell into the post-box and when I opened it I found that she had left me five hundred pounds a year for ever. Of the two—the vote and the money—the money, I own, seemed infinitely the more important. Before that I had made my living by cadging odd jobs from newspapers, by reporting a donkey show here or a wedding there; I had earned a few pounds by addressing envelopes, reading to old ladies, making artificial flowers, teaching the alphabet to small children in a kindergarten. Such were the chief occupations that were open to women before 1918. I need not, I am afraid, describe in any detail the hardness of the work, for you know perhaps women who have done it; nor the difficulty of living on the money when it was earned, for you may have tried. But what still remains with me as a worse infliction than either was the poison of fear and bitterness which those days bred in me. To begin with, always to be doing work that one did not wish to do, and to do it like a slave, flattering and fawning, not always necessarily perhaps, but it seemed necessary and the stakes were too great to run risks; and then the thought of that one gift which it was death to hide—a small one but dear to the possessor—perishing and with it myself, my soul—all this became like a rust eating away the bloom of the spring, destroying the tree at its heart. However, as I say, my aunt died; and whenever I change a ten-shilling note a little of that rust and corrosion is rubbed off; fear and bitterness go. Indeed, I thought, slipping the silver into my purse, it is remarkable, remembering the bitterness of those days, what a change of temper a fixed income will bring about. No force in the world can take from me my five hundred pounds. Food, house and clothing are mine for ever. Therefore not merely do effort and labour cease, but also hatred and bitterness. I need not hate any man; he cannot hurt me. I need not flatter any man; he has nothing to give me. So imperceptibly I found myself adopting a new attitude towards the other half of the human race. It was absurd to blame any class or any sex, as a whole. Great bodies of people are never responsible for what they do. They are driven by instincts which are not within their control. They too, the patriarchs, the professors, had endless difficulties, terrible drawbacks to contend with. Their education had been in some ways as faulty as my own. It had bred in them defects as great. True, they had money and power, but only at the cost of harbouring in their breasts an eagle, a vulture, for ever tearing the liver out and plucking at the lungs—the instinct for possession, the rage for acquisition which drives them to desire other people's fields and goods perpetually; to make frontiers and flags; battleships and poison gas; to offer up their own lives and their children's lives. Walk through the Admiralty Arch[3] (I had reached that monument), or any other avenue given up to trophies and cannon, and reflect upon the kind of glory celebrated there. Or watch in the spring sunshine the stockbroker and the great barrister going indoors to make money and more money and more money when it is a fact that five hundred pounds a year will keep one alive in the sunshine. These are unpleasant instincts to harbour, I reflected. They are bred of the conditions of life; of the lack of civilisation, I thought, looking at the statue of the Duke of Cambridge, and in particular at the feathers in his cocked hat, with a fixity that they have scarcely ever received before. And, as I realised these drawbacks, by degrees fear and bitterness modified themselves into pity and toleration; and then in a year or two, pity and toleration went, and the greatest release of all came, which is freedom to think of things in themselves. That building, for example, do I like it or not? Is that picture beautiful or not? Is that in my opinion a good book or a bad? Indeed my aunt's legacy unveiled the sky to me, and substituted for the large and imposing figure of a gentleman, which Milton recommended for my perpetual adoration, a view of the open sky.

So thinking, so speculating, I found my way back to my house by the river. Lamps were being lit and an indescribable change had come over London since the morning hour. It was as if the great machine after labouring all day had made with our help a few yards of something very exciting and beautiful—a fiery fabric flashing with red eyes, a tawny monster roaring with hot breath. Even the wind seemed flung like a flag as it lashed the houses and rattled the hoardings.

In my little street, however, domesticity prevailed. The house painter was descending his ladder; the nursemaid was wheeling the perambulator carefully in and out back to nursery tea; the coal-heaver was folding his empty

---

3. Between the Mall and Trafalgar Square in London, constructed 1906–11 to commemorate Britain's imperial successes.

sacks on top of each other; the woman who keeps the green-grocer's shop was adding up the day's takings with her hands in red mittens. But so engrossed was I with the problem you have laid upon my shoulders that I could not see even these usual sights without referring them to one centre. I thought how much harder it is now than it must have been even a century ago to say which of these employments is the higher, the more necessary. Is it better to be a coal-heaver or a nursemaid; is the charwoman who has brought up eight children of less value to the world than the barrister who has made a hundred thousand pounds? It is useless to ask such questions; for nobody can answer them. Not only do the comparative values of char-women and lawyers rise and fall from decade to decade, but we have no rods with which to measure them even as they are at the moment. I had been foolish to ask my professor to furnish me with "indisputable proofs" of this or that in his argument about women. Even if one could state the value of any one gift at the moment, those values will change; in a century's time very possibly they will have changed completely. Moreover, in a hundred years, I thought, reaching my own doorstep, women will have ceased to be the pro-tected sex. Logically they will take part in all the activities and exertions that were once denied them. The nursemaid will heave coal. The shop-woman will drive an engine. All assumptions founded on the facts observed when women were the protected sex will have disappeared—as, for example (here a squad of soldiers marched down the street), that women and clergymen and gardeners live longer than other people. Remove that protection, expose them to the same exertions and activities, make them soldiers and sailors and engine-drivers and dock labourers, and will not women die off so much younger, so much quicker, than men that one will say, "I saw a woman today," as one used to say, "I saw an aeroplane." Anything may happen when womanhood has ceased to be a protected occupation, I thought, opening the door. But what bearing has all this upon the subject of my paper, Women and Fiction? I asked, going indoors.

Chapter Three

It was disappointing not to have brought back in the evening some impor-tant statement, some authentic fact. Women are poorer than men because— this or that. Perhaps now it would be better to give up seeking for the truth, and receiving on one's head an avalanche of opinion hot as lava, discoloured as dish-water. It would be better to draw the curtains; to shut out distrac-tions; to light the lamp; to narrow the enquiry and to ask the historian, who records not opinions but facts, to describe under what conditions women lived, not throughout the ages, but in England, say in the time of Elizabeth.

For it is a perennial puzzle why no woman wrote a word of that extraor-dinary literature when every other man, it seemed, was capable of song or sonnet. What were the conditions in which women lived, I asked myself; for fiction, imaginative work that is, is not dropped like a pebble upon the ground, as science may be; fiction is like a spider's web, attached ever so lightly perhaps, but still attached to life at all four corners. Often the attach-ment is scarcely perceptible; Shakespeare's plays, for instance, seem to hang there complete by themselves. But when the web is pulled askew, hooked up at the edge, torn in the middle, one remembers that these webs are not spun in midair by incorporeal creatures, but are the work of suffering human beings, and are attached to grossly material things, like health and money and the houses we live in.

I went, therefore, to the shelf where the histories stand and took down one of the latest, Professor Trevelyan's *History of England.*[4] Once more I looked up Women, found "position of," and turned to the pages indicated. "Wife-beating," I read, "was a recognised right of man, and was practised without shame by high as well as low. . . . Similarly," the historian goes on, "the daughter who refused to marry the gentleman of her parents' choice was liable to be locked up, beaten and flung about the room, without any shock being inflicted on public opinion. Marriage was not an affair of personal affection, but of family avarice, particularly in the 'chivalrous' upper classes. . . . Betrothal often took place while one or both of the parties was in the cradle, and marriage when they were scarcely out of the nurses' charge." That was about 1470, soon after Chaucer's time. The next reference to the position of women is some two hundred years later, in the time of the Stuarts. "It was still the exception for women of the upper and middle class to choose their own husbands, and when the husband had been assigned, he was lord and master, so far at least as law and custom could make him. Yet even so," Professor Trevelyan concludes, "neither Shakespeare's women nor those of authentic seventeenth-century memoirs, like the Verneys and the Hutchinsons,[5] seem wanting in personality and character." Certainly, if we consider it, Cleopatra must have had a way with her; Lady Macbeth, one would suppose, had a will of her own; Rosalind,[6] one might conclude, was an attractive girl. Professor Trevelyan is speaking no more than the truth when he remarks that Shakespeare's women do not seem wanting in personality and character. Not being a historian, one might go even further and say that women have burnt like beacons in all the works of all the poets from the beginning of time—Clytemnestra, Antigone, Cleopatra, Lady Macbeth, Phèdre, Cressida, Rosalind, Desdemona, the Duchess of Malfi, among the dramatists; then among the prose writers: Millamant, Clarissa, Becky Sharp, Anna Karenina, Emma Bovary, Madame de Guermantes[7]—the names flock to mind, nor do they recall women "lacking in personality and character." Indeed, if woman had no existence save in the fiction written by men, one would imagine her a person of the utmost importance, very various; heroic and mean; splendid and sordid; infinitely beautiful and hideous in the extreme; as great as a man, some think even greater.[8] But this is woman in

4. G. M. Trevelyan's *History of England* (1926) long held its place as the standard one-volume history of the country.

5. "The ideal family life of the period [1640–50] that ended in such tragic political division has been recorded once for all in the *Memoirs of the Verney Family*" (Trevelyan, *History of England*). Lucy Hutchinson (b. 1628) wrote the biography of her husband, Col. John Hutchinson (1616–1684); it was first published in 1806.

6. These three Shakespearean heroines are, respectively, in *Antony and Cleopatra, Macbeth,* and *As You Like It.*

7. Characters in, respectively, Aeschylus's *Agamemnon;* Sophocles' *Antigone;* Shakespeare's *Antony and Cleopatra* and *Macbeth;* Racine's *Phèdre;* Shakespeare's *Troilus and Cressida, As You Like It,* and *Othello;* Webster's *The Duchess of*

Malfi; Congreve's *Way of the World;* Richardson's *Clarissa;* Thackeray's *Vanity Fair;* Tolstoy's *Anna Karenina;* Flaubert's *Madame Bovary;* and Proust's *A la recherche du temps perdu.*

8. "It remains a strange and almost inexplicable fact that in Athena's city, where women were kept in almost Oriental suppression as odalisques or drudges, the stage should yet have produced figures like Clytemnestra and Cassandra, Atossa and Antigone, Phèdre and Medea, and all the other heroines who dominate play after play of the 'misogynist' Euripides. But the paradox of this world where in real life a respectable woman could hardly show her face alone in the street, and yet on the stage woman equals or surpasses man, has never been satisfactorily explained. In modern tragedy the same predominance exists. At all events, a very cursory survey of Shakespeare's work

fiction. In fact, as Professor Trevelyan points out, she was locked up, beaten and flung about the room.

A very queer, composite being thus emerges. Imaginatively she is of the highest importance; practically she is completely insignificant. She pervades poetry from cover to cover; she is all but absent from history. She dominates the lives of kings and conquerors in fiction; in fact she was the slave of any boy whose parents forced a ring upon her finger. Some of the most inspired words, some of the most profound thoughts in literature fall from her lips; in real life she could hardly read, could scarcely spell, and was the property of her husband.

It was certainly an odd monster that one made up by reading the historians first and the poets afterwards—a worm winged like an eagle; the spirit of life and beauty in a kitchen chopping up suet. But these monsters, however amusing to the imagination, have no existence in fact. What one must do to bring her to life was to think poetically and prosaically at one and the same moment, thus keeping in touch with fact—that she is Mrs Martin, aged thirty-six, dressed in blue, wearing a black hat and brown shoes; but not losing sight of fiction either—that she is a vessel in which all sorts of spirits and forces are coursing and flashing perpetually. The moment, however, that one tries this method with the Elizabethan woman, one branch of illumination fails; one is held up by the scarcity of facts. One knows nothing detailed, nothing perfectly true and substantial about her. History scarcely mentions her. And I turned to Professor Trevelyan again to see what history meant to him. I found by looking at his chapter headings that it meant—

"The Manor Court and the Methods of Open-field Agriculture . . . The Cistercians and Sheep-farming . . . The Crusades . . . The University . . . The House of Commons . . . The Hundred Years' War . . . The Wars of the Roses . . . The Renaissance Scholars . . . The Dissolution of the Monasteries . . . Agrarian and Religious Strife . . . The Origin of English Sea-power . . . The Armada . . ." and so on. Occasionally an individual woman is mentioned, an Elizabeth, or a Mary; a queen or a great lady. But by no possible means could middle-class women with nothing but brains and character at their command have taken part in any one of the great movements which, brought together, constitute the historian's view of the past. Nor shall we find her in any collection of anecdotes. Aubrey[9] hardly mentions her. She never writes her own life and scarcely keeps a diary; there are only a handful of her letters in existence. She left no plays or poems by which we can judge her. What one wants, I thought—and why does not some brilliant student at Newnham or Girton supply it?—is a mass of information; at what age did she marry; how many children had she as a rule; what was her house like; had she a room to herself; did she do the cooking; would she be likely to have a servant? All these facts lie somewhere, presumably, in parish registers and account books; the life of the average Elizabethan woman must be scattered about somewhere, could one collect it and make a book of it. It would be ambitious beyond my daring, I thought, looking about the shelves for books that were

---

(similarly with Webster, though not with Marlowe or Jonson) suffices to reveal how this dominance, this initiative of women, persists from Rosalind to Lady Macbeth. So too in Racine; six of his tragedies bear their heroines' names; and what male characters of his shall we set against Hermione and Andromaque, Bérénice and Roxane, Phèdre and Athalie? So again with Ibsen; what men shall we match with Solveig and Nora, Hedda and Hilda Wangel and Rebecca West?"—F. L. Lucas, *Tragedy*, pp. 114–15 [Woolf's note].

9. John Aubrey (1626–1697), diarist.

not there, to suggest to the students of those famous colleges that they should re-write history, though I own that it often seems a little queer as it is, unreal, lop-sided; but why should they not add a supplement to history? calling it, of course, by some inconspicuous name so that women might figure there without impropriety? For one often catches a glimpse of them in the lives of the great, whisking away into the background, concealing, I sometimes think, a wink, a laugh, perhaps a tear. And, after all, we have lives enough of Jane Austen; it scarcely seems necessary to consider again the influence of the tragedies of Joanna Baillie[1] upon the poetry of Edgar Allan Poe; as for myself, I should not mind if the homes and haunts of Mary Russell Mitford[2] were closed to the public for a century at least. But what I find deplorable, I continued, looking about the bookshelves again, is that nothing is known about women before the eighteenth century. I have no model in my mind to turn about this way and that. Here am I asking why women did not write poetry in the Elizabethan age, and I am not sure how they were educated; whether they were taught to write; whether they had sitting-rooms to themselves; how many women had children before they were twenty-one; what, in short, they did from eight in the morning till eight at night. They had no money evidently; according to Professor Trevelyan they were married whether they liked it or not before they were out of the nursery, at fifteen or sixteen very likely. It would have been extremely odd, even upon this showing, had one of them suddenly written the plays of Shakespeare, I concluded, and I thought of that old gentleman, who is dead now, but was a bishop, I think, who declared that it was impossible for any woman, past, present, or to come, to have the genius of Shakespeare. He wrote to the papers about it. He also told a lady who applied to him for information that cats do not as a matter of fact go to heaven, though they have, he added, souls of a sort. How much thinking those old gentlemen used to save one! How the borders of ignorance shrank back at their approach! Cats do not go to heaven. Women cannot write the plays of Shakespeare.

Be that as it may, I could not help thinking, as I looked at the works of Shakespeare on the shelf, that the bishop was right at least in this; it would have been impossible, completely and entirely, for any woman to have written the plays of Shakespeare in the age of Shakespeare. Let me imagine, since facts are so hard to come by, what would have happened had Shakespeare had a wonderfully gifted sister, called Judith, let us say. Shakespeare himself went, very probably—his mother was an heiress—to the grammar school, where he may have learnt Latin—Ovid, Virgil and Horace—and the elements of grammar and logic. He was, it is well known, a wild boy who poached rabbits, perhaps shot a deer, and had, rather sooner than he should have done, to marry a woman in the neighbourhood, who bore him a child rather quicker than was right. That escapade sent him to seek his fortune in London. He had, it seemed, a taste for the theatre; he began by holding horses at the stage door. Very soon he got work in the theatre, became a successful actor, and lived at the hub of the universe, meeting everybody, knowing everybody, practising his art on the boards, exercising his wits in the streets, and even getting access to the palace of the queen. Meanwhile

1. Baillie (1762–1851), poet and dramatist.
2. Mitford (1787–1855), poet and novelist, best known for her sketches of country life.

his extraordinarily gifted sister, let us suppose, remained at home. She was as adventurous, as imaginative, as agog to see the world as he was. But she was not sent to school. She had no chance of learning grammar and logic, let alone of reading Horace and Virgil. She picked up a book now and then, one of her brother's perhaps, and read a few pages. But then her parents came in and told her to mend the stockings or mind the stew and not moon about with books and papers. They would have spoken sharply but kindly, for they were substantial people who knew the conditions of life for a woman and loved their daughter—indeed, more likely than not she was the apple of her father's eye. Perhaps she scribbled some pages up in an apple loft on the sly, but was careful to hide them or set fire to them. Soon, however, before she was out of her teens, she was to be betrothed to the son of a neighbouring wool-stapler.[3] She cried out that marriage was hateful to her, and for that she was severely beaten by her father. Then he ceased to scold her. He begged her instead not to hurt him, not to shame him in this matter of her marriage. He would give her a chain of beads or a fine petticoat, he said; and there were tears in his eyes. How could she disobey him? How could she break his heart? The force of her own gift alone drove her to it. She made up a small parcel of her belongings, let herself down by a rope one summer's night and took the road to London. She was not seventeen. The birds that sang in the hedge were not more musical than she was. She had the quickest fancy, a gift like her brother's, for the tune of words. Like him, she had a taste for the theatre. She stood at the stage door; she wanted to act, she said. Men laughed in her face. The manager—a fat, loose-lipped man—guffawed. He bellowed something about poodles dancing and women acting—no woman, he said, could possibly be an actress. He hinted—you can imagine what. She could get no training in her craft. Could she even seek her dinner in a tavern or roam the streets at midnight? Yet her genius was for fiction and lusted to feed abundantly upon the lives of men and women and the study of their ways. At last—for she was very young, oddly like Shakespeare the poet in her face, with the same grey eyes and rounded brows—at last Nick Greene the actor-manager took pity on her; she found herself with child by that gentleman and so—who shall measure the heat and violence of the poet's heart when caught and tangled in a woman's body?—killed herself one winter's night and lies buried at some cross-roads where the omnibuses now stop outside the Elephant and Castle.[4]

That, more or less, is how the story would run, I think, if a woman in Shakespeare's day had had Shakespeare's genius. But for my part, I agree with the deceased bishop, if such he was—it is unthinkable that any woman in Shakespeare's day should have had Shakespeare's genius. For genius like Shakespeare's is not born among labouring, uneducated, servile people. It was not born in England among the Saxons and the Britons. It is not born today among the working classes. How, then, could it have been born among women whose work began, according to Professor Trevelyan, almost before they were out of the nursery, who were forced to it by their parents and held to it by all the power of law and custom? Yet genius of a sort must have

3. A stapler is a dealer in staple goods (i.e., established goods in trade and marketing); hence a wool-stapler is a dealer in wool (one of the "staple" products of 16th-century England).

4. Suicides were buried at crossroads. The Elephant and Castle was a tavern south of the Thames where roads went off to different parts of southern England.

existed among women as it must have existed among the working classes. Now and again an Emily Brontë or a Robert Burns blazes out and proves its presence. But certainly it never got itself on to paper. When, however, one reads of a witch being ducked, of a woman possessed by devils, of a wise woman selling herbs, or even of a very remarkable man who had a mother, then I think we are on the track of a lost novelist, a suppressed poet, of some mute and inglorious[5] Jane Austen, some Emily Brontë who dashed her brains out on the moor or mopped and mowed about the highways crazed with the torture that her gift had put her to. Indeed, I would venture to guess that Anon, who wrote so many poems without signing them, was often a woman. It was a woman Edward Fitzgerald,[6] I think, suggested who made the ballads and the folk-songs, crooning them to her children, beguiling her spinning with them, or the length of the winter's night.

This may be true or it may be false—who can say?—but what is true in it, so it seemed to me, reviewing the story of Shakespeare's sister as I had made it, is that any woman born with a great gift in the sixteenth century would certainly have gone crazed, shot herself, or ended her days in some lonely cottage outside the village, half witch, half wizard, feared and mocked at. For it needs little skill in psychology to be sure that a highly gifted girl who had tried to use her gift for poetry would have been so thwarted and hindered by other people, so tortured and pulled asunder by her own contrary instincts, that she must have lost her health and sanity to a certainty. No girl could have walked to London and stood at a stage door and forced her way into the presence of actor-managers without doing herself a violence and suffering an anguish which may have been irrational—for chastity may be a fetish invented by certain societies for unknown reasons—but were none the less inevitable. Chastity had then, it has even now, a religious importance in a woman's life, and has so wrapped itself round with nerves and instincts that to cut it free and bring it to the light of day demands courage of the rarest. To have lived a free life in London in the sixteenth century would have meant for a woman who was poet and playwright a nervous stress and dilemma which might well have killed her. Had she survived, whatever she had written would have been twisted and deformed, issuing from a strained and morbid imagination. And undoubtedly, I thought, looking at the shelf where there are no plays by women, her work would have gone unsigned. That refuge she would have sought certainly. It was the relic of the sense of chastity that dictated anonymity to women even so late as the nineteenth century. Currer Bell, George Eliot, George Sand,[7] all the victims of inner strife as their writings prove, sought ineffectively to veil themselves by using the name of a man. Thus they did homage to the convention, which if not implanted by the other sex was liberally encouraged by them (the chief glory of a woman is not to be talked of, said Pericles,[8] himself a much-talked-of man), that publicity in women is detestable. Anonymity runs in their blood. The desire to be veiled still possesses them. They are not even now as concerned about the health of their fame as men are, and, speaking generally, will pass a tombstone or a signpost without feeling an irresistible desire to

---

5. An echo of Thomas Gray's famous line about "some mute inglorious Milton" in *Elegy Written in a Country Churchyard* (1751), line 59.
6. Poet and translator (1809–1883).

7. Male pseudonyms, respectively, of Charlotte Brontë, Marian Evans, and Amandine-Aurore-Lucie Dupin.
8. Athenian statesman (ca. 495–429 B.C.E.).

cut their names on it, as Alf, Bert or Chas. must do in obedience to their instinct, which murmurs if it sees a fine woman go by, or even a dog, Ce chien est à moi.[9] And, of course, it may not be a dog, I thought, remembering Parliament Square, the Sieges Allee[1] and other avenues; it may be a piece of land or a man with curly black hair. It is one of the great advantages of being a woman that one can pass even a very fine negress without wishing to make an Englishwoman of her.

That woman, then, who was born with a gift of poetry in the sixteenth century, was an unhappy woman, a woman at strife against herself. All the conditions of her life, all her own instincts, were hostile to the state of mind which is needed to set free whatever is in the brain. But what is the state of mind that is most propitious to the act of creation, I asked. Can one come by any notion of the state that furthers and makes possible that strange activity? Here I opened the volume containing the Tragedies of Shakespeare. What was Shakespeare's state of mind, for instance, when he wrote *Lear* and *Antony and Cleopatra*? It was certainly the state of mind most favourable to poetry that there has ever existed. But Shakespeare himself said nothing about it. We only know casually and by chance that he "never blotted a line."[2] Nothing indeed was ever said by the artist himself about his state of mind until the eighteenth century perhaps. Rousseau[3] perhaps began it. At any rate, by the nineteenth century self-consciousness had developed so far that it was the habit for men of letters to describe their minds in confessions and autobiographies. Their lives also were written, and their letters were printed after their deaths. Thus, though we do not know what Shakespeare went through when he wrote *Lear*, we do know what Carlyle went through when he wrote the *French Revolution*; what Flaubert went through when he wrote *Madame Bovary*; what Keats was going through when he tried to write poetry against the coming of death and the indifference of the world.

And one gathers from this enormous modern literature of confession and self-analysis that to write a work of genius is almost always a feat of prodigious difficulty. Everything is against the likelihood that it will come from the writer's mind whole and entire. Generally material circumstances are against it. Dogs will bark; people will interrupt; money must be made; health will break down. Further, accentuating all these difficulties and making them harder to bear is the world's notorious indifference. It does not ask people to write poems and novels and histories; it does not need them. It does not care whether Flaubert finds the right word or whether Carlyle scrupulously verifies this or that fact. Naturally, it will not pay for what it does not want. And so the writer, Keats, Flaubert, Carlyle, suffers, especially in the creative years of youth, every form of distraction and discouragement. A curse, a cry of agony, rises from those books of analysis and confession. "Mighty poets in their misery dead"[4]—that is the burden of their song. If anything comes through in spite of all this, it is a miracle, and probably no book is born entire and uncrippled as it was conceived.

---

9. This dog is mine (French).
1. Avenue of Victory, a busy thoroughfare in Berlin.
2. Ben Jonson, in *Timber*, writes, "I remember, the players have often mentioned it as an honour to Shakespeare that in his writing (whatsoever he

penned) he never blotted out a line."
3. Jean-Jacques Rousseau (1712–1778), early Romantic French philosopher and writer.
4. From Wordsworth's *Resolution and Independence*.

But for women, I thought, looking at the empty shelves, these difficulties were infinitely more formidable. In the first place, to have a room of her own, let alone a quiet room or a sound-proof room, was out of the question, unless her parents were exceptionally rich or very noble, even up to the beginning of the nineteenth century. Since her pin money, which depended on the good will of her father, was only enough to keep her clothed, she was debarred from such alleviations as came even to Keats or Tennyson or Carlyle, all poor men, from a walking tour, a little journey to France, from the separate lodging which, even if it were miserable enough, sheltered them from the claims and tyrannies of their families. Such material difficulties were formidable; but much worse were the immaterial. The indifference of the world which Keats and Flaubert and other men of genius have found so hard to bear was in her case not indifference but hostility. The world did not say to her as it said to them, Write if you choose; it makes no difference to me. The world said with a guffaw, Write? What's the good of your writing? Here the psychologists of Newnham and Girton might come to our help, I thought, looking again at the blank spaces on the shelves. For surely it is time that the effect of discouragement upon the mind of the artist should be measured, as I have seen a dairy company measure the effect of ordinary milk and Grade A milk upon the body of the rat. They set two rats in cages side by side, and of the two one was furtive, timid and small, and the other was glossy, bold and big. Now what food do we feed women as artists upon? I asked, remembering, I suppose, that dinner of prunes and custard. To answer that question I had only to open the evening paper and to read that Lord Birkenhead is of opinion—but really I am not going to trouble to copy out Lord Birkenhead's opinion upon the writing of women. What Dean Inge says I will leave in peace. The Harley Street specialist[5] may be allowed to rouse the echoes of Harley Street with his vociferations without raising a hair on my head. I will quote, however, Mr Oscar Browning, because Mr Oscar Browning was a great figure in Cambridge at one time, and used to examine the students at Girton and Newnham. Mr Oscar Browning was wont to declare "that the impression left on his mind, after looking over any set of examination papers, was that, irrespective of the marks he might give, the best woman was intellectually the inferior of the worst man." After saying that Mr Browning went back to his rooms—and it is this sequel that endears him and makes him a human figure of some bulk and majesty—he went back to his rooms and found a stable-boy lying on the sofa—"a mere skeleton, his cheeks were cavernous and sallow, his teeth were black, and he did not appear to have the full use of his limbs. . . . 'That's Arthur' [said Mr Browning]. 'He's a dear boy really and most high-minded.' " The two pictures always seem to me to complete each other. And happily in this age of biography the two pictures often do complete each other, so that we are able to interpret the opinions of great men not only by what they say, but by what they do.

But though this is possible now, such opinions coming from the lips of important people must have been formidable enough even fifty years ago. Let us suppose that a father from the highest motives did not wish his daughter to leave home and become writer, painter or scholar. "See what Mr Oscar

5. On Harley Street in London many medical specialists have their consulting rooms.

Browning says," he would say; and there was not only Mr Oscar Browning; there was the *Saturday Review*; there was Mr Greg[6]—the "essentials of a woman's being," said Mr Greg emphatically, "are that *they are supported by, and they minister to, men*"—there was an enormous body of masculine opinion to the effect that nothing could be expected of women intellectually. Even if her father did not read out loud these opinions, any girl could read them for herself; and the reading, even in the nineteenth century, must have lowered her vitality, and told profoundly upon her work. There would always have been that assertion—you cannot do this, you are incapable of doing that—to protest against, to overcome. Probably for a novelist this germ is no longer of much effect; for there have been women novelists of merit. But for painters it must still have some sting in it; and for musicians, I imagine, is even now active and poisonous in the extreme. The woman composer stands where the actress stood in the time of Shakespeare. Nick Greene, I thought, remembering the story I had made about Shakespeare's sister, said that a woman acting put him in mind of a dog dancing. Johnson repeated the phrase two hundred years later of women preaching. And here, I said, opening a book about music, we have the very words used again in this year of grace, 1928, of women who try to write music. "Of Mlle Germaine Tailleferre one can only repeat Dr Johnson's dictum concerning a woman preacher, transposed into terms of music. 'Sir, a woman's composing is like a dog's walking on his hind legs. It is not done well, but you are surprised to find it done at all.' "[7] So accurately does history repeat itself.

Thus, I concluded, shutting Mr Oscar Browning's life and pushing away the rest, it is fairly evident that even in the nineteenth century a woman was not encouraged to be an artist. On the contrary, she was snubbed, slapped, lectured and exhorted. Her mind must have been strained and her vitality lowered by the need of opposing this, of disproving that. For here again we come within range of that very interesting and obscure masculine complex which has had so much influence upon the woman's movement; that deep-seated desire, not so much that *she* shall be inferior as that *he* shall be superior, which plants him wherever one looks, not only in front of the arts, but barring the way to politics too, even when the risk to himself seems infinitesimal and the suppliant humble and devoted. Even Lady Bessborough, I remembered, with all her passion for politics, must humbly bow herself and write to Lord Granville Leveson-Gower:[8] ". . . notwithstanding all my violence in politics and talking so much on that subject, I perfectly agree with you that no woman has any business to meddle with that or any other serious business, farther than giving her opinion (if she is ask'd)." And so she goes on to spend her enthusiasm where it meets with no obstacle whatsoever upon that immensely important subject, Lord Granville's maiden speech in the House of Commons. The spectacle is certainly a strange one, I thought. The history of men's opposition to women's emancipation is more interesting perhaps than the story of that emancipation itself. An amusing book might be made of it if some young student at Girton or Newnham would

6. Sir W. W. Greg (1875–1959), bibliographer and literary scholar.
7. *A Survey of Contemporary Music*, Cecil Gray, p. 246 [Woolf's note].

8. Leveson-Gower (1773–1846). Lady Bessborough is Henrietta, countess of Bessborough (1761–1821).

collect examples and deduce a theory—but she would need thick gloves on her hands, and bars to protect her of solid gold.

But what is amusing now, I recollected, shutting Lady Bessborough, had to be taken in desperate earnest once. Opinions that one now pastes in a book labelled cock-a-doodle-dum and keeps for reading to select audiences on summer nights once drew tears, I can assure you. Among your grandmothers and great-grandmothers there were many that wept their eyes out. Florence Nightingale shrieked loud in her agony.[9] Moreover, it is all very well for you, who have got yourselves to college and enjoy sitting-rooms—or is it only bed-sitting-rooms?—of your own to say that genius should disregard such opinions; that genius should be above caring what is said of it. Unfortunately, it is precisely the men or women of genius who mind most what is said of them. Remember Keats. Remember the words he had cut on his tombstone.[1] Think of Tennyson; think—but I need hardly multiply instances of the undeniable, if very unfortunate, fact that it is the nature of the artist to mind excessively what is said about him. Literature is strewn with the wreckage of men who have minded beyond reason the opinions of others.

And this susceptibility of theirs is doubly unfortunate, I thought, returning again to my original enquiry into what state of mind is most propitious for creative work, because the mind of an artist, in order to achieve the prodigious effort of freeing whole and entire the work that is in him, must be incandescent, like Shakespeare's mind, I conjectured, looking at the book which lay open at *Antony and Cleopatra*. There must be no obstacle in it, no foreign matter unconsumed.

For though we say that we know nothing about Shakespeare's state of mind, even as we say that, we are saying something about Shakespeare's state of mind. The reason perhaps why we know so little of Shakespeare—compared with Donne or Ben Jonson or Milton—is that his grudges and spites and antipathies are hidden from us. We are not held up by some "revelation" which reminds us of the writer. All desire to protest, to preach, to proclaim an injury, to pay off a score, to make the world the witness of some hardship or grievance was fired out of him and consumed. Therefore his poetry flows from him free and unimpeded. If ever a human being got his work expressed completely, it was Shakespeare. If ever a mind was incandescent, unimpeded, I thought, turning again to the bookcase, it was Shakespeare's mind.

Chapter Four

That one would find any woman in that state of mind in the sixteenth century was obviously impossible. One has only to think of the Elizabethan tombstones with all those children kneeling with clasped hands; and their early deaths; and to see their houses with their dark, cramped rooms, to realise that no woman could have written poetry then. What one would expect to find would be that rather later perhaps some great lady would take advantage of her comparative freedom and comfort to publish something with her name to it and risk being thought a monster. Men, of course, are

9. See *Cassandra*, by Florence Nightingale, printed in *The Cause*, by R. Strachey [Woolf's note].

1. Here lies one whose name was writ in water.

not snobs, I continued, carefully eschewing "the arrant feminism" of Miss Rebecca West; but they appreciate with sympathy for the most part the efforts of a countess to write verse. One would expect to find a lady of title meeting with far greater encouragement than an unknown Miss Austen or a Miss Brontë at that time would have met with. But one would also expect to find that her mind was disturbed by alien emotions like fear and hatred and that her poems showed traces of that disturbance. Here is Lady Winchilsea,[2] for example, I thought, taking down her poems. She was born in the year 1661; she was noble both by birth and by marriage; she was childless; she wrote poetry, and one has only to open her poetry to find her bursting out in indignation against the position of women:

> How are we fallen! fallen by mistaken rules,
> And Education's more than Nature's fools;
> Debarred from all improvements of the mind,
> And to be dull, expected and designed;
> And if some one would soar above the rest,
> With warmer fancy, and ambition pressed,
> So strong the opposing faction still appears,
> The hopes to thrive can ne'er outweigh the fears.

Clearly her mind has by no means "consumed all impediments and become incandescent." On the contrary, it is harrassed and distracted with hates and grievances. The human race is split up for her into two parties. Men are the "opposing faction"; men are hated and feared, because they have the power to bar her way to what she wants to do—which is to write.

> Alas! a woman that attempts the pen,
> Such a presumptuous creature is esteemed,
> The fault can by no virtue be redeemed.
> They tell us we mistake our sex and way;
> Good breeding, fashion, dancing, dressing, play,
> Are the accomplishments we should desire;
> To write, or read, or think, or to enquire,
> Would cloud our beauty, and exhaust our time,
> And interrupt the conquests of our prime,
> Whilst the dull manage of a servile house
> Is held by some our utmost art and use.

Indeed she has to encourage herself to write by supposing that what she writes will never be published; to soothe herself with the sad chant:

> To some few friends, and to thy sorrows sing,
> For groves of laurel thou wert never meant;
> Be dark enough thy shades, and be thou there content.

Yet it is clear that could she have freed her mind from hate and fear and not heaped it with bitterness and resentment, the fire was hot within her. Now and again words issue of pure poetry:

> Nor will in fading silks compose,
> Faintly the inimitable rose.

2. Anne Finch, countess of Winchilsea (1661–1720); the quotations are from her poem *The Introduction*.

—they are rightly praised by Mr Murry,[3] and Pope, it is thought, remembered and appropriated those others:

> Now the jonquille o'ercomes the feeble brain;
> We faint beneath the aromatic pain.

It was a thousand pities that the woman who could write like that, whose mind was turned to nature and reflection, should have been forced to anger and bitterness. But how could she have helped herself? I asked, imagining the sneers and the laughter, the adulation of the toadies, the scepticism of the professional poet. She must have shut herself up in a room in the country to write, and been torn asunder by bitterness and scruples perhaps, though her husband was of the kindest, and their married life perfection. She "must have," I say, because when one comes to seek out the facts about Lady Winchilsea, one finds, as usual, that almost nothing is known about her. She suffered terribly from melancholy, which we can explain at least to some extent when we find her telling us how in the grip of it she would imagine:

> My lines decried, and my employment thought,
> An useless folly or presumptuous fault:

The employment, which was thus censured, was, as far as one can see, the harmless one of rambling about the fields and dreaming:

> My hand delights to trace unusual things,
> And deviates from the known and common way,
> Nor will in fading silks compose,
> Faintly the inimitable rose.

Naturally, if that was her habit and that was her delight, she could only expect to be laughed at; and, accordingly, Pope or Gay[4] is said to have satirised her "as a blue-stocking with an itch for scribbling." Also it is thought that she offended Gay by laughing at him. She said that his *Trivia* showed that "he was more proper to walk before a chair than to ride in one." But this is all "dubious gossip" and, says Mr Murry, "uninteresting." But there I do not agree with him, for I should have liked to have had more even of dubious gossip so that I might have found out or made up some image of this melancholy lady, who loved wandering in the fields and thinking about unusual things and scorned, so rashly, so unwisely, "the dull manage of a servile house." But she became diffuse, Mr Murry says. Her gift is all grown about with weeds and bound with briars. It had no chance of showing itself for the fine distinguished gift it was. And so, putting her back on the shelf, I turned to the other great lady, the Duchess whom Lamb loved, harebrained, fantastical Margaret of Newcastle,[5] her elder, but her contemporary. They were very different, but alike in this that both were noble and both childless, and both were married to the best of husbands. In both burnt the same passion for poetry and both are disfigured and deformed by the same causes. Open the Duchess and one finds the same outburst of rage, "Women

3. John Middleton Murry (1889–1957), English literary critic.
4. John Gay (1685–1732), English poet and playwright, author of the poem *Trivia, or The Art of Walking the Streets of London* (1716), mentioned below.
5. Margaret Lucas Cavendish, duchess of Newcastle (1623–1673), author of *Female Orations*, quoted below.

live like Bats or Owls, labour like Beasts, and die like Worms. . . ." Margaret too might have been a poet; in our day all that activity would have turned a wheel of some sort. As it was, what could bind, tame or civilise for human use that wild, generous, untutored intelligence? It poured itself out, higgledy-piggledy, in torrents of rhyme and prose, poetry and philosophy which stand congealed in quartos and folios that nobody ever reads. She should have had a microscope put in her hand. She should have been taught to look at the stars and reason scientifically. Her wits were turned with solitude and freedom. No one checked her. No one taught her. The professors fawned on her. At Court they jeered at her. Sir Egerton Brydges[6] complained of her coarseness—"as flowing from a female of high rank brought up in the Courts." She shut herself up at Welbeck alone.

What a vision of loneliness and riot the thought of Margaret Cavendish brings to mind! as if some giant cucumber had spread itself over all the roses and carnations in the garden and choked them to death. What a waste that the woman who wrote "the best bred women are those whose minds are civilest" should have frittered her time away scribbling nonsense and plunging ever deeper into obscurity and folly till the people crowded round her coach when she issued out. Evidently the crazy Duchess became a bogey to frighten clever girls with. Here, I remembered, putting away the Duchess and opening Dorothy Osborne's[7] letters, is Dorothy writing to Temple about the Duchess's new book. "Sure the poore woman is a little distracted, shee could never bee soe rediculous else as to venture at writeing book's and in verse too, if I should not sleep this fortnight I should not come to that."

And so, since no woman of sense and modesty could write books, Dorothy, who was sensitive and melancholy, the very opposite of the Duchess in temper, wrote nothing. Letters did not count. A woman might write letters while she was sitting by her father's sick-bed. She could write them by the fire whilst the men talked without disturbing them. The strange thing is, I thought, turning over the pages of Dorothy's letters, what a gift that untaught and solitary girl had for the framing of a sentence, for the fashioning of a scene. Listen to her running on:

"After dinner wee sitt and talk till Mr B. com's in question and then I am gon. the heat of the day is spent in reading or working and about sixe or seven a Clock, I walke out into a Common that lyes hard by the house where a great many young wenches keep Sheep and Cow's and sitt in the shades singing of Ballads; I goe to them and compare their voyces and Beauty's to some Ancient Shepherdesses that I have read of and finde a vaste difference there, but trust mee I think these are as innocent as those could bee. I talke to them, and finde they want nothing to make them the happiest People in the world, but the knoledge that they are soe. most commonly when we are in the middest of our discourse one looks aboute her and spyes her Cow's goeing into the Corne and then away they all run, as if they had wing's at theire heels. I that am not soe nimble stay behinde, and when I see them driveing home theire Cattle I think tis time for mee to retyre too. when I have supped I goe into the Garden and soe to the syde of a small River that runs by it where I sitt downe and wish you with mee. . . ."

6. English writer (1762–1837).
7. Later, Lady Temple (1627–1695), famous for her letters to her future husband.

One could have sworn that she had the makings of a writer in her. But "if I should not sleep this fortnight I should not come to that"—one can measure the opposition that was in the air to a woman writing when one finds that even a woman with a great turn for writing has brought herself to believe that to write a book was to be ridiculous, even to show oneself distracted. And so we come, I continued, replacing the single short volume of Dorothy Osborne's letters upon the shelf, to Mrs Behn.[8]

And with Mrs Behn we turn a very important corner on the road. We leave behind, shut up in their parks among their folios, those solitary great ladies who wrote without audience or criticism, for their own delight alone. We come to town and rub shoulders with ordinary people in the streets. Mrs Behn was a middle-class woman with all the plebeian virtues of humour, vitality and courage; a woman forced by the death of her husband and some unfortunate adventures of her own to make her living by her wits. She had to work on equal terms with men. She made, by working very hard, enough to live on. The importance of that fact outweighs anything that she actually wrote, even the splendid "A Thousand Martyrs I have made," or "Love in Fantastic Triumph sat," for here begins the freedom of the mind, or rather the possibility that in the course of time the mind will be free to write what it likes. For now that Aphra Behn had done it, girls could go to their parents and say, You need not give me an allowance; I can make money by my pen. Of course the answer for many years to come was, Yes, by living the life of Aphra Behn! Death would be better! and the door was slammed faster than ever. That profoundly interesting subject, the value that men set upon women's chastity and its effect upon their education, here suggests itself for discussion, and might provide an interesting book if any student at Girton or Newnham cared to go into the matter. Lady Dudley, sitting in diamonds among the midges of a Scottish moor, might serve for frontispiece. Lord Dudley, *The Times* said when Lady Dudley died the other day, "a man of cultivated taste and many accomplishments, was benevolent and bountiful, but whimsically despotic. He insisted upon his wife's wearing full dress, even at the remotest shooting-lodge in the Highlands; he loaded her with gorgeous jewels," and so on, "he gave her everything—always excepting any measure of responsibility." Then Lord Dudley had a stroke and she nursed him and ruled his estates with supreme competence for ever after. That whimsical despotism was in the nineteenth century too.

But to return. Aphra Behn proved that money could be made by writing at the sacrifice, perhaps, of certain agreeable qualities; and so by degrees writing became not merely a sign of folly and a distracted mind, but was of practical importance. A husband might die, or some disaster overtake the family. Hundreds of women began as the eighteenth century drew on to add to their pin money, or to come to the rescue of their families by making translations or writing the innumerable bad novels which have ceased to be recorded even in text-books, but are to be picked up in the fourpenny boxes in the Charing Cross Road.[9] The extreme activity of mind which showed itself in the later eighteenth century among women—the talking, and the meeting, the writing of essays on Shakespeare, the translating of the clas-

---

8. Aphra Behn (ca. 1640–1689), English poet and playwright, and author of *Oroonoko*.

9. A street in London famed for its bookshops.

sics—was founded on the solid fact that women could make money by writing. Money dignifies what is frivolous if unpaid for. It might still be well to sneer at "blue stockings with an itch for scribbling," but it could not be denied that they could put money in their purses. Thus, towards the end of the eighteenth century a change came about which, if I were rewriting history, I should describe more fully and think of greater importance than the Crusades or the Wars of the Roses. The middle-class woman began to write. For if *Pride and Prejudice* matters, and *Middlemarch* and *Villette* and *Wuthering Heights*[1] matter, then it matters far more than I can prove in an hour's discourse that women generally, and not merely the lonely aristocrat shut up in her country house among her folios and her flatterers, took to writing. Without those forerunners, Jane Austen and the Brontës and George Eliot could no more have written than Shakespeare could have written without Marlowe, or Marlowe without Chaucer, or Chaucer without those forgotten poets who paved the ways and tamed the natural savagery of the tongue. For masterpieces are not single and solitary births; they are the outcome of many years of thinking in common, of thinking by the body of the people, so that the experience of the mass is behind the single voice. Jane Austen should have laid a wreath upon the grave of Fanny Burney, and George Eliot done homage to the robust shade of Eliza Carter[2]—the valiant old woman who tied a bell to her bedstead in order that she might wake early and learn Greek. All women together ought to let flowers fall upon the tomb of Alphra Behn which is, most scandalously but rather appropriately, in Westminster Abbey, for it was she who earned them the right to speak their minds. It is she— shady and amorous as she was—who makes it not quite fantastic for me to say to you tonight: Earn five hundred a year by your wits.

Here, then, one had reached the early nineteenth century. And here, for the first time, I found several shelves given up entirely to the works of women. But why, I could not help asking, as I ran my eyes over them, were they, with very few exceptions, all novels? The original impulse was to poetry. The "supreme head of song" was a poetess. Both in France and in England the women poets precede the women novelists. Moreover, I thought, looking at the four famous names, what had George Eliot in common with Emily Brontë? Did not Charlotte Brontë fail entirely to understand Jane Austen? Save for the possibly relevant fact that not one of them had a child, four more incongruous characters could not have met together in a room—so much so that it is tempting to invent a meeting and a dialogue between them. Yet by some strange force they were all compelled, when they wrote, to write novels. Had it something to do with being born of the middle class, I asked; and with the fact, which Miss Emily Davies[3] a little later was so strikingly to demonstrate, that the middle-class family in the early nineteenth century was possessed only of a single sitting-room between them? If a woman wrote, she would have to write in the common sitting-room. And, as Miss Nightingale was so vehemently to complain,—"women never have an half hour . . . that they can call their own"—she was always interrupted. Still it would be easier to write prose and fiction there than to write poetry or a play. Less concentration is required. Jane Austen wrote like that to the end of her days.

---

1. Novels by, respectively, Jane Austen, George Eliot, Charlotte Brontë, and Emily Brontë.
2. English poet and translator. (1717–1806).

3. English educator (1830–1921), who established what was to become Girton College.

"How she was able to effect all this," her nephew writes in his Memoir, "is surprising, for she had no separate study to repair to, and most of the work must have been done in the general sitting-room, subject to all kinds of casual interruptions. She was careful that her occupation should not be suspected by servants or visitors or any persons beyond her own family party."[4] Jane Austen hid her manuscripts or covered them with a piece of blotting-paper. Then, again, all the literary training that a woman had in the early nineteenth century was training in the observation of character, in the analysis of emotion. Her sensibility had been educated for centuries by the influences of the common sitting-room. People's feelings were impressed on her; personal relations were always before her eyes. Therefore, when the middle-class woman took to writing, she naturally wrote novels, even though, as seems evident enough, two of the four famous women here named were not by nature novelists. Emily Brontë should have written poetic plays; the overflow of George Eliot's capacious mind should have spread itself when the creative impulse was spent upon history or biography. They wrote novels, however; one may even go further, I said, taking *Pride and Prejudice* from the shelf, and say that they wrote good novels. Without boasting or giving pain to the opposite sex, one may say that *Pride and Prejudice* is a good book. At any rate, one would not have been ashamed to have been caught in the act of writing *Pride and Prejudice*. Yet Jane Austen was glad that a hinge creaked, so that she might hide her manuscript before any one came in. To Jane Austen there was something discreditable in writing *Pride and Prejudice*. And, I wondered, would *Pride and Prejudice* have been a better novel if Jane Austen had not thought it necessary to hide her manuscript from visitors? I read a page or two to see; but I could not find any signs that her circumstances had harmed her work in the slightest. That, perhaps, was the chief miracle about it. Here was a woman about the year 1800 writing without hate, without bitterness, without fear, without protest, without preaching. That was how Shakespeare wrote, I thought, looking at *Antony and Cleopatra*; and when people compare Shakespeare and Jane Austen, they may mean that the minds of both had consumed all impediments; and for that reason we do not know Jane Austen and we do not know Shakespeare, and for that reason Jane Austen pervades every word that she wrote, and so does Shakespeare. If Jane Austen suffered in any way from her circumstances it was in the narrowness of life that was imposed upon her. It was impossible for a woman to go about alone. She never travelled; she never drove through London in an omnibus or had luncheon in a shop by herself. But perhaps it was the nature of Jane Austen not to want what she had not. Her gift and her circumstances matched each other completely. But I doubt whether that was true of Charlotte Brontë, I said, opening *Jane Eyre* and laying it beside *Pride and Prejudice*.

I opened it at chapter twelve and my eye was caught by the phrase, "Anybody may blame me who likes." What were they blaming Charlotte Brontë for, I wondered? And I read how Jane Eyre used to go up on to the roof when Mrs. Fairfax was making jellies and looked over the fields at the distant view. And then she longed—and it was for this that they blamed her—that "then I longed for a power of vision which might overpass that limit; which might

---

4. *Memoir of Jane Austen,* by her nephew, James Edward Austen-Leigh [Woolf's note].

reach the busy world, towns, regions full of life I had heard of but never seen: that then I desired more of practical experience than I possessed; more of intercourse with my kind, of acquaintance with variety of character than was here within my reach. I valued what was good in Mrs. Fairfax, and what was good in Adèle; but I believed in the existence of other and more vivid kinds of goodness, and what I believed in I wished to behold.

"Who blames me? Many, no doubt, and I shall be called discontented. I could not help it: the restlessness was in my nature; it agitated me to pain sometimes . . . .

"It is vain to say human beings ought to be satisfied with tranquillity: they must have action; and they will make it if they cannot find it. Millions are condemned to a stiller doom than mine, and millions are in silent revolt against their lot. Nobody knows how many rebellions ferment in the masses of life which people earth. Women are supposed to be very calm generally: but women feel just as men feel; they need exercise for their faculties and a field for their efforts as much as their brothers do; they suffer from too rigid a restraint, too absolute a stagnation, precisely as men would suffer; and it is narrow-minded in their more privileged fellow-creatures to say that they ought to confine themselves to making puddings and knitting stockings, to playing on the piano and embroidering bags. It is thoughtless to condemn them, or laugh at them, if they seek to do more or learn more than custom has pronounced necessary for their sex.

"When thus alone I not unfrequently heard Grace Poole's laugh. . . ."

That is an awkward break, I thought. It is upsetting to come upon Grace Poole all of a sudden. The continuity is disturbed. One might say, I continued, laying the book down beside *Pride and Prejudice,* that the woman who wrote those pages had more genius in her than Jane Austen; but if one reads them over and marks that jerk in them, that indignation, one sees that she will never get her genius expressed whole and entire. Her books will be deformed and twisted. She will write in a rage where she should write calmly. She will write foolishly where she should write wisely. She will write of herself where she should write of her characters. She is at war with her lot. How could she help but die young, cramped and thwarted?

One could not but play for a moment with the thought of what might have happened if Charlotte Brontë had possessed say three hundred a year—but the foolish woman sold the copyright of her novels outright for fifteen hundred pounds; had somehow possessed more knowledge of the busy world, and towns and regions full of life; more practical experience, and intercourse with her kind and acquaintance with a variety of character. In those words she puts her finger exactly not only upon her own defects as a novelist but upon those of her sex at that time. She knew, no one better, how enormously her genius would have profited if it had not spent itself in solitary visions over distant fields; if experience and intercourse and travel had been granted her. But they were not granted; they were withheld; and we must accept the fact that all those good novels, *Villette, Emma, Wuthering Heights, Middlemarch,* were written by women without more experience of life than could enter the house of a respectable clergyman; written too in the common sitting-room of that respectable house and by women so poor that they could not afford to buy more than a few quires of paper at a time upon which to write *Wuthering Heights* or *Jane Eyre.* One of them, it is true, George Eliot, escaped after much tribulation, but only to a secluded villa in St John's Wood.[5] And there she settled down in the shadow of the world's disapproval. "I wish it to be understood," she wrote, "that I should never invite any one to come and see me who did not ask for the invitation"; for was she not living in sin with a married man and might not the sight of her damage the chastity of Mrs Smith or whoever it might be that chanced to call? One must submit to the social convention, and be "cut off from what is called the world." At the same time, on the other side of Europe, there was a young man living freely with this gipsy or with that great lady; going to the wars; picking up unhindered and uncensored all that varied experience of human life which served him so splendidly later when he came to write his books. Had Tolstoi lived at the Priory in seclusion with a married lady "cut off from what is called the world," however edifying the moral lesson, he could scarcely, I thought, have written *War and Peace*.

But one could perhaps go a little deeper into the question of novel-writing and the effect of sex upon the novelist. If one shuts one's eyes and thinks of the novel as a whole, it would seem to be a creation owning a certain looking-glass likeness to life, though of course with simplifications and distortions innumerable. At any rate, it is a structure leaving a shape on the mind's eye, built now in squares, now pagoda shaped, now throwing out wings and arcades, now solidly compact and domed like the Cathedral of Saint Sofia at Constantinople. This shape, I thought, thinking back over certain famous novels, starts in one the kind of emotion that is appropriate to it. But that emotion at once blends itself with others, for the "shape" is not made by the relation of stone to stone, but by the relation of human being to human being. Thus a novel starts in us all sorts of antagonistic and opposed emotions. Life conflicts with something that is not life. Hence the difficulty of coming to any agreement about novels, and the immense sway that our private prejudices have upon us. On the one hand, we feel You—John the hero—must live, or I shall be in the depths of despair. On the other, we feel, Alas, John, you must die, because the shape of the book requires it. Life conflicts with something that is not life. Then since life it is in part, we judge it as life. James is the sort of man I most detest, one says. Or, This is a farrago of absurdity. I could never feel anything of the sort myself. The whole structure, it is obvious, thinking back on any famous novel, is one of infinite complexity, because it is thus made up of so many different judgments, of so many different kinds of emotion. The wonder is that any book so composed holds together for more than a year or two, or can possibly mean to the English reader what it means for the Russian or the Chinese. But they do hold together occasionally very remarkably. And what holds them together in these rare instances of survival (I was thinking of *War and Peace*) is something that one calls integrity, though it has nothing to do with paying one's bills or behaving honourably in an emergency. What one means by integrity, in the case of the novelist, is the conviction that he gives one that this is the truth. Yes, one feels, I should never have thought that this could be so; I have never known people behaving like that. But you have convinced me that so it is, so it happens. One holds every phrase, every scene to the light as one reads—for Nature seems, very oddly, to have provided us with an

5. A suburb in northwest London that developed in the 1840s.

inner light by which to judge of the novelist's integrity or disintegrity. Or perhaps it is rather that Nature, in her most irrational mood, has traced in invisible ink on the walls of the mind a premonition which these great artists confirm; a sketch which only needs to be held to the fire of genius to become visible. When one so exposes it and sees it come to life one exclaims in rapture, But this is what I have always felt and known and desired! And one boils over with excitement, and, shutting the book even with a kind of reverence as if it were something very precious, a stand-by to return to as long as one lives, one puts it back on the shelf, I said, taking *War and Peace* and putting it back in its place. If, on the other hand, these poor sentences that one takes and tests rouse first a quick and eager response with their bright colouring and their dashing gestures but there they stop: something seems to check them in their development: or if they bring to light only a faint scribble in that corner and a blot over there, and nothing appears whole and entire, then one heaves a sigh of disappointment and says, Another failure. This novel has come to grief somewhere.

And for the most part, of course, novels do come to grief somewhere. The imagination falters under the enormous strain. The insight is confused; it can no longer distinguish between the true and the false; it has no longer the strength to go on with the vast labour that calls at every moment for the use of so many different faculties. But how would all this be affected by the sex of the novelist, I wondered, looking at *Jane Eyre* and the others. Would the fact of her sex in any way interfere with the integrity of a woman novelist—that integrity which I take to be the backbone of the writer? Now, in the passages I have quoted from *Jane Eyre*, it is clear that anger was tampering with the integrity of Charlotte Brontë the novelist. She left her story, to which her entire devotion was due, to attend to some personal grievance. She remembered that she had been starved of her proper due of experience— she had been made to stagnate in a parsonage mending stockings when she wanted to wander free over the world. Her imagination swerved from indignation and we feel it swerve. But there were many more influences than anger tugging at her imagination and deflecting it from its path. Ignorance, for instance. The portrait of Rochester is drawn in the dark. We feel the influence of fear in it; just as we constantly feel an acidity which is the result of oppression, a buried suffering smouldering beneath her passion, a rancour which contracts those books, splendid as they are, with a spasm of pain.

And since a novel has this correspondence to real life, its values are to some extent those of real life. But it is obvious that the values of women differ very often from the values which have been made by the other sex; naturally, this is so. Yet it is the masculine values that prevail. Speaking crudely, football and sport are "important"; the worship of fashion, the buying of clothes "trivial." And these values are inevitably transferred from life to fiction. This is an important book, the critic assumes, because it deals with war. This is an insignificant book because it deals with the feelings of women in a drawing-room. A scene in a battlefield is more important than a scene in a shop—everywhere and much more subtly the difference of value persists. The whole structure, therefore, of the early nineteenth-century novel was raised, if one was a woman, by a mind which was slightly pulled from the straight, and made to alter its clear vision in deference to external authority. One has only to skim those old forgotten novels and listen to the tone of voice in which they are written to divine that the writer was meeting criticism; she was saying this by way of aggression, or that by way of conciliation. She was admitting that she was "only a woman," or protesting that she was "as good as a man." She met that criticism as her temperament dictated, with docility and diffidence, or with anger and emphasis. It does not matter which it was; she was thinking of something other than the thing itself. Down comes her book upon our heads. There was a flaw in the centre of it. And I thought of all the women's novels that lie scattered, like small pock-marked apples in an orchard, about the secondhand book shops of London. It was the flaw in the centre that had rotted them. She had altered her values in deference to the opinion of others.

But how impossible it must have been for them not to budge either to the right or to the left. What genius, what integrity it must have required in face of all that criticism, in the midst of that purely patriarchal society, to hold fast to the thing as they saw it without shrinking. Only Jane Austen did it and Emily Brontë. It is another feather, perhaps the finest, in their caps. They wrote as women write, not as men write. Of all the thousand women who wrote novels then, they alone entirely ignored the perpetual admonitions of the eternal pedagogue—write this, think that. They alone were deaf to that persistent voice, now grumbling, now patronising, now domineering, now grieved, now shocked, now angry, now avuncular, that voice which cannot let women alone, but must be at them, like some too conscientious governess, adjuring them, like Sir Egerton Brydges, to be refined; dragging even into the criticism of poetry criticism of sex;[6] admonishing them, if they would be good and win, as I suppose, some shiny prize, to keep within certain limits which the gentleman in question thinks suitable: ". . . female novelists should only aspire to excellence by courageously acknowledging the limitations of their sex."[7] That puts the matter in a nutshell, and when I tell you, rather to your surprise, that this sentence was written not in August 1828 but in August 1928, you will agree, I think, that however delightful it is to us now, it represents a vast body of opinion—I am not going to stir those old pools, I take only what chance has floated to my feet—that was far more vigorous and far more vocal a century ago. It would have needed a very stalwart young woman in 1828 to disregard all those snubs and chidings and promises of prizes. One must have been something of a firebrand to say to oneself, Oh, but they can't buy literature too. Literature is open to everybody. I refuse to allow you, Beadle though you are, to turn me off the grass. Lock up your libraries if you like; but there is no gate, no lock, no bolt that you can set upon the freedom of my mind.

But whatever effect discouragement and criticism had upon their writing— and I believe that they had a very great effect—that was unimportant compared with the other difficulty which faced them (I was still considering those early nineteenth-century novelists) when they came to set their thoughts on paper—that is that they had no tradition behind them, or one so short and partial that it was of little help. For we think back through our mothers if

---

6. "[She] has a metaphysical purpose, and that is a dangerous obsession, especially with a woman, for women rarely possess men's healthy love of rhetoric. It is a strange lack in the sex which is in other things more primitive and more materialistic."—*New Criterion*, June 1928 [Woolf's note].

7. "If, like the reporter, you believe that female novelists should only aspire to excellence by courageously acknowledging the limitations of their sex (Jane Austen [has] demonstrated how gracefully this gesture can be accomplished). . . ."—*Life and Letters*, August 1928 [Woolf's note].

we are women. It is useless to go to the great men writers for help, however much one may go to them for pleasure. Lamb, Browne, Thackeray, Newman, Sterne, Dickens, De Quincey—whoever it may be—never helped a woman yet, though she may have learnt a few tricks of them and adapted them to her use. The weight, the pace, the stride of a man's mind are too unlike her own for her to lift anything substantial from him successfully. The ape is too distant to be sedulous. Perhaps the first thing she would find, setting pen to paper, was that there was no common sentence ready for her use. All the great novelists like Thackeray and Dickens and Balzac have written a natural prose, swift but not slovenly, expressive but not precious, taking their own tint without ceasing to be common property. They have based it on the sentence that was current at the time. The sentence that was current at the beginning of the nineteenth century ran something like this perhaps: "The grandeur of their works was an argument with them, not to stop short, but to proceed. They could have no higher excitement or satisfaction than in the exercise of their art and endless generations of truth and beauty. Success prompts to exertion; and habit facilitates success." That is a man's sentence; behind it one can see Johnson, Gibbon and the rest. It was a sentence that was unsuited for a woman's use. Charlotte Brontë, with all her splendid gift for prose, stumbled and fell with that clumsy weapon in her hands. George Eliot committed atrocities with it that beggar description. Jane Austen looked at it and laughed at it and devised a perfectly natural, shapely sentence proper for her own use and never departed from it. Thus, with less genius for writing than Charlotte Brontë, she got infinitely more said. Indeed, since freedom and fullness of expression are of the essence of the art, such a lack of tradition, such a scarcity and inadequacy of tools, must have told enormously upon the writing of women. Moreover, a book is not made of sentences laid end to end, but of sentences built, if an image helps, into arcades or domes. And this shape too has been made by men out of their own needs for their own uses. There is no reason to think that the form of the epic or of the poetic play suits a woman any more than the sentence suits her. But all the older forms of literature were hardened and set by the time she became a writer. The novel alone was young enough to be soft in her hands— another reason, perhaps, why she wrote novels. Yet who shall say that even now "the novel" (I give it inverted commas to mark my sense of the words' inadequacy), who shall say that even this most pliable of all forms is rightly shaped for her use? No doubt we shall find her knocking that into shape for herself when she has the free use of her limbs; and providing some new vehicle, not necessarily in verse, for the poetry in her. For it is the poetry that is still denied outlet. And I went on to ponder how a woman nowadays would write a poetic tragedy in five acts—would she use verse—would she not use prose rather?

But these are difficult questions which lie in the twilight of the future. I must leave them, if only because they stimulate me to wander from my subject into trackless forests where I shall be lost and, very likely, devoured by wild beasts. I do not want, and I am sure that you do not want me, to broach that very dismal subject, the future of fiction, so that I will only pause here one moment to draw your attention to the great part which must be played in that future so far as women are concerned by physical conditions. The book has somehow to be adapted to the body, and at a venture one would say that women's books should be shorter, more concentrated, than those of men, and framed so that they do not need long hours of steady and uninterrupted work. For interruptions there will always be. Again, the nerves that feed the brain would seem to differ in men and women, and if you are going to make them work their best and hardest, you must find out what treatment suits them—whether these hours of lectures, for instance, which the monks devised, presumably, hundreds of years ago, suit them—what alternations of work and rest they need, interpreting rest not as doing nothing but as doing something but something that is different; and what should that difference be? All this should be discussed and discovered; all this is part of the question of women and fiction. And yet, I continued, approaching the bookcase again, where shall I find that elaborate study of the psychology of women by a woman? If through their incapacity to play football women are not going to be allowed to practise medicine——

Happily my thoughts were now given another turn.

Chapter Five

I had come at last, in the course of this rambling, to the shelves which hold books by the living; by women and by men; for there are almost as many books written by women now as by men. Or if that is not yet quite true, if the male is still the voluble sex, it is certainly true that women no longer write novels solely. There are Jane Harrison's books on Greek archaeology; Vernon Lee's books on aesthetics; Gertrude Bell's[8] books on Persia. There are books on all sorts of subjects which a generation ago no woman could have touched. There are poems and plays and criticism; there are histories and biographies, books of travel and books of scholarship and research; there are even a few philosophies and books about science and economics. And though novels predominate, novels themselves may very well have changed from association with books of a different feather. The natural simplicity, the epic age of women's writing, may have gone. Reading and criticism may have given her a wider range, a greater subtlety. The impulse towards autobiography may be spent. She may be beginning to use writing as an art, not as a method of self-expression. Among these new novels one might find an answer to several such questions.

I took down one of them at random. It stood at the very end of the shelf, was called *Life's Adventure*, or some such title, by Mary Carmichael,[9] and was published in this very month of October. It seems to be her first book, I said to myself, but one must read it as if it were the last volume in a fairly long series, continuing all those other books that I have been glancing at— Lady Winchilsea's poems and Aphra Behn's plays and the novels of the four great novelists. For books continue each other, in spite of our habit of judging them separately. And I must also consider her—this unknown woman—as the descendant of all those other women whose circumstances I have been glancing at and see what she inherits of their characteristics and restrictions.

8. English archaeologist and writer (1868–1926). Harrison (1850–1928), scholar and lecturer at Cambridge. Lee (1856–1935), essayist and art critic.

9. A work titled *Love's Creation* was published in London in 1928 under the name Marie Carmichael, the pseudonym for Marie Stopes, a crusader for birth control. The plot and characters resemble those mentioned by Woolf.

So, with a sigh, because novels so often provide an anodyne and not an antidote, glide one into torpid slumbers instead of rousing one with a burning brand, I settled down with a notebook and a pencil to make what I could of Mary Carmichael's first novel, *Life's Adventure*.

To begin with, I ran my eye up and down the page. I am going to get the hang of her sentences first, I said, before I load my memory with blue eyes and brown and the relationship that there may be between Chloe and Roger. There will be time for that when I have decided whether she has a pen in her hand or a pickaxe. So I tried a sentence or two on my tongue. Soon it was obvious that something was not quite in order. The smooth gliding of sentence after sentence was interrupted. Something tore, something scratched; a single word here and there flashed its torch in my eyes. She was "unhanding" herself as they say in the old plays. She is like a person striking a match that will not light, I thought. But why, I asked her as if she were present, are Jane Austen's sentences not of the right shape for you? Must they all be scrapped because Emma and Mr Woodhouse are dead? Alas, I sighed, that it should be so. For while Jane Austen breaks from melody to melody as Mozart from song to song, to read this writing was like being out at sea in an open boat. Up one went, down one sank. This terseness, this shortwindedness, might mean that she was afraid of something; afraid of being called "sentimental" perhaps; or she remembers that women's writing has been called flowery and so provides a superfluity of thorns; but until I have read a scene with some care, I cannot be sure whether she is being herself or some one else. At any rate, she does not lower one's vitality, I thought, reading more carefully. But she is heaping up too many facts. She will not be able to use half of them in a book of this size. (It was about half the length of *Jane Eyre*.) However, by some means or other she succeeded in getting us all—Roger, Chloe, Olivia, Tony and Mr Bigham—in a canoe up the river. Wait a moment, I said, leaning back in my chair, I must consider the whole thing more carefully before I go any further.

I am almost sure, I said to myself, that Mary Carmichael is playing a trick on us. For I feel as one feels on a switchback railway when the car, instead of sinking, as one has been led to expect, swerves up again. Mary is tampering with the expected sequence. First she broke the sentence; now she has broken the sequence. Very well, she has every right to do both these things if she does them not for the sake of breaking, but for the sake of creating. Which of the two it is I cannot be sure until she has faced herself with a situation. I will give her every liberty, I said, to choose what that situation shall be; she shall make it of tin cans and old kettles if she likes; but she must convince me that she believes it to be a situation; and then when she has made it she must face it. She must jump. And, determined to do my duty by her as reader if she would do her duty by me as writer, I turned the page and read . . . I am sorry to break off so abruptly. Are there no men present? Do you promise me that behind that red curtain over there the figure of Sir Chartres Biron is not concealed? We are all women, you assure me? Then I may tell you that the very next words I read were these—"Chloe liked Olivia . . ." Do not start. Do not blush. Let us admit in the privacy of our own society that these things sometimes happen. Sometimes women do like women.

"Chloe liked Olivia," I read. And then it struck me how immense a change was there. Chloe liked Olivia perhaps for the first time in literature. Cleopatra did not like Octavia. And how completely *Antony and Cleopatra* would have been altered had she done so! As it is, I thought, letting my mind, I am afraid, wander a little from *Life's Adventure,* the whole thing is simplified, conventionalised, if one dared say it, absurdly. Cleopatra's only feeling about Octavia is one of jealousy. Is she taller than I am? How does she do her hair? The play, perhaps, required no more. But how interesting it would have been if the relationship between the two women had been more complicated. All these relationships between women, I thought, rapidly recalling the splendid gallery of fictitious women, are too simple. So much has been left out, unattempted. And I tried to remember any case in the course of my reading where two women are represented as friends. There is an attempt at it in *Diana of the Crossways.* They are confidantes, of course, in Racine[1] and the Greek tragedies. They are now and then mothers and daughters. But almost without exception they are shown in their relation to men. It was strange to think that all the great women of fiction were, until Jane Austen's day, not only seen by the other sex, but seen only in relation to the other sex. And how small a part of a woman's life is that; and how little can a man know even of that when he observes it through the black or rosy spectacles which sex puts upon his nose. Hence, perhaps, the peculiar nature of woman in fiction; the astonishing extremes of her beauty and horror; her alternations between heavenly goodness and hellish depravity—for so a lover would see her as his love rose or sank, was prosperous or unhappy. This is not so true of the nineteenth-century novelists, of course. Woman becomes much more various and complicated there. Indeed it was the desire to write about women perhaps that led men by degrees to abandon the poetic drama which, with its violence, could make so little use of them, and to devise the novel as a more fitting receptacle. Even so it remains obvious, even in the writing of Proust,[2] that a man is terribly hampered and partial in his knowledge of women, as a woman in her knowledge of men.

Also, I continued, looking down at the page again, it is becoming evident that women, like men, have other interests besides the perennial interests of domesticity. "Chloe liked Olivia. They shared a laboratory together. . . ." I read on and discovered that these two young women were engaged in mincing liver, which is, it seems, a cure for pernicious anaemia: although one of them was married and had—I think I am right in stating—two small children. Now all that, of course, has had to be left out, and thus the splendid portrait of the fictitious woman is much too simple and much too monotonous. Suppose, for instance, that men were only represented in literature as the lovers of women, and were never the friends of men, soldiers, thinkers, dreamers; how few parts in the plays of Shakespeare could be allotted to them; how literature would suffer! We might perhaps have most of Othello; and a good deal of Antony; but no Caesar, no Brutus, no Hamlet, no Lear, no Jaques—literature would be incredibly impoverished, as indeed literature is impoverished beyond our counting by the doors that have been shut upon women. Married against their will, kept in one room, and to one occupation, how could a dramatist give a full or interesting or truthful account of them? Love

---

1. Jean Racine (1639–1699), French dramatist. "*Diana of the Crossways*": (1885) novel by the English author George Meredith (1828–1909).

2. Marcel Proust (1871–1922), French novelist and author of the seven-volume *A la recherche du temps perdu* (1913–27).

was the only possible interpreter. The poet was forced to be passionate or bitter, unless indeed he chose to "hate women," which meant more often than not that he was unattractive to them.

Now if Chloe likes Olivia and they share a laboratory, which of itself will make their friendship more varied and lasting because it will be less personal; if Mary Carmichael knows how to write, and I was beginning to enjoy some quality in her style; if she has a room to herself, of which I am not quite sure; if she has five hundred a year of her own—but that remains to be proved—then I think that something of great importance has happened.

For if Chloe likes Olivia and Mary Carmichael knows how to express it she will light a torch in that vast chamber where nobody has yet been. It is all half lights and profound shadows like those serpentine caves where one goes with a candle peering up and down, not knowing where one is stepping. And I began to read the book again, and read how Chloe watched Olivia put a jar on a shelf and say how it was time to go home to her children. That is a sight that has never been seen since the world began, I exclaimed. And I watched too, very curiously. For I wanted to see how Mary Carmichael set to work to catch those unrecorded gestures, those unsaid or half-said words, which form themselves, no more palpably than the shadows of moths on the ceiling, when women are alone, unlit by the capricious and coloured light of the other sex. She will need to hold her breath, I said, reading on, if she is to do it; for women are so suspicious of any interest that has not some obvious motive behind it, so terribly accustomed to concealment and suppression, that they are off at the flicker of an eye turned observingly in their direction. The only way for you to do it, I thought, addressing Mary Carmichael as if she were there, would be to talk of something else, looking steadily out of the window, and thus note, not with a pencil in a notebook, but in the shortest of shorthand, in words that are hardly syllabled yet, what happens when Olivia—this organism that has been under the shadow of the rock these million years—feels the light fall on it, and sees coming her way a piece of strange food—knowledge, adventure, art. And she reaches out for it, I thought, again raising my eyes from the page, and has to devise some entirely new combination of her resources, so highly developed for their purposes, so as to absorb the new into the old without disturbing the infinitely intricate and elaborate balance of the whole.

But, alas, I had done what I had determined not to do; I had slipped unthinkingly into praise of my own sex. "Highly developed"—"infinitely intricate"—such are undeniably terms of praise, and to praise one's own sex is always suspect, often silly; moreover, in this case, how could one justify it? One could not go to the map and say Columbus discovered America and Columbus was a woman; or take an apple and remark, Newton discovered the laws of gravitation and Newton was a woman; or look into the sky and say aeroplanes are flying overhead and aeroplanes were invented by women. There is no mark on the wall to measure the precise height of women. There are no yard measures, neatly divided into the fractions of an inch, that one can lay against the qualities of a good mother or the devotion of a daughter, or the fidelity of a sister, or the capacity of a housekeeper. Few women even now have been graded at the universities; the great trials of the professions, army and navy, trade, politics and diplomacy have hardly tested them. They remain even at this moment almost unclassified. But if I want to know all that a human being can tell me about Sir Hawley Butts, for instance, I have only to open Burke or Debrett[3] and I shall find that he took such and such a degree; owns a hall; has an heir; was Secretary to a Board; represented Great Britain in Canada; and has received a certain number of degrees, offices, medals and other distinctions by which his merits are stamped upon him indelibly. Only Providence can know more about Sir Hawley Butts than that.

When, therefore, I say "highly developed," "infinitely intricate," of women, I am unable to verify my words either in Whitaker, Debrett or the University Calendar. In this predicament what can I do? And I looked at the bookcase again. There were the biographies: Johnson and Goethe and Carlyle and Sterne and Cowper and Shelley and Voltaire and Browning and many others. And I began thinking of all those great men who have for one reason or another admired, sought out, lived with, confided in, made love to, written of, trusted in, and shown what can only be described as some need of and dependence upon certain persons of the opposite sex. That all these relationships were absolutely Platonic I would not affirm, and Sir William Joynson Hicks[4] would probably deny. But we should wrong these illustrious men very greatly if we insisted that they got nothing from these alliances but comfort, flattery and the pleasures of the body. What they got, it is obvious, was something that their own sex was unable to supply; and it would not be rash, perhaps, to define it further, without quoting the doubtless rhapsodical words of the poets, as some stimulus, some renewal of creative power which is in the gift only of the opposite sex to bestow. He would open the door of drawing-room or nursery, I thought, and find her among her children perhaps, or with a piece of embroidery on her knee—at any rate, the centre of some different order and system of life, and the contrast between this world and his own, which might be the law courts or the House of Commons, would at once refresh and invigorate; and there would follow, even in the simplest talk, such a natural difference of opinion that the dried ideas in him would be fertilised anew; and the sight of her creating in a different medium from his own would so quicken his creative power that insensibly his sterile mind would begin to plot again, and he would find the phrase or the scene which was lacking when he put on his hat to visit her. Every Johnson has his Thrale,[5] and holds fast to her for some such reasons as these, and when the Thrale marries her Italian music master Johnson goes half mad with rage and disgust, not merely that he will miss his pleasant evenings at Streatham, but that the light of his life will be "as if gone out."

And without being Dr Johnson or Goethe or Carlyle or Voltaire, one may feel, though very differently from these great men, the nature of this intricacy and the power of this highly developed creative faculty among women. One goes into the room—but the resources of the English language would be much put to the stretch, and whole flights of words would need to wing their way illegitimately into existence before a woman could say what happens when she goes into a room. The rooms differ so completely; they are calm

---

3. Annual reference works of genealogy and the peerage. Sir Hawley Butts, however, seems to be Woolf's invention.
4. Hicks (1865–1932), English Conservative politician and evangelical religious figure.
5. Hester Lynch Thrale (1741–1821), who with her husband, Henry, was for many years friend and hostess to Samuel Johnson at their home in Streatham Place. After Henry's death, she married an Italian musician, much to Johnson's distress; his reaction helped end their friendship.

or thunderous; open on to the sea, or, on the contrary, give on to a prison yard; are hung with washing; or alive with opals and silks; are hard as horsehair or soft as feathers—one has only to go into any room in any street for the whole of that extremely complex force of femininity to fly in one's face. How should it be otherwise? For women have sat indoors all these millions of years, so that by this time the very walls are permeated by their creative force, which has, indeed, so overcharged the capacity of bricks and mortar that it must needs harness itself to pens and brushes and business and politics. But this creative power differs greatly from the creative power of men. And one must conclude that it would be a thousand pities if it were hindered or wasted, for it was won by centuries of the most drastic discipline, and there is nothing to take its place. It would be a thousand pities if women wrote like men, or lived like men, or looked like men, for if two sexes are quite inadequate, considering the vastness and variety of the world, how should we manage with one only? Ought not education to bring out and fortify the differences rather than the similarities? For we have too much likeness as it is, and if an explorer should come back and bring word of other sexes looking through the branches of other trees at other skies, nothing would be of greater service to humanity; and we should have the immense pleasure into the bargain of watching Professor X rush for his measuring-rods to prove himself "superior."

Mary Carmichael, I thought, still hovering at a little distance above the page, will have her work cut out for her merely as an observer. I am afraid indeed that she will be tempted to become, what I think the less interesting branch of the species—the naturalist-novelist, and not the contemplative. There are so many new facts for her to observe. She will not need to limit herself any longer to the respectable houses of the upper middle classes. She will go without kindness or condescension, but in the spirit of fellowship into those small, scented rooms where sit the courtesan, the harlot and the lady with the pug dog. There they still sit in the rough and ready-made clothes that the male writer has had perforce to clap upon their shoulders. But Mary Carmichael will have out her scissors and fit them close to every hollow and angle. It will be a curious sight, when it comes, to see these women as they are, but we must wait a little, for Mary Carmichael will still be encumbered with that self-consciousness in the presence of "sin" which is the legacy of our sexual barbarity. She will still wear the shoddy old fetters of class on her feet.

However, the majority of women are neither harlots nor courtesans; nor do they sit clasping pug dogs to dusty velvet all through the summer afternoon. But what do they do then? and there came to my mind's eye one of those long streets somewhere south of the river whose infinite rows are innumerably populated. With the eye of the imagination I saw a very ancient lady crossing the street on the arm of a middle-aged woman, her daughter, perhaps, both so respectably booted and furred that their dressing in the afternoon must be a ritual, and the clothes themselves put away in cupboards with camphor, year after year, throughout the summer months. They cross the road when the lamps are being lit (for the dusk is their favourite hour), as they must have done year after year. The elder is close on eighty; but if one asked her what her life has meant to her, she would say that she remembered the streets lit for the battle of Balaclava, or had heard the guns fire in Hyde Park for the birth of King Edward the Seventh.[6] And if one asked her, longing to pin down the moment with date and season, but what were you doing on the fifth of April 1868, or the second of November 1875, she would look vague and say that she could remember nothing. For all the dinners are cooked; the plates and cups washed; the children set to school and gone out into the world. Nothing remains of it all. All has vanished. No biography or history has a word to say about it. And the novels, without meaning to, inevitably lie.

All these infinitely obscure lives remain to be recorded, I said, addressing Mary Carmichael as if she were present; and went on in thought through the streets of London feeling in imagination the pressure of dumbness, the accumulation of unrecorded life, whether from the women at the street corners with their arms akimbo, and the rings embedded in their fat swollen fingers, talking with a gesticulation like the swing of Shakespeare's words; or from the violet-sellers and match-sellers and old crones stationed under doorways; or from drifting girls whose faces, like waves in sun and cloud, signal the coming of men and women and the flickering lights of shop windows. All that you will have to explore, I said to Mary Carmichael, holding your torch firm in your hand. Above all, you must illumine your own soul with its profundities and its shallows, and its vanities and its generosities, and say what your beauty means to you or your plainness, and what is your relation to the everchanging and turning world of gloves and shoes and stuffs swaying up and down among the faint scents that come through chemists' bottles down arcades of dress material over a floor of pseudo-marble. For in imagination I had gone into a shop; it was laid with black and white paving; it was hung, astonishingly beautifully, with coloured ribbons. Mary Carmichael might well have a look at that in passing, I thought, for it is a sight that would lend itself to the pen as fittingly as any snowy peak or rocky gorge in the Andes. And there is the girl behind the counter too—I would as soon have her true history as the hundred and fiftieth life of Napoleon or seventieth study of Keats and his use of Miltonic inversion when old Professor Z and his like are now inditing. And then I went on very warily, on the very tips of my toes (so cowardly am I, so afraid of the lash that was once almost laid on my own shoulders), to murmur that she should also learn to laugh, without bitterness, at the vanities—say rather at the peculiarities, for it is a less offensive word—of the other sex. For there is a spot the size of a shilling at the back of the head which one can never see for oneself. It is one of the good offices that sex can discharge for sex—to describe that spot the size of a shilling at the back of the head. Think how much women have profited by the comments of Juvenal; by the criticism of Strindberg.[7] Think with what humanity and brilliancy men, from the earliest ages, have pointed out to women that dark place at the back of the head! And if Mary were very brave and very honest, she would go behind the other sex and tell us what she found there. A true picture of man as a whole can never be painted until a

6. In 1841 (since Woolf is writing in 1928, Edward's birth would actually have been before the birth of a woman "close on eighty"). The "battle of Balaclava," famous for the charge of the Light Brigade, occurred in 1854.
7. August Strindberg (1849–1912), Swedish playwright. Juvenal (ca. 60–136), Roman satirist.

woman has described that spot the size of a shilling. Mr Woodhouse and Mr Casaubon[8] are spots of that size and nature. Not of course that any one in their senses would counsel her to hold up to scorn and ridicule of set purpose—literature shows the futility of what is written in that spirit. Be truthful, one would say, and the result is bound to be amazingly interesting. Comedy is bound to be enriched. New facts are bound to be discovered.

However, it was high time to lower my eyes to the page again. It would be better, instead of speculating what Mary Carmichael might write and should write, to see what in fact Mary Carmichael did write. So I began to read again. I remembered that I had certain grievances against her. She had broken up Jane Austen's sentence, and thus given me no chance of pluming myself upon my impeccable taste, my fastidious ear. For it was useless to say, "Yes, yes, this is very nice; but Jane Austen wrote much better than you do," when I had to admit that there was no point of likeness between them. Then she had gone further and broken the sequence—the expected order. Perhaps she had done this unconsciously, merely giving things their natural order, as a woman would, if she wrote like a woman. But the effect was somehow baffling; one could not see a wave heaping itself, a crisis coming round the next corner. Therefore I could not plume myself either upon the depths of my feelings and my profound knowledge of the human heart. For whenever I was about to feel the usual things in the usual places, about love, about death, the annoying creature twitched me away, as if the important point were just a little further on. And thus she made it impossible for me to roll out my sonorous phrases about "elemental feelings," the "common stuff of humanity," "depths of the human heart," and all those other phrases which support us in our belief that, however clever we may be on top, we are very serious, very profound and very humane underneath. She made me feel, on the contrary, that instead of being serious and profound and humane, one might be—and the thought was far less seductive—merely lazy minded and conventional into the bargain.

But I read on, and noted certain other facts. She was no "genius"—that was evident. She had nothing like the love of Nature, the fiery imagination, the wild poetry, the brilliant wit, the brooding wisdom of her great predecessors, Lady Winchilsea, Charlotte Brontë, Jane Austen and George Eliot; she could not write with the melody and the dignity of Dorothy Osborne— indeed she was no more than a clever girl whose books will no doubt be pulped by the publishers in ten years' time. But, nevertheless, she had certain advantages which women of far greater gift lacked even half a century ago. Men were no longer to her "the opposing faction"; she need not waste her time railing against them; she need not climb on to the roof and ruin her peace of mind longing for travel, experience and a knowledge of the world and character that were denied her. Fear and hatred were almost gone, or traces of them showed only in a slight exaggeration of the joy of freedom, a tendency to the caustic and satirical, rather than to the romantic, in her treatment of the other sex. Then there could be no doubt that as a novelist she enjoyed some natural advantages of a high order. She had a sensibility that was very wide, eager and free. It responded to an almost imperceptible

8. The husband of the heroine in George Eliot's *Middlemarch*. Woodhouse is the father of the heroine in Jane Austen's *Emma*.

touch on it. It feasted like a plant newly stood in the air on every sight and sound that came its way. It ranged, too, very subtly and curiously, among almost unknown or unrecorded things; it lighted on small things and showed that perhaps they were not small after all. It brought buried things to light and made one wonder what need there had been to bury them. Awkward though she was and without the unconscious bearing of long descent which makes the least turn of the pen of a Thackeray or a Lamb delightful to the ear, she had—I began to think—mastered the first great lesson; she wrote as a woman, but as a woman who has forgotten that she is a woman, so that her pages were full of that curious sexual quality which comes only when sex is unconscious of itself.

All this was to the good. But no abundance of sensation or fineness of perception would avail unless she could build up out of the fleeting and the personal the lasting edifice which remains unthrown. I had said that I would wait until she faced herself with "a situation." And I meant by that until she proved by summoning, beckoning and getting together that she was not a skimmer of surfaces merely, but had looked beneath into the depths. Now is the time, she would say to herself at a certain moment, when without doing anything violent I can show the meaning of all this. And she would begin—how unmistakable that quickening is!—beckoning and summoning, and there would rise up in memory, half forgotten, perhaps quite trivial things in other chapters dropped by the way. And she would make their presence felt while some one sewed or smoked a pipe as naturally as possible, and one would feel, as she went on writing, as if one had gone to the top of the world and seen it laid out, very majestically, beneath.

At any rate, she was making the attempt. And as I watched her lengthening out for the test, I saw, but hoped that she did not see, the bishops and the deans, the doctors and the professors, the patriarchs and the pedagogues all at her shouting warning and advice. You can't do this and you shan't do that! Fellows and scholars only allowed on the grass! Ladies not admitted without a letter of introduction! Aspiring and graceful female novelists this way! So they kept at her like the crowd at a fence on the race-course, and it was her trial to take her fence without looking to right or left. If you stop to curse you are lost, I said to her; equally, if you stop to laugh. Hesitate or fumble and you are done for. Think only of the jump, I implored her, as if I had put the whole of my money on her back; and she went over it like a bird. But there was a fence beyond that and a fence beyond that. Whether she had the staying power I was doubtful, for the clapping and the crying were fraying to the nerves. But she did her best. Considering that Mary Carmichael was no genius, but an unknown girl writing her first novel in a bed-sitting-room, without enough of those desirable things, time, money and idleness, she did not do so badly, I thought.

Give her another hundred years, I concluded, reading the last chapter—people's noses and bare shoulders showed naked against a starry sky, for some one had twitched the curtain in the drawing-room—give her a room of her own and five hundred a year, let her speak her mind and leave out half that she now puts in, and she will write a better book one of these days. She will be a poet, I said, putting *Life's Adventure,* by Mary Carmichael, at the end of the shelf, in another hundred years' time.

Chapter Six

Next day the light of the October morning was falling in dusty shafts through the uncurtained windows, and the hum of traffic rose from the street. London then was winding itself up again; the factory was astir; the machines were beginning. It was tempting, after all this reading, to look out of the window and see what London was doing on the morning of the twenty-sixth of October 1928. And what was London doing? Nobody, it seemed, was reading *Antony and Cleopatra*. London was wholly indifferent, it appeared, to Shakespeare's plays. Nobody cared a straw—and I do not blame them—for the future of fiction, the death of poetry or the development by the average woman of a prose style completely expressive of her mind. If opinions upon any of these matters had been chalked on the pavement, nobody would have stooped to read them. The nonchalance of the hurrying feet would have rubbed them out in half an hour. Here came an errand-boy; here a woman with a dog on a lead. The fascination of the London street is that no two people are ever alike; each seems bound on some private affair of his own. There were the business-like, with their little bags; there were the drifters rattling sticks upon area railings; there were affable characters to whom the streets serve for clubroom, hailing men in carts and giving information without being asked for it. Also there were funerals to which men, thus suddenly reminded of the passing of their own bodies, lifted their hats. And then a very distinguished gentleman came slowly down a doorstep and paused to avoid collision with a bustling lady who had, by some means or other, acquired a splendid fur coat and a bunch of Parma violets. They all seemed separate, self-absorbed, on business of their own.

At this moment, as so often happens in London, there was a complete lull and suspension of traffic. Nothing came down the street; nobody passed. A single leaf detached itself from the plane tree at the end of the street, and in that pause and suspension fell. Somehow it was like a signal falling, a signal pointing to a force in things which one had overlooked. It seemed to point to a river, which flowed past, invisibly, round the corner, down the street, and took people and eddied them along, as the stream at Oxbridge had taken the undergraduate in his boat and the dead leaves. Now it was bringing from one side of the street to the other diagonally a girl in patent leather boots, and then a young man in a maroon overcoat; it was also bringing a taxi-cab; and it brought all three together at a point directly beneath my window; where the taxi stopped; and the girl and the young man stopped; and they got into the taxi; and then the cab glided off as if it were swept on by the current elsewhere.

The sight was ordinary enough; what was strange was the rhythmical order with which my imagination had invested it; and the fact that the ordinary sight of two people getting into a cab had the power to communicate something of their own seeming satisfaction. The sight of two people coming down the street and meeting at the corner seems to ease the mind of some strain, I thought, watching the taxi turn and make off. Perhaps to think, as I had been thinking these two days, of one sex as distinct from the other is an effort. It interferes with the unity of the mind. Now that effort had ceased and that unity had been restored by seeing two people come together and get into a taxi-cab. The mind is certainly a very mysterious organ, I reflected, drawing my head in from the window, about which nothing whatever is known, though we depend upon it so completely. Why do I feel that there are severances and oppositions in the mind, as there are strains from obvious causes on the body? What does one mean by "the unity of the mind," I pondered, for clearly the mind has so great a power of concentrating at any point at any moment that it seems to have no single state of being. It can separate itself from the people in the street, for example, and think of itself as apart from them, at an upper window looking down on them. Or it can think with other people spontaneously, as, for instance, in a crowd waiting to hear some piece of news read out. It can think back through its fathers or through its mothers, as I have said that a woman writing thinks back through her mothers. Again if one is a woman one is often surprised by a sudden splitting off of consciousness, say in walking down Whitehall,[9] when from being the natural inheritor of that civilisation, she becomes, on the contrary, outside of it, alien and critical. Clearly the mind is always altering its focus, and bringing the world into different perspectives. But some of these states of mind seem, even if adopted spontaneously, to be less comfortable than others. In order to keep oneself continuing in them one is unconsciously holding something back, and gradually the repression becomes an effort. But there may be some state of mind in which one could continue without effort because nothing is required to be held back. And this perhaps, I thought, coming in from the window, is one of them. For certainly when I saw the couple get into the taxi-cab the mind felt as if, after being divided, it had come together again in a natural fusion. The obvious reason would be that it is natural for the sexes to co-operate. One has a profound, if irrational, instinct in favour of the theory that the union of man and woman makes for the greatest satisfaction, the most complete happiness. But the sight of the two people getting into the taxi and the satisfaction it gave me made me also ask whether there are two sexes in the mind corresponding to the two sexes in the body, and whether they also require to be united in order to get complete satisfaction and happiness. And I went on amateurishly to sketch a plan of the soul so that in each of us two powers preside, one male, one female; and in the man's brain, the man predominates over the woman, and in the woman's brain, the woman predominates over the man. The normal and comfortable state of being is that when the two live in harmony together, spiritually cooperating. If one is a man, still the woman part of the brain must have effect; and a woman also must have intercourse with the man in her. Coleridge perhaps meant this when he said that a great mind is androgynous. It is when this fusion takes place that the mind is fully fertilised and uses all its faculties. Perhaps a mind that is purely masculine cannot create, any more than a mind that is purely feminine, I thought. But it would be well to test what one meant by man-womanly, and conversely by woman-manly, by pausing and looking at a book or two.

Coleridge certainly did not mean, when he said that a great mind is androgynous, that it is a mind that has any special sympathy with women; a mind that takes up their cause or devotes itself to their interpretation. Perhaps the androgynous mind is less apt to make these distinctions than the single-sexed mind. He meant, perhaps, that the androgynous mind is resonant and

9. London thoroughfare along which are located the chief offices of the British government.

porous; that it transmits emotion without impediment; that it is naturally creative, incandescent and undivided. In fact one goes back to Shakespeare's mind as the type of the androgynous, of the man-womanly mind, though it would be impossible to say what Shakespeare thought of women. And if it be true that it is one of the tokens of the fully developed mind that it does not think specially or separately of sex, how much harder it is to attain that condition now than ever before. Here I came to the books by living writers, and there paused and wondered if this fact were not at the root of something that had long puzzled me. No age can ever have been as stridently sex-conscious as our own; those innumerable books by men about women in the British Museum are a proof of it. The Suffrage campaign was no doubt to blame. It must have roused in men an extraordinary desire for self-assertion; it must have made them lay an emphasis upon their own sex and its characteristics which they would not have troubled to think about had they not been challenged. And when one is challenged, even by a few women in black bonnets, one retaliates, if one has never been challenged before, rather excessively. That perhaps accounts for some of the characteristics that I remember to have found here, I thought, taking down a new novel by Mr A, who is in the prime of life and very well thought of, apparently, by the reviewers. I opened it. Indeed, it was delightful to read a man's writing again. It was so direct, so straightforward after the writing of women. It indicated such freedom of mind, such liberty of person, such confidence in himself. One had a sense of physical well-being in the presence of this well-nourished, well-educated, free mind, which had never been thwarted or opposed, but had had full liberty from birth to stretch itself in whatever way it liked. All this was admirable. But after reading a chapter or two a shadow seemed to lie across the page. It was a straight dark bar, a shadow shaped something like the letter "I." One began dodging this way and that to catch a glimpse of the landscape behind it. Whether that was indeed a tree or a woman walking I was not quite sure. Back one was always hailed to the letter "I." One began to be tired of "I." Not but what this "I" was a most respectable "I"; honest and logical; as hard as a nut, and polished for centuries by good teaching and good feeding. I respect and admire that "I" from the bottom of my heart. But—here I turned a page or two, looking for something or other—the worst of it is that in the shadow of the letter "I" all is shapeless as mist. Is that a tree? No, it is a woman. But . . . she has not a bone in her body, I thought, watching Phoebe, for that was her name, coming across the beach. Then Alan got up and the shadow of Alan at once obliterated Phoebe. For Alan had views and Phoebe was quenched in the flood of his views. And then Alan, I thought, had passions; and here I turned page after page very fast, feeling that the crisis was approaching, and so it was. It took place on the beach under the sun. It was done very openly. It was done very vigorously. Nothing could have been more indecent. But . . . I had said "but" too often. One cannot go on saying "but." One must finish the sentence somehow, I rebuked myself. Shall I finish it, "But—I am bored!" But why was I bored? Partly because of the dominance of the letter "I" and the aridity, which, like the giant beech tree, it casts within its shade. Nothing will grow there. And partly for some more obscure reason. There seemed to be some obstacle, some impediment of Mr A's mind which blocked the fountain of creative energy and shored it within narrow limits. And remembering the lunch party at Oxbridge, and the cigarette ash and the Manx cat and Tennyson and Christina Rossetti all in a bunch, it seemed possible that the impediment lay there. As he no longer hums under his breath, "There has fallen a splendid tear from the passion-flower at the gate," when Phoebe crosses the beach, and she no longer replies, "My heart is like a singing bird whose nest is in a water'd shoot," when Alan approaches what can he do? Being honest as the day and logical as the sun, there is only one thing he can do. And that he does, to do him justice, over and over (I said, turning the pages) and over again. And that, I added, aware of the awful nature of the confession, seems somehow dull. Shakespeare's indecency uproots a thousand other things in one's mind, and is far from being dull. But Shakespeare does it for pleasure; Mr A, as the nurses say, does it on purpose. He does it in protest. He is protesting against the equality of the other sex by asserting his own superiority. He is therefore impeded and inhibited and self-conscious as Shakespeare might have been if he too had known Miss Clough and Miss Davies. Doubtless Elizabethan literature would have been very different from what it is if the woman's movement had begun in the sixteenth century and not in the nineteenth.

What, then, it amounts to, if this theory of the two sides of the mind holds good, is that virility has now become self-conscious—men, that is to say, are now writing only with the male side of their brains. It is a mistake for a woman to read them, for she will inevitably look for something that she will not find. It is the power of suggestion that one most misses, I thought, taking Mr B the critic in my hand and reading, very carefully and very dutifully, his remarks upon the art of poetry. Very able they were, acute and full of learning; but the trouble was, that his feelings no longer communicated; his mind seemed separated into different chambers; not a sound carried from one to the other. Thus, when one takes a sentence of Mr B into the mind it falls plump to the ground—dead; but when one takes a sentence of Coleridge into the mind, it explodes and gives birth to all kinds of other ideas, and that is the only sort of writing of which one can say that it has the secret of perpetual life.

But whatever the reason may be, it is a fact that one must deplore. For it means—here I had come to rows of books by Mr Galsworthy and Mr Kipling[1]—that some of the finest works of our greatest living writers fall upon deaf ears. Do what she will a woman cannot find in them that fountain of perpetual life which the critics assure her is there. It is not only that they celebrate male virtues, enforce male values and describe the world of men; it is that the emotion with which these books are permeated is to a woman incomprehensible. It is coming, it is gathering, it is about to burst on one's head, one begins saying long before the end. That picture will fall on old Jolyon's head; he will die of the shock; the old clerk will speak over him two or three obituary words; and all the swans on the Thames will simultaneously burst out singing. But one will rush away before that happens and hide in the gooseberry bushes, for the emotion which is so deep, so subtle, so symbolical to a man moves a woman to wonder. So with Mr Kipling's officers who turn their backs; and his Sowers who sow the Seed; and his Men who are alone with their Work; and the Flag—one blushes at all these capital

1. John Galsworthy (1867–1933) and Rudyard Kipling (1865–1936), English novelists.

letters as if one had been caught eavesdropping at some purely masculine orgy. The fact is that neither Mr Galsworthy nor Mr Kipling has a spark of the woman in him. Thus all their qualities seem to a woman, if one may generalise, crude and immature. They lack suggestive power. And when a book lacks suggestive power, however hard it hits the surface of the mind it cannot penetrate within.

And in that restless mood in which one takes books out and puts them back again without looking at them I began to envisage an age to come of pure, of self-assertive virility, such as the letters of professors (take Sir Walter Raleigh's letters, for instance) seem to forebode, and the rulers of Italy have already brought into being. For one can hardly fail to be impressed in Rome by the sense of unmitigated masculinity; and whatever the value of unmitigated masculinity upon the state, one may question the effect of it upon the art of poetry. At any rate, according to the newspapers, there is a certain anxiety about fiction in Italy. There has been a meeting of academicians whose object it is "to develop the Italian novel." "Men famous by birth, or in finance, industry or the Fascist corporations" came together the other day and discussed the matter, and a telegram was sent to the Duce[2] expressing the hope "that the Fascist era would soon give birth to a poet worthy of it." We may all join in that pious hope, but it is doubtful whether poetry can come out of an incubator. Poetry ought to have a mother as well as a father. The Fascist poem, one may fear, will be a horrid little abortion such as one sees in a glass jar in the museum of some county town. Such monsters never live long, it is said; one has never seen a prodigy of that sort cropping grass in a field. Two heads on one body do not make for length of life.

However, the blame for all this, if one is anxious to lay blame, rests no more upon one sex than upon the other. All seducers and reformers are responsible, Lady Bessborough when she lied to Lord Granville; Miss Davies when she told the truth to Mr Greg. All who have brought about a state of sex-consciousness are to blame, and it is they who drive me, when I want to stretch my faculties on a book, to seek it in that happy age, before Miss Davies and Miss Clough were born, when the writer used both sides of his mind equally. One must turn back to Shakespeare then, for Shakespeare was androgynous; and so was Keats and Sterne and Cowper and Lamb and Coleridge. Shelley perhaps was sexless. Milton and Ben Jonson had a dash too much of the male in them. So had Wordsworth and Tolstoi. In our time Proust was wholly androgynous, if not perhaps a little too much of a woman. But that failing is too rare for one to complain of it, since without some mixture of the kind the intellect seems to predominate and the other faculties of the mind harden and become barren. However, I consoled myself with the reflection that this is perhaps a passing phase; much of what I have said in obedience to my promise to give you the course of my thoughts will seem out of date; much of what flames in my eyes will seem dubious to you who have not yet come of age.

Even so, the very first sentence that I would write here, I said, crossing over to the writing-table and taking up the page headed Women and Fiction, is that it is fatal for any one who writes to think of their sex. It is fatal to be a man or woman pure and simple; one must be woman-manly or man-

---

2. "The leader," i.e., Mussolini.

womanly. It is fatal for a woman to lay the least stress on any grievance; to plead even with justice any cause; in any way to speak consciously as a woman. And fatal is no figure of speech; for anything written with that conscious bias is doomed to death. It ceases to be fertilised. Brilliant and effective, powerful and masterly, as it may appear for a day or two, it must wither at nightfall; it cannot grow in the minds of others. Some collaboration has to take place in the mind between the woman and the man before the act of creation can be accomplished. Some marriage of opposites has to be consummated. The whole of the mind must lie wide open if we are to get the sense that the writer is communicating his experience with perfect fullness. There must be freedom and there must be peace. Not a wheel must grate, not a light glimmer. The curtains must be close drawn. The writer, I thought, once his experience is over, must lie back and let his mind celebrate its nuptials in darkness. He must not look or question what is being done. Rather, he must pluck the petals from a rose or watch the swans float calmly down the river. And I saw again the current which took the boat and the undergraduate and the dead leaves; and the taxi took the man and the woman, I thought, seeing them come together across the street, and the current swept them away, I thought, hearing far off the roar of London's traffic, into that tremendous stream.

Here, then, Mary Beton ceases to speak. She has told you how she reached the conclusion—the prosaic conclusion—that it is necessary to have five hundred a year and a room with a lock on the door if you are to write fiction or poetry. She has tried to lay bare the thoughts and impressions that led her to think this. She has asked you to follow her flying into the arms of a Beadle, lunching here, dining there, drawing pictures in the British Museum, taking books from the shelf, looking out of the window. While she has been doing all these things, you no doubt have been observing her failings and foibles and deciding what effect they have had on her opinions. You have been contradicting her and making whatever additions and deductions seem good to you. That is all as it should be, for in a question like this truth is only to be had by laying together many varieties of error. And I will end now in my own person by anticipating two criticisms, so obvious that you can hardly fail to make them.

No opinion has been expressed, you may say, upon the comparative merits of the sexes even as writers. That was done purposely, because, even if the time had come for such a valuation—and it is far more important at the moment to know how much money women had and how many rooms than to theorise about their capacities—even if the time had come I do not believe that gifts, whether of mind or character, can be weighed like sugar and butter, not even in Cambridge, where they are so adept at putting people into classes and fixing caps on their heads and letters after their names. I do not believe that even the Table of Precedency which you will find in Whitaker's *Almanac* represents a final order of values, or that there is any sound reason to suppose that a Commander of the Bath will ultimately walk in to dinner behind a Master in Lunacy. All this pitting of sex against sex, of quality against quality; all this claiming of superiority and imputing of inferiority, belong to the private-school stage of human existence where there are "sides," and it is necessary for one side to beat another side, and of the utmost importance to walk up to a platform and receive from the hands of the Headmaster himself a highly ornamental pot. As people mature they cease to believe in sides or in Headmasters or in highly ornamental pots. At any rate, where books are concerned, it is notoriously difficult to fix labels of merit in such a way that they do not come off. Are not reviews of current literature a perpetual illustration of the difficulty of judgement? "This great book," "this worthless book," the same book is called by both names. Praise and blame alike mean nothing. No, delightful as the pastime of measuring may be, it is the most futile of all occupations, and to submit to the decrees of the measurers the most servile of attitudes. So long as you write what you wish to write, that is all that matters; and whether it matters for ages or only for hours, nobody can say. But to sacrifice a hair of the head of your vision, a shade of its colour, in deference to some Headmaster with a silver pot in his hand or to some professor with a measuring-rod up his sleeve, is the most abject treachery, and the sacrifice of wealth and chastity which used to be said to be the greatest of human disasters, a mere flea-bite in comparison.

Next I think that you may object that in all this I have made too much of the importance of material things. Even allowing a generous margin for symbolism, that five hundred a year stands for the power to contemplate, that a lock on the door means the power to think for oneself, still you may say that the mind should rise above such things; and that great poets have often been poor men. Let me then quote to you the words of your own Professor of Literature, who knows better than I do what goes to the making of a poet. Sir Arthur Quiller-Couch writes:[3]

"What are the great poetical names of the last hundred years or so? Coleridge, Wordsworth, Byron, Shelley, Landor, Keats, Tennyson, Browning, Arnold, Morris, Rossetti, Swinburne—we may stop there. Of these, all but Keats, Browning, Rossetti were University men; and of these three, Keats, who died young, cut off in his prime, was the only one not fairly well to do. It may seem a brutal thing to say, and it is a sad thing to say: but, as a matter of hard fact, the theory that poetical genius bloweth where it listeth, and equally in poor and rich, holds little truth. As a matter of hard fact, nine out of those twelve were University men: which means that somehow or other they procured the means to get the best education England can give. As a matter of hard fact, of the remaining three you know that Browning was well to do, and I challenge you that, if he had not been well to do, he would no more have attained to write Saul or The Ring and the Book than Ruskin would have attained to writing Modern Painters if his father had not dealt prosperously in business. Rossetti had a small private income; and, moreover, he painted. There remains but Keats; whom Atropos[4] slew young, as she slew John Clare in a mad-house, and James Thomson by the laudanum he took to drug disappointment. These are dreadful facts, but let us face them. It is—however dishonouring to us as a nation—certain that, by some fault in our commonwealth, the poor poet has not in these days, nor has had for two hundred years, a dog's chance. Believe me—and I have spent a great part of ten years in watching some three hundred and twenty elementary schools— we may prate of democracy, but actually, a poor child in England has little

---

3. The Art of Writing, by Sir Arthur Quiller-Couch [Woolf's note].

4. In Greek mythology, the Fate who cut the thread of life.

more hope than had the son of an Athenian slave to be emancipated into that intellectual freedom of which great writings are born."

Nobody could put the point more plainly. "The poor poet has not in these days, nor has had for two hundred years, a dog's chance . . . a poor child in England has little more hope than had the son of an Athenian slave to be emancipated into that intellectual freedom of which great writings are born." That is it. Intellectual freedom depends upon material things. Poetry depends upon intellectual freedom. And women have always been poor, not for two hundred years merely, but from the beginning of time. Women have had less intellectual freedom than the sons of Athenian slaves. Women, then, have not had a dog's chance of writing poetry. That is why I have laid so much stress on money and a room of one's own. However, thanks to the toils of those obscure women in the past, of whom I wish we knew more, thanks, curiously enough, to two wars, the Crimean which let Florence Nightingale out of her drawing-room, and the European War which opened the doors to the average woman some sixty years later, these evils are in the way to be bettered. Otherwise you would not be here tonight, and your chance of earning five hundred pounds a year, precarious as I am afraid that it still is, would be minute in the extreme.

Still, you may object, why do you attach so much importance to this writing of books by women when, according to you, it requires so much effort, leads perhaps to the murder of one's aunts, will make one almost certainly late for luncheon, and may bring one into very grave disputes with certain very good fellows? My motives, let me admit, are partly selfish. Like most uneducated Englishwomen, I like reading—I like reading books in the bulk. Lately my diet has become a trifle monotonous; history is too much about wars; biography too much about great men; poetry has shown, I think, a tendency to sterility, and fiction—but I have sufficiently exposed my disabilities as a critic of modern fiction and will say no more about it. Therefore I would ask you to write all kinds of books, hesitating at no subject however trivial or however vast. By hook or by crook, I hope that you will possess yourselves of money enough to travel and to idle, to contemplate the future or the past of the world, to dream over books and loiter at street corners and let the line of thought dip deep into the stream. For I am by no means confining you to fiction. If you would please me—and there are thousands like me—you would write books of travel and adventure, and research and scholarship, and history and biography, and criticism and philosophy and science. By so doing you will certainly profit the art of fiction. For books have a way of influencing each other. Fiction will be much the better for standing cheek by jowl with poetry and philosophy. Moreover, if you consider any great figure of the past, like Sappho, like the Lady Murasaki,[5] like Emily Brontë, you will find that she is an inheritor as well as an originator, and has come into existence because women have come to have the habit of writing naturally; so that even as a prelude to poetry such activity on your part would be invaluable.

But when I look back through these notes and criticise my own train of thought as I made them, I find that my motives were not altogether selfish.

5. Japanese writer, (978?–?1026) author of *The Tale of Genji*. Sappho (7th century B.C.E.), Greek lyric poet.

There runs through these comments and discursions the conviction—or is it the instinct?—that good books are desirable and that good writers, even if they show every variety of human depravity, are still good human beings. Thus when I ask you to write more books I am urging you to do what will be for your good and for the good of the world at large. How to justify this instinct or belief I do not know, for philosophic words, if one has not been educated at a university, are apt to play one false. What is meant by "reality"? It would seem to be something very erratic, very undependable—now to be found in a dusty road, now in a scrap of newspaper in the street, now in a daffodil in the sun. It lights up a group in a room and stamps some casual saying. It overwhelms one walking home beneath the stars and makes the silent world more real than the world of speech—and then there it is again in an omnibus in the uproar of Piccadilly. Sometimes, too, it seems to dwell in shapes too far away for us to discern what their nature is. But whatever it touches, it fixes and makes permanent. That is what remains over when the skin of the day has been cast into the hedge; that is what is left of past time and of our loves and hates. Now the writer, as I think, has the chance to live more than other people in the presence of this reality. It is his business to find it and collect it and communicate it to the rest of us. So at least I infer from reading *Lear* or *Emma* or *La Recherche du Temps Perdu*. For the reading of these books seems to perform a curious couching operation on the senses; one sees more intensely afterwards; the world seems bared of its covering and given an intenser life. Those are the enviable people who live at enmity with unreality; and those are the pitiable who are knocked on the head by the thing done without knowing or caring. So that when I ask you to earn money and have a room of your own, I am asking you to live in the presence of reality, an invigorating life, it would appear, whether one can impart it or not.

Here I would stop, but the pressure of convention decrees that every speech must end with a peroration. And a peroration addressed to women should have something, you will agree, particularly exalting and ennobling about it. I should implore you to remember your responsibilities, to be higher, more spiritual; I should remind you how much depends upon you, and what an influence you can exert upon the future. But those exhortations can safely, I think, be left to the other sex, who will put them, and indeed have put them, with far greater eloquence than I can compass. When I rummage in my own mind I find no noble sentiments about being companions and equals and influencing the world to higher ends. I find myself saying briefly and prosaically that it is much more important to be oneself than anything else. Do not dream of influencing other people, I would say, if I knew how to make it sound exalted. Think of things in themselves.

And again I am reminded by dipping into newspapers and novels and biographies that when a woman speaks to women she should have something very unpleasant up her sleeve. Women are hard on women. Women dislike women. Women—but are you not sick to death of the word? I can assure you that I am. Let us agree, then, that a paper read by a woman to women should end with something particularly disagreeable.

But how does it go? What can I think of? The truth is, I often like women. I like their unconventionality. I like their subtlety. I like their anonymity. I like—but I must not run on in this way. That cupboard there,—you say it holds clean table-napkins only; but what if Sir Archibald Bodkin were concealed among them? Let me then adopt a sterner tone. Have I, in the preceding words, conveyed to you sufficiently the warnings and reprobation of mankind? I have told you the very low opinion in which you were held by Mr Oscar Browning. I have indicated what Napoleon once thought of you and what Mussolini thinks now. Then, in case any of you aspire to fiction, I have copied out for your benefit the advice of the critic about courageously acknowledging the limitations of your sex. I have referred to Professor X and given prominence to his statement that women are intellectually, morally and physically inferior to men. I have handed on all that has come my way without going in search of it, and here is a final warning—from Mr John Langdon Davies.[6] Mr John Langdon Davies warns women "that when children cease to be altogether desirable, women cease to be altogether necessary." I hope you will make a note of it.

How can I further encourage you to go about the business of life? Young women, I would say, and please attend, for the peroration is beginning, you are, in my opinion, disgracefully ignorant. You have never made a discovery of any sort of importance. You have never shaken an empire or led an army into battle. The plays of Shakespeare are not by you, and you have never introduced a barbarous race to the blessings of civilisation. What is your excuse? It is all very well for you to say, pointing to the streets and squares and forests of the globe swarming with black and white and coffee-coloured inhabitants, all busily engaged in traffic and enterprise and love-making, we have had other work on our hands. Without our doing, those seas would be unsailed and those fertile lands a desert. We have borne and bred and washed and taught, perhaps to the age of six or seven years, the one thousand six hundred and twenty-three million human beings who are, according to statistics, at present in existence, and that, allowing that some had help, takes time.

There is truth in what you say—I will not deny it. But at the same time may I remind you that there have been at least two colleges for women in existence in England since the year 1866; that after the year 1880 a married woman was allowed by law to possess her own property; and that in 1919—which is a whole nine years ago—she was given a vote? May I also remind you that the most of the professions have been open to you for close on ten years now? When you reflect upon these immense privileges and the length of time during which they have been enjoyed, and the fact that there must be at this moment some two thousand women capable of earning over five hundred a year in one way or another, you will agree that the excuse of lack of opportunity, training, encouragement, leisure and money no longer holds good. Moreover, the economists are telling us that Mrs Seton has had too many children. You must, of course, go on bearing children, but, so they say, in twos and threes, not in tens and twelves.

Thus, with some time on your hands and with some book learning in your brains—you have had enough of the other kind, and are sent to college partly, I suspect, to be uneducated—surely you should embark upon another stage of your very long, very laborious and highly obscure career. A thousand pens are ready to suggest what you should do and what effect you will have. My

---

6. *A Short History of Women*, by John Langdon Davies [Woolf's note].

own suggestion is a little fantastic, I admit; I prefer, therefore, to put it in the form of fiction.

I told you in the course of this paper that Shakespeare had a sister; but do not look for her in Sir Sidney Lee's[7] life of the poet. She died young— alas, she never wrote a word. She lies buried where the omnibuses now stop, opposite the Elephant and Castle. Now my belief is that this poet who never wrote a word and was buried at the crossroads still lives. She lives in you and in me, and in many other women who are not here tonight, for they are washing up the dishes and putting the children to bed. But she lives; for great poets do not die; they are continuing presences; they need only the opportunity to walk among us in the flesh. This opportunity, as I think, it is now coming within your power to give her. For my belief is that if we live another century or so—I am talking of the common life which is the real life and not of the little separate lives which we live as individuals—and have five hundred a year each of us and rooms of our own; if we have the habit of freedom and the courage to write exactly what we think; if we escape a little from the common sitting-room and see human beings not always in their relation to each other but in relation to reality; and the sky, too, and the trees or whatever it may be in themselves; if we look past Milton's bogey,[8] for no human being should shut out the view; if we face the fact, for it is a fact, that there is no arm to cling to, but that we go alone and that our relation is to the world of reality and not only to the world of men and women, then the opportunity will come and the dead poet who was Shakespeare's sister will put on the body which she has so often laid down. Drawing her life from the lives of the unknown who were her forerunners, as her brother did before her, she will be born. As for her coming without that preparation, without that effort on our part, without that determination that when she is born again she shall find it possible to live and write her poetry, that we cannot expect, for that would be impossible. But I maintain that she would come if we worked for her, and that so to work, even in poverty and obscurity, is worth while.

1929

Professions for Women[1]

When your secretary invited me to come here, she told me that your Society is concerned with the employment of women and she suggested that I might tell you something about my own professional experiences. It is true I am a woman; it is true I am employed; but what professional experiences have I had? It is difficult to say. My profession is literature; and in that profession there are fewer experiences for women than in any other, with the exception of the stage—fewer, I mean, that are peculiar to women. For

7. Biographer and Shakespeare scholar (1859– 1926), author of *Life of William Shakespeare* (1898).
8. Milton, with his unhappy first marriage, his campaign for freedom of divorce, and his deliberate subordination of Eve to Adam in *Paradise Lost*,

was and often still is held to be (not altogether accurately) an example of what the present age calls a male chauvinist.
1. A paper read to the Women's Service League [Woolf's note].

the road was cut many years ago—by Fanny Burney, by Aphra Behn, by Harriet Martineau,[2] by Jane Austen, by George Eliot—many famous women, and many more unknown and forgotten, have been before me, making the path smooth, and regulating my steps. Thus, when I came to write, there were very few material obstacles in my way. Writing was a reputable and harmless occupation. The family peace was not broken by the scratching of a pen. No demand was made upon the family purse. For ten and sixpence one can buy paper enough to write all the plays of Shakespeare—if one has a mind that way. Pianos and models, Paris, Vienna, and Berlin, masters and mistresses, are not needed by a writer. The cheapness of writing paper is, of course, the reason why women have succeeded as writers before they have succeeded in the other professions.

But to tell you my story—it is a simple one. You have only got to figure to yourselves a girl in a bedroom with a pen in her hand. She had only to move that pen from left to right—from ten o'clock to one. Then it occurred to her to do what is simple and cheap enough after all—to slip a few of those pages into an envelope, fix a penny stamp in the corner, and drop the envelope into the red box at the corner. It was thus that I became a journalist; and my effort was rewarded on the first day of the following month—a very glorious day it was for me—by a letter from an editor containing a cheque for one pound ten shillings and sixpence. But to show you how little I deserve to be called a professional woman, how little I know of the struggles and difficulties of such lives, I have to admit that instead of spending that sum upon bread and butter, rent, shoes and stockings, or butcher's bills, I went out and bought a cat—a beautiful cat, a Persian cat, which very soon involved me in bitter disputes with my neighbours.

What could be easier than to write articles and to buy Persian cats with the profits? But wait a moment. Articles have to be about something. Mine, I seem to remember, was about a novel by a famous man. And while I was writing this review, I discovered that if I were going to review books I should need to do battle with a certain phantom. And the phantom was a woman, and when I came to know her better I called her after the heroine of a famous poem, The Angel in the House.[3] It was she who used to come between me and my paper when I was writing reviews. It was she who bothered and wasted my time and so tormented me that at last I killed her. You who come of a younger and happier generation may not have heard of her—you may not know what I mean by The Angel in the House. I will describe her as shortly as I can. She was intensely sympathetic. She was immensely charming. She was utterly unselfish. She excelled in the difficult arts of family life. She sacrificed herself daily. If there was chicken, she took the leg; if there was a draught she sat in it—in short she was so constituted that she never had a mind or a wish of her own, but preferred to sympathise always with the minds and wishes of others. Above all—I need not say it—she was pure. Her purity was supposed to be her chief beauty—her blushes, her great grace. In those days—the last of Queen Victoria—every house had its Angel. And when I came to write I encountered her with the very first words. The shadow of her wings fell on my page; I heard the rustling of her skirts in the

2. Economist, moralist, journalist, and novelist (1802–1876). Burney (1752–1840), author of *Evelina* and other novels. Behn (1640–1689), writer of romances and plays.
3. By Coventry Patmore (1823–1896), published 1854–62.

room. Directly, that is to say, I took my pen in my hand to review that novel by a famous man, she slipped behind me and whispered: 'My dear, you are a young woman. You are writing about a book that has been written by a man. Be sympathetic; be tender; flatter; deceive; use all the arts and wiles of our sex. Never let anybody guess that you have a mind of your own. Above all, be pure.' And she made as if to guide my pen. I now record the one act for which I take some credit to myself, though the credit rightly belongs to some excellent ancestors of mine who left me a certain sum of money—shall we say five hundred pounds a year?—so that it was not necessary for me to depend solely on charm for my living. I turned upon her and caught her by the throat. I did my best to kill her. My excuse, if I were to be had up in a court of law, would be that I acted in self-defence. Had I not killed her she would have killed me. She would have plucked the heart out of my writing. For, as I found, directly I put pen to paper, you cannot review even a novel without having a mind of your own, without expressing what you think to be the truth about human relations, morality, sex. And all these questions, according to the Angel of the House, cannot be dealt with freely and openly by women; they must charm, they must conciliate, they must—to put it bluntly—tell lies if they are to succeed. Thus, whenever I felt the shadow of her wing or the radiance of her halo upon my page, I took up the inkpot and flung it at her. She died hard. Her fictitious nature was of great assistance to her. It is far harder to kill a phantom than a reality. She was always creeping back when I thought I had despatched her. Though I flatter myself that I killed her in the end, the struggle was severe; it took much time that had better have been spent upon learning Greek grammar; or in roaming the world in search of adventures. But it was a real experience; it was an experience that was bound to befall all women writers at that time. Killing the Angel in the House was part of the occupation of a woman writer.

But to continue my story. The Angel was dead; what then remained? You may say that what remained was a simple and common object—a young woman in a bedroom with an inkpot. In other words, now that she had rid herself of falsehood, that young woman had only to be herself. Ah, but what is 'herself'? I mean, what is a woman? I assure you, I do not know. I do not believe that you know. I do not believe that anybody can know until she has expressed herself in all the arts and professions open to human skill. That indeed is one of the reasons why I have come here—out of respect for you, who are in process of showing us by your experiments what a woman is, who are in process of providing us, by your failures and successes, with that extremely important piece of information.

But to continue the story of my professional experiences. I made one pound ten and six by my first review; and I bought a Persian cat with the proceeds. Then I grew ambitious. A Persian cat is all very well, I said; but a Persian cat is not enough. I must have a motor-car. And it was thus that I became a novelist—for it is a very strange thing that people will give you a motor-car if you will tell them a story. It is a still stranger thing that there is nothing so delightful in the world as telling stories. It is far pleasanter than writing reviews of famous novels. And yet, if I am to obey your secretary and tell you my professional experiences as a novelist, I must tell you about a very strange experience that befell me as a novelist. And to understand it you must try first to imagine a novelist's state of mind. I hope I am not giving away professional secrets if I say that a novelist's chief desire is to be as unconscious as possible. He has to induce in himself a state of perpetual lethargy. He wants life to proceed with the utmost quiet and regularity. He wants to see the same faces, to read the same books, to do the same things day after day, month after month, while he is writing, so that nothing may break the illusion in which he is living—so that nothing may disturb or disquiet the mysterious nosings about, feelings round, darts, dashes, and sudden discoveries of that very shy and illusive spirit, the imagination. I suspect that this state is the same both for men and women. Be that as it may, I want you to imagine me writing a novel in a state of trance. I want you to figure to yourselves a girl sitting with a pen in her hand, which for minutes, and indeed for hours, she never dips into the inkpot. The image that comes to my mind when I think of this girl is the image of a fisherman lying sunk in dreams on the verge of a deep lake with a rod held out over the water. She was letting her imagination sweep unchecked round every rock and cranny of the world that lies submerged in the depths of our unconscious being. Now came the experience that I believe to be far commoner with women writers than with men. The line raced through the girl's fingers. Her imagination had rushed away. It had sought the pools, the depths, the dark places where the largest fish slumber. And then there was a smash. There was an explosion. There was foam and confusion. The imagination had dashed itself against something hard. The girl was roused from her dream. She was indeed in a state of the most acute and difficult distress. To speak without figure, she had thought of something, something about the body, about the passions which it was unfitting for her as a woman to say. Men, her reason told her, would be shocked. The consciousness of what men will say of a woman who speaks the truth about her passions had roused her from her artist's state of unconsciousness. She could write no more. The trance was over. Her imagination could work no longer. This I believe to be a very common experience with women writers—they are impeded by the extreme conventionality of the other sex. For though men sensibly allow themselves great freedom in these respects, I doubt that they realize or can control the extreme severity with which they condemn such freedom in women.

These then were two very genuine experiences of my own. These were two of the adventures of my professional life. The first—killing the Angel in the House—I think I solved. She died. But the second, telling the truth about my own experiences as a body, I do not think I solved. I doubt that any woman has solved it yet. The obstacles against her are still immensely powerful—and yet they are very difficult to define. Outwardly, what is simpler than to write books? Outwardly, what obstacles are there for a woman rather than for a man? Inwardly, I think, the case is very different; she has still many ghosts to fight, many prejudices to overcome. Indeed it will be a long time still, I think, before a woman can sit down to write a book without finding a phantom to be slain, a rock to be dashed against. And if this is so in literature, the freest of all professions for women, how is it in the new professions which you are now for the first time entering?

Those are the questions that I should like, had I time, to ask you. And indeed, if I have laid stress upon these professional experiences of mine, it is because I believe that they are, though in different forms, yours also. Even when the path is nominally open—when there is nothing to prevent a woman from being a doctor, a lawyer, a civil servant—there are many phantoms and obstacles, as I believe, looming in her way. To discuss and define them is I think of great value and importance; for thus only can the labour be shared, the difficulties be solved. But besides this, it is necessary also to discuss the ends and the aims for which we are fighting, for which we are doing battle with these formidable obstacles. Those aims cannot be taken for granted; they must be perpetually questioned and examined. The whole position, as I see it—here in this hall surrounded by women practising for the first time in history I know not how many different professions—is one of extraordinary interest and importance. You have won rooms of your own in the house hitherto exclusively owned by men. You are able, though not without great labour and effort, to pay the rent. You are earning your five hundred pounds a year. But this freedom is only a beginning; the room is your own, but it is still bare. It has to be furnished; it has to be decorated; it has to be shared. How are you going to furnish it, how are you going to decorate it? With whom are you going to share it, and upon what terms? These, I think are questions of the utmost importance and interest. For the first time in history you are able to ask them; for the first time you are able to decide for yourselves what the answers should be. Willingly would I stay and discuss those questions and answers—but not tonight. My time is up; and I must cease.

1942

From A Sketch of the Past[1]

[MOMENTS OF BEING AND NON-BEING]

—I begin: the first memory.

This was of red and purple flowers on a black ground—my mother's dress; and she was sitting either in a train or in an omnibus, and I was on her lap. I therefore saw the flowers she was wearing very close; and can still see purple and red and blue, I think, against the black; they must have been anemones, I suppose. Perhaps we were going to St Ives; more probably, for from the light it must have been evening, we were coming back to London. But it is more convenient artistically to suppose that we were going to St Ives, for that will lead to my other memory, which also seems to be my first memory, and in fact it is the most important of all my memories. If life has a base that it stands upon, if it is a bowl that one fills and fills and fills— then my bowl without a doubt stands upon this memory. It is of lying half asleep, half awake, in bed in the nursery at St Ives. It is of hearing the waves breaking, one, two, one, two, and sending a splash of water over the beach; and then breaking, one, two, one, two, behind a yellow blind. It is of hearing the blind draw its little acorn[2] across the floor as the wind blew the blind out. It is of lying and hearing this splash and seeing this light, and feeling,

1. The autobiographical essay from which this extract is taken was published in *Moments of Being*, ed. Jeanne Schulkind (1976). Woolf began it on April 18, 1939, as a relief from the labor of writing *Roger Fry: A Biography* (1940). The last date entered in the manuscript is November 17, 1940, some four months before her death. Under

the shadow of approaching war, she gropes back for the bright memories of childhood, especially those associated with the Stephens' summer home, Talland House, at St. Ives in Cornwall, the setting for her novel *To the Lighthouse*.
2. I.e., the acorn-shaped button on the end of the blind cord.

it is almost impossible that I should be here; of feeling the purest ecstasy I can conceive.

I could spend hours trying to write that as it should be written, in order to give the feeling which is even at this moment very strong in me. But I should fail (unless I had some wonderful luck); I dare say I should only succeed in having the luck if I had begun by describing Virginia herself.

Here I come to one of the memoir writer's difficulties—one of the reasons why, though I read so many, so many are failures. They leave out the person to whom things happened. The reason is that it is so difficult to describe any human being. So they say: "This is what happened"; but they do not say what the person was like to whom it happened. And the events mean very little unless we know first to whom they happened. Who was I then? Adeline Virginia Stephen, the second daughter of Leslie and Julia Prinsep Stephen, born on 25th January 1882, descended from a great many people, some famous, others obscure; born into a large connection, born not of rich parents, but of well-to-do parents, born into a very communicative, literate, letter writing, visiting, articulate, late nineteenth century world; so that I could if I liked to take the trouble, write a great deal here not only about my mother and father but about uncles and aunts, cousins and friends. But I do not know how much of this, or what part of this, made me feel what I felt in the nursery at St Ives. I do not know how far I differ from other people. That is another memoir writer's difficulty. Yet to describe oneself truly one must have some standard of comparison; was I clever, stupid, good looking, ugly, passionate, cold—? Owing partly to the fact that I was never at school, never competed in any way with children of my own age, I have never been able to compare my gifts and defects with other people's. But of course there was one external reason for the intensity of this first impression: the impression of the waves and the acorn on the blind; the feeling, as I describe it sometimes to myself, of lying in a grape and seeing through a film of semi-transparent yellow—it was due partly to the many months we spent in London. The change of nursery was a great change. And there was the long train journey; and the excitement. I remember the dark; the lights; the stir of the going up to bed.

But to fix my mind upon the nursery—it had a balcony; there was a partition, but it joined the balcony of my father's and mother's bedroom. My mother would come out onto her balcony in a white dressing gown. There were passion flowers growing on the wall; they were great starry blossoms, with purple streaks, and large green buds, part empty, part full.

If I were a painter I should paint these first impressions in pale yellow, silver, and green. There was the pale yellow blind; the green sea; and the silver of the passion flowers. I should make a picture that was globular; semi-transparent. I should make a picture of curved petals; of shells; of things that were semi-transparent; I should make curved shapes, showing the light through, but not giving a clear outline. Everything would be large and dim; and what was seen would at the same time be heard; sounds would come through this petal or leaf—sounds indistinguishable from sights. Sound and sight seem to make equal parts of these first impressions. When I think of the early morning in bed I also hear the caw of rooks[3] falling from a great

---

3. Black crows.

height. The sound seems to fall through an elastic, gummy air; which holds it up; which prevents it from being sharp and distinct. The quality of the air above Talland House seemed to suspend sound, to let it sink down slowly, as if it were caught in a blue gummy veil. The rooks cawing is part of the waves breaking—one, two, one, two—and the splash as the wave drew back and then it gathered again, and I lay there half awake, half asleep, drawing in such ecstasy as I cannot describe.

The next memory—all these colour-and-sound memories hang together at St Ives—was much more robust; it was highly sensual. It was later. It still makes me feel warm; as if everything were ripe; humming; sunny; smelling so many smells at once; and all making a whole that even now makes me stop—as I stopped then going down to the beach; I stopped at the top to look down at the gardens. They were sunk beneath the road. The apples were on a level with one's head. The gardens gave off a murmur of bees; the apples were red and gold; there were also pink flowers; and grey and silver leaves. The buzz, the croon, the smell, all seemed to press voluptuously against some membrane; not to burst it; but to hum round one such a complete rapture of pleasure that I stopped, smelt; looked. But again I cannot describe that rapture. It was rapture rather than ecstasy.

The strength of these pictures—but sight was always then so much mixed with sound that picture is not the right word—the strength anyhow of these impressions makes me again digress. Those moments—in the nursery, on the road to the beach—can still be more real than the present moment. This I have just tested. For I got up and crossed the garden. Percy was digging the asparagus bed; Louie was shaking a mat in front of the bedroom door.[4] But I was seeing them through the sight I saw here—the nursery and the road to the beach. At times I can go back to St Ives more completely than I can this morning. I can reach a state where I seem to be watching things happen as if I were there. That is, I suppose, that my memory supplies what I had forgotten, so that it seems as if it were happening independently, though I am really making it happen. In certain favourable moods, memories—what one has forgotten—come to the top. Now if this is so, is it not possible—I often wonder—that things we have felt with great intensity have an existence independent of our minds; are in fact still in existence? And if so, will it not be possible, in time, that some device will be invented by which we can tap them? I see it—the past—as an avenue lying behind; a long ribbon of scenes, emotions. There at the end of the avenue still, are the garden and the nursery. Instead of remembering here a scene and there a sound, I shall fit a plug into the wall;[5] and listen in to the past. I shall turn up August 1890. I feel that strong emotion must leave its trace; and it is only a question of discovering how we can get ourselves again attached to it, so that we shall be able to live our lives through from the start.

But the peculiarity of these two strong memories is that each was very simple. I am hardly aware of myself, but only of the sensation. I am only the container of the feeling of ecstasy, of the feeling of rapture. Perhaps this is characteristic of all childhood memories; perhaps it accounts for their strength. Later we add to feelings much that makes them more complex; and

---

4. The gardener and "daily help," respectively, at Monks House, the Woolfs' country home in Rod-   mell, Sussex.
5. I.e., as if plugging in a radio.

therefore less strong; or if not less strong, less isolated, less complete. But instead of analysing this, here is an instance of what I mean—my feeling about the looking-glass in the hall.

There was a small looking-glass in the hall at Talland House. It had, I remember, a ledge with a brush on it. By standing on tiptoe I could see my face in the glass. When I was six or seven perhaps, I got into the habit of looking at my face in the glass. But I only did this if I was sure that I was alone. I was ashamed of it. A strong feeling of guilt seemed naturally attached to it. But why was this so? One obvious reason occurs to me—Vanessa and I were both what was called tomboys; that is, we played cricket, scrambled over rocks, climbed trees, were said not to care for clothes and so on. Perhaps therefore to have been found looking in the glass would have been against our tomboy code. But I think that my feeling of shame went a great deal deeper. I am almost inclined to drag in my grandfather—Sir James, who once smoked a cigar, liked it, and so threw away his cigar and never smoked another. I am almost inclined to think that I inherited a streak of the puritan, of the Clapham Sect.[6] At any rate, the looking-glass shame has lasted all my life, long after the tomboy phase was over. I cannot now powder my nose in public. Everything to do with dress—to be fitted, to come into a room wearing a new dress—still frightens me; at least makes me shy, self-conscious, uncomfortable. "Oh to be able to run, like Julian Morrell,[7] all over the garden in a new dress", I thought not many years ago at Garsington; when Julian undid a parcel and put on a new dress and scampered round and round like a hare. Yet femininity was very strong in our family. We were famous for our beauty—my mother's beauty, Stella's beauty, gave me as early as I can remember, pride and pleasure. What then gave me this feeling of shame, unless it were that I inherited some opposite instinct? My father was spartan, ascetic, puritanical. He had I think no feeling for pictures; no ear for music; no sense of the sound of words. This leads me to think that my—I would say 'our' if I knew enough about Vanessa, Thoby and Adrian[8]—but how little we know even about brothers and sisters—this leads me to think that my natural love for beauty was checked by some ancestral dread. Yet this did not prevent me from feeling ecstasies and raptures spontaneously and intensely and without any shame or the least sense of guilt, so long as they were disconnected with my own body. I thus detect another element in the shame which I had in being caught looking at myself in the glass in the hall. I must have been ashamed or afraid of my own body. Another memory, also of the hall, may help to explain this. There was a slab outside the dining room door for standing dishes upon. Once when I was very small Gerald Duckworth lifted me onto this, and as I sat there he began to explore my body.[9] I can remember the feel of his hand going under my clothes; going firmly and steadily lower and lower. I remember how I hoped that he would stop; how I stiffened and wriggled as his hand approached my private parts. But it did not stop. His

6. In marrying Jane Catherine Venn, Woolf's grandfather, James Stephen, had allied himself with the heart of the so-called Clapham sect. John and Henry Venn, respectively rector and curate of Clapham in south London, were prominent members of this evangelical society that, in the early 19th century, was instrumental in bringing about the abolition of the slave trade.

7. Daughter of Philip Morrell, Member of Parliament, and his wife, Ottoline, the celebrated literary hostess. Garsington Manor was their house in Oxfordshire.

8. Woolf's brothers and sister.

9. Woolf's half-brother and the subject of her autobiographical essay 22 Hyde Park Gate, written in 1920 and published in Moments of Being (1978).

hand explored my private parts too. I remember resenting, disliking it—what is the word for so dumb and mixed a feeling? It must have been strong, since I still recall it. This seems to show that a feeling about certain parts of the body; how they must not be touched; how it is wrong to allow them to be touched; must be instinctive. It proves that Virginia Stephen was not born on the 25th January 1882, but was born many thousands of years ago; and had from the very first to encounter instincts already acquired by thousands of ancestresses in the past.

And this throws light not merely on my own case, but upon the problem that I touched on the first page; why it is so difficult to give any account of the person to whom things happen. The person is evidently immensely complicated. Witness the incident of the looking-glass. Though I have done my best to explain why I was ashamed of looking at my own face I have only been able to discover some possible reasons; there may be others; I do not suppose that I have got at the truth; yet this is a simple incident; and it happened to me personally; and I have no motive for lying about it. In spite of all this, people write what they call "lives" of other people; that is, they collect a number of events, and leave the person to whom it happened unknown. Let me add a dream; for it may refer to the incident of the looking-glass. I dreamt that I was looking in a glass when a horrible face—the face of an animal—suddenly showed over my shoulder. I cannot be sure if this was a dream, or if it happened. Was I looking in the glass one day when something in the background moved, and seemed to me alive? I cannot be sure. But I have always remembered the other face in the glass, whether it was a dream or a fact, and that it frightened me.

These then are some of my first memories. But of course as an account of my life they are misleading, because the things one does not remember are as important; perhaps they are more important. If I could remember one whole day I should be able to describe, superficially at least, what life was like as a child. Unfortunately, one only remembers what is exceptional. And there seems to be no reason why one thing is exceptional and another not. Why have I forgotten so many things that must have been, one would have thought, more memorable than what I do remember? Why remember the hum of bees in the garden going down to the beach, and forget completely being thrown naked by father into the sea? (Mrs Swanwick says she saw that happen.)[1]

This leads to a digression, which perhaps may explain a little of my own psychology; even of other people's. Often when I have been writing one of my so-called novels I have been baffled by this same problem; that is, how to describe what I call in my private shorthand—"non-being." Every day includes much more non-being than being. Yesterday for example, Tuesday the 18th of April, was [as] it happened a good day; above the average in "being." It was fine; I enjoyed writing these first pages; my head was relieved of the pressure of writing about Roger; I walked over Mount Misery[2] and along the river; and save that the tide was out, the country, which I notice very closely always, was coloured and shaded as I like—there were the wil-

---

1. In Mrs. Swanwick's autobiography, *I Have Been Young* (1935), she recalls having known Leslie Stephen at St. Ives: "We watched with delight his naked babies running about the beach or being towed into the sea between his legs, and their beautiful mother."
2. Two cottages on the hillside between Southease and Piddinghoe known locally as Mount Misery.

lows, I remember, all plumy and soft green and purple against the blue. I also read Chaucer with pleasure; and began a book—the memoirs of Madame de la Fayette—which interested me. These separate moments of being were however embedded in many more moments of non-being. I have already forgotten what Leonard and I talked about at lunch; and at tea; although it was a good day the goodness was embedded in a kind of non-descript cotton wool. This is always so. A great part of every day is not lived consciously. One walks, eats, sees things, deals with what has to be done; the broken vacuum cleaner; ordering dinner; writing orders to Mabel;[3] washing; cooking dinner; bookbinding. When it is a bad day the proportion of non-being is much larger. I had a slight temperature last week; almost the whole day was non-being. The real novelist can somehow convey both sorts of being. I think Jane Austen can; and Trollope; perhaps Thackeray and Dickens and Tolstoy. I have never been able to do both. I tried—in *Night and Day;* and in *The Years.*[4] But I will leave the literary side alone for the moment.

As a child then, my days, just as they do now, contained a large proportion of this cotton wool, this non-being. Week after week passed at St Ives and nothing made any dint upon me. Then, for no reason that I know about, there was a sudden violent shock; something happened so violently that I have remembered it all my life. I will give a few instances. The first: I was fighting with Thoby on the lawn. We were pommelling each other with our fists. Just as I raised my fist to hit him, I felt: why hurt another person? I dropped my hand instantly, and stood there, and let him beat me. I remember the feeling. It was a feeling of hopeless sadness. It was as if I became aware of something terrible; and of my own powerlessness. I slunk off alone, feeling horribly depressed. The second instance was also in the garden at St Ives. I was looking at the flower bed by the front door; "That is the whole," I said. I was looking at a plant with a spread of leaves; and it seemed suddenly plain that the flower itself was a part of the earth; that a ring enclosed what was the flower; and that was the real flower; part earth; part flower. It was a thought I put away as being likely to be very useful to me later. The third case was also at St Ives. Some people called Valpy had been staying at St Ives, and had left. We were waiting at dinner one night, when somehow I overheard my father or my mother say that Mr Valpy had killed himself. The next thing I remember is being in the garden at night and walking on the path by the apple tree. It seemed to me that the apple tree was connected with the horror of Mr Valpy's suicide. I could not pass it. I stood there looking at the grey-green creases of the bark—it was a moonlit night—in a trance of horror. I seemed to be dragged down, hopelessly, into some pit of absolute despair from which I could not escape. My body seemed paralysed.

These are three instances of exceptional moments. I often tell them over, or rather they come to the surface unexpectedly. But now that for the first time I have written them down, I realise something that I have never realised before. Two of these moments ended in a state of despair. The other ended, on the contrary, in a state of satisfaction. When I said about the flower "That is the whole," I felt that I had made a discovery. I felt that I had put away in my mind something that I should go back [to], to turn over and explore. It

---

3. Instructions to the Woolfs' maid.   4. Novels published in 1919 and 1938, respectively.

strikes me now that this was a profound difference. It was the difference in the first place between despair and satisfaction. This difference I think arose from the fact that I was quite unable to deal with the pain of discovering that people hurt each other; that a man I had seen had killed himself. The sense of horror held me powerless. But in the case of the flower I found a reason; and was thus able to deal with the sensation. I was not powerless. I was conscious—if only at a distance—that I should in time explain it. I do not know if I was older when I saw the flower than I was when I had the other two experiences. I only know that many of these exceptional moments brought with them a peculiar horror and a physical collapse; they seemed dominant; myself passive. This suggests that as one gets older one has a greater power through reason to provide an explanation; and that this explanation blunts the sledge-hammer force of the blow. I think this is true, because though I still have the peculiarity that I receive these sudden shocks, they are now always welcome; after the first surprise, I always feel instantly that they are particularly valuable. And so I go on to suppose that the shock-receiving capacity is what makes me a writer. I hazard the explanation that a shock is at once in my case followed by the desire to explain it. I feel that I have had a blow; but it is not, as I thought as a child, simply a blow from an enemy hidden behind the cotton wool of daily life; it is or will become a revelation of some order; it is a token of some real thing behind appearances; and I make it real by putting it into words. It is only by putting it into words that I make it whole; this wholeness means that it has lost its power to hurt me; it gives me, perhaps because by doing so I take away the pain, a great delight to put the severed parts together. Perhaps this is the strongest pleasure known to me. It is the rapture I get when in writing I seem to be discovering what belongs to what; making a scene come right; making a character come together. From this I reach what I might call a philosophy; at any rate it is a constant idea of mine; that behind the cotton wool is hidden a pattern; that we—I mean all human beings—are connected with this; that the whole world is a work of art; that we are parts of the work of art. *Hamlet* or a Beethoven quartet is the truth about this vast mass that we call the world. But there is no Shakespeare, there is no Beethoven; certainly and emphatically there is no God; we are the words; we are the music; we are the thing itself. And I see this when I have a shock.

This intuition of mine—it is so instinctive that it seems given to me, not made by me—has certainly given its scale to my life ever since I saw the flower in the bed by the front door at St Ives. If I were painting myself I should have to find some—rod, shall I say—something that would stand for the conception. It proves that one's life is not confined to one's body and what one says and does; one is living all the time in relation to certain background rods or conceptions. Mine is that there is a pattern hid behind the cotton wool. And this conception affects me every day. I prove this, now, by spending the morning writing, when I might be walking, running a shop, or learning to do something that will be useful if war comes. I feel that by writing I am doing what is far more necessary than anything else.

All artists I suppose feel something like this. It is one of the obscure elements in life that has never been much discussed. It is left out in almost all biographies and autobiographies, even of artists. Why did Dickens spend his entire life writing stories? What was his conception? I bring in Dickens partly because I am reading *Nicholas Nickleby* at the moment; also partly because it struck me, on my walk yesterday, that these moments of being of mine were scaffolding in the background; were the invisible and silent part of my life as a child. But in the foreground there were of course people; and these people were very like characters in Dickens. They were caricatures; they were very simple; they were immensely alive. They could be made with three strokes of the pen, if I could do it. Dickens owes his astonishing power to make characters alive to the fact that he saw them as a child sees them; as I saw Mr Wolstenholme; C. B. Clarke, and Mr Gibbs.

I name these three people because they all died when I was a child. Therefore they have never been altered. I see them exactly as I saw them then. Mr Wolstenholme was a very old gentleman who came every summer to stay with us. He was brown; he had a beard and very small eyes in fat cheeks; and he fitted into a brown wicker beehive chair as if it had been his nest. He used to sit in this beehive chair smoking and reading. He had only one characteristic—that when he ate plum tart he spurted the juice through his nose so that it made a purple stain on his grey moustache. This seemed enough to cause us perpetual delight. We called him "The Woolly One." By way of shading him a little I remember that we had to be kind to him because he was not happy at home; that he was very poor, yet once gave Thoby half a crown; that he had a son who was drowned in Australia; and I know too that he was a great mathematician. He never said a word all the time I knew him. But he still seems to me a complete character; and whenever I think of him I begin to laugh.

Mr Gibbs was perhaps less simple. He wore a tie ring; had a bald, benevolent head; was dry; neat; precise; and had folds of skin under his chin. He made father groan—"why can't you go—why can't you go?" And he gave Vanessa and myself two ermine skins, with slits down the middle out of which poured endless wealth—streams of silver. I also remember him lying in bed, dying; husky; in a night shirt; and showing us drawings by Retzsch.[5] The character of Mr Gibbs also seems to me complete and amuses me very much.

As for C. B. Clarke, he was an old botanist; and he said to my father "All you young botanists like Osmunda."[6] He had an aunt aged eighty who went for a walking tour in the New Forest. That is all—that is all I have to say about these three old gentlemen. But how real they were! How we laughed at them! What an immense part they played in our lives!

One more caricature comes into my mind; though pity entered into this one. I am thinking of Justine Nonon. She was immensely old. Little hairs sprouted on her long bony chin. She was a hunchback; and walked like a spider, feeling her way with her long dry fingers from one chair to another. Most of the time she sat in the arm-chair beside the fire. I used to sit on her knee; and her knee jogged up and down; and she sang in a hoarse cracked voice "Ron ron ron—et plon plon plon—" and then her knee gave and I was tumbled onto the floor. She was French; she had been with the Thackerays. She only came to us on visits. She lived by herself at Shepherd's Bush; and used to bring Adrian a glass jar of honey. I got the notion that she was extremely poor; and it made me uncomfortable that she brought this honey,

5. Friedrich Retzsch (1779–1857), German engraver.   6. Flowering ferns.

because I felt she did it by way of making her visit acceptable. She said too: "I have come in my carriage and pair"—which meant the red omnibus. For this too I pitied her; also because she began to wheeze; and the nurses said she would not live much longer; and soon she died. That is all I know about her; but I remember her as if she were a completely real person, with nothing left out, like the three old men.

Apr. 1939–Nov. 1940   1978

The Legacy

"For Sissy Miller." Gilbert Clandon, taking up the pearl brooch that lay among a litter of rings and brooches on a little table in his wife's drawing-room, read the inscription: "For Sissy Miller, with my love."

It was like Angela to have remembered even Sissy Miller, her secretary. Yet how strange it was, Gilbert Clandon thought once more, that she had left everything in such order—a little gift of some sort for every one of her friends. It was as if she had foreseen her death. Yet she had been in perfect health when she left the house that morning, six weeks ago; when she stepped off the kerb in Piccadilly[1] and the car had killed her.

He was waiting for Sissy Miller. He had asked her to come; he owed her, he felt, after all the years she had been with them, this token of consideration. Yes, he went on, as he sat there waiting, it was strange that Angela had left everything in such order. Every friend had been left some little token of her affection. Every ring, every necklace, every little Chinese box—she had a passion for little boxes—had a name on it. And each had some memory for him. This he had given her; this—the enamel dolphin with the ruby eyes— she had pounced upon one day in a back street in Venice. He could remember her little cry of delight. To him, of course, she had left nothing in particular, unless it were her diary. Fifteen little volumes, bound in green leather, stood behind him on her writing table. Ever since they were married, she had kept a diary. Some of their very few—he could not call them quarrels, say tiffs—had been about that diary. When he came in and found her writing, she always shut it or put her hand over it. "No, no, no," he could hear her say, "After I'm dead—perhaps." So she had left it him, as her legacy. It was the only thing they had not shared when she was alive. But he had always taken it for granted that she would outlive him. If only she had stopped one moment, and had thought what she was doing, she would be alive now. But she had stepped straight off the kerb, the driver of the car had said at the inquest. She had given him no chance to pull up. . . . Here the sound of voices in the hall interrupted him.

"Miss Miller, Sir," said the maid.

She came in. He had never seen her alone in his life, nor, of course, in tears. She was terribly distressed, and no wonder. Angela had been much more to her than an employer. She had been a friend. To himself, he thought, as he pushed a chair for her and asked her to sit down, she was scarcely distinguishable from any other woman of her kind. There were thousands of Sissy Millers—drab little women in black carrying attaché cases. But Angela,

1. Street in the center of London.

with her genius for sympathy, had discovered all sorts of qualities in Sissy Miller. She was the soul of discretion, so silent; so trustworthy, one could tell her anything, and so on.

Miss Miller could not speak at first. She sat there dabbing her eyes with her pocket handkerchief. Then she made an effort.

"Pardon me, Mr Clandon," she said.

He murmured. Of course he understood. It was only natural. He could guess what his wife had meant to her.

"I've been so happy here," she said, looking round. Her eyes rested on the writing table behind him. It was here they had worked—she and Angela. For Angela had her share of the duties that fall to the lot of the wife of a prominent politician. She had been the greatest help to him in his career. He had often seen her and Sissy sitting at that table—Sissy at the typewriter, taking down letters from her dictation. No doubt Miss Miller was thinking of that, too. Now all he had to do was to give her the brooch his wife had left her. A rather incongruous gift it seemed. It might have been better to have left her a sum of money, or even the typewriter. But there it was—"For Sissy Miller, with my love." And, taking the brooch, he gave it her with the little speech that he had prepared. He knew, he said, that she would value it. His wife had often worn it. . . . And she replied, as she took it, almost as if she too had prepared a speech, that it would always be a treasured possession. . . . She had, he supposed, other clothes upon which a pearl brooch would not look quite so incongruous. She was wearing the little black coat and skirt that seemed the uniform of her profession. Then he remembered—she was in mourning, of course. She too had had her tragedy—a brother, to whom she was devoted, had died only a week or two before Angela. In some accident was it? He could remember only Angela telling him; Angela, with her genius for sympathy, had been terribly upset. Meanwhile Sissy Miller had risen. She was putting on her gloves. Evidently she felt that she ought not to intrude. But he could not let her go without saying something about her future. What were her plans? Was there any way in which he could help her?

She was gazing at the table, where she had sat at her typewriter, where the diary lay. And, lost in her memories of Angela, she did not at once answer his suggestion that he should help her. She seemed for a moment not to understand. So he repeated:

"What are your plans, Miss Miller?"

"My plans? Oh, that's all right, Mr Clandon," she exclaimed. "Please don't bother yourself about me."

He took her to mean that she was in no need of financial assistance. It would be better, he realised, to make any suggestion of that kind in a letter. All he could do now was to say as he pressed her hand, "Remember, Miss Miller, if there's any way in which I can help you, it will be a pleasure. . . ." Then he opened the door. For a moment, on the threshold, as if a sudden thought had struck her, she stopped.

"Mr Clandon," she said, looking straight at him for the first time, and for the first time he was struck by the expression, sympathetic yet searching, in her eyes. "If at any time," she was saying, "there's anything I can do to help you, remember, I shall feel it, for your wife's sake, a pleasure. . . ."

With that she was gone. Her words and the look that went with them were unexpected. It was almost as if she believed, or hoped, that he would have need of her. A curious, perhaps a fantastic idea occurred to him as he returned to his chair. Could it be, that during all those years when he had scarcely noticed her, she, as the novelists say, had entertained a passion for him? He caught his own reflection in the glass as he passed. He was over fifty; but he could not help admitting that he was still, as the looking-glass showed him, a very distinguished-looking man.

"Poor Sissy Miller!" he said, half laughing. How he would have liked to share that joke with his wife! He turned instinctively to her diary. "Gilbert," he read, opening it at random, "looked so wonderful. . . ." It was as if she had answered his question. Of course, she seemed to say, you're very attractive to women. Of course Sissy Miller felt that too. He read on. "How proud I am to be his wife!" And he had always been very proud to be her husband. How often when they dined out somewhere he had looked at her across the table and said to himself, She is the loveliest woman here! He read on. That first year he had been standing for Parliament. They had toured his constituency.[2] "When Gilbert sat down the applause was terrific. The whole audience rose and sang: 'For he's a jolly good fellow.' I was quite overcome." He remembered that, too. She had been sitting on the platform beside him. He could still see the glance she cast at him, and how she had tears in her eyes. And then? He turned the pages. They had gone to Venice. He recalled that happy holiday after the election. "We had ices at Florians."[3] He smiled—she was still such a child, she loved ices. "Gilbert gave me a most interesting account of the history of Venice. He told me that the Doges[4] . . ." she had written it all out in her schoolgirl hand. One of the delights of travelling with Angela had been that she was so eager to learn. She was so terribly ignorant, she used to say, as if that were not one of her charms. And then—he opened the next volume—they had come back to London. "I was so anxious to make a good impression. I wore my wedding dress." He could see her now sitting next old Sir Edward; and making a conquest of that formidable old man, his chief. He read on rapidly, filling in scene after scene from her scrappy fragments. "Dined at the House of Commons.[5] . . . To an evening party at the Lovegroves. Did I realise my responsibility, Lady L. asked me, as Gilbert's wife?" Then as the years passed—he took another volume from the writing table—he had become more and more absorbed in his work. And she, of course, was more often alone. It had been a great grief to her, apparently, that they had had no children. "How I wish," one entry read, "that Gilbert had a son!" Oddly enough he had never much regretted that himself. Life had been so full, so rich as it was. That year he had been given a minor post in the government. A minor post only, but her comment was: "I am quite certain now that he will be Prime Minister!" Well, if things had gone differently, it might have been so. He paused here to speculate upon what might have been. Politics was a gamble, he reflected; but the game wasn't over yet. Not at fifty. He cast his eyes rapidly over more pages, full of the little trifles, the insignificant, happy, daily trifles that had made up her life.

He took up another volume and opened it at random. "What a coward I am! I let the chance slip again. But it seemed selfish to bother him about my own affairs, when he has so much to think about. And we so seldom have an evening alone." What was the meaning of that? Oh here was the explanation—it

---

2. Area represented by a Member of Parliament.
3. A café in the Piazza San Marco in Venice.
4. Chief magistrates in the Republic of Venice.
5. Lower House of the British Parliament.

referred to her work in the East End. "I plucked up courage and talked to Gilbert at last. He was so kind, so good. He made no objection." He remembered that conversation. She had told him that she felt so idle, so useless. She wished to have some work of her own. She wanted to do something—she had blushed so prettily, he remembered, as she said it sitting in that very chair—to help others. He had bantered her a little. Hadn't she enough to do looking after him, after her home? Still if it amused her of course he had no objection. What was it? Some district? Some committee? Only she must promise not to make herself ill. So it seemed that every Wednesday she went to Whitechapel. He remembered how he hated the clothes she wore on those occasions. But she had taken it very seriously it seemed. The diary was full of references like this: "Saw Mrs Jones. . . . She has ten children. . . . Husband lost his arm in an accident. . . . Did my best to find a job for Lily." He skipped on. His own name occurred less frequently. His interest slackened. Some of the entries conveyed nothing to him. For example: "Had a heated argument about socialism with B. M." Who was B. M.? He could not fill in the initials; some woman, he supposed, that she had met on one of her committees. "B. M. made a violent attack upon the upper classes. . . . I walked back after the meeting with B. M. and tried to convince him. But he is so narrow-minded." So B. M. was a man—no doubt one of those "intellectuals" as they call themselves, who are so violent, as Angela said, and so narrow-minded. She had invited him to come and see her apparently. "B. M. came to dinner. He shook hands with Minnie!" That note of exclamation gave another twist to his mental picture. B. M. it seemed wasn't used to parlourmaids; he had shaken hands with Minnie. Presumably he was one of those tame working men who air their views in ladies' drawing-rooms. Gilbert knew the type, and had no liking for this particular specimen, whoever B. M. might be. Here he was again. "Went with B. M. to the Tower of London. . . . He said revolution is bound to come. . . . He said we live in a Fool's Paradise." That was just the kind of thing B. M. would say—Gilbert could hear him. He could also see him quite distinctly—a stubby little man, with a rough beard, red tie, dressed as they always did in tweeds, who had never done an honest day's work in his life. Surely Angela had the sense to see through him? He read on. "B. M. said some very disagreeable things about . . ." The name was carefully scratched out. "I told him I would not listen to any more abuse of . . ." Again the name was obliterated. Could it have been his own name? Was that why Angela covered the page so quickly when he came in? The thought added to his growing dislike of B. M. He had had the impertinence to discuss him in this very room. Why had Angela never told him? It was very unlike her to conceal anything; she had been the soul of candour. He turned the pages, picking out every reference to B. M. "B. M. told me the story of his childhood. His mother went out charring.[6] . . . When I think of it, I can hardly bear to go on living in such luxury. . . . Three guineas for one hat!" If only she had discussed the matter with him, instead of puzzling her poor little head about questions that were much too difficult for her to understand! He had lent her books. Karl Marx. "The Coming Revolution." The initials B. M., B. M., B. M., recurred repeatedly. But why never the full name? There was an informality, an intimacy in the use of initials that was very unlike Angela. Had she

6. Working as a "charwoman" or house cleaner.

called him B. M. to his face? He read on. "B. M. came unexpectedly after dinner. Luckily, I was alone." That was only a year ago. "Luckily"—why luckily?—"I was alone." Where had he been that night? He checked the date in his engagement book. It had been the night of the Mansion House dinner.[7] And B. M. and Angela had spent the evening alone! He tried to recall that evening. Was she waiting up for him when he came back? Had the room looked just as usual? Were there glasses on the table? Were the chairs drawn close together? He could remember nothing—nothing whatever, nothing except his own speech at the Mansion House dinner. It became more and more inexplicable to him—the whole situation: his wife receiving an unknown man alone. Perhaps the next volume would explain. Hastily he reached for the last of the diaries—the one she had left unfinished when she died. There on the very first page was that cursed fellow again. "Dined alone with B. M. . . . He became very agitated. He said it was time we understood each other. . . . I tried to make him listen. But he would not. He threatened that if I did not . . ." the rest of the page was scored over. She had written "Egypt. Egypt. Egypt." over the whole page. He could not make out a single word; but there could be only one interpretation: the scoundrel had asked her to become his mistress. Alone in his room! The blood rushed to Gilbert Clandon's face. He turned the pages rapidly. What had been her answer? Initials had ceased. It was simply "he" now. "He came again. I told him I could not come to any decision. . . . I implored him to leave me." He had forced himself upon her in this very house? But why hadn't she told him? How could she have hesitated for an instant? Then: "I wrote him a letter." Then pages were left blank. Then there was this: "No answer to my letter." Then more blank pages; and then this. "He has done what he threatened." After that—what came after that? He turned page after page. All were blank. But there, on the very day before her death, was this entry: "Have I the courage to do it too?" That was the end.

Gilbert Clandon let the book slide to the floor. He could see her in front of him. She was standing on the kerb in Piccadilly. Her eyes stared; her fists were clenched. Here came the car. . . .

He could not bear it. He must know the truth. He strode to the telephone.

"Miss Miller!" There was silence. Then he heard someone moving in the room.

"Sissy Miller speaking"—her voice at last answered him.

"Who," he thundered, "is B. M.?"

He could hear the cheap clock ticking on her mantelpiece; then a long drawn sigh. Then at last she said:

"He was my brother."

He *was* her brother; her brother who had killed himself.

"Is there," he heard Sissy Miller asking, "anything that I can explain?"

"Nothing!" he cried. "Nothing!"

He had received his legacy. She had told him the truth. She had stepped off the kerb to rejoin her lover. She had stepped off the kerb to escape from him.

1940   1985

---

7. A banquet at the official residence of the lord mayor of London.

JAMES JOYCE
1882–1941

James Joyce was born in Dublin, son of a talented but feckless father who is accurately described by Stephen Dedalus in *A Portrait of the Artist as a Young Man* as a man who had in his time been "a medical student, an oarsman, a tenor, an amateur actor, a shouting politician, a small landlord, a small investor, a drinker, a good fellow, a storyteller, somebody's secretary, something in a distillery, a tax-gatherer, a bankrupt, and at present a praiser of his own past." The elder Joyce drifted steadily down the financial and social scale, his family moving from house to house, each one less genteel and more shabby than the previous. James Joyce's whole education was Catholic, from the age of six to the age of nine at Clongowes Wood College and from eleven to sixteen at Belvedere College, Dublin. Both were Jesuit institutions and were normal roads to the priesthood. He then studied modern languages at University College, Dublin.

From a comparatively early age Joyce regarded himself as a rebel against the shabbiness and Philistinism of Dublin. In his early youth he was very religious, but in his last year at Belvedere he began to reject his Catholic faith in favor of a literary mission that he saw as involving rebellion and exile. He refused to play any part in the nationalist or other popular activities of his fellow students, and he created some stir by his outspoken articles, one of which, on the Norwegian playwright Henrik Ibsen, appeared in the *Fortnightly Review* for April 1900. He taught himself Norwegian to be able to read Ibsen and to write to him. When an article by Joyce, significantly titled *The Day of the Rabblement,* was refused, on instructions of the faculty adviser, by the student magazine that had commissioned it, he had it printed privately. By 1902, when he received his A.B. degree, he was already committed to a career as exile and writer. For Joyce, as for his character Stephen Dedalus, the latter implied the former. To preserve his integrity, to avoid involvement in popular sentimentalities and dishonesties, and above all to be able to re-create with both total understanding and total objectivity the Dublin life he knew so well, he felt that he had to go abroad.

Joyce went to Paris after graduation, was recalled to Dublin by his mother's fatal illness, had a short spell there as a schoolteacher, then returned to the Continent in 1904 to teach English at Trieste and then at Zurich. He took with him Nora Barnacle, an uneducated Galway girl with no interest in literature; her native vivacity and peasant wit charmed Joyce, and the two lived in devoted companionship until Joyce's death, although they were not married until 1931. In 1920 Joyce settled in Paris, where he lived until December 1940, when the war forced him to take refuge in Switzerland; he died in Zurich a few weeks later.

Proud, obstinate, absolutely convinced of his genius, given to fits of sudden gaiety and of sudden silence, Joyce was not always an easy person to get along with, yet he never lacked friends, and throughout his thirty-six years on the Continent he was always the center of a literary circle. Life was hard at first. At Trieste he had very little money, and he did not improve matters by drinking heavily, a habit checked somewhat by his brother Stanislaus, who came out from Dublin to act (as Stanislaus put it much later) as his "brother's keeper." His financial position was much improved by the patronage of Mrs. Harold McCormick (Edith Rockefeller), who provided him with a monthly stipend from March 1917 until September 1919, when they quarreled, apparently because Joyce refused to submit to psychoanalysis by Carl Jung, who had been heavily endowed by her. The New York lawyer and art patron John Quinn, steered in Joyce's direction by Ezra Pound, also helped Joyce financially in 1917. A more permanent benefactor was the English feminist and editor Harriet Shaw Weaver, who not only subsidized Joyce generously from 1917 to the end of his life but occupied herself indefatigably with arrangements for publishing his work.

Joyce's almost lifelong exile from his native Ireland has something paradoxical about it. No writer has ever been more soaked in Dublin, its atmosphere, its history, its topography; in spite of doing most of his writing in Trieste, Zurich, and Paris, he wrote only and always about Dublin. He devised ways of expanding his accounts of Dublin, however, so that they became microcosms, small-scale models, of all human life, of all history, and of all geography. Indeed that was his life's work: to write about Dublin in such a way that he was writing about all of human experience.

Joyce began his career by writing a series of stories etching with extraordinary clarity aspects of Dublin life. But these stories—published as *Dubliners* in 1914—are more than sharp realistic sketches. In each, the detail is so chosen and organized that carefully interacting symbolic meanings are set up, and as a result, *Dubliners* is a book about human fate as well as a series of sketches of Dublin. Furthermore, the stories are presented in a particular order so that new meanings arise from the relation between them.

The last story in *Dubliners, The Dead,* was not part of the original draft of the book but was added later, at a time when Joyce was preoccupied with the nature of artistic objectivity. A series of jolting events frees the protagonist, Gabriel, from his possessiveness and egotism; the view he attains at the end is the mood of supreme neutrality that Joyce saw as the beginning of artistic awareness. It is the view of art developed by Stephen Dedalus in *A Portrait of the Artist as a Young Man. Dubliners* represents Joyce's first phase: he had to come directly to terms with the life he had rejected, to see it for what it was and for what it meant. Next, he had to come to terms with the meaning of his own development as a man dedicated to writing. He did this by weaving his autobiography into a novel so finely chiseled and carefully organized, so stripped of everything superfluous, that each word contributes to the presentation of the theme: the parallel movement toward art and toward exile. A part of Joyce's first draft has been posthumously published under the original title of *Stephen Hero* (1944): a comparison between it and the final version that Joyce gave to the world, *A Portrait of the Artist as a Young Man* (1916), will show how carefully Joyce reworked and compressed his material for maximum effect. The *Portrait* is not literally true as autobiography, although it has many autobiographical elements, but it is representatively true not only of Joyce but of the relation between the artist and society in the early twentieth century.

In the *Portrait* Stephen worked out a theory of art that considers that art moves from the lyrical form—which is the simplest, the personal expression of an instant of emotion—through the narrative form—no longer purely personal—to the dramatic— the highest and most nearly perfect form, where "the artist, like the God of creation, remains within or behind or beyond or above his handiwork, invisible, refined out of existence, indifferent, paring his fingernails." This view of art, which involves the objectivity, even the exile, of the artist (even though the artist uses only the materials provided for him or her by his or her own life), is related to that held by the poets of the 1890s. More widely, it is related to the rejection by the artist of the ordinary world of middle-class values and activities that we see equally, though in different ways, in Matthew Arnold's war against the Philistines and in the concept (very un-Arnoldian) of the artist as bohemian. Joyce's career belongs to that long chapter in the history of the arts in Western civilization that begins with the artist's declaring independence and ends with his or her feeling inevitable alienation. But if Joyce was alienated, as in certain ways he clearly was, he made his alienation serve his art: the kinds of writing represented by *Ulysses* and *Finnegans Wake* represent the most consummate craftsmanship put at the service of a humanely comic vision of all life. Some of Joyce's innovations in organization and style have been imitated by other writers, but these books are, and will probably remain, unique in our literature.

From the beginning, Joyce had trouble with the Philistines. Publication of *Dubliners* was held up for many years while he fought with both English and Irish publishers about certain words and phrases that they wished to eliminate. (It was one of the former who finally published the book.) His masterpiece *Ulysses* was banned in both Britain and America on its first appearance in 1922; its earlier serialization in an American magazine, *The Little Review* (March 1918–December 1920), had had to stop abruptly when the U.S. Post Office brought a charge of obscenity against it. Fortunately, Judge Woolsey's history-making decision in favor of *Ulysses* in a U.S. district court on December 6, 1933, resulted in the lifting of the ban and the free circulation of the work first in America and soon afterward in Britain.

ULYSSES

Ulysses is an account of one day in the lives of citizens of Dublin in the year 1904; it is thus the description of a limited number of events involving a limited number of people in a limited environment. Yet Joyce's ambition—which took him seven years to realize—is to make his action into a microcosm of all human experience. The events are not, therefore, told on a single level; the story is presented in such a manner that depth and implication are given to them and they become symbolic of the activity of the Individual in the World. The most obvious of the devices that Joyce employs to make clear the microcosmic aspect of his story is the parallel with Homer's *Odyssey:* every episode in *Ulysses* corresponds in some way to an episode in the *Odyssey.* Joyce regarded Homer's Ulysses as the most "complete" man in literature, a man who is shown in all his aspects—both coward and hero, cautious and reckless, weak and strong, husband and philanderer, father and son, dignified and ridiculous; so he makes his hero, Leopold Bloom, an Irish Jew, into a modern Ulysses and by so doing helps make him Everyman and make Dublin the world.

The book opens at eight o'clock on the morning of June 16, 1904. Stephen Dedalus (the same character we saw in the *Portrait,* but this is two years after our last glimpse of him there) had been summoned back to Dublin by his mother's fatal illness and now lives in an old military tower on the shore with Buck Mulligan, a rollicking medical student, and an Englishman called Haines. In the first three episodes of *Ulysses,* which concentrate on Stephen, he is built up as an aloof, uncompromising artist, rejecting all advances by representatives of the normal world, the incomplete man, to be contrasted later with the complete Leopold Bloom, who is much more "normal" and conciliatory. After tracing Stephen through his early-morning activities and learning the main currents of his mind, we go, in the fourth episode, to the home of Bloom. We follow closely his every activity: attending a funeral, transacting his business, eating his lunch, walking through the Dublin streets, worrying about his wife's infidelity with Blazes Boylan—and at each point the contents of his mind, including retrospect and anticipation, are presented to the reader, until all his past history is revealed. Finally, Bloom and Stephen, who have been just missing each other all day, get together. By this time it is late, and Stephen, who has been drinking with some medical students, is the worse for liquor. Bloom, moved by a paternal feeling toward Stephen (his own son had died in infancy and in a symbolic way Stephen takes his place), follows him during subsequent adventures in the role of protector. The climax of the book comes when Stephen, far gone in drink, and Bloom, worn out with fatigue, succumb to a series of hallucinations where their subconscious and unconscious come to the surface in dramatic form and their whole personalities are revealed with a completeness and a frankness unique in literature. Then Bloom takes the unresponsive Stephen home and gives him a meal. After Stephen's departure Bloom retires to bed—it is now two in the morning on June 17—while his wife, Molly, representing the principles of sex and reproduction on which all human life is based, closes the book with a long monologue in which her experiences as woman are remembered.

On the level of realistic description, *Ulysses* pulses with life and can be enjoyed for its evocation of early twentieth-century Dublin. On the level of psychological exploration, it gives a profound and moving presentation of the personality and consciousness of Leopold Bloom and (to a lesser extent) Stephen Dedalus. On the level of style, it exhibits the most fascinating linguistic virtuosity. On a deeper symbolic level, the novel explores the paradoxes of human loneliness and sociability (for Bloom is both Jew and Dubliner, both exile and citizen, just as all of us are in a sense both exiles and citizens), and it explores the problems posed by the relations between parent and child, between the generations, and between the sexes. At the same time, through its use of themes from Homer, Dante, and Shakespeare and from literature, philosophy, and history, the book weaves a subtle pattern of allusion and suggestion that illuminates many aspects of human experience. The more one reads *Ulysses* the more one finds in it, but at the same time one does not need to probe into the symbolic meaning to relish both its literary artistry and its human feeling. At the forefront stands Leopold Bloom, from one point of view, a frustrated and confused outsider in the society in which he moves, from another, a champion of kindness and justice whose humane curiosity about his fellows redeems him from mere vulgarity and gives the book its positive human foundation.

Readers who come to *Ulysses* with expectations about the way the story is to be presented derived from their reading of Victorian novels or even of such twentieth-century novelists as Conrad and Lawrence will find much that is at first puzzling. Joyce presents the consciousness of his characters directly, without any explanatory comment that tells the reader whose consciousness is being rendered (this is the stream of consciousness method). He may move, in the same paragraph and without any sign that he is making such a transition, from a description of a character's action—e.g., Stephen walking along the shore or Bloom entering a restaurant—to an evocation of the character's mental response to this action. That response is always multiple: it derives partly from the character's immediate situation and partly from the whole complex of attitudes that his past history has created in him. To suggest this multiplicity, Joyce may vary his style, from the flippant to the serious or from a realistic description to a suggestive set of images that indicate what might be called the general tone of the character's consciousness. Past and present mingle in the texture of the prose because they mingle in the texture of consciousness, and this mingling can be indicated by puns, by sudden breaks into a new kind of style or a new kind of subject matter, or by some other device for keeping the reader constantly in sight of the shifting, kaleidoscopic nature of human awareness. With a little experience, the reader learns to follow the implications of Joyce's shifts in manner and content—even to follow that at first sight bewildering passage in the "Proteus" episode in which Stephen does not go to visit his uncle and aunt but, passing the road that leads to their house, imagines the kind of conversation that would take place in his home *if* he had gone to visit his uncle and had then returned home and reported that he had done so. *Ulysses* must not be approached as though it were a novel written in a traditional manner; all preconceptions must be set aside and we must follow wherever the author leads us and let the language tell us what it has to say without our troubling whether language is being used "properly" or not.

FINNEGANS WAKE

Joyce's last work, *Finnegans Wake*, was published in 1939; it took more than fourteen years to write, and Joyce considered it his masterpiece. In *Ulysses* he had made the symbolic aspect of the novel at least as important as the realistic aspect, but in *Finnegans Wake* he gave up realism altogether. This vast story of a symbolic Irishman's cosmic dream develops by enormous reverberating puns a continuous expansion of meaning, the elements in the puns deriving from every conceivable source in history, literature, mythology, and Joyce's personal experience. The whole book being (on one level at least) a dream, Joyce invents his own dream language in which words are combined, distorted, created by fitting together bits of other words, used with several different meanings at once, often drawn from several different languages at once, and fused in all sorts of ways to achieve whole clusters of meaning simultaneously. In fact, so many echoing suggestions can be found in every word or phrase that a full annotation of even a few pages would require a large book. It has taken the cooperative work of a number of devoted readers to make clear the complex inter-actions of the multiple puns and pun clusters through which the ideas are projected, and every rereading reveals new meanings. It is true that many readers find the efforts of explication demanded by *Finegans Wake* too arduous; some, indeed, feel that the law of diminishing returns has now begun to operate, and that the effort of both author and reader is disproportionate. Nevertheless, the book has great beauty and fascination even for the casual reader. Students are advised to read aloud—or to listen to the record of Joyce reading aloud—the extract printed here to appreciate the degree to which the rhythms of the prose assist in conveying the meaning.

To an even greater extent than *Ulysses, Finnegans Wake* aims at embracing all of human history. The title is from an Irish-American ballad about Tom Finnegan, a hod carrier who falls off a ladder when drunk and is apparently killed, but who revives when during the wake (the watch by the dead body) someone spills whiskey on him. The theme of death and resurrection, of cycles of change coming round in the course of history, is central to *Finnegans Wake,* which derives one of its main principles of organization from the cyclical theory of history put forward in 1725 by the Italian philosopher Giambattista Vico. Vico held that history passes through four phases: the divine or theocratic, when people are governed by their awe of the supernatural; the aristocratic (the "heroic age" reflected in Homer and in *Beowulf*); the democratic and individualistic; and the final stage of chaos, a fall into confusion startles humanity back into supernatural reverence and starts the process once again. Joyce, like Yeats, saw his own generation as in the final stage awaiting the shock that will bring humans back to the first.

A mere account of the narrative line of *Finnegans Wake* cannot, of course, give any idea of the content of the work. If one explains that it opens with Finnegan's fall, then introduces his successor Humphrey Chimpden Earwicker, who is Everyman, and whose dream constitutes the novel; that he is presented as having guilt feelings about an indecency he committed (or may have committed) in Phoenix Park, Dublin; that his wife, Anna Livia Plurabelle or ALP (who is also Eve, Iseult, Ireland, the river Liffey), changes her role just as he does; that he has two sons, Shem and Shaun (or Jerry and Kevin), who represent introvert and extrovert, artist and practical man, creator and popularizer, and symbolize this basic dichotomy in human nature by all kinds of metamorphoses; and if one adds that, in the four books into which *Finnegans Wake* is divided (after Vico's pattern), actions comic or grotesque or sad or tender or desperate or passionate or terribly ordinary (and very often several of these things at the same time) take place with all the shifting meanings of a dream, so that characters change into others or into inanimate objects and the setting keeps shifting—if we explain all this, we still have said very little about what makes *Finnegans Wake* what it is. The dreamer, whose initials HCE indicate his universality ("Here Comes Every-body"), is at the same time a particular person, who keeps a pub in Chapelizod, a Dublin suburb on the river Liffey near Phoenix Park. His mysterious misdemeanor in Phoenix Park is in a sense Original Sin: Earwicker is Adam as well as a primeval giant, the Hill of Howth, the Great Parent ("Haveth Childers Everywhere" is another expansion of HCE), and Man in History. Other characters who flit and change through the book, such as the Twelve Customers (who are also twelve jurymen and public opinion) and the Four Old Men (who are also judges, the authors of the four Gospels, and the four elements), help weave the texture of multiple significance so characteristic of the work. But always it is the punning language, extending signifi-cance downward—rather than the plot, developing it lengthwise—that bears the main load of meaning.

Araby[1]

North Richmond Street, being blind, was a quiet street except at the hour when the Christian Brothers' School[2] set the boys free. An uninhabited house of two storeys stood at the blind end, detached from its neighbours in a square ground. The other houses of the street, conscious of decent lives within them, gazed at one another with brown imperturbable faces.

The former tenant of our house, a priest, had died in the back drawing-room. Air, musty from having been long enclosed, hung in all the rooms, and the waste room behind the kitchen was littered with old useless papers. Among these I found a few paper-covered books, the pages of which were curled and damp: *The Abbot*, by Walter Scott, *The Devout Communicant* and *The Memoirs of Vidocq*.[3] I liked the last best because its leaves were yellow. The wild garden behind the house contained a central apple-tree and a few straggling bushes under one of which I found the late tenant's rusty bicycle-pump. He had been a very charitable priest; in his will he had left all his money to institutions and the furniture of his house to his sister.

When the short days of winter came dusk fell before we had well eaten our dinners. When we met in the street the houses had grown sombre. The space of sky above us was the colour of ever-changing violet and towards it the lamps of the street lifted their feeble lanterns. The cold air stung us and we played till our bodies glowed. Our shouts echoed in the silent street. The career of our play brought us through the dark muddy lanes behind the houses where we ran the gantlet of the rough tribes from the cottages, to the back doors of the dark dripping gardens where odours arose from the ashpits, to the dark odorous stables where a coachman smoothed and combed the horse or shook music from the buckled harness. When we returned to the street light from the kitchen windows had filled the areas. If my uncle was seen turning the corner we hid in the shadow until we had seen him safely housed. Or if Mangan's sister came out on the doorstep to call her brother in to his tea we watched her from our shadow peer up and down the street. We waited to see whether she would remain or go in and, if she remained, we left our shadow and walked up to Mangan's steps resignedly. She was waiting for us, her figure defined by the light from the half-opened door. Her brother always teased her before he obeyed and I stood by the railings looking at her. Her dress swung as she moved her body and the soft rope of her hair tossed from side to side.

---

1. The third of the fifteen stories in *Dubliners*. This tale of the frustrated quest for beauty in the midst of drabness is both meticulously realistic in its handling of details of Dublin life and the Dublin scene and highly symbolic in that almost every image and incident suggests some particular aspect of the theme (e.g., the suggestion of the Holy Grail in the image of the chalice, mentioned in the fifth paragraph). Joyce was drawing on his own childhood recollections, and the uncle in the story is a reminiscence of Joyce's father. But in all the stories in *Dubliners* dealing with childhood, the child lives not with his parents but with an uncle and aunt—a symbol of that isolation and lack of proper relation between "consubstantial" (in the flesh) parents and children which is a major theme in Joyce's work.

2. The Joyce family moved to 17 North Richmond Street, Dublin, in 1894; and Joyce had earlier briefly attended the Christian Brothers' school a few doors away (the Christian Brothers are a Catholic religious community). The details of the house described here correspond exactly to those of number 17.

3. François Eugène Vidocq (1775–1857) had an extraordinary career as soldier, thief, chief of the French detective force, and private detective. *The Abbot* is a historical novel dealing with Mary, Queen of Scots. *The Devout Communicant* is a Catholic religious manual.

Every morning I lay on the floor in the front parlour watching her door. The blind was pulled down to within an inch of the sash so that I could not be seen. When she came out on the doorstep my heart leaped. I ran to the hall, seized my books and followed her. I kept her brown figure always in my eye and, when we came near the point at which our ways diverged, I quickened my pace and passed her. This happened morning after morning. I had never spoken to her, except for a few casual words, and yet her name was like a summons to all my foolish blood.

Her image accompanied me even in places the most hostile to romance. On Saturday evenings when my aunt went marketing I had to go to carry some of the parcels. We walked through the flaring streets, jostled by drunken men and bargaining women, amid the curses of labourers, the shrill litanies of shop-boys who stood on guard by the barrels of pigs' cheeks, the nasal chanting of street-singers, who sang a *come-all-you*[4] about O'Donovan Rossa, or a ballad about the troubles in our native land. These noises converged in a single sensation of life for me: I imagined that I bore my chalice safely through a throng of foes. Her name sprang to my lips at moments in strange prayers and praises which I myself did not understand. My eyes were often full of tears (I could not tell why) and at times a flood from my heart seemed to pour itself out into my bosom. I thought little of the future. I did not know whether I would ever speak to her or not or, if I spoke to her, how I could tell her of my confused adoration. But my body was like a harp and her words and gestures were like fingers running upon the wires.

One evening I went into the back drawing-room in which the priest had died. It was a dark rainy evening and there was no sound in the house. Through one of the broken panes I heard the rain impinge upon the earth, the fine incessant needles of water playing in the sodden beds. Some distant lamp or lighted window gleamed below me. I was thankful that I could see so little. All my senses seemed to desire to veil themselves and, feeling that I was about to slip from them, I pressed the palms of my hands together until they trembled, murmuring: *O love! O love!* many times.

At last she spoke to me. When she addressed the first words to me I was so confused that I did not know what to answer. She asked me was I going to *Araby*.[5] I forgot whether I answered yes or no. It would be a splendid bazaar, she said; she would love to go.

—And why can't you? I asked.

While she spoke she turned a silver bracelet round and round her wrist. She could not go, she said, because there would be a retreat that week in her convent.[6] Her brother and two other boys were fighting for their caps and I was alone at the railings. She held one of the spikes, bowing her head towards me. The light from the lamp opposite our door caught the white curve of her neck, lit up her hair that rested there and, falling, lit up the hand upon the railing. It fell over one side of her dress and caught the white border of a petticoat, just visible as she stood at ease.

—It's well for you, she said.

4. Street ballad, so called from its opening words. This one was about the 19th-century Irish nationalist Jeremiah Donovan, popularly known as O'Donovan Rossa.
5. The bazaar, described by its "official catalogue"

as a "Grand Oriental Fête," was actually held in Dublin on May 14–19, 1894.
6. I.e., her convent school. "Retreat": period of seclusion from ordinary activities devoted to religious exercises.

—If I go, I said, I will bring you something.

What innumerable follies laid waste my waking and sleeping thoughts after that evening! I wished to annihilate the tedious intervening days. I chafed against the work of school. At night in my bedroom and by day in the classroom her image came between me and the page I strove to read. The syllables of the word *Araby* were called to me through the silence in which my soul luxuriated and cast an Eastern enchantment over me. I asked for leave to go to the bazaar on Saturday night. My aunt was surprised and hoped it was not some Freemason affair.[7] I answered few questions in class. I watched my master's face pass from amiability to sternness; he hoped I was not beginning to idle. I could not call my wandering thoughts together. I had hardly any patience with the serious work of life which, now that it stood between me and my desire, seemed to me child's play, ugly monotonous child's play.

On Saturday morning I reminded my uncle that I wished to go to the bazaar in the evening. He was fussing at the hallstand, looking for the hat-brush, and answered me curtly:

—Yes, boy, I know.

As he was in the hall I could not go into the front parlour and lie at the window. I left the house in bad humour and walked slowly towards the school. The air was pitilessly raw and already my heart misgave me.

When I came home to dinner my uncle had not yet been home. Still it was early. I sat staring at the clock for some time and, when its ticking began to irritate me, I left the room. I mounted the staircase and gained the upper part of the house. The high cold empty gloomy rooms liberated me and I went from room to room singing. From the front window I saw my companions playing below in the street. Their cries reached me weakened and indistinct and, leaning my forehead against the cool glass, I looked over at the dark house where she lived. I may have stood there for an hour, seeing nothing but the brown-clad figure cast by my imagination, touched discreetly by the lamplight at the curved neck, at the hand upon the railings and at the border below the dress.

When I came downstairs again I found Mrs Mercer sitting at the fire. She was an old garrulous woman, a pawn-broker's widow, who collected used stamps for some pious purpose. I had to endure the gossip of the tea-table. The meal was prolonged beyond an hour and still my uncle did not come. Mrs Mercer stood up to go: she was sorry she couldn't wait any longer, but it was after eight o'clock and she did not like to be out late, as the night air was bad for her. When she had gone I began to walk up and down the room, clenching my fists. My aunt said:

—I'm afraid you may put off your bazaar for this night of Our Lord.

At nine o'clock I heard my uncle's latchkey in the halldoor. I heard him talking to himself and heard the hallstand rocking when it had received the weight of his overcoat. I could interpret these signs. When he was midway through his dinner I asked him to give me the money to go to the bazaar. He had forgotten.

—The people are in bed and after their first sleep now, he said.

---

7. His aunt shares her church's distrust of the Freemasons, an old European secret society, reputedly anti-Catholic.

I did not smile. My aunt said to him energetically:

—Can't you give him the money and let him go? You've kept him late enough as it is.

My uncle said he was very sorry he had forgotten. He said he believed in the old saying: *All work and no play makes Jack a dull boy.* He asked me where I was going and, when I had told him a second time he asked me did I know *The Arab's Farewell to his Steed.*[8] When I left the kitchen he was about to recite the opening lines of the piece to my aunt.

I held a florin[9] tightly in my hand as I strode down Buckingham Street towards the station. The sight of the streets thronged with buyers and glaring with gas recalled to me the purpose of my journey. I took my seat in a third-class carriage of a deserted train. After an intolerable delay the train moved out of the station slowly. It crept onward among ruinous houses and over the twinkling river. At Westland Row Station a crowd of people pressed to the carriage doors; but the porters moved them back, saying that it was a special train for the bazaar. I remained alone in the bare carriage. In a few minutes the train drew up beside an improvised wooden platform. I passed out on to the road and saw by the lighted dial of a clock that it was ten minutes to ten. In front of me was a large building which displayed the magical name.

I could not find any sixpenny entrance and, fearing that the bazaar would be closed, I passed in quickly through a turnstile, handing a shilling to a weary-looking man. I found myself in a big hall girdled at half its height by a gallery. Nearly all the stalls were closed and the greater part of the hall was in darkness. I recognized a silence like that which pervades a church after a service. I walked into the centre of the bazaar timidly. A few people were gathered about the stalls which were still open. Before a curtain, over which the words *Café Chantant*[1] were written in coloured lamps, two men were counting money on a salver. I listened to the fall of the coins.

Remembering with difficulty why I had come I went over to one of the stalls and examined porcelain vases and flowered tea-sets. At the door of the stall a young lady was talking and laughing with two young gentlemen. I remarked their English accents and listened vaguely to their conversation.

—O, I never said such a thing!

—O, but you did!

—O, but I didn't!

—Didn't she say that?

—Yes. I heard her.

—O, there's a . . . fib![2]

Observing me the young lady came over and asked me did I wish to buy anything. The tone of her voice was not encouraging; she seemed to have spoken to me out of a sense of duty. I looked humbly at the great jars that stood like eastern guards at either side of the dark entrance to the stall and murmured:

—No, thank you.

---

8. Once-popular sentimental poem by Caroline Norton.
9. A silver coin, now obsolete, worth two shillings.
1. Singing café (French; literal trans.); a café that provided musical entertainment, popular early in the 20th century.
2. A lie.

The young lady changed the position of one of the vases and went back to the two young men. They began to talk of the same subject. Once or twice the young lady glanced at me over her shoulder.

I lingered before her stall, though I knew my stay was useless, to make my interest in her wares seem the more real. Then I turned away slowly and walked down the middle of the bazaar. I allowed the two pennies to fall against the sixpence in my pocket. I heard a voice call from one end of the gallery that the light was out. The upper part of the hall was now completely dark.

Gazing up into the darkness I saw myself as a creature driven and derided by vanity; and my eyes burned with anguish and anger.

1905   1914

The Dead

Lily, the caretaker's daughter, was literally run off her feet. Hardly had she brought one gentleman into the little pantry behind the office on the ground floor and helped him off with his overcoat than the wheezy hall-door bell clanged again and she had to scamper along the bare hallway to let in another guest. It was well for her she had not to attend to the ladies also. But Miss Kate and Miss Julia had thought of that and had converted the bathroom upstairs into a ladies' dressing-room. Miss Kate and Miss Julia were there, gossiping and laughing and fussing, walking after each other to the head of the stairs, peering down over the banisters and calling down to Lily to ask her who had come.

It was always a great affair, the Misses Morkan's annual dance. Everybody who knew them came to it, members of the family, old friends of the family, the members of Julia's choir, any of Kate's pupils that were grown up enough and even some of Mary Jane's pupils too. Never once had it fallen flat. For years and years it had gone off in splendid style as long as anyone could remember; ever since Kate and Julia, after the death of their brother Pat, had left the house in Stoney Batter and taken Mary Jane, their only niece, to live with them in the dark gaunt house on Usher's Island, the upper part of which they had rented from Mr Fulham, the cornfactor[1] on the ground floor. That was a good thirty years ago if it was a day. Mary Jane, who was then a little girl in short clothes, was now the main prop of the household for she had the organ in Haddington Road.[2] She had been through the Academy and gave a pupils' concert every year in the upper room of the Antient Concert Rooms.[3] Many of her pupils belonged to better-class families on the Kingstown and Dalkey line. Old as they were, her aunts also did their share. Julia, though she was quite grey, was still the leading soprano in Adam and Eve's, and Kate, being too feeble to go about much, gave music lessons to beginners on the old square piano in the back room. Lily, the caretaker's daughter, did housemaid's work for them. Though their life was modest they believed in eating well; the best of everything: diamond-bone sirloins, three-

---

1. Grain merchant.
2. Haddington Road and Adam and Eve's are churches.

3. Concert hall in Dublin. The academy was the Royal Irish Academy of Music.

shilling tea and the best bottled stout.[4] But Lily seldom made a mistake in the orders so that she got on well with her three mistresses. They were fussy, that was all. But the only thing they would not stand was back answers.

Of course they had good reason to be fussy on such a night. And then it was long after ten o'clock and yet there was no sign of Gabriel and his wife. Besides they were dreadfully afraid that Freddy Malins might turn up screwed. They would not wish for worlds that any of Mary Jane's pupils should see him under the influence; and when he was like that it was sometimes very hard to manage him. Freddy Malins always came late but they wondered what could be keeping Gabriel: and that was what brought them every two minutes to the banisters to ask Lily had Gabriel or Freddy come.

—O, Mr Conroy, said Lily to Gabriel when she opened the door for him, Miss Kate and Miss Julia thought you were never coming. Good-night, Mrs Conroy.

—I'll engage they did, said Gabriel, but they forget that my wife here takes three mortal hours to dress herself.

He stood on the mat, scraping the snow from his goloshes, while Lily led his wife to the foot of the stairs and called out:

—Miss Kate, here's Mrs Conroy.

Kate and Julia came toddling down the dark stairs at once. Both of them kissed Gabriel's wife, said she must be perished alive and asked was Gabriel with her.

—Here I am as right as the mail, Aunt Kate! Go on up. I'll follow, called out Gabriel from the dark.

He continued scraping his feet vigorously while the three women went upstairs, laughing, to the ladies' dressing-room. A light fringe of snow lay like a cape on the shoulders of his overcoat and like toecaps on the toes of his goloshes; and, as the buttons of his overcoat slipped with a squeaking noise through the snow-stiffened frieze,[5] a cold fragrant air from out-of-doors escaped from crevices and folds.

—Is it snowing again, Mr Conroy? asked Lily.

She had preceded him into the pantry to help him off with his overcoat. Gabriel smiled at the three syllables she had given his surname and glanced at her. She was a slim, growing girl, pale in complexion and with hay-coloured hair. The gas in the pantry made her look still paler. Gabriel had known her when she was a child and used to sit on the lowest step nursing a rag doll.

—Yes, Lily, he answered, and I think we're in for a night of it.

He looked up at the pantry ceiling, which was shaking with the stamping and shuffling of feet on the floor above, listened for a moment to the piano and then glanced at the girl, who was folding his overcoat carefully at the end of a shelf.

—Tell me, Lily, he said in a friendly tone, do you still go to school?

—O no, sir, she answered. I'm done schooling this year and more.

—O, then, said Gabriel gaily, I suppose we'll be going to your wedding one of these fine days with your young man, eh?

The girl glanced back at him over her shoulder and said with great bitterness:

---

4. A dark brown malt liquor, akin to beer. 5. A kind of coarse woolen cloth.

—The men that is now is only all palaver and what they can get out of you.

Gabriel coloured as if he felt he had made a mistake and, without looking at her, kicked off his goloshes and flicked actively with his muffler at his patent-leather shoes.

He was a stout tallish young man. The high colour of his cheeks pushed upwards even to his forehead where it scattered itself in a few formless patches of pale red; and on his hairless face there scintillated restlessly the polished lenses and the bright gilt rims of the glasses which screened his delicate and restless eyes. His glossy black hair was parted in the middle and brushed in a long curve behind his ears where it curled slightly beneath the groove left by his hat.

When he had flicked lustre into his shoes he stood up and pulled his waistcoat down more tightly on his plump body. Then he took a coin rapidly from his pocket.

—O Lily, he said, thrusting it into her hands, it's Christmas-time, isn't it? Just . . . here's a little. . . .

He walked rapidly towards the door.

—O no, sir! cried the girl, following him. Really, sir, I wouldn't take it.

—Christmas-time! Christmas-time! said Gabriel, almost trotting to the stairs and waving his hand to her in deprecation.

The girl, seeing that he had gained the stairs, called out after him:

—Well, thank you, sir.

He waited outside the drawing-room door until the waltz should finish, listening to the skirts that swept against it and to the shuffling of feet. He was still discomposed by the girl's bitter and sudden retort. It had cast a gloom over him which he tried to dispel by arranging his cuffs and the bows of his tie. Then he took from his waistcoat pocket a little paper and glanced at the headings he had made for his speech. He was undecided about the lines from Robert Browning for he feared they would be above the heads of his hearers. Some quotation that they could recognise from Shakespeare or from the Melodies[6] would be better. The indelicate clacking of the men's heels and the shuffling of their soles reminded him that their grade of culture differed from his. He would only make himself ridiculous by quoting poetry to them which they could not understand. They would think that he was airing his superior education. He would fail with them just as he had failed with the girl in the pantry. He had taken up a wrong tone. His whole speech was a mistake from first to last, an utter failure.

Just then his aunts and his wife came out of the ladies' dressing-room. His aunts were two small plainly dressed old women. Aunt Julia was an inch or so taller. Her hair, drawn low over the tops of her ears, was grey; and grey also, with darker shadows, was her large flaccid face. Though she was stout in build and stood erect her slow eyes and parted lips gave her the appearance of a woman who did not know where she was or where she was going. Aunt Kate was more vivacious. Her face, healthier than her sister's, was all puckers and creases, like a shrivelled red apple, and her hair, braided in the same old-fashioned way, had not lost its ripe nut colour.

---

6. *Irish Melodies* by Dublin-born Thomas Moore (1779–1852), a collection of songs—including one called "O Ye Dead"—that was extremely popular in late-19th- and early-20th-century Ireland.

They both kissed Gabriel frankly. He was their favourite nephew, the son of their dead elder sister, Ellen, who had married T. J. Conroy of the Port and Docks.

—Gretta tells me you're not going to take a cab back to Monkstown to-night, Gabriel, said Aunt Kate.

—No, said Gabriel, turning to his wife we had quite enough of that last year, hadn't we. Don't you remember, Aunt Kate, what a cold Gretta got out of it? Cab windows rattling all the way, and the east wind blowing in after we passed Merrion. Very jolly it was. Greta caught a dreadful cold.

Aunt Kate frowned severely and nodded her head at every word.

—Quite right, Gabriel, quite right, she said. You can't be too careful.

—But as for Gretta there, said Gabriel, she'd walk home in the snow if she were let.

Mrs Conroy laughed.

—Don't mind him, Aunt Kate, she said. He's really an awful bother, what with green shades for Tom's eyes at night and making him do the dumb-bells, and forcing Eva to eat the stirabout[7] The poor child! And she simply hates the sight of it! . . . O, but you'll never guess what he makes me wear now!

She broke out into a peal of laughter and glanced at her husband, whose admiring and happy eyes had been wandering from her dress to her face and hair. The two aunts laughed heartily too, for Gabriel's solicitude was a stand-ing joke with them.

—Goloshes! said Mrs Conroy. That's the latest. Whenever it's wet under-foot I must put on my goloshes. To-night even he wanted me to put them on, but I wouldn't. The next thing he'll buy me will be a diving suit.

Gabriel laughed nervously and patted his tie reassuringly while Aunt Kate nearly doubled herself, so heartily did she enjoy the joke. The smile soon faded from Aunt Julia's face and her mirthless eyes were directed towards her nephew's face. After a pause she asked:

—And what are goloshes, Gabriel?

—Goloshes, Julia! exclaimed her sister. Goodness me, don't you know what goloshes are? You wear them over your . . . over your boots, Gretta, isn't it?

—Yes, said Mrs Conroy. Guttapercha things. We both have a pair now. Gabriel says everyone wears them on the continent.

—O, on the continent, murmured Aunt Julia, nodding her head slowly.

Gabriel knitted his brows and said, as if he were slightly angered:

—It's nothing very wonderful but Gretta thinks it very funny because she says the word reminds her of Christy Minstrels.[8]

—But tell me, Gabriel, said Aunt Kate, with brisk tact. Of course, you've seen about the room. Gretta was saying . . .

—O, the room is all right, replied Gabriel. I've taken one in the Gresham.[9]

—To be sure, said Aunt Kate, by far the best thing to do. And the children, Gretta, you're not anxious about them?

---

7. Porridge made by stirring oatmeal in boiling milk or water.
8. Originally the name of a troupe of entertainers imitating African Americans, founded by George Christy of New York. By Joyce's time the meaning had become extended to any group with blackened faces who sang what were known as Negro melo-dies to banjo accompaniment, interspersed with jokes.
9. The Gresham Hotel, still one of the best hotels in Dublin.

—O, for one night, said Mrs Conroy. Besides, Bessie will look after them.

—To be sure, said Aunt Kate again. What a comfort it is to have a girl like that, one you can depend on! There's that Lily, I'm sure I don't know what has come over her lately. She's not the girl she was at all.

Gabriel was about to ask his aunt some questions on this point but she broke off suddenly to gaze after her sister who had wandered down the stairs and was craning her neck over the banisters.

—Now, I ask you, she said, almost testily, where is Julia going? Julia! Julia! Where are you going?

Julia, who had gone halfway down one flight, came back and announced blandly:

—Here's Freddy.

At the same moment a clapping of hands and a final flourish of the pianist told that the waltz had ended. The drawing-room door was opened from within and some couples came out. Aunt Kate drew Gabriel aside hurriedly and whispered into his ear:

—Slip down, Gabriel, like a good fellow and see if he's all right, and don't let him up if he's screwed. I'm sure he's screwed. I'm sure he is.

Gabriel went to the stairs and listened over the banisters. He could hear two persons talking in the pantry. Then he recognised Freddy Malins' laugh. He went down the stairs noisily.

—It's such a relief, said Aunt Kate to Mrs Conroy, that Gabriel is here. I always feel easier in my mind when he's here. . . . Julia, there's Miss Daly and Miss Power will take some refreshment. Thanks for your beautiful waltz, Miss Daly. It made lovely time.

A tall wizen-faced man, with a stiff grizzled moustache and swarthy skin, who was passing out with his partner said:

—And may we have some refreshment, too, Miss Morkan?

—Julia, said Aunt Kate summarily, and here's Mr Browne and Miss Furlong. Take them in, Julia, with Miss Daly and Miss Power.

—I'm the man for the ladies, said Mr Browne, pursing his lips until his moustache bristled and smiling in all his wrinkles. You know, Miss Morkan, the reason they are so fond of me is—

He did not finish his sentence, but, seeing that Aunt Kate was out of earshot, at once led the three young ladies into the back room. The middle of the room was occupied by two square tables placed end to end, and on these Aunt Julia and the caretaker were straightening and smoothing a large cloth. On the sideboard were arrayed dishes and plates, and glasses and bundles of knives and forks and spoons. The top of the closed square piano served also as a sideboard for viands and sweets. At a smaller sideboard in one corner two young men were standing, drinking hop-bitters.

Mr Browne led his charges thither and invited them all, in jest, to some ladies' punch, hot, strong and sweet. As they said they never took anything strong he opened three bottles of lemonade for them. Then he asked one of the young men to move aside, and, taking hold of the decanter, filled out for himself a goodly measure of whisky. The young men eyed him respectfully while he took a trial sip.

—God help me, he said, smiling, it's the doctor's orders.

His wizened face broke into a broader smile, and the three young ladies laughed in musical echo to his pleasantry, swaying their bodies to and fro, with nervous jerks of their shoulders. The boldest said:

—O, now, Mr Browne, I'm sure the doctor never ordered anything of the kind.

Mr Browne took another sip of his whisky and said, with sidling mimicry:

—Well, you see, I'm like the famous Mrs Cassidy, who is reported to have said: *Now, Mary Grimes, if I don't take it, make me take it, for I feel I want it.*

His hot face had leaned forward a little too confidentially and he had assumed a very low Dublin accent so that the young ladies, with one instinct, received his speech in silence. Miss Furlong, who was one of Mary Jane's pupils, asked Miss Daly what was the name of the pretty waltz she had played; and Mr Browne, seeing that he was ignored, turned promptly to the two young men who were more appreciative.

A red-faced young woman, dressed in pansy, came into the room, excitedly clapping her hands and crying:

—Quadrilles![1] Quadrilles!

Close on her heels came Aunt Kate, crying:

—Two gentlemen and three ladies, Mary Jane!

—O, here's Mr Bergin and Mr Kerrigan, said Mary Jane. Mr Kerrigan, will you take Miss Power? Miss Furlong, may I get you a partner, Mr Bergin. O, that'll just do now.

—Three ladies, Mary Jane, said Aunt Kate.

The two young gentlemen asked the ladies if they might have the pleasure, and Mary Jane turned to Miss Daly.

—O, Miss Daly, you're really awfully good, after playing for the last two dances, but really we're so short of ladies to-night.

—I don't mind in the least, Miss Morkan.

—But I've a nice partner for you, Mr Bartell D'Arcy, the tenor. I'll get him to sing later on. All Dublin is raving about him.

—Lovely voice, lovely voice! said Aunt Kate.

As the piano had twice begun the prelude to the first figure Mary Jane led her recruits quickly from the room. They had hardly gone when Aunt Julia wandered slowly into the room, looking behind her at something.

—What is the matter, Julia? asked Aunt Kate anxiously. Who is it?

Julia, who was carrying in a column of table-napkins, turned to her sister and said, simply, as if the question had surprised her:

—It's only Freddy, Kate, and Gabriel with him.

In fact right behind her Gabriel could be seen piloting Freddy Malins across the landing. The latter, a young man of about forty, was of Gabriel's size and build, with very round shoulders. His face was fleshy and pallid, touched with colour only at the thick hanging lobes of his ears and at the wide wings of his nose. He had coarse features, a blunt nose, a convex and receding brow, tumid and protruded lips. His heavy-lidded eyes and the disorder of his scanty hair made him look sleepy. He was laughing heartily in a high key at a story which he had been telling Gabriel on the stairs and at the same time rubbing the knuckles of his left fist backwards and forwards into his left eye.

—Good-evening, Freddy, said Aunt Julia.

Freddy Malins bade the Misses Morkan good-evening in what seemed an offhand fashion by reason of the habitual catch in his voice and then, seeing

1. A square dance usually performed by four couples.

that Mr Browne was grinning at him from the sideboard, crossed the room on rather shaky legs and began to repeat in an undertone the story he had just told to Gabriel.

—He's not so bad, is he? said Aunt Kate to Gabriel.

Gabriel's brows were dark but he raised them quickly and answered:

—O no, hardly noticeable.

—Now, isn't he a terrible fellow! she said. And his poor mother made him take the pledge[2] on New Year's Eve. But come on, Gabriel, into the drawing-room.

Before leaving the room with Gabriel she signalled to Mr Browne by frowning and shaking her forefinger in warning to and fro. Mr Browne nodded in answer and, when she had gone, said to Freddy Malins:

—Now, then, Teddy, I'm going to fill you out a good glass of lemonade just to buck you up.

Freddy Malins, who was nearing the climax of his story, waved the offer aside impatiently but Mr Browne, having first called Freddy Malins' attention to a disarray in his dress, filled out and handed him a full glass of lemonade. Freddy Malins' left hand accepted the glass mechanically, his right hand being engaged in the mechanical readjustment of his dress. Mr Browne, whose face was once more wrinkling with mirth, poured out for himself a glass of whisky while Freddy Malins exploded, before he had well reached the climax of his story, in a kink of high-pitched bronchitic laughter and, setting down his untasted and overflowing glass, began to rub the knuckles of his left fist backwards and forwards into his left eye, repeating words of his last phrase as well as his fit of laughter would allow him.

Gabriel could not listen while Mary Jane was playing her Academy piece, full of runs and difficult passages, to the hushed drawing-room. He liked music but the piece she was playing had no melody for him and he doubted whether it had any melody for the other listeners, though they had begged Mary Jane to play something. Four young men, who had come from the refreshment-room to stand in the door-way at the sound of the piano, had gone away quietly in couples after a few minutes. The only persons who seemed to follow the music were Mary Jane herself, her hands racing along the key-board or lifted from it at the pauses like those of a priestess in momentary imprecation, and Aunt Kate standing at her elbow to turn the page.

Gabriel's eyes, irritated by the floor, which glittered with beeswax under the heavy chandelier, wandered to the wall above the piano. A picture of the balcony scene in *Romeo and Juliet* hung there and beside it was a picture of the two murdered princes in the Tower which Aunt Julia had worked in red, blue and brown wools when she was a girl. Probably in the school they had gone to as girls that kind of work had been taught, for one year his mother had worked for him as a birthday present a waistcoat of purple tabinet,[3] with little foxes' heads upon it, lined with brown satin and having round mulberry buttons. It was strange that his mother had had no musical talent though Aunt Kate used to call her the brains carrier of the Morkan family. Both she and Julia had always seemed a little proud of their serious and matronly

---

2. Sign a solemn promise not to drink alcohol. 3. A kind of poplin made chiefly in Ireland.

sister. Her photograph stood before the pierglass.[4] She held an open book on her knees and was pointing out something in it to Constantine who, dressed in a man-o'-war suit,[5] lay at her feet. It was she who had chosen the names for her sons for she was very sensible of the dignity of family life. Thanks to her, Constantine was now senior curate[6] in Balbriggan and, thanks to her, Gabriel himself had taken his degree in the Royal University. A shadow passed over his face as he remembered her sullen opposition to his marriage. Some slighting phrases she had used still rankled in his memory; she had once spoken of Gretta as being country cute and that was not true of Gretta at all. It was Gretta who had nursed her during all her last long illness in their house at Monkstown.

He knew that Mary Jane must be near the end of her piece for she was playing again the opening melody with runs of scales after every bar and while he waited for the end the resentment died down in his heart. The piece ended with a trill of octaves in the treble and a final deep octave in the bass. Great applause greeted Mary Jane as, blushing and rolling up her music nervously, she escaped from the room. The most vigorous clapping came from the four young men in the doorway who had gone away to the refreshment-room at the beginning of the piece but had come back when the piano had stopped.

Lancers[7] were arranged. Gabriel found himself partnered with Miss Ivors. She was a frank-mannered talkative young lady, with a freckled face and prominent brown eyes. She did not wear a low-cut bodice and the large brooch which was fixed in the front of her collar bore on it an Irish device.

When they had taken their places she said abruptly:

—I have a crow to pluck with you.

—With me? said Gabriel.

She nodded her head gravely.

—What is it? asked Gabriel, smiling at her solemn manner.

—Who is G. C.? answered Miss Ivors, turning her eyes upon him.

Gabriel coloured and was about to knit his brows, as if he did not understand, when she said bluntly:

—O, innocent Amy! I have found out that you write for *The Daily Express.* Now, aren't you ashamed of yourself?

—Why should I be ashamed of myself? asked Gabriel, blinking his eyes and trying to smile.

—Well, I'm ashamed of you, said Miss Ivors frankly. To say you'd write for a rag like that. I didn't think you were a West Briton.[8]

A look of perplexity appeared on Gabriel's face. It was true that he wrote a literary column every Wednesday in *The Daily Express,* for which he was paid fifteen shillings. But that did not make him a West Briton surely. The books he received for review were almost more welcome than the paltry cheque. He loved to feel the covers and turn over the pages of newly printed books. Nearly every day when his teaching in the college was ended he used to wander down the quays to the second-hand booksellers, to Hickey's on Bachelor's Walk, to Webb's, or Massey's on Aston's Quay, or to O'Clohissey's

---

4. Large tall mirror.
5. Sailor suit, favorite wear for children of both sexes early in the 20th century.
6. Clergyman appointed to assist a parish priest.

7. A square dance for four or more couples.
8. A pejorative term for one who denies a separate Irish nationality and sees Ireland as simply a western extension of Great Britain.

in the by-street. He did not know how to meet her charge. He wanted to say that literature was above politics. But they were friends of many years' standing and their careers had been parallel, first at the University and then as teachers: he could not risk a grandiose phrase with her. He continued blinking his eyes and trying to smile and murmured lamely that he saw nothing political in writing reviews of books.

When their turn to cross had come he was still perplexed and inattentive. Miss Ivors promptly took his hand in a warm grasp and said in a soft friendly tone:

—Of course, I was only joking. Come, we cross now.

When they were together again she spoke of the University question and Gabriel felt more at ease. A friend of hers had shown her his review of Browning's poems. That was how she had found out the secret: but she liked the review immensely. Then she said suddenly:

—O, Mr Conroy, will you come for an excursion to the Aran Isles[9] this summer? We're going to stay there a whole month. It will be splendid out in the Atlantic. You ought to come. Mr Clancy is coming, and Mr Kilkelly and Kathleen Kearney. It would be splendid for Gretta too if she'd come. She's from Connacht,[1] isn't she?

—Her people are, said Gabriel shortly.

—But you will come, won't you? said Miss Ivors, laying her warm hand eagerly on his arm.

—The fact is, said Gabriel, I have already arranged to go—

—Go where? asked Miss Ivors.

—Well, you know, every year I go for a cycling tour with some fellows and so—

—But where? asked Miss Ivors.

—Well, we usually go to France or Belgium or perhaps Germany, said Gabriel awkwardly.

—And why do you go to France and Belgium, said Miss Ivors, instead of visiting your own land?

—Well, said Gabriel, it's partly to keep in touch with the languages and partly for a change.

—And haven't you your own language to keep in touch with—Irish? asked Miss Ivors.

—Well, said Gabriel, if it comes to that, you know, Irish is not my language.

Their neighbours had turned to listen to the cross-examination. Gabriel glanced right and left nervously and tried to keep his good humour under the ordeal which was making a blush invade his forehead.

—And haven't you your own land to visit, continued Miss Ivors, that you know nothing of, your own people, and your own country?

—O, to tell you the truth, retorted Gabriel suddenly, I'm sick of my own country, sick of it!

—Why? asked Miss Ivors.

Gabriel did not answer for his retort had heated him.

—Why? repeated Miss Ivors.

9. Three small islands lying across the entrance to Galway Bay, on the west coast of Ireland.

1. Connacht (or Connaught) is a rural region in the west of Ireland.

They had to go visiting together and, as he had not answered her, Miss Ivors said warmly:

—Of course, you've no answer.

Gabriel tried to cover his agitation by taking part in the dance with great energy. He avoided her eyes for he had seen a sour expression on her face. But when they met in the long chain he was surprised to feel his hand firmly pressed. She looked at him from under her brows for a moment quizzically[2] until he smiled. Then, just as the chain was about to start again, she stood on tiptoe and whispered into his ear:

—West Briton!

When the lancers were over Gabriel went away to a remote corner of the room where Freddy Malins' mother was sitting. She was a stout feeble old woman with white hair. Her voice had a catch in it like her son's and she stuttered slightly. She had been told that Freddy had come and that he was nearly all right. Gabriel asked her whether she had had a good crossing. She lived with her married daughter in Glasgow and came to Dublin on a visit once a year. She answered placidly that she had had a beautiful crossing and that the captain had been most attentive to her. She spoke also of the beautiful house her daughter kept in Glasgow, and of all the nice friends they had there. While her tongue rambled on Gabriel tried to banish from his mind all memory of the unpleasant incident with Miss Ivors. Of course the girl or woman, or whatever she was, was an enthusiast but there was a time for all things. Perhaps he ought not to have answered her like that. But she had no right to call him a West Briton before people, even in joke. She had tried to make him ridiculous before people, heckling him and staring at him with her rabbit's eyes.

He saw his wife making her way towards him through the waltzing couples. When she reached him she said into his ear:

—Gabriel, Aunt Kate wants to know won't you carve the goose as usual. Miss Daly will carve the ham and I'll do the pudding.

—All right, said Gabriel.

—She's sending in the younger ones first as soon as this waltz is over so that we'll have the table to ourselves.

—Were you dancing? asked Gabriel.

—Of course I was. Didn't you see me? What words had you with Molly Ivors?

—No words. Why? Did she say so?

—Something like that. I'm trying to get that Mr D'Arcy to sing. He's full of conceit, I think.

—There were no words, said Gabriel moodily, only she wanted me to go for a trip to the west of Ireland and I said I wouldn't.

His wife clasped her hands excitedly and gave a little jump.

—O, do go, Gabriel, she cried. I'd love to see Galway again.

—You can go if you like, said Gabriel coldly.

She looked at him for a moment, then turned to Mrs Malins and said:

—There's a nice husband for you, Mrs Malins.

While she was threading her way back across the room Mrs Malins, without adverting to the interruption, went on to tell Gabriel what beautiful

2. Teasingly.

places there were in Scotland and beautiful scenery. Her son-in-law brought them every year to the lakes and they used to go fishing. Her son-in-law was a splendid fisher. One day he caught a fish, a beautiful big big fish, and the man in the hotel boiled it for their dinner.

Gabriel hardly heard what she said. Now that supper was coming near he began to think again about his speech and about the quotation. When he saw Freddy Malins coming across the room to visit his mother Gabriel left the chair free for him and retired into the embrasure of the window. The room had already cleared and from the back room came the clatter of plates and knives. Those who still remained in the drawing-room seemed tired of dancing and were conversing quietly in little groups. Gabriel's warm trembling fingers tapped the cold pane of the window. How cool it must be outside! How pleasant it would be to walk out alone, first along by the river and then through the park! The snow would be lying on the branches of the trees and forming a bright cap on the top of the Wellington Monument. How much more pleasant it would be there than at the supper-table!

He ran over the headings of his speech: Irish hospitality, sad memories, the Three Graces,[3] Paris, the quotation from Browning. He repeated to himself a phrase he had written in his review: *One feels that one is listening to a thought-tormented music.* Miss Ivors had praised the review. Was she sincere? Had she really any life of her own behind all her propagandism? There had never been any ill-feeling between them until that night. It unnerved him to think that she would be at the supper-table, looking up at him while he spoke with her critical quizzing eyes. Perhaps she would not be sorry to see him fail in his speech. An idea came into his mind and gave him courage. He would say, alluding to Aunt Kate and Aunt Julia: *Ladies and Gentlemen, the generation which is now on the wane among us may have had its faults but for my part I think it had certain qualities of hospitality, of humour, of humanity, which the new and very serious and hypereducated generation that is growing up around us seems to me to lack.* Very good: that was one for Miss Ivors. What did he care that his aunts were only two ignorant old women?

A murmur in the room attracted his attention. Mr Browne was advancing from the door, gallantly escorting Aunt Julia, who leaned upon his arm, smiling and hanging her head. An irregular musketry of applause escorted her also as far as the piano and then, as Mary Jane seated herself on the stool, and Aunt Julia, no longer smiling, half turned so as to pitch her voice fairly into the room, gradually ceased. Gabriel recognised the prelude. It was that of an old song of Aunt Julia's—*Arrayed for the Bridal.*[4] Her voice, strong and clear in tone, attacked with great spirit the runs which embellish the air and though she sang very rapidly she did not miss even the smallest of the grace notes. To follow the voice, without looking at the singer's face, was to feel and share the excitement of swift and secure flight. Gabriel applauded loudly with all the others at the close of the song and loud applause was borne in from the invisible supper-table. It sounded so genuine that a little colour struggled into Aunt Julia's face as she bent to replace in the music-

3. In Greek mythology, three goddesses—Aglaia, splendor; Euphrosyne, festivity; and Thalia, rejoicing—who together represented loveliness and joy. Gabriel is making a mental note to refer to his two aunts and Mary Jane in this complimentary way.
4. This old song (beginning "Arrayed for the bri-

dal, in beauty behold her") "is replete with long and complicated runs, requiring a sophisticated and gifted singer" (Bowen, *Musical Allusions in the Works of James Joyce,* 1974); the suggestion is that Aunt Julia was a really accomplished singer.

stand the old leather-bound songbook that had her initials on the cover. Freddy Malins, who had listened with his head perched sideways to hear her better, was still applauding when everyone else had ceased and talking animatedly to his mother who nodded her head gravely and slowly in acquiescence. At last, when he could clap no more, he stood up suddenly and hurried across the room to Aunt Julia whose hand he seized and held in both his hands, shaking it when words failed him or the catch in his voice proved too much for him.

—I was just telling my mother, he said, I never heard you sing so well, never. No, I never heard your voice so good as it is to-night. Now! Would you believe that now? That's the truth. Upon my word and honour that's the truth I never heard your voice sound so fresh and so . . . so clear and fresh, never.

Aunt Julia smiled broadly and murmured something about compliments as she released her hand from his grasp. Mr Browne extended his open hand towards her and said to those who were near him in the manner of a showman introducing a prodigy to an audience:

—Miss Julia Morkan, my latest discovery!

He was laughing very heartily at this himself when Freddy Malins turned to him and said:

—Well, Browne, if you're serious you might make a worse discovery. All I can say is I never heard her sing half so well as long as I am coming here. And that's the honest truth.

—Neither did I, said Mr Browne. I think her voice has greatly improved.

Aunt Julia shrugged her shoulders and said with meek pride:

—Thirty years ago I hadn't a bad voice as voices go.

—I often told Julia, said Aunt Kate emphatically, that she was simply thrown away in that choir. But she never would be said by me.

She turned as if to appeal to the good sense of the others against a refractory child while Aunt Julia gazed in front of her, a vague smile of reminiscence playing on her face.

—No, continued Aunt Kate, she wouldn't be said or led by anyone, slaving there in that choir night and day, night and day. Six o'clock on Christmas morning! And all for what?

—Well, isn't it for the honour of God, Aunt Kate? asked Mary Jane, twisting round on the piano-stool and smiling.

Aunt Kate turned fiercely on her niece and said:

—I know all about the honour of God, Mary Jane, but I think it's not at all honourable for the pope to turn out the women out of the choirs that have slaved there all their lives and put little whipper-snappers of boys over their heads. I suppose it is for the good of the Church if the pope does it. But it's not just, Mary Jane, and it's not right.

She had worked herself into a passion and would have continued in defence of her sister for it was a sore subject with her but Mary Jane, seeing that all the dancers had come back, intervened pacifically:

—Now, Aunt Kate, you're giving scandal to Mr Browne who is of the other persuasion.[5]

---

5. I.e., Protestant.

Aunt Kate turned to Mr Browne, who was grinning at this allusion to his religion, and said hastily:

—O, I don't question the pope's being right. I'm only a stupid old woman and I wouldn't presume to do such a thing. But there's such a thing as common everyday politeness and gratitude. And if I were in Julia's place I'd tell that Father Healy straight up to his face . . .

—And besides, Aunt Kate, said Mary Jane, we really are all hungry and when we are hungry we are all very quarrelsome.

—And when we are thirsty we are also quarrelsome, added Mr Browne.

—So that we had better go to supper, said Mary Jane, and finish the discussion afterwards.

On the landing outside the drawing-room Gabriel found his wife and Mary Jane trying to persuade Miss Ivors to stay for supper. But Miss Ivors, who had put on her hat and was buttoning her cloak, would not stay. She did not feel in the least hungry and she had already overstayed her time.

—But only for ten minutes, Molly, said Mrs Conroy. That won't delay you.

—To take a pick itself, said Mary Jane, after all your dancing.

—I really couldn't, said Miss Ivors.

—I am afraid you didn't enjoy yourself at all, said Mary Jane hopelessly.

—Ever so much, I assure you, said Miss Ivors, but you really must let me run off now.

—But how can you get home? asked Mrs Conroy.

—O, it's only two steps up the quay.

Gabriel hesitated a moment and said:

—If you will allow me, Miss Ivors, I'll see you home if you really are obliged to go.

But Miss Ivors broke away from them.

—I won't hear of it, she cried. For goodness sake go in to your suppers and don't mind me. I'm quite well able to take care of myself.

—Well, you're the comical girl, Molly, said Mrs Conroy frankly.

—*Beannacht libh*,[6] cried Miss Ivors, with a laugh, as she ran down the staircase.

Mary Jane gazed after her, a moody puzzled expression on her face, while Mrs Conroy leaned over the banisters to listen for the hall-door. Gabriel asked himself was he the cause of her abrupt departure. But she did not seem to be in ill humour: she had gone away laughing. He stared blankly down the staircase.

At that moment Aunt Kate came toddling out of the supper-room, almost wringing her hands in despair.

—Where is Gabriel? she cried. Where on earth is Gabriel? There's everyone waiting in there, stage to let, and nobody to carve the goose!

—Here I am, Aunt Kate! cried Gabriel, with sudden animation, ready to carve a flock of geese, if necessary.

A fat brown goose lay at one end of the table and at the other end, on a bed of creased paper strewn with sprigs of parsley, lay a great ham, stripped of its outer skin and peppered over with crust crumbs, a neat paper frill round its shin and beside this was a round of spiced beef. Between these rival ends ran parallel lines of side-dishes: two little minsters of jelly, red and yellow; a

6. Blessing on you (Gaelic; literal trans.); good-bye.

shallow dish full of blocks of blancmange and red jam, a large green leaf-shaped dish with a stalk-shaped handle, on which lay bunches of purple raisins and peeled almonds, a companion dish on which lay a solid rectangle of Smyrna figs, a dish of custard topped with grated nutmeg, a small bowl full of chocolates and sweets wrapped in gold and silver papers and a glass vase in which stood some tall celery stalks. In the centre of the table there stood, as sentries to a fruit-stand which upheld a pyramid of oranges and American apples, two squat old-fashioned decanters of cut glass, one containing port and the other dark sherry. On the closed square piano a pudding in a huge yellow dish lay in waiting and behind it were three squads of bottles of stout and ale and minerals, drawn up according to the colours of their uniforms, the first two black, with brown and red labels, the third and smallest squad white, with transverse green sashes.

Gabriel took his seat boldly at the head of the table and, having looked to the edge of the carver, plunged his fork firmly into the goose. He felt quite at ease now for he was an expert carver and liked nothing better than to find himself at the head of a well-laden table.

—Miss Furlong, what shall I send you? he asked. A wing or a slice of the breast?

—Just a small slice of the breast.

—Miss Higgins, what for you?

—O, anything at all, Mr Conroy.

While Gabriel and Miss Daly exchanged plates of goose and plates of ham and spiced beef Lily went from guest to guest with a dish of hot floury potatoes wrapped in a white napkin. This was Mary Jane's idea and she had also suggested apple sauce for the goose but Aunt Kate had said that plain roast goose without apple sauce had always been good enough for her and she hoped she might never eat worse. Mary Jane waited on her pupils and saw that they got the best slices and Aunt Kate and Aunt Julia opened and carried across from the piano bottles of stout and ale for the gentlemen and bottles of minerals for the ladies. There was a great deal of confusion and laughter and noise, the noise of orders and counter-orders, of knives and forks, of corks and glass-stoppers. Gabriel began to carve second helpings as soon as he had finished the first round without serving himself. Everyone protested loudly so that he compromised by taking a long draught of stout for he had found the carving hot work. Mary Jane settled down quietly to her supper but Aunt Kate and Aunt Julia were still toddling round the table, walking on each other's heels, getting in each other's way and giving each other unheeded orders. Mr Browne begged of them to sit down and eat their suppers and so did Gabriel but they said there was time enough so that, at last, Freddy Malins stood up and, capturing Aunt Kate, plumped her down on her chair amid general laughter.

When everyone had been well served Gabriel said, smiling:

—Now, if anyone wants a little more of what vulgar people call stuffing let him or her speak.

A chorus of voices invited him to begin his own supper and Lily came forward with three potatoes which she had reserved for him.

—Very well, said Gabriel amiably, as he took another preparatory draught, kindly forget my existence, ladies and gentlemen, for a few minutes.

He set to his supper and took no part in the conversation with which the table covered Lily's removal of the plates. The subject of talk was the opera company which was then at the Theatre Royal. Mr Bartell D'Arcy, the tenor, a dark-complexioned young man with a smart moustache, praised very highly the leading contralto of the company but Miss Furlong thought she had a rather vulgar style of production. Freddy Malins said there was a negro chieftain singing in the second part of the Gaiety pantomime who had one of the finest tenor voices he had every heard.

—Have you heard him? he asked Mr Bartell D'Arcy across the table.

—No, answered Mr Bartell D'Arcy carelessly.

—Because, Freddy Malins explained, now I'd be curious to hear your opinion of him. I think he has a grand voice.

—It takes Teddy to find out the really good things, said Mr Browne familiarly to the table.

—And why couldn't he have a voice too? asked Freddy Malins sharply. Is it because he's only a black?

Nobody answered this question and Mary Jane led the table back to the legitimate opera. One of her pupils had given her a pass for *Mignon*.[7] Of course it was very fine, she said, but it made her think of poor Georgina Burns. Mr Browne could go back farther still, to the old Italian companies that used to come to Dublin—Tietjens, Ilma de Murzka, Campanini, the great Trebelli, Giuglini, Ravelli, Aramburo. Those were the days, he said, when there was something like singing to be heard in Dublin. He told too of how the top gallery of the old Royal used to be packed night after night, of how one night an Italian tenor had sung five encores to *Let Me Like a Soldier Fall*,[8] introducing a high C every time, and of how the gallery boys would sometimes in their enthusiasm unyoke the horses from the carriage of some great *prima donna* and pull her themselves through the streets to her hotel. Why did they never play the grand old operas now, he asked, *Dinorah, Lucrezia Borgia?*[9] Because they could not get the voices to sing them: that was why.

—O, well, said Mr Bartell D'Arcy, I presume there are as good singers today as there were then.

—Where are they? asked Mr Browne defiantly.

—In London, Paris, Milan, said Mr Bartell d'Arcy warmly. I suppose Caruso,[1] for example, is quite as good, if not better than any of the men you have mentioned.

—Maybe so, said Mr Browne. But I may tell you I doubt it strongly.

—O, I'd give anything to hear Caruso sing, said Mary Jane.

—For me, said Aunt Kate, who had been picking a bone, there was only one tenor. To please me, I mean. But I suppose none of you ever heard of him.

—Who was he, Miss Morkan? asked Mr Bartell D'Arcy politely.

—His name, said Aunt Kate, was Parkinson. I heard him when he was in

7. Opera by Ambroise Thomas first produced in Paris in 1866 and in London in 1870.
8. This song, from the opera *Maritana* by W. Wallace (it actually begins "Yes! let me like a soldier fall"), ends on middle C; it would be a piece of exhibitionism to end on a high C, as Joyce's father, who had a good voice, used to do. Joyce's brother Stanislaus remembered the song as insufferable

rubbish. Mr. Browne is not to be taken seriously as a music critic.
9. An opera by Donizetti, first produced at La Scala, Milan, in 1833. *Dinorah* is an opera by Meyerbeer, first produced in Paris in 1859.
1. Enrico Caruso (1873–1921), the great Italian dramatic tenor.

his prime and I think he had then the purest tenor voice that was ever put into a man's throat.

—Strange, said Mr Bartell d'Arcy. I never even heard of him.

—Yes, yes, Miss Morkan is right, said Mr Browne. I remember hearing of old Parkinson but he's too far back for me.

—A beautiful pure sweet mellow English tenor, said Aunt Kate with enthusiasm.

Gabriel having finished, the huge pudding was transferred to the table. The clatter of forks and spoons began again. Gabriel's wife served out spoonfuls of the pudding and passed the plates down the table. Midway down they were held up by Mary Jane, who replenished them with raspberry or orange jelly or with blancmange and jam. The pudding was of Aunt Julia's making and she received praises for it from all quarters. She herself said that it was not quite brown enough.

—Well, I hope, Miss Morkan, said Mr Browne, that I'm brown enough for you because, you know, I'm all brown.

All the gentlemen, except Gabriel, ate some of the pudding out of compliment to Aunt Julia. As Gabriel never ate sweets the celery had been left for him. Freddy Malins also took a stalk of celery and ate it with his pudding. He had been told that celery was a capital thing for the blood and he was just then under doctor's care. Mrs Malins, who had been silent all through the supper, said that her son was going down to Mount Melleray in a week or so. The table then spoke of Mount Melleray, how bracing the air was down there, how hospitable the monks were and how they never asked for a penny-piece from their guests.

—And do you mean to say, asked Mr Browne incredulously, that a chap can go down there and put up there as if it were a hotel and live on the fat of the land and then come away without paying a farthing?

—O, most people give some donation to the monastery when they leave, said Mary Jane.

—I wish we had an institution like that in our Church, said Mr Browne candidly.

He was astonished to hear that the monks never spoke, got up at two in the morning and slept in their coffins. He asked what they did it for.

—That's the rule of the order, said Aunt Kate firmly.

—Yes, but why? asked Mr Browne.

Aunt Kate repeated that it was the rule, that was all. Mr Browne still seemed not to understand. Freddy Malins explained to him, as best he could, that the monks were trying to make up for the sins committed by all the sinners in the outside world. The explanation was not very clear for Mr Browne grinned and said:

—I like that idea very much but wouldn't a comfortable spring bed do them as well as a coffin?

—The coffin, said Mary Jane, is to remind them of their last end.

As the subject had grown lugubrious it was buried in a silence of the table during which Mrs Malins could be heard saying to her neighbour in an indistinct undertone:

—They are very good men, the monks, very pious men.

The raisins and almonds and figs and apples and oranges and chocolates and sweets were now passed about the table and Aunt Julia invited all the guests to have either port or sherry. At first Mr Bartell D'Arcy refused to take either but one of his neighbours nudged him and whispered something to him upon which he allowed his glass to be filled. Gradually as the last glasses were being filled the conversation ceased. A pause followed, broken only by the noise of the wine and by unsettlings of chairs. The Misses Morkan, all three, looked down at the tablecloth. Someone coughed once or twice and then a few gentlemen patted the table gently as a signal for silence. The silence came and Gabriel pushed back his chair and stood up.

The patting at once grew louder in encouragement and then ceased altogether. Gabriel leaned his ten trembling fingers on the tablecloth and smiled nervously at the company. Meeting a row of upturned faces he raised his eyes to the chandelier. The piano was playing a waltz tune and he could hear the skirts sweeping against the drawing-room door. People, perhaps, were standing in the snow on the quay outside, gazing up at the lighted windows and listening to the waltz music. The air was pure there. In the distance lay the park where the trees were weighted with snow. The Wellington Monument wore a gleaming cap of snow that flashed westward over the white field of Fifteen Acres.

He began:

—Ladies and Gentlemen.

—It has fallen to my lot this evening, as in years past, to perform a very pleasing task but a task for which I am afraid my poor powers as a speaker are all too inadequate.

—No, no! said Mr Browne.

—But, however that may be, I can only ask you to-night to take the will for the deed and to lend me your attention for a few moments while I endeavour to express to you in words what my feelings are on this occasion.

—Ladies and Gentlemen. It is not the first time that we have gathered together under this hospitable roof, around this hospitable board. It is not the first time that we have been the recipients—or perhaps, I had better say, the victims—of the hospitality of certain good ladies.

He made a circle in the air with his arm and paused. Everyone laughed or smiled at Aunt Kate and Aunt Julia and Mary Jane who all turned crimson with pleasure. Gabriel went on more boldly:

—I feel more strongly with every recurring year that our country has no tradition which does it so much honour and which it should guard so jealously as that of its hospitality. It is a tradition that is unique as far as my experience goes (and I have visited not a few places abroad) among the modern nations. Some would say, perhaps, that with us it is rather a failing than anything to be boasted of. But granted even that, it is, to my mind, a princely failing, and one that I trust will long be cultivated among us. Of one thing, at least, I am sure. As long as this one roof shelters the good ladies aforesaid—and I wish from my heart it may do so for many and many a long year to come—the tradition of genuine warm-hearted courteous Irish hospitality, which our forefathers have handed down to us and which we in turn must hand down to our descendants, is still alive among us.

A hearty murmur of assent ran round the table. It shot through Gabriel's mind that Miss Ivors was not there and that she had gone away discourteously: and he said with confidence in himself:

—Ladies and Gentlemen.

—A new generation is growing up in our midst, a generation actuated by new ideas and new principles. It is serious and enthusiastic for these new ideas and its enthusiasm, even when it is misdirected, is, I believe, in the main sincere. But we are living in a sceptical and, if I may use the phrase, a thought-tormented age: and sometimes I fear that this new generation, educated or hypereducated as it is, will lack those qualities of humanity, of hospitality, of kindly humour which belonged to an older day. Listening tonight to the names of all those great singers of the past it seemed to me, I must confess, that we were living in a less spacious age. Those days might, without exaggeration, be called spacious days: and if they are gone beyond recall let us hope, at least, that in gatherings such as this we shall still speak of them with pride and affection, still cherish in our hearts the memory of those dead and gone great ones whose fame the world will not willingly let die.

—Hear, hear! said Mr Browne loudly.

—But yet, continued Gabriel, his voice falling into a softer inflection, there are always in gatherings such as this sadder thoughts that will recur to our minds: thoughts of the past, of youth, of changes, of absent faces that we miss here to-night. Our path through life is strewn with many such sad memories: and were we to brood upon them always we could not find the heart to go on bravely with our work among the living. We have all of us living duties and living affections which claim, and rightly claim, our strenuous endeavours.

—Therefore, I will not linger on the past. I will not let any gloomy moralising intrude upon us here to-night. Here we are gathered together for a brief moment from the bustle and rush of our everyday routine. We are met here as friends, in the spirit of good-fellowship, as colleagues, also to a certain extent, in the true spirit of *camaraderie,* and as the guests of—what shall I call them?—the Three Graces of the Dublin musical world.

The table burst into applause and laughter at this sally. Aunt Julia vainly asked each of her neighbours in turn to tell her what Gabriel had said.

—He says we are the Three Graces, Aunt Julia, said Mary Jane.

Aunt Julia did not understand but she looked up, smiling, at Gabriel, who continued in the same vein:

—Ladies and Gentlemen.

—I will not attempt to play to-night the part that Paris played on another occasion. I will not attempt to choose between them. The task would be an invidious one and one beyond my poor powers. For when I view them in turn, whether it be our chief hostess herself, whose good heart, whose too good heart, has become a byword with all who know her, or her sister, who seems to be gifted with perennial youth and whose singing must have been a surprise and a revelation to us all to-night, or, last but not least, when I consider our youngest hostess, talented, cheerful, hard-working and the best of nieces, I confess, Ladies and Gentlemen, that I do not know to which of them I should award the prize.

Gabriel glanced down at his aunts and, seeing the large smile on Aunt Julia's face and the tears which had risen to Aunt Kate's eyes, hastened to his close. He raised his glass of port gallantly, while every member of the company fingered a glass expectantly, and said loudly:

—Let us toast them all three together. Let us drink to their health, wealth, long life, happiness and prosperity and may they long continue to hold the proud and self-won position which they hold in their profession and the position of honour and affection which they hold in our hearts.

All the guests stood up, glass in hand, and, turning towards the three seated ladies, sang in unison, with Mr Browne as leader:

> *For they are jolly gay fellows,*
> *For they are jolly gay fellows,*
> *For they are jolly gay fellows,*
> *Which nobody can deny.*

Aunt Kate was making frank use of her handkerchief and even Aunt Julia seemed moved. Freddy Malins beat time with his pudding-fork and the singers turned towards one another, as if in melodious conference, while they sang, with emphasis:

> *Unless he tells a lie,*
> *Unless he tells a lie.*

Then, turning once more towards their hostesses, they sang:

> *For they are jolly gay fellows,*
> *For they are jolly gay fellows,*
> *For they are jolly gay fellows,*
> *Which nobody can deny.*

The acclamation which followed was taken up beyond the door of the supper-room by many of the other guests and renewed time after time, Freddy Malins acting as officer with his fork on high.

The piercing morning air came into the hall where they were standing so that Aunt Kate said:

—Close the door, somebody. Mrs Malins will get her death of cold.

—Browne is out there, Aunt Kate, said Mary Jane.

—Browne is everywhere, said Aunt Kate, lowering her voice.

Mary Jane laughed at her tone.

—Really, she said archly, he is very attentive.

—He has been laid on here like the gas, said Aunt Kate in the same tone, all during the Christmas.

She laughed herself this time good-humouredly and then added quickly:

—But tell him to come in, Mary Jane, and close the door. I hope to goodness he didn't hear me.

At that moment the hall-door was opened and Mr Browne came in from the doorstep, laughing as if his heart would break. He was dressed in a long green overcoat with mock astrakhan cuffs and collar and wore on his head an oval fur cap. He pointed down the snow-covered quay from where the sound of shrill prolonged whistling was borne in.

—Teddy will have all the cabs in Dublin out, he said.

Gabriel advanced from the little pantry behind the office, struggling into his overcoat and, looking round the hall, said:

—Gretta not down yet?

—She's getting on her things, Gabriel, said Aunt Kate.

—Who's playing up there? asked Gabriel.

—Nobody. They're all gone.

—O no, Aunt Kate, said Mary Jane. Bartell D'Arcy and Miss O'Callaghan aren't gone yet.

—Someone is strumming at the piano, anyhow, said Gabriel.

Mary Jane glanced at Gabriel and Mr Browne and said with a shiver:

—It makes me feel cold to look at you two gentlemen muffled up like that. I wouldn't like to face your journey home at this hour.

—I'd like nothing better this minute, said Mr Browne stoutly, than a rattling fine walk in the country or a fast drive with a good spanking goer between the shafts.

—We used to have a very good horse and trap[2] at home, said Aunt Julia sadly.

—The never-to-be-forgotten Johnny, said Mary Jane, laughing.

Aunt Kate and Gabriel laughed too.

—Why, what was wonderful about Johnny? asked Mr Browne.

—The late lamented Patrick Morkan, our grandfather, that is, explained Gabriel, commonly known in his later years as the old gentleman, was a glueboiler.

—O, now, Gabriel, said Aunt Kate, laughing, he had a starch mill.

—Well, glue or starch, said Gabriel, the old gentleman had a horse by the name of Johnny. And Johnny used to work in the old gentleman's mill, walking round and round in order to drive the mill. That was all very well; but now comes the tragic part about Johnny. One fine day the old gentleman thought he'd like to drive out with the quality[3] to a military review in the park.

—The Lord have mercy on his soul, said Aunt Kate compassionately.

—Amen, said Gabriel. So the old gentleman, as I said, harnessed Johnny and put on his very best tall hat and his very best stock collar and drove out in grand style from his ancestral mansion somewhere near Back Lane, I think.

Everyone laughed, even Mrs Malins, at Gabriel's manner and Aunt Kate said:

—O now, Gabriel, he didn't live in Back Lane, really. Only the mill was there.

—Out from the mansion of his forefathers, continued Gabriel, he drove with Johnny. And everything went on beautifully until Johnny came in sight of King Billy's statue: and whether he fell in love with the horse King Billy sits on or whether he thought he was back again in the mill, anyhow he began to walk round the statue.

Gabriel paced in a circle round the hall in his goloshes amid the laughter of the others.

—Round and round he went, said Gabriel, and the old gentleman, who was a very pompous old gentleman, was highly indignant. *Go on, sir! What do you mean, sir? Johnny! Johnny! Most extraordinary conduct! Can't understand the horse!*

The peals of laughter which followed Gabriel's imitation of the incident were interrupted by a resounding knock at the hall-door. Mary Jane ran to

2. A two-wheeled horse-drawn carriage on springs.   3. People of rank or high social position.

open it and let in Freddy Malins. Freddy Malins, with his hat well back on his head and his shoulders humped with cold, was puffing and steaming after his exertions.

—I could only get one cab, he said.

—O, we'll find another along the quay, said Gabriel.

—Yes, said Aunt Kate. Better not keep Mrs Malins standing in the draught.

Mrs Malins was helped down the front steps by her son and Mr Browne and, after many manœuvres, hoisted into the cab. Freddy Malins clambered in after her and spent a long time settling her on the seat, Mr Browne helping him with advice. At last she was settled comfortably and Freddy Malins invited Mr Browne into the cab. There was a good deal of confused talk, and then Mr Browne got into the cab. The cabman settled his rug over his knees, and bent down for the address. The confusion grew greater and the cabman was directed differently by Freddy Malins and Mr Browne, each of whom had his head out through a window of the cab. The difficulty was to know where to drop Mr Browne along the route and Aunt Kate, Aunt Julia and Mary Jane helped the discussion from the doorstep with cross-directions and contradictions and abundance of laughter. As for Freddy Malins he was speechless with laughter. He popped his head in and out of the window every moment, to the great danger of his hat, and told his mother how the discussion was progressing till at last Mr Browne shouted to the bewildered cabman above the din of everybody's laughter:

—Do you know Trinity College?

—Yes, sir, said the cabman.

—Well, drive bang up against Trinity College gates, said Mr Browne, and then we'll tell you where to go. You understand now?

—Yes, sir, said the cabman.

—Make like a bird for Trinity College.

—Right, sir, cried the cabman.

The horse was whipped up and the cab rattled off along the quay amid a chorus of laughter and adieus.

Gabriel had not gone to the door with the others. He was in a dark part of the hall gazing up the staircase. A woman was standing near the top of the first flight, in the shadow also. He could not see her face but he could see the terracotta and salmonpink panels of her skirt which the shadow made appear black and white. It was his wife. She was leaning on the banisters, listening to something. Gabriel was surprised at her stillness and strained his ear to listen also. But he could hear little save the noise of laughter and dispute on the front steps, a few chords struck on the piano and a few notes of a man's voice singing.

He stood still in the gloom of the hall, trying to catch the air that the voice was singing and gazing up at his wife. There was grace and mystery in her attitude as if she were a symbol of something. He asked himself what is a woman standing on the stairs in the shadow, listening to distant music, a symbol of. If he were a painter he would paint her in that attitude. Her blue felt hat would show off the bronze of her hair against the darkness and the dark panels of her skirt would show off the light ones. *Distant Music* he would call the picture if he were a painter.

The hall-door was closed; and Aunt Kate, Aunt Julia and Mary Jane came down the hall, still laughing.

—Well, isn't Freddy terrible? said Mary Jane. He's really terrible.

Gabriel said nothing but pointed up the stairs towards where his wife was standing. Now that the hall-door was closed the voice and the piano could be heard more clearly. Gabriel held up his hand for them to be silent. The song seemed to be in the old Irish tonality and the singer seemed uncertain both of his words and of his voice. The voice, made plaintive by distance and by the singer's hoarseness, faintly illuminated the cadence of the air with words expressing grief:

> O, the rain falls on my heavy locks
> And the dew wets my skin,
> My babe lies cold . . .

—O, exclaimed Mary Jane. It's Bartell D'Arcy singing and he wouldn't sing all the night. O, I'll get him to sing a song before he goes.

—O do, Mary Jane, said Aunt Kate.

Mary Jane brushed past the others and ran to the staircase but before she reached it the singing stopped and the piano was closed abruptly.

—O, what a pity! she cried. Is he coming down, Gretta?

Gabriel heard his wife answer yes and saw her come down towards them. A few steps behind her were Mr Bartell D'Arcy and Miss O'Callaghan.

—O, Mr D'Arcy, cried Mary Jane, it's downright mean of you to break off like that when we were all in raptures listening to you.

—I have been at him all the evening, said Miss O'Callaghan, and Mrs Conroy too and he told us he had a dreadful cold and couldn't sing.

—O, Mr D'Arcy, said Aunt Kate, now that was a great fib to tell.

—Can't you see that I'm as hoarse as a crow? said Mr D'Arcy roughly.

He went into the pantry hastily and put on his overcoat. The others, taken aback by his rude speech, could find nothing to say. Aunt Kate wrinkled her brows and made signs to the others to drop the subject. Mr D'Arcy stood swathing his neck carefully and frowning.

—It's the weather, said Aunt Julia, after a pause.

—Yes, everybody has colds, said Aunt Kate readily, everybody.

—They say, said Mary Jane, we haven't had snow like it for thirty years; and I read this morning in the newspapers that the snow is general all over Ireland.

—I love the look of snow, said Aunt Julia sadly.

—So do I, said Miss O'Callaghan. I think Christmas is never really Christmas unless we have the snow on the ground.

—But poor Mr D'Arcy doesn't like the snow, said Aunt Kate, smiling.

Mr D'Arcy came from the pantry, full swathed and buttoned, and in a repentant tone told them the history of his cold. Everyone gave him advice and said it was a great pity and urged him to be very careful of his throat in the night air. Gabriel watched his wife who did not join in the conversation. She was standing right under the dusty fanlight and the flame of the gas lit up the rich bronze of her hair which he had seen her drying at the fire a few days before. She was in the same attitude and seemed unaware of the talk about her. At last she turned towards them and Gabriel saw that there was colour on her cheeks and that her eyes were shining. A sudden tide of joy went leaping out of his heart.

—Mr D'Arcy, she said, what is the name of that song you were singing?

—It's called *The Lass of Aughrim*,[4] said Mr D'Arcy, but I couldn't remember it properly. Why? Do you know it?

—*The Lass of Aughrim,* she repeated. I couldn't think of the name.

—It's a very nice air, said Mary Jane. I'm sorry you were not in voice to-night.

—Now, Mary Jane, said Aunt Kate, don't annoy Mr D'Arcy. I won't have him annoyed.

Seeing that all were ready to start she shepherded them to the door where good-night was said:

—Well, good-night, Aunt Kate, and thanks for the pleasant evening.

—Good-night, Gabriel. Good-night, Gretta!

—Good-night, Aunt Kate, and thanks ever so much. Good-night, Aunt Julia.

—O, good-night, Gretta, I didn't see you.

—Good-night, Mr D'Arcy. Good-night, Miss O'Callaghan.

—Good-night, Miss Morkan.

—Good-night, again.

—Good-night, all. Safe home.

—Good-night. Good-night.

The morning was still dark. A dull yellow light brooded over the houses and the river; and the sky seemed to be descending. It was slushy underfoot; and only streaks and patches of snow lay on the roofs, on the parapets of the quay and on the area railings. The lamps were still burning redly in the murky air and, across the river, the palace of the Four Courts stood out menacingly against the heavy sky.

She was walking on before him with Mr Bartell D'Arcy, her shoes in a brown parcel tucked under one arm and her hands holding her skirt up from the slush. She had no longer any grace of attitude but Gabriel's eyes were still bright with happiness. The blood went bounding along his veins; and the thoughts went rioting through his brain, proud, joyful, tender, valorous.

She was walking on before him so lightly and so erect that he longed to run after her noiselessly, catch her by the shoulders and say something foolish and affectionate into her ear. She seemed to him so frail that he longed to defend her against something and then to be alone with her. Moments of their secret life together burst like stars upon his memory. A heliotrope envelope was lying beside his breakfast-cup and he was caressing it with his hand. Birds were twittering in the ivy and the sunny web of the curtain was shimmering along the floor: he could not eat for happiness. They were standing on the crowded platform and he was placing a ticket inside the warm palm of her glove. He was standing with her in the cold, looking in through a grated window at a man making bottles in a roaring furnace. It was very cold. Her face, fragrant in the cold air, was quite close to his; and suddenly she called out to the man at the furnace:

—Is the fire hot, sir?

But the man could not hear her with the noise of the furnace. It was just as well. He might have answered rudely.

A wave of yet more tender joy escaped from his heart and went coursing

4. An Irish version of a ballad about a girl deserted by her lover whom she later tries to find, bringing the baby she had by him. Other versions are called *Love Gregory* and *Lord Gregory* (the name of the deserting lover), *The Lass of Lochryan,* and *The Lass of Ocram.*

in warm flood along his arteries. Like the tender fires of stars moments of their life together, that no one knew of or would ever know of, broke upon and illumined his memory. He longed to recall to her those moments, to make her forget the years of their dull existence together and remember only their moments of ecstasy. For the years, he felt, had not quenched his soul or hers. Their children, his writing, her household cares had not quenched all their souls' tender fire. In one letter that he had written to her then he had said: *Why is it that words like these seem to me so dull and cold? Is it because there is no word tender enough to be your name?*

Like distant music these words that he had written years before were borne towards him from the past. He longed to be alone with her. When the others had gone away, when he and she were in their room in the hotel, then they would be alone together. He would call her softly:

—Gretta!

Perhaps she would not hear at once: she would be undressing. Then something in his voice would strike her. She would turn and look at him. . . .

At the corner of Winetavern Street they met a cab. He was glad of its rattling noise as it saved him from conversation. She was looking out of the window and seemed tired. The others spoke only a few words, pointing out some building or street. The horse galloped along wearily under the murky morning sky, dragging his old rattling box after his heels, and Gabriel was again in a cab with her, galloping to catch the boat, galloping to their honeymoon.

As the cab drove across O'Connell[5] Bridge Miss O'Callaghan said:

—They say you never cross O'Connell Bridge without seeing a white horse.

—I see a white man this time, said Gabriel.

—Where? asked Mr Bartell D'Arcy.

Gabriel pointed to the statue, on which lay patches of snow. Then he nodded familiarly to it and waved his hand.

—Good-night, Dan, he said gaily.

When the cab drew up before the hotel Gabriel jumped out and, in spite of Mr Bartell D'Arcy's protest, paid the driver. He gave the man a shilling over his fare. The man saluted and said:

—A prosperous New Year to you, sir.

—The same to you, said Gabriel cordially.

She leaned for a moment on his arm in getting out of the cab and while standing at the curbstone, bidding the others good-night. She leaned lightly on his arm, as lightly as when she had danced with him a few hours before. He had felt proud and happy then, happy that she was his, proud of her grace and wifely carriage. But now, after the kindling again of so many memories, the first touch of her body, musical and strange and perfumed, sent through him a keen pang of lust. Under cover of her silence he pressed her arm closely to his side; and, as they stood at the hotel door, he felt that they had escaped from their lives and duties, escaped from home and friends and run away together with wild and radiant hearts to a new adventure.

An old man was dozing in a great hooded chair in the hall. He lit a candle in the office and went before them to the stairs. They followed him in silence,

5. Daniel O'Connell (1775–1847), Irish nationalist, statesman, and orator. His statue stands by O'Connell Bridge in Dublin.

their feet falling in soft thuds on the thickly carpeted stairs. She mounted the stairs behind the porter, her head bowed in the ascent, her frail shoulders curved as with a burden, her skirt girt tightly about her. He could have flung his arms about her hips and held her still for his arms were trembling with desire to seize her and only the stress of his nails against the palms of his hands held the wild impulse of his body in check. The porter halted on the stairs to settle his guttering candle. They halted too on the steps below him. In the silence Gabriel could hear the falling of the molten wax into the tray and the thumping of his own heart against his ribs.

The porter led them along a corridor and opened a door. Then he set his unstable candle down on a toilet-table and asked at what hour they were to be called in the morning.

—Eight, said Gabriel.

The porter pointed to the tap of the electric-light and began a muttered apology but Gabriel cut him short.

—We don't want any light. We have light enough from the street. And I say, he added, pointing to the candle, you might remove that handsome article, like a good man.

The porter took up his candle again, but slowly for he was surprised by such a novel idea. Then he mumbled good-night and went out. Gabriel shot the lock to.

A ghostly light from the street lamp lay in a long shaft from one window to the door. Gabriel threw his overcoat and hat on a couch and crossed the room towards the window. He looked down into the street in order that his emotion might calm a little. Then he turned and leaned against a chest of drawers with his back to the light. She had taken off her hat and cloak and was standing before a large swinging mirror, unhooking her waist.[6] Gabriel paused for a few moments, watching her, and then said:

—Gretta!

She turned away from the mirror slowly and walked along the shaft of light towards him. Her face looked so serious and weary that the words would not pass Gabriel's lips. No, it was not the moment yet.

—You looked tired, he said.

—I am a little, she answered.

—You don't feel ill or weak?

—No, tired: that's all.

She went on to the window and stood there, looking out. Gabriel waited again and then, fearing that diffidence was about to conquer him, he said abruptly:

—By the way, Gretta!

—What is it?

—You know that poor fellow Malins? he said quickly.

—Yes. What about him?

—Well, poor fellow, he's a decent sort of chap after all, continued Gabriel in a false voice. He gave me back that sovereign I lent him and I didn't expect it really. It's a pity he wouldn't keep away from that Browne, because he's not a bad fellow at heart.

6. Shirtwaist; a tailored blouse.

He was trembling now with annoyance. Why did she seem so abstracted? He did not know how he could begin. Was she annoyed, too, about something? If she would only turn to him or come to him of her own accord! To take her as she was would be brutal. No, he must see some ardour in her eyes first. He longed to be master of her strange mood.

—When did you lend him the pound? she asked, after a pause.

Gabriel strove to restrain himself from breaking out into brutal language about the sottish Malins and his pound. He longed to cry to her from his soul, to crush her body against his, to overmaster her. But he said:

—O, at Christmas, when he opened that little Christmas-card shop in Henry Street.

He was in such a fever of rage and desire that he did not hear her come from the window. She stood before him for an instant, looking at him strangely. Then, suddenly raising herself on tiptoe and resting her hands lightly on his shoulders, she kissed him.

—You are a very generous person, Gabriel, she said.

Gabriel, trembling with delight at her sudden kiss and at the quaintness of her phrase, put his hands on her hair and began smoothing it back, scarcely touching it with his fingers. The washing had made it fine and brilliant. His heart was brimming over with happiness. Just when he was wishing for it she had come to him of her own accord. Perhaps her thoughts had been running with his. Perhaps she had felt the impetuous desire that was in him and then the yielding mood had come upon her. Now that she had fallen to him so easily he wondered why he had been so diffident.

He stood, holding her head between his hands. Then, slipping one arm swiftly about her body and drawing her towards him, he said softly:

—Gretta dear, what are you thinking about?

She did not answer nor yield wholly to his arm. He said again, softly:

—Tell me what it is, Gretta. I think I know what is the matter. Do I know?

She did not answer at once. Then she said in an outburst of tears:

—O, I am thinking about that song, *The Lass of Aughrim*.

She broke loose from him and ran to the bed and, throwing her arms across the bed-rail, hid her face. Gabriel stood stock-still for a moment in astonishment and then followed her. As he passed in the way of the cheval-glass he caught sight of himself in full length, his broad, well-filled shirt-front, the face whose expression always puzzled him when he saw it in a mirror and his glimmering gilt-rimmed eyeglasses. He halted a few paces from her and said:

—What about the song? Why does that make you cry?

She raised her head from her arms and dried her eyes with the back of her hand like a child. A kinder note than he had intended went into his voice.

—Why, Gretta? he asked.

—I am thinking about a person long ago who used to sing that song.

—And who was the person long ago? asked Gabriel, smiling.

—It was a person I used to know in Galway when I was living with my grandmother, she said.

The smile passed away from Gabriel's face. A dull anger began to gather again at the back of his mind and the dull fires of his lust began to glow angrily in his veins.

—Someone you were in love with? he asked ironically.

—It was a young boy I used to know, she answered, named Michael Furey. He used to sing that song, *The Lass of Aughrim*. He was very delicate.

Gabriel was silent. He did not wish her to think that he was interested in this delicate boy.

—I can see him so plainly, she said after a moment. Such eyes as he had: big dark eyes! And such an expression in them—an expression!

—O then, you were in love with him? said Gabriel.

—I used to go out walking with him, she said, when I was in Galway.

A thought flew across Gabriel's mind.

—Perhaps that was why you wanted to go to Galway with that Ivors girl? he said coldly.

She looked at him and asked in surprise:

—What for?

Her eyes made Gabriel feel awkward. He shrugged his shoulders and said:

—How do I know! To see him perhaps.

She looked away from him along the shaft of light towards the window in silence.

—He is dead, she said at length. He died when he was only seventeen. Isn't it a terrible thing to die so young as that?

—What was he? asked Gabriel, still ironically.

—He was in the gasworks, she said.

Gabriel felt humiliated by the failure of his irony and by the evocation of this figure from the dead, a boy in the gasworks. While he had been full of memories of their secret life together, full of tenderness and joy and desire, she had been comparing him in her mind with another. A shameful consciousness of his own person assailed him. He saw himself as a ludicrous figure, acting as a pennyboy for his aunts, a nervous well-meaning sentimentalist, orating to vulgarians and idealising his own clownish lusts, the pitiable fatuous fellow he had caught a glimpse of in the mirror. Instinctively he turned his back more to the light lest she might see the shame that burned upon his forehead.

He tried to keep up his tone of cold interrogation but his voice when he spoke was humble and indifferent.

—I suppose you were in love with this Michael Furey, Gretta, he said.

—I was great with him at that time, she said.

Her voice was veiled and sad. Gabriel, feeling now how vain it would be to try to lead her whither he had purposed, caressed one of her hands and said, also sadly:

—And what did he die of so young, Gretta? Consumption, was it?

—I think he died for me, she answered.

A vague terror seized Gabriel at this answer as if, at that hour when he had hoped to triumph, some impalpable and vindictive being was coming against him, gathering forces against him in its vague world. But he shook himself free of it with an effort of reason and continued to caress her hand. He did not question her again for he felt that she would tell him of herself. Her hand was warm and moist: it did not respond to his touch but he continued to caress it just as he had caressed her first letter to him that spring morning.

—It was in the winter, she said, about the beginning of the winter when

I was going to leave my grandmother's and come up here to the convent. And he was ill at the time in his lodgings in Galway and wouldn't be let out and his people in Oughterard were written to. He was in decline, they said, or something like that. I never knew rightly.

She paused for a moment and sighed.

—Poor fellow, she said. He was very fond of me and he was such a gentle boy. We used to go out together, walking, you know, Gabriel, like the way they do in the country. He was going to study singing only for his health. He had a very good voice, poor Michael Furey.

—Well; and then? asked Gabriel.

—And then when it came to the time for me to leave Galway and come up to the convent he was much worse and I wouldn't be let see him so I wrote a letter saying I was going up to Dublin and would be back in the summer and hoping he would be better then.

She paused for a moment to get her voice under control and then went on:

—Then the night before I left I was in my grandmother's house in Nuns' Island, packing up, and I heard gravel thrown up against the window. The window was so wet I couldn't see so I ran downstairs as I was and slipped out the back into the garden and there was the poor fellow at the end of the garden, shivering.

—And did you not tell him to go back? asked Gabriel.

—I implored him to go home at once and told him he would get his death in the rain. But he said he did not want to live. I can see his eyes as well as well! He was standing at the end of the wall where there was a tree.

—And did he go home? asked Gabriel.

—Yes, he went home. And when I was only a week in the convent he died and he was buried in Oughterard where his people came from. O, the day I heard that, that he was dead!

She stopped, choking with sobs, and overcome by emotion, flung herself face downward on the bed, sobbing in the quilt. Gabriel held her hand for a moment longer, irresolutely, and then, shy of intruding on her grief, let it fall gently and walked quietly to the window.

She was fast asleep.

Gabriel, leaning on his elbow, looked for a few moments unresentfully on her tangled hair and half-open mouth, listening to her deep-drawn breath. So she had had that romance in her life: a man had died for her sake. It hardly pained him now to think how poor a part he, her husband, had played in her life. He watched her while she slept as though he and she had never lived together as man and wife. His curious eyes rested long upon her face and on her hair: and, as he thought of what she must have been then, in that time of her first girlish beauty, a strange friendly pity for her entered his soul. He did not like to say even to himself that her face was no longer beautiful but he knew that it was no longer the face for which Michael Furey had braved death.

Perhaps she had not told him all the story. His eyes moved to the chair over which she had thrown some of her clothes. A petticoat string dangled to the floor. One boot stood upright, its limp upper fallen down: the fellow of it lay upon its side. He wondered at his riot of emotions of an hour before.

From what had it proceeded? From his aunt's supper, from his own foolish speech, from the wine and dancing, the merry-making when saying good-night in the hall, the pleasure of the walk along the river in the snow. Poor Aunt Julia! She, too, would soon be a shade with the shade of Patrick Morkan and his horse. He had caught that haggard look upon her face for a moment when she was singing *Arrayed for the Bridal*. Soon, perhaps, he would be sitting in that same drawing-room, dressed in black, his silk hat on his knees. The blinds would be drawn down and Aunt Kate would be sitting beside him, crying and blowing her nose and telling him how Julia had died. He would cast about in his mind for some words that might console her, and would find only lame and useless ones. Yes, yes: that would happen very soon.

The air of the room chilled his shoulders. He stretched himself cautiously along under the sheets and lay down beside his wife. One by one they were all becoming shades. Better pass boldly into that other world, in the full glory of some passion, than fade and wither dismally with age. He thought of how she who lay beside him had locked in her heart for so many years that image of her lover's eyes when he had told her that he did not wish to live.

Generous tears filled Gabriel's eyes. He had never felt like that himself towards any woman but he knew that such a feeling must be love. The tears gathered more thickly in his eyes and in the partial darkness he imagined he saw the form of a young man standing under a dripping tree. Other forms were near. His soul had approached that region where dwell the vast hosts of the dead. He was conscious of, but could not apprehend, their wayward and flickering existence. His own identity was fading out into a grey impalpable world: the solid world itself which these dead had one time reared and lived in was dissolving and dwindling.

A few light taps upon the pane made him turn to the window. It had begun to snow again. He watched sleepily the flakes, silver and dark, falling obliquely against the lamplight. The time had come for him to set out on his journey westward. Yes, the newspapers were right: snow was general all over Ireland. It was falling on every part of the dark central plain, on the treeless hills, falling softly upon the Bog of Allen[7] and, farther westward, softly falling into the dark mutinous Shannon waves. It was falling, too, upon every part of the lonely churchyard on the hill where Michael Furey lay buried. It lay thickly drifted on the crooked crosses and headstones, on the spears of the little gate, on the barren thorns. His soul swooned slowly as he heard the snow falling faintly through the universe and faintly falling, like the descent of their last end, upon all the living and the dead.

1914

---

7. The name given to many separate peat bogs between the rivers Liffey (which runs through Dublin) and Shannon (which runs through the central plain of Ireland).

From Ulysses[1]

[PROTEUS][2]

Ineluctable modality of the visible: at least that if no more, thought through my eyes.[3] Signatures of all things[4] I am here to read, seaspawn and seawrack, the nearing tide, that rusty boot. Snotgreen, bluesilver, rust: coloured signs. Limits of the diaphane.[5] But he adds: in bodies. Then he was aware of them bodies before of them coloured. How? By knocking his sconce against them, sure. Go easy. Bald he was and a millionaire, *maestro di color che sanno.*[6] Limit of the diaphane in. Why in? Diaphane, adiaphane.[7] If you can put your five fingers through it, it is a gate, if not a door. Shut your eyes and see.

Stephen closed his eyes to hear his boots crush crackling wrack and shells. You are walking through it howsomever. I am, a stride at a time. A very short space of time through very short times of space. Five, six: the *Nacheinander.*[8] Exactly: and that is the ineluctable modality of the audible. Open your eyes. No. Jesus! If I fell over a cliff that beetles o'er his base,[9] fell through the *Nebeneinander*[1] ineluctably. I am getting on nicely in the dark. My ash sword hangs at my side. Tap with it: they do.[2] My two feet in his boots[3] are at the

---

1. *Ulysses* was first published in book form on Feb. 2, 1922, Joyce's fortieth birthday. The text given here has been collated with the 1932 Odyssey Press edition.
2. *Proteus* is so titled because of the deliberate analogies that exist between it and the description of Proteus in *Odyssey* 4. (Joyce did not title any of the episodes in *Ulysses,* but the names are his; he used them in correspondence and in talk with friends.)

In Homer's *Odyssey,* Proteus is the changing sea god who continually alters his shape: when Telemachus, the son of Ulysses, asks Menelaus for help in finding his father, Menelaus tells him that he encountered Proteus by the seashore on the island of Pharos "in front of Egypt," and that, by holding on to him while he changed from one shape to another, he was able to force him to tell what had happened to Ulysses and the other Greek heroes of the Trojan war. In Joyce's narrative, Stephen Dedalus (who, like Homer's Telemachus, is looking for a father, but not in the literal "consubstantial" sense) is walking by the Dublin shore alone, "along Sandymount strand," speculating on the shifting shapes of things and the possibility of knowing truth by mere appearances.

First Stephen meditates on the "modality of the visible" and on the mystical notion that God writes his signature on all His works; then on the "modality of the audible," closing his eyes and trying to know reality simply through the sense of hearing. As he continues his walk, the people and objects he sees mingle in his thoughts with memories of his past relations with his family, of his schooldays, his residence in Paris from where he was recalled by his mother's fatal illness, his feeling of guilt about his mother's death (he had refused to kneel down and pray at her bedside, because he considered it would be a betrayal of his integrity as an unbeliever), and a variety of speculations about life and reality often derived from mystical works he had read "in the stagnant bay of Marsh's library" (in Dublin). The highly theoretical, inquiring,

musing, speculating mind of Stephen is in sharp contrast to the practical, humane, sensual, concrete imagination of the book's real hero, Leopold Bloom, but there are also significant parallels between the streams of consciousness of the two. Some of the more important themes that emerge in Stephen's reverie are pointed out in the footnotes.
3. I.e., the sense of sight provides an unavoidable way ("ineluctable modality") of knowing reality, the knowledge thus provided being a kind of "thought through [the] eyes."
4. From Jakob Böhme (1575–1624), German mystic.
5. Transparency. Stephen is speculating on Aristotle's view of perception as developed in his *De Anima.*
6. There was a tradition that Aristotle was bald, with thin legs, small eyes, and a lisp. Aristotle is also traditionally supposed to have inherited considerable wealth and to have been presented with a fortune by his former pupil Alexander the Great. The Italian phrase is Dante's description of Aristotle in the *Inferno,* and means "the master of them that know."
7. What is not transparent (opposite of "diaphane").
8. "After one another." Stephen, with eyes shut, is now sensing reality through the sense of sound only: unlike sight, sound falls on the sense of hearing in chronological sequence, one sound after another.
9. "What if it tempt you toward the flood, my lord. / Or to the dreadful summit of the cliff / That beetles o'er his base into the sea" (*Hamlet* 1.4.69–71).
1. Beside one another.
2. Stephen is still walking with his eyes shut, tapping with his "ash sword" (the walking stick of ash wood he always carried), as "they" (i.e., blind people) do.
3. I.e., Buck Mulligan's. Stephen, lacking boots of his own, had borrowed a castoff pair of Mulligan's.

ends of my legs, *nebeneinander*. Sounds solid: made by the mallet of *Los demiurgos*.[4] Am I walking into eternity along Sandymount strand? Crush, crack, crik, crick. Wild sea money. Dominie[5] Deasy kens them a'.

> *Won't you come to Sandymount,*
> *Madeline the mare?*

Rhythm begins, you see. I hear. A catalectic tetrameter[6] of iambs marching. No, agallop: *deline the mare*.

Open your eyes now. I will. One moment. Has all vanished since? If I open and am for ever in the black adiaphane. *Basta!*[7] I will see if I can see.

See now. There all the time without you: and ever shall be, world without end.

They came down the steps from Leahy's terrace prudently, *Frauenzimmer*:[8] and down the shelving shore flabbily, their splayed feet sinking in the silted sand. Like me, like Algy,[9] coming down to our mighty mother. Number one swung lourdily[1] her midwife's bag, the other's gamp[2] poked in the beach. From the liberties, out for the day. Mrs Florence MacCabe, relict of the late Patk MacCabe,[3] deeply lamented, of Bride Street. One of her sisterhood lugged me squealing into life. Creation from nothing. What has she in the bag? A misbirth with a trailing navelcord, hushed in ruddy wool. The cords of all link back, strandentwining cable of all flesh. That is why mystic monks. Will you be as gods? Gaze in your *omphalos*. Hello. Kinch here. Put me on to Edenville. Aleph, alpha: nought, nought, one.[4]

Spouse and helpmate of Adam Kadmon: Heva,[5] naked Eve. She had no navel. Gaze. Belly without blemish, bulging big, a buckler of taut vellum, no, whiteheaped corn, orient and immortal, standing from everlasting to everlasting. Womb of sin.[6]

---

4. The Demiurge, or demiurgos, supernatural being who, according to the Gnostic philosophy, made the world in subordination to God. The mystical notion of the Demiurge who created the world haunts Stephen's mind; it is the Demiurge who writes his signature on created objects and whose mallet fashioned them. The world, sensed by the ear only, "sounds solid," as though made by the Demiurge's hammer. The ending *-os* gives the word the appearance of a Spanish plural, so Joyce whimsically writes "Los demiurgos," which in Spanish would be "the demiurges."
5. Schoolmaster. Mr. Deasy was the headmaster of the school where Stephen taught (the previous episode has shown Stephen teaching). "Kens them a' ": knows them all; Stephen is putting Deasy into a mock-Scottish folk song.
6. The first of the two lines of popular verse that have come into Stephen's head consists metrically of four iambic feet ("tetrameter") with the last foot unlike the first, not defective ("catalectic").
7. Enough! (Italian).
8. Here, midwives. Stephen sees them coming from Leahy's Terrace, which runs by the beach.
9. Algernon Charles Swinburne, who wrote: "I will go back to the great sweet mother, / Mother and lover of men, the sea. / I will go down to her, I and none other" (*The Triumph of Time*, lines 1–3).
1. Heavily (coined by Stephen from the French *lourd*). Stephen, like Joyce, had studied modern languages at University College, Dublin, and his preoccupation with words and languages is part of his character as potential literary artist.

2. Umbrella; and perhaps reference to Mrs. Gamp, the nurse in Dickens's *Martin Chuzzlewit*.
3. Stephen imagines the first midwife is called Mrs. MacCabe. "Relict": widow.
4. Stephen is speculating on the mystical significance of the navel cord, seeing it as linking the generations, the combined navel cords stretching back to Adam and Eve. A mystic gazed in his *omphalos* (navel) to make contact with the first man. Stephen thinks of himself ("Kinch," his nickname) calling up Adam in "Edenville" through his navel, using the line of linked navel cords as a telephone line. Adam's telephone number, "Aleph, alpha: nought, nought, one," begins with the first letters of the Hebrew and of the Greek alphabet to suggest the great primeval number.
5. Hebrew for Eve. Because she was not born in the regular way, but created from Adam's rib, she had no navel. "Adam Kadman": Adam the Beginner, so called in Hebrew cabalistic literature of the Middle Ages.
6. Stephen is led, through reflection on Eve's navelless "belly without blemish," to a recollection of the description of the original Eden (Paradise) by Thomas Traherne (ca. 1637–1674), from whose prose *Centuries of Meditation* he quotes: "The corn was orient and immortal wheat, which should never be reaped, nor was ever sown. I thought it had stood from everlasting to everlasting." But immediately afterward Stephen reflects that such language is inappropriate to Eve's body, as hers was the "womb of sin"—i.e., she first ate the fatal apple and brought forth sin.

Wombed in sin darkness I was too, made not begotten. By them, the man with my voice and my eyes and a ghostwoman with ashes on her breath.[7] They clasped and sundered, did the coupler's will. From before the ages He willed me and now may not will me away or ever. A *lex eterna*[8] stays about Him. Is that then the divine substance wherein Father and Son are consubstantial? Where is poor dear Arius[9] to try conclusions? Warring his life long on the contransmagnificandjewbangtantiality.[1] Illstarred heresiarch.[2] In a Greek watercloset he breathed his last: *euthanasia*. With beaded mitre and with crozier, stalled upon his throne, widower of a widowed see, with upstiffed omophorion, with clotted hinderparts.

Airs romped round him, nipping and eager airs. They are coming, waves. The whitemaned seahorses, champing, brightwindbridled, the steeds of Mananaan.[3]

I mustn't forget his letter for the press. And after? The Ship, half twelve. By the way go easy with that money like a good young imbecile. Yes, I must.[4]

His pace slackened. Here. Am I going to aunt Sara's or not? My consubstantial father's voice. Did you see anything of your artist brother Stephen lately? No? Sure he's not down in Strasburg terrace with his aunt Sally? Couldn't he fly a bit higher than that, eh? And and and and tell us Stephen, how is uncle Si? O weeping God, the things I married into. De boys up in de hayloft. The drunken little costdrawer and his brother, the cornet player. Highly respectable gondoliers. And skeweyed Walter sirring his father, no less. Sir. Yes, sir. No, sir. Jesus wept: and no wonder, by Christ.[5]

I pull the wheezy bell of their shuttered cottage: and wait. They take me for a dun, peer out from a coign of vantage.[6]

—It's Stephen, sir.

—Let him in. Let Stephen in.

A bolt drawn back and Walter welcomes me.

—We thought you were someone else.

In his broad bed nuncle Richie, pillowed and blanketed, extends over the

---

7. Stephen is haunted by thoughts of his mother in this guise.

8. Eternal law. God's eternal law, Stephen reflects, willed his birth from the beginning. He then goes on to speculate on the nature of the divine substance and whether God the Father and God the Son are of the same substance ("consubstantial").

9. Third-century theologian who "tried conclusions" on this matter, maintaining that Christ was less divine than God (Arius's views were condemned as heretical by the Council of Nicaea in 325).

1. Ironic "portmanteau word" made up of terms connected with the Arian controversy—"consubstantial," "transubstantial" (of a substance that changes into another)—and with the facts of Christ's nature (e.g., "Jew"; Jesus was a Jew, as Leopold Bloom in a later episode reminds an anti-Semitic Irishman).

2. Arch-heretic. Arius died suddenly in Constantinople in 336. He was never a bishop, and Stephen's image of him at the moment of death in full episcopal attire seems to combine recollections of other early "heresiarchs." In an earlier reverie Stephen had conjured up in his mind "a horde of heresies fleeing with mitres awry." These heretics

are connected in Stephen's mind with argument about the relation between God the Father and God the Son and so with the problem of the true nature of paternity, which haunts him constantly.

3. Mananaan MacLir, Celtic sea god; his steeds are the "whitemaned seahorses." ("White horses" is still the name in Britain for the white foam on top of waves.)

4. Mr. Deasy had given Stephen a letter to the press to be taken to the newspaper office. After that he has an appointment with Mulligan at The Ship, a tavern. "That money" is Mr. Deasy's last payment to him.

5. Stephen has been wondering whether to call on his uncle and aunt, Richie and Sara Goulding. He imagines his father interrogating him about the visit as if he had gone; he then pictures his cousins asking after his father, Simon Dedalus (his cousins' "uncle Si"). Simon is contemptuous of his wife's relations (Sara Goulding is his wife's sister). Stephen knows that any mention of them will bring on the familiar abuse of "the things I married into"—at best "highly respectable gondoliers" (from Gilbert and Sullivan's opera *The Gondoliers*). The scene that follows is also Stephen's purely imaginary picture of what the visit would be like.

6. Favorable corner.

hillock of his knees a sturdy forearm. Cleanchested. He has washed the upper moiety.

—Morrow, nephew.

He lays aside the lapboard whereon he drafts his bills of costs for the eyes of master Goff and master Shapland Tandy, filing consents and common searches and a writ of *Duces Tecum*.[7] A bogoak frame over his bald head: Wilde's *Requiescat*.[8] The drone of his misleading whistle brings Walter back.

—Yes, sir?

—Malt[9] for Richie and Stephen, tell mother. Where is she?

—Bathing Crissie, sir.

Papa's little bedpal. Lump of love.

—No, uncle Richie . . .

—Call me Richie. Damn your lithia water. It lowers. Whusky!

—Uncle Richie, really. . . .

—Sit down or by the law Harry I'll knock you down.

Walter squints vainly for a chair.

—He has nothing to sit down on, sir.

—He has nowhere to put it, you mug. Bring in our chippendale chair. Would you like a bite of something? None of your damned lawdeedaw air here: the rich of a rasher fried with a herring? Sure? So much the better. We have nothing in the house but backache pills.

All'erta![1] He drones bars of Ferrando's *aria di sortita*. The grandest number, Stephen, in the whole opera. Listen.

His tuneful whistle sounds again, finely shaded, with rushes of the air, his fists bigdrumming on his padded knees.

This wind is sweeter.

Houses of decay, mine, his and all. You told the Clongowes gentry you had an uncle a judge and an uncle a general in the army.[2] Come out of them, Stephen. Beauty is not there. Nor in the stagnant bay of Marsh's library where you read the fading prophecies of Joachim Abbas.[3] For whom? The hundredheaded rabble of the cathedral close.[4] A hater of his kind ran from them to the wood of madness, his mane foaming in the moon, his eyeballs stars. Houyhnhnm, horsenostrilled.[5] The oval equine faces, Temple, Buck Mulligan, Foxy Campbell. Lantern jaws. Abbas[6] father, furious dean, what offence laid fire to their brains? Paff! *Descende, calve, ut nimium decalveris.*[7] A garland of grey hair on his comminated head see him me clambering down

7. You shall take with you. Opening words of a search warrant. Goulding was a law clerk with Messrs. Goff and Tandy.

8. Poem by Oscar Wilde.

9. Whiskey.

1. Look out! The first words of the *aria di sortita* (aria sung by a character about to leave the stage) sung by Ferrando, captain of the guard, in Verdi's opera *Il Trovatore*.

2. Stephen, reflecting on the steady social decline of his family, is remembering that, while at school at Clongowes Wood College, he had pretended to have important relations.

3. Abbot Joachim of Floris (the monastery of San Giovanni in Fiore, Italy), 12th-century mystic and theologian, whose prophetic work *Expositio in Apocalypsin* Stephen (i.e., Joyce) had read in Marsh's Library.

4. I.e., the precinct of a cathedral (Marsh's Library is in the close of St. Patrick's Cathedral).

5. St. Patrick's Close has recalled Jonathan Swift (who was dean of St. Patrick's). Stephen remembers Swift's misanthropy (he was "a hater of his kind") and his creation of the Houyhnhnms (noble horses) in book 4 of *Gulliver's Travels*. Then he thinks of people he knew who have horse faces.

6. Literally: father.

7. Go down, bald-head, lest you become even balder. This sentence, from Joachim's *Concordia* of the Old and New Testaments, is based on the mocking cry of the children to the prophet Elisha (2 Kings 2.23: "Go up, thou bald head"); Joachim saw Elisha as a forerunner of St. Benedict—both had shaven or baldish heads. Stephen goes on to imagine the "comminated" (threatened) head of Joachim descending, clutching a "monstrance" (receptacle in which the Host [consecrated bread or wafer] is exposed for adoration), in the midst of a nightmare church service.

to the footpace (*descende*), clutching a monstrance, basiliskeyed. Get down, bald poll! A choir gives back menace and echo, assisting about the altar's horns, the snorted Latin of jackpriests moving burly in their albs, tonsured and oiled and gelded, fat with the fat of kidneys of wheat.

And at the same instant perhaps a priest round the corner is elevating it. Dringdring! And two streets off another locking it into a pyx.[8] Dringadring! And in a ladychapel another taking housel all to his own cheek. Dringdring! Down, up, forward, back. Dan Occam[9] thought of that, invincible doctor. A misty English morning the imp hypostasis tickled his brain. Bringing his host down and kneeling he heard twine with his second bell the first bell in the transept (he is lifting his) and, rising, heard (now I am lifting) their two bells (he is kneeling) twang in diphthong.

Cousin Stephen, you will never be a saint.[1] Isle of saints.[2] You were awfully holy, weren't you? You prayed to the Blessed Virgin that you might not have a red nose. You prayed to the devil in Serpentine avenue that the fubsy widow in front might lift her clothes still more from the wet street. O si, certo![3] Sell your soul for that, do, dyed rags pinned round a squaw. More tell me, more still! On the top of the Howth tram alone crying to the rain: *Naked women!* What about that, eh?

What about what? What else were they invented for?

Reading two pages apiece of seven books every night, eh? I was young. You bowed to yourself in the mirror, stepping forward to applause earnestly, striking face. Hurray for the Goddamned idiot! Hray! No-one saw: tell no-one. Books you were going to write with letters for titles. Have you read his F? O yes, but I prefer Q. Yes, but W is wonderful. O yes, W. Remember your epiphanies[4] on green oval leaves, deeply deep, copies to be sent if you died to all the great libraries of the world, including Alexandria? Someone was to read them there after a few thousand years, a mahamanvantara.[5] Pico della Mirandola[6] like. Ay, very like a whale.[7] When one reads these strange pages of one long gone one feels that one is at one with one who once . . .

The grainy sand had gone from under his feet. His boots trod again a damp crackling mast, razorshells, squeaking pebbles, that on the unnumbered pebbles beats, wood sieved by the shipworm, lost Armada. Unwholesome sand-flats waited to suck his treading soles, breathing upward sewage breath. He coasted them, walking warily. A porterbottle stood up, stogged to its waist, in the cakey sand dough. A sentinel: isle of dreadful thirst.[8] Broken hoops

---

8. Vessel in which the Host is kept. Stephen is imagining such a service, with himself officiating (he almost became a priest).

9. William of Occam or Ockham ("Dan" means "master"), 14th-century English theologian, who held that the individual thing is the reality and its name, the universal, an abstraction; he was concerned with hypostasis—the essential part of a thing as distinct from its attributes.

1. A parody of the words of Dryden to his distant relative Swift: Cousin, you will never make a poet.

2. Ireland was called "*insula sanctorum,*" (isle of saints) in the Middle Ages.

3. Oh yes, certainly!

4. Joyce's term for the prose poems he wrote as a young man. An epiphany, he said, was the sudden "revelation of the whatness of a thing"—of a gesture, a phrase, or a thought which he had experienced; he attempted to express, in the writing, the moment at which "the soul of the commonest object . . . seems to us radiant." Stephen's recollection of

early and exotic literary ambitions is drawn directly from Joyce's own ambitions at the same age.

5. Cycle of change and recurrence, in Indian mystical thought. It is connected in Stephen's mind with the constant ebb and flow of the sea by which he is walking.

6. Fifteenth-century mystical philosopher; his *Heptaplus* is a mystical account of the creation, much influenced by Jewish cabalistic thought.

7. Polonius to Hamlet (*Hamlet* 3.2.399) with reference to the changing shape of a cloud. The Protean theme of constant change, of ebb and flow, and of metempsychosis (i.e., transmigration of souls: a major theme in *Ulysses*), is working in Stephen's mind. The following sentence is a parody of an elegant, condescending modern essay on Pico or some other early mystic.

8. The atmosphere of the sandflats reminds Stephen of a desert island where people die of thirst. (The island of Pharos, where Menelaus found Proteus, was an "island of dreadful hunger.")

on the shore; at the land a maze of dark cunning nets; farther away chalk-scrawled backdoors and on the higher beach a dryingline with two crucified shirts. Ringsend: wigwams of brown steersmen and master mariners. Human shells.

He halted. I have passed the way to aunt Sara's. Am I not going there? Seems not. No-one about. He turned northeast and crossed the firmer sand towards the Pigeonhouse.[9]

—*Qui vous a mis dans cette fichue position?*

—*C'est le pigeon, Joseph.*

Patrice, home on furlough, lapped warm milk with me in the bar Mac-Mahon. Son of the wild goose, Kevin Egan of Paris. My father's a bird, he lapped the sweet *lait chaud* with pink young tongue, plump bunny's face. Lap, *lapin*. He hopes to win in the *gros lots*. About the nature of women he read in Michelet. But he must send me *La Vie de Jésus* by M. Léo Taxil. Lent it to his friend.[1]

—*C'est tordant, vous savez. Moi, je suis socialiste. Je ne crois pas en l'existence de Dieu. Faut pas le dire à mon père.*

—*Il croit?*

—*Mon père, oui.*

Schluss.[2] He laps.

My Latin quarter hat. God, we simply must dress the character. I want puce gloves. You were a student, weren't you? Of what in the other devil's name? Paysayenn. P. C. N., you know: *physiques, chimiques et naturelles.*[3] Aha. Eating your groatsworth of *mou en civet,*[4] fleshpots of Egypt, elbowed by belching cabmen. Just say in the most natural tone: when I was in Paris, *boul'Mich',*[5] I used to. Yes, used to carry punched tickets to prove an alibi if they arrested you for murder somewhere. Justice. On the night of the seventeenth of February 1904 the prisoner was seen by two witnesses. Other fellow did it: other me. Hat, tie, overcoat, nose. *Lui, c'est moi.*[6] You seem to have enjoyed yourself.

Proudly walking. Whom were you trying to walk like? Forget: a dispossessed. With mother's money order, eight shillings, the banging door of the post office slammed in your face by the usher. Hunger toothache. *Encore deux minutes.* Look clock. Must get. *Fermé.* Hired dog! Shoot him to bloody bits with a bang shotgun, bits man spattered walls all brass buttons. Bits all

9. The Pigeon House in Ringsend, an old structure built on a breakwater in Dublin Bay and which in the course of time has served a great variety of purposes, suggests to Stephen the Dove, which is the symbol of the Holy Spirit, and this in turn suggests an irreverent dialogue (supposedly between Joseph and Mary when Mary is found to be pregnant: "Who has got you into this wretched condition?" "It was the pigeon [i.e., the Holy Dove], Joseph"). This he had picked up in Paris from the blasphemous M. Léo Taxil, whose book *La Vie de Jésus* ("The Life of Jesus") is mentioned in the next paragraph.
1. Stephen had first met Léo Taxil through Patrice, the son of "Kevin Egan of Paris," who in real life was the exiled nationalist Joseph Casey. The phrase "my father's a bird" comes from *The Song of the Cheerful Jesus,* a blasphemous poem by Buck Mulligan (actually Oliver Gogarty, who really wrote the poem); Stephen recalls Patrice reciting

it as he drank warm milk ("*lait chaud*"), lapping it like a "*lapin*" (rabbit), and expressing the hope that he would win something substantial in the French national lottery (*gros lot:* "first prize"). Jules Michelet (1798–1874), French historian.
2. End. Conversation between Stephen and Patrice: "It's screamingly funny, you know. I'm a socialist myself. I don't believe in the existence of God. Mustn't tell my father." "He is a believer?" "My father, yes."
3. I.e., the faculty of physics, chemistry, and biology at the École de Médecine in Paris, where Stephen, like Joyce, took a premedical course for a short time. The faculty was popularly known as "P. C. N." (pronounced "Paysayenn").
4. Stew.
5. Popular Parisian abbreviation for the Boulevard Saint Michel.
6. "He is me"—a parody of Louis XIV's remark "*L'état c'est moi*" (I am the state).

khrrrrklak in place clack back. Not hurt? O, that's all right. Shake hands. See what I meant, see? O, that's all right. Shake a shake. O, that's all only all right.[7]

You were going to do wonders, what? Missionary to Europe after fiery Columbanus. Fiacre and Scotus on their creepystools[8] in heaven spilt from their pintpots, loudlatinlaughing: *Euge! Euge!*[9] Pretending to speak broken English as you dragged your valise, porter threepence, across the slimy pier at Newhaven. *Comment?* Rich booty you brought back; *Le Tutu*, five tattered numbers of *Pantalon Blanc et Culotte Rouge*,[1] a blue French telegram, curiosity to show:

—Mother dying come home father.[2]

The aunt thinks you killed your mother. That's why she won't.[3]

> Then here's a health to Mulligan's aunt
> And I'll tell you the reason why.
> She always kept things decent in
> The Hannigan famileye.

His feet marched in sudden proud rhythm over the sand furrows, along by the boulders of the south wall. He stared at them proudly, piled stone mammoth skulls. Gold light on sea, on sand, on boulders. The sun is there, the slender trees, the lemon houses.

Paris rawly waking, crude sunlight on her lemon streets. Moist pith of farls[4] of bread, the froggreen wormwood, her matin incense, court the air. Belluomo rises from the bed of his wife's lover's wife, the kerchiefed housewife is astir, a saucer of acetic acid in her hand. In Rodot's Yvonne and Madeleine newmake their tumbled beauties, shattering with gold teeth *chaussons* of pastry, their mouths yellowed with the *pus* of *flan breton*.[5] Faces of Paris men go by, their wellpleased pleasers, curled *conquistadores*.[6]

Noon slumbers. Kevin Egan rolls gunpowder cigarettes through fingers smeared with printer's ink,[7] sipping his green fairy as Patrice his white. About us gobblers fork spiced beans down their gullets. *Un demi setier!*[8] A jet of coffee steam from the burnished caldron. She serves me at his beck. *Il est irlandais. Hollandais? Non fromage. Deux irlandais, nous, Irlande, vous savez? Ah, oui!*[9] She thought you wanted a cheese *hollandais*. Your postprandial, do you know that word? Postprandial. There was a fellow I knew once in Barcelona, queer fellow, used to call it his postprandial. Well: *slainte!*[1] Around

7. A recollection of the occasion when, desperate for money, Stephen had received a money order for eight shillings from his mother. Afflicted with both hunger and toothache, he had gone to cash it at the post office—which was closed, even though, as he expostulated with the man at the door, there were still two minutes (*"encore deux minutes"*) until the official closing time. In his retrospective rage he imagines himself shooting the "hired dog" to bits, and then in a revulsion of feeling has a mental reconciliation with him.
8. Low stools. "Columbanus": 6th-century Irish missionary on the Continent. Fiacre was a 6th-century Irish saint. Duns Scotus (ca. 1265–1308), scholastic theologian and philosopher.
9. Well done!
1. Like the preceding name, name of French popular periodical.
2. This telegram was actually received by Joyce in Paris.

3. Stephen recalls Buck Mulligan's telling him that his (Mulligan's) aunt disapproved of Stephen because, by refusing to pray at his dying mother's bedside, he had hastened her death. Stephen then tries to laugh away his feeling of guilt by quoting mentally a (slightly parodied) verse of a popular song.
4. Thin circular cakes.
5. Memories of a restaurant in Paris. "*Chaussons*": pastry turnovers. "*Flan breton*": pastry filled with custard.
6. Conquerors (Spanish).
7. Egan (i.e., Joseph Casey) became a typesetter for the Parisian edition of the *New York Herald*.
8. Abusive Parisian slang for a liquid measure (about one-fourth of a liter)—here, presumably, of wine or beer.
9. He is Irish. Dutch? Not cheese. We are two Irishmen, Ireland, you understand? Oh, yes!
1. Your health! (Gaelic).

the slabbed tables the tangle of wined breaths and grumbling gorges. His breath hangs over our saucestained plates, the green fairy's fang thrusting between his lips. Of Ireland, the Dalcassians, of hopes, conspiracies, of Arthur Griffith now.[2] To yoke me as his yokefellow, our crimes our common cause. You're your father's son. I know the voice. His fustian shirt, sanguineflowered, trembles its Spanish tassels at his secrets. M. Drumont,[3] famous journalist, Drumont, know what he called queen Victoria? Old hag with the yellow teeth. *Vieille ogresse* with the *dents jaunes.* Maud Gonne, beautiful woman, *la Patrie,* M. Millevoye, Félix Faure,[4] know how he died? Licentious men. The *froeken, bonne à tout faire,*[5] who rubs male nakedness in the bath at Upsala. *Moi faire,* she said, *tous les messieurs.*[6] Not this *monsieur,* I said. Most licentious custom. Bath a most private thing. I wouldn't let my brother, not even my own brother, most lascivious thing. Green eyes, I see you. Fang, I feel. Lascivious people.

The blue fuse burns deadly between hands and burns clear. Loose tobacco shreds catch fire: a flame and acrid smoke light our corner. Raw facebones under his peep of day boy's hat. How the head centre got away, authentic version. Got up as a young bride, man, veil, orangeblossoms, drove out the road to Malahide. Did, faith. Of lost leaders, the betrayed, wild escapes. Disguises, clutched at, gone not here.[7]

Spurned lover. I was a strapping young gossoon[8] at that time, I tell you. I'll show you my likeness one day. I was, faith. Lover, for her love he prowled with colonel Richard Burke, tanist of his sept,[9] under the walls of Clerkenwell[1] and, crouching, saw a flame of vengeance hurl them upward in the fog. Shattered glass and toppling masonry. In gay Paree he hides, Egan of Paris, unsought by any save by me. Making his day's stations, the dingy printingcase, his three taverns, the Montmartre lair he sleeps short night in, *rue de la Goutte-d'Or,* damascened with flyblown faces of the gone. Loveless, landless, wifeless. She is quite nicey comfy without her outcast man,[2] madame in *rue Gît-le-Cœur,* canary and two buck lodgers. Peachy cheeks, a zebra skirt, frisky as a young thing's. Spurned and undespairing. Tell Pat[3] you saw me, won't you? I wanted to get poor Pat a job one time. *Mon fils,* soldier of France. I taught him to sing *The boys of Kilkenny are stout roaring blades.* Know that old lay? I taught Patrice that. Old Kilkenny: saint Canice, Strongbow's castle on the Nore.[4] Goes like this. O, O. He takes me, Napper Tandy,[5] by the hand.

---

2. Two extremes of Irish history. From the Dalcassian line came the early kings of Munster (from 300 C.E. on). Arthur Griffith (1872–1922) was an Irish revolutionary leader, founder of the Sinn Fein ("Ourselves Alone") movement.
3. Edouard Drumont (1844–1917), French politician and bitter anti-Semite.
4. Nineteenth-century French statesman. Maud Gonne, the beautiful actress and violent Irish nationalist whom Yeats loved. "*La Patrie*": journal edited by Lucien Millevoye, French nationalist deputy and Maud Gonne's lover.
5. Maid-of-all-work (French). "*Froeken*": fröken, unmarried woman or Miss (Swedish).
6. I do all the gentlemen (in broken French).
7. Another Protean theme of change. Egan had told Stephen of his cousin James Stephens's escape from prison disguised as a bride (Stephens was really the cousin of Casey, the original of Egan in this episode).

8. Boy.
9. Clan. "Tanist": successor-apparent to a Celtic chief.
1. District in east-central London. Stephen is recalling Egan's conversation about the Fenian violence in London that necessitated his fleeing to France.
2. I.e., Egan's wife, who is "quite nicey comfy" in the metaphorical "rue Gît-le-Cœur" (i.e., the street where the heart lies dead) back home in Ireland.
3. Patrice, Egan's son.
4. Kilkenny is called after the Irish Saint Canice (its Irish name is Cill Chainnigh), on the river Nore, where Strongbow (the second earl of Pembroke, who invaded Ireland in the 12th century), had his stronghold.
5. James Napper Tandy (1740–1803), Irish revolutionary hero of the song "The Wearing of the Green."

O, O the boys of
Kilkenny . . .

Weak wasting hand on mine. They have forgotten Kevin Egan, not he them. Remembering thee, O Sion.[6]

He had come nearer the edge of the sea and wet sand slapped his boots. The new air greeted him, harping in wild nerves, wind of wild air of seeds of brightness. Here, I am not walking out to the Kish lightship, am I? He stood suddenly, his feet beginning to sink slowly in the quaking soil. Turn back.

Turning, he scanned the shore south, his feet sinking again slowly in new sockets. The cold domed room of the tower[7] waits. Through the barbicans[8] the shafts of light are moving ever, slowly ever as my feet are sinking, creeping duskward over the dial floor. Blue dusk, nightfall, deep blue night. In the darkness of the dome they wait, their pushedback chairs, my obelisk valise, around a board of abandoned platters. Who to clear it? He has the key.[9] I will not sleep there when this night comes. A shut door of a silent tower, entombing their blind bodies, the panthersahib and his pointer.[1] Call: no answer. He lifted his feet up from the suck and turned back by the mole of boulders. Take all, keep all. My soul walks with me, form of forms. So in the moon's midwatches I pace the path above the rocks, in sable silvered, hearing Elsinore's tempting flood.[2]

The flood is following me. I can watch it flow past from here. Get back then by the Poolbeg road to the strand there. He climbed over the sedge and eely oarweeds and sat on a stool of rock, resting his ashplant in a grike.[3]

A bloated carcass of a dog lay lolled on bladderwrack. Before him the gunwale of a boat, sunk in sand. *Un coche ensablé*[4] Louis Veuillot called Gautier's[5] prose. These heavy sands are language tide and wind have silted here. And there, the stoneheaps of dead builders, a warren of weasel rats. Hide gold there. Try it. You have some. Sands and stones. Heavy of the past. Sir Lout's toys. Mind you don't get one bang on the ear. I'm the bloody well gigant rolls all them bloody well boulders, bones for my steppingstones. Feefawfum. I zmellz de bloodz oldz an Iridzman.[6]

A point, live dog, grew into sight running across the sweep of sand. Lord, is he going to attack me? Respect his liberty. You will not be master of others or their slave. I have my stick. Sit tight. From farther away, walking shoreward across from the crested tide, figures, two. The two maries. They have tucked it safe mong the bulrushes. Peekaboo. I see you. No, the dog. He is running back to them. Who?

Galleys of the Lochlanns[7] ran here to beach, in quest of prey, their blood-

---

6. Cf. Psalm 137.1 (in the King James Bible): "we wept, when we remembered Zion." But "Zion" in the Douay (Roman Catholic) Bible, is spelled "Sion," and the Book of Common Prayer has "When we remembered thee, O Sion."
7. Where Stephen lived with Buck Mulligan.
8. Outworks of a castle.
9. In the preceding episode, Mulligan asked for and got the key of the tower from Stephen.
1. I.e., Mulligan and the Englishman Haines, who lived with Stephen in the tower. Stephen thinks of them as calling for him in vain, because he has decided not to return.
2. Cf. *Hamlet* 1.2.242, where the ghost of Hamlet's murdered father is described as having a beard of "sable silver'd." Allusions to *Hamlet* occur often in *Ulysses*; in a later episode Stephen expounds the

theory that Shakespeare is to be identified not with Hamlet himself but with his betrayed father.
3. Chink, crevice.
4. A coach embedded in the sand.
5. Théophile Gautier, 19th-century French poet, novelist, and critic. Veuillot, 19th-century French journalist.
6. Stephen is thinking of the boulders on the shore as the work of a large but clumsy giant ("Sir Lout"). "They [Sir Lout and his family] were giants right enough. . . . My Sir Lout has rocks in his mouth instead of teeth. He articulates badly" (Joyce to Frank Budgen, reported in Budgen's *James Joyce and the Making of Ulysses*, 1934).
7. Scandinavians (Gaelic). Stephen is meditating on the Vikings who settled Dublin; it was here that they came ashore, he thinks.

beaked prows riding low on a molten pewter surf. Dane vikings, torcs of tomahawks aglitter on their breasts when Malachi wore the collar of gold. A school of turlehide whales stranded in hot noon, spouting, hobbling in the shallows. Then from the starving cagework city a horde of jerkined dwarfs, my people, with flayers' knives, running, scaling, hacking in green blubbery whalemeat. Famine, plague and slaughters. Their blood is in me, their lusts my waves. I moved among them on the frozen Liffey, that I, a changeling, among the spluttering resin fires. I spoke to no-one: none to me.

The dog's bark ran towards him, stopped, ran back.[8] Dog of my enemy. I just simply stood pale, silent, bayed about. *Terribilia meditans.*[9] A primrose doublet, fortune's knave, smiled on my fear. For that are you pining, the bark of their applause? Pretenders: live their lives. The Bruce's brother, Thomas Fitzgerald, silken knight, Perkin Warbeck, York's false scion, in breeches of silk of whiterose ivory, wonder of a day, and Lambert Simnel, with a tail of nans and sutlers, a scullion crowned.[1] All kings' sons. Paradise of pretenders then and now. He saved men from drowning[2] and you shake at a cur's yelping. But the courtiers who mocked Guido in Or san Michele were in their own house. House of . . . We don't want any of your medieval abstrusiosities. Would you do what he did? A boat would be near, a lifebuoy. *Natürlich,*[3] put there for you. Would you or would you not? The man that was drowned nine days ago off Maiden's rock. They are waiting for him now. The truth, spit it out. I would want to. I would try. I am not a strong swimmer. Water cold soft. When I put my face into it in the basin at Clongowes. Can't see! Who's behind me? Out quickly, quickly! Do you see the tide flowing quickly in on all sides, sheeting the lows of sands quickly, shellcocoacoloured? If I had land under my feet. I want his life still to be his, mine to be mine. A drowning man. His human eyes scream to me out of horror of his death. I . . . With him together down . . . I could not save her.[4] Waters: bitter death: lost.

A woman and a man. I see her skirties. Pinned up, I bet.

Their dog ambled about a bank of dwindling sand, trotting, sniffing on all sides. Looking for something lost in a past life. Suddenly he made off like a bounding hare, ears flung back, chasing the shadow of a lowskimming gull. The man's shrieked whistle struck his limp ears. He turned, bounded back, came nearer, trotted on twinkling shanks. On a field tenney a buck, trippant, proper, unattired.[5] At the lacefringe of the tide he halted with stiff forehoofs, seawardpointed ears. His snout lifted barked at the wavenoise, herds of seamorse. They serpented towards his feet, curling, unfurling many crests, every ninth, breaking, plashing, from far, from farther out, waves and waves.

Cocklepickers.[6] They waded a little way in the water and, stooping, soused their bags, and, lifting them again, waded out. The dog yelped running to

---

8. The dog in this and subsequent paragraphs keeps changing in appearance; he "is the mummer among beasts—the Protean animal" (Joyce to Budgen). Joyce himself was afraid of dogs.
9. Meditating terrible things.
1. Stephen is meditating on pretenders (i.e., false claimants): the names here are those of pretenders who have figured in English history. This is the Proteus theme again—disguises and changes.
2. Mulligan had saved a man from drowning.
3. Of course.
4. A man had been drowned off the coast, and his

body had not yet been recovered. As Stephen thinks of the horror of drowning he recalls once again his mother's death.
5. At this point in its constantly changing appearance the dog looks like a heraldic animal and is described in the language of heraldry. This sentence means: "On an orange-brown (tawny) background, a buck, tripping, in natural colors, without horns."
6. Stephen recognizes the man and woman on the beach as gypsy cockle pickers (cockles are edible shellfish, like mussels).

them, reared up and pawed them, dropping on all fours, again reared up at them with mute bearish fawning. Unheeded he kept by them as they came towards the drier sand, a rag of wolf's tongue redpanting from his jaws. His speckled body ambled ahead of them and then loped off at a calf's gallop. The carcass lay on his path. He stopped, sniffed, stalked round it, brother, nosing closer, went round it, sniffing rapidly like a dog all over the dead dog's bedraggled fell. Dogskull, dogsniff, eyes on the ground, moves to one great goal. Ah, poor dogsbody. Here lies poor dogsbody's body.

—Tatters! Outofthat, you mongrel.

The cry brought him skulking back to his master and a blunt bootless kick sent him unscathed across a spit of sand, crouched in flight. He slunk back in a curve. Doesn't see me. Along by the edge of the mole he lolloped, dawdled, smelt a rock and from under a cocked hindleg pissed against it. He trotted forward and, lifting his hindleg, pissed quick short at an unsmelt rock. The simple pleasures of the poor. His hindpaws then scattered sand: then his forepaws dabbled and delved. Something he buried there, his grandmother.[7] He rooted in the sand, dabbling, delving and stopped to listen to the air, scraped up the sand again with a fury of his claws, soon ceasing, a pard,[8] a panther, got in spousebreach,[9] vulturing the dead.

After he woke me last night same dream or was it? Wait. Open hallway. Street of harlots. Remember. Haroun al Raschid.[1] I am almosting it. That man led me, spoke. I was not afraid. The melon he had he held against my face. Smiled: creamfruit smell. That was the rule, said. In. Come. Red carpet spread. You will see who.

Shouldering their bags they trudged, the red Egyptians.[2] His blued feet out of turnedup trousers slapped the clammy sand, a dull brick muffler strangling his unshaven neck. With woman steps she followed: the ruffian and his strolling mort. Spoils[3] slung at her back. Loose sand and shellgrit crusted her bare feet. About her windraw face her hair trailed. Behind her lord his helpmate, bing awast, to Romeville.[4] When night hides her body's flaws calling under her brown shawl from an archway where dogs have mired. Her fancyman is treating two Royal Dublins in O'Loughlin's of Blackpitts. Buss her, wap in rogues' rum lingo, for, O, my dimber wapping dell.[5] A shefiend's whiteness under her rancid rags. Fumbally's lane that night: the tanyard smells.

> White thy fambles, red thy gan
> And thy quarrons dainty is.

---

7. Reference to a joke Stephen had made to his pupils in school that morning about "the fox burying his grandmother under a hollybush." This has many symbolic reverberations throughout *Ulysses*. The buried grandmother suggests Stephen's mother, the church, and Ireland (the "Poor old Woman"), while the hollybush, evergreen tree of life, represents resurrection in which, in spite of his religious disbelief, Stephen is much interested and about which (as about metempsychosis) he is continually brooding.
8. Leopard or panther.
9. I.e., begotten in adultery.
1. Stephen's dream of the famous Caliph of Baghdad, of the "street of harlots" and of his meeting a man with a melon, foreshadows his meeting later in the day with Leopold Bloom and his visit to the brothel area of Dublin.
2. I.e., gypsies. As Stephen watches the gypsy cockle pickers with their dog he imagines their vagabond life and recalls fragments of gypsy speech and of thieves' slang.
3. The association of gypsy ("Mort": free gypsy woman; harlot) with Egyptian reminds Stephen of the Israelites "spoiling the Egyptians" (Exodus 12.36).
4. Go away to London.
5. Seventeenth-century thieves' slang. "Buss": kiss. "Wap": copulate with. "Rum": good. "Dimber": pretty. "Wapping dell": whore.

> *Couch a hogshead with me then.*
> *In the darkmans clip and kiss.*[6]

Morose delectation Aquinas tunbelly calls this, *frate porcospino.*[7] Unfallen Adam rode and not rutted. Call away let him:[8] *thy quarrons dainty is.* Language no whit worse than his. Monkwords, marybeads jabber on their girdles: roguewords, tough nuggets patter in their pockets.

Passing now.

A side-eye at my Hamlet hat. If I were suddenly naked here as I sit? I am not. Across the sands of all the world, followed by the sun's flaming sword, to the west, trekking to evening lands. She trudges, schlepps, trains, drags, trascines her load.[9] A tide westering, moondrawn, in her wake. Tides, myriad-islanded, within her, blood not mine, *oinopa ponton,*[1] a winedark sea. Behold the handmaid of the moon. In sleep the wet sign calls her hour, bids her rise. Bridebed, childbed, bed of death, ghostcandled.[2] *Omnis caro ad te veniet.* He comes, pale vampire, through storm his eyes, his bat sails bloodying the sea, mouth to her mouth's kiss.[3]

Here. Put a pin in that chap, will you? My tablets.[4] Mouth to her kiss. No. Must be two of em. Glue 'em well. Mouth to her mouth's kiss.

His lips lipped and mouthed fleshless lips of air: mouth to her womb. Oomb, allwombing tomb.[5] His mouth moulded issuing breath, unspeeched: ooeeehah: roar of cataractic planets, globed, blazing, roaring wayawayaway-awayawayaway. Paper. The banknotes, blast them. Old Deasy's letter. Here. Thanking you for the hospitality tear the blank end off. Turning his back to the sun he bent over far to a table of rock and scribbled words.[6] That's twice I forgot to take slips from the library counter.

His shadow lay over the rocks as he bent, ending. Why not endless till the farthest star? Darkly they are there behind this light, darkness shining in the brightness, delta of Cassiopeia, worlds. Me sits there with his augur's rod of ash, in borrowed sandals, by day beside a livid sea, unbeheld, in violet night walking beneath a reign of uncouth stars.[7] I throw this ended shadow from me, manshape ineluctable, call it back. Endless, would it be mine, form of my form? Who watches me here? Who ever anywhere will read these written words? Signs on a white field. Somewhere to someone in your flutiest voice.

---

6. More thieves' slang. "Fambles": hands. "Gan": mouth. "Quarrons": body. "Couch a hogshead": come to bed. "Darkmans": night. "Clip": kiss. These four lines and some of the phrases in the preceding paragraph are quoted from a song of the period, "The Rogue's Delight in Praise of His Strolling Mort" (cf. n. 2 and n. 3, p. 2279).
7. Brother porcupine (Italian), a reference to the fat ("tunbelly") but prickly philosopher, St. Thomas Aquinas.
8. The gypsy is calling his dog.
9. All words suggesting moving or dragging. " 'I like that crescendo of verbs,' he [Joyce] said. 'The irresistible tug of the tides' " (Budgen).
1. Winedark sea (Homer).
2. He is thinking of his mother again. The following Latin (from the burial service) means: All flesh will come to thee.
3. Death comes like the Flying Dutchman in a

phantom ship to give the fatal kiss.
4. Cf. *Hamlet* 1.5.107: "My tables!"
5. Our understanding of Stephen's consciousness here can be illuminated with reference to Blake's poem *The Gates of Paradise*, which concludes: "The door of death I open found / And the worm weaving in the ground: / Thou'rt my mother from the womb, / Wife, sister, daughter, to the tomb." Cf. also *Romeo and Juliet* 2.3.9–10: "the earth that's nature's mother is her tomb. / What is her burying ground that is her womb."
6. Stephen tears off the blank end of Mr. Deasy's letter to the press and writes a poem that will be quoted later in the novel.
7. He imagines himself as the constellation Cassiopeia, supposed to represent the wife of Cepheus (an Ethiopian king) seated in a chair and holding up her arms. His ash walking stick he thinks of as an "augur's [Roman soothsayer's] rod of ash."

The good bishop of Cloyne[8] took the veil of the temple out of his shovel hat: veil of space with coloured emblems hatched on its field. Hold hard. Coloured on a flat: yes, that's right. Flat I see, then think distance, near, far, flat I see, east, back. Ah, see now. Falls back suddenly, frozen in stereoscope. Click does the trick. You find my words dark. Darkness is in our souls, do you not think? Flutier. Our souls, shamewounded by our sins, cling to us yet more, a woman to her lover clinging, the more the more.

She trusts me, her hand gentle, the longlashed eyes. Now where the blue hell am I bringing her beyond the veil?[9] Into the ineluctable modality of the ineluctable visuality. She, she, she. What she? The virgin at Hodges Figgis' window on Monday looking in for one of the alphabet books you were going to write. Keen glance you gave her. Wrist through the braided jess of her sunshade. She lives in Leeson park with a grief and kickshaws, a lady of letters. Talk that to some else, Stevie: a pickmeup. Bet she wears those curse of God stays suspenders and yellow stockings, darned with lumpy wool. Talk about apple dumplings, *piuttosto.*[1] Where are your wits?

Touch me. Soft eyes. Soft soft soft hand. I am lonely here. O, touch me soon, now. What is that word known to all men? I am quiet here alone. Sad too. Touch, touch me.

He lay back at full stretch over the sharp rocks, cramming the scribbled note and pencil into a pocket, his hat tilted down on his eyes. That is Kevin Egan's movement I made, nodding for his nap, sabbath sleep. *Et vidit Deus. Et erant valde bona.*[2] Alo! *Bonjour.* Welcome as the flowers in May. Under its leaf he watched through peacocktwittering lashes the southing sun. I am caught in this burning scene. Pan's hour, the faunal noon. Among gumheavy serpentplants, milkoozing fruits, where on the tawny waters leaves lie wide. Pain is far.

And no more turn aside and brood.[3]

His gaze brooded on his broadtoed boots, a buck's castoffs, *nebeneinander.* He counted the creases of rucked leather wherein another's foot had nested warm. The foot that beat the ground in tripudium, foot I dislove. But you were delighted when Esther Osvalt's shoe went on you: girl I knew in Paris. *Tiens, quel petit pied!*[4] Staunch friend, a brother soul: Wilde's love that dare not speak its name. He now will leave me. And the blame? As I am. As I am. All or not at all.

In long lassoes from the Cock lake the water flowed full, covering greengoldenly lagoons of sand, rising, flowing. My ashplant will float away. I shall wait. No, they will pass on, passing chafing against the low rocks, swirling, passing. Better get this job over quick. Listen: a fourworded wavespeech: seesoo, hrss, rsseeiss ooos. Vehement breath of waters amid seasnakes, rear-

---

8. George Berkeley (1685–1753), bishop of Cloyne (in Ireland), who argued that the external world has no objective reality but exists only in the mind of the perceiver. Stephen (as at the opening of this episode) is experimenting again with ways of sensing reality.
9. "She" is Psyche, the soul, whom he is bringing from "beyond the veil." But from metaphysical speculations on reality and the soul Stephen is led (by the Psyche association) to think of "the virgin at Hodges Figgis' [a bookseller's] window."
1. Rather, sooner.
2. Connecting two phrases from the Vulgate: "And

God saw" (Genesis 1.4) and "And they were very good" (Genesis 1.31).
3. The first line of the second (and last) stanza of Yeats's poem *Who Goes with Fergus?* which is often in Stephen's mind. The line expresses for him the mood of noontide stillness and of lotos eating in a lush Asian scene that overcomes him momentarily when he realizes that it is twelve o'clock, the hour of the Greek nature god Pan, "faunal noon." This Asian lotos-eating theme, which is associated also with Bloom, is important in the *Odyssey.*
4. Look, what a little foot!

ing horses, rocks. In cups of rocks it slops: flop, slop, slap: bounded in barrels.
And, spent, its speech ceases. It flows purling, widely flowing, floating foam-
pool, flower unfurling.

Under the upswelling tide he saw the writhing weeds lift languidly and
sway reluctant arms, hising up their petticoats,[5] in whispering water swaying
and upturning coy silver fronds. Day by day: night by night: lifted, flooded
and let fall. Lord, they are weary: and, whispered to, they sigh. Saint Ambrose
heard it, sigh of leaves and waves, waiting, awaiting the fullness of their
times, *diebus ac noctibus iniurias patiens ingemiscit.*[6] To no end gathered;
vainly then released, forthflowing, wending back: loom of the moon. Weary
too in sight of lovers, lascivious men, a naked woman shining in her courts,
she draws a toil of waters.

Five fathoms out there. Full fathom five thy father lies.[7] At one he said.
Found drowned. High water at Dublin bar. Driving before it a loose drift of
rubble, fanshoals of fishes, silly shells. A corpse rising salt-white from the
undertow, bobbing landward a pace a pace a porpoise. There he is. Hook it
quick. Sunk though he be beneath the watery floor. We have him. Easy now.

Bag of corpsegas sopping in foul brine. A quiver of minnows, fat of a
spongy titbit, flash through the slits of his buttoned trouserfly. God becomes
man becomes fish becomes barnacle goose becomes featherbed mountain.
Dead breaths I living breathe, tread dead dust, devour a urinous offal from
all dead. Hauled stark over the gunwhale he breathes upward the stench of
his green grave, his leprous nosehole snoring to the sun.

A seachange[8] this, brown eyes saltblue. Seadeath, mildest of all deaths
known to man. Old Father Ocean. *Prix de Paris:*[9] beware of imitations. Just
you give it a fair trial. We enjoyed ourselves immensely.

Come. I thirst. Clouding over. No black clouds anywhere, are there?[1]
Thunderstorm. Allbright he falls, proud lightning of the intellect, *Lucifer,
dico, qui nescit occasum.*[2] No. My cockle hat and staff and hismy sandal
shoon.[3] Where? To evening lands. Evening will find itself.

He took the hilt of his ashplant, lunging with it softly, dallying still. Yes,
evening will find itself in me, without me. All days make their end. By the
way next when is it? Tuesday will be the longest day. Of all the glad new
year, mother,[4] the rum tum tiddledy tum. Lawn Tennyson,[5] gentleman poet.
Già.[6] For the old hag with the yellow teeth. And Monsieur Drumont, gentleman journalist. *Già.* My teeth are very bad. Why, I wonder? Feel. That

---

5. A phrase from a vulgar song sung by Mulligan
earlier that morning.
6. Night and day he patiently groaned forth his
wrongs (St. Ambrose).
7. From Ariel's song (*The Tempest* 1.2.396). The
theme of the drowned man is important in this episode (cf. the drowned sailor in Eliot's *Waste Land*).
8. Another quotation from Ariel's song (*The Tempest*).
9. Prize of Paris. The reference is probably to the
Paris Exposition of 1889, where prizes were
awarded in various categories of food, etc.; the
prize-winning commodities bear the seal of the
prize on the label (hence, "beware of imitations").
Stephen mentally awards the prize to death by
drowning.
1. Stephen is looking up to make sure the sky does

not threaten a thunderstorm; like Joyce, he hates
thunder.
2. Lucifer, I say, who knows not his fall. Thunder
and lightning recall the fall of Lucifer.
3. From Ophelia's mad song (*Hamlet* 4.5.23–26):
"How should I your true-love know / From another
one? / By his cockle hat and staff / And his sandal
shoon." Ophelia, too, was drowned.
4. Cf. Tennyson, *The May Queen:* "You must wake
and call me early, call me early, mother dear; /
Tomorrow 'ill be the happiest time of all the glad
New Year."
5. Alfred, Lord Tennyson. A parody of the poet's
name, punning on "lawn tennis," attributed to
W. B. Yeats.
6. Of course!

one is going too. Shells. Ought I go to a dentist, I wonder, with what money? That one. Toothless Kinch, the superman. Why is that, I wonder, or does it mean something perhaps?

My handkerchief. He threw it. I remember. Did I not take it up?

His hand groped vainly in his pockets. No, I didn't. Better buy one.

He laid the dry snot picked from his nostril on a ledge of rock, carefully. For the rest let look who will.

Behind. Perhaps there is someone.

He turned his face over a shoulder, rere regardant.[7] Moving through the air high spars of a threemaster, her sails brailed up on the crosstrees,[8] homing, upstream, silently moving, a silent ship.

[LESTRYGONIANS][9]

Pineapple rock, lemon platt, butter scotch. A sugarsticky girl shovelling scoopfuls of creams for a christian brother. Some school treat. Bad for their tummies. Lozenge and comfit manufacturer to His Majesty the King. God. Save. Our. Sitting on his throne sucking red jujubes white.

A sombre Y. M. C. A. young man, watchful among the warm sweet fumes of Graham Lemon's, placed a throwaway in a hand of Mr Bloom.

Heart to heart talks.

Bloo . . . Me? No.

Blood of the Lamb.[1]

His slow feet walked him riverward, reading. Are you saved? All are washed in the blood of the lamb. God wants blood victim. Birth, hymen, martyr, war, foundation of a building, sacrifice, kidney burntoffering, druids' altars. Elijah is coming. Dr John Alexander Dowie,[2] restorer of the church in Zion, is coming.

7. Looking behind him (heraldic terminology). Stephen, as we leave him sitting by the shore, is described in a highly stylized, heraldic language.

8. When Budgen pointed out to Joyce that *crosstrees* was not the proper nautical term for the spars to which the sails are bent, Joyce thanked him but added: "But the word 'crosstrees' is essential. It comes in later on and I can't change it. After all, a yard is also a crosstree for the onlooking landlubber." Joyce later uses *crosstree* in a reference to the crucifixion of Christ, so that the suggestion here is of Stephen as both artist and martyr (as his name implies). But the ship is also a real ship, which arrived in Dublin on June 16, 1904.

9. It is lunchtime in Dublin and Leopold Bloom, as he walks through the city in no great hurry (for he likes to linger and watch what goes on around him), thinks of food. The Lestrygonians in book 10 of the *Odyssey* are cannibals, and throughout this episode there are suggestions of the slaughter of living creatures for food or of food as something disgusting, which make somewhat tenuous contact with Homer's description of the cannibals spearing Ulysses' men for food; the parallel is not, however, profound or very important. What is most important about this episode is that it shows us Bloom's consciousness responding to the sights and sounds of Dublin. His humane curiosity, his desire to learn and to improve the human lot, his sympathetic concern for Mrs. Breen and Mrs. Purefoy, his feeding the gulls, his recollections of a happier time

when his daughter was a baby and his relations with his wife, Molly, were thoroughly satisfactory, his interest in opera, his continuous shying away from thoughts of his wife's rendezvous with the dashing Blazes Boylan—all this helps to build up his character in depth and to differentiate him sharply from Stephen. Unlike Stephen, Bloom's interest in language is confined to simple puns and translations; his interest in poetry is obvious and sentimental; his interest in the nature of reality takes the form of half-forgotten fragments of science remaining in his mind from school days. Everything about him is concrete, practical, sensual, and middlebrow or lowbrow, as distinct from the abstract, theoretical, esoteric speculations of Stephen in the *Proteus* episode. For example, when Stephen saw seagulls, he speculated on Daedalus and on flying as a symbol of the artist going into exile; when Bloom sees them, he thinks they must be hungry and buys a bun to feed them. There are parallels between their two streams of consciousness. Bloom's thoughts, in a sense, include Stephen's but in a popularized and even vulgarized form.

1. Bloom has been handed a religious leaflet ("throwaway") containing the phrase "Blood of the Lamb." He at first mistakes "Blood" for "Bloom."

2. Dowie (1847–1907), Scottish-American evangelist who established the "Christian Catholic Apostolic Church in Zion" (i.e., Zion City, IL) in 1901.

Is coming! Is coming!! Is coming!!!
All heartily welcome.

Paying game. Torry and Alexander last year. Polygamy. His wife will put the stopper on that. Where was that ad some Birmingham firm the luminous crucifix. Our Saviour. Wake up in the dead of night and see him on the wall, hanging. Pepper's ghost idea.[3] Iron Nails Ran In.

Phosphorus it must be done with. If you leave a bit of codfish for instance. I could see the bluey silver over it. Night I went down to the pantry in the kitchen. Don't like all the smells in it waiting to rush out. What was it she[4] wanted? The Malaga raisins. Thinking of Spain. Before Rudy[5] was born. The phosphorescence, that bluey greeny. Very good for the brain.

From Butler's monument house corner he glanced along Bachelor's walk. Dedalus' daughter there still outside Dillon's auctionrooms. Must be selling off some old furniture. Knew her eyes at once from the father. Lobbing about waiting for him. Home always breaks up when the mother goes. Fifteen children he had. Birth every year almost. That's in their theology or the priest won't give the poor woman the confession, the absolution. Increase and multiply. Did you ever hear such an idea? Eat you out of house and home. No families themselves to feed. Living on the fat of the land. Their butteries and larders. I'd like to see them do the black fast Yom Kippur.[6] Crossbuns. One meal and a collation for fear he'd collapse on the altar. A housekeeper of one of those fellows if you could pick it out of her. Never pick it out of her. Like getting L s. d.[7] out of him. Does himself well. No guests. All for number one. Watching his water. Bring your own bread and butter. His reverence. Mum's the word.

Good Lord, that poor child's dress is in flitters. Underfed she looks too. Potatoes and marge, marge and potatoes. It's after they feel it. Proof of the pudding. Undermines the constitution.

As he set foot on O'Connell bridge a puffball of smoke plumed up from the parapet. Brewery barge with export stout. England. Sea air sours it, I heard. Be interesting some day get a pass through Hancock to see the brewery. Regular world in itself. Vats of porter, wonderful. Rats get in too. Drink themselves bloated as big as a collie floating. Dead drunk on the porter. Drink till they puke again like christians. Imagine drinking that! Rats: vats. Well of course if we knew all the things.

Looking down he saw flapping strongly, wheeling between the gaunt quay-walls, gulls. Rough weather outside. If I threw myself down? Reuben J's son must have swallowed a good bellyful of that sewage.[8] One and eightpence too much. Hhhhm. It's the droll way he comes out with the things. Knows how to tell a story too.

They wheeled lower. Looking for grub. Wait.

---

3. A dramatic troupe advertising themselves as "The original Pepper's Ghost! and Spectral Opera Company" was popular in the late 19th century; they seem to have specialized in ghostly special effects, possibly achieved through the use of phosphorescent material on their costumes.
4. I.e., Bloom's wife, Molly, born in Gibraltar.
5. Their son, who had died in infancy eleven years before.
6. Jewish Day of Atonement.

7. I.e., cash: L, s., d. are the abbreviations, respectively, for pounds, shillings, and pence.
8. Reuben J. Dodd, Dublin solicitor (lawyer), whose son had been rescued from the Liffey River by a man to whom Reuben J. had given two shillings as a reward—"one and eightpence too much," as Simon Dedalus had remarked to Bloom earlier that morning when they were discussing the incident. It is Dedalus's comment that Bloom is thinking of in the following sentences.

He threw down among them a crumpled paper ball. Elijah thirtytwo feet per sec is com.[9] Not a bit. The ball bobbed unheeded on the wake of swells, floated under by the bridgepiers. Not such damn fools. Also the day I threw that stale cake out of the Erin's King picked it up in the wake fifty yards astern. Live by their wits. They wheeled, flapping.

> The hungry famished gull
> Flaps o'er the waters dull.

That is how poets write, the similar sounds. But then Shakespeare has no rhymes: blank verse. The flow of the language it is. The thoughts. Solemn.

> Hamlet, I am thy father's spirit
> Doomed for a certain time to walk the earth.[1]

—Two apples a penny! Two for a penny!

His gaze passed over the glazed apples serried on her stand. Australians they must be this time of year. Shiny peels: polishes them up with a rag or a handkerchief.

Wait. Those poor birds.

He halted again and bought from the old applewoman two Banbury cakes for a penny and broke the brittle paste and threw its fragments down into the Liffey. See that? The gulls swooped silently two, then all from their heights, pouncing on prey. Gone. Every morsel.

Aware of their greed and cunning he shook the powdery crumb from his hands. They never expected that. Manna.[2] Live on fishy flesh they have to, all seabirds, gulls, seagoose. Swans from Anna Liffey[3] swim down here sometimes to preen themselves. No accounting for tastes. Wonder what kind is swanmeat. Robinson Crusoe had to live on them.

They wheeled, flapping weakly. I'm not going to throw any more. Penny quite enough. Lot of thanks I get. Not even a caw. They spread foot and mouth disease too. If you cram a turkey, say, on chestnutmeal it tastes like that. Eat pig like pig. But then why is it that saltwater fish are not salty? How is that?

His eyes sought answer from the river and saw a rowboat rock at anchor on the treacly swells lazily its plastered board.

Kino's
11 / —
Trousers[4]

Good idea that. Wonder if he pays rent to the corporation. How can you own water really? It's always flowing in a stream, never the same, which in the stream of life we trace. Because life is a stream. All kinds of places are good for ads. That quack doctor for the clap used to be stuck up in all the greenhouses. Never see it now. Strictly confidential. Dr Hy Franks. Didn't cost him a red like Maginni the dancing master self advertisement. Got fel-

---

9. I.e., Elijah is coming, accelerating at the rate of thirty-two feet per second per second, the acceleration rate of falling bodies. ("Elijah is coming" is the legend on the handbill Bloom is tossing away).
1. *Hamlet* 1.5.9–10 (slightly misquoted).
2. The divine food (small, round, and white) that the children of Israel ate in the wilderness (Exodus

16.14–15).
3. The Liffey flows from the Wicklow Mountains northeast and east to Dublin Bay.
4. I.e., eleven shillings ("11/-") for Kino's Trousers. Bloom is a canvasser for advertisements: he receives commissions from newspapers for getting tradesmen to place advertisements with them.

lows to stick them up or stick them up himself for that matter on the q.t. running in to loosen a button. Flybynight. Just the place too. POST NO BILLS. POST NO PILLS.[5] Some chap with a dose burning him.

If he . . .

O!

Eh?

No . . . No.

No, no. I don't believe it. He wouldn't surely?

No, no.[6]

Mr Bloom moved forward, raising his troubled eyes. Think no more about that. After one. Timeball on the ballastoffice is down. Dunsink time. Fascinating little book that is of Sir Robert Ball's. Parallax. I never exactly understood.[7] There's a priest. Could ask him. Par it's Greek: parallel, parallax. Met him pike hoses[8] she called it till I told her about the transmigration. O rocks!

Mr Bloom smiled O rocks at two windows of the ballastoffice. She's right after all. Only big words for ordinary things on account of the sound. She's not exactly witty. Can be rude too. Blurt out what I was thinking. Still I don't know. She used to say Ben Dollard had a base barreltone voice. He has legs like barrels and you'd think he was singing into a barrel. Now isn't that wit? They used to call him big Ben. Not half as witty as calling him base barreltone. Appetite like an albatross. Get outside of a baron of beef. Powerful man he was at stowing away number one Bass.[9] Barrel of Bass. See? It all works out.

A procession of whitesmocked men marched slowly towards him along the gutter, scarlet sashes across their boards. Bargains. Like that priest they are this morning: we have sinned: we have suffered. He read the scarlet letters on their five tall white hats: H. E. L. Y. S. Wisdom Hely's. Y lagging behind drew a chunk of bread from under his foreboard, crammed it into his mouth and munched as he walked. Our staple food. Three bob a day, walking along the gutters, street after street. Just keep skin and bone together, bread and skilly. They are not Boyl: no: M'Glade's men. Doesn't bring in any business either. I suggested to him about a transparent showcart with two smart girls sitting inside writing letters, copybooks, envelopes, blottingpaper. I bet that would have caught on. Smart girls writing something catch the eye at once. Everyone dying to know what she's writing. Get twenty of them round you if you stare at nothing. Have a finger in the pie. Women too. Curiosity. Pillar of salt. Wouldn't have it of course because he didn't think of it himself first. Or the inkbottle I suggested with a false stain of black celluloid. His ideas for ads like Plumtree's potted under the obituaries, cold meat department.

5. The revised text edited by John Kidd (1993) reads, POST NO BILLS. POST 110 PILLS. "Post no bills" can mean either "do not affix any posters" or "mail no accounts." Bloom is punning to himself on the quack doctor's advertising (by posting bills), collecting his money (by mailing accounts), and sending pills to patients by mail.
6. Blazes Boylan, flashy philanderer, is due to call on Molly Bloom that afternoon, to discuss the program of a concert that he is managing for her (Molly is a singer). Bloom knows that Boylan and his wife will commit adultery together. Here it suddenly occurs to him that Boylan might give Molly a "dose" of veneral disease, but he puts the thought from him as incredible.

7. The "timeball on the ballastoffice" registers the official time of the observatory at Dunsink. Noticing that the timeball is down, which means that it is after one o'clock, Bloom is reminded of the observatory, then of the Irish astronomer Sir Robert Ball's popular book on astronomy, The Story of the Heavens (1886), and of the astronomical term "parallax" he found in the book but "never exactly understood."
8. Molly's way of pronouncing metempsychosis. When Bloom had explained metempsychosis to her that morning, she had exclaimed "O rocks" at the pretentious term. He now mentally repeats "O rocks!" at the thought of the word parallax.
9. A popular British ale.

You can't lick 'em. What? Our envelopes. Hello! Jones, where are you going? Can't stop, Robinson, I am hastening to purchase the only reliable inkeraser *Kansell,* sold by Hely's Ltd, 85 Dame street. Well out of that ruck I am. Devil of a job it was collecting accounts of those convents. Tranquilla convent. That was a nice nun there, really sweet face. Wimple suited her small head. Sister? Sister? I am sure she was crossed in love by her eyes. Very hard to bargain with that sort of a woman. I disturbed her at her devotions that morning. But glad to communicate with the outside world. Our great day, she said. Feast of Our Lady of Mount Carmel. Sweet name too: caramel. She knew, I think she knew by the way she. If she had married she would have changed. I suppose they really were short of money. Fried everything in the best butter all the same. No lard for them. My heart's broke eating dripping. They like buttering themselves in and out. Molly tasting it, her veil up. Sister? Pat Claffey, the pawnbroker's daughter. It was a nun they say invented barbed wire.

He crossed Westmoreland street when apostrophe S had plodded by. Rover cycleshop. Those races are on today. How long ago is that? Year Phil Gilligan died. We were in Lombard street west. Wait, was in Thom's. Got the job in Wisdom Hely's year we married. Six years. Ten years ago: ninety-four he died, yes that's right the big fire at Arnott's. Val Dillon was lord mayor. The Glencree dinner. Alderman Robert O'Reilly emptying the port into his soup before the flag fell, Bobbob lapping it for the inner alderman. Couldn't hear what the band played. For what we have already received may the Lord make us. Milly[1] was a kiddy then. Molly had that elephantgrey dress with the braided frogs. Mantailored with selfcovered buttons. She didn't like it because I sprained my ankle first day she wore choir picnic at the Sugarloaf. As if that. Old Goodwin's tall hat done up with some sticky stuff. Flies' picnic too. Never put a dress on her back like it. Fitted her like a glove, shoulder and hips. Just beginning to plump it out well. Rabbitpie we had that day. People looking after her.

Happy. Happier then. Snug little room that was with the red wallpaper, Dockrell's, one and ninepence a dozen. Milly's tubbing night. American soap I bought: elderflower. Cosy smell of her bathwater. Funny she looked soaped all over. Shapely too. Now photography.[2] Poor papa's daguerreotype atelier he told me of. Hereditary taste.

He walked along the curbstone.

Stream of life. What was the name of that priestlylooking chap was always squinting in when he passed? Weak eyes, woman. Stopped in Citron's saint Kevin's parade. Pen something. Pendennis? My memory is getting. Pen . . . ? Of course it's years ago. Noise of the trams probably. Well, if he couldn't remember the dayfather's name that he sees every day.

Bartell d'Arcy was the tenor, just coming out then. Seeing her home after practice. Conceited fellow with his waxedup moustache. Gave her that song *Winds that blow from the south.*

Windy night that was I went to fetch her there was that lodge meeting on about those lottery tickets after Goodwin's concert in the supperroom or oakroom of the Mansion house. He and I behind. Sheet of her music blew out of my hand against the High school railings. Lucky it didn't. Thing like

---

1. Bloom's fifteen-year-old daughter.　　　　2. Milly is working at a photographer's.

that spoils the effect of a night for her. Professor Goodwin linking her in front. Shaky on his pins, poor old sot. His farewell concerts. Positively last appearance on any stage. May be for months and may be for never. Remember her laughing at the wind, her blizzard collar up. Corner of Harcourt road remember that gust. Brrfoo! Blew up all her skirts and her boa nearly smothered old Goodwin. She did get flushed in the wind. Remember when we got home raking up the fire and frying up those pieces of lap of mutton for her supper with the Chutney sauce she liked. And the mulled rum. Could see her in the bedroom from the hearth unclamping the busk of her stays: white.

Swish and soft flop her stays made on the bed. Always warm from her. Always liked to let her self out. Sitting there after till near two taking out her hairpins. Milly tucked up in beddyhouse. Happy. Happy. That was the night . . .

—O, Mr Bloom, how do you do?

—O, how do you do, Mrs Breen?[3]

—No use complaining. How is Molly those times? Haven't seen her for ages.

—In the pink, Mr Bloom said gaily, Milly has a position down in Mullingar, you know.

—Go away! Isn't that grand for her?

—Yes, in a photographer's there. Getting on like a house on fire. How are all your charges?

—All on the baker's list, Mrs Breen said.

How many has she? No other in sight.

—You're in black I see. You have no . . .

—No, Mr. Bloom said. I have just come from a funeral.

Going to crop up all day, I foresee. Who's dead, when and what did he die of? Turn up like a bad penny.

—O dear me, Mrs Breen said, I hope it wasn't any near relation.

May as well get her sympathy.

—Dignam, Mr Bloom said. An old friend of mine. He died quite suddenly, poor fellow. Heart trouble, I believe. Funeral was this morning.

> Your funeral's tomorrow
> While you're coming through the rye.
> Diddlediddle dumdum
> Diddlediddle . . .

—Sad to lose the old friends, Mrs Breen's womaneyes said melancholily. Now that's quite enough about that. Just quietly: husband.

—And your lord and master?

Mrs Breen turned up her two large eyes. Hasn't lost them anyhow.

—O, don't be talking, she said. He's a caution to rattlesnakes. He's in there now with his lawbooks finding out the law of libel. He has me heartscalded. Wait till I show you.

Hot mockturtle vapour and steam of newbaked jampuffs rolypoly poured out from Harrison's. The heavy noonreek tickled the top of Mr Bloom's gullet. Want to make good pastry, butter, best flour, Demerara sugar, or they'd taste it with the hot tea. Or is it from her? A barefoot arab stood over the

---

3. Mrs. Breen had been an old sweetheart of Bloom's.

grating, breathing in the fumes. Deaden the gnaw of hunger that way. Pleasure or pain is it? Penny dinner. Knife and fork chained to the table.

Opening her handbag, chipped leather, hatpin: ought to have a guard on
those things. Stick it in a chap's eye in the tram. Rummaging. Open. Money.
Please take one. Devils if they lose sixpence. Raise Cain. Husband barging.
Where's the ten shillings I gave you on Monday? Are you feeding your little
brother's family? Soiled handkerchief: medicinebottle. Pastille that was fell.
What is she? . . .

—There must be a new moon out, she said. He's always bad then.[4] Do
you know what he did last night?

Her hand ceased to rummage. Her eyes fixed themselves on him, wide in
alarm, yet smiling.

—What? Mr. Bloom asked.

Let her speak. Look straight in her eyes. I believe you. Trust me.

—Woke me up in the night, she said. Dream he had, a nightmare.

Indiges.

—Said the ace of spades[5] was walking up the stairs.

—The ace of spades! Mr Bloom said.

She took a folded postcard from her handbag.

—Read that, she said. He got it this morning.

—What is it? Mr Bloom asked, taking the card. U. P.?

—U.p.: up, she said. Someone taking a rise out of him. It's a great shame
for them whoever he is.

—Indeed it is, Mr Bloom said.

She took back the card, sighing.

—And now he's going round to Mr Menton's office. He's going to take an
action for ten thousand pounds, he says.

She folded the card into her untidy bag and snapped the catch.

Same blue serge dress she had two years ago, the nap bleaching. Seen its
best days. Wispish hair over her ears. And that dowdy toque: three old grapes
to take the harm out of it. Shabby genteel. She used to be a tasty dresser.
Lines round her mouth. Only a year or so older than Molly.

See the eye that woman gave her, passing. Cruel. The unfair sex.

He looked still at her, holding back behind his look his discontent. Pungent mockturtle oxtail mulligatawny. I'm hungry too. Flakes of pastry on the
gusset of her dress: daub of sugary flour stuck to her cheek. Rhubarb tart
with liberal fillings, rich fruit interior. Josie Powell that was. In Luke Doyle's
long ago, Dolphin's Barn, the charades. U.p.: up.

Change the subject.

—Do you ever see anything of Mrs Beaufoy, Mr Bloom asked.

—Mina Purefoy? she said.

Philip Beaufoy I was thinking. Playgoers' Club[6] Matcham often thinks of
the masterstroke. Did I pull the chain? Yes. The last act.

—Yes.

—I just called to ask on the way in is she over it. She's in the lying-in
hospital in Holles street. Dr Horne got her in. She's three days bad now.

---

4. Mr. Breen is mentally disturbed.
5. Symbol of death.
6. Bloom is thinking of the story *Matcham's Masterstroke*, by "Mr. Philip Beaufoy, Playgoers' Club,

London," which he had read in the toilet that
morning. He then mentally quotes the opening
sentence.

—O, Mr Bloom said. I'm sorry to hear that.

—Yes, Mrs Breen said. And a houseful of kids at home. It's a very stiff birth, the nurse told me.

—O, Mr Bloom said.

His heavy pitying gaze absorbed her news. His tongue clacked in compassion. Dth! Dth!

—I'm sorry to hear that, he said. Poor thing! Three days! That's terrible for her.

Mrs Breen nodded

—She was taken bad on the Tuesday . . .

Mr Bloom touched her funnybone gently, warning her.

—Mind! Let this man pass.

A bony form strode along the curbstone from the river, staring with a rapt gaze into the sunlight through a heavystringed glass. Tight as a skullpiece a tiny hat gripped his head. From his arm a folded dustcoat, a stick and an umbrella dangled to his stride.

—Watch him, Mr Bloom said. He always walks outside the lampposts. Watch!

—Who is he if it's a fair question? Mrs Breen asked. Is he dotty?

—His name is Cashel Boyle O'Connor Fitzmaurice Tisdall Farrell, Mr Bloom said smiling. Watch!

—He has enough of them, she said. Denis will be like that one of these days.

She broke off suddenly.

—There he is, she said. I must go after him. Goodbye. Remember me to Molly, won't you?

—I will, Mr Bloom said.

He watched her dodge through passers towards the shopfronts. Denis Breen in skimpy frockcoat and blue canvas shoes shuffled out of Harrison's hugging two heavy tomes to his ribs. Blown in from the bay. Like old times. He suffered her to overtake him without surprise and thrust his dull grey beard towards her, his loose jaw wagging as he spoke earnestly.

Meshuggah.[7] Off his chump.

Mr Bloom walked on again easily, seeing ahead of him in sunlight the tight skullpiece, the dangling stick, umbrella, dustcoat. Going the two days. Watch him! Out he goes again. One way of getting on in the world. And that other old mosey lunatic in those duds. Hard time she must have with him.

U.p.: up. I'll take my oath that's Alf Bergan or Richie Goulding. Wrote it for a lark in the Scotch house, I bet anything. Round to Menton's office. His oyster eyes staring at the postcard. Be a feast for the gods.

He passed the *Irish Times*. There might be other answers lying there. Like to answer them all. Good system for criminals. Code. At their lunch now. Clerk with the glasses there doesn't know me. O, leave them there to simmer. Enough bother wading through fortyfour of them. Wanted smart lady typist to aid gentleman in literary work. I called you naughty darling because I do not like that other world. Please tell me what is the meaning. Please tell me what perfume does your wife. Tell me who made the

---

7. Mad (Yiddish).

world.[8] The way they spring those questions on you. And the other one Lizzie Twigg.[9] My literary efforts have had the good fortune to meet with the approval of the eminent poet A. E. (Mr Geo. Russell).[1] No time to do her hair drinking sloppy tea with a book of poetry.

Best paper by long chalks for a small ad. Got the provinces now. Cook and general, exc cuisine, housemaid kept. Wanted live man for spirit counter. Resp. girl (R. C.) wishes to hear of post in fruit or pork shop. James Carlisle made that. Six and a half per cent dividend. Made a big deal on Coates's shares. Ca' canny. Cunning old Scotch hunks. All the toady news. Our gracious and popular vicereine.[2] Bought the *Irish Field* now. Lady Mountcashel has quite recovered after her confinement and rode out with the Ward Union staghounds at the enlargement yesterday at Rathoath. Uneatable fox. Pothunters too. Fear injects juices make it tender enough for them. Riding astride. Sit her horse like a man. Weightcarrying huntress. No sidesaddle or pillion for her, not for Joe. First to the meet and in at the death. Strong as a broodmare some of those horsey women. Swagger around livery stables. Toss off a glass of brandy neat while you'd say knife. That one at the Grosvenor this morning. Up with her on the car: wishswish. Stonewall or fivebarred gate put her mount to it. Think that pugnosed driver did it out of spite. Who is this she was like? O yes! Mrs Miriam Dandrade that sold me her old wraps and black underclothes in the Shelbourne hotel. Divorced Spanish American. Didn't take a feather out of her my handling them. As if I was her clotheshorse. Saw her in the viceregal party when Stubbs the park ranger got me in with Whelan of the *Express*. Scavenging what the quality left. High tea. Mayonnaise I poured on the plums thinking it was custard. Her ears ought to have tingled for a few weeks after. Want to be a bull for her. Born courtesan. No nursery work for her, thanks.

Poor Mrs Purefoy! Methodist husband. Method in his madness. Saffron bun and milk and soda lunch in the educational dairy. Eating with a stopwatch, thirtytwo chews to the minute. Still his muttonchop whiskers grew. Supposed to be well connected. Theodore's cousin in Dublin Castle. One tony relative in every family. Hardy annuals he presents her with. Saw him out at the Three Jolly Topers marching along bareheaded and his eldest boy carrying one in a marketnet. The squallers. Poor thing! Then having to give the breast year after year all hours of the night. Selfish those t.t's[3] are. Dog in the manger. Only one lump of sugar in my tea, if you please.

He stood at Fleet street crossing. Luncheon interval a sixpenny at Rowe's? Must look up that ad in the national library.[4] An eightpenny in the Burton. Better. On my way.

---

8. Cf. Marlowe's *The Tragical History of Doctor Faustus* 5, lines 237–44:
FAUSTUS. . . . Tell me who made the world?
MEPHASTOPHILIS. I will not.
. . . Think on hell Faustus, for thou art damned.
FAUSTUS. Think, Faustus, upon God, that made the world.
9. Bloom is mentally quoting a letter written to him by the typist Martha Clifford, with whom he is carrying on a purely epistolary love affair (she had misspelled *word* as *world*: "I do not like that other world"). Lizzie Twigg was one of the other typists who had answered his advertisement for a secretary "to aid gentleman in literary work" (Bloom's pretext for beginning such an affair).

1. Æ (George Russell, 1867–1935), the Irish poet mentioned as a reference by Lizzie Twigg when she answered Bloom's advertisement, is later encountered by Bloom with a woman who Bloom speculates might be Lizzie.
2. Wife of the viceroy, who represented the British Crown in Ireland; Bloom is thinking of the society column in the *Irish Times*.
3. Abbreviation of "teetotalers," total abstainers from alcohol.
4. Bloom's goal, on his walk through Dublin, is the National Library, where he wants to look up an advertisement in a back number of the *Kilkenny People*.

He walked on past Bolton's Westmoreland house. Tea. Tea. Tea. I forgot to tap Tom Kernan.[5]

Sss. Dth, dth, dth! Three days imagine groaning on a bed with a vinegared handkerchief round her forehead, her belly swollen out. Phew! Dreadful simply! Child's head too big: forceps. Doubled up inside her trying to butt its way out blindly, groping for the way out. Kill me that would. Lucky Molly got over hers lightly. They ought to invent something to stop that. Life with hard labour. Twilightsleep idea: queen Victoria was given that. Nine she had. A good layer. Old woman that lived in a shoe she had so many children. Suppose he was consumptive. Time someone thought about it instead of gassing about the what was it the pensive bosom of the silver effulgence. Flapdoddle to feed fools on. They could easily have big establishments. Whole thing quite painless out of all the taxes give every child born five quid at compound interest up to twentyone, five per cent is a hundred shillings and five tiresome pounds, multiply by twenty decimal system, encourage people to put by money save hundred and ten and a bit twentyone years want to work it out on paper come to a tidy sum, more than you think.

Not stillborn of course. They are not even registered. Trouble for nothing.

Funny sight two of them together, their bellies out. Molly and Mrs Moisel. Mothers' meeting. Phthisis retires for the time being, then returns. How flat they look after all of a sudden! Peaceful eyes. Weight off their mind. Old Mrs Thornton was a jolly old soul. All my babies, she said. The spoon of pap in her mouth before she fed them. O, that's nyumyum. Got her hand crushed by old Tom Wall's son. His first bow to the public. Head like a prize pumpkin. Snuffy Dr Murren. People knocking them up at all hours. For God's sake doctor. Wife in her throes. Then keep them waiting months for their fee. To attendance on your wife. No gratitude in people. Humane doctors, most of them.

Before the huge high door of the Irish house of parliament a flock of pigeons flew. Their little frolic after meals. Who will we do it on? I pick the fellow in black. Here goes. Here's good luck. Must be thrilling from the air. Apjohn, myself and Owen Goldberg up in the trees near Goose green playing the monkeys. Mackerel they called me.

A squad of constables debouched from College street, marching in Indian file. Goosestep. Foodheated faces, sweating helmets, patting their truncheons. After their feed with a good load of fat soup under their belts. Policeman's lot is oft a happy one.[6] They split up into groups and scattered, saluting towards their beats. Let out to graze. Best moment to attack one in pudding time. A punch in his dinner. A squad of others, marching irregularly, rounded Trinity railings, making for the station. Bound for their troughs. Prepare to receive cavalry. Prepare to receive soup.

He crossed under Tommy Moore's roguish finger. They did right to put him up over a urinal: meeting of the waters.[7] Ought to be places for women. Running into cakeshops. Settle my hat straight. *There is not in this wide world a vallee.* Great song of Julia Morkan's. Kept her voice up to the very last. Pupil of Michael Balfe's wasn't she?

He gazed after the last broad tunic. Nasty customers to tackle. Jack Power

5. A Dublin tea merchant and friend of Bloom's, whom Bloom had earlier intended to ask ("tap") for some tea.
6. Cf. W. S. Gilbert, *Pirates of Penzance*: "The policeman's lot is not a happy one."
7. *The Meeting of the Waters* was a famous poem by the much-loved Irish poet Thomas Moore (1779–1852), whose statue Bloom now passes.

could a tale unfold: father a G man. If a fellow gave them trouble being lagged they let him have it hot and heavy in the bridewell.[8] Can't blame them after all with the job they have especially the young hornies. That horsepoliceman the day Joe Chamberlain was given his degree in Trinity he got a run for his money.[9] My word he did! His horse's hoofs clattering after us down Abbey street. Luck I had the presence of mind to dive into Manning's or I was souped. He did come a wallop, by George. Must have cracked his skull on the cobblestones. I oughtn't to have got myself swept along with those medicals. And the Trinity jibs[1] in their mortarboards. Looking for trouble. Still I got to know that young Dixon who dressed that sting for me in the Mater and now he's in Holles street where Mrs Purefoy. Wheels within wheels. Police whistle in my ears still. All skedaddled. Why he fixed on me. Give me in charge. Right here it began.

—Up the Boers!

—Three cheers for De Wet![2]

—We'll hang Joe Chamberlain on a sourapple tree.

Silly billies: mob of young cubs yelling their guts out. Vinegar hill. The Butter exchange band. Few years' time half of them magistrates and civil servants. War comes on: into the army helterskelter: same fellows used to. Whether on the scaffold high.

Never know who you're talking to. Corny Kelleher he has Harvey Duff in his eye. Like that Peter or Denis or James Carey that blew the gaff on the invincibles. Member of the corporation too. Egging raw youths on to get in the know. All the time drawing secret service pay from the castle.[3] Drop him like a hot potato. Why those plainclothes men are always courting slaveys. Easily twig a man used to uniform. Squarepushing up against a backdoor. Maul her a bit. Then the next thing on the menu. And who is the gentleman does be visiting there? Was the young master saying anything? Peeping Tom through the keyhole. Decoy duck. Hotblooded young student fooling round her fat arms ironing.

—Are those yours, Mary?

—I don't wear such things . . . Stop or I'll tell the missus on you. Out half the night.

—There are great times coming, Mary. Wait till you see.

—Ah, get along with your great times coming.

Barmaids too. Tobaccoshopgirls.

James Stephens'[4] idea was the best. He knew them. Circles of ten so that a fellow couldn't round on more than his own ring. Sinn Fein.[5] Back out you get the knife. Hidden hand. Stay in. The firing squad. Turnkey's daughter got him out of Richmond, off from Lusk. Putting up in the Buckingham Palace hotel under their very noses. Garibaldi.[6]

You must have a certain fascination: Parnell. Arthur Griffith[7] is a squareheaded fellow but he has no go in him for the mob. Want to gas about our

---

8. Prison.

9. When Joseph Chamberlain, the British colonial secretary, came to Dublin to receive an honorary degree from Trinity College, a group of medical students rioted against him and against the Boer War.

1. Trinity College students.

2. Boer general.

3. I.e., from the British government, whose representative lived at Dublin Castle.

4. Irish nationalist revolutionary.

5. Irish revolutionary movement. The Gaelic words mean "Ourselves Alone."

6. Bloom is thinking of a variety of nationalist conspirators who escaped from danger, among them the 19th-century Italian patriot and general Giuseppe Garibaldi.

7. Founder of the Sinn Fein (1872–1922). Charles Stewart Parnell (1846–1891), Irish nationalist political leader.

lovely land. Gammon and spinach. Dublin Bakery Company's tearoom. Debating societies. That republicanism is the best form of government. That the language question should take precedence of the economic question. Have your daughters inveigling them to your house. Stuff them up with meat and drink. Michaelmas goose. Here's a good lump of thyme seasoning under the apron for you. Have another quart of goosegrease before it gets too cold. Halffed enthusiasts. Penny roll and a walk with the band. No grace for the carver. The thought that the other chap pays best sauce in the world. Make themselves thoroughly at home. Show us over those apricots, meaning peaches. The not far distant day. Home Rule sun rising up in the northwest.[8]

His smile faded as he walked, a heavy cloud hiding the sun slowly, shadowing Trinity's surly front. Trams passed one another, ingoing, outgoing, clanging. Useless words. Things go on same; day after day: squads of police marching out, back: trams in, out. Those two loonies mooching about. Dignam carted off. Mina Purefoy swollen belly on a bed groaning to have a child tugged out of her. One born every second somewhere. Other dying every second. Since I fed the birds five minutes. Three hundred kicked the bucket. Other three hundred born, washing the blood off, all are washed in the blood of the lamb, bawling maaaaaa.

Cityful passing away, other cityful coming, passing away too: other coming on, passing on. Houses, lines of houses, streets, miles of pavements, piledup bricks, stones. Changing hands. This owner, that. Landlord never dies they say. Other steps into his shoes when he gets his notice to quit. They buy the place up with gold and still they have all the gold. Swindle in it somewhere. Piled up in cities, worn away age after age. Pyramids in sand. Built on bread and onions. Slaves Chinese wall. Babylon. Big stones left. Round towers. Rest rubble, sprawling suburbs, jerrybuilt, Kerwan's mushroom houses built of breeze. Shelter for the night.

No-one is anything.

This is the very worst hour of the day. Vitality. Dull, gloomy: hate this hour. Feel as if I had been eaten and spewed.

Provost's house. The reverend Dr Salmon: tinned salmon. Well tinned in there. Wouldn't live in it if they paid me. Hope they have liver and bacon today. Nature abhors a vacuum.

The sun freed itself slowly and lit glints of light among the silverware in Walter Sexton's window opposite by which John Howard Parnell[9] passed, unseeing.

There he is: the brother. Image of him. Haunting face. Now that's a coincidence. Course hundreds of times you think of a person and don't meet him. Like a man walking in his sleep. No-one knows him. Must be a corporation meeting today. They say he never put on the city marshal's uniform since he got the job. Charley Beulger used to come out on his high horse, cocked hat, puffed, powdered and shaved. Look at the woebegone walk of him. Eaten a bad egg. Poached eyes on ghost. I have a pain. Great man's brother: his brother's brother. He'd look nice on the city charger. Drop into the D. B. C. probably for his coffee, play chess there. His brother used men as pawns. Let them all go to pot. Afraid to pass a remark on him. Freeze

8. Reference to Griffith's comment on the *Freeman* masthead, which showed the sun rising in the northwest from behind the Bank of Ireland. Bloom has a *Freeman* in his pocket.
9. Parnell's brother.

them up with that eye of his. That's the fascination: the name. All a bit touched. Mad Fanny and his other sister Mrs Dickinson driving about with scarlet harness. Bolt upright like surgeon M'Ardle. Still David Sheehy beat him for south Meath. Apply for the Chiltern Hundreds[1] and retire into public life. The patriot's banquet. Eating orangepeels in the park. Simon Dedalus said when they put him in parliament that Parnell would come back from the grave and lead him out of the House of Commons by the arm.

—Of the twoheaded octopus, one of whose heads is the head upon which the ends of the world have forgotten to come while the other speaks with a Scotch accent. The tentacles . . .

They passed from behind Mr Bloom along the curbstone. Beard and bicycle. Young woman.

And there he is too. Now that's really a coincidence: second time. Coming events cast their shadows before. With the approval of the eminent poet, Mr Geo Russell. That might be Lizzie Twigg with him.[2] A. E.: what does that mean? Initials perhaps. Albert Edward, Arthur Edmund, Alphonsus Eb Ed El Esquire. What was he saying? The ends of the world with a Scotch accent. Tentacles: octopus. Something occult: symbolism. Holding forth. She's taking it all in. Not saying a word. To aid gentleman in literary work.

His eyes followed the high figure in homespun, beard and bicycle, a listening woman at his side. Coming from the vegetarian. Only weggebobbles and fruit. Don't eat a beefsteak. If you do the eyes of that cow will pursue you through all eternity. They say it's healthier. Wind and watery though. Tried it. Keep you on the run all day. Bad as a bloater. Dreams all night. Why do they call that thing they gave me nutsteak? Nutarians. Fruitarians. To give you the idea you are eating rumpsteak. Absurd. Salty too. They cook in soda. Keep you sitting by the tap all night.

Her stockings are loose over her ankles. I detest that: so tasteless. Those literary etherial people they are all. Dreamy, cloudy, symbolistic. Esthetes they are. I wouldn't be surprised if it was that kind of food you see produces the like waves of the brain the poetical. For example one of those policemen sweating Irish stew into their shirts; you couldn't squeeze a line of poetry out of him. Don't know what poetry is even. Must be in a certain mood.

The dreamy cloudy gull
Waves o'er the waters dull.

He crossed at Nassau street corner and stood before the window of Yeates and Son, pricing the fieldglasses. Or will I drop into old Harris's and have a chat with young Sinclair? Wellmannered fellow. Probably at his lunch. Must get those old glasses of mine set right. Gœrz lenses six guineas. Germans making their way everywhere. Sell on easy terms to capture trade. Undercutting. Might chance on a pair in the railway lost property office. Astonishing the things people leave behind them in trains and cloakrooms. What do they be thinking about? Women too. Incredible. Last year travelling to Ennis

---

1. The Stewardship of the Chiltern Hundreds (a tract of land in central England owned by the British Crown) is by a legal figment held to be an office of profit under the Crown and is conferred on any Member of Parliament wishing to resign his seat, which by law he cannot do, so long as he is duly qualified. A Member of Parliament who accepts an office of profit under the Crown must vacate his seat.

2. Bloom wonders whether the woman with A. E. might be Lizzie Twigg and then goes on to speculate on the meaning of "A. E." and on Russell's mystical ideas.

had to pick up that farmer's daughter's bag and hand it to her at Limerick junction. Unclaimed money too. There's a little watch up there on the roof of the bank to test those glasses by.

His lids came down on the lower rims of his irides. Can't see it. If you imagine it's there you can almost see it. Can't see it.

He faced about and, standing between the awnings, held out his right hand at arm's length towards the sun. Wanted to try that often. Yes: completely. The tip of his little finger blotted out the sun's disk. Must be the focus where the rays cross. If I had black glasses. Interesting. There was a lot of talk about those sunspots when we were in Lombard street west. Terrific explosions they are. There will be a total eclipse this year: autumn some time.

Now that I come to think of it, that ball falls at Greenwich time. It's the clock is worked by an electric wire from Dunsink. Must go out there some first Saturday of the month. If I could get an introduction to professor Joly or learn up something about his family. That would do to: man always feels complimented. Flattery where least expected. Nobleman proud to be descended from some king's mistress. His foremother. Lay it on with a trowel. Cap in hand goes through the land. Not go in and blurt out what you know you're not to: what's parallax? Show this gentleman the door.

Ah.

His hand fell again to his side.

Never know anything about it. Waste of time. Gasballs spinning about, crossing each other, passing. Same old dingdong always. Gas, then solid, then world, then cold, then dead shell drifting around, frozen rock like that pineapple rock. The moon. Must be a new moon out, she said. I believe there is.

He went on by la maison Claire.

Wait. The full moon was the night we were Sunday fortnight exactly there is a new moon. Walking down by the Tolka. Not bad for a Fairview moon. She was humming. The young May moon she's beaming, love. He other side of her. Elbow, arm. He. Glowworm's la-amp is gleaming, love. Touch. Fingers. Asking. Answer. Yes.

Stop. Stop. If it was it was.[3] Must.

Mr Bloom, quickbreathing, slowlier walking passed Adam court.

With deep quiet relief, his eyes took note: this is street here middle of the day Bob Doran's bottle shoulders. On his annual bend, M'Coy said. They drink in order to say or do something or *cherchez la femme.*[4] Up in the Coombe with chummies and streetwalkers and then the rest of the year as sober as a judge.

Yes. Thought so. Sloping into the Empire. Gone. Plain soda would do him good. Where Pat Kinsella had his Harp theatre before Whitbread ran the Queen's.[5] Broth of a boy. Dion Boucicault[6] business with his harvestmoon face in a poky bonnet. Three Purty Maids from School. How time flies eh? Showing long red pantaloons under his skirts. Drinkers, drinking, laughed spluttering, their drink against their breath. More power, Pat. Coarse red: fun for drunkards: guffaw and smoke. Take off that white hat. His parboiled

---

3. Bloom is thinking again of his wife's infidelity.
4. Look for the woman (in the case).
5. The Queen's Theatre.

6. Irish-born American dramatist, manager, and actor.

eyes. Where is he now? Beggar somewhere. The harp that once did starve us all.[7]

I was happier then. Or was that I? Or am I now I? Twentyeight I was. She twentythree when we left Lombard street west something changed. Could never like it again after Rudy. Can't bring back time. Like holding water in your hand. Would you go back to then? Just beginning then. Would you? Are you not happy in your home, you poor little naughty boy? Wants to sew on buttons for me. I must answer. Write it in the library.

Grafton street gay with housed awnings lured his senses. Muslin prints silk, dames and dowagers, jingle of harnesses, hoofthuds lowringing in the baking causeway. Thick feet that woman has in the white stockings. Hope the rain mucks them up on her. Countrybred chawbacon. All the beef to the heels were in. Always gives a woman clumsy feet. Molly looks out of plumb.

He passed, dallying, the windows of Brown Thomas, silk mercers. Cascades of ribbons. Flimsy China silks. A tilted urn poured from its mouth a flood of bloodhued poplin: lustrous blood. The huguenots brought that here. *La causa è santa!*[8] *Tara tara.* Great chorus that. *Tara.* Must be washed in rainwater. Meyerbeer. *Tara: bom bom bom.*

Pincushions. I'm a long time threatening to buy one. Stick them all over the place. Needles in window curtains.

He bared slightly his left forearm. Scrape: nearly gone. Not today anyhow. Must go back for that lotion. For her birthday perhaps. Junejuly augseptember eighth. Nearly three months off. Then she mightn't like it. Women won't pick up pins. Say it cuts lo.

Gleaming silks, petticoats on slim brass rails, rays of flat silk stockings.

Useless to go back. Had to be. Tell me all.

High voices. Sunwarm silk. Jingling harnesses. All for a woman, home and houses, silkwebs, silver, rich fruits, spicy from Jaffa. Agendath Netaim.[9] Wealth of the world.

A warm human plumpness settled down on his brain. His brain yielded. Perfume of embraces all him assailed. With hungered flesh obscurely, he mutely craved to adore.

Duke street. Here we are. Must eat. The Burton. Feel better then.

He turned Combridge's corner, still pursued. Jingling hoofthuds. Perfumed bodies, warm, full. All kissed, yielded: in deep summer fields, tangled pressed grass, in trickling hallways of tenements, along sofas, creaking beds.

—Jack, love!

—Darling!

—Kiss me, Reggy!

—My boy!

—Love![1]

7. A reference to the lack of financial success of the Harp Theatre through a punning reworking (almost worthy of Stephen Dedalus) of Moore's famous *Harp That Once Through Tara's Halls.*
8. "The cause is sacred," chorus from Meyerbeer's opera *Les Huguenots*, which Bloom is recalling. The Huguenots were 16th- and 17th-century French Protestants, many of whom fled to Britain to escape persecution.
9. Planters' Company (Hebrew). Bloom recalls a leaflet, which he had seen that morning and is still

carrying in his pocket, advertising an early Zionist settlement
1. Sensual images are leading Bloom to imagine love scenes from a sentimental novel. The Lestrygonians had used "the handsome daughter of Lestrygonian Antiphates" as a decoy to lure Ulysses' men to her father, and Bloom is drawn by his sensual and sexual imagination to enter Burton's restaurant—only to be disgusted by the grossness of the atmosphere.

His heart astir he pushed in the door of the Burton restaurant. Stink gripped his trembling breath: pungent meatjuice, slop of greens. See the animals feed.

Men, men, men.

Perched on high stools by the bar, hats shoved back, at the tables calling for more bread no charge, swilling, wolfing gobfuls of sloppy food, their eyes bulging, wiping wetted moustaches. A pallid suetfaced young man polished his tumbler knife fork and spoon with his napkin. New set of microbes. A man with an infant's saucestained napkin tucked round him shovelled gurgling soup down his gullet. A man spitting back on his plate: halfmasticated gristle: no teeth to chewchewchew it. Chump chop from the grill. Bolting to get it over. Sad booser's eyes. Bitten off more than he can chew. Am I like that? See ourselves as others see us. Hungry man is an angry man. Working tooth and jaw. Don't! O! A bone! That last pagan king of Ireland Cormac in the schoolpoem choked himself at Sletty southward of the Boyne.[2] Wonder what he was eating. Something galoptious. Saint Patrick converted him to Christianity. Couldn't swallow it all however.

—Roast beef and cabbage.

—One stew.

Smells of men. His gorge rose. Spaton sawdust, sweetish warmish cigarettesmoke, reek of plug, spilt beer, men's beery piss, the stale of ferment.

Couldn't eat a morsel here. Fellow sharpening knife and fork, to eat all before him, old chap picking his tootles. Slight spasm, full, chewing the cud. Before and after. Grace after meals. Look on this picture then on that. Scoffing up stewgravy with sopping sippets of bread. Lick it off the plate, man! Get out of this.

He gazed round the stooled and tabled eaters, tightening the wings of his nose.

—Two stouts here.

—One corned and cabbage.

That fellow ramming a knifeful of cabbage down as if his life depended on it. Good stroke. Give me the fidgets to look. Safer to eat from his three hands. Tear it limb from limb. Second nature to him. Born with a silver knife in his mouth. That's witty, I think. Or no. Silver means born rich. Born with a knife. But then the allusion is lost.

An illgirt server gathered sticky clattering plates. Rock, the bailiff, standing at the bar blew the foamy crown from his tankard. Well up: it splashed yellow near his boot. A diner, knife and fork upright, elbows on table, ready for a second helping stared towards the food-lift across his stained square of newspaper. Other chap telling him something with his mouth full. Sympathetic listener. Table talk. I munched hum un thu Unchster Bunk un Munchday. Ha? Did you, faith?

Mr Bloom raised two fingers doubtfully to his lips. His eyes said:

—Not here. Don't see him.[3]

Out. I hate dirty eaters.

He backed towards the door. Get a light snack in Davy Byrne's. Stopgap. Keep me going. Had a good breakfast.

---

2. Bloom is recalling a "schoolpoem" about a legendary incident in Irish history.
3. He pretends he is looking for someone he can-

not see, so that he has an excuse to leave without eating.

—Roast and mashed here.

—Pint of stout.

Every fellow for his own, tooth and nail. Gulp. Grub. Gulp. Gobstuff.

He came out into clearer air and turned back towards Grafton street. Eat or be eaten. Kill! Kill!

Suppose that communal kitchen years to come perhaps. All trotting down with porringers and tommycans to be filled. Devour contents in the street. John Howard Parnell example the provost of Trinity every mother's son don't talk of your provosts and provost of Trinity women and children, cabmen, priests, parsons, fieldmarshals, archbishops. From Ailesbury road, Clyde road, artisans' dwellings north Dublin union, lord mayor in his gingerbread coach, old queen in a bathchair. My plate's empty. After you with our incorporated drinking cup. Like sir Philip Crampton's fountain. Rub off the microbes with your handkerchief. Next chap rubs on a new batch with his. Father O'Flynn would make hares of them all. Have rows all the same. All for number one. Children fighting for the scrapings of the pot. Want a souppot as big as the Phoenix park. Harpooning flitches and hindquarters out of it. Hate people all round you. City Arms hotel *table d'hôte* she called it. Soup, joint and sweet. Never know whose thoughts you're chewing. Then who'd wash up all the plates and forks? Might be all feeding on tabloids that time. Teeth getting worse and worse.

After all there's a lot in that vegetarian fine flavour of things from the earth garlic, of course, it stinks Italian organgrinders crisp of onions mushrooms truffles. Pain to animal too. Pluck and draw fowl. Wretched brutes there at the cattlemarket waiting for the poleaxe to split their skulls open. Moo. Poor trembling calves. Meh. Staggering bob. Bubble and squeak. Butchers' buckets wobble lights. Give us that brisket off the hook. Plup. Rawhead and bloody bones. Flayed glasseyed sheep hung from their haunches, sheepsnouts bloodypapered snivelling nosejam on sawdust. Top and lashers going out. Don't maul them pieces, young one.

Hot fresh blood they prescribe for decline. Blood always needed. Insidious. Lick it up smokinghot, thick sugary. Famished ghosts.

Ah, I'm hungry.

He entered Davy Byrne's. Moral pub. He doesn't chat. Stands a drink now and then. But in leapyear once in four. Cashed a cheque for me once.

What will I take now? He drew his watch. Let me see now. Shandygaff?

—Hello, Bloom, Nosey Flynn said from his nook.

—Hello, Flynn.

—How's things?

—Tiptop . . . Let me see. I'll take a glass of burgundy and . . . let me see.

Sardines on the shelves. Almost taste them by looking. Sandwich? Ham and his descendants mustered and bred there. Potted meats. What is home without Plumtree's potted meat? Incomplete. What a stupid ad! Under the obituary notices they stuck it. All up a plumtree. Dignam's potted mat. Cannibals would with lemon and rice. White missionary too salty. Like pickled pork. Expect the chief consumes the parts of honour. Ought to be tough from exercise. His wives in a row to watch the effect. *There was a right royal old nigger. Who ate or something the somethings of the reverend Mr Mac-Trigger.* With it an abode of bliss. Lord knows what concoction. Cauls mouldy tripes windpipes faked and minced up. Puzzle find the meat. Kosher.

No meat and milk together. Hygiene that was what they call now, Yom Kippur fast spring cleaning of inside. Peace and war depend on some fellow's digestion. Religions. Christmas turkeys and geese. Slaughter of innocents. Eat, drink and be merry. Then casual wards full after. Heads bandaged. Cheese digests all but itself. Mighty cheese.

—Have you a cheese sandwich?

—Yes, sir.

Like a few olives too if they had them. Italian I prefer. Good glass of burgundy; take away that. Lubricate. A nice salad, cool as a cucumber. Tom Kernan can dress. Puts gusto into it. Pure olive oil. Milly served me that cutlet with a sprig of parsley. Take one Spanish onion. God made food, the devil the cooks. Devilled crab.

—Wife well?

—Quite well, thanks . . . A cheese sandwich, then. Gorgonzola, have you?

—Yes, sir.

Nosey Flynn sipped his grog.

—Doing any singing those times?

Look at his mouth. Could whistle in his own ear. Flap ears to match. Music. Knows as much about it as my coachman. Still better tell him. Does no harm. Free ad.

—She's engaged for a big tour end of this month. You may have heard perhaps.

—No. O, that's the style. Who's getting it up?

The curate[4] served.

—How much is that?

—Seven d., sir . . . Thank you, sir.

Mr Bloom cut his sandwich into slender strips. *Mr MacTrigger.* Easier than the dreamy creamy stuff. *His five hundred wives. Had the time of their lives.*

—Mustard, sir?

—Thank you.

He studded under each lifted strip yellow blobs. *Their lives.* I have it. *It grew bigger and bigger and bigger.*

—Getting it up? he said. Well, it's like a company idea, you see. Part shares and part profits.

—Ay, now I remember, Nosey Flynn said, putting his hand in his pocket to scratch his groin. Who is this was telling me? Isn't Blazes Boylan mixed up in it?

A warm shock of air heat of mustard hanched on Mr Bloom's heart. He raised his eyes and met the stare of a bilious clock. Two. Pub clock five minutes fast. Time going on. Hands moving. Two. Not yet.[5]

His midriff yearned then upward, sank within him, yearned more longly, longingly.

Wine.

He smellsipped the cordial juice and, bidding his throat strongly to speed it, set his wineglass delicately down.

—Yes, he said. He's the organiser in point of fact.

No fear: no brains.

Nosey Flynn snuffled and scratched. Flea having a good square meal.

---

4. Bartender.   5. I.e., not yet time for Boylan to visit Molly.

—He had a good slice of luck, Jack Mooney was telling me, over that boxing match Myler Keogh won again that soldier in the Portobello barracks. By God, he had the little kipper down in the country Carlow he was telling me. . . .

Hope that dewdrop doesn't come down into his glass. No, snuffled it up.

—For near a month, man, before it came off. Sucking duck eggs by God till further orders. Keep him off the boose, see? O, by God, Blazes is a hairy chap.

Davy Byrne came forward from the hindbar in tuckstitched shirtsleeves, cleaning his lips with two wipes of his napkin. Herring's blush. Whose smile upon each feature plays with such and such replete. Too much fat on the parsnips.

—And here's himself and pepper on him, Nosey Flynn said. Can you give us a good one for the Gold cup?

—I'm off that, Mr Flynn, Davy Byrne answered. I never put anything on a horse.

—You're right there, Nosey Flynn said.

Mr Bloom ate his strips of sandwich, fresh clean bread, with relish of disgust, pungent mustard, the feety savour of green cheese. Sips of his wine soothed his palate. Not logwood that. Tastes fuller this weather with the chill off.

Nice quiet bar. Nice piece of wood in that counter. Nicely planed. Like the way it curves there.

—I wouldn't do anything at all in that line, Davy Byrne said. It ruined many a man, the same horses.

Vintners' sweepstake. Licensed for the sale of beer, wine and spirits for consumption on the premises. Heads I win tails you lose.

—True for you, Nosey Flynn said. Unless you're in the know. There's no straight sport going now. Lenehan gets some good ones. He's giving Sceptre today. Zinfandel's the favourite, lord Howard de Walden's, won at Epsom. Morny Cannon is riding him. I could have got seven to one against Saint Amant a fortnight before.

—That so? Davy Byrne said. . . .

He went towards the window and, taking up the petty cash book, scanned its pages.

—I could, faith, Nosey Flynn said, snuffling. That was a rare bit of horseflesh. Saint Frusquin was her sire. She won in a thunderstorm, Rothschild's filly, with wadding in her ears. Blue jacket and yellow cap. Bad luck to big Ben Dollard and his John O'Gaunt. He put me off it. Ay.

He drank resignedly from his tumbler, running his fingers down the flutes.

—Ay, he said, sighing.

Mr Bloom, champing standing, looked upon his sigh. Nosey numbskull. Will I tell him that horse Lenehan?[6] He knows already. Better let him forget. Go and lose more. Fool and his money. Dewdrop coming down again. Cold nose he'd have kissing a woman. Still they might like. Prickly beards they like. Dogs' cold noses. Old Mrs Riordan with the rumbling stomach's Skye terrier in the City Arms hotel. Molly fondling him in her lap. O, the big doggybowwowsywowsy!

Wine soaked and softened rolled pith of bread mustard a moment mawkish

6. Bloom is wondering whether to pass on a tip from Lenehan, who wrote for the racing paper *Sport*.

cheese. Nice wine it is. Taste it better because I'm not thirsty. Bath of course does that. Just a bite or two. Then about six o'clock I can. Six. Six. Time will be gone then. She . . .

Mild fire of wine kindled his veins. I wanted that badly. Felt so off colour. His eyes unhungrily saw shelves of tins, sardines, gaudy lobsters' claws. All the odd things people pick up for food. Out of shells, periwinkles with a pin, off trees, snails out of the ground the French eat, out of the sea with bait on a hook. Silly fish learn nothing in a thousand years. If you didn't know risky putting anything into your mouth. Poisonous berries. Johnny Magories. Roundness you think good. Gaudy colour warns you off. One fellow told another and so on. Try it on the dog first. Led on by the smell or the look. Tempting fruit. Ice cones. Cream. Instinct. Orangegroves for instance. Need artificial irrigation. Bleibtreustrasse.[7] Yes but what about oysters. Unsightly like a clot of phlegm. Filthy shells. Devil to open them too. Who found them out? Garbage, sewage they feed on. Fizz and Red bank oysters. Effect on the sexual. Aphrodis. He was in the Red bank this morning. Was he oyster old fish at table. Perhaps he young flesh in bed. No. June has no ar no oysters. But there are people like tainted game. Jugged hare. First catch your hare. Chinese eating eggs fifty years old, blue and green again. Dinner of thirty courses. Each dish harmless might mix inside. Idea for a poison mystery. That archduke Leopold was it. No. Yes, or was it Otto one of those Habsburgs? Or who was it used to eat the scruff off his own head? Cheapest lunch in town. Of course, aristocrats, then the others copy to be in the fashion. Milly too rock oil and flour. Raw pastry I like myself. Half the catch of oysters they throw back in the sea to keep up the price. Cheap. No-one would buy. Caviare. Do the grand. Hock in green glasses. Swell blowout. Lady this. Powdered bosom pearls. The élite. Crème de la crème.[8] They want special dishes to pretend they're. Hermit with a platter of pulse keep down the stings of the flesh. Know me come eat with me. Royal sturgeon. High sheriff, Coffey, the butcher, right to venisons of the forest from his ex.[9] Send him back the half of a cow. Spread I saw down in the Master of the Rolls' kitchen area. Whitehatted Chef like a rabbi. Combustible duck. Curly cabbage à la duchesse de Parme. Just as well to write it on the bill of fare so you can know what you've eaten too many drugs spoil the broth. I know it myself. Dosing it with Edwards' desicated soup. Geese stuffed silly for them. Lobsters boiled alive. Do ptake some ptarmigan. Wouldn't mind being a waiter in a swell hotel. Tips, evening dress, halfnaked ladies. May I tempt you to a little more filleted lemon sole, miss Dubedat? Yes, do bedad. And she did bedad. Huguenot name I expect that. A miss Dubedat lived in Killiney, I remember. Du, de la, French. Still it's the same fish, perhaps old Micky Hanlon of Moore street ripped the guts out of making money, hand over fist, finger in fishes' gills, can't write his name on a cheque, think he was painting the landscape with his mouth twisted. Moooikill A Aitcha Ha. Ignorant as a kish of brogues,[1] worth fifty thousand pounds.

Stuck on the pane two flies buzzed, stuck.

---

7. The Berlin street that contained the offices of the "Planters' Company."
8. Cream of the cream (i.e., the very best, socially).
9. All sturgeon caught in or off Britain were the property of the king, according to the ancient tra-

ditional rights to certain kinds of fish or game. Bloom goes on to imagine a Dublin butcher having a "right to venisons of the forest from his ex[cellency]"—i.e., the viceroy.
1. A basket of shoes.

Glowing wine on his palate lingered swallowed. Crushing in the winepress grapes of Burgundy. Sun's heat it is. Seems to a secret touch telling me memory. Touched his sense moistened remembered. Hidden under wild ferns on Howth. Below us bay sleeping sky. No sound. The sky. The bay purple by the Lion's head. Green by Drumleck. Yellowgreen towards Sutton. Fields of undersea, the lines faint brown in grass, buried cities. Pillowed on my coat she had her hair, earwigs in the heather scrub my hand under her nape, you'll toss me all. O wonder! Coolsoft with ointments her hand touched me, caressed: her eyes upon me did not turn away. Ravished over her I lay, full lips full open, kissed her mouth. Yum. Softly she gave me in my mouth the seedcake warm and chewed. Mawkish pulp her mouth had mumbled sweet and sour with spittle. Joy: I ate it: joy. Young life, her lips that gave me pouting. Soft, warm, sticky gumjelly lips. Flowers her eyes were, take me, willing eyes. Pebbles fell. She lay still. A goat. No-one. High on Ben Howth rhododendrons a nannygoat walking surefooted, dropping currants. Screened under ferns she laughed warmfolded. Wildly I lay on her, kissed her, eyes, her lips, her stretched neck, beating, woman's breasts full in her blouse of nun's veiling, fat nipples upright. Hot I tongued her. She kissed me. I was kissed. All yielding she tossed my hair. Kissed, she kissed me.[2]

Me. And me now.

Stuck, the flies buzzed.

His downcast eyes followed the silent veining of the oaken slab. Beauty: it curves: curves are beauty. Shapely goddesses, Venus, Juno: curves the world admires. Can see them library museum standing in the round hall, naked goddesses. Aids to digestion. They don't care what man looks. All to see. Never speaking, I mean to say to fellows like Flynn. Suppose she did Pygmalion and Galatea[3] what would she say first? Mortal! Put you in your proper place. Quaffing nectar at mess with gods, golden dishes, all ambrosial. Not like a tanner lunch we have, boiled mutton, carrots and turnips, bottle of Allsop. Nectar, imagine it drinking electricity: god's food. Lovely forms of women sculped Junonian. Immortal lovely. And we stuffing food in one hole and out behind: food, chyle, blood, dung, earth, food: have to feed it like stoking an engine. They have no. Never looked. I'll look today. Keeper won't see. Bend down let something see if she.

Dribbling a quiet message from his bladder came to go to do not to do there to do. A man and ready he drained his glass to the lees and walked, to men too they gave themselves, manly conscious, lay with men lovers, a youth enjoyed her, to the yard.

When the sound of his boots had ceased Davy Byrne said from his book:

—What is this he is? Isn't he in the insurance line?

—He's out of that long ago, Nosey Flynn said. He does canvassing for the *Freeman*.

—I know him well to see, Davy Byrne said. Is he in trouble?

—Trouble? Nosey Flynn said. Not that I heard of. Why?

2. Bloom is remembering when he first proposed to Molly, on the Hill of Howth, near Dublin, Molly also recalls this in the final "Penelope" episode, which is her soliloquy: "we were lying among the rhododendrons on Howth head in the gray tweed suit and his straw hat the day I got him to propose to me yes . . . my God after that long kiss I near lost my breath . . . I saw he understood or felt what a woman is and I knew I could always get round him and I gave him all the pleasure I could leading him on."

3. Pygmalion was the sculptor whose statue of Galatea came alive.

—I noticed he was in mourning.

—Was he? Nosey Flynn said. So he was, faith. I asked him how was all at home. You're right, by God. So he was.

—I never broach the subject, Davy Byrne said humanely, if I see a gentleman is in trouble that way. It only brings it up fresh in their minds.

—It's not the wife anyhow, Nosey Flynn said. I met him the day before yesterday and he coming out of that Irish farm dairy John Wyse Nolan's wife has in Henry street with a jar of cream in his hand taking it home to his better half. She's well nourished, I tell you. Plovers on toast.

—And is he doing for the *Freeman*? Davy Byrne said.

Nosey Flynn pursed his lips.

—He doesn't buy cream on the ads he picks up. You can make bacon of that.

—How so? Davy Byrne asked, coming from his book.

Nosey Flynn made swift passes in the air with juggling fingers. He winked.

—He's in the craft,[4] he said.

—Do you tell me so? Davy Byrne said.

—Very much so, Nosey Flynn said. Ancient free and accepted order. Light, life and love, by God. They give him a leg up. I was told that by a, well, I won't say who.

—Is that a fact?

—O, it's a fine order, Nosey Flynn said. They stick to you when you're down. I know a fellow was trying to get into it, but they're as close as damn it. By God they did right to keep the women out of it.

Davy Byrne smiledyawnednodded all in one:

—Iiiiiichaaaaaaach!

—There was one woman, Nosey Flynn said, hid herself in a clock to find out what they do be doing. But be damned but they smelt her out and swore her in on the spot a master mason. That was one of the Saint Legers of Doneraile.

Davy Byrne, sated after his yawn, said with tearwashed eyes:

—And is that a fact? Decent quiet man he is. I often saw him in here and I never once saw him, you know, over the line.

—God Almighty couldn't make him drunk, Nosey Flynn said firmly. Slips off when the fun gets too hot. Didn't you see him look at his watch? Ah, you weren't there. If you ask him to have a drink first thing he does he outs with the watch to see what he ought to imbibe. Declare to God he does.

—There are some like that, Davy Byrne said. He's a safe man, I'd say.

—He's not too bad, Nosey Flynn said, snuffling it up. He has been known to put his hand down too to help a fellow. Give the devil his due. O, Bloom has his good points. But there's one thing he'll never do.

His hand scrawled a dry pen signature beside his grog.

—I know, Davy Byrne said.

—Nothing in black and white, Nosey Flynn said.

Paddy Leonard and Bantam Lyons came in. Tom Rochford followed frowning, a plaining hand on his claret waistcoat.

—Day, Mr Byrne.

---

4. I.e., in the "free and accepted order" of Freemasons, one of the oldest European secret societies; it was not in good repute in predominantly Roman Catholic countries like Ireland.

—Day, gentlemen.

They paused at the counter.

—Who's standing? Paddy Leonard asked.

—I'm sitting anyhow, Nosey Flynn answered.

—Well, what'll it be? Paddy Leonard asked.

—I'll take a stone ginger, Bantam Lyons said.

—How much? Paddy Leonard cried. Since when, for God's sake? What's yours, Tom?

—How is the main drainage? Nosey Flynn asked, sipping.

For answer Tom Rochford pressed his hand to his breastbone and hiccupped.

—Would I trouble you for a glass of fresh water, Mr Byrne? he said.

—Certainly, sir.

Paddy Leonard eyed his alemates.

—Lord love a duck, he said, look at what I'm standing drinks to! Cold water and gingerpop! Two fellows that would suck whisky off a sore leg. He has some bloody horse up his sleeve for the Gold cup. A dead snip.

—Zinfandel is it? Nosey Flynn asked.

Tom Rochford spilt powder from a twisted paper into the water set before him.

—That cursed dyspepsia, he said before drinking.

—Breadsoda is very good, Davy Byrne said.

Tom Rochford nodded and drank.

—Is it Zinfandel?

—Say nothing, Bantam Lyons winked. I'm going to plunge five bob on my own.

—Tell us if you're worth your salt and be damned to you, Paddy Leonard said. Who gave it to you?

Mr Bloom on his way out raised three fingers in greeting.

—So long, Nosey Flynn said.

The others turned.

—That's the man now that gave it to me, Bantam Lyons whispered.

—Prrwht! Paddy Leonard said with scorn. Mr Byrne, sir, we'll take two of your small Jamesons[5] after that and a . . .

—Stone ginger, Davy Byrne added civilly.

—Ay, Paddy Leonard said. A suckingbottle for the baby.

Mr Bloom walked towards Dawson street, his tongue brushing his teeth smooth. Something green it would have to be: spinach say. Then with those Röntgen rays searchlight you could.

At Duke lane a ravenous terrier choked up a sick knuckly cud on the cobblestones and lapped it with new zest. Surfeit. Returned with thanks having fully digested the contents. First sweet then savoury. Mr Bloom coasted warily. Ruminants. His second course. Their upper jaw they move. Wonder if Tom Rochford will do anything with that invention of his. Wasting time explaining it to Flynn's mouth. Lean people long mouths. Ought to be a hall or a place where inventors could go in and invent free. Course then you'd have all the cranks pestering.

He hummed, prolonging in solemn echo, the closes of the bars:

5. Brand of Irish whiskey.

> *Don Giovanni, a cenar teco*
> *M'invitasti.*[6]

Feel better. Burgundy. Good pick me up. Who distilled first? Some chap in the blues. Dutch courage. That *Kilkenny People* in the national library now I must.

Bare clean closestools, waiting, in the window of William Miller, plumber, turned back his thoughts. They could: and watch it all the way down, swallow a pin sometimes come out of the ribs years after, tour round the body, changing biliary duct, spleen squirting liver, gastric juice coils of intestines like pipes. But the poor buffer would have to stand all the time with his insides entrails on show. Science.

—*A cenar teco.*

What does that *teco* mean? Tonight perhaps.

> *Don Giovanni, thou hast me invited*
> *To come to supper tonight,*
> *The rum the rumdum.*

Doesn't go properly.

Keyes: two months if I get Nannetti[7] to. That'll be two pounds ten, about two pounds eight. Three Hynes owes me. Two eleven. Prescott's ad. Two fifteen. Five guineas about. On the pig's back.

Could buy one of those silk petticoats for Molly, colour of her new garters. Today. Today. Not think.[8]

Tour the south then. What about English wateringplaces? Brighton, Margate. Piers by moonlight. Her voice floating out. Those lovely seaside girls. Against John Long's a drowsing loafer lounged in heavy thought, gnawing a crusted knuckle. Handy man wants job. Small wages. Will eat anything.

Mr Bloom turned at Gray's confectioner's window of unbought tarts and passed the reverend Thomas Connellan's bookstore. *Why I left the church of Rome?* Birds' Nest. Women run him. They say they used to give pauper children soup to change to protestants in the time of the potato blight. Society over the way papa went to for the conversion of poor jews. Same bait. *Why we left the church of Rome?*

A blind stripling stood tapping the curbstone with his slender cane. No tram in sight. Wants to cross.

—Do you want to cross? Mr Bloom asked.

The blind stripling did not answer. His wallface frowned weakly. He moved his head uncertainly.

—You're in Dawson street, Mr Bloom said. Molesworth street is opposite. Do you want to cross? There's nothing in the way.

The cane moved out trembling to the left. Mr Bloom's eye followed its line and saw again the dyeworks' van drawn up before Drago's. Where I saw his

---

6. Because Molly is a singer, Bloom is familiar with opera. Here he recalls the song sung by the Commendatore's statue in Mozart's *Don Giovanni* and translates accurately the Italian words he quotes, except for "*teco*" (with thee). This opera supplies some of the key themes in *Ulysses*, and the famous duet between Don Giovanni and Zerlina. "*Là ci darèm la mano*" (There we will join hands), haunts Bloom's mind continually throughout the day. It is on the program of Molly's concert that she is discussing with Boylan that afternoon, and Bloom associates it with her adultery with Boylan.
7. Proofreader and business manager of the *Freeman's Journal* and in charge of the advertising Bloom is trying to get for the paper. If he will add a complimentary reference to Keyes, a grocer, in a gossip column, Keyes promises to renew his advertisement, which means a commission for Bloom.
8. I.e., of Molly and Boylan.

brillantined hair just when I was. Horse drooping. Driver in John Long's. Slaking his drouth.

—There's a van there, Mr Bloom said, but it's not moving. I'll see you across. Do you want to go to Molesworth street?

—Yes, the stripling answered. South Frederick street.

—Come, Mr Bloom said.

He touched the thin elbow gently: then took the limp seeing hand to guide it forward.

Say something to him. Better not do the condescending. They mistrust what you tell them. Pass a common remark.

—The rain kept off.

No answer.

Stains on his coat. Slobbers his food, I suppose. Tastes all different for him. Have to be spoonfed first. Like a child's hand, his hand. Like Milly's was. Sensitive. Sizing me up I daresay from my hand. Wonder if he has a name. Van. Keep his cane clear of the horse's legs tired drudge get his doze. That's right. Clear. Behind a bull: in front of a horse.

—Thanks, sir.

Knows I'm a man. Voice.

—Right now? First turn to the left.

The blind stripling tapped the curbstone and went on his way, drawing his cane back, feeling again.

Mr Bloom walked behind the eyeless feet, a flatcut suit of herringbone tweed. Poor young fellow! How on earth did he know that van was there? Must have felt it. See things in their foreheads perhaps. Kind of sense of volume. Weight would he feel it if something was removed. Feel a gap. Queer idea of Dublin he must have, tapping his way round by the stones. Could he walk in a beeline if he hadn't that cane? Bloodless pious face like a fellow going in to be a priest.

Penrose! That was that chap's name.

Look at all the things they can learn to do. Read with their fingers. Tune pianos. Or we are surprised they have any brains. Why we think a deformed person or a hunchback clever if he says something we might say. Of course the other senses are more. Embroider. Plait baskets. People ought to help. Workbasket I could buy Molly's birthday. Hates sewing. Might take an objection. Dark men they call them.

Sense of smell must be stronger too. Smells on all sides bunched together. Each person too. Then the spring, the summer: smells. Tastes. They say you can't taste wines with your eyes shut or a cold in the head. Also smoke in the dark they say get no pleasure.

And with a woman, for instance. More shameless not seeing. That girl passing the Stewart institution, head in the air. Look at me. I have them all on. Must be strange not to see her. Kind of a form in his mind's eye. The voice temperature when he touches her with fingers must almost see the lines, the curves. His hands on her hair, for instance. Say it was black for instance. Good. We call it black. Then passing over her white skin. Different feel perhaps. Feeling of white.

Postoffice. Must answer.[9] Fag[1] today. Send her a postal order two shillings

9. Martha Clifford's letter.   1. Nuisance.

half a crown. Accept my little present. Stationer's just here too. Wait. Think over it.

With a gentle finger he felt ever so slowly the hair combed back above his ears. Again. Fibres of fine fine straw. Then gently his finger felt the skin of his right cheek. Downy hair there too. Not smooth enough. The belly is the smoothest. No-one about. There he goes into Frederick street. Perhaps to Levenston's dancing academy piano. Might be settling my braces.

Walking by Doran's public house he slid his hand between waistcoat and trousers and, pulling aside his shirt gently, felt a slack fold of his belly. But I know it's whitey yellow. Want to try in the dark to see.

He withdrew his hand and pulled his dress to.

Poor fellow! Quite a boy. Terrible. Really terrible. What dreams would he have, not seeing. Life a dream for him. Where is the justice being born that way. All those women and children excursion beanfeast burned and drowned in New York.[2] Holocaust. Karma they call that transmigration for sins you did in a past life the reincarnation met him pike hoses.[3] Dear, dear, dear. Pity of course: but somehow you can't cotton on to them someway.

Sir Frederick Falkiner going into the freemasons' hall. Solemn as Troy. After his good lunch in Earlsfort terrace. Old legal cronies cracking a magnum. Tales of the bench and assizes and annals of the bluecoat school.[4] I sentenced him to ten years. I suppose he'd turn up his nose at that stuff I drank. Vintage wine for them, the year marked on a dusty bottle. Has his own ideas of justice in the recorder's court. Wellmeaning old man. Police charge sheets crammed with cases get their percentage manufacturing crime. Sends them to the rightabout. The devil on moneylenders. Gave Reuben J. a great strawcalling. Now he's really what they call a dirty jew. Power those judges have. Crusty old topers in wigs. Bear with a sore paw. And may the Lord have mercy on your soul.

Hello, placard. Mirus bazaar. His excellency the lord lieutenant. Sixteenth today it is. In aid of funds for Mercer's hospital. The *Messiah* was first given for that. Yes. Handel. What about going out there. Ballsbridge. Drop in on Keyes. No use sticking to him like a leech. Wear out my welcome. Sure to know someone on the gate.

Mr Bloom came to Kildare street. First I must. Library.

Straw hat in sunlight. Tan shoes. Turnedup trousers. It is. It is.[5]

His heart quopped softly. To the right. Museum. Goddesses. He swerved to the right.

Is it? Almost certain. Won't look. Wine in my face. Why did I? Too heady. Yes, it is. The walk. Not see. Not see. Get on.

Making for the museum gate with long windy strides he lifted his eyes. Handsome building. Sir Thomas Deane designed. Not following me?

Didn't see me perhaps. Light in his eyes.

The flutter of his breath came forth in short sighs. Quick. Cold statues: quiet there. Safe in a minute.

---

2. This terrible disaster on an excursion steamer on a New York City river took place on June 15, 1904, and was reported in the Dublin papers on June 16.

3. I.e., metempsychosis. Bloom is remembering again their morning conversation on this subject, when Molly exclaimed, "O rocks!"

4. Sir Frederick Falkiner wrote the history of the "bluecoat school" in Oxmantown, Dublin. The Dublin bluecoat school was founded by Charles II for poor children.

5. Bloom catches a glimpse of Boylan and tries to avoid an encounter.

No, didn't see me. After two. Just at the gate.

My heart!

His eyes beating looked steadfastly at cream curves of stone. Sir Thomas Deane was the Greek architecture.

Look for something I.

His hasty hand went quick into a pocket, took out, read unfolded Agendath Netaim. Where did I?

Busy looking for.

He thrust back quickly Agendath.

Afternoon she said.

I am looking for that. Yes, that. Try all pockets. Handker. *Freeman.* Where did I? Ah, yes. Trousers. Purse. Potato. Where did I?

Hurry. Walk quietly. Moment more. My heart.

His hand looking for the where did I put found in his hip pocket soap lotion have to call tepid paper stuck. Ah, soap there! Yes. Gate.[6]

Safe!

1914–21   1922

Finnegans Wake

Finnegans Wake   Because the meanings in *Finnegans Wake* are developed not by action but by language—a great network of multiple puns that echo themes back and forth throughout the book—the careful reading of a single passage, even out of context, will convey more than any summary of the "plot" (some discussion of the general plan of the work is given in the Joyce headnote). The particular passage printed here was one of Joyce's favorites, and there exists a phonograph recording of it made by him. It consists of the closing pages of chapter 8 of book 1; the chapter was published separately as *Anna Livia Plurabelle* in 1928 and 1930, although the finished book omits this title.

The entire chapter is a dialogue, and the scene is the river Liffey: two washerwomen are washing in public the dirty linen of HCE and ALP (the "hero" and "heroine"; see headnote p. 2235) and gossiping as they work. As this excerpt opens, it is growing dark; things become gradually less and less distinct, so that the washerwomen cannot be sure what the objects seen in the dusk really are. As it grows darker, the river becomes wider (we get nearer its mouth) and the wind rises, so that the women have more and more difficulty hearing each other. At last, as night falls, they become part of the landscape, an elm tree and a stone on the river bank. Toward the end of the dialogue they ask to hear a tale of Shem and Shaun (HCE's two sons), and this question points the way to book 2, which opens with the two boys (metamorphosed for the moment into Glugg and Chuff) playing in front of the tavern in the evening.

A complete annotation of even this brief passage is, of course, a physical impossibility in this anthology. The notes that are provided are intended to indicate the nature of what Joyce does with language and to enable the reader to see what is going on. But there are all sorts of suggestions built up in the language that are not referred to in the notes: all readers will find some for themselves.

6. Anxious to avoid Boylan, Bloom pretends to admire the architecture of the Museum and National Library building and then pretends to be looking for something in his pockets, where he finds the "Agendath Netaim" leaflet. He continues to search desperately in his pockets to avoid looking up and seeing Boylan, discovers the potato he carries as a remedy against rheumatism and a cake of soap he had bought that morning (the soap reminds him that he must call at the chemist's to collect a face lotion he had ordered for Molly). At last he goes through the National Library gate and feels safe.

From Finnegans Wake

From *Anna Livia Plurabelle*

* * * Well, you know or don't you kennet[1] or haven't I told you every telling
has a taling and that's the he and the she of it. Look, look, the dusk is
growing! My branches lofty are taking root. And my cold cher's gone ashley.[2]
Fieluhr? Filou![3] What age is at? It saon[4] is late. 'Tis endless now senne[5] eye
or erewone[6] last saw Waterhouse's clogh.[7] They took it asunder, I hurd thum
sigh. When will they reassemble it? O, my back, my back, my bach![8] I'd want
to go to Aches-les-Pains.[9] Pingpong! There's the Belle for Sexaloitez![10] And
Concepta de Send-us-pray! Pang! Wring out the Clothes! Wring in the dew![11]
Godavari,[12] vert the showers![13] And grant thaya grace! Aman. Will we spread
them here now? Ay, we will. Flip! Spread on your bank and I'll spread mine
on mine. Flep! It's what I'm doing. Spread! It's churning chill. Der went[14] is
rising. I'll lay a few stones on the hostel sheets. A man and his bride embraced
between them. Else I'd have sprinkled and folded them only. And I'll tie my
butcher's apron here. It's suety yet. The strollers will pass it by. Six shifts,
ten kerchiefs, nine to hold to the fire and this for the code,[15] the convent
napkins, twelve, one baby's shawl. Good mother Jossiph[16] knows, she said.
Whose head? Mutter snores? Deataceas![17] Wharnow are alle her childer, say?
In kingdome gone or power to come or gloria be to them farther? Allalivial,
allalluvial![18] Some here, more no more, more again lost alla stranger.[19] I've
heard tell that same brooch of the Shannons[20] was married into a family in
Spain. And all the Dunders de Dunnes[21] in Markland's[22] Vineland beyond

---

1. Ken it ("know it") + Kennet (river in England).
Rivers in *Finnegans Wake* symbolize the flow of
life, and thousands of river names are suggested
throughout the book in allusive pun combinations,
as here.
2. "Cold cher": cold cheer (i.e., cold comfort) +
cold chair + (perhaps) culture. "Gone ashley":
gone to ashes. Going to ashes suggests the fiery
death and rebirth of the mythical phoenix: from
the ashes of the dead phoenix rises a new one.
Modern culture, which can provide only cold
cheer, is in the state of decay, the "going to ashes,"
which precedes the stage of rebirth into a new cultural cycle (according to Giambattista Vico's cyclical theory of history, which is important to
Finnegans Wake). "Gone ashley" also means
"turned into an ash tree" (i.e., it is so cold that the
speaker feels herself turning into a tree).
3. Pickpocket; thief (French). "Fieluhr": *Viel Uhr?*
(What's the time? German). From an old anecdote
of a German soldier and a French soldier shouting
at each other across the Rhine. They mishear each
other as the washerwomen will later.
4. Soon + Saône (river in France).
5. Since + Senne (river in Belgium).
6. E'er a one + *Erewhon* (novel by Samuel Butler—an anagram for *Nowhere*).
7. Waterhouse's clock, a well-known clock on
Dame Street, Dublin.
8. "Brook" (German) + "dear" (Welsh).
9. Cf. Aix-les-Bains, France.
10. "Sachselüte," a Zurich fertility rite (literally,
the ringing of six o'clock), which celebrates the
burial of winter.

11. Tennyson, *In Memoriam:* "Ring out the old,
ring in the new."
12. God of Eire + the name of a river in India.
13. "Vert": avert + *vert* ("green," French), for "the
showers" make grass green.
14. *Der Wind* ("the wind," German) + Derwent
(river in England).
15. Cold + code (i.e., the code in which the book
is written). The numbers in this sentence have special meanings indicated in other episodes.
16. Joseph + *joss* ("God," pidgin English) + gossip
(which derives from "god-sib," Middle English,
"godparent").
17. A play on Deo gratias ("thanks be to God") and
on Dea Tacita ("silent-goddess"), a name from
Roman mythology.
18. Multiple punning—Anna Livia + all alive +
la lluvia ("rain," Spanish) + alluvial—suggesting
the mother-river-fertility associations of ALP. At
least two other meanings are also present: All alive
O! (street cry of shellfish vendors) + Alleluia (Vulgate Latin form of "Hallelujah").
19. Cf. *à l'étranger* (abroad, French).
20. Ornament and branch of the Shannons (family and river).
21. The form of the name suggests an aristocratic
Anglo-Norman family. "Dunder" suggests thunder.
Dun is an Irish word meaning "hill," "fort on a hill."
22. Borderland + land of the mark (i.e., land of
money, or America; Markland's Vineland was one
of Leif Ericson's names for America). Both King
Mark of Cornwall (a character in the Tristan and
Iseult story) and Mark of the Gospels are primary
symbolic characters in *Finnegans Wake*.

the Brendan's herring pool[23] takes number nine in yangsee's[24] hats. And one of Biddy's[25] beads went bobbing till she rounded up lost histereve[26] with a marigold and a cobbler's candle in a side strain of a main drain of a manzinahurries[27] off Bachelor's Walk. But all that's left to the last of the Meaghers[28] in the loup[29] of the years prefixed and between is one kneebuckle and two hooks in the front. Do you tell me that now? I do in troth. Orara por Orbe and poor Las Animals![30] Ussa, Ulla, we're umbas[31]all! Mezha, didn't you hear it a deluge of times, ufer[32] and ufer, respund to spond?[33] You deed, you deed! I need, I need! It's that irrawaddyng[34] I've stoke in my aars. It all but husheth the lethest zswound. Oronoko![35] What's your trouble? Is that the great Finnleader[36] himself in his joakimono[37] on his statue riding the high horse there forehengist?[38] Father of Otters,[39] it is himself! Yonne there! Isset that? On Fallareen Common? You're thinking of Astley's Amphitheayter where the bobby restrained you making sugarstuck pouts to the ghostwhite horse of the Peppers.[40] Throw the cobwebs from your eyes, woman, and spread your washing proper! It's well I know your sort of slop. Flap! Ireland sober is Ireland stiff.[41] Lord help you, Maria, full of grease, the load is with me! Your prayers. I sonht zo![42] Madammangut! Were you lifting your elbow, tell us, glazy cheeks, in Conway's Carrigacurra canteen? Was I what, hobbledyhips?[43] Flop! Your rere gait's creakorheuman bitts your butts disagrees.[44] Amn't I up since the damp dawn, marthared mary allacook, with Corrigan's pulse and varicoarse veins, my pramaxle smashed, Alice Jane in decline and my oneeyed mongrel twice run over, soaking and bleaching boiler rags, and sweating cold, a widow like me, for to deck my tennis champion son, the laundryman with the lavandier flannels? You won your limpopo[45] limp from

23. The Atlantic Ocean. St. Brendan was an Irish monk who sailed out into the Atlantic to find the terrestrial paradise.

24. Yankees' + Yangtze (river in China). The de Dunnes have swollen heads now that they have emigrated to America.

25. Diminutive form of the name Bridget. St. Brigid (or Bridget) is a patron saint of Ireland. "Biddy" is also a term for an Irish maidservant.

26. Yester eve (last night) + eve of history. The sentence may be paraphrased: "Irish history got lost when she went off in a side branch of the main Roman Catholic church, and Biddy (i.e., Ireland) landed herself in the dirt." There are also Freudian implications here.

27. A urinal + Manzanares (river in Spain).

28. Thomas Francis Meagher, Irish patriot and revolutionary, who was transported to Van Diemen's Land in 1849 and escaped to America in 1852.

29. Loop + loup ("wolf" and also "solitary man," French). Cf. Wolfe Tone, the ill-fated Irish revolutionist.

30. Souls (Spanish) + the name of a river in Colorado. Ora pro nobis (pray for us; Latin) + Orara (river in New South Wales) + pro orbe (for the world; Latin) + Orbe (river in France). The entire sentence may be read: "Pray for us and for all souls."

31. Umbra (shade; Latin) + Umba (river in Africa). "Ussa," "Ulla," and "Mezha" are also river names; each contains a number of other meanings.

32. Bank (of river).

33. Spund (bung; German).

34. A multiple pun: Irrawady (river in Burma) + irritating + wadding. This and the following sentence may be paraphrased: "It's that wadding I've stuck in my ears. It hushes the least sound."

35. Oroonoko (novel by Aphra Behn about a "noble savage," published ca. 1678) + Orinoco (river in Venezuela).

36. Fionn mac Cumhail (Finn MacCool), legendary hero of ancient Ireland.

37. Comic kimono. Joki is the Finnish word for river; the name Joachim is perhaps also implied.

38. According to tradition, Hengist was the Jute invader of England (with Horsa), ca. 449; he founded the kingdom of Kent.

39. Father of Waters (i.e., the Mississippi) + Father of Orders (i.e., Saint Patrick).

40. Philip Astley's Royal Amphitheatre was a famous late 18th-century English circus, specializing in trained horses. "Pepper's Ghost" was a popular circus act. One of the washerwomen has been reproving the other, who thought she saw the great Finn himself riding his high horse, by telling her that once before she had to be restrained by a policeman for making "sugarstuck pouts" at a circus horse.

41. The temperance reformer Father Matthew had as his slogan "Ireland sober is Ireland free."

42. I thought so + Izonzo (river in Italy).

43. Hobbledehoy + wobbly hips.

44. The sentence is a punning discussion of her hard work and ailments.

45. A river in south Africa.

the husky[46] hussars when Collars and Cuffs was heir to the town and your slur gave the stink to Carlow.[47] Holy Scamander,[48] I sar[49] it again! Near the golden falls. Icis on us! Seints of light! Zezere![50] Subdue your noise, you hamble creature! What is it but a blackburry growth or the dwyergray ass them four old codgers[51] owns. Are you meanam[52] Tarpey and Lyons and Gregory?[53] I meyne now, thank all, the four of them, and the roar of them, that draves[54] that stray in the mist and old Johnny MacDougal along with them. Is that the Poolbeg flasher beyant,[55] pharphar, or a fireboat coasting nyar[56] the Kishtna[57] or a glow I behold within a hedge or my Garry come back from the Indes? Wait till the honeying of the lune,[58] love! Die eve, little eve, die![59] We see that wonder in your eye. We'll meet again, we'll part once more. The spot I'll seek if the hour you'll find. My chart shines high where the blue milk's upset. Forgivemequick. I'm going! Bubye! And you, pluck your watch, forgetmenot. Your evenlode.[60] So save to jurna's[61] end! My sights are swimming thicker on me by the shadows to this place. I sow[62] home slowly now by own way, moyvalley way. Towy[63] I too, rathmine.

Ah, but she was the queer old skeowsha[64] anyhow, Anna Livia, trinket-toes! And sure he was the quare old buntz too, Dear Dirty Dumpling,[65] foostherfather of fingalls[66] and dotthergills. Gammer and gaffer we're all their gangsters. Hadn't he seven dams to wive him? And every dam had her seven crutches. And every crutch had its seven hues.[67] And each hue had a differing cry. Sudds[68] for me and supper for you and the doctor's bill for Joe John. Befor! Bifur![69] He married his markets, cheap by foul, I know, like any Etrurian Catholic Heathen, in their pinky limony creamy birnies[70] and their turkiss indienne mauves. But at milkidmass[71] who was the spouse? Then all that was was fair. Tys Elvenland![72] Teems of times and happy returns. The seim anew.[73] Ordovico or viricordo. Anna was, Livia is, Plura-

---

46. Cf. *uisge* (whiskey, but literally "water [of life]," Gaelic).
47. I.e., "You got a slur on your reputation carrying on with soldiers in the Age of Elegance, and the scandal was all over Ireland" (ALP is being addressed and some of her many lovers are mentioned). "Carlow": a county in Ireland.
48. River near Troy, famous in classical legend.
49. I saw + Isar (river in Germany).
50. See there + Zezere (river in Portugal).
51. The Four Old Men, who represent, among other things, the authors of the Gospels, and the four elements.
52. Meaning + Menam (river in Thailand).
53. Tarpey, Lyons, Gregory, and MacDougal (next sentence) are the "four old codgers."
54. Drives + Drave (river in Hungary).
55. I.e., the Poolbeg Lighthouse beyond (this lighthouse is in Dublin Bay). "Pharphar": far far + Pharphar (river in Damascus) + *pharos* (lighthouse; Greek).
56. Near + Nyar (river in India).
57. City in ancient Mesopotamia, traditionally the ruling city after the Flood + Krishna (Hindu god of joy) + Kistna (river in India) + the Kish lightship (in Dublin Bay).
58. Loon (boy; Scottish) + *luna* (moon; Latin). "Honeying of the lune": honeymoon, etc.
59. From a children's game in which a swing is allowed to slow down to the refrain "She's dead, little Eva, little Eva, she's dead."

60. Evening load + Evenlode (river in England).
61. Journey + Jurna (river in Brazil).
62. Sow (river in England).
63. Name of a river in Wales. Moy is the name of an Irish river, and Moyvalley and Rathmine are names of Dublin suburbs.
64. Old timer, in Dublin.
65. "Dumpling" suggests Humpty Dumpty, whose fall is one of the many involved in the vastly symbolic fall of Finnegan. The phrase "Dear Dirty Dublin" occurs in *Ulysses.*
66. Blond and dark Scandinavian invaders of Ireland.
67. Colors of the rainbow (suggested a few lines later by "pinky limony creamy" and "turkiss indienne mauves"). In these sentences Joyce is parodying the nursery rhyme, "As I was going to St. Ives / I met a man with seven wives."
68. Suds (slang for beer) + soap suds + sudd (the floating vegetable matter that often obstructs navigation on the White Nile).
69. Bifurcated creature! This image of man as a forked being suggests HCE (cf. "Etrurian Catholic Heathen"). HCE's marital history, in his role as the Great Parent or generator, is one of the themes in this passage.
70. Coats of mail.
71. Milking time + Michaelmas (September 29).
72. 'Tis the land of Elves + Tys Elv (Norway).
73. The same again + Seim (river in Ireland).

belle's to be.[74] Northmen's thing made southfolk's place but howmulty plur-
ators made each one in person?[75] Latin me that, my trinity scholard, out of
eure sanscreed into oure eryan![76] *Hircus Civis Eblanensis!*[77] He had buckgoat
paps on him, soft ones for orphans. Ho,[78] Lord! Twins of his bosom. Lord
save us! And ho! Hey? What all men. Hot? His tittering daughters of.
Whawk?

Can't hear with the waters of. The chittering waters of. Flittering bats,
fieldmice bawk talk. Ho! Are you not gone ahome? What Thom Malone?
Can't hear with bawk of bats, all thim liffeying waters of. Ho, talk save us!
My foos won't moos.[79] I feel as old as yonder elm. A tale told of Shaun or
Shem? All Livia's daughter-sons. Dark hawks hear us. Night! Night! My ho
head halls. I feel as heavy as yonder stone. Tell me of John or Shaun? Who
were Shem and Shaun the living sons or daughters of? Night now! Tell me,
tell me, tell me, elm! Night night! Telmetale of stem or stone.[80] Beside the
rivering waters of, hitherandthithering waters of. Night!

1923–38   1939

74. The Ordovices were an ancient British tribe in
northern Wales, and Ordovician is a term for a geological period. "Ordovico" is also a pun on Vico and
his order of historical phases. Joyce is suggesting
the cyclical nature of things: the marital history of
HCE is the history of ever-renewing life ("the seim
anew"), and HCE's bride is Everywoman, past,
present, and future ("Anna was, Livia is, Plurabelle's to be"). "Viricordo" is another verbal twist
to Vico and his cycles, suggesting his *ricorso*
("recurrence," i.e., the fourth stage of the cycle
that brings back the first), as well as overtones from
the Latin *vir* (man) and *cor* (heart): the heart of
the individual beats on, through all phases of civilization.
75. This sentence may be paraphrased: "The
Northmen's assembly (thing) is now in Suffolk
Place, but how many ancestors went into the making of each one of us?"
76. I.e., out of your Sanskrit into your Aryan.

"Sanscreed" has further punning meanings: *sans*
screed (without script) + *sans* creed (without
faith). Thus the phrase can read: "out of your illit-
eracy or faithlessness into Irish" (Eire-an). I.e., the
greatest skeptic must pause in reverence before the
endless flow of life, represented by Irish history.
77. The Goat-Citizen of Dublin! (Latin). The goat
is the symbol of lust and so of fecundity; "*Eblanensis*" is the adjective form of Eblana, the name
given by the 3rd-century Alexandrian geographer
Ptolemy to what may have been the site of the
modern Dublin.
78. River (Chinese).
79. Move + *Moos* (moss, German). Her foot
("foos") won't move; it is also turning to moss.
80. Stone and elm tree are important symbols in
Finnegans Wake. Signifying permanence and
change, time and space, mercy and justice, they
undergo many changes of symbolic meaning
throughout the book.

D. H. LAWRENCE
1885–1930

David Herbert Lawrence was born in the Midland mining village of Eastwood, Not-
tinghamshire. His father was a miner; his mother, better educated than her husband
and self-consciously genteel, fought all her married life to lift her children out of the
working class. Lawrence was aware from an early age of the struggle between his
parents; he was very much on his mother's side during his childhood, resenting his
father's coarse and sometimes drunken behavior and allying himself with his mother's
delicacy and refinement. After the death of an elder brother he became the center of
his mother's emotional life and played in his own relation to her a loving and protective role. His mother's claims on him kept frustrating his relationships with women,
and the personal problems and conflicts that resulted are presented in his first really
distinguished novel, *Sons and Lovers* (1913), where, against a background of paternal

coarseness and vitality conflicting with maternal refinement and gentility, he sets the theme of the demanding mother who has given up the prospect of achieving a true emotional life with her husband and turns to her sons with a stultifying and possessive love. Many years later Lawrence came to feel that he had misjudged his father, whose coarseness represented after all a genuine vitality and some wholeness of personality, even if these qualities were impoverished and distorted by the civilization in which he lived.

Spurred on by his mother, Lawrence escaped through education from the mining world of his father. He won a scholarship to Nottingham high school and later, after working first as a clerk and then as an elementary-school teacher (1902–6), studied for two years at Nottingham University College, where he obtained his teacher's certificate in 1908. Meanwhile he was reading on his own a great deal of literature and some philosophy and was working on his first novel, encouraged (as he was in all his early writing) by Jessie Chambers, the "Miriam" of *Sons and Lovers*. His first published work was a group of poems that appeared in the *English Review* for November 1909. The following February the same periodical published his first short story. He was now regarded in London literary circles as a promising young writer; his first novel, *The White Peacock* (1910), was received with respect. From 1908 to 1912 he taught school in Croydon, a southern suburb of London, but he gave this up after falling in love with Frieda von Richthofen, the German wife of a professor of French at Nottingham. They went to Germany together and married in 1914, after Frieda had been divorced by her first husband.

Abroad with Frieda, Lawrence finished *Sons and Lovers*, the autobiographical novel at which he had been working off and on for years. The war brought them back to England, where Frieda's German origins and Lawrence's fierce objection to the war gave him trouble with the authorities. More and more—especially after the banning of his next novel, *The Rainbow*, in 1915—Lawrence came to feel that the forces of modern civilization were arrayed against him. As soon as he could leave England after the war he sought refuge in Italy, Australia, Mexico, then again in Italy, and finally in the south of France, often desperately ill, restlessly searching for an ideal, or at least a tolerable, community in which to live. He died of tuberculosis in the south of France on March 2, 1930, at the age of forty-four.

Shortly before his death he had written:

> Give me the moon at my feet
> Put my feet upon the crescent, like a Lord!
> O let my ankles be bathed in moonlight, that I may go
> sure and moon-shod, cool and bright-footed
> towards my goal.
>
> For the sun is hostile, now
> his face is like the red lion . . .

In these elemental images he invoked his end, a gesture at once heroic and desperate. It was typical of him to symbolize his passing with reference to the sun and moon, for Lawrence was at home with such cosmic images as no other English writer except Blake has ever been; he was at home, one might say, with the universe, with all that is deep-rooted and elemental in the Individual and Nature, and at constant war with the mechanical and artificial, with the constraints and hypocrisies that civilization imposes on our fundamental selves. His most characteristic writings are essentially a record in symbolic terms of his explorations of human individuality and of all that hindered it and all that might fulfill it, whether in the natural world or in the world of other individuals.

This is not what the English novel is generally supposed to do, and Lawrence, with new things to say and a new way of using the novel form, was not easily or quickly appreciated. His early novels, *The White Peacock, The Trespasser,* and even the original and impressive *Sons and Lovers,* were more conventional in style and treatment; they aroused contemporary interest and even acclaim, and it appeared that he might be on his way to becoming one of the acknowledged and popular Georgian novelists. But with the publication of *The Rainbow* in 1915 the true, original Lawrence first emerged clearly, and the critics turned away in bewilderment and condemnation. *The Rainbow* was suppressed as indecent a month after its publication, and the war between Lawrence and the world of timid convention was on. The rest of his life, during which he produced about a dozen more novels and many poems, short stories, sketches, and miscellaneous articles, was, in his own words, "a savage enough pilgrimage," marked by incessant struggle and by moments of frustration and despair. Lawrence was one of those artists who had to create the taste by which they could be appreciated. He had no gift for explaining his attitude and literary technique in simple expository prose. He could explain himself only by performing, by operating in his own way as an artist, letting the work of art speak with its own voice and pulse with its own life. When he tried to talk *about* his ideas, instead of projecting them symbolically in art, he was often irritatingly and vaguely rhetorical. "Sense of truth," "supreme impulse" are phrases characteristic of Lawrence's belief in intuition, in the dark forces of the inner self, that must not be allowed to be swamped by the rational faculties but must be brought into a harmonious relation with them. It was a point of view—or rather, a perception, a passionate insight—that could not be convincingly expressed in argument but demanded direct projection in art.

The genteel culture of Lawrence's mother came more and more to represent death for Lawrence. In much of his later work, and especially in some of his short stories, he sets the deadening restrictiveness of middle-class conventional living against the forces of liberation that are often represented by an outsider—a peasant, a gypsy, a worker, a primitive of some kind, someone free by circumstance or personal effort. The recurring theme of his short stories—which contain some of his best work—is the distortion of love by possessiveness or gentility or a false romanticism or a false conception of the life of the artist and the achievement of a living relation between a man and a woman against the pressure of class-feeling or tradition or habit or prejudice.

His two masterpieces, *The Rainbow* and *Women in Love* (both of which developed out of what was originally conceived as a single novel to be called *The Sisters*), are to be read as symbolic and dramatic poems in prose. In these novels Lawrence probes with both subtlety and power into various aspects of relationship—the relationship between humans and their environment, the relationship between the generations, the relationship between man and woman, the relationship between instinct and intellect, and above all the proper basis for the marriage relationship as he conceived it. Lawrence's view of marriage as a struggle derived from his own relationship with his strong-minded German-born wife, Frieda. There are more and bitterer lovers' quarrels in Lawrence's novels than anywhere else in English literature. Lawrence's "crockery-throwing" view of love could become tedious, except that, as he presents it, it is bound up with the deepest rhythms and most profound instincts of the man-woman relationship.

In *The Rainbow* and *Women in Love* Lawrence is developing a radically new kind of novel in which he explores kinds of human relationships with a combination of uncanny psychological precision and intense poetic feeling. They have an acute surface realism, a sharp sense of time and place, and brilliant topographical detail; and at the same time their high poetic symbolism, both of the total pattern of action and of incidents and objects within it, establishes a rhythm of meaning that is missed by those who read the novels with the conventional categories of "plot" and "characters" in mind. His next novel, *Aaron's Rod* (1922), is more uneven; in it Lawrence, employing many of his own experiences, explores problems of human relations under the question of moral and political leadership, which for a time obsessed him. He was concerned with the struggle for leadership in marriage as well as in politics. Two other novels on the theme of leadership, *Kangaroo* (1923), set in Australia, and *The Plumed Serpent* (1926), set in Mexico, similarly uneven, show him trying to give symbolic fictional form to his own problems and preoccupations. But *Kangaroo* in particular has its moments of uncanny perceptiveness, and it is extraordinary how Lawrence, drawing on his experiences during a short stay in Australia, was able to get beneath the skin of the country and evoke so much of the essential reality of both place and people.

It is hard to think of another English novelist whose best and most characteristic work makes such a disquieting assault on our normal patterns of thought and feeling. It is not simply that Lawrence is a rebel against convention—many writers have been that—or that his views are startling, though they sometimes are. It is rather that the whole response to life, and in particular to the problems posed by human relationships, that emerges from his novels and stories seems to come so profoundly from the deepest recesses of his being and, therefore, assault the deepest recesses of *our* being, that the challenge seems to go beyond that which is normally asserted by a work of art. It is difficult to escape the challenge; to make any attempt to respond fully to what he is saying is to be drawn into his world, forced to share his vision.

Although there are complex critical reasons for the posthumous triumph of this writer who was so much reviled in his lifetime, there is also a simple and striking reason that must not be forgotten. Lawrence had vision; he had a poetic sense of life; he had a keen ear and a piercing eye for every kind of vitality and color and sound in the world, for landscape—be it of England or Italy or New Mexico—for the individuality and concreteness of things in nature, and for the individuality and concreteness of people. His travel sketches are as impressive in their way as his novels; he seizes both on the symbolic incident and on the concrete reality, and each is interpreted in terms of the other. He looked at the world freshly, with his own eyes, avoiding formulas and clichés; and he forged for himself a kind of utterance that, at his best, was able to convey powerfully and vividly what his fresh, original vision showed him. This kind of originality has its drawbacks; he was sometimes shrill, sometimes repetitive, sometimes almost hysterical; some scenes in his novels are murky with unachieved symbolism or splutter with unresolved passion. But the great Lawrence remains.

This restless pilgrim with his uncanny perceptions into the depths of physical things, with his uncompromising honesty and originality in his view of human beings and the world, cannot be dismissed as merely a great eccentric. Nor is he a great prophet. He is essentially an artist; it is his *rendering* of life in his art, not his preaching about life's meaning, that matters.

Odour of Chrysanthemums

I

The small locomotive engine, Number 4, came clanking, stumbling down from Selston with seven full wagons. It appeared round the corner with loud threats of speed, but the colt that it startled from among the gorse,[1] which still flickered indistinctly in the raw afternoon, out-distanced it at a canter. A woman, walking up the railway line to Underwood, drew back into the hedge, held her basket aside, and watched the footplate of the engine advancing. The trucks[2] thumped heavily past, one by one, with slow inevitable movement, as she stood insignificantly trapped between the jolting black wagons

---

1. Also known as furze or whin, a prickly bush with yellow flowers common on heaths, moors, and hillsides all over Britain.
2. Open freight cars.

and the hedge; then they curved away towards the coppice[3] where the withered oak leaves dropped noiselessly, while the birds, pulling at the scarlet hips beside the track, made off into the dusk that had already crept into the spinney.[4] In the open, the smoke from the engine sank and cleaved to the rough grass. The fields were dreary and forsaken, and in the marshy strip that led to the whimsey,[5] a reedy pit-pond, the fowls had already abandoned their run among the alders, to roost in the tarred fowl-house. The pit-bank loomed up beyond the pond, flames like red sores licking its ashy sides, in the afternoon's stagnant light. Just beyond rose the tapering chimneys and the clumsy black headstocks of Brinsley Colliery.[6] The two wheels were spinning fast up against the sky, and the winding engine rapped out its little spasms. The miners were being turned up.

The engine whistled as it came into the wide bay of railway lines beside the colliery, where rows of trucks stood in harbour.

Miners, single, trailing and in groups, passed like shadows diverging home. At the edge of the ribbed level of sidings squat a low cottage, three steps down from the cinder track. A large bony vine clutched at the house, as if to claw down the tiled roof. Round the bricked yard grew a few wintry primroses. Beyond, the long garden sloped down to a bush-covered brook course. There were some twiggy apple trees, winter-crack trees, and ragged cabbages. Beside the path hung disheveled pink chrysanthemums, like pink cloths hung on bushes. A woman came stooping out of the felt-covered fowl-house, half-way down the garden. She closed and padlocked the door, then drew herself erect, having brushed some bits from her white apron.

She was a tall woman of imperious mien, handsome, with definite black eyebrows. Her smooth black hair was parted exactly. For a few moments she stood steadily watching the miners as they passed along the railway: then she turned towards the brook course. Her face was calm and set, her mouth was closed with disillusionment. After a moment she called:

"John!" There was no answer. She waited, and then said distinctly:

"Where are you?"

"Here!" replied a child's sulky voice from among the bushes. The woman looked piercingly through the dusk.

"Are you at that brook?" she asked sternly.

For answer the child showed himself before the raspberry-canes that rose like whips. He was a small, sturdy boy of five. He stood quite still, defiantly.

"Oh!" said the mother, conciliated. "I thought you were down at that wet brook—and you remember what I told you——"

The boy did not move or answer.

"Come, come on in," she said more gently, "it's getting dark. There's your grandfather's engine coming down the line!"

The lad advanced slowly, with resentful, taciturn movement. He was dressed in trousers and waistcoat of cloth that was too thick and hard for the size of the garments. They were evidently cut down from a man's clothes.

As they went slowly towards the house he tore at the ragged wisps of chrysanthemums and dropped the petals in handfuls along the path.

"Don't do that—it does look nasty," said his mother. He refrained, and

---

3. A wood of small trees or shrubs.
4. Copse, thicket.
5. Machine for raising ore or water from a mine.

6. Coal mine. "Headstocks" support revolving parts of a machine.

she, suddenly pitiful, broke off a twig with three or four wan flowers and held them against her face. When mother and son reached the yard her hand hesitated, and instead of laying the flower aside, she pushed it in her apron-band. The mother and son stood at the foot of the three steps looking across the bay of lines at the passing home of the miners. The trundle of the small train was imminent. Suddenly the engine loomed past the house and came to a stop opposite the gate.

The engine-driver, a short man with round grey beard, leaned out of the cab high above the woman.

"Have you got a cup of tea?" he said in a cheery, hearty fashion.

It was her father. She went in, saying she would mash.[7] Directly, she returned.

"I didn't come to see you on Sunday," began the little grey-bearded man.

"I didn't expect you," said his daughter.

The engine-driver winced; then, reassuming his cheery, airy manner, he said:

"Oh, have you heard then? Well, and what do you think——?"

"I think it is soon enough," she replied.

At her brief censure the little man made an impatient gesture, and said coaxingly, yet with dangerous coldness:

"Well, what's a man to do? It's no sort of life for a man of my years, to sit at my own hearth like a stranger. And if I'm going to marry again it may as well be soon as late—what does it matter to anybody?"

The woman did not reply, but turned and went into the house. The man in the engine-cab stood assertive, till she returned with a cup of tea and a piece of bread and butter on a plate. She went up the steps and stood near the footplate of the hissing engine.

"You needn't 'a' brought me bread an' butter," said her father. "But a cup of tea"—he sipped appreciatively—"it's very nice." He sipped for a moment or two, then: "I hear as Walter's got another bout[8] on," he said.

"When hasn't he?" said the woman bitterly.

"I heerd tell of him in the 'Lord Nelson' braggin' as he was going to spend that b—— afore he went: half a sovereign[9] that was."

"When?" asked the woman.

"A' Sat'day night—I know that's true."

"Very likely," she laughed bitterly. "He gives me twenty-three shillings."

"Aye, it's a nice thing, when a man can do nothing with his money but make a beast of himself!" said the grey-whiskered man. The woman turned her head away. Her father swallowed the last of his tea and handed her the cup.

"Aye, he sighed, wiping his mouth. "It's a settler,[1] it is——"

He put his hand on the lever. The little engine strained and groaned, and the train rumbled towards the crossing. The woman again looked across the metals. Darkness was settling over the spaces of the railway and trucks: the miners, in grey somber groups, were still passing home. The winding engine pulsed hurriedly, with brief pauses. Elizabeth Bates looked at the dreary flow of men, then she went indoors. Her husband did not come.

---

7. Steep the tea.
8. Session; i.e., bout of drinking.
9. Gold coin worth twenty shillings. Half a sover-

eign is worth ten. Lord Nelson is the name of a public house (pub).
1. Crushing (or final) blow.

The kitchen was small and full of firelight; red coals piled glowing up the chimney mouth. All the life of the room seemed in the white, warm hearth and the steel fender reflecting the red fire. The cloth was laid for tea; cups glinted in the shadows. At the back, where the lowest stairs protruded into the room, the boy sat struggling with a knife and a piece of white wood. He was almost hidden in the shadow. It was half-past four. They had but to await the father's coming to begin tea. As the mother watched her son's sullen little struggle with the wood, she saw herself in his silence and pertinacity; she saw the father in her child's indifference to all but himself. She seemed to be occupied by her husband. He had probably gone past his home, slunk past his own door, to drink before he came in, while his dinner spoiled and wasted in waiting. She glanced at the clock, then took the potatoes to strain them in the yard. The garden and fields beyond the brook were closed in uncertain darkness. When she rose with the saucepan, leaving the drain steaming into the night behind her, she saw the yellow lamps were lit along the high road that went up the hill away beyond the space of the railway lines and the field.

Then again she watched the men trooping home, fewer now and fewer.

Indoors the fire was sinking and the room was dark red. The woman put her saucepan on the hob, and set a batter-pudding near the mouth of the oven. Then she stood unmoving. Directly, gratefully, came quick young steps to the door. Someone hung on the latch a moment, then a little girl entered and began pulling off her outdoor things, dragging a mass of curls, just ripening from gold to brown, over her eyes with her hat.

Her mother chid her for coming late from school, and said she would have to keep her at home the dark winter days.

"Why, mother, it's hardly a bit dark yet. The lamp's not lighted, and my father's not home."

"No, he isn't. But it's a quarter to five! Did you see anything of him?"

The child became serious. She looked at her mother with large, wistful blue eyes.

"No, mother, I've never seen him. Why? Has he come up an' gone past, to Old Brinsley? He hasn't, mother, 'cos I never saw him."

"He'd watch that," said the mother bitterly, "he'd take care as you didn't see him. But you may depend upon it, he's seated in the 'Prince o' Wales.'[2] He wouldn't be this late."

The girl looked at her mother piteously.

"Let's have our teas, mother, should we?" said she.

The mother called John to table. She opened the door once more and looked out across the darkness of the lines. All was deserted: she could not hear the winding-engines.

"Perhaps," she said to herself, "he's stopped to get some ripping[3] done."

They sat down to tea. John, at the end of the table near the door, was almost lost in the darkness. Their faces were hidden from each other. The girl crouched against the fender slowly moving a thick piece of bread before the fire. The lad, his face a dusky mark on the shadow, sat watching her who was transfigured in the red glow.

2. Name of a pub.
3. Taking out or cutting away coal or stone (a mining and quarrying term).

"I do think it's beautiful to look in the fire," said the child.

"Do you?" said her mother. "Why?"

"It's so red, and full of little caves—and it feels so nice, and you can fair smell it."

"It'll want mending directly," replied her mother, "and then if your father comes he'll carry on and say there never is a fire when a man comes home sweating from the pit. A public-house is always warm enough."

There was silence till the boy said complainingly: "Make haste, our Annie."

"Well, I am doing! I can't make the fire do it no faster, can I?"

"She keeps wafflin' it about so's to make 'er slow," grumbled the boy.

"Don't have such an evil imagination, child," replied the mother.

Soon the room was busy in the darkness with the crisp sound of crunching. The mother ate very little. She drank her tea determinedly, and sat thinking. When she rose her anger was evident in the stern unbending of her head. She looked at the pudding in the fender, and broke out:

"It is a scandalous thing as a man can't even come home to his dinner! If it's crozzled up to a cinder I don't see why I should care. Past his very door he goes to get to a public-house, and here I sit with his dinner waiting for him——"

She went out. As she dropped piece after piece of coal on the red fire, the shadows fell on the walls, till the room was almost in total darkness.

"I canna see," grumbled the invisible John. In spite of herself, the mother laughed.

"You know the way to your mouth," she said. She set the dust pan outside the door. When she came again like a shadow on the hearth, the lad repeated, complaining sulkily:

"I canna see."

"Good gracious!" cried the mother irritably, "you're as bad as your father if it's a bit dusk!"

Nevertheless, she took a paper spill from a sheaf on the mantelpiece and proceeded to light the lamp that hung from the ceiling in the middle of the room. As she reached up, her figure displayed itself just rounding with maternity.

"Oh, mother——!" exclaimed the girl.

"What?" said the woman, suspended in the act of putting the lamp-glass over the flame. The copper reflector shone handsomely on her, as she stood with uplifted arm, turning to face her daughter.

"You've got a flower in your apron!" said the child, in a little rapture at this unusual event.

"Goodness me!" exclaimed the woman, relieved. "One would think the house was afire." She replaced the glass and waited a moment before turning up the wick. A pale shadow was seen floating vaguely on the floor.

"Let me smell!" said the child, still rapturously, coming forward and putting her face to her mother's waist.

"Go along, silly!" said the mother, turning up the lamp. The light revealed their suspense so that the woman felt it almost unbearable. Annie was still bending at her waist. Irritably, the mother took the flowers out from her apron-band.

"Oh, mother—don't take them out!" Annie cried, catching her hand and trying to replace the sprig.

"Such nonsense!" said the mother, turning away. The child put the pale chrysanthemums to her lips, murmuring:

"Don't they smell beautiful!"

Her mother gave a short laugh.

"No," she said, "not to me. It was chrysanthemums when I married him, and chrysanthemums when you were born, and the first time they ever brought him home drunk, he'd got brown chrysanthemums in his button-hole."

She looked at the children. Their eyes and their parted lips were wondering. The mother sat rocking in silence for some time. Then she looked at the clock.

"Twenty minutes to six!" In a tone of fine bitter carelessness she continued: "Eh, he'll not come now till they bring him. There he'll stick! But he needn't come rolling in here in his pit-dirt, for I won't wash him. He can lie on the floor——Eh, what a fool I've been, what a fool! And this is what I came here for, to this dirty hole, rats and all, for him to slink past his very door. Twice last week—he's begun now——"

She silenced herself and rose to clear the table.

While for an hour or more the children played, subduedly intent, fertile of imagination, united in fear of the mother's wrath, and in dread of their father's home-coming, Mrs Bates sat in her rocking chair making a "singlet" of thick cream-coloured flannel, which gave a dull wounded sound as she tore off the grey edge. She worked at her sewing with energy, listening to the children, and her anger wearied itself, lay down to rest, opening its eyes from time to time and steadily watching, its ears raised to listen. Sometimes even her anger quailed and shrank, and the mother suspended her sewing, tracing the footsteps that thudded along the sleepers outside; she would lift her head sharply to bid the children "hush," but she recovered herself in time, and the footsteps went past the gate, and the children were not flung out of their play-world.

But at last Annie sighed, and gave in. She glanced at her wagon of slippers, and loathed the game. She turned plaintively to her mother.

"Mother!"—but she was inarticulate.

John crept out like a frog from under the sofa. His mother glanced up.

"Yes," she said, "just look at those shirt-sleeves!"

The boy held them out to survey them, saying nothing. Then somebody called in a hoarse voice away down the line, and suspense bristled in the room, till two people had gone by outside, talking.

"It is time for bed," said the mother.

"My father hasn't come," wailed Annie plaintively. But her mother was primed with courage.

"Never mind. They'll bring him when he does come—like a log." She meant there would be no scene. "And he may sleep on the floor till he wakes himself. I know he'll not go to work to-morrow after this!"

The children had their hands and faces wiped with a flannel. They were very quiet. When they had put on their night-dresses, they said their prayers, the boy mumbling. The mother looked down at them, at the brown silken bush of intertwining curls in the nape of the girl's neck, at the little black head of the lad, and her heart burst with anger at their father, who caused all three such distress. The children hid their faces in her skirts for comfort.

When Mrs Bates came down, the room was strangely empty, with a tension of expectancy. She took up her sewing and stitched for some time without raising her head. Meantime her anger was tinged with fear.

II

The clock struck eight and she rose suddenly, dropping her sewing on her chair. She went to the stair-foot door, opened it, listening. Then she went out, locking the door behind her.

Something scuffled in the yard, and she started, though she knew it was only the rats with which the place was over-run. The night was very dark. In the great bay of railway lines, bulked with trucks, there was no trace of light, only away back she could see a few yellow lamps at the pit-top, and the red smear of the burning pit-bank on the night. She hurried along the edge of the track, then, crossing the converging lines, came to the stile by the white gates, whence she emerged on the road. Then the fear which had led her shrank. People were walking up to New Brinsley; she saw the lights in the houses; twenty yards farther on were the broad windows of the "Prince of Wales," very warm and bright, and the loud voices of men could be heard distinctly. What a fool she had been to imagine that anything had happened to him! He was merely drinking over there at the "Prince of Wales." She faltered. She had never yet been to fetch him, and she never would go. So she continued her walk towards the long straggling line of houses, standing back on the highway. She entered a passage between the dwellings.

"Mr Rigley?—Yes! Did you want him? No, he's not in at this minute."

The raw-boned woman leaned forward from her dark scullery and peered at the other, upon whom fell a dim light through the blind of the kitchen window.

"Is it Mrs Bates?" she asked in a tone tinged with respect.

"Yes. I wondered if your Master was at home. Mine hasn't come yet."

" 'Asn't 'e! Oh, Jack's been 'ome an' 'ad 'is dinner an' gone out. 'E's just gone for 'alf an hour afore bed-time. Did you call at the 'Prince of Wales'?"

"No——"

"No, you didn't like——! It's not very nice." The other woman was indulgent. There was an awkward pause. "Jack never said nothink about—about your Master," she said.

"No!—I expect he's stuck in there!"

Elizabeth Bates said this bitterly, and with recklessness. She knew that the woman across the yard was standing at her door listening, but she did not care. As she turned:

"Stop a minute! I'll just go an' ask Jack if 'e knows anythink," said Mrs Rigley.

"Oh no—I wouldn't like to put——!"

"Yes, I will, if you'll just step inside an' see as th' childer doesn't come downstairs and set theirselves afire."

Elizabeth Bates, murmuring a remonstrance, stepped inside. The other woman apologised for the state of the room.

The kitchen needed apology. There were little frocks and trousers and childish undergarments on the squab[4] and on the floor, and a litter of playthings everywhere. On the black American cloth[5] of the table were pieces of bread and cake, crusts, slops, and a teapot with cold tea.

"Eh, ours is just as bad," said Elizabeth Bates, looking at the woman, not at the house. Mrs Rigley put a shawl over her head and hurried out, saying: "I shanna be a minute."

The other sat, noting with faint disapproval the general untidiness of the room. Then she fell to counting the shoes of various sizes scattered over the floor. There were twelve. She sighed and said to herself: "No wonder!"— glancing at the litter. There came the scratching of two pairs of feet on the yard, and the Rigleys entered. Elizabeth Bates rose. Rigley was a big man, with very large bones. His head looked particularly bony. Across his temple was a blue scar, caused by a wound got in the pit, a wound in which the coal dust remained blue like tattooing.

" 'Asna 'e come whoam yit?" asked the man, without any form of greeting, but with deference and sympathy. "I couldna say wheer he is—'e's non ower theer!"—he jerked his head to signify the "Prince of Wales."

" 'E's 'appen gone up to th' Yew,"[6] said Mrs Rigley.

There was another pause. Rigley had evidently something to get off his mind:

"Ah left 'im finishin' a stint," he began. "Loose-all[7] 'ad bin gone about ten minutes when we com'n away, an' I shouted: 'Are ter comin', Walt?' an' 'e said: 'Go on, Ah shanna be but a'ef a minnit,' so we com'n ter th' bottom, me an' Bowers, thinkin' as 'e wor just behint, an' 'ud come up i' th' next bantle[8]——"

He stood perplexed, as if answering a charge of deserting his mate. Elizabeth Bates, now again certain of disaster, hastened to reassure him:

"I expect 'e's gone up to th' 'Yew Tree,' as you say. It's not the first time. I've fretted myself into a fever before now. He'll come home when they carry him."

"Ay, isn't it too bad!" deplored the other woman.

"I'll just step up to Dick's an' see if 'e is theer," offered the man, afraid of appearing alarmed, afraid of taking liberties.

"Oh, I wouldn't think of bothering you that far," said Elizabeth Bates, with emphasis, but he knew she was glad of his offer.

As they stumbled up the entry, Elizabeth Bates heard Rigley's wife run across the yard and open her neighbour's door. At this, suddenly all the blood in her body seemed to switch away from her heart.

"Mind!" warned Rigley. "Ah've said many a time as Ah'd fill up them ruts in this entry, sumb'dy 'll be breakin' their legs yit."

She recovered herself and walked quickly along with the miner.

"I don't like leaving the children in bed, and nobody in the house," she said.

---

4. Couch.
5. Oilcloth.
6. I.e., the Yew Tree (a pub).

7. Signal for end of work.
8. Group.

"No, you dunna!" he replied courteously. They were soon at the gate of the cottage.

"Well, I shanna be many minnits. Dunna you be frettin' now, 'e'll be all right," said the butty.[9]

"Thank you very much, Mr Rigley," she replied.

"You're welcome!" he stammered, moving away. "I shanna be many minnits."

The house was quiet. Elizabeth Bates took off her hat and shawl, and rolled back the rug. When she had finished, she sat down. It was a few minutes past nine. She was startled by the rapid chuff of the winding-engine at the pit, and the sharp whirr of the brakes on the rope as it descended. Again she felt the painful sweep of her blood, and she put her hand to her side, saying aloud: "Good gracious!—it's only the nine o'clock deputy[1] going down," rebuking herself.

She sat still, listening. Half an hour of this, and she was wearied out.

"What am I working myself up like this for?" she said pitiably to herself, "I s'll only be doing myself some damage."

She took out her sewing again.

At a quarter to ten there were footsteps. One person! She watched for the door to open. It was an elderly woman, in a black bonnet and a black woollen shawl—his mother. She was about sixty years old, pale, with blue eyes, and her face all wrinkled and lamentable. She shut the door and turned to her daughter-in-law peevishly.

"Eh, Lizzie, whatever shall we do, whatever shall we do!" she cried.

Elizabeth drew back a little, sharply.

"What is it, mother?" she said.

The elder woman seated herself on the sofa.

"I don't know, child, I can't tell you!"—she shook her head slowly. Elizabeth sat watching her, anxious and vexed.

"I don't know," replied the grandmother, sighing very deeply. "There's no end to my troubles, there isn't. The things I've gone through, I'm sure it's enough——!" She wept without wiping her eyes, the tears running.

"But, mother," interrupted Elizabeth, "what do you mean? What is it?"

The grandmother slowly wiped her eyes. The fountains of her tears were stopped by Elizabeth's directness. She wiped her eyes slowly.

"Poor child! Eh, you poor thing!" she moaned. "I don't know what we're going to do, I don't—and you as you are—it's a thing, it is indeed!"

Elizabeth waited.

"Is he dead?" she asked, and at the words her heart swung violently, though she felt a slight flush of shame at the ultimate extravagance of the question. Her words sufficiently frightened the old lady, almost brought her to herself.

"Don't say so, Elizabeth! We'll hope it's not as bad as that; no, may the Lord spare us that, Elizabeth. Jack Rigley came just as I was sittin' down to a glass afore going to bed, an' 'e said: ' 'Appen you'll go down th' line, Mrs. Bates. Walt's had an accident. 'Appen you'll go an' sit wi' 'er till we can get him home.' I hadn't time to ask him a word afore he was gone. An' I put my bonnet on an' come straight down, Lizzie. I thought to myself: 'Eh, that poor

---

9. Workmate (cf. "buddy"). Among English coal miners it has the meaning of "a supervisor intermediary between the employers and the men."
1. Minor coal-mine official.

blessed child, if anybody should come an' tell her of a sudden, there's no knowin' what'll 'appen to 'er.' You mustn't let it upset you, Lizzie—or you know what to expect. How long is it, six months—or is it five, Lizzie? Ay!"— the old woman shook her head—"time slips on, it slips on! Ay!"

Elizabeth's thoughts were busy elsewhere. If he was killed—would she be able to manage on the little pension and what she could earn?—she counted up rapidly. If he was hurt—they wouldn't take him to the hospital—how tiresome he would be to nurse!—but perhaps she'd be able to get him away from the drink and his hateful ways. She would—while he was ill. The tears offered to come to her eyes at the picture. But what sentimental luxury was this she was beginning? She turned to consider the children. At any rate she was absolutely necessary for them. They were her business.

"Ay!" repeated the old woman, "it seems but a week or two since he brought me his first wages. Ay—he was a good lad, Elizabeth, he was, in his way. I don't know why he got to be such a trouble, I don't. He was a happy lad at home, only full of spirits. But there's no mistake he's been a handful of trouble, he has! I hope the Lord'll spare him to mend his ways. I hope so, I hope so. You've had a sight o' trouble with him, Elizabeth, you have indeed. But he was a jolly enough lad wi' me, he was, I can assure you. I don't know how it is . . . ."

The old woman continued to muse aloud, a monotonous irritating sound, while Elizabeth thought concentratedly, startled once, when she heard the winding-engine chuff quickly, and the brakes skirr with a shriek. Then she heard the engine more slowly, and the brakes made no sound. The old woman did not notice. Elizabeth waited in suspense. The mother-in-law talked, with lapses into silence.

"But he wasn't your son, Lizzie, an' it makes a difference. Whatever he was, I remember him when he was little, an' I learned to understand him and to make allowances. You've got to make allowances for them——"

It was half-past ten, and the old woman was saying: "But it's trouble from beginning to end; you're never too old for trouble, never too old for that——" when the gate banged back, and there were heavy feet on the steps.

"I'll go, Lizzie, let me go," cried the old woman, rising. But Elizabeth was at the door. It was a man in pit-clothes.

"They're bringin' 'im, Missis," he said. Elizabeth's heart halted a moment. Then it surged on again, almost suffocating her.

"Is he—is it bad?" she asked.

The man turned away, looking at the darkness:

"The doctor says 'e'd been dead hours. 'E saw 'im i' th' lamp-cabin."

The old woman, who stood just behind Elizabeth, dropped into a chair, and folded her hands, crying: "Oh, my boy, my boy!"

"Hush!" said Elizabeth, with a sharp twitch of a frown. "Be still, mother, don't waken th' children: I wouldn't have them down for anything!"

The old woman moaned softly, rocking herself. The man was drawing away. Elizabeth took a step forward.

"How was it?" she asked.

"Well, I couldn't say for sure," the man replied, very ill at ease. " 'E wor finishin' a stint an' th' butties 'ad gone, an' a lot o' stuff come down atop 'n 'im."

"And crushed him?" cried the widow, with a shudder.

"No," said the man, "it fell at th' back of 'im. 'E wor under th' face an' it niver touched 'im. It shut 'im in. It seems 'e wor smothered."

Elizabeth shrank back. She heard the old woman behind her cry:

"What?—what did 'e say it was?"

The man replied, more loudly: " 'E wor smothered!"

Then the old woman wailed aloud, and this relieved Elizabeth.

"Oh, mother," she said, putting her hand on the old woman, "don't waken th' children, don't waken th' children."

She wept a little, unknowing, while the old mother rocked herself and moaned. Elizabeth remembered that they were bringing him home, and she must be ready. "They'll lay him in the parlour," she said to herself, standing a moment pale and perplexed.

Then she lighted a candle and went into the tiny room. The air was cold and damp, but she could not make a fire, there was no fireplace. She set down the candle and looked round. The candlelight glittered on the lustre-glasses, on the two vases that held some of the pink chrysanthemums, and on the dark mahogany. There was a cold, deathly smell of chrysanthemums in the room. Elizabeth stood looking at the flowers. She turned away, and calculated whether there would be room to lay him on the floor, between the couch and the chiffonier. She pushed the chairs aside. There would be room to lay him down and to step round him. Then she fetched the old red tablecloth, and another old cloth, spreading them down to save her bit of carpet. She shivered on leaving the parlour; so, from the dresser drawer she took a clean shirt and put it at the fire to air. All the time her mother-in-law was rocking herself in the chair and moaning.

"You'll have to move from there, mother," said Elizabeth. "They'll be bringing him in. Come in the rocker."

The old mother rose mechanically, and seated herself by the fire, continuing to lament. Elizabeth went into the pantry for another candle, and there, in the little pent-house under the naked tiles, she heard them coming. She stood still in the pantry doorway, listening. She heard them pass the end of the house, and come awkwardly down the three steps, a jumble of shuffling footsteps and muttering voices. The old woman was silent. The men were in the yard.

Then Elizabeth heard Matthews, the manager of the pit, say: "You go in first, Jim. Mind!"

The door came open, and the two women saw a collier backing into the room, holding one end of a stretcher, on which they could see the nailed pit-boots of the dead man. The two carriers halted, the man at the head stooping to the lintel of the door.

"Wheer will you have him?" asked the manager, a short, white-bearded man.

Elizabeth roused herself and came from the pantry carrying the unlighted candle.

"In the parlour," she said.

"In there, Jim!" pointed the manager, and the carriers backed round into the tiny room. The coat with which they had covered the body fell off as they awkwardly turned through the two doorways, and the women saw their man, naked to the waist, lying stripped for work. The old woman began to moan in a low voice of horror.

"Lay th' stretcher at th' side," snapped the manager, "an' put 'im on th' cloths. Mind now, mind! Look you now———!"

One of the men had knocked off a vase of chrysanthemums. He stared awkwardly, then they set down the stretcher. Elizabeth did not look at her husband. As soon as she could get in the room, she went and picked up the broken vase and the flowers.

"Wait a minute!" she said.

The three men waited in silence while she mopped up the water with a duster.

"Eh, what a job, what a job, to be sure!" the manager was saying, rubbing his brow with trouble and perplexity. "Never knew such a thing in my life, never! He'd no business to ha' been left. I never knew such a thing in my life! Fell over him clean as a whistle, an' shut him in. Not four foot of space, there wasn't—yet it scarce bruised him."

He looked down at the dead man, lying prone, half naked, all grimed with coal-dust.

" ' 'Sphyxiated,' the doctor said. It is the most terrible job I've ever known Seems as if it was done o' purpose. Clean over him, an' shut 'im in, like a mouse-trap"—he made a sharp, descending gesture with his hand.

The colliers standing by jerked aside their heads in hopeless comment.

The horror of the thing bristled upon them all.

Then they heard the girl's voice upstairs calling shrilly: "Mother, mother—who is it? Mother, who is it?"

Elizabeth hurried to the foot of the stairs and opened the door:

"Go to sleep!" she commanded sharply. "What are you shouting about? Go to sleep at once—there's nothing——"

Then she began to mount the stairs. They could hear her on the boards, and on the plaster floor of the little bedroom. They could hear her distinctly:

"What's the matter now?—what's the matter with you, silly thing?"—her voice was much agitated, with an unreal gentleness.

"I thought it was some men come," said the plaintive voice of the child. "Has he come?"

"Yes, they've brought him. There's nothing to make a fuss about. Go to sleep now, like a good child."

They could hear her voice in the bedroom, they waited whilst she covered the children under the bedclothes.

"Is he drunk?" asked the girl, timidly, faintly.

"No! No—he's not! He—he's asleep."

"Is he asleep downstairs?"

"Yes—and don't make a noise."

There was silence for a moment, then the men heard the frightened child again:

"What's that noise?"

"It's nothing, I tell you, what are you bothering for?"

The noise was the grandmother moaning. She was oblivious of everything, sitting on her chair rocking and moaning. The manager put his hand on her arm and bade her "Sh—sh! !"

The old woman opened her eyes and looked at him. She was shocked by this interruption, and seemed to wonder.

"What time is it?" the plaintive thin voice of the child, sinking back unhappily into sleep, asked this last question.

"Ten o'clock," answered the mother more softly. Then she must have bent down and kissed the children.

Matthews beckoned to the men to come away. They put on their caps and took up the stretcher. Stepping over the body, they tiptoed out of the house. None of them spoke till they were far from the wakeful children.

When Elizabeth came down she found her mother alone on the parlour floor, leaning over the dead man, the tears dropping on him.

"We must lay him out," the wife said. She put on the kettle, then returning knelt at the feet, and began to unfasten the knotted leather laces. The room was clammy and dim with only one candle, so that she had to bend her face almost to the floor. At last she got off the heavy boots and put them away.

"You must help me now," she whispered to the old woman. Together they stripped the man.

When they arose, saw him lying in the naïve dignity of death, the women stood arrested in fear and respect. For a few moments they remained still, looking down, the old mother whimpering. Elizabeth felt countermanded. She saw him, how utterly inviolable he lay in himself. She had nothing to do with him. She could not accept it. Stooping, she laid her hand on him, in claim. He was still warm, for the mine was hot where he had died. His mother had his face between her hands, and was murmuring incoherently. The old tears fell in succession as drops from wet leaves; the mother was not weeping, merely her tears flowed. Elizabeth embraced the body of her husband, with cheek and lips. She seemed to be listening, inquiring, trying to get some connection. But she could not. She was driven away. He was impregnable.

She rose, went into the kitchen where she poured warm water into a bowl, brought soap and flannel and a soft towel. "I must wash him," she said.

Then the old mother rose stiffy, and watched Elizabeth as she carefully washed his face, carefully brushing his big blond moustache from his mouth with the flannel. She was afraid with a bottomless fear, so she ministered to him. The old woman, jealous, said:

"Let me wipe him!"—and she kneeled on the other side drying slowly as Elizabeth washed, her big black bonnet sometimes brushing the dark head of her daughter-in-law. They worked thus in silence for a long time. They never forgot it was death, and the touch of the man's dead body gave them strange emotions, different in each of the women; a great dread possessed them both, the mother felt the lie was given to her womb, she was denied; the wife felt the utter isolation of the human soul, the child within her was a weight apart from her.

At last it was finished. He was a man of handsome body, and his face showed no traces of drink. He was blond, full-fleshed, with fine limbs. But he was dead.

"Bless him," whispered his mother, looking always at his face, and speaking out of sheer terror. "Dear lad—bless him!" She spoke in a faint, sibilant ecstasy of fear and mother love.

Elizabeth sank down again to the floor, and put her face against his neck, and trembled and shuddered. But she had to draw away again. He was dead, and her living flesh had no place against his. A great dread and weariness held her: she was so unavailing. Her life was gone like this.

"White as milk he is, clear as a twelve-month baby, bless him, the darling!" the old mother murmured to herself. "Not a mark on him, clear and clean and white, beautiful as ever a child was made," she murmured with pride. Elizabeth kept her face hidden.

"He went peaceful, Lizzie—peaceful as sleep. Isn't he beautiful, the lamb? Ay—he must ha' made his peace, Lizzie. 'Appen he made it all right, Lizzie, shut in there. He'd have time. He wouldn't look like this if he hadn't made his peace. The lamb, the dear lamb. Eh, but he had a hearty laugh. I loved to hear it. He had the heartiest laugh, Lizzie, as a lad——"

Elizabeth looked up. The man's mouth was fallen back, slightly open under the cover of the moustache. The eyes, half shut, did not show glazed in the obscurity. Life with its smoky burning gone from him, had left him apart and utterly alien to her. And she knew what a stranger he was to her. In her womb was ice of fear, because of this separate stranger with whom she had been living as one flesh. Was this what it all meant—utter, intact separateness, obscured by heat of living? In dread she turned her face away. The fact was too deadly. There had been nothing between them, and yet they had come together, exchanging their nakedness repeatedly. Each time he had taken her, they had been two isolated beings, far apart as now. He was no more responsible than she. The child was like ice in her womb. For as she looked at the dead man, her mind, cold and detached, said clearly: "Who am I? What have I been doing? I have been fighting a husband who did not exist. *He* existed all the time. What wrong have I done? What was that I have been living with? There lies the reality, this man." And her soul died in her for fear: she knew she had never seen him, he had never seen her, they had met in the dark and had fought in the dark, not knowing whom they met or whom they fought. And now she saw, and turned silent in seeing. For she had been wrong. She had said he was something he was not; she had felt familiar with him. Whereas he was apart all the while, living as she never lived, feeling as she never felt.

In fear and shame she looked at his naked body, that she had known falsely. And he was the father of her children. Her soul was torn from her body and stood apart. She looked at his naked body and was ashamed, as if she had denied it. After all, it was itself. It seemed awful to her. She looked at his face, and she turned her own face to the wall. For his look was other than hers, his way was not her way. She had denied him what he was—she saw it now. She had refused him as himself. And this had been her life, and his life. She was grateful to death, which restored the truth. And she knew she was not dead.

And all the while her heart was bursting with grief and pity for him. What had he suffered? What stretch of horror for this helpless man! She was rigid with agony. She had not been able to help him. He had been cruelly injured, this naked man, this other being, and she could make no reparation. There were the children—but the children belonged to life. This dead man had nothing to do with them. He and she were only channels through which life had flowed to issue in the children. She was a mother—but how awful she knew it now to have been a wife. And he, dead now, how awful he must have felt it to be a husband. She felt that in the next world he would be a stranger to her. If they met there, in the beyond, they would only be ashamed of what had been before. The children had come, for some mysterious reason, out of both of them. But the children did not unite them. Now he was dead, she knew how eternally he was apart from her, how eternally he had nothing more to do with her. She saw this episode of her life closed. They had denied each other in life. Now he had withdrawn. An anguish came over her. It was finished then: it had become hopeless between them long before he died. Yet he had been her husband. But how little!

"Have you got his shirt, 'Lizabeth?"

Elizabeth turned without answering, though she strove to weep and behave as her mother-in-law expected. But she could not, she was silenced. She went into the kitchen and returned with the garment.

"It is aired," she said, grasping the cotton shirt here and there to try. She was almost ashamed to handle him; what right had she or anyone to lay hands on him; but her touch was humble on his body. It was hard work to clothe him. He was so heavy and inert. A terrible dread gripped her all the while: that he could be so heavy and utterly inert, unresponsive, apart. The horror of the distance between them was almost too much for her—it was so infinite a gap she must look across.

At last it was finished. They covered him with a sheet and left him lying, with his face bound. And she fastened the door of the little parlour, lest the children should see what was lying there. Then, with peace sunk heavy on her heart, she went about making tidy the kitchen. She knew she submitted to life, which was her immediate master. But from death, her ultimate master, she winced with fear and shame.

1911, 1914

The Horse Dealer's Daughter

"Well, Mabel, and what are you going to do with yourself?" asked Joe, with foolish flippancy. He felt quite safe himself. Without listening for an answer, he turned aside, worked a grain of tobacco to the tip of his tongue, and spat it out. He did not care about anything, since he felt safe himself.

The three brothers and the sister sat round the desolate breakfast-table, attempting some sort of desultory consultation. The morning's post had given the final tap to the family fortunes, and all was over. The dreary dining-room itself, with its heavy mahogany furniture, looked as if it were waiting to be done away with.

But the consultation amounted to nothing. There was a strange air of ineffectuality about the three men, as they sprawled at table, smoking and reflecting vaguely on their own condition. The girl was alone, a rather short, sullen-looking young woman of twenty-seven. She did not share the same life as her brothers. She would have been good-looking, save for the impressive fixity of her face, "bull-dog," as her brothers called it.

There was a confused tramping of horses' feet outside. The three men all sprawled round in their chairs to watch. Beyond the dark holly bushes that separated the strip of lawn from the high-road, they could see a cavalcade of shire horses swinging out of their own yard, being taken for exercise. This was the last time. These were the last horses that would go through their hands. The young men watched with critical, callous look. They were all frightened at the collapse of their lives, and the sense of disaster in which they were involved left them no inner freedom.

Yet they were three fine, well-set fellows enough. Joe, the eldest, was a man of thirty-three, broad and handsome in a hot, flushed way. His face was red, he twisted his black moustache over a thick finger, his eyes were shallow and restless. He had a sensual way of uncovering his teeth when he laughed, and his bearing was stupid. Now he watched the horses with a glazed look of helplessness in his eyes, a certain stupor of downfall.

The great draught horses swung past. They were tied head to tail, four of them, and they heaved along to where a lane branched off from the high-road, planting their great hoofs floutingly in the fine black mud, swinging their great rounded haunches sumptuously, and trotting a few sudden steps as they were led into the lane, round the corner. Every movement showed a massive, slumbrous strength, and a stupidity which held them in subjection. The groom at the head looked back, jerking the leading rope. And the cavalcade moved out of sight up the lane, the tail of the last horse, bobbed up tight and stiff, held out taut from the swinging great haunches as they rocked behind the hedges in a motion-like sleep.

Joe watched with glazed hopeless eyes. The horses were almost like his own body to him. He felt he was done for now. Luckily he was engaged to a woman as old as himself, and therefore her father, who was steward of a neighbouring estate, would provide him with a job. He would marry and go into harness. His life was over, he would be a subject animal now.

He turned uneasily aside, the retreating steps of the horses echoing in his ears. Then, with foolish restlessness, he reached for the scraps of bacon-rind from the plates, and making a faint whistling sound, flung them to the terrier that lay against the fender. He watched the dog swallow them, and waited till the creature looked into his eyes. Then a faint grin came on his face, and in a high, foolish voice he said:

"You won't get much more bacon, shall you, you little b——?"

The dog faintly and dismally wagged its tail, then lowered its haunches, circled round, and lay down again.

There was another helpless silence at the table. Joe sprawled uneasily in his seat, not willing to go till the family conclave was dissolved. Fred Henry, the second brother, was erect, clean-limbed, alert. He had watched the passing of the horses with more *sang-froid*.[1] If he was an animal, like Joe, he was an animal which controls, not one which is controlled. He was master of any horse, and he carried himself with a well-tempered air of mastery. But he was not master of the situations of life. He pushed his coarse brown moustache upwards, off his lip, and glanced irritably at his sister, who sat impassive and inscrutable.

"You'll go and stop with Lucy for a bit, shan't you?" he asked. The girl did not answer.

"I don't see what else you can do," persisted Fred Henry.

"Go as a skivvy,"[2] Joe interpolated laconically.

The girl did not move a muscle.

"If I was her, I should go in for training for a nurse," said Malcolm, the

---

1. Cold blood (French, literal trans.); here, calm detachment.   2. Servant girl.

youngest of them all. He was the baby of the family, a young man of twenty-two, with a fresh, jaunty *museau*.[3]

But Mabel did not take any notice of him. They had talked at her and round her for so many years, that she hardly heard them at all.

The marble clock on the mantelpiece softly chimed the half-hour, the dog rose uneasily from the hearth-rug and looked at the party at the breakfast-table. But still they sat in an ineffectual conclave.

"Oh, all right," said Joe suddenly, apropos of nothing. "I'll get a move on."

He pushed back his chair, straddled his knees with a downward jerk, to get them free, in horsey fashion, and went to the fire. Still he did not go out of the room; he was curious to know what the others would do or say. He began to charge his pipe, looking down at the dog and saying in a high, affected voice:

"Going wi' me? Going wi' me are ter? Tha'rt goin' further than tha counts on just now, dost hear?"

The dog faintly wagged his tail, the man stuck out his jaw and covered his pipe with his hands, and puffed intently, losing himself in the tobacco, look-ing down all the while at the dog with an absent brown eye. The dog looked up at him in mournful distrust. Joe stood with his knees stuck out, in real horsey fashion.

"Have you had a letter from Lucy?" Fred Henry asked of his sister.

"Last week," came the neutral reply.

"And what does she say?"

There was no answer.

"Does she *ask* you to go and stop there?" persisted Fred Henry.

"She says I can if I like."

"Well, then, you'd better. Tell her you'll come on Monday."

This was received in silence.

"That's what you'll do then, is it?" said Fred Henry, in some exasperation.

But she made no answer. There was a silence of futility and irritation in the room. Malcolm grinned fatuously.

"You'll have to make up your mind between now and next Wednesday," said Joe loudly, "or else find yourself lodgings on the kerbstone."

The face of the young woman darkened, but she sat on immutable.

"Here's Jack Ferguson!" exclaimed Malcolm, who was looking aimlessly out of the window.

"Where?" exclaimed Joe loudly.

"Just gone past."

"Coming in?"

Malcolm craned his neck to see the gate.

"Yes," he said.

There was a silence. Mabel sat on like one condemned, at the head of the table. Then a whistle was heard from the kitchen. The dog got up and barked sharply. Joe opened the door and shouted:

"Come on."

After a moment a young man entered. He was muffled up in overcoat and a purple woollen scarf, and his tweed cap, which he did not remove, was pulled down on his head. He was of medium height, his face was rather long and pale, his eyes looked tired.

---

3. Muzzle (French); here, face.

"Hello, Jack! Well, Jack!" exclaimed Malcolm and Joe. Fred Henry merely said: "Jack."

"What's doing?" asked the newcomer, evidently addressing Fred Henry.

"Same. We've got to be out by Wednesday. Got a cold?"

"I have—got it bad, too."

"Why don't you stop in?"

"*Me* stop in? When I can't stand on my legs, perhaps I shall have a chance." The young man spoke huskily. He had a slight Scotch accent.

"It's a knock-out, isn't it," said Joe, boisterously, "if a doctor goes round croaking with a cold. Looks bad for the patients, doesn't it?"

The young doctor looked at him slowly.

"Anything the matter with *you*, then?" he asked sarcastically.

"Not as I know of. Damn your eyes, I hope not. Why?"

"I thought you were very concerned about the patients, wondered if you might be one yourself."

"Damn it, no, I've never been patient to no flaming doctor, and hope I never shall be," returned Joe.

At this point Mabel rose from the table, and they all seemed to become aware of her existence. She began putting the dishes together. The young doctor looked at her, but did not address her. He had not greeted her. She went out of the room with the tray, her face impassive and unchanged.

"When are you off then, all of you?" asked the doctor.

"I'm catching the eleven-forty," replied Malcolm. "Are you goin' down wi' th' trap, Joe?"

"Yes, I've told you I'm going down wi' th' trap, haven't I?"

"We'd better be getting her in then. So long Jack, if I don't see you before I go," said Malcolm, shaking hands.

He went out, followed by Joe, who seemed to have his tail between his legs.

"Well, this is the devil's own," exclaimed the doctor, when he was left alone with Fred Henry. "Going before Wednesday, are you?"

"That's the orders," replied the other.

"Where, to Northampton?"

"That's it."

"The devil!" exclaimed Ferguson, with quiet chagrin.

And there was silence between the two.

"All settled up, are you?" asked Ferguson.

"About."

There was another pause.

"Well, I shall miss yer, Freddy, boy," said the young doctor.

"And I shall miss thee, Jack," returned the other.

"Miss you like hell," mused the doctor.

Fred Henry turned aside. There was nothing to say. Mabel came in again, to finish clearing the table.

"What are *you* going to do, then, Miss Pervin?" asked Ferguson. "Going to your sister's, are you?"

Mabel looked at him with her steady, dangerous eyes, that always made him uncomfortable, unsettling his superficial ease.

"No," she said.

"Well, what in the name of fortune *are* you going to do? Say what you mean to do," cried Fred Henry, with futile intensity.

But she only averted her head, and continued her work. She folded the white table-cloth, and put on the chenille cloth.

"The sulkiest bitch that ever trod!" muttered her brother.

But she finished her task with perfectly impassive face, the young doctor watching her interestedly all the while. Then she went out.

Fred Henry stared after her, clenching his lips, his blue eyes fixing in sharp antagonism, as he made a grimace of sour exasperation.

"You could bray[4] her into bits, and that's all you'd get out of her," he said, in a small, narrowed tone.

The doctor smiled faintly.

"What's she *going* to do, then?" he asked.

"Strike me if *I* know!" returned the other.

There was a pause. Then the doctor stirred.

"I'll be seeing you tonight, shall I?" he said to his friend.

"Ay—where's it to be? Are we going over to Jessdale?"

"I don't know. I've got such a cold on me. I'll come round to the 'Moon and Stars,'[5] anyway."

"Let Lizzie and May miss their night for once, eh?"

"That's it—if I feel as I do now."

"All's one——"

The two young men went through the passage and down to the back door together. The house was large, but it was servantless now, and desolate. At the back was a small bricked house-yard and beyond that a big square, gravelled fine and red, and having stables on two sides. Sloping, dank, winter-dark fields stretched away on the open sides.

But the stables were empty. Joseph Pervin, the father of the family, had been a man of no education, who had become a fairly large horse dealer. The stables had been full of horses, there was a great turmoil and come-and-go of horses and of dealers and grooms. Then the kitchen was full of servants. But of late things had declined. The old man had married a second time, to retrieve his fortunes. Now he was dead and everything was gone to the dogs,[6] there was nothing but debt and threatening.

For months, Mabel had been servantless in the big house, keeping the home together in penury for her ineffectual brothers. She had kept house for ten years. But previously it was with unstinted means. Then, however brutal and coarse everything was, the sense of money had kept her proud, confident. The men might be foul-mouthed, the women in the kitchen might have had reputations, her brothers might have illegitimate children. But so long as there was money, the girl felt herself established, and brutally proud, reserved.

No company came to the house, save dealers and coarse men. Mabel had no associates of her own sex, after her sister went away. But she did not mind. She went regularly to church, she attended to her father. And she lived in the memory of her mother, who had died when she was fourteen, and whom she had loved. She had loved her father, too, in a different way, depending upon him, and feeling secure in him, until at the age of fifty-four, he married again. And then she had set hard against him. Now he had died and left them all hopelessly in debt.

4. Grind.
5. Name of a public house (pub).
6. Gone wrong (slang).

She had suffered badly during the period of poverty. Nothing, however, could shake the curious, sullen, animal pride that dominated each member of the family. Now, for Mabel, the end had come. Still she would not cast about her. She would follow her own way just the same. She would always hold the keys of her own situation. Mindless and persistent, she endured from day to day. Why should she think? Why should she answer anybody? It was enough that this was the end, and there was no way out. She need not pass any more darkly along the main street of the small town, avoiding every eye. She need not demean herself any more, going into the shops and buying the cheapest food. This was at an end. She thought of nobody, not even of herself. Mindless and persistent, she seemed in a sort of ecstasy to be coming nearer to her fulfilment, her own glorification, approaching her dead mother, who was glorified.

In the afternoon, she took a little bag, with shears and sponge and a small scrubbing-brush, and went out. It was a grey, wintry day, with saddened, dark green fields and an atmosphere blackened by the smoke of foundries not far off. She went quickly, darkly along the causeway, heeding nobody, through the town to the churchyard.

There she always felt secure, as if no one could see her, although as a matter of fact she was exposed to the stare of everyone who passed along under the churchyard wall. Nevertheless, once under the shadow of the great looming church, among the graves, she felt immune from the world, reserved within the thick churchyard wall as in another country.

Carefully she clipped the grass from the grave, and arranged the pinky-white, small chrysanthemums in the tin cross. When this was done, she took an empty jar from a neighbouring grave, brought water, and carefully, most scrupulously sponged the marble headstone and the coping-stone.

It gave her sincere satisfaction to do this. She felt in immediate contact with the world of her mother. She took minute pains, went through the park in a state bordering on pure happiness, as if in performing this task she came into a subtle, intimate connection with her mother. For the life she followed here in the world was far less real than the world of death she inherited from her mother.

The doctor's house was just by the church. Ferguson, being a mere hired assistant, was slave to the country-side. As he hurried now to attend to the out-patients in the surgery, glancing across the graveyard with his quick eye, he saw the girl at her task at the grave. She seemed so intent and remote, it was like looking into another world. Some mystical element was touched in him. He slowed down as he walked, watching her as if spellbound.

She lifted her eyes, feeling him looking. Their eyes met. And each looked away again at once, each feeling, in some way, found out by the other. He lifted his cap and passed on down the road. There remained distinct in his consciousness, like a vision, the memory of her face, lifted from the tomb-stone in the churchyard, and looking at him with slow, large, portentous eyes. It *was* portentous, her face. It seemed to mesmerise him. There was a heavy power in her eyes which laid hold of his whole being, as if he had drunk some powerful drug. He had been feeling weak and done before. Now the life came back into him, he felt delivered from his own fretted, daily self.

He finished his duties at the surgery as quickly as might be, hastily filling up the bottles of the waiting people with cheap drugs. Then, in perpetual haste, he set off again to visit several cases in another part of his round, before tea-time. At all times he preferred to walk if he could, but particularly when he was not well. He fancied the motion restored him.

The afternoon was falling. It was grey, deadened, and wintry, with a slow, moist, heavy coldness sinking in and deadening all the faculties. But why should he think or notice? He hastily climbed the hill and turned across the dark green fields, following the black cinder-track. In the distance, across a shallow dip in the country, the small town was clustered like smouldering ash, a tower, a spire, a heap of low, raw, extinct houses. And on the nearest fringe of the town, sloping into the dip, was Oldmeadow, the Pervins' house. He could see the stables and the outbuildings distinctly, as they lay towards him on the slope. Well, he would not go there many more times! Another resource would be lost to him, another place gone: the only company he cared for in the alien, ugly little town he was losing. Nothing but work, drudgery, constant hastening from dwelling to dwelling among the colliers and the iron-workers. It wore him out, but at the same time he had a craving for it. It was a stimulant to him to be in the homes of the working people, moving, as it were, through the innermost body of their life. His nerves were excited and gratified. He could come so near, into the very lives of the rough, inarticulate, powerfully emotional men and women. He grumbled, he said he hated the hellish hole. But as a matter of fact it excited him, the contact with the rough, strongly-feeling people was a stimulant applied direct to his nerves.

Below Oldmeadow, in the green, shallow, soddened hollow of fields, lay a square, deep pond. Roving across the landscape, the doctor's quick eye detected a figure in black passing through the gate of the field, down towards the pond. He looked again. It would be Mabel Pervin. His mind suddenly became alive and attentive.

Why was she going down there? He pulled up on the path on the slope above, and stood staring. He could just make sure of the small black figure moving in the hollow of the failing day. He seemed to see her in the midst of such obscurity, that he was like a clairvoyant, seeing rather with the mind's eye than with ordinary sight. Yet he could see her positively enough, whilst he kept his eye attentive. He felt, if he looked away from her, in the thick, ugly falling dusk, he would lose her altogether.

He followed her minutely as she moved, direct and intent, like something transmitted rather than stirring in voluntary activity, straight down the field towards the pond. There she stood on the bank for a moment. She never raised her head. Then she waded slowly into the water.

He stood motionless as the small black figure walked slowly and deliberately towards the centre of the pond, very slowly, gradually moving deeper into the motionless water, and still moving forward as the water got up to her breast. Then he could see her no more in the dusk of the dead afternoon.

"There!" he exclaimed. "Would you believe it?"

And he hastened straight down, running over the wet, soddened fields, pushing through the hedges, down into the depression of callous wintry obscurity. It took him several minutes to come to the pond. He stood on the bank, breathing heavily. He could see nothing. His eyes seemed to penetrate the dead water. Yes, perhaps that was the dark shadow of her black clothing beneath the surface of the water.

He slowly ventured into the pond. The bottom was deep, soft clay, he sank in, and the water clasped dead cold round his legs. As he stirred he could smell the cold, rotten clay that fouled up into the water. It was objectionable in his lungs. Still, repelled and yet not heeding, he moved deeper into the pond. The cold water rose over his thighs, over his loins, upon his abdomen. The lower part of his body was all sunk in the hideous cold element. And the bottom was so deeply soft and uncertain, he was afraid of pitching with his mouth underneath. He could not swim, and was afraid.

He crouched a little, spreading his hands under the water and moving them round, trying to feel for her. The dead cold pond swayed upon his chest. He moved again, a little deeper, and again, with his hands underneath, he felt all around under the water. And he touched her clothing. But it evaded his fingers. He made a desperate effort to grasp it.

And so doing he lost his balance and went under, horribly, suffocating in the foul earthy water, struggling madly for a few moments. At last, after what seemed an eternity, he got his footing, rose again into the air and looked around. He gasped, and knew he was in the world. Then he looked at the water. She had risen near him. He grasped her clothing, and drawing her nearer, turned to take his way to land again.

He went very slowly, carefully, absorbed in the slow progress. He rose higher, climbing out of the pond. The water was now only about his legs; he was thankful, full of relief to be out of the clutches of the pond. He lifted her and staggered on to the bank, out of the horror of wet, grey clay.

He laid her down on the bank. She was quite unconscious and running with water. He made the water come from her mouth, he worked to restore her. He did not have to work very long before he could feel the breathing begin again in her; she was breathing naturally. He worked a little longer. He could feel her live beneath his hands; she was coming back. He wiped her face, wrapped her in his overcoat, looked round into the dim, dark grey world, then lifted her and staggered down the bank and across the fields.

It seemed an unthinkably long way, and his burden so heavy he felt he would never get to the house. But at last he was in the stable-yard, and then in the house-yard. He opened the door and went into the house. In the kitchen he laid her down on the hearth-rug and called. The house was empty. But the fire was burning in the grate.

Then again he kneeled to attend to her. She was breathing regularly, her eyes were wide open and as if conscious, but there seemed something missing in her look. She was conscious in herself, but unconscious of her surroundings.

He ran upstairs, took blankets from a bed, and put them before the fire to warm. Then he removed her saturated, earthy-smelling clothing, rubbed her dry with a towel, and wrapped her naked in the blankets. Then he went into the dining room, to look for spirits. There was a little whisky. He drank a gulp himself, and put some into her mouth.

The effect was instantaneous. She looked full into his face, as if she had been seeing him for some time, and yet had only just become conscious of him.

"Dr. Ferguson?" she said.

"What?" he answered.

He was divesting himself of his coat, intending to find some dry clothing upstairs. He could not bear the smell of the dead, clayey water, and he was mortally afraid for his own health.

"What did I do?" she asked.

"Walked into the pond," he replied. He had begun to shudder like one sick, and could hardly attend to her. Her eyes remained full on him, he seemed to be going dark in his mind, looking back at her helplessly. The shuddering became quieter in him, his life came back to him, dark and unknowing, but strong again.

"Was I out of my mind?" she asked, while her eyes were fixed on him all the time.

"Maybe, for the moment," he replied. He felt quiet, because his strength had come back. The strange fretful strain had left him.

"Am I out of my mind now?" she asked.

"Are you?" he reflected a moment. "No," he answered truthfully. "I don't see that you are." He turned his face aside. He was afraid now, because he felt dazed, and felt dimly that her power was stronger than his, in this issue. And she continued to look at him fixedly all the time. "Can you tell me where I shall find some dry things to put on?" he asked.

"Did you dive into the pond for me?" she asked.

"No," he answered. "I walked in. But I went in overhead as well."

There was silence for a moment. He hesitated. He very much wanted to go upstairs to get into dry clothing. But there was another desire in him. And she seemed to hold him. His will seemed to have gone to sleep, and left him, standing there slack before her. But he felt warm inside himself. He did not shudder at all, though his clothes were sodden on him.

"Why did you?" she asked.

"Because I didn't want you to do such a foolish thing," he said.

"It wasn't foolish," she said, still gazing at him as she lay on the floor, with a sofa cushion under her head. "It was the right thing to do. I knew best, then."

"I'll go and shift these wet things," he said. But still he had not the power to move out of her presence, until she sent him. It was as if she had the life of his body in her hands, and he could not extricate himself. Or perhaps he did not want to.

Suddenly she sat up. Then she became aware of her own immediate condition. She felt the blankets about her, she knew her own limbs. For a moment it seemed as if her reason were going. She looked round, with wild eye, as if seeking something. He stood still with fear. She saw her clothing lying scattered.

"Who undressed me?" she asked, her eyes resting full and inevitable on his face.

"I did," he replied, "to bring you round."

For some moments she sat and gazed at him awfully, her lips parted.

"Do you love me, then?" she asked.

He only stood and stared at her, fascinated. His soul seemed to melt.

She shuffled forward on her knees, and put her arms round him, round his legs, as he stood there, pressing her breasts against his knees and thighs, clutching him with strange, convulsive certainty, pressing his thighs against her, drawing him to her face, her throat, as she looked up at him with flaring, humble eyes of transfiguration, triumphant in first possession.

"You love me," she murmured, in strange transport, yearning and triumphant and confident. "You love me. I know you love me, I know."

And she was passionately kissing his knees, through the wet clothing, passionately and indiscriminately kissing his knees, his legs, as if unaware of everything.

He looked down at the tangled wet hair, the wild, bare, animal shoulders. He was amazed, bewildered, and afraid. He had never thought of loving her. He had never wanted to love her. When he rescued her and restored her, he was a doctor, and she was a patient. He had had no single personal thought of her. Nay, this introduction of the personal element was very distasteful to him, a violation of his professional honour. It was horrible to have her there embracing his knees. It was horrible. He revolted from it, violently. And yet—and yet—he had not the power to break away.

She looked at him again, with the same supplication of powerful love, and that same transcendent, frightening light of triumph. In view of the delicate flame which seemed to come from her face like a light, he was powerless. And yet he had never intended to love her. He had never intended. And something stubborn in him could not give way.

"You love me," she repeated, in a murmur of deep, rhapsodic assurance. "You love me."

Her hands were drawing him, drawing him down to her. He was afraid, even a little horrified. For he had, really, no intention of loving her. Yet her hands were drawing him towards her. He put out his hand quickly to steady himself, and grasped her bare shoulder. A flame seemed to burn the hand that grasped her soft shoulder. He had no intention of loving her: his whole will was against his yielding. It was horrible. And yet wonderful was the touch of her shoulders, beautiful the shining of her face. Was she perhaps mad? He had a horror of yielding to her. Yet something in him ached also.

He had been staring away at the door, away from her. But his hand remained on her shoulder. She had gone suddenly very still. He looked down at her. Her eyes were now wide with fear, with doubt, the light was dying from her face, a shadow of terrible greyness was returning. He could not bear the touch of her eyes' question upon him, and the look of death behind the question.

With an inward groan he gave way, and let his heart yield towards her. A sudden gentle smile came on his face. And her eyes, which never left his face, slowly, slowly filled with tears. He watched the strange water rise in her eyes, like some slow fountain coming up. And his heart seemed to burn and melt away in his breast.

He could not bear to look at her any more. He dropped on his knees and caught her head with his arms and pressed her face against his throat. She was very still. His heart, which seemed to have broken, was burning with a kind of agony in his breast. And he felt her slow, hot tears wetting his throat. But he could not move.

He felt the hot tears wet his neck and the hollows of his neck, and he remained motionless, suspended through one of man's eternities. Only now it had become indispensable to him to have her face pressed close to him; he could never let her go again. He could never let her head go away from the close clutch of his arm. He wanted to remain like that for ever, with his heart hurting him in a pain that was also life to him. Without knowing, he was looking down on her damp, soft brown hair.

Then, as it were suddenly, he smelt the horrid stagnant smell of that water. And at the same moment she drew away from him and looked at him. Her eyes were wistful and unfathomable. He was afraid of them, and he fell to kissing her, not knowing what he was doing. He wanted her eyes not to have that terrible, wistful, unfathomable look.

When she turned her face to him again, a faint delicate flush was glowing, and there was again dawning that terrible shining of joy in her eyes, which really terrified him, and yet which he now wanted to see, because he feared the look of doubt still more.

"You love me?" she said, rather faltering.

"Yes." The word cost him a painful effort. Not because it wasn't true. But because it was too newly true, the *saying* seemed to tear open again his newly-torn heart. And he hardly wanted it to be true, even now.

She lifted her face to him, and he bent forward and kissed her on the mouth, gently, with the one kiss that is an eternal pledge. And as he kissed her his heart strained again in his breast. He never intended to love her. But now it was over. He had crossed over the gulf to her, and all that he had left behind had shrivelled and become void.

After the kiss, her eyes again slowly filled with tears. She sat still, away from him, with her face drooped aside, and her hands folded in her lap. The tears fell very slowly. There was complete silence. He too sat there motionless and silent on the hearth-rug. The strange pain of his heart that was broken seemed to consume him. That he should love her? That this was love! That he should be ripped open in this way! Him, a doctor! How they would all jeer if they knew! It was agony to him to think they might know.

In the curious naked pain of the thought he looked again to her. She was sitting there drooped into a muse. He saw a tear fall, and his heart flared hot. He saw for the first time that one of her shoulders was quite uncovered, one arm bare, he could see one of her small breasts; dimly, because it had become almost dark in the room.

"Why are you crying?" he asked, in an altered voice.

She looked up at him, and behind her tears the consciousness of her situation for the first time brought a dark look of shame to her eyes.

"I'm not crying, really," she said, watching him, half frightened.

He reached his hand, and softly closed it on her bare arm.

"I love you! I love you!" he said in a soft, low vibrating voice, unlike himself.

She shrank, and dropped her head. The soft, penetrating grip of his hand on her arm distressed her. She looked up at him.

"I want to go," she said. "I want to go and get you some dry things."

"Why?" he said. "I'm all right."

"But I want to go," she said. "And I want you to change your things."

He released her arm, and she wrapped herself in the blanket, looking at him, rather frightened. And still she did not rise.

"Kiss me," she said wistfully.

He kissed her, but briefly, half in anger.

Then, after a second, she rose nervously, all mixed up in the blanket. He watched her in her confusion as she tried to extricate herself and wrap herself up so that she could walk. He watched her relentlessly, as she knew. And as she went, the blanket trailing, and as he saw a glimpse of her feet and her white leg, he tried to remember her as she was when he had wrapped her in the blanket. But then he didn't want to remember, because she had been nothing to him then, and his nature revolted from remembering her as she was when she was nothing to him.

A tumbling muffled noise from within the dark house startled him. Then he heard her voice: "There are clothes." He rose and went to the foot of the stairs, and gathered up the garments she had thrown down. Then he came back to the fire, to rub himself down and dress. He grinned at his own appearance when he had finished.

The fire was sinking, so he put on coal. The house was now quite dark, save for the light of a street-lamp that shone in faintly from beyond the holly trees. He lit the gas with matches he found on the mantelpiece. Then he emptied the pockets of his own clothes, and threw all his wet things in a heap into the scullery. After which he gathered up her sodden clothes, gently, and put them in a separate heap on the copper-top in the scullery.

It was six o'clock on the clock. His own watch had stopped. He ought to go back to the surgery. He waited, and still she did not come down. So he went to the foot of the stairs and called:

"I shall have to go."

Almost immediately he heard her coming down. She had on her best dress of black voile, and her hair was tidy, but still damp. She looked at him—and in spite of herself, smiled.

"I don't like you in those clothes," she said.

"Do I look a sight?" he answered.

They were shy of one another.

"I'll make you some tea," she said.

"No, I must go."

"Must you?" And she looked at him again with the wide, strained, doubtful eyes. And again, from the pain of his breast, he knew how he loved her. He went and bent to kiss her, gently, passionately, with his heart's painful kiss.

"And my hair smells so horrible," she murmured in distraction. "And I'm so awful, I'm so awful! Oh no, I'm too awful." And she broke into bitter, heart-broken sobbing. "You can't want to love me, I'm horrible."

"Don't be silly, don't be silly," he said, trying to comfort her, kissing her, holding her in his arms. "I want you, I want to marry you, we're going to be married, quickly, quickly—to-morrow if I can."

But she only sobbed terribly, and cried:

"I feel awful. I feel awful. I feel I'm horrible to you."

"No, I want you, I want you," was all he answered, blindly, with that terrible intonation which frightened her almost more than her horror lest he should *not* want her.

1922

Why the Novel Matters

We have curious ideas of ourselves. We think of ourselves as a body with a spirit in it, or a body with a soul in it, or a body with a mind in it. *Mens sana in corpore sano.*[1] The years drink up the wine, and at last throw the bottle away, the body, of course, being the bottle.

It is a funny sort of superstition. Why should I look at my hand, as it so cleverly writes these words, and decide that it is a mere nothing compared to the mind that directs it? Is there really any huge difference between my hand and my brain? Or my mind? My hand is alive, it flickers with a life of its own. It meets all the strange universe in touch, and learns a vast number of things, and knows a vast number of things. My hand, as it writes these words, slips gaily along, jumps like a grasshopper to dot an *i*, feels the table rather cold, gets a little bored if I write too long, has its own rudiments of thought, and is just as much *me* as is my brain, my mind, or my soul. Why should I imagine that there is a *me* which is more *me* than my hand is? Since my hand is absolutely alive, me alive.

Whereas, of course, as far as I am concerned, my pen isn't alive at all. My pen *isn't me* alive. Me alive ends at my finger tips.

Whatever is me alive is me. Every tiny bit of my hands is alive, every little freckle and hair and fold of skin. And whatever is me alive is me. Only my finger-nails, those ten little weapons between me and an inanimate universe, they cross the mysterious Rubicon[2] between me alive and things like my pen, which are not alive, in my own sense.

So, seeing my hand is all alive, and me alive, wherein is it just a bottle, or a jug, or a tin can, or a vessel of clay, or any of the rest of that nonsense? True, if I cut it it will bleed, like a can of cherries. But then the skin that is cut, and the veins that bleed, and the bones that should never be seen, they are all just as alive as the blood that flows. So the tin can business, or vessel of clay, is just bunk.

And that's what you learn, when you're a novelist. And that's what you are very liable *not* to know, if you're a parson, or a philosopher, or a scientist, or a stupid person. If you're a parson, you talk about souls in heaven. If you're a novelist, you know that paradise is in the palm of your hand, and on the end of your nose, because both are alive; and alive, and man alive, which is more than you can say, for certain, of paradise. Paradise is after life, and I for one am not keen on anything that is *after* life. If you are a philosopher, you talk about infinity, and the pure spirit which knows all things. But if you pick up a novel, you realise immediately that infinity is just a handle to this self-same jug of a body of mine; while as for knowing, if I find my finger in the fire, I know that fire burns, with a knowledge so emphatic and vital, it leaves Nirvana[3] merely a conjecture. Oh, yes, my body, me alive, *knows,* and knows intensely. And as for the sum of all knowledge, it can't be anything more than an accumulation of all the things I know in the body, and you, dear reader, know in the body.

These damned philosophers, they talk as if they suddenly went off in steam, and were then much more important than they are when they're in their shirts. It is nonsense. Every man, philosopher included, ends in his own finger-tips. That's the end of his man alive. As for the words and thoughts

---

1. A healthy mind in a healthy body (Latin).
2. When Julius Caesar crossed the river Rubicon (near Rimini, Italy) in 49 B.C.E., in defiance of the Senate, he indicated his intention of advancing against Pompey and thus involving the country in civil war. Hence to "cross the Rubicon" means to take an important and irrevocable decision.
3. In Buddhist theology, the extinction of the self and its desires and the attainment of perfect beatitude.

and sighs and aspirations that fly from him, they are so many tremulations in the ether, and not alive at all. But if the tremulations reach another man alive, he may receive them into his life, and his life may take on a new colour, like a chameleon creeping from a brown rock on to a green leaf. All very well and good. It still doesn't alter the fact that the so-called spirit, the message or teaching of the philosopher or the saint, isn't alive at all, but just a tremulation upon the ether, like a radio message. All this spirit stuff is just tremulations upon the ether. If you, as man alive, quiver from the tremulation of the ether into new life, that is because you are man alive, and you take sustenance and stimulation into your alive man in a myriad ways. But to say that the message, or the spirit which is communicated to you, is more important than your living body, is nonsense. You might as well say that the potato at dinner was more important.

Nothing is important but life. And for myself, I can absolutely see life nowhere but in the living. Life with a capital L is only man alive. Even a cabbage in the rain is cabbage alive. All things that are alive are amazing. And all things that are dead are subsidiary to the living. Better a live dog than a dead lion. But better a live lion than a live dog. *C'est la vie!*

It seems impossible to get a saint, or a philosopher, or a scientist, to stick to this simple truth. They are all, in a sense, renegades. The saint wishes to offer himself up as spiritual food for the multitude. Even Francis of Assisi turns himself into a sort of angel-cake, of which anyone may take a slice. But an angel-cake is rather less than man alive. And poor St Francis might well apologise to his body, when he is dying: "Oh, pardon me, my body, the wrong I did you through the years!" It was no wafer, for others to eat.

The philosopher, on the other hand, because he can think, decides that nothing but thoughts matter. It is as if a rabbit, because he can make little pills, should decide that nothing but little pills matter. As for the scientist, he has absolutely no use for me so long as I am man alive. To the scientist, I am dead. He puts under the microscope a bit of dead me, and calls it me. He takes me to pieces, and says first one piece, and then another piece, is me. My heart, my liver, my stomach have all been scientifically me, according to the scientist; and nowadays I am either a brain, or nerves, or glands, or something more up-to-date in the tissue line.

Now I absolutely flatly deny that I am a soul, or a body, or a mind, or an intelligence, or a brain, or a nervous system, or a bunch of glands, or any of the rest of these bits of me. The whole is greater than the part. And therefore, I, who am man alive, am greater than my soul, or spirit, or body, or mind, or consciousness, or anything else that is merely a part of me. I am a man, and alive. I am man alive, and as long as I can, I intend to go on being man alive.

For this reason I am a novelist. And being a novelist, I consider myself superior to the saint, the scientist, the philosopher, and the poet, who are all great masters of different bits of man alive, but never get the whole hog.

The novel is the one bright book of life. Books are not life. They are only tremulations on the ether. But the novel as a tremulation can make the whole man alive tremble. Which is more than poetry, philosophy, science, or any other book-tremulation can do.

The novel is the book of life. In this sense, the Bible is a great confused novel. You may say, it is about God. But it is really about man alive. Adam,

Eve, Sarai, Abraham, Isaac, Jacob, Samuel, David, Bath-Sheba, Ruth, Esther, Solomon, Job, Isaiah, Jesus, Mark, Judas, Paul, Peter: what is it but man alive, from start to finish? Man alive, not mere bits. Even the Lord is another man alive, in a burning bush, throwing the tablets of stone at Moses's head.

I do hope you begin to get my idea, why the novel is supremely important, as a tremulation on the ether. Plato makes the perfect ideal being tremble in me. But that's only a bit of me. Perfection is only a bit, in the strange make-up of man alive. The Sermon on the Mount makes the selfless spirit of me quiver. But that, too, is only a bit of me. The Ten Commandments set the old Adam shivering in me, warning me that I am a thief and a murderer, unless I watch it. But even the old Adam is only a bit of me.

I very much like all these bits of me to be set trembling with life and the wisdom of life. But I do ask that the whole of me shall tremble in its wholeness, some time or other.

And this, of course, must happen in me, living.

But as far as it can happen from a communication, it can only happen when a whole novel communicates itself to me. The Bible—but *all* the Bible—and Homer, and Shakespeare: these are the supreme old novels. These are all things to all men. Which means that in their wholeness they affect the whole man alive, which is the man himself, beyond any part of him. They set the whole tree trembling with a new access of life, they do not just stimulate growth in one direction.

I don't want to grow in any one direction any more. And, if I can help it, I don't want to stimulate anybody else into some particular direction. A particular direction ends in a *cul-de-sac*. We're in a *cul-de-sac* at present.

I don't believe in any dazzling revelation, or in any supreme Word. "The grass withereth, the flower fadeth, but the Word of the Lord shall stand for ever." That's the kind of stuff we've drugged ourselves with. As a matter of fact, the grass withereth, but comes up all the greener for that reason, after the rains. The flower fadeth, and therefore the bud opens. But the Word of the Lord, being man-uttered and a mere vibration on the ether, becomes staler and staler, more and more boring, till at last we turn a deaf ear and it ceases to exist, far more finally than any withered grass. It is grass that renews its youth like the eagle, not any Word.

We should ask for no absolutes, or absolute. Once and for all and for ever, let us have done with the ugly imperialism of any absolute. There is no absolute good, there is nothing absolutely right. All things flow and change, and even change is not absolute. The whole is a strange assembly of apparently incongruous parts, slipping past one another.

Me, man alive, I am a very curious assembly of incongruous parts. My yea! of today is oddly different from my yea! of yesterday. My tears of to-morrow will have nothing to do with my tears of a year ago. If the one I love remains unchanged and unchanging, I shall cease to love her. It is only because she changes and startles me into change and defies my inertia, and is herself staggered in her inertia by my changing, that I can continue to love her. If she stayed put, I might as well love the pepper pot.

In all this change, I maintain a certain integrity. But woe betide me if I try to put my finger on it. If I say of myself, I am this, I am that!—then, if I stick to it, I turn into a stupid fixed thing like a lamp-post. I shall never know wherein lies my integrity, my individuality, my me. I *can* never know it. It is useless to talk about my ego. That only means that I have made up an *idea* of myself, and that I am trying to cut myself out to pattern. Which is no good. You can cut your cloth to fit your coat, but you can't clip bits off your living body, to trim it down to your idea. True, you can put yourself into ideal corsets. But even in ideal corsets, fashions change.

Let us learn from the novel. In the novel, the characters can do nothing but *live*. If they keep on being good, according to pattern, or bad, according to pattern, or even volatile, according to pattern, they cease to live, and the novel falls dead. A character in a novel has got to live, or it is nothing.

We, likewise, in life have got to live, or we are nothing.

What we mean by living is, of course, just as indescribable as what we mean by *being*. Men get ideas into their heads, of what they mean by Life, and they proceed to cut life out to pattern. Sometimes they go into the desert to seek God, sometimes they go into the desert to seek cash, sometimes it is wine, woman, and song, and again it is water, political reform, and votes. You never know what it will be next: from killing your neighbour with hideous bombs and gas that tears the lungs, to supporting a Foundlings' Home[4] and preaching infinite Love, and being co-respondent in a divorce.

In all this wild welter, we need some sort of guide. It's no good inventing Thou Shalt Nots!

What then? Turn truly, honourably to the novel, and see wherein you are man alive, and wherein you are dead man in life. You may love a woman as man alive, and you may be making love to a woman as sheer dead man in life. You may eat your dinner as man alive, or as a mere masticating corpse. As man alive you may have shot at your enemy. But as a ghastly simulacrum of life you may be firing bombs into men who are neither your enemies nor your friends, but just things you are dead to. Which is criminal, when the things happen to be alive.

To be alive, to be man alive, to be whole man alive: that is the point. And at its best, the novel, and the novel supremely, can help you. It can help you not to be dead man in life. So much of a man walks about dead and a carcass in the street and house, to-day: so much of women is merely dead. Like a pianoforte with half the notes mute.

But the novel you can see, plainly, when the man goes dead, the woman goes inert. You can develop an instinct for life, if you will, instead of a theory of right and wrong, good and bad.

In life, there is right and wrong, good and bad, all the time. But what is right in one case is wrong in another. And in the novel you see one man becoming a corpse, because of his so-called goodness, another going dead because of his so-called wickedness. Right and wrong is an instinct: but an instinct of the whole consciousness in a man, bodily, mental, spiritual at once. And only in the novel are *all* things given full play, or at least, they may be given full play, when we realize that life itself, and not inert safety, is the reason for living. For out of the full play of all things emerges the only thing that is anything, the wholeness of a man, the wholeness of a woman, man live, and live woman.

1936

---

4. Orphanage.

Love on the Farm[1]

What large, dark hands are those at the window
Grasping in the golden light
Which weaves its way through the evening wind
    At my heart's delight?

5 Ah, only the leaves! But in the west
I see a redness suddenly come
Into the evening's anxious breast—
    'Tis the wound of love goes home!

The woodbine creeps abroad
10 Calling low to her lover:
    The sunlit flirt who all the day
    Has poised above her lips in play
    And stolen kisses, shallow and gay
    Of pollen, now has gone away—
15   She woos the moth with her sweet, low word;
And when above her his moth-wings hover
Then her bright breast she will uncover
And yield her honey-drop to her lover.

Into the yellow, evening glow
20 Saunters a man from the farm below;
Leans, and looks in at the low-built shed
Where the swallow has hung her marriage bed.
    The bird lies warm against the wall.
    She glances quick her startled eyes
25   Towards him, then she turns away
    Her small head, making warm display
    Of red upon the throat. Her terrors sway
    Her out of the nest's warm, busy ball,
    Whose plaintive cry is heard as she flies
30   In one blue stoop from out the sties
    Into the twilight's empty hall.
Oh, water-hen, beside the rushes
Hide your quaintly scarlet blushes,
Still your quick tail, lie still as dead,
35 Till the distance folds over his ominous tread!

The rabbit presses back her ears,
Turns back her liquid, anguished eyes
And crouches low; then with wild spring
Spurts from the terror of *his* oncoming;
40 To be choked back, the wire ring
    Her frantic effort throttling:
    Piteous brown ball of quivering fears!

---

1. Called *Cruelty and Love* when first published in 1913 and *Love on the Farm* when it appeared in *Collected Poems* (1928).

Ah, soon in his large, hard hands she dies,
And swings all loose from the swing of his walk!
45 Yet calm and kindly are his eyes
And ready to open in brown surprise
Should I not answer to his talk
Or should he my tears surmise.

I hear his hand on the latch, and rise from my chair
50 Watching the door open; he flashes bare
His strong teeth in a smile, and flashes his eyes
In a smile like triumph upon me; then careless-wise
He flings the rabbit soft on the table board
And comes towards me: ah! the uplifted sword
55 Of his hand against my bosom! and oh, the broad
Blade of his glance that asks me to applaud
His coming! With his hand he turns my face to him
And caresses me with his fingers that still smell grim
Of the rabbit's fur! God, I am caught in a snare!
60 I know not what fine wire is round my throat;
I only know I let him finger there
My pulse of life, and let him nose like a stoat
Who sniffs with joy before he drinks the blood.

And down his mouth comes to my mouth! and down
65 His bright dark eyes come over me, like a hood
Upon my mind! his lips meet mine, and a flood
Of sweet fire sweeps across me, so I drown
Against him, die, and find death good.

1913, 1928

Piano[1]

Softly, in the dusk, a woman is singing to me;
Taking me back down the vista of years, till I see
A child sitting under the piano, in the boom of the tingling strings
And pressing the small, poised feet of a mother who smiles as she sings.

5 In spite of myself, the insidious mastery of song
Betrays me back, till the heart of me weeps to belong
To the old Sunday evenings at home, with winter outside
And hymns in the cozy parlour, the tinkling piano our guide.

So now it is vain for the singer to burst into clamour
10 With the great black piano appassionato. The glamour
Of childish days is upon me, my manhood is cast
Down in the flood of remembrance, I weep like a child for the past.

1918

---

1. For an earlier version of this poem, see "Poems in Process," in the appendices to this volume.

Tortoise Shell[1]

The Cross, the Cross
Goes deeper in than we know,
Deeper into life;
Right into the marrow
5   And through the bone.
Along the back of the baby tortoise
The scales are locked in an arch like a bridge,
Scale-lapping, like a lobster's sections
Or a bee's.
10   Then crossways down his sides
Tiger-stripes and wasp-bands.

Five, and five again, and five again,
And round the edges twenty-five little ones,
The sections of the baby tortoise shell.

15   Four, and a keystone;
Four, and a keystone;
Four, and a keystone;
Then twenty-four, and a tiny little keystone.

It needed Pythagoras[2] to see life playing with counters on the living back
20   Of the baby tortoise;
Life establishing the first eternal mathematical tablet
Not in stone, like the Judean Lord,[3] or bronze, but in life-clouded, life-rosy
     tortoise shell.

The first little mathematical gentleman
Stepping, wee mite, in his loose trousers
25   Under all the eternal dome of mathematical law.

Fives, and tens,
Threes and fours and twelves,
All the *volte face*[4] of decimals,
The whirligig of dozens and the pinnacle of seven.

30   Turn him on his back,
The kicking little beetle,
And there again, on his shell-tender, earth-touching belly,
The long cleavage of division, upright of the eternal cross
And on either side count five,
35   On each side, two above, on each side, two below
The dark bar horizontal.

The Cross!
It goes right through him, the sprottling° insect,   *sprawling*

1. The first of six poems known as the "Tortoise
sequence," first published in a volume called *Tor-
toises* in 1921.
2. Pythagoras (6th century B.C.E.), Greek mathematician and philosopher.
3. The God of the Jews who delivered the stone
tablets of the Law to Moses.
4. About-face (French).

Through his cross-wise cloven psyche,
40 Through his five-fold complex-nature.

So turn him over on his toes again;
Four pin-point toes, and a problematical thumb-piece,
Four rowing limbs, and one wedge-balancing head,
Four and one makes five, which is the clue to all mathematics.

45 The Lord wrote it all down on the little slate
Of the baby tortoise.
Outward and visible indication of the plan within,
The complex, manifold involvedness of an individual creature
Plotted out
50 On this small bird, this rudiment,
This little dome, this pediment
Of all creation,
This slow one.

                                                    1921

Tortoise Shout

I thought he was dumb,
I said he was dumb,
Yet I've heard him cry.

First faint scream,
5   Out of life's unfathomable dawn,
Far off, so far, like a madness, under the horizon's dawning rim,
Far, far off, far scream.

Tortoise *in extremis.*[1]

Why were we crucified into sex?
10 Why were we not left rounded off, and finished in ourselves.
As we began,
As he certainly began, so perfectly alone?

A far, was-it-audible scream,
Or did it sound on the plasm direct?

15 Worse than the cry of the new-born,
A scream,
A yell,
A shout,
A pæan,
20 A death-agony,
A birth-cry,

1. At the point of death (Latin).

A submission,
All, tiny, far away, reptile under the first dawn.

War-cry, triumph, acute-delight, death-scream reptilian,
25 Why was the veil torn?[2]
The silken shriek of the soul's torn membrane?
The male soul's membrane
Torn with a shriek half music, half horror.

Crucifixion.
30 Male tortoise, cleaving behind the hovel-wall of that dense female,
Mounted and tense, spread-eagle, outreaching out of the shell
In tortoise-nakedness,
Long neck, and long vulnerable limbs extruded, spread-eagle over her
        house-roof,
And the deep, secret, all-penetrating tail curved beneath her walls,
35 Reaching and gripping tense, more reaching anguish in uttermost tension
Till suddenly, in the spasm of coition, tupping like a jerking leap, and oh!
Opening its clenched face from his outstretched neck
And giving that fragile yell, that scream,
Super-audible,
40 From his pink, cleft, old-man's mouth,
Giving up the ghost,
Or screaming in Pentecost,[3] receiving the ghost.

His scream, and his moment's subsidence,
The moment of eternal silence,
45 Yet unreleased, and after the moment, the sudden, startling jerk of coition,
        and at once
The inexpressible faint yell—
And so on, till the last plasm of my body was melted back
To the primeval rudiments of life, and the secret.

So he tups,° and screams   mates
50 Time after time that frail, torn scream
After each jerk, the longish interval,
The tortoise eternity,
Age-long, reptilian persistence,
Heart-throb, slow heart-throb, persistent for the next spasm.

55 I remember, when I was a boy,
I heard the scream of a frog, which was caught with his foot in the mouth
        of an up-starting snake;
I remember when I first heard bull-frogs break into sound in the spring;
I remember hearing a wild goose out of the throat of night
Cry loudly, beyond the lake of waters;
60 I remember the first time, out of a bush in the darkness, a nightingale's
        piercing cries and gurgles startled the depths of my soul;

2. Cf. Matthew 27.50–51, describing Christ's death: "Jesus, when he had cried again with a loud voice, yielded up the ghost. And, behold, the veil [curtain] of the temple was rent in twain, from the top to the bottom; and the earth did quake, and the rocks rent."
3. The religious holiday celebrating the descent of the Holy Ghost on Christ's apostles.

I remember the scream of a rabbit as I went through a wood at midnight;
I remember the heifer in her heat, blorting and blorting through the hours,
    persistent and irrepressible;
I remember my first terror hearing the howl of weird, amorous cats;
I remember the scream of a terrified, injured horse, the sheet lightning,
65 And running away from the sound of a woman in labour, something like an
    owl whooing,
And listening inwardly to the first bleat of a lamb,
The first wail of an infant,
And my mother singing to herself,
And the first tenor singing of the passionate throat of a young
    collier,° who has long since drunk himself to death,   *coal miner*
70 The first elements of foreign speech
On wild dark lips.

And more than all these,
And less than all these,
This last,
75 Strange, faint coition yell
Of the male tortoise at extremity,
Tiny from under the very edge of the farthest far-off horizon of life.

The cross,
The wheel on which our silence first is broken,
80 Sex, which breaks up our integrity, our single inviolability, our deep silence,
Tearing a cry from us.

Sex, which breaks us into voice, sets us calling across the deeps, calling,
    calling for the complement,
Singing, and calling, and singing again, being answered, having found.
Torn, to become whole again, after long seeking for what is lost,
85 The cry from the tortoise as from Christ, the Osiris[4]-cry of abandonment,
That which is whole, torn asunder,
That which is in part, finding its whole again throughout the universe.

1921

Bavarian Gentians[1]

Not every man has gentians in his house
in soft September, at slow, sad Michaelmas.

Bavarian gentians, big and dark, only dark
darkening the daytime torchlike with the smoking blueness of Pluto's[2]
    gloom,

4. The Egyptian vegetation god was murdered by
his brother Set, who cut the corpse into fourteen
pieces and scattered them throughout Egypt. Osiris, like Christ, was resurrected, and became an
important ruler in the other world.
1. Keith Sagar challenges the accepted view that
this is the final version of the poem in "The Genesis

of 'Bavarian Gentians,' " *The D. H. Lawrence
Review* (Spring 1975): 47–53. He prefers the
longer version printed in *The Collected Poems of
D. H. Lawrence* (1964), ed. Vivian de Sola Pinto
and Warren Roberts, 975.
2. God of the underworld in classical mythology.
He was also called "Dis" (line 8).

5 ribbed and torchlike, with their blaze of darkness spread blue
down flattening into points, flattened under the sweep of white day
torch-flower of the blue-smoking darkness, Pluto's dark-blue daze,
black lamps from the halls of Dis, burning dark blue,
giving off darkness, blue darkness, as Demeter's pale lamps give off light,
10 lead me then, lead me the way.

Reach me a gentian, give me a torch
let me guide myself with the blue, forked torch of this flower
down the darker and darker stairs, where blue is darkened on blueness.
even where Persephone³ goes, just now, from the frosted September
15 to the sightless realm where darkness was awake upon the dark
and Persephone herself is but a voice
or a darkness invisible enfolded in the deeper dark
of the arms Plutonic, and pierced with the passion of dense gloom,
among the splendour of torches of darkness, shedding darkness on the lost
     bride and her groom.

1923

Snake

A snake came to my water-trough
On a hot, hot day, and I in pyjamas for the heat,
To drink there.

In the deep, strange-scented shade of the great dark carob-tree
5 I came down the steps with my pitcher
And must wait, must stand and wait, for there he was at the trough before
    me.

He reached down from a fissure in the earth-wall in the gloom
And trailed his yellow-brown slackness soft-bellied down, over the edge of
    the stone trough
And rested his throat upon the stone bottom,
10 And where the water had dripped from the tap, in a small clearness,
He sipped with his straight mouth,
Softly drank through his straight gums, into his slack long body,
Silently.

Someone was before me at my water-trough,
15 And I, like a second comer, waiting.

He lifted his head from his drinking, as cattle do,
And looked at me vaguely, as drinking cattle do,
And flickered his two-forked tongue from his lips, and mused a moment,
And stooped and drank a little more,

3. Bride of Pluto, who abducted her from the earth, and daughter of Demeter, goddess of the fruits of the earth (line 9). She was allowed to return to earth every spring but had to descend again to Hades in the autumn, "the frosted September." Demeter and Persephone were central figures in ancient fertility myths, where Persephone's annual descent and return were linked with the death and rebirth of vegetation.

20　　Being earth-brown, earth-golden from the burning bowels of the earth
　　　On the day of Sicilian July, with Etna smoking.

　　　The voice of my education said to me
　　　He must be killed,
　　　For in Sicily the black, black snakes are innocent, the gold are venomous.

25　　And voices in me said, If you were a man
　　　You would take a stick and break him now, and finish him off.

　　　But must I confess how I liked him,
　　　How glad I was he had come like a guest in quiet, to drink at my water-
　　　　　trough
　　　And depart peaceful, pacified, and thankless
30　　Into the burning bowels of this earth?

　　　Was it cowardice, that I dared not kill him?
　　　Was it perversity, that I longed to talk to him?
　　　Was it humility, to feel so honoured?
　　　I felt so honoured.

35　　And yet those voices:
　　　If you were not afraid, you would kill him!

　　　And truly I was afraid, I was most afraid,
　　　But even so, honoured still more
　　　That he should seek my hospitality
40　　From out the dark door of the secret earth.

　　　He drank enough
　　　And lifted his head, dreamily, as one who has drunken,
　　　And flickered his tongue like a forked night on the air, so black;
　　　Seeming to lick his lips,
45　　And looked around like a god, unseeing, into the air,
　　　And slowly turned his head,
　　　And slowly, very slowly, as if thrice adream
　　　Proceeded to draw his slow length curving round
　　　And climb the broken bank of my wall-face.

50　　And as he put his head into that dreadful hole,
　　　And as he slowly drew up, snake-easing his shoulders, and entered farther,
　　　A sort of horror, a sort of protest against his withdrawing into that horrid
　　　　black hole,
　　　Deliberately going into the blackness, and slowly drawing himself after,
　　　Overcame me now his back was turned.

55　　I looked round, I put down my pitcher,
　　　I picked up a clumsy log
　　　And threw it at the water-trough with a clatter.

　　　I think it did not hit him;
　　　But suddenly that part of him that was left behind convulsed in undigni-
　　　　fied haste,

60 Writhed like lightning, and was gone
Into the black hole, the earth-lipped fissure in the wall-front
At which, in the intense still noon, I stared with fascination.

And immediately I regretted it.
I thought how paltry, how vulgar, what a mean act!
65 I despised myself and the voices of my accursed human education.

And I thought of the albatross,[1]
And I wished he would come back, my snake.

For he seemed to me again like a king,
Like a king in exile, uncrowned in the underworld,
70 Now due to be crowned again.

And so, I missed my chance with one of the lords
Of life.
And I have something to expiate;
A pettiness.

1923

Cypresses[1]

Tuscan cypresses,
What is it?

Folded in like a dark thought,
For which the language is lost,
5   Tuscan cypresses,
Is there a great secret?
Are our words no good?

The undeliverable secret,
Dead with a dead race and a dead speech, and yet
10 Darkly monumental in you,
Etruscan cypresses.

Ah, how I admire your fidelity,
Dark cypresses!

Is it the secret of the long-nosed Etruscans?[2]
15 The long-nosed, sensitive-footed, subtly-smiling Etruscans,
Who made so little noise outside the cypress groves?

Among the sinuous, flame-tall cypresses
That swayed their length of darkness all around
Etruscan-dusky, wavering men of old Etruria:
20 Naked except for fanciful long shoes,

---

1. In Coleridge's *Ancient Mariner*.
1. Tall dark coniferous evergreen trees, associated with mourning.

2. The most important of the pre-Roman inhabitants of Italy.

Going with insidious, half-smiling quietness
And some of Africa's imperturbable sang-froid
About a forgotten business.

What business, then?
25   Nay, tongues are dead, and words are hollow as hollow seed-pods,
Having shed their sound and finished all their echoing
Etruscan syllables,
That had the telling.

Yet more I see you darkly concentrate,
30   Tuscan cypresses,
On one old thought:
On one old slim imperishable thought, while you remain
Etruscan cypresses;
Dusky, slim marrow-thought of slender, flickering men of Etruria,
35   Whom Rome called vicious.

Vicious, dark cypresses:
Vicious, you supple, brooding, softly-swaying pillars of dark flame.
Monumental to a dead, dead race
Embowered in you!

40   Were they then vicious, the slender, tender-footed
Long-nosed men of Etruria?
Or was their way only evasive and different, dark, like cypress-trees in a
      wind?

They are dead, with all their vices,
And all that is left
45   Is the shadowy monomania of some cypresses
And tombs.

The smile, the subtle Etruscan smile still lurking
Within the tombs,
Etruscan cypresses.

50   He laughs longest who laughs last;
Nay, Leonardo[3] only bungled the pure Etruscan smile.

What would I not give
To bring back the rare and orchid-like
Evil-yclept[4] Etruscan?
55   For as to the evil
We have only Roman word for it,
Which I, being a little weary of Roman virtue,
Don't hang much weight on.

For oh, I know, in the dust where we have buried
60   The silenced races and all their abominations,
We have buried so much of the delicate magic of life.

---

3. Leonardo da Vinci (1452–1519), Italian painter   *conda* has a famous mysterious smile.
whose portrait known as the *Mona Lisa* or *La Gio-*   4. Called (archaic).

There in the deeps
That churn the frankincense and ooze the myrrh,
Cypress shadowy,
65 Such an aroma of lost human life!

They say the fit survive,
But I invoke the spirits of the lost.
Those that have not survived, the darkly lost,
To bring their meaning back into life again,
70 Which they have taken away
And wrap inviolable in soft cypress-trees,
Etruscan cypresses.

Evil, what is evil?
There is only one evil, to deny life
75 As Rome denied Etruria
And mechanical America Montezuma[5] still.

                                                            Fiesole.

                                                                    1923

How Beastly the Bourgeois Is

How beastly the bourgeois is
especially the male of the species—

Presentable, eminently presentable—
shall I make you a present of him?

5 Isn't he handsome? Isn't he healthy? Isn't he a fine specimen?
Doesn't he look the fresh clean englishman, outside?
Isn't it god's own image? tramping his thirty miles a day
after partridges, or a little rubber ball?
wouldn't you like to be like that, well off, and quite the thing?

10 Oh, but wait!
Let him meet a new emotion, let him be faced with another man's need,
let him come home to a bit of moral difficulty, let life face him with a new
          demand on his understanding
and then watch him go soggy, like a wet meringue.
Watch him turn into a mess, either a fool or a bully.
15 Just watch the display of him, confronted with a new demand on his
          intelligence,
a new life-demand.

How beastly the bourgeois is
especially the male of the species—

5. Aztec war chief or emperor of ancient Mexico at the time of the Spanish conquest in the early 16th
century.

Nicely groomed, like a mushroom
20 standing there so sleek and erect and eyeable—
and like a fungus, living on the remains of bygone life
sucking his life out of the dead leaves of greater life than his own.

And even so, he's stale, he's been there too long.
Touch him, and you'll find he's all gone inside
25 just like an old mushroom, all wormy inside, and hollow
under a smooth skin and an upright appearance.

Full of seething, wormy, hollow feelings
rather nasty—
How beastly the bourgeois is!

30 Standing in their thousands, these appearances, in damp England
what a pity they can't all be kicked over
like sickening toadstools, and left to melt back, swiftly
into the soil of England.

1929

The Ship of Death[1]

I

Now it is autumn and the falling fruit
and the long journey towards oblivion.

The apples falling like great drops of dew
to bruise themselves an exit from themselves.

5   And it is time to go, to bid farewell
to one's own self, and find an exit
from the fallen self.

II

Have you built your ship of death, O have you?
O build your ship of death, for you will need it.

10 The grim frost is at hand, when the apples will fall
thick, almost thundrous, on the hardened earth.

And death is on the air like a smell of ashes!
Ah! can't you smell it?

And in the bruised body, the frightened soul
15 finds itself shrinking, wincing from the cold
that blows upon it through the orifices.

1. It was the practice of Vikings and other seafaring peoples to put dead chieftains on a ship, set fire to it, and send it out to sea (cf. *Beowulf*, lines 26–52). Other cultures buried their dead leaders in ships, provisioned with food and drink for their journey in the afterlife.

III

And can a man his own quietus make
with a bare bodkin?[2]

20   With daggers, bodkins, bullets, man can make
a bruise or break of exit for his life;
but is that a quietus, O tell me, is it quietus?

Surely not so! for how could murder, even self-murder
ever a quietus make?

IV

O let us talk of quiet that we know,
25   that we can know, the deep and lovely quiet
of a strong heart at peace!

How can we this, our own quietus, make?

V

Build then the ship of death, for you must take
the longest journey, to oblivion.

30   And die the death, the long and painful death
that lies between the old self and the new.

Already our bodies are fallen, bruised, badly bruised,
already our souls are oozing through the exit
of the cruel bruise.

35   Already the dark and endless ocean of the end
is washing in through the breaches of our wounds,
already the flood is upon us.

Oh build your ship of death, your little ark
and furnish it with food, with little cakes, and wine
40   for the dark flight down oblivion.

VI

Piecemeal the body dies, and the timid soul
has her footing washed away, as the dark flood rises.

We are dying, we are dying, we are all of us dying
and nothing will stay the death-flood rising within us
45   and soon it will rise on the world, on the outside world.

2. Cf. *Hamlet* 3.1.70–76: "For who would bear the whips and scorns of time, / . . . When he himself might
his quietus make / With a bare bodkin?"

We are dying, we are dying, piecemeal our bodies are dying
and our strength leaves us,
and our soul cowers naked in the dark rain over the flood,
cowering in the last branches of the tree of our life.

VII

50   We are dying, we are dying, so all we can do
is now to be willing to die, and to build the ship
of death to carry the soul on the longest journey.

A little ship, with oars and food
and little dishes, and all accoutrements
55   fitting and ready for the departing soul.

Now launch the small ship, now as the body dies
and life departs, launch out, the fragile soul
in the fragile ship of courage, the ark of faith
with its store of food and little cooking pans
60   and change of clothes,
upon the flood's black waste
upon the waters of the end
upon the sea of death, where still we sail
darkly, for we cannot steer, and have no port.

65   There is no port, there is nowhere to go
only the deepening blackness darkening still
blacker upon the soundless, ungurgling flood
darkness at one with darkness, up and down
and sideways utterly dark, so there is no direction any more
70   and the little ship is there; yet she is gone.
She is not seen, for there is nothing to see her by.
She is gone! gone! and yet
somewhere she is there.
Nowhere!

VIII

75   And everything is gone, the body is gone
completely under, gone, entirely gone.
The upper darkness is heavy as the lower,
between them the little ship
is gone
80   she is gone.

It is the end, it is oblivion.

IX

And yet out of eternity a thread
separates itself on the blackness,

a horizontal thread
85   that fumes a little with pallor upon the dark.

Is it illusion? or does the pallor fume
A little higher?
Ah wait, wait, for there's the dawn,
the cruel dawn of coming back to life
90   out of oblivion.

Wait, wait, the little ship
drifting, beneath the deathly ashy grey
of a flood-dawn.

Wait, wait! even so, a flush of yellow
95   and strangely, O chilled wan soul, a flush of rose.

A flush of rose, and the whole thing starts again.

X

The flood subsides, and the body, like a worn sea-shell
emerges strange and lovely.
And the little ship wings home, faltering and lapsing
100   on the pink flood,
and the frail soul steps out, into her house again
filling the heart with peace.

Swings the heart renewed with peace
even of oblivion.

105   Oh build your ship of death, oh build it!
for you will need it.
For the voyage of oblivion awaits you.

1929–30   1933

T. S. ELIOT
1888–1965

Thomas Stearns Eliot was born in St. Louis, Missouri, of New England stock. He entered Harvard in 1906 and was influenced there by the anti-Romanticism of Irving Babbitt and the philosophical and critical interests of George Santayana, as well as by the enthusiasm that prevailed in certain Harvard circles for Elizabethan and Jacobean literature, the Italian Renaissance, and Indian mystical philosophy. His philosophical studies included intensive work on the English idealist philosopher F. H. Bradley, on whom he eventually wrote his Harvard dissertation. (Bradley's emphasis on the private nature of individual experience, "a circle enclosed on the outside," had considerable influence on the private imagery of Eliot's poetry and on the view of the relation between the individual and other individuals reflected in much of his poetry.) Later, Eliot studied literature and philosophy in France and Germany, before going to England shortly after the outbreak of World War I in 1914. He studied Greek philosophy at Oxford, taught school in London, and then obtained a position with Lloyd's Bank. In 1915 he married an English writer, Vivienne Haigh-Wood, but the marriage was not a success. She was highly neurotic and in increasingly bad health. The strain told on Eliot, too. By November 1921 distress and worry had brought him to the verge of a nervous breakdown, and on medical advice, he went to recuperate in a Swiss sanitorium. Two months later he returned, pausing in Paris long enough to give Ezra Pound the manuscript of *The Waste Land*. Eliot left his wife in 1933; and she was eventually committed to a mental home, where she died in 1947. Ten years later he married again and, for the eight years that remained to him, at last knew happiness.

Eliot started writing literary and philosophical reviews soon after settling in London. He wrote for the *Athenaeum* and the *Times Literary Supplement*, among other periodicals, and was assistant editor of the *Egoist* from 1917 to 1919. In 1922 he founded the influential quarterly *Criterion*, which he edited until it ceased publication in 1939. His poetry first appeared in 1915, when *The Love Song of J. Alfred Prufrock* was printed in *Poetry* magazine (Chicago) and a few other short poems were published in the short-lived periodical *Blast*. His first published collection of poems was *Prufrock and Other Observations*, 1917; two other small collections followed in 1919 and 1920; in 1922 *The Waste Land* appeared, first in the *Criterion* in October, then in the *Dial* (in America) in November, and finally in book form. *Poems 1909–25* (1925) collected these earlier poems. Meanwhile he was also publishing collections of his critical essays, notably *The Sacred Wood* in 1920 and *Homage to John Dryden* in 1924. *For Lancelot Andrewes* followed in 1928 and in 1932 he included most of these earlier essays with some new ones in *Selected Essays*. In 1925 he joined the London publishing firm of Faber and Gwyer, becoming a director when the firm became Faber & Faber. He became a British subject and joined the Church of England in 1927.

"Our civilization comprehends great variety and complexity, and this variety and complexity, playing upon a refined sensibility, must produce various and complex results. The poet must become more and more comprehensive, more allusive, more indirect, in order to force, to dislocate if necessary, language into his meaning." This remark, from Eliot's essay *The Metaphysical Poets* (1921), gives one clue to his poetic method from *Prufrock* through *The Waste Land*. In the tradition of the Georgian poets who were active when he settled in London, he saw an exhausted poetic mode being employed, with no verbal excitement or original craftsmanship. He sought to make poetry more subtle, more suggestive, and at the same time more precise. He had learned from the imagists the necessity of clear and precise images, and he learned, too, from the philosopher-poet T. E. Hulme and from his early supporter and adviser Ezra Pound to fear romantic softness and to regard the poetic medium rather than the poet's personality as the important factor. At the same time, the "hard, dry" images advocated by Hulme were not enough for him; he wanted wit, allusiveness, irony. He saw in the Metaphysical poets how wit and passion could be combined, and he saw in the French symbolists how an image could be both absolutely precise in what it referred to physically and at the same time endlessly suggestive in the meanings it set up because of its relationship to other images. The combination of precision, symbolic suggestion, and ironic mockery in the poetry of the late-nineteenth-century French poet Jules Laforgue attracted and influenced him, and he was influenced too by other nineteenth-century French poets: by Théophile Gautier's artful carving of impersonal shapes of meaning; by Charles Baudelaire's strangely evocative explorations of the symbolic suggestions of objects and images; by the symbolist poets Paul Verlaine, Arthur Rimbaud, and Stéphane Mallarmé. He also found in the Jacobean dramatists a flexible blank verse with overtones of colloquial movement: Middleton, Tourneur, Webster, and others, taught him as much—in the way of verse movement, imagery, the counterpointing of the accent of conversation and the note of terror—as either the Metaphysicals or the French symbolists.

Hulme's protests against the Romantic concept of poetry fitted in well enough with what Eliot had learned from Irving Babbitt at Harvard; yet for all his severity with such poets as Shelley, for all his conscious cultivation of a classical viewpoint and his insistence on order and discipline rather than on mere self-expression in art, one side of Eliot's poetic genius is, in one sense of the word, Romantic. The symbolist influence on his imagery, his interest in the evocative and the suggestive, such lines as "And fiddled whisper music on those strings / And bats with baby faces in the violet light / Whistled, and beat their wings," and such recurring images as the hyacinth girl and the rose garden, all show what could be called a Romantic element in his poetry. But it is combined with a dry ironic allusiveness, a play of wit, and a colloquial element, which are not normally found in poets of the Romantic tradition.

Eliot's real novelty—and the cause of much bewilderment when his poems first appeared—was his deliberate elimination of all merely connective and transitional passages, his building up of the total pattern of meaning through the immediate juxtaposition of images without overt explanation of what they are doing, together with his use of oblique references to other works of literature (some of them quite obscure to most readers of his time). *Prufrock* presents a symbolic landscape where the meaning emerges from the mutual interaction of the images, and that meaning is enlarged by echoes, often ironic, of Hesiod and Dante and Shakespeare. *The Waste Land* is a series of scenes and images with no author's voice intervening to tell us where we are but with the implications developed through multiple contrasts and through analogies with older literary works often referred to in a distorted quotation or half-concealed allusion. Furthermore, the works referred to are not necessarily works that are central in the Western literary tradition: besides Dante and Shakespeare there are pre-Socratic philosophers; minor (as well as major) seventeenth-century poets and dramatists; works of anthropology, history, and philosophy; and other echoes of the poet's private reading. In a culture where there is no longer any assurance on the part of the poet that his or her public has a common cultural heritage, a common knowledge of works of the past, Eliot felt it necessary to build up his own body of references. It is this that marks the difference between Eliot's use of earlier literature and, say, Milton's. Both poets are difficult for the modern reader, who needs editorial assistance in recognizing and understanding many of the allusions—but Milton was drawing on a body of knowledge common to educated people in his day. Nevertheless, this aspect of Eliot can be exaggerated: the fact remains that the nature of his imagery together with the movement of his verse generally succeed in setting the tone he requires, in establishing the area of meaning to be developed, so that even a reader ignorant of most of the literary allusions can often get the feel of the poem and achieve some understanding of what it says.

Eliot's early poetry, until at least the middle 1920s, is mostly concerned in one way or another with the Waste Land, with aspects of the decay of culture in the modern Western world. After his formal acceptance of Anglican Christianity we find a penitential note in much of his verse, a note of quiet searching for spiritual peace, with considerable allusion to biblical, liturgical, and mystical religious literature and to Dante. *Ash Wednesday* (1930), a poem in six parts, much less fiercely concentrated in style than the earlier poetry, explores with gentle insistence a mood both penitential and questioning. The so-called Ariel poems (the title has nothing to do with their form or content) present or explore aspects of religious doubt or discovery or revelation, sometimes, as in *Marina*, using a purely secular imagery and sometimes, as in *Journey of the Magi*, drawing on biblical incident. In *Four Quartets* (of which the first, *Burnt Norton*, appeared in the *Collected Poems* of 1935, though all four were not completed until 1943, when they were published together) Eliot further explored essentially religious moods, dealing with the relation between time and eternity and the cultivation of that selfless passivity that can yield the moment of timeless revelation in the midst of time. The mocking irony, the savage humor, the deliberately startling juxtaposition of the sordid and the romantic give way in these later poems to a quieter poetic idiom, often still complexly allusive but never deliberately shocking.

Eliot's criticism was the criticism of a practicing poet who worked out in relation to his reading of older literature what he needed to hold and to admire. He lent the growing weight of his authority to that shift in literary taste that replaced Milton by Donne as the great seventeenth-century English poet and replaced Tennyson in the nineteenth century by Hopkins. His often-quoted description of the late seventeenth-century "dissociation of sensibility"—keeping wit and passion in separate compartments—which he saw as determining the course of English poetry throughout the eighteenth and nineteenth centuries, is both a contribution to the rewriting of English literary history and an explanation of what he was aiming at in his own poetry: the reestablishment of that *unified* sensibility he found in Donne and other early seventeenth-century poets and dramatists. His view of tradition, his dislike of the poetic exploitation of the author's own personality, his advocacy of what he called "orthodoxy," made him suspicious of what he considered eccentric geniuses such as Blake and D. H. Lawrence. On the other side, his dislike of the grandiloquent and his insistence on complexity and on the mingling of the formal with the conversational made him distrustful of the influence of Milton on English poetry. He considered himself "classicist in literature, royalist in politics, and Anglo-Catholic in religion" (*For Lancelot Andrewes*, 1928), in favor of order against chaos, tradition against eccentricity, authority against rampant individualism; yet his own poetry is in many respects untraditional and certainly highly individual in tone. His conservative and even authoritarian habit of mind alienated some who admire—and some whose own poetry has been much influenced by—his poetry.

Eliot's plays have all been, directly or indirectly, on religious themes. *Murder in the Cathedral* (1935) deals with the murder of Archbishop Thomas à Becket in an appropriately ritual manner, with much use of a chorus and with the central speech in the form of a sermon by the archbishop in his cathedral shortly before his murder. *The Family Reunion* (1939) deals with the problem of guilt and redemption in a modern upper-class English family; it makes a deliberate attempt to combine choric devices from Greek tragedy with a poetic idiom subdued to the accents of drawing-room conversation. In his three later plays, all written in the 1950s, *The Cocktail Party*, *The Confidential Clerk*, and *The Elder Statesman*, he achieved popular success by casting a serious religious theme in the form of a sophisticated modern social comedy, using a verse that is so conversational in movement that when spoken in the theater it does not sound like verse at all.

Critics differ on the degree to which Eliot succeeded in his last plays in combining box-office success with dramatic effectiveness. But there is no disagreement on his importance as one of the great renovators of the English poetic dialect, whose influence on a whole generation of poets, critics, and intellectuals generally was enormous. His range as a poet is limited, and his interest in the great middle ground of human experience (as distinct from the extremes of saint and sinner) deficient: but when in 1948 he was awarded the rare honor of the Order of Merit by King George VI and also gained the Nobel Prize in literature, his positive qualities were widely and fully recognized—his poetic cunning, his fine craftsmanship, his original accent, his historical and representative importance as *the* poet of the modern symbolist-Metaphysical tradition.

The Love Song of J. Alfred Prufrock[1]

S'io credesse che mia risposta fosse
a persona che mai tornasse al mondo,
questa fiamma staria senza più scosse.
Ma per cio cche giammai di questo fondo
non torno vivo alcun, s'i'odo il vero,
senza tema d'infamia ti rispondo.[2]

Let us go then, you and I,
When the evening is spread out against the sky
Like a patient etherised upon a table;
Let us go, through certain half-deserted streets,
5   The muttering retreats
Of restless nights in one-night cheap hotels
And sawdust restaurants with oyster shells:
Streets that follow like a tedious argument
Of insidious intent
10   To lead you to an overwhelming question. . .
Oh, do not ask, 'What is it?'
Let us go and make our visit.

In the room the women come and go
Talking of Michelangelo.

15   The yellow fog that rubs its back upon the window-panes,
The yellow smoke that rubs its muzzle on the window-panes
Licked its tongue into the corners of the evening,
Lingered upon the pools that stand in drains,
Let fall upon its back the soot that falls from chimneys,
20   Slipped by the terrace, made a sudden leap,
And seeing that it was a soft October night,
Curled once about the house, and fell asleep.

And indeed there will be time[3]
For the yellow smoke that slides along the street,
25   Rubbing its back upon the window-panes;
There will be time, there will be time
To prepare a face to meet the faces that you meet;
There will be time to murder and create,
And time for all the works and days of hands[4]
30   That lift and drop a question on your plate;
Time for you and time for me,

1. The title implies an ironic contrast between the romantic suggestions of "love song" and the dully prosaic name "J. Alfred Prufrock."
2. "If I thought that my reply would be to one who would ever return to the world, this flame would stay without further movement; but since none has ever returned alive from this depth, if what I hear is true, I answer you without fear of infamy" (Dante, *Inferno* 27.61–66). Guido da Montefeltro, shut up in his flame (the punishment given to false counselors), tells the shame of his evil life to Dante because he believes Dante will never return to earth to report it.
3. Cf. Andrew Marvell, *To His Coy Mistress*, line 1: "Had we but world enough, and time."
4. *Works and Days* is a poem about the farming year by Hesiod (8th century B.C.E.), Greek poet. Eliot's contrast is between useful agricultural labor and the futile "works and days of hands" engaged in meaningless social gesturing.

And time yet for a hundred indecisions,
And for a hundred visions and revisions,
Before the taking of a toast and tea.

35   In the room the women come and go
Talking of Michelangelo.

And indeed there will be time
To wonder, 'Do I dare?' and, 'Do I dare?'
Time to turn back and descend the stair,
40   With a bald spot in the middle of my hair—
(They will say: 'How his hair is growing thin!')
My morning coat, my collar mounting firmly to the chin,
My necktie rich and modest, but asserted by a simple pin—
(They will say: 'But how his arms and legs are thin!')
45   Do I dare
Disturb the universe?
In a minute there is time
For decisions and revisions which a minute will reverse.

For I have known them all already, known them all—
50   Have known the evenings, mornings, afternoons,
I have measured out my life with coffee spoons;
I know the voices dying with a dying fall[5]
Beneath the music from a farther room.
       So how should I presume?

55   And I have known the eyes already, known them all—
The eyes that fix you in a formulated phrase,
And when I am formulated, sprawling on a pin,
When I am pinned and wriggling on the wall,
Then how should I begin
60   To spit out all the butt-ends of my days and ways?
       And how should I presume?

And I have known the arms already, known them all—
Arms that are braceleted and white and bare
(But in the lamplight, downed with light brown hair!)
65   Is it perfume from a dress
That makes me so digress?
Arms that lie along a table, or wrap about a shawl.
       And should I then presume?
       And how should I begin?

• • •

70   Shall I say, I have gone at dusk through narrow streets
And watched the smoke that rises from the pipes
Of lonely men in shirt-sleeves, leaning out of windows? . . .

5. Ironic recollection of Orsino's speech in *Twelfth Night* 1.1.4: "That strain again! It had a dying fall."

I should have been a pair of ragged claws
Scuttling across the floors of silent seas.[6]

. . .

75 And the afternoon, the evening, sleeps so peacefully!
Smoothed by long fingers,
Asleep . . . tired . . . or it malingers,
Stretched on the floor, here beside you and me.
Should I, after tea and cakes and ices,
80 Have the strength to force the moment to its crisis?
But though I have wept and fasted, wept and prayed,
Though I have seen my head (grown slightly bald) brought in upon a
  platter,[7]
I am no prophet—and here's no great matter;
I have seen the moment of my greatness flicker,
85 And I have seen the eternal Footman hold my coat, and snicker,
And in short, I was afraid.

And would it have been worth it, after all,
After the cups, the marmalade, the tea,
Among the porcelain, among some talk of you and me,
90 Would it have been worth while,
To have bitten off the matter with a smile,
To have squeezed the universe into a ball[8]
To roll it toward some overwhelming question,
To say: 'I am Lazarus,[9] come from the dead,
95 Come back to tell you all, I shall tell you all'—
If one, settling a pillow by her head,
  Should say: 'That is not what I meant at all.
  That is not it, at all.'

And would it have been worth it, after all,
100 Would it have been worth while,
After the sunsets and the dooryards and the sprinkled streets,
After the novels, after the teacups, after the skirts that trail along the floor—
And this, and so much more?—
It is impossible to say just what I mean!
105 But as if a magic lantern threw the nerves in patterns on a screen:
Would it have been worth while
If one, settling a pillow or throwing off a shawl,
And turning toward the window, should say:
  'That is not it at all,
110 That is not what I meant, at all.'

. . .

---

6. I.e., he would have been better as a crab on the
ocean bed. Perhaps, too, the motion of a crab suggests futility and growing old. Cf. *Hamlet* 2.2.205–
206: "for yourself, sir, should be old as I am,
if, like a crab, you could go backward."
7. Like that of John the Baptist. See Mark 6.17–

28 and Matthew 14.3–11.
8. Cf., Marvell, *To His Coy Mistress,* lines 41–44:
"Let us roll all our strength and all / Our sweetness
up into one ball, / And tear our pleasures with
rough strife / Thorough the iron gates of life."
9. Cf. Luke 16.19–31 and John 11.1–44.

No! I am not Prince Hamlet, nor was meant to be;
Am an attendant lord, one that will do
To swell a progress,[1] start a scene or two,
Advise the prince; no doubt, an easy tool,
115 Deferential, glad to be of use,
Politic, cautious, and meticulous;
Full of high sentence,[2] but a bit obtuse;
At times, indeed, almost ridiculous—
Almost, at times, the Fool.

120   I grow old . . . I grow old . . .
I shall wear the bottoms of my trousers rolled.

    Shall I part my hair behind? Do I dare to eat a peach?
I shall wear white flannel trousers, and walk upon the beach.
I have heard the mermaids singing, each to each.

125 I do not think that they will sing to me.

I have seen them riding seaward on the waves
Combing the white hair of the waves blown back
When the wind blows the water white and black.

We have lingered in the chambers of the sea
130 By sea-girls wreathed with seaweed red and brown
Till human voices wake us, and we drown.

1910–11   1915, 1917

Sweeney Among the Nightingales

ὤμοι, πέπληγμαι καιρίαν πληγὴν ἔσω.[1]

Apeneck Sweeney spreads his knees
Letting his arms hang down to laugh,
The zebra stripes along his jaw
Swelling to maculate° giraffe.   *spotted, stained*

5 The circles of the stormy moon
Slide westward toward the River Plate,[2]
Death and the Raven drift above
And Sweeney guards the hornèd gate.[3]

Gloomy Orion and the Dog
10 Are veiled;[4] and hushed the shrunken seas;

1. In the Elizabethan sense of a state journey made by a royal or noble person. Elizabethan plays sometimes showed such "progresses" crossing the stage. Cf. Chaucer's *General Prologue* to *The Canterbury Tales,* line 308.
2. In its older meanings: "opinions," "sententiousness."
1. "Alas, I am struck with a mortal blow within" (Aeschylus, *Agamemnon,* line 1343). The voice of Agamemnon heard crying out from the palace as he is murdered by his wife, Clytemnestra.
2. Estuary on the South American coast between Argentina and Uruguay, formed by the Uruguay and Paraná rivers.
3. The gates of horn, in Hades, through which true dreams come to the upper world.
4. "Orion" and "the Dog" are the constellations. For Sweeney and his lady friend, the gate of vision

The person in the Spanish cape
Tries to sit on Sweeney's knees

Slips and pulls the table cloth
Overturns a coffee-cup,
15   Reorganized upon the floor
She yawns and draws a stocking up;

The silent man in mocha brown
Sprawls at the window-sill and gapes;
The waiter brings in oranges
20   Bananas figs and hothouse grapes;

The silent vertebrate in brown
Contracts and concentrates, withdraws;
Rachel *née* Rabinovitch
Tears at the grapes with murderous paws;

25   She and the lady in the cape
Are suspect, thought to be in league;
Therefore the man with heavy eyes
Declines the gambit, shows fatigue,

Leaves the room and reappears
30   Outside the window, leaning in,
Branches of wistaria
Circumscribe a golden grin;

The host with someone indistinct
Converses at the door apart,
35   The nightingales are singing near
The Convent of the Sacred Heart,

And sang within the bloody wood
When Agamemnon cried aloud[5]
And let their liquid siftings fall
40   To stain the stiff dishonoured shroud.

1918, 1919

The Waste Land

The Waste Land   This is a poem about spiritual dryness, about the kind of
existence in which no regenerating belief gives significance and value to people's daily
activities, sex brings no fruitfulness, and death heralds no resurrection. Eliot himself
gives one of the main clues to the theme and structure of the poem in a general note,

---

is blocked and the great myth-making constellations are "veiled."
5. Agamemnon was not murdered in a "bloody
wood," but in his bath. Eliot is here telescoping
Agamemnon's murder with the wood where Philomela, in Greek myth, was ravished by her sister's

husband, Terens (she was subsequently turned
into a nightingale), and also with the "bloody
wood" of Nemi, where in ancient times the old
priest was slain by his successor (as described in
the first chapter of Sir James Frazer's *Golden
Bough*).

in which he stated that "not only the title, but the plan and a good deal of the symbolism of the poem were suggested by Miss Jessie L. Weston's book on the Grail legend: *From Ritual to Romance*" (1920). He further acknowledged a general indebtedness to Sir James Frazer's *Golden Bough* (13 volumes, 1890–1915), "especially the . . . volumes *Adonis, Attis, Osiris*," in which Frazer deals with ancient vegetation myths and fertility ceremonies. Weston's study, drawing on material from Frazer and other anthropologists, traced the relationship of these myths and rituals to Christianity and most especially to the legend of the Holy Grail. She found an archetypal fertility myth in the story of the Fisher King whose death, infirmity, or impotence (there are many forms of the myth) brought drought and desolation to the land and failure of the power to reproduce themselves among both humans and beasts. This symbolic Waste Land can be revived only if a "questing knight" goes to the Chapel Perilous, situated in the heart of it, and there asks certain ritual questions about the Grail (or Cup) and the Lance—originally fertility symbols, female and male, respectively. The proper asking of these questions revives the king and restores fertility to the land. The relation of this original Grail myth to fertility cults and rituals found in many different civilizations, and represented by stories of a dying god who is later resurrected (e.g., Tammuz, Adonis, Attis), shows their common origin in a response to the cyclical movement of the seasons, with vegetation dying in winter to be resurrected again in the spring. Christianity, according to Weston, gave its own spiritual meaning to the myth; it "did not hesitate to utilize the already existing medium of instruction, but boldly identified the Deity of Vegetation, regarded as Life Principle, with the God of the Christian Faith." The Fisher King is related to the use of the fish symbol in early Christianity. Weston states "with certainty that the Fish is a Life symbol of immemorial antiquity, and that the title of Fisher has, from the earliest ages, been associated with the Deities who were held to be specially connected with the origin and preservation of Life." Eliot, following Weston, thus uses a great variety of mythological and religious material, both Occidental and Oriental, to paint a symbolic picture of the modern Waste Land and the need for regeneration. The terror of that life—its loneliness, emptiness, and irrational apprehensions—as well as its misuse of sexuality are vividly presented, but paradoxically, the poem ends with a benediction. Another significant general source for the poem is the composer Richard Wagner, some of whose operas (*Götterdämmerung* ["Twilight of the Gods"], *Parsifal, Das Rheingold,* and *Tristan und Isolde*) are drawn on.

The poem as published owed a great deal to the severe pruning of Ezra Pound; the original manuscript, with Pound's excisions and comments, provides fascinating information about the genesis and development of the poem. It was reproduced in facsimile in 1971, edited by Eliot's widow, Valerie Eliot, who also supplied notes supplementing those that Eliot himself added when the poem was first published in book form in 1925 and that are included with the present editors' footnotes to the poem.

The Waste Land

"Nam Sibyllam quidem Cumis ego ipse oculis meis vidi in ampulla pendere, et cum illi pueri dicerent: Σίβυλλα τί θέλεις; respondebat illa: ἀποθανεῖν θέλω."[1]

1. From the *Satyricon* of Petronius (1st century C.E.): "For once I myself saw with my own eyes the Sibyl at Cumae hanging in a cage, and when the boys said to her 'Sibyl, what do you want?' she replied, 'I want to die.' " (The Greek may be transliterated, "Síbylla tí théleis?" and "apothanéin thélo.") The Cumaean Sibyl was the most famous of the Sibyls, the prophetic old women of Greek mythology; she guided Aeneas through Hades in the *Aeneid*. She had been granted immortality by Apollo, but because she forgot to ask for perpetual youth, she shrank into withered old age and her authority declined.

FOR EZRA POUND

il miglior fabbro[2]

I. The Burial of the Dead[3]

April is the cruellest month, breeding
Lilacs out of the dead land, mixing
Memory and desire, stirring
Dull roots with spring rain.
5   Winter kept us warm, covering
Earth in forgetful snow, feeding
A little life with dried tubers.
Summer surprised us, coming over the Starnbergersee[4]
With a shower of rain; we stopped in the colonnade,
10 And went on in sunlight, into the Hofgarten,[5]
And drank coffee, and talked for an hour.
Bin gar keine Russin, stamm' aus Litauen, echt deutsch.[6]
And when we were children, staying at the arch-duke's,
My cousin's, he took me out on a sled,
15 And I was frightened. He said, Marie,
Marie, hold on tight. And down we went.
In the mountains, there you feel free.
I read, much of the night, and go south in the winter.

What are the roots that clutch, what branches grow
20 Out of this stony rubbish? Son of man,[7]
You cannot say, or guess, for you know only
A heap of broken images, where the sun beats,
And the dead tree gives no shelter, the cricket no relief,[8]
And the dry stone no sound of water. Only
25 There is shadow under this red rock,[9]
(Come in under the shadow of this red rock),
And I will show you something different from either
Your shadow at morning striding behind you
Or your shadow at evening rising to meet you;
30 I will show you fear in a handful of dust.

---

2. "The better craftsman," a tribute originally paid to the Provençal poet Arnaut Daniel in Dante's *Purgatorio* 26.117. Ezra Pound (1885–1972), American expatriate poet who was a key figure in the modern movement in poetry, helped Eliot with the final revisions.

3. The title comes from the Anglican burial service.

4. Lake a few miles south of Munich, where the "mad" King Ludwig II of Bavaria drowned in 1886 in mysterious circumstances. This romantic, melancholy king was a passionate admirer of Richard Wagner and especially of Wagner's opera *Tristan und Isolde*, which plays a significant part in *The Waste Land*. Ludwig's suffering of "death by water" in the Starnbergersee thus evokes a cluster of themes central to the poem. Eliot had met King Ludwig's second cousin Countess Marie Larisch and talked with her. Although he had probably not read the countess's book *My Past*, which discusses King Ludwig at length, he got information about her life and times from her in person, and the

remarks made in lines 7–17 are hers. They distill a sense of romantic decadence that Eliot associates with this period of European history. Line 17 is a translation of the opening of a Bavarian folksong celebrating King Ludwig and lamenting his drowning.

5. A small public park in Munich.

6. I am not Russian at all; I come from Lithuania, a true German

7. Cf. Ezekiel 2.1 [Eliot's note]. Here God is addressing Ezekiel. God continues, "stand upon thy feet, and I will speak unto thee."

8. Cf. Ecclesiastes 12.5 [Eliot's note]. The verse cited by Eliot is part of the preacher's picture of the desolation of old age, "when they shall be afraid of that which is high, and fears shall be in the way, and the almond tree shall flourish, and the grasshopper shall be a burden, and desire shall fail."

9. Cf. Isaiah 32.2: the "righteous king" "shall be . . . as rivers of water in a dry place, as the shadow of a great rock in a weary land."

Frisch weht der Wind
Der Heimat zu
Mein Irisch Kind,
Wo weilest du?[1]

35 'You gave me hyacinths first a year ago;
They called me the hyacinth girl.'
—Yet when we came back, late, from the Hyacinth garden,
Yours arms full, and your hair wet, I could not
Speak, and my eyes failed, I was neither
40 Living nor dead, and I knew nothing,
Looking into the heart of light, the silence.
Oed' und leer das Meer.[2]

Madame Sosostris,[3] famous clairvoyante,
Had a bad cold, nevertheless
45 Is known to be the wisest woman in Europe,
With a wicked pack of cards.[4] Here, said she,
Is your card, the drowned Phoenician Sailor,[5]
(Those are pearls that were his eyes. Look!)
Here is Belladonna,[6] the Lady of the Rocks,
50 The lady of situations.
Here is the man with three staves,[7] and here the Wheel,[8]
And here is the one-eyed merchant,[9] and this card,
Which is blank, is something he carries on his back,
Which I am forbidden to see. I do not find
55 The Hanged Man.[1] Fear death by water.

1. V. [see] *Tristan und Isolde,* 1, verses 5–8 [Eliot's note]. In Wagner's opera, a sailor recalls the girl he has left behind: "Fresh blows the wind to the homeland; my Irish child, where are you waiting?"
2. Id. [Ibid] 3, verse 24 [Eliot's note]. In act 3 of *Tristan und Isolde,* Tristan lies dying. He is waiting for Isolde to come to him from Cornwall, but a shepherd, appointed to watch for her sail, can only report, "Waste and empty is the sea."
3. A mock Egyptian name (suggested to Eliot by "Sesostris, the Sorceress of Ecbatana," the name assumed by a character in Aldous Huxley's novel *Crome Yellow* who dresses up as a gypsy to tell fortunes at a fair).
4. I.e., the deck of Tarot cards. The four suits of the Tarot pack, discussed by Jessie Weston in *From Ritual to Romance,* are the cup, lance, sword, and dish—the life symbols found in the Grail story. Weston noted that "today the Tarot has fallen somewhat into disrepute, being principally used for purposes of divination." Some of the cards mentioned in lines 46–56 are discussed by Eliot in his note to this passage: "I am not familiar with the exact constitution of the Tarot pack of cards, from which I have obviously departed to suit my own convenience. The Hanged Man, a member of the traditional pack, fits my purpose in two ways: because he is associated in my mind with the Hanged God of Frazer, and because I associate him with the hooded figure in the passage of the disciples to Emmaus in part 5. The Phoenician Sailor and the Merchant appear later; also the 'crowds of people,' and Death by Water is executed in part 4. The Man with Three Staves (an authentic member of the Tarot pack) I associate, quite arbitrarily, with the Fisher King himself."
5. See part 4. Phlebas the Phoenician and Mr.

Eugenides, the Smyrna merchant—both of whom appear later in the poem—are different phases of the same symbolic character, here identified as the "Phoenician Sailor." Mr. Eugenides exports "currants" (line 210); the drowned Phlebas floats in the "current" (line 315). The line that follows is from Shakespeare's *Tempest* (1.2.398). Ariel's song to the shipwrecked Ferdinand, who was "sitting on a bank / Weeping again the King my father's wrack," when "this music crept by me on the waters." The song is about the supposed drowning of Ferdinand's father, Alonso. *The Waste Land* contains many references to *The Tempest.* Ferdinand is associated with Phlebas and Mr. Eugenides and, therefore, with the "drowned Phoenician Sailor."
6. Beautiful lady. The word also suggests Madonna (the Virgin Mary) and, therefore, the Madonna of the Rocks (as in Leonardo da Vinci's painting); the rocks symbolize the church. Belladonna is also an eye cosmetic and a poison—the deadly nightshade. In the next line, the woman figure of the Virgin becomes "the lady of situations," foreshadowing the neurasthenic lady of intrigue in part 2.
7. Life-force symbol, associated by Eliot with the Fisher King.
8. I.e., the wheel of fortune, whose turning represents the reversals of human life.
9. I.e., Mr. Eugenides, "one-eyed" because the figure is in profile on the card and also as a suggestion of evil or crookedness.
1. On his card in the Tarot pack he is shown hanging from one foot from a T-shaped cross. He symbolizes the self-sacrifice of the fertility god who is killed in order that his resurrection may bring fertility once again to land and people.

I see crowds of people, walking round in a ring.
Thank you. If you see dear Mrs Equitone,
Tell her I bring the horoscope myself:
One must be so careful these days.

60   Unreal City,[2]
Under the brown fog of a winter dawn,
A crowd flowed over London Bridge, so many,[3]
I had not thought death had undone so many.
Sighs, short and infrequent, were exhaled,[4]
65   And each man fixed his eyes before his feet.
Flowed up the hill and down King William Street,
To where Saint Mary Woolnoth kept the hours
With a dead sound on the final stroke of nine.[5]
There I saw one I knew, and stopped him, crying: 'Stetson![6]
70   'You who were with me in the ships at Mylae![7]
'That corpse you planted last year in your garden,
'Has it begun to sprout?[8] Will it bloom this year?
'Or has the sudden frost disturbed its bed?
'Oh keep the Dog far hence, that's friend to men,
75   'Or with his nails he'll dig it up again![9]
'You! hypocrite lecteur!—mon semblable—mon frère!'[1]

II. A Game of Chess[2]

The Chair she sat in, like a burnished throne,[3]
Glowed on the marble, where the glass

2. Cf. Baudelaire: '*Fourmillante cité, cité pleine de rêves, / Où le spectre en plein jour raccroche le passant*' [Eliot's note]. The lines are quoted from *Les Sept Vieillards* ("The Seven Old Men") by Charles Baudelaire (1821–67); it is poem 93 of *Les Fleurs du Mal* ("The Flowers of Evil"). The lines may be translated: "Swarming city, city full of dreams, / Where the specter in broad daylight accosts the passerby."
3. Cf. Inferno 3.55–57 [Eliot's note]. The note goes on to quote Dante's lines, which may be translated: "So long a train of people, / that I should never have believed / That death had undone so many." Dante, just outside the gate of hell, has seen "the wretched souls of those who lived without disgrace and without praise." In his essay on Baudelaire, Eliot argued that in a sense it was better to be positively evil than to be neither good nor evil.
4. Cf. Inferno 4.25–27 [Eliot's note]. In Limbo, the first circle of hell, Dante has found the virtuous heathens, who lived before Christianity and are, therefore, eternally unable to achieve their desire of seeing God. Dante's lines, cited by Eliot, mean "Here, so far as I could tell by listening, / there was no lamentation except sighs, / which caused the eternal air to tremble."
5. A phenomenon which I have often noticed [Eliot's note]. St. Mary Woolnoth is a church in the "Unreal City" of London (the financial district); the crowd is flowing across London Bridge to work in the City.
6. Presumably representing the "average businessman."
7. The battle of Mylae (260 B.C.E.) in the First Punic War, which, in some measure like World War I, was fought for economic reasons.
8. A distortion of the ritual death of the fertility god.
9. Cf. the Dirge in Webster's *White Devil* [Eliot's note]. In the play by John Webster (d. 1625), the dirge, sung by Cornelia, has the lines "But keep the wolf far thence, that's foe to men, / For with his nails he'll dig them up again." Eliot makes the "wolf" into a "dog," which is not a foe but a friend to humans. There may be a reference to Sirius, the Dog Star, which is important in Egyptian mythology as heralding the fertilizing floods of the Nile (this is discussed by Weston).
1. V. Baudelaire, Preface to *Fleurs du Mal* [Eliot's note]. The passage is the last line of the introductory poem *Au Lecteur* ("To the Reader") in Baudelaire's *Fleurs du Mal*; it may be translated: "Hypocrite reader!—my likeness—my brother!" *Au Lecteur* describes man as sunk in stupidity, sin, and evil, but the worst in "each man's foul menagerie of sin" is boredom, the "*monstre délicat*"— "You know him, reader."
2. The title suggests two plays by Thomas Middleton (1580–1627): *A Game at Chess* and, more significant, *Women Beware Women*, which has a scene in which a mother-in-law is distracted by a game of chess while her daughter-in-law is seduced: every move in the chess game represents a move in the seduction.
3. Cf. *Antony and Cleopatra*, 2.2.190 [Eliot's note]. In Shakespeare's play, Enobarbus's famous description of the first meeting of Antony and Cleopatra begins, "The barge she sat in, like a burnish'd throne, / Burn'd on the water." Eliot's language in the opening lines of part 2 is full of ironic distortions of Enobarbus's speech.

Held up by standards wrought with fruited vines
80   From which a golden Cupidon peeped out
(Another hid his eyes behind his wing)
Doubled the flames of sevenbranched candelabra
Reflecting light upon the table as
The glitter of her jewels rose to meet it,
85   From satin cases poured in rich profusion.
In vials of ivory and coloured glass
Unstoppered, lurked her strange synthetic perfumes,
Unguent, powdered, or liquid—troubled, confused
And drowned the sense in odours; stirred by the air
90   That freshened from the window, these ascended
In fattening the prolonged candle-flames,
Flung their smoke into the laquearia,[4]
Stirring the pattern on the coffered ceiling.
Huge sea-wood fed with copper
95   Burned green and orange, framed by the coloured stone,
In which sad light a carvèd dolphin swam.
Above the antique mantel was displayed
As though a window gave upon the sylvan scene[5]
The change of Philomel,[6] by the barbarous king
100   So rudely forced; yet there the nightingale
Filled all the desert with inviolable voice
And still she cried, and still the world pursues,
'Jug Jug'[7] to dirty ears.
And other withered stumps of time
105   Were told upon the walls; staring forms
Leaned out, leaning, hushing the room enclosed.
Footsteps shuffled on the stair.
Under the firelight, under the brush, her hair
Spread out in fiery points
110   Glowed into words, then would be savagely still.

    'My nerves are bad tonight. Yes, bad. Stay with me.
'Speak to me. Why do you never speak. Speak.
   'What are you thinking of? What thinking? What?
'I never know what you are thinking. Think.'

115   I think we are in rats' alley[8]
Where the dead men lost their bones.

    'What is that noise?'
              The wind under the door.[9]

---

4. Laquearia. V. *Aeneid*, 1. 726 [Eliot's note]. *Laquearia* means "a paneled ceiling," and Eliot's note quotes the passage in the *Aeneid* that was his source for the word. The passage may be translated: "Blazing torches hang from the gold-paneled ceiling [*laquearibus aureis*], and torches conquer the night with flames." Virgil is describing the banquet given by Dido, queen of Carthage, for Aeneas, with whom she fell in love.
5. Sylvan scene. V. Milton, *Paradise Lost*, 4.140 [Eliot's note]. The phrase is part of the first description of Eden, which we see through Satan's eyes.

6. V. Ovid, *Metamorphoses*, 6, Philomela [Eliot's note]. The note is a reference to Ovid's version of the Greek myth of the rape of Philomela by "the barbarous king" Tereus, husband of her sister Procne. Philomela was transformed into a nightingale. Eliot's note for line 100 refers ahead to his elaboration of the nightingale's song.
7. Conventional representation of nightingale's song in Elizabethan poetry.
8. Cf. part 3, line 195 [Eliot's note].
9. Cf. Webster: 'Is the wind in that door still?' [Eliot's note]. The line cited in the note is from John Webster, *The Devil's Law Case* 3.2.162.

'What is that noise now? What is the wind doing?'
120   Nothing again nothing.

                                'Do
'You know nothing? Do you see nothing? Do you remember
'Nothing?'

      I remember
125   Those are pearls that were his eyes.
"Are you alive, or not? Is there nothing in your head?"
                                   But

O O O O that Shakespeherian Rag[1]—
It's so elegant
130   So intelligent
'What shall I do now? What shall I do?'
'I shall rush out as I am, and walk the street
'With my hair down, so. What shall we do tomorrow?
'What shall we ever do?'
135   The hot water at ten.
And if it rains, a closed car at four.
And we shall play a game of chess,[2]
Pressing lidless eyes and waiting for a knock upon the door.

      When Lil's husband got demobbed,[3] I said—
140   I didn't mince my words, I said to her myself,
HURRY UP PLEASE ITS TIME[4]
Now Albert's coming back, make yourself a bit smart.
He'll want to know what you done with that money he gave you
To get yourself some teeth. He did, I was there.
145   You have them all out, Lil, and get a nice set,
He said, I swear, I can't bear to look at you.
And no more can't I, I said, and think of poor Albert,
He's been in the army four years, he wants a good time,
And if you don't give it him, there's others will, I said.
150   Oh is there, she said. Something o' that, I said.
Then I'll know who to thank, she said, and give me a straight look.
HURRY UP PLEASE ITS TIME
If you don't like it you can get on with it, I said.
Others can pick and choose if you can't.
155   But if Albert makes off, it won't be for lack of telling.
You ought to be ashamed, I said, to look so antique.
(And her only thirty-one.)
I can't help it, she said, pulling a long face,
It's them pills I took, to bring it off, she said.
160   (She's had five already, and nearly died of young George.)
The chemist[5] said it would be all right, but I've never been the same

---

1. American ragtime song, which was a hit of Zieg-
feld's Follies in 1912.
2. Cf. the game of chess in Middleton's *Women
Beware Women* [Eliot's note]. The significance of
this chess game is discussed in 2nd n. 2, p. 2372.

3. British slang for "demobilized" (discharged
from the army).
4. The traditional call of the British bartender at
closing time.
5. Druggist. "To bring it off": to cause an abortion.

You *are* a proper fool, I said.
Well, if Albert won't leave you alone, there it is, I said,
What you get married for if you don't want children?
165 HURRY UP PLEASE ITS TIME
Well, that Sunday Albert was home, they had a hot gammon,°   *ham, bacon*
And they asked me in to dinner, to get the beauty of it hot—
HURRY UP PLEASE ITS TIME
HURRY UP PLEASE ITS TIME
170 Goonight Bill. Goonight Lou. Goonight May. Goonight.
Ta ta. Goonight. Goonight.
Good night, ladies, good night, sweet ladies, good night, good night.[6]

III. The Fire Sermon[7]

The river's tent is broken: the last fingers of leaf
Clutch and sink into the wet bank. The wind
175 Crosses the brown land, unheard. The nymphs are departed.
Sweet Thames, run softly, till I end my song.[8]
The river bears no empty bottles, sandwich papers,
Silk handkerchiefs, cardboard boxes, cigarette ends
Or other testimony of summer nights. The nymphs are departed.
180 And their friends, the loitering heirs of city directors;
Departed, have left no addresses.
By the waters of Leman I sat down and wept[9] . . .
Sweet Thames, run softly till I end my song,
Sweet Thames, run softly, for I speak not loud or long.
185 But at my back in a cold blast I hear[1]
The rattle of the bones, and chuckle spread from ear to ear.

A rat crept softly through the vegetation
Dragging its slimy belly on the bank
While I was fishing in the dull canal
190 On a winter evening round behind the gashouse
Musing upon the king my brother's wreck[2]
And on the king my father's death before him.
White bodies naked on the low damp ground
And bones cast in a little low dry garret,
195 Rattled by the rat's foot only, year to year.
But at my back from time to time I hear[3]
The sound of horns and motors, which shall bring

6. Cf. the mad Ophelia's departing words (*Hamlet* 4.5.72). Ophelia, too, met "death by water."
7. The Fire Sermon was preached by the Buddha against the fires of lust and other passions that destroy people and prevent their regeneration (see also n. 7, p. 2379).
8. V. Spenser, *Prothalamion* [Eliot's note]. Eliot's line is the refrain from Spenser's marriage song, which is also set by the Thames in London—but a very different Thames from the modern littered river.
9. Cf. Psalms 137.1, in which the exiled Hebrews mourn for their homeland: "By the rivers of Bab-

ylon, there we sat down, yea, we wept, when we remembered Zion." Lake Leman is another name for Lake Geneva; Eliot wrote *The Waste Land* in Lausanne, by that lake. The common noun *leman* is an archaic word meaning a lover, sweetheart, or mistress.
1. An ironic distortion of Andrew Marvell's *To His Coy Mistress*, lines 21–22: "But at my back I always hear / Time's wingèd chariot hurrying near." Cf. line 196.
2. Cf. *The Tempest*, 1.2 [Eliot's note]. See line 48.
3. Cf. Marvell, *To His Coy Mistress* [Eliot's note].

Sweeney to Mrs Porter in the spring.[4]
O the moon shone bright on Mrs Porter
200 And on her daughter
They wash their feet in soda water[5]
Et O ces voix d'enfants, chantant dans la coupole![6]

Twit twit twit
Jug jug jug jug jug jug
205 So rudely forc'd.
Tereu[7]

   Unreal City
Under the brown fog of a winter noon
Mr Eugenides, the Smyrna[8] merchant
210 Unshaven, with a pocket full of currants
C.i.f.[9] London: documents at sight,
Asked me in demotic° French   *popular*
To luncheon at the Cannon Street Hotel[1]
Followed by a weekend at the Metropole.

215   At the violet hour, when the eyes and back
Turn upward from the desk, when the human engine waits
Like a taxi throbbing waiting,
I Tiresias,[2] though blind, throbbing between two lives,

4. Cf. Day, *Parliament of Bees:* 'When of the sudden, listening, you shall hear, / A noise of horns and hunting, which shall bring / Actaeon to Diana in the spring, / Where all shall see her naked skin' [Eliot's note]. Actaeon was changed to a stag and hunted to death after he saw Diana, the goddess of chastity, bathing with her nymphs.
5. I do not know the origin of the ballad from which these lines are taken: it was reported to me from Sydney, Australia [Eliot's note]. One of the less bawdy versions of the song, which was popular among Australian troops in World War I, went as follows: "O the moon shines bright on Mrs. Porter / And on the daughter / Of Mrs. Porter. / They wash their feet in soda water / And so they oughter / To keep them clean."
6. V. Verlaine, *Parsifal* [Eliot's note]. The line is translated, "And O those children's voices singing in the dome!" Verlaine's sonnet describes Parsifal, the questing knight, resisting all sensual temptations to keep himself pure for the Grail; Wagner's Parsifal had his feet washed before entering the castle of the Grail.
7. A reference to Tereus, who "rudely forc'd" Philomela; it was also one of the conventional words for a nightingale's song in Elizabethan poetry. Cf. the song from John Lyly's *Alexander and Campaspe* (1564): "Oh, 'tis the ravished nightingale. / *Jug, jug, jug, jug, tereu!* she cries," and lines 100ff.
8. Seaport in western Turkey; here associated with Carthage and the ancient Phoenician and Syrian merchants (unlike those of modern Smyrna), who spread the old mystery cults. The sort of cult spread by Mr. Eugenides is indicated by his suggestion of "a weekend at the Metropole" (a luxury hotel at Brighton).
9. The currants were quoted at a price 'carriage and insurance free to London'; and the Bill of Lading etc. were to be handed to the buyer upon payment of the sight draft [Eliot's note].

1. Located near the station that was then chief terminus for travelers to the Continent, hence a favorite meeting place for businesspeople going or coming from abroad.
2. Tiresias, although a mere spectator and not indeed a 'character', is yet the most important personage in the poem, uniting all the rest. Just as the one-eyed merchant, seller of currants, melts into the Phoenician Sailor, and the latter is not wholly distinct from Ferdinand Prince of Naples, so all the women are one woman, and the two sexes meet in Tiresias. What Tiresias *sees*, in fact, is the substance of the poem. The whole passage from Ovid is of great anthropological interest [Eliot's note]. The note then quotes the Latin text of Ovid's *Metamorphoses* that tells the story of Tiresias's change of sex. The Latin may be translated: "[The story goes that once Jove, having drunk a great deal,] jested with Juno. He said, 'Your pleasure in love is really greater than that enjoyed by men.' She denied it; so they decided to seek the opinion of the wise Tiresias, for he knew both aspects of love. For once, with a blow of his staff, he had committed violence on two huge snakes as they copulated in the green forest; and—wonderful to tell—was turned from a man into a woman and thus spent seven years. In the eighth year he saw the same snakes again and said: 'If a blow struck at you is so powerful that it changes the sex of the giver, I will now strike at you again.' With these words she struck the snakes, and again became a man. So he was appointed arbitrator in the playful quarrel, and supported Jove's statement. It is said that Saturnia [i.e., Juno] was quite disproportionately upset, and condemned the arbitrator to perpetual blindness. But the almighty father (for no god may undo what has been done by another god), in return for the sight that was taken away, gave him the power to know the future and so lightened the penalty paid by the honor."

Old man with wrinkled female breasts, can see
220 At the violet hour, the evening hour that strives
Homeward, and brings the sailor home from sea,[3]
The typist home at teatime, clears her breakfast, lights
Her stove, and lays out food in tins.
Out of the window perilously spread
225 Her drying combinations touched by the sun's last rays,
On the divan are piled (at night her bed)
Stockings, slippers, camisoles, and stays.
I Tiresias, old man with wrinkled dugs
Perceived the scene, and foretold the rest—
230 I too awaited the expected guest.
He, the young man carbuncular,° arrives,   *pimply*
A small house agent's clerk, with one bold stare,
One of the low on whom assurance sits
As a silk hat on a Bradford[4] millionaire.
235 The time is now propitious, as he guesses,
The meal is ended, she is bored and tired,
Endeavours to engage her in caresses
Which still are unreproved, if undesired.
Flushed and decided, he assaults at once;
240 Exploring hands encounter no defence;
His vanity requires no response,
And makes a welcome of indifference.
(And I Tiresias have foresuffered all
Enacted on this same divan or bed;
245 I who have sat by Thebes[5] below the wall
And walked among the lowest of the dead.)
Bestows one final patronising kiss,
And gropes his way, finding the stairs unlit . . .

She turns and looks a moment in the glass,
250 Hardly aware of her departed lover;
Her brain allows one half-formed thought to pass:
'Well now that's done: and I'm glad it's over.'
When lovely woman stoops to folly and
Paces about her room again, alone,
255 She smoothes her hair with automatic hand,
And puts a record on the gramophone.[6]

---

3. This may not appear as exact as Sappho's lines, but I had in mind the 'longshore' or 'dory' fisherman, who returns at nightfall [Eliot's note]. Sappho's poem addressed Hesperus, the evening star, as the star that brings everyone home from work to evening rest; her poem is here distorted by Eliot. There is also an echo of Robert Louis Stevenson's *Requiem*, line 221: "Home is the sailor, home from sea".
4. Either the Yorkshire woolen manufacturing town, where many fortunes were made in World War I, or the pioneer oil town of Bradford, Pennsylvania, the home of one of Eliot's wealthy Harvard contemporaries, T. E. Hanley.

5. Tiresias lived in Thebes for many generations, where he witnessed the tragic fates of Oedipus and Creon; he prophesied in the marketplace by the wall of Thebes.
6. V. Goldsmith, the song in *The Vicar of Wakefield* [Eliot's note]. Olivia, a character in Oliver Goldsmith's novel, sings the following song when she returns to the place where she was seduced: "When lovely woman stoops to folly / And finds too late that men betray / What charm can soothe her melancholy, / What art can wash her guilt away? / The only art her guilt to cover, / To hide her shame from every eye, / To give repentance to her lover / And wring his bosom—is to die."

'This music crept by me upon the waters'[7]
And along the Strand, up Queen Victoria Street.
O City city, I can sometimes hear
260 Beside a public bar in Lower Thames Street,
The pleasant whining of a mandoline
And a clatter and a chatter from within
Where fishmen lounge at noon: where the walls
Of Magnus Martyr hold
265 Inexplicable splendour of Ionian white and gold.[8]

　　　　The river sweats[9]
　　　　Oil and tar
　　　　The barges drift
　　　　With the turning tide
270 　　　Red sails
　　　　Wide
　　　　To leeward, swing on the heavy spar.
　　　　The barges wash
　　　　Drifting logs
275 　　　Down Greenwich reach
　　　　Past the Isle of Dogs.[1]
　　　　　　　Weialala leia
　　　　　　　Wallala leialala

　　　　Elizabeth and Leicester[2]
280 　　　Beating oars
　　　　The stern was formed
　　　　A gilded shell
　　　　Red and gold
　　　　The brisk swell
285 　　　Rippled both shores
　　　　Southwest wind
　　　　Carried down stream
　　　　The peal of bells
　　　　White towers
290 　　　　　Weialala leia
　　　　　　　Wallala leialala

7. V. *The Tempest*, as above [Eliot's note]. Cf. line 48. The line is from Ferdinand's speech, continuing after "weeping again the King my father's wrack."
8. The interior of St Magnus Martyr is to my mind one of the finest among [Sir Christopher] Wren's interiors [Eliot's note]. In these lines, the "pleasant" music, the "fishmen" resting after labor, and the splendor of the church interior all suggest a world of true values, where work and relaxation are both real and take place in a context of religious meaning. It is but a momentary glimpse of an almost lost world.
9. The Song of the (three) Thames-daughters begins here. From line 292 to 306 inclusive they speak in turn. V. *Götterdämmerung*, 3.1: the Rhine-daughters [Eliot's note]. Eliot parallels the Thames-daughters with the Rhinemaidens in Wagner's opera *Götterdämmerung* ("The Twilight of the Gods") who lament that, with the gold of the

Rhine stolen, the beauty of the river is gone. The refrain in lines 277–78 is borrowed from Wagner.
1. Greenwich is a borough in London on the south side of the Thames; opposite is the Isle of Dogs (a peninsula): Eliot presumably intends a reference to the earlier theme of the Dog.
2. The fruitless love of Queen Elizabeth and the earl of Leicester (Robert Dudley) is recalled in Eliot's note: "V. [J. A.] Froude, *Elizabeth*, Vol. 1, ch. 4, letter of De Quadra to Philip of Spain: 'In the afternoon we were in a barge, watching the games on the river. (The queen) was alone with Lord Robert and myself on the poop, when they began to talk nonsense, and went so far that Lord Robert at last said, as I was on the spot there was no reason why they should not be married if the queen pleased.'" Queen Elizabeth was born in the old Greenwich House, by the river, where Greenwich Hospital now stands.

'Trams and dusty trees.
Highbury bore me. Richmond and Kew
Undid me.³ By Richmond I raised my knees
295   Supine on the floor of a narrow canoe.'

'My feet are at Moorgate,⁴ and my heart
Under my feet. After the event
He wept. He promised "a new start."
I made no comment. What should I resent?'

300   'On Margate⁵ Sands.
I can connect
Nothing with nothing.
The broken fingernails of dirty hands.
My people humble people who expect
305   Nothing.'
            la la

To Carthage then I came⁶

Burning burning burning burning⁷
O Lord Thou pluckest me out⁸
310   O Lord Thou pluckest

burning

IV. Death by Water⁹

Phlebas the Phoenician, a fortnight dead,
Forgot the cry of gulls, and the deep sea swell
And the profit and loss.
315   A current under sea

3. Cf. *Purgatorio,* 5.133 [Eliot's note]. The *Purgatorio* lines, which Eliot here parodies, may be translated: "Remember me, who am La Pia. / Siena made me, Maremma undid me." "Highbury": a residential London suburb. "Richmond": a pleasant part of London westward up the Thames, with boating and riverside hotels. "Kew": adjoining Richmond, has the famous Kew Gardens.
4. Underground (subway) station Eliot used daily while working at Lloyds Bank.
5. Popular seaside resort on Thames estuary.
6. V. St Augustine's *Confessions:* 'to Carthage then I came, where a caldron of unholy loves sang all about mine ears' [Eliot's note]. The passage from the *Confessions* quoted here occurs in St. Augustine's account of his youthful life of lust. Cf. line 92 and its note.
7. The complete text of the Buddha's Fire Sermon (which corresponds in importance to the Sermon on the Mount) from which these words are taken, will be found translated in the late Henry Clarke Warren's *Buddhism in Translation* (Harvard Oriental Series) [Eliot's note]. In the sermon, the Buddha instructs his priests that all things "are on fire. . . . The eye . . . is on fire; forms are on fire; eye-consciousness is on fire; impressions received by

the eye are on fire; and whatever sensation, pleasant, unpleasant, or indifferent, originates in dependence on impressions received by the eye, that also is on fire. And with what are these on fire? With the fire of passion, say I, with the fire of hatred, with the fire of infatuation." For Christ's Sermon on the Mount see Matthew 5–7.
8. "From St. Augustine's *Confessions* again. The collocation of these two representatives of eastern and western asceticism, as the culmination of this part of the poem, is not an accident" [Eliot's note]. Cf. also Zechariah 3.2, where God, rebuking Satan, speaks of Joshua the high priest as "a brand plucked out of the fire."
9. This section has been interpreted in two ways: either it signifies death by water without resurrection (water *misused*) or it symbolizes the sacrificial death that precedes rebirth. It is true that Phlebas is purged of his commercial interests and vanities when he suffers a sea change, and Weston tells of the annual casting into the sea at Alexandria of an effigy of the head of Adonis—to be taken out after seven days by jubilant celebrators of the cult. The majority of interpreters, however, see Phlebas's drowning as a death by water that brings no resurrection, although there is a strange sense of peace in the death. Cf. line 47 and n. 5, p. 2371.

Picked his bones in whispers. As he rose and fell
He passed the stages of his age and youth
Entering the whirlpool.
                        Gentile or Jew
320   O you who turn the wheel and look to windward,
      consider Phlebas, who was once handsome and tall as you.

V. What the Thunder Said[1]

      After the torchlight red on sweaty faces
      After the frosty silence in the gardens
      After the agony in stony places
325   The shouting and the crying
      Prison and palace and reverberation
      Of thunder of spring over distant mountains
      He who was living is now dead[2]
      We who were living are now dying
330   With a little patience

      Here is no water but only rock
      Rock and no water and the sandy road
      The road winding above among the mountains
      Which are mountains of rock without water
335   If there were water we should stop and drink
      Amongst the rock one cannot stop or think
      Sweat is dry and feet are in the sand
      If there were only water amongst the rock
      Dead mountain mouth of carious teeth that cannot spit
340   Here one can neither stand nor lie nor sit
      There is not even silence in the mountains
      But dry sterile thunder without rain
      There is not even solitude in the mountains
      But red sullen faces sneer and snarl
345   From doors of mudcracked houses
                              If there were water
            And no rock
            If there were rock
            And also water
350   And water
            A spring
            A pool among the rock
            If there were the sound of water only
            Not the cicada[3]

1. In the first part of part 5 three themes are employed: the journey to Emmaus, the approach to the Chapel Perilous (see Miss Weston's book), and the present decay of eastern Europe [Eliot's note]. The journey to Emmaus (see line 360 and n. 5, p. 2381) is a significant feature in the story of Christ, and in this section the Waste Land is more clearly related to that story. Christ is associated with the slain fertility god, but there is still no resurrection.

2. These lines, containing allusions to Christ's imprisonment and trial and to Gethsemane and Golgotha, suggest the hopeless day between Good Friday and Easter, between the Crucifixion and the Resurrection—associated with the death of the Fisher King.
3. Grasshopper. Cf. the prophecy of Ecclesiastes, "the grasshopper shall be a burden, and desire shall fail." Cf. also line 23 and n. 8, p. 2370.

355 And dry grass singing
  But sound of water over a rock
  Where the hermit thrush[4] sings in the pine trees
  Drip drop drip drop drop drop drop
  But there is no water

360 Who is the third who walks always beside you?[5]
  When I count, there are only you and I together
  But when I look ahead up the white road
  There is always another one walking beside you
  Gliding wrapped in a brown mantle, hooded
365 I do not know whether a man or a woman
  —But who is that on the other side of you?

  What is that sound high in the air[6]
  Murmur of maternal lamentation
  Who are those hooded hordes swarming
370 Over endless plains, stumbling in cracked earth
  Ringed by the flat horizon only
  What is the city over the mountains
  Cracks and reforms and bursts in the violet air
  Falling towers
375 Jerusalem Athens Alexandria
  Vienna London
  Unreal

  A woman drew her long black hair out tight
  And fiddled whisper music on those strings
380 And bats with baby faces in the violet light
  Whistled, and beat their wings
  And crawled head downward down a blackened wall
  And upside down in air were towers
  Tolling reminiscent bells, that kept the hours
385 And voices singing out of empty cisterns and exhausted wells.

  In this decayed hole among the mountains
  In the faint moonlight, the grass is singing
  Over the tumbled graves, about the chapel
  There is the empty chapel, only the wind's home.[7]
390 It has no windows, and the door swings,

---

4. This is . . . the hermit thrush which I have heard in Quebec County . . . Its 'water-dripping song' is justly celebrated [Eliot's note].

5. The following lines were stimulated by the account of one of the Antarctic expeditions (I forget which, but I think one of Shackleton's): it was related that the party of explorers, at the extremity of their strength, had the constant delusion that there was *one more member* than could actually be counted [Eliot's note]. This reminiscence is associated with the journey of Christ's disciples to Emmaus given in Luke 24.13–16: "And it came to pass, that, while they communed together and reasoned, Jesus himself drew near, and went with them. But their eyes were holden that they should not know him."

6. Eliot's note for lines 367–377 is: "Cf. Herman Hesse, *Blick ins Chaos* ["A Glimpse into Chaos"]." The note then quotes a passage from the German text, which is translated: "Already half of Europe, already at least half of Eastern Europe, on the way to Chaos, drives drunk in sacred infatuation along the edge of the precipice, sings drunkenly, as though hymn singing, as Dmitri Karamazov [in Dostoyevski's *Brothers Karamazov*] sang. The offended bourgeois laughs at the songs; the saint and the seer hear them with tears."

7. Suggesting the moment of near despair before the Chapel Perilous, when the questing knight sees nothing there but decay. This illusion of nothingness is the knight's final test.

Dry bones can harm no one.
Only a cock stood on the rooftree
Co co rico co co rico[8]
In a flash of lightning. Then a damp gust
395   Bringing rain

Ganga° was sunken, and the limp leaves   *Ganges River*
Waited for rain, while the black clouds
Gathered far distant, over Himavant.[9]
The jungle crouched, humped in silence.
400   Then spoke the thunder
    DA[1]
Datta: what have we given?
My friend, blood shaking my heart
The awful daring of a moment's surrender
405   Which an age of prudence can never retract
By this, and this only, we have existed
Which is not to be found in our obituaries
Or in memories draped by the beneficent spider[2]
Or under seals broken by the lean solicitor°   *lawyer*
410   In our empty rooms
    DA
Dayadhvam: I have heard the key[3]
Turn in the door once and turn once only
We think of the key, each in his prison
415   Thinking of the key, each confirms a prison
Only at nightfall, æthereal rumors
Revive for a moment a broken Coriolanus[4]
    DA
Damyata: The boat responded
420   Gaily, to the hand expert with sail and oar
The sea was calm, your heart would have responded
Gaily, when invited, beating obedient
To controlling hands

---

8. The crowing of the cock signals the departure of ghosts and evil spirits. Cf. *Hamlet* 1.1.157ff.
9. I.e., snowy mountain; the name of a peak in the Himalayas.
1. 'Datta, dayadhvam, damyata' (Give, sympathize, control). The fable of the meaning of the Thunder is found in the *Brihadaranyaka—Upanishad*, 5, 1 [Eliot's note]. The Hindu fable referred to is that of gods, men, and demons each in turn asking of their father Prajapati, "Speak to us, O Lord." To each he replied with the one syllable "DA," and each group interpreted it in a different way: "*Datta,*" to give alms; "*Dayadhvam,*" to have compassion; "*Damyata,*" to practice self-control. The fable concludes, "This is what the divine voice, the Thunder, repeats when he says: *DA, DA, DA:* 'Control yourselves; give alms; be compassionate.' Therefore one should practice these three things: self-control, alms-giving, and compassion."
2. Cf. Webster, *The White Devil*, 5.6: '. . . they'll remarry / Ere the worm pierce your winding-sheet, ere the spider / Make a thin curtain for your epitaphs' [Eliot's note].

3. Cf. *Inferno*, 33.46 [Eliot's note]. In this passage from the *Inferno* Ugolino recalls his imprisonment in the tower with his children, where they starved to death: "And I heard below the door of the horrible tower being locked up." Eliot implies that we cannot obey the command to sympathize because we are imprisoned within the circle of our own egotism. Eliot's note for this line goes on to quote F. H. Bradley, *Appearance and Reality*, p. 346, as follows: " 'My external sensations are no less private to myself than are my thoughts or my feelings. In either case my experience falls within my own circle, a circle closed on the outside; and, with all its elements alike, every sphere is opaque to the others which surround it. . . . In brief, regarded as an existence which appears in a soul, the whole world for each is peculiar and private to that soul.' "
4. Coriolanus, who acted out of pride rather than duty, is an obvious example of a man locked in the prison of his own self. He led the enemy against his native city out of injured pride (cf. Shakespeare, *Coriolanus*).

I sat upon the shore

425 Fishing,[5] with the arid plain behind me

Shall I at least set my lands in order?[6]

London Bridge is falling down falling down falling down[7]

Poi s'ascose nel foco che gli affina[8]

Quando fiam uti chelidon[9]—O swallow swallow[1]

430 *Le Prince d'Aquitaine à la tour abolie*[2]

These fragments I have shored against my ruins[3]

Why then Ile fit you. Hieronymo's mad againe.[4]

Datta. Dayadhvam. Damyata.

Shantih   shantih   shantih[5]

1921   1922

The Hollow Men

Mistah Kurtz—he dead.[1]
A penny for the Old Guy[2]

I

We are the hollow men
We are the stuffed men

---

5. V. Weston: *From Ritual to Romance*; chapter on the Fisher King [Eliot's note].

6. Cf. Isaiah 38.1: "Thus saith the Lord, Set thine house in order, for thou shalt die, and not live." The inclusive "I," who sits in the symbolic act of fishing (seeking salvation, regeneration, eternity) with the Waste Land behind him, wonders how far he can order his affairs.

7. One of the later lines of this nursery rhyme is "Take the key and lock her up, my fair lady."

8. V. *Purgatorio*, 26.148 [Eliot's note]. The note goes on to quote lines 145–148 of the *Purgatorio*, in which Arnaut Daniel, the Provençal poet, addresses Dante: " 'Now I pray you, by that virtue which guides you to the summit of the stairway, be mindful in due time of my pain.' " Then (in the line Eliot quotes here) "he hid himself in the fire which refines them." The purgatorial vision of refining fire—as distinct from the fires of lust—represents one of the hopeful fragments shored up by the seeker for regeneration and order.

9. V. *Pervigilium Veneris*. Cf. Philomela in parts 2 and 3 [Eliot's note]. The Latin phrase in the text means, "When shall I be as the swallow?" It comes from the *Pervigilium Veneris* ("Vigil of Venus"), an anonymous late Latin poem combining a hymn to Venus with a description of spring. In the last two stanzas of the *Pervigilium* occurs a recollection of the Tereus-Procne-Philomela myth (except that in this version the swallow is identified with Philomela); the anonymous poet's mood changes to one of sadness, combined with hope for renewal: "The maid of Tereus sings under the poplar shade, so that you would think musical trills of love came from her mouth and not a sister's complaint of a barbarous husband. . . . She sings, we are silent. When will my spring come? When shall I be as the swallow that I may cease to be silent? I have lost the Muse in silence, and Apollo regards me not."

1. Cf. Swinburne's *Itylus*, which begins, "Swallow, my sister, O sister swallow, / How can thine heart be full of spring?" and Tennyson's lyric in *The Princess*: "O Swallow, Swallow, flying, flying south."

2. V. Gerard de Nerval, Sonnet *El Desdichado* [Eliot's note]. The French line may be translated, "The Prince of Aquitaine in the ruined tower." One of the cards in the Tarot pack is "the tower struck by lightning."

3. This may refer to the whole poem—fragments assembled by the speaker in the attempt to come to terms with his situation.

4. V. Kyd's *Spanish Tragedy* [Eliot's note]. Subtitled "Hieronymo's Mad Again," Kyd's play (1594) is an early example of the Elizabethan tragedy of revenge. Hieronymo, driven mad by the murder of his son, has his revenge when he is asked to write a court entertainment. He replies, "Why then Ile fit you!" (i.e., accommodate you), and assigns the parts in the entertainment so that, in the course of the action, his son's murderers are killed.

5. Shantih. Repeated as here, a formal ending to an Upanishad. 'The Peace which passeth understanding' is our equivalent to this word [Eliot's note]. The Upanishads are poetic dialogues on Hindu metaphysics, written after the Vedas, the ancient Hindu scriptures, and in part commenting on them. The fact that the benediction is in a language so foreign to Western tradition may indicate that the solution is willed, not achieved.

1. From Joseph Conrad's *Heart of Darkness* (see p. 2010).

2. Every year on Nov. 5, British children build bonfires on which they burn a scarecrow effigy of the traitor Guido [Guy] Fawkes who, in 1605, attempted to blow up the Parliament buildings. For some days before this, they ask people in the streets for pennies with which to buy fireworks.

Leaning together
Headpiece filled with straw. Alas!
5 Our dried voices, when
We whisper together
Are quiet and meaningless
As wind in dry glass
Or rats' feet over broken glass
10 In our dry cellar[3]

Shape without form, shade without colour,
Paralysed force, gesture without motion;

Those who have crossed
With direct eyes, to death's other Kingdom
15 Remember us—if at all—not as lost
Violent souls, but only
As the hollow men
The stuffed men.

II

Eyes I dare not meet in dreams
20 In death's dream kingdom[4]
These do not appear:
There, the eyes are
Sunlight on a broken column
There, is a tree swinging
25 And voices are
In the wind's singing
More distant and more solemn
Than a fading star.

Let me be no nearer
30 In death's dream kingdom
Let me also wear
Such deliberate disguises
Rat's coat, crowskin, crossed staves
In a field[5]
35 Behaving as the wind behaves
No nearer—

Not that final meeting
In the twilight kingdom[6]

3. Cf. *The Waste Land,* lines 115 and 195.
4. At the end of Dante's *Purgatorio* and in *Paradiso*
4, he cannot meet the gaze of Beatrice (see Eliot's
1929 essay, *Dante*).
5. The traditional British scarecrow is made from
two sticks tied in the form of a cross (the vertical

one stuck in the ground), dressed in cast-off
clothes, and sometimes draped with dead vermin.
6. Perhaps a reference to Dante's meeting with
Beatrice after he has crossed the river Lethe. There
reminded of his sins, he is allowed to proceed to
Paradise (*Purgatorio* 30).

III

This is the dead land
40 This is cactus land
Here the stone images[7]
Are raised, here they receive
The supplication of a dead man's hand
Under the twinkle of a fading star.

45 Is it like this
In death's other kingdom
Waking alone
At the hour when we are
Trembling with tenderness
50 Lips that would kiss
Form prayers to broken stone.

IV

The eyes are not here
There are no eyes here
In this valley of dying stars
55 In this hollow valley
This broken jaw of our lost kingdoms

In this last of meeting places
We grope together
And avoid speech
60 Gathered on this beach of the tumid river[8]

Sightless, unless
The eyes reappear
As the perpetual star
Multifoliate rose[9]
65 Of death's twilight kingdom
The hope only
Of empty men.

V

Here we go round the prickly pear
Prickly pear prickly pear
70 *Here we go round the prickly pear*
At five o'clock in the morning.[1]

Between the idea
And the reality
Between the motion

---

7. Cf. *The Waste Land* line 22.
8. Dante's Acheron, which encircles Hell, and the Congo of Conrad's *Heart of Darkness*.
9. The image of heaven in Dante's *Paradiso* 32.

1. Parodic version of the children's rhyme ending "Here we go round the mulberry bush / On a cold and frosty morning."

75 And the act[2]
    Falls the Shadow[3]
            For Thine is the Kingdom[4]

    Between the conception
    And the creation
80 Between the emotion
    And the response
    Falls the Shadow
            Life is very long

    Between the desire
85 And the spasm
    Between the potency
    And the existence
    Between the essence
    And the descent
90 Falls the Shadow
            For Thine is the Kingdom

    For Thine is
    Life is
    For Thine is the

95 *This is the way the world ends*
    This is the way the world ends
    This is the way the world ends
    Not with a bang but a whimper.

1924–25   1925

Journey of the Magi[1]

    'A cold coming we had of it,
    Just the worst time of the year
    For a journey, and such a long journey:
    The ways deep and the weather sharp,
5   The very dead of winter.'[2]
    And the camels galled, sore-footed, refractory,
    Lying down in the melting snow.
    There were times we regretted
    The summer palaces on slopes, the terraces,

---

2. Cf. Shakespeare's *Julius Caesar* 2.1.63–5: "Between the acting of a dreadful thing / And the first motion, all the interim is / Like a phantasma or a hideous dream."
3. Cf. Ernest Dowson's *Non sum qualis eram bonae sub regno Cynarae*, lines 1–2: "Last night, ah, yesternight, betwixt her lips and mine / There fell thy shadow, Cynara!"
4. Cf. The Lord's Prayer.
1. One of the wise men who came from the east

to Jerusalem to do homage to the infant Jesus (Matthew 2.1–12) is recalling in old age the meaning of the experience.
2. Adapted from a passage in a Nativity sermon by the 17th-century divine Lancelot Andrewes: "A cold coming they had of it at this time of the year, just the worst time of the year to take a journey, and specially a long journey in. The ways deep, the weather sharp, the days short, the sun farthest off, *in solstitio brumali*, 'the very dead of winter.' "

10 And the silken girls bringing sherbet.
　Then the camel men cursing and grumbling
　And running away, and wanting their liquor and women,
　And the night-fires going out, and the lack of shelters,
　And the cities hostile and the towns unfriendly
15 And the villages dirty and charging high prices:
　A hard time we had of it.
　At the end we preferred to travel all night,
　Sleeping in snatches,
　With the voices singing in our ears, saying
20 That this was all folly.

　　Then at dawn we came down to a temperate valley,
　Wet, below the snow line, smelling of vegetation;
　With a running stream and a water mill beating the darkness,
　And three trees on the low sky.[3]
25 And an old white horse galloped away in the meadow.
　Then we came to a tavern with vine-leaves over the lintel,
　Six hands at an open door dicing for pieces of silver,[4]
　And feet kicking the empty wine-skins.
　But there was no information, and so we continued
30 And arrived at evening, not a moment too soon
　Finding the place; it was (you may say) satisfactory.

　　All this was a long time ago, I remember,
　And I would do it again, but set down
　This set down
35 This: were we led all that way for
　Birth or Death? There was a Birth, certainly,
　We had evidence and no doubt. I had seen birth and death,
　But had thought they were different; this Birth was
　Hard and bitter agony for us, like Death, our death.
40 We returned to our places, these Kingdoms,
　But no longer at ease here, in the old dispensation,
　With an alien people clutching their gods.
　I should be glad of another death.

1927

---

3. The "three trees" suggest the three crosses, with Christ crucified on the center one; the men "dicing for pieces of silver" (line 27) suggest the soldiers dicing for Christ's garments and Judas's betrayal of him for thirty pieces of silver.
4. "Why, for all of us, out of all that we have heard, seen, felt, in a lifetime, do certain images recur, charged with emotion, rather than others? . . . six ruffians seen through an open window playing cards at night at a small French railway junction where there was a water mill" (Eliot, *The Use of Poetry and the Use of Criticism*).

Marina[1]

Quis hic locus, quae regio, quae mundi plaga?[2]

What seas what shores what gray rocks and what islands
What water lapping the bow
And scent of pine and the woodthrush singing through the fog
What images return
5 O my daughter.

Those who sharpen the tooth of the dog, meaning
Death
Those who glitter with the glory of the hummingbird, meaning
Death
10 Those who sit in the sty of contentment, meaning
Death
Those who suffer the ecstasy of the animals, meaning
Death

Are become unsubstantial, reduced by a wind,
15 A breath of pine, and the woodsong fog
By this grace dissolved in place

What is this face, less clear and clearer
The pulse in the arm, less strong and stronger—
Given or lent? more distant than stars and nearer than the eye

20 Whispers and small laughter between leaves and hurrying feet
Under sleep, where all the waters meet.

Bowsprit cracked with ice and paint cracked with heat.
I made this, I have forgotten
And remember.
25 The rigging weak and the canvas rotten
Between one June and another September.
Made this unknowing, half conscious, unknown, my own.
The garboard strake[3] leaks, the seams need caulking.
This form, this face, this life
30 Living to live in a world of time beyond me; let me
Resign my life for this life, my speech for that unspoken,
The awakened, lips parted, the hope, the new ships.

What seas what shores what granite islands towards my timbers
And woodthrush calling through the fog
35 My daughter.

1930

---

1. Pericles' daughter in Shakespeare's *Pericles, Prince of Tyre:* she was born at sea, lost to her father, then as a young woman found by him again.
2. "What place is this, what country, what region of the world?" Spoken by Hercules on regaining sanity after having killed his children in his madness, in Seneca's *Hercules Furens* (The mad Her-

cules). This is a situation contrary to the one evoked in the poem. Eliot once wrote to a correspondent that he wished to achieve a "crisscross" between the scenes in the Senecan and the Shakespearean plays.
3. The planking nearest to the boat's keel—hence its most vital spot.

FROM FOUR QUARTETS

Little Gidding[1]

I

Midwinter spring is its own season
Sempiternal° though sodden towards sundown, *eternal, everlasting*
Suspended in time, between pole and tropic,
When the short day is brightest, with frost and fire,
5 The brief sun flames the ice, on pond and ditches,
In windless cold that is the heart's heat,
Reflecting in a watery mirror
A glare that is blindness in the early afternoon.
And glow more intense than blaze of branch, or brazier,
10 Stirs the dumb spirit: no wind, but pentecostal fire[2]
In the dark time of the year. Between melting and freezing
The soul's sap quivers. There is no earth smell
Or smell of living thing. This is the springtime
But not in time's covenant. Now the hedgerow
15 Is blanched for an hour with transitory blossom
Of snow, a bloom more sudden
Than that of summer, neither budding nor fading,
Not in the scheme of generation.
Where is the summer, the unimaginable
Zero summer?

20   If you came this way,
Taking the route you would be likely to take
From the place you would be likely to come from,
If you came this way in may time, you would find the hedges
White again, in May, with voluptuary sweetness.
25 It would be the same at the end of the journey,
If you came at night like a broken king,[3]
If you came by day not knowing what you came for,
It would be the same, when you leave the rough road
And turn behind the pig-sty to the dull façade
30 And the tombstone. And what you thought you came for
Is only a shell, a husk of meaning
From which the purpose breaks only when it is fulfilled

---

1. This is the fourth of Eliot's *Four Quartets,* four related poems each divided into five "movements" in a manner reminiscent of the structure of a quartet or a sonata and each dealing with some aspect of the relation of time and eternity, the meaning of history, the achievement of the moment of time-less insight. Although the *Four Quartets* constitute a unified sequence, they were each written separately and can be read as individual poems. "*Little Gidding* can be understood by itself, without reference to the preceding poems, which it yet so beautifully completes" (Helen Gardner). Each of the four is named after a place. Little Gidding is a village in Huntingdonshire where in 1625 Nicholas Ferrar established an Anglican religious community; it was broken up in 1647, toward the end of the civil war, by the victorious Puritans; the chapel, however, was rebuilt in the 19th century and still exists. Eliot wrote the poem in 1942, when he was taking his turn as a nighttime fire-watcher during the incendiary bombings of London in World War II, and he looks back at the history and meaning of Little Gidding from his own war experience in order to project its present significance.
2. On the Pentecost day after the death and resurrection of Christ, there appeared to His apostles "cloven tongues like as of fire . . . And they were all filled with the Holy Ghost" (Acts 2).
3. King Charles I visited Ferrar's community more than once and is said to have paid his last visit in secret after his final defeat at the battle of Naseby in the Civil War.

If at all. Either you had no purpose
Or the purpose is beyond the end you figured
35   And is altered in fulfilment. There are other places
Which also are the world's end, some at the sea jaws,
Or over a dark lake, in a desert or a city⁴—
But this is the nearest, in place and time,
Now and in England.

                    If you came this way,
40   Taking any route, starting from anywhere,
At any time or at any season,
It would always be the same: you would have to put off
Sense and notion. You are not here to verify,
Instruct yourself, or inform curiosity
45   Or carry report. You are here to kneel
Where prayer has been valid. And prayer is more
Than an order of words, the conscious occupation
Of the praying mind, or the sound of the voice praying.
And what the dead had no speech for, when living,
50   They can tell you, being dead: the communication
Of the dead is tongued with fire beyond the language of the living.
Here, the intersection of the timeless moment
Is England and nowhere. Never and always.

                              II

Ash on an old man's sleeve
55   Is all the ash the burnt roses leave.
Dust in the air suspended
Marks the place where a story ended.⁵
Dust inbreathed was a house—
The wall, the wainscot, and the mouse.
60   The death of hope and despair,
          This is the death of air.⁶

There are flood and drouth
Over the eyes and in the mouth,
Dead water and dead sand
65   Contending for the upper hand.
The parched eviscerate soil
Gapes at the vanity of toil,
          Laughs without mirth.
                    This is the death of earth.

4. "The 'sea jaws' [Eliot] associated with Iona and St. Columba and with Lindisfarne and St. Cuthbert: the 'dark lake' with the lake of Glendalough and St. Kevin's hermitage in County Wicklow: the desert with the hermits of the Thebaid and St. Antony: the city with Padua and the other St. Antony" (Gardner, *The Composition of Four Quartets*, p. 163).
5. Eliot wrote to a friend: "During the Blitz [bombing] the accumulated debris was suspended in the London air for hours after a bombing. Then it would slowly descend and cover one's sleeves and coat with a fine white ash."
6. "The death of air," like that of "earth" and of "water and fire" in the succeeding stanzas, recalls the theory of the creative strife of the four elements propounded by Heraclitus (Greek philosopher of 4th and 5th centuries B.C.E.): "Fire lives in the death of air; water lives in the death of earth; and earth lives in the death of water."

70 Water and fire succeed
  The town, the pasture, and the weed.
  Water and fire deride
  The sacrifice that we denied.
  Water and fire shall rot
75 The marred foundations we forgot,
  Of sanctuary and choir.
   This is the death of water and fire.

 In the uncertain hour before the morning[7]
  Near the ending of interminable night
80 At the recurrent end of the unending
 After the dark dove with the flickering tongue[8]
  Had passed below the horizon of his homing
  While the dead leaves still rattled on like tin
 Over the asphalt where no other sound was
85 Between three districts whence the smoke arose
  I met one walking, loitering and hurried
 As if blown towards me like the metal leaves
  Before the urban dawn wind unresisting.
  And as I fixed upon the down-turned face
90 That pointed scrutiny with which we challenge
  The first-met stranger in the waning dusk
  I caught the sudden look of some dead master
 Whom I had known, forgotten, half recalled
  Both one and many; in the brown baked features
95 The eyes of a familiar compound ghost[9]
 Both intimate and unidentifiable.
  So I assumed a double part, and cried
  And heard another's voice cry: "What! are *you* here?"
 Although we were not. I was still the same,
100 Knowing myself yet being someone other—
  And he a face still forming; yet the words sufficed
 To compel the recognition they preceded.
  And so, compliant to the common wind,
  Too strange to each other for misunderstanding,
105 In concord at this intersection time
  Of meeting nowhere, no before and after,
  We trod the pavement in a dead patrol.
 I said: 'The wonder that I feel is easy,
  Yet ease is cause of wonder. Therefore speak:
110 I may not comprehend, may not remember.'
 And he: 'I am not eager to rehearse
  My thought and theory which you have forgotten.
  These things have served their purpose: let them be.
 So with your own, and pray they be forgiven
115 By others, as I pray you to forgive

---

7. The pattern of indentation in the left margin of lines 78–149, their movement and elevated diction, are meant to suggest the *terza rima* of Dante's *Inferno.*
8. The German dive bomber.
9. This encounter with a ghost "compounded" of W. B. Yeats and his fellow Irishman Jonathan Swift is modeled on Dante's meeting with Brunetto Latini (*Inferno* 15), closing with a direct translation of Dante's cry of horrified recognition: "*Siete voi qui, ser Brunetto?*" Cf. also Shakespeare's Sonnet 86, line 9: "that affable familiar ghost."

Both bad and good. Last season's fruit is eaten
And the fullfed beast shall kick the empty pail.
For last year's words belong to last year's language
And next year's words await another voice.
120 But, as the passage now presents no hindrance
To the spirit unappeased and peregrine°   foreign, wandering
Between two worlds become much like each other,
So I find words I never thought to speak
In streets I never thought I should revisit
125 When I left my body on a distant shore.[1]
Since our concern was speech, and speech impelled us
To purify the dialect of the tribe[2]
And urge the mind to aftersight and foresight,
Let me disclose the gifts reserved for age
130 To set a crown upon your lifetime's effort.
First, the cold friction of expiring sense
Without enchantment, offering no promise
But bitter tastelessness of shadow fruit
As body and soul begin to fall asunder.
135 Second, the conscious impotence of rage[3]
At human folly, and the laceration
Of laughter at what ceases to amuse.[4]
And last, the rending pain of re-enactment
Of all that you have done, and been;[5] the shame
140 Of motives late revealed, and the awareness
Of things ill done and done to others' harm
Which once you took for exercise of virtue.
Then fools' approval stings, and honour stains.
From wrong to wrong the exasperated spirit
145 Proceeds, unless restored by that refining fire[6]
Where you must move in measure, like a dancer.'[7]
The day was breaking. In the disfigured street
He left me, with a kind of valediction,
And faded on the blowing of the horn.[8]

III

150 There are three conditions which often look alike
Yet differ completely, flourish in the same hedgerow:

1. Yeats died on Jan. 28, 1939, at Roquebrune in
the south of France.
2. A rendering of the line *"Donner un sens plus pur
aux mots de la tribu"* in Stéphane Mallarmé's sonnet *Le Tombeau d'Edgar Poe* (The tomb of Edgar
Poe).
3. Cf. Yeats's *The Spur:* "You think it horrible that
lust and rage / Should dance attention upon my
old age."
4. Cf. Yeats's *Swift's Epitaph* (translated from
Swift's own Latin): "Savage indignation there /
Cannot lacerate his breast."
5. Cf. Yeats's *The Man and the Echo:* "All that I
have said and done, / Now that I am old and ill, /
Turns into a question till / I lie awake night after
night / And never get the answer right. / Did that
play of mine send out / Certain men the English

shot?"
6. Cf. *The Waste Land,* line 428 and n. 8, p. 2383;
also the refining fire in Yeats's *Byzantium,* lines
25–32.
7. Cf. Yeats's *Among School Children,* line 64:
"How can we know the dancer from the dance?"
8. Cf. *Hamlet* 1.2.157: "It faded on the crowing of
the cock." The horn is the all-clear signal after an
air raid (the dialogue has taken place between the
dropping of the last bomb and the sounding of the
all clear). Eliot called the section that ends with
this line "the nearest equivalent to a canto of the
Inferno or *Purgatorio*" that he could achieve and
spoke of his intention to present "a parallel, by
means of contrast, between the *Inferno* and the
Purgatorio . . . and a hallucinated scene after an air
raid."

Attachment to self and to things and to persons, detachment
From self and from things and from persons; and, growing between
    them, indifference
Which resembles the others as death resembles life,
155 Being between two lives—unflowering, between
The live and the dead nettle.[9] This is the use of memory:
For liberation—not less of love but expanding
Of love beyond desire, and so liberation
From the future as well as the past. Thus, love of a country
160 Begins as attachment to our own field of action
And comes to find that action of little importance
Though never indifferent. History may be servitude,
History may be freedom. See, now they vanish,
The faces and places, with the self which, as it could, loved them,
165 To become renewed, transfigured, in another pattern.

Sin is Behovely, but
All shall be well, and
All manner of thing shall be well.[1]
If I think, again, of this place,
170 And of people, not wholly commendable,
Of no immediate kin or kindness,
But some of peculiar genius,
All touched by a common genius,
United in the strife which divided them;
175 If I think of a king at nightfall,[2]
Of three men, and more, on the scaffold
And a few who died forgotten
In other places, here and abroad,
And of one who died blind and quiet[3]
180 Why should we celebrate
These dead men more than the dying?
It is not to ring the bell backward
Nor is it an incantation
To summon the spectre of a Rose.
185 We cannot revive old factions
We cannot restore old policies
Or follow an antique drum.
These men, and those who opposed them
And those whom they opposed
190 Accept the constitution of silence
And are folded in a single party.
Whatever we inherit from the fortunate
We have taken from the defeated
What they had to leave us—a symbol:

---

9. Eliot wrote to a friend: "The dead nettle is the family of flowering plants of which the White Archangel is one of the commonest and closely resembles the stinging nettle and is found in its company."
1. A quotation from the 14th-century English mystic Dame Julian of Norwich: "Sin is behovabil [inevitable], but all shall be well and all shall be well and all manner of thing shall be well."
2. I.e., Charles I. He died "on the scaffold" in 1649, while his principal advisers, Archbishop Laud and Thomas Wentworth, earl of Strafford, were both executed earlier by the victorious parliamentary forces.
3. I.e., Milton.

195 A symbol perfected in death.
And all shall be well and
All manner of thing shall be well
By the purification of the motive
In the ground of our beseeching.[4]

IV

200 The dove descending breaks the air
With flame of incandescent terror
Of which the tongues declare
The one discharge from sin and error.
The only hope, or else despair
205   Lies in the choice of pyre or pyre—
   To be redeemed from fire by fire.

Who then devised the torment? Love.
Love is the unfamiliar Name
Behind the hands that wove
210 The intolerable shirt of flame[5]
Which human power cannot remove.
   We only live, only suspire
   Consumed by either fire or fire.

V

What we call the beginning is often the end
215 And to make an end is to make a beginning.
The end is where we start from. And every phrase
And sentence that is right (where every word is at home,
Taking its place to support the others,
The word neither diffident nor ostentatious,
220 And easy commerce of the old and the new,
The common word exact without vulgarity,
The formal word precise but not pedantic,
The complete consort[6] dancing together)
Every phrase and every sentence is an end and a beginning,
225 Every poem an epitaph. And any action
Is a step to the block, to the fire, down the sea's throat
Or to an illegible stone: and that is where we start.
We die with the dying:
See, they depart, and we go with them.
230 We are born with the dead:
See, they return, and bring us with them.
The moment of the rose and the moment of the yew-tree
Are of equal duration. A people without history
Is not redeemed from time, for history is a pattern

---

4. Dame Julian of Norwich was instructed in a vision that "the ground of our beseeching" is love.
5. Out of love for her husband, Hercules, Deianira gave him the poisoned shirt of Nessus. She had been told that it would increase his love for her, but instead it so corroded his flesh that in his agony he mounted a funeral pyre and burned himself to death.
6. Company, also harmony of sounds.

235 Of timeless moments. So, while the light fails
     On a winter's afternoon, in a secluded chapel
     History is now and England.

     With the drawing of this Love and the voice of this Calling[7]

     We shall not cease from exploration
240 And the end of all our exploring
     Will be to arrive where we started
     And know the place for the first time.
     Through the unknown, remembered gate
     When the last of earth left to discover
245 Is that which was the beginning;
     At the source of the longest river
     The voice of the hidden waterfall
     And the children in the apple tree
     Not known, because not looked for
250 But heard, half-heard, in the stillness
     Between two waves of the sea.[8]
     Quick now, here, now, always—
     A condition of complete simplicity
     (Costing not less than everything)
255 And all shall be well and
     All manner of thing shall be well
     When the tongues of flame are in-folded
     Into the crowned knot of fire
     And the fire and the rose are one.

1942   1942, 1943

Tradition and the Individual Talent[1]

1

In English writing we seldom speak of tradition, though we occasionally
apply its name in deploring its absence. We cannot refer to 'the tradition' or
to 'a tradition'; at most, we employ the adjective in saying that the poetry of
So-and-so is 'traditional' or even 'too traditional.' Seldom, perhaps, does the
word appear except in a phrase of censure. If otherwise, it is vaguely appro-
bative, with the implication, as to the work approved, of some pleasing
archæological reconstruction. You can hardly make the word agreeable to
English ears without this comfortable reference to the reassuring science of
archæology.

     Certainly the word is not likely to appear in our appreciations of living or
dead writers. Every nation, every race, has not only its own creative, but its
own critical turn of mind; and is even more oblivious of the shortcomings

7. This line is from the *Cloud of Unknowing*, an
anonymous 14th-century mystical work.
8. The voices of the children in the apple tree symbolize the sudden moment of insight. Cf. the conclusion to *Burnt Norton* (the first of the *Four
Quartets*), where the laughter of the children in the

garden has a like meaning: "Sudden in a shaft of
sunlight / Even while the dust moves / There rises
the hidden laughter / Of children in the foliage /
Quick now, here, now, always."
1. First published in the *Egoist* (1919) and later
collected in *The Sacred Wood* (1920).

and limitations of its critical habits than of those of its creative genius. We know, or think we know, from the enormous mass of critical writing that has appeared in the French language the critical method or habit of the French; we only conclude (we are such unconscious people) that the French are 'more critical' than we, and sometimes even plume ourselves a little with the fact, as if the French were the less spontaneous. Perhaps they are; but we might remind ourselves that criticism is as inevitable as breathing, and that we should be none the worse for articulating what passes in our minds when we read a book and feel an emotion about it, for criticizing our own minds in their work of criticism. One of the facts that might come to light in this process is our tendency to insist, when we praise a poet, upon those aspects of his work in which he least resembles anyone else. In these aspects or parts of his work we pretend to find what is individual, what is the peculiar essence of the man. We dwell with satisfaction upon the poet's difference from his predecessors, especially his immediate predecessors; we endeavour to find something that can be isolated in order to be enjoyed. Whereas if we approach a poet without this prejudice we shall often find that not only the best, but the most individual parts of his work may be those in which the dead poets, his ancestors, assert their immortality most vigorously. And I do not mean the impressionable period of adolescence, but the period of full maturity.

Yet if the only form of tradition, of handing down, consisted in following the ways of the immediate generation before us in a blind or timid adherence to its successes, 'tradition' should positively be discouraged. We have seen many such simple currents soon lost in the sand; and novelty is better than repetition. Tradition is a matter of much wider significance. It cannot be inherited, and if you want it you must obtain it by great labour. It involves, in the first place, the historical sense, which we may call nearly indispensable to any one who would continue to be a poet beyond his twenty-fifth year; and the historical sense involves a perception, not only of the pastness of the past, but of its presence; the historical sense compels a man to write not merely with his own generation in his bones, but with a feeling that the whole of the literature of Europe from Homer and within it the whole of the literature of his own country has a simultaneous existence and composes a simultaneous order. This historical sense, which is a sense of the timeless as well as of the temporal and of the timeless and of the temporal together, is what makes a writer traditional. And it is at the same time what makes a writer most acutely conscious of his place in time, of his own contemporaneity.

No poet, no artist of any art, has his complete meaning alone. His significance, his appreciation is the appreciation of his relation to the dead poets and artists. You cannot value him alone; you must set him, for contrast and comparison, among the dead. I mean this as a principle of æsthetic, not merely historical, criticism. The necessity that he shall conform, that he shall cohere, is not one-sided; what happens when a new work of art is created is something that happens simultaneously to all the works of art which preceded it. The existing monuments form an ideal order among themselves, which is modified by the introduction of the new (the really new) work of art among them. The existing order is complete before the new work arrives; for order to persist after the supervention of novelty, the *whole* existing order must be, if ever so slightly, altered; and so the relations, proportions, values of each work of art toward the whole are readjusted; and this is conformity between the old and the new. Whoever has approved this idea of order, of the form of European, of English literature will not find it preposterous that the past should be altered by the present as much as the present is directed by the past. And the poet who is aware of this will be aware of great difficulties and responsibilities.

In a peculiar sense he will be aware also that he must inevitably be judged by the standards of the past. I say judged, not amputated, by them; not judged to be as good as, or worse or better than, the dead; and certainly not judged by the canons of dead critics. It is a judgment, a comparison, in which two things are measured by each other. To conform merely would be for the new work not really to conform at all; it would not be new, and would therefore not be a work of art. And we do not quite say that the new is more valuable because it fits in; but its fitting in is a test of its value—a test, it is true, which can only be slowly and cautiously applied, for we are none of us infallible judges of conformity. We say: it appears to conform, and is perhaps individual, or it appears individual, and may conform; but we are hardly likely to find that it is one and not the other.

To proceed to a more intelligible exposition of the relation of the poet to the past: he can neither take the past as a lump, an indiscriminate bolus,[2] nor can he form himself wholly on one or two private admirations, nor can he form himself wholly upon one preferred period. The first course is inadmissible, the second is an important experience of youth, and the third is a pleasant and highly desirable supplement. The poet must be very conscious of the main current, which does not at all flow invariably through the most distinguished reputations. He must be quite aware of the obvious fact that art never improves, but that the material of art is never quite the same. He must be aware that the mind of Europe—the mind of his own country—a mind which he learns in time to be much more important than his own private mind—is a mind which changes, and that this change is a development which abandons nothing *en route,* which does not superannuate either Shakespeare, or Homer, or the rock drawing of the Magdalenian[3] draftsmen. That this development, refinement perhaps, complication certainly, is not, from the point of view of the artist, any improvement. Perhaps not even an improvement from the point of view of the psychologist or not to the extent which we imagine; perhaps only in the end based upon a complication in economics and machinery. But the difference between the present and the past is that the conscious present is an awareness of the past in a way and to an extent which the past's awareness of itself cannot show.

Someone said: 'The dead writers are remote from us because we *know* so much more than they did.' Precisely, and they are that which we know.

I am alive to a usual objection to what is clearly part of my programme for the *métier* of poetry. The objection is that the doctrine requires a ridiculous amount of erudition (pedantry), a claim which can be rejected by appeal to the lives of poets in any pantheon. It will even be affirmed that much learning deadens or perverts poetic sensibility. While, however, we persist in believing

2. A round mass of anything: a large pill.
3. The most advanced culture of the European

Paleolithic period (from discoveries at La Madeleine, France).

that a poet ought to know as much as will not encroach upon his necessary receptivity and necessary laziness, it is not desirable to confine knowledge to whatever can be put into a useful shape for examinations, drawing-rooms, or the still more pretentious modes of publicity. Some can absorb knowledge, the more tardy must sweat for it. Shakespeare acquired more essential history from Plutarch[4] than most men could from the whole British Museum. What is to be insisted upon is that the poet must develop or procure the consciousness of the past and that he should continue to develop this consciousness throughout his career.

What happens is a continual surrender of himself as he is at the moment to something which is more valuable. The progress of an artist is a continual self-sacrifice, a continual extinction of personality.

There remains to define this process of depersonalisation and its relation to the sense of tradition. It is in this depersonalization that art may be said to approach the condition of science. I, therefore, invite you to consider, as a suggestive analogy, the action which takes place when a bit of finely filiated[5] platinum is introduced into a chamber containing oxygen and sulphur dioxide.

II

Honest criticism and sensitive appreciation are directed not upon the poet but upon the poetry. If we attend to the confused cries of the newspaper critics and the susurrus[6] of popular repetition that follows, we shall hear the names of poets in great numbers; if we seek not Blue-book[7] knowledge but the enjoyment of poetry, and ask for a poem, we shall seldom find it. I have tried to point out the importance of the relation of the poem to other poems by other authors, and suggested the conception of poetry as a living whole of all the poetry that has ever been written. The other aspect of this Impersonal theory of poetry is the relation of the poem to its author. And I hinted, by an analogy, that the mind of the mature poet differs from that of the immature one not precisely in any valuation of 'personality,' not being necessarily more interesting, or having 'more to say,' but rather by being a more finely perfected medium in which special, or very varied, feelings are at liberty to enter into new combinations.

The analogy was that of the catalyst.[8] When the two gases previously mentioned are mixed in the presence of a filament of platinum, they form sulphurous acid. This combination takes place only if the platinum is present; nevertheless the newly formed acid contains no trace of platinum, and the platinum itself is apparently unaffected; has remained inert, neutral, and unchanged. The mind of the poet is the shred of platinum. It may partly or exclusively operate upon the experience of the man himself; but, the more perfect the artist, the more completely separate in him will be the man who suffers and the mind which creates; the more perfectly will the mind digest and transmute the passions which are its material.

The experience, you will notice, the elements which enter the presence of

---

4. Plutarch (1st century C.E.), Greek biographer of famous Greeks and Romans from whose work Shakespeare drew the plots of his Roman plays.
5. Drawn out like a thread.
6. Murmuring, buzzing (Latin).
7. British official government publication.
8. Substance that triggers a chemical change without itself being affected by the reaction.

the transforming catalyst, are of two kinds: emotions and feelings. The effect of a work of art upon the person who enjoys it is an experience different in kind from any experience not of art. It may be formed out of one emotion, or may be a combination of several; and various feelings, inhering for the writer in particular words or phrases or images, may be added to compose the final result. Or great poetry may be made without the direct use of any emotion whatever: composed out of feelings solely. Canto XV of the *Inferno* (Brunetto Latini)[9] is a working up of the emotion evident in the situation; but the effect, though single as that of any work of art, is obtained by considerable complexity of detail. The last quatrain gives an image, a feeling attaching to an image, which 'came,' which did not develop simply out of what precedes, but which was probably in suspension in the poet's mind until the proper combination arrived for it to add itself to.[1] The poet's mind is in fact a receptacle for seizing and storing up numberless feelings, phrases, images, which remain there until all the particles which can unite to form a new compound are present together.

If you compare several representative passages of the greatest poetry you see how great is the variety of types of combination, and also how completely any semi-ethical criterion of 'sublimity' misses the mark. For it is not the 'greatness,' the intensity, of the emotions, the components, but the intensity of the artistic process, the pressure, so to speak, under which the fusion takes place, that counts. The episode of Paolo and Francesca[2] employs a definite emotion, but the intensity of the poetry is something quite different from whatever intensity in the supposed experience it may give the impression of. It is no more intense, furthermore, than Canto XXVI,[3] the voyage of Ulysses, which has not the direct dependence upon an emotion. Great variety is possible in the process of transmutation of emotion: the murder of Agamemnon,[4] or the agony of Othello, gives an artistic effect apparently closer to a possible original than the scenes from Dante. In the *Agamemnon,* the artistic emotion approximates to the emotion of an actual spectator; in *Othello* to the emotion of the protagonist himself. But the difference between art and the event is always absolute; the combination which is the murder of Agamemnon is probably as complex as that which is the voyage of Ulysses. In either case there has been a fusion of elements. The ode of Keats contains a number of feelings which have nothing particular to do with the nightingale, but which the nightingale, partly, perhaps, because of its attractive name, and partly because of its reputation, served to bring together.

The point of view which I am struggling to attack is perhaps related to the metaphysical theory of the substantial unity of the soul: for my meaning is, that the poet has, not a 'personality' to express, but a particular medium, which is only a medium and not a personality, in which impressions and experiences combine in peculiar and unexpected ways. Impressions and experiences which are important for the man may take no place in the poetry,

9. Dante meets in Hell his old master Brunetto Latini, suffering eternal punishment for unnatural lust yet still loved and admired by Dante, who addresses him with affectionate courtesy (see n. 1, just below).

1. Dante's strange interview with Brunetto is over, and Brunetto moves off to continue his punishment: "Then he turned round, and seemed like one of those / Who run for the green cloth [in the footrace] at Verona / In the field; and he seemed among them / Not the loser but the winner."

2. Illicit lovers whom Dante meets in the second circle of Hell (*Inferno* 5) and at whose punishment and sorrows he swoons with pity.

3. Of the *Inferno.* Ulysses, suffering in Hell for "false counseling," tells Dante of his final voyage.

4. By his wife, Clytemnestra; the central action of Aeschylus's play *Agamemnon.*

and those which become important in the poetry may play quite a negligible part in the man, the personality.

I will quote a passage which is unfamiliar enough to be regarded with fresh attention in the light—or darkness—of these observations:

> And now methinks I could e'en chide myself
> For doating on her beauty, though her death
> Shall be revenged after no common action.
> Does the silkworm expend her yellow labours
> For thee? For thee does she undo herself?
> Are lordships sold to maintain ladyships
> For the poor benefit of a bewildering minute?
> Why does yon fellow falsify highways,
> And put his life between the judge's lips,
> To refine such a thing—keeps horse and men
> To beat their valours for her? . . .[5]

In this passage (as is evident if it is taken in its context) there is a combination of positive and negative emotions: an intensely strong attraction toward beauty and an equally intense fascination by the ugliness which is contrasted with it and which destroys it. This balance of contrasted emotion is in the dramatic situation to which the speech is pertinent, but that situation alone is inadequate to it. This is, so to speak, the structural emotion, provided by the drama. But the whole effect, the dominant tone, is due to the fact that a number of floating feelings, having an affinity to this emotion by no means superficially evident, have combined with it to give us a new art emotion.

It is not in his personal emotions, the emotions provoked by particular events in his life, that the poet is in any way remarkable or interesting. His particular emotions may be simple, or crude, or flat. The emotion in his poetry will be a very complex thing, but not with the complexity of the emotions of people who have very complex or unusual emotions in life. One error, in fact, of eccentricity in poetry is to seek for new human emotions to express; and in this search for novelty in the wrong place it discovers the perverse. The business of the poet is not to find new emotions, but to use the ordinary ones and, in working them up into poetry, to express feelings which are not in actual emotions at all. And emotions which he has never experienced will serve his turn as well as those familiar to him. Consequently, we must believe that 'emotion recollected in tranquillity'[6] is an inexact formula. For it is neither emotion, nor recollection, nor, without distortion of meaning, tranquility. It is a concentration, and a new thing resulting from the concentration, of a very great number of experiences which to the practical and active person would not seem to be experiences at all; it is a concentration which does not happen consciously or of deliberation. These experiences are not 'recollected,' and they finally unite in an atmosphere which is 'tranquil' only in that it is a passive attending upon the event. Of course this is not quite the whole story. There is a great deal, in the writing of poetry, which must be conscious and deliberate. In fact, the bad poet is usually unconscious where he ought to be conscious, and conscious where he ought to be unconscious.

---

5. From Cyril Tourneur, *The Revenger's Tragedy* 3.4 (1607).
6. Wordsworth's, *Preface to Lyrical Ballads* (2nd ed., 1800). Wordsworth said that poetry "takes its origin from emotion recollected in tranquility."

Both errors tend to make him 'personal.' Poetry is not a turning loose of emotion, but an escape from emotion; it is not the expression of personality, but an escape from personality. But, of course, only those who have personality and emotions know what it means to want to escape from these things.

III

ὁ δὲ νοῦζ ἴσωζ θειότερόν τι καὶ ἀπαθέζ ἐστιν.[7]

This essay proposes to halt at the frontier of metaphysics or mysticism, and confine itself to such practical conclusions as can be applied by the responsible person interested in poetry. To divert interest from the poet to the poetry is a laudable aim: for it would conduce to a juster estimation of actual poetry, good and bad. There are many people who appreciate the expression of sincere emotion in verse, and there is a smaller number of people who can appreciate technical excellence. But very few know when there is an expression of *significant* emotion, emotion which has its life in the poem and not in the history of the poet. The emotion of art is impersonal. And the poet cannot reach this impersonality without surrendering himself wholly to the work to be done. And he is not likely to know what is to be done unless he lives in what is not merely the present, but the present moment of the past, unless he is conscious, not of what is dead, but of what is already living.

1919, 1920

The Metaphysical Poets

By collecting these poems[1] from the work of a generation more often named than read, and more often read than profitably studied, Professor Grierson has rendered a service of some importance. Certainly the reader will meet with many poems already preserved in other anthologies, at the same time that he discovers poems such as those of Aurelian Townshend or Lord Herbert of Cherbury here included. But the function of such an anthology as this is neither that of Professor Saintsbury's admirable edition of Caroline poets nor that of the *Oxford Book of English Verse*. Mr. Grierson's book is in itself a piece of criticism and a provocation of criticism; and we think that he was right in including so many poems of Donne, elsewhere (though not in many editions) accessible, as documents in the case of 'metaphysical poetry.' The phrase has long done duty as a term of abuse or as the label of a quaint and pleasant taste. The question is to what extent the so-called metaphysicals formed a school (in our own time we should say a 'movement'), and how far this so-called school or movement is a digression from the main current.

Not only is it extremely difficult to define metaphysical poetry, but difficult

7. Aristotle's *De Anima* ("On the Soul") 1.4: "The mind is doubtless something more divine and unimpressionable."
1. *Metaphysical Lyrics and Poems of the Seven-* *teenth Century: Donne to Butler*. Selected and edited, with an Essay, by Herbert J. C. Grierson (1921). Eliot's essay was originally a review of this book in the London *Times Literary Supplement*.

to decide what poets practise it and in which of their verses. The poetry of Donne (to whom Marvell and Bishop King are sometimes nearer than any of the other authors) is late Elizabethan, its feeling often very close to that of Chapman. The 'courtly' poetry is derivative from Jonson, who borrowed liberally from the Latin; it expires in the next century with the sentiment and witticism of Prior. There is finally the devotional verse of Herbert, Vaughan, and Crashaw (echoed long after by Christina Rossetti and Francis Thompson); Crashaw, sometimes more profound and less sectarian than the others, has a quality which returns through the Elizabethan period to the early Italians. It is difficult to find any precise use of metaphor, simile, or other conceit, which is common to all the poets and at the same time important enough as an element of style to isolate these poets as a group. Donne, and often Cowley, employ a device which is sometimes considered characteristically 'metaphysical'; the elaboration (contrasted with the condensation) of a figure of speech to the furthest stage to which ingenuity can carry it. Thus Cowley develops the commonplace comparison of the world to a chess-board through long stanzas (*To Destiny*), and Donne, with more grace, in *A Valediction*,[2] the comparison of two lovers to a pair of compasses. But elsewhere we find, instead of the mere explication of the content of a comparison, a development by rapid association of thought which requires considerable agility on the part of the reader.

> On a round ball
> A workeman that hath copies by, can lay
> An Europe, Afrique, and an Asia,
> And quickly make that, which was nothing, All,
>> So doth each teare,
>> Which thee doth weare,
> A globe, yea world by that impression grow,
> Till thy tears mixt with mine doe overflow
> This world, by waters sent from thee, my heaven dissolved so.[3]

Here we find at least two connexions which are not implicit in the first figure, but are forced upon it by the poet: from the geographer's globe to the tear, and the tear to the deluge. On the other hand, some of Donne's most successful and characteristic effects are secured by brief words and sudden contrasts:

> A bracelet of bright hair about the bone,[4]

where the most powerful effect is produced by the sudden contrast of associations of 'bright hair' and of 'bone'. This telescoping of images and multiplied associations is characteristic of the phrase of some of the dramatists of the period which Donne knew: not to mention Shakespeare, it is frequent in Middleton, Webster, and Tourneur, and is one of the sources of the vitality of their language.

Johnson, who employed the term 'metaphysical poets', apparently having Donne, Cleveland, and Cowley chiefly in mind, remarks of them that 'the most heterogeneous ideas are yoked by violence together'.[5] The force of this

---

2. I.e., *A Valediction: Forbidding Mourning.*
3. Donne's *A Valediction: Of Weeping*, lines 10–18.
4. *The Relic,* line 6.
5. See Samuel Johnson's *Cowley.*

impeachment lies in the failure of the conjunction, the fact that often the ideas are yoked but not united; and if we are to judge of styles of poetry by their abuse, enough examples may be found in Cleveland to justify Johnson's condemnation. But a degree of heterogeneity of material compelled into unity by the operation of the poet's mind is omnipresent in poetry. We need not select for illustration such a line as:

> Notre âme est un trois-mâts cherchant son Icarie;[6]

we may find it in some of the best lines of Johnson himself (*The Vanity of Human Wishes*):

> His fate was destined to a barren strand,
> A petty fortress, and a dubious hand;
> He left a name at which the world grew pale,
> To point a moral, or adorn a tale.

where the effect is due to a contrast of ideas, different in degree but the same in principle, as that which Johnson mildly reprehended. And in one of the finest poems of the age (a poem which could not have been written in any other age), the *Exequy* of Bishop King, the extended comparison is used with perfect success: the idea and the simile become one, in the passage in which the Bishop illustrates his impatience to see his dead wife, under the figure of a journey:

> Stay for me there; I will not faile
> To meet thee in that hollow Vale.
> And think not much of my delay;
> I am already on the way,
> And follow thee with all the speed
> Desire can make, or sorrows breed.
> Each minute is a short degree,
> And ev'ry hour a step towards thee,
> At night when I betake to rest,
> Next morn I rise nearer my West
> Of life, almost by eight houres sail,
> Than when sleep breath'd his drowsy gale. . . .
> But heark! My Pulse, like a soft Drum
> Beats my approach, tells Thee I come;
> And slow howere my marches be,
> I shall at last sit down by Thee.

(In the last few lines there is that effect of terror which is several times attained by one of Bishop King's admirers, Edgar Poe.) Again, we may justly take these quatrains from Lord Herbert's Ode,[7] stanzas which would, we think, be immediately pronounced to be of the metaphysical school:

---

6. From Charles Baudelaire's *Le Voyage:* "Our soul is a three-masted ship searching for her Icarie"; Icarie is an imaginary utopia in *Voyage en Icarie,* 1840, a novel by the French socialist Etienne Cabet.

7. Lord Herbert of Cherbury (1583–1648), brother of George Herbert. The "Ode" is his *Ode upon a Question moved, whether Love should continue forever?*

> *So when from hence we shall be gone,*
> *And be no more, nor you, nor I,*
> *As one another's mystery,*
> *Each shall be both, yet both but one.*

> *This said, in her up-lifted face,*
> *Her eyes, which did that beauty crown,*
> *Were like two stars, that having faln down,*
> *Look up again to find their place:*

> *While such a moveless silent peace*
> *Did seize on their becalmed sense,*
> *One would have thought some influence*
> *Their ravished spirits did possess.*

There is nothing in these lines (with the possible exception of the stars, a simile not at once grasped, but lovely and justified) which fits Johnson's general observations on the metaphysical poets in his essay on Cowley. A good deal resides in the richness of association which is at the same time borrowed from and given to the word 'becalmed'; but the meaning is clear, the language simple and elegant. It is to be observed that the language of these poets is as a rule simple and pure; in the verse of George Herbert this simplicity is carried as far as it can go—a simplicity emulated without success by numerous modern poets. The *structure* of the sentences, on the other hand, is sometimes far from simple, but this is not a vice; it is a fidelity to thought and feeling. The effect, at its best, is far less artificial than that of an ode by Gray. And as this fidelity induces variety of thought and feeling, so it induces variety of music. We doubt whether, in the eighteenth century, could be found two poems in nominally the same metre, so dissimilar as Marvell's *Coy Mistress* and Crashaw's *Saint Teresa;* the one producing an effect of great speed by the use of short syllables, and the other an ecclesiastical solemnity by the use of long ones:

> *Love, thou art absolute sole lord*
> *Of life and death.*

If so shrewd and sensitive (though so limited) a critic as Johnson failed to define metaphysical poetry by its faults, it is worth while to inquire whether we may not have more success by adopting the opposite method: by assuming that the poets of the seventeenth century (up to the Revolution)[8] were the direct and normal development of the precedent age; and, without prejudicing their case by the adjective 'metaphysical', consider whether their virtue was not something permanently valuable, which subsequently disappeared, but ought not to have disappeared. Johnson has hit, perhaps by accident, on one of their peculiarities, when he observes that 'their attempts were always analytic'; he would not agree that, after the dissociation, they put the material together again in a new unity.

It is certain that the dramatic verse of the later Elizabethan and early Jacobean poets expresses a degree of development of sensibility which is not found in any of the prose, good as it often is. If we except Marlowe, a man

8. Of 1688; when James II was replaced by William and Mary.

of prodigious intelligence, these dramatists were directly or indirectly (it is at lest a tenable theory) affected by Montaigne. Even if we except also Jonson and Chapman, these two were probably erudite, and were notably men who incorporated their erudition into their sensibility: their mode of feeling was directly and freshly altered by their reading and thought. In Chapman especially there is a direct sensuous apprehension of thought, or a recreation of thought into feeling, which is exactly what we find in Donne:

> in this one thing, all the discipline
> Of manners and of manhood is contained;
> A man to join himself with th' Universe
> In his main sway, and make in all things fit
> One with that All, and go on, round as it;
> Not plucking from the whole his wretched part,
> And into straits, or into nought revert,
> Wishing the complete Universe might be
> Subject to such a rag of it as he;
> But to consider great Necessity.[9]

We compare this with some modern passage:

> No, when the fight begins within himself,
> A man's worth something. God stoops o'er his head,
> Satan looks up between his feet—both tug—
> He's left, himself, i' the middle; the soul wakes
> And grows. Prolong that battle through his life![1]

It is perhaps somewhat less fair, though very tempting (as both poets are concerned with the perpetuation of love by offspring), to compare with the stanzas already quoted from Lord Herbert's Ode the following from Tennyson:

> One walked between his wife and child,
> With measured footfall firm and mild,
> And now and then he gravely smiled.
> The prudent partner of his blood
> Leaned on him, faithful, gentle, good,
> Wearing the rose of womanhood.
> And in their double love secure,
> The little maiden walked demure,
> Pacing with downward eyelids pure.
> These three made unity so sweet,
> My frozen heart began to beat,
> Remembering its ancient heat.[2]

The difference is not a simple difference of degree between poets. It is something which had happened to the mind of England between the time of Donne or Lord Herbert of Cherbury and the time of Tennyson and Browning; it is the difference between the intellectual poet and the reflective poet. Tennyson and Browning are poets, and they think; but they do not feel their thought as immediately as the odour of a rose. A thought to Donne was an

9. From *The Revenge of Bussy d'Ambois* (4.1.137–146).
1. Robert Browning, *Bishop Blougram's Apology*,
lines 693–97.
2. *The Two Voices*, lines 412–23.

experience; it modified his sensibility. When a poet's mind is perfectly equipped for its work, it is constantly amalgamating disparate experience; the ordinary man's experience is chaotic, irregular, fragmentary. The latter falls in love, or reads Spinoza, and these two experiences have nothing to do with each other, or with the noise of the typewriter or the smell of cooking; in the mind of the poet these experiences are always forming new wholes.

We may express the difference by the following theory: The poets of the seventeenth century, the successors of the dramatists of the sixteenth, possessed a mechanism of sensibility which could devour any kind of experience. They are simple, artificial, difficult, or fantastic, as their predecessors were; no less nor more than Dante, Guido Cavalcanti, Guinicelli, or Cino.[3] In the seventeenth century a dissociation of sensibility set in, from which we have never recovered; and this dissociation, as is natural, was aggravated by the influence of the two most powerful poets of the century, Milton and Dryden. Each of these men performed certain poetic functions so magnificently well that the magnitude of the effect concealed the absence of others. The language went on and in some respects improved; the best verse of Collins, Gray, Johnson, and even Goldsmith satisfies some of our fastidious demands better than that of Donne or Marvell or King. But while the language became more refined, the feeling became more crude. The feeling, the sensibility, expressed in the *Country Churchyard* (to say nothing of Tennyson and Browning) is cruder than that in the *Coy Mistress*.

The second effect of the influence of Milton and Dryden followed from the first, and was therefore slow in manifestation. The sentimental age began early in the eighteenth century, and continued. The poets revolted against the ratiocinative, the descriptive; they thought and felt by fits, unbalanced; they reflected. In one or two passages of Shelley's *Triumph of Life*, in the second *Hyperion*, there are traces of a struggle toward unification of sensibility. But Keats and Shelley died, and Tennyson and Browning ruminated.

After this brief exposition of a theory—too brief, perhaps, to carry conviction—we may ask, what would have been the fate of the 'metaphysical' had the current of poetry descended in a direct line from them, as it descended in a direct line to them? They would not, certainly, be classified as metaphysical. The possible interests of a poet are unlimited; the more intelligent he is the better; the more intelligent he is the more likely that he will have interests: our only condition is that he turn them into poetry, and not merely meditate on them poetically. A philosophical theory which has entered into poetry is established, for its truth or falsity in one sense ceases to matter, and its truth in another sense is proved. The poets in question have, like other poets, various faults. But they were, at best, engaged in the task of trying to find the verbal equivalent for states of mind and feeling. And this means both that they are more mature, and that they wear better, than later poets of certainly not less literary ability.

It is not a permanent necessity that poets should be interested in philosophy, or in any other subject. We can only say that it appears likely that poets in our civilization, as it exists at present, must be *difficult*. Our civilization comprehends great variety and complexity, and this variety and complexity,

3. These last three poets, all of whom lived in the 13th century, were members of the Tuscan school of lyric love poets. Guido Guinicelli was hailed by Dante in the *Purgatorio* as "father of Italian poets." Cino da Pistoia was a friend of Dante and Petrarch.

playing upon a refined sensibility, must produce various and complex results. The poet must become more and more comprehensive, more allusive, more indirect, in order to force, to dislocate if necessary, language into his meaning. (A brilliant and extreme statement of this view, with which it is not requisite to associate oneself, is that of M Jean Epstein, *La Poésie d'aujourd'hui*.[4]) Hence we get something which looks very much like the conceit—we get, in fact, a method curiously similar to that of the 'metaphysical poets', similar also in its use of obscure words and of simple phrasing.

> *O géraniums diaphanes, guerroyeurs sortilèges,*
> *Sacrilèges monomanes!*
> *Emballages, dévergondages, douches! O pressoirs*
> *Des vendanges des grands soirs!*
> *Layettes aux abois,*
> *Thyrses au fond des bois!*
> *Transfusions, représailles,*
> *Relevailles, compresses et l'éternal potion,*
> *Angélus! n'en pouvoir plus*
> *De débâcles nuptiales! de débâcles nuptiales!*[5]

The same poet could write also simply:

> *Elle est bien loin, elle pleure,*
> *Le grand vent se lamente aussi*[6] . . .

Jules Laforgue, and Tristan Corbière[7] in many of his poems, are nearer to the 'school of Donne' than any modern English poet. But poets more classical than they have the same essential quality of transmuting ideas into sensations, of transforming an observation into a state of mind.

> *Pour l'enfant, amoureux de cartes et d'estampes,*
> *L'univers est égal à son vaste appétit.*
> *Ah, que le monde est grand à la clarté des lampes!*
> *Aux yeux du souvenir que le monde est petit!*[8]

In French literature the great master of the seventeenth century—Racine— and the great master of the nineteenth—Baudelaire—are in some ways more like each other than they are like anyone else. The greatest two masters of diction are also the greatest two psychologists, the most curious explorers of the soul. It is interesting to speculate whether it is not a misfortune that two of the greatest masters of diction in our language, Milton and Dryden, triumph with a dazzling disregard of the soul. If we continued to produce Miltons and Drydens it might not so much matter, but as things are it is a pity

---

4. Poetry of today (French).
5. From *Derniers vers X* ("Last Poems," 1890), by Jules Laforgue (1860–1887): "O transparent geraniums, warrior incantations, / Monomaniac sacrileges! / Packing materials, shamelessnesses, shower baths! O wine presses / Of great evening vintages! / Hard-pressed baby linen, / Thyrsis in the depths of the woods! / Transfusions, reprisals, / Churchings, compresses, and the eternal potion, / Angelus! no longer to be borne [are] / Catastrophic marriages! catastrophic marriages!" Eliot oddly sees a similarity between this kind of hysterical free association and the strictly ordered imagery of the Metaphysicals. But it is the combination of "obscure words and simple phrasing" that strikes him in both.
6. From *Derniers vers XI, Sur une défunte* ("On a Dead Woman"): "She is far away, she weeps / The great wind mourns also."
7. French symbolist poet (1845–1875).
8. From Baudelaire's *Le Voyage*: "For the child, in love with maps and prints, / The universe matches his vast appetite. / Ah, how big the world is by lamplight! How small the world is to the eyes of memory!"

that English poetry has remained so incomplete. Those who object to the 'artificiality' of Milton or Dryden sometimes tell us to 'look into our hearts and write.' But that is not looking deep enough; Racine or Donne looked into a good deal more than the heart. One must look into the cerebral cortex, the nervous system, and the digestive tracts.

May we not conclude, then, that Donne, Crashaw, Vaughan, Herbert and Lord Herbert, Marvell, King, Cowley at his best, are in the direct current of English poetry, and that their faults should be reprimanded by this standard rather than coddled by antiquarian affection? They have been enough praised in terms which are implicit limitations because they are 'metaphysical' or 'witty,' 'quaint' or 'obscure,' though at their best they have not these attributes more than other serious poets. On the other hand, we must not reject the criticism of Johnson (a dangerous person to disagree with) without having mastered it, without having assimilated the Johnsonian canons of taste. In reading the celebrated passage in his essay on Cowley we must remember that by wit he clearly means something more serious than we usually mean to-day; in his criticism of their versification we must remember in what a narrow discipline he was trained, but also how well trained; we must remember that Johnson tortures chiefly the chief offenders, Cowley and Cleveland. It would be a fruitful work, and one requiring a substantial book, to break up the classification of Johnson (for there has been none since) and exhibit these poets in all their difference of kind and of degree, from the massive music of Donne to the faint, pleasing tinkle of Aurelian Townshend—whose *Dialogue between a Pilgrim and Time* is one of the few regrettable omissions from the excellent anthology of Professor Grierson.

1921

KATHERINE MANSFIELD
1888–1923

Kathleen Mansfield Beauchamp was born in Wellington, New Zealand, daughter of a respected businessman who was later knighted. In 1903 the family came to London, where Kathleen and her sisters entered Queen's College, the first institution in England founded expressly for the higher education of women. The family returned to New Zealand, leaving the girls in London, but Mr. and Mrs. Beauchamp brought their daughters home in 1906. By this time Kathleen had written a number of poems, sketches, and stories; and after experimenting with different pen names, she eventually adopted that of Katherine Mansfield. She was restless and ambitious and chafed against the narrowness of middle-class life in New Zealand, at that time still very much a new country in the shadow of the British Empire.

In March 1907 her mother gave a garden party in their Wellington house; a fatal street accident to a neighbor living in a poor quarter nearby nearly spoiled the festive atmosphere of the day. (This was to form the basis of her story *The Garden Party*, but Laura's sensibility as portrayed in that story is subtler and finer than anything the author appears to have herself felt at that time. The story, like so much of Mansfield's reworking of her New Zealand experiences in her last years, represents a kind of atonement for her younger self.) In July 1908 she left again for London and never returned to New Zealand. Very much a rebel, she became involved in a number of love affairs and in 1909 suddenly married G. C. Bowden, a teacher of singing and elocution, but left him the same evening. Shortly afterward she became pregnant by another man and went to Germany to await the birth, but she had a miscarriage there. Her experiences in Germany are told in carefully observed sketches full of ironic detail in her first published book, *In a German Pension* (1911).

In 1910 she briefly resumed life with Bowden, who put her in touch with A. R. Orage, editor of the avant garde periodical *The New Age*. There she published a number of her stories and sketches. At the end of 1911 she met the critic John Middleton Murry, editor of *Rhythm*. She became involved with both Murry and *Rhythm* and lived with Murry fairly continuously for the rest of her life, marrying him in 1918 when Bowden finally divorced her. The Murrys became friendly with D. H. Lawrence and his wife, Frieda, but it was a strange relationship that developed into a hatred by Lawrence of both Mansfield and Murry. This is all part of a complicated story of literary and personal sensitivities and ambitions that involves many of the writers and artists of the day, but the important thing is that during all this time Mansfield was experimenting in technique and refining her art in an attempt to achieve a kind of short story that by precision of style and imagery and a symbolic patterning of incident would project insights into certain kinds of experience. The death in World War I in October 1915 of her much-loved younger brother sent her imagination back to their childhood days in New Zealand and in doing so gave a fresh charge and significance to her writing. Using her newly developed style with an ever greater subtlety and sensitivity, she now produced her best stories: *Prelude, Daughters of the Late Colonel, At the Bay,* and *The Garden Party*. With the publication of *The Garden Party and Other Stories* in February 1922, Mansfield's place as a master of the modern short story was ensured. But she was now gravely ill with tuberculosis and died suddenly in January 1923 at Fontainebleau, France, where she had gone to try to find a cure by adopting the methods of the controversial mystic George Ivanovich Gurdjieff.

Mansfield's life is one of the strangest stories in twentieth-century English literary history. Beginning in rebellion and ending in almost mystic acceptance, she proceeded through a variety of literary styles, but her best and most characteristic work was produced in the last years of her short life when she was able to combine incident, image, symbol, and structure in a way comparable with, yet interestingly different from, Joyce's method in *Dubliners. Daughters of the Late Colonel* shows her working characteristically through suggestion rather than explicit development, with the subdued elegiac sense of wasted lives providing a note of potential tragedy, although the surface is restrained comedy. The meaning is achieved most of all through the atmosphere, built up through the accumulation of small strokes, none of which seems in itself more than a piece of shrewdly observed realistic detail. The ability to manipulate time is another quality Mansfield shows in some of her best work: she makes particularly effective use of the unobtrusive flashback, where we find ourselves in an earlier phase of the action without quite knowing how we got there although fully aware of its relevance to the total action and atmosphere.

The Daughters of the Late Colonel

I

The week after was one of the busiest weeks of their lives. Even when they went to bed it was only their bodies that lay down and rested; their minds went on, thinking things out, talking things over, wondering, deciding, trying to remember where . . .

Constantia lay like a statue, her hands by her sides, her feet just overlapping each other, the sheet up to her chin. She stared at the ceiling.

'Do you think father would mind if we gave his top-hat to the porter?'

'The porter?' snapped Josephine. 'Why ever the porter? What a very extraordinary idea!'

'Because,' said Constantia slowly, 'he must often have to go to funerals. And I noticed at—at the cemetery that he only had a bowler.' She paused. 'I thought then how very much he'd appreciate a top-hat. We ought to give him a present, too. He was always very nice to father.'

'But,' cried Josephine, flouncing on her pillow and staring across the dark at Constantia, 'father's head!' And suddenly, for one awful moment, she nearly giggled. Not, of course, that she felt in the least like giggling. It must have been habit. Years ago, when they had stayed awake at night talking, their beds had simply heaved. And now the porter's head, disappearing, popped out, like a candle, under father's hat . . . . The giggle mounted, mounted; she clenched her hands; she fought it down; she frowned fiercely at the dark and said 'Remember' terribly sternly.

'We can decide tomorrow,' she sighed.

Constantia had noticed nothing; she sighed.

'Do you think we ought to have our dressing-gowns dyed as well?'

'Black?' almost shrieked Josephine.

'Well, what else?' said Constantia. 'I was thinking—it doesn't seem quite sincere, in a way, to wear black out of doors and when we're fully dressed, and then when we're at home—'

'But nobody sees us,' said Josephine. She gave the bedclothes such a twitch that both her feet became uncovered and she had to creep up the pillows to get them well under again.

'Kate does,' said Constantia. 'And the postman very well might.'

Josephine thought of her dark-red slippers, which matched her dressing-gown, and of Constantia's favourite indefinite green ones which went with hers. Black! Two black dressing-gowns and two pairs of black woolly slippers, creeping off to the bathroom like black cats.

'I don't think it's absolutely necessary,' said she.

Silence. Then Constantia said, 'We shall have to post the papers with the notice in them tomorrow to catch the Ceylon mail . . . . How many letters have we had up till now?'

'Twenty-three.'

Josephine had replied to them all, and twenty-three times when she came to 'We miss our dear father so much' she had broken down and had to use her handkerchief, and on some of them even to soak up a very light-blue tear with an edge of blotting-paper. Strange! She couldn't have put it on—but twenty-three times. Even now, though, when she said over to herself sadly 'We miss our dear father *so* much,' she could have cried if she'd wanted to.

'Have you got enough stamps?' came from Constantia.

'Oh, how can I tell?' said Josephine crossly. 'What's the good of asking me that now?'

'I was just wondering,' said Constantia mildly.

Silence again. There came a little rustle, a scurry, a hop.

'A mouse,' said Constantia.

'It can't be a mouse because there aren't any crumbs,' said Josephine.

'But it doesn't know there aren't,' said Constantia.

A spasm of pity squeezed her heart. Poor little thing! She wished she'd left a tiny piece of biscuit on the dressing-table. It was awful to think of it not finding anything. What would it do?

'I can't think how they manage to live at all,' she said slowly.

'Who?' demanded Josephine.

And Constantia said more loudly than she meant to, 'Mice.'

Josephine was furious. 'Oh, what nonsense, Con!' she said. 'What have mice got to do with it? You're asleep.'

'I don't think I am,' said Constantia. She shut her eyes to make sure. She was.

Josephine arched her spine, pulled up her knees, folded her arms so that her fists came under her ears, and pressed her cheek hard against the pillow.

II

Another thing which complicated matters was they had Nurse Andrews staying on with them that week. It was their own fault; they had asked her. It was Josephine's idea. On the morning—well, on the last morning, when the doctor had gone, Josephine had said to Constantia, 'Don't you think it would be rather nice if we asked Nurse Andrews to stay on for a week as our guest?'

'Very nice,' said Constantia.

'I thought,' went on Josephine quickly, 'I should just say this afternoon, after I've paid her, "My sister and I would be very pleased, after all you've done for us, Nurse Andrews, if you would stay on for a week as our guest." I'd have to put that in about being our guest in case—'

'Oh, but she could hardly expect to be paid!' cried Constantia.

'One never knows,' said Josephine sagely.

Nurse Andrews had, of course, jumped at the idea. But it was a bother. It meant they had to have regular sit-down meals at the proper times, whereas if they'd been alone they could just have asked Kate if she wouldn't have minded bringing them a tray wherever they were. And meal-times now that the strain was over were rather a trial.

Nurse Andrews was simply fearful about butter. Really they couldn't help feeling that about butter, at least, she took advantage of their kindness. And she had that maddening habit of asking for just an inch more bread to finish what she had on her plate, and then, at the last mouthful, absent-mindedly—of course it wasn't absent-mindedly—taking another helping. Josephine got very red when this happened, and she fastened her small, bead-like eyes on the tablecloth as if she saw a minute strange insect creeping through the web of it. But Constantia's long, pale face lengthened and set, and she gazed away—away—far over the desert, to where that line of camels unwound like a thread of wool . . . .

'When I was with Lady Tukes,' said Nurse Andrews, 'she had such a dainty little contrayvance for the buttah. It was a silvah cupid balanced on the—on the bordah of a glass dish, holding a tayny fork. And when you wanted some buttah you simply pressed his foot and he bent down and speared you a piece. It was quite a gayme.'

Josephine could hardly bear that. But 'I think those things are very extravagant' was all she said.

'But whey?' asked Nurse Andrews, beaming through her eyeglasses. 'No one, surely, would take more buttah than one wanted—would one?'

'Ring, Con,' cried Josephine. She couldn't trust herself to reply.

And proud young Kate, the enchanted princess, came in to see what the old tabbies wanted now. She snatched away their plates of mock something or other and slapped down a white terrified blancmange.

'Jam, please, Kate,' said Josephine kindly.

Kate knelt and burst open the sideboard, lifted the lid of the jam-pot, saw it was empty, put it on the table, and stalked off.

'I'm afraid,' said Nurse Andrews a moment later, 'there isn't any.'

'Oh, what a bother!' said Josephine. She bit her lip. 'What had we better do?'

Constantia looked dubious. 'We can't disturb Kate again,' she said softly.

Nurse Andrews waited, smiling at them both. Her eyes wandered, spying at everything behind her eyeglasses. Constantia in despair went back to her camels. Josephine frowned heavily—concentrated. If it hadn't been for this idiotic woman she and Con would, of course, have eaten their blancmange without. Suddenly the idea came.

'I know,' she said. 'Marmalade. There's some marmalade in the sideboard. Get it, Con.'

'I hope,' laughed Nurse Andrews—and her laugh was like a spoon tinkling against a medicine glass—'I hope it's not very bittah marmalayde.'

III

But, after all, it was not long now, and then she'd be gone for good. And there was no getting over the fact that she had been very kind to father. She had nursed him day and night at the end. Indeed, both Constantia and Josephine felt privately she had rather overdone the not leaving him at the very last. For when they had gone in to say goodbye Nurse Andrews had sat beside his bed the whole time, holding his wrist and pretending to look at her watch. It couldn't have been necessary. It was so tactless, too. Supposing father had wanted to say something—something private to them. Not that he had. Oh, far from it! He lay there, purple, a dark, angry purple in the face, and never even looked at them when they came in. Then, as they were standing there, wondering what to do, he had suddenly opened one eye. Oh, what a difference it would have made, what a difference to their memory of him, how much easier to tell people about it, if he had only opened both! But no—one eye only. It glared at them a moment and then . . . went out.

IV

It had made it very awkward for them when Mr Farolles, of St John's, called the same afternoon.

'The end was quite peaceful, I trust?' were the first words he said as he glided towards them through the dark drawing-room.

'Quite,' said Josephine faintly. They both hung their heads. Both of them felt certain that eye wasn't at all a peaceful eye.

'Won't you sit down?' said Josephine.

'Thank you, Miss Pinner,' said Mr Farolles gratefully. He folded his coat-tails and began to lower himself into father's armchair, but just as he touched it he almost sprang up and slid into the next chair instead.

He coughed. Josephine clasped her hands; Constantia looked vague.

'I want you to feel, Miss Pinner,' said Mr Farolles, 'and you, Miss Constantia, that I'm trying to be helpful. I want to be helpful to you both, if you will let me. These are the times,' said Mr Farolles, very simply and earnestly, 'when God means us to be helpful to one another.'

'Thank you very much, Mr Farolles,' said Josephine and Constantia.

'Not at all,' said Mr Farolles gently. He drew his kid gloves through his fingers and leaned forward. 'And if either of you would like a little Communion, either or both of you, here and now, you have only to tell me. A little Communion is often very help—a great comfort,' he added tenderly.

But the idea of a little Communion terrified them. What! In the drawing room by themselves—with no—no altar or anything! The piano would be much too high, thought Constantia, and Mr Farolles could not possibly lean over it with the chalice. And Kate would be sure to come bursting in and interrupt them, thought Josephine. And supposing the bell rang in the middle? It might be somebody important—about their mourning. Would they get up reverently and go out, or would they have to wait . . . in torture?

'Perhaps you will send round a note by your good Kate if you would care for it later,' said Mr Farolles.

'Oh yes, thank you very much!' they both said.

Mr Farolles got up and took his black straw hat from the round table.

'And about the funeral,' he said softly. 'I may arrange that—as your dear father's old friend and yours, Miss Pinner—and Miss Constantia?'

Josephine and Constantia got up too.

'I should like it to be quite simple,' said Josephine firmly, 'and not too expensive. At the same time, I should like—'

'A good one that will last,' thought dreamy Constantia, as if Josephine were buying a nightgown. But of course Josephine didn't say that. 'One suitable to our father's position.' She was very nervous.

'I'll run round to our good friend Mr Knight,' said Mr Farolles soothingly. 'I will ask him to come and see you. I am sure you will find him very helpful indeed.'

V

Well, at any rate, all that part of it was over, though neither of them could possibly believe that father was never coming back. Josephine had had a moment of absolute terror at the cemetery, while the coffin was lowered, to think that she and Constantia had done this thing without asking his permission. What would father say when he found out? For he was bound to find out sooner or later. He always did. 'Buried. You two girls had me buried?' She heard his stick thumping. Oh, what would they say? What possible excuse could they make? It sounded such an appallingly heartless thing to do. Such a wicked advantage to take of a person because he happened to be helpless at the moment. The other people seemed to treat it all as a matter of course. They were strangers; they couldn't be expected to understand that father was the very last person for such a thing to happen to. No, the entire blame for it all would fall on her and Constantia. And the expense, she thought, stepping into the tight-buttoned cab. When she had to show him the bills. What would he say then?

She heard him absolutely roaring, 'And do you expect me to pay for this gimcrack excursion of yours?'

'Oh,' groaned poor Josephine aloud, 'we shouldn't have done it, Con!'

And Constantia, pale as a lemon in all that blackness, said in a frightened whisper, 'Done what, Jug?'

'Let them bu-bury father like that,' said Josephine, breaking down and crying into her new, queer-smelling mourning handkerchief.

'But what else could we have done?' asked Constantia wonderingly. 'We couldn't have kept him unburied. At any rate, not in a flat that size.'

Josephine blew her nose; the cab was dreadfully stuffy.

'I don't know,' she said forlornly. 'It is all so dreadful. I feel we ought to have tried to, just for a time at least. To make perfectly sure. One thing's certain'—and her tears sprang out again—'father will never forgive us for this—never!'

VI

Father would never forgive them. That was what they felt more than ever when, two mornings later, they went into his room to go through his things. They had discussed it quite calmly. It was even down on Josephine's list of things to be done. Go through father's things and settle about them. But that was a very different matter from saying after breakfast:

'Well, are you ready, Con?'

'Yes, Jug—when you are.'

'Then I think we'd better get it over.'

It was dark in the hall. It had been a rule for years never to disturb father in the morning, whatever happened. And now they were going to open the door without knocking even . . . . Constantia's eyes were enormous at the idea; Josephine felt weak in the knees.

'You—you go first,' she gasped, pushing Constantia.

But Constantia said, as she always had said on those occasions, 'No, Jug, that's not fair. You're the eldest.'

Josephine was just going to say—what at other times she wouldn't have owned to for the world—what she kept for her very last weapon, 'But you're the tallest,' when they noticed that the kitchen door was open, and there stood Kate . . . .

'Very stiff,' said Josephine, grasping the door-handle and doing her best to turn it. As if anything ever deceived Kate!

It couldn't be helped. That girl was . . . Then the door was shut behind them, but—but they weren't in father's room at all. They might have suddenly walked through the wall by mistake into a different flat altogether. Was the door just behind them? They were too frightened to look. Josephine knew that if it was it was holding itself tight shut; Constantia felt that, like the doors in dreams, it hadn't any handle at all. It was the coldness which made it so awful. Or the whiteness—which? Everything was covered. The blinds were down, a cloth hung over the mirror, a sheet hid the bed, a huge fan of white paper filled the fireplace. Constantia timidly put out her hand; she almost expected a snowflake to fall. Josephine felt a queer tingling in her nose, as if her nose was freezing. Then a cab klop-klopped over the cobbles below, and the quiet seemed to shake into little pieces.

'I had better pull up a blind,' said Josephine bravely.

'Yes, it might be a good idea,' whispered Constantia.

They only gave the blind a touch, but it flew up and the cord flew after, rolling round the blind-stick, and the little tassel tapped as if trying to get free. That was too much for Constantia.

'Don't you think—don't you think we might put it off for another day?' she whispered.

'Why?' snapped Josephine, feeling, as usual, much better now that she knew for certain that Constantia was terrified. 'It's got to be done. But I do wish you wouldn't whisper, Con.'

'I didn't know I was whispering,' whispered Constantia.

'And why do you keep on staring at the bed?' said Josephine, raising her voice almost defiantly. 'There's nothing on the bed.'

'Oh, Jug, don't say so!' said poor Connie. 'At any rate, not so loudly.'

Josephine felt herself that she had gone too far. She took a wide swerve over to the chest of drawers, put out her hand, but quickly drew it back again.

'Connie!' she gasped, and she wheeled round and leaned with her back against the chest of drawers.

'Oh, Jug—what?'

Josephine could only glare. She had the most extraordinary feeling that she had just escaped something simply awful. But how could she explain to Constantia that father was in the chest of drawers? He was in the top drawer with his handkerchiefs and neckties, or in the next with his shirts and pyjamas, or in the lowest of all with his suits. He was watching there, hidden away—just behind the door-handle—ready to spring.

She pulled a funny old-fashioned face at Constantia, just as she used to in the old days when she was going to cry.

'I can't open,' she nearly wailed.

'No, don't, Jug,' whispered Constantia earnestly. 'It's much better not to. Don't let's open anything. At any rate, not for a long time.'

'But—but it seems so weak,' said Josephine, breaking down.

'But why not be weak for once, Jug?' argued Constantia, whispering quite fiercely. 'If it is weak.' And her pale stare flew from the locked writing-table— so safe—to the huge glittering wardrobe, and she began to breathe in a queer, panting way. 'Why shouldn't we be weak for once in our lives, Jug? It's quite excusable. Let's be weak—be weak, Jug. It's much nicer to be weak than to be strong.'

And then she did one of those amazingly bold things that she'd done about twice before in their lives: she marched over to the wardrobe, turned the key, and took it out of the lock. Took it out of the lock and held it up to Josephine, showing Josephine by her extraordinary smile that she knew what she'd done—she'd risked deliberately father being in there among his overcoats.

If the huge wardrobe had lurched forward, had crashed down on Constantia, Josephine wouldn't have been surprised. On the contrary, she would have thought it the only suitable thing to happen. But nothing happened. Only the room seemed quieter than ever, and bigger flakes of cold air fell on Josephine's shoulders and knees. She began to shiver.

'Come, Jug,' said Constantia, still with that awful callous smile; and Josephine followed just as she had that last time, when Constantia had pushed Benny into the round pond.

VII

But the strain told on them when they were back in the dining-room. They sat down, very shaky, and looked at each other.

'I don't feel I can settle to anything,' said Josephine, 'until I've had something. Do you think we could ask Kate for two cups of hot water?'

'I really don't see why we shouldn't,' said Constantia carefully. She was quite normal again. 'I won't ring. I'll go to the kitchen door and ask her.'

'Yes, do,' said Josephine, sinking down into a chair. 'Tell her, just two cups, Con, nothing else—on a tray.'

'She needn't even put the jug on, need she?' said Constantia, as though Kate might very well complain if the jug had been there.

'Oh, no, certainly not! The jug's not at all necessary. She can pour it direct out of the kettle,' cried Josephine, feeling that would be a labour-saving indeed.

Their cold lips quivered at the greenish brims. Josephine curved her small red hands round the cup; Constantia sat up and blew on the wavy stream, making it flutter from one side to the other.

'Speaking of Benny,' said Josephine.

And though Benny hadn't been mentioned Constantia immediately looked as though he had.

'He'll expect us to send him something of father's, of course. But it's so difficult to know what to send to Ceylon.'

'You mean things get unstuck so on the voyage,' murmured Constantia.

'No, lost,' said Josephine sharply. 'You know there's no post. Only runners.'

Both paused to watch a black man in white linen drawers running through the pale fields for dear life, with a large brown-paper parcel in his hands. Josephine's black man was tiny; he scurried along glistening like an ant. But there was something blind and tireless about Constantia's tall, thin fellow, which made him, she decided, a very unpleasant person indeed . . . . On the veranda, dressed all in white and wearing a cork helmet, stood Benny. His right hand shook up and down, as father's did when he was impatient. And behind him, not in the least interested, sat Hilda, the unknown sister-in-law. She swung in a cane rocker and flicked over the leaves of the *Tatler*.

'I think his watch would be the most suitable present,' said Josephine.

Constantia looked up; she seemed surprised.

'Oh, would you trust a gold watch to a native?'

'But of course I'd disguise it,' said Josephine. 'No one would know it was a watch.' She liked the idea of having to make a parcel such a curious shape that no one could possibly guess what it was. She even thought for a moment of hiding the watch in a narrow cardboard corset-box that she'd kept by her for a long time, waiting for it to come in for something. It was such beautiful firm cardboard. But, no, it wouldn't be appropriate for this occasion. It had lettering on it: *Medium Women's 28. Extra Firm Busks.* It would be almost too much of a surprise for Benny to open that and find father's watch inside.

'And of course it isn't as though it would be going—ticking, I mean,' said Constantia, who was still thinking of the native love of jewelery. 'At least,' she added, 'it would be very strange if after all that time it was.'

VIII

Josephine made no reply. She had flown off on one of her tangents. She had suddenly thought of Cyril. Wasn't it more usual for the only grandson to have the watch? And then dear Cyril was so appreciative and a gold watch meant so much to a young man. Benny, in all probability, had quite got out of the habit of watches; men so seldom wore waistcoats in those hot climates. Whereas Cyril in London wore them from year's end to year's end. And it would be so nice for her and Constantia, when he came to tea, to know it was there. 'I see you've got on grandfather's watch, Cyril.' It would be somehow so satisfactory.

Dear boy! What a blow his sweet, sympathetic little note had been! Of course they quite understood; but it was most unfortunate.

'It would have been such a point, having him,' said Josephine.

'And he would have enjoyed it so,' said Constantia, not thinking what she was saying.

However, as soon as he got back he was coming to tea with his aunties. Cyril to tea was one of their rare treats.

'Now, Cyril, you mustn't be frightened of our cakes. Your Auntie Con and I bought them at Buszard's this morning. We know what a man's appetite is. So don't be ashamed of making a good tea.'

Josephine cut recklessly into the rich dark cake that stood for her winter gloves or the soling and heeling of Constantia's only respectable shoes. But Cyril was most unmanlike in appetite.

'I say, Aunt Josephine, I simply can't. I've only just had lunch, you know.'

'Oh, Cyril, that can't be true! It's after four,' cried Josephine. Constantia sat with her knife poised over the chocolate-roll.

'It is, all the same,' said Cyril. 'I had to meet a man at Victoria,[1] and he kept me hanging about till . . . there was only time to get lunch and to come on here. And he gave me—phew'—Cyril put his hand to his forehead—'a terrific blow-out,' he said.

It was disappointing—today of all days. But still he couldn't be expected to know.

'But you'll have a meringue, won't you, Cyril?' said Aunt Josephine. 'These meringues were bought specially for you. Your dear father was so fond of them. We were sure you are, too.'

'I *am*, Aunt Josephine,' cried Cyril ardently. 'Do you mind if I take half to begin with?'

'Not at all, dear boy; but we mustn't let you off with that.'

'Is your dear father still so fond of meringues?' asked Auntie Con gently. She winced faintly as she broke through the shell of hers.

---

1. London railroad station, connecting with the Channel ports.

'Well, I don't quite know, Auntie Con,' said Cyril breezily.

At that they both looked up.

'Don't know?' almost snapped Josephine. 'Don't know a thing like that about your own father, Cyril?'

'Surely,' said Auntie Con softly.

Cyril tried to laugh it off. 'Oh, well,' he said, 'it's such a long time since—' He faltered. He stopped. Their faces were too much for him.

'Even *so*,' said Josephine.

And Auntie Con looked.

Cyril put down his teacup. 'Wait a bit,' he cried. 'Wait a bit, Aunt Josephine. What am I thinking of?'

He looked up. They were beginning to brighten. Cyril slapped his knee.

'Of course,' he said, 'it was meringues. How could I have forgotten? Yes, Aunt Josephine, you're perfectly right. Father's most frightfully keen on meringues.'

They didn't only beam. Aunt Josephine went scarlet with pleasure; Auntie Con gave a deep, deep sigh.

'And now, Cyril, you must come and see father,' said Josephine. 'He knows you were coming today.'

'Right,' said Cyril, very firmly and heartily. He got up from his chair; suddenly he glanced at the clock.

'I say, Auntie Con, isn't your clock a bit slow? I've got to meet a man at—at Paddington[2] just after five. I'm afraid I shan't be able to stay very long with grandfather.'

'Oh, he won't expect you to stay *very* long!' said Aunt Josephine.

Constantia was still gazing at the clock. She couldn't make up her mind if it was fast or slow. It was one or the other, she felt almost certain of that. At any rate, it had been.

Cyril still lingered. 'Aren't you coming along, Auntie Con?'

'Of course,' said Josephine, 'we shall all go. Come on, Con.'

IX

They knocked at the door, and Cyril followed his aunts into grandfather's hot, sweetish room.

'Come on,' said Grandfather Pinner. 'Don't hang about. What is it? What've you been up to?'

He was sitting in front of a roaring fire, clasping his stick. He had a thick rug over his knees. On his lap there lay a beautiful pale yellow silk handkerchief.

'It's Cyril, father,' said Josephine shyly. And she took Cyril's hand and led him forward.

'Good afternoon, grandfather,' said Cyril, trying to take his hand out of Aunt Josephine's. Grandfather Pinner shot his eyes at Cyril in the way he was famous for. Where was Auntie Con? She stood on the other side of Aunt Josephine; her long arms hung down in front of her; her hands were clasped. She never took her eyes off grandfather.

---

2. London railroad station, serving the west of England and Wales.

'Well,' said Grandfather Pinner, beginning to thump, 'what have you got to tell me?'

What had he, what had he got to tell him? Cyril felt himself smiling like a perfect imbecile. The room was stifling, too.

But Aunt Josephine came to his rescue. She cried brightly, 'Cyril says his father is still very fond of meringues, father dear.'

'Eh?' said Grandfather Pinner, curving his hand like a purple meringue-shell over one ear.

Josephine repeated, 'Cyril says his father is still very fond of meringues.'

'Can't hear,' said old Colonel Pinner. And he waved Josephine away with his stick, then pointed with his stick to Cyril. 'Tell me what she's trying to say,' he said.

(My God!) 'Must I?' said Cyril, blushing and staring at Aunt Josephine.

'Do, dear,' she smiled. 'It will please him so much.'

'Come on, out with it!' cried Colonel Pinner testily, beginning to thump again.

And Cyril leaned forward and yelled, 'Father's still very fond of meringues.'

At that Grandfather Pinner jumped as though he had been shot.

'Don't shout!' he cried. 'What's the matter with the boy? Meringues! What about 'em?'

'Oh, Aunt Josephine, must we go on?' groaned Cyril desperately.

'It's quite all right, dear boy,' said Aunt Josephine, as though he and she were at the dentist's together. 'He'll understand in a minute.' And she whispered to Cyril, 'He's getting a bit deaf, you know.' Then she leaned forward and really bawled at Grandfather Pinner, 'Cyril only wanted to tell you, father dear, that his father is still very fond of meringues.'

Colonel Pinner heard that time, heard and brooded, looking Cyril up and down.

'What an esstrordinary thing!' said old Grandfather Pinner. 'What an esstrordinary thing to come all this way here to tell me!'

And Cyril felt it *was*.

'Yes, I shall send Cyril the watch,' said Josephine.

'That would be very nice,' said Constantia. 'I seem to remember last time he came there was some little trouble about the time.'

X

They were interrupted by Kate bursting through the door in her usual fashion, as though she had discovered some secret panel in the wall.

'Fried or boiled?' asked the bold voice.

Fried or boiled? Josephine and Constantia were quite bewildered for the moment. They could hardly take it in.

'Fried or boiled what, Kate?' asked Josephine, trying to begin to concentrate.

Kate gave a loud sniff. 'Fish.'

'Well, why didn't you say so immediately?' Josephine reproached her gently. 'How could you expect us to understand, Kate? There are a great many things in this world, you know, which are fried or boiled.' And after such a display of courage she said quite brightly to Constantia, 'Which do you prefer, Con?'

'I think it might be nice to have it fried,' said Constantia. 'On the other hand, of course boiled fish is very nice. I think I prefer both equally well . . . Unless you . . . In that case—'

'I shall fry it,' said Kate, and she bounced back, leaving their door open and slamming the door of her kitchen.

Josephine gazed at Constantia; she raised her pale eyebrows until they rippled away into her pale hair. She got up. She said in a very lofty, imposing way, 'Do you mind following me me into the drawing-room, Constantia? I've something of great importance to discuss with you.'

For it was always to the drawing-room they retired when they wanted to talk over Kate.

Josephine closed the door meaningly. 'Sit down, Constantia,' she said, still very grand. She might have been receiving Constantia for the first time. And Con looked round vaguely for a chair, as though she felt indeed quite a stranger.

'Now the question is,' said Josephine, bending forward, 'whether we shall keep her or not.'

'That is the question,' agreed Constantia.

'And this time,' said Josephine firmly, 'we must come to a definite decision.'

Constantia looked for a moment as though she might begin going over all the other times, but she pulled herself together and said, 'Yes, Jug.'

'You see, Con,' explained Josephine, 'everything is so changed now.' Constantia looked up quickly. 'I mean,' went on Josephine, 'we're not dependent on Kate as we were.' And she blushed faintly. 'There's not father to cook for.'

'That is perfectly true,' agreed Constantia. 'Father certainly doesn't want any cooking now, whatever else—'

Josephine broke in sharply, 'You're not sleepy, are you, Con?'

'Sleepy, Jug?' Constantia was wide-eyed.

'Well, concentrate more,' said Josephine sharply, and she returned to the subject. 'What it comes to is, if we did'—and this she barely breathed, glancing at the door—'give Kate notice'—she raised her voice again—'we could manage our own food.'

'Why not?' cried Constantia. She couldn't help smiling. The idea was so exciting. She clasped her hands. 'What should we live on, Jug?'

'Oh, eggs in various forms!' said Jug, lofty again. 'And, besides, there are all the cooked foods.'

'But I've always heard,' said Constantia, 'they are considered so very expensive.'

'Not if one buys them in moderation,' said Josephine. But she tore herself away from this fascinating bypath and dragged Constantia after her.

'What we've got to decide now, however, is whether we really do trust Kate or not.'

Constantia leaned back. Her flat little laugh flew from her lips.

'Isn't it curious, Jug,' said she, 'that just on this one subject I've never been able to quite make up my mind?'

XI

She never had. The whole difficulty was to prove anything. How did one prove things, how could one? Suppose Kate had stood in front of her and deliberately made a face. Mightn't she very well have been in pain? Wasn't it impossible, at any rate, to ask Kate if she was making a face at her? If Kate answered 'No'—and of course she would say 'No'—what a position! How undignified! Then again Constantia suspected, she was almost certain that Kate went to her chest of drawers when she and Josephine were out, not to take things but to spy. Many times she had come back to find her amethyst cross in the most unlikely places, under her lace ties or on top of her evening Bertha.[3] More than once she had laid a trap for Kate. She had arranged things in a special order and then called Josephine to witness.

'You see, Jug?'

'Quite, Con.'

'Now we shall be able to tell.'

But, oh dear, when she did go to look, she was as far off from a proof as ever! If anything was displaced, it might so very well have happened as she closed the drawer; a jolt might have done it so easily.

'You come, Jug, and decide. I really can't. It's too difficult.'

But after a pause and a long glare Josephine would sigh. 'Now you've put the doubt into my mind, Con, I'm sure I can't tell myself.'

'Well, we can't postpone it again,' said Josephine. 'If we postpone it this time—'

XII

But at that moment in the street below a barrel-organ struck up. Josephine and Constantia sprang to their feet together.

'Run, Con,' said Josephine. 'Run quickly. There's sixpence on the—'

Then they remembered. It didn't matter. They would never have to stop the organ-grinder again. Never again would she and Constantia be told to make that monkey take his noise somewhere else. Never would sound that loud, strange bellow when father thought they were not hurrying enough. The organ-grinder might play there all day and the stick would not thump.

It never will thump again,
It never will thump again,

played the barrel-organ.

What was Constantia thinking? She had such a strange smile; she looked different. She couldn't be going to cry.

'Jug, Jug,' said Constantia softly, pressing her hands together. 'Do you know what day it is? It's Saturday. It's a week today, a whole week.'

A week since father died,
A week since father died,

cried the barrel-organ. And Josephine, too, forgot to be practical and sensible; she smiled faintly, strangely. On the Indian carpet there fell a square of

3. Detachable lace collar for low-necked dresses.

sunlight, pale red; it came and went and came—and stayed, deepened—until it shone almost golden.

'The sun's out,' said Josephine, as though it really mattered.

A perfect fountain of bubbling notes shook from the barrel-organ, round, bright notes, carelessly scattered.

Constantia lifted her big, cold hands as if to catch them, and then her hands fell again. She walked over to the mantelpiece to her favourite Buddha. And the stone and gilt image, whose smile always gave her such a queer feeling, almost a pain and yet a pleasant pain, seemed today to be more than smiling. He knew something; he had a secret. 'I know something that you don't know,' said her Buddha. Oh, what was it, what could it be? And yet she had always felt there was . . . something.

The sunlight pressed through the windows, thieved its way in, flashed its light over the furniture and the photographs. Josephine watched it. When it came to mother's photograph, the enlargement over the piano, it lingered as though puzzled to find so little remained of mother, except the ear-rings shaped like tiny pagodas and a black feather boa. Why did the photographs of dead people always fade so? wondered Josephine. As soon as a person was dead their photograph died too. But, of course, this one of mother was very old. It was thirty-five years old. Josephine remembered standing on a chair and pointing out that feather boa to Constantia and telling her that it was a snake that had killed their mother in Ceylon . . . . Would everything have been different if mother hadn't died? She didn't see why. Aunt Florence had lived with them until they had left school, and they had moved three times and had their yearly holiday and . . . and there'd been changes of servants, of course.

Some little sparrows, young sparrows they sounded, chirped on the window-ledge. *Yeep—eyeep—yeep.* But Josephine felt they were not sparrows, not on the window-ledge. It was inside her, that queer little crying noise. *Yeep—eyeep—yeep.* Ah, what was it crying, so weak and forlorn?

If mother had lived, might they have married? But there had been nobody for them to marry. There had been father's Anglo-Indian friends before he quarreled with them. But after that she and Constantia never met a single man except clergymen. How did one meet men? Or even if they'd met them, how could they have got to know men well enough to be more than strangers? One read of people having adventures, being followed, and so on. But nobody had ever followed Constantia and her. Oh yes, there had been one year at Eastbourne[4] a mysterious man at their boarding-house who had put a note on the jug of hot water outside their bedroom door! But by the time Connie had found it the steam had made the writing too faint to read; they couldn't even make out to which of them it was addressed. And he had left next day. And that was all. The rest had been looking after father and at the same time keeping out of father's way. But now? But now? The thieving sun touched Josephine gently. She lifted her face. She was drawn over to the window by gentle beams . . . .

Until the barrel-organ stopped playing Constantia stayed before the Buddha, wondering, but not as usual, not vaguely. This time her wonder was like longing. She remembered the times she had come in here, crept out of bed

---

4. Seaside resort on Sussex coast.

in her nightgown when the moon was full, and lain on the floor with her arms outstretched, as though she was crucified. Why? The big, pale moon had made her do it. The horrible dancing figures on the carved screen had leered at her and she hadn't minded. She remembered too how, whenever they were at the seaside, she had gone off by herself and got as close to the sea as she could, and sung something, something she had made up, while she gazed all over that restless water. There had been this other life, running out, bringing things home in bags, getting things on approval, discussing them with Jug, and taking them back to get more things on approval, and arranging father's trays and trying not to annoy father. But it all seemed to have happened in a kind of tunnel. It wasn't real. It was only when she came out of the tunnel into the moonlight or by the sea or into a thunderstorm that she really felt herself. What did it mean? What was it she was always wanting? What did it all lead to? Now? Now?

She turned away from the Buddha with one of her vague gestures. She went over to where Josephine was standing. She wanted to say something to Josephine, something frightfully important, about—about the future and what . . .

'Don't you think perhaps—' she began.

But Josephine interrupted her. 'I was wondering if now—' she murmured. They stopped; they waited for each either.

'Go on, Con,' said Josephine.

'No, no, Jug; after you,' said Constantia.

'No, say what you were going to say. You began,' said Josephine.

'I . . . I'd rather hear what you were going to say first,' said Constantia.

'Don't be absurd, Con.'

'Really, Jug.'

'Connie!'

'Oh, *Jug!*'

A pause. Then Constantia said faintly, 'I can't say what I was going to say, Jug, because I've forgotten what it was . . . that I was going to say.'

Josephine was silent for a moment. She stared at a big cloud where the sun had been. Then she replied shortly, 'I've forgotten too.'

1920   1922

The Garden Party

And after all the weather was ideal. They could not have had a more perfect day for a garden party if they had ordered it. Windless, warm, the sky without a cloud. Only the blue was veiled with a haze of light gold, as it is sometimes in early summer. The gardener had been up since dawn, mowing the lawns and sweeping them, until the grass and the dark flat rosettes where the daisy plants had been seemed to shine. As for the roses, you could not help feeling they understood that roses are the only flowers that impress people at garden parties; the only flowers that everybody is certain of knowing. Hundreds, yes, literally hundreds, had come out in a single night; the green bushes bowed down as though they had been visited by archangels.

Breakfast was not yet over before the men came to put up the marquee.

'Where do you want the marquee put, mother?'

'My dear child, it's no use asking me. I'm determined to leave everything to you children this year. Forget I am your mother. Treat me as an honoured guest.'

But Meg could not possibly go and supervise the men. She had washed her hair before breakfast, and she sat drinking her coffee in a green turban, with a dark wet curl stamped on each cheek. Jose, the butterfly, always came down in a silk petticoat and a kimono jacket.

'You'll have to go, Laura; you're the artistic one.'

Away Laura flew, still holding her piece of bread-and-butter. It's so delicious to have an excuse for eating out of doors, and besides, she loved having to arrange things; she always felt she could do it so much better than anybody else.

Four men in their shirt-sleeves stood grouped together on the garden path. They carried staves covered with rolls of canvas, and they had big tool-bags slung on their backs. They looked impressive. Laura wished now that she had not got the bread-and-butter, but there was nowhere to put it, and she couldn't possibly throw it away. She blushed and tried to look severe and even a little bit short-sighted as she came up to them.

'Good morning,' she said, copying her mother's voice. But that sounded so fearfully affected that she was ashamed, and stammered like a little girl, 'Oh—er—have you come—is it about the marquee?'

'That's right, miss,' said the tallest of the men, a lanky, freckled fellow, and he shifted his tool-bag, knocked back his straw hat and smiled down at her. 'That's about it.'

His smile was so easy, so friendly that Laura recovered. What nice eyes he had, small, but such a dark blue! And now she looked at the others, they were smiling too. 'Cheer up, we won't bite,' their smile seemed to say. How very nice workmen were! And what a beautiful morning! She mustn't mention the morning; she must be business-like. The marquee.

'Well, what about the lily-lawn? Would that do?'

And she pointed to the lily-lawn with the hand that didn't hold the bread-and-butter. They turned, they stared in the direction. A little fat chap thrust out his under-lip, and the tall fellow frowned.

'I don't fancy it,' said he. 'Not conspicuous enough. You see, with a thing like a marquee,' and he turned to Laura in his easy way, 'you want to put it somewhere where it'll give you a bang slap in the eye, if you follow me.'

Laura's upbringing made her wonder for a moment whether it was quite respectful of a workman to talk to her of bangs slap in the eye. But she did quite follow him.

'A corner of the tennis-court,' she suggested. 'But the band's going to be in one corner.'

'H'm, going to have a band, are you?' said another of the workmen. He was pale. He had a haggard look as his dark eyes scanned the tennis-court. What was he thinking?

'Only a very small band,' said Laura gently. Perhaps he wouldn't mind so much if the band was quite small. But the tall fellow interrupted.

'Look here, miss, that's the place. Against those trees. Over there. That'll do fine.'

Against the karakas. Then the karaka-trees would be hidden. And they were so lovely, with their broad, gleaming leaves, and their clusters of yellow fruit. They were like trees you imagined growing on a desert island, proud, solitary, lifting their leaves and fruits to the sun in a kind of silent splendour. Must they be hidden by a marquee?

They must. Already the men had shouldered their staves and were making for the place. Only the tall fellow was left. He bent down, pinched a sprig of lavender, put his thumb and forefinger to his nose and snuffed up the smell. When Laura saw that gesture she forgot all about the karakas in her wonder at him caring for things like that—caring for the smell of lavender. How many men that she knew would have done such a thing? Oh, how extraordinarily nice workmen were, she thought. Why couldn't she have workmen for friends rather than the silly boys she danced with and who came to Sunday night supper? She would get on much better with men like these.

It's all the fault, she decided, as the tall fellow drew something on the back of an envelope, something that was to be looped up or left to hang, of these absurd class distinctions. Well, for her part, she didn't feel them. Not a bit, not an atom . . . And now there came the chock-chock of wooden hammers. Some one whistled, some one sang out, 'Are you right there, matey?' 'Matey!' The friendliness of it, the—the—Just to prove how happy she was, just to show the tall fellow how at home she felt, and how she despised stupid conventions, Laura took a big bite of her bread-and-butter as she stared at the little drawing. She felt just like a work-girl.

'Laura, Laura, where are you? Telephone, Laura!' a voice cried from the house.

'Coming!' Away she skimmed, over the lawn, up the path, up the steps, across the veranda, and into the porch. In the hall her father and Laurie were brushing their hats ready to go to the office.

'I say, Laura,' said Laurie very fast, 'you might just give a squiz at my coat before this afternoon. See if it wants pressing.'

'I will,' said she. Suddenly she couldn't stop herself. She ran at Laurie and gave him a small, quick squeeze. 'Oh, I do love parties, don't you?' gasped Laura.

'Ra-ther,' said Laurie's warm, boyish voice, and he squeezed his sister too, and gave her a gentle push. 'Dash off to the telephone, old girl.'

The telephone. 'Yes, yes; oh yes. Kitty? Good morning, dear. Come to lunch? Do, dear. Delighted of course. It will only be a very scratch meal—just the sandwich crusts and broken meringue-shells and what's left over. Yes, isn't it a perfect morning? Your white? Oh, I certainly should. One moment—hold the line. Mother's calling.' And Laura sat back. 'What, mother? Can't hear.'

Mrs Sheridan's voice floated down the stairs. 'Tell her to wear that sweet hat she had on last Sunday.'

'Mother says you're to wear that sweet hat you had on last Sunday. Good. One o'clock. Bye-bye.'

Laura put back the receiver, flung her arms over her head, took a deep breath, stretched and let them fall. 'Huh,' she sighed, and the moment after the sigh she sat up quickly. She was still, listening. All the doors in the house seemed to be open. The house was alive with soft, quick steps and running voices. The green baize door that led to the kitchen regions swung open and shut with a muffled thud. And now there came a long, chuckling absurd sound. It was the heavy piano being moved on its stiff castors. But the air! If you stopped to notice, was the air always like this? Little faint winds were playing chase in at the tops of the windows, out at the doors. And there were two tiny spots of sun, one on the inkpot, one on a silver photograph frame, playing too. Darling little spots. Especially the one on the inkpot lid. It was quite warm. A warm little silver star. She could have kissed it.

The front door bell pealed, and there sounded the rustle of Sadie's print skirt on the stairs. A man's voice murmured; Sadie answered, careless, 'I'm sure I don't know. Wait. I'll ask Mrs Sheridan.'

'What is it, Sadie?' Laura came into the hall.

'It's the florist, Miss Laura.'

It was, indeed. There, just inside the door, stood a wide, shallow tray full of pots of pink lilies. No other kind. Nothing but lilies—canna lilies, big pink flowers, wide open, radiant, almost frighteningly alive on bright crimson stems.

'O-oh, Sadie!' said Laura, and the sound was like a little moan. She crouched down as if to warm herself at that blaze of lilies; she felt they were in her fingers, on her lips, growing in her breast.

'It's some mistake,' she said faintly. 'Nobody ever ordered so many. Sadie, go and find mother.'

But at that moment Mrs Sheridan joined them.

'It's quite right,' she said calmly. 'Yes, I ordered them. Aren't they lovely?' She pressed Laura's arm. 'I was passing the shop yesterday, and I saw them in the window. And I suddenly thought for once in my life I shall have enough canna lilies. The garden party will be a good excuse.'

'But I thought you said you didn't mean to interfere,' said Laura. Sadie had gone. The florist's man was still outside at his van. She put her arm round her mother's neck and gently, very gently, she bit her mother's ear.

'My darling child, you wouldn't like a logical mother, would you? Don't do that. Here's the man.'

He carried more lilies still, another whole tray.

'Bank them up, just inside the door, on both sides of the porch, please,' said Mrs Sheridan. 'Don't you agree, Laura?'

'Oh, I *do* mother.'

In the drawing-room Meg, Jose and good little Hans had at last succeeded in moving the piano.

'Now, if we put this chesterfield against the wall and move everything out of the room except the chairs, don't you think?'

'Quite.'

'Hans, move these tables into the smoking-room, and bring a sweeper to take these marks off the carpet and—one moment, Hans—' Jose loved giving orders to the servants, and they loved obeying her. She always made them feel they were taking part in some drama. 'Tell mother and Miss Laura to come here at once.'

'Very good, Miss Jose.'

She turned to Meg. 'I want to hear what the piano sounds like, just in case I'm asked to sing this afternoon. Let's try over "This life is Weary." '

Pom! Ta-ta-ta *Tee*-ta! The piano burst out so passionately that Jose's face changed. She clasped her hands. She looked mournfully and enigmatically at her mother and Laura as they came in.

> This Life is *Wee*-ary,
> A Tear—a Sigh.
> A Love that *Chan*-ges,
>   This Life is *Wee*-ary,
> A Tear—a Sigh.
> A Love that *Chan*-ges,
> And then . . . Good-bye!

But at the word 'Good-bye,' and although the piano sounded more desperate than ever, her face broke into a brilliant, dreadfully unsympathetic smile.

'Aren't I in good voice, mummy?' she beamed.

> This Life is *Wee*-ary,
> Hope comes to Die.
> A Dream—a *Wa*-kening.

But now Sadie interrupted them. 'What is it, Sadie?'

'If you please, m'm, cook says have you got the flags[1] for the sandwiches?'

'The flags for the sandwiches, Sadie?' echoed Mrs Sheridan dreamily. And the children knew by her face that she hadn't got them. 'Let me see.' And she said to Sadie firmly, 'Tell cook I'll let her have them in ten minutes.'

Sadie went.

'Now, Laura,' said her mother quickly. 'Come with me into the smoking-room. I've got the names[2] somewhere on the back of an envelope. You'll have to write them out for me. Meg, go upstairs this minute and take that wet thing off your head. Jose, run and finish dressing this instant. Do you hear me, children, or shall I have to tell your father when he comes home to-night? And—and, Jose, pacify cook if you do go into the kitchen, will you? I'm terrified of her this morning.'

The envelope was found at last behind the dining-room clock, though how it had got there Mrs Sheridan could not imagine.

'One of you children must have stolen it out of my bag, because I remember vividly—cream cheese and lemon-curd. Have you done that?'

'Yes.'

'Egg and—' Mrs Sheridan held the envelope away from her. 'It looks like mice. It can't be mice, can it?'

'Olive, pet,' said Laura, looking over her shoulder.

'Yes, of course, olive. What a horrible combination it sounds. Egg and olive.'

They were finished at last, and Laura took them off to the kitchen. She found Jose there pacifying the cook, who did not look at all terrifying.

'I have never seen such exquisite sandwiches,' said Jose's rapturous voice. 'How many kinds did you say there were, cook? Fifteen?'

'Fifteen, Miss Jose.'

'Well, cook, I congratulate you.'

Cook swept up crusts with the long sandwich knife and smiled broadly.

'Godber's has come,' announced Sadie, issuing out of the pantry. She had seen the man pass the window.

---

1. Little paper flags stuck in a plate of small triangular sandwiches indicating what is inside the sandwiches on each plate—an English custom adopted by the New Zealand middle class as a sign of gentility.

2. I.e., the names of the sandwich fillings to be written on each flag.

That meant the cream puffs had come. Godber's were famous for their cream puffs. Nobody ever thought of making them at home.

'Bring them in and put them on the table, my girl,' ordered cook.

Sadie brought them in and went back to the door. Of course Laura and Jose were far too grown-up to really care about such things. All the same, they couldn't help agreeing that the puffs looked very attractive. Very. Cook began arranging them, shaking off the extra icing sugar.

'Don't they carry one back to all one's parties?' said Laura.

'I suppose they do,' said practical Jose, who never liked to be carried back. 'They look beautifully light and feathery, I must say.'

'Have one each, my dears,' said cook in her comfortable voice. 'Yer ma won't know.'

Oh, impossible. Fancy cream puffs so soon after breakfast. The very idea made one shudder. All the same, two minutes later Jose and Laura were licking their fingers with that absorbed inward look that only comes from whipped cream.

'Let's go into the garden, out by the back way,' suggested Laura. 'I want to see how the men are getting on with the marquee. They're such awfully nice men.'

But the back door was blocked by cook, Sadie, Godber's man and Hans.

Something had happened.

'Tuk-tuk-tuk,' clucked cook like an agitated hen. Sadie had her hand clapped to her cheek as though she had toothache. Hans's face was screwed up in the effort to understand. Only Godber's man seemed to be enjoying himself; it was his story.

'What's the matter? What's happened?'

'There's been a horrible accident,' said cook. 'A man killed.'

'A man killed! Where? How? When?'

But Godber's man wasn't going to have his story snatched from under his very nose.

'Know those little cottages just below here, miss?' Know them? Of course, she knew them. 'Well, there's a young chap living there, name of Scott, a carter. His horse shied at a traction-engine, corner of Hawke Street this morning, and he was thrown out on the back of his head. Killed.'

'Dead!' Laura stared at Godber's man.

'Dead when they picked him up,' said Godber's man with relish. 'They were taking the body home as I come up here.' And he said to the cook, 'He's left a wife and five little ones.'

'Jose, come here.' Laura caught hold of her sister's sleeve and dragged her through the kitchen to the other side of the green baize door. There she paused and leaned against it. 'Jose!' she said, horrified, 'however are we going to stop everything?'

'Stop everything, Laura!' cried Jose in astonishment. 'What do you mean?'

'Stop the garden party, of course.' Why did Jose pretend?

But Jose was still more amazed. 'Stop the garden party? My dear Laura, don't be so absurd. Of course we can't do anything of the kind. Nobody expects us to. Don't be so extravagant.'

'But we can't possibly have a garden party with a man dead just outside the front gate.'

That really was extravagant, for the little cottages were in a lane to themselves at the very bottom of a steep rise that led up to the house. A broad road ran between. True, they were far too near. They were the greatest possible eyesore, and they had no right to be in that neighbourhood at all. They were little mean dwellings painted a chocolate brown. In the garden patches there was nothing but cabbage stalks, sick hens and tomato cans. The very smoke coming out of their chimneys was poverty-stricken. Little rags and shreds of smoke, so unlike the great silvery plumes that uncurled from the Sheridans' chimneys. Washerwomen lived in the lane and sweeps and a cobbler, and a man whose house-front was studded all over with minute bird-cages. Children swarmed. When the Sheridans were little they were forbidden to set foot there because of the revolting language and of what they might catch. But since they were grown up, Laura and Laurie on their prowls sometimes walked through. It was disgusting and sordid. They came out with a shudder. But still one must go everywhere; one must see everything. So through they went.

'And just think of what the band would sound like to that poor woman,' said Laura.

'Oh, Laura!' Jose began to be seriously annoyed. 'If you're going to stop a band playing every time some one has an accident, you'll lead a very strenuous life. I'm every bit as sorry about it as you. I feel just as sympathetic.' Her eyes hardened. She looked at her sister just as she used to when they were little and fighting together. 'You won't bring a drunken workman back to life by being sentimental,' she said softly.

'Drunk! Who said he was drunk?' Laura turned furiously on Jose. She said, just as they had used to say on those occasions, 'I'm going straight up to tell mother.'

'Do, dear,' cooed Jose.

'Mother, can I come into your room?' Laura turned the big glass door-knob.

'Of course, child. Why, what's the matter? What's given you such a colour?' And Mrs Sheridan turned round from her dressing-table. She was trying on a new hat.

'Mother, a man's been killed,' began Laura.

'Not in the garden?' interrupted her mother.

'No, no!'

'Oh, what a fright you gave me!' Mrs Sheridan sighed with relief, and took off the big hat and held it on her knees.

'But listen, mother,' said Laura. Breathless, half-choking, she told the dreadful story. 'Of course, we can't have our party, can we?' she pleaded. 'The band and everybody arriving. They'd hear us, mother; they're nearly neighbours!'

To Laura's astonishment her mother behaved just like Jose; it was harder to bear because she seemed amused. She refused to take Laura seriously.

'But, my dear child, use your common sense. It's only by accident we've heard of it. If some one had died there normally—and I can't understand how they keep alive in those poky little holes—we should still be having our party, shouldn't we?'

Laura had to say 'yes' to that, but she felt it was all wrong. She sat down on her mother's sofa and pinched the cushion frill.

'Mother, isn't it really terribly heartless of us?' she asked.

'Darling!' Mrs Sheridan got up and came over to her, carrying the hat. Before Laura could stop her she had popped it on. 'My child!' said her mother, 'the hat is yours. It's made for you. It's much too young for me. I have never seen you look such a picture. Look at yourself!' And she held up her hand-mirror.

'But, mother,' Laura began again. She couldn't look at herself; she turned aside.

This time Mrs Sheridan lost patience just as Jose had done.

'You are being very absurd, Laura,' she said coldly. 'People like that don't expect sacrifices from us. And it's not very sympathetic to spoil everybody's enjoyment as you're doing now.'

'I don't understand,' said Laura, and she walked quickly out of the room into her own bedroom. There, quite by chance, the first thing she saw was this charming girl in the mirror, in her black hat trimmed with gold daisies, and a long black velvet ribbon. Never had she imagined she could look like that. Is mother right? she thought. And now she hoped her mother was right. Am I being extravagant? Perhaps it was extravagant. Just for a moment she had another glimpse of that poor woman and those little children, and the body being carried into the house. But it all seemed blurred, unreal, like a picture in the newspaper. I'll remember it again after the party's over, she decided. And somehow that seemed quite the best plan . . .

Lunch was over by half past one. By half past two they were all ready for the fray. The green-coated band had arrived and was established in a corner of the tennis-court.

'My dear!' trilled Kitty Maitland, 'aren't they too like frogs for words? You ought to have arranged them round the pond with the conductor in the middle on a leaf.'

Laurie arrived and hailed them on his way to dress. At the sight of him Laura remembered the accident again. She wanted to tell him. If Laurie agreed with the others, then it was bound to be all right. And she followed him into the hall.

'Laurie!'

'Hallo!' He was half-way upstairs, but when he turned round and saw Laura he suddenly puffed out his cheeks and goggled his eyes at her. 'My word, Laura! You do look stunning,' said Laurie. 'What an absolutely topping hat!'

Laura said faintly 'Is it?' and smiled up at Laurie, and didn't tell him after all.

Soon after that people began coming in streams. The band struck up; the hired waiters ran from the house to the marquee. Wherever you looked there were couples strolling, bending to the flowers, greeting, moving on over the lawn. They were like bright birds that had alighted in the Sheridans' garden for this one afternoon, on their way to—where? Ah, what happiness it is to be with people who all are happy, to press hands, press cheeks, smile into eyes.

'Darling Laura, how well you look!'

'What a becoming hat, child!'

'Laura, you look quite Spanish. I've never seen you look so striking.'

And Laura, glowing, answered softly, 'Have you had tea? Won't you have an ice? The passion-fruit ices really are rather special.' She ran to her father and begged him. 'Daddy darling, can't the band have something to drink?'

And the perfect afternoon slowly ripened, slowly faded, slowly its petals closed.

'Never a more delightful garden party . . .' 'The greatest success . . .' 'Quite the most . . .'

Laura helped her mother with the goodbyes. They stood side by side in the porch till it was all over.

'All over, all over, thank heaven,' said Mrs Sheridan. 'Round up the others, Laura. Let's go and have some fresh coffee. I'm exhausted. Yes, it's been very successful. But oh, these parties, these parties! Why will you children insist on giving parties!' And they all of them sat down in the deserted marquee.

'Have a sandwich, daddy dear. I wrote the flag.'

'Thanks.' Mr Sheridan took a bite and the sandwich was gone. He took another. 'I suppose you didn't hear of a beastly accident that happened to-day?' he said.

'My dear,' said Mrs Sheridan, holding up her hand, 'we did. It nearly ruined the party. Laura insisted we should put it off.'

'Oh, mother!' Laura didn't want to be teased about it.

'It was a horrible affair all the same,' said Mr Sheridan. 'The chap was married too. Lived just below in the lane, and leaves a wife and half a dozen kiddies, so they say.'

An awkward little silence fell. Mrs Sheridan fidgeted with her cup. Really, it was very tactless of father . . .

Suddenly she looked up. There on the table were all those sandwiches, cakes, puffs, all un-eaten, all going to be wasted. She had one of her brilliant ideas.

'I know,' she said. 'Let's make up a basket. Let's send that poor creature some of this perfectly good food. At any rate, it will be the greatest treat for the children. Don't you agree? And she's sure to have neighbours calling in and so on. What a point to have it all ready prepared. Laura!' She jumped up. 'Get me the big basket out of the stairs cupboard.'

'But, mother, do you really think it's a good idea?' said Laura.

Again, how curious, she seemed to be different from them all. To take scraps from their party. Would the poor woman really like that?

'Of course! What's the matter with you today? An hour or two ago you were insisting on us being sympathetic, and now—'

Oh well! Laura ran for the basket. It was filled, it was heaped by her mother.

'Take it yourself, darling,' said she. 'Run down just as you are. No, wait, take the arum lilies too. People of that class are so impressed by arum lilies.'

'The stems will ruin her lace frock,' said practical Jose.

So they would. Just in time. 'Only the basket, then. And, Laura!'—her mother followed her out of the marquee—'don't on any account—'

'What mother?'

No, better not put such ideas into the child's head! 'Nothing! Run along.'

It was just growing dusky as Laura shut their garden gates. A big dog ran by like a shadow. The road gleamed white, and down below in the hollow the little cottages were in deep shade. How quiet it seemed after the after-noon. Here she was going down the hill to somewhere where a man lay dead, and she couldn't realize it. Why couldn't she? She stopped a minute. And it seemed to her that kisses, voices, tinkling spoons, laughter, the smell of crushed grass were somehow inside her. She had no room for anything else. How strange! She looked up at the pale sky, and all she thought was, 'Yes, it was the most successful.'

Now the broad road was crossed. The lane began, smoky and dark. Women in shawls and men's tweed caps hurried by. Men hung over the palings; the children played in the doorways. A low hum came from the mean little cottages. In some of them there was a flicker of light, and a shadow, crab-like, moved across the window. Laura bent her head and hurried on. She wished now she had put on a coat. How her frock shone! And the big hat with the velvet streamer—if only it was another hat! Were the people looking at her? They must be. It was a mistake to have come; she knew all along it was a mistake. Should she go back even now?

No, too late. This was the house. It must be. A dark knot of people stood outside. Beside the gate an old, old woman with a crutch sat in a chair, watching. She had her feet on a newspaper. The voices stopped as Laura drew near. The group parted. It was as though she was expected, as though they had known she was coming here.

Laura was terribly nervous. Tossing the velvet ribbon over her shoulder, she said to a woman standing by, 'Is this Mrs Scott's house?' and the woman, smiling queerly, said, 'It is, my lass.'

Oh, to be away from this! She actually said, 'Help me, God,' as she walked up the tiny path and knocked. To be away from those staring eyes, or to be covered up in anything, one of those women's shawls even. I'll just leave the basket and go, she decided. I shan't even wait for it to be emptied.

Then the door opened. A little woman in black showed in the gloom.

Laura said, 'Are you Mrs Scott?' But to her horror the woman answered, 'Walk in please, miss,' and she was shut in the passage.

'No,' said Laura, 'I don't want to come in. I only want to leave this basket. Mother sent—'

The little woman in the gloomy passage seemed not to have heard her. 'Step this way, please, miss,' she said in an oily voice, and Laura followed her.

She found herself in a wretched little low kitchen, lighted by a smoky lamp. There was a woman sitting before the fire.

'Em,' said the little creature who had let her in. 'Em! It's a young lady.' She turned to Laura. She said meaningly, 'I'm her sister, Miss. You'll excuse 'er, won't you?'

'Oh, but of course!' said Laura. 'Please, please don't disturb her. I—I only want to leave—'

But at that moment the woman at the fire turned round. Her face, puffed up, red, with swollen eyes and swollen lips, looked terrible. She seemed as though she couldn't understand why Laura was there. What did it mean? Why was this stranger standing in the kitchen with a basket? What was it all about? And the poor face puckered up again.

'All right, my dear,' said the other. 'I'll thenk the young lady.'

And again she began, 'You'll excuse her, miss, I'm sure,' and her face, swollen too, tried an oily smile.

Laura only wanted to get out, to get away. She was back in the passage.

The door opened. She walked straight through into the bedroom where the dead man was lying.

'You'd like a look at 'im, wouldn't you?' said Em's sister, and she brushed past Laura over to the bed. 'Don't be afraid, my lass,'—and now her voice sounded fond and sly, and fondly she drew down the sheet—' 'e looks a picture. There's nothing to show. Come along, my dear.'

Laura came.

There lay a young man, fast asleep—sleeping so soundly, so deeply, that he was far, far away from them both. Oh, so remote, so peaceful. He was dreaming. Never wake him up again. His head was sunk in the pillow, his eyes were closed; they were blind under the closed eyelids. He was given up to his dream. What did garden parties and baskets and lace frocks matter to him? He was far from all those things. He was wonderful, beautiful. While they were laughing and while the band was playing, this marvel had come to the lane. Happy . . . happy . . . All is well, said that sleeping face. This is just as it should be. I am content.

But all the same you had to cry, and she couldn't go out of the room without saying something to him. Laura gave a loud childish sob.

'Forgive my hat,' she said.

And this time she didn't wait for Em's sister. She found her way out of the door, down the path, past all those dark people. At the corner of the lane she met Laurie.

He stepped out of the shadow. 'Is that you, Laura?'

'Yes.'

'Mother was getting anxious. Was it all right?'

'Yes, quite. Oh, Laurie!' She took his arm, she pressed up against him.

'I say, you're not crying, are you?' asked her brother.

Laura shook her head. She was.

Laurie put his arm round her shoulder. 'Don't cry,' he said in his warm, loving voice. 'Was it awful?'

'No,' sobbed Laura. 'It was simply marvellous. But, Laurie—' She stopped, she looked at her brother. 'Isn't life,' she stammered, 'isn't life—' But what life was she couldn't explain. No matter. He quite understood.

'Isn't it, darling?' said Laurie.

1921   1922

HUGH MACDIARMID
1892–1978

Hugh MacDiarmid is the pen name of Christopher Murray Grieve, who was born in the Scottish border town of Langholm, son of a rural postman. After a short period of training as a teacher, he turned to journalism. In 1920–22 he brought out three volumes of new Scottish poetry by different hands, which he edited under the title *Northern Numbers, Being Representative Selections from Certain Living Scottish Poets.*

The aim of these volumes was to do for Scottish poetry what *Georgian Poetry* had done for English, although Grieve's own poetry had even at this stage little in common with anything that can be considered characteristically Georgian. MacDiarmid now became the champion of a Scottish Renaissance movement, to redeem Scottish culture from the sentimentality and pallid imitativeness that he saw as its chief faults.

The true emergence of "Hugh MacDiarmid" came with the publication of *Sangschaw* in 1925. The adoption of this pen name served notice that he associated himself with the Celtic element in Scottish history and culture, and later he was to associate Scotland with Ireland, Wales, and Cornwall as part of a Celtic ring of peoples who could produce an alternative culture to that of Anglo-Saxondom. But more significant than this new name was the kind of poetry he was now producing. This consisted largely of short lyrics in Scots, which is not a Celtic language at all (as Scottish Gaelic is) but the language originally identical with that spoken in northern England and developed into a powerful literary medium by the great medieval poets of Scotland, notably Robert Henryson and William Dunbar. The growth of standard English as the written language of Scotland drove the Scots language into the position of a spoken vernacular that was no longer a fully developed literary language. It was largely by concentration on the folk tradition that eighteenth-century Scottish poets, notably Robert Burns, were able to use Scots vigorously in their poetry. But in the nineteenth century the Burns tradition became debased and sentimentalized. MacDiarmid's great achievement was to recognize that the Scottish poetic tradition needed to be radically reshaped and that the decadent post-Burns tradition was beyond disciplining into a poetry of any maturity or originality.

To achieve a language for a creative Scottish poetry, MacDiarmid ransacked the rich vocabulary of Dunbar and Henryson and used it together with modern dialect Scots and standard English. This revived Scots, or "Lallans" (i.e., Lowland Scots) as it was often called, was unashamedly synthetic. Like Joyce, MacDiarmid had an enormous linguistic curiosity and wanted to increase the expressiveness of his poetic speech by every resource of vocabulary he could lay his hands on. In his later poetry, when he wrote in English, he ransacked the technical vocabularies of the sciences in the same spirit.

MacDiarmid's early Scots lyrics are brilliant poems, but they are miniatures, small and finely etched pieces, which avoid large pronouncements. In *A Drunk Man Looks at the Thistle* (1926), however, he builds up an epic statement about Scotland out of a series of related lyrics and passages of descriptive and reflective poetry. It can stand beside MacDiarmid's later long poem, written not in Scots but in his own special kind of English, *On a Raised Beach,* as one of his two masterpieces. To the disappointment of many who considered his Scots lyrics his finest achievement, MacDiarmid then turned more and more to what he called "the poetry of fact," trying to embrace, sometimes with an almost desperate use of enormous catalogs, all the new scientific and technological knowledge that the modern world had brought into being and to relate it to human awareness.

Perhaps the most remarkable example of MacDiarmid's later style is *In Memoriam James Joyce: from A Vision of a World Language* (1955). This is a poem of more than six thousand lines, written (more or less) in English, with an enormous number of quotations from and references to other languages and literatures. The movement of the verse is essentially colloquial, but the rise and fall of the sound and the carefully controlled shifts in tempo provide enough underlying formal pattern to prevent the poem from disintegrating into mere discursiveness. Its theme might be described as the essential kinship of everything in the world that is fully realized and properly possessed of its identity.

MacDiarmid is now generally recognized as the greatest Scottish poet since Burns (and some see him as greater than Burns) and one of a trilogy with Burns and Dunbar.

From A Drunk Man Looks at the Thistle

1. Farewell to Dostoevski

The wan leafs shak, atour° us like the snaw.   *around*
Here is the cavaburd[1] in which Earth's tint.°   *lost*
There's naebody but Oblivion and us,
Puir gangrel° buddies, waunderin' hameless in't.   *wanderer*

5   The stars are larochs° o' auld cottages,   *foundations*
And a' Time's glen is fu' o' blinnin'° stew.°   *blinding/storm*
Nae freen'ly lozen° skimmers:° and the wund° *window/gleams/wind*
Rises and separates even me and you.

I ken nae Russian and you ken nae Scots.
10   We canna tell oor voices frae the wund.
The snaw is seekin' everywhere: oor herts
At last like roofless ingles° it has f'und.   *hearths*

And gethers there in drift on endless drift,
Oor broken herts that it can never fill;
15   And still—its leafs like snaw, its growth like wund—
The thistle[2] rises and forever will!

                        1926

2. Yet Ha'e I Silence Left

Yet ha'e I Silence left, the croon° o' a'.   *crown*

No' her, wha on the hills langsyne° I saw   *long ago*
Liftin' a foreheid o' perpetual snaw.

No' her, wha in the how-dumb-deid o' nicht[3]
5   Kyths,[4] like Eternity in Time's despite.

No' her, withooten° shape, wha's name is Daith,° *without/death*
No' Him, unkennable° abies° to faith *unknowable/except*

—God whom, gin° e'er He saw a Man, 'ud be   *if*
E'en mair dumfooner'd[5] at the sicht° than he.   *sight*

10 —But Him, whom nocht° in man or Deity,   *nothing*
Or Daith or Dreid or Laneliness can touch,
Wha's deed owre often and has seen owre much.[6]

O I ha'e Silence left.

                        1926

---

1. Dense snowstorm.
2. The emblem of Scotland.
3. The still center of night.

4. Makes herself known, appears.
5. More dumbfounded.
6. Who has died too often and seen too much.

From In Memoriam James Joyce

We Must Look at the Harebell[1]

We must look at the harebell as if
We had never seen it before.
Remembrance gives an accumulation of satisfaction
Yet the desire for change is very strong in us
5 And change is in itself a recreation.
To those who take any pleasure
In flowers, plants, birds, and the rest
An ecological change is recreative.
(Come. Climb with me. Even the sheep are different
10 And of new importance.
The coarse-fleeced, hardy Herdwick,
The Hampshire Down, artificially fed almost from birth,
And butcher-fat from the day it is weaned,
The Lincoln-Longwool, the biggest breed in England,
15 With the longest fleece, and the Southdown
Almost the smallest—and between them thirty other breeds,
Some whitefaced, some black,
Some with horns and some without,
Some long-wooled, some short-wooled,
20 In England where the men, and women too,
Are almost as interesting as the sheep.)
Everything is different, everything changes,
Except for the white bedstraw which climbs all the way
Up from the valleys to the tops of the high passes
25 The flowers are all different and more precious
Demanding more search and particularity of vision.
Look! Here and there a pinguicula[2] eloquent of the Alps
Still keeps a purple-blue flower
On the top of its straight and slender stem.
30 Bog-asphodel, deep-gold, and comely in form,
The queer, almost diabolical, sundew,
And when you leave the bog for the stag moors and the rocks
The parsley fern—a lovelier plant
Than even the proud Osmunda Regalis[3]—
35 Flourishes in abundance
Showing off oddly contrasted fronds
From the cracks of the lichened stones.
It is pleasant to find the books
Describing it as "very local."
40 Here is a change indeed!
The universal *is* the particular.

1955

---

1. The Scottish bluebell, a blue flower with a bell-shaped blossom.
2. The butterwort, a genus of small herbs whose leaves secrete a sticky substance in which small insects are caught.
3. The flowering, or royal, fern; a plant with large fronds.

In the Children's Hospital

"Does it matter? Losing your legs?"
SIEGFRIED SASSOON

Now let the legless boy show the great lady
How well he can manage his crutches.
It doesn't matter though the Sister[1] objects,
"He's not used to them yet," when such is
5   The will of the Princess. Come, Tommy,[2]
Try a few desperate steps through the ward.
Then the hand of Royalty will pat your head
And life suddenly cease to be hard.
For a couple of legs are surely no miss
10   When the loss leads to such an honour as this!
One knows, when one sees how jealous the rest
Of the children are, it's been all for the best!—
But would the sound of your sticks on the floor
Thundered in her skull for evermore!

1935

Another Epitaph on an Army of Mercenaries[1]

It is a God-damned lie to say that these
Saved, or knew, anything worth any man's pride.
They were professional murderers and they took
Their blood money and impious risks and died.
5   In spite of all their kind some elements of worth
With difficulty persist here and there on earth.

1935

1. Head nurse in charge of a hospital ward.
2. Common name for British soldier but here just the actual name of the child.

1. Cf. A. E. Housman's *Epitaph on an Army of Mercenaries* (p. 2047), to which this is a response.

JEAN RHYS
1894?–1979

The novelist Jean Rhys was born Ella Gwendolen Rees Williams, the daughter of a Creole mother and a doctor of Welsh descent, on the island of Dominica in the West Indies. She was educated, first, at a convent school in Roseau, Dominica, and then, coming to England at the age of sixteen, at the Perse School in Cambridge. After studying for a term at the Academy of Dramatic Art in London, she worked as a chorus girl, film extra, and—during World War I—as a volunteer cook. In 1919 she left England to marry the first of three husbands and for many years lived abroad, mainly in Paris, where she began to write the stories of her first book, *The Left Bank: Sketches and Studies of Present-Day Bohemian Paris* (1927). This was published with an introduction by the established novelist and poet Ford Madox Ford. Ford was for a time her lover and, perceiving the link between her vulnerability as a person and her strength as a writer, spoke of her "terrifying insight . . . and passion for stating the case of the underdog."

Rhys's early "sketches"—such as *Mannequin*—were followed by *Postures* (1928, reprinted as *Quartet* in 1969); *After Leaving Mr. Mackenzie* (1930); *Voyage in the Dark* (1934), a semiautobiographical account of a nineteen-year-old chorus girl in London and on tour; and *Good Morning, Midnight* (1939), another first-person narrative of a lonely drifter, this time in Paris.

Returning to England, she wrote no more for many years until, following the enthusiastic reception of a radio adaptation of *Good Morning, Midnight* in 1958, she began her masterpiece, *Wide Sargasso Sea* (1966). In this, she returns to the Dominica of her childhood and, in a brilliant act of imaginative sympathy, re-creates herself as the nineteenth-century Creole heiress who would end her days as the first Mrs. Rochester, the mad woman in the attic of Charlotte Brontë's *Jane Eyre*.

As with all great writers, Rhys's voice is like no other, a voice well described by the critic A. Alvarez as "oddly youthful: light, clear, alert, casual and disabused, and uniquely concerned in simply telling the truth."

Mannequin

Twelve o'clock. Déjeuner chez Jeanne Veron, Place Vendôme.[1]

Anna, dressed in the black cotton, chemise-like garment of the mannequin off duty was trying to find her way along dark passages and down complicated flights of stairs to the underground room where lunch was served.

She was shivering, for she had forgotten her coat, and the garment that she wore was very short, sleeveless, displaying her rose-coloured stockings to the knee. Her hair was flamingly and honestly red; her eyes, which were very gentle in expression, brown and heavily shadowed with kohl; her face small and pale under its professional rouge. She was fragile, like a delicate child, her arms pathetically thin. It was to her legs that she owed this dazzling, this incredible opportunity.

Madame Veron, white-haired with black eyes, incredibly distinguished, who had given them one sweeping glance, the glance of the connoisseur, smiled imperiously and engaged her at an exceedingly small salary. As a beginner, Madame explained, Anna could not expect more. She was to wear the jeune fille[2] dresses. Another smile, another sharp glance.

Anna was conducted from the Presence by an underling who helped her to take off the frock she had worn temporarily for the interview. Aspirants for an engagement are always dressed in a model of the house.

She had spent yesterday afternoon in a delirium tempered by a feeling of exaggerated reality, and in buying the necessary make-up. It had been such a forlorn hope, answering the advertisement.

The morning had been dreamlike. At the back of the wonderfully decorated salons she had found an unexpected sombreness; the place, empty,

---

1. Lunch at Jeanne Vernon's house in the Vendôme square (French).   2. Young girls' (French).

would have been dingy and melancholy, countless puzzling corridors and staircases, a rabbit warren and a labyrinth. She despaired of ever finding her way.

In the mannequins' dressing-room she spent a shy hour making up her face—in an extraordinary and distinctive atmosphere of slimness and beauty; white arms and faces vivid with rouge; raucous voices and the smell of cosmetics; silken lingerie. Coldly critical glances were bestowed upon Anna's reflection in the glass. None of them looked at her directly. . . . A depressing room, taken by itself, bare and cold, a very inadequate conservatory for these human flowers. Saleswomen in black rushed in and out, talking in sharp voices; a very old woman hovered, helpful and shapeless, showing Anna where to hang her clothes, presenting to her the black garment that Anna was wearing, going to lunch. She smiled with professional motherliness, her little, sharp, black eyes travelling rapidly from la nouvelle's[3] hair to her ankles and back again.

She was Madame Pecard, the dresser.

Before Anna had spoken a word she was called away by a small boy in buttons to her destination in one of the salons: there, under the eye of a vendeuse,[4] she had to learn the way to wear the innocent and springlike air and garb of the jeune fille. Behind a yellow, silken screen she was hustled into a leather coat and paraded under the cold eyes of an American buyer. This was the week when the spring models are shown to important people from big shops all over Europe and America: the most critical week of the season. . . . The American buyer said that he would have that, but with an inch on to the collar and larger cuffs. In vain the saleswoman, in her best English with its odd Chicago accent, protested that that would completely ruin the chic of the model. The American buyer knew what he wanted and saw that he got it.

The vendeuse sighed, but there was a note of admiration in her voice. She respected Americans: they were not like the English, who, under a surface of annoying moroseness of manner, were notoriously timid and easy to turn round your finger.

'Was that all right?' Behind the screen one of the saleswomen smiled encouragingly and nodded. The other shrugged her shoulders. She had small, close-set eyes, a long thin nose and tight lips of the regulation puce colour. Behind her silken screen Anna sat on a high white stool. She felt that she appeared charming and troubled. The white and gold of the salon suited her red hair.

A short morning. For the mannequin's day begins at ten and the process of making up lasts an hour. The friendly saleswoman volunteered the information that her name was Jeannine, that she was in the lingerie, that she considered Anna rudement jolie,[5] that noon was Anna's lunch hour. She must go down the corridor and up those stairs, through the big salon then. . . . Anyone would tell her. But Anna, lost in the labyrinth, was too shy to ask her way. Besides, she was not sorry to have time to brace herself for the ordeal. She had reached the regions of utility and oilcloth: the decorative salons were far overhead. Then the smell of food—almost visible, it was so

---

3. The new girl's (French).
4. Saleswoman (French). "In buttons": in a uniform with two rows of buttons up the front of the

tunic. "Salons": rooms where clients are received.
5. Very pretty (French). "Lingerie": i.e., the lingerie department.

cloudlike and heavy—came to her nostrils, and high-noted, and sibilant, a buzz of conversation made her draw a deep breath. She pushed a door open.

She was in a big, very low-ceilinged room, all the floor space occupied by long wooden tables with no cloths. . . . She was sitting at the mannequins' table, gazing at a thick and hideous white china plate, a twisted tin fork, a wooden-handled stained knife, a tumbler so thick it seemed unbreakable.

There were twelve mannequins at Jeanne Veron's: six of them were lunching, the others still paraded, goddess-like, till their turn came for rest and refreshment. Each of the twelve was of a distinct and separate type: each of the twelve knew her type and kept to it, practising rigidly in clothing, manner, voice and conversation.

Round the austere table were now seated: Babette, the gamine, the traditional blonde enfant:[6] Mona, tall and darkly beautiful, the femme fatale, the wearer of sumptuous evening gowns. Georgette was the garçonne:[7] Simone with green eyes Anna knew instantly for a cat whom men would and did adore, a sleek, white, purring, long-lashed creature. . . . Eliane was the star of the collection.

Eliane was frankly ugly and it did not matter: no doubt Lilith,[8] from whom she was obviously descended, had been ugly too. Her hair was henna-tinted, her eyes small and black, her complexion bad under her thick make-up. Her hips were extraordinarily slim, her hands and feet exquisite, every movement she made was as graceful as a flower's in the wind. Her walk . . . But it was her walk which made her the star there and earned her a salary quite fabulous for Madame Veron's, where large salaries were not the rule. . . . Her walk and her 'chic of the devil' which lit an expression of admiration in even the cold eyes of American buyers.

Eliane was a quiet girl, pleasant-mannered. She wore a ring with a beautiful emerald on one long, slim finger, and in her small eyes were both intelligence and mystery.

Madame Pecard, the dresser, was seated at the head of the mannequin's table, talking loudly, unlistened to, and gazing benevolently at her flock.

At other tables sat the sewing girls, pale-faced, black-frocked—the workers, heroically gay, but with the stamp of labour on them: and the saleswomen. The mannequins, with their sensual, blatant charms and their painted faces were watched covertly, envied and apart.

Babette the blonde enfant was next to Anna, and having started the conversation with a few good, round oaths at the quality of the sardines, announced proudly that she could speak English and knew London very well. She began to tell Anna the history of her adventures in the city of coldness, dark and fogs. . . . She had gone to a job as a mannequin in Bond Street and the villainous proprietor of the shop having tried to make love to her and she being rigidly virtuous, she had left. And another job, Anna must figure to herself, had been impossible to get, for she, Babette, was too small and slim for the Anglo-Saxon idea of a mannequin.

She stopped to shout in a loud voice to the woman who was serving: 'Hé, my old one, don't forget your little Babette. . . .'

---

6. Child (French). "Gamine": young woman with an attractive urchinlike look (French).
7. Boylike woman (French). "Femme fatale": dangerously attractive woman (French).
8. An Assyrian demon, associated with the night; a vampire.

Opposite, Simone the cat and the sportive Georgette were having a low-voiced conversation about the triste-ness of a monsieur[9] of their acquaintance. 'I said to him,' Georgette finished decisively, 'Nothing to be done, my rabbit. You have not looked at me well, little one. In my place would you not have done the same?'

She broke off when she realized that the others were listening, and smiled in a friendly way at Anna.

She too, it appeared, had ambitions to go to London because the salaries were so much better there. Was it difficult? Did they really like French girls? Parisiennes?[1]

The conversation became general.

'The English boys are nice,' said Babette, winking one divinely candid eye. 'I had a chic type who used to take me to dinner at the Empire Palace. Oh, a pretty boy. . . .'

'It is the most chic restaurant in London,' she added importantly.

The meal reached the stage of dessert. The other tables were gradually emptying; the mannequins all ordered very strong coffee, several a liqueur. Only Mona and Eliane remained silent; Eliane, because she was thinking of something else; Mona, because it was her type, her genre to be haughty.

Her hair swept away from her white, narrow forehead and her small ears: her long earrings nearly touching her shoulders, she sipped her coffee with a disdainful air. Only once, when the blonde enfant, having engaged in a passage of arms with the waitress and got the worst of it was momentarily discomfited and silent, Mona narrowed her eyes and smiled an astonishingly cruel smile.

As soon as her coffee was drunk she got up and went out.

Anna produced a cigarette, and Georgette, perceiving instantly that here was the sportive touch, her genre,[2] asked for one and lit it with a devil-may-care air. Anna eagerly passed her cigarettes round, but the Mère[3] Pecard interfered weightily. It was against the rules of the house for the mannequins to smoke, she wheezed. The girls all lit their cigarettes and smoked. The Mère Pecard rumbled on: 'A caprice, my children. All the world knows that mannequins are capricious. Is it not so?' She appealed to the rest of the room.

As they went out Babette put her arm round Anna's waist and whispered: 'Don't answer Madame Pecard. We don't like her. We never talk to her. She spies on us. She is a camel.'

That afternoon Anna stood for an hour to have a dress draped on her. She showed this dress to a stout Dutch lady buying for the Hague,[4] to a beautiful South American with pearls, to a silver-haired American gentleman who wanted an evening cape for his daughter of seventeen, and to a hook-nosed, odd English lady of title who had a loud voice and dressed, under her furs, in a grey jersey and stout boots.

The American gentleman approved of Anna, and said so, and Anna gave him a passionately grateful glance. For, if the vendeuse Jeannine had been

---

9. Sadness of a gentleman (French).
1. Parisian women (French).
2. Style.

3. Mother (French, literal trans.); here older woman.
4. Capital of Holland.

uniformly kind and encouraging, the other, Madame Tienne, had been as uniformly disapproving and had once even pinched her arm hard.

About five o'clock Anna became exhausted. The four white and gold walls seemed to close in on her. She sat on her high white stool staring at a marvellous nightgown and fighting an intense desire to rush away. Anywhere! Just to dress and rush away anywhere, from the raking eyes of the customers and the pinching fingers of Irene.

'I will one day. I can't stick it,' she said to herself. 'I won't be able to stick it.' She had an absurd wish to gasp for air.

Jeannine came and found her like that.

'It is hard at first, hein?[5] . . . One asks oneself: Why? For what good? It is all idiot. We are all so. But we go on. Do not worry about Irene.' She whispered: 'Madame Veron likes you very much. I heard her say so.'

At six o'clock Anna was out in the rue de la Paix;[6] her fatigue forgotten, the feeling that now she really belonged to the great, maddening city possessed her and she was happy in her beautifully cut tailor-made and a beret.

Georgette passed her and smiled; Babette was in a fur coat.

All up the street the mannequins were coming out of the shops, pausing on the pavements a moment, making them as gay and as beautiful as beds of flowers before they walked swiftly away and the Paris night swallowed them up.

1968

On Not Shooting Sitting Birds[1]

There is no control over memory. Quite soon you find yourself being vague about an event which seemed so important at the time that you thought you'd never forget it. Or unable to recall the face of someone whom you could have sworn was there for ever. On the other hand, trivial and meaningless memories may stay with you for life. I can still shut my eyes and see Victoria grinding coffee on the pantry steps, the glass bookcase and the books in it, my father's pipe-rack, the leaves of the sandbox tree, the wallpaper of the bedroom in some shabby hotel, the hairdresser in Antibes.[2] It's in this way that I remember buying the pink milanese[3] silk underclothes, the assistant who sold them to me and coming into the street holding the parcel.

I had started out in life trusting everyone and now I trusted no one. So I had few acquaintances and no close friends. It was perhaps in reaction against the inevitable loneliness of my life that I'd find myself doing bold, risky, even outrageous things without hesitation or surprise. I was usually disappointed in these adventures and they didn't have much effect on me, good or bad, but I never quite lost the hope of something better or different.

---

5. Then (French exclamation).
6. Peace Street (French).
1. Game-bird hunters traditionally consider the shooting of sitting (rather than flying) birds shockingly unsporting.
2. Resort town on the south coast of France.
3. Made in Milan, Italy.

One day, I've forgotten now where, I met this young man who smiled at me and when we had talked a bit I agreed to have dinner with him in a couple of days' time. I went home excited, for I'd liked him very much, and began to plan what I should wear. I had a dress I quite liked, an evening cloak, shoes, stockings, but my underclothes weren't good enough for the occasion, I decided. Next day I went out and bought the milanese silk che-mise[4] and drawers.

So there we were seated at a table having dinner with a bedroom very obvious in the background. He was younger than I'd thought and stiffer and I didn't like him much after all. He kept eyeing me in such a wary, puzzled way. When we had finished our soup and the waiter had taken the plates away, he said: 'But you're a lady, aren't you?' exactly as he might have said, 'But you're really a snake or a crocodile, aren't you?'

'Oh no, not that you'd notice,' I said, but this didn't work. We looked glumly at each other across the gulf that had yawned between us.

Before I came to England I'd read many English novels and I imagined I knew all about the thoughts and tastes of various sorts of English people. I quickly decided that to distract or interest this man I must talk about shoot-ing.

I asked him if he knew the West Indies at all. He said no, he didn't and I told him a long story of having been lost in the Dominican forest when I was a child. This wasn't true. I'd often been in the woods but never alone. 'There are no parrots now,' I said, 'or very few. There used to be. There's a Domin-ican parrot in the zoo—have you ever seen it?—a sulky bird, very old I think. However, there are plenty of other birds and we do have shooting parties. Perdrix are very good to eat, but ramiers are rather bitter.'

Then I began describing a fictitious West Indian shooting party and all the time I talked I was remembering the real thing. An old shotgun leaning up in one corner of the room, the round table in the middle where we would sit to make cartridges, putting the shot in, ramming it down with a wad of paper. Gunpowder? There was that too, for I remember the smell. I suppose the boys were trusted to be careful.

The genuine shooting party consisted of my two brothers, who shared the shotgun, some hangers-on and me at the end of the procession, for then I couldn't bear to be left out of anything. As soon as the shooting was about to start I would stroll away casually and when I was out of sight run as hard as I could, crouch down behind a bush and put my fingers in my ears. It wasn't that I was sorry for the birds, but I hated and feared the noise of the gun. When it was all over I'd quietly join the others. I must have done this unobtrusively or probably my brothers thought me too insignificant to worry about, for no one ever remarked on my odd behaviour or teased me about it.

On and on I went, almost believing what I was saying, when he interrupted me. 'Do you mean to say that your brothers shot sitting birds?' His voice was cold and shocked.

I stared at him. How could I convince this man that I hadn't the faintest idea whether my brothers shot sitting birds or not? How could I explain now what really happened? If I did he'd think me a liar. Also a coward and there

---

4. Loose-fitting undergarment hanging straight from the shoulders.

he'd be right, for I was afraid of many things, not only the sound of gunfire. But by this time I wasn't sure that I liked him at all so I was silent and felt my face growing as stiff and unsmiling as his.

It was a most uncomfortable dinner. We both avoided looking at the bedroom and when the last mouthful was swallowed he announced that he was going to take me home. The way he said this rather puzzled me. Then I told myself that probably he was curious to see where I lived. Neither of us spoke in the taxi except to say, 'Well, goodnight.' 'Goodnight.'

I felt regretful when it came to taking off my lovely pink chemise, but I could still think: Some other night perhaps, another sort of man.

I slept at once.

1976

ROBERT GRAVES
1895–1985

Robert von Ranke Graves was born in London of partly Anglo-Irish and partly German descent—his great-uncle was the distinguished German historian Leopold von Ranke—but his voice is peculiarly English. He left Charterhouse School to go immediately into the army, serving in World War I until he was invalided out in 1917. After the war he went to Oxford, took a B.Litt. degree, and in 1926 began a brief period as professor of English at the Egyptian University in Cairo. In 1929 he published *Goodbye to All That*, an account of his experiences in the war, which, as he himself put it, "paid my debts and enabled me to set up in Majorca as a writer." He lived there with the American poet Laura Riding until, in 1936, the outbreak of the Spanish Civil War forced them to leave. He returned to Majorca, with his second wife, after World War II and remained there for the rest of his life.

Graves began as a Georgian poet, but from an early stage it was clear that he was a Georgian with a difference. The mingling of the colloquial and the visionary in his vocabulary, the accent of conversation underlying the regular rhythms of his stanzas, the tension between a romantic indulgence in emotion and a cool appraisal of its significance—these are qualities found even in his early poetry, although it is only in his later work that we find them more consistently employed and effectively disciplined. His best work combines the ironic and the visionary in a highly individual manner, and he is also capable of a down-to-earth poetry, often ironical and mocking in tone and dealing with simple domestic facts or the more annoying of personal relationships, which nevertheless is seen on further reading to reach out to ever wider and deeper implications. He himself said: "I write poems for poets, and satires or grotesques for wits. For people in general I write prose, and am content that they should be unaware that I do anything else. To write poems for other than poets is wasteful" (Foreword to *Poems 1938–45*). But this is mischievous exaggeration. "What Mr. Graves means," Lionel Trilling has observed, "is that, in our day, only poets can be counted on not to be misled by the lightness and clarity of his verse, by the irony and the humor; that only poets will be sufficiently aware of the tradition in which he writes, and of hearing the truth that lies not only in the doctrinal statements that the poem makes but also in the justice of its diction, in the pitch and tone of its voice" (*A Gathering of Fugitives*, p. 23).

Graves made his living by his prose, which is extensive and varied and includes, in addition to *Goodbye to All That,* a number of historical novels in which characters and events from the classical or biblical past are reconstructed in a lively modern idiom: the most notable of his historical novels are *I, Claudius* (1934), *Claudius the God* (1934), and *King Jesus* (1946). He was a good classical and biblical scholar, although an eccentric one. His interest in classical and biblical myth was closely related to his theory of poetry and of poetic inspiration, which he expressed in *The White Goddess* (1948), a study of mythology drawn from a great variety of sources but essentially original in its main emphases and interpretations. The book begins as a history of myth, develops into an attack on fashionable kinds of poetry, and ends with his own view of poetry. It preserves the secret wisdom of a people and derives from the great female inspirational principle that he called the White Goddess. Only a return to goddess worship and an abandonment of patriarchal in favor of matriarchal society can help modern poetry to recover its lost force, clarity, and mythic wisdom. There is often a note of willful exaggeration or mocking mischief in Graves's criticism: he loved to flutter the academic dovecotes.

Among the early influences on his poetry were the poet John Skelton (ca. 1460–1529), the ballads, Welsh and Irish heroic and popular poetry, and Thomas Hardy (one of the few poets surviving into his own lifetime whom he admired). In 1926 he met Laura Riding, who over the next fifteen years was to be his mistress, muse, mentor, and, some say, tormenter. They collaborated on various projects, including the influential critical work *A Survey of Modernist Poetry* (1927). But for Graves modernism was not represented by the later Yeats or by Pound or Eliot; it had more in common with the work of the American poets John Crowe Ransom, E. E. Cummings, and William Carlos Williams. In his own later poetry Graves became more and more the poet of personal relationships, especially of love between the sexes.

In successive editions of his poems he ruthlessly pruned away what he had come to dislike or believed to represent a phase of his poetic career that he had outgrown. He published more than seventeen volumes of poetry, of which *Collected Poems 1975* represented most of what he wanted to preserve. Its publication was the sign for clear critical affirmation, on both sides of the Atlantic, that Graves was a major English poet of our time.

Down, Wanton, Down!

Down, wanton, down! Have you no shame
That at the whisper of Love's name,
Or Beauty's, presto! up you raise
Your angry head and stand at gaze?

5   Poor bombard-captain, sworn to reach
The ravelin[1] and effect a breach—
Indifferent what you storm or why,
So be that in the breach you die![2]

Love may be blind, but Love at least
10   Knows what is man and what mere beast;
Or Beauty wayward, but requires
More delicacy from her squires.

---

1. Fortified projection from a castle wall.
2. A pun on the verb "to die," in the sense of "to achieve orgasm" (common from the 16th to the 18th centuries). Cf. Pope's *The Rape of the Lock*

5.77–78: "Nor feared the chief the unequal fight to try, / Who sought no more than on his fight to die."

Tell me, my witless, whose one boast
Could be your staunchness at the post,
When were you made a man of parts
To think fine and profess the arts?

Will many-gifted Beauty come
Bowing to your bald rule of thumb,
Or Love swear loyalty to your crown?
Be gone, have done! Down, wanton, down!

1933

Love Without Hope

Love without hope, as when the young bird-catcher
Swept off his tall hat to the Squire's own daughter,
So let the imprisoned larks escape and fly
Singing about her head, as she rode by.

1925

The Cool Web

Children are dumb to say how hot the day is,
How hot the scent is of the summer rose,
How dreadful the black wastes of evening sky,
How dreadful the tall soldiers drumming by.

But we have speech, to chill the angry day,
And speech, to dull the rose's cruel scent.
We spell away the overhanging night,
We spell away the soldiers and the fright.

There's a cool web of language winds us in,
Retreat from too much joy or too much fear:
We grow sea-green at last and coldly die
In brininess and volubility.

But if we let our tongues lose self-possession,
Throwing off language and its watery clasp
Before our death, instead of when death comes,
Facing the wide glare of the children's day,
Facing the rose, the dark sky and the drums,
We shall go mad no doubt and die that way.

1927

The Reader Over My Shoulder

You, reading over my shoulder, peering beneath
My writing arm—I suddenly feel your breath

Hot on my hand or on my nape,
So interrupt my theme, scratching these few
5 Words on the margin for you, namely you,
Too-human shape fixed in that shape:—

All the saying of things against myself
And for myself I have well done myself.
What now, old enemy, shall you do
10 But quote and underline, thrusting yourself
Against me, as ambassador of myself,
In damned confusion of myself and you?

For you in strutting, you in sycophancy,
Have played too long this other self of me,
15 Doubling the part of judge and patron
With that of creaking grind-stone to my wit.
Know me, have done: I am a proud spirit
And you for ever clay. Have done.

1938

To Juan at the Winter Solstice[1]

There is one story and one story only
That will prove worth your telling,
Whether as learned bard or gifted child;[2]
To it all lines or lesser gauds[3] belong
5 That startle with their shining
Such common stories as they stray into.

Is it of trees you tell, their months and virtues,[4]
Or strange beasts that beset you,
Of birds that croak at you the Triple will?[5]
10 Or of the Zodiac and how slow it turns
Below the Boreal Crown,[6]
Prison of all true kings that ever reigned?

Water to water, ark again to ark,
From woman back to woman:

1. Graves's "grammar of poetic myth," *The White Goddess* (1948; see the headnote, p. 2445), finds the only theme for true poetry in the story of the life cycle of the Sun God or Sun Hero, his marriage with the Goddess, and inevitable death at her hands or by her command. The poet's son Juan was born on December 21, 1945, one day before the winter solstice, which (being the time when the sun gives least heat and light to the north) is in many religions the birthday of the Sun Hero.
2. Graves has solved the riddle of the poem *The Battle of the Trees* by the Celtic bard Taliesin who, as a "gifted child," outmatched twenty-four experienced court poets.
3. The larger beads placed between the decades of "aves" in a Roman Catholic rosary (i.e., every

eleventh bead).
4. Graves cites, in addition to Taliesin's *The Battle of the Trees,* an ancient Druidic "tree-calendar" that describes the natural and magic properties of different trees and associates each with a different month or season.
5. The Goddess sometimes speaks through such "prophetic" birds as the owl and eagle and has been called the Triple Goddess because of her threefold aspect as Goddess of the Underworld, Earth, and Sky.
6. *Corona Borealis, . . .* which in Thracian-Libyan mythology carried to Bronze Age Britain, was the purgatory where Solar Heroes went after death [Graves's note]. The twelve signs of the turning zodiac correspond to the twelve months.

15 So each new victim treads unfalteringly
The never altered circuit of his fate,
Bringing twelve peers[7] as witness
Both to his starry rise and starry fall.[8]

Or is it of the Virgin's silver beauty,
20 All fish below the thighs?
She in her left hand bears a leafy quince;[9]
When with her right she crooks a finger, smiling,
How may the King hold back?
Royally then he barters life for love.

25 Or of the undying snake from chaos hatched,
Whose coils contain the ocean,
Into whose chops with naked sword he springs,
Then in black water, tangled by the reeds,
Battles three days and nights,
30 To be spewed up beside her scalloped shore?[1]

Much snow is falling, winds roar hollowly,
The owl hoots from the elder,
Fear in your heart cries to the loving-cup:
Sorrow to sorrow as the sparks fly upward.
35 The log groans and confesses:[2]
There is one story and one story only.

Dwell on her graciousness, dwell on her smiling,
Do not forget what flowers
The great boar trampled down in ivy time.[3]
40 Her brow was creamy as the crested wave,
Her sea-grey eyes were wild[4]
But nothing promised that is not performed.

1945

The White Goddess[1]

All saints revile her, and all sober men
Ruled by the God Apollo's golden mean—
In scorn of which we sailed to find her
In distant regions likeliest to hold her

7. Perhaps the twelve knights of King Arthur's round table, Christ's twelve apostles, or the twelve signs of the zodiac.
8. The king (or Solar Hero), reincarnated, reappears at the winter solstice floating in an ark on the water.
9. Two forms of the Goddess are Aphrodite, Greek goddess of love, whose emblem is the quince, and Rahab, the Hebraic sea goddess, who was depicted with a fish's tail.
1. The snake, Ophion, was created by the Goddess and mated with her. From their egg, the world was

hatched by the sun's rays. The king (or Solar Hero) must kill the snake to win the Goddess, but in Oct. the snake (perhaps reincarnated as the boar of line 39) must kill the king.
2. Cf. Job 5.7: "Man is born unto trouble, as the sparks fly upward." "The log is the Yule [or Christmas] log, burned at the year's end" [Graves's note].
3. Aphrodite's lover, Adonis, was killed by a boar.
4. Cf. Keats, La Belle Dame Sans Merci: A Ballad, line 16: "And her eyes were wild."
1. See headnote, p. 2445.

5   Whom we desired above all things to know,
  Sister of the mirage and echo.

  It was a virtue not to stay,
  To go our headstrong and heroic way
  Seeking her out at the volcano's head,
10   Among pack ice, or where the track had faded
  Beyond the cavern of the seven sleepers:[2]
  Whose broad high brow was white as any leper's,
  Whose eyes were blue, with rowan-berry lips,
  With hair curled honey-coloured to white hips.

15   Green sap of Spring in the young wood a-stir
  Will celebrate the Mountain Mother,
  And every song-bird shout awhile for her;
  But we are gifted, even in November
  Rawest of seasons, with so huge a sense
20   Of her nakedly worn magnificence
  We forget cruelty and past betrayal,
  Heedless of where the next bright bolt may fall.

1953

The Blue-Fly

Five summer days, five summer nights,
The ignorant, loutish, giddy blue-fly
Hung without motion on the cling peach,
Humming occasionally: "O my love, my fair one!"
5   As in the *Canticles*.[1]

Magnified one thousand times, the insect
Looks farcically human; laugh if you will!
Bald head, stage-fairy wings, blear eyes,
A caved-in chest, hairy black mandibles,
10   Long spindly thighs.

The crime was detected on the sixth day.
What then could be said or done? By anyone?
It would have been vindictive, mean and what-not
To swat that fly for being a blue-fly,
15   For debauch of a peach.

Is it fair, either, to bring a microscope
To bear on the case, even in search of truth?
Nature, doubtless, has some compelling cause
To glut the carriers of her epidemics—
20   Nor did the peach complain.

1952, 1953

---

2. Cf. Donne's, *The Good-Morrow*, line 4: "Or snorted we in the seven sleepers' den."

1. The biblical Song of Songs, or Song of Solomon.

A Slice of Wedding Cake

Why have such scores of lovely, gifted girls
    Married impossible men?
Simple self-sacrifice may be ruled out,
    And missionary endeavour, nine times out of ten.

5   Repeat "impossible men": not merely rustic,
        Foul-tempered or depraved
(Dramatic foils chosen to show the world
    How well women behave, and always have behaved).

Impossible men: idle, illiterate,
10   Self-pitying, dirty, sly,
For whose appearance even in City parks
    Excuses must be made to casual passers-by.

Has God's supply of tolerable husbands
    Fallen, in fact, so low?
15   Or do I always over-value woman
    At the expense of man?
           Do I?
             It might be so.

1959

STEVIE SMITH
1902–1971

Stevie Smith's real name was Florence Margaret Smith, but she was nicknamed "Stevie" after the famous jockey Steve Donoghue, because of her small stature. She was born in Hull, Yorkshire, but at the age of three went with her mother and sister to live with an aunt in Palmer's Green, an unfashionable and out-of-the-way suburb of London. She had a good high-school education, concentrating on French and the classics, but did not go on to a university. She obtained a position as secretary to the magazine-publishing firm of Newnes, Pearson, eventually becoming private secretary to the two directors of the firm, while continuing to live with her aunt, to whom she was devoted. When her aunt grew old and feeble Smith gave up her job to look after her, although she herself was often in ill health. At the same time she managed somehow to lead a lively social life in London and was known for the vividness and variety of her conversation at parties.

Stevie Smith first appeared as a novelist, with *Novel on Yellow Paper* (1936). This was followed by two further novels and nine volumes of poetry. It was *Novel on Yellow Paper* and her first volume of poetry, *A Good Time Was Had By All* (1937), that established her reputation, and her poems began to appear frequently in newspapers and periodicals.

Stevie Smith is one of the absolute originals of English literature, whose work fits into no category and shows none of the characteristic influences of the age. Sometimes she is reminiscent of Blake, sometimes of Ogden Nash, sometimes of Edward Lear, but her voice is always her own. Her language is sometimes simple and matter-of-fact, sometimes deliberately archaic (where it is often suggestive of old ballads), while her verse movement ranges from free conversational rhythms to traditional verse patterns, on occasion becoming—deliberately, with ironic effect—almost doggerel. The simple matter-of-fact speech can exist in the same poem as a more deliberately "poetic" language; in *Is It Wise?* for example, we encounter "a song of Melancholy," "a garland of sighs," "a martyr's dowry," and then the simple refrain "No, it is not wise." She illustrated many of her poems with quaint drawings ("doodles" as she called them) that have the same kind of oddity as the poetry. She was a religious skeptic who was at the same time fascinated by theological speculation, the language of the Bible, and religious experience. Her concern with death and suicide may seem morbid, but it was genuine, and in *Not Waving but Drowning* (published in the volume of that name in 1957) a deep pessimism is clothed in wit and even humor.

Is It Wise?

Is it wise
To hug misery
To make a song of Melancholy
To weave a garland of sighs
5   To abandon hope wholly?
No, it is not wise.

Is it wise
To love Mortality
To make a song of Corruptibility
10   A chain of linked lies
To bind Mutability?
No, it is not wise.

Is it wise
To endure
15   To call up Old Fury
And Pain for a martyr's dowry
When Death's a prize
Easy to carry?
No, it is not wise.

1937

Our Bog Is Dood

Our Bog is dood, our Bog is dood,
They lisped in accents mild,
But when I asked them to explain
They grew a little wild.
5   How do you know your Bog is dood
My darling little child?

We know because we wish it so
That is enough, they cried,
And straight within each infant eye
10   Stood up the flame of pride,
And if you do not think it so
You shall be crucified.

Then tell me, darling little ones,
What's dood, suppose Bog is?
15   Just what we think, the answer came,
Just what we think it is.
They bowed their heads. Our Bog is ours
And we are wholly his.

But when they raised them up again
20   They had forgotten me
Each one upon each other glared
In pride and misery
For what was dood, and what their Bog
They never could agree.

25   Oh sweet it was to leave them then,
And sweeter not to see,
And sweetest of all to walk alone
Beside the encroaching sea,
The sea that soon should drown them all,
30   That never yet drowned me.

1950

Not Waving but Drowning

Nobody heard him, the dead man,
But still he lay moaning:
I was much further out than you thought
And not waving but drowning.

5   Poor chap, he always loved larking
And now he's dead
It must have been too cold for him his heart gave way,
They said.

Oh, no no no, it was too cold always
10   (Still the dead one lay moaning)
I was much too far out all my life
And not waving but drowning.

1957

The New Age

Shall I tell you the signs of a New Age coming?
It is a sound of drubbing and sobbing
Of people crying, We are old, we are old
And the sun is going down and becoming cold
5   Oh sinful and sad and the last of our kind
If we turn to God now do you think He will mind?
Then they fall on their knees and begin to whine
That the state of Art itself presages decline
As if Art has anything or ever had
10   To do with civilization whether good or bad.
Art is wild as a cat and quite separate from civilization
But that is another matter that is not now under consideration.
Oh these people are fools with their sighing and sinning
Why should Man be at an end? he is hardly beginning.
15   This New Age will slip in under cover of their cries
And be upon them before they have opened their eyes.
Well, say geological time is a one-foot rule
Then Man's only been here about half an inch to play the fool
Or be wise if he likes, as he often has been
20   Oh heavens how these crying people spoil the beautiful geological scene.

1957

Thoughts About the Person from Porlock[1]

Coleridge received the Person from Porlock
And ever after called him a curse,
Then why did he hurry to let him in?
He could have hid in the house.

5   It was not right of Coleridge in fact it was wrong
(But often we all do wrong)
As the truth is I think he was already stuck
With Kubla Khan.

He was weeping and wailing: I am finished, finished,
10   I shall never write another word of it,
When along comes the Person from Porlock
And takes the blame for it.

It was not right, it was wrong,
But often we all do wrong.

• • •

15   May we inquire the name of the Person from Porlock?
Why, Porson, didn't you know?

1. See Coleridge, *Kubla Khan*, p. 439.

He lived at the bottom of Porlock Hill
So had a long way to go,

He wasn't much in the social sense
20 Though his grandmother was a Warlock,
One of the Ruthlandshire ones I fancy
And nothing to do with Porlock.

And he lived at the bottom of the hill as I said
And had a cat named Flo,
25 And had a cat named Flo.

I long for the Person from Porlock
To bring my thoughts to an end,
I am becoming impatient to see him
I think of him as a friend,

30 Often I look out of the window
Often I run to the gate
I think, He will come this evening,
I think it is rather late.

I am hungry to be interrupted
35 Forever and ever amen
O Person from Porlock come quickly
And bring my thoughts to an end.

I felicitate the people who have a Person from Porlock
To break up everything and throw it away
40 Because then there will be nothing to keep them
And they need not stay.

Why do they grumble so much?
He comes like a benison
They should be glad he has not forgotten them
45 They might have had to go on.

These thoughts are depressing I know. They are depressing,
I wish I was more cheerful, it is more pleasant,
Also it is a duty, we should smile as well as submitting
To the purpose of One Above who is experimenting
50 With various mixtures of human character which goes best,
All is interesting for him it is exciting, but not for us.
There I go again, Smile, smile, and get some work to do
Then you will be practically unconscious without positively having to go.

1962

Pretty

Why is the word pretty so underrated?
In November the leaf is pretty when it falls
The stream grows deep in the woods after rain
And in the pretty pool the pike stalks

5 He stalks his prey, and this is pretty too,
The prey escapes with an underwater flash
But not for long, the great fish has him now
The pike is a fish who always has his prey

And this is pretty. The water rat is pretty
10 His paws are not webbed, he cannot shut his nostrils
As the otter can and the beaver, he is torn between
The land and water, Not "torn," he does not mind.

The owl hunts in the evening and it is pretty
The lake water below him rustles with ice
15 There is frost coming from the ground, in the air mist
All this is pretty, it could not be prettier.

Yes, it could always be prettier, the eye abashes
It is becoming an eye that cannot see enough,
Out of the wood the eye climbs. This is prettier
20 A field in the evening, tilting up.

The field tilts to the sky. Though it is late
The sky is lighter than the hill field
All this looks easy but really it is extraordinary
Well, it is extraordinary to be so pretty.

25 And it is careless, and that is always pretty
This field, this owl, this pike, this pool are careless,
As Nature is always careless and indifferent
Who sees, who steps, means nothing, and this is pretty.

So a person can come along like a thief—pretty!—
30 Stealing a look, pinching the sound and feel,
Lick the icicle broken from the bank
And still say nothing at all, only cry pretty.

Cry pretty, pretty, pretty and you'll be able
Very soon not even to cry pretty
35 And so be delivered entirely from humanity
This is prettiest of all, it is very pretty.

1962

GEORGE ORWELL
1903–1950

George Orwell was the pseudonym of Eric Blair, who was born in India, where his father was a British civil servant. He was sent to private school in England, and won a scholarship to Eton, the foremost "public school" (i.e., private boarding school) in the country. It was at these schools that he first became conscious of the difference between his own background and the wealthy background of many of his schoolmates. On leaving school he joined the Imperial Police in Burma (both Burma and India were then still part of the British Empire). His service in Burma from 1922 to 1927 produced a sense of guilt about British colonialism and a feeling that he must make some kind of personal expiation for it. This he would later do with a fiercely antico-lonialist novel, *Burmese Days* (1934), and essays like *Shooting an Elephant* (1936). He returned to England determined to be a writer and adopted a pseudonym as one way of escaping from the class position in which his birth and education had placed him. He went to Paris to try to make a living by teaching while he made his first attempts at writing. His extremely difficult experience in Paris was followed by a spell as a tramp in England, and both experiences are vividly recorded in his first book, *Down and Out in Paris and London* (1933). Orwell did not have to suffer the dire poverty that he seems to have actually courted (he had influential friends who would have been glad to help him); he wanted, however, to learn about the life of the poor firsthand, partly out of humane curiosity, partly because, as he wrote, if he did so "part of my guilt would drop from me."

The Road to Wigan Pier (1937) discusses the experiences Orwell shared with the unemployed in the north of England. The book pleased neither the left nor the right, for by now Orwell was showing what was to become his characteristic independence of mind on political and social questions: he wrote of what he knew firsthand to be true and was contemptuous of ideologies. He never joined a political party but regarded himself as a man of the uncommitted and independent left. He took part on the Republican side in the Spanish Civil War, which broke out in 1936 when Franco raised his rebellion against the Republican government, and returned to write *Homage to Catalonia* (1938). This book strongly criticized the Communist part in the civil war and showed from his own experience how the Communist Party in Spain was out to destroy Anarchists, Trotskyists, and any others on the Republican side who were suspected of not toeing the Stalinist line; it aroused great indignation on the left in Britain and elsewhere, for leftists believed that they should solidly support the Soviet Union and the Communist Party as the natural leaders in the struggle against international fascism. Orwell never wavered in his belief that while profound social change was necessary and desirable in capitalist countries of the West, the so-called socialism established in Soviet Russia was a perversion of social-ism and a wicked tyranny. In *Animal Farm* (1945) he wrote an animal fable showing how such a perversion of socialism could develop, while in *Nineteen Eighty-Four* (1949), when he was an embittered man dying of tuberculosis, he wrote a savagely powerful novel depicting a totalitarian future in England where the government uses the language of socialism to cover a tyranny that systematically destroys the human spirit. In that dark vision of hell on earth, language has become one of the principal instruments of oppression. The Ministry of Truth is there concerned with the trans-mission of untruth, and the white face of its pyramidal structure proclaims in "New-speak" the three slogans of the party: "WAR IS PEACE / FREEDOM IS SLAVERY / IGNORANCE IS STRENGTH." Three years before Orwell formulated the concept of Newspeak, he had explored in one of his most influential essays, *Politics and the English Language* (1946), the decay of language and the ways in which it might be checked. The forty years that have passed since it was written have only confirmed the accuracy of its diagnosis and the value of its prescription.

It was Orwell's independent innocence of eye that made him both a permanent misfit politically and a brilliantly original writer. He was an outstanding journalist, and the essays he wrote regularly for the left-wing British journal *Tribune* and other periodicals include some of his best work.

Shooting an Elephant

In Moulmein, in Lower Burma, I was hated by large numbers of people—the only time in my life that I have been important enough for this to happen to me. I was sub-divisional police officer of the town, and in an aimless, petty kind of way anti-European feeling was very bitter. No one had the guts to raise a riot, but if a European woman went through the bazaars alone somebody would probably spit betel[1] juice over her dress. As a police officer I was an obvious target and was baited whenever it seemed safe to do so. When a nimble Burman tripped me up on the football field and the referee (another Burman) looked the other way, the crowd yelled with hideous laughter. This happened more than once. In the end the sneering yellow faces of young men that met me everywhere, the insults hooted after me when I was at a safe distance, got badly on my nerves. The young Buddhist priests were the worst of all. There were several thousands of them in the town and none of them seemed to have anything to do except stand on street corners and jeer at Europeans.

All this was perplexing and upsetting. For at that time I had already made up my mind that imperialism was an evil thing and the sooner I chucked up my job and got out of it the better. Theoretically—and secretly, of course—I was all for the Burmese and all against their oppressors, the British. As for the job I was doing, I hated it more bitterly than I can perhaps make clear. In a job like that you see the dirty work of Empire at close quarters. The wretched prisoners huddling in the stinking cages of the lock-ups, the grey, cowed faces of the long-term convicts, the scarred buttocks of the men who had been flogged with bamboos—all these oppressed me with an intolerable sense of guilt. But I could get nothing into perspective. I was young and ill-educated and I had had to think out my problems in the utter silence that is imposed on every Englishman in the East. I did not even know that the British Empire is dying, still less did I know that it is a great deal better than the younger empires that are going to supplant it. All I knew was that I was stuck between my hatred of the empire I served and my rage against the evil-spirited little beasts who tried to make my job impossible. With one part of my mind I thought of the British Raj as an unbreakable tyranny, as something clamped down, *in saecula saeculorum*,[2] upon the will of prostrate peoples; with another part I thought that the greatest joy in the world would be to drive a bayonet into a Buddhist priest's guts. Feelings like these are the normal by-products of imperialism; ask any Anglo-Indian official, if you can catch him off duty.

---

1. Leaf of a plant chewed as a delicacy in Burma and other Eastern countries. "Bazaars": Eastern marketplaces.

2. For ever and ever (Latin). "Raj": rule (Hindi).

One day something happened which in a roundabout way was enlighten-ing. It was a tiny incident in itself, but it gave me a better glimpse than I had had before of the real nature of imperialism—the real motives for which despotic governments act. Early one morning the sub-inspector at a police station the other end of the town rang me up on the phone and said that an elephant was ravaging the bazaar. Would I please come and do something about it? I did not know what I could do, but I wanted to see what was happening and I got on to a pony and started out. I took my rifle, an old .44 Winchester and much too small to kill an elephant, but I thought the noise might be useful *in terrorem*.[3] Various Burmans stopped me on the way and told me about the elephant's doings. It was not, of course, a wild elephant, but a tame one which had gone "must."[4] It had been chained up as tame elephants always are when their attack of "must" is due, but on the previous night it had broken its chain and escaped. Its mahout,[5] the only person who could manage it when it was in that state, had set out in pursuit, but he had taken the wrong direction and was now twelve hours' journey away, and in the morning the elephant had suddenly reappeared in the town. The Bur-mese population had no weapons and were quite helpless against it. It had already destroyed somebody's bamboo hut, killed a cow and raided some fruit-stalls and devoured the stock; also it had met the municipal rubbish van, and, when the driver jumped out and took to his heels, had turned the van over and inflicted violence upon it.

The Burmese sub-inspector and some Indian constables were waiting for me in the quarter where the elephant had been seen. It was a very poor quarter, a labyrinth of squalid bamboo huts, thatched with palm-leaf, wind-ing all over a steep hillside. I remember that it was a cloudy stuffy morning at the beginning of the rains. We began questioning the people as to where the elephant had gone, and, as usual, failed to get any definite information. That is invariably the case in the East; a story always sounds clear enough at a distance, but the nearer you get to the scene of events the vaguer it becomes. Some of the people said that the elephant had gone in one direc-tion, some said that he had gone in another, some professed not even to have heard of any elephant. I had almost made up my mind that the whole story was a pack of lies, when we heard yells a little distance away. There was a loud, scandalised cry of "Go away, child! Go away this instant!" and an old woman with a switch in her hand came round the corner of a hut, violently shooing away a crowd of naked children. Some more women followed, click-ing their tongues and exclaiming; evidently there was something there that the children ought not to have seen. I rounded the hut and saw a man's dead body sprawling in the mud. He was an Indian, a black Dravidian coolie,[6] almost naked, and he could not have been dead many minutes. The people said that the elephant had come suddenly upon him round the corner of the hut, caught him with its trunk, put its foot on his back and ground him into the earth. This was the rainy season and the ground was soft, and his face had scored a trench a foot deep and a couple of yards long. He was lying on his belly with arms crucified and head sharply twisted to one side. His face was coated with mud, the eyes wide open, the teeth bared and grinning with

3. To frighten it (Latin).
4. A state of dangerous frenzy to which certain animals are subject at irregular intervals.

5. Elephant driver (Hindi).
6. Hired laborer (disputed origin).

an expression of unendurable agony. (Never tell me, by the way, that the dead look peaceful. Most of the corpses I have seen looked devilish.) The friction of the great beast's foot had stripped the skin from his back as neatly as one skins a rabbit. As soon as I saw the dead man I sent an orderly to a friend's house nearby to borrow an elephant rifle. I had already sent back the pony, not wanting it to go mad with fright and throw me if it smelled the elephant.

The orderly came back in a few minutes with a rifle and five cartridges, and meanwhile some Burmans had arrived and told us that the elephant was in the paddy fields below, only a few hundred yards away. As I started forward practically the whole population of the quarter flocked out of their houses and followed me. They had seen the rifle and were all shouting excitedly that I was going to shoot the elephant. They had not shown much interest in the elephant when he was merely ravaging their homes, but it was different now that he was going to be shot. It was a bit of fun to them, as it would be to an English crowd; besides, they wanted the meat. It made me vaguely uneasy. I had no intention of shooting the elephant—I had merely sent for the rifle to defend myself if necessary—and it is always unnerving to have a crowd following you. I marched down the hill, looking and feeling a fool, with the rifle over my shoulder and an ever-growing army of people jostling at my heels. At the bottom, when you got away from the huts, there was a metalled road and beyond that a miry waste of paddy fields a thousand yards across, not yet ploughed but soggy from the first rains and dotted with coarse grass. The elephant was standing eighty yards from the road, his left side towards us. He took not the slightest notice of the crowd's approach. He was tearing up bunches of grass, beating them against his knees to clean them and stuffing them into his mouth.

I had halted on the road. As soon as I saw the elephant I knew with perfect certainty that I ought not to shoot him. It is a serious matter to shoot a working elephant—it is comparable to destroying a huge and costly piece of machinery—and obviously one ought not to do it if it can possibly be avoided. And at that distance, peacefully eating, the elephant looked no more dangerous than a cow. I thought then and I think now that his attack of "must" was already passing off; in which case he would merely wander harmlessly about until the mahout came back and caught him. Moreover, I did not in the least want to shoot him. I decided that I would watch him for a little while to make sure that he did not turn savage again, and then go home.

But at that moment I glanced round at the crowd that had followed me. It was an immense crowd, two thousand at the least and growing every minute. It blocked the road for a long distance on either side. I looked at the sea of yellow faces above the garish clothes—faces all happy and excited over this bit of fun, all certain that the elephant was going to be shot. They were watching me as they would watch a conjuror about to perform a trick. They did not like me, but with the magical rifle in my hands I was momentarily worth watching. And suddenly I realised that I should have to shoot the elephant after all. The people expected it of me and I had got to do it; I could feel their two thousand wills pressing me forward, irresistibly. And it was at this moment, as I stood there with the rifle in my hands, that I first grasped the hollowness, the futility of the white man's dominion in the East. Here was I, the white man with his gun, standing in front of the unarmed native crowd—seemingly the leading actor of the piece; but in reality I was only an absurd puppet pushed to and fro by the will of those yellow faces behind. I perceived in this moment that when the white man turns tyrant it is his own freedom that he destroys. He becomes a sort of hollow, posing dummy, the conventionalised figure of a sahib.[7] For it is the condition of his rule that he shall spend his life in trying to impress the "natives" and so in every crisis he has got to do what the "natives" expect of him. He wears a mask, and his face grows to fit it. I had got to shoot the elephant. I had committed myself to doing it when I sent for the rifle. A sahib has got to act like a sahib; he has got to appear resolute, to know his own mind and do definite things. To come all that way, rifle in hand, with two thousand people marching at my heels, and then to trail feebly away, having done nothing—no, that was impossible. The crowd would laugh at me. And my whole life, every white man's life in the East, was one long struggle not to be laughed at.

But I did not want to shoot the elephant. I watched him beating his bunch of grass against his knees, with that preoccupied grandmotherly air that elephants have. It seemed to me that it would be murder to shoot him. At that age I was not squeamish about killing animals, but I had never shot an elephant and never wanted to. (Somehow it always seems worse to kill a *large* animal.) Besides, there was the beast's owner to be considered. Alive, the elephant was worth at least a hundred pounds; dead, he would only be worth the value of his tusks—five pounds, possibly. But I had got to act quickly. I turned to some experienced-looking Burmans who had been there when we arrived, and asked them how the elephant had been behaving. They all said the same thing: he took no notice of you if you left him alone, but he might charge if you went too close to him.

It was perfectly clear to me what I ought to do. I ought to walk up to within, say, twenty-five yards of the elephant and test his behaviour. If he charged I could shoot, if he took no notice of me it would be safe to leave him until the mahout came back. But also I knew that I was going to do no such thing. I was a poor shot with a rifle and the ground was soft mud into which one would sink at every step. If the elephant charged and I missed him, I should have about as much chance as a toad under a steam-roller. But even then I was not thinking particularly of my own skin, only the watchful yellow faces behind. For at that moment, with the crowd watching me, I was not afraid in the ordinary sense, as I would have been if I had been alone. A white man mustn't be frightened in front of "natives"; and so, in general, he isn't frightened. The sole thought in my mind was that if anything went wrong those two thousand Burmans would see me pursued, caught, trampled on and reduced to a grinning corpse like that Indian up the hill. And if that happened it was quite probable that some of them would laugh. That would never do. There was only one alternative. I shoved the cartridges into the magazine and lay down on the road to get a better aim.

The crowd grew very still, and a deep, low, happy sigh, as of people who see the theatre curtain go up at last, breathed from innumerable throats. They were going to have their bit of fun after all. The rifle was a beautiful German thing with cross-hair sights. I did not then know that in shooting an elephant one should shoot to cut an imaginary bar running from ear-hole

---

7. White gentleman (Urdu).

to ear-hole. I ought therefore, as the elephant was sideways on, to have aimed straight at his ear-hole; actually I aimed several inches in front of this, thinking the brain would be further forward.

When I pulled the trigger I did not hear the bang or feel the kick—one never does when a shot goes home—but I heard the devilish roar of glee that went up from the crowd. In that instant, in too short a time, one would have thought, even for the bullet to get there, a mysterious, terrible change had come over the elephant. He neither stirred nor fell, but every line of his body had altered. He looked suddenly stricken, shrunken, immensely old, as though the frightful impact of the bullet had paralysed him without knocking him down. At last, after what seemed a long time—it might have been five seconds, I dare say—he sagged flabbily to his knees. His mouth slobbered. An enormous senility seemed to have settled upon him. One could have imagined him thousands of years old. I fired again into the same spot. At the second shot he did not collapse but climbed with desperate slowness to his feet and stood weakly upright, with legs sagging and head drooping. I fired a third time. That was the shot that did for him. You could see the agony of it jolt his whole body and knock the last remnant of strength from his legs. But in falling he seemed for a moment to rise, for as his hind legs collapsed beneath him he seemed to tower upwards like a huge rock toppling, his trunk reaching skyward like a tree. He trumpeted, for the first and only time. And then down he came, his belly towards me, with a crash that seemed to shake the ground even where I lay.

I got up. The Burmans were already racing past me across the mud. It was obvious that the elephant would never rise again, but he was not dead. He was breathing very rhythmically with long rattling gasps, his great mound of a side painfully rising and falling. His mouth was wide open—I could see far down into caverns of pale pink throat. I waited a long time for him to die, but his breathing did not weaken. Finally I fired my two remaining shots into the spot where I thought his heart must be. The thick blood welled out of him like red velvet, but still he did not die. His body did not even jerk when the shots hit him, the tortured breathing continued without a pause. He was dying, very slowly and in great agony, but in some world remote from me where not even a bullet could damage him further. I felt that I had got to put an end to that dreadful noise. It seemed dreadful to see the great beast lying there, powerless to move and yet powerless to die, and not even to be able to finish him. I sent back for my small rifle and poured shot after shot into his heart and down his throat. They seemed to make no impression. The tortured gasps continued as steadily as the ticking of a clock.

In the end I could not stand it any longer and went away. I heard later that it took him half an hour to die. Burmans were arriving with dahs[8] and baskets even before I left, and I was told they had stripped his body almost to the bones by the afternoon.

Afterwards, of course, there were endless discussions about the shooting of the elephant. The owner was furious, but he was only an Indian and could do nothing. Besides, legally I had done the right thing, for a mad elephant has to be killed, like a mad dog, if its owner fails to control it. Among the Europeans opinion was divided. The older men said I was right, the younger

---

8. Short heavy swords (Burmese).

men said it was a damn shame to shoot an elephant for killing a coolie, because an elephant was worth more than any damn Coringhee coolie. And afterwards I was very glad that the coolie had been killed; it put me legally in the right and it gave me a sufficient pretext for shooting the elephant. I often wondered whether any of the others grasped that I had done it solely to avoid looking a fool.

1936

Politics and the English Language

Most people who bother with the matter at all would admit that the English language is in a bad way, but it is generally assumed that we cannot by conscious action do anything about it. Our civilisation is decadent, and our language—so the argument runs—must inevitably share in the general collapse. It follows that any struggle against the abuse of language is a sentimental archaism, like preferring candles to electric light or hansom cabs to aeroplanes. Underneath this lies the half-conscious belief that language is a natural growth and not an instrument which we shape for our own purposes.

Now, it is clear that the decline of a language must ultimately have political and economic causes: it is not due simply to the bad influence of this or that individual writer. But an effect can become a cause, reinforcing the original cause and producing the same effect in an intensified form, and so on indefinitely. A man may take to drink because he feels himself to be a failure, and then fail all the more completely because he drinks. It is rather the same thing that is happening to the English language. It becomes ugly and inaccurate because our thoughts are foolish, but the slovenliness of our language makes it easier for us to have foolish thoughts. The point is that the process is reversible. Modern English, especially written English, is full of bad habits which spread by imitation and which can be avoided if one is willing to take the necessary trouble. If one gets rid of these habits one can think more clearly, and to think clearly is a necessary first step towards political regeneration: so that the fight against bad English is not frivolous and is not the exclusive concern of professional writers. I will come back to this presently, and I hope that by that time the meaning of what I have said here will have become clearer. Meanwhile, here are five specimens of the English language as it is now habitually written.

These five passages have not been picked out because they are especially bad—I could have quoted far worse if I had chosen—but because they illustrate various of the mental vices from which we now suffer. They are a little below the average, but are fairly representative samples. I number them so that I can refer back to them when necessary:

1. I am not, indeed, sure whether it is not true to say that the Milton who once seemed not unlike a seventeenth-century Shelley had not become, out of an experience ever more bitter in each year, more alien

(sic)[1] to the founder of that Jesuit sect which nothing could induce him to tolerate.

Professor Harold Laski (Essay in *Freedom of Expression*).

2. Above all, we cannot play ducks and drakes with a native battery of idioms which prescribes such egregious collocations of vocables as the Basic *put up with* for *tolerate* or *put at a loss* for *bewilder*.

Professor Lancelot Hogben *(Interglossa)*.

3. On the one side we have the free personality: by definition it is not neurotic, for it has neither conflict nor dream. Its desires, such as they are, are transparent, for they are just what institutional approval keeps in the forefront of consciousness; another institutional pattern would alter their number and intensity; there is little in them that is natural, irreducible, or culturally dangerous. But *on the other side,* the social bond itself is nothing but the mutual reflection of these self-secure integrities. Recall the definition of love. Is not this the very picture of a small academic? Where is there a place in this hall of mirrors for either personality or fraternity?

Essay on psychology in *Politics* (New York).

4. All the "best people" from the gentlemen's clubs, and all the frantic Fascist captains, united in common hatred of Socialism and bestial horror of the rising tide of the mass revolutionary movement, have turned to acts of provocation, to foul incendiarism, to medieval legends of poisoned wells, to legalise their own destruction to proletarian organisations, and rouse the agitated petty-bourgeoisie to chauvinistic fervour on behalf of the fight against the revolutionary way out of the crisis.

Communist pamphlet.

5. If a new spirit *is* to be infused into this old country, there is one thorny and contentious reform which must be tackled, and that is the humanisation and galvanisation of the BBC.[2] Timidity here will bespeak canker and atrophy of the soul. The heart of Britain may be sound and of strong beat, for instance, but the British lion's roar at present is like that of Bottom in Shakespeare's *Midsummer Night's Dream*—as gentle as any sucking dove. A virile new Britain cannot continue indefinitely to be traduced in the eyes, or rather ears, of the world by the effete languors of Langham Place, brazenly masquerading as "standard English." When the Voice of Britain is heard at nine o'clock,[3] better far and infinitely less ludicrous to hear aitches honestly dropped than the present priggish, inflated, inhibited, school-ma'amish arch braying of blameless bashful mewing maidens!

Letter in *Tribune*.

Each of these passages has faults of its own, but, quite apart from avoidable ugliness, two qualities are common to all of them. The first is staleness

---

1. Thus, i.e., that's the way it was written.
2. British Broadcasting Corporation.
3. During—and for some time after—World War

II, few programs had a larger audience than the evening nine o'clock news. Langham Place is the location of the BBC's main offices in London.

of imagery: the other is lack of precision. The writer either has a meaning and cannot express it, or he inadvertently says something else, or he is almost indifferent as to whether his words mean anything or not. This mixture of vagueness and sheer incompetence is the most marked characteristic of modern English prose, and especially of any kind of political writing. As soon as certain topics are raised, the concrete melts into the abstract and no one seems able to think of turns of speech that are not hackneyed: prose consists less and less of *words* chosen for the sake of their meaning, and more of *phrases* tacked together like the sections of a prefabricated hen-house. I list below, with notes and examples, various of the tricks by means of which the work of prose construction is habitually dodged:

Dying metaphors. A newly invented metaphor assists thought by evoking a visual image, while on the other hand a metaphor which is technically "dead" (e.g., *iron resolution*) has in effect reverted to being an ordinary word and can generally be used without loss of vividness. But in between these two classes there is a huge dump of worn-out metaphors which have lost all evocative power and are merely used because they save people the trouble of inventing phrases for themselves. Examples are: *Ring the changes on, take up the cudgels for, toe the line, ride roughshod over, stand shoulder to shoulder with, play into the hands of, no axe to grind, grist to the mill, fishing in troubled waters, rift within the lute, on the order of the day, Achilles' heel, swan song, hotbed.* Many of these are used without knowledge of their meaning (What is a "rift," for instance?), and incompatible metaphors are frequently mixed, a sure sign that the writer is not interested in what he is saying. Some metaphors now current have been twisted out of their original meaning without those who use them even being aware of the fact. For example, *toe the line* is sometimes written *tow the line.* Another example is *the hammer and the anvil,* now always used with the implication that the anvil gets the worst of it. In real life it is always the anvil that breaks the hammer, never the other way about: a writer who stopped to think what he was saying would be aware of this, and would avoid perverting the original phrase.

Operators, or *verbal false limbs.* These save the trouble of picking out appropriate verbs and nouns, and at the same time pad each sentence with extra syllables which give it an appearance of symmetry. Characteristic phrases are: *render inoperative, militate against, prove unacceptable, make contact with, be subjected to, give rise to, give grounds for, have the effect of, play a leading part (rôle) in, make itself felt, take effect, exhibit a tendency to, serve the purpose of,* etc etc. The keynote is the elimination of simple verbs. Instead of being a single word, such as *break, stop, spoil, mend, kill,* a verb becomes a *phrase,* made up of a noun or adjective tacked on to some general-purposes verb such as *prove, serve, form, play, render.* In addition, the passive voice is wherever possible used in preference to the active, and noun constructions are used instead of gerunds (*by examination of* instead of *by examining*). The range of verbs is further cut down by means of the *-ise* and *de-* formations, and banal statements are given an appearance of profundity by means of the *not un-* formation. Simple conjunctions and prepositions are replaced by such phrases as *with respect to, having regard to,* *the fact that, by dint of, in view of, in the interests of, on the hypothesis that;* and the ends of sentences are saved from anticlimax by such resounding commonplaces as *greatly to be desired, cannot be left out of account, a development to be expected in the near future, deserving of serious consideration, brought to a satisfactory conclusion,* and so on and so forth.

Pretentious diction. Words like *phenomenon, element, individual* (as noun), *objective, categorical, effective, virtual, basic, primary, promote, constitute, exhibit, exploit, utilise, eliminate, liquidate,* are used to dress up simple statements and give an air of scientific impartiality to biassed judgements. Adjectives like *epoch-making, epic, historic, unforgettable, triumphant, age-old, inevitable, inexorable, veritable,* are used to dignify the sordid processes of international politics, while writing that aims at glorifying war usually takes on an archaic colour, its characteristic words being: *realm, throne, chariot, mailed fist, trident, sword, shield, buckler, banner, jackboot, clarion.* Foreign words and expressions such as *cul de sac, ancien régime, deus ex machina, mutatis mutandis, status quo, Gleichschaltung, Weltanschauung,*[4] are used to give an air of culture and elegance. Except for the useful abbreviation *i.e., e.g.,* and *etc,* there is no real need for any of the hundreds of foreign phrases now current in English. Bad writers, and especially scientific, political and sociological writers, are nearly always haunted by the notion that Latin or Greek words are grander than Saxon ones, and unnecessary words like *expedite, ameliorate, predict, extraneous, deracinated, clandestine, sub-aqueous* and hundreds of others constantly gain ground from their Anglo-Saxon opposite numbers.[5] The jargon peculiar to Marxist writing (*hyena, hangman, cannibal, petty bourgeois, these gentry, lacquey, flunkey, mad dog, White Guard,* etc) consists largely of words and phrases translated from Russian, German or French; but the normal way of coining a new word is to use a Latin or Greek root with the appropriate affix and, where necessary, the *-ise* formation. It is often easier to make up words of this kind (*deregionalise, impermissible, extramarital, non-fragmentatory* and so forth) than to think up the English words that will cover one's meaning. The result, in general, is an increase in slovenliness and vagueness.

Meaningless words. In certain kinds of writing, particularly in art criticism and literary criticism, it is normal to come across long passages which are almost completely lacking in meaning.[6] Words like *romantic, plastic, values, human, dead, sentimental, natural, vitality,* as used in art criticism, are strictly meaningless, in the sense that they not only do not point to any discoverable object, but are hardly even expected to do so by the reader.

4. Respectively: dead end (French), former system of government (French), the god from the machine (Latin), with the necessary changes (Latin), the existing state of things (Latin), standardization of political institutions among authoritarian states (German), and philosophy of life (German).
5. An interesting illustration of this is the way in which the English flower names which were in use till very recently are being ousted by Greek ones, *snapdragon* becoming *antirrhinum, forget-me-not* becoming *myosotis,* etc. It is hard to see any practical reason for this change of fashion: it is probably due to an instinctive turning-away from the more homely word and a vague feeling that the Greek word is scientific [Orwell's note].
6. Example: "Comfort's catholicity of perception and image, strangely Whitmanesque in range, almost the exact opposite in aesthetic compulsion, continues to evoke that trembling atmospheric accumulative hinting at a cruel, an inexorably serene timelessness . . . Wrey Gardiner scores by aiming at simple bullseyes with precision. Only they are not so simple, and through this contented sadness runs more than the surface bitter-sweet of resignation." (*Poetry Quarterly.*) [Orwell's note].

When one critic writes, "The outstanding features of Mr X's work is its living quality," while another writes, "The immediately striking thing about Mr X's work is its peculiar deadness," the reader accepts this as a simple difference of opinion. If words like *black* and *white* were involved, instead of the jargon words *dead* and *living,* he would see at once that language was being used in an improper way. Many political words are similarly abused. The word *Fascism* has now no meaning except in so far as it signifies "something not desirable." The words *democracy, socialism, freedom, patriotic, realistic, justice,* have each of them several different meanings which cannot be reconciled with one another. In the case of a word like *democracy,* not only is there no agreed definition, but the attempt to make one is resisted from all sides. It is almost universally felt that when we call a country democratic we are praising it: consequently the defenders of every kind of régime claim that it is a democracy, and fear that they might have to stop using the word if it were tied down to any one meaning. Words of this kind are often used in a consciously dishonest way. That is, the person who uses them has his own private definition, but allows his hearer to think he means something quite different. Statements like *Marshal Pétain[7] was a true patriot, The Soviet press is the freest in the world, The Catholic Church is opposed to persecution,* are almost always made with intent to deceive. Other words used in variable meanings, in most cases more or less dishonestly, are: *class, totalitarian, science, progressive, reactionary, bourgeois, equality.*

Now that I have made this catalogue of swindles and perversions, let me give another example of the kind of writing that they lead to. This time it must of its nature be an imaginary one. I am going to translate a passage of good English into modern English of the worst sort. Here is a well-known verse from *Ecclesiastes:*

> I returned, and saw under the sun, that the race is not to the swift, nor the battle to the strong, neither yet bread to the wise, nor yet riches to men of understanding, nor yet favour to men of skill; but time and chance happeneth to them all.

Here it is in modern English:

> Objective consideration of contemporary phenomena compels the conclusion that success or failure in competitive activities exhibits no tendency to be commensurate with innate capacity, but that a considerable element of the unpredictable must invariably be taken into account.

This is a parody, but not a very gross one. Exhibit 3, above, for instance, contains several patches of the same kind of English. It will be seen that I have not made a full translation. The beginning and ending of the sentence follow the original meaning fairly closely, but in the middle the concrete illustrations—race, battle, bread—dissolve into the vague phrase "success or failure in competitive activities". This had to be so, because no modern writer of the kind I am discussing—no one capable of using phrases like "objective consideration of contemporary phenomena"—would ever tabulate his

---

7. French army officer and head of state of the Vichy government that collaborated with Germany in World War II.

thoughts in that precise and detailed way. The whole tendency of modern prose is away from concreteness. Now analyse these two sentences a little more closely. The first contains 49 words but only 60 syllables, and all its words are those of everyday life. The second contains 38 words of 90 syllables: 18 of its words are from Latin roots, and one from Greek. The first sentence contains six vivid images, and only one phrase ("time and chance") that could be called vague. The second contains not a single fresh, arresting phrase, and in spite of its 90 syllables it gives only a shortened version of the meaning contained in the first. Yet without a doubt it is the second kind of sentence that is gaining ground in modern English. I do not want to exaggerate. This kind of writing is not yet universal, and outcrops of simplicity will occur here and there in the worst-written page. Still, if you or I were told to write a few lines on the uncertainty of human fortunes, we should probably come much nearer to my imaginary sentence than to the one from *Ecclesiastes*.

As I have tried to show, modern writing at its worst does not consist in picking out words for the sake of their meaning and inventing images in order to make the meaning clearer. It consists in gumming together long strips of words which have already been set in order by someone else, and making the results presentable by sheer humbug. The attraction of this way of writing is that it is easy. It is easier—even quicker, once you have the habit—to say *In my opinion it is a not unjustifiable assumption that* than to say *I think*. If you use ready-made phrases, you not only don't have to hunt about for words; you also don't have to bother with the rhythms of your sentences, since these phrases are generally so arranged as to be more or less euphonious. When you are composing in a hurry—when you are dictating to a stenographer, for instance, or making a public speech—it is natural to fall into a pretentious, latinised style. Tags like *a consideration which we should do well to bear in mind* or *a conclusion to which all of us would readily assent* will save many a sentence from coming down with a bump. By using stale metaphors, similes and idioms, you save much mental effort, at the cost of leaving your meaning vague, not only for your reader but for yourself. This is the significance of mixed metaphors. The sole aim of a metaphor is to call up a visual image. When these images clash—as in *The Fascist octopus has sung its swan song, the jackboot is thrown into the melting-pot*—it can be taken as certain that the writer is not seeing a mental image of the objects he is naming; in other words he is not really thinking. Look again at the examples I gave at the beginning of this essay. Professor Laski (1) uses five negatives in 53 words. One of these is superfluous, making nonsense of the whole passage, and in addition there is the slip *alien* for akin, making further nonsense, and several avoidable pieces of clumsiness which increase the general vagueness. Professor Hogben (2) plays ducks and drakes with a battery which is able to write prescriptions, and, while disapproving of the everyday phrase *put up with*, is unwilling to look *egregious* up in the dictionary and see what it means. (3), if one takes an uncharitable attitude towards it, is simply meaningless: probably one could work out its intended meaning by reading the whole of the article in which it occurs. In (4) the writer knows more or less what he wants to say, but an accumulation of stale phrases chokes him like tea-leaves blocking a sink. In (5) words and meaning have almost parted company. People who write in this manner usually have a general emotional meaning—they dislike one thing and want to express solidarity with another—but they are not interested in the detail of what they are saying. A scrupulous writer, in every sentence that he writes, will ask himself at least four questions, thus: What am I trying to say? What words will express it? What image or idiom will make it clearer? Is this image fresh enough to have an effect? And he will probably ask himself two more: Could I put it more shortly? Have I said anything that is avoidably ugly? But you are not obliged to go to all this trouble. You can shirk it by simply throwing your mind open and letting the ready-made phrases come crowding in. They will construct your sentences for you—even think your thoughts for you, to a certain extent—and at need they will perform the important service of partially concealing your meaning even from yourself. It is at this point that the special connection between politics and the debasement of language becomes clear.

In our time it is broadly true that political writing is bad writing. Where it is not true, it will generally be found that the writer is some kind of rebel, expressing his private opinions, and not a "party line." Orthodoxy, of whatever colour, seems to demand a lifeless, imitative style. The political dialects to be found in pamphlets, leading articles, manifestos, White Papers and the speeches of Under-Secretaries[8] do, of course, vary from party to party, but they are all alike in that one almost never finds in them a fresh, vivid, home-made turn of speech. When one watches some tired hack on the platform mechanically repeating the familiar phrases—*bestial atrocities, iron heel, blood-stained tyranny, free peoples of the world, stand shoulder to shoulder*—one often has a curious feeling that one is not watching a live human being but some kind of dummy: a feeling which suddenly becomes stronger at moments when the light catches the speaker's spectacles and turns them into blank discs which seem to have no eyes behind them. And this is not altogether fanciful. A speaker who uses that kind of phraseology has gone some distance towards turning himself into a machine. The appropriate noises are coming out of his larynx, but his brain is not involved as it would be if he were choosing his words for himself. If the speech he is making is one that he is accustomed to make over and over again, he may be almost unconscious of what he is saying, as one is when one utters the responses in church. And this reduced state of consciousness, if not indispensable, is at any rate favourable to political conformity.

In our time, political speech and writing are largely the defence of the indefensible. Things like the continuance of British rule in India,[9] the Russian purges and deportations, the dropping of the atom bombs on Japan, can indeed be defended, but only by arguments which are too brutal for most people to face, and which do not square with the professed aims of political parties. Thus political language has to consist largely of euphemism, question-begging and sheer cloudy vagueness. Defenceless villages are bombarded from the air, the inhabitants driven out into the countryside, the cattle machine-gunned, the huts set on fire with incendiary bullets: this is called *pacification*. Millions of peasants are robbed of their farms and sent trudging along the roads with no more than they can carry: this is called

---

8. Senior British civil servants. "White Papers": official documents, each on a particular topic, issued by the British government.

9. This ended with the partition of the subcontinent in 1947.

transfer of population or *rectification of frontiers.* People are imprisoned for years without trial, or shot in the back of the neck or sent to die of scurvy in Arctic lumber camps: this is called *elimination of unreliable elements.* Such phraseology is needed if one wants to name things without calling up mental pictures of them. Consider for instance some comfortable English professor defending Russian totalitarianism. He cannot say outright, "I believe in killing off your opponents when you can get good results by doing so." Probably, therefore, he will say something like this:

> While freely conceding that the Soviet régime exhibits certain features which the humanitarian may be inclined to deplore, we must, I think, agree that a certain curtailment of the right to political opposition is an unavoidable concomitant of transitional periods, and that the rigours which the Russian people have been called upon to undergo have been amply justified in the sphere of concrete achievement.

The inflated style is itself a kind of euphemism. A mass of Latin words falls upon the facts like soft snow, blurring the outlines and covering up all the details. The great enemy of clear language is insincerity. When there is a gap between one's real and one's declared aims, one turns as it were instinctively to long words and exhausted idioms, like a cuttlefish squirting out ink. In our age there is no such thing as "keeping out of politics." All issues are political issues, and politics itself is a mass of lies, evasions, folly, hatred and schizophrenia. When the general atmosphere is bad, language must suffer. I should expect to find—this is a guess which I have not sufficient knowledge to verify—that the German, Russian and Italian languages have all deteriorated in the last ten or fifteen years, as a result of dictatorship.

But if thought corrupts language, language can also corrupt thought. A bad usage can spread by tradition and imitation, even among people who should and do know better. The debased language that I have been discussing is in some ways very convenient. Phrases like a *not unjustifiable assumption, leaves much to be desired, would serve no good purpose, a consideration which we should do well to bear in mind,* are a continuous temptation, a packet of aspirins always at one's elbow. Look back through this essay, and for certain you will find that I have again and again committed the very faults I am protesting against. By this morning's post I have received a pamphlet dealing with conditions in Germany. The author tells me that he "felt impelled" to write it. I open it at random, and here is almost the first sentence that I see: "(The Allies) have an opportunity not only of achieving a radical transformation of Germany's social and political structure in such a way as to avoid a nationalistic reaction in Germany itself, but at the same time of laying the foundations of a co-operative and unified Europe." You see, he "feels impelled" to write—feels, presumably, that he has something new to say—and yet his words, like cavalry horses answering the bugle, group themselves automatically into the familiar dreary pattern. This invasion of one's mind by ready-made phrases *(lay the foundations, achieve a radical transformation)* can only be prevented if one is constantly on guard against them, and every such phrase anaesthetises a portion of one's brain.

I said earlier that the decadence of our language is probably curable. Those who deny this would argue, if they produced an argument at all, that language merely reflects existing social conditions, and that we cannot influence its development by any direct tinkering with words and constructions. So far as the general tone or spirit of a language goes, this may be true, but it is not true in detail. Silly words and expressions have often disappeared, not through any evolutionary process but owing to the conscious action of a minority. Two recent examples were *explore every avenue* and *leave no stone unturned,* which were killed by the jeers of a few journalists. There is a long list of fly-blown metaphors which could similarly be got rid of if enough people would interest themselves in the job; and it should also be possible to laugh the *not un-* formation out of existence,[1] to reduce the amount of Latin and Greek in the average sentence, to drive out foreign phrases and strayed scientific words, and, in general, to make pretentiousness unfashionable. But all these are minor points. The defence of the English language implies more than this, and perhaps it is best to start by saying what it does *not* imply.

To begin with, it has nothing to do with archaism, with the salvaging of obsolete words and turns of speech, or with the setting-up of a "standard English" which must never be departed from. On the contrary, it is especially concerned with the scrapping of every word or idiom which has outworn its usefulness. It has nothing to do with correct grammar and syntax, which are of no importance so long as one makes one's meaning clear, or with the avoidance of Americanisms, or with having what is called a "good prose style." On the other hand it is not concerned with fake simplicity and the attempt to make written English colloquial. Nor does it even imply in every case preferring the Saxon word to the Latin one, though it does imply using the fewest and shortest words that will cover one's meaning. What is above all needed is to let the meaning choose the word, and not the other way about. In prose, the worst thing one can do with words is to surrender to them. When you think of a concrete object, you think wordlessly, and then, if you want to describe the thing you have been visualising, you probably hunt about till you find the exact words that seem to fit it. When you think of something abstract you are more inclined to use words from the start, and unless you make a conscious effort to prevent it, the existing dialect will come rushing in and do the job for you, at the expense of blurring or even changing your meaning. Probably it is better to put off using words as long as possible and get one's meaning as clear as one can through pictures or sensations. Afterwards one can choose—not simply *accept*—the phrases that will best cover the meaning, and then switch round and decide what impression one's words are likely to make on another person. This last effort of the mind cuts out all stale or mixed images, all prefabricated phrases, needless repetitions, and humbug and vagueness generally. But one can often be in doubt about the effect of a word or a phrase, and one needs rules that one can rely on when instinct fails. I think the following rules will cover most cases:

    i. Never use a metaphor, simile or other figure of speech which you are used to seeing in print.

    ii. Never use a long word where a short one will do.

    iii. If it is possible to cut a word out, always cut it out.

    iv. Never use the passive where you can use the active.

---

1. One can cure oneself of the *not un-* formation by memorising this sentence: *A not unblack dog was chasing a not unsmall rabbit across a not ungreen field* [Orwell's note].

v. Never use a foreign phrase, a scientific word or a jargon word if you can think of an everyday English equivalent.

vi. Break any of these rules sooner than say anything outright barbarous.

These rules sound elementary, and so they are, but they demand a deep change of attitude in anyone who has grown used to writing in the style now fashionable. One could keep all of them and still write bad English, but one could not write the kind of stuff that I quoted in those five specimens at the beginning of this article.

I have not here been considering the literary use of language, but merely language as an instrument for expressing and not for concealing or preventing thought. Stuart Chase and others have come near to claiming that all abstract words are meaningless, and have used this as a pretext for advocating a kind of political quietism. Since you don't know what Fascism is, how can you struggle against Fascism? One need not swallow such absurdities as this, but one ought to recognise that the present political chaos is connected with the decay of language, and that one can probably bring about some improvement by starting at the verbal end. If you simplify your English, you are freed from the worst follies of orthodoxy. You cannot speak any of the necessary dialects, and when you make a stupid remark its stupidity will be obvious, even to yourself. Political language—and with variations this is true of all political parties, from Conservatives to Anarchists—is designed to make lies sound truthful and murder respectable, and to give an appearance of solidity to pure wind. One cannot change this all in a moment, but one can at least change one's own habits, and from time to time one can even, if one jeers loudly enough, send some worn-out and useless phrase—some *jackboot, Achilles' heel, hotbed, melting pot, acid test, veritable inferno* or other lump of verbal refuse—into the dustbin where it belongs.

1946, 1947

SAMUEL BECKETT
1906–1989

Samuel Beckett, born near Dublin in what is now the Republic of Ireland, received a B.A. from Trinity College, Dublin, and, after teaching English at the École Normale Supérieure in Paris for two years, returned there to take his M.A. in 1931. He gave up teaching in 1932 to write, although, having produced an insightful essay on the early stages of James Joyce's *Finnegans Wake* in 1929, he also worked as Joyce's secretary and translator. From the mid-1940s he generally wrote in French and subsequently translated some of his work into an eloquent, Irish-inflected English. His early novels, *Murphy* (1938) and *Watt* (1953), and the trilogy, *Molloy* (1951), *Malone Dies* (1951), and *The Unnameable* (1953), have been hailed as masterpieces and precursors of postmodern fiction; but he is best known for his dramatic work, and in particular for *Waiting for Godot* (1953). He received the Nobel Prize for Literature in 1969.

Not much happens in a Beckett play; there is very little plot, very little incident,

and very little characterization. Characters engage in dialogue or dialectical monologues that go nowhere. There is no progression, no development, no resolution.
Rambling dialogue and repetitive actions enact the lack of a fixed center, of meaning,
of purpose, in the lives depicted. Yet the characters do persist in their habitual, almost
ritualistic, activities; they do go on talking, even if only to themselves. So long as there
is a stream of discourse, of thought and will, so long as there is a consciousness to
question its own meaning and purpose, there is life. In spite of a reiterated theme of
nonexistence, the characters go on existing—if minimally. In *Waiting for Godot*,
clownlike tramps wait for an arrival always expected yet constantly deferred. They
exist in a bleak landscape seemingly confined to one road, one tree; talking of moving
on, yet never leaving. Subsequent plays restrict the acting space to a room, to a
dustbin, to a mound in which the actor is buried; characters are physically confined
or disabled, until *Not I* presents the most minimal embodiment of human consciousness available to theatrical representation: a disembodied mouth.

In *Endgame*, irritable, resentful, spiteful characters talk of leaving, dying, or otherwise ending but simply continue in their peevish, complaining round. Like all of
Beckett's work, the play defies definitive interpretation. It draws on vaudeville and
other comic traditions but juxtaposes these with the intellectual and the grotesque.
Beckett's work shares this tragicomedic quality with Absurdist drama such as
Ionesco's *The Bald Soprano* (1958), which, like *Waiting for Godot* and *Endgame*,
disrupts the conventions of realist drama. The exaggerated symbolism of Absurdism
refuses to provide hierarchies of significance. Is the exfoliation of the tree in *Waiting
for Godot* deeply significant, or irrelevant? In *Endgame*, is it significant that Hamm
wears a close-fitting cap like that of a judge? Is the gaff symbolic of anything, or
merely a piece of flotsam from the wreckage of a life? We do not know; and our
attempts to determine or affix significance, constantly thwarted by the playful texts,
may represent our need to look for underlying meaning in a universe made up only
of surfaces. Like much Absurdist drama, Beckett's plays break and disrupt the conventions of realism to deny the audience the comfortable security of stability and to
draw attention to their own fictionality—but also to provide laughs, sometimes at the
audience's expense.

Endgame[1]

For Roger Blin

THE CHARACTERS

    NAGG
    NELL
    HAMM
    CLOV

Bare interior.
Grey light.
Left and right back, high up, two small windows, curtains drawn.
Front right, a door. Hanging near door, its face to wall, a picture.
Front left, touching each other, covered with an old sheet, two ashbins.
Centre, in an armchair on castors, covered with an old sheet, HAMM.
Motionless by the door, his eyes fixed on HAMM, CLOV. *Very red face.*
Brief tableau.

---

1. Translated by the author.

[CLOV *goes and stands under window left. Stiff, staggering walk. He looks up at window left. He turns and looks at window right. He goes and stands under window right. He looks up at window right. He turns and looks at window left. He goes out, comes back immediately with a small step-ladder, carries it over and sets it down under window left, gets up on it, draws back curtain. He gets down, takes six steps (for example) towards window right, goes back for ladder, carries it over and sets it down under window right, gets up on it, draws back curtain. He gets down, takes three steps towards window left, goes back for ladder, carries it over and sets it down under window left, gets up on it, looks out of window. Brief laugh. He gets down, takes one step towards window right, goes back for ladder, carries it over and sets it down under window right, gets up on it, looks out of window. Brief laugh. He gets down, goes with ladder towards ashbins, halts, turns, carries back ladder and sets it down under window right, goes to ashbins, removes sheet covering them, folds it over his arm. He raises one lid, stoops and looks into bin. Brief laugh. He closes lid. Same with other bin. He goes to* HAMM, *removes sheet covering him, folds it over his arm. In a dressing-gown, a stiff toque[2] on his head, a large blood-stained handkerchief over his face, a whistle hanging from his neck, a rug over his knees, thick socks on his feet,* HAMM *seems to be asleep.* CLOV *looks him over. Brief laugh. He goes to door, halts, turns towards auditorium.*]

CLOV [*Fixed gaze, tonelessly.*] Finished, it's finished, nearly finished, it must be nearly finished. [*Pause.*] Grain upon grain, one by one, and one day, suddenly, there's a heap, a little heap, the impossible heap. [*Pause.*] I can't be punished any more. [*Pause.*] I'll go now to my kitchen, ten feet by ten feet by ten feet, and wait for him to whistle me. [*Pause.*] Nice dimensions, nice proportions, I'll lean on the table, and look at the wall, and wait for him to whistle me.

[*He remains a moment motionless, then goes out. He comes back immediately, goes to window right, takes up the ladder and carries it out. Pause.* HAMM *stirs. He yawns under the handkerchief. He removes the handkerchief from his face. Very red face. Black glasses.*]

HAMM Me—[*He yawns.*]—to play.[3] [*He holds the handkerchief spread out before him.*] Old Stancher![4] [*He takes off his glasses, wipes his eyes, his face, the glasses, puts them on again, folds the handkerchief and puts it back neatly in the breast-pocket of his dressing-gown. He clears his throat, joins the tips of his fingers.*] Can there be misery—[*He yawns.*]—loftier than mine? No doubt. Formerly. But now? [*Pause.*] My father? [*Pause.*] My mother? [*Pause.*] My . . . dog? [*Pause.*] Oh I am willing to believe they suffer as much as such creatures can suffer. But does that mean their sufferings equal mine? No doubt. [*Pause.*] No, all is a—[*He yawns.*]—bsolute, [*Proudly.*] the bigger a man is the fuller he is. [*Pause. Gloomily.*] And the emptier. [*He sniffs.*] Clov! [*Pause.*] No, alone. [*Pause.*] What dreams! Those forests! [*Pause.*] Enough, it's time it ended, in the shelter too. [*Pause.*] And yet I hesitate, I hesitate to . . . to end. Yes, there it is, it's time it ended and yet I hesitate to—[*He yawns.*]—to end.

2. Small cap with no brim.
3. Hamm announces that it is his move, as it were in a game of chess, of which the final stage is called

the "endgame."
4. Handkerchief that stanches (checks the flow of) blood.

[*Yawns.*] God, I'm tired, I'd be better off in bed. [*He whistles. Enter* CLOV *immediately. He halts beside the chair.*]
You pollute the air! [*Pause.*] Get me ready, I'm going to bed.

CLOV   I've just got you up.

HAMM   And what of it?

CLOV   I can't be getting you up and putting you to bed every five minutes, I have things to do. [*Pause.*]

HAMM   Did you ever see my eyes?

CLOV   No.

HAMM   Did you never have the curiosity, while I was sleeping, to take off my glasses and look at my eyes?

CLOV   Pulling back the lids? [*Pause.*] No.

HAMM   One of these days I'll show them to you. [*Pause.*] It seems they've gone all white. [*Pause.*] What time is it?

CLOV   The same as usual.

HAMM   [*Gesture towards window right.*] Have you looked?

CLOV   Yes.

HAMM   Well?

CLOV   Zero.

HAMM   It'd need to rain.

CLOV   It won't rain. [*Pause.*]

HAMM   Apart from that, how do you feel?

CLOV   I don't complain.

HAMM   You feel normal?

CLOV   [*Irritably.*] I tell you I don't complain.

HAMM   I feel a little queer. [*Pause.*] Clov!

CLOV   Yes.

HAMM   Have you not had enough?

CLOV   Yes! [*Pause.*] Of what?

HAMM   Of this . . . this . . . thing.

CLOV   I always had. [*Pause.*] Not you?

HAMM   [*Gloomily.*] Then there's no reason for it to change.

CLOV   It may end. [*Pause.*] All life long the same questions, the same answers.

HAMM   Get me ready. [CLOV *does not move.*] Go and get the sheet. [CLOV *does not move.*] Clov!

CLOV   Yes.

HAMM   I'll give you nothing more to eat.

CLOV   Then we'll die.

HAMM   I'll give you just enough to keep you from dying. You'll be hungry all the time.

CLOV   Then we won't die. [*Pause.*] I'll go and get the sheet. [*He goes towards the door.*]

HAMM   No! [CLOV *halts.*] I'll give you one biscuit per day. [*Pause.*] One and a half. [*Pause.*] Why do you stay with me?

CLOV   Why do you keep me?

HAMM   There's no one else.

CLOV   There's nowhere else. [*Pause.*]

HAMM   You're leaving me all the same.

CLOV   I'm trying.

HAMM   You don't love me.

CLOV   No.

HAMM   You loved me once.

CLOV   Once!

HAMM   I've made you suffer too much. [*Pause.*] Haven't I?

CLOV   It's not that.

HAMM   [*Shocked.*] I haven't made you suffer too much?

CLOV   Yes!

HAMM   [*Relieved.*] Ah you gave me a fright! [*Pause. Coldly.*] Forgive me. [*Pause. Louder.*] I said, Forgive me.

CLOV   I heard you. [*Pause.*] Have you bled?

HAMM   Less. [*Pause.*] Is it not time for my pain-killer?

CLOV   No. [*Pause.*]

HAMM   How are your eyes?

CLOV   Bad.

HAMM   How are your legs?

CLOV   BAD.

HAMM   But you can move.

CLOV   Yes.

HAMM   [*Violently.*] Then move! [CLOV *goes to back wall, leans against it with his forehead and hands.*] Where are you?

CLOV   Here.

HAMM   Come back! [CLOV *returns to his place beside the chair.*] Where are you?

CLOV   Here.

HAMM   Why don't you kill me?

CLOV   I don't know the combination of the cupboard. [*Pause.*]

HAMM   Go and get two bicycle-wheels.

CLOV   There are no more bicycle-wheels.

HAMM   What have you done with your bicycle?

CLOV   I never had a bicycle.

HAMM   The thing is impossible.

CLOV   When there were still bicycles I wept to have one. I crawled at your feet. You told me to go to hell. Now there are none.

HAMM   And your rounds? When you inspected my paupers. Always on foot?

CLOV   Sometimes on horse. [*The lid of one of the bins lifts and the hands of* NAGG *appear, gripping the rim. Then his head emerges. Nightcap. Very white face.* NAGG *yawns, then listens.*] I'll leave you, I have things to do.

HAMM   In your kitchen?

CLOV   Yes.

HAMM   Outside of here it's death. [*Pause.*] All right, be off. [*Exit* CLOV. *Pause.*] We're getting on.

NAGG   Me Pap![5]

HAMM   Accursed progenitor![6]

NAGG   Me pap!

HAMM   The old folks at home! No decency left! Guzzle, guzzle, that's all they think of. [*He whistles. Enter* CLOV. *He halts beside the chair.*] Well! I thought you were leaving me.

CLOV   Oh not just yet, not just yet.

---

5. Mushy food.   6. Parent.

NAGG   Me pap!

HAMM   Give him his pap.

CLOV   There's no more pap.

HAMM   [*To* NAGG.] Do you hear that? There's no more pap. You'll never get any more pap.

NAGG   I want me pap!

HAMM   Give him a biscuit. [*Exit* CLOV.] Accursed fornicator! How are your stumps?

NAGG   Never mind me stumps. [*Enter* CLOV *with biscuit.*]

CLOV   I'm back again, with the biscuit. [*He gives biscuit to* NAGG *who fingers, it, sniffs it.*]

NAGG   [*Plaintively.*] What is it?

CLOV   Spratt's medium.[7]

NAGG   [*As before.*] It's hard! I can't!

HAMM   Bottle him! [CLOV *pushes* NAGG *back into the bin, closes the lid.*]

CLOV   [*Returning to his place beside the chair.*] If age but knew!

HAMM   Sit on him!

CLOV   I can't sit.

HAMM   True. And I can't stand.

CLOV   So it is.

HAMM   Every man his speciality. [*Pause.*] No phone calls? [*Pause.*] Don't we laugh?

CLOV   [*After reflection.*] I don't feel like it.

HAMM   [*After reflection.*] Not I. [*Pause.*] Clov!

CLOV   Yes.

HAMM   Nature has forgotten us.

CLOV   There's no more nature.

HAMM   No more nature! You exaggerate.

CLOV   In the vicinity.

HAMM   But we breathe, we change! We lose our hair, our teeth! Our bloom! Our ideals!

CLOV   Then she hasn't forgotten us.

HAMM   But you say there is none.

CLOV   [*Sadly.*] No one that ever lived ever thought so crooked as we.

HAMM   We do what we can.

CLOV   We shouldn't. [*Pause.*]

HAMM   You're a bit of all right,[8] aren't you?

CLOV   A smithereen.[9] [*Pause.*]

HAMM   This is slow work. [*Pause.*] Is it not time for my pain-killer?

CLOV   No. [*Pause.*] I'll leave you, I have things to do.

HAMM   In your kitchen?

CLOV   Yes.

HAMM   What, I'd like to know.

CLOV   I look at the wall.

HAMM   The wall! And what do you see on your wall? Mene, mene?[1] Naked bodies?

---

7. Brand name of a biscuit (cookie).
8. You're pretty good (British slang).
9. A little bit.
1. "Mene mene, tekel, upharsin": words written by

a heavenly hand on the wall during the feast of Balshazzar, king of Babylon. Translated as "Thou art weighed in the balance and found wanting," it foretells his ruin (Daniel 5.25–28).

CLOV   I see my light dying.

HAMM   Your light dying! Listen to that! Well, it can die just as well here, *your* light. Take a look at me and then come back and tell me what you think of *your* light. [*Pause.*]

CLOV   You shouldn't speak to me like that. [*Pause.*]

HAMM   [*Coldly.*] Forgive me. [*Pause. Louder.*] I said, Forgive me.

CLOV   I heard you. [*The lid of* NAGG's *bin lifts. His hands appear, gripping the rim. Then his head emerges. In his mouth the biscuit. He listens.*]

HAMM   Did your seeds come up?

CLOV   No.

HAMM   Did you scratch round them to see if they had sprouted?

CLOV   They haven't sprouted.

HAMM   Perhaps it's still too early.

CLOV   If they were going to sprout they would have sprouted. [*Violently.*] They'll never sprout! [*Pause.* NAGG *takes biscuit in his hand.*]

HAMM   This is not much fun. [*Pause.*] But that's always the way at the end of the day, isn't it, Clov?

CLOV   Always.

HAMM   It's the end of the day like any other day, isn't it, Clov?

CLOV   Looks like it. [*Pause.*]

HAMM   [*Anguished.*] What's happening, what's happening?

CLOV   Something is taking its course. [*Pause.*]

HAMM   All right, be off. [*He leans back in his chair, remains motionless.* CLOV *does not move, heaves a great groaning sigh.* HAMM *sits up.*] I thought I told you to be off.

CLOV   I'm trying. [*He goes to door, halts.*] Ever since I was whelped.[2] [*Exit* CLOV.]

HAMM   We're getting on.

  [*He leans back in his chair, remains motionless.* NAGG *knocks on the lid of the other bin. Pause. He knocks harder. The lid lifts and the hands of* NELL *appear, gripping the rim. Then her head emerges. Lace cap. Very white face.*]

NELL   What is it, my pet? [*Pause.*] Time for love?

NAGG   Were you asleep?

NELL   Oh no!

NAGG   Kiss me.

NELL   We can't.

NAGG   Try. [*Their heads strain towards each other, fail to meet, fall apart again.*]

NELL   Why this farce, day after day? [*Pause.*]

NAGG   I've lost me tooth.

NELL   When?

NAGG   I had it yesterday.

NELL   [*Elegiac.*[3]] Ah yesterday! [*They turn painfully towards each other.*]

NAGG   Can you see me?

NELL   Hardly. And you?

NAGG   What?

NELL   Can you see me?

---

2. Born (usually applied to puppies: whelps).   3. As though lamenting something lost.

NAGG   Hardly.

NELL   So much the better, so much the better.

NAGG   Don't say that. [*Pause.*] Our sight has failed.

NELL   Yes. [*Pause. They turn away from each other.*]

NAGG   Can you hear me?

NELL   Yes. And you?

NAGG   Yes. [*Pause.*] Our hearing hasn't failed.

NELL   Our what?

NAGG   Our hearing.

NELL   No. [*Pause.*] Have you anything else to say to me?

NAGG   Do you remember—

NELL   No.

NAGG   When we crashed on our tandem[4] and lost our shanks. [*They laugh heartily.*]

NELL   It was in the Ardennes. [*They laugh less heartily.*]

NAGG   On the road to Sedan.[5] [*They laugh still less heartily.*] Are you cold?

NELL   Yes, perished. And you?

NAGG   [*Pause.*] I'm freezing. [*Pause.*] Do you want to go in?

NELL   Yes.

NAGG   Then go in. [NELL *does not move*] Why don't you go in?

NELL   I don't know. [*Pause.*]

NAGG   Has he changed your sawdust?

NELL   It isn't sawdust. [*Pause. Wearily.*] Can you not be a little accurate, Nagg?

NAGG   Your sand then. It's not important.

NELL   It is important. [*Pause.*]

NAGG   It was sawdust once.

NELL   Once!

NAGG   And now it's sand. [*Pause.*] From the shore. [*Pause. Impatiently.*] Now it's sand he fetches from the shore.

NELL   Now it's sand.

NAGG   Has he changed yours?

NELL   No.

NAGG   Nor mine. [*Pause.*] I won't have it! [*Pause. Holding up the biscuit.*] Do you want a bit?

NELL   No. [*Pause.*] Of what?

NAGG   Biscuit. I've kept you half. [*He looks at the biscuit. Proudly.*] Three quarters. For you. Here. [*He proffers the biscuit.*] No? [*Pause.*] Do you not feel well?

HAMM   [*Wearily.*] Quiet, quiet, you're keeping me awake. [*Pause.*] Talk softer. [*Pause.*] If I could sleep I might make love. I'd go into the woods. My eyes would see . . . the sky, the earth. I'd run, run, they wouldn't catch me. [*Pause.*] Nature! [*Pause.*] There's something dripping in my head. [*Pause.*] A heart, a heart in my head. [*Pause.*]

NAGG   [*Soft.*] Do you hear him? A heart in his head! [*He chuckles cautiously.*]

---

4. A bicycle made for two.
5. Town in northern France where the French Army was defeated in 1870 during the Franco-

Prussian War. Ardennes is a forest in northern France, which was the scene of fierce fighting in both World Wars.

NELL   One mustn't laugh at those things, Nagg. Why must you always laugh at them?

NAGG   Not so loud!

NELL   [*Without lowering her voice.*] Nothing is funnier than unhappiness, I grant you that. But—

NAGG   [*Shocked.*] Oh!

NELL   Yes, yes, it's the most comical thing in the world. And we laugh, we laugh, with a will, in the beginning. But it's always the same thing. Yes, it's like the funny story we have heard too often, we still find it funny, but we don't laugh any more. [*Pause.*] Have you anything else to say to me?

NAGG   No.

NELL   Are you quite sure? [*Pause.*] Then I'll leave you.

NAGG   Do you not want your biscuit? [*Pause.*] I'll keep it for you. [*Pause.*] I thought you were going to leave me.

NELL   I am going to leave you.

NAGG   Could you give me a scratch before you go?

NELL   No. [*Pause.*] Where?

NAGG   In the back.

NELL   No. [*Pause.*] Rub yourself against the rim.

NAGG   It's lower down. In the hollow.

NELL   What hollow?

NAGG   The hollow! [*Pause.*] Could you not? [*Pause.*] Yesterday you scratched me there.

NELL   [*Elegiac.*] Ah yesterday!

NAGG   Could you not? [*Pause.*] Would you like me to scratch you? [*Pause.*] Are you crying again?

NELL   I was trying. [*Pause.*]

HAMM   Perhaps it's a little vein. [*Pause.*]

NAGG   What was that he said?

NELL   Perhaps it's a little vein.

NAGG   What does that mean? [*Pause.*] That means nothing. [*Pause.*] Will I tell you the story of the tailor?

NELL   No. [*Pause.*] What for?

NAGG   To cheer you up.

NELL   It's not funny.

NAGG   It always made you laugh. [*Pause.*] The first time I thought you'd die.

NELL   It was on Lake Como.[6] [*Pause.*] One April afternoon. [*Pause.*] Can you believe it?

NAGG   What?

NELL   That we once went out rowing on Lake Como. [*Pause.*] One April afternoon.

NAGG   We had got engaged the day before.

NELL   Engaged!

NAGG   You were in such fits that we capsized. By rights we should have been drowned.

---

6. Large lake in northern Italy.

NELL It was because I felt happy.

NAGG [*Indignant.*] It was not, it was not, it was my story and nothing else. Happy! Don't you laugh at it still? Every time I tell it. Happy!

NELL It was deep, deep. And you could see down to the bottom. So white. So clean.

NAGG Let me tell it again. [*Raconteur's voice.*] An Englishman, needing a pair of striped trousers in a hurry for the New Year festivities, goes to his tailor who takes his measurements. [*Tailor's voice.*] "That's the lot, come back in four days, I'll have it ready." Good. Four days later. [*Tailor's voice.*] "So sorry, come back in a week, I've made a mess of the seat." Good, that's all right, a neat seat can be very ticklish. A week later. [*Tailor's voice.*] "Frightfully sorry, come back in ten days. I've made a hash of the crotch." Good, can't be helped, a snug crotch is always a teaser. Ten days later. [*Tailor's voice.*] "Dreadfully sorry, come back in a fortnight, I've made a balls of the fly." Good, at a pinch, a smart fly is a stiff proposition. [*Pause. Normal voice.*] I never told it worse. [*Pause. Gloomy.*] I tell this story worse and worse. [*Pause. Raconteur's voice.*] Well, to make it short, the bluebells are blowing and he ballockses[7] the buttonholes. [*Customer's voice.*] "God damn you to hell, Sir, no, it's indecent, there are limits! In six days, do you hear me, six days, God made the world. Yes Sir, no less Sir, the WORLD! And you are not bloody well capable of making me a pair of trousers in three months!" [*Tailor's voice, scandalised.*] "But my dear Sir, my dear Sir, look—[*Disdainful gesture, disgustedly.*]—at the world—[*pause*] and look—[*Loving gesture, proudly.*]—at my TROUSERS!"

> [*Pause. He looks at* NELL *who has remained impassive, her eyes unseeing, breaks into a high forced laugh, cuts it short, pokes his head towards* NELL, *launches his laugh again.*]

HAMM Silence!

> [NAGG *starts, cuts short his laugh.*]

NELL You could see down to the bottom.

HAMM [*Exasperated.*] Have you not finished? Will you never finish? [*With sudden fury.*] Will this never finish? [NAGG *disappears into his bin, closes the lid behind him.* NELL *does not move. Frenziedly.*] My kingdom for a nightman![8] [*He whistles. Enter* CLOV.] Clear away this muck! Chuck it in the sea! [CLOV *goes to bins, halts.*]

NELL So white.

HAMM What? What's she blathering about? [CLOV *stoops, takes* NELL's *hand, feels her pulse.*]

NELL [*To* CLOV.] Desert! [CLOV *lets go her hand, pushes her back in the bin, closes the lid.*]

CLOV [*Returning to his place beside the chair.*] She has no pulse.

HAMM What was she drivelling about?

CLOV She told me to go away, into the desert.

HAMM Damn busybody! Is that all?

CLOV No.

HAMM What else?

---

7. Botches.
8. A collector of nightsoil (excrement). Cf. Shake-

speare's *Richard III* 5.4.7: "A horse! a horse! My kingdom for a horse!"

CLOV   I didn't understand.
HAMM   Have you bottled her?
CLOV   Yes.
HAMM   Are they both bottled?
CLOV   Yes.
HAMM   Screw down the lids. [CLOV *goes towards door.*] Time enough.
       [CLOV *halts.*] My anger subsides, I'd like to pee.
CLOV   [*With alacrity.*] I'll go and get the catheter. [*He goes towards door.*]
HAMM   Time enough. [CLOV *halts.*] Give me my pain-killer.
CLOV   It's too soon. [*Pause.*] It's too soon on top of your tonic, it wouldn't
       act.
HAMM   In the morning they brace you up and in the evening they calm
       you down. Unless it's the other way round. [*Pause.*] That old doctor, he's
       dead naturally?
CLOV   He wasn't old.
HAMM   But he's dead?
CLOV   Naturally. [*Pause.*] *You* ask *me* that? [*Pause.*]
HAMM   Take me for a little turn. [CLOV *goes behind the chair and pushes
       it forward.*] Not too fast! [CLOV *pushes chair.*] Right round the world!
       [CLOV *pushes chair.*] Hug the walls, then back to the centre again. [CLOV
       pushes chair.] I was right in the centre, wasn't I?
CLOV   [*Pushing.*] Yes.
HAMM   We'd need a proper wheel-chair. With big wheels. Bicycle wheels!
       [*Pause.*] Are you hugging?
CLOV   [*Pushing.*] Yes.
HAMM   [*Groping for wall.*] It's a lie! Why do you lie to me?
CLOV   [*Bearing closer to wall.*] There! There!
HAMM   Stop! [CLOV *stops chair close to back wall.* HAMM *lays his hand
       against wall.*] Old wall! [*Pause.*] Beyond is the . . . other hell. [*Pause. Vio-
       lently.*] Closer! Closer! Up against!
CLOV   Take away your hand. [HAMM *withdraws his hand.* CLOV *rams chair
       against wall.*] There! [HAMM *leans towards wall, applies his ear to it.*]
HAMM   Do you hear? [*He strikes the wall with his knuckles.*] Do you hear?
       Hollow bricks! [*He strikes again.*] All that's hollow! [*Pause. He straightens
       up. Violently.*] That's enough. Back!
CLOV   We haven't done the round.
HAMM   Back to my place! [CLOV *pushes chair back to centre.*] Is that my
       place?
CLOV   Yes, that's your place.
HAMM   Am I right in the centre?
CLOV   I'll measure it.
HAMM   More or less! More or less!
CLOV   [*Moving chair slightly.*] There!
HAMM   I'm more or less in the centre?
CLOV   I'd say so.
HAMM   You'd say so! Put me right in the centre!
CLOV   I'll go and get the tape.
HAMM   Roughly! Roughly! [CLOV *moves chair slightly.*] Bang in the centre!
CLOV   There! [*Pause.*]
HAMM   I feel a little too far to the left. [CLOV *moves chair slightly.*] Now

I feel a little too far to the right. [CLOV *moves chair slightly.*] I feel a little too far forward. [CLOV *moves chair slightly.*] Now I feel a little too far back. [CLOV *moves chair slightly.*] Don't stay there, [*I.e., behind the chair.*] you give me the shivers. [CLOV *returns to his place beside the chair.*]

CLOV   If I could kill him I'd die happy. [*Pause.*]

HAMM   What's the weather like?

CLOV   As usual.

HAMM   Look at the earth.

CLOV   I've looked.

HAMM   With the glass?

CLOV   No need of the glass.

HAMM   Look at it with the glass.

CLOV   I'll go and get the glass. [*Exit* CLOV.]

HAMM   No need of the glass! [*Enter* CLOV *with telescope.*]

CLOV   I'm back again, with the glass. [*He goes to window right, looks up at it.*] I need the steps.

HAMM   Why? Have you shrunk? [*Exit* CLOV *with telescope.*] I don't like that, I don't like that. [*Enter* CLOV *with ladder, but without telescope.*]

CLOV   I'm back again, with the steps. [*He sets down ladder under window right, gets up on it, realises he has not the telescope, gets down.*] I need the glass. [*He goes towards door.*]

HAMM   [*Violently.*] But you have the glass!

CLOV   [*Halting, violently.*] No, I haven't the glass! [*Exit* CLOV.]

HAMM   This is deadly. [*Enter* CLOV *with telescope. He goes towards ladder.*]

CLOV   Things are livening up. [*He gets up on ladder, raises the telescope, lets it fall.*] I did it on purpose. [*He gets down, picks up the telescope, turns it on auditorium.*] I see . . . a multitude . . . in transports . . . of joy.[9] [*Pause.*] That's what I call a magnifier. [*He lowers the telescope, turns towards* HAMM.] Well? Don't we laugh?

HAMM   [*After reflection.*] I don't.

CLOV   [*After reflection.*] Nor I. [*He gets up on ladder, turns the telescope on the without.*] Let's see. [*He looks, moving the telescope.*] Zero . . . [*He looks.*] . . . zero . . . [*He looks.*] . . . and zero.

HAMM   Nothing stirs. All is—

CLOV   Zer—

HAMM   [*Violently.*] Wait till you're spoke to! [*Normal voice.*] All is . . . all is . . . all is what? [*Violently.*] All is what?

CLOV   What all is? In a word? Is that what you want to know? Just a moment. [*He turns the telescope on the without, looks, lowers the telescope, turns towards* HAMM.] Corpsed. [*Pause.*] Well? Content?

HAMM   Look at the sea.

CLOV   It's the same.

HAMM   Look at the ocean! [CLOV *gets down, takes a few steps towards window left, goes back for ladder, carries it over and sets it down under window left, gets up on it, turns the telescope on the without, looks at length. He starts, lowers the telescope, examines it, turns it again on the without.*]

9. Cf. Revelation 7.9–10: "After this I beheld, and lo, a great multitude, which . . . cried with a loud voice . . . Salvation."

CLOV   Never seen anything like that!

HAMM   [*Anxious.*] What? A sail? A fin? Smoke?

CLOV   [*Looking.*] The light is sunk.

HAMM   [*Relieved.*] Pah! We all knew that.

CLOV   [*Looking.*] There was a bit left.

HAMM   The base.

CLOV   [*Looking.*] Yes.

HAMM   And now?

CLOV   [*Looking.*] All gone.

HAMM   No gulls?

CLOV   [*Looking.*] Gulls!

HAMM   And the horizon? Nothing on the horizon?

CLOV   [*Lowering the telescope, turning towards* HAMM, *exasperated.*] What in God's name could there be on the horizon? [*Pause.*]

HAMM   The waves, how are the waves?

CLOV   The waves? [*He turns the telescope on the waves.*] Lead.

HAMM   And the sun?

CLOV   [*Looking.*] Zero.

HAMM   But it should be sinking. Look again.

CLOV   [*Looking.*] Damn the sun.

HAMM   Is it night already then?

CLOV   [*Looking.*] No.

HAMM   Then what is it?

CLOV   [*Looking.*] Grey. [*Lowering the telescope, turning towards* HAMM, *louder.*] Grey! [*Pause. Still louder.*] GRREY! [*Pause. He gets down, approaches* HAMM *from behind, whispers in his ear.*]

HAMM   [*Starting.*] Grey! Did I hear you say grey?

CLOV   Light black. From pole to pole.

HAMM   You exaggerate. [*Pause.*] Don't stay there, you give me the shivers. [CLOV *returns to his place beside the chair.*]

CLOV   Why this farce, day after day?

HAMM   Routine. One never knows. [*Pause.*] Last night I saw inside my breast. There was a big sore.

CLOV   Pah! You saw your heart.

HAMM   No, it was living. [*Pause. Anguished.*] Clov!

CLOV   Yes.

HAMM   What's happening?

CLOV   Something is taking its course. [*Pause.*]

HAMM   Clov!

CLOV   [*Impatiently.*] What is it?

HAMM   We're not beginning to . . . to . . . mean something?

CLOV   Mean something! You and I, mean something! [*Brief laugh.*] Ah that's a good one!

HAMM   I wonder. [*Pause.*] Imagine if a rational being came back to earth, wouldn't he be liable to get ideas into his head if he observed us long enough. [*Voice of rational being.*] Ah, good, now I see what it is, yes, now I understand what they're at! [CLOV *starts, drops the telescope and begins to scratch his belly with both hands. Normal voice.*] And without going so far as that, we ourselves . . . [*With emotion.*] . . . we ourselves . . . at certain moments . . . [*Vehemently.*] To think perhaps it won't all have been for nothing!

CLOV [*Anguished, scratching himself.*] I have a flea!

HAMM A flea! Are there still fleas?

CLOV On me there's one. [*Scratching.*] Unless it's a crablouse.

HAMM [*Very perturbed.*] But humanity might start from there all over again! Catch him, for the love of God!

CLOV I'll go and get the powder. [*Exit* CLOV.]

HAMM A flea! This is awful! What a day! [*Enter* CLOV *with a sprinkling-tin.*]

CLOV I'm back again, with the insecticide.

HAMM Let him have it! [CLOV *loosens the top of his trousers, pulls it forward and shakes powder into the aperture. He stoops, looks, waits, starts, frenziedly shakes more powder, stoops, looks, waits.*]

CLOV The bastard!

HAMM Did you get him?

CLOV Looks like it. [*He drops the tin and adjusts his trousers.*] Unless he's laying doggo.

HAMM Laying! Lying you mean. Unless he's *lying* doggo.

CLOV Ah? One says lying? One doesn't say laying?

HAMM Use your head, can't you. If he was laying we'd be bitched.

CLOV Ah. [*Pause.*] What about that pee?

HAMM I'm having it.

CLOV Ah that's the spirit, that's the spirit! [*Pause.*]

HAMM [*With ardour.*] Let's go from here, the two of us! South! You can make a raft and the currents will carry us away, far away, to other . . . mammals!

CLOV God forbid!

HAMM Alone, I'll embark alone! Get working on that raft immediately. Tomorrow I'll be gone for ever.

CLOV [*Hastening towards door.*] I'll start straight away.

HAMM Wait! [CLOV *halts.*] Will there be sharks, do you think?

CLOV Sharks? I don't know. If there are there will be. [*He goes towards door.*]

HAMM Wait! [CLOV *halts.*] Is it not yet time for my pain-killer?

CLOV [*Violently.*] No! [*He goes towards door.*]

HAMM Wait! [CLOV *halts.*] How are your eyes?

CLOV Bad.

HAMM But you can see.

CLOV All I want.

HAMM How are your legs?

CLOV Bad.

HAMM But you can walk.

CLOV I come . . . and go.

HAMM In my house. [*Pause. With prophetic relish.*] One day you'll be blind, like me. You'll be sitting there, a speck in the void, in the dark, for ever, like me. [*Pause.*] One day you'll say to yourself, I'm tired, I'll sit down, and you'll go and sit down. Then you'll say, I'm hungry, I'll get up and get something to eat. But you won't get up. You'll say, I shouldn't have sat down, but since I have I'll sit on a little longer, then I'll get up and get something to eat. But you won't go up and you won't get anything to eat. [*Pause.*] You'll look at the wall a while, then you'll say, I'll close my eyes, perhaps have a little sleep, after that I'll feel better, and you'll close them. And when you open them again there'll be no wall any more. [*Pause.*] Infinite emptiness will be all around you, all the resurrected dead of all the ages wouldn't fill it, and there you'll be like a little bit of grit in the middle of the steppe.[1] [*Pause.*] Yes, one day you'll know what it is, you'll be like me, except that you won't have anyone with you, because you won't have had pity on anyone and because there won't be anyone left to have pity on. [*Pause.*]

CLOV   It's not certain. [*Pause.*] And there's one thing you forget.

HAMM   Ah?

CLOV   I can't sit down.

HAMM   [*Impatiently.*] Well you'll lie down then, what the hell! Or you'll come to a standstill, simply stop and stand still, the way you are now. One day you'll say, I'm tired, I'll stop. What does the attitude matter? [*Pause.*]

CLOV   So you all want me to leave you.

HAMM   Naturally.

CLOV   Then I'll leave you.

HAMM   You can't leave us.

CLOV   Then I won't leave you. [*Pause.*]

HAMM   Why don't you finish us? [*Pause.*] I'll tell you the combination of the cupboard if you promise to finish me.

CLOV   I couldn't finish you.

HAMM   Then you won't finish me. [*Pause.*]

CLOV   I'll leave you, I have things to do.

HAMM   Do you remember when you came here?

CLOV   No. Too small, you told me.

HAMM   Do you remember your father?

CLOV   [*Wearily.*] Same answer. [*Pause.*] You've asked me these questions millions of times.

HAMM   I love the old questions. [*With fervour.*] Ah the old questions, the old answers, there's nothing like them! [*Pause.*] It was I was a father to you.

CLOV   Yes. [*He looks at* HAMM *fixedly.*] You were that to me.

HAMM   My house a home for you.

CLOV   Yes. [*He looks about him.*] This was that for me.

HAMM   [*Proudly.*] But for me, [*Gesture towards himself.*] no father. But for Hamm, [*Gesture towards surroundings.*] no home. [*Pause.*]

CLOV   I'll leave you.

HAMM   Did you ever think of one thing?

CLOV   Never.

HAMM   That here we're down in a hole. [*Pause.*] But beyond the hills? Eh? Perhaps it's still green. Eh? [*Pause.*] Flora! Pomona! [*Ecstatically.*] Ceres![2] [*Pause.*] Perhaps you won't need to go very far.

CLOV   I can't go very far. [*Pause.*] I'll leave you.

HAMM   Is my dog ready?

CLOV   He lacks a leg.

---

1. Level grassy plain devoid of forest, especially in southeast Europe and Siberia.

2. In Roman mythology, respectively, the goddesses of flowers, fruit, and crops.

HAMM   Is he silky?

CLOV   He's a kind of Pomeranian.

HAMM   Go and get him.

CLOV   He lacks a leg.

HAMM   Go and get him! [*Exit* CLOV.] We're getting on. [*Enter* CLOV *holding by one of its three legs a black toy dog.*]

CLOV   Your dogs are here. [*He hands the dog to* HAMM *who feels it, fondles it.*]

HAMM   He's white, isn't he?

CLOV   Nearly.

HAMM   What do you mean, nearly? Is he white or isn't he?

CLOV   He isn't. [*Pause.*]

HAMM   You've forgotten the sex.

CLOV   [*Vexed.*] But he isn't finished. The sex goes on at the end. [*Pause.*]

HAMM   You haven't put on his ribbon.

CLOV   [*Angrily.*] But he isn't finished, I tell you! First you finish your dog and then you put on his ribbon! [*Pause.*]

HAMM   Can he stand?

CLOV   I don't know.

HAMM   Try. [*He hands the dog to* CLOV *who places it on the ground.*] Well?

CLOV   Wait! [*He squats down and tries to get the dog to stand on its three legs, fails, lets it go. The dog falls on its side.*]

HAMM   [*Impatiently.*] Well?

CLOV   He's standing.

HAMM   [*Groping for the dog.*] Where? Where is he? [CLOV *holds up the dog in a standing position.*]

CLOV   There. [*He takes* HAMM's hand and guides it towards the dog's head.]

HAMM   [*His hand on the dog's head.*] Is he gazing at me?

CLOV   Yes.

HAMM   [*Proudly.*] As if he were asking me to take him for a walk?

CLOV   If you like.

HAMM   [*As before.*] Or as if he were begging me for a bone. [*He withdraws his hand.*] Leave him like that, standing there imploring me. [CLOV *straightens up. The dog falls on its side.*]

CLOV   I'll leave you.

HAMM   Have you had your visions?

CLOV   Less.

HAMM   Is Mother Pegg's light on?

CLOV   Light! How could anyone's light be on?

HAMM   Extinguished!

CLOV   Naturally it's extinguished. If it's not on it's extinguished.

HAMM   No, I mean Mother Pegg.

CLOV   But naturally she's extinguished! [*Pause.*] What's the matter with you today?

HAMM   I'm taking my course. [*Pause.*] Is she buried?

CLOV   Buried! Who would have buried her?

HAMM   You.

CLOV   Me! Haven't I enough to do without burying people?

HAMM   But you'll bury me.

CLOV No I won't bury you. [*Pause.*]

HAMM She was bonny once, like a flower of the field. [*With reminiscent leer.*] And a great one for the men!

CLOV We too were bonny—once. It's a rare thing not to have been bonny—once. [*Pause.*]

HAMM Go and get the gaff.[3] [CLOV *goes to door, halts.*]

CLOV Do this, do that, and I do it. I never refuse. Why?

HAMM You're not able to.

CLOV Soon I won't do it any more.

HAMM You won't be able to any more. [*Exit* CLOV.] Ah the creatures, the creatures, everything has to be explained to them. [*Enter* CLOV *with gaff.*]

CLOV Here's your gaff. Stick it up. [*He gives the gaff to* HAMM *who, wielding it like a puntpole,[4] tries to move his chair.*]

HAMM Did I move?

CLOV No. [HAMM *throws down the gaff.*]

HAMM Go and get the oilcan.

CLOV What for?

HAMM To oil the castors.

CLOV I oiled them yesterday.

HAMM Yesterday! What does that mean? Yesterday!

CLOV [*Violently.*] That means that bloody awful day, long ago, before this bloody awful day. I use the words you taught me. If they don't mean anything any more, teach me others. Or let me be silent. [*Pause.*]

HAMM I once knew a madman who thought the end of the world had come. He was a painter—and engraver. I had a great fondness for him. I used to go and see him, in the asylum. I'd take him by the hand and drag him to the window. Look! There! All that rising corn! And there! Look! The sails of the herring fleet! All that loveliness! [*Pause.*] He'd snatch away his hand and go back into his corner. Appalled. All he had seen was ashes. [*Pause.*] He alone had been spared. [*Pause.*] Forgotten. [*Pause.*] It appears the case is . . . was not so . . . so unusual.

CLOV A madman! When was that?

HAMM Oh way back, way back, you weren't in the land of the living.

CLOV God be with the days! [*Pause.* HAMM *raises his toque.*]

HAMM I had a great fondness for him. [*Pause. He puts on his toque again.*] He was a painter—and engraver.

CLOV There are so many terrible things.

HAMM No, no, there are not so many now. [*Pause.*] Clov!

CLOV Yes.

HAMM Do you not think this has gone on long enough?

CLOV Yes! [*Pause.*] What?

HAMM This . . . this . . . thing.

CLOV I've always thought so. [*Pause.*] You not?

HAMM [*Gloomily.*] Then it's a day like any other day.

CLOV As long as it lasts. [*Pause.*] All life long the same inanities.

HAMM I can't leave you.

---

3. Barbed fishing spear.
4. Long pole, pushed against the bottom of a river to propel a punt (a shallow, flat-bottomed boat).

CLOV   I know. And you can't follow me. [*Pause.*]

HAMM   If you leave me how shall I know?

CLOV   [*Briskly.*] Well you simply whistle me and if I don't come running it means I've left you. [*Pause.*]

HAMM   You won't come and kiss me goodbye?

CLOV   Oh I shouldn't think so. [*Pause.*]

HAMM   But you might be merely dead in your kitchen.

CLOV   The result would be the same.

HAMM   Yes, but how would I know, if you were merely dead in your kitchen?

CLOV   Well . . . sooner or later I'd start to stink.

HAMM   You stink already. The whole place stinks of corpses.

CLOV   The whole universe.

HAMM   [*Angrily.*] To hell with the universe. [*Pause.*] Think of something.

CLOV   What?

HAMM   An idea, have an idea. [*Angrily.*] A bright idea!

CLOV   Ah good. [*He starts pacing to and fro, his eyes fixed on the ground, his hands behind his back. He halts.*] The pains in my legs! It's unbelievable! Soon I won't be able to think any more.

HAMM   You won't be able to leave me. [CLOV *resumes his pacing.*] What are you doing?

CLOV   Having an idea. [*He paces.*] Ah! [*He halts.*]

HAMM   What a brain! [*Pause.*] Well?

CLOV   Wait! [*He meditates. Not very convinced.*] Yes . . . [*Pause. More convinced.*] Yes! [*He raises his head.*] I have it! I set the alarm. [*Pause.*]

HAMM   This is perhaps not one of my bright days, but frankly—

CLOV   You whistle me. I don't come. The alarm rings. I'm gone. It doesn't ring. I'm dead. [*Pause.*]

HAMM   Is it working? [*Pause. Impatiently.*] The alarm, is it working?

CLOV   Why wouldn't it be working?

HAMM   Because it's worked too much.

CLOV   But it's hardly worked at all.

HAMM   [*Angrily.*] Then because it's worked too little!

CLOV   I'll go and see. [*Exit* CLOV. *Brief ring of alarm off. Enter* CLOV *with alarm-clock. He holds it against* HAMM's *ear and releases alarm. They listen to it ringing to the end. Pause.*] Fit to wake the dead! Did you hear it?

HAMM   Vaguely.

CLOV   The end is terrific!

HAMM   I prefer the middle. [*Pause.*] Is it not time for my pain-killer?

CLOV   No! [*He goes to door, turns.*] I'll leave you.

HAMM   It's time for my story. Do you want to listen to my story.

CLOV   No.

HAMM   Ask my father if he wants to listen to my story. [CLOV *goes to bins, raises the lid of* NAGG's, *stoops, looks into it. Pause. He straightens up.*]

CLOV   He's asleep.

HAMM   Wake him. [CLOV *stoops, wakes* NAGG *with the alarm. Unintelligible words.* CLOV *straightens up.*]

CLOV   He doesn't want to listen to your story.

HAMM   I'll give him a bon-bon.[5] [CLOV *stoops. As before.*]

---

5. Candy (French).

CLOV He wants a sugar-plum.

HAMM He'll get a sugar-plum. [CLOV *stoops. As before.*]

CLOV It's a deal. [*He goes towards door.* NAGG's *hands appear, gripping the rim. Then the head emerges.* CLOV *reaches door, turns.*] Do you believe in the life to come?

HAMM Mine was always that. [*Exit* CLOV.] Got him that time!

NAGG I'm listening.

HAMM Scoundrel! Why did you engender me?

NAGG I didn't know.

HAMM What? What didn't you know?

NAGG That it'd be you. [*Pause.*] You'll give me a sugar-plum?

HAMM After the audition.

NAGG You swear?

HAMM Yes.

NAGG On what?

HAMM My honour. [*Pause. They laugh heartily.*]

NAGG Two.

HAMM One.

NAGG One for me and one for—

HAMM One! Silence! [*Pause.*] Where was I? [*Pause. Gloomily.*] It's finished, we're finished. [*Pause.*] Nearly finished. [*Pause.*] There'll be no more speech. [*Pause.*] Something dripping in my head, ever since the fontanelles.[6] [*Stifled hilarity of* NAGG.] Splash, splash, always on the same spot. [*Pause.*] Perhaps it's a little vein. [*Pause.*] A little artery. [*Pause. More animated.*] Enough of that, it's story time, where was I? [*Pause. Narrative tone.*] The man came crawling towards me, on his belly. Pale, wonderfully pale and thin, he seemed on the point of—[*Pause. Normal tone.*] No, I've done that bit. [*Pause. Narrative tone.*] I calmly filled my pipe—the meerschaum, lit it with . . . let us say a vesta,[7] drew a few puffs. Aah! [*Pause.*] Well, what is it you want? [*Pause.*] It was an extraordinarily bitter day, I remember, zero by the thermometer. But considering it was Christmas Eve there was nothing . . . extra-ordinary about that. Seasonable weather, for once in a way. [*Pause.*] Well, what ill wind blows you my way? He raised his face to me, black with mingled dirt and tears. [*Pause. Normal tone.*] That should do it. [*Narrative tone.*] No, no, don't look at me, don't look at me. He dropped his eyes and mumbled something, apologies I presume. [*Pause.*] I'm a busy man, you know, the final touches, before the festivities, you know what it is. [*Pause. Forcibly.*] Come on now, what is the object of this invasion? [*Pause.*] It was a glorious bright day, I remember, fifty by the heliometer,[8] but already the sun was sinking down into the . . . down among the dead. [*Normal tone.*] Nicely put, that. [*Narrative tone.*] Come on now, come on, present your petition and let me resume my labours. [*Pause. Normal tone.*] There's English for you. Ah well . . . [*Narrative tone.*] It was then he took the plunge. It's my little one, he said. Tsstss, a little one, that's bad. My little boy, he said, as if the sex mattered. Where did he come from? He named the hole. A good half-day, on horse. What are you insinuating? That the place is still inhabited? No no, not a soul, except himself and

---

6. Membranous space in infant's skull at the angles of the parietal bones.

7. Vesta is the brand name of a type of match (from Vesta, Roman goddess of the hearth).

8. Literally, a sun meter.

the child—assuming he existed. Good. I enquired about the situation at Kov,[9] beyond the gulf. Not a sinner. Good. And you expect me to believe you have left your little one back there, all alone, and alive into the bargain? Come now! [*Pause.*] It was a howling wild day, I remember, a hundred by the anemometer.[1] The wind was tearing up the dead pines and sweeping them . . . away. [*Pause. Normal tone.*] A bit feeble, that. [*Narrative tone.*] Come on, man, speak up, what is you want from me, I have to put up my holly. [*Pause.*] Well to make it short it finally transpired that what he wanted from me was . . . bread for his brat? Bread? But I have no bread, it doesn't agree with me. Good. Then perhaps a little corn? [*Pause. Normal tone.*] That should do it. [*Narrative tone.*] Corn, yes, I have corn, it's true, in my granaries. But use your head. I give you some corn, a pound, a pound and a half, you bring it back to your child and you make him—if he's still alive—a nice pot of porridge, [NAGG *reacts.*] a nice pot and a half of porridge, full of nourishment. Good. The colours come back into his little cheeks—perhaps. And then? [*Pause.*] I lost patience. [*Violently.*] Use your head, can't you, use your head, you're on earth, there's no cure for that! [*Pause.*] It was an exceedingly dry day, I remember, zero by the hygrometer. Ideal weather, for my lumbago.[2] [*Pause. Violently.*] But what in God's name do you imagine? That the earth will awake in spring? That the rivers and seas will run with fish again? That there's manna in heaven still for imbeciles like you? [*Pause.*] Gradually I cooled down, sufficiently at least to ask him how long he had taken on the way. Three whole days. Good. In what condition he had left the child. Deep in sleep. [*Forcibly.*] But deep in what sleep, deep in what sleep already? [*Pause.*] Well to make it short I finally offered to take him into my service. He had touched a chord. And then I imagined already that I wasn't much longer for this world. [*He laughs. Pause.*] Well? [*Pause.*] Well? Here if you were careful you might die a nice natural death, in peace and comfort. [*Pause.*] Well? [*Pause.*] In the end he asked me would I consent to take in the child as well—if he were still alive. [*Pause.*] It was the moment I was waiting for. [*Pause.*] Would I consent to take in the child . . . [*Pause.*] I can see him still, down on his knees, his hands flat on the ground, glaring at me with his mad eyes, in defiance of my wishes. [*Pause. Normal tone.*] I'll soon have finished with this story. [*Pause.*] Unless I bring in other characters. [*Pause.*] But where would I find them? [*Pause.*] Where would I look for them? [*Pause. He whistles. Enter* CLOV.] Let us pray to God.

NAGG   Me sugar-plum!

CLOV   There's a rat in the kitchen!

HAMM   A rat! Are there still rats?

CLOV   In the kitchen there's one.

HAMM   And you haven't exterminated him?

CLOV   Half. You disturbed us.

HAMM   He can't get away?

CLOV   No.

HAMM   You'll finish him later. Let us pray to God.

9. Conceivably, the town of Kova in southern Siberia (except that it has no gulf); more probably, Hamm's invention.

1. A wind meter.
2. Rheumatic pain in lumbar region of the lower back. "Hygrometer": a moisture meter.

CLOV   Again!

NAGG   Me sugar-plum!

HAMM   God first! [*Pause.*] Are you right?

CLOV   [*Resigned.*] Off we go.

HAMM   [*To* NAGG.] And you?

NAGG   [*Clasping his hands, closing his eyes, in a gabble.*] Our Father which art—

HAMM   Silence! In silence! Where are your manners? [*Pause.*] Off we go. [*Attitudes of prayer. Silence. Abandoning his attitude, discouraged.*] Well?

CLOV   [*Abandoning his attitude.*] What a hope! And you?

HAMM   Sweet damn all! [*To* NAGG.] And you?

NAGG   Wait! [*Pause. Abandoning his attitude.*] Nothing doing!

HAMM   The bastard! He doesn't exist!

CLOV   Not yet.

NAGG   Me sugar-plum!

HAMM   There are no more sugar-plums! [*Pause.*]

NAGG   It's natural. After all I'm your father. It's true if it hadn't been me it would have been someone else. But that's no excuse. [*Pause.*] Turkish Delight,[3] for example, which no longer exists, we all know that, there is nothing in the world I love more. And one day I'll ask you for some, in return for a kindness, and you'll promise it to me. One must live with the times. [*Pause.*] Whom did you call when you were a tiny boy, and were frightened, in the dark? Your mother? No. Me. We let you cry. Then we moved you out of earshot, so that we might sleep in peace. [*Pause.*] I was asleep, as happy as a king, and you woke me up to have me listen to you. It wasn't indispensable, you didn't really need to have me listen to you. [*Pause.*] I hope the day will come when you'll really need to have me listen to you, and need to hear my voice, any voice. [*Pause.*] Yes, I hope I'll live till then, to hear you calling me like when you were a tiny boy, and were frightened, in the dark, and I was your only hope. [*Pause.* NAGG *knocks on lid of* NELL's *bin. Pause.*] Nell! [*Pause. He knocks louder. Pause. Louder.*] Nell! [*Pause.* NAGG *sinks back into his bin, closes the lid behind him. Pause.*]

HAMM   Our revels now are ended.[4] [*He gropes for the dog*] The dog's gone.

CLOV   He's not a real dog, he can't go.

HAMM   [*Groping.*] He's not there.

CLOV   He's lain down.

HAMM   Give him up to me. [CLOV *picks up the dog and gives it to* HAMM. HAMM *holds it in his arms. Pause.* HAMM *throws away the dog.*] Dirty brute! [CLOV *begins to pick up the objects lying on the ground.*] What are you doing?

CLOV   Putting things in order. [*He straightens up. Fervently.*] I'm going to clear everything away! [*He starts picking up again.*]

HAMM   Order!

CLOV   [*Straightening up.*] I love order. It's my dream. A world where all would be silent and still and each thing in its last place, under the last dust. [*He starts picking up again.*]

---

3. A sticky sweet candy (originally from Turkey).
4. Words spoken by Prospero in Shakespeare's *The Tempest* 4.1.148.

HAMM   [*Exasperated.*] What in God's name do you think you are doing?

CLOV   [*Straightening up.*] I'm doing my best to create a little order.

HAMM   Drop it! [CLOV *drops the objects he has picked up.*]

CLOV   After all, there or elsewhere. [*He goes towards door.*]

HAMM   [*Irritably.*] What's wrong with your feet?

CLOV   My feet?

HAMM   Tramp! Tramp!

CLOV   I must have put on my boots.

HAMM   Your slippers were hurting you? [*Pause.*]

CLOV   I'll leave you.

HAMM   No!

CLOV   What is there to keep me here?

HAMM   The dialogue. [*Pause.*] I've got on with my story. [*Pause.*] I've got on with it well. [*Pause. Irritably.*] Ask me where I've got to.

CLOV   Oh, by the way, your story?

HAMM   [*Surprised.*] What story?

CLOV   The one you've been telling yourself all your days.

HAMM   Ah you mean my chronicle?

CLOV   That's the one. [*Pause.*]

HAMM   [*Angrily.*] Keep going, can't you, keep going!

CLOV   You've got on with it, I hope.

HAMM   [*Modestly.*] Oh not very far, not very far. [*He sighs.*] There are days like that, one isn't inspired. [*Pause.*] Nothing you can do about it, just wait for it to come. [*Pause.*] No forcing, no forcing, it's fatal. [*Pause.*] I've got on with it a little all the same. [*Pause.*] Technique, you know. [*Pause. Irritably.*] I say I've got on with it a little all the same.

CLOV   [*Admiringly.*] Well I never! In spite of everything you were able to get on with it!

HAMM   [*Modestly.*] Oh not very far, you know, not very far, but nevertheless, better than nothing.

CLOV   Better than nothing! Is it possible?

HAMM   I'll tell you how it goes. He comes crawling on his belly—

CLOV   Who?

HAMM   What?

CLOV   Who do you mean, he?

HAMM   Who do I mean! Yet another.

CLOV   Ah him! I wasn't sure.

HAMM   Crawling on his belly, whining for bread for his brat. He's offered a job as gardener. Before—[CLOV *bursts out laughing.*] What is there so funny about that?

CLOV   A job as gardener!

HAMM   Is that what tickles you?

CLOV   It must be that.

HAMM   It wouldn't be the bread?

CLOV   Or the brat. [*Pause.*]

HAMM   The whole thing is comical, I grant you that. What about having a good guffaw the two of us together?

CLOV   [*After reflection.*] I couldn't guffaw again today.

HAMM   [*After reflection.*] Nor I. [*Pause.*] I continue then. Before accepting with gratitude he asks if he may have his little boy with him.

CLOV   What age?
HAMM   Oh tiny.
CLOV   He would have climbed the trees.
HAMM   All the little odd jobs.
CLOV   And then he would have grown up.
HAMM   Very likely. [*Pause.*]
CLOV   Keep going, can't you, keep going!
HAMM   That's all. I stopped there. [*Pause.*]
CLOV   Do you see how it goes on.
HAMM   More or less.
CLOV   Will it not soon be the end?
HAMM   I'm afraid it will.
CLOV   Pah! You'll make up another.
HAMM   I don't know. [*Pause.*] I feel rather drained. [*Pause.*] The prolonged
    creative effort. [*Pause.*] If I could drag myself down to the sea! I'd make
    a pillow of sand for my head and the tide would come.
CLOV   There's no more tide. [*Pause.*]
HAMM   Go and see is she dead. [CLOV *goes to bins, raises the lid of* NELL's,
    stoops, looks into it. Pause.]
CLOV   Looks like it. [*He closes the lid, straightens up.* HAMM *raises his toque.
    Pause. He puts it on again.*]
HAMM   [*With his hand to his toque.*] And Nagg? [CLOV *raises lid of* NAGG's
    bin, stoops, looks into it. Pause.]
CLOV   Doesn't look like it. [*He closes the lid, straightens up.*]
HAMM   [*Letting go his toque.*] What's he doing? [CLOV *raises lid of* NAGG's
    bin, stoops, looks into it. Pause.]
CLOV   He's crying. [*He closes lid, straightens up.*]
HAMM   Then he's living. [*Pause.*] Did you ever have an instant of happi-
    ness?
CLOV   Not to my knowledge. [*Pause.*]
HAMM   Bring me under the window. [CLOV *goes towards chair.*] I want to
    feel the light on my face. [CLOV *pushes chair.*] Do you remember, in the
    beginning, when you took me for a turn? You used to hold the chair too
    high. At every step you nearly tipped me out. [*With senile quaver.*] Ah
    great fun, we had, the two of us, great fun. [*Gloomily.*] And then we got
    into the way of it. [CLOV *stops the chair under window right.*] There
    already? [*Pause. He tilts back his head.*] Is it light?
CLOV   It isn't dark.
HAMM   [*Angrily*] I'm asking you is it light.
CLOV   Yes. [*Pause.*]
HAMM   The curtain isn't closed?
CLOV   No.
HAMM   What window is it?
CLOV   The earth.
HAMM   I knew it! [*Angrily.*] But there's no light there! The other! [CLOV
    stops the chair under window left. HAMM *tilts back his head.*] That's what
    I call light! [*Pause.*] Feels like a ray of sunshine. [*Pause.*] No?
CLOV   No.
HAMM   It isn't a ray of sunshine I feel on my face?
CLOV   No. [*Pause.*]

HAMM   Am I very white? [*Pause. Angrily.*] I'm asking you am I very white!

CLOV   Not more so than usual. [*Pause.*]

HAMM   Open the window.

CLOV   What for?

HAMM   I want to hear the sea.

CLOV   You wouldn't hear it.

HAMM   Even if you opened the window?

CLOV   No.

HAMM   Then it's not worth while opening it?

CLOV   No.

HAMM   [*Violently*] Then open it! [CLOV *gets up on the ladder, opens the window. Pause.*] Have you opened it?

CLOV   Yes. [*Pause.*]

HAMM   You swear you've opened it?

CLOV   Yes. [*Pause.*]

HAMM   Well . . . ! [*Pause.*] It must be very calm. [*Pause. Violently.*] I'm asking you is it very calm!

CLOV   Yes.

HAMM   It's because there are no more navigators. [*Pause.*] You haven't much conversation all of a sudden. Do you not feel well?

CLOV   I'm cold.

HAMM   What month are we? [*Pause.*] Close the window, we're going back. [CLOV *closes the window, gets down, pushes the chair back to its place, remains standing behind it, head bowed.*] Don't stay there, you give me the shivers! [CLOV *returns to his place beside the chair.*] Father! [*Pause. Louder.*] Father! [*Pause.*] Go and see did he hear me. [CLOV *goes to* NAGG's *bin, raises the lid, stoops. Unintelligible words.* CLOV *straightens up.*]

CLOV   Yes.

HAMM   Both times? [CLOV *stoops. As before.*]

CLOV   Once only.

HAMM   The first time or the second? [CLOV *stoops. As before.*]

CLOV   He doesn't know.

HAMM   It must have been the second.

CLOV   We'll never know. [*He closes lid.*]

HAMM   Is he still crying?

CLOV   No.

HAMM   The dead go fast. [*Pause.*] What's he doing?

CLOV   Sucking his biscuit.

HAMM   Life goes on. [CLOV *returns to his place beside the chair.*] Give me a rug. I'm freezing.

CLOV   There are no more rugs. [*Pause.*]

HAMM   Kiss me. [*Pause.*] Will you not kiss me?

CLOV   No.

HAMM   On the forehead.

CLOV   I won't kiss you anywhere. [*Pause.*]

HAMM   [*Holding out his hand.*] Give me your hand at least. [*Pause.*] Will you not give me your hand?

CLOV   I won't touch you. [*Pause.*]

HAMM   Give me the dog. [CLOV *looks round for the dog.*] No!

CLOV   Do you not want your dog?

HAMM   No.

CLOV   Then I'll leave you.

HAMM   [*Head bowed, absently.*] That's right. [CLOV *goes to door, turns.*]

CLOV   If I don't kill that rat he'll die.

HAMM   [*As before.*] That's right. [*Exit* CLOV. *Pause.*] Me to play. [*He takes out his handkerchief, unfolds it, holds it spread out before him.*] We're getting on. [*Pause.*] You weep, and weep, for nothing, so as not to laugh, and little by little . . . you begin to grieve. [*He folds the handkerchief, puts it back in his pocket, raises his head.*] All those I might have helped. [*Pause.*] Helped! [*Pause.*] Saved. [*Pause.*] Saved! [*Pause.*] The place was crawling with them! [*Pause. Violently.*] Use your head, can't you, use your head, you're on earth, there's no cure for that! [*Pause.*] Get out of here and love one another! Lick your neighbour as yourself![5] [*Pause. Calmer.*] When it wasn't bread they wanted it was crumpets. [*Pause. Violently.*] Out of my sight and back to your petting parties! [*Pause.*] All that, all that! [*Pause.*] Not even a real dog! [*Calmer.*] The end is in the beginning and yet you go on. [*Pause.*] Perhaps I could go on with my story, end it and begin another. [*Pause.*] Perhaps I could throw myself out on the floor. [*He pushes himself painfully off his seat, falls back again.*] Dig my nails into the cracks and drag myself forward with my fingers. [*Pause.*] It will be the end and there I'll be, wondering what can have brought it on and wondering what can have . . . [*He hesitates.*] . . . why it was so long coming. [*Pause.*] There I'll be, in the old shelter, alone against the silence and . . . [*He hesitates.*] . . . the stillness. If I can hold my peace, and sit quiet, it will be all over with sound, and motion, all over and done with. [*Pause.*] I'll have called my father and I'll have called my . . . [*He hesitates.*] . . . my son. And even twice, or three times, in case they shouldn't have heard me, the first time, or the second. [*Pause.*] I'll say to myself, He'll come back. [*Pause.*] And then? [*Pause.*] And then? [*Pause.*] He couldn't, he has gone too far. [*Pause.*] And then? [*Pause. Very agitated.*] All kinds of fantasies! That I'm being watched! A rat! Steps! Breath held and then . . . [*He breathes out.*] Then babble, babble, words, like the solitary child who turns himself into children, two, three, so as to be together, and whisper together, in the dark. [*Pause.*] Moment upon moment, pattering down, like the millet grains of . . . [*He hesitates.*] . . . that old Greek,[6] and all life long you wait for that to mount up to a life. [*Pause. He opens his mouth to continue, renounces.*] Ah let's get it over! [*He whistles. Enter* CLOV *with alarm-clock. He halts beside the chair.*] What? Neither gone nor dead?

CLOV   In spirit only.

HAMM   Which?

CLOV   Both.

HAMM   Gone from me you'd be dead.

CLOV   And vice versa.

HAMM   Outside of here it's death! [*Pause.*] And the rat?

5. Parody of Christ's instruction: "Thou shalt love thy neighbor as thyself" (Matthew 19.19).
6. Zeno of Elea (ca. 450 B.C.E.), a Greek philosopher famous for his paradoxes; e.g., "If a grain of millet falling makes no sound, how can a bushel of grains make any sound?" (reported by Aristotle in his *Physics* 5:250 a.19).

CLOV He's got away.

HAMM He can't go far. [*Pause. Anxious.*] Eh?

CLOV He doesn't need to go far. [*Pause.*]

HAMM Is it not time for my pain-killer?

CLOV Yes.

HAMM Ah! At last! Give it to me! Quick! [*Pause.*]

CLOV There's no more pain-killer. [*Pause.*]

HAMM [*Appalled.*] Good . . . ! [*Pause.*] No more pain-killer!

CLOV No more pain-killer. You'll never get any more pain-killer. [*Pause.*]

HAMM But the little round box. It was full!

CLOV Yes. But now it's empty. [*Pause.* CLOV *starts to move about the room. He is looking for a place to put down the alarm-clock.*]

HAMM [*Soft.*] What'll I do? [*Pause. In a scream.*] What'll I do? [CLOV *sees the picture, takes it down, stands it on the floor with its face to the wall, hangs up the alarm-clock in its place.*] What are you doing?

CLOV Winding up.

HAMM Look at the earth.

CLOV Again!

HAMM Since it's calling to you.

CLOV Is your throat sore? [*Pause.*] Would you like a lozenge? [*Pause.*] No. [*Pause.*] Pity. [CLOV *goes, humming, towards window right, halts before it, looks up at it.*]

HAMM Don't sing.

CLOV [*Turning towards* HAMM.] One hasn't the right to sing any more?

HAMM No.

CLOV Then how can it end?

HAMM You want it to end?

CLOV I want to sing.

HAMM I can't prevent you. [*Pause.* CLOV *turns towards window right.*]

CLOV What did I do with that steps? [*He looks around for ladder.*] You didn't see that steps? [*He sees it.*] Ah, about time. [*He goes towards window left.*] Sometimes I wonder if I'm in my right mind. Then it passes over and I'm as lucid as before. [*He gets up on ladder, looks out of window.*] Christ, she's under water! [*He looks.*] How can that be? [*He pokes forward his head, his hand above his eyes.*] It hasn't rained. [*He wipes the pane, looks. Pause.*] Ah what a fool I am! I'm on the wrong side! [*He gets down, takes a few steps towards window right.*] Under water! [*He goes back for ladder.*] What a fool I am! [*He carries ladder towards window right.*] Sometimes I wonder if I'm in my right senses. Then it passes off and I'm as intelligent as ever. [*He sets down ladder under window right, gets up on it, looks out of window. He turns towards* HAMM.] Any particular sector you fancy? Or merely the whole thing?

HAMM Whole thing.

CLOV The general effect? Just a moment. [*He looks out of window. Pause.*]

HAMM Clov.

CLOV [*Absorbed.*] Mmm.

HAMM Do you know what it is?

CLOV [*As before.*] Mmm.

HAMM I was never there. [*Pause.*] Clov!

CLOV [*Turning towards* HAMM, *exasperated.*] What is it?

HAMM   I was never there.

CLOV   Lucky for you. [*He looks out of window.*]

HAMM   Absent, always. It all happened without me. I don't know what's happened. [*Pause.*] Do you know what's happened? [*Pause.*] Clov!

CLOV   [*Turning towards* HAMM, *exasperated.*] Do you want me to look at this muckheap, yes or no?

HAMM   Answer me first.

CLOV   What?

HAMM   Do you know what's happened?

CLOV   When? Where?

HAMM   [*Violently.*] When! What's happened? Use your head, can't you! What has happened?

CLOV   What for Christ's sake does it matter? [*He looks out of window.*]

HAMM   I don't know. [*Pause.* CLOV *turns towards* HAMM.]

CLOV   [*Harshly.*] When old Mother Pegg asked you for oil for her lamp and you told her to get out to hell, you knew what was happening then, no? [*Pause.*] You know what she died of, Mother Pegg? Of darkness.

HAMM   [*Feebly.*] I hadn't any.

CLOV   [*As before.*] Yes, you had. [*Pause.*]

HAMM   Have you the glass?

CLOV   No, it's clear enough as it is.

HAMM   Go and get it. [*Pause.* CLOV *casts up his eyes, brandishes his fists. He loses balance, clutches on to the ladder. He starts to get down, halts.*]

CLOV   There's one thing I'll never understand. [*He gets down.*] Why I always obey you. Can you explain that to me?

HAMM   No. . . . Perhaps it's compassion. [*Pause.*] A kind of great compassion. [*Pause.*] Oh you won't find it easy, you won't find it easy. [*Pause.* CLOV *begins to move about the room in search of the telescope.*]

CLOV   I'm tired of our goings on, very tired. [*He searches.*] You're not sitting on it? [*He moves the chair, looks at the place where it stood, resumes his search.*]

HAMM   [*Anguished.*] Don't leave me there! [*Angrily* CLOV *restores the chair to its place.*] Am I right in the centre?

CLOV   You'd need a microscope to find this—[*He sees the telescope.*] Ah, about time. [*He picks up the telescope, gets up on the ladder, turns the telescope on the without.*]

HAMM   Give me the dog.

CLOV   [*Looking.*] Quiet!

HAMM   [*Angrily.*] Give me the dog! [CLOV *drops the telescope, clasps his hands to his head. Pause. He gets down precipitately, looks for the dog, sees it, picks it up, hastens towards* HAMM *and strikes him violently on the head with the dog.*]

CLOV   There's your dog for you! [*The dog falls to the ground. Pause.*]

HAMM   He hit me!

CLOV   You drive me mad, I'm mad!

HAMM   If you must hit me, hit me with the axe. [*Pause.*] Or with the gaff, hit me with the gaff. Not with the dog. With the gaff. Or with the axe. [CLOV *picks up the dog and gives it to* HAMM *who takes it in his arms.*]

CLOV   [*Imploringly.*] Let's stop playing!

HAMM   Never! [*Pause.*] Put me in my coffin.

CLOV   There are no more coffins.

HAMM   Then let it end! [CLOV *goes towards ladder.*] With a bang! [CLOV *gets up on ladder, gets down again, looks for telescope, sees it, picks it up, gets up ladder, raises telescope.*] Of darkness! And me? Did anyone ever have pity on me?

CLOV   [*Lowering the telescope, turning towards* HAMM.] What? [*Pause.*] Is it me you're referring to?

HAMM   [*Angrily.*] An aside, ape! Did you never hear an aside before? [*Pause.*] I'm warming up for my last soliloquy.

CLOV   I warn you. I'm going to look at this filth since it's an order. But it's the last time. [*He turns the telescope on the without.*] Let's see. [*He moves the telescope.*] Nothing . . . nothing . . . good . . . good . . . nothing . . . goo—[*He starts, lowers the telescope, examines it, turns it again on the without. Pause.*] Bad luck to it!

HAMM   More complications! [CLOV *gets down.*] Not an underplot, I trust. [CLOV *moves ladder nearer window, gets up on it, turns telescope on the without.*]

CLOV   [*Dismayed.*] Looks like a small boy!

HAMM   [*Sarcastic.*] A small . . . boy!

CLOV   I'll go and see. [*He gets down, drops the telescope, goes towards door, turns.*] I'll take the gaff. [*He looks for the gaff, sees it, picks it up, hastens towards door.*]

HAMM   No! [CLOV *halts.*]

CLOV   No? A potential procreator?

HAMM   If he exists he'll die there or he'll come here. And if he doesn't . . . [*Pause.*]

CLOV   You don't believe me? You think I'm inventing? [*Pause.*]

HAMM   It's the end, Clov, we've come to the end. I don't need you any more. [*Pause.*]

CLOV   Lucky for you. [*He goes towards door.*]

HAMM   Leave me the gaff. [CLOV *gives him the gaff, goes towards door, halts, looks at alarm-clock, takes it down, looks round for a better place to put it, goes to bins, puts it on lid of* NAGG's *bin. Pause.*]

CLOV   I'll leave you. [*He goes towards door.*]

HAMM   Before you go . . . [CLOV *halts near door.*] . . . say something.

CLOV   There is nothing to say.

HAMM   A few words . . . to ponder . . . in my heart.

CLOV   Your heart!

HAMM   Yes. [*Pause. Forcibly.*] Yes! [*Pause.*] With the rest, in the end, the shadows, the murmurs, all the trouble, to end up with. [*Pause.*] Clov. . . . He never spoke to me. Then, in the end, before he went, without my having asked him, he spoke to me. He said . . .

CLOV   [*Despairingly.*] Ah . . . !

HAMM   Something . . . from your heart.

CLOV   My heart!

HAMM   A few words . . . from your heart. [*Pause.*]

CLOV   [*Fixed gaze, tonelessly, towards auditorium.*] They said to me, That's love, yes, yes, not a doubt, now you see how—

HAMM   Articulate!

CLOV   [*As before.*] How easy it is. They said to me, That's friendship, yes,

yes, no question, you've found it. They said to me, Here's the place, stop, raise your head and look at all that beauty. That order! They said to me. Come now, you're not a brute beast, think upon these things and you'll see how all becomes clear. And simple! They said to me, What skilled attention they get, all these dying of their wounds.

HAMM Enough!

CLOV [As before.] I say to myself—sometimes, Clov, you must learn to suffer better than that if you want them to weary of punishing you—one day. I say to myself—sometimes, Clov, you must be there better than that if you want them to let you go—one day. But I feel too old, and too far, to form new habits. Good, it'll never end, I'll never go. [Pause.] Then one day, suddenly, it ends, it changes, I don't understand, it dies, or it's me, I don't understand, that either. I ask the words that remain—sleeping, waking, morning, evening. They have nothing to say. [Pause.] I open the door of the cell and go. I am so bowed I only see my feet, if I open my eyes, and between my legs a little trail of black dust. I say to myself that the earth is extinguished, though I never saw it lit. [Pause.] It's easy going. [Pause.] When I fall I'll weep for happiness. [Pause. He goes towards door.]

HAMM Clov! [CLOV halts, without turning.] Nothing. [CLOV moves on.] Clov! [CLOV halts, without turning.]

CLOV This is what we call making an exit.

HAMM I'm obliged to you, Clov. For your services.

CLOV [Turning, sharply.] Ah pardon, it's I am obliged to you.

HAMM It's we are obliged to each other. [Pause. CLOV goes towards door.] One thing more. [CLOV halts.] A last favour. [Exit CLOV.] Cover me with the sheet. [Long pause.] No? Good. [Pause.] Me to play. [Pause. Wearily.] Old endgame lost of old, play and lose and have done with losing. [Pause. More animated.] Let me see. [Pause.] Ah yes! [He tries to move the chair, using the gaff as before. Enter CLOV, dressed for the road. Panama hat, tweed coat, raincoat over his arm, umbrella, bag. He halts by the door and stands there, impassive and motionless, his eyes fixed on HAMM, till the end. HAMM gives up.] Good. [Pause.] Discard. [He throws away the gaff, makes to throw away the dog, thinks better of it.] Take it easy. [Pause.] And now? [Pause.] Raise hat. [He raises his toque.] Peace to our . . . arses. [Pause.] And put on again. [He puts on his toque.] Deuce. [Pause. He takes off his glasses.] Wipe. [He takes out his handkerchief and, without unfolding it, wipes his glasses.] And put on again. [He puts on his glasses, puts back the handkerchief in his pocket.] We're coming. A few more squirms like that and I'll call. [Pause.] A little poetry. [Pause.] You prayed—[Pause. He corrects himself.] You CRIED for night; it comes— [Pause. He corrects himself.] It FALLS: now cry in darkness. [He repeats, chanting.] You cried for night; it falls: now cry in darkness.[7] [Pause.] Nicely put, that. [Pause.] And now? [Pause.] Moments for nothing, now as always, time was never and time is over, reckoning closed and story ended. [Pause. Narrative tone.] If he could have his child with him. . . . [Pause.] It was the moment I was waiting for. [Pause.] You don't want to

---

7. Parody of a line from Baudelaire's poem *Meditation*, which can be translated as: "You were calling for evening; it falls; it is here."

abandon him? You want him to bloom while you are withering? Be there
to solace your last million last moments? [*Pause.*] He doesn't realize, all
he knows is hunger, and cold, and death to crown it all. But you! You
ought to know what the earth is like, nowadays. Oh I put him before his
responsibilities! [*Pause. Normal tone.*] Well, there we are, there I am,
that's enough. [*He raises the whistle to his lips, hesitates, drops it. Pause.*]
Yes, truly! [*He whistles. Pause. Louder. Pause.*] Good. [*Pause.*] Father!
[*Pause. Louder.*] Father! [*Pause.*] Good. [*Pause.*] We're coming. [*Pause.*]
And to end up with? [*Pause.*] Discard. [*He throws away the dog. He tears
the whistle from his neck.*] With my compliments. [*He throws whistle
towards auditorium. Pause. He sniffs. Soft.*] Clov! [*Long pause.*] No?
Good. [*He takes out the handkerchief.*] Since that's the way we're playing
it . . . [*He unfolds handkerchief.*] . . . let's play it that way . . . [*He
unfolds.*] . . . and speak no more about it . . . [*He finishes unfolding.*] . . .
speak no more. [*He holds handkerchief spread out before him.*] Old
stancher! [*Pause.*] You . . . remain. [*Pause. He covers his face with handkerchief, lowers his arms to armrests, remains motionless.*] [*Brief tableau.*]

CURTAIN

1958

W. H. AUDEN
1907–1973

Wystan Hugh Auden was born in York and educated at Gresham's School, Holt,
Norfolk, and Christ Church, Oxford. After leaving Oxford he taught school from 1930
to 1935 and later worked for a government film unit. His sympathies in the 1930s
were with the Left, like those of most intellectuals of his age, and he went to Spain
during the Civil War, intending to serve as an ambulance driver on the left-wing
Republican side. He found himself to his surprise, however, so disturbed by the sight
of the many Roman Catholic churches gutted and looted by the Republicans that he
returned to England without fulfilling his ambition. He traveled in Iceland and China
before coming to America in 1939; in 1946 he became an American citizen. He taught
at a number of American colleges and was professor of poetry at Oxford from 1956
to 1960.

Auden was the most active of the group of young English poets who, in the late
1920s and early 1930s, saw themselves bringing new techniques and attitudes to
English poetry. Stephen Spender (1909–1995) and Cecil Day Lewis (1904–1972)
were at the time the most prominent of the other members of the new school, which
soon afterward fell apart, each poet going his own separate way. Like all his generation, Auden learned poetic wit and irony from T. S. Eliot, and he also learned metrical
and verbal techniques from Gerard Manley Hopkins and from Wilfred Owen. His
English studies at Oxford familiarized him with the rhythms and long alliterative line
of Anglo-Saxon poetry as well as with the rapid and rollicking short lines (a sort of
inspired doggerel) of the poet John Skelton (ca. 1460–1529); both influenced his own
versification. He learned, too, from the songs of the English music hall and, later,
from American blues singers.

The Depression that hit America in 1929 hit England soon afterward, and Auden and his contemporaries looked out at an England of industrial stagnation and mass unemployment, seeing not the metaphorical Waste Land of Eliot but a more literal Waste Land of poverty and "depressed areas." His early poetry is much concerned with a diagnosis of the ills of his country. This diagnosis, conducted in a verse that combined deliberate irreverence and sometimes even clowning with a cunning verbal craftsmanship, drew on both Freud and Marx to show England now as a nation of neurotic invalids who must learn to "throw away their rugs" and now as the victim of an antiquated economic system. The liveliness and nervous force of this early poetry of Auden's made a great impression, even though an uncertainty about his audience led him to introduce purely private symbols, intelligible only to a few friends, in some of his poems.

Gradually, Auden learned to clarify his imagery and control his desire to shock, and he produced, in the years around 1940, some poems (such as *Lullaby*) of finely disciplined movement, pellucid clarity, and deep yet unsentimental feeling. At the same time he was developing a more complex view of the world, moving from his earlier diagnosis of modern ills in terms of Freud and Marx to a more religious view of personal responsibility and traditional value without, however, abandoning the ideas and terms he had learned from modern psychology. But he never lost his ear for popular speech or his ability to combine elements from popular art with an extreme technical formality. He was always the experimenter, particularly in ways of bringing together high artifice and a colloquial tone.

Some of Auden's most exciting work is found in his early volumes, *Poems* (1930) and *On This Island* (1937). *Another Time* (1940) shows greater control and less violence. Of his later volumes, *Nones* (1951) shows most clearly his characteristic ways of combining or alternating the grave and the flippant. For the first part of his career—the English and the early American phase—Auden was very much the poet of his times, first of the Depression and then of the Age of the Refugee. In the poems of this period he preferred to confront modern problems directly rather than to filter them, as Eliot did, through symbolic situations. The poems of the last phase of his career, notably those in *About the House* (1967) and *City without Walls* (1970), are increasingly personal in tone and combine an apparent air of offhand informality with remarkable technical skill in versification. Auden grew increasingly hostile to the modern world and skeptical of all remedies offered for modern ills: he took refuge in love and friendship, particularly the love and friendship he shared with Chester Kallmann; emotions grounded in an ever deepening but rarely obtrusive religious feeling. In the last year of his life he returned to England to live in Oxford, feeling the need to be part of a university community as a protection against loneliness. An uneven poet, a poet who in the opinion of some critics never quite fulfilled the enormous promise of his early work, Auden is nevertheless now generally recognized as one of the masters of twentieth-century English poetry, a thoughtful, seriously playful (if one may put it in this paradoxical way) poet whom more than one critic has compared with Dryden in his combination of lively intelligence and immense craftsmanship.

Petition

> Sir, no man's enemy, forgiving all
> But will his negative inversion, be prodigal:
> Send to us power and light, a sovereign touch[1]
> Curing the intolerable neural itch,
> 5   The exhaustion of weaning, the liar's quinsy,°   *tonsillitis*

---

1. The king's touch was often regarded as miraculous cure for disease (cf. "sovereign" as an adjective, meaning "supreme, all-dominating").

And the distortions of ingrown virginity.
Prohibit sharply the rehearsed response
And gradually correct the coward's stance;
Cover in time with beams those in retreat
10 That, spotted, they turn though the reverse were great;
Publish each healer that in city lives
Or country houses at the end of drives;
Harrow the house of the dead; look shining at
New styles of architecture, a change of heart.

Oct. 1929   1930

On This Island

Look, stranger, on this island now
The leaping light for your delight discovers,
Stand stable here
And silent be,
5   That through the channels of the ear
May wander like a river
The swaying sound of the sea.

Here at the small field's ending pause
When the chalk wall falls to the foam and its tall ledges
10 Oppose the pluck
And knock of the tide,
And the shingle scrambles after the suck-
-ing surf,
And the gull lodges
15 A moment on its sheer side.

Far off like floating seeds the ships
Diverge on urgent voluntary errands,
And the full view
Indeed may enter
20 And move in memory as now these clouds do,
That pass the harbour mirror
And all the summer through the water saunter.

1935   1936

Spain 1937[1]

Yesterday all the past. The language of size
Spreading to China along the trade routes; the diffusion
          Of the counting-frame and the cromlech;[2]
Yesterday the shadow-reckoning in the sunny climates.

1. Written when the Spanish Civil War was raging. The rebellion by General Franco's right-wing
army against the left-wing Spanish government,
which broke out in 1936 and provoked full-scale
civil war, was viewed by British liberal intellectuals
at the time as a testing struggle between fascism
and democracy. The poem first appeared separately in 1937, the proceeds of its sale going to
Medical Aid for Spain. This is Auden's revised version of 1940.
2. Ancient stone circle.

5   Yesterday the assessment of insurance by cards,
The divination of water; yesterday the invention
            Of cart-wheels and clocks, the taming of
Horses; yesterday the bustling world of the navigators.

    Yesterday the abolition of fairies and giants;
10 The fortress like a motionless eagle eyeing the valley,
            The chapel built in the forest;
Yesterday the carving of angels and of frightening gargoyles;

    The trial of heretics among the columns of stone;
Yesterday the theological feuds in the taverns
15   And the miraculous cure at the fountain;
Yesterday the Sabbath of Witches.[3] But to-day the struggle.

    Yesterday the installation of dynamos and turbines;
The construction of railways in the colonial desert;
            Yesterday the classic lecture
20 On the origin of Mankind. But to-day the struggle.

    Yesterday the belief in the absolute value of Greek;
The fall of the curtain upon the death of a hero;
            Yesterday the prayer to the sunset,
And the adoration of madmen. But to-day the struggle.

25 As the poet whispers, startled among the pines
Or, where the loose waterfall sings, compact, or upright
            On the crag by the leaning tower:
"O my vision. O send me the luck of the sailor."

    And the investigator peers through his instruments
30 At the inhuman provinces, the virile bacillus
            Or enormous Jupiter finished:
"But the lives of my friends. I inquire, I inquire."

    And the poor in their fireless lodgings dropping the sheets
Of the evening paper: "Our day is our loss. O show us
35   History the operator, the
Organizer, Time the refreshing river."

    And the nations combine each cry, invoking the life
That shapes the individual belly and orders
            The private nocturnal terror:
40 "Did you not found once the city state of the sponge,

    "Raise the vast military empires of the shark
And the tiger, establish the robin's plucky canton?°   *district*
            Intervene. O descend as a dove or
A furious papa or a mild engineer: but descend."

---

3. Convocation of witches in parody of Christian service.

45 And the life, if it answers at all, replies from the heart
And the eyes and the lungs, from the shops and squares of the city:
"O no, I am not the Mover,
Not to-day, not to you. To you I'm the

"Yes-man, the bar-companion, the easily-duped:
50 I am whatever you do; I am your vow to be
Good, your humorous story;
I am your business voice; I am your marriage.

"What's your proposal? To build the Just City? I will.
I agree. Or is it the suicide pact, the romantic
55 Death? Very well, I accept, for
I am your choice, your decision: yes, I am Spain."

Many have heard it on remote peninsulas,
On sleepy plains, in the aberrant fishermen's islands,
In the corrupt heart of the city;
60 Have heard and migrated like gulls or the seeds of a flower.

They clung like burrs to the long expresses that lurch
Through the unjust lands, through the night, through the alpine tunnel;
They floated over the oceans;
They walked the passes: they came to present their lives.

65 On that arid square, that fragment nipped off from hot
Africa, soldered so crudely to inventive Europe,
On that tableland scored by rivers,
Our fever's menancing shapes are precise and alive.

To-morrow, perhaps, the future: the research on fatigue
70 And the movements of packers; the gradual exploring of all the
Octaves of radiation;
To-morrow the enlarging of consciousness by diet and breathing.

To-morrow the rediscovery of romantic love;
The photographing of ravens; all the fun under
75 Liberty's masterful shadow;
To-morrow the hour of the pageant-master and the musician.

To-morrow for the young the poets exploding like bombs,
The walks by the lake, the winter of perfect communion;
To-morrow the bicycle races
80 Through the suburbs on summer evenings: but to-day the struggle.

To-day the inevitable increase in the chances of death;
The conscious acceptance of guilt in the fact of murder;
To-day the expending of powers
On the flat ephemeral pamphlet and the boring meeting.

85 To-day the makeshift consolations; the shared cigarette;
The cards in the candle-lit barn and the scraping concert,

The masculine jokes; to-day the
Fumbled and unsatisfactory embrace before hurting.

90 The stars are dead; the animals will not look:
We are left alone with our day, and the time is short and
                    History to the defeated
May say Alas but cannot help or pardon.

1937   1937, 1940

Musée des Beaux Arts[1]

About suffering they were never wrong,
The Old Masters: how well they understood
Its human position; how it takes place
While someone else is eating or opening a window or just walking dully along;
5 How, when the aged are reverently, passionately waiting
For the miraculous birth, there always must be
Children who did not specially want it to happen, skating
On a pond at the edge of the wood:
They never forgot
10 That even the dreadful martyrdom must run its course
Anyhow in a corner, some untidy spot
Where the dogs go on with their doggy life and the torturer's horse
Scratches its innocent behind on a tree.

In Brueghel's *Icarus*,[2] for instance: how everything turns away
15 Quite leisurely from the disaster; the ploughman may
Have heard the splash, the forsaken cry,
But for him it was not an important failure; the sun shone
As it had to on the white legs disappearing into the green
Water; and the expensive delicate ship that must have seen
20 Something amazing, a boy falling out of the sky,
Had somewhere to get to and sailed calmly on.

Dec. 1938   1940

Lullaby

Lay your sleeping head, my love,
Human on my faithless arm;
Time and fevers burn away
Individual beauty from
5 Thoughtful children, and the grave
Proves the child ephemeral:

1. Museum of Fine Arts. The reference is to the Museum of Fine Arts in Brussels, which contains Brueghel's *Icarus*.
2. Icarus was the son of Daedalus, the cunning craftsman of ancient legend. Together they flew on artificial wings fastened to their shoulders with wax, but Icarus ventured too near the sun, which melted the wax, and so he fell and perished. The painting of the fall of Icarus is by the Flemish painter Pieter Brueghel (ca. 1520–1569): Icarus's legs are disappearing into the sea in one corner of the picture, the rest of which has nothing to do with him.

But in my arms till break of day
Let the living creature lie,
Mortal, guilty, but to me
10   The entirely beautiful.

Soul and body have no bounds:
To lovers as they lie upon
Her tolerant enchanted slope
In their ordinary swoon,
15   Grave the vision Venus sends
Of supernatural sympathy,
Universal love and hope;
While an abstract insight wakes
Among the glaciers and the rocks
20   The hermit's carnal ecstasy.

Certainty, fidelity
On the stroke of midnight pass
Like vibrations of a bell,
And fashionable madmen raise
25   Their pedantic boring cry:
Every farthing[1] of the cost,
All the dreaded cards foretell,
Shall be paid, but from this night
Not a whisper, not a thought,
30   Not a kiss nor look be lost.

Beauty, midnight, vision dies:
Let the winds of dawn that blow
Softly round your dreaming head
Such a day of sweetness show
35   Eye and knocking heart may bless,
Find the mortal world enough;
Noons of dryness see you fed
By the involuntary powers,
Nights of insult let you pass
40   Watched by every human love.

Jan. 1937   1940

In Memory of W. B. Yeats

(d. Jan. 1939)

1

He disappeared in the dead of winter:
The brooks were frozen, the airports almost deserted,
And snow disfigured the public statues;
The mercury sank in the mouth of the dying day.

---

1. At one time the smallest and least valuable British coin.

5 What instruments we have agree
The day of his death was a dark cold day.

Far from his illness
The wolves ran on through the evergreen forests,
The peasant river was untempted by the fashionable quays;
10 By mourning tongues
The death of the poet was kept from his poems.

But for him it was his last afternoon as himself,
An afternoon of nurses and rumours;
The provinces of his body revolted,
15 The squares of his mind were empty,
Silence invaded the suburbs,
The current of his feeling failed: he became his admirers.

Now he is scattered among a hundred cities
And wholly given over to unfamiliar affections;
20 To find his happiness in another kind of wood[1]
And be punished under a foreign code of conscience.
The words of a dead man
Are modified in the guts of the living.

But in the importance and noise of to-morrow
25 When the brokers are roaring like beasts on the floor of the
    Bourse,°   *stock exchange*
And the poor have the sufferings to which they are fairly accustomed,
And each in the cell of himself is almost convinced of his freedom,
A few thousand will think of this day
As one thinks of a day when one did something slightly unusual.
30 What instruments we have agree
The day of his death was a dark cold day.

2

You were silly like us: your gift survived it all:
The parish of rich women, physical decay,
Yourself. Mad Ireland hurt you into poetry.
35 Now Ireland has her madness and her weather still,
For poetry makes nothing happen: it survives
In the valley of its making where executives
Would never want to tamper, flows on south
From ranches of isolation and the busy griefs,
40 Raw towns that we believe and die in; it survives,
A way of happening, a mouth.

3

Earth, receive an honoured guest:
William Yeats is laid to rest.

1. Cf. Dante's *Inferno* 1.1–3 (translated): "In the middle of the journey of our life I came to myself in a dark wood where the straight way was lost."

Let the Irish vessel lie
45   Emptied of its poetry.[2]

In the nightmare of the dark
All the dogs of Europe bark,
And the living nations wait,
Each sequestered in its hate;

50   Intellectual disgrace
Stares from every human face,
And the seas of pity lie
Locked and frozen in each eye.

Follow, poet, follow right
55   To the bottom of the night,
With your unconstraining voice
Still persuade us to rejoice;

With the farming of a verse
Make a vineyard of the curse,
60   Sing of human unsuccess
In a rapture of distress;

In the deserts of the heart
Let the healing fountain start,
In the prison of his days
65   Teach the free man how to praise.

Feb. 1939   1940, 1966

Their Lonely Betters

As I listened from a beach-chair in the shade
To all the noises that my garden made,
It seemed to me only proper that words
Should be withheld from vegetables and birds.

5   A robin with no Christian name ran through
The Robin-Anthem which was all it knew,
And rustling flowers for some third party waited
To say which pairs, if any, should get mated.

Not one of them was capable of lying,
10   There was not one which knew that it was dying
Or could have with a rhythm or a rhyme
Assumed responsibility for time.

2. Three stanzas that originally followed this were omitted in the 1966 edition of Auden's *Collected Shorter Poems* and thereafter: "Time that is intolerant / Of the brave and innocent, / And indifferent in a week / To a beautiful physique, // Worships language and forgives / Everyone by whom it lives; / Pardons cowardice, conceit, / Lays its honours at their feet. // Time that with this strange excuse / Pardoned Kipling and his views, / And will pardon Paul Claudel, / Pardons him for writing well." Kipling's views were imperialistic. Paul Claudel (1868–1955), French poet, dramatist, and diplomat, was an extreme right-winger in his political ideas. Yeats's own politics were at times antidemocratic and appeared to favor dictatorship.

Let them leave language to their lonely betters
Who count some days and long for certain letters;
15   We, too, make noises when we laugh or weep,
Words are for those with promises to keep.

1950   1951

In Praise of Limestone[1]

If it form the one landscape that we the inconstant ones
    Are consistently homesick for, this is chiefly
Because it dissolves in water. Mark these rounded slopes
    With their surface fragrance of thyme and, beneath,
5   A secret system of caves and conduits; hear the springs
    That spurt out everywhere with a chuckle
Each filling a private pool for its fish and carving
    Its own little ravine whose cliffs entertain
The butterfly and the lizard; examine this region
10   Of short distances and definite places:
What could be more like Mother or a fitter background
    For her son, for the flirtatious male who lounges
Against a rock in the sunlight, never doubting
    That for all his faults he is loved; whose works are but
15 Extensions of his power to charm? From weathered outcrop
    To hill-top temple, from appearing waters to
Conspicuous fountains, from a wild to a formal vineyard,
    Are ingenious but short steps that a child's wish
To receive more attention than his brothers, whether
20   By pleasing or teasing, can easily take.

Watch, then, the band of rivals as they climb up and down
    Their steep stone gennels[2] in twos and threes, at times
Arm in arm, but never, thank God, in step; or engaged
    On the shady side of a square at midday in
25 Voluble discourse, knowing each other too well to think
    There are any important secrets, unable
To conceive a god whose temper-tantrums are moral
    And not to be pacified by a clever line
Or a good lay: for, accustomed to a stone that responds,
30   They have never had to veil their faces in awe
Of a crater whose blazing fury could not be fixed;
    Adjusted to the local needs of valleys
Where everything can be touched or reached by walking,
    Their eyes have never looked into infinite space
35 Through the lattice-work of a nomad's comb;[3] born lucky,

1. The landscape of this poem derives from Auden's native Yorkshire. Cf. his *New Year Letter:* "I see the nature of my kind / As a locality I love / Those limestone moors that stretch from Brough / To Hexham on the Roman Wall / That is my symbol of us all."
2. Long narrow passages between houses (Yorkshire and northern English dialect); here passages between rocks.

3. The context suggests that this might be a popular name for a plant or tree (cf. "traveler's joy" and "traveler's palm"), but Auden is probably using the phrase quite literally to suggest that these people have never led a nomad's (wanderer's) life. The "nomad's comb" might be the fringe of unkempt hair through which the nomad peers at wild landscapes.

Their legs have never encountered the fungi
And insects of the jungle, the monstrous forms and lives
  With which we have nothing, we like to hope, in common.
So, when one of them goes to the bad, the way his mind works
40   Remains comprehensible: to become a pimp
Or deal in fake jewelry or ruin a fine tenor voice
  For effects that bring down the house, could happen to all
But the best and the worst of us . . .
                        That is why, I suppose,
  The best and worst never stayed here long but sought
45   Immoderate soils where the beauty was not so external,
  The light less public and the meaning of life
Something more than a mad camp. "Come!" cried the granite wastes,
  "How evasive is your humour, how accidental
Your kindest kiss, how permanent is death." (Saints-to-be
50   Slipped away sighing.) "Come!" purred the clays and gravels.
"On our plains there is room for armies to drill; rivers
  Wait to be tamed and slaves to construct you a tomb
In the grand manner: soft as the earth is mankind and both
  Need to be altered." (Intendant Caesars° rose and   *Roman emperors*
55   Left, slamming the door.) But the really reckless were fetched
  By an older colder voice, the oceanic whisper:
"I am the solitude that asks and promises nothing;
  That is how I shall set you free. There is no love;
There are only the various envies, all of them sad."

60   They were right, my dear, all those voices were right
And still are; this land is not the sweet home that it looks,
  Nor its peace the historical calm of a site
Where something was settled once and for all: A backward
  And dilapidated province, connected
65   To the big busy world by a tunnel, with a certain
  Seedy appeal, is that all it is now? Not quite:
It has a worldly duty which in spite of itself
  It does not neglect, but calls into question
All the Great Powers assume; it disturbs our rights. The poet,
70   Admired for his earnest habit of calling
The sun the sun, his mind Puzzle, is made uneasy
  By these marble statues which so obviously doubt
His antimythological myth; and these gamins,°   *urchins*
  Pursuing the scientist down the tiled colonnade
75   With such lively offers, rebuke his concern for Nature's
  Remotest aspects: I, too, am reproached, for what
And how much you know. Not to lose time, not to get caught,
  Not to be left behind, not, please! to resemble
The beasts who repeat themselves, or a thing like water
80   Or stone whose conduct can be predicted, these
Are our Common Prayer, whose greatest comfort is music
  Which can be made anywhere, is invisible,
And does not smell. In so far as we have to look forward
  To death as a fact, no doubt we are right: But if
85 Sins can be forgiven, if bodies rise from the dead,

These modifications of matter into
Innocent athletes and gesticulating fountains,
    Made solely for pleasure, make a further point:
The blessed will not care what angle they are regarded from,
90   Having nothing to hide. Dear, I know nothing of
Either, but when I try to imagine a faultless love
    Or the life to come, what I hear is the murmur
Of underground streams, what I see is a limestone landscape.

May 1948   1948, 1951

The Shield of Achilles[1]

    She looked over his shoulder
      For vines and olive trees,
    Marble well-governed cities
      And ships upon untamed seas,
5   But there on the shining metal
      His hands had put instead
    An artificial wilderness
      And a sky like lead.

    A plain without a feature, bare and brown,
10   No blade of grass, no sign of neighbourhood,
    Nothing to eat and nowhere to sit down,
      Yet, congregated on its blankness, stood
      An unintelligible multitude,
    A million eyes, a million boots in line,
15   Without expression, waiting for a sign.

    Out of the air a voice without a face
      Proved by statistics that some cause was just
    In tones as dry and level as the place:
      No one was cheered and nothing was discussed;
20   Column by column in a cloud of dust
    They marched away enduring a belief
    Whose logic brought them, somewhere else, to grief.

    She looked over his shoulder
      For ritual pieties,
25   White flower-garlanded heifers,
      Libation and sacrifice,[2]
    But there on the shining metal

---

1. In books 16 and 17 of Homer's *Iliad*, Achilles, the chief Greek hero in the war against Troy, lends his armor to his friend Patroclus and loses it when Patroclus is killed by the Trojan hero Hector. While Achilles is mourning for his friend, his mother, the goddess Thetis, goes to Mount Olympus to beg Hephaestos, god of fire, to forge new armor for Achilles. The splendid shield that Hephaestos then makes him is described in book 18 of the *Iliad* (lines 478–608). On it he depicts the heavens, the sea, and the earth represented by many scenes such as a city at peace and a city at war.

2. Cf. Keats, *Ode on a Grecian Urn*, lines 31–34: "Who are these coming to the sacrifice? / To what green altar, O mysterious priest, / Lead'st thou that heifer lowing at the skies, / And all her silken flanks with garlands drest?" "Libation": sacrifice of wine or other liquid.

Where the altar should have been,
She saw by his flickering forge-light
Quite another scene.

Barbed wire enclosed an arbitrary spot
  Where bored officials lounged (one cracked a joke)
And sentries sweated for the day was hot:
  A crowd of ordinary decent folk
Watched from without and neither moved nor spoke
As three pale figures were led forth and bound
To three posts driven upright in the ground.

The mass and majesty of this world, all
  That carries weight and always weighs the same
Lay in the hands of others; they were small
  And could not hope for help and no help came:
What their foes liked to do was done, their shame
Was all the worst could wish; they lost their pride
And died as men before their bodies died.

She looked over his shoulder
  For athletes at their games,
Men and women in a dance
  Moving their sweet limbs
Quick, quick, to music,
  But there on the shining shield
His hands had set no dancing-floor
  But a weed-choked field.

A ragged urchin, aimless and alone,
  Loitered about that vacancy; a bird
Flew up to safety from his well-aimed stone:
  That girls are raped, that two boys knife a third,
  Were axioms to him, who'd never heard
Of any world where promises were kept,
Or one could weep because another wept.

The thin-lipped armourer,
  Hephaestos, hobbled away,
Thetis of the shining breasts
  Cried out in dismay
At what the god had wrought
  To please her son, the strong
Iron-hearted man-slaying Achilles
  Who would not live long.

1952   1955

LOUIS MacNEICE
1907–1963

Born in Belfast, the son of a strong-willed Anglican rector (later to become a courageously independent bishop), Louis MacNeice illustrates Cyril Connolly's dictum that "the one golden recipe for Art is the ferment of an unhappy childhood working through a noble imagination." MacNeice's mother fell ill and died. "When I was five the black dreams came;/Nothing after was quite the same." Educated at Marlborough College and Merton College, Oxford, he became a lecturer in classics at Birmingham University and, later, at Bedford College, London. Following the breakup of his first marriage, he traveled to Iceland with his friend W. H. Auden, then to Spain on the eve of—and again during—the Spanish Civil War, and to the United States at the beginning of World War II. Returning to England in 1940, he joined the British Broadcasting Corporation as a feature writer and producer and, except for a year and a half spent in Athens as director of the British Institute, he worked for the BBC for the rest of his life.

He was a pioneer of radio drama, a notable playwright, a translator (of Aeschylus' *Agamemnon* and Goethe's *Faust*), and a literary critic. Best known as a poet, however, he was early and somewhat carelessly identified with the other Oxford poets, Auden, Spender, and Day Lewis; but just as he was never, like them, a Communist sympathizer, he never moved, as they did, to the political right. The consistency and integrity of the man characterizes his work. He delights in the surface of the world his senses apprehend and celebrates "the drunkenness of things being various," often (as in *Bagpipe Music*) with wit and a wild gaiety. But like his fellow Irishman Yeats, he knew that "Man is in love and loves what vanishes," and this knowledge informs his work with an underlying sense of sadness and, sometimes, tragedy: "All our games are funeral games." There is an openness, honesty, and a consistently high level of craftmanship in his poems that give them their special air of full realization: one never finds on a second reading that one has been taken in by an initial showiness. MacNeice is coming to be regarded more and more in England as second only to Auden among the poets of his generation.

Sunday Morning

Down the road someone is practising scales,
The notes like little fishes vanish with a wink of tails,
Man's heart expands to tinker with his car
For this is Sunday morning, Fate's great bazaar,
5   Regard these means as ends, concentrate on this Now,
And you may grow to music or drive beyond Hindhead[1] anyhow,
Take corners on two wheels until you go so fast
That you can clutch a fringe or two of the windy past,
That you can abstract this day and make it to the week of time
10   A small eternity, a sonnet self-contained in rhyme.

But listen, up the road, something gulps, the church spire
Opens its eight bells out, skulls' mouths which will not tire
To tell how there is no music or movement which secures
Escape from the weekday time. Which deadens and endures.

1933   1935

---

1. An upland district in Surrey popular for outings.

The Sunlight on the Garden

The sunlight on the garden
Hardens and grows cold,
We cannot cage the minute
Within its nets of gold,
When all is told   5
We cannot beg for pardon.

Our freedom as free lances
Advances towards its end;
The earth compels, upon it
Sonnets and birds descend;   10
And soon, my friend,
We shall have no time for dances.

The sky was good for flying
Defying the church bells
And every evil iron   15
Siren and what it tells:
The earth compels,
We are dying, Egypt, dying[1]

And not expecting pardon,
Hardened in heart anew,   20
But glad to have sat under
Thunder and rain with you,
And grateful too
For sunlight on the garden.

1937   1938

Bagpipe Music

It's no go the merrygoround, it's no go the rickshaw,
All we want is a limousine and a ticket for the peepshow.
Their knickers° are made of crêpe-de-chine,° their shoes   °panties/silky material
    are made of python,
Their halls are lined with tiger rugs and their walls with heads of bison.

John MacDonald found a corpse, put it under the sofa,   5
Waited till it came to life and hit it with a poker,
Sold its eyes for souvenirs, sold its blood for whisky,
Kept its bones for dumb-bells to use when he was fifty.

It's no go the Yogi-Man, it's no go Blavatsky,[1]
All we want is a bank balance and a bit of skirt in a taxi.   10

---

1. Cf. Antony's speech in Shakespeare's *Antony and Cleopatra* 4.15.41: "I am dying, Egypt, dying."
1. Madame Blavatsky (1831–1891), the famous theosophist whose ideas were popular in some quarters in Britain in the 1930s.

Annie MacDougall went to milk, caught her foot in the heather,
Woke to hear a dance record playing of Old Vienna.
It's no go your maidenheads, it's no go your culture,
All we want is a Dunlop tyre and the devil mend the puncture.

15   The Laird o' Phelps spent Hogmanay[2] declaring he was sober,
Counted his feet to prove the fact and found he had one foot over.
Mrs Carmichael had her fifth, looked at the job with repulsion,
Said to the midwife "Take it away; I'm through with overproduction."

It's no go the gossip column, it's no go the Ceilidh,[3]
20   All we want is a mother's help and a sugar-stick for the baby.

Willie Murray cut his thumb, couldn't count the damage,
Took the hide of an Ayrshire cow and used it for a bandage.
His brother caught three hundred cran[4] when the seas were lavish,
Threw the bleeders back in the sea and went upon the parish.[5]

25   It's no go the Herring Board, it's no go the Bible,
All we want is a packet of fags° when our hands are idle.   *cigarettes*

It's no go the picture palace, it's no go the stadium,
It's no go the country cot° with a pot of pink geraniums.   *cottage*
It's no go the Government grants, it's no go the elections,
30   Sit on your arse for fifty years and hang your hat on a pension.

It's no go my honey love, it's no go my poppet;
Work your hands from day to day, the winds will blow the profit.
The glass is falling hour by hour, the glass will fall forever,
But if you break the bloody glass you won't hold up the weather.

1937   1938

Soap Suds

This brand of soap has the same smell as once in the big
House he visited when he was eight: the walls of the bathroom open
To reveal a lawn where a great yellow ball rolls back through a hoop
To rest at the head of a mallet held in the hands of a child.[1]

5   And these were the joys of that house: a tower with a telescope;
Two great faded globes, one of the earth, one of the stars;
A stuffed black dog in the hall; a walled garden with bees;
A rabbit warren; a rockery; a vine under glass; the sea.

To which he has now returned. The day of course is fine
10   And a grown-up voice cries Play! The mallet slowly swings,

2. New Year's Eve.
3. A Scottish Gaelic word meaning a social evening spent in singing and story telling (pronounced
kaley).
4. A measure of fresh herrings, about 750 fish.

The Scottish herring industry failed in the 1930s;
the Herring Board (line 25) was a government
attempt to provide helpful direction.
5. I.e., "went on the county" (on relief).
1. The child is playing croquet.

Then crack, a great gong booms from the dog-dark hall and the ball
Skims forward through the hoop and then through the next and then

Through hoops where no hoops were and each dissolves in turn
And the grass has grown head-high and an angry voice cries Play!
15   But the ball is lost and the mallet slipped long since from the hands
Under the running tap that are not the hands of a child.

1961   1963

Star-Gazer

Forty-two years ago (to me if to no one else
The number is of some interest) it was a brilliant starry night
And the westward train was empty and had no corridors
So darting from side to side I could catch the unwonted sight
5   Of those almost intolerably bright
Holes, punched in the sky, which excited me partly because
Of their Latin names and partly because I had read in the textbooks
How very far off they were, it seemed their light
Had left them (some at least) long years before I was.

10   And this remembering now I mark that what
Light was leaving some of them at least then,
Forty-two years ago, will never arrive
In time for me to catch it, which light when
It does get here may find that there is not
15   Anyone left alive
To run from side to side in a late night train
Admiring it and adding noughts in vain.

Jan. 1963   1963

DYLAN THOMAS
1914–1953

Dylan Thomas was born in Swansea, Wales, and educated at Swansea Grammar
School. After working for a time as a newspaper reporter, he was "discovered" as a
poet in 1933 through a poetry contest in a popular newspaper. The following year his
Eighteen Poems caused considerable excitement because of the strange violence of
their imagery and their powerfully suggestive obscurity. It looked as though a new
kind of strength and romantic picturesqueness had been restored to English poetry
after the deliberately muted tones of T. S. Eliot and his followers. Thomas did not,
however, turn out to be the founder of a neo-Romantic movement, though some early
critics took him to be so. As his poetry became better known, and after he had clarified
the somewhat clotted imagery of his early style in his later volumes—*The Map of Love*
(1939), *Deaths and Entrances* (1946), *Collected Poems* (1953)—it became clear that
he was a master craftsman and not the shouting rhapsodist that some had taken him

to be. His images were most carefully ordered in a patterned sequence, and his major theme was the unity of all life, the continuing *process* of life and death and new life that linked the generations to each other. Thomas saw the workings of biology as a magical transformation producing unity out of diversity, and again and again in his poetry he sought a poetic ritual to celebrate this unity ("The force that through the green fuse drives the flower / Drives my green age"). He saw men and women locked in a round of identities—with the beginning of growth also the first movement toward death, the beginning of love leading to procreation, new growth, and so in turn to death again and to life again, and because of this view he comforted himself with the unity of humankind and nature, of past and present, of life and death, and so "refused to mourn the death of a child." In his best poems the closely woven imagery (deriving from the Bible, Welsh folklore and preaching, and Freud) is organized to present aspects of this theme. His more open-worked poems of reminiscence and autobiographical emotion, such as *Poem in October*, communicate more immediately to the reader through their fine lyrical feeling and compelling use of simple natural images. His autobiographical work *Portrait of the Artist as a Young Dog* and his radio play *Under Milk Wood* reveal a vividness of observation and a combination of violence and tenderness in expression that show he could handle prose as excitingly as verse.

Thomas was a brilliant talker (when he felt like it), a considerable drinker, a reckless and impulsive man whose short life was packed with emotional ups and downs. His poetry readings in the United States between 1950 and 1953 were enormous successes, in spite of his sometimes reckless antics. He died suddenly in New York, in November 1953, of what was diagnosed as "an insult to the brain," precipitated by alcohol. He acted the wild bohemian poet as that role had not been played since the 1890s; some thought this behavior wonderful, though others deplored it. He was a brilliant reader of his own and others' poems, and many people who do not normally read poetry were drawn to Thomas's by the magic of his own reading. After his premature death a reaction set in: some critics declared that he had been overrated as a poet because of the sensational role he had played in life. But a balanced view is now possible; it is clear that at his best he was an original poet of great power and beauty.

The Force That Through the Green Fuse
Drives the Flower

The force that through the green fuse drives the flower
Drives my green age; that blasts the roots of trees
Is my destroyer.
And I am dumb to tell the crooked rose
5   My youth is bent by the same wintry fever.

The force that drives the water through the rocks
Drives my red blood; that dries the mouthing streams
Turns mine to wax.
And I am dumb to mouth unto my veins
10   How at the mountain spring the same mouth sucks.

The hand that whirls the water in the pool[1]
Stirs the quicksand; that ropes the blowing wind
Hauls my shroud sail.
And I am dumb to tell the hanging man
15   How of my clay is made the hangman's lime.[2]

1. The hand of the angel who troubles the water of the pool Bethesda, thus rendering it curative, in John 5.1–4.

2. Quicklime was sometimes poured into the graves of victims of the public hangmen to accelerate decomposition.

The lips of time leech to the fountain head;
Love drips and gathers, but the fallen blood
Shall calm her sores.
And I am dumb to tell a weather's wind
20   How time has ticked a heaven round the stars.

And I am dumb to tell the lover's tomb
How at my sheet goes the same crooked worm.

1933

After the Funeral

(*In Memory of Ann Jones*)[1]

After the funeral, mule praises, brays,
Windshake of sailshaped ears, muffle-toed tap
Tap happily of one peg in the thick
Grave's foot, blinds down the lids, the teeth in black,
5   The spittled eyes, the salt ponds in the sleeves,
Morning smack of the spade that wakes up sleep,
Shakes a desolate boy who slits his throat
In the dark of the coffin and sheds dry leaves,
That breaks one bone to light with a judgment clout,
10   After the feast of tear-stuffed time and thistles
In a room with a stuffed fox and a stale fern,
I stand, for this memorial's sake, alone
In the snivelling hours with dead, humped Ann
Whose hooded, fountain heart once fell in puddles
15   Round the parched worlds of Wales and drowned each sun
(Though this for her is a monstrous image blindly
Magnified out of praise; her death was a still drop;
She would not have me sinking in the holy
Flood of her heart's fame; she would lie dumb and deep
20   And need no druid[2] of her broken body).
But I, Ann's bard on a raised hearth, call all
The seas to service that her wood-tongued virtue
Babble like a bellbuoy over the hymning heads,
Bow down the walls of the ferned and foxy woods
25   That her love sing and swing through a brown chapel,
Bless her bent spirit with four, crossing birds.
Her flesh was meek as milk, but this skyward statue
With the wild breast and blessed and giant skull
Is carved from her in a room with a wet window
30   In a fiercely mourning house in a crooked year.
I know her scrubbed and sour humble hands
Lie with religion in their cramp, her threadbare
Whisper in a damp word, her wits drilled hollow,
Her fist of a face died clenched on a round pain;

---

1. Ann Jones was Thomas's aunt; she lived at a
farmhouse called Fern Hill in the Welsh landscape
described in *Poem in October* and *Fern Hill*.

2. Priest of the ancient Celtic pagans (ancestors
of the modern Welsh).

35 And sculptured Ann is seventy years of stone.
These cloud-sopped, marble hands, this monumental
Argument of the hewn voice, gesture and psalm,
Storm me forever over her grave until
The stuffed lung of the fox twitch and cry Love
40 And the strutting fern lay seeds on the black sill.

1938, 1939

There Was a Saviour

There was a saviour
Rarer than radium,
Commoner than water, crueller than truth;
Children kept from the sun
5 Assembled at his tongue
To hear the golden note turn in a groove,
Prisoners of wishes locked their eyes
In the jails and studies of his keyless smiles.

The voice of children says
10 From a lost wilderness
There was calm to be done in his safe unrest,
When hindering man hurt
Man, animal, or bird
We hid our fears in that murdering breath,
15 Silence, silence to do, when earth grew loud,
In lairs and asylums of the tremendous shout.

There was glory to hear
In the churches of his tears,
Under his downy arm you sighed as he struck,
20 O you who could not cry
On to the ground when a man died
Put a tear for joy in the unearthly flood
And laid your cheek against a cloud-formed shell:
Now in the dark there is only yourself and myself.

25 Two proud, blacked brothers cry,
Winter-locked side by side,
To this inhospitable hollow year,
O we who could not stir
One lean sigh when we heard
30 Greed on man beating near and fire neighbour
But wailed and nested in the sky-blue wall
Now break a giant tear for the little known fall,

For the drooping of homes
That did not nurse our bones,
35 Brave deaths of only ones but never found,
Now see, alone in us,

Our own true strangers' dust
Ride through the doors of our unentered house.
Exiled in us we arouse the soft,
40   Unclenched, armless, silk and rough love that breaks all rocks.

1940

The Hunchback in the Park

The hunchback in the park
A solitary mister
Propped between trees and water
From the opening of the garden lock
5   That lets the trees and water enter
Until the Sunday sombre bell at dark

Eating bread from a newspaper
Drinking water from the chained cup
That the children filled with gravel
10   In the fountain basin where I sailed my ship
Slept at night in a dog kennel
But nobody chained him up.

Like the park birds he came early
Like the water he sat down
15   And Mister they called Hey mister
The truant boys from the town
Running when he had heard them clearly
On out of sound

Past lake and rockery
20   Laughing when he shook his paper
Hunchbacked in mockery
Through the loud zoo of the willow groves
Dodging the park keeper
With his stick that picked up leaves.

25   And the old dog sleeper
Alone between nurses and swans
While the boys among willows
Made the tigers jump out of their eyes
To roar on the rockery stones
30   And the groves were blue with sailors

Made all day until bell time
A woman figure without fault
Straight as a young elm
Straight and tall from his crooked bones
35   That she might stand in the night
After the locks and chains

All night in the unmade park
After the railings and shrubberies
The birds the grass the trees the lake
40 And the wild boys innocent as strawberries
Had followed the hunchback
To his kennel in the dark.

1941

Poem in October

It was my thirtieth year to heaven
Woke to my hearing from harbour and neighbour wood
   And the mussel pooled and the heron
      Priested shore
5   The morning beckon
With water praying and call of seagull and rook
And the knock of sailing boats on the net webbed wall
      Myself to set foot
      That second
10 In the still sleeping town and set forth.

My birthday began with the water-
Birds and the birds of the winged trees flying my name
   Above the farms and the white horses
      And I rose
15   In rainy autumn
And walked abroad in a shower of all my days.
High tide and the heron dived when I took the road
      Over the border
      And the gates
20 Of the town closed as the town awoke.

A springful of larks in a rolling
Cloud and the roadside bushes brimming with whistling
   Blackbirds and the sun of October
      Summery
25   On the hill's shoulder,
Here were fond climates and sweet singers suddenly
Come in the morning where I wandered and listened
      To the rain wringing
      Wind blow cold
30 In the wood faraway under me.

Pale rain over the dwindling harbour
And over the sea wet church the size of a snail
   With its horns through mist and the castle
      Brown as owls
35   But all the gardens
Of spring and summer were blooming in the tall tales
Beyond the border and under the lark full cloud.

There could I marvel
My birthday
40 Away but the weather turned around.

It turned away from the blithe country
And down the other air and the blue altered sky
Streamed again a wonder of summer
With apples
45 Pears and red currants
And I saw in the turning so clearly a child's
Forgotten mornings when he walked with his mother
Through the parables
Of sun light
50 And the legends of the green chapels

And the twice told fields of infancy
That his tears burned my cheeks and his heart moved in mine.
These were the woods the river and sea
Where a boy
55 In the listening
Summertime of the dead whispered the truth of his joy
To the trees and the stones and the fish in the tide.
And the mystery
Sang alive
60 Still in the water and singingbirds.

And there could I marvel my birthday
Away but the weather turned around. And the true
Joy of the long dead child sang burning
In the sun.
65 It was my thirtieth
Year to heaven stood there then in the summer noon
Though the town below lay leaved with October blood.
O may my heart's truth
Still be sung
70 On this high hill in a year's turning.

1945, 1946

Fern Hill[1]

Now as I was young and easy under the apple boughs
About the lilting house and happy as the grass was green,
The night above the dingle[2] starry,
Time let me hail and climb
5 Golden in the heydays of his eyes,
And honoured among wagons I was prince of the apple towns
And once below a time I lordly had the trees and leaves

---

1. Name of the Welsh farmhouse, home of Thomas's aunt Ann Jones, where he spent summer holidays as a boy.
2. Deep dell or hollow, usually wooded.

Trail with daisies and barley
Down the rivers of the windfall light.

10 And as I was green and carefree, famous among the barns
About the happy yard and singing as the farm was home,
In the sun that is young once only,
Time let me play and be
Golden in the mercy of his means,
15 And green and golden I was huntsman and herdsman, the calves
Sang to my horn, the foxes on the hills barked clear and cold,
And the sabbath rang slowly
In the pebbles of the holy streams.

All the sun long it was running, it was lovely, the hay
20 Fields high as the house, the tunes from the chimneys, it was air
And playing, lovely and watery
And fire green as grass.
And nightly under the simple stars
As I rode to sleep the owls were bearing the farm away,
25 All the moon long I heard, blessed among stables, the night-jars[3]
Flying with the ricks,° and the horses   haystacks
Flashing into the dark.

And then to awake, and the farm, like a wanderer white
With the dew, come back, the cock on his shoulder: it was all
30 Shining, it was Adam and maiden,[4]
The sky gathered again
And the sun grew round that very day.
So it must have been after the birth of the simple light
In the first, spinning place, the spellbound horses walking warm
35 Out of the whinnying green stable
On to the fields of praise.

And honoured among foxes and pheasants by the gay house
Under the new made clouds and happy as the heart was long,
In the sun born over and over,
40 I ran my heedless ways,
My wishes raced through the house high hay
And nothing I cared, at my sky blue trades, that time allows
In all his tuneful turning so few and such morning songs
Before the children green and golden
45 Follow him out of grace,

Nothing I cared, in the lamb white days, that time would take me
Up to the swallow thronged loft by the shadow of my hand,
In the moon that is always rising,
Nor that riding to sleep
50 I should hear him fly with the high fields
And wake to the farm forever fled from the childless land.
Oh as I was young and easy in the mercy of his means,

3. Species of bird.   4. Cf. Genesis 1.

Time held me green and dying
Though I sang in my chains like the sea.

1946

Do Not Go Gentle into That Good Night

Do not go gentle into that good night,
Old age should burn and rave at close of day;
Rage, rage against the dying of the light.

Though wise men at their end know dark is right,
5   Because their words had forked no lightning they
Do not go gentle into that good night.

Good men, the last wave by, crying how bright
Their frail deeds might have danced in a green bay,
Rage, rage against the dying of the light.

10 Wild men who caught and sang the sun in flight,
And learn, too late, they grieved it on its way,
Do not go gentle into that good night.

Grave men, near death, who see with blinding sight
Blind eyes could blaze like meteors and be gay,
15 Rage, rage against the dying of the light.

And you, my father, there on the sad height,
Curse, bless, me now with your fierce tears, I pray.
Do not go gentle into that good night.
Rage, rage against the dying of the light.

1951, 1952

Voices from World War II

There has long been a widespread impression—which the following pages may help to dispel—that World War II, unlike World War I, produced no notable poetry. Disappointment with the poets' failure to contribute to the war effort was voiced as early as December 1939, when a leading article in *The Times Literary Supplement* urged them to do their duty: "it is for the poets to sound the trumpet call . . . the monstrous threat to belief and freedom which we are fighting should urge new psalmists to fresh songs of deliverance." The biblical diction is revealing of the underlying expectation that the poets of 1940 would come forward, like those of 1914, to sanctify the cause with images of sacrifice derived from Christ's precedent and precept: "greater love hath no man than this, that a man lay down his life for his friends." Far from taking up trumpets, the poets responded bitterly—Day Lewis with a poem:

Where Are the War Poets?

> They who in folly or mere greed
> Enslaved religion, markets, laws,
> Borrow our language now and bid
> Us to speak up in freedom's cause.
>
> It is the logic of our times,
> No subject for immortal verse—
> That we who lived by honest dreams
> Defend the bad against the worse.

Stephen Spender responded with an essay in which he wrote: "At the beginning of the last war Rupert Brooke and others were 'trumpets singing to battle.' Why did not Rupert Brooke step forward 'young and goldenhaired' this time? No doubt, in part, precisely because one had done so last time. There is another reason: the poetry of the war of democracy versus fascism had already been written by English, French, Spanish, German and Italian émigré poets during the Spanish war."

With few exceptions, the British poets of the 1930s had been born shortly before the outbreak of World War I, and those who were to be the poets of World War II were born during that earlier conflict. They grew up not, as Rupert Brooke, in the sunlit peace of Georgian England, but amid wars and rumors of wars. They lived through the Depression and the rise of fascism. Introduced to the horrors of the last war—raised to mythic proportions by their fathers, uncles, and elder brothers—they were continually reminded of it by a flood of best-seller battle memoirs: Blunden's *Undertones of War* (1928), Graves's *Goodbye to All That* (1929), Sassoon's *Memoirs of an Infantry Officer* (1930) and *Sherston's Progress* (1936), and Jones's *In Parenthesis* (1937). By then another myth, that of the Next War, was taking even more terrifying shape. Western intellectuals' last hope for the 1930s rested with the ragged troops of the left-wing Spanish Republic in their civil war against the right-wing Spanish Army that had mutinied, in 1936, against the country's elected government. Democracy and fascism were at last in the open, fighting a war that many thought would determine not simply the future of Spain but the future of Europe. The conscience of the

2525

West was aroused as never since the Greek War of Independence against the Turks in 1821–29, in which Byron had lost his life. With the final defeat of the Spanish Republicans in 1938, the Next War ceased to be a myth so much as an all-but-inescapable certainty. At the start of Yeats's poem *Lapis Lazuli* (1938), hysterical women say:

> everybody knows or else should know
> That if nothing drastic is done
> Aeroplane and Zeppelin will come out,
> Pitch like King Billy bomb-balls in
> Until the town lie beaten flat.

World War I had been fought, for the most part, on the land, and its emblem in popular mythology was the trench. After the indiscriminate killing of civilians in a bombing raid—by German aircraft—on the Spanish town of Guernica in 1937, everybody knew or else should know that the emblem of the Next War would be the bomb, the fire from heaven.

So it proved. On September 1, 1939, Germany, in pursuit of imperial ambitions and without warning, launched a savage attack on Poland by land and air. Two days later, Britain and France declared war on Germany. By the end of the month, Germany and its ally Russia had between them defeated and partitioned Poland. It was then Russia's turn to attack Finland, and in April 1940, Germany invaded Denmark and Norway. For Britain and France, the period of inactivity that came to be known as "The Phoney War" ended in May, when the German Army overran Luxembourg and invaded The Netherlands and Belgium; their armored columns raced for the English Channel. Cut off, the British forces were evacuated by sea, with heavy losses, from Dunkirk and, in June, France signed an armistice with Germany. In August, as prelude to an invasion, the German *Luftwaffe* (Air Force) attacked England. Over the months that followed, the fighter pilots of the Royal Air Force (RAF) challenged the enemy bombers' nightly blitz of London and other major cities. The Battle of Britain, as it came to be called, cost the *Luftwaffe* twenty-three hundred planes and the RAF, nine hundred and caused the Germans to abandon their plans for invasion.

In 1941, at the end of *Between the Acts,* Virginia Woolf imagines the coming fury that would be a factor in her suicide. The village pageant of English history is over, and Mr. Streatfield's speech of thanks is interrupted: "A zoom severed it. Twelve aeroplanes in perfect formation like a flight of wild duck came overhead." The following year Edith Sitwell was to depict the blitz in *Still Falls the Rain* and T. S. Eliot, in part 2 of *Little Gidding.* The Battle of Britain, however, was not the only battle, and British poets were already responding to war on land and at sea as well as in the air. Some of their work shows the influence of their predecessors: Alun Lewis acknowledges a debt to Edward Thomas, whereas the diction and pararhyming of Keith Douglas's poems clearly owes something to Wilfred Owen's. Their voices, however, are their own, and the dominant mood of their poetry is strikingly unlike that from and about the trenches of the Western Front. Just as the heroics of 1914 were impossible in 1940 (although there was no lack of heroism), so too was the anti-propagandist indignation of a Siegfried Sassoon. Now that everybody knew about the Battle of the Somme, the bombing of Guernica, London, Dresden, who could be surprised by evidence of "Man's inhumanity to man"? In one of the more influential poetic manifestos of the twentieth century, Owen's draft preface to his poems, he had written: "All a poet can do today is warn. That is why the true poets must be truthful." His warnings and those of his contemporaries had been uttered in vain, but the poets of World War II knew they must be truthful, true to their wartime experience of boredom and brutality, true to their humanity, and above all, resistant to the murderous inhumanity of the machines.

EDITH SITWELL
1887–1964

Edith Sitwell and her younger brothers, the poet, essayist, and novelist Osbert and the poet, essayist, and art historian Sacheverel, constituted one of the most extraordinary literary families in the England of their time. Their father was an eccentric English baronet (whose character is brilliantly captured in Osbert's autobiography). Sitwell herself was an eccentrically gifted poet who objected to the subdued rural descriptions and reflections of the Georgian poets and reacted in favor of a highly abstract verbal clowning that exploited the sounds and rhythms and suggestions of words and phrases, often with remarkable pyrotechnic display. She edited and was a substantial contributor to the six "cycles" of *Wheels* (1916–21), in which she displayed her verbal and rhythmic virtuosity and encouraged others to follow her example. Her poem sequence *Façade* (1922), with its cunning exploration of rhymes and rhythms, was set to music by the composer Sir William Walton, whose intensely sympathetic setting of the words enhanced their impact in a remarkable way. The first performance in January 1922 was a sensation: Sitwell read the poems from behind a screen, and Walton conducted the orchestra.

But Sitwell was more than a juggler of colored balls. There is always a human meaning hinted at, sometimes with mocking laughter, sometimes with anguish, in her poetry, and in her later work she uses her shock tactics to attack the pettiness and philistinism of the life of high society of her time. Her last poems are much concerned with the horrors of war, the varieties of human suffering produced by modern civilization, and the healing powers of a faith in God combined with a sense of the richness and variety of nature. She never found a style in which this later attitude could be fully and distinctively rendered, so that while her last poems remain the most moving and sympathetic in terms of their subject matter, they are often less successful and certainly less exciting than the best of her earlier poems.

Still Falls the Rain

The Raids, 1940.[1] Night and Dawn

Still falls the Rain—
Dark as the world of man, black as our loss—
Blind as the nineteen hundred and forty nails
Upon the Cross.

5 Still falls the Rain
With a sound like the pulse of the heart that is changed to the hammer-
    beat
In the Potter's Field,[2] and the sound of the impious feet

---

1. During the Battle of Britain, the German air force carried out many raids on London, often with incendiary bombs (see lines 27 and 30).
2. Cf. Matthew 27.3–8: "Then Judas, which betrayed [Jesus], when he saw that he was condemned, repented himself, and brought back the 30 pieces of silver to the chief priests and elders, saying, I have sinned in that I betrayed innocent blood. But they said, What is that to us? see thou to it. And he cast down the pieces of silver into the sanctuary, and departed; and he went away and hanged himself. And the chief priests took the pieces of silver . . . and bought with them the potter's field, to bury strangers in. Wherefore that field was called, The field of blood, unto this day."

On the Tomb:
>   Still falls the Rain
In the Field of Blood where the small hopes breed and the human brain
10 Nurtures its greed, that worm with the brow of Cain.[3]

Still falls the Rain
At the feet of the Starved Man hung upon the Cross.
Christ that each day, each night, nails there, have mercy on us—
On Dives and on Lazarus:[4]
15 Under the Rain the sore and the gold are as one.

Still falls the Rain—
Still falls the Blood from the Starved Man's wounded Side:
He bears in His Heart all wounds,—those of the light that died,
The last faint spark
20 In the self-murdered heart, the wounds of the sad uncomprehending dark,
The wounds of the baited bear,[5]—
The blind and weeping bear whom the keepers beat
On his helpless flesh . . . the tears of the hunted hare.

Still falls the Rain—
25 Then—O Ile leape up to my God: who pulles me doune—
See, see where Christ's blood streames in the firmament:[6]
It flows from the Brow we nailed upon the tree
Deep to the dying, to the thirsting heart
That holds the fires of the world,—dark-smirched with pain
30 As Caesar's laurel crown.[7]

Then sounds the voice of One who like the heart of man
Was once a child who among beasts has lain—
"Still do I love, still shed my innocent light, my Blood, for thee."

1942

---

3. The first murderer (Genesis 4).
4. In Jesus' parable, the rich man Dives was sent to hell, while the leprous beggar Lazarus went to heaven (Luke 16.19–31). This is not the same Lazarus who was raised from the dead.
5. A medieval and Elizabethan sport in which dogs fought a bear chained to a post.

6. Faustus's despairing cry at the end of Marlowe's play, *Doctor Faustus*, when he realizes that he has been damned for his pact with Mephistopheles.
7. Traditionally worn by victorious generals, and perhaps here associated with Jesus' crown of thorns (Matthew 27.29).

HENRY REED

1914–1986

Henry Reed was born and educated in Birmingham, at the King Edward VI School and at Birmingham University, where he gained a first-class degree in classics (having taught himself Greek) and wrote an M.A. thesis on Thomas Hardy. Leaving the university in 1934, he tried teaching (like many other British writers of the 1930s) but, again like most of them, hated it and left to make his way as a free-lance writer and critic. During World War II, he served—"or rather *studied*," as he preferred to put it—in the Royal Army Ordnance Corps for a year. A notable mimic, he would entertain his friends with a comic imitation of a sergeant instructing new recruits. After a few performances, he noticed that the words of the weapon-training instructor, couched in the style of the military manual, fell into certain rhythmic patterns that fascinated him and eventually produced his *Lessons of the War*. The first of these, *Naming of Parts*, is probably the most anthologized poem prompted by World War II, and its fame has unfairly eclipsed his later work.

From 1942 to 1945 Reed worked as a cryptographer and translator at the Government Code and Cypher School at Bletchley. In the evenings he wrote much of his first radio play, an adaptation of Melville's *Moby Dick*, and many of the poems to be published in *A Map of Verona* (1946). After the war, he produced a number of other successful—and often funny—radio plays, verse translations of the Italian poet Giacomo Leopardi (1798–1837), and some more fine poems. Many of the best of these were found in manuscript at his death in 1986, and with the posthumous publication of his *Collected Poems* (1991), he emerged as a poet whose lifelong quest for lasting homosexual love—which he never found—led him through Edenic landscapes of desire, like the setting of *Naming of Parts*.

From Lessons of the War

To Alan Michell

Vixi duellis nuper idoneus
Et militavi non sine gloria[1]

1. Naming of Parts

Today we have naming of parts. Yesterday,
We had daily cleaning. And tomorrow morning,
We shall have what to do after firing. But today,
Today we have naming of parts. Japonica[2]
5 Glistens like coral in all of the neighbouring gardens,
    And today we have naming of parts.

This is the lower sling swivel. And this
Is the upper sling swivel, whose use you will see,
When you are given your slings. And this is the piling swivel,
10 Which in your case you have not got. The branches
Hold in the gardens their silent, eloquent gestures,
    Which in our case we have not got.

This is the safety-catch, which is always released
With an easy flick of the thumb. And please do not let me
15 See anyone using his finger. You can do it quite easy
If you have any strength in your thumb. The blossoms

---

1. "Lately I have lived in the midst of battles, creditably enough, / and have soldiered, not without glory." (Horace's *Odes* 3.26.1–2, with the letter *p* of *puellis*—girls—turned upside down to produce *duellis*—battles; an emendation, an exchange, that encapsulates the theme of the Lessons.)
2. A shrub with brilliant scarlet flowers.

Are fragile and motionless, never letting anyone see
    Any of them using their finger.

And this you can see is the bolt. The purpose of this
20 Is to open the breech, as you see. We can slide it
Rapidly backwards and forwards: we call this
Easing the spring.[3] And rapidly backwards and forwards
The early bees are assaulting and fumbling the flowers:
    They call it easing the Spring.

25 They call it easing the Spring: it is perfectly easy
If you have any strength in your thumb; like the bolt,
And the breech, and the cocking-piece, and the point of balance,
Which in our case we have not got; and the almond-blossom
Silent in all of the gardens and the bees going backwards and forwards,
30   For today we have naming of parts.

2. *Judging Distances*

Not only how far away, but the way that you say it
Is very important. Perhaps you may never get
The knack of judging a distance, but at least you know
How to report on a landscape: the central sector,
35 The right of arc and that, which we had last Tuesday,
    And at least you know

That maps are of time,[4] not place, so far as the army
Happens to be concerned—the reason being,
Is one which need not delay us. Again, you know
40 There are three kinds of tree, three only, the fir and the poplar,
And those which have bushy tops to; and lastly
    That things only seem to be things.

A barn is not called a barn, to put it more plainly,
Or a field in the distance, where sheep may be safely grazing.
45 You must never be over-sure. You must say, when reporting:
At five o'clock in the central sector is a dozen
Of what appear to be animals; whatever you do,
    Don't call the bleeders *sheep*.

I am sure that's quite clear; and suppose, for the sake of example,
50 The one at the end, asleep, endeavours to tell us
What he sees over there to the west, and how far away,
After first having come to attention. There to the west,
On the fields of summer the sun and the shadows bestow
    Vestments of purple and gold.

---

3. An operation that, by ejecting the bullets from the magazine of a rifle, takes the pressure off the magazine spring.
4. Military targets on a map or on the ground are sometimes indicated by taking a distinctive topographical feature, such as a tree, as the center of an imaginary clock. A target below and to the right of that would then be described (line 46) as "at five o'clock."

55 The still white dwellings are like a mirage in the heat,
And under the swaying elms a man and a woman
Lie gently together. Which is, perhaps, only to say
That there is a row of houses to the left of arc,
And that under some poplars a pair of what appear to be humans
60   Appear to be loving.

Well that, for an answer, is what we might rightly call
Moderately satisfactory only, the reason being,
Is that two things have been omitted, and those are important.
The human beings, now: in what direction are they,
65 And how far away, would you say? And do not forget
     There may be dead ground[5] in between.

There may be dead ground in between; and I may not have got
The knack of judging a distance; I will only venture
A guess that perhaps between me and the apparent lovers
70   (Who, incidentally, appear by now to have finished)
At seven o'clock from the houses, is roughly a distance
     Of about one year and a half.

                                                    1945

5. Military term for an area that cannot be reached by fire from a given weapon or a given point.

RICHARD HILLARY
1919–1943

Richard Hillary was born in Sydney, Australia, in 1919. He came to England after World War I with his father, who was in the Australian Treasury. In 1931 he went to Shrewsbury School and in 1937 to Trinity College, Oxford. He was at Oxford when the war broke out and, with other members of the Oxford Royal Air Force Volunteer Reserve (RAFVR), was soon in uniform:

> For myself [he wrote later], I was glad for purely selfish reasons. The war solved all problems of a career, and promised a chance of self-realization that would normally take years to achieve. As a fighter pilot I hoped for a concentration of amusement, fear, and exaltation which it would be impossible to experience in any other form of existence. I was not disappointed.

Hillary was one of the first pilots to be shot down in the Battle of Britain. Trapped in the blazing cockpit of his machine, he managed to struggle free and bailed out, after which he was picked up from the sea by a lifeboat and taken to Margate Hospital suffering from shock and severe burns to his face and hands. Then began a long period of surgical operations and a convalescence interrupted by further operations. It was during this period that he wrote his book *The Last Enemy* (1942). An autobiography in the tradition inaugurated by St. Augustine's *Confessions, The Last Enemy* traces the career of the fighter pilot from its highest point—his first "kill"—to the crisis at its lowest—his experience, on the ground, of the ugly results of the war in the air. As soon as Hillary had recovered sufficiently to use his hands, he badgered the authorities until he was allowed to return to operational flying. He was killed in active service in January 1943.

From The Last Enemy

I climbed into the cockpit of my plane and felt an empty sensation of suspense in the pit of my stomach. For one second time seemed to stand still and I stared blankly in front of me. I knew that that morning I was to kill for the first time. That I might be killed or in any way injured did not occur to me. Later, when we were losing pilots regularly, I did consider it in an abstract way when on the ground; but once in the air, never. I knew it could not happen to me. I suppose every pilot knows that, knows it cannot happen to him; even when he is taking off for the last time, when he will not return, he knows that he cannot be killed. I wondered idly what he was like, this man I would kill. Was he young, was he fat, would he die with the Fuehrer's name on his lips, or would he die alone, in that last moment conscious of himself as a man? I would never know. Then I was being strapped in, my mind automatically checking the controls, and we were off.

We ran into them at 18,000 feet, twenty yellow-nosed Messerschmitt 109's, about 500 feet above us. Our Squadron strength was eight, and as they came down on us we went into line astern and turned head on to them. Brian Carbury, who was leading the Section, dropped the nose of his machine, and I could almost feel the leading Nazi pilot push forward on his stick to bring his guns to bear. At the same moment Brian hauled hard back on his own control stick and led us over them in a steep climbing turn to the left. In two vital seconds they lost their advantage. I saw Brian let go a burst of fire at the leading plane, saw the pilot put his machine into a half roll, and knew that he was mine. Automatically, I kicked the rudder to the left to get him at right angles, turned the gun-button to "Fire," and let go in a four-second burst with full deflection. He came right through my sights and I saw the tracer[1] from all eight guns thud home. For a second he seemed to hang motionless; then a jet of red flame shot upwards and he spun out of sight.

For the next few minutes I was too busy looking after myself to think of anything, but when, after a short while, they turned and made off over the Channel,[2] and we were ordered to our base, my mind began to work again.

It had happened.

My first emotion was one of satisfaction, satisfaction at a job adequately done, at the final logical conclusion of months of specialised training. And then I had a feeling of the essential rightness of it all. He was dead and I was alive; it could so easily have been the other way round; and that would somehow have been right too. I realised in that moment just how lucky a fighter pilot is. He has none of the personalised emotions of the soldier, handed a rifle and bayonet and told to charge. He does not even have to

---

1. Shells whose flight is made visible by phosphorus coating.   2. English Channel between England and France.

share the dangerous emotions of the bomber pilot who night after night must experience that childhood longing for smashing things. The fighter pilot's emotions are those of the duellist—cool, precise, impersonal. He is privileged to kill well. For if one must either kill or be killed, as now one must, it should, I feel, be done with dignity. Death should be given the setting it deserves; it should never be a pettiness; and for the fighter pilot it never can be.

From this flight Broody Benson did not return.

* * *

"We'd be better off underground tonight, sir, and no mistake." It was my taxi-driver speaking.

"Nonsense," I said. "We couldn't be drinking this down there," and I took a long pull at my beer.

I was pushing the glass across the counter for a refill when we heard it[3] coming. The girl in the corner was still laughing and for the first time I heard her soldier speak. "Shut up!" he said, and the laugh was cut off like the sound track in a movie. Then everyone was diving for the floor. The barmaid (she was of considerable bulk) sank from view with a desperate slowness behind the counter and I flung myself tight up against the other side, my taxi-driver beside me. He still had his glass in his hand and the beer shot across the floor, making a dark stain and setting the sawdust afloat. The soldier too had made for the bar counter and wedged the girl on his inside. One of her shoes had nearly come off. It was an inch from my nose: she had a ladder in her stocking.

My hands were tight-pressed over my ears but the detonation deafened me. The floor rose up and smashed against my face, the swing-door tore off its hinges and crashed over a table, glass splinters flew across the room, and behind the bar every bottle in the place seemed to be breaking. The lights went out, but there was no darkness. An orange glow from across the street shone through the wall and threw everything into a strong relief.

I scrambled unsteadily to my feet and was leaning over the bar to see what had happened to the unfortunate barmaid when a voice said, "Anyone hurt?" and there was an A.F.S.[4] man shining a torch. At that everyone began to move, but slowly and reluctantly as though coming out of a dream. The girl stood white and shaken in a corner, her arm about her companion, but she was unhurt and had stopped talking. Only the barmaid failed to get up.

"I think there is someone hurt behind the bar," I said. The fireman nodded and went out, to return almost immediately with two stretcher-bearers who made a cursory inspection and discovered that she had escaped with no more than a severe cut on the head. They got her on to the stretcher and disappeared.

Together with the man in the A.F.S., the taxi-driver and I found our way out into the street. He turned to us almost apologetically. "If you have nothing very urgent on hand," he said, "I wonder if you'd help here for a bit. You see it was the house next to you that was hit and there's someone buried in there."

I turned and looked on a heap of bricks and mortar, wooden beams and

---

3. A bomb.   4. Auxiliary Fire Service.

doors, and one framed picture, unbroken. It was the first time that I had seen a building newly blasted. Often had I left the flat in the morning and walked up Piccadilly,[5] aware vaguely of the ominously tidy gap between two houses, but further my mind had not gone.

We dug, or rather we pushed, pulled, heaved, and strained, I somewhat ineffectually because of my hands; I don't know for how long, but I suppose for a short enough while. And yet it seemed endless. From time to time I was aware of figures round me: an A.R.P.[6] warden, his face expressionless under a steel helmet; once a soldier swearing savagely in a quiet monotone; and the taxi-driver, his face pouring sweat.

And so we came to the woman. It was her feet that we saw first, and whereas before we had worked doggedly, now we worked with a sort of frenzy, like prospectors at the first glint of gold. She was not quite buried, and through the gap between two beams we could see that she was still alive. We got the child out first. It was passed back carefully and with an odd sort of reverence by the warden, but it was dead. She must have been holding it to her in the bed when the bomb came.

Finally we made a gap wide enough for the bed to be drawn out. The woman who lay there looked middle-aged. She lay on her back and her eyes were closed. Her face, through the dirt and streaked blood, was the face of a thousand working women; her body under the cotton nightdress was heavy. The nightdress was drawn up to her knees and one leg was twisted under her. There was no dignity about that figure.

Around me I heard voices. "Where's the ambulance?" "For Christ's sake don't move her!" "Let her have some air!"

I was at the head of the bed, and looking down into that tired, blood-streaked, work-worn face I had a sense of complete unreality. I took the brandy flask from my hip pocket and held it to her lips. Most of it ran down her chin but a little flowed between those clenched teeth. She opened her eyes and reached out her arms instinctively for the child. Then she started to weep. Quite soundlessly, and with no sobbing, the tears were running down her cheeks when she lifted her eyes to mine.

"Thank you, sir," she said, and took my hand in hers. And then, looking at me again, she said after a pause, "I see they got you too."

Very carefully I screwed the top on to the brandy flask, unscrewed it once and screwed it on again, for I had caught it on the wrong thread. I put the flask into my hip pocket and did up the button. I pulled across the buckle on my great-coat and noticed that I was dripping with sweat. I pulled the cap down over my eyes and walked out into the street.

Someone caught me by the arm, I think it was the soldier with the girl, and said: "You'd better take some of that brandy yourself. You don't look too good"; but I shook him off. With difficulty I kept my pace to a walk, forcing myself not to run. For I wanted to run, to run anywhere away from that scene, from myself, from the terror that was inside me, the terror of something that was about to happen and which I had not the power to stop.

It started small, small but insistent deep inside of me, sharp as a needle, then welling up uncontrollable, spurting, flowing over, choking me. I was drowning, helpless in a rage that caught and twisted and hurled me on,

---

5. Street in the center of London.   6. Air-raid precautions.

mouthing in a blind unthinking frenzy. I heard myself cursing, the words pouring out, shrill, meaningless, and as my mind cleared a little I knew that it was the woman I cursed. Yes, the woman that I reviled, hating her that she should die like that for me to see, loathing that silly bloody twisted face that had said those words: "I see they got you too." That she should have spoken to me, why, oh Christ, to me? Could she not have died the next night, ten minutes later, or in the next street? Could she not have died without speaking, without raising those cow eyes to mine?

"I see they got you too." All humanity had been in those few words, and I had cursed her. Slowly the frenzy died in me, the rage oozed out of me, leaving me cold, shivering, and bitterly ashamed. I had cursed her, cursed her, I realized as I grew calmer, for she had been the one thing that my rage surging uncontrollably had had to fasten on, the one thing to which my mind, overwhelmed by the sense of something so huge and beyond the range of thought, could cling. Her death was unjust, a crime, an outrage, a sin against mankind—weak inadequate words which even as they passed through my mind mocked me with their futility.

That that woman should so die was an enormity so great that it was terrifying in its implications, in its lifting of the veil on possibilities of thought so far beyond the grasp of the human mind. It was not just the German bombs, or the German Air Force, or even the German mentality, but a feeling of the very essence of anti-life that no words could convey. This was what I had been cursing—in part, for I had recognised in that moment what it was that Peter[7] and the others had instantly recognised as evil and to be destroyed utterly. I saw now that it was not crime; it was Evil itself—something of which until then I had not even sensed the existence. And it was in the end, at bottom, myself against which I had raged, myself I had cursed. With awful clarity I saw myself suddenly as I was. Great God, that I could have been so arrogant!

1942

7. Peter Pease, Hillary's closest fighter-pilot friend, was shot down and killed in 1940.

KEITH DOUGLAS
1920–1944

Keith Douglas was born in Tunbridge Wells, the son of a regular army officer who had won the Military Cross in World War I and who, in 1927, deserted his wife and son. Byron had had a similar experience, with similar results. Both poets grew up as men of action with an almost obsessive interest in warfare. At the age of ten, Douglas wrote a poem about the Battle of Waterloo, and later, at Christ's Hospital School in London, he divided his leisure time between developing his precocious talents as poet and artist, riding, playing rugby football, and participating enthusiastically in the Officer Cadet Corps. Going on to Merton College, Oxford, he was tutored by Edmund Blunden, a distinguished soldier poet of World War I. In 1940, Douglas enlisted in a cavalry regiment that was soon obliged to exchange its horses for tanks and, in

August 1942, went into battle against Field Marshal Rommel's Africa Corps in the Egyptian desert. Forced to remain in reserve behind the lines, Douglas commandeered a truck and, in direct disobedience of orders, drove off to join his regiment.

His subsequent achievement as a poet and prose writer, author of a brilliant memoir of the desert campaign, *Alamein to Zem Zem* (1966), was to celebrate the last stand of the chivalric hero. His poem *Aristocrats* ends perhaps with a distant echo of Roland's horn, sounded in the Pass of Roncevalles at the end of the twelfth-century French chivalric epic *The Song of Roland*. Douglas's poem succeeds where most of the would-be heroic poems of 1914 and 1915 fail. It is sharply focused, acknowledging both the stupidity and the chivalry, the folly and the glamour of cavalrymen on mechanical mounts dueling in the desert. Douglas's language, finely responsive to his theme, fuses ancient and modern: his heroes are "gentle"—like Chaucer's "verray parfit gentil knight"—and at the same time "obsolescent."

Douglas survived the desert campaign to take part in the assault on the Normandy beaches, where, on June 6, 1944, he was killed.

Gallantry

The Colonel[1] in a casual voice
spoke into the microphone a joke
Which through a hundred earphones broke
into the ears of a doomed race.[2]

5   Into the ears of the doomed boy, the fool
whose perfectly mannered flesh fell
in opening the door for a shell
as he had learnt to do at school.

Conrad luckily survived the winter:
10 he wrote a letter to welcome
the auspicious spring: only his silken
intentions severed with a single splinter.

Was George fond of little boys?
We always suspected it,
15 but who will say: since George was hit
we never mention our surmise.

It was a brave thing the Colonel said,
but the whole sky turned too hot
and the three heroes never heard what
20 it was, gone deaf with steel and lead.

But the bullets cried with laughter,
the shells were overcome with mirth,
plunging their heads in steel and earth—
(the air commented in a whisper).

Apr. 1943   1949

---

1. Lt. Col. J. D. Player, killed in Tunisia, Enfidaville, February 1943, left £3,000 to the Beaufort Hunt, and directed that the incumbent of the living in his gift [i.e., the church whose vicar he was entitled to appoint] should be a 'man who approves of hunting, shooting, and all manly sports, which are the backbone of the nation.' [Douglas's note on one of the manuscripts of *Aristocrats*. Player was in fact killed in April.]
2. Cf. Owen, *Anthem for Doomed Youth* (p. 2066).

Vergissmeinnicht[1]

Three weeks gone and the combatants gone
returning over the nightmare ground
we found the place again, and found
the soldier sprawling in the sun.

5   The frowning barrel of his gun
overshadowing. As we came on
that day, he hit my tank with one
like the entry of a demon.

Look. Here in the gunpit spoil
10 the dishonoured picture of his girl
who has put: *Steffi. Vergissmeinnicht*
in a copybook gothic script.

We see him almost with content,
abased, and seeming to have paid
15 and mocked at by his own equipment
that's hard and good when he's decayed.

But she would weep to see today
how on his skin the swart° flies move;   *black*
the dust upon the paper eye
20 and the burst stomach like a cave.

For here the lover and killer are mingled
who had one body and one heart.
And death who had the soldier singled
has done the lover mortal hurt.

1943   1944

Aristocrats[1]

"I think I am becoming a God"[2]

The noble horse with courage in his eye
clean in the bone, looks up at a shellburst:
away fly the images of the shires[3]
but he puts the pipe back in his mouth.

5   Peter was unfortunately killed by an 88:[4]
it took his leg away, he died in the ambulance.
I saw him crawling on the sand; he said
It's most unfair, they've shot my foot off.

1. Forget me not (German).
1. Another version of this poem is entitled *Sportsmen*.
2. The dying words of Roman Emperor Vespasian were supposedly: "Alas! I suppose I am turning into a god."
3. Counties. Cf. Owen, *Anthem for Doomed Youth*, line 8 (p. 2067).
4. A German tank fitted with an eighty-eight-millimeter gun.

How can I live among this gentle
10   obsolescent breed of heroes, and not weep?
Unicorns, almost,
for they are falling into two legends
in which their stupidity and chivalry
are celebrated. Each, fool and hero, will be an immortal.

15   The plains were their cricket pitch[5]
and in the mountains the tremendous drop fences[6]
brought down some of the runners. Here then
under the stones and earth they dispose themselves,
I think with their famous unconcern.
20   It is not gunfire I hear but a hunting horn.[7]

Enfidaville, Tunisia, 1943   1946

From Alamein to Zem Zem

After we had been back in our position about a quarter of an hour, some-one on the right reported twelve enemy tanks advancing. A second report estimated twenty. Soon after this a very hot fire began to fall around us. Two petrol lorries were hit at once and began to blaze. The Germans came towards us out of the setting sun, firing, and supported by anti-tank and high-explosive fire. Some of the Crusaders,[1] Andrew's tank included, began reversing. I moved back myself, but it was obvious that we should soon get mixed up with the heavy tanks. I halted. Someone could be heard calling for smoke. Andrew was rating the squadron for bunching up and his own tank meanwhile avoided reversing into a Grant[2] more by luck than judgement. There was a certain amount of incipient panic apparent in some of the mes-sages coming over the air. The enemy fire grew more intense: it seemed incredible that only the two lorries had so far been hit. I crouched in the turret, expecting at any moment the crash which would bring our disinte-gration, seeing again the torn shell of the tank we had passed the previous evening—it seemed weeks ago. I could not see the enemy tanks any longer, and was not sure after so much reversing and milling around, exactly what the situation was. These were the intensest moments of physical fear, outside of dreams, I have ever experienced.

Control now instructed us: 'Open fire on the enemy. Range one zero zero zero.'[3] Give the buggers every round you've got. Over.' With, I think, some relief the various squadrons acknowledge: 'One O.K. off'; 'Two O.K. off'; 'Three O.K. off.' I ordered Evan to fire. 'I can't see a muckin' thing,' he protested. 'Never mind, you fire at a thousand as fast as I can load.' Every gun was now blazing away into the twilight, the regiment somewhat massed together, firing with every available weapon. I crammed shells into the six-pounder as fast as Evan could lay and fire it. Presently the deflector bag

---

5. Field on which the game of cricket is played.
6. Fences in the course of a steeplechase horse race.
7. See n. 1, p. 2536.

1. Low-lined tanks which were fast if mechani-cally unreliable [Douglas's comment].
2. A heavy tank.
3. One thousand yards.

CHARLES CAUSLEY / 2539

was full of shell cases, and Evan, who had now adjusted the Besa,[4] blazed off a whole belt without a stoppage, while I tossed out the empty cases, too hot to touch with a bare hand. The turret was full of fumes and smoke. I coughed and sweated; fear had given place to exhilaration. Twilight increased to near-darkness, and the air all round us gleamed with the different coloured traces of shells and bullets, brilliant graceful curves travelling from us to the enemy and from him towards us. The din was tremendously exciting. I could see a trail of machine-gun bullets from one of our heavy tanks passing a few yards to the left of my tank, on a level with my head. Above us whistled the shells of the seventy-fives. Overhead the trace of enemy shells could be seen mounting to the top of their flight where, as the shell tilted towards us, it disappeared. Red and orange bursts leapt up beside and in front of us.

Darkness ended the action as suddenly as it had begun; the petrol lorries alone blazed like beacons, answered by distant fires in the direction of the enemy. Gradually we found our way into leaguer,[5] creeping past the beacons after the dim shapes of our companions. My first day in action had been eventful enough: I felt as if I had been fighting for months.

1946

---

4. Popular name for a machine-gun manufactured by the Birmingham Small Arms Company. 5. Camp for armored vehicles.

CHARLES CAUSLEY
b. 1917

Born and educated in Launceston, Cornwall, where he still lives, Charles Causley followed the tradition of a seafaring people and served in the Royal Navy from 1940 to 1946. His experiences on a destroyer and an aircraft carrier had a catalytic effect on him as a poet. "It was Hitler who pushed a subject under my nose," he writes. "I think the event that affected me more than anything else in those years was the fact that the companion who had left my home-town with me for the navy in 1940 was later lost in a convoy to Russia. From the moment I heard this news, I found myself haunted by the words in the twenty-fourth chapter of St Matthew: 'Then shall two be in the field; the one shall be taken, and the other left.' If my poetry is 'about' anything, it is this."

Causley's Cornishness shows in his skillful use of verse forms and narrative strategies drawn from an oral folk tradition. He is a master of the ballad told in a voice that is at once impersonal—the voice of the anonymous early balladeers—and unmistakably his own. Causley's seeming simplicity, like theirs, can be misleading; his jaunty cadences, his spry interweaving of ancient and modern diction, heighten the poignancy of such elegies as are printed here.

From 1947 to 1976 he taught at a school in Cornwall. He has written many volumes of poems and several plays—some of both, with great success, for children.

At the British War Cemetery, Bayeux[1]

I walked where in their talking graves
And shirts of earth five thousand lay,
When history with ten feasts of fire
Had eaten the red air away.

5   I am Christ's boy, I cried, I bear
In iron hands the bread, the fishes.[2]
I hang with honey and with rose
This tidy wreck of all your wishes.

On your geometry of sleep
10   The chestnut and the fir-tree fly,
And lavender and marguerite
Forge with their flowers an English sky.

Turn now towards the belling town
Your jigsaws of impossible bone,
15   And rising read your rank of snow
Accurate as death upon the stone.

About your easy heads my prayers
I said with syllables of clay.
What gift, I asked, shall I bring now
20   Before I weep and walk away?

Take, they replied, the oak and laurel.[3]
Take our fortune of tears and live
Like a spendthrift lover. All we ask
Is the one gift you cannot give.

1957

Armistice Day

I stood with three comrades in Parliament Square[1]
November her freights of grey fire unloading,
No sound from the city upon the pale air
Above us the sea-bell eleven exploding.

5   Down by the bands and the burning memorial
Beats all the brass in a royal array,
But at our end we are not so sartorial:
Out of (as usual) the rig of the day.

---

1. Near the coast of northwest France, the scene
of heavy fighting following the Normandy landings
in June 1944.
2. Cf. Matthew 14.19–20.
3. Trees whose leaves are traditionally taken as
emblems of courage and victory, respectively.

1. An annual "Remembrance Sunday" service is
held at the Cenotaph, a stone memorial to the dead
of two world wars, in London's Parliament Square.
It includes a two-minute silence after the last
stroke of eleven o'clock.

Starry is wearing a split pusser's flannel[2]
10 Rubbed, as he is, by the regular tide;
Oxo the ducks[3] that he ditched in the Channel
In June, 1940 (when he was inside).

Kitty recalls his abandon-ship station,
Running below at the Old Man's salute[4]
15 And (with a deck-watch) going down for duration[5]
Wearing his oppo's pneumonia-suit.[6]

Comrades, for you the black captain of carracks[7]
Writes in Whitehall[8] his appalling decisions,
But as was often the case in the Barracks
20 Several ratings are not at Divisions.[9]

Into my eyes the stiff sea-horses stare,
Over my head sweeps the sun like a swan.
As I stand alone in Parliament Square
A cold bugle calls, and the city moves on.

1957

2. A torn navy-issue shirt.
3. Sailor's white tunic and trousers.
4. There is a British naval tradition whereby the Captain (Old Man) of a sinking ship goes down saluting.
5. I.e., for the duration of the war; a phrase common during World War II.

6. Canvas suit—belonging to his friend ("opposite number")—worn while painting the ship.
7. Large merchant ships equipped for warfare.
8. London street in which stands the Admiralty (navy headquarters).
9. I.e., noncommissioned sailors are absent from church parade, the religious service on board ship.

DORIS LESSING
b. 1919

Born in Persia of British parents, Doris Lessing (née Tayler) lived in southern Rhodesia (now Zimbabwe) from 1924 to 1949 before settling in England. Her five-novel sequence with the general title *Children of Violence* (beginning with *Martha Quest*, 1952) combines elements of psychological autobiography with powerful exploration of the relationship between black and white in southern Africa. Her combination of psychological introspection, political analysis, social documentary, and feminism gives a characteristic tone to her novels and short stories. These elements are effectively combined in her novel *The Golden Notebook* (1962), which explores the sexual problems of an independent woman in a man's world with unexhibitionist frankness while at the same time probing the political conscience of an ex-Communist and the needs and dilemmas of a creative writer. In the early 1970s, influenced by the writings of the renegade psychologist R. D. Laing and by the principles of Sufism (the mystical, ecstatic aspects of Islam), Lessing's realistic investigations of social issues took a mythic turn. In *Briefing for a Descent into Hell* (1971) and *The Memoirs of a Survivor* (1974) she explores the possibilities of myth and fantasy, restrained within a broadly realist context. In a series of novels with the general title *Canopus in Argos: Archives* (written between 1979 and 1983), she draws on her reading of the Old and New Testaments, the Apocrypha, and the Koran and borrows conventions from science fiction to describe the efforts of a superhuman, extraterrestrial race to guide human history. The novels convey the scope of human suffering in the twentieth century with an imaginative power that surmounts their sometimes proselytizing tone. On completion of this novel sequence, Lessing took the unusual step of publishing two pseudonymous novels (now known jointly as *The Diaries of Jane Somers*, 1983–84), in which she reverted to the realist mode with which she is most widely associated. *The Good Terrorist* (1985) is also written in the style of documentary realism, but a more recent novel, *The Fifth Child* (1988), combines elements of realism and fantasy, exploring the effect on a happy family of the birth of a genetically abnormal, non-human child. Her work in the 1990s has included two fearlessly honest volumes of autobiography, *Under My Skin* (1994) and *Walking in the Shade* (1997), and a series of short stories. Some of these stories—which deal with racial and social dilemmas as well as with loneliness, the claims of politics, the problems of aging (especially for women), the conflict between the generations, and a whole spectrum of problems of alienation and isolation—have a pungency and force that can be lacking in her more discursive novels. Lessing (she uses the name of her second husband, although both her marriages have been dissolved) is very much a writer of her time, deeply involved with the changing patterns of thought, feeling, and culture during the last forty years. A predominantly realist novelist, she has consistently explored and tested the boundaries of realist technique, without resort to formal experimentalism, and one feels that there is a fundamental continuity between her life and her work. The story printed here is taken from her volume of short stories *A Man and Two Women*.

To Room Nineteen

This is a story, I suppose, about a failure in intelligence: the Rawlings' marriage was grounded in intelligence.

They were older when they married than most of their married friends: in their well-seasoned late twenties. Both had had a number of affairs, sweet rather than bitter; and when they fell in love—for they did fall in love—had known each other for some time. They joked that they had saved each other "for the real thing." That they had waited so long (but not too long) for this real thing was to them a proof of their sensible discrimination. A good many of their friends had married young, and now (they felt) probably regretted lost opportunities; while others, still unmarried, seemed to them arid, self-doubting, and likely to make desperate or romantic marriages.

Not only they, but others, felt they were well matched: their friends' delight was an additional proof of their happiness. They had played the same roles, male and female, in this group or set, if such a wide, loosely connected, constantly changing constellation of people could be called a set. They had both become, by virtue of their moderation, their humour, and their abstinence from painful experience people to whom others came for advice. They could be, and were, relied on. It was one of those cases of a man and a woman linking themselves whom no one else had ever thought of linking, probably because of their similarities. But then everyone exclaimed: Of course! How right! How was it we never thought of it before!

And so they married amid general rejoicing, and because of their foresight and their sense for what was probable, nothing was a surprise to them.

Both had well-paid jobs. Matthew was a subeditor on a large London newspaper, and Susan worked in an advertising firm. He was not the stuff of which editors or publicised journalists are made, but he was much more than "a subeditor," being one of the essential background people who in fact steady, inspire and make possible the people in the limelight. He was content with this position. Susan had a talent for commercial drawing. She was humorous about the advertisements she was responsible for, but she did not feel strongly about them one way or the other.

Both, before they married, had had pleasant flats, but they felt it unwise to base a marriage on either flat, because it might seem like a submission of personality on the part of the one whose flat it was not. They moved into a new flat in South Kensington on the clear understanding that when their marriage had settled down (a process they knew would not take long, and was in fact more a humorous concession to popular wisdom than what was due to themselves) they would buy a house and start a family.

And this is what happened. They lived in their charming flat for two years, giving parties and going to them, being a popular young married couple, and then Susan became pregnant, she gave up her job, and they bought a house in Richmond. It was typical of this couple that they had a son first, then a daughter, then twins, son and daughter. Everything right, appropriate, and what everyone would wish for, if they could choose. But people did feel these two had chosen; this balanced and sensible family was no more than what was due to them because of their infallible sense for *choosing* right.

And so they lived with their four children in their gardened house in Richmond and were happy. They had everything they had wanted and had planned for.

And yet . . .

Well, even this was expected, that there must be a certain flatness. . . .

Yes, yes, of course, it was natural they sometimes felt like this. Like what?

Their life seemed to be like a snake biting its tail. Matthew's job for the sake of Susan, children, house, and garden—which caravanserai needed a well-paid job to maintain it. And Susan's practical intelligence for the sake of Matthew, the children, the house and the garden—which unit would have collapsed in a week without her.

But there was no point about which either could say: "For the sake of *this* is all the rest." Children? But children can't be a centre of life and a reason for being. They can be a thousand things that are delightful, interesting, satisfying, but they can't be a wellspring to live from. Or they shouldn't be. Susan and Matthew knew that well enough.

Matthew's job? Ridiculous. It was an interesting job, but scarcely a reason for living. Matthew took pride in doing it well; but he could hardly be expected to be proud of the newspaper: the newspaper he read, *his* newspaper, was not the one he worked for.

Their love for each other? Well, that was nearest it. If this wasn't a centre, what was? Yes, it was around this point, their love, that the whole extraordinary structure revolved. For extraordinary it certainly was. Both Susan and Matthew had moments of thinking so, of looking in secret disbelief at this thing they had created: marriage, four children, big house, garden, charwomen, friends, cars . . . and this *thing,* this entity, all of it had come into existence, been blown into being out of nowhere, because Susan loved Matthew and Matthew loved Susan. Extraordinary. So that was the central point, the wellspring.

And if one felt that it simply was not strong enough, important enough, to support it all, well whose fault was that? Certainly neither Susan's nor Matthew's. It was in the nature of things. And they sensibly blamed neither themselves nor each other.

On the contrary, they used their intelligence to preserve what they had created from a painful and explosive world: they looked around them, and took lessons. All around them, marriages collapsing, or breaking, or rubbing along (even worse, they felt). They must not make the same mistakes, they must not.

They had avoided the pitfall so many of their friends had fallen into—of buying a house in the country *for the sake of the children;* so that the husband became a weekend husband, a weekend father, and the wife always careful not to ask what went on in the town flat which they called (in joke) a bachelor flat. No, Matthew was a full-time husband, a full-time father, and at nights, in the big married bed in the big married bedroom (which had an attractive view of the river) they lay beside each other talking and he told her about his day, and what he had done, and whom he had met; and she told him about her day (not as interesting, but that was not her fault) for both knew of the hidden resentments and deprivations of the woman who has lived her own life—and above all, has earned her own living—and is now dependent on a husband for outside interests and money.

Nor did Susan make the mistake of taking a job for the sake of her independence, which she might very well have done, since her old firm, missing her qualities of humour, balance, and sense, invited her often to go back. Children needed their mother to a certain age, that both parents knew and agreed on; and when these four healthy wisely brought-up children were of the right age, Susan would work again, because she knew, and so did he, what happened to women of fifty at the height of their energy and ability, with grown-up children who no longer needed their full devotion.

So here was this couple, testing their marriage, looking after it, treating it like a small boat full of helpless people in a very stormy sea. Well, of course, so it was. . . . The storms of the world were bad, but not too close—which is not to say they were selfishly felt: Susan and Matthew were both well-informed and responsible people. And the inner storms and quicksands were understood and charted. So everything was all right. Everything was in order. Yes, things were under control.

So what did it matter if they felt dry, flat? People like themselves, fed on a hundred books (psychological, anthropological, sociological) could scarcely be unprepared for the dry, controlled wistfulness which is the distinguishing mark of the intelligent marriage. Two people, endowed with education, with discrimination, with judgement, linked together voluntarily from their will to be happy together and to be of use to others—one sees them everywhere, one knows them, one even is that thing oneself: sadness because so much is after all so little. These two, unsurprised, turned towards each other with even more courtesy and gentle love: this was life, that two people, no matter how carefully chosen, could not be everything to each other. In fact, even to say so, to think in such a way, was banal, they were ashamed to do it.

It was banal, too, when one night Matthew came home late and confessed he had been to a party, taken a girl home and slept with her. Susan forgave him, of course. Except that forgiveness is hardly the word. Understanding, yes. But if you understand something, you don't forgive it, you are the thing itself: forgiveness is for what you *don't* understand. Nor had he *confessed*— what sort of word is that?

The whole thing was not important. After all, years ago they had joked: Of course I'm not going to be faithful to you, no one can be faithful to one other person for a whole lifetime. (And there was the word *faithful*—stupid, all these words, stupid, belonging to a savage old world.) But the incident left both of them irritable. Strange, but they were both bad-tempered, annoyed. There was something unassimilable about it.

Making love splendidly after he had come home that night, both had felt that the idea that Myra Jenkins, a pretty girl met at a party, could be even relevant was ridiculous. They had loved each other for over a decade, would love each other for years more. Who, then, was Myra Jenkins?

Except, thought Susan, unaccountably bad-tempered, she was (is?) the first. In ten years. So either the ten years' fidelity was not important, or she isn't. (No, no, there is something wrong with this way of thinking, there must be.) But if she isn't important, presumably it wasn't important either when Matthew and I first went to bed with each other that afternoon whose delight even now (like a very long shadow at sundown) lays a long, wand-like finger over us. (Why did I say sundown?) Well, if what we felt that afternoon was not important, nothing is important, because if it hadn't been for what we felt, we wouldn't be Mr and Mrs Rawlings with four children, etc., etc. The whole thing is *absurd*—for him to have come home and told me was absurd. For him not to have told me was absurd. For me to care, or for that matter not to care, is absurd . . . and who is Myra Jenkins? Why, no one at all.

There was only one thing to do, and of course these sensible people did it: they put the thing behind them, and consciously, knowing what they were doing, moved forward into a different phase of their marriage, giving thanks for past good fortune as they did so.

For it was inevitable that the handsome, blond, attractive, manly man, Matthew Rawlings, should be at times tempted (oh, what a word!) by the attractive girls at parties she could not attend because of the four children; and that sometimes he would succumb (a word even more repulsive, if possible) and that she, a good-looking woman in the big well-tended garden at Richmond, would sometimes be pierced as by an arrow from the sky with bitterness. Except that bitterness was not in order, it was out of court. Did the casual girls touch the marriage? They did not. Rather it was they who knew defeat because of the handsome Matthew Rawlings' marriage body and soul to Susan Rawlings.

In that case why did Susan feel (though luckily not for longer than a few seconds at a time) as if life had become a desert, and that nothing mattered, and that her children were not her own?

Meanwhile her intelligence continued to assert that all was well. What if her Matthew did have an occasional sweet afternoon, the odd affair? For she knew quite well, except in her moments of aridity, that they were very happy, that the affairs were not important.

Perhaps that was the trouble? It was in the nature of things that the adventures and delights could no longer be hers, because of the four children and the big house that needed so much attention. But perhaps she was secretly wishing, and even knowing that she did, that the wildness and the beauty could be his. But he was married to her. She was married to him. They were married inextricably. And therefore the gods could not strike him with the real magic, not really. Well, was it Susan's fault that after he came home from an adventure he looked harassed rather than fulfilled? (In fact, that was how she knew he had been *unfaithful,* because of his sullen air, and his glances at her, similar to hers at him: What is it that I share with this person that shields all delight from me?) But none of it by anybody's fault. (But what did they feel ought to be somebody's fault?) Nobody's fault, nothing to be at fault, no one to blame, no one to offer or to take it . . . and nothing wrong, either, except that Matthew never was really struck, as he wanted to be, by joy; and that Susan was more and more often threatened by emptiness. (It was usually in the garden that she was invaded by this feeling: she was coming to avoid the garden, unless the children or Matthew were with her.) There was no need to use the dramatic words, unfaithful, forgive, and the rest: intelligence forbade them. Intelligence barred, too, quarrelling, sulking, anger, silences of withdrawal, accusations and tears. Above all, intelligence forbids tears.

A high price has to be paid for the happy marriage with the four healthy children in the large white gardened house.

And they were paying it, willingly, knowing what they were doing. When they lay side by side or breast to breast in the big civilised bedroom overlooking the wild sullied river, they laughed, often, for no particular reason; but they knew it was really because of these two small people, Susan and Matthew, supporting such an edifice on their intelligent love. The laugh comforted them; it saved them both, though from what, they did not know.

They were now both fortyish. The older children, boy and girl were ten and eight, at school. The twins, six, were still at home. Susan did not have nurses or girls to help her: childhood is short; and she did not regret the hard work. Often enough she was bored, since small children can be boring; she was often very tired; but she regretted nothing. In another decade, she would turn herself back into being a woman with a life of her own.

Soon the twins would go to school, and they would be away from home from nine until four. These hours, so Susan saw it, would be the preparation for her own slow emancipation away from the role of hub-of-the-family into woman-with-her-own-life. She was already planning for the hours of freedom when all the children would be "off her hands." That was the phrase used by Matthew and by Susan and by their friends, for the moment when the youngest child went off to school. "They'll be off your hands, darling Susan, and you'll have time to yourself." So said Matthew, the intelligent husband, who had often enough commended and consoled Susan, standing by her in spirit during the years when her soul was not her own, as she said, but her children's.

What it amounted to was that Susan saw herself as she had been at twenty-eight, unmarried; and then again somewhere about fifty, blossoming from the root of what she had been twenty years before. As if the essential Susan were in abeyance, as if she were in cold storage. Matthew said something like this to Susan one night: and she agreed that it was true—she did feel something like that. What, then, was this essential Susan? She did not know.

Put like that it sounded ridiculous, and she did not really feel it. Anyway, they had a long discussion about the whole thing before going off to sleep in each other's arms.

So the twins went off to their school, two bright affectionate children who had no problems about it, since their older brother and sister had trodden this path so successfully before them. And now Susan was going to be alone in the big house, every day of the school term, except for the daily woman who came in to clean.

It was now, for the first time in this marriage, that something happened which neither of them had foreseen.

This is what happened. She returned, at nine-thirty, from taking the twins to the school by car, looking forward to seven blissful hours of freedom. On the first morning she was simply restless, worrying about the twins "naturally enough" since this was their first day away at school. She was hardly able to contain herself until they came back. Which they did happily, excited by the world of school, looking forward to the next day. And the next day Susan took them, dropped them, came back, and found herself reluctant to enter her big and beautiful home because it was as if something was waiting for her there that she did not wish to confront. Sensibly, however, she parked the car in the garage, entered the house, spoke to Mrs Parkes the daily woman about her duties, and went up to her bedroom. She was possessed by a fever which drove her out again, downstairs, into the kitchen, where Mrs Parkes was making cake and did not need her, and into the garden. There she sat on a bench and tried to calm herself, looking at trees, at a brown glimpse of the river. But she was filled with tension, like a panic: as if an enemy was in the garden with her. She spoke to herself severely, thus: All this is quite natural. First, I spent twelve years of my adult life working, *living my own life*. Then I married, and from the moment I became pregnant for the first time I signed myself over, so to speak, to other people. To the children. Not for one moment in twelve years have I been alone, had time to myself. So now I have to learn to be myself again. That's all.

And she went indoors to help Mrs Parkes cook and clean, and found some sewing to do for the children. She kept herself occupied every day. At the end of the first term she understood she felt two contrary emotions. First: secret astonishment and dismay that during those weeks when the house was empty of children she had in fact been more occupied (had been careful to keep herself occupied) than ever she had been when the children were around her needing her continual attention. Second: that now she knew the house would be full of them, and for five weeks, she resented the fact she would never be alone. She was already looking back at those hours of sewing, cooking (but by herself), as at a lost freedom which would not be hers for five long weeks. And the two months of term which would succeed the five weeks stretched alluringly open to her—freedom. But what freedom—when in fact she had been so careful *not* to be free of small duties during the last weeks? She looked at herself, Susan Rawlings, sitting in a big chair by the window in the bedroom, sewing shirts or dresses, which she might just as well have bought. She saw herself making cakes for hours at a time in the big family kitchen: yet usually she bought cakes. What she saw was a woman alone, that was true, but she had not felt alone. For instance, Mrs Parkes was always somewhere in the house. And she did not like being in the garden at all, because of the closeness there of the enemy—irritation, restlessness, emptiness, whatever it was, which keeping her hands occupied made less dangerous for some reason.

Susan did not tell Matthew of these thoughts. They were not sensible. She did not recognize herself in them. What should she say to her dear friend and husband Matthew? "When I go into the garden, that is, if the children are not there, I feel as if there is an enemy there waiting to invade me." "What enemy, Susan darling?" "Well I don't know, really. . . ." "Perhaps you should see a doctor?"

No, clearly this conversation should not take place. The holidays began and Susan welcomed them. Four children, lively, energetic, intelligent, demanding: she was never, not for a moment of her day, alone. If she was in a room, they would be in the next room, or waiting for her to do something for them; or it would soon be time for lunch or tea, or to take one of them to the dentist. Something to do: five weeks of it, thank goodness.

On the fourth day of these so welcome holidays, she found she was storming with anger at the twins, two shrinking beautiful children who (and this is what checked her) stood hand in hand looking at her with sheer dismayed disbelief. This was their calm mother, shouting at them. And for what? They had come to her with some game, some bit of nonsense. They looked at each other, moved closer for support, and went off hand in hand, leaving Susan holding on to the windowsill of the living room, breathing deep, feeling sick. She went to lie down, telling the older children she had a headache. She heard the boy Harry telling the little ones: "It's all right, Mother's got a headache." She heard that *It's all right* with pain.

That night she said to her husband: "Today I shouted at the twins, quite unfairly." She sounded miserable, and he said gently: "Well, what of it?"

"It's more of an adjustment than I thought, their going to school."

"But Susie, Susie darling. . . ." For she was crouched weeping on the bed. He comforted her: "Susan, what is all this about? You shouted at them? What of it? If you shouted at them fifty times a day it wouldn't be more than the little devils deserve." But she wouldn't laugh. She wept. Soon he comforted her with his body. She became calm. Calm, she wondered what was wrong with her, and why she should mind so much that she might, just once, have behaved unjustly with the children. What did it matter? They had forgotten it all long ago: Mother had a headache and everything was all right.

It was a long time later that Susan understood that that night, when she had wept and Matthew had driven the misery out of her with his big solid body, was the last time, ever in their married life, that they had been—to use their mutual language—with each other. And even that was a lie, because she had not told him of her real fears at all.

The five weeks passed, and Susan was in control of herself, and good and kind, and she looked forward to the end of the holidays with a mixture of fear and longing. She did not know what to expect. She took the twins off to school (the elder children took themselves to school) and she returned to the house determined to face the enemy wherever he was, in the house, or the garden or—where?

She was again restless, she was possessed by restlessness. She cooked and sewed and worked as before, day after day, while Mrs Parkes remonstrated: "Mrs Rawlings, what's the need for it? I can do that, it's what you pay me for."

And it was so irrational that she checked herself. She would put the car into the garage, go up to her bedroom, and sit, hands in her lap, forcing herself to be quiet. She listened to Mrs Parkes moving around the house. She looked out into the garden and saw the branches shake the trees. She sat defeating the enemy, restlessness. Emptiness. She ought to be thinking about her life, about herself. But she did not. Or perhaps she could not. As soon as she forced her mind to think about Susan (for what else did she want to be alone for?) it skipped off to thoughts of butter or school clothes. Or it thought of Mrs Parkes. She realised that she sat listening for the movements of the cleaning woman, following her every turn, bend, thought. She followed her in her mind from kitchen to bathroom, from table to oven, and it was as if the duster, the cleaning cloth, the saucepan, were in her own hand. She would hear herself saying: No, not like that, don't put that there. . . . Yet she did not give a damn what Mrs Parkes did, or if she did it at all. Yet she could not prevent herself from being conscious of her, every minute. Yes, this was what was wrong with her: she needed, when she was alone, to be really alone, with no one near. She could not endure the knowledge that in ten minutes or in half an hour Mrs Parkes would call up the stairs: "Mrs Rawlings, there's no silver polish. Madam, we're out of flour."

So she left the house and went to sit in the garden where she was screened from the house by trees. She waited for the demon to appear and claim her, but he did not.

She was keeping him off, because she had not, after all, come to an end of arranging herself.

She was planning how to be somewhere where Mrs Parkes would not come after her with a cup of tea, or a demand to be allowed to telephone (always irritating since Susan did not care who she telephoned or how often), or just a nice talk about something. Yes, she needed a place, or a state of affairs, where it would not be necessary to keep reminding herself: In ten minutes I must telephone Matthew about . . . and at half past three I must leave early for the children because the car needs cleaning. And at ten o'clock tomorrow I must remember. . . . She was possessed with resentment that the seven hours of freedom in every day (during weekdays in the school term) were not free, that never, not for one second, ever, was she free from the pressure of time, from having to remember this or that. She could never forget herself; never really let herself go into forgetfulness.

Resentment. It was poisoning her. (She looked at this emotion and thought it was absurd. Yet she felt it.) She was a prisoner. (She looked at this thought too, and it was no good telling herself it was a ridiculous one.) She must tell Matthew—but what? She was filled with emotions that were utterly ridiculous, that she despised, yet that nevertheless she was feeling so strongly she could not shake them off.

The school holidays came round, and this time they were for nearly two months, and she behaved with a conscious controlled decency that nearly drove her crazy. She would lock herself in the bathroom, and sit on the edge of the bath, breathing deep, trying to let go into some kind of calm. Or she went up into the spare room, usually empty, where no one would expect her to be. She heard the children calling "Mother, Mother," and kept silent, feeling guilty. Or she went to the very end of the garden, by herself, and looked at the slow-moving brown river; she looked at the river and closed her eyes and breathed slow and deep, taking it into her being, into her veins.

Then she returned to the family, wife and mother, smiling and responsible, feeling as if the pressure of these people—four lively children and her husband—were a painful pressure on the surface of her skin, a hand pressing on her brain. She did not once break down into irritation during these holidays, but it was like living out a prison sentence, and when the children went back to school, she sat on a white stone seat near the flowing river, and she thought: It is not even a year since the twins went to school, since *they were off my hands* (What on earth did I think I meant when I used that stupid phrase?) and yet I'm a different person. I'm simply not myself. I don't understand it.

Yet she had to understand it. For she knew that this structure—big white house, on which the mortgage still cost four hundred a year, a husband, so good and kind and insightful, four children, all doing so nicely, and the garden where she sat, and Mrs Parkes the cleaning woman—all this depended on her, and yet she could not understand why, or even what it was she contributed to it.

She said to Matthew in their bedroom: "I think there must be something wrong with me."

And he said: "Surely not, Susan? You look marvelous—you're as lovely as ever."

She looked at the handsome blond man, with his clear, intelligent, blue-eyed face, and thought: Why is it I can't tell him? Why not? And she said: "I need to be alone more than I am."

At which he swung his slow blue gaze at her, and she saw what she had been dreading: Incredulity. Disbelief. And fear. An incredulous blue stare from a stranger who was her husband, as close to her as her own breath.

He said: "But the children are at school and off your hands."

She said to herself: I've got to force myself to say: Yes, but do you realise that I never feel free? There's never a moment I can say to myself: There's nothing I have to remind myself about, nothing I have to do in half an hour, or an hour, or two hours. . . .

But she said: "I don't feel well."

He said: "Perhaps you need a holiday."

She said, appalled: "But not without you, surely?" For she could not imagine herself going off without him. Yet that was what he meant. Seeing her face, he laughed, and opened his arms, and she went into them, thinking: Yes, yes, but why can't I say it? And what is it I have to say?

She tried to tell him, about never being free. And he listened and said: "But Susan, what sort of freedom can you possibly want—short of being dead! Am I ever free? I go to the office, and I have to be there at ten—all right, half past ten, sometimes. And I have to do this or that, don't I? Then I've got to come home at a certain time—I don't mean it, you know I don't—but if I'm not going to be back home at six I telephone you. When can I ever say to myself: I have nothing to be responsible for in the next six hours?"

Susan, hearing this, was remorseful. Because it was true. The good marriage, the house, the children, depended just as much on his voluntary bondage as it did on hers. But why did he not feel bound? Why didn't he chafe and become restless? No, there was something really wrong with her and this proved it.

And that word *bondage*—why had she used it? She had never felt marriage, or the children, as bondage. Neither had he, or surely they wouldn't be together lying in each other's arms content after twelve years of marriage.

No, her state (whatever it was) was irrelevant, nothing to do with her real good life with her family. She had to accept the fact that after all, she was an irrational person and to live with it. Some people had to live with crippled arms, or stammers, or being deaf. She would have to live knowing she was subject to a state of mind she could not own.

Nevertheless, as a result of this conversation with her husband, there was a new regime next holidays.

The spare room at the top of the house now had a cardboard sign saying: PRIVATE! DO NOT DISTURB! on it. (This sign had been drawn in coloured chalks by the children, after a discussion between the parents in which it was decided this was psychologically the right thing.) The family and Mrs Parkes knew this was "Mother's Room" and that she was entitled to her privacy. Many serious conversations took place between Matthew and the children about not taking Mother for granted. Susan overheard the first, between father and Harry, the older boy, and was surprised at her irritation over it. Surely she could have a room somewhere in that big house and retire into it without such a fuss being made? Without it being so solemnly discussed? Why couldn't she simply have announced: "I'm going to fit out the little top room for myself, and when I'm in it I'm not to be disturbed for anything short of fire"? Just that, and finished; instead of long earnest discussions. When she heard Harry and Matthew explaining it to the twins with Mrs Parkes coming in—"Yes, well, a family sometimes gets on top of a woman"—she had to go right away to the bottom of the garden until the devils of exasperation had finished their dance in her blood.

But now there was a room, and she could go there when she liked, she used it seldom: she felt even more caged there than in her bedroom. One day she had gone up there after a lunch for ten children she had cooked and served because Mrs Parkes was not there, and had sat alone for a while looking into the garden. She saw the children stream out from the kitchen and stand looking up at the window where she sat behind the curtains. They were all—her children and their friends—discussing Mother's Room. A few minutes later, the chase of children in some game came pounding up the stairs, but ended as abruptly as if they had fallen over a ravine, so sudden was the silence. They had remembered she was there, and had gone silent in a great gale of "Hush! Shhhhhh! Quiet, you'll disturb her. . . ." And they went tiptoeing downstairs like criminal conspirators. When she came down to make tea for them, they all apologised. The twins put their arms around her, from front and back, making a human cage of loving limbs, and promised it would never occur again. "We forgot, Mummy, we forgot all about it!"

What it amounted to was that Mother's Room, and her need for privacy, had become a valuable lesson in respect for other people's rights. Quite soon Susan was going up to the room only because it was a lesson it was a pity to drop. Then she took sewing up there, and the children and Mrs Parkes came in and out: it had become another family room.

She sighed, and smiled, and resigned herself—she made jokes at her own expense with Matthew over the room. That is, she did from the self she liked, she respected. But at the same time, something inside her howled with impatience, with rage. . . . And she was frightened. One day she found herself kneeling by her bed and praying: "Dear God, keep it away from me, keep him away from me." She meant the devil, for she now thought of it, not caring if she were irrational, as some sort of demon. She imagined him, or it, as a youngish man, or perhaps a middle-aged man pretending to be young. Or a man young-looking from immaturity? At any rate, she saw the young-looking face which, when she drew closer, had dry lines about mouth and eyes. He was thinnish, meagre in build. And he had a reddish complexion, and ginger hair. That was he—a gingery, energetic man, and he wore a reddish hairy jacket, unpleasant to the touch.

Well, one day she saw him. She was standing at the bottom of the garden, watching the river ebb past, when she raised her eyes and saw this person, or being, sitting on the white stone bench. He was looking at her, and grinning. In his hand was a long crooked stick, which he had picked off the ground, or broken off the tree above him. He was absent-mindedly, out of an absent-minded or freakish impulse of spite, using the stick to stir around in the coils of a blindworm or a grass snake (or some kind of snakelike creature: it was whitish and unhealthy to look at, unpleasant). The snake was twisting about, flinging its coils from side to side in a kind of dance of protest against the teasing prodding stick.

Susan looked at him thinking: Who is the stranger? What is he doing in our garden? Then she recognised the man around whom her terrors had crystallised. As she did so, he vanished. She made herself walk over to the bench. A shadow from a branch lay across thin emerald grass, moving jerkily over its roughness, and she could see why she had taken it for a snake, lashing and twisting. She went back to the house thinking: Right, then, so I've seen him with my own eyes, so I'm not crazy after all—there *is* a danger because I've seen him. He is lurking in the garden and sometimes even in the house, and he wants *to get into me and to take me over.*

She dreamed of having a room or a place, anywhere, where she could go and sit, by herself, no one knowing where she was.

Once, near Victoria, she found herself outside a news agent that had Rooms to Let advertised. She decided to rent a room, telling no one. Sometimes she could take the train in to Richmond and sit alone in it for an hour or two. Yet how could she? A room would cost three or four pounds a week, and she earned no money, and how could she explain to Matthew that she needed such a sum? What for? It did not occur to her that she was taking it for granted she wasn't going to tell him about the room.

Well, it was out of the question, having a room; yet she knew she must.

One day, when a school term was well established, and none of the children had measles or other ailments, and everything seemed in order, she did the shopping early, explained to Mrs Parkes she was meeting an old school friend, took the train to Victoria, searched until she found a small quiet hotel, and asked for a room for the day. They did not let rooms by the day, the manageress said, looking doubtful, since Susan so obviously was not the kind of woman who needed a room for unrespectable reasons. Susan made a long explanation about not being well, being unable to shop without frequent rests for lying down. At last she was allowed to rent the room provided she paid a full night's price for it. She was taken up by the manageress and a maid, both concerned over the state of her health . . . which must be pretty bad if, living at Richmond (she had signed her name and address in the register), she needed a shelter at Victoria.

The room was ordinary and anonymous, and was just what Susan needed. She put a shilling in the gas fire, and sat, eyes shut, in a dingy armchair with her back to a dingy window. She was alone. She was alone. She was alone. She could feel pressures lifting off her. First the sounds of traffic came very loud; then they seemed to vanish; she might even have slept a little. A knock on the door: it was Miss Townsend the manageress, bringing her a cup of tea with her own hands, so concerned was she over Susan's long silence and possible illness.

Miss Townsend was a lonely woman of fifty, running this hotel with all the rectitude expected of her, and she sensed in Susan the possibility of understanding companionship. She stayed to talk. Susan found herself in the middle of a fantastic story about her illness, which got more and more improbable as she tried to make it tally with the large house at Richmond, well-off husband, and four children. Suppose she said instead: Miss Townsend, I'm here in your hotel because I need to be alone for a few hours, above all *alone and with no one knowing where I am.* She said it mentally, and saw, mentally, the look that would inevitably come on Miss Townsend's elderly maiden's face. "Miss Townsend, my four children and my husband are driving me insane, do you understand that? Yes, I can see from the gleam of hysteria in your eyes that comes from loneliness controlled but only just contained that I've got everything in the world you've ever longed for. Well, Miss Townsend, I don't want any of it. You can have it, Miss Townsend. I wish I was absolutely alone in the world, like you. Miss Townsend, I'm besieged by seven devils, Miss Townsend, Miss Townsend, let me stay here in your hotel where the devils can't get me. . . ." Instead of saying all this, she described her anaemia, agreed to try Miss Townsend's remedy for it, which was raw liver, minced, between whole-meal bread, and said yes, perhaps it would be better if she stayed at home and let a friend do shopping for her. She paid her bill and left the hotel, defeated.

At home Mrs Parkes said she didn't really like it, no, not really, when Mrs Rawlings was away from nine in the morning until five. The teacher had telephoned from school to say Joan's teeth were paining her, and she hadn't known what to say; and what was she to make for the children's tea, Mrs Rawlings hadn't said.

All this was nonsense, of course. Mrs Parkes's complaint was that Susan had withdrawn herself spiritually, leaving the burden of the big house on her.

Susan looked back at her day of "freedom" which had resulted in her becoming a friend to the lonely Miss Townsend, and in Mrs Parkes's remonstrances. Yet she remembered the short blissful hour of being alone, really alone. She was determined to arrange her life, no matter what it cost, so that she could have that solitude more often. An absolute solitude, where no one knew her or cared about her.

But how? She thought of saying to her old employer: I want you to back me up in a story with Matthew that I am doing part-time work for you. The truth is that . . . but she would have to tell him a lie too, and which lie? She could not say: I want to sit by myself three or four times a week in a rented room. And besides, he knew Matthew, and she could not really ask him to tell lies on her behalf, apart from his being bound to think it meant a lover.

Suppose she really took a part-time job, which she could get through fast and efficiently, leaving time for herself. What job? Addressing envelopes? Canvassing?

And there was Mrs Parkes, working widow, who knew exactly what she was prepared to give to the house, who knew by instinct when her mistress withdrew in spirit from her responsibilities. Mrs Parkes was one of the servers of this world, but she needed someone to serve. She had to have Mrs Rawlings, her madam, at the top of the house or in the garden, so that she could come and get support from her: "Yes, the bread's not what it was when I was a girl. . . . Yes, Harry's got a wonderful appetite, I wonder where he puts it all. . . . Yes, it's lucky the twins are so much of a size, they can wear each other's shoes, that's a saving in these hard times. . . . Yes, the cherry jam from Switzerland is not a patch on the jam from Poland, and three times the price. . . ." And so on. That sort of talk Mrs Parkes must have, every day, or she would leave, not knowing herself why she left.

Susan Rawlings, thinking these thoughts, found that she was prowling through the great thicketed garden like a wild cat: she was walking up the stairs, down the stairs, through the rooms, into the garden, along the brown running river, back, up through the house, down again. . . . It was a wonder Mrs Parkes did not think it strange. But on the contrary, Mrs Rawlings could do what she liked, she could stand on her head if she wanted, provided she was *there*. Susan Rawlings prowled and muttered through her house, hating Mrs Parkes, hating poor Miss Townsend, dreaming of her hour of solitude in the dingy respectability of Miss Townsend's hotel bedroom, and she knew quite well she was mad. Yes, she was mad.

She said to Matthew that she must have a holiday. Matthew agreed with her. This was not as things had been once—how they had talked in each other's arms in the marriage bed. He had, she knew, diagnosed her finally as *unreasonable*. She had become someone outside himself that he had to manage. They were living side by side in this house like two tolerably friendly strangers.

Having told Mrs Parkes, or rather, asked for her permission, she went off on a walking holiday in Wales. She chose the remotest place she knew of. Every morning the children telephoned her before they went off to school, to encourage and support her, just as they had over Mother's Room. Every evening she telephoned them, spoke to each child in turn, and then to Matthew. Mrs Parkes, given permission to telephone for instructions or advice, did so every day at lunchtime. When, as happened three times, Mrs Rawlings was out on the mountainside, Mrs Parkes asked that she should ring back at such and such a time, for she would not be happy in what she was doing without Mrs Rawlings' blessing.

Susan prowled over wild country with the telephone wire holding her to her duty like a leash. The next time she must telephone, or wait to be telephoned, nailed her to her cross. The mountains themselves seemed trammelled by her unfreedom. Everywhere on the mountains, where she met no one at all, from breakfast time to dusk, excepting sheep, or a shepherd, she came face to face with her own craziness which might attack her in the broadest valleys, so that they seemed too small; or on a mountaintop from which she could see a hundred other mountains and valleys, so that they seemed too low, too small, with the sky pressing down too close. She would stand gazing at a hillside brilliant with ferns and bracken, jewelled with running water, and see nothing but her devil, who lifted inhuman eyes at her from where he leaned negligently on a rock, switching at his ugly yellow boots with a leafy twig.

She returned to her home and family, with the Welsh emptiness at the back of her mind like a promise of freedom.

She told her husband she wanted to have an *au pair* girl.

They were in their bedroom, it was late at night, the children slept. He sat, shirted and slippered, in a chair by the window, looking out. She sat brushing her hair and watching him in the mirror. A time-hallowed scene in the connubial bedroom. He said nothing, while she heard the arguments coming into his mind, only to be rejected because every one was *reasonable*.

"It seems strange to get one now, after all, the children are in school most of the day. Surely the time for you to have help was when you were stuck with them day and night. Why don't you ask Mrs Parkes to cook for you? She's even offered to—I can understand if you are tired of cooking for six people. But you know that an *au pair* girl means all kinds of problems, it's not like having an ordinary char in during the day. . . ."

Finally he said carefully: "Are you thinking of going back to work?"

"No," she said, "no, not really," She made herself sound vague, rather stupid. She went on brushing her black hair and peering at herself so as to be oblivious of the short uneasy glances her Matthew kept giving her. "Do you think we can't afford it?" she went on vaguely, not at all the old efficient Susan who knew exactly what they could afford.

"It's not that," he said, looking out of the window at dark trees, so as not to look at her. Meanwhile she examined a round, candid, pleasant face with clear dark brows and clear grey eyes. A sensible face. She brushed thick healthy black hair and thought: Yet that's the reflection of a madwoman. How very strange! Much more to the point if what looked back at me was the gingery green-eyed demon with his dry meagre smile. . . . Why wasn't Matthew agreeing? After all, what else could he do? She was breaking her part of the bargain and there was no way of forcing her to keep it: that her spirit, her soul, should live in this house, so that the people in it could grow like plants in water, and Mrs Parkes remain content in their service. In return for this, he would be a good loving husband, and responsible towards the children. Well, nothing like this had been true of either of them for a long time. He did his duty, perfunctorily; she did not even pretend to do hers. And he had become like other husbands, with his real life in his work and the people he met there, and very likely a serious affair. All this was her fault.

At last he drew heavy curtains, blotting out the trees, and turned to force her attention: "Susan, are you really sure we need a girl?" But she would not meet his appeal at all: She was running the brush over her hair again and again, lifting fine black clouds in a small hiss of electricity. She was peering in and smiling as if she were amused at the clinging hissing hair that followed the brush.

"Yes, I think it would be a good idea on the whole," she said, with the cunning of a madwoman evading the real point.

In the mirror she could see her Matthew lying on his back, his hands behind his head, staring upwards, his face sad and hard. She felt her heart (the old heart of Susan Rawlings) soften and call out to him. But she set it to be indifferent.

He said: "Susan, the children?" It was an appeal that *almost* reached her. He opened his arms, lifting them from where they had lain by his sides, palms up, empty. She had only to run across and fling herself into them, onto his hard, warm chest, and melt into herself, into Susan. But she could not. She would not see his lifted arms. She said vaguely: "Well, surely it'll be even better for them? We'll get a French or a German girl and they'll learn the language."

In the dark she lay beside him, feeling frozen, a stranger. She felt as if Susan had been spirited away. She disliked very much this woman who lay here, cold and indifferent beside a suffering man, but she could not change her.

Next morning she set about getting a girl, and very soon came Sophie Traub from Hamburg, a girl of twenty, laughing, healthy, blue-eyed, intending to learn English. Indeed, she already spoke a good deal. In return for a room—"Mother's Room"—and her food, she undertook to do some light cooking, and to be with the children when Mrs Rawlings asked. She was an intelligent girl and understood perfectly what was needed. Susan said: "I go off sometimes, for the morning or for the day—well, sometimes the children run home from school, or they ring up, or a teacher rings up. I should be here, really. And there's the daily woman. . . ." And Sophie laughed her deep fruity *Fräulein's* laugh, showed her fine white teeth and her dimples, and said: "You want some person to play mistress of the house sometimes, not so?"

"Yes, that is just so," said Susan, a bit dry, despite herself, thinking in secret fear how easy it was, how much nearer to the end she was than she thought. Healthy Fräulein Traub's instant understanding of their position proved this to be true.

The *au pair* girl, because of her own common sense, or (as Susan said to herself with her new inward shudder) because she had been *chosen* so well by Susan, was a success with everyone, the children liking her, Mrs Parkes forgetting almost at once that she was German, and Matthew finding her "nice to have around the house." For he was now taking things as they came, from the surface of life, withdrawn both as a husband and a father from the household.

One day Susan saw how Sophie and Mrs Parkes were talking and laughing in the kitchen, and she announced that she would be away until teatime. She knew exactly where to go and what she must look for. She took the District Line to South Kensington, changed to the Circle, got off at Paddington, and walked around looking at the smaller hotels until she was satisfied with one which had FRED'S HOTEL painted on windowpanes that needed cleaning. The façade was a faded shiny yellow, like unhealthy skin. A door at the end of a passage said she must knock; she did, and Fred appeared. He was not at all attractive, not in any way, being fattish, and run-down, and wearing a tasteless striped suit. He had small sharp eyes in a white creased face, and was quite prepared to let Mrs Jones (she chose the farcical name deliberately, staring him out) have a room three days a week from ten until six. Provided of course that she paid in advance each time she came? Susan produced fifteen shillings (no price had been set by him) and held it out, still fixing him with a bold unblinking challenge she had not known until then she could use at will. Looking at her still, he took up a ten-shilling note from her palm between thumb and forefinger, fingered it; then shuffled up two half crowns, held out his own palm with these bits of money displayed thereon, and let his gaze lower broodingly at them. They were standing in the passage, a red-shaded light above, bare boards beneath, and a strong smell of floor polish rising about them. He shot his gaze up at her over the still-extended palm, and smiled as if to say: What do you take me for? "I shan't," said Susan, "be using this room for the purposes of making money." He still waited. She added another five shillings, at which he nodded and said: "You pay, and I ask no questions." "Good," said Susan. He now went past her to the stairs, and there waited a moment: the light from the street door being in her eyes, she lost sight of him momentarily. Then she saw a sober-suited, white-faced, white-balding little man trotting up the stairs like a waiter, and she went after him. They proceeded in utter silence up the stairs of this house where no questions were asked—Fred's Hotel, which could afford the freedom for its visitors that poor Miss Townsend's hotel could not. The room was hideous. It had a single window, with thin green brocade curtains, a three-quarter bed that had a cheap green satin bedspread on it, a fireplace with a gas fire and a shilling meter by it, a chest of drawers, and a green wicker armchair.

"Thank you," said Susan, knowing that Fred (if this was Fred, and not George, or Herbert or Charlie) was looking at her not so much with curiosity, an emotion he would not own to, for professional reasons, but with a philosophical sense of what was appropriate. Having taken her money and shown her up and agreed to everything, he was clearly disapproving of her for coming here. She did not belong here at all, so his look said. (But she knew, already, how very much she did belong: the room had been waiting for her to join it.) "Would you have me called at five o'clock, please?" and he nodded and went downstairs.

It was twelve in the morning. She was free. She sat in the armchair, she simply sat, she closed her eyes and sat and let herself be alone. She was alone and no one knew where she was. When a knock came on the door she was annoyed, and prepared to show it: but it was Fred himself, it was five o'clock and he was calling her as ordered. He flicked his sharp little eyes over the room—bed, first. It was undisturbed. She might never have been in the room at all. She thanked him, said she would be returning the day after tomorrow, and left. She was back home in time to cook supper, to put the children to bed, to cook a second supper for her husband and herself later. And to welcome Sophie back from the pictures where she had gone with a friend. All these things she did cheerfully, willingly. But she was thinking all the time of the hotel room, she was longing for it with her whole being.

Three times a week. She arrived promptly at ten, looked Fred in the eyes, gave him twenty shillings, followed him up the stairs, went into the room, and shut the door on him with gentle firmness. For Fred, disapproving of her being here at all, was quite ready to let friendship, or at least acquaintanceship, follow his disapproval, if only she would let him. But he was content to go off on her dismissing nod, with the twenty shillings in his hand.

She sat in the armchair and shut her eyes.

What did she *do* in the room? Why, nothing at all. From the chair, when it had rested her, she went to the window, stretching her arms, smiling, treasuring her anonymity, to look out. She was no longer Susan Rawlings, mother of four, wife of Matthew, employer of Mrs Parkes and of Sophie Traub, with these and those relations with friends, schoolteachers, tradesmen. She no longer was mistress of the big white house and garden, owning clothes suitable for this and that activity or occasion. She was Mrs Jones, and she was alone, and she had no past and no future. Here I am, she thought, after all these years of being married and having children and playing those roles of responsibility—and I'm just the same. Yet there have been times I thought that nothing existed of me except the roles that went with being Mrs Matthew Rawlings. Yes, here I am, and if I never saw any of my family again, here I would still be . . . how very strange that is! And she leaned on the sill, and looked into the street, loving the men and women who passed, because she did not know them. She looked at the downtrodden buildings over the street, and at the sky, wet and dingy, or sometimes blue, and she felt she had never seen buildings or sky before. And then she went back to the chair, empty, her mind a blank. Sometimes she talked aloud, saying nothing—an exclamation, meaningless, followed by a comment about the floral pattern on the thin rug, or a stain on the green satin coverlet. For the most part, she wool-gathered—what word is there for it?—brooded, wandered, simply went dark, feeling emptiness run deliciously through her veins like the movement of her blood.

This room had become more her own than the house she lived in. One morning she found Fred taking her a flight higher than usual. She stopped, refusing to go up, and demanded her usual room, Number 19. "Well, you'll have to wait half an hour then," he said. Willingly she descended to the dark disinfectant-smelling hall, and sat waiting until the two, man and woman, came down the stairs, giving her swift indifferent glances before they hurried out into the street, separating at the door. She went up to the room, *her* room, which they had just vacated. It was no less hers, though the windows were set wide open, and a maid was straightening the bed as she came in.

After these days of solitude, it was both easy to play her part as mother and wife, and difficult—because it was so easy: she felt an impostor. She felt as if her shell moved here, with her family, answering to Mummy, Mother, Susan, Mrs Rawlings. She was surprised no one saw through her, that she wasn't turned out of doors, as a fake. On the contrary, it seemed the children loved her more; Matthew and she "got on" pleasantly, and Mrs Parkes was happy in her work under (for the most part, it must be confessed) Sophie Traub. At night she lay beside her husband, and they made love again, apparently just as they used to, when they were really married. But she, Susan, or the being who answered so readily and improbably to the name of Susan, was not there: she was in Fred's Hotel, in Paddington, waiting for the easing hours of solitude to begin.

Soon she made a new arrangement with Fred and with Sophie. It was for five days a week. As for the money, five pounds, she simply asked Matthew for it. She saw that she was not even frightened he might ask what for: he would give it to her, she knew that, and yet it was terrifying it could be so, for this close couple, these partners, had once known the destination of every shilling they must spend. He agreed to give her five pounds a week. She asked for just so much, not a penny more. He sounded indifferent about it. It was as if he were paying her, she thought: *paying her off*—yes, that was it. Terror came back for a moment, when she understood this, but she stilled it: things had gone too far for that. Now, every week, on Sunday nights, he gave her five pounds, turning away from her before their eyes could meet on the transaction. As for Sophie Traub, she was to be somewhere in or near the house until six at night, after which she was free. She was not to cook, or to clean, she was simply to be there. So she gardened or sewed, and asked friends in, being a person who was bound to have a lot of friends. If the children were sick, she nursed them. If teachers telephoned, she answered them sensibly. For the five daytimes in the school week, she was altogether the mistress of the house.

One night in the bedroom, Matthew asked: "Susan, I don't want to interfere—don't think that, please—but are you sure you are well?"

She was brushing her hair at the mirror. She made two more strokes on either side of her head, before she replied: "Yes, dear, I am sure I am well."

He was again lying on his back, his big blond head on his hands, his elbows angled up and part-concealing his face. He said: "Then Susan, I have to ask you this question, though you must understand, I'm not putting any sort of pressure on you." (Susan heard the word pressure with dismay, because this was inevitable, of course she could not go on like this.) "Are things going to go on like this?"

"Well," she said, going vague and bright and idiotic again, so as to escape: "Well, I don't see why not."

He was jerking his elbows up and down, in annoyance or in pain, and, looking at him, she saw he had got thin, even gaunt; and restless angry movements were not what she remembered of him. He said: "Do you want a divorce, is that it?"

At this, Susan only with the greatest difficulty stopped herself from laughing: she could hear the bright bubbling laughter she *would* have emitted, had she let herself. He could only mean one thing: she had a lover, and that was why she spent her days in London, as lost to him as if she had vanished to another continent.

Then the small panic set in again: she understood that he hoped she did have a lover, he was begging her to say so, because otherwise it would be too terrifying.

She thought this out, as she brushed her hair, watching the fine black stuff fly up to make its little clouds of electricity, hiss, hiss, hiss. Behind her head, across the room, was a blue wall. She realised she was absorbed in watching the black hair making shapes against the blue. She should be answering him. "Do *you* want a divorce, Matthew?"

He said: "That surely isn't the point, is it?"

"You brought it up, I didn't," she said, brightly, suppressing meaningless tinkling laughter.

Next day she asked Fred: "Have enquiries been made for me?"

He hesitated, and she said: "I've been coming here a year now. I've made no trouble, and you've been paid every day. I have a right to be told."

"As a matter of fact, Mrs Jones, a man did come asking."

"A man from a detective agency?"

"Well, he could have been, couldn't he?"

"I was asking you . . . well, what did you tell him?"

"I told him a Mrs Jones came every weekday from ten until five or six and stayed in Number Nineteen by herself."

"Describing me?"

"Well Mrs Jones, I had no alternative. Put yourself in my place."

"By rights I should deduct what that man gave you for the information."

He raised shocked eyes: she was not the sort of person to make jokes like this! Then he chose to laugh: a pinkish wet slit appeared across his white crinkled face: his eyes positively begged her to laugh, otherwise he might lose some money. She remained grave, looking at him.

He stopped laughing and said: "You want to go up now?"—returning to the familiarity, the comradeship, of the country where no questions are asked, on which (and he knew it) she depended completely.

She went up to sit in her wicker chair. But it was not the same. Her husband had searched her out. (The world had searched her out.) The pressures were on her. She was here with his connivance. He might walk in at any moment, here, into Room 19. She imagined the report from the detective agency: "A woman calling herself Mrs Jones, fitting the description of your wife (etc., etc., etc.), stays alone all day in room No. 19. She insists on this room, waits for it if it is engaged. As far as the proprietor knows she receives no visitors there, male or female." A report something on these lines, Matthew must have received.

Well of course he was right: things couldn't go on like this. He had put an end to it all simply by sending the detective after her.

She tried to shrink herself back into the shelter of the room, a snail pecked out of its shell and trying to squirm back. But the peace of the room had gone. She was trying consciously to revive it, trying to let go into the dark creative trance (or whatever it was) that she had found there. It was no use, yet she craved for it, she was as ill as a suddenly deprived addict.

Several times she returned to the room, to look for herself there, but instead she found the unnamed spirit of restlessness, a prickling fevered hunger for movement, an irritable self-consciousness that made her brain feel as if it had coloured lights going on and off inside it. Instead of the soft dark that had been the room's air, were now waiting for her demons that made her dash blindly about, muttering words of hate; she was impelling herself from point to point like a moth dashing itself against a windowpane, sliding to the bottom, fluttering off on broken wings, then crashing into the invisible barrier again. And again and again. Soon she was exhausted, and she told Fred that for a while she would not be needing the room, she was going on holiday. Home she went, to the big white house by the river. The middle of a weekday, and she felt guilty at returning to her own home when not expected. She stood unseen, looking in at the kitchen window. Mrs Parkes, wearing a discarded floral overall of Susan's, was stooping to slide something into the oven. Sophie, arms folded, was leaning her back against a cupboard and laughing at some joke made by a girl not seen before by Susan—a dark foreign girl, Sophie's visitor. In an armchair Molly, one of the twins, lay curled, sucking her thumb and watching the grownups. She must have some sickness, to be kept from school. The child's listless face, the dark circles under her eyes, hurt Susan: Molly was looking at the three grownups working and talking in exactly the same way Susan looked at the four through the kitchen window: she was remote, shut off from them.

But then, just as Susan imagined herself going in, picking up the little girl, and sitting in an armchair with her, stroking her probably heated forehead,

Sophie did just that: she had been standing on one leg, the other knee flexed, its foot set against the wall. Now she let her foot in its ribbon-tied red shoe slide down the wall, and stood solid on two feet, clapping her hands before and behind her, and sang a couple of lines in German, so that the child lifted her heavy eyes at her and began to smile. Then she walked, or rather skipped, over to the child, swung her up, and let her fall into her lap at the same moment she sat herself. She said "Hopla! Hopla! Molly . . ." and began stroking the dark untidy young head that Molly laid on her shoulder for comfort.

Well. . . . Susan blinked the tears of farewell out of her eyes, and went quietly up the house to her bedroom. There she sat looking at the river through the trees. She felt at peace, but in a way that was new to her. She had no desire to move, to talk, to do anything at all. The devils that had haunted the house, the garden, were not there; but she knew it was because her soul was in Room 19 in Fred's Hotel; she was not really here at all. It was a sensation that should have been frightening: to sit at her own bedroom window, listening to Sophie's rich young voice sing German nursery songs to her child, listening to Mrs Parkes clatter and move below, and to know that all this had nothing to do with her: she was already out of it.

Later, she made herself go down and say she was home: it was unfair to be here unannounced. She took lunch with Mrs Parkes, Sophie, Sophie's Italian friend Maria, and her daughter Molly, and felt like a visitor.

A few days later, at bedtime, Matthew said: "Here's your five pounds," and pushed them over at her. Yet he must have known she had not been leaving the house at all.

She shook her head, gave it back to him, and said, in explanation, not in accusation: "As soon as you knew where I was, there was no point."

He nodded, not looking at her. He was turned away from her: thinking, she knew, how best to handle this wife who terrified him.

He said: "I wasn't trying to . . . it's just that I was worried."

"Yes, I know."

"I must confess that I was beginning to wonder . . ."

"You thought that I had a lover?"

"Yes, I am afraid I did."

She knew that he wished she had. She sat wondering how to say: "For a year now I've been spending all my days in a very sordid hotel room. It's the place where I'm happy. In fact, without it I don't exist." She heard herself saying this, and understood how terrified he was that she might. So instead she said: "Well, perhaps you're not far wrong."

Probably Matthew would think the hotel proprietor lied: he would want to think so.

"Well," he said, and she could hear his voice spring up, so to speak, with relief: "in that case I must confess I've got a bit of an affair on myself."

She said, detached and interested: "Really? Who is she?" and saw Matthew's startled look because of this reaction.

"It's Phil. Phil Hunt."

She had known Phil Hunt well in the old unmarried days. She was thinking: No, she won't do, she's too neurotic and difficult. She's never been happy yet. Sophie's much better: Well Matthew will see that himself, as sensible as he is.

This line of thought went on in silence, while she said aloud: "It's no point in telling you about mine, because you don't know him."

Quick, quick, invent, she thought. Remember how you invented all that nonsense for Miss Townsend.

She began slowly, careful not to contradict herself: "His name is Michael"—(*Michael What?*)—"Michael Plant." (What a silly name!) "He's rather like you—in looks, I mean." And indeed, she could imagine herself being touched by no one but Matthew himself. "He's a publisher." (Really? Why?) "He's got a wife already and two children."

She brought out this fantasy, proud of herself.

Matthew said: "Are you two thinking of marrying?"

She said, before she could stop herself: "Good God, *no!*"

She realised, if Matthew wanted to marry Phil Hunt, that this was too emphatic, but apparently it was all right, for his voice sounded relieved as he said: "It is a bit impossible to imagine oneself married to anyone else, isn't it?" With which he pulled her to him, so that her head lay on his shoulder. She turned her face into the dark of his flesh, and listened to the blood pounding through her ears saying: I am alone, I am alone, I am alone.

In the morning Susan lay in bed while he dressed.

He had been thinking things out in the night, because now he said: "Susan, why don't we make a foursome?"

Of course, she said to herself, of course he would be bound to say that. If one is sensible, if one is reasonable, if one never allows oneself a base thought or an envious emotion, naturally one says: Let's make a foursome!

"Why not?" she said.

"We could all meet for lunch. I mean, it's ridiculous, you sneaking off to filthy hotels, and me staying late at the office, and all the lies everyone has to tell."

What on earth did I say his name was?—she panicked, then said: "I think it's a good idea, but Michael is away at the moment. When he comes back though—and I'm sure you two would like each other."

"He's away, is he? So that's why you've been . . ." Her husband put his hand to the knot of his tie in a gesture of male coquetry she would not before have associated with him; and he bent to kiss her cheek with the expression that goes with the words: Oh you naughty little puss! And she felt its answering look, naughty and coy, come onto her face.

Inside she was dissolving in horror at them both, at how far they had both sunk from honesty of emotion.

So now she was saddled with a lover, and he had a mistress! How ordinary, how reassuring, how jolly! And now they would make a foursome of it, and go about to theatres and restaurants. After all, the Rawlings could well afford that sort of thing, and presumably the publisher Michael Plant could afford to do himself and his mistress quite well. No, there was nothing to stop the four of them developing the most intricate relationship of civilised tolerance, all enveloped in a charming afterglow of autumnal passion. Perhaps they would all go off on holidays together? She had known people who did. Or perhaps Matthew would draw the line there? Why should he, though, if he was capable of talking about "foursomes" at all?

She lay in the empty bedroom, listening to the car drive off with Matthew in it, off to work. Then she heard the children clattering off to school to the accompaniment of Sophie's cheerfully ringing voice. She slid down into the hollow of the bed, for shelter against her own irrelevance. And she stretched out her hand to the hollow where her husband's body had lain, but found no comfort there: he was not her husband. She curled herself up in a small tight ball under the clothes: she could stay here all day, all week, indeed, all her life.

But in a few days she must produce Michael Plant, and—but how? She must presumably find some agreeable man prepared to impersonate a publisher called Michael Plant. And in return for which she would—what? Well, for one thing they would make love. The idea made her want to cry with sheer exhaustion. Oh no, she had finished with all that—the proof of it was that the words "make love," or even imagining it, trying hard to revive no more than the pleasures of sensuality, let alone affection, or love, made her want to run away and hide from the sheer effort of the thing. . . . Good Lord, why make love at all? Why make love with anyone? Or if you are going to make love, what does it matter who with? Why shouldn't she simply walk into the street, pick up a man and have a roaring sexual affair with him? Why not? Or even with Fred? What difference did it make?

But she had let herself in for it—an interminable stretch of time with a lover, called Michael, as part of a gallant civilised foursome. Well, she could not, and she would not.

She got up, dressed, went down to find Mrs Parkes, and asked her for the loan of a pound, since Matthew, she said, had forgotten to leave her money. She exchanged with Mrs Parkes variations on the theme that husbands are all the same, they don't think, and without saying a word to Sophie, whose voice could be heard upstairs from the telephone, walked to the underground, travelled to South Kensington, changed to the Inner Circle, got out at Paddington, and walked to Fred's Hotel. There she told Fred that she wasn't going on holiday after all, she needed the room. She would have to wait an hour, Fred said. She went to a busy tearoom-cum-restaurant around the corner, and sat watching the people flow in and out the door that kept swinging open and shut, watched them mingle and merge and separate, felt her being flow into them, into their movement. When the hour was up she left a half crown for her pot of tea, and left the place without looking back at it, just as she had left her house, the big, beautiful white house, without another look, but silently dedicating it to Sophie. She returned to Fred, received the key of No. 19, now free, and ascended the grimy stairs slowly, letting floor after floor fall away below her, keeping her eyes lifted, so that floor after floor descended jerkily to her level of vision, and fell away out of sight.

No. 19 was the same. She saw everything with an acute, narrow, checking glance: the cheap shine of the satin spread, which had been replaced carelessly after the two bodies had finished their convulsions under it; a trace of powder on the glass that topped the chest of drawers; an intense green shade in a fold of the curtain. She stood at the window, looking down, watching people pass and pass and pass until her mind went dark from the constant movement. Then she sat in the wicker chair, letting herself go slack. But she had to be careful, because she did not want, today, to be surprised by Fred's knock at five o'clock.

The demons were not here. They had gone forever, because she was buying her freedom from them. She was slipping already into the dark fructifying dream that seemed to caress her inwardly, like the movement of her blood . . . but she had to think about Matthew first. Should she write a letter for the coroner? But what should she say? She would like to leave him with the look on his face she had seen this morning—banal, admittedly, but at least confidently healthy. Well, that was impossible, one did not look like that with a wife dead from suicide. But how to leave him believing she was dying because of a man—because of the fascinating publisher Michael Plant? Oh, how ridiculous! How absurd! How humiliating! But she decided not to trouble about it, simply not to think about the living. If he wanted to believe she had a lover, he would believe it. And he *did* want to believe it. Even when he had found out that there was no publisher in London called Michael Plant, he would think: Oh poor Susan, she was afraid to give me his real name.

And what did it matter whether he married Phil Hunt or Sophie? Though it ought to be Sophie, who was already the mother of those children . . . and what hypocrisy to sit here worrying about the children, when she was going to leave them because she had not got the energy to stay.

She had about four hours. She spent them delightfully, darkly, sweetly, letting herself slide gently, gently, to the edge of the river. Then, with hardly a break in her consciousness, she got up, pushed the thin rug against the door, made sure the windows were tight shut, put two shillings in the meter, and turned on the gas. For the first time since she had been in the room she lay on the hard bed that smelled stale, that smelled of sweat and sex.

She lay on her back on the green satin cover, but her legs were chilly. She got up, found a blanket folded in the bottom of the chest of drawers, and carefully covered her legs with it. She was quite content lying there, listening to the faint soft hiss of the gas that poured into the room, into her lungs, into her brain, as she drifted off into the dark river.

1963

PHILIP LARKIN
1922–1985

Philip Larkin was born in Coventry; was educated at its King Henry VIII School and at St. John's College, Oxford; and was for many years librarian of the Hull University Library. He wrote the poems of his first book, *The North Ship* (1945), under Yeats's strong enchantment; but released by his discovery of Hardy's *Collected Poems*, Larkin found his own voice. Like Hardy, he wrote novels, *Jill* (1946) and *A Girl in Winter* (1947), and his poems have a novelist's sense of place and skill in the handling of direct speech. He was the dominant figure in what came to be known as "the Movement," a group of poets that included Kingsley Amis, Donald Davie, and Thom Gunn, whose work (in the words of Robert Conquest's introduction to his 1956 anthology *New Lines*) "is free from both mystical and logical compulsions and—like modern philosophy—is empirical in its attitude to all that comes."

No other poet presents the welfare-state world of postimperial Britain so vividly, so unsparingly, and in the last analysis so tenderly. Much has been written of Larkin's Hardyesque pessimism, his depiction of loneliness, age, and death; however, the many negatives in his poems imply positives, out of reach of the ironic and self-deprecating speaker, but available perhaps to others more fortunate, elsewhere. His output was small; but his four volumes of poetry and his controversial anthology *The Oxford Book of Twentieth-Century English Verse* (1973) testify to the continuing vitality of a native English tradition, the tradition of Chaucer, Wordsworth, and Hardy, distinct from (and, in Larkin's view, opposed to) the imported modernist tradition of Eliot and Pound.

Church Going

Once I am sure there's nothing going on
I step inside, letting the door thud shut.
Another church: matting, seats, and stone,
And little books; sprawlings of flowers, cut
5   For Sunday, brownish now; some brass and stuff
Up at the holy end; the small neat organ;
And a tense, musty, unignorable silence,
Brewed God knows how long. Hatless, I take off
My cycle-clips in awkward reverence,

10   Move forward, run my hand around the font.
From where I stand, the roof looks almost new—
Cleaned, or restored? Someone would know: I don't.
Mounting the lectern, I peruse a few
Hectoring large-scale verses, and pronounce
15   "Here endeth" much more loudly than I'd meant.
The echoes snigger briefly. Back at the door
I sign the book, donate an Irish sixpence,[1]
Reflect the place was not worth stopping for.

Yet stop I did: in fact I often do,
20   And always end much at a loss like this,
Wondering what to look for; wondering, too,
When churches fall completely out of use
What we shall turn them into, if we shall keep
A few cathedrals chronically on show,
25   Their parchment, plate and pyx[2] in locked cases,
And let the rest rent-free to rain and sheep.
Shall we avoid them as unlucky places?

Or, after dark, will dubious women come
To make their children touch a particular stone;
30   Pick simples° for a cancer; or on some   *medicinal herbs*
Advised night see walking a dead one?
Power of some sort or other will go on
In games, in riddles, seemingly at random;

---

1. An Irish sixpence has no value in England.   2. Box in which communion wafers are kept.

But superstition, like belief, must die,
35 And what remains when disbelief has gone?
Grass, weedy pavement, brambles, buttress, sky,

A shape less recognisable each week,
A purpose more obscure. I wonder who
Will be the last, the very last, to seek
40 This place for what it was; one of the crew
That tap and jot and know what rood-lofts[3] were?
Some ruin-bibber, randy for antique,
Or Christmas-addict, counting on a whiff
Of gown-and-bands and organ-pipes and myrrh?[4]
45 Or will he be my representative,

Bored, uninformed, knowing the ghostly silt
Dispersed, yet tending to this cross of ground
Through suburb scrub because it held unspilt
So long and equably what since is found
50 Only in separation—marriage, and birth,
And death, and thoughts of these—for which was built
This special shell? For, though I've no idea
What this accoutred frowsty barn is worth,
It pleases me to stand in silence here;

55 A serious house on serious earth it is,
In whose blent air all our compulsions meet,
Are recognised, and robed as destinies.
And that much never can be obsolete,
Since someone will forever be surprising
60 A hunger in himself to be more serious,
And gravitating with it to this ground,
Which, he once heard, was proper to grow wise in,
If only that so many dead lie round.

1954   1955

MCMXIV[1]

Those long uneven lines
Standing as patiently
As if they were stretched outside
The Oval or Villa Park,[2]
5 The crowns of hats, the sun
On moustached archaic faces
Grinning as if it were all
An August bank Holiday lark;

3. Galleries on top of carved screens separating
the nave of a church from the choir.
4. Gum resin, from trees of genus *Commiphora*,
used in the making of incense; one of three presents given by the Three Wise Men to the infant
Jesus. "Gown-and-bands": gown and decorative
collar worn by clergymen.
1. 1914, in Roman numerals, as incised on stone
memorials to the dead of World War I.
2. London cricket ground and Birmingham football ground.

And the shut shops, the bleached,
10 Established names on the sunblinds,
The farthings and sovereigns,[3]
And dark-clothed children at play
Called after kings and queens,
The tin advertisements
15 For cocoa and twist,° and the pubs   *tobacco*
Wide open all day;

And the countryside not caring:
The place-names all hazed over
With flowering grasses, and fields
20 Shadowing Domesday lines[4]
Under wheat's restless silence;
The differently-dressed servants
With tiny rooms in huge houses,
The dust behind limousines;

25 Never such innocence,
Never before or since,
As changed itself to past
Without a word—the men
Leaving the gardens tidy,
30 The thousands of marriages
Lasting a little while longer:
Never such innocence again.

1960   1964

Talking in Bed

Talking in bed ought to be easiest,
Lying together there goes back so far,
An emblem of two people being honest.

Yet more and more time passes silently.
5 Outside, the wind's incomplete unrest
Builds and disperses clouds about the sky,

And dark towns heap up on the horizon.
None of this cares for us. Nothing shows why
At this unique distance from isolation

10 It becomes still more difficult to find
Words at once true and kind,
Or not untrue and not unkind.

1960   1964

3. At that time, the least valuable and the most valuable British coins, respectively.
4. The still-visible boundaries of medieval farmers' long and narrow plots, ownership of which is recorded in William the Conqueror's *Domesday Book* (1085–86).

Ambulances

Closed like confessionals,[1] they thread
Loud noons of cities, giving back
None of the glances they absorb.
Light glossy grey, arms on a plaque,
5 They come to rest at any kerb:
All streets in time are visited.

Then children strewn on steps or road,
Or women coming from the shops
Past smells of different dinners, see
10 A wild white face that overtops
Red stretcher-blankets momently
As it is carried in and stowed,

And sense the solving emptiness
That lies just under all we do,
15 And for a second get it whole,
So permanent and blank and true.
The fastened doors recede. *Poor soul,*
They whisper at their own distress;

For borne away in deadened air
20 May go the sudden shut of loss
Round something nearly at an end,
And what cohered in it across
The years, the unique random blend
Of families and fashions, there

25 At last begin to loosen. Far
From the exchange of love to lie
Unreachable inside a room
The traffic parts to let go by
Brings closer what is left to come,
30 And dulls to distance all we are.

1961   1964

High Windows

When I see a couple of kids
And guess he's fucking her and she's
Taking pills or wearing a diaphragm,
I know this is paradise

5 Everyone old has dreamed of all their lives—
Bonds and gestures pushed to one side

---

1. Enclosed stalls in Roman Catholic churches in which priests hear confession.

Like an outdated combine harvester,
And everyone young going down the long slide

To happiness, endlessly. I wonder if
10   Anyone looked at me, forty years back,
And thought, *That'll be the life;*
No God any more, or sweating in the dark

About hell and that, or having to hide
What you think of the priest. He
15   *And his lot will all go down the long slide*
Like free bloody birds. And immediately

Rather than words comes the thought of high windows:
The sun-comprehending glass,
And beyond it, the deep blue air, that shows
20   Nothing, and is nowhere, and is endless.

1967   1974

Sad Steps[1]

Groping back to bed after a piss
I part thick curtains, and am startled by
The rapid clouds, the moon's cleanliness.

Four o'clock: wedge-shadowed gardens lie
5   Under a cavernous, a wind-picked sky.
There's something laughable about this,

The way the moon dashes through clouds that blow
Loosely as cannon-smoke to stand apart
(Stone-coloured light sharpening the roofs below)

10   High and preposterous and separate—
Lozenge of love! Medallion of art!
O wolves of memory! Immensements! No,

One shivers slightly, looking up there.
The hardness and the brightness and the plain
15   Far-reaching singleness of that wide stare

Is a reminder of the strength and pain
Of being young; that it can't come again,
But is for others undiminished somewhere.

1968   1974

---

1. Cf. Sir Philip Sidney's *Astrophil and Stella* 31: "With how sad steps, O Moon, thou climb'st the skies."

The Explosion

On the day of the explosion
Shadows pointed towards the pithead:°   *mine entrance*
In the sun the slagheap slept.

Down the lane came men in pitboots
5 Coughing oath-edged talk and pipe-smoke,
Shouldering off the freshened silence.

One chased after rabbits; lost them;
Came back with a nest of lark's eggs;
Showed them; lodged them in the grasses.

10 So they passed in beards and moleskins,
Fathers, brothers, nicknames, laughter,
Through the tall gates standing open.

At noon, there came a tremor; cows
Stopped chewing for a second; sun,
15 Scarfed as in a heat-haze, dimmed.

The dead go on before us, they
Are sitting in God's house in comfort,
We shall see them face to face—

Plain as lettering in the chapels
20 It was said, and for a second
Wives saw men of the explosion

Larger than in life they managed—
Gold as on a coin, or walking
Somehow from the sun towards them,

25 One showing the eggs unbroken.

1970   1974

Aubade[1]

I work all day, and get half-drunk at night.
Waking at four to soundless dark, I stare.
In time the curtain-edges will grow light.
Till then I see what's really always there:
5 Unresting death, a whole day nearer now,
Making all thought impossible but how
And where and when I shall myself die.
Arid interrogation: yet the dread

1. Music or poem announcing dawn.

Of dying, and being dead,
10   Flashes afresh to hold and horrify.

The mind blanks at the glare. Not in remorse
—The good not done, the love not given, time
Torn off unused—nor wretchedly because
An only life can take so long to climb
15   Clear of its wrong beginnings, and may never;
But at the total emptiness for ever,
The sure extinction that we travel to
And shall be lost in always. Not to be here,
Not to be anywhere,
20   And soon; nothing more terrible, nothing more true.

This is a special way of being afraid
No trick dispels. Religion used to try,
That vast moth-eaten musical brocade
Created to pretend we never die,
25   And specious stuff that says *No rational being*
Can fear a thing it will not feel, not seeing
That this is what we fear—no sight, no sound,
No touch or taste or smell, nothing to think with,
Nothing to love or link with,
30   The anaesthetic from which none come round.

And so it stays just on the edge of vision,
A small unfocused blur, a standing chill
That slows each impulse down to indecision.
Most things may never happen: this one will,
35   And realisation of it rages out
In furnace-fear when we are caught without
People or drink. Courage is no good:
It means not scaring others. Being brave
Lets no one off the grave.
40   Death is no different whined at than withstood.

Slowly light strengthens, and the room takes shape.
It stands plain as a wardrobe, what we know,
Have always known, know that we can't escape,
Yet can't accept. One side will have to go.
45   Meanwhile telephones crouch, getting ready to ring
In locked-up offices, and all the uncaring
Intricate rented world begins to rouse.
The sky is white as clay, with no sun.
Work has to be done.
50   Postmen like doctors go from house to house.

1977

NADINE GORDIMER
b. 1923

Perhaps more than the work of any other writer, the novels of Nadine Gordimer have given imaginative and moral shape to the recent history of South Africa. Since the publication of her first book, *The Lying Days* (1953), she has charted the changing patterns of response and resistance to apartheid with her exploration of the place of the European in Africa, her selection of representative themes and governing motifs for novels and short stories, and her accompanying shifts in ideological focus from a liberal to a more radical position. It was in recognition of this achievement, of having borne untiring and lucid narrative witness, that Gordimer was awarded the 1991 Nobel Prize for Literature.

Born in 1923 to Jewish immigrant parents in the South African mining town of Springs, Gordimer began writing early, from the beginning taking as her subject the pathologies and everyday realities of a racially divided society. Her decision to remain in Johannesburg through the years of political repression reflected her commitment to her subject and to her vision of a postapartheid future. In the years since apartheid was dismantled in 1994, Gordimer has continued to live and write in South Africa, and her recent novels, *None to Accompany Me* (1994) and *The House Gun* (1998), retain an uncompromising focus on the inhabitants of a racially fractured culture.

As her nonfictional essays suggest, Gordimer self-consciously places her writing within a tradition of European realism, most notably that defined by the Hungarian philosopher and critic Georg Lukács (1885–1971). Her concern—as shown in her incisive and highly acclaimed novels of the 1970s, *The Conservationist* (1974) and *Burger's Daughter* (1979)—is to evoke by way of the personal and the precisely observed particular a broader political and historical totality. It is this that gives her characters, and her novels themselves, their representativeness. As Gordimer has famously said, "politics is character in South Africa." Yet, throughout the long years of political polarization in that country and the banning of three of her own books, Gordimer has distanced herself from polemics and retained a firm humanist belief in what she variously describes as the objectivity and the inwardness of the writer. Although she has referred to an engagement with political reality as imperative and explores permutations of the question of engagement in novels like *Burger's Daughter* and *July's People* (1981), she nevertheless asserts the autonomy of the writer's perspective, "the last true judgment." Narrative for Gordimer helps define and clarify historical experience. Her keen sense of history as formation, and as demanding a continual rewriting, has ensured that her novels can be read as at once contemporary in their reference and symbolic of broader social and historical patterns, as in the paranoia surrounding the case of the buried black body on a white farm in *The Conservationist*, or in the psychosocial portrait of Rosa Burger in *Burger's Daughter*.

Gordimer has drawn criticism both for her apparent lack of attention to feminism in favor of race issues and for the wholeness and unfashionable completeness of her novels—their plottedness, meticulous scene paintings, fully realized characters. However, the searching symbolism and complexity of her narratives generally work against such judgments. As the following short story shows, a prominent feature of her writing is to give a number of different perspectives on a situation, in some cases most poignantly those of apartheid's supporters, and in this way to represent the broader anatomy of a diseased politics. Gordimer's subject, as she emphasizes, is much more than apartheid; it is the human being in history.

The Moment before the Gun Went Off

Marais Van der Vyver shot one of his farm labourers, dead. An accident, there are accidents with guns every day of the week—children playing a fatal game with a father's revolver in the cities where guns are domestic objects, nowadays, hunting mishaps like this one, in the country—but these won't be reported all over the world. Van der Vyver knows his will be. He knows that the story of the Afrikaner farmer—regional Party leader and Commandant of the local security commando—shooting a black man who worked for him will fit exactly *their* version of South Africa, it's made for them. They'll be able to use it in their boycott and divestment campaigns, it'll be another piece of evidence in their truth about the country. The papers at home will quote the story as it has appeared in the overseas press, and in the back-and-forth he and the black man will become those crudely-drawn figures on anti-apartheid banners, units in statistics of white brutality against the blacks quoted at the United Nations—he, whom they will gleefully be able to call "a leading member" of the ruling Party.

People in the farming community understand how he must feel. Bad enough to have killed a man, without helping the Party's, the government's, the country's enemies, as well. They see the truth of that. They know, reading the Sunday papers, that when Van der Vyver is quoted saying he is "terribly shocked," he will "look after the wife and children," none of those Americans and English, and none of those people at home who want to destroy the white man's power will believe him. And how they will sneer when he even says of the farm boy (according to one paper, if you can trust any of those reporters), "He was my friend, I always took him hunting with me." Those city and overseas people don't know it's true: farmers usually have one particular black boy they like to take along with them in the lands; you could call it a kind of friend, yes, friends are not only your own white people, like yourself, you take into your house, pray with in church and work with on the Party committee. But how can those others know that? They don't want to know it. They think all blacks are like the big-mouth agitators in town. And Van der Vyver's face, in the photographs, strangely opened by distress—everyone in the district remembers Marais Van der Vyver as a little boy who would go away and hide himself if he caught you smiling at him, and everyone knows him now as a man who hides any change of expression round his mouth behind a thick, soft moustache, and in his eyes by always looking at some object in hand, leaf of a crop fingered, pen or stone picked up, while concentrating on what he is saying, or while listening to you. It just goes to show what shock can do; when you look at the newspaper photographs you feel like apologising, as if you had stared in on some room where you should not be.

There will be an inquiry; there had better be, to stop the assumption of yet another case of brutality against farm workers, although there's nothing in doubt—an accident, and all the facts fully admitted by Van der Vyver. He made a statement when he arrived at the police station with the dead man in his bakkie.[1] Captain Beetge knows him well, of course; he gave him brandy. He was shaking, this big, calm, clever son of Willem Van der Vyver, who inherited the old man's best farm. The black was stone dead, nothing

---

1. Pickup truck.

to be done for him. Beetge will not tell anyone that after the brandy Van der Vyver wept. He sobbed, snot running onto his hands, like a dirty kid. The Captain was ashamed, for him, and walked out to give him a chance to recover himself.

Marais Van der Vyver left his house at three in the afternoon to cull a buck from the family of kudu[2] he protects in the bush areas of his farm. He is interested in wildlife and sees it as the farmers' sacred duty to raise game as well as cattle. As usual, he called at his shed workshop to pick up Lucas, a twenty-year-old farmhand who had shown mechanical aptitude and whom Van der Vyver himself had taught to maintain tractors and other farm machinery. He hooted, and Lucas followed the familiar routine, jumping onto the back of the truck. He liked to travel standing up there, spotting game before his employer did. He would lean forward, braced against the cab below him.

Van der Vyver had a rifle and .300 ammunition beside him in the cab. The rifle was one of his father's, because his own was at the gunsmith's in town. Since his father died (Beetge's sergeant wrote "passed on") no one had used the rifle and so when he took it from a cupboard he was sure it was not loaded. His father had never allowed a loaded gun in the house; he himself had been taught since childhood never to ride with a loaded weapon in a vehicle. But this gun was loaded. On a dirt track, Lucas thumped his fist on the cab roof three times to signal: look left. Having seen the white-ripple-marked flank of a kudu, and its fine horns raking through disguising bush, Van der Vyver drove rather fast over a pot-hole. The jolt fired the rifle. Upright, it was pointing straight through the cab roof at the head of Lucas. The bullet pierced the roof and entered Lucas's brain by way of his throat.

That is the statement of what happened. Although a man of such standing in the district, Van der Vyver had to go through the ritual of swearing that it was the truth. It has gone on record, and will be there in the archive of the local police station as long as Van der Vyver lives, and beyond that, through the lives of his children, Magnus, Helena and Karel—unless things in the country get worse, the example of black mobs in the towns spreads to the rural areas and the place is burned down as many urban police stations have been. Because nothing the government can do will appease the agitators and the whites who encourage them. Nothing satisfies them, in the cities: blacks can sit and drink in white hotels, now, the Immorality Act[3] has gone, blacks can sleep with whites. . . . It's not even a crime any more.

Van der Vyver has a high barbed security fence round his farmhouse and garden which his wife, Alida, thinks spoils completely the effect of her artificial stream with its tree-ferns beneath the jacarandas.[4] There is an aerial soaring like a flag-pole in the back yard. All his vehicles, including the truck in which the black man died, have aerials that swing their whips when the driver hits a pot-hole: they are part of the security system the farmers in the district maintain, each farm in touch with every other by radio, twenty-four hours out of twenty-four. It has already happened that infiltrators from over the border have mined remote farm roads, killing white farmers and their families out on their own property for a Sunday picnic. The pot-hole could

---

2. Large African antelope. The males have long, spirally twisted horns.
3. South African government act prohibiting sex-
ual relations between whites and other races.
4. Tropical trees with blue flowers.

have set off a land-mine, and Van der Vyver might have died with his farm boy. When neighbours use the communications system to call up and say they are sorry about "that business" with one of Van der Vyver's boys, there goes unsaid: it could have been worse.

It is obvious from the quality and fittings of the coffin that the farmer has provided money for the funeral. And an elaborate funeral means a great deal to blacks; look how they will deprive themselves of the little they have, in their lifetime, keeping up payments to a burial society so they won't go in boxwood to an unmarked grave. The young wife is pregnant (of course) and another little one, wearing red shoes several sizes too large, leans under her jutting belly. He is too young to understand what has happened, what he is witnessing that day, but neither whines nor plays about; he is solemn without knowing why. Blacks expose small children to everything, they don't protect them from the sight of fear and pain the way whites do theirs. It is the young wife who rolls her head and cries like a child, sobbing on the breast of this relative and that.

All present work for Van der Vyver or are the families of those who work; and in the weeding and harvest seasons, the women and children work for him, too, carried—wrapped in their blankets, on a truck, singing—at sunrise to the fields. The dead man's mother is a woman who can't be more than in her late thirties (they start bearing children at puberty) but she is heavily mature in a black dress between her own parents, who were already working for old Van der Vyver when Marais, like their daughter, was a child. The parents hold her as if she were a prisoner or a crazy woman to be restrained. But she says nothing, does nothing. She does not look up; she does not look at Van der Vyver, whose gun went off in the truck, she stares at the grave. Nothing will make her look up; there need be no fear that she will look up; at him. His wife, Alida, is beside him. To show the proper respect, as for any white funeral, she is wearing the navy-blue-and-cream hat she wears to church this summer. She is always supportive, although he doesn't seem to notice it; this coldness and reserve—his mother says he didn't mix well as a child—she accepts for herself but regrets that it has prevented him from being nominated, as he should be, to stand as the Party's parliamentary candidate for the district. He does not let her clothing, or that of anyone else gathered closely, make contact with him. He, too, stares at the grave. The dead man's mother and he stare at the grave in communication like that between the black man outside and the white man inside the cab the moment before the gun went off.

The moment before the gun went off was a moment of high excitement shared through the roof of the cab, as the bullet was to pass, between the young black man outside and the white farmer inside the vehicle. There were such moments, without explanation, between them, although often around the farm the farmer would pass the young man without returning a greeting, as if he did not recognize him. When the bullet went off what Van der Vyver saw was the kudu stumble in fright at the report and gallop away. Then he heard the thud behind him, and past the window saw the young man fall out of the vehicle. He was sure he had leapt up and toppled—in fright, like the buck. The farmer was almost laughing with relief, ready to tease, as he opened his door, it did not seem possible that a bullet passing through the roof could have done harm.

The young man did not laugh with him at his own fright. The farmer carried him in his arms, to the truck. He was sure, sure he could not be dead. But the young black man's blood was all over the farmer's clothes, soaking against his flesh as he drove.

How will they ever know, when they file newspaper clippings, evidence, proof, when they look at the photographs and see his face—guilty! guilty! they are right!—how will they know, when the police stations burn with all the evidence of what has happened now, and what the law made a crime in the past. How could they know that *they do not know*. Anything. The young black callously shot through the negligence of the white man was not the farmer's boy; he was his son.

1991

THOM GUNN
b. 1929

The son of a London journalist, Thomson Gunn was educated at University College School, London, then Trinity College, Cambridge, and Stanford University where he studied under the antimodernist, classically inclined poet Yvor Winters. In a poem addressed to Winters, he wrote: "You keep both Rule and Energy in view, / Much power in each, most in the balanced two." The poems of Gunn's *Fighting Terms* (1954) and *The Sense of Movement* (1957) aimed for the same balance. They were influenced by John Donne and the French philosopher Jean-Paul Sartre and introduced a modern Metaphysical poet able to give powerfully concrete expression to abstract ideas. He has said, "Most of my poems are ambivalent," and in the second half of *My Sad Captains* (1961), he began to move away from the will-driven heroes and the tight-fitting stanzas of his early work into more tentative explorations of experience and more supple syllabic or open verse forms. Moving from England to San Francisco, where he now lives, he experimented with LSD and moved also from poems presumably addressed to women to poems frankly homosexual. His most recent collection and the first for ten years, *The Man with Night Sweats* (1992), ends with a sequence of poems remarkable for their unflinching directness, compassion, and grace about the deaths of friends from AIDS. Gunn is a poet hard to classify but of rare intelligence and power in all his protean changes.

Considering the Snail

The snail pushes through a green
night, for the grass is heavy
with water and meets over
the bright path he makes, where rain
5   has darkened the earth's dark. He
moves in a wood of desire,

pale antlers barely stirring
as he hunts. I cannot tell
what power is at work, drenched there

10   with purpose, knowing nothing.
      What is a snail's fury? All
      I think is that if later

      I parted the blades above
      the tunnel and saw the thin
15   trail of broken white across
      litter, I would never have
      imagined the slow passion
      to that deliberate progress.

1956

A Map of the City

      I stand upon a hill and see
      A luminous country under me,
      Through which at two the drunk must weave;
      The transient's pause, the sailor's leave.

5   I notice, looking down the hill,
      Arms braced upon a window sill;
      And on the web of fire escapes
      Move the potential, the grey shapes.

      I hold the city here, complete:
10   And every shape defined by light
      Is mine, or corresponds to mine,
      Some flickering or some steady shine.

      This map is ground of my delight.
      Between the limits, night by night,
15   I watch a malady's advance,
      I recognize my love of chance.

      By the recurrent lights I see
      Endless potentiality,
      The crowded, broken, and unfinished!
20   I would not have the risk diminished.

1961

Black Jackets

      In the silence that prolongs the span
      Rawly of music when the record ends,
      The red-haired boy who drove a van
      In weekday overalls but, like his friends,

5   Wore cycle boots and jacket here
      To suit the Sunday hangout he was in,
      Heard, as he stretched back from his beer,
      Leather creak softly round his neck and chin.

Before him, on a coal-black sleeve
10 Remote exertion had lined, scratched, and burned
Insignia that could not revive
The heroic fall or climb where they were earned.

On the other drinkers bent together,
Concocting selves for their impervious kit,
15 He saw it as no more than leather
Which, taut across the shoulders grown to it,

Sent through the dimness of a bar
As sudden and anonymous hints of light
As those that shipping give, that are
20 Now flickers in the Bay, now lost in night.

He stretched out like a cat, and rolled
The bitterish taste of beer upon his tongue,
And listened to a joke being told:
The present was the things he stayed among.

25 If it was only loss he wore,
He wore it to assert, with fierce devotion,
Complicity and nothing more.
He recollected his initiation,

And one especially of the rites.
30 For on his shoulders they had put tattoos:
The group's name on the left, The Knights,
And on the right the slogan Born To Lose.

1961

My Sad Captains

One by one they appear in
the darkness: a few friends, and
a few with historical
names. How late they start to shine!
5 but before they fade they stand
perfectly embodied, all

the past lapping them like a
cloak of chaos. They were men
who, I thought, lived only to
10 renew the wasteful force they
spent with each hot convulsion.
They remind me, distant now.

True, they are not at rest yet,
but now that they are indeed

15 apart, winnowed from failures,
they withdraw to an orbit
and turn with disinterested
hard energy, like the stars.

1961

From the Wave

It mounts at sea, a concave wall
    Down-ribbed with shine,
And pushes forward, building tall
    Its steep incline.

5 Then from their hiding rise to sight
    Black shapes on boards
Bearing before the fringe of white
    It mottles towards.

Their pale feet curl, they poise their weight
10   With a learn'd skill.
It is the wave they imitate
    Keeps them so still.

The marbling bodies have become
    Half wave, half men,
15 Grafted it seems by feet of foam
    Some seconds, then,

Late as they can, they slice the face
    In timed procession:
Balance is triumph in this place,
20   Triumph possession.

The mindless heave of which they rode
    A fluid shelf
Breaks as they leave it, falls and, slowed,
    Loses itself.

25 Clear, the sheathed bodies slick as seals
    Loosen and tingle;
And by the board the bare foot feels
    The suck of shingle.

They paddle in the shallows still;
30   Two splash each other;
Then all swim out to wait until
    The right waves gather.

1971

DEREK WALCOTT
b. 1930

Derek Walcott was born on the island of St. Lucia in the British West Indies and educated there at St. Mary's College and at the University of the West Indies in Jamaica. He then moved to Trinidad, where he has worked as a book reviewer, art critic, playwright, and artistic director of a theater workshop. He has also been poet-in-residence at a number of American colleges and universities and is the recipient of a MacArthur Award.

At once flamboyant and disciplined, poems like his wittily titled *A Far Cry from Africa* proclaim his divided roots, as a black poet writing from within both the English literary tradition and the history of a subject people. He has since proved the truth of Yeats's statement that "out of our quarrel with ourselves we make poetry." Isolation is Walcott's theme; and as with Yeats, the writing and producing of plays has increased the emotional and dramatic range of his poetry. The movement of *Another Life* (1973) and *Midsummer* (1984) is freer, more flexible than that of earlier work, but Walcott's language still has the accuracy and energy that proclaim him—more than any of his American contemporaries—the natural heir of his friend Robert Lowell. His plays, like his poems, are infused with the spirit of syncretism, as in *Drums and Colours* (1958), which vividly conjoins Caribbean and European motifs. In constructing his popular play *O Babylon!* (1976), set among the Rastafarians of Jamaica, he described finding himself "at the center of a language poised between defiance and translation." In 1992, following the publication of his verse epic *Omeros*, which transposes elements of Homeric epic from the Aegean to the Caribbean, Walcott was awarded the Nobel Prize for Literature.

A Far Cry from Africa

A wind is ruffling the tawny pelt
Of Africa. Kikuyu,[1] quick as flies,
Batten upon the bloodstreams of the veldt.[2]
Corpses are scattered through a paradise.
5   Only the worm, colonel of carrion, cries:
"Waste no compassion on these separate dead!"
Statistics justify and scholars seize
The salients of colonial policy.
What is that to the white child hacked in bed?
10   To savages, expendable as Jews?

Threshed out by beaters,[3] the long rushes break
In a white dust of ibises whose cries
Have wheeled since civilization's dawn
From the parched river or beast-teeming plain.
15   The violence of beast on beast is read
As natural law, but upright man
Seeks his divinity by inflicting pain.
Delirious as these worried beasts, his wars

1. An east African tribe whose members, as Mau Mau fighters, conducted an eight-year terrorist campaign against British colonial settlers in Kenya.
2. Open country, neither cultivated nor forest (Afrikaans).
3. In big-game hunting, natives are hired to beat the brush, driving birds—such as ibises—and other animals into the open.

Dance to the tightened carcass of a drum,
20 While he calls courage still that native dread
Of the white peace contracted by the dead.

Again brutish necessity wipes its hands
Upon the napkin of a dirty cause, again
A waste of our compassion, as with Spain,[4]
25 The gorilla wrestles with the superman.
I who am poisoned with the blood of both,
Where shall I turn, divided to the vein?
I who have cursed
The drunken officer of British rule, how choose
30 Between this Africa and the English tongue I love?
Betray them both, or give back what they give?
How can I face such slaughter and be cool?
How can I turn from Africa and live?

1962

Nights in the Gardens of Port of Spain[1]

Night, the black summer, simplifies her smells
into a village; she assumes the impenetrable

musk of the negro, grows secret as sweat,
her alleys odorous with shucked oyster shells,

5 coals of gold oranges, braziers of melon.
Commerce and tambourines increase her heat.

Hellfire or the whorehouse: crossing Park Street,
a surf of sailors' faces crests, is gone

with the sea's phosphoresence; the boites-de-nuit[2]
10 tinkle like fireflies in her thick hair.

Blinded by headlamps, deaf to taxi klaxons,
she lifts her face from the cheap, pitch oil flare

towards white stars, like cities, flashing neon,
burning to be the bitch she must become.

15 As daylight breaks the coolie turns his tumbril[3]
of hacked, beheaded coconuts towards home.

1964

---

4. The Spanish Civil War (1936–39).
1. Capital of Trinidad, British West Indies.
2. Nightclubs (French).

3. Open cart used in the French Revolution to
carry victims to the guillotine.

The Glory Trumpeter

Old Eddie's face, wrinkled with river lights,
Looked like a Mississippi man's. The eyes,
Derisive and avuncular at once,
Swivelling, fixed me. They'd seen
5   Too many wakes, too many cathouse nights.
The bony, idle fingers on the valves
Of his knee-cradled horn could tear
Through "Georgia on My Mind" or "Jesus Saves"
With the same fury of indifference,
10 If what propelled such frenzy was despair.

Now, as the eyes sealed in the ashen flesh,
And Eddie, like a deacon at his prayer,
Rose, tilting the bright horn, I saw a flash
Of gulls and pigeons from the dunes of coal
15 Near my grandmother's barracks on the wharves,
I saw the sallow faces of those men
Who sighed as if they spoke into their graves
About the Negro in America. That was when
The Sunday comics sprawled out on her floor,
20 Sent from the States, had a particular odour,
A smell of money mingled with man's sweat.

And yet, if Eddie's features held our fate,
Secure in childhood I did not know then
A jesus-ragtime or gut-bucket blues
25 To the bowed heads of lean, compliant men
Back from the States in their funereal serge,
Black, rusty Homburgs[1] and limp waiters' ties
With honey accents and lard-coloured eyes
Was Joshua's ram's horn wailing for the Jews
30 Of patient bitterness or bitter siege.[2]

Now it was that as Eddie turned his back
On our young crowd out fêteing, swilling liquor,
And blew, eyes closed, one foot up, out to sea,
His horn aimed at those cities of the Gulf,
35 Mobile and Galveston and sweetly meted
The horn of plenty through a bitter cup,
In lonely exaltation blaming me
For all whom race and exile have defeated,
For my own uncle in America,
40 That living there I never could look up.

1964

---

1. Old-fashioned felt hats. "Funereal serge":
cheap dark suits.

2. At the fall of the city of Jericho (Joshua 6.1–
21).

From The Schooner *Flight*

1 Adios,[1] *Carenage*

In idle August, while the sea soft,
and leaves of brown islands stick to the rim
of this Caribbean, I blow out the light
by the dreamless face of Maria Concepcion
5   to ship as a seaman on the schooner *Flight*.
Out in the yard turning grey in the dawn,
I stood like a stone and nothing else move
but the cold sea rippling like galvanize
and the nail holes of stars in the sky roof,
10   till a wind start to interfere with the trees.
I pass me dry neighbour sweeping she yard
as I went downhill, and I nearly said:
"Sweep soft, you witch, 'cause she don't sleep hard,"
but the bitch look through me like I was dead.
15   A route taxi pull up, park-lights still on.
The driver size up my bags with a grin:
"This time, Shabine, like you really gone!"
I ain't answer the ass, I simply pile in
the back seat and watch the sky burn
20   above Laventille pink as the gown
in which the woman I left was sleeping,
and I look in the rearview and see a man
exactly like me, and the man was weeping
for the houses, the streets, the whole fucking island.
25   Christ have mercy on all sleeping things!
From that dog rotting down Wrightson Road
to when I was a dog on these streets;
if loving these islands must be my load,
out of corruption my soul takes wings,
30   But they had started to poison my soul
with their big house, big car, big-time bohbohl,
coolie, nigger, Syrian, and French Creole,
so I leave it for them and their carnival—
I taking a sea-bath, I gone down the road.
35   I know these islands from Monos to Nassau,
a rusty head sailor with sea-green eyes
that they nickname Shabine, the patois for
any red nigger, and I, Shabine, saw
when these slums of empire was paradise.
40   I'm just a red nigger who love the sea,
I had a sound colonial education,
I have Dutch, nigger, and English in me,
and either I'm nobody, or I'm a nation.

    But Maria Concepcion was all my thought
45   watching the sea heaving up and down

1. Goodbye (Spanish).

as the port side of dories, schooners, and yachts
was painted afresh by the strokes of the sun
signing her name with every reflection;
I knew when dark-haired evening put on
50 her bright silk at sunset, and, folding the sea,
sidled under the sheet with her starry laugh,
that there'd be no rest, there'd be no forgetting.
Is like telling mourners round the graveside
about resurrection, they want the dead back,
55 so I smile to myself as the bow rope untied
and the *Flight* swing seaward: "Is no use repeating
that the sea have more fish. I ain't want her
dressed in the sexless light of a seraph,
I want those round brown eyes like a marmoset, and
60 till the day when I can lean back and laugh,
those claws that tickled my back on sweating
Sunday afternoons, like a crab on wet sand."
As I worked, watching the rotting waves come
past the bow that scissor the sea like silk,
65 I swear to you all, by my mother's milk,
by the stars that shall fly from tonight's furnace,
that I loved them, my children, my wife, my home;
I loved them as poets love the poetry
that kills them, as drowned sailors the sea.

70 You ever look up from some lonely beach
and see a far schooner? Well, when I write
this poem, each phrase go be soaked in salt;
I go draw and knot every line as tight
as ropes in this rigging; in simple speech
75 my common language go be the wind,
my pages the sails of the schooner *Flight*.

1979

Midsummer

Certain things here[1] are quietly American—
that chain-link fence dividing the absent roars
of the beach from the empty ball park, its holes
muttering the word umpire instead of empire;
5 the gray, metal light where an early pelican
coasts, with its engine off, over the pink fire
of a sea whose surface is as cold as Maine's.
The light warms up the sides of white, eager Cessnas[2]
parked at the airstrip under the freckling hills
10 of St. Thomas. The sheds, the brown, functional hangar,
are like those of the Occupation in the last war.
The night left a rank smell under the casuarinas,[3]

1. I.e., in Trinidad.   3. Trees with jointed branches.
2. Make of small aircraft.

the villas have fenced-off beaches where the natives walk,
illegal immigrants from unlucky islands
15   who envy the smallest polyp its right to work.
Here the wetback crab and the mollusc are citizens,
and the leaves have green cards. Bulldozers jerk
and gouge out a hill, but we all know that the dust
is industrial and must be suffered. Soon—
20   the sea's corrugations are sheets of zinc
soldered by the sun's steady acetylene. This
drizzle that falls now is American rain,
stitching stars in the sand. My own corpuscles
are changing as fast. I fear what the migrant envies:
25   the starry pattern they make—the flag on the post office—
the quality of the dirt, the fealty changing under my foot.

1984

From Omeros

Chapter XXX

1

He yawned and watched the lilac horns of his island
lift the horizon.
                    "I know you ain't like to talk,"
the mate said, "but this morning I could use a hand.

Where your mind was whole night?"
                                    "Africa."
                                              "Oh? You walk?"
5   The mate held up his T-shirt, mainly a red hole,
and wriggled it on. He tested the bamboo pole

that trawled the skipping lure from the fast-shearing hull
with the Trade behind them.
                            "Mackerel running," he said.
"Africa, right! You get sunstroke, chief. That is all.

10   You best put that damn captain-cap back on your head."
All night he had worked the rods without any sleep,
watching Achille cradled in the bow; he had read

the stars and known how far out they were and how deep
the black troughs were and how long it took them to lift,
15   but he owed it to his captain, who took him on

when he was stale-drunk. He had not noticed the swift.
"You know what we ketch last night? One *mako* size 'ton,' "
using the patois for kingfish, blue albacore.

"Look by your foot."
                          The kingfish, steel-blue and silver,
20 lay fresh at his feet, its eye like a globed window
ringing with cold, its rim the circular river

of the current that had carried him back, with the spoon
bait in its jaw, the ton was his deliverer,
now its cold eye in sunlight was blind as the moon.

25 A grey lens clouded the gaze of the albacore
that the mate had gaffed and clubbed. It lay there, gaping,
its blue flakes yielding the oceanic colour

of the steel-cold depth from which it had shot, leaping,
stronger than a stallion's neck tugging its stake,
30 sounding, then bursting its trough, yawning at the lure

of a fishhook moon that was reeled in at daybreak
round the horizon's wrist. Tired of slapping water,
the tail's wedge had drifted into docility.

Achille had slept through the fight. Cradled at the bow
35 like a foetus, like a sea-horse, his memory
dimmed in the sun with the scales of the albacore.

"Look, land!" the mate said. Achille altered the rudder
to keep sideways in the deep troughs without riding
the crests, then he looked up at an old man-o'-war

40 tracing the herring-gulls with that endless gliding
that made it the sea-king.
                          "Them stupid gulls does fish
for him every morning. He himself don't catch none,

white slaves for a black king."
                          "When?" the mate said. "You wish."
"Look him dropping." Achille pointed. "Look at that son-
45 of-a-bitch stealing his fish for the whole fucking week!"

A herring-gull climbed with silver bent in its beak
and the black magnificent frigate met the gull
halfway with the tribute; the gull dropped the mackerel

but the frigate-bird caught it before it could break
the water and soared.
50   "The black bugger beautiful,
though!" The mate nodded, and Achille felt the phrase lift

his heart as high as the bird whose wings wrote the word
"Afolabe," in the letters of the sea-swift.
"The king going home," he said as he and the mate

55 watched the frigate steer into that immensity
 of seraphic space whose cumuli were a gate
 dividing for a monarch entering his city.

1990

TED HUGHES
1930–1998

Ted Hughes was born in Yorkshire, the son of one of seventeen men from a regiment of several hundred to return from Gallipoli in World War I, a tragedy that imprinted the imagination of the poet. He was educated at Mexborough Grammar School and Pembroke College, Cambridge, where in his last year he changed his course of study from English to archaeology and anthropology, pursuing his interest in the extravagant mythic structures that were later to inform his poetry. In 1956 he married the American poet Sylvia Plath, who committed suicide in 1963. As poets, they explored the world of raw sensation, Nature "red in tooth and claw," a world that Hughes's poems tended to view through the eye of the predator, Plath's through the eye of the victim. His early books, *The Hawk in the Rain* (1957) and *Lupercal* (1960), show the influence of D. H. Lawrence's *Birds, Beasts and Flowers* (1923), and Hughes's electrifying descriptions of jaguar, thrushes, and pike similarly generate metaphors that relate such creatures to forces underlying all animal and human experience. With *Crow* (1970) and *Gaudete* (1977) he abandoned at once the semblance of realism and the traditional metrical patterning of his early work, in the belief that "the very sound of metre calls up the ghosts of the past and it is difficult to sing one's own tune against that choir. It is easier to speak a language that raises no ghosts." Returning from the wilder shores of myth, Hughes showed in *Moortown* (1979), *Remains of Elmet* (1979), *River* (1983), and *Flowers and Insects* (1989) that he could render the natural world with a delicacy and tenderness as arresting as his earlier ferocity. Delicacy, tenderness, and, to a lesser degree, ferocity are again on display in his two last books: *Tales from Ovid* (1997), twenty-four passages brilliantly re-created—rather than translated—from the Roman poet Ovid's *Metamorphoses,* and *Birthday Letters* (1998), all but two of which are addressed to his late wife, Sylvia Plath. In perhaps the most moving and memorable sequence of poems Hughes wrote, he broke the dignified silence of thirty-five years to lift the curtain on the tragic drama of their marriage.

 In 1985 he succeeded the late John Betjeman as poet laureate of the United Kingdom and in 1998 was appointed a member of the Order of Merit, the first poet laureate to be so honored for almost half a century.

Wind

This house has been far out at sea all night,
The woods crashing through darkness, the booming hills,
Winds stampeding the fields under the window
Floundering black astride and blinding wet

5 Till day rose; then under an orange sky
The hills had new places, and wind wielded

Blade-light, luminous and emerald,
Flexing like the lens of a mad eye.

At noon I scaled along the house-side as far as
10 The coal-house door. I dared once to look up—
Through the brunt wind that dented the balls of my eyes
The tent of the hills drummed and strained its guyrope,

The fields quivering, the skyline a grimace,
At any second to bang and vanish with a flap:
15 The wind flung a magpie away and a black-
Back gull bent like an iron bar slowly. The house

Rang like some fine green goblet in the note
That any second would shatter it. Now deep
In chairs, in front of the great fire, we grip
20 Our hearts and cannot entertain book, thought,

Or each other. We watch the fire blazing,
And feel the roots of the house move, but sit on,
Seeing the window tremble to come in,
Hearing the stones cry out under the horizons.

1957

Relic

I found this jawbone at the sea's edge:
There, crabs, dogfish, broken by the breakers or tossed
To flap for half an hour and turn to a crust
Continue the beginning. The deeps are cold:
5 In that darkness camaraderie does not hold:

Nothing touches but, clutching, devours. And the jaws,
Before they are satisfied or their stretched purpose
Slacken, go down jaws; go gnawn bare. Jaws
Eat and are finished and the jawbone comes to the beach:
10 This is the sea's achievement; with shells,
Vertebrae, claws, carapaces, skulls.

Time in the sea eats its tail, thrives, casts these
Indigestibles, the spars of purposes
That failed far from the surface. None grow rich
15 In the sea. This curved jawbone did not laugh
But gripped, gripped and is now a cenotaph.[1]

1960

1. Monument to the dead.

Pike

Pike, three inches long, perfect
Pike in all parts, green tigering the gold.
Killers from the egg: the malevolent aged grin.
They dance on the surface among the flies.

5   Or move, stunned by their own grandeur,
Over a bed of emerald, silhouette
Of submarine delicacy and horror.
A hundred feet long in their world.

In ponds, under the heat-struck lily pads—
10   Gloom of their stillness:
Logged on last year's black leaves, watching upwards.
Or hung in an amber cavern of weeds

The jaws' hooked clamp and fangs
Not to be changed at this date;
15   A life subdued to its instrument;
The gills kneading quietly, and the pectorals.

Three we kept behind glass,
Jungled in weed: three inches, four,
And four and a half: fed fry° to them—   *young fish*
20   Suddenly there were two. Finally one

With a sag belly and the grin it was born with.
And indeed they spare nobody.
Two, six pounds each, over two feet long,
High and dry and dead in the willow-herb—

25   One jammed past its gills down the other's gullet:
The outside eye stared: as a vice locks—
The same iron in this eye
Though its film shrank in death.

A pond I fished, fifty yards across,
30   Whose lilies and muscular tench[1]
Had outlasted every visible stone
Of the monastery that planted them—

Stilled legendary depth:
It was as deep as England. It held
35   Pike too immense to stir, so immense and old
That past nightfall I dared not cast

But silently cast and fished
With the hair frozen on my head

---

1. Variety of freshwater fish.

For what might move, for what eye might move.
40 The still splashes on the dark pond,

Owls hushing the floating woods
Frail on my ear against the dream
Darkness beneath night's darkness had freed,
That rose slowly towards me, watching.

1959, 1960

Examination at the Womb-Door[1]

Who owns these scrawny little feet? *Death.*
Who owns this bristly scorched-looking face? *Death.*
Who owns these still-working lungs? *Death.*
Who owns this utility coat of muscles? *Death.*
5 Who owns these unspeakable guts? *Death.*
Who owns these questionable brains? *Death.*
All this messy blood? *Death.*
These minimum-efficiency eyes? *Death.*
This wicked little tongue? *Death.*
10 This occasional wakefulness? *Death.*

Given, stolen, or held pending trial?
Held.

Who owns the whole rainy, stony earth? *Death.*
Who owns all of space? *Death.*

15 Who is stronger than hope? *Death.*
Who is stronger than the will? *Death.*
Stronger than love? *Death.*
Stronger than life? *Death.*

But who is stronger than death?
                    Me, evidently.
20 Pass, Crow.

1970

Theology

No, the serpent did not
Seduce Eve to the apple.
All that's simply
Corruption of the facts.

5 Adam ate the apple.
Eve ate Adam.

---

1. The demonic hero of the Crow myth is interrogated by an unidentified questioner.

The serpent ate Eve.
This is the dark intestine.

The serpent, meanwhile,
10   Sleeps his meal off in Paradise—
Smiling to hear
God's querulous calling.

1967

The Seven Sorrows

The first sorrow of autumn
Is the slow goodbye
Of the garden who stands so long in the evening—
A brown poppy head,
5   The stalk of a lily,
And still cannot go.

The second sorrow
Is the empty feet
Of the pheasant who hangs from a hook with his brothers.
10   The woodland of gold
Is folded in feathers
With its head in a bag.

And the third sorrow
Is the slow goodbye
15   Of the sun who has gathered the birds and who gathers
The minutes of evening,
The golden and holy
Ground of the picture.

The fourth sorrow
20   Is the pond gone black
Ruined and sunken the city of water—
The beetle's palace,
The catacombs
Of the dragonfly.

25   And the fifth sorrow
Is the slow goodbye
Of the woodland that quietly breaks up its camp.
One day it's gone.
It has left only litter—
30   Firewood, tentpoles.

And the sixth sorrow
Is the fox's sorrow
The joy of the huntsman, the joy of the hounds,
The hooves that pound

35   Till earth closes her ear
      To the fox's prayer.

      And the seventh sorrow
      Is the slow goodbye
      Of the face with its wrinkles that looks through the window
40   As the year packs up
      Like a tatty fairground
      That came for the children.

                           1976

Daffodils

      Remember how we[1] picked the daffodils?
      Nobody else remembers, but I remember.
      Your daughter came with her armfuls, eager and happy,
      Helping the harvest. She has forgotten.
5   She cannot even remember you. And we sold them.
      It sounds like sacrilege, but we sold them.
      Were we so poor? Old Stoneman, the grocer,
      Boss-eyed, his blood-pressure purpling to beetroot
      (It was his last chance,
10   He would die in the same great freeze as you),
      He persuaded us. Every Spring
      He always bought them, sevenpence a dozen,
      'A custom of the house'.

      Besides, we still weren't sure we wanted to own
15   Anything. Mainly we were hungry
      To convert everything to profit.
      Still nomads—still strangers
      To our whole possession. The daffodils
      Were incidental gilding of the deeds,[2]
20   Treasure trove. They simply came,
      And they kept on coming.
      As if not from the sod but falling from heaven.
      Our lives were still a raid on our own good luck.
      We knew we'd live for ever. We had not learned
25   What a fleeting glance of the everlasting
      Daffodils are. Never identified
      The nuptial flight of the rarest ephemera[3]—
      Our own days!
               We thought they were a windfall.
      Never guessed they were a last blessing.
30   So we sold them. We worked at selling them
      As if employed on somebody else's

---

1. Ted Hughes is addressing his first wife, the American poet Sylvia Plath (1932–1963).
2. Document establishing legal possession of a house.
3. Insect that lives only a few days.

Flower-farm. You bent at it
In the rain of that April—your last April.
We bent there together, among the soft shrieks
35   Of their jostled stems, the wet shocks shaken
Of their girlish dance-frocks—
Fresh-opened dragonflies, wet and flimsy,
Opened too early.

We piled their frailty lights on a carpenter's bench,
40   Distributed leaves among the dozens—
Buckling blade-leaves, limber, groping for air, zinc-silvered—
Propped their raw butts in bucket water,
Their oval, meaty butts,
And sold them, sevenpence a bunch—

45   Wind-wounds, spasms from the dark earth,
With their odourless metals,
A flamy purification of the deep grave's stony cold
As if ice had a breath—

We sold them, to wither.
50   The crop thickened faster than we could thin it.
Finally, we were overwhelmed
And we lost our wedding-present scissors.

Every March since they have lifted again
Out of the same bulbs, the same
55   Baby-cries from the thaw,
Ballerinas too early for music, shiverers
In the draughty wings of the year.
On that same groundswell of memory, fluttering
They return to forget you stooping there
60   Behind the rainy curtains of a dark April,
Snipping their stems.

But somewhere your scissors remember. Wherever they are.
Here somewhere, blades wide open,
April by April
65   Sinking deeper
Through the sod—an anchor, a cross of rust.

                                                        1998

HAROLD PINTER
b. 1930

Harold Pinter is one of the most challenging and original of the many important playwrights who have emerged in Britain in the last half century. He was born and educated in East London, studied briefly at the Academy of Dramatic Art, and from the age of nineteen to the age of twenty-seven acted in a repertory company. His first play (in one act), *The Room,* was written and produced in 1957 and was followed immediately by *The Dumb Waiter* and *The Birthday Party,* his first real success. *The Caretaker* won the Evening Standard Drama Award for 1960 and the Page 1 Award of the Newspaper Guild of New York, the first of many prizes that include a Tony Award and the Whitbread Award in 1967 and the Shakespeare Prize in 1970. In addition to his work for theater and television, he has written a number of screenplays based on such novels as L. P. Hartley's *The Go-Between,* Marcel Proust's *A la Recherche du Temps Perdu,* John Fowles's *The French Lieutenant's Woman;* and he adapted his own play *Betrayal* for the screen.

Pinter's early work shows the influence of the "theater of the absurd," especially of Samuel Beckett and the French playwright Eugène Ionesco (1912–1994), but his vision rapidly established itself as more naturalistic and no less alarming than theirs. His territory is typically a room (refuge, prison cell, trap) symbolic of the world of its occupants. Into this, and into their ritualized relationship with its rules and taboos, comes a stranger on to whom—as on to a screen—the occupants project their deepest desires, guilts, neuroses. The breakdown that follows is mirrored in the breakdown of language. Pinter, who has a poet's ear for the rhythms of spoken English, is a master of these pauses, double entendres, and silences that communicate a secondary level of meaning often opposed to the first. He has said of language:

> The speech we hear is an indication of that which we don't hear. It is a necessary avoidance, a violent, sly, and anguished or mocking smoke screen which keeps the other in its true place. When true silence falls we are left with echo but are nearer nakedness. One way of looking at speech is to say that it is a constant stratagem to cover nakedness.

The critic Lois Gordon has well said that "one way of looking at Pinter's plays is to say that they are dramatic stratagems that uncover nakedness."

The Dumb Waiter

SCENE: *A basement room. Two beds, flat against the back wall. A serving hatch, closed, between the beds. A door to the kitchen and lavatory, left. A door to a passage, right.*

BEN *is lying on a bed, left, reading a paper.* GUS *is sitting on a bed, right, tying his shoelaces, with difficulty. Both are dressed in shirts, trousers and braces.*
Silence.
GUS *ties his laces, rises, yawns and begins to walk slowly to the door, left. He stops, looks down, and shakes his foot.*
BEN *lowers his paper and watches him.* GUS *kneels and unties his shoelace and slowly takes off the shoe. He looks inside it and brings out a flattened matchbox. He shakes it and examines it. Their eyes meet.* BEN *rattles his paper and reads.* GUS *puts the matchbox in his pocket and bends down to put on his shoe. He ties his lace, with difficulty.* BEN *lowers his paper and watches him.* GUS *walks*

to the door, left, stops, and shakes the other foot. He kneels, unties his shoelace, and slowly takes off the shoe. He looks inside it and brings out a flattened cigarette packet. He shakes it and examines it. Their eyes meet. BEN *rattles his paper and reads.* GUS *puts the packet in his pocket, bends down, puts on his shoe and ties the lace.*
　　He wanders off, left.
　　BEN *slams the paper down on the bed and glares after him. He picks up the paper and lies on his back, reading.*
　　Silence.
　　A lavatory chain is pulled twice off left, but the lavatory does not flush.
　　Silence.
　　GUS *re-enters, left, and halts at the door, scratching his head.*
　　BEN *slams down the paper.*

BEN　Kaw!
　　　[*He picks up the paper.*]
　　What about this? Listen to this!
　　　[*He refers to the paper.*]
　　A man of eighty-seven wanted to cross the road. But there was a lot of traffic, see? He couldn't see how he was going to squeeze through. So he crawled under a lorry.[1]
GUS　He what?
BEN　He crawled under a lorry. A stationary lorry.
GUS　No?
BEN　The lorry started and ran over him.
GUS　Go on!
BEN　That's what it says here.
GUS　Get away.
BEN　It's enough to make you want to puke, isn't it?
GUS　Who advised him to do a thing like that?
BEN　A man of eighty-seven crawling under a lorry!
GUS　It's unbelievable.
BEN　It's down here in black and white.
GUS　Incredible.
　　　[*Silence.*]
　　　[GUS *shakes his head and exits.* BEN *lies back and reads.*]
　　　[*The lavatory chain is pulled once off left, but the lavatory does not flush.*]
　　　[BEN *whistles at an item in the paper.*]
　　　[GUS *re-enters.*]
　　I want to ask you something.
BEN　What are you doing out there?
GUS　Well, I was just—
BEN　What about the tea?
GUS　I'm just going to make it.
BEN　Well, go on, make it.
GUS　Yes, I will. [*He sits in a chair. Ruminatively.*] He's laid on some very nice crockery this time, I'll say that. It's sort of striped. There's a white stripe.
　　　[BEN *reads.*]

1. Truck.

It's very nice. I'll say that.

[BEN *turns the page*.]

You know, sort of round the cup. Round the rim. All the rest of it's black, you see. Then the saucer's black, except for right in the middle, where the cup goes, where it's white.

[BEN *reads*.]

Then the plates are the same, you see. Only they've got a black stripe— the plates—right across the middle. Yes, I'm quite taken with the crockery.

BEN   [*Still reading*.] What do you want plates for? You're not going to eat.

GUS   I've brought a few biscuits.

BEN   Well, you'd better eat them quick.

GUS   I always bring a few biscuits. Or a pie. You know I can't drink tea without anything to eat.

BEN   Well, make the tea then, will you? Time's getting on.

[GUS *brings out the flattened cigarette packet and examines it*.]

GUS   You got any cigarettes? I think I've run out.

[*He throws the packet high up and leans forward to catch it*.]

I hope it won't be a long job, this one.

[*Aiming carefully, he flips the packet under his bed*.]

Oh, I wanted to ask you something.

BEN   [*Slamming his paper down*.] Kaw!

GUS   What's that?

BEN   A child of eight killed a cat!

GUS   Get away.

BEN   It's a fact. What about that, eh? A child of eight killing a cat!

GUS   How did he do it?

BEN   It was a girl.

GUS   How did she do it?

BEN   She—

[*He picks up the paper and studies it*.]

It doesn't say.

GUS   Why not?

BEN   Wait a minute. It just says—Her brother, aged eleven, viewed the incident from the toolshed.

GUS   Go on!

BEN   That's bloody ridiculous.

[*Pause*.]

GUS   I bet he did it.

BEN   Who?

GUS   The brother.

BEN   I think you're right.

[*Pause*.]

[*Slamming down the paper*.] What about that, eh? A kid of eleven killing a cat and blaming it on his little sister of eight! It's enough to—

[*He breaks off in disgust and seizes the paper*. GUS *rises*.]

GUS. What time is he getting in touch?

[BEN *reads*.]

What time is he getting in touch?

BEN   What's the matter with you? It could be any time. Any time.

GUS [*Moves to the foot of* BEN's *bed.*] Well, I was going to ask you something.

BEN What?

GUS Have you noticed the time that tank takes to fill?

BEN What tank?

GUS In the lavatory.

BEN No. Does it?

GUS Terrible.

BEN Well, what about it?

GUS What do you think's the matter with it?

BEN Nothing.

GUS Nothing?

BEN It's got a deficient ballcock, that's all.

GUS A deficient what?

BEN Ballcock.

GUS No? Really?

BEN That's what I should say.

GUS Go on! That didn't occur to me.

[GUS. *wanders to his bed and presses the mattress.*]

I didn't have a very restful sleep today, did you? It's not much of a bed. I could have done with another blanket too. [*He catches sight of a picture on the wall.*] Hello, what's this? [*Peering at it.*] "The First Eleven."[2] Cricketers. You seen this, Ben?

BEN [*Reading.*] What?

GUS The first eleven.

BEN What?

GUS There's a photo here of the first eleven.

BEN What first eleven?

GUS [*Studying the photo.*] It doesn't say.

BEN What about that tea?

GUS They all look a bit old to me.

[GUS *wanders downstage, looks out front, then all about the room.*]

I wouldn't like to live in this dump. I wouldn't mind if you had a window, you could see what it looked like outside.

BEN What do you want a window for?

GUS Well, I like to have a bit of a view, Ben. It whiles away the time.

[*He walks about the room.*]

I mean, you come into a place when it's still dark, you come into a room you've never seen before, you sleep all day, you do your job, and then you go away in the night again.

[*Pause.*]

I like to get a look at the scenery. You never get the chance in this job.

BEN You get your holidays, don't you?

GUS Only a fortnight.

BEN [*Lowering the paper.*] You kill me. Anyone would think you're working every day. How often do we do a job? Once a week? What are you complaining about?

---

2. A school's top team of cricketers.

GUS   Yes, but we've got to be on tap though, haven't we? You can't move out of the house in case a call comes.

BEN   You know what your trouble is?

GUS   What?

BEN   You haven't got any interests.

GUS   I've got interests.

BEN   What? Tell me one of your interests.

      [*Pause.*]

GUS   I've got interests.

BEN   Look at me. What have I got?

GUS   I don't know. What?

BEN   I've got my woodwork. I've got my model boats. Have you ever seen me idle? I'm never idle. I know how to occupy my time, to its best advantage. Then when a call comes, I'm ready.

GUS   Don't you ever get a bit fed up?

BEN   Fed up? What with?

      [*Silence.*]

      [BEN *reads.* GUS *feels in the pocket of his jacket, which hangs on the bed.*]

GUS   You got any cigarettes? I've run out.

      [*The lavatory flushes off left.*]

There she goes.

      [GUS *sits on his bed.*]

No, I mean, I say the crockery's good. It is. It's very nice. But that's about all I can say for this place. It's worse than the last one. Remember that last place we were in? Last time, where was it? At least there was a wireless there. No, honest. He doesn't seem to bother much about our comfort these days.

BEN   When are you going to stop jabbering?

GUS   You'd get rheumatism in a place like this, if you stay long.

BEN   We're not staying long. Make the tea, will you? We'll be on the job in a minute.

      [GUS *picks up a small bag by his bed and brings out a packet of tea. He examines it and looks up.*]

GUS   Eh, I've been meaning to ask you.

BEN   What the hell is it now?

GUS   Why did you stop the car this morning, in the middle of that road?

BEN   [*Lowering the paper.*] I thought you were asleep.

GUS   I was, but I woke up when you stopped. You did stop, didn't you?

      [*Pause.*]

In the middle of that road. It was still dark, don't you remember? I looked out. It was all misty. I thought perhaps you wanted to kip,[3] but you were sitting up dead straight, like you were waiting for something.

BEN   I wasn't waiting for anything.

GUS   I must have fallen asleep again. What was all that about then? Why did you stop?

BEN   [*Picking up the paper.*] We were too early.

---

3. Nap.

GUS Early? [*He rises.*] What do you mean? We got the call, didn't we, saying we were to start right away. We did. We shoved out on the dot. So how could we be too early?

BEN [*Quietly.*] Who took the call, me or you?

GUS You.

BEN We were too early.

GUS Too early for what?

    [*Pause.*]

You mean someone had to get out before we got in?

    [*He examines the bedclothes.*]

I thought these sheets didn't look too bright. I thought they ponged[4] a bit. I was too tired to notice when I got in this morning. Eh, that's taking a bit of a liberty, isn't it? I don't want to share my bed-sheets. I told you things were going down the drain. I mean, we've always had clean sheets laid on up till now. I've noticed it.

BEN How do you know those sheets weren't clean?

GUS What do you mean?

BEN How do you know they weren't clean? You've spent the whole day in them, haven't you?

GUS What, you mean it might be my pong? [*He sniffs sheets.*] Yes. [*He sits slowly on bed.*] It could be my pong, I suppose. It's difficult to tell. I don't really know what I pong like, that's the trouble.

BEN [*Referring to the paper.*] Kaw!

GUS Eh, Ben.

BEN Kaw!

GUS Ben.

BEN What?

GUS What town are we in? I've forgotten.

BEN I've told you. Birmingham.

GUS Go on!

    [*He looks with interest about the room.*]

That's in the Midlands. The second biggest city in Great Britain. I'd never have guessed.

    [*He snaps his fingers.*]

Eh, it's Friday today, isn't it? It'll be Saturday tomorrow.

BEN What about it?

GUS [*Excited.*] We could go and watch the Villa.[5]

BEN They're playing away.

GUS No, are they? Caarr! What a pity.

BEN Anyway, there's no time. We've got to get straight back.

GUS Well, we have done in the past, haven't we? Stayed over and watched a game, haven't we? For a bit of relaxation.

BEN Things have tightened up, mate. They're tightened up.

    [GUS *chuckles to himself.*]

GUS I saw the Villa get beat in a cup tie once. Who was it against now? White shirts. It was one-all at half time. I'll never forget it. Their oppo-

---

4. Smelled.
5. Aston Villa, popularly known simply as "the Villa," Birmingham's soccer team.

nents won by a penalty. Talk about drama. Yes, it was a disputed penalty. Disputed. They got beat two–one, anyway, because of it. You were there yourself.

BEN Not me.

GUS Yes, you were there. Don't you remember that disputed penalty?

BEN No.

GUS He went down just inside the area. Then they said he was just acting. I didn't think the other bloke touched him myself. But the referee had the ball on the spot.

BEN Didn't touch him! What are you talking about? He laid him out flat!

GUS Not the Villa. The Villa don't play that sort of game.

BEN Get out of it.

  [*Pause.*]

GUS Eh, that must have been here, in Birmingham.

BEN What must?

GUS The Villa. That must have been here.

BEN They were playing away.

GUS Because you know who the other team was? It was the Spurs. It was Tottenham Hotspur.[6]

BEN Well, what about it?

GUS We've never done a job in Tottenham.

BEN How do you know?

GUS I'd remember Tottenham.

  [BEN *turns on his bed to look at him.*]

BEN Don't make me laugh, will you?

  [BEN *turns back and reads.* GUS *yawns and speaks through his yawn.*]

GUS When's he going to get in touch?

  [*Pause.*]

  Yes, I'd like to see another football match. I've always been an ardent football fan. Here, what about coming to see the Spurs tomorrow?

BEN [*Tonelessly.*] They're playing away.

GUS Who are?

BEN The Spurs.

GUS Then they might be playing here.

BEN Don't be silly.

GUS If they're playing away they might be playing here. They might be playing the Villa.

BEN [*Tonelessly.*] But the Villa are playing away.

  [*Pause. An envelope slides under the door, right.* GUS *sees it. He stands, looking at it.*]

GUS Ben.

BEN Away. They're all playing away.

GUS Ben, look here.

BEN What?

GUS Look.

  [BEN *turns his head and sees the envelope. He stands.*]

BEN What's that?

GUS I don't know.

---

6. A soccer team; Tottenham is in north London.

BEN   Where did it come from?
GUS   Under the door.
BEN   Well, what is it?
GUS   I don't know.
       [*They stare at it.*]
BEN   Pick it up.
GUS   What do you mean?
BEN   Pick it up!
       [GUS *slowly moves towards it, bends and picks it up.*]
  What is it?
GUS   An envelope.
BEN   Is there anything on it?
GUS   No.
BEN   Is it sealed?
GUS   Yes.
BEN   Open it.
GUS   What?
BEN   Open it!
       [GUS *opens it and looks inside.*]
  What's in it?
       [GUS *empties twelve matches into his hand.*]
GUS   Matches.
BEN   Matches?
GUS   Yes.
BEN   Show it to me.
       [GUS *passes the envelope.* BEN *examines it.*]
  Nothing on it. Not a word.
GUS   That's funny, isn't it?
BEN   It came under the door?
GUS   Must have done.
BEN   Well, go on.
GUS   Go on where?
BEN   Open the door and see if you catch anyone outside.
GUS   Who, me?
BEN   Go on!
       [GUS *stares at him, puts the matches in his pocket, goes to his bed and
       brings a revolver from under the pillow. He goes to the door, opens it,
       looks out and shuts it.*]
GUS   No one.
       [*He replaces the revolver.*]
BEN   What did you see?
GUS   Nothing.
BEN   They must have been pretty quick.
       [GUS *takes the matches from pocket and looks at them.*]
GUS   Well, they'll come in handy.
BEN   Yes.
GUS   Won't they?
BEN   Yes, you're always running out, aren't you?
GUS   All the time.
BEN   Well, they'll come in handy then.

GUS   Yes.

BEN   Won't they?

GUS   Yes, I could do with them. I could do with them too.

BEN   You could, eh?

GUS   Yes.

BEN   Why?

GUS   We haven't any.

BEN   Well, you've got some now, haven't you?

GUS   I can light the kettle now.

BEN   Yes, you're always cadging matches. How many have you got there?

GUS   About a dozen.

BEN   Well, don't lose them. Red too. You don't even need a box.

[GUS *probes his ear with a match.*]

[*Slapping his hand.*] Don't waste them! Go on, go and light it.

GUS   Eh?

BEN   Go and light it.

GUS   Light what?

BEN   The kettle.

GUS   You mean the gas.

BEN   Who does?

GUS   You do.

BEN   [*His eyes narrowing.*] What do you mean, I mean the gas?

GUS   Well, that's what you mean, don't you? The gas.

BEN   [*Powerfully.*] If I say go and light the kettle I mean go and light the kettle.

GUS   How can you light a kettle?

BEN   It's a figure of speech! Light the kettle. It's a figure of speech!

GUS   I've never heard it.

BEN   Light the kettle! It's common usage!

GUS   I think you've got it wrong.

BEN   [*Menacing.*] What do you mean?

GUS   They say put on the kettle.

BEN   [*Taut.*] Who says?

[*They stare at each other, breathing hard.*]

[*Deliberately.*] I have never in all my life heard anyone say put on the kettle.

GUS   I bet my mother used to say it.

BEN   Your mother? When did you last see your mother?

GUS   I don't know, about—

BEN   Well, what are you talking about your mother for?

[*They stare.*]

Gus, I'm not trying to be unreasonable. I'm just trying to point out something to you.

GUS   Yes, but—

BEN   Who's the senior partner here, me or you?

GUS   You.

BEN   I'm only looking after your interests, Gus. You've got to learn, mate.

GUS   Yes, but I've never heard—

BEN   [*Vehemently.*] Nobody says light the gas! What does the gas light?

GUS   What does the gas—?

BEN   [*Grabbing him with two hands by the throat, at arm's length.*] THE KETTLE, YOU FOOL!

    [GUS *takes the hands from his throat.*]

GUS   All right, all right.

    [*Pause.*]

BEN   Well, what are you waiting for?

GUS   I want to see if they light.

BEN   What?

GUS   The matches.

    [*He takes out the flattened box and tries to strike.*]

No.

    [*He throws the box under the bed.*]

    [BEN *stares at him.*]

    [GUS *raises his foot.*]

Shall I try it on here?

    [BEN *stares.* GUS *strikes a match on his shoe. It lights.*]

Here we are.

BEN   [*Wearily.*] Put on the bloody kettle, for Christ's sake.

    [BEN *goes to his bed, but, realizing what he has said, stops and half turns. They look at each other.* GUS *slowly exits, left.* BEN *slams his paper down on the bed and sits on it, head in hands.*]

GUS   [*Entering.*] It's going.

BEN   What?

GUS   The stove.

    [GUS *goes to his bed and sits.*]

I wonder who it'll be tonight.

    [*Silence.*]

Eh, I've been wanting to ask you something.

BEN   [*Putting his legs on the bed.*] Oh, for Christ's sake.

GUS   No. I was going to ask you something.

    [*He rises and sits on* BEN's *bed.*]

BEN   What are you sitting on my bed for?

    [GUS *sits.*]

What's the matter with you? You're always asking me questions. What's the matter with you?

GUS   Nothing.

BEN   You never used to ask me so many damn questions. What's come over you?

GUS   No, I was just wondering.

BEN   Stop wondering. You've got a job to do. Why don't you just do it and shut up?

GUS   That's what I was wondering about.

BEN   What?

GUS   The job.

BEN   What job?

GUS   [*Tentatively.*] I thought perhaps you might know something.

    [BEN *looks at him.*]

I thought perhaps you—I mean—have you got any idea—who it's going to be tonight?

BEN   Who what's going to be?

[*They look at each other.*]

GUS [*At length.*] Who it's going to be.
     [*Silence.*]

BEN   Are you feeling all right?

GUS   Sure.

BEN   Go and make the tea.

GUS   Yes, sure.

     [GUS *exits, left,* BEN *looks after him. He then takes his revolver from under the pillow and checks it for ammunition.* GUS *re-enters.*]

  The gas has gone out.

BEN   Well, what about it?

GUS   There's a meter.[7]

BEN   I haven't got any money.

GUS   Nor have I.

BEN   You'll have to wait.

GUS   What for?

BEN   For Wilson.

GUS   He might not come. He might just send a message. He doesn't always come.

BEN   Well, you'll have to do without it, won't you?

GUS   Blimey.

BEN   You'll have a cup of tea afterwards. What's the matter with you?

GUS   I like to have one before.

     [BEN *holds the revolver up to the light and polishes it.*]

BEN   You'd better get ready anyway.

GUS   Well, I don't know, that's a bit much, you know, for my money.

     [*He picks up a packet of tea from the bed and throws it into the bag.*]

  I hope he's got a shilling, anyway, if he comes. He's entitled to have. After all, it's his place, he could have seen there was enough gas for a cup of tea.

BEN   What do you mean, it's his place?

GUS   Well, isn't it?

BEN   He's probably only rented it. It doesn't have to be his place.

GUS   I know it's his place. I bet the whole house is. He's not even laying on any gas now either.

     [GUS *sits on his bed.*]

  It's his place all right. Look at all the other places. You go to this address, there's a key there, there's a teapot, there's never a soul in sight—[*He pauses.*] Eh, nobody ever hears a thing, have you ever thought of that? We never get any complaints, do we, too much noise or anything like that? You never see a soul, do you?—except the bloke who comes. You ever noticed that? I wonder if the walls are soundproof. [*He touches the wall above his bed.*] Can't tell. All you do is wait, eh? Half the time he doesn't even bother to put in an appearance, Wilson.

BEN   Why should he? He's a busy man.

GUS   [*Thoughtfully.*] I find him hard to talk to, Wilson. Do you know that, Ben?

BEN   Scrub round it, will you?

---

7. One that controls the supply of gas and must be fed with shilling coins.

[*Pause.*]

GUS   There are a number of things I want to ask him. But I can never get round to it, when I see him.

    [*Pause.*]

    I've been thinking about the last one.

BEN   What last one?

GUS   That girl.

    [BEN *grabs the paper, which he reads.*]

    [*Rising, looking down at* BEN.] How many times have you read that paper?

    [BEN *slams the paper down and rises.*]

BEN   [*Angrily.*] What do you mean?

GUS   I was just wondering how many times you'd—

BEN   What are you doing, criticizing me?

GUS   No, I was just—

BEN   You'll get a swipe round your earhole if you don't watch your step.

GUS   Now look here, Ben—

BEN   I'm not looking anywhere [*He addresses the room.*] How many times have I—! A bloody liberty!

GUS   I didn't mean that.

BEN   You just get on with it, mate. Get on with it, that's all.

    [BEN *gets back on the bed.*]

GUS   I was just thinking about that girl, that's all.

    [GUS *sits on his bed.*]

    She wasn't much to look at, I know, but still. It was a mess though, wasn't it? What a mess. Honest, I can't remember a mess like that one. They don't seem to hold together like men, women. A looser texture, like. Didn't she spread, eh? She didn't half spread. Kaw! But I've been meaning to ask you.

    [BEN *sits up and clenches his eyes.*]

    Who clears up after we've gone? I'm curious about that. Who does the clearing up? Maybe they don't clear up. Maybe they just leave them there, eh? What do you think? How many jobs have we done? Blimey, I can't count them. What if they never clear anything up after we've gone.

BEN   [*Pityingly.*] You mutt. Do you think we're the only branch of this organization? Have a bit of common. They got departments for everything.

GUS   What, cleaners and all?

BEN   You birk!

GUS   No, it was that girl made me start to think—

    [*There is a loud clatter and racket in the bulge of wall between the beds, of something descending. They grab their revolvers, jump up and face the wall. The noise comes to a stop. Silence. They look at each other.* BEN *gestures sharply towards the wall.* GUS *approaches the wall slowly. He bangs it with his revolver. It is hollow.* BEN *moves to the head of his bed, his revolver cocked.* GUS *puts his revolver on his bed and pats along the bottom of the centre panel. He finds a rim. He lifts the panel. Disclosed is a serving-hatch, a "dumb waiter." A wide box is held by pulleys.* GUS *peers into the box. He brings out a piece of paper.*]

BEN   What is it?

GUS   You have a look at it.

BEN   Read it.

GUS   [*Reading.*] Two braised steak and chips. Two sago puddings. Two teas without sugar.

BEN   Let me see that. [*He takes the paper.*]

GUS   [*To himself.*] Two teas without sugar.

BEN   Mmnn.

GUS   What do you think of that?

BEN   Well—

    [*The box goes up,* BEN *levels his revolver.*]

GUS   Give us a chance! They're in a hurry, aren't they?

    [BEN *rereads the note.* GUS *looks over his shoulder.*]

That's a bit—that's a bit funny, isn't it?

BEN   [*Quickly.*] No, it's not funny. It probably used to be a café here, that's all. Upstairs. These places change hands very quickly.

GUS   A café?

BEN   Yes.

GUS   What, do you mean this was the kitchen, down here?

BEN   Yes, they change hands overnight, these places. Go into liquidation. The people who run it, you know, they don't find it a going concern, they move out.

GUS   You mean the people who ran this place didn't find it a going concern and moved out?

BEN   Sure.

GUS   WELL, WHO'S GOT IT NOW?

    [*Silence.*]

BEN   What do you mean, who's got it now?

GUS   Who's got it now? If they moved out, who moved in?

BEN   Well, that all depends—

    [*The box descends with a clatter and bang.* BEN *levels his revolver.* GUS *goes to the box and brings out a piece of paper.*]

GUS   [*Reading.*] Soup of the day. Liver and onions. Jam tart.

    [*A pause.* GUS *looks at* BEN. BEN *takes the note and reads it. He walks slowly to the hatch.* GUS *follows.* BEN *looks into the hatch but not up it.* GUS *puts his hand on* BEN's *shoulder.* BEN *throws if off.* GUS *puts his finger to his mouth. He leans on the hatch and swiftly looks up it.* BEN *flings him away in alarm.* BEN *looks at the note. He throws his revolver on the bed and speaks with decision.*]

BEN   We'd better send something up.

GUS   Eh?

BEN   We'd better send something up.

GUS   Oh! Yes. Yes. Maybe you're right.

    [*They are both relieved at the decision.*]

BEN   [*Purposefully.*] Quick! What have you got in that bag?

GUS   Not much.

    [GUS *goes to the hatch and shouts up it.*]

Wait a minute!

BEN   Don't do that!

    [GUS *examines the contents of the bag and brings them out, one by one.*]

GUS   Biscuits. A bar of chocolate. Half a pint of milk.

BEN   That all?

GUS Packet of tea.

BEN Good.

GUS We can't send the tea. That's all the tea we've got.

BEN Well, there's no gas. You can't do anything with it, can you?

GUS Maybe they can send us down a bob.[8]

BEN What else is there?

GUS [Reaching into bag.] One Eccles cake.[9]

BEN One Eccles cake?

GUS Yes.

BEN You never told me you had an Eccles cake.

GUS Didn't I?

BEN Why only one? Didn't you bring one for me?

GUS I didn't think you'd be keen.

BEN Well, you can't send up one Eccles cake, anyway.

GUS Why not?

BEN Fetch one of those plates.

GUS All right.

    [GUS goes towards the door, left, and stops.]

Do you mean I can keep the Eccles cake then?

BEN Keep it?

GUS Well, they don't know we've got it, do they?

BEN That's not the point.

GUS Can't I keep it?

BEN No, you can't. Get the plate.

    [GUS exits, left. BEN looks in the bag. He brings out a packet of crisps.[1]
    Enter GUS with a plate.]

[Accusingly, holding up the crisps.] Where did these come from?

GUS What?

BEN Where did these crisps come from?

GUS Where did you find them?

BEN [Hitting him on the shoulder.] You're playing a dirty game, my lad!

GUS I only eat those with beer!

BEN Well, where were you going to get the beer?

GUS I was saving them till I did.

BEN I'll remember this. Put everything on the plate.

    [They pile everything on to the plate. The box goes up without the plate.]

Wait a minute!

    [They stand.]

GUS It's gone up.

BEN It's all your stupid fault, playing about!

GUS What do we do now?

BEN We'll have to wait till it comes down.

    [BEN puts the plate on the bed, puts on his shoulder holster, and starts
    to put on his tie.]

You'd better get ready.

    [GUS goes to his bed, puts on his tie, and starts to fix his holster.]

GUS Hey, Ben.

---

8. A shilling (i.e., to insert in the gas meter).
9. A small cake originally made in the Lancashire

town of Eccles.
1. Potato chips.

BEN   What?

GUS   What's going on here?
       [*Pause.*]

BEN   What do you mean?

GUS   How can this be a café?

BEN   It used to be a café.

GUS   Have you seen the gas stove?

BEN   What about it?

GUS   It's only got three rings.

BEN   So what?

GUS   Well, you couldn't cook much on three rings, not for a busy place
       like this.

BEN   [*Irritably.*] That's why the service is slow!
       [BEN *puts on his waistcoat.*]

GUS   Yes, but what happens when we're not here? What do they do then?
       All these menus coming down and nothing going up. It might have been
       going on like this for years.
       [BEN *brushes his jacket.*]
       What happens when we go?
       [BEN *puts on his jacket.*]
       They can't do much business.
       [*The box descends. They turn about.* GUS *goes to the hatch and brings
       out a note.*]

GUS   [*Reading.*] Macaroni Pastitsio. Ormitha Macarounada.

BEN   What was that?

GUS   Macaroni Pastitsio. Ormitha macarounada.

BEN   Greek dishes.

GUS   No.

BEN   That's right.

GUS   That's pretty high class.

BEN   Quick before it goes up.
       [GUS *puts the plate in the box.*]

GUS   [*Calling up the hatch.*] Three McVitie and Price! One Lyons Red
       Label! One Smith's Crisps![2] One Eccles cake! One Fruit and Nut!

BEN   Cadbury's.[3]

GUS   [*Up the hatch.*] Cadbury's!

BEN   [*Handing the milk.*] One bottle of milk.

GUS   [*Up the hatch.*] One bottle of milk! Half a pint! [*He looks at the label*]
       Express Dairy! [*He puts the bottle in the box.*]
       [*The box goes up.*]
       Just did it.

BEN   You shouldn't shout like that.

GUS   Why not?

BEN   It isn't done.
       [BEN *goes to his bed.*]
       Well, that should be all right, anyway, for the time being.

GUS   You think so, eh?

---

2. Brands, respectively, of cookies, tea, and potato   3. A brand of chocolate bar.
chips.

BEN   Get dressed, will you? It'll be any minute now.

     [GUS *puts on his waistcoat.* BEN *lies down and looks up at the ceiling.*]

GUS   This is some place. No tea and no biscuits.

BEN   Eating makes you lazy, mate. You're getting lazy, you know that? You don't want to get slack on your job.

GUS   Who me?

BEN   Slack, mate, slack.

GUS   Who me? Slack?

BEN   Have you checked your gun? You haven't even checked your gun. It looks disgraceful, anyway. Why don't you ever polish it?

     [GUS *rubs his revolver on the sheet.* BEN *takes out a pocket mirror and straightens his tie.*]

GUS   I wonder where the cook is. They must have had a few, to cope with that. Maybe they had a few more gas stoves. Eh! Maybe there's another kitchen along the passage.

BEN   Of course there is! Do you know what it takes to make an Ormitha Macarounada?

GUS   No, what?

BEN   An Ormitha—! Buck your ideas up, will you?

GUS   Takes a few cooks, eh?

     [GUS *puts his revolver in its holster.*]

The sooner we're out of this place the better.

     [*He puts on his jacket.*]

Why doesn't he get in touch? I feel like I've been here years. [*He takes his revolver out of its holster to check the ammunition.*] We've never let him down though, have we? We've never let him down. I was thinking only the other day, Ben. We're reliable, aren't we?

     [*He puts his revolver back in its holster.*]

Still, I'll be glad when it's over tonight.

     [*He brushes his jacket.*]

I hope the bloke's not going to get excited tonight, or anything. I'm feeling a bit off. I've got a splitting headache.

     [*Silence.*]

     [*The box descends.* BEN *jumps up.*]

     [GUS *collects the note.*]

[*Reading.*] One Bamboo Shoots, Water Chestnuts, and Chicken. One Char Siu and Beansprouts.

BEN   Beansprouts?

GUS   Yes.

BEN   Blimey.

GUS   I wouldn't know where to begin.

     [*He looks back at the box. The packet of tea is inside it. He picks it up.*]

They've sent back the tea.

BEN   [*Anxious.*] What'd they do that for?

GUS   Maybe it isn't teatime.

     [*The box goes up. Silence.*]

BEN   [*Throwing the tea on the bed, and speaking urgently.*] Look here. We'd better tell them.

GUS   Tell them what?

BEN   That we can't do it, we haven't got it.

GUS   All right then.

BEN   Lend us your pencil. We'll write a note.

     [GUS, *turning for a pencil, suddenly discovers the speaking tube, which hangs on the right wall of the hatch facing his bed.*]

GUS   What's this?

BEN   What?

GUS   This.

BEN   [*Examining it.*] This? It's a speaking tube.

GUS   How long has that been there?

BEN   Just the job. We should have used it before, instead of shouting up there.

GUS   Funny I never noticed it before.

BEN   Well, come on.

GUS   What do you do?

BEN   See that? That's a whistle.

GUS   What, this?

BEN   Yes, take it out. Pull it out.

     [GUS *does so.*]

  That's it.

GUS   What do we do now?

BEN   Blow into it.

GUS   Blow?

BEN   It whistles up there if you blow. Then they know you want to speak. Blow.

     [GUS *blows. Silence.*]

GUS   [*Tube at mouth.*] I can't hear a thing.

BEN   Now you speak! Speak into it!

     [GUS *looks at* BEN, *then speaks into the tube.*]

GUS   The larder's bare!

BEN   Give me that!

     [*He grabs the tube and puts it to his mouth.*]

  [*Speaking with great deference.*] Good evening. I'm sorry to—bother you, but we just thought we'd better let you know that we haven't got anything left. We sent up all we had. There's no more food down here.

     [*He brings the tube slowly to his ear.*]

  What?

     [*To mouth.*]

  What?

     [*To ear. He listens. To mouth.*]

  No, all we had we sent up.

     [*To ear. He listens. to mouth.*]

  Oh, I'm very sorry to hear that.

     [*To ear. He listens. To* GUS.]

  The Eccles cake was stale.

     [*He listens. To* GUS.]

  The chocolate was melted.

     [*He listens. To* GUS.]

  The milk was sour.

GUS   What about the crisps?

BEN   [*Listening.*] The biscuits were mouldy.

[*He glares at* GUS. *Tube to mouth.*]

Well, we're sorry about that.

[*Tube to ear.*]

What?

[*To mouth.*]

What?

[*To ear.*]

Yes. Yes.

[*To mouth.*]

Yes certainly. Right away.

[*To ear. The voice has ceased. He hangs up the tube.*]

[*Excitedly.*] Did you hear that?

GUS   What?

BEN   You know what he said? Light the kettle! Not put on the kettle! Not light the gas! But light the kettle!

GUS   How can we light the kettle?

BEN   What do you mean?

GUS   There's no gas.

BEN   [*Clapping hand to head.*] Now what do we do?

GUS   What did he want us to light the kettle for?

BEN   For tea. He wanted a cup of tea.

GUS   *He* wanted a cup of tea! What about me? I've been wanting a cup of tea all night!

BEN   [*Despairingly.*] What do we do now?

GUS   What are we supposed to drink?

[BEN *sits on his bed, staring.*]

What about us?

[BEN *sits.*]

I'm thirsty too. I'm starving. And he wants a cup of tea. That beats the band, that does.

[BEN *lets his head sink on his chest.*]

I could do with a bit of sustenance myself. What about you? You look as if you could do with something too.

[GUS *sits on his bed.*]

We send him up all we've got and he's not satisfied. No, honest, it's enough to make the cat laugh. Why did you send him up all that stuff? [*Thoughtfully.*] Why did I send it up?

[*Pause.*]

Who knows what he's got upstairs? He's probably got a salad bowl. They must have something up there. They won't get much from down here. You notice they didn't ask for any salads? They've probably got a salad bowl up there. Cold meat, radishes, cucumbers. Watercress. Roll mops.

[*Pause.*]

Hardboiled eggs.

[*Pause.*]

The lot. They've probably got a crate of beer too. Probably eating my crisps with a pint of beer now. Didn't have anything to say about those crisps, did he? They do all right, don't worry about that. You don't think they're just going to sit there and wait for stuff to come up from down here, do you? That'll get them nowhere.

[*Pause.*]
They do all right.
[*Pause.*]
And he wants a cup of tea.
[*Pause.*]
That's past a joke, in my opinion.
[*He looks over at* BEN, *rises, and goes to him.*]
What's the matter with you? You don't look too bright. I feel like an Alka-
Seltzer myself.
[BEN *sits up.*]

BEN   [*In a low voice.*] Time's getting on.
GUS   I know. I don't like doing a job on an empty stomach.
BEN   [*Wearily.*] Be quiet a minute. Let me give you your instructions.
GUS   What for? We always do it the same way, don't we?
BEN   Let me give you your instructions.
     [GUS *sighs and sits next to* BEN *on the bed. The instructions are stated and repeated automatically.*]
    When we get the call, you go over and stand behind the door.
GUS   Stand behind the door.
BEN   If there's a knock on the door you don't answer it.
GUS   If there's a knock on the door I don't answer it.
BEN   But there won't be a knock on the door.
GUS   So I won't answer it.
BEN   When the bloke comes in—
GUS   When the bloke comes in—
BEN   Shut the door behind him.
GUS   Shut the door behind him.
BEN   Without divulging your presence.
GUS   Without divulging my presence.
BEN   He'll see me and come towards me.
GUS   He'll see you and come towards you.
BEN   He won't see you.
GUS   [*Absently.*] Eh?
BEN   He won't see you.
GUS   He won't see me.
BEN   But he'll see me.
GUS   He'll see you.
BEN   He won't know you're there.
GUS   He won't know you're there.
BEN   He won't know *you're* there.
GUS   He won't know I'm there.
BEN   I take out my gun.
GUS   You take out your gun.
BEN   He stops in his tracks.
GUS   He stops in his tracks.
BEN   If he turns round—
GUS   If he turns round—
BEN   You're there.
GUS   I'm here.
    [BEN *frowns and presses his forehead.*]

You've missed something out.

BEN   I know. What?

GUS   I haven't taken my gun out, according to you.

BEN   You take your gun out—

GUS   After I've closed the door.

BEN   After you've closed the door.

GUS   You've never missed that out before, you know that?

BEN   When he sees you behind him—

GUS   Me behind him—

BEN   And me in front of him—

GUS   And you in front of him—

BEN   He'll feel uncertain—

GUS   Uneasy.

BEN   He won't know what to do.

GUS   So what will he do?

BEN   He'll look at me and he'll look at you.

GUS   We won't say a word.

BEN   We'll look at him.

GUS   He won't say a word.

BEN   He'll look at us.

GUS   And we'll look at him.

BEN   Exactly.

       [*Pause.*]

GUS   What do we do if it's a girl?

BEN   We do the same.

GUS   Exactly the same?

BEN   Exactly.

       [*Pause.*]

GUS   We don't do anything different?

BEN   We do exactly the same.

GUS   Oh.

       [GUS *rises, and shivers.*]

Excuse me.

       [*He exits through the door on the left.* BEN *remains sitting on the bed, still.*]

       [*The lavatory chain is pulled once off left, but the lavatory does not flush.*]

       [*Silence.*]

       [GUS *re-enters and stops inside the door, deep in thought. He looks at* BEN, *then walks slowly across to his own bed. He is troubled. He stands, thinking. He turns and looks at* BEN. *He moves a few paces towards him.*]

[*Slowly in a low, tense voice.*] Why did he send us matches if he knew there was no gas?

       [*Silence.*]

       [BEN *stares in front of him.* GUS *crosses to the left side of* BEN, *to the foot of his bed, to get to his other ear.*]

Ben. Why did he send us matches if he knew there was no gas?

       [BEN *looks up.*]

Why did he do that?

BEN   Who?

GUS   Who sent us those matches?

BEN   What are you talking about?
        [GUS *stares down at him.*]
GUS   [*Thickly.*] Who is it upstairs?
BEN   [*Nervously.*] What's one thing to do with another?
GUS   Who is it, though?
BEN   What's one thing to do with another?
        [BEN *fumbles for his paper on the bed.*]
GUS   I asked you a question.
BEN   Enough!
GUS   [*With growing agitation.*] I asked you before. Who moved in? I asked
     you. You said the people who had it before moved out. Well, who moved
     in?
BEN   [*Hunched.*] Shut up.
GUS   I told you, didn't I?
BEN   [*Standing.*] Shut up!
GUS   [*Feverishly.*] I told you before who owned this place, didn't I? I told
     you.
        [BEN *hits him viciously on the shoulder.*]
     I told you who ran this place, didn't I?
        [BEN *hits him viciously on the shoulder.*]
   [*Violently.*] Well, what's he playing all these games for? That's what I
   want to know. What's he doing it for?
BEN   What games?
GUS   [*Passionately, advancing.*] What's he doing it for? We've been through
     our tests, haven't we? We got right through our tests, years ago, didn't
     we? We took them together, don't you remember, didn't we? We've
     proved ourselves before now, haven't we? We've always done our job.
     What's he doing all this for? What's the idea? What's he playing these
     games for?
        [*The box in the shaft comes down behind them. The noise is this time
        accompanied by a shrill whistle, as it falls.* GUS *rushes to the hatch and
        seizes the note.*]
   [*Reading.*] Scampi!
        [*He crumples the note, picks up the tube, takes out the whistle, blows
        and speaks.*]
   WE'VE GOT NOTHING LEFT! NOTHING! DO YOU UNDERSTAND?
        [BEN *seizes the tube and flings* GUS *away. He follows* GUS *and slaps him
        hard, back-handed, across the chest.*]
BEN   Stop it! You maniac!
GUS   But you heard!
BEN   [*Savagely.*] That's enough! I'm warning you!
        [*Silence.*]
        [BEN *hangs the tube. He goes to his bed and lies down. He picks up his
        paper and reads.*]
        [*Silence.*]
        [*The box goes up.*]
        [*They turn quickly, their eyes meet.* BEN *turns to his paper.*]
        [*Slowly* GUS *goes back to his bed, and sits.*]
        [*Silence.*]

[*The hatch falls back into place.*]

[*They turn quickly, their eyes meet.* BEN *turns back to his paper.*]

[*Silence.*]

[BEN *throws his paper down.*]

BEN   Kaw!

[*He picks up the paper and looks at it.*]

Listen to this!

[*Pause.*]

What about that, eh?

[*Pause.*]

Kaw!

[*Pause.*]

Have you ever heard such a thing?

GUS   [*Dully.*] Go on!

BEN   It's true.

GUS   Get away.

BEN   It's down here in black and white.

GUS   [*Very low.*] Is that a fact?

BEN   Can you imagine it.

GUS   It's unbelievable.

BEN   It's enough to make you want to puke, isn't it?

GUS   [*Almost inaudible.*] Incredible.

[BEN *shakes his head. He puts the paper down and rises. He fixes the revolver in his holster.*]

[GUS *stands up. He goes towards the door on the left.*]

BEN   Where are you going?

GUS   I'm going to have a glass of water.

[*He exits.* BEN *brushes dust off his clothes and shoes. The whistle in the speaking tube blows. He goes to it, takes the whistle out and puts the tube to his ear. He listens. He puts it to his mouth.*]

BEN   Yes.

[*To ear. He listens. To mouth.*]

Straight away. Right.

[*To ear. He listens. To mouth.*]

Sure we're ready.

[*To ear. He listens. To mouth.*]

Understood. Repeat. He has arrived and will be coming in straight away. The normal method to be employed. Understood.

[*To ear. He listens. To mouth.*]

Sure we're ready.

[*To ear. He listens. To mouth.*]

Right.

[*He hangs the tube up.*]

Gus!

[*He takes out a comb and combs his hair, adjusts his jacket to diminish the bulge of the revolver. The lavatory flushes off left.* BEN *goes quickly to the door, left.*]

Gus!

[*The door right opens sharply.* BEN *turns, his revolver leveled at the door.*]

[GUS *stumbles in.*]
[*He is stripped of his jacket, waistcoat, tie, holster, and revolver.*]
[*He stops, body stooping, his arms at his sides.*]
[*He raises his head and looks at* BEN.]
[*A long silence.*]
[*They stare at each other.*]

CURTAIN

1960

CHINUA ACHEBE
b. 1930

The most celebrated African novelist today is Chinua Achebe, whose *Things Fall Apart* (1958) permanently transformed the landscape of African fiction, both in his own continent and in the Western imagination. His novels, while steadfastly refusing to sentimentalize their Nigerian subjects, effectively challenged many of the West's entrenched impressions of African life and culture, replacing simplistic stereotypes with portrayals of a complex society still suffering from a legacy of Western colonial oppression.

Achebe was born in Ogidi, an Igbo-speaking town in eastern Nigeria, and educated—in English—at church schools and University College, Ibadan, where he subsequently taught (briefly) before joining the Nigerian Broadcasting Corporation in Lagos. He was director of external broadcasting from 1961 to 1966, and then launched a publishing company with Christopher Okigbo, a poet soon to die in the Nigerian civil war (1967–70). After the war, Achebe taught in the United States, before returning for a time to the University of Nigeria at Nsukka. Since 1990 Achebe has been Charles P. Stevenson Jr. Professor of Languages and Literature at Bard College.

A volume of Achebe's poems was joint winner of the Commonwealth Poetry Prize in 1972. He also has written short stories and essays, including an attack on corruption in Nigerian politics, *The Trouble with Nigeria* (1983). An extract from a more famous attack of another kind, his essay *"An Image of Africa: Racism in Conrad's Heart of Darkness,"* can be found on p. 2035 of this volume. Achebe is best known for his novels, however: *Things Fall Apart* (1958), *No Longer at Ease* (1960), *Arrow of God* (1964), *A Man of the People* (1966), and *Anthills of the Savannah* (1987). The first of these is a response to Joyce Cary's *Mr. Johnson* (1939), a novel famous in its day for its depiction of Nigerian tribal society. Cary had been a British district officer in Nigeria, and his account of the life and tragic death of a young African clerk, although well meaning, was written from an outsider's patronizing perspective. By contrast, Achebe's *Things Fall Apart,* written with an insider's understanding of the African world and its history, depicts the destruction of an individual, a family, and a culture at the moment of colonial incursion. Taking his title from W. B. Yeats's poem *The Second Coming* (p. 2106), Achebe shows how "the blood-dimmed tide is loosed" in a Nigerian village by European colonizers, drowning the ceremonies and innocence of the indigenous society. Achebe's hero, Okonkwo, is dignified and courageous, a noble figure, whereas Cary's Mr. Johnson was charming but undignified. Like other great tragic heroes, however, Okonkwo is flawed and falls through lack of the balance everywhere celebrated in Achebe's writings. *Things Fall Apart* is at once Okonkwo's tragedy and that of a complex tribal society, whose members speak a richly proverbial language that operates in the book as an image of all the beautiful and traditional structures that the white people will destroy.

PRONOUNCING GLOSSARY

The following list uses common English syllables and stress accents to provide rough equivalents of selected words whose pronunciation may be unfamiliar to the general reader. Most of the names in *Things Fall Apart* are pronounced basically as they would be in English (for example, Okonkwo as *oh-kon'-kwo*), except that Igbo (like other African languages and Chinese) is a tonal language and also uses high or low tones for individual syllables.

Chielo: *chee'-ay-loh*

egwugu: *eg-woog'-woo*

Erulu: *air-oo'loo*

Ezeani: *ez-ah'-nee*

Ezeugo: *e'-zoo-goh*

Idemili: *ee-day-mee'-lee*

Igbo: *ee'-boh*

Ikemefuna: *ee-kay-may'-foo-na*

mbari: *mbah'-ree*

Ndulue: *in'-doo-loo'-eh*

Nwakibie: *nwa'-kee-ee'-bee-yay*

Nwayieke: *nwah'-ee-eh'-kay*

Umuofia: *oo'-moo-off'-yah*

Things Fall Apart

Turning and turning in the widening gyre
The falcon cannot hear the falconer;
Things fall apart; the centre cannot hold;
Mere anarchy is loosed upon the world.
W. B. Yeats: 'The Second Coming'

Part One

CHAPTER ONE

Okonkwo[1] was well known throughout the nine villages and even beyond. His fame rested on solid personal achievements. As a young man of eighteen he had brought honour to his village by throwing Amalinze the Cat. Amalinze was the great wrestler who for seven years was unbeaten, from Umuofia to Mbaino.[2] He was called the Cat because his back would never touch the earth. It was this man that Okonkwo threw in a fight which the old men agreed was one of the fiercest since the founder of their town engaged a spirit of the wild for seven days and seven nights.

The drums beat and the flutes sang and the spectators held their breath. Amalinze was a wily craftsman, but Okonkwo was as slippery as a fish in water. Every nerve and every muscle stood out on their arms, on their backs and their thighs, and one almost heard them stretching to breaking point. In the end Okonkwo threw the Cat.

That was many years ago, twenty years or more, and during this time Okonkwo's fame had grown like a bush-fire in the harmattan.[3] He was tall

1. Man [*oko*] born on Nkwo Day; the name also suggests stubborn male pride.
2. Four settlements. Umuofia means children of the forest (literal trans.); but *ofia* ("forest") also

means "bush," or land untouched by European influence.
3. A dusty wind from the Sahara.

and huge, and his bushy eyebrows and wide nose gave him a very severe look. He breathed heavily, and it was said that, when he slept, his wives and children in their out-houses could hear him breathe. When he walked, his heels hardly touched the ground and he seemed to walk on springs, as if he was going to pounce on somebody. And he did pounce on people quite often. He had a slight stammer and whenever he was angry and could not get his words out quickly enough, he would use his fists. He had no patience with unsuccessful men. He had had no patience with his father.

Unoka,[4] for that was his father's name, had died ten years ago. In his day he was lazy and improvident and was quite incapable of thinking about tomorrow. If any money came his way, and it seldom did, he immediately bought gourds of palm-wine, called round his neighbours and made merry. He always said that whenever he saw a dead man's mouth he saw the folly of not eating what one had in one's lifetime. Unoka was, of course, a debtor, and he owed every neighbour some money, from a few cowries[5] to quite substantial amounts.

He was tall but very thin and had a slight stoop. He wore a haggard and mournful look except when he was drinking or playing on his flute. He was very good on his flute, and his happiest moments were the two or three moons after the harvest when the village musicians brought down their instruments, hung above the fireplace. Unoka would play with them, his face beaming with blessedness and peace. Sometimes another village would ask Unoka's band and their dancing egwugwu[6] to come and stay with them and teach them their tunes. They would go to such hosts for as long as three or four markets,[7] making music and feasting. Unoka loved the good fare and the good fellowship, and he loved this season of the year, when the rains had stopped and the sun rose every morning with dazzling beauty. And it was not too hot either, because the cold and dry harmattan wind was blowing down from the north. Some years the harmattan was very severe and a dense haze hung on the atmosphere. Old men and children would then sit round log fires, warming their bodies. Unoka loved it all, and he loved the first kites[8] that returned with the dry season, and the children who sang songs of welcome to them. He would remember his own childhood, how he had often wandered around looking for a kite sailing leisurely against the blue sky. As soon as he found one he would sing with his whole being, welcoming it back from its long, long journey, and asking it if it had brought home any lengths of cloth.

That was years ago, when he was young. Unoka, the grown-up, was a failure. He was poor and his wife and children had barely enough to eat. People laughed at him because he was a loafer, and they swore never to lend him any more money because he never paid back. But Unoka was such a man that he always succeeded in borrowing more, and piling up his debts.

One day a neighbour called Okoye[9] came in to see him. He was reclining

---

4. Home is supreme.
5. Glossy half-inch-long tan-and-white shells, collected in strings and used as money. A bag of twenty-four thousand cowries weighed about sixty pounds and, at the time of the story, was worth approximately £1 British.
6. Here, masked performers as part of musical entertainment.

7. Counting one important market day a week, roughly two English weeks. The Igbo week has four days: Eke, Oye, Afo, and Nkwo. Eke is a rest day and the main market day; Afo, a half day on the farm; and Oye and Nkwo, full work days.
8. A kind of hawk.
9. Man born on Oye Day; a generic "Everyman" name.

on a mud bed in his hut playing on the flute. He immediately rose and shook hands with Okoye, who then unrolled the goatskin which he carried under his arm, and sat down. Unoka went into an inner room and soon returned with a small wooden disc containing a kola nut, some alligator pepper and a lump of white chalk.[1]

"I have kola," he announced when he sat down, and passed the disc over to his guest.

"Thank you. He who brings kola brings life. But I think you ought to break it," replied Okoye passing back the disc.

"No, it is for you, I think," and they argued like this for a few moments before Unoka accepted the honour of breaking the kola. Okoye, meanwhile, took the lump of chalk, drew some lines on the floor, and then painted his big toe.[2]

As he broke the kola, Unoka prayed to their ancestors for life and health, and for protection against their enemies. When they had eaten they talked about many things: about the heavy rains which were drowning the yams, about the next ancestral feast and about the impending war with the village of Mbaino. Unoka was never happy when it came to wars. He was in fact a coward and could not bear the sight of blood. And so he changed the subject and talked about music, and his face beamed. He could hear in his mind's ear the blood-stirring and intricate rhythms of the *ekwe* and the *udu* and the *ogene*,[3] and he could hear his own flute weaving in and out of them, decorating them with a colourful and plaintive tune. The total effect was gay and brisk, but if one picked out the flute as it went up and down and then broke up into short snatches, one saw that there was sorrow and grief there.

Okoye was also a musician. He played on the *ogene*. But he was not a failure like Unoka. He had a large barn full of yams and he had three wives. And now he was going to take the Idemili title,[4] the third highest in the land. It was a very expensive ceremony and he was gathering all his resources together. That was in fact the reason why he had come to see Unoka. He cleared his throat and began:

"Thank you for the kola. You may have heard of the title I intend to take shortly."

Having spoken plainly so far, Okoye said the next half a dozen sentences in proverbs. Among the Ibo the art of conversation is regarded very highly, and proverbs are the palm-oil with which words are eaten. Okoye was a great talker and he spoke for a long time, skirting round the subject and then hitting it finally. In short, he was asking Unoka to return the two hundred cowries he had borrowed from him more than two years before. As soon as Unoka understood what his friend was driving at, he burst out laughing. He laughed loud and long and his voice rang out clear as the *ogene*, and tears

1. Signifies coolness and peace and is offered in rituals of hospitality so that the guest may draw his personal emblem on the floor. "Kola nut": a bitter, caffeine-rich nut that is broken and eaten ceremonially; it indicates life or vitality. "Alligator pepper": black pepper, known as the "pepper for kola" to distinguish it from cooking pepper, or chilies.
2. If the guest has taken the first title, he marks his big toe. Higher titles require different facial markings.
3. A bell-shaped gong made from two pieces of sheet iron. "Ekwe": a wooden drum, about three feet long, that produces high and low tones (as does the Igbo language). "Udu": a clay pot with a hole to one side of the neck opening; various resonant tones are produced when the hole is struck with one hand while the other hand covers or uncovers the top.
4. A title of honor named after the river god Idemili, to whom the python is sacred. "Barn": not a building, but a walled enclosure for the yam stacks (frames on which individual yams are tied, shaded with palm leaves, and exposed to circulating air).

stood in his eyes. His visitor was amazed, and sat speechless. At the end, Unoka was able to give an answer between fresh outbursts of mirth.

"Look at that wall," he said, pointing at the far wall of his hut, which was rubbed with red earth so that it shone. "Look at those lines of chalk;" and Okoye saw groups of short perpendicular lines drawn in chalk. There were five groups, and the smallest group had ten lines. Unoka had a sense of the dramatic and so he allowed a pause, in which he took a pinch of snuff and sneezed noisily, and then he continued: "Each group there represents a debt to someone, and each stroke is one hundred cowries. You see, I owe that man a thousand cowries. But he has not come to wake me up in the morning for it. I shall pay you, but not today. Our elders say that the sun will shine on those who stand before it shines on those who kneel under them. I shall pay my big debts first." And he took another pinch of snuff, as if that was paying the big debts first. Okoye rolled his goatskin and departed.

When Unoka died he had taken no title at all and he was heavily in debt. Any wonder then that his son Okonkwo was ashamed of him? Fortunately, among these people a man was judged according to his worth and not according to the worth of his father. Okonkwo was clearly cut out for great things. He was still young but he had won fame as the greatest wrestler in the nine villages. He was a wealthy farmer and had two barns full of yams, and had just married his third wife. To crown it all he had taken two titles and had shown incredible prowess in two inter-tribal wars. And so although Okonkwo was still young, he was already one of the greatest men of his time. Age was respected among his people, but achievement was revered. As the elders said, if a child washed his hands he could eat with kings. Okonkwo had clearly washed his hands and so he ate with kings and elders. And that was how he came to look after the doomed lad who was sacrificed to the village of Umu-ofia by their neighbours to avoid war and bloodshed. The ill-fated lad was called Ikemefuna.[5]

CHAPTER TWO

Okonkwo had just blown out the palm-oil lamp and stretched himself on his bamboo bed when he heard the *ogene* of the town-crier piercing the still night air. *Gome, gome, gome, gome,* boomed the hollow metal. Then the crier gave his message, and at the end of it beat his instrument again. And this was the message. Every man of Umuofia was asked to gather at the market-place tomorrow morning. Okonkwo wondered what was amiss, for he knew certainly that something was amiss. He had discerned a clear overtone of tragedy in the crier's voice, and even now he could still hear it as it grew dimmer and dimmer in the distance.

The night was very quiet. It was always quiet except on moonlight nights. Darkness held a vague terror for these people, even the bravest among them. Children were warned not to whistle at night for fear of evil spirits. Danger-ous animals became even more sinister and uncanny in the dark. A snake was never called by its name at night, because it would hear. It was called a string. And so on this particular night as the crier's voice was gradually swal-lowed up in the distance, silence returned to the world, a vibrant silence made more intense by the universal trill of a million million forest insects.

5. My strength should not be dissipated.

On a moonlight night it would be different. The happy voices of children playing in open fields would then be heard. And perhaps those not so young would be playing in pairs in less open places, and old men and women would remember their youth. As the Ibo say: "When the moon is shining the cripple becomes hungry for a walk."

But this particular night was dark and silent. And in all the nine villages of Umuofia a town-crier with his *ogene* asked every man to be present tomorrow morning. Okonkwo on his bamboo bed tried to figure out the nature of the emergency—war with a neighbouring clan? That seemed the most likely reason, and he was not afraid of war. He was a man of action, a man of war. Unlike his father he could stand the look of blood. In Umuofia's latest war he was the first to bring home a human head. That was his fifth head; and he was not an old man yet. On great occasions such as the funeral of a village celebrity he drank his palm-wine from his first human head.

In the morning the market-place was full. There must have been about ten thousand men there, all talking in low voices. At last Ogbuefi Ezeugo stood up in the midst of them and bellowed four times, *"Umuofia kwenu,"*[6] and on each occasion he faced a different direction and seemed to push the air with a clenched fist. And ten thousand men answered *"Yaa!"* each time. Then there was perfect silence. Ogbuefi Ezeugo was a powerful orator and was always chosen to speak on such occasions. He moved his hand over his white head and stroked his white beard. He then adjusted his cloth, which was passed under his right arm-pit and tied above his left shoulder.

"Umuofia kwenu," he bellowed a fifth time, and the crowd yelled in answer. And then suddenly like one possessed he shot out his left hand and pointed in the direction of Mbaino, and said through gleaming white teeth firmly clenched: "Those sons of wild animals have dared to murder a daughter of Umuofia." He threw his head down and gnashed his teeth, and allowed a murmur of suppressed anger to sweep the crowd. When he began again, the anger on his face was gone and in its place a sort of smile hovered, more terrible and more sinister than the anger. And in a clear unemotional voice he told Umuofia how their daughter had gone to market at Mbaino and had been killed. That woman, said Ezeugo, was the wife of Ogbuefi Udo,[7] and he pointed to a man who sat near him with a bowed head. The crowd then shouted with anger and thirst for blood.

Many others spoke, and at the end it was decided to follow the normal course of action. An ultimatum was immediately dispatched to Mbaino asking them to choose between war on the one hand, and on the other the offer of a young man and a virgin as compensation.

Umuofia was feared by all its neighbours. It was powerful in war and in magic, and its priests and medicine-men were feared in all the surrounding country. Its most potent war-medicine was as old as the clan itself. Nobody knew how old. But on one point there was general agreement—the active principle in that medicine had been an old woman with one leg. In fact, the medicine itself was called *agadi-nwayi*, or old woman. It had its shrine in the centre of Umuofia, in a cleared spot. And if anybody was so foolhardy as to

6. United Umuofia! An orator's call on the audience to respond as a group. "Ogbuefi": cow killer (literal trans.); indicates someone who has taken a high title (e.g., the Idemili title) for which the celebration ceremony requires the slaughter of a cow. "Ezeugo": a name denoting a priest or high initiate, someone who wears the eagle feather.
7. Peace.

pass by the shrine after dusk he was sure to see the old woman hopping about.

And so the neighbouring clans who naturally knew of these things feared Umuofia, and would not go to war against it without first trying a peaceful settlement. And in fairness to Umuofia it should be recorded that it never went to war unless its case was clear and just and was accepted as such by its Oracle—the Oracle of the Hills and the Caves. And there were indeed occasions when the Oracle had forbidden Umuofia to wage a war. If the clan had disobeyed the Oracle they would surely have been beaten, because their dreaded *agadi-nwayi* would never fight what the Ibo call *a fight of blame*.

But the war that now threatened was a just war. Even the enemy clan knew that. And so when Okonkwo of Umuofia arrived at Mbaino as the proud and imperious emissary of war, he was treated with great honour and respect, and two days later he returned home with a lad of fifteen and a young virgin. The lad's name was Ikemefuna, whose sad story is still told in Umuofia unto this day.

The elders, or *ndichie*, met to hear a report of Okonkwo's mission. At the end they decided, as everybody knew they would, that the girl should go to Ogbuefi Udo to replace his murdered wife. As for the boy, he belonged to the clan as a whole, and there was no hurry to decide his fate. Okonkwo was, therefore, asked on behalf of the clan to look after him in the interim. And so for three years Ikemefuna lived in Okonkwo's household.

Okonkwo ruled his household with a heavy hand. His wives, especially the youngest, lived in perpetual fear of his fiery temper, and so did his little children. Perhaps down in his heart Okonkwo was not a cruel man. But his whole life was dominated by fear, the fear of failure and of weakness. It was deeper and more intimate than the fear of evil and capricious gods and of magic, the fear of the forest, and of the forces of nature, malevolent, red in tooth and claw. Okonkwo's fear was greater than these. It was not external but lay deep within himself. It was the fear of himself, lest he should be found to resemble his father. Even as a little boy he had resented his father's failure and weakness, and even now he still remembered how he had suffered when a playmate had told him that his father was *agbala*. That was how Okonkwo first came to know that *agbala* was not only another name for a woman, it could also mean a man who had taken no title. And so Okonkwo was ruled by one passion—to hate everything that his father Unoka had loved. One of those things was gentleness and another was idleness.

During the planting season Okonkwo worked daily on his farms from cock-crow until the chickens went to roost. He was a very strong man and rarely felt fatigue. But his wives and young children were not as strong, and so they suffered. But they dared not complain openly. Okonkwo's first son, Nwoye,[8] was then twelve years old but was already causing his father great anxiety for his incipient laziness. At any rate, that was how it looked to his father, and he sought to correct him by constant nagging and beating. And so Nwoye was developing into a sad-faced youth.

Okonkwo's prosperity was visible in his household. He had a large compound enclosed by a thick wall of red earth. His own hut, or *obi*, stood

8. Child born on Oye Day.

immediately behind the only gate in the red walls. Each of his three wives had her own hut, which together formed a half moon behind the *obi*. The barn was built against one end of the red walls, and long stacks of yam stood out prosperously in it. At the opposite end of the compound was a shed for the goats, and each wife built a small attachment to her hut for the hens. Near the barn was a small house, the 'medicine house' or shrine where Okonkwo kept the wooden symbols of his personal god and of his ancestral spirits. He worshipped them with sacrifices of kola nut, food and palm-wine, and offered prayers to them on behalf of himself, his three wives and eight children.

So when the daughter of Umuofia was killed in Mbaino, Ikemefuna came into Okonkwo's household. When Okonkwo brought him home that day he called his most senior wife and handed him over to her.

"He belongs to the clan," he told her. "So look after him."

"Is he staying long with us?" she asked.

"Do what you are told, woman," Okonkwo thundered, and stammered. "When did you become one of the *ndichie* of Umuofia?"

And so Nwoye's mother took Ikemefuna to her hut and asked no more questions.

As for the boy himself, he was terribly afraid. He could not understand what was happening to him or what he had done. How could he know that his father had taken a hand in killing a daughter of Umuofia? All he knew was that a few men had arrived at their house, conversing with his father in low tones, and at the end he had been taken out and handed over to a stranger. His mother had wept bitterly, but he had been too surprised to weep. And so the stranger had brought him, and a girl, a long, long way from home, through lonely forest paths. He did not know who the girl was, and he never saw her again.

CHAPTER THREE

Okonkwo did not have the start in life which many young men usually had. He did not inherit a barn from his father. There was no barn to inherit. The story was told in Umuofia of how his father, Unoka, had gone to consult the Oracle of the Hills and the Caves to find out why he always had a miserable harvest.

The Oracle was called Agbala,[9] and people came from far and near to consult it. They came when misfortune dogged their steps or when they had a dispute with their neighbours. They came to discover what the future held for them or to consult the spirits of their departed fathers.

The way into the shrine was a round hole at the side of a hill, just a little bigger than the round opening into a hen-house. Worshippers and those who came to seek knowledge from the god crawled on their belly through the hole and found themselves in a dark, endless space in the presence of Agbala. No one had ever beheld Agbala, except his priestess. But no one who had ever crawled into his awful shrine had come out without the fear of his power. His priestess stood by the sacred fire which she built in the heart of

9. The Oracle is masculine, but his priestess, or Voice, is feminine.

the cave and proclaimed the will of the god. The fire did not burn with a flame. The glowing logs only served to light up vaguely the dark figure of the priestess.

Sometimes a man came to consult the spirit of his dead father or relative. It was said that when such a spirit appeared, the man saw it vaguely in the darkness, but never heard its voice. Some people even said that they had heard the spirits flying and flapping their wings against the roof of the cave.

Many years ago when Okonkwo was still a boy his father, Unoka, had gone to consult Agbala. The priestess in those days was a woman called Chika.[1] She was full of the power of her god, and she was greatly feared. Unoka stood before her and began his story.

"Every year," he said sadly, "before I put any crop in the earth, I sacrifice a cock to Ani, the owner of all land. It is the law of our fathers. I also kill a cock at the shrine of Ifejioku, the god of yams. I clear the bush and set fire to it when it is dry. I sow the yams when the first rain has fallen, and stake them when the young tendrils appear. I weed——"

"Hold your peace!" screamed the priestess, her voice terrible as it echoed through the dark void. "You have offended neither the gods nor your fathers. And when a man is at peace with his gods and his ancestors, his harvest will be good or bad according to the strength of his arm. You, Unoka, are known in all the clan for the weakness of your matchet and your hoe. When your neighbours go out with their axe to cut down virgin forests, you sow your yams on exhausted farms that take no labour to clear. They cross seven rivers to make their farms; you stay at home and offer sacrifices to a reluctant soil. Go home and work like a man."

Unoka was an ill-fated man. He had a bad *chi* or personal god, and evil fortune followed him to the grave, or rather to his death, for he had no grave. He died of the swelling which was an abomination to the earth goddess. When a man was afflicted with swelling in the stomach and the limbs he was not allowed to die in the house. He was carried to the Evil Forest and left there to die. There was the story of a very stubborn man who staggered back to his house and had to be carried again to the forest and tied to a tree. The sickness was an abomination to the earth, and so the victim could not be buried in her bowels. He died and rotted away above the earth, and was not given the first or the second burial. Such was Unoka's fate. When they carried him away, he took with him his flute.

With a father like Unoka, Okonkwo did not have the start in life which many young men had. He neither inherited a barn nor a title, nor even a young wife. But in spite of these disadvantages, he had begun even in his father's lifetime to lay the foundations of a prosperous future. It was slow and painful. But he threw himself into it like one possessed. And indeed he was possessed by the fear of his father's contemptible life and shameful death.

There was a wealthy man in Okonkwo's village who had three huge barns, nine wives and thirty children. His name was Nwakibie[2] and he had taken the highest but one title which a man could take in the clan. It was for this man that Okonkwo worked to earn his first seed yams.

---

1. Sky is supreme.

2. The child surpasses his neighbors.

He took a pot of palm-wine and a cock to Nwakibie. Two elderly neighbours were sent for, and Nwakibie's two grown-up sons were also present in his *obi*. He presented a kola nut and an alligator pepper, which was passed round for all to see and then returned to him. He broke it, saying: "We shall all live. We pray for life, children, a good harvest and happiness. You will have what is good for you and I will have what is good for me. Let the kite perch and let the egret perch too. If one says no to the other, let his wing break."

After the kola nut had been eaten Okonkwo brought his palm-wine from the corner of the hut where it had been placed and stood it in the centre of the group. He addressed Nwakibie, calling him 'Our father'.

"*Nna ayi*," he said. "I have brought you this little kola. As our people say, a man who pays respect to the great paves the way for his own greatness. I have come to pay you my respects and also to ask a favour. But let us drink the wine first."

Everybody thanked Okonkwo and the neighbours brought out their drinking horns from the goatskin bags they carried. Nwakibie brought down his own horn, which was fastened to the rafters. The younger of his sons, who was also the youngest man in the group, moved to the centre, raised the pot on his left knee and began to pour out the wine. The first cup went to Okonkwo, who must taste his wine before anyone else.[3] Then the group drank, beginning with the eldest man. When everyone had drunk two or three horns, Nwakibie sent for his wives. Some of them were not at home and only four came in.

"Is Anasi not in?" he asked them. They said she was coming. Anasi was the first[4] wife and the others could not drink before her, and so they stood waiting.

Anasi was a middle-aged woman, tall and strongly built. There was authority in her bearing and she looked every inch the ruler of the womenfolk in a large and prosperous family. She wore the anklet of her husband's titles, which the first wife alone could wear.

She walked up to her husband and accepted the horn from him. She then went down on one knee, drank a little and handed back the horn. She rose, called him by his name and went back to her hut. The other wives drank in the same way, in their proper order, and went away.

The men then continued their drinking and talking. Ogbuefi Idigo was talking about the palm-wine tapper, Obiako, who suddenly gave up his trade.

"There must be something behind it," he said, wiping the foam of wine from his moustache with the back of his left hand. "There must be a reason for it. A toad does not run in the daytime for nothing."

"Some people say the Oracle warned him that he would fall off a palm tree and kill himself," said Akukalia.

"Obiako has always been a strange one," said Nwakibie. "I have heard that many years ago, when his father had not been dead very long, he had gone to consult the Oracle. The Oracle said to him, 'Your dead father wants you to sacrifice a goat to him.' Do you know what he told the Oracle? He said, 'Ask my dead father if he ever had a fowl when he was alive.'" Everybody

---

3. A ceremonial gesture; one who gives wine tastes it first to show that it is not poisoned.

4. First or favorite wife—not always the same.

laughed heartily except Okonkwo, who laughed uneasily because, as the saying goes, an old woman is always uneasy when dry bones are mentioned in a proverb. Okonkwo remembered his own father.

At last the young man who was pouring out the wine held up half a horn of the thick, white dregs and said, "What we are eating is finished." "We have seen it," the others replied. "Who will drink the dregs?" he asked. "Whoever has a job in hand," said Idigo, looking at Nwakibie's elder son Igwelo with a malicious twinkle in his eye.

Everybody agreed that Igwelo should drink the dregs. He accepted the half-full horn from his brother and drank it. As Idigo had said, Igwelo had a job in hand because he had married his first wife a month or two before. The thick dregs of palm-wine were supposed to be good for men who were going in to their wives.

After the wine had been drunk Okonkwo laid his difficulties before Nwakibie.

"I have come to you for help," he said. "Perhaps you can already guess what it is. I have cleared a farm but have no yams to sow. I know what it is to ask a man to trust another with his yams, especially these days when young men are afraid of hard work. I am not afraid of work. The lizard that jumped from the high iroko tree to the ground said he would praise himself if no one else did. I began to fend for myself at an age when most people still suck at their mothers' breasts. If you give me some yam seeds I shall not fail you."

Nwakibie cleared his throat. "It pleases me to see a young man like you these days when our youth have gone so soft. Many young men have come to me to ask for yams but I have refused because I knew they would just dump them in the earth and leave them to be choked by weeds. When I say no to them they think I am hard-hearted. But it is not so. Eneke the bird[5] says that since men have learnt to shoot without missing, he has learnt to fly without perching. I have learnt to be stingy with my yams. But I can trust you. I know it as I look at you. As our fathers said, you can tell a ripe corn by its look. I shall give you twice four hundred yams. Go ahead and prepare your farm."

Okonkwo thanked him again and again and went home feeling happy. He knew that Nwakibie would not refuse him, but he had not expected he would be so generous. He had not hoped to get more than four hundred seeds. He would now have to make a bigger farm. He hoped to get another four hundred yams from one of his father's friends at Isiuzo.[6]

Share-cropping was a very slow way of building up a barn of one's own. After all the toil one only got a third of the harvest. But for a young man whose father had no yams, there was no other way. And what made it worse in Okonkwo's case was that he had to support his mother and two sisters from his meagre harvest. And supporting his mother also meant supporting his father. She could not be expected to cook and eat while her husband starved. And so at a very early age when he was striving desperately to build a barn through share-cropping Okonkwo was also fending for his father's house. It was like pouring grains of corn into a bag full of holes. His mother

---

5. Proverbial.

6. Head of the road; a small town.

and sisters worked hard enough, but they grew women's crops, like coco-yams, beans and cassava. Yam, the king of crops, was a man's crop.[7]

The year that Okonkwo took eight hundred seed-yams from Nwakibie was the worst year in living memory. Nothing happened at its proper time; it was either too early or too late. It seemed as if the world had gone mad. The first rains were late, and, when they came, lasted only a brief moment. The blazing sun returned, more fierce than it had ever been known, and scorched all the green that had appeared with the rains. The earth burned like hot coals and roasted all the yams that had been sown. Like all good farmers, Okonkwo had begun to sow with the first rains. He had sown four hundred seeds when the rains dried up and the heat returned. He watched the sky all day for signs of rain-clouds and lay awake all night. In the morning he went back to his farm and saw the withering tendrils. He had tried to protect them from the smouldering earth by making rings of thick sisal leaves around them. But by the end of the day the sisal rings were burnt dry and grey. He changed them every day, and prayed that the rain might fall in the night. But the drought continued for eight market weeks and the yams were killed.

Some farmers had not planted their yams yet. They were the lazy easygoing ones who always put off clearing their farms as long as they could. This year they were the wise ones. They sympathised with their neighbours with much shaking of the head, but inwardly they were happy for what they took to be their own foresight.

Okonkwo planted what was left of his seed-yams when the rains finally returned. He had one consolation. The yams he had sown before the drought were his own, the harvest of the previous year. He still had the eight hundred from Nwakibie and the four hundred from his father's friend. So he would make a fresh start.

But the year had gone mad. Rain fell as it had never fallen before. For days and nights together it poured down in violent torrents, and washed away the yam heaps. Trees were uprooted and deep gorges appeared everywhere. Then the rain became less violent. But it went on from day to day without a pause. The spell of sunshine which always came in the middle of the wet season did not appear. The yams put on luxuriant green leaves, but every farmer knew that without sunshine the tubers would not grow.

That year the harvest was sad, like a funeral, and many farmers wept as they dug up the miserable and rotting yams. One man tied his cloth to a tree branch and hanged himself.

Okonkwo remembered that tragic year with a cold shiver throughout the rest of his life. It always surprised him when he thought of it later that he did not sink under the load of despair. He knew he was a fierce fighter, but that year had been enough to break the heart of a lion.

"Since I survived that year," he always said, "I shall survive anything." He put it down to his inflexible will.

His father, Unoka, who was then an ailing man, had said to him during

---

7. Yams, a staple food in Western Africa, were a sacred crop generally cultivated only by men and eaten either roasted or boiled. "Coco-yams" (a brown root also called taro) and "cassava" (or manioc, which is refined in various ways to remove natural cyanide) were low-status root vegetables, prepared for eating by boiling and pounding.

that terrible harvest month: "Do not despair. I know you will not despair. You have a manly and a proud heart. A proud heart can survive a general failure because such a failure does not prick its pride. It is more difficult and more bitter when a man fails *alone*."

Unoka was like that in his last days. His love of talk had grown with age and sickness. It tried Okonkwo's patience beyond words.

CHAPTER FOUR

"Looking at a king's mouth," said an old man, "one would think he never sucked at his mother's breast." He was talking about Okonkwo, who had risen so suddenly from great poverty and misfortune to be one of the lords of the clan. The old man bore no ill-will towards Okonkwo. Indeed he respected him for his industry and success. But he was struck, as most people were, by Okonkwo's brusqueness in dealing with less successful men. Only a week ago a man had contradicted him at a kindred meeting which they held to discuss the next ancestral feast. Without looking at the man Okonkwo had said: "This meeting is for men." The man who had contradicted him had no titles. That was why he had called him a woman. Okonkwo knew how to kill a man's spirit.

Everybody at the kindred meeting took sides with Osugo[8] when Okonkwo called him a woman. The oldest man present said sternly that those whose palm-kernels were cracked for them by a benevolent spirit should not forget to be humble. Okonkwo said he was sorry for what he had said, and the meeting continued.

But it was really not true that Okonkwo's palm-kernels had been cracked for him by a benevolent spirit. He had cracked them himself. Anyone who knew his grim struggle against poverty and misfortune could not say he had been lucky. If ever a man deserved his success, that man was Okonkwo. At an early age he had achieved fame as the greatest wrestler in all the land. That was not luck. At the most one could say that his *chi* or personal god was good. But the Ibo people have a proverb that when a man says yes his *chi* says yes also. Okonkwo said yes very strongly; so his *chi* agreed. And not only his *chi* but his clan too, because it judged a man by the work of his hands. That was why Okonkwo had been chosen by the nine villages to carry a message of war to their enemies unless they agreed to give up a young man and a virgin to atone for the murder of Udo's wife. And such was the deep fear that their enemies had for Umuofia that they treated Okonkwo like a king and brought him a virgin who was given to Udo as wife, and the lad Ikemefuna.

The elders of the clan had decided that Ikemefuna should be in Okonkwo's care for a while. But no one thought it would be as long as three years. They seemed to forget all about him as soon as they had taken the decision.

At first Ikemefuna was very much afraid. Once or twice he tried to run away, but he did not know where to begin. He thought of his mother and his three-year-old sister and wept bitterly. Nwoye's mother was very kind to him and treated him as one of her own children. But all he said was: "When

8. Low-status (*osu*) person.

shall I go home?" When Okonkwo heard that he would not eat any food he came into the hut with a big stick in his hand and stood over him while he swallowed his yams, trembling. A few moments later he went behind the hut and began to vomit painfully. Nwoye's mother went to him and placed her hands on his chest and on his back. He was ill for three market weeks, and when he recovered he seemed to have overcome his great fear and sadness. He was by nature a very lively boy and he gradually became popular in Okonkwo's household, especially with the children. Okonkwo's son, Nwoye, who was two years younger, became quite inseparable from him because he seemed to know everything. He could fashion out flutes from bamboo stems and even from the elephant grass. He knew the names of all the birds and could set clever traps for the little bush rodents. And he knew which trees made the strongest bows.

Even Okonkwo himself became very fond of the boy—inwardly of course. Okonkwo never showed any emotion openly, unless it be the emotion of anger. To show affection was a sign of weakness; the only thing worth demonstrating was strength. He therefore treated Ikemefuna as he treated everybody else—with a heavy hand. But there was no doubt that he liked the boy. Sometimes when he went to big village meetings or communal ancestral feasts he allowed Ikemefuna to accompany him, like a son, carrying his stool and his goatskin bag. And, indeed, Ikemefuna called him father.

Ikemefuna came to Umuofia at the end of the carefree season between harvest and planting. In fact he recovered from his illness only a few days before the Week of Peace began. And that was also the year Okonkwo broke the peace, and was punished, as was the custom, by Ezeani, the priest of the earth goddess.

Okonkwo was provoked to justifiable anger by his youngest wife, who went to plait her hair at her friend's house and did not return early enough to cook the afternoon meal. Okonkwo did not know at first that she was not at home. After waiting in vain for her dish he went to her hut to see what she was doing. There was nobody in the hut and the fireplace was cold.

"Where is Ojiugo?" he asked his second wife, who came out of her hut to draw water from a gigantic pot in the shade of a small tree in the middle of the compound.

"She has gone to plait her hair."

Okonkwo bit his lips as anger welled up within him.

"Where are her children? Did she take them?" he asked with unusual coolness and restraint.

"They are here," answered his first wife, Nwoye's mother. Okonkwo bent down and looked into her hut. Ojiugo's children were eating with the children of his first wife.

"Did she ask you to feed them before she went?"

"Yes," lied Nwoye's mother, trying to minimise Ojiugo's thoughtlessness.

Okonkwo knew she was not speaking the truth. He walked back to his *obi* to await Ojiugo's return. And when she returned he beat her very heavily. In his anger he had forgotten that it was the Week of Peace. His first two wives ran out in great alarm pleading with him that it was the sacred week. But Okonkwo was not the man to stop beating somebody half-way through, not even for fear of a goddess.

Okonkwo's neighbours heard his wife crying and sent their voices over the compound walls to ask what was the matter. Some of them came over to see for themselves. It was unheard-of to beat somebody during the sacred week.

Before it was dusk Ezeani, who was the priest of the earth goddess, Ani, called on Okonkwo in his *obi*. Okonkwo brought out kola nut and placed it before the priest.

"Take away your kola nut. I shall not eat in the house of a man who has no respect for our gods and ancestors."

Okonkwo tried to explain to him what his wife had done, but Ezeani seemed to pay no attention. He held a short staff in his hand which he brought down on the floor to emphasise his points.

"Listen to me," he said when Okonkwo had spoken. "You are not a stranger in Umuofia. You know as well as I do that our forefathers ordained that before we plant any crops in the earth we should observe a week in which a man does not say a harsh word to his neighbour. We live in peace with our fellows to honour our great goddess of the earth without whose blessing our crops will not grow. You have committed a great evil." He brought down his staff heavily on the floor. "Your wife was at fault, but even if you came into your *obi* and found her lover on top of her, you would still have committed a great evil to beat her." His staff came down again. "The evil you have done can ruin the whole clan. The earth goddess whom you have insulted may refuse to give us her increase, and we shall all perish." His tone now changed from anger to command. "You will bring to the shrine of Ani tomorrow one she-goat, one hen, a length of cloth and a hundred cowries." He rose and left the hut.

Okonkwo did as the priest said. He also took with him a pot of palm-wine. Inwardly, he was repentant. But he was not the man to go about telling his neighbours that he was in error. And so people said he had no respect for the gods of the clan. His enemies said his good fortune had gone to his head. They called him the little bird *nza*[9] who so far forgot himself after a heavy meal that he challenged his *chi*.

No work was done during the Week of Peace. People called on their neighbours and drank palm-wine. This year they talked of nothing else but the *nso-ani*[1] which Okonkwo had committed. It was the first time for many years that a man had broken the sacred peace. Even the oldest men could only remember one or two other occasions somewhere in the dim past.

Ogbuefi Ezeudu, who was the oldest man in the village, was telling two other men who came to visit him that the punishment for breaking the Peace of Ani had become very mild in their clan.

"It has not always been so," he said. "My father told me that he had been told that in the past a man who broke the peace was dragged on the ground through the village until he died. But after a while this custom was stopped because it spoilt the peace which it was meant to preserve."

"Somebody told me yesterday," said one of the younger men, "that in some clans it is an abomination for a man to die during the Week of Peace."

"It is indeed true," said Ogbuefi Ezeudu. "They have that custom in Obo-

---

9. The one that talks back (literal trans.); a small aggressive bird. In the traditional story, it is easily defeated (alternatively, caught by a hawk) when it becomes bold enough to challenge its personal god.
1. Sin, abomination against the Earth goddess Ani.

doani.[2] If a man dies at this time he is not buried but cast into the Evil Forest. It is a bad custom which these people observe because they lack understanding. They throw away large numbers of men and women without burial. And what is the result? Their clan is full of the evil spirits of these unburied dead, hungry to do harm to the living."

After the Week of Peace every man and his family began to clear the bush to make new farms. The cut bush was left to dry and fire was then set to it. As the smoke rose into the sky kites appeared from different directions and hovered over the burning field in silent valediction. The rainy season was approaching when they would go away until the dry season returned.

Okonkwo spent the next few days preparing his seed-yams. He looked at each yam carefully to see whether it was good for sowing. Sometimes he decided that a yam was too big to be sown as one seed and he split it deftly along its length with his sharp knife. His eldest son, Nwoye, and Ikemefuna helped him by fetching the yams in long baskets from the barn and in counting the prepared seeds in groups of four hundred. Sometimes Okonkwo gave them a few yams each to prepare. But he always found fault with their effort, and he said so with much threatening.

"Do you think you are cutting up yams for cooking?" he asked Nwoye. "If you split another yam of this size, I shall break your jaw. You think you are still a child. I began to own a farm at your age. And you," he said to Ikemefuna, "do you not grow yams where you come from?"

Inwardly Okonkwo knew that the boys were still too young to understand fully the difficult art of preparing seed-yams. But he thought that one could not begin too early. Yam stood for manliness, and he who could feed his family on yams from one harvest to another was a very great man indeed. Okonkwo wanted his son to be a great farmer and a great man. He would stamp out the disquieting signs of laziness which he thought he already saw in him.

"I will not have a son who cannot hold up his head in the gathering of the clan. I would sooner strangle him with my own hands. And if you stand staring at me like that," he swore, "Amadiora[3] will break your head for you!"

Some days later, when the land had been moistened by two or three heavy rains, Okonkwo and his family went to the farm with baskets of seed-yams, their hoes and matchets, and the planting began. They made single mounds of earth in straight lines all over the field and sowed the yams in them.

Yam, the king of crops, was a very exacting king. For three or four moons it demanded hard work and constant attention from cock-crow till the chickens went back to roost. The young tendrils were protected from earth-heat with rings of sisal leaves. As the rains became heavier the women planted maize, melons and beans between the yam mounds. The yams were then staked, first with little sticks and later with tall and big tree branches. The women weeded the farm three times at definite periods in the life of the yams, neither early nor late.

And now the rains had really come, so heavy and persistent that even the

2. The town of the land (literal trans.); i.e., Any-town, Nigeria.

3. God of thunder and lightning.

village rain-maker no longer claimed to be able to intervene. He could not stop the rain now, just as he would not attempt to start it in the heart of the dry season, without serious danger to his own health. The personal dynamism required to counter the forces of these extremes of weather would be far too great for the human frame.

And so nature was not interfered with in the middle of the rainy season. Sometimes it poured down in such thick sheets of water that earth and sky seemed merged in one grey wetness. It was then uncertain whether the low rumbling of Amadiora's thunder came from above or below. At such times, in each of the countless thatched huts of Umuofia, children sat around their mother's cooking fire telling stories, or with their father in his *obi* warming themselves from a log fire, roasting and eating maize. It was a brief resting period between the exacting and arduous planting season and the equally exacting but light-hearted month of harvests.

Ikemefuna had begun to feel like a member of Okonkwo's family. He still thought about his mother and his three-year-old sister, and he had moments of sadness and depression. But he and Nwoye had become so deeply attached to each other that such moments became less frequent and less poignant. Ikemefuna had an endless stock of folk tales. Even those which Nwoye knew already were told with a new freshness and the local flavour of a different clan. Nwoye remembered this period very vividly till the end of his life. He even remembered how he had laughed when Ikemefuna told him that the proper name for a corn-cob with only a few scattered grains was *eze-agadi-nwayi*, or the teeth of an old woman. Nwoye's mind had gone immediately to Nwayieke, who lived near the udala tree.[4] She had about three teeth and was always smoking her pipe.

Gradually the rains became lighter and less frequent, and earth and sky once again became separate. The rain fell in thin, slanting showers through sunshine and quiet breeze. Children no longer stayed indoors but ran about singing:

> "The rain is falling, the sun is shining,
> Alone Nnadi[5] is cooking and eating."

Nwoye always wondered who Nnadi was and why he should live all by himself, cooking and eating. In the end he decided that Nnadi must live in that land of Ikemefuna's favourite story where the ant holds his court in splendour and the sands dance forever.

CHAPTER FIVE

The Feast of the New Yam was approaching and Umuofia was in a festival mood. It was an occasion for giving thanks to Ani, the earth goddess and the source of all fertility. Ani played a greater part in the life of the people than any other deity. She was the ultimate judge of morality and conduct. And what was more, she was in close communion with the departed fathers of the clan whose bodies had been committed to earth.

The Feast of the New Yam was held every year before the harvest began,

4. African star apple tree. "Nwayieke": Woman born on Eke Day.   5. Father is there or Father exists.

to honour the earth goddess and the ancestral spirits of the clan. New yams could not be eaten until some had first been offered to these powers. Men and women, young and old, looked forward to the New Yam Festival because it began the season of plenty—the new year. On the last night before the festival, yams of the old year were all disposed of by those who still had them. The new year must begin with tasty, fresh yams and not the shrivelled and fibrous crop of the previous year. All cooking-pots, calabashes and wooden bowls were thoroughly washed, especially the wooden mortar in which yam was pounded. Yam foo-foo[6] and vegetable soup was the chief food in the celebration. So much of it was cooked that, no matter how heavily the family ate or how many friends and relations they invited from neighbouring villages, there was always a huge quantity of food left over at the end of the day. The story was always told of a wealthy man who set before his guests a mound of foo-foo so high that those who sat on one side could not see what was happening on the other, and it was not until late in the evening that one of them saw for the first time his in-law who had arrived during the course of the meal and had fallen to on the opposite side. It was only then that they exchanged greetings and shook hands over what was left of the food.

The New Yam Festival was thus an occasion for joy throughout Umuofia. And every man whose arm was strong, as the Ibo people say, was expected to invite large numbers of guests from far and wide. Okonkwo always asked his wives' relations, and since he now had three wives his guests would make a fairly big crowd.

But somehow Okonkwo could never become as enthusiastic over feasts as most people. He was a good eater and he could drink one or two fairly big gourds of palm-wine. But he was always uncomfortable sitting around for days waiting for a feast or getting over it. He would be very much happier working on his farm.

The festival was now only three days away. Okonkwo's wives had scrubbed the walls and the huts with red earth until they reflected light. They had then drawn patterns on them in white, yellow and dark green. They then set about painting themselves with cam wood and drawing beautiful black patterns on their stomachs and on their backs. The children were also decorated, especially their hair, which was shaved in beautiful patterns. The three women talked excitedly about the relations who had been invited, and the children revelled in the thought of being spoilt by these visitors from motherland. Ikemefuna was equally excited. The New Yam Festival seemed to him to be a much bigger event here than in his own village, a place which was already becoming remote and vague in his imagination.

And then the storm burst. Okonkwo, who had been walking about aimlessly in his compound in suppressed anger, suddenly found an outlet.

"Who killed this banana tree?" he asked.

A hush fell on the compound immediately.

"Who killed this tree? Or are you all deaf and dumb?"

As a matter of fact the tree was very much alive. Okonkwo's second wife had merely cut a few leaves off it to wrap some food, and she said so. Without further argument Okonkwo gave her a sound beating and left her and her

6. A mashed, edible base that is shaped into balls with the fingers and then indented for cupping and eating soup.

only daughter weeping. Neither of the other wives dared to interfere beyond an occasional and tentative, "It is enough, Okonkwo," pleaded from a reasonable distance.

His anger thus satisfied, Okonkwo decided to go out hunting. He had an old rusty gun made by a clever blacksmith who had come to live in Umuofia long ago. But although Okonkwo was a great man whose prowess was universally acknowledged, he was not a hunter. In fact he had not killed a rat with his gun. And so when he called Ikemefuna to fetch his gun, the wife who had just been beaten murmured something about guns that never shot. Unfortunately for her, Okonkwo heard it and ran madly into his room for the loaded gun, ran out again and aimed at her as she clambered over the dwarf wall of the barn. He pressed the trigger and there was a loud report accompanied by the wail of his wives and children. He threw down the gun and jumped into the barn, and there lay the woman, very much shaken and frightened but quite unhurt. He heaved a heavy sigh and went away with the gun.

In spite of this incident the New Yam Festival was celebrated with great joy in Okonkwo's household. Early that morning as he offered a sacrifice of new yam and palm-oil to his ancestors he asked them to protect him, his children and their mothers in the new year.

As the day wore on his in-laws arrived from three surrounding villages, and each party brought with them a huge pot of palm-wine. And there was eating and drinking till night, when Okonkwo's in-laws began to leave for their homes.

The second day of the new year was the day of the great wrestling match between Okonkwo's village and their neighbours. It was difficult to say which the people enjoyed more—the feasting and fellowship of the first day or the wrestling contest of the second. But there was one woman who had no doubt whatever in her mind. She was Okonkwo's second wife, Ekwefi, whom he nearly shot. There was no festival in all the seasons of the year which gave her as much pleasure as the wrestling match. Many years ago when she was the village beauty Okonkwo had won her heart by throwing the Cat in the greatest contest within living memory. She did not marry him then because he was too poor to pay her bride-price. But a few years later she ran away from her husband and came to live with Okonkwo. All this happened many years ago. Now Ekwefi[7] was a woman of forty-five who had suffered a great deal in her time. But her love of wrestling contests was still as strong as it was thirty years ago.

It was not yet noon on the second day of the New Yam Festival. Ekwefi and her only daughter, Ezinma,[8] sat near the fireplace waiting for the water in the pot to boil. The fowl Ekwefi had just killed was in the wooden mortar. The water began to boil, and in one deft movement she lifted the pot from the fire and poured the boiling water on to the fowl. She put back the empty pot on the circular pad in the corner, and looked at her palms, which were black with soot. Ezinma was always surprised that her mother could lift a pot from the fire with her bare hands.

---

7. An abbreviation of "Do you have a cow?"; the cow being a symbol of wealth. Okonkwo would presumably have repaid Ekwefi's bride-price to her first husband.

8. True beauty (literal trans.), or goodness.

"Ekwefi," she said, "is it true that when people are grown up, fire does not burn them?" Ezinma, unlike most children, called her mother by her name.

"Yes," replied Ekwefi, too busy to argue. Her daughter was only ten years old but she was wiser than her years.

"But Nwoye's mother dropped her pot of hot soup the other day and it broke on the floor."

Ekwefi turned the hen over in the mortar and began to pluck the feathers.

"Ekwefi," said Ezinma, who had joined in plucking the feathers, "my eyelid is twitching."

"It means you are going to cry," said her mother.

"No," Ezinma said, "it is this eyelid, the top one."

"That means you will see something."

"What will I see?" she asked.

"How can I know?" Ekwefi wanted her to work it out herself.

"Oho," said Ezinma at last. "I know what it is—the wrestling match."

At last the hen was plucked clean. Ekwefi tried to pull out the horny beak but it was too hard. She turned round on her low stool and put the beak in the fire for a few moments. She pulled again and it came off.

"Ekwefi!" a voice called from one of the other huts. It was Nwoye's mother, Okonkwo's first wife.

"Is that me?" Ekwefi called back. That was the way people answered calls from outside. They never answered yes for fear it might be an evil spirit calling.

"Will you give Ezinma some fire to bring to me?" Her own children and Ikemefuna had gone to the stream.

Ekwefi put a few live coals into a piece of broken pot and Ezinma carried it across the clean-swept compound to Nwoye's mother.

"Thank you, Nma," she said. She was peeling new yams, and in a basket beside her were green vegetables and beans.

"Let me make the fire for you," Ezinma offered.

"Thank you, Ezigbo," she said. She often called her Ezigbo, which means "the good one."

Ezinma went outside and brought some sticks from a huge bundle of firewood. She broke them into little pieces across the sole of her foot and began to build a fire, blowing it with her breath.

"You will blow your eyes out," said Nwoye's mother, looking up from the yams she was peeling. "Use the fan." She stood up and pulled out the fan which was fastened into one of the rafters. As soon as she got up, the troublesome nanny-goat, which had been dutifully eating yam peelings, dug her teeth into the real thing, scooped out two mouthfuls and fled from the hut to chew the cud in the goats' shed. Nwoye's mother swore at her and settled down again to her peeling. Ezinma's fire was now sending up thick clouds of smoke. She went on fanning it until it burst into flames. Nwoye's mother thanked her and she went back to her mother's hut.

Just then the distant beating of drums began to reach them. It came from the direction of the *ilo*, the village playground. Every village had its own *ilo* which was as old as the village itself and where all the great ceremonies and dances took place. The drums beat the unmistakable wrestling dance—quick, light and gay, and it came floating on the wind.

Okonkwo cleared his throat and moved his feet to the beat of the drums.

It filled him with fire as it had always done from his youth. He trembled with the desire to conquer and subdue. It was like the desire for woman.

"We shall be late for the wrestling," said Ezinma to her mother.

"They will not begin until the sun goes down."

"But they are beating the drums."

"Yes. The drums begin at noon but the wrestling waits until the sun begins to sink. Go and see if your father has brought out yams for the afternoon."

"He has. Nwoye's mother is already cooking."

"Go and bring our own, then. We must cook quickly or we shall be late for the wrestling."

Ezinma ran in the direction of the barn and brought back two yams from the dwarf wall.

Ekwefi peeled the yams quickly. The troublesome nanny-goat sniffed about, eating the peelings. She cut the yams into small pieces and began to prepare a pottage, using some of the chicken.

At that moment they heard someone crying just outside their compound. It was very much like Obiageli,[9] Nwoye's sister.

"Is that not Obiageli weeping?" Ekwefi called across the yard to Nwoye's mother.

"Yes," she replied. "She must have broken her water-pot."

The weeping was now quite close and soon the children filed in, carrying on their heads various sizes of pots suitable to their years. Ikemefuna came first with the biggest pot, closely followed by Nwoye and his two younger brothers. Obiageli brought up the rear, her face streaming with tears. In her hand was the cloth pad on which the pot should have rested on her head.

"What happened?" her mother asked, and Obiageli told her mournful story. Her mother consoled her and promised to buy her another pot.

Nwoye's younger brothers were about to tell their mother the true story of the accident when Ikemefuna looked at them sternly and they held their peace. The fact was that Obiageli had been making *inyanga*[1] with her pot. She had balanced it on her head, folded her arms in front of her and began to sway her waist like a grown-up young lady. When the pot fell down and broke she burst out laughing. She only began to weep when they got near the iroko tree outside their compound.

The drums were still beating, persistent and unchanging. Their sound was no longer a separate thing from the living village. It was like the pulsation of its heart. It throbbed in the air, in the sunshine, and even in the trees, and filled the village with excitement.

Ekwefi ladled her husband's share of the pottage into a bowl and covered it. Ezinma took it to him in his *obi*.

Okonkwo was sitting on a goatskin already eating his first wife's meal. Obiageli, who had brought it from her mother's hut, sat on the floor waiting for him to finish. Ezinma placed her mother's dish before him and sat with Obiageli.

"Sit like a woman!" Okonkwo shouted at her. Ezinma brought her two legs together and stretched them in front of her.

"Father, will you go to see the wrestling?" Ezinma asked after a suitable interval.

9. Born to eat (born into prosperity).   1. Showing off.

"Yes," he answered. "Will you go?"

"Yes." And after a pause she said: "Can I bring your chair for you?"

"No, that is a boy's job." Okonkwo was specially fond of Ezinma. She looked very much like her mother, who was once the village beauty. But his fondness only showed on very rare occasions.

"Obiageli broke her pot today," Ezinma said.

"Yes, she has told me about it," Okonkwo said between mouthfuls.

"Father," said Obiageli, "people should not talk when they are eating or pepper may go down the wrong way."

"That is very true. Do you hear that, Ezinma? You are older than Obiageli but she has more sense."

He uncovered his second wife's dish and began to eat from it. Obiageli took the first dish and returned to her mother's hut. And then Nkechi came in, bringing the third dish. Nkechi was the daughter of Okonkwo's third wife.

In the distance the drums continued to beat.

CHAPTER SIX

The whole village turned out on the *ilo*, men, women and children. They stood round in a huge circle leaving the centre of the playground free. The elders and grandees of the village sat on their own stools brought there by their young sons or slaves. Okonkwo was among them. All others stood except those who came early enough to secure places on the few stands which had been built by placing smooth logs on forked pillars.

The wrestlers were not there yet and the drummers held the field. They too sat just in front of the huge circle of spectators, facing the elders. Behind them was the big and ancient silk-cotton tree which was sacred. Spirits of good children lived in that tree waiting to be born. On ordinary days young women who desired children came to sit under its shade.

There were seven drums and they were arranged according to their sizes in a long wooden basket. Three men beat them with sticks, working feverishly from one drum to another. They were possessed by the spirit of the drums.

The young men who kept order on these occasions dashed about, consulting among themselves and with the leaders of the two wrestling teams, who were still outside the circle, behind the crowd. Once in a while two young men carrying palm fronds ran round the circle and kept the crowd back by beating the ground in front of them or, if they were stubborn, their legs and feet.

At last the two teams danced into the circle and the crowd roared and clapped. The drums rose to a frenzy. The people surged forward. The young men who kept order flew around, waving their palm fronds. Old men nodded to the beat of the drums and remembered the days when they wrestled to its intoxicating rhythm.

The contest began with boys of fifteen or sixteen. There were only three such boys in each team. They were not the real wrestlers; they merely set the scene. Within a short time the first two bouts were over. But the third created a big sensation even among the elders who did not usually show their excitement so openly. It was as quick as the other two, perhaps even quicker. But very few people had ever seen that kind of wrestling before. As soon as the two boys closed in, one of them did something which no one could

2638 / Chinua Achebe

describe because it had been as quick as a flash. And the other boy was flat
on his back. The crowd roared and clapped and for a while drowned the
frenzied drums. Okonkwo sprang to his feet and quickly sat down again.
Three young men from the victorious boy's team ran forward, carried him
shoulder-high and danced through the cheering crowd. Everybody soon
knew who the boy was. His name was Maduka, the son of Obierika.[2]

The drummers stopped for a brief rest before the real matches. Their
bodies shone with sweat, and they took up fans and began to fan themselves.
They also drank water from small pots and ate kola nuts. They became ordinary human beings again, talking and laughing among themselves and with
others who stood near them. The air, which had been stretched taut with
excitement, relaxed again. It was as if water had been poured on the tightened skin of a drum. Many people looked around, perhaps for the first time,
and saw those who stood or sat next to them.

"I did not know it was you," Ekwefi said to the woman who had stood
shoulder to shoulder with her since the beginning of the matches.

"I do not blame you," said the woman. "I have never seen such a large
crowd of people. Is it true that Okonkwo nearly killed you with his gun?"

"It is true indeed, my dear friend. I cannot yet find a mouth with which
to tell the story."

"Your *chi* is very much awake, my friend. And how is my daughter,
Ezinma?"

"She has been very well for some time now. Perhaps she has come to stay."

"I think she has. How old is she now?"

"She is about ten years old."

"I think she will stay. They usually stay if they do not die before the age
of six."

"I pray she stays," said Ekwefi with a heavy sigh.

The woman with whom she talked was called Chielo.[3] She was the priestess of Agbala, the Oracle of the Hills and the Caves. In ordinary life Chielo
was a widow with two children. She was very friendly with Ekwefi and they
shared a common shed in the market. She was particularly fond of Ekwefi's
only daughter, Ezinma, whom she called "my daughter". Quite often she
bought bean-cakes and gave Ekwefi some to take home to Ezinma. Anyone
seeing Chielo in ordinary life would hardly believe she was the same person
who prophesied when the spirit of Agbala was upon her.

The drummers took up their sticks again and the air shivered and grew
tense like a tightened bow.

The two teams were ranged facing each other across the clear space. A
young man from one team danced across the centre to the other side and
pointed at whomever he wanted to fight. They danced back to the centre
together and then closed in.

There were twelve men on each side and the challenge went from one side
to the other. Two judges walked around the wrestlers and when they thought
they were equally matched, stopped them. Five matches ended in this way.
But the really exciting moments were when a man was thrown. The huge
voice of the crowd then rose to the sky and in every direction. It was even
heard in the surrounding villages.

2. The heart eats [enjoys] more.   3. Chi who plants.

The last match was between the leaders of the teams. They were among the best wrestlers in all the nine villages. The crowd wondered who would throw the other this year. Some said Okafo was the better man; others said he was not the equal of Ikezue.[4] Last year neither of them had thrown the other even though the judges had allowed the contest to go on longer than was the custom. They had the same style and one saw the other's plans beforehand. It might happen again this year.

Dusk was already approaching when their contest began. The drums went mad and the crowds also. They surged forward as the two young men danced into the circle. The palm fronds were helpless in keeping them back.

Ikezue held out his right hand. Okafo seized it, and they closed in. It was a fierce contest. Ikezue strove to dig in his right heel behind Okafo so as to pitch him backwards in the clever *ege* style. But the one knew what the other was thinking. The crowd had surrounded and swallowed up the drummers, whose frantic rhythm was no longer a mere disembodied sound but the very heart-beat of the people.

The wrestlers were now almost still in each other's grip. The muscles on their arms and their thighs and on their backs stood out and twitched. It looked like an equal match. The two judges were already moving forward to separate them when Ikezue, now desperate, went down quickly on one knee in an attempt to fling his man backwards over his head. It was a sad miscalculation. Quick as the lightning of Amadiora, Okafo raised his right leg and swung it over his rival's head. The crowd burst into a thunderous roar. Okafo was swept off his feet by his supporters and carried home shoulder-high. They sang his praise and the young women clapped their hands:

> "Who will wrestle for our village?
> Okafo will wrestle for our village.
> Has he thrown a hundred men?
> He has thrown four hundred men.
> Has he thrown a hundred Cats?
> He has thrown four hundred Cats.
> Then send him word to fight for us."

CHAPTER SEVEN

For three years Ikemefuna lived in Okonkwo's household and the elders of Umuofia seemed to have forgotten about him. He grew rapidly like a yam tendril in the rainy season, and was full of the sap of life. He had become wholly absorbed into his new family. He was like an elder brother to Nwoye, and from the very first seemed to have kindled a new fire in the younger boy. He made him feel grown-up; and they no longer spent the evenings in mother's hut while she cooked, but now sat with Okonkwo in his *obi*, or watched him as he tapped his palm tree for the evening wine. Nothing pleased Nwoye now more than to be sent for by his mother or another of his father's wives to do one of those difficult and masculine tasks in the home, like splitting wood, or pounding food. On receiving such a message through a younger brother or sister, Nwoye would feign annoyance and grumble aloud about women and their troubles.

Okonkwo was inwardly pleased at his son's development, and he knew it

4. Strength is complete (a boastful name).

was due to Ikemefuna. He wanted Nwoye to grow into a tough young man capable of ruling his father's household when he was dead and gone to join the ancestors. He wanted him to be a prosperous man, having enough in his barn to feed the ancestors with regular sacrifices. And so he was always happy when he heard him grumbling about women. That showed that in time he would be able to control his women-folk. No matter how prosperous a man was, if he was unable to rule his women and his children (and especially his women) he was not really a man. He was like the man in the song who had ten and one wives and not enough soup for his foo-foo.

So Okonkwo encouraged the boys to sit with him in his *obi*, and he told them stories of the land—masculine stories of violence and bloodshed. Nwoye knew that it was right to be masculine and to be violent, but somehow he still preferred the stories that his mother used to tell, and which she no doubt still told to her younger children—stories of the tortoise and his wily ways, and of the bird *eneke-nti-oba*[5] who challenged the whole world to a wrestling contest and was finally thrown by the cat. He remembered the story she often told of the quarrel between Earth and Sky long ago, and how Sky withheld rain for seven years, until crops withered and the dead could not be buried because the hoes broke on the stony Earth. At last Vulture was sent to plead with Sky, and to soften his heart with a song of the suffering of the sons of men. Whenever Nwoye's mother sang this song he felt carried away to the distant scene in the sky where Vulture, Earth's emissary, sang for mercy. At last Sky was moved to pity, and he gave to Vulture rain wrapped in leaves of coco-yam. But as he flew home his long talon pierced the leaves and the rain fell as it had never fallen before. And so heavily did it rain on Vulture that he did not return to deliver his message but flew to a distant land, from where he had espied a fire. And when he got there he found it was a man making a sacrifice. He warmed himself in the fire and ate the entrails.

That was the kind of story that Nwoye loved. But he now knew that they were for foolish women and children, and he knew that his father wanted him to be a man. And so he feigned that he no longer cared for women's stories. And when he did this he saw that his father was pleased, and no longer rebuked him or beat him. So Nwoye and Ikemefuna would listen to Okonkwo's stories about tribal wars, or how, years ago, he had stalked his victim, overpowered him and obtained his first human head. And as he told them of the past they sat in darkness or the dim glow of logs, waiting for the women to finish their cooking. When they finished, each brought her bowl of foo-foo and bowl of soup to her husband. An oil lamp was lit and Okonkwo tasted from each bowl, and then passed two shares to Nwoye and Ikemefuna.

In this way the moons and the seasons passed. And then the locusts came. It had not happened for many a long year. The elders said locusts came once in a generation, reappeared every year for seven years and then disappeared for another lifetime. They went back to their caves in a distant land, where they were guarded by a race of stunted men. And then after another lifetime these men opened the caves again and the locusts came to Umuofia.

---

5. The swallow with the ear of a crocodile [who is deaf] (literal trans.); a bird who proverbially flies without perching.

They came in the cold harmattan season after the harvests had been gathered, and ate up all the wild grass in the fields.

Okonkwo and the two boys were working on the red outer walls of the compound. This was one of the lighter tasks of the after-harvest season. A new cover of thick palm branches and palm leaves was set on the walls to protect them from the next rainy season. Okonkwo worked on the outside of the wall and the boys worked from within. There were little holes from one side to the other in the upper levels of the wall, and through these Okonkwo passed the rope, or *tie-tie*,[6] to the boys and they passed it round the wooden stays and then back to him; and in this way the cover was strengthened on the wall.

The women had gone to the bush to collect firewood, and the little children to visit their playmates in the neighbouring compounds. The harmattan was in the air and seemed to distil a hazy feeling of sleep on the world. Okonkwo and the boys worked in complete silence, which was only broken when a new palm frond was lifted on to the wall or when a busy hen moved dry leaves about in her ceaseless search for food.

And then quite suddenly a shadow fell on the world, and the sun seemed hidden behind a thick cloud. Okonkwo looked up from his work and wondered if it was going to rain at such an unlikely time of the year. But almost immediately a shout of joy broke out in all directions, and Umuofia, which had dozed in the noon-day haze, broke into life and activity.

"Locusts are descending," was joyfully chanted everywhere, and men, women and children left their work or their play and ran into the open to see the unfamiliar sight. The locusts had not come for many, many years, and only the old people had seen them before.

At first, a fairly small swarm came. They were the harbingers sent to survey the land. And then appeared on the horizon a slowly-moving mass like a boundless sheet of black cloud drifting towards Umuofia. Soon it covered half the sky, and the solid mass was now broken by tiny eyes of light like shining star-dust. It was a tremendous sight, full of power and beauty.

Everyone was now about, talking excitedly and praying that the locusts should camp in Umuofia for the night. For although locusts had not visited Umuofia for many years, everybody knew by instinct that they were very good to eat. And at last the locusts did descend. They settled on every tree and on every blade of grass; they settled on the roofs and covered the bare ground. Mighty tree branches broke away under them, and the whole country became the brown-earth colour of the vast, hungry swarm.

Many people went out with baskets trying to catch them, but the elders counselled patience till nightfall. And they were right. The locusts settled in the bushes for the night and their wings became wet with dew. Then all Umuofia turned out in spite of the cold harmattan, and everyone filled his bags and pots with locusts. The next morning they were roasted in clay pots and then spread in the sun until they became dry and brittle. And for many days this rare food was eaten with solid palm-oil.

Okonkwo sat in his *obi* crunching happily with Ikemefuna and Nwoye, and drinking palm-wine copiously, when Ogbuefi Ezeudu came in. Ezeudu was the oldest man in this quarter of Umuofia. He had been a great and

6. A creeper used as a rope to lash sections in building (pidgin English from "to tie").

fearless warrior in his time, and was now accorded great respect in all the clan. He refused to join in the meal, and asked Okonkwo to have a word with him outside. And so they walked out together, the old man supporting himself with his stick. When they were out of ear-shot, he said to Okonkwo:

"That boy calls you father. Do not bear a hand in his death." Okonkwo was surprised, and was about to say something when the old man continued:

"Yes, Umuofia has decided to kill him. The Oracle of the Hills and the Caves has pronounced it. They will take him outside Umuofia as is the custom, and kill him there. But I want you to have nothing to do with it. He calls you his father."

The next day a group of elders from all the nine villages of Umuofia came to Okonkwo's house early in the morning, and before they began to speak in low tones Nwoye and Ikemefuna were sent out. They did not stay very long, but when they went away Okonkwo sat still for a very long time supporting his chin in his palms. Later in the day he called Ikemefuna and told him that he was to be taken home the next day. Nwoye overheard it and burst into tears, whereupon his father beat him heavily. As for Ikemefuna, he was at a loss. His own home had gradually become very faint and distant. He still missed his mother and his sister and would be very glad to see them. But somehow he knew he was not going to see them. He remembered once when men had talked in low tones with his father; and it seemed now as if it was happening all over again.

Later, Nwoye went to his mother's hut and told her that Ikemefuna was going home. She immediately dropped the pestle with which she was grinding pepper, folded her arms across her breast and sighed, "Poor child".

The next day, the men returned with a pot of wine. They were all fully dressed as if they were going to be a big clan meeting or to pay a visit to a neighbouring village. They passed their cloths under the right arm-pit, and hung their goatskin bags and sheathed matchets over their left shoulders. Okonkwo got ready quickly and the party set out with Ikemefuna carrying the pot of wine. A deathly silence descended on Okonkwo's compound. Even the very little children seemed to know. Throughout that day Nwoye sat in his mother's hut and tears stood in his eyes.

At the beginning of their journey the men of Umuofia talked and laughed about the locusts, about their women, and about some effeminate men who had refused to come with them. But as they drew near to the outskirts of Umuofia silence fell upon them too.

The sun rose slowly to the centre of the sky, and the dry, sandy footway began to throw up the heat that lay buried in it. Some birds chirruped in the forests around. The men trod dry leaves on the sand. All else was silent. Then from the distance came the faint beating of the *ekwe*. It rose and faded with the wind—a peaceful dance from a distant clan.

"It is an *ozo* dance,"[7] the men said among themselves. But no one was sure where it was coming from. Some said Ezimili, others Abame or Aninta. They argued for a short while and fell into silence again, and the elusive dance rose and fell with the wind. Somewhere a man was taking one of the titles of his clan, with music and dancing and a great feast.

The footway had now become a narrow line in the heart of the forest. The

---

7. Part of the *ozo* rituals, the spiritual ceremonies that accompanied the taking of titles.

short trees and sparse undergrowth which surrounded the men's village began to give way to giant trees and climbers which perhaps had stood from the beginning of things, untouched by the axe and the bush-fire. The sun breaking through their leaves and branches threw a pattern of light and shade on the sandy footway.

Ikemefuna heard a whisper close behind him and turned round sharply. The man who had whispered now called out aloud, urging the others to hurry up.

"We still have a long way to go," he said. Then he and another man went before Ikemefuna and set a faster pace.

Thus the men of Umuofia pursued their way, armed with sheathed machets, and Ikemefuna, carrying a pot of palm-wine on his head, walked in their midst. Although he had felt uneasy at first, he was not afraid now. Okonkwo walked behind him. He could hardly imagine that Okonkwo was not his real father. He had never been fond of his real father, and at the end of three years he had become very distant indeed. But his mother and his three-year-old sister . . . of course she would not be three now, but six. Would he recognise her now? She must have grown quite big. How his mother would weep for joy, and thank Okonkwo for having looked after him so well and for bringing him back. She would want to hear everything that had happened to him in all these years. Could he remember them all? He would tell her about Nwoye and his mother, and about the locusts. . . . Then quite suddenly a thought came upon him. His mother might be dead. He tried in vain to force the thought out of his mind. Then he tried to settle the matter the way he used to settle such matters when he was a little boy. He still remembered the song:

> *Eze elina, elina!*
> > *Sala*
> *Eze ilikwa ya*
> *Ikwaba akwa oligholi*
> *Ebe Danda nechi eze*
> *Ebe Uzuzu nete egwu*
> > *Sala*[8]

He sang it in his mind, and walked to its beat. If the song ended on his right foot, his mother was alive. If it ended on his left, she was dead. No, not dead, but ill. It ended on the right. She was alive and well. He sang the song again, and it ended on the left. But the second time did not count. The first voice gets to Chukwu, or God's house. That was a favourite saying of children. Ikemefuna felt like a child once more. It must be the thought of going home to his mother.

One of the men behind him cleared his throat. Ikemefuna looked back, and the man growled at him to go on and not stand looking back. The way he said it sent cold fear down Ikemefuna's back. His hands trembled vaguely on the black pot he carried. Why had Okonkwo withdrawn to the rear? Ikemefuna felt his legs melting under him. And he was afraid to look back.

---

8. King don't eat, don't eat / Sala / King if you eat it / You will weep for the abomination / Where Danda installs a king / Where Uzuzu dances / Sala. "Sala": meaningless refrain. "Danda": the ant. "Uzuzu": sand. Ikemefuna reassures himself by singing his favorite song about the country where the "sands dance forever" (see p. 2636).

As the man who had cleared his throat drew up and raised his matchet, Okonkwo looked away. He heard the blow. The pot fell and broke in the sand. He heard Ikemefuna cry, "My father, they have killed me!" as he ran towards him. Dazed with fear, Okonkwo drew his matchet and cut him down. He was afraid of being thought weak.

As soon as his father walked in, that night, Nwoye knew that Ikemefuna had been killed, and something seemed to give way inside him, like the snapping of a tightened bow. He did not cry. He just hung limp. He had had the same kind of feeling not long ago, during the last harvest season. Every child loved the harvest season. Those who were big enough to carry even a few yams in a tiny basket went with grown-ups to the farm. And if they could not help in digging up the yams, they could gather firewood together for roasting the ones that would be eaten there on the farm. This roasted yam soaked in red palm-oil and eaten in the open farm was sweeter than any meal at home. It was after such a day at the farm during the last harvest that Nwoye had felt for the first time a snapping inside him like the one he now felt. They were returning home with baskets of yams from a distant farm across the stream when they had heard the voice of an infant crying in the thick forest. A sudden hush had fallen on the women, who had been talking, and they had quickened their steps. Nwoye had heard that twins were put in earthenware pots and thrown away in the forest, but he had never yet come across them. A vague chill had descended on him and his head had seemed to swell, like a solitary walker at night who passes an evil spirit on the way. Then something had given way inside him. It descended on him again, this feeling, when his father walked in, that night after killing Ikemefuna.

CHAPTER EIGHT

Okonkwo did not taste any food for two days after the death of Ikemefuna. He drank palm-wine from morning till night, and his eyes were red and fierce like the eyes of a rat when it was caught by the tail and dashed against the floor. He called his son, Nwoye, to sit with him in his *obi*. But the boy was afraid of him and slipped out of the hut as soon as he noticed him dozing.

He did not sleep at night. He tried not to think about Ikemefuna, but the more he tried the more he thought about him. Once he got up from bed and walked about his compound. But he was so weak that his legs could hardly carry him. He felt like a drunken giant walking with the limbs of a mosquito. Now and then a cold shiver descended on his head and spread down his body.

On the third day he asked his second wife, Ekwefi, to roast plantains for him. She prepared it the way he liked—with slices of oil-bean and fish.

"You have not eaten for two days," said his daughter Ezinma when she brought the food to him. "So you must finish this." She sat down and stretched her legs in front of her. Okonkwo ate the food absent-mindedly. 'She should have been a boy,' he thought as he looked at his ten-year-old daughter. He passed her a piece of fish.

"Go and bring me some cold water," he said. Ezinma rushed out of the hut, chewing the fish, and soon returned with a bowl of cool water from the earthen pot in her mother's hut.

Okonkwo took the bowl from her and gulped the water down. He ate a few more pieces of plantain and pushed the dish aside.

"Bring me my bag," he asked, and Ezinma brought his goatskin bag from the far end of the hut. He searched in it for his snuff-bottle. It was a deep bag and took almost the whole length of his arm. It contained other things apart from his snuff-bottle. There was a drinking horn in it, and also a drinking gourd, and they knocked against each other as he searched. When he brought out the snuff-bottle he tapped it a few times against his knee-cap before taking out some snuff on the palm of his left hand. Then he remembered that he had not taken out his snuff-spoon. He searched his bag again and brought out a small, flat, ivory spoon, with which he carried the brown snuff to his nostrils.

Ezinma took the dish in one hand and the empty water bowl in the other and went back to her mother's hut. 'She should have been a boy,' Okonkwo said to himself again. His mind went back to Ikemefuna and he shivered. If only he could find some work to do he would be able to forget. But it was the season of rest between the harvest and the next planting season. The only work that men did at this time was covering the walls of their compound with new palm fronds. And Okonkwo had already done that. He had finished it on the very day the locusts came, when he had worked on one side of the wall and Ikemefuna and Nwoye on the other.

'When did you become a shivering old woman,' Okonkwo asked himself, 'you, who are known in all the nine villages for your valour in war? How can a man who has killed five men in battle fall to pieces because he has added a boy to their number? Okonkwo, you have become a woman indeed.'

He sprang to his feet, hung his goatskin bag on his shoulder and went to visit his friend, Obierika.

Obierika was sitting outside under the shade of an orange tree making thatches from leaves of the raffia-palm. He exchanged greetings with Okonkwo and led the way into his *obi*.

"I was coming over to see you as soon as I finished that thatch," he said, rubbing off the grains of sand that clung to his thighs.

"Is it well?" Okonkwo asked.

"Yes," replied Obierika. "My daughter's suitor is coming today and I hope we will clinch the matter of the bride-price. I want you to be there."

Just then Obierika's son, Maduka, came into the *obi* from outside, greeted Okonkwo and turned towards the compound.

"Come and shake hands with me," Okonkwo said to the lad. "Your wrestling the other day gave me much happiness." The boy smiled, shook hands with Okonkwo and went into the compound.

"He will do great things," Okonkwo said. "If I had a son like him I should be happy. I am worried about Nwoye. A bowl of pounded yams can throw him in a wrestling match. His two younger brothers are more promising. But I can tell you, Obierika, that my children do not resemble me. Where are the young suckers that will grow when the old banana tree dies? If Ezinma had been a boy I would have been happier. She has the right spirit."

"You worry yourself for nothing," said Obierika. "The children are still very young."

"Nwoye is old enough to impregnate a woman. At his age I was already fending for myself. No, my friend, he is not too young. A chick that will grow into a cock can be spotted the very day it hatches. I have done my best to make Nwoye grow into a man, but there is too much of his mother in him."

'Too much of his grandfather,' Obierika thought, but he did not say it. The same thought also came to Okonkwo's mind. But he had long learnt how to lay that ghost. Whenever the thought of his father's weakness and failure troubled him he expelled it by thinking about his own strength and success. And so he did now. His mind went to his latest show of manliness.

"I cannot understand why you refused to come with us to kill that boy," he asked Obierika.

"Because I did not want to," Obierika replied sharply. "I had something better to do."

"You sound as if you question the authority and the decision of the Oracle, who said he should die."

"I do not. Why should I? But the Oracle did not ask me to carry out its decision."

"But someone had to do it. If we were all afraid of blood, it would not be done. And what do you think the Oracle would do then?"

"You know very well, Okonkwo, that I am not afraid of blood; and if anyone tells you that I am, he is telling a lie. And let me tell you one thing, my friend. If I were you I would have stayed at home. What you have done will not please the Earth. It is the kind of action for which the goddess wipes out whole families."

"The Earth cannot punish me for obeying her messenger," Okonkwo said. "A child's fingers are not scalded by a piece of hot yam which its mother puts into its palm."

"That is true," Obierika agreed. "But if the Oracle said that my son should be killed I would neither dispute it nor be the one to do it."

They would have gone on arguing had Ofoedu[9] not come in just then. It was clear from his twinkling eyes that he had important news. But it would be impolite to rush him. Obierika offered him a lobe of the kola nut he had broken with Okonkwo. Ofoedu ate slowly and talked about the locusts. When he finished his kola nut he said:

"The things that happen these days are very strange."

"What has happened?" asked Okonkwo.

"Do you know Ogbuefi Ndulue?"[1] Ofoedu asked.

"Ogbuefi Ndulue of Ire village," Okonkwo and Obierika said together.

"He died this morning," said Ofoedu.

"That is not strange. He was the oldest man in Ire," said Obierika.

"You are right," Ofoedu agreed. "But you ought to ask why the drum has not been beaten to tell Umuofia of his death."

"Why?" asked Obierika and Okonkwo together.

"That is the strange part of it. You know his first wife who walks with a stick?"

"Yes. She is called Ozoemena."[2]

"That is so," said Ofoedu. "Ozoemena was, as you know, too old to attend Ndulue during his illness. His younger wives did that. When he died this morning, one of these women went to Ozoemena's hut and told her. She rose from her mat, took her stick and walked over to the *obi*. She knelt on

9. The ancestors are our guide.
1. Life has arrived.

2. Another bad thing will not happen.

her knees and hands at the threshold and called her husband, who was laid on a mat. 'Ogbuefi Ndulue,' she called, three times, and went back to her hut. When the youngest wife went to call her again to be present at the washing of the body, she found her lying on the mat, dead."

"That is very strange indeed," said Okonkwo. "They will put off Ndulue's funeral until his wife has been buried."[3]

"That is why the drum has not been beaten to tell Umuofia."

"It was always said that Ndulue and Ozoemena had one mind," said Obierika. "I remember when I was a young boy there was a song about them. He could not do anything without telling her."

"I did not know that," said Okonkwo. "I thought he was a strong man in his youth."

"He was indeed," said Ofoedu.

Okonkwo shook his head doubtfully.

"He led Umuofia to war in those days," said Obierika.

Okonkwo was beginning to feel like his old self again. All that he required was something to occupy his mind. If he had killed Ikemefuna during the busy planting season or harvesting it would not have been so bad; his mind would have been centred on his work. Okonkwo was not a man of thought but of action. But in the absence of work, talking was the next best.

Soon after Ofoedu left, Okonkwo took up his goatskin bag to go.

"I must go home to tap my palm trees for the afternoon," he said.

"Who taps your tall trees for you?" asked Obierika.

"Umezulike," replied Okonkwo.

"Sometimes I wish I had not taken the *ozo* title," said Obierika. "It wounds my heart to see these young men killing palm trees in the name of tapping."

"It is so indeed," Okonkwo agreed. "But the law of the land must be obeyed."

"I don't know how we got that law," said Obierika. "In many other clans a man of title is not forbidden to climb the palm tree. Here we say he cannot climb the tall tree but he can tap the short ones standing on the ground. It is like Dimaragana, who would not lend his knife for cutting up dog-meat because the dog was taboo to him, but offered to use his teeth."

"I think it is good that our clan holds the *ozo* title in high esteem," said Okonkwo. "In those other clans you speak of, *ozo* is so low that every beggar takes it."

"I was only speaking in jest," said Obierika. "In Abame and Aninta the title is worth less than two cowries. Every man wears the thread of title on his ankle, and does not lose it even if he steals."

"They have indeed soiled the name of *ozo*," said Okonkwo as he rose to go.

"It will not be very long now before my in-laws come," said Obierika.

"I shall return very soon," said Okonkwo, looking at the position of the sun.

There were seven men in Obierika's hut when Okonkwo returned. The suitor was a young man of about twenty-five, and with him were his father

---

3. A wife dying shortly after her husband was sometimes considered guilty of his death, so the village preserves appearances by burying Ozoemena before announcing Ogbuefi Ndulue's death.

and uncle. On Obierika's side were his two elder brothers and Maduka, his sixteen-year-old son.

"Ask Akueke's mother to send us some kola nuts," said Obierika to his son. Maduka vanished into the compound like lightning. The conversation at once centred on him, and everybody agreed that he was as sharp as a razor.

"I sometimes think he is too sharp," said Obierika, somewhat indulgently. "He hardly ever walks. He is always in a hurry. If you are sending him on an errand he flies away before he has heard half of the message."

"You were very much like that yourself," said his eldest brother. "As our people say, 'When mother-cow is chewing grass its young ones watch its mouth.' Maduka has been watching your mouth."

As he was speaking the boy returned, followed by Akueke,[4] his half-sister, carrying a wooden dish with three kola nuts and alligator pepper. She gave the dish to her father's eldest brother and then shook hands, very shyly, with her suitor and his relatives. She was about sixteen and just ripe for marriage. Her suitor and his relatives surveyed her young body with expert eyes as if to assure themselves that she was beautiful and ripe.

She wore a coiffure which was done up into a crest in the middle of the head. Cam wood was rubbed lightly into her skin, and all over her body were black patterns drawn with *uli*.[5] She wore a black necklace which hung down in three coils just above her full, succulent breasts. On her arms were red and yellow bangles, and on her waist four or five rows of *jigida*, or waist-beads.

When she had shaken hands, or rather held out her hand to be shaken, she returned to her mother's hut to help with the cooking.

"Remove your *jigida* first," her mother warned as she moved near the fireplace to bring the pestle resting against the wall. "Every day I tell you that *jigida* and fire are not friends. But you will never hear. You grew your ears for decoration, not for hearing. One of these days your *jigida* will catch fire on your waist, and then you will know."

Akueke moved to the other end of the hut and began to remove the waist-beads. It had to be done slowly and carefully, taking each string separately, else it would break and the thousand tiny rings would have to be strung together again. She rubbed each string downwards with her palms until it passed the buttocks and slipped down to the floor around her feet.

The men in the *obi* had already begun to drink the palm-wine which Akueke's suitor had brought. It was a very good wine and powerful, for in spite of the palm fruit hung across the mouth of the pot to restrain the lively liquor, white foam rose and spilled over.

"That wine is the work of a good tapper," said Okonkwo.

The young suitor, whose name was Ibe, smiled broadly and said to his father: "Do you hear that?" He then said to the others: "He will never admit that I am a good tapper."

"He tapped three of my best palm trees to death," said his father, Ukegbu.

"That was about five years ago," said Ibe, who had begun to pour out the

---

4. Wealth of Eke (a divinity). Similar names built on *ako* ("wealth") connote riches and are associated with the idea of women as a form of exchangeable material wealth.
5. A liquid made from crushed seeds, which caused the skin to pucker temporarily. It was used to create black tattoolike decorations. "Cam wood": a shrub. The powdered red heartwood of the shrub was used as a cosmetic dye.

wine, "before I learnt how to tap." He filled the first horn and gave to his father. Then he poured out for the others. Okonkwo brought out his big horn from the goatskin bag, blew into it to remove any dust that might be there, and gave it to Ibe to fill.

As the men drank, they talked about everything except the thing for which they had gathered. It was only after the pot had been emptied that the suitor's father cleared his voice and announced the object of their visit.

Obierika then presented to him a small bundle of short broomsticks. Ukegbu counted them.

"They are thirty?" he asked.

Obierika nodded in agreement.

"We are at last getting somewhere," Ukegbu said, and then turning to his brother and his son he said: "Let us go out and whisper together." The three rose and went outside. When they returned Ukegbu handed the bundle of sticks back to Obierika. He counted them; instead of thirty there were now only fifteen. He passed them over to his eldest brother, Machi, who also counted them and said:

"We had not thought to go below thirty. But as the dog said, 'If I fall down for you and you fall down for me, it is play'. Marriage should be a play and not a fight; so we are falling down again." He then added ten sticks to the fifteen and gave the bundle to Ukegbu.

In this way Akueke's bride-price was finally settled at twenty bags of cowries. It was already dusk when the two parties came to this agreement.

"Go and tell Akueke's mother that we have finished," Obierika said to his son, Maduka. Almost immediately the woman came in with a big bowl of foo-foo. Obierika's second wife followed with a pot of soup, and Maduka brought in a pot of palm-wine.

As the men ate and drank palm-wine they talked about the customs of their neighbours.

"It was only this morning," said Obierika, "that Okonkwo and I were talking about Abame and Aninta, where titled men climb trees and pound foo-foo for their wives."

"All their customs are upside-down. They do not decide bride-price as we do, with sticks. They haggle and bargain as if they were buying a goat or a cow in the market."

"That is very bad," said Obierika's eldest brother. "But what is good in one place is bad in another place. In Umunso they do not bargain at all, not even with broomsticks. The suitor just goes on bringing bags of cowries until his in-laws tell him to stop. It is a bad custom because it always leads to a quarrel."

"The world is large," said Okonkwo. "I have even heard that in some tribes a man's children belong to his wife and her family."

"That cannot be," said Machi. "You might as well say that the woman lies on top of the man when they are making the children."

"It is like the story of white men who, they say, are white like this piece of chalk," said Obierika. He held up a piece of chalk, which every man kept in his *obi* and with which his guests drew lines on the floor before they ate kola nuts. "And these white men, they say, have no toes."[6]

---

6. They wear shoes.

"And have you never seen them?" asked Machi.

"Have you?" asked Obierika.

"One of them passes here frequently," said Machi. "His name is Amadi."

Those who knew Amadi laughed. He was a leper, and the polite name for leprosy was 'the white skin'.

CHAPTER NINE

For the first time in three nights, Okonkwo slept. He woke up once in the middle of the night and his mind went back to the past three days without making him feel uneasy. He began to wonder why he had felt uneasy at all. It was like a man wondering in broad daylight why a dream had appeared so terrible to him at night. He stretched himself and scratched his thigh where a mosquito had bitten him as he slept. Another one was wailing near his right ear. He slapped the ear and hoped he had killed it. Why do they always go for one's ears? When he was a child his mother had told him a story about it. But it was as silly as all women's stories. Mosquito, she had said, had asked Ear to marry him, whereupon Ear fell on the floor in uncontrollable laughter. "How much longer do you think you will live?" she asked. "You are already a skeleton." Mosquito went away humiliated, and any time he passed her way he told Ear that he was still alive.

Okonkwo turned on his side and went back to sleep. He was roused in the morning by someone banging on his door.

"Who is that?" he growled. He knew it must be Ekwefi. Of his three wives Ekwefi was the only one who would have the audacity to bang on his door.

"Ezinma is dying," came her voice, and all the tragedy and sorrow of her life were packed in those words.

Okonkwo sprang from his bed, pushed back the bolt on his door and ran into Ekwefi's hut.

Ezinma lay shivering on a mat beside a huge fire that her mother had kept burning all night.

"It is *iba*,"[7] said Okonkwo as he took his matchet and went into the bush to collect the leaves and grasses and barks of trees that went into making the medicine for *iba*.

Ekwefi knelt beside the sick child, occasionally feeling with her palm the wet, burning forehead.

Ezinma was an only child and the centre of her mother's world. Very often it was Ezinma who decided what food her mother should prepare. Ekwefi even gave her such delicacies as eggs, which children were rarely allowed to eat because such food tempted them to steal. One day as Ezinma was eating an egg Okonkwo had come in unexpectedly from his hut. He was greatly shocked and swore to beat Ekwefi if she dared to give the child eggs again. But it was impossible to refuse Ezinma anything. After her father's rebuke she developed an even keener appetite for eggs. And she enjoyed above all the secrecy in which she now ate them. Her mother always took her into their bedroom and shut the door.

Ezinma did not call her mother *Nne* like all children. She called her by her name, Ekwefi, as her father and other grown-up people did. The rela-

---

7. A fever accompanied by jaundice, probably caused by malaria.

tionship between them was not only that of mother and child. There was something in it like the companionship of equals, which was strengthened by such little conspiracies as eating eggs in the bedroom.

Ekwefi had suffered a good deal in her life. She had borne ten children and nine of them had died in infancy, usually before the age of three. As she buried one child after another her sorrow gave way to despair and then to grim resignation. The birth of her children, which should be a woman's crowning glory, because for Ekwefi mere physical agony devoid of promise. The naming ceremony after seven market weeks became an empty ritual. Her deepening despair found expression in the names she gave her children. One of them was a pathetic cry, Onwumbiko—'Death, I implore you.' But Death took no notice; Onwumbiko died in his fifteenth month. The next child was a girl, Ozoemena—'May it not happen again.' She died in her eleventh month, and two others after her. Ekwefi then became defiant and called her next child Onwuma—'Death may please himself.' And he did.

After the death of Ekwefi's second child, Okonkwo had gone to a medicine-man, who was also a diviner of the Afa Oracle,[8] to inquire what was amiss. This man told him that the child was an *ogbanje*, one of those wicked children who, when they died, entered their mothers' wombs to be born again.

"When your wife becomes pregnant again," he said, "let her not sleep in her hut. Let her go and stay with her people. In that way she will elude her wicked tormentor and break its evil cycle of birth and death."

Ekwefi did as she was asked. As soon as she became pregnant she went to live with her old mother in another village. It was there that her third child was born and circumcised on the eighth day. She did not return to Okonkwo's compound until three days before the naming ceremony. The child was called Onwumbiko.

Onwumbiko was not given proper burial when he died. Okonkwo had called in another medicine-man who was famous in the clan for his great knowledge about *ogbanje* children. His name was Okagbue Uyanwa. Okagbue was a very striking figure, tall, with a full beard and a bald head. He was light in complexion and his eyes were red and fiery. He always gnashed his teeth as he listened to those who came to consult him. He asked Okonkwo a few questions about the dead child. All the neighbours and relations who had come to mourn gathered round them.

"On what market-day was it born?" he asked.

"*Oye*," replied Okonkwo.

"And it died this morning?"

Okonkwo said yes, and only then realised for the first time that the child had died on the same market-day as it had been born. The neighbours and relations also saw the coincidence and said among themselves that it was very significant.

"Where do you sleep with your wife, in your *obi* or in her own hut?" asked the medicine-man.

"In her hut."

"In future call her into your *obi*."

The medicine-man then ordered that there should be no mourning for the

8. One who communicates with the clients' ancestors by reading patterns made by objects (e.g., seeds, teeth, shells) thrown on a flat surface.

dead child. He brought out a sharp razor from the goatskin bag slung from his left shoulder and began to mutilate the child. Then he took it away to bury in the Evil Forest, holding it by the ankle and dragging it on the ground behind him. After such treatment it would think twice before coming again, unless it was one of the stubborn ones who returned, carrying the stamp of their mutilation—a missing finger or perhaps a dark line where the medicine-man's razor had cut them.

By the time Onwumbiko died Ekwefi had become a very bitter woman. Her husband's first wife had already had three sons, all strong and healthy. When she had borne her third son in succession, Okonkwo had slaughtered a goat for her, as was the custom. Ekwefi had nothing but good wishes for her. But she had grown so bitter about her own *chi* that she could not rejoice with others over their good fortune. And so, on the day that Nwoye's mother celebrated the birth of her three sons with feasting and music, Ekwefi was the only person in the happy company who went about with a cloud on her brow. Her husband's wife took this for malevolence, as husband's wives were wont to. How could she know that Ekwefi's bitterness did not flow outwards to others but inwards into her own soul; that she did not blame others for their good fortune but her own evil *chi* who denied her any?

At last Ezinma was born, and although ailing she seemed determined to live. At first Ekwefi accepted her, as she had accepted others—with listless resignation. But when she lived on to her fourth, fifth and sixth years, love returned once more to her mother, and, with love, anxiety. She determined to nurse her child to health, and she put all her being into it. She was rewarded by occasional spells of health during which Ezinma bubbled with energy like fresh palm-wine. At such times she seemed beyond danger. But all of a sudden she would go down again. Everybody knew she was an *ogbanje*. These sudden bouts of sickness and health were typical of her kind. But she had lived so long that perhaps she had decided to stay. Some of them did become tired of their evil rounds of birth and death, or took pity on their mothers, and stayed. Ekwefi believed deep inside her that Ezinma had come to stay. She believed because it was that faith alone that gave her own life any kind of meaning. And this faith had been strengthened when a year or so ago a medicine-man had dug up Ezinma's *iyi-uwa*.[9] Everyone knew then that she would live because her bond with the world of *ogbanje* had been broken. Ekwefi was reassured. But such was her anxiety for her daughter that she could not rid herself completely of her fear. And although she believed that the *iyi-uwa* which had been dug up was genuine, she could not ignore the fact that some really evil children sometimes misled people into digging up a specious one.

But Ezinma's *iyi-uwa* had looked real enough. It was a smooth pebble wrapped in a dirty rag. The man who dug it up was the same Okagbue who was famous in all the clan for his knowledge in these matters. Ezinma had not wanted to co-operate with him at first. But that was only to be expected. No *ogbanje* would yield her secrets easily, and most of them never did because they died too young—before they could be asked questions.

"Where did you bury your *iyi-uwa*?" Okagbue had asked Ezinma. She was nine then and was just recovering from a serious illness.

---

9. Stone that forms the link between an *ogbanje* child and the spirit world. If the *iyi-uwa* is found and destroyed, the cycle is broken and the child will not die.

"What is *iyi-uwa*?" she asked in return.

"You know what it is. You buried it in the ground somewhere so that you can die and return again to torment your mother."

Ezinma looked at her mother, whose eyes, sad and pleading, were fixed on her.

"Answer the question at once," roared Okonkwo, who stood beside her. All the family were there and some of the neighbours too.

"Leave her to me," the medicine-man told Okonkwo in a cool, confident voice. He turned again to Ezinma. "Where did you bury your *iyi-uwa*?"

"Where they bury children," she replied, and the quiet spectators murmured to themselves.

"Come along then and show me the spot," said the medicine-man.

The crowd set out with Ezinma leading the way and Okagbue following closely behind her. Okonkwo came next and Ekwefi followed him. When she came to the main road, Ezinma turned left as if she was going to the stream.

"But you said it was where they bury children?" asked the medicine-man.

"No," said Ezinma, whose feeling of importance was manifest in her sprightly walk. She sometimes broke into a run and stopped again suddenly. The crowd followed her silently. Women and children returning from the stream with pots of water on their heads wondered what was happening until they saw Okagbue and guessed that it must be something to do with *ogbanje*. And they all knew Ekwefi and her daughter very well.

When she got to the big udala tree Ezinma turned left into the bush, and the crowd followed her. Because of her size she made her way through trees and creepers more quickly than her followers. The bush was alive with the tread of feet on dry leaves and sticks and the moving aside of tree branches. Ezinma went deeper and deeper and the crowd went with her. Then she suddenly turned round and began to walk back to the road. Everybody stood to let her pass and then filed after her.

"If you bring us all this way for nothing I shall beat sense into you," Okonkwo threatened.

"I have told you to let her alone. I know how to deal with them," said Okagbue.

Ezinma led the way back to the road, looked left and right and turned right. And so they arrived home again.

"Where did you bury your *iyi-uwa*?" asked Okagbue when Ezinma finally stopped outside her father's *obi*. Okagbue's voice was unchanged. It was quiet and confident.

"It is near that orange tree," Ezinma said.

"And why did you not say so, you wicked daughter of Akalogoli?" Okonkwo swore furiously. The medicine-man ignored him.

"Come and show me the exact spot," he said quietly to Ezinma.

"It is here," she said when they got to the tree.

"Point at the spot with your finger," said Okagbue.

"It is here," said Ezinma touching the ground with her finger. Okonkwo stood by, rumbling like thunder in the rainy season.

"Bring me a hoe," said Okagbue.

When Ekwefi brought the hoe, he had already put aside his goatskin bag and his big cloth and was in his underwear, a long and thin strip of cloth wound round the waist like a belt and then passed between the legs to be fastened to the belt behind. He immediately set to work digging a pit where

Ezinma had indicated. The neighbours sat around watching the pit becoming deeper and deeper. The dark top-soil soon gave way to the bright-red earth with which women scrubbed the floor and walls of huts. Okagbue worked tirelessly and in silence, his back shining with perspiration. Okonkwo stood by the pit. He asked Okagbue to come up and rest while he took a hand. But Okagbue said he was not tired yet.

Ekwefi went into her hut to cook yams. Her husband had brought out more yams than usual because the medicine-man had to be fed. Ezinma went with her and helped in preparing the vegetables.

"There is too much green vegetable," she said.

"Don't you see the pot is full of yams?" Ekwefi asked.

"And you know how leaves become smaller after cooking."

"Yes," said Ezinma, "that was why the snake-lizard killed his mother."

"Very true," said Ekwefi.

"He gave his mother seven baskets of vegetables to cook and in the end there were only three. And so he killed her," said Ezinma.

"That is not the end of the story."

"Oho," said Ezinma. "I remember now. He brought another seven baskets and cooked them himself. And there were again only three. So he killed himself too."

Outside the *obi* Okagbue and Okonkwo were digging the pit to find where Ezinma had buried her *iyi-uwa*. Neighbours sat around, watching. The pit was now so deep that they no longer saw the digger. They only saw the red earth he threw up mounting higher and higher. Okonkwo's son, Nwoye, stood near the edge of the pit because he wanted to take in all that happened.

Okagbue had again taken over the digging from Okonkwo. He worked, as usual, in silence. The neighbours and Okonkwo's wives were now talking. The children had lost interest and were playing.

Suddenly Okagbue sprang to the surface with the agility of a leopard.

"It is very near now," he said. "I have felt it."

There was immediate excitement and those who were sitting jumped to their feet.

"Call your wife and child," he said to Okonkwo. But Ekwefi and Ezinma had heard the noise and run out to see what it was.

Okagbue went back into the pit, which was now surrounded by spectators. After a few more hoe-fuls of earth he struck the *iyi-uwa*. He raised it carefully with the hoe and threw it to the surface. Some women ran away in fear when it was thrown. But they soon returned and everyone was gazing at the rag from a reasonable distance. Okagbue emerged and without saying a word or even looking at the spectators he went to his goatskin bag, took out two leaves and began to chew them. When he had swallowed them, he took up the rag with his left hand and began to untie it. And then the smooth, shiny pebble fell out. He picked it up.

"Is this yours?" he asked Ezinma.

"Yes," she replied. All the women shouted with joy because Ekwefi's troubles were at last ended.

All this had happened more than a year ago and Ezinma had not been ill since. And then suddenly she had begun to shiver in the night. Ekwefi brought her to the fireplace, spread her mat on the floor and built a fire. But she had got worse and worse. As she knelt by her, feeling with her palm the wet, burning forehead, she prayed a thousand times. Although her husband's wives were saying that it was nothing more than *iba*, she did not hear them.

Okonkwo returned from the bush carrying on his left shoulder a large bundle of grasses and leaves, roots and barks of medicinal trees and shrubs. He went into Ekwefi's hut, put down his load and sat down.

"Get me a pot," he said, "and leave the child alone."

Ekwefi went to bring the pot and Okonkwo selected the best from his bundle, in their due proportions, and cut them up. He put them in the pot and Ekwefi poured in some water.

"Is that enough?" she asked when she had poured in about half of the water in the bowl.

"A little more . . . I said a *little*. Are you deaf?" Okonkwo roared at her.

She set the pot on the fire and Okonkwo took up his matchet to return to his *obi*.

"You must watch the pot carefully," he said as he went, "and don't allow it to boil over. If it does its power will be gone." He went away to his hut and Ekwefi began to tend the medicine pot almost as if it was itself a sick child. Her eyes went constantly from Ezinma to the boiling pot and back to Ezinma.

Okonkwo returned when he felt the medicine had cooked long enough. He looked it over and said it was done.

"Bring a low stool for Ezinma," he said, "and a thick mat."

He took down the pot from the fire and placed it in front of the stool. He then roused Ezinma and placed her on the stool, astride the steaming pot. The thick mat was thrown over both. Ezinma struggled to escape from the choking and overpowering steam, but she was held down. She started to cry.

When the mat was at last removed she was drenched in perspiration. Ekwefi mopped her with a piece of cloth and she lay down on a dry mat and was soon asleep.

CHAPTER TEN

Large crowds began to gather on the village *ilo* as soon as the edge had worn off the sun's heat and it was no longer painful on the body. Most communal ceremonies took place at that time of the day, so that even when it was said that a ceremony would begin "after the midday meal" everyone understood that it would begin a long time later, when the sun's heat had softened.

It was clear from the way the crowd stood or sat that the ceremony was for men. There were many women, but they looked on from the fringe like outsiders. The titled men and elders sat on their stools waiting for the trials to begin. In front of them was a row of stools on which nobody sat. There were nine of them. Two little groups of people stood at a respectable distance beyond the stools. They faced the elders. There were three men in one group and three men and one woman in the other. The woman was Mgbafo and the three men with her were her brothers. In the other group were her husband, Uzowulu, and his relatives. Mgbafo and her brothers were as still as statues into whose faces the artist has moulded defiance. Uzowulu and his relative, on the other hand, were whispering together. It looked like whispering, but they were really talking at the top of their voices. Everybody in the crowd was talking. It was like the market. From a distance the noise was a deep rumble carried by the wind.

An iron gong sounded, setting up a wave of expectation in the crowd. Everyone looked in the direction of the *egwugwu*[1] house. *Gome, gome, gome, gome* went the gong, and a powerful flute blew a high-pitched blast. Then came the voices of the *egwugwu*, guttural and awesome. The wave struck the women and children and there was a backward stampede. But it was momentary. They were already far enough where they stood and there was room for running away if any of the *egwugwu* should go towards them.

The drum sounded again and the flute blew. The *egwugwu* house was now a pandemonium of quavering voices: *Aru oyim de de de dei!*[2] filled the air as the spirits of the ancestors, just emerged from the earth, greeted themselves in their esoteric language. The *egwugwu* house into which they emerged faced the forest, away from the crowd, who saw only its back with the many-coloured patterns and drawings done by specially chosen women at regular intervals. These women never saw the inside of the hut. No woman ever did. They scrubbed and painted the outside walls under the supervision of men. If they imagined what was inside, they kept their imagination to themselves. No woman ever asked questions about the most powerful and the most secret cult in the clan.

Aru oyim de de de dei! flew around the dark, closed hut like tongues of fire. The ancestral spirits of the clan were abroad. The metal gong beat continuously now and the flute, shrill and powerful, floated on the chaos.

And then the *egwugwu* appeared. The women and children sent up a great shout and took to their heels. It was instinctive. A woman fled as soon as an *egwugwu* came in sight. And when, as on that day, nine of the greatest masked spirits in the clan came out together it was a terrifying spectacle. Even Mgbafo took to her heels and had to be restrained by her brothers.

Each of the nine *egwugwu* represented a village of the clan. Their leader was called Evil Forest. Smoke poured out of his head.

The nine villages of Umuofia had grown out of the nine sons of the first father of the clan. Evil Forest represented the village of Umueru, or the children of Eru, who was the eldest of the nine sons.

"*Umuofia kwenu!*" shouted the leading *egwugwu*, pushing the air with his raffia arms. The elders of the clan replied, "*Yaa!*"

"*Umuofia kwenu!*"

"*Yaa!*"

"*Umuofia kwenu!*"

"*Yaa!*"

Evil Forest then thrust the pointed end of his rattling staff into the earth. And it began to shake and rattle, like something agitating with a metallic life. He took the first of the empty stools and the eight other *egwugwu* began to sit in order of seniority after him.

Okonkwo's wives, and perhaps other women as well, might have noticed that the second *egwugwu* had the springy walk of Okonkwo. And they might also have noticed that Okonkwo was not among the titled men and elders who sat behind the row of *egwugwu*. But if they thought these things they

---

1. Here the term refers to the village's highest spiritual and judicial authority, prominent men who, after putting on elaborate ceremonial costumes, embody the village's ancestral spirits.
2. Body of my friend, greetings!

kept them within themselves. The *egwugwu* with the springy walk was one of the dead fathers of the clan. He looked terrible with the smoked raffia body, a huge wooden face painted white except for the round hollow eyes and the charred teeth that were as big as a man's fingers. On his head were two powerful horns.

When all the *egwugwu* had sat down and the sound of the many tiny bells and rattles on their bodies had subsided, Evil Forest addressed the two groups of people facing them.

"Uzowulu's body, I salute you," he said. Spirits always addressed humans as 'bodies'. Uzowulu bent down and touched the earth with his right hand as a sign of submission.

"Our father, my hand has touched the ground," he said.

"Uzowulu's body, do you know me?" asked the spirit.

"How can I know you, father? You are beyond our knowledge."

Evil Forest then turned to the other group and addressed the eldest of the three brothers.

"The body of Odukwe, I greet you," he said, and Odukwe bent down and touched the earth. The hearing then began.

Uzowulu stepped forward and presented his case.

"That woman standing there is my wife, Mgbafo. I married her with my money and my yams. I do not owe my in-laws anything. I owe them no yams. I owe them no coco-yams. One morning three of them came to my house, beat me up and took my wife and children away. This happened in the rainy season. I have waited in vain for my wife to return. At last I went to my in-laws and said to them, 'You have taken back your sister. I did not send her away. You yourselves took her. The law of the clan is that you should return her bride-price.' But my wife's brothers said they had nothing to tell me. So I have brought the matter to the fathers of the clan. My case is finished. I salute you."

"Your words are good," said the leader of the *egwugwu*. "Let us hear Odukwe. His words may also be good."

Odukwe was short and thick-set. He stepped forward, saluted the spirits and began his story.

"My in-law has told you that we went to his house, beat him up and took our sister and her children away. All that is true. He told you that he came to take back her bride-price and we refused to give it him. That also is true. My in-law, Uzowulu, is a beast. My sister lived with him for nine years. During those years no single day passed in the sky without his beating the woman. We have tried to settle their quarrels time without number and on each occasion Uzowulu was guilty——"

"It is a lie!" Uzowulu shouted.

"Two years ago," continued Odukwe, "when she was pregnant, he beat her until she miscarried."

"It is a lie. She miscarried after she had gone to sleep with her lover."

"Uzowulu's body, I salute you," said Evil Forest, silencing him. "What kind of lover sleeps with a pregnant woman?" There was a loud murmur of approbation from the crowd. Odukwe continued:

"Last year when my sister was recovering from an illness, he beat her again so that if the neighbours had not gone in to save her she would have been killed. We heard of it, and did as you have been told. The law of Umuofia is that if a woman runs away from her husband her bride-price is returned. But in this case she ran away to save her life. Her two children belong to Uzowulu. We do not dispute it, but they are too young to leave their mother. If, on the other hand, Uzowulu should recover from his madness and come in the proper way to beg his wife to return she will do so on the understanding that if he ever beats her again we shall cut off his genitals for him."

The crowd roared with laughter. Evil Forest rose to his feet and order was immediately restored. A steady cloud of smoke rose from his head. He sat down again and called two witnesses. They were both Uzowulu's neighbours, and they agreed about the beating. Evil Forest then stood up, pulled out his staff and thrust it into the earth again. He ran a few steps in the direction of the women; they all fled in terror, only to return to their places almost immediately. The nine *egwugwu* then went away to consult together in their house. They were silent for a long time. Then the metal gong sounded and the flute was blown. The *egwugwu* had emerged once again from their underground home. They saluted one another and then reappeared on the *ilo*.

"*Umuofia kwenu!*" roared Evil Forest, facing the elders and grandees of the clan.

"*Yaa!*" replied the thunderous crowd; then silence descended from the sky and swallowed the noise.

Evil Forest began to speak and all the while he spoke everyone was silent. The eight other *egwugwu* were as still as statues.

"We have heard both sides of the case," said Evil Forest. "Our duty is not to blame this man or to praise that, but to settle the dispute." He turned to Uzowulu's group and allowed a short pause.

"Uzowulu's body, I salute you," he said.

"Our father, my hand has touched the ground," replied Uzowulu, touching the earth.

"Uzowulu's body, do you know me?"

"How can I know you, father? You are beyond our knowledge," Uzowulu replied.

"I am Evil Forest. I kill a man on the day that his life is sweetest to him."

"That is true," replied Uzowulu.

"Go to your in-laws with a pot of wine and beg your wife to return to you. It is not bravery when a man fights with a woman." He turned to Odukwe, and allowed a brief pause.

"Odukwe's body, I greet you," he said.

"My hand is on the ground," replied Odukwe.

"Do you know me?"

"No man can know you," replied Odukwe.

"I am Evil Forest, I am Dry-meat-that-fills-the-mouth, I am Fire-that-burns-without-faggots. If your in-law brings wine to you, let your sister go with him. I salute you." He pulled his staff from the hard earth and thrust it back.

"*Umuofia kwenu!*" he roared, and the crowd answered.

"I don't know why such a trifle should come before the *egwugwu*," said one elder to another.

"Don't you know what kind of man Uzowulu is? He will not listen to any other decision," replied the other.

As they spoke two other groups of people had replaced the first before the *egwugwu*, and a great land case began.

CHAPTER ELEVEN

The night was impenetrably dark. The moon had been rising later and later every night until now it was seen only at dawn. And whenever the moon forsook evening and rose at cock-crow the nights were as black as charcoal.

Ezinma and her mother sat on a mat on the floor after their supper of yam foo-foo and bitter-leaf soup. A palm-oil lamp gave out yellowish light. Without it, it would have been impossible to eat; one could not have known where one's mouth was in the darkness of that night. There was an oil lamp in all the four huts on Okonkwo's compound, and each hut seen from the others looked like a soft eye of yellow half-light set in the solid massiveness of night.

The world was silent except for the shrill cry of insects, which was part of the night, and the sound of wooden mortar and pestle as Nwayieke pounded her foo-foo. Nwayieke lived four compounds away, and she was notorious for her late cooking. Every woman in the neighbourhood knew the sound of Nwayieke's mortar and pestle. It was also part of the night.

Okonkwo had eaten from his wives' dishes and was now reclining with his back against the wall. He searched his bag and brought out his snuff-bottle. He turned it on to his left palm, but nothing came out. He hit the bottle against his knee to shake up the tobacco. That was always the trouble with Okeke's snuff. It very quickly went damp, and there was too much saltpetre in it. Okonkwo had not bought snuff from him for a long time. Idigo was the man who knew how to grind good snuff. But he had recently fallen ill.

Low voices, broken now and again by singing, reached Okonkwo from his wives' huts as each woman and her children told folk stories. Ekwefi and her daughter, Ezinma, sat on a mat on the floor. It was Ekwefi's turn to tell a story.

"Once upon a time," she began, "all the birds were invited to a feast in the sky. They were very happy and began to prepare themselves for the great day. They painted their bodies with red cam wood and drew beautiful patterns on them with *uli*.

"Tortoise saw all these preparations and soon discovered what it all meant. Nothing that happened in the world of the animals ever escaped his notice; he was full of cunning. As soon as he heard of the great feast in the sky his throat began to itch at the very thought. There was a famine in those days and Tortoise had not eaten a good meal for two moons. His body rattled like a piece of dry stick in his empty shell. So he began to plan how he would go to the sky."

"But he had no wings," said Ezinma.

"Be patient," replied her mother. "That is the story. Tortoise had no wings, but he went to the birds and asked to be allowed to go with them.

" 'We know you too well,' said the birds when they had heard him. 'You are full of cunning and you are ungrateful. If we allow you to come with us you will soon begin your mischief.'

" 'You do not know me,' said Tortoise. 'I am a changed man. I have learnt that a man who makes trouble for others is also making it for himself.'

"Tortoise had a sweet tongue, and within a short time all the birds agreed that he was a changed man, and they each gave him a feather, with which he made two wings.

"At last the great day came and Tortoise was the first to arrive at the meeting-place. When all the birds had gathered together, they set off in a body. Tortoise was very happy and voluble as he flew among the birds, and he was soon chosen as the man to speak for the party because he was a great orator.

" 'There is one important thing which we must not forget,' he said as they flew on their way. 'When people are invited to a great feast like this, they take new names for the occasion. Our hosts in the sky will expect us to honour this age-old custom.'

"None of the birds had heard of this custom but they knew that Tortoise, in spite of his failings in other directions, was a widely-travelled man who knew the customs of different peoples. And so they each took a new name. When they had all taken, Tortoise also took one. He was to be called *All of you.*

"At last the party arrived in the sky and their hosts were very happy to see them. Tortoise stood up in his many-coloured plumage and thanked them for their invitation. His speech was so eloquent that all the birds were glad they had brought him, and nodded their heads in approval of all he said. Their hosts took him as the king of the birds, especially as he looked somewhat different from the others.

"After kola nuts had been presented and eaten, the people of the sky set before their guests the most delectable dishes Tortoise had ever seen or dreamt of. The soup was brought out hot from the fire and in the very pot in which it had been cooked. It was full of meat and fish. Tortoise began to sniff aloud. There was pounded yam and also yam pottage cooked with palm-oil and fresh fish. There were also pots of palm-wine. When everything had been set before the guests, one of the people of the sky came forward and tasted a little from each pot. He then invited the birds to eat. But Tortoise jumped to his feet and asked: 'For whom have you prepared this feast?'

" 'For all of you,' replied the man.

"Tortoise turned to the birds and said: 'You remember that my name is *All of you.* The custom here is to serve the spokesman first and the others later. They will serve you when I have eaten.'

"He began to eat and the birds grumbled angrily. The people of the sky thought it must be their custom to leave all the food for their king. And so Tortoise ate the best part of the food and then drank two pots of palm-wine, so that he was full of food and drink and his body filled out in his shell.

"The birds gathered round to eat what was left and to peck at the bones he had thrown all about the floor. Some of them were too angry to eat. They chose to fly home on an empty stomach. But before they left each took back the feather he had lent to Tortoise. And there he stood in his hard shell full of food and wine but without any wings to fly home. He asked the birds to take a message for his wife, but they all refused. In the end Parrot, who had felt more angry than the others, suddenly changed his mind and agreed to take the message.

" 'Tell my wife,' said Tortoise, 'to bring out all the soft things in my house and cover the compound with them so that I can jump down from the sky without very great danger.'

"Parrot promised to deliver the message, and then flew away. But when he reached Tortoise's house he told his wife to bring out all the hard things in the house. And so she brought out her husband's hoes, matchets, spears, guns and even his cannon. Tortoise looked down from the sky and saw his wife bringing things out, but it was too far to see what they were. When all seemed ready he let himself go. He fell and fell and fell until he began to fear that he would never stop falling. And then like the sound of his cannon he crashed on the compound."

"Did he die?" asked Ezinma.

"No," replied Ekwefi. "His shell broke into pieces. But there was a great medicine-man in the neighbourhood. Tortoise's wife sent for him and he gathered all the bits of shell and stuck them together. That is why Tortoise's shell is not smooth."

"There is no song in the story," Ezinma pointed out.

"No," said Ekwefi. "I shall think of another one with a song. But it is your turn now."

"Once upon a time," Ezinma began, "Tortoise and Cat went to wrestle against Yams—no, that is not the beginning. Once upon a time there was a great famine in the land of animals. Everybody was lean except Cat, who was fat and whose body shone as if oil was rubbed on it . . ."

She broke off because at that very moment a loud and high-pitched voice broke the outer silence of the night. It was Chielo, the priestess of Agbala, prophesying. There was nothing new in that. Once in a while Chielo was possessed by the spirit of her god and she began to prophesy. But tonight she was addressing her prophecy and greetings to Okonkwo, and so everyone in his family listened. The folk stories stopped.

"*Agbala do-o-o-o! Agbala ekeneo-o-o-o,*"[3] came the voice like a sharp knife cutting through the night. "*Okonkwo! Agbala ekene gio-o-o-o! Agbala cholu ifu ada ya Ezinmao-o-o-o!*"[4]

At the mention of Ezinma's name Ekwefi jerked her head sharply like an animal that had sniffed death in the air. Her heart jumped painfully within her.

The priestess had now reached Okonkwo's compound and was talking with him outside his hut. She was saying again and again that Agbala wanted to see his daughter, Ezinma. Okonkwo pleaded with her to come back in the morning because Ezinma was now asleep. But Chielo ignored what he was trying to say and went on shouting that Agbala wanted to see his daughter. Her voice was as clear as metal, and Okonkwo's women and children heard from their huts all that she said. Okonkwo was still pleading that the girl had been ill of late and was asleep. Ekwefi quickly took her to their bedroom and placed her on their high bamboo bed.

The priestess suddenly screamed. "Beware, Okonkwo!" she warned. "Beware of exchanging words with Agbala. Does a man speak when a god speaks? Beware!"

3. Agbala wants something! Agbala greets.
4. Agbala greets you! Agbala wants to see his daughter Ezinma!

She walked through Okonkwo's hut into the circular compound and went straight towards Ekwefi's hut. Okonkwo came after her.

"Ekwefi," she called, "Agbala greets you. Where is my daughter, Ezinma? Agbala wants to see her."

Ekwefi came out from her hut carrying her oil lamp in her left hand. There was a light wind blowing, so she cupped her right hand to shelter the flame. Nwoye's mother, also carrying an oil lamp, emerged from her hut. Her children stood in the darkness outside their hut watching the strange event. Okonkwo's youngest wife also came out and joined the others.

"Where does Agbala want to see her?" Ekwefi asked.

"Where else but in his house in the hills and the caves?" replied the priestess.

"I will come with you, too," Ekwefi said firmly.

"*Tufia-a!*"[5] the priestess cursed, her voice cracking like the angry bark of thunder in the dry season. "How dare you, woman, to go before the mighty Agbala of your own accord? Beware, woman, lest he strike you in his anger. Bring me my daughter."

Ekwefi went into her hut and came out again with Ezinma.

"Come, my daughter," said the priestess. "I shall carry you on my back. A baby on its mother's back does not know that the way is long."

Ezinma began to cry. She was used to Chielo calling her 'my daughter'. But it was a different Chielo she now saw in the yellow half-light.

"Don't cry, my daughter," said the priestess, "lest Agbala be angry with you."

"Don't cry," said Ekwefi, "she will bring you back very soon. I shall give you some fish to eat." She went into the hut again and brought down the smoke-black basket in which she kept her dried fish and other ingredients for cooking soup. She broke a piece in two and gave it to Ezinma, who clung to her.

"Don't be afraid," said Ekwefi, stroking her head, which was shaved in places, leaving a regular pattern of hair. They went outside again. The priestess bent down on one knee and Ezinma climbed on her back, her left palm closed on her fish and her eyes gleaming with tears.

"*Agbala do-o-o-o! Agbala ekeneo-o-o-o!* . . ." Chielo began once again to chant greetings to her god. She turned round sharply and walked through Okonkwo's hut, bending very low at the eaves. Ezinma was crying loudly now, calling on her mother. The two voices disappeared into the thick darkness.

A strange and sudden weakness descended on Ekwefi as she stood gazing in the direction of the voices like a hen whose only chick has been carried away by a kite. Ezinma's voice soon faded away and only Chielo was heard moving farther and farther into the distance.

"Why do you stand there as though she had been kidnapped?" asked Okonkwo as he went back to his hut.

"She will bring her back soon," Nwoye's mother said.

But Ekwefi did not hear these consolations. She stood for a while, and then, all of a sudden, made up her mind. She hurried through Okonkwo's hut and went outside.

5. A curse in words meaning "spitting" or "clearing out," often accompanied by spitting.

"Where are you going?" he asked.

"I am following Chielo," she replied and disappeared in the darkness. Okonkwo cleared his throat, and brought out his snuff-bottle from the goat-skin bag by his side.

The priestess's voice was already growing faint in the distance. Ekwefi hurried to the main footpath and turned left in the direction of the voice. Her eyes were useless to her in the darkness. But she picked her way easily on the sandy footpath hedged on either side by branches and damp leaves. She began to run, holding her breasts with her hands to stop them flapping noisily against her body. She hit her left foot against an outcropped root, and terror seized her. It was an ill omen. She ran faster. But Chielo's voice was still a long way away. Had she been running too? How could she go so fast with Ezinma on her back? Although the night was cool, Ekwefi was beginning to feel hot from her running. She continually ran into the luxuriant weeds and creepers that walled in the path. Once she tripped up and fell. Only then did she realise, with a start, that Chielo had stopped her chanting. Her heart beat violently and she stood still. Then Chielo's renewed outburst came from only a few paces ahead. But Ekwefi could not see her. She shut her eyes for a while and opened them again in an effort to see. But it was useless. She could not see beyond her nose.

There were no stars in the sky because there was a rain-cloud. Fireflies went about with their tiny green lamps, which only made the darkness more profound. Between Chielo's outbursts the night was alive with the shrill tremor of forest insects woven into the darkness.

"Agbala do-o-o-o! . . . Agbala ekeneo-o-o-o! . . ." Ekwefi trudged behind, neither getting too near nor keeping too far back. She thought they must be going towards the sacred cave. Now that she walked slowly she had time to think. What would she do when they got to the cave? She would not dare to enter. She would wait at the mouth, all alone in that fearful place. She thought of all the terrors of the night. She remembered the night, long ago, when she had seen *Ogbu-agali-odu*, one of those evil essences loosed upon the world by the potent 'medicines' which the tribe had made in the distant past against its enemies but had now forgotten how to control. Ekwefi had been returning from the stream with her mother on a dark night like this when they saw its glow as it flew in their direction. They had thrown down their water-pots and lain by the roadside expecting the sinister light to descend on them and kill them. That was the only time Ekwefi ever saw *Ogbu-agali-odu*. But although it had happened so long ago, her blood still ran cold whenever she remembered that night.

The priestess's voice came at longer intervals now, but its vigour was undiminished. The air was cool and damp with dew. Ezinma sneezed. Ekwefi muttered, "Life to you." At the same time the priestess also said, "Life to you, my daughter." Ezinma's voice from the darkness warmed her mother's heart. She trudged slowly along.

And then the priestess screamed. "Somebody is walking behind me!" she said. "Whether you are spirit or man, may Agbala shave your head with a blunt razor! May he twist your neck until you see your heels!"

Ekwefi stood rooted to the spot. One mind said to her: 'Woman, go home before Agbala does you harm.' But she could not. She stood until Chielo had increased the distance between them and she began to follow again. She had already walked so long that she began to feel a slight numbness in the limbs and in the head. Then it occurred to her that they could not have been heading for the cave. They must have by-passed it long ago; they must be going towards Umuachi, the farthest village in the clan. Chielo's voice now came after long intervals.

It seemed to Ekwefi that the night had become a little lighter. The cloud had lifted and a few stars were out. The moon must be preparing to rise, its sullenness over. When the moon rose late in the night, people said it was refusing food, as a sullen husband refuses his wife's food when they have quarrelled.

"*Agbala do-o-o-o! Umuachi! Agbala ekene unuo-o-o!*" It was just as Ekwefi had thought. The priestess was now saluting the village of Umuachi. It was unbelievable, the distance they had covered. As they emerged into the open village from the narrow forest track the darkness was softened and it became possible to see the vague shape of trees. Ekwefi screwed her eyes up in an effort to see her daughter and the priestess, but whenever she thought she saw their shape it immediately dissolved like a melting lump of darkness. She walked numbly along.

Chielo's voice was now rising continuously, as when she first set out. Ekwefi had a feeling of spacious openness, and she guessed they must be on the village *ilo*, or playground. And she realised too with something like a jerk that Chielo was no longer moving forward. She was, in fact, returning. Ekwefi quickly moved away from her line of retreat. Chielo passed by, and they began to go back the way they had come.

It was a long and weary journey and Ekwefi felt like a sleep-walker most of the way. The moon was definitely rising, and although it had not yet appeared on the sky its light had already melted down the darkness. Ekwefi could now discern the figure of the priestess and her burden. She slowed down her pace so as to increase the distance between them. She was afraid of what might happen if Chielo suddenly turned round and saw her.

She had prayed for the moon to rise. But now she found the half-light of the incipient moon more terrifying than darkness. The world was now peopled with vague, fantastic figures that dissolved under her steady gaze and then formed again in new shapes. At one stage Ekwefi was so afraid that she nearly called out to Chielo for companionship and human sympathy. What she had seen was the shape of a man climbing a palm tree, his head pointing to the earth and his legs skywards. But at that very moment Chielo's voice rose again in her possessed chanting, and Ekwefi recoiled, because there was no humanity there. It was not the same Chielo who sat with her in the market and sometimes bought bean-cakes for Ezinma, whom she called her daughter. It was a different woman—the priestess of Agbala, the Oracle of the Hills and Caves. Ekwefi trudged along between two fears. The sound of her benumbed steps seemed to come from some other person walking behind her. Her arms were folded across her bare breasts. Dew fell heavily and the air was cold. She could no longer think, not even about the terrors of night. She just jogged along in a half-sleep, only waking to full life when Chielo sang.

At last they took a turning and began to head for the caves. From then on, Chielo never ceased in her chanting. She greeted her god in a multitude of names—the owner of the future, the messenger of earth, the god who cut a man down when his life was sweetest to him. Ekwefi was also awakened and her benumbed fears revived.

The moon was now up and she could see Chielo and Ezinma clearly. How a woman could carry a child of that size so easily and for so long was a miracle. But Ekwefi was not thinking about that. Chielo was not a woman that night.

"*Agbala do-o-o-o! Agbala ekeno-o-o-o! Chi negbu madu ubosi ndu ya nato ya uto daluo-o-o!* . . ."[6]

Ekwefi could already see the hills looming in the moonlight. They formed a circular ring with a break at one point through which the foot-track led to the centre of the circle.

As soon as the priestess stepped into this ring of hills her voice was not only doubled in strength but was thrown back on all sides. It was indeed the shrine of a great god. Ekwefi picked her way carefully and quietly. She was already beginning to doubt the wisdom of her coming. Nothing would happen to Ezinma, she thought. And if anything happened to her could she stop it? She would not dare to enter the underground caves. Her coming was quite useless, she thought.

As these things went through her mind she did not realise how close they were to the cave mouth. And so when the priestess with Ezinma on her back disappeared through a hole hardly big enough to pass a hen, Ekwefi broke into a run as though to stop them. As she stood gazing at the circular darkness which had swallowed them, tears gushed from her eyes, and she swore within her that if she heard Ezinma cry she would rush into the cave to defend her against all the gods in the world. She would die with her.

Having sworn that oath, she sat down on a stony ledge and waited. Her fear had vanished. She could hear the priestess's voice, all its metal taken out of it by the vast emptiness of the cave. She buried her face in her lap and waited.

She did not know how long she waited. It must have been a very long time. Her back was turned on the footpath that led out of the hills. She must have heard a noise behind her and turned round sharply. A man stood there with a matchet in his hand. Ekwefi uttered a scream and sprang to her feet.

"Don't be foolish," said Okonkwo's voice. "I thought you were going into the shrine with Chielo," he mocked.

Ekwefi did not answer. Tears of gratitude filled her eyes. She knew her daughter was safe.

"Go home and sleep," said Okonkwo. "I shall wait here."

"I shall wait too. It is almost dawn. The first cock has crowed."

As they stood there together, Ekwefi's mind went back to the days when they were young. She had married Anene because Okonkwo was too poor then to marry. Two years after her marriage to Anene she could bear it no longer and she ran away to Okonkwo. It had been early in the morning. The moon was shining. She was going to the stream to fetch water. Okonkwo's house was on the way to the stream. She went in and knocked at his door and he came out. Even in those days he was not a man of many words. He just carried her into his bed and in the darkness began to feel around her waist for the loose end of her cloth.

---

6. Agbala wants something! Agbala greets . . . God who kills a man on the day his life is so pleasant he give thanks!

CHAPTER TWELVE

On the following morning the entire neighbourhood wore a festive air because Okonkwo's friend, Obierika, was celebrating his daughter's *uri*. It was the day on which her suitor (having already paid the greater part of her bride-price) would bring palm-wine not only to her parents and immediate relatives but to the wide and extensive group of kinsmen called *umunna*. Everybody had been invited—men, women and children. But it was really a woman's ceremony and the central figures were the bride and her mother.

As soon as day broke, breakfast was hastily eaten and women and children began to gather at Obierika's compound to help the bride's mother in her difficult but happy task of cooking for a whole village.

Okonkwo's family was astir like any other family in the neighbourhood. Nwoye's mother and Okonkwo's youngest wife were ready to set out for Obierika's compound with all their children. Nwoye's mother carried a basket of coco-yams, a cake of salt and smoked fish which she would present to Obierika's wife. Okonkwo's youngest wife, Ojiugo, also had a basket of plantains and coco-yams and a small pot of palm-oil. Their children carried pots of water.

Ekwefi was tired and sleepy from the exhausting experiences of the previous night. It was not very long since they had returned. The priestess, with Ezinma sleeping on her back, had crawled out of the shrine on her belly like a snake. She had not as much as looked at Okonkwo and Ekwefi or shown any surprise at finding them at the mouth of the cave. She looked straight ahead of her and walked back to the village. Okonkwo and his wife followed at a respectful distance. They thought the priestess might be going to her house, but she went to Okonkwo's compound, passed through his *obi* and into Ekwefi's hut and walked into her bedroom. She placed Ezinma carefully on the bed and went away without saying a word to anybody.

Ezinma was still sleeping when everyone else was astir, and Ekwefi asked Nwoye's mother and Ojiugo to explain to Obierika's wife that she would be late. She had got ready her basket of coco-yams and fish, but she must wait for Ezinma to wake.

"You need some sleep yourself," said Nwoye's mother. "You look very tired."

As they spoke Ezinma emerged from the hut, rubbing her eyes and stretching her spare frame. She saw the other children with their water-pots and remembered that they were going to fetch water for Obierika's wife. She went back to the hut and brought her pot.

"Have you slept enough?" asked her mother.

"Yes," she replied. "Let us go."

"Not before you have had your breakfast," said Ekwefi. And she went into her hut to warm the vegetable soup she had cooked last night.

"We shall be going," said Nwoye's mother. "I will tell Obierika's wife that you are coming later." And so they all went to help Obierika's wife—Nwoye's mother with her four children and Ojiugo with her two.

As they trooped through Okonkwo's *obi* he asked: "Who will prepare my afternoon meal?"

"I shall return to do it," said Ojiugo.

Okonkwo was also feeling tired and sleepy, for although nobody else knew it, he had not slept at all last night. He had felt very anxious but did not show it. When Ekwefi had followed the priestess, he had allowed what he regarded as a reasonable and manly interval to pass and then gone with his matchet to the shrine, where he thought they must be. It was only when he had got there that it had occurred to him that the priestess might have chosen to go round the villages first. Okonkwo had returned home and sat waiting. When he thought he had waited long enough he again returned to the shrine. But the Hills and the Caves were as silent as death. It was only on his fourth trip that he had found Ekwefi, and by then he had become gravely worried.

Obierika's compound was as busy as an ant-hill. Temporary cooking tripods were erected on every available space by bringing together three blocks of sun-dried earth and making a fire in their midst. Cooking pots went up and down the tripods, and foo-foo was pounded in a hundred wooden mortars. Some of the women cooked the yams and the cassava, and others prepared vegetable soup. Young men pounded the foo-foo or split firewood. The children made endless trips to the stream.

Three young men helped Obierika to slaughter the two goats with which the soup was made. They were very fat goats, but the fattest of all was tethered to a peg near the wall of the compound. It was as big as a small cow. Obierika had sent one of his relatives all the way to Umuike to buy that goat. It was the one he would present alive to his in-laws.

"The market of Umuike is a wonderful place," said the young man who had been sent by Obierika to buy the giant goat. "There are so many people on it that if you threw up a grain of sand it would not find a way to fall to earth again."

"It is the result of a great medicine," said Obierika. "The people of Umuike wanted their market to grow and swallow up the markets of their neighbours. So they made a powerful medicine. Every market-day, before the first cock-crow, this medicine stands on the market-ground in the shape of an old woman with a fan. With this magic fan she beckons to the market all the neighbouring clans. She beckons in front of her and behind her, to her right and to her left."

"And so everybody comes," said another man, "honest men and thieves. They can steal your cloth from off your waist in that market."

"Yes," said Obierika. "I warned Nwankwo to keep a sharp eye and a sharp ear. There was once a man who went to sell a goat. He led it on a thick rope which he tied round his wrist. But as he walked through the market he realised that people were pointing at him as they do to a madman. He could not understand it until he looked back and saw that what he led at the end of the tether was not a goat but a heavy log of wood."

"Do you think a thief can do that kind of thing singlehanded?" asked Nwankwo.

"No," said Obierika. "They use medicine."

When they had cut the goats' throats and collected the blood in a bowl, they held them over an open fire to burn off the hair, and the smell of burning hair blended with the smell of cooking. Then they washed them and cut them up for the women who prepared the soup.

All this ant-hill activity was going smoothly when a sudden interruption came. It was a cry in the distance: *Oji odu achu ijiji-o-o!* (*The one that uses its tail to drive flies away!*) Every woman immediately abandoned whatever she was doing and rushed out in the direction of the cry.

"We cannot all rush out like that, leaving what we are cooking to burn in the fire," shouted Chielo, the priestess. "Three or four of us should stay behind."

"It is true," said another woman. "We will allow three or four women to stay behind."

Five women stayed behind to look after the cooking-pots, and all the rest rushed away to see the cow that had been let loose. When they saw it they drove it back to its owner, who at once paid the heavy fine which the village imposed on anyone whose cow was let loose on his neighbours' crops. When the women had exacted the penalty they checked among themselves to see if any woman had failed to come out when the cry had been raised.

"Where is Mgbogo?" asked one of them.

"She is ill in bed," said Mgbogo's next-door neighbour. "She has *iba*."

"The only other person is Udenkwo," said another woman, "and her child is not twenty-eight days yet."

Those women whom Obierika's wife had not asked to help her with the cooking returned to their homes, and the rest went back, in a body, to Obierika's compound.

"Whose cow was it?" asked the women who had been allowed to stay behind.

"It was my husband's," said Ezelagbo. "One of the young children had opened the gate of the cow-shed."

Early in the afternoon the first two pots of palm-wine arrived from Obierika's in-laws. They were duly presented to the women, who drank a cup or two each, to help them in their cooking. Some of it also went to the bride and her attendant maidens, who were putting the last delicate touches of razor to her coiffure and cam wood on her smooth skin.

When the heat of the sun began to soften, Obierika's son, Maduka, took a long broom and swept the ground in front of his father's *obi*. And as if they had been waiting for that, Obierika's relatives and friends began to arrive, every man with his goatskin bag hung on one shoulder and a rolled goatskin mat under his arm. Some of them were accompanied by their sons bearing carved wooden stools. Okonkwo was one of them. They sat in a half circle and began to talk of many things. It would not be long before the suitors came.

Okonkwo brought out his snuff-bottle and offered it to Ogbuefi Ezenwa, who sat next to him. Ezenwa[7] took it, tapped it on his knee-cap, rubbed his left palm on his body to dry it before tipping a little snuff into it. His actions were deliberate, and he spoke as he performed them:

"I hope our in-laws will bring many pots of wine. Although they come from a village that is known for being close-fisted, they ought to know that Akueke is the bride for a king."

"They dare not bring fewer than thirty pots," said Okonkwo. "I shall tell them my mind if they do."

---

7. King from childhood (strong praise).

At that moment Obierika's son, Maduka, led out the giant goat from the inner compound, for his father's relatives to see. They all admired it and said that that was the way things should be done. The goat was then led back to the inner compound.

Very soon after, the in-laws began to arrive. Young men and boys in single file, each carrying a pot of wine, came first. Obierika's relatives counted the pots as they came in. Twenty, twenty-five. There was a long break, and the hosts looked at each other as if to say, 'I told you.' Then more pots came. Thirty, thirty-five, forty, forty-five. The hosts nodded in approval and seemed to say, 'Now they are behaving like men.' Altogether there were fifty pots of wine. After the pot-bearers came Ibe, the suitor, and the elders of his family. They sat in a half-moon, thus completing a circle with their hosts. The pots of wine stood in their midst. Then the bride, her mother and half a dozen other women and girls emerged from the inner compound, and went round the circle shaking hands with all. The bride's mother led the way, followed by the bride and the other women. The married women wore their best cloths and the girls wore red and black waist-beads and anklets of brass.

When the women retired, Obierika presented kola nuts to his in-laws. His eldest brother broke the first one. "Life to all of us," he said as he broke it. "And let there be friendship between your family and ours."

The crowd answered: "Ee-e-e!"

"We are giving you our daughter today. She will be a good wife to you. She will bear you nine sons like the mother of our town."

"Ee-e-e!"

The oldest man in the camp of the visitors replied: "It will be good for you and it will be good for us."

"Ee-e-e!"

"This is not the first time my people have come to marry your daughter. My mother was one of you."

"Ee-e-e!"

"And this will not be the last, because you understand us and we understand you. You are a great family."

"Ee-e-e!"

"Prosperous men and great warriors." He looked in the direction of Okonkwo. "Your daughter will bear us sons like you."

"Ee-e-e!"

The kola was eaten and the drinking of palm-wine began. Groups of four or five men sat round with a pot in their midst. As the evening wore on, food was presented to the guests. There were huge bowls of foo-foo and steaming pots of soup. There were also pots of yam pottage. It was a great feast.

As night fell, burning torches were set on wooden tripods and the young men raised a song. The elders sat in a big circle and the singers went round singing each man's praise as they came before him. They had something to say for every man. Some were great farmers, some were orators who spoke for the clan; Okonkwo was the greatest wrestler and warrior alive. When they had gone round the circle they settled down in the centre, and girls came from the inner compound to dance. At first the bride was not among them. But when she finally appeared holding a cock in her right hand, a loud cheer rose from the crowd. All the other dancers made way for her. She presented the cock to the musicians and began to dance. Her brass anklets rattled as she danced and her body gleamed with cam wood in the soft yellow light. The musicians with their wood, clay and metal instruments went from song to song. And they were all gay. They sang the latest song in the village:

> "If I hold her hand
> She says, 'Don't touch!'
> If I hold her foot
> She says, 'Don't touch!'
> But when I hold her waist-beads
> She pretends not to know."

The night was already far spent when the guests rose to go, taking their bride home to spend seven market weeks with her suitor's family. They sang songs as they went, and on their way they paid short courtesy visits to prominent men like Okonkwo, before they finally left for their village. Okonkwo made a present of two cocks to them.

CHAPTER THIRTEEN

Go-di-di-go-go-di-go. Di-go-go-di-go. It was the *ekwe* talking to the clan. One of the things every man learned was the language of the hollowed-out wooden instrument. Diim! Diim! Diim! boomed the cannon at intervals.

The first cock had not crowed, and Umuofia was still swallowed up in sleep and silence when the *ekwe* began to talk, and the cannon shattered the silence. Men stirred on their bamboo beds and listened anxiously. Somebody was dead. The cannon seemed to rend the sky. Di-go-go-di-go-di-di-go-go floated in the message-laden night air. The faint and distant wailing of women settled like a sediment of sorrow on the earth. Now and again a full-chested lamentation rose above the wailing whenever a man came into the place of death. He raised his voice once or twice in manly sorrow and then sat down with the other men listening to the endless wailing of the women and the esoteric language of the *ekwe*. Now and again the cannon boomed. The wailing of the women would not be heard beyond the village, but the *ekwe* carried the news to all the nine villages and even beyond. It began by naming the clan: *Umuofia obodo dike*, 'the land of the brave.' *Umuofia obodo dike! Umuofia obodo dike!* It said this over and over again, and as it dwelt on it, anxiety mounted in every heart that heaved on a bamboo bed that night. Then it went nearer and named the village: *Iguedo[8] of the yellow grinding-stone!* It was Okonkwo's village. Again and again Iguedo was called and men waited breathlessly in all the nine villages. At last the man was named and people sighed "E-u-u, Ezeudu is dead". A cold shiver ran down Okonkwo's back as he remembered the last time the old man had visited him. "That boy calls you father," he had said. "Bear no hand in his death."

Ezeudu was a great man, and so all the clan was at his funeral. The ancient drums of death beat, guns and cannon were fired, and men dashed about in frenzy, cutting down every tree or animal they saw, jumping over walls and dancing on the roof. It was a warrior's funeral, and from morning till night warriors came and went in their age-groups. They all wore smoked raffia

8. The yellow grindstone.

skirts and their bodies were painted with chalk and charcoal. Now and again an ancestral spirit or *egwugwu* appeared from the underworld, speaking in a tremulous, unearthly voice and completely covered in raffia. Some of them were very violent, and there had been a mad rush for shelter earlier in the day when one appeared with a sharp matchet and was only prevented from doing serious harm by two men who restrained him with the help of a strong rope tied round his waist. Sometimes he turned round and chased those men, and they ran for their lives. But they always returned to the long rope he trailed behind. He sang, in a terrifying voice, that Ekwensu, or Evil Spirit, had entered his eye.

But the most dreaded of all was yet to come. He was always alone and was shaped like a coffin. A sickly odour hung in the air wherever he went, and flies went with him. Even the greatest medicine-men took shelter when he was near. Many years ago another *egwugwu* had dared to stand his ground before him and had been transfixed to the spot for two days. This one had only one hand and with it carried a basket full of water.

But some of the *egwugwu* were quite harmless. One of them was so old and infirm that he leaned heavily on a stick. He walked unsteadily to the place where the corpse was laid, gazed at it a while and went away again— to the underworld.

The land of the living was not far removed from the domain of the ances- tors. There was coming and going between them, especially at festivals and also when an old man died, because an old man was very close to the ances- tors. A man's life from birth to death was a series of transition rites which brought him nearer and nearer to his ancestors.

Ezeudu had been the oldest man in his village, and at his death there were only three men in the whole clan who were older, and four or five others in his own age-group. Whenever one of these ancient men appeared in the crowd to dance unsteadily the funeral steps of the tribe, younger men gave way and the tumult subsided.

It was a great funeral, such as befitted a noble warrior. As the evening drew near, the shouting and the firing of guns, the beating of drums and the brandishing and clanging of matchets increased.

Ezeudu had taken three titles in his life. It was a rare achievement. There were only four titles in the clan, and only one or two men in any generation ever achieved the fourth and highest. When they did, they became the lords of the land. Because he had taken titles, Ezeudu was to be buried after dark with only a glowing brand to light the sacred ceremony.

But before this quiet and final rite, the tumult increased tenfold. Drums beat violently and men leaped up and down in frenzy. Guns were fired on all sides and sparks flew out as matchets clanged together in warriors' salutes. The air was full of dust and the smell of gunpowder. It was then that the one-handed spirit came, carrying a basket full of water. People made way for him on all sides and the noise subsided. Even the smell of gunpowder was swallowed in the sickly smell that now filled the air. He danced a few steps to the funeral drums and then went to see the corpse.

"Ezeudu!" he called in his guttural voice. "If you had been poor in your last life I would have asked you to be rich when you come again. But you were rich. If you had been a coward, I would have asked you to bring courage. But you were a fearless warrior. If you had died young, I would have asked you to get life. But you lived long. So I shall ask you to come again the way you came before. If your death was the death of nature, go in peace. But if a man caused it, do not allow him a moment's rest." He danced a few more steps and went away.

The drums and the dancing began again and reached fever-heat. Darkness was around the corner, and the burial was near. Guns fired the last salute and the cannon rent the sky. And then from the centre of the delirious fury came a cry of agony and shouts of horror. It was as if a spell had been cast. All was silent. In the centre of the crowd a boy lay in a pool of blood. It was the dead man's sixteen-year-old son, who with his brothers and half-brothers had been dancing the traditional farewell to their father. Okonkwo's gun had exploded and a piece of iron had pierced the boy's heart.

The confusion that followed was without parallel in the tradition of Umuofia. Violent deaths were frequent, but nothing like this had ever happened.

The only course open to Okonkwo was to flee from the clan. It was a crime against the earth goddess to kill a clansman, and a man who committed it must flee from the land. The crime was of two kinds, male and female. Okonkwo had committed the female, because it had been inadvertent. He could return to the clan after seven years.

That night he collected his most valuable belongings into head-loads. His wives wept bitterly and their children wept with them without knowing why. Obierika and half a dozen other friends came to help and to console him. They each made nine or ten trips carrying Okonkwo's yams to store in Obierika's barn. And before the cock crowed Okonkwo and his family were fleeing to his motherland. It was a little village called Mbanta,[9] just beyond the borders of Mbaino.

As soon as the day broke, a large crowd of men from Ezeudu's quarter stormed Okonkwo's compound, dressed in garbs of war. They set fire to his houses, demolished his red walls, killed his animals and destroyed his barn. It was the justice of the earth goddess, and they were merely her messengers. They had no hatred in their hearts against Okonkwo. His greatest friend, Obierika, was among them. They were merely cleansing the land which Okonkwo had polluted with the blood of a clansman.

Obierika was a man who thought about things. When the will of the goddess had been done, he sat down in his *obi* and mourned his friend's calamity. Why should a man suffer so grievously for an offence he had committed inadvertently? But although he thought for a long time he found no answer. He was merely led into greater complexities. He remembered his wife's twin children, whom he had thrown away. What crime had they committed? The Earth had decreed that they were an offence on the land and must be destroyed. And *if* the clan did not exact punishment for an offence against the great goddess, her wrath was loosed on all the land and not just on the offender. As the elders said, if one finger brought oil it soiled the others.

9. Small town.

Part Two

CHAPTER FOURTEEN

Okonkwo was well received by his mother's kinsmen in Mbanta. The old man who received him was his mother's younger brother, who was now the eldest surviving member of that family. His name was Uchendu,[1] and it was he who had received Okonkwo's mother twenty and ten years before when she had been brought home from Umuofia to be buried with her people. Okonkwo was only a boy then and Uchendu still remembered him crying the traditional farewell: "Mother, mother, mother is going."

That was many years ago. Today Okonkwo was not bringing his mother home to be buried with her people. He was taking his family of three wives and eleven children to seek refuge in his motherland. As soon as Uchendu saw him with his sad and weary company he guessed what had happened, and asked no questions. It was not until the following day that Okonkwo told him the full story. The old man listened silently to the end and then said with some relief: "It is a female *ochu*."[2] And he arranged the requisite rites and sacrifices.

Okonkwo was given a plot of ground on which to build his compound, and two or three pieces of land on which to farm during the coming planting season. With the help of his mother's kinsmen he built himself an *obi* and three huts for his wives. He then installed his personal god and the symbols of his departed fathers. Each of Uchendu's five sons contributed three hundred seed-yams to enable their cousin to plant a farm, for as soon as the first rain came farming would begin.

At last the rain came. It was sudden and tremendous. For two or three moons the sun had been gathering strength till it seemed to breathe a breath of fire on the earth. All the grass had long been scorched brown, and the sands felt like live coals to the feet. Evergreen trees wore a dusty coat of brown. The birds were silenced in the forests, and the world lay panting under the live, vibrating heat. And then came the clap of thunder. It was an angry, metallic and thirsty clap, unlike the deep and liquid rumbling of the rainy season. A mighty wind arose and filled the air with dust. Palm trees swayed as the wind combed their leaves into flying crests like strange and fantastic coiffure.

When the rain finally came, it was in large, solid drops of frozen water which the people called "the nuts of the water of heaven". They were hard and painful on the body as they fell, yet young people ran about happily picking up the cold nuts and throwing them into their mouths to melt.

The earth quickly came to life and the birds in the forests fluttered around and chirped merrily. A vague scent of life and green vegetation was diffused in the air. As the rain began to fall more soberly and in smaller liquid drops, children sought for shelter, and all were happy, refreshed and thankful.

Okonkwo and his family worked very hard to plant a new farm. But it was like beginning life anew without the vigour and enthusiasm of youth, like learning to become left-handed in old age. Work no longer had for him the

---

1. The thought created by life.   2. Murder, manslaughter.

pleasure it used to have, and when there was no work to do he sat in a silent half-sleep.

His life had been ruled by a great passion—to become one of the lords of the clan. That had been his life-spring. And he had all but achieved it. Then everything had been broken. He had been cast out of his clan like a fish on to a dry, sandy beach, panting. Clearly his personal god or *chi* was not made for great things. A man could not rise beyond the destiny of his *chi*. The saying of the elders was not true—that if a man said yea his *chi* also affirmed. Here was a man whose *chi* said nay despite his own affirmation.

The old man, Uchendu, saw clearly that Okonkwo had yielded to despair and he was greatly troubled. He would speak to him after the *isa-ifi*[3] ceremony.

The youngest of Uchendu's five sons, Amikwu, was marrying a new wife. The bride-price had been paid and all but the last ceremony had been performed. Amikwu and his people had taken palm-wine to the bride's kinsmen about two moons before Okonkwo's arrival in Mbanta. And so it was time for the final ceremony of confession.

The daughters of the family were all there, some of them having come a long way from their homes in distant villages. Uchendu's eldest daughter had come from Obodo, nearly half a day's journey away. The daughters of Uchendu's brothers were also there. It was a full gathering of *umuada*,[4] in the same way as they would meet if a death occurred in the family. There were twenty-two of them.

They sat in a big circle on the ground and the bride sat in the centre with a hen in her right hand. Uchendu sat by her, holding the ancestral staff of the family. All the other men stood outside the circle, watching. Their wives watched also. It was evening and the sun was setting.

Uchendu's eldest daughter, Njide, asked the questions.

"Remember that if you do not answer truthfully you will suffer or even die at child-birth," she began. "How many men have lain with you since my brother first expressed the desire to marry you?"

"None," she replied simply.

"Answer truthfully," urged the other women.

"None?" asked Njide.

"None," she answered.

"Swear on this staff of my fathers," said Uchendu.

"I swear," said the bride.

Uchendu took the hen from her, slit its throat with a sharp knife and allowed some of the blood to fall on his ancestral staff.

From that day Amikwu took the young bride to his hut and she became his wife. The daughters of the family did not return to their homes immediately but spent two or three days with their kinsmen.

On the second day Uchendu called together his sons and daughters and his nephew, Okonkwo. The men brought their goatskin mats, with which

---

3. A ceremony to ascertain that a wife (here, a promised bride) had been faithful to her husband during a separation.
4. The daughters, who, according to Igbo custom,

married outside the clan, perform a special initiation upon returning home for important gatherings.

they sat on the floor, and the women sat on a sisal mat spread on a raised bank of earth. Uchendu pulled gently at his grey beard and gnashed his teeth. Then he began to speak, quietly and deliberately, picking his words with great care:

"It is Okonkwo that I primarily wish to speak to," he began. "But I want all of you to note what I am going to say. I am an old man and you are all children. I know more about the world than any of you. If there is any one among you who thinks he knows more let him speak up." He paused, but no one spoke.

"Why is Okonkwo with us today? This is not his clan. We are only his mother's kinsmen. He does not belong here. He is an exile, condemned for seven years to live in a strange land. And so he is bowed with grief. But there is just one question I would like to ask him. Can you tell me, Okonkwo, why it is that one of the commonest names we give our children is Nneka, or 'Mother is Supreme'? We all know that a man is the head of the family and his wives do his bidding. A child belongs to its father and his family and not to its mother and her family. A man belongs to his fatherland and not to his motherland. And yet we say Nneka—'Mother is Supreme.' Why is that?"

There was silence. "I want Okonkwo to answer me," said Uchendu.

"I do not know the answer," Okonkwo replied.

"You do not know the answer? So you see that you are a child. You have many wives and many children—more children than I have. You are a great man in your clan. But you are still a child, *my* child. Listen to me and I shall tell you. But there is one more question I shall ask you. Why is it that when a woman dies she is taken home to be buried with her own kinsmen? She is not buried with her husband's kinsmen. Why is that? Your mother was brought home to me and buried with my people. Why was that?"

Okonkwo shook his head.

"He does not know that either," said Uchendu, "and yet he is full of sorrow because he has come to live in his motherland for a few years." He laughed a mirthless laughter, and turned to his sons and daughters. "What about you? Can you answer my question?"

They all shook their heads.

"Then listen to me," he said and cleared his throat. "It's true that a child belongs to its father. But when a father beats his child, it seeks sympathy in its mother's hut. A man belongs to his fatherland when things are good and life is sweet. But when there is sorrow and bitterness he finds refuge in his motherland. Your mother is there to protect you. She is buried there. And that is why we say that mother is supreme. Is it right that you, Okonkwo, should bring to your mother a heavy face and refuse to be comforted? Be careful or you may displease the dead. Your duty is to comfort your wives and children and take them back to your fatherland after seven years. But if you allow sorrow to weigh you down and kill you, they will all die in exile." He paused for a long while. "These are now your kinsmen." He waved at his sons and daughters. "You think you are the greatest sufferer in the world. Do you know that men are sometimes banished for life? Do you know that men sometimes lose all their yams and even their children? I had six wives once. I have none now except that young girl who knows not her right from her left. Do you know how many children I have buried—children I begot in my youth and strength? Twenty-two. I did not hang myself, and I am still alive. If you think you are the greatest sufferer in the world ask my daughter, Akueni, how many twins she has borne and thrown away. Have you not heard the song they sing when a woman dies?

> " 'For whom is it well, for whom is it well?
> There is no one for whom it is well.'

"I have no more to say to you."

CHAPTER FIFTEEN

It was in the second year of Okonkwo's exile that his friend, Obierika, came to visit him. He brought with him two young men, each of them carrying a heavy bag on his head. Okonkwo helped them put down their loads. It was clear that the bags were full of cowries.

Okonkwo was very happy to receive his friend. His wives and children were very happy too, and so were his cousins and their wives when he sent for them and told them who his guest was.

"You must take him to salute our father," said one of the cousins.

"Yes," replied Okonkwo. "We are going directly." But before they went he whispered something to his first wife. She nodded, and soon the children were chasing one of their cocks.

Uchendu had been told by one of his grandchildren that three strangers had come to Okonkwo's house. He was therefore waiting to receive them. He held out his hands to them when they came into his *obi*, and after they had shaken hands he asked Okonkwo who they were.

"This is Obierika, my great friend. I have already spoken to you about him."

"Yes," said the old man, turning to Obierika. "My son has told me about you, and I am happy you have come to see us. I knew your father, Iweka. He was a great man. He had many friends here and came to see them quite often. Those were good days when a man had friends in distant clans. Your generation does not know that. You stay at home, afraid of your next-door neighbour. Even a man's motherland is strange to him nowadays." He looked at Okonkwo. "I am an old man and I like to talk. That is all I am good for now." He got up painfully, went into an inner room and came back with a kola nut.

"Who are the young men with you?" he asked as he sat down again on his goatskin. Okonkwo told him.

"Ah," he said. "Welcome, my sons." He presented the kola nut to them, and when they had seen it and thanked him, he broke it and they ate.

"Go into that room," he said to Okonkwo, pointing with his finger. "You will find a pot of wine there."

Okonkwo brought the wine and they began to drink. It was a day old, and very strong.

"Yes," said Uchendu after a long silence. "People travelled more in those days. There is not a single clan in these parts that I do not know very well. Aninta, Umuazu, Ikeocha, Elumelu, Abame—I know them all."

"Have you heard," asked Obierika, "that Abame is no more?"

"How is that?" asked Uchendu and Okonkwo together.

"Abame has been wiped out," said Obierika. "It is a strange and terrible story. If I had not seen the few survivors with my own eyes and heard their story with my own ears, I would not have believed. Was it not on an Eke day that they fled into Umuofia?" he asked his two companions, and they nodded their heads.

"Three moons ago," said Obierika, "on an Eke market-day a little band of fugitives came into our town. Most of them were sons of our land whose mothers had been buried with us. But there were some too who came because they had friends in our town, and others who could think of nowhere else open to escape. And so they fled into Umuofia with a woeful story." He drank his palm-wine, and Okonkwo filled his horn again. He continued:

"During the last planting season a white man had appeared in their clan."

"An albino," suggested Okonkwo.

"He was not an albino. He was quite different." He sipped his wine. "And he was riding an iron horse.[5] The first people who saw him ran away, but he stood beckoning to them. In the end the fearless ones went near and even touched him. The elders consulted their Oracle and it told them that the strange man would break their clan and spread destruction among them." Obierika again drank a little of his wine. "And so they killed the white man and tied his iron horse to their sacred tree because it looked as if it would run away to call the man's friends. I forgot to tell you another thing which the Oracle said. It said that other white men were on their way. They were locusts, it said, and that first man was their harbinger sent to explore the terrain. And so they killed him."

"What did the white man say before they killed him?" asked Uchendu.

"He said nothing," answered one of Obierika's companions.

"He said something, only they did not understand him," said Obierika. "He seemed to speak through his nose."

"One of the men told me," said Obierika's other companion, "that he repeated over and over again a word that resembled Mbaino. Perhaps he had been going to Mbaino and had lost his way."

"Anyway," resumed Obierika, "they killed him and tied up his iron horse. This was before the planting season began. For a long time nothing happened. The rains had come and yams had been sown. The iron horse was still tied to the sacred silk-cotton tree. And then one morning three white men led by a band of ordinary men like us came to the clan. They saw the iron horse and went away again. Most of the men and women of Abame had gone to their farms. Only a few of them saw these white men and their followers. For many market weeks nothing else happened. They have a big market in Abame on every other Afo day and, as you know, the whole clan gathers there. That was the day it happened. The three white men and a very large number of other men surrounded the market. They must have used a powerful medicine to make themselves invisible until the market was full. And they began to shoot. Everybody was killed, except the old and the sick who were at home and a handful of men and women whose *chi* were wide awake and brought them out of that market."[6] He paused.

5. Bicycle.
6. Achebe bases his account on a similar incident in 1905 when British troops massacred the town of Ahiara in reprisal for the death of a missionary.

"Their clan is now completely empty. Even the sacred fish in their mysterious lake have fled and the lake has turned the colour of blood. A great evil has come upon their land as the Oracle had warned."

There was a long silence. Uchendu ground his teeth together audibly. Then he burst out:

"Never kill a man who says nothing. Those men of Abame were fools. What did they know about the man?" He ground his teeth again and told a story to illustrate his point. "Mother Kite once sent her daughter to bring food. She went, and brought back a duckling. 'You have done very well,' said Mother Kite to her daughter, 'but tell me, what did the mother of this duckling say when you swooped and carried its child away?' 'It said nothing,' replied the young kite. 'It just walked away.' 'You must return the duckling,' said Mother Kite. 'There is something ominous behind the silence.' And so Daughter Kite returned the duckling and took a chick instead. 'What did the mother of this chick do?' asked the old kite. 'It cried and raved and cursed me,' said the young kite. 'Then we can eat the chick,' said her mother. 'There is nothing to fear from someone who shouts.' Those men of Abame were fools."

"They were fools," said Okonkwo after a pause. "They had been warned that danger was ahead. They should have armed themselves with their guns and their matchets even when they went to market."

"They have paid for their foolishness," said Obierika. "But I am greatly afraid. We have heard stories about white men who made the powerful guns and the strong drinks and took slaves away across the seas, but no one thought the stories were true."

"There is no story that is not true," said Uchendu. "The world has no end, and what is good among one people is an abomination with others. We have albinos among us. Do you not think that they came to our clan by mistake, that they have strayed from their way to a land where everybody is like them?"

Okonkwo's first wife soon finished her cooking and set before their guests a big meal of pounded yams and bitter-leaf soup. Okonkwo's son, Nwoye, brought in a pot of sweet wine tapped from the raffia palm.

"You are a big man now," Obierika said to Nwoye. "Your friend Anene asked me to greet you."

"Is he well?" asked Nwoye.

"We are all well," said Obierika.

Ezinma brought them a bowl of water with which to wash their hands. After that they began to eat and to drink the wine.

"When did you set out from home?" asked Okonkwo.

"We had meant to set out from my house before cock-crow," said Obierika. "But Nweke did not appear until it was quite light. Never make an early morning appointment with a man who has just married a new wife." They all laughed.

"Has Nweke married a wife?" asked Okonkwo.

"He has married Okadigbo's second daughter," said Obierika.

"That is very good," said Okonkwo. "I do not blame you for not hearing the cock crow."

When they had eaten, Obierika pointed at the two heavy bags.

"That is the money from your yams," he said. "I sold the big ones as soon as you left. Later on I sold some of the seed-yams and gave out others to share-croppers. I shall do that every year until you return. But I thought you would need the money now and so I brought it. Who knows what may happen tomorrow? Perhaps green men will come to our clan and shoot us."

"God will not permit it," said Okonkwo. "I do not know how to thank you."

"I can tell you," said Obierika. "Kill one of your sons for me."

"That will not be enough," said Okonkwo.

"Then kill yourself," said Obierika.

"Forgive me," said Okonkwo, smiling. "I shall not talk about thanking you any more."

CHAPTER SIXTEEN

When nearly two years later Obierika paid another visit to his friend in exile the circumstances were less happy. The missionaries had come to Umuofia. They had built their church there, won a handful of converts and were already sending evangelists to the surrounding towns and villages. That was a source of great sorrow to the leaders of the clan; but many of them believed that the strange faith and the white man's god would not last. None of his converts was a man whose word was heeded in the assembly of the people. None of them was a man of title. They were mostly the kind of people that were called *efulefu*, worthless, empty men. The imagery of an *efulefu* in the language of the clan was a man who sold his matchet and wore the sheath to battle. Chielo, the priestess of Agbala, called the converts the excrement of the clan, and the new faith was a mad dog that had come to eat it up.

What moved Obierika to visit Okonkwo was the sudden appearance of the latter's son, Nwoye, among the missionaries in Umuofia.

"What are you doing here?" Obierika had asked when after many difficulties the missionaries had allowed him to speak to the boy.

"I am one of them," replied Nwoye.

"How is your father?" Obierika asked, not knowing what else to say.

"I don't know. He is not my father," said Nwoye, unhappily.

And so Obierika went to Mbanta to see his friend. And he found that Okonkwo did not wish to speak about Nwoye. It was only from Nwoye's mother that he heard scraps of the story.

The arrival of the missionaries had caused a considerable stir in the village of Mbanta. There were six of them and one was a white man. Every man and woman came out to see the white man. Stories about these strange men had grown since one of them had been killed in Abame and his iron horse tied to the sacred silk-cotton tree. And so everybody came to see the white man. It was the time of the year when everybody was at home. The harvest was over.

When they had all gathered, the white man began to speak to them. He spoke through an interpreter who was an Ibo man, though his dialect was different and harsh to the ears of Mbanta. Many people laughed at his dialect and the way he used words strangely. Instead of saying 'myself' he always said 'my buttocks.'[7] But he was a man of commanding presence and the clansmen listened to him. He said he was one of them, as they could see from his colour and his language. The other four black men were also their brothers, although one of them did not speak Ibo. The white man was also their brother because they were all sons of God. And he told them about this new God, the Creator of all the world and all the men and women. He told them that they worshipped false gods, gods of wood and stone. A deep murmur went through the crowd when he said this. He told them that the true God lived on high and that all men when they died went before Him for judgment. Evil men and all the heathen who in their blindness bowed to wood and stone were thrown into a fire that burned like palm-oil. But good men who worshipped the true God lived for ever in His happy kingdom. "We have been sent by this great God to ask you to leave your wicked ways and false gods and turn to Him so that you may be saved when you die," he said.

"Your buttocks understand our language," said someone light-heartedly and the crowd laughed.

"What did he say?" the white man asked his interpreter. But before he could answer, another man asked a question: "Where is the white man's horse?" he asked. The Ibo evangelists consulted among themselves and decided that the man probably meant bicycle. They told the white man and he smiled benevolently.

"Tell them," he said, "that I shall bring many iron horses when we have settled down among them. Some of them will even ride the iron horse themselves." This was interpreted to them but very few of them heard. They were talking excitedly among themselves because the white man had said he was going to live among them. They had not thought about that.

At this point an old man said he had a question. "Which is this god of yours," he asked, "the goddess of the earth, the god of the sky, Amadiora of the thunderbolt, or what?"

The interpreter spoke to the white man and he immediately gave his answer. "All the gods you have named are not gods at all. They are gods of deceit who tell you to kill your fellows and destroy innocent children. There is only one true God and He has the earth, the sky, you and me and all of us."

"If we leave our gods and follow your god," asked another man, "who will protect us from the anger of our neglected gods and ancestors?"

"Your gods are not alive and cannot do you any harm," replied the white man. "They are pieces of wood and stone."

When this was interpreted to the men of Mbanta they broke into derisive laughter. These men must be mad, they said to themselves. How else could they say that Ani and Amadiora were harmless? And Idemili and Ogwugwu too? And some of them began to go away.

Then the missionaries burst into song. It was one of those gay and rollicking tunes of evangelism which had the power of plucking at silent and dusty chords in the heart of an Ibo man. The interpreter explained each verse to the audience, some of whom now stood enthralled. It was a story of brothers

7. The Igbo language has high and low tones so that the same word may have different meanings according to its pronunciation. Here, Achebe is probably referring to a famous pair of near-homonyms: *íké* ("strength") and *íkè* ("buttocks").

who lived in darkness and in fear, ignorant of the love of God. It told of one sheep out on the hills, away from the gates of God and from the tender shepherd's care.

After the singing the interpreter spoke about the Son of God whose name was Jesu Kristi. Okonkwo, who only stayed in the hope that it might come to chasing the men out of the village or whipping them, now said:

"You told us with your own mouth that there was only one god. Now you talk about his son. He must have a wife, then." The crowd agreed.

"I did not say He had a wife," said the interpreter, somewhat lamely.

"Your buttocks said he had a son," said the joker. "So he must have a wife and all of them must have buttocks."

The missionary ignored him and went on to talk about the Holy Trinity. At the end of it Okonkwo was fully convinced that the man was mad. He shrugged his shoulders and went away to tap his afternoon palm-wine.

But there was a young lad who had been captivated. His name was Nwoye, Okonkwo's first son. It was not the mad logic of the Trinity that captivated him. He did not understand it. It was the poetry of the new religion, something felt in the marrow. The hymn about brothers who sat in darkness and in fear seemed to answer a vague and persistent question that haunted his young soul—the question of the twins crying in the bush and the question of Ikemefuna who was killed. He felt a relief within as the hymn poured into his parched soul. The words of the hymn were like the drops of frozen rain melting on the dry palate of the panting earth. Nwoye's callow mind was greatly puzzled.

CHAPTER SEVENTEEN

The missionaries spent their first four or five nights in the market-place, and went into the village in the morning to preach the gospel. They asked who the king of the village was, but the villagers told them that there was no king. "We have men of high title and the chief priests and the elders," they said.

It was not very easy getting the men of high title and the elders together after the excitement of the first day. But the missionaries persevered, and in the end they were received by the rulers of Mbanta. They asked for a plot of land to build their church.

Every clan and village had its 'evil forest'. In it were buried all those who died of the really evil diseases, like leprosy and smallpox. It was also the dumping ground for the potent fetishes of great medicine-men when they died. An 'evil forest' was, therefore, alive with sinister forces and powers of darkness. It was such a forest that the rulers of Mbanta gave to the missionaries. They did not really want them in their clan, and so they made them that offer which nobody in his right senses would accept.

"They want a piece of land to build their shrine," said Uchendu to his peers when they consulted among themselves. "We shall give them a piece of land." He paused, and there was a murmur of surprise and disagreement. "Let us give them a portion of the Evil Forest. They boast about victory over death. Let us give them a real battlefield in which to show their victory." They laughed and agreed, and sent for the missionaries, whom they had asked to leave them for a while so that they might 'whisper together'. They offered them as much of the Evil Forest as they cared to take. And to their greatest amazement the missionaries thanked them and burst into song.

"They do not understand," said some of the elders. "But they will understand when they go to their plot of land tomorrow morning." And they dispersed.

The next morning the crazy men actually began to clear a part of the forest and to build their house. The inhabitants of Mbanta expected them all to be dead within four days. The first day passed and the second and third and fourth, and none of them died. Everyone was puzzled. And then it became known that the white man's fetish had unbelievable power. It was said that he wore glasses on his eyes so that he could see and talk to evil spirits. Not long after, he won his first three converts.

Although Nwoye had been attracted to the new faith from the very first day, he kept it secret. He dared not go too near the missionaries for fear of his father. But whenever they came, to preach in the open market-place or the village playground, Nwoye was there. And he was already beginning to know some of the simple stories they told.

"We have now built a church," said Mr Kiaga, the interpreter, who was now in charge of the infant congregation. The white man had gone back to Umuofia, where he built his headquarters and from where he paid regular visits to Mr Kiaga's congregation at Mbanta.

"We have now built a church," said Mr Kiaga, "and we want you all to come in every seventh day to worship the true God."

On the following Sunday, Nwoye passed and re-passed the little red-earth and thatch building without summoning enough courage to enter. He heard the voice of singing and although it came from a handful of men it was loud and confident. Their church stood on a circular clearing that looked like the open mouth of the Evil Forest. Was it waiting to snap its teeth together? After passing and re-passing by the church, Nwoye returned home.

It was well known among the people of Mbanta that their gods and ancestors were sometimes long-suffering and would deliberately allow a man to go on defying them. But even in such cases they set their limit at seven market weeks or twenty-eight days. Beyond that limit no man was suffered to go. And so excitement mounted in the village as the seventh week approached since the impudent missionaries built their church in the Evil Forest. The villagers were so certain about the doom that awaited these men that one or two converts thought it wise to suspend their allegiance to the new faith.

At last the day came by which all the missionaries should have died. But they were still alive, building a new red-earth and thatch house for their teacher, Mr Kiaga. That week they won a handful more converts. And for the first time they had a woman. Her name was Nneka, the wife of Amadi, who was a prosperous farmer. She was very heavy with child.

Nneka had had four previous pregnancies and childbirths. But each time she had borne twins, and they had been immediately thrown away. Her husband and his family were already becoming highly critical of such a woman and were not unduly perturbed when they found she had fled to join the Christians. It was a good riddance.

One morning Okonkwo's cousin, Amikwu, was passing by the church on his way from the neighbouring village, when he saw Nwoye among the Christians. He was greatly surprised, and when he got home he went straight to Okonkwo's hut and told him what he had seen. The women began to talk excitedly, but Okonkwo sat unmoved.

It was late afternoon before Nwoye returned. He went into the *obi* and saluted his father, but he did not answer. Nwoye turned round to walk into the inner compound when his father, suddenly overcome with fury, sprang to his feet and gripped him by the neck.

"Where have you been?" he stammered.

Nwoye struggled to free himself from the choking grip.

"Answer me," roared Okonkwo, "before I kill you!" He seized a heavy stick that lay on the dwarf wall and hit him two or three savage blows.

"Answer me!" he roared again. Nwoye stood looking at him and did not say a word. The women were screaming outside, afraid to go in.

"Leave that boy at once!" said a voice in the outer compound. It was Okonkwo's uncle, Uchendu. "Are you mad?"

Okonkwo did not answer. But he left hold of Nwoye, who walked away and never returned.

He went back to the church and told Mr Kiaga that he had decided to go to Umuofia, where the white missionary had set up a school to teach young Christians to read and write.

Mr Kiaga's joy was very great. "Blessed is he who forsakes his father and his mother for my sake," he intoned. "Those that hear my words are my father and my mother."

Nwoye did not fully understand. But he was happy to leave his father. He would return later to his mother and his brothers and sisters and convert them to the new faith.

As Okonkwo sat in his hut that night, gazing into a log fire, he thought over the matter. A sudden fury rose within him and he felt a strong desire to take up his matchet, go to the church and wipe out the entire vile and miscreant gang. But on further thought he told himself that Nwoye was not worth fighting for. Why, he cried in his heart, should he, Okonkwo, of all people, be cursed with such a son? He saw clearly in it the finger of his personal god or *chi*. For how else could he explain his great misfortune and exile and now his despicable son's behaviour? Now that he had time to think of it, his son's crime stood out in its stark enormity. To abandon the gods of one's father and go about with a lot of effeminate men clucking like old hens was the very depth of abomination. Suppose when he died all his male children decided to follow Nwoye's steps and abandon their ancestors? Okonkwo felt a cold shudder run through him at the terrible prospect, like the prospect of annihilation. He saw himself and his fathers crowding round their ancestral shrine waiting in vain for worship and sacrifice and finding nothing but ashes of bygone days, and his children the while praying to the white man's god. If such a thing were ever to happen, he, Okonkwo, would wipe them off the face of the earth.

Okonkwo was popularly called the "Roaring Flame." As he looked into the log fire he recalled the name. He was a flaming fire. How then could he have begotten a son like Nwoye, degenerate and effeminate? Perhaps he was not his son. No! he could not be. His wife had played him false. He would teach her! But Nwoye resembled his grandfather, Unoka, who was Okonkwo's father. He pushed the thought out of his mind. He, Okonkwo, was called a flaming fire. How could he have begotten a woman for a son? At Nwoye's age Okonkwo had already become famous throughout Umuofia for his wrestling and his fearlessness.

He sighed heavily, and as if in sympathy the smouldering log also sighed. And immediately Okonkwo's eyes were opened and he saw the whole matter clearly. Living fire begets cold, impotent ash. He sighed again, deeply.

CHAPTER EIGHTEEN

The young church in Mbanta had a few crises early in its life. At first the clan had assumed that it would not survive. But it had gone on living and gradually becoming stronger. The clan was worried, but not overmuch. If a gang of *efulefu* decided to live in the Evil Forest it was their own affair. When one came to think of it, the Evil Forest was a fit home for such undesirable people. It was true they were rescuing twins from the bush, but they never brought them into the village. As far as the villagers were concerned, the twins still remained where they had been thrown away. Surely the earth goddess would not visit the sins of the missionaries on the innocent villagers?

But on one occasion the missionaries had tried to overstep the bounds. Three converts had gone into the village and boasted openly that all the gods were dead and impotent and that they were prepared to defy them by burning all their shrines.

"Go and burn your mothers' genitals," said one of the priests. The men were seized and beaten until they streamed with blood. After that nothing happened for a long time between the church and the clan.

But stories were already gaining ground that the white man had not only brought a religion but also a government. It was said that they had built a place of judgment in Umuofia to protect the followers of their religion. It was even said that they had hanged one man who killed a missionary.

Although such stories were now often told they looked like fairy-tales in Mbanta and did not as yet affect the relationship between the new church and the clan. There was no question of killing a missionary here, for Mr Kiaga, despite his madness, was quite harmless. As for his converts, no one could kill them without having to flee from the clan, for in spite of their worthlessness they still belonged to the clan. And so nobody gave serious thought to the stories about the white man's government or the consequences of killing the Christians. If they became more troublesome than they already were they would simply be driven out of the clan.

And the little church was at that moment too deeply absorbed in its own troubles to annoy the clan. It all began over the question of admitting outcasts.

These outcasts, or *osu*, seeing that the new religion welcomed twins and such abominations, thought that it was possible that they would also be received. And so one Sunday two of them went into the church. There was an immediate stir; but so great was the work the new religion had done among the converts that they did not immediately leave the church when the outcasts came in. Those who found themselves nearest to them merely moved to another seat. It was a miracle. But it only lasted till the end of the service. The whole church raised a protest and were about to drive these people out, when Mr Kiaga stopped them and began to explain.

"Before God," he said, "there is no slave or free. We are all children of God and we must receive these our brothers."

"You do not understand," said one of the converts. "What will the heathen say of us when they hear that we receive *osu* into our midst? They will laugh."

"Let them laugh," said Mr Kiaga. "God will laugh at them on the judgment day. Why do the nations rage and the peoples imagine a vain thing? He that sitteth in the heavens shall laugh. The Lord shall have them in derision."

"You do not understand," the convert maintained. "You are our teacher, and you can teach us the things of the new faith. But this is a matter which we know." And he told him what an *osu* was.

He was a person dedicated to a god, a thing set apart—a taboo for ever, and his children after him. He could neither marry nor be married by the free-born. He was in fact an outcast, living in a special area of the village, close to the Great Shrine. Wherever he went he carried with him the mark of his forbidden caste—long, tangled and dirty hair. A razor was taboo to him. An *osu* could not attend an assembly of the free-born, and they, in turn, could not shelter under his roof. He could not take any of the four titles of the clan, and when he died he was buried by his kind in the Evil Forest. How could such a man be a follower of Christ?

"He needs Christ more than you and I," said Mr Kiaga.

"Then I shall go back to the clan," said the convert. And he went. Mr Kiaga stood firm, and it was his firmness that saved the young church. The wavering converts drew inspiration and confidence from his unshakable faith. He ordered the outcasts to shave off their long, tangled hair. At first they were afraid they might die.

"Unless you shave off the mark of your heathen belief I will not admit you into the church," said Mr Kiaga. "You fear that you will die. Why should that be? How are you different from other men who shave their hair? The same God created you and them. But they have cast you out like lepers. It is against the will of God, who has promised everlasting life to all who believe in His holy name. The heathen say you will die if you do this or that, and you are afraid. They also said I would die if I built my church on this ground. Am I dead? They said I would die if I took care of twins. I am still alive. The heathen speak nothing but falsehood. Only the word of our God is true."

The two outcasts shaved off their hair, and soon they were among the strongest adherents of the new faith. And what was more, nearly all the *osu* in Mbanta followed their example. It was in fact one of them who in his zeal brought the church into serious conflict with the clan a year later by killing the sacred python, the emanation of the god of water.

The royal python was the most revered animal in Mbanta and all the surrounding clans. It was addressed as 'Our Father', and was allowed to go wherever it chose, even into people's beds. It ate rats in the house and sometimes swallowed hens' eggs. If a clansman killed a royal python accidentally, he made sacrifices of atonement and performed an expensive burial ceremony such as was done for a great man. No punishment was prescribed for a man who killed the python knowingly. Nobody thought that such a thing could ever happen.

Perhaps it never did happen. That was the way the clan at first looked at it. No one had actually seen the man do it. The story had arisen among the Christians themselves.

But, all the same, the rulers and elders of Mbanta assembled to decide on their action. Many of them spoke at great length and in fury. The spirit of war was upon them. Okonkwo, who had begun to play a part in the affairs of his motherland, said that until the abominable gang was chased out of the village with whips there would be no peace.

But there were many others who saw the situation differently, and it was their counsel that prevailed in the end.

"It is not our custom to fight for our gods," said one of them. "Let us not presume to do so now. If a man kills the sacred python in the secrecy of his hut, the matter lies between him and the god. We did not see it. If we put ourselves between the god and his victim we may receive blows intended for the offender. When a man blasphemes, what do we do? Do we go and stop his mouth? No. We put our fingers into our ears to stop us hearing. That is a wise action."

"Let us not reason like cowards," said Okonkwo. "If a man comes into my hut and defæcates on the floor, what do I do? Do I shut my eyes? No! I take a stick and break his head. That is what a man does. These people are daily pouring filth over us, and Okeke says we should pretend not to see." Okonkwo made a sound full of disgust. This was a womanly clan, he thought. Such a thing could never happen in his fatherland, Umuofia.

"Okonkwo has spoken the truth," said another man. "We should do something. But let us ostracise these men. We would then not be held accountable for their abominations."

Everybody in the assembly spoke, and in the end it was decided to ostracise the Christians. Okonkwo ground his teeth in disgust.

That night a bell-man went through the length and breadth of Mbanta proclaiming that the adherents of the new faith were thenceforth excluded from the life and privileges of the clan.

The Christians had grown in number and were now a small community of men, women and children, self-assured and confident. Mr Brown, the white missionary, paid regular visits to them. "When I think that it is only eighteen months since the Seed was first sown among you," he said, "I marvel at what the Lord hath wrought."

It was Wednesday in Holy Week and Mr Kiaga had asked the women to bring red earth and white chalk and water to scrub the church for Easter; and the women had formed themselves into three groups for this purpose. They set out early that morning, some of them with their water-pots to the stream, another group with hoes and baskets to the village red-earth pit, and the others to the chalk quarry.

Mr Kiaga was praying in the church when he heard the women talking excitedly. He rounded off his prayer and went to see what it was all about. The women had come to the church with empty water-pots. They said that some young men had chased them away from the stream with whips. Soon after, the women who had gone for red earth returned with empty baskets. Some of them had been heavily whipped. The chalk women also returned to tell a similar story.

"What does it all mean?" asked Mr Kiaga, who was greatly perplexed.

"The village has outlawed us," said one of the women. "The bell-man announced it last night. But it is not our custom to debar anyone from the stream or the quarry."

Another woman said, "They want to ruin us. They will not allow us into the markets. They have said so."

Mr Kiaga was going to send into the village for his men-converts when he saw them coming on their own. Of course they had all heard the bell-man, but they had never in all their lives heard of women being debarred from the stream.

"Come along," they said to the women. "We will go with you to meet those cowards." Some of them had big sticks and some even matchets.

But Mr Kiaga restrained them. He wanted first to know why they had been outlawed.

"They say that Okoli killed the sacred python," said one man.

"It is false," said another. "Okoli told me himself that it was false."

Okoli was not there to answer. He had fallen ill on the previous night. Before the day was over he was dead. His death showed that the gods were still able to fight their own battles. The clan saw no reason then for molesting the Christians.

CHAPTER NINETEEN

The last big rains of the year were falling. It was the time for treading red earth with which to build walls. It was not done earlier because the rains were too heavy and would have washed away the heap of trodden earth; and it could not be done later because harvesting would soon set in, and after that the dry season.

It was going to be Okonkwo's last harvest in Mbanta. The seven wasted and weary years were at last dragging to a close. Although he had prospered in his motherland Okonkwo knew that he would have prospered even more in Umuofia, in the land of his fathers where men were bold and warlike. In these seven years he would have climbed to the utmost heights. And so he regretted every day of his exile. His mother's kinsmen had been very kind to him, and he was grateful. But that did not alter the facts. He had called the first child born to him in exile Nneka—'Mother is Supreme'—out of politeness to his mother's kinsmen. But two years later when a son was born he called him Nwofia—'Begotten in the Wilderness'.

As soon as he entered his last year in exile Okonkwo sent money to Obierika to build him two huts in his old compound where he and his family would live until he built more huts and the outside wall of his compound. He could not ask another man to build his own *obi* for him, nor the walls of his compound. Those things a man built for himself or inherited from his father.

As the last heavy rains of the year began to fall, Obierika sent word that the two huts had been built and Okonkwo began to prepare for his return, after the rains. He would have liked to return earlier and build his compound that year before the rains stopped, but in doing so he would have taken something from the full penalty of seven years. And that could not be. So he waited impatiently for the dry season to come.

It came slowly. The rain became lighter and lighter until it fell in slanting showers. Sometimes the sun shone through the rain and a light breeze blew. It was a gay and airy kind of rain. The rainbow began to appear, and sometimes two rainbows, like a mother and her daughter, the one young and beautiful, and the other an old and faint shadow. The rainbow was called the python of the sky.

Okonkwo called his three wives and told them to get things together for a great feast. "I must thank my mother's kinsmen before I go," he said.

Ekwefi still had some cassava left on her farm from the previous year. Neither of the other wives had. It was not that they had been lazy, but that they had many children to feed. It was therefore understood that Ekwefi would provide cassava for the feast. Nwoye's mother and Ojiugo would provide the other things like smoked fish, palm-oil and pepper for the soup. Okonkwo would take care of meat and yams.

Ekwefi rose early on the following morning and went to her farm with her daughter, Ezinma, and Ojiugo's daughter, Obiageli, to harvest cassava tubers. Each of them carried a long cane basket, a matchet for cutting down the soft cassava stem, and a little hoe for digging out the tuber. Fortunately, a light rain had fallen during the night and the soil would not be very hard.

"It will not take us long to harvest as much as we like," said Ekwefi.

"But the leaves will be wet," said Ezinma. Her basket was balanced on her head, and her arms folded across her breasts. She felt cold. "I dislike cold water dropping on my back. We should have waited for the sun to rise and dry the leaves."

Obiageli called her "Salt" because she said that she disliked water. "Are you afraid you may dissolve?"

The harvesting was easy, as Ekwefi had said. Ezinma shook every tree violently with a long stick before she bent down to cut the stem and dig out the tuber. Sometimes it was not necessary to dig. They just pulled the stump, and earth rose, roots snapped below, and the tuber was pulled out.

When they had harvested a sizeable heap they carried it down in two trips to the stream, where every woman had a shallow well for fermenting her cassava.

"It should be ready in four days or even three," said Obiageli. "They are young tubers."

"They are not all that young," said Ekwefi. "I planted the farm nearly two years ago. It is a poor soil and that is why the tubers are so small."

Okonkwo never did things by halves. When his wife Ekwefi protested that two goats were sufficient for the feast he told her that it was not her affair.

"I am calling a feast because I have the wherewithal. I cannot live on the bank of a river and wash my hands with spittle. My mother's people have been good to me and I must show my gratitude."

And so three goats were slaughtered and a number of fowls. It was like a wedding feast. There was foo-foo and yam pottage, egusi[8] soup and bitter-leaf soup and pots and pots of palm-wine.

All the *umunna*[9] were invited to the feast, all the descendants of Okolo, who had lived about two hundred years before. The oldest member of this extensive family was Okonkwo's uncle, Uchendu. The kola nut was given to

8. Melon seed, which is roasted, ground, and cooked in soup.

9. Children of the father (literal trans.); the clan (male).

him to break, and he prayed to the ancestors. He asked them for health and children. "We do not ask for wealth because he that has health and children will also have wealth. We do not pray to have more money but to have more kinsmen. We are better than animals because we have kinsmen. An animal rubs its itching flank against a tree, a man asks his kinsman to scratch him." He prayed especially for Okonkwo and his family. He then broke the kola nut and threw one of the lobes on the ground for the ancestors.

As the broken kola nuts were passed round, Okonkwo's wives and children and those who came to help them with the cooking began to bring out the food. His sons brought out the pots of palm-wine. There was so much food and drink that many kinsmen whistled in surprise. When all was laid out, Okonkwo rose to speak.

"I beg you to accept this little kola," he said. "It is not to pay you back for all you did for me in these seven years. A child cannot pay for its mother's milk. I have only called you together because it is good for kinsmen to meet."

Yam pottage was served first because it was lighter than foo-foo and because yam always came first. Then the foo-foo was served. Some kinsmen ate it with egusi soup and others with bitter-leaf soup. The meat was then shared so that every member of the *umunna* had a portion. Every man rose in order of years and took a share. Even the few kinsmen who had not been able to come had their shares taken out for them in due turn.

As the palm-wine was drunk one of the oldest members of the *umunna* rose to thank Okonkwo:

"If I say that we did not expect such a big feast I will be suggesting that we did not know how open-handed our son, Okonkwo, is. We all know him, and we expected a big feast. But it turned out to be even bigger than we expected. Thank you. May all you took out return again tenfold. It is good in these days when the younger generation consider themselves wiser than their sires to see a man doing things in the grand, old way. A man who calls his kinsmen to a feast does not do so to save them from starving. They all have food in their own homes. When we gather together in the moonlit village ground it is not because of the moon. Every man can see it in his own compound. We come together because it is good for kinsmen to do so. You may ask why I am saying all this. I say it because I fear for the younger generation, for you people." He waved his arm where most of the young men sat. "As for me, I have only a short while to live, and so have Uchendu and Unachukwu and Emefo. But I fear for you young people because you do not understand how strong is the bond of kinship. You do not know what it is to speak with one voice. And what is the result? An abominable religion has settled among you. A man can now leave his father and his brothers. He can curse the gods of his fathers and his ancestors, like a hunter's dog that suddenly goes mad and turns on his master. I fear for you; I fear for the clan." He turned again to Okonkwo and said, "Thank you for calling us together."

Part Three

CHAPTER TWENTY

Seven years was a long time to be away from one's clan. A man's place was not always there, waiting for him. As soon as he left, someone else rose and filled it. The clan was like a lizard; if it lost its tail it soon grew another.

Okonkwo knew these things. He knew that he had lost his place among the nine masked spirits who administered justice in the clan. He had lost the chance to lead his warlike clan against the new religion, which he was told, had gained ground. He had lost the years in which he might have taken the highest titles in the clan. But some of these losses were not irreparable. He was determined that his return should be marked by his people. He would return with a flourish, and regain the seven wasted years.

Even in his first year in exile he had begun to plan for his return. The first thing he would do would be to rebuild his compound on a more magnificent scale. He would build a bigger barn than he had had before and he would build huts for two new wives. Then he would show his wealth by initiating his sons into the *ozo* society. Only the really great men in the clan were able to do this. Okonkwo saw clearly the high esteem in which he would be held, and he saw himself taking the highest title in the land.

As the years of exile passed one by one it seemed to him that his *chi* might now be making amends for the past disaster. His yams grew abundantly, not only in his motherland but also in Umuofia, where his friend gave them out year by year to share-croppers.

Then the tragedy of his first son had occurred. At first it appeared as if it might prove too great for his spirit. But it was a resilient spirit, and in the end Okonkwo overcame his sorrow. He had five other sons and he would bring them up in the way of the clan.

He sent for the five sons and they came and sat in his *obi*. The youngest of them was four years old.

"You have all seen the great abomination of your brother. Now he is no longer my son or your brother. I will only have a son who is a man, who will hold his head up among my people. If any one of you prefers to be a woman, let him follow Nwoye now while I am alive so that I can curse him. If you turn against me when I am dead I will visit you and break your neck."

Okonkwo was very lucky in his daughters. He never stopped regretting that Ezinma was a girl. Of all his children she alone understood his every mood. A bond of sympathy had grown between them as the years had passed.

Ezinma grew up in her father's exile and became one of the most beautiful girls in Mbanta. She was called Crystal of Beauty, as her mother had been called in her youth. The young ailing girl who had caused her mother so much heartache had been transformed, almost overnight, into a healthy buoyant maiden. She had, it was true, her moments of depression when she would snap at everybody like an angry dog. These moods descended on her suddenly and for no apparent reason. But they were very rare and short-lived. As long as they lasted, she could bear no other person but her father.

Many young men and prosperous middle-aged men of Mbanta came to marry her. But she refused them all, because her father had called her one evening and said to her: "There are many good and prosperous people here, but I shall be happy if you marry in Umuofia when we return home."

That was all he had said. But Ezinma had seen clearly all the thought and hidden meaning behind the few words. And she had agreed.

"Your half-sister, Obiageli, will not understand me," Okonkwo said. "But you can explain to her."

Although they were almost the same age, Ezinma wielded a strong influence over her half-sister. She explained to her why they should not marry yet, and she agreed also. And so the two of them refused every offer of marriage in Mbanta.

"I wish she were a boy," Okonkwo thought within himself. She understood things so perfectly. Who else among his children could have read his thought so well? With two beautiful grown-up daughters his return to Umuofia would attract considerable attention. His future sons-in-law would be men of authority in the clan. The poor and unknown would not dare to come forth.

Umuofia had indeed changed during the seven years Okonkwo had been in exile. The church had come and led many astray. Not only the low-born and the outcast but sometimes a worthy man had joined it. Such a man was Ogbuefi Ugonna,[1] who had taken two titles, and who like a madman had cut the anklet of his titles and cast it away to join the Christians. The white missionary was very proud of him and he was one of the first men in Umuofia to receive the sacrament of Holy Communion, or Holy Feast as it was called in Ibo. Ogbuefi Ugonna had thought of the Feast in terms of eating and drinking, only more holy than the village variety. He had therefore put his drinking-horn into his goatskin bag for the occasion.

But apart from the church, the white men had also brought a government. They had built a court where the District Commissioner judged cases in ignorance. He had court messengers who brought men to him for trial. Many of these messengers came from Umuru on the bank of the Great River, where the white men first came many years before and where they had built the centre of their religion and trade and government. These court messengers were greatly hated in Umuofia because they were foreigners and also arrogant and high-handed. They were called *kotma*,[2] and because of their ash-coloured shorts they earned the additional name of Ashy-Buttocks. They guarded the prison, which was full of men who had offended against the white man's law. Some of these prisoners had thrown away their twins and some had molested the Christians. They were beaten in the prison by the *kotma* and made to work every morning clearing the government compound and fetching wood for the white Commissioner and the court messengers. Some of these prisoners were men of title who should be above such mean occupation. They were grieved by the indignity and mourned for their neglected farms. As they cut grass in the morning the younger men sang in time with the strokes of their matchets:

> "*Kotma* of the ash buttocks,
>   He is fit to be a slave.
> The white man has no sense,
>   He is fit to be a slave."

The court messengers did not like to be called Ashy-Buttocks, and they beat the men. But the song spread in Umuofia.

Okonkwo's head was bowed in sadness as Obierika told him these things.

"Perhaps I have been away too long," Okonkwo said, almost to himself. "But I cannot understand these things you tell me. What is it that has happened to our people? Why have they lost the power to fight?"

"Have you not heard how the white man wiped out Abame?" asked Obierika.

---

1. Father's honor (with the eagle feather).   2. Court messenger (pidgin English).

"I have heard," said Okonkwo. "But I have also heard that Abame people were weak and foolish. Why did they not fight back? Had they no guns and matchets? We would be cowards to compare ourselves with the men of Abame. Their fathers had never dared to stand before our ancestors. We must fight these men and drive them from the land."

"It is already too late," said Obierika sadly. "Our own men and our sons have joined the ranks of the stranger. They have joined his religion and they help to uphold his government. If we should try to drive out the white men in Umuofia we should find it easy. There are only two of them. But what of our own people who are following their way and have been given power? They would go to Umuru and bring the soldiers, and we would be like Abame." He paused for a long time and then said: "I told you on my last visit to Mbanta how they hanged Aneto."

"What has happened to that piece of land in dispute?" asked Okonkwo.

"The white man's court has decided that it should belong to Nnama's family, who had given much money to the white man's messengers and interpreter."

"Does the white man understand our custom about land?"

"How can he when he does not even speak our tongue? But he says that our customs are bad; and our own brothers who have taken up his religion also say that our customs are bad. How do you think we can fight when our own brothers have turned against us? The white man is very clever. He came quietly and peaceably with his religion. We were amused at his foolishness and allowed him to stay. Now he has won our brothers, and our clan can no longer act like one. He has put a knife on the things that held us together and we have fallen apart."

"How did they get hold of Aneto to hang him?" asked Okonkwo.

"When he killed Oduche in the fight over the land, he fled to Aninta to escape the wrath of the earth. This was about eight days after the fight, because Oduche had not died immediately from his wounds. It was on the seventh day that he died. But everybody knew that he was going to die and Aneto got his belongings together in readiness to flee. But the Christians had told the white man about the accident, and he sent his *kotma* to catch Aneto. He was imprisoned with all the leaders of his family. In the end Oduche died and Aneto was taken to Umuru and hanged. The other people were released, but even now they have not found the mouth with which to tell of their suffering."

The two men sat in silence for a long while afterwards.

CHAPTER TWENTY-ONE

There were many men and women in Umuofia who did not feel as strongly as Okonkwo about the new dispensation. The white man had indeed brought a lunatic religion, but he had also built a trading store and for the first time palm-oil and kernel[3] became things of great price, and much money flowed into Umuofia.

And even in the matter of religion there was a growing feeling that there

---

3. The red fleshy husk of the palm nut is crushed manually to produce cooking oil, leaving a fibrous residue along with hard kernels. The Europeans bought both the red oil and the kernels, from which they could extract a very fine oil by using machines.

might be something in it after all, something vaguely akin to method in the overwhelming madness.

This growing feeling was due to Mr Brown, the white missionary, who was very firm in restraining his flock from provoking the wrath of the clan. One member in particular was very difficult to restrain. His name was Enoch and his father was the priest of the snake cult. The story went around that Enoch had killed and eaten the sacred python, and that his father had cursed him.

Mr Brown preached against such excess of zeal. Everything was possible, he told his energetic flock, but everything was not expedient. And so Mr Brown came to be respected even by the clan, because he trod softly on its faith. He made friends with some of the great men of the clan and on one of his frequent visits to the neighbouring villages he had been presented with a carved elephant tusk, which was a sign of dignity and rank. One of the great men in that village was called Akunna[4] and he had given one of his sons to be taught the white man's knowledge in Mr Brown's school.

Whenever Mr Brown went to that village he spent long hours with Akunna in his *obi* talking through an interpreter about religion. Neither of them succeeded in converting the other but they learnt more about their different beliefs.

"You say that there is one supreme God who made heaven and earth," said Akunna on one of Mr Brown's visits. "We also believe in Him and call Him Chukwu. He made all the world and the other gods."

"There are no other gods," said Mr Brown. "Chukwu is the only God and all others are false. You carve a piece of wood—like that one" (he pointed at the rafters from which Akunna's carved *Ikenga*[5] hung), "and you call it a god. But it is still a piece of wood."

"Yes," said Akunna. "It is indeed a piece of wood. The tree from which it came was made by Chukwu, as indeed all minor gods were. But He made them for His messengers so that we could approach Him through them. It is like yourself. You are the head of your church."

"No," protested Mr Brown. "The head of my church is God Himself."

"I know," said Akunna, "but there must be a head in this world among men. Somebody like yourself must be the head here."

"The head of my church in that sense is in England."

"That is exactly what I am saying. The head of your church is in your country. He has sent you here as his messenger. And you have also appointed your own messengers and servants. Or let me take another example, the District Commissioner. He is sent by your king."

"They have a queen," said the interpreter on his own account.

"Your queen sends her messenger, the District Commissioner. He finds that he cannot do the work alone and so he appoints *kotma* to help him. It is the same with God, or Chukwu. He appoints the smaller gods to help Him because His work is too great for one person."

"You should not think of him as a person," said Mr Brown. "It is because you do so that you imagine He must need helpers. And the worst thing about it is that you give all the worship to the false gods you have created."

"That is not so. We make sacrifices to the little gods, but when they fail

---

4. Father's wealth.
5. A carved wooden figure with the horns of a ram that symbolized the strength of a man's right hand.

Every adult male kept an *Ikenga* in his personal shrine.

and there is no one else to turn to we go to Chukwu. It is right to do so. We approach a great man through his servants. But when his servants fail to help us, then we go to the last source of hope. We appear to pay greater attention to the little gods but that is not so. We worry them more because we are afraid to worry their Master. Our fathers knew that Chukwu was the Overlord and that is why many of them gave their children the name Chukwuka—'Chukwu is Supreme'."

"You said one interesting thing," said Mr Brown. "You are afraid of Chukwu. In my religion Chukwu is a loving Father and need not be feared by those who do His will."

"But we must fear Him when we are not doing Him will," said Akunna. "And who is to tell His will? It is too great to be known."

In this way Mr Brown learnt a good deal about the religion of the clan and he came to the conclusion that a frontal attack on it would not succeed. And so he built a school and a little hospital in Umuofia. He went from family to family begging people to send their children to his school. But at first they only sent their slaves or sometimes their lazy children. Mr Brown begged and argued and prophesied. He said that the leaders of the land in the future would be men and women who had learnt to read and write. If Umuofia failed to send her children to the school, strangers would come from other places to rule them. They could already see that happening in the Native Court, where the D.C. was surrounded by strangers who spoke his tongue. Most of these strangers came from the distant town of Umuru on the bank of the Great River where the white man first went.

In the end Mr Brown's arguments began to have an effect. More people came to learn in his school, and he encouraged them with gifts of singlets[6] and towels. They were not all young, these people who came to learn. Some of them were thirty years old or more. They worked on their farms in the morning and went to school in the afternoon. And it was not long before the people began to say that the white man's medicine was quick in working. Mr Brown's school produced quick results. A few months in it were enough to make one a court messenger or even a court clerk. Those who stayed longer became teachers; and from Umuofia labourers went forth into the Lord's vineyard. New churches were established in the surrounding villages and a few schools with them. From the very beginning religion and education went hand in hand.

Mr Brown's mission grew from strength to strength, and because of its link with the new administration it earned a new social prestige. But Mr Brown himself was breaking down in health. At first he ignored the warning signs. But in the end he had to leave his flock, sad and broken.

It was in the first rainy season after Okonkwo's return to Umuofia that Mr Brown left for home. As soon as he had learnt of Okonkwo's return five months earlier, the missionary had immediately paid him a visit. He had just sent Okonkwo's son, Nwoye, who was now called Isaac,[7] to the new training college for teachers in Umuru. And he had hoped that Okonkwo would be

6. Undershirts, T-shirts.
7. Son of Abraham, offered to God as a sacrifice (Genesis 22).

happy to hear of it. But Okonkwo had driven him away with the threat that if he came into his compound again, he would be carried out of it.

Okonkwo's return to his native land was not as memorable as he had wished. It was true his two beautiful daughters aroused great interest among suitors and marriage negotiations were soon in progress, but, beyond that, Umuofia did not appear to have taken any special notice of the warrior's return. The clan had undergone such profound change during his exile that it was barely recognisable. The new religion and government and the trading stores were very much in the people's eyes and minds. There were still many who saw these new institutions as evil, but even they talked and thought about little else, and certainly not about Okonkwo's return.

And it was the wrong year too. If Okonkwo had immediately initiated his two sons into the *ozo* society as he had planned he would have caused a stir. But the initiation rite was performed once in three years in Umuofia, and he had to wait for nearly two years for the next round of ceremonies.

Okonkwo was deeply grieved. And it was not just a personal grief. He mourned for the clan, which he saw breaking up and falling apart, and he mourned for the warlike men of Umuofia, who had so unaccountably become soft like women.

CHAPTER TWENTY-TWO

Mr Brown's successor was the Reverend James Smith, and he was a different kind of man. He condemned openly Mr Brown's policy of compromise and accommodation. He saw things as black and white. And black was evil. He saw the world as a battlefield in which the children of light were locked in mortal conflict with the sons of darkness. He spoke in his sermons about sheep and goats and about wheat and tares. He believed in slaying the prophets of Baal.

Mr Smith was greatly distressed by the ignorance which many of his flock showed even in such things as the Trinity and the Sacraments. It only showed that they were seeds sown on a rocky soil. Mr Brown had thought of nothing but numbers. He should have known that the kingdom of God did not depend on large crowds. Our Lord Himself stressed the importance of fewness. Narrow is the way and few the number. To fill the Lord's holy temple with an idolatrous crowd clamouring for signs was a folly of everlasting consequence. Our Lord used the whip only once in His life—to drive the crowd away from His church.

Within a few weeks of his arrival in Umuofia Mr Smith suspended a young woman from the church for pouring new wine into old bottles. This woman had allowed her heathen husband to mutilate her dead child. The child had been declared an *ogbanje*, plaguing its mother by dying and entering her womb to be born again. Four times this child had run its evil round. And so it was mutilated to discourage it from returning.

Mr Smith was filled with wrath when he heard of this. He disbelieved the story which even some of the most faithful confirmed, the story of really evil children who were not deterred by mutilation, but came back with all the scars. He replied that such stories were spread in the world by the Devil to lead men astray. Those who believed such stories were unworthy of the Lord's table.

There was a saying in Umuofia that as a man danced so the drums were beaten for him. Mr Smith danced a furious step and so the drums went mad. The over-zealous converts who had smarted under Mr Brown's restraining hand now flourished in full favour. One of them was Enoch, the son of the snake-priest who was believed to have killed and eaten the sacred python. Enoch's devotion to the new faith had seemed so much greater than Mr Brown's that the villagers called him The outsider who wept louder than the bereaved.

Enoch was short and slight of build, and always seemed in great haste. His feet were short and broad, and when he stood or walked his heels came together and his feet opened outwards as if they had quarrelled and meant to go in different directions. Such was the excessive energy bottled up in Enoch's small body that it was always erupting in quarrels and fights. On Sundays he always imagined that the sermon was preached for the benefit of his enemies. And if he happened to sit near one of them he would occasionally turn to give him a meaningful look, as if to say, 'I told you so'. It was Enoch who touched off the great conflict between church and clan in Umuofia which had been gathering since Mr Brown left.

It happened during the annual ceremony which was held in honour of the earth deity. At such times the ancestors of the clan who had been committed to Mother Earth at their death emerged again as *egwugwu* through tiny antholes.

One of the greatest crimes a man could commit was to unmask an *egwugwu* in public, or to say or do anything which might reduce its immortal prestige in the eyes of the uninitiated. And this was what Enoch did.

The annual worship of the earth goddess fell on a Sunday, and the masked spirits were abroad. The Christian women who had been to church could not therefore go home. Some of their men had gone out to beg the *egwugwu* to retire for a short while for the women to pass. They agreed and were already retiring, when Enoch boasted aloud that they would not dare to touch a Christian. Whereupon they all came back and one of them gave Enoch a good stroke of the cane, which was always carried. Enoch fell on him and tore off his mask. The other *egwugwu* immediately surrounded their desecrated companion, to shield him from the profane gaze of women and children, and led him away. Enoch had killed an ancestral spirit, and Umuofia was thrown into confusion.

That night the Mother of the Spirits walked the length and breadth of the clan, weeping for her murdered son. It was a terrible night. Not even the oldest man in Umuofia had ever heard such a strange and fearful sound, and it was never to be heard again. It seemed as if the very soul of the tribe wept for a great evil that was coming—its own death.

On the next day all the masked *egwugwu* of Umuofia assembled in the market-place. They came from all the quarters of the clan and even from the neighbouring villages. The dreaded Otakagu came from Imo, and Ekwensu, dangling a white cock, arrived from Uli. It was a terrible gathering. The eerie voices of countless spirits, the bells that clattered behind some of them, and the clash of matchets as they ran forwards and backwards and saluted one another, sent tremors of fear into every heart. For the first time in living memory the sacred bull-roarer was heard in broad daylight.

From the market-place the furious band made for Enoch's compound.

Some of the elders of the clan went with them, wearing heavy protections of charms and amulets. These were men whose arms were strong in *ogwu*, or medicine. As for the ordinary men and women, they listened from the safety of their huts.

The leaders of the Christians had met together at Mr Smith's parsonage on the previous night. As they deliberated they could hear the Mother of Spirits wailing for her son. The chilling sound affected Mr Smith, and for the first time he seemed to be afraid.

"What are they planning to do?" he asked. No one knew, because such a thing had never happened before. Mr Smith would have sent for the District Commissioner and his court messengers, but they had gone on tour on the previous day.

"One thing is clear," said Mr Smith. "We cannot offer physical resistance to them. Our strength lies in the Lord." They knelt down together and prayed to God for delivery.

"O Lord save Thy people," cried Mr Smith.

"And bless Thine inheritance," replied the men.

They decided that Enoch should be hidden in the parsonage for a day or two. Enoch himself was greatly disappointed when he heard this, for he had hoped that a holy war was imminent; and there were a few other Christians who thought like him. But wisdom prevailed in the camp of the faithful and many lives were thus saved.

The band of *egwugwu* moved like a furious whirlwind to Enoch's compound and with matchet and fire reduced it to a desolate heap. And from there they made for the church, intoxicated with destruction.

Mr Smith was in his church when he heard the masked spirits coming. He walked quietly to the door which commanded the approach to the church compound, and stood there. But when the first three or four *egwugwu* appeared on the church compound he nearly bolted. He overcame this impulse and instead of running away he went down the two steps that led up to the church and walked towards the approaching spirits.

They surged forward, and a long stretch of the bamboo fence with which the church compound was surrounded gave way before them. Discordant bells clanged, matchets clashed and the air was full of dust and weird sounds. Mr Smith heard a sound of footsteps behind him. He turned round and saw Okeke, his interpreter. Okeke had not been on the best of terms with his master since he had strongly condemned Enoch's behaviour at the meeting of the leaders of the church during the night. Okeke had gone as far as to say that Enoch should not be hidden in the parsonage, because he would only draw the wrath of the clan on the pastor. Mr Smith had rebuked him in very strong language, and had not sought his advice that morning. But now, as he came up and stood by him confronting the angry spirits, Mr Smith looked at him and smiled. It was a wan smile, but there was deep gratitude there.

For a brief moment the onrush of the *egwugwu* was checked by the unexpected composure of the two men. But it was only a momentary check, like the tense silence between blasts of thunder. The second onrush was greater than the first. It swallowed up the two men. Then an unmistakable voice rose above the tumult and there was immediate silence. Space was made around the two men, and Ajofia began to speak.

Ajofia was the leading *egwugwu* of Umuofia. He was the head and spokesman of the nine ancestors who administered justice in the clan. His voice was unmistakable and so he was able to bring immediate peace to the agitated spirits. He then addressed Mr Smith, and as he spoke clouds of smoke rose from his head.

"The body of the white man, I salute you," he said, using the language in which immortals spoke to men.

"The body of the white man, do you know me?" he asked.

Mr Smith looked at his interpreter, but Okeke, who was a native of distant Umuru, was also at a loss.

Ajofia laughed in his guttural voice. It was like the laugh of rusty metal. "They are strangers," he said, "and they are ignorant. But let that pass." He turned round to his comrades and saluted them, calling them the fathers of Umuofia. He dug his rattling spear into the ground and it shook with metallic life. Then he turned once more to the missionary and his interpreter.

"Tell the white man that we will not do him any harm," he said to the interpreter. "Tell him to go back to his house and leave us alone. We liked his brother who was with us before. He was foolish, but we liked him, and for his sake we shall not harm his brother. But this shrine which he built must be destroyed. We shall no longer allow it in our midst. It has bred untold abominations and we have come to put an end to it." He turned to his comrades. "Fathers of Umuofia, I salute you;" and they replied with one guttural voice. He turned again to the missionary. "You can stay with us if you like our ways. You can worship your own god. It is good that a man should worship the gods and the spirits of his fathers. Go back to your house so that you may not be hurt. Our anger is great but we have held it down so that we can talk to you."

Mr Smith said to his interpreter: "Tell them to go away from here. This is the house of God and I will not live to see it desecrated."

Okeke interpreted wisely to the spirits and leaders of Umuofia: "The white man says he is happy you have come to him with your grievances, like friends. He will be happy if you leave the matter in his hands."

"We cannot leave the matter in his hands because he does not understand our customs, just as we do not understand his. We say he is foolish because he does not know our ways, and perhaps he says we are foolish because we do not know his. Let him go away."

Mr Smith stood his ground. But he could not save his church. When the *egwugwu* went away the red-earth church which Mr Brown had built was a pile of earth and ashes. And for the moment the spirit of the clan was pacified.

CHAPTER TWENTY-THREE

For the first time in many years Okonkwo had a feeling that was akin to happiness. The times which had altered so unaccountably during his exile seemed to be coming round again. The clan which had turned false on him appeared to be making amends.

He had spoken violently to his clansmen when they had met in the marketplace to decide on their action. And they had listened to him with respect. It was like the good old days again, when a warrior was a warrior. Although they had not agreed to kill the missionary or drive away the Christians, they had agreed to do something substantial. And they had done it. Okonkwo was almost happy again.

For two days after the destruction of the church, nothing happened. Every man in Umuofia went about armed with a gun or a matchet. They would not be caught unawares, like the men of Abame.

Then the District Commissioner returned from his tour. Mr Smith went immediately to him and they had a long discussion. The men of Umuofia did not take any notice of this, and if they did, they thought it was not important. The missionary often went to see his brother white man. There was nothing strange in that.

Three days later the District Commissioner sent his sweet-tongued messenger to the leaders of Umuofia asking them to meet him in his headquarters. That also was not strange. He often asked them to hold such palavers, as he called them. Okonkwo was among the six leaders he invited.

Okonkwo warned the others to be fully armed. "An Umuofia man does not refuse a call," he said. "He may refuse to do what he is asked; he does not refuse to be asked. But the times have changed, and we must be fully prepared."

And so the six men went to see the District Commissioner, armed with their matchets. They did not carry guns, for that would be unseemly. They were led into the court-house where the District Commissioner sat. He received them politely. They unslung their goatskin bags and their sheathed matchets, put them on the floor, and sat down.

"I have asked you to come," began the Commissioner, "because of what happened during my absence. I have been told a few things but I cannot believe them until I have heard your own side. Let us talk about it like friends and find a way of ensuring that it does not happen again."

Ogbuefi Ekwueme[8] rose to his feet and began to tell the story.

"Wait a minute," said the Commissioner. "I want to bring in my men so that they too can hear your grievances and take warning. Many of them come from distant places and although they speak your tongue they are ignorant of your customs. James! Go and bring in the men." His interpreter left the court-room and soon returned with twelve men. They sat together with the men of Umuofia, and Ogbuefi Ekwueme began again to tell the story of how Enoch murdered an *egwugwu*.

It happened so quickly that the six men did not see it coming. There was only a brief scuffle, too brief even to allow the drawing of a sheathed matchet. The six men were handcuffed and led into the guardroom.

"We shall not do you any harm," said the District Commissioner to them later, "if only you agree to co-operate with us. We have brought a peaceful administration to you and your people so that you may be happy. If any man ill-treats you we shall come to your rescue. But we will not allow you to ill-treat others. We have a court of law where we judge cases and administer justice just as it is done in my own country under a great queen. I have brought you here because you joined together to molest others, to burn people's houses and their place of worship. That must not happen in the domin-

8. A person who does what he says (a praise name).

2700 / CHINUA ACHEBE

ion of our queen, the most powerful ruler in the world. I have decided that you will pay a fine of two hundred bags of cowries. You will be released as soon as you agree to this and undertake to collect that fine from your people. What do you say to that?"

The six men remained sullen and silent and the Commissioner left them for a while. He told the court messengers, when he left the guardroom, to treat the men with respect because they were the leaders of Umuofia. They said, "Yes, sir," and saluted.

As soon as the District Commissioner left, the head messenger, who was also the prisoners' barber, took down his razor and shaved off all the hair on the men's heads. They were still handcuffed, and they just sat and moped.

"Who is the chief among you?" the court messengers asked in jest. "We see that every pauper wears the anklet of title in Umuofia. Does it cost as much as ten cowries?"

The six men ate nothing throughout that day and the next. They were not even given any water to drink, and they could not go out to urinate or go into the bush when they were pressed. At night the messengers came in to taunt them and to knock their shaven heads together.

Even when the men were left alone they found no words to speak to one another. It was only on the third day, when they could no longer bear the hunger and the insults, that they began to talk about giving in.

"We should have killed the white man if you had listened to me," Okonkwo snarled.

"We could have been in Umuru now waiting to be hanged," someone said to him.

"Who wants to kill the white man?" asked a messenger who had just rushed in. Nobody spoke.

"You are not satisfied with your crime, but you must kill the white man on top of it." He carried a strong stick, and he hit each man a few blows on the head and back. Okonkwo was choked with hate.

As soon as the six men were locked up, court messengers went into Umuofia to tell the people that their leaders would not be released unless they paid a fine of two hundred and fifty bags of cowries.

"Unless you pay the fine immediately," said their headman, "we will take your leaders to Umuru before the big white man, and hang them."

This story spread quickly through the villages, and was added to as it went. Some said that the men had already been taken to Umuru and would be hanged on the following day. Some said that their families would also be hanged. Others said that soldiers were already on their way to shoot the people of Umuofia as they had done in Abame.

It was the time of the full moon. But that night the voice of children was not heard. The village *ilo* where they always gathered for a moon-play was empty. The women of Iguedo did not meet in their secret enclosure to learn a new dance to be displayed later to the village. Young men who were always abroad in the moonlight kept their huts that night. Their manly voices were not heard on the village paths as they went to visit their friends and lovers. Umuofia was like a startled animal with ears erect, sniffing the silent, ominous air and not knowing which way to run.

The silence was broken by the village crier beating his sonorous *ogene*. He called every man in Umuofia, from the Akakanma age-group upwards, to a meeting in the market-place after the morning meal. He went from one end of the village to the other and walked all its breadth. He did not leave out any of the main footpaths.

Okonkwo's compound was like a deserted homestead. It was as if cold water had been poured on it. His family was all there, but everyone spoke in whispers. His daughter Ezinma had broken her twenty-eight-day visit to the family of her future husband, and returned home when she heard that her father had been imprisoned, and was going to be hanged. As soon as she got home she went to Obierika to ask what the men of Umuofia were going to do about it. But Obierika had not been home since morning. His wives thought he had gone to a secret meeting. Ezinma was satisfied that something was being done.

On the morning after the village crier's appeal the men of Umuofia met in the market-place and decided to collect without delay two hundred and fifty bags of cowries to appease the white man. They did not know that fifty bags would go to the court messengers, who had increased the fine for that purpose.

CHAPTER TWENTY-FOUR

Okonkwo and his fellow prisoners were set free as soon as the fine was paid. The District Commissioner spoke to them again about the great queen, and about peace and good government. But the men did not listen. They just sat and looked at him and at his interpreter. In the end they were given back their bags and sheathed matchets and told to go home. They rose and left the court-house. They neither spoke to anyone nor among themselves.

The court-house, like the church, was built a little way outside the village. The footpath that linked them was a very busy one because it also led to the stream, beyond the court. It was open and sandy. Footpaths were open and sandy in the dry season. But when the rains came the bush grew thick on either side and closed in on the path. It was now dry season.

As they made their way to the village the six men met women and children going to the stream with their waterpots. But the men wore such heavy and fearsome looks that the women and children did not say 'nno' or 'welcome' to them, but edged out of the way to let them pass. In the village little groups of men joined them until they became a sizeable company. They walked silently. As each of the six men got to his compound, he turned in, taking some of the crowd with him. The village was astir in a silent, suppressed way.

Ezinma had prepared some food for her father as soon as news spread that the six men would be released. She took it to him in his *obi*. He ate absent-mindedly. He had no appetite; he only ate to please her. His male relations and friends had gathered in his *obi*, and Obierika was urging him to eat. Nobody else spoke, but they noticed the long stripes on Okonkwo's back where the warder's whip had cut into his flesh.

The village crier was abroad again in the night. He beat his iron gong and announced that another meeting would be held in the morning. Everyone knew that Umuofia was at last going to speak its mind about the things that were happening.

Okonkwo slept very little that night. The bitterness in his heart was now mixed with a kind of child-like excitement. Before he had gone to bed he had brought down his war dress, which he had not touched since his return from exile. He had shaken out his smoked raffia skirt and examined his tall feather head-gear and his shield. They were all satisfactory, he had thought.

As he lay on his bamboo bed he thought about the treatment he had received in the white man's court, and he swore vengeance. If Umuofia decided on war, all would be well. But if they chose to be cowards he would go out and avenge himself. He thought about wars in the past. The noblest, he thought, was the war against Isike. In those days Okudo[9] was still alive. Okudo sang a war song in a way that no other man could. He was not a fighter, but his voice turned every man into a lion.

'Worthy men are no more,' Okonkwo sighed as he remembered those days. 'Isike will never forget how we slaughtered them in that war. We killed twelve of their men and they killed only two of ours. Before the end of the fourth market week they were suing for peace. Those were days when men were men.'

As he thought of these things he heard the sound of the iron gong in the distance. He listened carefully, and could just hear the crier's voice. But it was very faint. He turned on his bed and his back hurt him. He ground his teeth. The crier was drawing nearer and nearer until he passed by Okonkwo's compound.

'The greatest obstacle in Umuofia,' Okonkwo thought bitterly, 'is that coward, Egonwanne.[1] His sweet tongue can change fire into cold ash. When he speaks he moves our men to impotence. If they had ignored his womanish wisdom five years ago, we would not have come to this.' He ground his teeth. 'Tomorrow he will tell them that our fathers never fought a "war of blame". If they listen to him I shall leave them and plan my own revenge.'

The crier's voice had once more become faint, and the distance had taken the harsh edge off his iron gong. Okonkwo turned from one side to the other and derived a kind of pleasure from the pain his back gave him. 'Let Egonwanne talk about a "war of blame" tomorrow and I shall show him my back and head.' He ground his teeth.

The market-place began to fill as soon as the sun rose. Obierika was waiting in his *obi* when Okonkwo came along and called him. He hung his goat-skin bag and his sheathed matchet on his shoulder and went out to join him. Obierika's hut was close to the road and he saw every man who passed to the market-place. He had exchanged greetings with many who had already passed that morning.

When Okonkwo and Obierika got to the meeting-place there were already so many people that if one threw up a grain of sand it would not find its way to the earth again. And many more people were coming from every quarter of the nine villages. It warmed Okonkwo's heart to see such strength of numbers. But he was looking for one man in particular, the man whose tongue he dreaded and despised so much.

"Can you see him?" he asked Obierika.

"Who?"

"Egonwanne," he said, his eyes roving from one corner of the huge market-

---

9. Great eagle feather (a praise name).   1. Wealth of a sibling.

place to the other. Most of the men were seated on goatskins on the ground. A few of them sat on wooden stools they had brought with them.

"No," said Obierika, casting his eyes over the crowd. "Yes, there he is, under the silk-cotton tree. Are you afraid he would convince us not to fight?"

"Afraid? I do not care what he does to *you*. I despise him and those who listen to him. I shall fight alone if I choose."

They spoke at the top of their voices because everybody was talking, and it was like the sound of a great market.

'I shall wait till he has spoken,' Okonkwo thought. 'Then I shall speak.'

"But how do you know he will speak against war?" Obierika asked after a while.

"Because I know he is a coward," said Okonkwo. Obierika did not hear the rest of what he said because at that moment somebody touched his shoulder from behind and he turned round to shake hands and exchange greetings with five or six friends. Okonkwo did not turn round even though he knew the voices. He was in no mood to exchange greetings. But one of the men touched him and asked about the people of his compound.

"They are well," he replied without interest.

The first man to speak to Umuofia that morning was Okika, one of the six who had been imprisoned. Okika was a great man and an orator. But he did not have the booming voice which a first speaker must use to establish silence in the assembly of the clan. Onyeka[2] had such a voice; and so he was asked to salute Umuofia before Okika began to speak.

"*Umuofia kwenu!*" he bellowed, raising his left arm and pushing the air with his open hand.

"*Yaa!*" roared Umuofia.

"*Umuofia kwenu!*" he bellowed again, and again and again, facing a new direction each time. And the crowd answered, "*Yaa!*"

There was immediate silence as though cold water had been poured on a roaring flame.

Okika sprang to his feet and also saluted his clansmen four times. Then he began to speak:

"You all know why we are here, when we ought to be building our barns or mending our huts, when we should be putting our compounds in order. My father used to say to me: 'Whenever you see a toad jumping in broad daylight, then know that something is after its life.' When I saw you all pouring into this meeting from all the quarters of our clan so early in the morning, I knew that something was after our life." He paused for a brief moment and then began again:

"All our gods are weeping. Idemili is weeping, Ogwugwu is weeping, Agbala is weeping, and all the others. Our dead fathers are weeping because of the shameful sacrilege they are suffering and the abomination we have all seen with our eyes." He stopped again to steady his trembling voice.

"This is a great gathering. No clan can boast of greater numbers or greater valour. But are we all here? I ask you: Are all the sons of Umuofia with us here?" A deep murmur swept through the crowd.

"They are not," he said. "They have broken the clan and gone their several ways. We who are here this morning have remained true to our fathers, but

2. "Who surpasses [God]?" (a rhetorical question).

our brothers have deserted us and joined a stranger to soil their fatherland. If we fight the stranger we shall hit our brothers and perhaps shed the blood of a clansman. But we must do it. Our fathers never dreamt of such a thing, they never killed their brothers. But a white man never came to them. So we must do what our fathers would never have done. Eneke the bird was asked why he was always on the wing and he replied: 'Men have learnt to shoot without missing their mark and I have learnt to fly without perching on a twig.' We must root out this evil. And if our brothers take the side of evil we must root them out too. And we must do it *now*. We must bale this water now that it is only ankle-deep. . . ."

At this point there was a sudden stir in the crowd and every eye was turned in one direction. There was a sharp bend in the road that led from the market-place to the white man's court, and to the stream beyond it. And so no one had seen the approach of the five court messengers until they had come round the bend, a few paces from the edge of the crowd. Okonkwo was sitting at the edge.

He sprang to his feet as soon as he saw who it was. He confronted the head messenger, trembling with hate, unable to utter a word. The man was fearless and stood his ground, his four men lined up behind him.

In that brief moment the world seemed to stand still, waiting. There was utter silence. The men of Umuofia were merged into the mute backcloth of trees and giant creepers, waiting.

The spell was broken by the head messenger. "Let me pass!" he ordered.

"What do you want here?"

"The white man whose power you know too well has ordered this meeting to stop."

In a flash Okonkwo drew his matchet. The messenger crouched to avoid the blow. It was useless. Okonkwo's matchet descended twice and the man's head lay beside his uniformed body.

The waiting backcloth jumped into tumultuous life and the meeting was stopped. Okonkwo stood looking at the dead man. He knew that Umuofia would not go to war. He knew because they had let the other messengers escape. They had broken into tumult instead of action. He discerned fright in that tumult. He heard voices asking: "Why did he do it?"

He wiped his matchet on the sand and went away.

CHAPTER TWENTY-FIVE

When the District Commissioner arrived at Okonkwo's compound at the head of an armed band of soldiers and court messengers he found a small crowd of men sitting wearily in the *obi*. He commanded them to come outside, and they obeyed without a murmur.

"Which among you is called Okonkwo?" he asked through his interpreter.

"He is not here," replied Obierika.

"Where is he?"

"He is not here!"

The Commissioner became angry and red in the face. He warned the men that unless they produced Okonkwo forthwith he would lock them all up. The men murmured among themselves, and Obierika spoke again.

"We can take you where he is, and perhaps your men will help us."

The Commissioner did not understand what Obierika meant when he said, "Perhaps your men will help us." One of the most infuriating habits of these people was their love of superfluous words, he thought.

Obierika with five or six others led the way. The Commissioner and his men followed, their firearms held at the ready. He had warned Obierika that if he and his men played any monkey tricks they would be shot. And so they went.

There was a small bush behind Okonkwo's compound. The only opening into this bush from the compound was a little round hole in the red-earth wall through which fowls went in and out in their endless search for food. The hole would not let a man through. It was to this bush that Obierika led the Commissioner and his men. They skirted round the compound, keeping close to the wall. The only sound they made was with their feet as they crushed dry leaves.

Then they came to the tree from which Okonkwo's body was dangling, and they stopped dead.

"Perhaps your men can help us bring him down and bury him," said Obierika. "We have sent for strangers from another village to do it for us, but they may be a long time coming."

The District Commissioner changed instantaneously. The resolute administrator in him gave way to the student of primitive customs.

"Why can't you take him down yourselves?" he asked.

"It is against our custom," said one of the men. "It is an abomination for a man to take his own life. It is an offence against the Earth, and a man who commits it will not be buried by his clansmen. His body is evil, and only strangers may touch it. That is why we ask your people to bring him down, because you are strangers."

"Will you bury him like any other man?" asked the Commissioner.

"We cannot bury him. Only strangers can. We shall pay your men to do it. When he has been buried we will then do our duty by him. We shall make sacrifices to cleanse the desecrated land."

Obierika, who had been gazing steadily at his friend's dangling body, turned suddenly to the District Commissioner and said ferociously: "That man was one of the greatest men in Umuofia. You drove him to kill himself; and now he will be buried like a dog. . . ." He could not say any more. His voice trembled and choked his words.

"Shut up!" shouted one of the messengers, quite unnecessarily.

"Take down the body," the Commissioner ordered his chief messenger, "and bring it and all these people to the court."

"Yes, sah," the messenger said, saluting.

The Commissioner went away, taking three or four of the soldiers with him. In the many years in which he had toiled to bring civilisation to different parts of Africa he had learnt a number of things. One of them was that a District Commissioner must never attend to such undignified details as cutting down a hanged man from the tree. Such attention would give the natives a poor opinion of him. In the book which he planned to write he would stress that point. As he walked back to the court he thought about that book. Every day brought him some new material. The story of this man who had killed a messenger and hanged himself would make interesting reading. One could almost write a whole chapter on him. Perhaps not a whole chapter but a reasonable paragraph, at any rate. There was so much else to include, and one must be firm in cutting out details. He had already chosen the title of the book, after much thought: *The Pacification of the Primitive Tribes of the Lower Niger*.

1958

ALICE MUNRO
b. 1931

Born in Wingham, Ontario, in 1931, Alice Munro has become one of the leading short-story writers of her generation. Her fiction combines spareness and realism—an uncompromising look at a panorama of faltering lives—with magisterial vision and expansiveness. Munro's signature approach to the short story, in which she uses a deceptively simple style to produce complex, layered, and emotionally engaging effects, has influenced many of her English-language contemporaries, both within and outside of Canada. In addition to one novel, *Lives of Girls and Women* (1972), she has published eight collections of short stories, including *Dance of the Happy Shades* (1968, from which the story here is taken), *Something I've Been Meaning to Tell You* (1974), *The Moons of Jupiter* (1982), *Friend of My Youth* (1990), and mostly recently *The Love of a Good Woman* (1998).

Many of Munro's stories are written in the first-person, often from the perspective of women whose voices and experiences suggest the author's own history. She was born Alice Anne Laidlaw to a poor family, and her parents' struggles within a variety of rural occupations continued throughout her childhood. She began writing in her teens and in 1949 enrolled in the University of Western Ontario; she left the university two years later, to marry and raise three daughters. Her first marriage ended in divorce in the late 1970s; sometime later she remarried and moved to Clinton, Ontario. Munro's stories are typically set in small towns where poverty stamps itself on all facets of life, and where women confront—often in a spirit that combines resignation with stubborn resistance—the triple binds of economic, gender, and cultural confinement. Through a precise and particular emphasis on setting and character, her fictions evoke a period in rural Canadian history in the decades following mid-century, when a sense of modernity and the promise of the future are often crowded out by the hardening nature of the past.

In an early writing, Munro describes an approach to the outside world that effectively captures her sense of the mystery within the ordinary—the hallmark of her realist style: "It seems as if there are feelings that have to be translated into a next-door language, which might blow them up and burst them altogether; or else they have to be let alone. The truth about them is always suspected, never verified, the light catches but doesn't define them. . . . Yet there is the feeling—I have the feeling—that at some level these things open; fragments, moments, suggestions, open, full of power." It is this aura of openness and suggestion, in the context of a riveting "next-door language," that gives Munro's stories their haunting aspect, their quality of movement, rippling and widening from the small scale to the magnificent. The story included here, *Walker Brothers Cowboy*, exemplifies her ability to imbue "fragments, moments, suggestions" with fullness and power, as we view through the eyes of a young girl both the pathos and the degradation of men and women who face the deadening quality of life in a cycle of promise and decay.

Walker Brothers Cowboy[1]

After supper my father says, "Want to go down and see if the Lake's still there?" We leave my mother sewing under the dining-room light, making clothes for me against[2] the opening of school. She has ripped up for this purpose an old suit and an old plaid wool dress of hers, and she has to cut and match very cleverly and also make me stand and turn for endless fittings, sweaty, itching from the hot wool, ungrateful. We leave my brother in bed in the little screened porch at the end of the front veranda, and sometimes he kneels on his bed and presses his face against the screen and calls mournfully, "Bring me an ice-cream cone!" but I call back, "You will be asleep," and do not even turn my head.

Then my father and I walk gradually down a long, shabby sort of street, with Silverwoods Ice Cream signs standing on the sidewalk, outside tiny, lighted stores. This is in Tuppertown, an old town on Lake Huron,[3] an old grain port. The street is shaded, in some places, by maple trees whose roots have cracked and heaved the sidewalk and spread out like crocodiles into the bare yards. People are sitting out, men in shirtsleeves and undershirts and women in aprons—not people we know but if anybody looks ready to nod and say, "Warm night," my father will nod too and say something the same. Children are still playing. I don't know them either because my mother keeps my brother and me in our own yard, saying he is too young to leave it and I have to mind him. I am not so sad to watch their evening games because the games themselves are ragged, dissolving. Children, of their own will, draw apart, separate into islands of two or one under the heavy trees, occupying themselves in such solitary ways as I do all day, planting pebbles in the dirt or writing in it with a stick.

Presently we leave these yards and houses behind; we pass a factory with boarded-up windows, a lumberyard whose high wooden gates are locked for the night. Then the town falls away in a defeated jumble of sheds and small junkyards, the sidewalk gives up and we are walking on a sandy path with burdocks, plantains, humble nameless weeds all around. We enter a vacant lot, a kind of park really, for it is kept clear of junk and there is one bench with a slat missing on the back, a place to sit and look at the water. Which is generally gray in the evening, under a lightly overcast sky, no sunsets, the horizon dim. A very quiet, washing noise on the stones of the beach. Further along, towards the main part of town, there is a stretch of sand, a water slide, floats bobbing around the safe swimming area, a lifeguard's rickety throne. Also a long dark-green building, like a roofed veranda, called the Pavilion, full of farmers and their wives, in stiff good clothes, on Sundays. That is the part of the town we used to know when we lived at Dungannon and came here three or four times a summer, to the Lake. That, and the docks where we would go and look at the grain boats, ancient, rusty, wallowing, making us wonder how they got past the breakwater let alone to Fort William.

Tramps hang around the docks and occasionally on these evenings wan-

---

1. A traveling salesman for a Canadian company that is probably modeled on the still-operating Watkins Products firm.
2. In time for.

3. One of the Great Lakes, bordering on Ontario and eastern Michigan. Place names are both real and invented.

der up the dwindling beach and climb the shifting, precarious path boys have made, hanging on to dry bushes, and say something to my father which, being frightened of tramps, I am too alarmed to catch. My father says he is a bit hard up himself. "I'll roll you a cigarette if it's any use to you," he says, and he shakes tobacco out carefully on one of the thin butterfly papers, flicks it with his tongue, seals it and hands it to the tramp, who takes it and walks away. My father also rolls and lights and smokes one cigarette of his own.

He tells me how the Great Lakes came to be. All where Lake Huron is now, he says, used to be flat land, a wide flat plain. Then came the ice, creeping down from the North, pushing deep into the low places. Like *that*— and he shows me his hand with his spread fingers pressing the rock-hard ground where we are sitting. His fingers make hardly any impression at all and he says, "Well, the old ice cap had a lot more power behind it than this hand has." And then the ice went back, shrank back towards the North Pole where it came from, and left its fingers of ice in the deep places it had gouged, and ice turned to lakes and there they were today. They were *new*, as time went. I try to see that plain before me, dinosaurs walking on it, but I am not able even to imagine the shore of the Lake when the Indians were there, before Tuppertown. The tiny share we have of time appalls me, though my father seems to regard it with tranquillity. Even my father, who sometimes seems to me to have been at home in the world as long as it has lasted, has really lived on this earth only a little longer than I have, in terms of all the time there has been to live in. He has not known a time, any more than I, when automobiles and electric lights did not at least exist. He was not alive when this century started. I will be barely alive—old, old—when it ends. I do not like to think of it. I wish the Lake to be always just a lake, with the safe-swimming floats marking it, and the breakwater and the lights of Tuppertown.

My father has a job, selling for Walker Brothers. This is a firm that sells almost entirely in the country, the back country. Sunshine, Boylesbridge, Turnaround—that is all his territory. Not Dungannon where we used to live, Dungannon is too near town and my mother is grateful for that. He sells cough medicine, iron tonic, corn plasters, laxatives, pills for female disorders, mouthwash, shampoo, liniment, salves, lemon and orange and raspberry concentrate for making refreshing drinks, vanilla, food coloring, black and green tea, ginger, cloves, and other spices, rat poison. He has a song about it, with these two lines:

> And have all liniments and oils,
> For everything from corns to boils. . . .

Not a very funny song, in my mother's opinion. A peddler's song, and that is what he is, a peddler knocking at backwoods kitchens. Up until last winter we had our own business, a fox farm. My father raised silver foxes and sold their pelts to the people who make them into capes and coats and muffs. Prices fell, my father hung on hoping they would get better next year, and they fell again, and he hung on one more year and one more and finally it was not possible to hang on anymore, we owed everything to the feed company. I have heard my mother explain this, several times, to Mrs. Oliphant, who is the only neighbor she talks to. (Mrs. Oliphant also has come down in the world, being a schoolteacher who married the janitor.) We poured all we had into it, my mother says, and we came out with nothing. Many people could say the same thing, these days, but my mother has no time for the national calamity, only ours. Fate has flung us onto a street of poor people (it does not matter that we were poor before; that was a different sort of poverty), and the only way to take this, as she sees it, is with dignity, with bitterness, with no reconciliation. No bathroom with a claw-footed tub and a flush toilet is going to comfort her, nor water on tap and sidewalks past the house and milk in bottles, not even the two movie theatres and the Venus Restaurant and Woolworths so marvellous it has live birds singing in its fan-cooled corners and fish as tiny as fingernails, as bright as moons, swimming in its green tanks. My mother does not care.

In the afternoons she often walks to Simon's Grocery and takes me with her to help carry things. She wears a good dress, navy blue with little flowers, sheer, worn over a navy-blue slip. Also a summer hat of white straw, pushed down on the side of the head, and white shoes I have just whitened on a newspaper on the back steps. I have my hair freshly done in long damp curls which the dry air will fortunately soon loosen, a stiff large hair ribbon on top of my head. This is entirely different from going out after supper with my father. We have not walked past two houses before I feel we have become objects of universal ridicule. Even the dirty words chalked on the sidewalk are laughing at us. My mother does not seem to notice. She walks serenely like a lady shopping, like a *lady* shopping, past the housewives in loose belt-less dresses torn under the arms. With me her creation, wretched curls and flaunting hair bow, scrubbed knees and white socks—all I do not want to be. I loathe even my name when she says it in public, in a voice so high, proud, and ringing, deliberately different from the voice of any other mother on the street.

My mother will sometimes carry home, for a treat, a brick of ice cream— pale Neapolitan; and because we have no refrigerator in our house we wake my brother and eat it at once in the dining room, always darkened by the wall of the house next door. I spoon it up tenderly, leaving the chocolate till last, hoping to have some still to eat when my brother's dish is empty. My mother tries then to imitate the conversations we used to have at Dungan-non, going back to our earliest, most leisurely days before my brother was born, when she would give me a little tea and a lot of milk in a cup like hers and we would sit out on the step facing the pump, the lilac tree, the fox pens beyond. She is not able to keep from mentioning those days. "Do you remem-ber when we put you in your sled and Major pulled you?" (Major our dog, that we had to leave with neighbors when we moved.) "Do you remember your sandbox outside the kitchen window?" I pretend to remember far less than I do, wary of being trapped into sympathy or any unwanted emotion.

My mother has headaches. She often has to lie down. She lies on my brother's narrow bed in the little screened porch, shaded by heavy branches. "I look up at that tree and I think I am at home," she says.

"What you need," my father tells her, "is some fresh air and a drive in the country." He means for her to go with him, on his Walker Brothers route.

That is not my mother's idea of a drive in the country.

"Can I come?"

"Your mother might want you for trying on clothes."

"I'm beyond sewing this afternoon," my mother says.

"I'll take her then. Take both of them, give you a rest."

What is there about us that people need to be given a rest from? Never mind. I am glad enough to find my brother and make him go to the toilet and get us both into the car, our knees unscrubbed, my hair unringleted. My father brings from the house his two heavy brown suitcases, full of bottles, and sets them on the back seat. He wears a white shirt, brilliant in the sunlight, a tie, light trousers belonging to his summer suit (his other suit is black, for funerals, and belonged to my uncle before he died), and a creamy straw hat. His salesman's outfit, with pencils clipped in the shirt pocket. He goes back once again, probably to say goodbye to my mother, to ask her if she is sure she doesn't want to come, and hear her say, "No. No thanks, I'm better just to lie here with my eyes closed." Then we are backing out of the driveway with the rising hope of adventure, just the little hope that takes you over the bump into the street, the hot air starting to move, turning into a breeze, the houses growing less and less familiar as we follow the shortcut my father knows, the quick way out of town. Yet what is there waiting for us all afternoon but hot hours in stricken farmyards, perhaps a stop at a country store and three ice-cream cones or bottles of pop, and my father singing? The one he made up about himself has a title—"The Walker Brothers Cowboy"—and it starts out like this:

> Old Ned Fields, he now is dead,
> So I am ridin' the route instead. . . .

Who is Ned Fields? The man he has replaced, surely, and if so he really is dead; yet my father's voice is mournful-jolly, making his death some kind of nonsense, a comic calamity. "Wisht I was back on the Rio Grande,[4] plungin' through the dusky sand." My father sings most of the time while driving the car. Even now, heading out of town, crossing the bridge and taking the sharp turn onto the highway, he is humming something, mumbling a bit of a song to himself, just tuning up, really, getting ready to improvise, for out along the highway we pass the Baptist Camp, the Vacation Bible Camp, and he lets loose:

> Where are the Baptists, where are the Bapists,
>   where are all the Baptists today?
> They're down in the water, in Lake Huron water,
>   with their sins all a-gittin' washed away."

My brother takes this for straight truth and gets up on his knees trying to see down to the Lake. "I don't see any Baptists," he says accusingly. "Neither do I, son," says my father. "I told you, they're down in the Lake."

No roads paved when we left the highway. We have to roll up the windows because of dust. The land is flat, scorched, empty. Bush lots at the back of the farms hold shade, black pine-shade like pools nobody can ever get to. We bump up a long lane and at the end of it what could look more unwelcoming, more deserted than the tall unpainted farmhouse with grass growing uncut

---

4. A large river that begins in Colorado and flows south, becoming the border between Mexico and the United States.

right up to the front door, green blinds down, and a door upstairs opening on nothing but air? Many houses have this door, and I have never yet been able to find out why. I ask my father and he says they are for walking in your sleep. *What?* Well, if you happen to be walking in your sleep and you want to step outside. I am offended, seeing too late that he is joking, as usual, but my brother says sturdily, "If they did that they would break their necks."

The 1930s. How much this kind of farmhouse, this kind of afternoon seem to me to belong to that one decade in time, just as my father's hat does, his bright flared tie, our car with its wide running board (an Essex, and long past its prime). Cars somewhat like it, many older, none dustier, sit in the farm-yards. Some are past running and have their doors pulled off, their seats removed for use on porches. No living things to be seen, chickens or cattle. Except dogs. There are dogs lying in any kind of shade they can find, dream-ing, their lean sides rising and sinking rapidly. They get up when my father opens the car door, he has to speak to them. "Nice boy, there's a boy, nice old boy." They quiet down, go back to their shade. He should know how to quiet animals, he has held desperate foxes with tongs around their necks. One gentling voice for the dogs and another, rousing, cheerful, for calling at doors. "Hello there, missus, it's the Walker Brothers man and what are you out of today?" A door opens, he disappears. Forbidden to follow, forbid-den even to leave the car, we can just wait and wonder what he says. Some-times trying to make my mother laugh, he pretends to be himself in a farm kitchen, spreading out his sample case. "Now then, missus, are you troubled with parasitic life? Your children's scalps, I mean. All those crawly little things we're too polite to mention that show up on the heads of the best of families? Soap alone is useless, kerosene is not too nice a perfume, but I have here—" Or else, "Believe me, sitting and driving all day the way I do I *know* the value of these fine pills. Natural relief. A problem common to old folks too, once their days of activity are over—How about you, Grandma?" He would wave the imaginary box of pills under my mother's nose and she would laugh finally, unwillingly. "He doesn't say that really, does he?" I said, and she said no of course not, he was too much of a gentleman.

One yard after another, then, the old cars, the pumps, dogs, views of gray barns and falling-down sheds and unturning windmills. The men, if they are working in the fields, are not in any fields that we can see. The children are far away, following dry creek beds or looking for blackberries, or else they are hidden in the house, spying at us through cracks in the blinds. The car seat has grown slick with our sweat. I dare my brother to sound the horn, wanting to do it myself but not wanting to get the blame. He knows better. We play I Spy, but it is hard to find many colors. Gray for the barns and sheds and toilets and houses, brown for the yard and fields, black or brown for the dogs. The rusting cars show rainbow patches, in which I strain to pick out purple or green; likewise I peer at doors for shreds of old peeling paint, maroon or yellow. We can't play with letters, which would be better, because my brother is too young to spell. The game disintegrates anyway. He claims my colors are not fair, and wants extra turns.

In one house no door opens, though the car is in the yard. My father knocks and whistles, calls, "Hullo there ! Walker Brothers man!" but there is not a stir of reply anywhere. This house has no porch, just a bare, slanting slab of cement on which my father stands. He turns around, searching the barnyard, the barn whose mow must be empty because you can see the sky through it, and finally he bends to pick up his suitcases. Just then a window is opened upstairs, a white pot appears on the sill, is tilted over and its contents splash down the outside wall. The window is not directly above my father's head, so only a stray splash would catch him. He picks up his suitcases with no particular hurry and walks, no longer whistling, to the car. "Do you know what that was?" I say to my brother. "*Pee.*" He laughs and laughs.

My father rolls and lights a cigarette before he starts the car. The window has been slammed down, the blind drawn, we never did see a hand or face. "Pee, pee," sings my brother ecstatically. "Somebody dumped down pee!" "Just don't tell your mother that," my father says. "She isn't liable to see the joke." "Is it in your song?" my brother wants to know. My father says no but he will see what he can do to work it in.

I notice in a little while that we are not turning in any more lanes, though it does not seem to me that we are headed home. "Is this the way to Sunshine?" I ask my father, and he answers, "No, ma'am, it's not." "Are we still in your territory?" He shakes his head. "We're going *fast,*" my brother says approvingly, and in fact we are bouncing along through dry puddle-holes so that all the bottles in the suitcases clink together and gurgle promisingly.

Another lane, a house, also unpainted, dried to silver in the sun.

"I thought we were out of your territory."

"We are."

"Then what are we going in here for?"

"You'll see."

In front of the house a short, sturdy woman is picking up washing, which had been spread on the grass to bleach and dry. When the car stops she stares at it hard for a moment, bends to pick up a couple more towels to add to the bundle under her arm, comes across to us and says in a flat voice, neither welcoming nor unfriendly, "Have you lost your way?"

My father takes his time getting out of the car. "I don't think so," he says. "I'm the Walker Brothers man."

"George Golley is our Walker Brothers man," the woman says, "and he was out here no more than a week ago. Oh, my Lord God," she says harshly, "it's you."

"It was, the last time I looked in the mirror," my father says.

The woman gathers all the towels in front of her and holds on to them tightly, pushing them against her stomach as if it hurt. "Of all the people I never thought to see. And telling me you were the Walker Brothers man."

"I'm sorry if you were looking forward to George Golley," my father says humbly.

"And look at me, I was prepared to clean the henhouse. You'll think that's just an excuse but it's true. I don't go round looking like this every day." She is wearing a farmer's straw hat, through which pricks of sunlight penetrate and float on her face, a loose, dirty print smock, and canvas shoes. "Who are those in the car, Ben? They're not yours?"

"Well, I hope and believe they are," my father says, and tells our names and ages. "Come on, you can get out. This is Nora, Miss Cronin. Nora, you better tell me, is it still Miss, or have you got a husband hiding in the woodshed?"

"If I had a husband that's not where I'd keep him, Ben," she says, and they both laugh, her laugh abrupt and somewhat angry. "You'll think I got no manners, as well as being dressed like a tramp," she says. "Come on in out of the sun. It's cool in the house."

We go across the yard ("Excuse me taking you in this way but I don't think the front door has been opened since Papa's funeral, I'm afraid the hinges might drop off"), up the porch steps, into the kitchen, which really is cool, high-ceilinged, the blinds of course down, a simple, clean, threadbare room with waxed worn linoleum, potted geraniums, drinking-pail and dipper, a round table with scrubbed oilcloth. In spite of the cleanness, the wiped and swept surfaces, there is a faint sour smell—maybe of the dishrag or the tin dipper or the oilcloth, or the old lady, because there is one, sitting in an easy chair under the clock shelf. She turns her head slightly in our direction and says, "Nora? Is that company?"

"Blind," says Nora in a quick explaining voice to my father. Then, "You won't guess who it is, Momma. Hear his voice."

My father goes to the front of her chair and bends and says hopefully, "Afternoon, Mrs. Cronin."

"Ben Jordan," says the old lady with no surprise. "You haven't been to see us in the longest time. Have you been out of the country?"

My father and Nora look at each other.

"He's married, Momma," says Nora cheerfully and aggressively. "Married and got two children and here they are." She pulls us forward, makes each of us touch the old lady's dry, cool hand while she says our names in turn. Blind! This is the first blind person I have ever seen close up. Her eyes are closed, the eyelids sunk away down, showing no shape of the eyeball, just hollows. From one hollow comes a drop of silver liquid, a medicine, or a miraculous tear.

"Let me get into a decent dress," Nora says. "Talk to Momma. It's a treat for her. We hardly ever see company, do we, Momma?"

"Not many makes it out this road," says the old lady placidly. "And the ones that used to be around here, our old neighbors, some of them have pulled out."

"True everywhere," my father says.

"Where's your wife then?"

"Home. She's not too fond of the hot weather, makes her feel poorly."

"Well." This is a habit of country people, old people, to say "well," meaning, "Is that so?" with a little extra politeness and concern.

Nora's dress, when she appears again—stepping heavily on Cuban heels down the stairs in the hall—is flowered more lavishly than anything my mother owns, green and yellow on brown, some sort of floating sheer crêpe, leaving her arms bare. Her arms are heavy, and every bit of her skin you can see is covered with little dark freckles like measles. Her hair is short, black, coarse and curly, her teeth very white and strong. "It's the first time I knew there was such a thing as green poppies," my father says, looking at her dress.

"You would be surprised all the things you never knew," says Nora, sending a smell of cologne far and wide when she moves and displaying a change of voice to go with the dress, something more sociable and youthful. "They're not poppies anyway, they're just flowers. You go and pump me some good cold water and I'll make these children a drink." She gets down from the cupboard a bottle of Walker Brothers Orange syrup.

"You telling me you were the Walker Brothers man!"

"It's the truth, Nora. You go and look at my sample cases in the car if you don't believe me. I got the territory directly south of here."

"Walker Brothers? Is that a fact? You selling for Walker Brothers?"

"Yes, ma'am."

"We always heard you were raising foxes over Dungannon way."

"That's what I was doing, but I kind of run out of luck in that business."

"So where're you living? How long've you been out selling?"

"We moved into Tuppertown. I been at it, oh, two, three months. It keeps the wolf from the door. Keeps him as far away as the back fence."

Nora laughs. "Well, I guess you count yourself lucky to have the work. Isabel's husband in Brantford, he was out of work the longest time. I thought if he didn't find something soon I was going to have them all land in here to feed, and I tell you I was hardly looking forward to it. It's all I can manage with me and Momma."

"Isabel married," my father says. "Muriel married too?"

"No, she's teaching school out West. She hasn't been home for five years. I guess she finds something better to do with her holidays. I would if I was her." She gets some snapshots out of the table drawer and starts showing him. "That's Isabel's oldest boy, starting school. That's the baby sitting in her carriage. Isabel and her husband. Muriel. That's her roommate with her. That's a fellow she used to go around with, and his car. He was working in a bank out there. That's her school, it has eight rooms. She teaches Grade Five." My father shakes his head. "I can't think of her any way but when she was going to school, so shy I used to pick her up on the road—I'd be on my way to see you—and she would not say one word, not even to agree it was a nice day."

"She's got over that."

"Who are you talking about?" says the old lady.

"Muriel. I said she's got over being shy."

"She was here last summer."

"No, Momma, that was Isabel. Isabel and her family were here last summer. Muriel's out West."

"I meant Isabel."

Shortly after this the old lady falls asleep, her head on the side, her mouth open. "Excuse her manners," Nora says. "It's old age." She fixes an afghan over her mother and says we can all go into the front room where our talking won't disturb her.

"You two," my father says. "Do you want to go outside and amuse yourselves?"

Amuse ourselves how? Anyway, I want to stay. The front room is more interesting than the kitchen, though barer. There is a gramophone and a pump organ and a picture on the wall of Mary, Jesus' mother—I know that much—in shades of bright blue and pink with a spiked band of light around her head. I know that such pictures are found only in the homes of Roman Catholics and so Nora must be one. We have never known any Roman Catholics at all well, never well enough to visit in their houses. I think of what my grandmother and my Aunt Tena, over in Dungannon, used to always say to indicate that somebody was a Catholic. *So-and-so digs with the wrong foot,* they would say. *She digs with the wrong foot.* That was what they would say about Nora.[5]

Nora takes a bottle, half full, out of the top of the organ and pours some of what is in it into the two glasses that she and my father have emptied of the orange drink.

"Keep it in case of sickness?" my father says.

"Not on your life," says Nora. "I'm never sick. I just keep it because I keep it. One bottle does me a fair time, though, because I don't care for drinking alone. Here's luck!" She and my father drink and I know what it is. Whisky. One of the things my mother has told me in our talks together is that my father never drinks whisky. But I see he does. He drinks whisky and he talks of people whose names I have never heard before. But after a while he turns to a familiar incident. He tells about the chamberpot that was emptied out the window. "Picture me there," he says, "hollering my heartiest. *Oh, lady, it's your Walker Brothers man, anybody home?*" He does himself hollering, grinning absurdly, waiting, looking up in pleased expectation, and then—oh, ducking, covering his head with his arms, looking as if he begged for mercy (when he never did anything like that, I was watching), and Nora laughs, almost as hard as my brother did at the time.

"That isn't true! That's not a word true!"

"Oh, indeed it is, ma'am. We have our heroes in the ranks of Walker Brothers. I'm glad you think it's funny," he says sombrely.

I ask him shyly, "Sing the song."

"What song? Have you turned into a singer on top of everything else?"

Embarrassed, my father says, "Oh, just this song I made up while I was driving around, it gives me something to do, making up rhymes."

But after some urging he does sing it, looking at Nora with a droll, apologetic expression, and she laughs so much that in places he has to stop and wait for her to get over laughing so he can go on, because she makes him laugh too. Then he does various parts of his salesman's spiel. Nora when she laughs squeezes her large bosom under her folded arms. "You're crazy," she says. "That's all you are." She sees my brother peering into the gramophone and she jumps up and goes over to him. "Here's us sitting enjoying ourselves and not giving you a thought, isn't it terrible?" she says. "You want me to put a record on, don't you? You want to hear a nice record? Can you dance? I bet your sister can, can't she?"

I say no. "A big girl like you and so good-looking and can't dance!" says Nora. "It's high time you learned. I bet you'd make a lovely dancer. Here, I'm going to put on a piece I used to dance to and even your daddy did, in his dancing days. You didn't know your daddy was a dancer, did you? Well, he is a talented man, your daddy!"

She puts down the lid and takes hold of me unexpectedly around the waist, picks up my other hand, and starts making me go backwards. "This is the way, now, this is how they dance. Follow me. This foot, see. One and one-two. One and one-two. That's fine, that's lovely, don't look at your feet! Follow me, that's right, see how easy? You're going to be a lovely dancer!

---

5. Relations between Protestants and Catholics within the Irish population in southern Ontario were often strained.

One and one-two. One and one-two. Ben, see your daughter dancing!" *Whispering while you cuddle near me, Whispering so no one can hear me . . .* [6]

Round and round the linoleum, me proud, intent, Nora laughing and moving with great buoyancy, wrapping me in her strange gaiety, her smell of whisky, cologne, and sweat. Under the arms her dress is damp, and little drops form along her upper lip, hang in the soft black hairs at the corners of her mouth. She whirls me around in front of my father—causing me to stumble, for I am by no means so swift a pupil as she pretends—and lets me go, breathless.

"Dance with me, Ben."

"I'm the world's worst dancer, Nora, and you know it."

"I certainly never thought so."

"You would now."

She stands in front of him, arms hanging loose and hopeful, her breasts, which a moment ago embarrassed me with their warmth and bulk, rising and falling under her loose flowered dress, her face shining with the exercise, and delight.

"Ben."

My father drops his head and says quietly, "Not me, Nora."

So she can only go and take the record off. "I can drink alone but I can't dance alone," she says. "Unless I am a whole lot crazier than I think I am."

"Nora," says my father, smiling. "You're not crazy."

"Stay for supper."

"Oh, no. We couldn't put you to the trouble."

"It's no trouble. I'd be glad of it."

"And their mother would worry. She'd think I'd turned us over in a ditch."

"Oh, well. Yes."

"We've taken a lot of your time now."

"Time," says Nora bitterly. "Will you come by ever again?"

"I will if I can," says my father.

"Bring the children. Bring your wife."

"Yes, I will," says my father. "I will if I can."

When she follows us to the car he says, "You come to see us too, Nora. We're right on Grove Street, left-hand side going in, that's north, and two doors this side—east—of Baker Street."

Nora does not repeat these directions. She stands close to the car in her soft, brilliant dress. She touches the fender, making an unintelligible mark in the dust there.

On the way home my father does not buy any ice cream or pop, but he does go into a country store and get a package of licorice, which he shares with us. She digs with the wrong foot, I think, and the words seem sad to me as never before, dark, perverse. My father does not say anything to me about not mentioning things at home, but I know, just from the thoughtfulness, the pause when he passes the licorice, that there are things not to be mentioned. The whisky, maybe the dancing. No worry about my brother, he does not notice enough. At most he might remember the blind lady, the picture of Mary.

6. From the popular song "Whispering," whose original 1920 recording was one of the first records to sell a million copies.

"Sing," my brother commands my father, but my father says gravely, "I don't know, I seem to be fresh out of songs. You watch the road and let me know if you see any rabbits."

So my father drives and my brother watches the road for rabbits and I feel my father's life flowing back from our car in the last of the afternoon, darkening and turning strange, like a landscape that has an enchantment on it, making it kindly, ordinary and familiar while you are looking at it, but changing it, once your back is turned, into something you will never know, with all kinds of weathers, and distances you cannot imagine.

When we get closer to Tuppertown the sky becomes gently overcast, as always, nearly always, on summer evenings by the Lake.

1968

GEOFFREY HILL
b. 1932

Geoffrey Hill, born in the Worcestershire village of Bromsgrove, educated at its high school and at Keble College, Oxford, has been a professor of English at Leeds University, a lecturer at Cambridge, and is now a professor at Boston University. As a boy, he was drawn to the Metaphysical poets' "fusion of intellectual strength with simple, sensuous, and passionate immediacy," and his own poems offer something of the same fusion, if seldom the same confident conclusions. What he has said of *Annunciations: 2* might have been said of many of his poems: "But I want the poem to have this dubious end; because I feel dubious; and the whole business is dubious." He is a religious poet, but a poet of religious doubt—an agnostic confronting the extremes of human experience, "man's inhumanity to man," on the cross and in the concentration camps—or delight in the abundance of the natural world: pain and pleasure alike rendered with a Keatsian richness and specificity. Distinctively resonant as is the voice of Hill's poems, they are consistently impersonal. Even when the poet's earlier self is conflated with that of Offa in *Mercian Hymns* (1971), subjectivity is dissolved in the objective projection of a historical imagination of great range and power. Although that book had been concerned at one level with what medieval historians called "the matter of Britain," a more recent collection, *Canaan* (1996), bleakly attempts to diagnose the matter *with* Britain (identifying the UK with "Canaan, the land of the Philistines," excoriated in the Bible). As one of the most ambitious poets now writing in English, Hill is at once one of the most difficult and one of the most rewarding.

In Memory of Jane Fraser

When snow like sheep lay in the fold
And winds went begging at each door,
And the far hills were blue with cold,
And a cold shroud lay on the moor,

5   She kept the siege. And every day
We watched her brooding over death

Like a strong bird above its prey.
The room filled with the kettle's breath.

Damp curtains glued against the pane
10 Sealed time away. Her body froze
As if to freeze us all, and chain
Creation to a stunned repose.

She died before the world could stir.
In March the ice unloosed the brook
15 And water ruffled the sun's hair.
Dead cones upon the alder shook.

1959

Requiem for the Plantagenet Kings[1]

For whom the possessed sea littered, on both shores,
Ruinous arms; being fired, and for good,
To sound the constitution of just wars,
Men, in their eloquent fashion, understood.

5 Relieved of soul, the dropping-back of dust,
Their usage, pride, admitted within doors;
At home, under caved chantries,[2] set in trust,
With well-dressed alabaster and proved spurs
They lie; they lie; secure in the decay
10 Of blood, blood-marks, crowns hacked and coveted,
Before the scouring fires of trial-day
Alight on men; before sleeked groin, gored head,
Budge through the clay and gravel, and the sea
Across daubed rock evacuates its dead.

1959

September Song[1]

born 19.6.32—deported 24.9.42

Undesirable you may have been, untouchable
you were not. Not forgotten
or passed over at the proper time.

---

1. Dynastic succession of 12th- to 15th-century English kings, beginning with Henry II, who was followed in turn by Richard I, John, Henry III, Edward I, Edward II, Edward III, and Richard II. They ruled not only over England but also over much of France ("on both shores"). The last Plantagenet king was Richard III, who was killed at the Battle of Bosworth on Aug. 22, 1485.

2. Chapels endowed for priests to sing masses for the souls of those who founded them. Many chantries have cavelike ceilings of vaulted stone and contain effigies—sometimes in alabaster—of their founders.

1. The poem is about the gassing of Jews in German extermination camps; Zyklon-B was the gas used. Hill's fellow poet Jon Silkin has drawn attention to the kind of wit involved in the subtitle, "where the natural event of birth is placed, simply, beside the human and murderous 'deported' as if the latter were of the same order and inevitability for the victim"; he discusses, too, "the irony of conjuncted meanings between 'undesirable' (touching on both sexual desire and racism) and 'untouchable,' which exploits a similar ambiguity but reverses the emphases," and is "unusually dense *and* simple."

As estimated, you died. Things marched,
5   sufficient, to that end.
Just so much Zyklon and leather, patented
terror, so many routine cries.

(I have made
an elegy for myself it
10   is true)[2]

September fattens on vines. Roses
flake from the wall. The smoke
of harmless fires drifts to my eyes.

This is plenty. This is more than enough.

1968

From Mercian Hymns[1]

6

The princes of Mercia were badger and raven. Thrall
to their freedom, I dug and hoarded. Orchards
fruited above clefts. I drank from honeycombs of
chill sandstone.

5   "A boy at odds in the house, lonely among brothers."
But I, who had none, fostered a strangeness; gave
myself to unattainable toys.

Candles of gnarled resin, apple-branches, the tacky
mistletoe. "Look" they said and again "look." But
10   I ran slowly; the landscape flowed away, back to
its source.

In the schoolyard, in the cloakrooms, the children
boasted their scars of dried snot; wrists and
knees garnished with impetigo.

7

Gasholders,[2] russet among fields. Milldams, marlpools[3]
that lay unstirring. Eel-swarms. Coagulations of
frogs: once, with branches and half-bricks, he

2. The critic Christopher Ricks has pointed out that Hill was born on 18.6.32 (June 18, 1932).
1. The historical Offa reigned over Mercia (and the greater part of England south of the Humber) in the years 757–96 C.E. During early medieval times he was already becoming a creature of legend. The Offa who figures in this sequence might perhaps most usefully be regarded as the presiding genius of the West Midlands, his dominion enduring from the middle of the 8th century until the middle of the 20th (and possibly beyond). The indication of such a timespan will, I trust, explain and to some extent justify a number of anachronisms [Hill's note].
2. Or gasometers, large metal receptacles for gas.
3. Pools in deposits of crumbling clay and chalk.

    battered a ditchful; then sidled away from the
5   stillness and silence.

Ceolred[4] was his friend and remained so, even after
    the day of the lost fighter: a biplane, already
    obsolete and irreplaceable, two inches of heavy
    snub silver. Ceolred let it spin through a hole
10   in the classroom-floorboards, softly, into the rat-
    droppings and coins.

After school he lured Ceolred, who was sniggering
    with fright, down to the old quarries, and flayed
    him. Then, leaving Ceolred, he journeyed for hours,
15   calm and alone, in his private derelict sandlorry
    named *Albion*.[5]

28

Processes of generation; deeds of settlement. The
    urge to marry well; wit to invest in the proper
    ties of healing-springs. Our children and our
    children's children, o my masters.

5   Tracks of ancient occupation. Frail ironworks rust-
    ing in the thorn-thicket. Hearthstones; charred
    lullabies. A solitary axe-blow that is the echo
    of a lost sound.

Tumult recedes as though into the long rain. Groves
10   of legendary holly; silverdark the ridged gleam.

30

And it seemed, while we waited, he began to walk to-
    wards us   he vanished

he left behind coins, for his lodging, and traces of
    red mud.

                                                    1971

---

4. A 9th-century bishop of Leicester, but the
name is here used as a characteristic Anglo-Saxon
Mercian name.

5. Albion was an old Celtic name for England; it
is also the name of a famous make of British truck.
"Sandlorry": sand truck.

From An Apology for the Revival of Christian Architecture in England

the spiritual, Platonic old England . . .
—STC, *Anima Poetae*[1]

"Your situation," said Coningsby, looking up
the green and silent valley, "is absolutely
poetic."

"I try sometimes to fancy," said Mr Millbank,
with a rather fierce smile, "that I am in the
New World."

—BENJAMIN DISRAELI,[2] *Coningsby*

9. The Laurel Axe

Autumn resumes the land, ruffles the woods
with smoky wings, entangles them. Trees shine
out from their leaves, rocks mildew to moss-green;
the avenues are spread with brittle floods.

5   Platonic England, house of solitudes,
rests in its laurels and its injured stone,
replete with complex fortunes that are gone,
beset by dynasties of moods and clouds.

It stands, as though at ease with its own world,
10   the mannerly extortions, languid praise,
all that devotion long since bought and sold,

the rooms of cedar and soft-thudding baize,[3]
tremulous boudoirs where the crystals kissed
in cabinets of amethyst and frost.

1978

---

1. I.e., an idealized orderly rural England. "STC":
Samuel Taylor Coleridge (1772–1834), English
poet and philosopher.
2. British novelist and statesman (1804–1881).
The "New World" referred to is that of an idealized
rural America.

3. Billiard rooms in British "stately homes." The
"soft-thudding baize" may refer either to the soft
green cloth covering billiard tables or to the door
traditionally covered with green baize dividing the
family side of the home from the servants' quarters.

V. S. NAIPAUL
b. 1932

Widely regarded as the most accomplished novelist from the English-speaking Caribbean, Vidiadhar Surajprasad Naipaul was born in Trinidad and educated at Queen's Royal College, Port of Spain, and at University College, Oxford. Settling in England, he became editor of the *Caribbean Voices* program for the BBC (1954–56) and fiction reviewer for the *New Statesman* (1957–61). The recipient of many major literary awards and prizes, including the Booker Prize in 1971 for *In a Free State,* he was knighted in 1990. He continues to live and write in England.

Naipaul's first three books, *The Mystic Masseur* (1957), *The Suffrage of Elvira* (1958), and *Miguel Street* (short stories, 1959), are comedies of manners, set in a Trinidad viewed with an exile's acute and ironic eye. If, as some critics believe, these early works present a starkly satiric vision, a more modulated tone appears in Naipaul's first major novel, the semiautobiographical *A House for Mr. Biswas* (1961). Following the declining fortunes of its gentle hero from cradle to grave, the novel traces the disintegration of a traditional way of life, on something approaching an epic scale, to produce what the critic Louis James has well described as "a tender tragi-comedy." Subsequent novels, including *The Mimic Men* (1967), *Guerrillas* (1973), and *The Enigma of Arrival* (1987), have continued to explore the desperate and destructive conditions facing individuals as they struggle with cultures in complicated states of transition and development.

Naipaul has produced essays on a variety of themes, including a travel narrative about the southern United States, *A Turn in the South* (1988), and two studies—what he calls "cultural explorations"—of Islam: *Among the Believers: An Islamic Journey* (1981) and *Beyond Belief: Islamic Excursions among the Converted Peoples* (1998). Like his novels, these writings range widely, carrying readers to Africa, England, the Indian subcontinent, the Middle East, South and North America. With the years, Naipaul's voice has become ever more compelling, his vision of the human condition darker and more pessimistic, as he brilliantly lays bare the insensitivities and disconnections that bedevil relations among individuals, races, and nations. Such tremendous disjunctions and dire consequences are revealed in *One Out of Many,* the second of three stories that, with two linking diary entries, make up *In a Free State,* an ironic, searching, bleak, yet emotionally engaging study of what it means to be enslaved and what it means to be free.

One Out of Many

I am now an American citizen and I live in Washington, capital of the world. Many people, both here and in India, will feel that I have done well. But.

I was so happy in Bombay. I was respected, I had a certain position. I worked for an important man. The highest in the land came to our bachelor chambers and enjoyed my food and showered compliments on me. I also had my friends. We met in the evenings on the pavement below the gallery of our chambers. Some of us, like the tailor's bearer[1] and myself, were domestics who lived in the street. The others were people who came to that bit of pavement to sleep. Respectable people; we didn't encourage riff-raff.

In the evenings it was cool. There were few passers-by and, apart from an occasional double-decker bus or taxi, little traffic. The pavement was swept

---

1. Servant.

and sprinkled, bedding brought out from daytime hiding-places, little oil-lamps lit. While the folk upstairs chattered and laughed, on the pavement we read newspapers, played cards, told stories and smoked. The clay pipe passed from friend to friend; we became drowsy. Except of course during the monsoon,[2] I preferred to sleep on the pavement with my friends, although in our chambers a whole cupboard below the staircase was reserved for my personal use.

It was good after a healthy night in the open to rise before the sun and before the sweepers came. Sometimes I saw the street lights go off. Bedding was rolled up; no one spoke much; and soon my friends were hurrying in silent competition to secluded lanes and alleys and open lots to relieve themselves. I was spared this competition; in our chambers I had facilities.[3]

Afterwards for half an hour or so I was free simply to stroll. I liked walking beside the Arabian Sea, waiting for the sun to come up. Then the city and the ocean gleamed like gold. Alas for those morning walks, that sudden ocean dazzle, the moist salt breeze on my face, the flap of my shirt, that first cup of hot sweet tea from a stall, the taste of the first leaf-cigarette.

Observe the workings of fate. The respect and security I enjoyed were due to the importance of my employer. It was this very importance which now all at once destroyed the pattern of my life.

My employer was seconded[4] by his firm to Government service and was posted to Washington. I was happy for his sake but frightened for mine. He was to be away for some years and there was nobody in Bombay he could second me to. Soon, therefore, I was to be out of a job and out of the chambers. For many years I had considered my life as settled. I had served my apprenticeship, known my hard times. I didn't feel I could start again. I despaired. Was there a job for me in Bombay? I saw myself having to return to my village in the hills, to my wife and children there, not just for a holiday but for good. I saw myself again becoming a porter during the tourist season, racing after the buses as they arrived at the station and shouting with forty or fifty others for luggage. Indian luggage, not this lightweight American stuff! Heavy metal trunks!

I could have cried. It was no longer the sort of life for which I was fitted. I had grown soft in Bombay and I was no longer young. I had acquired possessions, I was used to the privacy of my cupboard. I had become a city man, used to certain comforts.

My employer said, "Washington is not Bombay, Santosh. Washington is expensive. Even if I was able to raise your fare, you wouldn't be able to live over there in anything like your present style."

But to be barefoot in the hills, after Bombay! The shock, the disgrace! I couldn't face my friends. I stopped sleeping on the pavement and spent as much of my free time as possible in my cupboard among my possessions, as among things which were soon to be taken from me.

My employer said, "Santosh, my heart bleeds for you."

I said, "Sahib,[5] if I look a little concerned it is only because I worry about you. You have always been fussy, and I don't see how you will manage in Washington."

---

2. Rainy season.
3. I.e., a toilet.

4. Temporarily transferred.
5. Master (Urdu).

"It won't be easy. But it's the principle. Does the representative of a poor country like ours travel about with his cook? Will that create a good impression?"

"You will always do what is right, sahib."

He went silent.

After some days he said, "There's not only the expense, Santosh. There's the question of foreign exchange. Our rupee[6] isn't what it was."

"I understand, sahib. Duty is duty."

A fortnight later, when I had almost given up hope, he said, "Santosh, I have consulted Government. You will accompany me. Government has sanctioned, will arrange accommodation. But no expenses. You will get your passport and your P form. But I want you to think, Santosh. Washington is not Bombay."

I went down to the pavement that night with my bedding.

I said, blowing down my shirt, "Bombay gets hotter and hotter."

"Do you know what you are doing?" the tailor's bearer said. "Will the Americans smoke with you? Will they sit and talk with you in the evenings? Will they hold you by the hand and walk with you beside the ocean?"

It pleased me that he was jealous. My last days in Bombay were very happy.

I packed my employer's two suitcases and bundled up my own belongings in lengths of old cotton. At the airport they made a fuss about my bundles. They said they couldn't accept them as luggage for the hold because they didn't like the responsibility. So when the time came I had to climb up to the aircraft with all my bundles. The girl at the top, who was smiling at everybody else, stopped smiling when she saw me. She made me go right to the back of the plane, far from my employer. Most of the seats there were empty, though, and I was able to spread my bundles around and, well, it was comfortable.

It was bright and hot outside, cool inside. The plane started, rose up in the air, and Bombay and the ocean tilted this way and that. It was very nice. When we settled down I looked around for people like myself, but I could see no one among the Indians or the foreigners who looked like a domestic. Worse, they were all dressed as though they were going to a wedding and, brother, I soon saw it wasn't they who were conspicuous. I was in my ordinary Bombay clothes, the loose long-tailed shirt, the wide-waisted pants held up with a piece of string. Perfectly respectable domestic's wear, neither dirty nor clean, and in Bombay no one would have looked. But now on the plane I felt heads turning whenever I stood up.

I was anxious. I slipped off my shoes, tight even without the laces, and drew my feet up. That made me feel better. I made myself a little betel-nut[7] mixture and that made me feel better still. Half the pleasure of betel, though, is the spitting; and it was only when I had worked up a good mouthful that I saw I had a problem. The airline girl saw too. That girl didn't like me at all. She spoke roughly to me. My mouth was full, my cheeks were bursting, and I couldn't say anything. I could only look at her. She went and called a man in uniform and he came and stood over me. I put my shoes back on and swallowed the betel juice. It made me feel quite ill.

---

6. Indian currency, at this time worth ten cents.
7. Evergreen plant, the leaves of which are chewed in the East with areca-nut parings.

The girl and the man, the two of them, pushed a little trolley of drinks down the aisle. The girl didn't look at me but the man said, "You want a drink, chum?" He wasn't a bad fellow. I pointed at random to a bottle. It was a kind of soda drink, nice and sharp at first but then not so nice. I was worrying about it when the girl said, "Five shillings sterling or sixty cents U.S." That took me by surprise. I had no money, only a few rupees. The girl stamped, and I thought she was going to hit me with her pad when I stood up to show her who my employer was.

Presently my employer came down the aisle. He didn't look very well. He said, without stopping, "Champagne, Santosh? Already we are overdoing?" He went on to the lavatory. When he passed back he said, "Foreign exchange, Santosh! Foreign exchange!" That was all. Poor fellow, he was suffering too.

The journey became miserable for me. Soon, with the wine I had drunk, the betel juice, the movement and the noise of the aeroplane, I was vomiting all over my bundles, and I didn't care what the girl said or did. Later there were more urgent and terrible needs. I felt I would choke in the tiny, hissing room at the back. I had a shock when I saw my face in the mirror. In the fluorescent light it was the colour of a corpse. My eyes were strained, the sharp air hurt my nose and seemed to get into my brain. I climbed up on the lavatory seat and squatted. I lost control of myself. As quickly as I could I ran back out into the comparative openness of the cabin and hoped no one had noticed. The lights were dim now; some people had taken off their jackets and were sleeping. I hoped the plane would crash.

The girl woke me up. She was almost screaming. "It's you, isn't it? Isn't it?"

I thought she was going to tear the shirt off me. I pulled back and leaned hard on the window. She burst into tears and nearly tripped on her sari as she ran up the aisle to get the man in uniform.

Nightmare. And all I knew was that somewhere at the end, after the airports and the crowded lounges where everybody was dressed up, after all those take-offs and touchdowns, was the city of Washington. I wanted the journey to end but I couldn't say I wanted to arrive at Washington. I was already a little scared of that city, to tell the truth. I wanted only to be off the plane and to be in the open again, to stand on the ground and breathe and to try to understand what time of day it was.

At last we arrived. I was in a daze. The burden of those bundles! There were more closed rooms and electric lights. There were questions from officials.

"Is he diplomatic?"[8]

"He's only a domestic," my employer said.

"Is that his luggage? What's in that pocket?"

I was ashamed.

"Santosh," my employer said.

I pulled out the little packets of pepper and salt, the sweets, the envelopes with scented napkins, the toy tubes of mustard. Airline trinkets. I had been collecting them throughout the journey, seizing a handful, whatever my condition, every time I passed the galley.

"He's a cook," my employer said.

"Does he always travel with his condiments?"

---

8. In the Diplomatic Corps.

"Santosh, Santosh," my employer said in the car afterwards, "in Bombay it didn't matter what you did. Over here you represent your country. I must say I cannot understand why your behaviour has already gone so much out of character."

"I am sorry, sahib."

"Look at it like this, Santosh. Over here you don't only represent your country, you represent me."

For the people of Washington it was late afternoon or early evening, I couldn't say which. The time and the light didn't match, as they did in Bombay. Of that drive I remember green fields, wide roads, many motor cars travelling fast, making a steady hiss, hiss, which wasn't at all like our Bombay traffic noise. I remember big buildings and wide parks; many bazaar areas; then smaller houses without fences and with gardens like bush, with the hubshi[9] standing about or sitting down, more usually sitting down, everywhere. Especially I remember the hubshi. I had heard about them in stories and had seen one or two in Bombay. But I had never dreamt that this wild race existed in such numbers in Washington and were permitted to roam the streets so freely. O father, what was this place I had come to?

I wanted, I say, to be in the open, to breathe, to come to myself, to reflect. But there was to be no openness for me that evening. From the aeroplane to the airport building to the motor car to the apartment block to the elevator to the corridor to the apartment itself, I was forever enclosed, forever in the hissing, hissing sound of air-conditioners.

I was too dazed to take stock of the apartment. I saw it as only another halting place. My employer went to bed at once, completely exhausted, poor fellow. I looked around for my room. I couldn't find it and gave up. Aching for the Bombay ways, I spread my bedding in the carpeted corridor just outside our apartment door. The corridor was long: doors, doors. The illuminated ceiling was decorated with stars of different sizes; the colours were grey and blue and gold. Below that imitation sky I felt like a prisoner.

Waking, looking up at the ceiling, I thought just for a second that I had fallen asleep on the pavement below the gallery of our Bombay chambers. Then I realized my loss. I couldn't tell how much time had passed or whether it was night or day. The only clue was that newspapers now lay outside some doors. It disturbed me to think that while I had been sleeping, alone and defenceless, I had been observed by a stranger and perhaps by more than one stranger.

I tried the apartment door and found I had locked myself out. I didn't want to disturb my employer. I thought I would get out into the open, go for a walk. I remembered where the elevator was. I got in and pressed the button. The elevator dropped fast and silently and it was like being in the aeroplane again. When the elevator stopped and the blue metal door slid open I saw plain concrete corridors and blank walls. The noise of machinery was very loud. I knew I was in the basement and the main floor was not far above me. But I no longer wanted to try; I gave up ideas of the open air. I thought I would just go back up to the apartment. But I hadn't noted the number and didn't even know what floor we were on. My courage flowed out of me. I sat on the floor of the elevator and felt the tears come to my eyes. Almost without

---

9. Derogatory Indian term for African blacks (Persian).

noise the elevator door closed, and I found I was being taken up silently at great speed.

The elevator stopped and the door opened. It was my employer, his hair uncombed, yesterday's dirty shirt partly unbuttoned. He looked frightened.

"Santosh, where have you been at this hour of morning? Without your shoes."

I could have embraced him. He hurried me back past the newspapers to our apartment and I took the bedding inside. The wide window showed the early morning sky, the big city; we were high up, way above the trees.

I said, "I couldn't find my room."

"Government sanctioned," my employer said. "Are you sure you've looked?"

We looked together. One little corridor led past the bathroom to his bedroom; another, shorter corridor led to the big room and the kitchen. There was nothing else.

"Government sanctioned," my employer said, moving about the kitchen and opening cupboard doors. "Separate entrance, shelving. I have the correspondence." He opened another door and looked inside. "Santosh, do you think it is possible that this is what Government meant?"

The cupboard he had opened was as high as the rest of the apartment and as wide as the kitchen, about six feet. It was about three feet deep. It had two doors. One door opened into the kitchen; another door, directly opposite, opened into the corridor.

"Separate entrance," my employer said. "Shelving, electric light, power point, fitted carpet."

"This must be my room, sahib."

"Santosh, some enemy in Government has done this to me."

"Oh no, sahib. You mustn't say that. Besides, it is very big. I will be able to make myself very comfortable. It is much bigger than my little cubby-hole in the chambers. And it has a nice flat ceiling. I wouldn't hit my head."

"You don't understand, Santosh. Bombay is Bombay. Here if we start living in cupboards we give the wrong impression. They will think we all live in cupboards in Bombay."

"O sahib, but they can just look at me and see I am dirt."

"You are very good, Santosh. But these people are malicious. Still, if you are happy, then I am happy."

"I am very happy, sahib."

And after all the upset, I was. It was nice to crawl in that evening, spread my bedding and feel protected and hidden. I slept very well.

In the morning my employer said, "We must talk about money, Santosh. Your salary is one hundred rupees a month. But Washington isn't Bombay. Everything is a little bit more expensive here, and I am going to give you a Dearness Allowance. As from today you are getting one hundred and fifty rupees."

"Sahib."

"And I'm giving you a fortnight's pay in advance. In foreign exchange. Seventy-five rupees. Ten cents to the rupee, seven hundred and fifty cents. Seven fifty U.S. Here, Santosh. This afternoon you go out and have a little walk and enjoy. But be careful. We are not among friends, remember."

So at last, rested, with money in my pocket, I went out in the open. And of course the city wasn't a quarter as frightening as I had thought. The buildings weren't particularly big, not all the streets were busy, and there were many lovely trees. A lot of the *hubshi* were about, very wild-looking some of them, with dark glasses and their hair frizzed out, but it seemed that if you didn't trouble them they didn't attack you.

I was looking for a café or a tea-stall where perhaps domestics congregated. But I saw no domestics, and I was chased away from the place I did eventually go into. The girl said, after I had been waiting some time, "Can't you read? We don't serve hippies or bare feet here."

O father! I had come out without my shoes. But what a country, I thought, walking briskly away, where people are never allowed to dress normally but must forever wear their very best! Why must they wear out shoes and fine clothes for no purpose? What occasion are they honouring? What waste, what presumption! Who do they think is noticing them all the time?

And even while these thoughts were in my head I found I had come to a roundabout with trees and a fountain where—and it was like a fulfilment in a dream, not easy to believe—there were many people who looked like my own people. I tightened the string around my loose pants, held down my flapping shirt and ran through the traffic to the green circle.

Some of the *hubshi* were there, playing musical instruments and looking quite happy in their way. There were some Americans sitting about on the grass and the fountain and the kerb. Many of them were in rough, friendly-looking clothes; some were without shoes; and I felt I had been over hasty in condemning the entire race. But it wasn't these people who had attracted me to the circle. It was the dancers. The men were bearded, barefooted and in saffron robes, and the girls were in saris and canvas shoes that looked like our own Bata[1] shoes. They were shaking little cymbals and chanting and lifting their heads up and down and going round in a circle, making a lot of dust. It was a little bit like a Red Indian dance in a cowboy movie, but they were chanting Sanskrit words in praise of Lord Krishna.[2]

I was very pleased. But then a disturbing thought came to me. It might have been because of the half-caste appearance of the dancers; it might have been their bad Sanskrit pronunciation and their accent. I thought that these people were now strangers, but that perhaps once upon a time they had been like me. Perhaps, as in some story, they had been brought here among the *hubshi* as captives a long time ago and had become a lost people, like our own wandering gipsy folk, and had forgotten who they were. When I thought that, I lost my pleasure in the dancing; and I felt for the dancers the sort of distaste we feel when we are faced with something that should be kin but turns out not to be, turns out to be degraded, like a deformed man, or like a leper, who from a distance looks whole.

I didn't stay. Not far from the circle I saw a café which appeared to be serving bare feet. I went in, had a coffee and a nice piece of cake and bought a pack of cigarettes; matches they gave me free with the cigarettes. It was all right, but then the bare feet began looking at me, and one bearded fellow came and sniffed loudly at me and smiled and spoke some sort of gibberish, and then some others of the bare feet came and sniffed at me. They weren't unfriendly, but I didn't appreciate the behaviour; and it was a little fright-

---

1. I.e., the Bata Shoe Company. 2. Great Hindu deity.

ening to find, when I left the place, that two or three of them appeared to be following me. They weren't unfriendly, but I didn't want to take any chances. I passed a cinema; I went in. It was something I wanted to do anyway. In Bombay I used to go once a week.

And that was all right. The movie had already started. It was in English, not too easy for me to follow, and it gave me time to think. It was only there, in the darkness, that I thought about the money I had been spending. The prices had seemed to me very reasonable, like Bombay prices. Three for the movie ticket, one fifty in the café, with tip. But I had been thinking in rupees and paying in dollars. In less than an hour I had spent nine days' pay.

I couldn't watch the movie after that. I went out and began to make my way back to the apartment block. Many more of the *hubshi* were about now and I saw that where they congregated the pavement was wet, and dangerous with broken glass and bottles. I couldn't think of cooking when I got back to the apartment. I couldn't bear to look at the view. I spread my bedding in the cupboard, lay down in the darkness and waited for my employer to return.

When he did I said, "Sahib, I want to go home."

"Santosh, I've paid five thousand rupees to bring you here. If I send you back now, you will have to work for six or seven years without salary to pay me back."

I burst into tears.

"My poor Santosh, something has happened. Tell me what has happened."

"Sahib, I've spent more than half the advance you gave me this morning. I went out and had a coffee and cake and then I went to a movie."

His eyes went small and twinkly behind his glasses. He bit the inside of his top lip, scraped at his moustache with his lower teeth, and he said, "You see, you see. I told you it was expensive."

I understood I was a prisoner. I accepted this and adjusted. I learned to live within the apartment, and I was even calm.

My employer was a man of taste and he soon had the apartment looking like something in a magazine, with books and Indian paintings and Indian fabrics and pieces of sculpture and bronze statues of our gods. I was careful to take no delight in it. It was of course very pretty, especially with the view. But the view remained foreign and I never felt that the apartment was real, like the shabby old Bombay chambers with the cane chairs, or that it had anything to do with me.

When people came to dinner I did my duty. At the appropriate time I would bid the company goodnight, close off the kitchen behind its folding screen and pretend I was leaving the apartment. Then I would lie down quietly in my cupboard and smoke. I was free to go out; I had my separate entrance. But I didn't like being out of the apartment. I didn't even like going down to the laundry room in the basement.

Once or twice a week I went to the supermarket on our street. I always had to walk past groups of *hubshi* men and children. I tried not to look, but it was hard. They sat on the pavement, on steps and in the bush around their redbrick houses, some of which had boarded-up windows. They appeared to be very much a people of the open air, with little to do; even in the mornings some of the men were drunk.

Scattered among the *hubshi* houses were others just as old but with gas-lamps that burned night and day in the entrance. These were the houses of the Americans. I seldom saw these people; they didn't spend much time on the street. The lighted gas-lamp was the American way of saying that though a house looked old outside it was nice and new inside. I also felt that it was like a warning to the *hubshi* to keep off.

Outside the supermarket there was always a policeman with a gun. Inside, there were always a couple of *hubshi* guards with truncheons, and, behind the cashiers, some old *hubshi* beggar men in rags. There were also many young *hubshi* boys, small but muscular, waiting to carry parcels, as once in the hills I had waited to carry Indian tourists' luggage.

These trips to the supermarket were my only outings, and I was always glad to get back to the apartment. The work there was light. I watched a lot of television and my English improved. I grew to like certain commercials very much. It was in these commercials I saw the Americans whom in real life I so seldom saw and knew only by their gas-lamps. Up there in the apartment, with a view of the white domes and towers and greenery of the famous city, I entered the homes of the Americans and saw them cleaning those homes. I saw them cleaning floors and dishes. I saw them buying clothes and cleaning clothes, buying motor cars and cleaning motor cars. I saw them cleaning, cleaning.

The effect of all this television on me was curious. If by some chance I saw an American on the street I tried to fit him or her into the commercials; and I felt I had caught the person in an interval between his television duties. So to some extent Americans have remained to me, as people not quite real, as people temporarily absent from television.

Sometimes a *hubshi* came on the screen, not to talk of *hubshi* things, but to do a little cleaning of his own. That wasn't the same. He was too different from the *hubshi* I saw on the street and I knew he was an actor. I knew that his television duties were only make-believe and that he would soon have to return to the street.

One day at the supermarket, when the *hubshi* girl took my money, she sniffed and said, "You always smell sweet, baby."

She was friendly, and I was at last able to clear up that mystery, of my smell. It was the poor country weed I smoked. It was a peasant taste of which I was slightly ashamed, to tell the truth; but the cashier was encouraging. As it happened, I had brought a quantity of the weed with me from Bombay in one of my bundles, together with a hundred razor blades, believing both weed and blades to be purely Indian things. I made an offering to the girl. In return she taught me a few words of English. "Me black and beautiful"[3] was the first thing she taught me. Then she pointed to the policeman with the gun outside and taught me: "He pig."

My English lessons were taken a stage further by the *hubshi* maid who worked for someone on our floor in the apartment block. She too was attracted by my smell, but I soon began to feel that she was also attracted by my smallness and strangeness. She herself was a big woman, broad in the face, with high cheeks and bold eyes and lips that were full but not pendulous. Her largeness disturbed me; I found it better to concentrate on her

---

3. Cf. Song of Solomon 1.5: "I am black, but comely."

face. She misunderstood; there were times when she frolicked with me in a violent way. I didn't like it, because I couldn't fight her off as well as I would have liked and because in spite of myself I was fascinated by her appearance. Her smell mixed with the perfumes she used could have made me forget myself.

She was always coming into the apartment. She disturbed me while I was watching the Americans on television. I feared the smell she left behind. Sweat, perfume, my own weed: the smells lay thick in the room, and I prayed to the bronze gods my employer had installed as living-room ornaments that I would not be dishonoured. Dishonoured, I say; and I know that this might seem strange to people over here, who have permitted the *hubshi* to settle among them in such large numbers and must therefore esteem them in certain ways. But in our country we frankly do not care for the *hubshi*. It is written in our books, both holy and not so holy, that it is indecent and wrong for a man of our blood to embrace the *hubshi* woman. To be dishonoured in this life, to be born a cat or a monkey or a *hubshi* in the next!

But I was falling. Was it idleness and solitude? I was found attractive: I wanted to know why. I began to go to the bathroom of the apartment simply to study my face in the mirror. I cannot easily believe it myself now, but in Bombay a week or a month could pass without my looking in the mirror; then it wasn't to consider my looks but to check whether the barber had cut off too much hair or whether a pimple was about to burst. Slowly I made a discovery. My face was handsome. I had never thought of myself in this way. I had thought of myself as unnoticeable, with features that served as identification alone.

The discovery of my good looks brought its strains. I became obsessed with my appearance, with a wish to see myself. It was like an illness. I would be watching television, for instance, and I would be surprised by the thought: are you as handsome as that man? I would have to get up and go to the bathroom and look in the mirror.

I thought back to the time when these matters hadn't interested me, and I saw how ragged I must have looked, on the aeroplane, in the airport, in that café for bare feet, with the rough and dirty clothes I wore, without doubt or question, as clothes befitting a servant. I was choked with shame. I saw, too, how good people in Washington had been, to have seen me in rags and yet to have taken me for a man.

I was glad I had a place to hide. I had thought of myself as a prisoner. Now I was glad I had so little of Washington to cope with: the apartment, my cupboard, the television set, my employer, the walk to the supermarket, the *hubshi* woman. And one day I found I no longer knew whether I wanted to go back to Bombay. Up there, in the apartment, I no longer knew what I wanted to do.

I became more careful of my appearance. There wasn't much I could do. I bought laces for my old black shoes, socks, a belt. Then some money came my way. I had understood that the weed I smoked was of value to the *hubshi* and the bare feet; I disposed of what I had, disadvantageously as I now know, through the *hubshi* girl at the supermarket. I got just under two hundred dollars. Then, as anxiously as I had got rid of my weed, I went out and bought some clothes.

I still have the things I bought that morning. A green hat, a green suit. The suit was always too big for me. Ignorance, inexperience; but I also remember the feeling of presumption. The salesman wanted to talk, to do his job. I didn't want to listen. I took the first suit he showed me and went into the cubicle and changed. I couldn't think about size and fit. When I considered all that cloth and all that tailoring I was proposing to adorn my simple body with, that body that needed so little, I felt I was asking to be destroyed. I changed back quickly, went out of the cubicle and said I would take the green suit. The salesman began to talk; I cut him short; I asked for a hat. When I got back to the apartment I felt quite weak and had to lie down for a while in my cupboard.

I never hung the suit up. Even in the shop, even while counting out the precious dollars, I had known it was a mistake. I kept the suit folded in the box with all its pieces of tissue paper. Three or four times I put it on and walked about the apartment and sat down on chairs and lit cigarettes and crossed my legs, practising. But I couldn't bring myself to wear the suit out of doors. Later I wore the pants, but never the jacket. I never bought another suit; I soon began wearing the sort of clothes I wear today, pants with some sort of zippered jacket.

Once I had had no secrets from my employer; it was so much simpler not to have secrets. But some instinct told me now it would be better not to let him know about the green suit or the few dollars I had, just as instinct had already told me I should keep my growing knowledge of English to myself.

Once my employer had been to me only a presence. I used to tell him then that beside him I was as dirt. It was only a way of talking, one of the courtesies of our language, but it had something of truth. I meant that he was the man who adventured in the world for me, that I experienced the world through him, that I was content to be a small part of his presence. I was content, sleeping on the Bombay pavement with my friends, to hear the talk of my employer and his guests upstairs. I was more than content, late at night, to be identified among the sleepers and greeted by some of those guests before they drove away.

Now I found that, without wishing it, I was ceasing to see myself as part of my employer's presence, and beginning at the same time to see him as an outsider might see him, as perhaps the people who came to dinner in the apartment saw him. I saw that he was a man of my own age, around thirty-five; it astonished me that I hadn't noticed this before. I saw that he was plump, in need of exercise, that he moved with short, fussy steps; a man with glasses, thinning hair, and that habit, during conversation, of scraping at his moustache with his teeth and nibbling at the inside of his top lip; a man who was frequently anxious, took pains over his work, was subjected at his own table to unkind remarks by his office colleagues; a man who looked as uneasy in Washington as I felt, who acted as cautiously as I had learned to act.

I remember an American who came to dinner. He looked at the pieces of sculpture in the apartment and said he had himself brought back a whole head from one of our ancient temples; he had got the guide to hack it off.

I could see that my employer was offended. He said, "But that's illegal."

"That's why I had to give the guide two dollars. If I had a bottle of whisky he would have pulled down the whole temple for me."

My employer's face went blank. He continued to do his duties as host but he was unhappy throughout the dinner. I grieved for him.

Afterwards he knocked on my cupboard. I knew he wanted to talk. I was in my underclothes but I didn't feel underdressed, with the American gone. I stood in the door of my cupboard; my employer paced up and down the small kitchen; the apartment felt sad.

"Did you hear that person, Santosh?"

I pretended I hadn't understood, and when he explained I tried to console him. I said, "Sahib, but we know these people are Franks and barbarians."

"They are malicious people, Santosh. They think that because we are a poor country we are all the same. They think an official in Government is just the same as some poor guide scraping together a few rupees to keep body and soul together, poor fellow."

I saw that he had taken the insult only in a personal way, and I was disappointed. I thought he had been thinking of the temple.

A few days later I had my adventure. The *hubshi* woman came in, moving among my employer's ornaments like a bull. I was greatly provoked. The smell was too much; so was the sight of her armpits. I fell. She dragged me down on the couch, on the saffron spread which was one of my employer's nicest pieces of Punjabi folk-weaving. I saw the moment, helplessly, as one of dishonour. I saw her as Kali,[4] goddess of death and destruction, coal-black, with a red tongue and white eyeballs and many powerful arms. I expected her to be wild and fierce; but she added insult to injury by being very playful, as though, because I was small and strange, the act was not real. She laughed all the time. I would have liked to withdraw, but the act took over and completed itself. And then I felt dreadful.

I wanted to be forgiven, I wanted to be cleansed, I wanted her to go. Nothing frightened me more than the way she had ceased to be a visitor in the apartment and behaved as though she possessed it. I looked at the sculpture and the fabrics and thought of my poor employer, suffering in his office somewhere.

I bathed and bathed afterwards. The smell would not leave me. I fancied that the woman's oil was still on that poor part of my poor body. It occurred to me to rub it down with half a lemon. Penance and cleansing; but it didn't hurt as much as I expected, and I extended the penance by rolling about naked on the floor of the bathroom and the sitting-room and howling. At last the tears came, real tears, and I was comforted.

It was cool in the apartment; the air-conditioning always hummed; but I could see that it was hot outside, like one of our own summer days in the hills. The urge came upon me to dress as I might have done in my village on a religious occasion. In one of my bundles I had a dhoti[5]-length of new cotton, a gift from the tailor's bearer that I had never used. I draped this around my waist and between my legs, lit incense sticks, sat down cross-legged on the floor and tried to meditate and become still. Soon I began to feel hungry. That made me happy; I decided to fast.

Unexpectedly my employer came in. I didn't mind being caught in the attitude and garb of prayer; it could have been so much worse. But I wasn't expecting him till late afternoon.

"Santosh, what has happened?"

Pride got the better of me. I said, "Sahib, it is what I do from time to time."

---

4. Great Hindu deity.　　5. Loincloth (Hindi).

But I didn't find merit in his eyes. He was far too agitated to notice me properly. He took off his lightweight fawn jacket, dropped it on the saffron spread, went to the refrigerator and drank two tumblers of orange juice, one after the other. Then he looked out at the view, scraping at his moustache.

"Oh, my poor Santosh, what are we doing in this place? Why do we have to come here?"

I looked with him. I saw nothing unusual. The wide window showed the colours of the hot day: the pale-blue sky, the white, almost colourless, domes of famous buildings rising out of dead-green foliage; the untidy roofs of apartment blocks where on Saturday and Sunday mornings people sunbathed; and, below, the fronts and backs of houses on the tree-lined street down which I walked to the supermarket.

My employer turned off the air-conditioning and all noise was absent from the room. An instant later I began to hear the noises outside: sirens far and near. When my employer slid the window open the roar of the disturbed city rushed into the room. He closed the window and there was near-silence again. Not far from the supermarket I saw black smoke, uncurling, rising, swiftly turning colourless. This was not the smoke which some of the apartment blocks gave off all day. This was the smoke of a real fire.

"The *hubshi* have gone wild, Santosh. They are burning down Washington."

I didn't mind at all. Indeed, in my mood of prayer and repentance, the news was even welcome. And it was with a feeling of release that I watched and heard the city burn that afternoon and watched it burn that night. I watched it burn again and again on television; and I watched it burn in the morning. It burned like a famous city and I didn't want it to stop burning. I wanted the fire to spread and spread and I wanted everything in the city, even the apartment block, even the apartment, even myself, to be destroyed and consumed. I wanted escape to be impossible; I wanted the very idea of escape to become absurd. At every sign that the burning was going to stop I felt disappointed and let down.

For four days my employer and I stayed in the apartment and watched the city burn. The television continued to show us what we could see and what, whenever we slid the window back, we could hear. Then it was over. The view from our window hadn't changed. The famous buildings stood; the trees remained. But for the first time since I had understood that I was a prisoner I found that I wanted to be out of the apartment and in the streets.

The destruction lay beyond the supermarket. I had never gone into this part of the city before, and it was strange to walk in those long wide streets for the first time, to see trees and houses and shops and advertisements, everything like a real city, and then to see that every signboard on every shop was burnt or stained with smoke, that the shops themselves were black and broken, that flames had burst through some of the upper windows and scorched the red bricks. For mile after mile it was like that. There were *hubshi* groups about, and at first when I passed them I pretended to be busy, minding my own business, not at all interested in the ruins. But they smiled at me and I found I was smiling back. Happiness was on the faces of the *hubshi*. They were like people amazed they could do so much, that so much lay in their power. They were like people on holiday. I shared their exhilaration.

The idea of escape was a simple one, but it hadn't occurred to me before. When I adjusted to my imprisonment I had wanted only to get away from Washington and to return to Bombay. But then I had become confused. I had looked in the mirror and seen myself, and I knew it wasn't possible for me to return to Bombay to the sort of job I had had and the life I had lived. I couldn't easily become part of someone else's presence again. Those evening chats on the pavement, those morning walks: happy times, but they were like the happy times of childhood: I didn't want them to return.

I had taken, after the fire, to going for long walks in the city. And one day, when I wasn't even thinking of escape, when I was just enjoying the sights and my new freedom of movement, I found myself in one of those leafy streets where private houses had been turned into business premises. I saw a fellow countryman superintending the raising of a signboard on his gallery. The signboard told me that the building was a restaurant, and I assumed that the man in charge was the owner. He looked worried and slightly ashamed, and he smiled at me. This was unusual, because the Indians I had seen on the streets of Washington pretended they hadn't seen me; they made me feel that they didn't like the competition of my presence or didn't want me to start asking them difficult questions.

I complimented the worried man on his signboard and wished him good luck in his business. He was a small man of about fifty and he was wearing a double-breasted suit with old-fashioned wide lapels. He had dark hollows below his eyes and he looked as though he had recently lost a little weight. I could see that in our country he had been a man of some standing, not quite the sort of person who would go into the restaurant business. I felt at one with him. He invited me in to look around, asked my name and gave his. It was Priya.

Just past the gallery was the loveliest and richest room I had ever seen. The wallpaper was like velvet; I wanted to pass my hand over it. The brass lamps that hung from the ceiling were in a lovely cut-out pattern and the bulbs were of many colours. Priya looked with me, and the hollows under his eyes grew darker, as though my admiration was increasing his worry at his extravagance. The restaurant hadn't yet opened for customers and on a shelf in one corner I saw Priya's collection of good-luck objects: a brass plate with a heap of uncooked rice, for prosperity; a little copybook and a little diary pencil, for good luck with the accounts; a little clay lamp, for general good luck.

"What do you think, Santosh? You think it will be all right?"

"It is bound to be all right, Priya."

"But I have enemies, you know, Santosh. The Indian restaurant people are not going to appreciate me. All mine, you know, Santosh. Cash paid. No mortgage or anything like that. I don't believe in mortgages. Cash or nothing."

I understood him to mean that he had tried to get a mortgage and failed, and was anxious about money.

"But what are you doing here, Santosh? You used to be in Government or something?"

"You could say that, Priya."

"Like me. They have a saying here. If you can't beat them, join them. I joined them. They are still beating me." He sighed and spread his arms on the top of the red wall-seat. "Ah, Santosh, why do we do it? Why don't we renounce and go and meditate on the riverbank?" He waved about the room. "The yemblems[6] of the world, Santosh. Just yemblems."

I didn't know the English word he used, but I understood its meaning; and for a moment it was like being back in Bombay, exchanging stories and philosophies with the tailor's bearer and others in the evening.

"But I am forgetting, Santosh. You will have some tea or coffee or something?"

I shook my head from side to side to indicate that I was agreeable, and he called out in a strange harsh language to someone behind the kitchen door.

"Yes, Santosh. Yem-*blems*!" And he sighed and slapped the red seat hard.

A man came out from the kitchen with a tray. At first he looked like a fellow countryman, but in a second I could tell he was a stranger.

"You are right," Priya said, when the stranger went back to the kitchen. "He is not of Bharat. He is a Mexican. But what can I do? You get fellow countrymen, you fix up their papers and everything. And then? Then they run away. Run-run-runaway. Crooks this side, crooks that side, I can't tell you. Listen, Santosh. I was in cloth business before. Buy for fifty rupees that side, sell for fifty dollars this side. Easy. But then. Caftan, everybody wants caftan. Caftanaftan, I say, I will settle your caftan. I buy one thousand, Santosh. Delays India-side,[7] of course. They come one year later. Nobody wants caftan then. We're not organized, Santosh. We don't do enough consumer research. That's what the fellows at the embassy tell me. But if I do consumer research, when will I do my business? The trouble, you know, Santosh, is that this shopkeeping is not in my blood. The damn thing goes *against* my blood. When I was in cloth business I used to hide sometimes for shame when a customer came in. Sometimes I used to pretend I was a shopper myself. Consumer research! These people make us dance, Santosh. You and I, we will renounce. We will go together and walk beside Potomac and meditate."

I loved his talk. I hadn't heard anything so sweet and philosophical since the Bombay days. I said, "Priya, I will cook for you, if you want a cook."

"I feel I've known you a long time, Santosh. I feel you are like a member of my own family. I will give you a place to sleep, a little food to eat and a little pocket money, as much as I can afford."

I said, "Show me the place to sleep."

He led me out of the pretty room and up a carpeted staircase. I was expecting the carpet and the new paint to stop somewhere, but it was nice and new all the way. We entered a room that was like a smaller version of my employer's apartment.

"Built-in cupboards and everything, you see, Santosh."

I went to the cupboard. It had a folding door that opened outward. I said, "Priya, it is too small. There is room on the shelf for my belongings. But I don't see how I can spread my bedding inside here. It is far too narrow."

He giggled nervously. "Santosh, you are a joker. I feel that we are of the same family already."

Then it came to me that I was being offered the whole room. I was stunned.

---

6. Emblems.
7. In India. "Caftan": long loose tunic or shirt (Turkish).

Priya looked stunned too. He sat down on the edge of the soft bed. The dark hollows under his eyes were almost black and he looked very small in his double-breasted jacket. "This is how they make us dance over here, Santosh. You say staff quarters and they say staff quarters. This is what they mean."

For some seconds we sat silently, I fearful, he gloomy, meditating on the ways of this new world.

Someone called from downstairs, "Priya!"

His gloom gone, smiling in advance, winking at me, Priya called back in an accent of the country, "Hi, Bab!"

I followed him down.

"Priya," the American said, "I've brought over the menus."

He was a tall man in a leather jacket, with jeans that rode up above thick white socks and big rubber-soled shoes. He looked like someone about to run in a race. The menus were enormous; on the cover there was a drawing of a fat man with a moustache and a plumed turban, something like the man in the airline advertisements.

"They look great, Bab."

"I like them myself. But what's that, Priya? What's that shelf doing there?"

Moving like the front part of a horse, Bab walked to the shelf with the rice and the brass plate and the little clay lamp. It was only then that I saw that the shelf was very roughly made.

Priya looked penitent and it was clear he had put the shelf up himself. It was also clear he didn't intend to take it down.

"Well, it's yours," Bab said. "I suppose we had to have a touch of the East somewhere. Now, Priya—"

"Money-money-money, is it?" Priya said, racing the words together as though he was making a joke to amuse a child. "But, Bab, how can *you ask me* for money? Anybody hearing you would believe that this restaurant is mine. But this restaurant isn't mine, Bab. This restaurant is yours."

It was only one of our courtesies, but it puzzled Bab and he allowed himself to be led to other matters.

I saw that, for all his talk of renunciation and business failure, and for all his jumpiness, Priya was able to cope with Washington. I admired this strength in him as much as I admired the richness of his talk. I didn't know how much to believe of his stories, but I liked having to guess about him. I liked having to play with his words in my mind. I liked the mystery of the man. The mystery came from his solidity. I knew where I was with him. After the apartment and the green suit and the *hubshi* woman and the city burning for four days, to be with Priya was to feel safe. For the first time since I had come to Washington I felt safe.

I can't say that I moved in. I simply stayed. I didn't want to go back to the apartment even to collect my belongings. I was afraid that something might happen to keep me a prisoner there. My employer might turn up and demand his five thousand rupees. The *hubshi* woman might claim me for her own; I might be condemned to a life among the *hubshi*. And it wasn't as if I was leaving behind anything of value in the apartment. The green suit I was even happy to forget. But.

Priya paid me forty dollars a week. After what I was getting, three dollars and seventy-five cents, it seemed a lot; and it was more than enough for my needs. I didn't have much temptation to spend, to tell the truth. I knew that my old employer and the *hubshi* woman would be wondering about me in their respective ways and I thought I should keep off the streets for a while. That was no hardship; it was what I was used to in Washington. Besides, my days at the restaurant were pretty full; for the first time in my life I had little leisure.

The restaurant was a success from the start, and Priya was fussy. He was always bursting into the kitchen with one of those big menus in his hand, saying in English, "Prestige job, Santosh, prestige." I didn't mind. I liked to feel I had to do things perfectly; I felt I was earning my freedom. Though I was in hiding, and though I worked every day until midnight, I felt I was much more in charge of myself than I had ever been.

Many of our waiters were Mexicans, but when we put turbans on them they could pass. They came and went, like the Indian staff. I didn't get on with these people. They were frightened and jealous of one another and very treacherous. Their talk amid the biryanis and the pillaus was all of papers and green cards. They were always about to get green cards or they had been cheated out of green cards or they had just got green cards. At first I didn't know what they were talking about. When I understood I was more than depressed.

I understood that because I had escaped from my employer I had made myself illegal in America. At any moment I could be denounced, seized, jailed, deported, disgraced. It was a complication. I had no green card; I didn't know how to set about getting one; and there was no one I could talk to.

I felt burdened by my secrets. Once I had none; now I had so many. I couldn't tell Priya I had no green card. I couldn't tell him I had broken faith with my old employer and dishonoured myself with a *hubshi* woman and lived in fear of retribution. I couldn't tell him that I was afraid to leave the restaurant and that nowadays when I saw an Indian I hid from him as anxiously as the Indian hid from me. I would have felt foolish to confess. With Priya, right from the start, I had pretended to be strong; and I wanted it to remain like that. Instead, when we talked now, and he grew philosophical, I tried to find bigger causes for being sad. My mind fastened on to these causes, and the effect of this was that my sadness became like a sickness of the soul.

It was worse than being in the apartment, because now the responsibility was mine and mine alone. I had decided to be free, to act for myself. It pained me to think of the exhilaration I had felt during the days of the fire; and I felt mocked when I remembered that in the early days of my escape I had thought I was in charge of myself.

The year turned. The snow came and melted. I was more afraid than ever of going out. The sickness was bigger than all the causes. I saw the future as a hole into which I was dropping. Sometimes at night when I awakened my body would burn and I would feel the hot perspiration break all over.

I leaned on Priya. He was my only hope, my only link with what was real. He went out; he brought back stories. He went out especially to eat in the restaurants of our competitors.

He said, "Santosh, I never believed that running a restaurant was a way to God. But it is true. I eat like a scientist. Every day I eat like a scientist. I feel I have already renounced."

This was Priya. This was how his talk ensnared me and gave me the bigger causes that steadily weakened me. I became more and more detached from the men in the kitchen. When they spoke of their green cards and the jobs they were about to get I felt like asking them: Why? Why?

And every day the mirror told its own tale. Without exercise, with the sickening of my heart and my mind, I was losing my looks. My face had become pudgy and sallow and full of spots; it was becoming ugly. I could have cried for that, discovering my good looks only to lose them. It was like a punishment for my presumption, the punishment I had feared when I bought the green suit.

Priya said, "Santosh, you must get some exercise. You are not looking well. Your eyes are getting like mine. What are you pining for? Are you pining for Bombay or your family in the hills?"

But now, even in my mind, I was a stranger in those places.

Priya said one Sunday morning, "Santosh, I am going to take you to see a Hindi movie today. All the Indians of Washington will be there, domestics and everybody else."

I was very frightened. I didn't want to go and I couldn't tell him why. He insisted. My heart began to beat fast as soon as I got into the car. Soon there were no more houses with gas-lamps in the entrance, just those long wide burnt-out *hubshi* streets, now with fresh leaves on the trees, heaps of rubble on bulldozed, fenced-in lots, boarded-up shop windows, and old smoke-stained signboards announcing what was no longer true. Cars raced along the wide roads; there was life only on the roads. I thought I would vomit with fear.

I said, "Take me back, *sahib*."

I had used the wrong word. Once I had used the word a hundred times a day. But then I had considered myself a small part of my employer's presence, and the word was not servile; it was more like a name, like a reassuring sound, part of my employer's dignity and therefore part of mine. But Priya's dignity could never be mine; that was not our relationship. Priya I had always called Priya; it was his wish, the American way, man to man. With Priya the word was servile. And he responded to the word. He did as I asked; he drove me back to the restaurant. I never called him by his name again.

I was good-looking; I had lost my looks. I was a free man; I had lost my freedom.

One of the Mexican waiters came into the kitchen late one evening and said, "There is a man outside who wants to see the chef."

No one had made this request before, and Priya was at once agitated. "Is he an American? Some enemy has sent him here. Sanitary-anitary, health-ealth, they can inspect my kitchens at any time."

"He is an Indian," the Mexican said.

I was alarmed. I thought it was my old employer; that quiet approach was like him. Priya thought it was a rival. Though Priya regularly ate in the restuarants of his rivals he thought it unfair when they came to eat in his. We both went to the door and peeked through the glass window into the dimly lit dining-room.

"Do you know that person, Santosh?"

"Yes, sahib."

It wasn't my old employer. It was one of his Bombay friends, a big man in

Government, whom I had often served in the chambers. He was by himself and seemed to have just arrived in Washington. He had a new Bombay hair-cut, very close, and a stiff dark suit, Bombay tailoring. His shirt looked blue, but in the dim multi-coloured light of the dining-room everything white looked blue. He didn't look unhappy with what he had eaten. Both his elbows were on the curry-spotted tablecloth and he was picking his teeth, half clos-ing his eyes and hiding his mouth with his cupped left hand.

"I don't like him," Priya said. "Still, big man in Government and so on. You must go to him, Santosh."

But I couldn't go.

"Put on your apron, Santosh. And that chef's cap. Prestige. You must go, Santosh."

Priya went out to the dining-room and I heard him say in English that I was coming.

I ran up to my room, put some oil on my hair, combed my hair, put on my best pants and shirt and my shining shoes. It was so, as a man about town rather than as a cook, I went to the dining-room.

The man from Bombay was as astonished as Priya. We exchanged the old courtesies, and I waited. But, to my relief, there seemed little more to say. No difficult questions were put to me; I was grateful to the man from Bombay for his tact. I avoided talk as much as possible. I smiled. The man from Bombay smiled back. Priya smiled uneasily at both of us. So for a while we were, smiling in the dim blue-red light and waiting.

The man from Bombay said to Priya, "Brother, I just have a few words to say to my old friend Santosh."

Priya didn't like it, but he left us.

I waited for those words. But they were not the words I feared. The man from Bombay didn't speak of my old employer. We continued to exchange courtesies. Yes, I was well and he was well and everybody else we knew was well; and I was doing well and he was doing well. That was all. Then, secre-tively, the man from Bombay gave me a dollar. A dollar, ten rupees, an enormous tip for Bombay. But, from him, much more than a tip: an act of graciousness, part of the sweetness of the old days. Once it would have meant so much to me. Now it meant so little. I was saddened and embarrassed. And I had been anticipating hostility!

Priya was waiting behind the kitchen door. His little face was tight and serious, and I knew he had seen the money pass. Now, quickly, he read my own face, and without saying anything to me he hurried out into the dining-room.

I heard him say in English to the man from Bombay, "Santosh is a good fellow. He's got his own room with bath and everything. I am giving him a hundred dollars a week from next week. A thousand rupees a week. This is a first-class establishment."

A thousand chips a week! I was staggered. It was much more than any man in Government got, and I was sure the man from Bombay was also staggered, and perhaps regretting his good gesture and that precious dollar of foreign exchange.

"Santosh," Priya said, when the restaurant closed that evening, "that man was an enemy. I knew it from the moment I saw him. And because he was an enemy I did something very bad, Santosh."

"Sahib."

"I lied, Santosh. To protect you. I told him, Santosh, that I was going to give you seventy-five dollars a week after Christmas."

"Sahib."

"And now I have to make that lie true. But, Santosh, you know that is money we can't afford. I don't have to tell you about overheads and things like that. Santosh, I will give you sixty."

I said, "Sahib, I couldn't stay on for less than a hundred and twenty-five."

Priya's eyes went shiny and the hollows below his eyes darkened. He giggled and pressed out his lips. At the end of that week I got a hundred dollars. And Priya, good man that he was, bore me no grudge.

Now here was a victory. It was only after it happened that I realized how badly I had needed such a victory, how far, gaining my freedom, I had begun to accept death not as the end but as the goal. I revived. Or rather, my senses revived. But in this city what was there to feed my senses? There were no walks to be taken, no idle conversations with understanding friends. I could buy new clothes. But then? Would I just look at myself in the mirror? Would I go walking, inviting passers-by to look at me and my clothes? No, the whole business of clothes and dressing up only threw me back into myself.

There was a Swiss or German woman in the cake-shop some doors away, and there was a Filipino woman in the kitchen. They were neither of them attractive, to tell the truth. The Swiss or German could have broken my back with a slap, and the Filipino, though young, was remarkably like one of our older hill women. Still, I felt I owed something to the senses, and I thought I might frolic with these women. But then I was frightened of the responsibility. Goodness, I had learned that a woman is not just a roll and a frolic but a big creature weighing a hundred-and-so-many pounds who is going to be around afterwards.

So the moment of victory passed, without celebration. And it was strange, I thought, that sorrow lasts and can make a man look forward to death, but the mood of victory fills a moment and then is over. When my moment of victory was over I discovered below it, as if waiting for me, all my old sickness and fears: fear of my illegality, my former employer, my presumption, the *hubshi* woman. I saw then that the victory I had had was not something I had worked for, but luck; and that luck was only fate's cheating, giving an illusion of power.

But that illusion lingered, and I became restless. I decided to act, to challenge fate. I decided I would no longer stay in my room and hide. I began to go out walking in the afternoons. I gained courage; every afternoon I walked a little farther. It became my ambition to walk to that green circle with the fountain where, on my first day out in Washington, I had come upon those people in Hindu costumes, like domestics abandoned a long time ago, singing their Sanskrit gibberish and doing their strange Red Indian dance. And one day I got there.

One day I crossed the road to the circle and sat down on a bench. The *hubshi* were there, and the bare feet, and the dancers in saris and the saffron robes. It was mid-afternoon, very hot, and no one was active. I remembered how magical and inexplicable that circle had seemed to me the first time I saw it. Now it seemed so ordinary and tired: the roads, the motor cars, the shops, the trees, the careful policemen: so much part of the waste and futility that was our world. There was no longer a mystery. I felt I knew where everybody had come from and where those cars were going. But I also felt that everybody there felt like me, and that was soothing. I took to going to the circle every day after the lunch rush and sitting until it was time to go back to Priya's for the dinners.

Late one afternoon, among the dancers and the musicians, the *hubshi* and the bare feet, the singers and the police, I saw her. The *hubshi* woman. And again I wondered at her size; my memory had not exaggerated. I decided to stay where I was. She saw me and smiled. Then, as if remembering anger, she gave me a look of great hatred; and again I saw her as Kali, many-armed, goddess of death and destruction. She looked hard at my face; she considered my clothes. I thought: is it for this I bought these clothes? She got up. She was very big and her tight pants made her much more appalling. She moved towards me. I got up and ran. I ran across the road and then, not looking back, hurried by devious ways to the restaurant.

Priya was doing his accounts. He always looked older when he was doing his accounts, not worried, just older, like a man to whom life could bring no further surprises. I envied him.

"Santosh, some friend brought a parcel for you."

It was a big parcel wrapped in brown paper. He handed it to me, and I thought how calm he was, with his bills and pieces of paper, and the pen with which he made his neat figures, and the book in which he would write every day until that book was exhausted and he would begin a new one.

I took the parcel up to my room and opened it. Inside there was a cardboard box; and inside that, still in its tissue paper, was the green suit.

I felt a hole in my stomach. I couldn't think. I was glad I had to go down almost immediately to the kitchen, glad to be busy until midnight. But then I had to go up to my room again, and I was alone. I hadn't escaped; I had never been free. I had been abandoned. I was like nothing; I had made myself nothing. And I couldn't turn back.

In the morning Priya said, "You don't look very well, Santosh."

His concern weakened me further. He was the only man I could talk to and I didn't know what I could say to him. I felt tears coming to my eyes. At that moment I would have liked the whole world to be reduced to tears. I said, "Sahib, I cannot stay with you any longer."

They were just words, part of my mood, part of my wish for tears and relief. But Priya didn't soften. He didn't even look surprised. "Where will you go, Santosh?"

How could I answer his serious question?

"Will it be different where you go?"

He had freed himself of me. I could no longer think of tears. I said, "Sahib, I have enemies."

He giggled. "You are a joker, Santosh. How can a man like yourself have enemies? There would be no profit in it. *I* have enemies. It is part of your happiness and part of the equity of the world that you cannot have enemies. That's why you can run-run-runaway." He smiled and made the running gesture with his extended palm.

So, at last, I told him my story. I told him about my old employer and my escape and the green suit. He made me feel I was telling him nothing he hadn't already known. I told him about the *hubshi* woman. I was hoping for some rebuke. A rebuke would have meant that he was concerned for my honour, that I could lean on him, that rescue was possible.

But he said, "Santosh, you have no problems. Marry the *hubshi*. That will automatically make you a citizen. Then you will be a free man."

It wasn't what I was expecting. He was asking me to be alone forever. I said, "Sahib, I have a wife and children in the hills at home."

"But this is your home, Santosh. Wife and children in the hills, that is very nice and that is always there. But that is over. You have to do what is best for you here. You are alone here. *Hubshi-ubshi*, nobody worries about that here, if that is your choice. This isn't Bombay. Nobody looks at you when you walk down the street. Nobody cares what you do."

He was right. I was a free man; I could do anything I wanted. I could, if it were possible for me to turn back, go to the apartment and beg my old employer for forgiveness. I could, if it were possible for me to become again what I once was, go to the police and say, "I am an illegal immigrant here. Please deport me to Bombay." I could run away, hang myself, surrender, confess, hide. It didn't matter what I did, because I was alone. And I didn't know what I wanted to do. It was like the time when I felt my senses revive and I wanted to go out and enjoy and I found there was nothing to enjoy.

To be empty is not to be sad. To be empty is to be calm. It is to renounce. Priya said no more to me; he was always busy in the mornings. I left him and went up to my room. It was still a bare room, still like a room that in half an hour could be someone else's. I had never thought of it as mine. I was frightened of its spotless painted walls and had been careful to keep them spotless. For just such a moment.

I tried to think of the particular moment in my life, the particular action, that had brought me to that room. Was it the moment with the *hubshi* woman, or was it when the American came to dinner and insulted my employer? Was it the moment of my escape, my sight of Priya in the gallery, or was it when I looked in the mirror and bought the green suit? Or was it much earlier, in that other life, in Bombay, in the hills? I could find no one moment; every moment seemed important. An endless chain of action had brought me to that room. It was frightening; it was burdensome. It was not a time for new decisions. It was time to call a halt.

I lay on the bed watching the ceiling, watching the sky. The door was pushed open. It was Priya.

"My goodness, Santosh! How long have you been here? You have been so quiet I forgot about you."

He looked about the room. He went into the bathroom and came out again.

"Are you all right, Santosh?"

He sat on the edge of the bed and the longer he stayed the more I realized how glad I was to see him. There was this: when I tried to think of him rushing into the room I couldn't place it in time; it seemed to have occurred only in my mind. He sat with me. Time became real again. I felt a great love for him. Soon I could have laughed at his agitation. And later, indeed, we laughed together.

I said, "Sahib, you must excuse me this morning. I want to go for a walk. I will come back about tea time."

He looked hard at me, and we both knew I had spoken truly.

"Yes, yes, Santosh. You go for a good long walk. Make yourself hungry with walking. You will feel much better."

Walking, through streets that were now so simple to me, I thought how nice it would be if the people in Hindu costumes in the circle were real. Then I might have joined them. We would have taken to the road; at midday we would have halted in the shade of big trees; in the late afternoon the sinking sun would have turned the dust clouds to gold; and every evening at some village there would have been welcome, water, food, a fire in the night. But that was a dream of another life. I had watched the people in the circle long enough to know that they were of their city; that their television life awaited them; that their renunciation was not like mine. No television life awaited me. It didn't matter. In this city I was alone and it didn't matter what I did.

As magical as the circle with the fountain the apartment block had once been to me. Now I saw that it was plain, not very tall, and faced with small white tiles. A glass door; four tiled steps down; the desk to the right, letters and keys in the pigeonholes; a carpet to the left, upholstered chairs, a low table with paper flowers in the vase; the blue door of the swift, silent elevator. I saw the simplicity of all these things. I knew the floor I wanted. In the corridor, with its illuminated star-decorated ceiling, an imitation sky, the colours were blue, grey and gold. I knew the door I wanted. I knocked.

The *hubshi* woman opened. I saw the apartment where she worked. I had never seen it before and was expecting something like my old employer's apartment, which was on the same floor. Instead, for the first time, I saw something arranged for a television life.

I thought she might have been angry. She looked only puzzled. I was grateful for that.

I said to her in English, "Will you marry me?"

And there, it was done.

"It is for the best, Santosh," Priya said, giving me tea when I got back to the restaurant. "You will be a free man. A citizen. You will have the whole world before you."

I was pleased that he was pleased.

So I am now a citizen, my presence is legal, and I live in Washington. I am still with Priya. We do not talk together as much as we did. The restaurant is one world, the parks and green streets of Washington are another, and every evening some of these streets take me to a third. Burnt-out brick houses, broken fences, overgrown gardens; in a levelled lot between the high brick walls of two houses, a sort of artistic children's playground which the *hubshi* children never use; and then the dark house in which I now live.

Its smells are strange, everything in it is strange. But my strength in this house is that I am a stranger. I have closed my mind and heart to the English language, to newspapers and radio and television, to the pictures of *hubshi* runners and boxers and musicians on the wall. I do not want to understand or learn any more.

I am a simple man who decided to act and see for himself, and it is as though I have had several lives. I do not wish to add to these. Some afternoons I walk to the circle with the fountain. I see the dancers but they are separated from me as by glass. Once, when there were rumours of new burnings, someone scrawled in white paint on the pavement outside my house: *Soul Brother.* I understand the words; but I feel, brother to what or to whom? I was once part of the flow, never thinking of myself as a presence. Then I looked in the mirror and decided to be free. All that my freedom has brought me is the knowledge that I have a face and have a body, that I must feed this body and clothe this body for a certain number of years. Then it will be over.

1971

EDNA O'BRIEN
b. 1932

Edna O'Brien was born in the village of Tuamgraney, County Clare, Ireland, and was educated at the National School in Scarrif, the Convent of Mercy at Longrea, and the Pharmaceutical College in Dublin. Her 1951 marriage was dissolved in 1964. She has two sons.

The Irish novelist Frank Tuohy wrote in an essay about James Joyce that, while Joyce in *Dubliners* and *A Portrait of the Artist as a Young Man* was the first Irish Roman Catholic to make his experience and his surroundings recognizable, "the world of Nora Barnacle [the Dublin chambermaid who became Joyce's wife] had to wait for the fiction of Edna O'Brien." Growing up under the shadow of violent fathers, both women turned for comfort to their suffering mothers, and both had their first experience of a world outside the family in a convent school like that depicted in O'Brien's *Sister Imelda*. Much of her fiction, like much of Joyce's, has an autobiographical element; and the story printed here, in its delineation of a troubled awakening to sexuality and shame, adolescent love in conflict with the love of God, invites comparison with his *Portrait of the Artist*. Like Joyce again, O'Brien had to escape from Mother Ireland (the title of her 1976 history of her country), Mother Church, and her own overloved mother, to find the necessary freedom in which to write. She moved to London in 1959, and in her first month of exile wrote her first novel, *The Country Girls* (1960). The two that followed this—*The Lonely Girl* (1962) and *Girls in Their Married Bliss* (1964)—were reissued as *The Country Girls Trilogy and Epilogue* (1987). She has published seven other novels, including *August Is a Wicked Month* (1965), *The High Road* (1988), *Time and Tide* (1992), and *House of Splendid Isolation* (1994); as well as three collections of short stories and *A Fanatic Heart: Selected Stories* (1984). She has also written plays for the stage and television, several screenplays, and works of nonfiction.

Love, in its combustible mixture of pleasure and pain, profit and loss, remains her principal theme—typically, the committed love of a lonely woman for an uncommitted man. The men in her fiction are sometimes shadowy stereotypes of deviousness or brutality, but what gives her work its power is her depiction—in a style as simple as Joyce's is complex—of women as sufferers and survivors.

Sister Imelda

Sister Imelda did not take classes on her first day back in the convent but we spotted her in the grounds after the evening Rosary.[1] Excitement and curiosity impelled us to follow her and try to see what she looked like, but she thwarted us by walking with head bent and eyelids down. All we could be certain of was that she was tall and limbre and that she prayed while she walked. No looking at nature for her, or no curiosity about seventy boarders in gaberdine coats and black shoes and stockings. We might just as well have been crows, so impervious was she to our stares and to abortive attempts at trying to say "Hello, Sister."

We had returned from our long summer holiday and we were all wretched. The convent, with its high stone wall and green iron gates enfolding us again, seemed more of a prison than ever—for after our spell in the outside world we all felt very much older and more sophisticated, and my friend Baba and I were dreaming of our final escape, which would be in a year. And so, on that damp autumn evening when I saw the chrysanthemums and saw the new nun intent on prayer I pitied her and thought how alone she must be, cut off from her friends and conversation, with only God as her intangible spouse.

The next day she came into our classroom to take geometry. Her pale, slightly long face I saw as formidable, but her eyes were different, being blue-black and full of verve. Her lips were very purple, as if she had put puce pencil on them. They were the lips of a woman who might sing in a cabaret, and unconsciously she had formed the habit of turning them inward, as if she, too, was aware of their provocativeness. She had spent the last four years—the same span that Baba and I had spent in the convent—at the university in Dublin, where she studied languages. We couldn't understand how she had resisted the temptations of the hectic world and willingly come back to this. Her spell in the outside world made her different from the other nuns; there was more bounce in her walk, more excitement in the way she tackled teaching, reminding us that it was the most important thing in the world as she uttered the phrase "Praise be the Incarnate World." She began each day's class by reading from Cardinal Newman,[2] who was a favourite of hers. She read how God dwelt in light unapproachable, and how with Him there was neither change nor shadow of alteration. It was amazing how her looks changed. Some days, when her eyes were flashing, she looked almost profane and made me wonder what events inside the precincts of the convent caused her to be suddenly so excited. She might have been a girl going to a dance, except for her habit.

"Hasn't she wonderful eyes," I said to Baba. That particular day they were like blackberries, large and soft and shiny.

"Something wrong in her upstairs department," Baba said, and added that with makeup Imelda would be a cinch.[3]

"Still, she has a vocation!" I said, and even aired the idiotic view that I

---

1. The recitation of prayers, each associated with a bead in a string of beads known in the Roman Catholic Church as a rosary.
2. John Henry Newman (1801–1890), Roman

Catholic cardinal and theologian, author of *Apologia Pro Vita Sua*.
3. Beauty (slang for "a sure thing").

might have one. At certain moments it did seem enticing to become a nun, to lead a life unspotted by sin, never to have to have babies, and to wear a ring that singled one out as the Bride of Christ. But there was the other side to it, the silence, the gravity of it, having to get up two or three times a night to pray and, above all, never having the opportunity of leaving the confines of the place except for the funeral of one's parents. For us boarders it was torture, but for the nuns it was nothing short of doom. Also, we could complain to each other, and we did, food being the source of the greatest grumbles. Lunch was either bacon and cabbage or a peculiar stringy meat followed by tapioca pudding; tea consisted of bread dolloped with lard and occasionally, as a treat, fairly green rhubarb jam, which did not have enough sugar. Through the long curtainless windows we saw the conifer trees and a sky that was scarcely ever without the promise of rain or a downpour.

She was a right lunatic, then, Baba said, having gone to university for four years and willingly come back to incarceration, to poverty, chastity, and obedience. We concocted scenes of agony in some Dublin hostel, while a boy, or even a young man, stood beneath her bedroom window throwing up chunks of clay or whistles or a supplication. In our version of it he was slightly older than her, and possibly a medical student, since medical students had a knack with women, because of studying diagrams and skeletons. His advances, like those of a sudden storm, would intermittently rise and overwhelm her, and the memory of these sudden flaying advances of his would haunt her until she died, and if ever she contracted fever, these secrets would out. It was also rumoured that she possessed a fierce temper and that, while a postulant,[4] she had hit a girl so badly with her leather strap that the girl had to be put to bed because of wounds. Yet another black mark against Sister Imelda was that her brother Ambrose had been sued by a nurse for breach of promise.[5]

That first morning when she came into our classroom and modestly introduced herself, I had no idea how terribly she would infiltrate my life, how in time she would be not just one of those teachers or nuns but rather a special one, almost like a ghost who passed the boundaries of common exchange and who crept inside one, devouring so much of one's thoughts, so much of one's passion, invading the place that was called one's heart. She talked in a low voice, as if she did not want her words to go beyond the bounds of the wall, and constantly she stressed the value of work both to enlarge the mind and to discipline the thought. One of her eyelids was red and swollen, as if she was getting a sty. I reckoned that she overmortified[6] herself by not eating at all. I saw in her some terrible premonition of sacrifice which I would have to emulate. Then, in direct contrast, she absently held the stick of chalk between her first and second fingers, the very same as if it were a cigarette, and Baba whispered to me that she might have been a smoker when in Dublin. Sister Imelda looked down sharply at me and said what was the secret and would I like to share it, since it seemed so comical. I said, "Nothing, Sister, nothing," and her dark eyes exuded such vehemence that I prayed she would never have occasion to punish me.

4. Candidate for admission into a religious order or community.
5. Broken promise of marriage (formerly grounds for litigation).
6. Punished herself excessively (as in paragraph below) for her real or imagined sins.

November came and the tiled walls of the recreation hall oozed moisture and gloom. Most girls had sore throats and were told to suffer this inconvenience to mortify themselves in order to lend a glorious hand in that communion of spirit that linked the living with the dead. It was the month of the Suffering Souls in Purgatory, and as we heard of their twofold agony, the yearning for Christ and the ferocity of the leaping flames that burned and charred their poor limbs, we were asked to make acts of mortification. Some girls gave up jam or sweets and some gave up talking, and so in recreation time they were like dummies making signs with thumb and finger to merely say "How are you?" Baba said that saner people were locked in the lunatic asylum, which was only a mile away. We saw them in the grounds, pacing back and forth, with their mouths agape and dribble coming out of them, like melting icicles. Among our many fears was that one of those lunatics would break out and head straight for the convent and assault some of the girls.

Yet in the thick of all these dreads I found myself becoming dreadfully happy. I had met Sister Imelda outside of class a few times and I felt that there was an attachment between us. Once it was in the grounds, when she did a reckless thing. She broke off a chrysanthemum and offered it to me to smell. It had no smell, or at least only something faint that suggested autumn, and feeling this to be the case herself, she said it was not a gardenia, was it? Another time we met in the chapel porch, and as she drew her shawl more tightly around her body, I felt how human she was, and prey to the cold.

In the classroom things were not so congenial between us. Geometry was my worst subject, indeed, a total mystery to me. She had not taught more than four classes when she realised this and threw a duster at me in a rage. A few girls gasped as she asked me to stand up and make a spectacle of myself. Her face had reddened, and presently she took out her handkerchief and patted the eye which was red and swollen. I not only felt a fool but felt in imminent danger of sneezing as I inhaled the smell of chalk that had fallen onto my gym frock.[7] Suddenly she fled from the room, leaving us ten minutes free until the next class. Some girls said it was a disgrace, said I should write home and say I had been assaulted. Others welcomed the few minutes in which to gabble. All I wanted was to run after her and say that I was sorry to have caused her such distemper, because I knew dimly that it was as much to do with liking as it was with dislike. In me then there came a sort of speechless tenderness for her, and I might have known that I was stirred.

"We could get her defrocked,"[8] Baba said, and elbowed me in God's name to sit down.

That evening at Benediction[9] I had the most overwhelming surprise. It was a particularly happy evening, with the choir nuns in full soaring form and the rows of candles like so many little ladders to the golden chalice[1] that glittered all the more because of the beams of fitful flame. I was full of tears when I discovered a new holy picture had been put in my prayer book, and before I dared look on the back to see who had given it to me, I felt and guessed that this was no ordinary picture from an ordinary girl friend, that

---

7. Costume worn for gymnastics.
8. Expelled from a religious order or community.
9. Short service, ending with a blessing.

1. Drinking cup, containing wine, used in the Roman Catholic mass.

this was a talisman and a peace offering from Sister Imelda. It was a pale-blue picture, so pale that it was almost gray, like the down of a pigeon, and it showed a mother looking down on the infant child. On the back, in her beautiful ornate handwriting, she had written a verse:

> *Trust Him when dark doubts assail thee,*
> *Trust Him when thy faith is small,*
> *Trust Him when to simply trust Him*
> *Seems the hardest thing of all.*

This was her atonement. To think that she had located the compartment in the chapel where I kept my prayer book and to think that she had been so naked as to write in it and give me a chance to boast about it and to show it to other girls. When I thanked her next day, she bowed but did not speak. Mostly the nuns were on silence and only permitted to talk during class.

In no time I had received another present, a little miniature prayer book with a leather cover and gold edging. The prayers were in French and the lettering so minute it was as if a tiny insect had fashioned them. Soon I was publicly known as her pet. I opened the doors for her, raised the blackboard two pegs higher (she was taller than other nuns), and handed out the exercise books which she had corrected. Now in the margins of my geometry propositions I would find "Good" or "Excellent," when in the past she used to splash "Disgraceful." Baba said it was foul to be a nun's pet and that any girl who sucked up to a nun could not be trusted.

About a month later Sister Imelda asked me to carry her books up four flights of stairs to the cookery kitchen. She taught cookery to a junior class. As she walked ahead of me, I thought how supple she was and how thoroughbred, and when she paused on the landing to look out through the long curtainless window, I too paused. Down below, two women in suede boots were chatting and smoking as they moved along the street with shopping baskets. Nearby a lay nun[2] was on her knees scrubbing the granite steps, and the cold air was full of the raw smell of Jeyes Fluid. There was a potted plant on the landing, and Sister Imelda put her fingers in the earth and went "Tch tch tch," saying it needed water. I said I would water it later on. I was happy in my prison then, happy to be near her, happy to walk behind her as she twirled her beads and bowed to the servile nun. I no longer cried for my mother, no longer counted the days on a pocket calendar until the Christmas holidays.

"Come back at five," she said as she stood on the threshold of the cookery kitchen door. The girls, all in white overalls, were arranged around the long wooden table waiting for her. It was as if every girl was in love with her. Because, as she entered, their faces broke into smiles, and in different tones of audacity they said her name. She must have liked cookery class, because she beamed and called to someone, anyone, to get up a blazing fire. then she went across to the cast-iron stove and spat on it to test its temperature. It was hot, because her spit rose up and sizzled.

When I got back later, she was sitting on the edge of the table swaying

---

2. One who has taken the habit and vows of a religious order but is employed in manual labor and excused other duties.

her legs. There was something reckless about her pose, something defiant. It seemed as if any minute she would take out a cigarette case, snap it open, and then archly offer me one. The wonderful smell of baking made me realise how hungry I was, but far more so, it brought back to me my own home, my mother testing orange cakes with a knitting needle and letting me lick the line of half-baked dough down the length of the needle. I wondered if she had supplanted my mother, and I hoped not, because I had aimed to outstep my original world and take my place in a new and hallowed one.

"I bet you have a sweet tooth," she said, and then she got up, crossed the kitchen, and from under a wonderful shining silver cloche[3] she produced two jam tarts with a crisscross design on them where the pastry was latticed over the dark jam. They were still warm.

"What will I do with them?" I asked.

"Eat them, you goose," she said, and she watched me eat as if she herself derived some peculiar pleasure from it, whereas I was embarrassed about the pastry crumbling and the bits of blackberry jam staining my lips. She was amused. It was one of the most awkward yet thrilling moments I had lived, and inherent in the pleasure was the terrible sense of danger. Had we been caught, she, no doubt, would have had to make massive sacrifice. I looked at her and thought how peerless and how brave, and I wondered if she felt hungry. She had a white overall over her black habit and this made her warmer and freer, and caused me to think of the happiness that would be ours, the laissez-faire[4] if we were away from the convent in an ordinary kitchen doing something easy and customary. But we weren't. It was clear to me then that my version of pleasure was inextricable from pain, that they existed side by side and were interdependent, like the two forces of an electric current.

"Had you a friend when you were in Dublin at university?" I asked daringly.

"I shared a desk with a sister from Howth and stayed in the same hostel," she said.

But what about boys? I thought, and what of your life now and do you long to go out into the world? But could not say it.

We knew something about the nuns' routine. It was rumoured that they wore itchy wool underwear, ate dry bread for breakfast, rarely had meat, cakes, or dainties, kept certain hours of strict silence with each other, as well as constant vigil on their thoughts; so that if their minds wandered to the subject of food or pleasure, they would quickly revert to thoughts of God and their eternal souls. They slept on hard beds with no sheets and hairy blankets. At four o'clock in the morning while we slept, each nun got out of bed, in her habit—which was also her death habit—and chanting, they all flocked down the wooden stairs like ravens, to fling themselves on the tiled floor of the chapel. Each nun—even the Mother Superior—flung herself in total submission, saying prayers in Latin and offering up the moment to God. Then silently back to their cells for one more hour of rest. It was not difficult to imagine Sister Imelda face downward, arms outstretched, prostrate on the tiled floor. I often heard their chanting when I wakened suddenly from a nightmare, because, although we slept in a different building, both adjoined, and if one wakened one often heard that monotonous Latin chanting, long before the birds began, long before our own bell summoned us to rise at six.

---

3. Bell-shaped cover with a handle on top.   4. Lack of interference (French).

"Do you eat nice food?" I asked.

"Of course," she said, and smiled. She sometimes broke into an eager smile, which she did much to conceal.

"Have you ever thought of what you will be?" she asked.

I shook my head. My design changed from day to day.

She looked at her man's silver pocket watch, closed the damper[5] of the range, and prepared to leave. She checked that all the wall cupboards were locked by running her hand over them.

"Sister," I called, gathering enough courage at last—we must have some secret, something to join us together—"what colour hair have you?"

We never saw the nuns' hair, or their eyebrows, or ears, as all that part was covered by a stiff white wimple.[6]

"You shouldn't ask such a thing," she said, getting pink in the face, and then she turned back and whispered, "I'll tell you on your last day here, provided your geometry has improved."

She had scarcely gone when Baba, who had been lurking behind some pillar, stuck her head in the door and said, "Christsake, save me a bit." She finished the second pastry, then went around looking in kitchen drawers. Because of everything being locked, she found only some castor sugar in a china shaker. She ate a little and threw the remainder into the dying fire, so that it flared up for a minute with a yellow spluttering flame. Baba showed her jealousy by putting it around the school that I was in the cookery kitchen every evening, gorging cakes with Sister Imelda and telling tales.

I did not speak to Sister Imelda again in private until the evening of our Christmas theatricals. She came to help us put on makeup and get into our stage clothes and fancy headgear. These clothes were kept in a trunk from one year to the next, and though sumptuous and strewn with braiding and gold, they smelled of camphor.[7] Yet as we donned them we felt different, and as we sponged pancake makeup onto our faces, we became saucy and emphasized these new guises by adding dark pencil to the eyes and making the lips bright carmine. There was only one tube of lipstick and each girl clamoured for it. The evening's entertainment was to comprise scenes from Shakespeare and laughing sketches. I had been chosen to recite Mark Antony's lament over Caesar's body,[8] and for this I was to wear a purple toga,[9] white knee-length socks, and patent buckle shoes. The shoes were too big and I moved in them as if in clogs. She said to take them off, to go barefoot. I realised that I was getting nervous and that in an effort to memorize my speech, the words were getting all askew and flying about in my head, like the separate pieces of a jigsaw puzzle. She sensed my panic and very slowly put her hand on my face and enjoined me to look at her. I looked into her eyes, which seemed fathomless, and saw that she was willing me to be calm and obliging me to be master of my fears, and I little knew that one day she would have to do the same as regards the swoop of my feelings for her. As we continued to stare I felt myself becoming calm and the words were restored to me in their right and fluent order. The lights were being lowered out in the recreation hall, and we knew now that all the nuns had arrived, had settled

5. Lever regulating the draft in a coal-burning kitchen stove.
6. Headdress, usually of linen.
7. Acrid-smelling substance used to keep moths and insects from stored clothes.
8. From *Julius Caesar* 3.2.73–107.
9. Long and flowing robe worn by Roman citizens in time of peace.

themselves down, and were eagerly awaiting this annual hotchpotch of amateur entertainment. There was that fearsome hush as the hall went dark and the few spotlights were turned on. She kissed her crucifix and I realised that she was saying a prayer for me. Then she raised her arm as if depicting the stance of a Greek goddess; walking onto the stage, I was fired by her ardour.

Baba could say that I bawled like a bloody bull, but Sister Imelda, who stood in the wings, said that temporarily she had felt the streets of Rome, had seen the corpse of Caesar, as I delivered those poignant, distempered lines. When I came off stage she put her arms around me and I was encased in a shower of silent kisses. After we had taken down the decorations and put the fancy clothes back in the trunk, I gave her two half-pound boxes of chocolates—bought for me illicitly by one of the day girls—and she gave me a casket made from the insides of match boxes and covered over with gilt paint and gold dust. It was like holding moths and finding their powder adhering to the fingers.

"What will you do on Christmas Day, Sister?" I said.

"I'll pray for you," she said.

It was useless to say, "Will you have turkey?" or "Will you have plum pudding?" or "Will you loll in bed?" because I believed that Christmas Day would be as bleak and deprived as any other day in her life. Yet she was radiant as if such austerity was joyful. Maybe she was basking in some secret realization involving her and me.

On the cold snowy afternoon three weeks later when we returned from our holidays, Sister Imelda came up to the dormitory to welcome me back. All the other girls had gone down to the recreation hall to do barn dances and I could hear someone banging on the piano. I did not want to go down and clump around with sixty other girls, having nothing to look forward to, only tea and the Rosary and early bed. The beds were damp after our stay at home, and when I put my hand between the sheets, it was like feeling dew but did not have the freshness of outdoors. What depressed me further was that I had seen a mouse in one of the cupboards, seen its tail curl with terror as it slipped away into a crevice. If there was one mouse, there were God knows how many, and the cakes we hid in secret would not be safe. I was still unpacking as she came down the narrow passage between the rows of iron beds and I saw in her walk such agitation.

"Tut, tut, tut, you've curled your hair," she said, offended.

Yes, the world outside was somehow declared in this perm, and for a second I remembered the scalding pains the trickles of ammonia dribbled down my forehead and then the joy as the hairdresser said that she would make me look like Movita, a Mexican star. Now suddenly that world and those aspirations seemed trite and I wanted to take a brush and straighten my hair and revert to the dark gawky sombre girl that I had been. I offered her iced queen cakes that my mother had made, but she refused them and said she could only stay a second. She lent me a notebook of hers, which she had had as a pupil, and into which she had copied favourite quotations, some religious, some not. I read at random:

> Twice or thrice had I loved thee,
> Before I knew thy face or name.

> So in a voice, so in a shapeless flame,
> Angels affect us oft . . . .[1]

"Are you well?" I asked.

She looked pale. It may have been the day, which was wretched and grey with sleet, or it may have been the white bedspreads, but she appeared to be ailing.

"I missed you," she said.

"Me too," I said.

At home, gorging, eating trifle at all hours, even for breakfast, having little ratafias[2] to dip in cups of tea, fitting on new shoes and silk stockings, I wished that she could be with us, enjoying the fire and the freedom.

"You know it is not proper for us to be so friendly."

"It's not wrong," I said.

I dreaded that she might decide to turn away from me, that she might stamp on our love and might suddenly draw a curtain over it, a black crepe curtain that would denote its death. I dreaded it and knew it was going to happen.

"We must not become attached," she said, and I could not say we already were, no more than I could remind her of the day of the revels and the intimacy between us. Convents were dungeons and no doubt about it.

From then on she treated me as less of a favourite. She said my name sharply in class, and once she said if I must cough, could I wait until class had finished. Baba was delighted, as were the other girls, because they were glad to see me receding in her eyes. Yet I knew that the crispness was part of her love, because no matter how callously she looked at me, she would occasionally soften. Reading her notebook helped me, and I copied out her quotations into my own book, trying as accurately as possible to imitate her handwriting.

But some little time later when she came to supervise our study one evening, I got a smile from her as she sat on the rostrum looking down at us all. I continued to look up at her and by slight frowning indicated that I had a problem with my geometry. She beckoned to me lightly and I went up, bringing my copybook and the pen. Standing close to her, and also because her wimple was crooked, I saw one of her eyebrows for the first time. She saw that I noticed it and said did that satisfy my curiosity. I said not really. She said what else did I want to see, her swan's neck perhaps, and I went scarlet. I was amazed that she would say such a thing in the hearing of other girls, and then she said a worse thing, she said that G. K. Chesterton[3] was very forgetful and had once put on his trousers backward. She expected me to laugh. I was so close to her that a rumble in her stomach seemed to be taking place in my own, and about this she also laughed. It occurred to me for one terrible moment that maybe she had decided to leave the convent, to jump over the wall. Having done the theorem for me, she marked it "100 out of 100" and then asked if I had any other problems. My eyes filled with tears, I wanted her to realise that her recent coolness had wrought havoc with my nerves and my peace of mind.

"What is it?" she said.

---

1. John Donne, *Air and Angels,* lines 1–4.
2. Flavored cake or biscuit.
3. English Catholic essayist, critic, novelist, and poet (1874–1936).

I could cry, or I could tremble to try to convey the emotion, but I could not tell her. As if on cue, the Mother Superior came in and saw this glaring intimacy and frowned as she approached the rostrum.

"Would you please go back to your desk," she said, "and in future kindly allow Sister Imelda to get on with her duties."

I tiptoed back and sat with head down, bursting with fear and shame. Then she looked at a tray on which the milk cups were laid, and finding one cup of milk untouched, she asked which girl had not drunk her milk.

"Me, sister," I said, and I was called up to drink it and stand under the clock as a punishment. The milk was tepid and dusty, and I thought of cows on the fairs days at home and the farmers hitting them as they slid and slithered over the muddy streets.

For weeks I tried to see my nun in private; I even lurked outside doors where I knew she was due, only to be rebuffed again and again. I suspected the Mother Superior had warned her against making a favourite of me. But I still clung to a belief that a bond existed between us and that her coldness and even some glares which I had received were a charade, a mask. I would wonder how she felt alone in bed and what way she slept and if she thought of me, or refusing to think of me, if she dreamed of me as I did of her. She certainly got thinner, because her nun's silver ring slipped easily and sometimes unavoidably off her marriage finger. It occurred to me that she was having a nervous breakdown.

One day in March the sun came out, the radiators were turned off, and, though there was a lashing wind, we were told that officially spring had arrived and that we could play games. We all trooped up to the games field and, to our surprise, saw that Sister Imelda was officiating that day. The daffodils in the field tossed and turned; they were a very bright shocking yellow, but they were not as fetching as the little timid snowdrops that trembled in the wind. We played rounders,[4] and when my turn came to hit the ball with the long wooden pound, I crumbled and missed, fearing that the ball could hit me.

"Champ . . ." said Baba, jeering.

After three such failures Sister Imelda said that if I liked I could sit and watch, and when I was sitting in the greenhouse swallowing my shame, she came in and said that I must not give way to tears, because humiliation was the greatest test of Christ's love, or indeed *any* love.

"When you are a nun you will know that," she said, and instantly I made up my mind that I would be a nun and that though we might never be free to express our feelings, we would be under the same roof, in the same cloister, in mental and spiritual conjunction all our lives.

"Is it very hard at first?" I said.

"It's awful," she said, and she slipped a little medal into my gym-frock pocket. It was warm from being in her pocket, and as I held it, I knew that once again we were near and that in fact we had never severed. Walking down from the playing field to our Sunday lunch of mutton and cabbage, everyone chattered to Sister Imelda. The girls milled around her, linking her, trying to hold her hand, counting the various keys on her bunch of keys, and asking impudent questions.

---

4. Game, very like baseball, played in England mainly by girls.

"Sister, did you ever ride a motorbicycle?"

"Sister, did you ever wear seamless stockings?"

"Sister, who's your favourite film star—male?"

"Sister, what's your favourite food?"

"Sister, if you had a wish, what would it be?"

"Sister, what do you do when you want to scratch your head?"

Yes, she had ridden a motorbicycle, and she had worn silk stockings, but they were seamed. She liked bananas best, and if she had a wish, it would be to go home for a few hours to see her parents and her brother.

That afternoon as we walked through the town, the sight of closed shops with porter[5] barrels outside and mongrel dogs did not dispel my refound ecstasy. The medal was in my pocket, and every other second I would touch it for confirmation. Baba saw a Swiss roll in a confectioner's window laid on a doily and dusted with castor sugar, and it made her cry out with hunger and rail against being in a bloody reformatory, surrounded by drips and mopes. On impulse she took her nail file out of her pocket and dashed across to the window to see if she could cut the glass. The prefect[6] rushed up from the back of the line and asked Baba if she wanted to be locked up.

"I am anyhow," Baba said, and sawed at one of her nails, to maintain her independence and vent her spleen. Baba was the only girl who could stand up to a prefect. When she felt like it, she dropped out of a walk, sat on a stone wall, and waited until we all came back. She said that if there was one thing more boring than studying it was walking. She used to roll down her stockings and examine her calves and say that she could see varicose veins coming from this bloody daily walk. Her legs, like all our legs, were black from the dye of the stockings; we were forbidden to bathe, because baths were immoral. We washed each night in an enamel basin beside our beds. When girls splashed cold water onto their chests, they let out cries, though this was forbidden.

After the walk we wrote home. We were allowed to write home once a week; our letters were always censored. I told my mother that I had made up my mind to be a nun, and asked if she could send me bananas when a batch arrived at our local grocery shop. That evening, perhaps as I wrote to my mother on the ruled white paper, a telegram arrived which said that Sister Imelda's brother had been killed in a van while on his way home from a hurling[7] match. The Mother Superior announced it, and asked us to pray for his soul and write letters of sympathy to Sister Imelda's parents. We all wrote identical letters, because in our first year at school we had been given specimen letters for various occasions, and we all referred back to our specimen letter of sympathy.

Next day the town hire-car drove up to the convent, and Sister Imelda, accompanied by another nun, went home for the funeral. She looked as white as a sheet, with eyes swollen, and she wore a heavy knitted shawl over her shoulders. Although she came back that night (I stayed awake to hear the car), we did not see her for a whole week, except to catch a glimpse of her back, in the chapel. When she resumed class, she was peaky and distant, making no reference at all to her recent tragedy.

The day the bananas came I waited outside the door and gave her a bunch

---

5. Beer.
6. Senior pupil authorized to maintain discipline.

7. Game, having similarities with hockey and lacrosse, played in Ireland.

wrapped in tissue paper. Some were still a little green, and she said that Mother Superior would put them in the glasshouse to ripen. I felt that Sister Imelda would never taste them; they would be kept for a visiting priest or bishop.

"Oh, Sister, I'm sorry about your brother," I said in a burst.

"It will come to us all, sooner or later," Sister Imelda said dolefully.

I dared to touch her wrist to communicate my sadness. She went quickly, probably for fear of breaking down. At times she grew irritable and had a boil on her cheek. She missed some classes and was replaced in the cookery kitchen by a younger nun. She asked me to pray for her brother's soul and to avoid seeing her alone. Each time as she came down a corridor toward me, I was obliged to turn the other way. Now Baba or some other girl moved the blackboard two pegs higher and spread her shawl, when wet, over the radiator to dry.

I got flu and was put to bed. Sickness took the same bleak course, a cup of hot senna[8] delivered in person by the head nun, who stood there while I drank it, tea at lunchtime with thin slices of brown bread (because it was just after the war,[9] food was still rationed, so the butter was mixed with lard and had white streaks running through it and a faintly rancid smell), hours of just lying there surveying the empty dormitory, the empty iron beds with white counterpanes on each one, and metal crucifixes laid on each white, frilled pillow slip. I knew that she would miss me and hoped that Baba would tell her where I was. I counted the number of tiles from the ceiling to the head of my bed, thought of my mother at home on the farm mixing hen food, thought of my father, losing his temper perhaps and stamping on the kitchen floor with nailed boots, and I recalled the money owing for my school fees and hoped that Sister Imelda would never get to hear of it. During the Christmas holiday I had seen a bill sent by the head nun to my father which said, "Please remit this week without fail." I hated being in bed causing extra trouble and therefore reminding the head nun of the unpaid liability. We had no clock in the dormitory, so there was no way of guessing the time, but the hours dragged.

Marigold, one of the maids, came to take off the counterpanes at five and brought with her two gifts from Sister Imelda—an orange and a pencil sharpener. I kept the orange peel in my hand, smelling it, and planning how I would thank her. Thinking of her I fell into a feverish sleep and was wakened when the girls came to bed at ten and switched on the various ceiling lights.

At Easter Sister Imelda warned me not to give her chocolates, so I got her a flashlamp instead and spare batteries. Pleased with such a useful gift (perhaps she read her letters in bed), she put her arms around me and allowed one cheek to adhere but not to make the sound of a kiss. It made up for the seven weeks of withdrawal, and as I drove down the convent drive with Baba, she waved to me, as she had promised, from the window of her cell.

In the last term at school, studying was intensive because of the examinations which loomed at the end of June. Like all the other nuns, Sister Imelda thought only of these examinations. She crammed us with knowledge, lost her temper every other day, and gritted her teeth whenever the blackboard was too greasy to take the imprint of the chalk. If ever I met her

---

8. Laxative. 9. World War II.

in the corridor, she asked if I knew such and such a thing, and coming down from Sunday games, she went over various questions with us. The fateful examination day arrived and we sat at single desks supervised by some strange woman from Dublin. Opening a locked trunk, she took out the pink examination papers and distributed them around. Geometry was on the fourth day. When we came out from it, Sister Imelda was in the hall with all the answers, so that we could compare our answers with hers. Then she called me aside and we went up toward the cookery kitchen and sat on the stairs while she went over the paper with me, question for question. I knew that I had three right and two wrong, but did not tell her so.

"It is black," she said then, rather suddenly. I thought she meant the dark light where we were sitting.

"It's cool, though," I said.

Summer had come; our white skins baked under the heavy uniform, and dark violet pansies bloomed in the convent grounds. She looked well again, and her pale skin was once more unblemished.

"My hair," she whispered, "is black." And she told me how she had spent her last night before entering the convent. She had gone cycling with a boy and ridden for miles, and they'd lost their way up a mountain, and she became afraid she would be so late home that she would sleep it out the next morning. It was understood between us that I was going to enter the convent in September and that I could have a last fling, too.

Two days later we prepared to go home. There were farewells and outlandish promises, and autograph books signed, and girls trudging up the recreation hall, their cases bursting open with clothes and books. Baba scattered biscuit crumbs in the dormitory for the mice and stuffed all her prayer books under a mattress. Her father promised to collect us at four. I had arranged with Sister Imelda secretly that I would meet her in one of the summerhouses around the walks, where we would spend our last half hour together. I expected that she would tell me something of what my life as a postulant would be like. But Baba's father came an hour early. He had something urgent to do later and came at three instead. All I could do was ask Marigold to take a note to Sister Imelda.

> Remembrance is all I ask,
> But if remembrance should prove a task,
> Forget me.

I hated Baba, hated her busy father, hated the thought of my mother standing in the doorway in her good dress, welcoming me home at last. I would have become a nun that minute if I could.

I wrote to my nun that night and again the next day and then every week for a month. Her letters were censored, so I tried to convey my feelings indirectly. In one of her letters to me (they were allowed one letter a month) she said that she looked forward to seeing me in September. But by September Baba and I had left for the university in Dublin. I stopped writing to Sister Imelda then, reluctant to tell her that I no longer wished to be a nun.

In Dublin we enrolled at the college where she had surpassed herself. I saw her maiden name on a list, for having graduated with special honours, and for days was again sad and remorseful. I rushed out and bought batteries for the flashlamp I'd given her, and posted them without any note enclosed. No mention of my missing vocation, no mention of why I had stopped writing.

One Sunday about two years later, Baba and I were going out to Howth on a bus. Baba had met some businessmen who played golf there and she had done a lot of scheming to get us invited out. The bus was packed, mostly mothers with babies and children on their way to Dollymount Strand.[1] We drove along the coast road and saw the sea, bright green and glinting in the sun, and because of the way the water was carved up into millions of little wavelets, its surface seemed like an endless heap of dark-green broken bottles. Near the shore the sand looked warm and was biscuit-coloured. We never swam or sunbathed, we never did anything that was good for us. Life was geared to work and to meeting men, and yet one knew that mating could only lead to one's being a mother and hawking obstreperous children out to the seaside on Sunday. "They know not what they do" could surely be said of us.

We were very made up; even the conductor seemed to disapprove and snapped at having to give change of ten shillings. For no reason at all I thought of our makeup rituals before the school play and how innocent it was in comparison, because now our skins were smothered beneath layers of it and we never took it off at night. Thinking of the convent, I suddenly thought of Sister Imelda, and then, as if prey to a dream, I heard the rustle of serge,[2] smelled the Jeyes Fluid and the boiled cabbage, and saw her pale shocked face in the months after her brother died. Then I looked around and saw her in earnest, and at first thought I was imagining things. But no, she had got on accompanied by another nun and they were settling themselves in the back seat nearest the door. She looked older, but she had the same aloof quality and the same eyes, and my heart began to race with a mixture of excitement and dread. At first it raced with a prodigal strength, and then it began to falter and I thought it was going to give out. My fear of her and my love came back in one fell realisation. I would have gone through the window except that it was not wide enough. The thing was how to escape her. Baba gurgled with delight, stood up, and in the most flagrant way looked around to make sure that it was Imelda. She recognised the other nun as one with the nickname of Johnny who taught piano lessons. Baba's first thought was revenge, as she enumerated the punishments they had meted out to us and said how nice it would be to go back and shock them and say, "Mud in your eye, Sisters," or "Get lost," or something worse. Baba could not understand why I was quaking, no more than she could understand why I began to wipe off the lipstick. Above all, I knew that I could not confront them.

"You're going to have to," Baba said.

"I can't," I said.

It was not just my attire; it was the fact of my never having written and of my broken promise. Baba kept looking back and said they weren't saying a word and that children were gawking at them. It wasn't often that nuns travelled in buses, and we speculated as to where they might be going.

"They might be off to meet two fellows," Baba said, and visualised them in the golf club getting blotto and hoisting up their skirts. For me it was no

---

1. A beach in Dublin.   2. Woolen fabric.

laughing matter. She came up with a strategy: it was that as we approached our stop and the bus was still moving, I was to jump up and go down the aisle and pass them without even looking. She said most likely they would not notice us, as their eyes were lowered and they seemed to be praying.

"I can't run down the bus," I said. There was a matter of shaking limbs and already a terrible vertigo.

"You're going to," Baba said, and though insisting that I couldn't, I had already begun to rehearse an apology. While doing this, I kept blessing myself over and over again, and Baba kept reminding me that there was only one more stop before ours. When the dreadful moment came, I jumped up and put on my face what can only be called an apology of a smile. I followed Baba to the rear of the bus. But already they had gone. I saw the back of their two sable, identical figures with their veils being blown wildly about in the wind. They looked so cold and lost as they hurried along the pavement and I wanted to run after them. In some way I felt worse than if I had confronted them. I cannot be certain what I would have said. I knew that there is something sad and faintly distasteful about love's ending, particularly love that has never been fully realized. I might have hinted at that, but I doubt it. In our deepest moments we say the most inadequate things.

1981

FLEUR ADCOCK
b.1934

Kareen Fleur Adcock was born in Papakura, New Zealand, and was educated at Victoria University in Wellington. Twice briefly married and the mother of two children, she has worked mainly as a librarian, first in New Zealand and then in London, where she joined the Foreign and Commonwealth Office in 1963. The following year, her first book of poems, *The Eye of the Hurricane,* was published. Her *Selected Poems* (1983) drew on that and four other collections, and she has since published four others—*The Incident Book* (1986), *Meeting the Comet* (1988), *Time Zones* (1991), and *Looking Back* (1997)—as well as three anthologies and two books of translations. One of a growing number of Commonwealth poets whose work is enriching English literature, Adcock simultaneously reflects the decorum and distanced violence of life in the predominantly white former Dominions. Her poetic voice is at once soft-spoken—traditional, even, on occasions, old-fashioned—and outspoken, especially on sexual matters. Much of the voltage of her best poems is generated by the opposition of these two poles, frequently in situations involving the juxtaposition of a calm daylight world and a dark dream in which "something angry, or nightmarish, or discomforting leaps out."

The Ex-Queen Among the Astronomers

They serve revolving saucer eyes,
dishes of stars; they wait upon

huge lenses hung aloft to frame
the slow procession of the skies.

5   They calculate, adjust, record,
watch transits, measure distances.
They carry pocket telescopes
to spy through when they walk abroad.

Spectra[1] possess their eyes; they face
10 upwards, alert for meteorites,
cherishing little glassy worlds:
receptacles for outer space.

But she, exile, expelled, ex-queen,
swishes among the men of science
15 waiting for cloudy skies, for nights
when constellations can't be seen.

She wears the rings he let her keep;
she walks as she was taught to walk
for his approval, years ago.
20 His bitter features taunt her sleep.

And so when these have laid aside
their telescopes, when lids are closed
between machine and sky, she seeks
terrestrial bodies to bestride.

25 She plucks this one or that among
the astronomers, and is become
his canopy, his occultation;[2]
she sucks at earlobe, penis, tongue

mouthing the tubes of flesh; her hair
30 crackles, her eyes are comet-sparks.
She brings the distant briefly close
above his dreamy abstract stare.

1979

Poem Ended by a Death

They will wash all my kisses and fingerprints off you
and my tearstains—I was more inclined to weep
in those wild-garlicky days—and our happier stains,
thin scales of papery silk . . . Fuck that for a cheap
5 opener; and false too—any such traces
you pumiced away yourself, those years ago

---

1. Images retained for a time on the retina of the eye when turned away after gazing fixedly at bright objects.
2. Concealment of a heavenly body behind the body of the earth.

when you sent my letters back, in the week I married
that anecdotal ape. So start again. So:

They will remove the tubes and drips and dressings
10 which I censor from my dreams. They will, it is true,
wash you; and they will put you into a box.
After which whatever else they may do
won't matter. This is my laconic style.
You praised it, as I praised your intricate pearled
15 embroideries; these links laced us together,
plain and purl across the ribs of the world . . .

1979

The Soho Hospital for Women

1

Strange room, from this angle:
white door open before me,
strange bed, mechanical hum, white lights.
There will be stranger rooms to come.

5 As I almost slept I saw the deep flower opening
and leaned over into it, gratefully.
It swimmingly closed in my face. I was not ready.
It was not death, it was acceptance.

•

Our thin patient cat died purring,
10 her small triangular head tilted back,
the nurse's fingers caressing her throat,
my hand on her shrunken spine; the quick needle.

That was the second death by cancer.
The first is not for me to speak of.
15 It was telephone calls and brave letters
and a friend's hand bleeding under the coffin.

•

Doctor, I am not afraid of a word.
But neither do I wish to embrace that visitor,
to engulf it as Hine-Nui-te-Po
20 engulfed Maui;[1] that would be the way of it.

And she was the winner there: her womb crushed him.
Goddesses can do these things.
But I have admitted the gloved hands and the speculum[2]
and must part my ordinary legs to the surgeon's knife.

1. Supernatural hero in Polynesian mythology,
Maui the sun-snarer, fire-stealer, monster-slayer,
entered the womb of Hine, sleeping goddess of the
underworld, in search of immortality. He intended
to depart through her mouth, but when his bird

companion laughed at the sight, Hine awoke and
crushed Maui to death.
2. Surgical instrument for dilating orifices of the
body to facilitate examination or operation.

2

25 Nellie has only one breast
    ample enough to make several.
    Her quilted dressing-gown softens
    to semi-doubtful this imbalance
    and there's no starched vanity
30 in our abundant ward-mother:
    her silvery hair's in braids, her slippers
    loll, her weathered smile holds true.
    When she dresses up in her black
    with her glittering marcasite brooch on
35 to go for the weekly radium treatment
    she's the bright star of the taxi-party—
    whatever may be growing under her ribs.

                                           •

    Doris hardly smokes in the ward—
    and hardly eats more than a dreamy spoonful—
40 but the corridors and bathrooms
    reek of her Players Number 10,
    and the drug-trolley pauses
    for long minutes by her bed.
    Each week for the taxi-outing
45 she puts on her skirt again
    and has to pin the slack waistband
    more tightly over her scarlet sweater.
    Her face, a white shadow through smoked glass,
    lets Soho display itself unregarded.

                                           •

50 Third in the car is Mrs Golding
    who never smiles. And why should she?

3

    The senior consultant on his rounds
    murmurs in so subdued a voice
    to the students marshalled behind
55 that they gather in, forming a cell,
    a cluster, a rosette around him
    as he stands at the foot of my bed
    going through my notes with them,
    half-audibly instructive, grave.

60 The slight ache as I strain forward
    to listen still seems imagined.

    Then he turns his practised smile on me:
    "How are you this morning?" "Fine,
    very well, thank you." I smile too.
65 And possibly all that murmurs within me
    is the slow dissolving of stitches.

4

I am out in the supermarket choosing—
this very afternoon, this day—
picking up tomatoes, cheese, bread,

70 things I want and shall be using
to make myself a meal, while they
eat their stodgy suppers in bed:

Janet with her big freckled breasts,
her prim Scots voice, her one friend,
75 and never in hospital before,

who came in to have a few tests
and now can't see where they'll end;
and Coral in the bed by the door

who whimpered and gasped behind a screen
80 with nurses to and fro all night
and far too much of the day;

pallid, bewildered, nineteen.
And Mary, who will be all right
but gradually. And Alice, who may.

85 Whereas I stand almost intact,
giddy with freedom, not with pain.
I lift my light basket, observing

how little I needed in fact;
and move to the checkout, to the rain,
90 to the lights and the long street curving.

1979

TONY HARRISON
b. 1937

Tony Harrison is a true (in the double sense of genuine and faithful) working-class poet. He was born in Leeds and educated at its grammar school and university, where he studied classics. As a lecturer in English at Ahmadu Bello University in northern Nigeria, he translated (with fellow poet James Simmons) Aristophanes' *Lysistrata* into the pidgin English of the Hausa people while, at the same time, writing poems in the voices of working-class British expatriates. He is a free-lance poet, who has been resident dramatist at the National Theatre in London and has undertaken commissions for the Metropolitan Opera in New York.

Like Philip Larkin and Geoffrey Hill, Harrison has a strong sense of history, but his perspective is more political and his politics are the politics of the exploited and oppressed. His poems give speech to the speechless—the two uncles of *Heredity*, a bereaved father unable to articulate his grief, a terrified convict—exposing their predicaments with passion and indignation. Printed here are seven "sonnets," as Harrison (following the example of George Meredith's *Modern Love*) calls his sixteen-line poems, from a long work in progress called *The School of Eloquence*. Each is a small stage on which he brings himself and the dead dramatically to life, as on the larger stage of the British National Theatre he has given new life to Old Masters in his verse adaptations of Molière's *The Misanthrope* (1973), Racine's *Phèdre* (*Phaedra Britannica* 1975), and Aeschylus' *The Oresteia* (1981). The filmed version of his poem *v.* won the Royal Television Society's Award for 1987, and his film *Black Daisies for the Bride* won the Prix Italia in 1994.

Heredity

How you became a poet's a mystery!
Wherever did you get your talent from?

I say: I had two uncles, Joe and Harry—
one was a stammerer, the other dumb.

1978

National Trust[1]

Bottomless pits. There's one in Castleton,[2]
and stout upholders of our law and order
one day thought its depth worth wagering on
and borrowed a convict hush-hush from his warder
5 and winched him down; and back, flayed, grey, mad, dumb.

Not even a good flogging made him holler!

O gentlemen, a better way to plumb
the depths of Britain's dangling a scholar,
say, here at the booming shaft at Towanroath,[3]
10 now National Trust, a place where they got tin,
those gentlemen who silenced the men's oath
and killed the language that they swore it in.

The dumb go down in history and disappear
and not one gentleman's been brought to book:

15 *Mes den hep tavas a-gollas y dyr*

(Cornish)—
            "the tongueless man gets his land took."

1978

---

1. A British association to preserve places of natural beauty or buildings of architectural or historical importance.
2. In the Derby coalfields.
3. A tin mine in Cornwall.

Book Ends

I

Baked the day she suddenly dropped dead
we chew it slowly that last apple pie.

Shocked into sleeplessness you're scared of bed.
We never could talk much, and now don't try.

5 *You're like book ends, the pair of you,* she'd say,
Hog that grate, say nothing, sit, sleep, stare . . .

The "scholar" me, you, worn out on poor pay,
only our silence made us seem a pair.

Not as good for staring in, blue gas,
10 too regular each bud, each yellow spike.

A night you need my company to pass
and she not here to tell us we're alike!

Your life's all shattered into smithereens.

Back in our silences and sullen looks,
15 for all the Scotch we drink, what's still between's
not the thirty or so years, but books, books, books.

1978

II

The stone's too full. The wording must be terse.
There's scarcely room to carve the FLORENCE on it—

Come on, it's not as if we're wanting verse.
It's not as if we're wanting a whole sonnet!

5 After tumblers of neat *Johnny Walker*
(I think that both of us were on our third)

you said you'd always been a clumsy talker
and couldn't find another, shorter word
for "beloved" or for "wife" in the inscription,
10 but not too clumsy that you can't still cut:

You're supposed to be the bright boy at description
and you can't tell them what the fuck to put!

I've got to find the right words on my own.

I've got the envelope that he'd been scrawling,
15   mis-spelt, mawkish, stylistically appalling
but I can't squeeze more love into their stone.

1981

Long Distance

I

Your bed's got two wrong sides. Your life's all grouse.°   *grumble*
I let your phone-call take its dismal course:

Ah can't stand it no more, this empty house!

Carrots choke us wi'out your mam's white sauce!

5   *Them sweets you brought me, you can have 'em back.*
Ah'm diabetic now. Got all the facts.
(The diabetes comes hard on the track
of two coronaries and cataracts.)

Ah've allus liked things sweet! But now ah push
10   *food down mi throat! Ah'd sooner do wi'out.*
And t'only reason now for beer 's to flush
(so t'dietician said) mi kidneys out.

When I come round, they'll be laid out, the sweets,
Lifesavers, my father's New World treats,
15   still in the big brown bag, and only bought
rushing through JFK[1] as a last thought.

1981

II

Though my mother was already two years dead
Dad kept her slippers warming by the gas,
put hot water bottles her side of the bed
and still went to renew her transport pass.

5   You couldn't just drop in. You had to phone.
He'd put you off an hour to give him time
to clear away her things and look alone
as though his still raw love were such a crime.

He couldn't risk my blight of disbelief
10   though sure that very soon he'd hear her key
scrape in the rusted lock and end his grief.
He *knew* she'd just popped out to get the tea.

---

1. A New York airport.

I believe life ends with death, and that is all.
You haven't both gone shopping; just the same,
15   in my new black leather phone book there's your name
and the disconnected number I still call.

1981

Turns

I thought it made me look more "working class"
(as if a bit of chequered cloth could bridge that gap!)
I did a turn in it before the glass.
My mother said: *It suits you, your dad's cap.*
5   (She preferred me to wear suits and part my hair:
You're every bit as good as that lot are!)

All the pension queue[1] came out to stare.
Dad was sprawled beside the postbox (still VR),[2]
his cap turned inside up beside his head,
10   smudged H A H in purple Indian ink
and Brylcreem slicks displayed so folk might think
he wanted charity for dropping dead.

He never begged. For nowt!° Death's reticence   *nothing*
crowns his life's, and *me*, I'm opening my trap
15   to busk[3] the class that broke him for the pence
that splash like brackish tears into our cap.

1981

Marked with D.[1]

When the chilled dough of his flesh went in an oven
not unlike those he fuelled all his life,
I thought of his cataracts ablaze with Heaven
and radiant with the sight of his dead wife,
5   light streaming from his mouth to shape her name,
"not Florence and not Flo but always Florrie."
I thought how his cold tongue burst into flame
but only literally, which makes me sorry,
sorry for his sake there's no Heaven to reach.
10   I get it all from Earth my daily bread
but he hungered for release from mortal speech
that kept him down, the tongue that weighed like lead.

---

1. Line of retired people waiting for their pension (social security) payments.
2. Sidewalk mailbox dating from the reign of Queen Victoria and carrying the initials of her name and Latin title: Victoria Regina.
3. Take around the hat; i.e., solicit money for street entertainment (from members of the middle class, in this case).

1. Cf. the anonymous nursery rhyme: "Pat-a-cake, pat-a-cake, baker's man / Bake me a cake as fast as you can/ Pat it and prick it, and mark it with B, / Put it in the oven for baby and me."

The baker's man that no-one will see rise
and England made to feel like some dull oaf
15   is smoke, enough to sting one person's eyes
and ash (not unlike flour) for one small loaf.

1981

ANITA DESAI
b. 1937

The daughter of a Bengali father and a German mother, Anita Desai was born in Musoori, northern India, in 1937, and went to school and university in Delhi. Her background and upbringing have given her a bifocal vision of India, enabling her to paint a complex portrait of richness and squalor, of a present infused with the legacy of the past, through both Indian and foreign eyes. The author of a short story collection and eight novels, including *Fire on the Mountain* (1977), *Clear Light of Day* (1980), and *In Custody* (1984), Desai has become a leading voice in what is now regarded as a literary renaissance in contemporary India.

The critic Bruce King has said that Desai writes "novels about what men do and novels about what women feel." Her men are sharply and often satirically observed, like David, the scholar of her story printed here; but her specialty is the unfolding of middle-class women's lives as they come to terms with, and sometimes overcome, the constrictions and handicaps of a male-dominated society. Her novels and stories alike focus on a life at a crucial stage and, as both a skilled architect of narrative structures and an accomplished stylist, she has a particular gift for showing the transformation of that life. So Pat, the American gypsy of *Scholar and Gypsy*, escaping from the heat and horrors of Bombay, finds in the hills not only a rural landscape more congenial than the congested city but an inner strength and spiritual life she could not have imagined before. In a countermovement of elegant chiasmus (a rhetorical figure derived from the Greek term for the letter X, or a cross-over), the scholar loses his way as the gypsy finds hers. The economy of this double transformation is typical of Desai's mature work, which manages to present a tragic vision of difficult lives within a literary topography that incorporates both comedy and a biting critique of human limitation.

Scholar and Gypsy

Her first day in Bombay wilted her. If she stepped out of the air-conditioned hotel room, she drooped, her head hung, her eyes glazed, she felt faint. Once she was back in it, she fell across her bed as though she had been struck by calamity, was extinguished, and could barely bring herself to believe that she had, after all, survived. Sweating, it seemed to her that life, energy, hope were all seeping out of her, flowing down a drain, gurgling ironically.

'But you knew it would be hot,' David said, not being able to help a sense of disappointment in her. He had bought himself crisp bush-shirts of madras cotton and open Kolhapur sandals. He was drinking more than was his habit, it was true, but it did not seem to redden and coarsen him as it did her. He looked so right, so fitting on the Bombay streets, striding over the coconut shells and betel-stained[1] papers and the fish scales and lepers' stumps. 'You could hardly come to India and expect it to be cool, Pat.'

'Hot, yes,' she moaned, 'but not—not *killing*. Not so like death. I feel half-dead, David, sometimes *quite* dead.'

'Shall we go and have a gin-and-lime in the bar?'

She tried that since it seemed to do him so much good. But the bar in the hotel was so crowded, the people there were so large and vital and forceful in their brilliant clothes and with their metallic voices and their eyes that flashed over her like barbers' shears, cutting and exposing, that she felt crushed rather than revived.

David attracted people like a magnet—with his charm, his nonchalance, his grace, he did it so well, so smoothly, his qualities worked more efficiently than any visiting card system—and they started going to parties. It began to seem to her that this was the chief occupation of people in Bombay—going to parties. She was always on the point of collapse when she arrived at one: the taxi invariably stank, the driver's hair dripped oil, and then the sights and scenes they passed on the streets, the congestion and racket of the varied traffic, the virulent cinema posters, the blazing colours of women's clothing, the profusion of toys and decorations of coloured paper and tinsel, the radios and loudspeakers never tuned to less than top volume, and amongst them flower sellers, pilgrims, dancing monkeys and performing bears . . . that there should be such poverty, such disease, such filth, and that out of it boiled so much vitality, such irrepressible life, seemed to her unnatural and sinister—it was as if chaos and evil triumphed over reason and order. Then the parties they went to were all very large ones. The guests all wore brilliant clothes and jewellery, and their eyes and teeth flashed with such primitive lust as they eyed her slim, white-sheathed blonde self, that the sensation of being caught up and crushed, crowded in and choked sent her into corners where their knees pushed into her, their hands slid over her back, their voices bored into her, so that when she got back to the hotel, on David's arm, she was more like a corpse than an American globe-trotter.

Folding her arms about her, she muttered at the window, 'I never expected them to be so primitive. I thought it would all be modern, up-to-date. Not this—this wild jungle stuff.'

He was pouring himself a night-cap and splashed it in genuine surprise. 'What do you mean? We've only been seeing the modern and up-to-date. These people would be at home at any New York cocktail party—'

'No,' she burst out, hugging herself tightly. 'No, they would *not*. They haven't the polish, the smoothness, the softness. David, they're *not* civilised. They're still a primitive people. When I see their eyes I see how primitive they are. When they touch me, I feel frightened—I feel I'm in danger.'

He looked at her with apprehension. They had drunk till it was too late to eat and now he was hungry, tired. He found her exhausting. He would have liked to sit back comfortably in that air-conditioned cool, to go over the party, to discuss the people they had met, to share his views with her. But she

---

1. Stained with the red juice spat out by those chewing *pan* (Hindi), the leaf of the evergreen betel plant.

seemed launched in some other direction, she was going alone and he did not want to be drawn into her deep wake. 'You're very imaginative tonight,' he said lightly, playing with the bottle-opener and not looking at her. 'Here was I, disappointed at finding them so westernised. I would have liked them a bit more primitive—at least for the sake of my thesis. Now look at the Gidwanis. Did you ever think an Indian wife would be anything like Gidwani's wife—what was her name?'

'Oh, she was terrible, terrible,' Pat whispered, shuddering, as she thought of the vermilion sari tied below the navel, of the uneven chocolate-smooth expanse of belly and the belt of little silver bells around it. She didn't care to remember the dance she had danced with David on the floor of the night-club. She had never even looked at the woman's face, she had kept her eyes lowered and not been able to go any further than that black navel. If that was not primitive, what could David, a sociology student, mean by the word?

It was at the Gidwanis' dinner later that week that she collapsed. She had begun to feel threatened, menaced, the moment they entered that flat. Leaving behind them the betel-stained walls of the elevator shaft, the servant boys asleep on mats in the passage, the cluster of watchmen and chauffeurs playing cards under the unshaded bulb in the lobby, they had stepped onto a black marble floor that glittered like a mirror and reflected the priceless statuary that sailed on its surface like ships of stone. Scarlet and vermilion ixora[2] in pots. Menservants in stiffly starched uniform. Jewels, enamel, brocade and gold. Gidwani with a face like an amiable baboon's, immediately sliding a soft hand across her back. His wife's chocolate pudding belly with the sari slipping suggestively about her hips. Pat shrank and shrank. Her lips felt very dry and she licked and licked them, nervously. She lost David's arm. Her feet in their sandals seemed to swell grotesquely. She sat at the table, her head slanting. She saw David looking at her concernedly. The manservant's stomach pushed against her shoulder as he lowered the dishes for her. The dishes smelt, she wondered of what—oil, was it, or goat's meat? It was not conducive to appetite. Her fork slipped. The table slipped. She had fainted. They were all crying, shoving, crowding. She pushed at them with her hands in panic.

'David, get me out, get me out,' she blubbered, trying to free herself of them.

Later, sitting at the foot of her bed, 'We'd better leave,' he said sadly. Was it Gidwani's wife's belly that saddened him, she wondered. It was not a sight that one could forget, or discard, or deny. 'Delhi's said to be dryer,' he said, 'not so humid. It'll be better for you.'

'But your thesis, David?' she wept, repentantly. 'Will you be able to work on it there?'

'I suppose so,' he said gloomily, looking down at her, shrunk into something small on the bed, paler and fainter each day that she spent in the wild jungles of the city of Bombay.

Delhi was dryer. It was dry as a skeleton. Yellow sand seethed and stormed, then settled on wood, stone, flesh and skin, brittle and gritty as powdered

2. Small trees.

bone. Trees stood leafless. Red flowers blazed on their black branches, golden and purple ones burgeoned. Beggars drowsed in their shade, stretched unrecognizable limbs at her. I will pull myself together, Pat said, walking determinedly through the piled yellow dust, I must pull myself together. Her body no longer melted, it did not ooze and seep out of her grasp any more. It was dry, she would hold herself upright, she would look into people's eyes when they spoke to her and smile pleasantly—like David, she thought. But the dust inside her sandals made her feet drag. If she no longer melted, she burnt. She felt the heat strike through to her bones. Even her eyes, protected by giant glare glasses, seemed on fire. She thought she would shrivel up like a piece of paper under a magnifying glass held to reflect the sun. Rubbing her fingers together, she made a scraping, papery sound. Her hair was full of sand.

'But you can't let climate get you down, dear,' David said softly, in order to express tenderness that he hardly felt any longer, seeing her suffer so unbeautifully, her feet dusty, her hair stringy, her face thin and appalled. 'Climate isn't *important*, Pat—rise above it, there's so much *else*. Try to concentrate on *that*.' He wanted to help her. It made things so difficult for him if she wouldn't come along but kept drifting off loosely in some other direction, obliging him to drop things and go after her since she seemed so uncontrolled, dangerously so. He couldn't meet people, work on his thesis, do anything. He had never imagined she could be a burden—not the companion and fellow gypsy she had so fairly promised to be. She came of plain, strong farmer stock—she ought to have some of that blood in her, strong, simple and capable. Why wasn't she capable? He held his hand to her temple—it throbbed hard. They sat sipping iced coffee in a very small, very dark restaurant that smelt, somehow, of railway soot.

'I must try,' she said, flatly and without conviction.

That afternoon she went round the antique shops of New Delhi, determined to take an interest in Indian art and culture. She left the shopping arcade after an hour, horror rising in her throat like vomit. She felt pursued by the primitive, the elemental and barbaric, and kept rubbing her fingers together nervously, recalling those great heavy bosoms of bronze and stone, the hips rounded and full as water-pots, the flirtatious little bells on ankles and bellies, the long, sly eyes that curved out of the voluptuous stone faces, not unlike those of the shopkeepers themselves with their sibilant, inviting voices. Then the gods they showed her, named for her, with their flurry of arms, their stamping feet, their blazing, angered eyes and flying locks, all thunder and lightning, revenge and menace. Scraping the papery tips of her fingers together, she hurried through the dust back to the hotel. Back on her bed, she wept into her pillow for the lost home, for apple trees and cows, for red barns and swallows, for icecream sodas and drive-in movies, all that was innocent and sweet and lost, lost, lost.

'I'm just not sophisticated enough for you,' she gulped over the iced lemon tea David brought her. It was the first time she mentioned the disparity in their backgrounds—it had never seemed to matter before. Laying it bare now was like digging the first rift between them, the first division of raw, red clay. It frightened them both. 'I expect you knew about such things—you must have learnt them in college. You know I only went to high school and stayed home after that—'

'Darling,' he said, with genuine pain and tenderness, and could not go on. His tastes would not allow him to, or his scruples: the vulgarity appalled him as much as the pain. 'Do take a shower and have a shampoo, Pat. We're going out—'

'No, no, no,' she moaned in anguish, putting away the iced tea and falling onto her pillow.

'But to quite different people this time, Pat. To see a social worker—I mean, Sharma's wife is a social worker. She'll show you something quite different. I know it'll interest you.'

'I couldn't bear it,' she wept, playing with the buttons of her dress like a child.

But they did prove different. The Delhi intellectual was poorer than the Bombay intellectual, for one thing. He lived in a small, airless flat with white-washed walls and a divan and bits of folk art. He served dinner in cheap, bright ceramic ware. Of course there was the inevitable long-haired intellectual—either journalist or professor—who sat cross-legged on the floor and held forth, abusively, on the crassness of the Americans, to David's delight and Pat's embarrassment. But Sharma's wife was actually a new type, to Pat. She was a genuine social worker, trained, and next morning, having neatly tucked the night before under the divan, she took Pat out to see a milk centre, a crèche, a nursery school, clinics and dispensaries, some housed in cow sheds, others in ruined tombs. Pat saw workers' babies asleep like cocoons in hammocks slung from tin sheds on building sites; she saw children with kohl-rimmed eyes solemnly eating their free lunches out of brass containers, and schools where children wrote painstakingly on wooden boards with reed pens and the teacher sneezed brown snuff sneezes at her. It was different in content. It was the same in effect. Her feet dragged, dustier by the hour. Her hair was like string on her shoulders. When she met David in the evening, at the hotel, he was red from the sun, like a well-ripened tomato, longing to talk, to tell, to ask and question, while she drooped tired, dusty, stringy, dry, trying to revive herself, for his sake, with little sips of some iced drink but feeling quite surely that life was shrivelling up inside her. She never spoke of apple trees or barns, of popcorn or drug stores, but he saw them in her eyes, more remote and faint every day. Her eyes had been so blue, now they were fading, as if the memory, the feel of apple trees and apples were fading from her. He panicked.

'We'd better go to the hills for a while,' he said: he did not want murder on his hands. 'Sharma said June is bad, very bad, in Delhi. He says everyone who can goes to the hills. Well, we can. Let's go, Pat.'

She looked at him dumbly with her fading eyes, and tried to smile. She thought of the way the child at the hospital had smiled after the doctor had finished painting her burns with gentian violet[3] and given her a plastic doll. It had been a cheap, cracked pink plastic doll and the child had smiled at it through the gentian violet, its smile stamped in, or cut out, in that face still taut with pain, as by a machine. Pat had known that face would always be in pain, and the smile would always be cut out as by the machine of charity, mechanically. The plastic doll and the gentian violet had been incidental.

At the airlines office, the man could only find them seats on the plane to Manali, in the Kulu Valley. To Manali they went.

---

3. A purple dye used as disinfectant.

Not, however, by plane, for there were such fierce sandstorms sweeping through Delhi that day that no planes took off, and they went the three hundred miles by bus instead. The sandstorm did not spare the highway or the bus—it tore through the cracked windows and buried passengers and seats under the yellow sand of the Rajasthan desert. The sun burnt up the tin body of the bus till it was a great deal hotter inside than out in the sun. Pat sat stone-still, as though she had been beaten unconscious, groping with her eyes only for a glimpse of a mango grove or an avenue of banyans, instinctively believing she would survive only if she could find and drink in their dark, damp shade. David kept his eyes tightly shut behind his glare glasses. Perspiration poured from under his hair down his face, cutting rivers through the map of dust. The woman in the seat behind his was sick all the way up the low hills to Bilaspur. In front of him a small child wailed without stop while its mother ate peanuts and jovially threw the shells over her shoulder into his lap. The bus crackled with sand, peanut shells and explosive sounds from the protesting engine. There was a stench of diesel oil, of vomit, of perspiration and stale food such as he had never believed could exist—it was so thick. The bus was long past its prime but rattled, roared, shook and vibrated all the way through the desert, the plains, the hills, to Mandi where it stopped for a tea-break in a rest house under some eucalyptus trees in which cicadas trilled hoarsely. Then it plunged, bent on suicide, into the Beas river gorge.

After one look down the vertical cliff-side of slipping, crumbling slate ending in the wild river tearing through the narrow gorge in a torrent of ice-green and white spray, David's head fell back against the seat, lolled there loosely, and he muttered 'This is the end, Pat, my girl, I'm afraid it's the end.'

'But it's cooler,' fluted a youthful voice in a rising inflection, and David's head jerked with foolish surprise. Who had spoken? He turned to his wife and found her leaning out of the window, her strings of hair flying back at him in the breeze. She turned to him her excited face—dust-grimed and wan but with its eyes alive and observant. 'I can feel the spray—*cold* spray, David. It's better than a shower or air-conditioning or even a drink. Do just feel it.'

But he was too baffled and stunned and slain to feel anything at all. He sat slumped, not daring to watch the bus take the curves of that precarious path hewn through cliffs of slate, poised above the river that hurtled and roared over the black rocks and dashed itself against the mountainside. He was not certain what exactly would happen—whether the overhanging slate would come crashing down upon them, burying them alive, or if they would lurch headlong into the Beas and be dashed to bits on the rocks—but he had no doubt that it would be one or the other. In the face of this certainty, Pat's untimely revival seemed no more than a pathetic footnote.

To Pat, being fanned to life by that spray-spotted breeze, no such possibility occurred. She was watching the white spray rise and spin over the ice-green river and break upon the gleaming rocks, looking out for small sandy coves where pink oleanders bloomed and banana trees hung their limp green flags, exclaiming with delight at the small birds that skimmed the river like foam—feeling curiosity, pleasure and amusement stir in her for the first time since she had landed in India. She no longer heard the retching of the woman behind them or the faint mewing of the exhausted child in front. Peanut shells slipped into her shoes and out of them. The stench of fifty perspiring passengers was lost in the freshness of the mountains. Up on the ridge, if she craned her neck, she could see the bunched needles of pine trees flash-ing.

When they emerged from the gorge into the sunlight, apricot-warm and mild, of the Kulu valley, she sat back with a contented sigh and let the bus carry them alongside the now calm and wide river Beas, through orchards in which little apples knobbled the trees, past flocks of royal mountain goats and their blanketed shepherds striding ahead with the mountaineer's swing, up into the hills of Manali, its deodar forests indigo in the evening air and the snow-streaked rocks of the Rohtang Pass hovering above them, an incredible distance away.

Then they were disgorged, broken sandals, shells, hair, rags, children and food containers, into the Manali bazaar, and the bus conductor swung him-self onto the roof of the bus and hurled down their bags and boxes. David was on his knees, picking up the pieces of his broken suitcase and holding them together. The crying child was fed hot fritters his father had fetched from a wayside food stall. The vomiting woman squatted, holding her head in her hands, and a *pai*[4] dog sniffed at her in curiosity and consolation. A big handsome man with a pigtail and a long turquoise ear-ring came up to Pat with an armful of red puppies, his teeth flashing in a cajoling smile. 'Fifty *rupees*,' he murmured, and raised it to 'Eighty' as soon as Pat reached out to fondle the smallest of them. Touts and pimps, ubiquitously small and greasy, piped around David 'Moonlight Hotel, plumbing and flush toilet,' and 'Hotel Paradise, non-vegetarian and best view, sir.'

David, holding his suitcase in his arms, looked over the top of their heads and at the mountain peaks, as if for succour. Then his face tilted down at them palely and he shook his head, his eyes quite empty. 'Let's go, Pat,' he sighed, and she followed him up through the bazaar for he had, of course, made bookings and they had rooms at what had been described to them as an 'English boarding house.'

It was on the hillside, set in a sea of apple trees, and they had to walk through the bazaar to it, nudging past puppy-sellers, women who had spread amber and coral and bronze prayer bells on the pavement, stalls in which huge pans of milk boiled and steamed and fritters jumped up and hissed, and holiday crowds that stood about eating, talking and eyeing the newcom-ers.

'Jesus,' David said in alarm, 'the place is full of hippies.'

Pat looked at the faces they passed then and saw that the crowd outside the baker's was indeed one of fair men and women, even if they seemed to be beggars. Some were dressed like Indian gurus, in loincloths or saffron robes, with beads around their necks, others as gypsies in pantaloons or spangled skirts, some in plain rags and tatters. All were barefoot and had packs on their backs, and one or two had silent, stupefied babies astride their hips. 'Why,' she said, watching one woman with a child approach an Indian couple with her empty hand outstretched, 'they might be Americans!' David shuddered and turned up a dusty path that went between the deodar trees to the red-roofed building of the boarding house. But several hippies were climbing the same path, not to the boarding house but vanishing into the forest, or crossing the wooden bridge over the river into the meadows beyond. Americans, Europeans, here in Manali, at the end of the world—what were

4. Ownerless mongrel (Hindi).

they doing? she wondered. Well, what was *she* doing? Ah, she'd come to try and live again. She threw back her shoulders and took in lungfuls of the clear, cold air and it washed through her like water, cleansing and pure. Someone in a red cap was sawing wood outside the boarding house, she saw, and blue smoke curled out of its chimney as in a Grandma Moses painting. There was a sound of a rushing stream below. A cuckoo called. Above the tips of the immense deodars the sky was a clear turquoise, an evening colour, without heat although still distilled with sunlight. Dog roses bloomed open and white on the hillside. She tried to clasp David's arm with joy but he was holding onto the suitcase which had broken its locks and burst open and he could not spare her a finger.

'But David,' she coaxed, 'it's going to be lovely.'

'I'm glad,' he said, white-lipped, and pitched the suitcase onto the wooden veranda at the feet of the proprietor who sat benignly as a Buddha[5] on a wooden upright chair, in a white pullover and string cap, gazing down at them with an expression of pity under his bland welcome.

The room was clean, although bare but for two white iron bedsteads and a dressing table with a small yellow mirror. Its window overlooked a yard in which brown hens pecked and climbed onto over-turned buckets and wood piles, and wild daisies bloomed, as white and yellow as fresh bread and butter, around a water pump. The bathroom had no tub but a very well-polished brass bucket, a green plastic mug and, holy of holies, a flush toilet that worked, however reluctantly and complainingly. The proprietor, apple-cheeked and woolly—was he an Anglo-Indian, European or Indian? Pat could not tell—sent them tea and Glaxo biscuits on a tin tray. They sat on the bed and drank the black, bitter tea, sighing 'Well, it's *hot*.'

But Pat could not stay still. Once she had examined the drawers of the dressing table and read scraps from the old newspaper with which they were lined, turned on the taps in the bathroom and washed, changed into her Delhi slippers and drunk her tea, she wanted to go out and 'Explore!' David looked longingly at the clean white, although thin and darned, sheets stretched on the beds and the hairy brown blanket so competently tucked in, but she was adamant.

'We can't waste a minute,' she said urgently, for some unknown reason. 'We mustn't waste this lovely evening.'

He did not see how it would be wasted if they were to lie down on their clean beds, wait for hot water to be brought for their baths and then sleep, but realized it would be somehow craven and feeble for him to say so when she stood at the window with something strong and active in the swing of her hips and a fervour in her newly pink and washed face that he had almost forgotten was once her natural expression—in a different era, a different land.

'We're surrounded by apple trees,' she enticed him, 'and I think, I *think* I heard a cuckoo.'

'Why not?' he grumbled, and followed her out onto the wooden veranda where the proprietor continued to look comfortable on that upright chair, and down the garden path to the road that took them into the forest.

It was a deodar forest. The trees were so immensely old and tall that while

5. Seated statue of The Enlightened One, title given to the founder of the Buddhist religion, Sakyamuni, Gautema, or Siddartha, who flourished in northern India in the 5th century B.C.E.

the lower boughs already dipped their feet into the evening, the tops still brushed the late sunlight, and woolly yellow beams slanted through the black trunks as through the pillars of a shadowy cathedral. The turf was soft and uneven under their feet, wild iris bloomed in clumps and ferns surrounded rocks that were conspicuously stranded here and there. Pat fell upon the wild stawberries that grew with a careless luxuriance—small, seed-ridden ones she found sweet. The few people they passed, village men and women wrapped in white Kulu blankets with handsome stripes, had faces that were brown and russet, calm and pleasant, although they neither smiled nor greeted Pat and David, merely observed them in passing. Pat liked them for that—for not whining or wheedling or begging or sneering as the crowds in Bombay and Delhi had done—but simply conferring on them a status not unlike their own. 'Such independence,' she glowed, 'so self-contained. True mountain people, you know.'

David looked at her a little fearfully, not having noted such a surge of Vermont pride in his country wife before. 'Do you feel one of them yourself?' he asked, a little tentatively.

He was startled by the positive quality of the laugh that rang out of her, by the way she threw out her arms in an open embrace. 'Why, *sure*,' she cried, explosively, and sprang over a small stream that ran over the moss like a trickle of mercury. 'Look, here's dear old Jack in the pulpit,' she cried, darting at some ferns from which protruded that rather sinister gentleman, striped and hooded, David thought, like a silent cobra. She plucked it and strode on, her hair no longer like string but like drawn toffee, now catching fire in the sunbeams, now darkening in the shade. After a while, she remarked 'It isn't much like the friendly Vermont woods, really. It's more like a grand medieval cathedral, isn't it?'

'An observation several before you have made on forests,' he remarked, a trifle drily. 'Is one permitted to sit in your cathedral or can one only kneel?' he asked, lowering himself onto a rock. 'Jesus, is my bottom sore from that bus ride.'

She laughed, threw the Jack in the pulpit into his lap and flung herself on the grass at his feet. And so they might have stopped and talked and laughed a bit before going back to an English supper and their fresh, clean beds but, swinging homewards hand-in-hand, they came suddenly upon a strange edifice on a slope in the forest, like a great pagoda built of wood, heavy and dark timber, rough-hewn and sculpted as a stone temple might be, with trees rearing about it in the twilight, shaggy and dark, like Himalayan bears.

'Could it be a temple?' Pat wondered, for the temples she had so far seen had been bursting at the seams with loud pilgrims and busy beggars and priests, affairs of garish paint and plaster, clatter of bells and malodorous marigolds. A still temple in a silent forest—she had quite lost hope of finding such a thing in this overpopulated land.

'We might go in,' David said since she was straining at his hand and, after hovering at the threshold for a bit, they slipped off their sandals and crossed its high wooden plinth.

It was very much darker inside, like a cave scooped out of a tree trunk. The floor, however, was of clay, hard-packed and silky. A shelf of rock projected from the dark wall and a lamp hung from it with a few flowers bright around its wick. It had that minute been blown out by a tall woman with an appropriately wooden face who wore her hair in a tight plait around her head. She lifted her hand, swung only once but vigorously a large bell, and left with a quick stride, barely glancing at them as she went. They bent to study the stone slab beneath the gently smoking lamp and could only just make out the outline of a giant footprint on it. That was all by way of an image and there were neither offerings nor money-box, neither priest nor pilgrim around.

They came out in silence and walked away slowly, as though afraid something would jump out at them from it, or from the forest—they were so much a part of each other, that forest and its temple.

Finally they emerged from the trees and were within sight of the red roof and chimney pot of the English boarding house amongst its apple trees, far below the snow-streaked black ridges of the mountain pass, still pale and luminous against the darkening sky, at once threatening and protective in its attitude, like an Indian god.

'I'm sure I've never seen anything like that before,' Pat murmured then.

'What, not even in Vermont?' he teased, but received no answer.

They ate their dinner in silence, Pat hugely although reflectively, while David sipped a cup of soup and felt as peevish as a neglected invalid.

Perhaps it was only the smallness of Manali—barely a town, merely an overgrown village, a place for shepherds to halt on their way up to the Pass and over it to Lahaul, and apple growers to load their fruit onto lorries bound for the plains, suddenly struck and swollen by a seasonal avalanche of tourists and their vehicles—that led Pat so quickly to know it and feel it as home. It presented no difficulty, as other Indian towns of her acquaintance had, it was innocent and open and if it did not clamorously and cravenly invite, it did not shut its doors either—it had none to shut. It lay in the cup of the valley, the river and forest to one side, bright paddy fields and apple orchards to the other, open and sunlit, small and easy.

She bought herself a cloth bag to sling over her shoulder and with it strode down the single street of Manali in her friendly squeaking sandals. She stopped at the baker's for ginger biscuits and to smile, somewhat tentatively, at the hippies who stood barefoot at the door, begging for loaves of bread from Indian tourists who seemed as embarrassed as stupefied to discover that it was not only Indians who could beg, and always gave them far more than they did to poorer Indian beggars. She eyed the vegetable stalls and the baskets of ripe fruit on the pavements with envy, wishing she could set up house and do her own marketing. This walk through the bazaar invariably took her to the Tibetan quarter, a smelly lane that took off to one side. Pat could not explain why she had to visit it daily. David refused to accompany her after one visit. He could not face the open drain that one had to jump over in order to enter one of its shops. He could not face the yellow *pai* dogs and the abjectly filthy children one had to pass, nor the extraordinary odour of the shops in which sweaty castaway woollens discarded by returning mountaineers and impecunious hippies made soft furry mountains along with Tibetan rugs, exquisitely chased silver candlesticks and bronze icons that democratically lived together with tawdry plastic and glass jewellery, all presided over by stolid women with faces carved intricately out of hard wood. So David thought them. To Pat they were wise and inscrutable old ladies who parted with objects of great value at pathetically low prices. Pushing through old dresses and woollen pullovers that hung from the rafters, she knelt on worn rugs and shuffled through the baubles and beads in order to pick out a lama carved in wood with the elegance of extreme simplicity, bits of turquoise, a ball of amber like solidified honey, a string of prayer beads as cool as river pebbles between her fingers . . .

'Junk, junk, junk,' David groaned as she spread them out on the bed for him to see. 'Couldn't you walk in some other direction? Must it be that bloody bazaar every day?'

'It isn't,' she protested. 'I walk all over. Just come with me and I'll show you,' she offered, but rather indifferently, and he saw that she did not care at all if he came with her or not, while in Bombay or Delhi she would have cared passionately. This needled him into closing his typewriter, laying his papers in the dressing table drawer and coming with her for once, stepping gingerly over the goat droppings and puddles in the yard, out onto the dusty road.

He found she did know, as she had claimed to, every path and stream and orchard in the place for miles, and was determined to prove it to him. To his horror, she even waved and beamed at the drug-struck, meditative hippies as they swung past the Happy Café where they invariably gathered to eat, talk, play on flutes and gaze into space in that dim, dusty interior where a chart hung on the wall offering the *table d'hôte*:[6] daily it was Brown Rice, Beans and Custard. What hippy had carried his macroculture to Manali, David wondered, pinning it to the wall above the counter where flies circled plates of yellow sweetmeats and Britannia Biscuit packets? The faces of the pale Europeans who gathered there seemed to him distressingly vacant, their postures defeated and vague, but when he mentioned this to Pat, she was scornful.

'You're just making up your mind about them without really looking,' she claimed. 'Now look at that man in white robes—doesn't he look like Christ? And it isn't just the bone structure. And see that young man who's always laughing? That's his pet loris[7] on his shoulder. There's another I see in that bazaar sometimes, who has a pet eagle, but he lives way off in the mountains. It's true they don't talk much—but you often see them laugh. Or else they just sit and think. Isn't that beautiful, to be able to do that? I think it's beautiful.'

'I think they're stoned,' he said, happy to leave the Happy Café to its shadowy, macrocultural bliss and climb the steep hill into the deodar forest. 'Lord, must we go to the temple *again*?' he moaned, as she led him forward, having already seen it till he could no longer keep his yawns from cracking his jaws apart while he had again to sit outside, on some excruciating roots, and wait for his wife to pay it a ritual visit. He was not really sure what she did in there, nor did he wish to know. Surely she didn't pray? No, she came out looking much too jolly for that.

But no, today she was taking him for a walk and for a walk she would take him, she said, with that new positivism in her jaw-line and swing of her arms that he rather feared. She led him along a stream in which a man and a woman in gypsy dress—and bald patch, and red curls, respectively—were scrubbing some incredibly blackened pots and pans, like children at play—

---

6. Fixed-price meal in a hotel.   7. Small, slender, tailless lemur.

'Aren't they charming?' Pat enquired, as if of a painted landscape tastefully peopled with just a few rural figures, and David retorted 'Damn vagabonds'—and down lanes that wound through orchards overhung with apricot trees from which fruit dropped ripe and soft onto the stones under their feet, past farm houses screened by daisies and day lilies from which issued bursts, sometimes of tubercular coughing and sometimes of abstract, atonal music, both curiously foreign, and then uphill, beside a stream that leaped over the rocks like a startled hare, white and flashing between ferns and boulders, to a village of large, square stone and wood houses—the ground floors smaller, built solidly of square blocks of stone, the upper floors larger, their elaborately carved wooden balconies overhanging the courtyards in which cows ate the apricots swept up in hills for them, and children climbed crackling haystacks. Apricot trees festooned with unhealthy-looking mistletoe shaded that village and Pat stopped to ask an old man in a blue cap if he had some to sell. They waited in his courtyard, amongst dung pats and milk pails, standing close to the stone wall to let a herd of mountain goats go by, silk-shawled, tip-tapping and bleat-voiced as a party of tipsy ladies, while the man climbed his tree and plucked them a capful. Eating them out of their pockets—they proved not quite ripe and not as sweet as those sold in the bazaar, but Pat wouldn't say so and David did—they continued uphill, out of the village (David glimpsed a lissome[8] brunette in purple robes and Biblical sandals climbing down to the stream but averted his eyes) into the deodar forest again. David was so grateful for its blue shade, and so overfull with bucolic scenes and apricots, that he was ready to sprawl. His wife sprang on ahead, calling, and then he saw her destination. Another temple. He might have known.

Catching up with her, he found Pat fondling the ears of a big tawny dog that had come barking out of the temple courtyard, with familiarity and a wag of its royal tail. 'We can't go in, it's shut,' she reassured him, 'but do see,' she coaxed, and led him through the courtyard and eventually he had to admit that even as Kulu temples went, this one in Nasogi was a pearl. It was no larger than Hansel and Gretel's hut, its roof sloping steeply to the ground, edged with carved icicles of wood. Its doors and beams were massive, but every bit was elegantly carved and fitted. There was a paved courtyard opening into others, all open and inviting, possibly for pilgrims, and around it a grandeur of trees. David lowered himself onto a root, put his arms around his knees, tilted his head to one side and said 'Well yes, you have something here, Pat, I'll give that to you.'

She glowed. 'I think it's most magical spot on earth, if you'd like to know.'

'Aren't you funny?' he commented. 'I take you the length and breadth of India, I show you palaces and museums, jewels and tiger skins—and all the time you were hankering after a forest and an orchard and a village. Little Gretchen you, little Martha, hmm?'

'Do you think that's all I see in it?' she enquired, and he did not quite like, quite trust her sudden gravity that had something too set about it, too extreme, like that of a fanatic. But what was she being so fanatical about—the country life? A mountain idyll? Surely that was obtainable and possible without fanaticism.

She gave only a hint—it was obvious she had thought nothing out yet,

8. Lithe, agile.

however much she had felt. 'This isn't like the rest of India, Dave. It's come to me as a relief, as an escape from India. You know, down in those horrible cities, I'd gotten to think of India as one horrible temple, bursting, *crawling* with people—people on their knees, *hopeless* people—and those horrible idols towering over them with their hundred legs and hundred heads—all *horrible* . . .' (David, tiring of that one adjective, clicked his tongue like an impatient pedagogue, making her veer, only slightly, then return to her track, sifting dry deodar needles through nervous brown fingers) . . . 'and then, to walk through the forest and come upon this—this little shrine—it's like escaping from all those Hindu horrors—it's like coming out into the open and breathing naturally again, without fear. That's what I feel here, you know,' she said with a renewed burst of confidence, '—without *fear*. And you can see that's something I share with, or perhaps have just learnt from, the mountain people here. That's what I admire so in them, in the Tibetans. I don't mean the ones down in the bazaar—those are just like the greasy Indian masses, whining and cajoling and sneering—oh, *horrible*—but the ones one sees on the mountain roads. They're upright, they're honest, independent. They have such a strong swing and a stride to their walk—they walk like gods amongst those crawling, cringing masses. And they haven't those furtive Indian faces either—eyes sliding this way and that, expressions showing and then closing up—*their* faces are all open, and they laugh and sing. All they have is a black old kettle and a pack of wood on their backs, rope sandals and a few sheep, but they laugh and sing and go striding up the mountains like—like lords. I watch them all the time, I admire them, you know, and I got to thinking what makes them so different? I wondered if it was their religion. I feel, being Buddhists, they're different from the Hindus, and it must be something in their belief that gives them this—this fearlessness. When I come to this shrine and sit and think things out quietly, I can see where they get their strength from, and their joy . . .'

But here he could stand it no longer. 'Pat, Pat,' he cried, jumping up and striking his sides. 'You're all confused, Pat, you're so muddled, so hopelessly muddled! My dear, addled wife, Pat!'

She frowned and squinted, her fist closed on a handful of needles, ceased to sift them. 'What do you mean?' she asked, in a tight, closed voice.

'What do I mean? Don't you know? You're sitting outside a *Hindu* shrine, this is a *Hindu* temple, and you're making it out to be a source of Buddhist strength and serenity! Don't you even know that the Kulu Valley has a Hindu population, and the shrines you see here are Hindu shrines?' He whooped with laughter, he pulled her to her feet and dragged her homeward, laughing so much that every time she opened her mouth to protest, he drowned her out with his roars of derision. In the end, that laughter gave him a headache.

He tired of his thesis—the notes he had collected while in Bombay and Delhi and the typescript he was now preparing—long before it was done. The whole job had begun to seem totally irrelevant. Ramming the cover onto the little flat Olivetti,[9] he pushed his legs out so that the waste-paper basket went sprawling, and yawned angrily. The cock on the woodpile at the window caught his eye and gave a wicked wink, but David looked away almost without registering it. Where was Pat?

9. Brand of typewriter.

That was the perennial question these days. Pat was never there. What was more, he no longer asked her where she had been when she appeared for meals or to throw herself down on the bed for the night, her feet raw and dirty from walking in sandals, her cloth bag flung onto the floor. (Once he saw a ragged copy of the Dhammapada[1] slip out of it and hastily looked away: the idea of his poor, addled wife poring over ancient Buddhist texts embarrassed him acutely.) He merely eyed her with accusation and with distaste: she was playing a rôle he had not engaged her to play, she was making a fool of herself, she was embarrassing him, she was absolutely outrageous. As she grew browner from the outdoor life and her limbs sturdier from the exercize, it seemed to him she was losing the fragility, the gentleness that he had loved in her, that she was growing into some tough, sharp countrywoman who might very well carry loads, chop wood, haul water and harvest, but was scarcely fit to be his wife—his, David's, the charming and socially graceful young David of Long Island upbringing—and her movements were marked by rough angles that jarred on him, her voice, when she bothered at all to reply to his vague questions, was brusque and abrupt. It was clear there was no meeting-point between them any more—he would have considered it lowering in status to make a move towards her and she clearly had no interest in meeting him half-way, or anywhere.

He had not cared for the answers she had given him when he had first, mistakenly, asked. On coming upon her one morning, while slouching through the bazaar to post a packet of letters, in, of all places, the Happy Café, round-shouldered on a bench, drinking something cloudy out of a thick glass, in the company of those ragged pilgrims with the incongruously fair heads, he had questioned her with some heat.

'Yes, they're friends of mine,' she shrugged, standing with her new stolidity in the centre of the room to which he had insisted on taking her back. 'I could have told you about them earlier if you'd asked. There's no need for you to spy.'

'Don't be ridiculous,' he snapped. 'Spy on *you*? What for? Why should it interest me what you do with yourself while I'm slogging away in here—'

'Then why ask?' she snapped back.

His curiosity was larger than his distaste in the beginning. Over dinner he asked her the questions he had earlier resolved not to ask and, pleased with the big plateful of food before her, she had talked pleasantly about the Californian couple she had taken up with, and told him the story of their erratic and precipitous voyage from the forests of Big Sur to those of the Kulu Valley, via Afghanistan and Nepal, in search of a guru they had indeed found but now discarded in favour of communal life, vegetarianism and *bhang* which seemed to them a smooth and gentle path to earthly nirvana.[2]

'Nirvana on earth!' he snorted. 'That's a contradiction in terms, don't you know?' Then, seeing her nostrils flare dangerously, went on hastily, but no more wisely, 'Is that what you were drinking down there in that joint, Pat?'

She gave a whoop of delight on seeing the pudding—caramel custard—and buried her nose in a plateful with greed. 'Gee, all this walking makes me hungry,' she apologized, 'and sleepy. Jesus, *how* sleepy.' She went straight to bed.

1. "Words of Doctrine," an anthology of basic Buddhist teachings.
2. In Buddhist theology, the extinction of individ-
ual existence and the absorption of the soul in the supreme spirit. "*Bhang*": leaves of the Indian hemp, used as a narcotic.

On another and even more uncomfortable occasion, he had found her while out taking the air after a particularly dull and boring day at the typewriter, in the park in front of the Moonlight Hotel and Rama's Bakery where the hippies were wont to gather, some even to sleep at night, rolled in their blankets on the grass. One of the Indian gurus who held court there was seated, lotus style, under a sun-dressed lime tree, with an admiring crowd of fair and tattered hippies about him, his wife Pat as cross-legged, as smiling and as tattered as the rest. He was too far away to hear what they were saying but it seemed more as if they were bandying jokes—what jokes could East and West possibly share?—than meditating or discoursing on theology. What particularly anguished him was the sight of the Indian tourists who had made an outer circle around this central core of seekers of nirvana and bliss-through-*bhang*, as if this were one of the sights of the Kulu Valley that they had paid to see. They stood about with incredulous faces, smiling uneasily, exchanging whispered asides with one another, exactly as if they were watching some disquieting although amusing play. There was condescension and, in some cases, pity in their expressions and attitudes that he could not bear to see directed at his fellow fair-heads, much less at his own wife. He turned and almost raced back to the boarding house.

That evening he had tried to question her again but she was tired, vague, merely brushed the hair from her face and murmured 'Yes, that's Guru Dina Nath. He's so sweet—so gay—so—' and went up to bed. He sniffed the air in the room suspiciously. Was it *bhang*? But he wouldn't know what it smelt like if it were. He imagined it would be sweetish and the air in their room was sour, acid. He wrenched the window open, with violence, hoping to wake her. It did not.

The day he gave up questioning her or pursuing her was when she came in, almost prancing, he thought, like some silly mare, burbling, 'Do you remember Nasogi, David? That darling village where we ate apricots? You remember its temple like a little dolls' house? Well, I met some folks who live in a commune right next to it—a big attic over a cow shed actually, but it overlooks the temple and has an orchard all around it, so it's real nice. Edith—she's from Harlem—took me across, and I had coffee with some of them—'

'Sure it was coffee?' he snarled and, turning his back, hurled himself at the typewriter with such frenzy that she could not make herself heard. She sat on her bed, chewing her lip for a while, then got up and went out again. What she had planned to say to him was put away, like an unsuccessful gift.

She kept out of his way after that, and made no further attempts to take him along with her on the way to nirvana. When, at breakfast, he told her, 'It's time I got back to Delhi. I've got more material to research down there and I can't sit here in your valley and contemplate the mountains any more. I plan to book some seats on that plane for Delhi.'

She was shocked, although she made a stout attempt to disguise it, and he was gratified to see this. 'When d'you want to leave?' she asked, spitting a plum seed into her fist.

'Next Monday, I think,' he said.

She said nothing and disappeared for the rest of the day. She was out again before he'd emerged from his bath next morning, and he had to go down to the bus depot by himself, hating every squalid step of the way: the rag market where Tibetans sold stained and soiled imported clothes to avid Indian tourists and played dice in the dust while waiting for customers, the street where snot-gobbed urchins raced and made puppies scream, only just managing to escape from under roaring lorries and stinking buses. He directed looks of fury at the old beggar without a nose or fingers who solicited him for alms and at the pig-tailed Tibetan with one turquoise ear-ring who tried to sell him a mangey pup. 'We're going to get out of here,' he ground out at them through his teeth, and they smiled at him with every encouragement. The booking office was, however, not yet open for business and he was obliged to wait outside the bus depot which was the filthiest spot in the whole bazaar. He stood slouching against a wooden pillar, watching a half-empty bus push through a herd of worriedly bleating sheep and then come up, boiling and steaming, its green-painted, rose-wreathed sides almost falling apart with the effort. It groaned the last few yards of the way and expired at his feet, with a hiss of steam that made its bonnet rise inches into the air.

The driver, a wiry young Sikh who had hung his turban on a peg by the seat and wore only a purple handkerchief over his top-knot, leaped out and raced around to fling open the bonnet before the contraption exploded. His assistant, who had jumped down from the back door and vanished into the nearest shop, a grocer's, now came running out with an enamel jug of water which the driver grabbed from his hands and, before David's incredulous eyes, threw onto the radiator.

The next thing that David knew was that an explosion of steam and boiling water had hit him, hit the driver, the assistant and he didn't know how many bystanders—he couldn't see, he flung his hands to his face, but too late, he was on fire, he was howling—everyone was howling. Someone grabbed his shoulders, someone shouted 'Sir, sir, are you blind? Are you blind?' and he roared 'Yes, damn you, I'm blind, *blind.*' And where was Pat, his bloody useless wife, where was *she*? Here was he, blinded, scalded, being dragged through the streets by strangers, madmen, all trying to carry him, all babbling as at a universal holocaust.

'There, try opening your eyes now. I think you can, son, just try it,' a blessedly American voice spoke, and prised away his hands from his face. In his desperation to see the owner of this blessed voice, David allowed his hands to be loosed from his face and actually opened his eyes—an act he had never thought to perform again—and gazed upon the American doctor with the auburn sideburns and the shirt of blue and brown checked wool as at a vision of St Michael at the golden gates. 'That's wonderful, just wonderful,' beamed the gorgeous man, solid and middle-aged and wondrously square. 'You haven't lost your eyes, see. Now let me just paint those burns for you and you'll leave here as fit as a fiddle, see if you don't . . .' So he burbled on, in that rich, heavy voice from the Middle West, and David sat back as helpless as a baby, and felt those large dry hands with their strong growth of ginger hair gently dab at his face, bringing peace and blessing in their wake. He was the American mission hospital doctor but to David he was God himself on an inspection visit mercifully timed to coincide with David's accident.

It was David's accident. He quite forgot to ask about the driver or his brainless help or the hapless bystanders who had been standing too close to the boiling radiator. He merely sat there, limp and helpless, feeling the doctor's voice flow over him like a stream of American milk. And then he was actually handed a glass of milk—Horlicks, the doctor called it, sweet and hot, and he sipped it with bowed head like a child, afraid he would cry now that the agony was over and the convalescence so sweetly begun.

'It's the shock,' the doctor was saying kindly. 'Your eyes are quite safe, son, and the burns are superficial—luckily—it's just the shock,' and he patted David on the back with those ginger-tufted hands that were so square and sure. 'We see all kinds of accidents up here, you know. Yesterday it was one of those crazy hippies who had to be brought in on a stretcher. He'd fallen off a mountain. Now can you credit that? A grown man just going and falling off a mountain like he was a kid? He'd broken both legs, see. I had to send my assistant with him to Delhi. They'll have quite a time getting him on his feet again but the Holy Family Hospital tries its best. Still,' he added, in the considerate manner of one who knows how to deal with a patient, 'yours sure is the most *unnecessary* accident we've had, I'll say that,' he declared, filling David with sweet pride. Bowing his head, he sipped his milk and drank in the doctor's kindly gossip. He tried to say 'Yeah, those hippies—they shouldn't be allowed—I don't see how they're allowed—' but his voice died away and the doctor shrugged tolerantly and laughed. 'It takes all kinds, you know, but they really are kids, they shouldn't be allowed out of their mamma's sight. How about another drink of Horlicks? You think you can walk home now? Feel okay, son?' David would have given a great deal to say he was not okay at all, that he couldn't possibly walk home, that he wanted to stay and tell the doctor all about Pat, how she had practically deserted him, and about the unsavoury friends she had made here. He wanted to ask him to speak to Pat, reason with her, return his wife to him, return his former life to him. It made him weep, almost, to think that he was expected to get up and walk out. He threw a look of anguish at the doctor as he was seen down the rickety stairs to the bus depot, and did not realize that no one could make out his expression through that coating of gentian violet that coloured his entire face, neck and ears with an extraordinary neon glow.

'My God, what's up with *you*?' screamed Pat when she came in, hours later, and was struck still by shock.

He glared at her, exulting at having elicited such a response from her. But a minute later he saw that she had collapsed against the door frame, not with shock, but with laughter.

'What have you *done*, Dave?' she squealed. 'What made you do *that*?'

Harsh words were exchanged then. David, having lost his tight-lipped control (that morning's sweet Horlicks had washed it away) demanded roughly where she had been when he was standing in the sun to buy tickets and getting scalded and very nearly blinded in the process. Didn't she care about him, he wanted to know, and what *did* she care about at all now? And she, revolted, she said, by his egoism and conceit that didn't allow him to see beyond the tip of his nose—what was wrong with him that he couldn't move out of the way of a bus, for Christ's sake, didn't it just show that he saw nothing, noticed nothing outside himself?—told him what she cared about. She had found a place for herself in the commune at Nasogi. It was what she was meant for, she realized—not going to parties with David, but to live with other men and women who shared her beliefs. They were going to live the simple life, wash themselves and their dishes in a stream, cook brown rice and lentils, pray and meditate in the forest and, at the end, perhaps, become Buddhists—'A Buddhist, you crackpot? In a Hindu temple?' he spluttered—but she continued calmly that she was sure to find, in the end, something that could not be found on the cocktail rounds of Delhi, Bombay or even, for that matter, Long Island, but that she was positive existed here, in the forest, on the mountains.

'What cocktail rounds? Are you trying to imply I'm a social gadabout, not a serious student of sociology, working on a thesis on which my entire career is based?'

'Working on a thesis?' she screeched derisively. 'Sociology? The idea of you, Dave, when you've never so much as looked, I mean really looked, into the soul, the *prana*, of the next man—is just too,—' she spluttered to a stop, wildly threw her hair about her face and burst out. 'You, you don't even know it's possible to find Buddha in a Hindu temple. Why, you can find him in a church, a forest, anywhere. Do you think he's as narrow-minded as *you?*' she flung at him, and the explosiveness with which this burst from her showed how his derision had cut into her, how it had festered in her.

The English boarding house was treated to much more hurling of American abuse that night, to throwing around of suitcases, to sounds of packing and dramatic partings and exits, and many heads leant out of the windows into the chalky moonlight to see Pat set off, striding through the daisy-spattered yard in her newly acquired hippy rags that whipped against her legs as she marched off, bag and prayer beads in hand, with never a backward look. There was no one, however, but the proprietor, bland and inscrutable as ever, to see David off next morning making a quieter, neater and sadder departure for Delhi, unconventional only on account of the brilliant purple hue of his face.

If the truth were to be told, he felt greater regret at having to arrive in Delhi with a face like a painted baboon's than to arrive without his wife.

1978

TOM STOPPARD
b. 1937

Tom Stoppard was born in Czechoslovakia, emigrated to Singapore (where his father died), and came to England in 1946. On his mother's remarriage, he took his stepfather's name of Stoppard. Leaving Pocklington School in Yorkshire at seventeen, he became a journalist, wrote a novel, and in 1962 his two short plays, *The Dissolution of Dominic Boot* and *M Is for Moon among Other Things*, were broadcast on the radio. The British theater had been dominated for a decade by realistic "kitchen sink" dramas when Stoppard's *Rosencrantz and Guildenstern are Dead* (1966) appeared and was hailed as a major theatrical event. Critics recognized a debt to *Waiting for Godot*, but where Samuel Beckett had focused on the hopelessness of his two abandoned characters, Stoppard celebrates the gaiety and perverse vitality that can be generated from despair.

Stoppard frequently uses plays by other playwrights as launching pads for his own: Rosencrantz and Guildenstern step out of the shadows of Shakespeare's *Hamlet*, and the plot of Stoppard's *Travesties* (1974) is entwined with that of Oscar Wilde's *The Importance of Being Earnest*. Past and present are again entwined, though not intertextually, in his masterpiece, *Arcadia* (1993), which explores the nature of Nature, Classical and Romantic theories of landscape gardening, literary history and historians, truth and time, and the disruptive influence of sex on human orbits—"the attraction which Newton left out." Stoppard's most recent plays have been *Indian Ink* (1993) and *The Invention of Love* (1997), which brings together in one galaxy A. E. Housman, Moses Jackson, Oscar Wilde, and a sparkling constellation of High Victorian worthies.

In a different but no less witty mode, *The Real Inspector Hound* (1968) parodies the classic country-house murder-mystery play. Stoppard's hilarious spoof parallels Agatha Christie's play *The Mousetrap*. An extratheatrical dimension is added by the subplot satirizing the pomposities of theater critics. When the lives of Birdboot and Moon become entangled with those of the characters in the play they are supposedly reviewing, we are treated to a brilliant demonstration of one of Stoppard's recurrent themes, the indistinct frontier between Life and Art. He has said:

> I write plays because writing dialogue is the only respectable way of contradicting yourself. I'm the kind of person who embarks on an endless leapfrog down the great moral issues. I put a position, rebut it, refute the rebuttal, and rebut the refutation.

Stoppard shared an Oscar for the screenplay of *Shakespeare in Love* (1998) and has also written for radio and television, alternating—sometimes in the same work—between a serious handling of political themes and arabesques of exuberant fantasy. As he says: "I never quite know whether I want to be a serious artist or a siren."

The Real Inspector Hound

The first thing is that the audience appear to be confronted by their own reflection in a huge mirror. Impossible. However, back there in the gloom—not at the footlights—a bank of plush seats and pale smudges of faces. (The total effect having been established, it can be progressively faded out as the play goes on, until the front row remains to remind us of the rest and then, finally, merely two seats in that row—one of which is now occupied by MOON[1] *Between* MOON *and the auditorium is an acting area which represents, in as realistic an idiom as possible, the drawing-room of Muldoon Manor. French windows[2] at one side. A telephone fairly well upstage (i.e., towards* MOON). *The* BODY *of a man lies sprawled face down on the floor in front of a large settee. This settee must be of a size and design to allow it to be wheeled over the body, hiding it completely. Silence. The room. The* BODY. MOON.

MOON *stares blankly ahead. He turns his head to one side then the other, then up, then down—waiting. He picks up his programme and reads the front cover. He turns over the page and reads.*

---

1. Stoppard told Kenneth Tynan: "Moon is a person to whom things happen. Boot is rather more aggressive."

2. A pair of windows, reaching to the ground, that open like doors between room and garden.

He turns over the page and reads.
He turns over the page and reads.
He turns over the page and reads.
He looks at the back cover and reads.
He puts it down and crosses his legs and looks about. He stares front. Behind him and to one side, barely visible, a man enters and sits down: BIRDBOOT.

Pause. MOON *picks up his programme, glances at the front cover and puts it down impatiently. Pause. . . . Behind him there is the crackle of a chocolate-box, absurdly loud.* MOON *looks round. He and* BIRDBOOT *see each other. They are clearly known to each other. They acknowledge each other with constrained waves.* MOON *looks straight ahead.* BIRDBOOT *comes down to join him.*

Note: *Almost always,* MOON *and* BIRDBOOT *converse in tones suitable for an auditorium, sometimes a whisper. However good the acoustics might be, they will have to have microphones where they are sitting. The effect must be not of sound picked up, amplified and flung out at the audience, but of sound picked up, carried, and gently dispersed around the auditorium.*

Anyway, BIRDBOOT, *with a box of Black Magic,*[3] *makes his way down to join* MOON *and plumps himself down next to him, plumpish middle-aged* BIRDBOOT *and younger taller, less-relaxed* MOON.

BIRDBOOT   [*Sitting down; conspiratorially.*] Me and the lads[4] have had a meeting in the bar and decided it's first-class family entertainment but if it goes on beyond half-past ten it's self-indulgent—pass it on . . . [*And laughs jovially.*] I'm on my own tonight, don't mind if I join you?

MOON   Hello, Birdboot.

BIRDBOOT   Where's Higgs?

MOON   I'm standing in.

MOON AND BIRDBOOT   Where's Higgs?

MOON   Every time.

BIRDBOOT   What?

MOON   It is as if we only existed one at a time, combining to achieve continuity. I keep space warm for Higgs. My presence defines his absence, his absence confirms my presence, his presence precludes mine. . . . When Higgs and I walk down this aisle together to claim our common seat, the oceans will fall into the sky and the trees will hang with fishes.

BIRDBOOT   [*He has not been paying attention, looking around vaguely, now catches up.*] Where's Higgs?

MOON   The very sight of me with a complimentary ticket[5] is enough. The streets are impassable tonight, the country is rising and the cry goes up from hill to hill—Where—is—Higgs? [*Small pause.*] Perhaps he's dead at last, or trapped in a lift somewhere, or succumbed to amnesia, wandering the land with his turn-ups[6] stuffed with ticket-stubs. [BIRDBOOT *regards him doubtfully for a moment.*]

BIRDBOOT   Yes. . . . Yes, well I didn't bring Myrtle tonight—not exactly her cup of tea, I thought, tonight.

MOON   Over her head, you mean?

BIRDBOOT   Well, no—I mean it's a sort of a *thriller*, isn't it?

---

3. Brand of chocolates.
4. I.e., the other theater critics.

5. As issued to a theater critic.
6. Trouser leg cuffs.

MOON   Is it?

BIRDBOOT   That's what I heard. Who killed thing?—no one will leave the house.

MOON   I suppose so. Underneath.

BIRDBOOT   *Underneath?!?* It's a whodunnit, man!—Look at it!
[*They look at it. The room. The* BODY. *Silence.*]
   Has it started yet?

MOON   Yes.
[*Pause. They look at it.*]

BIRDBOOT   Are you sure?

MOON   It's a pause.

BIRDBOOT   You can't start with a *pause!* If you want my opinion there's total panic back there. [*Laughs and subsides.*] Where's Higgs tonight, then?

MOON   It will follow me to the grave and become my epitaph—Here lies Moon the second string: where's Higgs? . . . Sometimes I dream of revolution, a bloody *coup d'etat*[7] by the second rank—troupes of actors slaughtered by their understudies, magicians sawn in half by indefatigably smiling glamour girls, cricket teams wiped out by marauding bands of twelfth men[8]—I dream of champions chopped down by rabbit-punching sparring partners while eternal bridesmaids turn and rape the bridegrooms over the sausage rolls and parliamentary private secretaries plant bombs in the Minister's Humber[9]—comedians die on provincial stages, robbed of their feeds[1] by mutely triumphant stooges[2]—
   —and—march—
   —an army of assistants and deputies, the seconds-in-command, the runners-up, the right-hand men—storming the palace gates wherein the second son has already mounted the throne having committed regicide with a croquet-mallet—stand-ins of the world stand up!—
[*Beat.*][3] Sometimes I dream of Higgs.
[*Pause.* BIRDBOOT *regards him doubtfully. He is at a loss, and grasps reality in the form of his box of chocolates.*]

BIRDBOOT   [*Chewing into mike.*] Have a chocolate!

MOON   What kind?

BIRDBOOT   [*Chewing into mike.*] Black Magic.

MOON   No thanks.
[*Chewing stops dead.*]
[*Of such tiny victories and defeats. . . .*]

BIRDBOOT   I'll give you a tip, then. Watch the girl.

MOON   You think she did it?

BIRDBOOT   No, no—the *girl,* watch her.

MOON   What girl?

BIRDBOOT   You won't know her, I'll give you a nudge.

MOON   *You* know her, do you?

BIRDBOOT   [*Suspiciously, bridling.*] What's *that* supposed to mean?

MOON   I beg your pardon?

---

7. Revolution (French).
8. Reserve players on cricket teams with eleven members.
9. (Make of) car assigned to a government minis-

ter.
1. Cue lines.
2. Foils or subordinate partners.
3. Short pause.

BIRDBOOT I'm trying to tip you a wink—give you a nudge as good as a tip—for God's sake, Moon, what's the matter with you?—you could do yourself some good, spotting her first time out—she's new, from the provinces,[4] going straight to the top. I don't want to put words into your mouth but a word from us and we could make her.

MOON I suppose you've made dozens of them, like that.

BIRDBOOT [*Instantly outraged.*] I'll have you know I'm a family man devoted to my homely but good-natured wife, and if you're suggesting—

MOON No, no—

BIRDBOOT —A man of my scrupulous morality—

MOON I'm sorry—

BIRDBOOT —falsely besmirched.

MOON Is that her?

[*For* MRS DRUDGE *has entered.*]

BIRDBOOT —don't be absurd, wouldn't be seen dead with the old—ah.

[MRS DRUDGE *is the char,[5] middle-aged, turbanned. She heads straight for the radio, dusting on the trot.*]

MOON [*Reading his programme.*] Mrs Drudge the Help.

RADIO [*Without preamble, having been switched on by* MRS DRUDGE] We interrupt our programme for a special police message.

[MRS DRUDGE *stops to listen.*]

The search still goes on for the escaped madman who is on the run in Essex.

MRS DRUDGE [*Fear and dismay.*] Essex!

RADIO County police led by Inspector Hound have received a report that the man has been seen in the desolate marshes around Muldoon Manor.

[*Fearful gasp from* MRS DRUDGE.]

The man is wearing a darkish suit with a lightish shirt. He is of medium height and build and youngish. Anyone seeing a man answering to his description and acting suspiciously, is advised to phone the nearest police station.

[*A man answering this description has appeared behind* MRS DRUDGE. *He is acting suspiciously. He creeps in. He creeps out.* MRS DRUDGE *does not see him. He does not see the body.*]

That is the end of the police message.

[MRS DRUDGE *turns off the radio and resumes her cleaning. She does not see the body. Quite fortuitously, her view of the body is always blocked, and when it isn't she has her back to it. However, she is dusting and polishing her way towards it.*]

BIRDBOOT So that's what they say about me, is it?

MOON What?

BIRDBOOT Oh, I know what goes on behind my back—sniggers—slanders—hole-in-corner innuendo— What have you heard?

MOON Nothing.

BIRDBOOT [*Urbanely.*] Tittle tattle. Tittle, my dear fellow, tattle. I take no notice of it—the sly envy of scandal mongers—I can afford to ignore them, I'm a respectable married man—

MOON Incidentally——

---

4. Working in theaters outside London.   5. Charwoman, house cleaner.

BIRDBOOT Water off a duck's back, I assure you.

MOON Who was that lady I saw you with last night?

BIRDBOOT [*Unexpectedly stung into fury.*] How dare you! [*More quietly.*] How dare you. Don't you come here with your slimy insinuations! My wife Myrtle understands perfectly well that a man of my critical standing is obliged occasionally to mingle with the world of the footlights, simply by way of keeping *au fait*[6] with the latest——

MOON I'm sorry——

BIRDBOOT That a critic of my scrupulous integrity should be vilified and pilloried in the stocks[7] of common gossip——

MOON Ssssh——

BIRDBOOT I have nothing to hide!—why, if this should reach the ears of my beloved Myrtle——

MOON Can I have a chocolate?

BIRDBOOT What? Oh——[*Mollified.*] Oh yes—my dear fellow—yes, let's have a chocolate——No point in—yes, good show. [*Pops chocolate into his mouth and chews.*] Which one do you fancy?—Cherry? Strawberry? Coffee cream? Turkish delight?

MOON I'll have montelimar.
          [*Chewing stops.*]

BIRDBOOT Ah. Sorry. [*Just missed that one.*]

MOON Gooseberry fondue?

BIRDBOOT No.

MOON Pistacchio fudge? Nectarine cluster? Hickory nut praline? Chateau Neuf du Pape '55 cracknell?

BIRDBOOT I'm afraid not. . . . Caramel?

MOON Yes, all right.

BIRDBOOT Thanks very much. [*He gives* MOON *a chocolate. Pause.*] Incidentally, old chap, I'd be grateful if you didn't mention—I mean, you know how these misunderstandings get about. . . .

MOON What?

BIRDBOOT The fact is, Myrtle simply doesn't *like* the theatre. . . .
          [*He tails off hopelessly.* MRS DRUDGE, *whose discovery of the body has been imminent, now—by way of tidying the room—slides the couch over the corpse, hiding it completely. She resumes dusting and humming.*]

MOON By the way, congratulations, Birdboot.

BIRDBOOT What?

MOON At the Theatre Royal. Your entire review reproduced in neon!

BIRDBOOT [*Pleased.*] Oh . . . that old thing.

MOON You've seen it, of course.

BIRDBOOT [*Vaguely.*] Well, I was passing. . . .

MOON I definitely intend to take a second look when it has settled down.

BIRDBOOT As a matter of fact I have a few colour transparencies—I don't know whether you'd care to . . . ?

MOON Please, please—love to, love to. . . .

---

6. In touch (French).
7. Slandered and abused. The pillory was a wooden framework with holes for the head and hands of an offender condemned to be exposed to public ridicule; the stocks was a similar framework with holes for feet and occasionally hands in which offenders were confined in a sitting position.

[BIRDBOOT *hands over a few colour slides and a battery-powered viewer which* MOON *holds up to his eyes as he speaks.*]

Yes . . . yes . . . lovely . . . awfully sound. It has scale, it has colour, it is, in the best sense of the word, electric. Large as it is, it is a small masterpiece—I would go so far as to say—kinetic[8] without being pop, and having said that, I think it must be said that here we have a review that adds a new dimension to the critical scene. I urge you to make haste to the Theatre Royal, for this is the stuff of life itself. [*Handing back the slides, morosely.*] All I ever got was "Unforgettable" on the posters for . . . What was it?

BIRDBOOT   Oh—yes—I know. . . . Was that you? I thought it was Higgs.

[*The phone rings.* MRS DRUDGE *seems to have been waiting for it do so and for the last few seconds has been dusting it with an intense concentration. She snatches it up.*]

MRS DRUDGE   [*Into phone.*] Hello, the drawing-room of Lady Muldoon's country residence one morning in early spring? . . . He*llo*!—the draw——Who? Who did you wish to speak to? I'm afraid there is no one of that name here, this is all very mysterious and I'm sure it's leading up to something, I hope nothing is amiss for we, that is Lady Muldoon and her houseguests, are here cut off from the world, including Magnus, the wheelchair-ridden half-brother of her ladyship's husband Lord Albert Muldoon who ten years ago went out for a walk on the cliffs and was never seen again—and all alone, for they had no children.

MOON   Derivative,[9] of course.

BIRDBOOT   But quite sound.

MRS DRUDGE   Should a stranger enter our midst, which I very much doubt, I will tell him you called. Good-bye.

[*She puts down the phone and catches sight of the previously seen suspicious character who has now entered again, more suspiciously than ever, through the french windows. He senses her stare, freezes, and straightens up.*]

SIMON   Ah!—hello there! I'm Simon Gascoyne, I hope you don't mind, the door was open so I wandered in. I'm a friend of Lady Muldoon, the lady of the house, having made her acquaintance through a mutual friend, Felicity Cunningham, shortly after moving into this neighbourhood just the other day.

MRS DRUDGE   I'm Mrs Drudge. I don't live in but I pop in on my bicycle when the weather allows to help in the running of charming though somewhat isolated Muldoon Manor. Judging by the time [*she glances at the clock*] you did well to get here before high water cut us off for all practical purposes from the outside world.

SIMON   I took the short cut over the cliffs and followed one of the old smugglers' paths through the treacherous swamps that surround this strangely inaccessible house.

MRS DRUDGE   Yes, many visitors have remarked on the topographical quirk in the local strata whereby there are no roads leading from the Manor, though there *are* ways of getting *to* it, weather allowing.

8. In motion.
9. I.e., of such other plays as Agatha Christie's *The Mousetrap.*

SIMON   Yes, well I must say it's a lovely day so far.

MRS DRUDGE   Ah, but now that the cuckoo-beard is in bud there'll be fog before the sun hits Foster's Ridge.

SIMON   I say, it's wonderful how you country people really know weather.

MRS DRUDGE   [*Suspiciously.*] Know whether what?

SIMON   [*Glancing out of the window.*] Yes, it does seem to be coming on a bit foggy.

MRS DRUDGE   The fog is very treacherous around here—it rolls off the sea without warning, shrouding the cliffs in a deadly mantle of blind man's buff.[1]

SIMON   Yes, I've heard it said.

MRS DRUDGE   I've known whole week-ends when Muldoon Manor, as this lovely old Queen Anne[2] House is called, might as well have been floating on the pack ice for all the good it would have done phoning the police. It was on such a week-end as this that Lord Muldoon who had lately brought his beautiful bride back to the home of his ancestors, walked out of this house ten years ago, and his body was never found.

SIMON   Yes, indeed, poor Cynthia.

MRS DRUDGE   His name was Albert.

SIMON   Yes indeed, poor Albert. But tell me, is Lady Muldoon about?

MRS DRUDGE   I believe she is playing tennis on the lawn with Felicity Cunningham.

SIMON   [*Startled.*] Felicity Cunningham?

MRS DRUDGE   A mutual friend, I believe you said. A happy chance. I will tell them you are here.

SIMON   Well, I can't really stay as a matter of fact—please don't disturb them—I really should be off.

MRS DRUDGE   They would be very disappointed. It is some time since we have had a four for pontoon bridge[3] at the Manor, and I don't play cards myself.

SIMON   There is another guest, then?

MRS DRUDGE   Major Magnus, the crippled half-brother of Lord Muldoon who turned up out of the blue from Canada just the other day, completes the house-party.

[MRS DRUDGE *leaves on this,* SIMON *is undecided.*]

MOON   [*Ruminating quietly.*] I think I must be waiting for Higgs to die.

BIRDBOOT   What?

MOON   Half afraid that I will vanish when he does.

[*The phone rings.* SIMON *picks it up.*]

SIMON   Hello?

MOON   I wonder if it's the same for Puckeridge?

BIRDBOOT AND SIMON   [*Together.*] Who?

MOON   Third string.

BIRDBOOT   Your stand-in?

MOON   Does he wait for Higgs and I to write each other's obituary—does he dream——?

---

1. A game in which a blindfolded person has to catch and identify others not blindfolded.
2. Built in the reign of Queen Anne (1702–14), or in the architectural style of that period.

3. Pontoon (otherwise *vingt-et-un*) and bridge are two quite different card games. A pontoon bridge, crossing a river, is supported by a line of barges, rafts, or hollow metal cylinders.

SIMON   To whom did you wish to speak?

BIRDBOOT   What's he like?

MOON   Bitter.

SIMON   There is no one of that name here.

BIRDBOOT   No—as a critic, what's Puckeridge like as a critic?

MOON   [*Laughs poisonously.*] Nobody knows——

SIMON   You must have got the wrong number!

MOON   —there's always been me and Higgs.

> [SIMON *replaces the phone and paces nervously. Pause.* BIRDBOOT *consults his programme.*]

BIRDBOOT   Simon Gascoyne. It's not him, of course.

MOON   What?

BIRDBOOT   I said it's not him.

MOON   Who is it, then?

BIRDBOOT   My guess is Magnus.

MOON   In disguise, you mean?

BIRDBOOT   What?

MOON   You think he's Magnus in disguise?

BIRDBOOT   I don't think you're concentrating, Moon.

MOON   I thought you said——

BIRDBOOT   You keep chattering on about Higgs and Puckeridge—what's the matter with you?

MOON   [*Thoughtfully.*] I wonder if they talk about me . . . ?

> [*A strange impulse makes* SIMON *turn on the radio.*]

RADIO   Here is another police message. Essex county police are still searching in vain for the madman who is at large in the deadly marshes of the coastal region. Inspector Hound who is masterminding the operation, is not available for comment but it is widely believed that he has a secret plan. . . . Meanwhile police and volunteers are combing the swamps with loud-hailers, shouting, "Don't be a madman, give yourself up." That is the end of the police message.

> [SIMON *turns off the radio. He is clearly nervous.* MOON *and* BIRDBOOT *are on separate tracks.*]

BIRDBOOT   [*Knowingly.*] Oh yes. . . .

MOON   Yes, I should think my name is seldom off Puckeridge's lips . . . sad, really. I mean, it's no life at all, a stand-in's stand-in.

BIRDBOOT   Yes . . . yes. . . .

MOON   Higgs never gives me a second thought. I can tell by the way he nods.

BIRDBOOT   Revenge, of course.

MOON   What?

BIRDBOOT   Jealousy.

MOON   Nonsense—there's nothing *personal* in it——

BIRDBOOT   The paranoid grudge——

MOON   [*Sharply first, then starting to career . . .*] It is merely that it is not enough to wax at another's wane,[4] to be held in reserve, to be on hand, on call, to step in or not at all, the substitute—the near offer—the tem-

---

4. Increase and decrease, respectively. Cf. Isaac Watts's hymn *Jesus shall reign where'er the sun*, lines 3–4: "His kingdom stretch from shore to shore, / Till moons shall wax and wane no more."

porary-acting—for I am Moon, continuous Moon, in my own shoes, Moon in June, April, September and no member of the human race keeps warm my bit of space—yes, I can tell by the way he nods.

BIRDBOOT   Quite mad, of course.

MOON   What?

BIRDBOOT   The answer lies out there in the swamps.

MOON   Oh.

BIRDBOOT   The skeleton in the cupboard is coming home to roost.

MOON   Oh yes. [*He clears his throat . . . for both he and* BIRDBOOT *have a "public" voice, a critic voice which they turn on for sustained pronouncements of opinion.*] Already in the opening stages we note the classic impact of the catalystic figure—the outsider—plunging through to the centre of an ordered world and setting up the disruptions—the shock waves—which unless I am much mistaken, will strip these comfortable people—these crustaceans in the rock pool of society—strip them of their shells and leave them exposed as the trembling raw meat which, at heart, is all of us. But there is more to it than that——

BIRDBOOT   I agree—keep your eye on Magnus.

[*A tennis ball bounces through the french windows, closely followed by* FELICITY, *who is in her twenties. She wears a pretty tennis outfit, and carries a racket.*]

FELICITY   [*Calling behind her.*] Out!

[*It takes her a moment to notice* SIMON *who is standing shiftily to one side.* MOON *is stirred by a memory.*]

MOON   I say, Birdboot. . . .

BIRDBOOT   That's the one.

FELICITY   [*Catching sight of* SIMON.] You!

[FELICITY'*s manner at the moment is one of great surprise but some pleasure.*]

SIMON   [*Nervously.*] Er, yes—hello again.

FELICITY   What are you doing here?

SIMON   Well, I. . . .

MOON   She's——

BIRDBOOT   Sssh. . . .

SIMON   No doubt you're surprised to see me.

FELICITY   Honestly, darling, you really are extraordinary.

SIMON   Yes, well, here I am.

FELICITY   You must have been desperate to see me—I mean, I'm *flattered*, but couldn't it wait till I got back?

SIMON   [*Bravely.*] There is something you don't know.

FELICITY   What is it?

SIMON   Look, about the things I said—it may be that I got carried away a little—we both did——

FELICITY   [*Stiffly.*] What are you trying to say?

SIMON   I love another!

FELICITY   I see.

SIMON   I didn't make any promises—I merely——

FELICITY   You don't have to say any more——

SIMON   Oh, I didn't want to hurt you——

FELICITY   Of all the nerve!

SIMON   Well, I——
FELICITY   You philandering coward——
SIMON   Let me explain——
FELICITY   This is hardly the time and place—you think you can barge in anywhere, whatever I happen to be doing——
SIMON   But I want you to know that my admiration for you is sincere—I don't want you to think that I didn't mean those things I said——
FELICITY   I'll kill you for this, Simon Gascoyne!
   [*She leaves in tears, passing* MRS DRUDGE *who has entered in time to overhear her last remark.*]
MOON   It was her.
BIRDBOOT   I told you—straight to the top——
MOON   No, no——
BIRDBOOT   Sssh. . . .
SIMON   [*To* MRS DRUDGE.] Yes, what is it?
MRS DRUDGE   I have come to set up the card table, sir.
SIMON   I don't think I can stay.
MRS DRUDGE   Oh, Lady Muldoon *will* be disappointed.
SIMON   Does she know I'm here?
MRS DRUDGE   Oh yes, sir, I just told her and it put her in quite a tizzy.
SIMON   Really? . . . Well, I suppose now that I've cleared the air. . . . Quite a tizzy, you say . . . really . . . really . . .
   [*He and* MRS DRUDGE *start setting up for card game.* MRS DRUDGE *leaves when this is done.*]
MOON   Felicity!—she's the one.
BIRDBOOT   Nonsense—red herring.
MOON   I mean, it was *her*!
BIRDBOOT   [*Exasperated.*] *What* was?
MOON   That lady I saw you with last night!
BIRDBOOT   [*Inhales with fury.*] Are you suggesting that a man of my scrupulous integrity would trade his pen for a mess of potage?![5] Simply because in the course of my profession I happen to have struck up an acquaintance—to have, that is, a warm regard, if you like, for a fellow toiler in the vineyard of greasepaint—I find it simply intolerable to be pillified and villoried——
MOON   I never implied——
BIRDBOOT   —to find myself the object of uninformed malice, the petty slanders of little men——
MOON   I'm sorry——
BIRDBOOT   —to suggest that my good opinion in a journal of unimpeachable integrity is at the disposal of the first coquette who gives me what I want——
MOON   Sssssh——
BIRDBOOT   A ladies' man! . . . Why, Myrtle and I have been together now for—Christ!—who's *that*?
   [*Enter* LADY CYNTHIA MULDOON *through french windows. A beautiful*

---

5. In the Old Testament, Esau sold his birthright for "a mess of pottage" (dish of soup); see Genevan Bible, Genesis 25.

woman in her thirties. She wears a cocktail dress, is formally coiffured, and carries a tennis racket.]

[*Her effect on* BIRDBOOT *is also impressive. He half rises and sinks back agape.*]

CYNTHIA [*Entering.*] Simon!

[*A dramatic freeze between her and* SIMON.]

MOON   Lady Muldoon.

BIRDBOOT   No, I mean—who *is* she?

SIMON   [*Coming forward.*] Cynthia!

CYNTHIA   Don't say anything for a moment—just hold me.

[*He seizes her and glues his lips to hers, as they say. While their lips are glued——*]

BIRDBOOT   She's *beautiful*—a vision of eternal grace, a poem . . .

MOON   I think she's got her mouth open.

[CYNTHIA *breaks away dramatically.*]

CYNTHIA   We can't go on meeting like this!

SIMON   We have nothing to be ashamed of!

CYNTHIA   But darling, this is madness!

SIMON   Yes!—I am mad with love for you!

CYNTHIA   Please—remember where we are!

SIMON   Cynthia, I love you!

CYNTHIA   Don't—I love Albert!

SIMON   He's dead! [*Shaking her.*] Do you understand me—Albert's dead!

CYNTHIA   No—I'll never give up hope! Let me go! We are not free!

SIMON   I don't care, we were meant for each other—had we but met in time.

CYNTHIA   You're a cad, Simon! You will use me and cast me aside as you have cast aside so many others.

SIMON   No, Cynthia!—you can make me a better person!

CYNTHIA   You're ruthless—so strong, so cruel——

[*Ruthlessly he kisses her.*]

MOON   The son she never had, projected in this handsome stranger and transformed into lover—youth, vigour, the animal, the athlete as aesthete—breaking down the barriers at the deepest level of desire.

BIRDBOOT   By jove, I think you're right. Her mouth *is* open.

[CYNTHIA *breaks away.* MRS DRUDGE *has entered.*]

CYNTHIA   Stop—can't you see you're making a fool of yourself!

SIMON   I'll kill anyone who comes between us!

CYNTHIA   Yes, what is it, Mrs Drudge?

MRS DRUDGE   Should I close the windows, my lady? The fog is beginning to roll off the sea like a deadly——

CYNTHIA   Yes, you'd better. It looks as if we're in for one of those days. Are the cards ready?

MRS DRUDGE   Yes, my lady.

CYNTHIA   Would you tell Miss Cunningham we are waiting.

MRS DRUDGE   Yes, my lady.

CYNTHIA   And fetch the Major down.

MRS DRUDGE   I think I hear him coming downstairs now. [*As she leaves.*]

[*She does: the sound of a wheelchair approaching down several flights*]

of stairs with landings in between. It arrives bearing MAGNUS *at about
15 m.p.h., knocking* SIMON *over violently.*]

CYNTHIA Simon!

MAGNUS [*Roaring.*] Never had a chance! Ran under the wheels!

CYNTHIA Darling, are you all right?

MAGNUS I have witnesses!

CYNTHIA Oh, Simon—say something!

SIMON [*Sitting up suddenly.*] I'm most frightfully sorry.

MAGNUS [*Shouting yet.*] How long have you been a pedestrian?

SIMON Ever since I could walk.

CYNTHIA Can you walk now . . . ?

　　　　[SIMON *rises and walks.*]

　　Thank God! Magnus, this is Simon Gascoyne.

MAGNUS What's he doing here?

CYNTHIA He just turned up.

MAGNUS Really? How do you like it here?

SIMON [*To* CYNTHIA.] I could stay for ever.

　　　　[FELICITY *enters.*]

FELICITY So—you're still here.

CYNTHIA Of course he's still here. We're going to play cards. There's no
need to introduce you two, is there, for I recall now that you, Simon,
met me through Felicity, our mutual friend.

FELICITY Yes, Simon is an old friend, though not as old as you, Cynthia
dear.

SIMON Yes, I haven't seen Felicity since——

FELICITY Last night.

CYNTHIA Indeed? Well, you deal, Felicity. Simon, you help me with the
sofa. Will you partner Felicity, Magnus, against Simon and me?

MAGNUS [*Aside.*] Will Simon and you always be partnered against me,
Cynthia?

CYNTHIA What do you mean, Magnus?

MAGNUS You are a damned attractive woman, Cynthia.

CYNTHIA Please! Please! Remember Albert!

MAGNUS Albert's dead, Cynthia—and you are still young. I'm sure he
would have wished that you and I——

CYNTHIA No, Magnus, this is not to be!

MAGNUS It's Gascoyne, isn't it? I'll kill him if he comes between us!

CYNTHIA [*Calling.*] Simon!

　　　　[*The sofa is shoved towards the card table, once more revealing the
　　　　corpse, though not to the players.*]

BIRDBOOT Simon's for the chop[6] all right.

CYNTHIA Right! Who starts?

MAGNUS I do. No bid.

CYNTHIA Did I hear you say you saw Felicity last night, Simon?

SIMON Did I—Ah yes, yes, quite—your turn, Felicity.

FELICITY I've had my turn, haven't I, Simon?—now, it seems, it's Cynthia's turn.

---

6. Will be cut down (slang).

CYNTHIA That's my trick, Felicity dear.

FELICITY Hell hath no fury like a woman scorned,[7] Simon.

SIMON Yes, I've heard it said.

FELICITY So I hope you have not been cheating, Simon.

SIMON [Standing up and throwing down his cards.] No, Felicity, it's just that I hold the cards![8]

CYNTHIA Well done, Simon!

[MAGNUS pays SIMON, while CYNTHIA deals.]

FELICITY Strange how Simon appeared in the neighbourhood from nowhere. We know so little about him.

SIMON It doesn't always pay to show your hand!

CYNTHIA Right! Simon, it's your opening on the minor bid.[9]

[SIMON plays.]

CYNTHIA Hm, let's see. . . . [Plays.]

FELICITY I hear there's a dangerous madman on the loose.

CYNTHIA Simon?

SIMON Yes—yes—sorry. [Plays.]

CYNTHIA I meld.

FELICITY Yes—personally, I think he's been hiding out in the deserted cottage [Plays.] on the cliffs.

SIMON Flush!

CYNTHIA No! Simon—your luck's in tonight!

FELICITY We shall see—the night is not over yet, Simon Gascoyne! [She exits.]

[MAGNUS pays SIMON again.]

SIMON [To MAGNUS.] So you're the crippled half-brother of Lord Muldoon who turned up out of the blue from Canada just the other day, are you? It's taken you a long time to get here. What did you do—walk? Oh, I say, I'm most frightfully sorry!

MAGNUS Care for a spin round the rose garden, Cynthia?

CYNTHIA No, Magnus, I must talk to Simon.

SIMON My round, I think, Major.

MAGNUS You think so?

SIMON Yes, Major—I do.

MAGNUS There's an old Canadian proverb handed down from the Bladfoot Indians, which says: He who laughs last laughs longest.

SIMON Yes, I've heard it said.

[SIMON turns away to CYNTHIA.]

MAGNUS Well, I think I'll go and oil my gun.[1] [He exits.]

CYNTHIA I think Magnus suspects something. And Felicity . . . Simon, was there anything between you and Felicity?

SIMON No, no—it's over between her and me, Cynthia—it was a mere passing fleeting thing we had—but now that I have found you——

CYNTHIA If I find that you have been untrue to me—if I find that you have falsely seduced me from my dear husband Albert—I will kill you, Simon Gascoyne!

---

7. Cf. Congreve, The Mourning Bride 3.7: "Heaven has no rage, like love to hatred turned, / Nor Hell a fury, like a woman scorned."
8. Have the advantage (slang).

9. Term used in certain card games, as also "meld" and "flush," below.
1. Go to the lavatory (slang).

[MRS DRUDGE *has entered silently to witness this. On this tableau, pregnant with significance, the act ends, the body still undiscovered. Perfunctory applause.*]

[MOON *and* BIRDBOOT *seem to be completely preoccupied, becoming audible, as it were.*]

MOON Camps it around the Old Vic in his opera cloak and passes me the tat.[2]

BIRDBOOT Do you believe in love at first sight?

MOON It's not that I think I'm a better critic——

BIRDBOOT I feel my whole life changing——

MOON I am but it's not that.

BIRDBOOT Oh, the world will laugh at me, I know. . . .

MOON It is not that they are much in the way of shoes to step into. . . .

BIRDBOOT . . . call me an infatuated old fool. . . .

MOON . . . . They are not.

BIRDBOOT . . . . condemn me. . . .

MOON He is standing in my light, that is all.

BIRDBOOT . . . betrayer of my class . . .

MOON . . . an almost continuous eclipse, interrupted by the phenomenon of moonlight.

BIRDBOOT I don't care, I'm a goner.

MOON And I dream. . . .

BIRDBOOT The Blue Angel[3] all over again.

MOON . . . of the day his temperature climbs through the top of his head. . . .

BIRDBOOT Ah, the sweet madness of love . . .

MOON . . . of the spasm on the stairs. . . .

BIRDBOOT Myrtle, farewell . . .

MOON . . . dreaming of the stair he'll never reach——

BIRDBOOT . . . for I only live but once. . . .

MOON Sometimes I dream that I've killed him.

BIRDBOOT What?

MOON What?

[*They pull themselves together.*]

BIRDBOOT Yes . . . yes. . . . A beautiful performance, a collector's piece. I shall say so.

MOON A very promising debut. I'll put in a good word.

BIRDBOOT It would be as hypocritical of me to withhold praise on grounds of personal feelings, as to withhold censure.

MOON You're right. Courageous.

BIRDBOOT Oh, I know what people will say——There goes Birdboot buttering up his latest——

MOON Ignore them——

BIRDBOOT But I rise above that——The fact is I genuinely believe her performance to be one of the summits in the range of contemporary theatre.

MOON Trim-buttocked, that's the word for her.

2. Leaves me the drudgery (*tat* is slang for rubbish or junk). "Old Vic": famous London theater.
3. A novel (1932) by Heinrich Mann, adapted as a film starring Marlene Dietrich, which tells of an old man's infatuation for a heartless young singer.

BIRDBOOT   —the radiance, the inner sadness——

MOON   Does she actually come across with it?

BIRDBOOT   The part as written is a mere cypher but she manages to make Cynthia a real person——

MOON   *Cynthia?*

BIRDBOOT   And should she, as a result, care to meet me over a drink, simply by way of er—thanking me, as it were——

MOON   Well, you fickle old bastard!

BIRDBOOT   [*Aggressively.*] Are you suggesting . . . ?

   [BIRDBOOT *shudders to a halt and clears his throat.*]

BIRDBOOT   Well now—shaping up quite nicely, wouldn't you say?

MOON   Oh yes, yes. A nice trichotomy⁴ of forces. One must reserve judgement of course, until the confrontation, but I think it's pretty clear where we're heading.

BIRDBOOT   I agree. It's Magnus a mile off.

   [*Small pause.*]

MOON   What's Magnus a mile off?

BIRDBOOT   If we knew that we wouldn't be here.

MOON   [*Clears throat.*] Let me at once say that it has *élan* while at the same time avoiding *éclat.*⁵ Having said that, and I think it must be said, I am bound to ask—does this play know where it is going?

BIRDBOOT   Well, it seems open and shut to me, Moon—Magnus is not what he pretends to be and he's got his next victim marked down——

MOON   Does it, I repeat, declare its affiliations? There are moments, and I would not begrudge it this, when the play, if we can call it that, and I think on balance we can, aligns itself uncompromisingly on the side of life. *Je suis,* it seems to be saying, *ergo sum.*⁶ But is that enough? I think we are entitled to ask. For what in fact is this play concerned with? It is my belief that here we are concerned with what I have referred to elsewhere as the nature of identity. I think we are entitled to ask—and here one is irresistibly reminded of Voltaire's cry, *"Voila!"*⁷—I think we are entitled to ask—*Where is God?*

BIRDBOOT   [*Stunned.*] Who?

MOON   Go-od.

BIRDBOOT   [*Peeping furtively into his programme.*] God?

MOON   I think we are entitled to ask.

   [*The phone rings.*]

   [*The set re-illumines to reveal* CYNTHIA, FELICITY, *and* MAGNUS *about to take coffee, which is being taken round by* MRS DRUDGE. SIMON *is missing. The body lies in position.*]

MRS DRUDGE   [*Into phone.*] The same, half an hour later? . . . No, I'm sorry—there's no one of that name here. [*She replaces phone and goes round with coffee. To* CYNTHIA.] Black or white, my lady?

CYNTHIA   White please.

   [MRS DRUDGE *pours.*]

MRS DRUDGE   [*To* FELICITY.] Black or white, miss?

4. Division into three.
5. Brilliant display (French). *"Élan"*: vivacity (French).
6. Cf. Descartes' *Le Discourse de la Methode:* *"Cogito, ergo sum"* (I think, therefore I am—

Latin). *"Je suis"*: I am (French).
7. The French philosopher and author François Marie Arouet de Voltaire is not on record as saying any such thing.

FELICITY   White please.
      [MRS DRUDGE *pours.*]
MRS DRUDGE   [*To* MAGNUS.] Black or white, Major?
MAGNUS   White please.
      [*Ditto.*]
MRS DRUDGE   [*To* CYNTHIA.] Sugar, my lady?
CYNTHIA   Yes please.
      [*Puts sugar in.*]
MRS DRUDGE   [*To* FELICITY.] Sugar, miss?
FELICITY   Yes please.
      [*Ditto.*]
MRS DRUDGE   [*To* MAGNUS.] Sugar, Major?
MAGNUS   Yes please.
      [*Ditto.*]
MRS DRUDGE   [*To* CYNTHIA.] Biscuit, my lady?
CYNTHIA   No thank you.
BIRDBOOT   [*Writing elaborately in his notebook.*] The second act, however,
   fails to fulfil the promise. . . .
FELICITY   If you ask me, there's something funny going on.
      [MRS DRUDGE's *approach to* FELICITY *makes* FELICITY *jump to her feet
      in impatience. She goes to the radio while* MAGNUS *declines his biscuit,
      and* MRS DRUDGE *leaves.*]
RADIO   We interrupt our programme for a special police message. The
   search for the dangerous madman who is on the loose in Essex has now
   narrowed to the immediate vicinity of Muldoon Manor. Police are ham-
   pered by the deadly swamps and the fog, but believe that the madman
   spent last night in a deserted cottage on the cliffs. The public is advised
   to stick together and make sure none of their number is missing. That
   is the end of the police message.
      [FELICITY *turns off the radio nervously. Pause.*]
CYNTHIA   Where's Simon?
FELICITY   Who?
CYNTHIA   Simon. Have you seen him?
FELICITY   No.
CYNTHIA   Have you, Magnus?
MAGNUS   No.
CYNTHIA   Oh.
FELICITY   Yes, there's something foreboding in the air, it is as if one of
   us——
CYNTHIA   Oh, Felicity, the house is locked up tight—no one can get in—
   and the police are practically on the doorstep.
FELICITY   I don't know—it's just a feeling.
CYNTHIA   It's only the fog.
MAGNUS   Hound will never get through on a day like this.
CYNTHIA   [*Shouting at him.*] Fog!
FELICITY   He means the Inspector.
CYNTHIA   Is he bringing a dog?
FELICITY   Not that I know of.
MAGNUS   —never get through the swamps. Yes, I'm afraid the madman
   can show his hand in safety now.
      [*A mournful baying hooting is heard in the distance, scary.*]

CYNTHIA   What's that?!

FELICITY   [*Tensely.*] It sounded like the cry of a gigantic hound![8]

MAGNUS   Poor devil!

CYNTHIA   Ssssh!

[*They listen. The sound is repeated, nearer.*]

FELICITY   There it is again!

CYNTHIA   It's coming this way—it's right outside the house!

[MRS DRUDGE *enters.*]

MRS DRUDGE   Inspector Hound!

CYNTHIA   A *police* dog?

[*Enter* INSPECTOR HOUND. *On his feet are his swamp boots. These are two inflatable—and inflated—pontoons with flat bottoms about two feet across. He carries a foghorn.*]

HOUND   Lady Muldoon?

CYNTHIA   Yes.

HOUND   I came as soon as I could. Where shall I put my foghorn and my swamp boots?

CYNTHIA   Mrs Drudge will take them out. Be prepared, as the Force's[9] motto has it, eh, Inspector? How very resourceful!

HOUND   [*Divesting himself of boots and foghorn.*] It takes more than a bit of weather to keep a policeman from his duty.

[MRS DRUDGE *leaves with chattels. A pause.*]

CYNTHIA   Oh—er, Inspector Hound—Felicity Cunningham, Major Magnus Muldoon.

HOUND   Good evening.

[*He and* CYNTHIA *continue to look expectantly at each other.*]

CYNTHIA AND HOUND   [*Together.*] Well?—Sorry——

CYNTHIA   No, do go on.

HOUND   Thank you. Well, tell me about it in your own words—take your time, begin at the beginning and don't leave anything out.

CYNTHIA   I beg your pardon?

HOUND   Fear nothing. You are in safe hands now. I hope you haven't touched anything.

CYNTHIA   I'm afraid I don't understand.

HOUND   I'm Inspector Hound.

CYNTHIA   Yes.

HOUND   Well, what's it all about?

CYNTHIA   I really have no idea.

HOUND   How did it begin?

CYNTHIA   What?

HOUND   The . . . thing.

CYNTHIA   What thing?

HOUND   [*Rapidly losing confidence but exasperated.*] The trouble!

CYNTHIA   There hasn't *been* any trouble!

HOUND   Didn't you phone the police?

CYNTHIA   No.

FELICITY   I didn't.

---

8. Cf. Sir Arthur Conan Doyle, *Hound of the Bas-kervilles:* "Mr. Holmes, they were the footprints of a gigantic hound!"

9. "Be prepared" is the motto of the Boy Scouts, not the British police force.

MAGNUS   What for?

HOUND   I see. [*Pause.*] This puts me in a very difficult position. [*A steady pause.*] Well, I'll be getting along, then. [*He moves towards the door.*]

CYNTHIA   I'm terribly sorry.

HOUND   [*Stiffly.*] That's perfectly all right.

CYNTHIA   Thank you so much for coming.

HOUND   Not at all. You never know, there might have been a serious matter.

CYNTHIA   Drink?

HOUND   More serious than that, even.

CYNTHIA   [*Correcting.*] Drink before you go?

HOUND   No thank you. [*Leaves.*]

CYNTHIA   [*Through the door.*] I do hope you find him.

HOUND   [*Reappearing at once.*] Find who, Madam?—out with it!

CYNTHIA   I thought you were looking for the lunatic.

HOUND   And what do you know about that?

CYNTHIA   It was on the radio.

HOUND   Was it, indeed? Well, that's what I'm here about, really. I didn't want to mention it because I didn't know how much you knew. No point in causing unnecessary panic, even with a murderer in our midst.

FELICITY   Murderer, did you say?

HOUND   Ah—so that was not on the radio?

CYNTHIA   Whom has he murdered, Inspector?

HOUND   Perhaps no one—yet. Let us hope we are in time.

MAGNUS   You believe he is in our midst, Inspector?

HOUND   I do. If anyone of you have recently encountered a youngish good-looking fellow in a smart suit, white shirt, hatless, well-spoken—someone possibly claiming to have just moved into the neighbourhood, someone who on the surface seems as sane as you or I, then now is the time to speak!

FELICITY   I——

HOUND   Don't interrupt!

FELICITY   Inspector——

HOUND   Very well.

CYNTHIA   No. Felicity!

HOUND   Please, Lady Cynthia, we are all in this together. I must ask you to put yourself completely in my hands.

CYNTHIA   Don't, Inspector. I love Albert.

HOUND   I don't think you quite grasp my meaning.

MAGNUS   Is one of us in danger, Inspector?

HOUND   Didn't it strike you as odd that on his escape the madman made a beeline for Muldoon Manor? It is my guess that he bears a deep-seated grudge against someone in this very house! Lady Muldoon—where is your husband?

CYNTHIA   My husband?—you don't mean——?

HOUND   I don't know—but I have a reason to believe that one of you is the real McCoy![1]

1. The genuine article (slang).

FELICITY The real what?

HOUND William Herbert McCoy who as a young man, meeting the madman in the street and being solicited for sixpence for a cup of tea, replied, "Why don't you do a decent day's work, you shifty old bag of horse manure," in Canada all those many years ago and went on to make his fortune. [*He starts to pace intensely.*] The madman was a mere boy at the time but he never forgot that moment, and thenceforth carried in his heart the promise of revenge! [*At which point he finds himself standing on top of the corpse. He looks down carefully.*]

HOUND Is there anything you have forgotten to tell me?

[*They all see the corpse for the first time.*]

FELICITY So the madman has struck!

CYNTHIA Oh—it's horrible—horrible——

HOUND Yes, just as I feared. Now you see the sort of man you are protecting.

CYNTHIA I can't believe it!

FELICITY I'll have to tell him, Cynthia—Inspector, a stranger of that description has indeed appeared in our midst—Simon Gascoyne. Oh, he had charm, I'll give you that, and he took me in completely. I'm afraid I made a fool of myself over him, and so did Cynthia.

HOUND Where is he now?

MAGNUS He must be around the house—he couldn't get away in these conditions.

HOUND You're right. Fear naught, Lady Muldoon—I shall apprehend the man who killed your husband.

CYNTHIA My husband? I don't understand.

HOUND Everything points to Gascoyne.

CYNTHIA But who's that? [*The corpse.*]

HOUND Your husband.

CYNTHIA No, it's not.

HOUND Yes, it is.

CYNTHIA I tell you it's not.

HOUND *I'm* in charge of this case!

CYNTHIA But that's not my husband.

HOUND Are you sure?

CYNTHIA For goodness sake!

HOUND Then who is it?

CYNTHIA I don't know.

HOUND Anybody?

FELICITY I've never seen him before.

MAGNUS Quite unlike anybody I've ever met.

HOUND This case is becoming an utter shambles.

CYNTHIA But what are we going to do?

HOUND [*Snatching the phone.*] I'll phone the police!

CYNTHIA But you are the police!

HOUND Thank God I'm here—the lines have been cut!

CYNTHIA You mean——?

HOUND Yes!—we're on our own, cut off from the world and in grave danger!

FELICITY You mean——?

HOUND   Yes!—I think the killer will strike again!

MAGNUS   You mean——?

HOUND   Yes! One of us ordinary mortals thrown together by fate and cut off by the elements, is the murderer! He must be found—search the house!

> [*All depart speedily in different directions leaving a momentarily empty stage.* SIMON *strolls on.*]

SIMON   [*Entering, calling.*] Anyone about?—funny. . . .

> [*He notices the corpse and is surprised. He approaches it and turns it over. He stands up and looks about in alarm.*]

BIRDBOOT   This is where Simon gets the chop.

> [*There is a shot.* SIMON *falls dead.*]
>
> [INSPECTOR HOUND *runs on and crouches down by* SIMON's *body.* CYNTHIA *appears at the french windows. She stops there and stares.*]

CYNTHIA   What happened, Inspector?!

> [HOUND *turns to face her.*]

HOUND   He's dead. . . . Simon Gascoyne, I presume. Rough justice even for a killer—unless—unless—We assumed that the body could not have been lying there before Simon Gascoyne entered the house . . . but . . . [*he slides the sofa over the body*] there's your answer. And now—who killed Simon Gascoyne? And why?

> [*"Curtain," freeze, applause, exeunt.*]

MOON   Why not?

BIRDBOOT   Exactly. Good riddance.

MOON   Yes, getting away with murder must be quite easy provided that one's motive is sufficiently inscrutable.

BIRDBOOT   Fickle young pup! He was deceiving her right, left and centre.

MOON   [*Thoughtfully.*] Of course. I'd still have Puckeridge behind *me*——

BIRDBOOT   She needs someone steadier, more mature——

MOON   —And if I could, so could he——

BIRDBOOT   Yes, I know of this rather nice hotel, very discreet, run by a man of the world——

MOON   Uneasy lies the head that wears the crown.[2]

BIRDBOOT   Breakfast served in one's room and no questions asked.

MOON   Does Puckeridge dream of me?

BIRDBOOT   [*Pause.*] Hello—what's happened?

MOON   What? Oh yes—what do you make of it, so far?

BIRDBOOT   [*Clears throat.*] It is at this point that the play for me comes alive. The groundwork has been well and truly laid, and the author has taken the trouble to learn from the masters of the genre. He has created a real situation, and few will doubt his ability to resolve it with a startling denouement. Certainly that is what it so far lacks, but it has a beginning, a middle and I have no doubt it will prove to have an end. For this let us give thanks, and double thanks for a good clean show without a trace of smut. But perhaps even all this would be for nothing were it not for a performance which I consider to be one of the summits in the range of contemporary theatre. In what is possibly the finest Cynthia since the war——

2. *2 Henry IV* 3.1.31.

MOON   If we examine this more closely, and I think close examination is the least tribute that this play deserves, I think we will find that within the austere framework of what is seen to be on one level a country-house week-end, and what a useful symbol that is, the author has given us— yes, I will go far—he has given us the human condition——

BIRDBOOT   More talent in her little finger——

MOON   An uncanny ear that might have belonged to a Van Gogh[3]——

BIRDBOOT   —a public scandal that the Birthday Honours[4] to date have neglected——

MOON   Faced as we are with such ubiquitous obliquity, it is hard, it is hard indeed, and therefore I will not attempt, to refrain from invoking the names of Kafka, Sartre, Shakespeare, St. Paul, Beckett, Birkett, Pinero, Pirandello, Dante, and Dorothy L. Sayers.[5]

BIRDBOOT   A rattling good evening out. I was held.

[*The phone starts to ring on the empty stage.* MOON *tries to ignore it.*]

MOON   Harder still——Harder still if possible——Harder still if it is possible to be——Neither do I find it easy——Dante and Dorothy L. Sayers. Harder still——

BIRDBOOT   Others taking part included—*Moon!*

[*For* MOON *has lost patience and is bearing down on the ringing phone. He is frankly irritated.*]

MOON   [*Picking up phone, barks.*] Hel-lo! [*Pause, turns to* BIRDBOOT, *quietly.*] It's for you. [*Pause.*]

[BIRDBOOT *gets up. He approaches cautiously.* MOON *gives him the phone and moves back to his seat.* BIRDBOOT *watches him go. He looks round and smiles weakly, expiating himself.*]

BIRDBOOT   [*Into phone.*] Hello. . . . [*Explosion.*] Oh, for God's sake, Myrtle!—I've told you never to phone me at work! [*He is naturally embarrassed, looking about with surreptitious fury.*] What? Last night? Good God, woman, this is hardly the time to—I assure you, Myrtle, there is absolutely nothing going on between me and—I took her to dinner simply by way of keeping *au fait* with the world of the paint and the motley[6]— —Yes, I promise——Yes, I do——Yes, I *said* yes—I *do*—and you are mine too, Myrtle—darling—I can't—[*Whispers.*] *I'm not alone*—[*Up.*] No, she's not!—[*He looks around furtively, licks his lips and mumbles.*] All *right!* I love your little pink ears and you are my own fluffy bunny-boo——Now for God's sake——Good-bye, Myrtle—[*Puts down phone.*]

[BIRDBOOT *mops his brow with his handkerchief. As he turns, a tennis ball bounces in through the french windows, followed by* FELICITY, *as before, in tennis outfit. The lighting is as it was. Everything is as it was. It is, let us say, the same moment of time.*]

FELICITY   [*Calling.*] Out! [*She catches sight of* BIRDBOOT *and is amazed.*] You!

---

3. The painter Vincent Van Gogh, in his madness, severed his ear and sent it to his brother.
4. Titles given on the British sovereign's official birthday.
5. British detective story writer and translator of Dante's *Divine Comedy*. Franz Kafka, German novelist of Czech origin. Jean-Paul Sartre, French philosopher and writer. William Shakespeare, English playwright. St. Paul of Tarsus, Christian apostle. Samuel Beckett, Irish playwright and novelist. Lord Birkett of Ulverston, lord justice of British Court of Appeal. Sir Arthur Pinero, British dramatist. Luigi Pirandello, Italian dramatist. Dante Alighieri, Italian poet.
6. I.e., theater (literally, greasepaint and the particolored costume of the jester).

BIRDBOOT   Er, yes—hello again.

FELICITY   What are you doing here?!

BIRDBOOT   Well, I . . .

FELICITY   Honestly, darling, you really are extraordinary——

BIRDBOOT   Yes, well, here I am. [*He looks round sheepishly.*]

FELICITY   You must have been desperate to see me—I mean, I'm flattered, but couldn't it wait till I got back?

BIRDBOOT   No, no, you've got it all wrong——

FELICITY   What is it?

BIRDBOOT   And about last night—perhaps I gave you the wrong impression—got carried away a bit, perhaps——

FELICITY   [*Stiffly.*] What are you trying to say?

BIRDBOOT   I want to call it off.

FELICITY   I see.

BIRDBOOT   I didn't promise anything—and the fact is, I have my reputation—people do talk——

FELICITY   You don't have to say any more——

BIRDBOOT   And my wife, too—I don't know how she got to hear of it, but——

FELICITY   Of all the nerve! To march in here and——

BIRDBOOT   I'm sorry you had to find out like this—the fact is I didn't mean it this way——

FELICITY   You philandering coward!

BIRDBOOT   I'm sorry—but I want you to know that I meant those things I said—oh yes—shows brilliant promise—I shall say so——

FELICITY   I'll kill you for this, Simon Gascoyne!

[*She leaves in tears, passing* MRS DRUDGE *who has entered in time to overhear her last remark.*]

BIRDBOOT   [*Wide-eyed.*] Good God. . . .

MRS DRUDGE   I have come to set up the card table, sir.

BIRDBOOT   [*Wildly.*] I can't stay for a game of *cards*!

MRS DRUDGE   Oh, Lady Muldoon *will* be disappointed.

BIRDBOOT   You mean . . . you mean, she wants to meet me . . . ?

MRS DRUDGE   Oh yes, sir, I just told her and it put her in quite a tizzy.

BIRDBOOT   Really? Yes, well, a man of my influence is not to be sneezed at—I think I have some small name for the making of reputations—mmm, yes, quite a tizzy, you say?

[MRS DRUDGE *is busied with the card table.* BIRDBOOT *stands marooned and bemused for a moment.*]

MOON   [*From his seat.*] Birdboot!—[*A tense whisper.*]. Birdboot!

[BIRDBOOT *looks round vaguely.*]

What the hell are you doing?

BIRDBOOT   Nothing.

MOON   Stop making an ass of yourself. Come back.

BIRDBOOT   Oh, I know what you're thinking—but the fact is I genuinely consider her performance to be one of the summits——

[CYNTHIA *enters as before.* MRS DRUDGE *has gone.*]

CYNTHIA   Darling!

BIRDBOOT   Ah, good evening—may I say that I genuinely consider——

CYNTHIA   Don't say anything for a moment—just hold me.

[*She falls into his arms.*]

BIRDBOOT All right! [*They kiss.*] My God!—she *does* have her mouth open!
Dear lady, from the first moment I saw you, I felt my whole life changing—

CYNTHIA [*Breaking free.*] We can't go on meeting like this!

BIRDBOOT I am not ashamed to proclaim nightly my love for you!—but
fortunately that will not be necessary——I know of a very good hotel,
discreet—run by a man of the world——

CYNTHIA But darling, this is madness!

BIRDBOOT Yes! I am mad with love.

CYNTHIA Please!—remember where we are!

BIRDBOOT I don't care! Let them think what they like, I love you!

CYNTHIA Don't—I love Albert!

BIRDBOOT He's dead. [*Shaking her.*] Do you understand me—Albert's
dead!

CYNTHIA No—I'll never give up hope! Let me go! We are not free!

BIRDBOOT You mean Myrtle? She means nothing to me—nothing!—she's
all cocoa and blue nylon fur slippers—not a spark of creative genius in
her whole slumping knee-length-knickered body——

CYNTHIA You're a cad, Simon! You will use me and cast me aside as you
have cast aside so many others!

BIRDBOOT No, Cynthia—now that I have found you——

CYNTHIA You're ruthless—so strong—so cruel——

[BIRDBOOT *seizes her in an embrace, during which* MRS DRUDGE *enters,
and* MOON's *fevered voice is heard.*]

MOON Have you taken leave of your tiny mind?

[CYNTHIA *breaks free.*]

CYNTHIA Stop—can't you see you're making a fool of yourself!

MOON She's right.

BIRDBOOT [*To* MOON.] You keep out of this.

CYNTHIA Yes, what is it, Mrs Drudge?

MRS DRUDGE Should I close the windows, my lady? The fog——

CYNTHIA Yes, you'd better.

MOON Look, they've got your number——

BIRDBOOT I'll leave in my own time, thank you very much.

MOON It's the finish of you, I suppose you know that——

BIRDBOOT I don't need your twopenny Grubb Street prognostications[7]—
I have found something bigger and finer——

MOON [*Bemused, to himself.*] If only it were Higgs. . . .

CYNTHIA . . . And fetch the Major down.

MRS DRUDGE I think I hear him coming down stairs now.

[*She leaves. The sound of a wheelchair's approach as before.* BIRDBOOT
*prudently keeps out of the chair's former path but it enters from the next
wing down and knocks him flying. A babble of anguish and protestation.*]

CYNTHIA Simon—say something!

BIRDBOOT That reckless bastard [*as he sits up*].

CYNTHIA Thank God!——

---

7. Forecasts of literary hack. Grub Street in London was inhabited by hack writers in the 17th and 18th
centuries.

MAGNUS What's *he* doing here?

CYNTHIA He just turned up.

MAGNUS Really? How do you like it here?

BIRDBOOT I couldn't take it night after night.

[FELICITY *enters.*]

FELICITY So—you're still here.

CYNTHIA Of course he's still here. We're going to play cards. There is no need to introduce you two, is there, for I recall now that you, Simon, met me through Felicity, our mutual friend.

FELICITY Yes, Simon is an old friend——

BIRDBOOT Ah—yes—well, I like to give young up and comers the benefit of my—er—Of course, she lacks technique as yet——

FELICITY Last night.

BIRDBOOT I'm not talking about last night!

CYNTHIA Indeed? Well, you deal, Felicity. Simon, you help me with the sofa.

BIRDBOOT [*To* MOON.] Did you see that? Tried to kill me. I told you it was Magnus—not that it *is* Magnus.

MOON Who did it, you mean?

BIRDBOOT What?

MOON You think it's not Magnus who did it?

BIRDBOOT Get a grip on yourself, Moon—the facts are staring you in the face. He's after Cynthia for one thing.

MAGNUS It's Gascoyne, isn't it?

BIRDBOOT Over my dead body!

MAGNUS If he comes between us . . .

MOON [*Angrily.*] For God's sake sit down!

CYNTHIA Simon!

BIRDBOOT She needs me, Moon. I've got to make up a four.[8]

[CYNTHIA *and* BIRDBOOT *move the sofa as before, and they all sit at the table.*]

CYNTHIA Right! Who starts?

MAGNUS I do. I'll dummy for a no-bid ruff and double my holding on South's queen. [*While he moves cards.*]

CYNTHIA Did I hear you say you saw Felicity last night, Simon?

BIRDBOOT Er—er——

FELICITY Pay twenty-ones or trump my contract. [*Discards.*] Cynthia's turn.

CYNTHIA I'll trump your contract with five dummy no-trumps there [*discards*], and I'll move West's rook for the re-bid with a banker ruff on his second trick there. [*Discards.*] Simon?

BIRDBOOT Would you mind doing that again?

CYNTHIA And I'll ruff your dummy with five no-bid trumps there, [*discards*] and I support your re-bid with a banker for the solo ruff in the dummy trick there. [*Discards.*]

BIRDBOOT [*Standing up and throwing down his cards.*] And I call your bluff!

---

8. For a game of cards. In what follows, the players employ a nonsensical medley of terms from a variety of card games, interspersed with terms from chess ("rook," "king's gambit," "check"), roulette ("Faites vos jeux." "Rien ne va plus." "Rouge et noir"), and cricket ("How's that?" "Not out").

CYNTHIA Well done, Simon!

[MAGNUS *pays* BIRDBOOT *while* CYNTHIA *deals.*]

FELICITY Strange how Simon appeared in the neighbourhood from nowhere, we know so little about him.

CYNTHIA Right, Simon, it's your opening on the minor bid. Hmm. Let's see. I think I'll overbid the spade convention with two no-trumps and King's gambit offered there—[*discards*] and West's dummy split double to Queen's Bishop four there!

MAGNUS [*As he plays cards.*] Faites vos jeux. Rien ne va plus. Rouge et noir.[9] Zero.

CYNTHIA Simon?

BIRDBOOT [*Triumphant, leaping to his feet.*] And I call your bluff!

CYNTHIA [*Imperturbably.*] I meld.

FELICITY I huff.

MAGNUS I ruff.

BIRDBOOT I bluff.

CYNTHIA Twist.

FELICITY Bust.

MAGNUS Check.

BIRDBOOT Snap.

CYNTHIA How's that?

FELICITY Not out.

MAGNUS Double top.

BIRDBOOT Bingo!

CYNTHIA No! Simon—your luck's in tonight.

FELICITY We shall see—the night is not over yet, Simon Gascoyne! [*She quickly exits.*]

BIRDBOOT [*Looking after* FELICITY.] Red herring—smell it a mile off. [*To* MAGNUS.] Oh, yes, she's as clean as a whistle, I've seen it a thousand times. And I've seen you before too, haven't I? Strange—there's something about you——

MAGNUS Care for a spin round the rose garden, Cynthia?

CYNTHIA No, Magnus, I must talk to Simon.

BIRDBOOT There's nothing for you there, you know.

MAGNUS You think so?

BIRDBOOT Oh, yes, she knows which side her bread is buttered. I am a man not without a certain influence among those who would reap the limelight—she's not going to throw me over for a heavily disguised cripple.

MAGNUS There's an old Canadian proverb——

BIRDBOOT Don't give me that—I tumbled to you right from the start— oh, yes, you chaps are not as clever as you think. . . . Sooner or later you make your mistake. . . . Incidentally, where was it I saw you? . . . I've definitely——

MAGNUS [*Leaving.*] Well, I think I'll go and oil my gun. [*Exits.*]

BIRDBOOT [*After* MAGNUS.] Double bluff!—[*To* CYNTHIA.] I've seen it a thousand times.

CYNTHIA I think Magnus suspects something. And Felicity? Simon, was there anything between you and Felicity?

---

9. Place your bets. No more betting. Red and black (French).

BIRDBOOT   No, no—that's all over now. I merely flattered her a little over
a drink, told her she'd go far, that sort of thing. Dear me, the fuss that's
been made over a simple flirtation——

CYNTHIA   [As MRS DRUDGE enters behind.] If I find you have falsely
seduced me from my dear husband Albert, I will kill you, Simon Gascoyne!

> [The "CURTAIN" as before. MRS DRUDGE and CYNTHIA leave. BIRDBOOT
> starts to follow them.]

MOON   Birdboot!

> [BIRDBOOT stops.]

MOON   For God's sake pull yourself together.

BIRDBOOT   I can't help it.

MOON   What do you think you're doing? You're turning it into a complete
farce!

BIRDBOOT   I know, I know—but I can't live without her. [He is making
erratic neurotic journeys about the stage.] I shall resign my position, of
course. I don't care I'm a gonner, I tell you——[He has arrived at the
body. He looks at it in surprise, hesitates, bends and turns it over.]

MOON   Birdboot, think of your family, your friends—your high standing
the world of letters—I say, what are you doing?

> [BIRDBOOT is staring at the body's face.]

Birdboot . . . leave it alone. Come and sit down—what's the matter with
you?

BIRDBOOT   [Dead-voiced.] It's Higgs.

MOON   What?

BIRDBOOT   It's Higgs.

> [Pause.]

MOON   Don't be silly.

BIRDBOOT   I tell you it's Higgs!

> [MOON half rises. Bewildered.]

I don't understand. . . . He's dead.

MOON   Dead?

BIRDBOOT   Who would want to . . . ?

MOON   He must have been lying there all the time. . . .

BIRDBOOT   . . . kill Higgs?

MOON   But what's he doing here? I was standing in tonight. . . .

BIRDBOOT   [Turning.] Moon? . . .

MOON   [In wonder, quietly.] So it's me and Puckeridge now.

BIRDBOOT   Moon . . . ?

MOON   [Faltering.] But I swear I. . . .

BIRDBOOT   I've got it——

MOON   But I didn't——

BIRDBOOT   [Quietly.] My God . . . so that was it. . . . [Up.] Moon—now I
see——

MOON   —I swear I didn't——

BIRDBOOT   Now—finally—I see it all——

> [There is a shot and BIRDBOOT falls dead.]

MOON   Birdboot! [He runs on, to BIRDBOOT's body.]

> [CYNTHIA appears at the french windows. She stops and stares. All as
> before.]

CYNTHIA   Oh my God—what happened, Inspector?

MOON   [*Almost to himself.*] He's dead. . . . [*He rises.*] That's a bit rough, isn't it?—A bit extreme!—He may have had his faults—I admit he was a fickle old . . . Who did this, and why?

> [MOON *turns to face her. He stands up and makes swiftly for his seat. Before he gets there he is stopped by the sound of voices.*]
>
> [SIMON *and* HOUND *are occupying the critics' seats.*]
>
> [MOON *freezes.*]

SIMON   To say that it is without pace, point, focus, interest, drama, wit or originality is to say simply that it does not happen to be my cup of tea. One has only to compare this ragbag with the masters of the genre to see that here we have a trifle that is not my cup of tea at all.

HOUND   I'm sorry to be blunt but there is no getting away from it. It lacks pace. A complete ragbag.

SIMON   I will go further. Those of you who were fortunate enough to be at the Comedie Française[1] on Wednesday last, will not need to be reminded that hysterics are no substitute for *éclat*.

HOUND   It lacks *élan*.

SIMON   Some of the cast seem to have given up acting altogether, apparently aghast, with every reason, at finding themselves involved in an evening that would, and indeed will, make the angels weep.[2]

HOUND   I am not a prude but I fail to see any reason for the shower of filth and sexual allusion foisted on to an unsuspecting public in the guise of modernity at all costs. . . .

> [*Behind* MOON, FELICITY, MAGNUS, *and* MRS DRUDGE *have made their entrances, so that he turns to face their semicircle.*]

MAGNUS   [*Pointing to* BIRDBOOT's *body.*] Well, Inspector, is this your man?

MOON   [*Warily.*] . . . Yes. . . . Yes. . . .

CYNTHIA   It's Simon . . .

MOON   Yes . . . yes . . . poor. . . . [*Up.*] Is this some kind of a joke?

MAGNUS   If it is, Inspector, it's in very poor taste.

> [MOON *pulls himself together and becomes galvanic, a little wild, in grief for* BIRDBOOT.]

MOON   All right! I'm going to find out who did this! I want everyone to go to the positions they occupied when the shot was fired—[*They move; hysterically.*]. No one will leave the house! [*They move back.*]

MAGNUS   I think we all had the opportunity to fire the shot, Inspector——

MOON   [*Furious.*] I am not——

MAGNUS   —but which of us would want to?

MOON   Perhaps you, Major Magnus!

MAGNUS   Why should I want to kill him?

MOON   Because he was on to you—yes, he tumbled you right from the start—and you shot him just when he was about to reveal that you killed—[MOON *points, pauses and then crosses to* Higgs's *body and falters*]—killed—[*He turns* Higgs *over.*]—this . . . chap.

MAGNUS   But what motive would there be for killing him? [*Pause.*] Who is this chap? [*Pause.*] Inspector?

1. State Theater in Paris, France.
2. Cf. *Measure for Measure* 2.2.117–22: "But man, proud man, / . . . like an angry ape / Plays such fantastic tricks before high heaven / As makes the angels weep."

MOON [*Rising.*] I don't know. Quite unlike anyone I've ever met. [*Long pause.*] Well . . . now . . .

MRS DRUDGE Inspector?

MOON [*Eagerly.*] Yes? Yes, what is it, dear lady?

MRS DRUDGE Happening to enter this room earlier in the day to close the windows, I chanced to overhear a remark made by the deceased Simon Gascoyne to her ladyship, viz.—"I will kill anyone who comes between us."

MOON Ah—yes—well, that's it, then. This . . . chap . . . [*Pointing.*] was obviously killed by [*Pointing.*] er . . . by [*Pause.*] Simon.

CYNTHIA But he didn't come between us!

MAGNUS And who, then, killed Simon?

MRS DRUDGE Subsequent to that reported remark, I also happened to be in earshot of a remark made by Lady Muldoon to the deceased, to the effect, "I will kill you, Simon Gascoyne!" I hope you don't mind my mentioning it.

MOON Not at all. I'm glad you did. It is from these chance remarks that we in the force build up our complete picture before moving in to make the arrest. It will not be long now, I fancy, and I must warn you, Lady Muldoon that anything you say——

CYNTHIA Yes!—I hated Simon Gascoyne, for he had me in his power!— But I didn't kill him!

MRS DRUDGE Prior to that, Inspector, I also chanced to overhear a remark made by Miss Cunningham, no doubt in the heat of the moment, but it stuck in my mind as these things do, viz., "I will kill you for this, Simon Gascoyne!"

MOON Ah! The final piece of the jigsaw! I think I am now in a position to reveal the mystery. This man [*The corpse.*] was, of course, McCoy, the Canadian who, as we heard, meeting Gascoyne in the street and being solicited for sixpence for a toffee apple, smacked him across the ear, with the cry, "How's that for a grudge to harbour, you sniffling little workshy!"[3] all those many years ago. Gascoyne bided his time, but in due course tracked McCoy down to this house, having, on the way, met, in the neighbourhood, a simple ambitious girl from the provinces. He was charming, persuasive—told her, I have no doubt, that she would go straight to the top—and she, flattered by his sophistication, taken in by his promises to see her all right[4] on the night, gave in to his simple desires. Perhaps she loved him. We shall never know. But in the very hour of her promised triumph, his eye fell on another—yes, I refer to Lady Cynthia Muldoon. From the moment he caught sight of her there was no other woman for him—he was in her spell, willing to sacrifice anything, even you, Felicity Cunningham. It was only today—unexpectedly finding him here—that you learned the truth. There was a bitter argument which ended with your promise to kill him—a promise that you carried out in this very room at your first opportunity! And I must warn you that anything you say——

FELICITY But it doesn't make sense!

MOON Not at first glance, *perhaps.*

---

3. Idler.   4. Look after her (slang).

MAGNUS   Could not Simon have been killed by the same person who killed McCoy?

FELICITY   But why should any of us want to kill a perfect stranger?

MAGNUS   Perhaps he was not a stranger to *one* of us.

MOON   [*Faltering.*] But Simon was the madman, wasn't he?

MAGNUS   We only have your word for that, Inspector. We only have your word for a lot of things. For instance—McCoy. Who is he? Is his name McCoy? Is there any truth in that fantastic and implausible tale of the insult inflicted in the Canadian streets? Or is there something else, something quite unknown to us, behind all this? Suppose for a moment that the madman, having killed this unknown stranger for private and inscrutable reasons of his own, was disturbed before he could dispose of the body, so having cut the telephone wires he decided to return to the scene of the crime, masquerading as—Police Inspector Hound!

MOON   But . . . I'm not mad . . . I'm almost sure I'm not mad. . . .

MAGNUS   . . . only to discover that in the house was a man, Simon Gascoyne, who recognized the corpse as a man against whom you had held a deep-seated grudge——!

MOON   But I didn't kill—I'm almost sure I——

MAGNUS   I put it to you!—are you the real Inspector Hound?!

MOON   You know damn well I'm not! What's it all about?

MAGNUS   I thought as much.

MOON   I only dreamed . . . sometimes I dreamed——

CYNTHIA   So it was you!

MRS DRUDGE   The madman!

FELICITY   The killer!

CYNTHIA   Oh, it's horrible, horrible.

MRS DRUDGE   The stranger in our midst!

MAGNUS   Yes, we had a shrewd suspicion he would turn up here—and he walked into the trap!

MOON   What *trap*?

MAGNUS   I am not the real Magnus Muldoon!—It was a mere subterfuge!—and [*Standing up and removing his moustaches.*] I now reveal myself as——

CYNTHIA   You mean——?

MAGNUS   Yes!—I am the real Inspector Hound!

MOON   [*Pause.*] Puckeridge!

MAGNUS   [*With pistol.*] Stand where you are, or I shoot!

MOON   [*Backing.*] Puckeridge! You killed Higgs—and Birdboot tried to tell me——

MAGNUS   Stop in the name of the law!

[MOON *turns to run.* MAGNUS *fires.* MOON *drops to his knees.*]

I have waited a long time for this moment.

CYNTHIA   So you are the real Inspector Hound.

MAGNUS   Not only that!—I have been leading a double life—at *least*!

CYNTHIA   You mean——?

MAGNUS   Yes!—It's been ten long years, but don't you know me?

CYNTHIA   You mean——?

MAGNUS   Yes!—it is me, Albert!—who lost his memory and joined the force, rising by merit to the rank of Inspector, his past blotted out—until

fate cast him back into the home he left behind, back to the beautiful
woman he had brought here as his girlish bride—in short, my darling,
my memory has returned and your long wait is over!

CYNTHIA   Oh, Albert!

    [*They embrace.*]

MOON   [*With a trace of admiration.*] Puckeridge . . . you cunning bastard.

    [MOON *dies.*]

THE END

1968

LES MURRAY

b. 1938

Leslie Allan Murray was born at Nabiac on the north coast of New South Wales,
Australia, and grew up on a dairy farm at nearby Bunyah. He was educated at Taree
High School and the University of Sydney, where he studied modern languages. After
military service with the Royal Australian Naval Reserve, he worked as a translator
in the Australian National University, Canberra, and as an officer in the prime minister's department. Since 1971, he has been a full-time writer.

Noonday Axeman, one of several remarkable poems in Murray's first book, *The Ilex
Tree* (1965), made audible a distinctive voice and defined one of his principal projects:

> Though I myself run to the cities, I will forever
> be coming back here to walk, knee-deep in ferns,
> up and away from this metropolitan century,
>
> to remember my ancestors, axemen, dairymen, horse-breakers,
> now coffined in silence, down with their beards and dreams,
> who, unwilling or rapt, despairing or very patient,
> made what amounts to a human breach in the silence,
>
> made of their lives the rough foundation of legends—
> men must have legends, else they will die of strangeness. . . .

Remaining true to his roots in the Australian "outback" (despite the globe-trotting
expected of a major poet in the late twentieth century), Murray has emerged as a
powerful celebrant of the natural world. His substantial *Collected Poems* (1998) is
dedicated "to the glory of God" and bears witness to a staunch and highly individual
Roman Catholicism. As one might expect of a religious poet, his celebration of Nature
includes human nature and reveals a sensibility generously attuned to the hopes and
fears, hurts and happinesses of ordinary lives. As the Nobel laureate Derek Walcott
has said of Murray's work: "There is no poetry in the English language so rooted in
its sacredness, so broad-leafed in its pleasures, and yet so intimate and conversational."

Noonday Axeman

Axe-fall, echo and silence. Noonday silence.
Two miles from here, it is the twentieth century:
cars on the bitumen,[1] powerlines vaulting the farms.
Here, with my axe, I am chopping into the stillness.

5   Axe-fall, echo and silence. I pause, roll tobacco,
twist a cigarette, lick it. All is still.
I lean on my axe. A cloud of fragrant leaves
hangs over me moveless, pierced everywhere by sky.

Here, I remember all of a hundred years:
10   candleflame, still night, frost and cattle bells,
the draywheels'[2] silence final in our ears,
and the first red cattle spreading through the hills

and my great-great-grandfather here with his first sons,
who would grow old, still speaking with his Scots accent,
15   having never seen those highlands that they sang of.
A hundred years. I stand and smoke in the silence.

A hundred years of clearing, splitting, sawing,
a hundred years of timbermen, ringbarkers, fencers
and women in kitchens, stoking loud iron stoves
20   year in, year out, and singing old songs to their children

have made this silence human and familiar
no farther than where the farms rise into foothills,
and, in that time, how many have sought their graves
or fled to the cities, maddened by this stillness?

25   Things are so wordless. These two opposing scarves
I have cut in my red-gum squeeze out jewels of sap
and stare. And soon, with a few more axe-strokes,
the tree will grow troubled, tremble, shift its crown

and, leaning slowly, gather speed and colossally
30   crash down and lie between the standing trunks.
And then, I know, of the knowledge that led my forebears
to drink and black rage and wordlessness, there will be silence.

After the tree falls, there will reign the same silence
as stuns and spurs us, enraptures and defeats us,
35   as seems to some a challenge, and seems to others
to be waiting here for something beyond imagining.

---

1. Name given to various inflammable mineral substances, here probably asphalt.   2. Wheels of a long, heavy cart.

Axe-fall, echo and silence. Unhuman silence.
A stone cracks in the heat. Through the still twigs, radiance
stings at my eyes. I rub a damp brow with a handkerchief
40 and chop on into the stillness. Axe-fall and echo.

The great mast murmurs now. The scarves in its trunk
crackle and squeak now, crack and increase as the hushing
weight of high branches heels outward, and commences
tearing and falling, and the collapse is tremendous.

45 Twigs fly, leaves puff and subside. The severed trunk
slips off its stump and drops along its shadow.
And then there is no more. The stillness is there
as ever. And I fall to lopping branches.

Axe-fall, echo and silence. It will be centuries
50 before many men are truly at home in this country,
and yet, there have always been some, in each generation,
there have always been some who could live in the presence of silence.

And some, I have known them, men with gentle broad hands,
who would die if removed from these unpeopled places,
55 some again I have seen, bemused and shy in the cities,
you have built against silence, dumbly trudging through noise

past the railway stations, looking up through the traffic
at the smoky halls, dreaming of journeys, of stepping
down from the train at some upland stop to recover
60 the crush of dry grass underfoot, the silence of trees.

Axe-fall, echo and silence. Dreaming silence.
Though I myself run to the cities, I will forever
be coming back here to walk, knee-deep in ferns,
up and away from this metropolitan century,

65 to remember my ancestors, axemen, dairymen, horse-breakers,
now coffined in silence, down with their beards and dreams,
who, unwilling or rapt, despairing or very patient,
made what amounts to a human breach in the silence,

made of their lives the rough foundation of legends—
70 men must have legends, else they will die of strangeness—
then died in their turn, each, after his own fashion,
resigned or agonized, from silence into great silence.

Axe-fall, echo and axe-fall. Noonday silence.
Though I go to the cities, turning my back on these hills,
75 for the talk and dazzle of cities, for the sake of belonging
for months and years at a time to the twentieth century,

the city will never quite hold me. I will be always
coming back here on the up-train, peering, leaning

out of the window to see, on far-off ridges,
80   the sky between the trees, and over the racket
of the rails to hear the echo and the silence.

I shoulder my axe and set off home through the stillness.

1965

Morse

Tuckett. Bill Tuckett. Telegraph operator, Hall's Creek,
which is way out back of the Outback, but he stuck it,
quite likely liked it, despite heat, glare, dust and the lack
of diversion or doctors. Come disaster you trusted to luck,
5   ingenuity and pluck. This was back when nice people said pluck,
the sleevelink and green eyeshade epoch.
                         Faced, though, like Bill Tuckett
with a man needing surgery right on the spot, a lot
would have done their dashes. It looked hopeless (dot dot dot)
Lift him up on the table, said Tuckett, running the key hot
10 till Head Office turned up a doctor who coolly instructed
up a thousand miles of wire, as Tuckett advanced slit by slit
with a safety razor blade, pioneering on into the wet,
copper-wiring the rivers off, in the first operation conducted
along dotted lines, with rum drinkers gripping the patient:
d-d-dash it, take care, Tuck!
15   And the vital spark stayed unshorted.
Yallah! breathed the camelmen. Tuckett, you did it, you did it!
cried the spattered la-de-dah jodhpur-wearing Inspector of Stock.
We imagine, some weeks later, a properly laconic
convalescent averring Without you, I'd have kicked the bucket . . .

20 From Chungking to Burrenjuck, morse keys have mostly gone silent
and only old men meet now to chit-chat in their electric
bygone dialect. The last letter many will forget
is dit-dit-dit-dah, V for Victory. The coders' hero had speed,
resource and a touch. So ditditdit daah for Bill Tuckett.

1983

SEAMUS HEANEY
b. 1939

Seamus Heaney was born into a Roman Catholic family in the Protestant north of
Ireland (or Ulster), and grew up on a farm in County Derry bordered on one side by
a stream that marked the frontier with the predominantly Roman Catholic Irish

Republic (or Eire) to the south. He won scholarships first to St. Columb's College, a Catholic boarding school, and then to Queen's University in Protestant Belfast. There he became one of a lively group of young poets that included Michael Longley and Derek Mahon, writing with the encouragement of two faculty poets, Laurence Lerner and Philip Hobsbaum. He has been Boylston Professor of Rhetoric and Oratory at Harvard and Professor of Poetry at Oxford.

With *Digging*, placed appropriately as the first poem of his first book, Heaney defined his territory. He dug into his memory, uncovering first his father and then, going deeper, his grandfather. In this and many later poems, his concern has been— like Tony Harrison's—to give a voice to the silent and oppressed. In 1967, his political preoccupations were brought into sharper focus by his reading of *The Bog People* by P. V. Glob, a Danish archaeologist. This opened his eyes—as Jessie L. Weston's *From Ritual to Romance* had opened Eliot's—to deeper levels of mythic and historical congruence. He writes of *The Bog People*:

> It was chiefly concerned with preserved bodies of men and women found in the bogs of Jutland, naked, strangled or with their throats cut, disposed under the peat since early Iron Age times. The author . . . argues convincingly that a number of these, and in particular, the Tollund Man, whose head is now preserved near Aarhus in the museum of Silkeburg, were ritual sacrifices to the Mother Goddess, the goddess of the ground who needed new bridegrooms each winter to bed with her in her sacred place, in the spring. Taken in relation to the tradition of Irish political martyrdom for the cause whose icon is Kathleen Ni Houlihan [mythic figure emblematic of Mother Ireland], this is more than an archaic barbarous rite: it is an archetypal pattern. And the unforgettable photographs of these victims blended in my mind with photographs of atrocities, past and present, in the long rites of Irish political and religious struggles.

Heaney's perception that the Irish "bog is a memory bank," in that it preserves everything thrown into it, produced the powerful bog poems of *North* (1975). By then, feeling constrained by the role of political poet being thrust on him, he had crossed the border to live in the Irish Republic. The troubles of Ireland continue to surface in the poems he has written since, but the richer harmonies of *Field Work* (1979), *Station Island* (1984), *The Haw Lantern* (1987), *Seeing Things* (1991), and *The Spirit Level* (1996) confirm the wisdom of his decision to move south and the truth of Robert Lowell's judgment that Heaney is "the best Irish poet since W. B. Yeats." His *Opened Ground: Poems 1966–1996* ends with "Crediting Poetry," the speech with which he accepted the 1995 Nobel Prize, awarded to him, in the words of the Swedish Academy of Letters, for his "words of lyrical beauty and ethical depth." Heaney is also a noteworthy translator; his verse translation of *Beowulf* appears in volume 1 of this anthology.

Digging

Between my finger and my thumb
The squat pen rests; snug as a gun.

Under my window, a clean rasping sound
When the spade sinks into gravelly ground:
5 My father, digging. I look down

Till his straining rump among the flowerbeds
Bends low, comes up twenty years away

Stooping in rhythm through potato drills[1]
Where he was digging.

10 The coarse boot nestled on the lug, the shaft
Against the inside knee was levered firmly.
He rooted out tall tops, buried the bright edge deep
To scatter new potatoes that we picked
Loving their cool hardness in our hands.

15 By God, the old man could handle a spade.
Just like his old man.

My grandfather cut more turf[2] in a day
Than any other man on Toner's bog.
Once I carried him milk in a bottle
20 Corked sloppily with paper. He straightened up
To drink it, then fell to right away
Nicking and slicing neatly, heaving sods
Over his shoulder, going down and down
For the good turf. Digging.

25 The cold smell of potato mould, the squelch and slap
Of soggy peat, the curt cuts of an edge
Through living roots awaken in my head.
But I've no spade to follow men like them.

Between my finger and my thumb
30 The squat pen rests.
I'll dig with it.

1966

The Forge

All I know is a door into the dark.
Outside, old axles and iron hoops rusting;
Inside, the hammered anvil's short-pitched ring,
The unpredictable fantail of sparks
5 Or hiss when a new shoe toughens in water.
The anvil must be somewhere in the centre,
Horned as a unicorn, at one end square,
Set there immoveable: an altar
Where he expends himself in shape and music.
10 Sometimes, leather-aproned, hairs in his nose,
He leans out on the jamb, recalls a clatter
Of hoofs where traffic is flashing in rows;
Then grunts and goes in, with a slam and flick
To beat real iron out, to work the bellows.

1969

---

1. Small furrows in which seeds are sown.
2. Slabs of peat that, when dried, are a common domestic fuel in Ireland.

Punishment[1]

I can feel the tug
of the halter at the nape
of her neck, the wind
on her naked front.

5   It blows her nipples
to amber beads,
it shakes the frail rigging
of her ribs.

I can see her drowned
10   body in the bog,
the weighing stone,
the floating rods and boughs.

Under which at first
she was a barked sapling
15   that is dug up
oak-bone, brain-firkin:°   *small cask*

her shaved head
like a stubble of black corn,
her blindfold a soiled bandage,
20   her noose a ring

to store
the memories of love.
Little adultress,
before they punished you

25   you were flaxen-haired,
undernourished, and your
tar-black face was beautiful.
My poor scapegoat,

I almost love you
30   but would have cast, I know,
the stones of silence.
I am the artful voyeur

---

1. In 1951 the peat-stained body of a young girl, who lived in the late 1st century C.E., was recovered from a bog in Windeby, Germany. As P. V. Glob describes her in *The Bog People*, she "lay naked in the hole in the peat, a bandage over the eyes and a collar round the neck. The band across the eyes was drawn tight and had cut into the neck and the base of the nose. We may feel sure that it had been used to close her eyes to this world. There was no mark of strangulation on the neck, so that it had not been used for that purpose." Her hair "had been shaved off with a razor on the left side of the head. . . . When the brain was removed the convolutions and folds of the surface could be clearly seen [Glob reproduces a photograph of her brain]. . . . this girl of only fourteen had had an inadequate winter diet. . . . To keep the young body under, some birch branches and a big stone were laid upon her." According to the Roman historian Tacitus, the Germanic peoples punished adulterous women by shaving off their hair and then scourging them out of the village or killing them. Today, her "betraying sisters" are sometimes shaved, stripped, tarred, and handcuffed by the IRA to the railings of Belfast in punishment for keeping company with British soldiers.

of your brain's exposed
and darkened combs,
35 your muscles' webbing
and all your numbered bones:

I who have stood dumb
when your betraying sisters,
cauled in tar,
40 wept by the railings,

who would connive
in civilized outrage
yet understand the exact
and tribal, intimate revenge.

1975

Casualty

1

He would drink by himself
And raise a weathered thumb
Towards the high shelf,
Calling another rum
5 And blackcurrant, without
Having to raise his voice,
Or order a quick stout°   strong, dark beer
By a lifting of the eyes
And a discreet dumb-show
10 Of pulling off the top;
At closing time would go
In waders and peaked cap
Into the showery dark,
A dole-kept[1] breadwinner
15 But a natural for work.
I loved his whole manner,
Sure-footed but too sly,
His deadpan sidling tact,
His fisherman's quick eye
20 And turned observant back.
Incomprehensible
To him, my other life.
Sometimes, on his high stool,
Too busy with his knife
25 At a tobacco plug
And not meeting my eye
In the pause after a slug[2]
He mentioned poetry.
We would be on our own

1. I.e., receiving unemployment benefits.   2. Of liquor.

30 And, always politic
    And shy of condescension,
    I would manage by some trick
    To switch the talk to eels
    Or lore of the horse and cart
35 Or the Provisionals.[3]

    But my tentative art
    His turned back watches too:
    He was blown to bits
    Out drinking in a curfew
40 Others obeyed, three nights
    After they shot dead
    The thirteen men in Derry.
    PARAS THIRTEEN, the walls said,
    BOGSIDE NIL.[4] That Wednesday
45 Everybody held
    His breath and trembled.

                2

    It was a day of cold
    Raw silence, wind-blown
    Surplice and soutane:[5]
50 Rained-on, flower-laden
    Coffin after coffin
    Seemed to float from the door
    Of the packed cathedral
    Like blossoms on slow water.
55 The common funeral
    Unrolled its swaddling band,[6]
    Lapping, tightening
    Till we were braced and bound
    Like brothers in a ring.

60 But he would not be held
    At home by his own crowd
    Whatever threats were phoned,
    Whatever black flags waved.
    I see him as he turned
65 In that bombed offending place,
    Remorse fused with terror
    In his still knowable face,
    His cornered outfaced stare
    Blinding in the flash.

70 He had gone miles away
    For he drank like a fish

---

3. The Provisional Branch of the IRA.
4. This graffito records—in the form of a football match score—that the British Army's Parachute Regiment had killed thirteen people, and the Roman Catholic inhabitants of Londonderry's Bogside district, none.
5. Vestments worn by Roman Catholic priests.
6. Long cloth in which babies were once wrapped to restrain them.

Nightly, naturally
Swimming towards the lure
Of warm lit-up places,
75 The blurred mesh and murmur
Drifting among glasses
In the gregarious smoke.
How culpable was he
That last night when he broke
80 Our tribe's complicity?[7]
"Now you're supposed to be
An educated man,"
I hear him say. "Puzzle me
The right answer to that one."

3

85 I missed his funeral,
Those quiet walkers
And sideways talkers
Shoaling out of his lane
To the respectable
90 Purring of the hearse . . .
They move in equal pace
With the habitual
Slow consolation
Of a dawdling engine,
95 The line lifted, hand
Over fist, cold sunshine
On the water, the land
Banked under fog: that morning
I was taken in his boat,
100 The screw° purling, turning   *propellor*
Indolent fathoms white,
I tasted freedom with him.
To get out early, haul
Steadily off the bottom,
105 Dispraise the catch, and smile
As you find a rhythm
Working you, slow mile by mile,
Into your proper haunt
Somewhere, well out, beyond . . .

110 Dawn-sniffing revenant,[8]
Plodder through midnight rain,
Question me again.

1979

---

7. The Roman Catholic community's agreement to obey the curfew (of lines 39–40).

8. One returned from the dead.

The Skunk

Up, black, striped and damasked like the chasuble[1]
At a funeral mass, the skunk's tail
Paraded the skunk. Night after night
I expected her like a visitor.

5   The refrigerator whinnied into silence.
My desk light softened beyond the verandah.
Small oranges loomed in the orange tree.
I began to be tense as a voyeur.

After eleven years I was composing
10   Love-letters again, broaching the word "wife"
Like a stored cask, as if its slender vowel
Had mutated into the night earth and air

Of California. The beautiful, useless
Tang of eucalyptus spelt your absence.
15   The aftermath of a mouthful of wine
Was like inhaling you off a cold pillow.

And there she was, the intent and glamorous,
Ordinary, mysterious skunk,
Mythologized, demythologized,
20   Snuffing the boards five feet beyond me.

It all came back to me last night, stirred
By the sootfall of your things at bedtime,
Your head-down, tail-up hunt in a bottom drawer
For the black plunge-line nightdress.

1979

From Station Island[1]

12

Like a convalescent, I took the hand
stretched down from the jetty, sensed again
an alien comfort as I stepped on ground
to find the helping hand still gripping mine,

1. Sleeveless vestment worn by the priest celebrating mass, its color regulated by the feast of the day.
1. *Station Island* is a sequence of dream encounters with familiar ghosts, set on Station Island on Lough Derg in Co. Donegal. The island is also known as St. Patrick's Purgatory because of a tradition that Patrick was the first to establish the penitential vigil of fasting and praying which still constitutes the basis of the three-day pilgrimage. Each unit of the contemporary pilgrim's exercises is called a 'station,' and a large part of each station involves walking barefoot and praying round the 'beds,' stone circles which are said to be the remains of early medieval monastic cells [Heaney's note]. In this last section of the poem, the familiar ghost is that of Heaney's countryman James Joyce.

5   fish-cold and bony, but whether to guide
or to be guided I could not be certain

for the tall man in step at my side
seemed blind, though he walked straight as a rush
upon his ash plant,[2] his eyes fixed straight ahead.

10   Then I knew him in the flesh
out there on the tarmac among the cars,
wintered hard and sharp as a blackthorn bush.

His voice eddying with the vowels of all rivers[3]
came back to me, though he did not speak yet,
15   a voice like a prosecutor's or a singer's,

cunning,[4] narcotic, mimic, definite
as a steel nib's downstroke, quick and clean,
and suddenly he hit a litter basket

with his stick, saying, "Your obligation
20   is not discharged by any common rite.
What you must do must be done on your own

so get back in harness. The main thing is to write
for the joy of it. Cultivate a work-lust
that imagines its haven like your hands at night

25   dreaming the sun in the sunspot of a breast.
You are fasted now, light-headed, dangerous.
Take off from here. And don't be so earnest,

let others wear the sackcloth and the ashes.[5]
Let go, let fly, forget.
30   You've listened long enough. Now strike your note."

It was as if I had stepped free into space
alone with nothing that I had not known
already. Raindrops blew in my face

as I came to. "Old father, mother's son,
35   there is a moment in Stephen's diary
for April the thirteenth, a revelation

set among my stars—that one entry
has been a sort of password in my ears,
the collect of a new epiphany,[6]

---

2. Walking stick made of ash. Joyce was almost blind.
3. The Anna Livia Plurabelle episode of *Finnegans Wake* (p. 2310) resounds with the names of many rivers.
4. "The only arms I allow myself to use—silence, exile, and cunning" (Joyce, *Portrait of the Artist as*

a Young Man).
5. As worn by penitents in biblical times and later.
6. Manifestation of a superhuman being, as of the infant Jesus to the Magi (Matthew 2). In the Christian calendar, the Feast of the Epiphany is January 6. "Collect": short prayer assigned to a particular day.

40   the Feast of the Holy Tundish."[7] "Who cares,"
he jeered, "any more? The English language
belongs to us. You are raking at dead fires,

a waste of time for somebody your age.
That subject people stuff is a cod's° game,   *fool's*
45   infantile, like your peasant pilgrimage.

You lose more of yourself than you redeem
doing the decent thing. Keep at a tangent.
When they make the circle wide, it's time to swim

out on your own and fill the element
50   with signatures on your own frequency,
echo soundings, searches, probes, allurements,

elver-gleams[8] in the dark of the whole sea."
The shower broke in a cloudburst, the tarmac
fumed and sizzled. As he moved off quickly

55   the downpour loosed its screens round his straight walk.

1984

The Sharping Stone[1]

In an apothecary's° chest of drawers,   *pharmacist's*
Sweet cedar that we'd purchased second hand,
In one of its weighty deep-sliding recesses
I found the sharping stone that was to be
5   Our gift to him. Still in its wrapping paper.
Like a baton of black light I'd failed to pass.

•

Airless cinder-depths. But all the same,
The way it lay there, it wakened something too . . .
I thought of us that evening on the logs,
10   Flat on our backs, the pair of us, parallel,
Supported head to heel, arms straight, eyes front,
Listening to the rain drip off the trees
And saying nothing, braced to the damp bark.
What possessed us? The bare, lopped loveliness
15   Of those two winter trunks, the way they seemed
Prepared for launching, at right angles across
A causeway of short fence-posts set like rollers.
Neither of us spoke. The puddles waited.
The workers had gone home, saws fallen silent.

---

7. See the end of James Joyce's *Portrait of the Artist as a Young Man* [Heaney's note]: "*13 April:* That
tundish [funnel] has been on my mind for a long
time. I looked it up and find it English and good
old blunt English too. Damn the dean of studies

and his funnel! What did he come here for to teach
us his own language or to learn it from us? Damn
him one way or the other!"
8. Gleams as of young eels.
1. Whetstone for sharpening metal blades.

20   And next thing down we lay, babes in the wood,
      Gazing up at the flood-face of the sky
      Until it seemed a flood was carrying us
      Out of the forest park, feet first, eyes front,
      Out of November, out of middle age,
25   Together, out, across the Sea of Moyle.[2]

•

      Sarcophage des époux.[3] In terra cotta.
      Etruscan couple shown side by side,
      Recumbent on left elbows, husband pointing
      With his right arm and watching where he points,
30   Wife in front, her earrings in, her braids
      Down to her waist, taking her sexual ease.
      He is all eyes, she is all brow and dream,
      Her right forearm and hand held out as if
      Some bird she sees in her deep inward gaze
35   Might be about to roost there. Domestic
      Love, the artist thought, warm tones and property,
      The frangibility of terra cotta . . .
      Which is how they figured on the colour postcard
      (*Louvre, Département des Antiquités*)[4]
40   That we'd sent him once, then found among his things.

•

      He loved inspired mistakes: his Spanish grandson's
      English transliteration, thanking him
      For a boat trip: 'That was a marvellous
      Walk on the water, granddad.' And indeed
45   He walked on air himself, never more so
      Than when he had been widowed and the youth
      In him, the athlete who had wooed her—
      Breasting tapes and clearing the high bars—
      Grew lightsome once again. Going at eighty
50   On the bendiest roads, going for broke
      At every point-to-point[5] and poker-school,
      'He commenced his wild career' a second time
      And not a bother on him. Smoked like a train
      And took the power mower in his stride.
55   Flirted and vaunted. Set fire to his bed.
      Fell from a ladder. Learned to microwave.

•

      So set the drawer on freshets[6] of thaw water
      And place the unused sharping stone inside it:
      To be found next summer on a riverbank
60   Where scythes once hung all night in alder trees
      And mowers played dawn scherzos[7] on the blades,

---

2. Channel between the northwestern coast of County Antrim in Ireland and the southwestern coast of Scotland.
3. Coffin for a married couple.
4. Department of Antiquities, the Louvre Museum, Paris, in which this Etruscan funerary statue, known as *The Cerveteri Couple,* is to be found.
5. Horse race over jumps.
6. Surges of water.
7. Vigorous light and playful musical composition.

Their arms like harpists' arms, one drawing towards,
One sweeping the bright rim of the extreme.

1996

J. M. COETZEE
b. 1940

John Michael Coetzee was born in Cape Town, South Africa, and went to school and university in that city. Earning his Ph.D. at the University of Texas at Austin, he worked in computing for some years before being appointed, first, assistant professor and, subsequently, Butler Professor of English at the State University of New York at Buffalo. In 1984, he returned to South Africa as professor of general literature at the University of Cape Town.

The central concern of Coetzee's fiction—the oppressive nature of colonialism—made its appearance with his first book, *Dusklands* (1974). This consists of two novellas, one set in the U.S. State Department during the Vietnam War, the other in southern Africa two hundred years earlier. The central protagonists of these seemingly different stories—Eugene Dawn, an expert in psychological warfare, and Jacobus Coetzee, an explorer and pioneer—are shown to be engaged in similar projects, each leading to oppression and murder. Since then, he has published six novels, including *In the Heart of the Country* (1977), *Life and Times of Michael K* (1983), and *The Master of Petersburg* (1994), as well as essays and criticism on a number of themes.

Coetzee is at once a passionate political novelist and an intensely literary one, both qualities emerging in his most compelling indictment of colonialism to date, *Waiting for the Barbarians* (1980). This novel takes its title and theme from a well-known poem by the Greek poet Constantine Cavafy (1863–1933), which ends (in Rae Dalven's translation):

> . . . night is here but the barbarians have not come.
> Some people arrived from the frontiers,
> And they said that there are no longer any barbarians.
>
> And now what shall become of us without any barbarians?
> Those people were a kind of solution.

The unspecified empire of Coetzee's novel is said (by its fascist rulers) to be threatened by barbarians who never appear, that threat holding it together against its real enemies, those within. The narrator is poised uneasily between the two. A well-meaning but weak liberal magistrate in charge of a frontier post, he is unable to protect his harmless prisoners from his brutal colleague, Colonel Joll.

From Waiting for the Barbarians

Today, only four days after the departure of the expedition, the first of the Colonel's prisoners arrive. From my window I watch them cross the square between their mounted guards, dusty, exhausted, cringing already from the spectators who crowd about them, the skipping children, the barking dogs. In the shade of the barracks wall the guards dismount; at once the prisoners squat down to rest, save for a little boy who stands on one leg, his arm on his mother's shoulder, staring back curiously at the onlookers. Someone brings a bucket of water and a ladle. They drink thirstily, while the crowd grows and presses in so tight around them that I can no longer see. Impatiently I wait for the guard who now pushes his way through the crowd and crosses the barracks yard.

'How do you explain this?' I shout at him. He bows his head, fumbles at his pockets. 'These are fishing people! How can you bring them back here?'

He holds out a letter. I break the seal and read: 'Please hold these and succeeding detainees incommunicado for my return.' Beneath his signature the seal is repeated, the seal of the Bureau[1] which he has carried with him into the desert and which, if he perished, I would doubtless have to send out a second expedition to recover.

'The man is ridiculous!' I shout. I storm about the room. One should never disparage officers in front of men, fathers in front of children, but towards this man I discover no loyalty in my heart. 'Did no one tell him these are fishing people? It is a waste of time bringing them here! You are supposed to help him track down thieves, bandits, invaders of the Empire! Do these people look like a danger to the Empire?' I fling the letter at the window.

The crowd parts before me till I stand at the centre confronting the dozen pathetic prisoners. They flinch before my anger, the little boy sliding into his mother's arms. I gesture to the guards: 'Clear a way and bring these people into the barracks yard!' They herd the captives along; the barracks gate closes behind us. 'Now explain yourselves,' I say; 'did no one tell him these prisoners are useless to him? Did no one tell him the difference between fishermen with nets and wild nomad horsemen with bows? Did no one tell him they don't even speak the same language?'

One of the soldiers explains. 'When they saw us coming they tried to hide in the reeds. They saw horsemen coming so they tried to hide. So the officer, the Excellency, ordered us to take them in. Because they were hiding.'

I could curse with vexation. A policeman! The reasoning of a policeman! 'Did the Excellency say why he wanted them brought back here? Did he say why he could not ask them his questions out there?'

'None of us could speak their language, sir.'

Of course not! These river people are aboriginal, older even than the nomads. They live in settlements of two or three families along the banks of the river, fishing and trapping for most of the year, paddling to the remote southern shores of the lake in the autumn to catch redworms and dry them, building flimsy reed shelters, groaning with cold through the winter, dressing in skins. Living in fear of everyone, skulking in the reeds, what can they possibly know of a great barbarian enterprise against the Empire?

I send one of the men to the kitchen for food. He comes back with a loaf of yesterday's bread which he offers to the oldest prisoner. The old man accepts the bread reverentially in both hands, sniffs it, breaks it, passes the lumps around. They stuff their mouths with this manna,[2] chewing fast, not raising their eyes. A woman spits masticated bread into her palm and feeds her baby. I motion for more bread. We stand watching them eat as though they are strange animals.

---

1. Government department. "Incommunicado": without allowing them to communicate with anyone.
2. Food from heaven (Exodus 16).

'Let them stay in the yard,' I tell their guards. 'It will be inconvenient for us, but there is nowhere else. If it gets cold tonight I will make another arrangement. See that they are fed. Give them something to do to keep their hands busy. Keep the gate closed. They will not run away but I do not want idlers coming in to stare at them.'

So I check my anger and do as the Colonel instructs: I hold his useless prisoners 'incommunicado' for him. And in a day or two these savages seem to forget they ever had another home. Seduced utterly by the free and plentiful food, above all by the bread, they relax, smile at everyone, move about the barracks yard from one patch of shade to another, doze and wake, grow excited as mealtimes approach. Their habits are frank and filthy. One corner of the yard has become a latrine where men and women squat openly and where a cloud of flies buzzes all day. ('Give them a spade!' I tell the guards; but they do not use it.) The little boy, grown quite fearless, haunts the kitchen, begging sugar from the maids. Aside from bread, sugar and tea are great novelties to them. Every morning they get a small block of pressed tea-leaves which they boil up in a four-gallon pail on a tripod over a fire. They are happy here; indeed unless we chase them away they may stay with us forever, so little does it seem to have taken to lure them out of a state of nature. I spend hours watching them from the upstairs window (other idlers have to watch through the gate). I watch the women picking lice, combing and plaiting each other's long black hair. Some of them have fits of harsh dry coughing. It is striking that there are no children in the group but the baby and the little boy. Did some of them, the nimble, the wakeful, after all succeed in escaping from the soldiers? I hope so. I hope that when we return them to their homes along the river they will have many far-fetched stories to tell their neighbours. I hope that the history of their captivity enters their legends, passed down from grandfather to grandson. But I hope too that memories of the town, with its easy life and its exotic foods, are not strong enough to lure them back. I do not want a race of beggars on my hands.

For a few days the fisherfolk are a diversion, with their strange gabbling, their vast appetites, their animal shamelessness, their volatile tempers. The soldiers lounge in the doorways watching them, making obscene comments about them which they do not understand, laughing; there are always children with their faces pressed to the bars of the gate; and from my window I stare down, invisible behind the glass.

Then, all together, we lose sympathy with them. The filth, the smell, the noise of their quarrelling and coughing become too much. There is an ugly incident when a soldier tries to drag one of their women indoors, perhaps only in play, who knows, and is pelted with stones. A rumour begins to go the rounds that they are diseased, that they will bring an epidemic to the town. Though I make them dig a pit in the corner of the yard and have the nightsoil[3] removed, the kitchen staff refuse them utensils and begin to toss them their food from the doorway as if they were indeed animals. The soldiers lock the door to the barracks hall, the children no longer come to the gate. Someone flings a dead cat over the wall during the night and causes an uproar. Through the long hot days they moon about the empty yard. The baby cries and coughs, cries and coughs till I flee for refuge to the farthest

---

3. Excrement.

corner of my apartment. I write an angry letter to the Third Bureau, unsleeping guardian of the Empire, denouncing the incompetence of one of its agents. 'Why do you not send people with experience of the frontier to investigate frontier unrest?' I write. Wisely I tear up the letter. If I unlock the gate in the dead of night, I wonder, will the fisherfolk sneak away? But I do nothing. Then one day I notice that the baby has stopped crying. When I look from the window it is nowhere to be seen. I send a guard to search and he finds the little corpse under its mother's clothes. She will not yield it up, we have to tear it away from her. After this she squats alone all day with her face covered, refusing to eat. Her people seem to shun her. Have we violated some custom of theirs, I wonder, by taking the child and burying it? I curse Colonel Joll for all the trouble he has brought me, and for the shame too.

Then in the middle of the night he is back. Bugle-calls from the ramparts break into my sleep, the barracks hall erupts in uproar as the soldiers go scrambling for their weapons. My head is confused, I am slow in dressing, by the time I emerge on to the square the column is already passing through the gates, some of the men riding, some leading their mounts. I stand back while the onlookers crowd around, touching and embracing the soldiers, laughing with excitement ('All safe!' someone shouts), until coming up in the middle of the column I see what I have been dreading: the black carriage, then the shuffling group of prisoners roped together neck to neck, shapeless figures in their sheepskin coats under the silver moonlight, then behind them the last of the soldiers leading the carts and pack-horses. As more and more people come running up, some with flaming torches, and the babble mounts, I turn my back on the Colonel's triumph and make my way back to my rooms. This is the point at which I begin to see the disadvantages of living, as I have chosen to do, in the rambling apartment over the storerooms and kitchen intended for the military commandant we have not had for years, rather than in the attractive villa with geraniums in the windows which falls to the lot of the civil magistrate. I would like to be able to stop my ears to the noises coming from the yard below, which has now, it appears, become permanently a prison yard. I feel old and tired, I want to sleep. I sleep whenever I can nowadays and, when I wake up, wake reluctantly. Sleep is no longer a healing bath, a recuperation of vital forces, but an oblivion, a nightly brush with annihilation. Living in the apartment has become bad for me, I think; but not only that. If I lived in the magistrate's villa on the quietest street in town, holding sittings of the court on Mondays and Thursdays, going hunting every morning, occupying my evenings in the classics, closing my ears to the activities of this upstart policeman, if I resolved to ride out the bad times, keeping my own counsel, I might cease to feel like a man who, in the grip of the undertow, gives up the fight, stops swimming, and turns his face towards the open sea and death. But it is the knowledge of how contingent my unease is, how dependent on a baby that wails beneath my window one day and does not wail the next, that brings the worst shame to me, the greatest indifference to annihilation. I know somewhat too much; and from this knowledge, once one has been infected, there seems to be no recovering. I ought never to have taken my lantern to see what was going on in the hut by the granary. On the other hand, there was no way, once I had picked up the lantern, for me to put it down again. The knot loops in upon itself; I cannot find the end.

All the next day the Colonel spends sleeping in his room at the inn, and the staff have to tiptoe about their duties. I try to pay no attention to the new batch of prisoners in the yard. It is a pity that all the doors of the barracks block as well as the stairway leading up to my apartment open on to the yard. I hurry out in the early-morning light, occupy myself all day with municipal rents, dine in the evening with friends. On the way home I meet the young lieutenant who accompanied Colonel Joll into the desert and congratulate him on his safe return. 'But why did you not explain to the Colonel that the fishing people could not possibly help him in his inquiries?' He looks embarrassed. 'I spoke to him,' he tells me, 'but all he said was, "Prisoners are prisoners". I decided it was not my place to argue with him.'

The next day the Colonel begins his interrogations. Once I thought him lazy, little more than a bureaucrat with vicious tastes. Now I see how mistaken I was. In his quest for the truth he is tireless. The questioning starts in the early morning and is still going on when I return after dark. He has enlisted the aid of a hunter who has shot pigs up and down the river all his life and knows a hundred words of the fisherfolk's language. One by one the fisherfolk are taken into the room where the Colonel has established himself, to be asked whether they have seen movements of strange horsemen. Even the child is questioned: 'Have strangers visited your father during the night?' (I guess, of course, at what passes in that room, at the fear, the bewilderment, the abasement.) The prisoners are returned not to the yard but to the main barracks hall: the soldiers have been turned out, quartered on the town. I sit in my rooms with the windows shut, in the stifling warmth of a windless evening, trying to read, straining my ears to hear or not to hear sounds of violence. Finally at midnight the interrogations cease, there is no more banging of doors or tramping of feet, the yard is silent in the moonlight, and I am at liberty to sleep.

* * *

Then, in my office at the courthouse, a visitor is announced. Colonel Joll, wearing his dark eyeshades indoors, enters and sits down opposite me. I offer him tea, surprised at how steady my hand is. He is leaving, he says. Should I try to conceal my joy? He sips his tea, sitting carefully upright, inspecting the room, the shelves upon shelves of papers bundled together and tied with ribbon, the record of decades of humdrum administration, the small bookcase of legal texts, the cluttered desk. He has completed his inquiries for the time being, he says, and is in a hurry to return to the capital and make his report. He has an air of sternly controlled triumph. I nod my understanding. 'Anything that I can do to facilitate your journey . . .' I say. There is a pause. Then into the silence, like a pebble into a pool, I drop my question.

'And your inquiries, Colonel, among the nomad peoples and the aboriginals—have they been as successful as you wished?'

He places his fingers together tip to tip before he answers. I have the feeling that he knows how much his affectations irritate me. 'Yes, Magistrate, I can say that we have had some success. Particularly when you consider that similar investigations are being carried out elsewhere along the frontier in a co-ordinated fashion.'

'That is good. And can you tell us whether we have anything to fear? Can we rest securely at night?'

The corner of his mouth crinkles in a little smile. Then he stands up, bows, turns, and leaves. Early next morning he departs accompanied by his small escort, taking the long east road back to the capital. Throughout a trying period he and I have managed to behave towards each other like civilized people. All my life I have believed in civilized behaviour; on this occasion, however, I cannot deny it, the memory leaves me sick with myself.

My first action is to visit the prisoners. I unlock the barracks hall which has been their jail, my senses already revolting at the sickly smell of sweat and ordure, and throw the doors wide open. 'Get them out of there!' I shout at the half-dressed soldiers who stand about watching me as they eat their porridge. From the gloom inside the prisoners stare apathetically back. 'Go in there and clean up that room!' I shout. 'I want everything cleaned up! Soap and water! I want everything as it was before!' The soldiers hurry to obey; but why is my anger directed at them, they must be asking. Into the daylight emerge the prisoners, blinking, shielding their eyes. One of the women has to be helped. She shakes all the time like an old person, though she is young. There are some too sick to stand up.

I last saw them five days ago (if I can claim ever to have seen them, if I ever did more than pass my gaze over their surface absently, with reluctance). What they have undergone in these five days I do not know. Now herded by their guards they stand in a hopeless little knot in the corner of the yard, nomads and fisherfolk together, sick, famished, damaged, terrified. It would be best if this obscure chapter in the history of the world were terminated at once, if these ugly people were obliterated from the face of the earth and we swore to make a new start, to run an empire in which there would be no more injustice, no more pain. It would cost little to march them out into the desert (having put a meal in them first, perhaps, to make the march possible), to have them dig, with their last strength, a pit large enough for all of them to lie in (or even to dig it for them!), and, leaving them buried there forever and forever, to come back to the walled town full of new intentions, new resolutions. But that will not be my way. The new men of Empire are the ones who believe in fresh starts, new chapters, clean pages; I struggle on with the old story, hoping that before it is finished it will reveal to me why it was that I thought it worth the trouble. Thus it is that, administration of law and order in these parts having today passed back to me, I order that the prisoners be fed, that the doctor be called in to do what he can, that the barracks return to being a barracks, that arrangements be made to restore the prisoners to their former lives as soon as possible, as far as possible.

1980

EAVAN BOLAND
b. 1944

Eavan Boland was born in Dublin, the youngest daughter of an Irish diplomat and his wife, Frances Kelly, the painter, but grew up mainly in London, where her father was Irish ambassador, and in New York, where he was his country's representative at the United Nations. She returned to Ireland, however, to study—and then to teach—English at Trinity College, Dublin, and subsequently her family moved to the United States, where she now is professor of English and director of the Creative Writing Program at Stanford University.

Boland has said (in her 1994 Ronald Duncan lecture): "I am an Irish poet. A woman poet. In the first category I enter the tradition of the English language at an angle. In the second, I enter my own tradition at an even more steep angle." Since Boland is an academically gifted woman who spent more of her formative years abroad than in Ireland, her poetic tradition may be said to be as much European as Irish—her early work includes verse translations from (or, as she prefers to say, "after") Horace, Mayakovsky, and Nelly Sachs—but a growing determination to speak for Ireland can be seen in the titles of her books: *In Her Own Image* (1980), *Night Feed* (1982), *The Journey and Other Poems* (1987), *Outside History: Selected Poems 1980–1990* (1990), *In a Time of Violence* (1994), and *The Lost Land* (1998). If her interweaving of private life and public life, to produce a national narrative, a "herstory" along the lines of the magisterial "histories" of Yeats and Heaney, has yet to attain their visionary intensity, her strengths—an eye for symbolic detail, an ear for musical structure—show to best advantage when she writes as a woman rather than a spokeswoman.

Approaching the bloody history of Easter 1916, for example, from an oblique angle (rather than head-on in the bardic manner of Yeats's *Easter 1916*) in *The Dolls Museum in Dublin*, Boland gives us a brilliant impressionist picture of Ascendancy Dublin, as reflected in Anglo-Irish eyes and those of the dolls only the Anglo-Irish could afford, on the eve of the uprising that would precipitate the decline and fall of their ascendancy.

That the Science of Cartography[1] Is Limited

—and not simply by the fact that this shading of
forest cannot show the fragrance of balsam,
the gloom of cypresses
is what I wish to prove.

5   When you and I were first in love we drove
to the borders of Connacht[2]
and entered a wood there.

Look down you said: this was once a famine road.

I looked down at ivy and the scutch grass
10   rough-cast stone had
disappeared into as you told me
in the second winter of their ordeal, in

1847, when the crop[3] had failed twice,
Relief Committees gave
15   the starving Irish such roads to build.

Where they died, there the road ended

---

1. Mapmaking.
2. Western province of Ireland.

3. Of potatoes, staple diet of Irish peasants in the 19th century.

and ends still and when I take down
the map of this island, it is never so
I can say here is
20   the masterful, the apt rendering of

the spherical as flat, nor
an ingenious design which persuades a curve
into a plane,
but to tell myself again that

25   the line which says woodland and cries hunger
and gives out among sweet pine and cypress,
and finds no horizon

will not be there.

1994

The Dolls Museum in Dublin

The wounds are terrible. The paint is old.
The cracks along the lips and on the cheeks
cannot be fixed. The cotton lawn[1] is soiled.
The arms are ivory dissolved to wax.

5   Recall the Quadrille. Hum the waltz.
Promenade on the yacht-club terraces.
Put back the lamps in their copper holders,
the carriage wheels on the cobbled quays.

And recreate Easter in Dublin.[2]
10   Booted officers. Their mistresses.
Sunlight criss-crossing College Green.
Steam hissing from the flanks of horses.

Here they are. Cradled and cleaned,
held close in the arms of their owners.
15   Their cold hands clasped by warm hands,
their faces memorized like perfect manners.

The altars are mannerly with linen.
The lilies are whiter than surplices.[3]
The candles are burning and warning:
20   Rejoice, they whisper. After sacrifice.

Horse-chestnuts hold up their candles.
The Green is vivid with parasols.

1. Usually fine linen, but also, as here, fine cotton.
2. What became known as the "Easter Rising"
began on Easter Monday, 1916, when fifteen hundred Irish Nationalists seized key points in Dublin
and an Irish Republic was proclaimed from the
General Post Office. See W. B. Yeats's *Easter 1916*
(p. 2104).
3. White linen vestments worn over cassocks.

Sunlight is pastel and windless.
The bar of the Shelbourne[4] is full.

25 Laughter and gossip on the terraces.
Rumour and alarm at the barracks.
The Empire is summoning its officers.
The carriages are turning: they are turning back.

Past children walking with governesses,
30 Looking down, cossetting their dolls,
then looking up as the carriage passes,
the shadow chilling them. Twilight falls.

It is twilight in the dolls' museum. Shadows
remain on the parchment-coloured waists,
35 are bruises on the stitched cotton clothes,
are hidden in the dimples on the wrists.

The eyes are wide. They cannot address
the helplessness which has lingered in
the airless peace of each glass case:
40 to have survived. To have been stronger than

a moment. To be the hostages ignorance
takes from time and ornament from destiny. Both.
To be the present of the past. To infer the difference
with a terrible stare. But not feel it. And not know it.

1994

The Lost Land

I have two daughters.

They are all I ever wanted from the earth.

Or almost all.

I also wanted one piece of ground:

5 One city trapped by hills. One urban river.
An island in its element.

So I could say *mine. My own.*
And mean it.

Now they are grown up and far away

---

4. Large Dublin hotel.

10 and memory itself
has become an emigrant,
wandering in a place
where love dissembles itself as landscape:

Where the hills
15 are the colours of a child's eyes,
where my children are distances, horizons:

At night,
on the edge of sleep,
I can see the shore of Dublin Bay.
20 Its rocky sweep and its granite pier.

Is this, I say
how they must have seen it,
backing out on the mailboat at twilight,

shadows falling
25 on everything they had to leave?
And would love forever?
And then

I imagine myself
at the landward rail of that boat
30 searching for the last sight of a hand.

I see myself
on the underworld side of that water,
the darkness coming in fast, saying
all the names I know for a lost land:

35 *Ireland. Absence. Daughter.*

1998

CRAIG RAINE
b. 1944

In an autobiographical essay, *A Silver Plate,* Craig Raine introduces his father: "a painter and decorator, plumber, electrician, publican and boxer, . . . a Spiritualist and a faith healer." From this splendidly indecorous figure he inherited an exuberant eye for the oddity of the world and its inhabitants.

Raine was born in Shildon, County Durham, and educated at Barnard Castle School and Exeter College, Oxford. For some years he was a lecturer at that university; then, from 1981 to 1991, he was poetry editor (as T. S. Eliot was) at the influential publishing house of Faber & Faber; and he is now a Fellow of New College, Oxford.

He is married to the niece of the great Russian poet Boris Pasternak, and Raine's dazzling metaphoric sequences probably owe something to this aspect of Pasternak's early poetry. Each tries to avoid the pronoun *I*—so often intrusive in the poems of others—and relies instead on the operations of an eye brilliantly equipped to make surprising connections. Where Pasternak sees crows "like charred pears / Windfallen from their branching skies," Raine shows us how "the arum lilies fold / back napkins monogrammed in gold." The writer he most admires, however, is James Joyce, and he said in an interview:

> One of Joyce's pupils in Trieste recalled that Joyce used to make his students go away and describe, say, an oil lamp: the student coined the phrase "descriptive lust" to evoke Joyce's aim. That's what I'm interested in. . . . I'm not interested in writing poems which end with thumping statements; I'm interested in making objects. I think poems are machines in the sense that Baudelaire called Delacroix's paintings machines; they have to work as artistic objects.

Raine's poems are flamboyant, self-conscious (for all their avoidance of the pronoun *I*), and witty, but they delight in the world, and when they work, they help us to delight in it. We see it, as never before, with the eye of the Martian in the poem that launched the "Martian School" of poetry.

The Onion, Memory

Divorced, but friends again at last,
we walk old ground together
in bright blue uncomplicated weather.
We laugh and pause
5   to hack to bits these tiny dinosaurs,
prehistoric, crenallated, cast
between the tractor ruts in mud.

On the green, a junior Douglas Fairbanks,[1]
swinging on the chestnut's unlit chandelier,
10   defies the corporation spears[2]—
a single rank around the bole,°   *tree trunk*
rusty with blood.
Green, tacky phalluses curve up, romance.
A gust—the old flag blazes on its pole.

15   In the village bakery
the pasty babies pass
from milky slump to crusty cadaver,
from crib to coffin—without palaver.
All's over in a flash,
20   too silently . . .

Tonight the arum lilies fold
back napkins monogrammed in gold,
crisp and laundered fresh.
Those crustaceous gladioli, on the sly,

---

1. Film actor famous for his swashbuckling daredevil exploits in the 1920s and 1930s.

2. Spiked fence put up by the town corporation.

25 reveal the crimson flower-flesh
    inside their emerald armour plate.
    The uncooked herrings blink a tearful eye.
    The candles palpitate.
    The Oistrakhs[3] bow and scrape
30 in evening dress, on Emi-tape.[4]

    Outside the trees are bending over backwards
    to please the wind: the shining sword
    grass flattens on its belly.
    The white-thorn's frillies offer no resistance.
35 In the fridge, a heart-shaped jelly
    strives to keep a sense of balance.

    I slice up the onions. You sew up a dress.
    This is the quiet echo—flesh—
    white muscle on white muscle,
40 intimately folded skin,
    finished with a satin rustle.
    One button only to undo, sewn up with shabby thread.
    It is the onion, memory,
    that makes me cry.

45 Because there's everything and nothing to be said,
    the clock with hands held up before its face,
    stammers softly on, trying to complete a phrase—
    while we, together and apart,
    repeat unfinished gestures got by heart.

50 And afterwards, I blunder with the washing on the line—
    headless torsos, faceless lovers, friends of mine.

                                                              1978

A Martian Sends a Postcard Home

    Caxtons[1] are mechanical birds with many wings
    and some are treasured for their markings—

    they cause the eyes to melt
    or the body to shriek without pain.

5   I have never seen one fly, but
    sometimes they perch on the hand.

    Mist is when the sky is tired of flight
    and rests its soft machine on ground:

---

3. David and Igor Oistrakh, celebrated Russian
violinists.
4. A popular British brand of audiotape.
1. I.e., books, which William Caxton (ca. 1422–

1491) was the first to print in English. In the next
couplet the Martian observes the effects of books
on their readers, but does not know the word for
cry or *laugh*.

then the world is dim and bookish
10 like engravings under tissue paper.

Rain is when the earth is television.
It has the property of making colours darker.

Model T[2] is a room with the lock inside—
a key° is turned to free the world   *ignition key*

15 for movement, so quick there is a film
to watch for anything missed.

But time is tied to the wrist
or kept in a box, ticking with impatience.

In homes, a haunted apparatus sleeps,
20 that snores when you pick it up.

If the ghost cries, they carry it
to their lips and soothe it to sleep

with sounds. And yet, they wake it up
deliberately, by tickling with a finger.

25 Only the young are allowed to suffer
openly. Adults go to a punishment room

with water but nothing to eat.
They lock the door and suffer the noises

alone. No one is exempt
30 and everyone's pain has a different smell.

At night, when all the colours die,
they hide in pairs

and read about themselves—
in colour, with their eyelids shut.

1979

2. I.e., the automobile.

SALMAN RUSHDIE
b. 1947

The most influential novelist to have come from India is the last fifty years is Ahmed Salman Rushdie, whose dynamic narratives—stories of magic, suffering, and the vitality of human beings in the grip of history—have helped generate the literary renaissance flowering in India today. Born in Bombay two months before the partition of the Indian subcontinent and educated at Cathedral School, Bombay, Rugby School, Warwickshire, and King's College, Cambridge, Rushdie eventually settled in England, working as an actor and as a freelance advertising copywriter (1970–80).

His first novel, *Grimus* (1979), passed unnoticed, but his second, *Midnight's Children* (1981), announced the arrival of a major writer. Taking its title from those who were born—two months later than its author—around midnight on August 15, 1947, when the state of Pakistan was born, *Midnight's Children* is a work of prodigious prodigality, a Dickensian cornucopia as richly fertile in character and incident as the subcontinent that is its setting. The book's triumphant progress across the world culminated in it being adjudged "the Booker of Bookers," the best novel to have won Britain's premier fiction prize in its first twenty-five years. Rushdie has said that "we're all radio-active with history," and the books that have followed *Midnight's Children* have again shown a form of "magic realism"—learned from such Latin American writers as Borges and García Márquez—deployed in the service of a powerful political-historical imagination.

In 1988, Rushdie found himself at the perilous center of a real, rather than a magic-realist, political-historical storm. His novel *The Satanic Verses* was judged by senior religious figures in Iran to have blasphemed the Prophet Mohammad, founder of the Muslim faith, and a *fatwa* (a proclamation calling for his death) was pronounced. He was obliged to go into hiding, and for almost a decade lived under round-the-clock protection from British Secret Service agents, while governments argued for and against the lifting of the *fatwa*, and the author himself became symbolic of the vulnerability of the intellectual in the face of fundamentalism. The *fatwa* was lifted in 1998, allowing Rushdie to reappear in public, but his life remains under constant threat. He is his own best critic and has defended his book in an essay, *In Good Faith* (1990):

> If *The Satanic Verses* is anything, it is a migrant's-eye view of the world. It is written from the very experience of uprooting, disjuncture and metamorphosis (slow or rapid, painful or pleasurable) that is the migrant condition, and from which, I believe, can be derived a metaphor for all humanity.
>
> Standing at the centre of the novel is a group of characters most of whom are British Muslims, or not particularly religious persons of Muslim background, struggling with just the sort of great problems of hybridization and ghettoization, of reconciling the old and the new. Those who oppose the novel most vociferously today are of the opinion that intermingling with a different culture will inevitably weaken and ruin their own. I am of the opposite opinion. *The Satanic Verses* celebrates hybridity, impurity, intermingling, the transformation that comes of new and unexpected combinations of human beings, cultures, ideas, politics, movies, songs. It rejoices in mongrelization and fears the absolutism of the Pure. *Mélange*, hotchpotch, a bit of this and a bit of that is *how newness enters the world*. It is the great possibility that mass migration gives the world, and I have tried to embrace it. *The Satanic Verses* is for change-by-fusion, change-by-conjoining. It is a love-song to our mongrel selves.

An earlier story had invoked the Prophet uncontroversially. *The Prophet's Hair* is at once a moral fable in the tradition of *The Thousand and One Nights* and a magic-realist extravaganza, packed with incident, poetic detail ("water to which the cold of the night had given the cloudy consistency of wild honey"), and humor, all brilliantly interwoven at breakneck speed. Salman Rushdie is the Scheherazade of the twentieth century.

The Prophet's[1] Hair

Early in the year 19—, when Srinagar[2] was under the spell of a winter so fierce it could crack men's bones as if they were glass, a young man upon whose cold-pinked skin there lay, like a frost, the unmistakable sheen of wealth was to be seen entering the most wretched and disreputable part of the city, where the houses of wood and corrugated iron seemed perpetually on the verge of losing their balance, and asking in low, grave tones where he might go to engage the services of a dependably professional burglar. The young man's name was Atta, and the rogues in that part of town directed him gleefully into ever darker and less public alleys, until in a yard wet with the blood of a slaughtered chicken he was set upon by two men whose faces he never saw, robbed of the substantial bank-roll which he had insanely brought on his solitary excursion, and beaten within an inch of his life.

Night fell. His body was carried by anonymous hands to the edge of the lake, whence it was transported by shikara[3] across the water and deposited, torn and bleeding, on the deserted embankment of the canal which led to the gardens of Shalimar. At dawn the next morning a flower-vendor was rowing his boat through water to which the cold of the night had given the cloudy consistency of wild honey when he saw the prone form of young Atta, who was just beginning to stir and moan, and on whose now deathly pale skin the sheen of wealth could still be made out dimly beneath an actual layer of frost.

The flower-vendor moored his craft and by stooping over the mouth of the injured man was able to learn the poor fellow's address, which was mumbled through lips that could scarcely move; whereupon, hoping for a large tip, the hawker rowed Atta home to a large house on the shores of the lake, where a beautiful but inexplicably bruised young woman and her distraught, but equally handsome mother, neither of whom, it was clear from their eyes, had slept a wink from worrying, screamed at the sight of their Atta—who was the elder brother of the beautiful young woman—lying motionless amidst the funereally stunted winter blooms of the hopeful florist.

The flower-vendor was indeed paid off handsomely, not least to ensure his silence, and plays no further part in our story. Atta himself, suffering terribly from exposure as well as a broken skull, entered a coma which caused the city's finest doctors to shrug helplessly. It was therefore all the more remarkable that on the very next evening the most wretched and disreputable part

---

1. The Prophet Mohammed, founder of the Muslim religion, was born in Mecca about 570 and died in 632.

2. Capital of the state of Kashmir.
3. Long swift Kashmiri boat.

of the city received a second unexpected visitor. This was Huma, the sister of the unfortunate young man, and her question was the same as her brother's, and asked in the same low, grave tones:

'Where may I hire a thief?'

The story of the rich idiot who had come looking for a burglar was already common knowledge in those insalubrious gullies, but this time the young woman added: 'I should say that I am carrying no money, nor am I wearing any jewellery items. My father has disowned me and will pay no ransom if I am kidnapped; and a letter has been lodged with the Deputy Commissioner of Police, my uncle, to be opened in the event of my not being safe at home by morning. In that letter he will find full details of my journey here, and he will move Heaven and Earth to punish my assailants.'

Her exceptional beauty, which was visible even through the enormous welts and bruises disfiguring her arms and forehead, coupled with the oddity of her inquiries, had attracted a sizable group of curious onlookers, and because her little speech seemed to them to cover just about everything, no one attempted to injure her in any way, although there were some raucous comments to the effect that it was pretty peculiar for someone who was trying to hire a crook to invoke the protection of a high-up policeman uncle.

She was directed into ever darker and less public alleys until finally in a gully as dark as ink an old woman with eyes which stared so piercingly that Huma instantly understood she was blind motioned her through a doorway from which darkness seemed to be pouring like smoke. Clenching her fists, angrily ordering her heart to behave normally, Huma followed the old woman into the gloom-wrapped house.

The faintest conceivable rivulet of candlelight trickled through the darkness; following this unreliable yellow thread (because she could no longer see the old lady), Huma received a sudden sharp blow to the shins and cried out involuntarily, after which she at once bit her lip, angry at having revealed her mounting terror to whoever or whatever waited before her, shrouded in blackness.

She had, in fact, collided with a low table on which a single candle burned and beyond which a mountainous figure could be made out, sitting cross-legged on the floor. 'Sit, sit,' said a man's calm, deep voice, and her legs, needing no more flowery invitation, buckled beneath her at the terse command. Clutching her left hand in her right, she forced her voice to respond evenly:

'And you, sir, will be the thief I have been requesting?'

Shifting its weight very slightly, the shadow-mountain informed Huma that all criminal activity originating in this zone was well organised and also centrally controlled, so that all requests for what might be termed freelance work had to be channelled through this room.

He demanded comprehensive details of the crime to be committed, including a precise inventory of items to be acquired, also a clear statement of all financial inducements being offered with no gratuities excluded, plus, for filing purposes only, a summary of the motives for the application.

At this, Huma, as though remembering something, stiffened both in body and resolve and replied loudly that her motives were entirely a matter for herself; that she would discuss details with no one but the thief himself; but that the rewards she proposed could only be described as 'lavish'.

'All I am willing to disclose to you, sir, since it appears that I am on the premises of some sort of employment agency, is that in return for such lavish rewards I must have the most desperate criminal at your disposal a man for whom life holds no terrors, not even the fear of God.

'The worst of fellows, I tell you—nothing less will do!'

At this a paraffin storm-lantern was lighted, and Huma saw facing her a grey-haired giant down whose left cheek ran the most sinister of scars, a cicatrice in the shape of the letter *sín* in the Nastaliq[4] script. She was gripped by the insupportably nostalgic notion that the bogeyman of her childhood nursery had risen up to confront her, because her ayah[5] had always forestalled any incipient acts of disobedience by threatening Huma and Atta: 'You don't watch out and I'll send that one to steal you away—that Sheikh[6] Sín, the Thief of Thieves!'

Here, grey-haired but unquestionably scarred, was the notorious criminal himself—and was she out of her mind, were her ears playing tricks, or had he truly just announced that, given the stated circumstances, he himself was the only man for the job?

Struggling hard against the newborn goblins of nostalgia, Huma warned the fearsome volunteer that only a matter of extreme urgency and peril would have brought her unescorted into these ferocious streets.

'Because we can afford no last-minute backings-out,' she continued, 'I am determined to tell you everything, keeping back no secrets whatsoever. If, after hearing me out, you are still prepared to proceed, then we shall do everything in our power to assist you, and to make you rich.'

The old thief shrugged, nodded, spat. Huma began her story.

Six days ago, everything in the household of her father, the wealthy money-lender Hashim, had been as it always was. At breakfast her mother had spooned khichri[7] lovingly on to the moneylender's plate; the conversation had been filled with those expressions of courtesy and solicitude on which the family prided itself.

Hashim was fond of pointing out that while he was not a godly man he set great store by 'living honourably in the world'. In that spacious lakeside residence, all outsiders were greeted with the same formality and respect, even those unfortunates who came to negotiate for small fragments of Hashim's large fortune, and of whom he naturally asked an interest rate of over seventy per cent, partly, as he told his khichri-spooning wife, 'to teach these people the value of money; let them only learn that, and they will be cured of this fever of borrowing borrowing all the time—so you see that if my plans succeed, I shall put myself out of business!'

In their children, Atta and Huma, the moneylender and his wife had suc-

4. A Persian cursive script, characterized by rounded forms and elongated horizontal strokes.
5. Child's nurse (Anglo-Indian, from Portuguese).
6. Chief (Arabic).
7. Rice and lentils cooked together (Hindi).

cessfully sought to inculcate the virtues of thrift, plain dealing and a healthy independence of spirit. On this, too, Hashim was fond of congratulating himself.

Breakfast ended; the family members wished one another a fulfilling day. Within a few hours, however, the glassy contentment of that household, of that life of porcelain delicacy and alabaster sensibilities, was to be shattered beyond all hope of repair.

The moneylender summoned his personal shikara and was on the point of stepping into it when, attracted by a glint of silver, he noticed a small vial[8] floating between the boat and his private quay. On an impulse, he scooped it out of the glutinous water.

It was a cylinder of tinted glass cased in exquisitely wrought silver, and Hashim saw within its walls a silver pendant bearing a single strand of human hair.

Closing his fist around this unique discovery, he muttered to the boatman that he'd changed his plans, and hurried to his sanctum, where, behind closed doors, he feasted his eyes on his find.

There can be no doubt that Hashim the moneylender knew from the first that he was in possession of the famous relic of the Prophet Muhammad, that revered hair whose theft from its shrine at Hazratbal mosque the previous morning had created an unprecedented hue and cry in the valley.

The thieves—no doubt alarmed by the pandemonium, by the procession through the streets of endless ululating[9] crocodiles of lamentation, by the riots, the political ramifications and by the massive police search which was commanded and carried out by men whose entire careers now hung upon the finding of this lost hair—had evidently panicked and hurled the vial into the gelatine bosom of the lake.

Having found it by a stroke of great good fortune, Hashim's duty as a citizen was clear: the hair must be restored to its shrine, and the state to equanimity and peace.

But the moneylender had a different notion.

All around him in his study was the evidence of his collector's mania. There were enormous glass cases full of impaled butterflies from Gulmarg, three dozen scale models in various metals of the legendary cannon Zamzama,[1] innumerable swords, a Naga spear, ninety-four terracotta camels of the sort sold on railway station platforms, many samovars,[2] and a whole zoology of tiny sandalwood animals, which had originally been carved to serve as children's bathtime toys.

'And after all,' Hashim told himself, 'the Prophet would have disapproved mightily of this relic-worship. He abhorred the idea of being deified! So, by keeping this hair from its distracted devotees, I perform—do I not?—a finer service than I would by returning it! Naturally, I don't want it for its religious value . . . I'm a man of the world, of this world. I see it purely as a secular

---

8. Small, cylindrical glass container.
9. Howling.
1. Cf. Rudyard Kipling's *Kim* (p. 1): "The gun Zam-Zammah on her brick platform opposite the old Ajaib-Gher—the Wonder House, as the natives call the Lahore Museum."
2. Apparatus for making tea (Russian for self-boiler).

object of great rarity and blinding beauty. In short, it's the silver vial I desire, more than the hair.

'They say there are American millionaires who purchase stolen art masterpieces and hide them away—they would know how I feel. I must, must have it!'

Every collector must share his treasures with one other human being, and Hashim summoned—and told—his only son Atta, who was deeply perturbed but, having been sworn to secrecy, only spilled the beans when the troubles became too terrible to bear.

The youth excused himself and left his father alone in the crowded solitude of his collections. Hashim was sitting erect in a hard, straight-backed chair, gazing intently at the beautiful vial.

It was well known that the moneylender never ate lunch, so it was not until evening that a servant entered the sanctum[3] to summon his master to the dining-table. He found Hashim as Atta had left him. The same, and not the same—for now the moneylender looked swollen, distended. His eyes bulged even more than they always had, they were red-rimmed, and his knuckles were white.

He seemed to be on the point of bursting! As though, under the influence of the misappropriated relic, he had filled up with some spectral fluid which might at any moment ooze uncontrollably from his every bodily opening.

He had to be helped to the table, and then the explosion did indeed take place.

Seemingly careless of the effect of his words on the carefully constructed and fragile constitution of the family's life, Hashim began to gush, to spume long streams of awful truths. In horrified silence, his children heard their father turn upon his wife, and reveal to her that for many years their marriage had been the worst of his afflictions. 'An end to politeness!' he thundered. 'An end to hypocrisy!'

Next, and in the same spirit, he revealed to his family the existence of a mistress; he informed them also of his regular visits to paid women. He told his wife that, far from being the principal beneficiary of his will, she would receive no more than the eighth portion which was her due under Islamic law. Then he turned upon his children, screaming at Atta for his lack of academic ability—'A dope! I have been cursed with a dope!'—and accusing his daughter of lasciviousness, because she went around the city barefaced, which was unseemly for any good Muslim girl to do. She should, he commanded, enter purdah[4] forthwith.

Hashim left the table without having eaten and fell into the deep sleep of a man who has got many things off his chest, leaving his children stunned, in tears, and the dinner going cold on the sideboard under the gaze of an anticipatory bearer.[5]

At five o'clock the next morning the moneylender forced his family to rise, wash and say their prayers. From then on, he began to pray five times daily

---

3. Private room.
4. Area of certain traditional Indian houses in which Hindu or Muslim women live secluded from the sight of men outside their family circle.
5. Servant.

for the first time in his life, and his wife and children were obliged to do likewise.

Before breakfast, Huma saw the servants, under her father's direction, constructing a great heap of books in the garden and setting fire to it. The only volume left untouched was the Qur'an,[6] which Hashim wrapped in a silken cloth and placed on a table in the hall. He ordered each member of his family to read passages from this book for at least two hours per day. Visits to the cinema were forbidden. And if Atta invited male friends to the house, Huma was to retire to her room.

By now, the family had entered a state of shock and dismay; but there was worse to come.

That afternoon, a trembling debtor arrived at the house to confess his inability to pay the latest instalment of interest owed, and made the mistake of reminding Hashim, in somewhat blustering fashion, of the Qur'an's strictures against usury. The moneylender flew into a rage and attacked the fellow with one of his large collection of bullwhips.

By mischance, later the same day a second defaulter came to plead for time, and was seen fleeing Hashim's study with a great gash in his arm, because Huma's father had called him a thief of other men's money and had tried to cut off the wretch's right hand with one of the thirty-eight kukri knives[7] hanging on the study walls.

These breaches of the family's unwritten laws of decorum alarmed Atta and Huma, and when, that evening, their mother attempted to calm Hashim down, he struck her on the face with an open hand. Atta leapt to his mother's defence and he, too, was sent flying.

'From now on,' Hashim bellowed, 'there's going to be some discipline around here!'

The moneylender's wife began a fit of hysterics which continued throughout that night and the following day, and which so provoked her husband that he threatened her with divorce, at which she fled to her room, locked the door and subsided into a raga[8] of sniffling. Huma now lost her composure, challenged her father openly, and announced (with that same independence of spirit which he had encouraged in her) that she would wear no cloth over her face; apart from anything else, it was bad for the eyes.

On hearing this, her father disowned her on the spot and gave her one week in which to pack her bags and go.

By the fourth day, the fear in the air of the house had become so thick that it was difficult to walk around. Atta told his shock-numbed sister: 'We are descending to gutter-level—but I know what must be done.'

That afternoon, Hashim left home accompanied by two hired thugs to extract the unpaid dues from his two insolvent clients. Atta went immediately to his father's study. Being the son and heir, he possessed his own key to the

---

6. Muslims' sacred book: collection of the Prophet Muhammad's oral revelations.
7. Curved knives broadening toward the point

(Hindi).
8. Musical improvisation (Sanskrit).

moneylender's safe. This he now used, and removing the little vial from its hiding-place, he slipped it into his trouser pocket and re-locked the safe door.

Now he told Huma the secret of what his father had fished out of Lake Dal, and exclaimed: 'Maybe I'm crazy—maybe the awful things that are happening have made me cracked—but I am convinced there will be no peace in our house until this hair is out of it.'

His sister at once agreed that the hair must be returned, and Atta set off in a hired shikara to Hazratbal mosque. Only when the boat had delivered him into the throng of the distraught faithful which was swirling around the desecrated shrine did Atta discover that the relic was no longer in his pocket. There was only a hole, which his mother, usually so attentive to household matters, must have overlooked under the stress of recent events.

Atta's initial surge of chagrin was quickly replaced by a feeling of profound relief.

'Suppose', he imagined, 'that I had already announced to the mullahs[9] that the hair was on my person! They would never have believed me now—and this mob would have lynched me! At any rate, it has gone, and that's a load off my mind.' Feeling more contented than he had for days, the young man returned home.

Here he found his sister bruised and weeping in the hall; upstairs, in her bedroom, his mother wailed like a brand-new widow. He begged Huma to tell him what had happened, and when she replied that their father, returning from his brutal business trip, had once again noticed a glint of silver between boat and quay, had once again scooped up the errant relic, and was consequently in a rage to end all rages, having beaten the truth out of her—then Atta buried his face in his hands and sobbed out his opinion, which was that the hair was persecuting them, and had come back to finish the job.

It was Huma's turn to think of a way out of their troubles.

While her arms turned black and blue and great stains spread across her forehead, she hugged her brother and whispered to him that she was determined to get rid of the hair *at all costs*—she repeated this last phrase several times.

'The hair', she then declared, 'was stolen from the mosque; so it can be stolen from this house. But it must be a genuine robbery, carried out by a bona-fide thief, not by one of us who are under the hair's thrall—by a thief so desperate that he fears neither capture nor curses.'

Unfortunately, she added, the theft would be ten times harder to pull off now that their father, knowing that there had already been one attempt on the relic, was certainly on his guard.

'Can you do it?'

Huma, in a room lit by candle and storm-lantern, ended her account with one further question: 'What assurances can you give that the job holds no terrors for you still?'

The criminal, spitting, stated that he was not in the habit of providing

9. Muslims learned in Islamic theology and sacred law.

references, as a cook might, or a gardener, but he was not alarmed so easily, certainly not by any children's djinni of a curse. Huma had to be content with this boast, and proceeded to describe the details of the proposed burglary.

'Since my brother's failure to return the hair to the mosque, my father has taken to sleeping with his precious treasure under his pillow. However, he sleeps alone, and very energetically; only enter his room without waking him, and he will certainly have tossed and turned quite enough to make the theft a simple matter. When you have the vial, come to my room,' and here she handed Sheikh Sín a plan of her home, 'and I will hand over all the jewellery owned by my mother and myself. You will find . . . it is worth . . . that is, you will be able to get a fortune for it . . .'

It was evident that her self-control was weakening and that she was on the point of physical collapse.

'Tonight,' she burst out finally. 'You must come tonight!'

No sooner had she left the room than the old criminal's body was convulsed by a fit of coughing: he spat blood into an old vanaspati[1] can. The great Sheikh, the 'Thief of Thieves', had become a sick man, and every day the time drew nearer when some young pretender to his power would stick a dagger in his stomach. A lifelong addiction to gambling had left him almost as poor as he had been when, decades ago, he had started out in this line of work as a mere pickpocket's apprentice; so in the extraordinary commission he had accepted from the moneylender's daughter he saw his opportunity of amassing enough wealth at a stroke to leave the valley for ever, and acquire the luxury of a respectable death which would leave his stomach intact.

As for the Prophet's hair, well, neither he nor his blind wife had ever had much to say for prophets—that was one thing they had in common with the moneylender's thunderstruck clan.

It would not do, however, to reveal the nature of this, his last crime, to his four sons. To his consternation, they had all grown up to be hopelessly devout men, who even spoke of making the pilgrimage to Mecca some day. 'Absurd!' their father would laugh at them. 'Just tell me how you will go?' For, with a parent's absolutist love, he had made sure they were all provided with a lifelong source of high income by crippling them at birth, so that, as they dragged themselves around the city, they earned excellent money in the begging business.

The children, then, could look after themselves.

He and his wife would be off soon with the jewel-boxes of the moneylender's women. It was a timely chance indeed that had brought the beautiful bruised girl into his corner of the town.

That night, the large house on the shore of the lake lay blindly waiting, with silence lapping at its walls. A burglar's night: clouds in the sky and mists on the winter water. Hashim the moneylender was asleep, the only member of his family to whom sleep had come that night. In another room, his son Atta

---

1. Brand of clarified butter.

lay deep in the coils of his coma with a blood-clot forming on his brain, watched over by a mother who had let down her long greying hair to show her grief, a mother who placed warm compresses on his head with gestures redolent of impotence. In a third bedroom Huma waited, fully dressed, amidst the jewel-heavy caskets of her desperation.

At last a bulbul[2] sang softly from the garden below her window and, creeping downstairs, she opened a door to the bird, on whose face there was a scar in the shape of the Nastaliq letter *sín*.

Noiselessly, the bird flew up the stairs behind her. At the head of the staircase they parted, moving in opposite directions along the corridor of their conspiracy without a glance at one another.

Entering the moneylender's room with professional ease, the burglar, Sín, discovered that Huma's predictions had been wholly accurate. Hashim lay sprawled diagonally across his bed, the pillow untenanted by his head, the prize easily accessible. Step by padded step, Sín moved towards the goal.

It was at this point that, in the bedroom next door, young Atta sat bolt upright in his bed, giving his mother a great fright, and without any warning—prompted by goodness knows what pressure of the blood-clot upon his brain—began screaming at the top of his voice:

'Thief! Thief! Thief!'

It seems probable that his poor mind had been dwelling, in these last moments, upon his own father; but it is impossible to be certain, because having uttered these three emphatic words the young man fell back upon his pillow and died.

At once his mother set up a screeching and a wailing and a keening and a howling so earsplittingly intense that they completed the work which Atta's cry had begun—that is, her laments penetrated the walls of her husband's bedroom and brought Hashim wide awake.

Sheikh Sín was just deciding whether to dive beneath the bed or brain the moneylender good and proper when Hashim grabbed the tiger-striped swordstick which always stood propped up in a corner beside his bed, and rushed from the room without so much as noticing the burglar who stood on the opposite side of the bed in the darkness. Sín stooped quickly and removed the vial containing the Prophet's hair from its hiding-place.

Meanwhile Hashim had erupted into the corridor, having unsheathed the sword inside his cane. In his right hand he held the weapon and was waving it about dementedly. His left hand was shaking the stick. A shadow came rushing towards him through the midnight darkness of the passageway and, in his somnolent anger, the moneylender thrust his sword fatally through its heart. Turning up the light, he found that he had murdered his daughter, and under the dire influence of this accident he was so overwhelmed by remorse that he turned the sword upon himself, fell upon it and so extinguished his life. His wife, the sole surviving member of the family, was driven mad by the general carnage and had to be committed to an asylum for the insane by her brother, the city's Deputy Commissioner of Police.

2. Asian song thrush.

Sheikh Sín had quickly understood that the plan had gone awry.

Abandoning the dream of the jewel-boxes when he was but a few yards from its fulfilment, he climbed out of Hashim's window and made his escape during the appalling events described above. Reaching home before dawn, he woke his wife and confessed his failure. It would be necessary, he whispered, for him to vanish for a while. Her blind eyes never opened until he had gone.

The noise in the Hashim household had roused their servants and even managed to awaken the night-watchman, who had been fast asleep as usual on his charpoy by the street-gate. They alerted the police, and the Deputy Commissioner himself was informed. When he heard of Huma's death, the mournful officer opened and read the sealed letter which his niece had given him, and instantly led a large detachment of armed men into the light-repellent gullies of the most wretched and disreputable part of the city.

The tongue of a malicious cat-burglar named Huma's fellow-conspirator; the finger of an ambitious bank-robber pointed at the house in which he lay concealed; and although Sín managed to crawl through a hatch in the attic and attempt a roof-top escape, a bullet from the Deputy Commissioner's own rifle penetrated his stomach and brought him crashing messily to the ground at the feet of Huma's enraged uncle.

From the dead thief's pocket rolled a vial of tinted glass, cased in filigree silver.

The recovery of the Prophet's hair was announced at once on All-India Radio. One month later, the valley's holiest men assembled at the Hazratbal mosque and formally authenticated the relic. It sits to this day in a closely guarded vault by the shores of the loveliest of lakes in the heart of the valley which was once closer than any other place on earth to Paradise.

But before our story can properly be concluded, it is necessary to record that when the four sons of the dead Sheikh awoke on the morning of his death, having unwittingly spent a few minutes under the same roof as the famous hair, they found that a miracle had occurred, that they were all sound of limb and strong of wind, as whole as they might have been if their father had not thought to smash their legs in the first hours of their lives. They were, all four of them, very properly furious, because the miracle had reduced their earning powers by 75 per cent, at the most conservative estimate; so they were ruined men.

Only the Sheikh's widow had some reason for feeling grateful, because although her husband was dead she had regained her sight, so that it was possible for her to spend her last days gazing once more upon the beauties of the valley of Kashmir.

1981

JAMES FENTON
b. 1949

Born in Lincoln, James Fenton was educated at Durham Chorister School and at Magdalen College, Oxford, where he won the Newdigate Prize for Poetry. He returned to Oxford to follow Seamus Heaney as Professor of Poetry from 1994 to 1999. He has worked as a literary and political journalist for the *New Statesman* and as drama critic for *The Sunday Times*. In the 1970s he was a foreign correspondent in Germany, Cambodia, and Vietnam. Firsthand experience of human suffering gives authority to such a poem as *A German Requiem,* his elegy for the German Jews killed by the Nazis in World War II—an authority all too often lacking in poems on such subjects written secondhand. Part of the poignancy of his *Requiem* stems from the grimly comic detail of the transferred nameplates, a touch typical of a poet who never lapses into portentous solemnity.

The texture of Fenton's poems is rich in factual detail and enlivened by wit. He has written some very funny light verse and nonsense poems, and the tonal range of his work is matched by—indeed, made possible by—a technical range that can encompass, with equal assurance, open forms and the greatest complexities of rhyme and meter.

A German Requiem

It is not what they built. It is what they knocked down.
It is not the houses. It is the spaces between the houses.
It is not the streets that exist. It is the streets that no longer exist.
It is not your memories which haunt you.
5   It is not what you have written down.
It is what you have forgotten, what you must forget.
What you must go on forgetting all your life.
And with any luck oblivion should discover a ritual.
You will find out that you are not alone in the enterprise.
10   Yesterday the very furniture seemed to reproach you.
Today you take your place in the Widow's Shuttle.[1]

           •

The bus is waiting at the southern gate
To take you to the city of your ancestors
Which stands on the hill opposite, with gleaming pediments,
15   As vivid as this charming square, your home.
Are you shy? You should be. It is almost like a wedding,
The way you clasp your flowers and give a little tug at your veil. Oh,
The hideous bridesmaids, it is natural that you should resent them
Just a little, on this first day.
20   But that will pass, and the cemetery is not far.
Here comes the driver, flicking a toothpick into the gutter,
His tongue still searching between his teeth.
See, he has not noticed you. No one has noticed you.
It will pass, young lady, it will pass.

           •

---

1. Popular name for bus going to the cemetery.

25   How comforting it is, once or twice a year,
      To get together and forget the old times.
      As on those special days, ladies and gentlemen,
      When the boiled shirts[2] gather at the graveside
      And a leering waistcoat approaches the rostrum.
30   It is like a solemn pact between the survivors.
      The mayor has signed it on behalf of the freemasonry.[3]
      The priest has sealed it on behalf of all the rest.
      Nothing more need be said, and it is better that way—

·

      The better for the widow, that she should not live in fear of surprise,
35   The better for the young man, that he should move at liberty between the
         armchairs,
      The better that these bent figures who flutter among the graves
      Tending the nightlights and replacing the chrysanthemums
      Are not ghosts,
      That they shall go home.
40   The bus is waiting, and on the upper terraces
      The workmen are dismantling the houses of the dead.

·

      But when so many had died, so many and at such speed,
      There were no cities waiting for the victims.
      They unscrewed the name-plates from the shattered doorways
45   And carried them away with the coffins.
      So the squares and parks were filled with the eloquence of young cemeteries:
      The smell of fresh earth, the improvised crosses
      And all the impossible directions in brass and enamel.

·

      "Doctor Gliedschirm, skin specialist, surgeries 14–16 hours or by appoint-
         ment."
50   Professor Sargnagel was buried with four degrees, two associate member-
         ships
      And instructions to tradesmen to use the back entrance.
      Your uncle's grave informed you that he lived on the third floor, left.
      You were asked please to ring, and he would come down in the lift°   *elevator*
      To which one needed a key . . .

·

55   Would come down, would ever come down
      With a smile like thin gruel, and never too much to say.
      How he shrank through the years.
      How you towered over him in the narrow cage.[4]
      How he shrinks now . . .

·

2. (Men wearing) dress shirts with starched fronts.
3. Fraternity for mutual help, called "Free and Accepted Masons," which has elaborate secret rituals.
4. Of the wire-screened elevator.

60 But come. Grief must have its term? Guilt too, then.
And it seems there is no limit to the resourcefulness of recollection.
So that a man might say and think:
When the world was at its darkest,
When the black wings passed over the rooftops[5]
65 (And who can divine His purposes?) even then
There was always, always a fire in this hearth.
You see this cupboard? A priest-hole![6]
And in that lumber-room whole generations have been housed and fed.
Oh, if I were to begin, if I were to begin to tell you
70 The half, the quarter, a mere smattering of what we went through!

•

His wife nods, and a secret smile,
Like a breeze with enough strength to carry one dry leaf
Over two pavingstones, passes from chair to chair.
Even the enquirer is charmed.
75 He forgets to pursue the point.
It is not what he wants to know.
It is what he wants not to know.
It is not what they say.
It is what they do not say.

1981

Wind

This is the wind, the wind in a field of corn.
Great crowds are fleeing from a major disaster
Down the long valleys, the green swaying wadis,[1]
Down through the beautiful catastrophe of wind.

5 Families, tribes, nations and their livestock
Have heard something, seen something. An expectation
Or a gigantic misunderstanding has swept over the hilltop
Bending the ear of the hedgerow with stories of fire and sword.

I saw a thousand years pass in two seconds.
10 Land was lost, languages rose and divided.
This lord went east and found safety.
His brother sought Africa and a dish of aloes.[2]

Centuries, minutes later, one might ask
How the hilt of a sword wandered so far from the smithy.
15 And somewhere they will sing: "Like chaff we were borne
In the wind." This is the wind in a field of corn.

1983

---

5. Cf. Exodus 12.27: "It is the sacrifice of the
Lord's passover, who passed over the houses of the
children of Israel in Egypt, when he smote the
Egyptians, and delivered our houses."
6. A secret hiding place for a Roman Catholic
priest during periods of persecution.
1. Rocky watercourse, dry except in the rainy season (in North Africa, etc.).
2. Plant with leaves yielding a bitter juice.

PAUL MULDOON
b. 1951

Paul Muldoon was born in Portadown, County Armagh, Northern Ireland, the eldest child of parents he has likened to the Morels in D. H. Lawrence's *Sons and Lovers*: his father a navvy, farm worker, mushroom grower; his mother a schoolmistress, who introduced him to many of the books that appear in his poems. He grew up in "a little enclave of Roman Catholics living within the predominantly Protestant parish of Loughgall, the village where the Orange Order was founded in 1795." Despite inheriting strong Republican sympathies, he depicts the Catholic Church unsympathetically, even going so far as to state that there is "a very fine line between organized religion and organized crime." He was educated at the primary school in Collegelands (where his mother taught), St. Patrick's College, Armagh, and Queen's University, Belfast, where he was tutored by Seamus Heaney and came to know such other poets of the "Belfast Group" as Derek Mahon and Michael Longley. On leaving university, he worked as a radio and television producer for the BBC in Belfast until, in the mid-1980s, he became a freelance writer and moved to the United States, where he currently teaches at Princeton University.

Muldoon's first published poems were written in Irish, and although he soon switched to English, Irish words and phrases would continue to appear in his work. As with many other Irish poets, America soon began to loom large in his imagination. Excited by American films, he adopted and adapted cinematic techniques in such hectic, hallucinatory narrative poems as *Immram* and *The More a Man Has the More a Man Wants*. Other poems parallel the plight of American Indians with that of Northern Irish Catholics. His earliest literary influence was Robert Frost's "strong, classic, lyric line. But the most important thing . . . was his mischievous, shy, multi-layered quality under the surface." It would be hard to improve on that last sentence as a description of Muldoon's own mature style, the expression of an omnivorous imagination that—in *Milkweed and Monarch*, for example—mixes together a memory of his parents' Collegelands grave with the remembered tastes of dill and tarragon, memories of the fur of an American sea otter, a pickled gherkin, Monarch butterflies, the Irish Cliffs of Moher, and a Russian samovar into a kaleidoscopic pattern that is at once moving, musically satisfying, and a brilliant postmodern variation on the ancient poetic form of villanelle (with the repetition of its first and third lines).

Gathering Mushrooms

The rain comes flapping through the yard
like a tablecloth that she hand-embroidered.
My mother has left it on the line.
It is sodden with rain.
5   The mushroom shed is windowless, wide,
its high-stacked wooden trays
hosed down with formaldehyde.[1]
And my father has opened the Gates of Troy[2]
to that first load of horse manure.
10   Barley straw. Gypsum.[3] Dried blood. Ammonia.
Wagon after wagon
blusters in, a self-renewing gold-black dragon

1. Formic-acid antiseptic.
2. City besieged by the Greeks in Homer's *Iliad*. Its walls could not be destroyed from without, and it was finally captured only by a trick.
3. Hydrated calcium sulfate, used for making plaster of Paris.

we push to the back of the mind.
We have taken our pitchforks to the wind.

15 All brought back to me that September evening
fifteen years on. The pair of us
tripping through Barnett's fair demesne°   *domain*
like girls in long dresses
after a hail-storm.
20 We might have been thinking of the fire-bomb
that sent Malone House sky-high
and its priceless collection of linen
sky-high.
We might have wept with Elizabeth McCrum.
25 We were thinking only of psilocybin.[4]
You sang of the maid you met on the dewy grass—
And she stooped so low gave me to know
it was mushrooms she was gathering O.

He'll be wearing that same old donkey-jacket[5]
30 and the sawn-off waders.
He carries a knife, two punnets,[6] a bucket.
He reaches far into his own shadow.
We'll have taken him unawares
and stand behind him, slightly to one side.
35 He is one of those ancient warriors
before the rising tide.
He'll glance back from under his peaked cap
without breaking rhythm:
his coaxing a mushroom—a flat or a cup—
40 the nick against his right thumb;
the bucket then, the punnet to left or right,
and so on and so forth till kingdom come.

We followed the overgrown tow-path by the Lagan.
The sunset would deepen through cinnamon
45 to aubergine,
the wood-pigeon's concerto for oboe and strings,
allegro, blowing your mind.
And you were suddenly out of my ken, hurtling
towards the ever-receding ground,
50 into the maw
of a shimmering green-gold dragon.
You discovered yourself in some outbuilding
with your long-lost companion, me,
though my head had grown into the head of a horse
55 that shook its dirty-fair mane
and spoke this verse:

Come back to us. However cold and raw, your feet
were always meant

---

4. Hallucinogenic drug made from mushrooms.   6. Small shallow baskets for fruit or vegetables.
5. Strong jacket with leather shoulder patches.

to negotiate terms with bare cement.
60   Beyond this concrete wall is a wall of concrete
and barbed wire. Your only hope
is to come back. If sing you must, let your song
tell of treading your own dung,
let straw and dung give a spring to your step.
65   If we never live to see the day we leap
into our true domain,
lie down with us now and wrap
yourself in the soiled grey blanket of Irish rain
that will, one day, bleach itself white.
70   Lie down with us and wait.

1983

Milkweed and Monarch

As he knelt by the grave of his mother and father
the taste of dill, or tarragon—
he could barely tell one from the other—

filled his mouth. It seemed as if he might smother.
5   Why should he be stricken
with grief, not for his mother and father,

but a woman slinking from the fur of a sea-otter
in Portland, Maine, or, yes, Portland, Oregon—
he could barely tell one from the other—

10   and why should he now savour
the tang of her, her little pickled gherkin,
as he knelt by the grave of his mother and father?

                                        •

He looked about. He remembered her palaver
on how both earth and sky would darken—
15   "You could barely tell one from the other"—

while the Monarch butterflies passed over
in their milkweed-hunger: "A wing-beat, some reckon,
may trigger off the mother and father

of all storms, striking your Irish Cliffs of Moher
20   with the force of a hurricane."
Then: "Milkweed and Monarch 'invented' each other."

                                        •

He looked about. Cow's-parsley in a samovar.[1]
He'd mistaken his mother's name, "Regan", for "Anger":
as he knelt by the grave of his mother and father
25   he could barely tell one from the other.

1994

1. Russian tea urn.

Poems in Process

In all ages, some poets have claimed that their poems were not willed but were inspired, whether by a muse, by divine visitation, or by sudden emergence from the author's subconscious mind. But as the poet Richard Aldington has remarked, "genius is not enough; one must also work." The working manuscripts of the greatest writers show that, however involuntary the origin of a poem, vision was usually followed by laborious revision before the work achieved the seeming inevitability of its final form.

Although some earlier poetic manuscripts have survived, it was not until the nineteenth century that the working drafts of poets began to be widely preserved, and so remain abundantly available. The examples from major poets that are transcribed here represent various stages in the composition of a poem, and a variety of procedures by individual poets. The selections from Blake, Byron, Shelley, and Keats are drafts that were written, emended, crossed out, and rewritten in the heat of first invention; while poems by Wordsworth, Hopkins, and Yeats are shown in successive stages of revision over an extended period of time. Shelley's *O World, O Life, O Time* originated in a few key nouns, together with an abstract rhythmic pattern that was only later fleshed out with words, while Yeats's *After Long Silence* began as a prose sketch that gradually and laboriously was reshaped into a metric and stanzaic form. Still other poems—Tennyson's *The Lady of Shalott*, Yeats's *The Sorrow of Love*—were subjected to radical revision long after the initial versions had been committed to print. In all these examples we look on as poets, no matter how rapidly they achieve a result they are willing to let stand, carry on their inevitably tentative efforts to meet the multiple requirements of meaning, syntax, meter, sound pattern, and the constraints imposed by a chosen stanza. And because these are all very good poets, the seeming conflict between the necessities of significance and form results not in the distortion but in the perfecting of the poetic statement.

Our transcriptions from the poets' drafts attempt to reproduce, as accurately as the change from script to print will allow, the appearance of the original manuscript page. A poet's first attempt at a line or phrase is reproduced in larger type, the emendations in smaller type. The line numbers in the headings that identify an excerpt are those of the final form of the complete poem, as reprinted in this anthology, above.

SELECTED BIBLIOGRAPHY

Autograph Poetry in the English Language, 2 vols., 1973, compiled by P. J. Croft, reproduces and transcribes one or more pages of manuscript in the poet's own hand, from the 14th century to the late twentieth century. Volume 1 includes Blake and Burns; volume 2 includes many of the other poets represented in this volume of *The Norton Anthology of English Literature*, from Wordsworth to Dylan Thomas. Books that discuss the process of composition and revision, with examples from the manuscripts and printed versions of poems, are Charles D. Abbott, ed., *Poets at Work*, 1948; Phyllis Bartlett, *Poems in Process*, 1951; A. F. Scott, *The Poet's Craft*, 1957; George Bornstein, *Poetic Remaking: The Art of Browning, Yeats, and Pound*, 1988. In

Word for Word: A Study of Authors' Alterations,
1965, Wallace Hildick analyzes the composition
of prose fiction as well as poems; a shorter version, *Word for Word: The Rewriting of Fiction,*
1965, discusses the revision of novels by George
Eliot, Samuel Butler, Hardy, Lawrence, James,
and Woolf. *Byron's "Don Juan,"* ed. T. G. Steffan
and W. W. Pratt, 4 vols., 1957, transcribes the
manuscript drafts; the Cornell Wordsworth, in
process, reproduces, transcribes, and discusses
various versions of Wordsworth's poems from
the first manuscript drafts to the final publication in his lifetime, and the Cornell Yeats, also
in process, does the same for Yeats. For facsim-

iles and transcripts of Keats's poems, see *John
Keats: Poetry Manuscripts at Harvard,* ed. Jack
Stillinger, 1990. Jon Stallworthy, *Between the
Lines: Yeats's Poetry in the Making,* 1963, reproduces and analyzes the sequential drafts of a
number of Yeats's major poems. Valerie Eliot
has edited T. S. Eliot's *The Waste Land: A Facsimile and Transcript of the Original Drafts
Including the Annotations of Ezra Pound,* 1971,
while Dame Helen Gardner has transcribed and
analyzed the manuscript drafts of Eliot's *Four
Quartets* in *The Composition of Four Quartets,*
1978.

WILLIAM BLAKE
The Tyger[1]

[*First Draft*]

The Tyger

1 Tyger Tyger burning bright
In the forests of the night
What immortal hand or eye
~~Dare Could frame~~ thy fearful symmetry

  Burnt in
2 ~~In what distant~~ deeps or skies
~~The cruel Burnt the fire~~ of thine eyes
On what wings dare he aspire
What the hand dare sieze the fire

3 And what shoulder & what art
Could twist the sinews of thy heart
And when thy heart began to beat
What dread hand & what dread feet

 ~~Could fetch it from the furnace deep~~
 ~~And in thy horrid ribs dare steep~~
 ~~In the well of sanguine woe~~
 ~~In what clay & what mould~~
 ~~Were thy eyes of fury rolld~~

  ~~Where~~   ~~where~~
4 ~~What~~ the hammer ~~what~~ the chain
In what furnace was thy brain

---

1. These drafts have been taken from a notebook
used by William Blake, called the Rossetti MS
because it was once owned by Dante Gabriel Rossetti, the Victorian poet and painter; David V. Erd-

man's edition of *The Notebook of William Blake*
(1973) contains a photographic facsimile. The
stanza and line numbers were written by Blake in
the manuscript.

dread grasp

What the anvil what the arm arm grasp clasp
Dare Could its deadly terrors clasp grasp clasp

6 Tyger Tyger burning bright
In the forests of the night
What immortal hand & eye

frame
Dare form thy fearful symmetry

[*Trial Stanzas*]

Burnt in distant deeps ok skies
The cruel fire of thine eye,
Could heart descend or wings aspire
What the hand dare sieze the fire

dare he smile laugh
5 3 And did he laugh his work to see

ankle
What the shoulder what the knee

Dare
4 Did he who made the lamb make thee
1 When the stars threw down their spears
2 And waterd heaven with their tears

[*Second Full Draft*]

Tyger Tyger burning bright
In the forests of the night
What Immortal hand & eye
Dare frame thy fearful symmetry

And what shoulder & what art
Could twist the sinews of thy heart
And when thy heart began to beat
What dread hand & what dread feet

When the stars threw down their spears
And waterd heaven with their tears
Did he smile his work to see
Did he who made the lamb make thee

Tyger Tyger burning bright
In the forests of the night
What immortal hand & eye
Dare frame thy fearful symmetry

[*Final Version, 1794*][2]

The Tyger

Tyger Tyger, burning bright,
In the forests of the night;
What immortal hand or eye,
Could frame thy fearful symmetry?

In what distant deeps or skies
Burnt the fire of thine eyes!
On what wings dare he aspire?
What the hand, dare sieze the fire?

And what shoulder, & what art,
Could twist the sinews of thy heart?
And when thy heart began to beat,
What dread hand? & what dread feet?

What the hammer? what the chain,
In what furnace was thy brain?
What the anvil? what dread grasp,
Dare its deadly terrors clasp?

When the stars threw down their spears
And water'd heaven with their tears:
Did he smile his work to see?
Did he who made the Lamb make thee?

Tyger, Tyger burning bright,
In the forests of the night:
What immortal hand or eye,
Dare frame thy fearful symmetry?

WILLIAM WORDSWORTH

She dwelt among the untrodden ways

[*Version in a Letter to Coleridge,
December 1798 or January 1799*][1]

My hope was one, from cities far
    Nursed on a lonesome heath:
Her lips were red as roses are,
    Her hair a woodbine wreath.

She lived among the untrodden ways
    Beside the springs of Dove,

---

2. As published in *Songs of Experience*.
1. Printed in Ernest de Selincourt's *Early Letters of William and Dorothy Wordsworth* (1935). By deleting two stanzas, and making a few verbal changes, Wordsworth achieved the terse published form of his great dirge.

A maid whom there were none to praise,
  And very few to love;

A violet by a mossy stone
  Half-hidden from the eye!
Fair as a star when only one
  Is shining in the sky!

And she was graceful as the broom
  That flowers by Carron's side;[2]
But slow distemper checked her bloom,
  And on the Heath she died.

Long time before her head lay low
  Dead to the world was she:
But now she's in her grave, and Oh!
  The difference to me!

[*Final Version, 1800*][3]

Song

She dwelt among th' untrodden ways
  Beside the springs of Dove,
A Maid whom there were none to praise
  And very few to love.

A Violet by a mossy stone
  Half-hidden from the Eye!
—Fair, as a star when only one
  Is shining in the sky!

She *liv'd* unknown, and few could know
  When Lucy ceas'd to be;
But she is in her Grave, and Oh!
  The difference to me.

LORD BYRON

From Don Juan[1]

[*First Draft: Canto 3, Stanza 9*]

~~Life is a play and men~~
  All tragedies are finished by a death,
  All Comedies are ended by a marriage,
~~For Life can go no further.~~

---

2. The Carron is a river in northwestern Scotland. "Broom" (preceding line) is a shrub with long slender branches and yellow flowers.
3. As published in the second edition of *Lyrical Ballads*.

1. Reproduced from transcripts made of Byron's manuscripts in T. G. Steffan and W. W. Pratt, *Byron's "Don Juan"* (1957). The stanzas were published by Byron in their emended form.

~~These two form the last gasp of Passion's breath~~
~~All further is a blank—I won't disparage~~
~~That holy state—but certainly beneath~~
The Sun—of human things
~~These two are levellers, and human breath~~
~~So~~ ~~These point the epigram of human breath;~~
~~Or any~~ The future states of both are left to faith,
~~Though Life and love I like not to disparage~~
~~The~~ For authors ~~think~~ description might disparage
      fear
~~'Tis strange that poets never try to wreathe~~ [sic?]
~~With enth~~ ~~'Tis strange that poets of the Catholic faith~~
~~Ne'er go beyond—and~~ ~~but seem to dread miscarriage~~
~~So dramas close with death or settlement for life~~
~~Veiling~~ ~~Leaving the future states of Love and Life~~
~~The paradise beyond like that of life~~
~~And ne'er describing either~~
~~To more conjecture of a devil~~ ~~and~~ ~~or wife~~
~~And don't say much of paradise or wife~~
The worlds to come of both—~~&~~ or fall beneath,
And ~~all~~ ~~both the worlds would blame them for miscarriage~~
And then both worlds would punish their miscarriage—
~~So leaving both with priest & prayerbook ready~~
So leaving ~~Clerg~~ both ~~a~~ each their Priest and prayerbook ready,
They say no more of death or of the Lady.

[First Draft: Canto 14, Stanza 95]

    quote   seldom
Alas! ~~I speak by~~ Experience—~~never~~ yet
~~I had a paramour—and I've had many~~
         ~~some small~~
~~To whom I did not cause a deep~~ regret—
~~Whom I had not some reason to regret~~
~~For Whom—I did not feel myself~~ a Zany—
Alas! by all experience, seldom yet
(I merely quote what I have heard from many)
Had lovers not some reason to regret
The passion which made Solomon a Zany.
~~I also had a wife~~—not to forget—
I've also seen some wives—not to forget—
The marriage state—the best or worst of any—
    were   paragons
Who ~~was~~ the very ~~paragon~~ of wives,
Yet made the misery of ~~both our~~ lives.
      ~~many~~
      ~~several~~
      ~~of~~ at least two

PERCY BYSSHE SHELLEY

The three stages of this poem labeled "First Draft" are scattered through one of Shelley's notebooks, now in the Huntington Library, San Marino, California; these drafts have been transcribed and analyzed by Bennett Weaver, "Shelley Works Out the Rhythm of *A Lament*," *PMLA* 47 (1932): 570–76. They show Shelley working with fragmentary words and phrases, and simultaneously with a wordless pattern of pulses that marked out the meter of the single lines and the shape of the lyric stanzas. Shelley left this draft unfinished.

Apparently at some later time, Shelley returned to the poem and wrote what is here called the "Second Draft"; from this he then made, on a second page, a revised fair copy that provided the text that Mary Shelley published in 1824, after the poet's death. These two manuscript pages are now in the Bodleian Library, Oxford; the first page is photographically reproduced and discussed by John Carter and John Sparrow, "Shelley, Swinburne, and Housman," *Times Literary Supplement*, November 21, 1968, pp. 1318–19.

O World, O Life, O Time

[*First Draft, Stage 1*]

Ah time, oh night, oh day
~~Ni nal ni na, na ni~~
~~Ni na ni na, ni na~~
Oh life O death, O time
    Time a di
~~Never Time~~
Ah time, a time O-time
    ~~Time!~~

[*First Draft, Stage 2*]

Oh time, oh night oh day
~~O day oh night, alas~~
  ~~O~~ Death time night ~~oh~~
Oh, Time
Oh time o night oh day

[*First Draft, Stage 3*]

Na na, na na ná na
Nă nă na na na—nă nă
    Nă nă nă nă nā nā
Na na nă nă nâ ă na

Na na na—nă nă—na na
  Na na na na—na na na na na
Na na na na na.
    Na na
Na na na na na
    Na na
Na na na na na ˇ na!

Oh time, oh night, o day
        alas
  O day ~~serenest,~~ o day
  O day alas the day
That thou shouldst sleep when we awake to say

O time time—o death—o day
O day, o death life is far from thee
O thou wert never free
For death is now with thee
~~And life is far from~~
O death, o day for life is far from thee

[*Second Draft*]¹

Out of the day & night   I am
A joy has taken flight   despair
Fresh spring & summer   & winter hoar
Fill my faint heart with grief, but with
                                delight
          No more—o never more!

~~Wo~~
     O World, o life, o time
     ~~Will ye~~ On whose last steps I climb
Trembling at those which I have trod² before
When will return the glory of yr prime
          No more   Oh never more

Out of the day & night
A joy has taken flight—
                    autumn
~~From~~ Green spring, & ~~summer gra~~³ & winter hoar

[FAIR COPY]

O World   o Life   o Time
On whose last steps I climb
Trembling at that where I had stood before
When will return the glory of yr prime?
          No more, o never more

2

Out of the day & night
A joy has taken flight
Fresh spring & summer   ⁴ & winter hoar

1. Shelley apparently wrote the first stanza of this draft low down on the page, and ran out of space after crowding in the third line of the second stanza; he then, in a lighter ink, wrote a revised form of the whole of the second stanza at the top of the page. In this revision, he left a space after "summer" in line 3, indicating that he planned an insertion that would fill out the four-foot meter of this line, and so make it match the five feet in the corresponding line of the first stanza.

In the upper right-hand corner of this manuscript page Shelley wrote "I am despair"—seemingly to express his bleak mood at the time he wrote the poem.

For this draft and information, and for the transcript of the fair copy that follows, the editors are indebted to Donald H. Reiman.

2. Shelley at first wrote "trod," then overwrote that with "stood." In the following line, Shelley at first wrote "yr," then overwrote "thy."
3. Not clearly legible; it is either "gra" or "gre." A difference in the ink from the rest of the line indicates that Shelley, having left a blank space, later started to fill it in, but thought better of it and crossed out the fragmentary insertion.
4. This fair copy of the second draft retains, and even enlarges, the blank space, indicating that Shelley still hasn't made up his mind what to insert after the word "summer." We may speculate, by reference to the fragmentary version of this stanza in the second draft, that he had in mind as possibilities either an adjective, "gray" or "green," or else the noun "autumn." Mary Shelley closed up this space when she published the poem in 1824, with

Move my faint heart with grief but with delight
No more, o, never more

JOHN KEATS

From The Eve of St. Agnes[1]

[*Stanza 26*]

But soon his heart revives—her prayers said
She ~~lays aside her neck~~ pearled
    strips her hair of all its ∧ wreathes pearl
~~Unclasps her bosom jewels~~
~~And twist it in one knot upon her head~~

                   ~~soon~~
But soon his heart revives—her praying done,
Of all its wreathed pearl she strips her hair
Unclasps her warmed jewels one by one
     her bursting
Loosens ~~the boddice from her~~
     ~~her Boddice lace string~~
     ~~her Boddice and her bosom bar~~
     her

[HERE KEATS BEGINS A NEW SHEET]

Loosens ~~her fragrant boddice and doth bare~~
~~Her~~

26

  Anon
~~But soon~~ his heart revives—her praying done,
               frees:
Of all its wreathe'd pearl her hair she ~~strips~~
Unclasps her warmed jewels one by one
            by degrees
          to her knees
Loosens her fragrant boddice: ~~and down slips~~
Her sweet attire ~~falls light creeps down by~~
     creeps rusteling to her knees
    Mermaid   in sea weed
Half hidden like ~~a Syren of the Sea~~
~~And more melodious~~
        dreaming
She stands awhile in ∧ thought; and sees
          on
In fancy fair Saint Agnes ~~in~~ her bed
But dares not look behind or all the charm is ~~f~~ dead

---

the result that editors, following her version, have until very recently printed this line as though Shelley had intended it to be one metric foot shorter than the corresponding line of stanza 1.

1. Transcribed from what is probably the best known of all manuscripts, that which contains Keats's first draft of all but the first seven stanzas of *The Eve of St. Agnes;* it is now in the Houghton Library, Harvard University. Keats's published version of the poem, above, contains some further changes in wording.

[*Stanza 30*]

But
~~And still she slept.~~
And still she slept an azure-lidded sleep
In blanched linen, smooth and lavender'd
While he from frorth the closet brough a heap
    fruits
Of candied ~~sweets~~ ~~sweets, with~~
    apple Quince and plumb and gourd
          creamed
With jellies soother than the ~~dairy~~ curd
    tinct
And lucent syrups ~~smooth~~ with ciannamon
~~And sugar'd dates from that oer Euphrates fard~~
      ~~in Brigantine transferred~~
Manna and daites in ~~Brigtine transferd~~
       ~~and manna wild transferd~~
~~And Manna wild and Bragantine~~
          sugar'd dates transferred

argosy

~~In Brigantino from Fez~~
From fez—and spiced danties every one
   ~~glutted~~
From ~~wealthy~~ Samarchand to cedard lebanon
   silken

To Autumn[2]

Season of Mists and mellow fruitfulness
  Close bosom friend of the naturring sun;
Conspiring with him how to load and bless
    The Vines with fruit that round the thatch eves run
      To bend with apples the moss'd Cottage trees
      And fill all furuits with sweeness to the core
        To swell the gourd, and plump the hazle shells
    With a white kernel; to set budding more
    And still more later flowers for the bees
    Until they think wam days with never cease
      For Summer has o'erbrimm'd their clammy cells—

          oft amid thy stores?
Who hath not seen thee? ~~for thy haunts are many~~
        abroad
  Sometimes whoeever seeks ~~for thee~~ may find
Thee sitting careless on a granary floorr
  Thy hair soft lifted by the winnowing wind

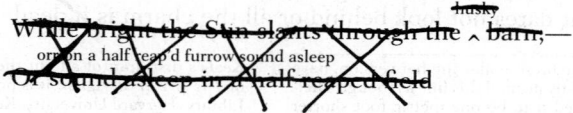

                  husky
~~While bright the Sun slants through the barn,—~~
    or on a half reap'd furrow sound asleep
~~Or sound asleep in a half reaped field~~

2. From an untitled manuscript—apparently Keats's first draft of the poem—in the Houghton Library, Harvard University. The many pen-slips and errors in spelling indicate that Keats wrote rapidly, in a state of creative excitement. Keats made a few further changes before publishing the poem in the form included in the selections above.

~~Dos'd with read poppies, while thy reeping hook~~
~~Spares form Some slumbrous~~
~~minutes while warm slumpers creep~~
Or on a half reap'd furrow sound asleep
Dos'd with the fume of poppies, while thy hook
Spares the next swath and all its twined flowers
~~Spares for some slumbrous minutes the next swath;~~
And sometimes like a gleans thost dost keep
Steady thy laden head across the brook;
Or by a Cyder-press with patent look
Thou watchest the last oozing hours by hours

Where are the songs of Sping? Aye where are they?
Think not of them thou hast thy music too—
   barred   bloom
While ~~a gold~~ clouds ~~gilds~~ the soft-dying day
And
~~And~~ Touch~~ing the~~ the stibble plains ∧ rosy hue—
Then in a waiful quire the small gnats mourn
Among the river sallows, ~~on the~~ borne afots
Or sinking as the light wind lives and dies;
And full grown Lambs loud bleat from hilly bourn,
Hedge crickets sing, and now again full soft
The Redbreast whistles from a garden croft:
~~And now flock still~~
And Gather'd Swallows twiter in the Skies—

ALFRED, LORD TENNYSON
From The Lady of Shalott[1]

[*Version of 1832*]

PART THE FIRST.

On either side the river lie
Long fields of barley and of rye,
That clothe the wold, and meet the sky.
And thro' the field the road runs by
      To manytowered Camelot.
The yellowleavèd waterlily,
The greensheathèd daffodilly,
Tremble in the water chilly,
      Round about Shallot.

Willows whiten, aspens shiver,
The sunbeam-showers break and quiver

1. First published in Tennyson's *Poems* of 1832 (dated 1833 on the title page). The volume was severely criticized by some reviewers; partly in response to this criticism, Tennyson radically revised a number of the poems, including *The Lady of Shalott*, before reprinting them in his *Poems* (1842).
  Parts 1 and 4 are reproduced here in the version of 1832. The final form of the poem reprinted in the selections from Tennyson, above, differs from the revised version that Tennyson published in 1842 only in line 157, which in 1842 read: "A corse between the houses high"; Tennyson changed the line to "Dead-pale between the houses high" in 1855.

In the stream that runneth ever
By the island in the river,
   Flowing down to Camelot.
Four gray walls and four gray towers
Overlook a space of flowers,
And the silent isle imbowers
   The Lady of Shallot.

Underneath the bearded barley,
The reaper, reaping late and early,
Hears her ever chanting cheerly,
Like an angel, singing clearly,
   O'er the stream of Camelot.
Piling the sheaves in furrows airy,
Beneath the moon, the reaper weary
Listening whispers, " 'tis the fairy
   Lady of Shalott."

The little isle is all inrailed
With a rose-fence, and overtrailed
With roses: by the marge unhailed
The shallop flitteth silkensailed,
   Skimming down to Camelot.
A pearlgarland winds her head:
She leaneth on a velvet bed,
Full royally apparellèd,
   The Lady of Shalott.

    * * *

PART THE FOURTH.

In the stormy eastwind straining
The pale-yellow woods were waning,
The broad stream in his banks complaining,
Heavily the low sky raining
   Over towered Camelot:
Outside the isle a shallow boat
Beneath a willow lay afloat,
Below the carven stern she wrote,
   THE LADY OF SHALOTT.

A cloudwhite crown of pearl she dight.
All raimented in snowy white
That loosely flew, (her zone in sight,
Clasped with one blinding diamond bright,)
   Her wide eyes fixed on Camelot,
Though the squally eastwind keenly
Blew, with folded arms serenely
By the water stood the queenly
   Lady of Shalott.

With a steady, stony glance—
Like some bold seer in a trance,
Beholding all his own mischance,
Mute, with a glassy countenance—
        She looked down to Camelot.
It was the closing of the day,
She loosed the chain, and down she lay,
The broad stream bore her far away,
        The Lady of Shalott.

As when to sailors while they roam,
By creeks and outfalls far from home,
Rising and dropping with the foam,
From dying swans wild warblings come,
        Blown shoreward; so to Camelot
Still as the boathead wound along
The willowy hills and fields among,
They heard her chanting her deathsong,
        The Lady of Shalott.

A longdrawn carol, mournful, holy,
She chanted loudly, chanted lowly,
Till her eyes were darkened wholly,
And her smooth face sharpened slowly
        Turned to towered Camelot:
For ere she reached upon the tide
The first house by the waterside,
Singing in her song she died,
        The Lady of Shalott.

Under tower and balcony,
By gardenwall and gallery,
A pale, pale corpse she floated by,
Deadcold, between the houses high.
        Dead into towered Camelot.
Knight and burgher, lord and dame,
To the plankèd wharfage came:
Below the stern they read her name,
        "The Lady of Shalott."

They crossed themselves, their stars they blest,
Knight, ministrel, abbot, squire and guest.
There lay a parchment on her breast,
That puzzled more than all the rest,
        The wellfed wits at Camelot.
"The web was woven curiously
The charm is broken utterly,
Draw near and fear not—this is I,
        The Lady of Shalott."

From Tithonus[2]

[*Lines 1–10*]

[TRINITY COLLEGE MANUSCRIPT]

Ay me! Ay me! the woods decay & fall

~~The stars blaze out & never rise again~~.

the

The vapours weep their substance to ground
Man comes & tills the earth & lies beneath
And after many summers dies the ~~rose~~ swan
Me only fatal immortality
Consumes: I wither slowly in thine arms:
Here at the quiet limit of the world

e   yet

A white-haired shade roaming like a dream
The ever-silent spaces of the East
Far-folded mists & gleaming halls of morn.

[HEATH MANUSCRIPT]

Tithon

Ay me! ay me! the woods decay and fall,
The vapours weep their substance to the ground,
Man comes and tills the earth and lies beneath,
And after many summers dies the rose.
Me only fatal immortality
Consumes: I wither slowly in thine arms,
Here at the quiet limit of the world,
A white-haired shadow roaming like a dream
The ever-silent spaces of the East,
Far-folded mists, and gleaming halls of morn.

[AS PRINTED IN 1864]

Tithonus

The woods decay, the woods decay and fall,
The vapours weep their burthen to the ground,
Man comes and tills the field and lies beneath,
And after many a summer dies the swan.
Me only cruel immortality
Consumes: I wither slowly in thine arms,
Here at the quiet limit of the world,
A white-haired shadow roaming like a dream

---

2. Three manuscript drafts of *Tithonus* are extant. Two are in Tennyson's Notebooks Nos. 20 and 21, at Trinity College, Cambridge; a third one, written 1833, is in the Commonplace Book compiled by Tennyson's friend J. M. Heath, which is in the Fitzwilliam Museum at Cambridge University. According to Tennyson's editor, Christopher Ricks, the Heath version is later than those in the Trinity Manuscripts. The transcriptions here of Tenny-son's opening lines are from the first draft (Trinity College manuscript, Notebook 20), and from the Heath manuscript, where the poem is titled "Tithon." These are followed by the final version of *Tithonus* that Tennyson published in 1864. As late as in the edition of 1860, the opening words had remained "Ay me! ay me!" and "field" (line 3) had remained "earth."

The ever-silent spaces of the East,
Far-folded mists, and gleaming halls of morn.

GERARD MANLEY HOPKINS
Thou art indeed just, Lord[1]

*Justus quidem tu es, Domine, si disputem tecum; verumtamen
justa loquar ad te: quare via impiorum prosperatur?* etc.
—Jer. xii 1.

March 17 1889

Lord, if I
Thou art indeed just, ~~were I to~~ contend
         sir,   plead
With thee; but, ~~Lord~~, so what I ~~speak~~ is just.

Why do sinners' ways prosper? and why must

Disappointment all I endeavour end?
Wert thou my enemy, O thou my friend,
How wouldst thou worse, I wonder, than thou dost
                    O the sots and   of
Defeat, thwart me? ~~Ah! sots, revellers~~, thralls to lust
Do in   that
In spare hours ~~do~~ more thrive than I ~~who~~ spend,
       great   See,
Sir, ~~my~~ life on thy cause. ~~Look~~, banks and brakes
Now, leavèd   lacèd they are
~~Leavèd~~ how thick! ~~broidered all~~ again
                 look
With fretty chervil, ~~now~~, and fresh wind shakes
Them; birds build—but not I build; no, but strain,
Time's eunuch, and not breed one work that wakes.
    Mine, O   send my
~~Then send~~, thou lord of life, ~~these~~ roots ~~their~~ rain.

WILLIAM BUTLER YEATS

Yeats usually composed very slowly and with painful effort. He tells us in his *Autobiography* that "five or six lines in two or three laborious hours were a day's work, and I longed for somebody to interrupt me." His manuscripts show the slow evolution of his best poems, which sometimes began with a prose sketch, were then versified, and

1. From a manuscript in the Bodleian Library, Oxford University; it is a clean copy, made after earlier drafts, which Hopkins goes on to revise further. Differences in the ink show that the emendation "lacèd they are" (line 10) was made during the first writing, but that the other verbal changes were made later. The interlinear markings are Hopkins's metrical indicators; he explains their sig-

nificance in the "Author's Preface," included in *Poems of Gerard Manley Hopkins* (1970), ed. W. H. Gardner and N. H. MacKenzie.
   The epigraph is from the Vulgate translation of Jeremiah 12.1; a literal translation of the Latin is "Thou art indeed just, Lord, [even] if I plead with Thee; nevertheless I will speak what is just to Thee: Why does the way of the wicked prosper? etc."

underwent numerous revisions. In many instances, even after the poems had been published, Yeats continued to revise them, sometimes drastically, in later printings.

The Sorrow of Love[1]

[Manuscript, 1891][2]

The quarrel of the sparrows in the eaves,
The full round moon and the star-laden sky,
The song of the ever-singing leaves,
Had hushed away earth's old and weary cry.

And then you came with those red mournful lips,
And with you came the whole of the world's tears,
And all the sorrows of her labouring ships,
And all the burden of her million years.

And now the angry sparrows in the eaves,
The withered moon, the white stars in the sky,
The wearisome loud chanting of the leaves,
Are shaken with earth's old and weary cry.

[First Printed Version, 1892][3]

The quarrel of the sparrows in the eaves,
    The full round moon and the star-laden sky,
And the loud song of the ever-singing leaves
    Had hid away earth's old and weary cry.

And then you came with those red mournful lips,
    And with you came the whole of the world's tears,
And all the sorrows of her labouring ships,
    And all burden of her myriad years.

And now the sparrows warring in the eaves,
    The crumbling moon, the white stars in the sky,
And the loud chanting of the unquiet leaves,
    Are shaken with earth's old and weary cry.

[Final Printed Version, 1925][4]

The brawling of a sparrow in the eaves,
The brilliant moon and all the milky sky,

---

1. Originally composed in Yeats's Pre-Raphaelite mode of the early 1890s, *The Sorrow of Love* was one of his most popular poems. Nonetheless, some thirty years after publication, Yeats rewrote the lyric to give it the greater precision and the colloquial vigor of his poetic style in the 1920s.
2. Manuscript version composed in October 1891, as transcribed by Jon Stallworthy, *Between the Lines: Yeats's Poetry in the Making* (Oxford University Press, 1963), pp. 47–48.
3. From Yeats's *The Countess Kathleen and Various Legends and Lyrics* (1892). In a corrected page proof for this printing, now in the Garvan Collection of the Yale University Library, lines 7–8 originally read: "And all the sorrows of his labouring ships, / And all the burden of his married years." Also, in lines 4 and 12, the adjective was "bitter"

instead of "weary." In his *Poems* (1895), Yeats inserted the missing "the" in line 8, and changed "sorrows" (line 7) to "trouble"; "burden" (line 8) to "trouble"; and "crumbling moon" (line 10) to "curd-pale moon."
4. From *Early Poems and Stories* (1925). Yeats wrote in his *Autobiography* (New York, 1938), p. 371, that "in later years" he had "learnt that occasional prosaic words gave the impression of an active man speaking," so that "certain words must be dull and numb. Here and there in correcting my early poems I have introduced such numbness and dullness, turned, for instance, 'the curd-pale moon' into the 'brilliant moon,' that all might seem, as it were, remembered with indifference, except some one vivid image." Yeats, however, did not recall his emendations accurately. He had in 1925 altered

And all that famous harmony of leaves,
Had blotted out man's image and his cry.

A girl arose that had red mournful lips
And seemed the greatness of the world in tears,
Doomed like Odysseus and the labouring ships
And proud as Priam murdered with his peers;

Arose, and on the instant clamorous eaves,
A climbing moon upon an empty sky,
And all that lamentation of the leaves,
Could but compose man's image and his cry.

Leda and the Swan[5]

[First Version]

Annunciation

Now can the swooping Godhead have his will
Yet hovers, though her helpless thighs are pressed
By the webbed toes; and that all powerful bill
Has suddenly bowed her face upon his breast.
How can those terrified vague fingers push
The feathered glory from her loosening thighs?
All the stretched body's laid on that white rush

       strange
And feels the ~~strong~~ heart beating where it lies
A shudder in the loins engenders there
The broken wall, the burning roof and tower
And Agamemnon dead. . . .

                 Being so caught up
Did nothing pass before her in the air?
Did she put on his knowledge with his power
Before the indifferent beak could let her drop
                 Sept 18 1923

  swooping
The ~~trembl~~ godhead is half hovering still,
  climbs
Yet ~~climbs~~ upon her trembling body pressed
  webbed
By the toes; & ~~through~~ that all powerful bill
      ~~thrown~~ bowed
Has suddenly ~~bowed~~ her face upon his breast.

"the full round moon" (line 2) to "the brilliant moon," and "the curd-pale moon" (line 10, version of 1895) to "a climbing moon."
5. From Yeats's manuscript *Journal*, Sections 248 and 250. This *Journal*, including facsimiles and transcriptions of the drafts of *Leda and the Swan*, has been published in W. B. Yeats, *Memoirs*, ed. Denis Donoghue (Macmillan, London, 1972).
  The first version, entitled *Annunciation*, seems to be a clean copy of earlier drafts; Yeats went on to revise it further, especially the opening octave.

Neither of the other two complete drafts, each of which Yeats labeled "Final Version," was in fact final. Yeats himself crossed out the first draft. The second, although Yeats published it in 1924, was subjected to further revision before he published the poem in *The Tower* (1928), in the final form reprinted in the selections from Yeats, above.
  Yeats's handwriting is hasty and very difficult to decipher. The readings of some words, in the manuscripts both of this poem and of *After Long Silence*, below, are uncertain.

How can those terrified vague fingers push
The feathered glory from her loosening thighs

                 laid
All the stretched body ~~leans~~ on that white rush
               or
~~Her falling body thrown on the white~~ white rush

Can feel etc
or Her body can but lean on the white rush

      But mounts until her trembling thighs are pressed[6]
  ~~B~~
      By the webbed toes; & that all powerful bill
      Has suddenly bowed her head on his breast

Final Version

Can hold

Annunciation

The swooping godhead is half hovering still
But mounts, until her trembling thighs are pressed
By the webbed toes, & that all powerful bill
~~Has hung~~ her helpless body
~~Has suddenly bowed her head up~~on his breast.
How can those terrified vague fingers push
The feathered glory from her loosening thighs?
~~How~~ now its body ~~leans~~ on
~~With her body laid on the white rush~~
     all the stretched body laid on the white rush
and ~~Can~~ feel the strange heart beating where it lies?
A shudder in the loins engenders there
The broken wall, the burning roof & tower
And Agamemnon dead . . .
                  Being mastered so
                  ~~Being so caught up~~
  So
~~And~~ mastered by the brute blood of the air
                 ~~Being mastered so~~
~~Did nothing pass before her in the air?~~
Did she put on his knowledge with his power
Before the indifferent beak could let her drop.
               WBY. Sept 18 1923

    swoop
A ~~rush~~ upon great wings & hovering still
~~He sinks until~~
~~He has sunk on her down, & her hair~~
~~The great bird sinks, till~~
The bird descends, & her frail ~~thigh~~ thighs are pressed
By the webbed toes, & that all

6. This passage is written across the blank page opposite the first version; Yeats drew a line indicating that it was to replace the revised lines 2–4, which he had written below the first version.

Now ~~all~~ that, her body's ~~laid~~ on that white rush[7]
~~All the stretched body, laid on~~ that white rush
~~Now that whole~~
~~Now that her body on the white rush~~
Can fee

Final Version

Leda & the Swan

A rush, a sudden wheel and
~~A swoop upon great wings & hovering still~~
     sinks down   bare frail
stet The bird ~~descends~~ & her ~~frail~~ thighs are pressed
By the ~~toes~~ webbed toes, & that all powerful bill
     laid
Has ~~driven~~ her helpless face upon his breast.
How can those terrified vague fingers push
The feathered glory from her loosening thighs?
         s laid
All the stretched body ~~laid~~ on that white rush
And ~~feel~~ feels the strange heart beating where it lies.
A shudder in the loins engenders there
The broken wall, the burning roof & tower
And Agamemnon dead.
            Being so caught up
So mastered by the ~~br~~ brute blood of the air
Did she put on his knowledge with his power
Before the indifferent beak could let her drop.

After Long Silence[8]

[Draft 1]

Subject

Your hair is white
My hair is white
Come let us talk of love
What other theme do we know
When we were young

---

7. Written on the blank page across from the complete version, with an arrow indicating that it was a revision of the seventh line.

8. The drafts of *After Long Silence* are interspersed with other materials on seven pages of a manuscript book, begun in 1928, which includes a number of additional poems that were published in *The Winding Stair and Other Poems* (1933). It begins, like many of Yeats's poems, with a prose sketch, and is labeled simply "Subject." It then passes through a tentative versified stage (Draft 2) in which Yeats sets down four complete lines and a set of possible rhyme words; is subjected to various drafts and revisions; and concludes with the final text that Yeats published in 1933. Yeats did not add the title *After Long Silence* until he wrote out a fair copy for his typist at some time after August 14, 1931.

David R. Clark, "After 'Silence,' The 'Supreme Theme': Eight Lines of Yeats," includes photocopies and transcripts of the drafts of this poem, together with a discussion of its biographical occasion and its interpretation (in *Myth and Reality in Irish Literature,* ed. Joseph Ronsley [Waterloo, Canada, 1977], pp. 149–73).

We were in love with one another
~~A O~~ And therefore ignorant

[Draft 2]

Those   s
~~Your~~ other lover being dead & gone

                                           friendly light
                                           hair is white

                     ~~on love descant~~   descant
Upon the ~~sole theme~~ supreme theme of art &   song
Wherein there's theme so fitting for the aged.   ;young
We loved each other & were ignorant

[Draft 3]

~~Th~~
   Once more I have kissed your hand & it is right—
   All other lovers being estranged or dead
   The heavy curtain drawn the candle light
   Waging a doubtful battle with the shade
                                   discant,
   ~~We call our wisdom up upon our wisdom & descant~~
   ~~Upon the supreme theme of art & song.~~
   Decrepitude increases wisdom—young
   We loved each other & were ignorant ignor   ignorant

[Draft 4]

Un
~~The~~ friendly lamplight hidden by its shade
~~And shutters clapped upon the deepening night—~~
~~The candle hidden by its friendly shade~~
Those curtains drawn upon the deepening night—

~~The curtains drawn on the unfriendly night~~
That we descant & yet again descant
         supreme theme
Upon the ~~supreme theme~~ of ~~art & song~~ art & song—
Bodily decrepitude is wisdom—young

[Final MS Version]

Speech after long silence; ~~/~~ it is right—

                         or
All other lovers being estranged & dead,
               hid
Unfriendly lamp-light ~~hid~~ under its shade,
                upon
The curtain's drawn ~~upon~~ unfriendly night—
That we descant & yet again descant
Upon the supreme theme of art & song,

Bodily decrepitude is wisdom~~M~~; young
We loved each other & were ignorant

Nov
~~Oct~~ 1929

D. H. LAWRENCE
The Piano[1]

Somewhere beneath that piano's superb sleek black
Must hide my mother's piano, little and brown, with
      the back
        stood close to
That ~~was against~~ the wall, and the front's faded silk, both torn
And the keys with little hollows, that my mother's fingers
      had worn.

Softly, in the shadows, a woman is singing to me
Quietly, through the years I have crept back to see
A child sitting under the piano, in the boom of the
      shaking ~~tingling~~ strings
Pressing the little poised feet of the mother who smiles
      as she sings

The full throated woman has chosen a winning, living[2]
      song
And surely the heart that is in me must belong
To the old Sunday evenings, when darkness wandered
      outside
And hymns gleamed on our warm lips, as we watched
      mother's fingers glide

        is
Or is this my sister at home in the old front room
Singing love's first surprised gladness, alone in
      the gloom.
She will start when she sees me, and blushing,
      spread out her hands
To cover my mouth's raillery, till I'm bound in
      heart-spun
      her shame's ~~pleading~~ bands.

1. Transcribed from a notebook in which Lawrence at first entered various academic assignments while he was a student at the University College of Nottingham, 1906–8, but then used to write drafts of some of his early poems. These were probably composed in the period from 1906 to 1910. The text reproduced here was revised and published with the title *Piano* in Lawrence's *New Poems*, 1918. A comparison of this draft with *Piano*, reprinted above, will show that Lawrence eliminated the first and fourth stanzas (as well as the last two lines of the third stanza); revised the remaining three stanzas, sometimes radically; and most surprisingly, reversed his original conclusion.

As Lawrence himself explained his revisions of some of his early poems, they "had to be altered, where sometimes the hand of commonplace youth had been laid on the mouth of the demon. It is not for technique that these poems are altered: it is to say the real say."

For transcriptions and discussions of this and other poems in Lawrence's early notebook, see Vivian de Sola Pinto, "D.H. Lawrence: Letter-Writer and Craftsman in Verse," in *Renaissance and Modern Studies* 1 (1957): 5–34.

2. A conjectural reading; the word is not clearly legible.

A woman is singing me a wild Hungarian
    air
And her arms, and her bosom and the whole
    of her soul is bare
And the great black piano is clamouring as my
    mother's never could clamour
            my mother's [   ]³ tunes are
And ~~the tunes of the past is~~ devoured of this music's
    ravaging glamour.

3. An undecipherable word is crossed out here.

Selected Bibliographies

The Selected Bibliographies consist of a list of Suggested General Readings on English literature, followed by bibliographies for each of the literary periods in this volume. For ease of reference, the authors within each period are arranged in alphabetical order. Entries for certain classes of writings (e.g., "The Rise and Fall of Empire") are included, in alphabetical order, within the listings for individual authors.

SUGGESTED GENERAL READINGS

Histories of England and of English Literature

New research and new perspectives have made even the most distinguished of the comprehensive, general histories written in past generations seem outmoded. Innovative research in social, cultural, and political history has made it difficult to write a single, coherent account of England from the Middle Ages to the present, let alone to accommodate in a unified narrative the complex histories of Scotland, Ireland, and Wales. Readers who wish to explore the historical matrix out of which the works of literature collected in this anthology emerged are advised to consult the studies of particular periods listed in the appropriate sections of this bibliography. The multivolume *Oxford History of England* is useful, as are the three-volume *Peoples of the British Isles: A New History*, ed. Stanford Lehmberg, 1992, and the nine-volume *Cambridge Cultural History of Britain*, ed. Boris Ford, 1992. Albert Baugh et al., *A Literary History of England*, rev. 1967, remains a convenient source of factual materials about authors, works, and chronology. Given the cultural centrality of London, readers may find Roy Porter's *London: A Social History*, 1994, valuable. Similar observations may be made about literary history. In the light of such initiatives as women's studies, new historicism, and postcolonialism, the range of authors deemed most significant has expanded in recent years, along with the geographical and conceptual boundaries of literature in English. Attempts to capture in a unified account the great sweep of literature from *Beowulf* to late last night have largely given way to studies of individual genres, carefully delimited time periods, and specific authors. For these more focused accounts, see the listings by period.

Among the large-scale literary surveys, *The Cambridge Guide to Literature in English*, 1993, is useful, as is *The Penguin History of Literature*.

The Feminist Companion to Literature in English, ed. Virginia Blain, Isobel Grundy, and Patricia Clements, 1990, is an important resource, and the editorial materials in *The Norton Anthology of Literature by Women* 2nd ed., 1996, ed. Sandra M. Gilbert and Susan Gubar, constitute a concise history and set of biographies of women authors since the Middle Ages. *Annals of English Literature, 1475–1950*, rev. 1961, lists important publications year by year, together with the significant literary events for each year. David Daiches, *A Critical History of English Literature*, 2 vols., rev. 1970, provides a running literary appreciation.

Helpful treatments and surveys of English meter, rhyme, and stanza forms are Paul Fussell Jr., *Poetic Meter and Poetic Form*, rev. 1979; Donald Wesling, *The Chances of Rhyme: Device and Modernity*, 1980; Derek Attridge, *The Rhythms of English Poetry*, 1982; Charles O. Hartman, *Free Verse: An Essay in Prosody*, 1983; John Hollander, *Vision and Resonance: Two Senses of Poetic Form*, rev. 1985; and Robert Pinsky, *The Sounds of Poetry: A Brief Guide*, 1998.

On the development of the novel as a form, see Ian Watt, *The Rise of the Novel*, 1957; *The Columbia History of the British Novel*, ed. John Richetti, 1994; and Margaret Doody, *The True Story of the Novel*, 1996. On women novelists and readers, see Nancy Armstrong, *Desire and Domestic Fiction: A Political History of the Novel*, 1987; and Catherine Gallagher, *Nobody's Story: The Vanishing Acts of Women Writers in the Marketplace, 1670–1820*, 1994.

On the history of playhouse design, see Richard Leacroft, *The Development of the English Playhouse: An Illustrated Survey of Theatre Building in England from Medieval to Modern Times*, 1988. For a survey of the plays that have appeared on these and other stages, see Allardyce Nicoll, *British Drama*, rev. 1962, and the eight-volume *Revels His-*

tory of Drama in English, gen. eds. Clifford Leech and T. W. Craik, 1975–83.

On some of the key intellectual currents that are at once reflected in and shaped by English literature, Arthur T. Lovejoy's classic studies *The Great Chain of Being,* 1936, and *Essays in the History of Ideas,* 1948, remain valuable, along with such works as Lovejoy and George Boas, *Primitivism and Related Ideas in Antiquity,* 1935; Ernst Kantowicz, *The King's Two Bodies: A Study in Medieval Political Theology,* 1957, new ed. 1997; Richard Popkin, *The History of Skepticism from Erasmus to Descartes,* 1960; M. H. Abrams, *Natural Supernaturalism: Tradition and Revolution in Romantic Literature,* 1971; and Michel Foucault, *Madness and Civilization: A History of Insanity in the Age of Reason,* Eng. trans. 1965, and *The Order of Things: An Archaeology of the Human Sciences,* Eng. trans. 1970.

Reference Works

The single most important tool for the study of literature in English is the *Oxford English Dictionary,* 2nd ed., 1989, also available on CD-ROM. The *OED* is written on historical principles: that is, it attempts not only to describe current word use but also to record the history and development of the language from its origins before the Norman conquest to the present. It thus provides, for familiar as well as archaic and obscure words, the widest possible range of meanings and uses, organized chronologically and illustrated with quotations. Beyond the *OED* there are many other valuable dictionaries, such as *The American Heritage Dictionary, The Oxford Dictionary of Etymology,* and an array of reference works from *The Cambridge Encyclopedia of the English Language,* ed. David Crystal, 1995, to guides to specialized vocabularies, slang, regional dialects, and the like.

There is a steady flow of new editions of most major and many minor writers in English, along with a ceaseless outpouring of critical appraisals and scholarship. The *MLA International Bibliography* (also on line) is the best way to keep abreast of the most recent work and to conduct bibliographic searches. *The New Cambridge Bibliography of English Literature,* George Watson, 1969–77, updated shorter ed. 1981, is a valuable guide to the huge body of earlier literary criticism and scholarship. *A Guide to English and American Literature,* ed. F. W. Bateson and Harrison Meserole, rev. 1976, is a selected list of editions, as well as scholarly and critical treatments. Further bibliographical aids are described in Arthur G. Kennedy, *A Concise Bibliography for Students of English,* rev. 1972; Richard D. Altick and Andrew Wright, *Selective Bibliography for the Study of English and American Literature* rev. 1979, and James L. Harner, *Literary Research Guide,* rev. 1998.

For compact biographies of English authors, see the multivolume *Dictionary of National Biography,* ed. Leslie Stephen and Sidney Lee, 1885–1900, with supplements that carry the work to 1980; con-

densed biographies will be found in the *Concise Dictionary of National Biography,* 2 parts (1920, 1988). Handy reference books of authors, works, and various literary terms and allusions are *The Oxford Companion to the Theatre,* Phyllis Hartnoll, rev. 1990; *Princeton Encyclopedia of Poetry and Poetics,* ed. Alex Preminger and others, rev. 1993; and *The Oxford Companion to English Literature,* ed. Margaret Drabble, rev. 1998. Low-priced handbooks that define and illustrate literary concepts and terms are *The Penguin Dictionary of Literary Terms and Literary Theory,* ed. J. A. Cuddon, 1991; W. F. Thrall and Addison Hibbard, *A Handbook to Literature,* ed. C. Hugh Holman, rev. 1992; *Critical Terms for Literary Study,* ed. Frank Lentricchia and Thomas McLaughlin, rev. 1995; and M. H. Abrams, *A Glossary of Literary Terms,* rev. 1992. On Greek and Roman background, see G. M. Kirkwood, *A Short Guide to Classical Mythology,* 1959; *The Oxford Classical Dictionary,* rev. 1996; and *The Oxford Companion to Classical Literature,* ed. M. C. Howatson and Ian Chilvers, rev. 1993.

Literary Criticism and Theory

Three volumes of the *Cambridge History of Literary Criticism* have been published, 1989–: *Classical Criticism,* ed. George A. Kennedy; *The Eighteenth Century,* ed. H. B. Nisbet and Claude Rawson, and *From Formalism to Poststructuralism,* ed. Raman Selden. See also M. H. Abrams, *The Mirror and the Lamp: Romantic Theory and the Critical Tradition,* 1953; William K. Wimsatt and Cleanth Brooks, *Literary Criticism: A Short History,* 1957; George Watson, *The Literary Critics,* 1962; René Wellek, *A History of Modern Criticism: 1750–1950,* 9 vols., 1955–1993; Frank Lentricchia, *After the New Criticism,* 1980; and *Redrawing the Boundaries: The Transformation of English and American Literary Studies,* ed. Stephen Greenblatt and Giles Gunn, 1992. Raman Selden, Peter Widdowson, and Peter Brooker have written *A Reader's Guide to Contemporary Literary Theory,* 1997.

The following is a selection of books in literary criticism that have been notably influential in shaping modern approaches to English literature and literary forms: Lionel Trilling, *The Liberal Imagination,* 1950; T. S. Eliot, *Selected Essays,* 3rd ed. 1951, and *On Poetry and Poets,* 1957; Erich Auerbach, *Mimesis: The Representation of Reality in Western Literature,* 1953; William Empson, *Seven Types of Ambiguity,* 3rd ed., 1953; William K. Wimsalt, *The Verbal Icon,* 1954; Northrop Frye, *Anatomy of Criticism,* 1957; Wayne C. Booth, *The Rhetoric of Fiction,* 1961, rev. ed. 1983; W. J. Bate, *The Burden of the Past and the English Poet,* 1970; Harold Bloom, *The Anxiety of Influence,* 1973; and Paul de Man, *Allegories of Reading,* 1979.

René Wellek and Austin Warren, *Theory of Literature,* rev. 1970, is a useful introduction to the variety of scholarly and critical approaches to literature up to the time of its publication. Jonathan Culler's *Literary Theory: A Very Short Introduction,* 1997, discusses recurrent issues and debates. Modern feminist literary criticism was fashioned by such works as Particia Meyers Spacks, *The Female Imagination*, 1975; Ellen Moers, *Literary Women*, 1976; Elaine Showalter, *A Literature of Their Own*, 1977; and Sandra Gilbert and Susan Gubar, *The Madwoman in the Attic*, 1979. More recent studies include Jane Gallop, *The Daughter's Seduction: Feminism and Psychoanalysis*, 1982; Gayatri Chakravorty Spivak, *In Other Worlds: Essays in Cultural Politics*, 1987; Sandra Gilbert and Susan Gubar, *No Man's Land: The Place of the Woman Writer in the Twentieth Century*, 2 vols., 1988–89; Barbara Johnson, *A World of Difference*, 1989; Judith Butler, *Gender Trouble*, 1990; and the critical views sampled in Elaine Showalter, *The New Feminist Criticism*, 1985; *Feminist Literary Theory: A Reader*, ed. Mary Eagleton, 2nd ed., 1995; and *Feminisms: An Anthology of Literary Theory and Criticism*, ed. Robyn R. Warhol and Diane Price Herndl, 2nd ed. 1997. Gay and lesbian studies and criticism are represented in *The Lesbian and Gay Studies Reader*, ed. Henry Abelove, Michele Barale, and David Halperin, 1993, and by such books as Eve Sedgwick, *Between Men: English Literature and Male Homosocial Desire*, 1985, and *Epistemology of the Closet*, 1990; Diana Fuss, *Essentially Speaking: Feminism, Nature, and Difference*, 1989; and Gregory Woods, *A History of Gay Literature: The Male Tradition*, 1998. Convenient introductions to structuralist literary criticism include Robert Scholes, *Structuralism in Literature: An Introduction*, 1974, and Jonathan Culler, *Structuralist Poetics*, 1975. The poststructuralist challenges to this approach are discussed in Jonathan Culler, *On Deconstruction*,

1982; Fredric Jameson, *Poststructuralism; or the Cultural Logic of Late Capitalism*, 1991; John McGowan, *Postmodernism and Its Critics*, 1991; and *Beyond Structuralism*, ed. Wendell Harris, 1996. New historicism is represented in Stephen Greenblatt, *Learning to Curse*, 1990, and in the essays collected in *The New Historicism*, ed. Harold Veeser, 1989, and *New Historical Literary Study: Essays on Reproducing Texts, Representing History*, ed. Jeffrey N. Cox and Larry J. Reynolds, 1993. The related social and historical dimension of texts is discussed in Jerome McGann, *Critique of Modern Textual Criticism*, 1983, and D. F. McKenzie, *Bibliography and Sociology of Texts*, 1986. Characteristic of new historicism is an expansion of the field of literary interpretation extended still further in cultural studies; for a broad sampling of the range of interests, see *The Cultural Studies Reader*, ed. Simon During, 1993, and *A Cultural Studies Reader: History, Theory, Practice*, ed. Jessica Munns and Gita Rajan, 1997. This expansion of the field is similarly reflected in postcolonial studies: see *The Post-Colonial Studies Reader*, ed. Bill Ashcroft, Gareth Griffiths, and Helen Tiffin, 1995, and such influential books as Ranajit Guha and Gayatri Chakravorti Spivak, *Selected Subaltern Studies*, 1988; Edward Said, *Culture and Imperialism*, 1993; and Homi Bhabha, *The Location of Culture*, 1994.

Anthologies representing a range of recent approaches include *Modern Criticism and Theory*, ed. David Lodge, 1988, and *Contemporary Literary Criticism*, ed. Robert Con Davis and Ronald Schlieffer, rev. 1998.

THE ROMANTIC PERIOD

Bibliographies
The most convenient starting points are the surveys by Frank Jordan and others in *The English Romantic Poets, a Review of Research and Criticism*, rev. 1985, on Blake, Wordsworth, Coleridge, Byron, Shelley, and Keats; and Carolyn W. Houtchens and Lawrence H. Houtchens, *The English Romantic Poets and Essayists*, rev. 1966, on Blake, the lesser poets, and the principal essayists. Annual bibliographies of publications about these writers are to be found in *ELH*, 1937–49; *Philological Quarterly*, 1950–64; *English Language Notes*, 1965–79; and *The Romantic Movement: A Selective and Critical Bibliography*, ed. David V. Erdman, 1980–. See also the topical bibliographies in *The Cambridge Companion to British Romanticism*, ed. Stuart Curran, 1993.

Political and Social, and Intellectual Backgrounds
Succinct treatments of the political and social events in this period are the relevant chapters of G. M. Trevelyan, *British History of the Nineteenth Century*, 2nd ed., 1937, and *English Social History*, 1942. More detailed histories are Asa Briggs, *The

Making of Modern England: 1783–1867, 1959; J. Steven Watson, *The Reign of George III, 1760–1815*, 1960; E. P. Thompson, *The Making of the English Working Class*, 1963, and *Customs in Common*, 1991; Marilyn Butler, *Romantics, Rebels, and Reactionaries: English Literature and Its Background, 1760–1830*, 1982; and M. J. Daunton, *Progress and Poverty: An Economic and Social History of Britain, 1700–1850*, 1995. See also Carl Woodring, *Politics in English Romantic Poetry*, 1970; James Chandler, *England in 1819: The Politics of Literary Culture and the Case of Romantic Historicism*, 1998; and the separate essays in *Romanticism, Race, and Imperial Culture, 1780–1834*, ed. Alan Richardson and Sonia Hofkosh, 1996.

For English literary relations to the French Revolution, see *The Debate on the French Revolution, 1789–1800*, 2nd ed., ed. Alfred Cobban, 1960; Howard Mumford Jones, *Revolution and Romanticism*, 1974; Ronald Paulson, *Representations of Revolution (1789–1820)*, 1983; *Burke, Paine, Godwin, and the Revolution Controversy*, ed. Marilyn Butler, 1984; H. T. Dickinson, *British Radicalism and the French Revolution, 1789–1815*, 1985; Seamus Deane, *The French Revolution and Enlightenment*

9–1832, 1988; Barton R. Friedman, *istory: English Writers on the French* 1988; Simon Bainbridge, *Napoleon and ɔmanticism*, 1995; Kevin Gilmartin, *Print The Press and Radical Opposition in Early ʐenth-Century England*, 1996; *The French Revolution and British Culture*, ed. Ceri Crossley and Ian Small, 1989; and *The French Revolution and British Popular Politics*, ed. Mark Philp, 1991.

Illuminating analyses of important intellectual movements will be found in A. O. Lovejoy's *The Great Chain of Being*, 1936, chapters 9 and 10, and *Essays in the History of Ideas*, 1948. Other particularly useful works on intellectual history are Basil Willey, *Nineteenth Century Studies: Coleridge to Matthew Arnold*, 1949; Hoxie Neale Fairchild, *Religious Trends in English Poetry*, of which vol. 3 (1949) deals with 1780–1830; H. W. Piper, *The Active Universe: Pantheism and the Concept of Imagination in the English Romantic Poets*, 1962; and James Engell, *The Creative Imagination: Enlightenment to Romanticism*, 1981. Marilyn Gaull, *English Romanticism: The Human Context*, 1988; and Robert M. Ryan, *The Romantic Reformation: Religious Politics in English Literature, 1789–1824*, 1997. On Romantic literature in its social matrix, see Raymond Williams, *Culture and Society, 1780–1950*, 1960; Jon Klancher, *The Making of English Reading Audiences, 1790–1832*, 1987; Alan Richardson, *Literature, Education, and Romanticism: Reading as Social Practice, 1780–1832*, 1994; and Lee Erickson, *The Economy of Literary Form: English Literature and the Industrialization of Publishing, 1800–1850*, 1996.

Literary History and Criticism

Among the histories of Romantic literature are W. L. Renwick's rather inadequate *English Literature, 1789–1815*, 1963; Ian Jack, *English Literature, 1815–1832*, 1963; and J. R. de J. Jackson, *Poetry of the Romantic Period*, 1980. Mario Praz, *The Romantic Agony*, 2nd ed., 1951, treats Satansim, sadism, vampirism, and others of the more exotic literary interests of the time; G. R. Thompson has edited *The Gothic Imagination: Essays in Dark Romanticism*, 1974; and Peter L. Thorslev Jr.'s *The Byronic Hero: Types and Prototypes*, 1962, discusses the solitary or alienated hero in other writers, as well as Byron; see also Frank Kermode, *Romantic Image*, 1957, on the concept of the poet at odds with society, from the Romantic period to Yeats. Douglas Bush, *Mythology and the Romantic Tradition in English Poetry*, 1937, is so broad in its range that it constitutes an excellent survey of Romantic poetry in general. Wilson Knight, *The Starlit Dome*, 1941, is an influential early example of the approach to Romantic poets by the analysis of characteristic patterns of imagery. Harold Bloom, *The Visionary Company*, rev. 1971, which relates these poets to the prophetic tradition of Spenser and Milton, includes brief and stimulating commentaries on many of the important poems; Bloom, *The Ringers in the Tower*, 1971, consists of essays on both nine-

teenth- and twentieth-century "Romantic" writers. David Perkins treats Wordsworth, Shelley, and Keats, in *The Quest for Permanence*, 1959; and Northrop Frye presents an archetypal overview in *A Study of English Romanticism*, 1968. In *Natural Supernaturalism: Tradition and Revolution in Romantic Literature*, 1971, and more recently in *The Correspondent Breeze: Essays on English Romanticism*, 1984, M. H. Abrams deals with persistent themes, concepts, and designs in English and German Romantic literature, and stresses their relation both to the biblical tradition and to the intellectual ambiance of a revolutionary age. Other useful books to be noted are Thomas Weiskel, *The Romantic Sublime: Studies in the Structure and Psychology of Transcendence*, 1976; Anne K. Mellor, *English Romantic Irony*, 1980; Thomas McFarland, *Romanticism and the Forms of Ruin: Wordsworth, Coleridge, and Modalities of Fragmentation*, 1981; Jerome J. McGann, *The Romantic Ideology*, 1983; Charles J. Rzepka, *The Self as Mind: Vision and Identity in Wordsworth, Coleridge, and Keats*, 1986; Clifford Siskin, *The Historicity of Romantic Discourse*, 1988; Peter J. Manning, *Reading Romantics: Texts and Contexts*, 1990; William H. Galperin, *The Return of the Visible in British Romanticism*, 1993; and Jerome McGann, *The Poetics of Sensibility: A Revolution in Literary Style*, 1996. *English Romantic Poets: Modern Essays in Criticism*, ed. M. H. Abrams, 1975, is a collection of representative essays by influential contemporary critics; *Romanticism and Consciousness: Essays in Criticism*, 1970, focuses on some prominent topics in Romantic literature. See also the essays in *Romantic Poetry: Recent Revisionary Criticism*, Kroeber and Gene W. Ruoff, 1993. For critical opinions of the poets during their own lifetime, see Donald H. Reiman, *The Romantics Reviewed: Contemporary Reviews of British Romantic Writers*, 9 vols., 1972.

Following are studies of various forms of Romantic literature. On literary criticism: M. H. Abrams, *The Mirror and the Lamp: Romantic Theory and the Critical Tradition*, 1953; René Wellek, *A History of Modern Criticism: 1750–1950*, vol. 2, *The Romantic Age*, 1955. On poetic genres: Stuart Curran, *Poetic Form and British Romanticism*, 1986, and Susan J. Wolfson, *Formal Charges: The Shaping of Poetry in British Romanticism*, 1997. On the fragment: Marjorie Levinson, *The Romantic Fragment Poem*, 1986. On narrative poetry: Karl Kroeber, *Romantic Narrative Art*, 1960, and Brian Wilkie, *Romantic Poets and Epic Tradition*, 1965. On the novel: Ernest A. Baker, *The History of the English Novel*, vol. 6, 1961; Montague Summers, *The Gothic Quest: A History of the Gothic Novel*, 1938; and Robert Kiely, *The Romantic Novel in England*, 1972. On drama: Allardyce Nicoll, *History of Early Nineteenth-Century Drama, 1800–50*, 2 vols., rev. 1955. On the essay: William F. Bryan and Ronald S. Crane, Introduction, *The English Familiar Essay*, 1916; Marie H. Law, *The English Familiar Essay in the Early Nineteenth Century*, 1934. See also Annette Wheeler Cafarelli, *Prose in the Age of Poets:*

Romanticism and Biographical Narrative from Johnson to De Quincey, 1990.

On women writers of the period, see Sandra M. Gilbert and Susan Gubar, *The Madwoman in the Attic: The Woman Writer and the Nineteenth-Century Literary Imagination*, 1979; Mary Poovey, *The Proper Lady and the Woman Writer: Ideology as Style in the Works of Mary Wollstonecraft, Mary Shelley, and Jane Austen*, 1984; Margaret Homans, *Bearing the Word: Language and Female Experience in Nineteenth-Century Women's Writing*, 1986; Marlon B. Ross, *The Contours of Masculine Desire: Romanticism and the Rise of Women's Poetry*, 1989; Gary Kelly, *Women, Writing, and Revolution, 1790–1827*, 1993; Anne K. Mellor, *Romanticism and Gender*, 1993; Judith Pascoe, *Romantic Theatricality: Gender, Poetry, and Spectatorship*, 1997; *Romanticism and Feminism*, ed. Anne K. Mellor, 1988; *Re-Visioning Romanticism: British Women Writers, 1776–1837*, ed. Carol Shiner Wilson and Joel Haefner, 1994; and *Romantic Women Writers: Voices and Countervoices*, ed. Paula R. Feldman and Theresa M. Kelley, 1995.

Joanna Baillie

The most useful collected edition is *The Dramatic and Poetical Works*, 1851; the most recent full-scale biography is Margaret S. Carhart's dissertation, *The Life and Work of Joanna Baillie*, 1923. For recent commentary, see Anne K. Mellor, "Joanna Baillie and the Counter-Public Sphere," *Studies in Romanticism* 1994; Andrea Henderson, "Passion and Fashion in Joanna Baillie's 'Introductory Discourse,'" *PMLA*, 1997; and Catherine B. Burroughs, *Closet Stages: Joanna Baillie and the Theater Theory of British Romantic Women Writers*, 1997.

Anna Letitia Barbauld

The Poems of Anna Letitia Barbauld, ed. William McCarthy and Elizabeth Kraft, 1994, is now the standard edition. For biography, see Betsy Rodgers, *Georgian Chronicle: Mrs. Barbauld and Her Family*, 1958. Among recent critical essays, see Julie Ellison, "The Politics of Fancy in the Age of Sensibility," in *Re-Visioning Romanticism*, ed. Wilson and Haefner, 1994; William Keach, "A Regency Prophecy and the End of Anna Barbauld's Career," *Studies in Romanticism*, 1994; Isobel Armstrong, "The Gush of the Feminine," in *Romantic Women Writers*, ed. Feldman and Kelley, 1995; and William McCarthy, "Repression, Desire, and Gender in Anna Letitia Barbauld's Early Poems," also in Feldman and Kelley.

William Blake

The beautifully printed *The Complete Writings of William Blake*, ed. Geoffrey Keynes, 1957, has been replaced as the scholar's edition by *The Poetry and Prose of William Blake*, ed. David Erdman and Harold Bloom, rev. 1982, which includes painstaking textual notes and brief commentaries on many of the poems. Erdman also prepared a modernized text of all Blake's verse, with copious explanatory notes by W. H. Stevenson, *The Poems of William Blake*

(Longman-Norton Annotated English Poets), 1971. A useful annotated selection of *Blake's Poetry and Designs* has been edited by Mary Lynn Johnson and John E. Grant, 1979. There is a *Life of William Blake* by Mona Wilson, 1927, rev. 1948, and Raymond Lister's *William Blake: An Introduction to the Man and His Work*, 1968; but the first full account, Alexander Gilchrist's *The Life of William Blake*, which appeared in 1863, has been a source book for all later biographers and is available (edited and supplemented by Ruthven Todd) in Everyman's Library, 1945. The most recent biographies are James King's *William Blake: His Life*, 1991, and Peter Ackroyd's *Blake*, 1996. See also *A Concordance to the Writings of William Blake*, ed. David V. Erdman, 1967.

The modern era of the scholarly explication of Blake symbolism was begun by S. Foster Damon's *William Blake: His Philosophy and Symbols*, 1924; the same scholar also published a *Blake Dictionary: The Ideas and Symbols of William Blake*, 1965. Among later books, some of the most useful are Northrop Frye's classic analysis of Blake's moral allegory, *Fearful Symmetry*, 1947; Mark Schorer's study of Blake's characteristic union of political, moral, and religious radicalism, *William Blake: The Politics of Vision*, 1946; David V. Erdman's investigation of the relation of Blake's poetry to the historical events of his time, *Blake: Prophet against Empire*, rev. 1969; Peter Fisher's exposition of Blake's thought, *The Valley of Vision*, 1961; Harold Bloom's commentaries on the individual poems, *Blake's Apocalypse: A Study in Poetic Argument*, 1963; Thomas R. Frosch, *The Awakening of Albion: The Renovation of the Body in the Poetry of William Blake*, 1973; J. A. Wittreich, *Angel of Apocalypse: Blake's Idea of Milton*, 1975; W. J. T. Mitchell, *Blake's Composite Art: A Study of the Illuminated Poetry*, 1978; Leopold Damrosch Jr., *Symbol and Truth in Blake's Myth*, 1980; Robert N. Essick, *William Blake and the Language of Albion*, 1989; Morris Eaves, *The Counter-Arts Conspiracy: Art and Identity in the Age of Blake*, 1992; and E. P. Thompson, *Witness against the Beast: William Blake and the Moral Law*, 1993.

H. M. Margoliouth, *William Blake*, 1951, and Martin K. Nurmi, *William Blake*, 1976, are useful general introductions to the man and his work. Studies emphasizing the shorter poems are Hazard Adams, *William Blake: A Reading of the Shorter Poems*, 1963; Robert F. Gleckner, *The Piper and the Bard*, 1959; E. D. Hirsch Jr., *Innocence and Experience: An Introduction to Blake*, 1964; and Brian Wilkie, *Blake's Thel and Oothoon*, 1990. *Blake's Sublime Allegory*, ed. Stuart Curran and Joseph Anthony Wittreich Jr., 1973, includes essays by various scholars on the major prophecies, *The Four Zoas*, *Milton*, and *Jerusalem*. On Blake's graphic work see David Bindman, *Blake as an Artist*, 1977; Robert N. Essick, *William Blake, Printmaker*, 1980; Morris Eaves, *William Blake's Theory of Art*, 1982; and Joseph Vicomi, *Blake and the Idea of the Book*, 1993. There is a large and growing list of books that

2885

of them in color) Blake's etched
,s, and engravings; especially useful
,inated Blake, ed. David V. Erdman,
,ich the subtitle describes the contents:
"All ot william Blake's Illuminated Works with a
Plate-by-Plate Commentary," and Erdman's reproduction, with transcripts and commentary, of The
Notebooks of William Blake, rev. 1977. The Blake
Trust has issued a splendid series of color reproductions of a number of Blake's illuminated works,
in expensive limited editions, printed by the Trianon
Press.

Robert Burns
The standard references for Burns's poems are the
Centenary Edition, ed. W. E. Henley and T. F.
Henderson, 4 vols., 1896–97, and The Poems and
Songs of Robert Burns, ed. James Kinsley, 3 vols.,
1968. A good one-volume edition is that by James
Kinsley, Oxford Standard Authors. 1969. J. De Lan-
cey Ferguson has given us a reliable edition of The
Letters of Robert Burns, 2 vols., 1931 (2nd ed., ed.
G. Ross Roy, 1985) and a brilliant portrait of Burns,
Pride and Passion, 1939. The most recent among
many biographies are James Mackay, A Biography
of Robert Burns, 1992; Ian McIntyre, Dirt and Deity:
A Life of Robert Burns, 1995; and Hugh Douglas,
Robert Burns: The Tinder Heart, 1996. David
Daiches, Robert Burns, 1950, provides a critical
analysis of the major poems, and Thomas Crawford,
Burns: A Study of the Poems and Songs, 1960, is a
detailed and comprehensive commentary. See also
Raymond Bentman, Robert Burns, 1987, and Robert
Burns and Cultural Authority, ed. Robert Crawford,
1997.

George Gordon, Lord Byron
For the poetry, the standard is Lord Byron: The
Complete Poetical Works, ed. Jerome J. McGann, 7
vols., 1980–93; for the letters, Byron's Letters and
Journals, ed. Leslie A. Marchand, 12 vols., 1973–
82 (with a supplementary volume in 1994); Marchand has also edited the one-volume Selected Letters and Journals, 1982. Ernest J. Lovell Jr., His Very
Self and Voice, 1954, is a compilation of Byron's
conversations. The standard biography, a circumstantial and objective narrative, is Marchand,
Byron: A Biography, 3 vols., 1957; a one-volume
condensation by Marchand is Byron: A Portrait,
1970. See also Louis Crompton, Byron and Greek
Love: Homophobia in 19th-Century England, 1985.

Among the many useful books on Byron as poet
are Andrew Rutherford, Byron: A Critical Study,
1961; Peter L. Thorslev Jr., The Byronic Hero,
1962; Jerome J. McGann, Fiery Dust: Byron's Poetic
Development, 1968; Paul G. Trueblood, Lord
Byron, rev. 1977; Peter J. Manning, Byron and His
Fictions, 1978; Frederick L. Beaty, Byron the Sati-
rist, 1985; Caroline Franklin, Byron's Heroines,
1992; and Jerome Christensen, Lord Byron's
Strength: Romantic Writing and Commercial
Society, 1993. See also Critical Essays on Lord
Byron, ed. Robert F. Gleckner, 1991, and Rereading
Byron, ed. Alice Levine and Robert N. Keane, 1993.

The variorum edition of Don Juan by Truman
Guy Steffan and Willis W. Pratt, 4 vols., 1957, provides an elaborate record of changes that Byron
made in his manuscripts; the first volume, by Steffan, is an extended commentary on the poem. Other
discussions of Byron's masterpiece include George
M. Ridenour, The Style of "Don Juan," 1960; Jerome
J. McGann, "Don Juan" in Context, 1976; Peter W.
Graham, "Don Juan" and Regency England, 1990;
and Moyra Haslett, Byron's "Don Juan" and the Don
Juan Legend, 1997.

John Clare
The most recent scholarly presentation of Clare's
poems is the series of Oxford English Texts volumes
under the general editorship of Eric Robinson: Later
Poems, 2 vols., 1984; Early Poems, 1989; and Poems
of the Middle Period, 2 vols. to date, 1996 (with
three more to come). Robinson and his associate
David Powell have also produced an Oxford Standard Authors John Clare, 1984. J. W. Tibble's two-
volume edition The Poems of John Clare, 1935, is
still useful. J. W. Tibble and Anne Tibble have written Clare: His Life and Poetry, rev. 1972, and edited
both Clare's Prose, 1951, and his Letters, also 1951.
The essays on Clare by J. M. Murry, collected in his
John Clare and Other Studies, 1959, indicate the
sudden leap forward of Clare's reputation when he
was "rediscovered" in the 1920s. For more recent
commentary, see John Barrell, The Idea of Landscape and the Sense of Place, 1730–1840: An
Approach to the Poetry of John Clare, 1972; Mark
Storey, The Poetry of John Clare: A Critical Introduction, 1974; Greg Crosson, A Relish for Eternity:
The Process of Divinization in the Poetry of John
Clare, 1976; and John Clare in Context, ed. Hugh
Haughton, Adam Phillips, and Geoffrey Summerfield, 1994.

Samuel Taylor Coleridge
The Complete Works, ed. W. G. T. Shedd, 7 vols.,
1853, hitherto the most inclusive collection of
Coleridge's works, is being superseded by The Collected Works under the general editorship of Kathleen Coburn: thirteen of the projected sixteen
volumes have now appeared, beginning in 1969.
E. H. Coleridge, Complete Poetical Works, 2 vols.,
1912 (with a one-volume edition of Poetical Works
by the same editor in the Oxford Standard Authors
series), remains the standard, though it will shortly
be replaced by J. C. C. Mays's edition of the poems
and plays in volume 16 of the Collected Works. The
most fully annotated edition of Biographia Literaria
is that by James Engell and W. Jackson Bate, 2 vols.
1983 (vol. 7 of the Collected Works).

Richard Holmes, Coleridge: Early Visions, 1989,
and Coleridge: Darker Reflections, 1998, together
constitute the most recent biography, following
close upon Rosemary Ashton, The Life of Samuel
Taylor Coleridge: A Critical Biography, 1987. The
definitive edition of Coleridge's Collected Letters is
edited by E. L. Griggs, 6 vols., 1956–71; see also
Selected Letters, ed. H. J. Jackson, 1987. The first
four volumes of Coleridge's Notebooks are available,
meticulously edited by Kathleen Coburn and associates, 1957–.

There are good short studies of the life and works by Walter Jackson Bate, *Coleridge*, 1968, and, with emphasis on the philosophical and religious writings, by Basil Willey, *Samuel Taylor Coleridge*, 1972. H. M. Margoliouth has described the most fruitful literary association on record in his *Wordsworth and Coleridge, 1795–1834*, 1953; more sophisticated studies are Paul Magnuson, *Coleridge and Wordsworth: A Lyrical Dialogue*, 1988, and Gene W. Ruoff, *Wordsworth and Coleridge: The Making of the Major Lyrics, 1802–1804*, 1989. The best older critique of Coleridge as poet is Humphry House, *Coleridge*, 1953. More recent studies include Max F. Schulz, *The Poetic Voices of Coleridge*, 1963; George Watson, *Coleridge the Poet*, 1966; Paul Magnuson, *Coleridge's Nightmare Poetry*, 1974; Reeve Parker, *Coleridge's Meditative Art*, 1975; Kelvin Everest, *Coleridge's Secret Ministry*, 1979; M. H. Abrams, *The Correspondent Breeze*, 1984; and Morton D. Paley, *Coleridge's Later Poetry*, 1996. *The Road to Xanadu*, by J. L. Lowes, 1927, rev. 1930, which investigates the sources and composition of *The Ancient Mariner* and *Kubla Khan*, has achieved the status of a critical classic. Discussion of Coleridge as critic will be found in M. H. Abrams, *The Mirror and the Lamp*, 1953; René Wellek, *A History of Modern Criticism, 1750–1950*, vol. 2, 1955; Richard Harter Fogle, *The Idea of Coleridge's Criticism*, 1962; and J. A. Appleyard, *Coleridge's Philosophy of Literature*, 1965. Norman Fruman, *Coleridge, the Damaged Archangel*, 1971, collects all the charges and evidence concerning Coleridge's "plagiarism." Among the excellent studies of Coleridge's philosophical, theological, and moral interests and achievements are Richard Haven, *Patterns of Consciousness*, 1969; Thomas McFarland's important and wide-ranging study of *Coleridge and the Pantheist Tradition*, 1969; Owen Barfield, *What Coleridge Thought*, 1971; and Lawrence S. Lockridge, *Coleridge the Moralist*, 1977. Recent studies of his political views include Nicholas Roe, *Wordsworth and Coleridge: The Radical Years*, 1988; John Morrow, *Coleridge's Political Thought*, 1990; and Patrick J. Keane, *Coleridge's Submerged Politics*, 1994. On opium, dreaming, and Coleridge's poetry, see Elisabeth Schneider, *Coleridge, Opium and "Kubla Khan,"* 1953; Alethea Hayter, *Opium and the Romantic Imagination*, 1968; M. H. Abrams, *The Milk of Paradise*, rev. 1970; and Jennifer Ford, *Coleridge on Dreaming: Romanticism, Dreams and the Medical Imagination*, 1998. On his developing reputation, see *Coleridge: The Critical Heritage*, ed. J. R. de J. Jackson, 2 vols., 1970, 1991. Modern essays in criticism have been collected by, among others, Kathleen Coburn, *Coleridge*, 1967; John Beer, *Coleridge's Variety*, 1974; Frederick Burwick, *Coleridge's "Biographia Literaria": Text and Meaning*, 1989; and Leonard Orr, *Critical Essays*, 1994.

Thomas De Quincey

The Collected Writings, ed. David Masson, 14 vols., 1889–90, although incomplete, is still the standard edition; other essays will be found in *Uncollected Writings*, ed. James Hogg, 2 vols., 1890, [ ] *humous Writings*, ed. A. H. Japp, 2 vols., 1[ ] There are numerous books of selections fr[ ] Quincey, and *The Confessions of an English O[ ] Eater* has been frequently reprinted. The [ ] recent full-scale biography is Grevel Lindop's [ ] *Opium-Eater: A Life of Thomas De Quincey*, 198[ ] For the effect of opium addiction on De Quincey writings, see Alethea Hayter, *Opium and the Romantic Imagination*, 1968, and M. H. Abrams, *The Milk of Paradise*, rev. 1970. Recent critical studies include John Barrell, *The Infection of Thomas De Quincey: A Psychopathology of Imperialism*, 1991; Alina Clej, *A Genealogy of the Modern Self: Thomas De Quincey and the Intoxication of Writing*, 1995; Charles J. Rzepka, *Sacramental Commodities: Gift, Text, and the Sublime in De Quincey*, 1995; and Margaret Russett, *De Quincey's Romanticism: Canonical Minority and the Forms of Transmission*, 1997.

William Hazlitt

The Complete Works of William Hazlitt, 21 vols., 1930–34, has been well edited by P. P. Howe; the final volume includes an overall index, as well as an index of Hazlitt's quotations. Useful selections of Hazlitt's writings are *Selected Essays*, ed. Geoffrey Keynes, 1930, and *Hazlitt on English Literature*, ed. Jacob Zeitlin, 1913. P. P. Howe's largely factual *Life of William Hazlitt*, 1947, has been superseded by Catherine M. Maclean's *Born under Saturn*, 1944, and by Herschel Baker's comprehensive study of his thought and writings, *William Hazlitt*, 1962. The most detailed biographies are Ralph M. Wardle, *Hazlitt*, 1971, and Stanley Jones, *Hazlitt: A Life, from Winterslow to Frith Street*, 1989. For the correspondence, see *The Letters of William Hazlitt*, ed. Herschel M. Sikes, 1978. On Hazlitt as a critic of literature and the arts, see René Wellek, *A History of Modern Criticism, 1750–1950*, vol. 2, 1955; Herschel Baker, *William Hazlitt*, 1962; John Kinnaird, *William Hazlitt: Critic of Power*, 1978; and David Bromwich, *Hazlitt: The Mind of a Critic*, 1983.

Felicia Dorothea Hemans

The best complete edition is *The Poetical Works of Felicia Dorothea Hemans*, 1914; a modern selection is in progress under the editorship of Gary Kelly. For criticism, see Peter W. Trinder, *Mrs. Hemans*, 1984; Angela Leighton, *Victorian Women Poets: Writing against the Heart*, 1992; Isobel Armstrong, *Victorian Poetry*, 1993; Tricia Lootens, "Hemans and Home," *PMLA*, 1994; Nanora Sweet, "Hemans and the Post-Napoleonic Moment," in *At the Limits of Romanticism*, ed. Mary A. Favret and Nicola J. Watson, 1994; Susan J. Wolfson, "Felicia Hemans and the Dilemma of Gender," in *Re-Visioning Romanticism*, ed. Wilson and Haefner, 1994; Paula R. Feldman, "Felicia Hemans and the Literary Marketplace," *Keats-Shelley Journal*, 1997.

John Keats

The standard edition of the poetry is Jack Stillinger, *The Poems of John Keats*, 1978. Miriam Allott, *The Poems of John Keats*, 1970, is copiously annotated.

.er E. Rollins, *The Letters of John Keats*, 2 vols., 58, provides exact texts based on the manuscripts. The most frequently cited biographies are Walter Jackson Bate, *John Keats*, 1963; Robert Gittings, *John Keats*, 1968; and Aileen Ward, *John Keats: The Making of a Poet*, rev. 1986. A good shorter life is Douglas Bush, *John Keats*, 1966; Andrew Motion, full-scale *Keats*, 1997, is the most recent.

Among the many critical studies, the following are especially useful: C. D. Thorpe, *The Mind of John Keats*, 1926 (on Keats's thought); M. R. Ridley, *Keats' Craftsmanship*, 1933 (based on the revisions in Keats's manuscripts); Earl Wasserman, *The Finer Tone*, 1953 (a close analysis of the major poems); David Perkins, *The Quest for Permanence*, 1959; Walter Evert, *Aesthetic and Myth in the Poetry of Keats*, 1965; Jack Stillinger, *The Hoodwinking of Madeline and Other Essays on Keats's Poems*, 1971; Stuart Sperry, *Keats the Poet*, 1973; Christopher Ricks's lively and wide-ranging study of *Keats and Embarrassment*, 1974; Robert M. Ryan's analysis of Keats's personal creed, *Keats: The Religious Sense*, 1976; Ronald A. Sharp, *Keats, Skepticism, and the Religion of Beauty*, 1979; Helen Vendler, *The Odes of John Keats*, 1983; Leon Waldoff, *Keats and the Silent Work of Imagination*, 1985; Susan J. Wolfson. *The Questioning Presence: Wordsworth, Keats, and the Interrogative Mode in Romantic Poetry*, 1986; John Barnard, *John Keats*, 1987; Marjorie Levinson, *Keats's Life of Allegory*, 1988; Daniel P. Watkins, *Keats's Poetry and the Poetics of Imagination*, 1989; Nicholas Roe, *John Keats and the Culture of Dissent*, 1997; *The Persistence of Poetry: Bicentennial Essays on Keats*, ed. Robert M. Ryan and Ronald A. Sharp, 1998. For other commentary on the odes, consult Jack Wright Rhodes, *Keats's Major Odes: An Annotated Bibliography of the Criticism*, 1984; and on *The Eve of St. Agnes*, Jack Stillinger's *Reading "The Eve of St. Agnes,"* 1999. For the poet's nineteenth-century reputation, see *Keats: The Critical Heritage*, ed. G. M. Matthews, 1971. Recent collections of essays include *Critical Essays on John Keats*, ed. Hermione de Almeida, 1990, and *Keats and History*, ed. Nicholas Roe, 1995.

Charles Lamb

We are indebted to E. V. Lucas for the standard *Works of Charles and Mary Lamb*, 7 vols., 1903–5; for the standard edition of their *Letters*, 3 vols., 1935; and for the standard *Life of Charles Lamb*, 2 vols., rev. 1921. Three volumes of a new edition of *The Letters of Charles and Mary Anne Lamb*, by Edwin W. Marrs Jr. have appeared, 1975–78. Winifred F. Courtney, *Young Charles Lamb, 1775–1802*, 1982, is the first volume of a new biography. For commentary, see Fred V. Randall, *The World of Elia: Charles Lamb's Essayistic Romanticism*, 1975; George L. Barnett, *Charles Lamb*, 1976; and Jane Aaron, *A Double Singleness: Gender and the Writing of Charles and Mary Lamb*, 1991. On Lamb's critical writings, see René Wellek, *History of Modern Criticism*, vol. 2, 1955.

Letitia Elizabeth Landon

For scholarly texts, consult *Letitia Elizabeth Landon: Selected Writings*, ed. Jerome McGann and Daniel Riess, 1997. Laman Blanchard, *Life and Literary Remains of L. E. L.*, 1841, is still a valuable biographical source. For criticism, see Angela Leighton, *Victorian Women Poets: Writing against the Heart*, 1992; Isobel Armstrong, *Victorian Poetry*, 1993; Glennis Stephenson, *Letitia Landon: The Woman behind L. E. L.*, 1995; and Judith Pascoe, *Romantic Theatricality*, 1997.

Walter Savage Landor

The Complete Works have been edited by T. E. Welby and Stephen Wheeler, 16 vols., 1927–36, and the poems alone by Stephen Wheeler in 3 vols., 1937. A more reliable edition of the prose writings is by C. G. Crump, 2 vols., 1891–93. The official biography is *Walter Savage Landor*, by his friend John Forster, 2 vols., 1869; a more interesting life is R. H. Super's *Landor: A Biography*, 1954. For criticism, see Malcolm Elwin, *Landor: A Replevin*, 1958; chapter 7 in Douglas Bush, *Mythology and the Romantic Tradition*, 1937; and Robert Pinsky, *Landor's Poetry*, 1968.

Thomas Moore

Consult *Poetical Works*, ed. A. D. Godley, 1910; a selection of *Lyrics and Satires*, ed. Sean O'Faolain, 1929; *Memoirs, Journals, and Correspondence*, ed. Lord John Russell, 8 vols., 1853–56; and *The Journal*, ed. Wilfred S. Owen, 6 vols., 1983–91. The best biography is Howard M. Jones's lively *The Harp That Once—A Chronicle of the Life of Thomas Moore*, 1937.

Mary Robinson

For scholarly texts and critical apparatus, we now have *Mary Robinson: Selected Poems*, ed. Judith Pascoe, 1999. The fullest biography is Robert Bass, *The Green Dragoon: The Lives of Banastre Tarleton and Mary Robinson*, 1957. For commentary, consult Stuart Curran, "Mary Robinson's *Lyrical Tales* in Context," in *Re-Visioning Romanticism*, ed. Wilson and Haefner, 1994; Linda H. Peterson, "Mary Robinson's *Memoirs* and the Origins of the Woman Artist's Autobiography," also in Wilson and Haefner; Jerome J. McGann, "Mary Robinson and the Myth of Sappho," *Modern Language Quarterly*, 1995; and Judith Pascoe, *Romantic Theatricality*, 1997.

Sir Walter Scott

Scott's novels have been often reprinted, both collectively and individually, and most of the best ones are available in cheap editions. A new scholarly edition of the complete Waverley Novels is in progress, general editor David Hewitt. A useful collection of the *Poetical Works* is that in the Oxford Standard Authors, ed. J. L. Robertson, 1904. The letters have been edited by H. J. C. Grierson in 12 vols., 1932–37, and the *Journal* has been edited by W. E. K. Anderson, 1972. The official *Memoirs of the Life of Sir Walter Scott* by Scott's son-in-law, J. G. Lockhart, 7 vols., 1837–38, is a classic; its facts and evaluations are supplemented by H. J. C. Grierson's *Sir*

Walter Scott, Bart., 1938, and by the full-scale biography, Edgar Johnson's Sir Walter Scott: The Great Unknown, 2 vols., 1970. For commentary, see David Daiches, Sir Walter Scott and His World, 1971; George McMaster, Scott and Society, 1981; Jane Millgate, Walter Scott: The Making of the Novelist, 1984; John MacQueen, The Rise of the Historical Novel, 1989; Ina Ferris, The Achievement of Literary Authority: Gender, History, and the Waverley Novels, 1991; and Ian Duncan, Modern Romance and Transformations of the Novel: The Gothic, Scott, Dickens, 1992.

Mary Wollstonecraft Shelley

At last we have a collected edition, The Novels and Selected Works of Mary Shelley, ed. Nora Crook, 8 vols., 1996. For separate texts of Frankenstein, see especially the editions by James Rieger, 1974, and J. Paul Hunter, 1996, both of which have reliable texts, a record of changes from the first to the third editions of 1818 and 1831, and much useful supplementary material. Charles E. Robinson has meticulously edited The "Frankenstein" Notebooks, 2 vols., 1996. Another fine novel, The Last Man, has been reprinted in an edition by Hugh J. Luke Jr., 1965. Mathilda, a novella of 1819 that the author left in manuscript, was printed for the first time by Elizabeth Nitchie, 1959. The short fictional writings have been edited by Charles E. Robinson, Mary Shelley: Collected Tales and Stories. 1976. Her prefaces and notes to her husband's poems are conveniently accessible in Oxford Standard Authors, The Complete Poetical Works of Percy Bysshe Shelley, ed. Thomas Hutchinson, and rev. G. M. Matthews, 1970. Betty T. Bennett has edited The Letters of Mary Wollstonecraft Shelley, 3 vols., 1980–88. Frederick L. Jones, Mary Shelley's Journal, 1947, has been replaced by a new edition of The Journals ed. Paula R. Feldman and Diana Scott-Kilvert, 2 vols., 1987. Older lives, still readable, include R. Glynn Grylls, Mary Shelley: A Biography, 1938; Muriel Spark, Child of Light: A Reassessment of Mary Shelley, 1951; and Elizabeth Nitchie, Mary Shelley, Author of "Frankenstein," 1953. Among more recent biographical and critical studies are William A. Walling, Mary Shelley, 1972; Paul A. Cantor, Creature and Creator: Myth-Making and English Romanticism, 1984; Mary Poovey, The Proper Lady and the Woman Writer, 1984; William R. Veeder, Mary Shelley and Frankenstein: The Fate of Androgyny, 1986; Chris Baldick, In Frankenstein's Shadow: Myth, Monstrosity, and Nineteenth-Century Writing, 1987; Anne K. Mellor, Mary Shelley: Her Life, Her Fiction, Her Monsters, 1988; William St. Clair, The Shelleys and the Godwins: The Biography of a Family, 1989; Emily W. Sunstein, Mary Shelley: Romance and Reality, 1989; Johanna M. Smith, Mary Shelley, 1996; and the essays collected in The Endurance of Frankenstein, ed. George Levine and U. C. Knoepflmacher, 1979; The Other Mary Shelley: Beyond "Frankenstein," ed. Audrey A. Fisch, Anne K. Mellor, and Esther H. Schor, 1993; and Critical Essays on Mary Wollstonecraft Shelley, ed. Mary Lowe-Evans, 1998.

Percy Bysshe Shelley

The nearest to a complete collection of Shelley's writings is The Complete Works, ed. Roger Ingpen and Walter E. Peck, 10 vols., 1926–30. The most widely used single-volume edition of the poems has been that in the Oxford Standard Authors, ed. Thomas Hutchinson and rev. G. M. Matthews, 1970. Shelley's Prose was collected by David Lee Clark in 1954; and The Letters were edited by Frederick L. Jones in 2 vols., 1964. Because of the erratic way in which Shelley's poems and essays were published, all the collected editions are faulty; Shelley's writings are now in the process of being revised and reprinted by a number of editors. Neville Rogers's edition of The Complete Poetical Works, of which two volumes are in print, 1972–, has been severely criticized by scholars. The best texts are those in The Lyrics of Shelley, edited and sensitively interpreted by Judith Chernaik, 1972; and in the large selection of Shelley's Poetry and Prose, A Norton Critical Edition, ed. Donald H. Reiman and Sharon B. Powers, 1977, which also includes a collection of critical essays on Shelley.

The classic life is Newman Ivey White, Shelley, 2 vols., 1940, which is also available in a condensed single volume, Portrait of Shelley, 1945. Richard Holmes's Shelley: The Pursuit, 1974, is not so detailed as White's biography, but provides a vivid sense of Shelley as a human being. Kenneth Neill Cameron, in The Young Shelley, 1950, and in the sequel, Shelley: The Golden Years, 1974, emphasizes the development of Shelley's radical social and political thinking. C. E. Pulos, The Deep Truth: A Study of Shelley's Scepticism, 1954, emphasizes the philosophic skepticism at the center of his idealism.

Shelley's Major Poetry, by Carlos Baker, 1948, provides analyses of the longer poems that stress their ideational content; Carl H. Grabo, in A Newton among Poets, 1930, and Desmond King-Hele, in Shelley: His Thought and Work, 1960, deal with Shelley's conversion of scientific knowledge into poetic images. The Imagery of Keats and Shelley, by Richard H. Fogle, 1949, analyzes the stylistic qualities of Shelley's poetry.

As early as 1900, W. B. Yeats, in "The Philosophy of Shelley's Poetry" (reprinted in Essays, 1924), dealt with Shelley as one of the great symbolist poets. More recent treatments of Shelley's symbolic imagery are Peter Butter, Shelley's Idols of the Cave, 1954, and Harold Bloom's innovative study, Shelley's Mythmaking, 1959, which puts Shelley in the line of visionary poets whose imaginative processes were instinctively mythopoeic. Earl Wasserman's Shelley: A Critical Reading, 1971, is a series of close readings of Shelley's most important poems and essays. Other useful critiques are Milton Wilson, Shelley's Later Poetry, 1959; R. G. Woodman, The Apocalyptic Tradition in the Poetry of Shelley, 1964; Stuart Curran's study of Shelley's Annus Mirabilis: The Maturing of an Epic Vision, 1975; Timothy

Webb, *Shelley: A Voice Not Understood*, 1977; William Keach, *Shelley's Style*, 1984; Stuart M. Sperry, *Shelley's Major Verse: The Narrative and Dramatic Poetry*, 1988; Stephen C. Behrendt, *Shelley and His Audiences*, 1989; Donald Reiman, *Percy Bysshe Shelley*, rev. 1990, and Susan Wolfson, *Formal Charges*, 1997. Charles Robinson discusses the personal and poetic relations of Byron and Shelley: *The Snake and the Eagle Wreathed in Fight*, 1975. *Shelley*, ed. George M. Ridenour, 1965, is an anthology of modern critical essays.

Charlotte Smith

The Poems of Charlotte Smith, ed. Stuart Curran, 1993, is the standard edition. The fullest biography is Florence May Anna Hilbish's dissertation, *Charlotte Smith, Poet and Novelist*, 1941. For commentary, see Judith Phillips Stanton, "Charlotte Smith's 'Literary Business,' " *The Age of Johnson*, 1987; Stuart Curran, "Charlotte Smith and British Romanticism," *South Central Review*, 1994; and Judith Pascoe, "Female Botanists and the Poetry of Charlotte Smith," in *Re-Visioning Romanticism*, ed. Wilson and Haefner, 1994.

Mary Wollstonecraft

There is a collected edition, *The Works of Mary Wollstonecraft*, ed. Janet Todd and Marilyn Butler, 7 vols., 1989. Todd has also edited *A Wollstonecraft Anthology*, 1989, and *Mary Wollstonecraft: Political Writings*, 1993. The most important reprints of single works are *A Vindication of the Rights of Men*, facsimile edition by Eleanor Louise Nicholes, 1960; *A Vindication of the Rights of Woman*, in both the annotated edition by Ulrich H. Hardt, 1982, and a Norton Critical Edition by Carol H. Poston, 1988; *Letters Written during a Short Residence in Sweden, Norway, and Denmark*, ed. Carol H. Poston, 1976; and a reprint in a single volume (ed. Gary Kelly, 1976) of her two novels, the early *Mary, A Fiction*, and *The Wrongs of Woman; or Maria*, which she left unfinished at her death. Ralph Wardle has edited *Collected Letters of Mary Wollstonecraft*, 1979.

Biographers rely for many facts on William Godwin's candid *Memoirs of the Author of "A Vindication of the Rights of Woman,"* 1798. The first modern critical biography is Ralph Wardle's *Mary Wollstonecraft*, 1951; see also Eleanor Flexner, *Mary Wollstonecraft: A Biography*, 1972; Claire Tomlin's *The Life and Death of Mary Wollstonecraft*, 1974; and Emily Sunstein's *A Different Face: The Life of Mary Wollstonecraft*, 1975. Recent studies include Moira Ferguson and Janet Todd, *Mary Wollstonecraft*, 1984; Mary Poovey, *The Proper Lady and the Woman Writer*, 1984; Jennifer Lorch, *Mary Wollstonecraft: The Making of a Radical Feminist*, 1990; Gary Kelly, *Revolutionary Feminism: The Mind and Career of Mary Wollstonecraft*, 1992; and Virginia Sapiro, *A Vindication of Political Virtue: The Political Theory of Mary Wollstonecraft*, 1992.

Dorothy Wordsworth

For the journals, the best editions are *Journals of Dorothy Wordsworth*, ed. Mary Moorman, 1971, and *The Grasmere Journals*, ed. Pamela Woof, 1991. For the poems, consult the appendix of Susan M. Levin's critical study, *Dorothy Wordsworth and Romanticism*, 1987. Dorothy Wordsworth's letters are collected with those of her brother in *The Letters of William and Dorothy Wordsworth*, rev. Chester L. Shaver and others, 8 vols., 1967–93; there is a one-volume selection of her *Letters*, ed. Alan G. Hill, 1985. The 1933 biography by Ernest de Selincourt has been superseded by Robert Gittings and Jo Manton, *Dorothy Wordsworth*, 1985. See also Catherine Macdonald Maclean, *Dorothy Wordsworth, the Early Years*, 1932; Elizabeth Hardwick, *Seduction and Betrayal*, 1974; and Margaret Homans, *Women Writers and Poetic Identity: Dorothy Wordsworth, Emily Brontë, and Emily Dickinson*, 1980.

William Wordsworth

Ernest de Selincourt edited *The Poetical Works* (with Helen Darbishire), 5 vols., 1940–49, and the variorum edition of *The Prelude*, with the texts of 1805 and 1850 on facing pages (rev. Helen Darbishire, 1959). *The Letters of William and Dorothy Wordsworth*, ed. de Selincourt, have been revised by C. L. Shaver, Mary Moorman, and Alan G. Hill, 7 vols., 1967–92. The 1805 and 1850 *Preludes* on facing pages, together with the "Two-Part *Prelude*" of 1799, various manuscript fragments of *The Prelude*, and a selection of recent critical essays on the poem, are available in *The Prelude: 1799, 1805, 1850*. A Norton Critical Edition, ed. Jonathan Wordsworth, M. H. Abrams, and Stephen Gill, 1979. Wordsworth's poems in one volume were edited for The Oxford Authors by Stephen Gill (1984). A series, the Cornell Wordsworth, general ed. Stephen Parrish, begun in 1975 and now close to completion, prints texts of the poems, together with variant readings from the manuscripts (which are reproduced and transcribed) through the final printings in Wordsworth's lifetime. W. J. B. Owen and Jane Worthington Smyser have edited *The Prose Works*, 3 vols., 1974, and there is a *Selected Prose*, ed. John O. Hayden, 1988. Owen has also printed from his edition a convenient collection of *Wordsworth's Literary Criticism*, 1974. Mary Moorman, *William Wordsworth*, vol. 1, rev. 1968; vol. 2, 1965, has been superseded by Stephen Gill's reliable *William Wordsworth: A Life* (1984) and by Kenneth B. Johnston's lively and well-researched, if at times speculative, *The Hidden Wordsworth* (1988), whose emphases are indicated by its subtitle: *Poet, Lover, Rebel, Spy*. Mark L. Reed's dating of Wordsworth's poems, manuscripts, and the events of his daily life, has reached two volumes, *Wordsworth: The Chronology of the Early Years*, 1967, and *The Chronology of the Middle Years*, 1975.

Walter Raleigh, *Wordsworth*, 1903; Helen Darbishire, *The Poet Wordsworth*, 1950; and Carl Woodring, *Wordsworth*, 1965, are useful introductions to Wordsworth's poetry. Paul D. Sheats has written a study of the early poems, *The Making of Wordsworth's Poetry, 1785–1798*, 1973. Modern interest in *Lyrical Ballads* is shown in Stephen M.

Parrish, *The Art of the "Lyrical Ballads,"* 1973; Mary Jacobus, *Tradition and Experiment in Wordsworth's "Lyrical Ballads,"* 1798, 1976; John E. Jordan, *Why the "Lyrical Ballads"*? 1976; and Don H. Bialostosky, *Making Tales,* 1984. Herbert Lindenberger, *On Wordsworth's "Prelude,"* 1963, explores Wordsworth's major achievement; Richard J. Onorato deals with it from a psychoanalytic standpoint in *The Character of the Poet: Wordsworth in "The Prelude,"* 1971; and Mary Jacobus from a feminist standpoint in *Romanticism, Writing, and Sexual Difference: Essays on "The Prelude,"* 1989. Aspects of Wordsworth's thought are explored by James A. W. Heffernan, *Wordsworth's Theory of Poetry,* 1969, and Geoffrey Durrant, *Wordsworth and the Great System,* 1970. Prominent critical studies of Wordsworth's poetry are John Jones, *The Egotistical Sublime,* 1954; David Perkins, *Wordsworth and the Poetry of Sincerity,* 1964; Geoffrey Hartman's impressive study of *Wordsworth's Poetry, 1787–1814,* 1964; James H. Averill, *Wordsworth and the*

Poetry of Human Suffering, 1980; Kenneth R. Johnston, *Wordsworth and "The Recluse,"* 1984; Marjorie Levinson, *Wordsworth's Great Period Poems,* 1986; Susan J. Wolfson, *The Questioning Presence: Wordsworth, Keats, and the Interrogative Mode in Romantic Poetry,* 1986; David Simpson, *Wordsworth's Historical Imagination,* 1987; Nicholas Roe, *Wordsworth and Coleridge: The Radical Years,* 1988; Theresa M. Kelley, *Wordsworth's Revisionary Aesthetics,* 1988; William H. Galperin, *Revision and Authority in Wordsworth,* 1989; Alan Liu, *Wordsworth, The Sense of History* (1989); Peter J. Manning, *Reading Romantics,* 1990; Judith W. Page, *Wordsworth and the Cultivation of Women,* 1994. The range and diversity of critical studies are represented in *Wordsworth: A Collection of Critical Essays,* ed. M. H. Abrams, 1972; *The Age of William Wordsworth: Critical Essays on the Romantic Tradition,* ed. Kenneth R. Johnston and Gene W. Ruoff, 1987; and *Critical Essays on William Wordsworth,* ed. George Gilpin, 1990.

THE VICTORIAN AGE

Studies of the Victorian age and its point of view include Richard D. Altick, *Victorian People and Ideas: A Companion for the Modern Reader of Victorian Literature,* 1973; Patrick Brantlinger, *Rule of Darkness: British Literature and Imperialism, 1830–1914,* 1988; Asa Briggs, *The Age of Improvement,* 1962; W. L. Burn, *The Age of Equipoise: A Study of the Mid-Victorian Generation,* 1964; Jerome Buckley, *The Victorian Temper,* 1951; David Cannadine, *The Decline and Fall of the British Aristocracy,* 1990; A. Dwight Culler, *The Victorian Mirror of History,* 1986; Robin Gilmour, *The Victorian Period: The Intellectual and Cultural Context of Victorian Literature, 1830–1890,* 1993; Walter E. Houghton, *The Victorian Frame of Mind, 1830–1870,* 1957; *Victorian Britain: An Encyclopedia,* ed. Sally Mitchell, 1988; David Newsome, *The Victorian World Picture: Perceptions and Introspections in a World of Change,* 1997; Mary Poovey, *Making a Social Body: British Cultural Formation, 1830–1864,* 1995; Richard L. Stein, *Victoria's Year: English Literature and Culture, 1837–38,* 1988; F. M. L. Thompson, *The Rise of Respectable Society: A Social History of Victorian Britain, 1830–1900,* 1988; and G. M. Young, *Victorian England: Portrait of an Age,* 1936 (republished in 1977 with 215 pages of explanatory notes by George Kitson Clark). Young's essay is a brilliant synthesis, but it can be incomprehensible to readers who are not yet adequately familiar with the history of the age. Such readers should consult David Thomson's *England in the Nineteenth Century,* 1950, or Derek Beales, *From Castlereagh to Gladstone: 1815–1885,* 1970.

Studies of special aspects of the age include James Eli Adams, *Dandies and Desert Saints: Styles of Victorian Masculinity,* 1995; Richard Altick, *The English Common Reader,* 1957; Asa Briggs, *Victo-*

rian Things, 1989; Jerome Buckley, *The Triumph of Time,* 1966; Peter Gay, *The Bourgeois Experience: From Victoria to Freud,* 2 vols., 1984–86; Mark Girouard, *The Return to Camelot,* 1981; Bruce Haley, *The Healthy Body and Victorian Culture,* 1978; Steven Marcus, *The Other Victorians: A Study of Sexuality and Pornography in Mid-Nineteenth-Century England,* 1964; Herbert Sussman, *Victorians and the Machine,* 1968; E. P. Thompson, *The Making of the English Working Class,* 1963; Frank M. Turner, *The Greek Heritage in Victorian Britain,* 1981; *The Victorian City,* ed. H. J. Dyos and Michael Wolff, 2 vols., 1973; Jeffrey Weeks, *Sex, Politics and Society: The Regulation of Sexuality Since 1800,* 1981; and Michael Wheeler, *Death and the Future Life in Victorian Literature and Theology,* 1991. For pictures and paintings of the Victorian scene, see Jeremy Maas, *Victorian Painters,* 1969. Also revealing are the illustrations for Henry Mayhew, *London Labour and London Poor,* originally published 1851, reprinted 1967, and Gustav Doré, *London: A Pilgrimage,* originally published 1872 and reprinted 1970. *Nature and the Victorian Imagination,* ed. U. C. Knoepflmacher and G. B. Tennyson, 1977; *Victorian Types, Victorian Shadows: Biblical Typology in Victorian Literature, Art, and Thought,* George Landow, 1980; and *Victorian Literature and the Victorian Visual Imagination,* ed. Carol T. Christ and John O. Jordan, 1995, feature valuable treatments of literature and the visual arts.

Studies of Victorian literature include Isobel Armstrong, *Victorian Poetry: Poetry, Poetics, and Politics,* 1993; Harold Bloom, *The Ringers in the Tower,* 1971; William E. Buckler, *The Victorian Imagination,* 1980; Douglas Bush, *Mythology and the Romantic Tradition,* 1937; Raymond Chapman,

The Sense of the Past in Victorian Literature, 1986; Carol T. Christ, *The Finer Optic: The Aesthetic of Particularity in Victorian Poetry*, 1975, and *Victorian and Modern Poetics*, 1984; Peter Allan Dale, *The Victorian Critic and the Idea of History*, 1977; Oliver Elton, *A Survey of English Literature*, 1920, vols. 3 and 4; Avrom Fleischman, *Figures of Autobiography: The Language of Self in Victorian and Modern England*, 1983; Pauline Fletcher, *Gardens and Grim Ravines . . . Landscape in Victorian Poetry*, 1983; George Ford, *Keats and the Victorians*, 1944; Hilary Fraser with David Brown, *English Prose of the Nineteenth Century*, 1997; E. D. H. Johnson, *The Alien Vision of Victorian Poetry*, 1952; Robert Langbaum, *The Poetry of Experience*, 1957; John P. McGowan, *Representation and Revelation: Victorian Realism from Carlyle to Yeats*, 1986; Dorothy Mermin, *The Audience in the Poem*, 1983; J. Hillis Miller, *The Disappearance of God: Five Nineteenth-Century Writers*, 1963; John R. Reed, *Victorian Conventions*, 1975; W. David Shaw, *The Lucid Veil: Poetic Truth in the Victorian Age*, 1987; René Wellek, *A History of Modern Criticism*, vol. 4, 1965. Helpful collections of critical essays have been compiled by Robert Preyer in his *Victorian Literature: Selected Essays*, 1965; Isobel Armstrong, *The Major Victorian Poets: Reconsiderations*, 1969; and by Michael Timko in *Victorian Poetry*, Spring 1978. Especially noteworthy is *The Art of Victorian Prose*, ed. George Levine and William Madden, 1968.

For the status of women in Victorian life and literature, see Nina Auerbach, *Woman and the Demon*, 1982, and *Romantic Imprisonment*, 1985; Deirdre David, *Rule Britannia: Women, Empire, and Victorian Writing*, 1996; Sandra Gilbert and Susan Gubar, *The Madwoman in the Attic*, 1979; Elizabeth Helsinger, Robin Lauterbach Sheets, and William Veeder, *The Woman Question*, 3 vols., 1980; Margaret Homans, *Bearing the Word: Language and Female Experience in Nineteenth-Century Women's Writing*, 1986; Elizabeth Langland, *Nobody's Angels: Middle Class Women and Domestic Ideology in Victorian Culture*, 1995; Angela Leighton, *Victorian Women Poets: Writing against the Heart*, 1992; Dorothy Mermin, *Godiva's Ride: Women of Letters in England, 1830–1880*, 1993; Ellen Moers, *Literary Women*, 1976; Mary Poovey, *Uneven Developments: The Ideological Work of Gender in Mid-Victorian England*, 1988; Eve Kosofsky Sedgwick, *Between Men: English Literature and Male Homosexual Desire*, 1985; Elaine Showalter, *A Literature of Their Own*, 1977; and Martha Vicinus, ed., *Suffer and Be Still*, 1972, *A Widening Sphere*, 1977, and *Ever Yours, Florence Nightingale, Selected Letters* (with Bea Nergaard), 1989.

For classified or annotated lists of other books and articles, see *The Victorian Poets: A Guide to Research*, ed. F. E. Faverty, rev. 1968; *Victorian Fiction: A Guide to Research*, ed. Lionel Stevenson, 1964; *Victorian Fiction: A Second Guide to Research*, ed. George H. Ford, 1978; *Victorian Prose: A Guide to Research*, ed. David J. DeLaura,
1973; Sharon W. Propas, *Victorian Studies: A Research Guide*, 1992; and Laurence W. Mazzeno, *Victorian Poetry: An Annotated Bibliography*, 1995.

For developments in prose fiction during the period, see Lionel Stevenson, *The English Novel: A Panorama*, 1960, and for introductions to individual novelists, see *Victorian Novelists before 1885*, ed. Ira Nadel and William Fredeman, *Dictionary of Literary Biography*, vol. 21, 1983. For special critical issues, see Peter Brooks, *Reading for the Plot: Design and Intention in Narrative*, 1984; Joseph W. Childers, *Novel Possibilities: Fiction and the Formation of Early Victorian Culture*, 1995; Catherine Gallagher, *The Industrial Reformation of English Fiction: Social Discourse and Narrative Form, 1832–1867*, 1985; Peter Garrett, *The Victorian Multiplot Novel*, 1980; George Levine, *The Realistic Imagination*, 1981; D. A. Miller, *The Novel and the Police*, 1988; J. Hillis Miller, *The Form of Victorian Fiction*, 1968; Robert M. Polhemus, *Erotic Faith*, 1990; and Donald Stone, *The Romantic Impulse in Victorian Fiction*, 1980.

Matthew Arnold

The standard edition of Arnold's poetry is the elaborately annotated *Poems of Arnold*, ed. Miriam Allott, 1979. Cecil Lang is editing *The Letters of Matthew Arnold*, 1996–. H. F. Lowry has edited *The Letters of Arnold to . . . Clough*, 1932. R. H. Super has produced an authoritative edition of *The Complete Prose Works*, 11 vols., 1960–77. For a study of those prose works, see William Robbins's *The Ethical Idealism of Matthew Arnold*, 1959, and Joseph Carroll's *The Cultural Theory of Matthew Arnold*, 1982.

The most satisfactory biography is Park Honan's *Matthew Arnold: A Life*, 1981, but see also Nicholas Murray, *A Life of Matthew Arnold*, 1996. Lionel Trilling's excellent *Matthew Arnold*, 1949, remains a standard critical and biographical study, but see also Dwight Culler's *Imaginative Reason*, 1966, and G. Robert Stange's *The Poet as Humanist*, 1967. For two centenary assessments, see Stefan Collini, *Arnold*, 1988, and David G. Riede, *Matthew Arnold and the Betrayal of Language*, 1988. Two investigations of Arnold's literary and intellectual background are Leon Gottfried, *Matthew Arnold and the Romantics*, 1983, and Ruth apRoberts, *Arnold and God*, 1983. See also Kenneth Allott, *Matthew Arnold*, 1975, and the selection of essays edited by Harold Bloom, *Matthew Arnold*, 1987.

Emily Brontë

The Complete Poems were first edited by C. W. Hatfield in 1941. A more recent edition is *The Poems of Emily Bronte*, ed. Derek Roper and Edward Chitham, 1995. Information about the Gondal narrative is supplied by Fannie R. Ratchford's *The Brontës' Web of Childhood*, 1941, and *Gondal's Queen, A Novel in Verse*, 1955. The most satisfactory biography is Edward Chitham, *A Life of Emily Brontë*, 1988. Several of the essays in *The Art of Emily Brontë*, ed. Anne Smith, 1977, and in Thomas John Winnifrith, *Critical Essays on Emily Bronte*, 1997, are devoted to the poetry, as is Margaret Homans,

Women Writers and Poetic Identity, 1980. Also see Irene Taylor, *Holy Ghosts: The Male Muses of Emily and Charlotte Brontë*, 1990. William M. Sale, Jr., and Richard J. Dunn have edited the Norton Critical Edition of *Wuthering Heights*, 3rd ed., 1990.

Elizabeth Barrett Browning
The standard *Complete Works* were edited by Charlotte Porter and Helen Clarke, 6 vols., 1900. Margaret Reynolds has edited a Norton Critical Edition of *Aurora Leigh*, 1996, and Julia Markus had edited *Casa Guidi Windows*, 1977. Of a projected forty-volume collection, *The Brownings' Correspondence*, ed. Philip Kelley and Ronald Hudson (1984–), fourteen volumes have been published. The best critical biography is Dorothy Mermin's *Elizabeth Barrett Browning: The Origins of a New Poetry*, 1989. See also Angela Leighton, *Elizabeth Barrett Browning*, 1986. Interesting recent discussions of Barrett Browning can be found in Ellen Moers, *Literary Women*, 1976; Sandra Gilbert and Susan Gubar, *The Madwoman in the Attic*, 1979; Deirdre David, *Intellectual Women and Victorian Patriarchy*, 1987; Helen Cooper, *Elizabeth Barrett Browning, Woman and Artist*, 1988; and Marjorie Stone, *Elizabeth Barrett Browning*, 1995.

Robert Browning
A standard edition is *The Complete Works of Robert Browning, with Variant Readings and Annotations*, ed. Roma A. King Jr., et al., 9 vols., 1969–89. Five volumes of a projected seven-volume annotated edition of the poetry only, *The Poetical Works of Robert Browning*, have appeared, edited by Ian Jack, Margaret Smith, and Robert Inglesfield, 1983–95. John Woolford and Daniel Karlin have also edited *The Poems of Browning*, 1991, two volumes of which have appeared. A convenient two-volume collection of the poems edited by John Pettigrew and Thomas J. Collins was published in 1981. For the Brownings' correspondence, see entry under **Elizabeth Barrett Browning**. The standard biography is *The Book, the Ring, and the Poet*, William Irvine and Park Honan, 1974; also see Clyde de L. Ryals, *The Life of Robert Browning: A Critical Biography*. Gertrude Reese Hudson provides a study of his critical reception in *Robert Browning's Literary Life*, 1993. W. C. DeVane's *A Browning Handbook*, rev. 1955, is a compilation of factual data concerning each of Browning's poems: sources, composition, and reputation. Further information is supplied by Norman B. Crowell, *A Reader's Guide to Robert Browning*, 1972, which also offers simplified summaries of critical discussions for twenty-three monologues.

The critical assessments in G. K. Chesterton's *Robert Browning*, 1903, are colorfully expressed and often shrewd. Robert Langbaum's *The Poetry of Experience* relates Browning's monologues to some of the main developments in modern literature. See also Roma A. King Jr., *The Bow and the Lyre*, 1957; W. O. Raymond, *The Infinite Moment*, 1965; Donald Hair, *Browning's Experiments with Genre*, 1972; Ian Jack, *Browning's Major Poetry*, 1973; Herbert Tucker, *Browning's Beginnings*, 1980; Loy Martin, *Browning's Dramatic Monologues and the Post-*

Romantic Subject, 1985; and Joseph Bristow, *Robert Browning*, 1991. Useful collections of essays include *The Browning Critics*, ed. Boyd Litzinger and K. L. Knickerbocker, 1965; *Robert Browning: A Collection of Critical Essays*, ed. Philip Drew, 1966; *Browning: The Critical Heritage*, ed. Boyd Litzinger and Donald Smalley, 1970; *Robert Browning*, ed. Isobel Armstrong, 1974; *Robert Browning: A Collection of Critical Essays*, ed. Harold Bloom and Adrienne Munich, 1979; and *Critical Essays on Robert Browning*, ed. Mary Ellis Gibson, 1992.

Thomas Carlyle
The *Works* have been edited by H. D. Traill, 30 vols., 1898–1901. Twenty-one volumes of the *Collected Letters*, projected to extend to thirty volumes, have been published since 1971 (ed. by C. R. Sanders et al.). C. F. Harrold's edition of *Sartor Resartus*, 1937, is helpful concerning Carlyle's debt to German literature, as is Louis Cazamian's *Carlyle*, 1932, concerning his religious background. J. A. Froude, *Thomas Carlyle*, 1882–84, for years the standard biography, has been replaced by Fred Kaplan, *Thomas Carlyle*, 1983. Recommended studies of Carlyle's thought are Emery Neff, *Carlyle and Mill*, 1926; Philip Rosenberg, *The Seventh Hero: Thomas Carlyle and the Theory of Radical Activism*, 1974; Ruth apRoberts, *The Ancient Dialect: Thomas Carlyle and Comparative Religion*, 1988; and Chris Vanden Bossche, *Carlyle and the Search for Authority*, 1991. That he has affinities with twentieth-century "mythmakers" such as D. H. Lawrence is argued by Albert J. LaValley in *Carlyle and the Idea of the Modern*, 1968. John Holloway's *The Victorian Sage*, 1953, includes a chapter analyzing Carlyle's rhetoric. George B. Tennyson, *Sartor Called Resartus*, 1965, is an important critical study. See also George Levine, *The Boundaries of Fiction*, 1968, on Carlyle, Macaulay, and Newman, and the collection of essays edited by K. J. Fielding and Rodger L. Tarr, *Carlyle Past and Present*, 1976. Tarr has also compiled *Thomas Carlyle: A Descriptive Bibliography*, 1990.

Lewis Carroll
The standard edition is *The Complete Writings of Lewis Carroll*, 1939. A highly recommended selection is *Alice in Wonderland*, a Norton Critical Edition, ed. Donald J. Gray, 2nd ed., 1992. For his life see Morton N. Cohen, *Lewis Carroll: A Biography*, 1995. See also William Empson. *Some Versions of Pastoral*, 1935. For a variety of recent critical views, see *Soaring with the Dodo: Essays on Lewis Carroll's Life and Art*, ed. Edward Giuliano and James R. Kincaid, 1982, and *Lewis Carroll*, ed. Harold Bloom, 1987. Francis Huxley's *The Raven and the Writing Desk*, 1976, is a brilliant and idiosyncratic discussion of Carroll's work.

Arthur Hugh Clough
The Poems were edited by H. F. Lowry, A. L. F. Norrington, and F. L. Mulhauser, 1951. In 1974 Mulhauser edited a revised edition, with some poems previously omitted. Mulhauser was also editor of *The Correspondence*, 1957. See also *The*

Oxford Diaries, ed. Anthony Kenny, 1990. *A. H. Clough: The Uncommitted Mind*, Katherine Chorley, 1962, is a lively but frequently misleading study. *The Poetry of Clough*, Walter Houghton, 1963, contends that Clough is a major satirical poet. On Clough's religious and intellectual background, see Anthony Kenny, *God and Two Poets: Arthur Hugh Clough and Gerard Manley Hopkins*, 1988, and Paul Veyriras, *A. H. Clough*, 1965 (in French). See also the judicious study by Robindra Biswas, *Arthur Hugh Clough: Towards a Reconsideration*, 1972.

Mary Elizabeth Coleridge

The only edition of Coleridge's poetry is *Collected Poems.*, ed. Theresa Whistler, 1954. A posthumous collection of selections from her stories and journals is contained in *Gathered Leaves from the Prose of Mary E. Coleridge*, with a memoir by Edith Sichel, 1910. Sandra M. Gilbert and Susan Gubar, *The Madwoman in the Attic*, 1979, contains a discussion of *The Other Side of a Mirror*.

Charles Dickens

The standard modern edition of Dickens's works is The Clarendon Edition, 1966–. Norton Critical Editions exist for *Bleak House*, ed. George Ford and Sylvere Monod, 1977; *David Copperfield*, ed. Jerome H. Buckley, 1990; *Great Expectations*, ed. Edgar Rosenberg, 1999; *Hard Times*, ed. George Ford and Sylvere Monod, 1990; and *Oliver Twist*, ed. Fred Kaplan, 1993. A modern edition of *The Letters of Charles Dickens*, ed. Madeline House et al., 1965–, is in progress.

Two classic biographies are John Forster, *The Life of Charles Dickens*, 2 vols., 1876, and Edward Johnson, *Charles Dickens*, 2 vols., 1952. For modern biographies, see Fred Kaplan, *Dickens: A Biography*, 1988, and Peter Ackroyd, *Dickens*, 1990. *Dickens: Interviews and Recollections*, 2 vols., Philip Collins, ed., 1981, is another biographical source.

Classic early studies include George Gissing, *Charles Dickens: A Critical Study*, 1903; G. K. Chesterton, *Charles Dickens*, 1906; Edmund Wilson, "Dickens: The Two Scrooges," in his *The Wound and the Bow*, 1952; and George Orwell, "Charles Dickens," in his *A Collection of Essays*, 1954. For modern critical studies see John Carey, *Here Comes Dickens*, 1974; Philip Collins, *Dickens and Crime*, 1962; George H. Ford, *Dickens and His Readers*, 1955; Robert Garis, *The Dickens Theatre*, 1965; Steven Marcus, *Dickens: From Pickwick to Dombey*, 1965; J. Hillis Miller, *Charles Dickens: The World of His Novels*, 1958; Alexander Welsh, *The City of Dickens*, 1971; Angus Wilson, *The World of Charles Dickens*, 1970. Critical responses to Dickens are collected in *Dickens: The Critical Heritage*, ed. Philip Collins, 1971, and *Charles Dickens*, ed. Stephen Wall, 1970. For a collection of modern essays, see *Charles Dickens*, ed. Harold Bloom, 1987.

Ernest Dowson

The standard modern edition of Dowson's poems is *The Poetry of Ernest Dowson*, ed. Desmond Flower, 1st American ed., 1970. Much lively and illuminating comment on Dowson will be found in W. B. Yeats's *Autobiography*, 1955. *Ernest Dowson*, by J. M. Longaker, 1944, and *Ernest Dowson*, by T. B. Swann, 1965, are critical biographies; a short chapter on Dowson in *Essays in Criticism and Research*, by Geoffrey Tillotson, 1967, assesses his relationship with other poets. See also *Letters of Ernest Dowson*, ed. Desmond Flower and Henry Maas, 1967.

See also entries under **The Nineties.**

George Eliot

There is no twentieth-century standard edition of Eliot's complete works. The collected edition of the works, corrected by Eliot, is the Cabinet Edition, 20 vols., 1878–80. Of modern editions, the *Essays* are edited by Thomas Pinney, 1963, and *The George Eliot Letters* are edited by Gordon S. Haight, 9 vols., 1954–78. Margaret Harris and Judith Johnston have edited *The Journals of George Eliot*, 1999. Five of the eight novels have been published in annotated Clarendon editions. Bert G. Hornback has edited the Norton Critical Edition of *Middlemarch*, 1977, and Carol Christ has edited *The Mill on the Floss* for the same series. The best critical biography is Ruby V. Redinger, *George Eliot: The Emergent Self*, 1975; Gordon Haight's *George Eliot: A Biography*, 1968, remains the most exhaustive account of her life. See also Rosemary Ashton, *George Eliot: A Life*, 1997; Rosemarie Bodenheimer, *The Real Life of Mary Ann Evans: George Eliot, Her Letters and Fiction*, 1994; and Frederick R. Karl, *George Eliot, Voice of a Century: A Biography*, 1995.

Good introductions to Eliot's fiction are Joan Bennett, *George Eliot: Her Mind and Her Art*, 1948, and Joseph Wiesenfarth's essay in *Victorian Novelists before 1885*, ed. Ira Nadel and William Fredeman, *Dictionary of Literary Biography*, vol. 21, 1983. F. R. Leavis's influential discussion of Eliot in *The Great Tradition*, 1948, revived critical interest in Eliot's work in this century. See also Dorothea Barrett, *Vocation and Desire: George Eliot's Heroines*, 1989; Gillian Beer, *George Eliot*, 1986; David Carroll, *George Eliot and the Conflict of Interpretations: A Reading of the Novels*, 1992; Deirdre David, *Intellectual Women and Victorian Patriarchy: Harriet Martineau, Elizabeth Barrett Browning, George Eliot*, 1987; W. J. Harvey, *The Art of George Eliot*, 1962; U. C. Knoepflmacher, *George Eliot's Early Novels: The Limits of Realism*, 1968; Alexander Welsh, *George Eliot and Blackmail*, 1985. Barbara Hardy, *Novels of George Eliot: A Study in Form*, 1959, and two collections of essays, *Critical Essays on George Eliot*, 1970, and *Particularities: Readings in George Eliot*, 1982, are standard critical works. Other collections include *George Eliot: The Critical Heritage*, ed. David Carroll, 1971; a special issue of *Nineteenth Century Fiction*, "George Eliot 1880–1980," ed. U. C. Knoepflmacher and George Levine, 1980; and *George Eliot*, ed. Harold Bloom, 1986. An especially useful reference work is George

Levine, *An Annotated Critical Bibliography of George Eliot*, 1988.

Michael Field

Michael Field's poetry has not been collected. Individual volumes are titled *Long Ago*, 1889; *Sight and Song*, 1892; *Underneath the Bough, A Book of Verses*, 1893; *Wild Honey From Various Thyme*, 1908; *Mystic Trees*, 1913; *Dedicated: An Early Work of Michael Field*, 1914; *Whym Chow: Flame of Love*, 1914; *The Wattlefold: Unpublished Poems*, 1930. *Works and Days: From the Journal of Michael Field*, ed. T. and D. C. Sturge Moore, 1933, contains selections from the diaries. For critical commentary, see Angela Leighton, *Victorian Women Poets*, 1992, and a special issue of *Victorian Poetry, Women Poets 1830–1894*.

Edward FitzGerald

George Bentham edited *The Variorum Edition of the . . . Writings of Edward FitzGerald*, 7 vols., 1902; a critical edition of the *Rubaiyat* has been edited by Christopher Decker, 1997. See also the *Letters*, ed. A. McKinley Terhune, 4 vols., 1980. The biography, by Robert Bernard Martin, is *With Friends Possessed: A Life of Edward FitzGerald*, 1985.

Elizabeth Gaskell

The standard edition of Gaskell's fiction is the Knutsford Edition, ed. A. W. Ward, 8 vols, 1906–20; the best modern editions are by Penguin. A modern edition exists of *The Letters of Mrs. Gaskell*, ed. J. A. V. Chapple and Arthur Pollard, rev. 1997. Biographies include Winifred Gerin, *Elizabeth Gaskell*, 1980, and Jenny Uglow, *Elizabeth Gaskell: A Habit of Stories*, 1993. For critical studies see W. A. Craik, *Elizabeth Gaskell and the English Provincial Novel*, 1975; Angus Easson, *Elizabeth Gaskell*, 1979; Angus Easson, ed., *Elizabeth Gaskell: The Critical Heritage*, 1991; Hilary M. Schor, *Scheherezade in the Marketplace: Elizabeth Gaskell and the Victorian Novel*, 1992; and Patsy Stoneman, *Elizabeth Gaskell*, 1987.

W. S. Gilbert

Gilbert's librettos for Sullivan in their finally revised form comprise *The Complete Plays of Gilbert and Sullivan*, 1976. The earliest published versions, often substantially different from those performed today, are reprinted in Reginald Allen, *The First Night Gilbert and Sullivan*, 1958. Earlier works by Gilbert include *The Bab Ballads*, ed. James Ellis, 1970, and *Gilbert Before Sullivan: Six Comic Plays*, 1967, ed. Jane W. Stedman, 1967. Hesketh Pearson's *Gilbert: His Life and Strife*, 1957, is the best modern biography. A sampling of Gilbert criticism is offered by John B. Hones in *W. S. Gilbert: A Century of Scholarship and Commentary*, 1970. See also Alan Fischler, *Modified Rapture: Comedy in W. S. Gilbert's Savoy Operas*, 1991.

William Ernest Henley

The standard edition, which includes essays and plays as well as poetry, is *The Works of William Ernest Henley*, 7 vols., 1970 (reprint of 1908 edition). See B. Ifor Evans, *English Poetry in the Later Nineteenth Century*, 1933, chapter 12, and Jerome H. Buckley, *William Ernest Henley: A Study of the "Counter-Decadence" of the Nineties*, 1945. Also useful on Henley as a figure of the Nineties is a study by André Guillaume, *William Ernest Henley et son groupe*, 1973.

See also entries under **The Nineties.**

Gerard Manley Hopkins

Robert Bridges edited the first (posthumous) edition of Hopkins's poems in 1918, which has been the nucleus of all subsequent editions. The most recent is *The Poetical Works of Gerard Manley Hopkins*, ed. Norman H. MacKenzie, 1990. In addition to the poems, Hopkins's letters and parts of his notebooks have been published: *The Letters of Gerard Manley Hopkins to Robert Bridges* and *The Correspondence of G. M. Hopkins and Richard Watson Dixon*, ed. C. C. Abbot, 2 vols., 1935; *Further Letters of Gerard Manley Hopkins*, ed. C. C. Abbott, 1938, rev. 1956; *The Journals and Papers of Gerard Manley Hopkins*, ed. Humphry House and Graham Storey, 1969; and *The Sermons and Devotional Writings of Gerard Manley Hopkins*, ed. Christopher Devlin, 1959. A helpful introduction to these works is Norman H. MacKenzie, *A Reader's Guide to Gerard Manley Hopkins*, 1981.

The two best biographies are Robert Bernard Martin, *Gerard Manley Hopkins: A Very Private Life*, 1991, and Norman White, *Hopkins: A Literary Biography*, 1992. Some useful critical studies are W. H. Gardner, *G. M. Hopkins: A Study of Poetic Idiosyncrasy in Relation to Poetic Tradition*, 2 vols., 1944, 1949; Paul L. Mariani, *A Commentary on the Complete Poems of Gerard Manley Hopkins*, 1970; Alison Sulloway, *Gerard Manley Hopkins and the Victorian Temper*, 1972; Daniel Harris, *Inspirations Unbidden: The "Terrible Sonnets" of Gerard Manley Hopkins*, 1982; Walter J. Ong, *Hopkins, the Self, and God*, 1986; and Virginia Ridley Ellis, *Gerard Manley Hopkins and the Language of Mystery*, 1991. Two good collections of critical essays are *Hopkins*, ed. Geoffrey Hartmann, 1966, and *Hopkins Among the Poets: Studies in Modern Responses to Gerard Manley Hopkins*, ed. Richard F. Giles, 1985.

Thomas Henry Huxley

The Life and Letters of Thomas Henry Huxley, Leonard Huxley, 2 vols., 1900, is the standard biography. William Irvine, *Apes, Angels, and Victorians*, 1955, is lively and informative. See also Harold Cyril Bibby, *Scientist Extraordinary: The Life and Scientific Work of Thomas Henry Huxley*, 1972.

Rudyard Kipling

The Sussex Edition of the complete works, 35 vols., 1937–39, is the standard complete edition. *Rudyard Kipling's Verse: Definitive Edition*, 1940, must now be supplemented by *Early Verse by Rudyard Kipling, 1879–1889: Unpublished, Uncollated and Rarely Collected Poems*, ed. Andrew Rutherford, 1986. T. S. Eliot has edited, with an appreciative and discerning introduction, *A Choice of Kipling's Verse*, 1941. Thomas Pinney edited *The Letters of Rudyard Kipling* (1872–99), 3 vols., 1988–96. Charles E. Carrington's *Rudyard Kipling*, 1955, is the official biography, but three others are worthy of note: J. I. M. Stewart, *Rudyard Kipling*, 1966; Philip Mason, *Kipling: The Glass, the Shadow, and the Fire*, 1975, an informative account of Kipling's complex relationship with India; and Angus Wilson, *The Strange Ride of Rudyard Kipling*, 1978, a judicious and readable interpretation of Kipling's life and attitudes. Three important midcentury critics have written interesting essays on Kipling: Edmund Wilson in *The Wound and the Bow*, 1941; George Orwell in *Critical Essays*, 1946; and Lionel Trilling in *The Liberal Imagination*, 1950. Studies of his fiction include Helen Pike Bauer, *Rudyard Kipling: A Study of the Short Fiction*, 1994; Elliot L. Gilbert, *The Good Kipling: Studies in the Short Story*, 1971; Sandra Kemp, *Kipling's Hidden Narratives*, 1987; Mark Paffard, *Kipling's Indian Fiction*, 1989; and Zohreh T. Sullivan, *Narratives of Empire: Fictions of Rudyard Kipling*, 1992. Peter Keating has written a study of his poetry, *Kipling the Poet*, 1994. There are a number of useful collections of critical essays: *Kipling's Mind and Art*, ed. Andrew Rutherford, 1964; *Kipling and the Critics*, ed. E. L. Gilbert, 1965; Roger Lancelyn Green, *Kipling: The Critical Heritage*, 1971; *Rudyard Kipling*, ed. John Gross, 1972 and *Critical Essays on Rudyard Kipling*, ed. Harold Orel, 1989.

See also entries under **The Nineties.**

Edward Lear

The Complete Nonsense, ed. Holbrook Jackson, 1947; Ina Rae Hark, *Edward Lear*, 1982; Elizabeth Sewell, *The Field of Nonsense*, 1952. Edward Gorey's *Gorey x 3*, 1976, provides delightful illustrations for Lear's verse-narratives. See also Thomas Byrom, *Nonsense and Wonder: The Poems and Cartoons of Edward Lear*, 1978.

Light Verse

Interesting collections of light verse include *Parodies: An Anthology from Chaucer to Beerbohm*, ed. Dwight Macdonald, 1969; *The Oxford Book of Light Verse*, ed. W. H. Auden, 1938; and *The New Oxford Book of Light Verse*, ed. Kingsley Amis, 1978.

See also entries under **Lewis Carroll, W. S. Gilbert,** and **Edward Lear.**

George Meredith

Phyllis Bartlett's edition of the *Poems*, 1978, supersedes G. M. Trevelyan's edition of 1928. *The Letters*, ed., C. L. Cline, were published in three volumes in 1970. See Lionel Stevenson, *The Ordeal of George Meredith*, 1953; C. Day Lewis, *Introduction to Modern Love*, 1948; and Norman Kelvin, *A Troubled Eden*, 1961. A Norton Critical Edition of his novel, *The Egoist*, was edited by Robert M. Adams in 1979.

John Stuart Mill

The *Collected Works*, ed. John Robson et al., were published in twenty-seven volumes, 1963–90. *Mill: The Spirit of the Age, On Liberty, The Subjection of Women* has been edited by Alan Ryan in the Norton Critical Editions, 1998. Ann P. Robson and John M. Robson have edited *Sexual Equality: Writings by John Stuart Mill, Harriet Taylor Mill, and Helen Taylor*, 1994. *The Life of J. S. Mill* by M. St. J. Packe, 1954, is the standard biography. Studies include A. W. Benn, *The History of English Rationalism in the Nineteenth Century*, 2 vols., 1906; Janice Carlisle, *John Stuart Mill and the Writing of Character*, 1991; Maurice Cowling, *Mill and Liberalism*, 1963; *J. S. Mill: On Liberty in Focus*, ed. John Gray and G. W. Smith, 1991; *A Cultivated Mind: Essays on J. S. Mill Presented to John M. Robson*, ed. Michael Laine, 1991; Emery Neff, *Carlyle and Mill*, 1926; John Robson, *The Improvement of Mankind*, 1968; Alan Ryan, *John Stuart Mill*, 1970; and *Mill: A Collection of Critical Essays*, ed. J. B. Schneewind, 1968.

William Morris

Collected Works, 24 vols., 1910–15; *The Collected Letters of William Morris*, ed. Norman Kelvin, 4 vols., 1984–96; Biographies include J. W. Mackail, *The Life of William Morris*, 2 vols, 1899; Philip Henderson, *William Morris, His Life, Work and Friends*, 1967; and Fiona MacCarthy, *William Morris: A Life for Our Time*, 1995. Also see George Bernard Shaw, *William Morris, As I Knew Him*, 1936; *William Morris: The Critical Heritage*, ed. Peter Faulkner, 1973; Jerome McGann, *Black Riders: The Visible Language of Modernism*, 1993; and Carole Silver, *The Romance of William Morris*, 1982. E. P. Thompson's Marxist approach in *William Morris: Romantic to Revolutionary*, 1977, offers the best study of Morris's politics.

John Henry Cardinal Newman

The forty-one volumes of Newman's works were published over a period of years, but no standard edition has as yet appeared. His *Letters and Diaries*, on the other hand, have been collected and edited by C. S. Dessain et al., 31 vols., 1961–84. For a useful text, with criticism, of *Apologia pro Vita Sua*, see David J. DeLaura, Norton Critical Edition, 1968. For Newman's religious background and development, see Charles F. Harold, *John Henry Newman*, 1945, and for a comprehensive study see Sheridan Gilley, *Newman and His Age*, 1990. His literary skill is analyzed in John Holloway, *The Victorian Sage*, 1953, chapter 6, and Walter E. Houghton, *The Art of Newman's "Apologia,"* 1945. Especially recommended is Dwight Culler, *The Imperial Intellect*, 1955. William Robbins, *The Newman Brothers*, 1966, develops an interesting contrast between Newman and his free-thinking brother, Francis Newman.

The Nineties

On the special qualities of the literature of the 1890s, see *Edwardians and Late Victorians*, ed. Richard Ellmann, 1960. See also Holbrook Jackson, *The Eighteen Nineties*, 1913, rev. 1976; Graham Hough, *The Last Romantics*, 1947; R. K. R. Thornton, *The Decadent Dilemma*, 1983; John R. Reed, *Decadent Style*, 1985; Linda C. Dowling, *Language and Decadence in the Victorian Fin de Siecle*, 1986;

Richard Dellamora, *Masculine Desire: The Sexual Politics of Victorian Aestheticism*, 1990; Elaine Showalter, *Sexual Anarchy: Gender and Culture at the Fin de Siecle*, 1990; Karl Beckson, *London in the 1890's: A Cultural History*, 1992; *The 1890's: An Encyclopedia of British Literature, Art, and Culture*, ed. G. A. Cevasco, 1993; and Rhonda K. Garelick, *Rising Star: Dandyism, Gender, and Performance in the Fin de Siecle*, 1998. Three useful anthologies are *An Anthology of "Nineties" Verse*, ed. A. J. A. Symons, 1928; *Aesthetes and Decadents of the 1890's: An Anthology of British Poetry and Prose*, ed. K. Beckson, 1966; and *Poetry of the Nineties*, ed. R. K. R. Thornton, 1971.

See also entries under **Ernest Dowson, William Ernest Henley, Rudyard Kipling, Walter Pater, Francis Thompson,** and **Oscar Wilde.**

Walter Pater

Works, 10 vols., 1910, and see also Donald Hill's annotated edition of *The Renaissance*, 1980. Thomas Wright, *The Life of Walter Pater*, 2 vols., 1907, is a standard but unreliable source. More satisfactory is Michael Levey, *The Case of Walter Pater*, 1978. A book-length study of Pater by Wolfgang Iser was published in Germany in 1960 and translated in 1987 as *Walter Pater: The Aesthetic Moment*. Critical essays include T. S. Eliot's "Arnold and Pater" in *Selected Essays 1917–32*, 1932; U. C. Knoepflmacher, *Religious Humanism and the Victorian Novel*, 1965; David J. DeLaura, *Hebrew and Hellene in Victorian England: Newman, Arnold, and Pater*, 1969; Carolyn Williams, *Transfigured World: Walter Pater's Aesthetic Historicism*, 1989; and Denis Donoghue, *Walter Pater: Lover of Strange Souls*, 1995. A collection of essays is *Walter Pater: Modern Critical Views*, ed. Harold Bloom, 1985. Highly recommended is Laurence Evans's chapter on Pater in *Victorian Prose: A Guide to Research*, ed. David J. DeLaura, 1973.

See also entries under **The Nineties.**

Christina Rossetti

The standard variorum edition is *The Complete Poems of Christina Rossetti*, ed. R. W. Crump, 3 vols., 1979–90. The first volume of *The Letters of Christina Rossetti*, ed. Anthony H. Harrison, 1997, has been published. See also *Selected Prose of Christina Rossetti*, ed. David A. Kent and P. G. Stanwood, 1998. Two recent biographies are Kathleen Jones, *Learning Not to Be First: The Life of Christina Rossetti*, 1991, and Jan Marsh, *Christina Rossetti: A Writer's Life*, 1995. Virginia Woolf's *Second Common Reader*, 1932, contains an essay on the poet. Dolores Rosenblum's *Christina Rossetti: The Poetry of Endurance*, 1986, and Antony H. Harrison's *Christina Rossetti in Context*, 1988, are good book-length studies of the poetry. David Kent has edited a collection of critical essays, *The Achievement of Christina Rossetti*, 1987.

Dante Gabriel Rossetti

Rossetti's *Works* were edited by W. M. Rossetti, 1911, and *The Letters* by Oswald Doughty and J. R. Wahl, 4 vols., 1965–67 (an incomplete collection).

See Oswald Doughty, *D. G. Rossetti: A Victorian Romantic*, 1960, and Lionel Stevenson, *The Pre-Raphaelite Poets*, 1973. Also recommended are Joan Rees, *The Poetry of Dante Gabriel Rossetti*, 1981; and David Riede, *Dante Gabriel Rossetti and the Limits of Victorian Vision*, 1983, and *Dante Gabriel Rossetti Revisited*, 1992. *The Rossetti Archieve*, ed. Jerome McGann, is an on-line edition currently in progress (jefferson.village.edu/rossetti/rossetti. html).

John Ruskin

The Works were edited by E. T. Cook and Alexander Wedderburn, 39 vols., 1903–12. Cook's early biography of Ruskin, 1911, has been superseded by John Dixon Hunt, *The Wider Sea: A Life of John Ruskin*, 1982, and by Tim Hilton, *John Ruskin: The Early Years*, 1985, the first of two projected volumes. An interesting digest of his aesthetic theories was compiled by Joan Evans in *The Lamp of Beauty: Writings on Art by John Ruskin*, 1958. Also recommended are R. H. Wilenski, *John Ruskin*, 1933; John D. Rosenberg, *The Darkening Glass*, 1961; George P. Landow, *The Aesthetic and Critical Theories of John Ruskin*, 1971; Elizabeth Helsinger, *Ruskin and the Art of the Beholder*, 1982; and Linda M. Austin, *The Practical Ruskin: Economics and Audience in the Late Work*, 1991. See also Robert Hewison, ed., *New Approaches to Ruskin*, 1981.

Bernard Shaw

The first volume of *The Collected Works of Bernard Shaw*, in the Ayot St. Lawrence Edition, 30 vols., appeared in 1930. *Collected Plays with Their Prefaces*, 7 vols., 1975, contains the fully revised texts of all the published plays, together with historical data and miscellaneous Shavian pronouncements on each play. There is a Norton Critical Edition, *Bernard Shaw's Plays*, ed. Warren Sylvester Smith, 1970. Selections of prose include *Bernard Shaw, Selected Prose*, ed. Diarmuid Russell, 1952; *Plays and Players*, ed. A. C. Ward, 1952; *The Nondramatic Literary Criticism of Bernard Shaw*, ed. Stanley Weintraub, 1972; *Shaw on Music*, ed. Eric Bentley, 1972; and *Bernard Shaw on Language*, ed. Abraham Tauber, 1963. The *Collected Letters of Bernard Shaw*, ed. Dan H. Laurence, 1965–, collects his voluminous correspondence.

The standard biography is Michael Holroyd, *Bernard Shaw*, 4 vols, 1988–93. Also of interest is Hesketh Pearson, *George Bernard Shaw: His Life and Personality*, 1963. Other biographical sources are *Shaw: An Autobiography, Selected from His Writings*, 2 vols., ed. Stanley Weintraub, 1969–70, and *Shaw: Interviews and Recollections*, ed. A. M. Gibbs, 1990.

Critical studies include Eric Bentley, *Bernard Shaw: A Reconsideration*, 1947; Charles A. Carpenter, *Bernard Shaw and the Art of Destroying Ideals*, 1969; Louis Crompton, *Shaw the Dramatist*, 1969; *Shaw and Politics*, ed. T. F. Evans, 1991; J. Ellen Gainor, *Shaw's Daughters: Dramatic and Narrative Constructions of Gender*, 1991; Gareth Griffith, *Socialism and Superior Brains: The Political Thought of Bernard Shaw*, 1992; and Sally Peters,

Bernard Shaw: The Ascent of the Superman, 1996. Two useful collections of essays are *George Bernard Shaw*, ed. Harold Bloom, 1987, and *Critical Essays on George Bernard Shaw*, ed. Elsie B. Adams, 1991.

Algernon Charles Swinburne

Complete Works, ed. E. W. Gosse and T. J. Wise, 20 vols., 1925–27, and *The Swinburne Letters*, ed. Cecil Y. Lang, 6 vols., 1959–62. Rikky Rooksby, *A. C. Swinburne: A Poet's Life*, 1997, is the best biography. For an attack on Swinburne's shortcomings as a poet, see A. E. Housman's essay of 1910, first published in *American Scholar*, Winter 1969–70. For more sympathetic readings see the special Swinburne issue of *Victorian Poetry*, Spring-Summer 1971, and also see Jerome J. McGann, *Swinburne: An Experiment in Criticism*, 1972; David Riede, *Swinburne: A Study of Romantic Mythmaking*, 1978; Margot K. Louis, *Swinburne and His Gods: The Roots and Growth of an Agnostic Poetry*, 1990; the chapter on Swinburne in Camille Paglia, *Sexual Personae*, 1990; and *The Whole Music of Passion: New Essays on Swinburne*, ed. Rikky Rooksby and Nicholas Shrimpton, 1993.

Alfred, Lord Tennyson

Tennyson's *Works* were edited by his son Hallam, Lord Tennyson, in 9 vols., 1907–8. The *Poems* in one volume were edited by Christopher Ricks in 1969 and extensively revised in three volumes in 1988. Norton Critical Editions of Tennyson's work are *Tennyson's Poetry*, ed. Robert W. Hill, Jr., 1972, and *In Memoriam*, ed. Robert H. Ross, 1974. *In Memoriam* has been edited by Susan Shatto and Marion Shaw, 1982. Three volumes of *The Letters of Alfred, Lord Tennyson*, to 1870, were edited by Cecil Y. Lang and Edgar F. Shannon, 1981–90. Hallam Tennyson's *Alfred, Lord Tennyson: A Memoir*, 2 vols., 1897, is a mine of anecdotes and valuable information. *The Tennyson Archive*, ed. Christopher Ricks and Aidan Day, 23 vols., 1987–89, is a monumental production concerning the manuscripts. The standard biography is Robert Martin, *Tennyson*, 1980. Sir Harold Nicolson, *Tennyson*, 1923, a critical study more than a biography, gives a lively but distorted assessment of Tennyson's achievement. A number of critical studies have successively corrected Nicolson's oversights and have variously demonstrated that Tennyson is one of the finest of poets. These include Jerome H. Buckley, *Tennyson: The Growth of a Poet*, 1961; Christopher Ricks, *Tennyson*, 1972; F. E. L. Priestley, *Language and Structure in Tennyson's Poetry*, 1973; James R. Kincaid, *Tennyson's Major Poems: The Comic and Ironic Patterns*, 1975; W. David Shaw, *Tennyson's Style*, 1976; and, most especially to be recommended, A. Dwight Culler, *The Poetry of Tennyson* 1977. See also Daniel Albright, *Tennyson: The Muses' Tug-of-War*, 1986; Alan Sinfield, *Alfred Tennyson*, 1986; Herbert F. Tucker, *Tennyson and the Doom of Romanticism*, 1988; Donald S. Hair, *Tennyson's Language*, 1991; and Gerhard Joseph, *Tennyson and the Text: The Weaver's Shuttle*, 1992.

Some of the most interesting discussions are in introductory essays to Tennyson's poems by T. S. Eliot, 1936; W. H. Auden, 1944; H. Marshall McLuhan, 1956; Jerome Buckley, 1958; and George MacBeth, 1971. Also useful are A. C. Bradley, *A Commentary on Tennyson's "In Memoriam,"* 1901; E. D. H. Johnson, *The Alien Vision of Victorian Poetry*, 1952; *Critical Essays on the Poetry of Tennyson*, ed. John Kilham, 1960; and Herbert F. Tucker, *Critical Essays on Alfred Lord Tennyson*, 1993. Book-length studies of the *Idylls* have been published by Clyde de L. Ryals, 1967, John R. Reed, 1969, and John D. Rosenberg, 1973. A collection of critical essays on *In Memoriam* was edited by John Dixon Hunt, 1970; and Timothy Peltason has published a study of the poem, *Reading In Memoriam*, 1985.

Francis Thompson

Complete Poetical Works was edited by Wilfred Meynell, 3 vols., 1913. Biographies are Paul van K. Thompson, *Francis Thompson*, 1961, and Brigid M. Boardman, *Between Heaven and Charing Cross: The Life of Francis Thompson*, 1988. For a general introduction, see Beverly Taylor, *Francis Thompson*, 1987.

See also entries under **The Nineties.**

Oscar Wilde

There is no standard complete edition, but a convenient one-volume collection is *The Complete Works of Oscar Wilde*, 1989. Rupert Hart-Davis has edited the *Letters*, 1962, and its supplement, *More Letters*, 1985. The standard biography is Richard Ellmann, *Oscar Wilde*, 1988. See also the psychoanalytic biography by Melissa Knox, *Oscar Wilde: A Long and Lovely Suicide*, 1994. Earlier biographies include Hesketh Pearson, *The Life of Oscar Wilde: His Life and Wit*, 1946, and H. Montgomery Hyde, *Oscar Wilde: A Biography*, 1975. *Oscar Wilde, a Pictorial Biography*, by Wilde's son, Vyvyan Holland, 1960, has splendid photographs of Wilde and his contemporaries and also provides a concise factual account of his life. The essays by Ian Fletcher and John Stokes in *Anglo-Irish Literature: A Review of Research*, 1976, and *Recent Research on Anglo-Irish Writers*, 1983 (both ed. Richard J. Finneran), provide a full-scale guide to editions of Wilde and studies of his life and work.

Oscar Wilde: A Collection of Critical Essays, ed. Richard Ellmann, 1969, is valuable for its coverage of responses to Wilde by other writers such as Yeats and Shaw. *Oscar Wilde: The Critical Heritage*, ed. Karl Beckson, 1970, is especially helpful with regard to the plays; it covers the period 1881–1927. For an account of the contemporary reception of Wilde, see Regina Gagnier, *Idylls of the Marketplace: Oscar Wilde and the Victorian Public*, 1986. See also Camille Paglia, *Sexual Personae*, 1990; *Critical Essays on Oscar Wilde*, ed. Regina Gagnier, 1991; Ed Cohen, *Talk on the Wilde Side: Toward a Genealogy of Discourse on Male Sexualities*, 1993; Gary Schmidgall, *The Stranger Wilde: Interpreting Oscar*, 1994; Lawrence Damson, *Wilde's Intentions:*

The Artist in His Criticism, 1997; The Cambridge Companion to Oscar Wilde, ed. Peter Raby, 1997; and Karl Beckson, The Oscar Wilde Encyclopedia, 1998. Harold Bloom has edited two anthologies of

critical essays: Oscar Wilde: Modern Critical Views, 1985, and Oscar Wilde's The Importance of Being Earnest: Modern Critical Interpretations, 1988. See also entries under The Nineties.

THE TWENTIETH CENTURY

Martin Gilbert, A History of the Twentieth Century, vol. 1, 1900–33, 1997, and vol. 2, 1933–51, 1998, offers a richly informative and readable account of the first half-century; while Peter Conrad, Modern Times, Modern Places, 1998, skillfully interweaves the history of the period with its artistic and intellectual movements.

The social and political background is well covered in Paul Fussell, The Great War and Modern Memory, 1975, and Wartime: Understanding and Behaviour in the Second World War, 1989; Robert Graves and Alan Hodge, The Long Week-End: A Social History of Great Britain, 1918–1939, 1940; The Baldwin Age, ed. John Raymond, 1960; Julian Symons, The Thirties, rev, 1975; Samuel Hynes, The Auden Generation: Literature and Politics in England in the 1930s, 1976, and A War Imagined: The First World War and British Culture, 1990; Hugh Thomas, The Spanish Civil War, 1986; Valentine Cunningham, British Writers of the Thirties, 1988; Malcolm Bradbury, The Social Context of Modern English Literature, 1971; and The Twentieth-Century Mind: History, Ideas, and Literature in Britain, 3 vols., ed. C. B. Cox and A. E. Dyson, 1972, all of which include useful bibliographies.

The following critical works deal with general aspects of modern English literature: Stephen Spender, The Struggle of the Modern, 1963; C. K. Stead, The New Poetic: Yeats to Eliot, 1964, and Pound, Yeats, Eliot, and the Modernists, 1986, M. L. Rosenthal and Sally M. Gall, The Modern Poetic Sequence: The Genius of Modern Poetry, 1983; The Modern Tradition: Backgrounds of Modern Literature, ed. Richard Ellmann and Charles Feidelson, 1965; Irving Howe, The Idea of the Modern, 1968; Hugh Kenner, The Pound Era, 1971; Modernism 1890–1930, ed. Malcolm Bradbury and James McFarlane, 1976; Robert Hughes, The Shock of the New, 1981; Carol T. Christ, Victorian and Modern Poetics, 1984; Sanford Schwartz, The Matrix of Modernism: Pound, Eliot and Early Twentieth-Century Thought, 1985; Maud Ellmann, The Poetics of Impersonality: T. S. Eliot and Ezra Pound, 1987; Perry Meisel, The Myth of the Modern: A Study in British Literature and Criticism after 1850, 1987; James Longenbach, Stone Cottage: Pound, Yeats, and Modernism, 1988; John Bayley, The Short Story: Henry James to Elizabeth Bowen, 1988; Sandra Gilbert and Susan Gubar, No Man's Land: The Place of the Woman Writer in the Twentieth Century, 3 vols., 1988–; George Watson, British Literature since 1945, 1991; and Joseph Bristow, Effeminate England: Homoerotic Writing after 1885, 1995.

Useful reference books include John L. Somer and Barbara Eck Cooper, American and British Literature 1945–1975: An Annotated Bibliography of Contemporary Scholarship, 1980; An Annotated Critical Bibliography of Modernism, ed. Alistair Davies, 1982; Contemporary Dramatists, 5th ed., ed. K. A. Berney, 1993; Contemporary Novelists, 4th ed., ed. D. L. Kirkpatrick and James Vinson, 1986; Contemporary Poets, ed. Thomas Riggs, 1996; The Oxford Companion to Twentieth-Century Poetry, ed. Ian Hamilton, 1994; and The Oxford Companion to Irish Literature, ed. Robert Welch, 1996.

See also entries for The Rise and Fall of Empire, Voices from World War I, and Voices from World War II.

Chinua Achebe

Achebe's first novel, Things Fall Apart, published in 1958, was the first of three known collectively as The African Trilogy. The others, No Longer at Ease and Arrow of God, were published in 1960 and 1964, respectively. A Man of the People was published in 1966, and Anthills of the Savannah in 1987. Collections of short stories include The Sacrificial Egg and Other Stories, 1962, and Girls at War and Other Stories, 1972. A collection of poems, Beware, Soul-Brother, and Other Poems, was published in 1971, and revised and enlarged the following year. Nonfiction writing includes Morning Yet on Creation Day: Essays, 1975; The Trouble with Nigeria, 1983; Hopes and Impediments: Selected Essays 1965–1987, 1988; The University and the Leadership Factor in Nigerian Politics, 1988, and Beyond Hunger in Africa: Conventional Wisdom and a Vision of Africa in 2057, 1990. For children he has written Chike and the River, 1966; How the Leopard Got his Claws, 1976, and The Flute and the Drum, 1977. He was editor of The Heinemann Book of Contemporary African Short Stories, 1992, and coeditor of The Insider: Stories of War and Peace from Nigeria, 1971, and of African Short Stories, 1985. For his life see Chinua Achebe: A Biography, ed. Ezenwa Ohaeto, 1997, and B. M. Okpu, Chinua Achebe: A Bibliography, 1984.

Critical material includes Arthur Ravenscroft, Chinua Achebe, 1977; C. L. Innes, Chinua Achebe, 1990; Kole Omotoso, Achebe or Soyinka? A Study in Contrasts, 1996; David Carroll, Chinua Achebe: Novelist, Poet, Critic, 2nd rev. ed. 1990; Simon Gikandi, Reading Chinua Achebe: Language and Ideology in Fiction, 1991; and G. D. Killam, The Novels of Chinua Achebe, Studies in African Literature Series, rev. ed. 1977. Useful contextual information is provided by Robert M. Wren, Achebe's

World: The Historical and Cultural Context of the Novels of Chinua Achebe, 1980, and Emmanuel Meziemadu Okoye, *The Traditional Religion and Its Encounter with Christianity in Achebe's Novels*, 1987. A collection of essays celebrating Achebe's achievement, *Chinua Achebe: A Celebration*, ed. Kirsten Holst Petersen and Anna Rutherford, was published in 1991. Critical studies of Achebe's *Things Fall Apart* include Christopher Heywood, *Chinua Achebe*, Things Fall Apart: *A Critical View*, 1985; Solomon Ogbede Iyasere, *Understanding* Things Fall Apart: *Selected Essays and Criticism*, 1998; and Kate Turkington, *Chinua Achebe*, Things Fall Apart, 1977. A useful section on Achebe as a postcolonial writer appears in Michael Parker, *Postcolonial Literatures: Achebe, Ngugi, Desai, Walcott*, 1995.

Fleur Adcock

Selected Poems, 1983, includes work from *The Eye of the Hurricane*, 1964; *Tigers*, 1967; *High Tide in the Garden*, 1971; *The Scenic Route*, 1974; and *The Inner Harbour*, 1979. She has since published three books of poetry: *The Incident Book*, 1986; *Time-Zones*, 1991, and *Looking Back*, 1997. Adcock has also translated medieval Latin secular poetry in *The Virgin and the Nightingale*, 1983, and selections from the work of two Romanian poets: Grete Tartler (*Orient Express*, 1989) and Daniela Crasnaru (*Letters from Darkness*, 1991). She has edited *The Oxford Book of Contemporary New Zealand Poetry*, 1982, and *The Faber Book of Twentieth Century Women's Poetry*, 1987, and is the coeditor, with Jacqueline Simms, of *The Oxford Book of Creatures*, 1995.

She has contributed an autobiographical essay to *Contemporary Authors: Autobiography Series*, 23 (1996). There is an article on her work by Bill Ruddock in *Critical Quarterly*, 26, (1984), and a full-length study by Julian Stannard, *Fleur Adcock in Context: From Movement to Martians*, 1997.

W. H. Auden

W. H. Auden: Collected Poems, ed. Edward Mendelson, 1976, contains all the poems that the author wished to preserve, in the texts that received his final approval. *The English Auden, Poems, Essays and Dramatic Writings, 1927–1939*, ed. Edward Mendelson, 1977, reprints in their original versions all the poems Auden published in book form during the 1930s, together with some previously unpublished and uncollected poems and a selection of Auden's early prose writings. The definitive collected edition of his works now proceeds, under the editorship of Edward Mendelson, *Plays and Other Dramatic Writings by W. H. Auden, 1928–1938*, 1989; *Libretti, and Other Dramatic Writings 1939–1973*, 1993; and *Prose and Travel Books in Prose and Verse*, Vol. 1, *1926–1938*, 1996. The precanonical poems are available in *Juvenilia 1922–1928*, ed. Katherine Bucknell, 1994. *The Dyer's Hand and Other Essays*, 1968, brings together a selection of his stimulating literary-critical articles, lectures, and reviews. *Forewords and Afterwards*, 1973, is a comparable collection. Auden edited a number of anthologies, including (with Norman

Pearson) *Poets of the English Language*, 5 vols., 1950; (with Noah Greenberg and Chester Kallman) *An Elizabethan Songbook*, 1955; and *The Elder Edda: A Selection*, 1969. The best critical studies are M. K. Spears, *The Poetry of W. H. Auden*, 1963; Justin Replogle, *Auden's Poetry*, 1969; Edward Mendelson, *Early Auden*, 1981; Edward Callan, *Auden: A Carnival of Intellect*, 1983; Stan Smith, *W. H. Auden*, 1985; Lucy McDiarmid, *Auden's Apologies for Poetry*, 1990; and Edward Mendelson, *Later Auden*, 1999. John Fuller, *W. H. Auden: A Commentary*, 1998, provides a commentary on Auden's poetry and drama in chronological order; and Samuel Hynes, *The Auden Generation: Literature and Politics in England in the 1930s*, 1976, is an illuminating study of Auden and his contemporaries in their historical context. The most comprehensive biography is Humphrey Carpenter, *W. H. Auden: A Biography*, 1981, but that by Richard Davenport-Hines, 1995, is a strongly conceived and thematic study. The standard bibliography is by Edward Mendelson and B. C. Bloomfield, 2nd ed., 1972, updated in *Auden Studies*, ed. Katherine Bucknell and Nicholas Jenkins, of which three volumes have so far appeared, 1990, 1994, and 1995.

Samuel Beckett

The standard biography is James Knowlson, *Doomed to Fame: The Life of Samuel Beckett*, 1996, but see also Anthony Cronin, *Samuel Beckett: The Last Modernist*, 1996, and *Conversations with and about Beckett*, ed. Mel Gussow, 1996. On the biographical background to the early work, see John Pilling, *Beckett before Godot*, 1998. Hugh Kenner, *A Reader's Guide to Samuel Beckett*, 1973, and A. Alvarez, *Samuel Beckett*, 1973, are good introductions to his work. On the plays, see Ruby Cohn, *Just Play: Beckett's Theatre*, 1980; Beryl Fletcher and John Fletcher, *A Student's Guide to the Plays of Samuel Beckett*, 1985; and, for the later drama, Rosemary Pountney, *Theatre of Shadows: Samuel Beckett's Drama 1956–1976*, 1998. On the fiction, see Ray Federman, *Journey to Chaos: Samuel Beckett's Early Fiction*, 1965; Rubin Rabinovitz, *Innovation in Samuel Beckett's Fiction*, 1992; and Bob Cochran, *Samuel Beckett: A Study of the Short Fiction*, 1992. On the later work in general, see Steven Connor, *Samuel Beckett: Repetition Theory and Text*, 1986; and Enoch Brater, *Beyond Minimalism: Beckett's Late Style in the Theatre*, 1987, and *The Drama in the Text: Beckett's Late Fiction*, 1994. Among many good general studies are *The Cambridge Companion to Beckett*, ed. John Pilling, 1994; Vivian Mercier, *Beckett/Beckett*, 1977; and Christopher Ricks, *Beckett's Dying Words*, 1993. Also very useful is *Samuel Beckett: The Critical Heritage*, ed. Lawrence Graver and Ray Federman, 1979. There is a Beckett Archive at the University of Reading, and the twice-yearly *Journal of Beckett Studies* began publication in 1976.

Eavan Boland

Boland's first published poems appeared in the pamphlet *23 Poems*, 1962, and her first full-length volume was *New Territory: Poems*, 1967. This was followed by *The War Horse: Poems*, 1975; *In Her Own Image*, 1980; and *Night Feed: Poems*, 1982. Her first volume to be published in Britain was *The Journey and Other Poems*, 1987, which was followed two years later by her *Selected Poems*, 1989. More recent volumes include *Outside History*, 1990; *In a Time of Violence*, 1994; and *Collected Poems*, 1995.

Rupert Brooke
The Poetical Works, 2nd ed., 1970, and *The Letters*, 1968, are both edited by G. L. Keynes. *The Prose* is edited by Christopher Hassall, 1956, who wrote the standard biography, *Rupert Brooke*, 1964. *Song of Love: The Letters of Rupert Brooke and Noel Olivier* is edited by Pippa Harris, 1991, and *Friends & Apostles: The Correspondence of Rupert Brooke and James Strachey* was written by Keith Hale, 1998. There is a group portrait, Paul Delany, *The Neopagans: Friendship and Love in the Rupert Brooke Circle*, 1987; and critical discussions in Walter de la Mare, "Rupert Brooke and the Intellectual Imagination," in his *Pleasures and Speculations*, 1940; John H. Johnston, *English Poetry of the First World War*, 1964; Bernard Bergonzi, *Heroes' Twilight*, 1965; and *Rupert Brooke: A Reappraisal and Selection from His Writings, Some Hitherto Unpublished*, ed. Timothy Rogers, 1971.

See entries under **Voices from World War I**.

May Wedderburn Cannan
Cannan published three collections of poems—*In War Time*, 1917, *The Splendid Days*, 1919, and *The House of Hope*, 1923—and a novel, *The Lonely Generation*, 1934. Her unfinished autobiography, *Grey Ghosts and Voices*, appeared posthumously in 1976.

See entries under **Voices from World War I**.

Charles Causley
Causley's many publications include his *Collected Poems, 1951–97*, 1997, as well as plays, short stories, and anthologies. There is critical discussion of his poetry in Elizabeth Jennings, *Poetry Today 1957–60*, 1961; Anthony Thwaite, *Poetry Today 1960–73*, 1973; Vernon Scannell, *Not Without Glory: Poets of the Second World War*, 1976; Edward Levy, "The Poetry of Charles Causley," in *PN Review* 5.2, 1978; Michael Schmidt, *An Introduction to 50 Modern British Poets*, 1979, and *Causley at Seventy*, ed. Harry Chambers, 1987.

See also under entries for **Voices from World War II**.

J. M. Coetzee
Coetzee's *Dusklands*, 1974, consists of two linked novellas. It was followed by the novels *In the Heart of the Country*, 1977, published as *From the Heart of the Country* in the United States; *Waiting for the Barbarians*, 1980; *Life and Times of Michael K.*, 1983; *Foe*, 1986; *Age of Iron*, 1990; and *The Master of Petersburg*, 1994. His nonfiction writing includes *Truth in Autobiography*, 1984; *White Writing: On the Culture of Letters in South Africa*, 1988; *Doubling the Point: Essays and Interviews*, 1992, and *Giving Offense: Essays on Censorship*, 1996. Kevin Goddard, John Read and Teresa Dovey, *J. M. Coet-*

zee: A Bibliography, 1990, is comprehensive of the work to 1990. The most inclusive overview of Coetzee's fiction to date is Dominic Head, *J. M. Coetzee*, 1997, although Dick Penner, *Countries of the Mind: The Fiction of J. M. Coetzee*, 1989, is illuminative of work up to and including *Foe*. Coetzee is examined as a specifically South African writer in David Attwell, *J. M. Coetzee: South Africa and the Politics of Writing*, 1993, and Susan VanZanten Gallagher, *A Story of South Africa: J. M. Coetzee's Fiction in Context*, 1991. More specialized is Claudia Egerer, *Fictions of Inbetweenness*, 1997. An impressive essay dedicated to *Foe* is Derek Attridge, "Oppressive Silence: J. M. Coetzee's *Foe* and the Politics of the Canon" in *Decolonizing Tradition: New Views of Twentieth Century "British" Literary Canon*, ed. Karen R. Lawrence, 1992.

Joseph Conrad
The standard edition of Conrad's works is *The Uniform Edition of the Works of Joseph Conrad*, 22 vols., 1923–38, rpt. 1946–55 as the *Collected Edition of the Works of Joseph Conrad*. Useful critical essays and notes to the novels are provided by the Norton Critical Editions of *Heart of Darkness*, 3rd ed., ed. Robert Kimbrough, 1987; *Lord Jim*, ed. Thomas C. Moser, 1968; and *The Nigger of the "Narcissus,"* ed. Robert Kimbrough, 1979. The Modern Library edition of *Nostromo*, 1951, also contains an illuminating introductory essay by Robert Penn Warren. Five volumes of Conrad's letters to 1916 have been published as *The Collected Letters of Joseph Conrad*, ed. Frederick R. Karl and Laurence Davies, 1983–96, and *Letters from Joseph Conrad*, ed. Edward Garnett, 1928, and are supplemented by material in *Joseph Conrad's Letters to R. B. Cunninghame Graham*, ed. C. T. Watts, 1969. Letters concerning as well as by Conrad are collected in *A Portrait in Letters: Correspondence to and about Conrad*, ed. John H. Stape and Owen Knowles, 1996. The most comprehensive biographies are John Batchelor, *The Life of Joseph Conrad: A Critical Biography*, 1993; Frederick Karl, *Joseph Conrad: The Three Lives: A Biography*, 1979; Zdzislaw Najder, *Joseph Conrad: A Chronicle*, 1983, and Cedric Watts, *Joseph Conrad: A Literary Life*, 1989. Memoirs of Conrad include Jessie Conrad, *Joseph Conrad As I Knew Him*, 1926, and *Joseph Conrad and His Circle*, 1935, and Ford Madox Ford, *Joseph Conrad: A Personal Remembrance*, 1989. See also material collected in *Joseph Conrad: Interviews and Recollections*, ed. Martin Ray, 1990. The standard bibliography is *Joseph Conrad: An Annotated Bibliography*, ed. Bruce Teets, 1990.

Robert Hampson, *Joseph Conrad: Betrayal and Identity*, 1992, looks at Conrad's early work, whereas Garry Geddes, *Conrad's Later Novels*, 1980, and Thomas Moser, *Joseph Conrad, Achievement and Decline*, 1957, look at the later work. Studies of the political novels include Eloise Knapp Hay, *The Political Novels of Joseph Conrad*, rev. ed. 1981; Clare Rosenfield, *Paradise of Snakes*, 1967; and Avrom Fleishman, *Conrad's Politics: Community and Anarchy in the Fiction of Joseph Conrad*,

1967. A feminist perspective is offered by Heliéna Krenn, *Conrad's Lingard Trilogy: Empire, Race and Women in the Malay Novels*, 1990, and Ruth Nadelhaft, *Joseph Conrad*, 1991. Conrad is examined through postcolonial theories in Gail Fincham and Myrtle Hooper, *Under Postcolonial Eyes: Joseph Conrad after Empire*, 1996, and Christopher L. GoGwilt, *The Invention of the West: Joseph Conrad and the Double-Mapping of Europe and Empire*, 1995. Also important are John Batchelor, *Lord Jim*, 1988; *Joseph Conrad*, ed. Harold Bloom, 1986; *Joseph Conrad: Critical Assessments*, 4 vols, ed. Keith Carabine, 1992; Peter J. Glassman, *Language and Being: Joseph Conrad and the Literature of Personality*, 1976; Albert J. Guerard, *Conrad the Novelist*, 1958; Jakob Lothe, *Conrad's Narrative Method*, 1989; *Conrad on Film*, ed. Gene M. Moore, 1997; Zdzislaw Najder, *Conrad in Perspective: Essays on Art and Fidelity*, 1997; *Joseph Conrad*, Longman Critical Reader Series, ed. Andrew Michael Roberts, 1998; Edward Said, *Joseph Conrad and the Fiction of Autobiography*, 1966; Daniel R. Schwarz, *Conrad: Almayer's Folly Through Under Western Eyes*, 1980; *Conrad: The Critical Heritage*, ed. Norman Sherry, 1973; *The Cambridge Companion to Joseph Conrad*, ed. J. H. Stape, 1996; Daphna Erdinast Vulcan, *Joseph Conrad and the Modern Temper*, 1991; Ian Watt, *Conrad in the Nineteenth Century*, 1981 (a monumental work, but concerned only with the period before 1900); Cedric Watts, *A Preface to Conrad*, 1982; Anthony Winner, *Culture and Irony: Studies in Joseph Conrad's Major Novels*, 1988, and Mark A. Wollaeger, *Joseph Conrad and the Fictions of Skepticism*, 1990. Important essays on Conrad's work can be found in Dorothy Van Ghent, *The English Novel: Form and Function*, 1953; Warwick Gould, *Modernist Writers and the Marketplace*, 1996; Frederic Jameson, *The Political Unconscious: Narrative as a Socially Symbolic Act*, 1981, and Vincent P. Pecora, *Self and Form in Modern Narrative*, 1989.

Anita Desai

Among Desai's earliest works are *Cry, the Peacock*, 1963, and *Voices in the City*, 1965. Later fiction includes *Bye-Bye, Blackbird*, 1971; *Where Shall We Go This Summer?*, 1975; *Fire on the Mountain*, 1977; *The Peacock Garden*, 1979; *Clear Light of Day*, 1980; *In Custody*, 1984; *Baumgartner's Bombay*, 1988, and *Journey to Ithaca*, 1995. She has also written collections of short stories, including *Games at Twilight, and Other Stories*, 1978, and children's fiction, including *The Village by the Sea: An Indian Family Story*, 1982. Kunj Bala Goel provides analysis of the structure and style of Desai's writing in *Language and Theme in Anita Desai's Fiction*, 1989, and overviews of the works can be found in Radhe Shyam Sharma, *Anita Desai*, Indian Writers Series, 1981; Madhusudan Prasad, *Anita Desai the Novelist*, 1981, and *Perspectives on Anita Desai*, ed. R. K. Srivastava, 1984. More recent critical works include Usha Bande, *The Novels of Anita Desai: A Study in Character and Conflict*, 1988; Jasbir Jain, *Stairs to

the Attic: The Novels of Anita Desai*, 1989, and *The Fiction of Anita Desai*, ed. R. K. Dhawan, 1989. There are sections on Desai in Fawzia Afzal-Khan, *Cultural Imperialism and the Indo-English Novel: Genre and Ideal in R. K. Narajan, Anita Desai, Kamala Markandaya and Salman Rushdie*, 1993, and *Postcolonial Literatures: Achebe, Ngugi, Desai, Walcott*, ed. Michael Parker and Roger Starkey, 1995.

Keith Douglas

The Complete Poems of Keith Douglas. 3rd ed., 1998, his memoir of the Desert War, *Alamein to Zem Zem*, rev. 1979, and *Keith Douglas: A Prose Miscellany*, 1985, were all edited by Desmond Graham, who also wrote *Keith Douglas, 1920–1944: A Biography*. Further critical discussion of Douglas's poems is to be found in Vernon Scannell, *Not Without Glory: Poets of the Second World War*, 1976.

See entries under **Voices from World War II.**

T. S. Eliot

The fullest one-volume collections of Eliot's poetry are *Collected Poems, 1909–1963*, 1963, and *The Complete Poems and Plays*, including *Poems Written in Early Youth*, 1969. *The Waste Land: A Facsimile and Transcript of the Original Drafts including the Annotations of Ezra Pound*, ed. Valerie Eliot, 1971, is an indispensable tool for study of *The Waste Land*. See also *Inventions of the March Hare, Poems 1909–17*, ed. Christopher Ricks, 1996. Eliot's most important critical essays are to be found in *The Sacred Wood: Essays on Poetry and Criticism*, 1921; *The Use of Poetry and the Use of Criticism: Studies in the Relation of Criticism to Poetry in England*, 1923; *Notes Towards the Definition of Culture*, 1948; *On Poetry and Poets*, 1957; *To Criticize the Critic and Other Writings*, 1965; and *The Varieties of Metaphysical Poetry*, ed. Ronald Schuchard, 1993. Helen Gardner, *The Composition of Four Quartets*, 1978, describes the growth of the poem from the drafts, and includes new information on its sources.

In the absence of a full-scale biography, one is the more grateful for *Notes on Some Figures behind T. S. Eliot*, Herbert Howarth, 1965; *T. S. Eliot: The Man and His Work*, ed. Allen Tate, 1967; Ronald Bush, *T. S. Eliot: A Study in Character and Style*, 1984; Peter Ackroyd, *T. S. Eliot*, 1984; *The Letters of T. S. Eliot*, Vol. 1: *1898–1922*, ed. Valerie Eliot, 1988; and Lyndall Gordon, *T. S. Eliot: An Imperfect Life*, 1998.

Among the many books on Eliot, F. O. Matthiessen, *The Achievement of T. S. Eliot*, rev. ed. 1947, has the enthusiasm of a pioneer work; Helen Gardner, *The Art of T. S. Eliot*, 1950, is a perceptive critical study of his poetry; B. C. Southam, *A Student's Guide to the Selected Poems of T. S. Eliot*, rev. ed., 1994, and *T. S. Eliot: The Critical Heritage*, 2 vols, ed. Michael Grant, 1982, are useful reference sources for students, and Grover Smith Jr., *T. S. Eliot's Poetry and Plays*, 1956, goes through the poems and plays in an exhaustive manner. More specialized studies include *The Making of T. S.

Eliot's Plays, Martin Browne, 1969; *Eliot in His Time*, ed. A. Walton Litz, 1973; A. D. Moody, *Thomas Stearns Eliot, Poet*, 1979; Grover Smith, "*The Waste Land*," 1983; Louis Menand, *Discovering Modernism: T. S. Eliot and His Context*, 1987; Robert Crawford, *The Savage and the City in the Work of T. S. Eliot*, 1987; Richard Shusterman, *T. S. Eliot and the Philosophy of Criticism*, 1988; Maud Ellmann, *The Poetics of Impersonality*, 1988; Jeffrey M. Perl, *Scepticism and Modern Enmity: Before and after Eliot*, 1989; Eric Sigg, *The American T. S. Eliot: A Study of the Early Writings*, 1989; Ronald Bush, *T. S. Eliot, The Modernist in History*, 1991; Manju Jain, *T. S. Eliot and American Philosophy: The Harvard Years*, 1992; Gail McDonald, *Learning to Be Modern: Pound, Eliot, and the American University*, 1993; Frank Lentricchia, *Modernist Quartet*, 1994; and Anthony Julius, *T. S. Eliot, Anti-Semitism, and Literary Form*, 1995.

James Fenton

The Memory of War: Poems 1968–1982, 1982, contains a selection from Fenton's previous book, *Terminal Moraine*, 1972, and pamphlets, notably *A German Requiem*, 1981, as well as poems previously uncollected. He has since published *Children in Exile*, 1984, *Manila Envelope*, 1989, *Out of Danger*, 1993, and a prose book, *All the Wrong Places: Adrift in the Politics of Asia*, 1988; and contributed an interview to the *Poetry Review* 72.2 (June 1982).

E. M. Forster

Forster's five major novels—*Where Angels Fear to Tread*, 1905; *The Longest Journey*, 1907; *A Room With a View*, 1910; *Howards End*, 1910; and *A Passage to India*, 1924—are available in various editions. The best and most recent is the Abinger Edition of Forster's works, ed. Oliver Stallybrass and Elizabeth Heine, which will eventually include all Forster's writings. A sixth novel, *Maurice*, was finished in 1914 but published posthumously in 1971. A homosexual romance, it adds nothing to Forster's reputation as a novelist. *The Collected Tales of E. M. Forster* appeared in 1947, *The Life to Come and Other Stories* posthumously in 1972. *Abinger Harvest*, a collection of some eighty essays, was published in 1927, *Two Cheers for Democracy*, a second collection, in 1951. Forster's casual but provocative study of fictional technique, *Aspects of the Novel*, appeared in 1927. His biography of his aunt, *Marianne Thornton*, 1956, is an illuminating contribution to Victorian social history.

There is a candid biography, *E. M. Forster: A Life*, vols. 1 and 2, 1977, 1978, by P. N. Furbank, who, with Mary Lago, edited Forster's *Selected Letters*, vols. 1 and 2, 1983, 1985. Philip Gardner has edited *E. M. Forster's Commonplace Book*, 1986, and *E. M. Forster: The Critical Heritage*, 1973; and P. J. Kirkpatrick has published *A Bibliography of E. M. Forster*, 1986.

Among the many critical studies of Forster's work, of particular interest are Lionel Trilling, *E. M. Forster*, 2nd rev. ed., 1965; Frederick Crews, *E. M. Forster: The Perils of Humanism*, 1962; Wilfred

Stone, *The Cave and the Mountain: A Study of E. M. Forster*, 1966; G. K. Das, *E. M. Forster's India*, 1977; and Barbara Rosecrance, *Forster's Narrative Vision*, 1982.

Nadine Gordimer

Gordimer's work includes the novels *The Lying Days*, 1953; *The Late Bourgeois World*, 1966; *A Guest of Honour*, 1971; *A World of Strangers*, 1976; *The Conservationist*, 1976; *Burger's Daughter*, 1979; *July's People*, 1981; *A Sport of Nature*, 1987; *My Son's Story*, 1990; *None to Accompany Me*, 1994; and *The House Gun*, 1998. The short-story collections are *Six Feet of the Country*, 1956; *Some Monday for Sure*, 1976; *A Soldier's Embrace*, 1980; *Something Out There*, 1984; and *Jump*, 1991. She has also published two collections of nonfiction essays, *The Essential Gesture: Writing, Politics and Places*, ed. Stephen Clingman, and *Writing and Being*, 1995. Critical accounts of her work include Michael Wade, *Nadine Gordimer*, 1978; Stephen Clingman, *The Novels of Nadine Gordimer: History from the Inside*, 1986; a chapter in Abdul R. JanMohamed, *Manichean Aesthetics: The Politics of Literature in Colonial Africa*, 1983; Judie Newman, *Nadine Gordimer*, 1988; *Critical Essays on Nadine Gordimer*, ed. Rowland Smith, 1990; *The Later Fiction of Nadine Gordimer*, ed. Bruce King, 1993; and Andrew V. Ettin, *Betrayals of the Body Politic: The Literary Commitments of Nadine Gordimer*, 1993.

Robert Graves

Robert Graves: The Complete Poems in three volumes, 1995, 1997, 1999 is the most recent and complete editions of his twelve hundred poems. Edited by his wife, Beryl Graves, and by Dunstan Ward, these volumes contain relevant bibliographical and textual notes. *Collected Poems 1975*, 1975, has a biographical introduction by James McKinley. Of Graves's many prose works, the most relevant to a study of his poetry are *Good-bye to All That*, rev. 1957, an autobiography written when he was thirty-three; *The Common Asphodel: Collected Essays on Poetry*, 1949; *On Poetry: Collected Talks and Essays*, 1969; *The White Goddess*, 1948, enlarged ed., 1966; and *In Broken Images: Selected Letters of Robert Graves, 1914–1946*, 1982, and *Between Moon and Moon: Selected Letters of Robert Graves, 1946–1972*, 1984, both edited by Paul O'Prey. Martin Seymour Smith, *Robert Graves: His Life and Works*, 2nd ed. 1995; Richard Perceval Graves, *Robert Graves: The Assault Heroic 1895–1926*, 1986, *Robert Graves—The Years with Laura, 1926–1940*, 1990, and *Robert Graves and the White Goddess 1940–1985*, 1995; and Miranda Seymour, *Robert Graves: Life on the Edge*, 1995, are indispensable biographies. There is also Fred H. Higginson and William Proctor Williams, *A Bibliography of the Writings of Robert Graves*, 2nd ed., 1988.

The most perceptive critical studies are Douglas Day, *Swifter Than Reason, The Poetry and Criticism of Robert Graves*, 1963; Michael Kirkham, *The Poetry of Robert Graves*, 1969; *Robert Graves*, ed. Harold Bloom, 1987; D. N. G. Carter, *Robert*

The Lasting Poetic Achievement, 1989; and ...ck J. Quinn, *The Great War and the Missing ...use: The Early Writings of Robert Graves and Siegfried Sassoon*, 1994.

Thom Gunn

Gunn's publications include *Fighting Terms*, 1954, rev. 1962; *The Sense of Movement*, 1957; *The Misanthrope*, 1958; *My Sad Captains*, 1961; *Touch*, 1967; *Positives*, 1967; *Poems 1950–1966*, 1969; *Moly*, 1971; *Jack Straw's Castle*, 1975; *Selected Poems 1950–1975*, 1979; *Lament*, 1985; *The Hurtless Trees*, 1986; *Undesirables*, 1988; and *The Man with Night Sweats*, 1992. Gunn contributed an interview to *Viewpoints: Poets in Conversation with John Haffenden*, 1981, and Clive Wilmer has edited Gunn's *The Occasions of Poetry: Essays in Criticism and Autobiography*, 1985. There is some critical discussion of his poetry in John Press, *Rule and Energy: Trends in British Poetry since the Second World War*, 1963, and *British Poetry since 1960: A Critical Survey*, ed. Michael Schmidt and Grevel Lindop, 1972. *PN Review*, 70 (1989), devoted chiefly to Gunn, contains useful discussion of his work; and George Bixby, *Thom Gunn: A Bibliography 1940–1978*, 1979, lists interviews as well as poems and articles.

Ivor Gurney

Two collections of poems were published in Gurney's lifetime: *Severn and Somme*, 1917, and *War's Embers*, 1919, but he left at his death some seven hundred unpublished poems. The most comprehensive selection of his work is the *Collected Poems of Ivor Gurney*, ed. P. J. Kavanagh, 1983. A selection of his *War Letters* has been edited by R. K. R. Thornton, 1983, and there is a good biography, Michael Hurd, *The Ordeal of Ivor Gurney*, 1978. Critical discussion of Gurney's poetry is to be found in Jon Silkin, *Out of Battle*, 1972, and Paul Fussell, *The Great War and Modern Memory*, 1975.

See entries under **Voices from World War I.**

Thomas Hardy

Hardy published over a dozen volumes of poetry in his lifetime; *The Collected Poems* were issued in one volume in 1932; and *The Complete Poetical Works of Thomas Hardy*, ed. Samuel Hynes, in three volumes in 1982–85. There are several collected editions of Hardy's complete work, notably the Wessex Edition, 21 vols., 1912–14, and the Mellstock Edition, 37 vols., 1919–20. Many of the novels are in paperbound editions; among the most notable are the Norton Critical Editions of *Jude the Obscure*, ed. Norman Page, 1978; *The Mayor of Casterbridge*, ed. James K. Robinson, 1977; *The Return of the Native*, ed. James Gindin, 1969; and *Tess of the D'Urbervilles*, 3rd ed., ed. Scott Elledge, 1990.

The best biographies are Robert Gittings, *Young Thomas Hardy*, 1975, and *Thomas Hardy's Later Years*, 1978; Michael Millgate, *Thomas Hardy: A Biography*, 1982; and Paul Turner, *The Life of Thomas Hardy*, 1998. Michael Millgate and R. Purdy have edited *The Collected Letters of Thomas Hardy*, 7 vols., 1978–88. Millgate has also edited *Selected Letters*, 1990, and Harold Orel has edited *Thomas Hardy's Personal Writings: Prefaces, Literary Opinions, Reminiscences*, 1990.

The Hardy Centennial Number of *The Southern Review*, 1940, was influential in shaping Hardy's critical reputation: the special Hardy issues of *Agenda*, 1970, and *Victorian Poetry*, 1979, are notable. *Hardy: A Collection of Critical Essays*, ed. Albert Guerard, 1963, treats both the prose and the poetry, as do J. Hillis Miller, *Thomas Hardy: Distance and Desire*, 1970; Jean R. Brooks, *Thomas Hardy: The Poetic Structure*, 1971; John Bayley, *An Essay on Hardy*, 1978; *Thomas Hardy After Fifty Years*, ed. Lance St. John Butler, 1977; and *Thomas Hardy: The Writer and His Background*, ed. Norman Page, 1980, which contains a useful bibliography. Ian Gregor, *The Great Web: The Form of Hardy's Major Fiction*, 1974, and *Critical Approaches to the Fiction of Thomas Hardy*, ed. Dale Kramer, 1979, provide good discussions of Hardy's novels. Samuel Hynes, *The Pattern of Hardy's Poetry*, 1956, remains sound and useful; Donald Davie, *Thomas Hardy and British Poetry*, 1973, is worth consulting. Paul Zeitlow, *Moments of Vision: The Poetry of Thomas Hardy*, 1974; Tom Paulin, *Thomas Hardy: The Poetry of Perception*, 1975; *The Poetry of Thomas Hardy*, ed. Patricia Clements and Juliet Grindle, 1980; William Earl Buckler, *The Poetry of Thomas Hardy: A Study in Art and Ideas*, 1983; and Dennis Taylor, *Hardy's Metres and Victorian Prosody*, 1988, contain good criticism of the poetry; J. O. Bailey, *The Poetry of Thomas Hardy*, 1970, and F. B. Pinion, *A Commentary on the Poems of Thomas Hardy*, 1976, are helpful on individual poems.

Tony Harrison

The second, expanded edition of Harrison's *Selected Poems*, 1987, contains representative selections from earlier collections, as well as new material, and there have been two subsequent collections, *A Cold Coming: Gulf War Poems*, 1991, and *The Gaze of the Gorgon*, 1992. There have been two collections of dramatic verse: *Theatre Works 1973–1985*, 1986, and *Plays 3*, 1996; and the uncollected plays: *The Misanthrope*, 1973; *Phaedra Britannica*, 1975; *Bow Down*, 1977; *The Trackers of Oxyrhynchus*, 1990; *The Common Chorus*, 1992; *Square Rounds*, 1992, and *The Prince's Play*, 1996. His television and film work includes *Black Daisies for the Bride*, 1993; *Prometheus*, 1998, and the collection *The Shadow of Hiroshima*, 1995. A bibliography (to 1987) was edited by John Kaiser. Biographical material appears in Joe Kelleher, *Tony Harrison*, British Council Writers and Their Work series, 1996. Criticism of Harrison's work includes an anthology of articles, *Bloodaxe Critical Anthologies 1: Tony Harrison*, ed. Neil Astley, 1991; a collection of essays, *Tony Harrison: Loiner*, ed. S. Byrne, 1997; S. Byrne, *H, v. & O: The Poetry of Tony Harrison*, 1998, and Luke Spencer, *The Poetry of Tony Harrison*, 1994.

Seamus Heaney

Open Ground: Poems 1966–1996, 1998, includes selections from Heaney's earlier collections *Death of a Naturalist*, 1966; *Door into the Dark*, 1969;

Wintering Out, 1972; *North*, 1975; *Field Work*, 1979; *Sweeney Astray*, 1983; *Station Island*, 1984; *The Haw Lantern*, 1987; *Seeing Things*, 1991, and *The Spirit Level*, 1996. He has published three collections of essays: *Preoccupations: Selected Prose, 1968–1978*, 1980; *The Government of the Tongue*, 1988; and *The Redress of Poetry: Oxford Lectures*, 1995. Heaney's verse translation of *Beowulf* (2000) is available in volume 1 of *The Norton Anthology of English Literature*, Seventh Edition. A biography, Michael Parker, *Seamus Heaney: The Making of the Poet*, was published in 1993. Critical and biographical studies include Blake Morrison, *Seamus Heaney*, 1982; Neil Corcoran, *Seamus Heaney: A Faber Study Guide*, 1986; Elmer Andrews, *The Poetry of Seamus Heaney: All the Reams of Whisper*, 1988; Thomas C. Foster, *Seamus Heaney*, 1989; H. Hart, *Seamus Heaney: Poet of Contrary Progressions*, 1992; Bernard O'Donoghue *Seamus Heaney*, 1994; J. W. Foster, *The Achievement of Seamus Heaney*, 1995; and Helen Vendler, *Seamus Heaney*, 1998. Collections of critical essays include *Seamus Heaney*, ed. Harold Bloom, 1988; *Seamus Heaney: A Collection of Critical Essays*, ed. Elmer Andrews, 1992; *The Art of Seamus Heaney*, 3rd ed., ed. Tony Curtis, 1994; and *Critical Essays on Seamus Heaney*, ed. Robert F. Garratt, 1995. Also indispensable is Michael J. Durkan and Rand Brandes, *Seamus Heaney: A Reference Guide*, 1996.

Geoffrey Hill

Hill's first three collections of poems—*For the Unfallen*, 1959; *King Log*, 1968; and *Mercian Hymns*, 1971—were published together in the United States under the title *Somewhere Is Such a Kingdom*, with an introduction by Harold Bloom, 1975. This has been followed by *Tenebrae*, 1978, *The Mystery of the Charity of Charles Péguy*, 1983, *Selected Poems*, 1986; *New and Collected Poems 1952–1992*, 1994; *Canaan*, 1997; and *The Triumph of Love*, 1998. Two collections of prose pieces are *The Lords of Limit: Essays on Literature and Ideas*, 1984, and *The Enemy Country: Words, Contexture, and Other Circumstances of Language*, 1991. There is an interview with Hill in *Viewpoints: Poets in Conversation with John Haffenden*, 1981. The best critical studies are Vincent Sherry, *The Uncommon Tongue: The Poetry and Criticism of Geoffrey Hill*, 1986, and Henry Hart, *The Poetry of Geoffrey Hill*, 1986. Jon Silkin contributed a chapter-length account of Hill's poetry to *British Poetry since 1960: A Critical Survey*, ed. Michael Schmidt and Grevel Lindop, 1972, and there are good critical essays in *Agenda*, Geoffrey Hill Special Issue, 17.1 (Spring 1979); Christopher Ricks, *The Force of Poetry*, 1984; and *Geoffrey Hill: Essays on His Work*, ed. Peter Robinson, 1986.

Richard Hillary

Richard Hillary's autobiographical *The Last Enemy*, 1942, was published in the United States as *Falling Through Space* and was collected, with two other stories of World War II aviation—Guy Gibson, *Enemy Coast Ahead*, and Paul Brickhill, *Reach for the Sky*—as *Great World War II Air Stories* in 1985. Secondary

material on Richard Hillary is largely biographical rather than critical, and includes Michael Burn, *Mary and Richard: The Story of Richard Hillary and Mary Booker*, 1988; Lovat Dickson, *Richard Hillary*, 1950; Terence J. Kean, *The Last Enemy: The Story of Flight Lieutenant R. H. Hillary, R.A.F., One of the Few*, 1993, and a section in Sebastian Faulks, *The Fatal Englishman: Three Short Lives*, 1997.

A. E. Housman

A. E. Housman: Collected Poems and Selected Prose, ed. Christopher Ricks, 1988; and *The Poems of A. E. Housman*, ed. Archie Burnett, 1997, are the best editions of his work. *The Letters of A. E. Housman* were edited by Henry Maas in 1971. The best biography is Norman Page, *A. E. Housman*, 1983. The best criticism is to be found in *A Collection of Critical Essays*, ed. Christopher Ricks, 1968, and John Bayley, *Housman's Poems*, 1992.

Ted Hughes

Hughes's many books of poems include *The Hawk in the Rain*, 1957; *Lupercal*, 1960; *Wodwo*, 1967; *Crow*, 1970, rev. ed. 1972; *Season Songs*, 1976; *Gaudete*, 1977; *Cave Birds*, 1978; *Moortown*, 1979; *Remains of Elmet*, 1979; *River*, 1983; *Flowers and Insects*, 1986; *Wolfwatching*, 1989; *Capriccio: Poems*, 1990; *Rain-Charm for the Duchy and Other Laureate Poems*, 1992; *New Selected Poems, 1957–1994*, 1995; *Tales from Ovid*, 1997, and *Birthday Letters*, 1998. His prose writings include *Poetry in the Making*, 1969; *Shakespeare and the Goddess of Complete Being*, 1992; and *Winter Pollen: Occasional Prose*, 1994. He translated Seneca's *Oedipus*, 1969; edited selections from Shakespeare, Coleridge, Dickinson, and Keith Douglas; and wrote extensively and very successfully for children.

Keith Sagar, *The Art of Ted Hughes*, 2nd ed., 1978, offers a detailed critical account of his work as well as a comprehensive bibliography of writings by and about him. More recent criticism includes Terry Gifford and Neil Roberts, *Ted Hughes: A Critical Study*, 1981, and Thomas West, *Ted Hughes*, 1985.

David Jones

Jones's long poems, *In Parenthesis*, 1937, and *The Anathémata*, 1952, are both available in paperback, as is *Introducing David Jones: A Selection of His Writings*, ed. John Matthias, with a preface by Stephen Spender, 1980. This includes poems from Jones's last collection, *The Sleeping Lord and Other Fragments*, 1974. His letters are available in *Dai Great-Coat: A Self-Portrait of David Jones in His Letters*, ed. René Hague, 1980; Thomas Dilworth, *Inner Necessities: The Letters of David Jones to Desmond Chute*, 1984; and Ruth Pryor, *David Jones: Letters to Vernon Watkins*, 1976. Some of Jones's more important prose is to be found in *Epoch and Artist: Selected Writings*, 1959, and *The Dying Gaul and Other Writings*, 1978, both edited by Harman Grisewood. Publication details of his shorter poems, prose writings, and the secondary literature on his work are listed in the bibliography to David Blamires, *David Jones: Artist and Writer*, 1971. That book; Jeremy Hooker, *David Jones: An Exploratory* _e Writings_, 1975; Thomas Dilworth, _The_ _f Meaning in the Poetry of David Jones_, ; and Jonathan Miles and Derek Shiel, _David_ _..es: The Maker Unmade_, 1996, are the most comprehensive critical studies to date. There are chapter-length discussions of _In Parenthesis_ in John H. Johnston, _English Poetry of the First World War_, 1964; Bernard Bergonzi, _Heroes' Twilight_, 1965; and Jon Silkin, _Out of Battle_, 1972.

See entries under **Voices from World War I.**

James Joyce
The most reliable edition of _Ulysses_, 1922, is _Ulysses: A Critical and Synoptic Edition_, 3 vols, ed. Hans Walter Gabler with Wolfhard Steppe and Claus Melchoir, 1984 and rev. ed., 1986. Annotated editions of _Dubliners_, 1914, and _A Portrait of the Artist as a Young Man_, 1916, are available in Viking, Penguin, and Oxford World's Classics editions. The Oxford World's Classics edition of _Ulysses_, ed. Jeri Johnson, 1993, uses the 1922 text and has the most exhaustive notes and supportive critical material. An edition of _Stephen Hero_, the novel that became the basis for _Portrait_, was edited by John J. Slocum and Herbert Cahoon, 1955. There is no textually reliable edition of _Finnegans Wake_, but currently available editions include those of Faber, Minerva, Palladin, and Penguin. _The Portable James Joyce_, ed. H. Levin, 1968, is useful. For Joyce's critical writing see _Critical Writings of James Joyce_, ed. Richard Ellmann and Ellsworth Mason, 1959, and for his poems and shorter pieces, _James Joyce: Poems and Shorter Writings_, ed. Richard Ellmann, A. Walton Litz, and John Whittier Ferguson, 1991. _The Letters of James Joyce_, 3 vols., has been edited by Stuart Gilbert and Richard Ellmann, 1957–66, and a selection is available, ed. Richard Ellmann, 1975. The standard bibliography of Joyce's work is _A Bibliography of James Joyce_, ed. John J. Slocum and Herbert Cahoon, 2nd ed., 1971, and Thomas Jackson Rice, _James Joyce: A Guide to Research_, 1982, is a helpful bibliography of the secondary literature.

The standard biography is Richard Ellmann, _James Joyce_, 3rd rev. ed., 1983. Also useful are Sylvia Beach, _Shakespeare and Company_, 1959; Stanislaus Joyce, _The Complete Dublin Diary of Stanislaus Joyce_, 1971, and _My Brother's Keeper: James Joyce's Early Years_, ed. Richard Ellmann, 1958; Brenda Maddox, _Nora: A Biography of Nora Joyce_, 1988; E. H. Mikhail, _James Joyce: Interviews and Recollections_, 1990; _Portraits of the Artist in Exile: Recollections of James Joyce by Europeans_, ed. Willard Potts, rpt. 1986; and Arthur Power, _Conversations with James Joyce_, rpt. 1982.

Good general accounts of Joyce's work can be found in _The Cambridge Companion to James Joyce_, ed. Derek Attridge, 1990; _A Companion to Joyce Studies_, ed. Zack Bowen and James F. Carens, 1984; _James Joyce: The Critical Heritage_, 2 vols., ed. Robert H. Deming, 1970; Richard Ellmann, _The Consciousness of Joyce_, 1977; Hugh Kenner, _Dublin's Joyce_, 1955, and _Joyce's Voices_, 1978; Colin MacCabe, _James Joyce and the Revolution of the_

Word, 1978; _James Joyce: New Perspectives_, ed. Colin MacCabe, 1982; Vicki Mahaffey, _Reauthorizing Joyce_, 1988; Patrick Parrinder, _James Joyce_, 1984; C. H. Peake, _James Joyce: The Citizen and the Artist_, 1976; and Jean-Michel Rabaté, _James Joyce: Authorized Reader_, 1991.

More specialized studies include _Post-Structuralist Joyce: Essays from the French_, ed. Derek Attridge and Daniel Ferrer, 1984; Samuel Beckett et al., _Our Exagmination Round His Factification for Incamination of Work in Progress_, rpt. 1972; Richard Brown, _James Joyce and Sexuality_, 1985; Kevin J. H. Dettmar, _The Illicit Joyce of Postmodernism: Reading against the Grain_, 1996; Patrick McGee, _Paperspace: Style as Ideology in Joyce_, 1988; Dominic Manganiello, _Joyce's Politics_, 1980; Margot Norris, _Joyce's Web: The Social Unraveling of Modernism_, 1992; Fritz Senn, _Joyce's Dislocations: Essays on Reading as Translation_, 1984; and Robert E. Spoo, _James Joyce and the Language of History: Daedalus's Nightmare._

Critical studies of _Dubliners_ and _A Portrait of the Artist as a Young Man_ include _Twentieth-Century Interpretations of_ Dubliners: _A Collection of Critical Essays_, ed. P. K. Garrett, 1968; _James Joyce's Dubliners: Critical Essays_, ed. Clive Hart, 1968; and Maud Ellmann, "Disremembering Daedalus: _A Portrait of the Artist as a Young Man_," in _Untying the Text: A Post-Structuralist Reader_, ed. Robert Young, 1981.

Among the most helpful of many critical studies of _Ulysses_ are Frank Budgen, _James Joyce and the Making of_ Ulysses, rpt. 1972; Edna Duffy, _The Subaltern Ulysses_, 1994; Maud Ellmann, "The Ghosts of Ulysses," in _James Joyce: The Artist and the Labyrinth_, ed. Augustine Martin, 1990; Richard Ellmann, _Ulysses on the Liffey_, rev. rpt. 1974; Marilyn French, _The Book as World: James Joyce's_ Ulysses, 1976; Don Gifford with Robert J. Seidman, _Ulysses Annotated: Notes for Joyce's_ Ulysses, rev. ed. 1988; Stuart Gilbert, _James Joyce's_ Ulysses: _A Study_, rev. ed., 1952; Michael Groden, _Ulysses in Progress_, 1977; _James Joyce's_ Ulysses: _Critical Essays_, ed. Clive Hart and David Hayman, 1974; David Hayman, Ulysses: _The Mechanics of Meaning_, rev. ed. 1982; Hugh Kenner, _Ulysses_, rev. ed. 1987; Karen Lawrence, _The Odyssey of Style in_ Ulysses, 1981; James H. Maddox, _Joyce's_ Ulysses _and the Assault upon Character_, 1978; William Schutte, _Joyce and Shakespeare_, 1957; Michael Seidel, _Epic Geography: James Joyce's_ Ulysses, 1976; Ulysses: _Fifty Years_, ed. Thomas F. Staley, rpt. 1974; and Weldon Thornton, _Allusions in_ Ulysses, 1973. David Pierce, _James Joyce's Ireland_, 1992, provides other useful background material.

Notes and drafts for the novel are examined in Philip Herring, _Joyce's Notes and Early Drafts for_ Ulysses: _Selections from the Buffalo Collection_, 1977, and _Joyce's_ Ulysses _Notesheets in the British Museum_, 1972.

The best studies of _Finnegans Wake_ include James S. Atherton, _The Books at the Wake: A Study of Literary Allusions in James Joyce's_ Finnegans Wake, 2nd ed. 1974; John Bishop, _Joyce's Book of_ the Dark: Finnegans Wake, 1986; Kimberly J. Devlin, Wandering and Return in Finnegans Wake: An Integrative Approach to Joyce's Fictions, 1991; Adaline Glasheen, A Third Census of Finnegans Wake: An Index of the Characters and Their Roles, 1977; Clive Hart, Structure and Motif in Finnegans Wake, 1962, and A Concordance to Finnegans Wake, rev. ed. 1974; Thomas C. Hofheinz, Joyce and the Invention of Irish History: Finnegans Wake in Context, 1995; and Roland McHugh, Annotations to Finnegans Wake, 1980.

Philip Larkin

Larkin's Collected Poems, ed. Anthony Thwaite, 1988, contains a number of hitherto unpublished poems in addition to the contents of his four collections: The North Ship, 1945, rev. 1966; The Less Deceived, 1955; The Whitsun Weddings, 1964 and High Windows, 1974. Thwaite has also edited Selected Letters of Philip Larkin, 1940–1985, 1992. Larkin published two early novels: Jill, 1946, and A Girl in Winter, 1947; a collection of essays on jazz: All That Jazz: A Record Diary, 1961–68, 1970; and Required Writing: Miscellaneous Pieces, 1955–1982, 1983, containing recollections, interviews, and essays on literature and jazz. He edited The Oxford Book of Twentieth-Century English Verse, 1973, and contributed an interview to Viewpoints: Poets in Conversation with John Haffenden, 1981. The standard biography is Andrew Motion, Philip Larkin: A Writer's Life, 1993. David Timms, Philip Larkin, 1973, was the first full-length study of his poetry. Andrew Tolley, Larkin at Work, 1998, offers a useful "study of Larkin's mode of composition as seen in his notebooks," and there are good critical essays in Phoenix: Philip Larkin Issue, 11/12 (Autumn and Winter 1973/4); Larkin at Sixty, ed. Anthony Thwaite, 1982; and Philip Larkin, ed. Stephen Regan, 1998.

D. H. Lawrence

The definitive Cambridge Edition of the Works of Lawrence is now almost complete. The seven volumes of his Letters, edited by James Boulton and others, were issued by Cambridge between 1979 and 1993. The best edition of Lawrence's poetry remains the third edition of The Complete Poems, ed. V. de Sola Pinto and W. Roberts, 1972. The Penguin paperback texts of the novels and shorter fiction are based on the Cambridge editions, and Oxford World's Classics have also issued useful paperback editions of The White Peacock, Sons and Lovers, The Rainbow, Women in Love, and certain other works.

The standard biography is the Cambridge triptych: John Worthen, D. H. Lawrence: The Early Years 1885–1912, 1991; Mark Kinkead-Weekes, D. H. Lawrence: Triumph to Exile 1912–1922, 1996; and David Ellis, D. H. Lawrence: Dying Game 1922–1930, 1998.

Pioneering critical studies include F. R. Leavis, D. H. Lawrence: Novelist, 1956; Graham Hough, The Dark Sun, 1957; H. M. Daleski, The Forked Flame, 1965; George Ford, Double Measure, 1965;

and Colin Clarke, River of Dissolution: D. H. Lawrence and English Romanticism, 1969. Some more recent valuable analyses are D. H. Lawrence: The Critical Heritage, ed. R. P. Draper, 1970; Emile Delavenay, D. H. Lawrence: The Man and His Work: The Formative Years, 1885–1919, trans. Katherine M. Delavenay, 1972; Sandra Gilbert, Acts of Attention: The Poems of D. H. Lawrence, 1972; Frank Kermode, Lawrence, 1973; Alastair Niven, D. H. Lawrence: The Novels, 1978; John Worthen, D. H. Lawrence and the Idea of the Novel, 1979; Paul Delaney, D. H. Lawrence's Nightmare: The Writer and His Circle in the Years of the Great War, 1979; Aidan Burns, Nature and Culture in D. H. Lawrence, 1980; Graham Holderness, D. H. Lawrence: History, Ideology and Fiction, 1982; Hilary Simpson, D. H. Lawrence and Feminism, 1982; Sheila Macleod, Lawrence's Men and Women, 1985; Cornelia Nixon, Lawrence's Leadership Politics and the Turn against Women, 1986; Daniel Schneider, The Consciousness of D. H. Lawrence: An Intellectual Biography, 1986; Christopher Heywood, D. H. Lawrence: New Studies, 1987; Colin Milton, Lawrence and Nietzsche: A Study in Influence, 1987; D. H. Lawrence: New Studies, ed. Colin Milton, 1988; M. J. Lockwood, A Study of the Poems of D. H. Lawrence: Thinking in Poetry, 1988; The Challenge of D. H. Lawrence, ed. Michael Squires and Keith Cushman, 1990; Tony Pinkney, D. H. Lawrence and D. H. Lawrence and Modernism, 1990; Rethinking Lawrence, ed. Keith Brown, 1990; Michael Black, D. H. Lawrence: The Early Philosophical Works: A Commentary, 1991; Barbara Mensch, D. H. Lawrence and the Authoritarian Personality, 1991; Charles Ross, Women in Love: A Novel of Mythic Realism, 1991; Michael Bell, D. H. Lawrence: Language and Being, 1992; D. H. Lawrence: A Critical Reader, ed. Peter Widdowson, 1992; Anne Fernihough, D. H. Lawrence: Aesthetics and Ideology, 1993; and Robert Montgomery, The Visionary D. H. Lawrence: Beyond Philosophy and Art, 1994. An essential reference tool is Paul Poplawski, D. H. Lawrence: A Reference Companion, 1996.

Doris Lessing

Lessing's first novel, The Grass Is Singing, 1950, was followed two years later by the first of the Children of Violence quintet, whose remaining volumes appeared between 1954 and 1969, during which time she published one of her best-known works, The Golden Notebook, 1962. Her other fiction includes Briefing for a Descent into Hell, 1971; Memoirs of a Survivor, 1975; the monumental Canopus in Argus Archives sequence (published between 1979 and 1983); The Diaries of Jane Somers, 1983; The Diary of a Good Neighbour, 1984; The Good Terrorist, 1985; The Fifth Child, 1988, a graphic novel in verse, Playing the Game, 1995; Love, Again, 1996; and Mara and Dann, 1999. Her short stories were collected in two volumes in 1978. Under My Skin: The First Volume of My Autobiography, to 1949, was published in 1994, and Walking

..e: The Second Volume of My Autobiog-
?49 to 1962, in 1998. The Doris Lessing
..r, 1989, contains her own selections from her
..ion, while A Small Personal Voice: Essays,
Reviews, Interviews, ed. Paul Schleuter, 1974, is a
selection of her nonfiction essays.

Michael Thorpe, Doris Lessing's Africa, 1978,
examines the influence of Lessing's home continent
on her work, and more general critical studies
include Paul Scheuter, The Novelistic Vision of
Doris Lessing: Breaking the Forms of Consciousness,
The Novels of Doris Lessing, 1973; Doris Lessing:
Critical Essays, ed. Annis Pratt and L. S. Dembo,
1974; Mary Ann Singleton, The Fiction of Doris Lessing, 1977; Notebooks/memoirs/archives: Reading
and Rereading Doris Lessing, ed. Jenny Taylor,
1982; Lorna Sage, Doris Lessing, 1983; Betsy
Draine, Substance under Pressure: Artistic Coher-
ence and Evolving Form, 1983; Mona Knapp, Doris
Lessing, 1984; Doris Lessing, ed. Harold Bloom,
1986; Critical Essays on Doris Lessing, ed. Claire
Sprague and Virginia Tiger, 1986; and Gayle
Greene, Doris Lessing: The Poetics of Change, 1994.
Jeannette King, Doris Lessing, 1989, takes a more
theoretical approach to Lessing's work, as does
Claire Sprague, Rereading Doris Lessing: Narrative
Patterns of Doubling and Repetition, 1987. Useful
reference works on Lessing's work are Selma R.
Burkom, Doris Lessing: A Checklist of Primary and
Secondary Sources, 1973, and Dee Seligman, Doris
Lessing: An Annotated Bibliography of Criticism,
1980.

Hugh MacDiarmid

Michael Grieve and W. R. Aitken have edited Hugh
MacDiarmid: The Complete Poems, 2 vols, 1985,
rev. ed. 1994. His Selected Poems and Selected
Prose were both published in 1992. An autobiography, Lucky Poet, was published in 1943, and Gordon Wright, MacDiarmid: An Illustrated Biography,
1977, covers eighty-five years of the poet's life in
photographs, caricatures, poems, press-cuttings,
and other documents. Alan Bold has written Mac-
Diarmid: A Critical Biography, 1988, and MacDiarmid: The Terrible Crystal, 1983, a helpful study of
MacDiarmid's main themes and attitudes. Catherine Kerrigan, Whaur Extremes Meet, 1983, and
Harvey Oxenhorn, Elemental Things: The Poetry of
Hugh MacDiarmid, 1984, provide perceptive critical discussions of the early and middle poetry.

The best general account of MacDiarmid and his
poetry is Kenneth Buthlay, Hugh MacDiarmid, rev.
1982. A good account of the Scottish cultural background and of MacDiarmid's part in Scottish literary movements is Duncan Glen, Hugh MacDiarmid
and the Scottish Renaissance, 1964. Hugh Mac-
Diarmid, A Festschrift, ed. K. D. Duval and Sydney
Goodsir Smith, 1962, contains fifteen essays by different hands on aspects of his life and work and is
the most important single critical book on Mac-
Diarmid. Hugh MacDiarmid: A Critical Survey, ed.
Duncan Glen, 1972, also contains fifteen essays by
different critics, together with a comprehensive bibliography.

Louis MacNeice

The Collected Poems, 1967, and MacNeice's posthumously published unfinished autobiography, The
Strings Are False, 1966, were both edited by E. R.
Dodds. MacNeice made verse translations of Aeschylus's Agamemnon, 1937, and, with E. L. Stahl,
of Goethe's Faust (an abridged version of parts 1
and 2), 1951. His Clark Lectures at Cambridge
were published as Varieties of Parable, 1963. Alan
Heuser has edited Selected Literary Criticism of
Louis MacNeice, 1987, and Selected Prose of Louis
MacNeice, 1990; and A Bibliography of the Works
of Louis MacNeice, ed. C. M. Armitage and Neil
Clark, 1973, lists most of his many other publications. There is a biography, Louis MacNeice,
1995, by Jon Stallworthy; Barbara Coulton, Louis
MacNeice in the BBC, 1980, is a biographical and
critical study of his work for radio; and Louis Mac-
Neice and this Influence, ed. Kathleen Devine and
Alan J. Peacock, 1998, brings together some useful
papers, and critical essays supplement personal recollections of friends and relatives in Time Was
Away, ed. Terence Brown, 1974.

Critical studies include Terence Brown, Louis
MacNeice: The Skeptical Vision, 1975; William T.
McKinnon, Apollo's Blended Dream: A Study of the
Poetry of Louis MacNeice, 1971 (which includes a
useful selective bibliography of books and articles
by and about MacNeice); Robyn Marsack, The Cave
of Making: The Poetry of Louis MacNeice, 1982, and
Edna Longley, Louis MacNeice: A Study 1988.

Katherine Mansfield

There is a convenient complete one-volume edition
of Katherine Mansfield's stories, The Short Stories
of Katherine Mansfield, 1937. Her Journal was
edited by Middleton Murry in 1954; The Critical
Writings of Katherine Mansfield, by Clare Hanson,
1987; Poems of Katherine Mansfield, by Vincent
O'Sullivan, 1988; The Collected Letters of Katherine
Mansfield, by Vincent O'Sullivan and Margaret
Scott, 1984; and The Katherine Mansfield Notebooks, 2 vols., by Scott, 1998. The best biographies
are Anthony Alpers, The Life of Katherine Mansfield,
2nd ed., 1979, and Claire Tomalin, Katherine
Mansfield: A Secret Life, 1987.

Critical studies include Marvin Magalener, The
Fiction of Katherine Mansfield, 1971; Ian A. Gor-
don, Undiscovered Country: The New Zealand Sto-
ries of Katherine Mansfield, 1974; Clare Hanson and
Andrew Gurr, Katherine Mansfield, 1981; C. A.
Hankin, Katherine Mansfield and Her Confessional
Stories, 1983; Kate Fullbrook, Katherine Mansfield,
1986; Critical Essays on Katherine Mansfield, ed.
Rhoda B. Nathan, 1993; and The Critical Response
to Katherine Mansfield, ed. Jan Pilditch, 1996.

Paul Muldoon

Muldoon's earliest volumes of poetry were Knowing
My Place, 1971; New Weather, 1973; Spirit of
Dawn, 1975; Mules, 1977, and Names and
Addresses, 1978. Better known are Why Brownlee
Left, 1980; Quoof, 1983, and Meeting the British,
1987, although during this period he also published
Immram, 1980; Out of Siberia, 1982, and The Wish-

bone, 1984. More recent volumes include *Madoc: a Mystery*, 1990; *The Prince of the Quotidian*, 1994; *The Annals of Chile*, 1994; *Kerry Slides*, 1996; *Noctuary of Narcissus Batt*, 1997, and *Hay*, 1997. An opera libretto, *Shining Brow*, was published in 1993, and a play, *Six Honest Serving Men*, in 1995. He has published two volumes of poetry for children, *The O-O's Party: New Year's Eve*, 1981, and *The Last Thesaurus*, 1995. His *Selected Poems 1968–1986* appeared in 1986 and *New Selected Poems 1968–1994* in 1994. Muldoon was the editor of *The Scrake of Dawn: Poems by Young People from Northern Ireland*, 1979; *The Faber Book of Contemporary Irish Poetry*, 1986; *The Essential Byron*, 1989, and *The Faber Book of Beasts*, 1997. His translations of poems by Nuala Ni Dhomhnaill, *The Astrakhan Coat*, were published in 1992. An introduction to and overview of Muldoon's poetry is provided by Tim Kendall, *Paul Muldoon*, 1996, which includes criticism of later poetry necessarily absent from Alan Jenkins, *Paul Muldoon*, 1988. Perhaps the definitive work is Clair Wills, *Reading Paul Muldoon*, 1998. Also useful are the extensive sections on Muldoon in Wills, "The Lie of the Land: Language, Imperialism and Trade in Paul Muldoon's 'Meeting the British,'" in *The Chosen Ground: Essays on the Contemporary Poetry of Northern Ireland*, ed. Neil Corcoran, 1992.

Alice Munro
Munro's work includes *The Love of a Good Woman*, 1998, *Open Secrets*, 1994, *Friend of My Youth*, 1990, *The Progress of Love*, 1986, *The Moons of Jupiter*, 1983, *The Beggar Maid*, 1979, *Who Do You Think You Are?*, 1978, *Something I've Been Meaning to Tell You . . .*, 1974, *Lives of Girls and Women*, 1973, and *Dance of the Happy Shades and Other Stories*, 1973. Critical accounts and interpretations of her work include *Alice Munro*, Ann Howells, 1998; *The Influence of Painting on Five Canadian Writers*, John Cooke, 1996; *The Tumble of Reason: Alice Munro's Discourse of Absence*, Ajay Heble, 1994; *The Other Country: Patterns in the Writing of Alice Munro*, James Carscallen, 1993; *Figuring Grief: Gallant, Munro, and the Poetics of Elegy*, Karen E. Smythe, 1992; *Mothers and Other Clowns: The Stories of Alice Munro*, Magdalene Redekop, 1992; *Dance of the Sexes: Art and Gender in the Fiction of Alice Munro*, Beverly Jean Rasporich, 1990; *Alice Munro*, E. D. Blodgett, 1988; *Alice Munro: Paradox and Parallel*, W. R. Martin, 1987; *Probable Fictions: Alice Munro's Narrative Acts*, ed. Louis K. MacKendrick, 1983. A biographical account of her life and fiction is *Alice Munro: A Double Life*, Catherine Sheldrick Ross, 1992.

Les Murray
Murray's early volumes of poetry include *The Weatherboard Cathedral*, 1969; *Poems against Economics*, 1972, and *Lunch & Counter Lunch*, 1974. A first *Selected Poems: The Vernacular Republic*, appeared in 1976, and was followed by further volumes, including *Ethnic Radio*, 1977; *Embodi-*

ment and Incarnation, 1982; *Equanimities*, 1982; *The People's Otherworld*, 1983; *The Gravy in Images*, 1987; *The Daylight Moon*, 1988; *Dog Fox Field*, 1991; *Subhuman Redneck Poems*, 1993; *Translations from the Natural World*, 1993, and *Fredy Neptune*, 1998. An updated *The Vernacular Republic: Poems 1961–1981*, was published in 1982, and *Collected Poems* in 1991. *Persistence in Folly*, 1984, is a prose memoir. A verse novel, *The Boys who Stole the Funeral: a Novel Sequence*, was published in 1989. Murray's essays and reviews have been collected in *The Peasant Mandarin*, 1978; *Blocks and Tackles: Articles and Essays 1982–1990*, 1990, and *The Paperbark Tree: Selected Prose*, 1992. Murray was the editor of *The New Oxford Book of Australian Verse*, 1986, which was reprinted in an expanded edition in 1991, of *The Anthology of Australian Religious Poetry*, 1991, and of *Fivefathers: Five Australian Poets of the Preacademic Era*, 1994. An introduction to Murray's work, which places it in the context of Australian poetry, is Laurence Bourke, *A Vivid Steady State: Les Murray and Australian Poetry*, 1992, and a collection of essays on Murray's work, *Counterbalancing Light: Essays on Les Murray*, ed. Carmel Gaffney, was published in 1997.

V. S. Naipaul
Naipaul's early, comic novels are *The Mystic Masseur*, 1957; *The Suffrage of Elvira*, 1958; *Miguel Street*, 1959, and *A House for Mr Biswas*, 1961. *Mr Stone and the Knights Companion*, 1963, *The Mimic Men*, 1967, and the collection of stories, *A Flag on the Island*, 1967, introduced more broadly political themes that were continued by *In a Free State*, 1971, *Guerrillas*, 1975, and *A Congo Diary*, 1980. More epic in its scope is *A Bend in the River*, 1979. More recent fiction includes *The Enigma of Arrival: A Novel in Five Sections*, 1987. Naipaul has also produced a great deal of journalism and travel writing, often concerned with the same political themes as his fiction, including *The Middle Passage: Impressions of Five Societies, British, French and Dutch, in the West Indies and South America*, 1962; *An Area of Darkness*, 1964; *The Return of Eva Peron: With The Killings in Trinidad*, 1966; *The Loss of El Dorado: A History*, 1969; *The Overcrowded Barracoon and Other Articles*, 1972; *India: A Wounded Civilization*, 1977; *Among the Believers: An Islamic Journey*, 1981; and *India: A Million Mutinies Now*, 1990. His most recent work is *A Way in the World: A Sequence*, 1994, and *Beyond Belief: Islamic Excursions among the Converted Peoples*, 1998. Introductions to Naipaul's work are provided by Paul Theroux, *V. S. Naipaul: An Introduction to His Work*, 1972; Landeg White, *V. S. Naipaul, A Critical Introduction*, 1975; Peter Hughes, *V. S. Naipaul*, 1988, and Peggy Nightingale, *Journey Through Darkness: The Writing of V. S. Naipaul*, 1987. Judith Levy examines the autobiographical element in Naipaul's writing in *V. S. Naipaul: Displacement and Autobiography*, 1995, as does Timothy Weiss, *On the Margins: The Art of Exile in V. S. Naipaul*, 1992. A more comprehensive study

...ing, *V. S. Naipaul*, 1993. Postcolonial
..f Naipaul's work are examined in R. Nixon,
...n *Calling: V. S. Naipaul, Postcolonial Man-
...n*, 1992.

Edna O'Brien

O'Brien's work includes her trilogy *The Country
Girls*, 1960, *The Lonely Girl*, 1962, and *Girls in
Their Married Bliss*, 1964, reissued as *The Country
Girls Trilogy and Epilogue*, 1987; and seven other
novels: *August Is a Wicked Month*, 1965, *Casualties
of Peace*, 1966, *Zee & Co*, 1971, *Night*, 1972, *The
High Road*, 1988, *Time and Tide*, 1992, and *House
of Splendid Isolation*, 1994. She has written three
collections of stories—*The Love Object*, 1968, *Mrs
Reinhardt and Other Stories*, 1978, *Lantern Slides*,
1990—and two plays: *A Pagan Place*, 1973, and *Virginia*, 1981. *A Fanatic Heart: Selected Stories* was
published in 1984, and she has compiled *Tales for
the Telling: Irish Folk and Fairy Stories*, 1988.

Critical accounts of her work include Grace Eck-
ley, *Edna O'Brien*, 1974; Raymonde Popot, "Edna
O'Brien's Paradise Lost," in *Cahiers Irlandais* 4–5
(1976); Lotus Snow, " 'That Trenchant Childhood
Route?': Quest in Edna O'Brien's Novels," in *Eire*
14.1 (1979); and Darcy O'Brien, "Edna O'Brien: A
Kind of Irish Childhood," in *Twentieth-Century
Women Novelists*, ed. Thomas Staley, 1982.

George Orwell

Following Orwell's autobiographical *Down and Out
in Paris and London*, 1933, his first novel, *Burmese
Days*, 1934, was also based on his own experiences,
and he continued to employ his own experience of
life below the poverty line in his journalism, essays,
and fiction, which were all vehicles for political and
social commentary. His second and third novels, *A
Clergyman's Daughter*, 1935, and *Keep the Aspidis-
tra Flying*, 1936, were followed by the nonfiction
works *The Road to Wigan Pier*, 1937, and *Homage
to Catalonia*, 1938. In 1939 he published another
novel, *Coming Up for Air*, which was followed by
Inside the Whale, 1940, and other works, including
a collection of essays, *The Lion and the Unicorn:
Socialism and the English Genius*, 1941; *Shooting
an Elephant*, 1950; *England Your England*, 1953;
and *Such, Such Were the Joys*, 1953. The four-
volume *Collected Essays, Journalism and Letters*, ed.
S. Orwell and I. Angus, was issued in paperback in
1968. Orwell is, however, best known for two works
of fiction: *Animal Farm*, 1945, and *Nineteen Eighty-
four*, 1949. The standard edition of his writing is
The Complete Works of George Orwell, 20 vols, ed.
Peter Davison, 1998. The standard bibliography is
Gillian Fenwick, *George Orwell: A Bibliography*,
'8.

major biographies are Bernard Crick, *George
` Life*, 1980; Michael Shelden, *Orwell: The
'iography*, 1991; and Peter Hobley Dav-
  * Literary Life*, 1996. Other works
  ohical material include Arthur
  vn Orwell, 1972, and P. Stan-
  Irwell: The Transformation,
  cles of Conscience, 1968,

compares the lives and work of Orwell and Arthur
Koestler.

The range of criticism of Orwell's work includes
R. J. Voorhees, *The Paradox of George Orwell*, 1961;
"Nineteen Eighty-four," ed. I. Howe, 1963; E. M.
Thomas, *Orwell*, 1965; G. Woodcock, *The Crystal
Spirit*, 1967; *George Orwell: A Collection of Critical
Essays*, ed. Raymond Williams, 1974; Alan Sandi-
son, *The Last Man in Europe*, 1974; *George Orwell:
The Critical Heritage*, ed. J. Meyers, 1975; *Critical
Essays on George Orwell*, ed. Bernard Oldsey and
Joseph Browne, 1986; *George Orwell*, ed. Harold
Bloom; 1987; Peter Buitenhuis and Ira Bruce
Nadal, *George Orwell: A Reassessment*, 1988; and
Alok Rai, *Orwell and the Politics of Despair: A Crit-
ical Study of the Writings of George Orwell*, 1990.
Works that examine Orwell and the social and his-
torical context of his life and work include *The
World of George Orwell*, ed. M. Gross, 1971; J. Mey-
ers, *A Reader's Guide to Orwell*, 1975; P. Lewis, *The
Road to 1984*, 1981; L. Hunter, *George Orwell, The
Search for a Voice*, 1984; and Patrick Reilly, *George
Orwell: The Age's Adversary*, 1986.

Wilfred Owen

*The Complete Poems and Fragments of Wilfred
Owen*, 2 vols., 1983, and *The Poems of Wilfred
Owen*, 1985, both edited by Jon Stallworthy, are the
standard scholarly edition and the standard reader's
edition, respectively. Jon Stallworthy, *Wilfred
Owen*, 1974, is the standard biography. Major
sources of biographical information are *The Collected Letters*, ed. Harold Owen and John Bell,
1967, and Harold Owen, *Journey from Obscurity:
Memoirs of the Owen Family*, vol. 1: 1963, vol. 2:
1964, and vol. 3: 1965. The best critical studies are
D. S. R. Welland, *Wilfred Owen*, 2nd ed., 1978;
Sven Bäckman, *Tradition Transformed: Studies in
the Poetry of Wilfred Owen*, 1979; Desmond Graham, *The Truth of War: Owen, Blunden and Rosenberg*, 1984; Dominic Hibberd, *Owen the Poet*, 1988;
and Arthur E. Lane, *An Adequate Response: The
War Poetry of Wilfred Owen and Siegfried Sassoon*,
1972.

See entries under **Voices from World War I.**

Harold Pinter

Pinter's plays, poetry, and selected prose have been
published in paperback in *Complete Works*, vol. 1:
1976, vol. 2: 1977, vol. 3: 1978, vol. 4: 1981; and
in *Collected Poems and Prose*, 1986. A number of
his screenplays have also been published: *Five
Screenplays*, 1971; *The Proust Screenplay*, written
with the collaboration of Joseph Losey and Barbara
Bray, 1977; and *The French Lieutenant's Woman
and Other Screenplays*, 1982. Recent publications
include *Mountain Language*, 1988; *The Heat of the
Day*, 1989; and *The Dwarfs: A Novel*, 1990. There
is a critical biography, Michael Billington, *The Life
and Work of Harold Pinter*, 1996.

Critical studies of his work include Walter Kerr,
Harold Pinter. 1967; Lois G. Gordon, *Stratagems to
Uncover Nakedness: The Dramas of Harold Pinter*,
1969; James R. Hollis, *Harold Pinter: The Poetics of*

Silence, 1970; Arlene Sykes, *Harold Pinter*, 1970; *Pinter: A Collection of Critical Essays*, ed. Arthur Ganz, 1972; Simon Trussler, *The Plays of Harold Pinter: An Assessment*, 1973; William Baker and Stephen Ely Tabachnick, *Harold Pinter*, 1973; Austin E. Quigley, *The Pinter Problem*, 1975; Martin Esslin, *Pinter: A Study of His Plays*, expanded 2nd ed., 1976; Bernard F. Dukore, *Where Laughter Stops: Pinter's Tragicomedy*, 1976; Steve H. Gale, *Butter's Going Up: A Critical Analysis of Harold Pinter's Work*, 1977; Arnold P. Hinchcliffe, *Harold Pinter*, rev. 1981; and Guido Almansi and Simon Henderson, *Harold Pinter*, 1983.

Craig Raine
Raine has published six collections of poems: *The Onion, Memory*, 1978; *A Martian Sends a Postcard Home*, 1979; *A Free Translation*, 1981; *Rich*, 1984; *History: The Home Movie*, 1994; and *Clay. Whereabouts Unknown*, 1996; a volume of critical essays, *Haydn and the Valve Trumpet*, 1990; and two adaptations for the stage: *The Electrification of the Soviet Union*, 1986, an opera libretto based on a novella by Pasternak, and *1953*, 1990, a version of Racine's *Andromaque*. He contributed an interview to *Viewpoints: Poets in Conversation with John Haffenden*, 1981.

Henry Reed
Reed's *Collected Poems*, edited with a biographical and critical introduction by Jon Stallworthy, 1991, contains not only the contents of his one published volume of poetry, *A Map of Verona*, 1947, but many uncollected and some unpublished poems. The best of his radio plays are to be found in *The Streets of Pompeii and Other Plays for Radio*, 1971, and *Hilda Tablet and Others: Four Pieces for Radio*, 1971. There is a critical account of his poetry in Vernon Scannell, *Not Without Glory: Poets of the Second World War*, 1976.

See entries under **Voices from World War II.**

Jean Rhys
The Left Bank: Sketches and Studies of Present-day Bohemian Paris was Rhys's first collection of short stories, published, with an introduction by Ford Madox Ford, in 1927. Her second collection, *Postures*, which appeared a year later, is better known as *Quartet*, under which title it was republished in 1969. She published regularly between 1930 and 1939, producing *After Leaving Mr. Mackenzie*, 1930, *Voyage in the Dark*, 1934, and *Good Morning, Midnight*, 1939, but then nothing until 1969 and *Wide Sargasso Sea*. Two further collections of short stories followed: *Tigers Are Better Looking*, 1968, and *Sleep It Off, Lady*, 1976, as well as an unfinished autobiography, *Smile Please*, 1979. A selection of her letters, edited by Francis Wyndham and Diana Melly, was published five years after her death. A memoir of Rhys appears in David Plante, *Difficult Women: A Memoir of Three*, 2nd edn 1983, but more comprehensive is Carole Angier's work of biographical criticism, *Jean Rhys: Life and Work*, 1990. There is also a bibliography: Elgin W. Mel-

lown, *Jean Rhys: A Descriptive and Annotated Bibliography*, 1984. A useful general exposition of Rhys's work is Coral Ann Howells, *Jean Rhys*, 1991, which supersedes Thomas F. Staley, *Jean Rhys: A Critical Study*, 1979, and Peter Wolfe, *Jean Rhys*, 1980. Louis James, *Jean Rhys*, Critical Studies of Caribbean Writers Series, 1978, considers her as a Caribbean writer, whereas Creole history, landscape, and characters in her work, particularly *Wide Sargasso Sea*, are examined in Veronica M. Gregg, *Jean Rhys's Historical Imagination: Reading and Writing the Creole*, 1995. Nancy R. Harrison examines her novels and stories as women's writing in *Jean Rhys and the Novel as Women's Text*, 1988, as does Helen Nebeker, *Jean Rhys, Woman in Passage: A Critical Study of the Novels of Jean Rhys*, 1981. Her shorter fiction is analyzed in Cheryl Alexander Malcolm and David Malcolm, *Jean Rhys: A Study of the Short Fiction*, 1996. Sections on Rhys are included in Judith Kegan Gardiner, *Rhys, Stead, Lessing and the Politics of Empathy*, 1989; Margaret Paul Joseph, *Caliban in Exile: The Outsider in Caribbean Fiction*, Contributions to the Study of World Literature Series, 1992; and Deborah Kelly, *The Unspeakable Mother: Forbidden Discourse in Jean Rhys and H. D.*, Reading Women Writing Series, 1989. In *The Ladies and the Mammies: Jane Austen and Jean Rhys*, 1983, Selma James studies *Wide Sargasso Sea* in depth.

The Rise and Fall of Empire
The history of the rise and crisis of the First British Empire is most fully discussed in *The Oxford History of the British Empire*, Vol. 1: *The Origins of Empire: British Overseas Enterprise to the Close of the Eighteenth Century*, ed. Nicholas Canny, 1998, and Vol. 2: *The Eighteenth Century*, ed. P. J. Marshall, 1998; and the history of the Second British Empire is well covered by *The Age of Empire 1875–1914*, E. J. Hobsbawm, 1975. The most readable account of the rise and fall of both empires is James Morris's trilogy: *Heaven's Command*, 1973, *Pax Britannica*, 1968, and *Farewell the Trumpets: An Imperial Retreat*, 1978. This is usefully complemented by *The Cambridge Illustrated History of the British Empire*, ed. P. J. Marshall, 1996.

J. A. Hobson, *Imperialism*, 1902, the most important pioneering analysis of its subject, provided much of the ammunition for V. I. Lenin's even more influential critique, *Imperialism: The Highest Stage of Capitalism*, published in Russian in 1916. The most influential subsequent critiques have been Frantz Fanon, *Black Skin, White Masks*, trans. Charles Lam Markmann, 1952; *The Wretched of the Earth*, trans. Constance Farrington, 1961; and *Studies in a Dying Colonialism*, 1989; and Edward Said, *Orientalism*, 1987, and *Culture and Imperialism*, 1993. Other important studies include B. J. Moore-Gilbert, *Kipling and "Orientalism,"* 1986; *"Race," Writing, and Difference*, ed. Henry Louis Gates Jr., 1986; Bill Ashcroft, Gareth Griffiths, and Helen Tiffin, *The Empire Writes Back: Theory and Practice in Post-Colonial Literatures*, 1989; Robert

...te Mythologies: Writing History and the *...90;* Aijaz Ahmad, *In Theory: Classes,* *...s, Literatures,* 1992; Anne McClintock, *Im-* *...al Leather: Race, Gender and Sexuality in the* *...olonial Contest,* 1995. The best introductions for students are Peter Childs and Patrick Williams, *An Introduction to Postcolonial Theory,* 1997; and Elleke Boehmer, *Colonial and Postcolonial Literature,* 1995, and *Empire Writing: An Anthology of Colonial Literature 1870–1918.*

See also entries under **Chinua Achebe, J. M. Coetzee, Anita Desai, E. M. Forster, Nadine Gordimer, Katherine Mansfield, Les Murray, V. S. Naipaul, George Orwell, Jean Rhys, Salman Rushdie,** and **Derek Walcott.**

Isaac Rosenberg

The Collected Works of Isaac Rosenberg: Poetry, Prose, Letters, Paintings and Drawings, with a foreword by Siegfried Sassoon, edited with an introduction and notes by Ian Parsons, 1979, is the standard edition. There are three critical biographies: Jean Liddiard, *Isaac Rosenberg: The Half Used Life,* 1975; Jean Moorcraft Wilson. *Isaac Rosenberg: Poet and Painter,* 1975; and Joseph Cohen. *Journey to the Trenches: The Life of Isaac Rosenberg, 1890–1918,* 1975. Critical discussion of Rosenberg's poetry will be found in John H. Johnston, *English Poetry of the First World War: A Study in the Evolution of Lyric and Narrative Form,* 1964; Jon Silkin, *Out of Battle: The Poetry of the Great War,* 1972; and Desmond Graham. *The Truth of War: Owen, Rosenberg and Blunden,* 1984.

See entries under **Voices from World War I.**

Salman Rushdie

Rushdie's first full-length work of fiction was the magic realist *Grimus: a Novel,* 1975, followed by *Midnight's Children,* 1981; *Shame,* 1983; and *The Satanic Verses,* 1988. He has also written a story for children, *Haroun and the Sea of Stories,* 1990. His nonfiction writing includes *The Jaguar Smile: A Nicaraguan Journey,* 1987, and a collection of essays, *Imaginary Homelands: Essays and Criticism, 1981–1991,* 1991, and he was coeditor, with Elizabeth West, of *The Vintage Book of Indian Writing, 1947–1997,* 1997. More recent publications include *In Good Faith,* 1990; *The Wizard of Oz,* 1992; *East, West,* 1994; *The Moor's Last Sigh,* 1995; and *The Ground Beneath Her Feet,* 1999. Some of the most useful of the abundant critical material on Rushdie's writing includes Linwood Taylor Antrim, *History, Nation, Faith: Salman Rushdie and the Reconstruction of Transcendence,* 1998; Catherine Cundy, *Salman Rushdie,* 1997; Jena Habegger, *Salman Rushdie and the Fictive Nature of Reality,* 1998; James Harrison, *Salman Rushdie,* 1992; Margareta Petersson, *Unending Metamorphoses: Myth, Satire and Religion in Salman Rushdie's Novels,* 1996. Works that focus on the controversy surrounding Rushdie's *Satanic Verses,* and his relationship with Islam, include Lisa Appignanesi, *The Rushdie File,* 1989; Umar Azam, *Rushdie's Satanic Verses: An Islamic Response,* 1990; Daniel Easterman, *New Jerusalems: Reflections on Islam, Funda-* *mentalism and the Rushdie Affair,* 1992; Jorgen S. Nielsen, *The "Rushdie Affair": A Documentation,* 1989; and Malise Ruthven, *A Satanic Affair: Salman Rushdie and the Wrath of Islam,* rev. ed. 1991. The section on Rushdie in Fawzia Afzal-Khan, *Cultural Imperialism and the Indo-English Novel: Genre and Ideology in R. K. Narayan, Anita Desai, Kamala Markandaya, and Salman Rushdie,* 1993, considers him as a postcolonial writer.

Siegfried Sassoon

The War Poems of Siegfried Sassoon, 1983, have been well edited by Rupert Hart-Davis, who also edited his *Diaries, 1920–1922,* 1981; *Diaries 1915–1918,* 1983; and *Diaries, 1923–1925,* 1985. These should be read in conjunction with Sassoon's prose works: *Memoirs of an Infantry Officer,* 1930; *Sherston's Progress,* 1936; and *Siegfried's Journey,* 1945. All are discussed in Michael Thorpe, *Siegfried Sassoon: A Critical Study,* 1966, and Paul Fussell, *The Great War and Modern Memory,* 1975. Jean Moorcroft Wilson has published the first volume of a biography: *Siegfried Sassoon: The Making of a War Poet, 1896–1918.* The poetry is considered in Bernard Bergonzi, *Heroes' Twilight: A Study of the Literature of the Great War,* 1965; John H. Johnston, *English Poetry of the First World War: A Study in the Evolution of Lyric and Narrative Form,* 1964; Jon Silkin, *Out of Battle: The Poetry of the Great War,* 1972; Arthur E. Lane, *An Adequate Response: The War Poetry of Wilfred Owen and Siegfried Sassoon,* 1972; and Patrick J. Quinn, *The Great War and the Missing Muse: The Early Writings of Robert Graves and Siegfried Sassoon,* 1994.

See also entries under **Voices from World War I.**

Edith Sitwell

In addition to more than thirty volumes of poetry, culminating in *Collected Poems,* 1993, and *Selected Poems,* with an introduction by John Lehmann, 1965, Edith Sitwell produced a variety of critical and other prose works. These include *Alexander Pope,* 1930; *The English Eccentrics,* rev. 1957; *Aspects of Modern Poetry,* 1934; *A Poet's Notebook,* 1950; and *Taken Care Of: An Autobiography,* 1965. John Lehmann and Derek Parker edited *Edith Sitwell: Selected Letters, 1919–1964,* and Lehmann has written an informative account of her family and background in *A Nest of Tigers: Edith, Osbert and Sacheverell Sitwell in Their Times,* 1968. The standard biography is Victoria Glendinning, *Edith Sitwell: A Unicorn Among the Lions,* 1983; and there is critical discussion of her work in J. D. Brophy, *Edith Sitwell: The Symbolist Order,* 1968; John Press, *A Map of Modern English Verse,* 1969; K. Rexroth, "Poets Old and New: Edith Sitwell," in *Assays,* 1961; and E. Salter, *The Last Years of a Rebel: A Memoir of Edith Sitwell,* 1967.

Stevie Smith

Smith's *Selected Poems,* 1962; *Collected Poems,* 1976; and *Me Again: Uncollected Writings of Stevie Smith,* ed. Jack Barbera and William McBrien, 1981, reproduce many of her drawings, which she often printed with the poems. She also wrote three novels: *Novel on Yellow Paper*, 1936; *Over the Frontier*, 1938; and *The Holiday*, 1949.

There are two biographies: one by Barbera and McBrien, 1985; the other by Frances Spalding, 1988; and two interviews, in *The Poet Speaks*, ed. Peter Orr, 1966, and Kay Dick, *Ivy and Stevie*, 1971, that are worth consulting. Also useful are Calvin Bedient, *Eight Contemporary Poets*, 1974; Philip Larkin, "Frivolous and Vulnerable," in his *Required Writing: Miscellaneous Pieces, 1955–1982*, 1983; Christopher Ricks, "Stevie Smith: The Art of Sinking in Poetry," in his *The Force of Poetry*, 1984; and Sanford Sternlicht, *In Search of Stevie Smith*, 1991.

Tom Stoppard

Stoppard's published plays include *Enter a Free Man*, 1968; *Rosencrantz and Guildenstern Are Dead*, 1967; *The Real Inspector Hound*, 1968; *A Separate Peace*, 1969; *After Magritte*, 1971; *Jumpers*, 1972; *Travesties*, 1975; *Dirty Linen, and Newfound-land*, 1976; *The Fifteen Minute Hamlet*, 1976; *Every Good Boy Deserves Favour, and Professional Foul*, 1978; *If You're Glad I'll Be Frank*, rev. 1978; *Hapgood: A Play*, 1988; *Artist Descending a Staircase*, 1988; *Arcadia*, 1993; *Indian Ink*, 1994; and *The Invention of Love*, 1997. He has also published screenplays, radio and television plays, a novel, and short stories. Critical studies of his work include C. W. E. Bigsby, *Tom Stoppard*, 1976; Ronald Hayman, *Tom Stoppard*, 1997; Victor L. Cahn, *Beyond Absurdity: The Plays of Tom Stoppard*, 1979; Felicia Hardison Londré, *Tom Stoppard*, 1981; Anthony Jenkins, *The Theatre of Tom Stoppard*, 1990; and Paul Delaney, *Tom Stoppard in Conversation*, 1994.

Dylan Thomas

The *Collected Poems*, ed. Walford Davies and Ralph Ward, 1988, is the standard edition of Thomas's poetry. He also wrote the autobiographical prose *Portrait of the Artist as a Young Dog*, 1940; *Adventures in the Skin Trade*, 1955; a radio play, *Under Milk Wood*, 1954, which has proved a great popular success; and *Quite Early One Morning*, 1954, a collection of stories, essays, and minor pieces. Paul Ferris edited *The Collected Letters of Dylan Thomas* in 1985, and *The Notebooks of Dylan Thomas* was edited by Ralph N. Maud in 1967. Maud, *Entrances to Dylan Thomas's Poetry*, 1963; William York Tindall, *A Reader's Guide to Dylan Thomas*, 1962; and William T. Moynahan, *The Craft and Art of Dylan Thomas*, 1966, are good introductions to the workings of the poet's mind. R. B. Kershner, *Dylan Thomas: The Poet and His Critics*, 1976, is an evaluation of criticism with a useful bibliography, and *Critical Essays on Dylan Thomas*, ed. Georg Gaston, 1989, offers more recent critical perspectives. John Ackerman has compiled *A Dylan Thomas Companion*, 1991, and written *Thomas: His Life and Work*, 1996. Constantine Fitzgibbon, *The Life of Dylan Thomas*, 1965, and Paul Ferris, *Dylan Thomas: A Biography*, 1977, are good biographies, Bill Read, *The Days of Dylan Thomas*, 1964, supplements a straightforward narrative with many photographs.

Edward Thomas

The Collected Poems of Edward Thomas, ed. R. George Thomas, 1978, is the standard scholarly edition, but also available are the plain-text *Collected Poems*, ed. Walter de la Mare, 1974, and *Selected Poems*, 1964. Edna Langley has edited *A Language not to be betrayed: Selected prose of Edward Thomas*, 1981, and R. George Thomas edited *Edward Thomas: Selected Letters*, 1996. The best studies of Thomas's life and work are William Cooke, *Edward Thomas: A Critical Biography*, 1970; R. George Thomas, *Edward Thomas*, 1972; and Andrew Motion, *The Poetry of Edward Thomas*, 1980. Also of biographical and critical importance are *Letters from Edward Thomas to Gordon Bottomley*, ed. R. George Thomas, 1968; *The Diary of Edward Thomas: 1 January–8 April 1917*, with an introduction by Roland Gant, 1977; the moving memoirs of the poet's wife, Helen Thomas, *As It Was* and *World Without End*, 1956; and Eleanor Farjeon, *Edward Thomas: The Last Four Years*, 1958.

See entries under **Voices from World War I.**

Voices from World War I

The best anthologies are *Up the Line to Death: The War Poets, 1914–1918*, ed. Brian Gardner, 1964; *Men Who March Away: Poems of the First World War*, ed. I. M. Parsons, 1965; *The Penguin Book of First World War Poetry*, ed. Jon Silkin, 2nd ed., 1981; and *The Penguin Book of First World War Prose* ed. Jan Glover and Jon Silkin, 1990. The poems are set in much-needed new perspectives by M. van Wyk Smith, *Drummer Hodge: The Poetry of the Anglo-Boer War, 1899–1902*, 1978, and Samuel Hynes, *A War Imagined: The First World War and British Culture*, 1990. Bernard Bergonzi, *Heroes' Twilight: A Study of the Literature of the Great War*, 1965, is a balanced introduction to both the poetry and the literary prose of the period, while one of the many strengths of Paul Fussell, *The Great War and Modern Memory*, 1975, is a range of reference that includes nonliterary as well as literary writing. John H. Johnston, *English Poetry of the First World War: A Study in the Evolution of Lyric and Narrative Form*, 1964; Jon Silkin, *Out of Battle: The Poetry of the Great War*, 1972; Desmond Graham, *The Truth of War: Owen, Rosenberg and Blunden*, 1984; and Hugh Cecil, *The Flower of Battle: British Fiction Writers of the First World War*, 1998, are more conventional critical studies. The British experience is usefully set in an international context by Patrick Bridgwater, *The German Poets of the First World War*, 1985; *The Lost Voices of World War I*, ed. Tim Cross, 1988; and Frank Field, *British and French Writers of the First World War*, 1991.

See also entries under **Rupert Brooke, May Wedderburn Cannan, Ivor Gurney, David Jones, Wilfred Owen, Isaac Rosenberg, Siegfried Sassoon,** and **Edward Thomas.**

Voices from World War II

The best anthologies are *The Poetry of War, 1939–45*, ed. Ian Hamilton, 1965, and *The Terrible Rain: The War Poets, 1939–45*, ed. Brian Gardner, 1966; and the fullest critical accounts of this poetry are

...nnell, *Not Without Glory: Poets of the World War*, 1976, and Linda M. Shines, *Poetry of the Second World War*, 1985. Paul ...sell, *Wartime: Understanding and Behaviour in ...ne Second World War*, 1989, is a useful contextual study.

See also entries under **Charles Causley, Keith Douglas, Richard Hillary, Henry Reed**, and **Edith Sitwell**.

Derek Walcott
Walcott's plays include *Dream on Monkey Mountain*, 1971; *The Joker of Seville*, 1978, and *O Babylon!*, 1978; and *Three Plays: The Last Carnival; Beef, No Chicken; A Branch of the Blue Nile*, 1986. He is better known for his poetry collections: *In a Green Night: Poems 1948–60*, 1960; *The Castaway and Other Poems*, 1965; *The Gulf and Other Poems*, 1969; *Another Life*, 1973; *Sea Grapes*, 1976; *The Fortunate Traveller*, 1981; *Midsummer*, 1984; *The Arkansas Testament*, 1988; *Omeros*, 1991; *The Bounty*, 1997. "The Poet in the Theatre," Derek Walcott's Ronald Duncan Lecture, was published in 1990. The standard bibliography is *Derek Walcott, The Primary Sources: An Annotated Bibliography of His Works*, ed. Irma E. Goldstraw, 1984. Critical studies of Walcott's writing include Edward Baugh, *Derek Walcott: Memory and Vision: Another Life*, 1978; Robert D. Hamner, *Critical Perspectives on Derek Walcott*, 1993, and Rei Terada, *Derek Walcott's Poetry: American Mimicry*, 1992. Useful sections on Walcott's work can be found in Tejumola Olaniyan, *Scars of Conquest—Masks of Resistance: The Invention of Cultural Identities in African, African-American, and Caribbean Drama*, 1995, and *Postcolonial Literatures: Achebe, Ngugi, Desai, Walcott*, ed. Michael Parker and Roger Starkey, 1995.

Virginia Woolf
The ten novels, *A Room of One's Own*, and *Three Guineas* are all available in paperback. *The Complete Shorter Fiction* has been edited by Susan Dick, 1985, and *The Essays*, 3 vols., by Andrew McNeillie, 1986–88. Useful selections of her essays edited by Rachel Bowlby, in Penguin paperbacks, are *The Crowded Dance of Modern Life* and *A Woman's Essays*. *The Diary of Virginia Woolf*, 5 vols., ed. Anne Olivier Bell and Andrew McNeillie, 1977–84, and *The Letters of Virginia Woolf*, 6 vols., ed. Nigel Nicolson and Joanne Trautmann, 1975–80, provide commentary on Woolf's life and work. For her early development, see *A Passionate Apprentice: The Early Journals, 1897–1909*, ed. Mitchell A. Leaska, 1990. *Moments of Being*, ed. Jeanne Schulkind, 1976, rev. 1989, contains her autobiographical writings. Her stories are collected in *The Complete Shorter Fiction of Virginia Woolf*, ed. Susan Dick, 1989.

Hermione Lee, *Virginia Woolf*, 1996, offers the fullest and most balanced account of her life and work; Quentin Bell, *Virginia Woolf*, 2 vols., 1972, is still an invaluable firsthand portrait; Phyllis Rose, *Woman of Letters: A Life of Virginia Woolf*, 1978, focuses on her feminism; and Lyndall Gordon, *Virginia Woolf: A Writer's Life*, 1984, shows Woolf's creative use of her own experience. Louise A. DeSalvo, *Virginia Woolf: The Impact of Childhood Sexual Abuse on Her Life and Work*, 1989, offers a revised picture of Woolf's childhood and its effect on her writing. Of interest also are Leonard Woolf's five volumes of autobiography, *Sowing*, 1960; *Growing*, 1961; *Beginning Again*, 1964; *Downhill All the Way*, 1967; *The Journey Not the Arrival Matters*, 1975; and *Letters of Leonard Woolf*, ed. Frederic Spotts, 1989. See also *Bloomsbury Group*, ed. S. P. Rosenbaum, 1975.

Perceptive critical studies include David Daiches, *Virginia Woolf*, rev. 1963; Joan Bennett, *Virginia Woolf: Her Art as a Novelist*, 2nd ed., 1964; H. Lee, *The Novels of Virginia Woolf*, 1977; Avrom Fleishman, *Virginia Woolf: A Critical Reading*, 1975; *New Feminist Essays on Virginia Woolf*, ed. Jane Marcus, 1981; *Virginia Woolf: New Critical Essays*, ed. Patricia Clements and Isobel Grundy, 1983; Alex Zwerdling, *Virginia Woolf and the Real World*, 1986; Rachel Bowlby, *Virginia Woolf: Feminist Destinations*, 1988, rev. 1997; Elizabeth Abel, *Virginia Woolf and the Fictions of Psychoanalysis*, 1989; John Mepham, *Virginia Woolf: A Literary Life*, 1991; Gillian Beer, *Virginia Woolf: The Common Ground*, 1996; Juliet Dusinberre, *Virginia Woolf's Renaissance*, 1997.

William Butler Yeats
In addition to poems and verse plays, Yeats published essays, stories, and autobiographical writings, and produced editions of William Blake (with Edwin Ellis) and of some poems of Spenser. He also edited *The Oxford Book of Modern Verse*, 1936. The major editions of his poems and plays are *The Variorum Edition of the Poems*, ed. Peter Allt and Russell K. Alspach, 1957, corrected 3rd printing, 1966, and *The Variorum Edition of the Plays*, ed. Russell K. Alspach, 1966, corrected 2nd printing, 1966. *Yeats's Poems*, ed. and annotated A. Norman Jeffares with an appendix by Warwick Gould, is the most satisfactory paperback edition. The fullest and most representative selection of the voluminous correspondence is *The Letters of W. B. Yeats*, ed. Allan Wade, 1954. This will be superseded by a multivolume edition, of which the first three volumes have appeared: *The Collected Letters of W. B. Yeats*, ed. John Kelly, 1986–. Yeats's mystical work *A Vision* was first published in 1925; a much-revised edition appeared in 1937. His autobiographical writings are combined in *The Autobiography of W. B. Yeats*, 1938–. Neither the first draft of Yeats's *Autobiography* nor his *Journals* were published until 1972, when Denis Donoghue edited them under the title *Memoirs*. *Mythologies*, 1959, contains the bulk of Yeats's prose fiction; *Essays and Introductions*, 1961, the most important of his critical prose; and *Explorations*, 1962, miscellaneous prose pieces not readily available elsewhere. John P. Frayne has edited *Uncollected Prose by W. B. Yeats*, 2 vols., 1970 and 1975, and William H. O'Donnell, *W. B. Yeats: Prefaces and Introductions*, 1988.

A. N. Jeffares, *W. B. Yeats: A New Biography*,

1989, is the best of the one-volume biographies, but will be superseded by Roy Foster, *W. B. Yeats: A Life*, vol. I of which was published in 1997.

The critical literature on Yeats is more extensive than that on any other twentieth-century poet, and the best guide to this is "W. B. Yeats" in *Anglo-Irish Literature: A Review of Research*, ed. Richard J. Finneran, 1976. Denis Donoghue, *Yeats*, 1971, is the most satisfactory of many short introductory studies, though less substantial than *Yeats: The Man and the Masks*, 1948, and *The Identity of Yeats*, 2nd ed., 1964, both by Richard Ellmann and still the best general accounts of Yeats's work. *The Permanence of Yeats*, ed. James Hall and Martin Steinmann, 1950; *Yeats: A Collection of Critical Essays*, ed. John Unterecker, 1963; *In Excited Reverie*, ed. A. N. Jef-

fares and K. G. W. Cross, 1965; and *Critical Essays on W. B. Yeats*, ed. Richard Finneran, 1987, are four of several useful collections of critical essays. The most helpful commentaries are A. N. Jeffares, *A New Commentary on the Poems of W. B. Yeats*, 1984, and *A Commentary on The Collected Plays of W. B. Yeats*, 1975. Specialized critical studies of important areas of Yeats's work are Thomas Parkinson, *W. B. Yeats, Self Critic: A Study of His Early Verse*, 1951, rpt. 1971 with *The Later Poetry* and a new foreword; Jon Stallworthy, *Between the Lines: W. B. Yeats's Poetry in the Making*, 1963, corrected 2nd imp., 1965; and Thomas R. Whitaker, *Swan and Shadow: Yeats's Dialogue with History*, 1964; and Michael J. Sidnell, *Yeats's Poetry and Poetics*, 1996.

Geographic Nomenclature: England, Great Britain, The United Kingdom

The British Isles refers to the prominent group of islands off the northwest coast of Europe, especially to the two largest, **Great Britain** and **Ireland**. At present these comprise two sovereign states: **The Republic of Ireland**, or **Eire**, and **The United Kingdom of Great Britain and Northern Ireland**—known for short as **The United Kingdom** or **The U.K.** Most of the smaller islands are part of **The U.K.** but a few, like the **Isle of Man** and the tiny **Channel Islands**, are very largely independent. **The U.K.** is often loosely referred to as "**Britain**" or "**Great Britain**" and is sometimes simply called "**England.**" The latter usage, though technically inaccurate and occasionally confusing, is common among Englishmen as well as foreigners, though, for obvious reasons, it is rarely heard among the inhabitants of the other countries of **The U.K.**—**Scotland**, **Wales**, and **Northern Ireland** (sometimes called **Ulster**). England is by far the most populous part of the kingdom, as well as the seat of its capital, London.

From the first to the fifth century C.E. most of what is now **England** and **Wales** was a province of the Roman Empire called **Britain** (in Latin, **Britannia**). After the fall of Rome, much of the island was invaded and settled by peoples from northern Germany and Denmark speaking what we now call Old English. They are collectively known as the Anglo-Saxons, and the word **England** is related to the first element of their name. By the time of the Norman Conquest (1066) most of the kingdoms founded by the Anglo-Saxons and subsequent Viking invaders had coalesced into the kingdom of **England**, which, in the latter Middle Ages, conquered and largely absorbed the neighboring Celtic kingdom of **Wales**. In 1603 James VI of **Scotland** inherited the island's other throne as James I of **England**, and for the next hundred years—except for the brief period of Puritan rule—**Scotland** and **England** (with **Wales**) were two kingdoms under a single king. In 1707 the Act of Union welded them together as **The United Kingdom of Great Britain**, which, upon the incorporation of **Ireland** in 1801, became **The United Kingdom of Great Britain and Ireland**. With the division of Ireland and the establishment of **The Irish Free State** after World War I, this name was modified to its present form. In 1949 **The Irish Free State** became **The Republic of Ireland**; and in 1997 **Scotland** voted to restore the separate parliament it had relinquished in 1707, without, however, ceasing to be part of **The United Kingdom**.

The **British Isles** are further divided into counties, which in **Great Britain** are also known as shires. This word, with its vowel shortened in pronunciation, forms the suffix in the names of many counties, such as **Yorkshire, Wiltshire, Somersetshire**.

The Latin names **Britannia (Britain), Caledonia (Scotland)**, and **Hibernia (Ireland)** are sometimes used in poetic diction; so too is **Britain**'s ancient Celtic name, **Albion**. Because of its accidental resemblance to *albus* (Latin for "white"), **Albion** is especially associated with the chalk cliffs which seem to gird much of the English coast like defensive walls.

The **British Empire** took its name from **The British Isles** because it was created not only by the **English** but by the **Irish, Scots**, and **Welsh**, as well as by civilians and servicemen from other constituent countries of the Empire.

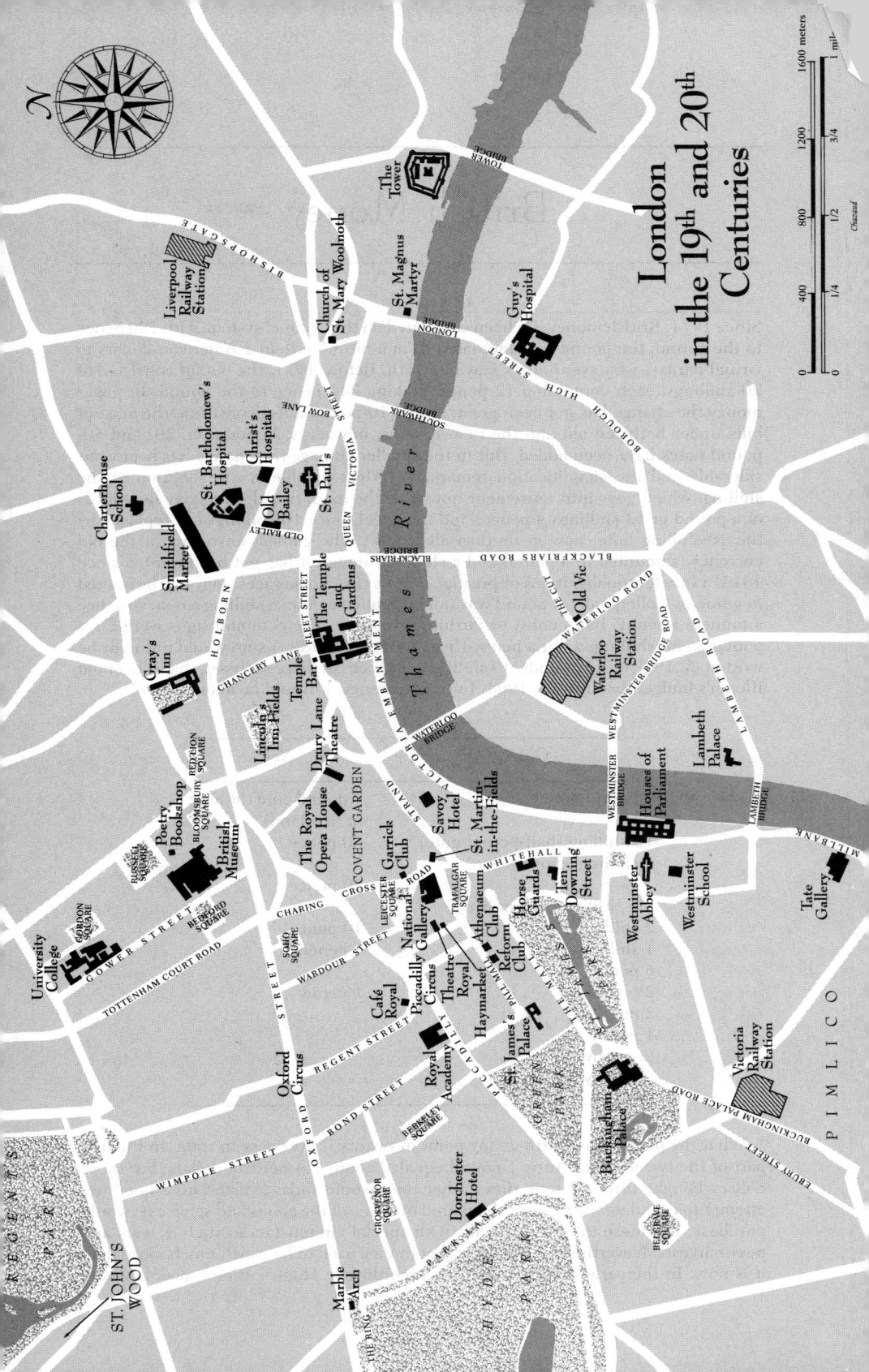

British Money

Since 1971, British money has been calculated on the decimal system, with 100 pence to the pound; the pound has fluctuated from a bit more than 2 American dollars to virtual parity—whatever dollars may be worth. Before 1971, the pound consisted of 20 shillings, each containing 12 pence, making 240 pence to the pound. In paper money the change has not been great; 5- and 10-pound notes constitute the mass of bills under both the old and the new systems; nowadays, in addition, 20- and 50-pound notes have been added. But in the smaller coinage the change has been considerable and the simplification remarkable. Most notable is the abolition of the shilling, which goes into retirement now with the mark (worth in its day two-thirds of a pound or 13 shillings 4 pence) and the angel (once 10 shillings but replaced by the 10-shilling note, now in its turn abolished). The guinea, an oddity of the old currency, amounted to a pound and a shilling; though it has not been minted since 1813, a very few quality items or prestige awards (like horse races) may still be quoted in guineas. Colloquially, a pound was (and is) called a quid; a shilling a bob; sixpence a tanner; a penny, half-penny, or farthing, a copper. The common signs were £ for pound, s. for shilling, d. for a penny (from Latin *denarius*). A sum would normally be written £2.19.3, i.e., 2 pounds, 19 shillings, 3 pence. In Joyce's *Ulysses*, that is Leopold Bloom's budget for June 16, 1904. In new currency, it would be about £2.96.

Old	New
1 pound note	1 pound coin (or note in Scotland)
10 shilling (half-pound note)	50 pence
5 shilling (crown)	
	20 pence
2½ shilling (half crown)	
2 shilling (florin)	10 pence
1 shilling	5 pence
6 pence	
2½ pence	1 penny
2 pence	
1 penny	
½ penny	
¼ penny (farthing)	

What the pound was worth at any point in history is ever easy to state. In the first part of the twentieth century, 1 pound equaled about 5 American dollars; but those dollars bought three or four times what they would today. Historians sometimes attempt to calculate the value of the pound in terms of the goods and services it would purchase, but these too vary radically with special circumstances such as wars and poor harvests. Nevertheless, it is clear that money used to be worth much more than it is now. In the early sixteenth century, according to Hugh Latimer, people would say, "Oh, he's a rich man, he's worth £500." Four centuries later, Virginia Woolf argued that £500 a year (along with a room of one's own) was the bare minimum necessary for a woman to be able to write. Whatever Latimer meant by "rich," or Woolf by "necessary," it is clear that the value of the pound had declined drastically over this period, as it has continued to do in the course of the twentieth century. In Britain today, a worker on minimum wage earns more than £500 a month, an income associated with severe poverty.

In the Anglo-Saxon period, the silver penny was the biggest coin in general circulation; 4 of them would buy a sheep. Peasants and craftsmen before the Black Death of the fourteenth century made at most 2 or 3 pence a day—an annual income of £3 or £4; after the onset of the plague, wages nearly doubled, due to the shortage of laborers. Throughout the medieval period, kings and commoners worried less about inflation than about the debasement of the silver currency. In 1124, dozens of mint-masters had their right hands chopped off on Christmas Day for issuing inferior coinage. In the early sixteenth century, under Henry VIII and his son Edward VI, the silver content of coins fell as low as 25 percent. Elizabeth I considered the revaluation of the silver coinage to be one of her greatest achievements as queen. Nevertheless, her reign was marked by sustained inflation of prices, caused in part by the influx of gold and silver from the New World, and in part by the rising population.

In the Elizabethan era, admission to the public theaters cost a penny for those who stood throughout the performance. Playwrights were paid about £6 for each play, so to make a living a writer had to be prolific (or, like Shakespeare, own shares in the theater company). In the same period, 40 pounds a year in independent income (generally rent from lands) was the minimum requirement for a justice of the peace; it marked the threshold of gentry status and was also the sum fixed by King James I at which a man could be forced to accept knighthood (paying a fee to the crown). In 1661, following further inflation, Samuel Pepys calculated his worth at a modest £650 just after he had begun working for the navy; five years later, that good bourgeois was worth more than £6000, and his annual income was about £3000. Of course, he was working for most of this income. Pepys was a rising official and would become a very important one; but he never achieved a title or even knighthood because the smell of commerce had never been washed from his money by possession of land.

Various writers provide examples of the incomes of rich and poor in the eighteenth and nineteenth centuries. Joseph Andrews (in Fielding's novel, published 1742) worked as a footman in the house of Lady Booby for £8 a year; in addition, he got his room, board, and livery, plus the occasional tip. Among the comfortable classes, Mr. Bennet of Jane Austen's *Price and Prejudice* (1813) enjoyed an income of £2000 a year (with a family of five nonearning females to support), while Mr. Darcy had close to £10,000, nearing the level of the aristocracy. In his deepest degradation David Copperfield (of Dickens's 1850 novel) worked in the warehouse of Murdstone & Grinby for 6 or 7 shillings a week (£15 to £18 a year). Mr. Murdstone paid extra for his lodging and laundry, but even so the boy was bitterly impoverished, though he had only himself to feed. When his father died, his mother was thought to be pretty well taken care of with £105 a year, less than £9 per month. Even in 1888, Annie Besant reports workers in Bryant and May's match factory made 4 to 9 shillings a week and paid for their own lodging—this, in the words of Ada Nield Chew, was not a living wage, but "a lingering, dying wage." Far removed from this world is Jack Worthing in Wilde's comedy *The Importance of Being Earnest* (1895), who receives £7000 or £8000 a year from investments and has a country house with about fifteen hundred acres attached to it, though it yields no income worth talking about.

While incomes have risen enormously over the centuries, and the value of the pound declined accordingly, the gap between rich and poor has remained. So too has the gap between the country and the city: London has always been very expensive, and elsewhere a small income goes further. To a large extent, one's position in terms of class and geography determines not only what money can buy but what it means.

We have only to contrast Jack Worthing's vague estimate of his income with the factory workers' exact sense of the value of a shilling. As Woolf acknowledged, having a purse with the power "to breed ten-shilling notes automatically," changes one's view of money and of the world. Perhaps it is because British currency has been so important in shaping people's views of themselves and their society that many Britons are reluctant to let it go. The question of whether the United Kingdom should relinquish the pound and the penny to join the single European currency (the Euro) is a matter of fierce and prolonged debate. For some, the pound, far more than the flag, is an enduring symbol of the nation. Whether or not one holds this view, it can at least be said that over the centuries the pound has undergone as many crises and transformations as the nation itself.

The British Baronage

The English monarchy is in principle hereditary, though at times during the Middle Ages the rules were subject to dispute. In general, authority passes from father to eldest surviving son, from daughters in order of seniority if there is no son, to a brother if there are no children, and in default of direct descendants to collateral lines (cousins, nephews, nieces) in order of closeness. There have been breaks in the order of succession (1066, 1399, 1688), but so far as possible the usurpers have always sought to paper over the break with a legitimate, i.e., a hereditary claim. When a queen succeeds to the throne and takes a husband, he does not become king unless he is in the line of blood succession; rather, he is named prince consort, as Albert was to Victoria. He may father kings, but is not one himself.

The original Saxon nobles were the king's thanes, ealdormen, or earls, who provided the king with military service and counsel in return for booty, gifts, or landed estates. William the Conqueror, arriving from France, where feudalism was fully developed, considerably expanded this group. In addition, as the king distributed the lands of his new kingdom, he also distributed dignities to men who became known collectively as "the baronage." "Baron" in its root meaning signifies simply "man," and barons were the king's men. As the title was common, a distinction was early made between greater and lesser barons, the former gradually assuming loftier and more impressive titles. The first English "duke" was created in 1337; the title of "marquess," or "marquis" (pronounced "markwis"), followed in 1385, and "viscount" ("vyekount") in 1440. Though "earl" is the oldest title of all, it now comes between a marquess and a viscount in order of dignity and precedence, and the old term "baron" now designates a rank just below viscount. "Baronets" were created in 1611 as a means of raising revenue for the crown (the title could be purchased for about £1000); they are marginal nobility and do not sit in the House of Lords.

Kings and queens are addressed as "Your Majesty," princes and princesses as "Your Highness," the other hereditary nobility as "My Lord" or "Your Lordship." Peers receive their titles either by inheritance (like Lord Byron, the sixth baron of that line) or from the monarch (like Alfred Lord Tennyson, created first Baron Tennyson by Victoria). The children, even of a duke, are commoners unless they are specifically granted some other title or inherit their father's title from him. A peerage can be forfeited by act of attainder, as for example when a lord is convicted of treason; and, when forfeited, or lapsed for lack of a successor, can be bestowed on another family. Thus Robert Cecil was made in 1605 first earl of Salisbury in the third creation, the first creation dating from 1149, the second from 1337, the title having been in abeyance since 1539. Titles descend by right of succession and do not depend on tenure of land; thus, a title does not always indicate where a lord dwells or holds power. Indeed, noble titles do not always refer to a real place at all. At Prince Edward's marriage in 1999, the queen created him earl of Wessex, although the old kingdom of Wessex has had no political existence since the Anglo-Saxon period, and the name was all but forgotten until it was resurrected by Thomas Hardy as the setting of his novels. (This is perhaps but one of many ways in which the world of the aristocracy increasingly resembles the realm of literature.)

The king and queen Prince and princess	(These are all of the royal line.)

Duke and duchess Marquess and marchioness Earl and countess Viscount and viscountess Baron and baroness Baronet and lady	(These may or may not be of the royal line, but are ordinarily remote from the succession.)

Scottish peers sat in the parliament of Scotland, as English peers did in the parliament of England, till at the Act of Union (1707) Scots peers were granted sixteen seats in the English House of Lords, to be filled by election. Similarly, Irish peers, when the Irish parliament was abolished in 1801, were granted the right to elect twenty-eight of their number to the House of Lords in Westminster. (Now that the Republic of Ireland is a separate nation, of course, this no longer applies.) The House of Lords still retains some power to influence or delay legislation. But this upper house is now being reformed. All or most of the hereditary peers are to be expelled, while recipients of nonhereditary Life Peerages will remain and vote as before.

Below the peerage the chief title of honor is "knight." Knighthood, which is not hereditary, is generally a reward for services rendered. A knight (Sir John Black) is addressed, using his first name, as "Sir John"; his wife, using the last name, is "Lady Black"—unless she is the daughter of an earl or nobleman of higher rank, in which case she will be "Lady Arabella." The female equivalent of a knight bears the title of "Dame."

Though the word itself comes from the Anglo-Saxon *cniht*, there seems to be some doubt as to whether knighthood amounted to much before the arrival of the Normans. The feudal system required military service as a condition of land tenure, and a man who came to serve his king at the head of an army of tenants required a title of authority and badges of identity—hence the title of knighthood and the coat of arms. During the Crusades, when men were far removed from their land (or had even sold it in order to go on crusade), more elaborate forms of fealty sprang up that soon expanded into orders of knighthood. The Templars, Hospitallers, Knights of the Teutonic Order, Knights of Malta, and Knights of the Golden Fleece were but a few of these companionships; not all of them were available at all times in England.

Gradually, with the rise of centralized government and the decline of feudal tenures, military knighthood became obsolete, and the rank largely honorific; sometimes, as under James I, it degenerated into a scheme of the royal government for making money. For hundreds of years after its establishment in the fourteenth century, the Order of the Garter was the only English order of knighthood, an exclusive courtly companionship. Then, during the late seventeenth, the eighteenth, and the nineteenth centuries, a number of additional orders were created, with names such as the Thistle, Saint Patrick, the Bath, Saint Michael and Saint George, plus a number of special Victorian and Indian orders. They retain the terminology, ceremony, and dignity of knighthood, but the military implications are vestigial.

Although the British Empire now belongs to history, appointments to the Order of the British Empire continue to be conferred for services to that empire at home or abroad. Such honors (commonly referred to as "gongs") are granted by the monarch in her New Year's and Birthday lists, but the decisions are now made by the government in power. In recent years there have been efforts to popularize and democratize the dispensation of honors, with recipients including rock stars and actors. But this does not prevent large sectors of British society from regarding both knighthood and the peerage as largely irrelevant to modern life.

The Royal Lines of England and Great Britain

England

SAXONS AND DANES

Egbert, king of Wessex	802–839
Ethelwulf, son of Egbert	839–858
Ethelbald, son of Ethelwulf	858–860
Ethelbert, second son of Ethelwulf	860–866
Ethelred I, third son of Ethelwulf	866–871
Alfred the Great, fourth son of Ethelwulf	871–899
Edward the Elder, son of Alfred	899–924
Athelstan the Glorious, son of Edward	924–940
Edmund I, third son of Edward	940–946
Edred, fourth son of Edward	946–955
Edwy the Fair, son of Edmund	955–959
Edgar the Peaceful, second son of Edmund	959–975
Edward the Martyr, son of Edgar	975–978 (murdered)
Ethelred II, the Unready, second son of Edgar	978–1016
Edmund II, Ironside, son of Ethelred II	1016–1016
Canute the Dane	1016–1035
Harold I, Harefoot, natural son of Canute	1035–1040
Hardecanute, son of Canute	1040–1042
Edward the Confessor, son of Ethelred II	1042–1066
Harold II, brother-in-law of Edward	1066–1066 (died in battle)

HOUSE OF NORMANDY

William I the Conqueror	1066–1087
William II, Rufus, third son of William I	1087–1100 (shot from ambush)
Henry I, Beauclerc, youngest son of William I	1100–1135

HOUSE OF BLOIS

Stephen, son of Adela, daughter of William I	1135–1154

HOUSE OF PLANTAGENET

Henry II, son of Geoffrey Plantagenet by Matilda, daughter of Henry I	1154–1189
Richard I, Coeur de Lion, son of Henry II	1189–1199
John Lackland, son of Henry II	1199–1216
Henry III, son of John	1216–1272
Edward I, Longshanks, son of Henry III	1272–1307
Edward II, son of Edward I	1307–1327
Edward III of Windsor, son of Edward II	1327–1377
Richard II, grandson of Edward III	1377–1400

HOUSE OF LANCASTER

Henry IV, son of John of Gaunt, son of Edward III	1399–1413
Henry V, Prince Hal, son of Henry IV	1413–1422
Henry VI, son of Henry V	1422–1471 (deposed)

HOUSE OF YORK

Edward IV, great-great-grandson of Edward III	1461–1483
Edward V, son of Edward IV	1483–1483 (murdered)
Richard III, Crookback	1483–1485 (died in battle)

HOUSE OF TUDOR

Henry VII, married daughter of Edward IV	1485–1509
Henry VIII, son of Henry VII	1509–1547
Edward VI, son of Henry VIII	1547–1553
Mary I, "Bloody," daughter of Henry VIII	1553–1558
Elizabeth I, daughter of Henry VIII	1558–1603

HOUSE OF STUART

James I (James VI of Scotland)	1603–1625
Charles I, son of James I	1625–1649 (executed)

COMMONWEALTH & PROTECTORATE

Council of State	1649–1653
Oliver Cromwell, Lord Protector	1653–1658
Richard Cromwell, son of Oliver	1658–1660 (resigned)

HOUSE OF STUART (RESTORED)

Charles II, son of Charles I	1660–1685
James II, second son of Charles I	1685–1688

(INTERREGNUM, 11 DECEMBER 1688 TO 13 FEBRUARY 1689)

William III of Orange, by Mary, daughter of Charles I	1685–1701
and Mary II, daughter of James II	–1694
Anne, second daughter of James II	1702–1714

Great Britain

HOUSE OF HANOVER

George I, son of Elector of Hanover and Sophia, granddaughter of James I	1714–1727
George II, son of George I	1727–1760
George III, grandson of George II	1760–1820
George IV, son of George III	1820–1830
William IV, third son of George III	1830–1837
Victoria, daughter of Edward, fourth son of George III	1837–1901

HOUSE OF SAXE-COBURG AND GOTHA

Edward VII, son of Victoria   1901–1910

HOUSE OF WINDSOR (NAME ADOPTED 17 JULY 1917)

George V, second son of Edward VII 1910–1936
Edward VIII, eldest son of George V 1936–1936 (abdicated)
George VI, second son of George V 1936–1952
Elizabeth II, daughter of George VI 1952–

Religions in England

Religious distinctions and denominations are important in British social history, hence deeply woven into the nation's literature. The numerous (over three hundred) British churches and sects divide along a scale from high to low, depending on the amount of authority they give to the church or the amount of liberty they concede to the individual conscience. At one end of the scale is the Roman Catholic Church, asserting papal infallibility, universal jurisdiction, and the supreme importance of hierarchy as guide and intercessor. For political and social reasons, Catholicism struck deep roots in Ireland but in England was the object of prolonged, bitter hatred on the part of Protestants from the Reformation through the nineteenth century. The Established English (Anglican) Episcopal church has been the official national church since the sixteenth century; it enjoys the support (once direct and exclusive, now indirect and peripheral) of the national government. Its creed is defined by Thirty-Nine Articles, but these are intentionally vague, so there are numerous ways of adhering to the Church of England. Roughly and intermittently, the chief classes of Anglicans have been known as High Church (with its highest portion calling itself Anglo-Catholic); Broad Church, or Latitudinarian (when they get so broad that they admit anyone believing in God, they may be known as Deists, or some may leave the church altogether and be known as Unitarians); and Low Church, whose adherents may stay in the English church and yet come close to shaking hands with Presbyterians or Methodists. These various groups may be arranged, from the High down to the Low Church, in direct relation to the amount of ritual each prefers and in the degree of authority conceded to the upper clergy—and in inverse relation to the importance ascribed to a saving faith directly infused by God into an individual conscience.

All English Protestants who decline to subscribe to the English established church are classed as Dissenters or Nonconformists; for a time in the sixteenth and seventeenth centuries, they were also known as Puritans. (Nowadays, though Puritanism has less distinct theological meaning, it marks a distinct character type; because of his passionate emphasis on individual conscience and moral economy, Bernard Shaw was a prototypical Puritan.) The Presbyterians model their church government on that established by John Calvin in the Swiss city of Geneva. It has no bishops, and therefore is more democratic for the clergy; but it gains energy by associating lay elders with clergymen in matters of social discipline and tends to be strict with the ungodly. From its first reformation the Scottish Kirk was fixed on the Presbyterian model. During the civil wars of the seventeenth century, a great many sects sprang up on the left wing of the Presbyterians, most of them touched by Calvinism but some rebelling against it; a few of these still survive. The Independents became our modern Congregationalists; the Quakers are still Quakers, as Baptists are still Baptists, though multiply divided. But many of the sects flourished and perished within the space of a few years. Among these now vanished groups were the Shakers (though a few groups still exist in America), the Seekers, the Ranters, the Anabaptists, the Muggletonians, the Fifth Monarchy Men, the Family of Love, the Sweet Singers of Israel, and many others, forgotten by all except scholars. During the eighteenth and nineteenth centuries, new sects arose, supplanting old ones; the Methodists, under John and Charles Wesley, became numerous and important, taking root particularly in Wales. (The three "subject" nationalities, Ireland, Scotland, and Wales, thus turned three different ways to avoid the Anglican church.) With the passage of time a small number of Swedenborgians sprang up, followers of the Swedish mystic Emanuel Swedenborg—to be followed by the Plymouth Brethren, Christian Scientists, Jehovah's Witnesses, and countless other nineteenth-century groups. All these sects constantly grow, shrink, split, and occasionally disappear as they succeed or fail in attracting new converts.

Within the various churches and sects, independent of them all but amazingly persistent, there has always survived a stream of esoteric or hermetic thought—a belief in occult powers, and sometimes in magic also, exemplified by the pseudosciences of astrology and alchemy but taking many other forms as well. From the mythical Egyptian seer Hermes Trismegistus through Paracelsus, Cornelius Agrippa, Giordano Bruno, Jakob Boehme, the society of Rosicrucians, and a hundred other shadowy figures, the line can be traced to William Blake and William Butler Yeats, who both in their different ways brought hermetic Protestantism close to its ultimate goal, a mystic church of a single consciousness, poised within its mind-elaborated cosmos.

Christianity is not, of course, the only religion present on the British Isles. The few Jews in medieval England were regarded as resident aliens, as were those in other European countries. In 1290 all English Jews who refused baptism were expelled from the kingdom, and officially, there were no Jews living in England between that time and the mid-1650s, when Cromwell encouraged Jewish merchants to settle in London. A considerable number of east European Jews emigrated to England in the first half of the twentieth century (many as refugees), but the country's Jewish population as a whole remains quite small (less than half a million). Hardly any Muslims or Hindus lived in the U.K. before the dissolution of the Empire shortly after World War II. Today both religions have a large and growing representation among excolonial immigrants and their children.

Poetic Forms and
Literary Terminology

Systematic literary theory and criticism in English began in the sixteenth century, at a time when the standard education for upper-class students emphasized the study of the classical languages and literatures. As a consequence, the English words that were introduced to describe meter, figures of speech, and literary genres often derive from Latin and Greek roots.

RHYTHM AND METER

Verse is generally distinguished from prose as a more compressed and more regularly rhythmic form of statement. This approximate truth underlines the importance of **meter** in poetry, as the means by which rhythm is measured and described.

In Latin and Greek, meter was established on a **quantitative** basis, by the regular alternation of long and short syllables (that is, syllables classified according to the time taken to pronounce them). Outside of a few experiments (and the songs of Thomas Campion), this system has never proved congenial to Germanic languages such as English, which distinguish, instead, between **stressed** and **unstressed,** or accented and unaccented syllables. Two varieties of accented stress may be distinguished. On the one hand, there is the natural stress pattern of words themselves; *sýllable* is accented on the first syllable, *deplórable* on the second, and so on. Then there is the sort of stress that indicates rhetorical emphasis. If the sentence "You went to Greece?" is given a pronounced accent on the last word, it implies "Greece (of all places)?" If the accent falls on the first word, it implies "you (of all people)?" The meter of poetry—that is, its rhythm—is ordinarily built up out of a regular recurrence of accents, whether established as **word accents** or **rhetorical accents;** once started, it has (like all rhythm) a tendency to persist in the reader's mind.

The unit that is repeated to give steady rhythm to a poem is called a **foot;** in English it usually consists of accented and unaccented syllables in one of five fairly simple patterns:

The **iambic foot** (or **iamb**) consists of an unstressed followed by a stressed syllable, as in *uníte, repeát,* or *insíst.* Most English verse falls naturally into the iambic pattern.

The **trochaic foot** (**trochee**) inverts this order; it is a stressed followed by an unstressed syllable—for example, *únit, réaper,* or *ínstant.*

The **anapestic foot** (**anapest**) consists of two unstressed syllables followed by a stressed syllable, as in *intercéde, disarránged,* or *Caméroon.*

The **dactylic foot** (**dactyl**) consists of a stressed syllable followed by two unstressed syllables, as in *Wáshington, Écuador,* or *ápplejack.*

The **spondaic foot** (**spondee**) consists of two successive stressed syllables, as in *heartbreak, headline,* or *Kashmir.*

In all the examples above, word accent and the quality of the metrical foot coincide exactly. But the metrical foot may well consist of several words, or, on the other hand, one word may well consist of several metrical feet. *Phótolithógraphy* consists of two dactyls in a single word; *dárk and with spóts on it*, though it consists of six words rather than one, is also two dactyls. When we read a piece of poetry with the intention of discovering its underlying metrical pattern, we are said to **scan** it—that is, we go through it line by line, indicating by conventional signs which are the accented and which the unaccented syllables within the feet. We also count the number of feet in each line; a line is, formally, also called a **verse** (from Latin *versus*, which means one "row" of metrical feet). Verse lengths are conventionally described in terms derived from the Greek:

Monometer: one foot (of rare occurrence)
Dimeter: two feet (also rare)
Trimeter: three feet
Tetrameter: four feet
Pentameter: five feet
Hexameter: six feet (six iambic feet make what is called an **Alexandrine**)
Heptameter: seven feet (also rare)

Samuel Johnson wrote a little parody of simpleminded poets which can be scanned this way:

> Ĭ pút m̆y hát ŭpón m̆y héad
> Ănd wálked ĭntó thĕ Stránd
> Ănd thére Ĭ mét ănóthĕr mán
> Whŏse hát wăs ín hĭs hánd.

The poem is iambic in rhythm, alternating tetrameter and trimeter in the length of the verse-lines. The fact that it scans so nicely is, however, no proof that it is good poetry. Quite the contrary. Many of poetry's most subtle effects are achieved by establishing an underlying rhythm and then varying it by means of a whole series of devices, some dramatic and expressive, others designed simply to lend variety and interest to the verse. A well-known sonnet of Shakespeare's (*116*) begins,

> Let me not to the marriage of true minds
> Admit impediments. Love is not love
> Which alters when it alteration finds,
> Or bends with the remover to remove.

It is possible to read the first line of this poem as mechanical iambic pentameter:

Lĕt mé nŏt tó thĕ márriăge óf trŭe mińds

But of course nobody ever reads it that way, except to make a point; read with normal English accent and some sense of what it is saying, the line would form a pattern something like this:

Lét mĕ nŏt tŏ thĕ márriăge ŏf trúe mińds

which is neither pentameter nor in any way iambic. The second line is a little more iambic, but, read expressively also falls short of pentameter:

Ădmít ĭmpédĭmeňts. Lóve ĭs nŏt lóve

Only in the third and fourth lines of the sonnet do we get verses that read as five iambic feet.

The fact is that perfectly regular metrical verse is easy to write and dull to read. Among the devices in common use for varying too regular a pattern are the insertion of a trochaic foot among iambics, especially at the opening of a line, where the soft first syllable of the iambic foot often needs stiffening (see line 1 of the sonnet above); the more or less free addition of extra unaccented syllables; and the use of **caesura,** or strong grammatical pause within a line (conventionally indicated, in scanning, by the sign ‖). The second line of the sonnet above is a good example of caesura:

Admit impediments. ‖ Love is not love

The strength of the caesura, and its placing in the line, may be varied to produce striking variations of effect. More broadly, the whole relation between the poem's sound and rhythm-patterns and its pattern as a sequence of assertions (phrases, clauses, sentences) may be manipulated by the poet. Sometimes the statements fit neatly within the lines, so that each line ends with a strong mark of punctuation; they are then known as **end-stopped lines.** Sometimes the sense flows over the ends of the lines, creating **run-on lines;** this process is also known, from the French, as **enjambment** (literally, "straddling").

End-stopped lines (Marlowe, *Hero and Leander*, lines 45–48):

> So lovely fair was Hero, Venus' nun,
> As Nature wept, thinking she was undone,
> Because she took more from her than she left
> And of such wondrous beauty her bereft.

Run-on lines (Keats, *Endymion* 1.89–93):

> Full in the middle of this pleasantness
> There stood a marble altar, with a tress
> Of flowers budded newly; and the dew
> Had taken fairy fantasies to strew
> Daisies upon the sacred sward, . . .

Following the example of such poets as Blake, Rimbaud, and Whitman, many twentieth-century poets have undertaken to write what is called **free** verse—that is, verse which has neither a fixed metrical foot nor (conse-quently) a fixed number of feet in its lines, but which depends for its rhythm on a pattern of cadences, or the rise and fall of the voice in utterance, or the pattern indicated to the reader's eye by the breaks between the verse lines. As in traditional versification, free verse is printed in short lines instead of with the continuity of prose; it differs from such versification, however, by the fact that its stressed syllables are not organized into a regular metric sequence.

SENSE AND SOUND

The words of which poetic lines—whether free or traditional—are composed cause them to have different sounds and produce different effects. Polysyl-lables, being pronounced fast, often cause a line to move swiftly; monosyl-lables, especially when heavy and requiring distinct accents, may cause it to move heavily, as in Milton's famous line (*Paradise Lost* 2.621):

> Rocks, caves, lakes, fens, bogs, dens, and shades of death

Poetic assertions are often dramatized and reinforced by means of **allitera-tion**—that is, the use of several nearby words or stressed syllables beginning with the same consonant. When Shakespeare writes (*Sonnet 64*),

> Ruin hath taught me thus to ruminate
> That Time will come and take my love away,

the alliterative *r*'s and rich internal echoes of the first line contrast with the sharp anxiety and directness of the alliterative *t*'s in the second. When Dry-den starts *Absalom and Achitophel* with the couplet,

> In pious times, ere priestcraft did begin,
> Before polygamy was made a sin,

the satiric undercutting is strongly reinforced by the triple alliteration that links *"pious"* with *"priestcraft"* and *"polygamy."*

Assonance, or repetition of the same or similar vowel sounds within a passage (usually in accented syllables), also serves to enrich it, as in two lines from Keats's *Ode on Melancholy*:

> For shade to shade will come too drowsily,
> And drown the wakeful anguish of the soul.

It is clear that the round, hollow tones of "drowsily," repeated in "drown" and darkening to the full *o*-sound of "soul," have much to do with the effect of the passage. A related device is **consonance**, or the repetition of a pattern of consonants with changes in the intervening vowels—for example: *linger, longer, languor; rider, reader, raider, ruder.*

The use of words that seem to reproduce the sounds they designate (known as **onomatopoeia**) has been much attempted, from Virgil's galloping horse—

Quadrupedante putrem sonitu quatit ungula campum—

through Tennyson's account, in *The Princess*, of

> The moan of doves in immemorial elms,
> And murmuring of innumerable bees—

to many poems in the present day.

RHYME AND STANZA

Rhyme consists of a repetition of accented sounds in words, usually those falling at the end of verse lines. If the rhyme sound is the very last syllable of the line (*rebound, sound*), the rhyme is called **masculine;** if the accented syllable is followed by an unaccented syllable (*hounding, bounding*), the rhyme is called **feminine**. Rhymes amounting to three or more syllables, like forced rhymes, generally have a comic effect in English, and have been freely used for this purpose, e.g., by Byron (*intellectual, henpecked-you-all*). Rhymes occurring within a single line are called **internal;** for instance, the Mother Goose rhyme "Mary, Mary, quite contrary," or from Coleridge's *Ancient Mariner* ("We were the first that ever burst / Into that silent sea"). **Eye rhymes** are words used as rhymes that look alike but actually sound different (for example, *alone, done; remove, love*); **off rhymes** (sometimes called **partial, imperfect,** or **slant rhymes**) are occasionally the result of pressing exigencies or lack of skill, but are also, at times, used deliberately by modern poets for special effects. For instance, a poem by Wilfred Owen (*Strange Meeting*) contains such paired words (which Owen called "pararhymes") as *years / yours* or *tigress / progress*.

Blank verse is unrhymed iambic pentameter; until the recent advent of free verse, it was the only unrhymed measure to achieve general popularity in English. Though first used by the earl of Surrey in translating Virgil's *Aeneid*, blank verse was during the sixteenth century employed primarily in plays; *Paradise Lost* was one of the first nondramatic poems in English to use it. But Milton's authority and his success were so great that during the eighteenth and nineteenth centuries blank verse came to be used for a great variety of discursive, descriptive, and philosophical poems—besides remaining the standard metrical form for epics. Thomson's *Seasons*, Cowper's *Task*, Wordsworth's *Prelude*, and Tennyson's *Idylls of the King* were all written in blank verse.

A **stanza** is a recurring unit of a poem, consisting of a number of verses. Certain poems (for example, Dryden's *Alexander's Feast*) have stanzas comprising a variable number of verses, of varying lengths. Others are more regular, and are identified by particular names.

The simplest form of stanza is the **couplet;** it is two lines rhyming together. A single couplet considered in isolation is sometimes called a **distich;** when it expresses a complete thought, ending with a terminal mark of punctuation such as a semicolon or period, it is called a **closed couplet.** The development of very regular end-stopped couplets, their use in so-called heroic tragedies, and their consequent acquisition of the name **heroic couplets** took place for the most part during the mid-seventeenth century. The heroic couplet was the principal form in English neoclassical poems.

Another traditional and challenging form of couplet is the **tetrameter, or four-beat couplet.** All rhymed couplets are hard to manage without monotony; and since, in addition, a four-beat line is hard to divide by caesura without splitting it into two tick-tock dimeters, tetrameter couplets have posed a perpetual challenge to poets, and still provide an admirable finger-exercise for aspiring versifiers. An instance of tetrameter couplets managed with marvelous variety, complexity, and expressiveness is Marvell's *To His Coy Mistress*:

> Thou by the Indian Ganges' side
> Shouldst rubies find; I by the tide
> Of Humber would complain. I would
> Love you ten years before the Flood,
> And you should, if you please, refuse
> Till the conversion of the Jews.

English has not done much with rhymes grouped in threes, but has borrowed from Italian the form known as **terza rima,** in which Dante composed his *Divine Comedy*. This form consists of linked groups of three rhymes according to the following pattern: *aba bcb cdc ded*, etc. Shelley's *Ode to the West Wind* is composed in stanzas of *terza rima*, the poem as a whole ending with a couplet.

Quatrains are stanzas of four lines; the lines usually rhyme alternately, *abab*, or in the second and fourth lines, *abcb*. When they alternate tetrameter and trimeter lines, as in Johnson's little poem about men in hats (above), or as in *Sir Patrick Spens*, they are called **ballad stanza.** Dryden's *Annus Mirabilis* and Gray's *Elegy Written in a Country Churchyard* are in **heroic quatrains;** these rhyme alternately *abab*, and employ five-stress iambic verse throughout. Tennyson used for *In Memoriam* a tetrameter quatrain rhymed *abba*, and FitzGerald translated *The Rubáiyát of Omar Khayyám* into a pentameter quatrain rhymed *aaba*; but these forms have not been widely adopted.

Chaucer's *Troilus and Criseide* is the premier example in English of **rhyme royal,** a seven-line iambic pentameter stanza consisting essentially of a quatrain dovetailed onto two couplets, according to the rhyme scheme *ababbcc* (the fourth line serves both as the final line of the quatrain and as the first line of the first couplet). Closely akin to rhyme royal, but differentiated by an extra *a*-rhyme between the two *b*-rhymes, is **ottava rima,** that is, an eight-line stanza rhyming *abababcc*. As its name suggests, ottava rima is of Italian origin; it was first used in English by Wyatt. Its final couplet, being less prepared for than in rhyme royal, and usually set off as a separate verbal unit, is capable of manifesting a witty snap, for which Byron found good use in *Don Juan*.

The longest and most intricate stanza generally used for narrative purposes in English is that devised by Edmund Spenser for *The Faerie Queene*. The **Spenserian stanza** has nine lines rhyming *ababbcbcc*; the first eight lines are pentameter, the last line an Alexandrine. Slow-moving, intricate of pattern, and very demanding in its rhyme scheme (the *b*-sound recurs four times, the *c*-sound three), the Spenserian stanza has nonetheless appealed widely to poets who seek a rich and complicated metrical form. Keats's *Eve of St. Agnes* and Shelley's *Adonais* are brilliantly successful nineteenth-century examples of its use.

The **sonnet,** originally a stanza of Italian origin that has developed into an independent lyric form, is usually defined nowadays as fourteen lines of iambic pentameter. None of the elements in this definition is absolute and in earlier centuries there were sonnets in hexameters (the first of Sidney's *Astrophil and Stella*), and sonnets of as many as twenty lines (Milton's *On the New Forcers of Conscience*). Most, however, approximate the definition. Most Elizabethan sonnets dealt with love; and some poets, like Sidney, Spenser, and Shakespeare, imitated Petrarch in grouping together their sonnets dealing with a particular lady or situation. The term for these gatherings is **sonnet sequences;** the extent to which they tell a sequential story, and the extent to which such stories are autobiographical, vary greatly. Since Elizabethan times, the sonnet has been applied to a wide range of subject matters—religious, political, satiric, moral, and philosophic.

In blank verse or irregularly rhymed verse, where stanzaic divisions do not exist or are indistinct, the poetry sometimes falls into **verse paragraphs,** which are in effect divisions of sense like prose paragraphs. This division can be clearly seen in Milton's *Lycidas* and *Paradise Lost*. An intermediate form, clearly stanzaic but with stanzas of varying patterns of line-length and rhyme, is illustrated by Spenser's *Epithalamion*; in this instance, the division into stanzas is reinforced by a **refrain,** which is simply a line repeated at the end of each stanza. Ballads also customarily have refrains; for example, the refrain of *Lord Randall* is

> mother, make my bed soon,
> For I'm weary wi' hunting, and fain wald lie down.

FIGURATIVE LANGUAGE

The act of bringing words together into rich and vigorous poetic lines is complex and demanding, chiefly because so many variables require control. There is the "thought" of the lines, their verbal texture, their emotional resonance, the developing perspective of the reader—all these to be managed at once. One of the poet's chief resources toward this end is figurative language. Here, as in matters of meter, one may distinguish a great variety of devices, some of which we use in everyday speech without special awareness of their names and natures. When we say someone eats "like a horse" or "like a bird," we are using a **simile,** that is, a comparison marked out by a specific word of likening—"like" or "as." When we omit the word of comparison but imply a likeness—as in the sentence "That hog has guzzled all the champagne"—we are making use of **metaphor.** The **epic simile,** frequent in epic poetry, is an extended simile in which the thing compared is described as an object in its own right, beyond its point of likeness with the main subject. Milton starts to compare Satan to Leviathan, but concludes his simile with the story of a sailor who moored his ship by mistake, one night, to a whale (*Paradise Lost* 1.200–208). Metaphors and similes have been distinguished according to their special effects; they may be, for instance, violent, comic, degrading, decorative, or ennobling.

When we speak of "forty head of cattle" or ask someone to "lend a hand" with a job, we are using **synecdoche,** a figure that substitutes the part for the whole. When we speak of a statement coming "from the White House," or a man much interested in "the turf," (that is, the race-course), we are using **metonymy,** or the substitution of one term for another with which it is closely associated. **Antithesis** is a device for placing opposing ideas in grammatical parallel, as, for example, in the following passage from Alexander Pope's *Rape of the Lock* (5.25–30), where there are more examples of antithesis than there are lines:

> But since, alas! frail beauty must decay,
> Curled or uncurled, since locks will turn to gray;
> Since painted, or not painted, all shall fade,
> And she who scorns a man must die a maid;
> What then remains but well our power to use,
> And keep good humor still whate'er we lose?

Irony is a verbal device that implies an attitude quite different from (and often opposite to) that which is literally expressed. In Pope's *The Rape of the Lock* (4.131–32), after poor Sir Plume has stammered an incoherent request to return the stolen lock of hair, the Baron answers ironically:

> "It grieves me much," replied the Peer again,
> "Who speaks so well should ever speak in vain."

And when Donne "proves," in *The Canonization*, that he and his mistress are going to found a new religion of love, he seems to be inviting us to take a subtly ironic attitude toward religion as well as love.

Because it is easy to see through, **hyperbole,** or willful exaggeration, is a favorite device of irony—which is not to say that it may not be "serious" as well. When she hears that a young man is "dying for love" of her, a sensible young woman does not accept this statement literally, but it may convey a serious meaning to her nonetheless. The **pun,** or play on words (known to the learned, sometimes, as **paronomasia**), may also be serious or comic in intent; witness, for example, the famous series of puns on Donne's name in his *Hymn to God the Father.* **Oxymoron** is a conjunction of two terms that in ordinary use are contraries or incompatible—for instance, Milton's famous description of hell as containing "darkness visible" (*Paradise Lost* 1.63). A **paradox** is a statement that seems absurd but turns out to have rational meaning after all, usually in some unexpected sense; Donne speaks of fear being great courage and high valor (*Satire* 3, line 16), and turns out to mean that fear of God is greater courage than any earthly bravery. A **conceit** is a far-fetched and unusually elaborate comparison. Writing in the fourteenth century, the Italian poet Petrarch popularized a great number of conceits handy for use in love poetry, and readily adapted by his English imitators. Wyatt, for example, is using **Petrarchan conceits** when he compares love to a warrior, or the lover's state to that of a storm-tossed ship; and a hundred other sonneteers developed the themes of the lady's stony heart, incendiary glances, and so forth. On the other hand, the **metaphysical conceit** was a more intellectualized, many-leveled comparison, giving a strong sense of the poet's ingenuity in overcoming obstacles—for instance, Donne's comparison of separated lovers to the legs of a compass (A *Valediction: Forbidding Mourning*) or Herbert's comparison of devotion to a pulley, in the poem of that name.

Personification (or in the term derived from Latin **prosopopoeia**) is the attribution of human qualities to an inanimate object (for example, the Sea) or an abstract concept (Freedom); a special variety of it is called (in a term of John Ruskin's invention) the **pathetic fallacy.** When we speak of leaves "dancing" or a lake "smiling," we attribute human traits to nonhuman objects. Ruskin thought this was false and therefore "morbid"; modern criticism tends to view the practice as artistically and morally neutral. A more formal and abstract variety of personification is **allegory,** in which a narrative (such as *Pilgrim's Progress*) is constructed by representing general concepts (Faithfulness, Sin, Despair) as persons who act out the plot. A **fable** (like Chaucer's *The Nun's Priest's Tale*) represents beasts behaving like humans; a **parable** is a brief story, or simply an observation, with strong moral application; and an **exemplum** is a story told to illustrate a point in a sermon.

A special series of devices, nearly obsolete today, used to be available to poets who could count on readers trained in the classics. These were the devices of **classical allusion**—that is, reference to the mythology (stories about the actions of gods and other supernatural beings) of the Greeks and Romans. In their simplest form, the classic **myths** used to provide a repertoire of agreeable stage properties, and a convenient shorthand for expressing emotional attitudes. Picturesque creatures like centaurs, satyrs, and sphinxes, heroes and heroines like Hector and Helen, and the whole pantheon of Olympic deities could be used to make ready reference to a great many aspects of human nature. One does not have to explain the problems of a man who is "cleaning the Augean stables"; if he is afflicted with an "Achilles' heel," or is assailing "Hydra-headed difficulties," his state is clear. These descriptive phrases, making **allusion** to mythological stories, suggest in a phrase situations that would normally require cumbersome explanations. But because it used to be taken for granted that the classical mythology was the common possession of all educated readers, the classic myths entered into English literature as early as Chaucer. In poets like Spenser and Milton, classical allusion becomes a kind of enormously learned game, in which the poet seeks to make his points as indirectly as possible. For instance, Spenser writes in the *Epithalamion*, lines 328–29:

> Lyke as when Jove with fayre Alcmena lay,
> When he begot the great Tirynthian groome.

The mere mention of Alcmena in the first line suggests, to the informed reader, Hercules, the son of Jupiter (Jove) by Alcmena. Spenser's problem in the second line is to find a way of referring to him that is neither redundant nor heavy-handed. "Tirynthian" reminds the reader of Hercules' long connection with the city of Tiryns, stretching our minds (as it were) across his whole career; and "groome" compresses references to a man-child, a servant, and a bridegroom, all of which apply to different aspects of Hercules' history. Thus, far from simply avoiding redundancy, Spenser has enriched, for the reader who possesses the classical information, the whole texture of his verse, thought, and feeling.

SCHOOLS

Literary scholars and critics often group together in **schools** writers who share stylistic traits or thematic concerns. Whether they considered themselves a group doesn't much matter; although in some cases—for example, the Imagists or the Beat poets—the writers themselves have identified themselves as belonging to a group. None of the **Romantic poets** knew they were being romantic, although Hazlitt, Shelley, and other writers of the time recognized shared features that they called "the spirit of the age." The followers of Spenser are known as **Spenserians;** they knew they admired and to some extent wrote like Spenser, but didn't realize that made them a group. **Cavalier** poets are set decisively apart from **Metaphysical** poets, though pretty surely none of the two-dozen-odd men involved knew that was what they were. And so with the **Gothic novelists,** and the so-called **Graveyard School** of the eighteenth century; these schools are generally grouped, defined, and named by scholars and critics after the event.

Intellectual affinities have led some writers to be classified under the names of the philosophical schools of Greece and Rome. These are chiefly the **Epicureans,** who specify that the aim of life and the source of value is pleasure; the **Stoics,** who emphasize stern virtue and the dignified endurance of what cannot be avoided; and the **Skeptics,** who doubt that anything can be known for certain. These categories are useful as capsule descriptions, but they aren't very tidy, as they are omissive, overlap one another, and cut across other categories. Dryden is an author strongly tinged with skepticism, but many of his poems suggest an unabashed epicureanism. *The Vanity of Human Wishes*, by Samuel Johnson, is the classic poem in English of stoic philosophy, but it also expresses a particularly strong coloring of Christian humanism.

TERMS OF LITERARY ART

The following section defines frequently used literary terms, especially frequently used terms that are closely related or tend to be mistaken for each other.

Allegory, Symbol, Emblem, Type. Allegory is a narrative in which the agents, and sometimes also the setting, are personified concepts or character-types, and the plot represents a doctrine or thesis. John Bunyan's *Pilgrim's Progress*, for example, allegorizes the Christian doctrine of salvation by narrating how the character named Christian, warned by Evangelist, flees the City of Destruction and makes his laborious way to the Celestial City; en route he meets such characters as Faithful and the Giant Despair, and passes through places like the Slough of Despond and Vanity Fair. A literary **symbol** is the representation of an object or event which has a further range of reference beyond itself. Examples of sustainedly symbolic poems are William Blake's *The Sick Rose* and William Butler Yeats's *Sailing to Byzantium*. In the sixteenth and seventeenth centuries, an **emblem** was an enigmatic picture of a physical object, to which was attached a motto and a verse explaining its significance. In present-day usage, an emblem is any object which is widely understood to signify an abstract concept; thus a dove is an emblem of peace, and a cross, of Christianity. In what was once a widespread Christian mode of biblical interpretation, a **type** was a person or event in the Old Testament which was regarded as historically real, but also as "prefiguring" a person or event in the New Testament. Thus Adam was often said to be a type of Christ, and the act of Moses in liberating the children of Israel was said to prefigure Christ in freeing men from Satan.

Baroque and **Mannerist** are terms imported into literary study from the history of art, and applied by analogy. Michelangelo is a **baroque** artist; he holds great masses in powerful dynamic tension, his style is heavily ornamented and restless. In these respects he is sometimes compared to Milton. El Greco is a **mannerist,** whose gaunt and distorted figures often seem to be laboring under great spiritual stress, whose light seems to be focused in spots against a dark background. He has been compared to Donne. Analogies of this sort are occasionally suggestive, but can readily deteriorate into parallels that are forced and nominal rather than substantial.

Bathos. See **Pathos,** the **Sublime,** and **Bathos.**

Burlesque and **Mock Heroic** differ in that the former makes its subject ludicrous by directly cutting it down, the latter by inflating it. In Pope's mock-heroic *Dunciad*, the figure of Dulness (Colley Cibber) is given inappropriately heroic dimensions; in Butler's burlesque *Hudibras*, the knightly hero is characterized by low and vulgar attributes, and persistently engages in inappropriately low behavior. Burlesque contributed to the development of the English novel; and during the nineteenth century, when formal drama tended to be stagy and melodramatic, a vigorous burlesque stage flourished in England, making fun of the classics. See **Imitation** and **Parody.**

Catastrophe and **Catharsis.** The **catastrophe** is the conclusion of a play; the word means "down-turning," and is usually applied only to tragedies, in which a frequent kind of catastrophe is the death of the protagonist. (A term for the precipitating final scene that applies both to tragedy and to comedy is **denouement,** which in French means "unknotting.") **Catharsis** in Greek signifies "purgation" or "purification." In Aristotle's *Poetics*, the special effect of tragedy is the "catharsis" of the "emotions of pity and fear" that have been aroused in the audience by the events of the drama.

Chiasmus and **Zeugma.** **Chiasmus** is an inversion of the word order in two parallel phrases, as in John Denham's *Cooper's Hill*: "Strong without rage, without o'erflowing full." **Zeugma** is the use of a single verb or adjective to control two nouns, as in Pope's *The Rape of the Lock*: "Or stain her honor, or her new brocade."

Classic and **Neoclassic.** See **Gothic, Classic, Neoclassic.**

Convention and **Tradition.** **Conventions** are agreed-upon artistic procedures peculiar to an art form. None of Shakespeare's contemporaries spoke blank verse in everyday life, but characters in his plays do, and the audience accepts it—as the audience at an opera accepts that characters will sing arias to express their feelings. A **tradition** consists of beliefs, attitudes, and ways of representing things that is widely shared by writers over a span of time; it generally includes a number of conventions.

Didactic poetry is designed to teach a branch of knowledge, or to embody in fictional form a moral, religious, or philosophical doctrine. The term is not derogatory. John Milton's *Paradise Lost*, for example, can be called didactic, insofar as it is organized, as Milton claimed in his invocation, to "assert Eternal Providence / And justify the ways of God to men." In the eighteenth century, a number of poets wrote didactic poems called **georgics** (modeled on the Roman Virgil's *Georgics* on rural life and farming), which described such applied arts as making cider or running a sugar plantation.

Dramatic irony and **Dramatic monologue** are quite different literary modes. In **dramatic irony** a stage character says something that has one meaning for him, but quite another for the audience who possesses relevant knowledge that the speaker lacks. The **dramatic monologue** is a form that was perfected by Robert Browning in such poems as *My Last Duchess* and *The Bishop Orders His Tomb*. In it, the poetic speaker unintentionally reveals to the reader his character and temperament by what he says, usually to another person whose presence we infer from the utterance of the speaker.

Eclogue. See **Pastorals**.

Emblem. See **Allegory, Symbol, Emblem, Type**.

Epigram, Epigraph, Epitaph. An **epigram** is a short, witty statement in verse or prose. One of Oscar Wilde's characters remarks, "I can resist everything, except temptation." An **epigraph** is an apposite quotation placed at the beginning of a book or a section of it. An **epitaph** is a brief statement about someone who has died; usually, it is intended to be inscribed on a tombstone.

Eulogy and **Elegy.** The **eulogy** is a work of praise, in prose or poetry, for a person either very distinguished or recently dead. In its usual modern sense, an **elegy** is a formal, and usually long, poetic lament for someone who has died. In an extended sense, the term is also used to designate poems on the transience of earthly things (such as the Old English *The Seafarer*) or poetic meditations on mortality (such as Thomas Gray's *Elegy Written in a Country Churchyard*).

Euphemism and **Euphuism. Euphemism,** or "fine speech," is a verbal device for avoiding an unpleasant concept or expression, as when, instead of saying a person "died," we say he "passed away." Euphues was the hero of a prose romance (published 1579–80) by John Lyly; his adventures are recounted in a mannered style full of puns, alliteration, and antithetical "points." Under the name of **Euphuism** this courtly style enjoyed a brief vogue in the Elizabethan era.

Fancy and **Imagination.** The distinction between these two mental powers was central to the literary theory of S. T. Coleridge. **Fancy** (a word directly derived by contraction from "fantasy") was defined by Coleridge as the power of combining several known properties into new combinations; **imagination,** on the other hand, was the faculty of using such properties to create an integral whole that is entirely new.

Folios, Quartos, etc., are terms used to specify the size of book pages. To make a **folio,** a sheet of paper (14" × 20" or larger) is folded just once (producing thereby four pages); **quartos** are folded twice (producing eight pages). Shakespeare's plays were first printed in quartos (often in several different editions), but when they were collected together, in 1623, they appeared as the First Folio edition.

Genre, Decorum. A **genre** is an established literary form or type, such as stage comedy, the picaresque novel, the epic, the sonnet. Works belonging to a certain genre tend to represent certain characters and events, and to seek a similar effect. **Decorum,** in literary criticism—where it was a central concept from the Renaissance through the eighteenth century—designates the requirement that there should be a propriety, or fitness, in the way that the character, actions, and style are matched to each other in a particular genre. Low characters, actions, and style, for example, were thought appropriate for satire, while epic demanded characters of high estate, engaged in great actions, and speaking in an appropriately high style.

Gothic, Classic, Neoclassic. These terms are used to distinguish prominent tendencies in literature and the other arts. The term **Gothic** originally referred to the Goths, an early Germanic tribe, then came to signify "medieval." In the eighteenth century "Gothic" connoted primitive and irregular work, possessing the qualities of the relatively barbaric North. **Gothic novels** were a very popular type of prose fiction, inaugurated by Horace Walpole's *Castle of Otranto* (1764), usually set in a medieval castle, which aimed to evoke chilling terror from their readers. **Classic** implies lucid, rational, and orderly works, such as are usually attributed to the writers and thinkers in the classic era of the Greeks and Romans. **Neoclassic**— a term often applied to the period in England from 1660 through most of the eighteenth century—implies an ideal of life, art, and thought deliberately modeled on Greek and Roman examples.

Heroic poems, Heroic drama, Heroic couplets. Because they concentrate on the figure of a typical hero (Achilles, Aeneas), epic poems were frequently called "**heroic.**" Trying to transfer epic grandeur to the stage, playwrights of the Restoration period wrote what was called **heroic drama,** but usually achieved only grandiosity. The stately iambic pentameter couplets in which they made their characters speak became known as **heroic couplets.**

Humor. See **Wit** and **Humor.**

Humors and **Temperaments** are psychological terms used by Renaissance writers. It was believed that every person's constitution contained four basic humors: the **choleric** (bile), the **sanguine** (blood), the **phlegmatic** (phlegm), and the **melancholy** (black bile). The **temperament,** or mixture, of these four humors was held to determine both a person's physical condition and a person's type of character. When a particular humor predominated, it pushed the character in that direction: choler = anger; sanguine = geniality; phlegm = cold torpor; and melancholy = gloomy self-absorption.

Imagination. See **Fancy** and **Imagination.**

Imitation and **Parody** are forms in which a literary work refers back to a predecessor. In the eighteenth century, an "imitation" was a poem that deliberately echoed an older work, but adapted it to subject matter in the writer's own era, usually with a satirical aim directed against that subject matter; Alexander Pope, for example, wrote a number of satires on contemporary life that he entitled *Imitations of Horace*. A **parody** imitates the characteristic style and other features of a particular literary work—or else of a particular literary type—but in such a way as to satirize that work, by making it either amusing or ridiculous. *Northanger Abbey* (1818) by Jane Austen was a good-humored parody of the popular horror-narratives known as gothic novels. (See **Burlesque** and **Gothic**.)

Irony, Sarcasm. **Irony** and **sarcasm** are both ways of saying one thing but implying something sharply different, often opposite; they differ, however, in the way they go about doing so. **Sarcasm** is a broad and taunting form of using apparent praise in order in fact to denigrate. The patriarch Job is bitterly sarcastic when he replies to his would-be comforters (12.2), "No doubt but ye are the people, and wisdom shall die with you." On the other hand, Jane Austen, in the first sentence of *Pride and Prejudice*, overstates the case just enough to make it drily **ironic** when she writes, "It is a truth universally acknowledged, that a single man in possession of a good fortune, must be in want of a wife." (See **Irony,** in the section "Figurative Language," above.)

Legend. See **Myth** and **Legend**.

Logic. See **Rhetoric** and **Logic**.

Masque. The **Masque,** which flourished during the reigns of Elizabeth I, James I, and Charles I, was an elaborate court entertainment that combined poetic drama, music, song, dance, and splendid costumes and settings. For a discussion of the English masque, see the introduction to Jonson's *Pleasure Reconciled to Virtue*.

Myth and **Legend.** **Myths** are hereditary narratives that purport to account, in supernatural terms, for why the world is as it is, and why people act as they do; they also often provide the rules by which people conduct their lives. Myths often spring up to explain rituals, the original meanings of which have been forgotten. A system of related myths is called a **mythology**—a body of supernatural narratives believed to be true by a particular cultural group. The term "myth" is frequently extended to a set of supernatural narratives that are developed by individual poets such as William Blake and W. B. Yeats. Three great mythologies that have been exploited by poets long after they ceased to be believed are the classical (Greek and Roman), the Celtic, and the Germanic. A **legend** is an old and popularly repeated story, of which the protagonist is not supernatural, but a human being. If a hereditary story concerns supernatural beings who are not gods, and the story is not part of a systematic mythology, it is usually classified as a **folktale**.

Naturalism. See **Realism** and **Naturalism**.

Neo-Classic. See **Gothic, Classic, Neoclassic**.

Novel. See **Romance, Novel**.

Ode. A long lyric poem serious in subject and treatment, written in an elevated style and, usually, in an elaborate stanza. See the discussion of English odes in the headnote to Jonson's *Ode on Cary and Morison*.

Pastoral, Eclogue, and **Pastoral Elegy.** **Pastorals** (from the Latin word for "shepherd") are deliberately conventional poems that project a cultivated poet's nostalgic image of the peace and simplicity of the life of shepherds and other rural folk in an idealized natural setting. The form was established by the Greek poet Theocritus in the third century B.C.E.; it is sometimes also called an **eclogue**, which was the title that the Roman poet Virgil gave to his collection of pastorals. The pastorals by Theocritus and later classical poets often included a poem in which a shepherd mourns the death of a fellow shepherd; from these poems developed the highly conventional **pastoral elegy**, a type that includes such great laments as Milton's *Lycidas* and Shelley's *Adonais*. *Lycidas* is also an example of the extension of the classical pastoral to a Christian range of reference, by way of the use of the term "pastor" (shepherd) for a parish priest or minister and the frequent representation of Christ as "the Good Shepherd."

Pathos, the Sublime, and Bathos. In Greek, **pathos** signified deep feeling, especially suffering; in modern criticism, it is used in a more limited way to signify a scene or passage designed to evoke the feelings of pity or sympathetic sorrow from an audience. An example is the passage in which King Lear is briefly reunited with his daughter Cordelia, beginning

> Pray, do not mock me.
> I am a very foolish fond old man . . .

In the first century the Greek rhetorician Longinus wrote a treatise *On the Sublime*, in which he proposed that sublimity ("loftiness") is the greatest of stylistic qualities in literature; the effect of the sublime on the reader is *elestasis* ("transport"). In 1757 Edmund Burke published a highly influential treatise on *The Sublime and Beautiful*, in which he distinguished the sublime from the beautiful, not as a stylistic quality, but as the representation of objects that are vast, obscure, and powerful, which evoke from the reader a "delightful horror" that combines pleasure and terror. **Bathos** (Greek for "depth") was used by Pope, in a parodic parallel to Longinus' "sublime," to signify an unintentional descent in literature, when an author, straining to be passionate or elevated, overshoots the mark and falls into the trivial or the ridiculous.

Poetic diction, Poetic license, Poetic justice. Poetic diction denotes a distinctive language used by a poet which is not current in the discourse of the age; an example is the deliberately archaic language of Spenser's *The Faerie Queene*. In modern critical discussion, the term is applied especially to the style of eighteenth-century poets who, according to the reigning principle of decorum (see **Decorum**), believed that a poet must adapt the level of his diction to the dignity of the high genres of epic, tragedy, and ode. The results were such phrases as "the finny tribe" for "fish" and "the bleating kind" for "sheep." **Poetic license** designates the freedom of a poet or other literary writer to depart, for special effects, from the norms of common discourse and of literal or historical truth. Examples: the use of archaic words, meter, and rhyme, and the use of other literary conventions. (See **Convention**.) **Poetic justice** was coined by Thomas Rymer, in the later seventeenth century, to denote his claim that a narrative or drama should, at the end, distribute rewards and punishments in proportion to the virtues and vices of each character. No important critic since Rymer has adopted this doctrine, except in a highly qualified way.

Quarto. See **Folios, Quartos.**

Realism and **Naturalism** are both terms applied to prose fictions that aim at a faithful representation of actual existence; they differ, however, in the aspects of that existence that they represent and in the manner in which they represent them. The realistic novel attempts to give the effect of representing ordinary life as it commonly occurs. Realistic novelists such as George Eliot in England and William Dean Howells in America present everyday characters experiencing ordinary events, rendered in great detail. **Naturalism,** which the French novelist Émile Zola developed in the 1870s and later, is based on the philosophy that a human being is merely a higher-order animal, whose character and behavior are determined by heredity and environment. Zola, followed by such later naturalistic novelists as the Americans Frank Norris and Theodore Dreiser, typically represents characters who inherit such compulsive instincts as greed and the sexual drive and are shaped by the social and economic forces of family, class, and the milieu into which they are born. Naturalistic novelists also often display an almost medical candor in describing human activities and bodily functions largely unmentioned in earlier fiction.

Rhetoric and **Logic. Rhetoric** was developed by Greek and Roman theorists as the art of using all available means of persuading an audience, either by speech or in writing; it had a great influence on literary criticism in the Renaissance and through the eighteenth century. Rhetorical theorists developed a detailed analysis of figures of speech, largely as effective means to the overall aim of persuasion. In the present century, however, the analysis of such figures has been excerpted from this rhetorical context and made an independent and central concern of language theorists and literary critics. See **Figurative language. Logic** is the study of the principles of reasoning. Logic may be used to persuade an audience, but it does not, like rhetoric, avail itself of all means of persuasion, emotional as well as rational; instead, logic limits itself to a concern with the formal procedures of reasoning from sound premises to valid conclusions.

Romance and **Novel.** Medieval **romances** were verse narratives of adventure, usually about a knightly hero on a quest to gain a lady's favor, who encounters both natural tribulations and supernatural marvels. The term "romance" has since come to be opposed to realism (see **Realism and Naturalism**) and is applied to prose fictions that represent characters and events which are more picturesque, fantastic, adventurous, or heroic than one encounters in ordinary life. The **novel,** as distinguished from the prose romance, undertakes to be a more realistic representation of common life and social relationships and tends to avoid the fantastic, the fabulous, and the realm of high derring-do. (See **Realism.**)

Sarcasm. See **Irony, Sarcasm.**

Satire designates literary forms which diminish or derogate a subject by making it ridiculous and by evoking toward it amusement, or scorn, or indignation. In **formal satire,** such as Alexander Pope's *Moral Essays,* the satire is accomplished in a direct, first-person address, either to the audience or to a listener within the work. **Indirect satire** is not a direct address, but is cast in the form of a fictional narrative, as in Swift's *Gulliver's Travels* or Byron's *Don Juan.* For a discussion of the backgrounds of English satire, see the introduction to Donne's *Satire 3.*

Sublime. See **Pathos, the Sublime,** and **Bathos.**

Symbol. See **Allegory, Symbol, Emblem, Type.**

Tradition. See **Convention** and **Tradition.**

Type. See **Allegory, Symbol, Emblem, Type.**

Wit and **Humor,** in their present use, designate elements in a literary work which are designed to amuse or to excite mirth in the reader or audience. **Wit,** through the seventeenth century, had a broad range of meanings, including general intelligence, mental acuity, and ingenuity in literary invention, especially in a brilliant and paradoxical style. From this last application there derived the most common present use of "wit" to denote a kind of verbal expression that is brief, deft, and contrived to produce a shock of comic surprise; a characteristic form of wit, in this sense, is the epigram. (See **Epigram.**) **Humor** goes back to the ancient theory of the four humors and the application of the term "humorous" to a comically eccentric character who has an imbalance of the humors in his or her temperament. (See **Humors** and **Temperament.**) As we now use the word, **humor** is ascribed both to a comic utterance and to the comic appearance or behavior of a literary character. A humorous utterance, unlike a witty utterance, need not be intended to be comic by the speaker, and is not cast in the neat epigrammatic form of a witty saying. In Shakespeare's *Twelfth Night,* for example, Malvolio's utterances, as well as his appearance and behavior, are all found humorous by the audience, but his utterances are never witty and are humorous despite his own very solemn intentions.

Zeugma. See **Chiasmus** and **Zeugma.**

PERMISSIONS ACKNOWLEDGMENTS

Chinua Achebe: THINGS FALL APART. Copyright © 1958 by Chinua Achebe. First published by William Heinemann Ltd., 1958. Reprinted by permission of Reed Consumer Books, London. Excerpt from *An Image of Africa: Racism in Conrad's HEART OF DARKNESS* from HOPES AND IMPEDIMENTS: SELECTED ESSAYS. Copyright by Chinua Achebe. Reprinted by permission of the author.

Fleur Adcock: from FLEUR ADCOCK: SELECTED POEMS (1983). Reprinted by permission of Oxford University Press.

W. H. Auden: *Petition* ("Sir, no man's enemy") and *Spain 1937* from THE ENGLISH AUDEN by W. H. Auden, edited by Edward Mendelson. Copyright © 1934, 1940 and renewed 1962, 1968 by W. H. Auden. Reprinted by permission of Random House, Inc., and Faber & Faber Ltd. *On This Island, Musee des Beaux Arts, Lullaby, In Memory of W. B. Yeats, Their Lonely Betters, In Praise of Limestone, The Shield of Achilles,* and an excerpt from *New Year Letter,* all from W. H. AUDEN: COLLECTED POEMS by W. H. Auden, edited by Edward Mendelson. Copyright © 1937, 1940, 1951, 1952 and renewed 1965, 1968 by W. H. Auden. Reprinted by permission of Random House, Inc., and Faber & Faber Ltd.

Samuel Beckett: *Endgame.* Copyright © 1958 by Samuel Beckett; copyright renewed © 1986 by Samuel Beckett. Used by permission of Grove/Atlantic, Inc., and Faber & Faber Ltd.

Annie Besant: *The White Slavery of London Match Workers* from STRONG-MINDED WOMEN by Janet H. Murray. Copyright © 1982 by Janet H. Murray. Reprinted by permission of Pantheon Books, a division of Random House, Inc., and the author.

William Blake: Poems from THE COMPLETE POETRY AND PROSE OF WILLIAM BLAKE, edited by David V. Erdman, copyright © 1965, 1981, Doubleday & Company. Blake engravings: reproduced from the Lessing J. Rosenwald Collection, Library of Congress.

Eavan Boland: *That the Science of Cartography Is Limited, The Dolls Museum in Dublin,* and *The Pomegranate* from IN A TIME OF VIOLENCE by Eavan Boland. Copyright © 1994 by Eavan Boland. Reprinted by permission of W. W. Norton & Company, Inc., and Carcanet Press Ltd.

Emily Brontë: All poems from THE COMPLETE POEMS OF EMILY JANE BRONTË, by C. W. Hatfield, copyright © 1941 by Columbia University Press. Reprinted with the permission of the publisher.

Lord Byron: Selections as indicated from LORD BYRON: THE COMPLETE POETICAL WORKS edited by Jerome J. McGann (Vol I. 1980). Reprinted by permission of Oxford University Press. Letters are reprinted by permission of the publisher from BYRON'S LETTERS AND JOURNALS, Volumes I–VII, edited by Leslie A. Marchand, Cambridge, Mass.: The Belknap Press of Harvard University Press: Copyright © Editorial 1973, 1975, 1976, 1977 by Leslie A. Marchand.

Robert Burns: Selections from THE POEMS AND SONGS OF ROBERT BURNS, edited by James Kinsley (1968). Reprinted by permission of Oxford University Press.

May Cannan: Excerpt from GRAY GHOSTS AND VOICES and *Rouen* from IN WAR TIME, POEMS. Reprinted by permission of James Cannan Slater.

Charles Causeley: *At the British Cemetery, Bayeux,* and *Armistice Day* from UNION STREET. Reprinted by permission of David Higham Associates.

Constantine Cavafy: Excerpt from *Expecting the Barbarians* from THE COMPLETE POEMS OF C. P. CAVAFY. Copyright © 1961 and renewed 1989 by Rae Dalven, translator. Reprinted by permission of Harcourt, Inc., and the Hogarth Press on the behalf of the Estate of C. P. Cavafy.

Ada Nield Chew: Extract from THE LIFE AND WRITINGS OF A WORKING WOMAN by Ada Nield Chew. Published by Virago Press, London. Reprinted by permission.

John Clare: *Mouse's Nest* and *Pastoral Poetry* from THE POEMS OF JOHN CLARE, edited by J. W. Tibble (J. M. Dent). Reprinted by permission of Orion Publishing Group Ltd. *The Nightingale's Nest* from SELECTED POEMS AND PROSE OF JOHN CLARE edited by Eric Robinson and Geoffrey Summerfield. Reproduced with permission of Curtis Brown Ltd, London, on behalf of Eric Robinson. Copyright Eric Robinson 1984, 1967. All other poems from THE LATER POEMS OF JOHN CLARE 1837–1864 edited by Eric Robinson and David Powell. Reproduced with permission of Curtis Brown Ltd, London, on behalf of Eric Robinson. Copyright Eric Robinson 1984, 1967.

J. M. Coetzee: Excerpt from WAITING FOR THE BARBARIANS by J. M. Coetzee. Copyright © 1980 by J. M. Coetzee. Used by permission of Viking Penguin, a division of Penguin Putnam, Inc., and Secker and Warburg.

Samuel Taylor Coleridge: Excerpt from COLERIDGE'S SHAKESPEAREAN CRITICISM, edited by Thomas M. Raysor. Copyright © 1930 by the President and Fellows of Harvard College, 1958 by Thomas M. Raysor. Selections reprinted by permission of the editor.

Anita Desai: *Scholar and Gypsy* from GAMES AT TWILIGHT. Copyright © 1978, Anita Desai. Reproduced by permission of the author c/o Rogers, Coleridge &White Ltd., 20 Powis Mews, London W11 1JN.

Keith Douglas: Excerpt from FROM ALAMEIN TO ZEM ZEM, edited by Desmond Graham. Reprinted by permission of Faber & Faber Ltd. *Gallantry, Vergissmeinnicht,* and *Aristocrats* from THE COMPLETE POEMS OF KEITH DOUGLAS, edited by Desmond Graham (1978). © Marie J. Douglas, 1978. Reprinted by permission of Faber & Faber Ltd.

George Eliot: Excerpt from THE MILL ON THE FLOSS, Riverside Edition, edited by Gorden Haight. Copyright © 1961 by Houghton Mifflin Company. Used with permission.

Derek Walcott: *A Far Cry from Africa*, XXVII of *Midsummer*, *Nights in the Gardens of Port of Spain*, and *The Glory Trumpeter* all from THE COLLECTED POEMS 1948–1984 by Derek Walcott. Copyright © 1986 by Derek Walcott. XXX from OMEROS by Derek Walcott. Copyright © 1990 by Derek Walcott. All reprinted by permission of Farrar, Straus & Giroux, Inc., and Faber & Faber Ltd. Excerpt of 77 lines of *The Schooner Flight* from THE COLLECTED POEMS 1948–1984 by Derek Walcott. Copyright © 1986 by Derek Walcott. Reprinted by permission of Farrar, Straus & Giroux, Inc., and Jonathan Cape.

Oscar Wilde: *De Profundis* from THE LETTERS OF OSCAR WILDE, edited by Sir Rupert Hart-Davis and Merlin Holland. Letters © 1962 by Vyvyan Holland. © 1985, 1990, 2000 by Merlin Holland. Editorial matter © 1962, 1985 by Rupert Hart-Davis, © 2000 by Rupert Hart-Davis and Merlin Holland. Reprinted by permission of Henry Holt & Company, LLC, and Fourth Estate Ltd.

Mary Wollstonecraft: Reprinted from LETTERS WRITTEN DURING A SHORT RESIDENCE IN SWEDEN, NORWAY, AND DENMARK by Mary Wollstonecraft, edited by Carol H. Poston, by permission of the University of Nebraska Press. Copyright © 1976 by the University of Nebraska Press. From A VINDICATION OF THE RIGHTS OF WOMAN: A NORTON CRITICAL EDITION, Second Edition, by Mary Wollstonecraft, edited by Carol H. Poston. Copyright © 1988, 1975 by W. W. Norton & Company, Inc. Reprinted by permission of W. W. Norton & Company, Inc.

Virginia Woolf: *The Mark on the Wall* and *The Legacy*. From A HAUNTED HOUSE AND OTHER SHORT STORIES by Virginia Woolf, copyright 1944 and renewed 1972 by Harcourt, Inc. *Modern Fiction* from THE COMMON READER by Virginia Woolf, copyright 1925 by Harcourt, Inc., and renewed 1953 by Leonard Woolf. *Professions for Women* from THE DEATH OF THE MOTH AND OTHER ESSAYS by Virginia Woolf, copyright 1942 by Harcourt, Inc., and renewed 1970 by Marjorie T. Parsons, Executrix. A ROOM OF ONE'S OWN by Virginia Woolf, copyright © 1929 by Harcourt Brace & Company and renewed 1957 by Leonard Woolf. All reprinted by permission of the publisher and The Society of Authors as the Literary Representative of the Estate of Virginia Woolf. Excerpt from *A Sketch from the Past* in MOMENTS OF BEING by Virginia Woolf, copyright © 1976 by Quentin Bell and Angelica Garnett, reprinted by permission of Harcourt, Inc., and the Hogarth Press on the behalf of the Executors of the Virginia Woolf Estate.

Dorothy Wordsworth: Selections as indicated from THE GRASMERE JOURNALS, edited by Pamela Woof (1991). Reprinted by permission of Oxford University Press. *Grasmere—A Fragment* and *Thoughts on My Sick Bed* from DOROTHY WORDSWORTH AND ROMANTICISM. Reprinted by permission of The Wordsworth Trust, Dove Cottage, Grasmere.

William Wordsworth: Reprinted from William Wordsworth: THE RUINED COTTAGE AND THE PEDLAR. Edited by James A. Butler. Copyright © 1978 by Cornell University. Reprinted from William Wordsworth: THE FOURTEEN-BOOK PRELUDE. Edited by W. J. B. Owen. Copyright © 1985 by Cornell University. Both used by permission of the publisher, Cornell University Press.

W. B. Yeats: *The Madness of King Goll, The Stolen Child, Down by the Salley Gardens, The Rose of the World, The Lake Isle of Innisfree, The Sorrow of Love, When You Are Old, Who Goes With Fergus?, The Man Who Dreamed of Faeryland, The Secret Rose, The Folly of Being Comforted, Adam's Curse, No Second Troy, The Fascination of What's Difficult, September 1913, To a Shade, A Coat, The Wild Swans at Coole*, and *In Memory of Major Robert Gregory*, all from THE POEMS OF W. B. YEATS: A NEW EDITION, edited by Richard J. Finneran. Reprinted by permission of A. P. Watt on the behalf of Michael B. Yeats. *Easter 1916, The Second Coming,* and *A Prayer for My Daughter*, reprinted with the permission of Simon & Schuster and A. P. Watt on the behalf of Michael B. Yeats from THE POEMS OF W. B. YEATS: A NEW EDITION, edited by Richard J. Finneran. Copyright © 1924 by Macmillan Publishing Company, renewed 1952 by Bertha Georgie Yeats. *Leda and the Swan* reprinted with the permission of Simon & Schuster and A. P. Watt on the behalf of Michael B. Yeats from THE POEMS OF W. B. YEATS: A NEW EDITION, edited by Richard J. Finneran. Copyright © 1928 by Macmillan Publishing Company; copyright renewed © 1956 by Georgie Yeats. *A Dialogue of Self and Soul, For Anne Gregory, Byzantium, Crazy Jane Talks with the Bishop,* and *After Long Silence* reprinted with the permission of Simon & Schuster and A. P. Watt on the behalf of Michael B. Yeats from THE POEMS OF W. B. YEATS: A NEW EDITION, edited by Richard J. Finneran. Copyright © 1933 by Macmillan Publishing Company; copyright renewed © 1961 by Bertha Georgie Yeats. *Lapis Lazuli, Long-Legged Fly, The Circus Animals' Desertion,* and *Under Ben Bulben* reprinted with the permission of Simon & Schuster and A. P. Watt on the behalf of Michael B. Yeats from THE POEMS OF W. B. YEATS: A NEW EDITION, edited by Richard J. Finneran. Copyright 1940 by Georgie Yeats; copyright renewed © 1968 by Bertha Georgie Yeats, Michael Butler Yeats, and Anne Yeats. Excerpts from REVERIES OVER CHILDHOOD AND YOUTH and THE TREMBLING OF THE VEIL. Reprinted by permission of A. P. Watt on the behalf of Michael B. Yeats. *The Sorrow of Love* (transcription of first printed version) from BETWEEN THE LINES: YEATS'S POETRY IN THE MAKING by Jon Stallworthy (1963). Reprinted by permission of Oxford University Press.

Index

About suffering they were never wrong, 2505

Abt Vogler, 1410

Achebe, Chinua, 2035, 2616

'A cold coming we had of it, 2386

Adam's Curse, 2097

Adcock, Fleur, 2759

Adlestrop, 2051

Adonais, 772

A flower was offered to me, 55

After Death, 1585

After Long Silence, 2117

After the burial-parties leave, 1893

After the Funeral, 2518

Afton Water, 108

A girl, 1743

Agnosticism and Christianity, 1566

Ah, Are You Digging on My Grave?, 1946

Ah, did you once see Shelley plain, 1365

Ah, what avails the sceptered race, 493

Ah! changed and cold, how changed and
very cold!, 1585

Ah Sun-flower, 55

Ah! why, because the dazzling sun, 1421

Alamein to Zem Zem, 2538

Alastor; or, The Spirit of Solitude, 702

Alexander Pope, 547

Alfoxden Journal, The, 385

A little black thing among the snow, 52

All I know is a door into the dark, 2820

All Nature seems at work. Slugs leave their
lair—, 467

All Religions Are One, 41

All saints revile her, and all sober men,
2448

Alton Locke, 1710

Ambulances, 2568

America: A Prophecy, 146

Am I alone, 1676

Among School Children, 2111

And did those feet, 85

And has the remnant of my life, 399

—and not simply by the fact that this shading of, 2835

Andrea del Sarto, 1385

And rise, O moon, from yonder down, 1279

Angel in the House, The, 1723

An old, mad, blind, despised, and dying
King, 728

Another Epitaph on an Army of Mercenaries,
2437

Anthem for Doomed Youth, 2066

Apeneck Sweeney spreads his knees, 2367

Apologia Pro Poemate Meo, 2067

Apologia Pro Vita Sua, 1128

Apology for the Revival of Christian Architecture in England, An, 2721

Apple-Gathering, An, 1587

Appreciations, 1645

April is the cruellest month, breeding, 2370

Araby, 2236

A Red, Red Rose, 115

Aristocrats, 2537

Armistice Day, 2540

Arnold, Matthew, 1471

As from their ancestral oak, 728

As he knelt by the grave of his mother and
father, 2858

As I listened from a beach-chair in the
shade, 2508

——A simple Child, 224

As Kingfishers Catch Fire, 1652

Ask Me No More, 1227

A slumber did my spirit seal, 254

A snake came to my water-trough, 2352

A Song: "Men of England," 727

A Sonnet is a moment's monument—, 1580

A square, squat room (a cellar on promotion), 1746

As the Team's Head Brass, 2053

A sudden blow; the great wings beating still,
2110

Atalanta in Calydon, 1623

At Francis Allen's on the Christmas eve—,
1217

At the British War Cemetery, Bayeux, 2540

Aubade, 2570

Auden, W. H., 2500

Auld Lang Syne, 108

Aurora Leigh, 1180

Autobiography (Martineau), 1725

Autobiography (Mill), 1166

Autumn resumes the land, ruffles the
woods, 2721

Ave Atque Vale, 1631

'Ave you 'eard o' the Widow at Windsor,
1889

A wind is ruffling the tawny pelt, 2580

Axe-fall, echo and silence. Noonday silence,
2816

Ay, gaze upon her rose-wreathed hair, 1040

Bagpipe Music, 2514

Baillie, Joanna, 209

Baked the day she suddenly dropped dead,
2765

Barbauld, Anna Letitia, 24

Bavarian Gentians, 2351

Beckett, Samuel, 2471

Behold her, single in the field, 293

Believe me, if all those endearing young charms, 527

Below the thunders of the upper deep, 1201

Beneath an old wall, that went round an old castle, 94

Bent double, like old beggars under sacks, 2069

Besant, Annie, 1715

Besant, Walter, 1738

Between my finger and my thumb, 2819

Binsey Poplars, 1654

Biographia Literaria, 467

Birthday, A, 1587

Bishop Orders His Tomb at Saint Praxed's Church, The, 1359

Black Jackets, 2577

Blake, William, 35, 144

"Blame not thyself too much," I said, "nor blame, 1229

Blessed Damozel, The, 1574

Blue-Fly, The, 2449

Boland, Eavan, 2834

Book Ends, 2765

Book of Thel, The, 59

Bottomless pits, There's one in Castleton, 2764

Bradley, Katherine, 1742

Break, Break, Break, 1216

Breaks of Day in the Trenches, 2062

Bright star, would I were stedfast as thou art, 845

Bright wanderer, fair coquette of Heaven, 788

Broken Appointment, A, 1936

Brontë, Emily, 1418

Brooke, Rupert, 2049

Browning, Elizabeth Barrett, 1173

Browning, Robert, 1345

Buried Life, The, 1480

Burke, Edmund, 121

Burns, Robert, 99

But, knowing now that they would have her speak, 1606

But do not let us quarrel any more, 1385

Byron, Lord (George Gordon), 551

By this he knew she wept with waking eyes, 1570

Byzantium, 2115

Caliban upon Setebos, 1402

Cannan, May Wedderburn, 2074

Cardinal Newman, 1604

Carlyle, Thomas, 1066

[Carlyle's Portraits of His Contemporaries], 1070

[*Carrion Comfort*], 1656

Carroll, Lewis, 1666

Carthusians, 1895

Casablanca, 815

Cassandra, 1734

Casualty, 2822

Causley, Charles, 2539

Caxtons are mechanical birds with many wings, 2840

Certain things here are quietly American—, 2584

Channel Firing, 1944

Charge of the Light Brigade, The, 1280

Cherry Trees, The, 2053

Chestnut Casts His Flambeaux, The, 2046

Chew, Ada Nield, 1717

Childe Harold's Pilgrimage, 563

"Childe Roland to the Dark Tower Came," 1367

Children are dumb to say how hot the day is, 2446

Chimney Sweeper, The (Songs of Experience), 52

Chimney Sweeper, The (Songs of Innocence), 46

Choruses from Hellas, 769

Christabel, 441

Christ's Hospital Five-and-Thirty Years Ago, 495

Church Going, 2565

Circus Animals' Desertion, The, 2120

Clare, John, 802

Clock a Clay, 809

Clod & the Pebble, The, 51

Closed like confessionals, they thread, 2568

Cloud, The, 763

Cloud-puffball, torn tufts, tossed pillows flaunt forth, then chevy on the air-, 1658

Clough, Arthur Hugh, 1451

Coat, A, 2100

Cobwebs, 1585

Coetzee, J. M., 2829

Cold Are the Crabs, 1665

Cold in the earth, and the deep snow piled above thee!, 1421

Coleridge, Mary Elizabeth, 1861

Coleridge, Samuel Taylor, 153, 416

Coleridge received the Person from Porlock, 2453

Come, balmy Sleep! tired nature's soft resort!, 33

Come, dear children, let us away, 1475

Come down, O Christ, and help me! reach thy hand, 1750

Come Down, O Maid!, 1228

Coming of Arthur, The, 1282

Composed upon Westminster Bridge, September 3, 1802, 296

Comrades, leave me here a little, while as yet 'tis early morn, 1219

Confessions of an English Opium-Eater, 530

Conrad, Joseph, 1952

Considering the Snail, 2576

Convergence of the Twain, The, 1945

Cool Web, The, 2446

Cooper, Edith, 1742

"Courage!" he said, and pointed toward the land, 1208

Crazy Jane Talks with the Bishop, 2116

Critic as Artist, The, 1752

Crossing the Bar, 1304
Cruelty has a Human Heart, 59
Cry of the Children, The, 1174
Culture and Anarchy, 1528
Cynara, 1893
Cypresses, 2354

Daffodils, 2592
Danny Deever, 1888
Darkling Thrush, The, 1937
Darkness, 559
Darwin, Charles, 1679, 1686
Daughters of the Late Colonel, The, 2409
Dead, The, 2240
Dead before Death, 1585
Dead Man's Dump, 2064
DEAD! One of them shot by the sea in the east, 1195
Defence of Poetry, A, 789
Defense of Guenevere, 1606
Dejection: An Ode, 459
De Profundis, 1805
De Quincey, Thomas, 529
Desai, Anita, 2768
Descent of Man, The, 1686
Descriptive Sketches, 150
Dialogue of Self and Soul, A, 2113
Dickens, Charles, 1333, 1711
Digging, 2819
Dirge, A, 786
Disabled, 2071
Discourse on the Love of Our Country, A, 118
Divine Image, A, 59
Divine Image, The, 47
Divorced, but friends again at last, 2839
Does the road wind up-hill all the way?, 1589
Dolls Museum in Dublin, The, 2836
Don Juan, 621
Do Not Go Gentle into That Good Night, 2524
Douglas, Keith, 2535
Dover Beach, 1492
Down, Wanton, Down!, 2445
Down by the Salley Gardens, 2091
Downhill I came, hungry, and yet not starved, 2052
Down the road someone is practising scales, 2513
Dowson, Ernest, 1894
Do ye hear the children weeping, O my brothers, 1174
Drummer Hodge, 1937
Drunk Man Looks at the Thistle, A, 2435
Dulce Et Decorum Est, 2069
Dumb Waiter, The, 2594
Duns Scotus's Oxford, 1654
During Wind and Rain, 1950

Eagle: A Fragment, The, 1219
Earth, ocean, air, beloved brotherhood!, 704
Earth has not any thing to show more fair, 296
Earth rais'd up her head, 50
Earth's Answer, 50
Easter 1916, 2104
Easter 1916 Proclamation of an Irish Republic, 2023
Ecchoing Green, The, 43
Elegiac Stanzas, 294
Eliot, George, 1454
Eliot, T. S., 2360
Ellis, Sarah Stickney, 1721
Endgame, 2472
Endymion: A Poetic Romance, 829
Engels, Friedrich, 1702
England in 1819, 728
England's Dead, 813
Eolian Harp, The, 419
Epic, The [Morte d'Arthur], 1217
Epilogue, 1279
Epistle Containing the Strange Medical Experience of Karshish, the Arab Physician, An, 1396
Epi-strauss-ium, 1452
Epitaph, 467
Epitaph on an Army of Mercenaries, 2047
Ere on my bed my limbs I lay, 462
Eros, 1745
E Tenebris, 1750
Evening morning over Rouen, hopeful, high, courageous morning, 2074
Eve of St. Agnes, The, 834
Everyone Sang, 2057
Everyone suddenly burst out singing, 2057
Examination at the Womb-Door, 2590
Excursion, The, 151
Explosion, The, 2570
Expostulation and Reply, 227
Ex-Queen Among the Astronomers, The, 2759
Extempore Effusion upon the Death of James Hogg, 299

Fall of Hyperion: A Dream, A, 873
Fanatics have their dreams, wherewith they weave, 875
Far Cry from Africa, A, 2580
Far-off, most secret, and inviolate Rose, 2095
Fascination of What's Difficult, The, 2098
Father and Son, 1694
Fear death?—to feel the fog in my throat, 1409
Felix Randal, 1655
Felix Randal the farrier, O is he dead then? my duty all ended, 1655
Fenton, James, 2853
Fern Hill, 2522
Field, Michael, 1742
Finnegans Wake, 2309
FitzGerald, Edward, 1304
Five summer days, five summer nights, 2449

Flower in the Crannied Wall, 1304
Flow gently, sweet Afton, among thy green braes, 108
Fly, The, 53
Folly of Being Comforted, The, 2096
For Anne Gregory, 2115
Force That Through the Green Fuse Drives the Flower, The, 2517
Forge, The, 2820
Forsaken Merman, The, 1475
Forster, E. M., 2131
Forty-two years ago (to me if to no one else), 2516
For whom the possessed sea littered, on both shores, 2718
Four Quartets, 2389
Fra Lippo Lippi, 1373
Frankenstein, 905
French Revolution: A Poem in Seven Books, The, 145
French Revolution, The, 1103
Friend of the wise! and teacher of the good!, 464
From low to high doth dissolution climb, 298
"From the abstraction I was roused,—and how?, 151
From the Wave, 2579
From Wynyard's Gap the livelong day, 1939
Frost at Midnight, 457
Function of Criticism at the Present Time, The, 1514
Futility, 2071

Gallantry, 2536
Garden of Love, The, 56
Garden of Proserpine, 1628
Garden Party, The, 2423
Gaskell, Elizabeth, 1318
Gathering Mushrooms, 2856
General, The, 2056
German Requiem, A, 2853
Germ of new life, whose powers expanding slow, 28
Gilbert, W. S., 1674
[Girl, A], 1743
Glory be to God for dappled things—, 1653
Glory of Women, 2057
Glory Trumpeter, The, 2582
Go, for they call you, shepherd, from the hill, 1486
Goblin Market, 1589
God of our fathers, known of old—, 1892
God's Grandeur, 1651
Goethe in Weimar sleeps, and Greece, 1482
"Good-morning: good-morning!" the General said, 2056
Gordimer, Nadine, 2572
Gosse, Sir Edmund, 1693
Grammarian's Funeral, A, 1392
Grasmere Journals, The, 387
Graves, Robert, 2444
Great Social Evil, The, 1728

Great Towns, The, 1703
Green grow the rashes, 99
Grey Ghosts and Voices, 2076
Groping along the tunnel, step by step, 2056
Groping back to bed after a piss, 2569
Grow old along with me!, 1413
Gr-r-r—there go, my heart's abhorrence!, 1350
Gunn, Thom, 2576
Gurney, Ivor, 2060

Had she come all the way for this, 1614
Hail to thee, blithe Spirit!, 765
Half a league, half a league, 1280
Hap, 1934
Hard Times, 1711
Hardy, Thomas, 1916
Harlot's House, The, 1750
Harp that once through Tara's halls, The, 527
Harrison, Tony, 2763
Haunted Beach, The, 96
Ha! whare ye gaun, ye crowlan ferlie!, 106
Haystack in the Floods, The, 1614
Hazlitt, William, 509
Heaney, Seamus, 2818
Hear the voice of the Bard!, 48
Heart of Darkness, 1957
Heart of Midlothian, The, 402
He clasps the crag with crooked hands, 1219
He disappeared in the dead of winter, 2506
Hélas, 1749
He loved the brook's soft sound, 810
Hemans, Felicia Dorothea, 812
He Never Expected Much, 1951
Henley, William Ernest, 1746
Here, where the world is quiet, 1628
Heredity, 2764
He sat in a wheeled chair, waiting for dark, 2071
He's gone, and all our plans, 2060
He stood among a crowd at Dromahair, 2094
He would drink by himself, 2822
He yawned and watched the lilac horns of his island, 2585
High Windows, 2568
Hill, Geoffrey, 2717
Hillary, Richard, 2531
Hobson, John Atkinson, 2020
Hollow Men, The, 2383
Holy Thursday (Songs of Experience), 51
Holy Thursday (Songs of Innocence), 47
Holy Willie's Prayer, 102
Homes of England, The, 817
Home-Thoughts, from Abroad, 1358
Home-Thoughts, from the Sea, 1358
Hopkins, Gerard Manley, 1648
Horse Dealer's Daughter, The, 2330
Hound of Heaven, The, 1857
House of Life, The, 1580

Housman, A. E., 2041
How Beastly the Bourgeois Is, 2356
How changed is here each spot man makes or fills!, 1498
How I Became a Socialist, 1618
How Pleasant to Know Mr. Lear, 1663
How They Brought the Good News from Ghent to Aix, 1356
How you became a poet's a mystery!, 2764
Hughes, Ted, 2587
Human Abstract, The, 57
[Humpty Dumpty's Explication of Jabberwocky], 1667
Hunchback in the Park, The, 2520
Hunting of the Snark, The, 1672
Hurrahing in Harvest, 1653
Huxley, Leonard, 1690
Huxley, Thomas Henry, 1558
Hyenas, The, 1893
Hymn to Intellectual Beauty, 723
Hymn to Proserpine, 1625

I, too, saw God through mud,—, 2067
I Am, 808
I am poor brother Lippo, by your leave!, 1373
I am—yet what I am, none cares or knows, 808
I arise from dreams of thee, 729
I askèd a thief, 85
I bring fresh showers for the thirsting flowers, 763
I can feel the tug, 2821
I caught this morning morning's minion, king-, 1652
Idea of a University, The, 1121
Idylls of the King, 1282
If but some vengeful god would call to me, 1934
If from the public way you turn your steps, 270
If in the month of dark December, 555
If I should die, think only this of me, 2050
If it form the one landscape that we the inconstant ones, 2509
I fled Him, down the nights and down the days, 1857
I found a ball of grass among the hay, 807
I found this jawbone at the sea's edge, 2588
If you have revisited the town, thin Shade, 2100
If You're Anxious for to Shine in the High Aesthetic Line, 1676
I had a dream, which was not all a dream, 559
I have heard that hysterical women say, 2117
I have lived long enough, having seen one thing, that love hath an end, 1625
I have met them at close of day, 2104
"I have no name, 48
I have two daughters, 2837

I have walked a great while over the snow, 1862
I heard a thousand blended notes, 226
I hid my love when young while I, 810
I leant upon a coppice gate, 1937
I'll tell thee everything I can, 1667
I Look into My Glass, 1936
I lost the love of heaven above, 807
I love thee, mournful, sober-suited Night!, 33
I made my song a coat, 2100
Image of Africa: Racism in Conrad's Heart of Darkness, An, 2035
I met a traveller from an antique land, 725
I met the Bishop on the road, 2116
I'm Happiest When Most Away, 1419
Impercipient, The, 1935
Importance of Being Earnest, The, 1761
Impression du Matin, 1749
In an apothecary's chest of drawers, 2827
In an Artist's Studio, 1586
In a solitude of the sea, 1945
Indian Girl's Song, The [The Indian Serenade], 729
I never said I loved you, John, 1601
Infant Joy, 48
Infant Sorrow, 57
In Hospital, 1746
In idle August, while the sea soft, 2583
In Memoriam A. H. H., 1230
In Memoriam James Joyce, 2436
In Memory of Jane Fraser, 2717
In Memory of Major Robert Gregory, 2102
In Memory of W. B. Yeats, 2506
In Parenthesis, 2079
In Praise of Limestone, 2509
In Progress, 1603
In summer's mellow midnight, 1420
In the Children's Hospital, 2437
In the cowslip's peeps I lie, 809
In the dungeon crypts idly did I stray, 1423
In the silence that prolongs the span, 2577
In the sweet shire of Cardigan, 222
In this lone, open glade I lie, 1484
In Time of "The Breaking of Nations," 1951
Introduction (Songs of Experience), 49
Introduction (Songs of Innocence), 43
Invictus, 1747
Invite to Eternity, An, 808
I peeled bits o'straw and I got switches too, 811
I plucked pink blossoms from mine apple tree, 1587
I said—Then, dearest, since 'tis so, 1382
I sat before my glass one day, 1861
I sat on cushioned otter-skin, 2088
Is It Wise?, 2451
Isolation. To Marguerite, 1478
I sought a theme and sought for it in vain, 2120
I sprang to the stirrup, and Joris, and he, 1356
I stand upon a hill and see, 2577

Is there, for honest Poverty, 116
Is there a solitary wretch who hies, 34
Is this a holy thing to see, 51
I stood with three comrades in Parliament Square, 2540
I tell my secret? No, indeed, not I, 1588
I thought he was dumb, 2349
I thought it made me look more "working class," 2767
It is a land with neither night nor day, 1585
It is an ancient Mariner, 423
It is not what they built. It is what they knocked down, 2853
It little profits that an idle king, 1213
It mounts at sea, a concave wall, 2579
I travelled among unknown men, 254
It seemed that out of battle I escaped, 2070
——It seems a day, 258
It seems I have no tears left. They should have fallen——, 2052
It's no go the merrygoround, it's no go the rickshaw, 2514
It was a beauteous evening, 297
[*It was deep April, and the morn*], 1744
It was my thirtieth year to heaven, 2521
I've taken my fun where I've found it, 1890
I Wake and Feel the Fell of Dark, Not Day, 1657
I walked where in their talking graves, 2540
I walk through the long schoolroom questioning, 2111
I wandered lonely as a cloud, 284
I wander thro' each charter'd street, 56
I was angry with my friend, 58
I was thy neighbor once, thou rugged Pile!, 294
I went to the Garden of Love, 56
I will arise and go now, and go to Innisfree, 2092
I wonder do you feel today, 1390
I work all day, and get half-drunk at night, 2570

Jabberwocky, 1666
January, 1795, 93
January 22nd, Missolonghi, 562
Joan of Arc: An Epic Poem, 148
Jock of Hazeldean, 415
Jones, David, 2078
Journal (Hopkins), 1659
Journey of the Magi, 2386
Joyce, James, 2231
Jumblies, The, 1664
Just for a handful of silver he left us, 1355

Karshish, the picker-up of learning's crumbs, 1396
Keats, John, 823
Kingsley, Charles, 1710
Kipling, Rudyard, 1863
Kraken, The, 1201
Kubla Khan, 439

La Belle Dame sans Merci: A Ballad, 845
Laboratory, The, 1353
Ladies, The, 1890
Lady, we would behold thee moving bright, 1744
Lady of Shalott, The, 1204
Lake Isle of Innisfree, The, 2092
Lamb, Charles, 494
Lamb, The, 45
Lamia, 856
Landing of the Pilgrim Fathers in New England, 814
Landon, Letitia Elizabeth, 1034
Landor, Walter Savage, 492
Lapis Lazuli, 2117
Larkin, Philip, 2564
Last Enemy, The, 2532
Last night, ah, yesternight, betwixt her lips and mine, 1893
Last Ride Together, The, 1382
Later Life, 1603
Latest Decalogue, The, 1452
Lawrence, D. H., 2313
Lay your sleeping head, my love, 2505
Lear, Edward, 1662
Lectures on Art, 2019
Lectures on Shakespeare, 486
Leda and the Swan, 2110
Legacy, The, 2226
Leodogran, the King of Cameliard, 1282
Lessing, Doris, 2541
Lessons of the War, 2529
Letters (George Gordon, Lord Byron), 689
    to Douglas Kinnaird, 695
    to John Cam Hobhouse and Douglas Kinnaird, 693
    to Leigh Hunt, 689
    to Percy Bysshe Shelley, 697
    to Thomas Moore, 691
Letters (Keats), 886
    to Benjamin Bailey, 887
    to Charles Brown, 902
    to Fanny Brawne, 900
    to George and Georgiana Keats, 896
    to George and Thomas Keats, 889
    to John Hamilton Reynolds, 890, 892
    to John Taylor, 891
    to Percy Bysshe Shelley, 901
    to Richard Woodhouse, 894
Letters Written in Sweden, Norway, and Denmark, 192
Let us begin and carry up this corpse, 1392
Life, 31
Life and Letters of Thomas Henry Huxley, The, 1690
Life! I know not what thou art, 31
Life's Parallels, A, 1603
Light flows our war of mocking words, and yet, 1480
Like a convalescent, I took the hand, 2825
Limerick, 1663
Lines Composed a Few Miles above Tintern Abbey, 235

Lines Written in Early Spring, 226
Lines Written in Kensington Gardens, 1484
Lines Written in the Bay of Lerici, 788
Literature and Science, 1545
Little Black Boy, The, 45
Little Fly, 53
Little Gidding, 2389
Little Lamb, who made thee?, 45
Little Shroud, The, 1041
Living Wage for Factory Girls at Crewe, 5
    May 1984, A, 1717
Lochinvar, 413
Locksley Hall, 1219
London, 56
London, 1802, 297
London Labour and the London Poor, 1714
London's Summer Morning, 92
Long Distance, 2766
Long-Legged Fly, 2119
Look, stranger, on this island now, 2502
Look at the stars! look, look up at the skies!,
    1651
Lost Land, The, 2837
Lost Leader, The, 1355
Lotos-Eaters, The, 1208
Louse Hunting, 2063
Love among the Ruins, 1365
Loveliest of Trees, 2042
Love on the Farm, 2346
"Love seeketh not Itself to please, 51
Love's Last Lesson, 1037
Love Song of J. Alfred Prufrock, The, 2364
Love Without Hope, 2446
Lucifer in Starlight, 1572
Lullaby, 2505

Macaulay, Thomas Babington, 1697
MacDiarmid, Hugh, 2433
MacNeice, Louis, 2513
Madness of King Goll, The, 2088
Maids, not to you my mind doth change,
    1742
[Maids, not to you my mind doth change],
    1742
Manfred, 588
Mannequin, 2438
Mansfield, Katherine, 2408
Man Who Dreamed of Faeryland, The, 2094
Man Who Would Be King, The, 1865
Map of the City, A, 2577
Márgarét, áre you gríeving, 1655
Margaret Fuller and Mary Wollstonecraft,
    1456
Mariana, 1202
Marina, 2388
Marked with D., 2767
Mark on the Wall, The, 2143
Marriage of Heaven and Hell, The, 72
Martian Sends a Postcard Home, A, 2840
Martineau, Harriet, 1725
Matthew and Mark and Luke and holy
    John, 1452
Mayhew, Henry, 1714

MCMXIV, 2566
Meeting at Night, 1362
Memoirs of an Infantry Officer, 2058
Memorabilia, 1365
Memorial Verses, 1482
Men of England, wherefore plough, 727
Mercian Hymns, 2719
Meredith, George, 1570
Metaphysical Poets, The, 2401
Michael, 270
Midsummer, 2584
Milkweed and Monarch, 2858
Mill, John Stuart, 1137
Mill on the Floss, The, 1469
Milton! thou should'st be living at this hour,
    297
Miners, 2068
Mock on, Mock on, Voltaire, Rousseau, 84
Modern Fiction, 2148
Modern Love, 1570
Modern Painters, 1428
Moment before the Gun Went Off, The,
    2573
Mont Blanc, 720
Moore, Thomas, 527
Morning and evening, 1589
Morris, James, 2027
Morris, William, 1605
Morse, 2818
Mother, I cannot mind my wheel, 492
Mother and Poet, 1195
Motions and Means, on land and sea at
    war, 299
Mouse's Nest, 807
Move him into the sun—, 2071
Mrs. Warren's Profession, 1810
Much have I travell'd in the realms of gold,
    826
Mulcahy, Richard, 2025
Muldoon, Paul, 2856
Mulock, Dinah Maria, 1732
Munro, Alice, 2706
Murray, Les, 2815
Musée des Beaux Arts, 2505
Music, when soft voices die, 768
Mutability (Shelley), 701
Mutability (Wordsworth), 298
My aspens dear, whose airy cages quelled,
    1654
My First Acquaintance with Poets, 513
My first thought was, he lied in every word,
    1367
My heart aches, and a drowsy numbness
    pains, 849
My heart is like a singing bird, 1587
My heart leaps up, 285
My Last Duchess, 1352
My mother bore me in the southern wild,
    45
My mother groand! my father wept., 57
My pensive Sara! thy soft cheek reclined,
    419
My Pretty Rose Tree, 55

My Sad Captains, 2578
My Sister's Sleep, 1578
MY SOUL, I summon to the winding ancient stair, 2113
My spirit is too week—mortality, 828

Naipaul, V. S., 2722
National Trust, 2764
Nehru, Jawaharlal, 2034
Nests in Elms, 1745
Neutral Tones, 1935
Never on this side of the grave again, 1603
Never pain to tell thy love, 84
"Never shall a young man, 2115
New Age, The, 2453
Newman, John Henry Cardinal, 1119
Night, the black summer, simplifies her smells, 2580
Nightingale, Florence, 1734
Nightingale's Nest, The, 803
Nights in the Gardens of Port of Spain, 2580
Night-Wind, The, 1420
No, no, go not to Lethe, neither twist, 853
"No, Thank You, John," 1601
No, the serpent did not, 2590
Nobly, nobly Cape Saint Vincent to the northwest died away, 1358
Nobody heard him, the dead man, 2452
No Coward Soul Is Mine, 1424
Noonday Axeman, 2816
No Second Troy, 2098
Not, I'll not, carrion comfort, Despair, not feast on thee, 1656
Not every man has gentians in his house, 2351
Nothing is so beautiful in Spring—, 1652
Not Waving but Drowning, 2452
Now as I was young and easy under the apple boughs, 2522
Now it is autumn and the falling fruit, 2357
Now let the legless boy show the great lady, 2437
No Worst, There Is None, 1657
Now Sleeps the Crimson Petal, 1227
Now that I, tying thy glass mask tightly, 1353
Now that we're almost settled in our house, 2102
Nudes—stark and glistening, 2063
Nurse's Song (Songs of Experience), 52
Nurse's Song (Songs of Innocence), 48
Nutting, 258

O Autumn, laden with fruit, and stained, 40
O'Brien, Edna, 2745
Ode: Intimations of Immortality, 286
Ode on a Grecian Urn, 851
Ode on Indolence, 854
Ode on Melancholy, 853
Ode to a Nightingale, 849
Ode to Duty, 292
Ode to Psyche, 847
Ode to the West Wind, 730

Odour of Chrysanthemums, 2316
O Eros of the mountains, of the earth, 1745
O for ten years, that I may overwhelm, 827
O Goddess! hear these tuneless numbers, wrung, 847
O golden-tongued Romance, with serene lute!, 833
Oh, Galuppi, Baldassaro, this is very sad to find!, 1363
Oh, talk not to me of a name great in story—, 561
Oh, thou! in Hellas deem'd of heav'nly birth, 564
Oh, to be in England, 1358
Oh, what could the ladye's beauty match, 1035
Old China, 505
Old Eddie's face, wrinkled with river lights, 2582
Old Nurse's Story, The, 1319
"O 'Melia, my dear, this does everything crown!, 1938
Omeros, 2585
O my Luve's like a red, red rose, 115
On a starred night Prince Lucifer uprose, 1572
On Being Cautioned against Walking on an Headland Overlooking the Sea, Because It Was Frequented by a Lunatic, 34
Once I am sure there's nothing going on, 2565
Once more the storm is howling, and half hid, 2107
On Donne's Poetry, 466
One by one they appear in, 2578
One face looks out from all his canvases, 1586
On either side of the river lie, 1204
One morn before me were three figures seen, 854
One Out of Many, 2722
One that is ever kind said yesterday, 2096
One We Knew, 1942
On First Looking into Chapman's Homer, 826
On Gusto, 510
Onion, Memory, The, 2839
On Liberty, 1146
Only a man harrowing clods, 1951
On Man, on Nature, and on Human Life, 301
On Not Shooting Sitting Birds, 2442
On Passing the New Menin Gate, 2057
On Seeing the Elgin Marbles, 828
On Sitting Down to Read King Lear *Once Again*, 833
On the day of the explosion, 2570
On the Knocking at the Gate of Macbeth, 543
On the steps of the Louvre; like a voice of God following a storm, the Abbe follow'd, 145

[*On the Treaty between Great Britain and Ireland*], 2025
On the Western Circuit, 1918
On This Island, 2502
On Wenlock Edge, 2043
Origin of Species, The, 1679
O Rose, thou art sick, 52
Orwell, George, 2456
O soft embalmer of the still midnight, 847
O there is a blessing in this gentle breeze, 305
Other Side of a Mirror, The, 1861
O thou, with dewy locks, who lookest down, 39
Our Bog Is Dood, 2451
Out of the night that covers me, 1747
O weary Champion of the Cross, lie still, 1604
Owen, Wilfred, 2066
Owen's Letters to His Mother, 2072
O what can ail thee, knight at arms, 845
O wild West Wind, thou breath of Autumn's being, 730
Owl, The, 2052
O World, O Life, O Time, 769
O young Lochinvar is come out of the west, 413
Ozymandias, 725

Paine, Thomas, 133
Pains of Sleep, The, 462
Parting at Morning, 1362
[*Partition of India, The*], 2028
Passage to India, A, 2133
Passing of Arthur, The, 1293
Past and Present, 1110
Pastoral Poesy, 805
Past ruined Ilion, 493
Pater, Walter, 1636
Patmore, Coventry, 1723
Pavement slipp'ry, people sneezing, 93
Peasant Poet, The, 810
Petition, 2501
Piano, 2347
Pied Beauty, 1653
Pike, 2589
Pinter, Harold, 2594
Piping down the valleys wild, 43
Pity would be no more, 57
Poem Ended by a Death, 2760
Poem in October, 2521
Poet of Nature, thou hast wept to know, 701
Poison Tree, A, 58
Political Significance of Imperialism, The, 2021
Politics and the English Language, 2462
Poor Singing Dame, The, 94
Porphyria's Lover, 1349
Poverty Knock, 1713
Prayer for My Daughter, A, 2107
Preface to Lyrical Ballads, 238
Preface to Poems (Arnold), 1504

Preface to The Nigger of the "Narcissus," 1954
Prelude, The, 303
Present State of Europe Compared with Antient Prophecies, 143
Press'd by the Moon, mute arbitress of tides, 34
Pretty, 2455
Price, Richard, 118
Priestly, Joseph, 142
Prisoner: A Fragment, The, 1423
Professions for Women, 2214
Prometheus Unbound, 732
Promise me no promises, 1602
Promises Like Pie-Crust, 1602
Prophet's Hair, The, 2843
Prospectus on The Recluse, 301
Prospice, 1409
Proud Ladye, The, 1035
Proud Maisie, 415
Punishment, 2821

Queen Mab: A Philosophical Poem, 157
Queen's Reign, The, 1738

Rabbi Ben Ezra, 1413
Rain, 2053
Rain, midnight rain, nothing but the wild rain, 2053
Raine, Craig, 2838
Rapt in the visionary theme!, 98
Reader Over My Shoulder, The, 2446
Real Inspector Hound, The, 2786
Rear-Guard, The, 2056
Recessional, 1892
Reed, Henry, 2528
Reflections on the Revolution in France, 122
Relic, 2588
Religious Musings, 153
Remember how we picked the daffodils?, 2592
Remembrance, 1421
Renaissance, The, 1638
Requiem for the Plantagenet Kings, 2718
Resolution and Independence, 280
Returning, We Hear the Larks, 2063
Revenge, 1040
Reveries over Childhood and Youth, 2124
Review of Southey's Colloquies, A, 1697
Rhys, Jean, 2437
Rights of Man, 133
Rights of Woman, The, 27
Rime of the Ancient Mariner, The, 422
Robert Bruce's March to Bannockburn, 114
Robinson, Mary, 91
Room of One's Own, A, 2153
Rose Aylmer, 493
Rosenberg, Isaac, 2061
Rose of the World, The, 2092
Rossetti, Christina, 1583
Rossetti, Dante Gabriel, 1573
Rouen, 2074
Rough wind, that moanest loud, 786

Round the cape of a sudden came the sea, 1362
Rubáiyát of Omar Khayyám, The, 1305
Ruined Cottage, The, 259
Ruined Maid, The, 1938
Rushdie, Salman, 2842
Ruskin, John, 1425, 2018

Sad Steps, 2569
Sailing to Byzantium, 2109
St. Agnes, Eve—Ah, bitter chill it was!, 834
Sartor Resartus, 1077
Sassoon, Siegfried, 2054
Say Not the Struggle Nought Availeth, 1453
Say over again, and yet once over again, 1179
Scholar and Gypsy, 2768
Scholar Gypsy, The, 1485
Schooner Flight, The, 2583
Science and Culture, 1559
Scots, wha hae wi' Wallace bled, 114
Scott, Sir Walter, 401
Seasons of mists and mellow fruitfulness, 872
Sea View, The, 35
Second Coming, The, 2106
Secret Rose, The, 2095
"See, here's the workbox, little wife, 1949
September 1913, 2099
September Song, 2718
Seven Sorrows, The, 2591
Shall I strew on the rose or rue or laurel, 1631
Shall I tell you the signs of a New Age coming?, 2453
Sharping Stone, The, 2827
Shaw, Bernard, 1808
She dwelt among the untrodden ways, 252
She fell asleep on Christmas Eve, 1578
She Hears the Storm, 1943
Shelley, Mary Wollstonecraft, 903
Shelley, Percy Bysshe, 156, 698
She looked over his shoulder, 2511
She put him on a snow-white shroud, 1041
She sat and sang alway, 1584
She told how they used to form for the country dances—, 1942
She walks in beauty, 556
Shield of Achilles, The, 2511
Ship of Death, The, 2357
Shooting an Elephant, 2457
Should auld acquaintance be forgot, 108
Sick Rose, The, 52
Silent One, The, 2061
Silly Novels by Lady Novelists, 1461
Simon Lee, 222
Sir, no man's enemy, forgiving all, 2501
Sister Imelda, 2746
Sitwell, Edith, 2527
Sketch of the Past, A, 2218
Skunk, The, 2825
Sleep and Poetry, 827
Sleeping at Last, 1604

Slice of Wedding Cake, A, 2450
slumber did my spirit seal, A, 254
Smith, Charlotte, 32
Smith, Stevie, 2450
Snake, 2352
So, we'll go no more a roving, 559
Soap Suds, 2515
Softly, in the dusk, a woman is singing to me, 2347
Soho Hospital for Women, The, 2761
Soldier, The, 2050
Soliloquy of the Spanish Cloister, 1350
Solitary Reaper, The, 293
Sombre the night is, 2063
Something this foggy day, a something which, 1603
Song: For a' that and a' that, 116
Song: Woo'd and married and a', 217
Song [I hid my love when young while I], 810
Song [I peeled bits o'straws and I got switches too], 811
Song ("She sat and sang alway"), 1584
Songs of Experience, 49
Songs of Innocence, 43
Song ("When I am dead, my dearest"), 1584
Sonnets from the Portuguese, 1179
Sonnet to Sleep, 847
Son of the ocean isle!, 813
Sorrow of Love, The, 2093
Southey, Robert, 1467
Spain 1937, 2502
Speech after long silence; it is right, 2117
Spirit's Return, A, 818
Splendor Falls, The, 1226
Spring, 1652
Spring and Fall, 1655
Standing aloof in giant ignorance, 834
Stanzas for Music, 558
Stanzas from the Grande Chartreuse, 1493
Stanzas Written in Dejection—December 1818, near Naples, 726
Stanzas Written on the Road between Florence and Pisa, 561
Star-Gazer, 2516
Starlight Night, The, 1651
Stars, 1421
Statesman's Manual, The, 489
Station Island, 2825
Steamboats, Viaducts, and Railways, 299
Stern Daughter of the Voice of God, 292
Still Falls the Rain, 2527
Stolen Child, The, 2090
Stones of Venice, The, 1432
Stop, Christian Passer-by!—Stop, child of God, 467
Stoppard, Tom, 2785
Storm-Cloud of the Nineteenth Century, The, 1443
Strange fits of passion have I known, 251
Strange Meeting, 2070
Strange room, from this angle, 2761
Strong Son of God, immortal Love, 1231

Study of Poetry, The, 1534

Subjection of Women, The, 1155

Summer ends now; now, barbarous in beauty, the stooks rise, 1653

Summer Evening's Meditation, A, 24

Sunday Morning, 2513

Sunlight on the Garden, The, 2514

Sunset and evening star, 1304

Surprised by joy, 298

Surprised by joy—impatient as the Wind, 298

Swear by what the sages spoke, 2121

Sweeney Among the Nightingales, 2367

Sweet and Low, 1225

Swiftly walk o'er the western wave, 767

Swinburne, Algernon Charles, 1621

Table Turned, The, 228

Talking in Bed, 2567

Tam o' Shanter: A Tale, 109

"Teach it me, if you can,—forgetfulness, 1037

Tears, 2052

Tears, Idle Tears, 1226

Tennyson, Alfred, Lord, 1198

Ten years ago it seemed impossible, 1603

Terence, This Is Stupid Stuff, 2044

"Terence, this is stupid stuff, 2044

That civilization may not sink, 2119

That is no country for old men. The young, 2109

That Nature Is a Heraclitean Fire and of the Comfort of the Resurrection, 1658

That night your great guns, unawares, 1944

That's my last Duchess painted on the wall, 1352

That story which the bold Sir Bedivere, 1293

That the Science of Cartography Is Limited, 2835

That with this bright believing band, 1935

The awful shadow of some unseen Power, 723

The Bishop tells us: "When the boys come back, 2055

The blessed damozel leaned out, 1574

The boy stood on the burning deck, 815

The brawling of a sparrow in the eaves, 2093

The breaking waves dash'd high, 814

The bride she is winsome and bonny, 217

The cherry trees bend over and are shedding, 2053

The chestnut casts his flambeaux, and the flowers, 2046

The cock, warm roosting 'mid his feather'd mates, 210

The Colonel in a casual voice, 2536

The Cross, the Cross, 2348

The curtains were half drawn, the floor was swept, 1585

The darkness crumbles away, 2062

The everlasting universe of things, 720

The fascination of what's difficult, 2098

The first sorrow of autumn, 2591

The force that through the green fuse drives the flower, 2517

The frost performs its secret ministry, 457

The garlands fade that Spring so lately wove, 33

The gray sea and the long black land, 1362

The harp that once through Tara's halls, 527

The hunchback in the park, 2520

Their Lonely Betters, 2508

The love that breeds, 1743

The morning comes, the night decays, the watchmen leave their stations, 146

The Muses are turned gossips; they have lost, 29

Then, land!-then, England! oh, the frosty cliffs, 1180

Then in her triumph spoke the Fairy Queen, 157

The noble horse with courage in his eye, 2537

Theology, 2590

The plunging limbers over the shattered track, 2064

The princes of Mercia were badger and raven. Thrall, 2719

The rain comes flapping through the yard, 2856

The rain set early in tonight, 1349

There be none of Beauty's daughters, 558

"There is a Thorn—it looks so old, 229

There Is No Natural Religion, 41

There is one story and one story only, 2447

There was a roaring in the wind all night, 280

There Was a Saviour, 2519

There was a time in former years—, 1943

There was a time when meadow, grove, and stream, 287

There was a whispering in my hearth, 2068

The rooks are cawing up and down the trees!, 1745

These, in the day when heaven was falling, 2047

The sea is calm tonight, 1492

"These are the Daemons that pervert the power, 148

The snail pushes through a green, 2576

The splendor falls on castle walls, 1226

The stately Homes of England, 817

The Sun does arise, 43

The Sun is warm, the sky is clear, 726

The sunlight on the garden, 2514

The sun was shining on the sea, 1670

The Thames nocturne of blue and gold, 1749

The time I've lost in wooing, 528

The time you won your town the race, 2042

The trees are in their autumn beauty, 2101

The unpurged images of day recede, 2115

The upland shepherd, as reclined he lies, 35

The wan leafs shak, atour, us like the snaw, 2435

The wind flapped loose, the wind was still, 1579

The woods decay, the woods decay and fall, 1215

The world is charged with the grandeur of God, 1651

The world is too much with us; late and soon, 297

The wounds are terrible. The paint is old, 2836

"They," 2055

They Are Not Long, 1895

They are not long, the weeping and the laughter, 1895

They roused him with muffins—they roused him with ice—, 1672

They say that Hope is happiness, 557

They serve revolving saucer eyes, 2759

They sing their dearest songs—, 1950

They throw in Drummer Hodge, to rest, 1937

They went to sea in a sieve, they did, 1664

They will wash all my kisses and finger-prints off you, 2760

Things Fall Apart, 2617

This brand of soap has the same smell as once in the big, 2515

This house has been far out at sea all night, 2587

This is the wind, the wind in a field of corn, 2855

This Lime-Tree Bower My Prison, 420

—Tho' Liberty shall soon, indignant, raise, 150

Thomas, Dylan, 2516

Thomas, Edward, 2051

Thompson, Francis, 1856

Thorn, The, 229

Those long uneven lines, 2566

Thou Art Indeed Just, Lord, 1658

Thou fair-hair'd angel of the evening, 40

Thoughts About the Person from Porlock, 2453

Thoughts on My Sick-Bed, 399

Thou large-brained woman and large-hearted man, 1178

Thou shalt have one God only; who, 1452

Thou still unravish'd bride of quietness, 851

Three sang of love together; one with lips, 1586

Three weeks gone and the combatants gone, 2537

Three Woe-Trumpets, The, 140

Three years she grew, 252

Through Alpine meadows soft-suffused, 1493

Through what long heaviness, assayed in what strange fire, 1895

Thyrsis, 1498

Thy voice prevails—dear friend, my gentle friend!, 818

time I've lost in wooing, The, 528

'Tis past! The sultry tyrant of the south, 24

'Tis the middle of the night by the castle clock, 442

'Tis time this heart should be unmoved, 562

Tithonus, 1215

To a Little Invisible Being Who Is Expected Soon to Become Visible, 28

To a Louse, 106

To a Mouse, 105

To an Athlete Dying Young, 2042

To a Shade, 2100

To a Sky-Lark, 765

To Autumn (Blake), 40

To Autumn (Keats), 872

Toccata of Galuppi's, A, 1363

To Christina Rossetti, 1744

Today we have naming of parts. Yesterday, 2529

To drift with every passion till my soul, 1749

To George Sand, 1178

To His Love, 2060

To Homer, 834

To Jane (The keen stars were twinkling), 787

To Juan at the Winter Solstice, 2447

The keen stars were twinkling, 787

To Marguerite—Continued, 1479

To Mercy, Pity, Peace, and Love, 47

To ——— [Music, when soft voices die], 768

To Night (Shelley), 767

To Night (Smith), 33

To Room Nineteen, 2542

Tortoise Shell, 2348

Tortoise Shout, 2349

To Sidmouth and Castlereagh, 728

To Sleep, 33

To Spring, 39

To the Evening Star, 40

To the Poet Coleridge, 98

To Tirzah, 58

Towery city and branchy between towers, 1654

To William Wordsworth, 464

To Wordsworth, 701

Tradition and the Individual Talent, 2395

Trampwoman's Tragedy, A, 1939

Trembling of the Veil, The, 2127

Triad, A, 1586

True genius, but true woman! dost deny, 1178

True poesy is not in words, 805

Tryst with Destiny, 2034

Tuckett. Bill Tuckett. Telegraph operator, Hall's Creek, 2818

Turning and turning in the widening gyre, 2106

Turns, 2767

Tuscan cypresses, 2354

'Twas brillig, and the slithy toves, 1666

'Twas on a Holy Thursday, their innocent faces clean, 47

'Twas summer and the sun was mounted high, 259
Twenty years hence, 493
Two April Mornings, The, 256
Two in the Campagna, 1390
Two Letters on Sight and Vision, 88
Tyger, The, 54

Ulysses (Joyce), 2269
Ulysses (Tennyson), 1213
Unbosoming, 1743
Under Ben Bulben, 2121
Under the Waterfall, 1947
Undesirable you may have been, untouchable, 2718
Up, black, striped and damasked like the chasuble, 2825
Up-Hill, 1589
Upon a lonely desart Beach, 96
Upon a time, before the faery broods, 857
Up! quit thy bower, 217
Up this green woodland ride let's softly rove, 803
Up! up! my Friend, and quit your books, 228

Vanity, saith the preacher, vanity, 1359
Vergissmeinnicht, 2537
Vindication of the Rights of Men, A, 128
Vindication of the Rights of Woman, The, 166
Vision, A, 807
Vision of the Last Judgment, A, 86
Visions of the Daughters of Albion, 64
Visit to Newgate, A, 1335
Voice, The, 1949

Waiting for the Barbarians, 2829
Wake! For the Sun, who scattered into flight, 1305
Walcott, Derek, 2580
Walk, The, 1948
Walker Brothers Cowboy, 2707
Walrus and the Carpenter, The, 1670
Washing-Day, 29
Waste Land, The, 2368
We are as clouds that veil the midnight moon, 701
We Are Seven, 224
We caught the tread of dancing feet, 1750
Wee, sleeket, cowran, tim'rous beastie, 105
Well, they are gone, and here must I remain, 421
Well, World, you have kept faith with me, 1951
Well! If the Bard was weather-wise, who made, 459
We must look at the harebell as if, 2436
We sat together at one summer's end, 2097
We stood by a pond that winter day, 1935
We walked along, while bright and red, 256
We were apart, yet, day by day, 1478

"What are the bugles blowin' for?" said Files-on-Parade, 1888
Whate'er is Born of Mortal Birth, 58
What Is Poetry?, 1139
What large, dark hands are those at the window, 2346
What need you, being come to sense, 2099
What passing-bells for these who die as cattle?, 2066
What seas what shores what gray rocks and what islands, 2388
When a man hath no freedom to fight for at home, 561
When Britain Really Ruled the Waves, 1678
When chapman billies leave the street, 109
"Whenever I plunge my arm, like this, 1947
When first, descending from the moorlands, 299
When I, Good Friends, Was Called to the Bar, 1675
When I am dead, my dearest, 1584
When I have fears that I may cease to be, 833
When I have fears that I may cease to be, 833
When I see a couple of kids, 2568
When I Was One-and-Twenty, 2042
When my mother died I was very young, 46
When snow like sheep lay in the fold, 2717
When the chilled dough of his flesh went into an oven, 2767
When the hounds of spring are on winter's traces, 1623
When the lamp is shattered, 786
When the lamp is shattered, 786
When the voices of children are heard on the green, 52
When we two parted, 557
When You Are Old, 2093
Where dips the rocky highland, 2090
Where the quiet-colored end of evening smiles, 1365
White Goddess, The, 2448
White Knight's Song, The, 1668
" 'White Slavery' of London Match Workers, The," 1715
Who died on the wires, and hung there, one of two—, 2061
Who dreamed that beauty passes like a dream?, 2092
Who Goes with Fergus?, 2094
Who had not wak'd to list the busy sounds, 92
Who owns these scrawny little feet? Death, 2590
Who will go drive with Fergus now, 2094
Who will remember, passing through this Gate, 2057
"Why, William, on the old grey stone, 227
Why did I laugh tonight? No voice will tell, 844
Why have such scores of lovely, gifted girls, 2450

Why is the word pretty so underrated?, 2455
Why should I blame her that she filled my days, 2098
Why the Novel Matters, 2341
"Why weep ye by the tide, ladie?, 415
Widow at Windsor, The, 1889
Wilde, Oscar, 1747
Wild Swans at Coole, The, 2101
['Will sprawl, now that the heat of day is best, 1403
Wilt thou go with me, sweet maid, 808
Winchester, Elhanan, 139
Wind (Fenton), 2855
Wind (Hughes), 2587
Windhover, The, 1652
Winter: My Secret, 1588
Winter's Day, A, 210
Witch, The, 1862
With blackest moss the flower-plots, 1202
With Donne, whose muse on dromedary trots, 466
With Rue My Heart Is Laden, 2044
Wollstonecraft, Mary, 128, 163
Woman much missed, how you call to me, call to me, 1949
["*Woman's Cause is Man's, The"*], 1229
Woman's Thoughts About Women, A, 1732
Women of England: Their Social Duties and Domestic Habits, The, 1721
Woodspurge, The, 1579
Woolf, Virginia, 2141

Wordsworth, Dorothy, 383
Wordsworth, William, 149, 219
Workbox, The, 1949
Work without Hope, 467
World is too much with us, The, 297
Worlds on worlds are rolling ever, 769
Would that the structure brave, the manifold music I build, 1410
Written after Swimming from Sestos to Abydos, 555
Written at the Close of Spring, 33
Written in the Church-Yard at Middleton at Sussex, 34

Yeats, William Butler, 2085
Yes, injured Woman! rise, assert thy right!, 27
Yes, I remember Adlestrop—, 2051
Yes! in the sea of life enisled, 1479
Yesterday all the past. The language of size, 2502
You, reading over my shoulder, peering beneath, 2446
You did not come, 1936
You did not walk with me, 1948
You love us when we're heroes, home on leave, 2057
Your bed's got two wrong sides. Your life's all grouse, 2766
"You seem very clever at explaining words, Sir" said Alice. "Would you, 1667

Themes — almost all   styles

• ephiphany   allusions
                                      ambiguity
• questioning social   Joyce   ellusive (invasive
  conciousness   = Eliot   intanglement)
                      Yeats
                      Conrad   stream of
                      Wolf   conciousness in some
• National / Global identity - Conrad
  (gender roles   - Joyce   (TTL,) ?
                       - Yeats
                       - Eliot

• declining outlook

                    Conrad, Wolf
• Light / Dark   Joyce

• realization of family & society

• Modernity
• technology for destruction
                            — Yeats
, return to poetic tradition   Eliot

, pessimistic

• fuility   (useless or vain)

, questions moral ,   →Yeats
• philosphical meaning   Conrad
    of literary action   Eliot

• Objections to rational
           public discourse

• smallness of man — Wolf

• Personal agony &
    political catastrophe